D MAP PAGES

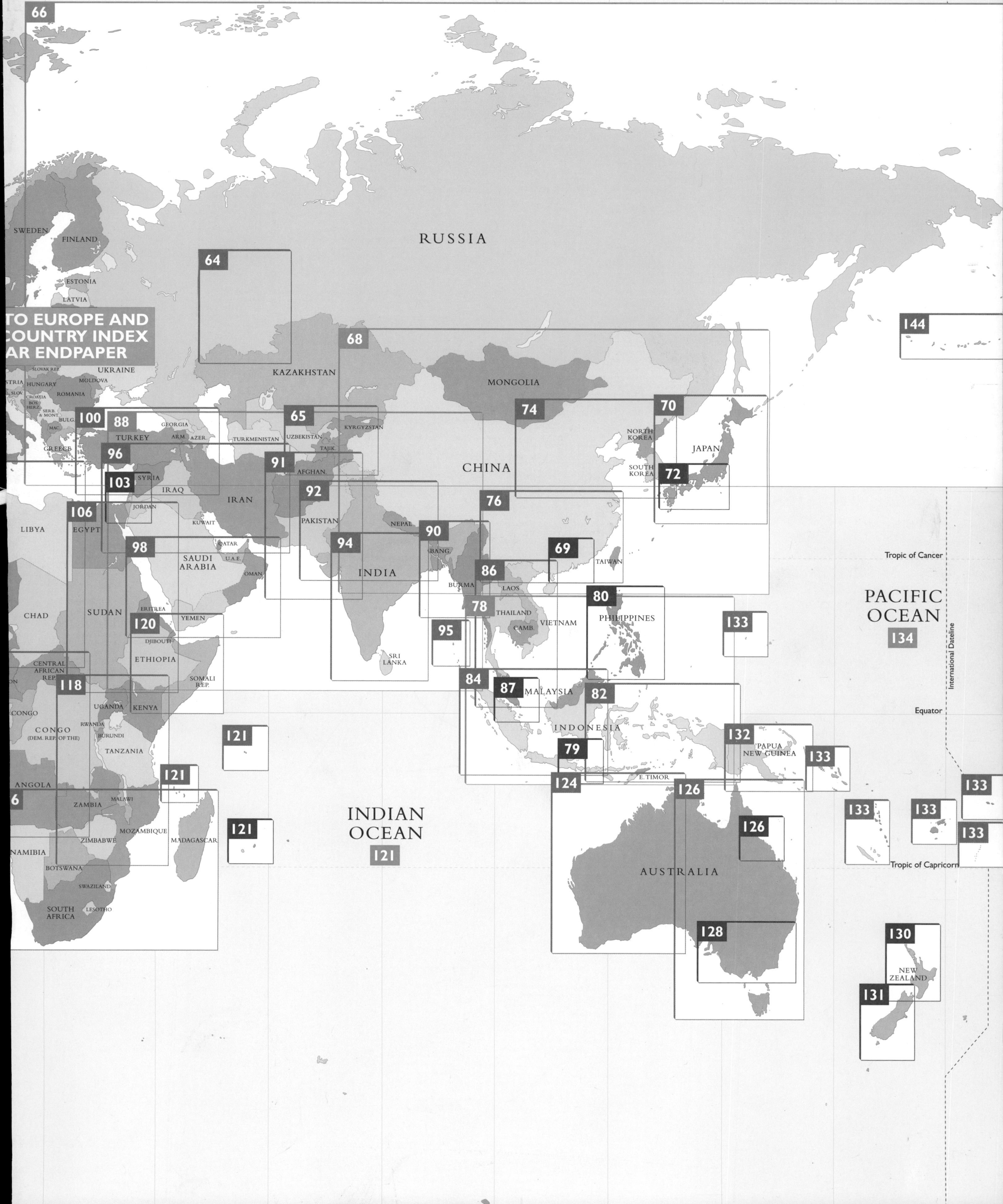
66
SWEDEN
FINLAND
ESTONIA
LATVIA
RUSSIA
64
TO EUROPE AND
COUNTRY INDEX
AR ENDPAPER
SLOVAK REP.
UKRAINE
STRIA
HUNGARY
MOLDOVA
SLOV.
CROATIA
ROMANIA
BOS.-HERZ.
SERB. & MONT.
BULG.
MAC.
GREECE
100
88
TURKEY
GEORGIA
ARM.
AZER.
KAZAKHSTAN
68
65
UZBEKISTAN
TURKMENISTAN
KYRGYZSTAN
TAJIK.
MONGOLIA
74
70
NORTH KOREA
SOUTH KOREA
JAPAN
72
CHINA
96
103
SYRIA
IRAQ
91
AFGHAN.
92
IRAN
JORDAN
KUWAIT
PAKISTAN
NEPAL
76
90
106
LIBYA
EGYPT
98
QATAR
U.A.E.
SAUDI ARABIA
OMAN
94
INDIA
BANG.
69
TAIWAN
86
BURMA
LAOS
80
PHILIPPINES
78
THAILAND
CAMB.
VIETNAM
144
Tropic of Cancer
PACIFIC OCEAN
134
133
CHAD
SUDAN
ERITREA
YEMEN
120
DJIBOUTI
ETHIOPIA
95
SRI LANKA
CENTRAL AFRICAN REP.
118
SOMALI REP.
84
87
MALAYSIA
82
International Dateline
Equator
UGANDA
KENYA
CONGO
CONGO (DEM. REP. OF THE)
RWANDA
BURUNDI
TANZANIA
121
INDONESIA
79
132
PAPUA NEW GUINEA
133
ANGOLA
MALAWI
ZAMBIA
E. TIMOR
124
126
INDIAN OCEAN
121
MOZAMBIQUE
ZIMBABWE
MADAGASCAR
NAMIBIA
BOTSWANA
SWAZILAND
SOUTH AFRICA
LESOTHO
AUSTRALIA
126
133
133
133
Tropic of Capricorn
128
130
NEW ZEALAND
131

PHILIP'S

ATLAS OF THE WORLD

COMPREHENSIVE EDITION

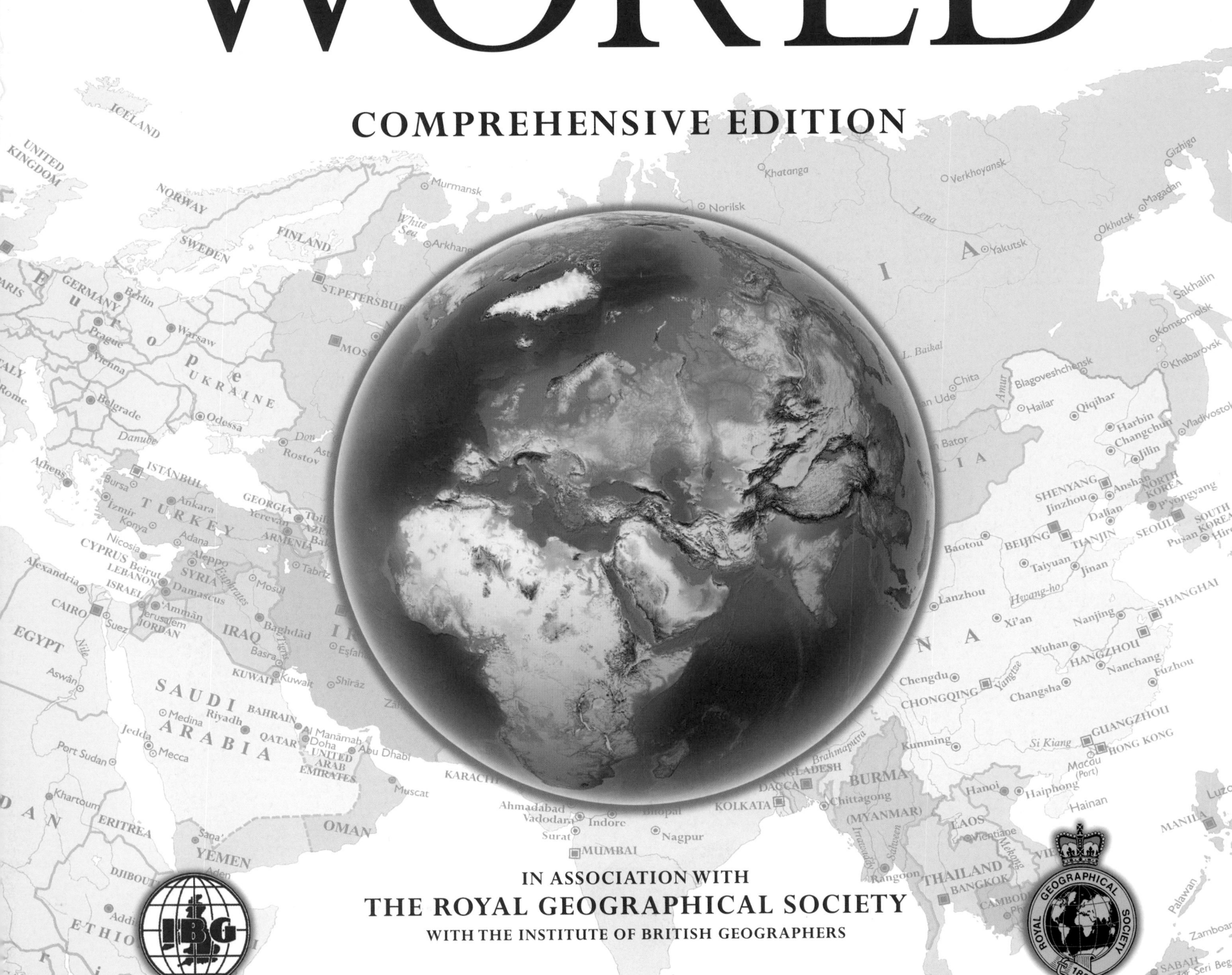

IN ASSOCIATION WITH

THE ROYAL GEOGRAPHICAL SOCIETY

WITH THE INSTITUTE OF BRITISH GEOGRAPHERS

ACKNOWLEDGEMENTS

IMAGES OF EARTH (PAGES IX–XXIV)
All satellite images in this section courtesy of NPA Group Limited, Edenbridge, Kent, UK (www.satmaps.com)

THE GAZETTEER OF NATIONS
TEXT Keith Lye

INTRODUCTION TO WORLD GEOGRAPHY
PICTURE ACKNOWLEDGEMENTS
Alamy /*Peter Bowater* 36
Corbis /*Jay Dickman* 47 (bottom left), /*Royalty-Free* 27, 32, 35, /*Vince Streano* 39, /*Liba Taylor* 42, /*David Turnley* 47 (bottom right)
NASA/GSFC 22 (bottom left and right), /*Cathy Clerbaux, NCAR Atmospheric Chemistry Division* 21 (bottom right)
NOAO/AURA/NSF/Todd Boroson 2
NPA Group 9, 13, 18, 48, /*Image provided by the USGS EROS Data Center Satellite Systems Branch* 23
Science Photo Library /*Earth Satellite Corporation* 20

STAR CHARTS
Wil Tirion

CARTOGRAPHY BY PHILIP'S

CITY MAPS
PAGE 11, DUBLIN: The town plan of Dublin is based on Ordnance Survey Ireland by permission of the Government Permit Number 7735. © Ordnance Survey Ireland and Government of Ireland.

Ordnance Survey
PAGE 11, EDINBURGH, and PAGE 15, LONDON: This product includes mapping data licensed from Ordnance Survey® with the permission of the Controller of Her Majesty's Stationery Office. © Crown copyright 2004. All rights reserved. Licence number 100011710.

VECTOR DATA: Courtesy of Gräfe and Unser Verlag GmbH, München, Germany (city centre maps of Bangkok, Beijing, Cape Town, Jerusalem, Mexico City, Moscow, Singapore, Sydney, Tokyo and Washington D.C.)

Published in Great Britain in 2004 by Philip's, a division of Octopus Publishing Group Ltd, 2–4 Heron Quays, London E14 4JP

ISBN-13 978-0-540-08603-0
ISBN-10 0-540-08603-7

A CIP catalogue record for this book is available from the British Library.

Printed in Spain

Details of other Philip's titles and services can be found on our website at: **www.philips-maps.co.uk**

FOREWORD

PHILIP'S HAVE BEEN MAPPING the world since 1834. The *Atlas of the World* is the flagship of the Philip's range, an authoritative and serious reference work and one of the finest atlases available anywhere in the world. The atlas incorporates computer-derived maps that have been produced using the very latest in digital cartographic techniques.

Philip's Atlas of the World has been devised with the help of a panel of specialist geography consultants from the United Kingdom and the United States, whose specialities range from the history of cartography, urban and social geography, epidemiology and the European Union to biogeography and applied geomorphology. The result of their valuable input can be seen in the wealth of maps and data contained in the '*Introduction to World Geography*' section of this atlas.

Country names are shown in conventional English form and are those that are in common usage. They are the forms used by publications such as *Newsweek* and *The Washington Post,* and by the BBC and the British Foreign Office. Alternative country names appear in brackets on the maps where space permits – for example, Burma (Myanmar) – and are cross-referenced in the index, for example, Côte d'Ivoire = Ivory Coast.

SPECIALIST GEOGRAPHY CONSULTANTS

PHILIP'S are grateful to the following people for acting as specialist geography consultants on the '*Introduction to World Geography*' front section:

Professor D. Brunsden Kings College, University of London, UK
Dr C. Clarke Oxford University, UK
Professor P. Haggett University of Bristol, UK
Professor M-L. Hsu University of Minnesota, Minnesota, USA
Professor K. McLachlan Geopolitical and International Boundaries Research Centre, School of Oriental and African Studies, University of London, UK
Professor M. Monmonier Syracuse University, New York, USA
Professor M. J. Tooley University of St Andrews, UK
Dr T. Unwin Royal Holloway, University of London, UK

PHILIP'S would also like to thank
Keith Lye
Robin Scagell
Dr I. S. Evans Durham University, UK
Dr Andrew Tatham The Royal Geographical Society

PHILIP'S World Atlases are published in association with THE ROYAL GEOGRAPHICAL SOCIETY (with THE INSTITUTE OF BRITISH GEOGRAPHERS).

The Society was founded in 1830 and given a Royal Charter in 1859 for 'the advancement of geographical science'. It holds historical collections of national and international importance, many of which relate to the Society's association with and support for scientific exploration and research from the 19th century onwards. It was pivotal in establishing geography as a teaching and research discipline in British universities close to the turn of the century, and has played a key role in geographical and environmental education ever since.

Today the Society is a leading world centre for geographical learning – supporting education, teaching, research and expeditions, and promoting public understanding of the subject. The Society welcomes those interested in geography as members. For further information, please visit the website at: **www.rgs.org**

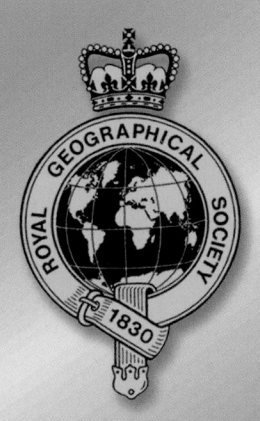

Philip's World Maps

The reference maps which form the main body of this atlas have been prepared in accordance with the highest standards of international cartography to provide an accurate and detailed representation of the Earth. The scales and projections used have been carefully chosen to give balanced coverage of the world, while emphasizing the most densely populated and economically significant regions. A hallmark of Philip's mapping is the use of hill shading and relief colouring to create a graphic impression of landforms: this makes the maps exceptionally easy to read. However, knowledge of the key features employed in the construction and presentation of the maps will enable the reader to derive the fullest benefit from the atlas.

Map Sequence

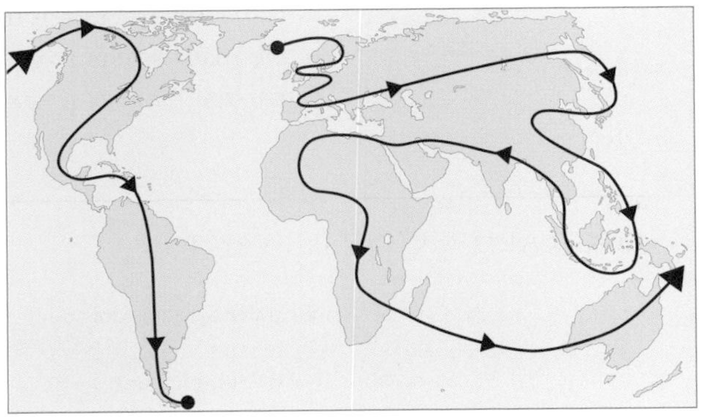

The atlas covers the Earth continent by continent: first Europe; then its land neighbour Asia (mapped north before south, in a clockwise sequence), then Africa, Australia and Oceania, North America and South America. This is the classic arrangement adopted by most cartographers since the 16th century. For each continent, there are maps at a variety of scales. First, physical relief and political maps of the whole continent; then a series of larger-scale maps of the regions within the continent, each followed, where required, by still larger-scale maps of the most important or densely populated areas. The governing principle is that by turning the pages of the atlas, the reader moves steadily from north to south through each continent, with each map overlapping its neighbours.

Map Presentation

With very few exceptions (for example, for the Arctic and Antarctic), the maps are drawn with north at the top, regardless of whether they are presented upright or sideways on the page. In the borders will be found the map title; a locator diagram showing the area covered; continuation arrows showing the page numbers for maps of adjacent areas; the scale; the projection used; the degrees of latitude and longitude; and the letters and figures used in the index for locating place names and geographical features. Physical relief maps also have a height reference panel identifying the colours used for each layer of contouring.

Map Symbols

Each map contains a vast amount of detail which can only be conveyed clearly and accurately by the use of symbols. Points and circles of varying sizes locate and identify the relative importance of towns and cities; different styles of type are employed for administrative, geographical and regional place names to aid identification. A variety of pictorial symbols denote landforms such as glaciers, marshes and coral reefs, and man-made structures including roads, railways, airports and canals. International borders are shown by red lines. Where neighbouring countries are in dispute, for example in parts of the Middle East, the maps show the *de facto* boundary between nations, regardless of the legal or historical situation. The symbols are explained on the first page of the World Maps section of the atlas.

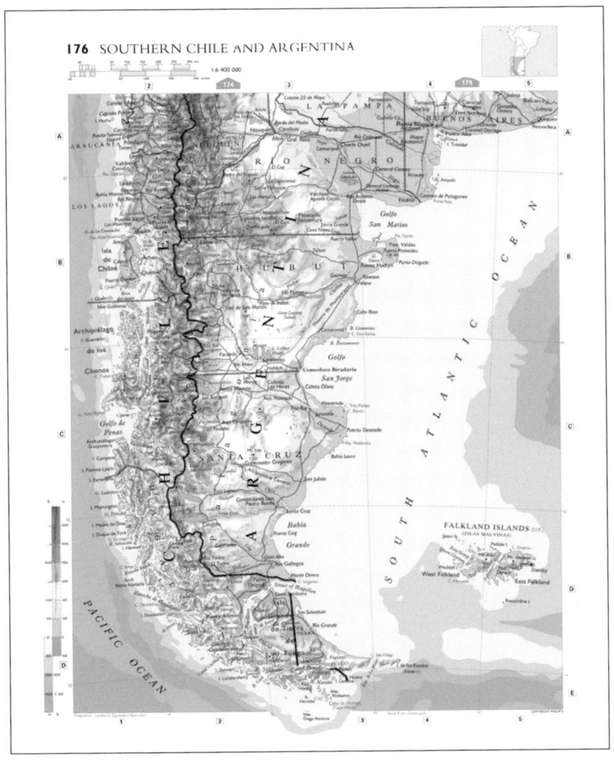

Map Scales

1:16 000 000
1 inch = 252 statute miles

The scale of each map is given in the numerical form known as the 'representative fraction'. The first figure is always one, signifying one unit of distance on the map; the second figure, usually in millions, is the number by which the map unit must be multiplied to give the equivalent distance on the Earth's surface. Calculations can easily be made in centimetres and kilometres, by dividing the Earth units figure by 100 000 (i.e. deleting the last five 0s). Thus 1:1 000 000 means 1 cm = 10 km. The calculation for inches and miles is more laborious, but 1 000 000 divided by 63 360 (the number of inches in a mile) shows that 1:1 000 000 means approximately 1 inch = 16 miles. The table below provides distance equivalents for scales down to 1:50 000 000.

LARGE SCALE		
1:1 000 000	1 cm = 10 km	1 inch = 16 miles
1:2 500 000	1 cm = 25 km	1 inch = 39.5 miles
1:5 000 000	1 cm = 50 km	1 inch = 79 miles
1:6 000 000	1 cm = 60 km	1 inch = 95 miles
1:8 000 000	1 cm = 80 km	1 inch = 126 miles
1:10 000 000	1 cm = 100 km	1 inch = 158 miles
1:15 000 000	1 cm = 150 km	1 inch = 237 miles
1:20 000 000	1 cm = 200 km	1 inch = 316 miles
1:50 000 000	1 cm = 500 km	1 inch = 790 miles
SMALL SCALE		

Measuring Distances

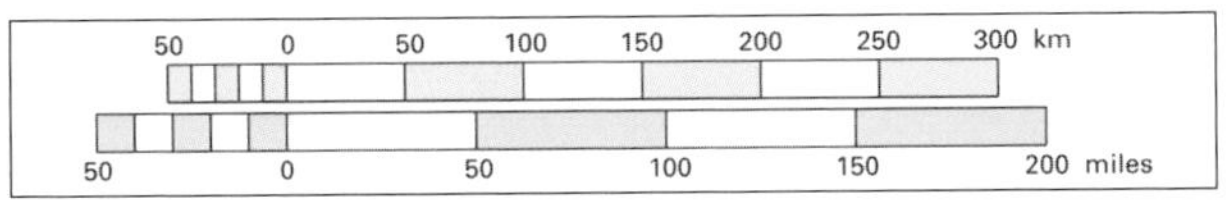

Although each map is accompanied by a scale bar, distances cannot always be measured with confidence because of the distortions involved in portraying the curved surface of the Earth on a flat page. As a general rule, the larger the map scale, the more accurate and reliable will be the distance measured. On small-scale maps such as those of the world and of entire continents, measurement may only be accurate along the 'standard parallels', or central axes, and should not be attempted without considering the map projection.

Map Projections

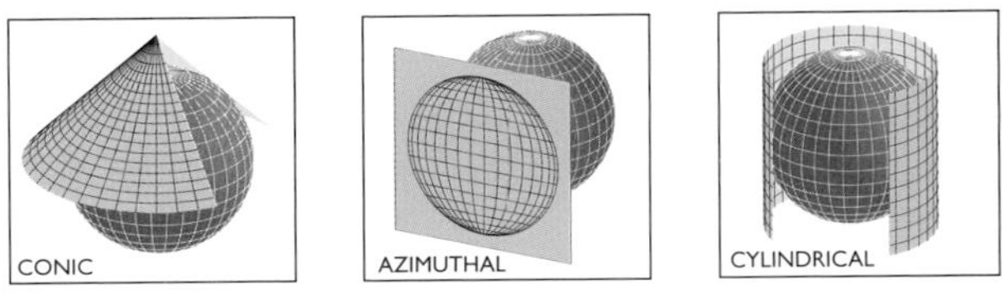

Unlike a globe, no flat map can give a true scale representation of the world in terms of area, shape and position of every region. Each of the numerous systems that have been devised for projecting the curved surface of the Earth on to a flat page involves the sacrifice of accuracy in one or more of these elements. The variations in shape and position of landmasses such as Alaska, Greenland and Australia, for example, can be quite dramatic when different projections are compared.

For this atlas, the guiding principle has been to select projections that involve the least distortion of size and distance. The projection used for each map is noted in the border. Most fall into one of three categories – conic, azimuthal or cylindrical – whose basic concepts are shown above. Each involves plotting the forms of the Earth's surface on a grid of latitude and longitude lines, which may be shown as parallels, curves or radiating spokes.

Latitude and Longitude

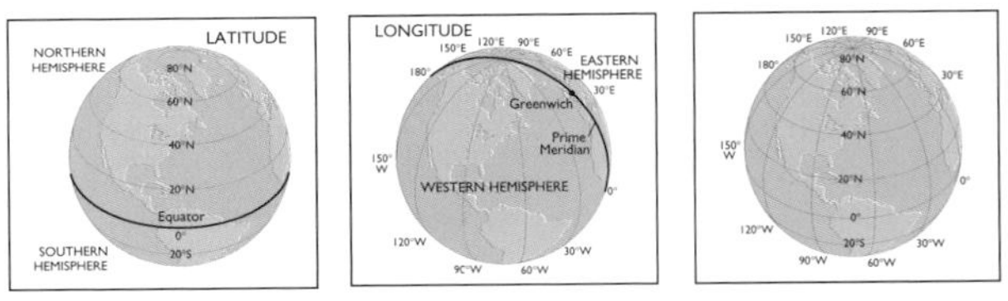

Accurate positioning of individual points on the Earth's surface is made possible by reference to the geometrical system of latitude and longitude. Latitude parallels are drawn west–east around the Earth and numbered by degrees north and south of the Equator, which is designated 0° of latitude. Longitude meridians are drawn north–south and numbered by degrees east and west of the prime meridian, 0° of longitude, which passes through Greenwich in England. By referring to these coordinates and their subdivisions of minutes (1/60th of a degree) and seconds (1/60th of a minute), any place on Earth can be located to within a few hundred metres. Latitude and longitude are indicated by blue lines on the maps; they are straight or curved according to the projection employed. Reference to these lines is the easiest way of determining the relative positions of places on different maps, and for plotting compass directions.

Name Forms

For ease of reference, both English and local name forms appear in the atlas. Oceans, seas and countries are shown in English throughout the atlas; country names may be abbreviated to their commonly accepted form (e.g. Germany, not The Federal Republic of Germany). Conventional English forms are also used for place names on the smaller-scale maps of the continents. However, local name forms are used on all large-scale and regional maps, with the English form given in brackets only for important cities – the large-scale map of Russia and Central Asia thus shows Moskva (Moscow). For countries which do not use a Roman script, place names have been transcribed according to the systems adopted by the British and US Geographic Names Authorities. For China, the Pin Yin system has been used, with some more widely known forms appearing in brackets, as with Beijing (Peking). Both English and local names appear in the index, the English form being cross-referenced to the local form.

Contents

World Statistics

Countries vi
Cities vii
Physical Dimensions viii

Images of Earth

Vancouver, Canada ix
Los Angeles, USA x
New York, USA xi
River Amazon, Brazil xii
Santiago, Chile xiii
London, UK xiv
IJsselmeer, Netherlands xv
Naples, Italy xvi
Strait of Gibraltar xvii
Cairo, Egypt xviii
Western Cape, South Africa xix
Tehran, Iran xx
Karachi, Pakistan xxi
Tokyo, Japan xxii
Sydney, Australia xxiii
Christchurch, New Zealand xxiv

The Gazetteer of Nations

An A–Z Gazetteer of Countries 1–32

Introduction to World Geography

The Universe 2–3
The Solar System 4–5
Time and Motion 6–7
Oceans 8–9
Geology 10–11
Landforms 12–13
Atmosphere and Weather 14–15
Climate 16–17
Water and Vegetation 18–19
The Natural Environment 20–21
People and the Environment 22–23
Population 24–25
Cities 26–27
The Human Family 28–29
Conflict and Co-operation 30–31
Agriculture 32–33
Energy 34–35
Minerals 36–37
Manufacturing 38–39
Trade 40–41
Health 42–43
Wealth 44–45
Standards of Living 46–47

City Maps

Amsterdam 2
Athens 2
Atlanta 3
Baghdad 3
Bangkok 3
Barcelona 4
Beijing 4
Berlin 5
Boston 6
Brussels 6
Budapest 7
Buenos Aires 7
Cairo 7
Calcutta (Kolkata) 8
Canton 8
Cape Town 8
Chicago 9
Copenhagen 10
Delhi 10
Dublin 11
Edinburgh 11
Helsinki 12
Hong Kong 12
Istanbul 12
Jakarta 13
Jerusalem 13
Johannesburg 13
Karachi 14
Lagos 14
Lisbon 14
London 15
Los Angeles 16
Lima 16
Madrid 17
Manila 17
Melbourne 17
Mexico City 18
Miami 18
Milan 18
Montreal 19
Moscow 19
Mumbai 20
Munich 20
New York 21
Osaka 22
Oslo 22
Paris 23
Prague 24
Rio de Janeiro 24
Rome 25
San Francisco 25
St Petersburg 26
Santiago 26
São Paulo 26
Seoul 26
Shanghai 27
Singapore 27
Stockholm 28
Sydney 28
Tokyo 29
Tehran 30
Tianjin 30
Toronto 30
Vienna 31
Warsaw 31
Washington 32
Wellington 32

Index to City Maps

Index to City Maps 33–39

World Maps

The World

Map Symbols 1
The World: Physical 2–3
1:76 000 000
The World: Political 4–5
1:76 000 000
Arctic Ocean 6
1:28 000 000
Antarctica 7
1:28 000 000
Atlantic Ocean 8
1:41 000 000
Islands of the Atlantic 9
Bermuda 1:400 000
New Providence Island 1:400 000
Madeira 1:800 000
Azores 1:1 600 000
Canary Islands 1:1 600 000
Falkland Islands 1:6 400 000
Ascension Island 1:400 000
St Helena 1:400 000
Cape Verde Islands 1:8 000 000
Greenland 10
1:10 000 000
Iceland 11
1:2 000 000

Europe

Europe: Physical 12
1:16 000 000
Europe: Political 13
1:16 000 000
Scandinavia 14–15
1:4 000 000
Iceland 1:4 000 000
Denmark and Southern Sweden 16–17
1:2 000 000
Southern Norway 18
1:2 000 000
British Isles 19
1:4 000 000
England and Wales 20–21
1:1 600 000
Scotland 22
1:1 600 000
Ireland 23
1:1 600 000
Netherlands, Belgium and Luxembourg 24
1:2 000 000
France 25
1:4 000 000
Northern France 26–27
1:2 000 000
Southern France 28–29
1:2 000 000
Germany 30–31
1:2 000 000
Switzerland 32–33
1:800 000
Austria, Czech Republic and Slovak Republic 34–35
1:2 000 000
Central Europe 36–37
1:4 000 000
Mediterranean Islands 38–39
Ibiza, Majorca, Minorca 1:800 000
Malta 1:400 000
Corfu 1:800 000
Rhodes 1:800 000
Levkas, Zante, Cephalonia 1:800 000
Crete 1:1 000 000
Cyprus 1:1 000 000
Eastern Spain 40–41
1:2 000 000
Western Spain and Portugal 42–43
1:2 000 000
Northern Italy, Slovenia and Croatia 44–45
1:2 000 000
Southern Italy 46–47
1:2 000 000
Southern Greece and Western Turkey 48–49
1:2 000 000
Serbia and Montenegro, Bulgaria and Northern Greece 50–51
1:2 000 000
Hungary, Romania and the Lower Danube 52–53
1:2 000 000
Poland and the Southern Baltic 54–55
1:2 000 000
Eastern Europe and Turkey 56–57
1:8 000 000
Baltic States, Belarus and Ukraine 58–59
1:4 000 000
The Volga Basin and the Caucasus 60–61
1:4 000 000

Asia

Asia: Physical 62
1:40 000 000

Asia: Political 63
1:40 000 000

Southern Urals 64
1:4 000 000

Central Asia 65
1:4 000 000

Russia and Central Asia 66–67
1:16 000 000

China and the Far East 68–69
1:12 000 000
Hong Kong and Macau 1:800 000

Japan 70–71
1:4 000 000
Ryukyu Islands 1:4 000 000

Southern Japan 72–73
1:2 000 000

Northern China and Korea 74–75
1:4 800 000

Southern China 76–77
1:4 800 000

Indonesia and the Philippines 78–79
1:10 000 000
Java and Madura 1:6 000 000
Bali 1:1 600 000

Philippines 80–81
1:3 200 000

Eastern Indonesia 82–83
1:5 600 000

Western Indonesia 84–85
1:5 600 000

Mainland South-east Asia 86–87
1:4 800 000
Ko Phuket 1:800 000
Ko Samui 1:800 000
Pinang 1:800 000
Singapore 1:800 000

Southern Asia and the Middle East 88–89
1:14 000 000

Bangladesh, North-eastern India and Burma 90
1:4 800 000

Afghanistan and Pakistan 91
1:5 600 000

Northern India and Nepal 92–93
1:4 800 000

Southern India and Sri Lanka 94–95
1:4 800 000
Lakshadweep Islands 1:4 800 000
Andaman and Nicobar Islands 1:4 800 000

The Middle East 96–97
1:5 600 000

Southern Arabian Peninsula 98–99
1:5 600 000

Turkey and Transcaucasia 100–101
1:4 000 000

Arabia and the Horn of Africa 102
1:12 000 000

The Near East 103
1:2 000 000

Africa

Africa: Physical 104
1:33 600 000

Africa: Political 105
1:33 600 000

The Nile Valley 106–107
1:6 400 000
The Nile Delta 1:3 200 000

Central North Africa 108–109
1:6 400 000

North-west Africa 110–111
1:6 400 000

West Africa 112–113
1:6 400 000

Central Africa 114–115
1:6 400 000
São Tomé and Príncipe 1:6 400 000

Southern Africa 116–117
1:6 400 000
Madagascar 1:6 400 000

East Africa 118–119
1:6 400 000

The Horn of Africa 120
1:6 400 000

Indian Ocean 121
1:40 000 000
Comoros 1:6 400 000
Seychelles 1:2 000 000
Réunion 1:2 000 000
Mauritius 1:2 000 000

Australia and Oceania

Australia and Oceania: Physical and Political 122–123
1:16 000 000

Western Australia 124–125
1:6 400 000

Eastern Australia 126–127
1:6 400 000
Whitsunday Group 1:2 000 000
Tasmania 1:6 400 000

South-east Australia 128–129
1:3 200 000

New Zealand – North Island 130
1:2 800 000

New Zealand – South Island 131
1:2 800 000
Chatham Islands 1:2 800 000

Papua New Guinea 132
1:5 200 000

Islands of the South-west Pacific 133
1:4 000 000
Fiji 1:4 000 000
Vanuatu 1:4 000 000
Solomon Islands 1:4 000 000
Tonga 1:4 000 000
Guam 1:4 000 000
Tahiti and Moorea 1:4 000 000
Samoan Islands 1:4 000 000
New Caledonia 1:4 000 000

Pacific Ocean 134–135
1:43 200 000

North America

North America: Physical 136
1:28 000 000

North America: Political 137
1:28 000 000

Canada 138–139
1:12 000 000
Alaska 1:24 000 000

Eastern Canada 140–141
1:5 600 000

Western Canada 142–143
1:5 600 000

Alaska 144
1:8 000 000

Hawaii 145
1:2 000 000
Oahu 1:500 000

United States 146–147
1:9 600 000
Hawaii 1:8 000 000

Eastern United States 148–149
1:4 800 000

North-eastern United States 150–151
1:2 000 000

South-eastern United States 152–153
1:2 000 000

Middle United States 154–155
1:4 800 000

Chicago and the Midwest 156–157
1:2 000 000

Western United States 158–159
1:4 800 000

Central and Southern California and Western Washington 160–161
1:2 000 000

Mexico 162–163
1:6 400 000

Central America and the West Indies 164–165
1:6 400 000
Jamaica 1:2 400 000
Guadeloupe 1:1 600 000
Martinique 1:1 600 000
Puerto Rico 1:2 400 000
Virgin Islands 1:1 600 000
St Lucia 1:800 000
Barbados 1:800 000

South America

South America: Physical 166
1:28 000 000

South America: Political 167
1:28 000 000

South America – North-west 168–169
1:6 400 000
Trinidad and Tobago 1:2 000 000

Eastern Brazil 170–171
1:6 400 000

South America – West 172–173
1:6 400 000
Galapagos Islands 1:3 200 000
Easter Island 1:400 000

Central South America 174–175
1:6 400 000

Southern Chile and Argentina 176
1:6 400 000

Geographical Glossary 177–178

Index to World Maps 179–304

World: Regions in the News 305

WORLD STATISTICS: COUNTRIES

This alphabetical list includes the principal countries and territories of the world. If a territory is not completely independent, the country it is associated with is named. The area figures give the total area of land, inland water and ice. The population figures are 2003 estimates where available. The annual income is the Gross Domestic Product per capita† in US dollars. The figures are the latest available, usually 2002 estimates.

Country/Territory	Area km^2 Thousands	Area miles^2 Thousands	Population Thousands	Capital	Annual Income US $
Afghanistan	652	252	28,717	Kabul	700
Albania	28.7	11.1	3,582	Tirana	4,400
Algeria	2,382	920	32,819	Algiers	5,400
American Samoa (US)	0.20	0.08	70	Pago Pago	8,000
Andorra	0.47	0.18	69	Andorra La Vella	19,000
Angola	1,247	481	10,766	Luanda	1,700
Anguilla (UK)	0.10	0.04	13	The Valley	8,600
Antigua & Barbuda	0.44	0.17	68	St John's	11,000
Argentina	2,780	1,074	38,741	Buenos Aires	10,500
Armenia	29.8	11.5	3,326	Yerevan	3,600
Aruba (Netherlands)	0.19	0.07	71	Oranjestad	28,000
Australia	7,741	2,989	19,732	Canberra	26,900
Austria	83.9	32.4	8,188	Vienna	27,900
Azerbaijan	86.6	33.4	7,831	Baku	3,700
Azores (Portugal)	2.2	0.86	236	Ponta Delgada	15,000
Bahamas	13.9	5.4	297	Nassau	15,300
Bahrain	0.69	0.27	667	Manama	15,100
Bangladesh	144	55.6	138,448	Dhaka	1,800
Barbados	0.43	0.17	277	Bridgetown	15,000
Belarus	208	80.2	10,322	Minsk	8,700
Belgium	30.5	11.8	10,289	Brussels	29,200
Belize	23.0	8.9	266	Belmopan	4,900
Benin	113	43.5	7,041	Porto-Novo	1,100
Bermuda (UK)	0.05	0.02	64	Hamilton	35,200
Bhutan	47.0	18.1	2,140	Thimphu	1,300
Bolivia	1,099	424	8,586	La Paz/Sucre	2,500
Bosnia-Herzegovina	51.2	19.8	3,989	Sarajevo	1,900
Botswana	582	225	1,573	Gaborone	8,500
Brazil	8,514	3,287	182,033	Brasília	7,600
Brunei	5.8	2.2	358	Bandar Seri Begawan	18,600
Bulgaria	111	42.8	7,538	Sofia	6,500
Burkina Faso	274	106	13,228	Ouagadougou	1,100
Burma (= Myanmar)	677	261	42,511	Rangoon	1,700
Burundi	27.8	10.7	6,096	Bujumbura	500
Cambodia	181	69.9	13,125	Phnom Penh	1,600
Cameroon	475	184	15,746	Yaoundé	1,700
Canada	9,971	3,850	32,207	Ottawa	29,300
Canary Is. (Spain)	7.2	2.8	1,682	Las Palmas/Santa Cruz	19,900
Cape Verde Is.	4.0	1.6	412	Praia	1,400
Cayman Is. (UK)	0.26	0.10	42	George Town	35,000
Central African Republic	623	241	3,684	Bangui	1,200
Chad	1,284	496	9,253	Ndjaména	1,000
Chile	757	292	15,665	Santiago	10,100
China	9,597	3,705	1,286,975	Beijing	4,700
Colombia	1,139	440	41,662	Bogotá	6,100
Comoros	2.2	0.86	633	Moroni	700
Congo	342	132	2,954	Brazzaville	900
Congo (Dem. Rep. of the)	2,345	905	56,625	Kinshasa	600
Cook Is. (NZ)	0.24	0.09	21	Avarua	5,000
Costa Rica	51.1	19.7	3,896	San José	8,300
Croatia	56.5	21.8	4,422	Zagreb	9,800
Cuba	111	42.8	11,263	Havana	2,700
Cyprus	9.3	3.6	772	Nicosia	13,200
Czech Republic	78.9	30.5	10,249	Prague	15,300
Denmark	43.1	16.6	5,384	Copenhagen	28,900
Djibouti	23.2	9.0	457	Djibouti	1,300
Dominica	0.75	0.29	70	Roseau	5,400
Dominican Republic	48.5	18.7	8,716	Santo Domingo	6,300
East Timor	14.9	5.7	998	Dili	500
Ecuador	284	109	13,710	Quito	3,200
Egypt	1,001	387	74,719	Cairo	4,000
El Salvador	21.0	8.1	6,470	San Salvador	4,600
Equatorial Guinea	28.1	10.8	510	Malabo	2,700
Eritrea	118	45.4	4,362	Asmara	700
Estonia	45.1	17.4	1,409	Tallinn	11,000
Ethiopia	1,104	426	66,558	Addis Ababa	700
Færoe Is. (Denmark)	1.4	0.54	46	Tórshavn	22,000
Fiji Islands	18.3	7.1	869	Suva	5,600
Finland	338	131	5,191	Helsinki	25,800
France	552	213	60,181	Paris	26,000
French Guiana (France)	90.0	34.7	187	Cayenne	14,400
French Polynesia (France)	4.0	1.5	262	Papeete	5,000
Gabon	268	103	1,322	Libreville	6,500
Gambia, The	11.3	4.4	1,501	Banjul	1,800
Gaza Strip (OPT)*	0.36	0.14	1,275	–	600
Georgia	69.7	26.9	4,934	Tbilisi	3,200
Germany	357	138	82,398	Berlin	26,200
Ghana	239	92.1	20,468	Accra	2,000
Gibraltar (UK)	0.006	0.002	28	Gibraltar Town	17,500
Greece	132	50.9	10,666	Athens	19,100
Greenland (Denmark)	2,176	840	56	Nuuk (Godthåb)	20,000
Grenada	0.34	0.13	89	St George's	5,000
Guadeloupe (France)	1.7	0.66	440	Basse-Terre	9,000
Guam (US)	0.55	0.21	164	Agana	21,000
Guatemala	109	42.0	13,909	Guatemala City	3,900
Guinea	246	94.9	9,030	Conakry	2,100
Guinea-Bissau	36.1	13.9	1,361	Bissau	700
Guyana	215	83.0	702	Georgetown	3,800
Haiti	27.8	10.7	7,528	Port-au-Prince	1,400
Honduras	112	43.3	6,670	Tegucigalpa	2,500
Hong Kong (China)	1.1	0.42	7,394	–	27,200
Hungary	93.0	35.9	10,045	Budapest	13,300
Iceland	103	39.8	281	Reykjavik	30,200
India	3,287	1,269	1,049,700	New Delhi	2,600
Indonesia	1,905	735	234,893	Jakarta	3,100
Iran	1,648	636	68,279	Tehran	6,800
Iraq	438	169	24,683	Baghdad	2,400
Ireland	70.3	27.1	3,924	Dublin	29,300
Israel	20.6	8.0	6,117	Jerusalem	19,500
Italy	301	116	57,998	Rome	25,100
Ivory Coast (= Côte d'Ivoire)	322	125	16,962	Yamoussoukro	1,400
Jamaica	11.0	4.2	2,696	Kingston	3,800
Japan	378	146	127,214	Tokyo	28,700
Jordan	89.3	34.5	5,460	Amman	4,300
Kazakhstan	2,725	1,052	16,764	Astana	7,200
Kenya	580	224	31,639	Nairobi	1,100
Kiribati	0.73	0.28	99	Tarawa	800
Korea, North	121	46.5	22,466	Pyŏngyang	1,000
Korea, South	99.3	38.3	48,289	Seoul	19,600
Kuwait	17.8	6.9	2,183	Kuwait City	17,500
Kyrgyzstan	200	77.2	4,893	Bishkek	2,900
Laos	237	91.4	5,922	Vientiane	1,800
Latvia	64.6	24.9	2,349	Riga	8,900
Lebanon	10.4	4.0	3,728	Beirut	4,800
Lesotho	30.4	11.7	1,862	Maseru	2,700
Liberia	111	43.0	3,317	Monrovia	1,000
Libya	1,760	679	5,499	Tripoli	6,200
Liechtenstein	0.16	0.06	33	Vaduz	25,000
Lithuania	65.2	25.2	3,593	Vilnius	8,400
Luxembourg	2.6	1.0	454	Luxembourg	48,900
Macau (China)	0.02	0.007	470	–	18,500
Macedonia (FYROM)	25.7	9.9	2,063	Skopje	5,100
Madagascar	587	227	16,980	Antananarivo	800
Madeira (Portugal)	0.78	0.30	241	Funchal	22,700
Malawi	118	45.7	11,651	Lilongwe	600
Malaysia	330	127	23,093	Kuala Lumpur/Putrajaya	8,800
Maldives	0.30	0.12	330	Malé	3,900
Mali	1,240	479	11,626	Bamako	900
Malta	0.32	0.12	400	Valletta	17,200
Marshall Is.	0.18	0.07	56	Majuro	1,600
Martinique (France)	1.1	0.43	426	Fort-de-France	10,700
Mauritania	1,026	396	2,913	Nouakchott	1,700
Mauritius	2.0	0.79	1,210	Port Louis	10,100
Mayotte (France)	0.37	0.14	178	Mamoundzou	600
Mexico	1,958	756	104,908	Mexico City	8,900
Micronesia, Fed. States of	0.70	0.27	108	Palikir	2,000
Moldova	33.9	13.1	4,440	Chişinău	2,600
Monaco	0.001	0.0004	32	Monaco	27,000
Mongolia	1,567	605	2,712	Ulan Bator	1,900
Montserrat (UK)	0.10	0.04	9	Plymouth	3,400
Morocco	447	172	31,689	Rabat	3,900
Mozambique	802	309	17,479	Maputo	1,100
Namibia	824	318	1,927	Windhoek	6,900
Nauru	0.02	0.008	13	Yaren District	5,000
Nepal	147	56.8	26,470	Katmandu	1,400
Netherlands	41.5	16.0	16,151	Amsterdam/The Hague	27,200
Netherlands Antilles (Neths)	0.80	0.31	216	Willemstad	11,400
New Caledonia (France)	18.6	7.2	211	Nouméa	14,000
New Zealand	271	104	3,951	Wellington	20,100
Nicaragua	130	50.2	5,129	Managua	2,200
Niger	1,267	489	11,059	Niamey	800
Nigeria	924	357	133,882	Abuja	900
Northern Mariana Is. (US)	0.46	0.18	80	Saipan	12,500
Norway	324	125	4,546	Oslo	33,000
Oman	310	119	2,807	Muscat	8,300
Pakistan	796	307	150,695	Islamabad	2,000
Palau	0.46	0.18	20	Koror	9,000
Panama	75.5	29.2	2,961	Panamá	6,200
Papua New Guinea	463	179	5,296	Port Moresby	2,100
Paraguay	407	157	6,037	Asunción	4,300
Peru	1,285	496	28,410	Lima	5,000
Philippines	300	116	84,620	Manila	4,600
Poland	323	125	38,623	Warsaw	9,700
Portugal	88.8	34.3	10,102	Lisbon	19,400
Puerto Rico (US)	8.9	3.4	3,886	San Juan	11,100
Qatar	11.0	4.2	817	Doha	20,100
Réunion (France)	2.5	0.97	755	St-Denis	5,600
Romania	238	92.0	22,272	Bucharest	7,600
Russia	17,075	6,593	144,526	Moscow	9,700
Rwanda	26.3	10.2	7,810	Kigali	1,200
St Kitts & Nevis	0.26	0.10	39	Basseterre	8,800
St Lucia	0.54	0.21	162	Castries	5,400
St Vincent & Grenadines	0.39	0.15	117	Kingstown	2,900
Samoa	2.8	1.1	178	Apia	5,600
San Marino	0.06	0.02	28	San Marino	34,600
São Tomé & Príncipe	0.96	0.37	176	São Tomé	1,200
Saudi Arabia	2,150	830	24,294	Riyadh	11,400
Senegal	197	76.0	10,580	Dakar	1,500
Serbia & Montenegro	102	39.4	10,656	Belgrade	2,200
Seychelles	0.46	0.18	80	Victoria	7,800
Sierra Leone	71.7	27.7	5,733	Freetown	500
Singapore	0.68	0.26	4,609	Singapore	25,200
Slovak Republic	49.0	18.9	5,430	Bratislava	12,400
Slovenia	20.3	7.8	1,936	Ljubljana	19,200
Solomon Is.	28.9	11.2	509	Honiara	1,700
Somalia	638	246	8,025	Mogadishu	600
South Africa	1,221	471	42,769	C. Town/Pretoria/Bloem.	10,000
Spain	498	192	40,217	Madrid	21,200
Sri Lanka	65.6	25.3	19,742	Colombo	3,700
Sudan	2,506	967	38,114	Khartoum	1,400
Suriname	163	63.0	435	Paramaribo	3,400
Swaziland	17.4	6.7	1,161	Mbabane	4,800
Sweden	450	174	8,878	Stockholm	26,000
Switzerland	41.3	15.9	7,319	Bern	32,000
Syria	185	71.5	17,586	Damascus	3,700
Taiwan	36.0	13.9	22,603	Taipei	18,000
Tajikistan	143	55.3	6,864	Dushanbe	1,300
Tanzania	945	365	35,922	Dodoma	600
Thailand	513	198	64,265	Bangkok	7,000
Togo	56.8	21.9	5,429	Lomé	1,400
Tonga	0.65	0.25	108	Nuku'alofa	2,200
Trinidad & Tobago	5.1	2.0	1,104	Port of Spain	10,000
Tunisia	164	63.2	9,925	Tunis	6,800
Turkey	775	299	68,109	Ankara	7,300
Turkmenistan	488	188	4,776	Ashkhabad	6,700
Turks & Caicos Is. (UK)	0.43	0.17	19	Cockburn Town	9,600
Tuvalu	0.03	0.01	11	Fongafale	1,100
Uganda	241	93.1	25,633	Kampala	1,200
Ukraine	604	233	48,055	Kiev	4,500
United Arab Emirates	83.6	32.3	2,485	Abu Dhabi	22,100
United Kingdom	242	93.4	60,095	London	25,500
United States of America	9,629	3,718	290,343	Washington, DC	36,300
Uruguay	175	67.6	3,413	Montevideo	7,900
Uzbekistan	447	173	25,982	Tashkent	2,600
Vanuatu	12.2	4.7	199	Port-Vila	2,900
Vatican City	0.0004	0.0002	1	Vatican City	N/A
Venezuela	912	352	24,655	Caracas	5,400
Vietnam	332	128	81,625	Hanoi	2,300
Virgin Is. (UK)	0.15	0.06	22	Road Town	16,000
Virgin Is. (US)	0.35	0.13	125	Charlotte Amalie	19,000
Wallis & Futuna Is. (France)	0.20	0.08	16	Mata-Utu	2,000
West Bank (OPT)*	5.9	2.3	2,237	–	800
Western Sahara	266	103	262	El Aaiún	N/A
Yemen	528	204	19,350	Sana	800
Zambia	753	291	10,307	Lusaka	800
Zimbabwe	391	151	12,577	Harare	2,100

*OPT = Occupied Palestinian Territory N/A = Not available

† Gross Domestic Product per capita has been measured using the purchasing power parity method. This enables comparisons to be made between countries through their purchasing power (in US dollars), showing real price levels of goods and services rather than using currency exchange rates.

World Statistics: Cities

This list shows the principal cities with more than 750,000 inhabitants. The figures are taken from the most recent census or estimate available, usually 2000, and as far as possible are the population of the metropolitan area or urban agglomeration (for example, greater New York, Mexico or Paris). All the figures are in thousands. Local name forms have been used for the smaller cities (for example, Thessaloniki).

AFGHANISTAN	
Kabul	2,602
ALGERIA	
Algiers	1,722
ANGOLA	
Luanda	2,697
ARGENTINA	
Buenos Aires	12,024
Córdoba	1,368
Rosario	1,279
Mendoza	934
San Miguel de Tucumán	792
ARMENIA	
Yerevan	1,407
AUSTRALIA	
Sydney	4,086
Melbourne	3,466
Brisbane	1,627
Perth	1,381
Adelaide	1,096
AUSTRIA	
Vienna	1,807
AZERBAIJAN	
Baku	1,792
BANGLADESH	
Dhaka	12,519
Chittagong	3,651
Khulna	1,442
Rajshahi	1,035
BELARUS	
Minsk	1,717
BELGIUM	
Brussels	964
BOLIVIA	
La Paz	1,487
Santa Cruz	1,035
Cochabamba	797
BRAZIL	
São Paulo	17,962
Rio de Janeiro	10,652
Belo Horizonte	4,224
Pôrto Alegre	3,757
Recife	3,346
Salvador	3,238
Fortaleza	3,066
Curitiba	2,562
Brasília	2,051
Campinas	1,434
Belém	1,658
Manaus	1,467
Santos	1,270
Goiânia	1,117
São José dos Campos	972
São Luís	968
Maceió	886
Teresina	848
Campo Grande	821
Natal	806
BULGARIA	
Sofia	1,187
BURKINA FASO	
Ouagadougou	831
BURMA (MYANMAR)	
Rangoon	4,393
Mandalay	770
CAMBODIA	
Phnom Penh	1,070
CAMEROON	
Douala	1,642
Yaoundé	1,420
CANADA	
Toronto	4,881
Montréal	3,511
Vancouver	2,079
Ottawa	1,107
Calgary	972
Edmonton	957
CHILE	
Santiago	5,467
CHINA	
Shanghai	12,887
Beijing	10,839
Tianjin	9,156
Hong Kong	6,860
Wuhan	5,169
Chongqing	4,900
Shenyang	4,828
Guangzhou	3,893
Chengdu	3,294
Xi'an	3,123
Changchun	3,093
Harbin	2,928
Nanjing	2,740
Zibo	2,675
Dalian	2,628
Jinan	2,568
Guiyang	2,533
Linyi	2,498
Taiyuan	2,415
Qingdao	2,316
Zhengzhou	2,070
Zaozhuang	2,048
Liupanshui	2,023
Handan	1,996
Jinxi	1,821
Lu'an	1,818
Hangzhou	1,780
Tianmen	1,779
Changsha	1,775
Wanxian	1,759
Lanzhou	1,730
Nanchang	1,722
Kunming	1,701
Yantai	1,681
Tangshan	1,671
Xuzhou	1,636
Xiantao	1,614
Shijiazhuang	1,603
Heze	1,600
Yancheng	1,562
Yulin	1,558
Xinghua	1,556
Tai'an	1,503
Pingxiang	1,502
Anshan	1,453
Luoyang	1,451
Jilin	1,435
Qiqihar	1,435
Suining (Sichuan)	1,428
Ürümqi	1,415
Fushun	1,413
Fuzhou	1,397
Neijiang	1,393
Changde	1,374
Zhanjiang	1,368
Huainan	1,354
Yiyang	1,343
Xintai	1,325
Baotou	1,319
Dongguan	1,319
Nanning	1,311
Weifang	1,287
Wenzhou	1,269
Hefei	1,242
Huaian	1,232
Yueyang	1,213
Suqian	1,189
Tianshui	1,187
Suzhou	1,183
Shantou	1,176
Ningbo	1,173
Yuzhou	1,173
Datong	1,165
Jingmen	1,153
Leshan	1,137
Shenzhen	1,131
Wuxi	1,127
Xiaoshan	1,124
Zaoyang	1,121
Yixing	1,108
Yongzhou	1,097
Chifeng	1,087
Huzhou	1,077
Daqing	1,076
Zigong	1,072
Mianyang	1,065
Nanchong	1,055
Fuyu	1,025
Jining (Shandong)	1,019
Hohhot	978
Xinyi (Guangdong)	973
Benxi	957
Jixi	949
Liuzhou	928
Xiangxiang	908
Yichun (Heilongjiang)	904
Xianyang	896
Linqing	891
Changzhou	886
Zhangjiagang	886
Zhangjiakou	880
Jiamusi	874
Yichun (Jiangxi)	871
Zhaotong	851
Yuyao	848
Jinzhou	834
Xuanzhou	823
Huaibei	814
Xinyu	808
Mudanjiang	801
Hengyang	799
Jiaxing	791
Anshun	789
Fuxin	785
Tongliao	785
Hunjiang	772
Kaifeng	769
COLOMBIA	
Bogotá	6,771
Medellín	2,866
Cali	2,233
Barranquilla	1,683
Bucaramanga	937
Cartagena	845
Cúcuta	772
CONGO	
Brazzaville	1,306
CONGO (DEM. REP.)	
Kinshasa	5,054
Lubumbashi	965
Mbuji-Mayi	806
COSTA RICA	
San José	961
CROATIA	
Zagreb	1,067
CUBA	
Havana	2,256
CZECH REPUBLIC	
Prague	1,203
DENMARK	
Copenhagen	1,332
DOMINICAN REPUBLIC	
Santo Domingo	2,563
Santiago de los Caballeros	804
ECUADOR	
Guayaquil	2,118
Quito	1,616
EGYPT	
Cairo	9,462
Alexandria	3,506
Shubrâ el Kheima	937
EL SALVADOR	
San Salvador	1,341
ETHIOPIA	
Addis Ababa	2,645
FINLAND	
Helsinki	937
FRANCE	
Paris	9,630
Lyons	1,353
Marseilles	1,290
Lille	991
Nice	889
Toulouse	761
Bordeaux	754
GEORGIA	
Tbilisi	1,406
GERMANY	
Berlin	3,387
Hamburg	1,705
Munich	1,195
Cologne	963
GHANA	
Accra	1,868
GREECE	
Athens	3,116
Thessaloniki	789
GUATEMALA	
Guatemala	3,242
GUINEA	
Conakry	1,232
HAITI	
Port-au-Prince	1,769
HONDURAS	
Tegucigalpa	949
HUNGARY	
Budapest	1,819
INDIA	
Mumbai (Bombay)	16,086
Kolkata (Calcutta)	13,058
Delhi	12,441
Chennai (Madras)	6,353
Bangalore	5,567
Hyderabad	5,445
Ahmedabad	4,427
Pune (Poona)	3,655
Surat	2,699
Kanpur	2,641
Jaipur	2,259
Lucknow	2,221
Nagpur	2,089
Patna	1,658
Indore	1,597
Vadodara	1,465
Bhopal	1,425
Coimbatore	1,420
Ludhiana	1,368
Cochin (Kochi)	1,340
Visakhapatnam	1,309
Agra	1,293
Varanasi	1,199
Madurai	1,187
Meerut	1,143
Nashik	1,117
Jabalpur	1,100
Jamshedpur	1,081
Asansol	1,065
Bhilainagar-Durg	1,049
Dhanbad	1,046
Allahabad	1,035
Faridabad	1,018
Vijayawada	999
Rajkot	974
Amritsar	955
Srinagar	954
Ghaziabad	928
Trivandrum	885
Calicut (Kozhikode)	875
Aurangabad	868
Gwalior	855
Solapur	853
Ranchi	844
Tiruchchirapalli	837
Jodhpur	833
Guwahati	797
Chandigarh	791
Hubli-Dharwad	776
Mysore	776
INDONESIA	
Jakarta	11,018
Bandung	3,409
Surabaya	2,461
Medan	1,879
Palembang	1,422
Ujung Pandang	1,051
Bandar Lampung	915
Malang	787
Semarang	787
Tegal	762
Bogor	761
IRAN	
Tehran	6,979
Mashhad	1,990
Esfahan	1,381
Tabriz	1,274
Karaj	1,200
Shiraz	1,124
Qom	888
Ahvaz	871
Bakhtaran	771
IRAQ	
Baghdad	4,865
Basra	1,338
Mosul	1,131
Irbil	840
IRELAND	
Dublin	985
ISRAEL	
Tel Aviv-Yafo	2,001
ITALY	
Rome	2,649
Milan	1,183
Naples	993
Turin	857
IVORY COAST	
Abidjan	3,790
JAPAN	
Tokyo	12,064
Yokohama	6,427
Osaka	2,599
Nagoya	2,172
Sapporo	1,922
Kobe	1,493
Kyoto	1,468
Fukuoka	1,341
Kawasaki	1,250
Hiroshima	1,126
Kitakyushu	1,011
Sendai	1,008
Chiba	887
Sakai	792
JORDAN	
Amman	1,148
KAZAKHSTAN	
Almaty	1,130
KENYA	
Nairobi	2,233
KOREA, NORTH	
Pyŏngyang	3,124
Hamhung	821
KOREA, SOUTH	
Seoul	9,888
Pusan	3,830
Inch'on	2,884
Taegu	2,675
Taejŏn	1,522
Kwangju	1,379
Sŏngnam	1,353
Ulsan	1,340
Ansan	984
Puch'on	900
Suwŏn	876
P'ohang	790
KUWAIT	
Kuwait	879
LATVIA	
Riga	811
LEBANON	
Beirut	2,070
LIBYA	
Tripoli	1,733
Benghazi	829
MADAGASCAR	
Antananarivo	1,603
MALAYSIA	
Kuala Lumpur	1,379
MALI	
Bamako	1,114
MEXICO	
Mexico City	18,066
Guadalajara	3,697
Monterrey	3,267
Puebla	1,888
Toluca	1,455
Tijuana	1,297
León	1,293
Ciudad Juárez	1,239
Torreón	1,012
San Luis Potosí	857
Mérida	849
Querétaro	798
Mexicali	771
Culiacán	750
MONGOLIA	
Ulan Bator	764
MOROCCO	
Casablanca	3,357
Rabat	1,616
Fès	907
Marrakesh	822
MOZAMBIQUE	
Maputo	1,094
NEPAL	
Katmandu	1,176
NETHERLANDS	
Amsterdam	1,105
Rotterdam	1,078
NEW ZEALAND	
Auckland	1,102
NICARAGUA	
Managua	1,009
NIGER	
Niamey	775
NIGERIA	
Lagos	8,665
Ibadan	1,549
Ogbomosho	809
NORWAY	
Oslo	779
PAKISTAN	
Karachi	10,032
Lahore	5,452
Faisalabad	2,142
Rawalpindi	1,521
Gujranwala	1,325
Multan	1,263
Hyderabad	1,221
Peshawar	1,066
Islamabad	791
PANAMA	
Panamá	1,173
PARAGUAY	
Asunción	1,262
PERU	
Lima	7,443
PHILIPPINES	
Manila	9,950
Davao	1,146
POLAND	
Warsaw	1,626
Lódz	815
PORTUGAL	
Lisbon	3,861
Porto	1,940
PUERTO RICO	
San Juan	2,217
ROMANIA	
Bucharest	2,001
RUSSIA	
Moscow	8,367
Saint Petersburg	4,635
Nizhniy Novgorod	1,332
Novosibirsk	1,321
Yekaterinburg	1,218
Omsk	1,174
Samara	1,132
Ufa	1,102
Kazan	1,063
Chelyabinsk	1,045
Perm	1,014
Rostov	1,012
Volgograd	1,000
Voronezh	918
Saratov	881
Ulyanovsk	864
Krasnoyarsk	840
Togliatti	771
SAUDI ARABIA	
Riyadh	3,180
Jedda	1,490
Mecca	770
SENEGAL	
Dakar	2,078
SERBIA AND MONTENEGRO	
Belgrade	1,673
SIERRA LEONE	
Freetown	822
SINGAPORE	
Singapore	4,131
SOMALIA	
Mogadishu	1,162
SOUTH AFRICA	
Johannesburg	2,950
Cape Town	2,930
Durban	2,391
Pretoria	1,590
Port Elizabeth	1,006
SPAIN	
Madrid	3,017
Barcelona	1,527
SUDAN	
Khartoum	2,742
SWEDEN	
Stockholm	1,612
Gothenburg	778
SWITZERLAND	
Zürich	939
SYRIA	
Aleppo	2,229
Damascus	2,144
Homs	811
TAIWAN	
Taipei	2,550
Kaohsiung	1,463
T'aichung	950
TANZANIA	
Dar es Salaam	2,115
THAILAND	
Bangkok	7,372
TUNISIA	
Tunis	1,892
TURKEY	
Istanbul	8,953
Ankara	3,203
Izmir	2,250
Bursa	1,184
Adana	1,133
Gaziantep	862
Konya	761
UGANDA	
Kampala	1,213
UKRAINE	
Kiev	2,621
Kharkov	1,521
Dnepropetrovsk	1,122
Donetsk	1,065
Odessa	1,027
Zaporozhye	863
Lvov	794
UNITED ARAB EMIRATES	
Abu Dhabi	928
Dubai	886
UNITED KINGDOM	
London	8,089
Birmingham	2,373
Manchester	2,353
Liverpool	852
Glasgow	832
UNITED STATES OF AMERICA	
New York	17,800
Los Angeles	11,789
Chicago	8,308
Philadelphia	5,149
Miami	4,919
Dallas–Fort Worth	4,146
Boston	4,032
Washington	3,934
Detroit	3,903
Houston	3,823
Atlanta	3,500
San Francisco	3,229
Phoenix	2,907
Seattle	2,712
San Diego	2,674
Minneapolis–St Paul	2,389
St Louis	2,078
Baltimore	2,076
Tampa–St Petersburg	2,062
Denver	1,985
Cleveland	1,787
Pittsburgh	1,753
Portland	1,583
San Jose	1,538
San Bernardino	1,507
Cincinnati	1,503
Norfolk–Virginia Beach	1,394
Sacramento	1,393
Kansas City	1,362
San Antonio	1,328
Las Vegas	1,314
Milwaukee	1,309
Indianapolis	1,219
Providence	1,175
Orlando	1,157
Columbus	1,133
New Orleans	1,009
Buffalo	977
Memphis	972
Austin	902
Stamford	889
Salt Lake City	888
Jacksonville	882
Louisville	864
Hartford	852
Richmond	819
Charlotte	759
URUGUAY	
Montevideo	1,324
UZBEKISTAN	
Tashkent	2,148
VENEZUELA	
Caracas	3,153
Maracaibo	1,901
Valencia	1,893
Maracay	1,100
Ciudad Guayana	966
Barquisimeto	923
VIETNAM	
Ho Chi Minh City	4,619
Hanoi	3,751
Haiphong	1,676
YEMEN	
Sana'	1,327
ZAMBIA	
Lusaka	1,653
ZIMBABWE	
Harare	1,791
Bulawayo	824

WORLD STATISTICS: PHYSICAL DIMENSIONS

Each topic list is divided into continents and within a continent the items are listed in order of size. The bottom part of many of the lists is selective in order to give examples from as many different countries as possible. The order of the continents is the same as in the atlas, beginning with Europe and ending with South America. The figures are rounded as appropriate.

World, Continents, Oceans

	km^2	$miles^2$	%
The World	509,450,000	196,672,000	–
Land	149,450,000	57,688,000	29.3
Water	360,000,000	138,984,000	70.7
Asia	44,500,000	17,177,000	29.8
Africa	30,302,000	11,697,000	20.3
North America	24,241,000	9,357,000	16.2
South America	17,793,000	6,868,000	11.9
Antarctica	14,100,000	5,443,000	9.4
Europe	9,957,000	3,843,000	6.7
Australia & Oceania	8,557,000	3,303,000	5.7
Pacific Ocean	179,679,000	69,356,000	49.9
Atlantic Ocean	92,373,000	35,657,000	25.7
Indian Ocean	73,917,000	28,532,000	20.5
Arctic Ocean	14,090,000	5,439,000	3.9

Ocean Depths

Atlantic Ocean	m	ft
Puerto Rico (Milwaukee) Deep	9,220	30,249
Cayman Trench	7,680	25,197
Gulf of Mexico	5,203	17,070
Mediterranean Sea	5,121	16,801
Black Sea	2,211	7,254
North Sea	660	2,165

Indian Ocean	m	ft
Java Trench	7,450	24,442
Red Sea	2,635	8,454

Pacific Ocean	m	ft
Mariana Trench	11,022	36,161
Tonga Trench	10,882	35,702
Japan Trench	10,554	34,626
Kuril Trench	10,542	34,587

Arctic Ocean	m	ft
Molloy Deep	5,608	18,399

Mountains

Europe		m	ft
Elbrus	*Russia*	5,642	18,510
Mont Blanc	*France/Italy*	4,807	15,771
Monte Rosa	*Italy/Switzerland*	4,634	15,203
Dom	*Switzerland*	4,545	14,911
Liskamm	*Switzerland*	4,527	14,852
Weisshorn	*Switzerland*	4,505	14,780
Taschorn	*Switzerland*	4,490	14,730
Matterhorn/Cervino	*Italy/Switzerland*	4,478	14,691
Mont Maudit	*France/Italy*	4,465	14,649
Dent Blanche	*Switzerland*	4,356	14,291
Nadelhorn	*Switzerland*	4,327	14,196
Grandes Jorasses	*France/Italy*	4,208	13,806
Jungfrau	*Switzerland*	4,158	13,642
Grossglockner	*Austria*	3,797	12,457
Mulhacén	*Spain*	3,478	11,411
Zugspitze	*Germany*	2,962	9,718
Olympus	*Greece*	2,917	9,570
Triglav	*Slovenia*	2,863	9,393
Gerlachovka	*Slovak Republic*	2,655	8,711
Galdhöpiggen	*Norway*	2,468	8,100
Kebnekaise	*Sweden*	2,117	6,946
Ben Nevis	*UK*	1,343	4,406

Asia		m	ft
Everest	*China/Nepal*	8,850	29,035
K2 (Godwin Austen)	*China/Kashmir*	8,611	28,251
Kanchenjunga	*India/Nepal*	8,598	28,208
Lhotse	*China/Nepal*	8,516	27,939
Makalu	*China/Nepal*	8,481	27,824
Cho Oyu	*China/Nepal*	8,201	26,906
Dhaulagiri	*Nepal*	8,172	26,811
Manaslu	*Nepal*	8,156	26,758
Nanga Parbat	*Kashmir*	8,126	26,660
Annapurna	*Nepal*	8,078	26,502
Gasherbrum	*China/Kashmir*	8,068	26,469
Broad Peak	*China/Kashmir*	8,051	26,414
Xixabangma	*China*	8,012	26,286
Kangbachen	*India/Nepal*	7,902	25,925
Trivor	*Pakistan*	7,720	25,328
Pik Kommunizma	*Tajikistan*	7,495	24,590
Demavend	*Iran*	5,604	18,386
Ararat	*Turkey*	5,165	16,945
Gunong Kinabalu	*Malaysia (Borneo)*	4,101	13,455
Fuji-San	*Japan*	3,776	12,388

Africa		m	ft
Kilimanjaro	*Tanzania*	5,895	19,340
Mt Kenya	*Kenya*	5,199	17,057
Ruwenzori (Margherita)	*Ug./Congo (D.R.)*	5,109	16,762
Ras Dashan	*Ethiopia*	4,620	15,157
Meru	*Tanzania*	4,565	14,977
Karisimbi	*Rwanda/Congo (D.R.)*	4,507	14,787
Mt Elgon	*Kenya/Uganda*	4,321	14,176
Batu	*Ethiopia*	4,307	14,130
Toubkal	*Morocco*	4,165	13,665
Mt Cameroon	*Cameroon*	4,070	13,353

Oceania		m	ft
Puncak Jaya	*Indonesia*	5,029	16,499
Puncak Trikora	*Indonesia*	4,750	15,584
Puncak Mandala	*Indonesia*	4,702	15,427
Mt Wilhelm	*Papua New Guinea*	4,508	14,790
Mauna Kea	*USA (Hawaii)*	4,205	13,796
Mauna Loa	*USA (Hawaii)*	4,169	13,681
Aoraki Mt Cook	*New Zealand*	3,753	12,313
Mt Kosciuszko	*Australia*	2,230	7,316

North America		m	ft
Mt McKinley (Denali)	*USA (Alaska)*	6,194	20,321
Mt Logan	*Canada*	5,959	19,551
Pico de Orizaba	*Mexico*	5,610	18,405
Mt St Elias	*USA/Canada*	5,489	18,008
Popocatepetl	*Mexico*	5,452	17,887
Mt Foraker	*USA (Alaska)*	5,304	17,401
Ixtaccihuatl	*Mexico*	5,286	17,342
Lucania	*Canada*	5,227	17,149
Mt Steele	*Canada*	5,073	16,644
Mt Bona	*USA (Alaska)*	5,005	16,420
Mt Whitney	*USA*	4,418	14,495
Tajumulco	*Guatemala*	4,220	13,845
Chirripó Grande	*Costa Rica*	3,837	12,589
Pico Duarte	*Dominican Rep.*	3,175	10,417

South America		m	ft
Aconcagua	*Argentina*	6,962	22,841
Bonete	*Argentina*	6,872	22,546
Ojos del Salado	*Argentina/Chile*	6,863	22,516
Pissis	*Argentina*	6,779	22,241
Mercedario	*Argentina/Chile*	6,770	22,211
Huascaran	*Peru*	6,768	22,204
Llullaillaco	*Argentina/Chile*	6,723	22,057
Nudo de Cachi	*Argentina*	6,720	22,047
Yerupaja	*Peru*	6,632	21,758
Sajama	*Bolivia*	6,542	21,463
Chimborazo	*Ecuador*	6,267	20,561
Pico Colon	*Colombia*	5,800	19,029
Pico Bolivar	*Venezuela*	5,007	16,427

Antarctica		m	ft
Vinson Massif		4,897	16,066
Mt Kirkpatrick		4,528	14,855

Rivers

Europe		km	miles
Volga	*Caspian Sea*	3,700	2,300
Danube	*Black Sea*	2,850	1,770
Ural	*Caspian Sea*	2,535	1,575
Dnepr (Dnipro)	*Black Sea*	2,285	1,420
Kama	*Volga*	2,030	1,260
Don	*Black Sea*	1,990	1,240
Petchora	*Arctic Ocean*	1,790	1,110
Oka	*Volga*	1,480	920
Dnister (Dniester)	*Black Sea*	1,400	870
Vyatka	*Kama*	1,370	850
Rhine	*North Sea*	1,320	820
N. Dvina	*Arctic Ocean*	1,290	800
Elbe	*North Sea*	1,145	710

Asia		km	miles
Yangtze	*Pacific Ocean*	6,380	3,960
Yenisey–Angara	*Arctic Ocean*	5,550	3,445
Huang He	*Pacific Ocean*	5,464	3,395
Ob–Irtysh	*Arctic Ocean*	5,410	3,360
Mekong	*Pacific Ocean*	4,500	2,795
Amur	*Pacific Ocean*	4,400	2,730
Lena	*Arctic Ocean*	4,400	2,730
Irtysh	*Ob*	4,250	2,640
Yenisey	*Arctic Ocean*	4,090	2,540
Ob	*Arctic Ocean*	3,680	2,285
Indus	*Indian Ocean*	3,100	1,925
Brahmaputra	*Indian Ocean*	2,900	1,800
Syrdarya	*Aral Sea*	2,860	1,775
Salween	*Indian Ocean*	2,800	1,740
Euphrates	*Indian Ocean*	2,700	1,675
Amudarya	*Aral Sea*	2,540	1,575

Africa		km	miles
Nile	*Mediterranean*	6,670	4,140
Congo	*Atlantic Ocean*	4,670	2,900
Niger	*Atlantic Ocean*	4,180	2,595
Zambezi	*Indian Ocean*	3,540	2,200
Oubangi/Uele	*Congo (D.R.)*	2,250	1,400
Kasai	*Congo (D.R.)*	1,950	1,210
Shaballe	*Indian Ocean*	1,930	1,200
Orange	*Atlantic Ocean*	1,860	1,155
Cubango	*Okavango Delta*	1,800	1,120
Limpopo	*Indian Ocean*	1,600	995
Senegal	*Atlantic Ocean*	1,600	995

Australia		km	miles
Murray–Darling	*Southern Ocean*	3,750	2,330
Darling	*Murray*	3,070	1,905
Murray	*Southern Ocean*	2,575	1,600
Murrumbidgee	*Murray*	1,690	1,050

North America		km	miles
Mississippi–Missouri	*Gulf of Mexico*	6,020	3,740
Mackenzie	*Arctic Ocean*	4,240	2,630
Mississippi	*Gulf of Mexico*	3,780	2,350
Missouri	*Mississippi*	3,780	2,350
Yukon	*Pacific Ocean*	3,185	1,980
Rio Grande	*Gulf of Mexico*	3,030	1,880
Arkansas	*Mississippi*	2,340	1,450
Colorado	*Pacific Ocean*	2,330	1,445
Red	*Mississippi*	2,040	1,270
Columbia	*Pacific Ocean*	1,950	1,210
Saskatchewan	*Lake Winnipeg*	1,940	1,205

South America		km	miles
Amazon	*Atlantic Ocean*	6,450	4,010
Paraná–Plate	*Atlantic Ocean*	4,500	2,800
Purus	*Amazon*	3,350	2,080
Madeira	*Amazon*	3,200	1,990
São Francisco	*Atlantic Ocean*	2,900	1,800
Paraná	*Plate*	2,800	1,740
Tocantins	*Atlantic Ocean*	2,750	1,710
Paraguay	*Paraná*	2,550	1,580
Orinoco	*Atlantic Ocean*	2,500	1,550
Pilcomayo	*Paraná*	2,500	1,550
Araguaia	*Tocantins*	2,250	1,400

Lakes

Europe		km^2	$miles^2$
Lake Ladoga	*Russia*	17,700	6,800
Lake Onega	*Russia*	9,700	3,700
Saimaa system	*Finland*	8,000	3,100
Vänern	*Sweden*	5,500	2,100

Asia		km^2	$miles^2$
Caspian Sea	*Asia*	371,800	143,550
Lake Baykal	*Russia*	30,500	11,780
Aral Sea	*Kazakhstan/Uzbekistan*	28,687	11,086
Tonlé Sap	*Cambodia*	20,000	7,700
Lake Balqash	*Kazakhstan*	18,500	7,100

Africa		km^2	$miles^2$
Lake Victoria	*East Africa*	68,000	26,000
Lake Tanganyika	*Central Africa*	33,000	13,000
Lake Malawi/Nyasa	*East Africa*	29,600	11,430
Lake Chad	*Central Africa*	25,000	9,700
Lake Turkana	*Ethiopia/Kenya*	8,500	3,300
Lake Volta	*Ghana*	8,500	3,300

Australia		km^2	$miles^2$
Lake Eyre	*Australia*	8,900	3,400
Lake Torrens	*Australia*	5,800	2,200
Lake Gairdner	*Australia*	4,800	1,900

North America		km^2	$miles^2$
Lake Superior	*Canada/USA*	82,350	31,800
Lake Huron	*Canada/USA*	59,600	23,010
Lake Michigan	*USA*	58,000	22,400
Great Bear Lake	*Canada*	31,800	12,280
Great Slave Lake	*Canada*	28,500	11,000
Lake Erie	*Canada/USA*	25,700	9,900
Lake Winnipeg	*Canada*	24,400	9,400
Lake Ontario	*Canada/USA*	19,500	7,500
Lake Nicaragua	*Nicaragua*	8,200	3,200

South America		km^2	$miles^2$
Lake Titicaca	*Bolivia/Peru*	8,300	3,200
Lake Poopo	*Bolivia*	2,800	1,100

Islands

Europe		km^2	$miles^2$
Great Britain	*UK*	229,880	88,700
Iceland	*Atlantic Ocean*	103,000	39,800
Ireland	*Ireland/UK*	84,400	32,600
Novaya Zemlya (N.)	*Russia*	48,200	18,600
Sicily	*Italy*	25,500	9,800
Corsica	*France*	8,700	3,400

Asia		km^2	$miles^2$
Borneo	*South-east Asia*	744,360	287,400
Sumatra	*Indonesia*	473,600	182,860
Honshu	*Japan*	230,500	88,980
Sulawesi (Celebes)	*Indonesia*	189,000	73,000
Java	*Indonesia*	126,700	48,900
Luzon	*Philippines*	104,700	40,400
Hokkaido	*Japan*	78,400	30,300

Africa		km^2	$miles^2$
Madagascar	*Indian Ocean*	587,040	226,660
Socotra	*Indian Ocean*	3,600	1,400
Réunion	*Indian Ocean*	2,500	965

Oceania		km^2	$miles^2$
New Guinea	*Indonesia/Papua NG*	821,030	317,000
New Zealand (S.)	*Pacific Ocean*	150,500	58,100
New Zealand (N.)	*Pacific Ocean*	114,700	44,300
Tasmania	*Australia*	67,800	26,200
Hawaii	*Pacific Ocean*	10,450	4,000

North America		km^2	$miles^2$
Greenland	*Atlantic Ocean*	2,175,600	839,800
Baffin Is.	*Canada*	508,000	196,100
Victoria Is.	*Canada*	212,200	81,900
Ellesmere Is.	*Canada*	212,000	81,800
Cuba	*Caribbean Sea*	110,860	42,800
Hispaniola	*Dominican Rep./Haiti*	76,200	29,400
Jamaica	*Caribbean Sea*	11,400	4,400
Puerto Rico	*Atlantic Ocean*	8,900	3,400

South America		km^2	$miles^2$
Tierra del Fuego	*Argentina/Chile*	47,000	18,100
Falkland Is. (E.)	*Atlantic Ocean*	6,800	2,600

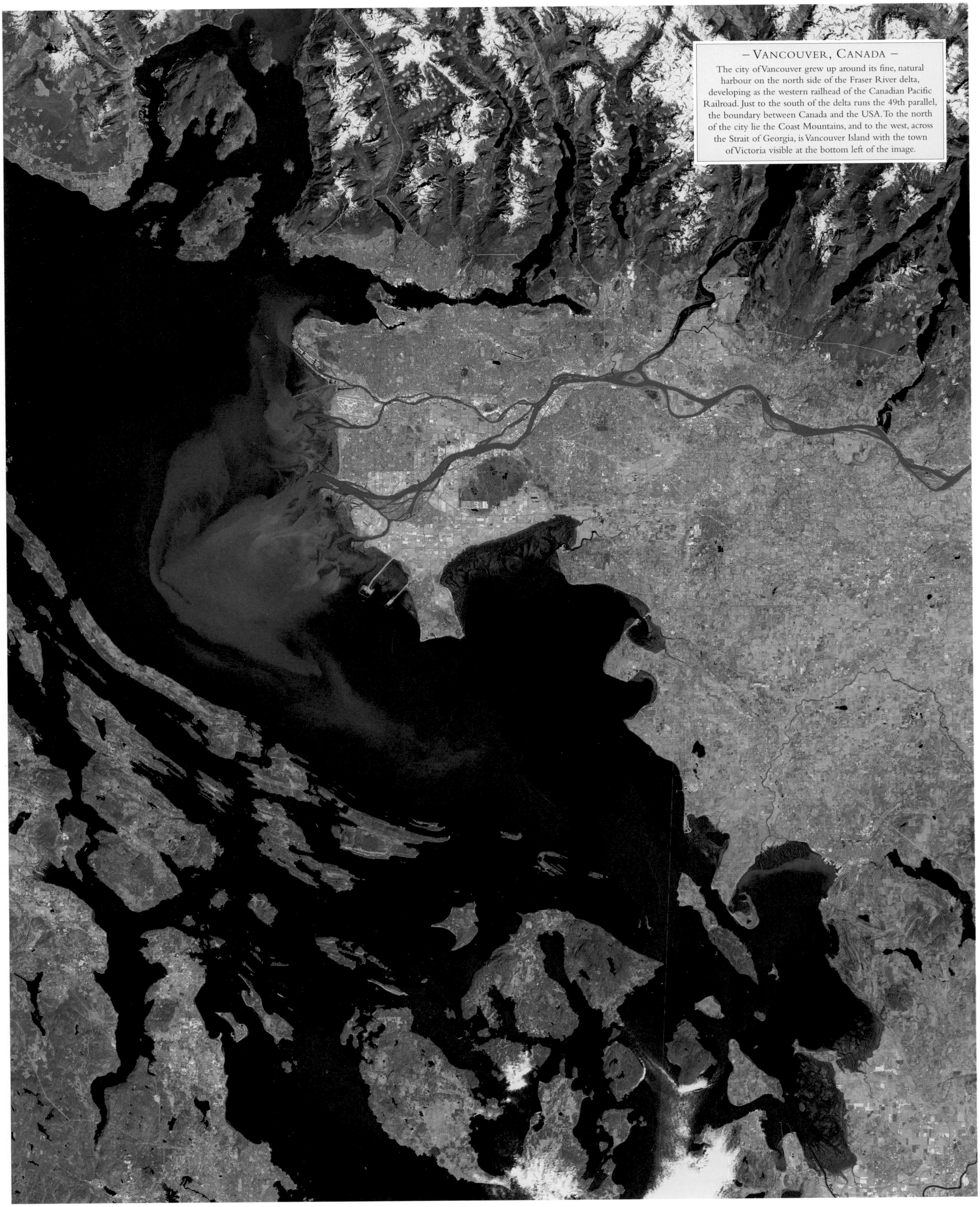

– VANCOUVER, CANADA –

The city of Vancouver grew up around its fine, natural harbour on the north side of the Fraser River delta, developing as the western railhead of the Canadian Pacific Railroad. Just to the south of the delta runs the 49th parallel, the boundary between Canada and the USA. To the north of the city lie the Coast Mountains, and to the west, across the Strait of Georgia, is Vancouver Island with the town of Victoria visible at the bottom left of the image.

– Los Angeles, USA –

The sprawling urban area of Greater LA covers most of the area to the south of the San Gabriel Mountains, which run across the top of the image. The population of the whole area is over 14 million people. Jutting into the left-hand side of the image, just below centre, the darker colours of the eastern end of the Santa Monica range can be seen; the centre of the city proper is just to the south-east of the end of the range. On its southern slopes lie Beverly Hills and Hollywood, with the San Fernando Valley to the north.

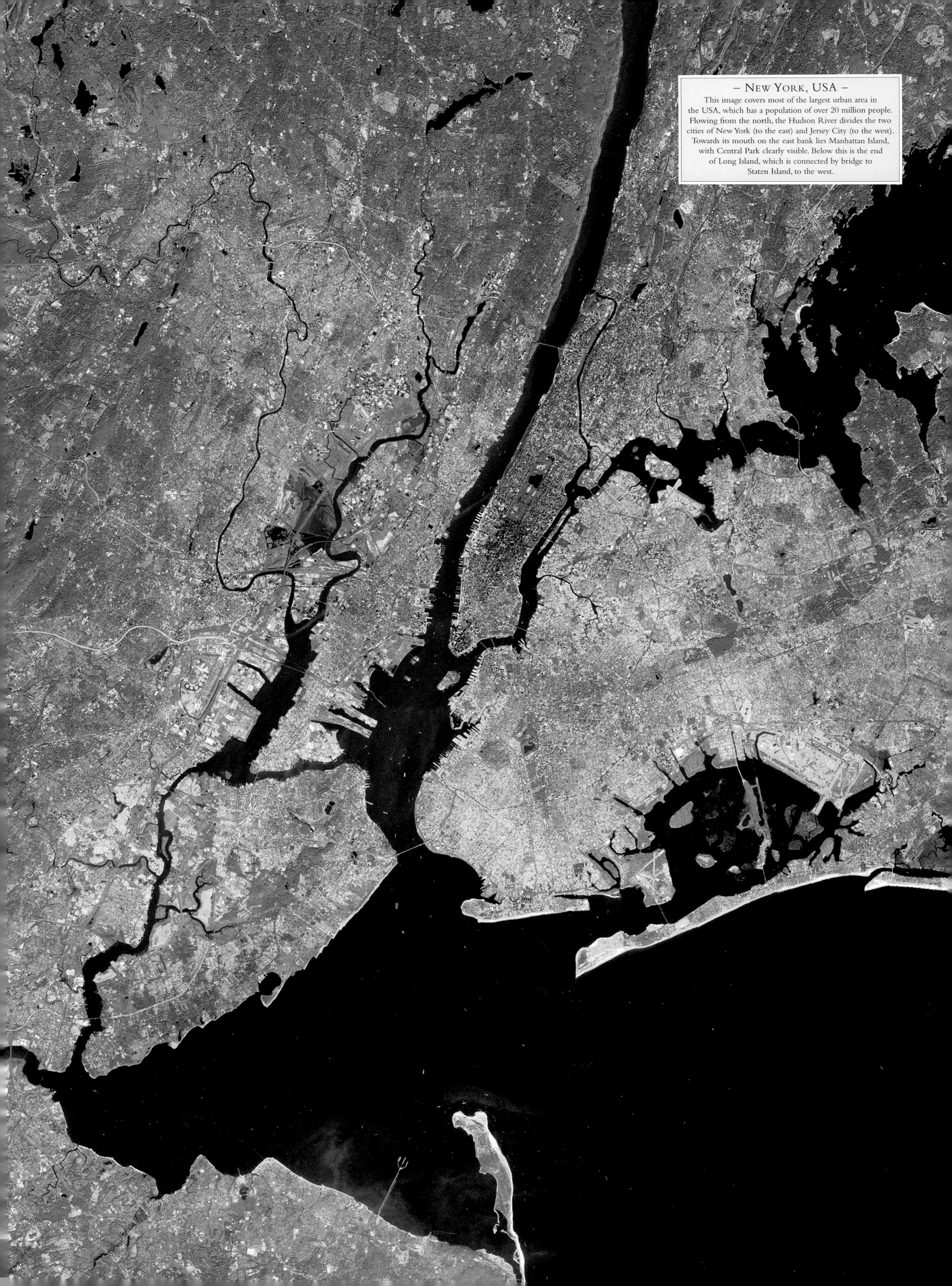

– New York, USA –

This image covers most of the largest urban area in the USA, which has a population of over 20 million people. Flowing from the north, the Hudson River divides the two cities of New York (to the east) and Jersey City (to the west). Towards its mouth on the east bank lies Manhattan Island, with Central Park clearly visible. Below this is the end of Long Island, which is connected by bridge to Staten Island, to the west.

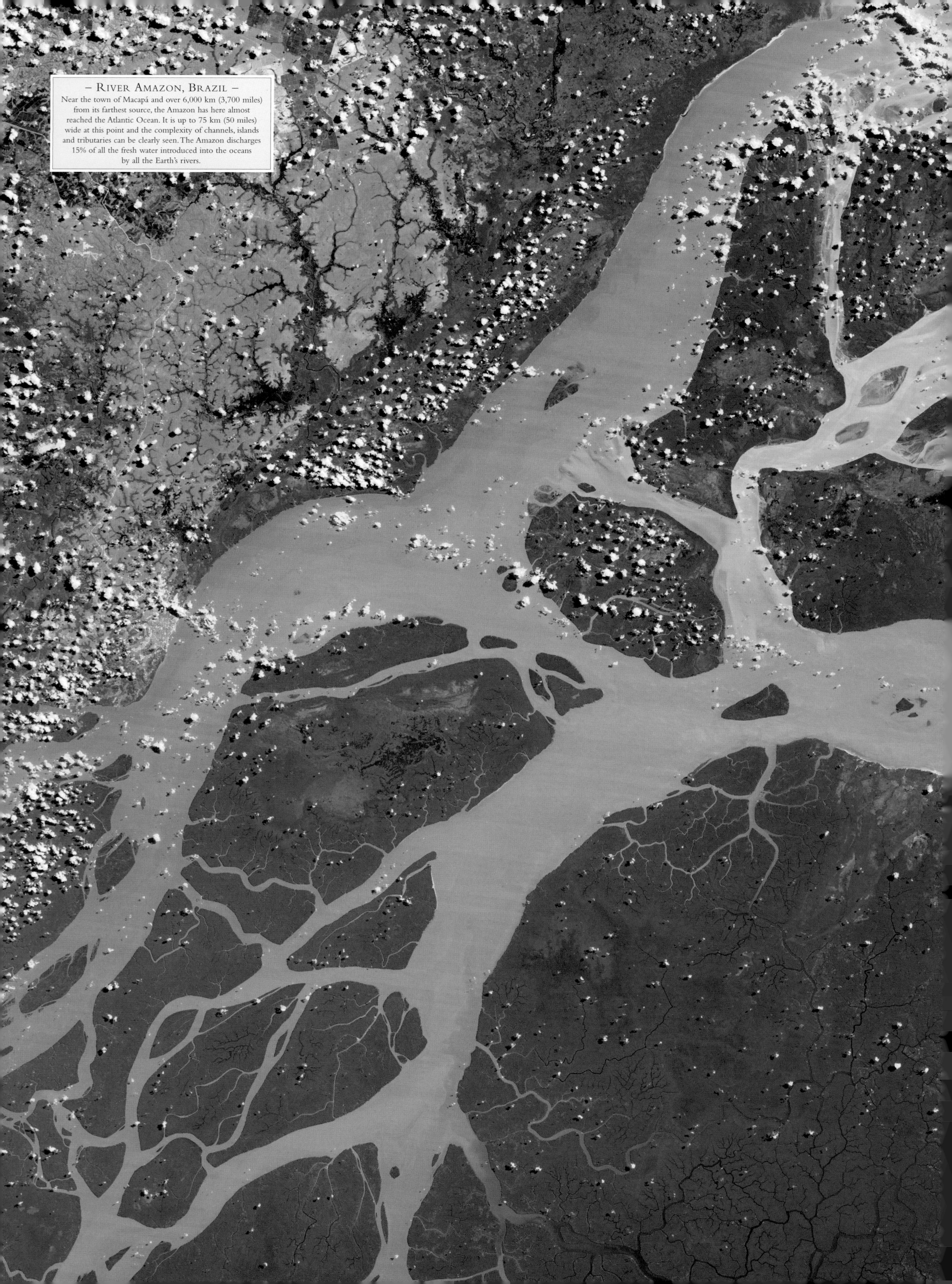

– River Amazon, Brazil –

Near the town of Macapá and over 6,000 km (3,700 miles) from its farthest source, the Amazon has here almost reached the Atlantic Ocean. It is up to 75 km (50 miles) wide at this point and the complexity of channels, islands and tributaries can be clearly seen. The Amazon discharges 15% of all the fresh water introduced into the oceans by all the Earth's rivers.

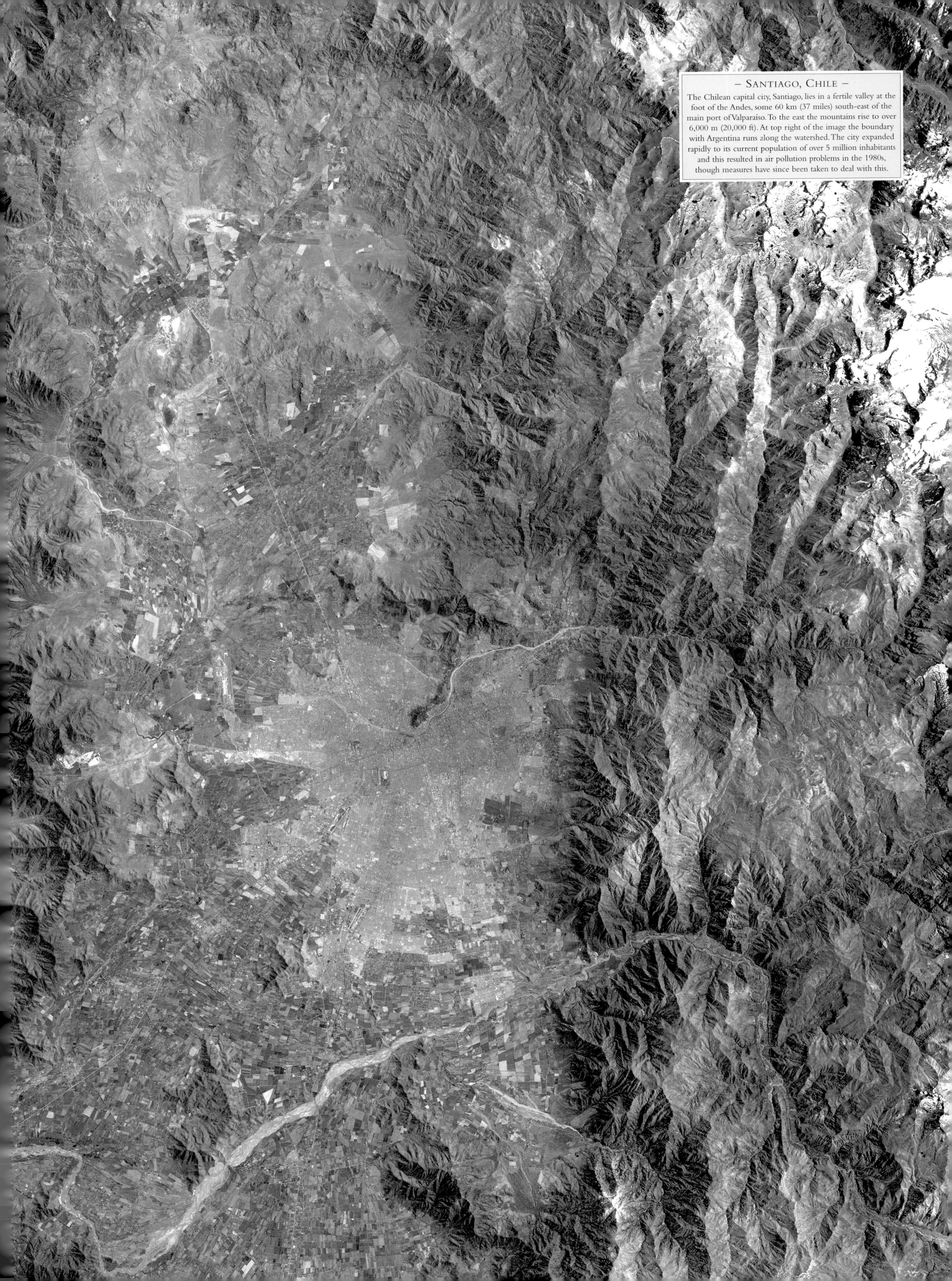

– Santiago, Chile –

The Chilean capital city, Santiago, lies in a fertile valley at the foot of the Andes, some 60 km (37 miles) south-east of the main port of Valparaíso. To the east the mountains rise to over 6,000 m (20,000 ft). At top right of the image the boundary with Argentina runs along the watershed. The city expanded rapidly to its current population of over 5 million inhabitants and this resulted in air pollution problems in the 1980s, though measures have since been taken to deal with this.

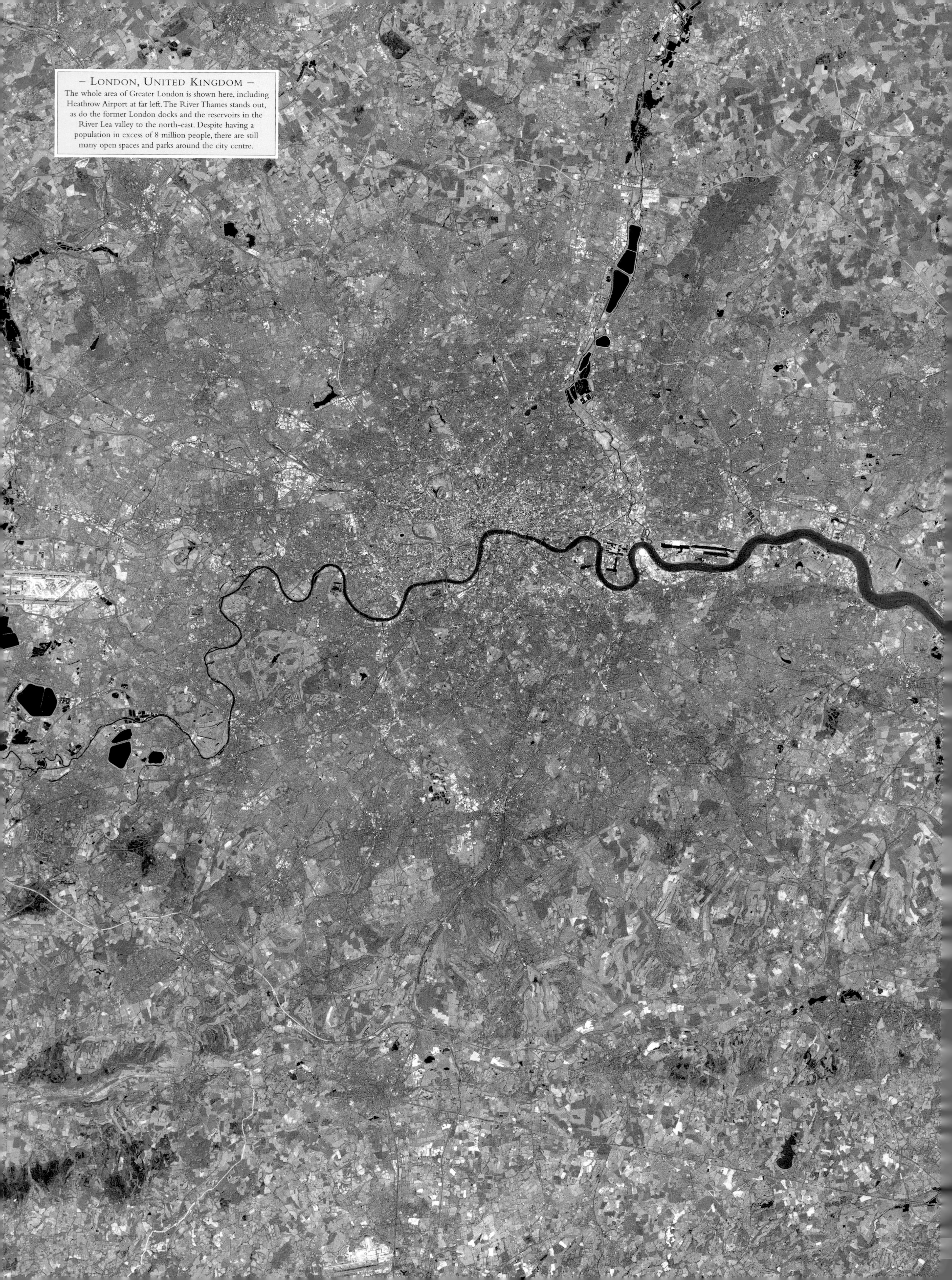

– London, United Kingdom –

The whole area of Greater London is shown here, including Heathrow Airport at far left. The River Thames stands out, as do the former London docks and the reservoirs in the River Lea valley to the north-east. Despite having a population in excess of 8 million people, there are still many open spaces and parks around the city centre.

– IJSSELMEER, NETHERLANDS –

This unique feature was created in the 13th century when the sea breached a protective sand bar, flooding all the low-lying land. The remnants of the bar can still be seen as the chain of Frisian Islands at the top of the image. Reclamation on a large scale started in 1932 with the completion of the causeway in the north. Since then four 'polders' have been drained and reclaimed. The city of Amsterdam is situated at bottom left.

– NAPLES, ITALY –

The city, situated in the north-eastern corner of the Bay of Naples, has a population in excess of 1 million inhabitants. The cone of the active volcano Vesuvius, 1,281 m (4,200 ft) high, dominates the bay. Evidence of other volcanic activity can also be seen to the west of the town in the area known as the Phlegraean Fields. Pompei, once buried by its lava, lies near the mountains to the south-east. On the southern peninsula is the town of Sorrento, and beyond, the island of Capri.

– Strait of Gibraltar –

The strait separates the Mediterranean Sea (to the right) from the Atlantic Ocean, and the continent of Europe (above) from Africa. At its narrowest eastern end, shown in the image, the strait is only 13 km (8 miles) wide. On the Spanish side, the deep inlet of Algeciras Bay stands out, with the British naval base at Gibraltar on the tip of its eastern peninsula, beneath the Rock. The Moroccan port of Tangier is at the bottom left of the image.

– Cairo, Egypt –

The largest city in Africa with almost 10 million inhabitants, Cairo evolved on the eastern bank of the River Nile, near its delta. This image clearly shows the differences between the arid desert areas to the south-east and south-west, the fertile lands of the Nile flood plain, and the urban area itself. The shadows of the Pyramids on the Giza Plateau can be seen on the left-hand edge of the cultivated area, below where the road crosses it.

– Western Cape, South Africa –

Cape Town sits to the bottom left of this image, with the Cape Peninsula running south-east to the Cape of Good Hope. Inland from the fertile coastal plain, where most of South Africa's wine is produced, is the rugged interior of the Great Karoo where parallel mountain ranges are dissected by river valleys.

– Tehran, Iran –

On the sheltered southern slopes of the Elburz (Alborz) Mountains, the street layout of Tehran, the capital city of Iran, can be clearly seen towards the bottom left-hand side of this image. However, it is the dissected parallel ridges of the mountains and the spectacular snow-covered peak of Demavend which dominate this scene. At 5,604 m (18,386 ft), the peak is the highest in the Middle East and is an extinct volcanic cone with no recorded historic eruptions, although there are still active hot springs on its slopes.

– KARACHI, PAKISTAN –

The largest city in Pakistan with over 10 million inhabitants, Karachi is the administrative headquarters of Sind province and is also the commercial and industrial capital of the whole country. To its south lie the mangrove swamps of the vast delta of the River Indus, 210 km (130 miles) wide where it flows into the Arabian Sea. To the north and east of the city are the dry, hot Sind plains, which are subject to a mean annual rainfall of only 125–250 mm (5–10 inches).

– TOKYO, JAPAN –

At the head of Tokyo Bay, the city, with its satellites of Kawasaki and Yokohama, forms one of the world's most densely populated areas with over 20 million people. Owing to the shortage of space, much development has taken place on areas reclaimed from the sea. One of these is Haneda International Airport, whose runway pattern is clearly visible at the mouth of the Tama River. The Tokyo Bay bridge/tunnel projects into the Bay from the eastern shore.

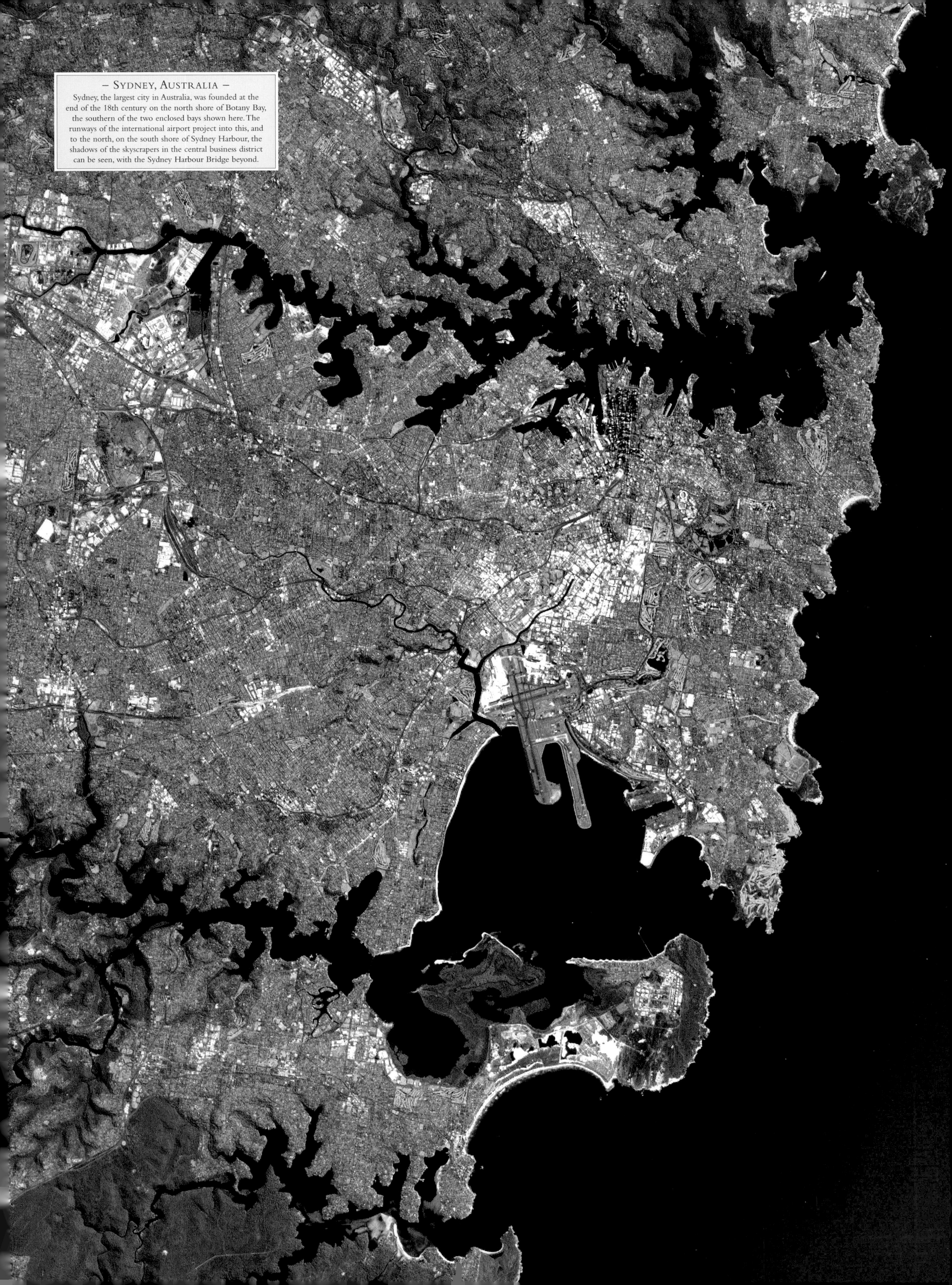

– Sydney, Australia –

Sydney, the largest city in Australia, was founded at the end of the 18th century on the north shore of Botany Bay, the southern of the two enclosed bays shown here. The runways of the international airport project into this, and to the north, on the south shore of Sydney Harbour, the shadows of the skyscrapers in the central business district can be seen, with the Sydney Harbour Bridge beyond.

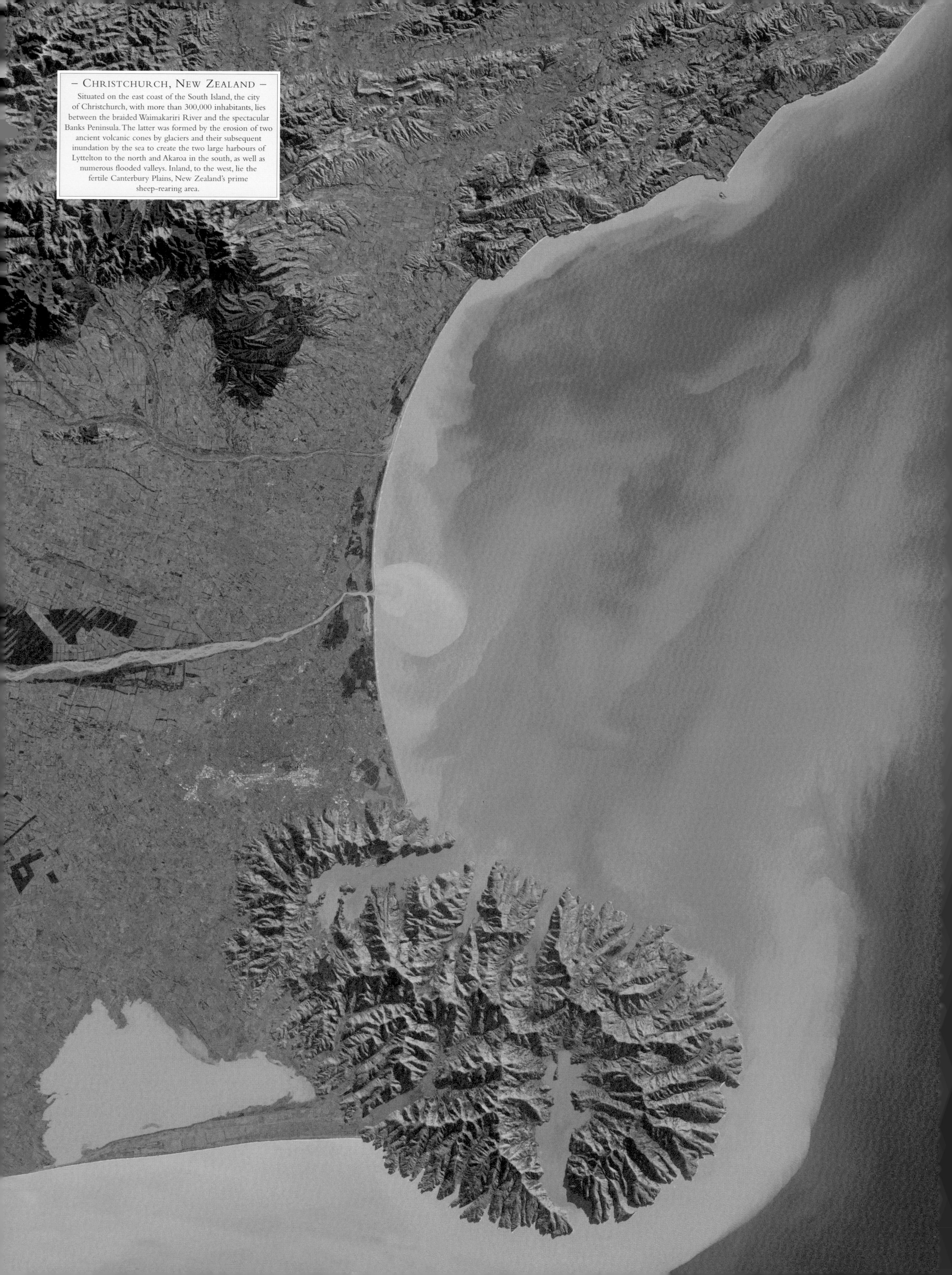

– Christchurch, New Zealand –

Situated on the east coast of the South Island, the city of Christchurch, with more than 300,000 inhabitants, lies between the braided Waimakariri River and the spectacular Banks Peninsula. The latter was formed by the erosion of two ancient volcanic cones by glaciers and their subsequent inundation by the sea to create the two large harbours of Lyttelton to the north and Akaroa in the south, as well as numerous flooded valleys. Inland, to the west, lie the fertile Canterbury Plains, New Zealand's prime sheep-rearing area.

THE GAZETTEER OF NATIONS

AFGHANISTAN

GEOGRAPHY The Republic of Afghanistan is a landlocked, mountainous country in southern Asia. The central highlands reach a height of more than 7,000 m [22,966 ft] in the east and make up nearly three-quarters of Afghanistan. The main range is the Hindu Kush, which is cut by deep, fertile valleys.

In winter, northerly winds bring cold, snowy weather to the mountains, but summers are hot and dry.

POLITICS & ECONOMY The modern history of Afghanistan began in 1747, when the various tribes in the area united for the first time. In the 19th century, Russia and Britain struggled for control of the country. Following Britain's withdrawal in 1919, Afghanistan became fully independent. Soviet troops invaded Afghanistan in 1979 to support a socialist regime in Kabul, but they withdrew in 1989. By the early 21st century, a group called the Taliban ('Islamic students') controlled 90% of the country. In 2001, following the refusal of the Taliban government to hand over the terrorist leader Osama bin Laden, an international force invaded Afghanistan. In 2002, a coalition government was set up under Hamid Karzai. A draft constitution was approved in 2004, but periodic conflict has dogged economic recovery.

Afghanistan is a poor country and more then 60% of its people are farmers or nomadic herders. Natural gas is produced, together with some coal, copper, gold, precious stones and salt.

AREA 652,090 sq km [251,772 sq mi] **POPULATION** 28,717,000
CAPITAL (POPULATION) Kabul (1,565,000)
GOVERNMENT Transitional **ETHNIC GROUPS** Pashtun (Pathan) 44%, Tajik 25%, Hazara 10%, Uzbek 8%, others 13%
LANGUAGES Pashtu, Dari/Persian (both official), Uzbek
RELIGIONS Islam (Sunni Muslim 84%, Shi'ite Muslim 15%), others 1%
CURRENCY Afghani = 100 puls

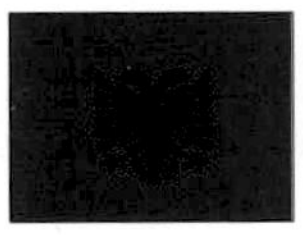

ALBANIA

GEOGRAPHY The Republic of Albania lies in the Balkan peninsula, facing the Adriatic Sea. About 70% of the land is mountainous, but most Albanians live in the west on the coastal lowlands.

The coastal areas of Albania experience a typical Mediterranean climate, with fairly dry, sunny summers and cool, moist winters. The mountains have a severe climate, with heavy winter snowfalls.

POLITICS & ECONOMY Albania is one of Europe's poorest nations. A former Communist country, Albania adopted a multi-party system in the early 1990s. The change proved difficult. But after elections in 1997, a socialist government committed to a market system took office. In 2001, the stability of the region was threatened when Albanian-speaking Kosovars and Macedonians, many of whom favoured the creation of a greater Albania, fought with government forces in north-western Macedonia.

In 2001, agriculture employed more than 60% of the people. Since 1991, private ownership of land has been encouraged, replacing the former state farm and collective system. Albania has some minerals. Chromite, copper and nickel are exported.

AREA 28,748 sq km [11,100 sq mi] **POPULATION** 3,582,000
CAPITAL (POPULATION) Tirana (300,000) **GOVERNMENT** Multiparty republic **ETHNIC GROUPS** Albanian 95%, Greek 3%, Macedonian, Vlachs, Gypsy **LANGUAGES** Albanian (official) **RELIGIONS** Many people say they are non-believers; of the believers, 70% follow Islam and 30% follow Christianity (Orthodox 20%, Roman Catholic 10%)
CURRENCY Lek = 100 qindars

ALGERIA

GEOGRAPHY The People's Democratic Republic of Algeria is Africa's second largest country after Sudan. Most Algerians live in the north, on the fertile coastal plains and hill country bordering the Mediterranean Sea. Four-fifths of Algeria is in the Sahara. The coast has a Mediterranean climate, but the arid Sahara is hot by day and cool at night.

POLITICS & ECONOMY France ruled Algeria from 1830 until 1962, when the socialist FLN (National Liberation Front) formed a one-party government. Following the recognition of opposition parties in 1989, a Muslim group, the FIS (Islamic Salvation Front), won an election in 1991. The FLN cancelled the elections and civil conflict broke out. About 100,000 people were killed in the 1990s. In 1999, following the withdrawal of the other candidates who alleged fraud, Abdelaziz Bouteflika, who was assumed to be favoured by the army, was elected president. Though Bouteflika's peace offensive reduced the violence, sporadic conflict continued. Bouteflika was re-elected in 2004.

Algeria is a developing country, whose chief resources are oil and natural gas, which were discovered in the Sahara in 1956. The natural gas reserves are among the world's largest, and gas and oil account for 90% of Algeria's exports. Cement, iron and steel, textiles and vehicles are manufactured. Barley, citrus fruits, dates, potatoes and wheat are the major crops.

AREA 2,381,741 sq km [919,590 sq mi] **POPULATION** 32,819,000
CAPITAL (POPULATION) Algiers (2,562,000)
GOVERNMENT Socialist republic **ETHNIC GROUPS** Arab-Berber 99%
LANGUAGES Arabic and Berber (official), French **RELIGIONS** Sunni Muslim 99% **CURRENCY** Algerian dinar = 100 centimes

AMERICAN SAMOA

An 'unincorporated territory' of the United States, American Samoa lies in the south-central Pacific Ocean.

AREA 199 sq km [77 sq mi]
POPULATION 70,000 **CAPITAL** Pago Pago

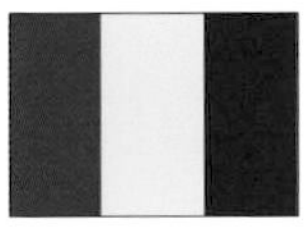

ANDORRA

A mini-state situated in the Pyrenees Mountains, Andorra is a co-principality whose main activity is tourism. Most Andorrans live in the six valleys (the Valls) that drain into the River Valira.

AREA 468 sq km [181 sq mi]
POPULATION 69,000 **CAPITAL** Andorra La Vella

ANGOLA

GEOGRAPHY The Republic of Angola is a large country in south-western Africa. Much of the country is part of the plateau that forms most of southern Africa, with a narrow coastal plain in the west.

Angola has a tropical climate, with temperatures of over 20°C [68°F] throughout the year, though the highest areas are cooler. The coast is dry, but the rainfall increases to the north and east.

POLITICS & ECONOMY Bantu-speaking people settled in Angola in the 13th century and later founded large kingdoms, such as the Kongo and Mbundu. Portugal controlled the coastal slave trade from the 17th century and extended their control inland in the 19th century. Angola became independent from Portugal in 1975, after which rival nationalist groups struggled for power. Despite a cease-fire in the mid-1990s, conflict finally ended in 2002, when the rebel leader, Jonas Savimbi, was killed in action and his successors negotiated peace.

Angola is a developing country, where 70% of the people are poor farmers. The main food crops are cassava and maize. Coffee is exported. Angola has important oil reserves and oil is exported. Angola also produces diamonds and has reserves of copper, manganese and phosphates.

AREA 1,246,700 sq km [481,351 sq mi] **POPULATION** 10,766,000
CAPITAL (POPULATION) Luanda (2,500,000)
GOVERNMENT Multiparty republic
ETHNIC GROUPS Ovimbundu 37%, Kimbundu 25%, Bakongo 13%, others 25% **LANGUAGES** Portuguese (official), many others
RELIGIONS Traditional beliefs 47%, Roman Catholic 38%, Protestant 15%
CURRENCY Kwanza = 100 lwei

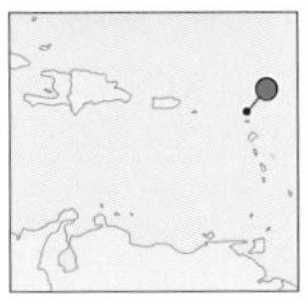

ANGUILLA

Formerly part of St Kitts and Nevis, Anguilla, the most northerly of the Leeward Islands, became a British dependency (now a British overseas territory) in 1980. The main source of revenue is now tourism, although lobster still accounts for half the island's exports.

AREA 96 sq km [37 sq mi]
POPULATION 13,000 **CAPITAL** The Valley

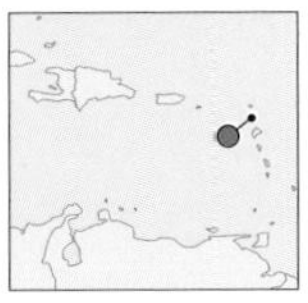

ANTIGUA & BARBUDA

A former British dependency in the Caribbean, Antigua and Barbuda became independent in 1981. Tourism is the main industry, though sugar is an important product.

AREA 442 sq km [171 sq mi]
POPULATION 68,000 **CAPITAL** St John's

ARGENTINA

GEOGRAPHY The Argentine Republic is South America's second largest and the world's eighth largest country. The high Andes range in the west contains Mount Aconcagua, the highest peak in the Americas. In southern Argentina, the Andes Mountains overlook Patagonia, a plateau region. In east-central Argentina lies a fertile plain called the pampas.

The climate varies from subtropical in the north to temperate in the south. Rainfall is abundant in the north-east but lower to the west and south. Patagonia is largely desert.

POLITICS & ECONOMY The earliest people were American Indians, but 86% of the people are now of European ancestry. Spain took control in the 16th century and ruled until 1816. Argentina later suffered from instability and periods of military rule. In 1982, Argentina's military regime invaded the Falkland (Malvinas) Islands, but Britain regained the territory later that year. Civilian rule was restored in 1983 and, in 1994, Argentina adopted a new constitution.

The World Bank classifies Argentina as an 'upper-middle-income' developing country. About 90% of the people live in urban areas. Manufactures include food products, cars, electrical equipment and textiles. Oil is the chief natural resource and the chief farm products are beef, maize and wheat. Oil is exported, together with meat, wheat, maize, vegetable oils, hides and skins, and wool. In 1991, Argentina, Brazil, Paraguay and Uruguay set up an alliance, Mercosur, aimed at creating a common market. However, in late 2001, a severe economic crisis threatened anarchy, though, by late 2003, there were signs of recovery.

AREA 2,780,400 sq km [1,073,512 sq mi] **POPULATION** 38,741,000
CAPITAL (POPULATION) Buenos Aires (2,965,000)
GOVERNMENT Federal republic **ETHNIC GROUPS** European 97%, Mestizo, Amerindian **LANGUAGES** Spanish (official)
RELIGIONS Roman Catholic 92%, Protestant 2%, Jewish 2%, others **CURRENCY** Argentine peso = 10,000 australs

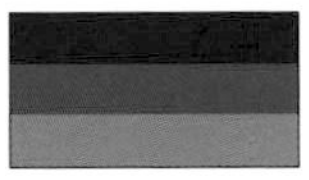

ARMENIA

GEOGRAPHY The Republic of Armenia is a landlocked country in south-western Asia. Most of Armenia consists of a rugged plateau, criss-crossed by long faults (cracks). Movements along the faults cause earthquakes. The highest point is Mount Aragats, at 4,090 m [13,419 ft] above sea level.

The height of the land, which averages 1,500 m [4,920 ft] above sea level gives rise to severe winters and cool summers. The highest peaks are snow-capped, but the total yearly rainfall is generally low.

POLITICS & ECONOMY In 1920, Armenia became a Communist republic and, in 1922, it became, with Azerbaijan and Georgia, part of the Transcaucasian Republic within the Soviet Union. But the three territories became separate Soviet Socialist Republics in 1936. After the break-up of the Soviet Union in 1991, Armenia became an independent republic. Fighting broke out over Nagorno-Karabakh, an area enclosed by Azerbaijan where the majority of the people are Armenians. In 1992, Armenia occupied the territory between it and Nagorno-Karabakh. A cease-fire agreed in 1994 left Armenia in control of about 20% of Azerbaijan's land area. Talks aimed at settling the dispute failed in 2001.

The World Bank classifies Armenia as a 'lower-middle-income' economy. The conflict has badly damaged the economy, but the government has encouraged free enterprise, selling farmland and government-owned businesses.

AREA 29,800 sq km [11,506 sq mi] **POPULATION** 3,326,000
CAPITAL (POPULATION) Yerevan (1,249,000)
GOVERNMENT Multiparty republic **ETHNIC GROUPS** Armenian 93%, Russian 2%, Azeri 1%, others (mostly Kurds) 4%
LANGUAGES Armenian (official) **RELIGIONS** Armenian Apostolic 94%
CURRENCY Dram = 100 couma

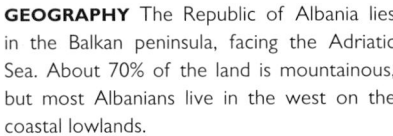

NOTE: This alphabetical list includes the principal countries and territories of the world. The area figures give the total area of land, inland water and ice. The population figures are 2003 estimates where available. The capital city population is for the 'city proper' (rather than its urban agglomeration) where available, using the latest census or estimate.

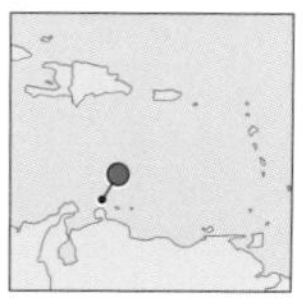

ARUBA

Formerly part of the Netherlands Antilles, Aruba (the most western of the Lesser Antilles) became a separate self-governing Dutch territory in 1986.

AREA 193 sq km [75 sq mi]
POPULATION 71,000 **CAPITAL** Oranjestad

AUSTRALIA

GEOGRAPHY The Commonwealth of Australia, the world's sixth largest country, is also a continent. Australia is the flattest of the continents and the main highland area is in the east. Here the Great Dividing Range separates the eastern coastal plains from the Central Plains. This range extends from the Cape York Peninsula to Victoria in the far south. The longest rivers, the Murray and Darling, drain the south-eastern part of the Central Plains. The Western Plateau makes up two-thirds of Australia. A few mountain ranges break the monotony of the generally flat landscape.

Only 10% of Australia has an average yearly rainfall of more than 1,000 mm [39 in]. These areas include the tropical north, where Darwin is situated, the north-east coast, and the south-east, where Sydney is located. The interior is dry, and water is quickly evaporated in the heat.

POLITICS & ECONOMY The Aboriginal people of Australia entered the continent from South-east Asia more than 50,000 years ago. The first European explorers were Dutch in the 17th century, but they did not settle. In 1770, the British Captain Cook explored the east coast and, in 1788, the first British settlement was established for convicts on the site of what is now Sydney. Australia has strong ties with the British Isles. But in the last 50 years, people from other parts of Europe and, most recently, from Asia have settled in Australia. Ties with Britain were also weakened by Britain's membership of the European Union. Many Australians believe that they should become more involved with the nations of eastern Asia and the Americas rather than with Europe. In 1999, Australians voted to retain the country's status as a monarchy by a vote of about 55% to 45%. In 2003, Australian troops joined the coalition force led by the United States in invading Iraq and overthrowing Saddam Hussein.

Australia is a prosperous country. Crops can be grown on only 6% of the land, but dry pasture covers another 58%. Yet the country remains a major producer and exporter of farm products, particularly cattle, wheat and wool. Grapes grown for wine-making are also important. The country is a major producer of minerals, including bauxite, coal, copper, diamonds, gold, iron ore, manganese, nickel, silver, tin, tungsten and zinc. Australia also produces oil and natural gas. Metals, minerals and farm products account for the bulk of exports. Australia's imports are mostly manufactured goods, especially machinery, though industry is now important, especially the manufacture of consumer goods.

AREA 7,741,220 sq km [2,988,885 sq mi] **POPULATION** 19,732,000
CAPITAL (POPULATION) Canberra (309,000) **GOVERNMENT** Federal constitutional monarchy **ETHNIC GROUPS** Caucasian 92%, Asian 7%, Aboriginal 1% **LANGUAGES** English (official)
RELIGIONS Roman Catholic 26%, Anglican 26%, other Christian 24%, non-Christian 24% **CURRENCY** Australian dollar = 100 cents

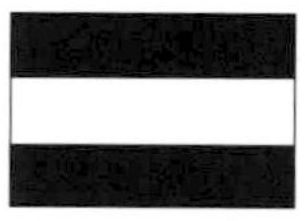

AUSTRIA

GEOGRAPHY Austria is a landlocked country in Europe. Northern Austria contains the valley of the River Danube, which flows from Germany to the Black Sea, and the Vienna basin. Southern Austria contains ranges of the Alps, their highest point at Grossglockner, 3,797 m [12,457 ft] above sea level.

The climate is influenced by westerly and easterly winds. Moist westerly winds bring rain and snow, and moderate temperatures. Dry easterly winds bring cold weather in winter and hot weather in summer.

POLITICS & ECONOMY Formerly part of the monarchy of Austria-Hungary, which collapsed in 1918, Austria was annexed by Germany in 1938. After World War II, the Allies partitioned and occupied the country. In 1955, Austria became a neutral federal republic. It joined the European Union on 1 January 1995, but was a focus of controversy when, in 2000, a coalition government was formed by the right-wing People's Party and the extreme right-wing Freedom Party. The Freedom Party lost much of its support in 2002, but it remained part of the ruling coalition.

Austria has a highly developed economy, with plenty of hydroelectric power and some oil, gas and coal reserves. The country's leading economic activity is manufacturing metals and metal products. Crops are grown on 18% of the land, and another 24% is pasture. Dairy and livestock farming are the leading activities. Major crops include barley, potatoes, rye, sugar beet and wheat. Tourism is a major activity in this scenic country.

AREA 83,859 sq km [32,378 sq mi] **POPULATION** 8,188,000
CAPITAL (POPULATION) Vienna (1,560,000) **GOVERNMENT** Federal republic **ETHNIC GROUPS** Austrian 90%, Croatian, Slovene, others
LANGUAGES German (official) **RELIGIONS** Roman Catholic 78%, Protestant 5%, Islam and others 17% **CURRENCY** Euro = 100 cents

AZERBAIJAN

GEOGRAPHY The Azerbaijani Republic is a country in the south-west of Asia, facing the Caspian Sea to the east. It includes an area called the Naxçivan Autonomous Republic, which is completely cut off from the rest of Azerbaijan by Armenian territory. The Caucasus Mountains border Russia in the north.

Azerbaijan has hot summers and cool winters. The plains are fairly dry, but the mountains are rainy.

POLITICS & ECONOMY After the Russian Revolution of 1917, attempts were made to form a Transcaucasian Federation made up of Armenia, Azerbaijan and Georgia. When this failed, Azerbaijanis set up an independent state. But Russian forces occupied the area in 1920. In 1922, the Communists set up a Transcaucasian Republic consisting of Armenia, Azerbaijan and Georgia under Russian control. In 1936, the three areas became separate Soviet Socialist Republics within the Soviet Union. In 1991, following the break-up of the Soviet Union, Azerbaijan became an independent nation. After independence, the country's economic progress was slow, partly because of the conflict with Armenia over the enclave of Nagorno-Karabakh, a region in Azerbaijan where the majority of people are Armenians. A cease-fire in 1994 left Armenia in control of about 20% of Azerbaijan's area, including Nagorno-Karabakh. Attempts to resolve the problem failed in 2001.

In the mid-1990s, the World Bank classified Azerbaijan as a 'lower-middle-income' economy. Yet by the late 1990s, the enormous oil reserves in the Baku area, on the Caspian Sea and in the sea itself, held out great promise for the future. Oil extraction and manufacturing, including oil refining and the production of chemicals, machinery and textiles, are now the most valuable activities.

AREA 86,600 sq km [33,436 sq mi] **POPULATION** 7,831,000
CAPITAL (POPULATION) Baku (1,792,000) **GOVERNMENT** Federal multiparty republic **ETHNIC GROUPS** Azeri 90%, Dagestani 3%, Russian, Armenian, others **LANGUAGES** Azerbaijani (official), Russian, Armenian **RELIGIONS** Islam 93%, Russian Orthodox 2%, Armenian Orthodox 2% **CURRENCY** Azerbaijani manat = 100 gopik

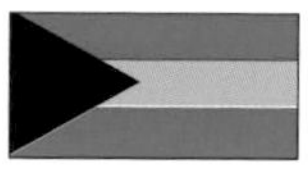
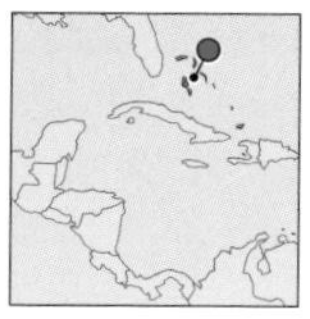

BAHAMAS

A coral-limestone archipelago off the coast of Florida, the Bahamas became independent from Britain in 1973, and has since developed strong ties with the United States. Tourism and banking are major activities.

AREA 13,878 sq km [5,358 sq mi]
POPULATION 297,000 **CAPITAL** Nassau

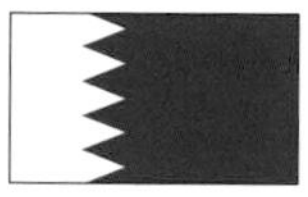
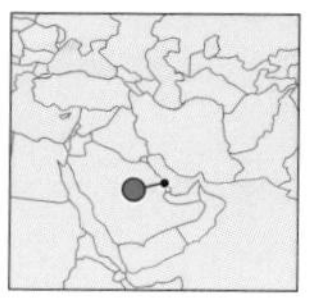

BAHRAIN

The Kingdom of Bahrain, an island nation in the Persian Gulf, became independent from the UK in 1971. Oil accounts for 80% of its exports.

AREA 694 sq km [268 sq mi]
POPULATION 667,000 **CAPITAL** Manama

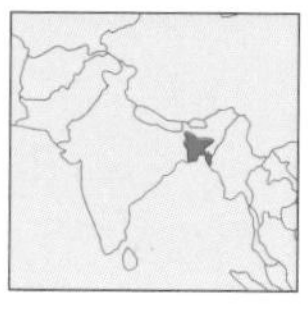

BANGLADESH

GEOGRAPHY The People's Republic of Bangladesh is one of the world's most densely populated countries. Apart from hilly regions in the far north-east and south-east, most of the land is flat and covered by fertile alluvium spread over the land by the Ganges, Brahmaputra and Meghna rivers. These rivers overflow when they are swollen by the annual monsoon rains. Floods also occur along the coast, 575 km [357 mi] long, when cyclones (hurricanes) drive seawater inland. Bangladesh has a tropical monsoon climate. Dry northerly winds blow in winter, but, in summer, moist winds from the south bring monsoon rains. Heavy monsoon rains cause floods. In 1998, about two-thirds of the entire country was submerged, causing great suffering.

POLITICS & ECONOMY In 1947, British India was partitioned between the mainly Hindu India and the Muslim Pakistan. Pakistan consisted of two parts, West and East Pakistan, which were separated by about 1,600 km [1,000 mi] of Indian territory. Differences developed between West and East Pakistan. In 1971, the East Pakistanis rebelled. After a nine-month civil war, they declared East Pakistan to be a separate nation named Bangladesh.

Bangladesh is one of the world's poorest countries. Its economy depends mainly on agriculture, which employs over half the population. Bangladesh is the world's fourth largest producer of rice.

AREA 143,998 sq km [55,598 sq mi] **POPULATION** 138,448,000
CAPITAL (POPULATION) Dhaka (3,839,000)
GOVERNMENT Multiparty republic **ETHNIC GROUPS** Bengali 98%, tribal groups **LANGUAGES** Bengali (official), English
RELIGIONS Islam 83%, Hinduism 16% **CURRENCY** Taka = 100 paisas

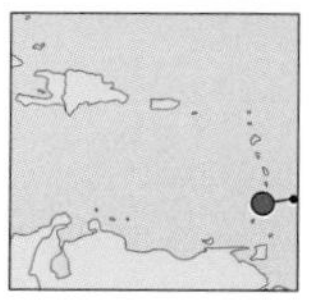

BARBADOS

The most easterly Caribbean country, Barbados became independent from the UK in 1960. A densely populated island, Barbados is prosperous by comparison with most Caribbean countries.

AREA 430 sq km [166 sq mi]
POPULATION 277,000 **CAPITAL** Bridgetown

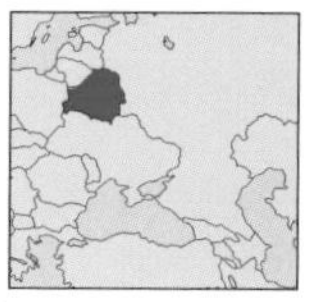

BELARUS

GEOGRAPHY The Republic of Belarus is a landlocked country in Eastern Europe. The land is low-lying and mostly flat. In the south, much of the land is marshy and this area contains Europe's largest marsh and peat bog, the Pripet Marshes. The climate is affected by both the moderating influence of the Baltic Sea and continental conditions to the east. The winters are cold and the summers warm.

POLITICS & ECONOMY In 1918, Belarus (White Russia) became an independent republic, but Russia invaded the country and, in 1919, a Communist state was set up. In 1922, Belarus became a founder republic of the Soviet Union. In 1991, Belarus again became an independent republic, though Belarus continued to support reunification with Russia. In 1998, Belarus and Russia set up a 'union state', with plans to have a common currency, a customs union, and common foreign and defence policies. But any surrender of sovereignty was not expected. In 2003, the Russian President Vladimir Putin agreed to deepen ties with Belarus, but also stated that he did not wish to create anything like the Soviet Union.

The World Bank classifies Belarus as an 'upper-middle-income' economy. Like other former republics of the Soviet Union, it faces many problems in turning from Communism to a free-market economy.

AREA 207,600 sq km [80,154 sq mi] **POPULATION** 10,322,000
CAPITAL (POPULATION) Minsk (1,677,000)
GOVERNMENT Multiparty republic **ETHNIC GROUPS** Belarusian 81%, Russian 11%, Polish, Ukrainian, others **LANGUAGES** Belarusian, Russian (both official) **RELIGIONS** Eastern Orthodox 80%, others 20% **CURRENCY** Belarusian rouble = 100 kopecks

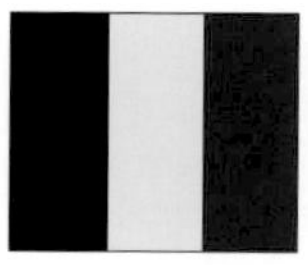
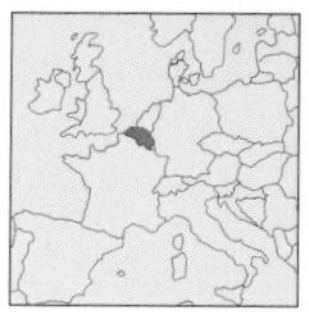

BELGIUM

GEOGRAPHY The Kingdom of Belgium is a densely populated country in western Europe. Behind the coastline on the North Sea, which is 63 km [39 mi] long, lie its coastal plains. Central Belgium consists of low plateaux and the only highland region is the Ardennes in the south-east.

Belgium has a cool, temperate climate. Moist winds from the Atlantic Ocean bring fairly heavy rain, especially in the Ardennes. In January and February much snow falls on the Ardennes.

POLITICS & ECONOMY In 1815, Belgium and the Netherlands united as the 'low countries', but Belgium became independent in 1830. Belgium's economy was weakened by the two World

Wars, but, from 1945, the country recovered quickly, first through collaboration with the Netherlands and Luxembourg, which formed a customs union called Benelux, and later through its membership of the European Union.

A central political problem in Belgium has been the tension between the Dutch-speaking Flemings and the French-speaking Walloons. In the 1970s, the government divided the country into three economic regions: Dutch-speaking Flanders, French-speaking Wallonia and bilingual Brussels. In 1993, Belgium adopted a federal constitution, with each region having its own parliament. Elections under this system were held in 1995, 1999 and 2003.

Belgium is a major trading nation, with a highly developed economy. Most of the materials needed for manufacturing are imported. Its main products include chemicals, processed food and steel. The textile industry is important. It has existed since medieval times in the Belgian province of Flanders. In 2002, the parliament voted to phase out the use of nuclear energy by 2025.

Agriculture employs only 2% of the people, but Belgian farmers produce most of the food needed by the people. Barley and wheat are the chief crops, followed by flax, hops, potatoes and sugar beet, but the most valuable activities are dairy farming and livestock rearing.

AREA 30,528 sq km [11,787 sq mi]
POPULATION 10,289,000
CAPITAL (POPULATION) Brussels (136,000)
GOVERNMENT Federal constitutional monarchy
ETHNIC GROUPS Belgian 89% (Fleming 58%, Walloon 31%), others 11% **LANGUAGES** Dutch, French, German (all official)
RELIGIONS Roman Catholic 75%, others 25%
CURRENCY Euro = 100 cents

BELIZE

GEOGRAPHY Behind the southern coastal plain, the land rises to the Maya Mountains, which reach 1,120 m [3,674 ft] at Victoria Peak. The north is mostly low-lying and swampy. Temperatures are high all year round, while the average annual rainfall ranges from 1,300 mm [51 in] in the north to over 3,800 mm [150 in] in the south. Hurricanes sometimes occur. One in 2001 killed 22 people and left 12,000 homeless.

POLITICS & ECONOMY From 1862, Belize (then called British Honduras) was a British colony. Full independence was achieved in 1981, but Guatemala, which had claimed the area since the early 19th century, opposed Belize's independence and British troops remained to prevent a possible invasion. In 1983, Guatemala reduced its claim to the southern fifth of Belize. Improved relations in the early 1990s led Guatemala to recognize Belize's independence and, in 1992, Britain agreed to withdraw its troops from the country.

The World Bank classifies Belize as a 'lower-middle-income' developing country. Its economy is based on agriculture and sugar cane is the chief commercial crop and export. Other crops include bananas, beans, citrus fruits, maize and rice. Forestry, fishing and tourism are other important activities.

AREA 22,966 sq km [8,867 sq mi] **POPULATION** 266,000
CAPITAL (POPULATION) Belmopan (8,000)
GOVERNMENT Constitutional monarchy **ETHNIC GROUPS** Mestizo 49%, Creole 25%, Mayan Indian 11%, Garifuna 6%, others 9%
LANGUAGES English (official), Spanish, Creole
RELIGIONS Roman Catholic 50%, Protestant 27%, others
CURRENCY Belizean dollar = 100 cents

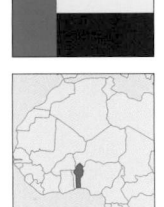

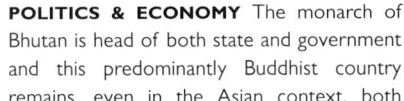

BENIN

GEOGRAPHY The Republic of Benin is one of Africa's smallest countries. It extends north–south for about 620 km [390 mi]. Lagoons line the short coastline, and the country has no natural harbours.

Benin has a hot, wet climate. The average annual temperature on the coast is about 25°C [77°F], and the average rainfall is about 1,330 mm [52 in]. The inland plains are wetter than the coast.

POLITICS & ECONOMY After slavery was ended in the 19th century, the French began to gain influence in the area. Benin became self-governing in 1958 and fully independent in 1960. After much instability and many changes of government, a military group took over in 1972. The country, renamed Benin in 1975, became a one-party socialist state. Socialism was abandoned in 1989. Multiparty elections were held in the 1990s and the early 2000s.

Benin is a poor developing country. About 70% of the people earn their living by farming, though many remain at subsistence level. The chief exports include cotton, petroleum and palm products. Cocoa, coffee, groundnuts (peanuts), tobacco and shea nuts are also grown for export.

AREA 112,622 sq km [43,483 sq mi] **POPULATION** 7,041,000
CAPITAL (POPULATION) Porto-Novo (233,000)
GOVERNMENT Multiparty republic **ETHNIC GROUPS** Fon, Adja, Bariba, Yoruba, Fulani **LANGUAGES** French (official), Fon, Adja, Yoruba
RELIGIONS Traditional beliefs 50%, Christianity 30%, Islam 20%
CURRENCY CFA franc = 100 centimes

BERMUDA

A group of about 150 small islands situated 920 km [570 mi] east of the USA. Bermuda remains Britain's oldest overseas territory, but it has a long tradition of self-government.

AREA 53 sq km [21 sq mi]
POPULATION 64,000 **CAPITAL** Hamilton

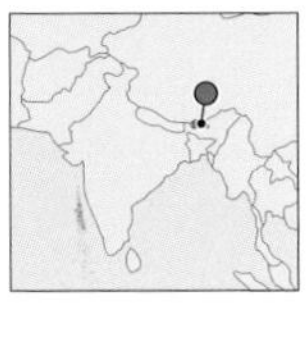

BHUTAN

GEOGRAPHY A mountainous, isolated Himalayan country located between India and Tibet. The climate is similar to that of Nepal, being dependent on altitude and affected by monsoonal winds.

POLITICS & ECONOMY The monarch of Bhutan is head of both state and government and this predominantly Buddhist country remains, even in the Asian context, both conservative and poor. Bhutan is the world's most 'rural' country, with about 87% of the population dependent on agriculture and only 7% living in towns.

AREA 47,000 sq km [18,147 sq mi] **POPULATION** 2,140,000
CAPITAL (POPULATION) Thimphu (35,000)
GOVERNMENT Constitutional monarchy **ETHNIC GROUPS** Bhutanese 50%, Nepalese 35% **LANGUAGES** Dzongkha (official) **RELIGIONS** Buddhism 75%, Hinduism 25% **CURRENCY** Ngultrum = 100 chetrum

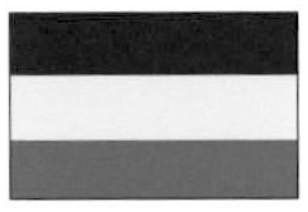

BOLIVIA

GEOGRAPHY The Republic of Bolivia is a landlocked country which straddles the Andes Mountains in central South America. The Andes rise to a height of 6,542 m [21,464 ft] at Nevado Sajama in the west.

About 40% of Bolivians live on a high plateau called the Altiplano in the Andean region, while the sparsely populated east is essentially a vast lowland plain.

The Bolivian climate is greatly affected by altitude, with the Andean peaks permanently snow-covered, and the eastern plains remaining hot and humid.

POLITICS & ECONOMY American Indians have lived in Bolivia for at least 10,000 years. The main groups today are the Aymara and Quechua people.

In the last 50 years, Bolivia, an independent country since 1825, has been ruled by a succession of civilian and military governments, which violated human rights. Constitutional government was restored in 1982. From the 1980s, Bolivia has pursued economic reforms and free-market policies.

Bolivia is one of the poorest countries in South America. It has several natural resources, including tin, silver and natural gas, but the chief activity is agriculture, which employs 47% of the people. Coca, which is used to make cocaine, is exported illegally. In 2002–3, the production of coca plummeted, causing much social unrest and ethnic tensions. The government hoped that oil and gas would soon replace coca as the chief export.

AREA 1,098,581 sq km [424,162 sq mi] **POPULATION** 8,586,000
CAPITAL (POPULATION) La Paz (seat of government, 940,000); Sucre (legal capital/seat of judiciary, 177,000)
GOVERNMENT Multiparty republic **ETHNIC GROUPS** Mestizo 30%, Quechua 30%, Aymara 25%, White 15% **LANGUAGES** Spanish, Aymara, Quechua (all official) **RELIGIONS** Roman Catholic 95%
CURRENCY Boliviano = 100 centavos

BOSNIA-HERZEGOVINA

GEOGRAPHY The Republic of Bosnia-Herzegovina is one of the five republics to emerge from the former Federal People's Republic of Yugoslavia. Much of the country is mountainous or hilly, with an arid limestone plateau in the south-west. The River Sava, which forms most of the northern border with Croatia, is a tributary of the River Danube. Because of the country's odd shape, the coastline is limited to a short stretch of 20 km [13 mi] on the Adriatic coast.

A Mediterranean climate, with dry, sunny summers and moist, mild winters, prevails only near the coast. Inland, the weather is more severe, with hot, dry summers and bitterly cold, snowy winters.

POLITICS & ECONOMY In 1918, Bosnia-Herzegovina became part of the Kingdom of the Serbs, Croats and Slovenes, which was renamed Yugoslavia in 1929. Germany occupied the area during World War II (1939–45). From 1945, Communist governments ruled Yugoslavia as a federation containing six republics, one of which was Bosnia-Herzegovina. In the 1980s, the country faced problems as Communist policies proved unsuccessful and differences arose between ethnic groups.

In 1990, free elections were held in Bosnia-Herzegovina and the non-Communists won a majority. A Muslim, Alija Izetbegovic, was elected president. In 1991, Croatia and Slovenia, other parts of the former Yugoslavia, declared themselves independent. In 1992, Bosnia-Herzegovina held a vote on independence. Most Bosnian Serbs boycotted the vote, while the Muslims and Bosnian Croats voted in favour. Many Bosnian Serbs, opposed to independence, started a war against the non-Serbs. They soon occupied more than two-thirds of the land. The Bosnian Serbs were accused of 'ethnic cleansing' – that is, the killing or expulsion of other ethnic groups from Serb-occupied areas. The war was later extended when Croat forces seized other parts of the country.

In 1995, the conflict was resolved. Under an agreement, the country's boundaries were maintained, but the territory was divided into two self-governing provinces, one Bosnian-Serb and the other Muslim-Croat, under a central unified government. At first, the country's future seemed uncertain. But, by 2004, its main problems were economic rather than political.

The economy of Bosnia-Herzegovina, the least developed of the six republics of the former Yugoslavia apart from Macedonia, was shattered by the war in the early 1990s. Before the war, manufactures were the main exports, including electrical, machinery and transport equipment, and textiles. Farm products include fruits, maize, tobacco, vegetables and wheat, but food has to be imported.

AREA 51,197 sq km [19,767 sq mi] **POPULATION** 3,989,000
CAPITAL (POPULATION) Sarajevo (529,000)
GOVERNMENT Federal republic **ETHNIC GROUPS** Bosnian 48%, Serb 37%, Croat 14% **LANGUAGES** Bosnian, Serbian, Croatian
RELIGIONS Islam 40%, Serbian Orthodox 31%, Roman Catholic 15%, others 14% **CURRENCY** Convertible marka = 100 convertible pfenniga

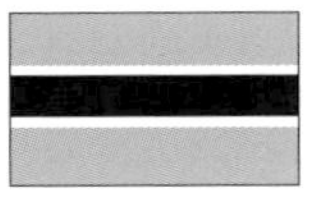
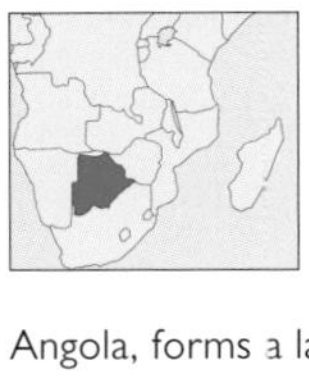

BOTSWANA

GEOGRAPHY The Republic of Botswana is a landlocked country in southern Africa. The Kalahari, a semi-desert area covered mostly by grasses and thorn scrub, covers much of the country. Most of the south has no permanent streams. But large depressions in the north are inland drainage basins. In one of them, the Okavango River, which rises in Angola, forms a large, swampy delta.

Temperatures are high in the summer months (October to April), but the winter months are much cooler. In winter, night-time temperatures sometimes drop below freezing point. The average annual rainfall ranges from over 400 mm [16 in] in the east to less than 200 mm [8 in] in the south-west.

POLITICS & ECONOMY The earliest inhabitants of the region were the San, who are also called Bushmen. They had a nomadic way of life, hunting wild animals and collecting wild plant foods.

Britain ruled the area as the Bechuanaland Protectorate between 1885 and 1966. When the country became independent, it was renamed Botswana. Since then, the country has been a stable, multiparty democracy. However, a major setback occurred in the early 21st century, when health officials announced that around 25% of the people were infected with HIV/AIDS. In 1966, Botswana was extremely poor, depending on meat and live cattle for its exports. But the discovery of minerals, including coal, cobalt, copper, diamonds and nickel, has boosted the economy. About 17% of the people now depend on agriculture, raising cattle and growing crops. Industries include the processing of farm products.

AREA 581,730 sq km [224,606 sq mi] **POPULATION** 1,573,000
CAPITAL (POPULATION) Gaborone (186,000)
GOVERNMENT Multiparty republic **ETHNIC GROUPS** Tswana (or Setswana) 79%, Kalanga 11%, Basarwa 3%, others
LANGUAGES English (official), Setswana **RELIGIONS** Traditional beliefs 85%, Christianity 15% **CURRENCY** Pula = 100 thebe

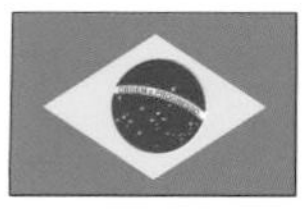

BRAZIL

GEOGRAPHY The Federative Republic of Brazil is the world's fifth largest country. It contains three main regions. The Amazon basin in the north covers more than half of Brazil. The Amazon, the world's second longest river, has a far greater volume than any other river. The second region, the north-east, consists of a coastal plain and the *sertão*, which is the name for the inland plateaux and hill country. The main river in this region is the São Francisco.

The third region is made up of the plateaux in the south-east. This region, which covers about a quarter of the country, is the most developed and densely populated part of Brazil. Its main river is the Paraná, which flows south through Argentina.

Manaus has high temperatures all through the year. The rainfall is heavy, though the period from June to September is drier than the rest of the year. The capital, Brasília, and the city Rio de Janeiro also have tropical climates, with much more marked dry seasons than Manaus. The far south has a temperate climate. The north-eastern interior is the driest region, with an average annual rainfall of only 250 mm [10 in] in places. The rainfall is also unreliable and severe droughts are common in this region.

POLITICS & ECONOMY The Portuguese explorer Pedro Alvarez Cabral claimed Brazil for Portugal in 1500. With Spain occupied in western South America, the Portuguese began to develop their colony, which was more than 90 times as big as Portugal. To do this, they enslaved many local Amerindian people and introduced about 4 million African slaves. Brazil declared itself an independent empire in 1822 and a republic in 1889. From the 1930s, Brazil faced periods of military rule and widespread corruption. Civilian rule was restored in 1985. Brazil adopted a new constitution in 1988.

The United Nations has described Brazil as a 'Rapidly Industrializing Country', or RIC. Its total volume of production is one of the largest in the world. But many people, including poor farmers and residents of the *favelas* (city slums), do not share in the country's fast economic growth. Widespread poverty, together with high inflation and unemployment led to the election as president of left-winger Luiz Inácio Lula da Silva (popularly known as 'Lula') in 2002. In office, he adopted a pragmatic approach to Brazil's many problems, but his popularity continued.

Industry is the most important economic sector. Brazil is among the world's top producers of bauxite, chrome, diamonds, gold, iron ore, manganese and tin. It is also a major manufacturing country. Its products include aircraft, cars, chemicals, processed food, including raw sugar, iron and steel, paper and textiles.

Brazil is one of the world's leading farming countries and agriculture employs 22% of the people. Coffee is a major export. Other leading products include bananas, citrus fruits, cocoa, maize, rice, soybeans and sugar cane. Brazil is also the top producer of eggs, meat and milk in South America.

Forestry is a major industry, though many people fear that the exploitation of the rainforests, with 1.5% to 4% of Brazil's forest being destroyed every year, is a disaster for the entire world.

AREA 8,514,215 sq km [3,287,338 sq mi] **POPULATION** 182,033,000
CAPITAL (POPULATION) Brasília (2,016,000)
GOVERNMENT Federal republic
ETHNIC GROUPS White 55%, Mulatto 38%, Black 6%, others 1% **LANGUAGES** Portuguese (official)
RELIGIONS Roman Catholic 80%
CURRENCY Real = 100 centavos

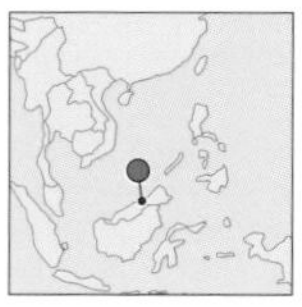

BRUNEI

The Islamic Sultanate of Brunei, a British protectorate until 1984, lies on the north coast of Borneo. The climate is tropical and rainforests cover large areas. Brunei is a prosperous country because of its oil and natural gas production, and the Sultan is said to be among the world's richest men.

AREA 5,765 sq km [2,226 sq mi] **POPULATION** 358,000
CAPITAL (POPULATION) Bandar Seri Begawan (50,000)

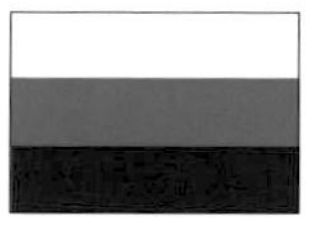
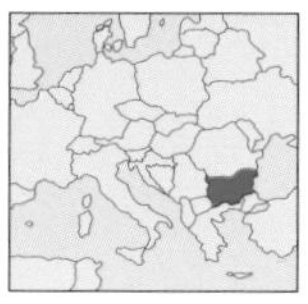

BULGARIA

GEOGRAPHY The Republic of Bulgaria is a country in the Balkan peninsula, facing the Black Sea in the east. The heart of Bulgaria is mountainous. The main ranges are the Balkan Mountains in the centre and the Rhodope (or Rhodopi) Mountains in the south.

Summers are hot and winters are cold, though seldom severe. The rainfall is moderate.

POLITICS & ECONOMY Ottoman Turks ruled Bulgaria from 1396 and ethnic Turks still form a sizeable minority in the country. In 1879, Bulgaria became a monarchy, and in 1908 it became fully independent. Bulgaria was an ally of Germany in World War I (1914–18) and again in World War II (1939–45). In 1944, Soviet troops invaded Bulgaria and, after the war, the monarchy was abolished and the country became a Communist ally of the Soviet Union. In the late 1980s, reforms in the Soviet Union led Bulgaria's government to introduce a multiparty system in 1990. A non-Communist government was elected in 1991, the first free elections in 44 years. Throughout the 1990s, Bulgaria faced many problems. In 2001, a coalition led by the former King Siméon, who had left Bulgaria in 1948, won the elections. Siméon became prime minister. In 2004, Bulgaria became a member of the North Atlantic Treaty Organization.

According to the World Bank, Bulgaria in the 1990s was a 'lower-middle-income' developing country. Bulgaria has some deposits of minerals, including brown coal, manganese and iron ore. But manufacturing is the leading activity, though, in the early 1990s, much of its industrial plant was out of date. Leading products include chemicals, processed foods, metal products, machinery and textiles. Manufactures are the leading exports.

AREA 110,912 sq km [42,823 sq mi] **POPULATION** 7,538,000
CAPITAL (POPULATION) Sofia (1,139,000) **GOVERNMENT** Multiparty republic **ETHNIC GROUPS** Bulgarian 84%, Turkish 9%, Gypsy 5%, Macedonian, Armenian, others **LANGUAGES** Bulgarian (official), Turkish **RELIGIONS** Bulgarian Orthodox 83%, Islam 12%, Roman Catholic 2%, others **CURRENCY** Lev = 100 stotinki

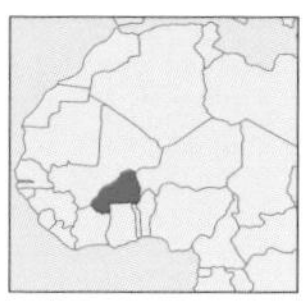

BURKINA FASO

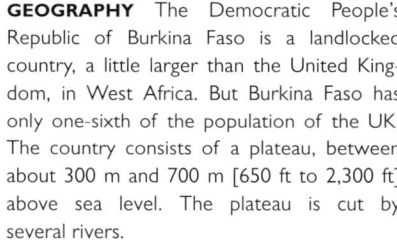

GEOGRAPHY The Democratic People's Republic of Burkina Faso is a landlocked country, a little larger than the United Kingdom, in West Africa. But Burkina Faso has only one-sixth of the population of the UK. The country consists of a plateau, between about 300 m and 700 m [650 ft to 2,300 ft] above sea level. The plateau is cut by several rivers.

The capital city, Ouagadougou, in central Burkina Faso, has high temperatures throughout the year. Most of the rain falls between May and September, but the rainfall is erratic and droughts are common.

POLITICS & ECONOMY The people of Burkina Faso are divided into two main groups. The Voltaic group includes the Mossi, who form the largest single group, and the Bobo. The French conquered the Mossi capital of Ouagadougou in 1897 and they made the area a protectorate. In 1919, the area became a French colony called Upper Volta. After independence in 1960, Upper Volta became a one-party state. But it was unstable – military groups seized power several times and political killings took place. In 1984, the country's name was changed to Burkina Faso. In 1991 and 1998, the former military leader, Captain Blaise Compaoré, was elected president, but the military continued to play an important part in the government.

Burkina Faso is one of the world's 20 poorest countries and has become very dependent on foreign aid. Most of Burkina Faso is dry with thin soils. The country's main food crops are beans, maize, millet, rice and sorghum. Cotton, groundnuts and shea nuts, whose seeds produce a fat used to make cooking oil and soap, are grown for sale abroad. Livestock are also an important export.

The country has few resources and manufacturing is on a small scale. There are some deposits of manganese, zinc, lead and nickel in the north of the country, but there is not yet a good enough transport system there. Many young men seek jobs abroad in Ghana and Ivory Coast. The money they send home to their families is important to the country's economy.

AREA 274,000 sq km [105,791 sq mi] **POPULATION** 13,228,000
CAPITAL (POPULATION) Ouagadougou (637,000)
GOVERNMENT Multiparty republic **ETHNIC GROUPS** Mossi 40%, Gurunsi, Senufo, Lobi, Bobo, Mande, Fulani **LANGUAGES** French (official), Mossi, Fulani **RELIGIONS** Islam 50%, traditional beliefs 40%, Christianity 10% **CURRENCY** CFA franc = 100 centimes

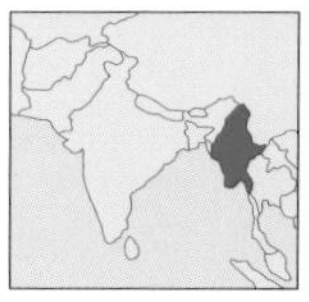

BURMA (MYANMAR)

GEOGRAPHY The Union of Burma is now officially known as the Union of Myanmar; its name was changed in 1989. Mountains border the country in the east and west, with the highest mountains in the north. Burma's highest mountain is Hkakabo Razi, which is 5,881 m [19,294 ft] high. Between these ranges is central Burma, which contains the fertile valleys of the Irrawaddy and Sittang rivers. The Irrawaddy delta on the Bay of Bengal is one of the world's leading rice-growing areas. Burma also includes the long Tenasserim coast in the south-east.

Burma has a tropical monsoon climate. There are three seasons. The rainy season runs from late May to mid-October. A cool, dry season follows, between late October and the middle part of February. The hot season lasts from late February to mid-May, though temperatures remain high during the humid rainy season.

POLITICS & ECONOMY Many groups settled in Burma in ancient times. Some, called the hill peoples, live in remote mountain areas where they have retained their own cultures. The ancestors of the country's main ethnic group today, the Burmese, arrived in the 9th century AD.

Britain conquered Burma in the 19th century and made it a province of British India. But, in 1937, the British granted Burma limited self-government. Japan conquered Burma in 1942, but the Japanese were driven out in 1945. Burma became a fully independent country in 1948.

Revolts by Communists and various hill people led to instability in the 1950s. In 1962, Burma became a military dictatorship and, in 1974, a one-party state. Attempts to control minority liberation movements and the opium trade led to repressive rule. The National League for Democracy led by Aung San Suu Kyi won the elections in 1990, but the military continued their repressive rule throughout the 1990s, earning Burma the reputation for having one of the world's worst human rights records. Its admission to ASEAN (Association of South-east Asian Nations) in 1997 may have implied regional recognition of the regime. However, the European Union continued to voice its concerns over human rights abuses. The opposition leader Aung San Suu Kyi was released in 2002, but she was soon placed under 'protective custody'.

Agriculture is the main activity, employing 66% of the people. The chief crop is rice. Maize, pulses, oilseeds and sugar cane are other major products. Forestry is important. Teak and rice together make up about two-thirds of the total value of the exports. Burma has many mineral resources, though they are mostly undeveloped, but the country is famous for its precious stones, especially rubies. Manufacturing is mostly on a small scale.

AREA 676,578 sq km [261,227 sq mi] **POPULATION** 42,511,000
CAPITAL (POPULATION) Rangoon (2,513,000) **GOVERNMENT** Military regime **ETHNIC GROUPS** Burman 68%, Shan 9%, Karen 7%, Rakhine 4%, Chinese, Indian, Mon **LANGUAGES** Burmese (official); minority ethnic groups have their own languages **RELIGIONS** Buddhism 89%, Christianity, Islam **CURRENCY** Kyat = 100 pyas

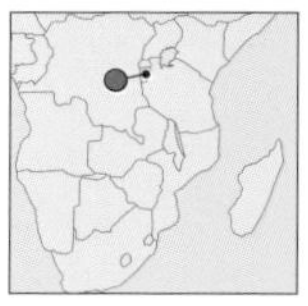

BURUNDI

GEOGRAPHY The Republic of Burundi is the fifth smallest country in mainland Africa. It is also the second most densely populated after its northern neighbour, Rwanda. Part of the Great African Rift Valley, which runs throughout eastern Africa into south-western Asia, lies in western Burundi. It includes part of Lake Tanganyika.

Bujumbura, the capital city, lies on the shore of Lake Tanganyika. It has a warm climate. A dry season occurs from June to September, but the other months are fairly rainy. The mountains and plateaux to the east are cooler and wetter, but the rainfall generally decreases to the east.

POLITICS & ECONOMY The Twa, a pygmy people, were the first known inhabitants of Burundi. About 1,000 years ago, the Hutu, a people who speak a Bantu language, gradually began to settle the area, pushing the Twa into remote areas.

From the 15th century, the Tutsi, a cattle-owning people from the north-east, gradually took over the country. The Hutu, though greatly outnumbering the Tutsi, were forced to serve the Tutsi overlords.

Germany conquered the area that is now Burundi and Rwanda in the late 1890s. The area, called Ruanda-Urundi, was taken by Belgium during World War I (1914–18). In 1961, the people of Urundi voted to become a monarchy, while the people of Ruanda voted to become a republic. The two territories became fully independent as Burundi and Rwanda in 1962. After 1962, the rivalries between the Hutu and Tutsi led to periodic outbreaks of fighting. The Tutsi monarchy was ended in 1966 and Burundi became a republic. Instability continued with coups and massacres as Tutsis and Hutus fought against each other. Following a power-sharing agreement in 2001, further conflict threatened the holding of elections in 2004.

Burundi is one of the world's ten poorest countries. About 93% of the people are farmers who live mostly at subsistence level. The main food crops are beans, cassava, maize and sweet potatoes. Cattle, goats and sheep are raised and fishing is also important. However, Burundi has to import food.

AREA 27,834 SQ KM [10,747 SQ MI] **POPULATION** 6,096,000 **CAPITAL (POPULATION)** BUJUMBURA (235,000) **GOVERNMENT** REPUBLIC **ETHNIC GROUPS** HUTU 85%, TUTSI 14%, TWA (PYGMY) 1% **LANGUAGES** FRENCH AND KIRUNDI (BOTH OFFICIAL) **RELIGIONS** ROMAN CATHOLIC 62%, TRADITIONAL BELIEFS 23%, ISLAM 10%, PROTESTANT 5% **CURRENCY** BURUNDI FRANC = 100 CENTIMES

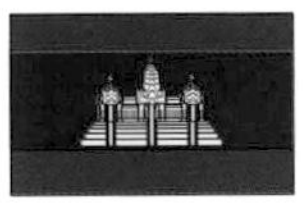

CAMBODIA

GEOGRAPHY The Kingdom of Cambodia is a country in South-east Asia. Low mountains border the country except in the south-east. But most of Cambodia consists of plains drained by the River Mekong, which enters Cambodia from Laos in the north and exits through Vietnam in the south-east. The north-west contains Tonlé Sap (or Great Lake). In the dry season, this lake drains into the River Mekong. But in the wet season, the level of the Mekong rises and water flows in the opposite direction from the river into Tonlé Sap – the lake then becomes the largest freshwater lake in Asia.

Cambodia has a tropical monsoon climate, with high temperatures throughout the year. The dry season, when winds blow from the north or north-east, runs from November to April. During the rainy season (May to October), moist winds blow from the south or south-east. The high humidity and heat often make conditions unpleasant. Rainfall is heaviest near the coast, and rather lower inland.

POLITICS & ECONOMY From 802 to 1432, the Khmer people ruled a great empire, which reached its peak in the 12th century. The Khmer capital was at Angkor. The Hindu stone temples built there and at nearby Angkor Wat form the world's largest group of religious buildings. France ruled the country between 1863 and 1954, when the country became an independent monarchy. But the monarchy was abolished in 1970 and Cambodia became a republic.

In 1970, US and South Vietnamese troops entered Cambodia but left after destroying North Vietnamese Communist camps in the east. The country became involved in the Vietnamese War, and then in a civil war as Cambodian Communists of the Khmer Rouge organization fought for power. The Khmer Rouge took over Cambodia in 1975 and launched a reign of terror in which between 1 million and 2.5 million people were killed. In 1979, Vietnamese and Cambodian troops overthrew the Khmer Rouge government. But fighting continued between factions. Vietnam withdrew in 1989, and in 1991 Prince Sihanouk was recognized as head of state. Elections were held in May 1993, and in September 1993 the monarchy was restored. Sihanouk again became king. In 1997, the prime minister, Prince Norodom Ranariddh, was deposed, so ending four years of democratic rule. Further elections were held in 1998 and, in 2001, the government set up courts to try leaders of the Khmer Rouge.

Cambodia is a poor country whose economy has been wrecked by war. Until the 1970s, the country's farmers produced most of the food needed by the people. But by 1986, it was only able to supply 80% of its needs. Farming is the main activity and rice, rubber and maize are major products. Manufacturing is almost non-existent, apart from rubber processing and a few factories producing items for sale in Cambodia.

AREA 181,035 SQ KM [69,898 SQ MI] **POPULATION** 13,125,000 **CAPITAL (POPULATION)** PHNOM PENH (1,000,000) **GOVERNMENT** CONSTITUTIONAL MONARCHY **ETHNIC GROUPS** KHMER 90%, VIETNAMESE 5%, CHINESE 1%, OTHERS **LANGUAGES** KHMER (OFFICIAL), FRENCH, ENGLISH **RELIGIONS** BUDDHISM 95%, OTHERS 5% **CURRENCY** RIEL = 100 SEN

CAMEROON

GEOGRAPHY The Republic of Cameroon in West Africa got its name from the Portuguese word *camarões*, or prawns. This name was used by Portuguese explorers who fished for prawns along the coast. Behind the narrow coastal plains on the Gulf of Guinea, the land rises to a series of plateaux, with a mountainous region in the south-west where the volcano Mount Cameroon is situated. In the north, the land slopes down towards the Lake Chad basin.

The rainfall is heavy, especially in the highlands. The rainiest months near the coast are June to September. The rainfall decreases to the north and the far north has a hot, dry climate. Temperatures are high on the coast, whereas the inland plateaux are cooler.

POLITICS & ECONOMY Germany lost Cameroon during World War I (1914–18). The country was then divided into two parts, one ruled by Britain and the other by France. In 1960, French Cameroon became the independent Cameroon Republic. In 1961, after a vote in British Cameroon, part of the territory joined the Cameroon Republic to become the Federal Republic of Cameroon. The other part joined Nigeria. In 1972, Cameroon became a unitary state called the United Republic of Cameroon. It adopted the name Republic of Cameroon in 1984, but the country had two official languages. In 1995, partly to placate English-speaking people, Cameroon became the 52nd member of the Commonwealth.

Like most countries in tropical Africa, Cameroon's economy is based on agriculture, which employs 74% of the people. The chief food crops include cassava, maize, millet, sweet potatoes and yams. The country also has plantations to produce such crops as cocoa and coffee for export.

Cameroon is fortunate in having some oil, the country's chief export, and bauxite. Although Cameroon has few manufacturing and processing industries, its mineral exports and its self-sufficiency in food production make it one of the better-off countries in tropical Africa.

AREA 475,442 SQ KM [183,568 SQ MI] **POPULATION** 15,746,000 **CAPITAL (POPULATION)** YAOUNDÉ (649,000) **GOVERNMENT** MULTIPARTY REPUBLIC **ETHNIC GROUPS** CAMEROON HIGHLANDERS 31%, BANTU 27%, KIRDI 11%, FULANI 10%, OTHERS **LANGUAGES** FRENCH AND ENGLISH (BOTH OFFICIAL) **RELIGIONS** CHRISTIANITY 40%, TRADITIONAL BELIEFS 40%, ISLAM 20% **CURRENCY** CFA FRANC = 100 CENTIMES

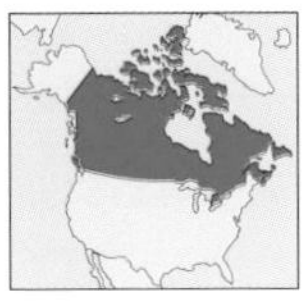

CANADA

GEOGRAPHY Canada is the world's second largest country after Russia. It is thinly populated, however, with much of the land too cold or too mountainous for human settlement. Most Canadians live within 300 km [186 mi] of the southern border.

Western Canada is rugged. It includes the Pacific ranges and the mighty Rocky Mountains. East of the Rockies are the interior plains. In the north lie the bleak Arctic islands, while to the south lie the densely populated lowlands around lakes Erie and Ontario and in the St Lawrence River valley.

Canada has a cold climate. In winter, temperatures fall below freezing point throughout most of Canada. But the south-western coast has a relatively mild climate. Along the Arctic Circle, mean temperatures are below freezing for seven months a year.

Western and south-eastern Canada experience high rainfall, but the prairies are dry with 250 mm to 500 mm [10 in to 20 in] of rain every year.

POLITICS & ECONOMY Canada's first people, the ancestors of the Native Americans, or Indians, arrived in North America from Asia around 40,000 years ago. Later arrivals were the Inuit (Eskimos), who also came from Asia. Europeans reached the Canadian coast in 1497 and a race began between Britain and France for control of the territory.

France gained an initial advantage, and the French founded Québec in 1608. But the British later occupied eastern Canada. In 1867, Britain passed the British North America Act, which set up the Dominion of Canada, which was made up of Québec, Ontario, Nova Scotia and New Brunswick. Other areas were added, the last being Newfoundland in 1949. Canada fought alongside Britain in both World Wars and many Canadians feel close ties with Britain. Canada is a constitutional monarchy, and the British monarch is Canada's head of state.

Rivalries between French- and English-speaking Canadians continue. In 1995, Québeckers voted against a move to make Québec a sovereign state. The majority was less than 1% and this issue seems unlikely to disappear. Another problem concerns the rights of the Aboriginal minorities, who would like to have more say in the running of their own affairs. To this end, in 1999, Canada created a new territory called Nunavut for the Inuit population in the north. Nunavut covers approximately 64% of what was formerly the eastern part of Northwest Territories.

Canada is a highly developed and prosperous country. Although farmland covers only 8% of the country, Canadian farms are highly productive. Canada is one of the world's leading producers of barley, wheat, meat and milk. Forestry and fishing are other important industries. It is rich in natural resources, especially oil and natural gas, and is a major exporter of minerals. The country also produces copper, gold, iron ore, uranium and zinc. Manufacturing is highly developed, especially in the cities where 79% of the people live. Canada has many factories that process farm and mineral products. It also produces cars, chemicals, electronic goods, machinery, paper and timber products.

AREA 9,970,610 SQ KM [3,849,653 SQ MI] **POPULATION** 32,207,000 **CAPITAL (POPULATION)** OTTAWA (774,000) **GOVERNMENT** FEDERAL MULTIPARTY CONSTITUTIONAL MONARCHY **ETHNIC GROUPS** BRITISH ORIGIN 28%, FRENCH ORIGIN 23%, OTHER EUROPEAN 15%, AMERINDIAN/INUIT 2%, OTHERS **LANGUAGES** ENGLISH AND FRENCH (BOTH OFFICIAL) **RELIGIONS** ROMAN CATHOLIC 46%, PROTESTANT 36%, JUDAISM, ISLAM, HINDUISM **CURRENCY** CANADIAN DOLLAR = 100 CENTS

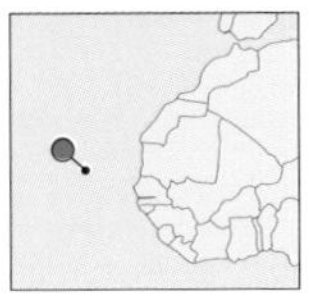

CAPE VERDE

Cape Verde consists of ten large and five small islands, and is situated 560 km [350 mi] west of Dakar in Senegal. The islands have a tropical climate, with high temperatures all year round. Cape Verde became independent from Portugal in 1975 and is rated as a 'low-income' developing country by the World Bank.

AREA 4,033 SQ KM [1,557 SQ MI] **POPULATION** 412,000 **CAPITAL** PRAIA

CAYMAN ISLANDS

The Cayman Islands are an overseas territory of the UK, consisting of three low-lying islands. Financial services are the main economic activity and the islands offer a secret tax haven to many companies and banks.

AREA 264 SQ KM [102 SQ MI] **POPULATION** 42,000 **CAPITAL** GEORGE TOWN

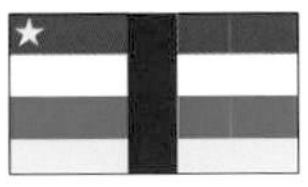

CENTRAL AFRICAN REPUBLIC

GEOGRAPHY The Central African Republic is a remote, landlocked country in the heart of Africa. It consists mostly of a plateau lying between 600 m and 800 m [1,970 ft to 2,620 ft] above sea level. The Ubangi drains the south, while the Chari (or Shari) River flows from the north to the Lake Chad basin. The climate is warm throughout the year, while the annual average rainfall in the capital Bangui totals 1,574 mm [62 in]. The north is drier, with an average annual rainfall of about 800 mm [31 in].

POLITICS & ECONOMY France set up an outpost at Bangui in 1899 and ruled the country as a colony from 1894. Known as Ubangi-Shari, the country was ruled by France as part of French Equatorial Africa until it gained independence in 1960.

Central African Republic became a one-party state in 1962, but army officers seized power in 1966. The head of the army, Jean-Bedel Bokassa, made himself emperor in 1976. The country was renamed the Central African Empire, but after a brutal reign, the tyrannical Bokassa was overthrown in a military coup in 1979. The country again became a republic.

The country adopted a new, multiparty constitution in 1991. Multiparty elections were held in 1993 and 1998. However, an army uprising began in 2002, culminating in the overthrow by a military coup of the elected President Patassé in 2003. He was succeeded by General François Bezize.

The World Bank classifies Central African Republic as a 'low-income' developing country. Over 80% of the people are farmers, and most of them produce little more than they need to feed their families. The main crops are bananas, maize, manioc, millet and yams. Coffee, cotton, timber and tobacco are produced for export, mainly on commercial plantations. The country's development has been impeded by its remote position, its poor transport system and its untrained workforce. The country depends heavily on aid, especially from France.

AREA 622,984 SQ KM [240,534 SQ MI] **POPULATION** 3,684,000 **CAPITAL (POPULATION)** BANGUI (553,000) **GOVERNMENT** MULTIPARTY REPUBLIC **ETHNIC GROUPS** BAYA 33%, BANDA 27%, MANDJIA 13%, SARA 10%, MBOUM 7%, MBAKA 4%, OTHERS **LANGUAGES** FRENCH (OFFICIAL), SANGHO **RELIGIONS** TRADITIONAL BELIEFS 35%, PROTESTANT 25%, ROMAN CATHOLIC 25%, ISLAM 15% **CURRENCY** CFA FRANC = 100 CENTIMES

CHAD

GEOGRAPHY The Republic of Chad is a landlocked country in north-central Africa. It is Africa's fifth largest country and is over twice the size of France, the country which once ruled it as a colony.

Ndjamena in central Chad has a hot, tropical climate, with a marked dry season from November to April. The south of the country is wetter, with an average yearly rainfall of around 1,000 mm [39 in]. The burning-hot desert in the north has an average yearly rainfall of less than 130 mm [5 in].

POLITICS & ECONOMY Chad straddles two worlds. The north is populated by Muslim Arab and Berber peoples, while black Africans, who follow traditional beliefs or who have converted to Christianity, live in the south. French explorers were active in the area in the late 19th century. France made Chad a colony in 1902.

Since becoming independent in 1960, Chad has been hit by ethnic conflict. The 1970s were marked by civil war and coups. Chad and Libya were in dispute over the northern Aozou Strip but, in 1994, the International Court of Justice ruled against Libya's claim over the area. A new constitution was adopted in 1997, but rebellions and conflict in several areas marred the country's progress.

Hit by drought and civil war, Chad is one of the world's poorest countries. Farming, fishing and livestock raising employ 83% of the people. Groundnuts, millet, rice and sorghum are major food crops in the south, but the chief export crop is cotton. Chad has few manufacturing industries, but its oil reserves hold out hope for development. The production of oil began in 2003.

AREA 1,284,000 sq km [495,752 sq mi] **POPULATION** 9,253,000
CAPITAL (POPULATION) Ndjamena (530,000)
GOVERNMENT Multiparty republic **ETHNIC GROUPS** 200 distinct groups: mostly Muslim in the north and centre; mostly Christian or animist in the south **LANGUAGES** French and Arabic (both official), many others **RELIGIONS** Islam 51%, Christianity 35%, animist 7%
CURRENCY CFA franc = 100 centimes

CHILE

GEOGRAPHY The Republic of Chile stretches about 4,260 km [2,650 mi] from north to south, although the maximum east–west distance is only about 430 km [267 mi]. The high Andes Mountains form Chile's eastern borders with Argentina and Bolivia. To the west are basins and valleys, with coastal uplands overlooking the shore. Most people live in the central valley, where Santiago is situated.

Santiago has a Mediterranean climate, with hot, dry summers from November to March and mild, moist winters from April to October. The Atacama Desert in the north is one of the world's driest places, while southern Chile is cold and stormy.

POLITICS & ECONOMY Amerindian people reached the southern tip of South America 8,000 years ago. In 1520, Portuguese navigator Ferdinand Magellan was the first European to sight Chile. The country became a Spanish colony in the 1540s. Chile became independent in 1818. During a war (1879–83), it gained mineral-rich areas from Peru and Bolivia.

In 1970, Salvador Allende became the first Communist leader to be elected democratically. He was overthrown in 1973 by army officers, who were supported by the CIA. General Augusto Pinochet then ruled as a dictator. A new constitution was introduced in 1981 and elections were held in 1989. In 2000, a socialist, Ricardo Lagos, was elected president. Pinochet, who had been charged with presiding over acts of torture, was found to be too ill to stand trial in 2001.

The World Bank classifies Chile as a 'lower-middle-income' developing country. Mining is important, especially copper production. Minerals dominate exports. The most valuable activity is manufacturing; products include processed foods, metals, iron and steel, transport equipment and textiles. The chief crop is wheat, while beans, fruits, maize and livestock products are also important. Chile's fishing industry is one of the world's largest.

AREA 756,626 sq km [292,133 sq mi] **POPULATION** 15,665,000
CAPITAL (POPULATION) Santiago (4,789,000)
GOVERNMENT Multiparty republic **ETHNIC GROUPS** Mestizo 95%, Amerindian 3% **LANGUAGES** Spanish (official)
RELIGIONS Roman Catholic 89%, Protestant 11%
CURRENCY Chilean peso = 100 centavos

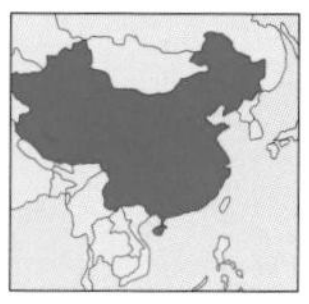

CHINA

GEOGRAPHY The People's Republic of China is the world's third largest country. Most people live in the east – on the coastal plains or in the fertile valleys of the Huang He (Hwang Ho or Yellow River), the Chang Jiang (Yangtze Kiang), which is Asia's longest river at 6,380 km [3,960 mi], and the Xi Jiang (Si Kiang). Western China is thinly populated. It includes the bleak Tibetan plateau which is bounded by the Himalaya, the world's highest mountain range. Other ranges include the Kunlun Shan, the Altun Shan and the Tian Shan. Deserts include the Gobi Desert along the Mongolian border and the Taklimakan Desert in the far west.

Beijing has cold winters and warm summers with moderate rainfall. To the south, Shanghai has milder winters and more rain. The south-east has a wet, subtropical climate, but the west has a severe climate. Lhasa has very cold winters and a low rainfall.

POLITICS & ECONOMY China is one of the world's oldest civilizations, going back 3,500 years. Under the Han dynasty (202 BC to AD 220), the Chinese empire was as large as the Roman empire. Mongols conquered China in the 13th century, but Chinese rule was restored in 1368. The Manchu people of Mongolia ruled the country from 1644 to 1912, when the country became a republic.

War with Japan (1937–45) was followed by civil war between the nationalists and the Communists. The Communists triumphed in 1949, setting up the People's Republic of China. In the 1980s, following the death of the revolutionary leader Mao Zedong (Mao Tse-tung) in 1976, China encouraged formerly forbidden policies, namely private enterprise and foreign investment. But the Communist leaders have not permitted political freedom. Opponents are still harshly treated, while attempts to negotiate some degree of autonomy for Tibet have been rejected.

China's economy has expanded greatly since the 1970s, with many Communist policies being abandoned. Foreign investors have help to set up many new industries in the east. Between 1989 and 2002, the economy grew by an average of 9.3% per year. With its cheap labour, trained managers and engineers, China has overtaken Japan to become the fourth largest exporter to the United States. It has benefited from the return of Hong Kong in 1997 and its admission to the World Trade Organization (WTO) in 2001. China would also like to regain the prosperous island of Taiwan, also a member of the WTO, but this seems unlikely in the near future. In 2004, the government announced plans to slow down economic growth by diverting resources to the rural poor, who had become relatively disadvantaged by the economic boom.

Despite its recent success, China remains a poor country. In the late 1990s, agriculture still employed nearly half of the people, although only 10% of the land is farmed. Products include rice, sweet potatoes, tea and wheat, and many fruits and vegetables. Livestock farming, especially pig rearing, is important. Resources include coal, iron ore, and other metals. Manufactures include cement, chemicals, fertilizers, machinery, telecommunications and recording equipment, and textiles. China is now a major producer of consumer goods, including air-conditioners, cameras, hard-disk drives and computer monitors, refrigerators, television sets and washing machines.

AREA 9,596,961 sq km [3,705,387 sq mi]
POPULATION 1,286,975,000 **CAPITAL (POPULATION)** Beijing (7,362,000) **GOVERNMENT** Single-party Communist republic
ETHNIC GROUPS Han Chinese 92%, many others
LANGUAGES Mandarin Chinese (official) **RELIGIONS** Atheist (official)
CURRENCY Renminbi yuan = 10 jiao = 100 fen

COLOMBIA

GEOGRAPHY The Republic of Colombia, in north-eastern South America, is the only country in the continent to have coastlines on both the Pacific and the Caribbean Sea. Colombia also contains the northernmost ranges of the Andes Mountains.

There is a tropical climate in the lowlands, but the altitude greatly affects the climate of the Andes. The capital, Bogotá, which stands on a plateau in the eastern Andes at about 2,800 m [9,200 ft] above sea level, has mild temperatures throughout the year. The rainfall is heavy, especially on the Pacific coast.

POLITICS & ECONOMY Amerindian people have lived in Colombia for thousands of years. But today, only a small proportion of the people are of unmixed Amerindian ancestry. Mestizos (people of mixed white and Amerindian ancestry) form the largest group, followed by whites and mulattos (people of mixed European and African ancestry).

Spaniards opened up the area in the early 16th century. They set up a territory known as the Vice-royalty of the New Kingdom of Granada, including Colombia, Ecuador, Panama and Venezuela. In 1819, the area became independent, but Ecuador and Venezuela soon split away, followed by Panama in 1903. Instability has marked its recent history. Political rivalries led to civil wars in 1899–1902 and 1949–57, when a coalition government was formed. The coalition ended in 1986 when the Liberal Party was elected. Colombia faces economic and security problems, notably combating left-wing guerrillas and right-wing paramilitaries, while controlling a large illicit drug industry. In the early 2000s, the US provided aid to help Colombia fight drug-trafficking. Colombia exports oil, coffee and chemicals.

AREA 1,138,914 sq km [439,735 sq mi] **POPULATION** 41,662,000
CAPITAL (POPULATION) Bogotá (6,545,000) **GOVERNMENT** Multiparty republic **ETHNIC GROUPS** Mestizo 58%, White 20%, Mulatto 14%, Black 4% **LANGUAGES** Spanish (official) **RELIGIONS** Roman Catholic 90% **CURRENCY** Colombian peso = 100 centavos

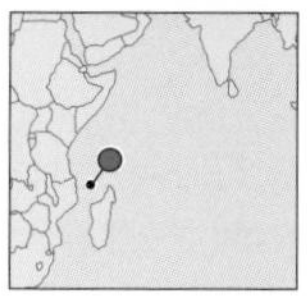

COMOROS

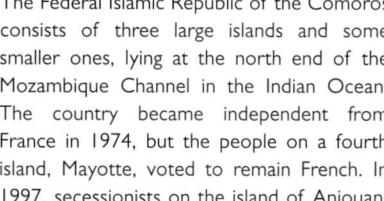

The Federal Islamic Republic of the Comoros consists of three large islands and some smaller ones, lying at the north end of the Mozambique Channel in the Indian Ocean. The country became independent from France in 1974, but the people on a fourth island, Mayotte, voted to remain French. In 1997, secessionists on the island of Anjouan, who favoured a return to French rule, defeated forces from Grand Comore and, in 1998, they voted overwhelmingly to break away from the Comoros. Most people are subsistence farmers, although cash crops such as coconuts, coffee, cocoa and spices are also produced. The main exports are cloves, perfume oils and vanilla.

AREA 2,235 sq km [863 sq mi] **POPULATION** 633,000 **CAPITAL** Moroni

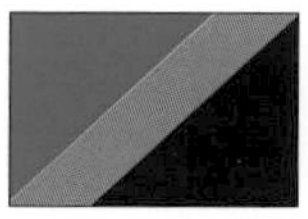
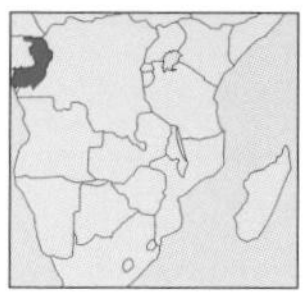

CONGO

GEOGRAPHY The Republic of Congo is a country on the River Congo in west-central Africa. The Equator runs through the centre of the country. Congo has a narrow coastal plain on which its main port, Pointe Noire, stands. Behind the plain are uplands through which the River Niari has carved a fertile valley. Central Congo consists of high plains. The north contains large swampy areas in the valleys of the tributaries of the River Congo.

Congo has a hot, wet equatorial climate. Brazzaville has a dry season between June and September. The coast is drier and cooler than the rest of Congo, because of the cold offshore Benguela ocean current.

POLITICS & ECONOMY Part of the huge Kongo kingdom between the 15th and 18th centuries, the coast of the Congo later became a centre of the European slave trade. The area came under French protection in 1880. It was later governed as part of a larger region called French Equatorial Africa. The country remained under French control until 1960.

Congo became a one-party state in 1964 and a military group took over the government in 1968. In 1970, Congo declared itself a Communist country, though it continued to seek aid from Western countries. The government officially abandoned its Communist policies in 1990. Multiparty elections were held in 1992, but the elected president, Pascal Lissouba, was overthrown in 1997 by former president Denis Sassou-Nguesso. Civil war again occurred in January 1999, but peace was restored. In 2002, Sassou-Nguesso was elected president.

The World Bank classifies Congo as a 'lower-middle-income' developing country. Agriculture is the most important activity, employing more than 60% of the people. But many farmers produce little more than they need to feed their families. Major food crops include bananas, cassava, maize and rice, while the leading cash crops are coffee and cocoa. Congo's main exports are oil (which makes up 90% of the total) and timber. Manufacturing is relatively unimportant at the moment, still hampered by poor transport links, but it is gradually being developed.

AREA 342,000 sq km [132,046 sq mi] **POPULATION** 2,954,000
CAPITAL (POPULATION) Brazzaville (938,000)
GOVERNMENT Military regime **ETHNIC GROUPS** Kongo 48%, Sangha 20%, Teke 17%, M'Bochi 12% **LANGUAGES** French (official), many others **RELIGIONS** Christianity 50%, animist 48%, Islam 2%
CURRENCY CFA franc = 100 centimes

CONGO (DEM. REP. OF THE)

GEOGRAPHY The Democratic Republic of the Congo, formerly known as Zaïre, is the world's 12th largest country. Much of the country lies within the drainage basin of the huge River Congo. The river reaches the sea along the country's coastline, which is 40 km [25 mi] long. Mountains rise in the east, where the country's borders run through lakes Tanganyika, Kivu, Edward and Albert. The equatorial region has high temperatures and heavy rainfall throughout the year.

POLITICS & ECONOMY Pygmies were the first inhabitants of the region, with Portuguese navigators not reaching the coast until 1482, but the interior was not explored until the late 19th century. In 1885, the country, called Congo Free State, became the personal property of King Léopold II of Belgium. In 1908, the country became a Belgian colony.

The Belgian Congo became independent in 1960 and was renamed Zaïre in 1971. Ethnic rivalries caused instability until 1965, when the country became a one-party state, ruled by President Mobutu. The government allowed the formation of political parties in 1990, but elections were repeatedly postponed. In 1996, fighting broke out in eastern Zaïre, as the Tutsi–Hutu conflict in Burundi and Rwanda spilled over. The rebel leader Laurent Kabila took power in 1997, ousting Mobutu and renaming the country. A rebellion against Kabila broke out in 1998. Rwanda and Uganda supported the rebels, while Angola, Chad, Namibia and Zimbabwe assisted Kabila. A peace treaty was signed in 1999, but fighting continued. Kabila was assassinated in 2001. His son, Major-General Joseph Kabila, who became president, worked to end a war which, by early 2003, had claimed over 2 million lives. But unrest continued and a failed coup occurred in March 2004.

The World Bank classifies the Democratic Republic of the Congo as a 'low-income' developing country, despite its reserves of copper, the main export, and other minerals. Agriculture, mainly at subsistence level, employs 63% of the people.

AREA 2,344,858 sq km [905,350 sq mi] **POPULATION** 56,625,000
CAPITAL (POPULATION) Kinshasa (4,665,000)
GOVERNMENT Single-party republic
ETHNIC GROUPS Over 200; the largest are Mongo, Luba, Kongo, Mangbetu-Azande
LANGUAGES French (official), tribal languages
RELIGIONS Roman Catholic 50%, Protestant 20%, Islam 10%, others
CURRENCY Congolese franc = 100 centimes

COSTA RICA

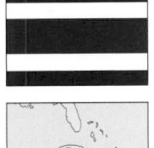

GEOGRAPHY The Republic of Costa Rica in Central America has coastlines on both the Pacific Ocean and also on the Caribbean Sea. Central Costa Rica consists of mountain ranges and plateaux with many volcanoes.

The coolest months are December and January. The north-east trade winds bring heavy rain to the Caribbean coast. There is less rainfall in the highlands and on the Pacific coastlands.

POLITICS & ECONOMY Christopher Columbus reached the Caribbean coast in 1502 and rumours of treasure soon attracted many Spaniards to settle in the country. Spain ruled the country until 1821, when Spain's Central American colonies broke away to join Mexico in 1822. In 1823, the Central American states broke with Mexico and set up the Central American Federation. Later, this large union broke up and Costa Rica became fully independent in 1838.

From the late 19th century, Costa Rica experienced a number of revolutions, with periods of dictatorship and periods of democracy. In 1948, following a revolt, the armed forces were abolished. Since 1948, Costa Rica has enjoyed a long period of stable democracy, which many in Latin America admire and envy.

Costa Rica is classified by the World Bank as a 'lower-middle-income' developing country and one of the most prosperous countries in Central America. There are high educational standards and a high average life expectancy (about 74 years for men and 79 years for women). Agriculture employs 19% of the people. Costa Rica's natural resources include its forests, but it lacks minerals apart from some bauxite and manganese. Manufacturing is increasing. The United States is Costa Rica's main trading partner. Tourism is a fast-growing industry.

AREA 51,100 sq km [19,730 sq mi] **POPULATION** 3,896,000
CAPITAL (POPULATION) San José (337,000) **GOVERNMENT** Multiparty republic **ETHNIC GROUPS** White (including Mestizo) 94%, Black 3%, Amerindian 1%, Chinese 1%, others **LANGUAGES** Spanish (official), English **RELIGIONS** Roman Catholic 76%, Evangelical 14%
CURRENCY Costa Rican colón = 100 céntimos

CROATIA

GEOGRAPHY The Republic of Croatia was one of the six republics that made up the former Communist country of Yugoslavia until it became independent in 1991. The region bordering the Adriatic Sea is called Dalmatia. It includes the coastal ranges, which contain large areas of bare limestone. Most of the rest of the country consists of the fertile Pannonian plains.

The coastal area has a typical Mediterranean climate, with hot, dry summers and mild, moist winters. Inland, the climate becomes more continental. Winters are cold, while temperatures often soar to 38°C [100°F] in the summer months.

POLITICS & ECONOMY Slav people settled in the area around 1,400 years ago. In 803, Croatia became part of the Holy Roman empire and the Croats soon adopted Christianity. Croatia was an independent kingdom in the 10th and 11th centuries. In 1102, the king of Hungary also became king of Croatia, creating a union that lasted 800 years. In 1526, part of Croatia came under the Turkish Ottoman empire, while the rest came under the Austrian Habsburgs.

After Austria–Hungary was defeated in World War I (1914–18), Croatia became part of the new Kingdom of the Serbs, Croats and Slovenes. This kingdom was renamed Yugoslavia in 1929. Germany occupied Yugoslavia during World War II (1939–45). Croatia was proclaimed independent, but it was really ruled by the invaders.

After the war, Communists took power with Josip Broz Tito as the country's leader. Despite ethnic differences between the people, Tito held Yugoslavia together until his death in 1980. In the 1980s, economic and ethnic problems, including a deterioration in relations with Serbia, threatened stability. In the 1990s, Yugoslavia split into five nations, one of which was Croatia, which declared itself independent in 1991.

After Serbia supplied arms to Serbs living in Croatia, war broke out between the two republics, causing great damage. Croatia lost more than 30% of its territory. But in 1992, the United Nations sent a peacekeeping force to Croatia, which effectively ended the war with Serbia.

In 1992, when war broke out in Bosnia-Herzegovina, Bosnian Croats occupied parts of the country. But in 1994, Croatia helped to end Croat–Muslim conflict in Bosnia-Herzegovina and, in 1995, after retaking some areas occupied by Serbs, it helped to draw up the Dayton Peace Accord, ending the civil war. The wars in the early 1990s disrupted the economy. But in the early 21st century, stability, which is so vital to the valuable tourist industry, seemed to be returning, although early accession to European Union membership was ruled out in 2003. Manufactures are Croatia's main exports.

AREA 56,538 sq km [21,829 sq mi] **POPULATION** 4,422,000
CAPITAL (POPULATION) Zagreb (779,000) **GOVERNMENT** Multiparty republic **ETHNIC GROUPS** Croat 90%, Serb 5%, others **LANGUAGES** Croatian 96% **RELIGIONS** Roman Catholic 88%, Orthodox 4%, Islam 1%, others **CURRENCY** Kuna = 100 lipas

CUBA

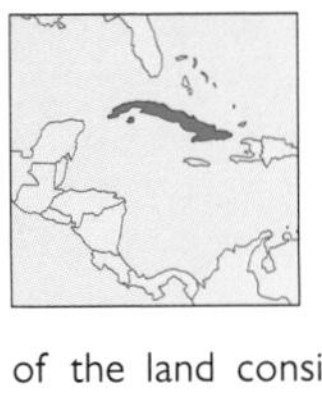

GEOGRAPHY The Republic of Cuba is the largest island country in the Caribbean Sea. It consists of one large island, Cuba, the Isle of Youth (Isla de la Juventud) and about 1,600 small islets. Mountains and hills cover about a quarter of Cuba. The highest mountain range, the Sierra Maestra in the south-east, reaches 2,000 m [6,562 ft] above sea level. The rest of the land consists of gently rolling country or coastal plains, crossed by fertile valleys carved by the short, mostly shallow and narrow rivers.

Cuba lies in the tropics. But sea breezes moderate the temperature, warming the land in winter and cooling it in summer.

POLITICS & ECONOMY Christopher Columbus discovered the island in 1492 and Spaniards began to settle there from 1511. Spanish rule ended in 1898, when the United States defeated Spain in the Spanish–American War. American influence in Cuba remained strong until 1959, when revolutionary forces under Fidel Castro overthrew the dictatorial government of Fulgencio Batista.

The United States opposed Castro's policies, when he turned to the Soviet Union for assistance. In 1961, Cuban exiles attempting an invasion were defeated. In 1962, the US learned that nuclear missile bases armed by the Soviet Union had been established in Cuba. The US ordered the Soviet Union to remove the missiles and bases and, after a few days, when many people feared that a world war might break out, the Soviet Union agreed to the American demands.

Cuba's relations with the Soviet Union remained strong until 1991, when the Soviet Union was broken up. The loss of Soviet aid greatly damaged Cuba's economy, but Castro maintained his left-wing policies. In 2000, the United States lifted its food embargo on Cuba, but Cuba again came under fire in 2003 following the arrests of 78 opponents of the regime.

The government runs Cuba's economy and owns 70% of the farmland. Agriculture is important and sugar is the chief export, followed by refined nickel ore. Other exports include cigars, citrus fruits, fish, medical products and rum.

Before 1959, US companies owned most of Cuba's manufacturing industries. But under Fidel Castro, they became government property. After the collapse of Communist governments in the Soviet Union and its allies, Cuba worked to increase its trade with Latin America and China.

AREA 110,861 sq km [42,803 sq mi] **POPULATION** 11,263,000
CAPITAL (POPULATION) Havana (2,192,000)
GOVERNMENT Socialist republic
ETHNIC GROUPS Mulatto 51%, White 37%, Black 11%
LANGUAGES Spanish (official) **RELIGIONS** Christianity
CURRENCY Cuban peso = 100 centavos

CYPRUS

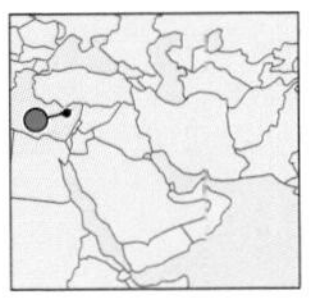

GEOGRAPHY The Republic of Cyprus is an island nation in the north-eastern Mediterranean Sea. Geographers regard it as part of Asia, but it resembles southern Europe in many ways. Its scenic mountain ranges include the southern Troodos Mountains, which reach 1,951 m [6,401 ft] at Mount Olympus, and the Kyrenia range in the north. Between them lies the Mesaoria plain. The climate is Mediterranean, with typically hot, dry summers and mild, moist winters. But the island's proximity to south-western Asia gives it a hotter climate than places in the western Mediterranean.

POLITICS & ECONOMY Greeks settled on Cyprus around 3,200 years ago. From AD 330, the island was part of the Byzantine empire. In the 1570s, Cyprus became part of the Turkish Ottoman empire. Turkish rule continued until 1878 when Cyprus was leased to Britain. Britain annexed the island in 1914 and proclaimed it a colony in 1925.

In the 1950s, Greek Cypriots, who made up four-fifths of the population, began a campaign for *enosis* (union) with Greece. Their leader was the Greek Orthodox Archbishop Makarios. A secret guerrilla force called EOKA attacked the British, who exiled Makarios. Cyprus became an independent country in 1960, although Britain retained two military bases. Independent Cyprus had a constitution which provided for power-sharing between the Greek and Turkish Cypriots. But the constitution proved unworkable and fighting broke out between the two communities. In 1964, the United Nations sent in a peacekeeping force, but communal clashes recurred in 1967.

In 1974, Cypriot forces led by Greek officers overthrew Makarios. This led Turkey to invade northern Cyprus, a territory occupying about 40% of the island. Many Greek Cypriots fled from the north, which, in 1979, was proclaimed the Turkish Republic of Northern Cyprus. The only country to recognize this state was Turkey. The United Nations regarded Cyprus as a single unit under the Greek-Cypriot government in the south. In 2002, the European Union invited Cyprus to become a member in 2004. In April 2004, the people voted on a UN plan to reunify the island. The Turkish-Cypriots voted in favour, but the Greek-Cypriots voted against. Hence, only the south was admitted to EU membership on 1 May 2004.

Cyprus got its name from the Greek word *kypros*, meaning copper. But little copper remains and the chief minerals today are asbestos and chromium. However, the most valuable activity in Cyprus is tourism. Manufactures include cement, clothes, footwear, tiles and wine.

In the early 1990s, the United Nations reclassified Cyprus as a developed rather than a developing country, reflecting the rapid economic progress in the south. But the north lagged far behind the prosperous Greek-Cypriot south.

AREA 9,251 sq km [3,572 sq mi] **POPULATION** 772,000
CAPITAL (POPULATION) Nicosia (198,000)
GOVERNMENT Multiparty republic **ETHNIC GROUPS** Greek Cypriot 77%, Turkish Cypriot 18%, others **LANGUAGES** Greek and Turkish (both official), English **RELIGIONS** Greek Orthodox 78%, Islam 18%
CURRENCY Cypriot pound = 100 cents

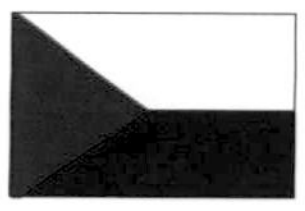

CZECH REPUBLIC

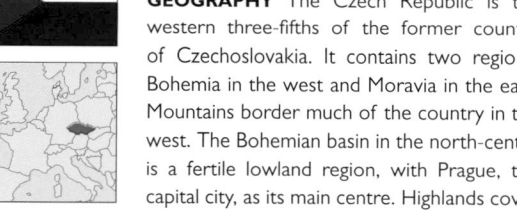

GEOGRAPHY The Czech Republic is the western three-fifths of the former country of Czechoslovakia. It contains two regions: Bohemia in the west and Moravia in the east. Mountains border much of the country in the west. The Bohemian basin in the north-centre is a fertile lowland region, with Prague, the capital city, as its main centre. Highlands cover much of the centre of the country, with lowlands in the south-east.

The climate is influenced by its landlocked position in east-central Europe. Prague has warm, sunny summers and cold winters. The average rainfall is moderate, with 500 mm to 750 mm [20 in to 30 in] every year in lowland areas.

POLITICS & ECONOMY After World War I (1914–18), Czechoslovakia was created. Germany seized the country in World War II (1939–45). In 1948, Communist leaders took power and Czechoslovakia was allied to the Soviet Union. When democratic reforms were introduced in the Soviet Union in the late 1980s, the Czechs also demanded reforms. Free elections were held in 1990, but differences between the Czechs and Slovaks led to the partitioning of the country on 1 January 1993. The Czech Republic became a member of NATO in 1999. In 2003, 77% of Czechs voted in favour of their country becoming a member of the European Union. This took place on 1 May 2004.

Under Communist rule the Czech Republic became one of the most industrialized parts of Eastern Europe. The country has deposits of coal, uranium, iron ore, magnesite, tin and zinc. Manufacturing employs about 29% of the Czech Republic's entire workforce. Farming is also important. Under Communism, the government owned the land, but private ownership is now being restored. The country was admitted into the OECD in 1995.

AREA 78,866 sq km [30,450 sq mi] **POPULATION** 10,249,000
CAPITAL (POPULATION) Prague (1,193,000)
GOVERNMENT Multiparty republic **ETHNIC GROUPS** Czech 81%, Moravian 13%, Slovak 3%, Polish, German, Silesian, Gypsy, Hungarian, Ukrainian **LANGUAGES** Czech (official) **RELIGIONS** Atheist 40%, Roman Catholic 39%, Protestant 4%, Orthodox 3%, others
CURRENCY Czech koruna = 100 haler

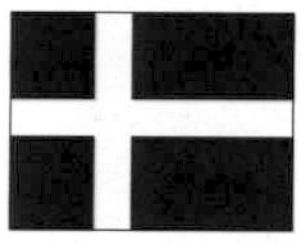

DENMARK

GEOGRAPHY The Kingdom of Denmark is the smallest country in Scandinavia. It consists of a peninsula, called Jutland (or Jylland), which is joined to Germany, and more than 400 islands, 89 of which are inhabited. The land is flat and mostly covered by rocks dropped there by huge ice sheets during the last Ice Age. The highest point in Denmark is on Jutland. It is only 173 m [568 ft] above sea level. Denmark has a mild, moist climate, except during cold spells in winter when The Sound between Sjælland and Sweden may freeze over.

POLITICS & ECONOMY Danish Vikings terrorized much of Western Europe for about 300 years after AD 800. In the late 14th century, Denmark formed a union with Norway and Sweden (which included Finland). Sweden broke away in 1523, while Denmark lost Norway to Sweden in 1814. After 1945, Denmark became a member of the North Atlantic Treaty Organization. It joined the European Union in 1973, though it did not adopt the euro in 2000. The Danes enjoy a high standard of living, but the country's welfare programmes are extremely costly.

Denmark has some oil and gas and the economy is highly developed. Manufacturing employs about 16% of the people. Products include furniture, processed food, machinery, television sets and textiles. Farms cover about three-quarters of the land. Farming employs only 3% of the people, but it is highly scientific. Meat and dairy farming are the chief activities.

AREA 43,094 sq km [16,639 sq mi] **POPULATION** 5,384,000
CAPITAL (POPULATION) Copenhagen (499,000) **GOVERNMENT** Parliamentary monarchy **ETHNIC GROUPS** Scandinavian, Inuit, Færoese **LANGUAGES** Danish (official), English, Færoese **RELIGIONS** Evangelical Lutheran 95% **CURRENCY** Danish krone = 100 øre

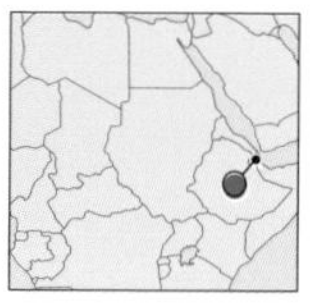

DJIBOUTI

GEOGRAPHY The Republic of Djibouti in eastern Africa occupies a strategic position where the Red Sea meets the Gulf of Aden. Djibouti has one of the world's hottest and driest climates.

POLITICS & ECONOMY France set up a territory called French Somaliland in 1888. Its capital, Djibouti, became important when a railway was built to Addis Ababa and Djibouti became the main outlet for Ethiopian trade. In 1967, France renamed the dependency the French Territory of the Afars and Issas, but it was renamed Djibouti on independence in 1977. It became a one-party state in 1981, but a new constitution (1992) permitted four parties which had to maintain a balance between the country's ethnic groups. Conflict between the Afars and Issas flared up in 1992 and 1993, but a peace agreement was signed in 1994.

Djibouti is a poor country. Its economy is based largely on the revenue it gets from its port and the railway to Addis Ababa.

AREA 23,200 sq km [8,958 sq mi] **POPULATION** 457,000
CAPITAL (POPULATION) Djibouti (317,000) **GOVERNMENT** Multiparty republic **ETHNIC GROUPS** Somali 60%, Afar 35% **LANGUAGES** Arabic and French (both official) **RELIGIONS** Islam 94%, Christianity 6%
CURRENCY Djiboutian franc = 100 centimes

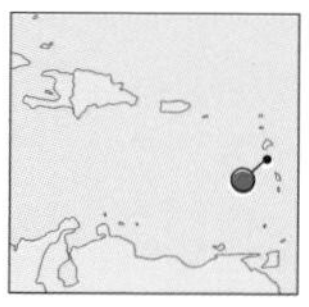

DOMINICA

The Commonwealth of Dominica, a former British colony, became independent in 1978. The island has a mountainous spine and less than 10% of the land is cultivated. But agriculture employs 18% of the people. The manufacture of coconut-based soap is important, while tourism and mining are other economic activities.

AREA 751 sq km [290 sq mi] **POPULATION** 70,000 **CAPITAL** Roseau

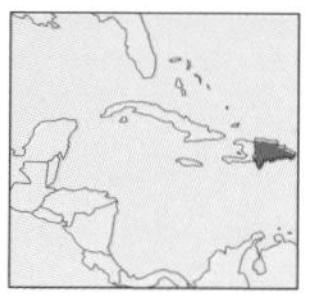

DOMINICAN REPUBLIC

GEOGRAPHY Second largest of the Caribbean nations in both area and population, the Dominican Republic shares the island of Hispaniola with Haiti, with the Dominican Republic occupying the eastern two-thirds. The country is mountainous, and the generally hot and humid climate eases with altitude.

POLITICS & ECONOMY In 1492, Christopher Columbus landed on Hispaniola and Spaniards soon settled the island, followed by the French who occupied the western third of the island (which is now Haiti). The island was held by Haitians from 1822 until 1844, when the Dominican Republic was established. Civil war broke out in 1966 but US intervention ended the conflict. Since 1966, the young democracy has survived violent elections under the watchful eye of the United States.

The Dominican Republic is a developing country and agriculture is the chief activity. Sugar cane, rice, bananas and cocoa are leading crops. Food processing is also important and some ferronickel is produced.

AREA 48,511 sq km [18,730 sq mi] **POPULATION** 8,716,000
CAPITAL (POPULATION) Santo Domingo (2,061,000)
GOVERNMENT Multiparty republic **ETHNIC GROUPS** Mulatto 73%, White 16%, Black 11% **LANGUAGES** Spanish (official) **RELIGIONS** Roman Catholic 95% **CURRENCY** Dominican peso = 100 centavos

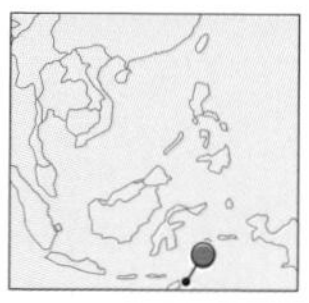

EAST TIMOR

The Republic of East Timor became fully independent and the world's newest country on 20 May 2002. The land is mainly rugged. Temperatures are generally high and the rainfall is moderate. Portugal ruled the area from the late 19th century, when it was called Portuguese Timor. Portugal withdrew in 1975 and Indonesia seized the area. Guerrilla activity mounted under Indonesian rule and, in 1999, the people voted for independence. Agriculture is the main activity. East Timor is heavily dependent on foreign aid. Offshore oil and natural gas deposits hold out hope for the future, though the ownership of some of the oilfields is disputed with Australia.

AREA 14,874 sq km [5,743 sq mi] **POPULATION** 998,000 **CAPITAL** Dili

ECUADOR

GEOGRAPHY The Republic of Ecuador straddles the Equator on the west coast of South America. Three ranges of the high Andes Mountains form the backbone of the country. Between the towering, snow-capped peaks of the mountains, some of which are volcanoes, lie a series of high plateaux, or basins. Nearly half of Ecuador's population lives on these plateaux.

The climate in Ecuador depends on the height above sea level. Though the coastline is cooled by the cold Peruvian Current, temperatures are between 23°C and 25°C [73°F to 77°F] all through the year. In Quito, at 2,500 m [8,200 ft] above sea level, temperatures are 14°C to 15°C [57°F to 59°F], though the city is just south of the Equator.

POLITICS & ECONOMY The Inca people of Peru conquered much of what is now Ecuador in the late 15th century. They introduced their language, Quechua, which is widely spoken today. Spanish forces defeated the Incas in 1533 and took control of Ecuador. The country became independent in 1822, following the defeat of a Spanish force in a battle near Quito.

In the 19th and 20th centuries, Ecuador suffered from political instability, while successive governments failed to tackle the country's social and economic problems. A war with Peru in 1941 led to a loss of territory. Disputes continued until 1995, but a border agreement was signed in January 1998. Economic crises in the early 21st century led the government to abolish the sucre, its official currency, and replace it with the US dollar.

The World Bank classifies Ecuador as a 'lower-middle-income' developing country. Agriculture employs 30% of the people and bananas, cocoa and coffee are all important crops. Fishing, forestry, mining and manufacturing are other activities.

AREA 283,561 sq km [109,483 sq mi] **POPULATION** 13,710,000
CAPITAL (POPULATION) Quito (1,648,000)
GOVERNMENT Multiparty republic
ETHNIC GROUPS Mestizo (mixed White/Amerindian) 65%, Amerindian 25%, White 7%, Black 3%
LANGUAGES Spanish (official), Quechua
RELIGIONS Roman Catholic 95%
CURRENCY US dollar = 100 cents

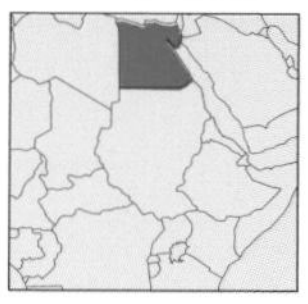

EGYPT

GEOGRAPHY The Arab Republic of Egypt is Africa's second largest country by population after Nigeria, though it ranks 13th in area. Most of Egypt is desert. Almost all the people live either in the Nile Valley and its fertile delta or along the Suez Canal, the artificial waterway between the Mediterranean and Red seas. This canal shortens the sea journey between the United Kingdom and India by 9,700 km [6,027 mi]. Recent attempts have been made to irrigate parts of the western desert and thus redistribute the rapidly growing Egyptian population into previously uninhabited regions.

Apart from the Nile Valley, Egypt has three other main regions. The Western and Eastern deserts are parts of the Sahara. The Sinai peninsula (Es Sina), to the east of the Suez Canal, is a mountainous desert region, geographically within Asia. It contains Egypt's highest peak, Gebel Katherina (2,637 m [8,650 ft]); few people live in this area.

Egypt is a dry country. The low rainfall occurs, if at all, in winter and the country is one of the sunniest places on Earth.

POLITICS & ECONOMY Ancient Egypt, which was founded about 5,000 years ago, was one of the great early civilizations. Throughout the country, pyramids, temples and richly decorated tombs are memorials to its great achievements.

After Ancient Egypt declined, the country came under successive foreign rulers. Arabs occupied Egypt in AD 639–42. They introduced the Arabic language and Islam. Their influence was so great that most Egyptians now regard themselves as Arabs.

Egypt came under British rule in 1882, but it gained partial independence in 1922, becoming a monarchy. The monarchy was abolished in 1952, when Egypt became a republic. The creation of Israel in 1948 led Egypt into a series of wars in 1948–9, 1956, 1967 and 1973. Since the late 1970s, Egypt has sought for peace. In 1979, Egypt signed a peace treaty with Israel and regained the Sinai region which it had lost in a war in 1967. Extremists opposed contacts with Israel and, in 1981, President Sadat, who had signed the treaty, was assassinated.

While Egypt plays a major part in Arab affairs, most of its people are poor. Some Islamic fundamentalists, who dislike Western influences on their way of life, have resorted to violence. In the

1990s, attacks on foreign visitors caused a decline in the valuable tourist industry, as also did the events of 11 September 2001 and the subsequent 'war against terrorism'. In 1999, Hosni Mubarak, president since 1981, was himself attacked by extremists, but he was re-elected to a fourth term in office.

Egypt is Africa's second most industrialized country after South Africa, but most people are poor. Oil and textiles are the main exports.

AREA 1,001,449 sq km [386,659 sq mi] **POPULATION** 74,719,000
CAPITAL (POPULATION) Cairo (6,801,000)
GOVERNMENT Republic
ETHNIC GROUPS Egyptians/Bedouins/Berbers 99%
LANGUAGES Arabic (official), French, English
RELIGIONS Islam (mainly Sunni Muslim) 94%, Christianity (mainly Coptic Christian) and others 6%
CURRENCY Egyptian pound = 100 piastres

EL SALVADOR

GEOGRAPHY The Republic of El Salvador is the only country in Central America which does not have a coast on the Caribbean Sea. El Salvador has a narrow coastal plain along the Pacific Ocean. Behind the coastal plain, the coastal range is a zone of rugged mountains, including volcanoes, which overlooks a densely populated inland plateau. Beyond the plateau, the land rises to the sparsely populated interior highlands. The coast has a hot, tropical climate. Inland the climate is moderated by the altitude. Rain falls on practically every afternoon between May and October.

POLITICS & ECONOMY Amerindians have lived in El Salvador for thousands of years. The ruins of Mayan pyramids built between AD 100 and 1000 are still found in the western part of the country. Spanish soldiers conquered the area in 1524 and 1525, and Spain ruled until 1821. In 1823, all the Central American countries, except for Panama, set up a Central American Federation. But El Salvador withdrew in 1840 and declared its independence in 1841. El Salvador suffered from instability throughout the 19th century. The 20th century saw a more stable government, but from 1931 military dictatorships alternated with elected governments.

The country remained poor. In the 1970s, protesters demanded that the government introduce reforms to help the poor. Kidnappings and murders committed by left- and right-wing groups caused instability. A civil war broke out in 1979 between the US-backed government forces and left-wing guerrillas. In 12 years, more than 750,000 people died and many were made homeless. A cease-fire was agreed in 1992 and democratic elections were held in 1993, 1999 and 2003. By 2003, the economy had shown signs of recovery, but the World Bank still classifies El Salvador as a 'lower-middle-income' economy.

About three-quarters of the country is farmed. Coffee, grown in the highlands, is the main export, followed by sugar and cotton, which grow on the coastal lowlands. Fishing for lobsters and shrimps is important, but manufacturing is on a small scale.

AREA 21,041 sq km [8,124 sq mi] **POPULATION** 6,470,000
CAPITAL (POPULATION) San Salvador (473,000)
GOVERNMENT Republic **ETHNIC GROUPS** Mestizo (mixed White and Amerindian) 90%, White 9%, Amerindian 1%
LANGUAGES Spanish (official) **RELIGIONS** Roman Catholic 83%
CURRENCY US dollar = 100 cents

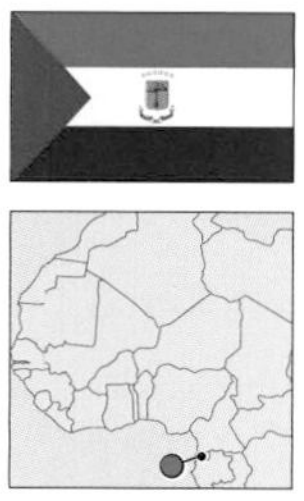

EQUATORIAL GUINEA

GEOGRAPHY The Republic of Equatorial Guinea is a small republic in west-central Africa. It consists of a mainland territory which makes up 90% of the land area, called Rio Muni, between Cameroon and Gabon, and five offshore islands in the Bight of Bonny, the largest of which is Bioko. The island of Annobon lies 560 km [350 mi] south-west of Rio Muni. Rio Muni consists mainly of hills and plateaux behind the coastal plains.

The climate is hot and humid. Bioko is mountainous, with the land rising to 3,008 m [9,869 ft], and hence it is particularly rainy. However, there is a marked dry season between the months of December and February. Mainland Rio Muni has a similar climate, though the rainfall diminishes inland.

POLITICS & ECONOMY Portuguese navigators reached the area in 1471. In 1778, Portugal granted Bioko, together with rights over Rio Muni, to Spain.

In 1959, Spain made Bioko and Rio Muni provinces of overseas Spain and, in 1963, it gave the provinces a degree of self-government. Equatorial Guinea became independent in 1968.

The first president of Equatorial Guinea, Francisco Macias Nguema, proved to be a tyrant. He was overthrown in 1979 and a group of officers, led by Lieutenant-Colonel Teodoro Obiang Nguema Mbasogo, set up a Supreme Military Council to rule the country. In 1991, the people voted to set up a multiparty democracy. Elections were held in the 1990s, but accusations of human rights abuses continued.

Agriculture employs more than half of the people and the most valuable crop is coffee. Oil has been produced since 1966 and, by 2002, it accounted for about 60% of the country's gross national product.

AREA 28,051 sq km [10,830 sq mi] **POPULATION** 510,000
CAPITAL (POPULATION) Malabo (30,000) **GOVERNMENT** Multiparty republic (transitional) **ETHNIC GROUPS** Bubi (on Bioko), Fang (in Rio Muni) **LANGUAGES** Spanish and French (both official)
RELIGIONS Christianity **CURRENCY** CFA franc = 100 centimes

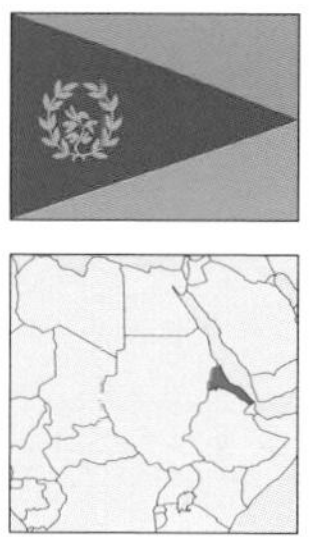

ERITREA

GEOGRAPHY The State of Eritrea consists of a hot, dry coastal plain facing the Red Sea, with a fairly mountainous area in the centre. Most people live in the cooler highland area.

POLITICS & ECONOMY From the 1st century AD, Eritrea was part of the ancient Kingdom of Axum, which adopted Christianity in the 4th century AD. It began to decline in the 7th century. The Ottoman Turks took over the area in the 16th century and it became an Italian colony in the 1880s. The Italians were driven out in 1941 and, in 1952, it became part of Ethiopia.

A guerrilla struggle launched in 1961 ended in 1993, when Eritrea became independent. Economic recovery was hampered by conflict with Yemen over three islands in the Red Sea. In 1988–9, clashes occurred along the border with Ethiopia. A peace agreement was signed in 2000, but arguments again broke out in 2003 over the proposed redrawing of the boundaries.

The main economic activities are farming and livestock rearing. The few manufacturing industries are based mainly in Asmara.

AREA 117,600 sq km [45,405 sq mi] **POPULATION** 4,362,000
CAPITAL (POPULATION) Asmara (358,000) **GOVERNMENT** Transitional government **ETHNIC GROUPS** Tigrinya 50%, Tigre and Kunama 40%, Afar 4%, Saho 3%, others **LANGUAGES** Afar, Arabic, Tigre and Kunama, Tigrinya **RELIGIONS** Islam, Coptic Christian, Roman Catholic **CURRENCY** Nakfa = 100 cents

ESTONIA

GEOGRAPHY The Republic of Estonia is the smallest of the three states on the Baltic Sea, which were formerly part of the Soviet Union, but which became independent in the early 1990s. Estonia consists of a generally flat plain which was covered by ice sheets during the Ice Age. The land is strewn with moraine (rocks deposited by the ice).

The country is dotted with more than 1,500 small lakes. The large Lake Peipus (Chudskoye Ozero) and the River Narva together make up much of Estonia's eastern border with Russia. Estonia also has more than 800 islands, which together make up about a tenth of the country. The largest island is Saaremaa (Sarema). Despite its northerly position, Estonia has a fairly mild climate because of the moderating effects of the sea.

POLITICS & ECONOMY The ancestors of the Estonians, who are related to the Finns, settled in the area several thousand years ago. German crusaders, known as the Teutonic Knights, introduced Christianity in the early 13th century. By the 16th century, German noblemen owned much of the land in Estonia. In 1561, Sweden took the northern part of the country and Poland the south. From 1625, Sweden controlled the entire country until Sweden handed it over to Russia in 1721.

Estonian nationalists campaigned for their independence from around the mid-19th century. Finally, Estonia was proclaimed independent in 1918. In 1919, the government began to break up the large estates and distribute land among the peasants.

In 1939, Germany and the Soviet Union agreed to take over parts of Eastern Europe. In 1940, Soviet forces occupied Estonia, but they were driven out by the Germans in 1941. Soviet troops returned in 1944 and Estonia became one of the 15 Soviet Socialist Republics of the Soviet Union. The Estonians strongly opposed Soviet rule. Many of them were deported to Siberia.

Political changes in the Soviet Union in the late 1980s led to renewed demands for freedom. In 1990, the Estonian government declared the country independent and, finally, the Soviet Union recognized this act in September 1991, shortly before the Soviet Union was dissolved. Estonia adopted a new constitution in 1992, when multiparty elections were held for a new national assembly. In 1993, Estonia negotiated an agreement with Russia to withdraw its troops.

Under Soviet rule, Estonia was the most prosperous of the three Baltic states. Since 1988, Estonia has worked to restructure its economy. Turning increasingly to the West, it became a member of both the North Atlantic Treaty Organization and the European Union in 2004. Estonia's resources include oil shale and its forests. Industries produce fertilizers, processed food, machinery, petrochemical products, wood products and textiles. Agriculture and fishing are also important activities.

AREA 45,100 sq km [17,413 sq mi] **POPULATION** 1,409,000
CAPITAL (POPULATION) Tallinn (418,000) **GOVERNMENT** Multiparty republic **ETHNIC GROUPS** Estonian 65%, Russian 28%, Ukrainian 3%, Belarusian 2%, Finnish 1% **LANGUAGES** Estonian (official), Russian
RELIGIONS Lutheran, Russian and Estonian Orthodox, Methodist, Baptist, Roman Catholic **CURRENCY** Estonian kroon = 100 senti

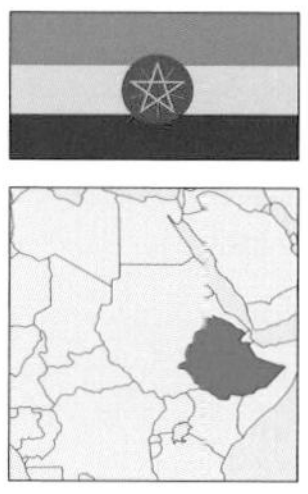

ETHIOPIA

GEOGRAPHY Ethiopia is a landlocked country in north-eastern Africa. The land is mainly mountainous, though there are extensive plains in the east, bordering southern Eritrea, and in the south, bordering Somalia. The highlands are divided into two blocks by an arm of the Great Rift Valley which runs throughout eastern Africa. North of the Rift Valley, the land is especially rugged, rising to 4,620 m [15,157 ft] at Ras Dashen. South-east of Ras Dashen is Lake Tana, source of the River Abay (Blue Nile).

The climate in Ethiopia is greatly affected by the altitude. Addis Ababa, at 2,450 m [8,000 ft], has an average yearly temperature of 20°C [68°F]. The rainfall is generally more than 1,000 mm [39 in]. But the lowlands bordering the Eritrean coast are hot.

POLITICS & ECONOMY Ethiopia was the home of an ancient monarchy, which became Christian in the 4th century. In the 7th century, Muslims gained control of the lowlands, but Christianity survived in the highlands. Ethiopia resisted attempts to colonize it, but Italy invaded the country in 1935. The Italians were driven out in 1941 during World War II.

In 1952, Eritrea, on the Red Sea coast, was federated with Ethiopia. But in 1961, Eritrean nationalists demanded their freedom and began a struggle that ended in their independence in 1993. Clashes along the border with Eritrea occurred in 1998 and 1999, but a peace agreement was signed in 2000, though a disagreement arose in 2003 about the status of Badme, the village where the conflict began. Some Ethiopian minorities would like self-government and, in 1995, the country was divided into nine provinces, each with its own regional assembly.

Ethiopia is one of the world's poorest countries, particularly in the 1970s and 1980s when it was plagued by civil war and famine caused partly by long droughts. Many richer countries have sent aid (money and food) to help the Ethiopian people. Agriculture remains the leading activity.

AREA 1,104,300 sq km [426,370 sq mi] **POPULATION** 66,558,000
CAPITAL (POPULATION) Addis Ababa (2,424,000) **GOVERNMENT** Federation of nine provinces **ETHNIC GROUPS** Oromo 40%, Amhara and Tigre 32%, Sidamo 9%, Shankella 6%, Somali 6%, others
LANGUAGES Amharic (official), many others **RELIGIONS** Islam 47%, Ethiopian Orthodox 40%, traditional beliefs 12%
CURRENCY Birr = 100 cents

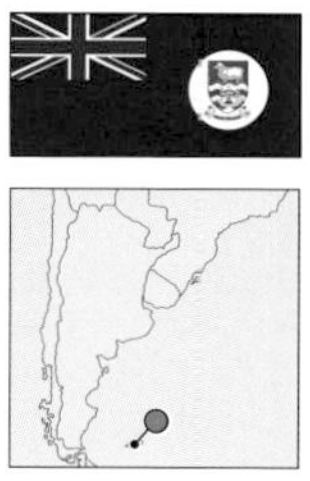

FALKLAND ISLANDS

Comprising two main islands and over 200 small islands, the Falkland Islands (or the Islas Malvinas, as they are called in Argentina) lie 480 km [300 mi] from South America. Sheep farming is the main activity, though the search for oil and diamonds holds out hope for the future of this harsh and virtually treeless environment.

AREA 12,173 sq km [4,700 sq mi] **POPULATION** 3,000
CAPITAL (POPULATION) Stanley (1,600)

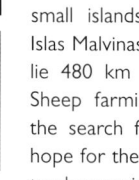

FÆROE ISLANDS

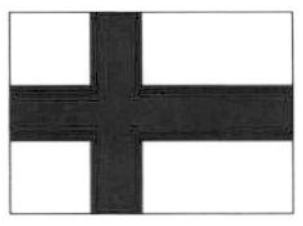

The Færoe Islands are a group of 18 volcanic islands and some reefs in the North Atlantic Ocean. The islands have been Danish since the 1380s, but they became largely self-governing in 1948. In 1998, the government of the Færoes announced its intention to become independent of Denmark.

AREA 1,399 SQ KM [540 SQ MI]
POPULATION 46,000 **CAPITAL** TÓRSHAVN

FIJI ISLANDS

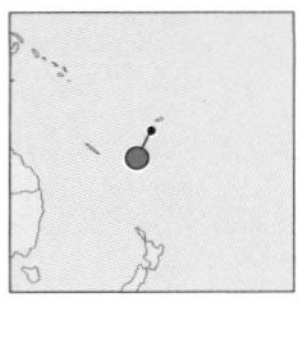

The Fiji Islands (the official name of Fiji since 1998) is a republic consisting of more than 800 Melanesian islands, the biggest being Viti Levu and Vanua Levu. The climate is tropical. A former British colony, Fiji became independent in 1970. Its recent history has been marred by efforts by ethnic Fijians to impose their rule, stopping members of the ethnic Indian community from holding senior cabinet posts. This action provoked international criticism.

AREA 18,274 SQ KM [7,056 SQ MI] **POPULATION** 869,000 **CAPITAL** SUVA

FINLAND

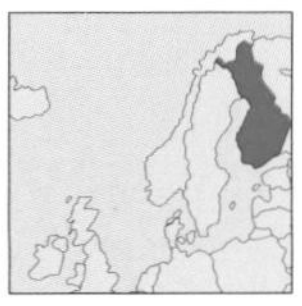

GEOGRAPHY The Republic of Finland is a beautiful country in northern Europe. In the south, behind the coastal lowlands where most Finns live, lies a region of sparkling lakes worn out by ice sheets in the Ice Age. The thinly populated northern uplands cover about two-fifths of the country.

Helsinki, the capital city, has warm summers, but the average temperatures between the months of December and March are below freezing point. Snow covers the land in winter. The north has less precipitation than the south, but it is much colder.

POLITICS & ECONOMY Between 1150 and 1809, Finland was under Swedish rule. The close links between the countries continue today. Swedish remains an official language in Finland and many towns have Swedish as well as Finnish names.

In 1809, Finland became a grand duchy of the Russian empire. It finally declared itself independent in 1917, after the Russian Revolution and the collapse of the Russian empire. But during World War II (1939–45), the Soviet Union declared war on Finland and took part of Finland's territory. Finland allied itself with Germany, but it lost more land to the Soviet Union at the end of the war.

After World War II, Finland became a neutral country and negotiated peace treaties with the Soviet Union. Finland also strengthened its relations with other northern European countries and became an associate member of the European Free Trade Association (EFTA) in 1961. Finland became a full member of EFTA in 1986, but in 1992, along with most of its fellow EFTA members, it applied for membership of the European Union, which it finally achieved on 1 January 1995. On 1 January 2002, the euro became Finland's sole official unit of currency.

Forests are Finland's most valuable resource, and forestry accounts for about 35% of the country's exports. The chief manufactures are wood products, pulp and paper. Since World War II, Finland has set up many other industries, producing such things as machinery and transport equipment. Its economy has expanded rapidly, but there has been a large increase in the number of unemployed people.

AREA 338,145 SQ KM [130,558 SQ MI] **POPULATION** 5,191,000
CAPITAL (POPULATION) HELSINKI (549,000)
GOVERNMENT MULTIPARTY REPUBLIC **ETHNIC GROUPS** FINNISH 93%, SWEDISH 6% **LANGUAGES** FINNISH AND SWEDISH (BOTH OFFICIAL)
RELIGIONS EVANGELICAL LUTHERAN 89% **CURRENCY** EURO = 100 CENTS

FRANCE

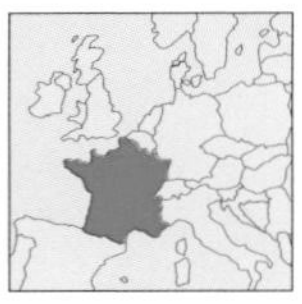

GEOGRAPHY The Republic of France is the largest country in Western Europe. The scenery is extremely varied. The Vosges Mountains overlook the Rhine valley in the north-east, the Jura Mountains and the Alps form the borders with Switzerland and Italy in the south-east, while the Pyrenees straddle France's border with Spain. The only large highland area entirely within France is the Massif Central between the Rhône-Saône valley and the basin of Aquitaine in southern France.

Brittany (Bretagne) and Normandy (Normande) form a scenic hill region. Fertile lowlands cover most of northern France, including the densely populated Paris basin. Another major lowland area, the Aquitanian basin, is in the south-west, while the Rhône-Saône valley and the Mediterranean lowlands are in the south-east.

The climate of France varies from west to east and from north to south. The west comes under the moderating influence of the Atlantic Ocean, giving generally mild weather. To the east, summers are warmer and winters colder. The climate also becomes warmer as one travels from north to south. The Mediterranean Sea coast has hot, dry summers and mild, moist winters. The Alps, Jura and Pyrenees mountains have snowy winters. Winter sports centres are found in all three areas. Large glaciers occupy high valleys in the Alps.

POLITICS & ECONOMY The Romans conquered France (then called Gaul) in the 50s BC. Roman rule began to decline in the fifth century AD and, in 486, the Frankish realm (as France was called) became independent under a Christian king, Clovis. In 800, Charlemagne, who had been king since 768, became emperor of the Romans. He extended France's boundaries, but, in 843, his empire was divided into three parts and the area of France contracted. After the Norman invasion of England in 1066, large areas of France came under English rule, but this was finally ended in 1453.

France later became a powerful monarchy. But the French Revolution (1789–99) ended absolute rule by French kings. In 1799, Napoleon Bonaparte took power and fought a series of brilliant military campaigns before his final defeat in 1815. The monarchy was restored until 1848, when the Second Republic was founded. In 1852, Napoleon's nephew became Napoleon III, but the Third Republic was established in 1875. France was the scene of much fighting during World War I (1914–18) and World War II (1939–45), causing great loss of life and much damage to the economy.

In 1946, France adopted a new constitution, establishing the Fourth Republic. But political instability and costly colonial wars slowed France's post-war recovery. In 1958, Charles de Gaulle was elected president and he introduced a new constitution, giving the president extra powers and inaugurating the Fifth Republic.

Since the 1960s, France has made rapid economic progress, becoming one of the most prosperous nations in the European Union. But France's government faced a number of problems, including unemployment, pollution and the growing number of elderly people, who find it difficult to live when inflation rates are high. One social problem concerns the presence in France of large numbers of immigrants from Africa and southern Europe, many of whom live in poor areas.

A socialist government was elected in 1997 and, in 2002, the euro, the single European currency, became France's sole official unit of currency. However, in 2002, centre-right parties defeated the socialists. France has a long record of independence in foreign affairs and, in 2003, it angered the United States and some of its European allies by opposing the invasion of Iraq.

France is one of the world's most developed countries. Its natural resources include its fertile soil, together with deposits of bauxite, coal, iron ore, oil and natural gas, and potash. France is also one of the world's top manufacturing nations, and it has often innovated in bold and imaginative ways. The TGV and hypermarkets are typical examples. Paris is a world centre of fashion industries, but France has many other industrial towns and cities. Major manufactures include aircraft, cars, chemicals, electronic and metal products, machinery, processed food, steel and textiles.

Agriculture employs about 2% of the people, but France is the largest producer of farm products in Western Europe, producing most of the food it needs. Wheat is the leading crop and livestock farming is of major importance. Fishing and forestry are leading industries, while tourism is a major activity.

AREA 551,500 SQ KM [212,934 SQ MI] **POPULATION** 60,181,000
CAPITAL (POPULATION) PARIS (2,152,000) **GOVERNMENT** MULTIPARTY REPUBLIC **ETHNIC GROUPS** CELTIC, LATIN, ARAB, TEUTONIC, SLAVIC
LANGUAGES FRENCH (OFFICIAL) **RELIGIONS** ROMAN CATHOLIC 85%, ISLAM 8%, OTHERS **CURRENCY** EURO = 100 CENTS

FRENCH GUIANA

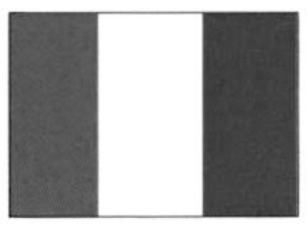

GEOGRAPHY French Guiana is the smallest country in mainland South America. The coastal plain is swampy in places, but some dry areas are cultivated. Inland lies a plateau, with the low Tumachumac Mountains in the south. Most of the rivers run north towards the Atlantic Ocean.

French Guiana has a hot, equatorial climate, with high temperatures throughout the year. The rainfall is heavy, especially between December and June, but it is dry between August and October. The north-east trade winds blow constantly across the country.

POLITICS & ECONOMY The first people to live in what is now French Guiana were Amerindians. Today, only a few of them survive in the interior. The first Europeans to explore the coast arrived in 1500, and they were followed by adventurers seeking El Dorado, the mythical city of gold. Cayenne was founded in 1637 by a group of French merchants. The area became a French colony in the late 17th century.

France used the colony as a penal settlement for political prisoners from the times of the French Revolution in the 1790s. From the 1850s to 1945, the country became notorious as a place where prisoners were harshly treated. Many of them died, unable to survive in the tropical conditions.

In 1946, French Guiana became an overseas department of France, and in 1974 it also became an administrative region. An independence movement developed in the 1980s, but most people want to retain their links with France and continue to obtain financial aid to develop their territory.

Although it has rich forest and mineral resources, such as bauxite (aluminium ore), French Guiana is a developing country. It depends greatly on France for money to run its services and the government is the country's biggest employer. Since 1968, Kourou in French Guiana, the European Space Agency's rocket-launching site, has earned money for France by sending communications satellites into space.

AREA 90,000 SQ KM [34,749 SQ MI] **POPULATION** 187,000
CAPITAL (POPULATION) CAYENNE (51,000) **GOVERNMENT** OVERSEAS DEPARTMENT OF FRANCE **ETHNIC GROUPS** BLACK OR MULATTO 66%, EAST INDIAN/CHINESE AND AMERINDIAN 12%, WHITE 12%, OTHERS 10%
LANGUAGES FRENCH (OFFICIAL) **RELIGIONS** ROMAN CATHOLIC
CURRENCY EURO = 100 CENTS

FRENCH POLYNESIA

French Polynesia consists of 130 islands, scattered over 4 million sq km [1.5 million sq mi] of the Pacific Ocean. Tribal chiefs in the area agreed to a French protectorate in 1843. They gained increased autonomy in 1984, but the links with France ensure a high standard of living.

AREA 4,000 SQ KM [1,544 SQ MI]
POPULATION 262,000 **CAPITAL** PAPEETE

GABON

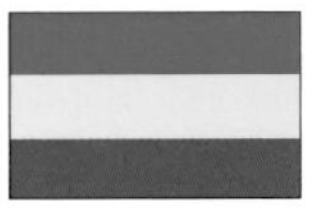

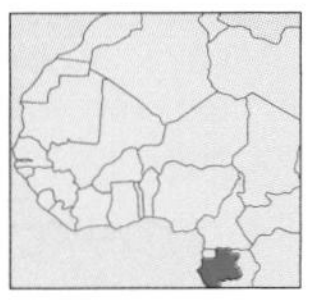

GEOGRAPHY The Gabonese Republic lies on the Equator in west-central Africa. In area, it is a little larger than the United Kingdom, with a coastline 800 km [500 mi] long. Behind the narrow, partly lagoon-lined coastal plain, the land rises to hills, plateaux and mountains divided by deep valleys carved by the River Ogooué and its tributaries.

Most of Gabon has an equatorial climate, with high temperatures and humidity throughout the year. The rainfall is heavy and the skies are often cloudy.

POLITICS & ECONOMY Gabon became a French colony in the 1880s, but it achieved full independence in 1960. In 1964, an attempted coup was put down when French troops intervened and crushed the revolt. In 1967, Bernard-Albert Bongo, who later renamed himself El Hadj Omar Bongo, became president. He declared Gabon a one-party state in 1968. Opposition parties were legalized in 1991, but Bongo was re-elected president in 1993. In 2003, the constitution was changed, enabling Bongo to stand as president as many times as he wished.

Gabon's natural resources include its forests, oil and gas deposits, manganese and uranium. Its mineral deposits make it one of Africa's better-off countries. But agriculture still employs two-fifths of the people and many farmers produce little more than they need to support their families.

AREA 267,668 SQ KM [103,347 SQ MI] **POPULATION** 1,322,000
CAPITAL (POPULATION) LIBREVILLE (362,000)
GOVERNMENT MULTIPARTY REPUBLIC
ETHNIC GROUPS FOUR MAJOR BANTU TRIBES: FANG, BAPOUNOU, NZEBI AND OBAMBA **LANGUAGES** FRENCH (OFFICIAL), FANG, MYENE, NZEBI, BAPOUNOU/ESCHIRA, BANDJABI
RELIGIONS CHRISTIANITY 75%, ANIMIST, ISLAM
CURRENCY CFA FRANC = 100 CENTIMES

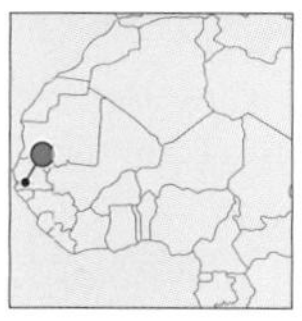

GAMBIA, THE

GEOGRAPHY The Republic of The Gambia is the smallest country in mainland Africa. It consists of a narrow strip of land bordering the River Gambia. The Gambia is almost entirely enclosed by Senegal, except along the short Atlantic coastline.

The Gambia has hot and humid summers, but the winter temperatures (November to May) drop to around 16°C [61°F]. In the summer, moist south-westerlies bring rain, which is heaviest on the coast.

POLITICS & ECONOMY English traders bought rights to trade on the River Gambia in 1588, and in 1664 the English established a settlement on an island in the river estuary. In 1765, the British founded Senegambia, which included parts of The Gambia and Senegal. In 1783, Britain handed this colony over to France. In the 19th century, Britain and France discussed the exchange of The Gambia for some other French territory, but an agreement was reached and Britain made The Gambia a British colony in 1888.

The Gambia achieved independence in 1965 and it became a republic in 1970. Relations between the English-speaking Gambians and the French-speaking Senegalese are a major political issue. In 1981, an attempted coup in The Gambia was put down with the help of Senegalese troops. In 1982, The Gambia and Senegal set up a defence alliance, called the Confederation of Senegambia. But this alliance was dissolved in 1989. In 1994, a military group overthrew the president, Sir Dawda Jawara, who fled into exile. Captain Yahya Jammeh, who took power, was elected president in 1996 and re-elected in 2001.

Agriculture employs more than 50% of the people. The main food crops include cassava, millet and sorghum, but groundnuts and groundnut products are the chief exports. Tourism is a growing industry.

AREA 11,295 sq km [4,361 sq mi] **POPULATION** 1,501,000
CAPITAL (POPULATION) Banjul (42,000)
GOVERNMENT Military regime
ETHNIC GROUPS Mandinka 42%, Fula 18%, Wolof 16%, Jola 10%, Serahuli 9%, others
LANGUAGES English (official), Mandinka, Wolof, Fula
RELIGIONS Islam 90%, Christianity 9%, traditional beliefs 1%
CURRENCY Dalasi = 100 butut

GEORGIA

GEOGRAPHY Georgia is a country on the borders of Europe and Asia, facing the Black Sea. The land is rugged with the Caucasus Mountains forming its northern border. The highest mountain in this range, Mount Elbrus (5,633 m [18,481 ft]), lies over the border with Russia.border in Russia.

The Black Sea plains have hot summers and mild winters. The rainfall is heavy, though inland areas are drier.

POLITICS & ECONOMY The first Georgian state was set up nearly 2,500 years ago. But for much of its history, the area was ruled by various conquerors. Christianity was introduced in AD 330. Georgia freed itself of foreign rule in the 11th and 12th centuries, but Mongol armies attacked in the 13th century. From the 16th to the 18th centuries, Iran and the Turkish Ottoman empire struggled for control of the area, and in the late 18th century Georgia sought the protection of Russia and, by the early 19th century, Georgia was part of the Russian empire. After the Russian Revolution of 1917, Georgia declared its independence, but Russia invaded, making the country part of the Soviet regime. Georgia declared itself independent in 1991. It became a separate country when the Soviet Union was dissolved in December 1991.

Georgia contains three regions containing minority peoples: Abkhazia in the north-west, South Ossetia in north-central Georgia, and Adjaria (also spelled Adzharia) in the south-west. Civil war broke out in South Ossetia in the early 1990s, while fierce fighting continued in Abkhazia until the late 1990s. In 2000, Georgia agreed to recognize Adjaria's autonomy in the country's constitution. In 2002, Russian and Georgian troops attacked Chechen rebels in Pankisi Gorge in north-eastern Georgia. The USA also alleged that terrorists from Afghanistan and elsewhere were hiding in the area. In 2004, civil war threatened when Adjaria unsuccessfully challenged the authority of President Mikhail Saakashvili.

Georgia is a developing country. Agriculture is important. Major products include barley, citrus fruits, grapes for wine-making, maize, tea, tobacco and vegetables. Food processing and silk and perfume-making are other important activities. Sheep and cattle are reared.

AREA 69,700 sq km [26,911 sq mi] **POPULATION** 4,934,000
CAPITAL (POPULATION) Tbilisi (1,268,000)
GOVERNMENT Multiparty republic **ETHNIC GROUPS** Georgian 70%, Armenian 8%, Russian 6%, Azeri 6%, Ossetian 3%, Greek 2%, Abkhaz 2%, others 3% **LANGUAGES** Georgian (official), Russian
RELIGIONS Georgian Orthodox 65%, Islam 11%, Russian Orthodox 10%, Armenian Apostolic 8%
CURRENCY Lari = 100 tetri

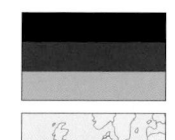

GERMANY

GEOGRAPHY The Federal Republic of Germany is the fourth largest country in Western Europe, after France, Spain and Sweden. The North German plain borders the North Sea in the north-west and the Baltic Sea in the north-east. Major rivers draining the plain include the Weser, Elbe and Oder.

The central highlands include the Harz Mountains, the Thuringian Forest (Thüringer Wald), the Ore Mountains (Erzgebirge), and the Bohemian Forest (Böhmerwald) on the Czech border. The Bavarian Alps in the south contain Germany's highest peak, Zugspitze, at 2,963 m [9,721 ft] above sea level. The Black Forest (Schwarzwald) in the south-west overlooks the River Rhine. North-western Germany has a mild climate, but the Baltic coasts are cooler. To the south, the climate becomes more continental, especially in the highlands. The precipitation is greatest on the uplands, with snow in winter.

POLITICS & ECONOMY Germany and its allies were defeated in World War I (1914–18) and the country became a republic. Adolf Hitler came to power in 1933 and ruled as a dictator. His order to invade Poland led to the start of World War II (1939–45), which ended with Germany in ruins.

In 1945, Germany was divided into four military zones. In 1949, the American, British and French zones were amalgamated to form the Federal Republic of Germany (West Germany), while the Soviet zone became the German Democratic Republic (East Germany), a Communist state. Berlin, which had also been partitioned, became a divided city. West Berlin was part of West Germany, while East Berlin became the capital of East Germany. Bonn was the capital of West Germany.

Tension between East and West mounted during the Cold War, but West Germany rebuilt its economy quickly. In East Germany, the recovery was less rapid. In the late 1980s, reforms in the Soviet Union led to unrest in East Germany. Free elections were held in East Germany in 1990 and, on 3 October 1990, Germany was reunited.

The united Germany adopted West Germany's official name, the Federal Republic of Germany. In the 1990s, the government faced many problems, especially those arising from the re-structuring of the economy of the former East Germany. In 1999, the parliament moved from Bonn to the reconstructed Reichstag building in Berlin. In 2003, Germany opposed the invasion of Iraq, incurring criticism from the United States.

West Germany's 'economic miracle' after World War II was greatly helped by foreign aid. Today, Germany is one of the world's top economic powers. Manufacturing is the mainstay of the economy and manufactured goods are the chief exports. Cars and other vehicles, cement, chemicals, computers, electrical equipment, processed food, machinery, scientific instruments, ships, steel, textiles and tools are manufactured. Germany has some coal, potash and rock salt deposits, but it imports many industrial raw materials. Germany also imports food. Leading products include fruits, grapes for wine-making, potatoes, sugar beet and vegetables. Livestock include beef and dairy cattle.

AREA 357,022 sq km [137,846 sq mi] **POPULATION** 82,398,000
CAPITAL (POPULATION) Berlin (3,387,000)
GOVERNMENT Federal multiparty republic **ETHNIC GROUPS** German 92%, Turkish 3%, Serbo-Croatian, Italian, Greek, Polish, Spanish
LANGUAGES German (official) **RELIGIONS** Protestant (mainly Lutheran) 34%, Roman Catholic 34%, Islam 4%, others
CURRENCY Euro = 100 cents

GHANA

GEOGRAPHY The Republic of Ghana faces the Gulf of Guinea in West Africa. This hot country, just north of the Equator, was formerly called the Gold Coast. Behind the thickly populated southern coastal plains, which are lined with lagoons, lies a plateau region in the south-west.

Accra has a hot, tropical climate. Rain occurs all through the year, though Accra is drier than areas inland.

POLITICS & ECONOMY Portuguese explorers reached the area in 1471 and named it the Gold Coast. The area became a centre of the slave trade in the 17th century. The slave trade was ended in the 1860s and, gradually, the British took control of the area. After independence in 1957, attempts were made to develop the economy by creating large state-owned manufacturing industries. But debt and corruption, together with falls in the price of cocoa, the chief export, caused economic problems. This led to instability and frequent coups. In 1981, power was invested in a Provisional National Defence Council, led by Flight-Lieutenant Jerry Rawlings.

The government steadied the economy and introduced several new policies, including the relaxation of government controls. In 1992, the government introduced a new constitution, which allowed for multiparty elections. Rawlings was elected president in 1992 and 1996, but he retired in 2002. He was succeeded as president by John Ageykum Kufuor. The World Bank classifies Ghana as a 'low-income' developing country. Most people are poor and farming employs 55% of the population.

AREA 238,533 sq km [92,098 sq mi] **POPULATION** 20,468,000
CAPITAL (POPULATION) Accra (949,000) **GOVERNMENT** Republic
ETHNIC GROUPS Akan 44%, Moshi-Dagomba 16%, Ewe 13%, Ga 8%, Gurma 3%, Yoruba 1% **LANGUAGES** English (official), Akan, Moshi-Dagomba, Ewe, Ga **RELIGIONS** Christianity 63%, traditional beliefs 21%, Islam 16% **CURRENCY** Cedi = 100 pesewas

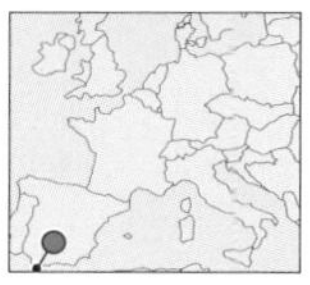

GIBRALTAR

Gibraltar occupies a strategic position on the south coast of Spain where the Mediterranean meets the Atlantic. It was recognized as a British possession in 1713 and, despite Spanish claims, its population has consistently voted to retain its contacts with Britain.

AREA 6 sq km [2.3 sq mi]
POPULATION 28,000 **CAPITAL** Gibraltar Town

GREECE

GEOGRAPHY The Hellenic Republic, as Greece is officially called, is a rugged country situated at the southern end of the Balkan peninsula. Olympus, at 2,917 m [9,570 ft] is the highest peak. Islands make up about a fifth of the land.

Low-lying areas in Greece have mild, moist winters and hot, dry summers. The east coast has more than 2,700 hours of sunshine a year and only about half of the rainfall of the west. The mountains have a much more severe climate, with snow on the higher slopes in winter.

POLITICS & ECONOMY Around 2,500 years ago, Greece became the birthplace of Western civilization and Ancient Greek ruins and art still attract millions of tourists to the country. The first civilization, the Minoan, was centred on Crete. It flourished between about 3000 and 1400 BC. Following the end of the related Mycaenean period on the mainland (1580–1100 BC), a 'dark age' lasted until about 800 BC. But from 750 BC, Greeks became rich traders and the city-state of Athens reached its peak in 461–431 BC. Greece became a Roman province in 146 BC and, in AD 365, it became part of the Byzantine Empire.

The Byzantine empire fell to the Turks in 1453. But Greece became an independent monarchy in 1830. After World War II (1939–45), when Germany ruled Greece, a civil war broke out between Greek Communists and nationalists. It ended in 1949 and a military dictatorship seized power in 1967. The monarchy was abolished in 1973 and democracy was restored in 1974. Greece joined the European Community (now the European Union) in 1981 and, on 1 January 2002, the euro became the sole unit of currency in Greece.

Greece is one of the EU's less economically developed members. Manufactured products include processed food, cement, chemicals, metal products, textiles and tobacco. Greece also mines lignite (brown coal), bauxite and chromite. Farmland covers about a third of the country and grazing land another 40%. Crops include barley, grapes for wine-making, dried fruits, olives, potatoes, sugar beet and wheat. Livestock farming is also important. Greece's beaches and ancient ruins make the country a major tourist destination.

AREA 131,957 sq km [50,949 sq mi] **POPULATION** 10,666,000
CAPITAL (POPULATION) Athens (772,000)
GOVERNMENT Multiparty republic **ETHNIC GROUPS** Greek 98%
LANGUAGES Greek (official) **RELIGIONS** Greek Orthodox 98%
CURRENCY Euro = 100 cents

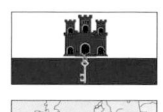

GREENLAND

Greenland is the world's largest island. Settlements are confined to the coast, because an ice sheet covers four-fifths of the land. Greenland became a Danish possession in 1380. Full internal self-government was granted in 1981 and, in 1997, Danish place names were superseded by Inuit forms. However, Greenland remains heavily dependent on Danish subsidies.

AREA 2,175,600 SQ KM [838,999 SQ MI] **POPULATION** 56,000
CAPITAL (POPULATION) NUUK (GODTHÅB) (14,000)

GRENADA

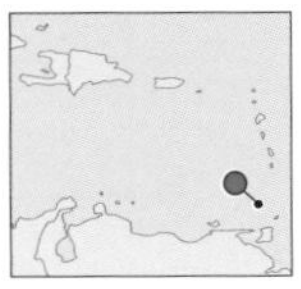

The most southerly of the Windward Islands in the Caribbean Sea, Grenada became independent from the UK in 1974. A military group seized power in 1983, when the prime minister was killed. US troops intervened and restored order and constitutional government.

AREA 344 SQ KM [133 SQ MI]
POPULATION 89,000 **CAPITAL** ST GEORGE'S

GUADELOUPE

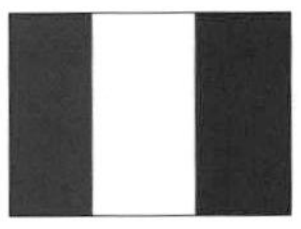
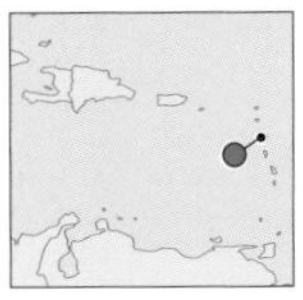

Guadeloupe is a French overseas department which includes seven Caribbean islands, the largest of which is Basse-Terre. French aid has helped to mantain a reasonable standard of living for the people.

AREA 1,705 SQ KM [658 SQ MI]
POPULATION 440,000 **CAPITAL** BASSE-TERRE

GUAM

Guam, a strategically important 'unincorporated territory' of the USA, is the largest of the Mariana Islands in the Pacific Ocean. It is composed of a coralline limestone plateau.

AREA 549 SQ KM [212 SQ MI]
POPULATION 164,000 **CAPITAL** AGANA

GUATEMALA

GEOGRAPHY The Republic of Guatemala in Central America contains a thickly populated mountain region, with fertile soils. The mountains, which run in an east–west direction, contain many volcanoes, some of which are active. Volcanic eruptions and earthquakes are common in the highlands. South of the mountains lie the thinly populated Pacific coastlands, while a large inland plain occupies the north.

The lowlands of Guatemala are hot and rainy, but the central highlands are cooler and drier. Guatemala City has a pleasant. warm climate with a dry season between November and April.

POLITICS & ECONOMY Much of what is now Guatemala was part of the Maya empire which thrived between AD 300 and 900. Spain ruled the area from the 1520s until 1821. In 1823, Guatemala joined the Central American Federation. But it became fully independent in 1839. Instability and periodic violence have marred its progress since independence.

Guatemala has a long-standing claim over Belize, but this was reduced in 1983 to the southern fifth of the country. Violence became widespread in Guatemala from the early 1960s, because of the conflict between left-wing groups, including many Amerindians, and government forces. A peace accord was signed in 1996, ending a war that had lasted 36 years and claimed perhaps 200,000 lives.

Guatemala is ranked as a 'lower-middle-income' economy. Agriculture employs 56% of the population. Coffee, sugar, bananas and beef are exported and the spice cardamom and cotton are also important. Maize is the main food crop.

AREA 108,889 SQ KM [42,042 SQ MI] **POPULATION** 13,909,000
CAPITAL (POPULATION) GUATEMALA CITY (1,007,000)
GOVERNMENT REPUBLIC **ETHNIC GROUPS** LADINO (MIXED HISPANIC AND AMERINDIAN) 55%, AMERINDIAN 43%, OTHERS 2%
LANGUAGES SPANISH (OFFICIAL), AMERINDIAN LANGUAGES
RELIGIONS CHRISTIANITY, INDIGENOUS MAYAN BELIEFS
CURRENCY US DOLLAR; QUETZAL = 100 CENTAVOS

GUINEA

GEOGRAPHY The Republic of Guinea faces the Atlantic Ocean in West Africa. A flat, swampy plain borders the coast. Behind this plain, the land rises to a plateau region called Fouta Djalon. The Upper Niger plains, named after one of Africa's longest rivers, the Niger, which rises there, are in the north-east.

Guinea has a tropical climate and Conakry, on the coast, has heavy rains between May and November. This is also the coolest period in the year. During the dry season, hot, dry harmattan winds blow south-westwards from the Sahara Desert.

POLITICS & ECONOMY Guinea came under the influence of several medieval African states, including Ancient Ghana and Ancient Mali. France began to control the area in the late 19th century. Guinea became independent in 1958. Its leaders pursued socialist policies but resorted to repressive measures to hold on to power. A military regime under Lansana Conté took over in 1984, but a multiparty system was restored in 1992. Conté was elected president in 1993 and re-elected in 1998 and 2002. From the late 1990s, Guinea was drawn into the conflicts taking place in Liberia and Sierra Leone.

Guinea is a 'low-income' developing country. Its resources include bauxite (aluminium ore), diamonds, gold, iron ore and uranium. Bauxite and alumina (processed bauxite) account for more than half of the exports. Agriculture employs 78% of the people, but most farmers are poor. Manufactures include alumina, processed food and textiles.

AREA 245,857 SQ KM [94,925 SQ MI] **POPULATION** 9,030,000
CAPITAL (POPULATION) CONAKRY (1,508,000)
GOVERNMENT MULTIPARTY REPUBLIC
ETHNIC GROUPS PEUHL 40%, MALINKE 30%, SOUSSOU 20%, OTHERS 10% **LANGUAGES** FRENCH (OFFICIAL)
RELIGIONS ISLAM 85%, CHRISTIANITY 8%, TRADITIONAL BELIEFS 7%
CURRENCY GUINEAN FRANC = 100 CAURIS

GUINEA-BISSAU

GEOGRAPHY The Republic of Guinea-Bissau, formerly known as Portuguese Guinea, is a small country in West Africa. The land is mostly low-lying, with a broad, swampy coastal plain and many flat offshore islands, including the Bijagós Archipelago.

The country has a tropical climate, with one dry season (December to May) and a rainy season from June to November.

POLITICS & ECONOMY Portuguese explorers reached Guinea-Bissau in 1446 and the area became a centre of the slave trade. From 1836, Portugal administered Guinea-Bissau with the Cape Verde Islands but, in 1879, the territories were separated. Guinea-Bissau became a separate colony called Portuguese Guinea. But economic development in the colony was slow.

In 1956, African nationalists in Portuguese Guinea and Cape Verde founded the African Party for the Independence of Guinea and Cape Verde (PAIGC). Because Portugal seemed determined to hang on to its overseas territories, the PAIGC began a guerrilla war in 1963. By 1968, it held two-thirds of the country. In 1972, a rebel National Assembly, elected by the people in the PAIGC-controlled area, voted to make the country independent as Guinea-Bissau.

In 1974, newly independent Guinea-Bissau faced many problems arising from its under-developed economy and its lack of trained people to work in the administration. One objective of the leaders of Guinea-Bissau was to unite their country with Cape Verde. But, in 1980, army leaders overthrew Guinea-Bissau's government. The Revolutionary Council, which took over, opposed unification with Cape Verde. Guinea-Bissau ceased to be a one-party state in 1991 and multiparty elections were held in 1994. Civil war broke out in 1998 and a military coup occurred in May 1999. In elections in 1999 and 2000, Kumba Ialá was elected president, but he was removed in a coup in 2003.

Guinea-Bissau is a poor country. Agriculture employs 77% of the people, but most farming is at subsistence level. Major crops include beans,coconuts, groundnuts, maize and rice.

AREA 36,125 SQ KM [13,948 SQ MI] **POPULATION** 1,361,000
CAPITAL (POPULATION) BISSAU (200,000)
GOVERNMENT 'INTERIM' GOVERNMENT
ETHNIC GROUPS BALANTA 30%, FULA 20%, MANJACA 14%, MANDINGA 13%, PAPEL 7% **LANGUAGES** PORTUGUESE (OFFICIAL), CRIOULO
RELIGIONS TRADITIONAL BELIEFS 50%, ISLAM 45%, CHRISTIANITY 5%
CURRENCY CFA FRANC = 100 CENTIMES

GUYANA

GEOGRAPHY The Co-operative Republic of Guyana is a country facing the Atlantic Ocean in north-eastern South America. The coastal plain is flat and much of it is below sea level.

The climate is hot and humid, though the interior highlands are cooler than the coast. The rainfall is heavy, occurring on more than 200 days a year.

POLITICS & ECONOMY Britain gained control of the area in 1814 and ruled British Guiana until it became independent as Guyana in 1966. A black lawyer, Forbes Burnham, was the first prime minister. Under a new constitution adopted in 1980, the president's powers were increased. Burnham became president and served in this post until he died in 1985. He was succeeded by Hugh Desmond Hoyte, who was defeated in 1993 by an ethnic Indian, Cheddi Jagan. Jagan died in 1997 and was succeeded by his wife, Janet. In 1999, Bharat Jagdeo was elected president. He was re-elected in 2001.

Guyana is a poor country. Its resources include gold, bauxite (aluminium ore) and other minerals, forests and fertile soils. Sugar cane and rice are leading crops. Guyana has potential for producing hydroelectricity from its many rivers.

AREA 214,969 SQ KM [83,000 SQ MI] **POPULATION** 702,000
CAPITAL (POPULATION) GEORGETOWN (150,000)
GOVERNMENT MULTIPARTY REPUBLIC
ETHNIC GROUPS EAST INDIAN 50%, BLACK 36%, AMERINDIAN 7%, OTHERS **LANGUAGES** ENGLISH (OFFICIAL), CREOLE, HINDI, URDU
RELIGIONS CHRISTIANITY 50%, HINDUISM 35%, ISLAM 10%, OTHERS
CURRENCY GUYANESE DOLLAR = 100 CENTS

HAITI

GEOGRAPHY The Republic of Haiti occupies the western third of Hispaniola in the Caribbean. The land is mainly mountainous. The climate is hot and humid, though the northern highlands, with about 200 mm [79 in], have more than twice as much rainfall as the southern coast.

POLITICS & ECONOMY Visited by Christopher Columbus in 1492, Haiti was later developed by the French. The African slaves revolted in 1791 and the country became independent in 1804.

Since independence, Haiti has suffered from instability, violence and dictatorial rule. Elections in 1990 returned Jean-Bertrand Aristide as president, but he was overthrown in 1991. Following US intervention, he returned in 1994. In 1995, René Préval was elected president, but Aristide was again elected president in 2000 but, in 2004, he was forced to flee the country after massive public protests. Agriculture employs more than half of the people. Cocoa, coffee and sugar cane are grown.

AREA 27,750 SQ KM [10,714 SQ MI] **POPULATION** 7,528,000
CAPITAL (POPULATION) PORT-AU-PRINCE (917,000)
GOVERNMENT MULTIPARTY REPUBLIC **ETHNIC GROUPS** BLACK 95%, MULATTO/WHITE 5% **LANGUAGES** FRENCH AND CREOLE (BOTH OFFICIAL)
RELIGIONS ROMAN CATHOLIC 80%, VOODOO
CURRENCY GOURDE = 100 CENTIMES

HONDURAS

GEOGRAPHY The Republic of Honduras is the second largest country in Central America. The northern coast on the Caribbean Sea extends more than 600 km [373 mi], but the Pacific coast in the south-east is only about 80 km [50 mi] long. Honduras has a tropical climate, but the highlands are cooler. The rainiest months are between May and November. Hurricanes often hit the north coast. Hurricane Mitch in 1998 caused the worst destruction in modern times.

POLITICS & ECONOMY Western Honduras was part of the Maya empire which flourished between AD 300 and 900. Christopher Columbus claimed the area for Spain in 1502 and Spain ruled from 1625 until 1821. Honduras became part of the Central American Federation but withdrew in 1838.

In the 1890s, American companies developed plantations to grow bananas. They soon became the country's chief source of income and Honduras became known as a 'banana republic'. But instability slowed economic progress. In 1969, Honduras fought a short 'Soccer War' with El Salvador. The war was sparked off by the treatment of fans in a World Cup soccer series, though the real reason was that Salvadoreans in Honduras had been forced to give up land. Since 1980, civilian governments have ruled Honduras, but the military remain influential.

Honduras is a developing country. Its few resources include silver, lead and zinc. Agriculture is the main activity. Bananas and coffee are exported and maize is the chief food crop. Honduras is one of Central America's least industrialized countries. Products include processed food, textiles and wood products.

AREA 112,088 sq km [43,277 sq mi] **POPULATION** 6,670,000
CAPITAL (POPULATION) Tegucigalpa (850,000)
GOVERNMENT Republic **ETHNIC GROUPS** Mestizo 90%, Amerindian 7%, Black (including Black Carib) 2%, White 1% **LANGUAGES** Spanish (official), Amerindian dialects **RELIGIONS** Roman Catholic 97%
CURRENCY Honduran lempira = 100 centavos

HUNGARY

GEOGRAPHY The Hungarian Republic is a landlocked country in central Europe. The land is mostly low-lying and drained by the Danube (Duna) and its tributary, the Tisza. Most of the land east of the Danube belongs to a region called the Great Plain (Nagyalföld), which covers about half of Hungary.

Hungary lies far from the moderating influence of the sea. As a result, summers are warmer and sunnier, and the winters colder than in Western Europe.

POLITICS & ECONOMY Hungary entered World War II (1939–45) in 1941, as an ally of Germany, but the Germans occupied the country in 1944. The Soviet Union invaded Hungary in 1944 and, in 1946, the country became a republic. The Communists gradually took over the government, taking complete control in 1949. From 1949, Hungary was an ally of the Soviet Union. In 1956, Soviet troops crushed an anti-Communist revolt. But in the 1980s, reforms in the Soviet Union led to the growth of anti-Communist groups in Hungary. In 1989, Hungary adopted a new constitution making it a multiparty state. Elections held in 1990 led to a victory for the non-Communist Democratic Forum. In 2002, the Hungarian Socialist Party, in alliance with the liberal Free Democrats, won a majority in parliament. In 2004, Hungary became a member of both the North Atlantic Treaty Organization and the European Union.

Before World War II, Hungary's economy was based mainly on agriculture. But the Communists set up many manufacturing industries. The new factories were owned by the government, as also was most of the land. However, from the late 1980s, the government has worked to increase private ownership. This change of policy caused many problems, including inflation and high rates of unemployment. Manufacturing is the chief activity. Major products include aluminium, chemicals, and electrical and electronic goods.

AREA 93,032 sq km [35,920 sq mi] **POPULATION** 10,045,000
CAPITAL (POPULATION) Budapest (1,825,000)
GOVERNMENT Multiparty republic
ETHNIC GROUPS Magyar 90%, Gypsy, German, Serb, Romanian, Slovak **LANGUAGES** Hungarian (official)
RELIGIONS Roman Catholic 68%, Calvinist 20%, Lutheran 5%, others **CURRENCY** Forint = 100 fillér

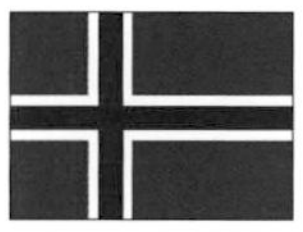
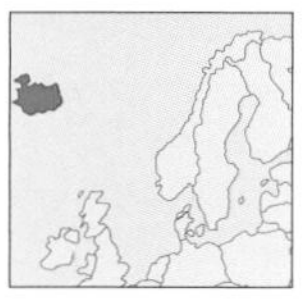

ICELAND

GEOGRAPHY The Republic of Iceland, in the North Atlantic Ocean, is closer to Greenland than Scotland. Iceland sits astride the Mid-Atlantic Ridge. It is slowly getting wider as the ocean is being stretched apart by continental drift.

Iceland has around 200 volcanoes, and eruptions are frequent. An eruption under the Vatnajökull ice cap in 1996 created a subglacial lake which subsequently burst, causing severe flooding. Geysers and hot springs are other common volcanic features. Ice caps and glaciers cover about an eighth of the land. The only habitable regions are the coastal lowlands.

Although it lies far to the north, Iceland's climate is moderated by the warm waters of the Gulf Stream. The port of Reykjavik is ice-free all the year round.

POLITICS & ECONOMY Norwegian Vikings colonized Iceland in AD 874, and in 930 the settlers founded the world's oldest parliament, the Althing.

Iceland united with Norway in 1262. But when Norway united with Denmark in 1380, Iceland came under Danish rule. Iceland became a self-governing kingdom, united with Denmark, in 1918. It became a fully independent republic in 1944, following a referendum in which 97% of the people voted to break their country's ties with Denmark.

Iceland has played an important part in European affairs and is a member of the North Atlantic Treaty Organization. Conflict with Britain over fishing rights have occurred since Iceland extended its territorial waters in the 1970s. Other fishing disputes with Norway, Russia and others continued in the 1990s.

Iceland has few resources besides the fishing grounds which surround it. Fishing and fish processing are major industries which dominate Iceland's overseas trade. Barely 1% of the land is used to grow crops, mainly root vegetables and fodder for livestock, but 23% of the country is used for grazing sheep and cattle. Vegetables and fruits are grown in greenhouses heated by water from hot springs.

AREA 103,000 sq km [39,768 sq mi] **POPULATION** 281,000
CAPITAL (POPULATION) Reykjavik (108,000)
GOVERNMENT Multiparty republic
ETHNIC GROUPS Icelandic 97%, Danish 1%
LANGUAGES Icelandic (official) **RELIGIONS** Evangelical Lutheran 87%, other Protestant 4%, Roman Catholic 2%, others
CURRENCY Icelandic króna = 100 aurar

INDIA

GEOGRAPHY The Republic of India is the world's seventh largest country. In population, it ranks second only to China. The north is mountainous, with mountains and foothills of the Himalayan range. Rivers, such as the Brahmaputra and Ganges (Ganga), rise in the Himalaya and flow across the fertile northern plains. Southern India consists of a large plateau, called the Deccan. The Deccan is bordered by two mountain ranges, the Western Ghats and the Eastern Ghats.

India has three main seasons. The cool season runs from October to February. The hot season runs from March to June. The rainy monsoon season starts in the middle of June and continues into September. Delhi has a moderate rainfall, with about 640 mm [25 in] a year. The south-western coast and the north-east have far more rain. Darjeeling in the north-east has an average annual rainfall of 3,040 mm [120 in]. But parts of the Thar Desert in the north-west have only 50 mm [2 in] of rain per year.

POLITICS & ECONOMY In southern India, most of the people are descendants of the dark-skinned Dravidians, who were among India's earliest people. Most northerners are descendants of lighter-skinned Aryans who arrived around 3,500 years ago.

India was the birthplace of several major religions, including Hinduism, Buddhism and Sikhism. Islam was introduced from about AD 1000. The Muslim Mughal empire was founded in 1526. From the 17th century, Britain began to gain influence. From 1858 to 1947, India was ruled as part of the British empire. An independence movement began after the Sepoy Rebellion (1857–9) and, in 1885, the Indian National Congress was formed. In 1920, Mohandas K. Gandhi became its leader and it soon became a mass movement. When independence was finally achieved in 1947, British India was divided into modern India and Muslim Pakistan. Partition was marred by mass slaughter as Hindus and Sikhs fled from Pakistan, and Indian Muslims poured into Pakistan. In the ensuing disputes, some 1 million people were killed.

Although India has 15 major languages and hundreds of minor ones, together with many religions, the country remains the world's largest democracy. It has faced many problems, especially with Pakistan, over the disputed territory of Jammu and Kashmir. Two wars in 1965 and 1972 failed to alter greatly the 1948 cease-fire lines. In the late 1980s, Kashmiri nationalists in the Indian-controlled area waged a campaign, demanding either integration into Pakistan or independence. India sent in troops and accused Pakistan of intervention. In the 1990s, Pakistani-backed guerrillas fought to break India's hold on the Srinigar valley, Kashmir's most populous region. The tense situation was further aggravated by the testing of nuclear devices by both India and Pakistan in 1998. In 2003–4, India and Pakistan launched a series of peace moves, raising hopes of an agreement, though conflict continued on the ground.

The World Bank classifies India as a 'low-income' developing country. To boost the economy, the right-wing coalition government, led by the Hindu Bharatiya Janata Party, introduced free-enterprise policies in the 1990s. But the victory in 2004 of a left-wing coalition, led by the Congress Party, led to fears that economic reform might be halted.

Agriculture employs 64% of the people. Crops include rice, wheat, millet, sorghum, peas and beans. India has more cattle than any other country. Milk is produced, but Hindus do not eat beef. Resources include coal, iron ore and oil. Manufacturing has expanded greatly since 1947. Iron and steel, machinery, refined petroleum, textiles and transport equipment are major products.

AREA 3,287,263 sq km [1,269,212 sq mi] **POPULATION** 1,049,700,000
CAPITAL (POPULATION) New Delhi (295,000)
GOVERNMENT Multiparty federal republic
ETHNIC GROUPS Indo-Aryan (Caucasoid) 72%, Dravidian (Aboriginal) 25% others (mainly Mongoloid) 3%
LANGUAGES Hindi, English, Telugu, Bengali, Marathi, Tamil, Urdu, Gujarati, Malayalam, Kannada, Oriya, Punjabi, Assamese, Kashmiri, Sindhi and Sanskrit are all official languages
RELIGIONS Hinduism 82%, Islam 12%, Christianity 2%, Sikhism 2%, Buddhism and others **CURRENCY** Indian rupee = 100 paisa

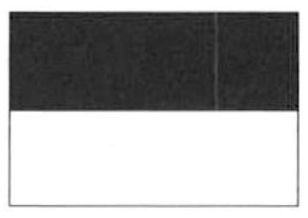

INDONESIA

GEOGRAPHY The Republic of Indonesia is an island nation in South-east Asia. In all, Indonesia contains about 13,600 islands, less than 6,000 of which are inhabited. Three-quarters of the country is made up of five main areas: the islands of Sumatra, Java and Sulawesi (Celebes), together with Kalimantan (southern Borneo) and Irian Jaya (western New Guinea). The islands are generally mountainous and volcanic. The larger islands have extensive coastal lowlands. The climate is hot and humid, with a high rainfall. Only Java and the Sunda Islands have relatively dry seasons.

POLITICS & ECONOMY Indonesia is the world's most populous Muslim nation, though Islam was introduced as recently as the 15th century. The Dutch became active in the area in the early 17th century and Indonesia became a Dutch colony in 1799. After a long struggle, the Netherlands recognized Indonesia's independence in 1949. The economy has expanded, but ethnic and religious conflict have slowed down economic progress. In the early 21st century, Indonesia was facing many problems, arising from widespread corruption in the government and the army. Separatists were operating in Aceh province in northern Sumatra and in West Papua (formerly Irian Jaya), Christian-Muslim clashes led to loss of life in the Moluccas, and East (formerly Portuguese) Timor became an independent country in May 2002. In October 2002, terrorists bombed a night club in Bali, killing more than 180 people. Another suicide bombing took place in Jakarta in 2004.

Indonesia is a developing country. Its resources include oil, natural gas, tin and other minerals, its fertile volcanic soils and its forests. Oil and gas are major exports. Timber, textiles, rubber, coffee and tea are also exported. The principal food crop is rice. Manufacturing is increasing, particularly on Java.

AREA 1,904,569 sq km [735,354 sq mi] **POPULATION** 234,893,000
CAPITAL (POPULATION) Jakarta (9,374,000)
GOVERNMENT Multiparty republic
ETHNIC GROUPS Javanese 45%, Sundanese 14%, Madurese 7%, coastal Malays 7%, approximately 300 others
LANGUAGES Bahasa Indonesian (official), many others
RELIGIONS Islam 88%, Roman Catholic 3%, Hinduism 2%, Buddhism 1%
CURRENCY Indonesian rupiah = 100 sen

IRAN

GEOGRAPHY The Republic of Iran contains a barren central plateau which covers about half of the country. It includes the Dasht-e-Kavir (Great Salt Desert) and the Dasht-e-Lut (Great Sand Desert). The Elburz Mountains north of the plateau contain Iran's highest peak, Damavand, while narrow lowlands lie between the mountains and the Caspian Sea. West of the plateau are the Zagros Mountains, beyond which the land descends to the plains bordering the Persian Gulf.

Much of Iran has a severe, dry climate, with hot summers and cold winters. In Tehran, rain falls on only about 30 days in the year and the annual temperature range is more than 25°C [45°F]. The climate in the lowlands, however, is generally milder.

POLITICS & ECONOMY Iran was called Persia until 1935. The empire of Ancient Persia flourished between 550 and 350 BC, when it fell to Alexander the Great. Islam was introduced in AD 641.

Britain and Russia competed for influence in the area in the 19th century, and in the early 20th century the British began to develop the country's oil resources. In 1925, the Pahlavi family took power.

Reza Khan became shah (king) and worked to modernize the country. The Pahlavi dynasty was ended in 1979 when a religious leader, Ayatollah Ruhollah Khomeini, made Iran an Islamic republic. In 1980–8, Iran and Iraq fought a war over disputed borders. Khomeini died in 1989, but his fundamentalist views and anti-Western attitudes continued to dominate politics. In 1997, Mohammad Khatami, a liberal, was elected president, but conservative clerics made actual reform difficult. In 2003–4, Iran was in dispute with the international community over its nuclear energy programme.

Iran's prosperity is based on its oil production and oil accounts for 95% of the country's exports. However, the economy was severely damaged by the Iran–Iraq war in the 1980s. Oil revenues have been used to develop a growing manufacturing sector. Agriculture is important even though farms cover only a tenth of the land. The main crops are wheat and barley. Livestock farming and fishing are other important activities, although Iran has to import much of the food it needs.

AREA 1,648,195 SQ KM [636,368 SQ MI] **POPULATION** 68,279,000
CAPITAL (POPULATION) TEHRAN (7,723,000)
GOVERNMENT ISLAMIC REPUBLIC **ETHNIC GROUPS** PERSIAN 51%, AZERI 24%, GILAKI AND MAZANDARANI 8%, KURD 7%, ARAB 3%, LUR 2%, BALUCHI 2%, TURKMEN 2% **LANGUAGES** PERSIAN 58%, TURKIC 26%, KURDISH **RELIGIONS** ISLAM (SHI'ITE MUSLIM 89%)
CURRENCY IRANIAN RIAL = 100 DINARS

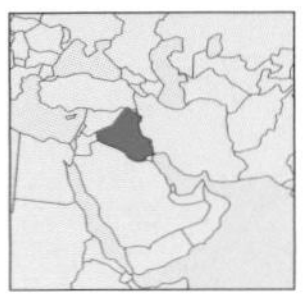

IRAQ

GEOGRAPHY The Republic of Iraq is a south-west Asian country at the head of the Persian Gulf. Rolling deserts cover western and south-western Iraq, with part of the Zagros Mountains in the north-east, where farming can be practised without irrigation. The northern plains, across which flow the rivers Euphrates (Nahr al Furat) and Tigris (Nahr Dijlah), are dry. But the southern plains, including Mesopotamia, and the delta of the Shatt al Arab, the river formed south of Al Qurnah by the combined Euphrates and Tigris, contain irrigated farmland, together with marshes.

The climate of Iraq ranges from temperate in the north to subtropical in the south. Baghdad, in central Iraq, has cool winters, with occasional frosts, and hot summers. The rainfall is generally low.

POLITICS & ECONOMY Mesopotamia was the home of several great civilizations, including Sumer, Babylon and Assyria. It later became part of the Persian empire. Islam was introduced in AD 637 and Baghdad became the brilliant capital of the powerful Arab empire. But Mesopotamia declined after the Mongols invaded it in 1258. From 1534, Mesopotamia became part of the Turkish Ottoman empire. Britain invaded the area in 1916. In 1921, Britain renamed the country Iraq and set up an Arab monarchy. Iraq finally became independent in 1932.

By the 1950s, oil dominated Iraq's economy. In 1952, Iraq agreed to take 50% of the profits of the foreign oil companies. This revenue enabled the government to pay for welfare services and development projects. But many Iraqis felt that they should benefit more from their oil. Since 1958, when army officers killed the king and made Iraq a republic, Iraq has undergone turbulent times. In the 1960s, the Kurds, who live in northern Iraq and also in Iran, Turkey, Syria and Armenia, asked for self-rule. The government rejected their demands and war broke out. A peace treaty was signed in 1975, but conflict has continued.

In 1979, Saddam Hussein became Iraq's president. Under his leadership, Iraq invaded Iran in 1980, starting an eight-year war. Iraqi Kurds supported Iran and the Iraqi government attacked Kurdish villages with poison gas. In 1990, Iraqi troops occupied Kuwait, but an international force drove them out in 1991. Since 1991, Iraqi troops have attacked Shi'ite Marsh Arabs and Kurds. In 1998, Iraq's failure to permit UN inspectors, charged with disposing of Iraq's deadliest weapons, access to suspect sites led to the Western bombardment of Iraqi military sites. Another major offensive occurred in February 2001. In 2002 and 2003, pressure mounted on Iraq to dispose of its alleged weapons of mass destruction. In March 2003, a coalition force, headed by the United States, invaded Iraq. However, continuing conflict, even after the capture of Saddam Hussein in December 2003, put the planned transition to a democratic government in jeopardy.

Civil war, war damage in 1991 and 2003, UN sanctions and mismanagement have all contributed to economic chaos. Oil remains Iraq's main resource, but a UN trade embargo in 1990 halted oil exports. Farmland, including pasture, covers about a fifth of the land. Products include barley, cotton, dates, fruit, livestock, wheat and wool, but Iraq still has to import food. Industries include oil refining and the manufacture of petrochemicals and consumer goods.

AREA 438,317 SQ KM [169,234 SQ MI] **POPULATION** 24,683,000
CAPITAL (POPULATION) BAGHDAD (5,605,000)
GOVERNMENT REPUBLIC **ETHNIC GROUPS** ARAB 77%, KURDISH 19%, ASSYRIAN AND OTHERS **LANGUAGES** ARABIC (OFFICIAL), KURDISH (OFFICIAL IN KURDISH AREAS), ASSYRIAN, ARMENIAN **RELIGIONS** ISLAM 97%, CHRISTIANITY AND OTHERS **CURRENCY** NEW IRAQI DINAR

IRELAND

GEOGRAPHY The Republic of Ireland occupies five-sixths of the island of Ireland. The country consists of a large lowland region surrounded by a broken rim of low mountains. The uplands include the Mountains of Kerry where Carrauntoohill, Ireland's highest peak at 1,041 m [3,415 ft], is situated. The River Shannon is the longest in the British Isles. It flows through three large lakes, loughs Allen, Ree and Derg.

Ireland has a mild, rainy climate influenced by the warm Gulf Stream current, whose effects are greatest in the west. However, Dublin in the east is cooler than places on the west coast.

POLITICS & ECONOMY In 1801, the Act of Union created the United Kingdom of Great Britain and Ireland. But Irish discontent intensified in the 1840s when a potato blight caused a famine in which a million people died and nearly a million emigrated. Britain was blamed for not having done enough to help. In 1916, an uprising in Dublin was crushed, but between 1919 and 1922 civil war occurred. In 1922, the Irish Free State was created as a Dominion in the British Commonwealth. But Northern Ireland remained part of the UK.

Ireland became a republic in 1949. Since then, Irish governments have sought to develop the economy, and it was for this reason that Ireland joined the European Community in 1973. In 1998, Ireland took part in the negotiations to produce a constitutional settlement in Northern Ireland. As part of the agreement, Ireland agreed to give up its constitutional claim on Northern Ireland. But the agreement proved difficult to implement.

Major farm products in Ireland include barley, cattle and dairy products, pigs, potatoes, poultry, sheep, sugar beet and wheat, while fishing provides another valuable source of food. Farming is now profitable, aided by European Union grants, but manufacturing is the leading economic sector. Many factories produce food and beverages. Chemicals and pharmaceuticals, electronic equipment, machinery, paper and textiles are also important.

AREA 70,273 SQ KM [27,132 SQ MI] **POPULATION** 3,924,000
CAPITAL (POPULATION) DUBLIN (482,000)
GOVERNMENT MULTIPARTY REPUBLIC **ETHNIC GROUPS** IRISH 94%
LANGUAGES IRISH (GAELIC) AND ENGLISH (BOTH OFFICIAL)
RELIGIONS ROMAN CATHOLIC 92%, PROTESTANT 3%
CURRENCY EURO = 100 CENTS

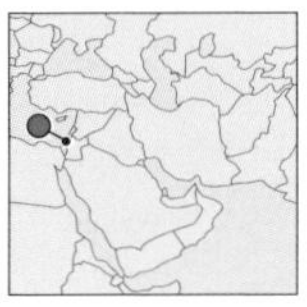

ISRAEL

GEOGRAPHY The State of Israel is a small country in the eastern Mediterranean. It includes a fertile coastal plain, where Israel's main industrial cities, Haifa (Hefa) and Tel Aviv-Jaffa are situated. Inland lie the Judaeo-Galilean highlands, which run from northern Israel to the northern tip of the Negev Desert. To the east lies part of the Great Rift Valley which contains the River Jordan, the Sea of Galilee and the Dead Sea. Summers are hot and dry. Winters on the coast are mild and moist, but the rainfall decreases from west to east and from north to south.

POLITICS & ECONOMY Israel is part of a region called Palestine. Some Jews have always lived in the area, though most modern Israelis are descendants of immigrants who began to settle there from the 1880s. Britain ruled Palestine from 1917. Large numbers of Jews escaping Nazi persecution arrived in the 1930s, provoking an Arab uprising against British rule. In 1947, the UN agreed to partition Palestine into an Arab and a Jewish state. Fighting broke out after Arabs rejected the plan. The State of Israel came into being in May 1948, but fighting continued into 1949. Other Arab-Israeli wars in 1956, 1967 and 1973 led to land gains for Israel.

In 1978, Israel signed a treaty with Egypt which led to the return of the occupied Sinai peninsula to Egypt in 1979. But conflict continued between Israel and the PLO (Palestine Liberation Organization). In 1993, the PLO and Israel agreed to establish Palestinian self-rule in two areas: the occupied Gaza Strip, and in the town of Jericho in the occupied West Bank. The agreement was extended in 1995 to include more than 30% of the West Bank. Israel's prime minister, Yitzhak Rabin, was assassinated in 1995. In 1996, his successor, Simon Peres, was defeated by the right-wing Benjamin Netanyahu, under whom the peace process stalled. In 1999, the left-wing Ehud Barak defeated Netanyahu and revived the peace process. But, following violence between the Palestinians and Israeli forces, Barak resigned. In 2001, Barak was defeated by the right-wing Ariel Sharon, who adopted a hardline policy against the Palestinians. In 2003, after Sharon won re-election, the United States exerted pressure on him to agree to the setting up of a Palestinian state.

Israel's most valuable activity is manufacturing and the country's products include chemicals, electronic equipment, fertilizers, military equipment, plastics, processed food, scientific instruments and textiles. Fruits and vegetables are leading exports.

AREA 20,600 SQ KM [7,954 SQ MI] **POPULATION** 6,117,000
CAPITAL (POPULATION) JERUSALEM (685,000)
GOVERNMENT MULTIPARTY REPUBLIC **ETHNIC GROUPS** JEWISH 80%, ARAB AND OTHERS 20% **LANGUAGES** HEBREW AND ARABIC (BOTH OFFICIAL)
RELIGIONS JUDAISM 80%, ISLAM (MOSTLY SUNNI) 14%, CHRISTIANITY 2%, DRUZE AND OTHERS 2% **CURRENCY** NEW ISRAELI SHEKEL = 100 AGORAT

ITALY

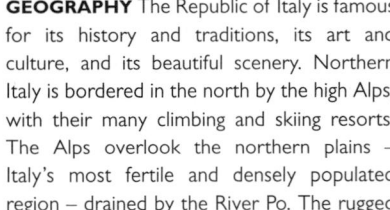

GEOGRAPHY The Republic of Italy is famous for its history and traditions, its art and culture, and its beautiful scenery. Northern Italy is bordered in the north by the high Alps, with their many climbing and skiing resorts. The Alps overlook the northern plains – Italy's most fertile and densely populated region – drained by the River Po. The rugged Apennines form the backbone of southern Italy. Bordering the range are scenic hilly areas and coastal plains. Southern Italy contains a string of volcanoes, stretching from Vesuvius, through the Lipari Islands, to Etna on Sicily, the largest Mediterranean island. Northern Italy has cold, often snowy, winters, but the summer months are warm and sunny, with brief summer thunderstorms. Rainfall is abundant. The south has mild, moist winters and warm, dry summers.

POLITICS & ECONOMY Magnificent ruins throughout Italy testify to the glories of the ancient Roman Empire, which was founded, according to legend, in 753 BC. It reached its peak in the AD 100s. It finally collapsed in the 400s, although the Eastern Roman empire, also called the Byzantine empire, survived for another 1,000 years.

In the Middle Ages, Italy was split into many tiny states. These states made a great contribution to the revival of art and learning, called the Renaissance, in the 14th to 16th centuries. Beautiful cities, such as Florence (Firenze) and Venice (Venézia), testify to the artistic achievements of this period.

Italy finally became a united kingdom in 1861, although the Papal Territories (a large area ruled by the Roman Catholic Church) was not added until 1870. The Pope and his successors disputed the takeover of the Papal Territories. The dispute was finally resolved in 1929, when the Vatican City was set up in Rome as a fully independent state.

Italy fought in World War I (1914–18) alongside the Allies – Britain, France and Russia. In 1922, the dictator Benito Mussolini, leader of the Fascist party, took power. Under Mussolini, Italy conquered Ethiopia. During World War II (1939–45), Italy at first fought on Germany's side against the Allies. But in late 1943, Italy declared war on Germany. Italy became a republic in 1946. It has played an important part in European affairs. It was a founder member of the North Atlantic Treaty Organization (NATO) in 1949 and also of what has now become the European Union in 1958.

After the setting up of the European Union, Italy's economy developed quickly. But the country faced many problems. For example, much of the economic development was in the north. This forced many people to leave the poor south to find jobs in the north or abroad. Social problems, corruption at high levels of society, and a succession of weak coalition governments all contributed to instability. Elections in 1996 were won by the left-wing Olive Tree alliance led by Romano Prodi, who was replaced in 1998 by an ex-Communist, Massimo d'Alema, who tried but failed to introduce a two-party system. In 2001, a centre-right coalition won a substantial majority in parliament and its leader, media tycoon Silvio Berlusconi, became prime minister.

Only 50 years ago, Italy was a mainly agricultural society. But today it is a leading industrial power. It lacks mineral resources, and imports most of the raw materials used in industry. Manufactures include textiles and clothing, processed food, machinery, cars and chemicals. The chief industrial region is in the north-west.

Farmland covers around 42% of the land, pasture 17%, and forest and woodland 22%. Major crops include citrus fruits, grapes which are used to make wine, olive oil, sugar beet and vegetables. Livestock farming is important, though meat is imported.

AREA 301,318 sq km [116,339 sq mi] **POPULATION** 57,998,000
CAPITAL (POPULATION) Rome (2,460,000)
GOVERNMENT Multiparty republic **ETHNIC GROUPS** Italian 94%, German, French, Albanian, Slovene, Greek **LANGUAGES** Italian (official), German, French, Slovene **RELIGIONS** Predominantly Roman Catholic **CURRENCY** Euro = 100 cents

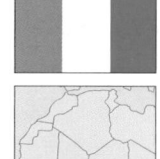

IVORY COAST

GEOGRAPHY The Republic of the Ivory Coast, in West Africa, is officially known as Côte d'Ivoire. The south-east coast is bordered by sand bars that enclose lagoons. The south-west coast is lined by rocky cliffs.

Ivory Coast has a hot and humid tropical climate, with high temperatures all year. The south has two rainy seasons: between May and July, and from October to November. Inland, the rainfall decreases and the north has one dry and one rainy season.

POLITICS & ECONOMY From 1895, Ivory Coast was governed as part of French West Africa, a massive union which also included what are now Benin, Burkina Faso, Guinea, Mali, Mauritania, Niger and Senegal. In 1946, Ivory Coast became a territory in the French Union.

Ivory Coast became fully independent in 1960. Its first president, Félix Houphouët-Boigny, became the longest serving head of state in Africa with an uninterrupted period in office which ended with his death in 1993. Houphouët-Boigny, a pro-Western leader, made Ivory Coast a one-party state. In 1983, the National Assembly voted to make Yamoussoukro, the president's birthplace, the new capital. In 1999, a military coup occurred, but civilian rule was restored in 2000, when Laurent Gbagbo was elected president. An army rebellion began in September 2002. It continued into 2003 when a power-sharing coalition was set up, including members from rebel groups.

Agriculture employs about half of the people, and farm products make up nearly half the value of the exports. Manufacturing has grown in importance since 1960; products include fertilizers, processed food, refined oil, textiles and timber.

AREA 322,463 sq km [124,503 sq mi] **POPULATION** 16,962,000
CAPITAL (POPULATION) Yamoussoukro (107,000)
GOVERNMENT Multiparty republic **ETHNIC GROUPS** Akan 42%, Voltaiques 18%, Northern Mandes 16%, Krous 11%, Southern Mandes 10% **LANGUAGES** French (official), many native dialects **RELIGIONS** Islam 40%, Christianity 30%, traditional beliefs 30%
CURRENCY CFA franc = 100 centimes

JAMAICA

GEOGRAPHY Third largest of the Caribbean islands, half of Jamaica lies above 300 m [1,000 ft] and moist south-east trade winds bring rain to the central mountain range.

The 'cockpit country' in the north-west of the island is an inaccessible limestone area of steep broken ridges and isolated basins.

POLITICS & ECONOMY Britain took Jamaica from Spain in the 17th century, and the island did not gain its independence until 1962. Some economic progress was made by the socialist government in the 1980s, but migration and unemployment remain high. Farming is the leading activity and sugar cane is the main crop, though bauxite production provides much of the country's income. Jamaica has some industries and tourism is a major industry.

AREA 10,991 sq km [4,244 sq mi] **POPULATION** 2,696,000
CAPITAL (POPULATION) Kingston (104,000)
GOVERNMENT Constitutional monarchy
ETHNIC GROUPS Black 91%, Mixed 7%, East Indian 1%
LANGUAGES English (official), patois English
RELIGIONS Protestant 61%, Roman Catholic 4%
CURRENCY Jamaican dollar = 100 cents

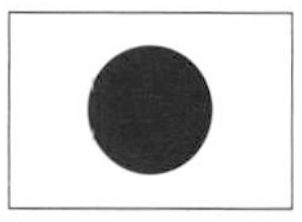

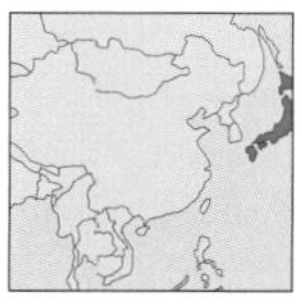

JAPAN

GEOGRAPHY Japan's four largest islands – Honshu, Hokkaido, Kyushu and Shikoku – make up 98% of the country. But Japan contains thousands of small islands. The four largest islands are mainly mountainous, while many of the small islands are the tips of volcanoes. Japan has more than 150 volcanoes, about 60 of which are active. Volcanic eruptions, earthquakes and tsunamis (destructive sea waves triggered by underwater earthquakes and eruptions) are common because the islands lie in an unstable part of our planet, where continental plates are always on the move. One powerful recent earthquake killed more than 5,000 people in Kobe in 1995.

The climate of Japan varies greatly from north to south. Hokkaido in the north has cold, snowy winters. At Sapporo, temperatures below –20°C [4°F] have been recorded between December and March. But summers are warm, with temperatures sometimes exceeding 30°C [86°F]. Rain falls throughout the year, though Hokkaido is one of the driest parts of Japan. Tokyo has higher rainfall and temperatures, while the southern islands of Shikoku and Kyushu have warm temperate climates. Summers are long and hot. Winters are cold.

POLITICS & ECONOMY In the late 19th century, Japan began a programme of modernization. Under its new imperial leaders, it began to look for lands to conquer. In 1894–5, it fought a war with China and, in 1904–5, it defeated Russia. Soon its overseas empire included Korea and Taiwan. In 1930, Japan invaded Manchuria (north-east China) and, in 1937, it began a war against China. In 1941, Japan launched an attack on the US base at Pearl Harbor in Hawaii. This drew both Japan and the United States into World War II.

Japan surrendered in 1945 when the Americans dropped atomic bombs on two cities, Hiroshima and Nagasaki. The United States occupied Japan until 1952. During this period, Japan adopted a democratic constitution. The emperor, who had previously been regarded as a god, became a constitutional monarch. Power was vested in the prime minister and cabinet, who are chosen from the Diet (elected parliament).

From the 1960s, Japan experienced many changes as the country rapidly built up new industries. By the early 1990s, Japan had become the world's second richest economic power after the US. But economic success has brought problems. For example, the rapid growth of cities has led to housing shortages and pollution. Another problem is that the proportion of people over 65 years of age is steadily increasing.

Japan has the world's second highest gross domestic product (GDP) after the United States. [The GDP is the total value of all goods and services produced in a country in one year.] The most important sector of the economy is industry. Yet Japan has to import most of the raw materials and fuels it needs for its industries. Its success is based on its use of the latest technology, its skilled and hard-working labour force, its vigorous export policies and its comparatively small government spending on defence. Manufactures dominate its exports, which include machinery, electrical and electronic equipment, vehicles and transport equipment, iron and steel, chemicals, textiles and ships. However, from the late 1990s, Japan experienced an economic slowdown, which merged in a recession in the early 21st century.

Japan is one of the world's top fishing nations and fish is an important source of protein. Because the land is so rugged, only 15% of the country can be farmed. Yet Japan produces about 70% of the food it needs. Rice is the chief crop, taking up about half of the total farmland. Other major products include fruits, sugar beet, tea and vegetables. Livestock farming has increased since the 1950s.

AREA 377,829 sq km [145,880 sq mi] **POPULATION** 127,214,000
CAPITAL (POPULATION) Tokyo (8,130,000)
GOVERNMENT Constitutional monarchy
ETHNIC GROUPS Japanese 99%, Chinese, Korean, Brazilian and others
LANGUAGES Japanese (official) **RELIGIONS** Shintoism and Buddhism 84% (most Japanese consider themselves to be both Shinto and Buddhist), others **CURRENCY** Yen = 100 sen

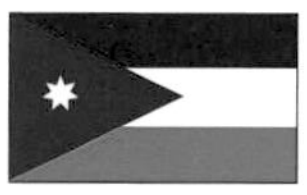

JORDAN

GEOGRAPHY The Hashemite Kingdom of Jordan is an Arab country in south-western Asia. The Great Rift Valley in the west contains the River Jordan and the Dead Sea, which Jordan shares with Israel. East of the Rift Valley is the Transjordan plateau, where most Jordanians live. To the east and south lie vast areas of desert.

Amman has a much lower rainfall and longer dry season than the Mediterranean lands to the west. The Transjordan plateau, on which Amman stands, is a transition zone between the Mediterranean climate zone and the desert climate to the east.

POLITICS & ECONOMY In 1921, Britain created a territory called Transjordan east of the River Jordan. In 1923, Transjordan became self-governing, but Britain retained control of its defences, finances and foreign affairs. This territory became fully independent as Jordan in 1946. Jordan has suffered from instability arising from the Arab–Israeli conflict since the creation of the State of Israel in 1948. After the first Arab–Israeli War in 1948–9, Jordan acquired East Jerusalem and a fertile area called the West Bank. In 1967, Israel occupied this area. In Jordan, the presence of Palestinian refugees led to civil war in 1970–1.

In 1974, Arab leaders declared that the PLO (Palestine Liberation Organization) was the sole representative of the Palestinian people. In 1988, King Hussein of Jordan renounced Jordan's claims to the West Bank and passed responsibility for it to the PLO. Opposition parties were legalized in 1991 and elections were held in 1993. In October 1994, Jordan and Israel signed a peace treaty, ending a state of war that had lasted more than 40 years. Jordan's King Hussein commanded respect for his role in Middle Eastern affairs until his death in 1999. He was succeeded by his eldest son, who became Abdullah II. As king, he continued Jordan's efforts to further the Israel–Palestinian peace process. He also supported the US-declared war on terrorism.

Jordan lacks natural resources, apart from phosphates and potash, and the economy depends substantially on aid. The World Bank classifies Jordan as a 'lower-middle-income' developing country. Because of the dry climate, less than 6% of the land is farmed or used as pasture. Jordan has an oil refinery and manufactures include cement, pharmaceuticals, processed food, fertilizers and textiles.

AREA 89,342 sq km [34,495 sq mi] **POPULATION** 5,460,000
CAPITAL (POPULATION) Amman (1,253,000)
GOVERNMENT Constitutional monarchy **ETHNIC GROUPS** Arab 98%, of which Palestinians make up roughly half **LANGUAGES** Arabic (official) **RELIGIONS** Islam (mostly Sunni) 94%, Christianity (mostly Greek Orthodox) 6% **CURRENCY** Jordanian dinar = 1,000 fils

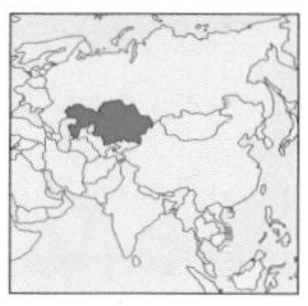

KAZAKHSTAN

GEOGRAPHY Kazakhstan is a large country in west-central Asia. In the west, the Caspian Sea lowlands include the Karagiye depression, which reaches 132 m [433 ft] below sea level. The lowlands extend eastwards through the Aral Sea area. The north contains high plains, but the highest land is along the eastern and southern borders. These areas include parts of the Altai and Tian Shan mountain ranges. Eastern Kazakhstan contains several freshwater lakes, the largest of which is Lake Balkhash. The water in the rivers has been used for irrigation, causing ecological problems. For example, the Aral Sea, deprived of water, shrank from 66,900 sq km [25,830 sq mi] in 1960 to 33,642 sq km [12,989 sq mi] in 1993. Large areas are now barren desert.

Kazakhstan lies far from the moderating influence of the oceans and it has an extreme climate. Winters are cold and snow covers the land for about 100 days at Almaty. The rainfall is generally low.

POLITICS & ECONOMY After the Russian Revolution of 1917, many Kazakhs wanted to make their country independent. But the Communists prevailed and in 1936 Kazakhstan became a republic of the Soviet Union, called the Kazakh Soviet Socialist Republic. During World War II and also after the war, the Soviet government moved many people from the west into Kazakhstan. From the 1950s, people were encouraged to work on a 'Virgin Lands' project, which involved bringing large areas of grassland under cultivation.

Reforms in the Soviet Union in the 1980s led to its break-up in December 1991. Kazakhstan maintained contacts with Russia through the Commonwealth of Independent States (CIS). In 1997, the government moved its capital from Almaty to Aqmola (later renamed Astana), a town in the Russian-dominated north. It hoped that this would bring some Kazakh identity to the area. In the early 21st century, Kazakhstan's economy was in better shape than any other of the Central Asian ex-Soviet republics. However, its President Nursultan Nazarbaev was criticized for cracking down on political dissent and independent newspapers.

The World Bank classifies Kazakhstan as a 'lower-middle-income' developing country. Livestock farming, especially sheep and cattle, is an important activity, and major crops include barley, cotton, rice and wheat. The country is rich in mineral resources, including coal and oil reserves, together with bauxite, copper, lead, tungsten and zinc. Manufactures include chemicals, food products, machinery and textiles. Oil is exported via a pipeline through Russia; however, to reduce dependence on Russia, Kazakhstan signed an agreement in 1997 to build a new pipeline to China. Other exports include metals, chemicals, grain, wool and meat.

AREA 2,724,900 sq km [1,052,084 sq mi] **POPULATION** 16,764,000
CAPITAL (POPULATION) Astana (322,000) **GOVERNMENT** Multiparty republic **ETHNIC GROUPS** Kazakh 53%, Russian 30%, Ukrainian 4%, German 2%, Uzbek 2% **LANGUAGES** Kazakh (official); Russian, the former official language, is widely spoken **RELIGIONS** Islam 47%, Russian Orthodox 44% **CURRENCY** Tenge = 100 tiyn

KENYA

GEOGRAPHY The Republic of Kenya is a country in East Africa which straddles the Equator. Behind the narrow coastal plain on the Indian Ocean, the land rises to high plains and highlands, broken by volcanic mountains, including Mount Kenya, the country's highest peak at 5,199 m [17,057 ft]. Crossing the country is an arm of the Great Rift Valley, on the floor of which are several lakes, including Baringo, Magadi, Naivasha, Nakuru and, on the northern frontier, Lake Turkana (formerly Lake Rudolf).

Mombasa on the coast is hot and humid. But inland, the climate is moderated by the height of the land. As a result, Nairobi, in the thickly populated south-western highlands, has summer temperatures which are 10°C [18°F] lower than Mombasa. Nights can be cool, but temperatures do not fall below freezing. Nairobi's main rainy season is from April to May, with 'little rains' in November and December. However, only about 15% of the country has a reliable rainfall of 800 mm [31 in].

POLITICS & ECONOMY The Kenyan coast has been a trading centre for more than 2,000 years. Britain took over the coast in 1895 and soon extended its influence inland. In the 1950s, a secret movement, called Mau Mau, launched an armed struggle against British rule. Although Mau Mau was eventually defeated, Kenya became independent in 1963.

Many Kenyans felt that Kenya should have a strong central government, and Kenya was a one-party state for much of the time since 1963. But democracy was restored in the early 1990s and elections were held in 1992, 1997 and 2002. In 1999, Kenya, with Tanzania and Uganda, set up an East African Community, which aimed to create a customs union, a common market, a monetary union, and, ultimately, a political union.

According to the United Nations, Kenya is a 'low-income' developing country. Agriculture employs about 80% of the people, but many Kenyans are subsistence farmers, growing little more than they need to support their families. The chief food crop is maize. The main cash crops and leading exports are coffee and tea. Manufactures include chemicals, leather and footwear, processed food, petroleum products and textiles.

AREA 580,367 sq km [224,080 sq mi] **POPULATION** 31,639,000
CAPITAL (POPULATION) Nairobi (2,143,000)
GOVERNMENT Multiparty republic **ETHNIC GROUPS** Kikuyu 22%, Luhya 14%, Luo 13%, Kalenjin 12%, Kamba 11%, others
LANGUAGES Kiswahili and English (both official)
RELIGIONS Protestant 45%, Roman Catholic 33%, traditional beliefs 10%, Islam 10% **CURRENCY** Kenyan shilling = 100 cents

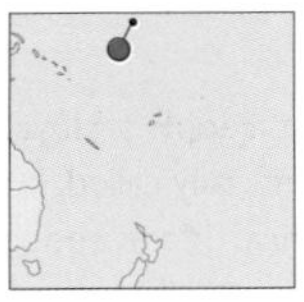

KIRIBATI

The Republic of Kiribati comprises three groups of corall atolls scattered over about 5 million sq km [2 million sq mi]. Kiribati straddles the equator and temperatures are high and the rainfall is abundant.

Formerly part of the British Gilbert and Ellice Islands, Kiribati became independent in 1979. The main export is copra and the country depends heavily on foreign aid.

AREA 726 sq km [280 sq mi] **POPULATION** 99,000 **CAPITAL** Tarawa

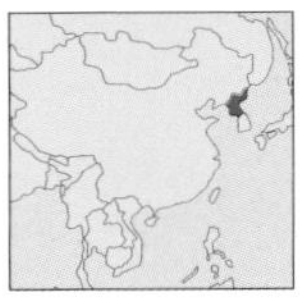

KOREA, NORTH

GEOGRAPHY The Democratic People's Republic of Korea occupies the northern part of the Korean peninsula which extends south from north-eastern China. Mountains form the heart of the country, with the highest peak, Paektu-san, reaching 2,744 m [9,003 ft] on the northern border.

North Korea has a fairly severe climate, with bitterly cold winters when winds blow from across central Asia, bringing snow and freezing conditions. In summer, moist winds from the oceans bring rain.

POLITICS & ECONOMY North Korea was created in 1945, when the peninsula, which had been a Japanese colony since 1910, was divided into two parts. Soviet forces occupied the north, with US forces in the south. Soviet occupation led to a Communist government being established in 1948 under the leadership of Kim Il Sung. He initiated a Stalinist regime in which he assumed the role of dictator, and a personality cult developed around him. He was to become the world's most durable Communist leader.

The Korean War began in June 1950 when North Korean troops invaded the south. North Korea, aided by China and the Soviet Union, fought with South Korea, which was supported by troops from the United States and other UN members. The war ended in July 1953. An armistice was signed but no permanent peace treaty was agreed. The end of the Cold War in the late 1990s eased the situation. North and South Korea joined the United Nations in 1991 and they made several agreements, including one in which they agreed not to use force against each other. However, North Korea remained as isolated as ever.

In 1993, North Korea began a new international crisis by announcing that it was withdrawing from the Nuclear Non-Proliferation Treaty. This led to suspicions that North Korea, which had signed the Treaty in 1985, was developing its own nuclear weapons. Kim Il Sung, who had ruled as a virtual dictator from 1948 until his death in 1994, was succeeded by his son, Kim Jong Il. In the early 2000s, attempts were made to reconcile the two Koreas, though the prospect of reunification seemed remote. In 2003, North Korea's relations with the United States deteriorated sharply when the US accused North Korea of developing nuclear weapons.

North Korea's resources include coal, copper, iron ore, lead, tin tungsten and zinc. Under Communism, the country developed heavy, state-owned industries. Manufactures include chemicals, iron and steel, machinery, processed food and textiles. Agriculture employs 32% of the people and rice is the chief crop. Economic mismanagement and successive floods in 1995 and 1996, and a drought in 1997, caused severe famine.

AREA 120,538 sq km [46,540 sq mi] **POPULATION** 22,466,000
CAPITAL (POPULATION) Pyŏngyang (2,725,000)
GOVERNMENT Single-party people's republic
ETHNIC GROUPS Korean 99%
LANGUAGES Korean (official)
RELIGIONS Buddhism and Confucianism
CURRENCY North Korean won = 100 chon

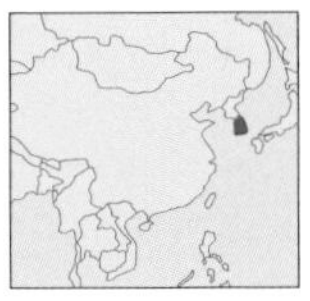

KOREA, SOUTH

GEOGRAPHY The Republic of Korea, as South Korea is officially known, occupies the southern part of the Korean peninsula. Mountains cover much of the country. The southern and western coasts are major farming regions. Many islands are found along the west and south coasts. The largest of these is Cheju-do, which contains South Korea's highest peak, Halla-San, which rises to 1,950 m [6,398 ft].

Like North Korea, South Korea is chilled in winter by cold, dry winds blowing from central Asia. Snow often covers the mountains in the east. The summers are hot and wet, especially in July and August.

POLITICS & ECONOMY After Japan's defeat in World War II (1939–45), North Korea was occupied by troops from the Soviet Union, while South Korea was occupied by United States forces. Attempts to reunify Korea failed and, in 1948, a National Assembly was elected in South Korea. This Assembly created the Republic of Korea, while North Korea became a Communist state. North Korean troops invaded the South in June 1950, sparking off the Korean War (1950–3).

In the 1950s, South Korea had a weak economy, which had been further damaged by the destruction caused by the Korean War. From the 1960s to the 1980s, South Korean governments worked to industrialize the economy. The governments were dominated by military leaders, who often used authoritarian methods and flouted human rights. In 1987, a new constitution was approved, enabling presidential elections to be held every five years. In 1991, South and North Korea became members of the United Nations and they signed agreements, including one in which they agreed not to use force against each other. Tensions continued, though hopes were raised when negotiations between the two countries took place in the early 21st century.

The World Bank classifies South Korea as an 'upper-middle-income' developing country. It is also one of the world's fastest growing industrial economies. The country's resources include coal and tungsten, and its main manufactures are processed food and textiles. Since partition, heavy industries have been built up, making chemicals, fertilizers, iron and steel, and ships. South Korea has also developed the production of such things as computers, cars and television sets. But, in late 1997, the expansion of the economy was halted by a market crash which affected many of the booming economies of eastern Asia. However, South Korea recovered faster than any other country in the region.

Farming remains important in South Korea. Rice is the chief crop, together with fruits, grains and vegetables, while fishing provides a major source of protein.

AREA 99,268 sq km [38,327 sq mi] **POPULATION** 48,289,000
CAPITAL (POPULATION) Seoul (10,231,000)
GOVERNMENT Multiparty republic **ETHNIC GROUPS** Korean 99%
LANGUAGES Korean (official) **RELIGIONS** No affiliation 46%, Christianity 26%, Buddhism 26%, Confucianism 1%
CURRENCY South Korean won = 100 chon

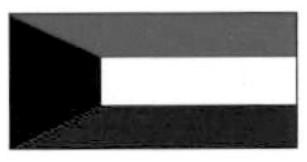

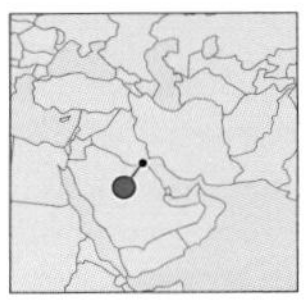

KUWAIT

The State of Kuwait at the north end of the Persian Gulf is an emirate (ruled by an emir or amir). The land is low-lying and largely desert. Summer temperatures are high but winters are cooler. The rainfall is low.

POLITICS & ECONOMY British influence began in 1775 and, in 1899, the local ruler concluded a treaty with Britain, agreeing to support British interests in return for British protection. Kuwait became independent in 1961. Its revenue from its oil exports made it highly prosperous. Iraq invaded Kuwait in 1990 and much damage was inflicted in 1991 when Kuwait was liberated by a coalition force. In the 1990s, reforms were introduced to make the country more democratic and raise the status of women. However, conservative Islamists, who opposed the reforms, won elections in 2003.

AREA 17,818 sq km [6,880 sq mi] **POPULATION** 2,183,000
CAPITAL (POPULATION) Kuwait City (29,000)

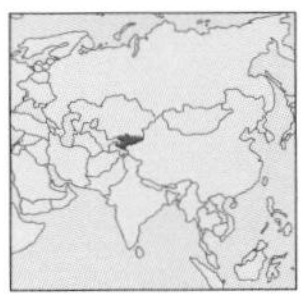

KYRGYZSTAN

GEOGRAPHY The Republic of Kyrgyzstan is a landlocked country between China, Tajikistan, Uzbekistan and Kazakhstan. The country is mountainous, with spectacular scenery. The highest mountain, Pik Pobedy in the Tian Shan range, reaches 7,439 m [24,406 ft] in the east. The lowlands have warm summers and cold winters. But January temperatures in the mountains plummet to –28°C [–18°F]. Kyrgyzstan has a low annual rainfall.

POLITICS & ECONOMY In 1876, Kyrgyzstan became a province of Russia and Russian settlement in the area began. In 1916, Russia crushed a rebellion among the Kyrgyz, and many subsequently fled to China. In 1922, the area became an autonomous oblast (self-governing region) of the newly formed Soviet Union but, in 1936, it became one of the Soviet Socialist Republics. Under Communist rule, local customs and religious worship were suppressed, but education and health services were greatly improved.

In 1991, Kyrgyzstan became an independent country following the break-up of the Soviet Union. The Communist party was dissolved, but the country maintained ties with Russia through an organization called the Commonwealth of Independent States. Kyrgyzstan adopted a new constitution in 1994 and parliamentary elections were held in 1995. In the early 21st century, many people were alarmed when Islamic guerrillas sought to set up an Islamic state in the Fergana valley, where Kyrgyzstan borders Tajikistan and Uzbekistan.

In the early 1990s, when Kyrgyzstan was working to reform its economy, the World Bank classified it as a 'lower-middle-income' developing country. Agriculture, especially livestock rearing, is the chief activity. The chief products include cotton, eggs, fruits, grain, tobacco, vegetables and wool. But food must be imported. Industries are mainly concentrated around the capital Bishkek.

AREA 199,900 sq km [77,181 sq mi] **POPULATION** 4,893,000
CAPITAL (POPULATION) Bishkek (753,000) **GOVERNMENT** Multiparty republic **ETHNIC GROUPS** Kyrgyz 65%, Russian 13%, Uzbek 13%
LANGUAGES Kyrgyz and Russian (both official) **RELIGIONS** Islam 75%, Russian Orthodox 20% **CURRENCY** Som = 100 tyiyn

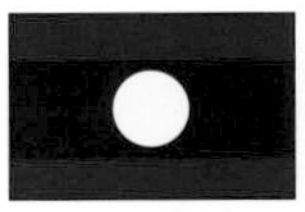

LAOS

GEOGRAPHY The Lao People's Democratic Republic is a landlocked country in South-east Asia. Mountains and plateaux cover much of the country. Most people live on the plains bordering the River Mekong and its tributaries. This river, one of Asia's longest, forms much of the country's north-western and south-western borders.

Laos has a tropical monsoon climate.

Winters are dry and sunny, with winds blowing in from the north-east. The temperatures rise until April, when the wind directions are reversed and moist south-westerly winds reach Laos, heralding the start of the wet monsoon season.

POLITICS & ECONOMY France made Laos a protectorate in the late 19th century and ruled it as part of French Indo-China, a region which also included Cambodia and Vietnam. Laos became a member of the French Union in 1948 and an independent kingdom in 1954.

After independence, Laos suffered from instability caused by a long power struggle between royalist government forces and a pro-Communist group called the Pathet Lao. A civil war broke out in 1960 and continued into the 1970s. The Pathet Lao took control in 1975 and the king abdicated. Laos then came under the influence of Communist Vietnam, which had used Laos as a supply base during the Vietnam War (1957–75). From the early 1980s, the economy deteriorated and opposition appeared when bombings occurred in Vientiane in 2000. They were attributed to rebels in the minority Hmong tribe or to politicians who wanted faster economic reforms.

Laos is one of the world's poorest countries. Agriculture employs about 76% of the people, compared with 7% in industry and 17% in services. Rice is the main crop, and timber and coffee are both exported. But the most valuable export is electricity, which is produced at hydroelectric power stations on the River Mekong and is exported to Thailand. Laos also produces opium.

AREA 236,800 SQ KM [91,428 SQ MI] **POPULATION** 5,922,000
CAPITAL (POPULATION) VIENTIANE (528,000)
GOVERNMENT SINGLE-PARTY REPUBLIC
ETHNIC GROUPS LAO LOUM 68%, LAO THEUNG 22%, LAO SOUNG 9%
LANGUAGES LAO (OFFICIAL), FRENCH, ENGLISH **RELIGIONS** BUDDHISM 60%, TRADITIONAL BELIEFS AND OTHERS 40% **CURRENCY** KIP = 100 AT

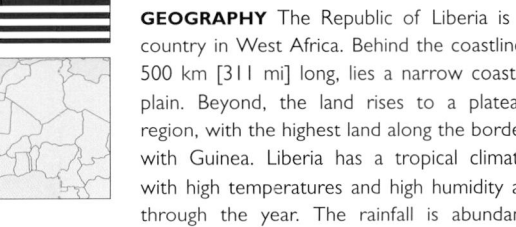

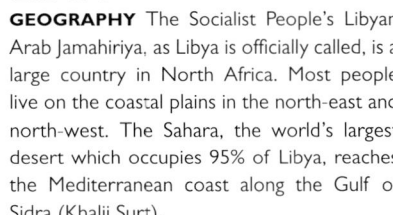

LATVIA

GEOGRAPHY The Republic of Latvia is one of three states on the south-eastern corner of the Baltic Sea which were ruled as parts of the Soviet Union between 1940 and 1991. Latvia consists mainly of flat plains separated by low hills, composed of moraine (ice-worn rocks).

Riga has warm summers, but the winter months (from December to March) are subzero. In the winter, the sea often freezes over. The rainfall is moderate and it occurs throughout the year, with light snow in winter.

POLITICS & ECONOMY In 1800, Russia was in control of Latvia, but Latvians declared their independence after World War I. In 1940, under a German-Soviet pact, Soviet troops occupied Latvia, but they were driven out by the Germans in 1941. Soviet troops returned in 1944 and Latvia became part of the Soviet Union. Under Soviet rule, many Russian immigrants settled in Latvia and many Latvians feared that the Russians would become the dominant ethnic group.

In the late 1980s, when reforms were being introduced in the Soviet Union, Latvia's government ended absolute Communist rule and made Latvian the official language. In 1990, it declared the country to be independent, an act which was finally recognized by the Soviet Union in September 1991.

Latvia held its first free elections to its parliament (the Saeima) in 1993. Voting was limited only to citizens of Latvia on 17 June 1940 and their descendants. This meant that about 34% of Latvian residents were unable to vote. In 1994, Latvia restricted the naturalization of non-Latvians, including many Russian settlers, who were not allowed to vote or own land. However, in 1998, the government agreed that all children born since independence should have automatic citizenship. Its cultivation of closer ties to the West was realized in 2004 when Latvia was admitted to membership of both the North Atlantic Treaty Organization and the European Union.

The World Bank classifies Latvia as a 'lower-middle-income' country and, in the 1990s, it faced many problems in turning its economy into a free-market system. Products include electronic goods, farm machinery, fertilizers, processed food, plastics, radios and vehicles. Latvia produces only about a tenth of the electricity it needs. It imports the rest from Belarus, Russia and Ukraine.

AREA 64,600 SQ KM [24,942 SQ MI] **POPULATION** 2,349,000
CAPITAL (POPULATION) RIGA (793,000)
GOVERNMENT MULTIPARTY REPUBLIC
ETHNIC GROUPS LATVIAN 58%, RUSSIAN 30%, BELARUSIAN, UKRAINIAN, POLISH, LITHUANIAN **LANGUAGES** LATVIAN (OFFICIAL), LITHUANIAN, RUSSIAN **RELIGIONS** LUTHERAN, ROMAN CATHOLIC, RUSSIAN ORTHODOX
CURRENCY LATVIAN LAT = 10 SANTIMI

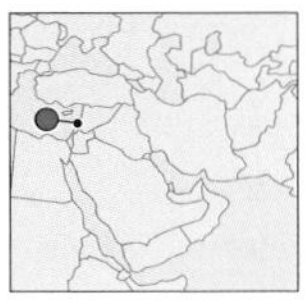

LEBANON

GEOGRAPHY The Republic of Lebanon is a country on the eastern shores of the Mediterranean Sea. Behind the coastal plain are the rugged Lebanon Mountains (Jabal Lubnan), which rise to 3,088 m [10,131 ft]. Another range, the Anti-Lebanon Mountains (Al Jabal Ash Sharqi), form the eastern border with Syria. Between the two ranges is the Bekaa (Beqaa) Valley, a fertile farming region.

The Lebanese coast has the hot, dry summers and mild, wet winters that are typical of many Mediterranean lands. Inland, onshore winds bring heavy rain to the western slopes of the mountains in the winter months, with snow at the higher altitudes.

POLITICS & ECONOMY Lebanon was ruled by Turkey from 1516 until World War I. France ruled the country from 1923, but Lebanon became independent in 1946. After independence, the Muslims and Christians agreed to share power, and Lebanon made rapid economic progress. But from the late 1950s, development was slowed by periodic conflict between Sunni and Shia Muslims, Druze and Christians. The situation was further complicated by the presence of Palestinian refugees who used bases in Lebanon to attack Israel.

In 1975, civil war broke out as private armies representing the many factions struggled for power. This led to intervention by Israel in the south and Syria in the north. UN peacekeeping forces arrived in 1978, but bombings, assassinations and kidnappings became almost everyday events in the 1980s. From 1991, Lebanon enjoyed an uneasy peace. But, Israel continued to occupy an area in the south. In the 1990s, Israel launched several attacks on pro-Iranian Hezbollah guerrillas in Lebanon, but all Israeli troops were withdrawn in May 2000.

Lebanon's civil war almost destroyed valuable trade and financial services that had been Lebanon's chief source of income, together with tourism. Manufacturing, formerly a major activity, was badly hit.

AREA 10,400 SQ KM [4,015 SQ MI] **POPULATION** 3,728,000
CAPITAL (POPULATION) BEIRUT (1,148,000)
GOVERNMENT MULTIPARTY REPUBLIC **ETHNIC GROUPS** ARAB 95%, ARMENIAN 4%, OTHERS **LANGUAGES** ARABIC (OFFICIAL), FRENCH, ENGLISH, ARMENIAN **RELIGIONS** ISLAM 70%, CHRISTIANITY 30%
CURRENCY LEBANESE POUND = 100 PIASTRES

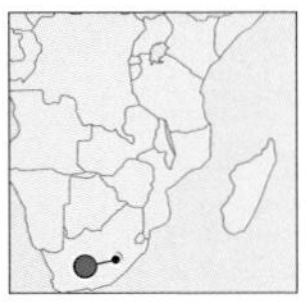

LESOTHO

GEOGRAPHY The Kingdom of Lesotho is a landlocked country, completely enclosed by South Africa. The land is mountainous, rising to 3,482 m [11,424 ft] on the north-eastern border. The Drakensberg range covers most of the country.

The climate of Lesotho is greatly affected by the altitude, because most of the country lies above 1,500 m [4,921 ft]. Summers are warm but winters are cold. The rainfall averages about 700 mm [28 in].

POLITICS & ECONOMY The Basotho nation was founded in the 1820s by King Moshoeshoe I, who united various groups fleeing from tribal wars in southern Africa. Britain made the area a protectorate in 1868 and, in 1871, placed it under the British Cape Colony in South Africa. But in 1884, Basutoland, as the area was called, was reconstituted as a British protectorate, where whites were not allowed to own land.

The country finally became independent in 1966 as the Kingdom of Lesotho, with Moshoeshoe II, great-grandson of Moshoeshoe I, as its king. Since independence, Lesotho has suffered instability. The military seized power in 1986 and stripped Moshoeshoe II of his powers in 1990, installing his son, Letsie III, as monarch. After elections in 1993, Moshoeshoe II was restored to office in 1995. But after his death in a car crash in 1996, Letsie III again became king. In 1998, an army revolt, following an election in which the ruling party won 79 out of the 80 seats, caused much damage to the economy, despite the intervention of a South African force. Lesotho also faces a health crisis. By 2003, an estimated 31% of all adults were infected with the HIV virus.

Lesotho is a 'low-income' developing country. It lacks natural resources. Agriculture, mainly at subsistence level, light manufacturing and money sent home by Basotho working abroad are the main sources of income.

AREA 30,355 SQ KM [11,720 SQ MI] **POPULATION** 1,862,000
CAPITAL (POPULATION) MASERU (109,000)
GOVERNMENT CONSTITUTIONAL MONARCHY
ETHNIC GROUPS SOTHO 99% **LANGUAGES** SESOTHO AND ENGLISH (BOTH OFFICIAL) **RELIGIONS** CHRISTIANITY 80%, TRADITIONAL BELIEFS 20%
CURRENCY LOTI = 100 LISENTE

LIBERIA

GEOGRAPHY The Republic of Liberia is a country in West Africa. Behind the coastline, 500 km [311 mi] long, lies a narrow coastal plain. Beyond, the land rises to a plateau region, with the highest land along the border with Guinea. Liberia has a tropical climate with high temperatures and high humidity all through the year. The rainfall is abundant all year round, but there is a particularly wet period from June to November. The rainfall generally increases from east to west.

POLITICS & ECONOMY In the late 18th century, some white Americans in the United States wanted to help freed black slaves to return to Africa. In 1816, they set up the American Colonization Society, which bought land in what is now Liberia.

In 1822, the Society landed former slaves at a settlement on the coast which they named Monrovia. In 1847, Liberia became a fully independent republic with a constitution much like that of the United States. For many years, the Americo-Liberians controlled the country's government. US influence remained strong and the American Firestone Company, which ran Liberia's rubber plantations, was especially influential. Foreign companies were also involved in exploiting Liberia's mineral resources, including its huge iron-ore deposits.

In 1980, a military group composed of people from the local population killed the Americo-Liberian president, William R. Tolbert. An army sergeant, Samuel K. Doe, was made president of Liberia. Elections held in 1985 resulted in victory for Doe. From 1989, the country was plunged into civil war between various ethnic groups. Doe was assassinated in 1990 and the struggle with rebel groups continued. West African peacekeeping forces arrived in Liberia and, in 1995, a cease-fire was agreed. A council of state, composed of former warlords, was set up and, in 1997, one of the warlords, Charles Taylor, was elected president. A cease-fire followed in 1998, but unrest continued. Another cease-fire was declared in 2003. Soon afterwards, Taylor resigned and went into exile.

Liberia's civil war devastated its economy. Three out of every four people depend on agriculture, though many of them grow little more than they need to feed their families. Major food crops include cassava, rice and sugar cane, while rubber, cocoa and coffee are exported. But the most valuable export is iron ore.

Liberia also obtains revenue from its 'flag of convenience', which is used by about one-sixth of the world's commercial shipping, exploiting low taxes.

AREA 111,369 SQ KM [43,000 SQ MI] **POPULATION** 3,317,000
CAPITAL (POPULATION) MONROVIA (421,000)
GOVERNMENT MULTIPARTY REPUBLIC **ETHNIC GROUPS** INDIGENOUS AFRICAN TRIBES 95% (INCLUDING KPELLE, BASSA, GREBO, GIO, KRU, MANO)
LANGUAGES ENGLISH (OFFICIAL), ETHNIC LANGUAGES
RELIGIONS CHRISTIANITY 40%, ISLAM 20%, TRADITIONAL BELIEFS AND OTHERS 40% **CURRENCY** LIBERIAN DOLLAR = 100 CENTS

LIBYA

GEOGRAPHY The Socialist People's Libyan Arab Jamahiriya, as Libya is officially called, is a large country in North Africa. Most people live on the coastal plains in the north-east and north-west. The Sahara, the world's largest desert which occupies 95% of Libya, reaches the Mediterranean coast along the Gulf of Sidra (Khalij Surt).

The coastal plains in the north-east and north-west have Mediterranean climates, with hot, dry summers and mild, sometimes wet winters. Inland, the average yearly rainfall drops to 100 mm [4 in] or less.

POLITICS & ECONOMY Italy took over Libya in 1911, but lost it during World War II. Britain and France jointly ruled Libya until 1951, when the country became an independent kingdom.

In 1969, a military group headed by Colonel Muammar Gaddafi deposed the king and set up a military government. Under Gaddafi, the government took control of the economy and used money from oil exports to finance welfare services and development projects. Gaddafi was criticized for supporting terrorist groups around the world, and Libya became isolated from the mid-1980s. In 1998, he tried to restore Libya's reputation by surrendering for trial two Libyans suspected of planting a bomb on a PanAm plane which exploded over the Scottish town of Lockerbie in 1988. In 2001, one of the Libyans was found guilty and the other acquitted of the bombing. In 2003, Libya announced that it would pay compensation to victims of the bombing. In 2004, in a further attempt to lose its pariah status in international affairs, Libya declared that it was ending the production of all weapons of mass destruction, a move welcomed by Western nations.

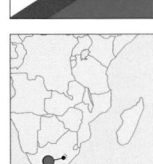

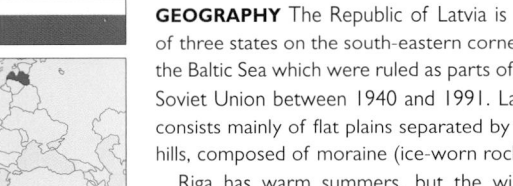

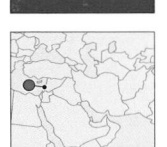

The discovery of oil and natural gas in 1959 led to a transformation of Libya's economy. This formerly poor country soon became Africa's richest in terms of its per capita income. But it remains a developing country, because oil accounts for nearly all its export revenues. Agriculture is important, although Libya imports food. Crops include barley, citrus fruits, dates, olives, potatoes and wheat, while cattle, sheep and poultry are raised. Libya has oil refineries and petrochemical plants. Other manufactures include cement and steel.

AREA 1,759,540 SQ KM [679,358 SQ MI] **POPULATION** 5,499,000 **CAPITAL (POPULATION)** TRIPOLI (1,500,000) **GOVERNMENT** SINGLE-PARTY SOCIALIST STATE **ETHNIC GROUPS** LIBYAN ARAB AND BERBER 97% **LANGUAGES** ARABIC (OFFICIAL), BERBER **RELIGIONS** ISLAM (SUNNI MUSLIM) 97% **CURRENCY** LIBYAN DINAR = 1,000 DIRHAMS

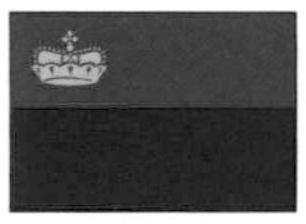

LIECHTENSTEIN

The tiny Principality of Liechtenstein is sandwiched between Switzerland and Austria. The River Rhine flows along its western border, while Alpine peaks rise in the east and south. The climate is relatively mild. Since 1924, Liechtenstein has been in a customs union with Switzerland. Taxation is low and the country is a haven for foreign companies. In 2003, the people voted to give their head of state, Prince Hans Adam II, sovereign powers. However, he later announced that he planned to retire from politics and hand over to his heir, Prince Alois, although Hans Adam II would remain head of state.

AREA 160 SQ KM [62 SQ MI] **POPULATION** 33,000 **CAPITAL** VADUZ

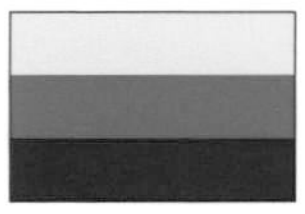

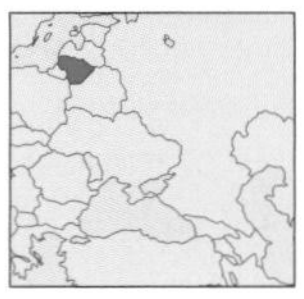

LITHUANIA

GEOGRAPHY The Republic of Lithuania is the southernmost of the three Baltic states which were ruled as part of the Soviet Union between 1940 and 1991. Much of the land is flat or gently rolling, with the highest land in the south-east.

Winters are cold and summers warm. The annual rainfall in the west is about 630 mm [25 in]. Eastern areas are drier.

POLITICS & ECONOMY The Lithuanian people were united into a single nation in the 12th century, and later joined a union with Poland. In 1795, Lithuania came under Russian rule. After World War I (1914–18), Lithuania declared itself independent, and in 1920 it signed a peace treaty with the Russians, though Poland held Vilnius until 1939. In 1940, the Soviet Union occupied Lithuania, but the Germans invaded in 1941. Soviet forces returned in 1944, and Lithuania was integrated into the Soviet Union. In 1988, when the Soviet Union was introducing reforms, the Lithuanians demanded independence. Their language is one of the oldest in the world, and the country was always the most homogenous of the Baltic states, staunchly Catholic and resistant of attempts to suppress their culture. Pro-independence groups won the national elections in 1990 and, in 1991, the Soviet Union recognized Lithuania's independence.

Since 1991, Lithuania has sought to reform its economy and introduce a private enterprise system. Lithuania has also drawn closer to the West and, in 2004, it became a member of both the North Atlantic Treaty Organization and the European Union.

The World Bank classifies Lithuania as a 'lower-middle-income' developing country. Lithuania lacks natural resources, but manufacturing, based on imported materials, is the most valuable activity.

AREA 65,200 SQ KM [25,174 SQ MI] **POPULATION** 3,593,000 **CAPITAL (POPULATION)** VILNIUS (578,000) **GOVERNMENT** MULTIPARTY REPUBLIC **ETHNIC GROUPS** LITHUANIAN 80%, RUSSIAN 9%, POLISH 7%, BELARUSIAN 2% **LANGUAGES** LITHUANIAN (OFFICIAL), RUSSIAN, POLISH **RELIGIONS** MAINLY ROMAN CATHOLIC **CURRENCY** LITAS = 100 CENTAI

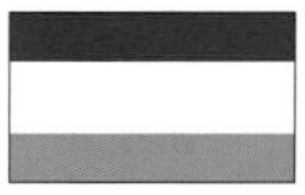

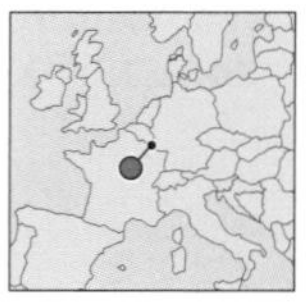

LUXEMBOURG

GEOGRAPHY The Grand Duchy of Luxembourg is one of the smallest and oldest countries in Europe. The north belongs to an upland region which includes the Ardenne in Belgium and Luxembourg, and the Eifel highlands in Germany.

Luxembourg has a temperate climate. The south has warm summers and autumns, when grapes ripen in sheltered south-eastern valleys. Winters are sometimes severe, especially in upland areas.

POLITICS & ECONOMY Germany occupied Luxembourg in World Wars I and II. In 1944–5, northern Luxembourg was the scene of the famous Battle of the Bulge. In 1948, Luxembourg joined Belgium and the Netherlands in a union called Benelux and, in the 1950s, it was one of the six founders of what is now the European Union. Luxembourg has played a major role in Europe. Its capital contains the headquarters of several international agencies, including the European Coal and Steel Community and the European Court of Justice. The city is also a major financial centre.

Luxembourg has iron-ore reserves and is a major steel producer. It also has many high-technology industries, producing electronic goods and computers. Steel and other manufactures, including chemicals, rubber products, glass and aluminium, dominate the country's exports. Other major activities include tourism and financial services.

AREA 2,586 SQ KM [998 SQ MI] **POPULATION** 454,000 **CAPITAL (POPULATION)** LUXEMBOURG (77,000) **GOVERNMENT** CONSTITUTIONAL MONARCHY (GRAND DUCHY) **ETHNIC GROUPS** LUXEMBOURGER 71%, PORTUGUESE, ITALIAN, FRENCH, BELGIAN, SLAVS **LANGUAGES** LUXEMBOURGISH (OFFICIAL), FRENCH, GERMAN **RELIGIONS** ROMAN CATHOLIC 87%, OTHERS 13% **CURRENCY** EURO = 100 CENTS

MACEDONIA (FYROM)

GEOGRAPHY The Republic of Macedonia is a country in south-eastern Europe, which was once one of the six republics that made up the former Federal People's Republic of Yugoslavia. This landlocked country is largely mountainous or hilly. Macedonia has hot summers, though highland areas are cooler. Winters are cold and snowfalls are often heavy. The climate is fairly continental in character and rain occurs throughout the year.

POLITICS & ECONOMY Until the 20th century, Macedonia's history was closely tied to a larger area, also called Macedonia, which included parts of northern Greece and south-western Bulgaria. This region reached its peak in power at the time of Philip II (382–336 BC) and his son Alexander the Great (336–323 BC). After Alexander's death, his empire was split up and it gradually declined. The area became a Roman province in the 140s BC and part of the Byzantine Empire from AD 395. In the 6th century, Slavs from eastern Europe settled in the area, followed by the Bulgars from central Asia in the 9th century. The Byzantine Empire regained control in 1018, but Serbia took Macedonia in the early 14th century. In 1371, the Ottoman Turks conquered the area and ruled it for more than 500 years. In 1913, at the end of the Balkan Wars, the area was divided between Serbia, Bulgaria and Greece. At the end of World War I, Serbian Macedonia became part of the Kingdom of the Serbs. Croats and Slovenes, which was renamed Yugoslavia in 1929. After World War II, Yugoslavia became a Communist country under ex-partisan leader Josip Broz Tito.

Tito died in 1980 and, in the early 1990s, the country broke up into five separate republics. Macedonia declared its independence in September 1991. Greece objected to this territory using the name Macedonia, which it considered to be a Greek name. It also objected to a symbol on Macedonia's flag and a reference in the constitution to the desire to reunite the three parts of the old Macedonia.

Macedonia adopted a new clause in its constitution rejecting any Macedonian claims on Greek territory and, in 1993, the United Nations accepted the new republic as a member under the name of The Former Yugoslav Republic of Macedonia (FYROM).

By the end of 1993, all the countries of the EU, except Greece, were establishing diplomatic relations with the FYROM. In 1995, Greece lifted its trade ban, when Macedonia agreed to redesign its flag and remove territorial claims from its constitution. In 2001, fighting along the Kosovo border spilled over into north-western Macedonia. It was attributed to nationalists who want to create a Great Albania, including part of Macedonia. The uprising ended when the Macedonian government gave its Albanian-speakers increased rights.

The World Bank describes Macedonia as a 'lower-middle-income' developing country. Manufactures dominate the country's exports. Macedonia mines coal, but imports all its oil and natural gas. The country is self-sufficient in its basic food needs.

AREA 25,713 SQ KM [9,928 SQ MI] **POPULATION** 2,063,000 **CAPITAL (POPULATION)** SKOPJE (430,000) **GOVERNMENT** MULTIPARTY REPUBLIC **ETHNIC GROUPS** MACEDONIAN 64%, ALBANIAN 25%, TURKISH 4%, ROMANIAN 3%, SERB 2% **LANGUAGES** MACEDONIAN AND ALBANIAN (OFFICIAL) **RELIGIONS** MACEDONIAN ORTHODOX 70%, ISLAM 29% **CURRENCY** MACEDONIAN DENAR = 100 PARAS

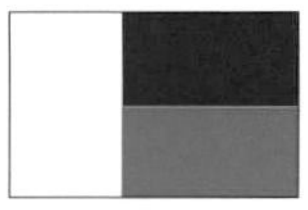

MADAGASCAR

GEOGRAPHY The Democratic Republic of Madagascar, in south-eastern Africa, is an island nation, which has a larger area than France. Behind the narrow coastal plains in the east lies a highland zone, mostly between 610 m and 1,220 m [2,000 ft to 4,000 ft] above sea level. Broad plains border the Mozambique Channel in the west.

Temperatures in the highlands are moderated by the altitude. The winters (from April to September) are dry, but heavy rains occur in summer. The eastern coastlands are warm and humid. The west is drier and the south and south-west are hot and dry.

POLITICS & ECONOMY People from South-east Asia began to settle on Madagascar around 2,000 years ago. Subsequent influxes from Africa and Arabia added to the island's diverse heritage, culture and language.

French troops defeated a Malagasy army in 1895 and Madagascar became a French colony. In 1960, it achieved full independence as the Malagasy Republic. In 1972, army officers seized control and, in 1975, under the leadership of Lieutenant-Commander Didier Ratsiraka, the country was renamed Madagascar. Parliamentary elections were held in 1977, but Ratsiraka remained president of a one-party socialist state. In 2002, the country came close to civil war when Ratsiraka and his opponent, Marc Ravalomanana, both claimed victory in presidential elections. Ravalomanana was eventually recognized as president and Ratsiraka went into exile.

Madagascar is one of the world's poorest countries. The land has been badly eroded because of the cutting down of the forests and overgrazing of the grasslands. Farming, fishing and forestry employ about 80% of the people. The country's food crops include bananas, cassava, rice and sweet potatoes. Coffee is the leading export.

AREA 587,041 SQ KM [226,657 SQ MI] **POPULATION** 16,980,000 **CAPITAL (POPULATION)** ANTANANARIVO (1,250,000) **GOVERNMENT** REPUBLIC **ETHNIC GROUPS** MERINA, BETSIMISARAKA, BETSILEO, TSIMIHETY, SAKALAVA AND OTHERS **LANGUAGES** MALAGASY AND FRENCH (BOTH OFFICIAL) **RELIGIONS** TRADITIONAL BELIEFS 52%, CHRISTIANITY 41%, ISLAM 7% **CURRENCY** MALAGASY FRANC = 100 CENTIMES

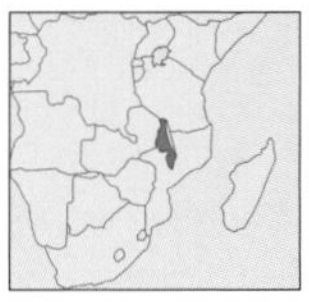

MALAWI

GEOGRAPHY The Republic of Malawi includes part of Lake Malawi, which is drained by the River Shire, a tributary of the River Zambezi. The land is mostly mountainous. The highest peak, Mulanje, reaches 3,000 m [9,843 ft] in the south-east.

While the low-lying areas of Malawi are hot and humid all year round, the uplands have a pleasant climate. Lilongwe, at about 1,100 m [3,609 ft] above sea level, has a warm and sunny climate. Frosts sometimes occur in July and August, in the middle of the long dry season.

POLITICS & ECONOMY Malawi, then called Nyasaland, became a British protectorate in 1891. In 1953, Britain established the Federation of Rhodesia and Nyasaland, which also included what are now Zambia and Zimbabwe. Black African opposition, led in Nyasaland by Dr Hastings Kamuzu Banda, led to the dissolution of the federation in 1963. In 1964, Nyasaland became independent as Malawi, with Banda as prime minister. Banda became president when the country became a republic in 1966 and, in 1971, he was made president for life. Banda ruled autocratically through the only party, the Malawi Congress Party. A multiparty system was restored in 1993. Banda and his party were defeated in elections in 1993. Bakili Muluzi became president and was re-elected in 1999. In 2004, Muluzi's nominee, Bingu wa Mutharika, was elected president.

Malawi is one of the world's poorest countries. More than 80% of the people are farmers, but many grow little more than they need to feed their families.

AREA 118,484 SQ KM [45,747 SQ MI] **POPULATION** 11,651,000 **CAPITAL (POPULATION)** LILONGWE (440,000) **GOVERNMENT** MULTIPARTY REPUBLIC **ETHNIC GROUPS** CHEWA, NYANJA, TONGA, TUMBUKA, LOMWE, YAO, NGONI AND OTHERS **LANGUAGES** CHICHEWA AND ENGLISH (BOTH OFFICIAL) **RELIGIONS** PROTESTANT 55%, ROMAN CATHOLIC 20%, ISLAM 20% **CURRENCY** MALAWIAN KWACHA = 100 TAMBALA

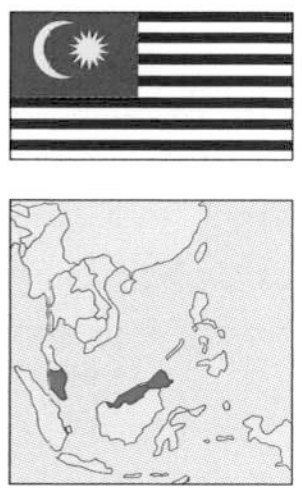

MALAYSIA

GEOGRAPHY The Federation of Malaysia consists of two main parts. Peninsular Malaysia, which is joined to mainland Asia, contains about 80% of the population. The other main regions, Sabah and Sarawak, are in northern Borneo, an island which Malaysia shares with Indonesia. Behind the coastal lowlands, the interior is mountainous.

Malaysia has a hot equatorial climate. The temperatures are high all through the year, though the mountains are much cooler than the lowland areas. The rainfall is heavy throughout the year.

POLITICS & ECONOMY Around 1,200 years ago, Indian traders introduced Hinduism and Buddhism into the Malay peninsula, while Arabs introduced Islam in the 15th century. Portuguese traders reached Melaka in 1509, but the Dutch took over in 1641. Britain became established in the area in 1786.

Japan occupied the area during World War II (1939–45), but the area reverted to British rule in 1945. In the 1940s and 1950s, Communist guerrillas battled unsuccessfully for power. Malaya (Peninsular Malaysia) became independent in 1957. Malaysia was created in 1963, when Malaya, Singapore, Sabah and Sarawak agreed to unite, but Singapore withdrew in 1965.

From 1981, under the leadership of Dr Mahathir bin Mohamad, Malaysia achieved rapid economic progress. However, together with other countries in eastern Asia, it experienced an economic recession in 1997. In response to the crisis, the government ordered the repatriation of many temporary foreign workers and initiated a series of austerity measures aimed at restoring confidence and avoiding the chronic debt problems affecting some other Asian countries. Mahathir bin Mohamad retired in 2003 and was succeeded as prime minister by Abdullah Ahmad Bud.

The World Bank classifies Malaysia as an 'upper-middle-income' developing country. Palm oil, rubber and tin are major products. Manufactures include cars, chemicals, a wide range of electronic goods, plastics, textiles, rubber and wood products.

AREA 329,758 SQ KM [127,320 SQ MI] **POPULATION** 23,093,000 **CAPITAL (POPULATION)** KUALA LUMPUR (1,145,000); PUTRAJAYA (ADMINISTRATIVE CAPITAL AWAITING COMPLETION) **GOVERNMENT** FEDERAL CONSTITUTIONAL MONARCHY **ETHNIC GROUPS** MALAY AND OTHER INDIGENOUS GROUPS 58%, CHINESE 24%, INDIAN 8%, OTHERS **LANGUAGES** MALAY (OFFICIAL), CHINESE, ENGLISH **RELIGIONS** ISLAM, BUDDHISM, DAOISM, HINDUISM, CHRISTIANITY, SIKHISM **CURRENCY** RINGGIT = 100 CENTS

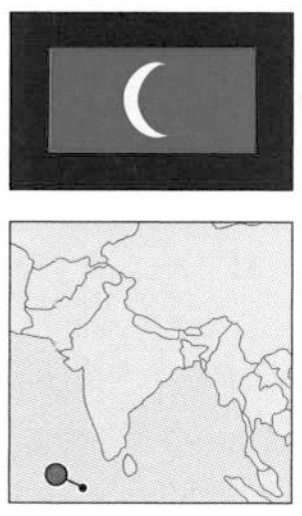

MALDIVES

The Republic of the Maldives consists of about 1,200 low-lying coral islands, south of India. The highest point is 24 m [79 ft], but most of the land is only 1.8 m [6 ft] above sea level. The islands became a British territory in 1887 and independence was achieved in 1965. Tourism and fishing are the main industries.

AREA 298 SQ KM [115 SQ MI] **POPULATION** 330,000 **CAPITAL** MALÉ

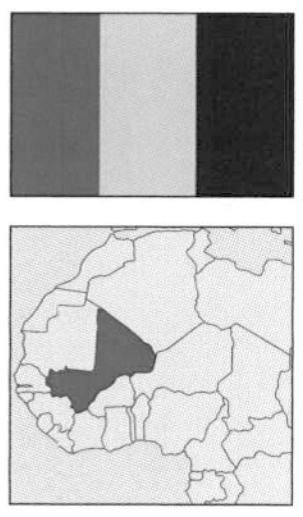

MALI

GEOGRAPHY The Republic of Mali is a landlocked country in northern Africa. The land is generally flat, with the highest land in the north. Northern Mali is hot and practically rainless. The south has enough rain for farming.

POLITICS & ECONOMY Between the 4th and 16th centuries, Mali was part of three African empires – ancient Ghana, ancient Mali and Songhay. However, after 1591, when Songhay was defeated by Morocco, the area was divided into small kingdoms. France ruled the area, then known as French Sudan, from 1893 until the country became independent as Mali in 1960.

The first socialist government was overthrown in 1968 by an army group led by Moussa Traoré, but he was ousted in 1991. Multiparty democracy was restored in 1992 and Alpha Oumar Konaré was elected president. Konaré stood down in 2002 and Ahmadou Toure, who had restored democracy in 1992, was elected president.

Mali is one of the world's poorest countries and 70% of the land is desert or semi-desert. Only about 2% of the land is used for growing crops, while 25% is used for grazing animals. Despite this, agriculture employs nearly 80% of the people, many of whom subsist by nomadic livestock rearing.

AREA 1,240,192 SQ KM [478,838 SQ MI] **POPULATION** 11,626,000 **CAPITAL (POPULATION)** BAMAKO (1,016,000) **GOVERNMENT** MULTIPARTY REPUBLIC **ETHNIC GROUPS** MANDE 50% (BAMBARA, MALINKE, SONINKE), PEUL 17%, VOLTAIC 12%, SONGHAI 6%, TUAREG AND MOOR 10%, OTHERS **LANGUAGES** FRENCH (OFFICIAL), MANY AFRICAN LANGUAGES **RELIGIONS** ISLAM 90%, TRADITIONAL BELIEFS 9%, CHRISTIANITY 1% **CURRENCY** CFA FRANC = 100 CENTIMES

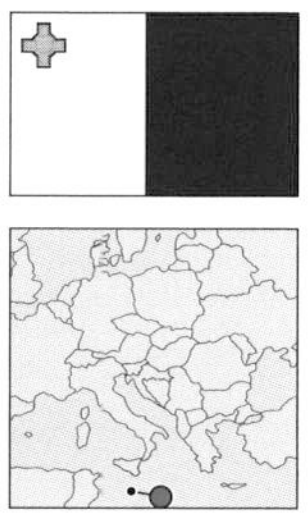

MALTA

GEOGRAPHY The Republic of Malta consists of two main islands, Malta and Gozo, a third, much smaller island called Comino lying between the two large islands and two islets. The climate is typically Mediterranean, with hot, dry summers and mild, moist winters.

POLITICS & ECONOMY Malta has fascinating Stone and Bronze age remains. The islands later came under Phoenician, Greek, Carthaginian, Roman and Arab rule. In about 1090, Malta came under the Norman kings of Sicily and, from 1530, the Knights Hospitallers (also called the Knights of St John of Jerusalem). France took the islands in 1798, but the British drove them out in 1800. British rule was officially recognized in 1815.

During World War I (1914–18), Malta was an important naval base. In World War II (1939–45), Italian and German aircraft bombed the islands. In recognition of the islanders' bravery, the British King George VI awarded the George Cross to Malta in 1942. In 1953, Malta became a base for NATO (North Atlantic Treaty Organization). Malta became independent in 1964 and a republic in 1974. In 1979, Malta ceased to be a British military base and all British forces withdrew. Malta was declared a neutral country in the 1980s. It became a member of the European Union on 1 May 2004.

The World Bank classifies Malta as an 'upper-middle-income' developing country. It lacks natural resources, and most people work in the former naval dockyards, which are now used for commercial shipbuilding and repair, in manufacturing industries and in the tourist industry.

Manufactures include chemicals, processed food and chemicals. Farming is difficult, because of the rocky soils. Crops include barley, fruits, potatoes and wheat. Malta also has a small fishing industry.

AREA 316 SQ KM [122 SQ MI] **POPULATION** 400,000 **CAPITAL (POPULATION)** VALLETTA (9,000) **GOVERNMENT** MULTIPARTY REPUBLIC **ETHNIC GROUPS** MALTESE 96%, BRITISH 2% **LANGUAGES** MALTESE AND ENGLISH (BOTH OFFICIAL) **RELIGIONS** ROMAN CATHOLIC 98% **CURRENCY** MALTESE LIRA = 100 CENTS

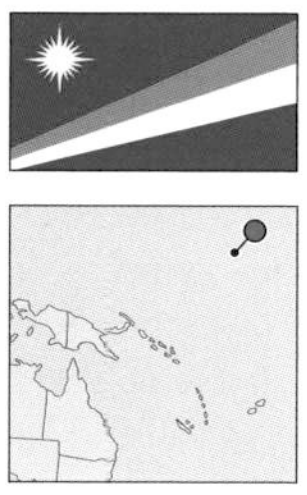

MARSHALL ISLANDS

The Republic of the Marshall Islands, a former US territory, became fully independent in 1991. This island nation, lying north of Kiribati in a region known as Micronesia, is heavily dependent on US aid. The main activities are agriculture and tourism.

AREA 181 SQ KM [70 SQ MI] **POPULATION** 56,000 **CAPITAL** MAJURO

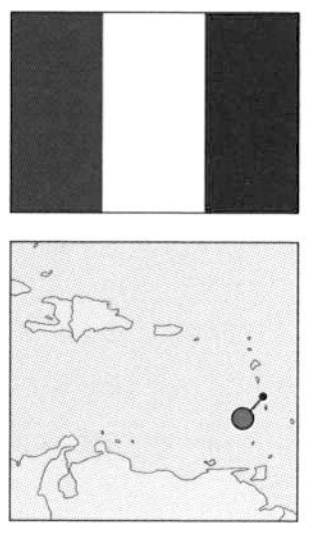

MARTINIQUE

Martinique, a volcanic island nation in the Caribbean, was colonized by France in 1635. It became a French overseas department in 1946. Tourism and agriculture are major activities. About 70% of Martinique's gross domestic product is provided by the French government, allowing for a good standard of living.

AREA 1,102 SQ KM [425 SQ MI] **POPULATION** 426,000 **CAPITAL** FORT-DE-FRANCE

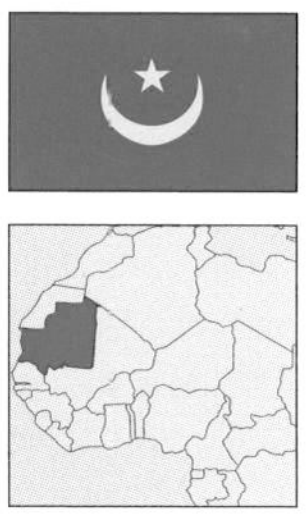

MAURITANIA

GEOGRAPHY The Islamic Republic of Mauritania in north-western Africa is nearly twice the size of France. But France has more than 28 times as many people. Part of the world's largest desert, the Sahara, covers northern Mauritania and most Mauritanians live in the south-west.

The amount of rainfall and the length of the rainy season increase from north to south. Much of the land is desert, with dry north-east and easterly winds throughout the year. But south-westerly winds bring summer rain to the south.

POLITICS & ECONOMY Originally part of the great African empires of Ghana and Mali, France set up a protectorate in Mauritania in 1903, attempting to exploit the trade in gum arabic. The country became a territory of French West Africa and a French colony in 1920. French West Africa was a huge territory, which included present-day Benin, Burkina Faso, Guinea, Ivory Coast, Mali, Niger and Senegal, as well as Mauritania. In 1958, Mauritania became a self-governing territory in the French Union and it became fully independent in 1960.

In 1976, Spain withdrew from Spanish (now Western) Sahara, a territory bordering Mauritania to the north. Morocco occupied the northern two-thirds of this territory, while Mauritania took the rest. But Saharan guerrillas belonging to POLISARIO (the Popular Front for the Liberation of Saharan Territories) began an armed struggle for independence. In 1979, Mauritania withdrew from the southern part of Western Sahara, which was then occupied by Morocco. Democracy was restored after a new constitution was adopted in 1991. In 2003, the government cracked down on Islamic militants and other critics of the government.

The World Bank classifies Mauritania as a 'low-income' developing country. Agriculture employs 38% of the people. Some are herders who move around with herds of cattle and sheep, though recent droughts forced many farmers to seek aid in the cities.

AREA 1,025,520 SQ KM [395,953 SQ MI] **POPULATION** 2,913,000 **CAPITAL (POPULATION)** NOUAKCHOTT (735,000) **GOVERNMENT** MULTIPARTY ISLAMIC REPUBLIC **ETHNIC GROUPS** MIXED MOOR/BLACK 40%, MOOR 30%, BLACK 30% **LANGUAGES** ARABIC AND WOLOF (BOTH OFFICIAL), FRENCH **RELIGIONS** ISLAM **CURRENCY** OUGUIYA = 5 KHOUMS

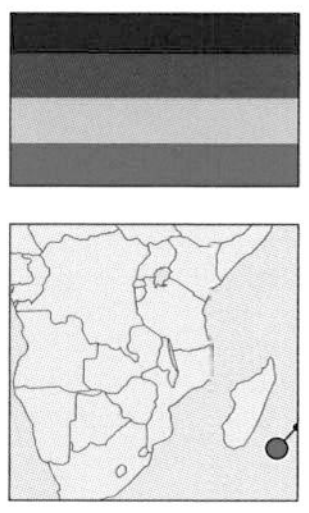

MAURITIUS

The Republic of Mauritius, an Indian Ocean nation lying east of Madagascar, was previously ruled by France and Britain until it achieved independence in 1968. It became a republic in 1992. Sugar production is in decline but tourism is vital to the economy.

AREA 2,040 SQ KM [788 SQ MI] **POPULATION** 1,210,000 **CAPITAL** PORT LOUIS

MEXICO

GEOGRAPHY The United Mexican States, as Mexico is officially named, is the world's most populous Spanish-speaking country. Much of the land is mountainous, although most people live on the central plateau. Mexico contains two large peninsulas, Lower (or Baja) California in the north-west and the flat Yucatán peninsula in the south-east.

The climate varies according to the altitude. The resort of Acapulco on the south-west coast has a dry and sunny climate. Mexico City, at about 2,300 m [7,546 ft] above sea level, is much cooler. Most rain occurs between June and September. The rainfall decreases north of Mexico City and northern Mexico is mainly arid.

POLITICS & ECONOMY In the mid-19th century, Mexico lost land to the United States, and between 1910 and 1921 violent revolutions created chaos.

Reforms were introduced in the 1920s and, in 1929, the Institutional Revolutionary Party (PRI) was formed. The PRI ruled Mexico effectively as a one-party state until it was finally defeated in 2001. The new president, Vicente Fox, faced many problems, including unemployment and rapid urbanization especially around Mexico City, demands for indigenous rights by Amerindian groups, and illegal emigration to the United States.

The World Bank classifies Mexico as an 'upper-middle-income' developing country. Agriculture is important. Food crops include beans, maize, rice and wheat, while cash crops include coffee, cotton, fruits and vegetables. Beef cattle, dairy cattle and other livestock are raised and fishing is also important.

But oil and oil products are the chief exports, while manufacturing is the most valuable activity. Mexico is the world's leading silver producer, and it also mines copper, gold, lead, zinc and other minerals. Many factories near the northern border assemble goods, such as car parts and electrical products, for US companies. These factories are called *maquiladoras*. Hope for the future lies in increasing economic co-operation with the USA and Canada through NAFTA (North American Free Trade Association), which came into being on 1 January 1994.

AREA 1,958,201 sq km [756,061 sq mi] **POPULATION** 104,908,000
CAPITAL (POPULATION) Mexico City (8,236,000)
GOVERNMENT Federal republic
ETHNIC GROUPS Mestizo 60%, Amerindian 30%, White 9%
LANGUAGES Spanish (official)
RELIGIONS Roman Catholic 90%, Protestant 6%
CURRENCY Mexican peso = 100 centavos

MICRONESIA

The Federated States of Micronesia, a former US territory covering a vast area in the western Pacific Ocean, became fully independent in 1991. The main export is copra. Fishing and tourism are also important.

AREA 702 sq km [271 sq mi]
POPULATION 108,000 **CAPITAL** Palikir

MOLDOVA

GEOGRAPHY The Republic of Moldova is a small country sandwiched between Ukraine and Romania. It was formerly one of the 15 republics that made up the Soviet Union. Much of the land is hilly and the highest areas are near the centre of the country.

Moldova has a moderately continental climate, with warm summers and fairly cold winters when temperatures dip below freezing point. Most of the rain comes in the warmer months.

POLITICS & ECONOMY In the 14th century, the Moldavians formed a state called Moldavia. It included part of Romania and Bessarabia (now the modern country of Moldova). The Ottoman Turks took the area in the 16th century, but in 1812 Russia took over Bessarabia. In 1861, Moldavia and Walachia united to form Romania. Russia retook southern Bessarabia in 1878.

After World War I (1914–18), all of Bessarabia was returned to Romania, but the Soviet Union did not recognize this act. From 1944, the Moldovan Soviet Socialist Republic was part of the Soviet Union.

In 1989, the Moldovans asserted their independence and ethnicity by making Romanian the official language and, at the end of 1991, Moldova became an independent country. In 1992, fighting occurred between Moldovans and Russians in Trans-Dniester, a mainly Russian-speaking area east of the River Dniester. The first multiparty elections were held in 1994, when a proposal to unite with Romania was rejected. Economic problems made the government unpopular and, in 2001, Moldova became the first former Soviet state to return the Communist party to power in a general election. The new government adopted many Russification policies, proclaiming Russian an official language.

In terms of its GNP per capita, Moldova is Europe's poorest country. Agriculture is the leading activity and products include fruits, maize, tobacco and wine. Moldova has few natural resources and it imports materials and fuels for its industries. Light industries, such as food processing and factories making household appliances, are increasing.

AREA 33,851 sq km [13,070 sq mi] **POPULATION** 4,440,000
CAPITAL (POPULATION) Chişinău (658,000)
GOVERNMENT Multiparty republic
ETHNIC GROUPS Moldovan/Romanian 65%, Ukrainian 14%, Russian 13%, others
LANGUAGES Moldovan/Romanian and Russian (official)
RELIGIONS Eastern Orthodox 98%
CURRENCY Moldovan leu = 100 bani

MONACO

The tiny Principality of Monaco consists of a narrow strip of coastline and a rocky peninsula on the French Riviera. Its considerable wealth is derived largely from banking, finance, gambling and tourism. Monaco's citizens do not pay any state tax. Its attractions include the Monte Carlo casino and such sporting events as the Monte Carlo Rally and the Monaco Grand Prix.

AREA 1 sq km [0.4 sq mi] **POPULATION** 32,000 **CAPITAL** Monaco

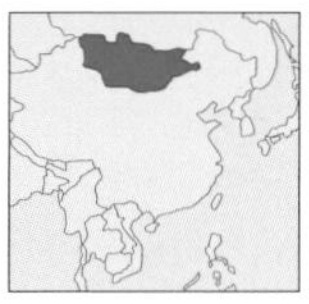

MONGOLIA

GEOGRAPHY The State of Mongolia is the world's largest landlocked country. It consists mainly of high plateaux, with the Gobi Desert in the south-east.

Ulan Bator lies on the northern edge of a desert plateau. It has bitterly cold winters. Summer temperatures are moderated by the altitude.

POLITICS & ECONOMY In the 13th century, Genghis Khan united the Mongolian peoples and built up a great empire. Under his grandson, Kublai Khan, the Mongol empire extended from Korea and China to eastern Europe and present-day Iraq.

The Mongol empire broke up in the late 14th century. In the early 17th century, Inner Mongolia came under Chinese control, and by the late 17th century Outer Mongolia had become a Chinese province. In 1911, the Mongolians drove the Chinese out of Outer Mongolia and made the area a Buddhist kingdom. But in 1924, under Russian influence, the Communist Mongolian People's Republic was set up. From the 1950s, Mongolia supported the Soviet Union in its disputes with China. In 1990, the people demonstrated for more freedom, and free elections in June 1990 resulted in victory for the Mongolian People's Revolutionary Party, which was composed of Communists. Communist rule ended in 1996, when the Democratic Union coalition won power. But the Communists regained power in 2000, though they were expected to continue free-market policies.

The World Bank classifies Mongolia as a 'lower-middle-income' developing country. Most people were once nomads, who moved around with their herds of sheep, cattle, goats and horses. Under Communist rule, most people were moved into permanent homes on government-owned farms. But livestock and animal products remain leading exports. The Communists also developed industry, especially the mining of coal, copper, gold, molybdenum, tin and tungsten, and manufacturing. Minerals and fuels now account for around half of Mongolia's exports.

AREA 1,566,500 sq km [604,826 sq mi] **POPULATION** 2,712,000
CAPITAL (POPULATION) Ulan Bator (760,000)
GOVERNMENT Multiparty republic **ETHNIC GROUPS** Khalkha Mongol 85%, Kazakh 6% **LANGUAGES** Khalkha Mongolian (official), Turkic, Russian **RELIGIONS** Tibetan Buddhist Lamaism 96%
CURRENCY Tugrik = 100 möngös

MONTSERRAT

Monserrat is a British overseas territory in the Caribbean Sea. The climate is tropical and hurricanes often cause much damage. Intermittent eruptions of the Soufrière Hills volcano between 1995 and 1998, and again in 2003, led to the emigration of many people and the virtual destruction of Plymouth, the capital, in the south.

AREA 102 sq km [39 sq mi] **POPULATION** 9,000 (prior to the volcanic activity) **CAPITAL** Plymouth

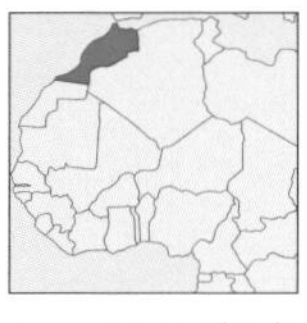

MOROCCO

GEOGRAPHY The Kingdom of Morocco lies in north-western Africa. Its name comes from the Arabic Maghreb-el-Aksa, meaning 'the farthest west'. Behind the western coastal plain the land rises to a broad plateau and ranges of the Atlas Mountains. The High (Haut) Atlas contains the highest peak, Djebel Toubkal, at 4,165 m [13,665 ft]. East of the mountains, the land descends to the Sahara. The Canaries Current cools the Atlantic coast. Inland, summers are hot and dry. Winters are mild, with moderate rainfall. Snow often falls on the High Atlas Mountains.

POLITICS & ECONOMY The original people of Morocco were the Berbers. But in the 680s, Arab invaders introduced Islam and the Arabic language. By the early 20th century, France and Spain controlled Morocco, which became an independent kingdom in 1956. Although Morocco is a constitutional monarchy, King Hassan II ruled the country in a generally authoritarian way from the time of his accession to the throne in 1961 to his death in 1999. His son and successor, Mohamed VI, faced several problems, including the future of Western Sahara, which Hassan II had claimed for Morocco. In 2003, Morocco faced another problem when Islamic suicide bombers blew up a hotel in Casablanca.

Morocco is classified as a 'lower-middle-income' developing country. It is the world's third largest producer of phosphate rock, which is used to make fertilizer. One of the reasons why Morocco wants to keep Western Sahara is that it, too, has large phosphate reserves. Farming employs 34% of Moroccans. Chief crops include barley, beans, citrus fruits, maize, olives, sugar beet and wheat. Processed phosphates are exported, but most of Morocco's manufactures are for home consumption. Fishing and tourism are also important.

AREA 446,550 sq km [172,413 sq mi] **POPULATION** 31,689,000
CAPITAL (POPULATION) Rabat (1,220,000)
GOVERNMENT Constitutional monarchy
ETHNIC GROUPS Arab-Berber 99%
LANGUAGES Arabic (official), Berber dialects, French
RELIGIONS Islam 99% **CURRENCY** Moroccan dirham = 100 centimes

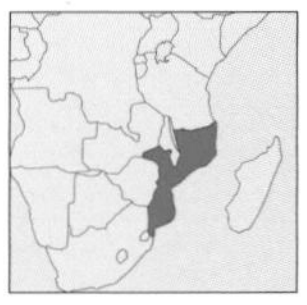

MOZAMBIQUE

GEOGRAPHY The Republic of Mozambique borders the Indian Ocean in south-eastern Africa. The coastal plains are narrow in the north but broaden in the south. Inland lie plateaux and hills, which make up another two-fifths of Mozambique.

Mozambique has a mostly tropical climate. The capital Maputo, which lies outside the tropics, has hot and humid summers, though the winters are mild and fairly dry.

POLITICS & ECONOMY In 1885, when the European powers divided Africa, Mozambique was recognized as a Portuguese colony. But black African opposition to European rule gradually increased. In 1961, the Front for the Liberation of Mozambique (FRELIMO) was founded to oppose Portuguese rule. In 1964, FRELIMO launched a guerrilla war, which continued for ten years. Mozambique became independent in 1975.

After independence, Mozambique became a one-party state. Its government aided African nationalists in Rhodesia (now Zimbabwe) and South Africa. But the white governments of these countries helped an opposition group, the Mozambique National Resistance Movement (RENAMO) to lead an armed struggle against Mozambique's government. Civil war, combined with droughts, caused much suffering in the 1980s. In 1989, FRELIMO declared that it had dropped its Communist policies and ended one-party rule. The war ended in 1992 and multiparty elections in 1994 heralded more stable conditions. In 1995 Mozambique became the 53rd member of the Commonwealth.

In the early 1990s, the UN rated Mozambique as one of the world's poorest countries. The second half of the 1990s saw a surge in economic growth, but huge floods in 2000 and 2001 proved to be a major setback. About 80% of the people are poor and agriculture is the main activity. Crops include cassava, cotton, maize, rice and tea.

AREA 801,590 sq km [309,494 sq mi] **POPULATION** 17,479,000
CAPITAL (POPULATION) Maputo (1,015,000)
GOVERNMENT Multiparty republic **ETHNIC GROUPS** Indigenous tribal groups (Shangaan, Chokwe, Manyika, Sena, Makua, others) 99%
LANGUAGES Portuguese (official), many others
RELIGIONS Traditional beliefs 50%, Christianity 30%, Islam 20%
CURRENCY Metical = 100 centavos

NAMIBIA

GEOGRAPHY The Republic of Namibia was formerly ruled by South Africa, which called it South West Africa. The country became independent in 1990. The coastal region contains the arid Namib Desert, which is virtually uninhabited. Inland is a central plateau, bordered by a rugged spine of mountains stretching north–south. Eastern Namibia contains part of the Kalahari Desert, a semi-desert area which extends into Botswana. Namibia is a warm and arid country. Lying at 1,700 m [5,500 ft] above sea level, Windhoek has an average annual rainfall of about 370 mm [15 in], often occurring during thunderstorms in the hot summer months.

POLITICS & ECONOMY During World War I, South African troops defeated the Germans who ruled what is now Namibia. After World War II, many people challenged South Africa's right to govern the territory and a civil war began in the 1960s between African guerrillas and South African troops. A cease-fire was agreed in 1989 and Namibia became independent in 1990. In the 1990s, the government pursued a policy of 'national reconciliation'. An enclave on the coast, called Walvis Bay (Walvisbaai), remained part of South Africa until 1994, when it was transferred to Namibia. In 1999, a secessionist group staged an unsuccessful uprising in the Caprivi Strip. In 2003–4, the government announced that it planned to speed up land reform by transferring farmland from white to black Namibians.

Namibia has reserves of diamonds, uranium, zinc and copper. Minerals make up 80% of the exports, though agriculture employs about 40% of the people. Sea fishing is important, but overfishing has reduced the yields of the fishing fleet. The country has few industries, but tourism is expanding.

AREA 824,292 SQ KM [318,259 SQ MI] **POPULATION** 1,927,000
CAPITAL (POPULATION) Windhoek (147,000)
GOVERNMENT Multiparty republic **ETHNIC GROUPS** Ovambo 50%, Kavango 9%, Herero 7%, Damara 7%, White 6%, Nama 5%
LANGUAGES English (official), Afrikaans, German, indigenous dialects **RELIGIONS** Christianity 90% (Lutheran 51%)
CURRENCY Namibian dollar = 100 cents

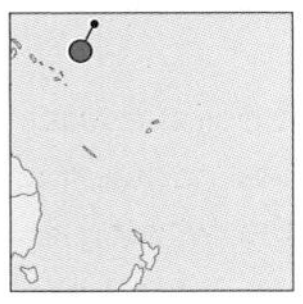

NAURU

Nauru is the world's smallest republic, located in the western Pacific Ocean, close to the equator. Independent since 1968, Nauru's prosperity is based on phosphate mining, but the reserves are running out.

AREA 21 SQ KM [8 SQ MI]
POPULATION 13,000 **CAPITAL** Yaren

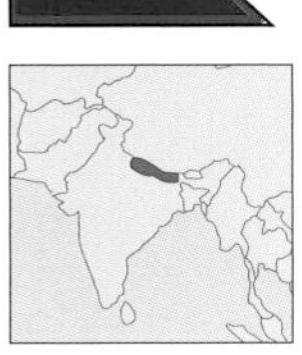

NEPAL

GEOGRAPHY Over three-quarters of Nepal lies in the Himalayan region, culminating in the world's highest peak (Mount Everest, or Chomolongma in Nepali) at 8,850 m [29,035 ft]. As a result, climatic conditions vary widely according to the altitude.

POLITICS & ECONOMY Nepal was united in the late 18th century, although its complex topography has ensured that it remains a diverse patchwork of peoples. From the mid-19th century to 1951, power was held by the royal Rana family. Attempts to introduce a democratic system in the 1950s failed. The first democratic elections in 32 years were held in 1991, but, by the early 21st century, Nepal faced many problems, including an uprising by Maoist guerrillas. In 2003, a brief cease-fire was agreed, but fighting continued in 2004. In 2001, King Birendra and other royal family members were shot dead by Crown Prince Dipendra in a family dispute.

Agriculture remains the chief activity in this overwhelmingly rural country and the government is heavily dependent on aid. Tourism, centred around the high Himalaya, grows in importance each year, although Nepal was closed to foreigners until 1951. There are also ambitious plans to exploit the hydroelectric potential offered by the ferocious Himalayan rivers.

AREA 147,181 SQ KM [56,827 SQ MI] **POPULATION** 26,470,000
CAPITAL (POPULATION) Katmandu (695,000)
GOVERNMENT Constitutional monarchy **ETHNIC GROUPS** Brahman, Chetri, Newar, Gurung, Magar, Tamang, Sherpa and others
LANGUAGES Nepali (official), local languages
RELIGIONS Hinduism 86%, Buddhism 8%, Islam 4%
CURRENCY Nepalese rupee = 100 paisa

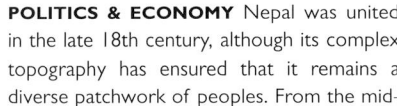

NETHERLANDS

GEOGRAPHY The Netherlands lies at the western end of the North European Plain, which extends to the Ural Mountains in Russia. Except for the far south-eastern corner, the Netherlands is flat and about 40% lies below sea level at high tide. To prevent flooding, the Dutch have built dykes (sea walls) to hold back the waves. Large areas which were once under the sea, but which have been reclaimed, are called polders. Because of its position on the North Sea, the Netherlands has a temperate climate, with mild, rainy winters.

POLITICS & ECONOMY Before the 16th century, the area that is now the Netherlands was under a succession of foreign rulers, including the Romans, the Germanic Franks, the French and the Spanish. The Dutch declared their independence from Spain in 1581 and their status was finally recognized by Spain in 1648. In the 17th century, the Dutch built up a great overseas empire, especially in South-east Asia. But in the early 18th century, the Dutch lost control of the seas to England.

France controlled the Netherlands from 1795 to 1813. In 1815, the Netherlands, then containing Belgium and Luxembourg, became an independent kingdom. Belgium broke away in 1830 and Luxembourg followed in 1890.

The Netherlands was neutral in World War I (1914–18), but was occupied by Germany in World War II (1939–45). After the war, the Netherlands Indies became independent as Indonesia. The Netherlands became active in West European affairs. With Belgium and Luxembourg, it formed a customs union called Benelux in 1948. In 1949, it joined NATO (the North Atlantic Treaty Organization), and the European Coal and Steel Community (ECSC) in 1953. In 1957, it became a founder member of the European Economic Community (now the European Union) and, in 2002, it adopted the euro as its sole unit of currency. In 2002, an anti-immigration group made sweeping gains in national elections. It joined a coalition government, which collapsed later that year. The group's vote collapsed in new elections in 2003.

The Netherlands is a highly industrialized country and industry and commerce are the most valuable activities. Its resources include natural gas, some oil, salt and china clay. But the Netherlands imports many of the materials needed by its industries and it is, therefore, a major trading country. Industrial products are wide-ranging, including aircraft, chemicals, electronic equipment, machinery, textiles and vehicles. Agriculture employs only 5% of the people, but scientific methods are used and yields are high. Dairy farming is the leading farming activity. Major products include barley, flowers and bulbs, potatoes, sugar beet and wheat.

AREA 41,526 SQ KM [16,033 SQ MI] **POPULATION** 16,151,000
CAPITAL (POPULATION) Amsterdam (729,000); The Hague (seat of government, 440,000)
GOVERNMENT Constitutional monarchy
ETHNIC GROUPS Dutch 83%, Indonesian, Turkish, Moroccan and others **LANGUAGES** Dutch (official), Frisian
RELIGIONS Roman Catholic 31%, Protestant 21%, Islam 4%, others
CURRENCY Euro = 100 cents

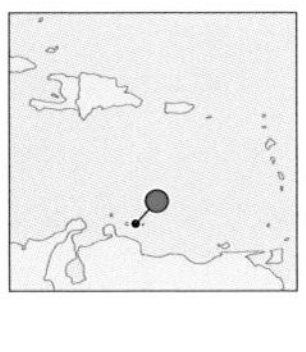

NETHERLANDS ANTILLES

The Netherlands Antilles consists of two different island groups; one off the coast of Venezuela, and the other at the northern end of the Leeward Islands, some 800 km [500 mi] away. They remain a self-governing Dutch territory. The island of Aruba was once part of the territory, but it broke away in 1986. Oil refining and tourism are important activities.

AREA 800 SQ KM [309 SQ MI] **POPULATION** 216,000 **CAPITAL** Willemstad

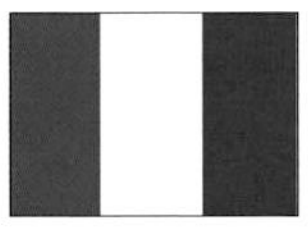

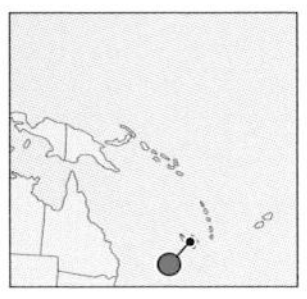

NEW CALEDONIA

New Caledonia is the most southerly of the Melanesian countries in the Pacific. A French possession since 1853 and an Overseas Territory since 1958. In 1998, France announced an agreement with local Melanesians that a vote on independence would be postponed until 2014. The country is rich in mineral resources, especially nickel.

AREA 18,575 SQ KM [7,172 SQ MI] **POPULATION** 211,000 **CAPITAL** Nouméa

NEW ZEALAND

GEOGRAPHY New Zealand lies about 1,600 km [994 mi] south-east of Australia. It consists of two main islands and several other small ones. Much of North Island is volcanic. Active volcanoes include Ngauruhoe and Ruapehu. Hot springs and geysers are common, and steam from the ground is used to produce electricity. The Southern Alps, which contain the country's highest peak Aoraki Mount Cook at 3,753 m [12,313 ft], form the backbone of South Island. The island also has some large, fertile plains.

Auckland in the north has a warm, humid climate throughout the year. Wellington has cooler summers, while in Dunedin, in the south-east, temperatures sometimes dip below freezing in winter. The rainfall is heaviest on the western highlands.

POLITICS & ECONOMY Evidence suggests that early Maori settlers arrived in New Zealand more than 1,000 years ago. The Dutch navigator Abel Tasman reached New Zealand in 1642, but his discovery was not followed up. In 1769, the British Captain James Cook rediscovered the islands. In the early 19th century, British settlers arrived and, in 1840, under the Treaty of Waitangi, Britain took possession of the islands. From the 1870s, the Maoris were gradually integrated into colonial society.

In 1907, New Zealand became a self-governing dominion in the British Commonwealth. The country's economy developed quickly and the people became increasingly prosperous. However, after Britain joined the European Economic Community in 1973, New Zealand's exports to Britain shrank and the country had to reassess its economic and defence strategies and seek new markets. The world recession led the government to cut back on welfare spending in the 1990s. The preservation of Maori culture and Maori rights are also major issues. Ties with Britain have been gradually reduced. In 2003, the parliament voted to end the right of legal appeal to the Privy Council in London, one of New Zealand's last ties with its imperial past.

New Zealand's economy has traditionally depended on agriculture, but manufacturing now employs twice as many people as agriculture. Meat and dairy products are the most valuable farm products. Sheep rearing has declined as the area under cattle, deer and vines has increased. Crops include barley, fruits, potatoes, other vegetables and wheat. Fishing is also important.

AREA 270,534 SQ KM [104,453 SQ MI] **POPULATION** 3,951,000
CAPITAL (POPULATION) Wellington (167,000)
GOVERNMENT Constitutional monarchy
ETHNIC GROUPS New Zealand European 74%, New Zealand Maori 10%, Polynesian 4% **LANGUAGES** English and Maori (both official) **RELIGIONS** Anglican 24%, Presbyterian 18%, Roman Catholic 15%, others
CURRENCY New Zealand dollar = 100 cents

NICARAGUA

GEOGRAPHY The Republic of Nicaragua is a large country in Central America. In the east is a broad plain bordering the Caribbean Sea. The plain is drained by rivers that flow from the Central Highlands. The fertile western Pacific region contains about 40 volcanoes, many of which are active, and earthquakes are common.

Nicaragua has a tropical climate. Managua is hot throughout the year and there is a marked rainy season from May to October. In October 1998, Hurricane Mitch caused great devastation in Nicaragua. The Central Highlands and Caribbean region are cooler and wetter. The wettest region is the humid Caribbean plain.

POLITICS & ECONOMY In 1502, Christopher Columbus claimed the area for Spain, which ruled Nicaragua until 1821. By the early 20th century, the United States had considerable influence in the country and, in 1912, US forces entered Nicaragua to protect US interests. From 1927 to 1933, rebels under General Augusto César Sandino, tried to drive US forces out of the country. In 1933, US marines set up a Nicaraguan army, the National Guard, to help to defeat the rebels. Its leader, Anastasio Somoza Garcia, had Sandino murdered in 1934 and, from 1937, Somoza ruled as a dictator.

In the mid-1970s, many people began to protest against Somoza's rule. Many joined a guerrilla force, called the Sandinista National Liberation Front, named after General Sandino. The rebels defeated the Somoza regime in 1979. In the 1980s, the US-supported forces, called the 'Contras', launched a campaign against the Sandinista government. The US government opposed the Sandinista regime, under Daniel José Ortega Saavedra, claiming that it was a Communist dictatorship. A coalition, the National Opposition Union, defeated the Sandinistas in elections in 1990. In 1996 and again in 2001, the Sandinista candidate Daniel Ortega was defeated in presidential elections.

In the early 1990s, Nicaragua faced many problems in rebuilding its shattered economy. Agriculture is the main activity, employing nearly half of the people. Coffee, cotton, sugar and bananas are grown for export, while rice is the main food crop.

AREA 130,000 SQ KM [50,193 SQ MI] **POPULATION** 5,129,000
CAPITAL (POPULATION) Managua (1,107,000)
GOVERNMENT Multiparty republic
ETHNIC GROUPS Mestizo 69%, White 17%, Black 9%, Amerindian 5%
LANGUAGES Spanish (official)
RELIGIONS Roman Catholic 85%, Protestant
CURRENCY Córdoba oro (gold córdoba) = 100 centavos

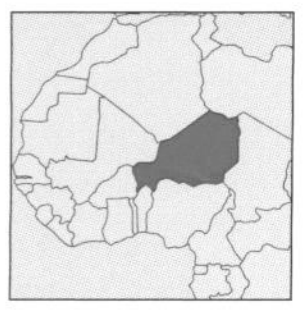

NIGER

GEOGRAPHY The Republic of Niger is a landlocked nation in north-central Africa. The northern plateaux lie in the Sahara Desert, while Central Niger contains the rugged Aïr Mountains. The most fertile, densely populated region is the Niger valley in the south-west.

Niger has a tropical climate and the south has a rainy season between June and September. The north is practically rainless.

POLITICS & ECONOMY Since independence in 1960, Niger, a French territory from 1900, has suffered severe droughts. Food shortages and the collapse of the traditional nomadic way of life of some of Niger's people have caused political instability. After a period of military rule, a multiparty constitution was adopted in 1992, but the military again seized power in 1996. Later that year, the coup leader, Colonel Ibrahim Barre Mainassara, was elected president. He was assassinated in 1999, but parliamentary rule was rapidly restored and Tandja Mamadou was elected president later in the year.

Niger's chief resource is uranium and the country is the fourth largest producer. In 2003, accusations that Niger supplied uranium to Iraq for its nuclear programme proved to be baseless. Some tin and tungsten are also mined, though other mineral reserves are largely untouched. Despite its resources, Niger is one of the world's poorest countries. Farming employs 76% of the people, but only 3% of the land can be used for crops and 8% for grazing.

AREA 1,267,000 sq km [489,189 sq mi] **POPULATION** 11,059,000
CAPITAL (POPULATION) Niamey (732,000)
GOVERNMENT Multiparty republic **ETHNIC GROUPS** Hausa 56%, Djerma 22%, Tuareg 8%, Fula 8%, others **LANGUAGES** French (official), Hausa, Djerma **RELIGIONS** Islam 80%, indigenous beliefs, Christianity **CURRENCY** CFA franc = 100 centimes

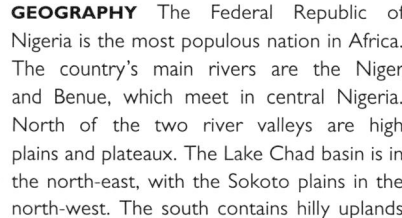

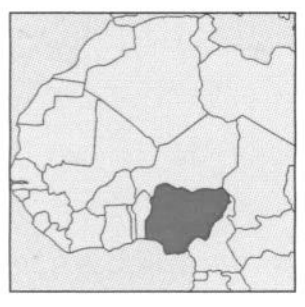

NIGERIA

GEOGRAPHY The Federal Republic of Nigeria is the most populous nation in Africa. The country's main rivers are the Niger and Benue, which meet in central Nigeria. North of the two river valleys are high plains and plateaux. The Lake Chad basin is in the north-east, with the Sokoto plains in the north-west. The south contains hilly uplands and plains. The south has a hot, rainy climate. The north is drier and often hotter than the south.

POLITICS & ECONOMY Nigeria has a long artistic tradition. Major cultures include the Nok (500 BC to AD 200), the Ife, a major Yoruba culture which developed about 1,000 years ago, and the Benin (15th to 17th centuries). Britain gradually extended its influence over the area in the second half of the 19th century.

Nigeria became independent in 1960 and a federal republic in 1963. A federal constitution dividing the country into regions was necessary because Nigeria contains more than 250 ethnic and linguistic groups, as well as several religious ones. Local rivalries have long been a threat to national unity, and six new states were created in 1996 in an attempt to overcome this. Civil war occurred between 1967 and 1970, when the people of the south-east attempted unsuccessfully to secede during the Biafran War. Between 1960 and 1998, Nigeria had only nine years of civilian government.

In 1998–9, civilian rule was restored. A former general, Olusegun Obasanjo, was elected president and he was re-elected in 2003. His government faced many problems, including religious clashes in the north, where several states adopted *sharia* (Islamic law). In 2004, the government declared that it had put down an uprising in the north-east aimed at creating a Muslim state.

Nigeria is a developing country with great potential. Its chief natural resource is oil, which accounts for most of its exports. Agriculture employs 43% of the people and the country is a major producer of cocoa, palm oil and palm kernels, groundnuts (peanuts) and rubber. Industry is increasing and manufactures include cement, chemicals, fertilizers, textiles and timber.

AREA 923,768 sq km [356,667 sq mi] **POPULATION** 133,882,000
CAPITAL (POPULATION) Abuja (339,000)
GOVERNMENT Federal multiparty republic
ETHNIC GROUPS Hausa and Fulani 29%, Yoruba 21%, Ibo (or Igbo) 18%, Ijaw 10%, Kanuri 4%, many others
LANGUAGES English (official), Hausa, Yoruba, Ibo
RELIGIONS Islam 50%, Christianity 40%, traditional beliefs 10%
CURRENCY Naira = 100 kobo

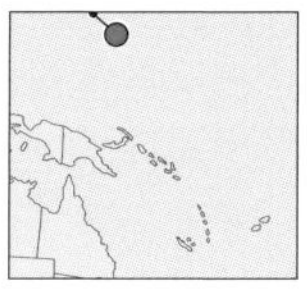

NORTHERN MARIANA ISLANDS

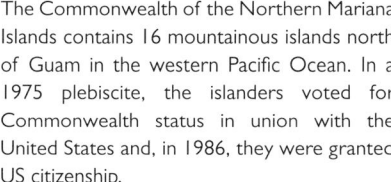

The Commonwealth of the Northern Mariana Islands contains 16 mountainous islands north of Guam in the western Pacific Ocean. In a 1975 plebiscite, the islanders voted for Commonwealth status in union with the United States and, in 1986, they were granted US citizenship.

AREA 464 sq km [179 sq mi] **POPULATION** 80,000 **CAPITAL** Saipan

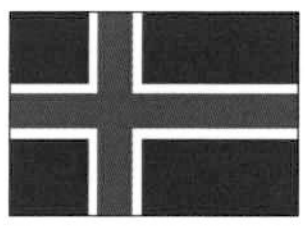

NORWAY

GEOGRAPHY The Kingdom of Norway forms the western part of the rugged Scandinavian peninsula. The deep inlets along the highly indented coastline were worn out by glaciers during the Ice Age. The warm North Atlantic Drift off the coast of Norway moderates the climate, with mild winters and cool summers. Nearly all the ports are ice-free throughout the year. Inland, winters are colder and snow cover lasts for at least three months a year.

POLITICS & ECONOMY Between about AD 800 and 1100, Norwegian Vikings ravaged western Europe. In 1380, Norway was united with Denmark. But in 1814, Denmark handed Norway over to Sweden, though it kept Norway's colonies – Greenland, Iceland and the Færoe Islands. Norway briefly became independent, but Swedish forces defeated the Norwegians and Norway had to accept Sweden's king as its ruler. The union with Sweden ended in 1903.

Germany occupied Norway during World War II (1939–45). Norway recovered quickly after the war and it now has one of the world's highest standards of living. In 1960, Norway and six other countries formed the European Free Trade Association (EFTA). In 1994, the Norwegians voted against joining the European Union.

Norway's chief resources and exports are oil and natural gas which come from wells under the North Sea. Farmland covers only 3% of the land. Dairy farming and meat production are important, but Norway has to import food. Norway has many industries powered by cheap hydroelectricity.

AREA 323,877 sq km [125,049 sq mi] **POPULATION** 4,546,000
CAPITAL (POPULATION) Oslo (513,000)
GOVERNMENT Constitutional monarchy
ETHNIC GROUPS Norwegian 97%
LANGUAGES Norwegian (official)
RELIGIONS Evangelical Lutheran 86%
CURRENCY Norwegian krone = 100 ore

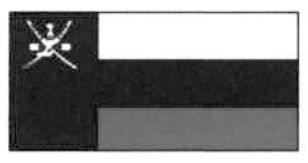

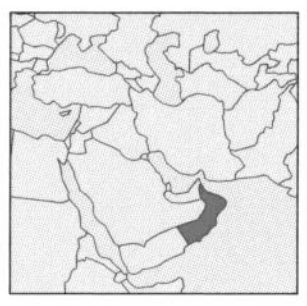

OMAN

GEOGRAPHY The Sultanate of Oman occupies the south-eastern corner of the Arabian peninsula. It also includes the tip of the Musandam peninsula, overlooking the strategic Strait of Hormuz.

Oman has a hot tropical climate. In Muscat, temperatures may reach 47°C [117°F] in the summer months.

POLITICS & ECONOMY British influence in Oman dates back to the end of the 18th century, but the country became fully independent in 1971. Since then, using revenue from oil, which was discovered in 1964, the absolute ruler, Qaboos ibn Said, and his government have sought to modernize the country. In 2000, Oman held its first direct elections to its consultative parliament. Unusually for the Gulf region, two women were returned.

The World Bank classifies Oman as an 'upper-middle-income' country. Oil accounts for the bulk of the exports, while huge natural gas deposits were discovered in 1991. However, agriculture remains important. Major crops include alfalfa, bananas, coconuts, dates, limes, tobacco, vegetables and wheat. Some cattle are raised and fishing, especially for sardines, is important. But Oman still has to import food.

AREA 309,500 sq km [119,498 sq mi] **POPULATION** 2,807,000
CAPITAL (POPULATION) Muscat (41,000)
GOVERNMENT Monarchy with consultative council
ETHNIC GROUPS Arab, Baluchi, Indian, Pakistani
LANGUAGES Arabic (official), Baluchi, English
RELIGIONS Islam (mainly Ibadhi), Hinduism
CURRENCY Omani rial = 100 baizas

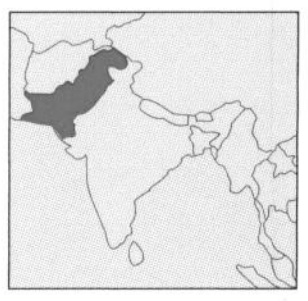

PAKISTAN

GEOGRAPHY The Islamic Republic of Pakistan contains high mountains, fertile plains and rocky deserts. The Karakoram range, which contains K2, the world's second highest peak, lies in the northern part of Jammu and Kashmir, which is occupied by Pakistan but claimed by India. Other mountains rise in the west. Plains, drained by the River Indus and its tributaries, occupy much of eastern Pakistan. Arid areas include the Thar Desert and the Baluchistan plateau. Most of Pakistan has hot summers and mild winters, though the mountains have cold winters. The rainfall is generally sparse.

POLITICS & ECONOMY Pakistan was the site of the Indus Valley civilization which developed about 4,500 years ago. But Pakistan's modern history dates from 1947, when British India was divided into India and Pakistan. Muslim Pakistan was divided into two parts: East and West Pakistan, but East Pakistan broke away in 1971 to become Bangladesh. In 1948–9, 1965 and 1971, Pakistan and India clashed over Kashmir. In 1998, Pakistan responded in kind to India's nuclear weapon tests but, in 2003–4, Pakistan and India raised hopes of a settlement in Kashmir.

Pakistan has been subject to several periods of military rule, but elections in 1988 led to Benazir Bhutto becoming prime minister. She was removed from office in 1990, but she returned as prime minister between 1993 and 1996. In 1997, Narwaz Sharif was elected prime minister, but a military coup in 1999 brought General Pervez Musharraf to power. In 2001, Pakistan supported the Western assault on Taliban forces in Afghanistan. In 2002, voters agreed to extend Musharraf's term in office by five years. In 2004, the government's moves towards democratization and its support for the international coalition against terrorism led the Commonwealth to restore Pakistan as a member.

According to the World Bank, Pakistan is a 'low-income' developing country. The economy is based on farming or rearing goats and sheep. Agriculture employs nearly half the people. Major crops include cotton, fruits, rice, sugar cane and wheat.

AREA 796,095 sq km [307,372 sq mi] **POPULATION** 150,695,000
CAPITAL (POPULATION) Islamabad (529,000)
GOVERNMENT Military regime **ETHNIC GROUPS** Punjabi, Sindhi, Pashtun (Pathan), Baluchi, Muhajir
LANGUAGES Urdu (official), many others
RELIGIONS Islam 97%, Christianity, Hinduism
CURRENCY Pakistani rupee = 100 paisa

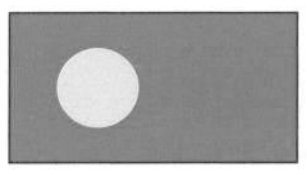

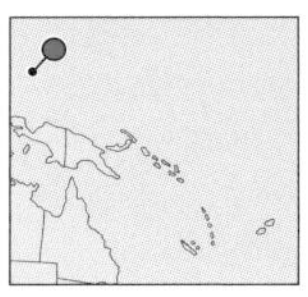

PALAU

The Republic of Palau became fully independent in 1994, after the USA refused to accede to a 1979 referendum that declared this island nation a nuclear-free zone. In December 1994 Palau joined the United Nations. The economy relies heavily on US aid, tourism, fishing and subsistence agriculture. The main crops include cassava, coconuts and copra.

AREA 459 sq km [177 sq mi] **POPULATION** 20,000 **CAPITAL** Koror

PANAMA

GEOGRAPHY The Republic of Panama forms an isthmus linking Central America to South America. The Panama Canal, which is 81.6 km [50.7 mi] long, cuts across the isthmus. It has made the country a major transport centre.

Panama has a tropical climate. Temperatures are high, though the mountains are much cooler than the coastal plains. The main rainy season is between May and December.

POLITICS & ECONOMY Christopher Columbus landed in Panama in 1502 and Spain soon took the area. In 1821, Panama became independent from Spain and a province of Colombia.

In 1903, Colombia refused a request by the United States to build a canal. Panama then revolted against Colombia, and became independent. The United States then began to build the canal, which was opened in 1914. The United States administered the Panama Canal Zone, a strip of land along the canal. But many Panamanians resented US influence and, in 1979, the Canal Zone was returned to Panama. Control of the canal itself was handed over by the USA to Panama on 31 December 1999.

Panama's government has changed many times since independence, and there have been periods of military dictatorships. In 1983, General Manuel Antonio Noriega became Panama's leader. In 1988, two US grand juries in Florida indicted

Noriega on charges of drug trafficking. In 1989, Noriega was apparently defeated in a presidential election, but the government declared the election invalid. After the killing of a US marine, US troops entered Panama and arrested Noriega, who was convicted by a Miami court of drug offences in 1992. However, Panama held national elections in 1994. In 1999, Mireya Moscoso became Panama's first woman president. In 2003–4, she was criticized for failing to curb corruption and provide more jobs.

The World Bank classifies Panama as a 'lower-middle-income' developing country. The Panama Canal is an important source of revenue and it generates many jobs in commerce, trade, manufacturing and transport. Away from the Canal, the main activity is agriculture, which employs 18% of the people.

AREA 75,517 sq km [29,157 sq mi] **POPULATION** 2,961,000 **CAPITAL (POPULATION)** Panamá (484,000) **GOVERNMENT** Multiparty republic **ETHNIC GROUPS** Mestizo 70%, Black and Mulatto 14%, White 10%, Amerindian 6% **LANGUAGES** Spanish (official), English **RELIGIONS** Roman Catholic 85%, Protestant 15% **CURRENCY** US dollar; Balboa = 100 centésimos

PAPUA NEW GUINEA

GEOGRAPHY Papua New Guinea is an independent country in the Pacific Ocean, north of Australia. It is part of a Pacific island region called Melanesia. Papua New Guinea includes the eastern part of New Guinea, the Bismarck Archipelago, the northern Solomon Islands, the D'Entrecasteaux Islands and the Louisiade Archipelago. The land is largely mountainous.

Papua New Guinea has a tropical climate, with high temperatures throughout the year. Most of the rain occurs during the monsoon season (from December to April), when the north-westerly winds blow. Winds blow from the south-east during the dry season.

POLITICS & ECONOMY The Dutch took western New Guinea (now part of Indonesia) in 1828, but it was not until 1884 that Germany took north-eastern New Guinea and Britain took the south-east. In 1906, Britain handed the south-east over to Australia. It then became known as the Territory of Papua. When World War I broke out in 1914, Australia took German New Guinea and, in 1921, the League of Nations gave Australia a mandate to rule the area, which was named the Territory of New Guinea.

Japan invaded New Guinea in 1942, but the Allies reconquered the area in 1944. In 1949, Papua and New Guinea were combined into the Territory of Papua and New Guinea. Papua New Guinea became fully independent in 1975.

Since independence, the government has worked to develop its mineral reserves. One of the most valuable mines was on Bougainville, in the northern Solomon Islands. But the people of Bougainville demanded a larger share in the profits of the mine. Conflict broke out, the mine was closed and the Bougainville Revolutionary Army proclaimed the island independent. But their attempted secession was not recognized internationally. A final peace settlement, giving the island local autonomy, was agreed in 2001.

The World Bank classifies Papua New Guinea as a 'lower-middle-income' developing country. Agriculture employs three out of every four people, many of whom produce little more than they need to feed their families. Minerals, notably copper and gold, are the most valuable exports.

AREA 462,840 sq km [178,703 sq mi] **POPULATION** 5,296,000 **CAPITAL (POPULATION)** Port Moresby (193,000) **GOVERNMENT** Constitutional monarchy **ETHNIC GROUPS** Papuan, Melanesian, Micronesian **LANGUAGES** English (official), Melanesian Pidgin; more than 700 indigenous languages **RELIGIONS** Traditional beliefs 34%, Roman Catholic 22%, Lutheran 16% **CURRENCY** Kina = 100 toea

PARAGUAY

GEOGRAPHY The Republic of Paraguay is a landlocked country and rivers, notably the Paraná, Pilcomayo (Brazo Sur) and Paraguay, form most of its borders. A flat region called the Gran Chaco lies in the north-west, while the south-east contains plains, hills and plateaux. Northern Paraguay lies in the tropics, while the south is subtropical. Most of the country has a warm, humid climate.

POLITICS & ECONOMY In 1776, Paraguay became part of a large colony called the Vice-royalty of La Plata, with Buenos Aires as the capital. Paraguayans opposed this move and the country declared its independence in 1811.

For many years, Paraguay was torn by internal strife and conflict with its neighbours. A war against Brazil, Argentina and Uruguay (1865–70) led to the deaths of more than half of Paraguay's population, and a great loss of territory.

General Alfredo Stroessner took power in 1954 and ruled as a dictator. His government imprisoned many opponents. Stroessner was overthrown in 1989. However, the return of democracy in the 1990s and 2000s often seemed precarious because of rivalries between politicians and army leaders, together with economic problems arising partly from the severe problems experienced in neighbouring Argentina and Brazil.

The World Bank classifies Paraguay as a 'lower-middle-income' developing country. Farming and forestry are important. Paraguay produces hydroelectricity and exports power to its neighbours.

AREA 406,752 sq km [157,047 sq mi] **POPULATION** 6,037,000 **CAPITAL (POPULATION)** Asunción (547,000) **GOVERNMENT** Multiparty republic **ETHNIC GROUPS** Mestizo 95% **LANGUAGES** Spanish and Guaraní (both official) **RELIGIONS** Roman Catholic 90%, Protestant **CURRENCY** Guaraní = 100 céntimos

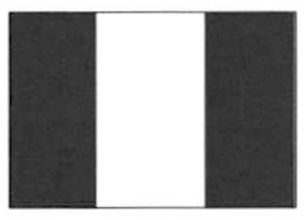

PERU

GEOGRAPHY The Republic of Peru lies in the tropics in western South America. A narrow coastal plain borders the Pacific Ocean in the west. Inland are ranges of the Andes Mountains, which rise to 6,768 m [22,205 ft] at Mount Huascarán, an extinct volcano. East of the Andes lies the Amazon basin.

Lima, on the coastal plain, has an arid climate. The coastal region is chilled by the cold, offshore Humboldt Current. The rainfall increases inland and many mountains in the high Andes are snow-capped.

POLITICS & ECONOMY Spanish conquistadors conquered Peru in the 1530s. In 1820, an Argentinian, José de San Martín, led an army into Peru and declared it independent. But Spain still held large areas. In 1823, the Venezuelan Simon Bolívar led another army into Peru and, in 1824, one of his generals defeated the Spaniards at Ayacucho. The Spaniards surrendered in 1826. Peru suffered much instability throughout the 19th century.

Instability continued in the 20th century. In 1980, when civilian rule was restored, a left-wing group called the Sendero Luminoso, or the 'Shining Path', began guerrilla warfare against the government. In 1990, Alberto Fujimori, son of Japanese immigrants, became president. In 1992, he suspended the constitution and dismissed the legislature. The guerrilla leader, Abimael Guzmán, was arrested in 1992, but instability continued. Following his victory in disputed presidential elections in 2000, Fujimori resigned and sought sanctuary in Japan. In 2001, Alejandro Toledo became the first Peruvian of Amerindian descent to be elected president. He faced many problems, including, in 2003, a resurgence in activity by the Shining Path guerrillas.

The World Bank classifies Peru as a 'lower-middle-income' developing country. Major food crops include beans, maize, potatoes and rice. Fish products are exported, but the most valuable export is copper. Peru also produces lead, silver, zinc and iron ore.

AREA 1,285,216 sq km [496,222 sq mi] **POPULATION** 28,410,000 **CAPITAL (POPULATION)** Lima (5,681,000) **GOVERNMENT** Transitional republic **ETHNIC GROUPS** Amerindian 45%, Mestizo 37%, White 15% **LANGUAGES** Spanish and Quechua (both official), Aymara, other Amazonian languages **RELIGIONS** Roman Catholic 90% **CURRENCY** New sol = 100 centavos

PHILIPPINES

GEOGRAPHY The Republic of the Philippines is an island country in south-eastern Asia. It includes about 7,100 islands, of which 2,770 are named and about 1,000 are inhabited. Luzon and Mindanao, the two largest islands, make up more than two-thirds of the country. The land is mainly mountainous.

The country has a hot tropical climate. The dry season runs from December to April. The rest of the year is wet. Much of the rainfall comes from the typhoons which periodically strike the east coast.

POLITICS & ECONOMY The first European to reach the Philippines was the Portuguese navigator Ferdinand Magellan in 1521. Spanish explorers claimed the region in 1565 when they established a settlement on Cebu. The Spaniards ruled the country until 1898, when the United States took over at the end of the Spanish–American War. Japan invaded the Philippines in 1941, but US forces returned in 1944. The country became fully independent as the Republic of the Philippines in 1946.

Since independence, the country's problems have included armed uprisings by left-wing guerrillas demanding land reform, and Muslim separatist groups, crime, corruption and unemployment. The dominant figure in recent times was Ferdinand Marcos, who ruled in a dictatorial manner from 1965 to 1986. His successors were Corazon Aquino (1986–92), Fidel Ramos (1992–8), and Joseph Estrada, who resigned following accusations of corruption. He was succeeded by Vice-President Gloria Arroyo. In 2003, her government had to put down a military rebellion as well as combating Muslim terrorists and Islamic separatists.

The Philippines is a developing country which has a 'lower-middle-income' economy. Agriculture employs 33% of the people. The main foods are rice and maize, while such crops as bananas, cocoa, coconuts, coffee, sugar cane and tobacco are all grown commercially. Manufacturing now plays an increasingly important role in the economy.

AREA 300,000 sq km [115,830 sq mi] **POPULATION** 84,620,000 **CAPITAL (POPULATION)** Manila (1,581,000) **GOVERNMENT** Multiparty republic **ETHNIC GROUPS** Christian Malay 92%, Muslim Malay 4%, Chinese and others **LANGUAGES** Filipino (Tagalog) and English (both official), Spanish, many others **RELIGIONS** Roman Catholic 83%, Protestant 9%, Islam 5% **CURRENCY** Philippine peso = 100 centavos

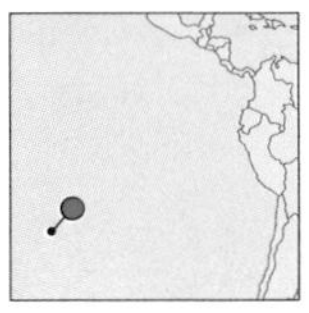

PITCAIRN

Pitcairn Island is a British overseas territory in the Pacific Ocean. Its inhabitants are descendants of the original settlers – nine mutineers from HMS *Bounty* and 18 Tahitians who arrived in 1790.

AREA 55 sq km [21 sq mi] **POPULATION** 50 **CAPITAL** Adamstown

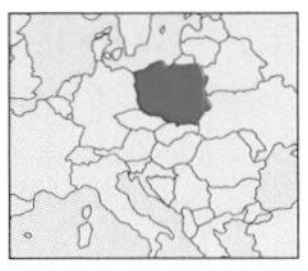

POLAND

GEOGRAPHY The Republic of Poland faces the Baltic Sea and, behind its lagoon-fringed coast, lies a broad plain. A plateau lies in the south-east, while the Sudeten Highlands straddle part of the border with the Czech Republic. Part of the Carpathian Range (the Tatra) lies in the south-east.

Poland's climate is influenced by its position in Europe. Warm, moist air masses come from the west, while cold air masses come from the north and east. Summers are warm, but winters are cold and snowy.

POLITICS & ECONOMY Poland's boundaries have changed several times in the last 200 years, partly as a result of its geographical location between the powers of Germany and Russia. It disappeared from the map in the late 18th century, when a Polish state called the Grand Duchy of Warsaw was set up. But in 1815, the country was partitioned, between Austria, Prussia and Russia. Poland became independent in 1918, but in 1939 it was divided between Germany and the Soviet Union. The country again became independent in 1945, when it lost land to Russia but gained some from Germany. Communists took power in 1948, but opposition mounted and eventually became focused through an organization called Solidarity.

Solidarity was led by a trade unionist, Lech Walesa. A coalition government was formed between Solidarity and the Communists in 1989. In 1990, the Communist party was dissolved and Walesa became president. But Walesa faced many problems in turning Poland towards a market economy. In presidential elections in 1995, Walesa was defeated by ex-Communist Aleksander Kwasniewski. However, Kwasniewski continued to follow westwards-looking policies and he was re-elected president in 2000. Poland joined the North Atlantic Treaty Organization in 1999 and, on 1 May 2004, it became a member of the European Union.

Poland has large reserves of coal and deposits of various minerals which are used in its factories. Manufactures include chemicals, processed food, machinery, ships, steel and textiles.

AREA 323,250 sq km [124,807 sq mi] **POPULATION** 38,623,000 **CAPITAL (POPULATION)** Warsaw (1,615,000) **GOVERNMENT** Multiparty republic **ETHNIC GROUPS** Polish 97%, Belarusian, Ukrainian, German **LANGUAGES** Polish (official) **RELIGIONS** Roman Catholic 95%, Eastern Orthodox **CURRENCY** Zloty = 100 groszy

PORTUGAL

GEOGRAPHY The Republic of Portugal is the most westerly of Europe's mainland countries. The land rises from the coastal plains on the Atlantic Ocean to the western edge of the huge plateau, or Meseta, which occupies most of the Iberian peninsula. The climate is moderated by winds blowing from the Atlantic Ocean. Summers are cooler and winters are milder than in other Mediterranean lands. Portugal also contains two autonomous regions, the Azores and Madeira island groups.

POLITICS & ECONOMY Portugal became a separate country, independent of Spain, in 1143. In the 15th century, Portugal led the 'Age of European Exploration'. This led to the growth of a large Portuguese empire, with colonies in Africa, Asia and, most valuable of all, Brazil in South America. Portuguese power began to decline in the 16th century and, between 1580 and 1640, Portugal was ruled by Spain. Portugal lost Brazil in 1822 and, in 1910, Portugal became a republic. Instability hampered progress and army officers seized power in 1926. In 1928, they chose Antonio de Salazar to be minister of finance. He became prime minister in 1932 and ruled as a dictator from 1933.

Salazar ruled until 1968, but his successor, Marcello Caetano, was overthrown in 1974 by a group of army officers. The new government made most of Portugal's remaining colonies independent. Free elections were held in 1978. Portugal joined the European Community (now the European Union) in 1986 and, on 1 January 2002, the euro replaced the escudo as Portugal's sole official unit of currency.

Agriculture and fishing were the mainstays of the economy until the mid-20th century, when manufacturing became the most valuable activity. The timber industry received a major setback in 2003 when forest fires caused enormous damage.

AREA 88,797 sq km [34,285 sq mi] **POPULATION** 10,102,000
CAPITAL (POPULATION) Lisbon (663,000)
GOVERNMENT Multiparty republic **ETHNIC GROUPS** Portuguese 99%
LANGUAGES Portuguese (official) **RELIGIONS** Roman Catholic 94%, Protestant **CURRENCY** Euro = 100 cents

PUERTO RICO

The Commonwealth of Puerto Rico, a mainly mountainous island, is the easternmost of the Greater Antilles chain. The climate is hot and wet. Puerto Rico is a dependent territory of the USA and the people are US citizens. In 1998, 50.2% of the population voted in a referendum on possible statehood to maintain the status quo.

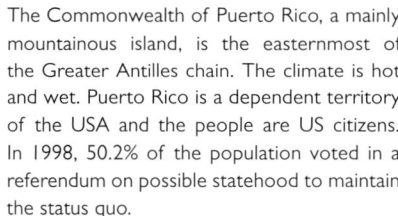

Puerto Rico is the most industrialized country in the Caribbean. Tax exemptions attract US companies to the island and manufacturing is expanding. The chief exports are chemicals and chemical products, machinery and food.

AREA 8,875 sq km [3,427 sq mi] **POPULATION** 3,886,000
CAPITAL (POPULATION) San Juan (422,000)

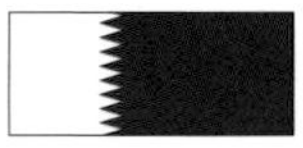

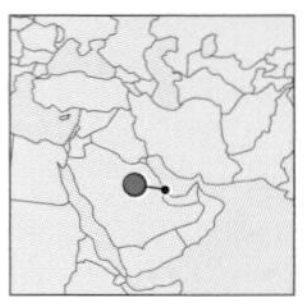

QATAR

The State of Qatar occupies a low, barren peninsula that extends northwards from the Arabian peninsula into the Persian Gulf. The climate is hot and dry. Qatar became a British protectorate in 1916, but it became fully independent in 1971. Oil, first discovered in 1939, is the mainstay of the economy of this prosperous nation.

AREA 11,000 sq km [4,247 sq mi] **POPULATION** 817,000 **CAPITAL** Doha

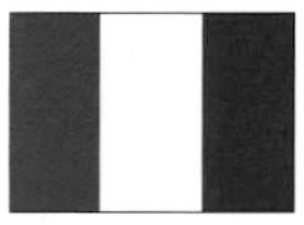

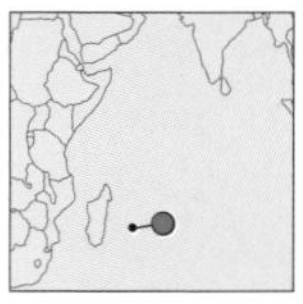

RÉUNION

Réunion is a French overseas department in the Indian Ocean. The land is mainly mountainous, though the lowlands are intensely cultivated. Sugar and sugar products are the main exports, but French aid, given to the island in return for its use as a military base, is important to the economy.

AREA 2,510 sq km [969 sq mi]
POPULATION 755,000 **CAPITAL** St-Denis

ROMANIA

GEOGRAPHY Romania is a country on the Black Sea in eastern Europe. Eastern and southern Romania form part of the Danube river basin. The delta region, near the mouths of the Danube, where the river flows into the Black Sea, is one of Europe's finest wetlands. The southern part of the coast contains several resorts. The heart of the country is called Transylvania. It is ringed in the east, south and west by scenic mountains which are part of the Carpathian mountain system. Romania has hot summers and cold winters. The rainfall is heaviest in spring and early summer.

POLITICS & ECONOMY From the late 18th century, the Turkish empire began to break up. The modern history of Romania began in 1861 when Walachia and Moldavia united. After World War I (1914–18), Romania, which had fought on the side of the victorious Allies, obtained large areas, including Transylvania, where most people were Romanians. This almost doubled the country's size and population. In 1939, Romania lost territory to Bulgaria, Hungary and the Soviet Union. Romania fought alongside Germany in World War II, and Soviet troops occupied the country in 1944. Hungary returned northern Transylvania to Romania in 1945, but Bulgaria and the Soviet Union kept former Romanian territory. In 1947, Romania officially became a Communist country.

In 1990, Romania held its first free elections since the end of World War II. The National Salvation Front, led by Ion Iliescu and containing many former Communist leaders, won a large majority. A new constitution, approved in 1991, made the country a democratic republic. Elections held under this constitution in 1992 again resulted in victory for Ion Iliescu, whose party was renamed the Party of Social Democracy (PDSR) in 1993. But the government faced many problems. In 1996, the centre-right Democratic Convention defeated the PDSR, led by Emil Constantinescu, who became president. But Iliescu was re-elected president in 2000. Romania's desire to establish good relations with the West were rewarded when it became a member of the North Atlantic Treaty Organization in 2004.

According to the World Bank, Romania is a 'lower-middle-income' economy. Under Communist rule, industry, including mining and manufacturing, became more important than agriculture.

AREA 238,391 sq km [92,043 sq mi] **POPULATION** 22,272,000
CAPITAL (POPULATION) Bucharest (2,016,000)
GOVERNMENT Multiparty republic
ETHNIC GROUPS Romanian 89%, Hungarian 7%, Roma 2%, Ukrainian **LANGUAGES** Romanian (official), Hungarian, German **RELIGIONS** Eastern Orthodox 87%, Protestant 7%, Roman Catholic 5% **CURRENCY** Leu = 100 bani

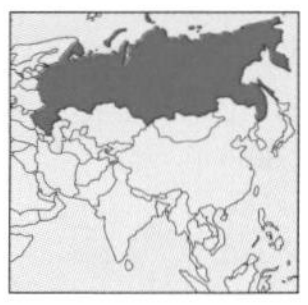

RUSSIA

GEOGRAPHY Russia is the world's largest country. About 25% lies west of the Ural Mountains in European Russia, where 80% of the population lives. It is mostly flat or undulating, but the land rises to the Caucasus Mountains in the south, where Russia's highest peak, Elbrus, at 5,633 m [18,481 ft], is found. Asian Russia, or Siberia, contains vast plains and plateaux, with mountains in the east and south. The Kamchatka peninsula in the far east has many active volcanoes. Russia contains many of the world's longest rivers, including the Yenisey-Angara and the Ob-Irtysh. It also includes part of the world's largest inland body of water, the Caspian Sea, and Lake Baikal, the world's deepest lake.

Moscow has a continental climate with cold and snowy winters and warm summers. Siberia has a harsher, drier climate.

POLITICS & ECONOMY In the 9th century AD, a state called Kievan Rus was formed by a group of people called the East Slavs. Kiev, now capital of Ukraine, became a major trading centre, but, in 1237, Mongol armies conquered Russia and destroyed Kiev. Russia was part of the Mongol empire until the late 15th century. Under Mongol rule, Moscow became the leading Russian city.

In the 16th century, Moscow's grand prince was retitled 'tsar'. The first tsar, Ivan the Terrible, expanded Russian territory. In 1613, after a period of civil war, Michael Romanov became tsar, founding a dynasty which ruled until 1917. In the early 18th century, Tsar Peter the Great began to westernize Russia and, by 1812, when Napoleon failed to conquer the country, Russia was a major European power. But during the 19th century, many Russians demanded reforms and discontent was widespread.

In World War I (1914–18), the Russian people suffered great hardships and, in 1917, Tsar Nicholas II was forced to abdicate. In November 1917, the Bolsheviks seized power under Vladimir Lenin. In 1922, the Bolsheviks set up a new nation, the Union of Soviet Socialist Republics (also called the USSR or the Soviet Union).

From 1924, Joseph Stalin introduced a socialist economic programme, suppressing all opposition. In 1939, the Soviet Union and Germany signed a non-aggression pact, but Germany invaded the Soviet Union in 1941. Soviet forces pushed the Germans back, occupying eastern Europe. They reached Berlin in May 1945. From the late 1940s, tension between the Soviet Union and its allies and Western nations developed into a 'Cold War'. This continued until 1991, when the Soviet Union was dissolved.

The Soviet Union collapsed because of the failure of its economic policies. From 1991, President Boris Yeltsin introduced democratic and economic reforms. Yeltsin retired in 1999 and, in 2000, was succeeded by Vladimir Putin. Putin has sought to develop increasing contacts with the West. He was re-elected by a landslide majority in 2004 and he supported the US-declared 'war on terrorism', though he opposed the war on Iraq in 2003. But he was unable to halt the ongoing conflict in Chechenia, which claimed the lives of more than 4,500 Russian soldiers in 1999–2002. This conflict reveals that Russia's sheer size and ethnic diversity makes national unity difficult to achieve.

Russia's economy was thrown into disarray after the collapse of the Soviet Union, and in the early 1990s the World Bank described Russia as a 'lower-middle-income' economy. Russia was admitted to the Council of Europe in 1997, essentially to discourage instability in the Caucasus. More significantly still, Boris Yeltsin was invited to attend the G7 summit in Denver in 1997. The summit became known as 'the Summit of the Eight' and it appeared that Russia will now be included in future meetings of the world's most powerful economies. Industry is the most valuable activity, though, under Communist rule, manufacturing was less efficient than in the West, and the emphasis was on heavy industry. Today, light industries producing consumer goods are becoming important. Russia's abundant resources include oil and natural gas, coal, timber, metal ores and hydroelectric power.

Most farmland is still government-owned or run as collectives. Russia is a major producer of farm products, though it imports grains. Major crops include barley, flax, fruits, oats, rye, potatoes, sugar beet, sunflower seeds, vegetables and wheat.

AREA 17,075,400 sq km [6,592,812 sq mi] **POPULATION** 144,526,000
CAPITAL (POPULATION) Moscow (8,297,000) **GOVERNMENT** Federal multiparty republic **ETHNIC GROUPS** Russian 82%, Tatar 4%, Ukrainian 3%, Chuvash 1%, more than 100 others
LANGUAGES Russian (official), many others
RELIGIONS Mainly Russian Orthodox, Islam, Judaism
CURRENCY Russian ruble = 100 kopeks

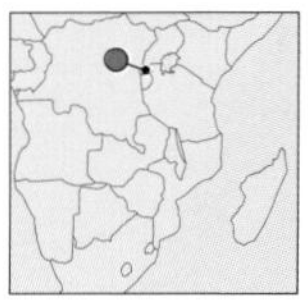

RWANDA

GEOGRAPHY The Republic of Rwanda is a small, landlocked country in east-central Africa. Lake Kivu and the River Ruzizi in the Great African Rift Valley form the country's western border.

Kigali stands on the central plateau of Rwanda. Here, temperatures are moderated by the altitude. The rainfall is abundant, but much heavier rain falls on the western mountains.

POLITICS & ECONOMY Germany conquered the area, called Ruanda-Urundi, in the 1890s. However, Belgium occupied the region during World War I (1914–18) and ruled it until 1961, when the people of Ruanda voted for their country to become a republic, called Rwanda. This decision followed a rebellion by the majority Hutu people against the Tutsi monarchy. About 150,000 deaths resulted from this conflict. Many Tutsis fled to Uganda, where they formed a rebel army. Burundi became independent as a monarchy, though it became a republic in 1966. Relations between Hutus and Tutsis continued to cause friction. Civil war broke out in 1994 and in 1996 the conflict spilled over into Congo (then Zaïre). Paul Kagame, Rwanda's effective leader since 1994, was elected president in 2000. His aim was to create unity.

According to the World Bank, Rwanda is a 'low-income' developing country. Most people are poor farmers. Food crops include bananas, beans, cassava and sorghum. Some cattle are raised.

AREA 26,338 sq km [10,169 sq mi] **POPULATION** 7,810,000
CAPITAL (POPULATION) Kigali (234,000)
GOVERNMENT Republic **ETHNIC GROUPS** Hutu 84%, Tutsi 15%, Twa 1% **LANGUAGES** French, English and Kinyarwanda (all official) **RELIGIONS** Roman Catholic 57%, Protestant 26%, Adventist 11%, Islam 5% **CURRENCY** Rwandan franc = 100 centimes

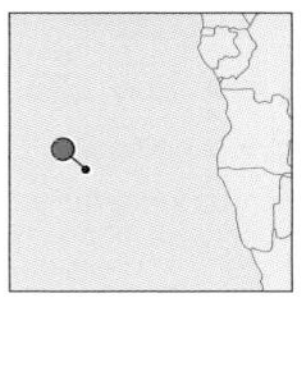

ST HELENA

St Helena, which became a British colony in 1834, is an isolated volcanic island in the south Atlantic Ocean. Now a British overseas territory, it is also the administrative centre of Ascension and Tristan da Cunha.

AREA 122 sq km [47 sq mi]
POPULATION 5,000 **CAPITAL** Jamestown

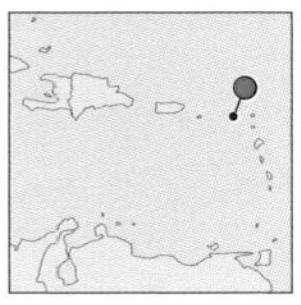

ST KITTS AND NEVIS

The Federation of St Kitts and Nevis comprises two well-watered volcanic islands, with mountains rising to around 1,000 m [3,300 ft]. The islands were the first in the Caribbean to be colonized by Britain (in 1623 and 1628), and they became an independent country in 1983. In 1998, a vote for the secession of Nevis fell short of the two-thirds majority required. Tourism has replaced sugar as the principal earner.

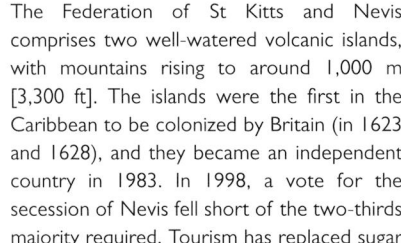

AREA 261 sq km [101 sq mi] **POPULATION** 39,000
CAPITAL (POPULATION) Basseterre (12,000)

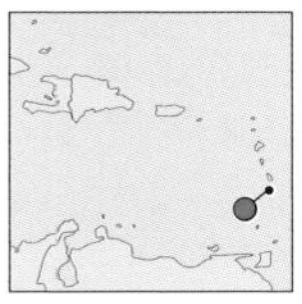

ST LUCIA

St Lucia, which became independent from Britain in 1979, is a mountainous, forested island of extinct volcanoes. It exports bananas and coconuts, and now attracts many tourists.

AREA 539 sq km [208 sq mi]
POPULATION 162,000 **CAPITAL** Castries

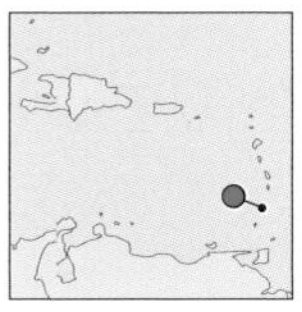

ST VINCENT AND THE GRENADINES

St Vincent and the Grenadines achieved its independence from Britain in 1979. Tourism is growing, but the territory is less prosperous than its neighbours.

AREA 388 sq km [150 sq mi]
POPULATION 117,000 **CAPITAL** Kingstown

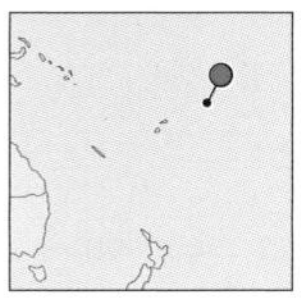

SAMOA

The Independent State of Samoa (formerly Western Samoa) comprises two islands in the South Pacific Ocean. Governed by New Zealand from 1920, the territory became independent in 1962. Exports include coconut cream and beer.

AREA 2,831 sq km [1,093 sq mi]
POPULATION 178,000 **CAPITAL** Apia

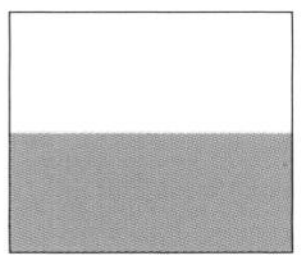

SAN MARINO

San Marino in northern Italy has been independent since 885 and a republic since the 14th century. It is the world's oldest republic. It has a friendship and co-operation treaty with Italy dating back to 1862. The state is governed by an elected council and has its own legal system. It has no armed forces and the police are 'hired' from the Italian constabulary. The chief occupations are tourism, limestone quarrying, textiles and wine-making.

AREA 61 sq km [24 sq mi] **POPULATION** 28,000 **CAPITAL** San Marino

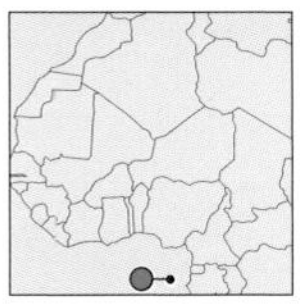

SÃO TOMÉ AND PRÍNCIPE

The Democratic Republic of São Tomé and Príncipe, a mountainous island territory west of Gabon, became a Portuguese colony in 1522. Following independence in 1975, the islands became a one-party Marxist state, but multiparty elections were held in 1991.

AREA 964 sq km [372 sq mi] **POPULATION** 176,000 **CAPITAL** São Tomé

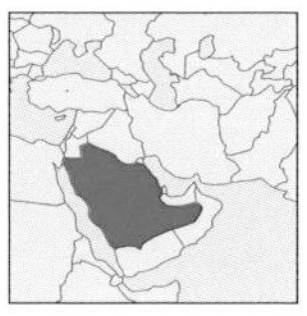

SAUDI ARABIA

GEOGRAPHY The Kingdom of Saudi Arabia occupies about three-quarters of the Arabian peninsula in south-west Asia. Deserts cover most of the land. Mountains border the Red Sea plains in the west. In the north is the sandy Nafud Desert (An Nafud). In the south is the Rub' al Khali (the 'Empty Quarter'), one of the world's bleakest deserts.

Saudi Arabia has a hot, dry climate. In the summer months, the temperatures in Riyadh often exceed 40°C [104°F], though the nights are cool.

POLITICS & ECONOMY Saudi Arabia contains the two holiest places in Islam – Mecca (or Makka), the birthplace of the Prophet Muhammad in AD 570, and Medina (Al Madinah) where Muhammad went in 622. These places are visited by many pilgrims.

Saudi Arabia was poor until the oil industry began to operate on the eastern plains in 1933. Oil revenues have been used to develop the country and Saudi Arabia has given aid to poorer Arab nations. The monarch has supreme authority and Saudi Arabia has no formal constitution. In the first Gulf War (1980–8), Saudi Arabia supported Iraq against Iran. But when Iraq invaded Kuwait in 1990, it joined the international alliance to drive Iraq's forces out of Kuwait in 1991. In 2001, relations with the US became strained after the terrorist attacks on 11 September 2001, partly because many alleged terrorists were Saudi nationals. Saudi Arabia denounced the attacks and, in 2004, a bombing occurred in Riyadh and the government cracked down on al Qaida suspects.

Saudi Arabia has about 25% of the world's known oil reserves and oil products make up about 90% of its exports. Agriculture remains important. Irrigation and desalination schemes have increased crop production.

AREA 2,149,690 sq km [829,995 sq mi] **POPULATION** 24,294,000
CAPITAL (POPULATION) Riyadh (3,000,000)
GOVERNMENT Absolute monarchy with consultative assembly
ETHNIC GROUPS Arab 90%, Afro-Asian 10%
LANGUAGES Arabic (official)
RELIGIONS Islam 100%
CURRENCY Saudi riyal = 100 halalas

SENEGAL

GEOGRAPHY The Republic of Senegal is on the north-west coast of Africa. The volcanic Cape Verde (Cap Vert), on which Dakar stands, is the most westerly point in Africa. Plains cover most of Senegal, though the land rises gently in the south-east.

Dakar has a tropical climate, with a short rainy season between July and October.

POLITICS & ECONOMY In 1882, Senegal became a French colony, and from 1895 it was ruled as part of French West Africa, the capital of which, Dakar, developed as a major port and city.

In 1959, Senegal joined French Sudan (now Mali) to form the Federation of Mali. But Senegal withdrew in 1960 and became the separate Republic of Senegal. Its first president, Léopold Sédar Senghor, served until 1981, when he was succeeded by Abdou Diouf. However, in 2000, Diouf was defeated in elections by Abdoulaye Wade. In 2003, conflict occurred in Casamance region in the south, where separatists wanted independence.

Senegal and The Gambia have always enjoyed close relations despite their differing French and British traditions. In 1981, Senegalese troops put down an attempted coup in The Gambia and, in 1982, the two countries set up a defence alliance, called the Confederation of Senegambia. But this confederation was dissolved in 1989.

According to the World Bank, Senegal is a 'lower-middle-income' developing country. It was badly hit in the 1960s and 1970s by droughts, which caused starvation. Agriculture still employs 81% of the population though many farmers produce little more than they need to feed their families. Food crops include groundnuts, millet and rice. Phosphates are the country's chief resource, but Senegal also refines oil which it imports from Gabon and Nigeria. Dakar is a busy port and has many industries.

AREA 196,722 sq km [75,954 sq mi] **POPULATION** 10,580,000
CAPITAL (POPULATION) Dakar (880,000)
GOVERNMENT Multiparty republic
ETHNIC GROUPS Wolof 44%, Pular 24%, Serer 15%
LANGUAGES French (official), tribal languages
RELIGIONS Islam 94%, Christianity (mainly Roman Catholic) 5%, traditional beliefs 1%
CURRENCY CFA franc = 100 centimes

SERBIA AND MONTENEGRO

GEOGRAPHY Serbia and Montenegro are two of the six republics which made up the country of Yugoslavia until it broke up in the early 1990s. From the early 1990s, Serbia and Montenegro were known as the Federal Republic of Yugoslavia. But, in 2003, the two republics became semi-independent and adopted the name of the Union of Serbia and Montenegro.

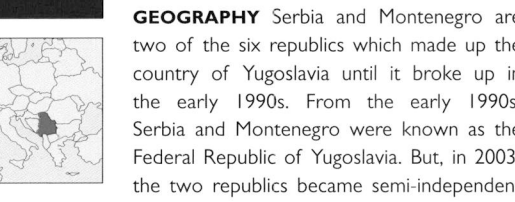

Behind the coastline on the Adriatic Sea lies an upland region, including the Dinaric Alps and part of the Balkan Mountains. The Pannonian plains, which are drained by the River Danube, are in the north. The coast has a Mediterranean climate. The interior highlands have bitterly cold winters and cool summers. The wettest season is the summer, but there is also plenty of sunshine.

POLITICS & ECONOMY People who became known as the South Slavs began to move into the region around 1,500 years ago. Each group, including the Serbs and Croats, founded its own state. But, by the 15th century, foreign countries controlled the region. Serbia and Montenegro were under the Turkish Ottoman empire.

In the 19th century, many Slavs worked for independence and Slavic unity. In 1914, Austria-Hungary declared war on Serbia, blaming it for the assassination of Archduke Francis Ferdinand of Austria–Hungary. This led to World War I and the defeat of Austria–Hungary. In 1918, the South Slavs united in the Kingdom of the Serbs, Croats and Slovenes, which consisted of Bosnia-Herzegovina, Croatia, Dalmatia, Montenegro, Serbia and Slovenia. The country was renamed Yugoslavia in 1929. Germany occupied Yugoslavia during World War II, but partisans, including a Communist force led by Josip Broz Tito, fought the invaders.

From 1945, the Communists controlled the country, which was called the Federal People's Republic of Yugoslavia. But after Tito's death in 1980, the country faced many problems. In 1990, non-Communist parties were permitted and non-Communists won majorities in elections in all but Serbia and Montenegro, where Socialists (former Communists) won control. Yugoslavia split apart in 1991–2 with Bosnia-Herzegovina, Croatia, Macedonia and Slovenia proclaiming their independence. The two remaining republics of Serbia and Montenegro became the new Yugoslavia.

Fighting broke out in Croatia and Bosnia-Herzegovina as rival groups struggled for power. In 1992, the United Nations withdrew recognition of Yugoslavia because of its failure to halt atrocities committed by Serbs living in Croatia and Bosnia. In 1995, Yugoslavia was involved in the talks that led to the Dayton Peace Accord, which brought peace to Bosnia-Herzegovina. But the issue of Yugoslav repression of minorities flared up again in 1998 in Kosovo, a province where the majority are ethnic Albanians. In response to Serb ethnic cleansing, NATO forces began an offensive against Yugoslavia. A Serb withdrawal was agreed in June 1999. Many Montenegrins wanted to secede and set up their own nation separate from Serbia. In 2003, Serbia and Montenegro set up a loose union, giving both republics semi-independence, and the name Yugoslavia passed into history. Montenegro agreed not to secede from this union for at least three years.

Under Communist rule, manufacturing became increasingly important in Yugoslavia. But in the early 1990s, the World Bank described what is now Serbia and Montenegro as a 'lower-middle-income' economy. Resources include bauxite, coal, copper and other metals, oil and natural gas. Manufactures, which form the main exports, include aluminium, machinery, plastics, steel, textiles and vehicles. Farming remains important. Crops include fruits, maize, potatoes, tobacco and wheat. Cattle, pigs and sheep are raised.

AREA 102,173 sq km [39,449 sq mi] **POPULATION** 10,656,000
CAPITAL (POPULATION) Belgrade (1,594,000)
GOVERNMENT Federal republic
ETHNIC GROUPS Serb 62%, Albanian 17%, Montenegrin 5%, Hungarian 3%, others
LANGUAGES Serbian (official), Albanian
RELIGIONS Orthodox 65%, Islam 19%, Roman Catholic 4%, others
CURRENCY New dinar = 100 paras

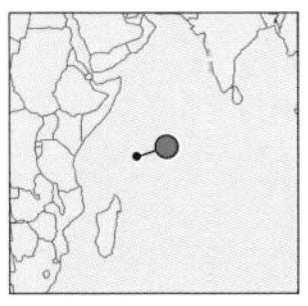

SEYCHELLES

The Republic of Seychelles in the western Indian Ocean achieved independence from Britain in 1976. Coconuts are the main cash crop, and fishing and tourism are important to the country's economy.

AREA 455 sq km [176 sq mi]
POPULATION 80,000 **CAPITAL** Victoria

SIERRA LEONE

GEOGRAPHY The Republic of Sierra Leone in West Africa is about the same size as the Republic of Ireland. The coast contains several deep estuaries in the north, with lagoons in the south. The most prominent feature is the mountainous Freetown (or Sierra Leone) peninsula.

Sierra Leone has a tropical climate, with heavy rainfall between April and November.

POLITICS & ECONOMY A former British territory, Sierra Leone became independent in 1961 and a republic in 1971. It became a one-party state in 1978, but, in 1991, the people voted for the restoration of democracy. The military seized power in 1992 and a civil war caused much destruction in 1994–5. Elections in 1996 were followed by another military coup. In 1998, the West African Peace Force restored the deposed President Ahmed Tejan Kabbah. In 1999, a peace agreement followed further conflict. As part of this agreement, Foday Sankoh, one of the rebel leaders, became vice-president. However, he was arrested in 2000 and charged with war crimes. Conflict resumed, but another cease-fire was agreed. In 2004, President Kabbah declared a successful end to disarmament in Sierra Leone.

The World Bank classifies Sierra Leone as a 'low-income' developing country Agriculture employs 60% of the people, though farming is mostly at subsistence level. The chief exports are minerals, including diamonds, bauxite and rutile (titanium ore). The country has few manufacturing industries.

AREA 71,740 sq km [27,699 sq mi] **POPULATION** 5,733,000
CAPITAL (POPULATION) Freetown (470,000)
GOVERNMENT Single-party republic **ETHNIC GROUPS** Native African tribes 90% **LANGUAGES** English (official), Mende, Temne, Krio
RELIGIONS Islam 60%, traditional beliefs 30%, Christianity 10%
CURRENCY Leone = 100 cents

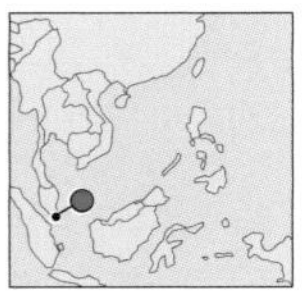

SINGAPORE

GEOGRAPHY The Republic of Singapore is an island country at the southern tip of the Malay peninsula. It consists of the large Singapore Island and 58 small islands, 20 of which are inhabited. Singapore has a hot, humid climate. Temperatures are high and rainfall is heavy throughout the year.

POLITICS & ECONOMY In 1819, Sir Thomas Stamford Raffles (1781–1826), agent of the British East India Company, made a treaty with the Sultan of Johor allowing the British to build a settlement on Singapore Island. Singapore soon became the leading British trading centre in South-east Asia and it later became a naval base. Japanese forces seized the island in 1942, but British rule was restored in 1945.

In 1963, Singapore became part of the Federation of Malaysia, which also included Malaya and the territories of Sabah and Sarawak on Borneo. In 1965, Singapore broke away and became independent.

The People's Action Party (PAP) has ruled Singapore since 1959. Its leader, Lee Kuan Yew, served as prime minister from 1959 until 1990, when he resigned and was succeeded by Goh Chok Tong. Under the PAP, the economy has expanded rapidly, though some considered its rule rather dictatorial. However, in 2004, Singapore began to relax some of its strict laws on public behaviour.

The World Bank classifies Singapore as a 'high-income' economy. A skilled workforce has created a fast-growing economy, but the recession in 1997–8 was a setback. Trade and finance are leading activities. Manufactures include electronic products, machinery, scientific instruments, textiles and ships. Singapore has a large oil refinery. Petroleum products and manufactures are the main exports.

AREA 683 sq km [264 sq mi] **POPULATION** 4,609,000
CAPITAL (POPULATION) Singapore City (3,894,000)
GOVERNMENT Multiparty republic
ETHNIC GROUPS Chinese 77%, Malay 14%, Indian 8%
LANGUAGES Chinese, Malay, Tamil and English (all official)
RELIGIONS Buddhism, Islam, Christianity, Hinduism
CURRENCY Singapore dollar = 100 cents

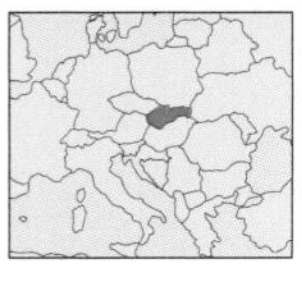

SLOVAK REPUBLIC

GEOGRAPHY The Slovak Republic is a predominantly mountainous country, consisting of part of the Carpathian range. The highest peak is Gerlachovka in the Tatra Mountains, which reaches 2,655 m [8,711 ft]. The south is a fertile lowland.

The Slovak Republic has cold winters and warm summers. Kosice, in the east, has average temperatures ranging from –3°C [27°F] in January to 20°C [68°F] in July. The highland areas are much colder. Snow or rain falls throughout the year. Kosice has an average annual rainfall of 600 mm [24 in], the wettest months being July and August.

POLITICS & ECONOMY Slavic peoples settled in the region in the 5th century AD. They were subsequently conquered by Hungary, beginning a millennium of Hungarian rule and suppression of Slovak culture.

In 1867, Hungary and Austria united to form Austria–Hungary, of which the present-day Slovak Republic was a part. Austria–Hungary collapsed at the end of World War I (1914–18). The Czech and Slovak people then united to form a new nation, Czechoslovakia. But Czech domination led to resentment by many Slovaks. In 1939, the Slovak Republic declared itself independent, but Germany occupied the country. At the end of World War II, the Slovak Republic again became part of Czechoslovakia.

The Communist party took control in 1948. In the 1960s, many people sought reform, but they were crushed by the Russians. In the late 1980s, demands for democracy mounted and a non-Communist government took office in 1990. Elections in 1992 led to victory for the Movement for a Democratic Slovakia headed by a former Communist and nationalist, Vladimir Meciar, and the independent Slovak Republic came into existence on 1 January 1993.

Independence raised national aspirations among Slovakia's Magyar-speaking community, but relations with Hungary deteriorated when the Magyars felt that administrative changes under-represented them politically. The government also made Slovak the only official language. The government's autocratic rule and human rights record provoked international criticism. In 1998, Meciar's party was defeated and Mikulas Dzurinda replaced Meciar as prime minister. The government continued to strengthen its ties with the West and, in 2004, it became a member of both the North Atlantic Treaty Organization and the European Union.

Before 1948, the Slovak Republic's economy was based on farming, but Communist governments developed manufacturing industries, producing such things as chemicals, machinery, steel and weapons. Since the late 1980s, many state-run businesses have been handed over to private owners.

AREA 49,012 sq km [18,924 sq mi] **POPULATION** 5,430,000
CAPITAL (POPULATION) Bratislava (449,000)
GOVERNMENT Multiparty republic
ETHNIC GROUPS Slovak 86%, Hungarian 11%
LANGUAGES Slovak (official), Hungarian
RELIGIONS Roman Catholic 60%, Protestant 8%, Orthodox 4%, others **CURRENCY** Slovak koruna = 100 halierov

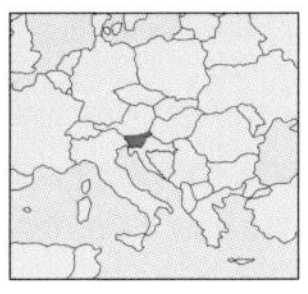

SLOVENIA

GEOGRAPHY The Republic of Slovenia was one of the six republics which made up the former Yugoslavia. Much of the land is mountainous, rising to 2,863 m [9,393 ft] at Mount Triglav in the Julian Alps (Julijske Alpe) in the north-west. Central Slovenia contains the limestone Karst region. The Postojna caves near Ljubljana are among the largest in Europe.

The coast has a mild Mediterranean climate, but inland the climate is more continental. The mountains are snow-capped in winter.

POLITICS & ECONOMY In the last 2,000 years, the Slovene people have been independent as a nation for less than 50 years. The Austrian Habsburgs ruled over the region from the 13th century until World War I. Slovenia became part of the Kingdom of the Serbs, Croats and Slovenes (later called Yugoslavia) in 1918. During World War II, Slovenia was invaded and partitioned between Italy, Germany and Hungary, but, after the war, Slovenia again became part of Yugoslavia.

From the late 1960s, some Slovenes demanded independence, but the central government opposed the break-up of the country. In 1990, when Communist governments had collapsed throughout Eastern Europe, elections were held and a non-Communist coalition government was set up. Slovenia then declared itself independent. This led to fighting between Slovenes and the federal army, but Slovenia did not become a battlefield like other parts of the former Yugoslavia. The European Community recognized Slovenia's independence in 1992. The electors returned a coalition led by the Liberal Democrats in 1992, 1996 and 2000. In 2004, it achieved two of its major objectives in becoming a member of both the North Atlantic Treaty Organization and the European Union.

The reform of the formerly state-run economy caused problems for Slovenia. However, it has enjoyed considerable economic progress, with one of Europe's fastest growing economies. In 1992, the World Bank classified Slovenia's economy as 'upper-middle-income'.

Manufacturing is the leading activity and manufactures are the main exports. Manufactures include chemicals, machinery and transport equipment, metal goods and textiles. Slovenia mines some iron ore, lead, lignite and mercury. Agriculture and forestry employ 10% of the people. Fruits, maize, potatoes and wheat are major crops, and many farmers raise animals.

AREA 20,256 sq km [7,821 sq mi] **POPULATION** 1,936,000
CAPITAL (POPULATION) Ljubljana (264,000)
GOVERNMENT Multiparty republic
ETHNIC GROUPS Slovene 92%, Croat 1%, Serb, Hungarian, Bosniak
LANGUAGES Slovenian (official), Serbo-Croatian
RELIGIONS Mainly Roman Catholic
CURRENCY Tolar = 100 stotin

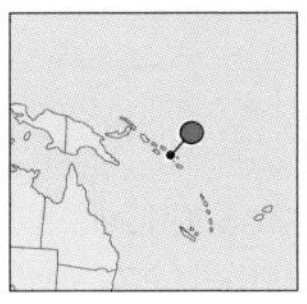

SOLOMON ISLANDS

The Solomon Islands, a chain of mainly volcanic islands in the Pacific Ocean, were a British territory between 1893 and 1978. The chain extends for some 2,250 km [1,400 mi]. They were the scene of fierce fighting during World War II. Most people are Melanesians, and the islands have a young population profile, with half the people aged under 20. Fish, coconuts and cocoa are leading products, though development is hampered by mountainous, forested terrain.

AREA 28,896 sq km [11,157 sq mi] **POPULATION** 509,000
CAPITAL (POPULATION) Honiara (49,000)

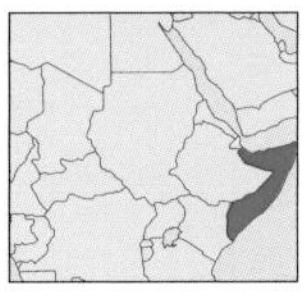

SOMALIA

GEOGRAPHY The Somali Democratic Republic, or Somalia, is in a region known as the 'Horn of Africa'. It is more than twice the size of Italy, the country which once ruled the southern part of Somalia. The most mountainous part of the country is in the north, behind the narrow coastal plains that border the Gulf of Aden.

Rainfall is light throughout Somalia. The wettest regions are the south and the northern mountains, but droughts often occur. Temperatures are high on the low plateaux and plains.

POLITICS & ECONOMY European powers became interested in the Horn of Africa in the 19th century. In 1884, Britain made the northern part of what is now Somalia a protectorate, while Italy took the south in 1905. The new boundaries divided the Somalis into five areas: the two Somalilands, Djibouti (which was taken by France in the 1880s), Ethiopia and Kenya. Since then, many Somalis have wanted to create a Greater Somalia. Italy invaded British Somaliland in 1940, but was defeated in 1941. Britain ruled both Somalilands until 1950, when the United Nations asked Italy to take over the former Italian Somaliland for ten years. In 1960, the two Somalilands became independent in a united Somalia.

Somalia has faced many problems. Economic difficulties led a military group to seize power in 1969. In the 1970s, Somalia supported an uprising of Somali-speaking people in the Ogaden region of Ethiopia. But, in 1988, Somalia and Ethiopia signed a peace treaty. In the 1990s, Somalia gradually broke apart. In 1991, the people in what was once British Somaliland set up the 'Somaliland Republic', but it failed to get international recognition. The north-east, called Puntland, also seceded, while the south was riven by clan warfare. US troops sent into the south by the UN in 1993 were forced to withdraw in 1994 and clan fighting continued. A three-year transitional government set up in 2000 failed to bring peace and, in 2004, further talks took place in Kenya, following the calling of a truce between the rival clans.

Somalia is a developing country, whose economy has been shattered by drought, floods and war. Many Somalis are nomads who raise livestock. Live animals, meat, and hides and skins are exported, followed by bananas grown in the wetter south. Other crops include citrus fruits, cotton, maize and sugar cane. Mining and manufacturing are relatively unimportant in the economy.

AREA 637,657 sq km [246,199 sq mi] **POPULATION** 8,025,000
CAPITAL (POPULATION) Mogadishu (900,000) **GOVERNMENT** Single-party republic, military dominated **ETHNIC GROUPS** Somali 85%, Bantu, Arab **LANGUAGES** Somali (official), Arabic **RELIGIONS** Islam (Sunni Muslim) **CURRENCY** Somali shilling = 100 cents

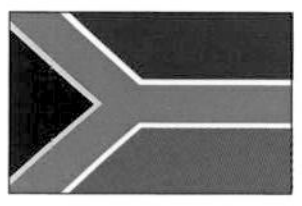
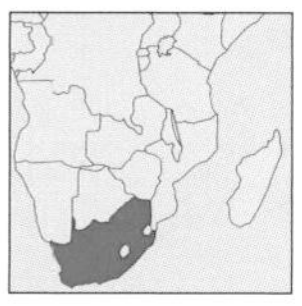

SOUTH AFRICA

GEOGRAPHY The Republic of South Africa is made up largely of the southern part of the huge plateau which makes up most of southern Africa. The highest peaks are in the Drakensberg range, which is formed by the uplifted rim of the plateau. The coastal plains include part of the Namib Desert in the north-west. Most of South Africa has a mild, sunny climate. Much of the coastal strip, including Cape Town, has warm, dry summers and mild, rainy winters. Inland, large areas are arid.

POLITICS & ECONOMY Early inhabitants in South Africa were the Khoisan. In the last 2,000 years, Bantu-speaking people moved into the area. Their descendants include the Zulu, Xhosa, Sotho and Tswana. The Dutch founded a settlement at the Cape in 1652, but Britain took over in the early 19th century, making the area a colony. The Dutch, called Boers or Afrikaners, resented British rule and moved inland. Rivalry between the groups led to Anglo-Boer Wars in 1880–1 and 1899–1902.

In 1910, the country was united as the Union of South Africa. In 1948, the National Party won power and introduced a policy known as apartheid, under which non-whites had no votes and their human rights were strictly limited. In 1990, Nelson Mandela, leader of the African National Congress (ANC), was released from prison. Multiracial elections were held in 1994 and Mandela became president. After Mandela's retirement in 1999, his successor, Thabo Mbeki, led the ANC to victory in national elections. In 2004, the ANC won again by a landslide. Taking almost 70% of the vote, it was far ahead of its nearest rival, the Democratic Alliance, which polled only 13%. However, the government faced massive problems of poverty and under-development, and maintaining national unity. South Africa also faces a major health crisis, with about 11% of its people infected with the HIV virus. It has the greatest number of infected people in the world, estimated by the UN in 2003 to be around 5 million.

South Africa is Africa's most developed country. However, most of the black people are poor, with low standards of living. Natural resources include diamonds, gold and many other metals. Mining and manufacturing are the most valuable activities.

AREA 1,221,037 sq km [471,442 sq mi] **POPULATION** 42,769,000
CAPITAL (POPULATION) Cape Town (legislative, 855,000); Pretoria (administrative, 692,000); Bloemfontein (judiciary, 350,000)
GOVERNMENT Multiparty republic **ETHNIC GROUPS** Black 76%, White 13%, Coloured 9%, Asian 2% **LANGUAGES** Afrikaans, English, Ndebele, Pedi, Sotho, Swazi, Tsonga, Tswana, Venda, Xhosa and Zulu (all official) **RELIGIONS** Christianity 68%, Islam 2%, Hinduism 1% **CURRENCY** Rand = 100 cents

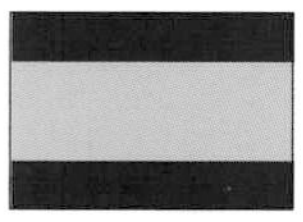

SPAIN

GEOGRAPHY The Kingdom of Spain is the second largest country in Western Europe after France. It shares the Iberian peninsula with Portugal. A large plateau, called the Meseta, covers most of Spain. Much of the Meseta is flat, but it is crossed by several mountain ranges, called sierras.

The northern highlands include the Cantabrian Mountains (Cordillera Cantabrica) and the high Pyrenees, which form Spain's border with France. But Mulhacén, the highest peak on the Spanish mainland, is in the Sierra Nevada in the south-east. Spain also contains fertile coastal plains. Other major lowlands are the Ebro river basin in the north-east and the Guadalquivir river basin in the south-west. Spain also includes the Balearic Islands in the Mediterranean Sea and the Canary Islands off the north-west coast of Africa.

The Meseta has a continental climate, with hot summers and cold winters, when temperatures often fall below freezing point. Snow frequently covers the mountain ranges on the Meseta. The Mediterranean coasts have hot, dry summers and mild winters.

POLITICS & ECONOMY In the 16th century, Spain became a world power. At its peak, it controlled much of Central and South America, parts of Africa and the Philippines in Asia. Spain began to decline in the late 16th century. Its sea power was destroyed by a British fleet in the Battle of Trafalgar (1805). By the 20th century, it was a poor country.

Spain became a republic in 1931, but the republicans were defeated in the Spanish Civil War (1936–9). General Francisco Franco (1892–1975) became the country's dictator, though, technically, it was a monarchy. When Franco died, the monarchy was restored. Prince Juan Carlos became king.

Spain has several groups with their own languages and cultures. Some of these people want to run their own regional affairs. In the northern Basque region, some nationalists have waged a terrorist campaign. A truce in 1998 was ended in 1999 when talks failed to produce results. In 2003, Spain's Supreme Court voted to ban Batasuna, the Basque separatist party.

Since the 1970s, regional parliaments with a considerable degree of autonomy have been set up in the Basque Country (called Euskadi in the indigenous language and Pais Vasco in Spanish), in Catalonia in the north-east, and in Galicia in the north-west. In March 2004, train bombings killed about 200 people in Madrid. But this was the work of al Qaida, not of Basque separatists. Following the bombings, the opposition socialists swept to power in national elections.

The revival of Spain's economy, which was shattered by the Civil War, began in the 1950s and 1960s, especially through the growth of tourism and manufacturing. Since the 1950s, Spain has changed from a poor country, dependent on agriculture, to a fairly prosperous industrial nation.

By 2001, agriculture employed 6% of the people, as compared with industry at 18%, and services, including tourism, at 76%. Arable and grazing land make up about two-thirds of Spain, while forest covers most of the rest of the land. Major crops include barley, citrus fruits, grapes for wine-making, olives, potatoes and wheat. Apart from some high-grade iron ore in the north, Spain lacks natural resources. But it has many manufacturing industries. Products include cars, chemicals, clothing, electronics, processed food, metal goods, steel and textiles.

AREA 497,548 sq km [192,103 sq mi] **POPULATION** 40,217,000
CAPITAL (POPULATION) Madrid (2,939,000)
GOVERNMENT Constitutional monarchy
ETHNIC GROUPS Composite of Mediterranean and Nordic types
LANGUAGES Castilian Spanish (official) 74%, Catalan 17%, Galician 7%, Basque 2%
RELIGIONS Roman Catholic 94%, others
CURRENCY Euro = 100 cents

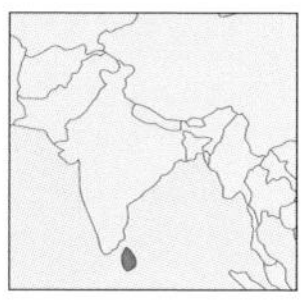

SRI LANKA

GEOGRAPHY The Democratic Socialist Republic of Sri Lanka is an island nation, separated from the south-east coast of India by the Palk Strait. The land is mostly low-lying, but a mountain region dominates the south-central part of the country.

The western part of Sri Lanka has a wet equatorial climate. Temperatures are high and the rainfall is heavy. Eastern Sri Lanka is drier than the west of the country.

POLITICS & ECONOMY From the early 16th century, Ceylon (as Sri Lanka was then known) was ruled successively by the Portuguese, Dutch and British. Independence was achieved in 1948 and the country was renamed Sri Lanka in 1972.

After independence, rivalries between the two main ethnic groups, the Sinhalese and Tamils, marred progress. In the 1950s, the government made Sinhala the official language. Following protests, the prime minister made provisions for Tamil to be used in some areas. In 1959, the prime minister was assassinated by a Sinhalese extremist and he was succeeded by Sirimavo Bandanaraike, the world's first woman prime minister.

Conflict between Tamils and Sinhalese continued in the 1970s and 1980s. In 1987, India helped to engineer a cease-fire. Indian troops arrived to enforce the agreement, but withdrew in 1990 after failing to subdue the main guerrilla group, the Tamil Tigers, who wanted to set up an independent Tamil homeland in northern Sri Lanka. In 1993, the country's president was assassinated by a suspected Tamil separatist. Offensives against the Tamil Tigers continued until hopes of peace were raised in 2002, with the signing of a cease-fire. But a power struggle broke out in 2003 between President Chandrika Kumaratunga and the prime minister, whom she accused of being soft in the peace talks. In a snap election in 2004, the president's United People's Freedom Alliance became the largest party in parliament. The peace process appeared stalled.

Sri Lanka is classed as a 'low-income' economy. Agriculture employs about 33% of the people. Coconuts, rubber and tea are exported, but rice is the main food crop. Factories process farm products and manufacture textiles.

AREA 65,610 sq km [25,332 sq mi] **POPULATION** 19,742,000
CAPITAL (POPULATION) Colombo (642,000)
GOVERNMENT Multiparty republic
ETHNIC GROUPS Sinhalese 74%, Tamil 18%, Moor 7%
LANGUAGES Sinhala and Tamil (both official)
RELIGIONS Buddhism 70%, Hinduism 15%, Christianity 8%, Islam 7%
CURRENCY Sri Lankan rupee = 100 cents

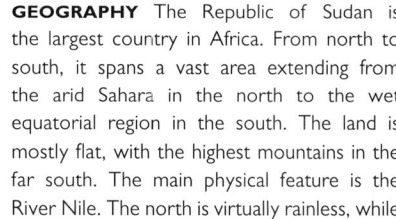

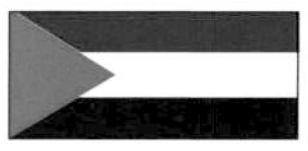
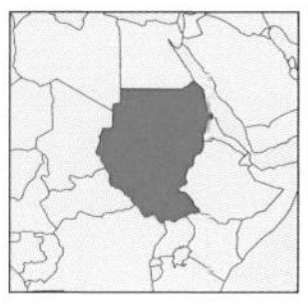

SUDAN

GEOGRAPHY The Republic of Sudan is the largest country in Africa. From north to south, it spans a vast area extending from the arid Sahara in the north to the wet equatorial region in the south. The land is mostly flat, with the highest mountains in the far south. The main physical feature is the River Nile. The north is virtually rainless, while the south has a wet equatorial climate.

POLITICS & ECONOMY In the 19th century, Egypt gradually took over Sudan. In 1881, a Muslim religious teacher, the Mahdi ('divinely appointed guide'), led an uprising. Britain and Egypt put the rebellion down in 1898. In 1899, they agreed to rule Sudan jointly as a condominium. After independence in 1952, the black Africans in the south, who were either Christians or followers of traditional religions, feared domination by the Muslim north. They objected to Arabic becoming the sole official language and, in 1964, civil war broke out. The war ended in 1972, when the south was granted regional self-government.

In 1983, the announcement that Islamic law would apply throughout Sudan sparked off further resistance from the rebel Sudan People's Liberation Army (SPLA) in the south. In 1998, Sudan's government announced that it accepted the idea of a referendum in the south. By 2004, talks that had started in 2002 held out hopes of peace. However, in 2004, conflict flared up in the western region of Darfur, where militias supported by government troops were accused of atrocities against the local people. Thousands of refugees fled into Chad.

Sudan is classed as a 'low-income' developing country. Agriculture employs 60% of the people and cotton is the chief crop. Minerals include oil, the most valuable export, chromium, gold and gypsum. Manufacturing is concerned mainly with processing local products.

AREA 2,505,813 sq km [967,494 sq mi] **POPULATION** 38,114,000
CAPITAL (POPULATION) Khartoum (947,000)
GOVERNMENT Military regime **ETHNIC GROUPS** Black 52%, Arab 39%, Beja 6%, others **LANGUAGES** Arabic (official), Nubian, Ta Bedawie **RELIGIONS** Islam 70%, traditional beliefs 25%
CURRENCY Sudanese dinar = 10 Sudanese pounds

SURINAME

GEOGRAPHY The Republic of Suriname is sandwiched between French Guiana and Guyana in north-eastern South America. The narrow coastal plain was once swampy, but it has been drained and now consists mainly of farmland. Inland lie hills and low mountains, which rise to 1,280 m [4,199 ft].

Suriname has a hot, wet and humid climate. Temperatures are high throughout the year.

POLITICS & ECONOMY In 1667, the British handed Suriname to the Dutch in return for New Amsterdam, an area that is now the state of New York. Slave revolts and Dutch neglect hampered development. In the early 19th century, Britain and the Netherlands disputed the ownership of the area. The British gave up their claims in 1813. Slavery was abolished in 1863 and, soon afterwards, Indian and Indonesian labourers were introduced to work on the plantations. Suriname became fully independent in 1975, but the economy was weakened when thousands of skilled people emigrated from Suriname to the Netherlands. Following a coup in 1980, Suriname was ruled by a military dictator, Dési Bouterse. The adoption of a new constitution led to the restoration of democracy in 1988, though another military coup occurred in 1990. Elections were held in 1996, but instability, deteriorating relations with the Netherlands and economic problems continued. In 1999, Bouterse was convicted in absentia in the Netherlands of having led a cocaine-trafficking ring during and after his tenure in office.

The World Bank classifies Suriname as an 'upper-middle-income' developing country. Its economy is based on mining and metal processing. Suriname is a leading producer of bauxite, from which the metal aluminium is made.

AREA 163,265 sq km [63,037 sq mi] **POPULATION** 435,000
CAPITAL (POPULATION) Paramaribo (216,000)
GOVERNMENT Multiparty republic
ETHNIC GROUPS Hindustani/East Indian 37%, Creole (mixed White and Black) 31%, Javanese 15%, Black 10%, Amerindian 2%, Chinese 2%, others **LANGUAGES** Dutch (official), Sranang Tonga
RELIGIONS Hinduism 27%, Protestant 25%, Roman Catholic 23%, Islam 20% **CURRENCY** Surinamese guilder = 100 cents

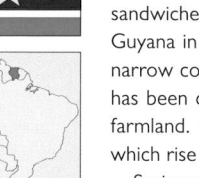

SWAZILAND

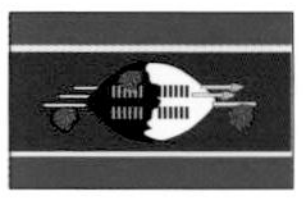

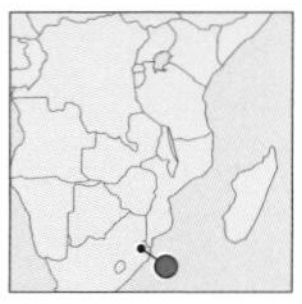

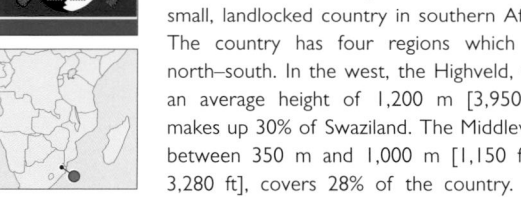

GEOGRAPHY The Kingdom of Swaziland is a small, landlocked country in southern Africa. The country has four regions which run north–south. In the west, the Highveld, with an average height of 1,200 m [3,950 ft], makes up 30% of Swaziland. The Middleveld, between 350 m and 1,000 m [1,150 ft to 3,280 ft], covers 28% of the country. The Lowveld, with an average height of 270 m [886 ft], covers another 33%. Finally, the Lebombo Mountains reach 800 m [2,600 ft] along the eastern border. The Lowveld is almost tropical, with average temperatures of 22°C [72°F] and low rainfall. The altitude moderates the climate in the west.

POLITICS & ECONOMY In 1894, Britain and the Boers of South Africa agreed to put Swaziland under the control of the South African Republic (the Transvaal). But at the end of the Anglo–Boer War (1899–1902), Britain took control of the country. In 1968, when Swaziland became fully independent as a constitutional monarchy, the head of state was King Sobhuza II. Sobhuza died in 1982 and was succeeded by one of his sons, Prince Makhosetive, who, in 1986, was installed as King Mswati III. Elections in 1993 and 1998, in which political parties were banned, failed to satisfy protesters who opposed the absolute monarchy. But Mswati continued to rule by decree. In 2003, he announced that democracy was not suitable for the Swazi people.

The World Bank classifies Swaziland as a 'lower-middle-income' developing country. Agriculture employs 50% of the people, and farm products and processed foods, including soft drink concentrates, sugar, wood pulp, citrus fruits and canned fruit, are the leading exports. Many farmers live at subsistence level. Swaziland is heavily dependent on South Africa and the two countries are linked through a customs union. Swaziland shares two major problems with South Africa – the widespread poverty and the high incidence of HIV/AIDS.

AREA 17,364 sq km [6,704 sq mi] **POPULATION** 1,161,000
CAPITAL (POPULATION) Mbabane (38,000)
GOVERNMENT Monarchy **ETHNIC GROUPS** African 97%, European 3% **LANGUAGES** Siswati and English (both official)
RELIGIONS Zionist (a mix of Christianity and traditional beliefs) 40%, Roman Catholic 20%, Islam 10% **CURRENCY** Lilangeni = 100 cents

SWEDEN

GEOGRAPHY The Kingdom of Sweden is the largest of the countries of Scandinavia in both area and population. It shares the Scandinavian peninsula with Norway. The western part of the country, along the border with Norway, is mountainous. The highest point is Kebnekaise, which reaches 2,117 m [6,946 ft] in the north-west.

The climate of Sweden becomes more severe from south to north. Stockholm has cold winters and cool summers. The far south is much milder.

POLITICS & ECONOMY Swedish Vikings plundered areas to the south and east between the 9th and 11th centuries. Sweden, Denmark and Norway were united in 1397, but Sweden regained its independence in 1523. In 1809, Sweden lost Finland to Russia, but, in 1814, it gained Norway from Denmark. The union between Sweden and Norway was dissolved in 1905. Sweden was neutral in World Wars I and II. Since 1945, Sweden has become a prosperous country. In 1995, it joined the European Union. However, many people were sceptical about the advantages of EU membership and Sweden did not adopt the euro, the single EU currency, in 1999.

Sweden has wide-ranging welfare services. But many people are concerned about the high cost of these services and the high taxes they must pay. In 1991, the Social Democrats, who had built up the welfare state, were defeated. They were re-elected in 1994. In 2003, the government held a referendum on replacing the country's currency with the EU's unit of currency, the euro, but the electorate rejected the proposal.

Sweden is a highly developed industrial country. Major products include steel and steel goods. Steel is used in the engineering industry to manufacture aircraft, cars, machinery and ships. Sweden has some of the world's richest iron ore deposits. They are located near Kiruna in the far north. But most of this ore is exported, and Sweden imports most of the materials needed by its industries. Sweden also has a major forestry industry. Development of hydroelectricity has made up for the lack of oil and coal. In 1996, a decision was taken to decommission all of Sweden's nuclear power stations. This is said to be one of the boldest and most expensive environmental pledges ever made by a government.

AREA 449,964 sq km [173,731 sq mi] **POPULATION** 8,878,000
CAPITAL (POPULATION) Stockholm (744,000)
GOVERNMENT Constitutional monarchy **ETHNIC GROUPS** Swedish 91%, Finnish, Sami **LANGUAGES** Swedish (official), Finnish, Sami
RELIGIONS Lutheran 87%, Roman Catholic, Orthodox
CURRENCY Swedish krona = 100 öre

SWITZERLAND

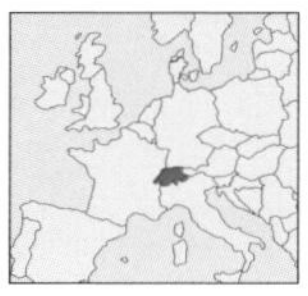

GEOGRAPHY The Swiss Confederation is a landlocked country in Western Europe. Much of the land is mountainous. The Jura Mountains lie along Switzerland's western border with France, while the Swiss Alps make up about 60% of the country in the south and east. Four-fifths of the people of Switzerland live on the fertile Swiss plateau, which contains most of Switzerland's large cities.

The climate of Switzerland varies greatly according to the height of the land. The plateau region has a central European climate with warm summers, but cold and snowy winters. Rain occurs all through the year. The rainiest months are in summer.

POLITICS & ECONOMY In 1291, three small cantons (states) united to defend their freedom against the Habsburg rulers of the Holy Roman Empire. They were Schwyz, Uri and Unterwalden, and they called the confederation they formed 'Switzerland'. Switzerland expanded and, in the 14th century, defeated Austria in three wars of independence. After a defeat by the French in 1515, the Swiss adopted a policy of neutrality, which they still follow. In 1815, the Congress of Vienna expanded Switzerland to 22 cantons and guaranteed its neutrality. Switzerland's 23rd canton, Jura, was created in 1979 from part of Bern. Neutrality combined with the vigour and independence of its people have made Switzerland prosperous. In 1993 and again in 2001, the Swiss people voted against starting negotiations to join the European Union. However, in 2002, the Swiss voted by a narrow majority to join the United Nations.

Although lacking in natural resources, Switzerland is a wealthy, industrialized country. Many workers are highly skilled. Major products include chemicals, electrical equipment, machinery and machine tools, precision instruments, processed food, watches and textiles. Farmers produce about three-fifths of the country's food – the rest is imported. Livestock raising, especially dairy farming, is the chief agricultural activity. Crops include fruits, potatoes and wheat. Tourism and banking are also important. Swiss banks attract investors from all over the world.

AREA 41,284 sq km [15,940 sq mi] **POPULATION** 7,319,000
CAPITAL (POPULATION) Bern (124,000) **GOVERNMENT** Federal republic **ETHNIC GROUPS** German 65%, French 18%, Italian 10%, Romansch 1%, others **LANGUAGES** French, German, Italian and Romansch (all official) **RELIGIONS** Roman Catholic 46%, Protestant 40% **CURRENCY** Swiss franc = 100 centimes

SYRIA

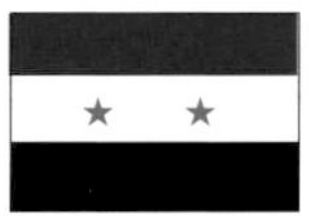

GEOGRAPHY The Syrian Arab Republic is a country in south-western Asia. The narrow coastal plain is overlooked by a low mountain range which runs north–south. Another range, the Jabal ash Sharqi, runs along the border with Lebanon. South of this range is the Golan Heights, which Israel has occupied since 1967.

The coast has a Mediterranean climate, with dry, warm summers and wet, mild winters. The low mountains cut off Damascus from the sea. It has less rainfall than the coastal areas. To the east, the land becomes drier.

POLITICS & ECONOMY After the collapse of the Turkish Ottoman empire in World War I, Syria was ruled by France. Since independence in 1946, Syria has been involved in the Arab–Israeli wars and, in 1967, it lost a strategic border area, the Golan Heights, to Israel. In 1970, Lieutenant-General Hafez al-Assad took power, establishing a stable but repressive regime. In 1999, Syria had talks with Israel concerning the future of the Golan Heights. These talks formed part of an attempt to establish a peace settlement for the entire east Mediterranean region. Following the death of Assad in 2000, his son, Bashar Assad, succeeded him.

The World Bank classifies Syria as a 'lower-middle-income' developing country. But it has great potential for development. Its main resources are oil, hydroelectricity from the dam at Lake Assad, and fertile land. Oil is the main export; farm products, textiles and phosphates are also important. Agriculture employs about 29% of the workforce.

AREA 185,180 sq km [71,498 sq mi] **POPULATION** 17,586,000
CAPITAL (POPULATION) Damascus (1,394,000)
GOVERNMENT Multiparty republic **ETHNIC GROUPS** Arab 90%, Kurdish, Armenian, others **LANGUAGES** Arabic (official), Kurdish, Armenian **RELIGIONS** Sunni Muslim 74%, other Islam 16%
CURRENCY Syrian pound = 100 piastres

TAIWAN

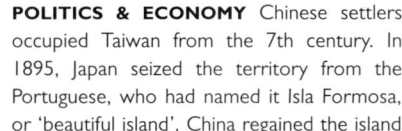

GEOGRAPHY High mountain ranges run down the length of the island, with dense forest in many areas. The climate is warm, moist and suitable for agriculture.

POLITICS & ECONOMY Chinese settlers occupied Taiwan from the 7th century. In 1895, Japan seized the territory from the Portuguese, who had named it Isla Formosa, or 'beautiful island'. China regained the island after World War II. In 1949, it became the refuge of the Nationalists who had been driven out of China by the Communists. They set up the Republic of China, which, with US help, began to expand its economy. Today, it produces a wide range of manufactured goods.

In the early 21st century, the Taiwanese declared full nationhood for Taiwan. But the government of mainland China threatened to attack the territory if it did not accept the fact that it was a self-governing province of China. But re-unification seemed a remote prospect.

AREA 36,000 sq km [13,900 sq mi] **POPULATION** 22,603,000
CAPITAL (POPULATION) Taipei (2,634,000)
GOVERNMENT Unitary multiparty republic
ETHNIC GROUPS Taiwanese 84%, mainland Chinese 14%
LANGUAGES Mandarin Chinese (official), Min, Hakka
RELIGIONS Buddhism, Taoism, Confucianism
CURRENCY New Taiwan dollar = 100 cents

TAJIKISTAN

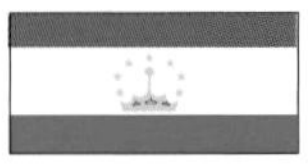

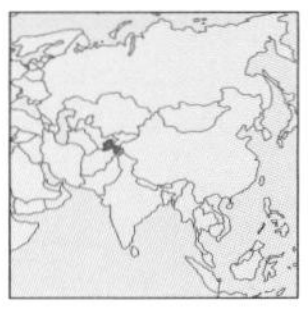

GEOGRAPHY The Republic of Tajikistan is one of the five central Asian republics that formed part of the former Soviet Union. Only 7% of the land is below 1,000 m [3,280 ft], while almost all of eastern Tajikistan is above 3,000 m [9,840 ft]. The highest point is Communism Peak (Pik Kommunizma), which reaches 7,495 m [24,590 ft]. The main ranges are the westwards extension of the Tian Shan Range in the north and the snow-capped Pamirs in the south-east. Earthquakes are common throughout the country. The climate is continental, with hot, dry summers in the lower valleys and bitterly cold winters, especially in the mountains.

POLITICS & ECONOMY Russia conquered parts of Tajikistan in the late 19th century and, by 1920, Russia took complete control. In 1924, Tajikistan became part of the Uzbek Soviet Socialist Republic, but, in 1929, it was expanded, taking in some areas populated by Uzbeks, becoming the Tajik Soviet Socialist Republic.

While the Soviet Union began to introduce reforms during the 1980s, many Tajiks demanded freedom. In 1989, the Tajik government made Tajik the official language instead of Russian and, in 1990, it stated that its local laws overruled Soviet laws. Tajikistan became fully independent in 1991, following the break-up of the Soviet Union. In 1992, civil war broke out between the government, which was run by former Communists, and an alliance of democrats and Islamic forces. A cease-fire was agreed in 1996 and, in 1997, opposition leaders were brought into the government. Presidential elections were held in 1999. In 2003, changes to the constitution enabled Emomali Rakhmanov, Tajikistan's president since 1994, to serve two more seven-year terms in office after elections in 2006.

The World Bank classifies Tajikistan as a 'low-income' developing country. Agriculture, mainly on irrigated land, is the main activity and cotton is the chief product. Other crops include fruits, grains and vegetables. The country has large hydroelectric power resources and it produces aluminium.

AREA 143,100 sq km [55,521 sq mi] **POPULATION** 6,864,000
CAPITAL (POPULATION) Dushanbe (529,000)
GOVERNMENT Transitional democracy
ETHNIC GROUPS Tajik 65%, Uzbek 25%, Russian
LANGUAGES Tajik (official), Russian
RELIGIONS Islam (Sunni Muslim 85%)
CURRENCY Somoni = 100 dirams

TANZANIA

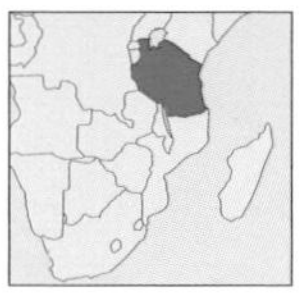

GEOGRAPHY The United Republic of Tanzania consists of the former mainland country of Tanganyika and the island nation of Zanzibar, which also includes the island of Pemba. Behind a narrow coastal plain, most of Tanzania is a plateau, which is broken by arms of the Great African Rift Valley. In the west, this valley contains lakes Nyasa and Tanganyika. The highest peak is Kilimanjaro, Africa's tallest mountain.

The coast has a hot and humid climate, with the greatest rainfall in April and May. The inland plateaux and mountains are cooler and less humid.

POLITICS & ECONOMY Mainland Tanganyika became a German territory in the 1880s, while Zanzibar and Pemba became a British protectorate in 1890. Following Germany's defeat in World War I, Britain took over Tanganyika, which remained a British territory until its independence in 1961. In 1964, Tanganyika and Zanzibar united to form the United Republic of Tanzania. The country's president, Julius Nyerere, pursued socialist policies of self-help (*ujamaa*) and egalitarianism. Many of its social reforms were successful, though the country failed to make economic progress. Nyerere resigned as president in 1985, although he retained much influence until his death in 1999. His successors, Ali Hassan Mwinyi and, from 1995, Benjamin Mkapa, introduced more liberal economic policies.

Tanzania is one of the world's poorest countries. Crops are grown on only 4.2% of the land, yet agriculture employs 80% of the people. Food crops include bananas, cassava, maize, millet and rice.

AREA 945,090 sq km [364,899 sq mi] **POPULATION** 35,922,000
CAPITAL (POPULATION) Dodoma (204,000)
GOVERNMENT Multiparty republic
ETHNIC GROUPS Native African 99% (of which 95% are Bantu consisting of more than 130 tribes)
LANGUAGES Swahili (Kiswahili) and English (both official)
RELIGIONS Islam 35% (99% in Zanzibar), traditional beliefs 35%, Christianity 30%
CURRENCY Tanzanian shilling = 100 cents

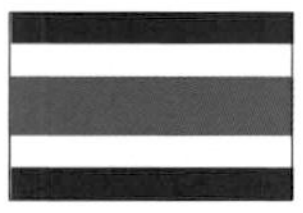

THAILAND

GEOGRAPHY The Kingdom of Thailand is one of the ten countries in South-east Asia. The highest land is in the north, where Doi Inthanon, the highest peak, reaches 2,595 m [8,514 ft]. The Khorat plateau, in the north-east, makes up about 30% of the country and is the most heavily populated part of Thailand. In the south, Thailand shares the finger-like Malay peninsula with Burma and Malaysia.

Thailand has a tropical climate. Monsoon winds from the south-west bring heavy rains between the months of May and October. The rainfall in Bangkok is lower than in many other parts of South-east Asia, because mountains shelter the central plains from the rain-bearing winds.

POLITICS & ECONOMY The first Thai state was set up in the 13th century. By 1350, it included most of what is now Thailand. European contact began in the early 16th century. But, in the late 17th century, the Thais, fearing interference in their affairs, forced all Europeans to leave. This policy continued for 150 years. In 1782, a Thai General, Chao Phraya Chakkri, became king, founding a dynasty which continues today. The country became known as Siam, and Bangkok became its capital. From the mid-19th century, contacts with the West were restored. In World War I, Siam supported the Allies against Germany and Austria-Hungary. But in 1941, the country was conquered by Japan and became its ally. However, after the end of World War II, it became an ally of the United States.

After 1967, when Thailand became a member of ASEAN (Association of South-east Asian Nations), its economy expanded rapidly, especially in manufacturing and service industries. However, in 1997, it suffered a recession along with other eastern Asian economies. Thailand's political stability was disturbed in 2003, when several suspected Islamic militants were arrested. In 2004, more than 100 people died in clashes between Muslims and the police in southern Thailand.

Agriculture employs about two-fifths of the people and it remains an important sector of the economy. Rice is the chief crop. Cassava, cotton, maize, rubber, sugar cane and tobacco are also grown. Tin and some other minerals are produced, but the chief exports are manufactures and food products. Tourism is another major source of income.

AREA 513,115 sq km [198,114 sq mi] **POPULATION** 64,265,000
CAPITAL (POPULATION) Bangkok (6,320,000)
GOVERNMENT Constitutional monarchy
ETHNIC GROUPS Thai 75%, Chinese 14%, others 11%
LANGUAGES Thai (official), English, ethnic and regional dialects
RELIGIONS Buddhism 95%, Islam, Christianity
CURRENCY Baht = 100 satang

TOGO

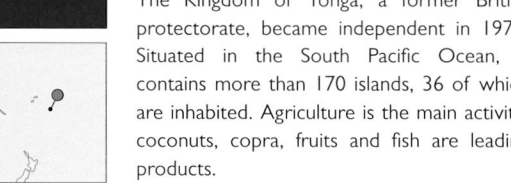

GEOGRAPHY The Republic of Togo is a long, narrow country in West Africa. From north to south, it extends about 500 km [311 mi]. Its coastline on the Gulf of Guinea is only 64 km [40 mi] long and it is only 145 km [90 mi] at its widest point.

Togo has high temperatures all through the year. The main wet season is from March to July, with a minor wet season in October and November.

POLITICS & ECONOMY Togo became a German protectorate in 1884 but, in 1919, Britain took over the western third of the territory, while France took over the eastern two-thirds. In 1956, the people of British Togoland voted to join Ghana, while French Togoland became an independent republic in 1960.

A military regime took power in 1963. In 1967, General Gnassingbe Eyadema became head of state and suspended the constitution. Under a new constitution adopted in 1992, multiparty elections were held in 1994. However, in 1998, paramilitary policies stopped the count in the presidential elections when it became clear that Eyadema had been defeated. As a result, the leading opposition parties boycotted the elections in 1999 and 2002.

Togo is a poor, developing country. Farming employs 67% of the people and major food crops include cassava, maize, millet and yams. The leading export is phosphate rock, which is used to make fertilizers.

AREA 56,785 sq km [21,925 sq mi] **POPULATION** 5,429,000
CAPITAL (POPULATION) Lomé (658,000)
GOVERNMENT Multiparty republic **ETHNIC GROUPS** Native African 99% (largest tribes are Ewe, Mina and Kabre) **LANGUAGES** French (official), African languages **RELIGIONS** Traditional beliefs 51%, Christianity 29%, Islam 20% **CURRENCY** CFA franc = 100 centimes

TONGA

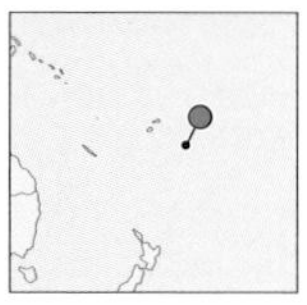

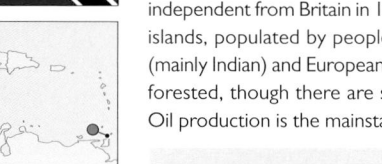

The Kingdom of Tonga, a former British protectorate, became independent in 1970. Situated in the South Pacific Ocean, it contains more than 170 islands, 36 of which are inhabited. Agriculture is the main activity; coconuts, copra, fruits and fish are leading products.

AREA 650 sq km [251 sq mi] **POPULATION** 108,000 **CAPITAL** Nuku'alofa

TRINIDAD AND TOBAGO

The Republic of Trinidad and Tobago became independent from Britain in 1962. These tropical islands, populated by people of African, Asian (mainly Indian) and European origin, are hilly and forested, though there are some fertile plains. Oil production is the mainstay of the economy.

AREA 5,130 sq km [1,981 sq mi]
POPULATION 1,104,000 **CAPITAL** Port-of-Spain

TUNISIA

GEOGRAPHY The Republic of Tunisia is the smallest country in North Africa. The mountains in the north are an eastwards and comparatively low extension of the Atlas Mountains. To the north and east of the mountains lie fertile plains, especially between Sfax, Tunis and Bizerte. In the south, low-lying regions contain a vast salt pan, called the Chott Djerid, and part of the Sahara Desert.

Northern Tunisia has a Mediterranean climate, with dry, sunny summers, and mild winters with a moderate rainfall. The average yearly rainfall decreases towards the south.

POLITICS & ECONOMY In 1881, France established a protectorate over Tunisia and ruled the country until 1956. The new parliament abolished the monarchy and declared Tunisia to be a republic in 1957, with the nationalist leader, Habib Bourguiba, as president. His government introduced many reforms, including votes for women, but various problems arose, including unemployment among the middle class and fears that Western values introduced by tourists might undermine Muslim values. In 1987, the prime minister Zine el Abidine Ben Ali removed Bourguiba and succeeded him as president. In 2002, the bombing of a synagogue on Djerba, believed to be the work of al Qaida, led to a major crackdown on dissidents.

The World Bank classifies Tunisia as a 'middle-income' developing country. The main resources and chief exports are phosphates and oil. Most industries are concerned with food processing. Agriculture employs 21% of the people; major crops being barley, dates, grapes, olives and wheat. Fishing is important, as is tourism.

AREA 163,610 sq km [63,170 sq mi] **POPULATION** 9,925,000
CAPITAL (POPULATION) Tunis (702,000) **GOVERNMENT** Multiparty republic **ETHNIC GROUPS** Arab 98%, European 1% **LANGUAGES** Arabic (official), French **RELIGIONS** Islam 98%, Christianity 1%, others **CURRENCY** Tunisian dinar = 1,000 millimes

TURKEY

GEOGRAPHY The Republic of Turkey lies in two continents. European Turkey, also called Thrace, lies west of a waterway linking the Mediterranean and Black seas. Most of Asian Turkey consists of plateaux and mountains, which rise to 5,165 m [16,945 ft] at Mount Ararat (Agri Dagi) near the border with Armenia. Earthquakes are common. Central Turkey has a dry climate, with hot, sunny summers and cold winters. The west has a Mediterranean climate, but the Black Sea coast has cooler summers.

POLITICS & ECONOMY In AD 330, the Roman empire moved its capital to Byzantium, which it renamed Constantinople. Constantinople became capital of the East Roman (or Byzantine) empire in 395. Muslim Seljuk Turks from central Asia invaded Anatolia in the 11th century. In the 14th century, another group of Turks, the Ottomans, conquered the area. In 1453, the Ottoman Turks took Constantinople, which they called Istanbul. The Ottomans built up a vast empire which finally collapsed during World War I (1914–18). Turkey became a republic in 1923. Its leader, Mustafa Kemal, or Atatürk ('father of the Turks') began to modernize and secularize the country.

Since the 1940s, Turkey has sought to strengthen its ties with Western powers. It joined NATO (North Atlantic Treaty Organization) in 1951 and it applied to join the European Economic Community in 1987. But Turkey's conflict with Greece, together with its invasion of northern Cyprus in 1974, have led many Europeans to treat Turkey's aspirations with caution. Political instability, military coups, conflict with Kurdish nationalists in eastern Turkey and concern about the country's record on human rights are other problems. Turkey has enjoyed democracy since 1983, though, in 1998, the government banned the Islamist Welfare Party, which it accused of violating secular principles. In 1999, the Muslim Virtue Party (successor to Islamist Welfare Party) lost ground. The largest numbers of parliamentary seats were won by the ruling Democratic Left Party and the far-right National Action Party. However, in the elections in 2002, the moderate Islamic Justice and Development Party (AKP) won 362 of the 500 seats in parliament, while none of the parties in the former ruling coalition won 10% of the vote. In 2003, Turkey opened its airspace to American aircraft during the Iraq war. Turkey hopes to join the European Union and, in 2003–4, it supported attempts to reunify Cyprus prior to that island's admission to the EU.

The World Bank classifies Turkey as a 'lower-middle-income' developing country. Agriculture employs 40% of the people, and barley, cotton, fruits, maize, tobacco and wheat are major crops. Livestock farming is important and wool is a leading product. Turkey produces chromium, but manufacturing is the chief activity. Manufactures include processed farm products and textiles, cars, fertilizers, iron and steel, machinery, metal products and paper products.

AREA 774,815 sq km [299,156 sq mi] **POPULATION** 68,109,000
CAPITAL (POPULATION) Ankara (2,984,000)
GOVERNMENT Multiparty republic **ETHNIC GROUPS** Turkish 80%, Kurdish 20% **LANGUAGES** Turkish (official), Kurdish, Arabic
RELIGIONS Islam (mainly Sunni Muslim) 99%
CURRENCY Turkish lira = 100 kurus

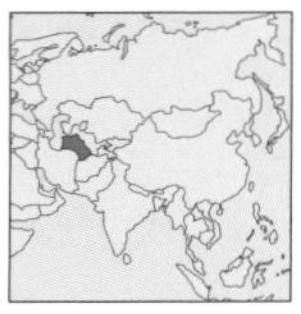

TURKMENISTAN

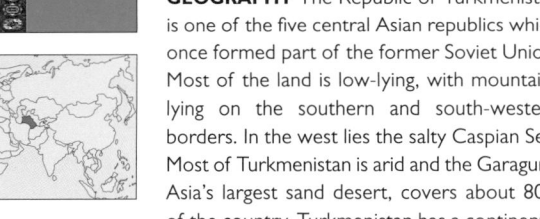

GEOGRAPHY The Republic of Turkmenistan is one of the five central Asian republics which once formed part of the former Soviet Union. Most of the land is low-lying, with mountains lying on the southern and south-western borders. In the west lies the salty Caspian Sea. Most of Turkmenistan is arid and the Garagum, Asia's largest sand desert, covers about 80% of the country. Turkmenistan has a continental climate, with average annual rainfall varying from 80 mm [3 in] in the desert to 300 mm [12 in] in the mountains. Summer months are hot, but winter temperatures drop well below freezing point.

POLITICS & ECONOMY Just over 1,000 years ago, Turkic people settled in the lands east of the Caspian Sea and the name 'Turkmen' comes from this time. Mongol armies conquered the area in the 13th century and Islam was introduced in the 14th century. Russia took over the area in the 1870s and 1880s. After the Russian Revolution of 1917, the area came under Communist rule and, in 1924, it became the Turkmen Soviet Socialist Republic. The Communists strictly controlled all aspects of life and discouraged religion. But they improved such services as education, health, housing and transport.

In the 1980s, when the Soviet Union began to introduce reforms, the Turkmen began to demand more freedom. In 1990, the Turkmen government stated that its laws overruled Soviet laws. In 1991, Turkmenistan became fully independent after the break-up of the Soviet Union. But the country kept ties with Russia through the Commonwealth of Independent States (CIS).

In 1992, Turkmenistan adopted a new constitution, allowing for the setting up of political parties, providing that they were not ethnic or religious in character. But, effectively, Turkmenistan remained a one-party state and, in 1992, Saparmurad Niyazov, the former Communist and now Democratic Party leader, was the only candidate. In 1994, a referendum prolonged Niyazov's term of office to 2002, while, in 1999, the parliament declared him president for life. In 2002, Niyazov survived an attempt on his life.

Faced with many economic problems, Turkmenistan began to look south rather than to the CIS for support. As part of this policy, it joined the Economic Co-operation Organization which had been set up in 1985 by Iran, Pakistan and Turkey. In 1996, the completion of a rail link from Turkmenistan to the Iranian coast was seen as a highly significant step for the future economic development of Central Asia.

Turkmenistan's chief resources are oil and natural gas, but the main activity is agriculture, with cotton, grown on irrigated land, as the main crop. Grain and vegetables are also important. Manufactures include cement, glass, petrochemicals and textiles.

AREA 488,100 SQ KM [188,455 SQ MI] **POPULATION** 4,776,000 **CAPITAL (POPULATION)** ASHKHABAD (521,000) **GOVERNMENT** SINGLE-PARTY REPUBLIC **ETHNIC GROUPS** TURKMEN 85%, UZBEK 5%, RUSSIAN 4% **LANGUAGES** TURKMEN (OFFICIAL), RUSSIAN, UZBEK **RELIGIONS** ISLAM 89%, EASTERN ORTHODOX 9% **CURRENCY** TURKMEN MANAT = 100 TENESI

TURKS AND CAICOS ISLANDS

The Turks and Caicos Islands, a British territory in the Caribbean since 1776, are a group of about 30 islands. Fishing and tourism are major activities.

AREA 430 SQ KM [166 SQ MI]
POPULATION 19,000 **CAPITAL** COCKBURN TOWN

TUVALU

Tuvalu, formerly called the Ellice Islands, was a British territory from the 1890s until it became independent in 1978. It consists of nine low-lying coral atolls in the southern Pacific Ocean. Copra is the chief export.

AREA 26 SQ KM [10 SQ MI]
POPULATION 11,000 **CAPITAL** FONGAFALE

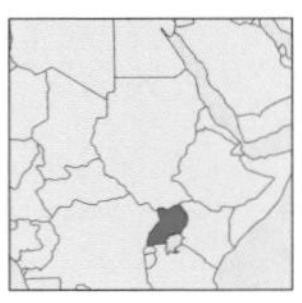

UGANDA

GEOGRAPHY The Republic of Uganda is a landlocked country on the East African plateau. It contains part of Lake Victoria, Africa's largest lake and a source of the River Nile, which occupies a shallow depression in the plateau.

The equator runs through Uganda and the country is warm throughout the year, though the high altitude moderates the temperature. The wettest regions are the lands to the north of Lake Victoria, where Kampala is situated, and the western mountains, especially the high Ruwenzori range.

POLITICS & ECONOMY Little is known of the early history of Uganda. When Europeans first reached the area in the 19th century, many of the people were organized in kingdoms, the most powerful of which was Buganda, the home of the Baganda people. Britain took over the country between 1894 and 1914, and ruled it until independence in 1962.

In 1967, Uganda became a republic and Buganda's Kabaka (king), Sir Edward Mutesa II, was made president. But tensions between the Kabaka and the prime minister, Apollo Milton Obote, led to the dismissal of the Kabaka in 1966. Obote also abolished the traditional kingdoms, including Buganda. Obote was overthrown in 1971 by an army group led by General Idi Amin Dada. Amin ruled as a dictator. He forced most of the Asians who lived in Uganda to leave the country and had many of his opponents killed.

In 1978, a border dispute between Uganda and Tanzania led Tanzanian troops to enter Uganda. With help from Ugandan opponents of Amin, they overthrew Amin's government. In 1980, Obote led his party to victory in national elections. But after charges of fraud, Obote's opponents began guerrilla warfare. A military group overthrew Obote in 1985, though strife continued until 1986, when Yoweri Museveni's National Resistance Movement seized power. In 1993, Museveni restored the traditional kingdoms, including Buganda where a new Kabaka was crowned. Museveni held elections in 1994 but political parties were not allowed. Museveni was elected president in 1996 and 2001. In 2003, the president announced that multiparty democracy would be restored, but he gave no date for the change.

The strife since the 1960s has greatly damaged the economy, but the economy grew during a period of stability in the 1990s. The situation worsened when Uganda intervened militarily in Congo (then Zaïre) in 1998. Agriculture dominates the economy, employing 80% of the people. The chief export is coffee.

AREA 241,038 SQ KM [93,065 SQ MI] **POPULATION** 25,633,000
CAPITAL (POPULATION) KAMPALA (774,000)
GOVERNMENT REPUBLIC IN TRANSITION
ETHNIC GROUPS BAGANDA 17%, ANKOLE 8%, BASOGO 8%, ITESO 8%, BAKIGA 7%, LANGI 6%, RWANDA 6%, BAGISU 5%, ACHOLI 4%, LUGBARA 4% AND OTHERS
LANGUAGES ENGLISH AND SWAHILI (BOTH OFFICIAL), GANDA
RELIGIONS ROMAN CATHOLIC 33%, PROTESTANT 33%, TRADITIONAL BELIEFS 18%, ISLAM 16%
CURRENCY UGANDAN SHILLING = 100 CENTS

UKRAINE

GEOGRAPHY Ukraine is the second largest country in Europe after Russia. It was formerly part of the Soviet Union, which split apart in 1991. This mostly flat country faces the Black Sea in the south. The Crimean peninsula includes a highland region overlooking Yalta. Ukraine has warm summers, but the winters are cold, becoming more severe from west to east. In the summer, the east of the country is often warmer than the west. The heaviest rainfall occurs in the summer.

POLITICS & ECONOMY Kiev was the original capital of the early Slavic civilization known as Kievan Rus. In the 17th and 18th centuries, parts of Ukraine came under Polish and Russian rule. But Russia gained most of Ukraine in the late 18th century. In 1918, Ukraine became independent, but in 1922 it became part of the Soviet Union. Millions of people died in the 1930s as a result of Soviet policies, while millions more died during the Nazi occupation (1941–4).

In the 1980s, Ukrainian people demanded more say over their affairs. The country became independent in 1991. Leonid Kuchma, who became president in 1994, came under fire in the early 2000s for maladministration and for his alleged involvement in the murder of a journalist. In 2003, Ukraine's Supreme Court ruled that Kuchma could not be prosecuted for crimes committed while in office and the Constitutional Court ruled that he could stand for a third term as president.

The World Bank classifies Ukraine as a 'lower-middle-income' economy. Agriculture is important. Crops include wheat and sugar beet, which are the major exports, together with barley, maize, potatoes, sunflowers and tobacco. Livestock rearing and fishing are also important industries.

Manufacturing is the chief economic activity. Major manufactures include iron and steel, machinery and vehicles. Ukraine has large coalfields. The country imports oil and natural gas, but it has hydroelectric and nuclear power stations. In 1986, an accident at the Chernobyl (Chornobyl) nuclear power plant caused widespread nuclear radiation. The plant was finally closed in 2001.

AREA 603,700 SQ KM [233,089 SQ MI] **POPULATION** 48,055,000
CAPITAL (POPULATION) KIEV (2,590,000)
GOVERNMENT MULTIPARTY REPUBLIC
ETHNIC GROUPS UKRAINIAN 78%, RUSSIAN 17%, BELARUSIAN, MOLDOVAN, BULGARIAN, HUNGARIAN, POLISH
LANGUAGES UKRAINIAN (OFFICIAL), RUSSIAN
RELIGIONS MOSTLY UKRAINIAN ORTHODOX
CURRENCY HRYVNIA = 100 KOPIYKAS

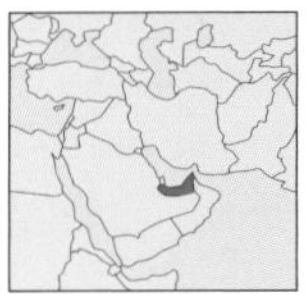

UNITED ARAB EMIRATES

The United Arab Emirates were formed in 1971 when the seven Trucial States of the Persian Gulf (Abu Dhabi, Dubai, Sharjah, Ajman, Umm al Qawayn, Ra's al Khaymah and Al Fujayrah) opted to join together and form an independent country. The economy of this hot and dry country depends on oil production, and oil revenues give the United Arab Emirates one of the highest per capita GNPs in Asia.

AREA 83,600 SQ KM [32,278 SQ MI] **POPULATION** 2,485,000
CAPITAL (POPULATION) ABU DHABI (363,000)

UNITED KINGDOM

GEOGRAPHY The United Kingdom (or UK) is a union of four countries. Three of them – England, Scotland and Wales – make up Great Britain. The fourth country is Northern Ireland. The Isle of Man and the Channel Islands, including Jersey and Guernsey, are not part of the UK. They are self-governing British dependencies.

The land is highly varied. Much of Scotland and Wales is mountainous, and the highest peak is Scotland's Ben Nevis at 1,343 m [4,406 ft]. England has some highland areas, including the Cumbrian Mountains (or Lake District) and the Pennine range in the north. But England also has large areas of fertile lowland. Northern Ireland is also a mixture of lowlands and uplands. It contains the UK's largest lake, Lough Neagh.

The UK has a mild climate, influenced by the warm Gulf Stream which flows across the Atlantic from the Gulf of Mexico, then past the British Isles. Moist winds from the south-west bring rain, but the rainfall decreases from west to east. Winds from the east and north bring cold weather in winter.

POLITICS & ECONOMY In ancient times, Britain was invaded by many peoples, including Iberians, Celts, Romans, Angles, Saxons, Jutes, Norsemen, Danes, and Normans, who arrived in 1066. The evolution of the United Kingdom spanned hundreds of years. The Normans finally overcame Welsh resistance in 1282, when King Edward I annexed Wales and united it with England. Union with Scotland was achieved by the Act of Union of 1707. This created a country known as the United Kingdom of Great Britain.

Ireland came under Norman rule in the 11th century, and much of its later history was concerned with a struggle against English domination. In 1801, Ireland became part of the United Kingdom of Great Britain and Ireland. But in 1921, southern Ireland broke away to become the Irish Free State. Most of the people in the Irish Free State were Roman Catholics. In Northern Ireland, where the majority of the people were Protestants, most people wanted to remain citizens of the United Kingdom. As a result, the country's official name changed to the United Kingdom of Great Britain and Northern Ireland.

The modern history of the UK began in the 18th century when the British empire began to develop, despite the loss in 1783 of its 13 North American colonies which became the core of the modern United States. The other major event occurred in the late 18th century, when the UK became the first country to industrialize its economy.

The British empire broke up after World War II (1939–45), though the UK still administers many small, mainly island, territories around the world. The empire was transformed into the Commonwealth of Nations, a free association of independent countries which numbered 54 in 2001.

The UK has retained an important world role. For example, in 2001, it played a prominent role in creating a broad alliance to counter international terrorism following the attacks on the United

States. It was also a prominent member of the coalition force which invaded Iraq in 2003. However, the UK has recognized that its economic future lies within Europe. It became a member of the European Economic Community (now the European Union) in 1973. In the early 21st century, most people accepted the importance of the EU to the UK's economic future. But some feared a loss of British identity should the EU ever evolve into a political federation.

The UK is a major industrial and trading nation. It lacks natural resources apart from coal, iron ore, oil and natural gas, and has to import most of the materials it needs for its industries. The UK also has to import food, because it produces only about two-thirds of the food it needs. In the first half of the 20th century, Britain was a major exporter of cars, ships, steel and textiles. But many industries have suffered from competition from other countries, with lower labour costs. Today, industries have to use high-technology in order to compete on the world market.

The UK is one of the world's most urbanized countries, and agriculture employs only 1% of the people. Production is high because of the use of scientific methods and modern machinery. However, in the early 21st century, especially following the outbreak of foot-and-mouth disease in 2001, questions were raised about the future of rural industries. Major crops include barley, potatoes, sugar beet and wheat. Sheep are the leading livestock, but beef and dairy cattle, pigs and poultry are also important. Fishing is another major activity and the UK is one of the largest fishing countries in the EU. Important catches include cod, haddock, plaice and mackerel.

Service industries play a major part in the UK's economy. Financial and insurance services bring in much-needed foreign exchange, while tourism has become a major earner.

AREA 241,857 sq km [93,381 sq mi] **POPULATION** 60,095,000
CAPITAL (POPULATION) London (8,089,000)
GOVERNMENT Constitutional monarchy
ETHNIC GROUPS English 82%, Scottish 10%, Irish 2%, Welsh 2%, Ulster 2%, West Indian, Indian, Pakistani and others **LANGUAGES** English (official), Welsh, Gaelic
RELIGIONS Christianity (Anglican, Roman Catholic, Presbyterian, Methodist), Islam, Sikhism, Hinduism, Judaism
CURRENCY Pound sterling = 100 pence

UNITED STATES OF AMERICA

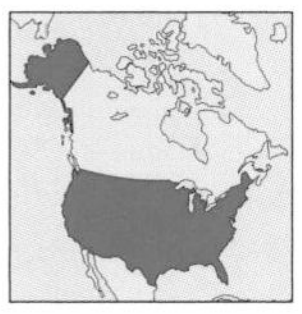

GEOGRAPHY The United States of America is the world's fourth largest country in area and the third largest in population. It contains 50 states, 48 of which lie between Canada and Mexico, plus Alaska in north-western North America, and Hawaii, a group of volcanic islands in the North Pacific Ocean. Densely populated coastal plains lie to the east and south of the Appalachian Mountains. The central lowlands drained by the Mississippi–Missouri rivers stretch from the Appalachians to the Rocky Mountains in the west. The Pacific region contains fertile valleys, separated by mountain ranges.

The climate varies greatly, ranging from the Arctic cold of Alaska to the intense heat of Death Valley, a bleak desert in California. Of the 48 states between Canada and Mexico, winters are cold and snowy in the north, but mild in the south, a region which is often called the 'Sun Belt'.

POLITICS & ECONOMY The first people in North America, the ancestors of the Native Americans (or American Indians) arrived perhaps 40,000 years ago from Asia. Although Vikings probably reached North America 1,000 years ago, European exploration proper did not begin until the late 15th century.

The first Europeans to settle in large numbers were the British, who founded settlements on the eastern coast in the early 17th century. British rule ended in the War of ndependence (1775–83). The country expanded in 1803 when a vast territory in the south and west was acquired through the Louisiana Purchase, while the border with Mexico was fixed in the mid-19th century. The Civil War (1861–5) ended slavery and the serious threat that the nation might split into two parts. In the late 19th century, the West was opened up, while immigrants flooded in from Europe and elsewhere.

During the late 19th and early 20th centuries, industrialization led to the United States becoming the world's leading economic superpower and a pioneer in science and technology. It took on the mantle of the champion of Western democracy and, following the break-up of the former Soviet Union, it became the world's only superpower. But the attacks on the country on 11 September 2001 revealed its vulnerability to terrorists and rogue states. The response was vigorous. In 2001, it attacked the Taliban government in Afghanistan, which was protecting al Qaida terrorists. Then, in 2003, it led a coalition force to invade Iraq and overthrow the repressive regime of Saddam Hussein. However, it met with considerable resistance even after the capture of Saddam Hussein in December 2003.

The United States has the world's largest economy in terms of the total value of its production. Although agriculture employs only about 2% of the people, farming is highly mechanized and scientific, and the United States leads the world in farm production. Major products include beef and dairy cattle, together with such crops as cotton, fruits, groundnuts, maize, potatoes, soybeans, tobacco and wheat.

The country's natural resources include oil, natural gas and coal. There are also a wide range of metal ores which are used in manufacturing industries, together with timber, especially from the forests of the Pacific north-west. Manufacturing is the single most important activity, employing about 14% of the population. Major products include vehicles, food products, chemicals, machinery, printed goods, metal products and scientific instruments. California is now the leading manufacturing state. Many southern states, petroleum rich and climatically favoured, have also become highly prosperous in recent years.

AREA 9,629,091 sq km [3,717,792 sq mi] **POPULATION** 290,343,000
CAPITAL (POPULATION) Washington, DC (572,000)
GOVERNMENT Federal republic
ETHNIC GROUPS White 77%, African American 13%, Asian 4%, Amerindian 2%, others **LANGUAGES** English (official), Spanish, more than 30 others **RELIGIONS** Protestant 56%, Roman Catholic 28%, Islam 2%, Judaism 2%
CURRENCY US dollar = 100 cents

URUGUAY

GEOGRAPHY Uruguay is South America's second smallest independent country after Suriname. The land consists mainly of flat plains and hills. The River Uruguay, which forms the country's western border, flows into the Río de la Plata, a large estuary which leads into the South Atlantic Ocean.

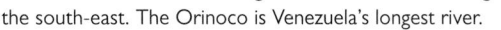

Uruguay has a mild climate, with rain in every month, though droughts sometimes occur. Summers are pleasantly warm, especially near the coast. The weather remains relatively mild throughout the winter.

POLITICS & ECONOMY In 1726, Spanish settlers founded Montevideo in order to halt the Portuguese gaining influence in the area. By the late 18th century, Spaniards had settled in most of the country. Uruguay became part of a colony called the Vice-royalty of La Plata, which also included Argentina, Paraguay, and parts of Bolivia, Brazil and Chile. In 1820 Brazil annexed Uruguay, ending Spanish rule. In 1825, Uruguayans, supported by Argentina, began a struggle for independence. Finally, in 1828, Brazil and Argentina recognized Uruguay as an independent republic. Social and economic developments were slow in the 19th century, but, from 1903, Uruguay became stable and democratic.

From the 1950s, economic problems caused unrest. Terrorist groups, notably the Tupumaros, carried out murders and kidnappings. The army crushed the Tupumaros in 1972, but the army took over the government in 1973. Military rule continued until 1984 when elections were held. In the early 21st century, Uruguay faced many economic problems, many of which were the result of the economic crisis in its neighbour, Argentina, and its imposition of banking controls.

The World Bank classifies Uruguay as an 'upper-middle-income' developing country. Agriculture employs only 4% of the people, but farm products, notably hides and leather goods, beef and wool, are the leading exports, while the leading manufacturing industries process farm products. The main crops include maize, potatoes, wheat and sugar beet. Uruguay depends largely on hydroelectric power for energy and exports electricity to Argentina.

AREA 175,016 sq km [67,574 sq mi] **POPULATION** 3,413,000
CAPITAL (POPULATION) Montevideo (1,303,000)
GOVERNMENT Multiparty republic
ETHNIC GROUPS White 88%, Mestizo 8%, Mulatto or Black 4%
LANGUAGES Spanish (official)
RELIGIONS Roman Catholic 66%, Protestant 2%, Judaism 1%
CURRENCY Uruguayan peso = 100 centésimos

UZBEKISTAN

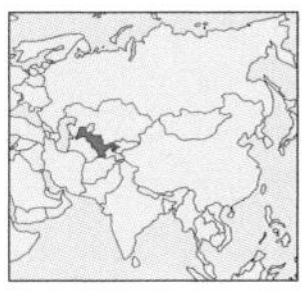

GEOGRAPHY The Republic of Uzbekistan is one of the five republics in Central Asia which were once part of the Soviet Union. Plains cover most of western Uzbekistan, with highlands in the east. The main rivers, the Amu (or Amu Darya) and Syr (or Syr Darya), drain into the Aral Sea. So much water has been taken from these rivers to irrigate the land that the Aral Sea has now shrunk to about a quarter of its size in 1960. The dried-up lake area has become desert, like much of the rest of the country. Uzbekistan has a continental climate with cold winters and hot summers. The west is extremely arid, with an average annual rainfall of about 200 mm [8 in].

POLITICS & ECONOMY Russia took the area in the 19th century. After the Russian Revolution of 1917, the Communists took over and, in 1924, they set up the Uzbek Soviet Socialist Republic. Under Communism, all aspects of Uzbek life were controlled and religious worship was discouraged. But education, health, housing and transport were improved. In the late 1980s, the people demanded more freedom and, in 1990, the government stated that its laws overruled those of the Soviet Union. Uzbekistan became independent in 1991 when the Soviet Union broke up, but it retained links with Russia through the Commonwealth of Independent States. Islam Karimov, leader of the People's Democratic Party (formerly the Communist Party), was elected president in December 1991. In 1992–3, many opposition leaders were arrested because the government said that they threatened national stability. In 1994–5, the PDP was victorious in national elections and, in 1995, a referendum extended Karimov's term in office until 2000, when he was again re-elected. In 2001, Karimov declared his support for the United States in combating terrorist bases in Afghanistan. But, in 2004, the United States criticized Uzbekistan for its suppression of democracy and human rights abuses.

The World Bank classifies Uzbekistan as a 'lower-middle-income' developing country and the government still controls most economic activity. The country produces coal, copper, gold, oil and natural gas.

AREA 447,400 sq km [172,741 sq mi] **POPULATION** 25,982,000
CAPITAL (POPULATION) Tashkent (2,143,000)
GOVERNMENT Socialist republic **ETHNIC GROUPS** Uzbek 80%, Russian 5%, Tajik 5%, Kazakh 3%, Tatar 2%, Kara-Kalpak 2%
LANGUAGES Uzbek (official), Russian **RELIGIONS** Islam 88%, Eastern Orthodox 9% **CURRENCY** Uzbekistani sum = 100 tiyin

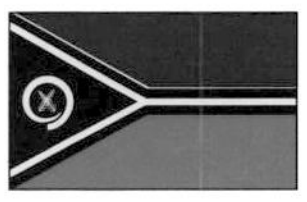

VANUATU

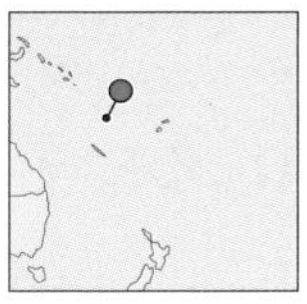

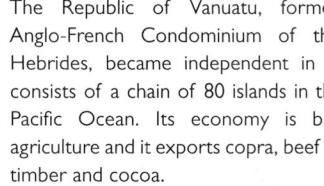

The Republic of Vanuatu, formerly the Anglo-French Condominium of the New Hebrides, became independent in 1980. It consists of a chain of 80 islands in the South Pacific Ocean. Its economy is based on agriculture and it exports copra, beef and veal, timber and cocoa.

AREA 12,189 sq km [4,706 sq mi]
POPULATION 199,000 **CAPITAL** Port-Vila

VATICAN CITY

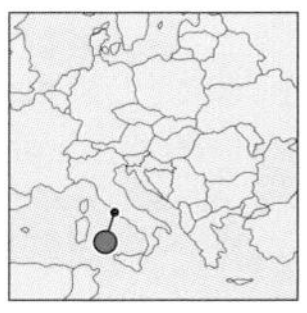

Vatican City State, the world's smallest independent nation, is an enclave on the west bank of the River Tiber in Rome. It forms an independent base for the Holy See, the governing body of the Roman Catholic Church.

AREA 0.44 sq km [0.17 sq mi]
POPULATION 1,000

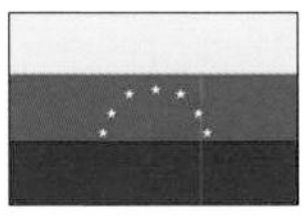

VENEZUELA

GEOGRAPHY The Bolivarian Republic of Venezuela, in northern South America, contains the Maracaibo lowlands around the oil-rich Lake Maracaibo in the west. Andean ranges enclose the lowlands and extend across most of northern Venezuela. The Orinoco river basin, containing tropical grasslands called *llanos*, lies between the northern highlands and the Guiana Highlands in the south-east. The Orinoco is Venezuela's longest river.

Venezuela has a tropical climate. Temperatures are high

throughout the year on the lowlands, though the mountains are much cooler. The rainfall is heaviest in the mountains. But much of the country has a marked dry season between December and April.

POLITICS & ECONOMY In the early 19th century, Venezuelans, such as Simón Bolívar and Francisco de Miranda, began a struggle against Spanish rule. Venezuela declared its independence in 1811. But it only became truly independent in 1821, when the Spanish were defeated in a battle near Valencia.

The development of Venezuela in the 19th and the first half of the 20th centuries was marred by instability, violence and periods of harsh dictatorial rule. But Venezuela has had elected governments since 1958. The country has greatly benefited from its oil resources which were first exploited in 1917. In 1960, Venezuela helped to form OPEC (the Organization of Petroleum Exporting Countries) and, in 1976, the government of Venezuela took control of the entire oil industry. In 1999, Hugo Chavez, who had staged an unsuccessful coup in 1992, was elected president. Chavez survived an attempted coup in April 2002 and a crippling general strike staged by his opponents between December 2002 and February 2003.

The World Bank classifies Venezuela as an 'upper-middle-income' developing country. Oil accounts for 80% of the exports. Other exports include bauxite and aluminium, iron ore and farm products. Agriculture employs 9% of people and cattle ranching is important; dairy cattle and poultry are also raised. Major crops include bananas, cassava, citrus fruits, coffee and rice. The chief industry is petroleum refining. Other manufactures include aluminium, cement, processed food, steel and textiles.

AREA 912,050 sq km [352,143 sq mi] **POPULATION** 24,655,000
CAPITAL (POPULATION) Caracas (1,823,000) **GOVERNMENT** Federal republic **ETHNIC GROUPS** Spanish, Italian, Portuguese, Arab, German, African, indigenous people **LANGUAGES** Spanish (official), indigenous dialects **RELIGIONS** Roman Catholic 96%
CURRENCY Bolívar = 100 céntimos

VIETNAM

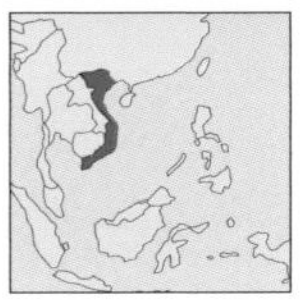

GEOGRAPHY The Socialist Republic of Vietnam occupies an S-shaped strip of land facing the South China Sea in South-east Asia. The coastal plains include two densely populated, fertile delta regions: the Red (Hong) delta facing the Gulf of Tonkin in the north, and the Mekong delta in the south.

Vietnam has a tropical climate, though the driest months of January to March are a little cooler than the wet, hot summer months, when monsoon winds blow from the south-west. Typhoons (cyclones or hurricanes) sometimes hit the coast, causing extensive flooding and much damage.

POLITICS & ECONOMY China dominated Vietnam for a thousand years before AD 939, when a Vietnamese state was founded. The French took over the area between the 1850s and 1880s. They ruled Vietnam as part of French Indo-China, which also included Cambodia and Laos.

Japan conquered Vietnam during World War II (1939–45). In 1946, war broke out between a nationalist group, called the Vietminh, and the French colonial government. France withdrew in 1954 and Vietnam was divided into a Communist North Vietnam, led by the Vietminh leader, Ho Chi Minh, and a non-Communist South.

A force called the Viet Cong rebelled against South Vietnam's government in 1957 and a war began, which gradually increased in intensity. The United States aided the South, but after it withdrew in 1975, South Vietnam surrendered. In 1976, the united Vietnam became a Socialist Republic.

Vietnamese troops intervened in Cambodia in 1978 to defeat the Communist Khmer Rouge government, but it withdrew its troops in 1989. In the 1990s, Vietnam began to introduce reforms. In 1995, the United States opened an embassy in Hanoi and, in 2000, a major trade pact was agreed by the countries.

The World Bank classifies Vietnam as a 'low-income' developing country and agriculture employs 67% of the population. The main food crop is rice. The country also produces chromium, oil (which was discovered off the south coast in 1986), phosphates and tin.

AREA 331,689 sq km [128,065 sq mi] **POPULATION** 81,625,000
CAPITAL (POPULATION) Hanoi (1,074,000)
GOVERNMENT Socialist republic
ETHNIC GROUPS Vietnamese 87%, Chinese, Hmong, Thai, Khmer, Cham, mountain groups **LANGUAGES** Vietnamese (official), English, Chinese **RELIGIONS** Buddhism, Christianity, indigenous beliefs
CURRENCY Dong = 10 hao = 100 xu

VIRGIN ISLANDS, BRITISH

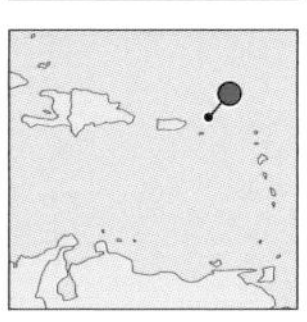

The British Virgin Islands, the most northerly of the Lesser Antilles, are a British overseas territory, with a substantial measure of self-government.

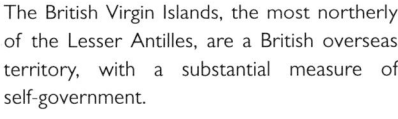

AREA 151 sq km [58 sq mi]
POPULATION 22,000 **CAPITAL** Road Town

VIRGIN ISLANDS, US

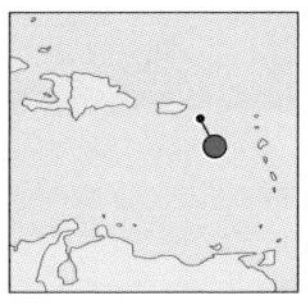

The Virgin Islands of the United States, a group of three islands and 65 small islets, are a self-governing US territory. Purchased from Denmark in 1917, its residents are US citizens and they elect a non-voting delegate to the US House of Representatives.

AREA 347 sq km [134 sq mi]
POPULATION 125,000 **CAPITAL** Charlotte Amalie

WALLIS AND FUTUNA

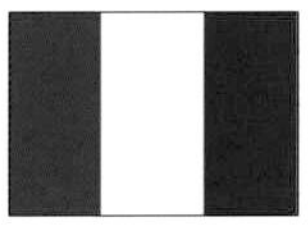

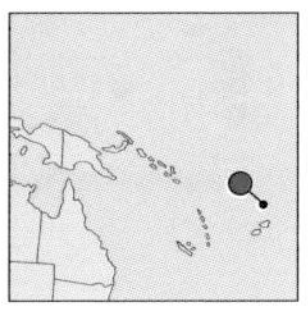

Wallis and Futuna, in the South Pacific Ocean, is the smallest and the poorest of France's overseas territories. French aid remains vital to an economy based on subsistence agriculture.

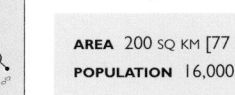

AREA 200 sq km [77 sq mi]
POPULATION 16,000 **CAPITAL** Mata-Utu

YEMEN

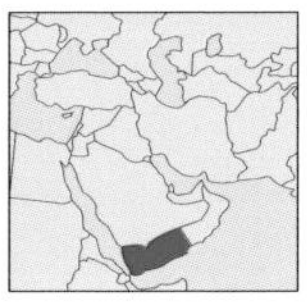

GEOGRAPHY The Republic of Yemen faces the Red Sea and the Gulf of Aden in the south-western corner of the Arabian peninsula. Behind the narrow coastal plain along the Red Sea, the land rises to a mountain region called High Yemen. The climate ranges from hot and often humid conditions on the coast to the cooler highlands. Most of the country is arid. The south coasts are particularly hot and humid.

POLITICS & ECONOMY After World War I, northern Yemen, which had been ruled by Turkey, began to evolve into a separate state from the south, where Britain was in control. Britain withdrew in 1967 and a left-wing government took power in the south. In North Yemen, the monarchy was abolished in 1962 and the country became a republic.

Clashes occurred between the traditionalist Yemen Arab Republic in the north and the formerly British Marxist People's Democratic Republic of Yemen but, in 1990, the two Yemens merged to form a single country. Further conflict occurred in 1994, when southern secessionist forces were defeated. In 1998 and 1999, militants in the Aden-Abyan Islamic army sought to destabilize the country. In 2000, suicide bombers, thought to be part of the al Qaida network, steered a craft into a US destroyer in Aden harbour, killing 17 sailors, while, in 2002, three American missionaries were shot in a hospital in the south.

The World Bank classifies Yemen as a 'low-income' developing country. Agriculture employs up to 50% of the people. Herders raise sheep and other animals, while farmers grow such crops as barley, fruits, wheat and vegetables in highland valleys and around oases. Cash crops include coffee and cotton.

Imported oil is refined at Aden and petroleum extraction began in the north-west in the 1980s. Handicrafts, leather goods and textiles are manufactured. Remittances from Yemenis abroad are a major source of revenue.

AREA 527,968 sq km [203,848 sq mi] **POPULATION** 19,350,000
CAPITAL (POPULATION) Sana' (954,000) **GOVERNMENT** Multiparty republic **ETHNIC GROUPS** Predominantly Arab **LANGUAGES** Arabic (official) **RELIGIONS** Islam **CURRENCY** Yemeni rial = 100 fils

ZAMBIA

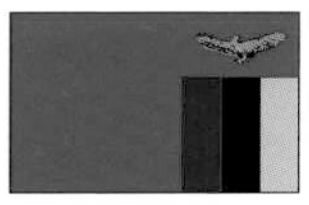

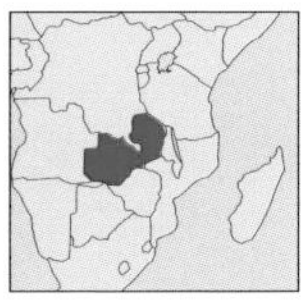

GEOGRAPHY The Republic of Zambia is a landlocked country in southern Africa. Zambia lies on the plateau that makes up most of southern Africa. Much of the land is between 900 m and 1,500 m [2,950 ft to 4,920 ft] above sea level. The Muchinga Mountains in the north-east rise above this flat land. Lakes include Bangweulu, which is entirely within Zambia, together with parts of lakes Mweru and Tanganyika in the north. Zambia lies in the tropics, but temperatures are moderated by the altitude.

POLITICS & ECONOMY European contact with Zambia began in the 19th century, when the explorer David Livingstone crossed the River Zambezi. In the 1890s, the British South Africa Company, set up by Cecil Rhodes (1853–1902), the British financier and statesman, made treaties with local chiefs and gradually took over the area. In 1911, the Company named the area Northern Rhodesia. In 1924, Britain took over the government of the country.

In 1953, Britain formed a federation of Northern Rhodesia, Southern Rhodesia (now Zimbabwe) and Nyasaland (now Malawi). Because of African opposition, the federation was dissolved in 1963 and Northern Rhodesia became independent as Zambia in 1964. Kenneth Kaunda became president and one-party rule was introduced in 1972. However, a new constitution was adopted in 1990 and, in 1991, Kaunda's party was defeated and Frederick Chiluba became president. Chiluba was re-elected in 1996. Chiluba stood down in 2001 and his party's candidate, Levy Mwanawasa, was elected president.

Copper, the main resource, accounted for 55% of the exports in 2001. Zambia also produces cobalt, lead, zinc and gemstones. Agriculture employs 69% of the people, as compared with 4% in industry and mining. Food crops include cassava, fruits and vegetables, maize, millet and sorghum, while cash crops include coffee, sugar cane and tobacco.

AREA 752,618 sq km [290,586 sq mi] **POPULATION** 10,307,000
CAPITAL (POPULATION) Lusaka (1,270,000)
GOVERNMENT Multiparty republic **ETHNIC GROUPS** Native African (Bemba, Tonga, Maravi/Nyanja) **LANGUAGES** English (official), Bemba, Kaonda, Nyanja and about 70 others **RELIGIONS** Christianity 70%, Islam, Hinduism **CURRENCY** Zambian kwacha = 100 ngwee

ZIMBABWE

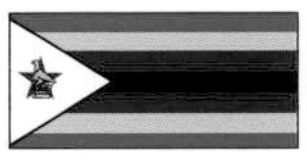

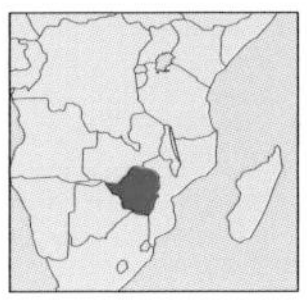

GEOGRAPHY The Republic of Zimbabwe is a landlocked country in southern Africa. Most of the country lies on a high plateau between the Zambezi and Limpopo rivers between 900 m and 1,500 m [2,950 ft to 4,920 ft] above sea level. From October to March, the weather is hot and wet, but in the winter, daily temperatures can vary greatly.

POLITICS & ECONOMY The Shona people became dominant in the region about 1,000 years ago. The British South Africa Company, under the statesman Cecil Rhodes (1853–1902), occupied the area in the 1890s, after obtaining mineral rights from local chiefs. The area was named Rhodesia and later Southern Rhodesia. It became a self-governing British colony in 1923. Between 1953 and 1963, Southern and Northern Rhodesia (now Zambia) were joined to Nyasaland (Malawi) in the Central African Federation.

In 1965, the European government of Southern Rhodesia (then called Rhodesia) declared their country independent but Britain refused to accept this. Finally, after a civil war, the country became legally independent in 1980, though rivalries between the Shona and Ndebele people threatened stability. Order was restored when the Shona prime minister, Robert Mugabe, brought his Ndebele rivals into his government. In 1987, Mugabe became the country's executive president and, in 1991, the government renounced its Marxist ideology. Mugabe was re-elected president in 1990 and 1996. During the late 1990s, Mugabe threatened to seize white-owned farms without paying compensation to the owners. Despite international pressure, landless 'war veterans' began to occupy white farms. The situation worsened in the early 2000s, resulting in violence and murder. In 2002, Mugabe was re-elected president amid accusations of electoral irregularities. The Commonwealth suspended Zimbabwe's membership for 12 months. However, in 2003, violence against Mugabe's opponents continued and, in 2004, the European Union renewed its sanctions against the country.

The World Bank classifies Zimbabwe as a 'low-income' developing country. The country has valuable mineral resources and mining accounts for a fifth of the country's exports. Agriculture employs 26% of working people. Maize is the chief food crop, while cash crops include cotton, sugar and tobacco. Cattle ranching is another important activity.

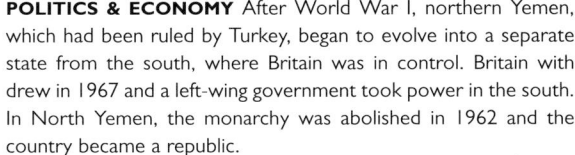

AREA 390,757 sq km [150,871 sq mi] **POPULATION** 12,577,000
CAPITAL (POPULATION) Harare (1,189,000)
GOVERNMENT Multiparty republic **ETHNIC GROUPS** Shona 82%, Ndebele 14%, other African groups 2%, mixed and Asian 1%
LANGUAGES English (official), Shona, Ndebele
RELIGIONS Christianity, traditional beliefs
CURRENCY Zimbabwean dollar = 100 cents

Introduction to World Geography

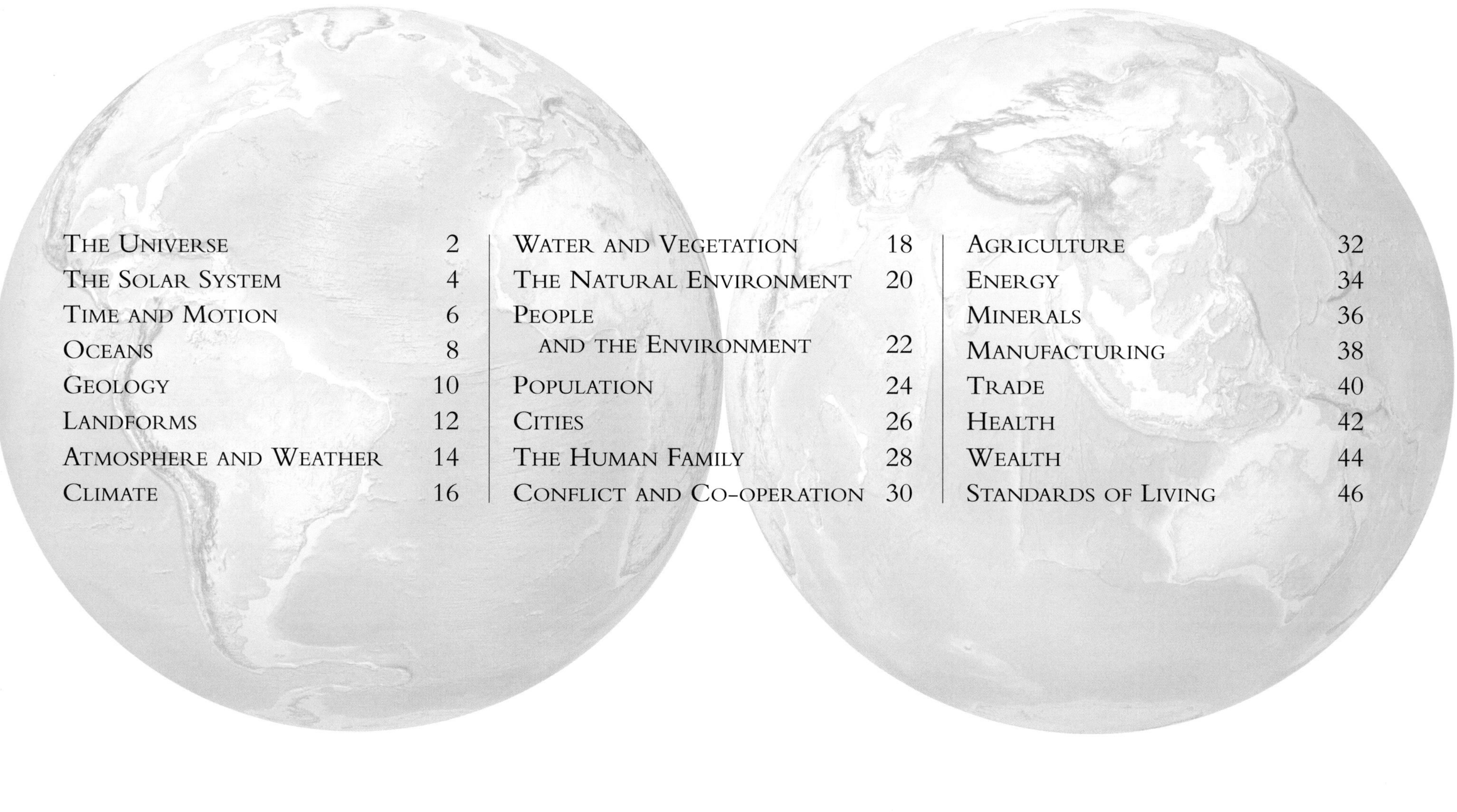

The Universe	2
The Solar System	4
Time and Motion	6
Oceans	8
Geology	10
Landforms	12
Atmosphere and Weather	14
Climate	16
Water and Vegetation	18
The Natural Environment	20
People and the Environment	22
Population	24
Cities	26
The Human Family	28
Conflict and Co-operation	30
Agriculture	32
Energy	34
Minerals	36
Manufacturing	38
Trade	40
Health	42
Wealth	44
Standards of Living	46

THE UNIVERSE

For more information:
4 Orbits of the planets
Planetary data

About 13.7 billion years ago, time and space began with the most colossal explosion in cosmic history: the so-called 'Big Bang' that is believed to have initiated the Universe. According to current theory, in the first millionth of a second of its existence it expanded from a dimensionless point of infinite mass and density into a fireball about 30 billion kilometres across – and it has been expanding ever since.

It took almost a million years for the primal fireball to cool enough for atoms to form. They were mostly hydrogen, still the most abundant material in the Universe. But the new matter was not evenly distributed around the young Universe, and a few billion years later atoms in relatively dense regions began to cling together under the influence of gravity, forming distinct masses of gas separated by vast expanses of empty space. To begin with, these first proto-galaxies were dark places: the Universe had cooled. But gravitational attraction continued, condensing matter into coherent lumps inside the galactic gas clouds. About 3 billion years later, some of these masses had contracted so much that internal pressure produced the high temperatures necessary to bring about nuclear fusion: the first stars were born.

There were several generations of stars, each feeding on the wreckage of its extinct predecessors as well as the original galactic gas swirls. With each new generation, progressively larger atoms were forged in stellar furnaces and the galaxy's range of elements, once restricted to hydrogen, grew larger. About 9 billion years after the Big Bang, a star formed on the outskirts of our galaxy with enough matter left over to create a retinue of planets. Nearly 5 billion years after that, human beings evolved.

The Sun is one of more than 100 billion stars in the home galaxy alone. Our galaxy, in turn, forms part of a local group of approximately 30 similar structures, some much larger than our own; there are at least 100 billion other galaxies in the Universe as a whole. The most distant ever observed, a highly energetic galactic core designated as quasar RD J030117+002025, lies about 13 billion light-years away.

LIFE OF A STAR

For most of its existence, a star produces energy by the nuclear fusion of hydrogen into helium at its core. The duration of this hydrogen-burning period – known as the *main sequence* – depends on the star's mass; the greater the mass, the higher the core temperatures and the sooner the star's supply of hydrogen is exhausted. Dim, dwarf stars consume their hydrogen slowly, eking it out over 1,000 billion years or more. The Sun, like other stars of its mass, should spend about 10 billion years on the main sequence; since it was formed less than 5 billion years ago, it still has half its life left.

Once all a star's core hydrogen has been fused into helium, nuclear activity moves outwards into layers of unconsumed hydrogen. For a time, energy production sharply increases: the star grows hotter and expands enormously, turning into a so-called red giant. Its energy output will increase a thousandfold, and it will swell to a hundred times its present diameter.

After a few hundred million years, helium in the core will become sufficiently compressed to initiate a new cycle of nuclear fusion: from helium to carbon. The star will contract somewhat, before beginning its last expansion, in the Sun's case engulfing the Earth and perhaps Mars. In this bloated condition, the Sun's outer layers will break off into space, leaving a tiny inner core, mainly of carbon, that shrinks progressively under the force of its own gravity: dwarf stars can attain a density more than 10,000 times that of normal matter, with crushing surface gravities to match. Gradually, the nuclear fires will die down, and the Sun will reach its terminal stage: a black dwarf, emitting insignificant amounts of energy.

Black holes

However, stars more massive than the Sun may undergo another transformation. The additional mass allows gravitational collapse to continue indefinitely: eventually, all the star's remaining matter shrinks to a point, and its density approaches infinity – a state that will not permit even subatomic structures to survive.

The star has become a *black hole*: an anomalous 'singularity' in the fabric of space and time. Although vast coruscations of radiation will be emitted by any matter falling into its grasp, the singularity itself has an escape velocity that exceeds the speed of light, and nothing can ever be released from it. Within the boundaries of the black hole, the laws of physics are suspended, but no physicist can ever observe the extraordinary events that may occur.

GALACTIC STRUCTURES

▲ M51, the Whirlpool Nebula, comprises the large spiral galaxy NGC5194 and its smaller, barred companion NGC5195. M51 was the first astronomical object in which a spiral structure was identified, in 1845. Although smaller and less massive than our own Galaxy, M51 is much brighter, due to recent star formation.

Many of the Universe's 100 billion galaxies show clear structural patterns, originally classified by the American astronomer Edwin Hubble in 1925. Spiral galaxies like our own have a central, almost spherical bulge and a surrounding disk composed of spiral arms. Barred spirals have a central bar of stars across the nucleus, with spiral arms trailing from the ends of the bar. Elliptical galaxies have a uniform appearance, ranging from a flattened disk to a near sphere. Most galaxies, however, have no obvious structure at all. Galaxies also vary enormously in size, from dwarf galaxies only 2,000 light-years across to great assemblies of stars 80 or more times larger.

THE HOME GALAXY

The Sun and its planets are located in one of the spiral arms of the Galaxy, a little less than 28,000 light-years from the galactic centre and orbiting around it in a period of 200 million years. The centre is invisible from the Earth, masked by vast, light-absorbing clouds of interstellar dust.

The Galaxy is probably around 12 billion years old and, like other spiral galaxies, has three distinct regions. The central bulge is about 30,000 light-years in diameter. The disk in which the Sun is located is not much more than 1,000 light-years thick, but approximately 100,000 light-years from end to end. Around the Galaxy is the halo, a spherical zone 300,000 light-years across, studded with globular star clusters and sprinkled with individual suns.

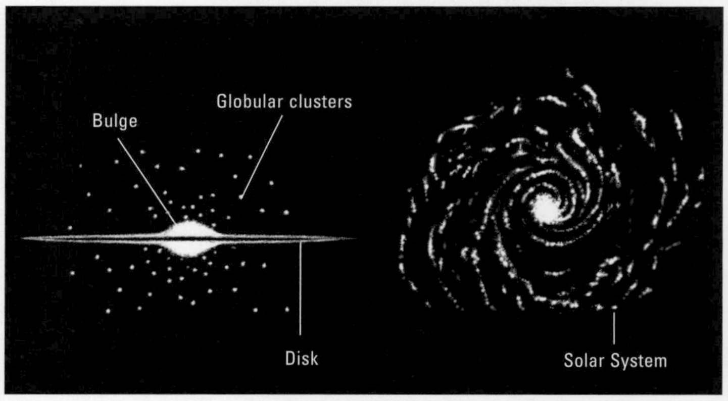

THE END OF THE UNIVERSE

The likely fate of the Universe is disputed. One theory (*top of diagram, below*) dictates that the expansion begun at the time of the Big Bang will continue 'indefinitely', with ageing galaxies moving further and further apart in an immense, dark graveyard.

Alternatively, gravity may overcome the expansion (*bottom of diagram*). Galaxies will fall back together until everything is again concentrated at a single point, followed by a new Big Bang and a new expansion, in an endlessly repeated cycle.

The first theory is supported by the amount of visible matter in the Universe; the second theory assumes that there is enough dark material in the Universe to bring about the gravitational collapse.

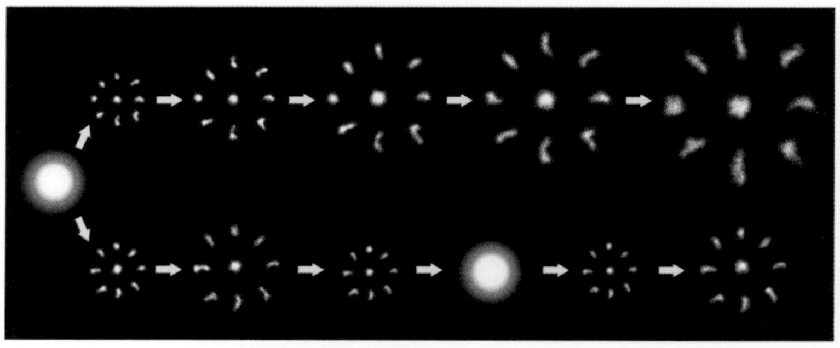

THE NEAREST STARS

The 22 nearest stars, excluding the Sun, with their distance from Earth in light-years*

Proxima Centauri	4.25	UV Ceti A	8.7	Epsilon Indi	11.2
Alpha Centauri A	4.3	UV Ceti B	8.7	Groombridge 34A	11.2
Alpha Centauri B	4.3	Ross 154	9.4	Groombridge 34B	11.2
Barnard's Star	6.0	Ross 248	10.3	L789-6	11.2
Wolf 359	7.8	Epsilon Eridani	10.7	Procyon A	11.4
Lalande 21185	8.3	Ross 128	10.9	Procyon B	11.4
Sirius A	8.7	61 Cygni A	11.1		
Sirius B	8.7	61 Cygni B	11.1		

Many of the nearest stars, like Alpha Centauri A and B, are double stars, orbiting about their common centre of gravity and to all intents and purposes equidistant from Earth. Many of them are dim objects, with no name other than the designation given to them by the astronomers who first investigated them. However, they include Sirius, the brightest star in the sky, and Procyon, the seventh brightest. Both are far larger than the Sun; of the nearest stars, only Epsilon Eridani is similar in size and luminosity.

* A light-year equals approximately 9,500,000,000,000 kilometres

NORTHERN HEAVENS

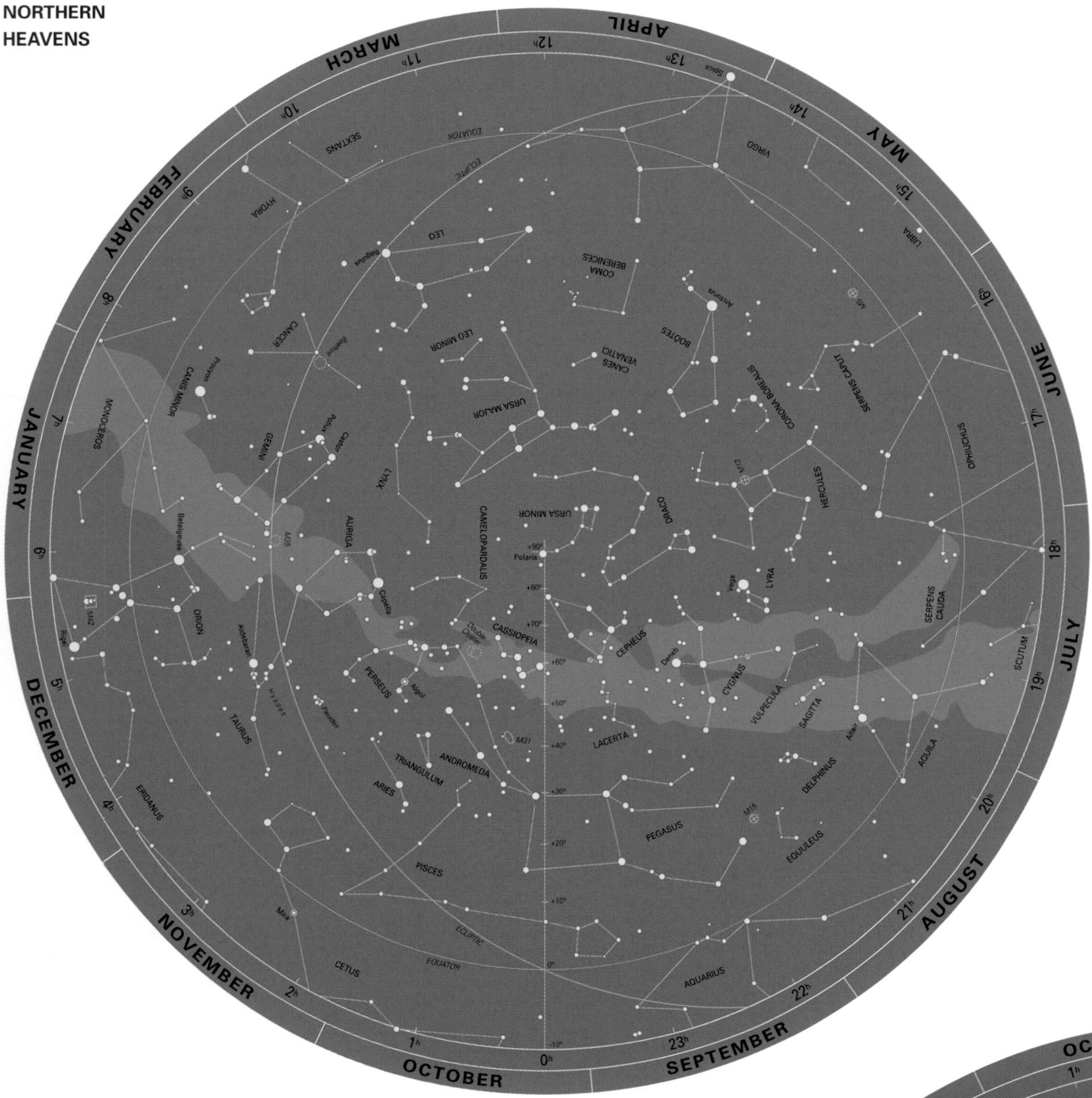

THE CONSTELLATIONS

The constellations and their English names

Andromeda	Andromeda	Lacerta	Lizard
Antlia	Air Pump	Leo	Lion
Apus	Bird of Paradise	Leo Minor	Little Lion
Aquarius	Water Carrier	Lepus	Hare
Aquila	Eagle	Libra	Scales
Ara	Altar	Lupus	Wolf
Aries	Ram	Lynx	Lynx
Auriga	Charioteer	Lyra	Lyre
Boötes	Herdsman	Mensa	Table
Caelum	Chisel	Microscopium	Microscope
Camelopardalis	Giraffe	Monoceros	Unicorn
Cancer	Crab	Musca	Fly
Canes Venatici	Hunting Dogs	Norma	Level
Canis Major	Great Dog	Octans	Octant
Canis Minor	Little Dog	Ophiuchus	Serpent Bearer
Capricornus	Goat	Orion	Orion
Carina	Keel	Pavo	Peacock
Cassiopeia	Cassiopeia	Pegasus	Winged Horse
Centaurus	Centaur	Perseus	Perseus
Cepheus	Cepheus	Phoenix	Phoenix
Cetus	Whale	Pictor	Easel
Chamaeleon	Chameleon	Pisces	Fishes
Circinus	Compasses	Piscis Austrinus	Southern Fish
Columba	Dove	Puppis	Ship's Stern
Coma Berenices	Berenice's Hair	Pyxis	Mariner's Compass
Corona Australis	Southern Crown	Reticulum	Net
Corona Borealis	Northern Crown	Sagitta	Arrow
Corvus	Crow	Sagittarius	Archer
Crater	Cup	Scorpius	Scorpion
Crux	Southern Cross	Sculptor	Sculptor
Cygnus	Swan	Scutum	Shield
Delphinus	Dolphin	Serpens	Serpent
Dorado	Swordfish	Sextans	Sextant
Draco	Dragon	Taurus	Bull
Equuleus	Little Horse	Telescopium	Telescope
Eridanus	Eridanus	Triangulum	Triangle
Fornax	Furnace	Triangulum Australe	Southern Triangle
Gemini	Twins	Tucana	Toucan
Grus	Crane	Ursa Major	Great Bear
Hercules	Hercules	Ursa Minor	Little Bear
Horologium	Clock	Vela	Sails
Hydra	Water Snake	Virgo	Virgin
Hydrus	Sea Serpent	Volans	Flying Fish
Indus	Indian	Vulpecula	Fox

SOUTHERN HEAVENS

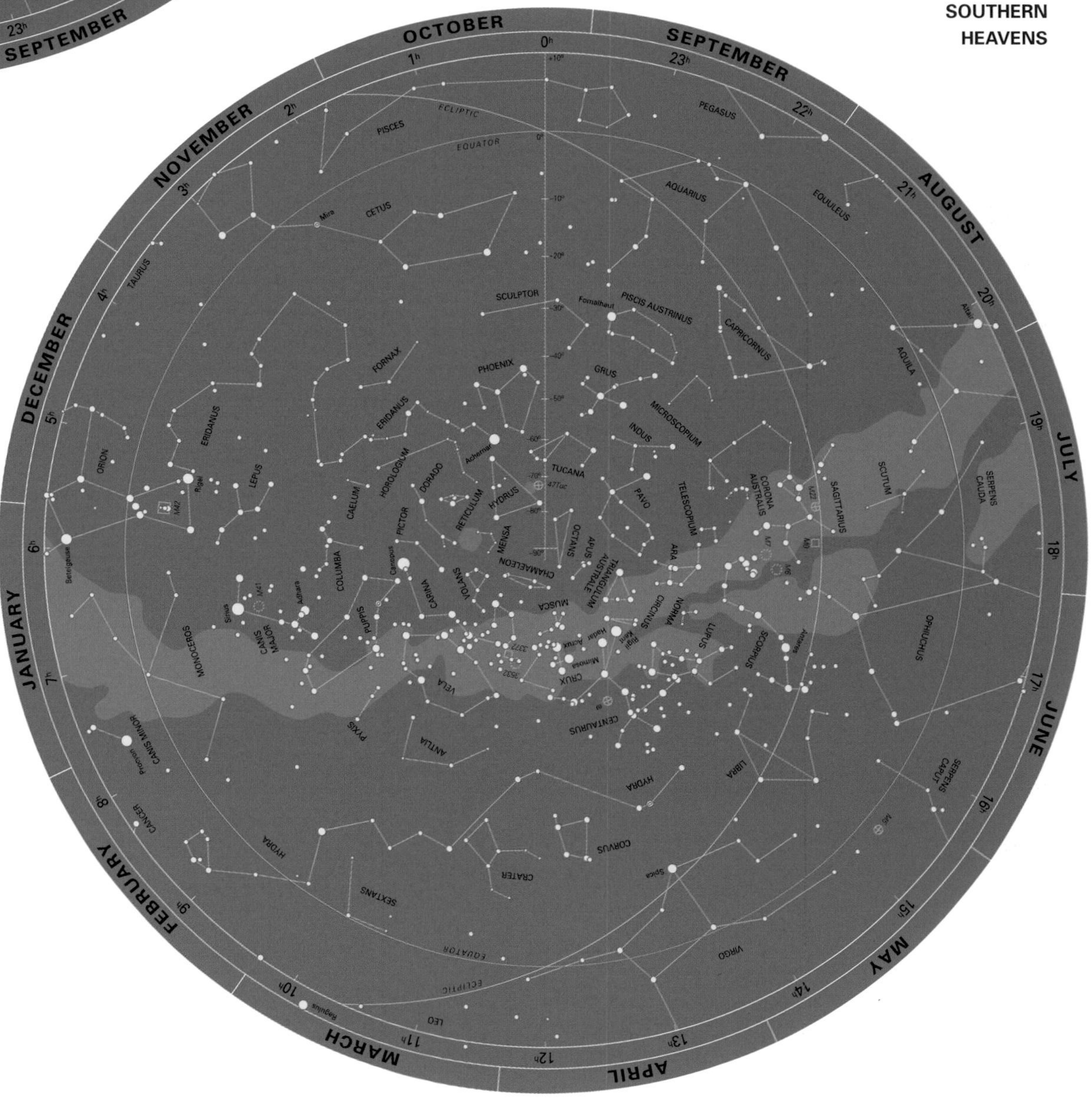

Star charts are drawn as projections of a vast, hollow sphere with the observer in the middle. Each circle on this page represents slightly more than one hemisphere, centred on the north and south celestial poles respectively – projections of the Earth's poles in the heavens. At the present era, the north pole is marked by the star Polaris; the south pole has no such convenient reference point.

Astronomical co-ordinates are normally given in terms of 'Right Ascension' for longitude and 'Declination' for latitude or altitude. Since the stars appear to rotate around the Earth once every 24 hours, Right Ascension is measured eastwards – anticlockwise – in hours and minutes and is marked around the edge of the map. One hour is equivalent to 15 angular degrees; zero on the scale is the point at which the Sun crosses the celestial equator at the spring equinox, known to astronomers as the 'First Point of Aries'. Unlike the Sun, stars always rise and set at the same point on the horizon. Declination measures (in degrees) a star's angular distance above or below the celestial equator and is marked on the vertical line.

Using the maps

First choose the one for your hemisphere and hold it with the month at the bottom. The stars in the lower part of the map are then due south (or north, in the southern hemisphere) at about 1 AM local time, not allowing for summer or daylight saving time. Their exact position above the horizon depends on your latitude. The closer to the Equator you live, the higher in the sky these stars will appear. Some additional stars from the map for the other hemisphere will be visible in the lower sky.

Stars near the top of the map will be below the opposite horizon at this date and time, but will be visible at other times of the night and year. The sky appears to move anticlockwise around the celestial pole during the course of the day (clockwise in the southern hemisphere), so the same stars will be visible at 11 PM a month earlier.

STAR MAGNITUDES

Apparent visual magnitudes

The magnitude scale of star brightnesses is developed from the system used by the Ancient Greeks in which the brightest stars were first magnitude and the faintest visible to the naked eye were sixth. Today the scale has a mathematical basis and extends, at the brightest end, through to negative magnitudes.

The Milky Way is shown in light blue on these charts.

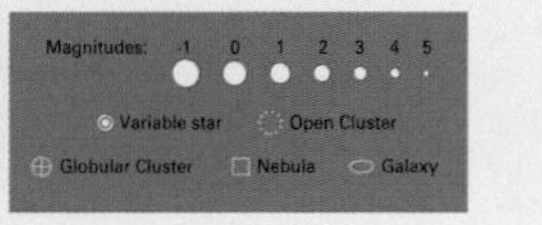

The Solar System

For more information:

2 The Home Galaxy
6 The seasons
Day and night
7 The Moon

Lying 28,000 light-years from the centre of one of billions of galaxies that comprise the observable Universe, our Solar System contains nine planets and their moons, innumerable asteroids and comets, and a miscellany of dust and gas, all tethered by the immense gravitational field of the Sun, the middling-sized star whose thermonuclear furnaces provide them all with heat and light.

The Solar System was formed about 4,600 million years ago, when a spinning cloud of gas, mostly hydrogen but seeded with other heavier elements, condensed enough to ignite a nuclear reaction and create a star. The Sun still accounts for almost 99.9% of the system's total mass.

By composition as well as distance, the planetary array divides quite neatly in two: an inner system of four small, solid planets, including the Earth, and an outer system, from Jupiter to Neptune, of four much larger planets composed of lighter materials, such as gas, liquid and ice. Between the two groups lies a scattering of rocky asteroids, numbering perhaps as many as 45,000. These may be debris left over from the formation of the inner Solar System. The outermost planet, Pluto, may simply be the largest of a number of bodies composed of rock and ice orbiting beyond Neptune, similarly left over from the formation of the outer Solar System.

Much of the early history of science is the story of people trying to make sense of the errant points of light that were all they knew of the planets. Now, men have themselves stood on the Earth's Moon, space probes have landed on Mars and Venus, and orbiting radars have mapped far distant landscapes with astonishing accuracy, transforming our knowledge of our celestial environment.

In the 1980s, the Voyager space probes skimmed all four major planets of the outer Solar System, bringing new revelations with each close approach. And in July 2004, the Cassini-Huygens spacecraft will begin a detailed four-year tour of Saturn, its moons (in particular Titan) and its rings. Only Pluto, inscrutably distant in an orbit that takes it 50 times the Earth's distance from the Sun, remains unvisited by our messengers.

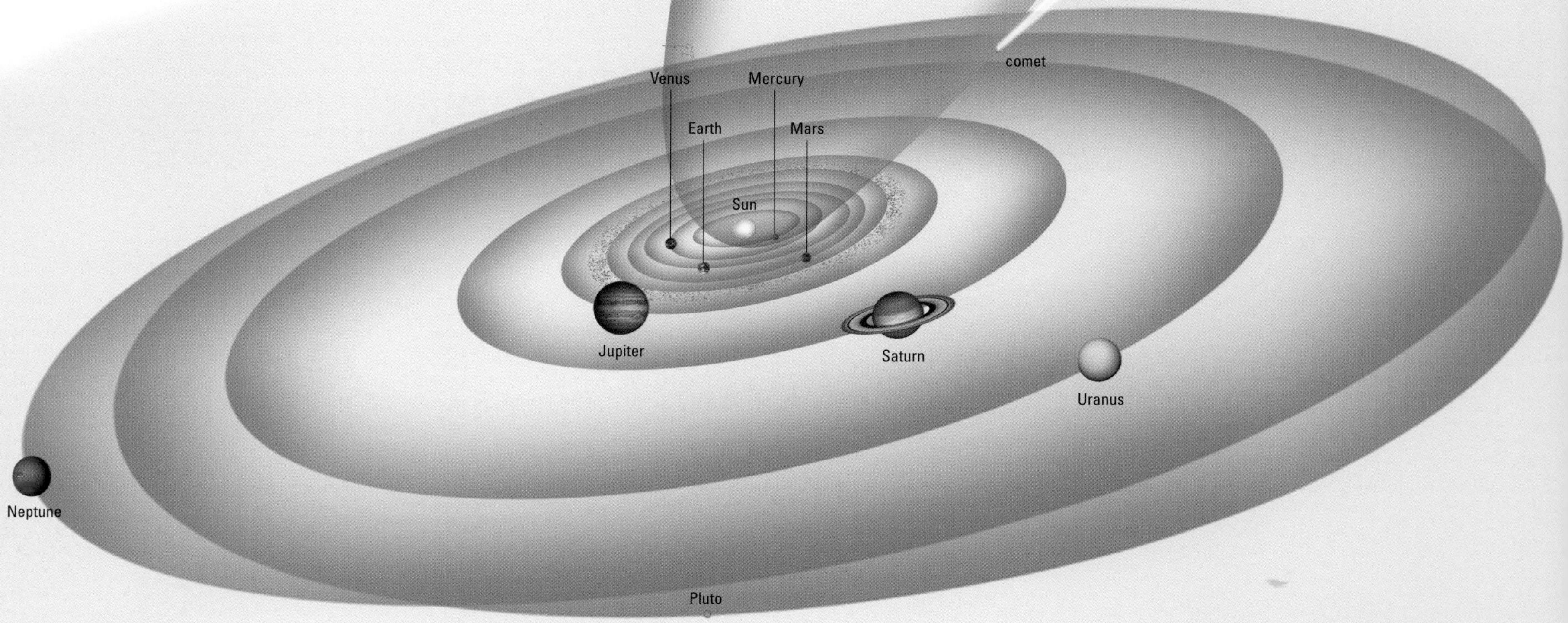

ORBITS OF THE PLANETS

The diagram above (*not drawn to scale*) shows the Solar System from the viewpoint of an observer a few light-hours distant in the direction of the constellation Hercules. Seen from such a position, above the plane of the ecliptic, all the planets revolve about the Sun in an anticlockwise direction. The perspective view exaggerates the elliptical form of all the planetary orbits: only Pluto and Mercury follow paths that deviate noticeably from circularity.

Near perihelion – its closest approach to the Sun – Pluto actually passes inside the orbit of Neptune, an event that last occurred in 1983. Pluto did not regain its station as the Sun's outermost planet until February 1999. In fact, Pluto comes closer to the Sun than Neptune for only a relatively brief 15-year period in the course of its 247.7-year orbit. The tilt of their respective orbits means that Neptune and Pluto will never collide with each other.

PLANETARY DATA

	Mean distance from Sun (million km)	Mass (Earth = 1)	Period of orbit (Earth days/years)	Period of rotation (Earth days)	Equatorial diameter (km)	Average density (water = 1)	Surface gravity (Earth = 1)	Escape velocity (km/sec)	Number of known satellites
Sun	*–*	*332,946*	*–*	*25.4*	*1,392,000*	*1.41*	*27.9*	*617.5*	*–*
Mercury	57.9	0.055	87.97d	58.67	4,878	5.44	0.38	4.25	0
Venus	108.2	0.815	224.7d	243.00	12,104	5.25	0.90	10.36	0
Earth	149.6	1.0	365.3d	1.00	12,756	5.52	1.00	11.18	1
Mars	227.9	0.11	687.0d	1.028	6,794	3.94	0.38	5.03	2
Jupiter	778	317.9	11.86y	0.411	143,884	1.33	2.64	59.60	63
Saturn	1,427	95.2	29.46y	0.427	120,536	0.71	1.16	35.60	31
Uranus	2,870	14.6	84.01y	0.748	51,118	1.27	0.79	21.10	27
Neptune	4,497	17.2	164.8y	0.710	50,538	1.77	0.98	24.60	13
Pluto	5,900	0.002	247.7y	6.39	2,324	2.02	0.06	1.20	1

Planetary days are given in sidereal time – that is, with respect to the stars rather than the Sun. Most of the information in the table was confirmed by spacecraft and often obtained from photographs and other data transmitted back to the Earth.

In the case of Pluto, however, only Earthbound observations have been made, and no spacecraft will encounter it until well into the 21st century. Given the planet's small size and great distance, figures for its diameter and rotation period have only recently been confirmed.

Pluto is not massive enough to account for the perturbations in the orbits of Uranus and Neptune that led to its discovery in 1930, but it is now widely believed that these perturbations can be explained away as observational errors made by the earlier observers.

THE PLANETS

Mercury is the closest planet to the Sun and hence the fastest-moving. It is very hot, with a cratered, wrinkled surface very similar to that of Earth's Moon. It is small and has no gravity, hence there is no significant atmosphere.

Venus has much the same physical dimensions as Earth. Its dense atmosphere is composed of 97% carbon dioxide resulting in a runaway greenhouse effect that makes the Venusian surface, at 477°C, the hottest of all the planets in the Solar System. Radar mapping shows the land to be relatively level, with volcanic regions whose sulphurous discharges explain the sulphuric-acid rains reported by soft-landing space probes before they succumbed to Venus' fierce climate.

Earth seen from space is easily the most beautiful of the inner planets; it is also, and more objectively, the largest, as well as the only home of known life. Living things are the main reason why the Earth is able to retain a substantial proportion of corrosive and highly reactive oxygen in its atmosphere, a state of affairs that contradicts the laws of chemical equilibrium; the oxygen in turn supports the life that constantly regenerates it.

Mars, smaller and cooler than the Earth, is nevertheless the most likely planet other than Earth where life may have formed, though whether life could thrive in its current cold, dry and thin atmosphere is doubtful. The ice caps are mainly frozen carbon dioxide, though data from NASA's probe Mars Odyssey, launched in 2001, suggests that vast reservoirs of water ice may lie a few centimetres beneath the surface over much of the planet. But the surface itself is a dustbowl, where occasional storms whirl dust high into the atmosphere.

Jupiter masses almost three times as much as all the other planets combined; had it scooped up rather more matter during its formation, it might have evolved into a small companion star for the Sun. The planet is mostly gas, under intense pressure in the lower atmosphere above a core of fiercely compressed hydrogen and helium. The upper layers form strikingly-coloured rotating belts, the outward sign of the intense storms created by Jupiter's rapid diurnal rotation. Close approaches by spacecraft have shown an orbiting ring system and discovered several previously unknown moons: Jupiter has at least 63 moons, though many are extremely small.

Saturn is structurally similar to Jupiter, rotating fast enough to produce an obvious bulge at its equator. It is composed of 89% hydrogen and 11% helium, and has wind velocities in the outer atmosphere of 500 m/sec. Ever since the invention of the telescope, however, Saturn's rings have been the feature that has attracted most observers. Voyager probes in 1980 and 1981 sent back detailed pictures that showed them to be composed of thousands of separate ringlets, each in turn made up of tiny icy particles.

Uranus was unknown to the ancients. Although it is faintly visible to the naked eye, it was not discovered until 1781. Its interior is largely water, with an atmosphere of hydrogen, helium and some methane, which gives the planet its blue-green colour. Observations in 1977 suggested the presence of a faint ring system, amply confirmed when Voyager 2 swung past the planet in 1986.

Neptune is always more than 4,000 million km from Earth, and despite its diameter of over 50,000 km, it can only be seen by telescope. Its discovery in 1846 was the result of mathematical predictions by astronomers seeking to explain irregularities in the orbit of Uranus, but until Voyager 2 closed with the planet in 1989, very little was known of it. Like Uranus, it has a ring system; recent observations have revealed a total of 13 moons.

Pluto is the most mysterious of the solar planets, if only because even the most powerful telescopes can scarcely resolve it from a point of light to a disk. It was discovered as recently as 1930, as the result of perturbations in the orbits of the two then outermost planets. Its small size, as well as its eccentric and highly tilted orbit, has led to suggestions that it is a former satellite of Neptune, somehow liberated from its primary. In 1978 Pluto was found to have a moon of its own, Charon, apparently half the size of Pluto itself.

Diagrams not drawn to scale

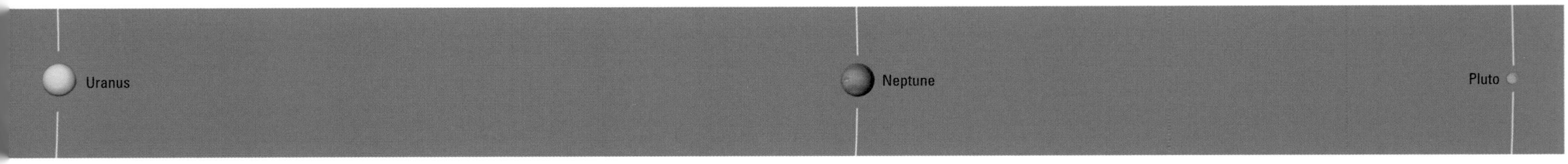

Time and Motion

For more information:

4 Orbits of the planets
9 Ocean currents
14 Circulation of the air
16 Climate

The basic unit of time measurement is the day, that is, one rotation of the Earth on its axis. Our present calendar is based on the solar year of 365.24 days, the time taken by the Earth to orbit the Sun.

Calendars based on the movements of the Sun and Moon have been used since ancient times. The average length of the year, according to the Julian Calendar introduced by Julius Caesar, was about 11 minutes too long. The cumulative error was rectified in 1582 by the Gregorian Calendar, when Pope Gregory XIII decreed that the day following 4 October was 15 October, and in that century years did not count as leap years unless they were divisible by 400. England finally adopted the reformed calendar in 1752, when it was 11 days behind the European mainland.

The rotation of the Earth on its axis causes day and night. Because the Earth rotates through 360° every 24 hours, the world is divided into 24 time zones centred on lines of longitude at 15° longitude.

The tilt of the Earth's axis, which is also called the 'obliquity of the ecliptic', accounts for the seasons which are so familiar in the middle latitudes. However, geological evidence shows that, over long periods of time, climates change, and the advances and retreats of the ice during the Pleistocene Ice Age may have been caused by regular variations in the Earth's tilt, its orbit around the Sun, and changes in the season when it is closest to the Sun (perihelion).

THE SEASONS

Seasons occur because the Earth's axis is tilted at an angle of approximately 23½°. When the northern hemisphere is tilted to a maximum extent towards the Sun, on 21 June, the Sun is overhead at the Tropic of Cancer (latitude 23½° North). This is midsummer, or the summer solstice, in the northern hemisphere.

On 22 or 23 September, the Sun is overhead at the Equator, and day and night are of equal length throughout the world. This is the autumnal equinox in the northern hemisphere.

On 21 or 22 December, the Sun is overhead at the Tropic of Capricorn (23½° South), the winter solstice in the northern hemisphere. The overhead Sun then tracks north until, on 21 March, it is overhead at the Equator. This is the spring (vernal) equinox in the northern hemisphere.

In the southern hemisphere, the seasons are the reverse of those in the north.

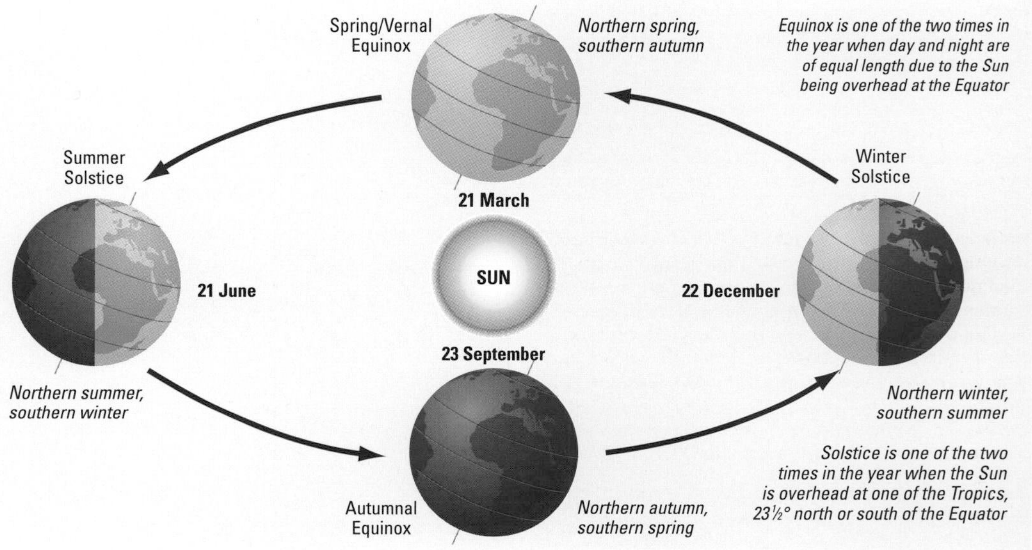

DAY AND NIGHT

The Sun appears to rise in the east, reach its highest point at noon, and then set in the west, to be followed by night. In reality, it is not the Sun that is moving but the Earth rotating from west to east. The moment when the Sun's upper limb first appears above the horizon is termed sunrise; the moment when the Sun's upper limb disappears below the horizon is sunset.

At the summer solstice in the northern hemisphere (21 June), the Arctic has total daylight and the Antarctic total darkness. The opposite occurs at the winter solstice (21 or 22 December). At the Equator, the length of day and night are almost equal all year.

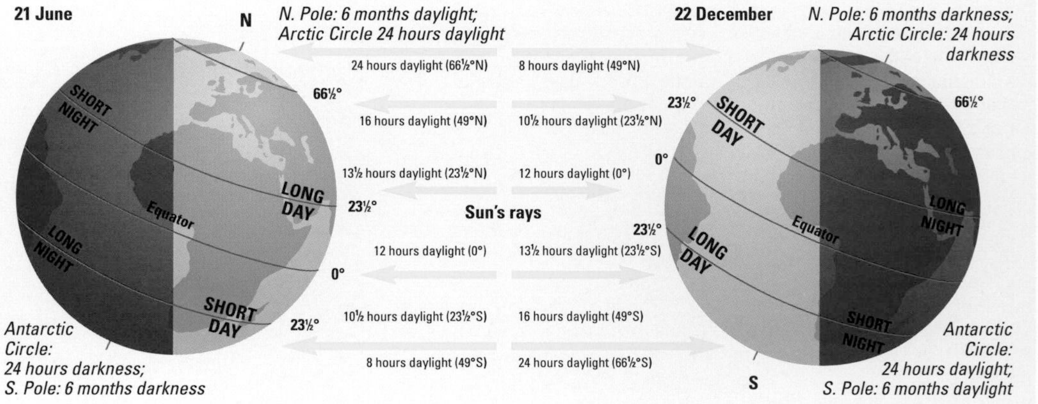

EARTH DATA

Aphelion (maximum distance from Sun):	152,007,016 km	**Length of year:**	365 days, 5 hours, 48 minutes, 46 seconds of mean solar time	**Polar circumference:**	40,009 km
Perihelion (minimum distance from Sun):	147,000,830 km	**Superficial area:**	510,000,000 sq km	**Equatorial diameter:**	12,756.8 km
Angle of tilt (obliquity of the ecliptic):	23° 27′ 08″	**Land surface:**	149,000,000 sq km (29.2%)	**Polar diameter:**	12,713.8 km
Length of year – solar tropical (equinox to equinox):	365.24 days	**Water surface:**	361,000,000 sq km (70.8%)	**Equatorial radius:**	6,378.4 km
		Equatorial circumference:	40,077 km	**Polar radius:**	6,356.9 km
				Volume of the Earth:	$1,083,230 \times 10^6$ cu km
				Mass of the Earth:	5.9×10^{21} tonnes

SUNRISE AND SUNSET

The term 'equinox' comes from the Latin for 'equal night'. At the spring and autumnal equinoxes, the Sun is vertically overhead at midday at the Equator and all places on Earth have 12 hours of darkness and 12 hours of daylight. The graphs showing sunrise and sunset show that these occasions occur on 21 March and on 22 or 23 September. The graphs also show that, because the Sun remains high in the sky at the Equator throughout the year, the length of day and night there remains roughly the same throughout the year, with sunrise around 6 AM and sunset around 6 PM.

The further north or south one travels, the greater the difference between the number of hours of daylight and darkness. For example, the graph (*right*) shows that at latitude 60°N sunrise varies from just after 9 AM in midwinter (on 22 or 23 December) to about 2.30 AM in midsummer (around the summer solstice on 21 June). By contrast, the second graph (*far right*) shows that sunset at latitude 60°N occurs at about 2.45 PM in midwinter and 9.20 PM in midsummer.

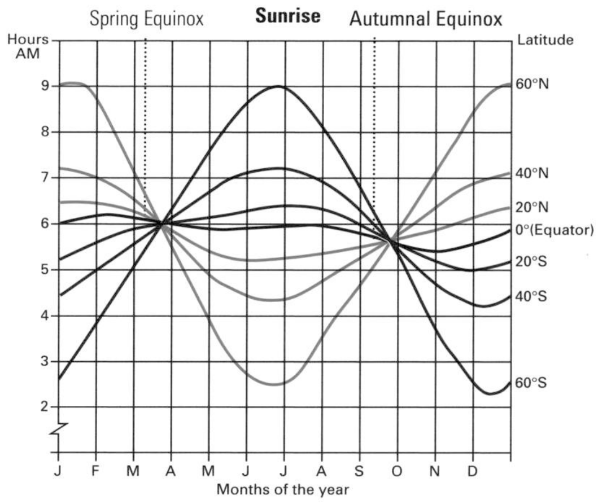

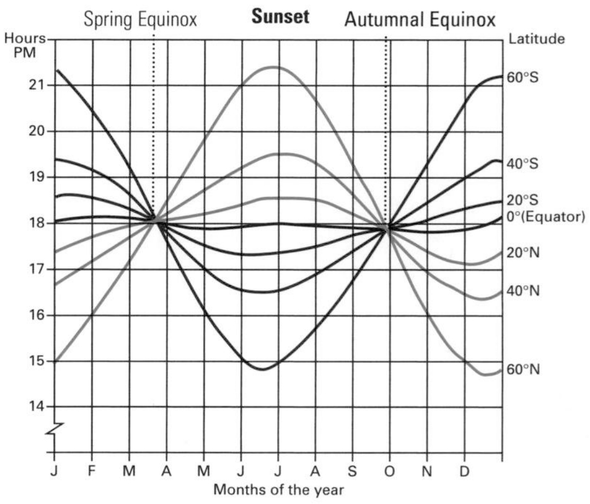

THE MOON

The Moon rotates more slowly than the Earth, making one complete turn on its axis in just over 27 days. Since this corresponds to its period of revolution around the Earth, the Moon always presents the same hemisphere or face to us, and we never see 'the dark side'. The interval between one full Moon and the next (and between new Moons) is about 29½ days – a lunar month. The apparent changes in the shape of the Moon are caused by its changing position in relation to the Earth; like the planets, it produces no light of its own and shines only by reflecting the rays of the Sun.

PHASES OF THE MOON

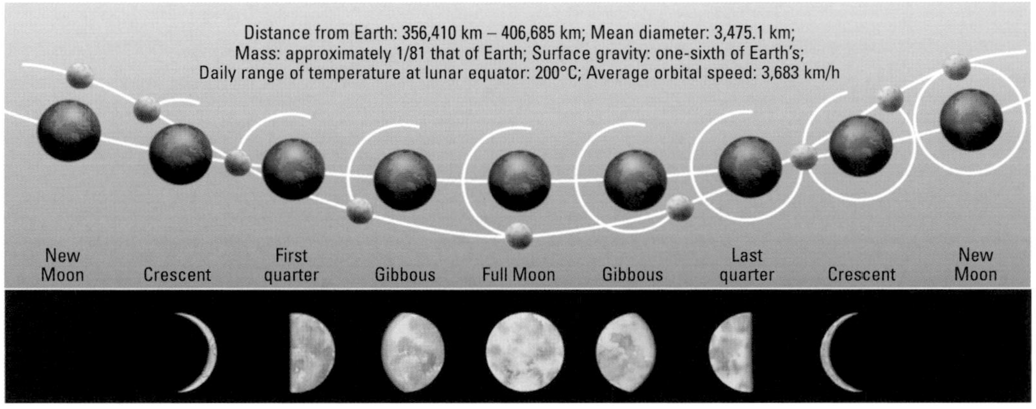

MOON DATA

Distance from Earth

The Moon orbits at a mean distance of 384,199 km, at an average speed of 3,683 km/h in relation to the Earth.

Size and mass

The average diameter of the Moon is 3,475 km. It is 400 times smaller than the Sun but is about 400 times closer to the Earth, so we see them as the same size. The Moon has a mass of $7{,}348 \times 10^{19}$ tonnes, with a density 3.344 times that of water.

Visibility

Only 59% of the Moon's surface is directly visible from Earth. Reflected light takes 1.25 seconds to reach Earth – compared to 8 minutes 27.3 seconds for light to reach us from the Sun.

Temperature

With the Sun overhead, the temperature on the lunar equator can reach 117.2°C [243°F]. At night it can sink to −162.7°C [−261°F].

ECLIPSES

When the Moon passes between the Sun and the Earth it causes a partial eclipse of the Sun (1) if the Earth passes through the Moon's outer shadow (P), or a total eclipse (2) if the inner cone shadow crosses the Earth's surface. In a lunar eclipse, the Earth's shadow crosses the Moon and, again, provides either a partial or total eclipse.

Eclipses of the Sun and the Moon do not occur every month because of the 5° difference between the plane of the Moon's orbit and the plane in which the Earth moves. In the 1990s, only 14 lunar eclipses were possible – for example, seven partial and seven total. Each was visible only from certain, and variable, parts of the world. The same period witnessed 13 solar eclipses – six partial (or annular) and seven total.

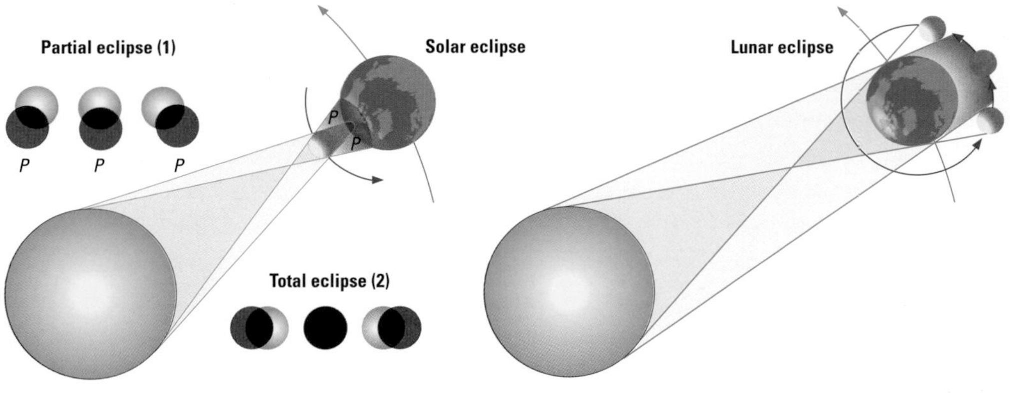

TIDES

The daily rise and fall of the ocean's tides are the result of the gravitational pull of the Moon and that of the Sun, though the effect of the latter is not as strong as that of the Moon. This effect is greatest on the hemisphere facing the Moon and causes a tidal 'bulge'. When the Sun, Earth and Moon are in line, Spring tides occur: high tide reaches the highest values, and low tide falls to low levels. When lunar and solar forces are least coincidental with the Sun and Moon at an angle (near the Moon's first and third quarters), Neap tides occur, which have a small tidal range.

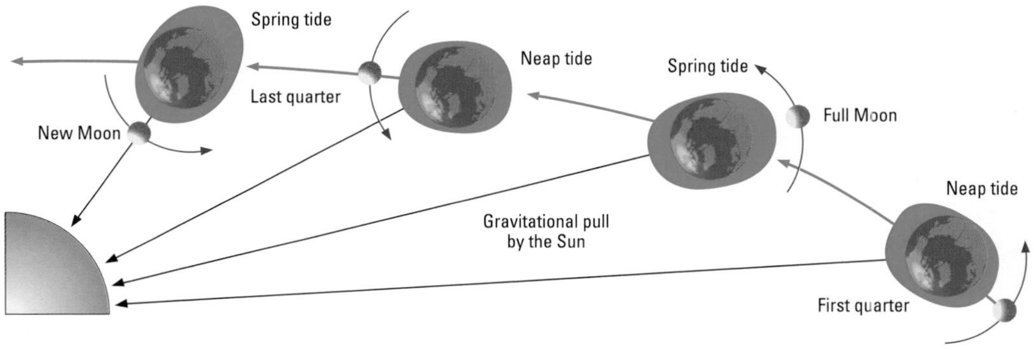

TIME ZONES

The Earth rotates through 360° in 24 hours, and so moves 15° every hour. The world is divided into 24 standard time zones, each centred on lines of longitude at 15° intervals. At the centre of the first zone is the Prime meridian or Greenwich meridian. All places to the west of Greenwich are one hour behind for every 15° of longitude; places to the east are ahead by one hour for every 15°.

International Date Line

When it is 12 noon at the Greenwich meridian, 180° east it is midnight of the same day – while 180° west the day is just beginning. To overcome this, the International Date Line was established, approximately following the 180° meridian. Thus, if you were to travel eastwards from Japan (140°E) to Samoa (170°W), you would pass from Sunday night into Sunday morning.

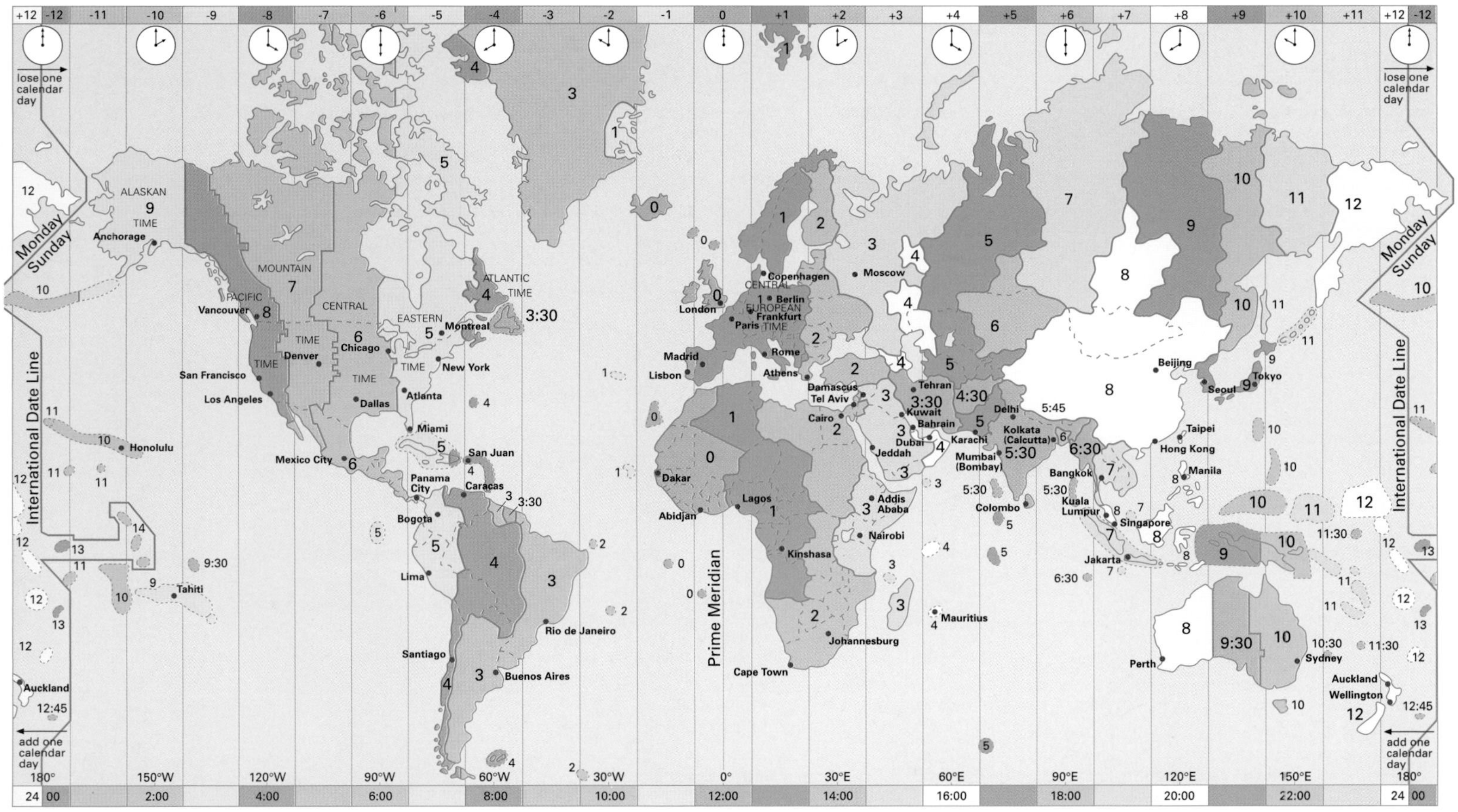

Projection: Mercator

10 Hours slow or fast of UT or Co-ordinated Universal Time

Zones using UT (GMT)

Zones slow of UT (GMT)

International boundaries

Zones fast of UT (GMT)

Half-hour zones

Time zone boundaries

International Date Line

Actual Solar Time when time at Greenwich is 12:00 (noon)

Note: Certain of the above time zones are affected by the incidence of 'Summer Time' in countries where it is adopted.

Oceans

For more information:

7 Tides
10 Plate tectonics
14 Atmosphere
18 Hydrological cycle
Water distribution
19 Watersheds
23 Water pollution
41 World shipping

The last 40 years have been described as the 'Space Age', but another exciting and perhaps even more important area of discovery, proceeding at the same time, has been the exploration of the oceans which cover more than 70% of our planet. Studies of the ocean floor and oceanic islands have revealed features that help to explain how continents move, and how the movements are related to earthquakes and volcanic activity.

Manned submersibles have established that life exists even in the deepest trenches, where the pressure reaches 1,000 atmospheres, the equivalent of the force of 1 tonne bearing down on every square centimetre. Further exploration in the pitch-black environment of the ocean ridges has revealed strange forms of marine life around scalding hot vents. The creatures include giant tubeworms, blind shrimps, and bacteria, some of which are genetically very different from any other known life forms. In 1996, an analysis of one micro-organism revealed that at least half of its 1,700 or so genes were hitherto unknown. This environment, which is based on chemicals, not sunlight, may resemble the places where life on Earth first began.

Another vital area of contemporary research concerns the interactions between the oceans and the atmosphere, as exemplified in the El Niño–Southern Oscillation (ENSO) cycle, and the bearing that these have on climatic change (*see below*).

Most geographers divide the world's ocean waters into four areas: the Pacific, Atlantic, Indian and Arctic oceans. The most active zone in the oceans is the sunlit upper layer, where the water is moved around by wind-blown currents. It is the home of most sea life and acts as a membrane through which the ocean breathes, absorbing great quantities of carbon dioxide and partly exchanging it for oxygen.

As the depth increases, so light fades and temperatures fall until just before 1,000 metres where there is a marked temperature change at the thermocline, the boundary between the warm surface zone and the cold deep zone. Below the thermocline, slow currents are caused by density differences between bodies of water with varying temperatures and salinity.

LIFE IN THE OCEANS

An imaginary profile of the typical coastal and oceanic zones is shown, with a selection of the life forms that might occur in the waters off the Pacific Coast of Central America. The animals illustrated are not drawn to scale as the range of sizes is too great. Most marine life is confined to the first 200 metres, the upper sunlit (photic) zone, where sunlight can still penetrate. Plant and animal plankton, the basis of life in the oceans, occur in great quantities in all zones.

In the pelagic environment (open sea), vertical gradients, including those of light, temperature and salinity, determine the distribution of organisms. From the tidal zone at the coastline, the continental shelf, geologically still part of the continental landmass, drops gently to about 200 metres – the sunlit zone. At the end of the shelf, the seabed falls away in the steeper angle of the continental slope. The subsequent descent to the deep-ocean floor, known as the continental rise, is more gentle, with gradients between 1 in 100 and 1 in 700 until the abyssal plains and hills between 2,500 and 6,000 metres below the surface.

The deep-sea floor contains seamounts, some of which are capped by coral reefs, ocean ridges – the longest mountain chains on Earth – and deep-ocean trenches, especially in the Pacific Ocean where six trenches reach depths of more than 10,000 metres, including the 11,022-metre deep Mariana Trench.

Each of these zones contains a distinctive community of species adapted to the different conditions of salinity, temperature and light intensity. Indeed, a few organisms have been found even in the abyssal darkness of the great ocean trenches.

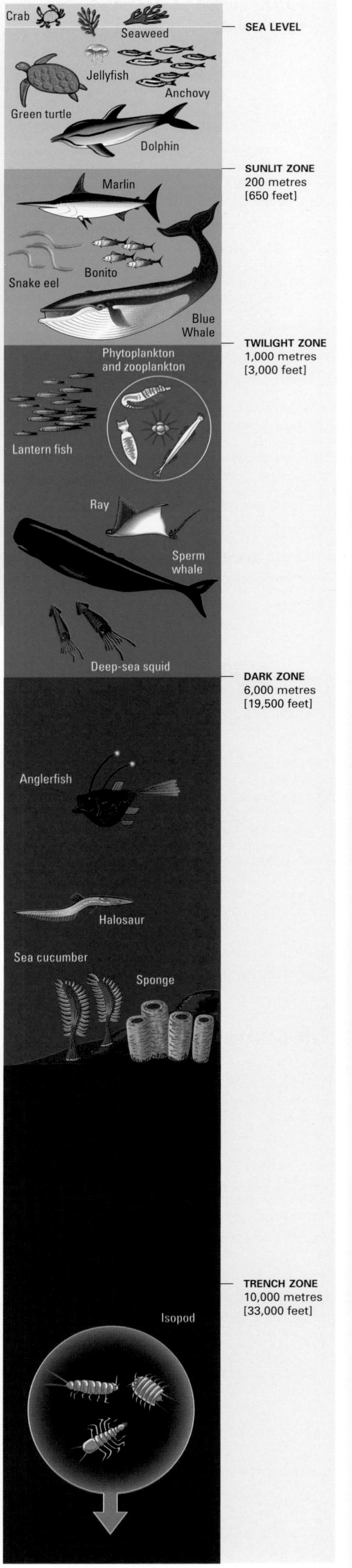

ATOLL BUILDING

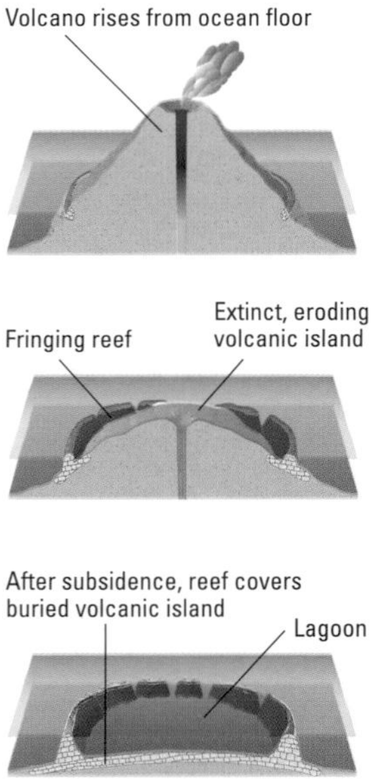

A coral atoll usually begins existence as a bare volcanic peak, thrusting above the surface of the ocean. A colony of coral – organisms with calcium carbonate skeletons – forms itself in the shallow water around the peak. The volcano is eroded and slowly sinks, leaving the coral forming a ring of hard limestone around its remnant. In time, the barrier reef of an atoll is all that remains.

EL NIÑO PHENOMENON

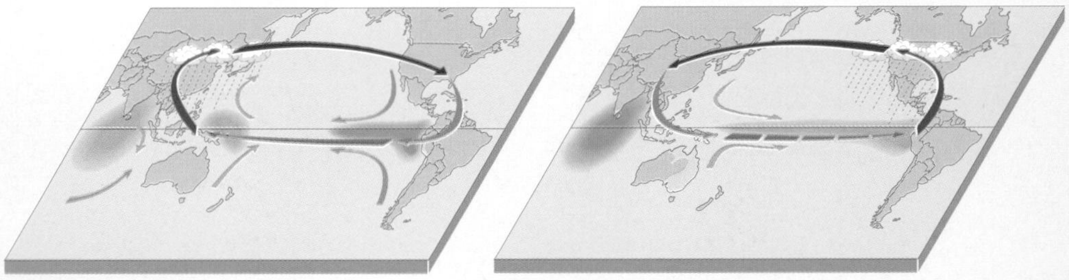

Normal year – Walker Circulation Cell | **El Niño event**

The importance of the ocean–atmosphere interaction is nowhere more dramatically demonstrated than in the El Niño phenomenon of the southern Pacific Ocean. Under normal conditions, called La Niña, cold, nutrient-rich water rises to the surface and spreads westwards. In the western Pacific, sea surface temperatures reach 28°C or more and warm air rises, creating a low-pressure air system and causing heavy rains. The rising air spreads out and some of it descends over South America and the eastern Pacific, creating a high-pressure air system from which winds blow westwards. This rotating system is called a Walker Circulation Cell.

An El Niño event is characterized by a reversal of currents. The upwelling of cold water off South America is greatly reduced and surface water temperatures rise, causing a drastic reduction in fish life. The heaviest rainfall is over the eastern Pacific, while South-east Asia is drier than usual.

During an intense El Niño, the effects of the current and wind reversals affect the weather around the world. In 1982–3, the monsoon rainfall was reduced in Australia and South-east Asia, while in 1983–4 a severe drought occurred in the Sahel, south of the Sahara, and also in southern Africa. The south-east coast of the United States suffered storms and heavy rainfall, and even Europe experienced changes in weather patterns, possibly as a result of consequent changes in the course of the jet stream.

Scientists have found evidence that the frequency of the El Niño event, which normally occurs every three to seven years, and lasts between 12–18 months, may have increased in recent years. Another intense El Niño occurred in 1997–8, with resultant freak weather conditions across the entire Pacific region.

We do not fully understand the causes of the El Niño event, though some researchers are investigating possible connections between major volcanic eruptions in the tropical Pacific region, the ENSO cycle and atmospheric circulation.

OCEAN CURRENTS

JANUARY CURRENTS AND TEMPERATURES

(Northern Hemisphere: winter)

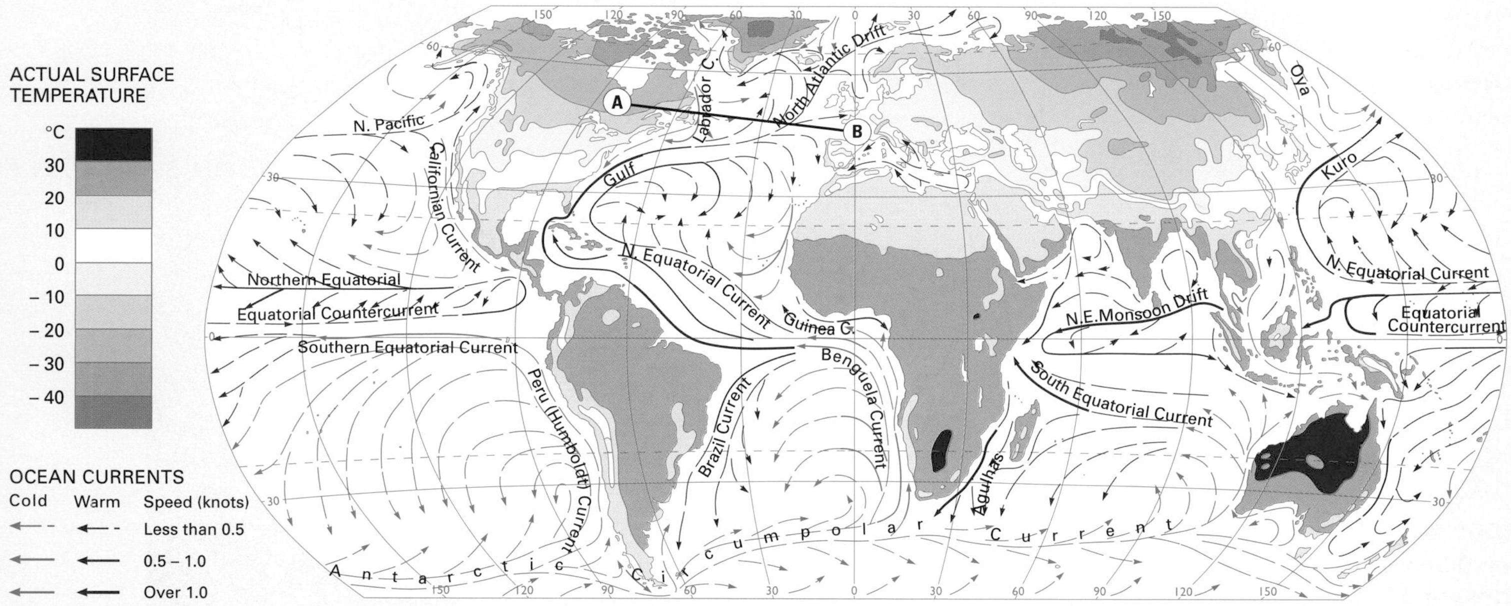

A ——— B Location of the Atlantic Ocean profile shown bottom left

JULY CURRENTS AND TEMPERATURES

(Northern Hemisphere: summer)

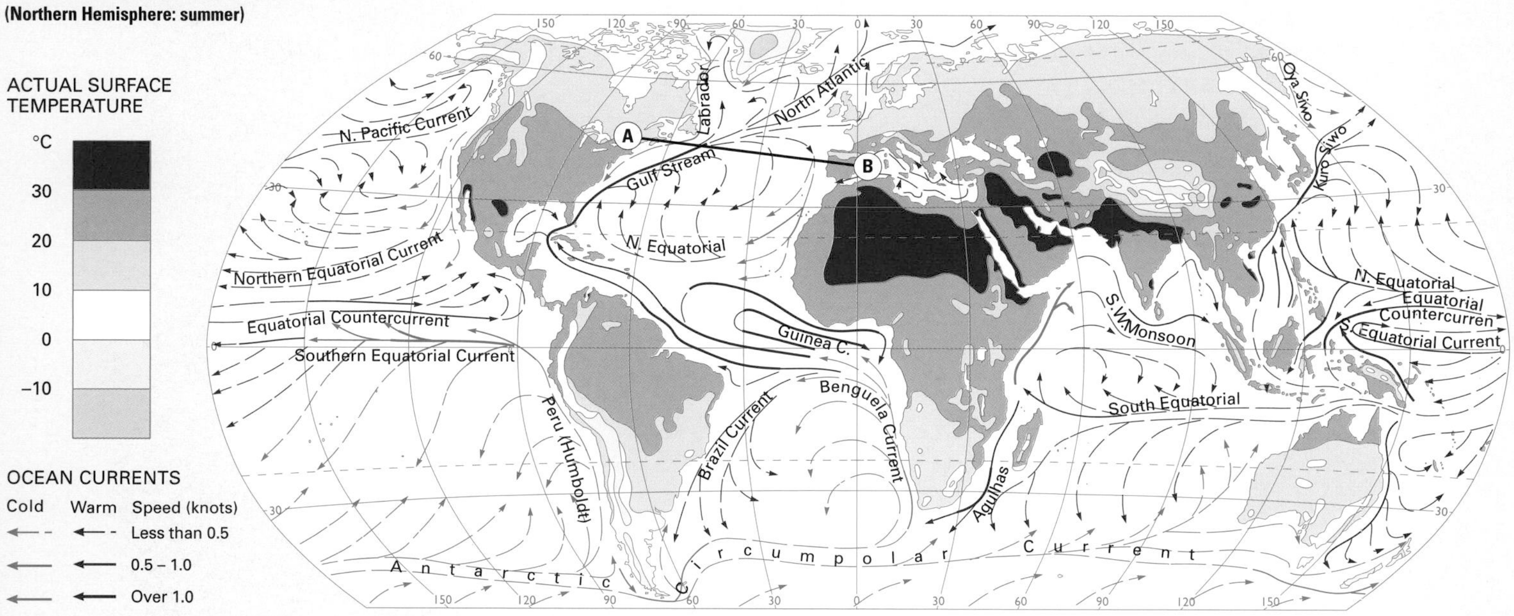

Moving immense quantities of energy as well as billions of tonnes of water every hour, the ocean currents are a vital part of the great heat engine that drives the Earth's climate. They themselves are produced by a twofold mechanism. At the surface, winds push huge masses of water before them; in the deep ocean, below an abrupt temperature gradient that separates the churning surface waters from the still depths, density variations cause slow vertical movements.

Coriolis effect

The pattern of circulation of the great surface currents is determined by the displacement known as the *Coriolis effect*. As the Earth turns, the vast mass of ocean water is deflected to one side. The deflection is most obvious near the Equator, where the Earth's surface is spinning eastwards at 1,700 km/h; currents moving polewards are curved clockwise in the northern hemisphere and anti-clockwise in the southern hemisphere.

Ocean currents

The result is a system of spinning circles known as 'gyres'. Warm currents move constantly from the Equator towards the poles, while cold water moves in the reverse direction. In this way, ocean currents act like a thermostat, helping to regulate temperatures around the world.

Depending on the annual movements of the prevailing wind belts, some currents on or near the Equator may reverse their direction in the course of the year, a variation on which Asia's monsoon rains depend and whose occasional failure has brought disaster to millions of people.

TOPOGRAPHY OF THE OCEAN FLOOR

Profile of the Atlantic Ocean

The deep-ocean floor was once believed to be flat, but sonar readings have shown that it is no more uniform than the surface of the continents. The profile (*below*) shows some of the features on the Atlantic Ocean floor between Massachusetts in North America and Gibraltar (*for location of profile, see maps above*).

Around the continents are shallow continental shelves composed of rocks that are less dense than the underlying oceanic crust. The continents end at the top of the steep continental slope, which descends to the abyss via the continental rise, made up of sediments washed down from the continental shelves.

The abyss contains large plains overlain by oozes but broken by volcanic seamounts and guyots (flat-topped seamounts), a few of which reach the surface as islands. The Mid-Atlantic Ridge contains a rift valley where new crustal rock is being formed as the plates on either side move apart.

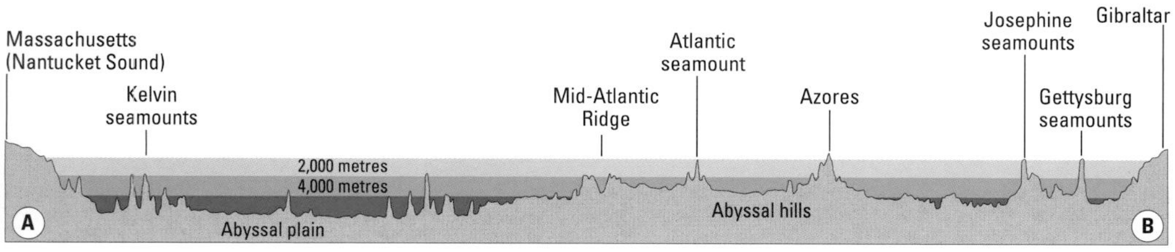

Topography of the ocean floor around Australia

In the image on the right, land areas are shown in grey, with shaded relief. The colours represent sea depths, with red representing the shallowest areas, through yellow and green to dark blue (the deepest).

The data for the sea topography are from the Seasat radar satellite. The deep blue area in the upper left is the Java Trench, which forms the boundary between the Indian-Australian plate and the Eurasian plate. In the top right, the New Guinea trench, which has a maximum depth of 9,103 metres, forms the border of the Indian-Australian and Pacific plates. Alongside the trenches are volcanic islands formed from magma, created as the edge of the Indian-Australian plate is subducted and melted.

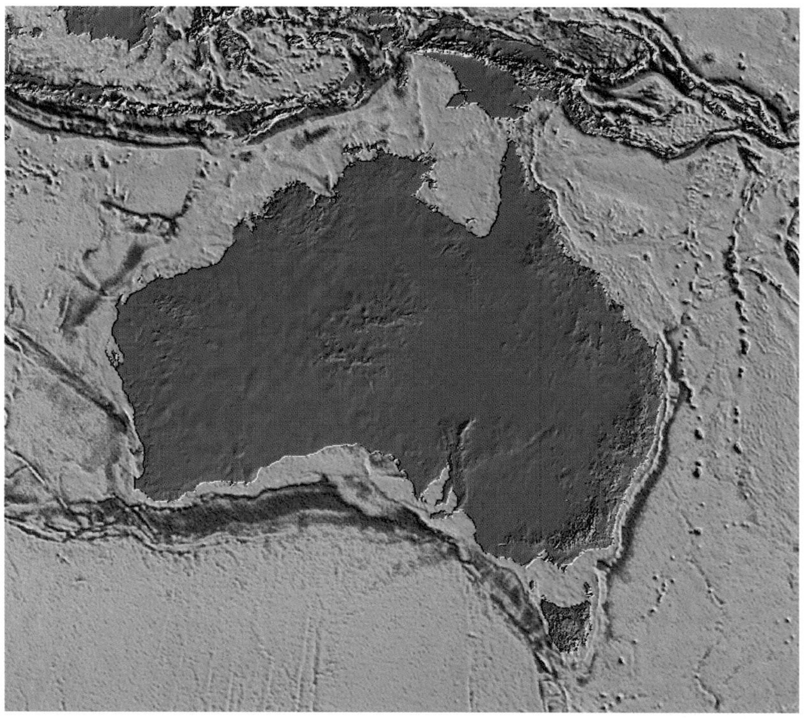

Geology of the Earth

For more information:
12 Types of rock
Mountain building
13 Surface processes
21 The carbon cycle
36 Minerals

Every year, earthquakes and volcanic eruptions cause much destruction throughout the world. Such phenomena were once thought to be unconnected, but since the late 1960s, scientists have understood that these events are surface manifestations of the tremendous forces operating in the Earth's interior that are slowly but constantly changing the face of our planet.

The Earth is divided into three zones. The crust, a brittle, low-density zone, overlies the dense mantle. Separating the crust from the mantle is a distinct boundary called the Mohorovičić (or Moho) discontinuity. Enclosed by the mantle is the Earth's core, which consists mainly of iron and nickel.

Temperatures inside the Earth range from about 870°C in the upper mantle to perhaps 5,000°C in the core. Heat creates convection currents in a semi-molten part of the mantle called the asthenosphere. Above the asthenosphere is the lithosphere, a solid layer about 70 km thick, consisting of the crust and part of the mantle. The lithosphere is divided into rigid plates, moved around by the currents in the asthenosphere, a process named plate tectonics.

The Earth was formed around 4.6 billion years ago. Lighter elements floated towards the surface, where they formed crustal rocks. The oldest rocks so far discovered are about 4 billion years old, while the oldest fossils occur in rocks formed around 3.5 billion years ago. An explosion of life occurred at the start of the Cambrian period, 570 million years ago. The fossil record since the start of the Cambrian has enabled scientists to piece together the story of life on Earth.

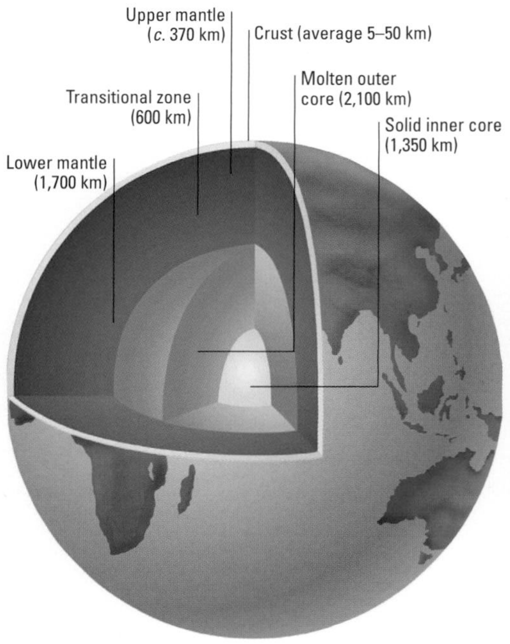

CONTINENTAL DRIFT

Trench
Rift
New ocean floor
Zones of slippage

In 1915, Alfred Wegener produced a series of world maps proposing that, around 200 million years ago, the continents had been joined together in a super-continent that he called Pangaea. This landmass started to break up about 180 million years ago and the parts drifted to their present positions. In the 1950s and 1960s, evidence from studies of the ocean floor suggested that the low-density continents rest on huge slow-moving plates. The arrows on the present-day world map (*below*) show that the continents are still on the move.

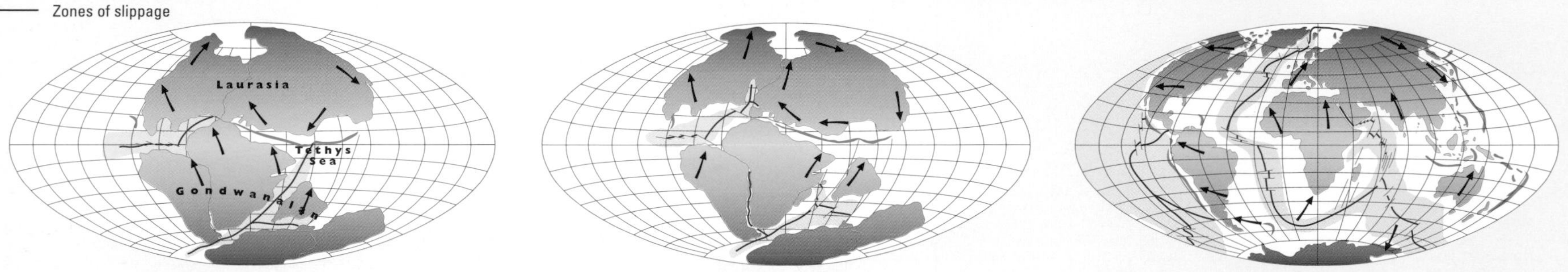

180 million years ago | 135 million years ago | Present day

DISTRIBUTION OF VOLCANOES

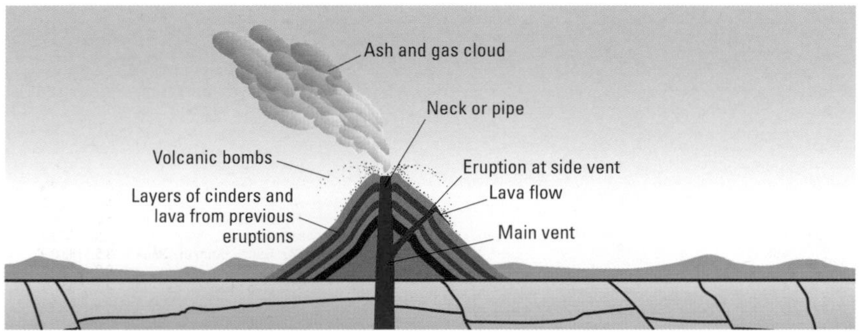

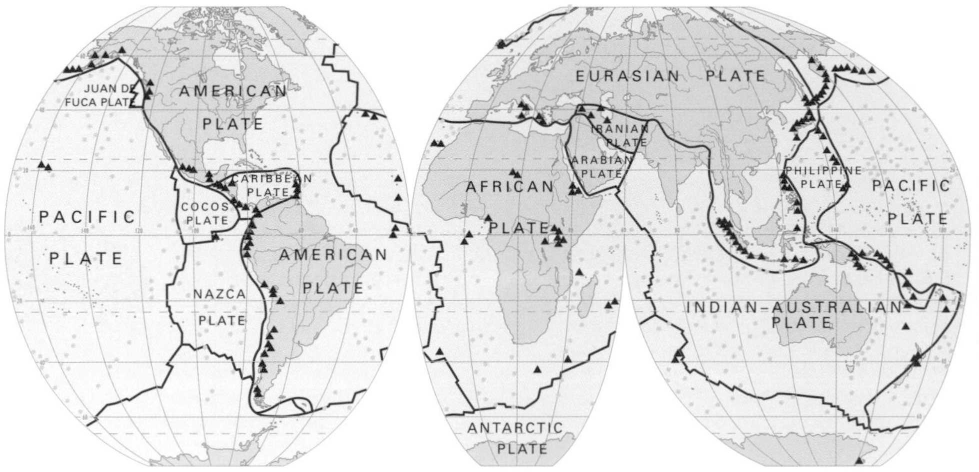

Volcanoes occur when hot liquefied rock beneath the Earth's crust is pushed up by pressure to the surface as molten lava. There are some 550 known active volcanoes, around 20 of which are erupting at any one time.

- Submarine volcanoes
- ▲ Land volcanoes active since 1700
- — Boundaries of tectonic plates

PLATE TECTONICS

The huge ridges that run through the oceans represent boundaries between plates. Here plates are diverging and molten magma from the mantle rises along a central rift valley to form new crustal rock. These ocean ridges, which are active zones where earthquakes and volcanic eruptions are common, are called constructive plate margins. Destructive plate margins, which occur when two plates converge, are marked by deep-ocean trenches as one plate is forced under the other. The descending plate is melted to produce the magma that fuels volcanoes alongside the trenches. Movements of descending plates are often sudden, triggering earthquakes in overlying continental areas.

Sea-floor spreading in the Atlantic Ocean and plate collision

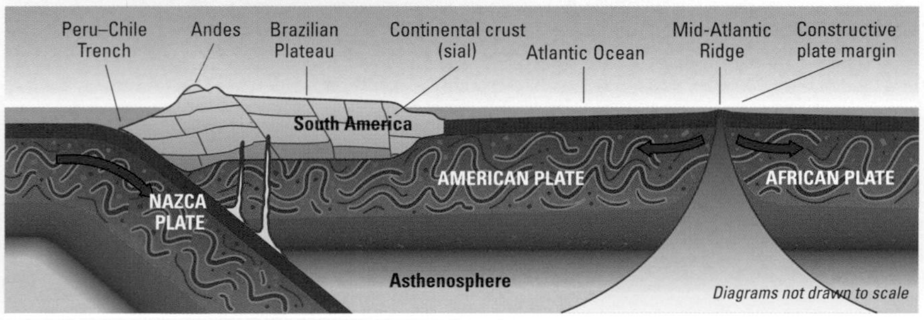

Sea-floor spreading in the Indian Ocean and continental plate collision

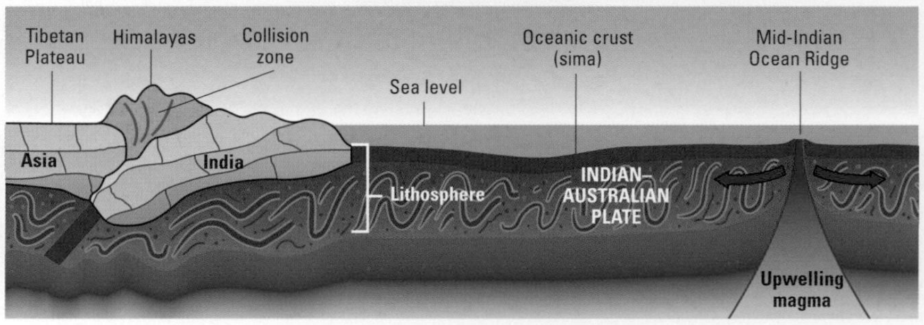

GEOLOGICAL TIME

Time, in millions of years before the present, is shown on a sliding scale, greatly compressed in the distant past.

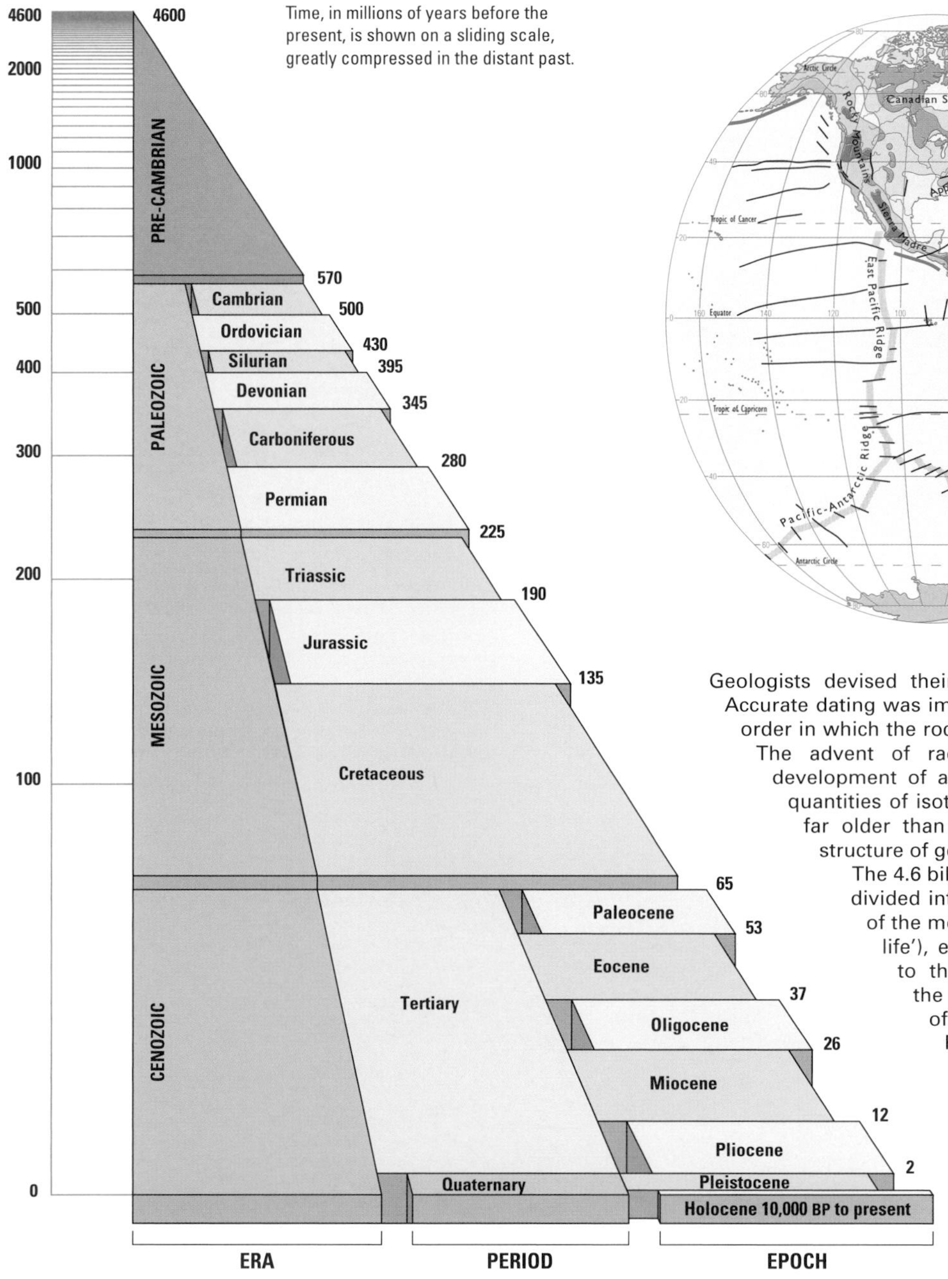

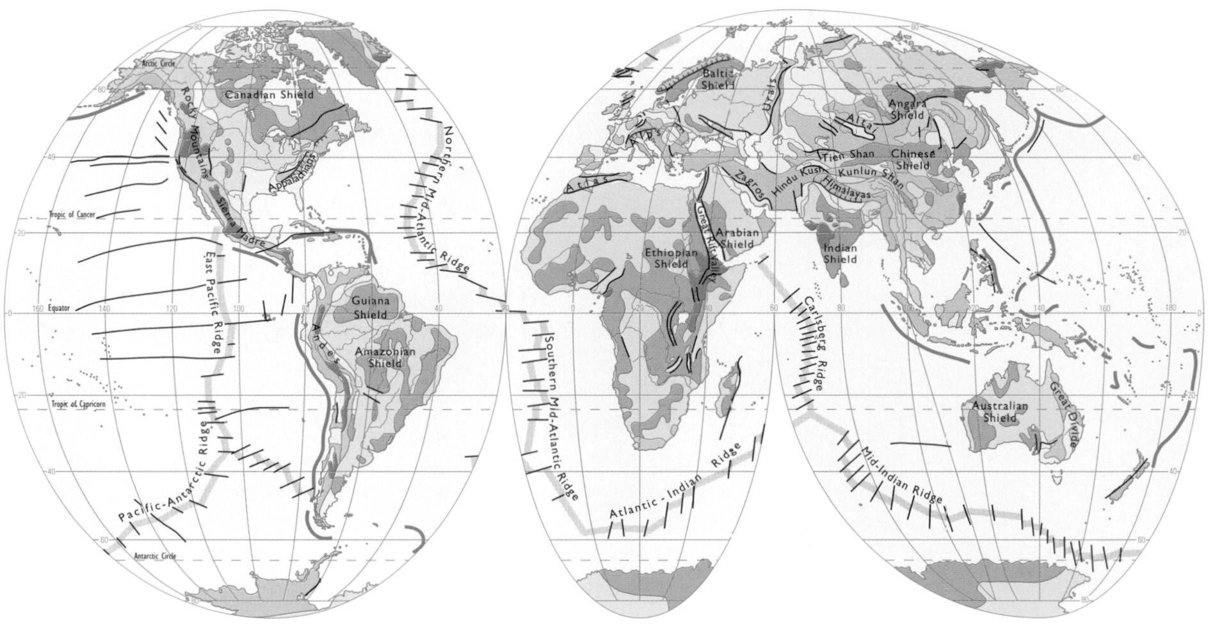

Geologists devised their timescale on the basis of relative, not calendar, ages. Accurate dating was impossible and estimates were often bitterly disputed, but the order in which the rocks were formed could be deduced from careful observation. The advent of radioactive dating – culminating in the 1950s with the development of a mass spectrometer capable of accurately measuring tiny quantities of isotopes – appears to have settled the arguments. The Earth is far older than geologists first imagined, but their painstakingly-created structure of geological time has withstood the advent of high technology.

The 4.6 billion (4,600 million) years since the formation of the Earth are divided into four great eras, further split into periods and, in the case of the most recent era, epochs. The present era is the Cenozoic ('new life'), extending backwards through 'middle life' and 'ancient life' to the Pre-Cambrian, named after the Latin word for Wales, the location of some of the earliest known fossils. Most of the Earth's geological history is encompassed by the Pre-Cambrian: though traces of ancient life have since been found, it was largely the proliferation of fossils from the beginning of the Paleozoic era onwards, some 570 million years ago, which first allowed precise subdivisions to be made.

Like the Cambrian, most are named after regions exemplifying a period's geology. Others – such as the Carboniferous ('coal-bearing') or the Cretaceous ('chalk-bearing') – are more directly descriptive.

- Pre-Cambrian shields
- Sedimentary cover on Pre-Cambrian shields
- Paleozoic (Caledonian and Hercynian) folding
- Sedimentary cover on Paleozoic folding
- Mesozoic folding
- Sedimentary cover on Mesozoic folding
- Cenozoic (Alpine) folding
- Sedimentary cover on Cenozoic folding
- Intensive Mesozoic and Cenozoic vulcanism
- Principal faults
- Oceanic marginal troughs
- Mid-oceanic ridges
- Overthrust faults

EARTHQUAKES

Earthquake magnitude is usually rated according to either the Richter or the Modified Mercalli scale, both devised by seismologists in the 1930s. The Richter scale measures absolute earthquake power with mathematical precision: each step upwards represents a tenfold increase in the amplitude of the shockwave. Theoretically, there is no upper limit, but the largest earthquakes measured have been rated at between 8.8 and 8.9. The 12-point Mercalli scale, based on observed effects, is often more meaningful, ranging from I (earthquakes noticed only by seismographs) to XII (total destruction); intermediate points include V (people awakened at night; unstable objects overturned), VII (collapse of ordinary buildings; chimneys and monuments fall), and IX (conspicuous cracks in ground; serious damage to reservoirs).

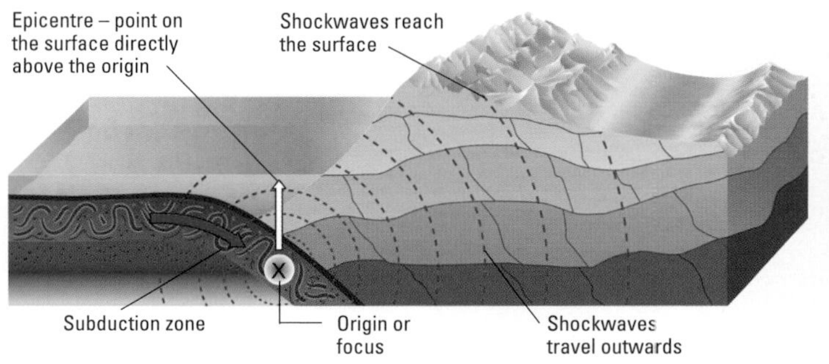

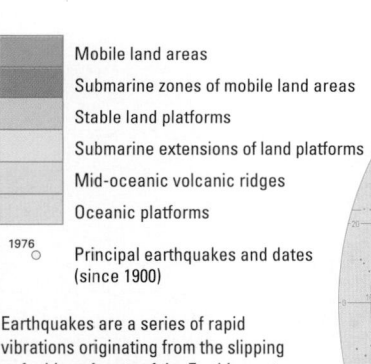

- Mobile land areas
- Submarine zones of mobile land areas
- Stable land platforms
- Submarine extensions of land platforms
- Mid-oceanic volcanic ridges
- Oceanic platforms
- 1976 ○ Principal earthquakes and dates (since 1900)

Earthquakes are a series of rapid vibrations originating from the slipping or faulting of parts of the Earth's crust when stresses within build up to breaking point. They usually happen at depths varying from 8 km to 30 km. Severe earthquakes cause extensive damage when they take place in populated areas, destroying structures and severing communications. Most initial loss of life occurs due to secondary causes such as falling masonry, fires and flooding.

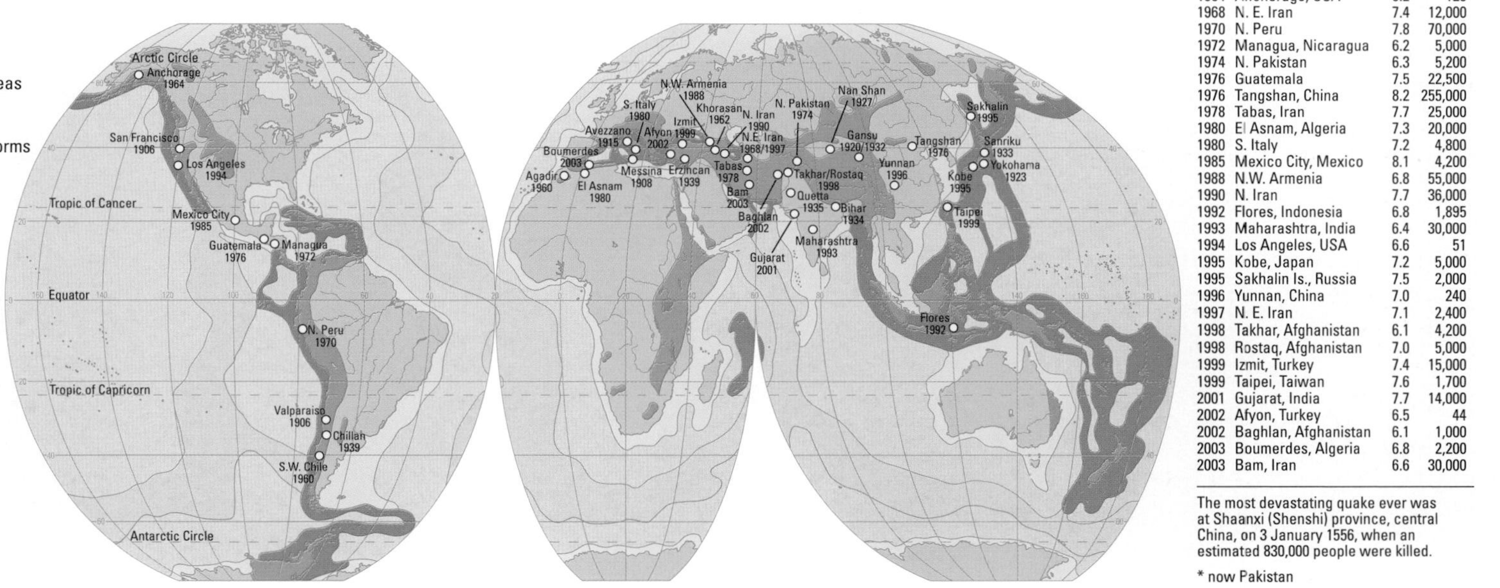

Notable Earthquakes Since 1900

Year	Location	Mag.	Deaths
1906	San Francisco, USA	8.3	3,000
1906	Valparaiso, Chile	8.6	22,000
1908	Messina, Italy	7.5	83,000
1915	Avezzano, Italy	7.5	30,000
1920	Gansu (Kansu), China	8.6	180,000
1923	Yokohama, Japan	8.3	143,000
1927	Nan Shan, China	8.3	200,000
1932	Gansu (Kansu), China	7.6	70,000
1933	Sanriku, Japan	8.9	2,990
1934	Bihar, India/Nepal	8.4	10,700
1935	Quetta, India*	7.5	60,000
1939	Chillan, Chile	8.3	28,000
1939	Erzincan, Turkey	7.9	30,000
1960	S. W. Chile	9.5	2,200
1960	Agadir, Morocco	5.8	12,000
1962	Khorasan, Iran	7.1	12,230
1964	Anchorage, USA	9.2	125
1968	N. E. Iran	7.4	12,000
1970	N. Peru	7.8	70,000
1972	Managua, Nicaragua	6.2	5,000
1974	N. Pakistan	6.3	5,200
1976	Guatemala	7.5	22,500
1976	Tangshan, China	8.2	255,000
1978	Tabas, Iran	7.7	25,000
1980	El Asnam, Algeria	7.3	20,000
1980	S. Italy	7.2	4,800
1985	Mexico City, Mexico	8.1	4,200
1988	N.W. Armenia	6.8	55,000
1990	N. Iran	7.7	36,000
1992	Flores, Indonesia	6.8	1,895
1993	Maharashtra, India	6.4	30,000
1994	Los Angeles, USA	6.6	51
1995	Kobe, Japan	7.2	5,000
1995	Sakhalin Is., Russia	7.5	2,000
1996	Yunnan, China	7.0	240
1997	N. E. Iran	7.1	2,400
1998	Takhar, Afghanistan	6.1	4,200
1998	Rostaq, Afghanistan	7.0	5,000
1999	Izmit, Turkey	7.4	15,000
1999	Taipei, Taiwan	7.6	1,700
2001	Gujarat, India	7.7	14,000
2002	Afyon, Turkey	6.5	44
2002	Baghlan, Afghanistan	6.1	1,000
2003	Boumerdes, Algeria	6.8	2,200
2003	Bam, Iran	6.6	30,000

The most devastating quake ever was at Shaanxi (Shenshi) province, central China, on 3 January 1556, when an estimated 830,000 people were killed.

* now Pakistan

LANDFORMS

For more information:
8 Oceans
10 The Earth's structure
Plate tectonics
Volcanoes
11 Geological time
18 Hydrological cycle
37 Structural regions

The theory of plate tectonics has offered new insights into how the Earth works, elucidating mysteries concerning continental drift, volcanic eruptions and earthquakes. It has also contributed to our understanding of how collisions between plates can squeeze up layers of sediments on seabeds, forming fold mountain ranges, such as the Himalayas.

Yet even as mountains rise, natural forces are wearing them away. In hot, dry climates, mechanical weathering (a result of rapid temperature changes) causes the outer layers of rocks to peel away, while, in cold mountain regions, boulders are prised apart when water freezes in cracks in rocks. Chemical weathering is responsible for hollowing out limestone caves and decomposing granites.

Climatic conditions have a great bearing on the principal agent of erosion in any particular area. Running water is most important in moist temperate regions. In cold regions, ice is the major agent of erosion, and in many mountain ranges, U-shaped valleys are evidence of the erosive power of valley glaciers. Ice sheets moulded much of the Earth's surface during the Ice Ages, the most recent of which, in the northern hemisphere, ended only 10,000 years ago. Polar climates also shape the scenery of the periglacial areas that border bodies of ice. Such areas are subject to constant freeze-thaw action, which creates such features as pingos (domed mounds).

Climatic change has also affected many of the landforms in hot deserts, which were shaped by running water at a time when the deserts enjoyed much wetter climates. However, the major agent of erosion in deserts today is wind-blown sand, which erodes rock strata to form mushroom-shaped rocks and caves.

The surface of the Earth is under constant assault from tectonic processes and the agents of erosion. The products of erosion, fragments of rock such as sand, are deposited to form sedimentary rocks. Metamorphic rocks are created when igneous or sedimentary rocks are buried and metamorphosed by heat and pressure. Eventually the rocks are recycled to form magma, which rises upwards to start the rock cycle all over again.

THE ROCK CYCLE

James Hutton first proposed the rock cycle in the late 1700s after he observed the slow but steady effects of erosion.

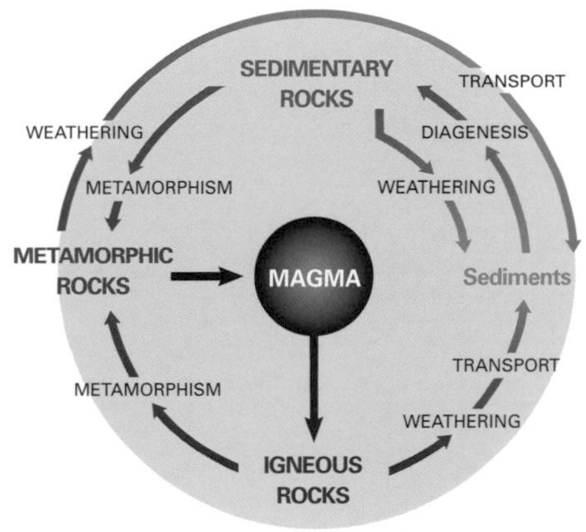

Rocks are divided into three types, according to the way in which they are formed:

Igneous rocks, including granite and basalt, are formed when magma cools inside the Earth's crust or on the surface.

Metamorphic rocks, such as slate, marble and quartzite, are formed below the Earth's surface by the compression or baking of existing rocks.

Sedimentary rocks, like sandstone and limestone, are formed on the surface of the Earth from the remains of living organisms and eroded fragments of older rocks.

MOUNTAIN BUILDING

Mountains are formed when pressures on the Earth's crust caused by continental drift become so intense that the surface buckles or cracks. This happens where oceanic crust is subducted by continental crust or, more dramatically, where two tectonic plates collide: the Rockies, Andes, Alps, Urals and Himalayas resulted from such impacts. These are known as fold mountains because they were formed by the compression of the rocks. The Himalayas were formed from the folded former sediments of the Tethys Sea, which was trapped in the collision zone between the Indian-Australian and Eurasian plates.

The other main mountain-building processes occur when the crust fractures to create faults, allowing rock to be forced upwards in large blocks, or when the pressure of magma within the crust forces the surface to bulge into a dome, or erupts to form a volcano.

Large mountain ranges may reveal a combination of these features. The Alps, for example, have been compressed so violently that the folds are fragmented by numerous faults and intrusions of molten igneous rock.

Over millions of years, even the greatest mountain ranges can be reduced by the agents of erosion (especially rivers) to a low, rugged landscape known as a peneplain.

Types of faults: Faults occur where the crust is being stretched or compressed so violently that the rock strata break in a horizontal or vertical movement. They are classified by the direction in which the blocks of rock have moved. A normal fault results when a vertical movement causes the surface to break apart; compression causes a reverse fault. Horizontal movement causes shearing, known as a strike-slip fault. When the rock breaks in two places, the central block may be pushed up in a horst fault, or sink (creating a rift valley) in a graben fault.

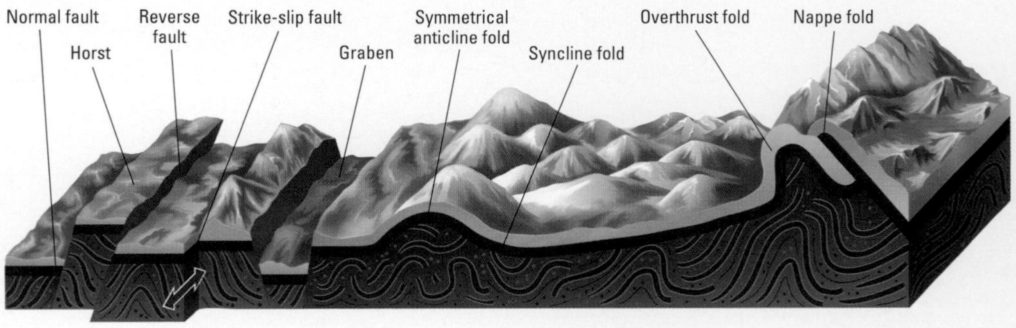

Types of fold: Folds occur when rock strata are squeezed and compressed. They are common, therefore, at destructive plate margins and where plates have collided, forcing the rocks to buckle into mountain ranges. Geographers give different names to the degrees of fold that result from continuing pressure on the rock. A simple fold may be symmetric, with even slopes on either side, but as the pressure builds up, one slope becomes steeper and the fold becomes asymmetric. Later, the ridge or 'anticline' at the top of the fold may slide over the lower ground or 'syncline' to form a recumbent fold. Eventually, the rock strata may break under the pressure to form an overthrust and finally a nappe fold.

CONTINENTAL GLACIATION

Many landforms in the northern hemisphere were shaped by ice sheets and meltwater during the Pleistocene Ice Age, which began about 2 million years ago. During the Ice Age, the ice sheets periodically advanced and retreated. The first map (*below left*) shows the ice cover at its greatest extent about 200,000 years BP (before the present), when it covered about 30% of the land surface, as compared with 10% today. About 18,000 years BP, the ice covered most of Canada and extended as far south as the Bristol Channel in England. Around the ice sheets, land areas experienced periglacial conditions.

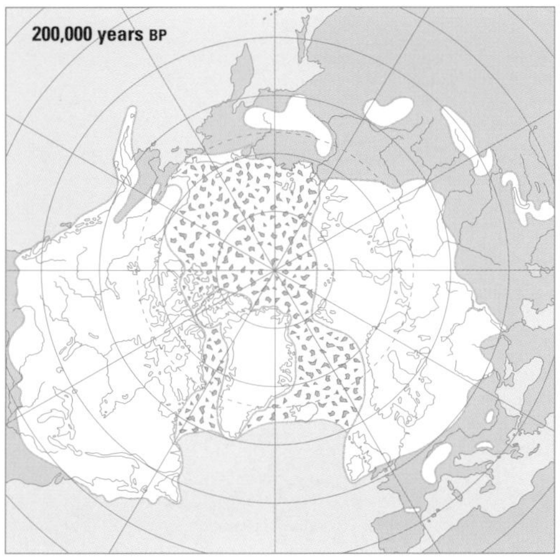

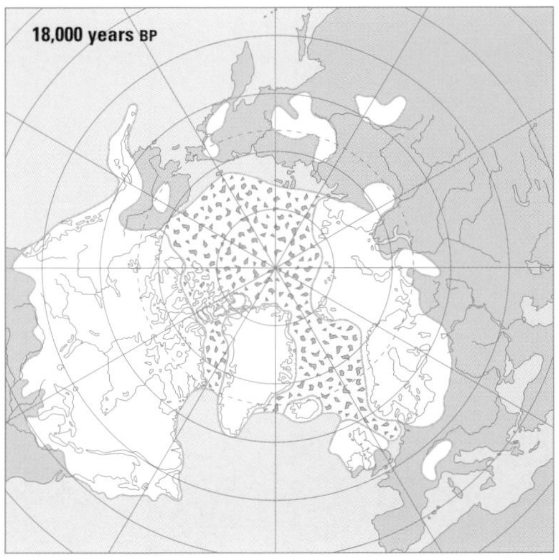

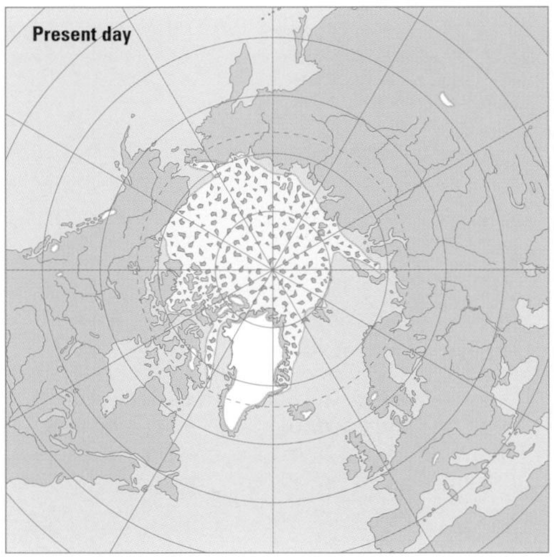

NATURAL LANDFORMS

Natural landforms reflect the influence of plate tectonics, through mountain-building and the generation of new rocks from the Earth's interior, together with the agents of erosion – running water, ice, winds and coastal waves. Over millions of years, mountains are gradually eroded, with the eroded material redistributed, usually at lower levels. The resultant landforms reflect the major forces that have been at work, as well as the underlying geology, the climatic conditions, which often vary over time, and the vegetation cover. The study of these processes and the landforms they create is called geomorphology. The stylized diagram (*below*) shows some major natural landforms found in the mid-latitudes.

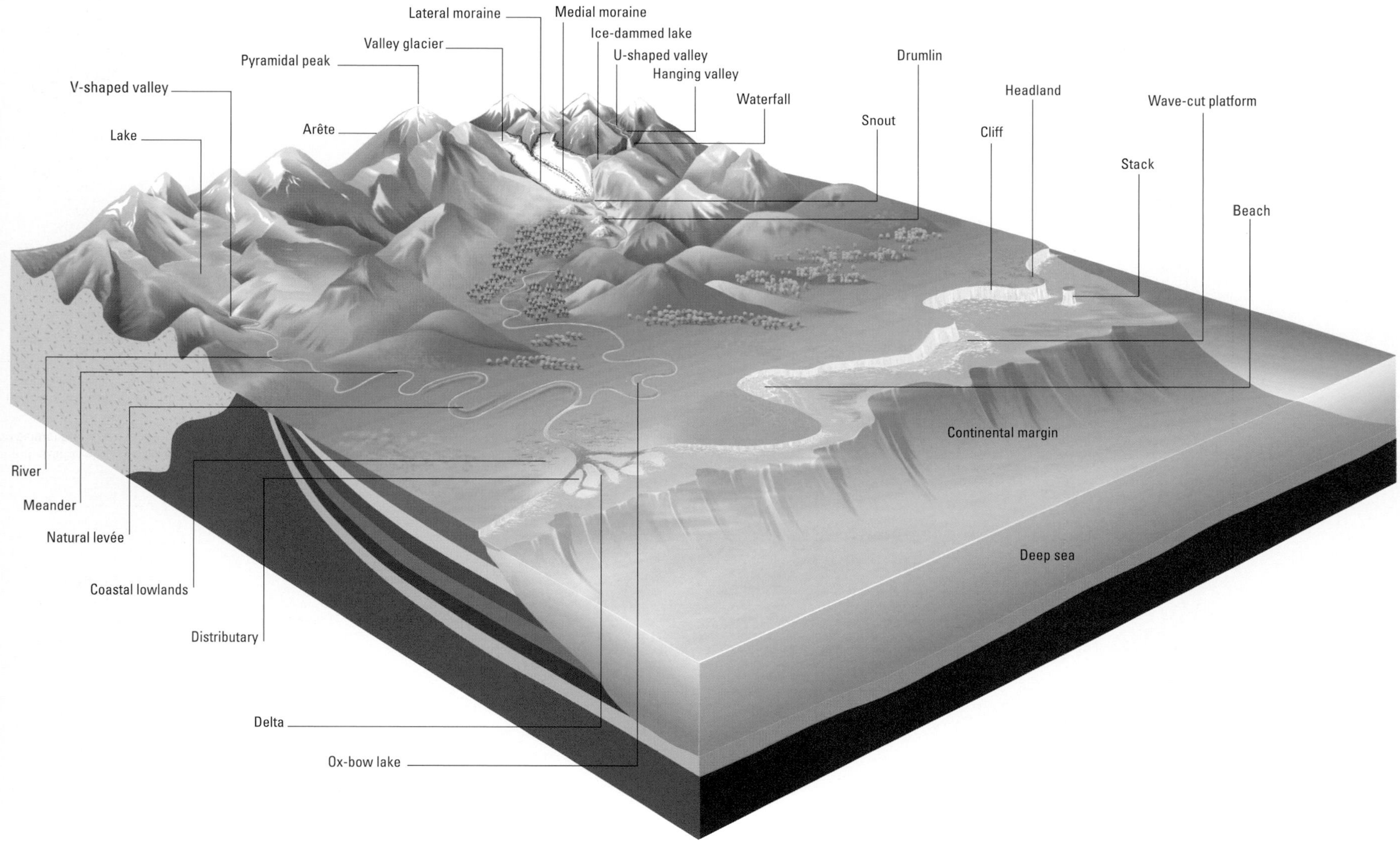

SURFACE PROCESSES

Catastrophic changes to landforms are caused periodically by such phenomena as avalanches, landslides and volcanic eruptions, but most of the processes that shape the Earth's surface operate extremely slowly in human terms.

Chemical weathering is at its greatest in warm, humid regions, while mechanical weathering (the physical break-up of rocks) predominates in cold mountain or hot desert regions. The most familiar type of chemical weathering is caused by the reaction of rainwater containing dissolved carbon dioxide on limestone; this leads to the creation of labyrinthine cave networks dissolved by groundwater. Mechanical weathering includes frost action, while in hot deserts, rapid temperature changes cause the outer layers of rocks to expand and contract until they crack and peel away, a process called exfoliation.

Running water is probably the world's leading agent of erosion and transportation. The energy of a river depends on several factors, including its velocity and volume, and its erosive power is at its peak when it is in full flood, sweeping soil, pebbles and even boulders along its course, cutting downwards into the bedrock or widening its valley.

Sea waves also exert tremendous erosive power during storms, when they hurl pebbles and large rocks against the shore, undercutting cliffs and hollowing out caves. Headlands are often attacked on both sides, forming caves, then a natural arch and eventually an isolated stack.

Glacier ice forms in mountain hollows, called cirques, and spills out to form valley glaciers, which transport rocks shattered by frost action. As a glacier moves, rocks embedded in the base and sides scrape away bedrock, eroding steep-sided, flat-bottomed, U-shaped valleys. Evidence of past glaciation in mountain regions includes cirques, knife-edged ridges, or arêtes, and pyramidal peaks, or horns.

DESERT LANDFORMS

Deserts are defined as places with an average annual precipitation of 250 mm [10 inches] per year, though places with a higher rainfall and a high evaporation rate may also qualify as deserts.

The three types of desert landforms are known by their Arabic names, a reflection of the fact that the Sahara in North Africa is the world's largest desert. Sand desert, called *erg*, covers about one-fifth of the world's deserts. The rest is divided between *hammada* (areas of bare rock) and *reg* (broad plains covered by loose gravel or pebbles).

The shapes of dunes in sand deserts reflect the character of local winds. Where winds are constant in direction, the sand often piles up in crescent-shaped dunes, called *barchans*. Barchans are constantly on the move and their forward march, unless halted by vegetation, may overwhelm settlements at oases. *Seif* dunes, named after the Arabic word for 'sword', are long ridges of sand that lie parallel to the direction of the wind, but where winds are variable, the sand sheets are often featureless.

Wind-blown sand is an effective agent of erosion, but because of the weight of sand grains, this type of erosion is confined to within approximately 2 metres [7 feet] of the land surface, creating caves and mushroom-shaped rocks.

In assessing desert landforms, it is important to remember that other processes were at work in the past when the climate was very different from today. For example, cave paintings suggest that the Sahara had a much wetter climate after the end of the Ice Age and only began to dry up after about 5000 BC. However, human action, including overgrazing and the cutting down of trees for firewood, can turn a grassland region into desert – a process known as desertification.

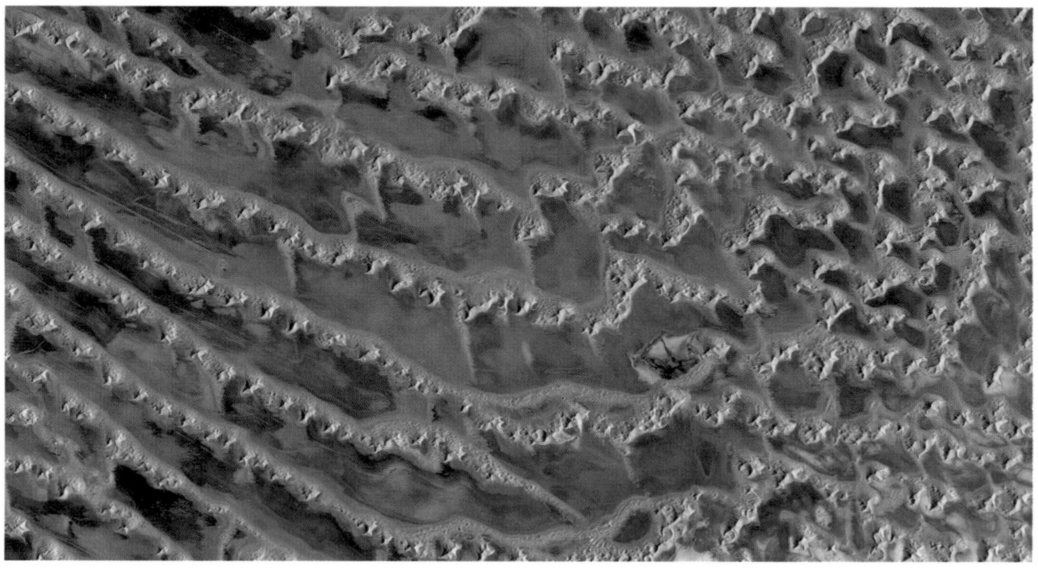

◀ This false-colour satellite image of part of the Rub' al Khali, or 'Empty Quarter', in Saudi Arabia shows part of the world's largest sand sea (*erg*), which covers almost 600,000 sq km [232,000 sq miles]. Showing many different types of sand dune, the image enhances the difference in colour between the dune sand and the inter-dune areas, which have a higher clay composition. The blue 'eye' is a partially flooded clay basin (*playa*).

The Atmosphere

For more information:
- 9 Ocean currents
- 17 Beaufort wind scale
  - Climate change
  - Monsoon
- 21 Solar energy
  - Greenhouse effect
- 22 Greenhouse power
- 23 Acid rain

The atmosphere is a meteor shield, a radiation deflector, a thermal blanket and a source of chemical energy for the Earth's diverse life forms. Five-sixths of its mass is in the lowest layer, the troposphere, which ranges in thickness from 18–10 km between the Equator and the poles. Powered by the Sun, the air is always on the move, flowing generally from high- to low-pressure areas. The troposphere is the layer where virtually all weather phenomena, including clouds, precipitation and winds, occur. Above the troposphere is the stratosphere, which contains the important ozone layer and extends to about 50 km above the Earth's surface. Beyond 100 km, atmospheric density is lower than most laboratory vacuums.

STRUCTURE OF THE ATMOSPHERE

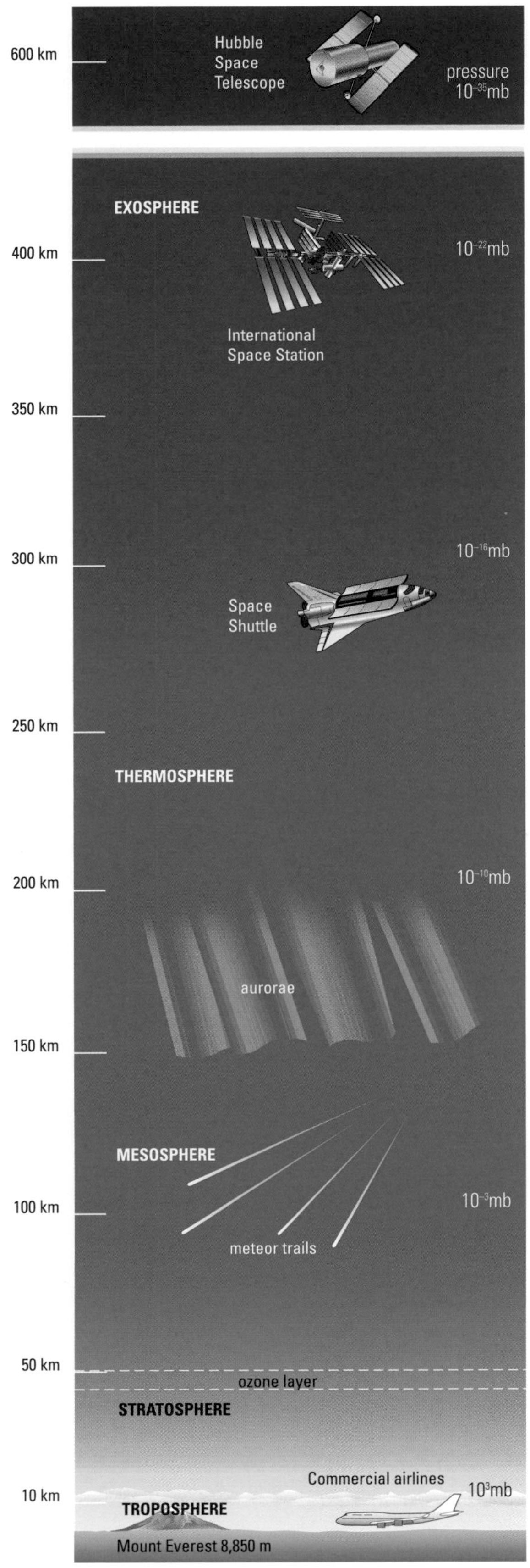

CIRCULATION OF THE AIR

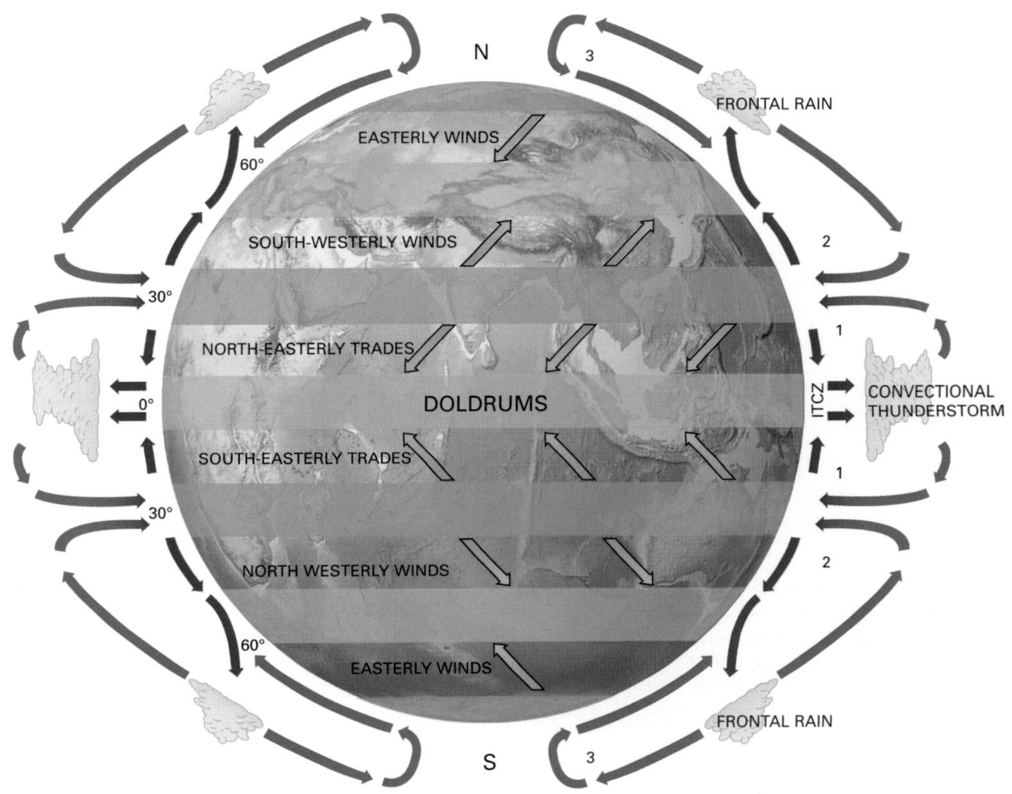

- High pressure
- Low pressure
- Warm air
- **1** Hadley Cell
- **2** Ferrel Cell
- **3** Polar Cell
- Cold air
- Surface winds
- Clouds
- **ITCZ** Intertropical convergence zone

FRONTAL SYSTEMS

Depressions, or cyclones, form along the polar front where dense polar easterlies meet warm subtropical westerlies. Depressions occur when warm air flows into waves in the polar front, while cold air flows in behind it, creating rotating air systems that bring changeable weather.

Along the warm front (the boundary on the ground between the warm and cold air), the warm air flows upwards over the cold air, producing a sequence of clouds that help forecasters to predict a depression's advance. Along the cold front, the advancing cold air forces warm air to rise steeply. Towering cumulonimbus clouds form in the rising air.

When the cold front overtakes the warm front, the warm air is pushed above ground level to form an occluded front. Cloud and rain persist along occlusions until temperatures equalize, the air mixes, and the depression dies out.

Depressions with these distinctive features are known as 'frontal'. The diagram below shows a cross-section through a depression and the associated cloud types and weather conditions that may be experienced.

CHEMICAL COMPOSITION

Gaseous composition of the principal atmospheric layers

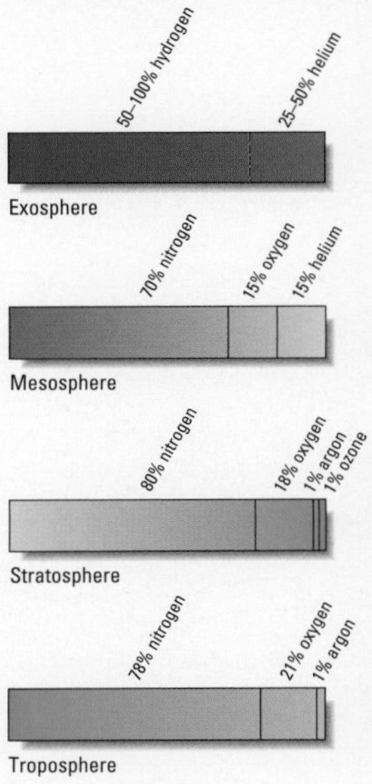

Helium vanishes with increasing altitude. Above 2,400 km the exosphere is almost entirely composed of hydrogen.

The high energy of mesospheric gas gives it a notional temperature of more than 2,000°C, although its density is negligible.

Stratospheric air contains enough ozone to make it poisonous, although it is in any case too rarified to breathe.

The narrowest of all the layers, this thin region contains about 85% of the atmosphere's total mass and almost all of its water vapour. It is also the realm of the Earth's weather.

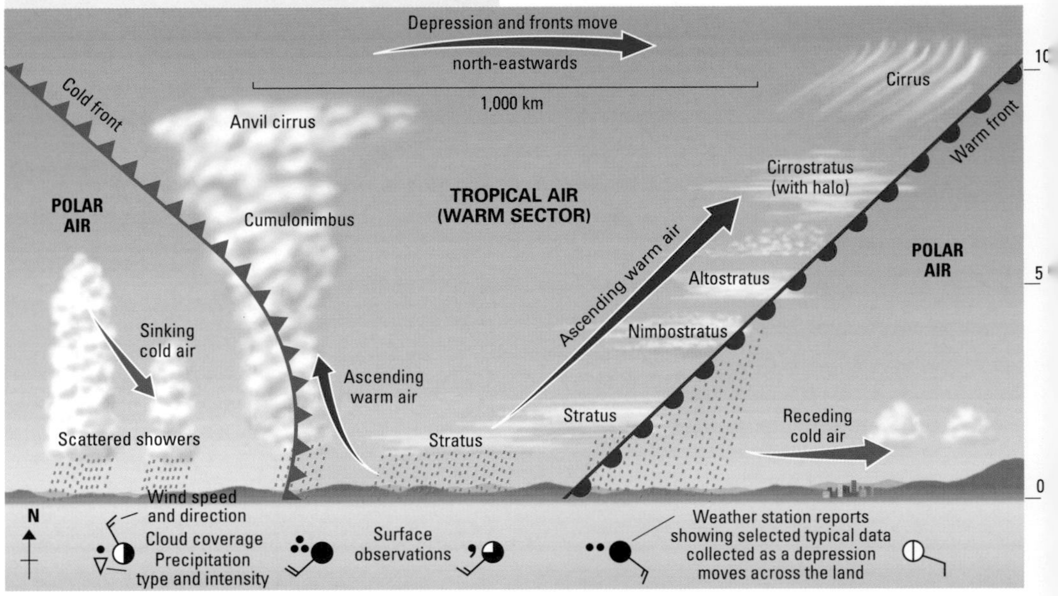

AIR MASSES

Air masses are bodies of air whose characteristics are broadly the same over a large area. Around the Equator, where the Sun's heat creates relatively high surface temperatures, warm air rises to create a zone of low pressure called the doldrums. The air cools and finally spreads out towards the poles. Around latitudes 30° north and south, the air sinks back to the surface, becoming warmer as it descends and creating zones of high pressure called the horse latitudes.

The high- and low-pressure zones are both areas of comparative calm, but between them lie the prevailing trade wind belts. Air also flows north and south from the high-pressure horse latitudes and these airflows meet up with cold, dense air flowing from the poles along the polar front.

This basic circulatory system is complicated by the Coriolis effect, brought about by the spinning Earth. Because of the Coriolis effect, the prevailing winds do not flow directly north–south but are deflected to the right in the northern hemisphere and to the left in the southern. Along the polar front, depressions form where the polar easterlies meet the westerlies.

The first classification of clouds was developed by a London chemist, Luke Howard, in 1803, and it was later modified by the World Meteorological Organization. The main types are divided into three groups according to their altitude, and into subgroups according to their shape, which vary from hairlike filaments (cirrus), heaps or piles (cumulus), and layers (stratus). Each cloud carries some kind of message, though not always a clear one, to weather forecasters.

CLASSIFICATION OF CLOUDS

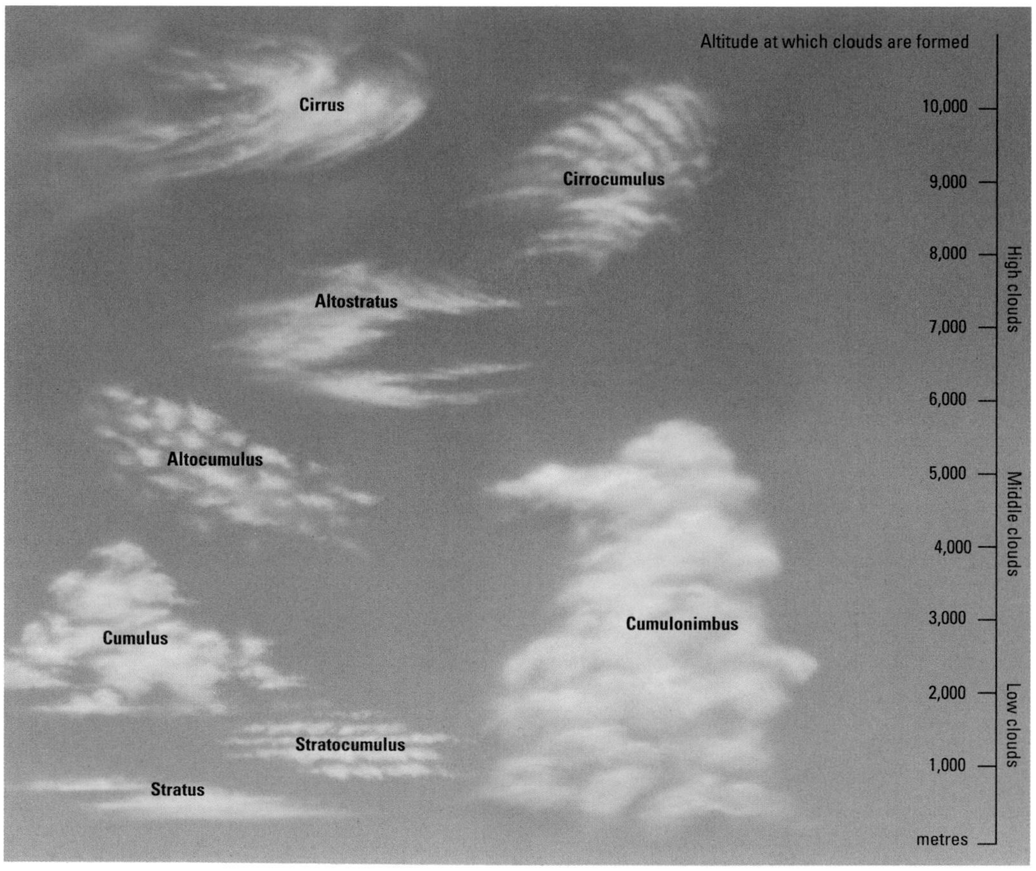

Clouds form when damp, usually rising, air is cooled. Thus they form when a wind rises to cross hills or mountains; when a mass of air rises over, or is pushed up by, another mass of denser air; or when local heating of the ground causes convection currents.

The types of clouds are classified according to altitude as high, middle or low. The high ones, composed of ice crystals, are cirrus, cirrostratus and cirrocumulus.

The middle clouds are altostratus – a grey or bluish striated, fibrous or uniform sheet producing light drizzle – and altocumulus, a thicker and fluffier version of cirrocumulus.

Low clouds include nimbostratus, a dark grey layer that brings rain or snow; cumulus, a detached heap, dark at the base; stratus, which forms dull, overcast skies at low levels; and stratocumulus, which consists of fluffy greyish-white layers.

Cumulonimbus, associated with storms and rains, heavy and dense with a flat base and a high, fluffy outline, can be tall enough to occupy middle as well as low altitudes.

PRESSURE AND SURFACE WINDS

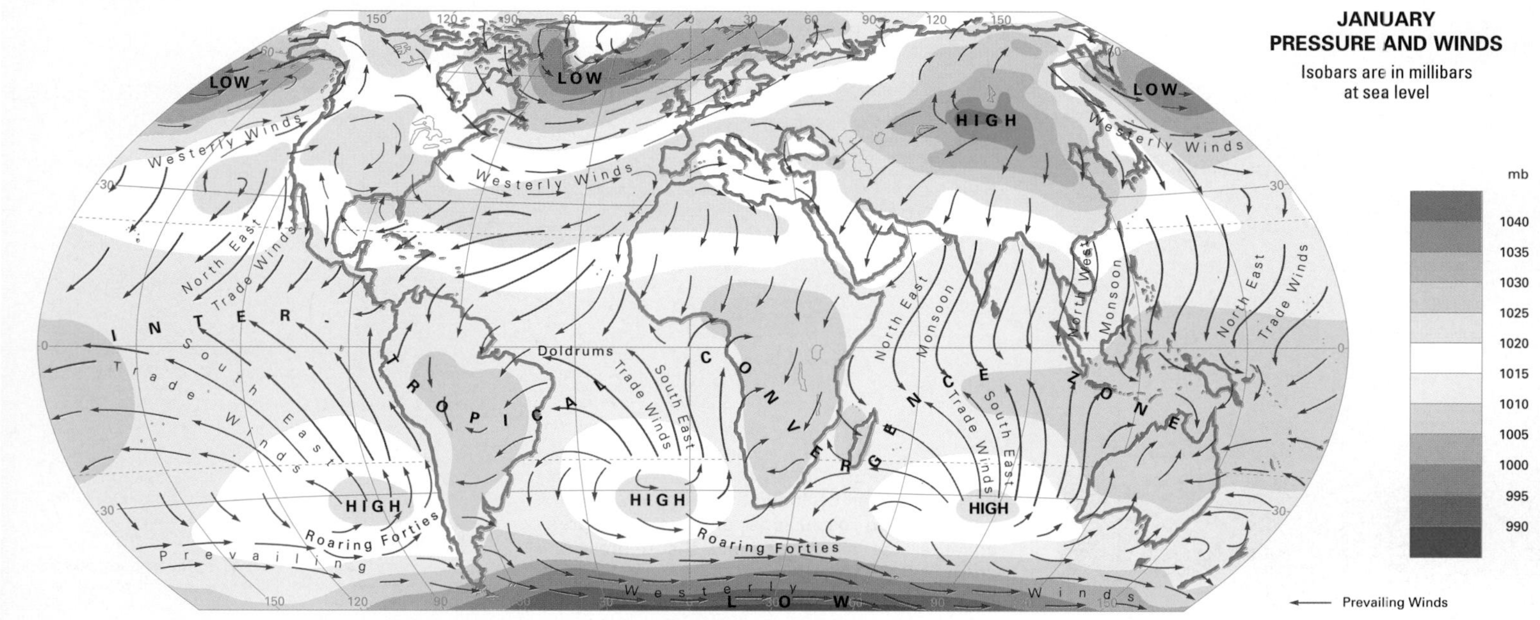

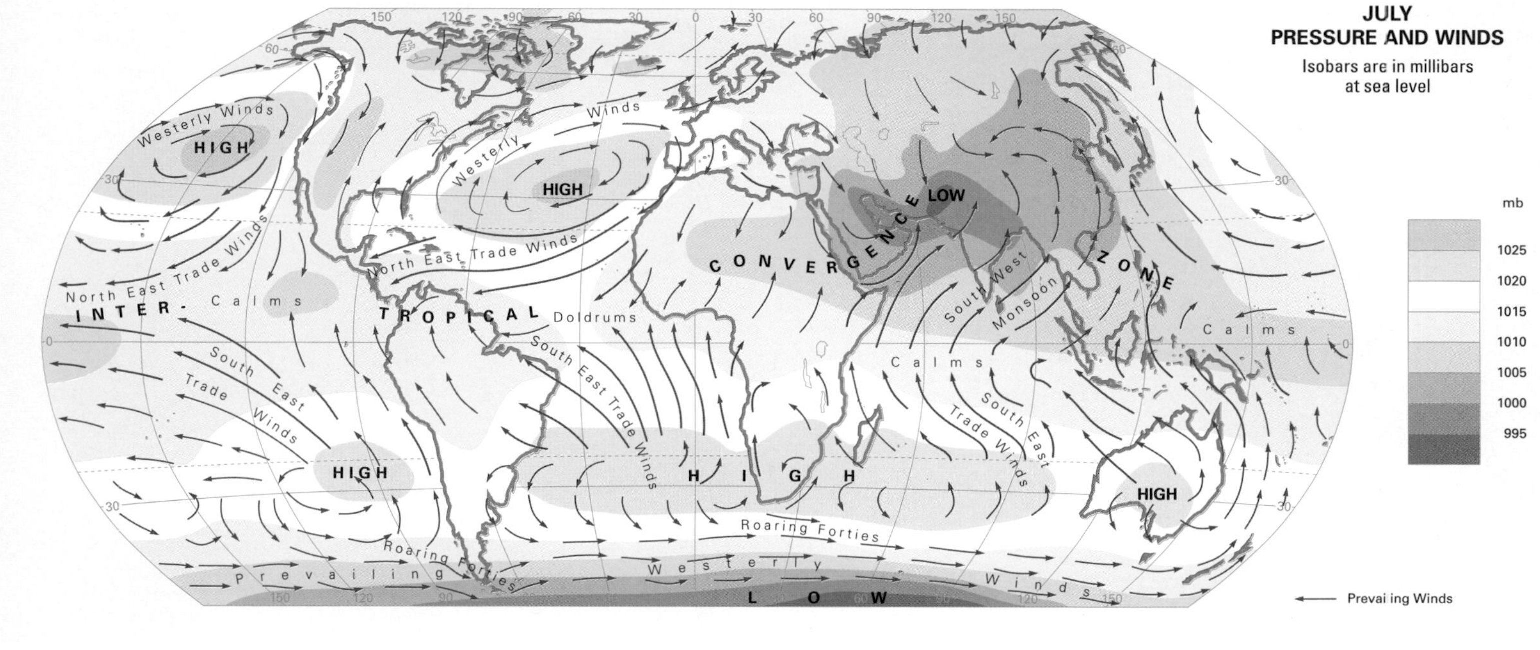

CLIMATE RECORDS

Pressure and winds

Highest barometric pressure:
Agata, Siberia, 1,083.8 mb at altitude 262 m [862 ft], 31 December 1968.

Lowest barometric pressure:
Typhoon Tip, 480 km [300 mi] west of Guam, Pacific Ocean, 870 mb, 12 October 1979.

Highest recorded wind speed:
Mt Washington, New Hampshire, USA, 371 km/h [231 mph], 12 April 1934. This is three times as strong as hurricane force on the Beaufort Scale.

Windiest place:
Commonwealth Bay, George V Coast, Antarctica, where gales frequently reach over 320 km/h [200 mph].

Worst recorded storm:
Bangladesh (then East Pakistan) cyclone*, 13 November 1970 – over 300,000 dead or missing. The 1991 cyclone, Bangladesh's and the world's second worst in terms of loss of life, killed an estimated 138,000 people.

Worst recorded tornado:
Missouri/Illinois/Indiana, USA, 18 March 1925 – 792 deaths. The tornado was only 275 m [300 yds] wide.

* *Tropical cyclones are known as hurricanes in Central and North America, as typhoons in the Far East, and as willy-willies in northern Australia.*

Climate

For more information:

9 Ocean currents
14 Circulation of the air
15 Classification of clouds
Pressure and winds
18 Hydrological cycle
19 Natural vegetation
21 Greenhouse effect
22 Global warming

Weather is the day-to-day or hour-to-hour condition of the air, while climate is weather in the long term – the seasonal pattern of hot and cold, wet and dry, averaged over a long period.

Most classifications of climate are based on a system developed in the early 19th century by Vladimir Köppen, a Russian meteorologist. Using a code based on letters and a classification centred on two main features, temperature and precipitation, he identified five main climatic types: tropical (A), dry (B), warm temperate (C), cold temperate (D), and polar (E). A highland mountain climate (H) was added later to account for the variety of altitudinal climatic zones on high mountains. Each of these main regions was then further subdivided.

Latitude is a major factor in determining climate, but other factors add to the complexity. These include the differential heating of land and sea, the distance from the sea, the effect of mountains on winds, and the influence of ocean currents. For example, New York City, Naples and the Gobi Desert share almost the same latitude, but their climates are very different.

During the last Ice Age, the Earth underwent alternating cold periods, called glacials, separated by warm interglacials. The Milankovich theory suggests such cycles may be caused by variations in the Earth's path around the Sun, changing from almost circular to elliptical every 95,000 years, and variations in the Earth's tilt from 21.5° to 24.5° every 42,000 years. Another factor is that the Earth is now closest to the Sun in the middle of winter in the northern hemisphere and furthest away in summer. But 12,000 years ago, at the height of the last glacial period, the northern winter fell with the Sun at its most distant.

Studies of these cycles suggest that we are now in an interglacial with a new glacial period on the way. However, scientists believe that global warming, largely a result of burning fossil fuels and deforestation, may be occurring much faster than the great, slow cycles of the Solar System.

Tropical rainy climates
All mean monthly temperatures above 18°C.

Af	Rainforest climate
Am	Monsoon climate
Aw	Savanna climate

Dry climates
Low rainfall combined with a wide range of temperatures

BS	Steppe climate
BW	Desert climate

Warm temperate rainy climates
The mean temperature is below 18°C but above –3°C and that of the warmest month is over 10°C.

Cw	Dry winter climate
Cs	Dry summer climate
Cf	Climate with no dry season

Cold temperate rainy climates
The mean temperature of the coldest month is below –3°C but that of the warmest month is still over 10°C.

Dw	Dry winter climate
Df	Climate with no dry season

Polar climates
The mean temperature of the warmest month is below 10°C, giving permanently frozen subsoil.

ET	Tundra climate

The mean temperature of the warmest month is below 0°C, giving permanent ice and snow.

EF	Polar climate

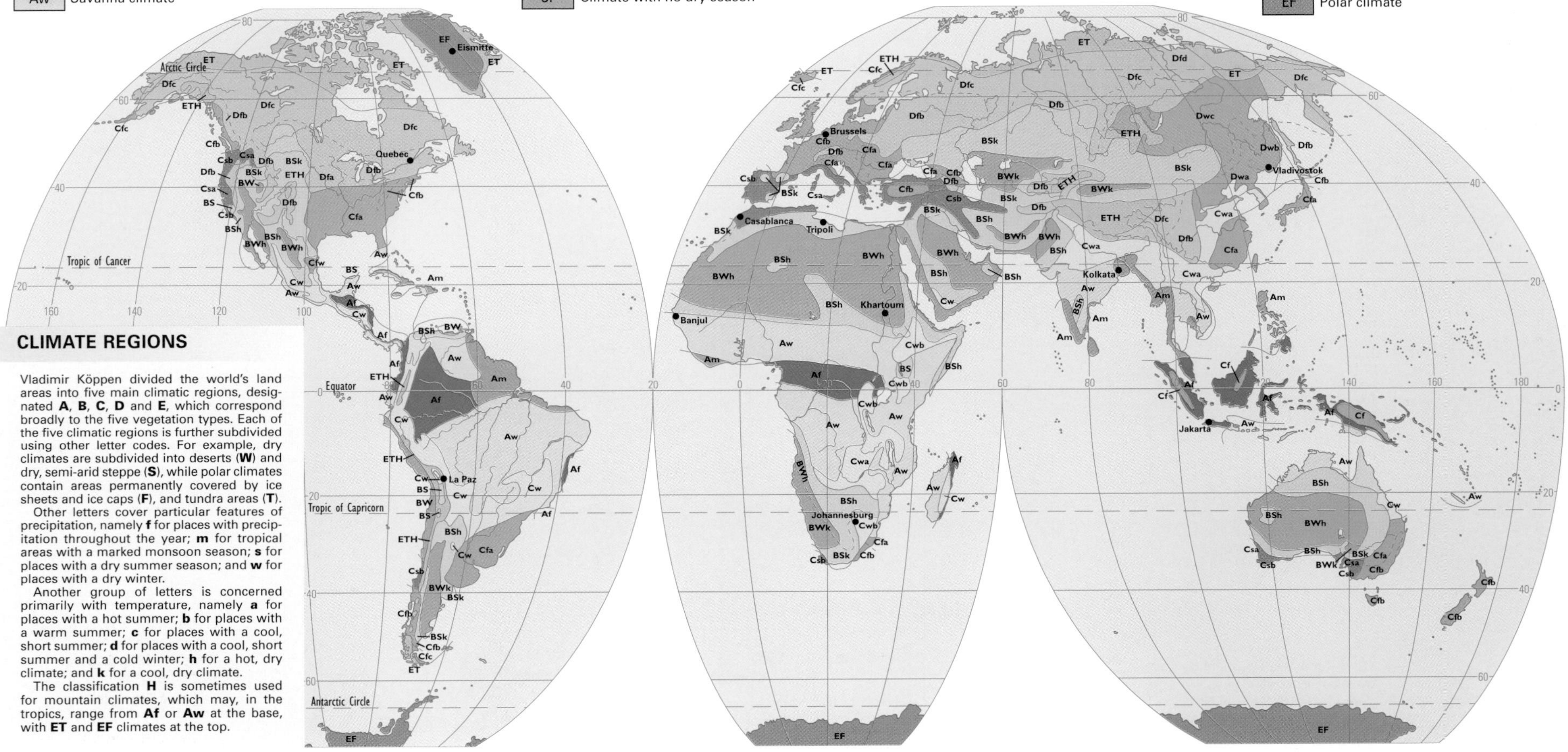

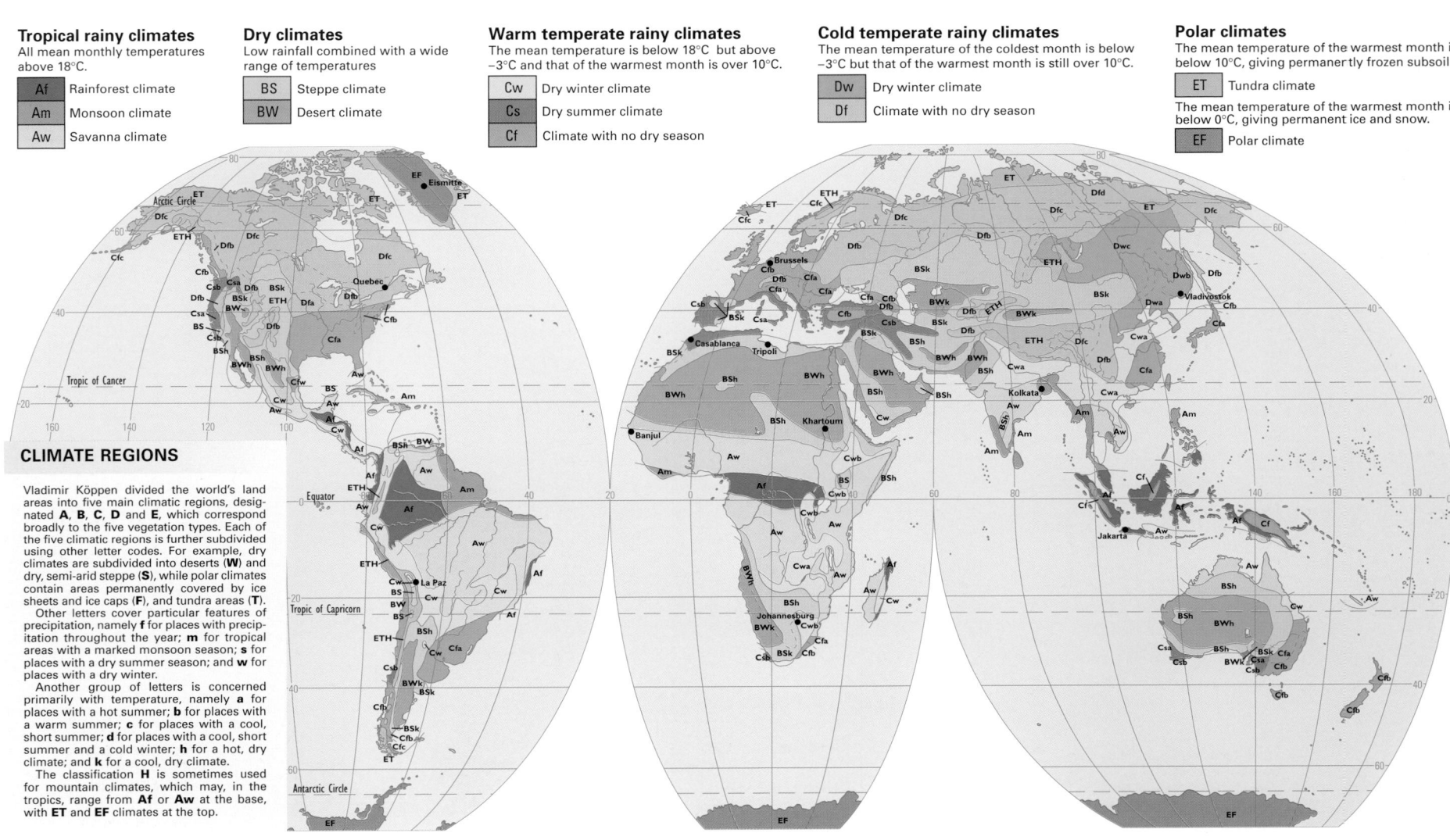

CLIMATE REGIONS

Vladimir Köppen divided the world's land areas into five main climatic regions, designated **A**, **B**, **C**, **D** and **E**, which correspond broadly to the five vegetation types. Each of the five climatic regions is further subdivided using other letter codes. For example, dry climates are subdivided into deserts (**W**) and dry, semi-arid steppe (**S**), while polar climates contain areas permanently covered by ice sheets and ice caps (**F**), and tundra areas (**T**).

Other letters cover particular features of precipitation, namely **f** for places with precipitation throughout the year; **m** for tropical areas with a marked monsoon season; **s** for places with a dry summer season; and **w** for places with a dry winter.

Another group of letters is concerned primarily with temperature, namely **a** for places with a hot summer; **b** for places with a warm summer; **c** for places with a cool, short summer; **d** for places with a cool, short summer and a cold winter; **h** for a hot, dry climate; and **k** for a cool, dry climate.

The classification **H** is sometimes used for mountain climates, which may, in the tropics, range from **Af** or **Aw** at the base, with **ET** and **EF** climates at the top.

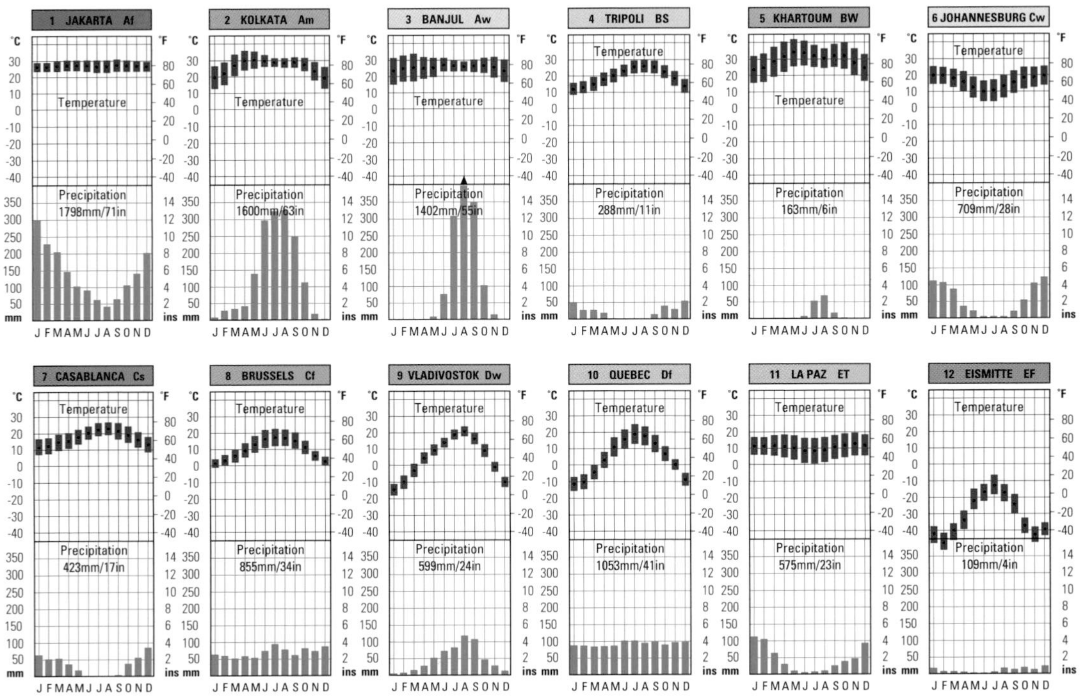

CLIMATE AND WEATHER TERMS

Anticyclone: area of high pressure with light winds and generally quiet weather.
Absolute humidity: amount of water vapour contained in a given volume of air.
Cloud cover: amount of cloud in the sky; measured in oktas (from 1–8), with 0 clear, and 8 total cover.
Condensation: the conversion of water vapour, or moisture in the air, into liquid.
Cyclone: violent storm resulting from anticlockwise rotation of winds in the northern hemisphere and clockwise in the southern: called hurricane in North America, typhoon in the Far East.
Depression: area of low pressure. The pressure gradient is towards the centre.
Dew: water droplets condensed out of the air after the ground has cooled at night.
Dew point: temperature at which air becomes saturated (reaches a relative humidity of 100%) at a constant pressure.
Drizzle: precipitation where drops are less than 0.5 mm [0.02 in] in diameter.
Evaporation: conversion of water from liquid into vapour or moisture in the air.
Front: the dividing line between two air masses.
Frost: dew that has frozen when the air temperature falls below freezing point.
Hail: frozen rain; small balls of ice, often falling during thunderstorms.
Hoar frost: formed on objects when the dew point is below freezing point.
Humidity: amount of moisture in the air.
Isobar: cartographic line connecting places of equal atmospheric pressure.
Isotherm: cartographic line connecting places of equal temperature.
Lightning: massive electrical discharge released in thunderstorm from cloud to cloud or cloud to ground, the result of the top becoming positively charged and the bottom negatively charged.
Precipitation: measurable rain, snow, sleet or hail.
Prevailing wind: most common direction of wind at a given location.
Rain: precipitation of liquid particles with diameter larger than 0.5 mm [0.02 in].
Relative humidity: amount of water vapour contained in a given volume of air at a given temperature.
Snow: formed when water vapour condenses below freezing point.
Thunder: sound produced by the rapid expansion of air heated by lightning.
Tornado: severe funnel-shaped storm that twists as hot air spins vertically (waterspout at sea).
Whirlwind: rapidly rotating column of air, only a few metres across, made visible by dust.

CLIMATE CHANGE

Human factors, such as the emission of greenhouse gases through the burning of fossil fuels and deforestation, have contributed to global warming. The histogram (*below*) shows in blue the average global temperatures from 1860 to 1996. The red line is a 10-year running average. Overall, there is an upwards trend, particularly so since the 1970s, when global warming became a matter of concern in scientific circles. The large year-to-year changes indicate the Earth's natural climatic variability and the influence of such factors as major volcanic eruptions.

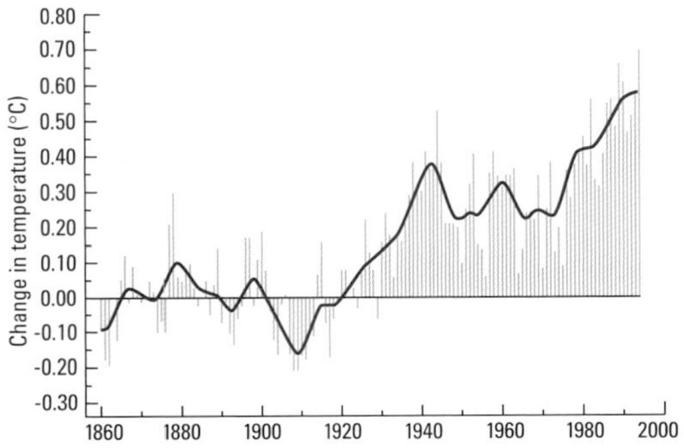

Data from the Hadley Centre for Climate Research and Prediction

BEAUFORT WIND SCALE

Named after Admiral Sir Francis Beaufort, the 19th-century British naval officer who devised it, the Beaufort Scale assesses wind speed according to its effects. It was originally designed as an aid for sailors, but has since been adapted for use on the land. It is used internationally.

Scale	Wind speed km/h	Wind speed mph	Effect
0	0–1	0–1	**Calm** Smoke rises vertically
1	1–5	1–3	**Light air** Wind direction shown only by smoke drift
2	6–11	4–7	**Light breeze** Wind felt on face; leaves rustle; vanes moved by wind
3	12–19	8–12	**Gentle breeze** Leaves and small twigs in constant motion; wind extends small flag
4	20–28	13–18	**Moderate** Raises dust and loose paper; small branches move
5	29–38	19–24	**Fresh** Small trees in leaf sway; crested wavelets on inland waters
6	39–49	25–31	**Strong** Large branches move; difficult to use umbrellas; overhead wires whistle
7	50–61	32–38	**Near gale** Whole trees in motion; difficult to walk against wind
8	62–74	39–46	**Gale** Twigs break from trees; walking very difficult
9	75–88	47–54	**Strong gale** Slight structural damage
10	89–102	55–63	**Storm** Trees uprooted; serious structural damage
11	103–117	64–72	**Violent storm** Widespread damage
12	118+	73+	**Hurricane**

THE MONSOON

Monsoon is the term given to the seasonal reversal of wind direction, most noticeably in South-east Asia. It results from a combination of factors: the extreme heating and cooling of large landmasses in relation to the less marked changes in temperature of the adjacent seas; the northwards movement of the Intertropical Convergence Zone (ITCZ); and the effect of the Himalayas on the circulation of the air.

In March, winds blow outwards from the mainland. But as the Sun and the ITCZ move northwards, the land is intensely heated, and a low-pressure system develops. The south-east trade winds change direction and are sucked into the interior to become south-westerlies, bringing heavy rain. By November, the Sun and the ITCZ have again moved south and the wind directions are again reversed. Cool winds blow from the Asian interior to the sea, losing any moisture on the Himalayas before descending to the coast.

TEMPERATURE

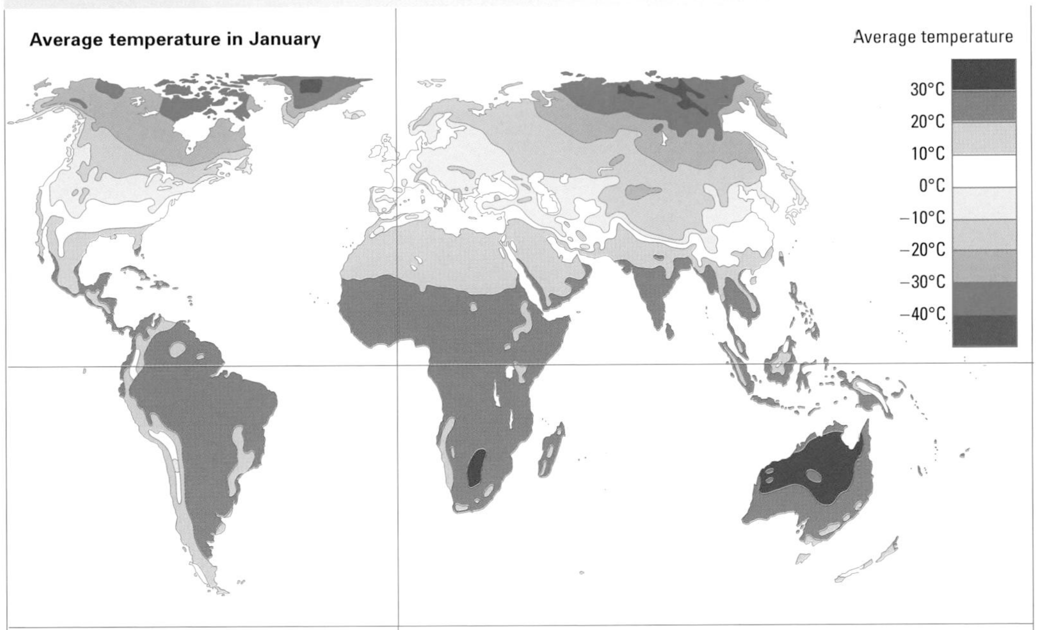

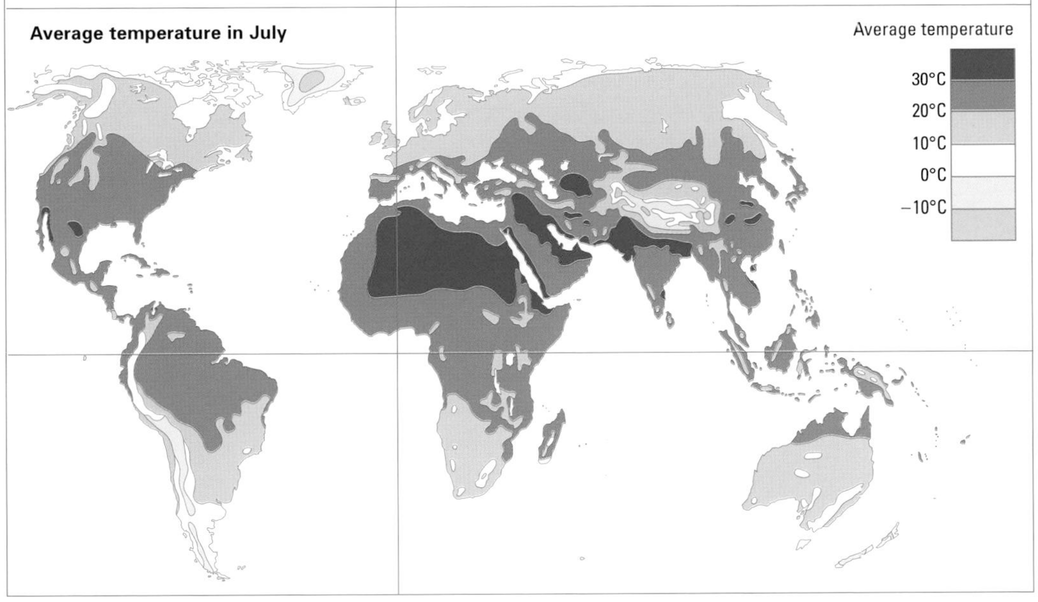

PRECIPITATION (RAINFALL AND SNOW)

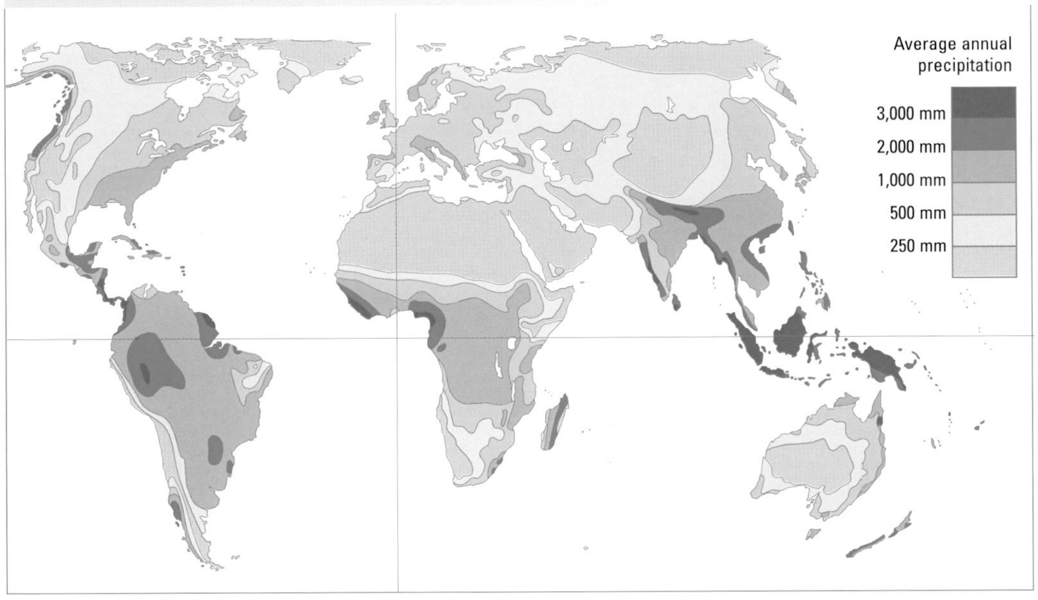

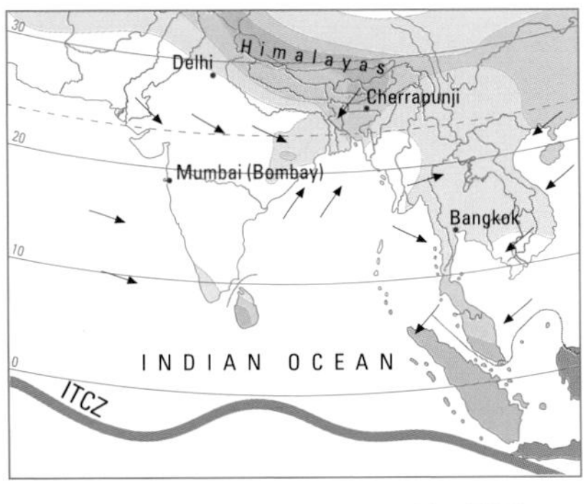

March – Start of the hot, dry season. The ITCZ is over the southern Indian Ocean.

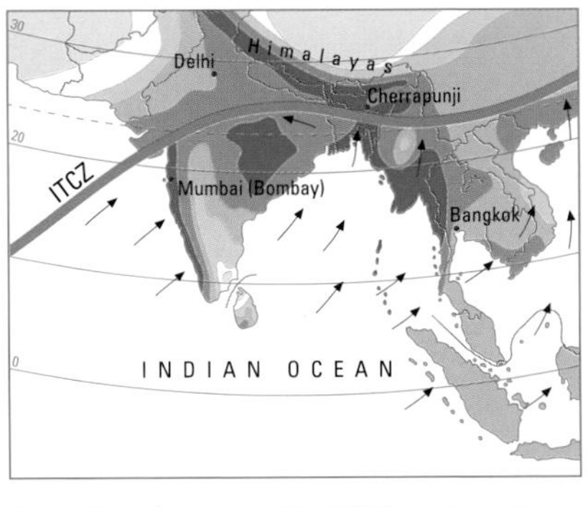

July – The rainy season. The ITCZ has migrated northwards; winds blow onshore.

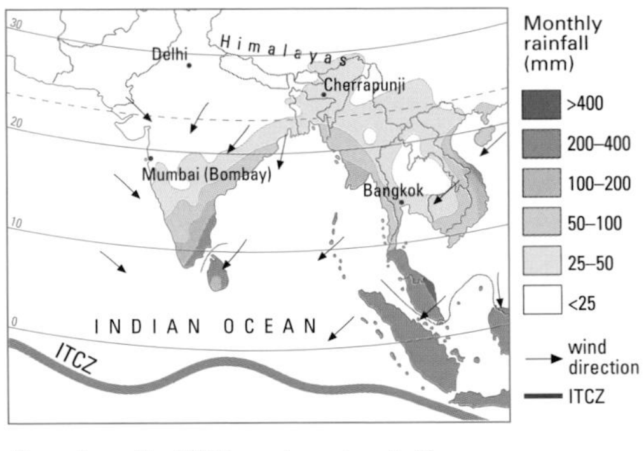

November – The ITCZ has returned south. The offshore winds are cool and dry.

CLIMATE RECORDS

TEMPERATURE

Highest recorded temperature:
Al Aziziyah, Libya, 58°C [136.4°F], 13 September 1922.

Highest mean annual temperature:
Dallol, Ethiopia, 34.4°C [94°F], 1960–6.

Longest heatwave:
Marble Bar, W. Australia, 162 days over 38°C [100°F], 23 October 1923 to 7 April 1924.

Lowest recorded temperature (outside poles):
Verkhoyansk, Siberia, −68°C [−90°F], 6 February 1933. Verkhoyansk also registered the greatest annual range of temperature: −70°C to 37°C [−94°F to 98°F].

Lowest mean annual temperature:
Polus Nedostupnosti, Pole of Cold, Antarctica, −57.8°C [−72°F].

PRECIPITATION

Driest place:
Calama, N. Chile: no recorded rainfall in 400 years to 1971.

Wettest place (average):
Tututendo, Colombia: mean annual rainfall 11,770 mm [463.4 in].

Wettest place (12 months):
Cherrapunji, Meghalaya, N.E. India, 26,470 mm [1,040 in], August 1860 to August 1861. Cherrapunji also holds the record for rainfall in one month: 2,930 mm [115 in], July 1861. (*See Monsoon maps below.*)

Wettest place (24 hours):
Cilaos, Réunion, Indian Ocean, 1,870 mm [73.6 in], 15–16 March 1952.

Heaviest hailstones:
Gopalganj, Bangladesh, up to 1.02 kg [2.25 lb], 14 April 1986 (killed 92 people).

Heaviest snowfall (continuous):
Bessans, Savoie, France, 1,730 mm [68 in] in 19 hours, 5–6 April 1969.

Heaviest snowfall (season/year):
Paradise Ranger Station, Mt Rainier, Washington, USA, 31,102 mm [1,224.5 in], 19 February 1971 to 18 February 1972.

Water and Vegetation

For more information:

16 Climate regions
17 Precipitation
20 Biodiversity
23 Water pollution
Deforestation

Without the hydrological cycle, by which water is constantly recycled between the oceans, the atmosphere and the land, the continents would be barren. Precipitation enables plants to grow and soils to form, creating the world's natural vegetation regions and the ecosystems that support animal life.

Running water also plays a major role in shaping landforms. Yet in many parts of the world, people do not have safe water to drink and suffer from diseases caused by water-borne organisms and pollution. In 2002, an estimated 1 billion people lacked access to safe water and 2.6 billion people lacked basic sanitation.

Experts argue that world demand for water is increasing at about twice the rate of population growth. It is predicted that, by 2025, half the world's population will face water shortages. This could lead to conflict and even boundary wars – 300 major rivers cross national frontiers and access to their water is likely to be disputed.

THE HYDROLOGICAL CYCLE

The world's water balance is regulated by the constant recycling of water between the oceans, the atmosphere and the land. The movement of water between these three reservoirs is known as the *hydrological cycle*. The oceans play a vital role in the hydrological cycle: 74% of the total precipitation falls over the oceans and 84% of the total evaporation comes from the oceans. Water vapour in the atmosphere circulates around the planet, transporting energy as well as the water itself. When the vapour cools, it falls as rain or snow. The whole cycle is driven by the Sun.

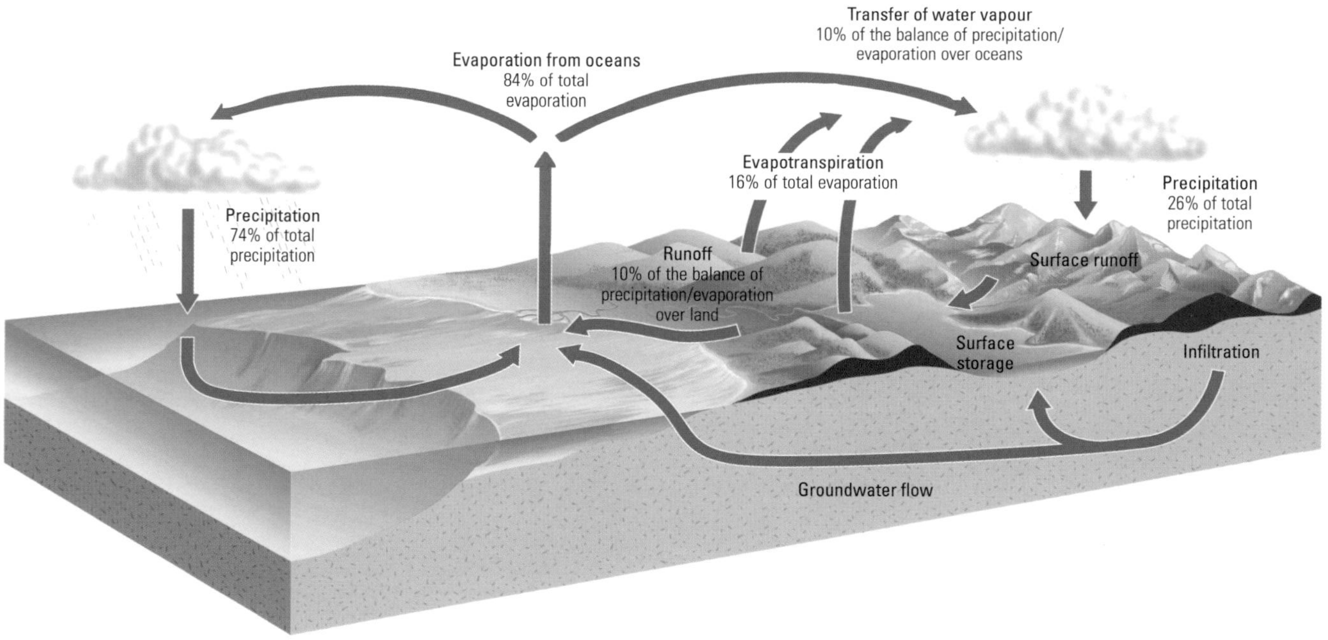

WATER DISTRIBUTION

The distribution of planetary water, by percentage. Oceans and ice caps together account for more than 99% of the total; the breakdown of the remainder is estimated.

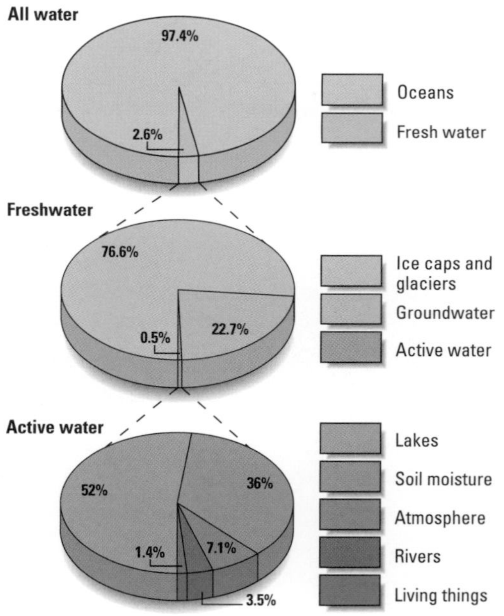

Almost all the world's water is 3,000 million years old, and all of it cycles endlessly through the hydrosphere, though at different rates. Water vapour circulates over days, even hours; deep-ocean water circulates over millennia; and ice-cap water remains solid for millions of years.

ANNUAL SEDIMENT YIELD

Around 20% of all land-derived sediment is carried by three Asian rivers: the Brahmaputra, the Huang He (Yellow River), and the Ganges. Together, these three rivers carry up to 3,206 million tonnes of sediment each year into the oceans. Sediment yield is affected by runoff and vegetation cover, and is steadily increasing due to large-scale deforestation, most notably in South-east Asia and the Amazon basin. In these regions, deforesting the slopes allows the heavy tropical rains to wash away whatever thin and fragile soil there is, leading to severe erosion of the land.

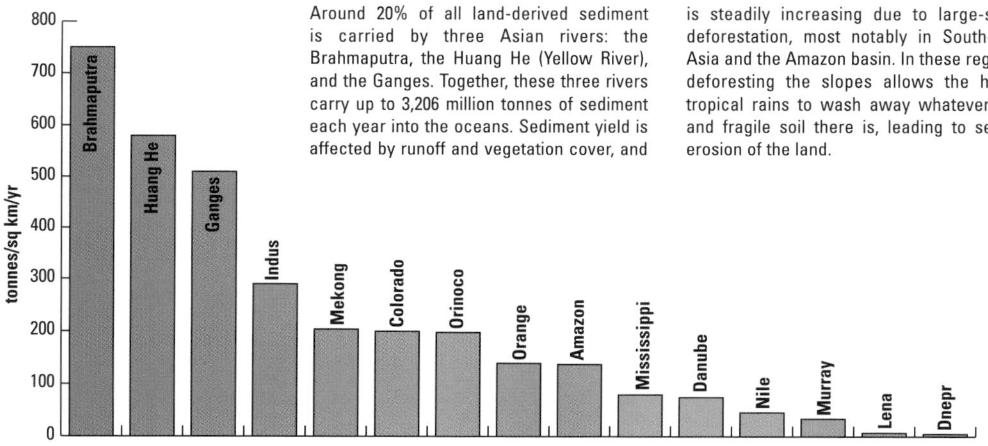

WATER RUNOFF

Annual freshwater runoff by continent in cubic kilometres

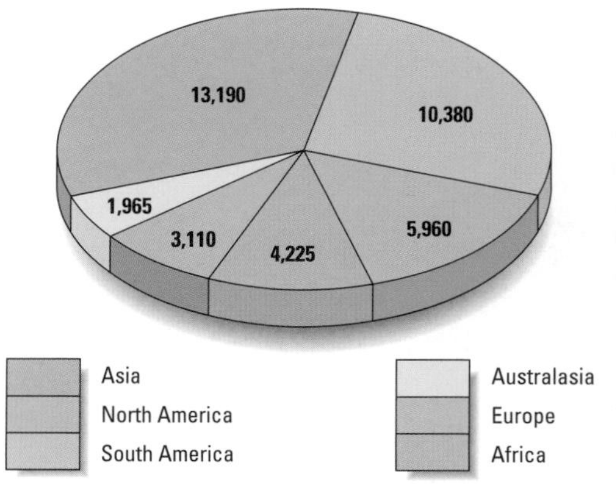

► The River Amazon is the world's second-longest river (after the River Nile), draining the vast rainforest basin of northern South America. The Amazon carries by far the greatest volume of water of any river in the world: the average rate of discharge is approximately 95,000 cu m [3,355,000 cu ft] per second, nearly three times as much as its nearest rival, the Congo. The flow is so great that its silt discolours the water up to 200 km [125 miles] into the Atlantic. At approximately 7 million sq km [2.7 million sq miles], the Amazon basin comprises nearly 40% of the whole of South America.

WATERSHEDS

The map below shows the world's major rivers, with the ranking of the 20 longest rivers shown in square brackets after their name, led by the Nile [1] and the Amazon [2].

The map shows the direction of freshwater flow on a continental scale, whereas the water runoff chart on the facing page indicates the quantities involved annually.

The rate of runoff varies seasonally and is affected by the surface vegetation and climate. Most of the world's major rivers discharge into the Atlantic Ocean.

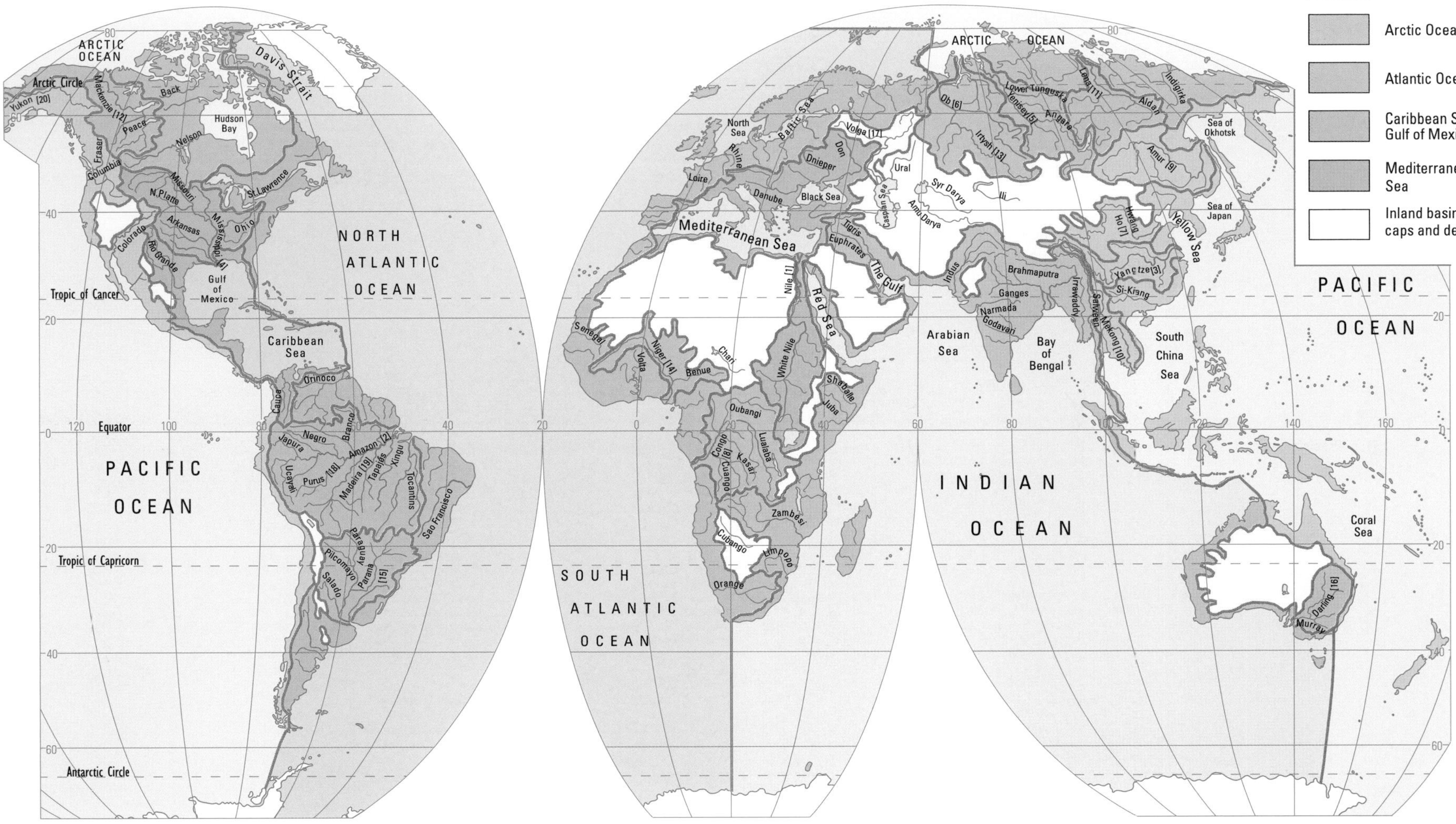

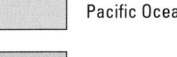

Where the rivers run

- Pacific Ocean
- Indian Ocean
- Arctic Ocean
- Atlantic Ocean
- Caribbean Sea–Gulf of Mexico
- Mediterranean Sea
- Inland basins, ice caps and deserts

NATURAL VEGETATION

The map below illustrates the natural 'climax vegetation' of a region, as dictated by its climate and topography. In most cases, human agricultural activity has drastically altered the pattern of the vegetation. Western Europe, for example, lost most of its broadleaf forests many centuries ago, while elsewhere irrigation has turned some natural semi-deserts into productive land. The various vegetation regions support different kinds of animals and wildlife, and, in an undisturbed state, they are highly developed biological communities, or 'biomes'.

The blue line on the map represents the northern limit of tree growth, and the red lines indicate the northern and southern limits of palm growth.

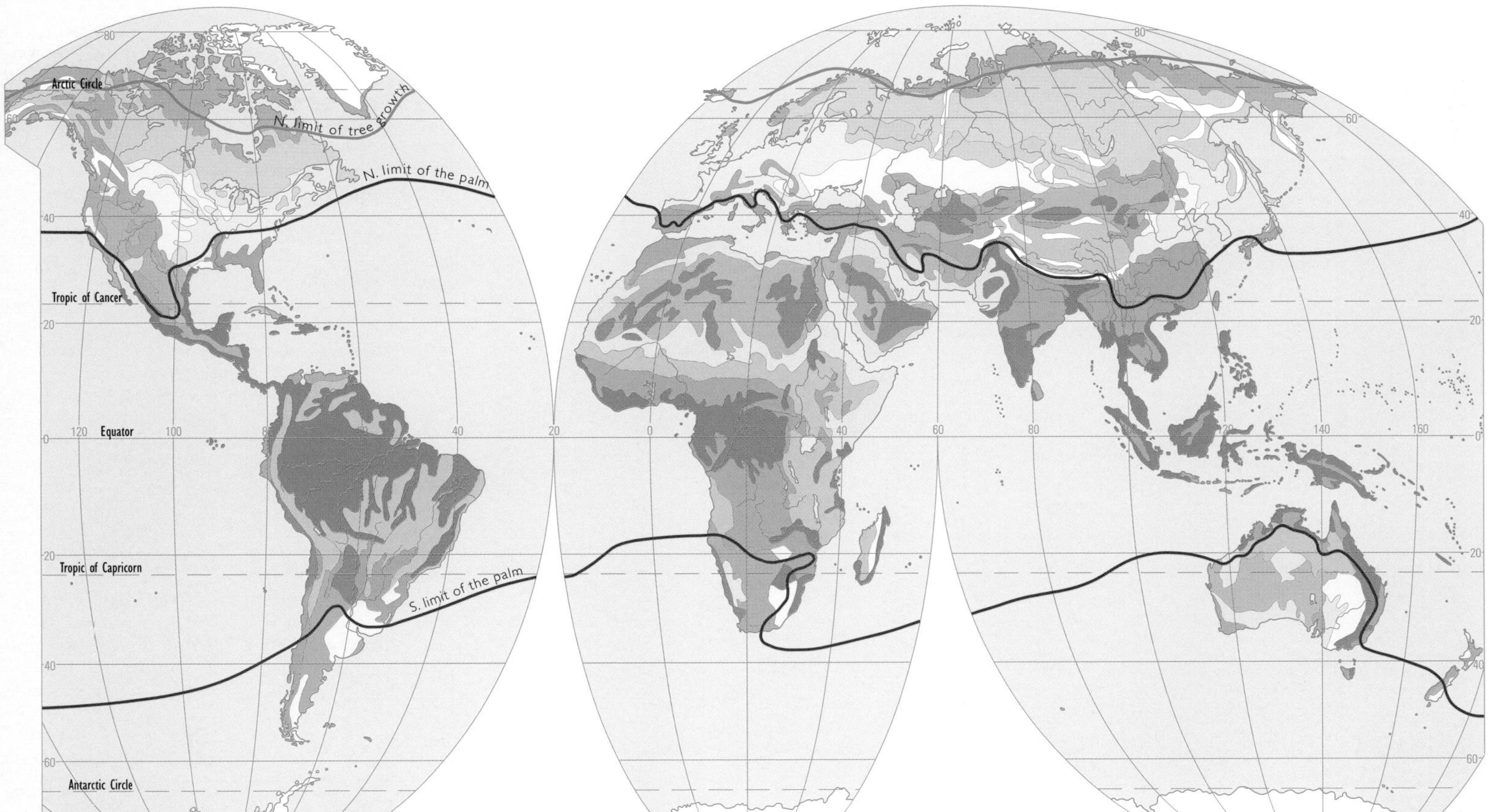

- Tropical rainforest
- Subtropical and temperate rainforest
- Monsoon woodland and open jungle
- Subtropical and temperate woodland, scrub and bush
- Tropical savanna, with low trees and bush
- Tropical savanna and grasslands
- Dry semi-desert, with shrub and grass
- Desert shrub
- Desert
- Dry steppe and shrub
- Temperate grasslands, prairie and steppe
- Mediterranean hardwood forest and scrub
- Temperate deciduous forest and meadow
- Temperate deciduous and coniferous forest
- Northern coniferous forest (taïga)
- Mountainous forest, mainly coniferous
- High plateau steppe and tundra
- Arctic tundra
- Polar and mountainous ice desert

The Natural Environment

For more information:

8 Oceans
14 Atmosphere
19 Natural vegetation
22 Carbon dioxide
Greenhouse power
Global warming
23 Acid rain
Desertification
Deforestation
Water pollution

Recent discoveries of life forms in some of the world's most hostile environments, such as around the black smokers along the ocean ridges, prepared the way for the announcement by NASA scientists in 1996 that they had found microfossils in a Martian meteorite. But other scientists were sceptical, believing them to be natural mineral structures and not evidence of extraterrestrial life.

Until further evidence is available, the Earth remains the only planet where we know for sure that life exists. According to the fossil record, life on Earth appeared at least 3,500 million years ago. Since then, it has evolved from its primitive beginnings to its modern biodiversity, including millions of plants, animals and micro-organisms. Living organisms have not only adapted to the environment, but they have also changed their environment to suit themselves. For example, the Earth's early atmosphere contained little oxygen, but the emergence of multi-celled, oxygen-producing algae, around 2,000 million years ago, led to the creation of an oxygen-rich atmosphere. This enabled land animals to populate the ancient continents.

The amount of the greenhouse-gas carbon dioxide in the atmosphere would steadily increase from its present 0.03% were it not for plants. Without them, the Earth's atmosphere would, in a few million years, be similar to that of Venus, where surface temperatures reach 477°C. The Earth has evolved into a complex control system, sensing and reacting to changes and tending always to maintain the balance it has achieved.

Much discussion has centred on how that balance changes. Only recently, scientists were suggesting that we may be living in an interglacial stage of the Pleistocene Ice Age. Since the 1980s, however, predictions of future climate patterns have concentrated more on global warming, caused by pollution that has led to an increase in greenhouse gases in the atmosphere. Interference in the natural cycles that control the environment may have consequences that are hard to predict.

Furthermore, we are currently experiencing a period of mass extinction of species, causing a rapid reduction in our planet's biodiversity. In 2002, a report by the International Union for the Conservation of Nature listed 11,167 organisms facing extinction. This was 121 more than in 2000.

THREATENED MAMMALS

The map shows the percentage of mammal species classified as threatened in 2002. Many scientists believe we are currently experiencing a period of mass extinction of species, rivalling five other periods in the past half a billion years. Among the most threatened mammals today are elephants, primates and rhinoceroses.

Over 50%
25 – 50%
10 – 25%
5 – 10%
Under 5%
No data available

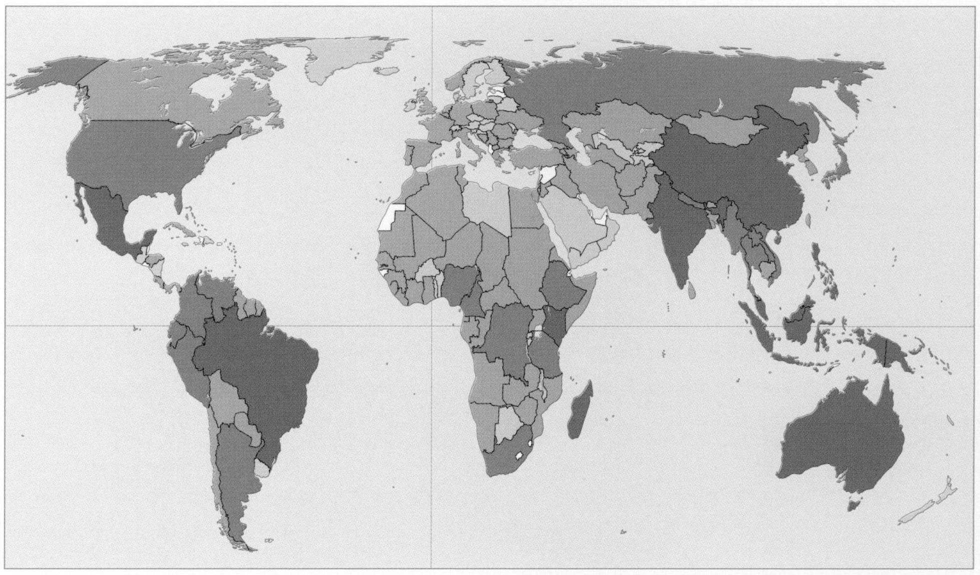

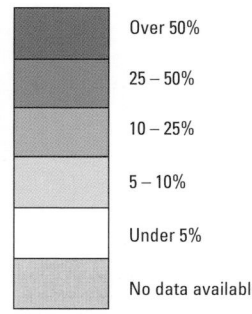

BIODIVERSITY IN CALIFORNIA, USA

This false-colour satellite image of central California shows San Francisco lying just below the entrance to San Francisco Bay, with Oakland on the far side and San Jose to the south-east. California, nicknamed the Golden State, is the third largest state in the United States and the most populous.

Due to its varied terrain and climate, California has a wide range of diverse habitats within a relatively small area. East of the forested Coast Ranges (the grey and red areas just inland from the bay) lies the fertile Central Valley, which appears as a red-and-blue chequerboard. In the north-west and south-west of the state (*not shown here*) lie parts of the Basin and Range region, much of which is desert. It includes Death Valley, which contains the country's lowest point on land, at 86 metres below sea level.

Natural vegetation

Forests cover about 40% of California and they include bristlecone pines, thought to be the oldest living things on Earth, together with coastal redwoods, the world's tallest trees. Wildlife is still abundant, though some species, such as the rare California condor, are on the endangered list.

The state has achieved much to protect its biodiversity. It contains eight of the 56 national parks in the United States. Two of them, Death Valley and Joshua Tree, were designated national parks as recently as 1994, as part of a conservation measure, including the protection of large areas of wilderness in the deserts.

California has vast resources and, were it a separate nation, it would rank among the world's ten most productive in terms of the total value of its goods and services. This means that, like the United States as a whole, it has resources, which many developing countries lack, to finance conservation measures. For example, the World Conservation Union reported in 1996 that 8% of mammals were threatened in the United States, as compared with 32% in the Philippines and 44% in Madagascar, two countries where habitat destruction has been proceeding on a large scale.

THE EARTH'S ENERGY BALANCE

Apart from a modest quantity of internal heat from its molten core, the Earth receives all of its energy from the Sun. If the planet is to remain at a constant temperature, it must reradiate exactly as much energy as it receives. Even a minute surplus would lead to a warmer Earth, a deficit to a cooler one. The temperature at which thermal equilibrium is reached depends on many factors, including the relative brightness of the Earth (its index of reflectivity, called the 'albedo') and the heat-trapping capacity of the atmosphere (the 'greenhouse effect').

Most of the Sun's energy arrives in the form of short-wave radiation. Some of the energy is reflected straight back into space, while some is absorbed by the atmosphere or by the Earth itself. Absorbed energy heats the Earth and its atmosphere alike, but since its temperature is much lower than that of the Sun, the outgoing energy is emitted at longer infrared wavelengths.

The diagram (*right*) shows short-wave radiation in yellow, with long-wave radiation in orange.

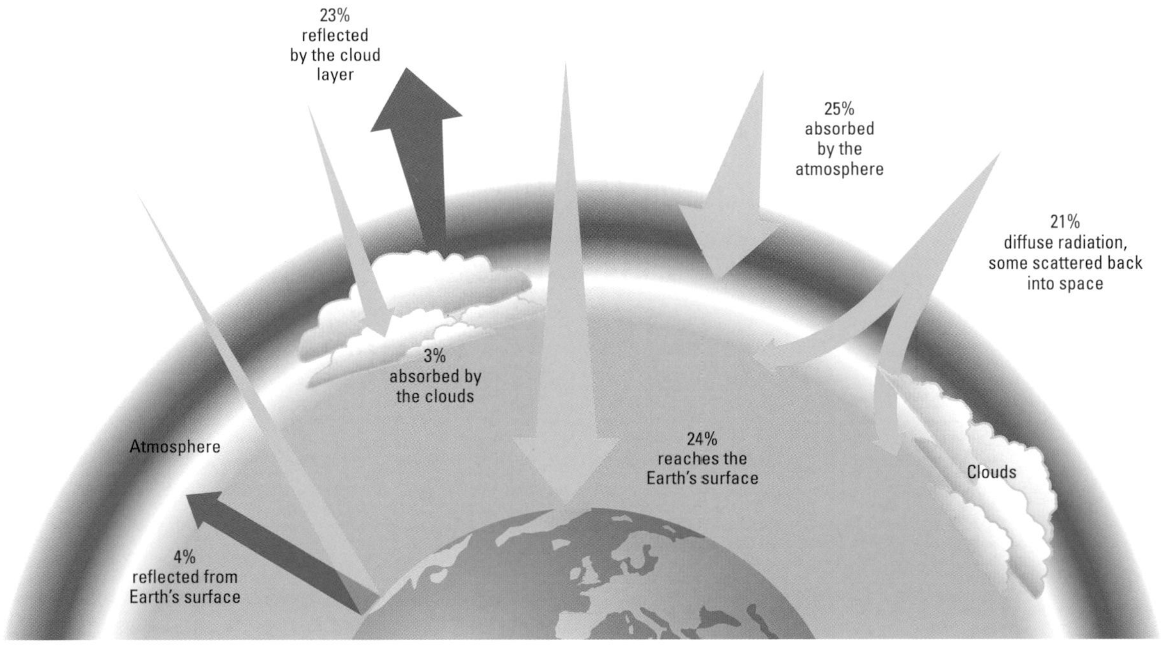

THE GREENHOUSE EFFECT

Constituting less than 1% of the atmosphere, the natural greenhouse gases (water vapour, carbon dioxide, methane, nitrous oxide and ozone) have a disproportionate effect on the Earth's climate, and even its habitability. Like the glass panes in a greenhouse, the gases are transparent to most incoming short-wave radiation, which passes freely to heat the planet beneath. But when the warmed Earth retransmits that energy, in the form of longer-wave infrared radiation, the gases function as an opaque shield, preventing some of it from escaping, so that the planetary surface (like the interior of a greenhouse) stays relatively hot.

Over the last 150 years, there has been a gradual increase in the levels of greenhouse gases (with the exception of water vapour, which remains a constant in the system). Current predictions suggest that there could be a further rise of 1.5–4.5°C by the year 2100. A serious reduction in the greenhouse gases would be just as damaging, though. A total absence of carbon dioxide, for example, would leave the planet with a temperature roughly 33°C colder than it is at present.

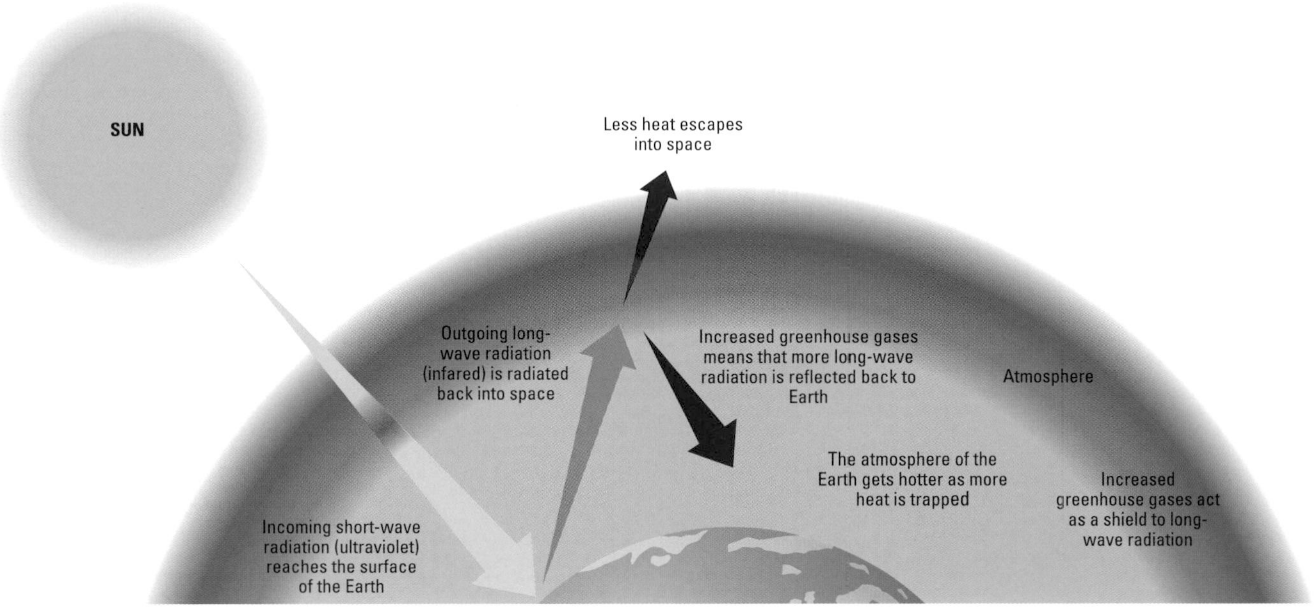

THE CARBON CYCLE

The Earth has a huge supply of carbon, only a small quantity of which is in the form of carbon dioxide. Of that, around 98% is dissolved in the sea; the fraction circulating in the air amounts to only 340 parts per million of the atmosphere, where its capacity as a greenhouse gas is the key regulator of the planetary temperature.

Living things, however, circulate carbon. Plants absorb carbon dioxide from the atmosphere and the carbon is then returned to circulation when the plants die, or is passed up the food chain to the herbivores, and then to the carnivores that feed on them. As organisms at each of these trophic levels die, they decay, releasing the carbon, which then combines once more with the oxygen released during life. However, a small proportion of carbon is removed almost permanently, buried beneath mud on land or at sea, sinking as dead matter to the ocean floor. In time, it is slowly compressed into sedimentary rocks, such as limestone and chalk.

The carbon cycle has continued for a very long time. However, human beings have found a way to release fixed carbon at a faster rate than existing global systems can recirculate it. It has taken only a few human generations to deplete the fossil fuels that represent many millions of years of carbon accumulation.

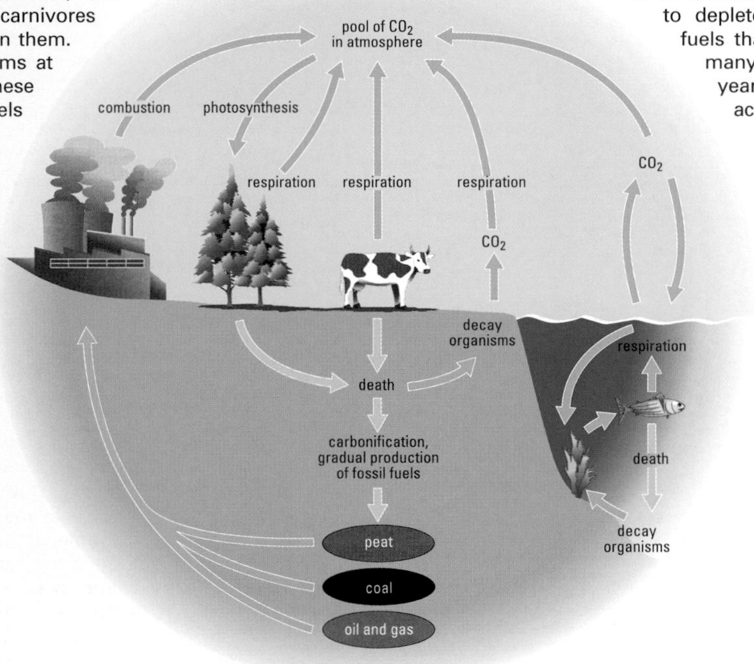

CARBON MONOXIDE CONCENTRATION

A colourless, odourless and poisonous gas, carbon monoxide (CO) is formed during the incomplete combustion of fossil fuels, occurring, for example, in coal gas and the exhaust fumes of cars. It is a major air pollutant and is now regulated by many world nations. The images below show the seasonal amounts and geographical sources of atmospheric carbon monoxide in the spring and summer months. Progressively higher levels of carbon monoxide are shown in green, yellow, orange and red, while the blue areas have little or no atmospheric carbon monoxide.

Carbon monoxide can remain in the atmosphere for up to several months and can affect air quality in regions that are a long way from the original source of the pollution emissions.

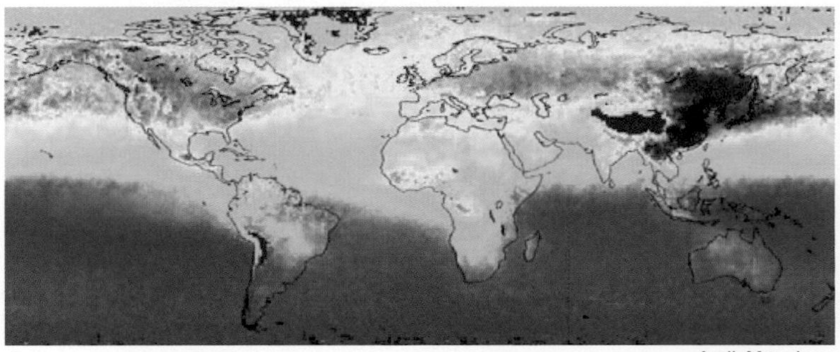

April, May, June

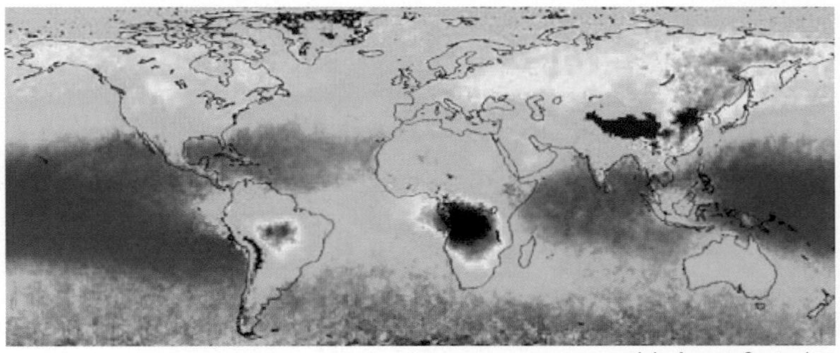

July, August, September

Carbon monoxide concentration (parts per billion by volume)

0 50 100 150 200 >250 no data

People and the Environment

For more information:

8 Oceans
14 Atmosphere
16 Climate
21 Greenhouse effect
26 Urban pollution

In 1996, the Intergovernmental Panel on Climate Change issued a report stating that 'The balance of evidence suggests a discernible human influence on global climate through emissions of carbon dioxide and other greenhouse gases.' The report acknowledged that average global temperatures had risen by about 0.5°C since the mid-19th century, though there were still reasons for caution on attributing this entirely to actions taken by humans.

Human interference with nature is nothing new, at least since people turned from hunting and gathering to agriculture more than 10,000 years ago. At first, human actions seemed to have no ill effects because the systems that regulate the global environment were able to absorb damage. But from the late 18th century, the Industrial Revolution and the population explosion have caused massive pollution that threatens to overwhelm the Earth's ability to cope.

The 20th century experienced many disasters, including the dumping of industrial wastes in rivers and seas, accidents at nuclear power stations, and the creation of acid rain through the release of sulphur dioxides and nitrous oxides by the burning of fossil fuels. The release of greenhouse gases are held to be the main reason for global warming, while CFCs (chlorofluorocarbons) have damaged the ozone layer in the stratosphere, the planet's screen against ultraviolet radiation.

In December 1998, an international conference in Kyoto, Japan, reached an agreement to reduce the emission of greenhouse gases by 5.2% by 2012. But, in the early 21st century, the United States, which produces about a third of all emissions, opposed the Kyoto protocol.

Global warming will lead to melting ice sheets and the flooding of fertile coastal plains. Computer models suggest that it might affect ocean currents so that northwestern Europe, which owes its mild climate to the Gulf Stream, could expect bitterly cold winters. Some models have also suggested that cloud cover could increase, reflecting more solar energy back into space and thus start a new Ice Age.

In many tropical areas, deforestation is making productive land barren, while in the dry grasslands bordering deserts, the removal of plant cover is causing desertification. But human ingenuity can respond to this crisis in planet management.

GLOBAL WARMING

High atmospheric concentrations of heat-absorbing gases appear to be causing a rise in average temperatures worldwide – up to 1.5°C [3°F] by the year 2020, according to some estimates. Global warming is likely to bring about a rise in sea levels that may flood some of the world's densely populated coastal areas.

Evidence of global warming is attributed mainly to the 'greenhouse effect', caused by the emission of certain gases, notably carbon dioxide, into the atmosphere (*see page 21*). Despite international action to control emissions of some greenhouse gases, carbon dioxide levels are still rising.

Carbon dioxide emissions in tonnes (latest available year)

Over 50 million
5 – 50 million
0.5 – 5 million
Under 0.5 million
No data available

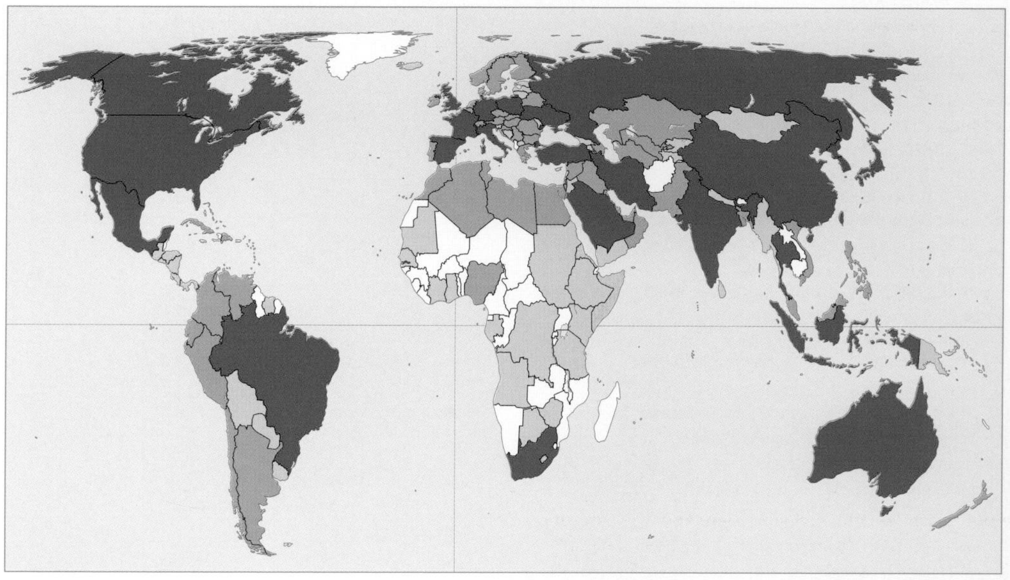

GREENHOUSE POWER

Relative contributions to the 'greenhouse effect' by the major heat-absorbing gases in the atmosphere
The chart combines greenhouse potency and volume. Carbon dioxide has a greenhouse potential of only 1, but its concentration of 350 parts per million makes it predominate. CFC 12, with 25,000 times the absorption capacity of CO_2, is present only as 0.00044 ppm.

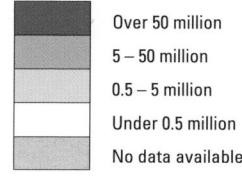

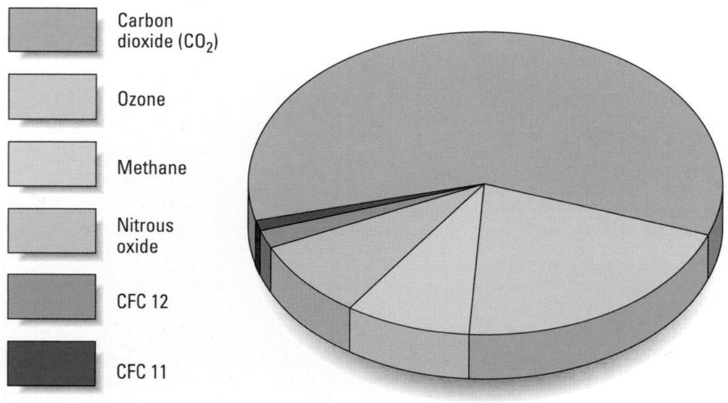

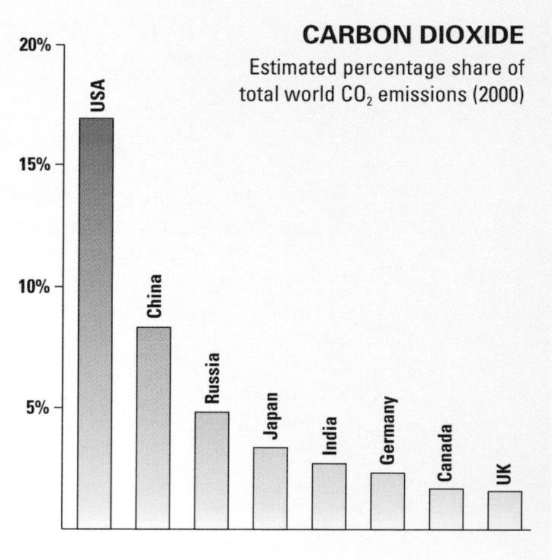

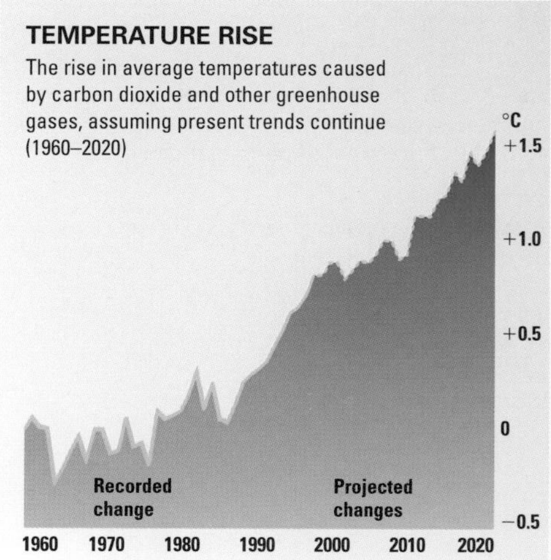

THE THINNING OZONE LAYER

Total atmospheric ozone concentration in the southern and northern hemispheres (Dobson Units, 2000)
In 1985, scientists working in Antarctica discovered a thinning of the ozone layer, commonly known as an 'ozone hole'. This caused immediate alarm because the ozone layer absorbs most of the Sun's dangerous ultraviolet radiation, which is believed to cause an increase in skin cancer, cataracts and damage to the immune system.

Since 1985, ozone depletion has increased and, by 2002, the ozone hole over the South Pole was estimated to be three times as large as the USA. The false-colour images (*right*) show the total atmospheric ozone concentration in the southern hemisphere (in September 2000) and the northern hemisphere (in March 2000) with the ozone hole clearly identifiable at the centre. The data is from the Tiros weather satellite. The colours represent the ozone concentration in Dobson Units (DU).

Scientists agree that ozone depletion is caused by CFCs, a group of manufactured chemicals used in air-conditioning systems and refrigerators. In a 1987 treaty most industrial nations agreed to phase out CFCs and a complete ban on most CFCs was agreed after the end of 1995. However, scientists believe that the chemicals will remain in the atmosphere for 50 to 100 years. As a result, ozone depletion will continue for many years.

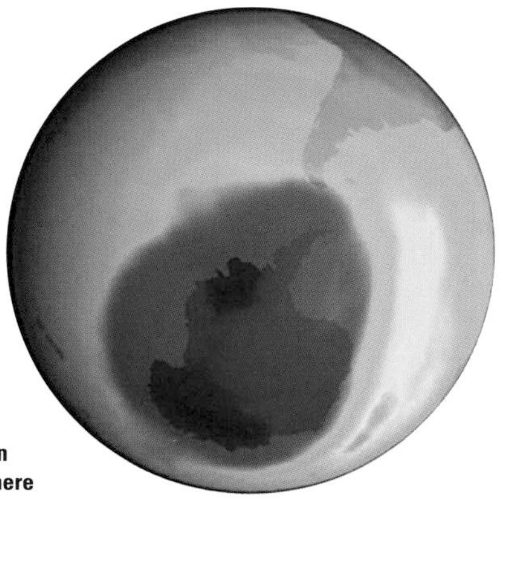

Southern hemisphere

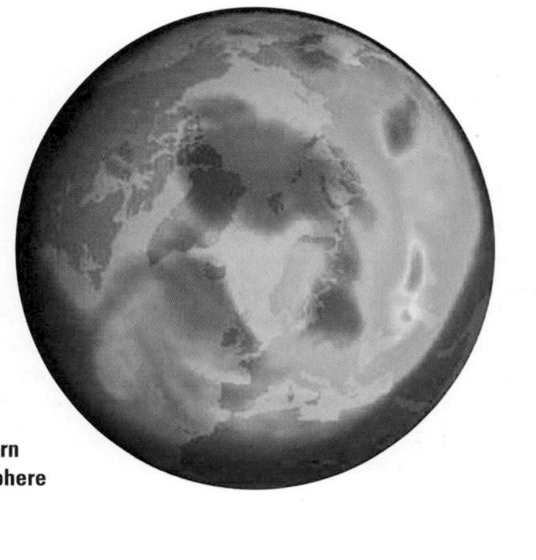

Northern hemisphere

WORLD POLLUTION

Acid rain and sources of acidic emissions (latest available year)
Acid rain is caused by high levels of sulphur and nitrogen in the atmosphere. They combine with water vapour and oxygen to form acids (H_2SO_4 and HNO_3) which fall as precipitation.

- Regions where sulphur and nitrogen oxides are released in high concentrations, mainly from fossil fuel combustion
- • Major cities with high levels of air pollution (including nitrogen and sulphur emissions)

Areas of heavy acid deposition
pH numbers indicate acidity, decreasing from a neutral 7. Normal rain, slightly acid from dissolved carbon dioxide, never exceeds a pH of 5.6.

- pH less than 4.0 (most acidic)
- pH 4.0 to 4.5
- pH 4.5 to 5.0
- Areas where acid rain is a potential problem

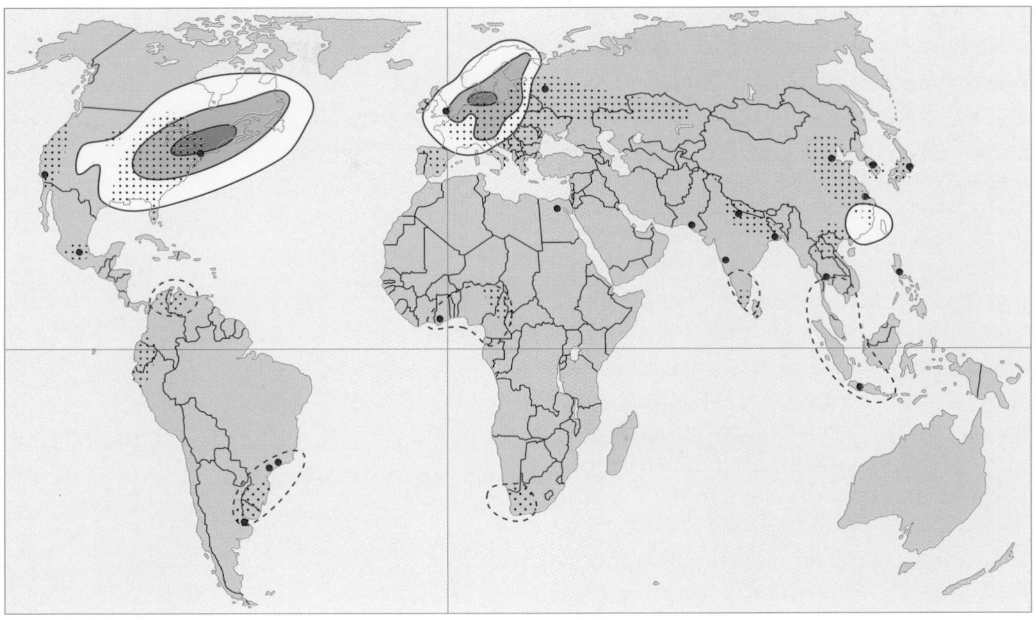

WATER POLLUTION

- Severely polluted sea areas and lakes
- Polluted sea areas and lakes
- Areas of frequent oil pollution by shipping
- ◣ Major oil tanker spills
- ▲ Major oil rig blow-outs
- ▼ Offshore dumpsites for industrial and municipal waste
- —— Severely polluted rivers and estuaries

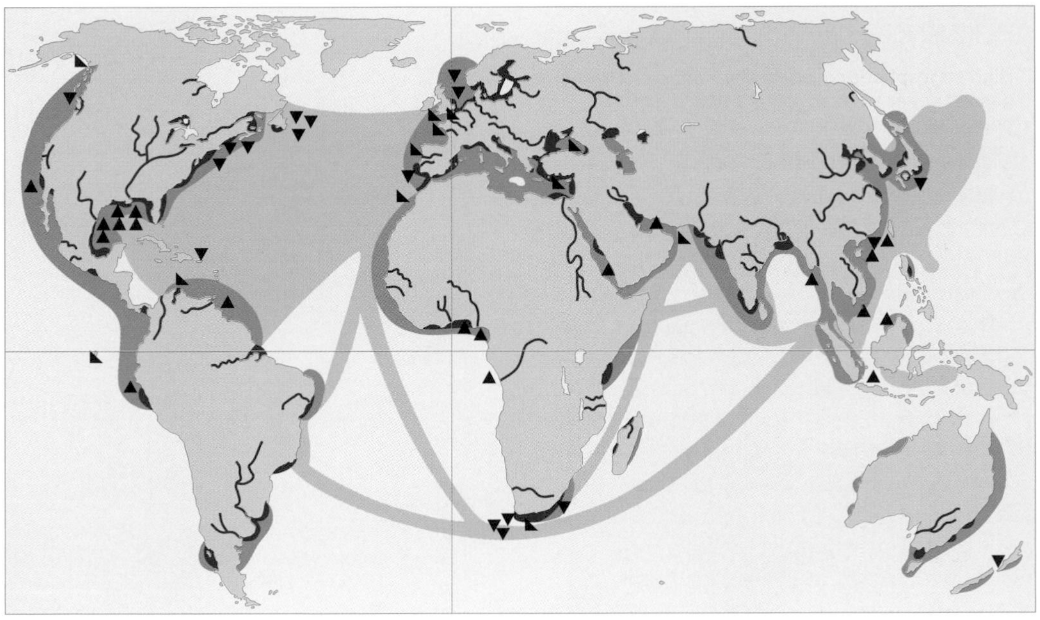

In December 2002, oil slicks from the 77,000-tonne *Prestige* tanker, which broke up off Spain, caused environmental damage to the north coast of Spain and, in 2003, to the south-west coast of France. This was a small incident by comparison with some earlier events, such as the collision between the *Atlantic Empress* and the *Aegean Captain* in July 1979. This was the worst tanker incident ever, polluting the Caribbean with 1,890,000 barrels of crude oil.

Oil spills, however, declined in the 1980s, from a peak of 750,000 tonnes in 1979 to less than 50,000 tonnes in 1990. The most notorious spill of that period – when the *Exxon Valdez* ran aground in Prince William Sound, Alaska, in March 1989 – released only 267,000 barrels, a relatively small amount when compared with the 2,500,000 barrels spilled during the Gulf War of 1991. Oil spillage, poisoned rivers, and domestic sewage have in recent years badly contaminated parts of the oceans.

DESERTIFICATION

- Existing deserts
- Areas with a high risk of desertification
- Areas with a moderate risk of desertification
- Former areas of rainforest
- Existing rainforest

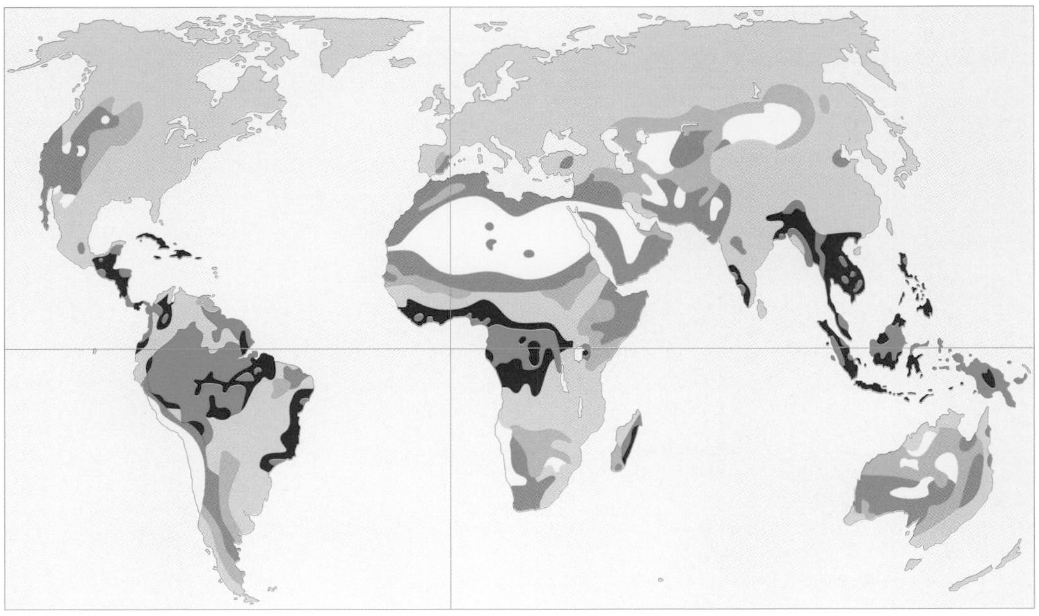

DEFORESTATION

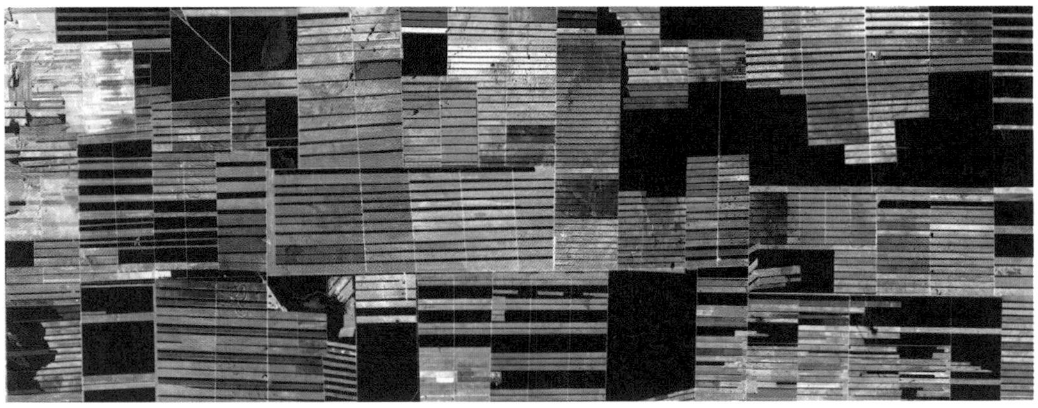

Bolivia has over 250,000 sq km [100,000 sq miles] of dry tropical forest, home to animals such as jaguars and ocelots. It is, however, being cleared at a rate of over 2% per annum. This false-colour image shows an area that has been almost completely cleared. The darkest areas are remnants of the original forest, some retained as wind breaks between newly created arable fields, growing such crops as soybeans.

Where deforestation occurs, there is an immediate danger that the vital topsoil will be eroded by wind or by rain. Proposals to clear large regions of the Amazonian rainforests, which play a key role in maintaining the Earth's oxygen balance, could cause an environmental catastrophe.

ANTARCTICA

The vast Antarctic ice sheet, containing some 70% of the Earth's fresh water, plays a crucial role in the circulation of the atmosphere and oceans, and hence the Earth's climate. The frozen southern continent is also the last remaining wilderness – the largest area to remain free from human colonization.

Various countries have pressed territorial claims over sections of Antarctica, spurred in recent years by its known and suspected mineral wealth: enough iron ore to supply the world at present levels for 200 years, large oil reserves and, probably, the biggest coal deposits on Earth.

The 1961 Antarctic Treaty set aside the area for peaceful uses only, guaranteeing freedom of scientific investigation, banning waste disposal and nuclear testing, and suspending the issue of territorial rights. By 1990, the original 12 signatories had grown to 25; a further 15 nations were granted observer status in subsequent deliberations.

In July 1991, a new accord banned all mineral exploration for a further 50 years. The ban can only be rescinded if all the present signatories, plus a majority of any future adherents, agree.

While the treaty has always lacked a formal mechanism for enforcement, it is firmly underwritten by public concern generated by the efforts of environmental pressure groups such as Greenpeace, which have campaigned vigorously to have Antarctica declared a 'World Park'.

However, from the mid-1990s, the continent appeared to be under threat from global warming, which some scientists believe was the cause of the break-up of ice shelves along the Antarctic peninsula. Rising temperatures have also disturbed the breeding patterns of Adelie penguins.

Population

For more information:

26 Urbanization of the Earth
Urban population
27 Largest cities
33 Food and population
44 Wealth and population

In 8000 BC, following the development of agriculture, the world had an estimated population of 8 million and by AD 1000 it was about 300 million. The onset of the Industrial Revolution in the late 18th century led to a population explosion. The 1,000 million mark was passed by 1850, it doubled by the 1920s, and doubled again to 4,000 million by 1975.

In the 1990s, demographers estimated that the world's population, which passed the 6 billion mark in 1999, would reach 8.9 billion by 2050 and only level out in 2200, at a peak of around 11 billion. However, in the early 21st century, after the rate of population growth had shown signs of decline, the Institute for Applied Systems Analysis suggested that the world's population might peak at about 9 billion in 2070. Whatever the global projections, everyone agreed that the greatest population growth would be in the developing countries.

The developing world includes what the World Bank (2001) describes as low-income economies (average per capita GNP of US $420), lower-middle-income economies (average per capita GNP of US $1,200) and upper-middle-income economies (average per capita GNP of US $4,870). Most developing countries are in Africa, Asia and Latin America. The developed world, made up of high-income, industrialized economies (average per capita GNP of US $26,440), contains Australasia, most of Europe and North America, and Japan.

In developing countries, a high proportion of the population is young and so these countries face high expenditure on health and education. In developed countries, the population pyramids are becoming top-heavy, with increasingly ageing populations.

LARGEST NATIONS

The world's most populous nations, in millions (2003 est.)

1.	China	1,287
2.	India	1,050
3.	USA	290
4.	Indonesia	235
5.	Brazil	182
6.	Pakistan	151
7.	Russia	145
8.	Bangladesh	138
9.	Nigeria	134
10.	Japan	127
11.	Mexico	105
12.	Philippines	85
13.	Germany	82
14.	Vietnam	82
15.	Egypt	75
16.	Iran	68
17.	Turkey	68
18.	Ethiopia	67
19.	Thailand	64
20.	France	60
21.	UK	60
22.	Italy	58
23.	Congo (Dem.Rep.)	57
24.	South Korea	48
25.	Ukraine	48

MOST CROWDED NATIONS

Population per square kilometre (2003 est.)

1.	Monaco	32,000
2.	Singapore	6,778
3.	Vatican City	2,500
4.	Malta	1,250
5.	Maldives	1,100
6.	Bahrain	967
7.	Bangladesh	961
8.	Nauru	650
9.	Barbados	644
10.	Taiwan	628

LEAST CROWDED NATIONS

Population per square kilometre (2003 est.)

1.	Mongolia	1.7
2.	Namibia	2.3
3.	Australia	2.5
4.	Suriname	2.7
5.	Iceland	2.7
6.	Botswana	2.7
7.	Mauritania	2.8
8.	Libya	3.1
9.	Canada	3.2
10.	Guyana	3.3

POPULATION DENSITY

The places marked on the map reflect the size of the urban agglomerations and conurbations, rather than the actual city limits. San Francisco itself, for example, has an official population of less than a million people.

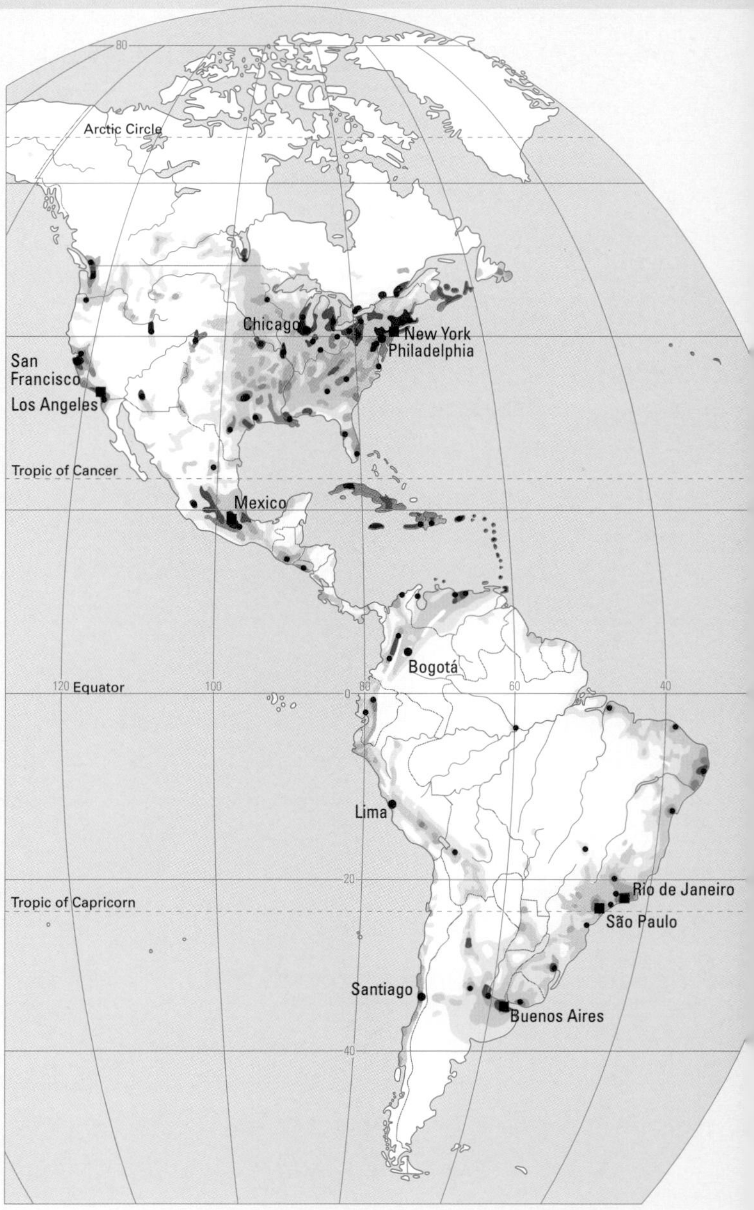

Inhabitants per square kilometre

- Over 200
- 100 – 200
- 50 – 100
- 25 – 50
- 6 – 25
- 3 – 6
- 1 – 3
- Under 1

Urban population

- ■ Over 10,000,000
- ● 5,000,000 – 10,000,000
- • 1,000,000 – 5,000,000

POPULATION CHANGE 1990–2000

The population change for the years 1990–2000

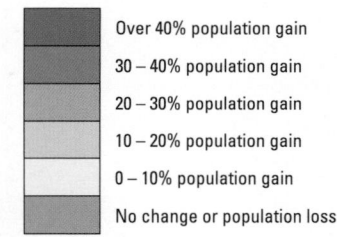

- Over 40% population gain
- 30 – 40% population gain
- 20 – 30% population gain
- 10 – 20% population gain
- 0 – 10% population gain
- No change or population loss

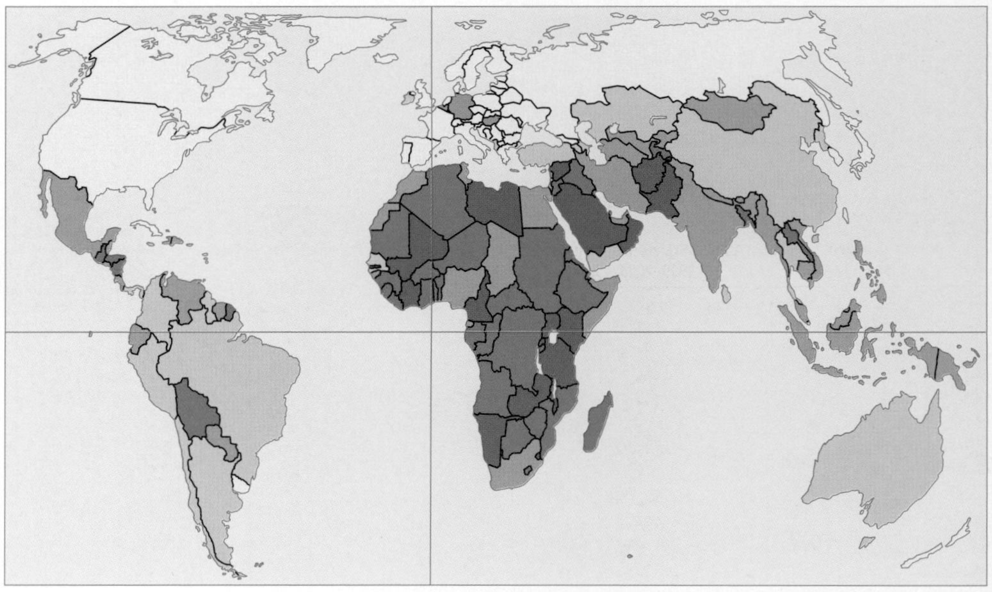

Top 5 countries		Bottom 5 countries	
Kuwait	+75.9%	Belgium	–0.1%
Namibia	+62.5%	Hungary	–0.2%
Afghanistan	+60.1%	Grenada	–2.4%
Mali	+55.5%	German	–3.2%
Tanzania	+54.6%	Tonga	–3.2%

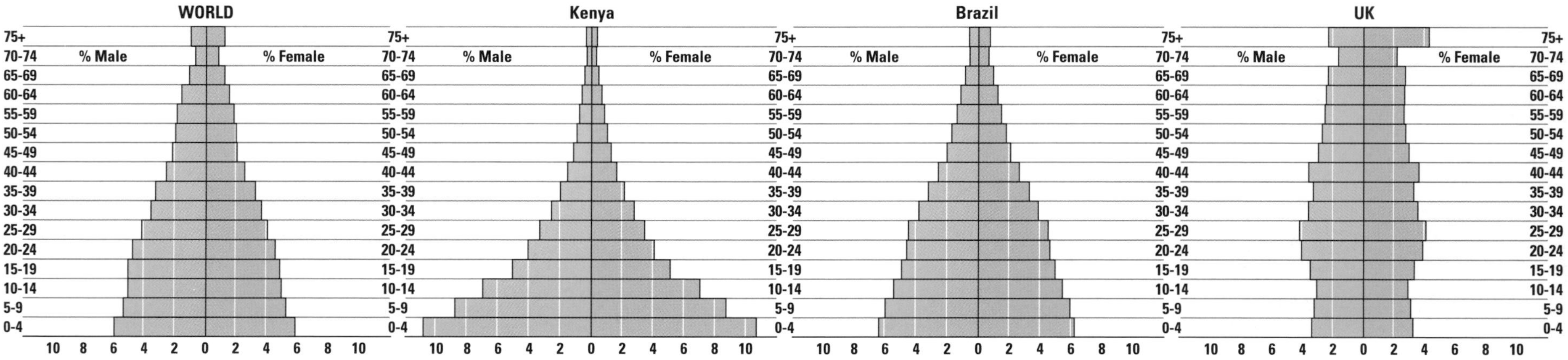

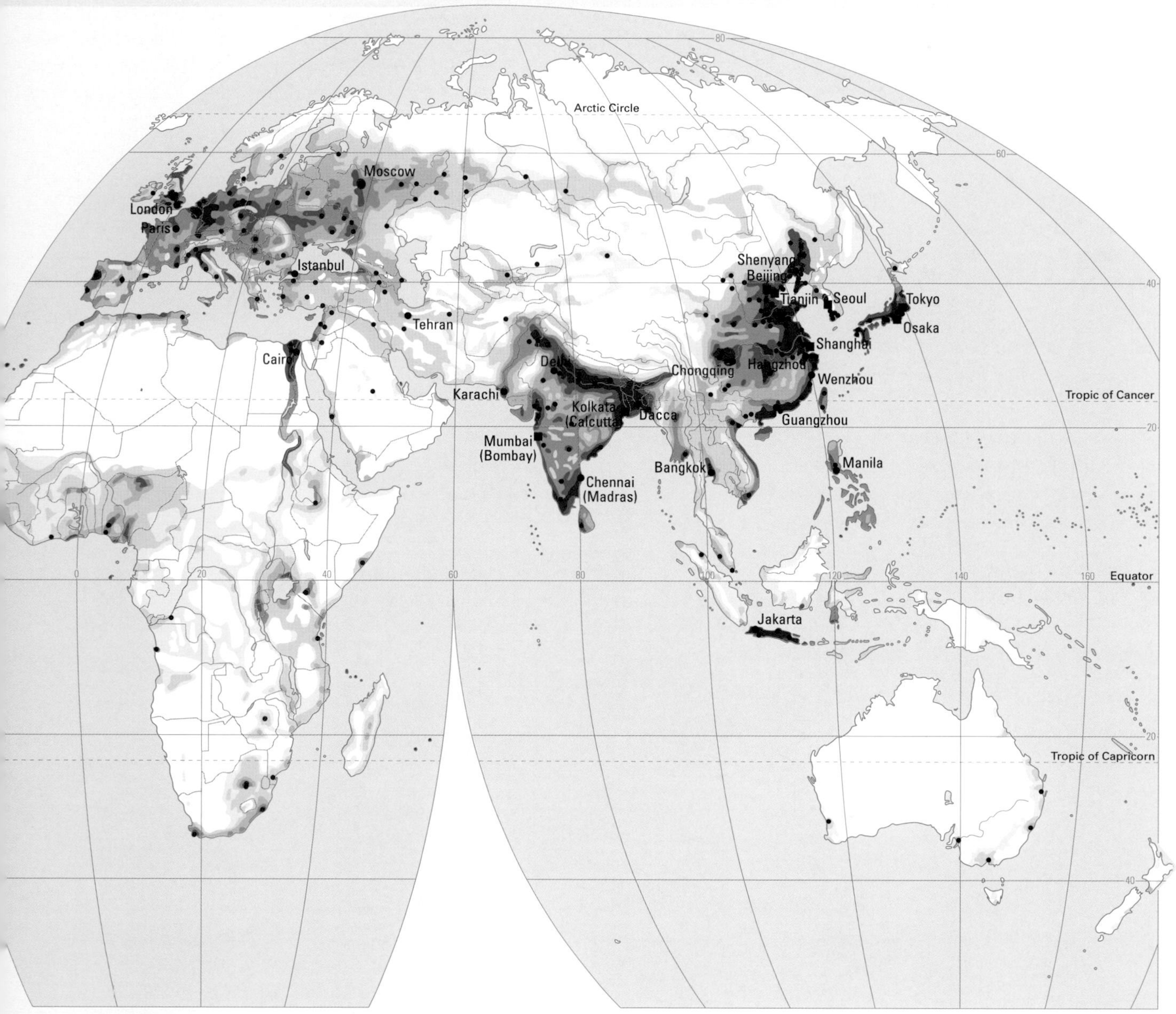

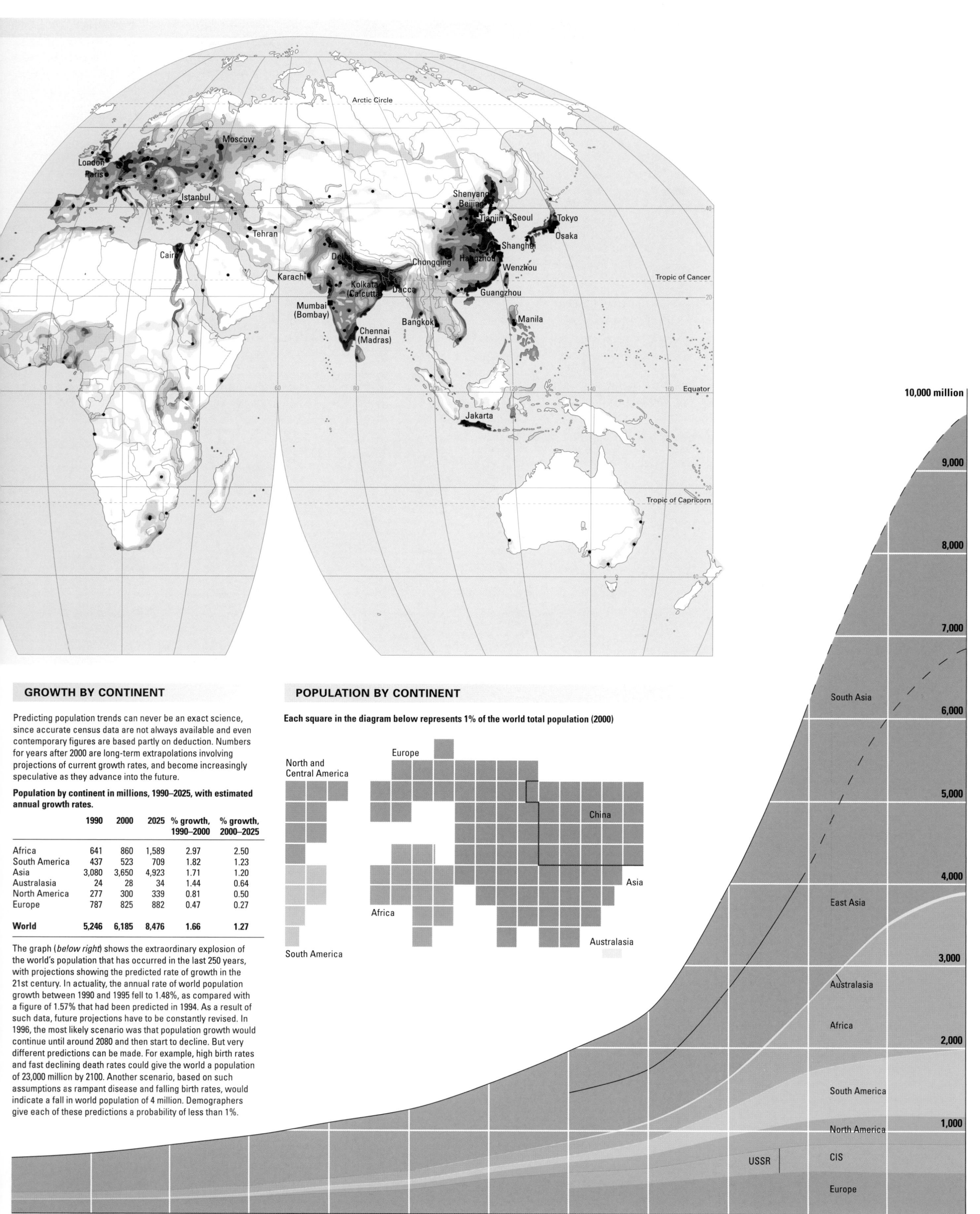

GROWTH BY CONTINENT

Predicting population trends can never be an exact science, since accurate census data are not always available and even contemporary figures are based partly on deduction. Numbers for years after 2000 are long-term extrapolations involving projections of current growth rates, and become increasingly speculative as they advance into the future.

Population by continent in millions, 1990–2025, with estimated annual growth rates.

	1990	2000	2025	% growth, 1990–2000	% growth, 2000–2025
Africa	641	860	1,589	2.97	2.50
South America	437	523	709	1.82	1.23
Asia	3,080	3,650	4,923	1.71	1.20
Australasia	24	28	34	1.44	0.64
North America	277	300	339	0.81	0.50
Europe	787	825	882	0.47	0.27
World	**5,246**	**6,185**	**8,476**	**1.66**	**1.27**

The graph (*below right*) shows the extraordinary explosion of the world's population that has occurred in the last 250 years, with projections showing the predicted rate of growth in the 21st century. In actuality, the annual rate of world population growth between 1990 and 1995 fell to 1.48%, as compared with a figure of 1.57% that had been predicted in 1994. As a result of such data, future projections have to be constantly revised. In 1996, the most likely scenario was that population growth would continue until around 2080 and then start to decline. But very different predictions can be made. For example, high birth rates and fast declining death rates could give the world a population of 23,000 million by 2100. Another scenario, based on such assumptions as rampant disease and falling birth rates, would indicate a fall in world population of 4 million. Demographers give each of these predictions a probability of less than 1%.

POPULATION BY CONTINENT

Each square in the diagram below represents 1% of the world total population (2000)

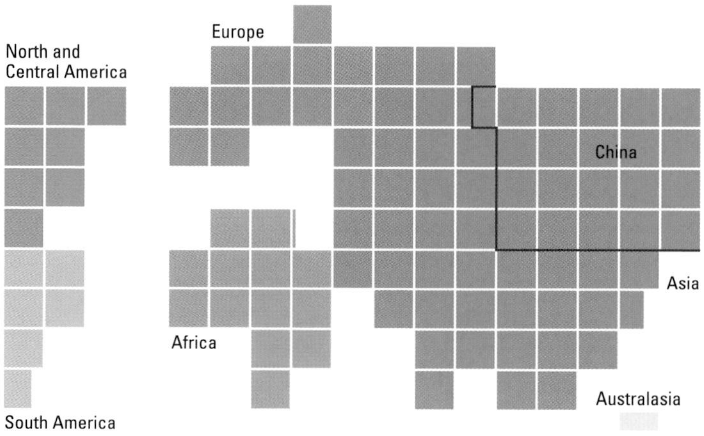

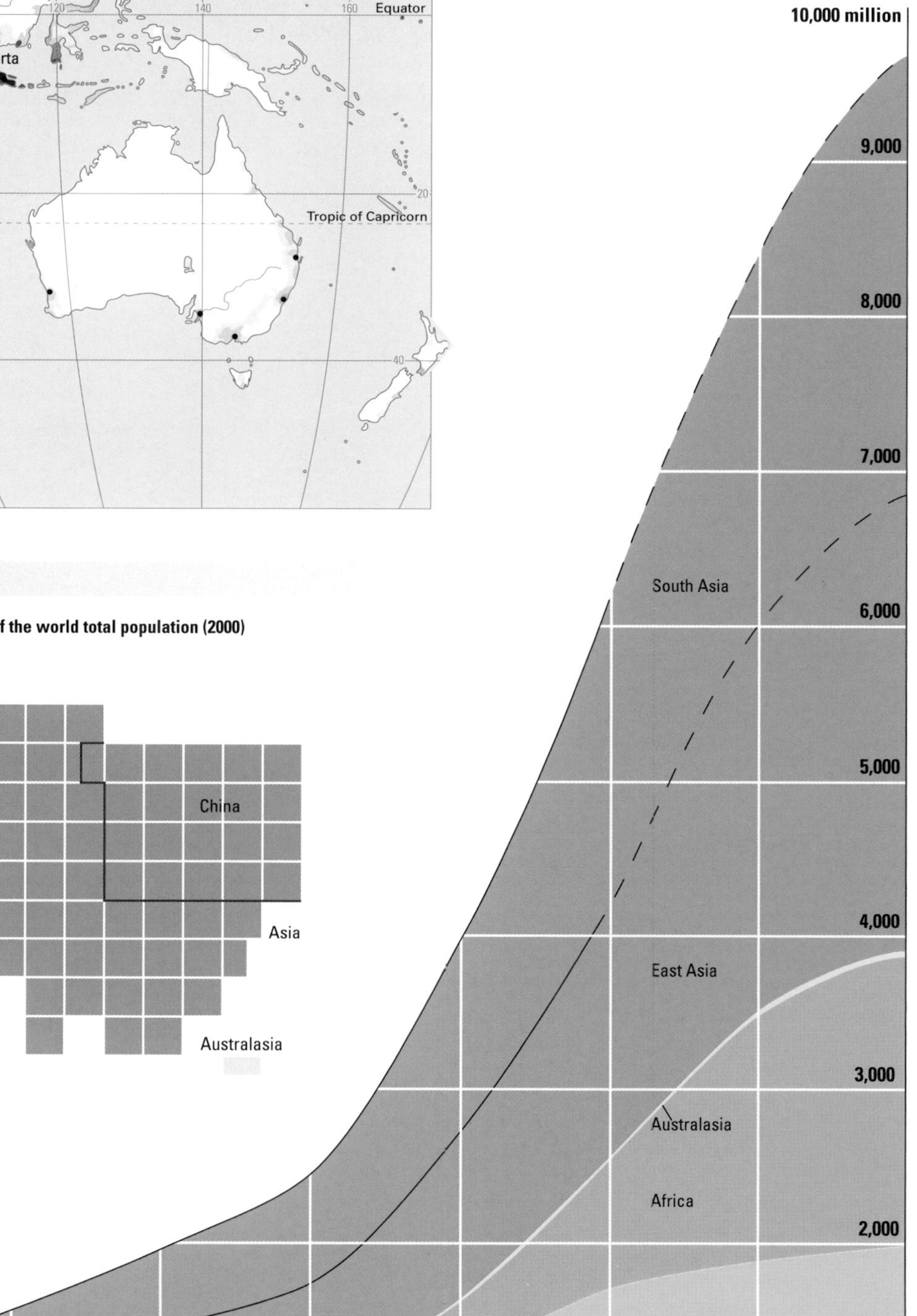

Cities

For more information:
18 Water distribution
24 Population density
41 The great ports

Following the development of agriculture more than 10,000 years ago, people began to live in farming villages. Around 5,500 years ago, the world's first cities appeared in the lower Tigris and Euphrates valleys in Mesopotamia. Cities were founded in Ancient Egypt around 5,000 years ago and in China around 3,600 years ago. By contrast with the villages, most people in the early cities were not engaged in farming. Instead, they worked in craft industries, in government services, in religion and in trade. The cities became centres of early civilizations and, through trade, their influence spread far and wide. However, they were dependent on the surrounding farming communities for their food and other materials.

In 1750, prior to the start of the Industrial Revolution, barely 3% of the world's population lived in urban areas. By 1850, London and Paris had more than a million people, and, by 1900, 14% of the world's population lived in cities. By 1950, the world had 83 cities with more than a million people, and by 1996 there were 280; by 2015, experts predict there will be more than 500. New York City was the only city with a population in excess of 10 million in 1950; by 2015, experts predict there will be 27 such cities worldwide, the majority located in the developing world.

However, predictions have to be constantly revised in light of new data. For example, in the late 1990s, demographers calculated that urban areas then accounted for 50% of the world's population. But after much lower census figures emerged for many cities in the early 21st century, the estimated date by which half of the world's population would be living in cities was pushed back to 2007.

Urbanization is greatest in industrialized countries. For example, in 2000, 77.2% of the people in the United States lived in urban areas. However, in low-income countries, which contained nearly 60% of the world's population in the late 1990s, only 28% lived in urban areas.

The rapid rate of urbanization has created many social problems, especially in cities that have been unable to provide enough jobs and services for the new arrivals. Many of the new city dwellers come from rural areas and take time to adjust to urban life and employment possibilities.

A typical city in a developing country contains millions of people living, often illegally, in shanty towns (or 'informal settlements'), while thousands live on the streets. Yet many of these shanty towns are healthier than the industrial cities of 19th-century Europe and North America. Indeed, surveys have shown that migrants to cities in developing countries are less likely to face poverty than they are in rural areas, while benefiting from greater access to healthcare services and education.

Modern cities face many problems today, including pollution, crime, and unemployment. Yet, given competent central and local government, they are capable of generating the wealth they need to solve them, as well as making a major contribution to the nation's economy.

URBAN POPULATION

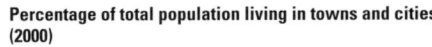

Percentage of total population living in towns and cities (2000)

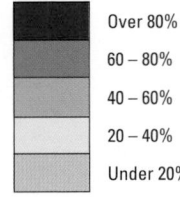

- Over 80%
- 60 – 80%
- 40 – 60%
- 20 – 40%
- Under 20%

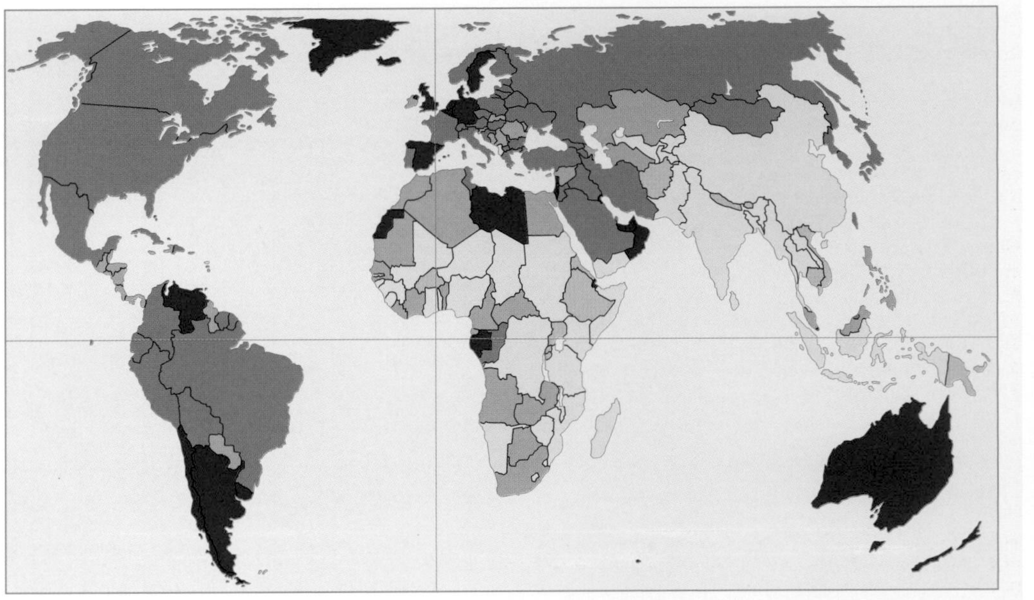

Most urbanized		Least urbanized	
Belgium	97%	Rwanda	6%
W. Sahara	96%	Bhutan	7%
Singapore	93%	East Timor	7%
UAE	93%	Burundi	9%
Iceland	93%	Nepal	11%

THE URBANIZATION OF THE EARTH

City-building, 1850–2000; each white spot represents a city of at least 1 million inhabitants

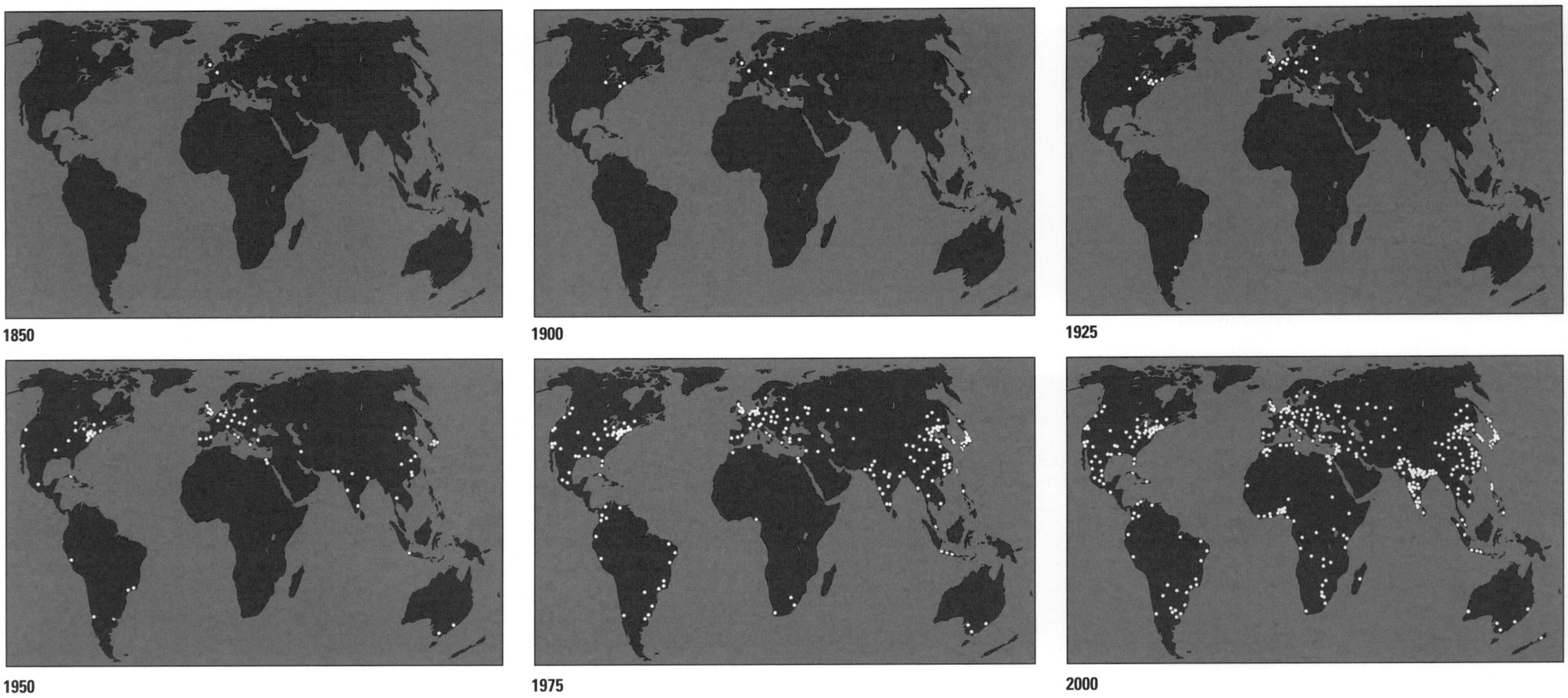

EXPANDING CITIES

These graphs show the projected growth of some of the world's megacities between 1950 and 2015. New York City, the world's largest city in 1950, reached a peak in 1970, but it has since experienced periods of negative growth. London's population also declined between 1970 and 1985, before resuming a modest rate of increase.

In both cases, the divergence from world trends is explained in part by counting methods. Each lies at the centre of a great agglomeration, and definitions of the 'city limits' may vary over time. Also, in developing countries, many areas around the megacities, which are counted as urban, are in fact rural in character.

The rates of city population growth in developing countries have also often been overestimated. For example, it was once predicted that Kolkata (Calcutta) would have a population of 40 million by the late 1990s. The reason why many estimates have proven incorrect is partly explained by a new trend, namely that rapid urban growth is now greatest, in some regions, in the smaller cities. For example, the main expansion in West Bengal is no longer in Kolkata (Calcutta), but in a rash of small cities across the state.

The growth of some of the world's largest cities in millions, 1950–2015

Comparisons of city populations over time are problematic due to changes in the definition of the city limits. These figures attempt to take such changes into consideration. The figure for London is the metropolitan region.

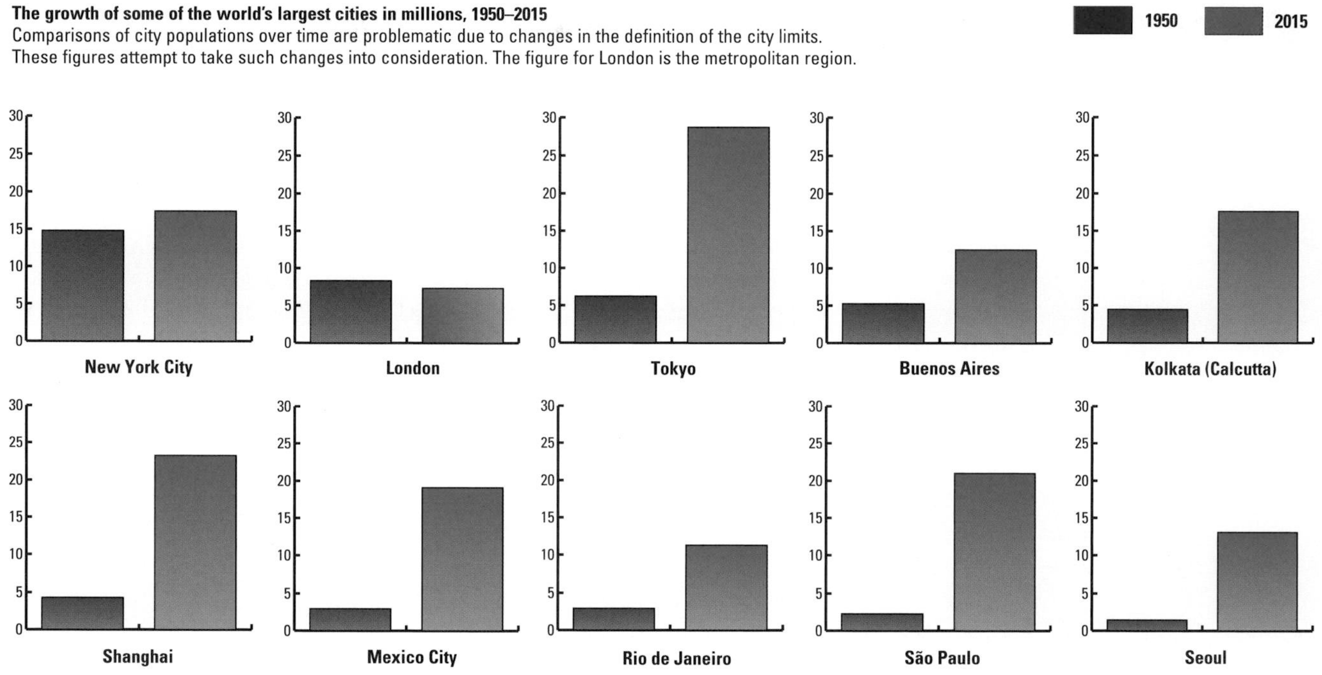

CITIES IN DANGER

In mid-2002, a 'brown haze', stretching 3 km [2 mi] high, covered much of southern Asia. Caused mainly by the burning of coal and biomass, it caused respiratory diseases and many deaths. Alarm concerning urban air pollution had been expressed much earlier, but controls since the 1980s had proved difficult to enforce and expensive to introduce.

Those cities taking part in the United Nation's Global Environment Monitoring System frequently show dangerous levels of pollutants, ranging from soot to sulphur dioxide and photo-chemical smog. Air in the majority of cities without such sampling equipment is likely to be at least as bad. Traffic, a major source of air pollution worldwide, loses Thailand's workforce 44 working days each year.

URBAN HOUSING NEEDS

Urbanization in most developing countries has been proceeding so rapidly that local governments have been unable to provide the necessary services and housing to meet demand.

In some cities, many people make their homes in squatter settlements, which are frequently without power, water and sanitation. Yet these communities are often a dynamic part of the city's economy, while their inhabitants sometimes take the initiative in setting up their own local government and self-help associations.

Some of the world's richest cities also have a homeless underclass, although calculating the numbers of people involved is problematic. Yet it is the case that homelessness and unemployment are currently affecting an increasing number of people in the developed world.

LARGEST CITIES

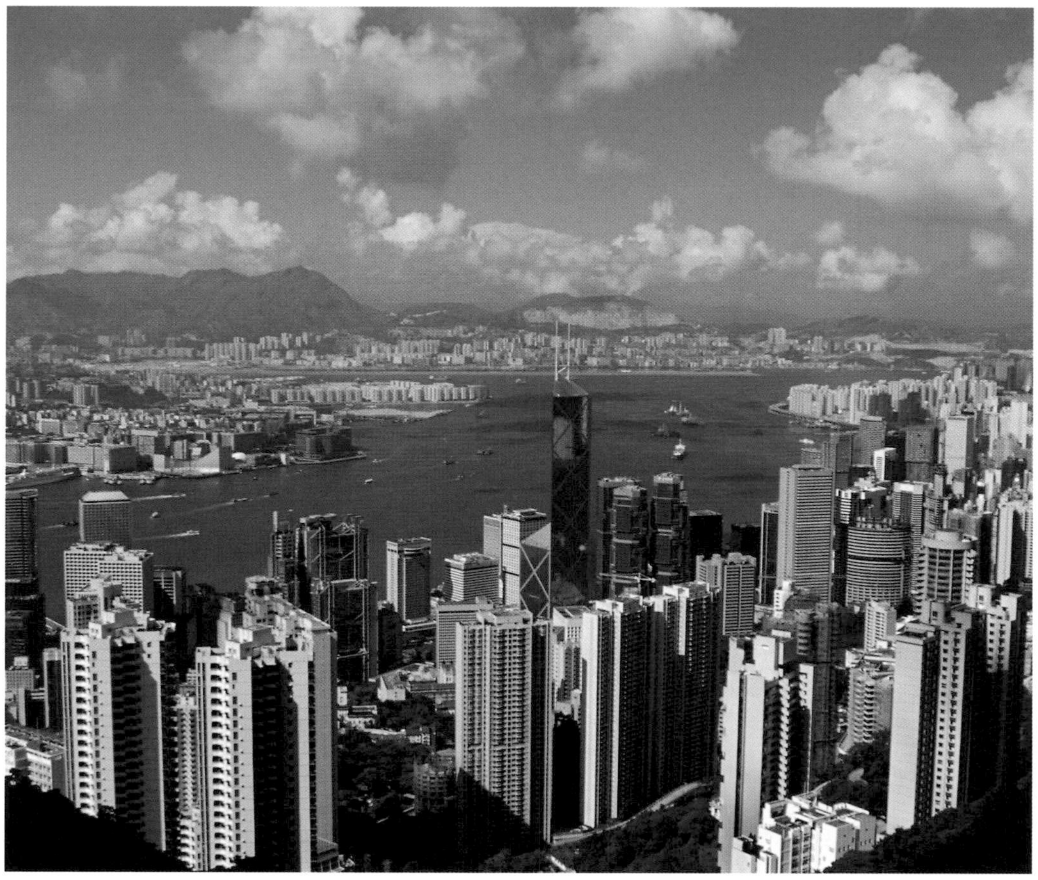

◀ The business district of Hong Kong City is located on the northern shore of Hong Kong Island. The cluster of modern high-rise buildings reflects the financial success of this tiny region, which has one of the strongest economies in Asia.

Early in the 21st century for the first time in history, the majority of the world's population will live in cities. Below is a list of all the cities with more than 10 million inhabitants, based on estimates for the year 2015.

1. Tokyo–Yokohama	28.7
2. Mumbai (Bombay)	27.4
3. Lagos	24.1
4. Shanghai	23.2
5. Jakarta	21.5
6. São Paulo	21.0
7. Karachi	20.6
8. Beijing	19.6
9. Dhaka	19.2
10. Mexico City	19.1
11. Kolkata (Calcutta)	17.6
12. Delhi	17.5
13. New York City	17.4
14. Tianjin	17.1
15. Manila	14.9
16. Cairo	14.7
17. Los Angeles	14.5
18. Seoul	13.1
19. Buenos Aires	12.5
20. Istanbul	12.1
21. Rio de Janeiro	11.3
22. Lahore	10.9
23. Hyderabad	10.6
24. Bangkok	10.4
25. Osaka	10.2
26. Lima	10.1
27. Tehran	10.0

The city populations above are based on urban agglomerations rather than legal city limits. In some cases, where two adjacent cities have merged into one concentration, such as Tokyo–Yokohama, they have been regarded as a single unit.

URBAN ADVANTAGES

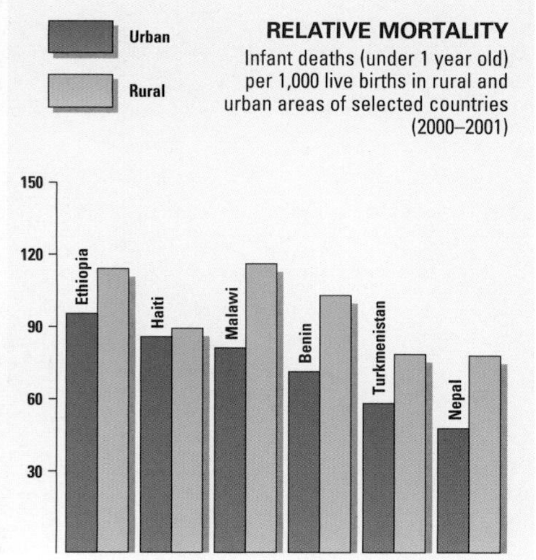

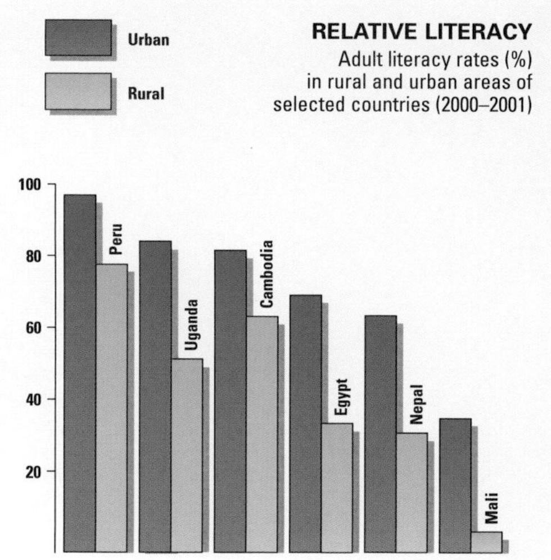

Despite overcrowding and poor housing, living standards in the developing world's cities are almost invariably better than in the surrounding countryside. Resources – financial, material and administrative – are concentrated in the towns, which are usually also the centres of political activity and pressure. Governments – frequently unstable, and rarely established on a solid democratic base – are usually more responsive to urban discontent than to rural misery.

In many developing countries, especially in Africa, food prices are kept artificially low, thus appeasing the underemployed urban masses at the expense of agricultural development.

This imbalance encourages further citywards migration, helping to account for the astonishing rate of post-1950 urbanization and putting great strain on the ability of many nations to provide even modest improvements for their people.

THE HUMAN FAMILY

For more information:
24 Population density
30 The world's refugees
War since 1945
31 United Nations
International organizations

Racial, language and religious differences have led to appalling acts of inhumanity throughout history. Yet, strictly speaking, all human beings belong to one species, *Homo sapiens*, which has no subspecies. The differences between the three racial types which most people identify – Caucasoid, Mongoloid and Negroid – reflect not so much evolutionary differences as long periods of separation.

Migration has recently mingled the various groups to an unprecedented extent, and most nations now have some degree of racial mixing. For example, the USA has often been called a melting pot, because of the large numbers of people from various geographical locations which make up the population. The country has no official language but, until recently, English was spoken by the vast majority of the people. But in recent years, some of the immigrants from Mexico, Cuba and other parts of Latin America have not learned English and speak only Spanish. This development disturbs those Americans who believe that the use of English binds the nation together, and several states have passed laws stating that English is their only official language.

Language is fundamental to human culture. Because definitions of languages vary, estimates of the total number range from 3,000 to 6,000, although most are spoken by only a few people. Chinese is spoken by more people as a first language than any other, while English ranks second, but English is the leading international language, because so many people speak it as their second tongue.

Like language, religion encourages cohesion in single human groups and it satisfies a deep human need by assigning people a place in a divinely ordered world. Religion is a way in which a culture can express its individuality. For example, the rise of Islamic fundamentalism in the late 20th century was partly an expression of resentment that secular Western values were being imposed on Muslims.

WORLD MIGRATION

The greatest voluntary migration was the colonization of North America by 30–35 million European settlers during the 19th century. The greatest forced migration involved 9–11 million Africans taken as slaves to America between 1550 and 1860. The migrations shown on the map below are mostly international, as population movements within borders are not usually recorded. Many of the statistics are necessarily estimates as so many refugees and migrant workers enter countries illegally and unrecorded. Emigrants may have a variety of motives for leaving, thus making it difficult to distinguish between voluntary and involuntary migrations.

Foreign born, as a % of total population (latest year)
- More than 7.5%
- 3 – 7.5%
- 1.5 – 3%
- Less than 1.5%
- No available data

Migration — 1500 – 1914: Voluntary, Involuntary; Since 1914: Voluntary, Involuntary
- Over 2,000,000 people
- 1 – 2,000,000 people
- 500,000 – 1,000,000 people
- Under 500,000 people

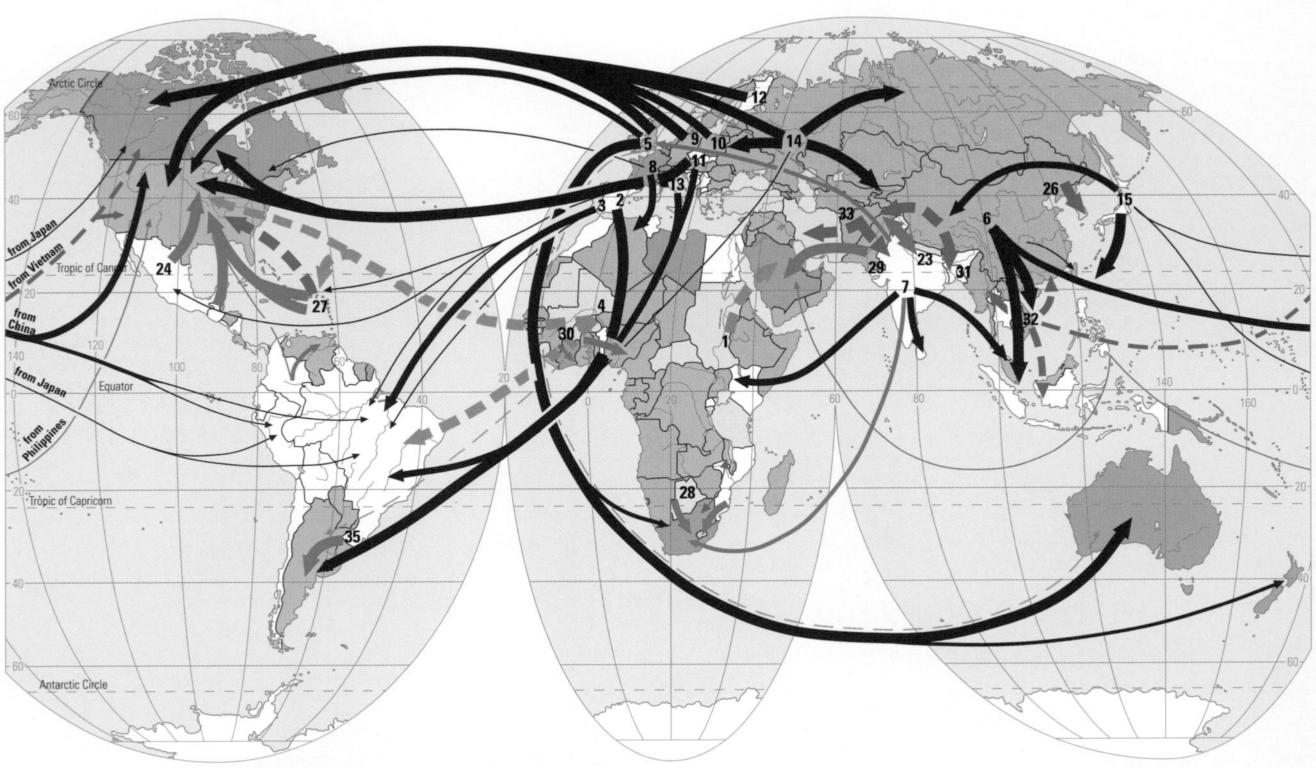

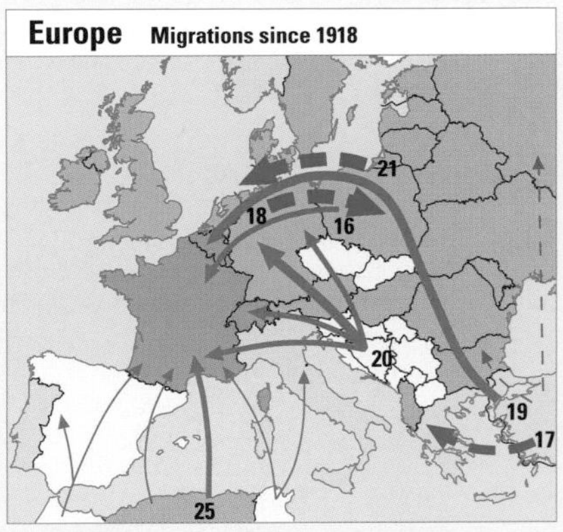

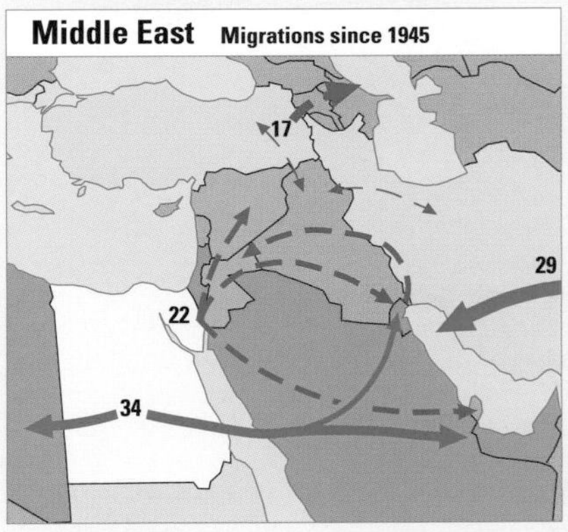

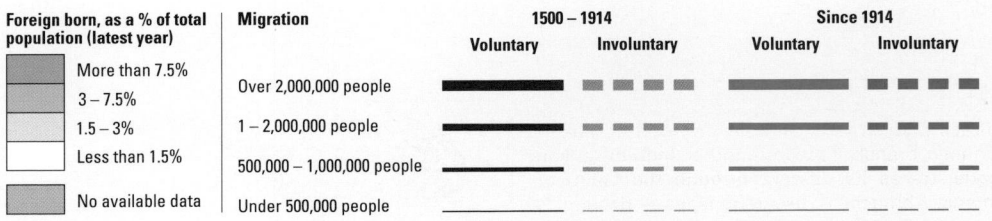

Major world migrations since 1500 (over 1 million people)

1. North and East African slaves to Arabia (4.3m) ... 1500–1900
2. Spanish to South and Central America (2.3m) ... 1530–1914
3. Portuguese to Brazil (1.4m) ... 1530–1914
4. West African slaves to South America (4.6m) ... 1550–1860
   to Caribbean (4m) ... 1580–1860
   to North/Central America (1m) ... 1650–1820
5. British and Irish to North America (13.5m) ... 1620–1914
   to Australasia and South Africa (3m) ... 1790–1914
6. Chinese to South-east Asia (22m) ... 1820–1914
   to North America (1m) ... 1880–1914
7. Indian migrant workers (3m) ... 1850–1914
8. French to North Africa (1.5m) ... 1850–1914
9. Germans to North America (5m) ... 1850–1914
10. Poles to North America (3.6m) ... 1850–1914
11. Austro-Hungarians to North America (3.2m) ... 1850–1914
    to Western Europe (3.4m) ... 1850–1914
    to South America (1.8m) ... 1850–1914
12. Scandinavians to North America (2.7m) ... 1850–1914
13. Italians to North America (5m) ... 1860–1914
    to South America (3.7m) ... 1860–1914
14. Russians to North America (2.2m) ... 1880–1914
    to Western Europe (2.2m) ... 1880–1914
    to Siberia (6m) ... 1880–1914
    to Central Asia (4m) ... 1880–1914
15. Japanese to Eastern Asia, South-east Asia and America (8m) ... 1900–1914
16. Poles to Western Europe (1m) ... 1920–1940
17. Greeks and Armenians from Turkey (1.6m) ... 1922–1923
18. European Jews to extermination camps (5m) ... 1940–1944
19. Turks to Western Europe (1.9m) ... 1940–
20. Yugoslavs to Western Europe (2m) ... 1940–
21. Germans to Western Europe (9.8m) ... 1945–1947
22. Palestinian refugees (2m) ... 1947–
23. Indian and Pakistani refugees (15m) ... 1947
24. Mexicans to North America (9m) ... 1950–
25. North Africans to Western Europe (1.1m) ... 1950–
26. Korean refugees (5m) ... 1950–1954
27. Latin Americans and West Indians to North America (4.7m) ... 1960–
28. Migrant workers to South Africa (1.5m) ... 1960–
29. Indians and Pakistanis to The Gulf (2.4m) ... 1970–
30. Migrant workers to Nigeria and Ivory Coast (3m) ... 1970–
31. Bangladeshi and Pakistani refugees (2m) ... 1972
32. Vietnamese and Cambodian refugees (1.5m) ... 1975–
33. Afghan refugees (6.1m) ... 1979–
34. Egyptians to The Gulf and Libya (2.9m) ... 1980–
35. Migrant workers to Argentina (2m) ... 1980–
36. Mozambique refugees (1.7m) ... 1985–
37. Yugoslav/Balkan refugees (1.7m) ... 1992–
38. Rwanda/Burundi refugees (2.6m) ... 1994–

BUILDING THE USA

US Immigration, 1920 and 2000

For decades the USA was the magnet that attracted millions of immigrants, notably from Central and Eastern Europe, the flow peaking in the early years of the 20th century. By the mid-1990s the proportion of immigrants had increased again to pre-World War II rates, reaching almost 10% by 2000. However, the balance of origin had swung from Europe to Latin America and Asia, as the graphs indicate.

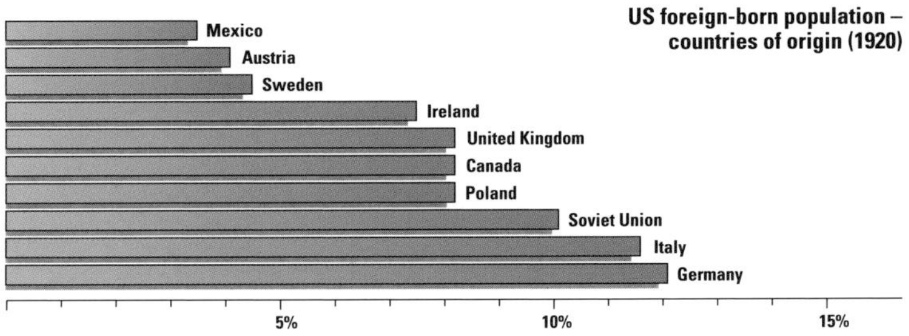

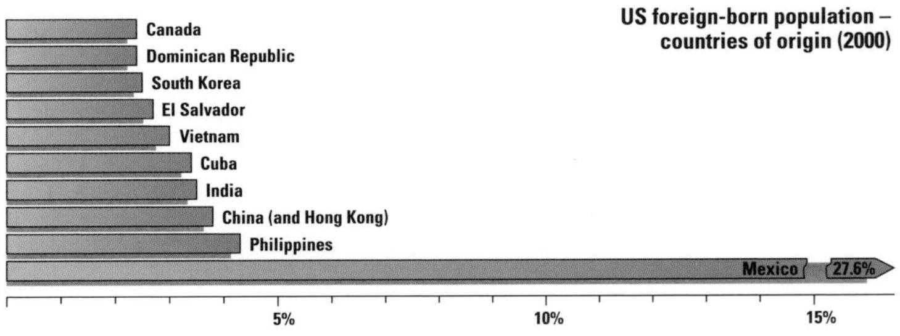

PREDOMINANT LANGUAGES

INDO-EUROPEAN FAMILY

- 1 Balto-Slavic group (incl. Russian, Ukrainian)
- 2 Germanic group (incl. English, German)
- 3 Celtic group
- 4 Greek
- 5 Albanian
- 6 Iranian group
- 7 Armenian
- 8 Romance group (incl. Spanish, Portuguese, French, Italian)
- 9 Indo-Aryan group (incl. Hindi, Bengali, Urdu, Punjabi, Marathi)
- 10 **CAUCASIAN FAMILY**

AFRO-ASIATIC FAMILY

- 11 Semitic group (incl. Arabic)
- 12 Kushitic group
- 13 Berber group
- 14 **KHOISAN FAMILY**
- 15 **NIGER-CONGO FAMILY**
- 16 **NILO-SAHARAN FAMILY**
- 17 **URALIC FAMILY**

ALTAIC FAMILY

- 18 Turkic group (incl. Turkish)
- 19 Mongolian group
- 20 Tungus-Manchu group
- 21 Japanese and Korean

SINO-TIBETAN FAMILY

- 22 Sinitic (Chinese) languages (incl. Mandarin, Wu, Yue)
- 23 Tibetic-Burmic languages
- 24 **TAI FAMILY**

AUSTRO-ASIATIC FAMILY

- 25 Mon-Khmer group
- 26 Munda group
- 27 Vietnamese
- 28 **DRAVIDIAN FAMILY** (incl. Telugu, Tamil)
- 29 **AUSTRONESIAN FAMILY** (incl. Malay-Indonesian, Javanese)
- 30 **OTHER LANGUAGES**

First-language speakers, in millions (1999)

Mandarin Chinese	885m
Spanish	332m
English	322m
Bengali	189m
Hindi	182m
Portuguese	170m
Russian	170m
Japanese	125m
German	98m
Wu Chinese	77m
Javanese	76m
Korean	75m
French	72m
Vietnamese	68m
Yue Chinese	66m
Marathi	65m
Tamil	63m
Turkish	59m
Urdu	58m

Languages form a kind of tree of development, splitting from a few ancient proto-tongues into branches that have grown apart and further divided with the passage of time. English and Hindi, for example, both belong to the great Indo-European family, although the relationship is only apparent after much analysis and comparison with non-Indo-European languages such as Chinese or Arabic. Hindi is part of the Indo-Aryan subgroup, whereas English is a member of Indo-European's Germanic branch. French, another Indo-European tongue, traces its descent through the Latin, or Romance, branch. A few languages – Basque is one example – have no apparent links with any other, living or dead. Most modern languages, of course, have acquired enormous quantities of vocabulary from each other.

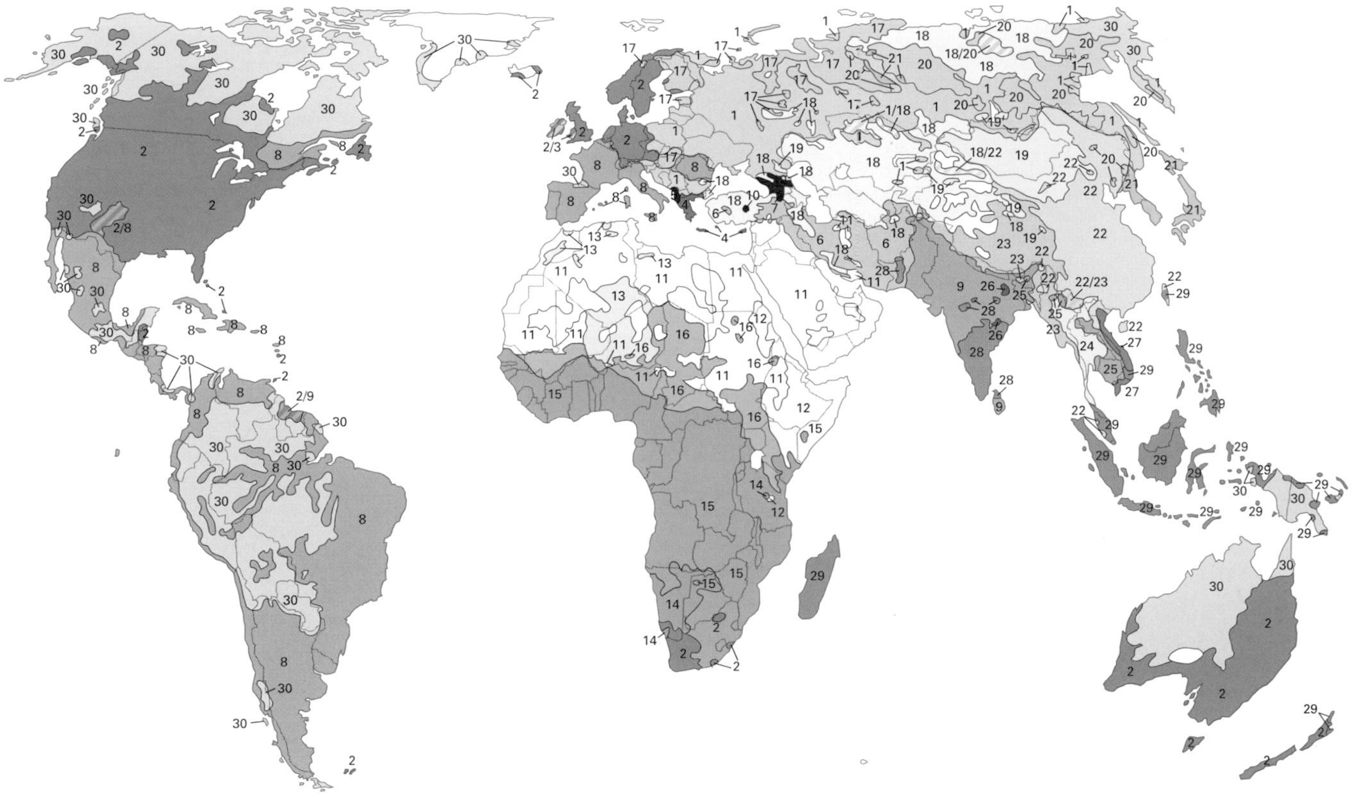

DISTRIBUTION OF LIVING LANGUAGES

The figures refer to the number of languages currently in use in the regions shown

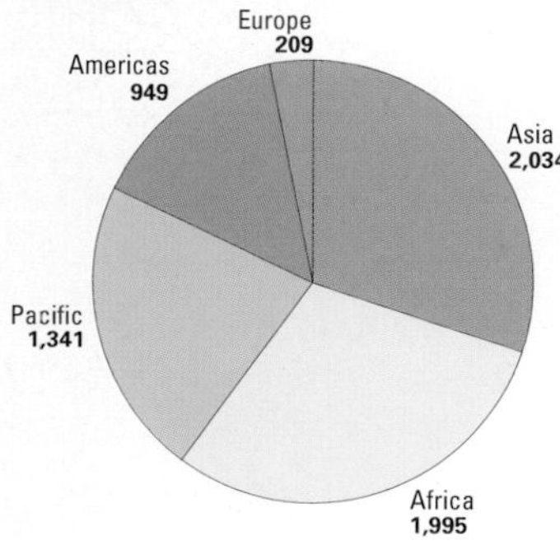

PREDOMINANT RELIGIONS

- Roman Catholicism
- Orthodox and other Eastern Churches
- Protestantism
- Sunni Islam
- Shia Islam
- Buddhism
- Hinduism
- Confucianism
- Judaism
- Shintoism
- Tribal Religions

Religions are not as easily mapped as the physical contours of the land. Divisions are often blurred and frequently overlapping: most nations include people of many different faiths – or no faith at all. Some religions, like Islam and Christianity, have proselytes worldwide; others, like Hinduism and Confucianism, are restricted to a particular area, though modern migrations have taken some Indians and Chinese very far from their cultural origins. It is also difficult to show the degree to which religion controls daily life: Christian Western Europe, for example, is now far less dominated by its religion than are the Islamic nations of the Middle East. Similarly, figures for the major faiths' adherents make no distinction between nominal believers enrolled at birth and those for whom religion is a vital part of their existence.

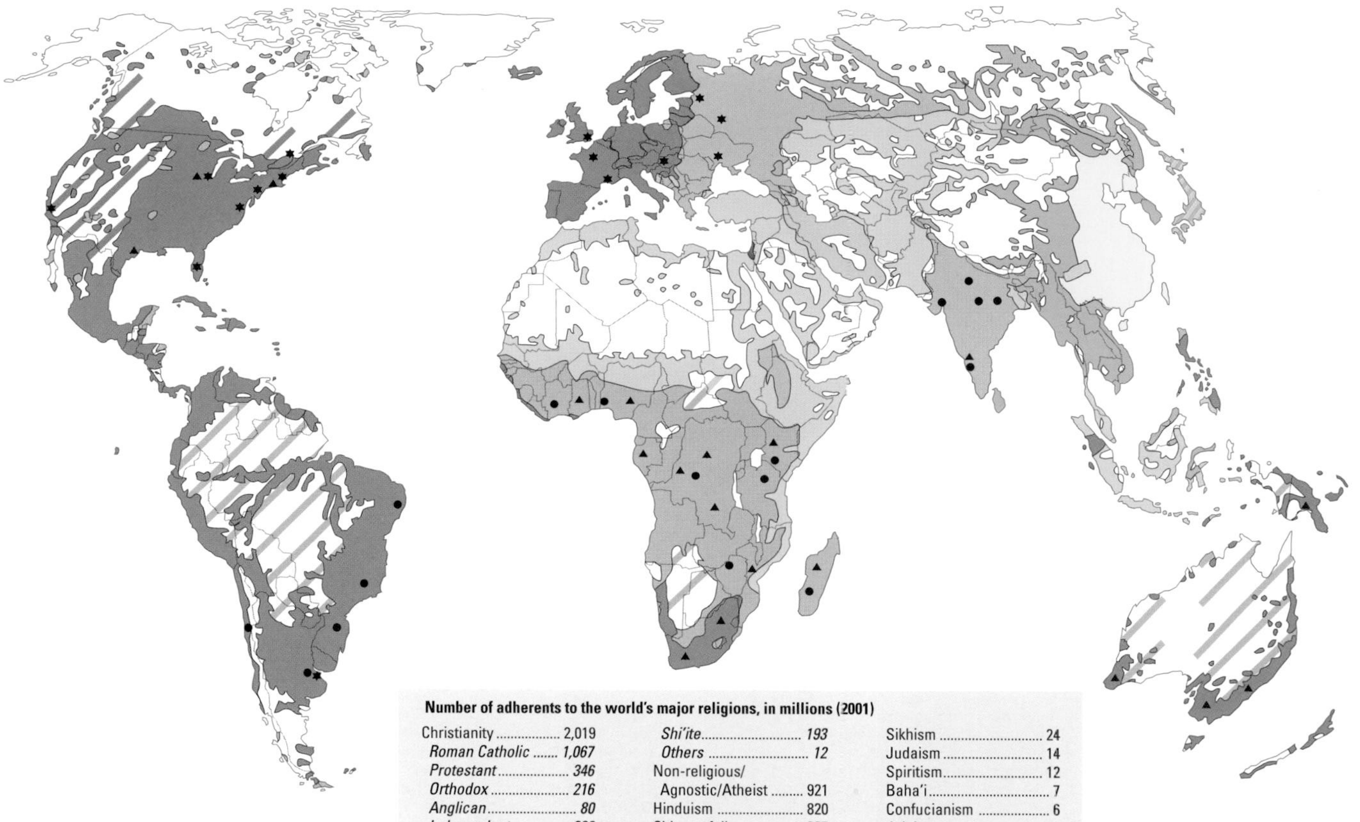

Number of adherents to the world's major religions, in millions (2001)

Christianity	2,019
Roman Catholic	*1,067*
Protestant	*346*
Orthodox	*216*
Anglican	*80*
Independent	*392*
Others	*139*
Islam	1,207
Sunni	*1,002*
Shi'ite	*193*
Others	*12*
Non-religious/ Agnostic/Atheist	921
Hinduism	820
Chinese folk	387
Buddhism	362
Ethnic religions	242
New religions	103
Sikhism	24
Judaism	14
Spiritism	12
Baha'i	7
Confucianism	6
Jainism	4
Shintoism	3

Conflict and Co-operation

For more information:
28 Migration
29 Religion

The 20th century witnessed two world wars, followed by a Cold War which several times threatened to erupt into a third world war, fought with nuclear weapons. The Cold War was marked by a great number of conflicts. Some were colonial wars, as the empires of the first half of the century fell apart, some were border wars, and some were civil wars. All the wars have caused great suffering among civilians, many of whom were forced to join the ranks of the world's refugees.

In the late 1980s, many people hoped that the end of the Cold War, following the collapse of Communist regimes in the former Soviet Union and Eastern Europe, would herald a new era of international stability. Instead, old ethnic and religious antagonisms surfaced in many areas, leading to civil war in such places as Chechenia, in Russia, and the former Yugoslavia. Nationalist rivalries, suppressed under Communist rule, replaced ideological factors as the major cause of conflict.

War is a very human activity, with no real equivalent in any other species. Yet humans also function well when they co-operate. Evolution has made this so. Hunter-gatherers in co-operative bands were far more effective than animals that prowled. Agriculture, urbanization and industrialization all depend on the ability of humans to co-operate.

The creation of the United Nations in 1945 held out hope that the world's nations, tired of war, would have the means to control humanity's aggressive instincts. Although the UN lacks the power to halt conflicts, it has often helped to achieve negotiation. Economic pressures have led to another kind of co-operation, resulting in the creation of common markets and economic unions, such as ASEAN in South-east Asia, the European Union, and NAFTA in North America.

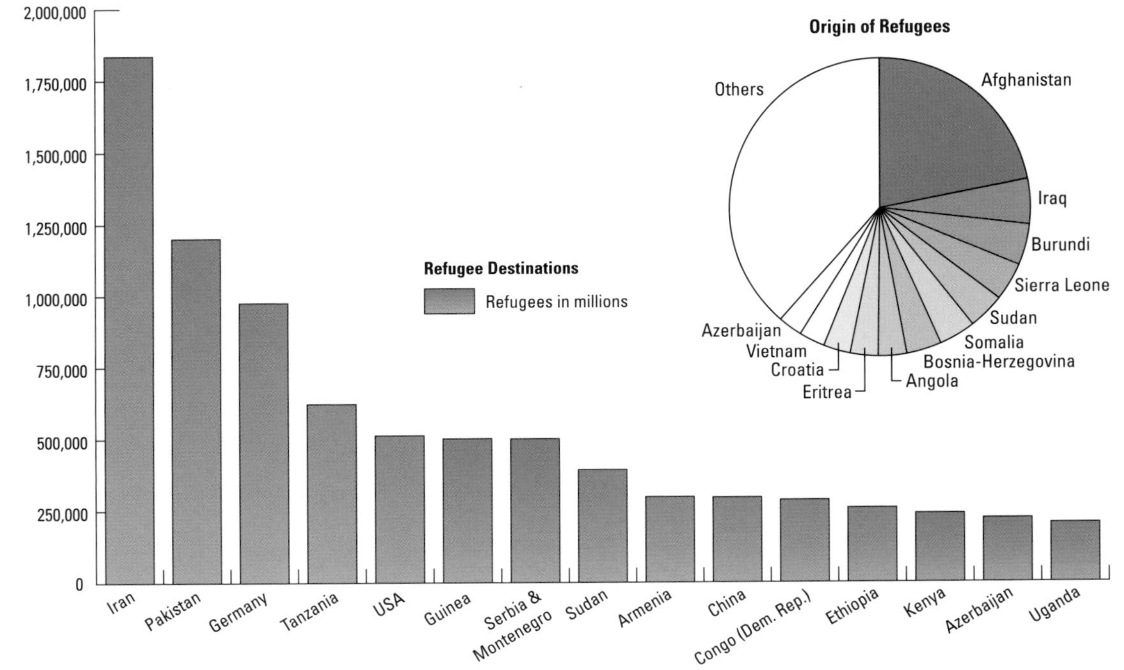

THE WORLD'S REFUGEES

Refugees by host nation (bar-chart, left) and by nation of origin (pie-chart, left) (2000). The source is the United Nations High Commission for Refugees (UNHCR). The 3.2 million Palestinian refugees living in Jordan, Syria, Lebanon, Gaza and the West Bank fall under the mandate of United Nations Relief and Works Agency (UNRWA) and are not included on the graphs.

The pie-chart shows the origins of the world's refugees, while the bar-chart below shows their destinations. According to the United Nations High Commission for Refugees (UNHCR) in 2000 there were 12.1 million refugees. However, the UNHCR definition of a refugee, 'a person who has left or remains outside their own country because they have a well-founded fear of persecution, or because their safety is threatened by events seriously disturbing public order', does not include people who are in a refugee-like situation but who have not been formally recognized. In 2000, there were a further 5.3 million people who were internally displaced, and a total 'population of concern' 21.1 million people, worldwide.

All but a few who cross international boundaries seek asylum in neighbouring countries, which are often the least equipped to deal with them. Lacking any rights or power, they frequently become an unwelcome burden to their hosts. Usually, the best any refugee can hope for is rudimentary food and shelter in temporary camps. Many Palestinians have been forced to live in camps since 1948.

WAR SINCE 1945

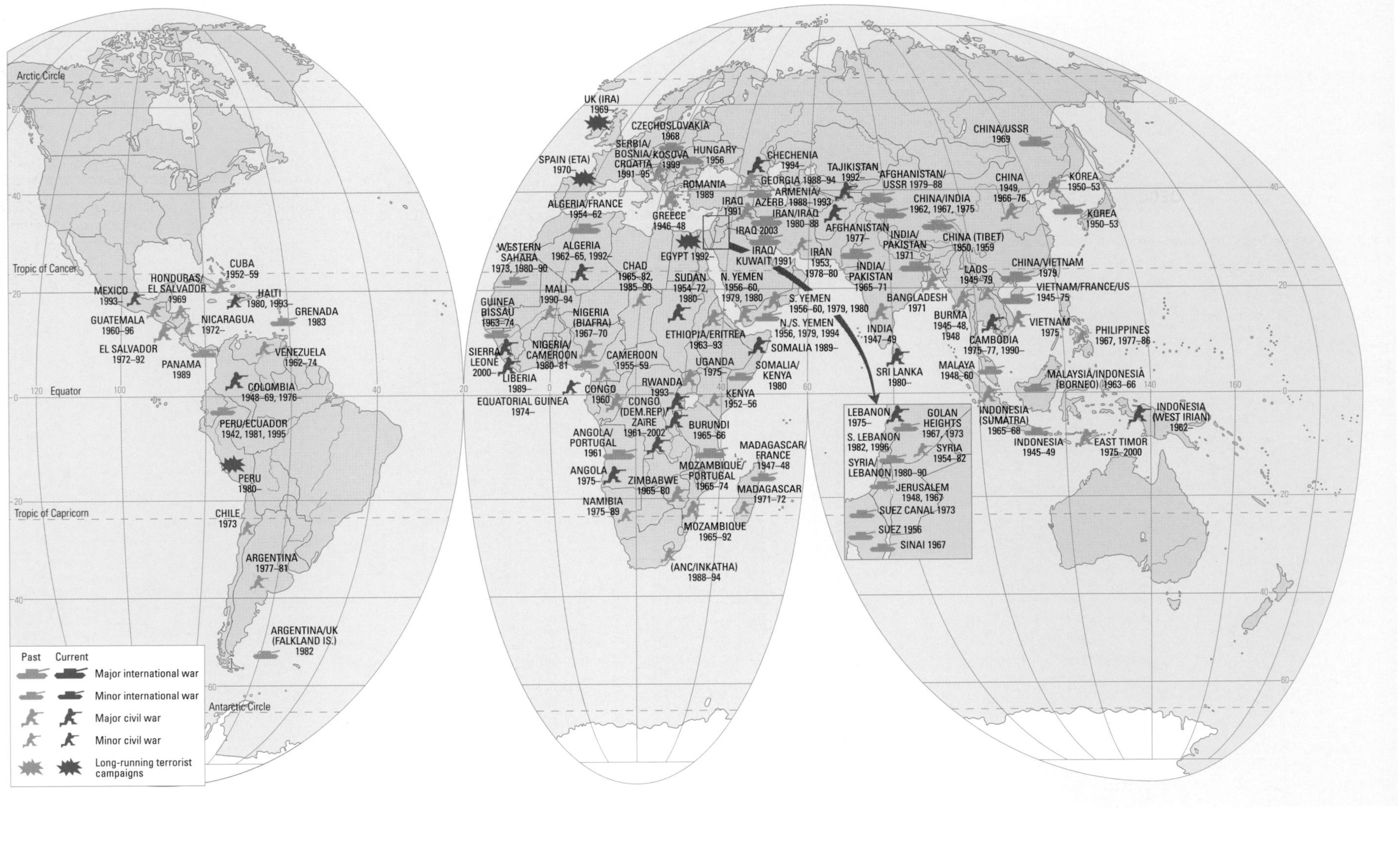

INTERNATIONAL ORGANIZATIONS

OAS Organization of American States (formed in 1948). It aims to promote social and economic co-operation between countries in the developed North America and developing Latin America.
EFTA European Free Trade Organization (founded 1960). Since Austria, Finland, Portugal and Sweden left to join the EU, it has four members: Iceland, Liechtenstein, Norway and Switzerland.
EU European Union (evolved from the European Community in 1993). Cyprus, the Czech Republic, Estonia, Hungary, Latvia, Lithuania, Malta, Poland, the Slovak Republic and Slovenia joined the EU in May 2004. The other 15 members of the EU are Austria, Belgium, Denmark, Finland, France, Germany, Greece, Ireland, Italy, Luxembourg, Netherlands, Portugal, Spain, Sweden and the UK – together they aim to integrate economies, co-ordinate social developments and bring about political union. Bulgaria and Romania are expected to join in 2007.
AU The African Union was set up in 2002, taking over from the Organization of African Unity (1963). It has 53 members. Working languages are Arabic, English, French and Portuguese.
COLOMBO PLAN (formed in 1951) Its 25 members aim to promote economic and social development in Asia and the Pacific.

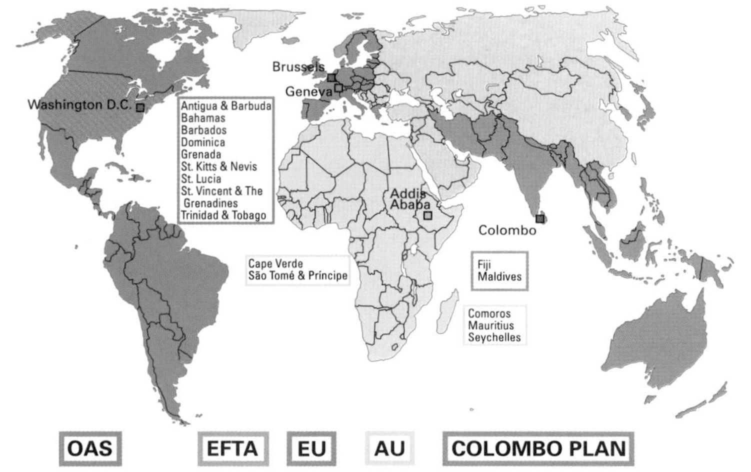

G8 Group of eight leading industrialized nations, comprising Canada, France, Germany, Italy, Japan, Russia, the UK and the USA. Periodic meetings are held to discuss major world issues, such as world recessions.
OECD Organization for Economic Co-operation and Development (formed in 1961). It comprises 30 major free-market economies. The 'G8' is its 'inner group' of leading industrial nations, comprising Canada, France, Germany, Italy, Japan, Russia, the UK and the USA.
ACP African-Caribbean-Pacific (formed in 1963). Members enjoy economic ties with the EU.
OPEC Organization of Petroleum Exporting Countries (formed in 1960). It controls about three-quarters of the world's oil supply. Gabon formally withdrew from OPEC in August 1996.
CIS The Commonwealth of Independent States (formed in 1991) comprises the countries of the former Soviet Union except for Estonia, Latvia and Lithuania.

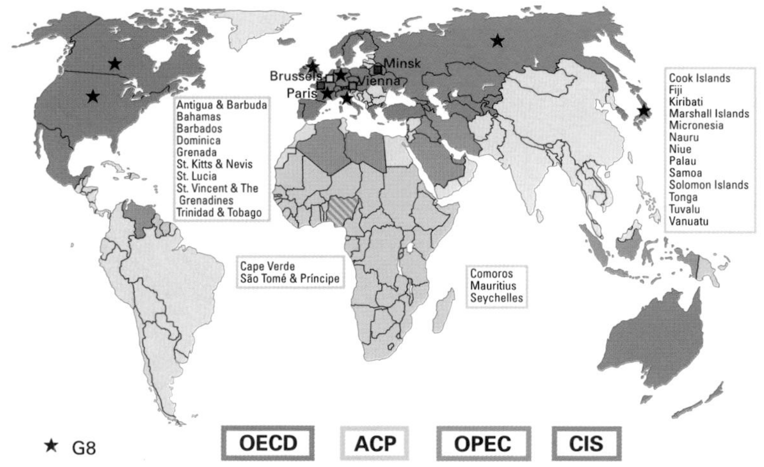

NATO North Atlantic Treaty Organization (formed in 1949). It continues despite the winding up of the Warsaw Pact in 1991. Bulgaria, Estonia, Latvia, Lithuania, Romania, the Slovak Republic and Slovenia became members in 2004.
LAIA The Latin American Integration Association (formed in 1980) superceded the Latin American Free Trade Association formed in 1961. Its aim is to promote freer regional trade.
ARAB LEAGUE (1945) Aims to promote economic, social, political and military co-operation. There are 22 member nations.
COMMONWEALTH The Commonwealth of Nations evolved from the British Empire. Pakistan was suspended in 1999, but reinstated in 2004. Zimbabwe was suspended in 2002 and, in response to its continued suspension, Zimbabwe left the Commonwealth in December 2003. It now comprises 16 Queen's realms, 31 republics and 6 indigenous monarchies, giving a total of 53 member states.
ASEAN Association of South-east Asian Nations (formed in 1967). Cambodia joined in 1999.

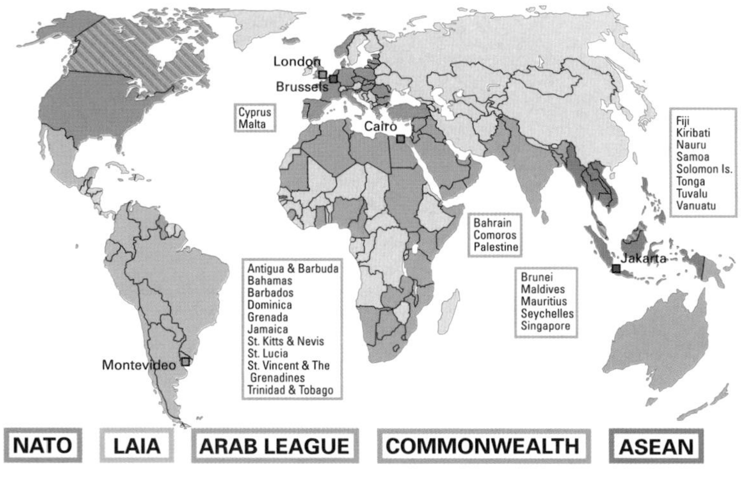

UNITED NATIONS

The United Nations Organization was born as World War II drew to its conclusion. Six years of strife had strengthened the world's desire for peace, but an effective international organization was needed to help achieve it. That body would replace the League of Nations which, since its inception in 1920, had failed to curb the aggression of at least some of its member nations. At the United Nations Conference on International Organization held in San Francisco, the United Nations Charter was drawn up. Ratified by the Security Council and signed by the 51 original members, it came into effect on 24 October 1945.

The Charter set out the aims of the organization: to maintain peace and security, and develop friendly relations between nations; to achieve international co-operation in solving economic, social, cultural and humanitarian problems; to promote respect for human rights and fundamental freedoms; and to harmonize the activities of nations in order to achieve these common goals.

The United Nations has five principal organs:

The General Assembly The forum at which member nations discuss moral and political issues affecting world development, peace and security meets annually in September, under a newly-elected President whose tenure lasts one year. Any member can bring business to the agenda, and each member nation has one vote.

The Security Council A legislative and executive body, the Security Council is the primary instrument for establishing and maintaining international peace by attempting to settle disputes between nations. It has the power to dispatch UN forces, and member nations undertake to provide armed forces, assistance and facilities. The Security Council has ten temporary members elected by the General Assembly for two-year terms, and five permanent members – China, France, Russia, the UK and the USA.

The Economic and Social Council By far the largest United Nations executive, the Council operates as a conduit between the General Assembly and the many United Nations agencies it instructs to implement Assembly decisions, and whose work it co-ordinates. The Council also commissions studies on economic conditions, collects data and makes recommendations to the Assembly.

The Secretariat This is the staff of the United Nations, and its task is to administer the policies and programmes of the UN and its organs, and assist and advise the Head of the Secretariat, the Secretary-General – a full-time, non-political appointment made by the General Assembly.

The Trusteeship Council This no longer administers any of the original 11 trust territories as they are all now independent.

The International Court of Justice (the World Court) The World Court is the judicial organ of the United Nations. It deals only with United Nations disputes and all members are subject to its jurisdiction. There are 15 judges, elected for nine-year terms by the General Assembly and the Security Council.

The social and humanitarian operations of the UN include:

United Nations Development Programme (UNDP) Plans and funds projects to help developing countries make better use of their resources.
United Nations International Childrens' Fund (UNICEF) Created at the General Assembly's first session in 1945 to help children in the aftermath of World War II, it now provides basic health care and aid worldwide.
Food and Agriculture Organization (FAO) Aims to raise living standards and nutrition levels in rural areas by improving food production and distribution.
United Nations Educational, Scientific and Cultural Organization (UNESCO) Promotes international co-operation through broader and better education.
World Health Organization (WHO) Promotes and provides for better health care, public and environmental health and medical research.

United Nations agencies are involved in many aspects of international trade, safety and security:

International Maritime Organization (IMO) Promotes unity amongst merchant shipping, especially in regard to safety, marine pollution and standardization.
International Labour Organization (ILO) Seeks to improve labour conditions and promote productive employment to raise living standards.
World Meteorological Organization (WMO) Promotes co-operation in weather observation, reporting and forecasting.
World Trade Organization (WTO) On 1 January 1995 the WTO replaced GATT. It advocates a common code of conduct and its aim is the liberalization of world trade.
Disarmament Commission Considers and makes recommendations to the General Assembly on disarmament issues.
International Atomic Energy Agency (IAEA) Fosters development of peaceful uses for nuclear energy and establishes safety standards.

The World Bank comprises three United Nations agencies:

International Monetary Fund (IMF) Cultivates international monetary co-operation and the expansion of trade.
International Bank for Reconstruction and Development (IBRD) Provides funds and technical assistance to developing countries.
International Finance Corporation (IFC) Encourages the growth of productive private enterprise in less developed countries.

Membership There are two independent states which are not members of the UN – Taiwan and Vatican City. Official languages are Chinese, English, French, Russian, Spanish and Arabic.

Funding The UN regular budget for 2002 was US $1.3 billion. Contributions are assessed by the members' ability to pay, with the maximum 22% of the total (USA's share), the minimum 0.01%. The EU pays over 37% of the budget.

Peacekeeping The UN has been involved in 54 peacekeeping operations worldwide since 1948.

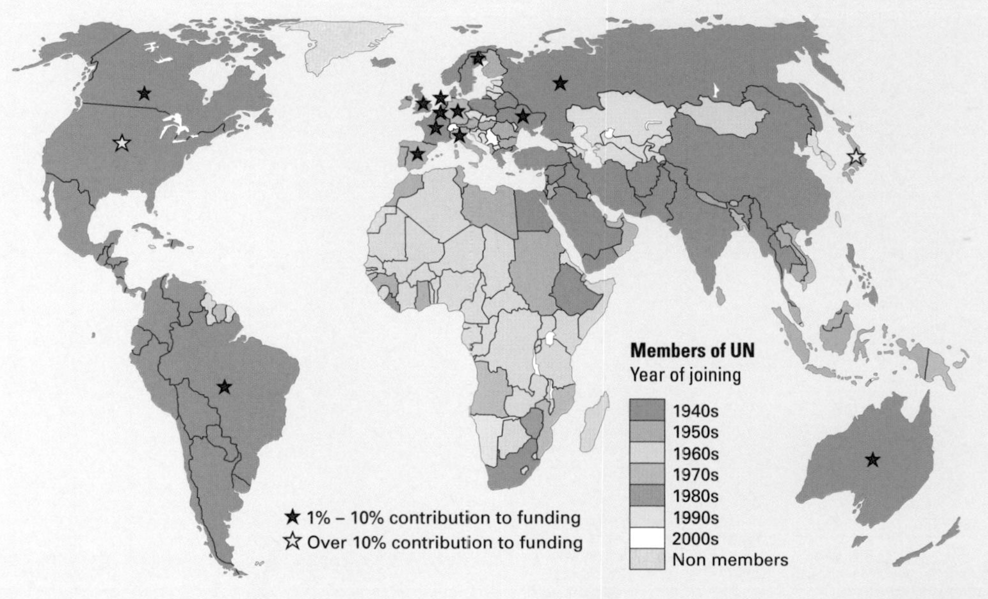

AGRICULTURE

For more information:
16 Climate regions
17 Temperature and precipitation
18 Water distribution
19 Natural vegetation
38 Division of employment

When harvests are bad and world grain reserves fall, an old debate is revived, namely whether the population explosion will cause major food crises in the 21st century. Experts estimate that 3 billion tonnes of cereals will be needed to feed the world's population in 25 years' time, as compared with 1.9 billion tonnes at present. To expand food production to this extent, some argue, will place great strain on the environment.

Other experts, however, argue that there should be no food crises. World grain production tripled between 1950 and 1990, largely as a result of the Green Revolution, during which genetically improved, high-yield varieties of maize, rice and wheat, the world's three leading staple crops, were developed.

These new varieties have helped many developing countries achieve food surpluses and prevent widespread starvation. Some people, however, oppose the use of genetically modified crops. In 2002, with severe droughts causing widespread starvation, Zambia and Zimbabwe both refused large maize donations from the USA because they might be genetically modified.

The only region of the world which seems likely to suffer food shortages in the 21st century is sub-Saharan Africa, where in the late 1990s the average daily calorie intake was 6% less than what was needed and where the population is expected to double in 20 years. Improved land management and a huge increase in global trade, especially in food distribution, is necessary if sub-Saharan Africans are not to go hungry.

The development of agriculture more than 10,000 years ago transformed human existence more than any other major advance. By supporting larger populations, it led to the growth of early civilizations and later it sustained people in the industrial cities that sprang up in the 19th century.

Today, agricultural production varies a great deal between the developed world, where it is highly mechanized and employs few people, such as 2% of the workforce in the United States, and the developing world, such as sub-Saharan Africa, where it employs 66% of the workforce. Many Africans are engaged in subsistence farming, providing the basic needs of their families but not contributing to the national economy. Much of Africa also suffers from economic mismanagement, as well as civil war and corruption.

Political problems have also affected food production in other parts of the world. The former USSR had much excellent farmland, but the failure of the collectives and state farms to maintain sufficiently high levels of production helped to bring about the collapse of Communism.

Farmers are under pressure not only to maintain high levels of production but also to increase them. However, the cultivation of marginal areas is one of the prime causes of soil erosion and desertification.

► The wheat harvest – photographed in Oregon, USA. Wheat, corn, rye, oats and barley are grown in temperate regions, whereas rice, millet, sorghum and maize require more tropical climates. Cereal cultivation was the basis of early civilizations, and, with the development of high-yielding strains, remains the world's most important food source today.

LAND USE

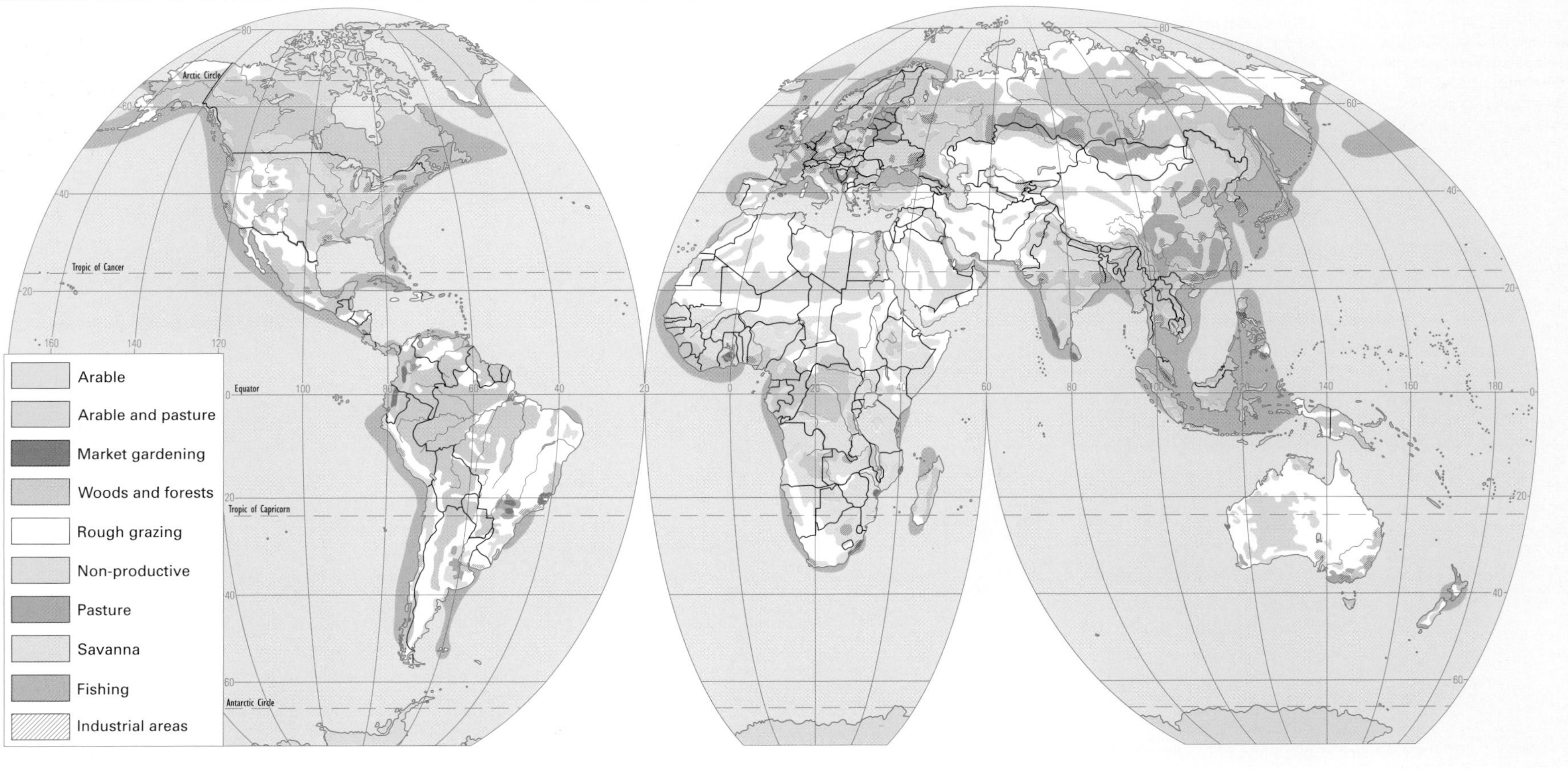

STAPLE CROPS

Wheat: Grown in a range of climates, with most varieties – including the highest-quality bread wheats – requiring temperate conditions. Mainly used in baking, it is also used for pasta and breakfast cereals.

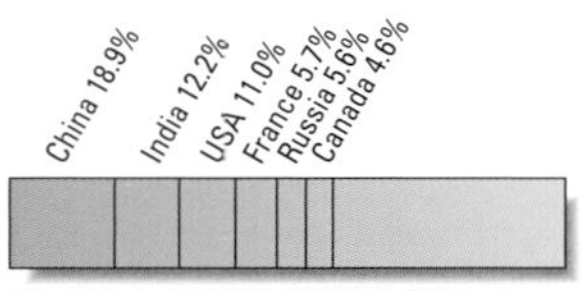

World total (2000): 576,317,000 tonnes

Maize: Originating in the New World and still an important human food in Africa and Latin America, in the developed world it is processed into breakfast cereals, oil, starches and adhesives. It is also used for animal feed.

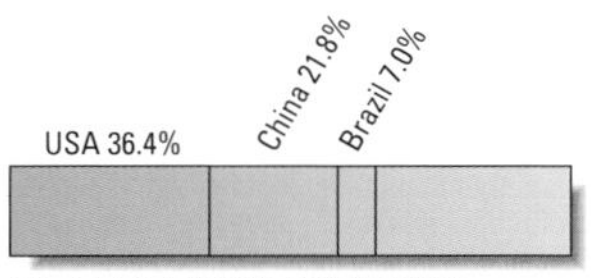

World total (2000): 590,791,000 tonnes

Oats: Most widely used to feed livestock, but eaten by humans as oatmeal or porridge. Oats have a beneficial effect on the cardiovascular system, and human consumption is likely to increase.

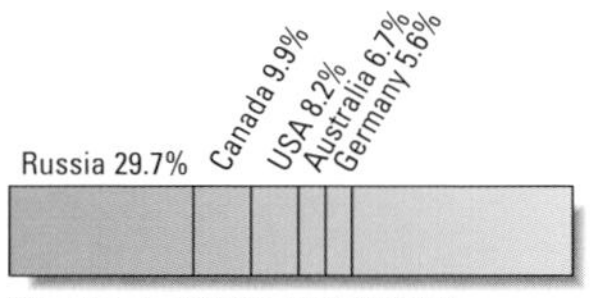

World total (2000): 25,953,000 tonnes

Millet: The name covers a number of small-grained cereals, members of the grass family with a short growing season. Used to produce flour, meal and animal feed, and fermented to make beer, especially in Africa.

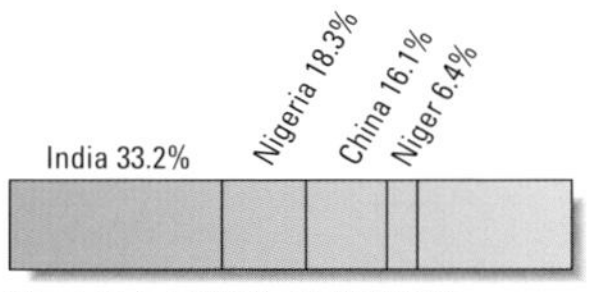

World total (2000): 27,255,000 tonnes

Rice: Thrives on the high humidity and temperatures of the Far East, where it is the traditional staple food of half the human race. Usually grown standing in water, rice responds well to continuous cultivation, with three or four crops annually.

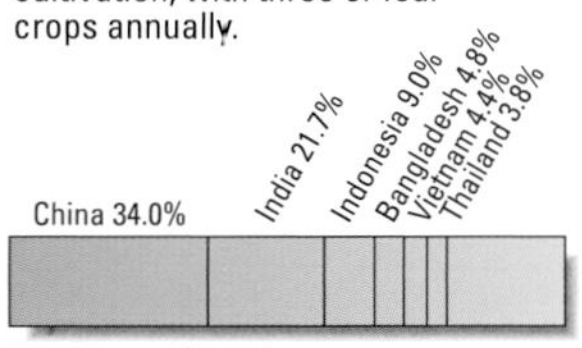

World total (2000): 598,852,000 tonnes

Potatoes: The most important of the edible tubers, potatoes grow in well-watered, temperate areas. Though weight for weight less nutritious than grain, they are a human staple as well as an important animal feed.

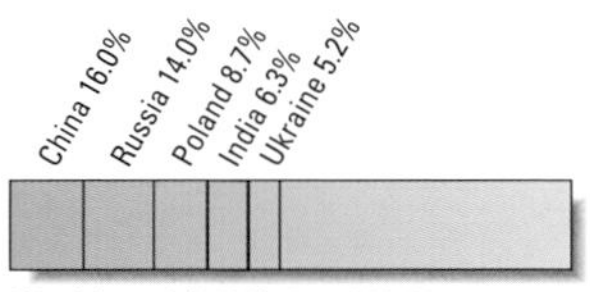

World total (2000): 311,288,000 tonnes

Soya: Beans from soya bushes (soybeans) are very high (30–40%) in protein. Most are processed into oil and proprietary protein foods. Consumption since 1950 has tripled, mainly due to the health-conscious developed world.

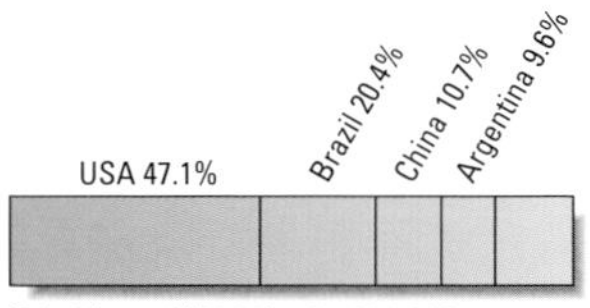

World total (2000): 161,993,000 tonnes

Cassava: A tropical shrub that needs high rainfall (over 1,000 mm annually) and a 10–30 month growing season to produce its large, edible tubers. Used as flour by humans, as cattle feed and in industrial starches.

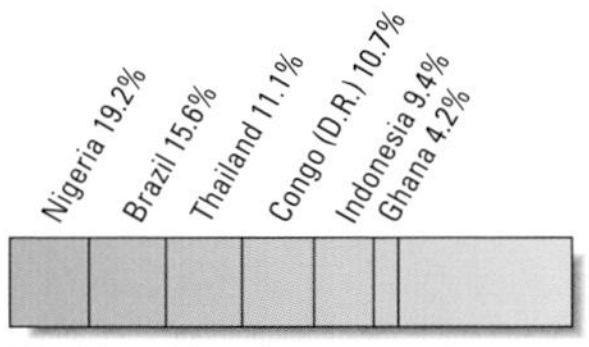

World total (2000): 172,737,000 tonnes

SUGARS

Sugar cane: Confined to tropical regions, cane sugar accounts for the bulk of international trade in sugar. Most is produced as a foodstuff, but some countries, notably Brazil and South Africa, distil sugar cane to make motor fuels.

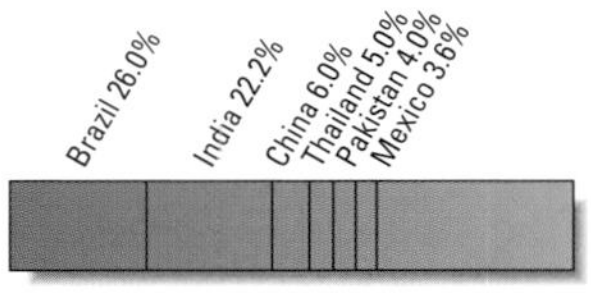

World total (2000): 1,278,093,000 tonnes

Sugar beet: Closely related to the beetroot, sugar beet's yield after processing is indistinguishable from cane sugar. It is replacing sugar-cane imports in Europe, to the detriment of the developing countries that rely on it as a major cash crop.

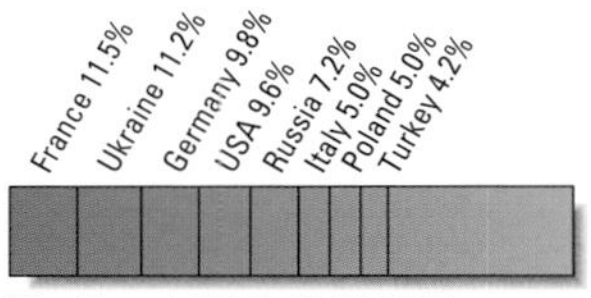

World total (2000): 244,780,000 tonnes

CEREALS & TUBERS

Cereals: These are grasses with starchy, edible seeds; every important civilization has depended on them as a source of food. The major cereal grains contain about 10% protein and 75% carbohydrate. Grain contributes more than any other group of foods to the energy and protein content of the human diet.

Starchy tuber crops or root crops: Second in importance after cereals as staple foods; easily cultivated, they provide high yields for little effort.

FOOD & POPULATION

Comparison of food production and population by continent

The left column indicates the % of world food production and the right shows population in proportion.

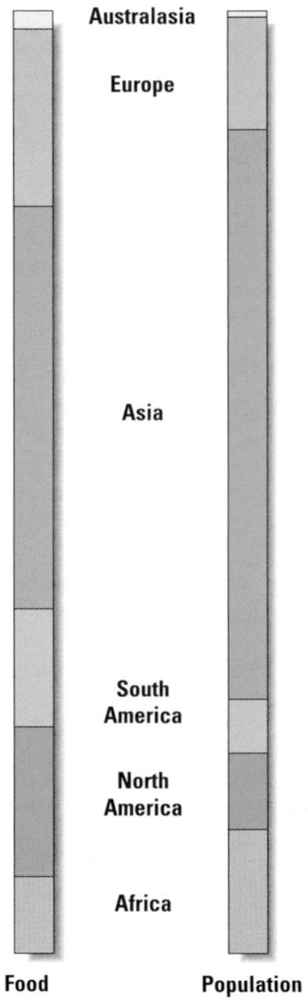

AGRICULTURAL POPULATION

Percentage of the total population dependent on agriculture for their livelihood (2000)

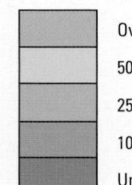

- Over 75% dependent
- 50 – 75% dependent
- 25 – 50% dependent
- 10 – 25% dependent
- Under 10% dependent

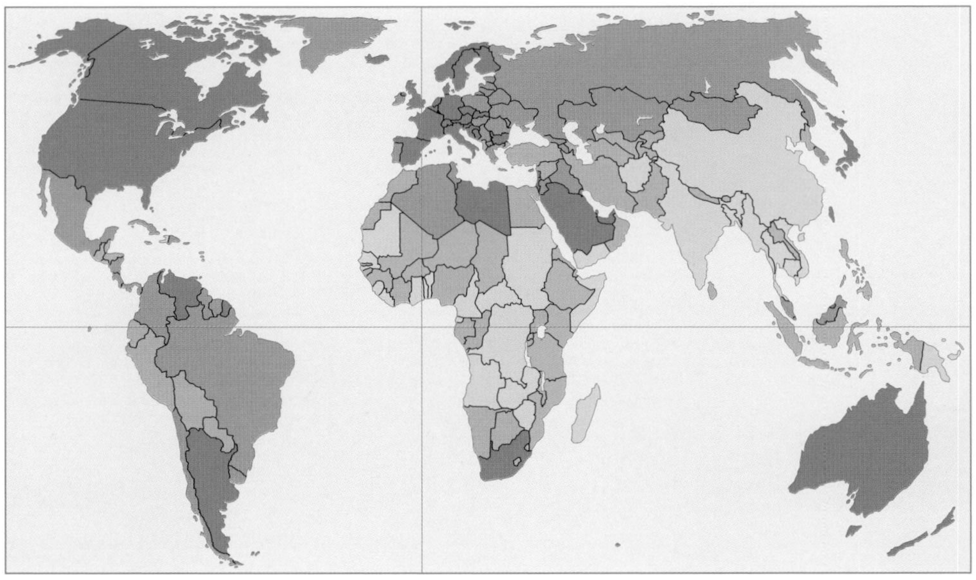

Top 5 countries		Bottom 5 countries	
Bhutan	93.7%	Singapore	0.1%
Nepal	93.0%	Brunei	0.7%
Burkina Faso	92.3%	Bahrain	1.0%
Burundi	90.4%	Kuwait	1.1%
Rwanda	90.3%	Qatar	1.3%

ANIMAL PRODUCTS

Traditionally, food animals subsisted on land unsuitable for cultivation, supporting agricultural production with their fertilizing dung. But free-ranging animals grow slowly and yield less meat than those more intensively reared; the demands of urban markets in the developed world have encouraged the growth of factory-like production methods.

A large proportion of staple crops, especially cereals, are fed to animals – an inefficient way to produce protein, but one likely to continue as long as people value meat and dairy products in their diet.

Cheese: Least perishable of all dairy products, cheese is milk fermented with selected bacterial strains to produce a foodstuff with a potentially immense range of flavours and textures. The vast majority of cheeses are made from cow's milk, although sheep and goat cheeses are highly prized.

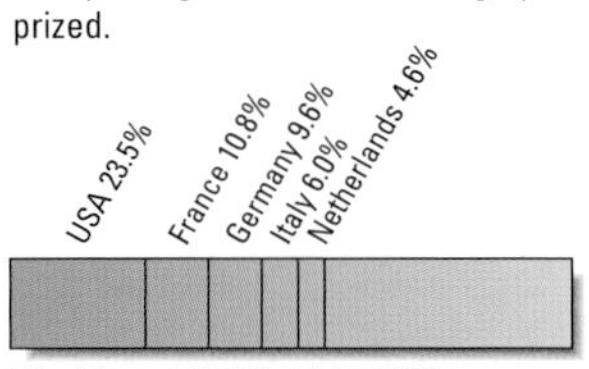

World total (2000): 16,045,000 tonnes

Beef and Veal: Most beef and veal is reared for home markets, and the top five producers are also the biggest consumers. The United States produces nearly a quarter of the world's beef and eats even more.

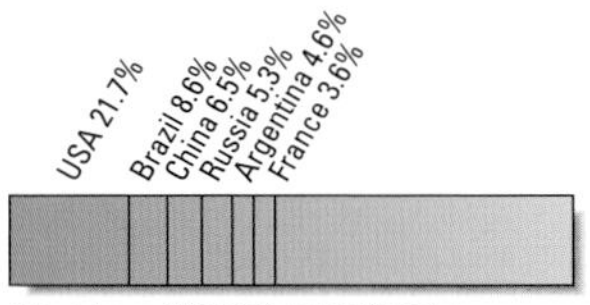

World total (2000): 57,170,000 tonnes

Milk: Many human groups, including most Asians, find raw milk indigestible after infancy, and it is often only the starting point for other dairy products such as butter, cheese and yoghurt. Most world production comes from cows, but sheep's milk and goats' milk are also important.

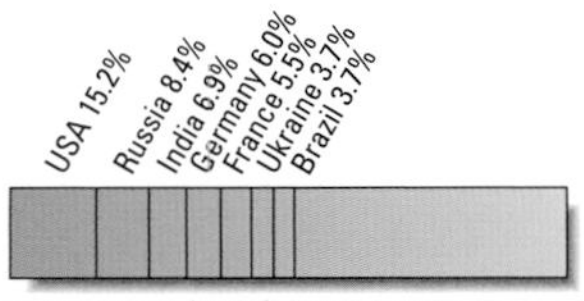

World total (2000): 2,504,000 tonnes

Butter: A traditional source of vitamin A as well as calories, butter has lost much popularity in the developed world for health reasons, although it remains a valuable food. Most butter from India, the world's largest producer, is clarified into ghee, which has religious as well as nutritional importance.

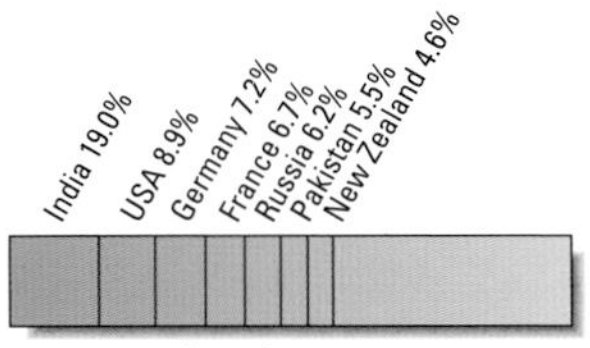

World total (2000): 7,049,000 tonnes

Pork: Although pork is forbidden to many millions, notably Muslims, on religious grounds, more is produced than any other meat in the world, mainly because it is the cheapest. It accounts for about 90% of China's meat output, although the per capita meat consumption is relatively low.

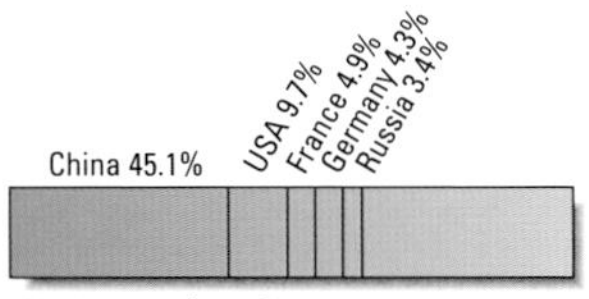

World total (2000): 90,909,000 tonnes

CRISIS IN AFRICA

Each year 40 million people, almost half of whom are children, die from starvation and related diseases. In 2000, 600 million people worldwide were estimated to be suffering from malnutrition. Africa suffers from more natural disasters than any other continent; pests such as locusts destroy crops, and tropical storms and floods ruin harvests. Famines periodically affect parts of Africa causing widespread hardship, even though enough food is produced worldwide to feed everyone.

A major phenomenon that affects the weather over tropical and subtropical regions areas around the world is called El Niño *(see page 8)*. It occurs when there is unusual warming in the tropical eastern Pacific Ocean, causing changes in the wind and pressure systems. Normal years are called La Niña. El Niño years included 1973–4, 1982–3, 1986–7, 1992, 1997–8, and 2002.

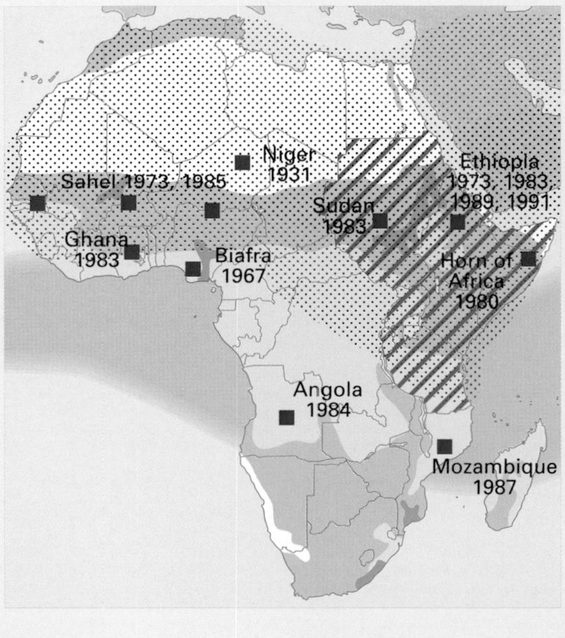

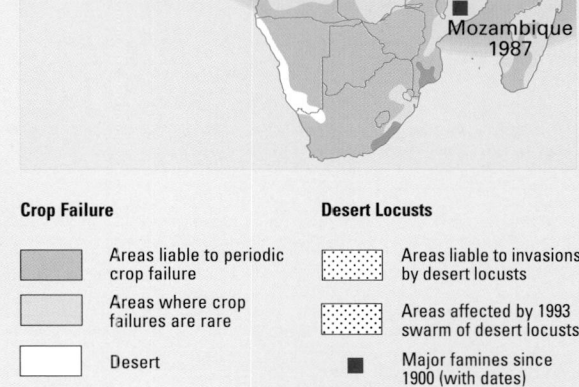

- Ocean areas affected by El Niño and La Niña temperature fluctuations
- Countries affected by 4 years of continuous drought, 1996–2000
- Areas liable to flood

Crop Failure

- Areas liable to periodic crop failure
- Areas where crop failures are rare
- Desert

Desert Locusts

- Areas liable to invasions by desert locusts
- Areas affected by 1993 swarm of desert locusts
- Major famines since 1900 (with dates)

ENERGY

For more information:

21 The carbon cycle
22 Global warming
Carbon dioxide
Greenhouse power
23 Water pollution
36 Minerals
41 World shipping

Every year, the world's energy consumption is about the equivalent of what would come from burning 9,000 million tonnes of oil (9,000 MtOe) – a 20-fold increase since 1850. Two-fifths of this total actually comes from burning oil and most of the rest comes from coal and natural gas.

The oil crises in the 1970s precipitated concern over dependence on finite fossil fuels as the primary source of energy, and growing environmental awareness has added impetus to the search for alternative energy resources. Fossil fuel combustion damages the environment through the release of gases and particulate matter, but two other major sources of energy, hydroelectricity and nuclear power, are also controversial. Hydroelectricity production involves flooding large areas to create reservoirs, while nuclear power stations generate dangerous radioactive wastes and can cause major disasters. Significantly, by 2002, five European countries – Belgium, Germany, the Netherlands, Spain and Sweden – had plans to phase out the use of nuclear energy.

Alternative energy resources may soon provide a much larger proportion of the world's energy consumption. Solar and wind energy may become important in such countries as China and India, while tidal, wave and geothermal energy all have potential in appropriate areas. Experts calculate that solar power could, in theory, supply between five and ten times the present electricity supply of developing countries.

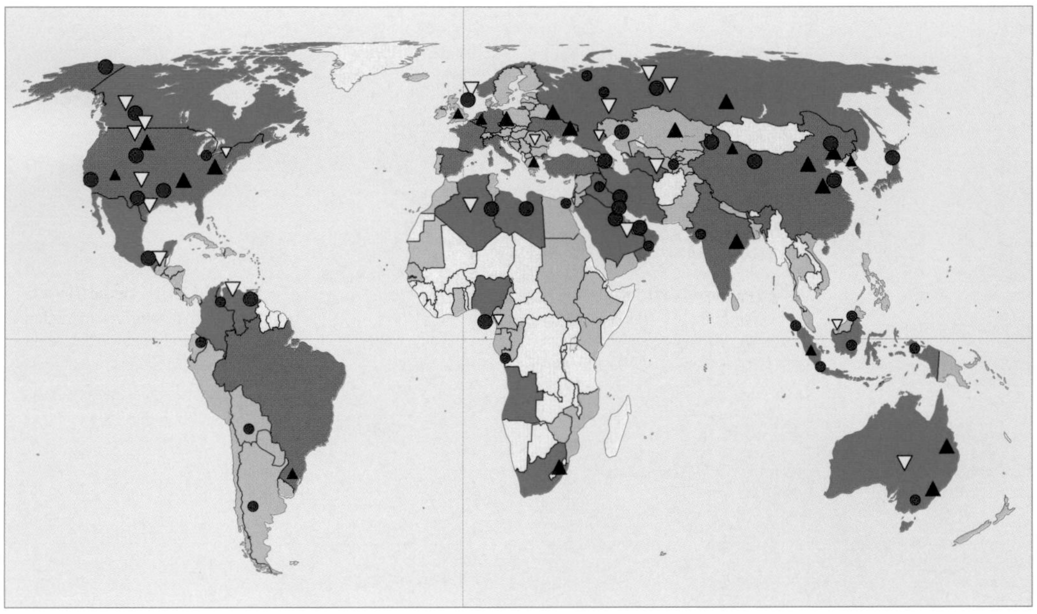

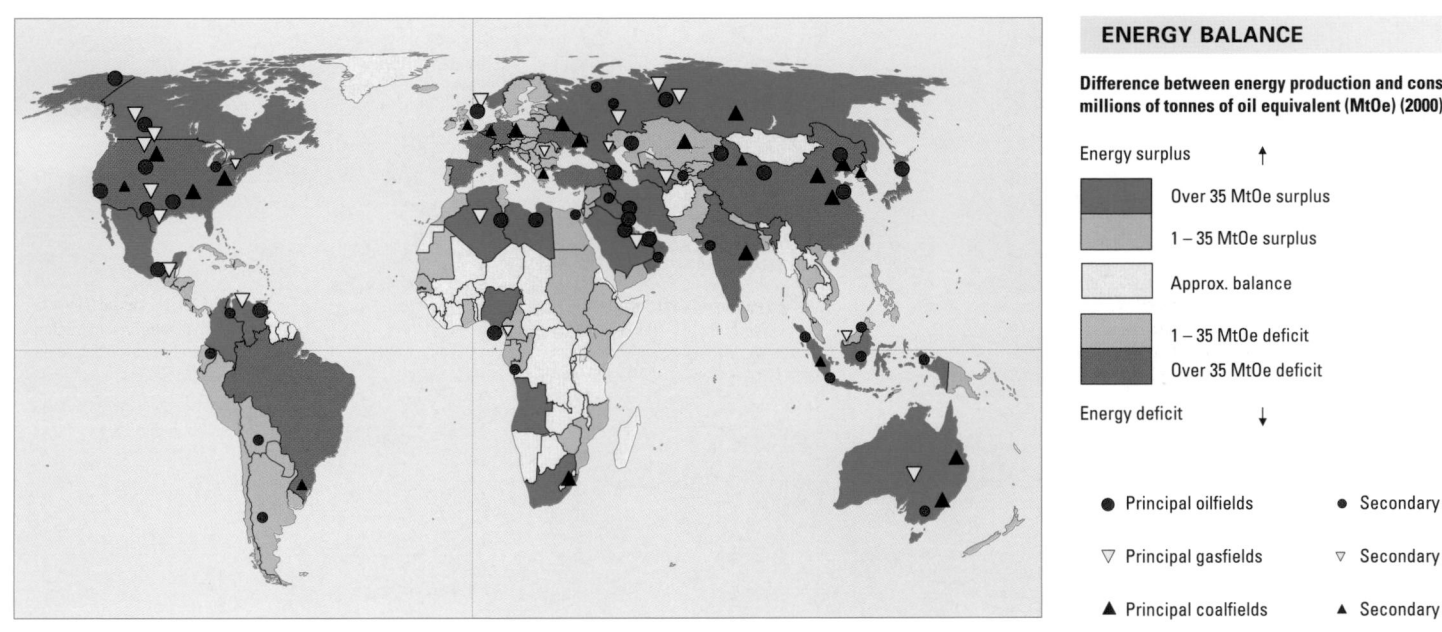

ENERGY BALANCE

Difference between energy production and consumption in millions of tonnes of oil equivalent (MtOe) (2000)

Energy surplus ↑

- Over 35 MtOe surplus
- 1 – 35 MtOe surplus
- Approx. balance
- 1 – 35 MtOe deficit
- Over 35 MtOe deficit

Energy deficit ↓

- ● Principal oilfields
- • Secondary oilfields
- ▽ Principal gasfields
- ▿ Secondary gasfields
- ▲ Principal coalfields
- ▴ Secondary coalfields

ENERGY CONSUMPTION

Energy consumed by world regions, measured in million tonnes of oil equivalent in 2001. Total world consumption was 9,125 MtOe. Only energy from oil, gas, coal, nuclear and hydroelectric sources are included. Excluded are fuels such as wood, peat, animal waste, wind, solar and geothermal which, though important in some countries, are unreliably documented in terms of consumption statistics.

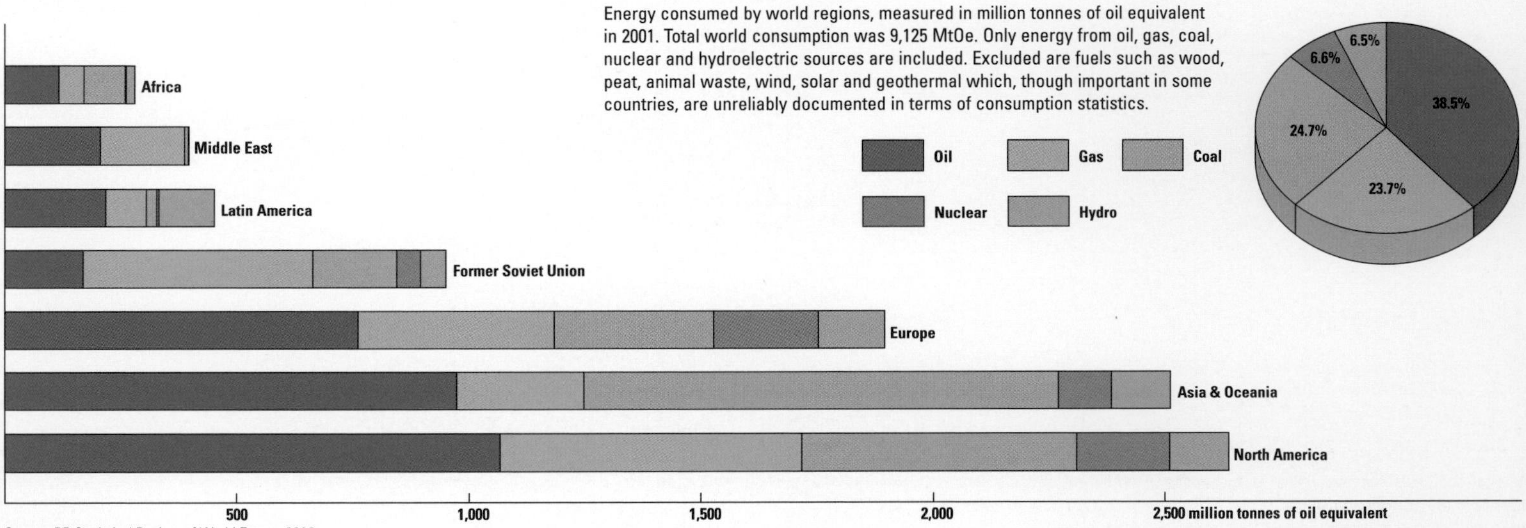

Source: BP Statistical Review of World Energy 2002

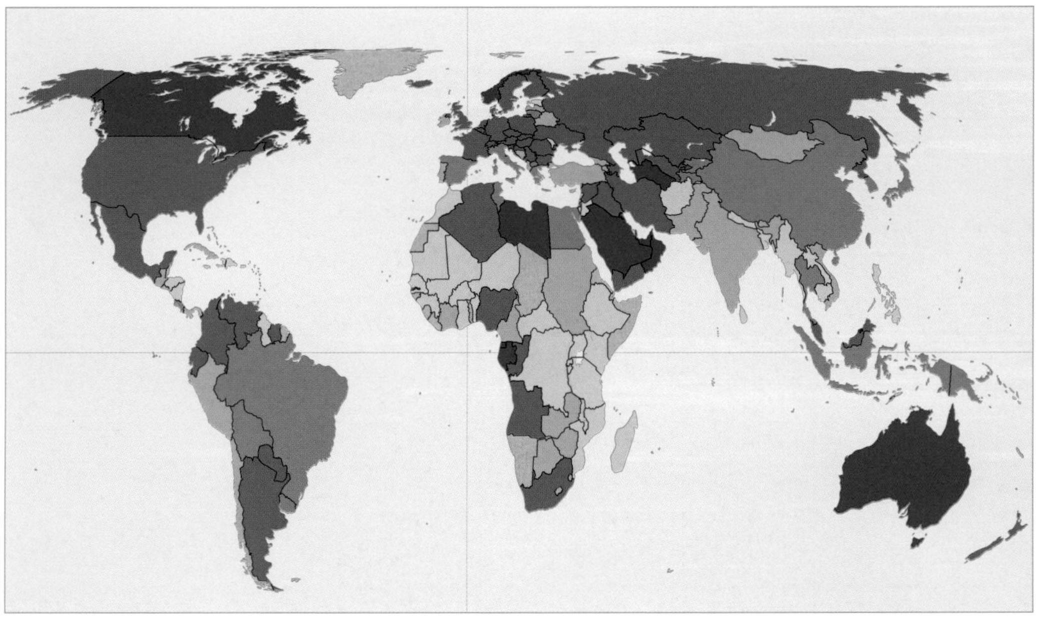

ENERGY PRODUCTION

Energy production in tonnes of oil equivalent per capita (2000)

- Over 10
- 1 – 10
- 0.5 – 1
- 0.1 – 0.5
- Under 0.1
- No data available

In developing countries traditional fuels are still very important. These so-called biomass fuels include wood, charcoal and dried dung. The pie-chart (*right*) highlights the importance of biomass in terms of energy consumption in Nigeria. Collecting fuelwood can be a time-consuming task, sometimes taking all day.

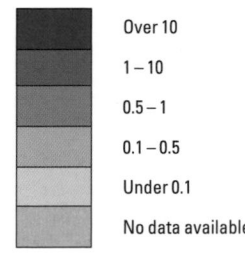

Nigeria

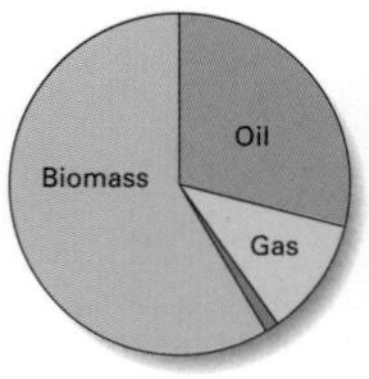

OIL MOVEMENTS

Major world movements of oil in millions of tonnes (2001)

1. Middle East to Asia (not China or Japan)	316.7
2. Middle East to Japan	208.8
3. Former Soviet Union to Europe	181.2
4. Middle East to Europe	176.2
5. Middle East to USA	138.0
6. South and Central America to USA	126.3
7. North Africa to Europe	96.9
8. Canada to USA	88.0
9. Mexico to USA	70.8
10. West Africa to USA	68.1
11. Europe to USA	46.2
12. Middle East to Africa	41.0
13. West Africa to Asia (not China or Japan)	36.9
14. West Africa to Europe	34.9
15. Middle East to China	34.2
16. Asia (not China) to Japan	34.2
Total world imports	**2,159,300,000 tonnes**

◀ With many of the world's onshore oilfields reaching their maturity, exploration and production in ever-deeper ocean waters is taking place to try to satisfy demand. The current deepest production well is in 1,829 m [6,004 ft] of water, offshore of Brazil. However, exploration wells off the coasts of Angola and Nigeria are already being drilled in water 2,438 m [8,000 ft] deep, and it is believed that wells in 3,048 m [10,000 ft] of water will soon be developed.

ENERGY RESERVES

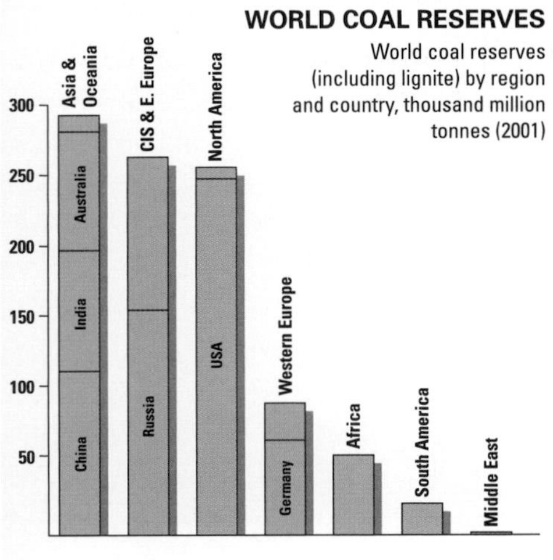

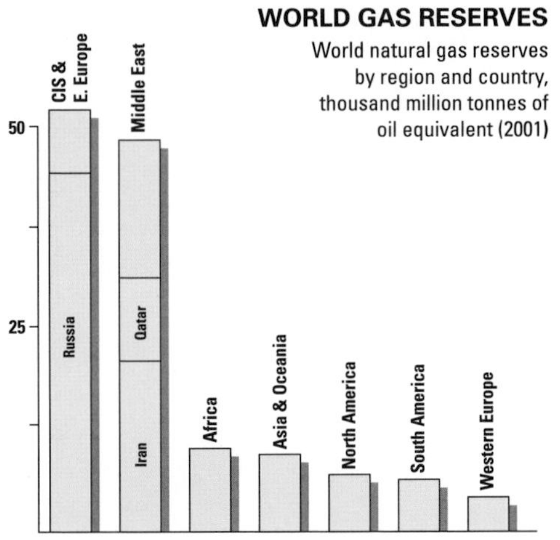

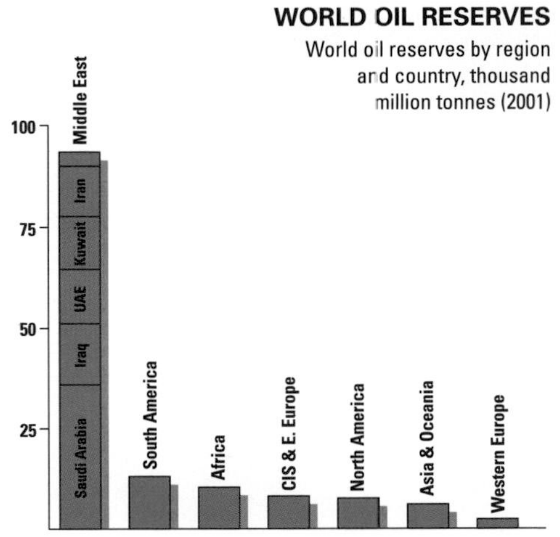

NUCLEAR POWER

Major producers by percentage of world total (2000) and by percentage of domestic electricity generation (1999)

Country	% of world total production	Country	% of nuclear as proportion of domestic electricity
1. USA	30.5%	1. Lithuania	76.1%
2. France	15.7%	2. France	75.1%
3. Japan	12.6%	3. Belgium	58.2%
4. Germany	6.7%	4. Slovak Rep.	47.5%
5. Russia	4.6%	5. Sweden	44.2%
6. South Korea	4.1%	6. Ukraine	41.6%
7. UK	3.8%	7. Bulgaria	41.4%
8. Canada	2.9%	8. South Korea	39.1%
9. Ukraine	2.8%	9. Hungary	38.1%
= Sweden	2.8%	10. Slovenia	35.9%

Although the 1980s were a bad time for the nuclear power industry (major projects ran over budget and fears of long-term environmental damage were heavily reinforced by the 1986 disaster at Chernobyl), the industry picked up in the early 1990s. Whilst the number of reactors is still increasing, however, orders for new plants have shrunk. In 1997, the Swedish government began to decommission the country's 12 nuclear power plants.

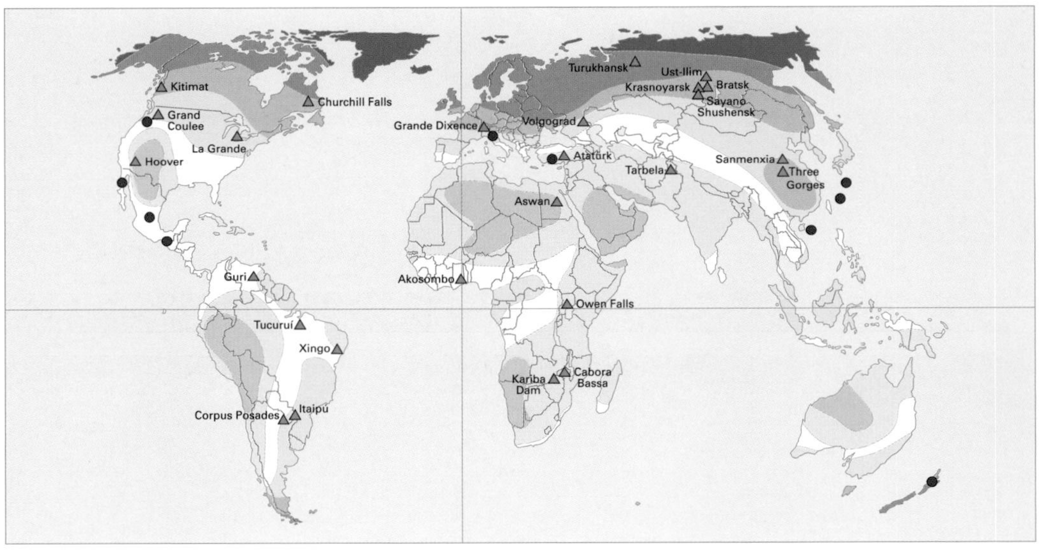

RENEWABLE ENERGY

Average annual solar irradiance in kWh/m², with selected major hydroelectric and geothermal power stations

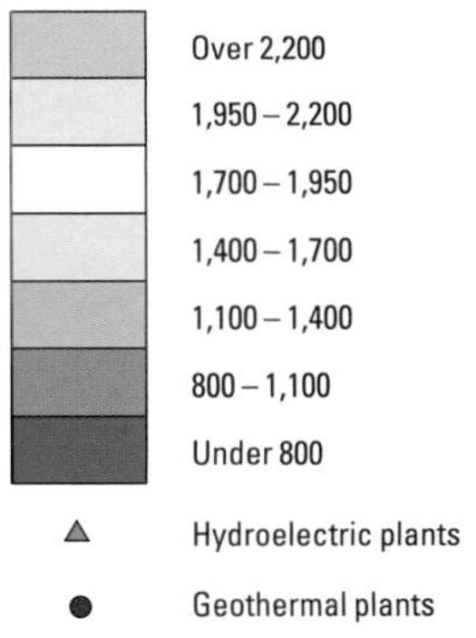

HYDROELECTRICITY

Major producers by percentage of world total (2000) and by percentage of domestic electricity generation (1999)

Country	% of world total production	Country	% of hydroelectric as proportion of domestic electricity
1. Canada	13.1%	1. Bhutan	99.9%
2. USA	12.0%	2. Paraguay	99.8%
3. Brazil	11.1%	= Zambia	99.8%
4. China	8.5%	4. Norway	99.1%
5. Russia	6.1%	5. Ethiopia	98.1%
6. Norway	4.6%	6. Congo (Rep. Dem.)	97.9%
7. Japan	3.3%	7. Tajikistan	97.8%
8. India	3.1%	8. Cameroon	97.3%
9. France	2.8%	9. Albania	97.2%
10. Sweden	2.7%	= Laos	97.2%

Countries heavily reliant on hydroelectricity are usually small and non-industrial: a high proportion of hydroelectric power more often reflects a modest energy budget than vast hydroelectric resources. The USA, for instance, produces only 8.5% of its power requirements from hydroelectricity; yet that 8.5% amounts to more than three times the hydropower generated by most of Africa.

ALTERNATIVE ENERGY RESOURCES

Solar: Each year the Sun bestows upon the Earth almost a million times as much energy as is locked up in all the planet's oil reserves, but only an insignificant fraction is trapped and used commercially. In a few installations around the world, mirrors focus the Sun's rays on to boilers, whose steam generates electricity by spinning turbines.

Wind: Caused by uneven heating of the Earth, winds are themselves a form of solar energy. Windmills have been long used for wind power; recent models, often arranged in banks on wind-swept high ground or off coastlines, usually generate electricity. Wind-power figures are given in the table (*right*) – it is the world's fastest growing energy source. In 2002, Germany, the USA, Spain and Denmark produced nearly 16,000 MW.

Tidal: The energy from tides is potentially enormous, although only a few installations have so far been built to exploit it. In theory at least, waves and currents could also provide almost unimaginable power, and the thermal differences in the ocean depths are another huge well of potential energy. But work on extracting it is still at the experimental stage.

Geothermal: The Earth's temperature rises by 1°C for every 30 metres descent, with much steeper temperature gradients in geologically active areas. El Salvador, for example, produces 39% of its electricity from geothermal power stations, whilst the USA is the world's leading producer. Some of the oldest and most successful applications are in Iceland, where 86% of all households are heated by geothermal energy.

Biomass: The oldest of human fuels ranges from animal dung, still burned in cooking fires in much of North Africa and elsewhere, to sugar-cane plantations feeding high-technology distilleries to produce ethanol for motor-vehicle engines. In Brazil and South Africa, plant ethanol provides up to 25% of motor fuel. Throughout the developing world, most biomass energy comes from firewood: although accurate figures are impossible to obtain, it may yield as much as 10% of the world's total energy consumption.

WIND POWER

World wind energy generating capacity, in megawatts

1980	10
1982	90
1984	600
1986	1,270
1988	1,580
1989	1,730
1990	1,930
1991	2,170
1992	2,510
1993	3,050
1994	3,710
1995	4,820
1996	6,115
1997	7,630
1998	9,600

Wind power is the fastest growing source of energy. Between 1998 and 2002, world production more than doubled.

Minerals

For more information:

10 Geology
39 Patterns of production
41 World shipping

The use of metals played a vital part in the evolving technologies of early peoples. Copper first came into use around 10,000 years ago, bronze about 5,000 years ago, and iron 3,300 years ago. In the early stages of the Industrial Revolution, the location of coal, iron ore and water power usually determined the location of new industries. But due to continuing improvements in transport, including oil pipelines, industries can now be located almost anywhere.

Minerals are distributed unevenly and some industrial countries, lacking their own mineral resources, import most of the raw materials they need. Some imports come from mineral-rich countries, such as Australia, but others come from developing countries, especially in Africa and South America. Most developing countries export unprocessed ores, losing out on the higher revenues gained from exporting metals.

Most minerals come from land deposits, because undersea deposits, with the exception of oil reserves under the continental shelves, have been inaccessible. But shortages of terrestrial minerals may one day encourage exploitation of the ocean floor.

► An aerial view of gold mine excavations in Zimbabwe, for extraction both above and below ground. Once a major producer of gold, Zimbabwe's gold mining industry has greatly declined in recent years as a result of political and social unrest.

URANIUM

Uranium was first discovered by the German chemist Martin Klaproth in 1789. In its pure state, uranium is an immensely heavy, white metal. But although spent uranium is employed as a projectile in anti-missile cannons, where its mass ensures a lethal punch, its main use is as a fuel in nuclear reactors, and in nuclear weaponry.

Uranium is very scarce: the main source is the rare ore pitchblende, which itself contains only 0.2% uranium oxide. This blackish, lustrous ore occurs in quartz veins. Only a minute fraction of that is the radioactive U^{235} isotope, though so-called breeder reactors can transmute the more common U^{238} into highly radioactive plutonium.

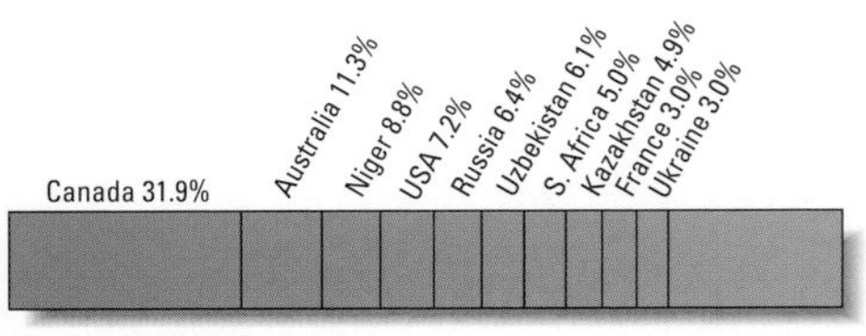

World total (2000): 34,746 tonnes

DIAMOND

Most of the world's diamond is found in kimberlite, or 'blue ground', a basic peridotite rock; erosion may wash the diamond from its kimberlite matrix and deposit it with sand or gravel on river beds. Only a small proportion of the world's diamond, the most flawless, is cut into gemstones – 'diamonds'; most are used in industry, where the material's remarkable hardness and abrasion resistance finds a use in cutting tools, drills and dies. Australia produced 31.6% of the world's total in 2000. The other main producers are the Democratic Republic of the Congo (24.7%), Russia (20%), South Africa (10.5%) and Botswana (8.5%). Natural diamonds now account for less than 10% of all industrial diamond output. Synthetic diamond production in centres such as Ireland, Japan, Russia and the USA far exceeds it.

METALS

*** Figures for aluminium are for refined metal; all other figures refer to ore production**

The world's leading producers of aluminium ore (bauxite) in 2000 were as follows:

1.	Australia	38.6%
2.	Guinea	11.8%
3.	Brazil	10.4%
4.	Jamaica	8.8%
5.	China	6.3%
6.	India	4.9%
7.	Venezuela	3.5%
8.	Suriname	3.1%
9.	Russia	3.1%
10.	Guyana	2.6%

The figures shown above are in stark contrast to the figures showing aluminium production (*see above right*). Australia, for example, produces 38.6% of the world's bauxite but only 5.9% of aluminium. Guinea and Jamaica account for over 20% of the bauxite mined but have no smelters and export virtually all of it to countries like the USA and Canada.

Aluminium: Produced mainly from its oxide, bauxite, which yields 25% of its weight in aluminium. The cost of refining and production is often too high for producer-countries to bear, so bauxite is largely exported. Lightweight and corrosion resistant, aluminium alloys are widely used in aircraft, vehicles, cans and packaging.

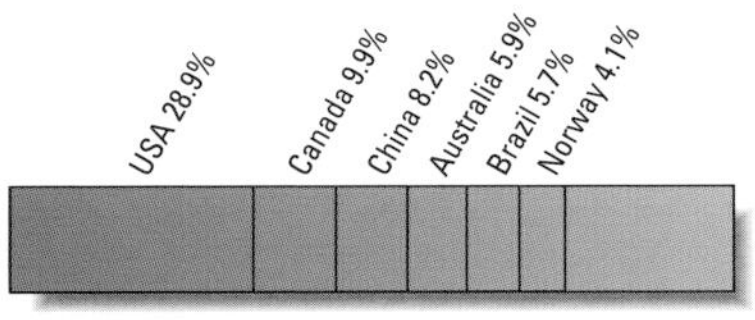

World total (2000): 23,900,000 tonnes*

Copper: Derived from low-yielding sulphide ores, copper is an important export for several developing countries. An excellent conductor of heat and electricity, it forms part of most electrical items, and is used in the manufacture of brass and bronze. Major importers include Japan and Germany.

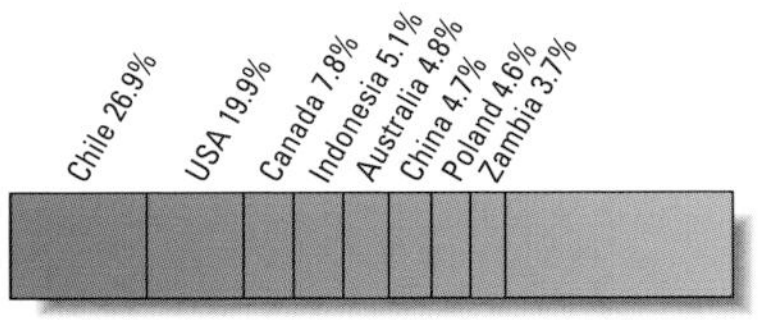

World total (2000): 12,900,000 tonnes*

Lead: A soft metal, obtained mainly from galena (lead sulphide), which occurs in veins associated with iron, zinc and silver sulphides. Its use in vehicle batteries accounts for the USA's prime consumer status; lead is also made into sheeting and piping. Its use as an additive to paints and petrol is decreasing.

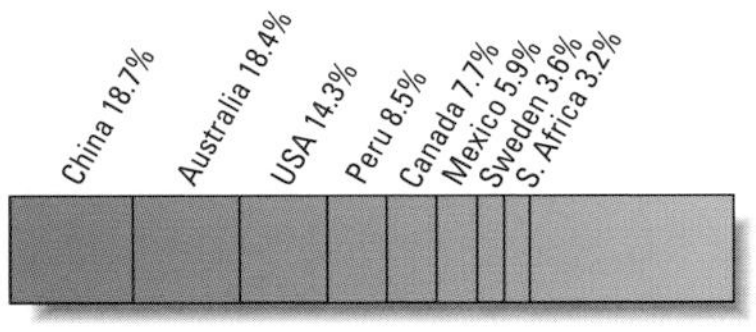

World total (2000): 2,980,000 tonnes*

Mercury: The only metal that is liquid at normal temperatures, most is derived from its sulphide, cinnabar, found only in small quantities in volcanic areas. Apart from its value in thermometers and other instruments, most mercury production is used in anti-fungal and anti-fouling preparations, and to make detonators.

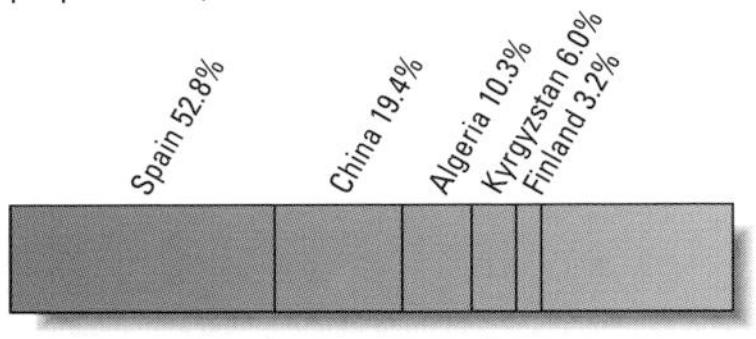

World total (2000): 1,800 tonnes*

Tin: Soft, pliable and non-toxic, used to coat 'tin' (tin-plated steel) cans, in the manufacture of foils and in alloys. The principal tin-bearing mineral is cassiterite (SnO_2), found in ore formed from molten rock. Producers and refiners were hit by a price collapse in 1991.

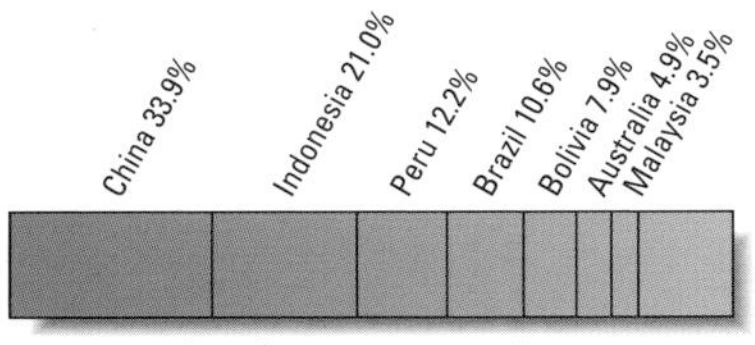

World total (2000): 200,000 tonnes*

Zinc: Often found in association with lead ores, zinc is highly resistant to corrosion, and about 40% of the refined metal is used to plate sheet steel, particularly vehicle bodies – a process known as galvanizing. Zinc is also used in dry batteries, paints and dyes.

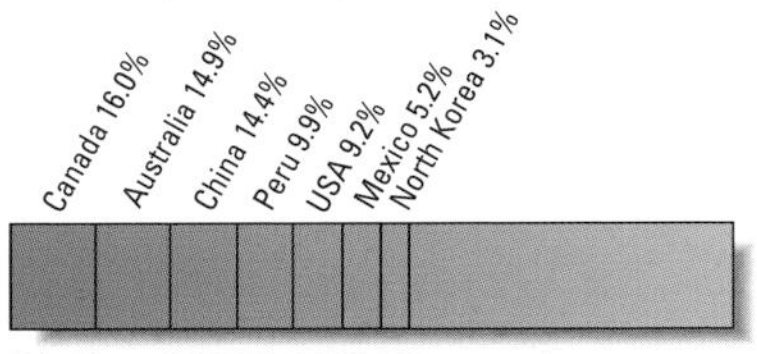

World total (2000): 8,000,000 tonnes*

Gold: Regarded for centuries as the most valuable metal in the world and used to make coins, gold is still recognized as the monetary standard. A soft metal, it is alloyed to make jewellery; the electronics industry values its corrosion resistance and conductivity.

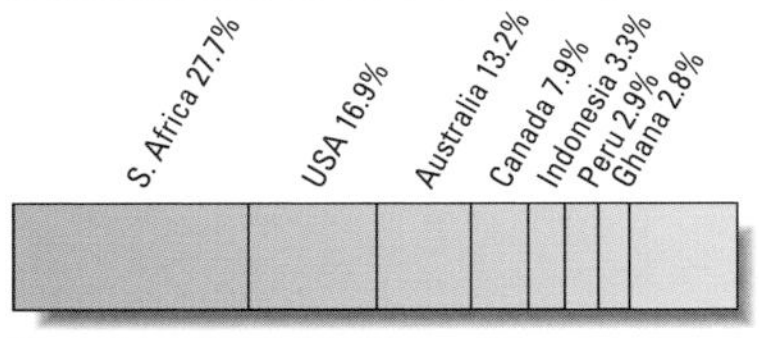

World total (2000): 2,445 tonnes*

Silver: Most silver comes from ores mined and processed for other metals (including lead and copper). Pure or alloyed with harder metals, it is used for jewellery and ornaments. Industrial use includes dentistry, electronics, photography and as a chemical catalyst.

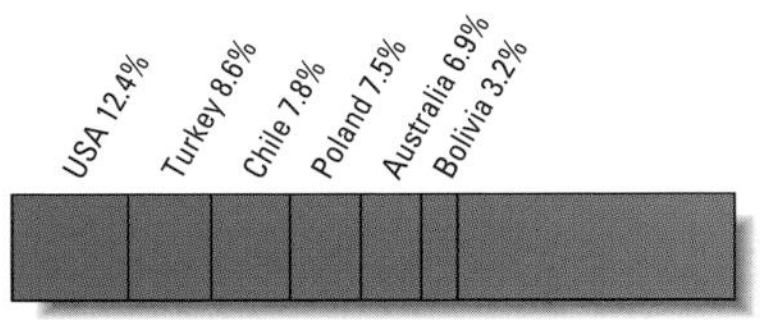

World total (2000): 17,900 tonnes*

DISTRIBUTION OF MINERALS

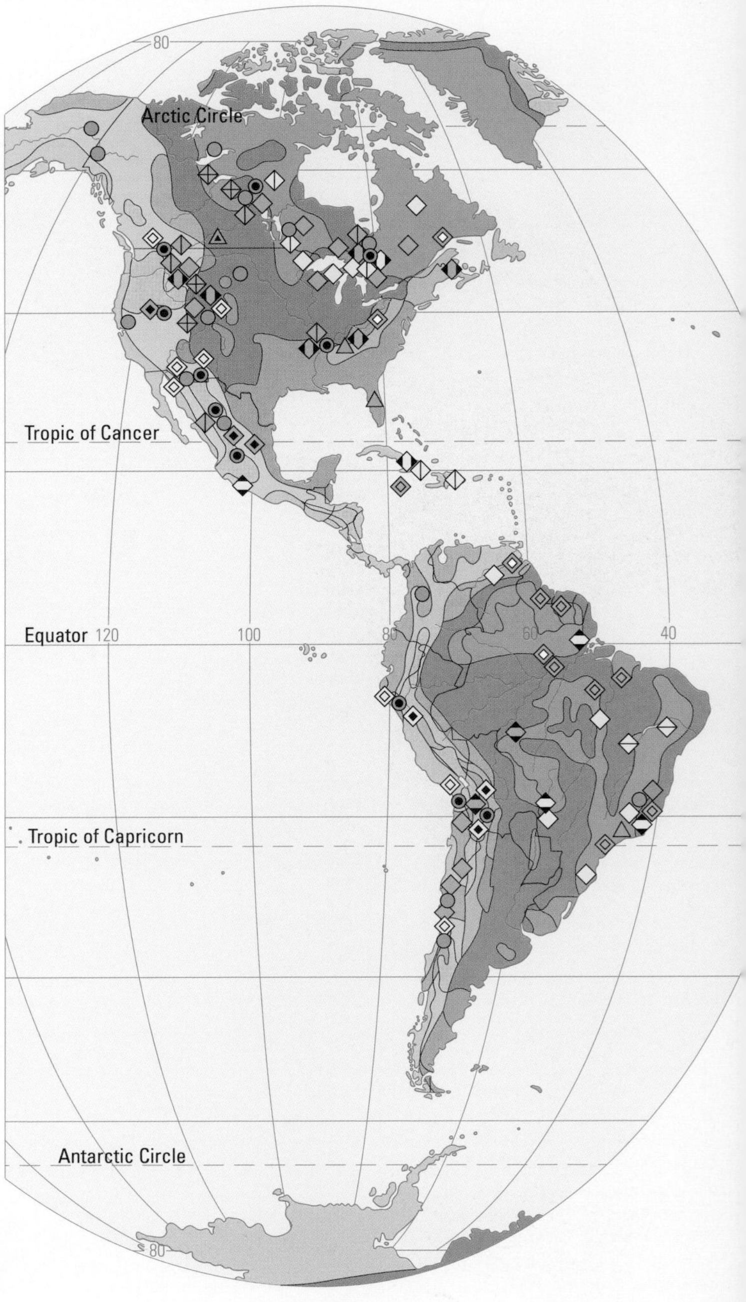

IRON ORE

Ever since the art of high-temperature smelting was discovered, some time in the second millennium BC, iron has been by far the most important metal known to man. The earliest iron ploughs transformed primitive agriculture and led to the first human population explosion, while iron weapons – or the lack of them – ensured the rise or fall of entire cultures.

Widely distributed around the world, iron ores usually contain 25–60% iron; blast furnaces process the raw product into pig-iron, which is then alloyed with carbon and other minerals to produce steels of various qualities. From the time of the Industrial Revolution, steel has been almost literally the backbone of modern civilization, the prime structural material on which all else is built.

Iron smelting usually developed close to the sources of ore and, later, to the coalfields that fuelled the furnaces. Today, most ore comes from a few richly-endowed locations where large-scale mining is possible.

Iron and steel plants are generally built at coastal sites so that giant ore carriers, which account for a sizeable proportion of the world's merchant fleet, can easily discharge their cargoes.

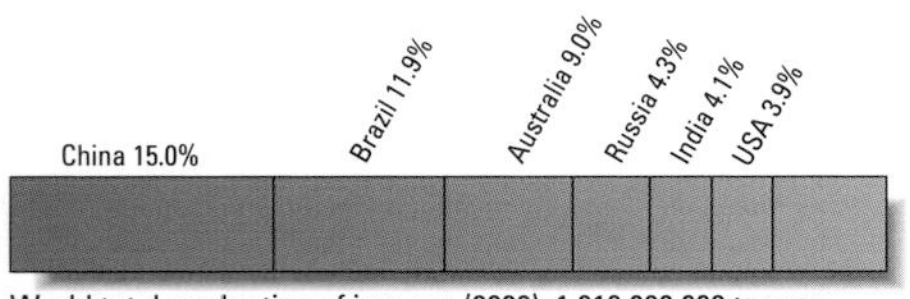

World total production of iron ore (2000): 1,010,000,000 tonnes

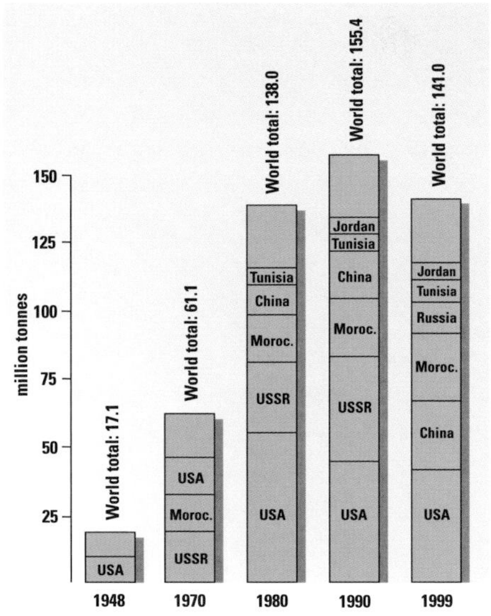

World production of phosphates in millions of tonnes (1999): Phosphate production is vital to the economies of several small countries. Nauru, for example, is heavily dependent on phosphate exports – the island has one of the world's richest deposits. In 1999, 500,000 tonnes were mined, employing 1,000 people. In Togo, earnings from phosphate exports have superseded all agricultural exports.

Percentage of total world phosphate production (1999)

1. USA	28.8%	7. Brazil	2.9%
2. China	17.8%	8. Israel	2.9%
3. Morocco	17.0%	9. South Africa	2.1%
4. Russia	7.9%	10. Syria	1.5%
5. Tunisia	5.7%	11. Senegal	1.3%
6. Jordan	4.3%	12. India	1.2%

World production of pig-iron (2000): All countries with an annual output of more than 1 million tonnes are shown

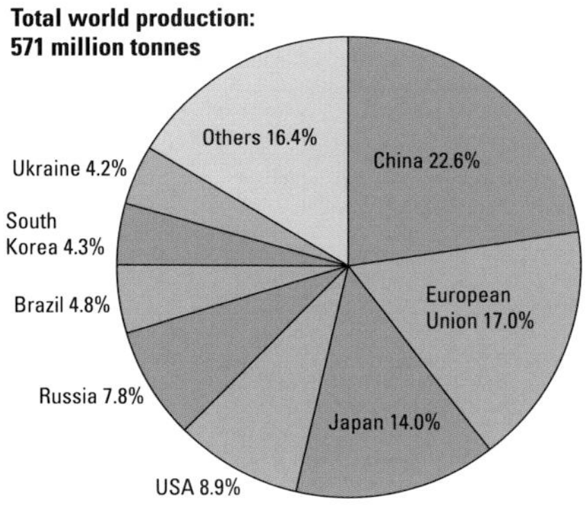

Manganese: In its pure state, manganese is a hard, brittle metal. Alloyed with chrome, iron and nickel, it produces abrasion-resistant steels; manganese-aluminium alloys are light but tough. Found in batteries and inks, manganese is also used in glass production. Manganese ores are frequently found in the same location as sedimentary iron ores. Pyrolusite (MnO_2) and psilomelane are the main economically-exploitable sources.

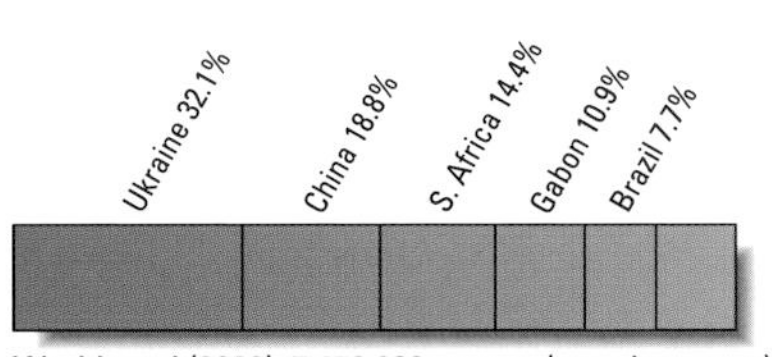

World total (2000): 7,450,000 tonnes (metal content)

Chromium: Most of the world's chromium production is alloyed with iron and other metals to produce steels with various different properties. Combined with iron, nickel, cobalt and tungsten, chromium produces an exceptionally hard steel, resistant to heat; chrome steels are used for many household items where utility must be matched with appearance – cutlery, for example. Chromium is also used in the production of refractory bricks, and its salts for tanning and dyeing leather and cloth.

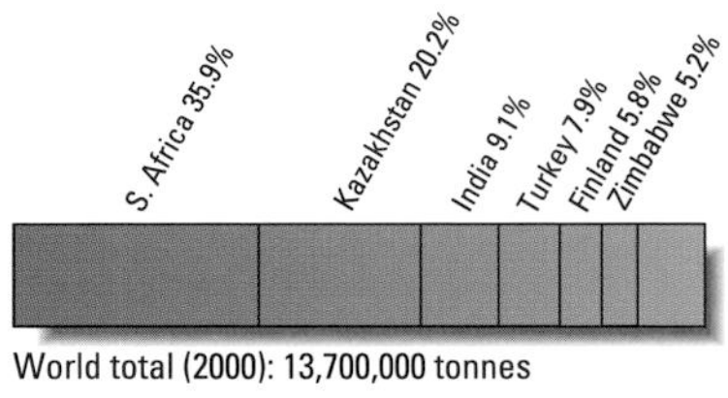

World total (2000): 13,700,000 tonnes

Nickel: Combined with chrome and iron, nickel produces stainless and high-strength steels; similar alloys go to make magnets and electrical heating elements. Nickel combined with copper is widely used to make coins; cupro-nickel alloy is very resistant to corrosion. Its ores yield only modest quantities of nickel – 0.5% to 3% – but also contain copper, iron and small amounts of precious metals. Japan, USA, UK, Germany and France are the principal importers.

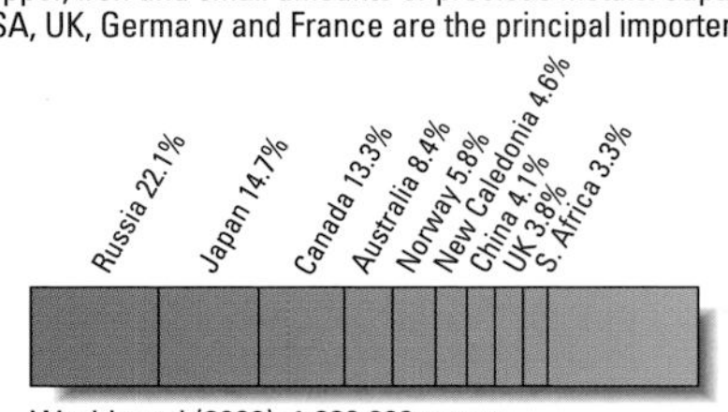

World total (2000): 1,230,000 tonnes

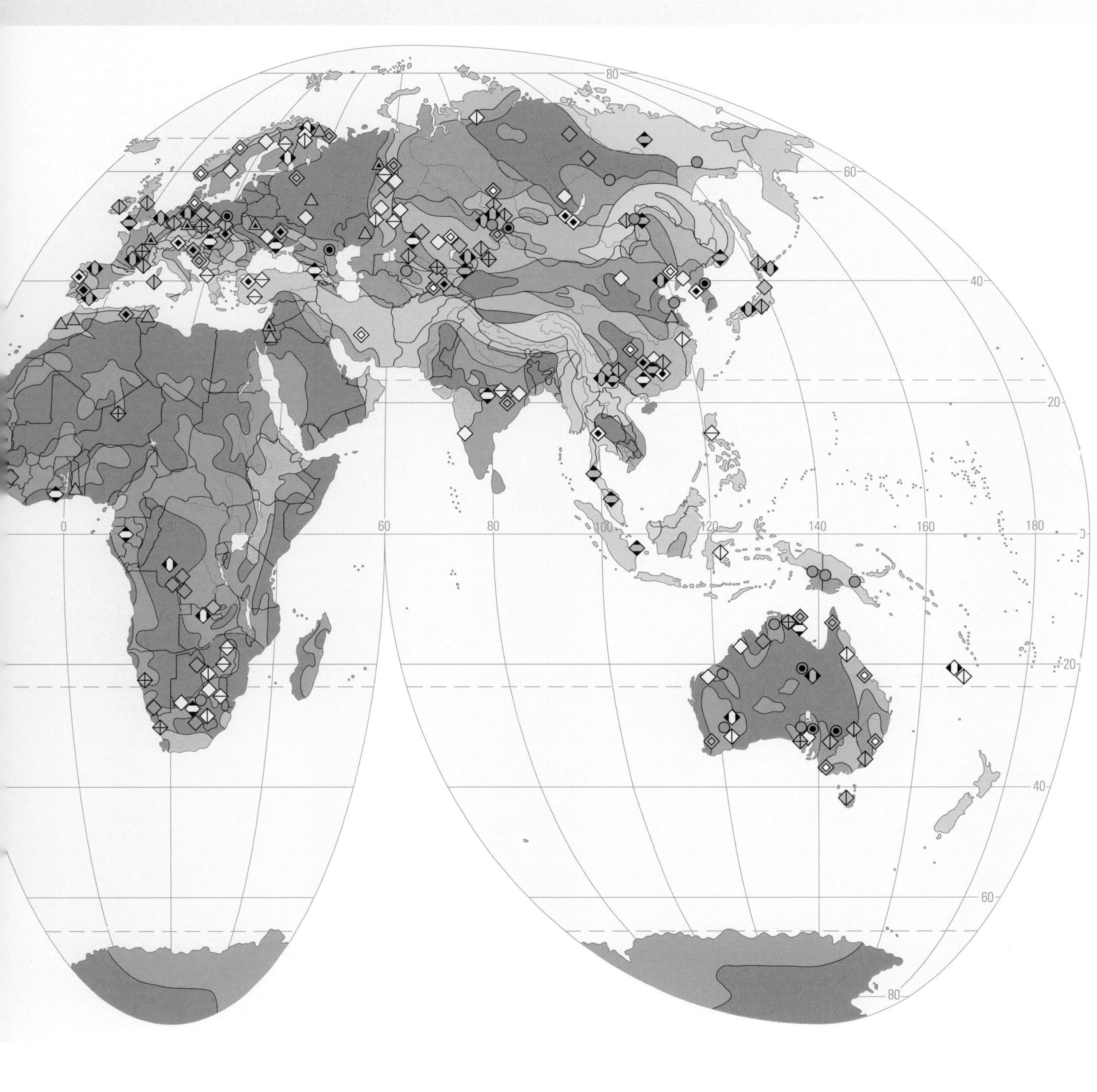

STRUCTURAL REGIONS

- Pre-Cambrian shields
- Sedimentary cover on Pre-Cambrian shields
- Paleozoic (Caledonian and Hercynian) folding
- Sedimentary cover on Paleozoic folding
- Mesozoic folding
- Sedimentary cover on Mesozoic folding
- Cenozoic (Alpine) folding
- Sedimentary cover on Cenozoic folding
- Intensive Mesozoic and Cenozoic vulcanism

DISTRIBUTION

Iron and ferro-alloys

- Chrome
- Cobalt
- Iron ore
- Manganese
- Molybdenum
- Nickel ore
- Tungsten

Non-ferrous metals

- Bauxite (Aluminium)
- Copper
- Lead
- Mercury
- Tin
- Zinc
- Uranium

Precious metals and stones

- Diamonds
- Gold
- Silver

Fertilizers

- Phosphates
- Potash

MANUFACTURING

For more information:
18 Water distribution
32 Land use
36 Minerals
37 Iron and ferro-alloys
40 Major exports
Traded products

The Industrial Revolution which began in Britain in the late 18th century, represented a major technological advance in the evolution of human society. It enabled a group of countries to become prosperous by replacing expensive human labour with increasingly sophisticated machinery. In economic terms, manufacturing is the transformation of raw materials, energy, labour and machines into finished goods, which have a higher value than the various elements used in production.

The economies of countries can be compared by reference to their per capita Gross National Products (or per capita GNPs), namely, the total value of goods and services produced in a country in a year, divided by the population.

The industrialized, or developed, countries accounted for 15% of the world's population in 2000 with an average per capita GNP of more than US $25,000. On the other hand, low-income developing countries, with small industrial sectors, accounted for 34% of the world's population. Their per capita GNPs are less than $755, with some as low as $200.

Kenya, with its low-income economy, had a per capita GNP in 2000 of US $350. Agriculture employs 19% of the people, industry 18% and services 64%. The main industries are the processing of agricultural imports and import substitution (making such necessities as cement, footwear and textiles). Heavy industry plays only a small part. By contrast, Germany had a per capita GNP in 2000 of $25,120. Agriculture employs only 2% of the population, with 30% in industry and 68% in services. Germany's industrial sector differs greatly from Kenya's, with its emphasis on vehicles, machinery, chemicals and electronics.

Since the 1970s, some former developing countries in eastern Asia achieved rapid economic growth through industrialization. Despite setbacks in the late 1990s, they demonstrated that a developing industrial sector can transform an economy, which starts off with certain advantages, such as low labour costs. But economic success also depends on such factors as education to provide skills, and regulations that attract foreign investors. China, whose economy grew by more than 9% per year between 1989 and 2002, satisfies many of these criteria, though its record on human rights leaves much to be desired.

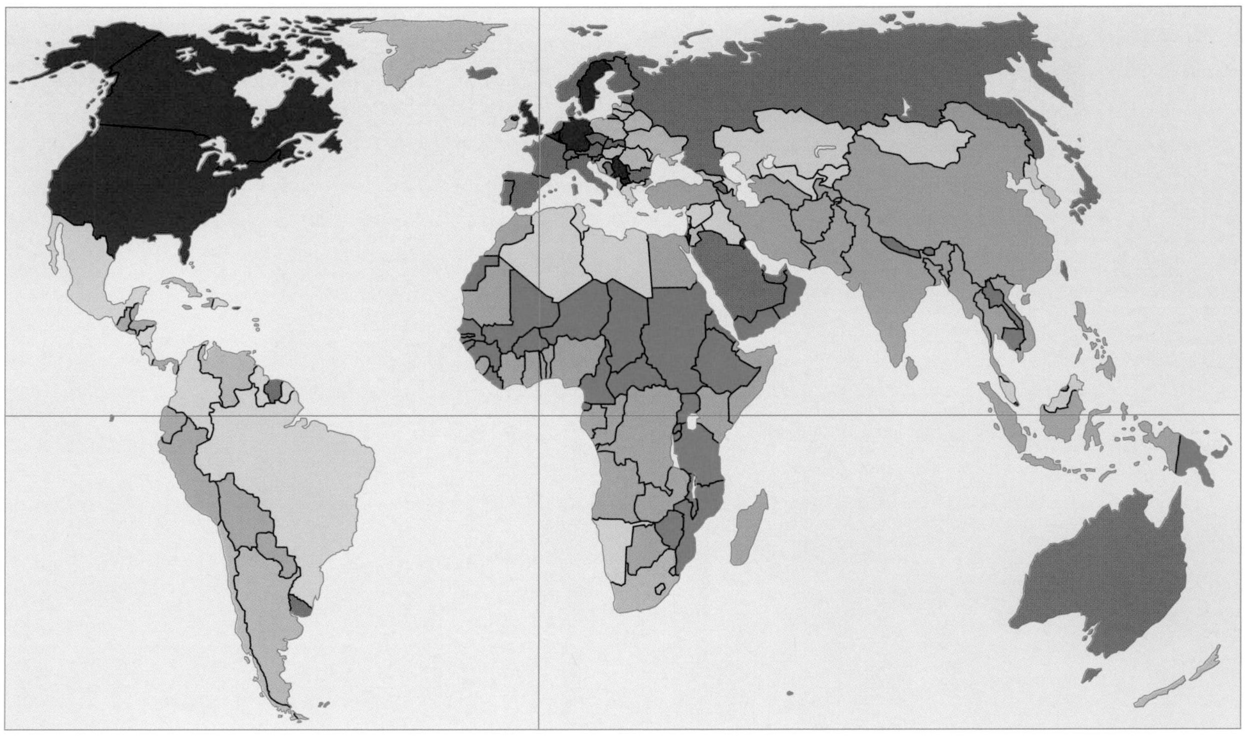

EMPLOYMENT

The number of workers employed in manufacturing for every 100 workers engaged in agriculture (latest available year)

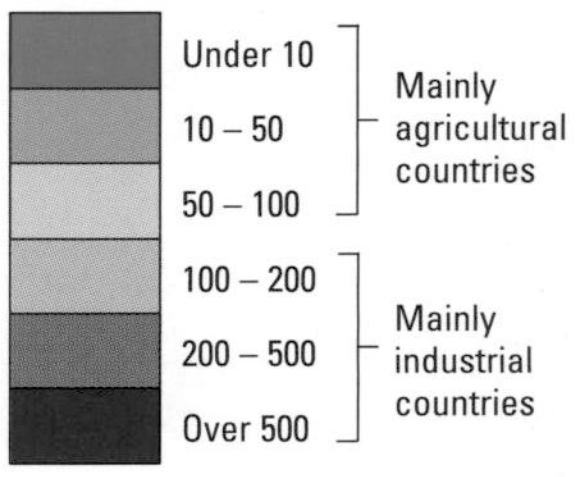

Selected countries (latest available year)

Singapore	8,860
UK	1,270
Belgium	820
Germany	800
Kuwait	767
Bahrain	660
USA	657
Israel	633

DIVISION OF EMPLOYMENT

Distribution of workers between agriculture, industry and services, selected countries (latest available year)

The six countries selected illustrate the usual stages of economic development, from dependence on agriculture through industrial growth to the expansion of the service sector.

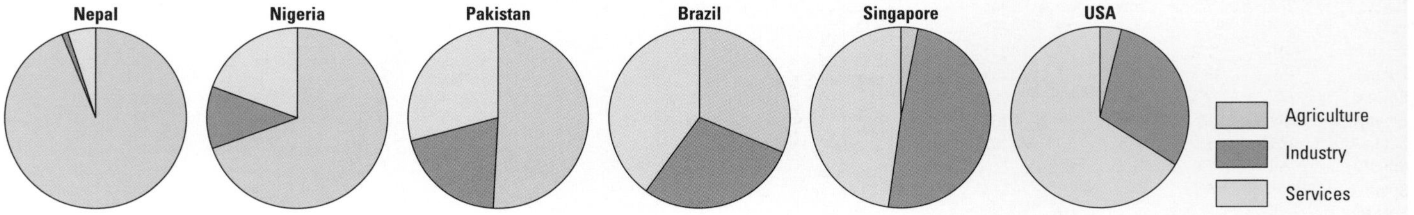

THE WORKFORCE

Percentages of men and women between 15 and 64 in employment, selected countries (latest available year)

The figures include employees and the self-employed, who in developing countries are often subsistence farmers. People in full-time education are excluded. Because of the population age structure in developing countries, the employed population has to support a far larger number of non-workers than its industrial equivalent. For example, more than 52% of Kenya's people are under 15, an age group that makes up less than a tenth of the UK population.

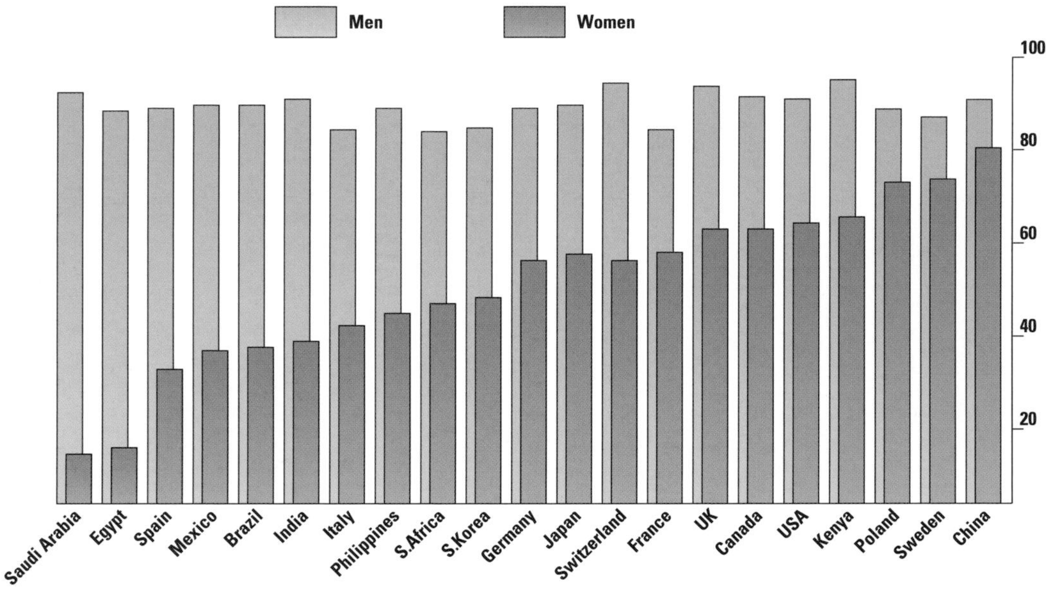

WEALTH CREATION

The Gross National Income (GNI) of the world's largest economies, US $ million (2001)

1.	USA	9,900,724	21.	Austria	194,463
2.	Japan	4,574,164	22.	Hong Kong	176,157
3.	Germany	1,947,951	23.	Turkey	168,335
4.	UK	1,451,442	24.	Denmark	166,345
5.	France	1,377,389	25.	Poland	163,907
6.	China	1,130,984	26.	Norway	160,577
7.	Italy	1,123,478	27.	Saudi Arabia	149,932
8.	Canada	661,881	28.	Indonesia	144,731
9.	Spain	586,874	29.	South Africa	125,486
10.	Mexico	550,456	30.	Greece	124,553
11.	Brazil	528,503	31.	Finland	124,171
12.	India	474,323	32.	Thailand	120,871
13.	South Korea	447,698	33.	Venezuela	117,169
14.	Netherlands	385,401	34.	Iran	112,855
15.	Australia	383,291	35.	Portugal	109,156
16.	Switzerland	266,503	36.	Israel	104,128
17.	Argentina	260,994	37.	Egypt	99,406
18.	Russia	253,413	38.	Singapore	99,404
19.	Belgium	239,779	39.	Ireland	88,385
20.	Sweden	225,894	40.	Malaysia	86,510

INDUSTRIAL OUTPUT

Industrial output (mining, manufacturing, construction, energy and water production), US $ billion (latest available year)

1.	Japan	1,941	21.	Sweden	73
2.	USA	1,808	22.	Saudi Arabia	67
3.	Germany	780	=	Thailand	67
4.	France	415	24.	Mexico	65
5.	UK	354	25.	Turkey	51
6.	Italy	337	26.	Denmark	50
7.	China	335	27.	Finland	46
8.	Brazil	255	=	Poland	46
9.	South Korea	196	29.	Norway	44
10.	Spain	187	30.	Malaysia	37
11.	Canada	174	=	Portugal	37
12.	Russia	131	32.	Ukraine	34
13.	Netherlands	107	33.	Greece	33
14.	Australia	98	34.	Singapore	30
15.	Switzerland	96	35.	Venezuela	29
16.	India	94	=	Israel	29
17.	Argentina	87	37.	Chile	24
18.	Belgium	83	=	Colombia	24
=	Indonesia	83	=	Hong Kong	24
20.	Austria	79	=	Philippines	24

INDUSTRY AND TRADE

Manufactured goods (including machinery and transport) as a percentage of total exports (1999)

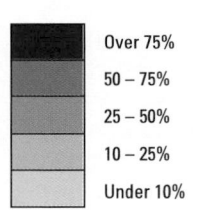

- Over 75%
- 50 – 75%
- 25 – 50%
- 10 – 25%
- Under 10%

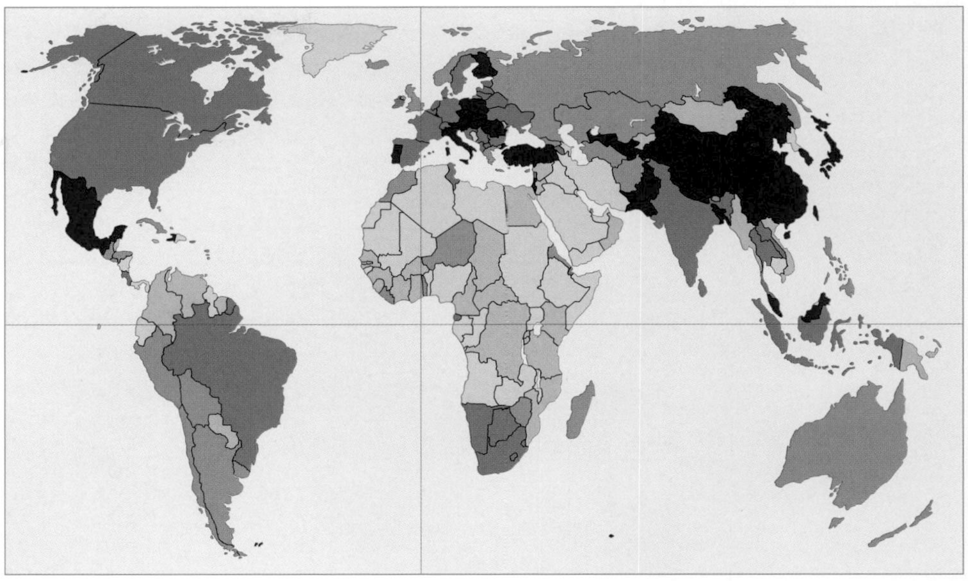

Countries most dependent on the export of manufactured goods

Malta	91%
Bangladesh	90%
China	90%
Japan	88%
South Korea	83%
Luxembourg	83%
Pakistan	83%

PATTERNS OF PRODUCTION

Breakdown of industrial output by value, selected countries (latest available year)

	Food & agric. products	Textiles & clothing	Machinery & transport	Chemicals	Other
Algeria	26%	20%	11%	1%	41%
Argentina	24%	10%	16%	12%	37%
Australia	18%	7%	21%	8%	45%
Austria	17%	8%	25%	6%	43%
Belgium	19%	8%	23%	13%	36%
Brazil	15%	12%	24%	9%	40%
Burkina Faso	62%	18%	2%	1%	17%
Canada	15%	7%	25%	9%	44%
Denmark	22%	6%	23%	10%	39%
Egypt	20%	27%	13%	10%	31%
Finland	13%	6%	24%	7%	50%
France	18%	7%	33%	9%	33%
Germany	12%	5%	38%	10%	36%
Greece	20%	22%	14%	7%	38%
Hungary	6%	11%	37%	11%	35%
India	11%	16%	26%	15%	32%
Indonesia	23%	11%	10%	10%	47%
Iran	13%	22%	22%	7%	36%
Ireland	28%	7%	20%	15%	28%
Israel	13%	10%	28%	8%	42%
Italy	7%	13%	32%	10%	38%
Japan	10%	6%	38%	10%	37%
Kenya	35%	12%	14%	9%	29%
Malaysia	21%	5%	23%	14%	37%
Mexico	24%	12%	14%	12%	39%
Netherlands	19%	4%	28%	11%	38%
New Zealand	26%	10%	16%	6%	43%
Norway	21%	3%	26%	7%	44%
Pakistan	34%	21%	8%	12%	25%
Philippines	40%	7%	7%	10%	35%
Poland	15%	16%	30%	6%	33%
Portugal	17%	22%	16%	8%	38%
Singapore	6%	5%	46%	8%	36%
South Africa	14%	8%	17%	11%	49%
South Korea	15%	17%	24%	9%	35%
Spain	17%	9%	22%	9%	43%
Sweden	10%	2%	35%	8%	44%
Thailand	30%	17%	14%	6%	33%
Turkey	20%	14%	15%	8%	43%
UK	14%	6%	32%	11%	36%
USA	12%	5%	35%	10%	38%
Venezuela	23%	8%	9%	11%	49%

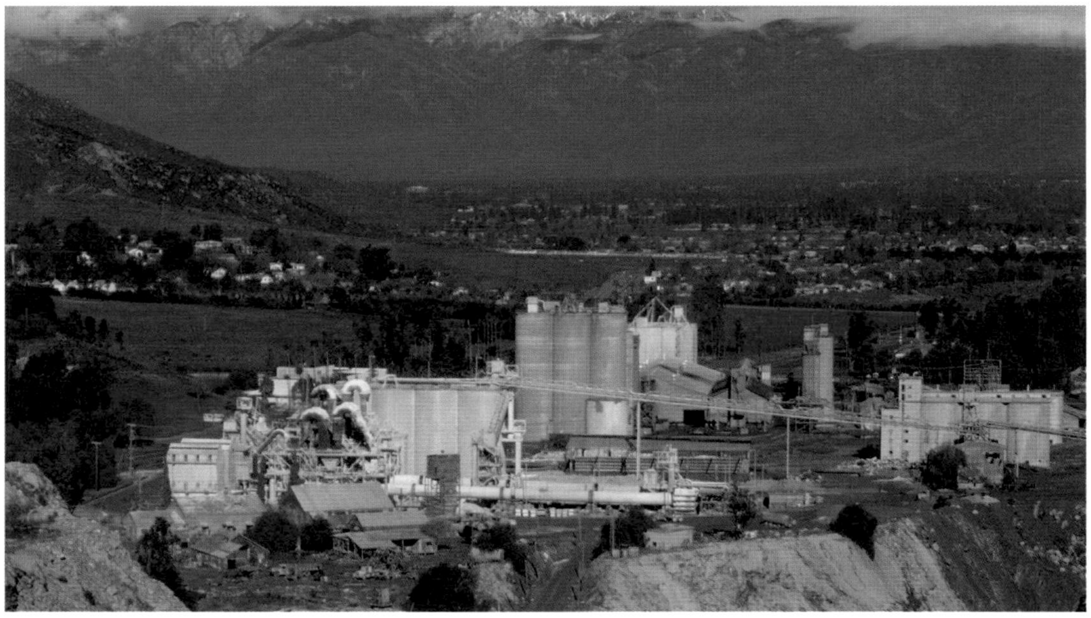

◀ This photograph shows a cement-manufacturing plant in Riverside, California, USA. Cement production figures are often an indicator of the relative prosperity of a country, since they show the construction of roads, dams and other infrastructure projects (*see the graph below*).

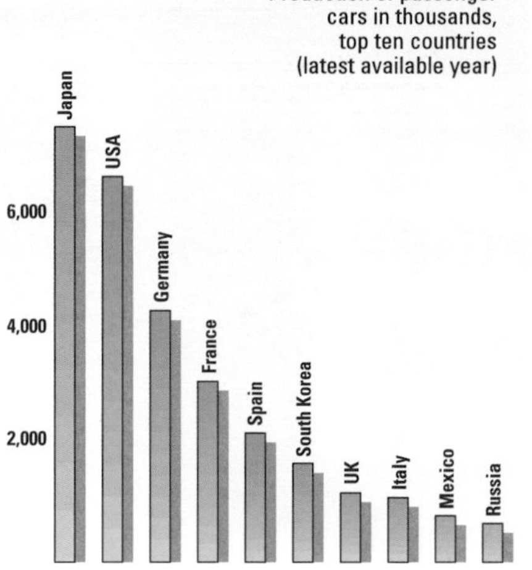

AUTOMOBILES
Production of passenger cars in thousands, top ten countries (latest available year)

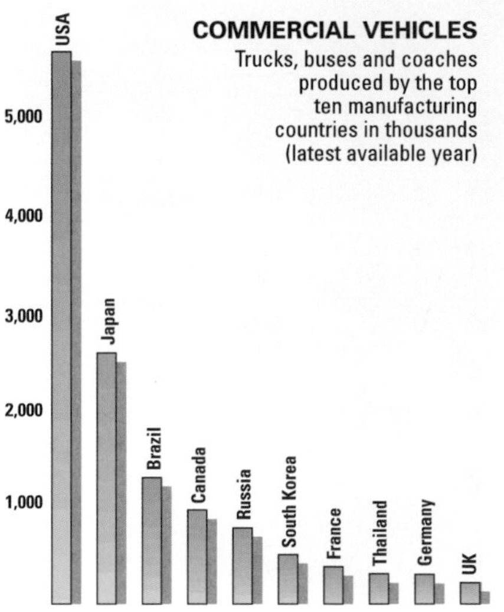

COMMERCIAL VEHICLES
Trucks, buses and coaches produced by the top ten manufacturing countries in thousands (latest available year)

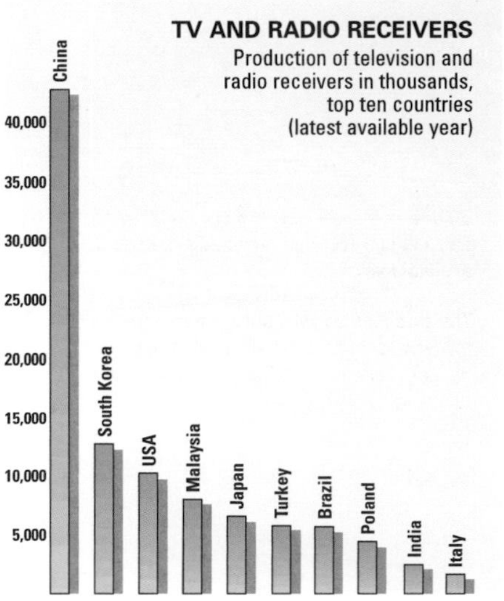

TV AND RADIO RECEIVERS
Production of television and radio receivers in thousands, top ten countries (latest available year)

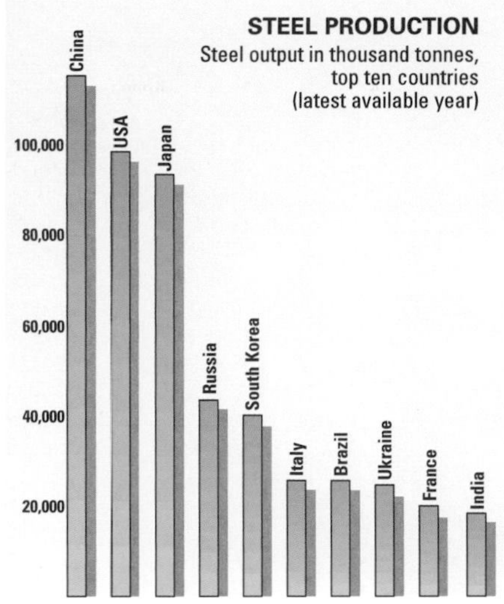

STEEL PRODUCTION
Steel output in thousand tonnes, top ten countries (latest available year)

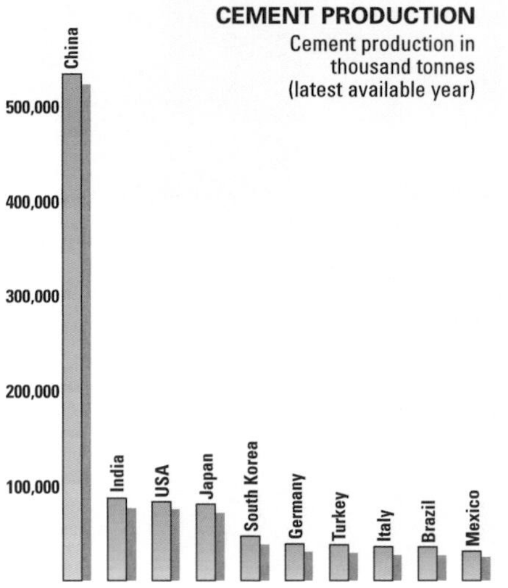

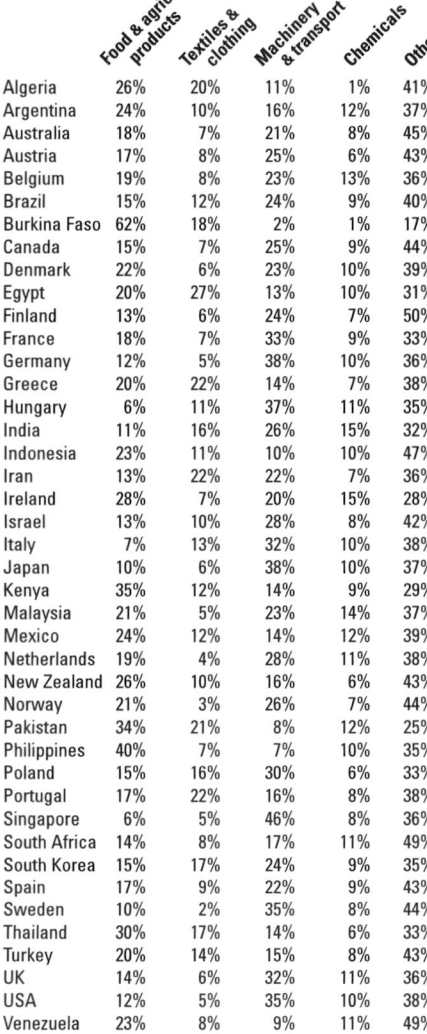

CEMENT PRODUCTION
Cement production in thousand tonnes (latest available year)

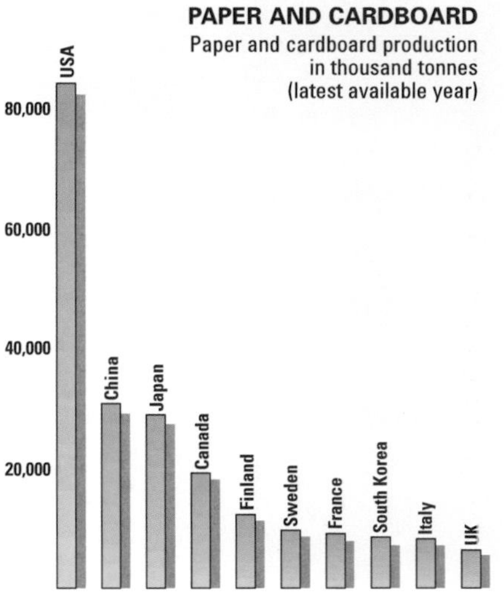

PAPER AND CARDBOARD
Paper and cardboard production in thousand tonnes (latest available year)

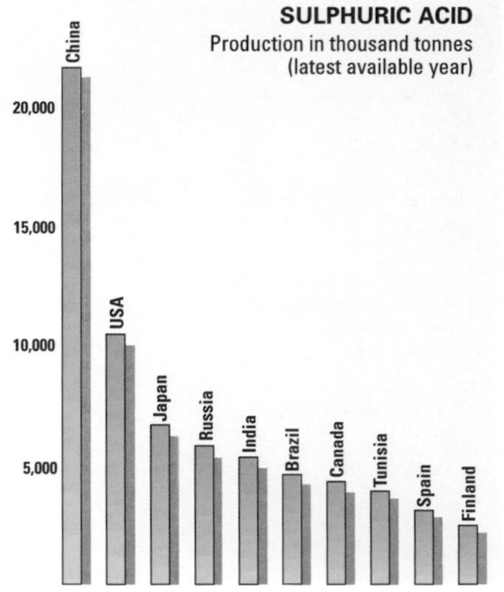

SULPHURIC ACID
Production in thousand tonnes (latest available year)

TRADE

For more information:

31 International organizations
35 Movements of oil
36 Minerals
38 Wealth creation
39 Industry and trade
45 Air travel and tourism
Inflation

Trade played a vital role in the growth of early civilizations and it was later a spur to European exploration and colonization. The colonial powers grew rich by exporting cheap manufactures, such as clothing and footwear, while obtaining primary products from their colonies.

From the late 19th century to the early 1950s, as transport technology improved, primary products, especially oil in the later stages of this period, dominated world trade. However, since that time, manufactures have become the chief commodities in world trade, which is dominated by the industrialized countries. Nearly half of all world trade flows between the developed market economies of the European Union, the United States and Japan, although a number of Asian economies, notably China, Malaysia, Singapore, South Korea, Taiwan and Thailand, increased their share in the 1990s.

China's remarkable economic growth meant that, by 2002, it had overtaken Japan to become the fourth biggest exporter to the United States. China's low production costs, especially its cheap labour, was estimated to be one-twentieth of those of Japan, making its high-quality exports highly competitive in price. Growth in world trade is regarded as a sign of economic health, as is a favourable balance of trade (or trade surplus) in any country.

WORLD TRADE

Percentage share of total world exports by value (2000)

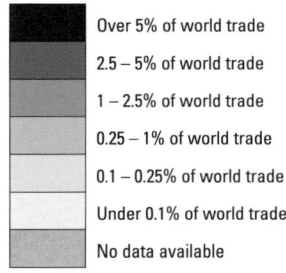

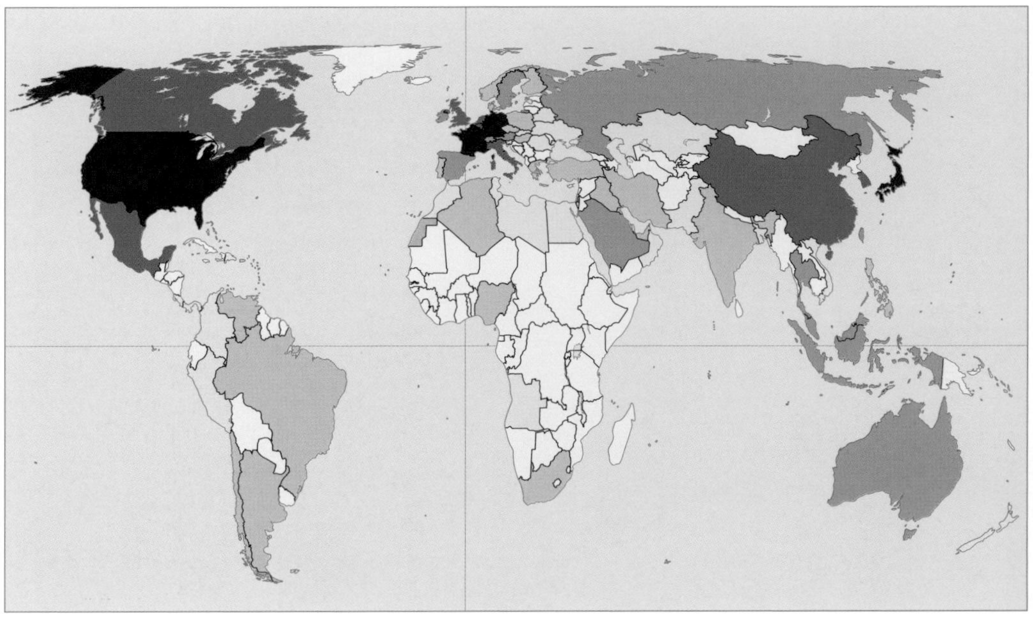

International trade is dominated by a handful of powerful maritime nations. The members of 'G8' (Canada, France, Germany, Italy, Japan, Russia, the United Kingdom and the United States) account for more than half the total. The majority of nations contribute less than a quarter of 1% to the worldwide total of exports. The countries of the European Union account for 35%, whereas the Pacific Rim nations account for over 50%.

DEPENDENCE ON TRADE

Exports as a percentage of GDP (2001)

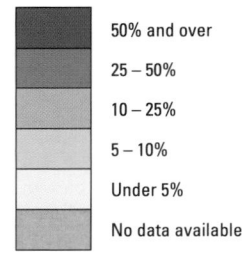

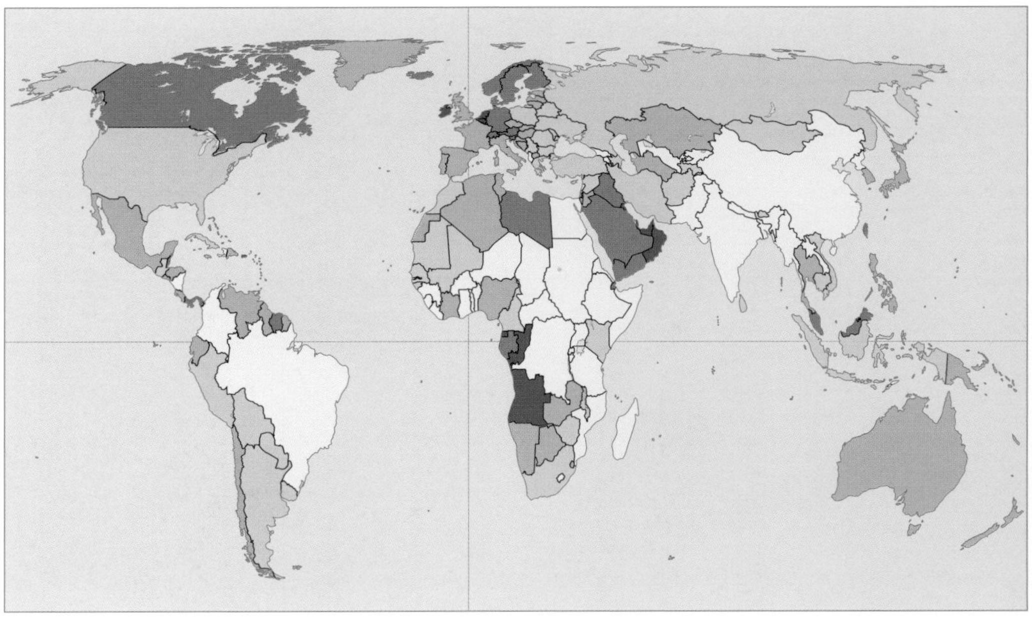

The character of world trade has changed a great deal in the last 50 years or so. While many developing countries still remain heavily dependent on exporting mineral ores, fossil fuels or farm products, such as coffee or cocoa, world trade is now dominated by manufactured goods. Since the 1980s, high-tech products, such as computer equipment, telecommunications gear and transistors, have become increasingly important.

TRADED PRODUCTS

Major manufactures traded by value, in millions of US $ (2000)

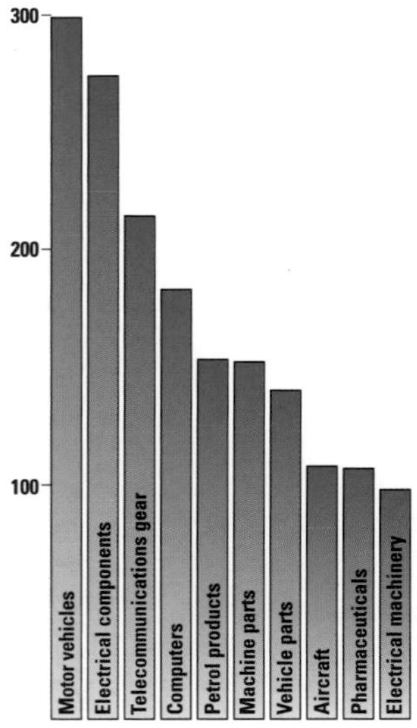

MAJOR EXPORTS

Leading manufactured items and their exporters (2000)

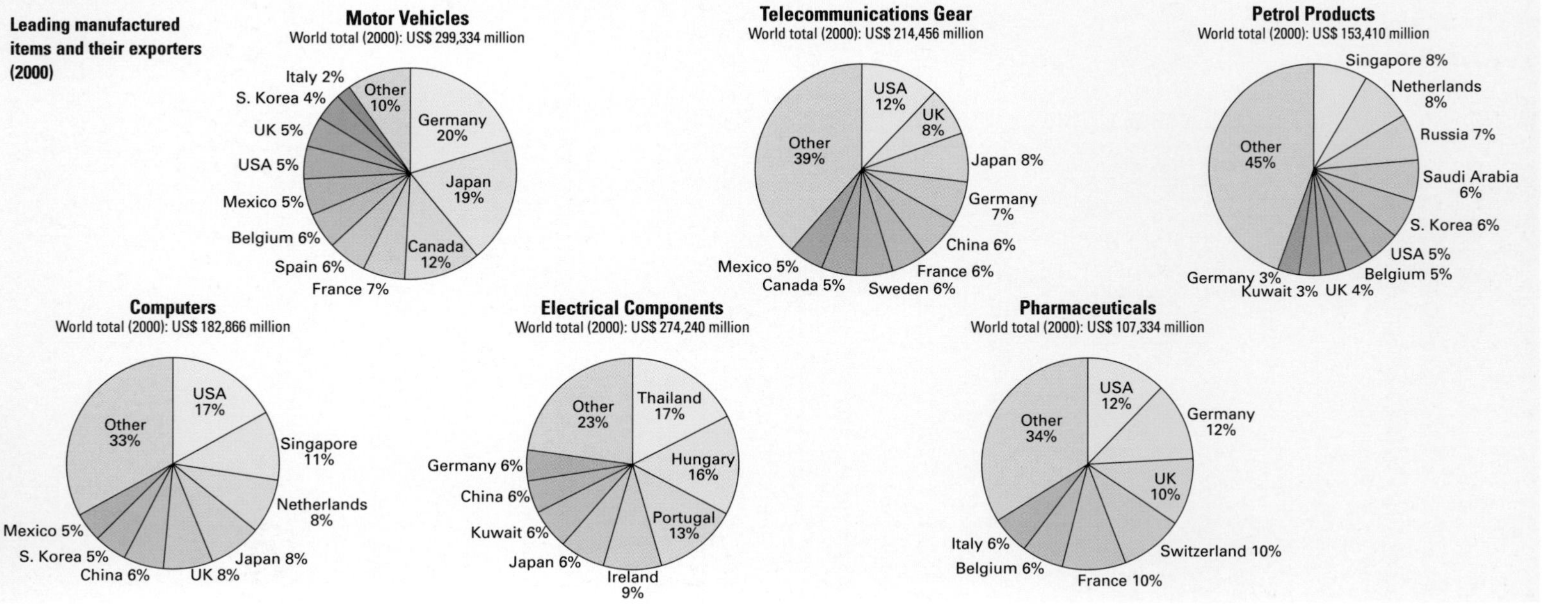

WORLD SHIPPING

While ocean passenger traffic is relatively modest nowadays, sea transport still carries most of the world's trade. Oil and bulk carriers make up the majority of the world fleet, although the general cargo category is the fastest growing. Two innovations have revolutionized sea transport. The first is the development of the roll-on/roll-off (Ro-Ro) method where lorries or even trains loaded with freight are driven straight on to the ship, thus saving time. The second is containerization in which goods are packed into containers (the dimensions of which are fixed) at the factory, driven to the port, and loaded on board by specialist machinery.

Almost 30% of world shipping today sails under a 'flag of convenience', whereby owners take advantage of low taxes by registering their vessels in a foreign country the ships will never see, notably Panama and Liberia.

▲ Shanghai is the largest port in China, lying on the Yangtze River, which is navigable for over 1,000 km [600 miles]. In this image more modern shipping can be seen alongside smaller traditional craft, which are used to trans-ship cargoes to smaller ports.

MERCHANT FLEETS

Merchant fleets in thousand gross registered tonnage (2000). Although a large number of vessels are registered in Liberia and Panama, they are not part of the national fleet

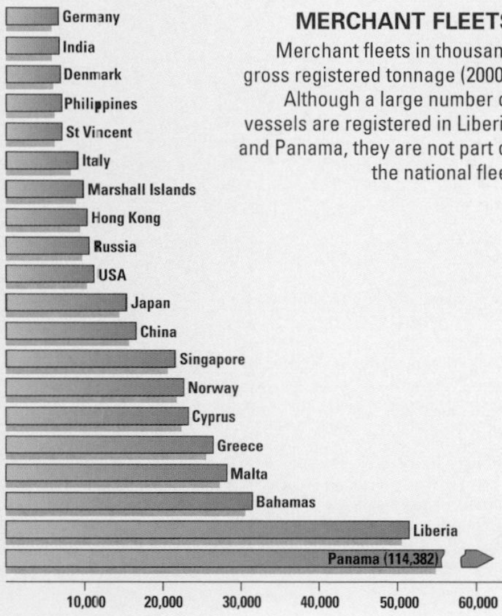

THE GREAT PORTS

Total cargo traffic, in million tonnes (2000)

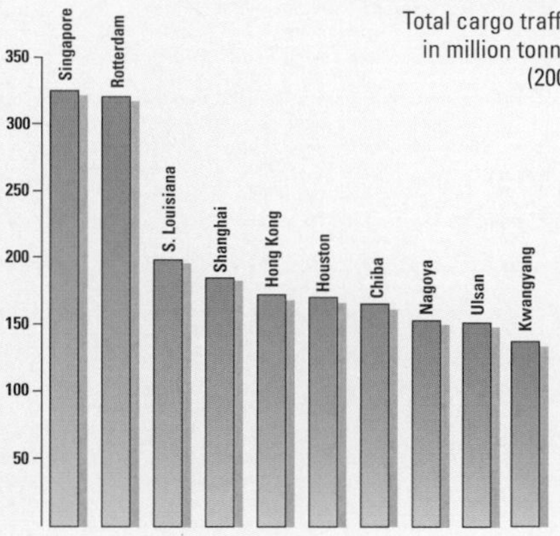

TYPES OF VESSELS

World merchant fleet by type of vessel and deadweight tonnage (2000)

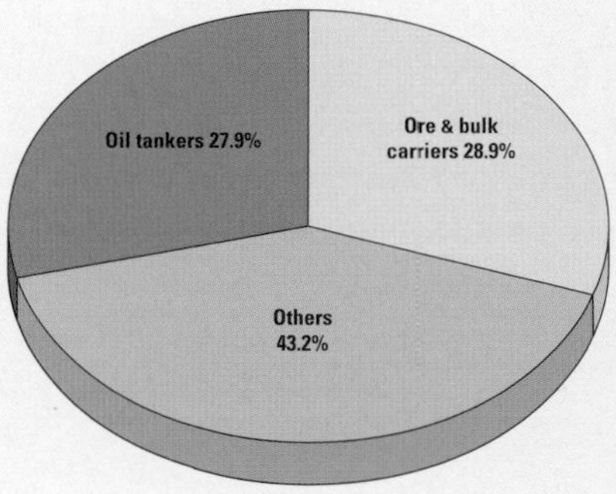

TRADE IN PRIMARY PRODUCTS

Primary products (excluding fuels, metals and minerals) as a percentage of total export value (2000)

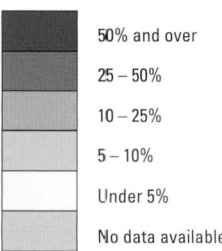

- 50% and over
- 25 – 50%
- 10 – 25%
- 5 – 10%
- Under 5%
- No data available

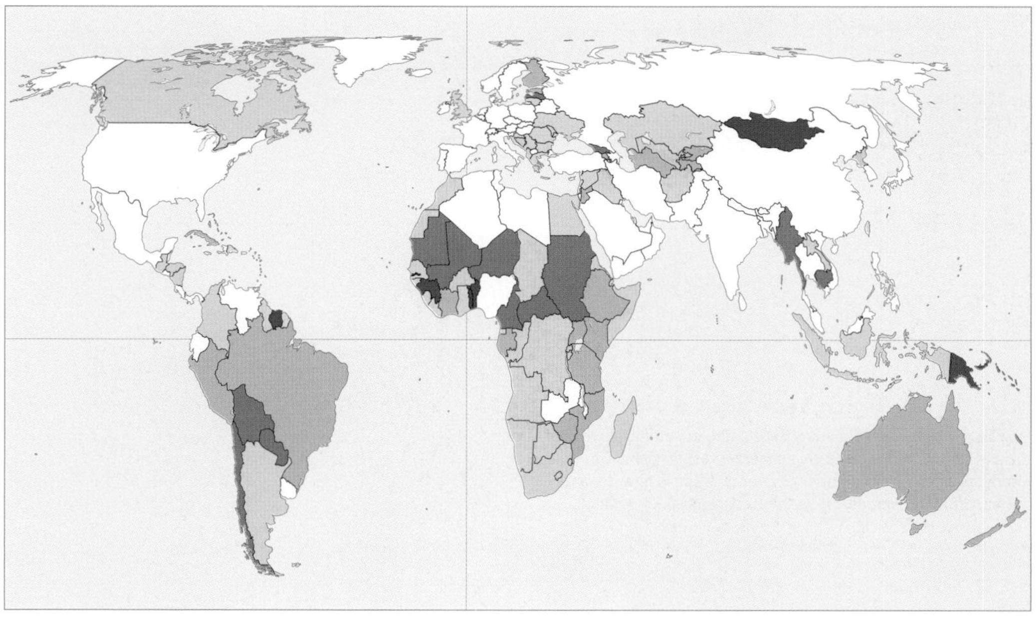

Primary products are raw materials or partly processed products that form the basis for manufacturing. They are the necessary requirements of industries and include agricultural products, minerals and timber, as well as many semi-manufactured goods such as cotton, which has been spun but not woven, wood pulp or flour. Many developed countries have few natural resources and rely on imports for the majority of their primary products. The countries of South-east Asia export hardwoods to the rest of the world, while many South American countries are heavily dependent on coffee exports.

BALANCE OF TRADE

Value of exports in proportion to the value of imports (2000)

Imports exceed exports by:

- More than 40%
- 10 – 40%
- 10% either side
- 10 – 40%
- More than 40%%

Exports exceed imports by:

- No data available

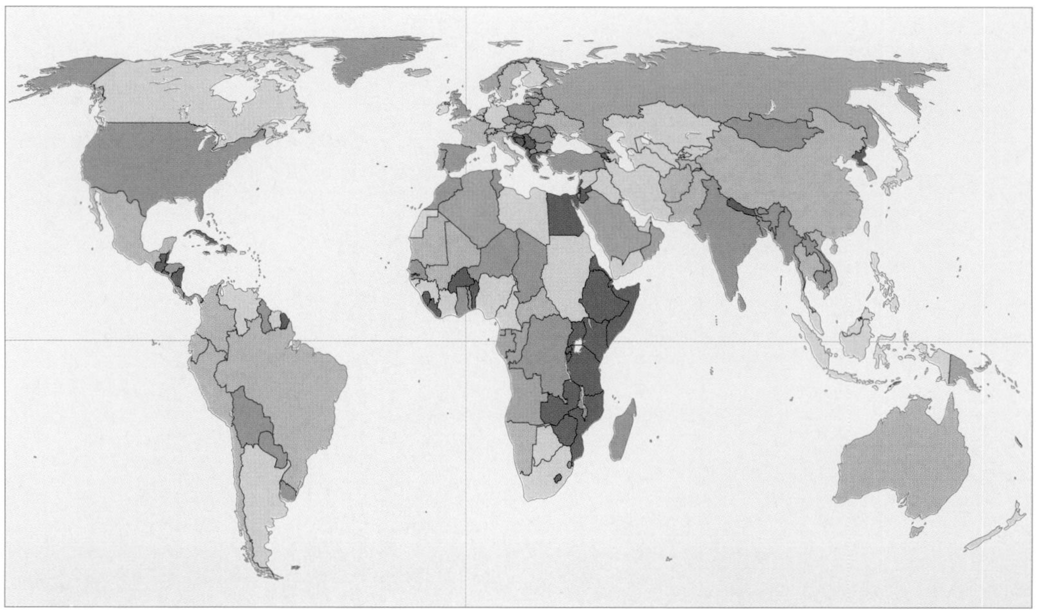

The total world trade balance should amount to zero, since exports must equal imports on a global scale. In practice, though, at least US $100 billion in exports go unrecorded, leaving the world with an apparent deficit and many countries in a better position than public accounting reveals. However, a favourable trade balance is not necessarily a sign of prosperity: many poorer countries must maintain a high surplus in order to service debts, and do so by restricting imports below the levels needed to sustain successful economies.

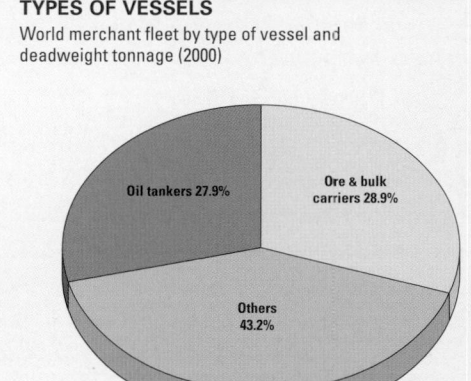

HEALTH

For more information:

18 Water distribution
27 Urban pollution
Urban advantages
33 Crisis in Africa
Food and population
47 Distribution of spending

Until the late 1990s, when the full extent of the AIDS crisis emerged, average life expectancies at birth were rising almost everywhere. By 2000, they ranged from 78 years in high income economies to 47 in sub-Saharan Africa. These figures represented an enormous advance on the situation in 1880, when citizens of Berlin had an estimated life expectancy of 30 years.

The ravages of AIDS have been greatest in southern Africa. One of the worst affected countries is Botswana, where nearly 40% of the adult population were thought to be infected by 2002. In Botswana, life expectancies were expected to fall to 27 years in 2010 instead of an original estimate of 74 years. However, in much of the world, average life expectancies are still increasing. The rises are attributed to improvements in agriculture and, hence, nutrition, as well as health education, improved sanitation and the quality of drinking water, together with advances in medicine.

Besides AIDS, the people of the developing world are subject to another affliction – malnutrition. The map below shows that in most of Africa, Asia and Latin America, the average daily calorie supply per person is so low as to cause malnutrition. Malnutrition is a serious condition – among pregnant women it causes high rates of child mortality.

Deficiency diseases occur when people do not have a balanced diet. Protein deficiency causes stunting and kwashiorkor, which can be fatal, especially among young children, while vitamin deficiencies cause such illnesses as beri beri, pellagra, scurvy and rickets. Iron deficiency causes anaemia, while a lack of iodine causes mental retardation.

Infectious diseases, in association with deficient diets, continue to affect people in developing countries. Around the turn of the century, a WHO report stated that infectious diseases cause over 16 million deaths a year. Most of the victims are young and otherwise fit people in developing countries. The major killers are AIDS, cholera, dysentery, malaria, measles, pneumonia, respiratory infections, tuberculosis and typhoid.

Infectious diseases are much less important as causes of death in developed countries, where cancer and circulatory diseases, such as atherosclerosis and hypertension, which cause strokes and heart attacks, are the most common causes of fatality. Because these diseases tend to kill older people, they are relatively less important in the developing countries where people have shorter lifespans.

Harmful habits are also generally practiced more by the rich than the poor. For example, smoking is an important cause of death in developed countries, while high alcohol consumption has bad effects on health.

▲ Almost 17% of the world's population does not have access to safe water (the diagram at the bottom left-hand corner of this page shows how this breaks down by continent). This places a huge strain on the millions of mainly women and children who have to walk, collect and carry drinkable water in order to survive. UNICEF is dedicated to help improve this situation and to react swiftly in the case of emergencies such as civil war, as with the case of this man in Liberia.

FOOD CONSUMPTION

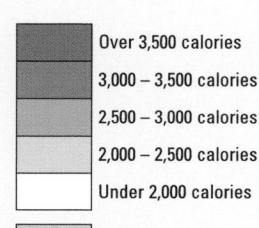

Average daily food intake in calories per person (2000)

- Over 3,500 calories
- 3,000 – 3,500 calories
- 2,500 – 3,000 calories
- 2,000 – 2,500 calories
- Under 2,000 calories
- No data available

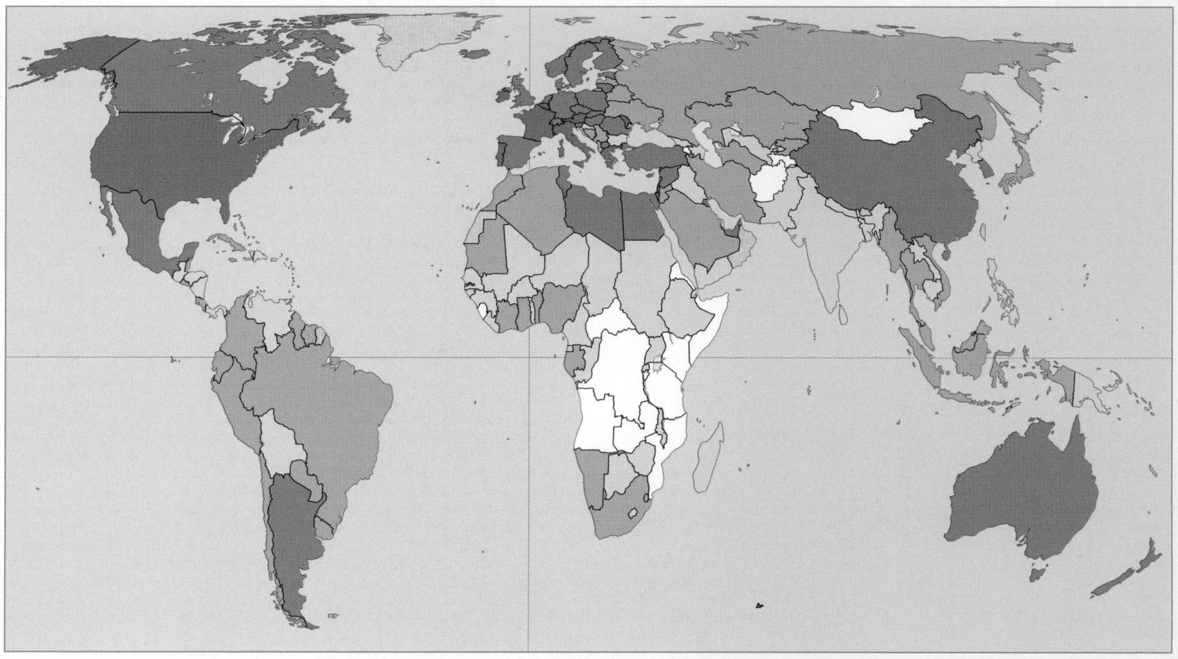

The daily food intake rated adequate by the World Health Organization is between 2,300 and 2,500 calories per day. Approximately 6 million children under the age of 5 years die of starvation each year, the vast majority in Africa. In 2000, the FAO estimated that 840 million people were undernourished, contrasting sharply with the overconsumption of food in some Western cultures.

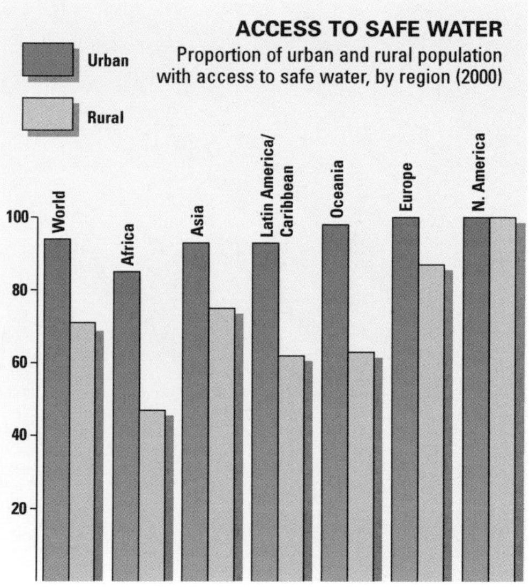

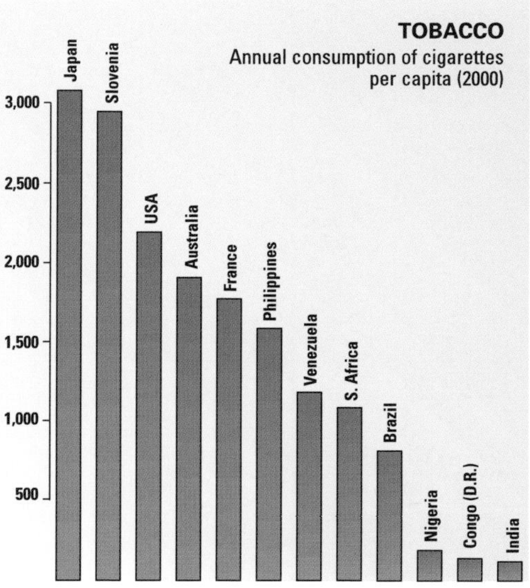

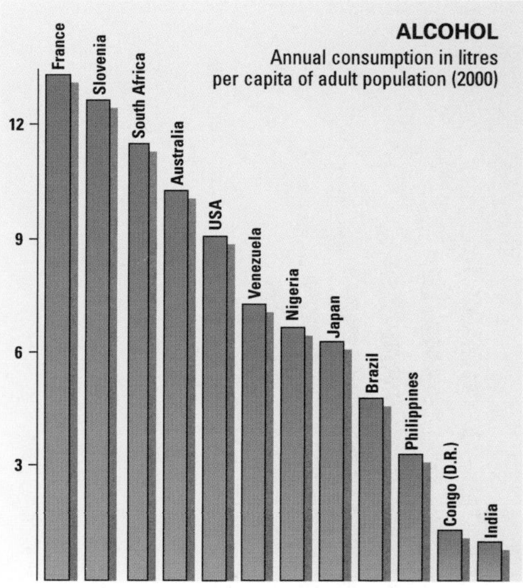

INFANT MORTALITY

Number of babies who died under the age of one, per 1,000 births (2000)

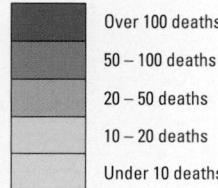

- Over 100 deaths
- 50 – 100 deaths
- 20 – 50 deaths
- 10 – 20 deaths
- Under 10 deaths

Highest infant mortality

Afghanistan	137 deaths
Western Sahara	134 deaths
Malawi	131 deaths

Lowest infant mortality

Iceland	5 deaths
Finland	4 deaths
Japan	4 deaths

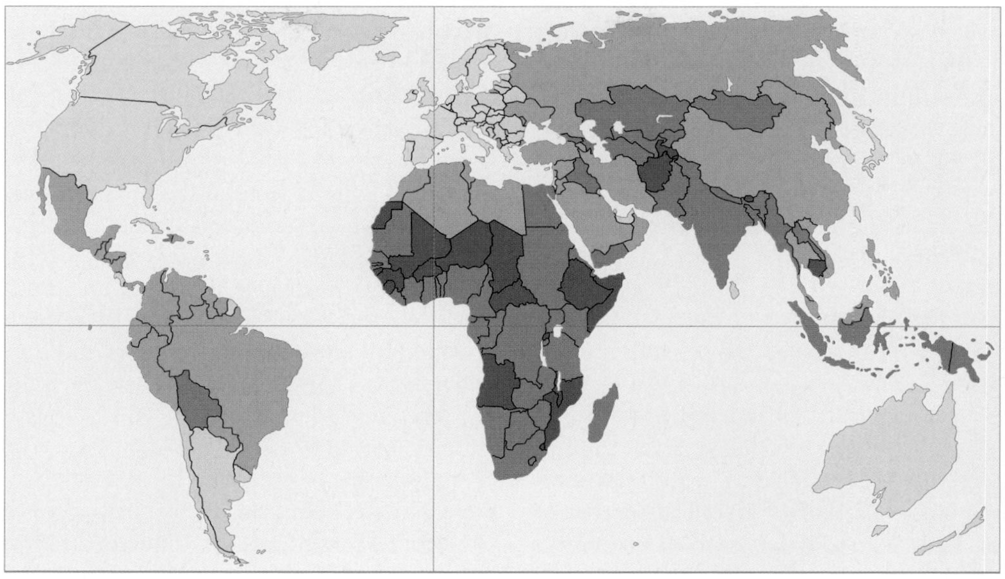

THE AIDS CRISIS

The Acquired Immune Deficiency Syndrome (AIDS) was first identified in 1981 when American doctors found otherwise healthy young men succumbing to rare infections. By 1984 the cause had been traced to the Human Immunodeficiency Virus (HIV), which can remain dormant for many years and perhaps indefinitely: only half of those known to carry the virus in 1981 had developed AIDS ten years later.

In Western countries in the 1990s, most AIDS deaths were among male homosexuals or needle-sharing drug-users. However, the disease is spreading fastest among heterosexual men and women, which is its usual vector in the developing world where most of its victims live.

In 2002, 25 million people had already died of AIDS and another 42 million were infected with the HIV virus. Around 30 million of them live in Africa. In some southern African countries, more than a third of the population carries the virus. In South Africa, which has the largest number of HIV infections, about 6 million people were expected to die of the disease between 2002 and 2012.

AIDS also has other serious consequences. A report by UNAIDS and UNICEF stated that the number of children orphaned by AIDS rose threefold between 1996 and 2002, reaching an all-time high of 13.4 million.

AIDS

Cases reported in 1999

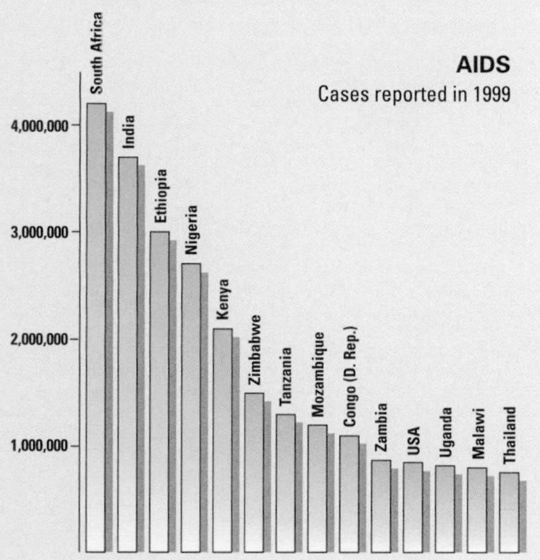

MEDICAL PROVISION

Doctors per 100,000 population, selected countries (2000)

Although the ratio of people to doctors gives a good approximation of a country's health provision, it is not an absolute indicator. Raw numbers may mask inefficiency and other weaknesses: the high proportion of physicians in Hungary, for example, has not prevented infant mortality rates more than twice as high as in the United Kingdom.

The definition of a doctor also varies from nation to nation. As well as registered medical practitioners, it may include trained medical assistants – an especially important category in developing countries, where they provide many of the same services as fully qualified physicians, including simple operations.

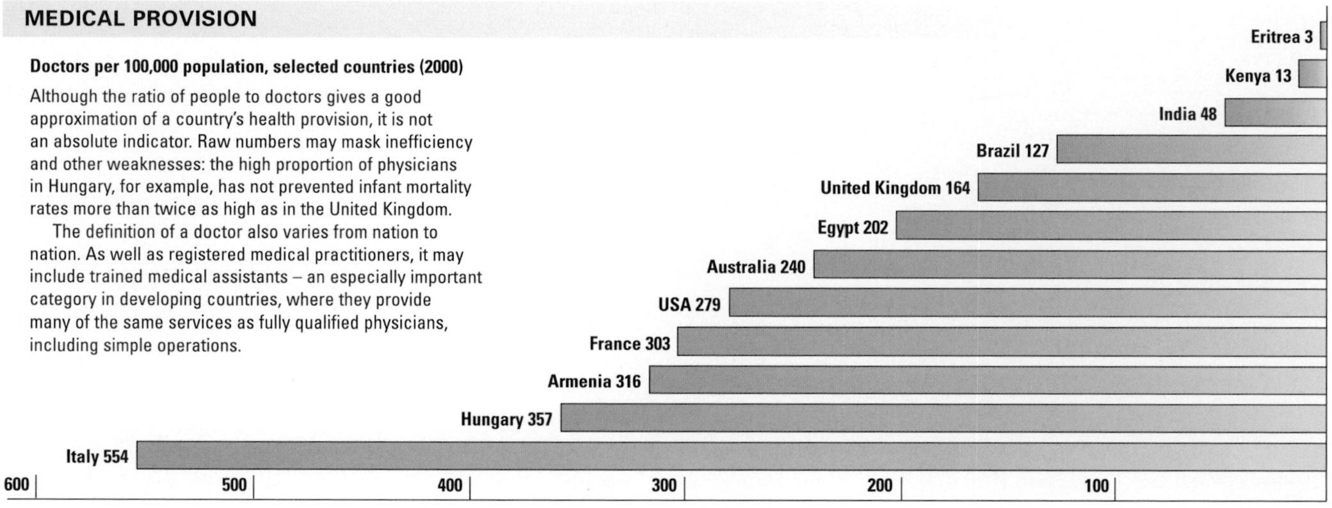

CAUSES OF DEATH

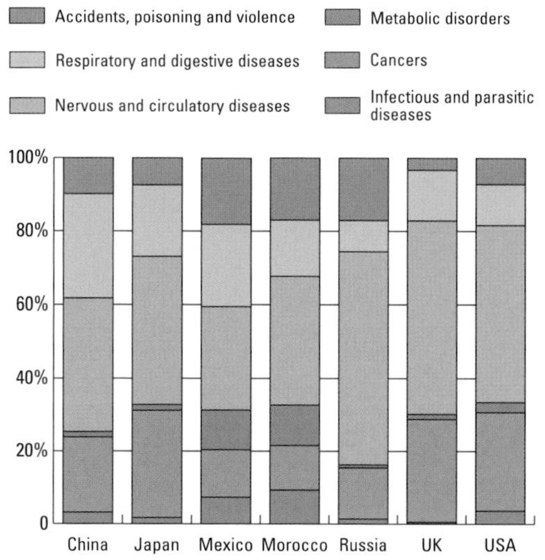

EXPENDITURE ON HEALTH

Public health expenditure per capita, in US $ (latest available year)

Countries with the highest spending		Countries with the lowest spending	
USA	$4,271	Mozambique	$8
Switzerland	$3,857	Tanzania	$8
Norway	$3,182	Sierra Leone	$8
Denmark	$2,785	Indonesia	$8
Luxembourg	$2,731	Chad	$7
Iceland	$2,701	Laos	$6
Germany	$2,697	Niger	$5
France	$2,288	Madagascar	$5
Japan	$2,243	Burundi	$5
Netherlands	$2,173	Ethiopia	$4

The allocation of limited funds for health care in developing countries is rarely evenly spread – the quality of treatment can vary enormously from place to place within the same country. Urban dwellers tend to have much better access to health provisions than those living in rural areas.

SANITATION

Percentage of population with access to sanitation services, selected countries (latest available year)

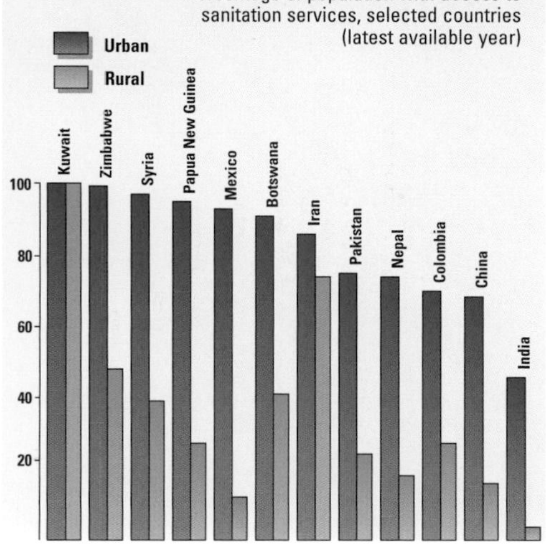

MALARIA

Cases of malaria per 100,000 people exposed to malaria-infected environments, selected countries* (latest available year)

data not available for Africa where 80% of malaria cases occur

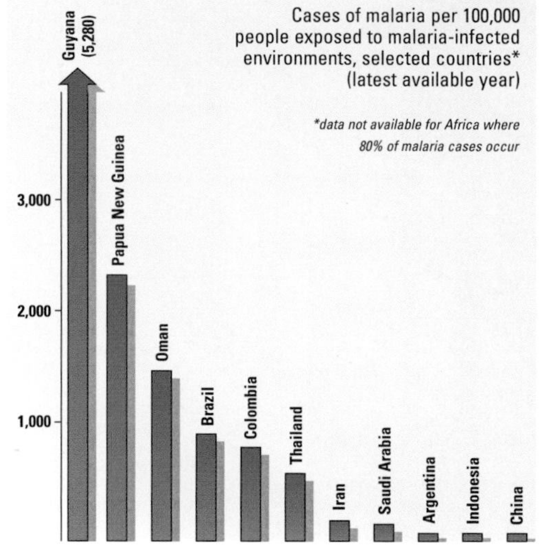

CIRCULATORY DISEASE IN EUROPE

Diseases of the circulatory system per 100,000 people (latest available year)

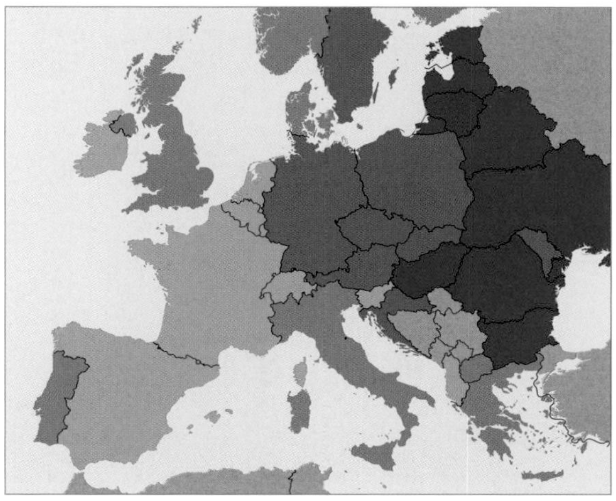

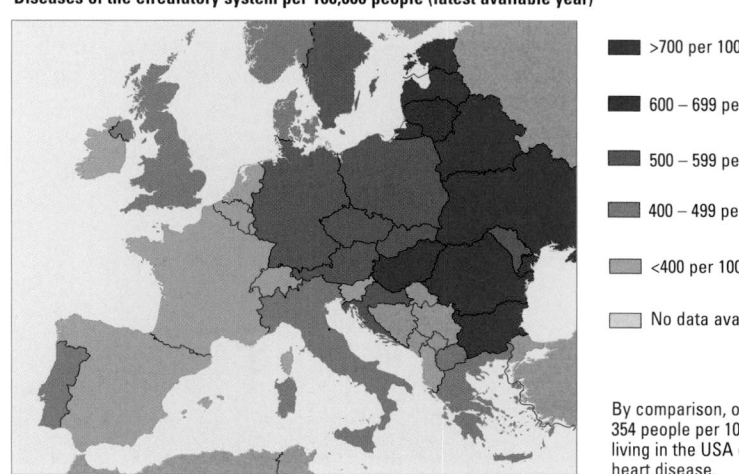

- >700 per 100,000
- 600 – 699 per 100,000
- 500 – 599 per 100,000
- 400 – 499 per 100,000
- <400 per 100,000
- No data available

By comparison, over 354 people per 100,000 living in the USA die of heart disease.

WEALTH

For more information:

38 Wealth creation
39 Industrial output
40 World trade
Major exports
41 Balance of trade
47 Distribution of spending

Perhaps the most glaring differences in the world today are those between the rich and the poor. The World Bank divides countries into three main groups based on average economic production expressed in terms of per capita GNP (Gross National Product). They are the low-income economies, including most African countries and much of Asia; the middle-income economies, including most of Latin America and most of the former USSR; and the high-income economies of Canada, the United States, Western Europe, Japan and Australia.

Per capita GNPs are a measure of the total goods and services produced by a country divided by the population, and then converted into US dollars at official exchange rates. They are useful indicators of a country's prosperity, though, like all statistics, they must be treated with care. For example, the prices for goods and services in China are far cheaper than they are in the United States. China's per capita GNP in 2000 was $840 (as compared with $34,100 in the USA), but the PPP (Purchasing Power Parity) estimate of China's per capita GNP was considerably higher at $3,920. Another problem with per capita GNPs is that they are averages, which often conceal wide internal variations.

The pattern of poverty varies from region to region. In Latin America, much progress has been made through industrialization, though startling inequalities still exist between rich and poor. China and other countries in eastern Asia, including South Korea and Taiwan, have followed Japan's example in pursuing export-led industrial policies. The success of China's Special Economic Zones, where foreign investment is encouraged, has led to a huge rise in China's per capita GNP.

Solutions to poverty in Africa are much harder to find because of its high population growth, civil wars, natural disasters and high inflation rates. Although Africa receives more aid than any other continent, aid is only a partial solution. Much aid has been wasted on overambitious projects, in the servicing of huge national debts, or lost by inexperienced or corrupt governments. One initiative in some African countries has been to improve the infrastructure and develop tourism, creating employment and providing much-needed foreign currency. But tourism alone cannot solve the problems of under-development.

The International Monetary Fund and the World Bank argue that real economic progress in Africa will be achieved only when African countries create market-friendly economies that encourage trade through export-led manufacturing, while at the same time strictly controlling public spending on welfare, the civil service and other areas.

CONTINENTAL SHARES

Shares of population and of wealth (GNP) by continent

These generalized continental figures show the startling difference between rich and poor, but mask the successes or failures of individual countries. Japan, for example, with less than 4% of Asia's population, produces almost 70% of the continent's output. Within countries, the difference between rich and poor can also be startling. In Brazil, for example, the richest 20% of the population own 60% of the wealth.

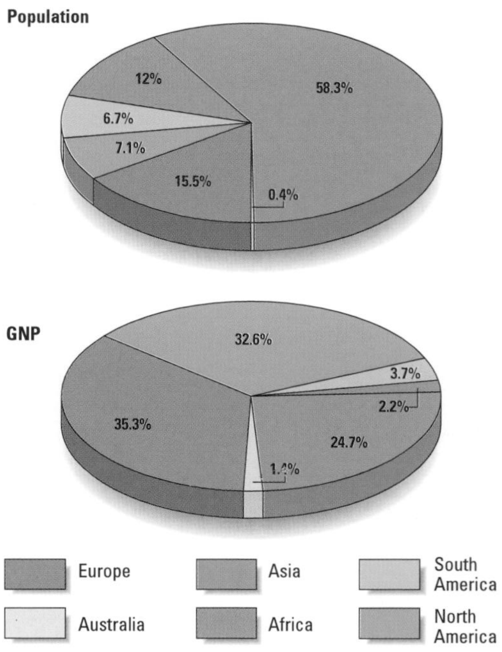

LEVELS OF INCOME

Gross National Income per capita: the value of total production divided by the population (2000)

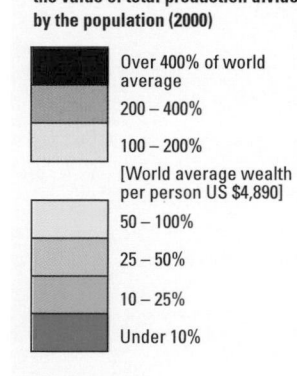

- Over 400% of world average
- 200 – 400%
- 100 – 200%

[World average wealth per person US $4,890]

- 50 – 100%
- 25 – 50%
- 10 – 25%
- Under 10%

Top 5 countries

Luxembourg	$42,060
Switzerland	$38,140
Japan	$35,620
Norway	$34,530
Bermuda	$34,470

Bottom 5 countries

Ethiopia	$100
Burundi	$110
Sierra Leone	$130
Eritrea	$170
Malawi	$170

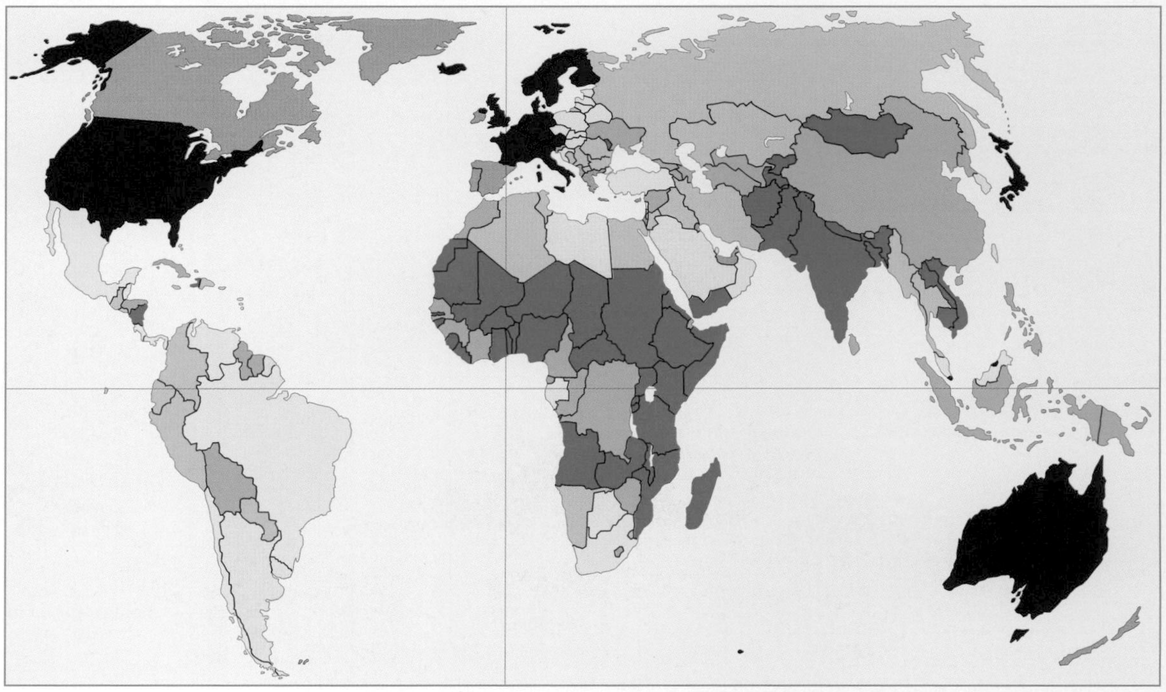

INDICATORS

The gap between the world's rich and poor is now so great that it is difficult to illustrate on a single graph. Within each income group (as defined by the World Bank), however, comparisons have some meaning. The wealth gap in many developing countries, though, is wide, with a small, rich class and a large, impoverished majority, while many high-income countries contain an underclass of unemployed and homeless people.

HIGH INCOME

Number of cars, internet users and mobile phones for each 1,000 people, selected high income countries (2000)

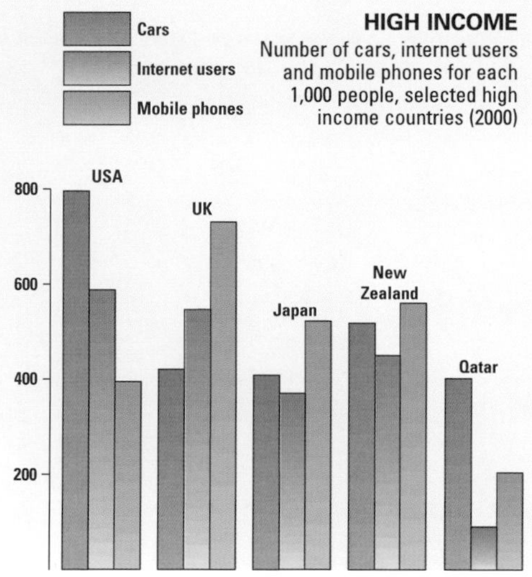

MIDDLE INCOME

Number of cars, internet users and mobile phones for each 1,000 people, selected middle income countries (2000)

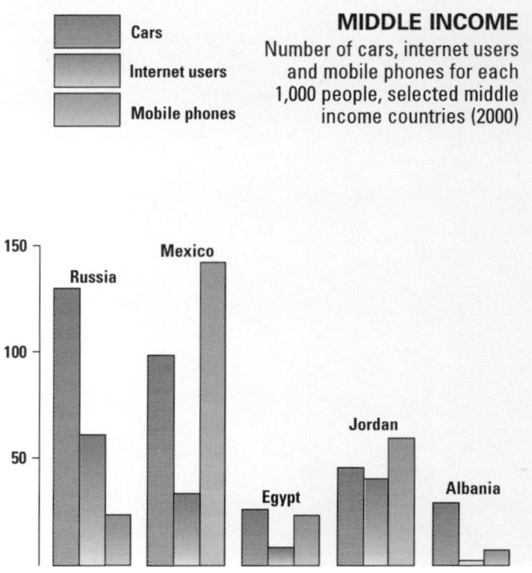

LOW INCOME

Number of cars, internet users and mobile phones for each 1,000 people, selected low income countries (2000)

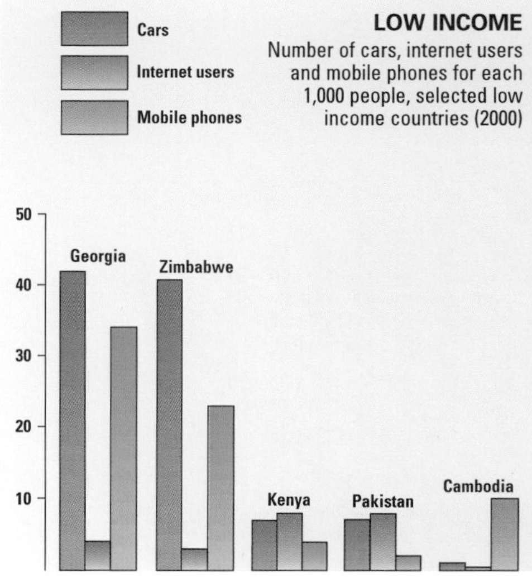

STATE FINANCE

Inflation rates (*shown on the map, right*) are an indication of a country's financial stability and, usually, of its prosperity. Annual inflation rates above 20% are usually marked by slow or even negative growth of the GNP. Above 50%, it becomes hyperinflation and an economy is left reeling.

In the late 1980s and early 1990s, many high-income countries had to contend with annual inflation rates of 10% or more, while Japan, the growth leader, had an average inflation rate of just 1.3% between 1985 and 1994.

Market-friendly policies, including low taxes and state spending, liberal trade policies and a warm welcome for foreign investors, are major factors in countries that have enjoyed rapid economic growth in the decades since 1980. For example, the setting up of Special Economic Zones in eastern China has led to a spectacular rise in that country's per capita GNP.

Other successful countries include South Korea and Singapore, although an Asian market crash in 1997 temporarily halted the dramatic economic expansion of these countries.

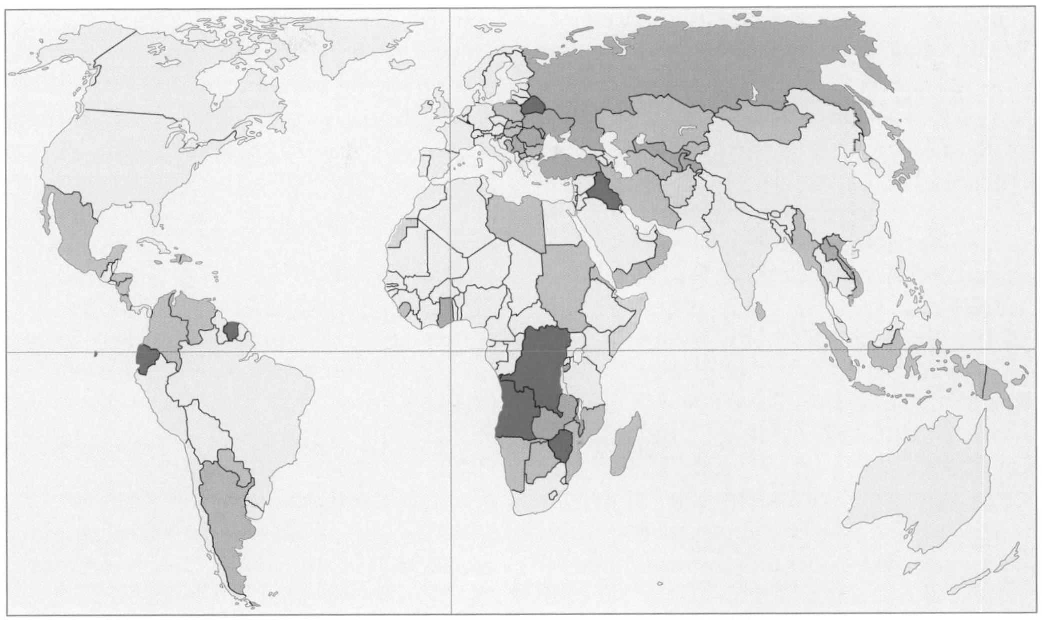

INFLATION

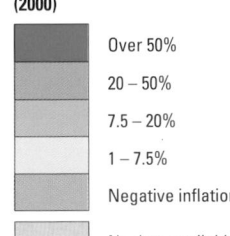

Average annual rate of inflation (2000)

- Over 50%
- 20 – 50%
- 7.5 – 20%
- 1 – 7.5%
- Negative inflation
- No data available

Highest average inflation

Congo (Dem. Rep.)	1,423%
Angola	740%
Turkmenistan	407%

Lowest average inflation

Antigua and Barbuda	–11.5%
Argentina*	–3.1%
Bahrain	–0.1%

* During 2002, Argentina experienced a sharp rise in inflation which is not reflected on this map.

GROWTH IN GNI

GNI per capita annual growth rate (1998–9)

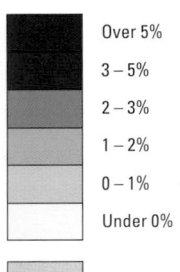

- Over 5%
- 3 – 5%
- 2 – 3%
- 1 – 2%
- 0 – 1%
- Under 0%
- No data available

Countries with highest growth rates

Equatorial Guinea	15.0%
Mozambique	10.0%
Palau	10.0%
South Korea	10.0%
Guinea-Bissau	9.5%

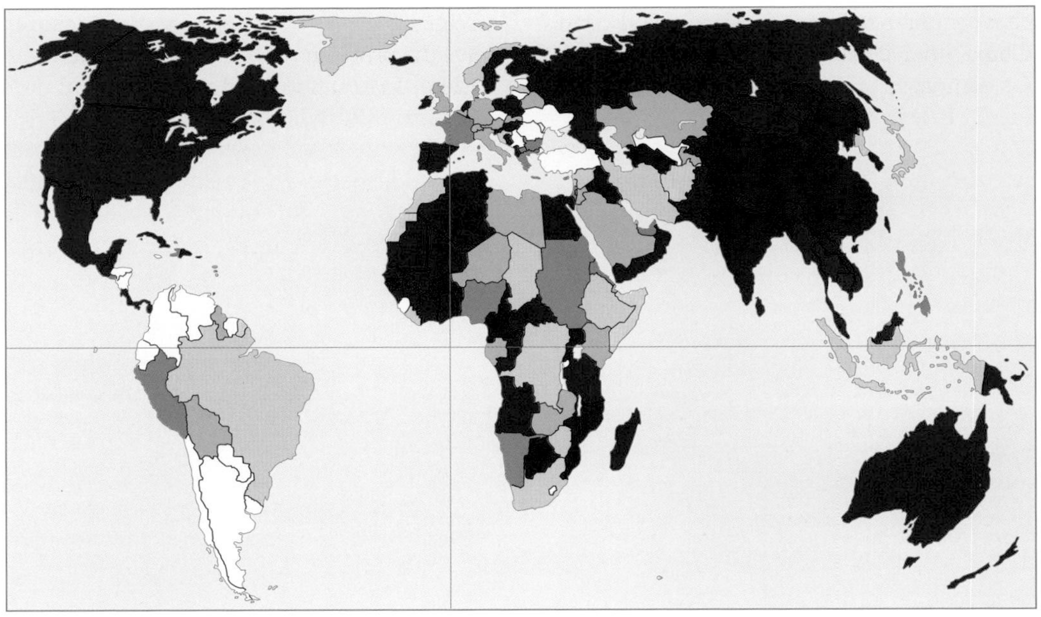

WORLD AIR TRAVEL

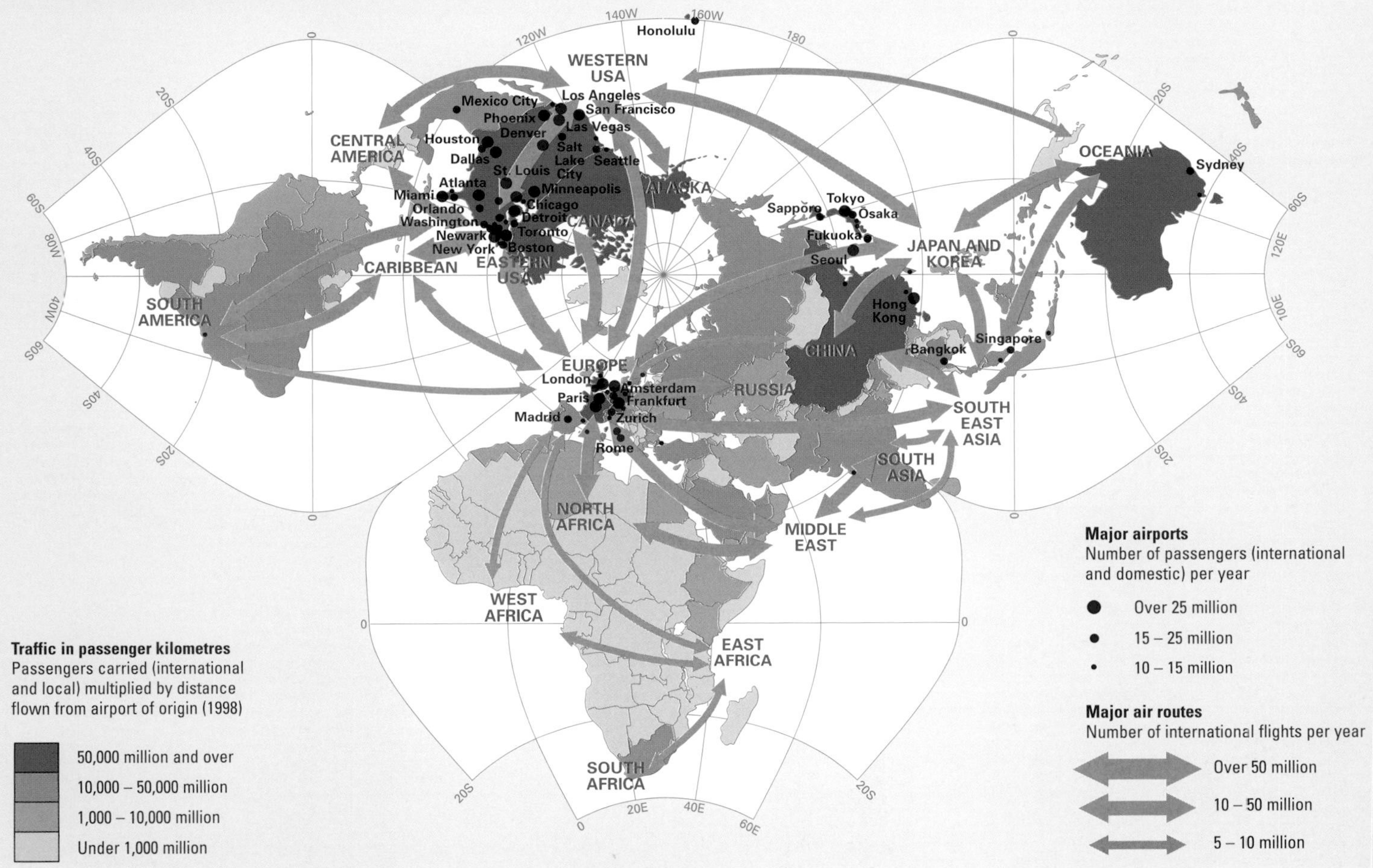

Leisure and tourism is the world's second largest industry in terms of revenue generated. Small economies in attractive areas are often completely dominated by tourism: in some Caribbean islands, tourist spending provides over 90% of the total income and is the biggest foreign exchange earner. In cash terms, the USA is the world leader: its 2000 earnings exceeded US $82 billion, though that sum amounted to approximately 0.9% of its total GDP. Of the 51 million visitors to the USA, 29% came from Canada and 20% from Mexico. Germany spends the most on overseas tourism; this amounts to over US $50,000 million. The next biggest spenders are the USA, Japan and the UK.

The world's busiest airport in terms of total number of passengers is Atlanta (76.9 million passengers in 2002); the busiest international airport is London's Heathrow.

WORLD'S BUSIEST AIRPORTS

Total passengers in millions (2002)

1.	Atlanta Hartsfield Intl. (ATL)	76.9
2.	Chicago O'Hare Intl. (ORD)	66.6
3.	London Heathrow (LHR)	63.3
4.	Tokyo Haneda (HND)	61.1
5.	Los Angeles Intl. (LAX)	56.2
6.	Dallas/Fort Worth Intl. (DFW)	52.8
7.	Frankfurt Intl. (FRA)	48.5
8.	Paris Charles de Gaulle (CDG)	48.4
9.	Amsterdam Schiphol (AMS)	40.7
10.	Denver Intl. (DEN)	35.7

Standards of Living

For more information:

18 Water supply
24 Population density
26 Urban population
27 Urban advantages
30 World's refugees
War since 1945
38 Employment
The workforce
43 Infant mortality
44 Wealth

Wealth is a basic factor in determining standards of living. Everywhere, the rich have more of everything, including higher average life expectancies, while the poor have to spend most of their income on basic human needs, such as food and clothing. Yet poverty and wealth are relative terms: slum dwellers living on social security in an industrial society feel their poverty acutely, but have far more resources than an average African living in a rural area.

In 1990 the United Nations Development Programme published its first Human Development Index (HDI), an attempt to construct a comparative scale by which a simplified form of well-being might be measured. The HDI, expressed as a value between 0 and 0.999, combines figures for life expectancy and literacy with a wealth scale, based on Purchasing Power Parity.

The world's countries are divided into three groups, those with a high HDI (0.800 and above); those with a medium HDI (0.500 to 0.799); and those with a low HDI (below 0.500). In 2002, Norway was top in the world rankings and Sierra Leone was bottom. In fact, of the 36 countries with a low HDI, 29 were from Africa, six from Asia, plus Haiti from the Caribbean. Besides having low per capita GNPs, the average life expectancy in these countries was 59 years, while the adult literacy rate was 58%. By comparison, the average life expectancy at birth in countries in the high HDI group was 78 years, while the literacy rate was 98%.

Comparisons between countries with similar per capita GNPs reveal the effects of government actions. For example, the World Bank classifies both India and China as low-income economies, but India's HDI at 0.577 is much lower than that of China, at 0.726. This reflects not only China's economic progress in the 1980s and 1990s, but also differences in average life expectancies (63 years in India and 70 years in China), and adult literacy rates (52% in India and 82% in China).

Disparities in standards of living exist not only between countries but also between individuals, groups and regions within countries. For example, income distribution figures for 1995 show that, in the United States, the poorest 20% of households received less than 4% of the income.

Other contrasts exist in developing countries between rural communities, where incomes are low and basic services are often in short supply, and urban areas, where even those living in slums are generally better off than their rural neighbours. Other striking differences exist between men and women. For example, while adult literacy rates for men and women living in developed countries are more or less the same, large differences exist in many developing countries. In 2001, in countries in the lowest HDI category, only 64% of women were literate, as compared with 73% of men.

Female education is a factor in population control, especially as women's fertility rates appear to fall in direct proportion to the amount of secondary education they receive. This point was acknowledged in 1994 by the UN Population Fund, which defined four main objectives relating to women and population control: the reduction of maternal, infant and child mortality; better education, especially for girls; universal access to reproductive health services; and gender equality.

Statistical analysis presents many problems of interpretation, especially when trying to define such intangible factors as a sense of well-being. For example, education helps create wealth; but are rich countries wealthy because their people are well educated, or are they well educated because they are rich?

HUMAN DEVELOPMENT INDEX

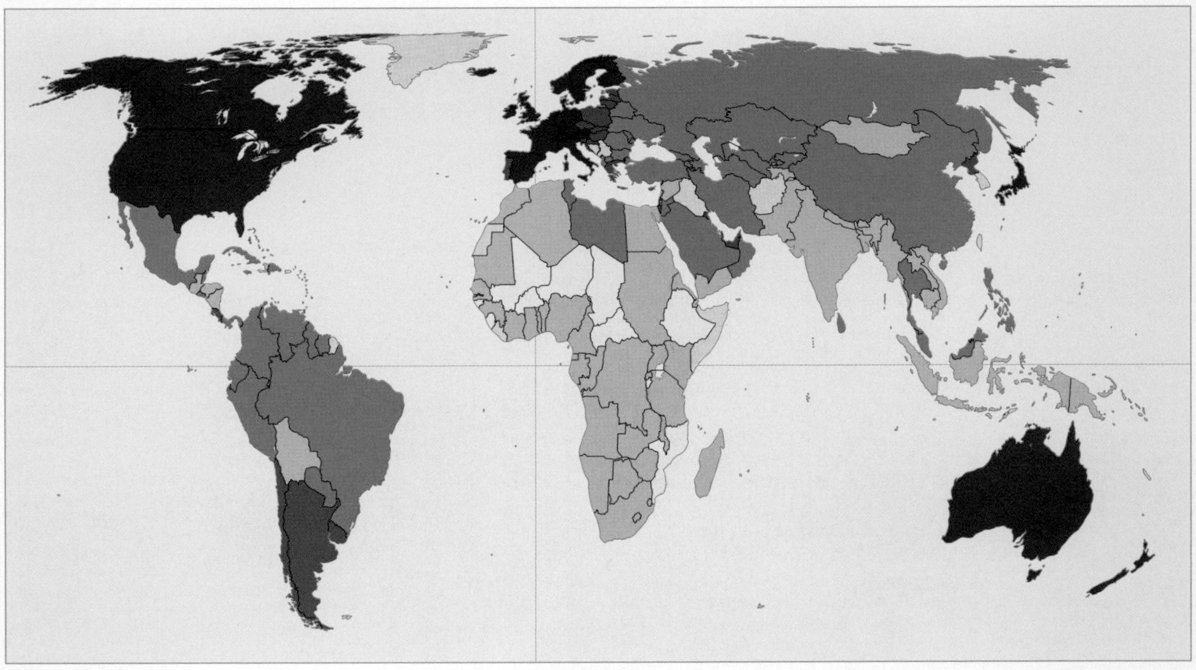

The Human Development Index (HDI), calculated by the UN Development Programme (UNDP), gives a value to countries using indicators of life expectancy, education and standards of living in 2000. Higher values show more developed countries.

- 0.9 and over
- 0.8 – 0.9
- 0.7 – 0.8
- 0.4 – 0.7
- Under 0.4
- No data available

Highest values

Norway	0.942
Sweden	0.941
Canada	0.940
USA	0.939
Belgium	0.939

Lowest values

Sierra Leone	0.275
Niger	0.277
Burundi	0.313
Mozambique	0.322
Burkina Faso	0.325

EDUCATION

The developing countries made great efforts in the 1970s and 1980s to bring at least a basic education to their people. In all but the poorest nations, primary school enrolments rose above 60%. However, figures often include teenagers or young adults, and there are still 300 million children worldwide who receive no schooling at all. A lack of resources has restricted the development of secondary and higher education. Most primary school education is free in the poorer countries, but fees are often paid for secondary and higher education, thus heightening the differences between rich and poor.

PRIMARY

Percentage of age group in primary school, selected countries (2000)

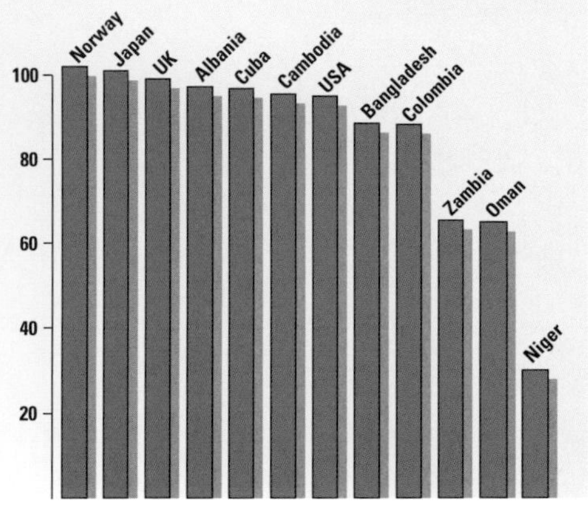

SECONDARY

Percentage of age group in secondary school, selected countries (2000)

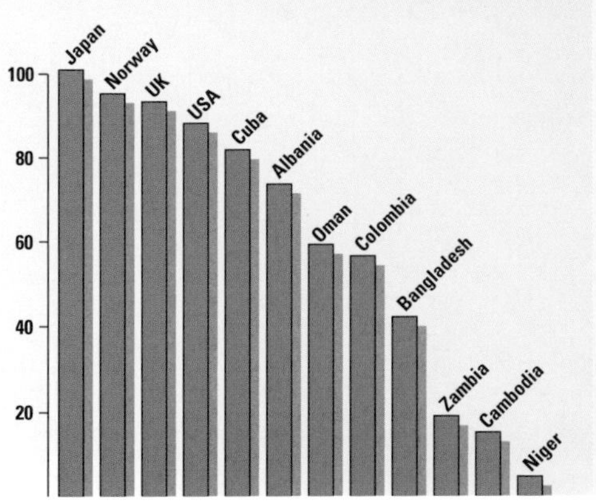

HIGHER

Percentage of age group in higher education, selected countries (2000)

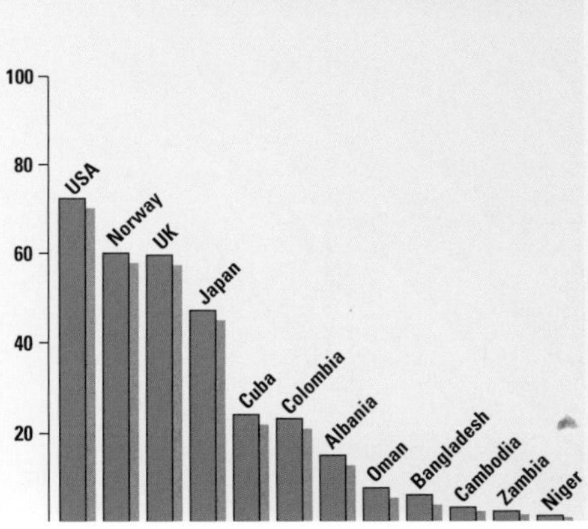

DISTRIBUTION OF SPENDING

Percentage share of household spending (latest available year)

A high proportion of the average income of households in developing nations is spent on basic needs such as food and clothing. In most Western countries food and clothing account for less than 25% of expenditure.

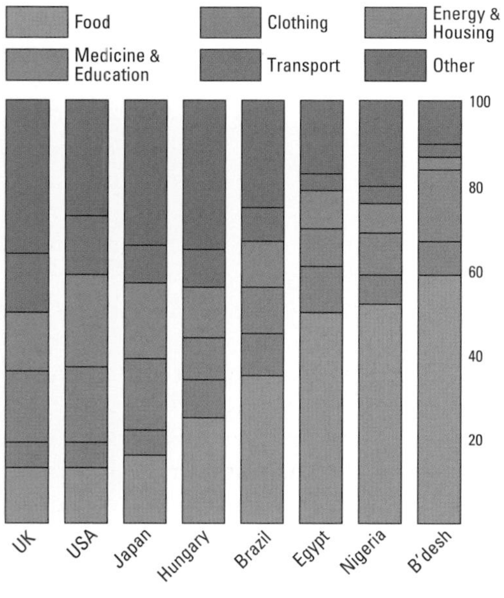

STANDARDS OF LIVING IN THE USA BY RACE, AGE AND RELIGION

A comparison of measures of income and education, by selected characteristics (2001–2)

Median income per household (US $), by age and region

15–24 years	28,196
25–34 years	45,086
35–44 years	53,320
45–54 years	58,045
55–64 years	45,864
65 years and over	23,118
North-east	45,716
Mid-west	43,834
South	38,904
West	45,687

Per capita income (US $), by race and Hispanic origin of householder

ALL RACES	22,851
White	24,127
Black	14,953
Asian and Pacific Is.	24,277
Hispanic (any race)	13,003

The poorest 20% of households received just 3.6% of the income, whereas the richest 20% received 48.2%.

Percentage of persons aged 25 and over who have completed High School, by race or origin

ALL RACES	1975	62.5
	2001	84.1
White	1975	64.5
	2001	84.4
Black	1975	42.5
	2001	78.7
Hispanic	1975	37.9
	2001	57.0

FERTILITY AND EDUCATION

Fertility rates compared with female education, selected countries (1995–2000)

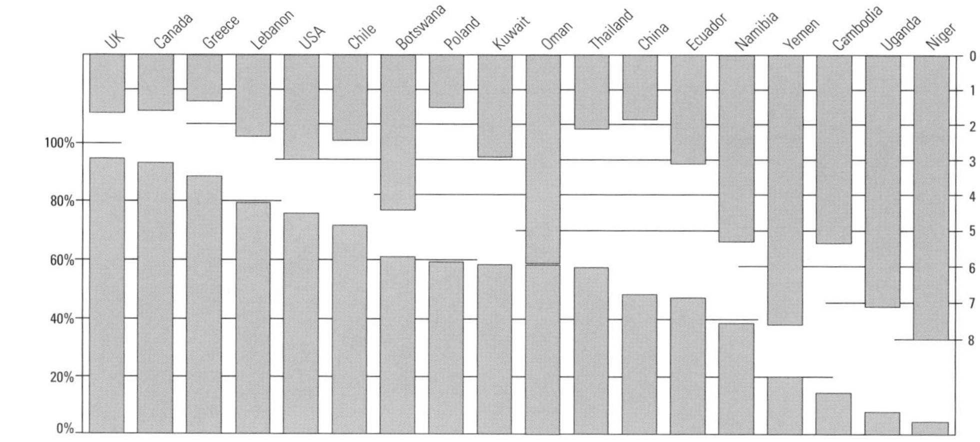

Access to secondary education is closely linked to low fertility rates in developed countries. By contrast, in many developing countries, women's lives are dominated by agriculture, or they lack access to secondary and higher education for cultural reasons, as in Muslim countries. Such disparities are reflected in women's parliamentary representation which is only one-seventh that of men, despite the emergence of such figures as Mrs Indira Gandhi, India's former prime minister. Female wages are also, on average, only two-thirds of those of men.

Fertility rate: average number of children borne per woman

Percentage of females aged 12–17 in secondary education

GENDER DEVELOPMENT INDEX

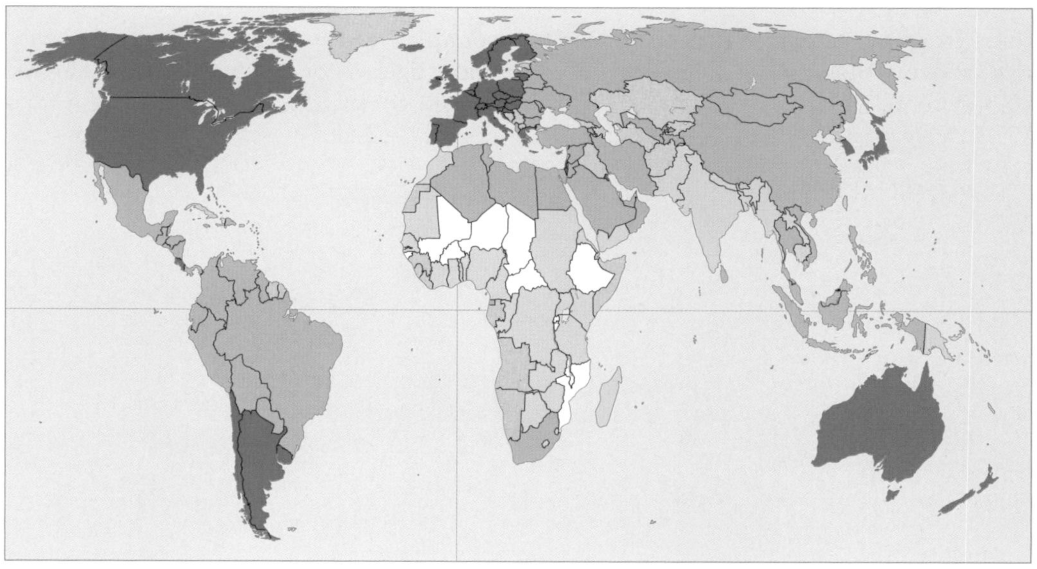

The Gender Development Index (GDI) shows economic and social differences between men and women by using various UNDP indicators (2002). Countries with higher values of GDI have more equality between men and women.

- 0.8 and over
- 0.6 – 0.8
- 0.4 – 0.6
- Under 0.4
- No data available

Highest values

Norway	0.941
Australia	0.938
Canada	0.938
USA	0.937

Lowest values

Niger	0.263
Burundi	0.306
Mozambique	0.307
Burkina Faso	0.312

REGIONAL INEQUALITY IN ITALY

The southern part of Italy, known as the *Mezzogiorno*, has been described as one of the poorest parts of the European Union. It is identifiable on the map (*right*) as all the regions with a GDP per capita of less than US $12,000 (including the two islands of Sicily and Sardinia), plus Abruzzi whose capital is L'Aquila.

The *Mezzogiorno* region suffers from a lack of energy resources, minerals, industry, commerce, services and skilled labour. As a result, standards of living in the region are well below the rest of Italy. Employment is predominantly agricultural and small-scale.

The north of Italy accounts for 60% of the population but 80% of the GDP, whereas the *Mezzogiorno* accounts for 40% of the population and only 20% of the GDP. Manpower surpluses in the south led to emigration to other parts of Europe and the Americas.

It has also led, especially in the last 50 years, to inter-regional migration from the islands and the southern mainland to the north. The main regions attracting migrants are the north-west (the prosperous Liguria–Piedmont–Lombardy triangle, with its great industrial cities of Genoa, Milan and Turin) and the Venetia region in the north-east.

As a result, the north has experienced much higher population growth rates than the rest of Italy.

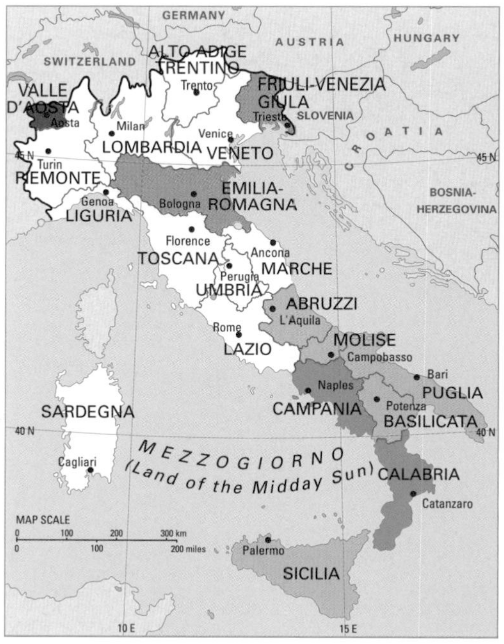

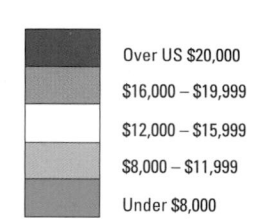

Gross Domestic Product (GDP) per capita in Italy, by region (1999)

- Over US $20,000
- $16,000 – $19,999
- $12,000 – $15,999
- $8,000 – $11,999
- Under $8,000

The average GNI (Gross National Income) per capita for Italy was US $20,170. By comparison, the GNI for the UK was $23,590; for the USA $31,910; and for the EU $22,250.

The number of inhabitants per doctor, another social indicator, varies from less than 500 in the north-west of Italy to over 800 in the far south (the *Mezzogiorno*), with a national average of 607.

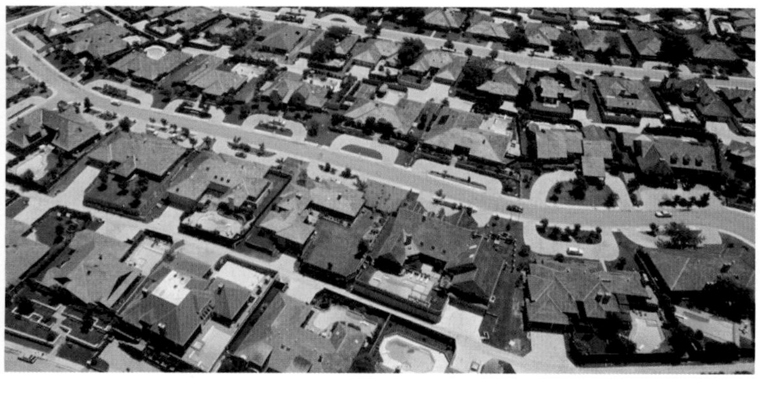

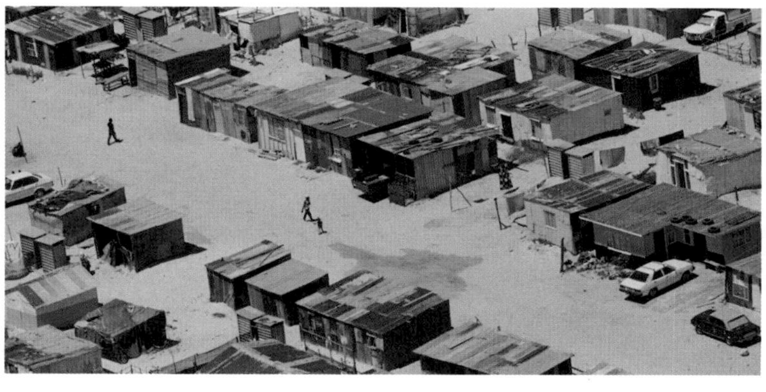

◀ These two images illustrate the reality of suburban life for people at either end of the economic scale. On the far left is part of a huge area of 'tract housing' in California, where large houses of a similar design are laid out by a developer, complete with gardens, drives and swimming pools. On the right is a much more haphazard arrangement of home-built, rudimentary shelters, many without sanitation and most with no electricity in Crossroads Township, outside Cape Town in South Africa.

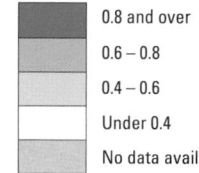

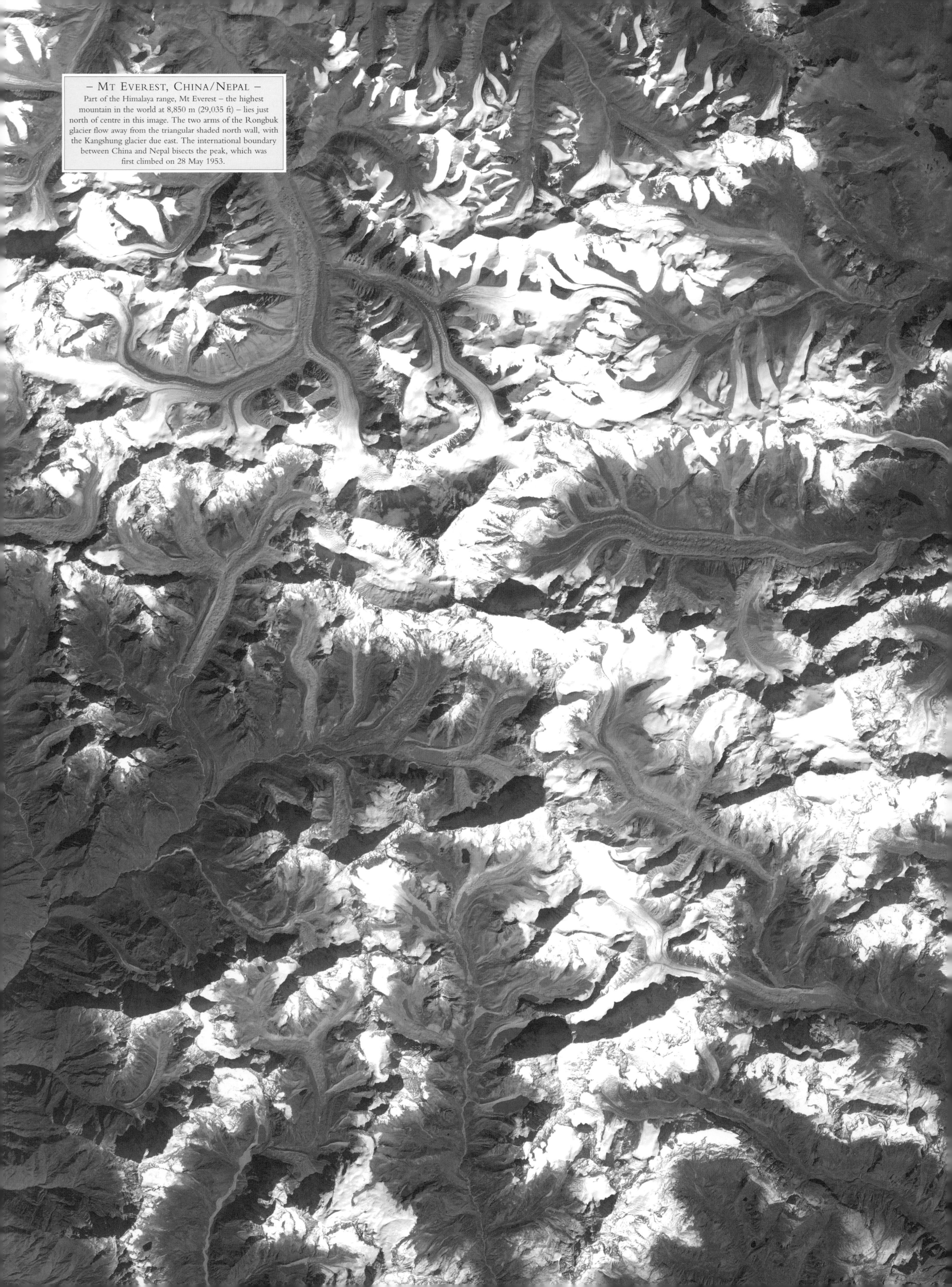

– Mt Everest, China/Nepal –

Part of the Himalaya range, Mt Everest – the highest mountain in the world at 8,850 m (29,035 ft) – lies just north of centre in this image. The two arms of the Rongbuk glacier flow away from the triangular shaded north wall, with the Kangshung glacier due east. The international boundary between China and Nepal bisects the peak, which was first climbed on 28 May 1953.

CITY MAPS

Amsterdam	2	Copenhagen	10	Manila	17	St Petersburg	26
Athens	2	Delhi	10	Melbourne	17	Santiago	26
Atlanta	3	Dublin	11	Mexico City	18	São Paulo	26
Baghdad	3	Edinburgh	11	Miami	18	Seoul	26
Bangkok	3	Helsinki	12	Milan	18	Shanghai	27
Barcelona	4	Hong Kong	12	Montréal	19	Singapore	27
Beijing	4	Istanbul	12	Moscow	19	Stockholm	28
Berlin	5	Jakarta	13	Mumbai	20	Sydney	28
Boston	6	Jerusalem	13	Munich	20	Tokyo	29
Brussels	6	Johannesburg	13	New York	21	Tehran	30
Budapest	7	Karachi	14	Osaka	22	Tianjin	30
Buenos Aires	7	Lagos	14	Oslo	22	Toronto	30
Cairo	7	Lisbon	14	Paris	23	Vienna	31
Calcutta (Kolkata)	8	London	15	Prague	24	Warsaw	31
Canton	8	Los Angeles	16	Rio de Janeiro	24	Washington	32
Cape Town	8	Lima	16	Rome	25	Wellington	32
Chicago	9	Madrid	17	San Francisco	25	Index	33–39

CITY MAPS

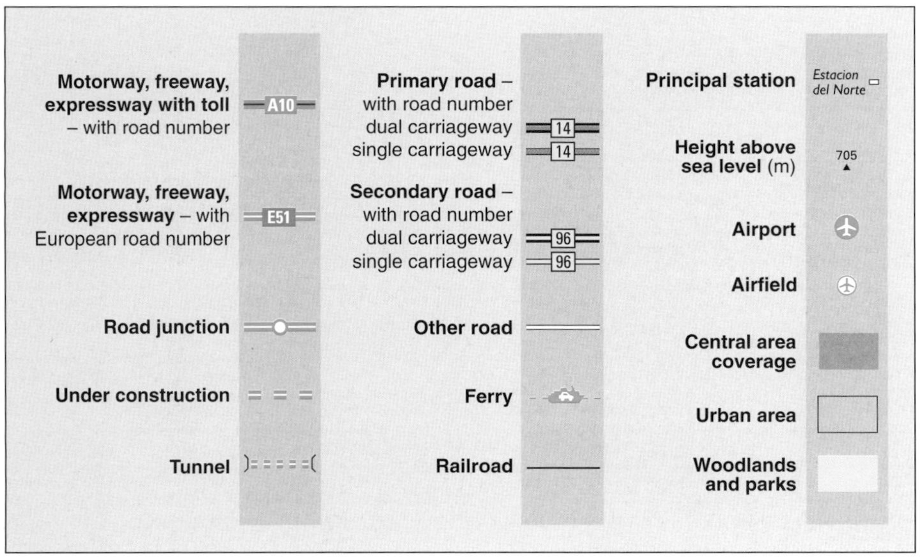

CENTRAL AREA MAPS

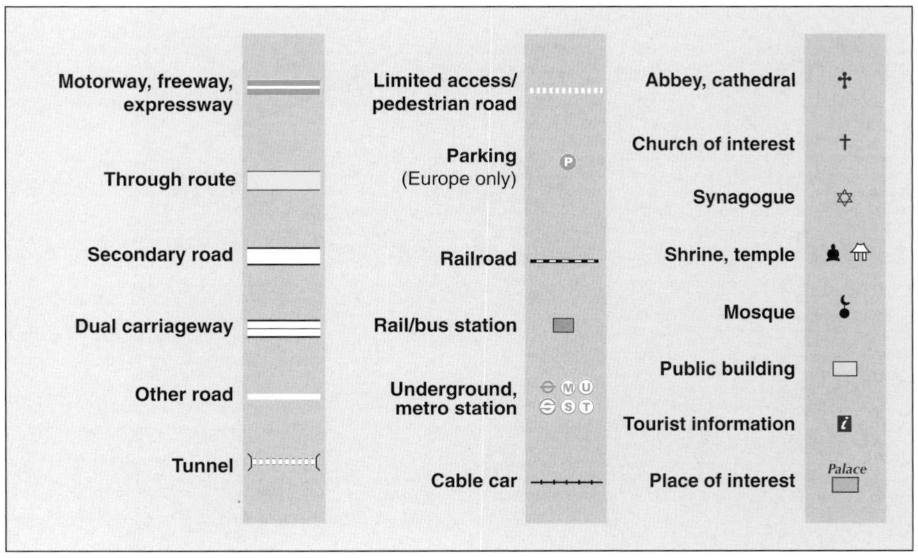

AMSTERDAM

0 km 5
0 miles 3

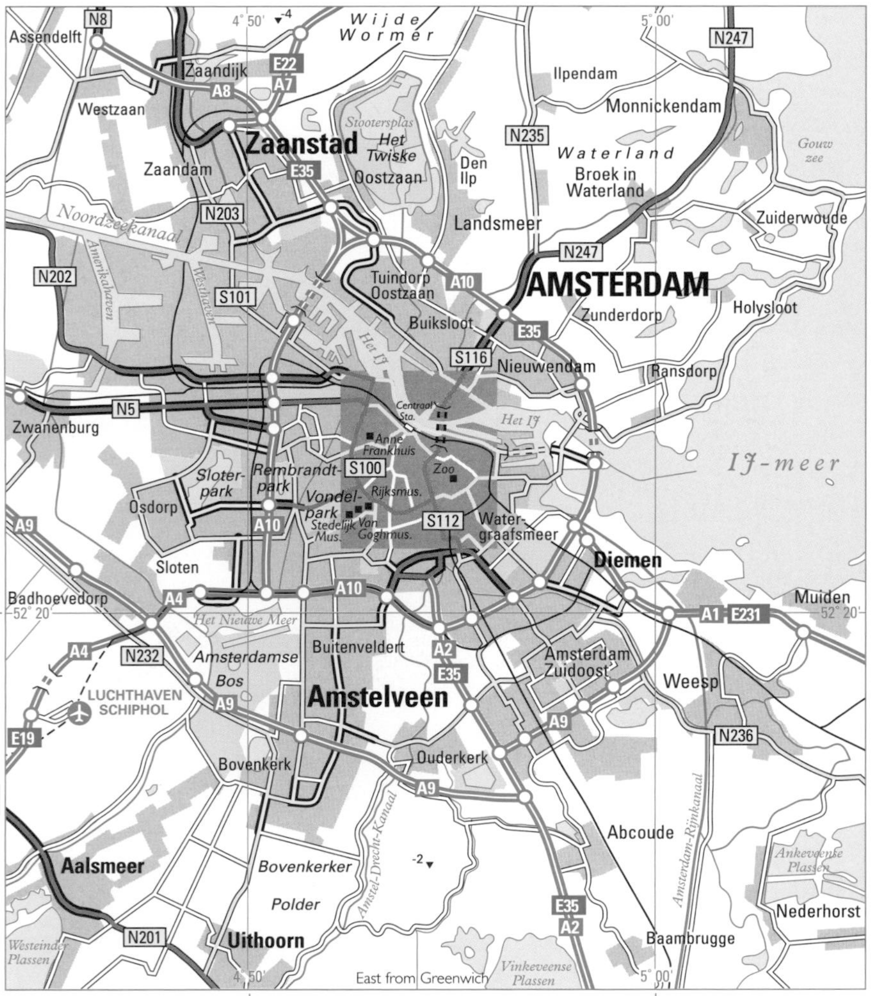

1 2 3

CENTRAL AMSTERDAM

0 km 1
0 miles 0.5

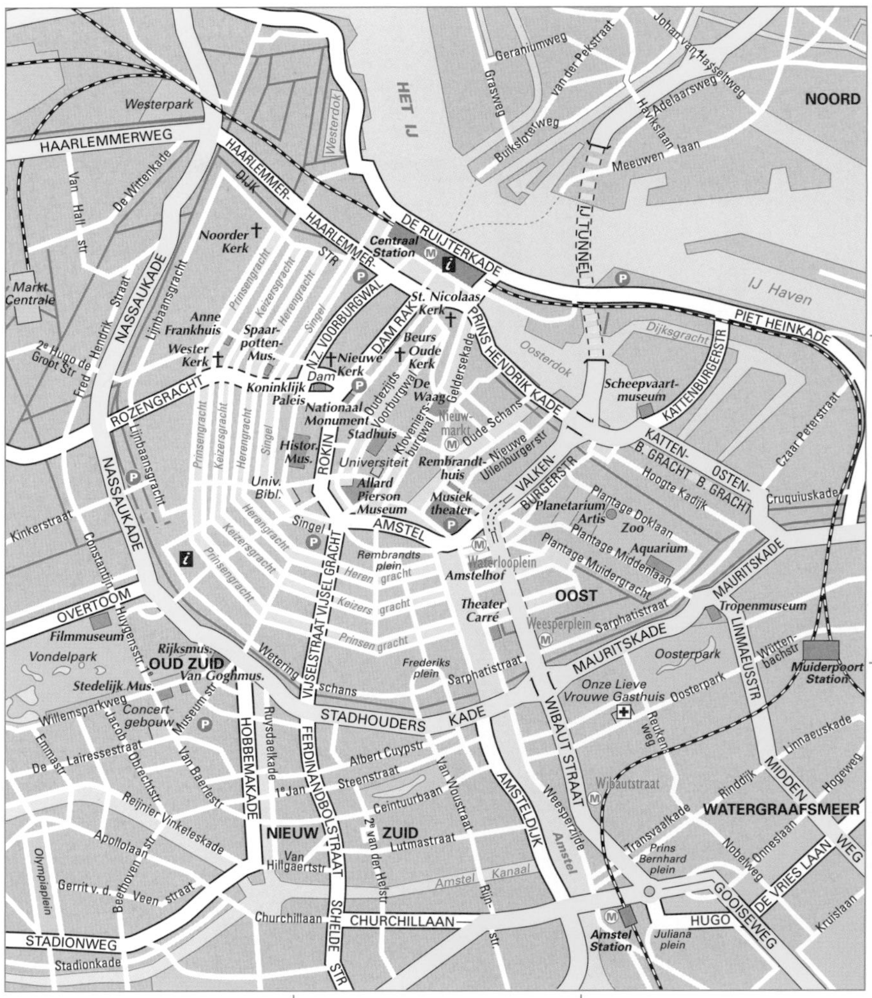

1 2 3

ATHENS

0 km 5
0 miles 3

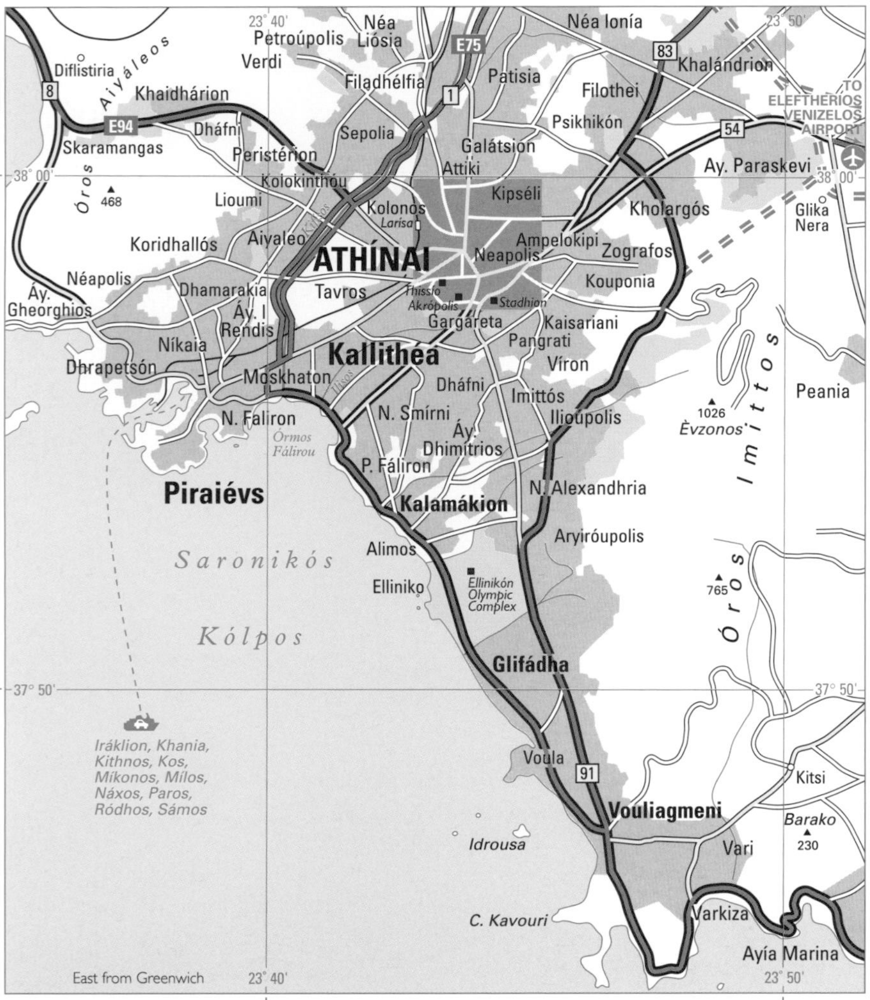

1 2 3

CENTRAL ATHENS

0 km 1
0 miles 0.5

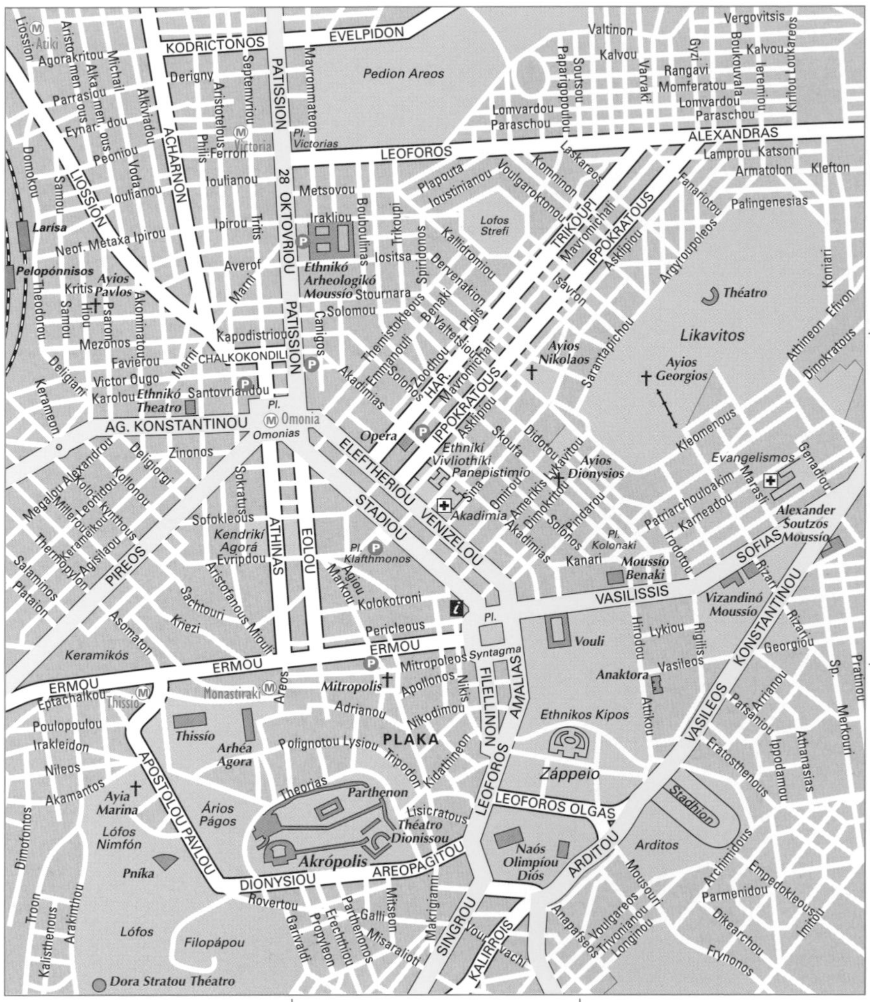

1 2 3

ATLANTA

0 km 5
0 miles 3

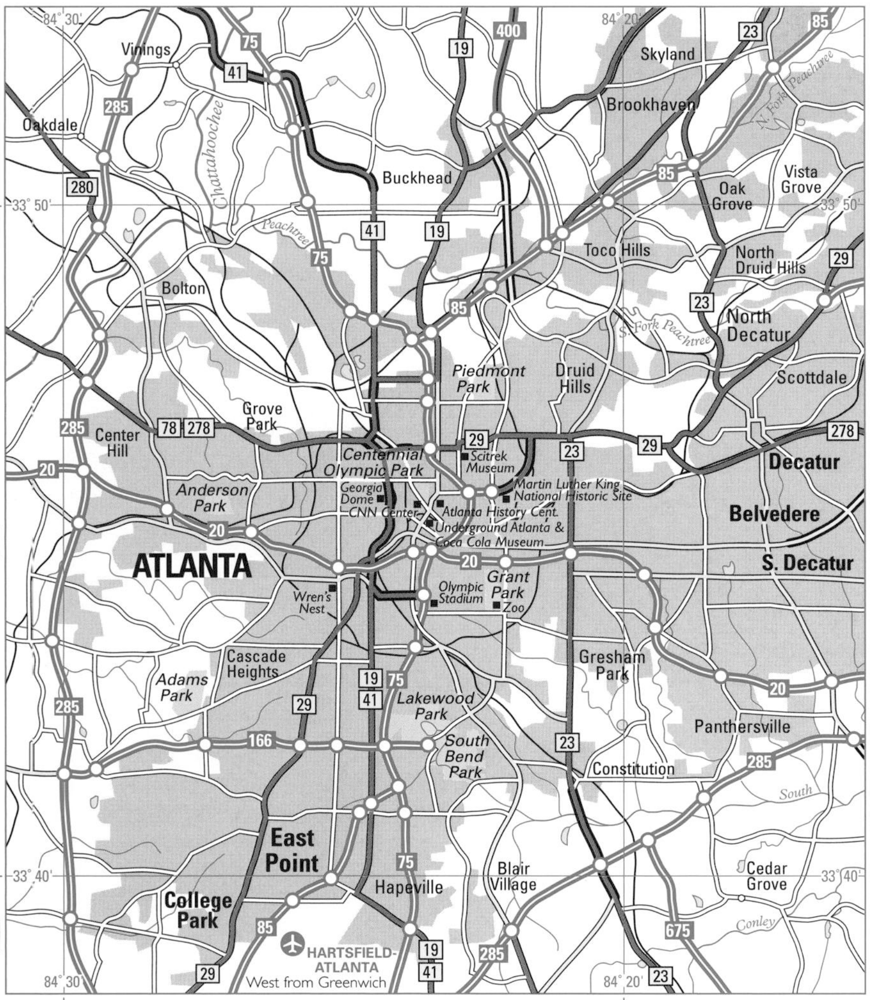

BAGHDAD

0 km 5
0 miles 3

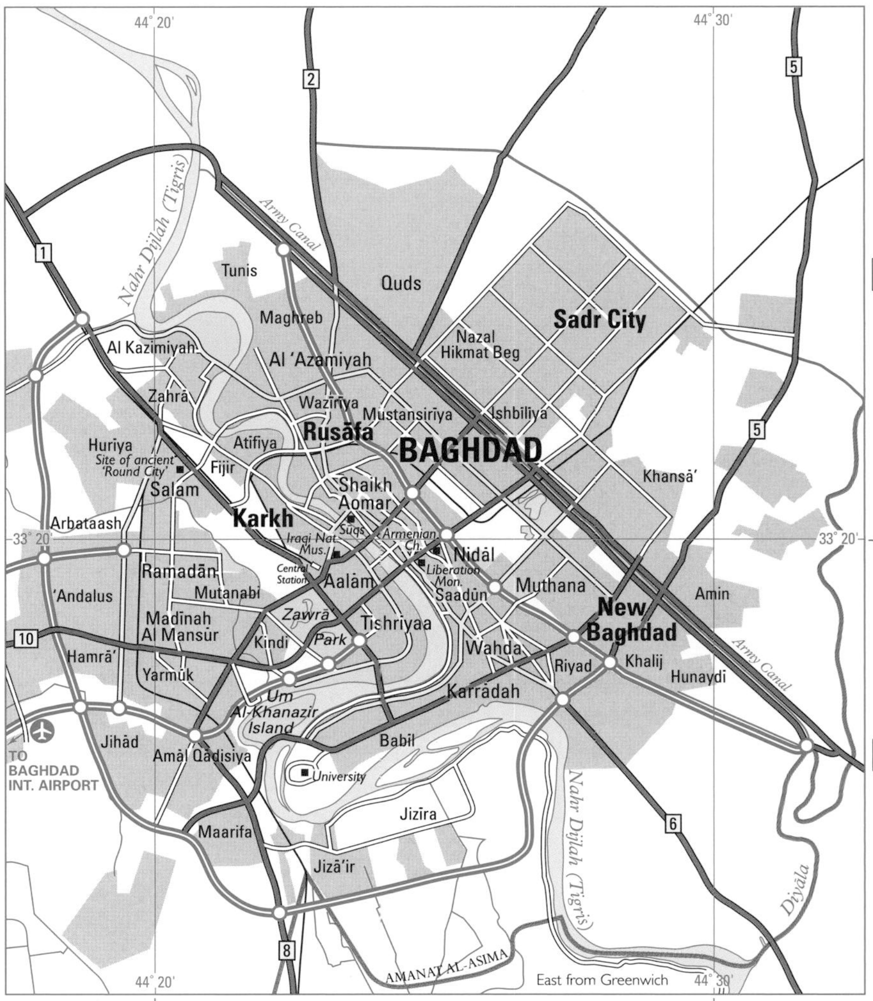

BANGKOK

0 km 5
0 miles 3

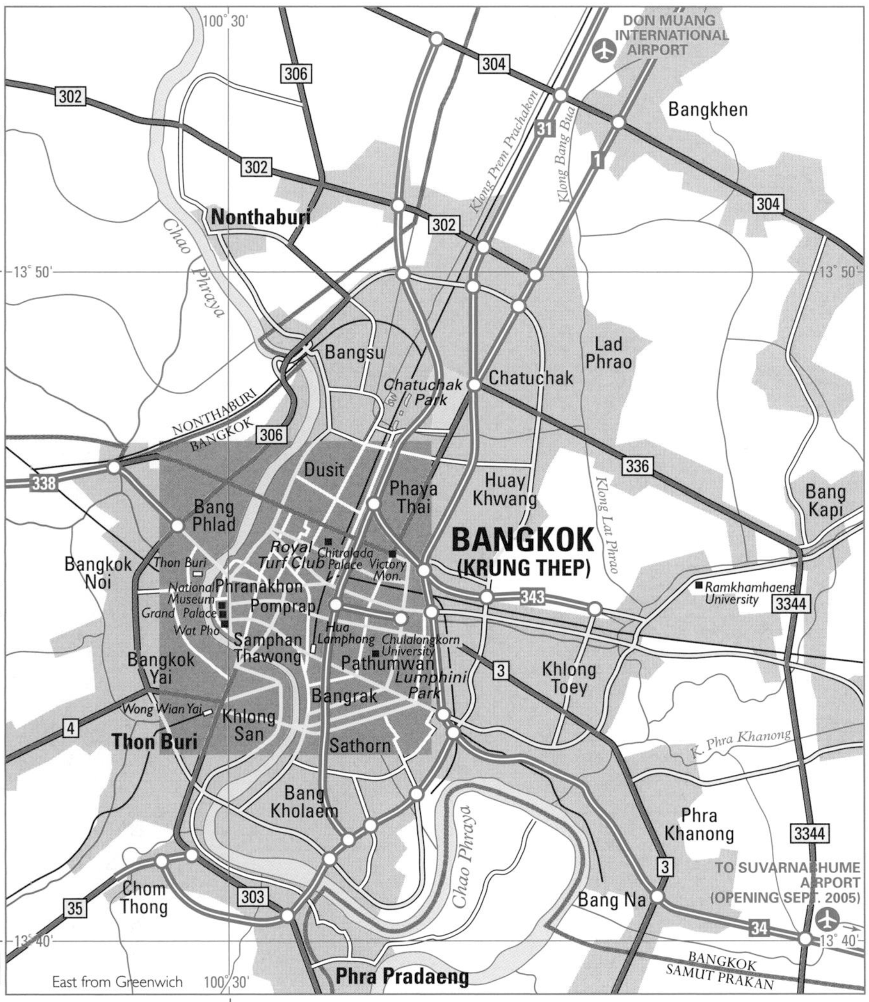

CENTRAL BANGKOK

0 km 2
0 miles 1

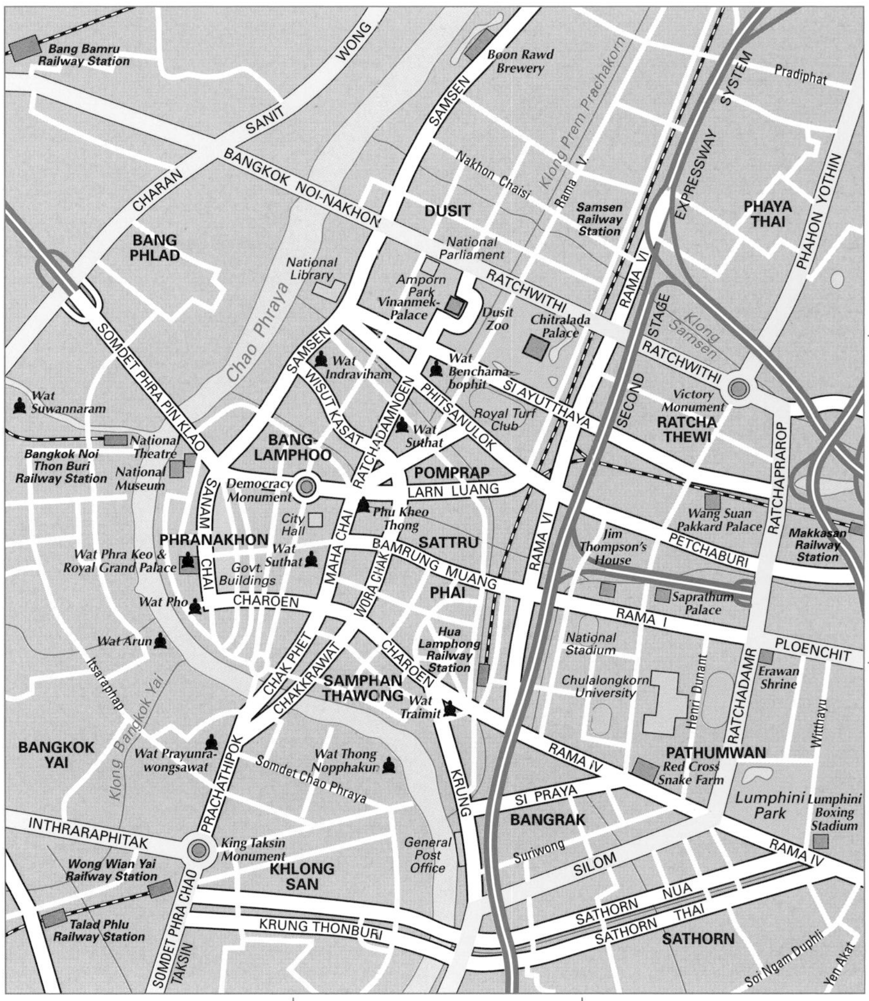

BARCELONA

0 km 5
0 miles 3

CENTRAL BARCELONA

0 km 1
0 miles 0.5

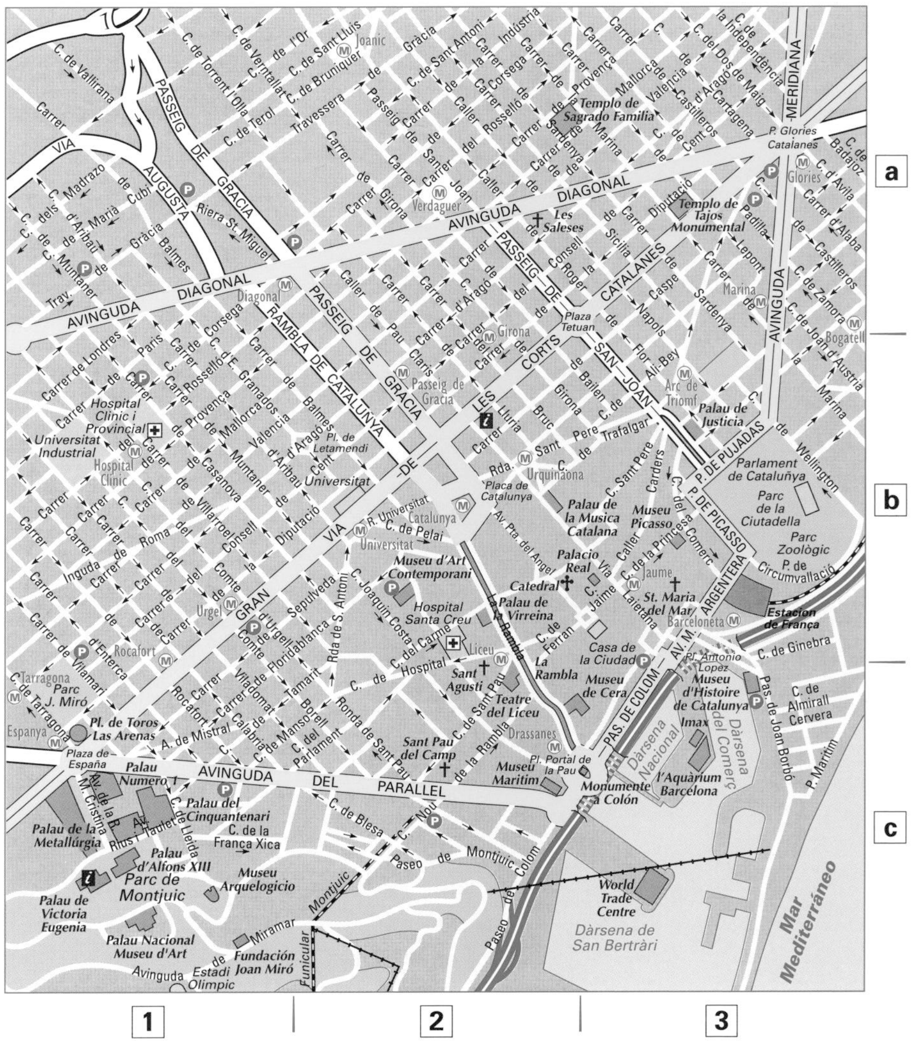

BEIJING

0 km 5
0 miles 3

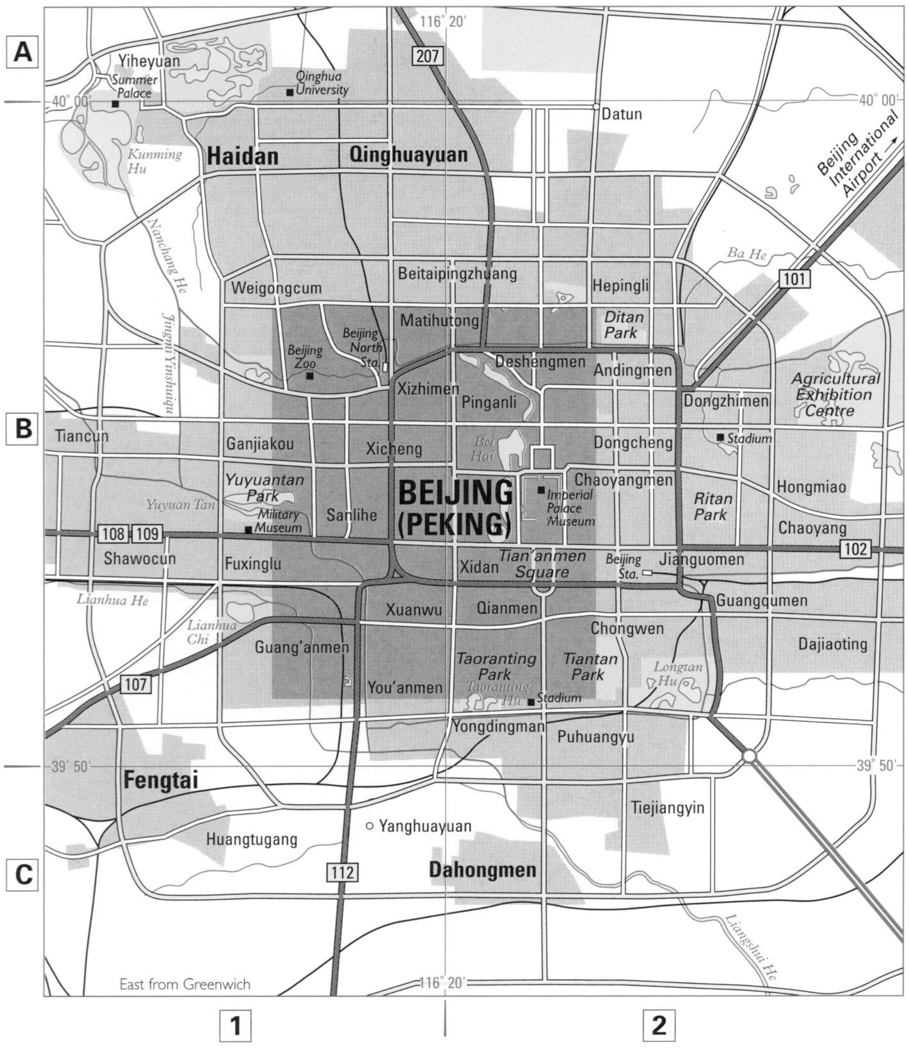

CENTRAL BEIJING

0 km 2
0 miles 1

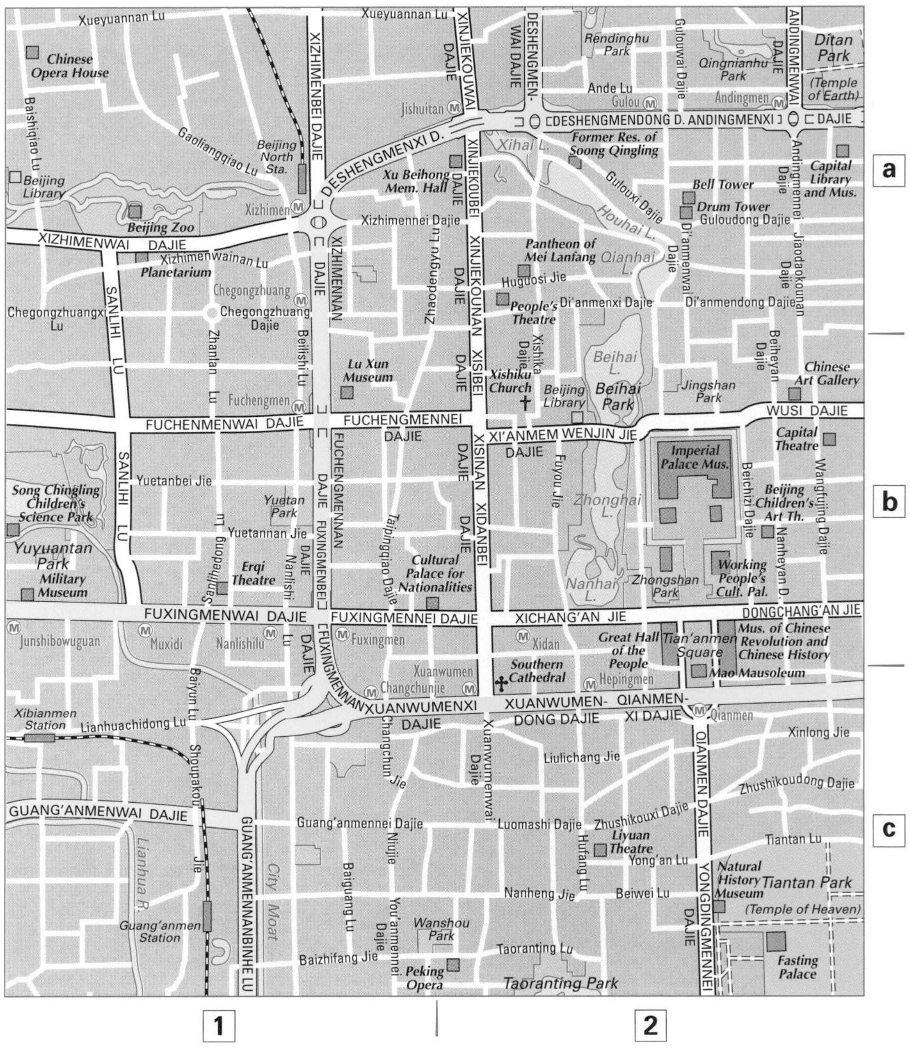

BERLIN

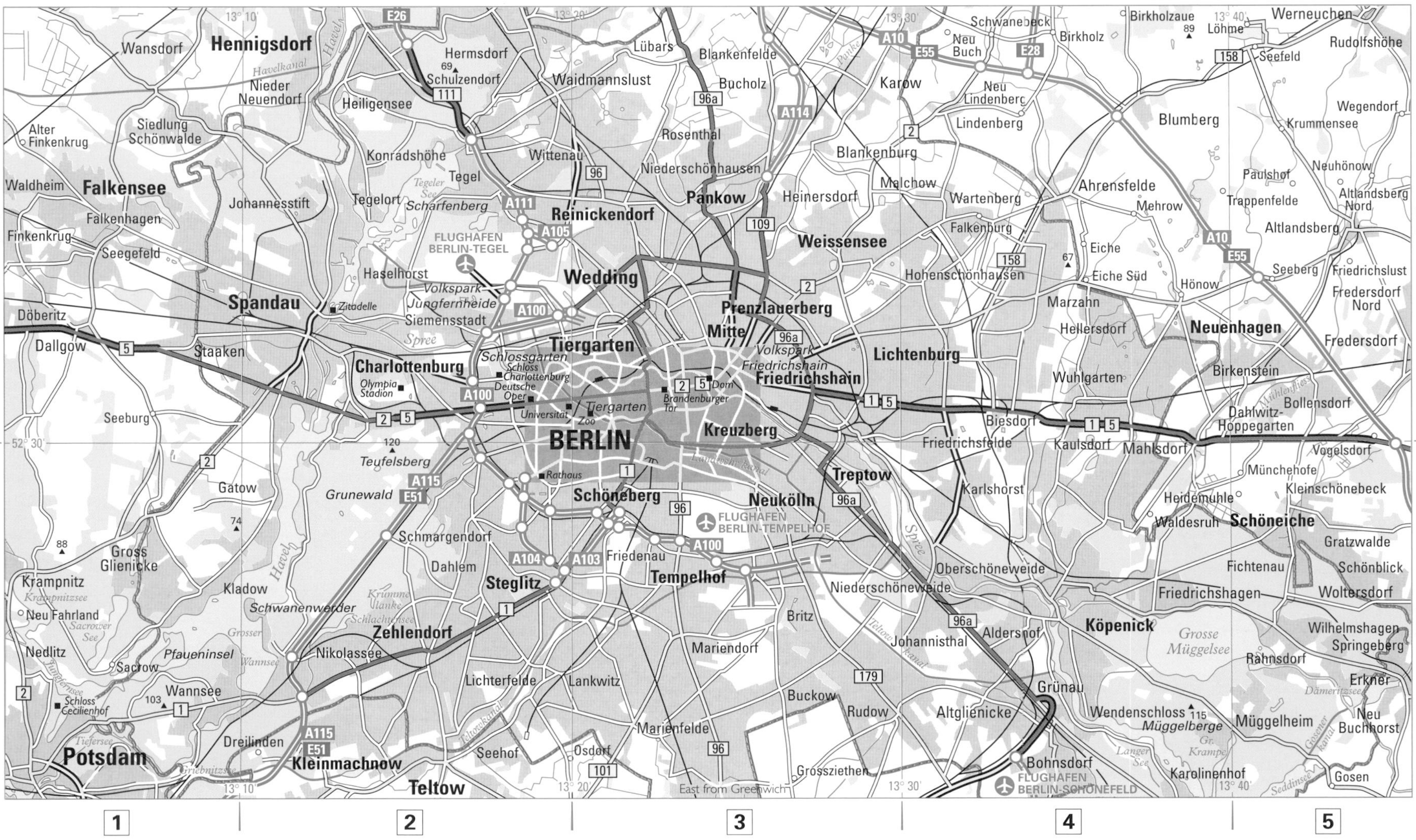
0 km 5
0 miles 3
Hennigsdorf
Wansdorf
Nieder Neuendorf
Heiligensee
Hermsdorf
Schulzendorf
Lübars
Waidmannslust
Blankenfelde
Bucholz
Karow
Schwanebeck
Neu Buch
Birkholz
Birkholzaue
Löhme
Werneuchen
Seefeld
Rudolfshöhe
Alter Finkenkrug
Siedlung Schönwalde
Konradshöhe
Tegel
Wittenau
Rosenthal
Niederschönhausen
Blankenburg
Neu Lindenberg
Lindenberg
Blumberg
Wegendorf
Krummensee
Waldheim
Falkensee
Johannesstift
Tegelort
Scharfenberg
Reinickendorf
Pankow
Heinersdorf
Malchow
Wartenberg
Ahrensfelde
Mehrow
Paulshof
Trappenfelde
Neuhönow
Altlandsberg Nord
Finkenkrug
Falkenhagen
Seegefeld
FLUGHAFEN BERLIN-TEGEL
Weissensee
Falkenburg
Eiche
Eiche Süd
Altlandsberg
Haselhorst
Volkspark Jungfernheide
Siemensstadt
Wedding
Hohenschönhausen
Hönow
Seeberg
Fredersdorf Nord
Friedrichslust
Spandau
Zitadelle
Prenzlauerberg
Marzahn
Döberitz
Dallgow
Staaken
Tiergarten
Mitte
Volkspark Friedrichshain
Friedrichshain
Lichtenberg
Hellersdorf
Neuenhagen
Fredersdorf
Charlottenburg
Schlossgarten
Schloss Charlottenburg
Olympia Stadion
Deutsche Oper
Universität
Zoo
Brandenburger Tor
Dom
Wuhlgarten
Birkenstein
Bollensdorf
Seeburg
BERLIN
Kreuzberg
Biesdorf
Friedrichsfelde
Kaulsdorf
Mahlsdorf
Dahlwitz-Hoppegarten
Vogelsdorf
Teufelsberg
Rathaus
Treptow
Karlshorst
Münchehofe
Kleinschönebeck
Gatow
Grunewald
Schöneberg
Neukölln
Heidemühle
Waldesruh
Schöneiche
FLUGHAFEN BERLIN-TEMPELHOF
Schmargendorf
Gratzwalde
Krampnitz
Gross Glienicke
Dahlem
Friedenau
Tempelhof
Oberschöneweide
Fichtenau
Schönblick
Kladow
Steglitz
Niederschöneweide
Friedrichshagen
Woltersdorf
Neu Fahrland
Schwanenwerder
Zehlendorf
Britz
Köpenick
Grosse Müggelsee
Wilhelmshagen
Nedlitz
Nikolassee
Pfaueninsel
Mariendorf
Johannisthal
Adlershof
Springeberg
Sacrow
Wannsee
Lichterfelde
Lankwitz
Buckow
Rudow
Grünau
Rahnsdorf
Erkner
Schloss Cecilienhof
Marienfelde
Altglienicke
Wendenschloss
Müggelberge
Müggelheim
Neu Buchhorst
Potsdam
Dreilinden
Kleinmachnow
Seehof
Osdorf
Grossziethen
Bohnsdorf
FLUGHAFEN BERLIN-SCHÖNEFELD
Karolinenhof
Gosen
Teltow
East from Greenwich
A
B
1
2
3
4
5

CENTRAL BERLIN

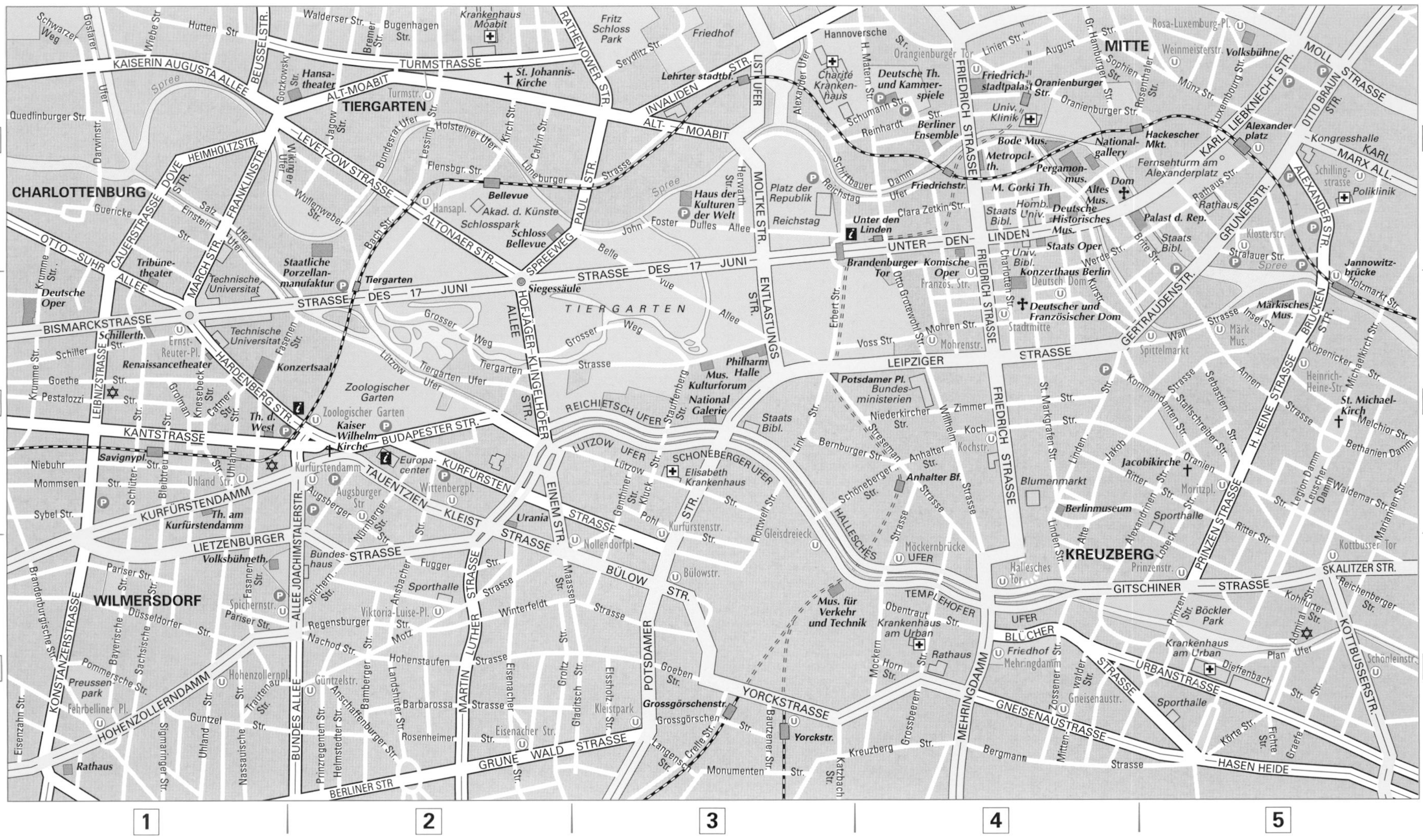
0 km 1
0 miles 0.5
MITTE
TIERGARTEN
CHARLOTTENBURG
WILMERSDORF
KREUZBERG
KAISERIN AUGUSTA ALLEE
TURMSTRASSE
ALT-MOABIT
INVALIDEN STR.
Hansa-theater
St. Johannis-Kirche
Lehrter stadtbf.
Charité Krankenhaus
Deutsche Th. und Kammer-spiele
Friedrich-stadtpalast
Oranienburger Str.
Volksbühne
Bellevue
Akad. d. Künste
Schloss Bellevue
Haus der Kulturen der Welt
Platz der Republik
Reichstag
Berliner Ensemble
Bode Mus.
Metropol-th.
Pergamon-mus.
National-gallery
Hackescher Mkt.
Alexander platz
Fernsehturm am Alexanderplatz
Friedrichstr.
M. Gorki Th.
Altes Mus.
Dom
Palast d. Rep.
Unter den Linden
UNTER DEN LINDEN
Deutsches Historisches Mus.
Staats Oper
Brandenburger Tor
Komische Oper
Konzerthaus Berlin
Deutscher und Französischer Dom
STRASSE DES 17 JUNI
Siegessäule
TIERGARTEN
Staatliche Porzellan-manufaktur
Tribüne-theater
Technische Universität
Deutsche Oper
BISMARCKSTRASSE
Schillerth.
Renaissancetheater
Konzertsaal
HARDENBERG STR.
Zoologischer Garten
Th. d. West
Kaiser Wilhelm Kirche
Europa-center
Philharm Halle
Mus. Kulturforum
National Galerie
Staats Bibl.
LEIPZIGER STRASSE
Potsdamer Pl.
Bundes-ministerien
Anhalter Bf.
KANTSTRASSE
BUDAPESTER STR.
REICHPIETSCH UFER
KURFÜRSTENDAMM
Th. am Kurfürstendamm
TAUENTZIEN
KURFÜRSTEN
Urania
Elisabeth Krankenhaus
SCHÖNEBERGER UFER
Jannowitz-brücke
Märkisches Mus.
St. Michael-Kirch
Jacobikirche
Blumenmarkt
Berlinmuseum
Spittelmarkt
GITSCHINER STRASSE
SKALITZER STR.
Volksbühneth.
LIETZENBURGER STRASSE
BÜLOW STR.
Mus. für Verkehr und Technik
Krankenhaus am Urban
Böckler Park
Krankenhaus am Urban
HOHENZOLLERNDAMM
YORCKSTRASSE
GNEISENAUSTRASSE
MEHRINGDAMM
URBANSTRASSE
Grossgörschenstr.
Yorckstr.
Rathaus
GRUNE WALD STRASSE
BERLINER STR.
HASEN HEIDE
a
b
c
1
2
3
4
5

BOSTON

0 km 5
0 miles 3

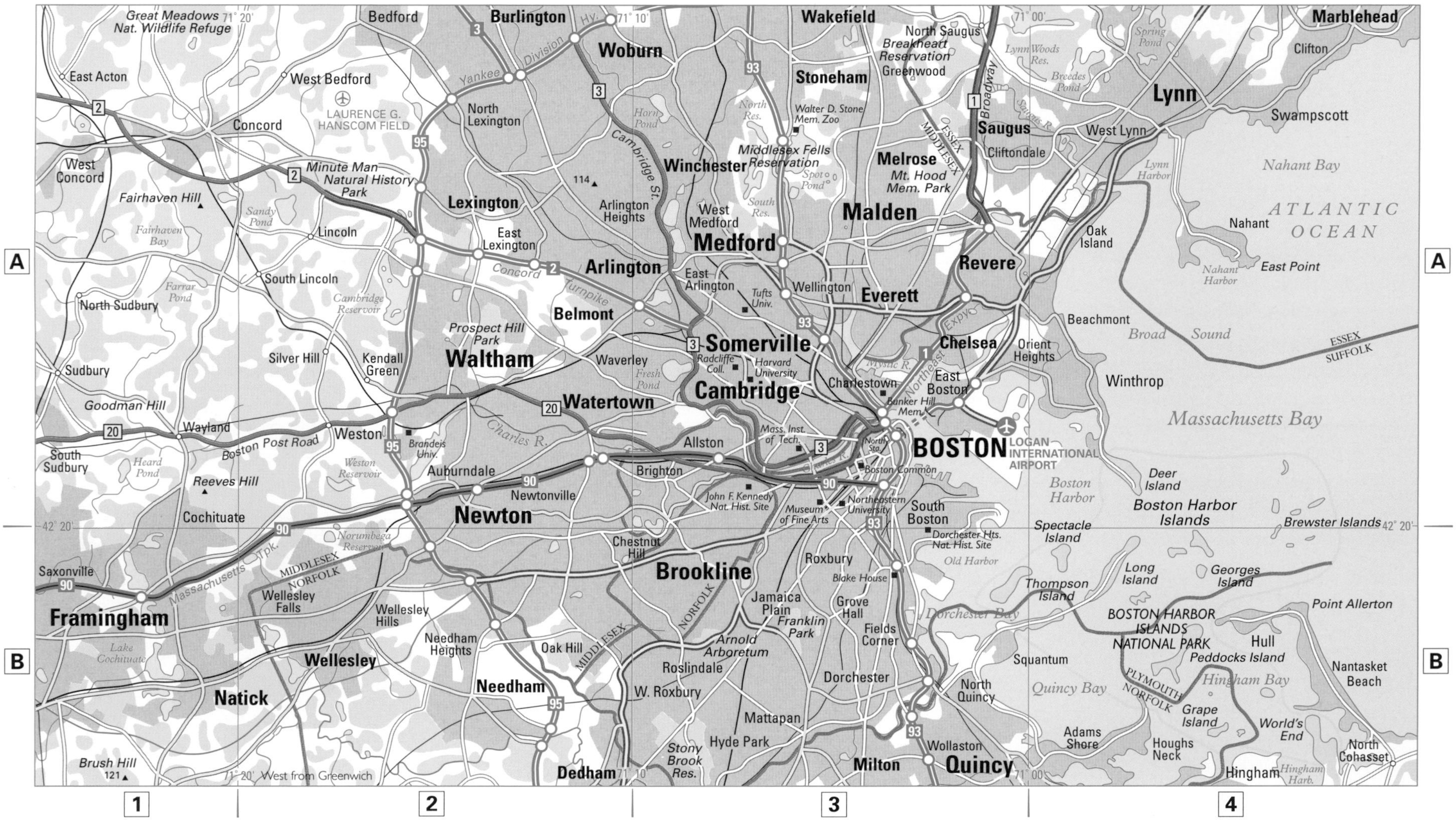

BRUSSELS

0 km 5
0 miles 3

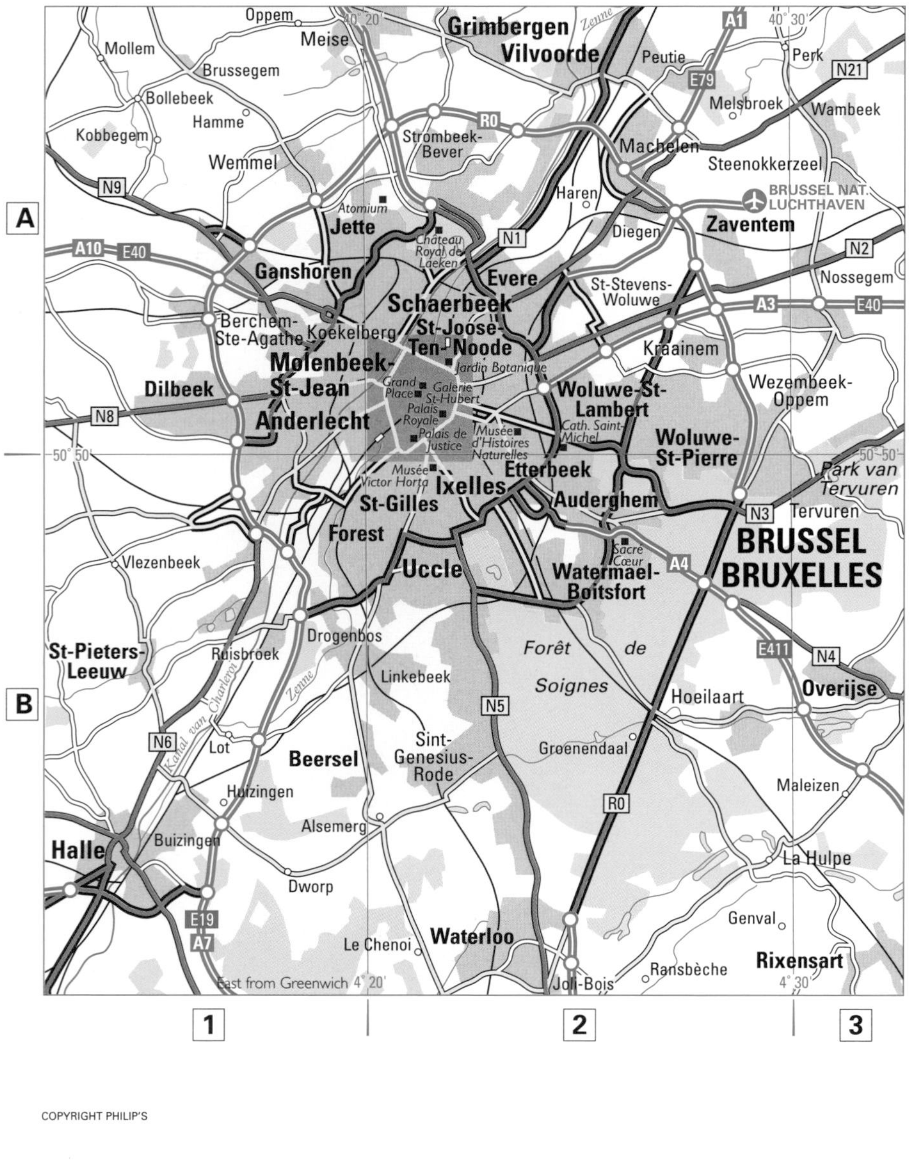

CENTRAL BRUSSELS

0 km 1
0 miles 0.5

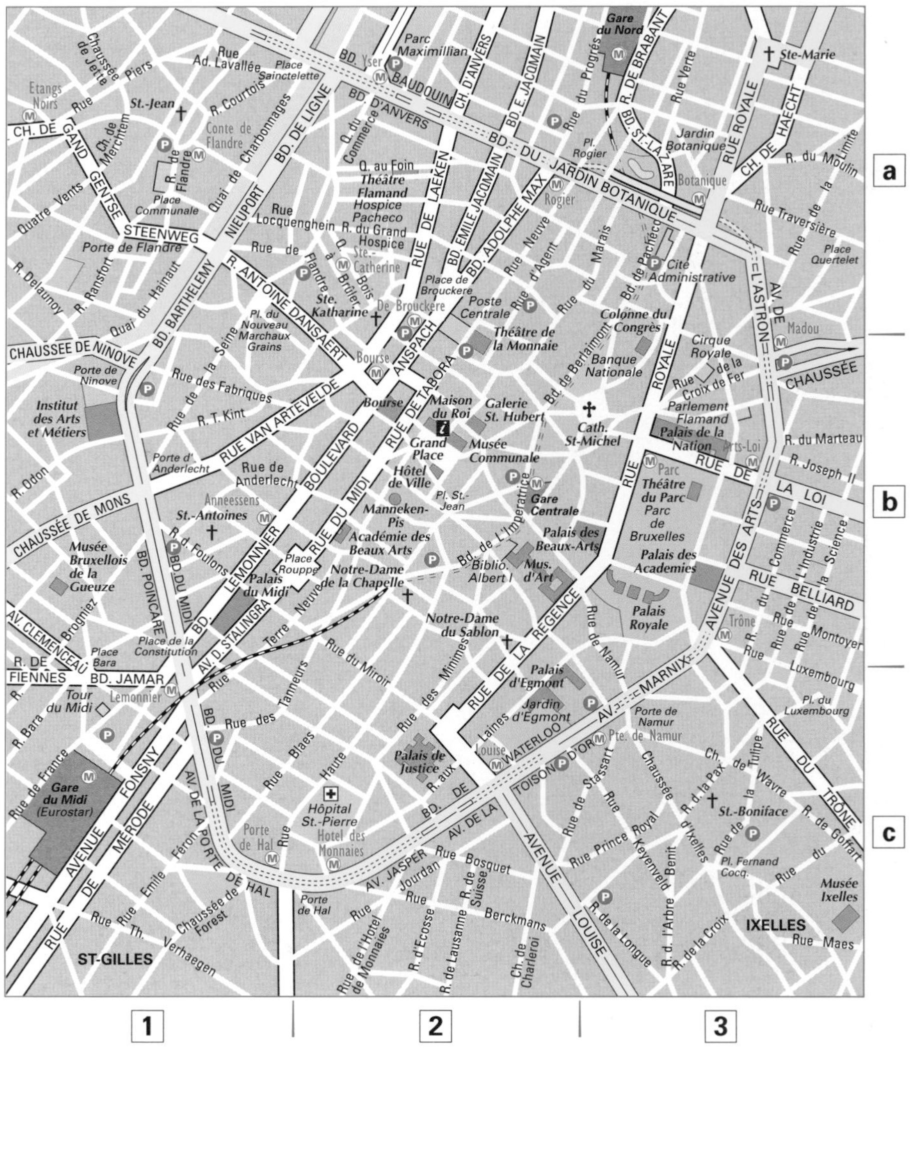

BUDAPEST

0 km 5 / 0 miles 3

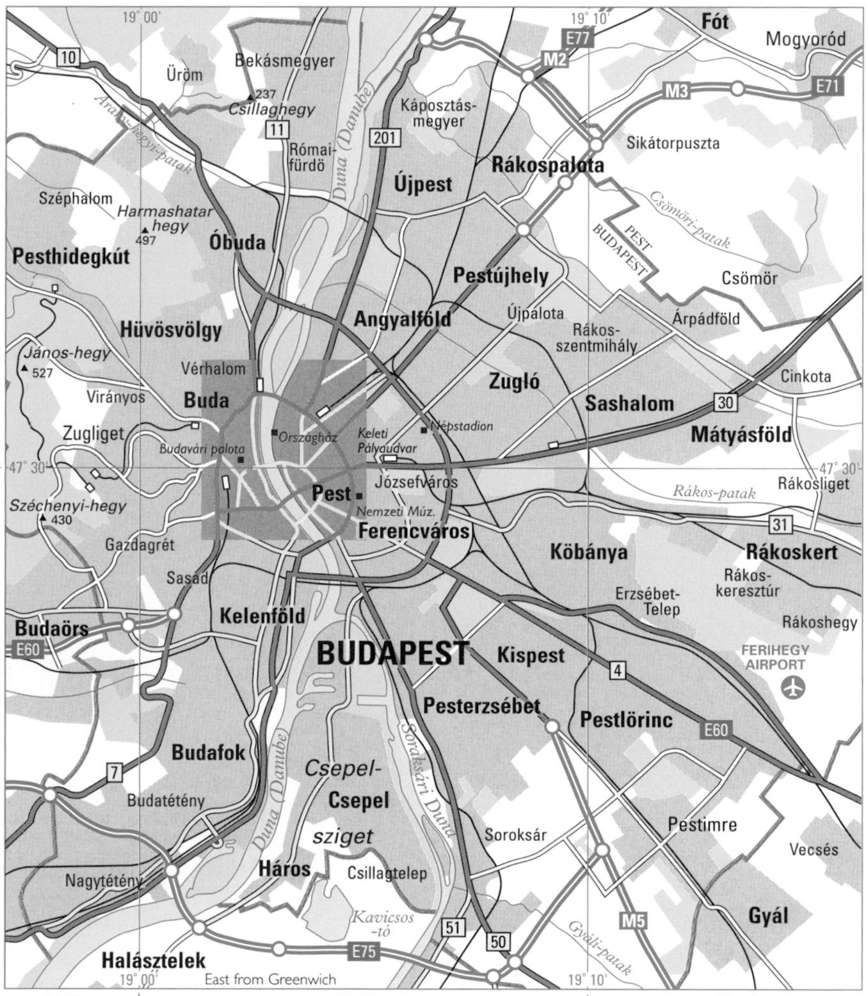

CENTRAL BUDAPEST

0 km 1 / 0 miles 0.5

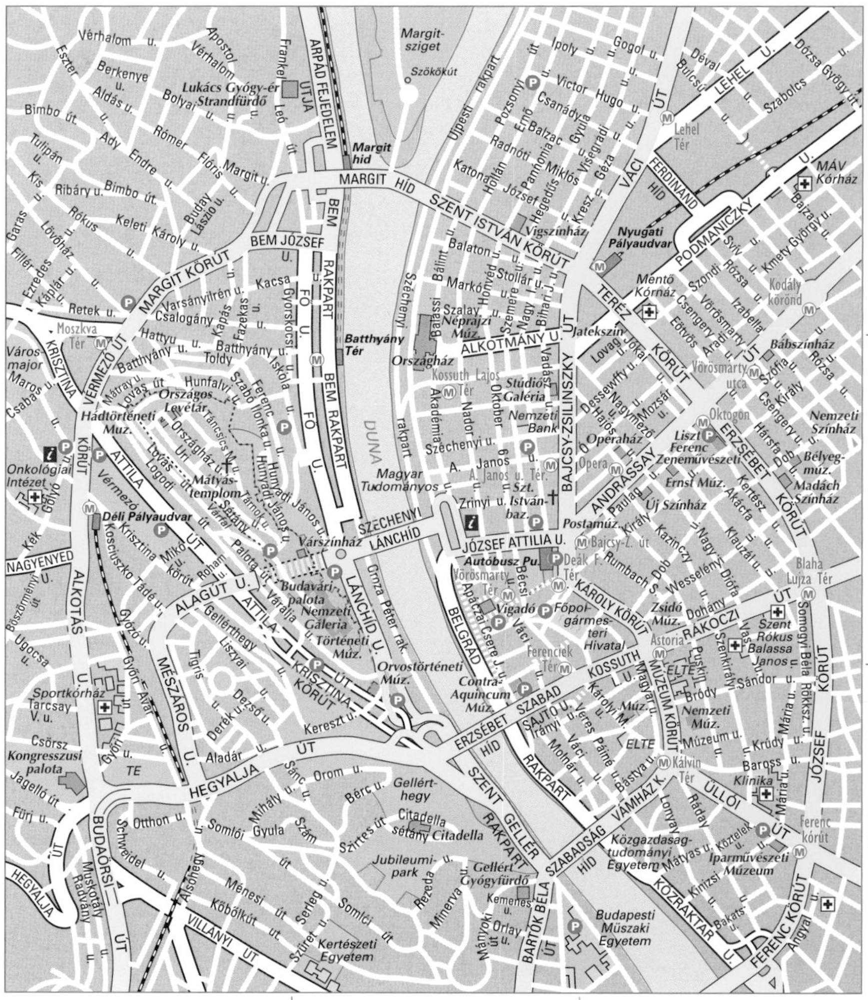

BUENOS AIRES

0 km 5 / 0 miles 3

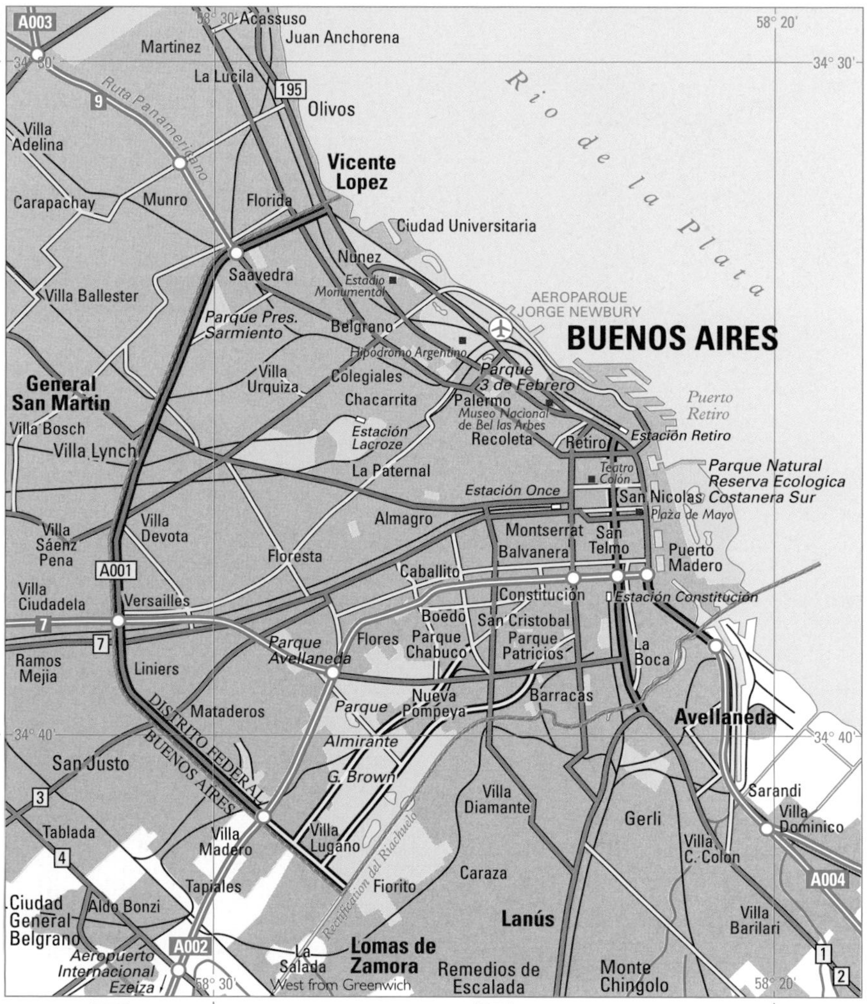

CAIRO

0 km 5 / 0 miles 3

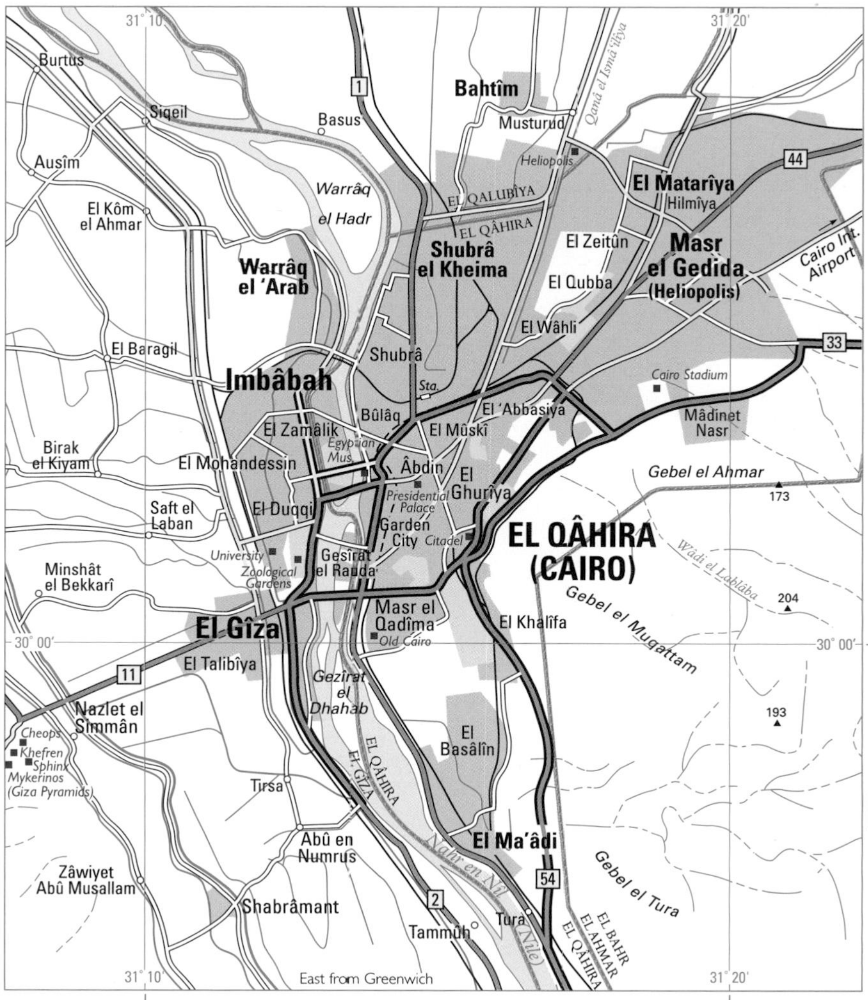

CALCUTTA (KOLKATA)

0 km 5
0 miles 3

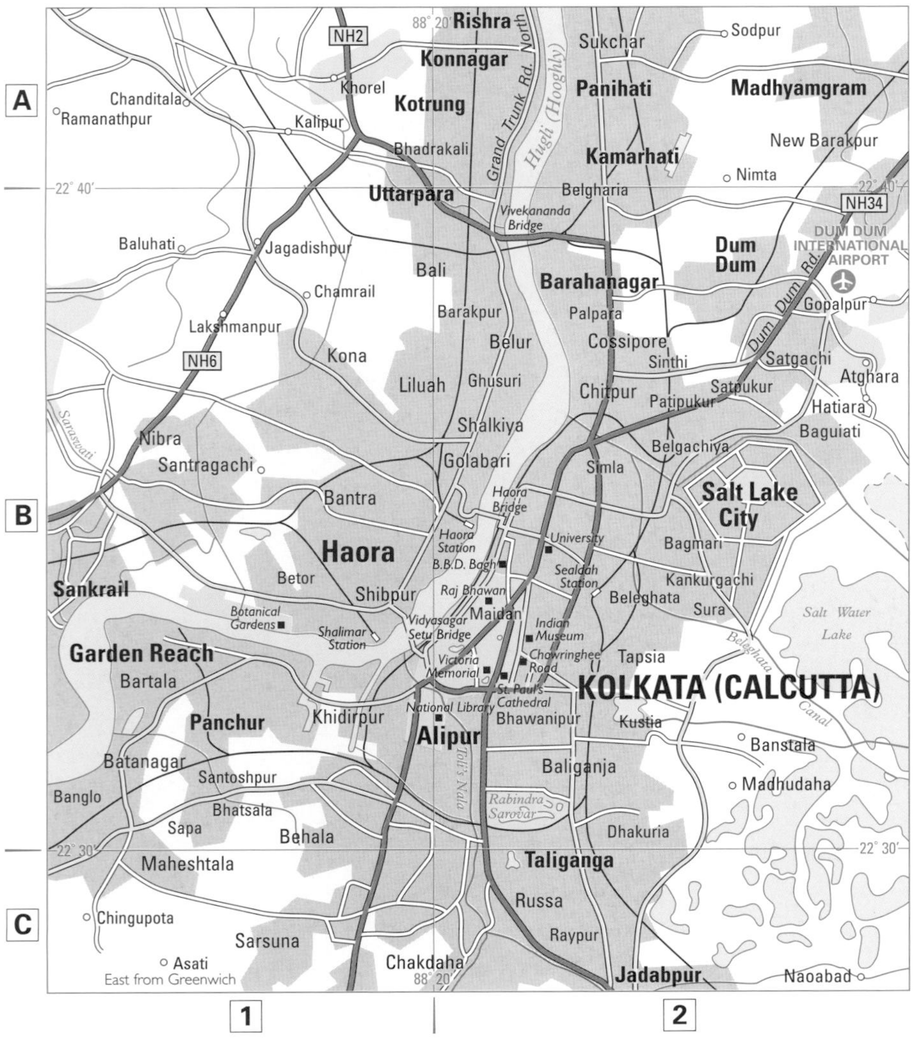

CANTON

0 km 5
0 miles 3

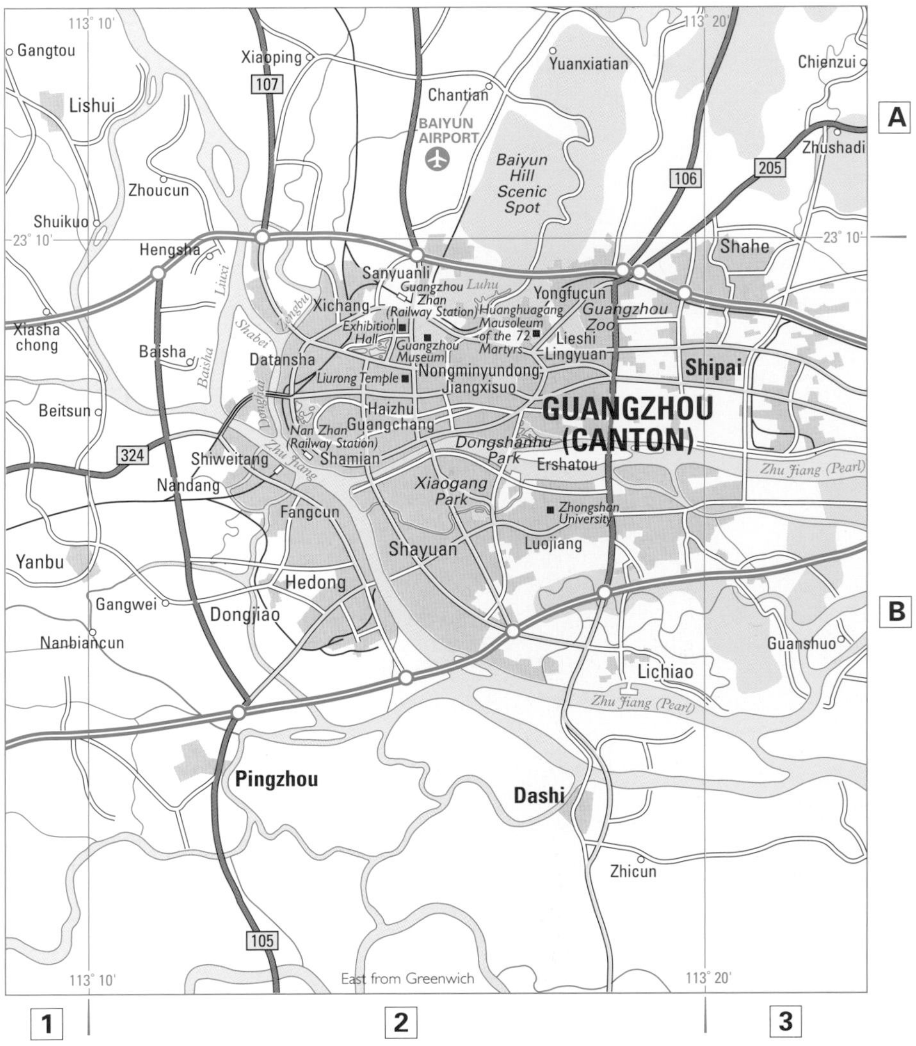

CAPE TOWN

0 km 5
0 miles 3

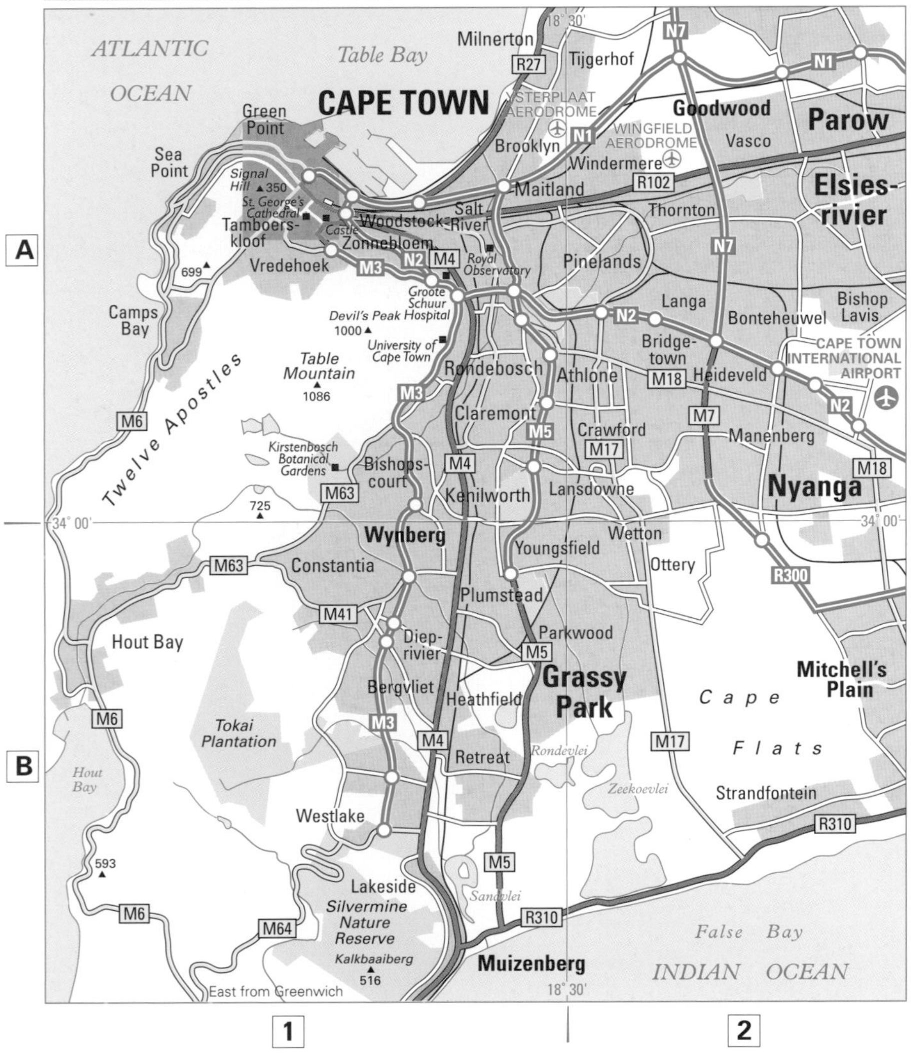

CENTRAL CAPE TOWN

0 km 0.5
0 miles 0.25

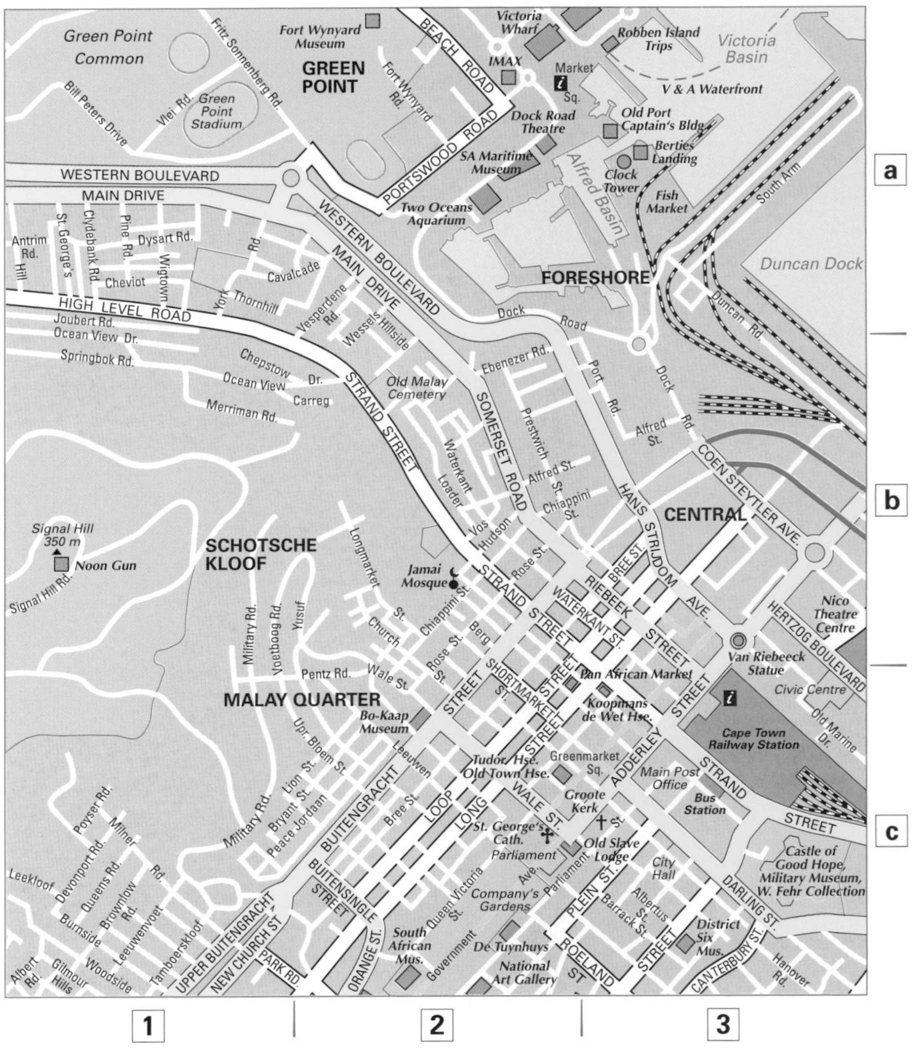

CHICAGO

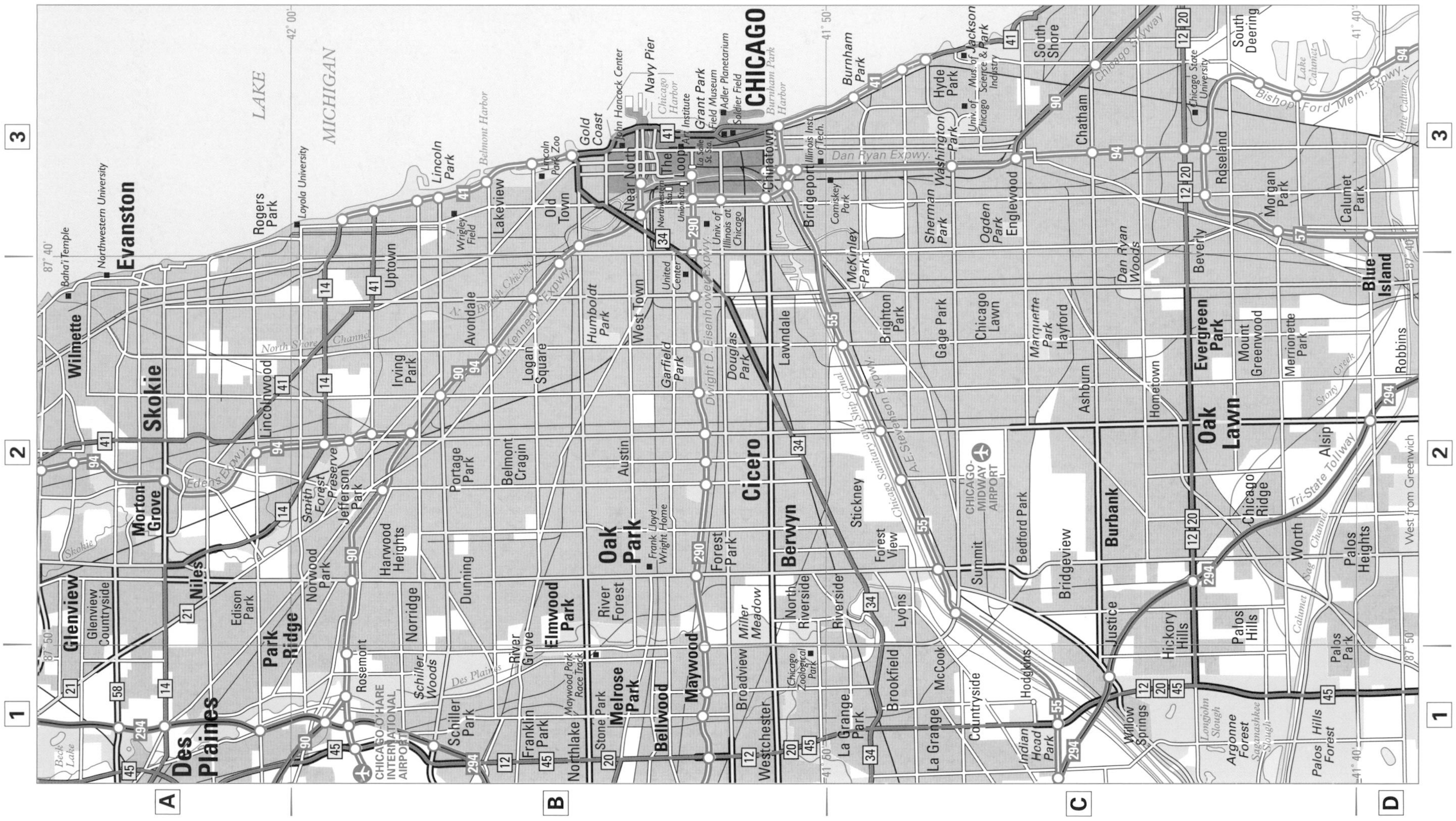
0 km 5
0 miles 3
LAKE
MICHIGAN
Evanston
Wilmette
Skokie
Morton Grove
Glenview
Niles
Park Ridge
Des Plaines
Rogers Park
Uptown
Lincoln Park
Lakeview
Old Town
Gold Coast
Near North
The Loop
CHICAGO
Chinatown
Bridgeport
Navy Pier
Grant Park
Hyde Park
Jackson Park
South Shore
Chatham
Englewood
Washington Park
Beverly
Roseland
Morgan Park
Calumet Park
Blue Island
Evergreen Park
Oak Lawn
Burbank
Cicero
Berwyn
Oak Park
Austin
Humboldt Park
Logan Square
Irving Park
Avondale
Portage Park
Belmont Cragin
Harwood Heights
Norridge
Dunning
Elmwood Park
River Forest
Melrose Park
Maywood
Bellwood
Forest Park
Westchester
Riverside
Brookfield
La Grange
La Grange Park
Lyons
McCook
Summit
Countryside
Hodgkins
Stickney
Bridgeview
Justice
Hickory Hills
Palos Hills
Palos Heights
Palos Park
Worth
Chicago Ridge
Alsip
Robbins
Garfield Park
Douglas Park
Lawndale
McKinley Park
Brighton Park
Gage Park
Chicago Lawn
Marquette Park
Ashburn
Hometown
Mount Greenwood
Merrionette Park
South Deering
Sherman Park
Ogden Park
Burnham Park
Rosemont
Franklin Park
Northlake
Stone Park
Schiller Park
River Grove
Edison Park
Norwood Park
Jefferson Park
Lincolnwood
CHICAGO O'HARE INTERNATIONAL AIRPORT
CHICAGO MIDWAY AIRPORT
A
B
C
D
1
2
3

CENTRAL CHICAGO

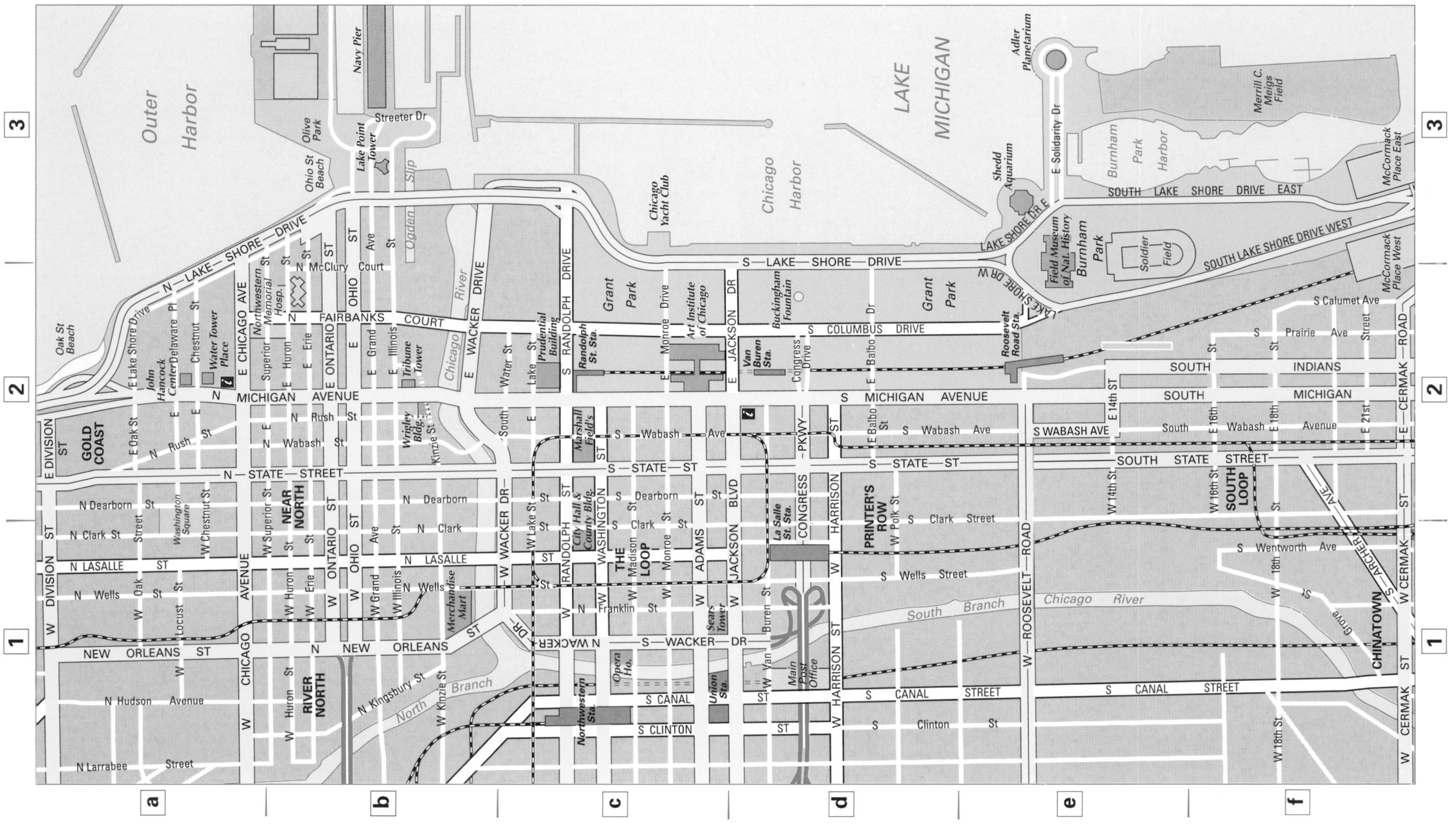
0 km 1
0 miles 0.5
LAKE MICHIGAN
Outer Harbor
Chicago Harbor
Burnham Park Harbor
Navy Pier
Adler Planetarium
Shedd Aquarium
Merrill C. Meigs Field
McCormack Place East
McCormack Place West
Field Museum of Nat. History
Soldier Field
Burnham Park
Grant Park
Buckingham Fountain
Art Institute of Chicago
Chicago Yacht Club
GOLD COAST
NEAR NORTH
RIVER NORTH
THE LOOP
PRINTER'S ROW
SOUTH LOOP
CHINATOWN
N LAKE SHORE DRIVE
S LAKE SHORE DRIVE
MICHIGAN AVENUE
STATE STREET
WACKER DRIVE
ROOSEVELT ROAD
CERMAK ROAD
CONGRESS PKWY
Chicago River
South Branch
North Branch
Sears Tower
Union Sta.
Northwestern Sta.
Main Post Office
a
b
c
d
e
f
1
2
3

COPENHAGEN

0 km 5
0 miles 3

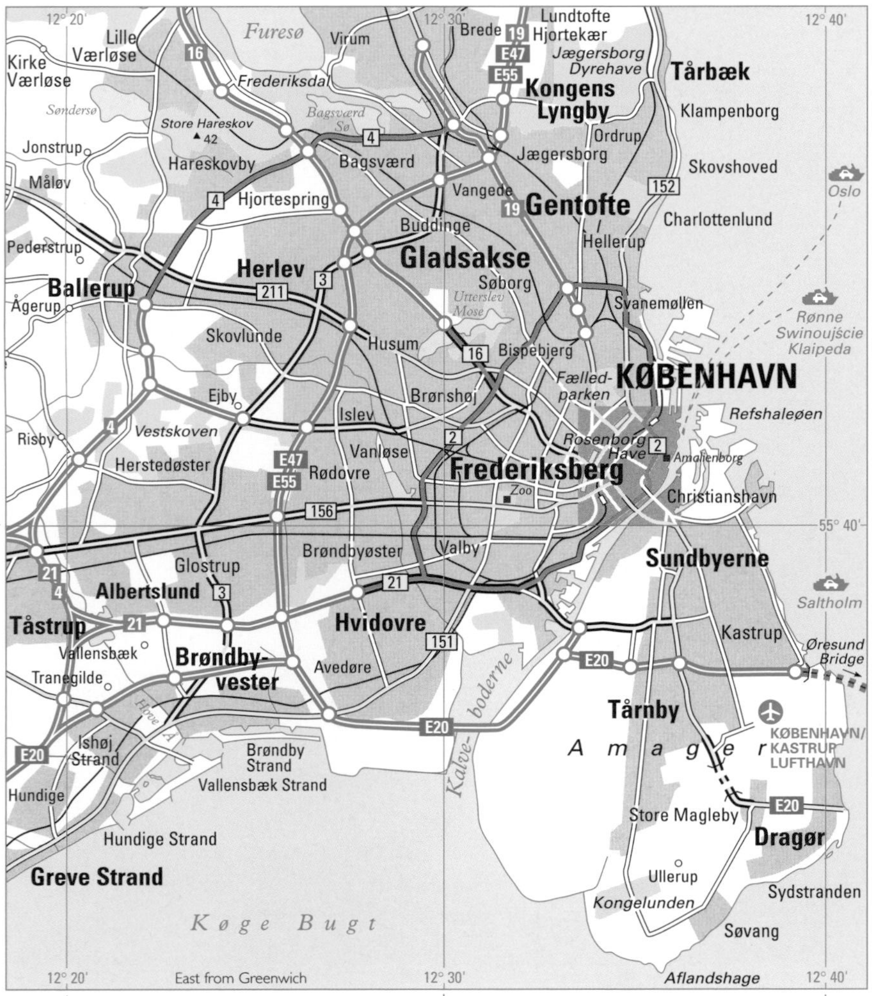

CENTRAL COPENHAGEN

0 km 0.5
0 miles 0.25

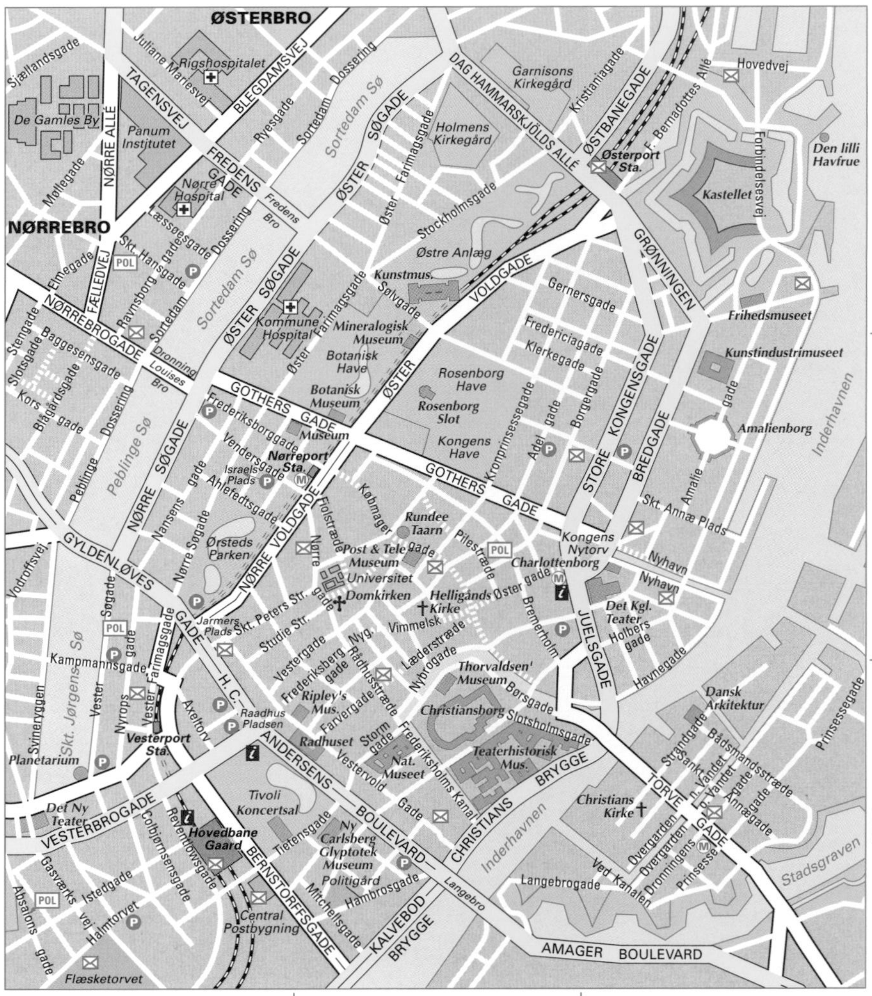

DELHI

0 km 5
0 miles 3

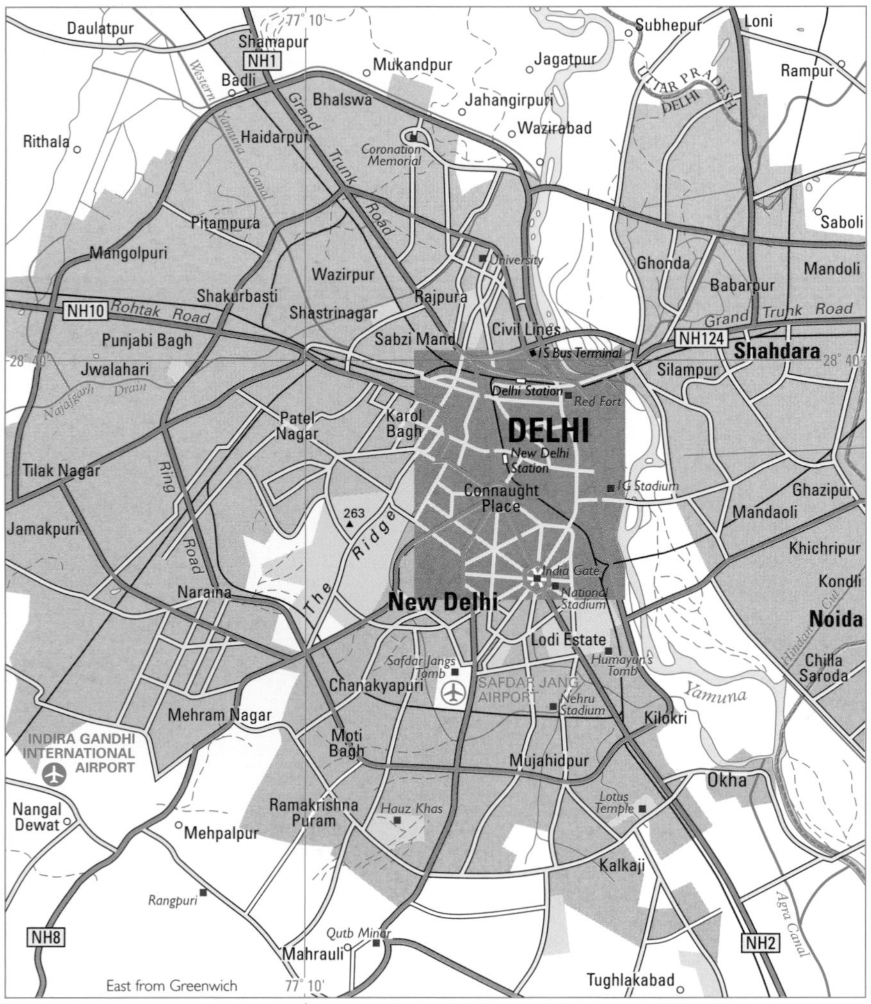

CENTRAL DELHI

0 km 2
0 miles 1

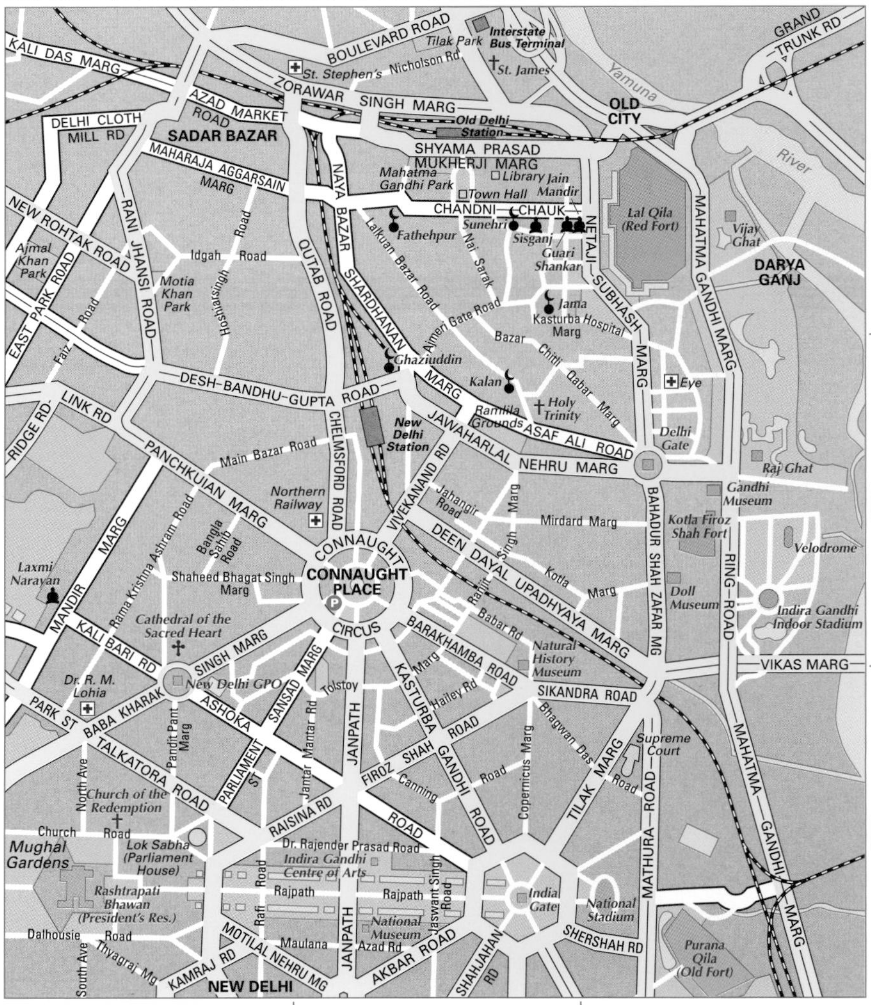

DUBLIN

0 km 5
0 miles 3

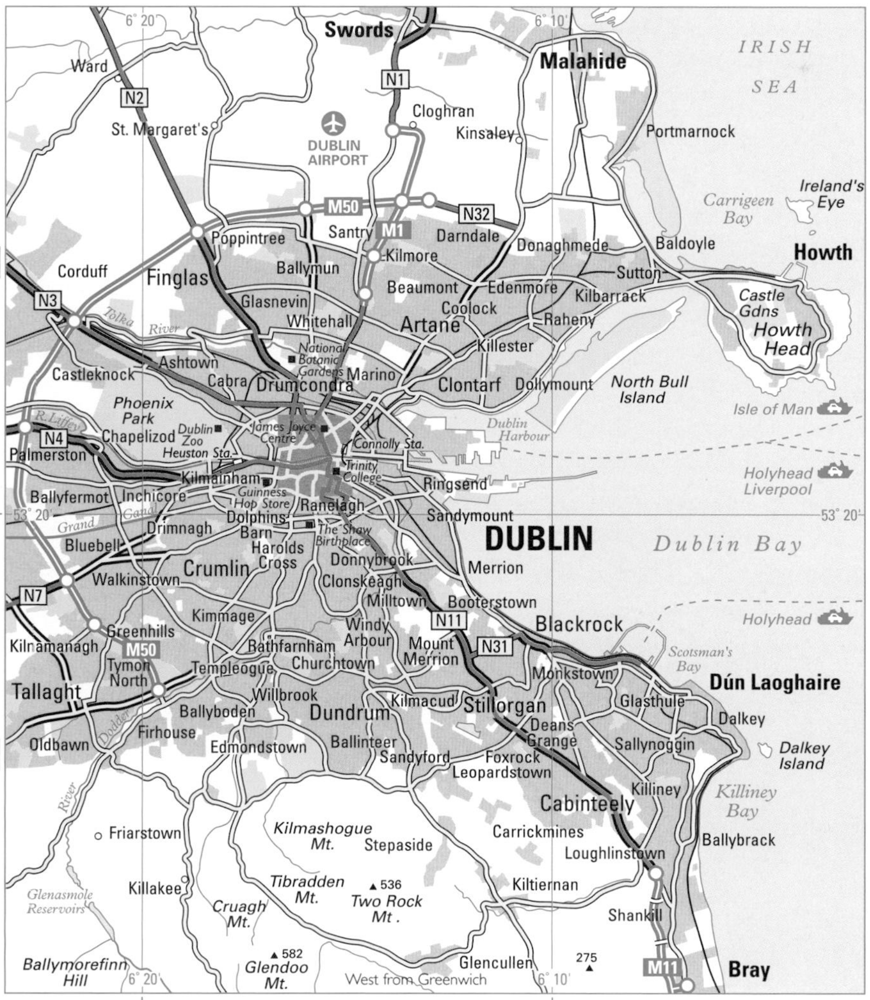

CENTRAL DUBLIN

0 km 0.5
0 miles 0.25

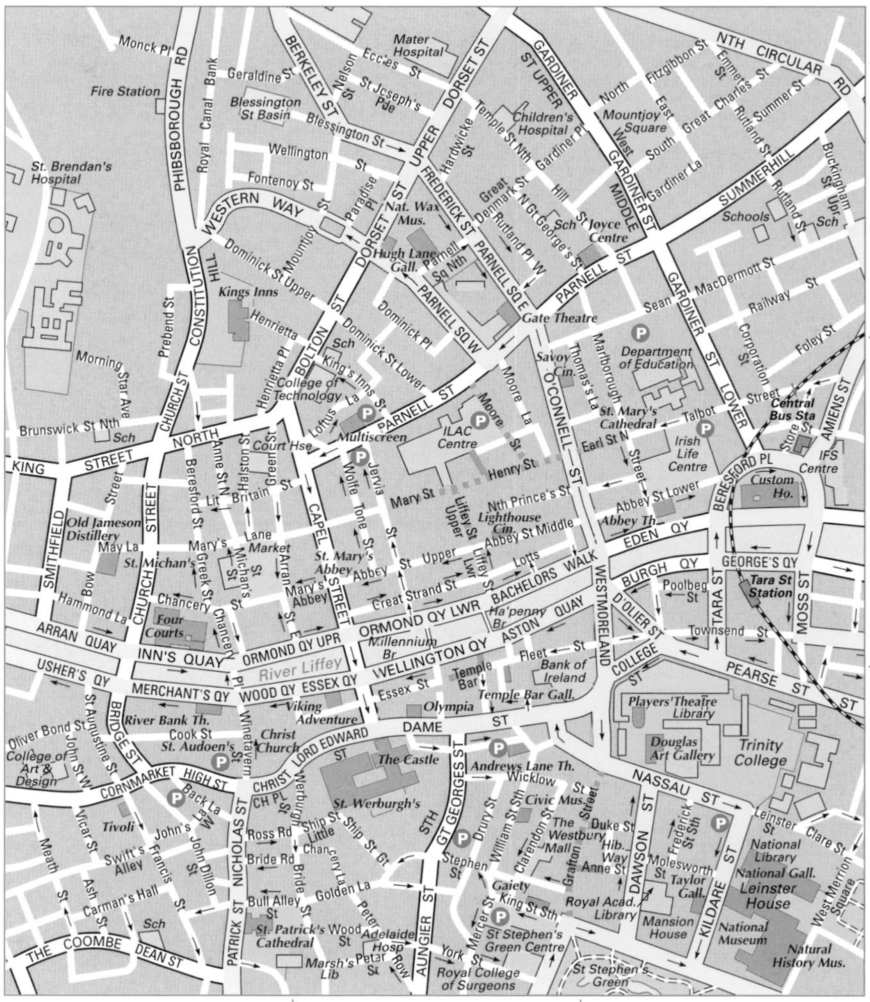

EDINBURGH

0 km 5
0 miles 3

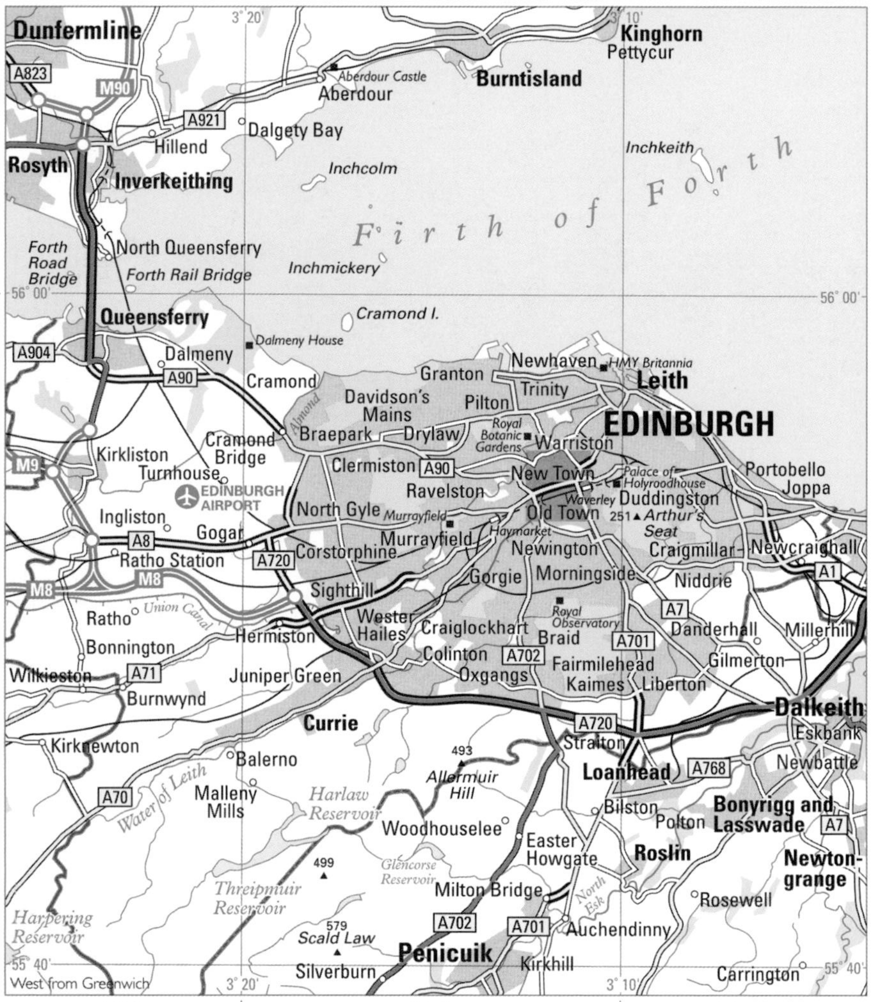

CENTRAL EDINBURGH

0 km 0.5
0 miles 0.25

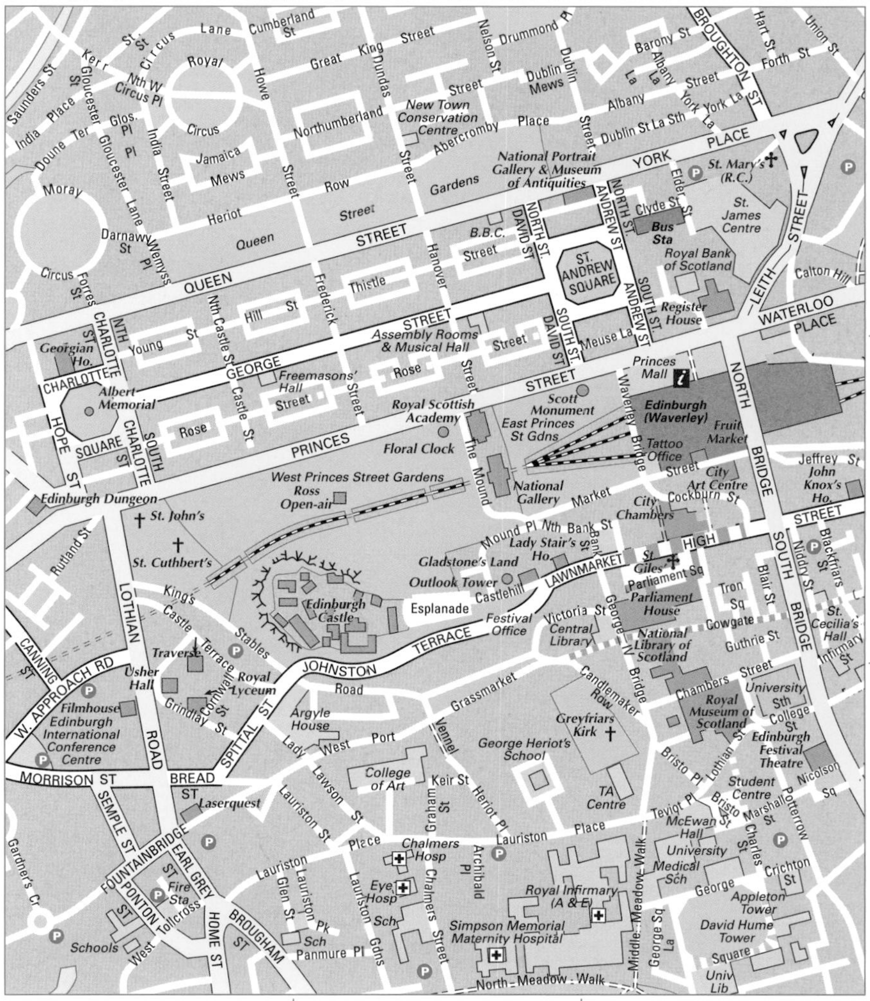

HELSINKI

0 km 5
0 miles 3

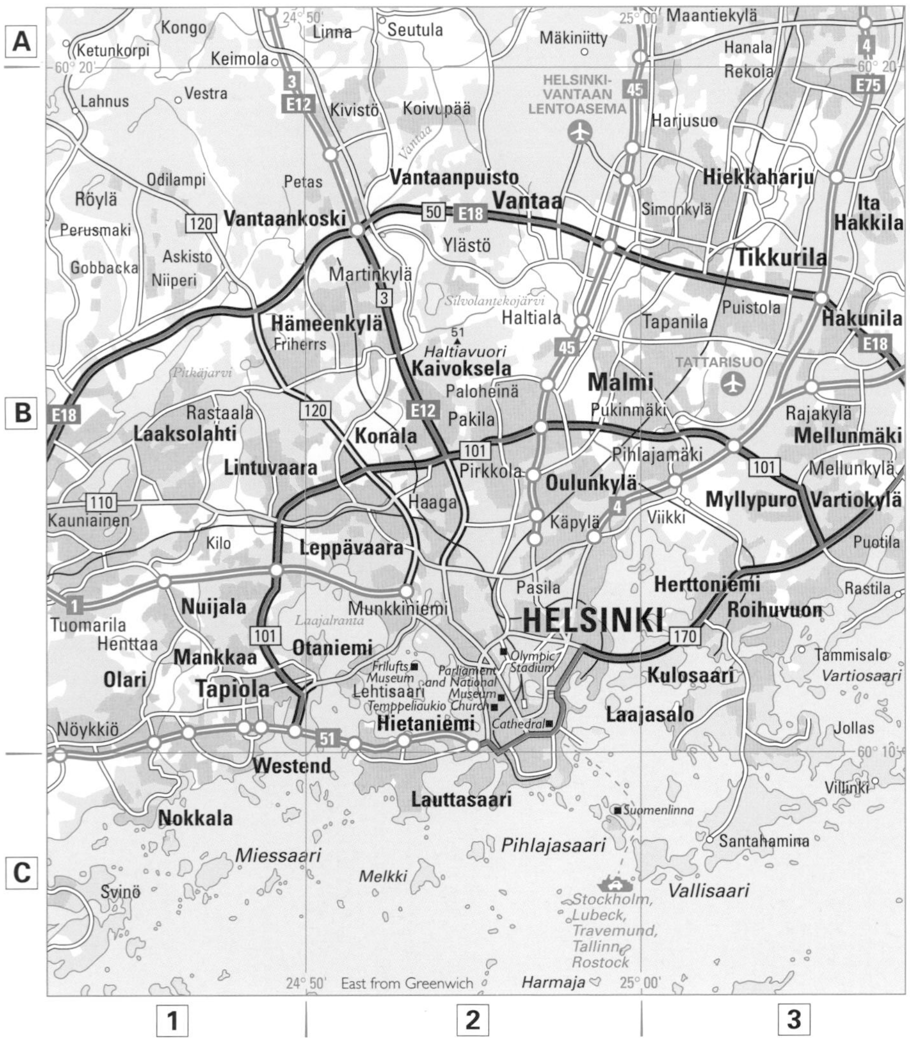

ISTANBUL

0 km 5
0 miles 3

HONG KONG

0 km 5
0 miles 3

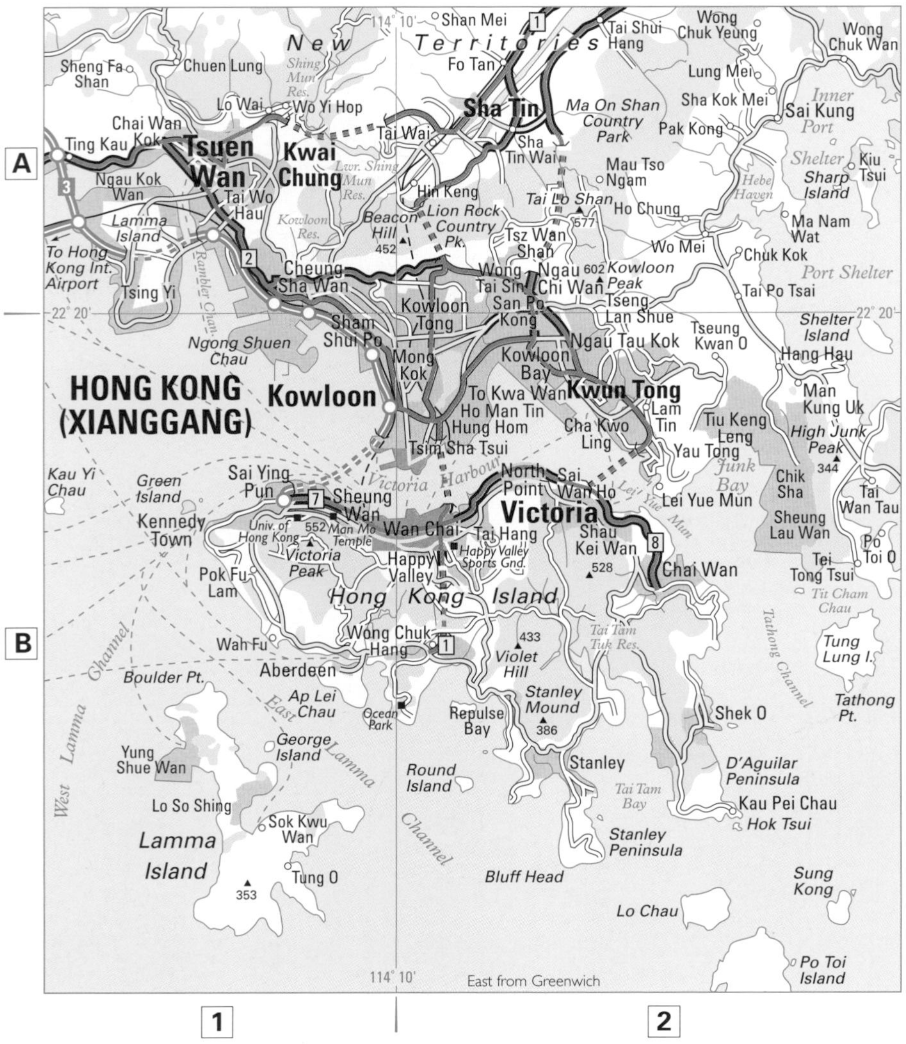

CENTRAL HONG KONG

0 km 0.5
0 miles 0.25

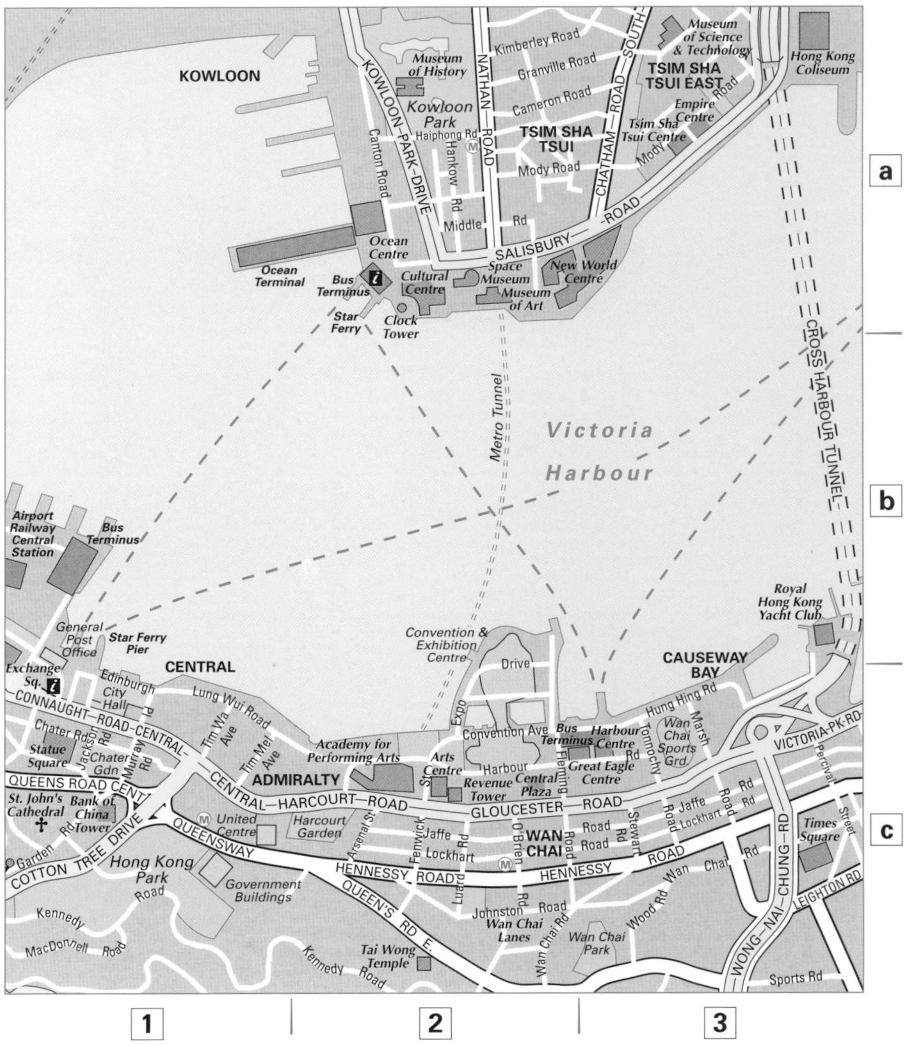

JERUSALEM

0 km 5
0 miles 3

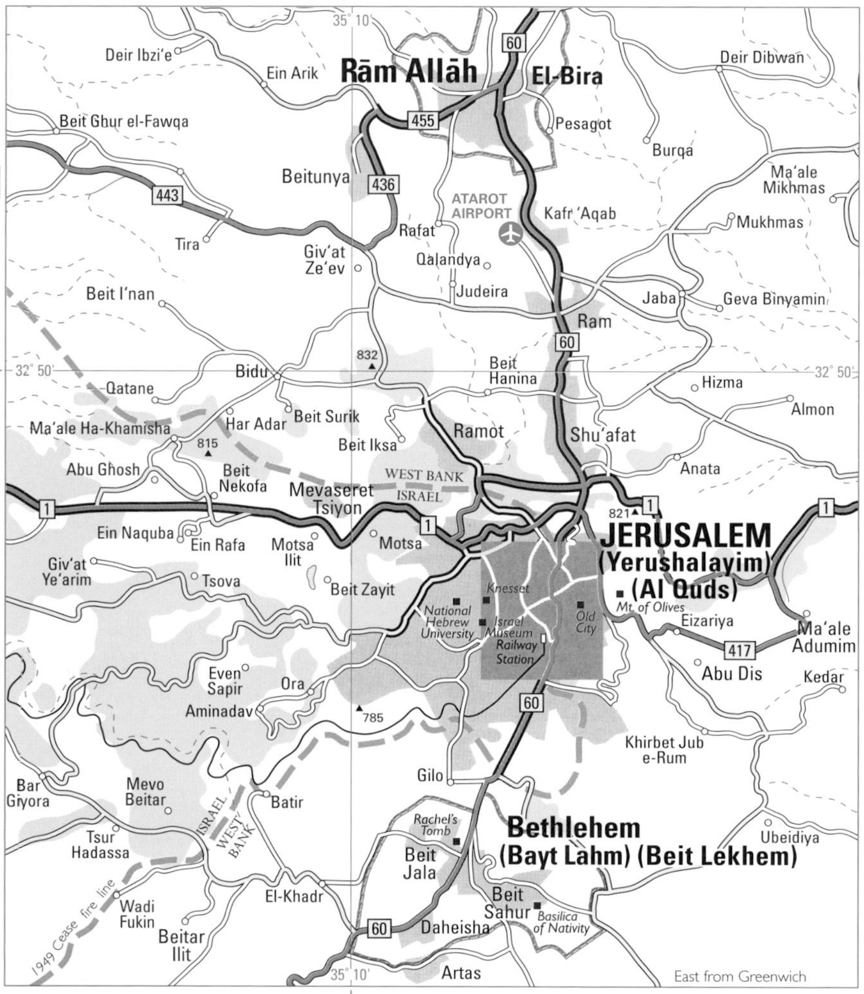

CENTRAL JERUSALEM

0 km 1
0 miles 0.5

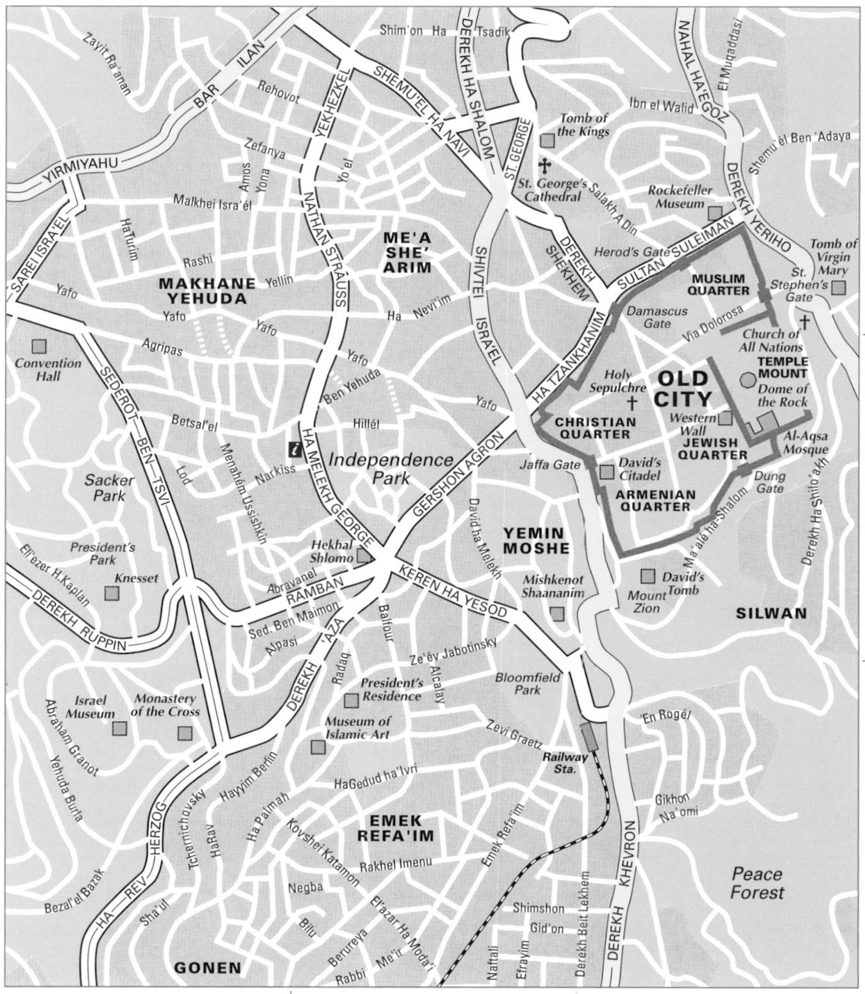

JAKARTA

0 km 5
0 miles 3

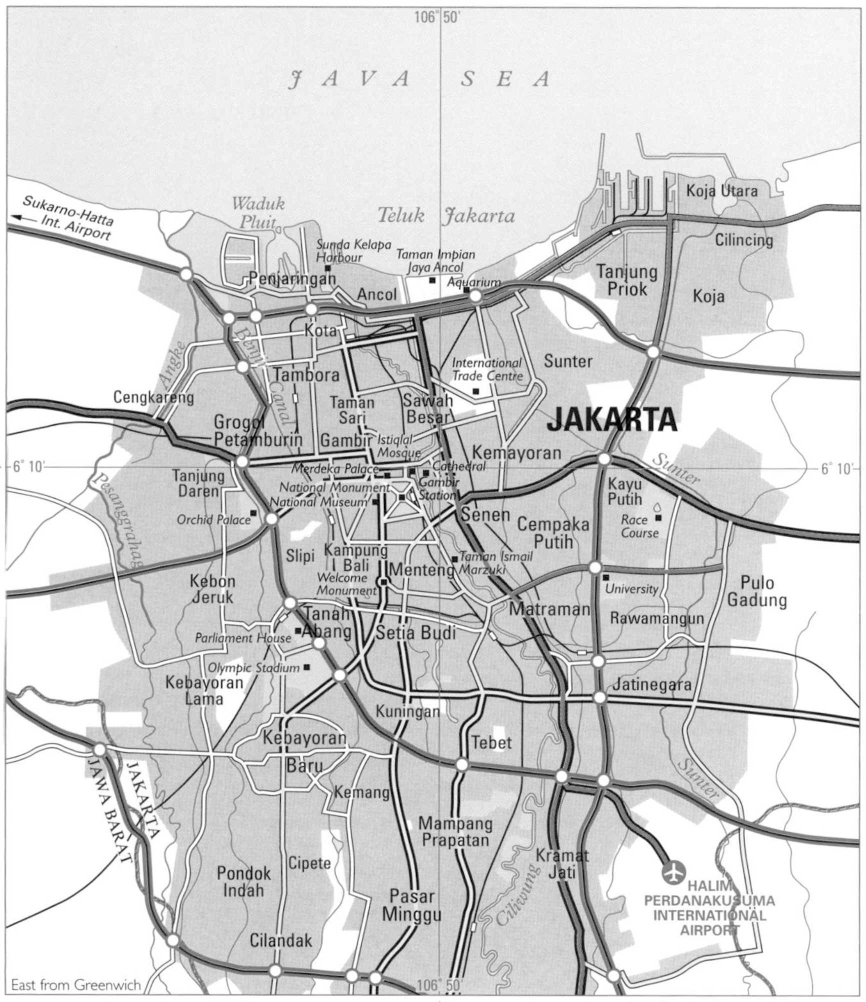

JOHANNESBURG

0 km 5
0 miles 3

KARACHI

0 km 5
0 miles 3

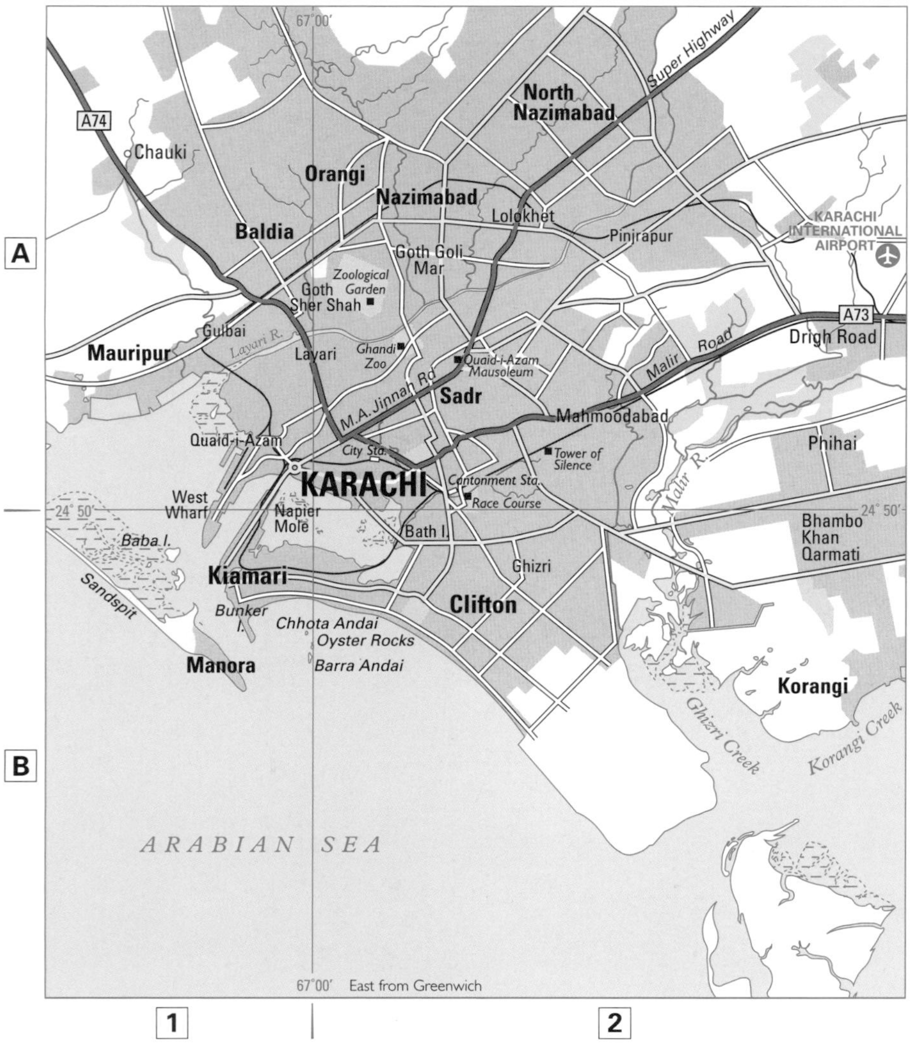

LAGOS

0 km 5
0 miles 3

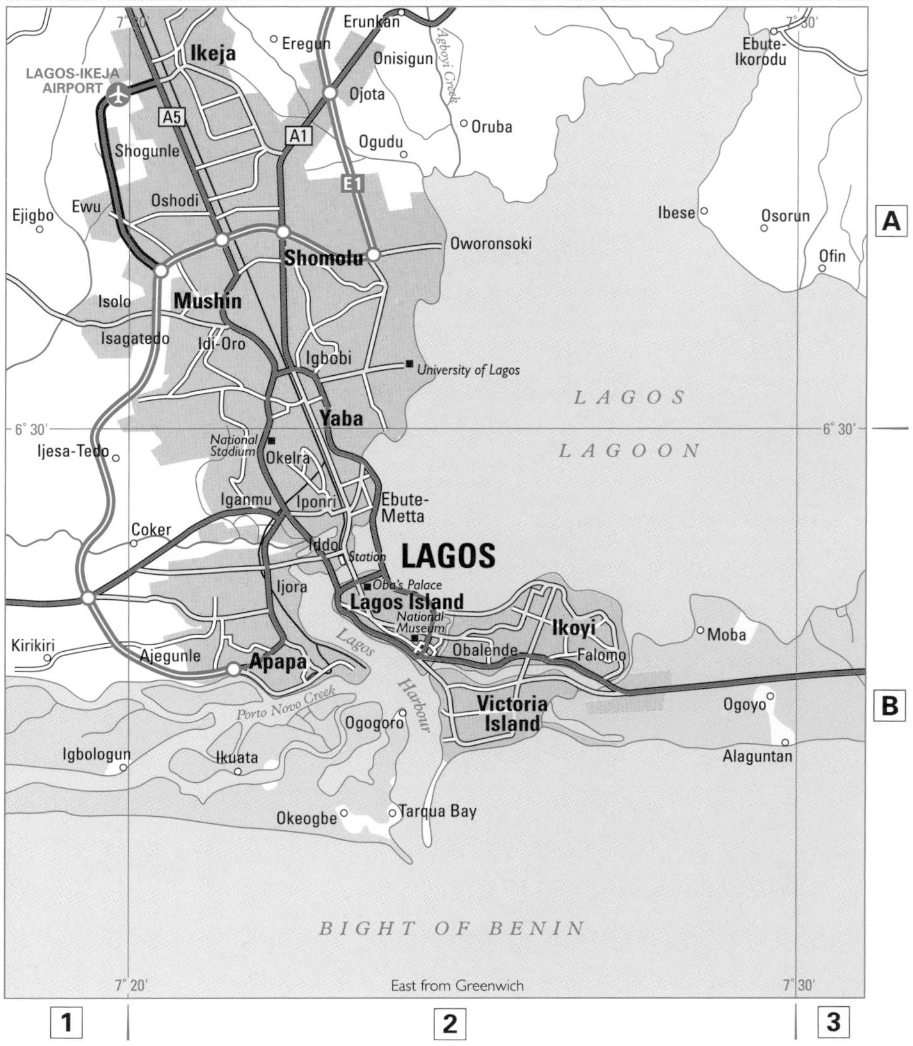

LISBON

0 km 5
0 miles 3

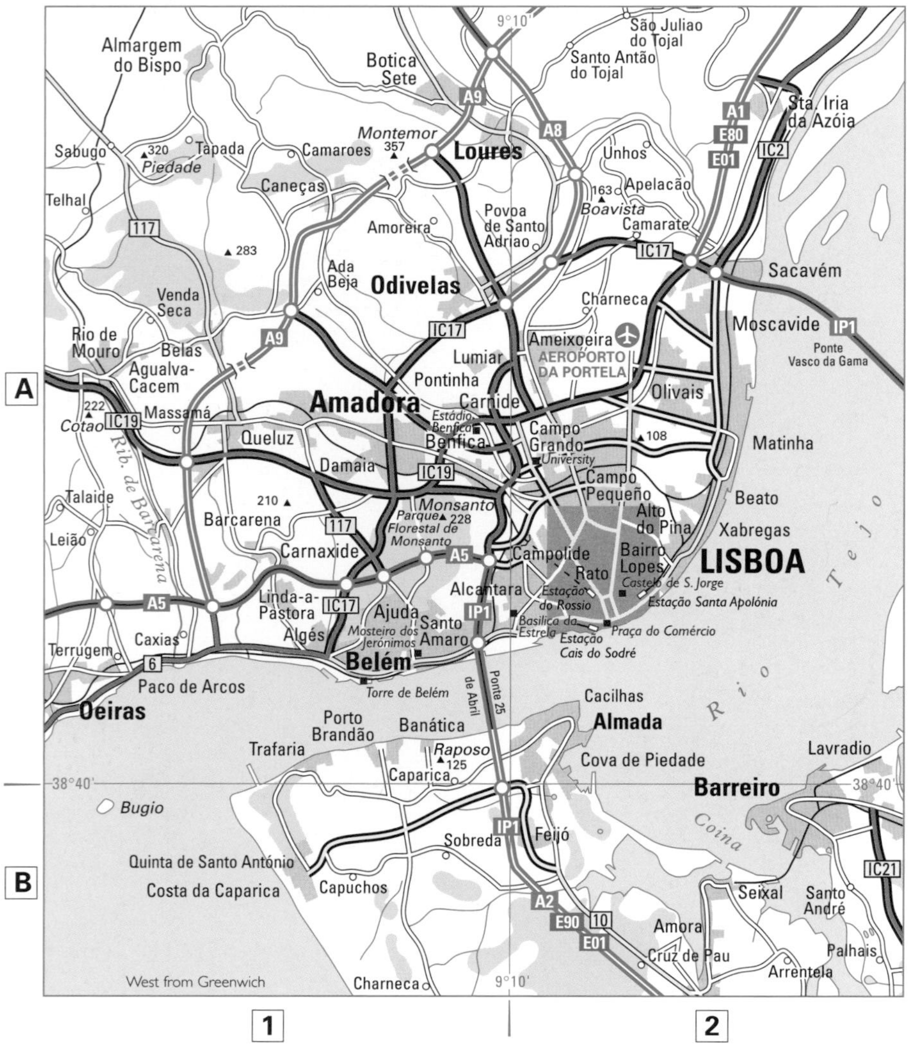

CENTRAL LISBON

0 km 1
0 miles 0.5

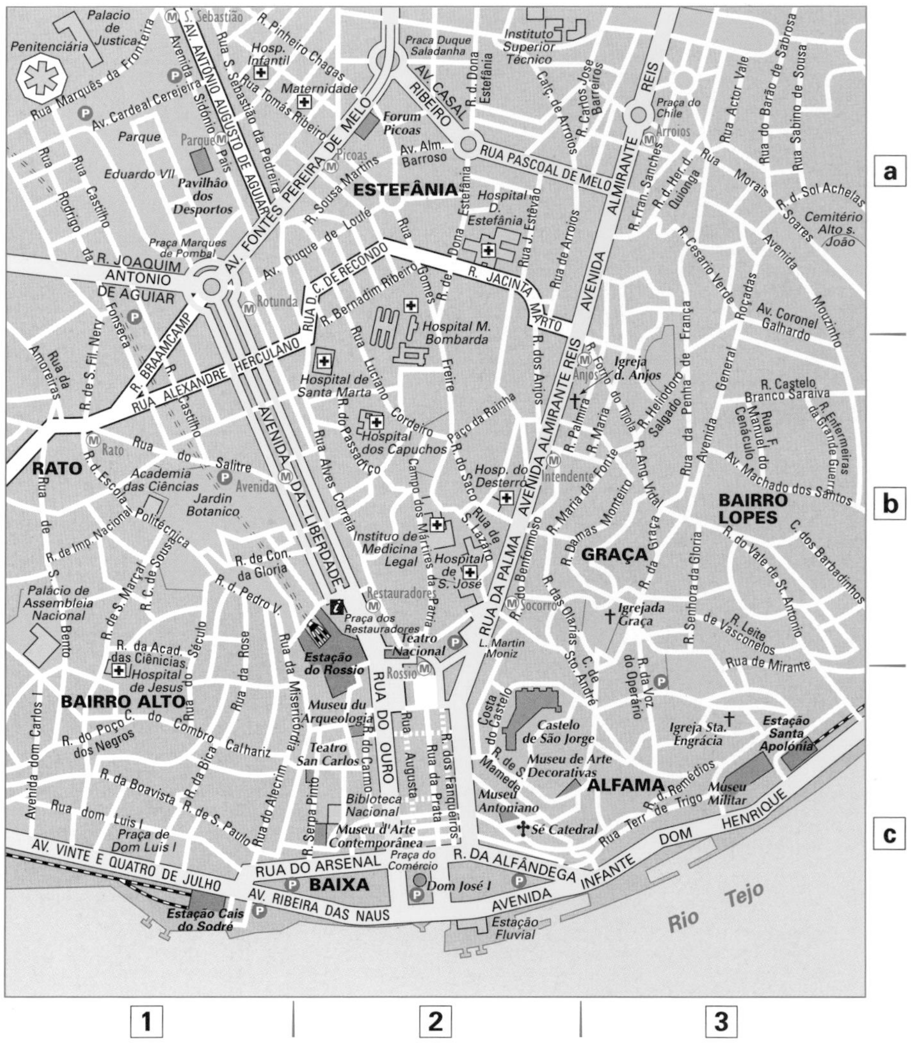

LONDON

0 km 5
0 miles 3

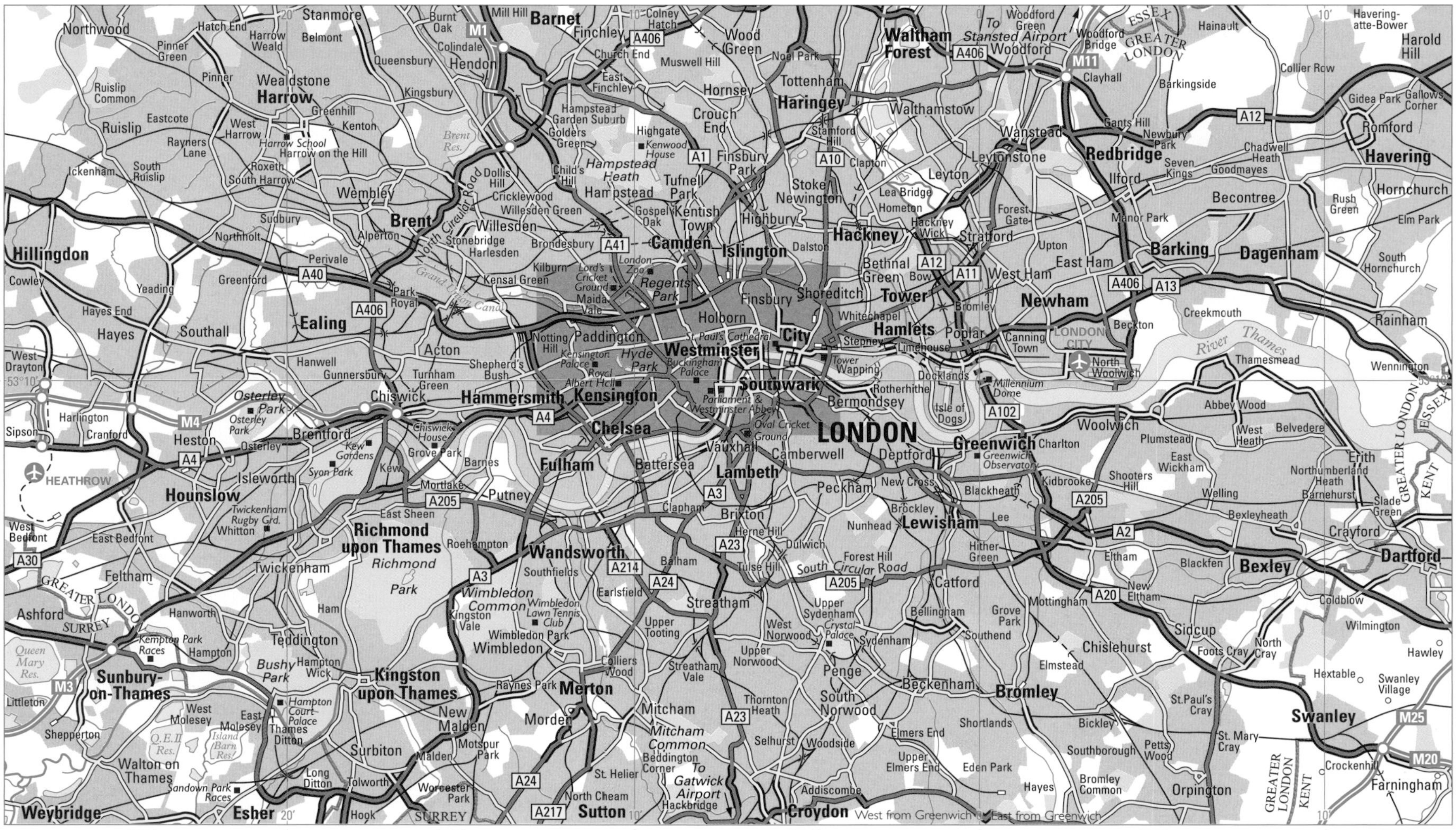

CENTRAL LONDON

0 km 2
0 miles 1

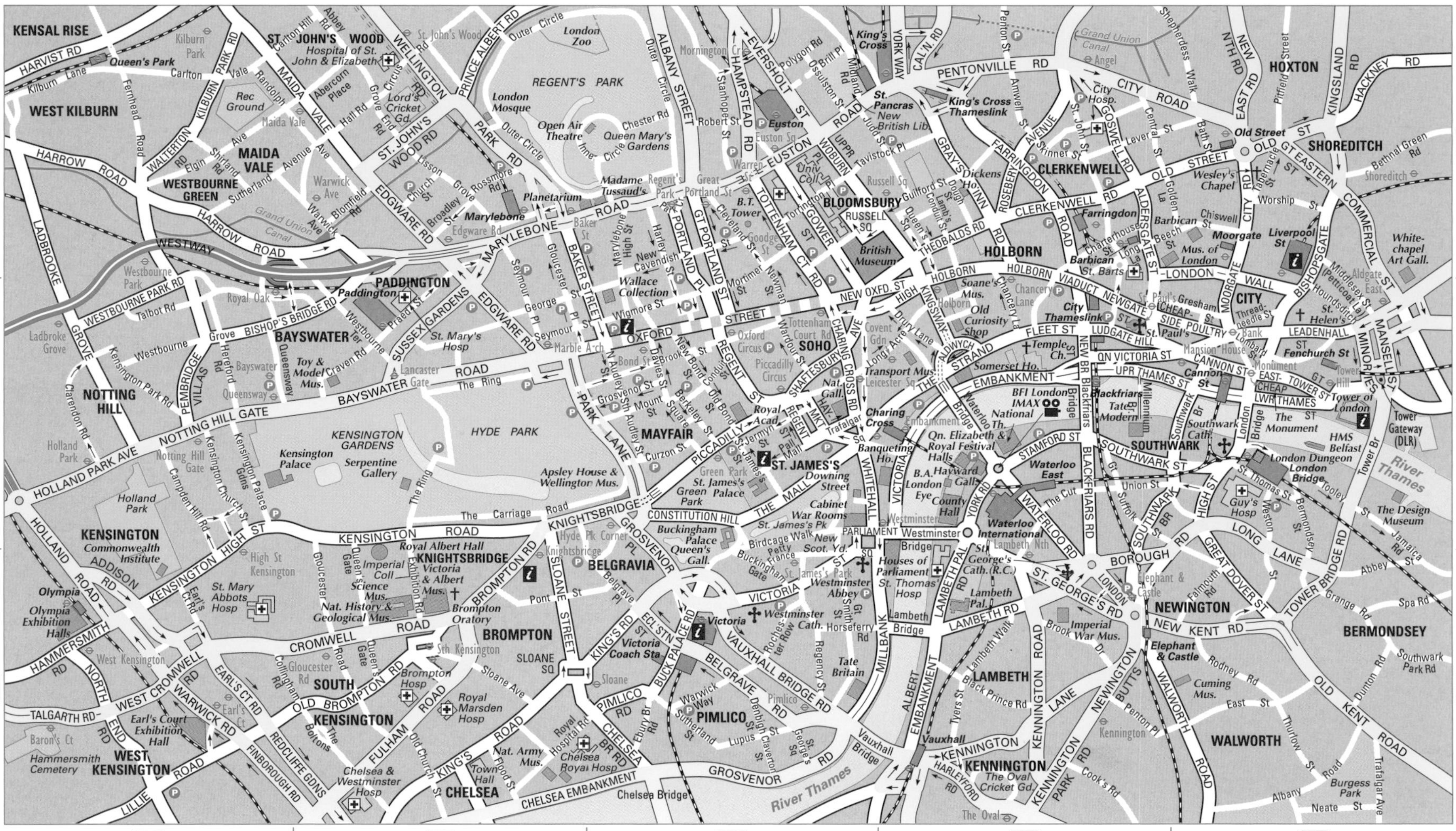

LOS ANGELES

0 km 5
0 miles 3

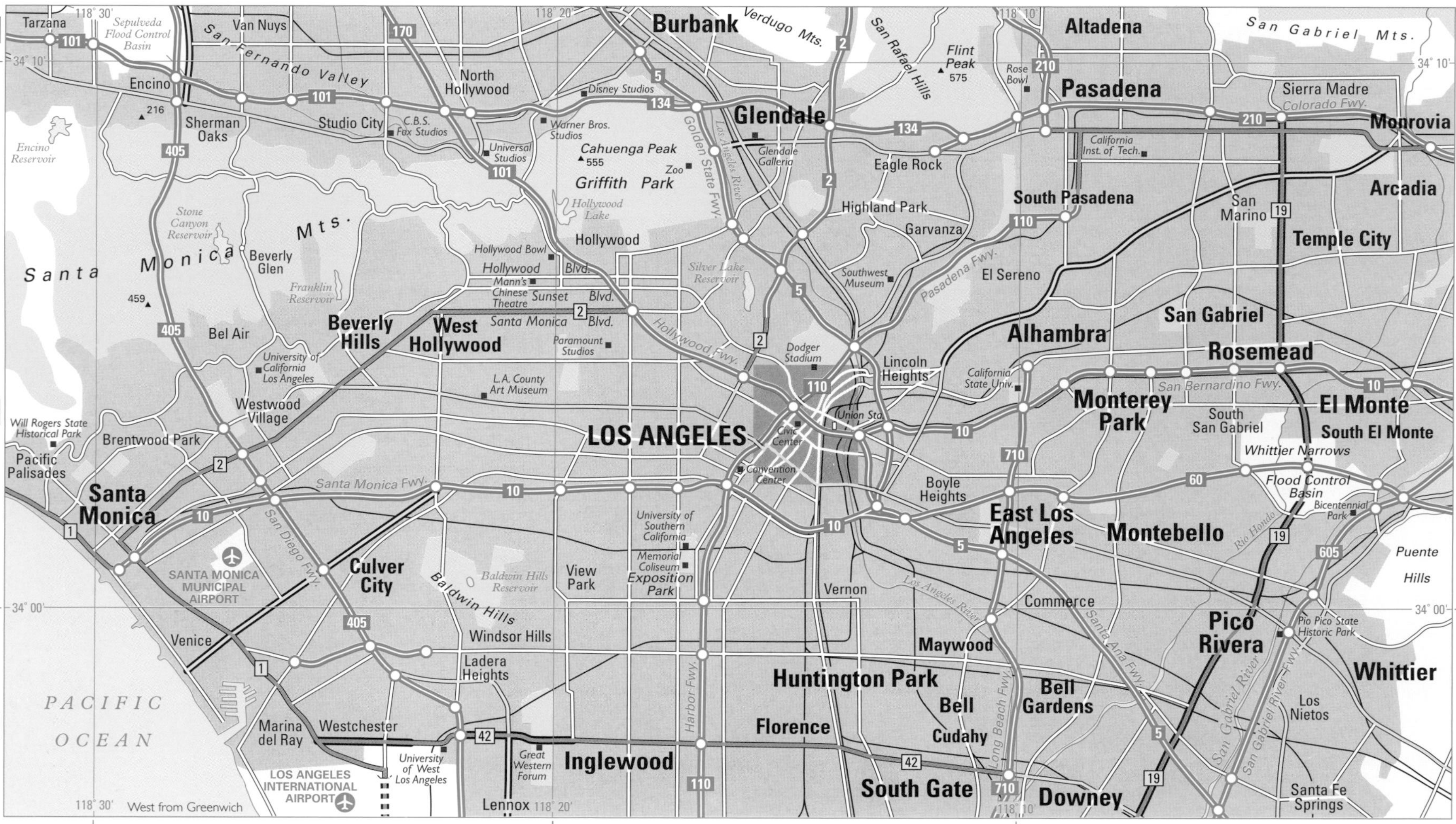

LIMA

0 km 5
0 miles 3

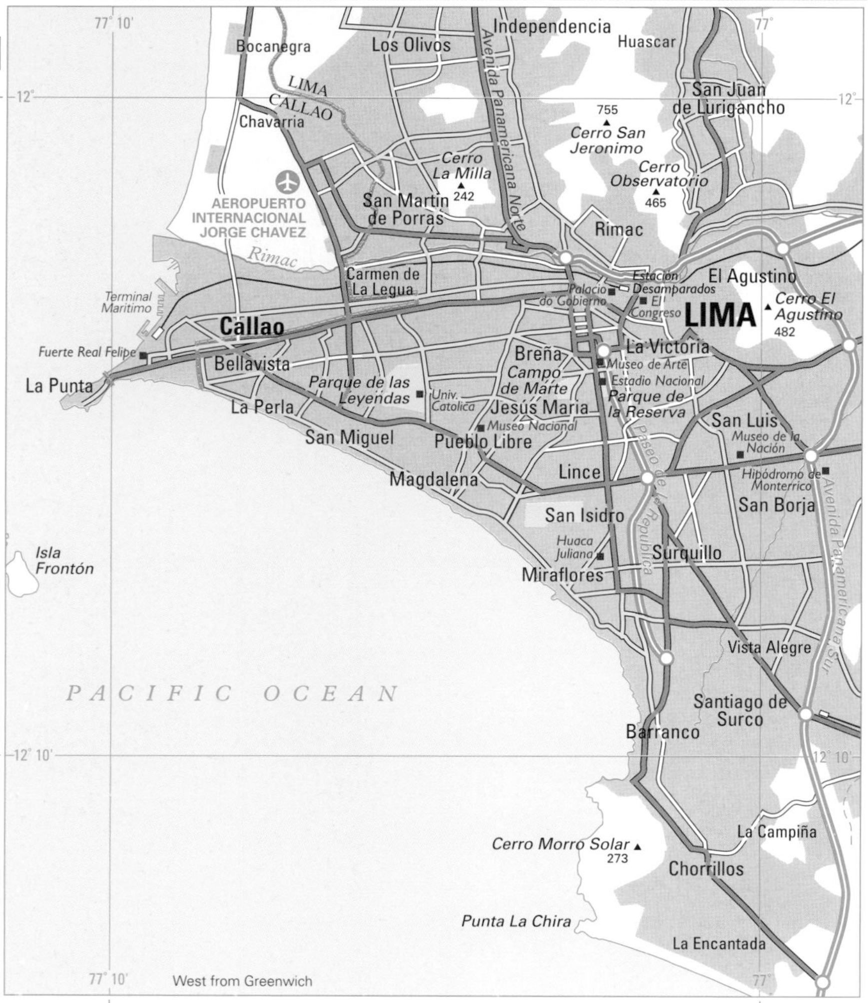

CENTRAL LOS ANGELES

0 km 1
0 miles 0.5

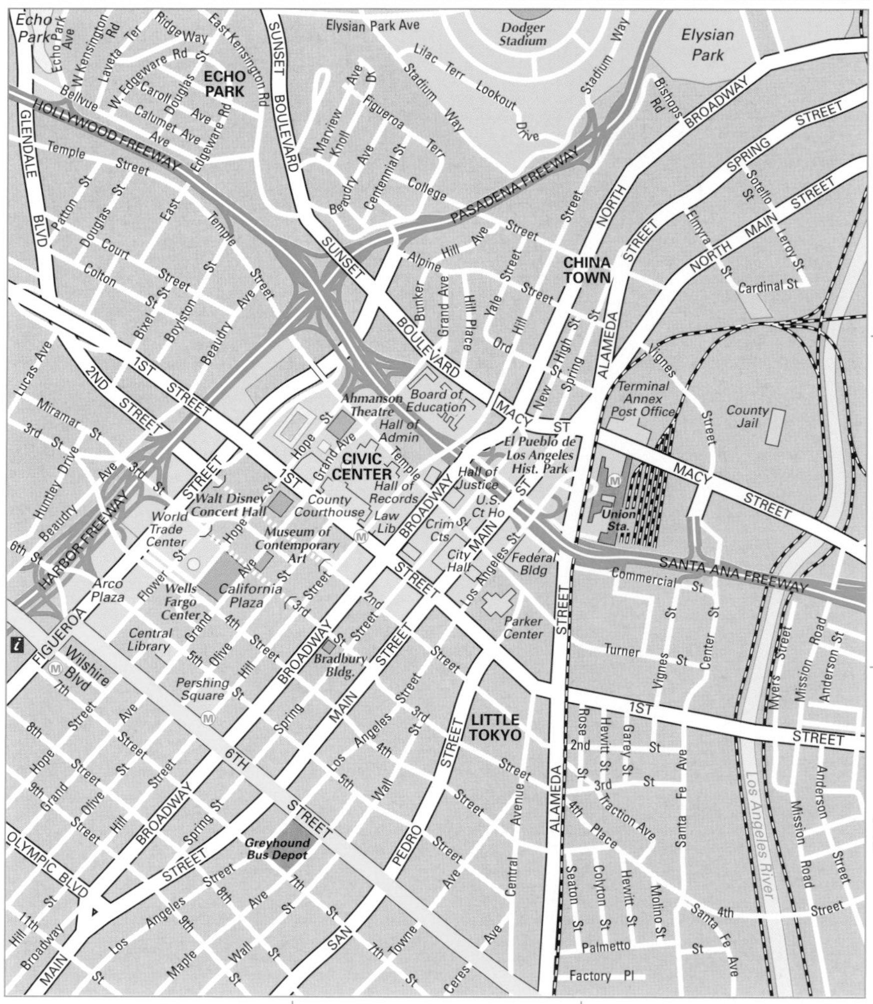

MADRID

0 km 5
0 miles 3

A
B
C

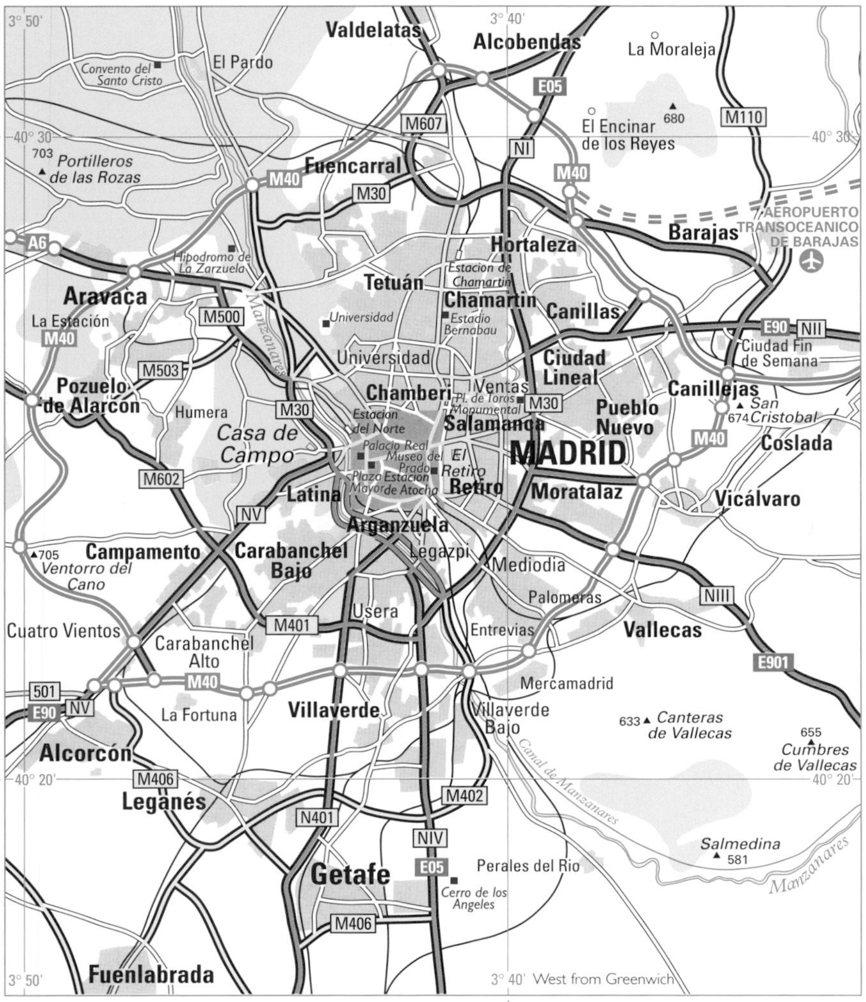

1 2

CENTRAL MADRID

0 km 1
0 miles 0.5

a
b
c

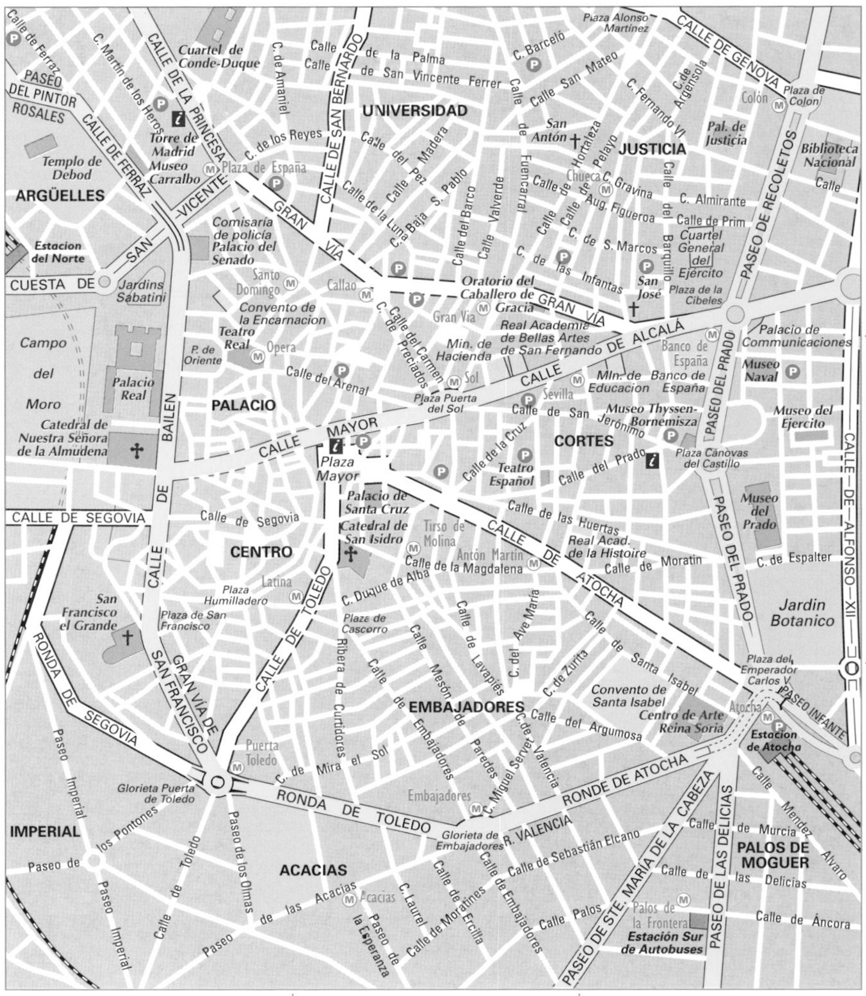

1 2 3

MANILA

0 km 5
0 miles 3

A
B
C

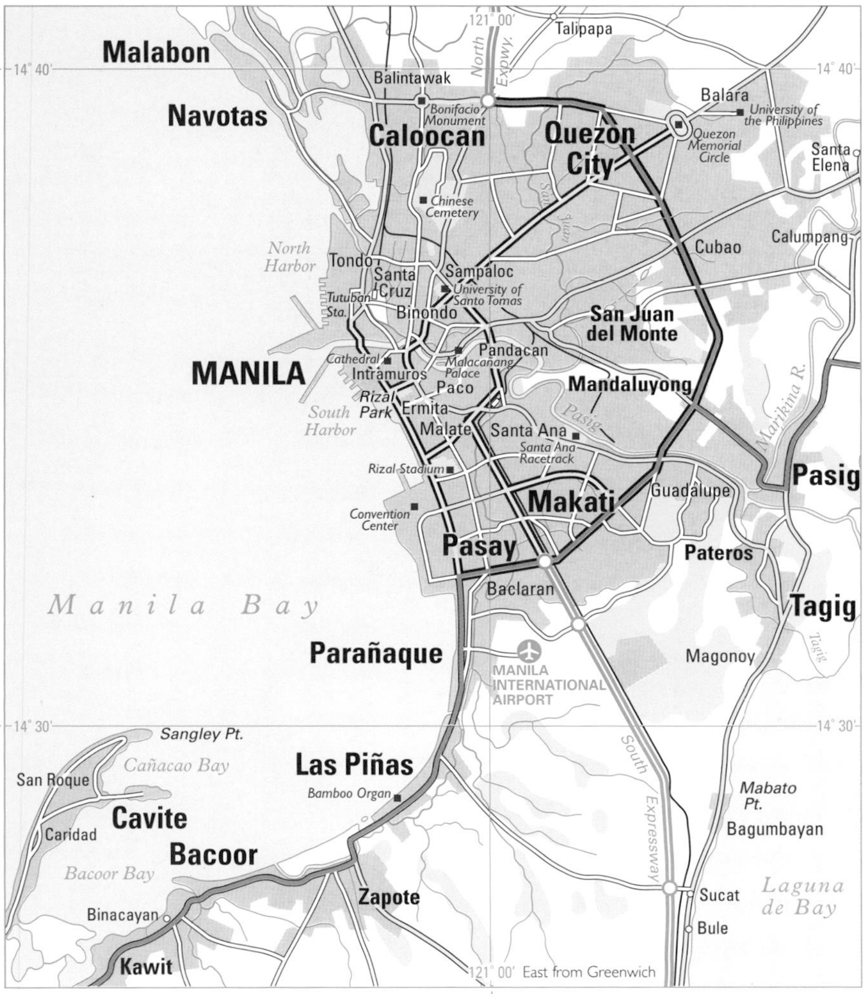

1 2

MELBOURNE

0 km 5
0 miles 3

A
B

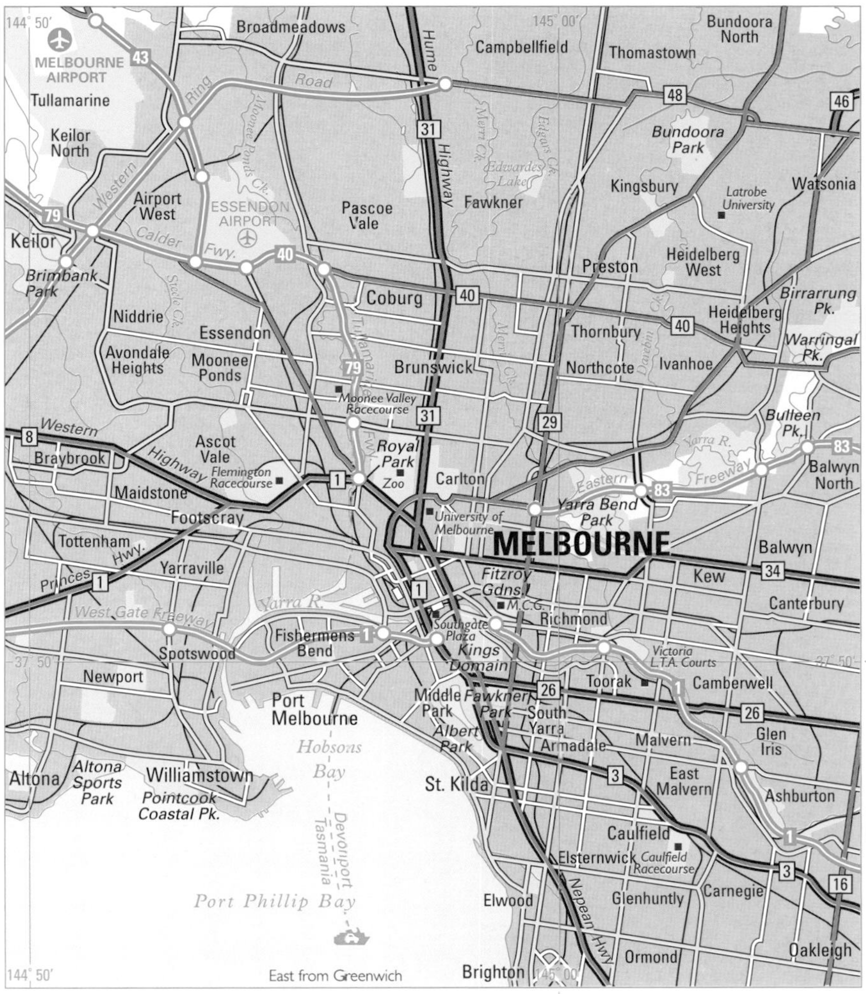

1 2

MEXICO CITY

0 km 5
0 miles 3

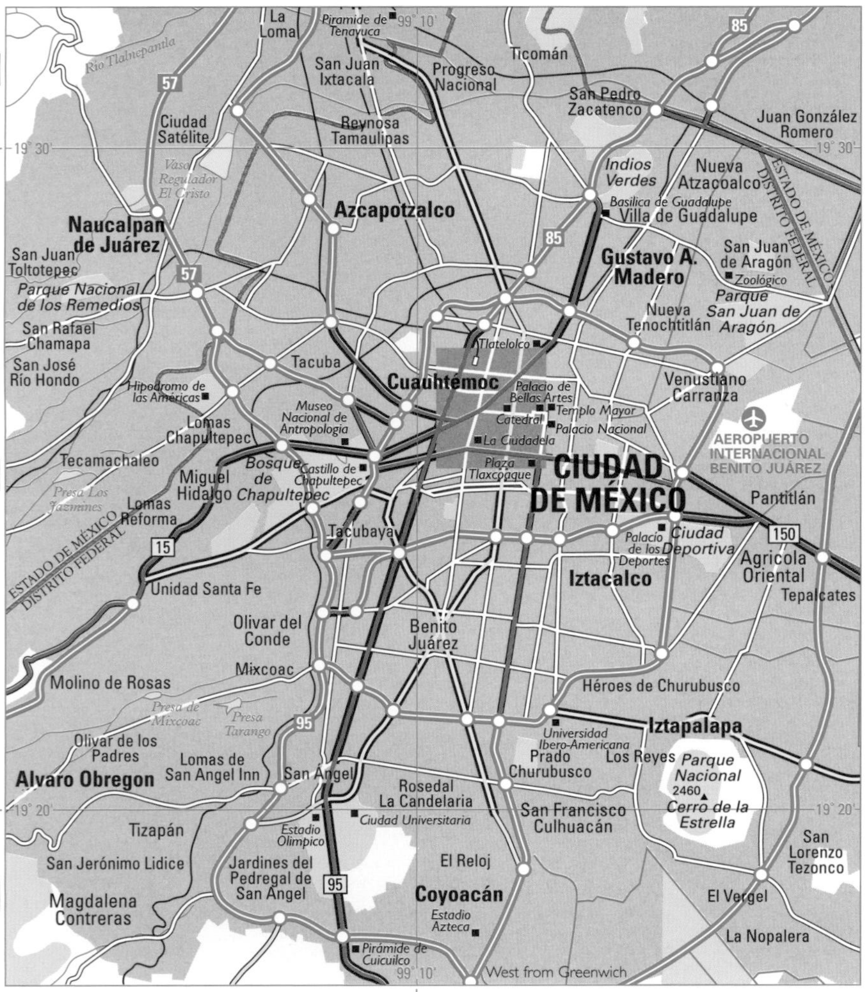

CENTRAL MEXICO CITY

0 km 1
0 miles 0.5

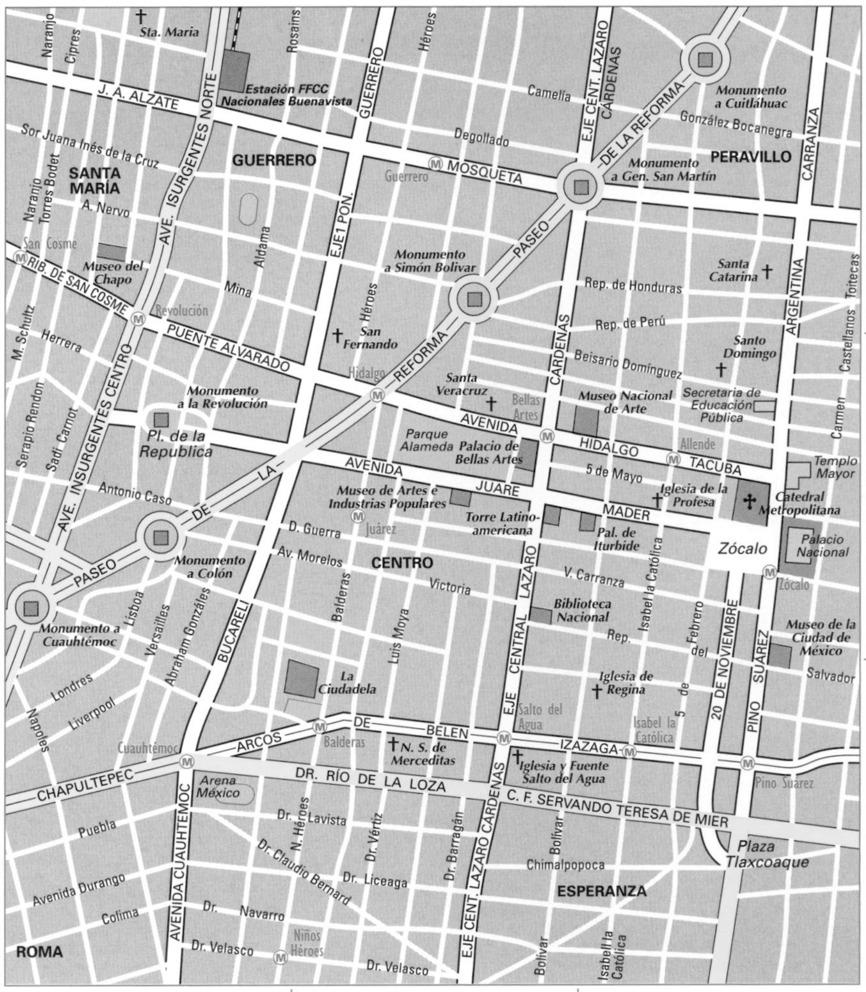

MIAMI

0 km 5
0 miles 3

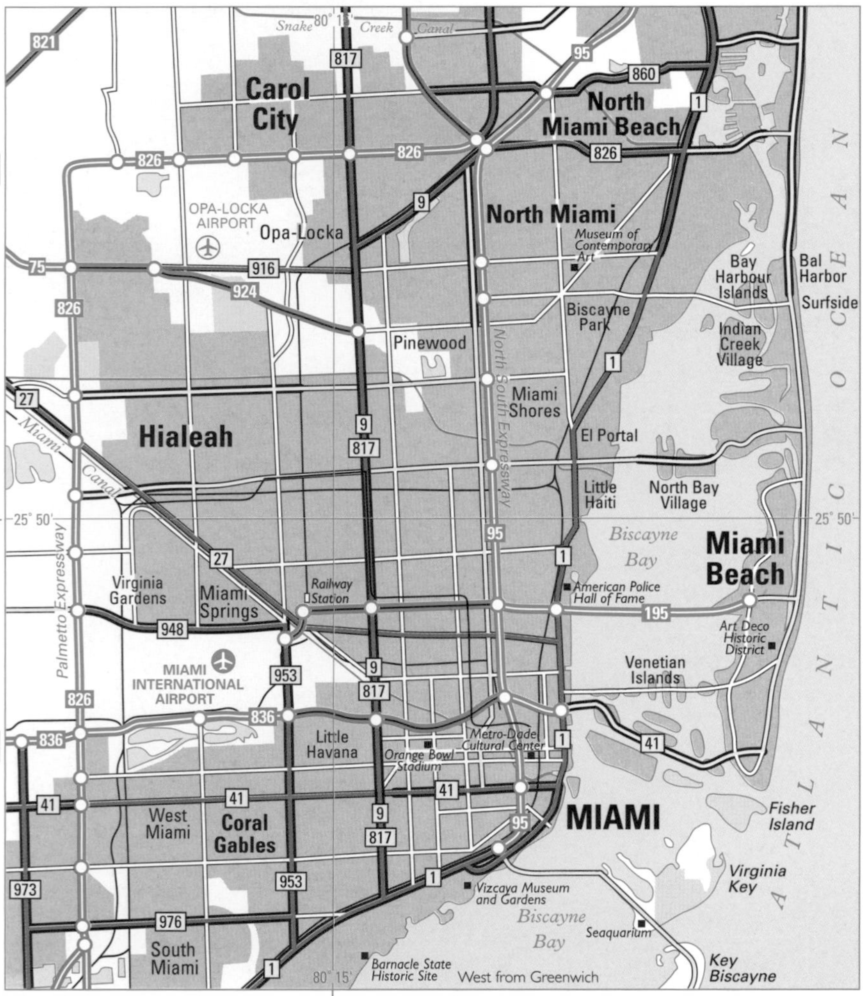

MILAN

0 km 5
0 miles 3

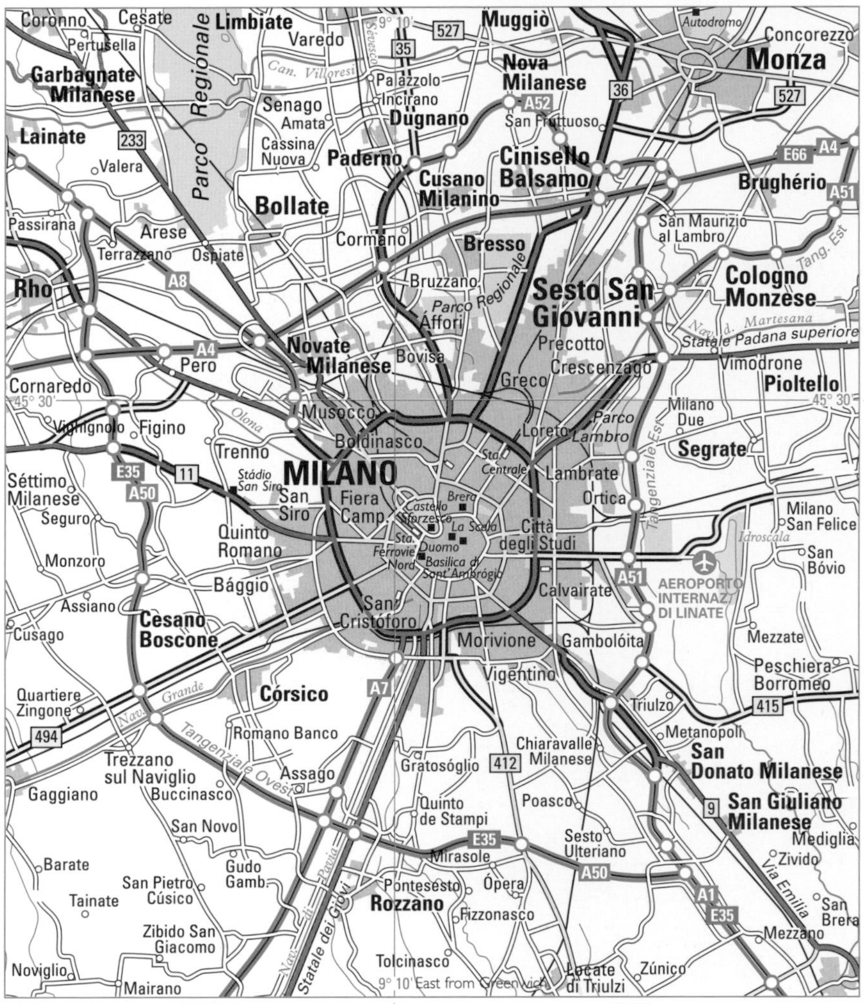

MOSCOW

0 km 5
0 miles 3

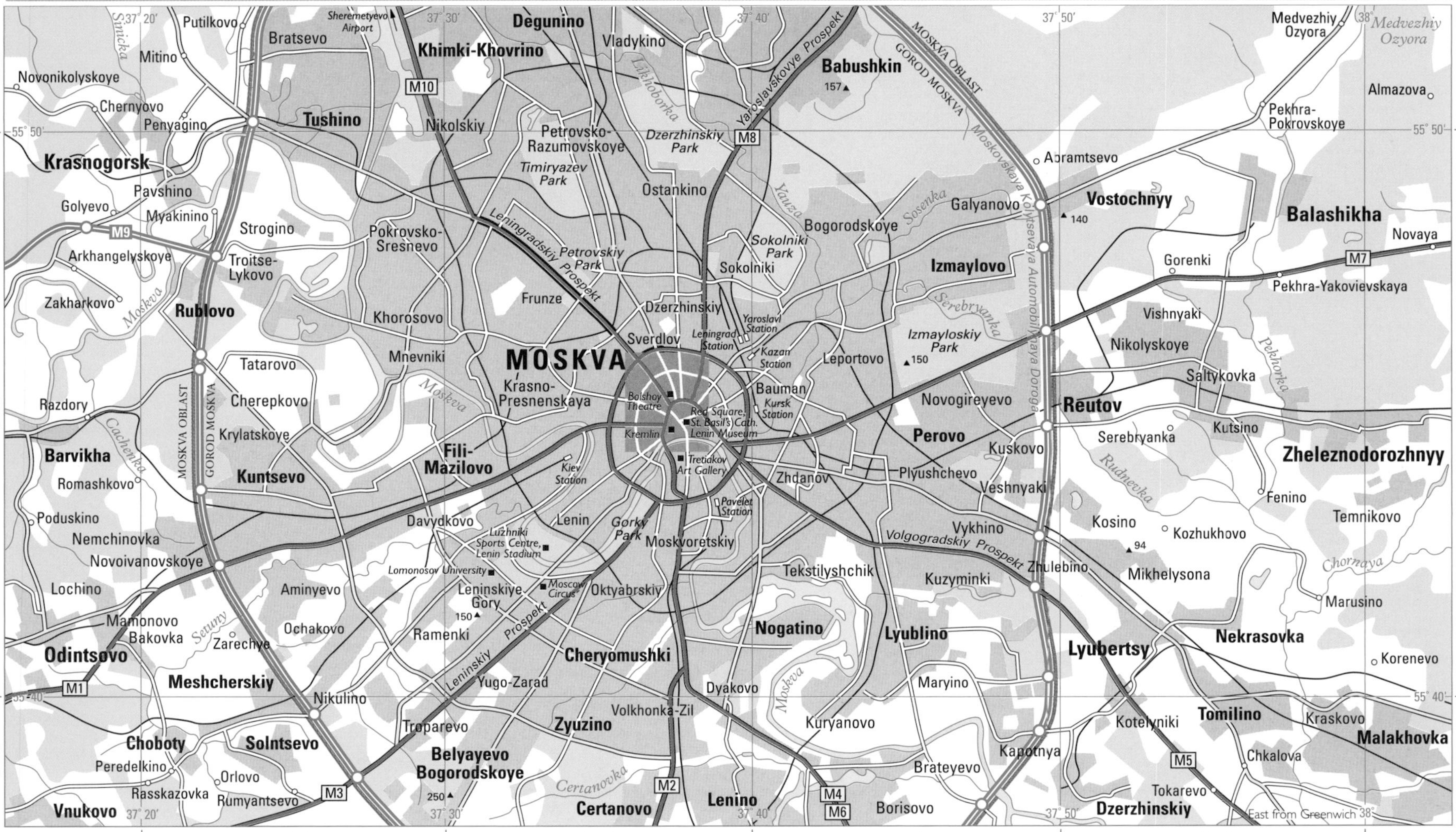

MONTRÉAL

0 km 5
0 miles 3

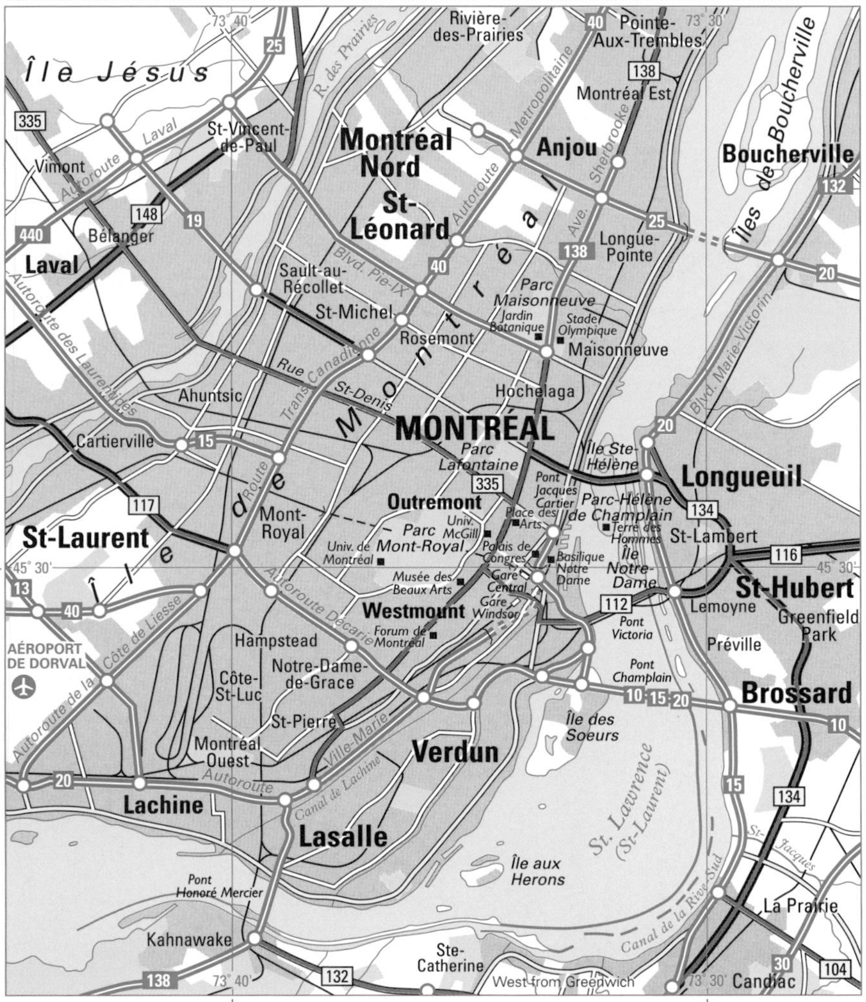

CENTRAL MOSCOW

0 km 1
0 miles 0.5

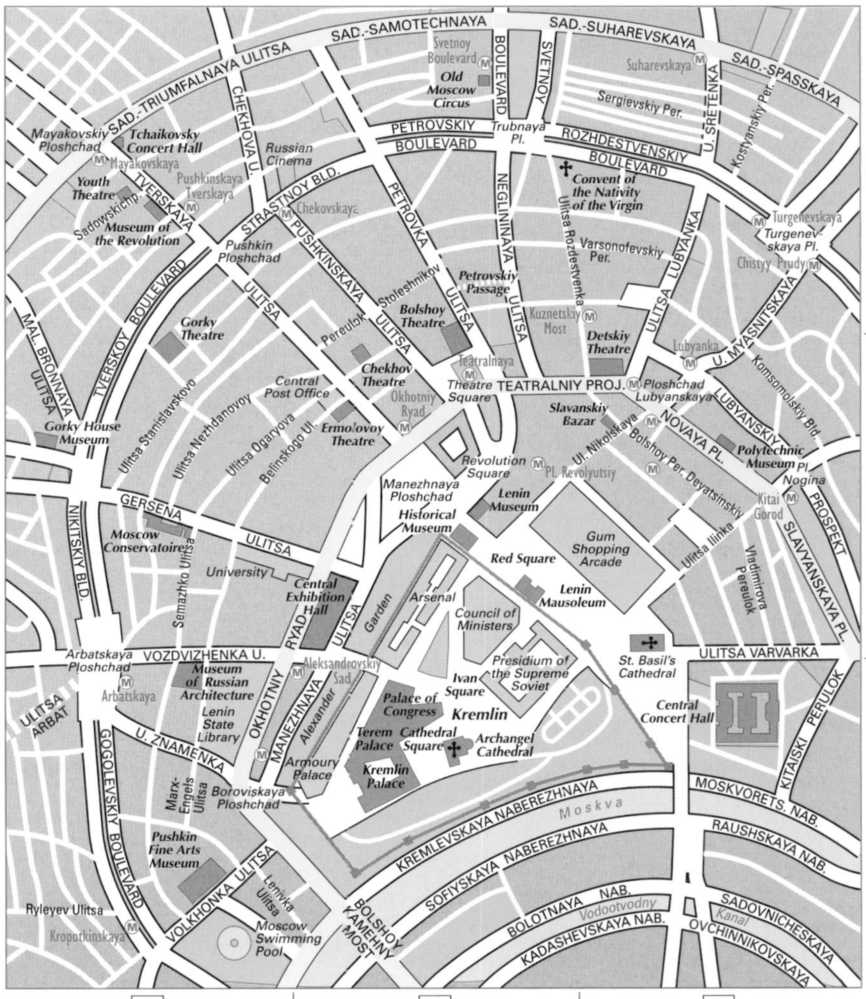

MUMBAI

0 km 5
0 miles 3

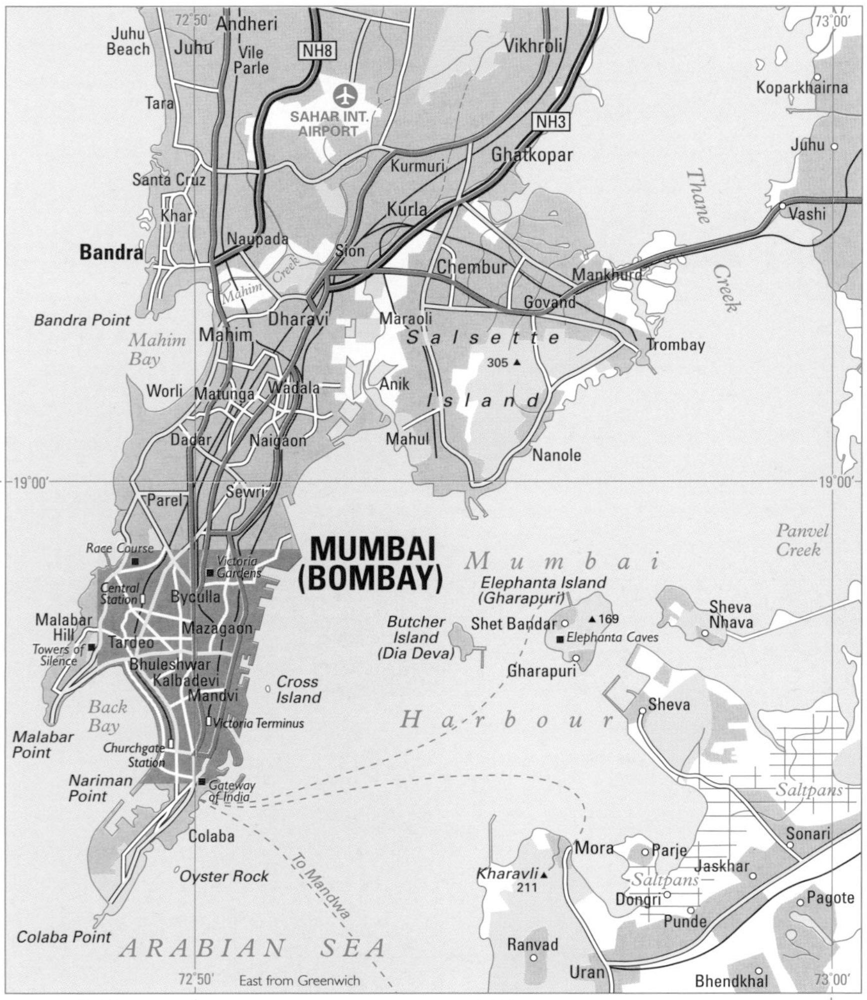

CENTRAL MUMBAI

0 km 2
0 miles 1

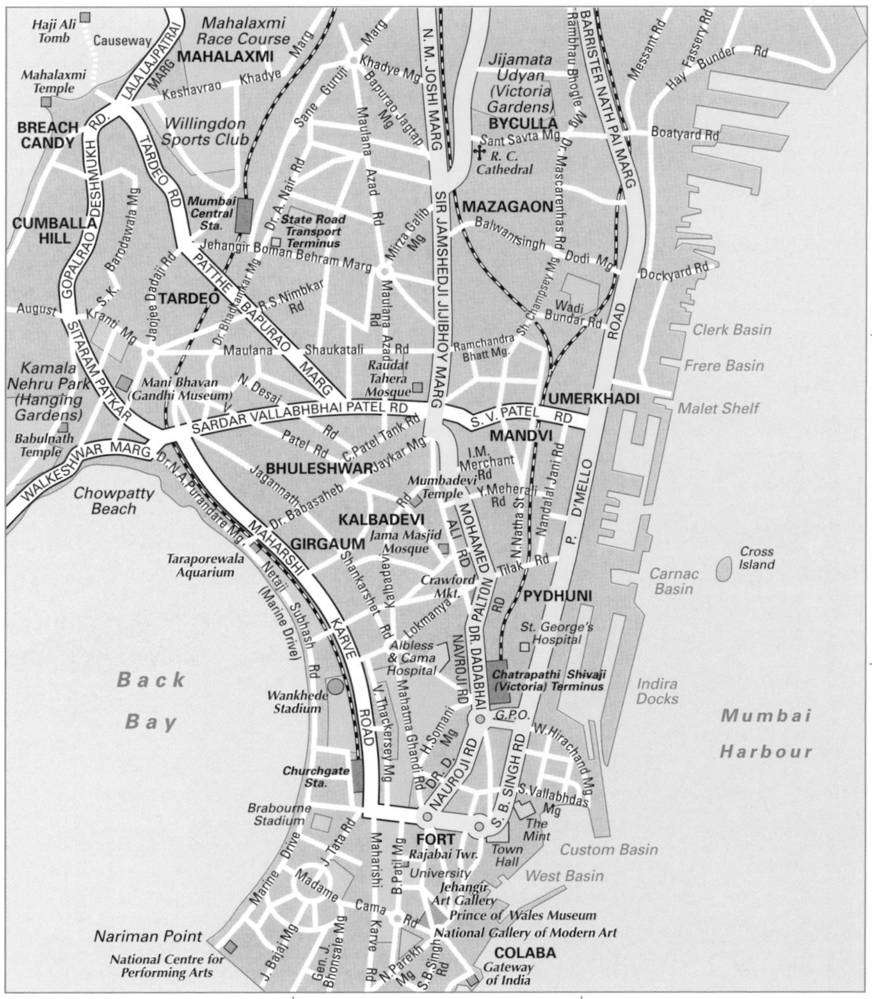

MUNICH

0 km 5
0 miles 3

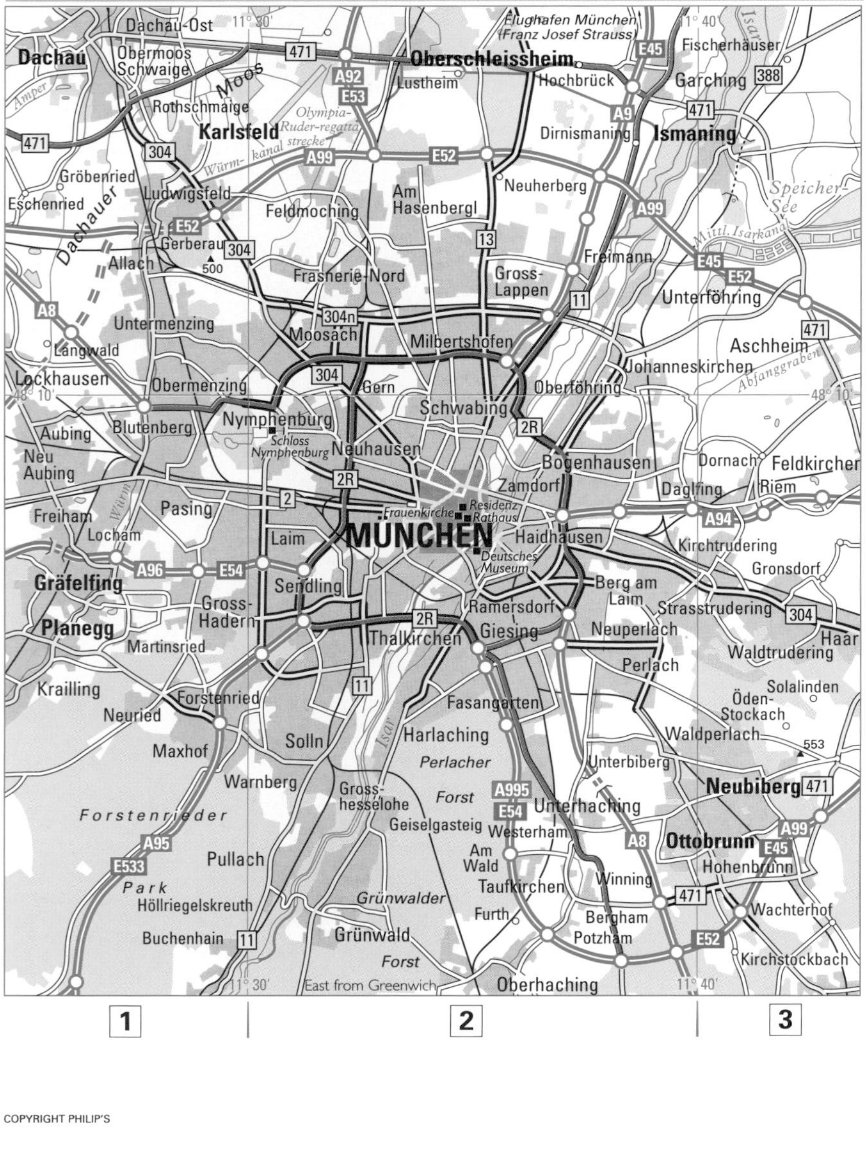

CENTRAL MUNICH

0 km 1
0 miles 0.5

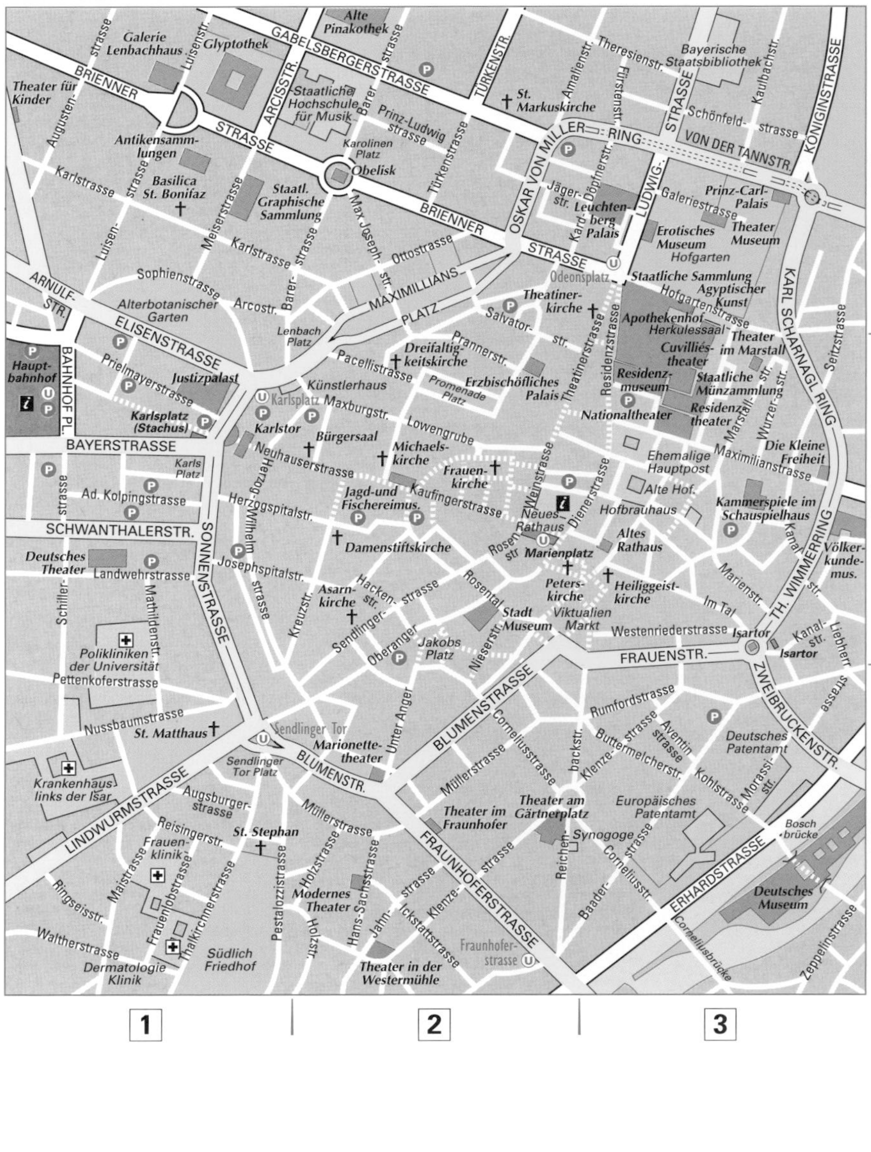

NEW YORK

0 km 5
0 miles 3

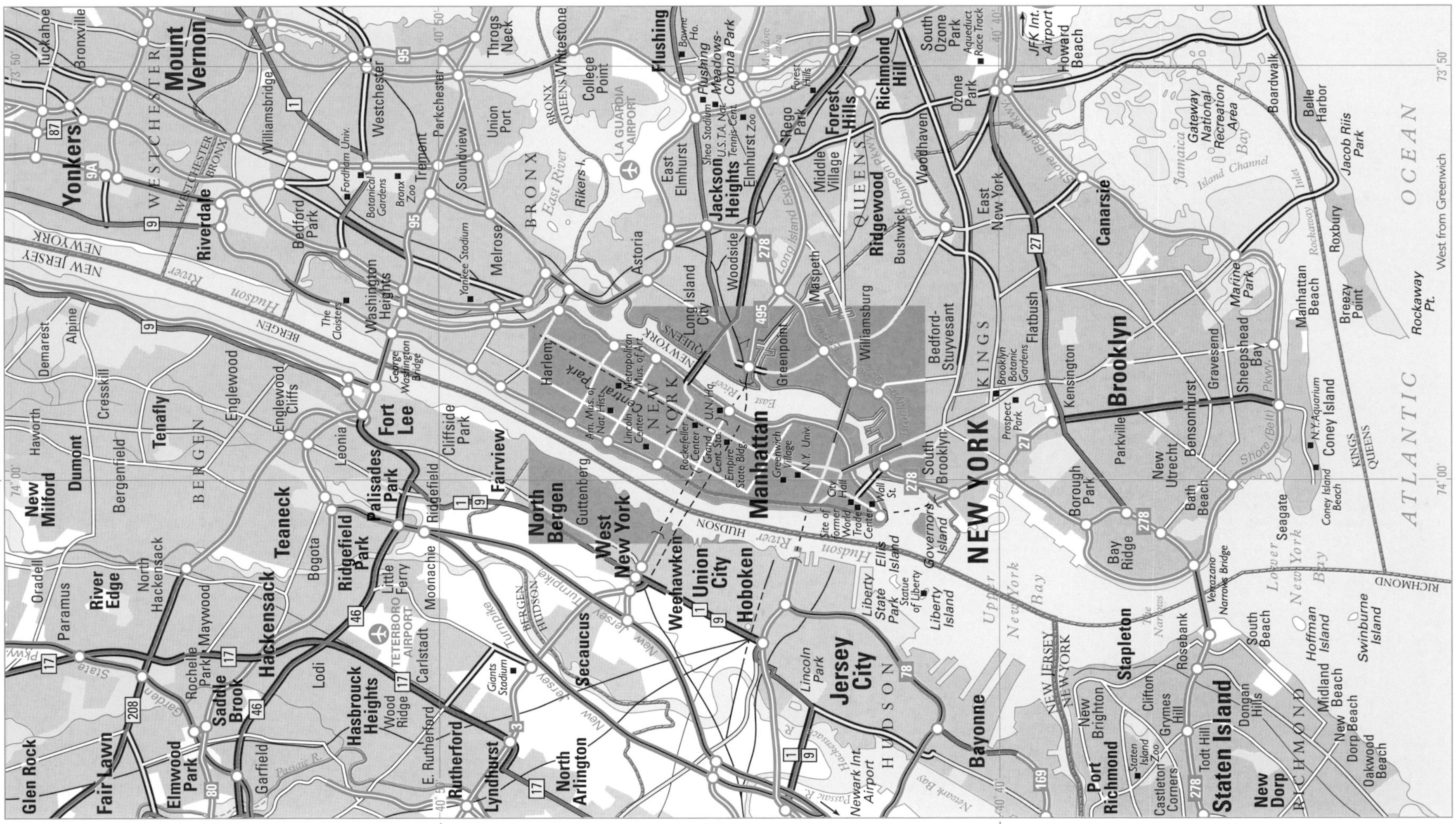

CENTRAL NEW YORK

0 km 2
0 miles 1

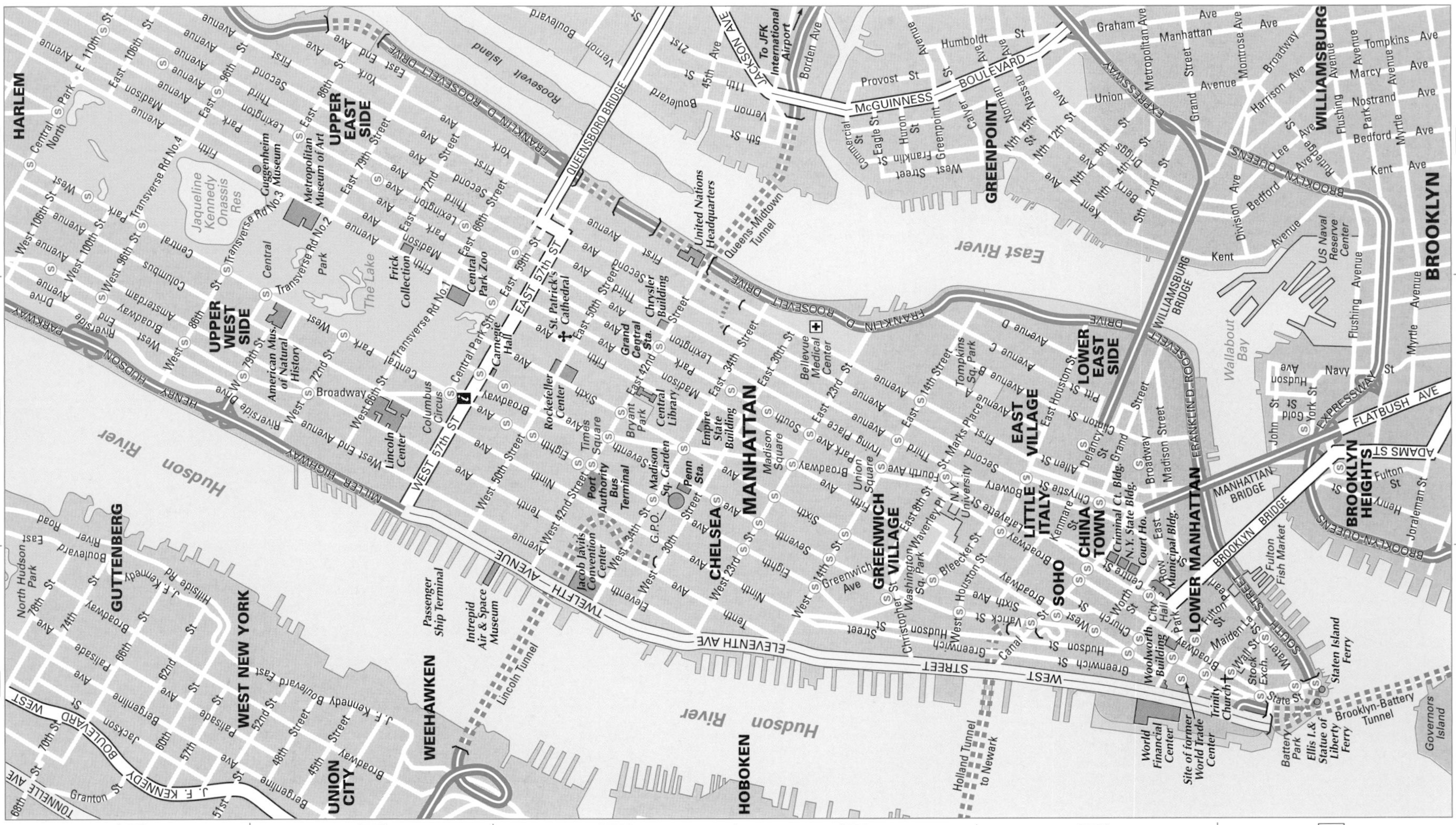

OSAKA

0 km 5
0 miles 3

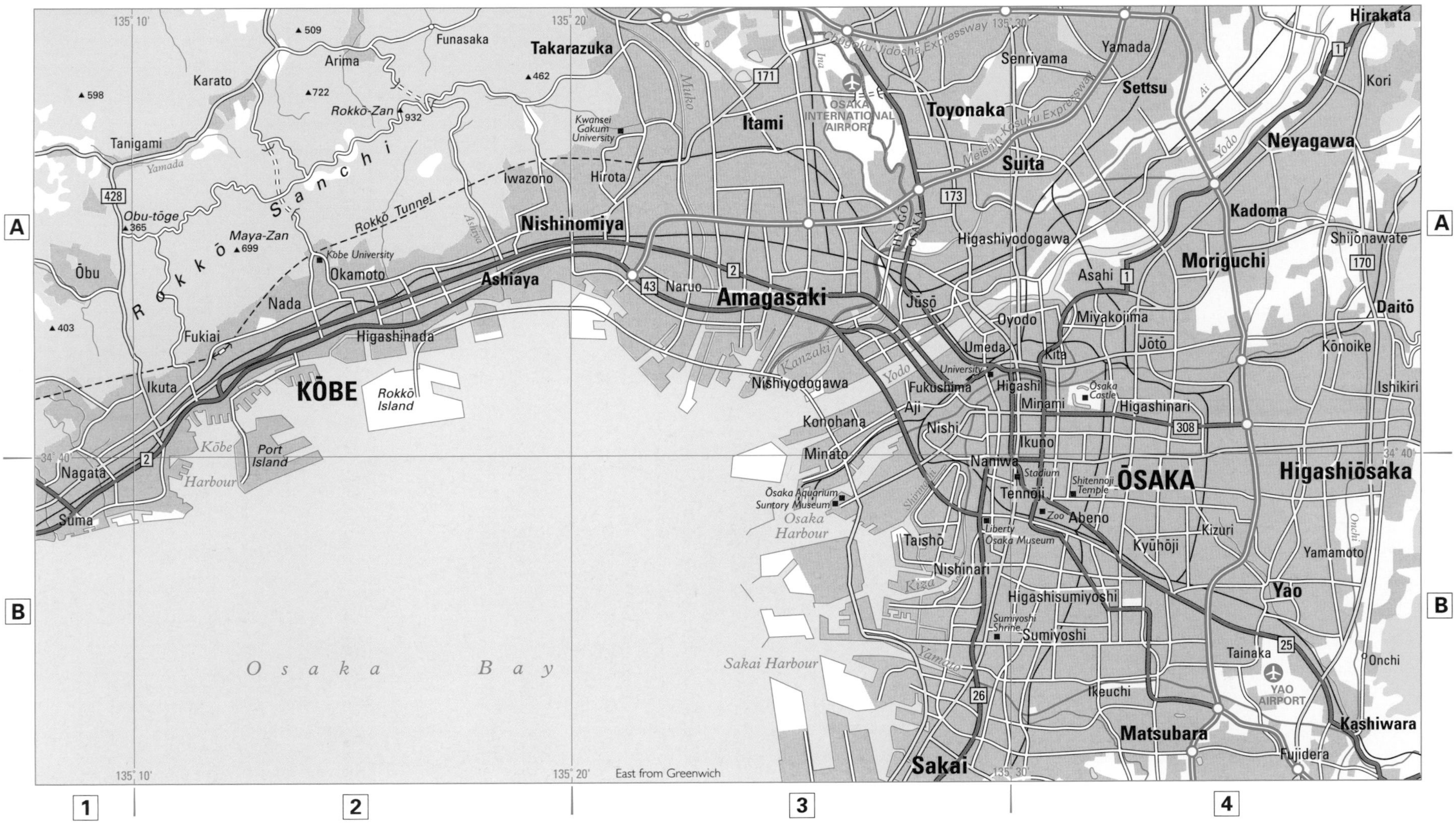

OSLO

0 km 5
0 miles 3

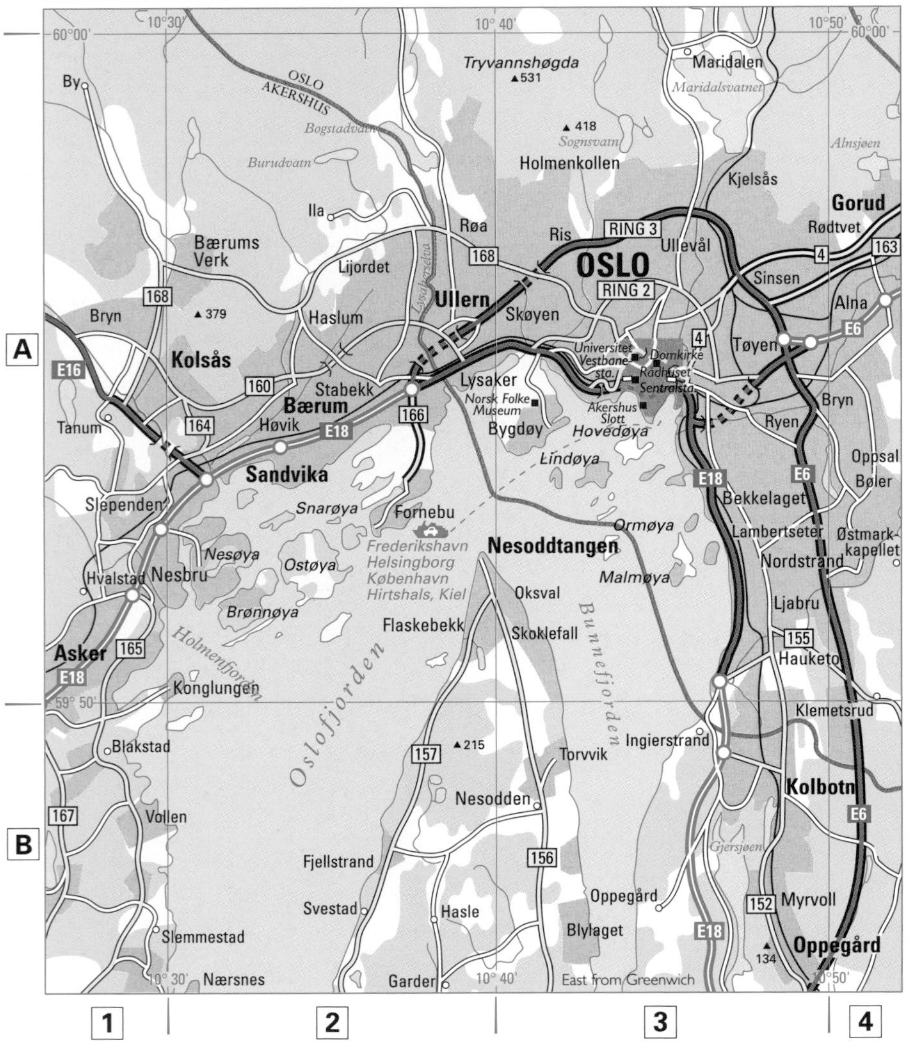

CENTRAL OSLO

0 km 0.5
0 miles 0.25

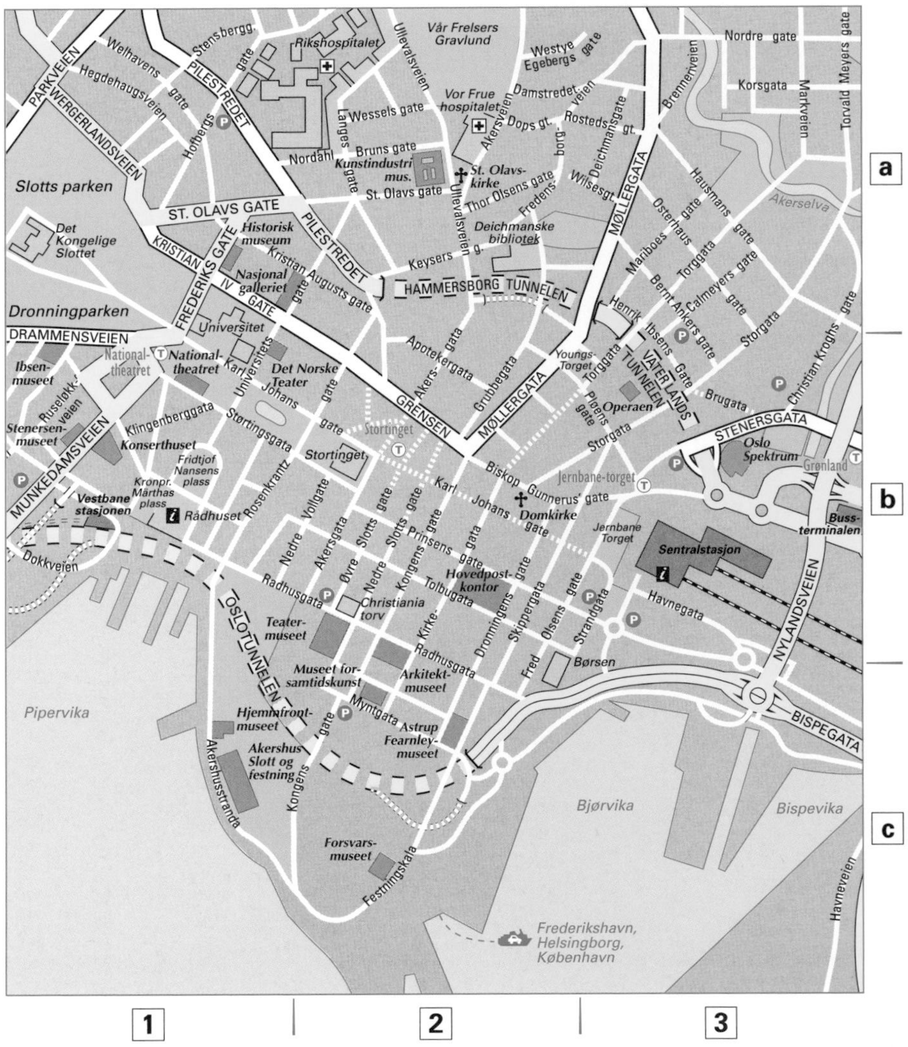

PARIS

0 km 5
0 miles 3

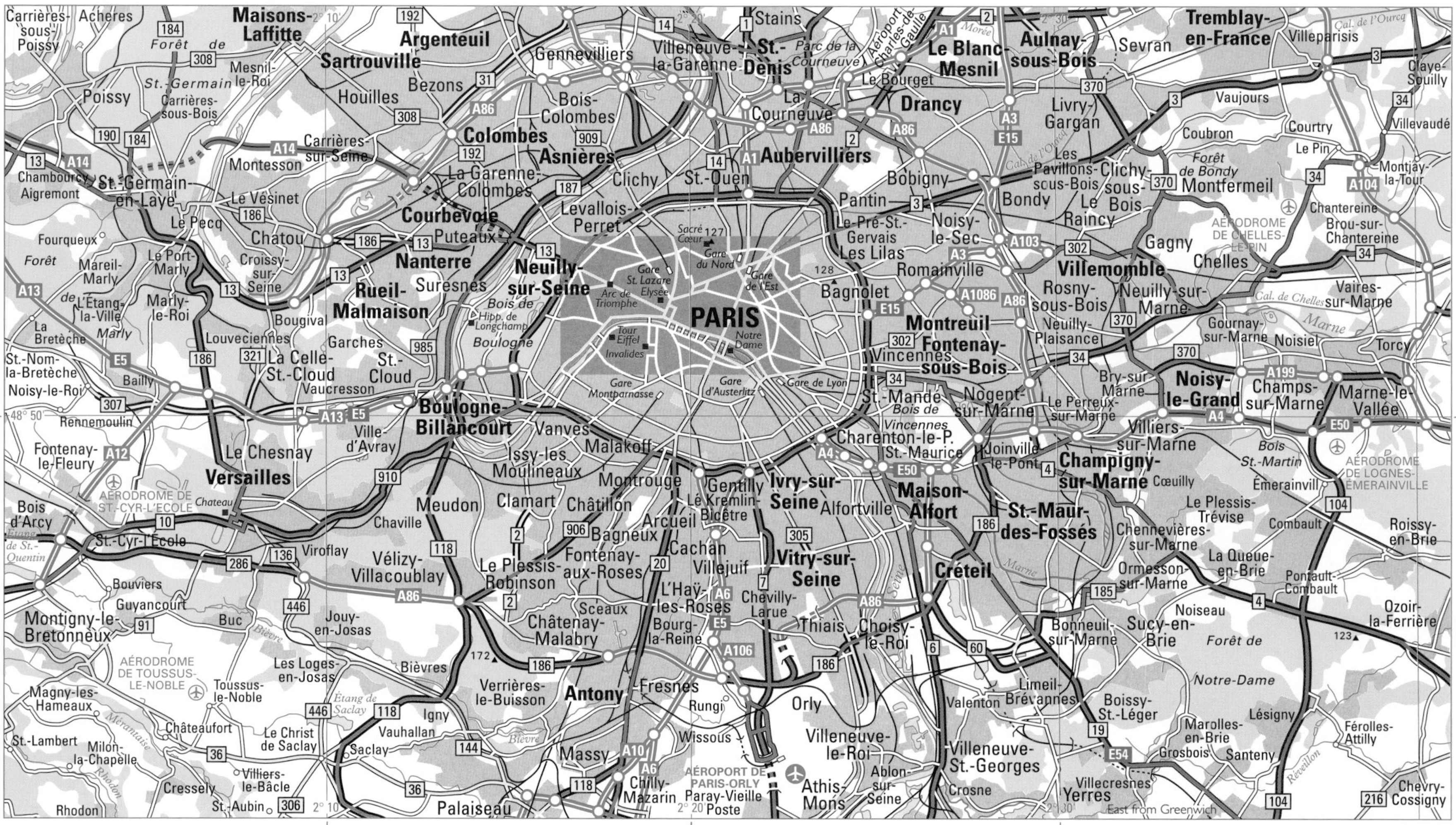
A
B
1
2
3
4
Carrières-sous-Poissy
Achères
Maisons-Laffitte
Argenteuil
Sartrouville
Houilles
Bezons
Poissy
Gennevilliers
Villeneuve-la-Garenne
Stains
St.-Denis
Le Blanc-Mesnil
Aulnay-sous-Bois
Sevran
Tremblay-en-France
Villeparisis
Claye-Souilly
Le Bourget
Drancy
Livry-Gargan
Vaujours
La Courneuve
Colombes
Bois-Colombes
Asnières
Aubervilliers
Coubron
Courtry
Villevaudé
St.-Germain-en-Laye
Chambourcy
Aigremont
Le Vésinet
Le Pecq
Montesson
Carrières-sur-Seine
La Garenne-Colombes
Clichy
St.-Ouen
Bobigny
Les Pavillons-sous-Bois
Clichy-sous-Bois
Montfermeil
Le Pin
Montjay-la-Tour
Bondy
Le Raincy
Pantin
Courbevoie
Levallois-Perret
Chatou
Puteaux
Le Pré-St.-Gervais
Les Lilas
Noisy-le-Sec
Gagny
Chelles
Chantereine
Brou-sur-Chantereine
Fourqueux
Le Port-Marly
Croissy-sur-Seine
Nanterre
Neuilly-sur-Seine
Romainville
Villemomble
Mareil-Marly
Rueil-Malmaison
Suresnes
Bagnolet
Rosny-sous-Bois
Neuilly-sur-Marne
Vaires-sur-Marne
L'Étang-la-Ville
Marly-le-Roi
Bougival
Louveciennes
PARIS
Montreuil
Neuilly-Plaisance
Gournay-sur-Marne
Noisiel
Torcy
La Bretèche
St.-Nom-la-Bretèche
Noisy-le-Roi
Bailly
La Celle-St.-Cloud
Garches
Vaucresson
St.-Cloud
Boulogne
Vincennes
Fontenay-sous-Bois
Bry-sur-Marne
Noisy-le-Grand
Champs-sur-Marne
Marne-la-Vallée
Rennemoulin
Boulogne-Billancourt
Vanves
St.-Mandé
Nogent-sur-Marne
Le Perreux-sur-Marne
Fontenay-le-Fleury
Le Chesnay
Ville-d'Avray
Issy-les-Moulineaux
Malakoff
Charenton-le-P.
St.-Maurice
Joinville-le-Pont
Villiers-sur-Marne
Champigny-sur-Marne
Versailles
Montrouge
Gentilly
Ivry-sur-Seine
Maison-Alfort
Bois d'Arcy
Meudon
Clamart
Châtillon
Le Kremlin-Bicêtre
Alfortville
St.-Maur-des-Fossés
Le Plessis-Trévise
Émerainville
Chaville
Bagneux
Arcueil
Cachan
Villejuif
Vitry-sur-Seine
Chennevières-sur-Marne
Combault
Roissy-en-Brie
St.-Cyr-l'École
Viroflay
Vélizy-Villacoublay
Le Plessis-Robinson
Fontenay-aux-Roses
L'Haÿ-les-Roses
Chevilly-Larue
Créteil
Ormesson-sur-Marne
La Queue-en-Brie
Pontault-Combault
Bouviers
Guyancourt
Montigny-le-Bretonneux
Buc
Jouy-en-Josas
Sceaux
Châtenay-Malabry
Bourg-la-Reine
Thiais
Choisy-le-Roi
Bonneuil-sur-Marne
Sucy-en-Brie
Noiseau
Ozoir-la-Ferrière
Les Loges-en-Josas
Bièvres
Verrières-le-Buisson
Antony
Fresnes
Rungis
Orly
Limeil-Brévannes
Valenton
Boissy-St.-Léger
Magny-les-Hameaux
Toussus-le-Noble
Châteaufort
Le Christ de Saclay
Igny
Vauhallan
Saclay
Massy
Wissous
Villeneuve-le-Roi
Villeneuve-St.-Georges
Marolles-en-Brie
Lésigny
Férolles-Attilly
St.-Lambert
Milon-la-Chapelle
Villiers-le-Bâcle
Cressely
Rhodon
St.-Aubin
Palaiseau
Chilly-Mazarin
Paray-Vieille Poste
Athis-Mons
Ablon-sur-Seine
Crosne
Yerres
Villecresnes
Grosbois
Santeny
Chevry-Cossigny
AÉROPORT DE PARIS-ORLY
AÉRODROME DE ST.-CYR-L'ÉCOLE
AÉRODROME DE TOUSSUS-LE-NOBLE
AÉRODROME DE CHELLES-LE-PIN
AÉRODROME DE LOGNES-ÉMERAINVILLE
Seine
Marne
East from Greenwich

CENTRAL PARIS

0 km 1
0 miles 0.5

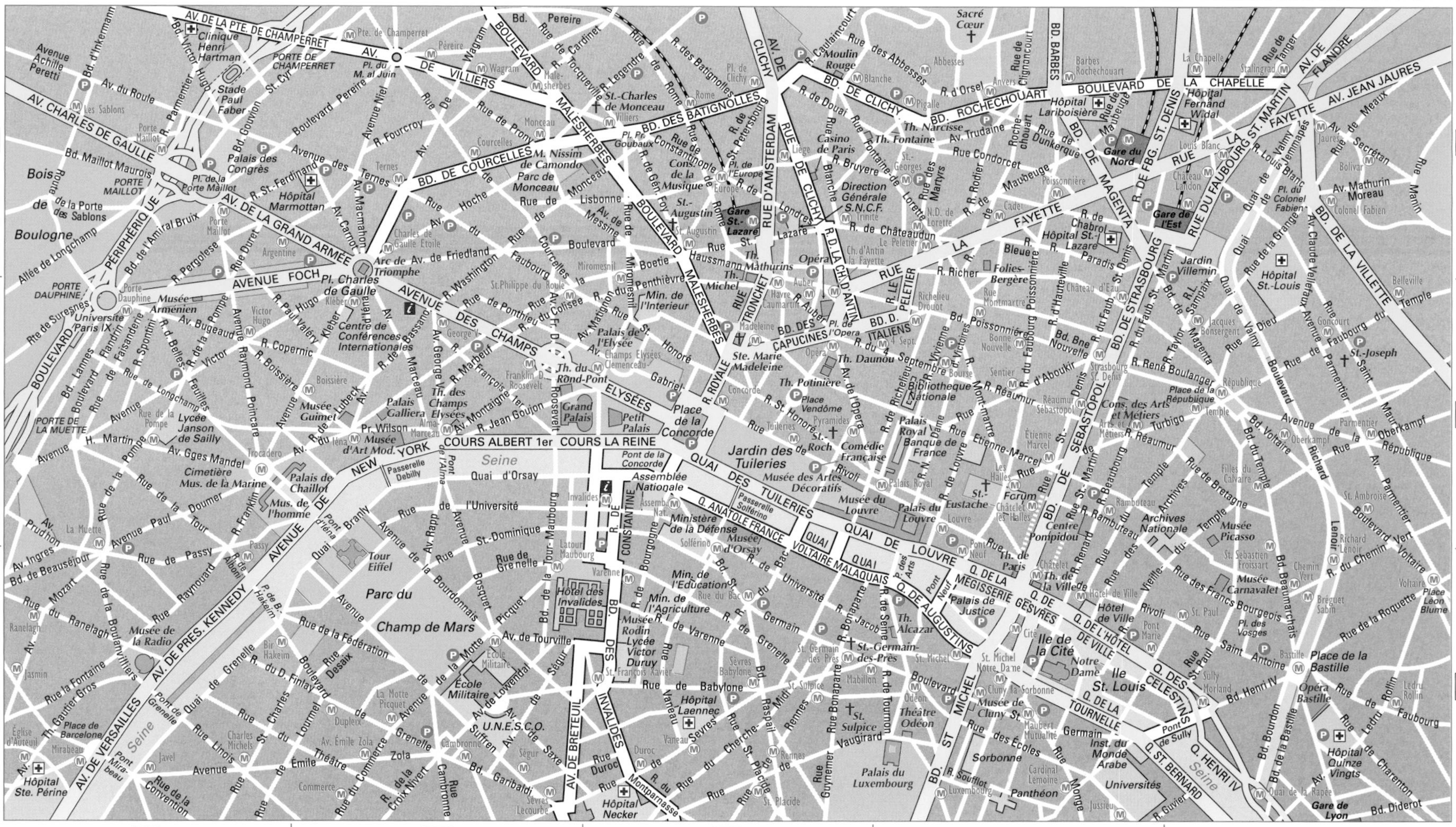
a
b
c
1
2
3
4
5
Bois de Boulogne
AVENUE FOCH
Pl. Charles de Gaulle
Arc de Triomphe
AVENUE DES CHAMPS ELYSÉES
Palais des Congrès
Gare St. Lazare
Gare du Nord
Gare de l'Est
Opéra
Place de la Concorde
Jardin des Tuileries
Musée du Louvre
Grand Palais
Petit Palais
Seine
Tour Eiffel
Parc du Champ de Mars
Hôtel des Invalides
École Militaire
U.N.E.S.C.O.
Musée d'Orsay
Assemblée Nationale
Centre Pompidou
Forum
Île de la Cité
Notre-Dame
Île St. Louis
Place de la Bastille
Opéra Bastille
Musée Picasso
Musée Carnavalet
Palais du Luxembourg
Sorbonne
Panthéon
Institut du Monde Arabe
Gare de Lyon
Moulin Rouge
Sacré Cœur
BOULEVARD DE LA CHAPELLE
BD. DE ROCHECHOUART
BD. DE CLICHY
BD. DES BATIGNOLLES
BD. DE COURCELLES
BOULEVARD MALESHERBES
AV. DE LA GRANDE ARMÉE
AV. CHARLES DE GAULLE
BD. DE MAGENTA
BD. DE STRASBOURG
BD. DE SÉBASTOPOL
BD. ST. MICHEL
AV. DE VERSAILLES
AV. DE PRES. KENNEDY
QUAI D'ORSAY
QUAI DES TUILERIES
QUAI DU LOUVRE
Parc de Monceau
Place Vendôme
Palais Royal
Hôpital Necker
Hôpital St. Louis
Hôpital Lariboisière

PRAGUE

0 km 5
0 miles 3

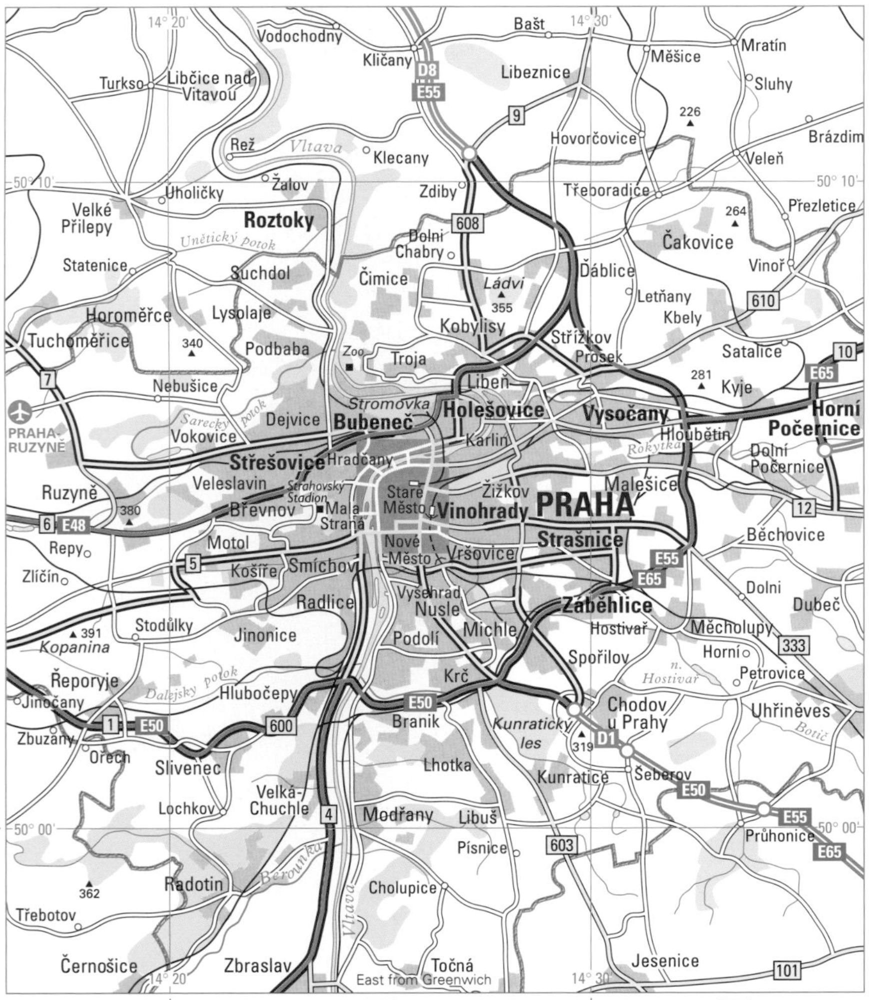

CENTRAL PRAGUE

0 km 1
0 miles 0.5

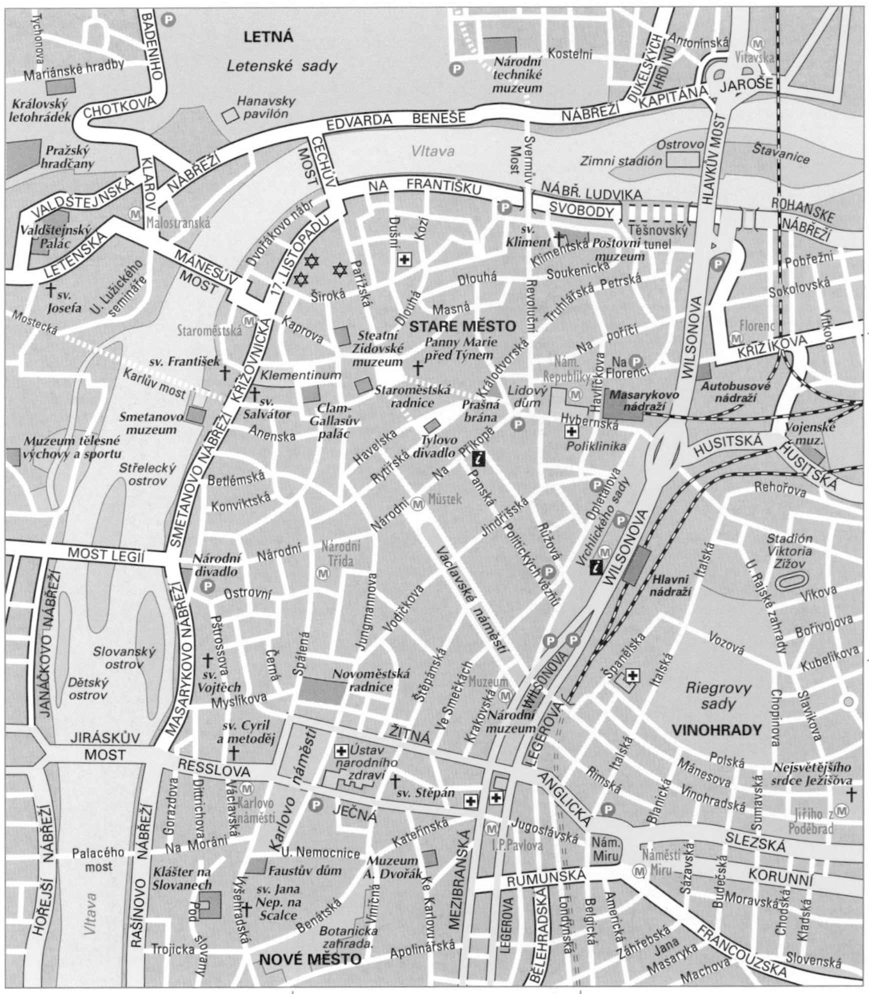

RIO DE JANEIRO

0 km 5
0 miles 3

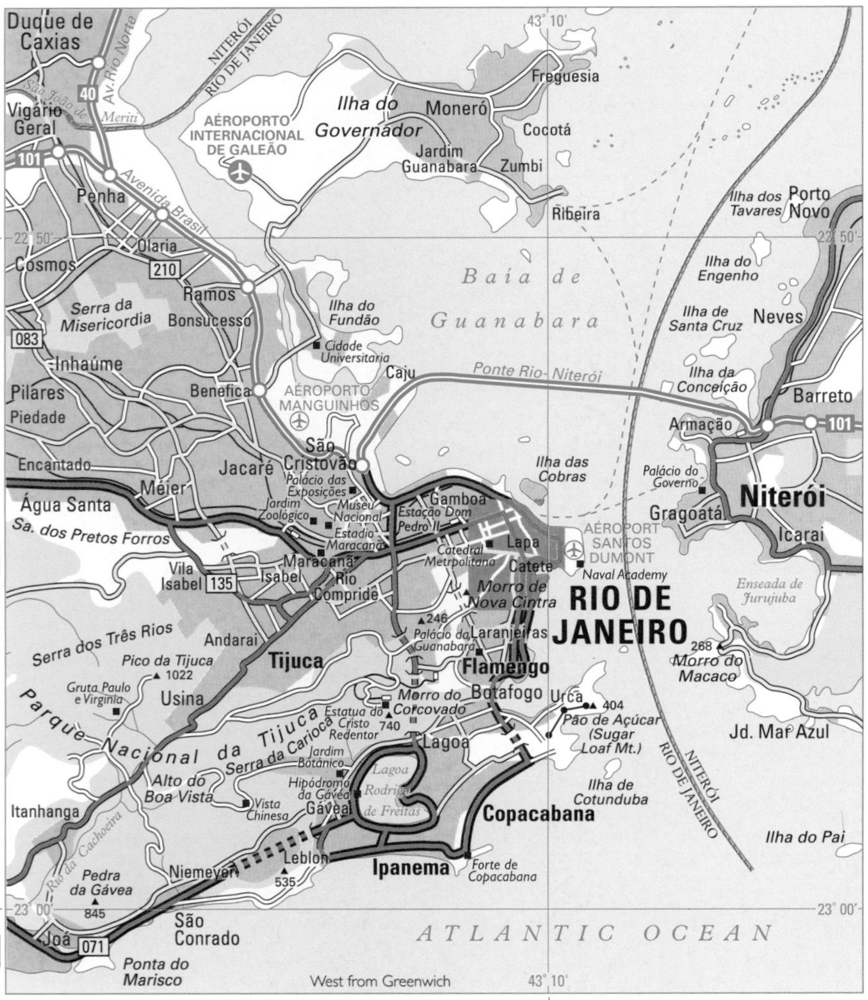

CENTRAL RIO DE JANEIRO

0 km 0.25
0 miles 0.125

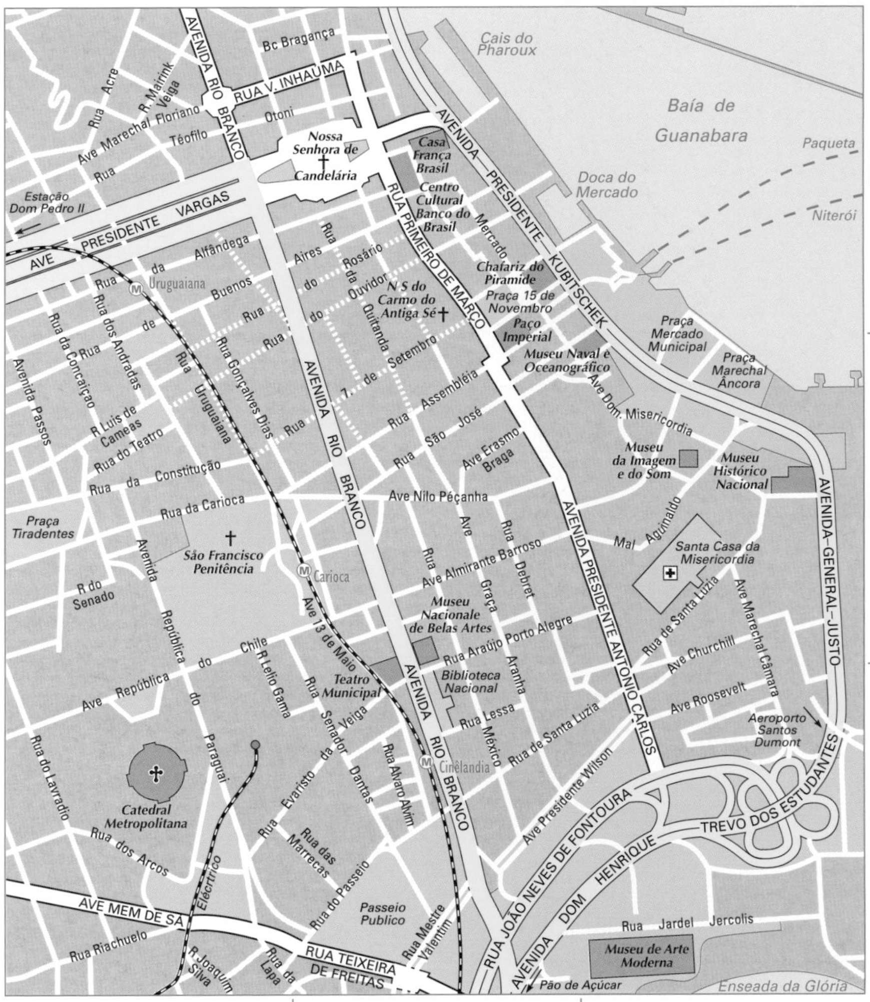

ROME

0 km 5
0 miles 3

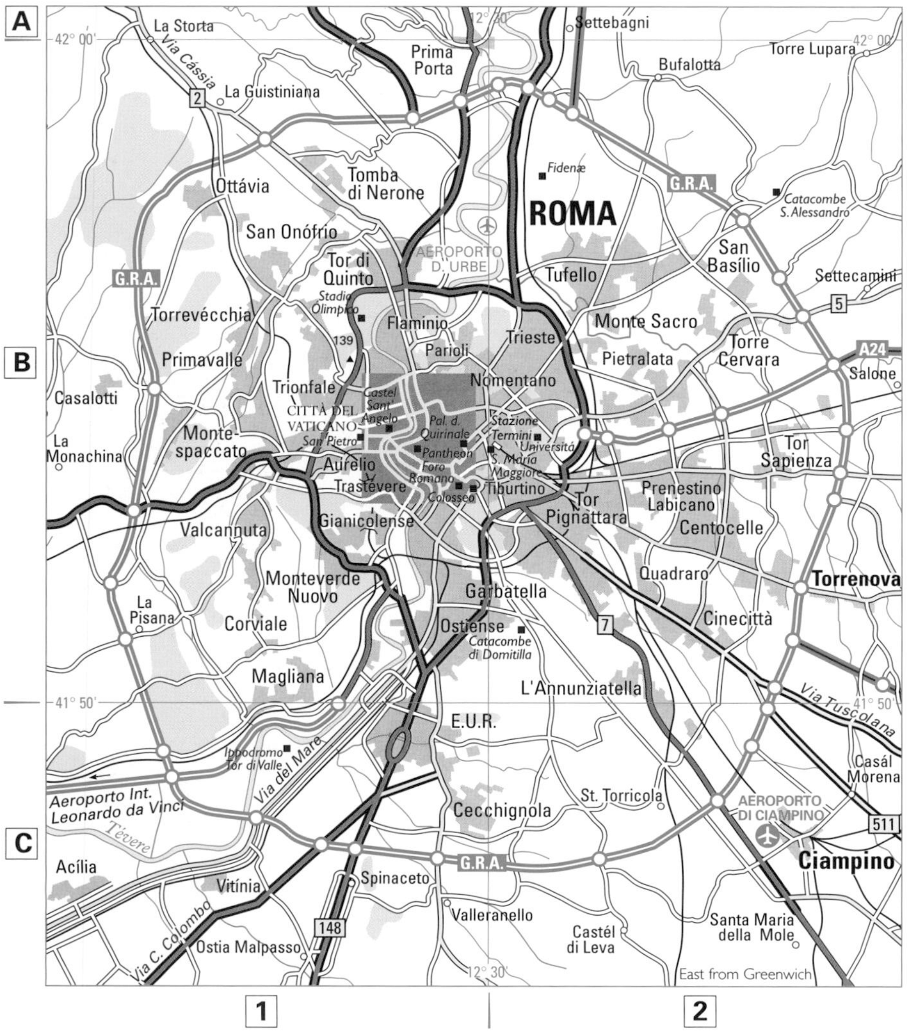

CENTRAL ROME

0 km 1
0 miles 0.5

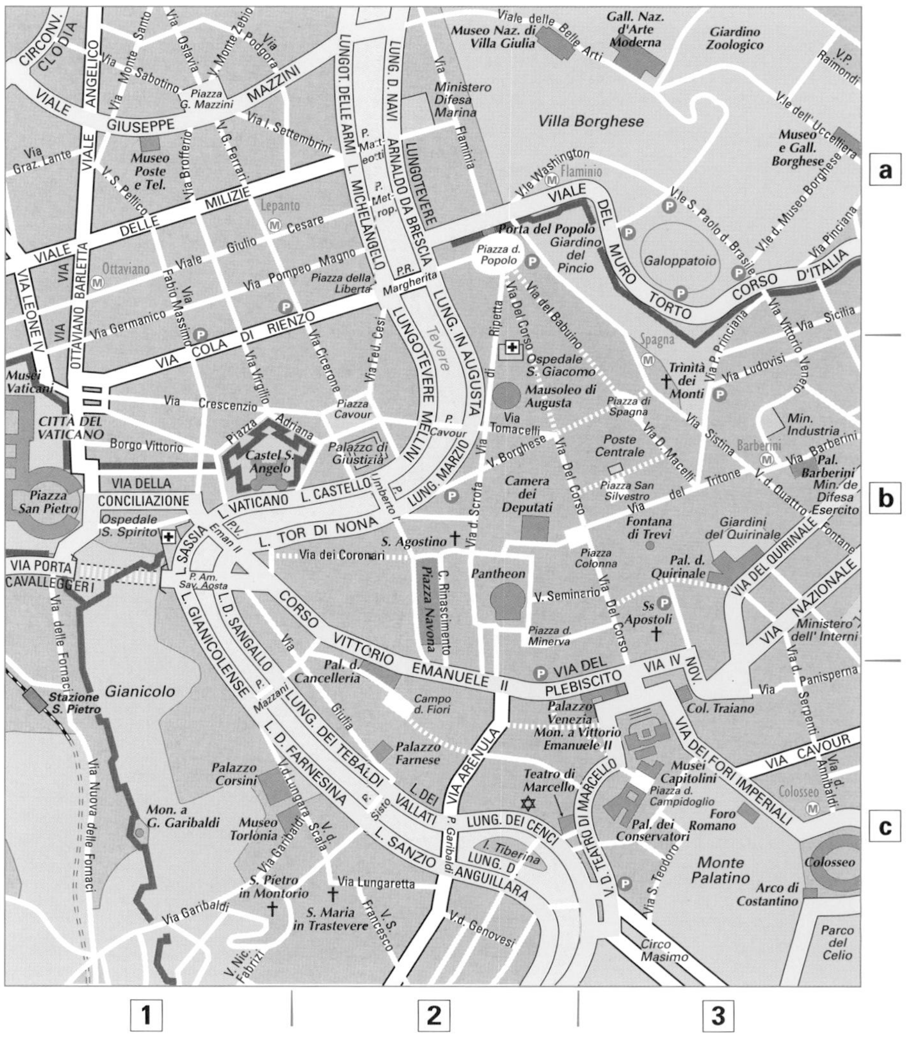

SAN FRANCISCO

0 km 5
0 miles 3

CENTRAL SAN FRANCISCO

0 km 0.25
0 miles 0.125

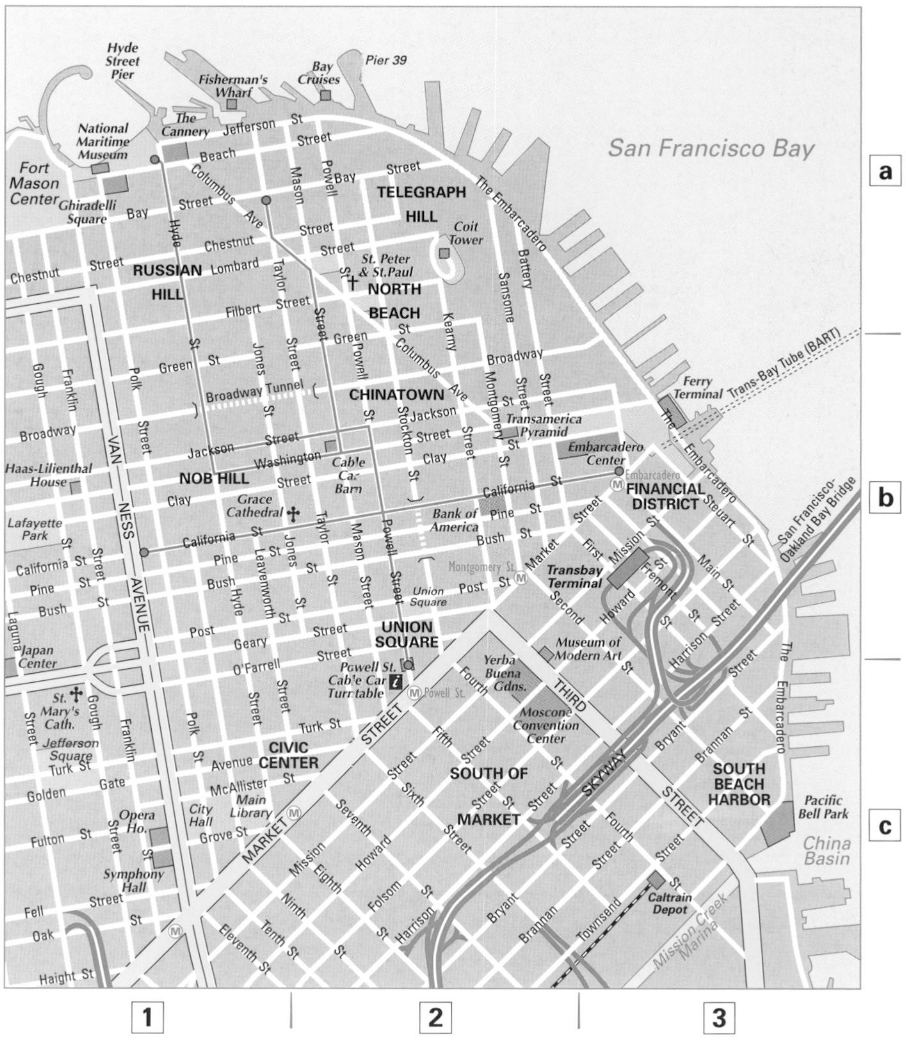

ST. PETERSBURG

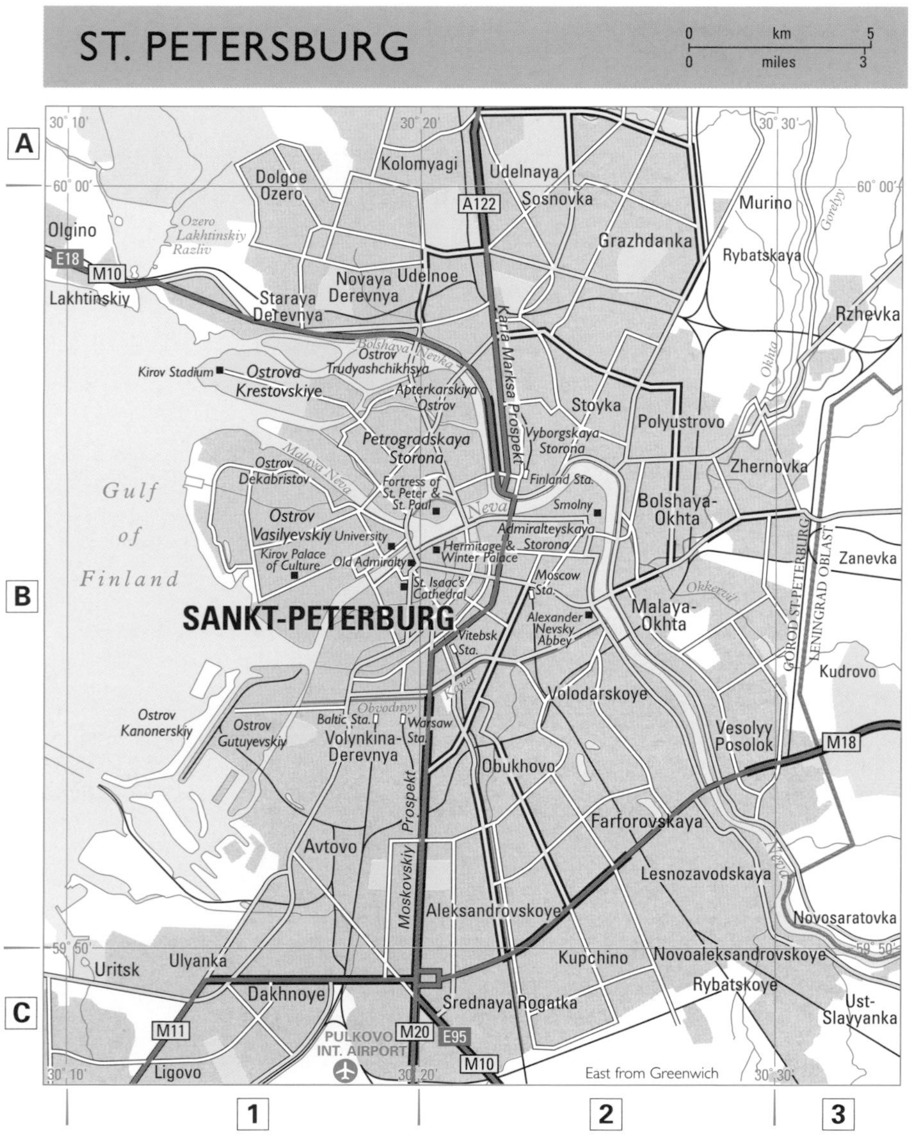
0 km 5
0 miles 3
A
B
C
1
2
3
30° 10'
30° 20'
30° 30'
60° 00'
59° 50'
Kolomyagi
Udelnaya
Sosnovka
Murino
Dolgoe Ozero
A122
Olgino
Ozero Lakhtinskiy Razliv
E18
M10
Lakhtinskiy
Grazhdanka
Rybatskaya
Novaya Derevnya
Udelnoe
Staraya Derevnya
Karla Marksa Prospekt
Rzhevka
Kirov Stadium
Ostrova Krestovskiye
Apterkarskiy Ostrov
Stoyka
Polyustrovo
Petrogradskaya Storona
Vyborgskaya Storona
Zhernovka
Ostrov Dekabristov
Fortress of St. Peter & St. Paul
Finland Sta.
Smolny
Bolshaya-Okhta
Gulf of Finland
Ostrov Vasilyevskiy
University
Kirov Palace of Culture
Old Admiralty
Hermitage & Winter Palace
Admiralteyskaya Storona
Moscow Sta.
St. Isaac's Cathedral
Zanevka
SANKT-PETERBURG
Alexander Nevsky Abbey
Malaya-Okhta
Vitebsk Sta.
Kudrovo
Ostrov Kanonerskiy
Ostrov Gutuyevskiy
Baltic Sta.
Warsaw Sta.
Volynkina-Derevnya
Volodarskoye
Vesolyy Posolok
M18
Obukhovo
Moskovskiy Prospekt
Farforovskaya
Avtovo
Lesnozavodskaya
Aleksandrovskoye
Novosaratovka
Uritsk
Ulyanka
Kupchino
Novoaleksandrovskoye
Dakhnoye
Rybatskoye
Srednaya Rogatka
Ust-Slavyanka
M11
M20
E95
PULKOVO INT. AIRPORT
M10
Ligovo
East from Greenwich
GOROD ST PETERBURG
LENINGRAD OBLAST

SANTIAGO

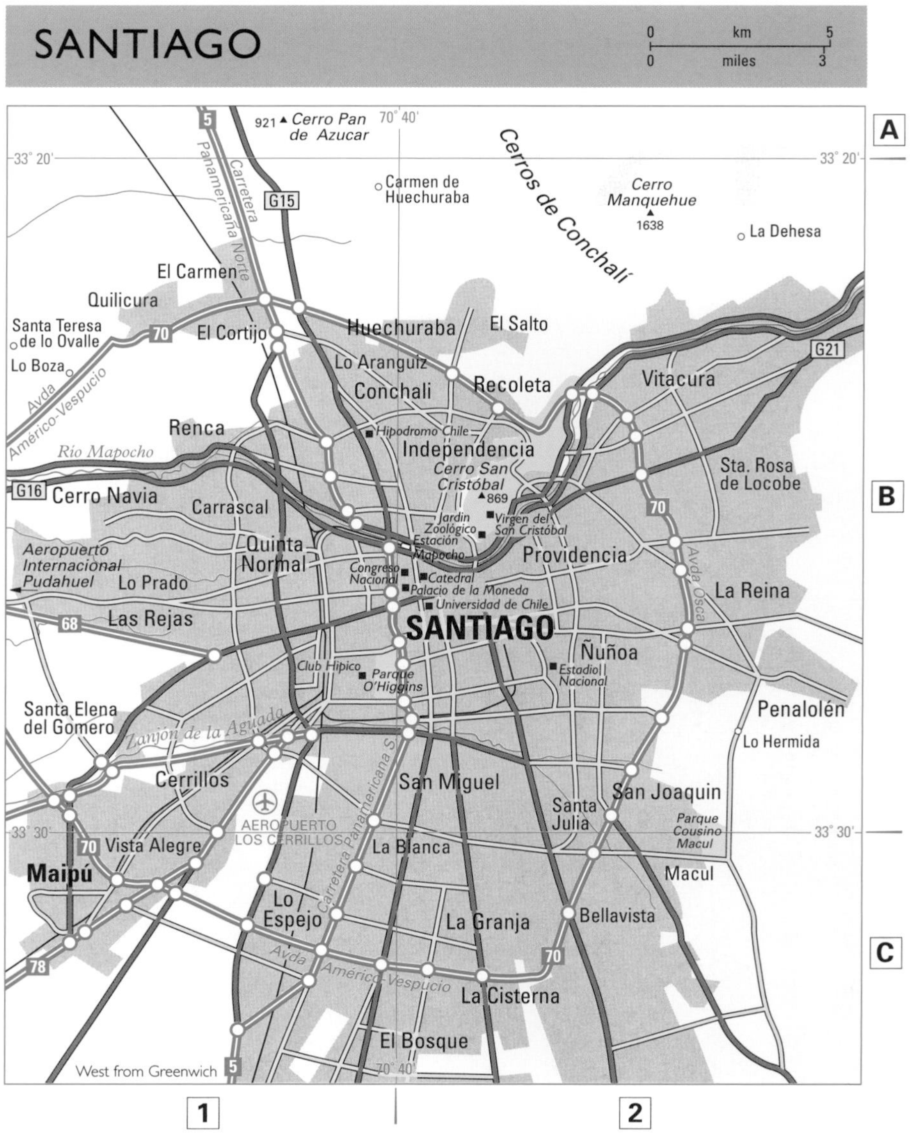
0 km 5
0 miles 3
A
B
C
1
2
921 Cerro Pan de Azucar
70° 40'
33° 20'
33° 30'
Carretera Panamericana Norte
Carmen de Huechuraba
Cerros de Conchalí
Cerro Manquehue 1638
La Dehesa
G15
El Carmen
Quilicura
Santa Teresa de lo Ovalle
El Cortijo
Huechuraba
El Salto
Lo Boza
Lo Aranguiz
Conchali
Recoleta
Vitacura
G21
Avda. Américo-Vespucio
Renca
Hipodromo Chile
Independencia
Cerro San Cristóbal 869
Rio Mapocho
Sta. Rosa de Locobe
G16
Cerro Navia
Carrascal
Jardin Zoológico
Estación Mapocho
Virgen del San Cristóbal
Aeropuerto Internacional Pudahuel
Lo Prado
Quinta Normal
Congreso Nacional
Catedral
Palacio de la Moneda
Universidad de Chile
Providencia
La Reina
Las Rejas
68
SANTIAGO
Ñuñoa
Club Hípico
Parque O'Higgins
Estadio Nacional
Santa Elena del Gomero
Zanjón de la Aguada
Penalolén
Lo Hermida
Cerrillos
San Miguel
San Joaquin
AEROPUERTO LOS CERRILLOS
Santa Julia
Parque Cousino Macul
Vista Alegre
La Blanca
Macul
Maipú
Lo Espejo
La Granja
Bellavista
78
Avda. Américo-Vespucio
La Cisterna
El Bosque
West from Greenwich

SÃO PAULO

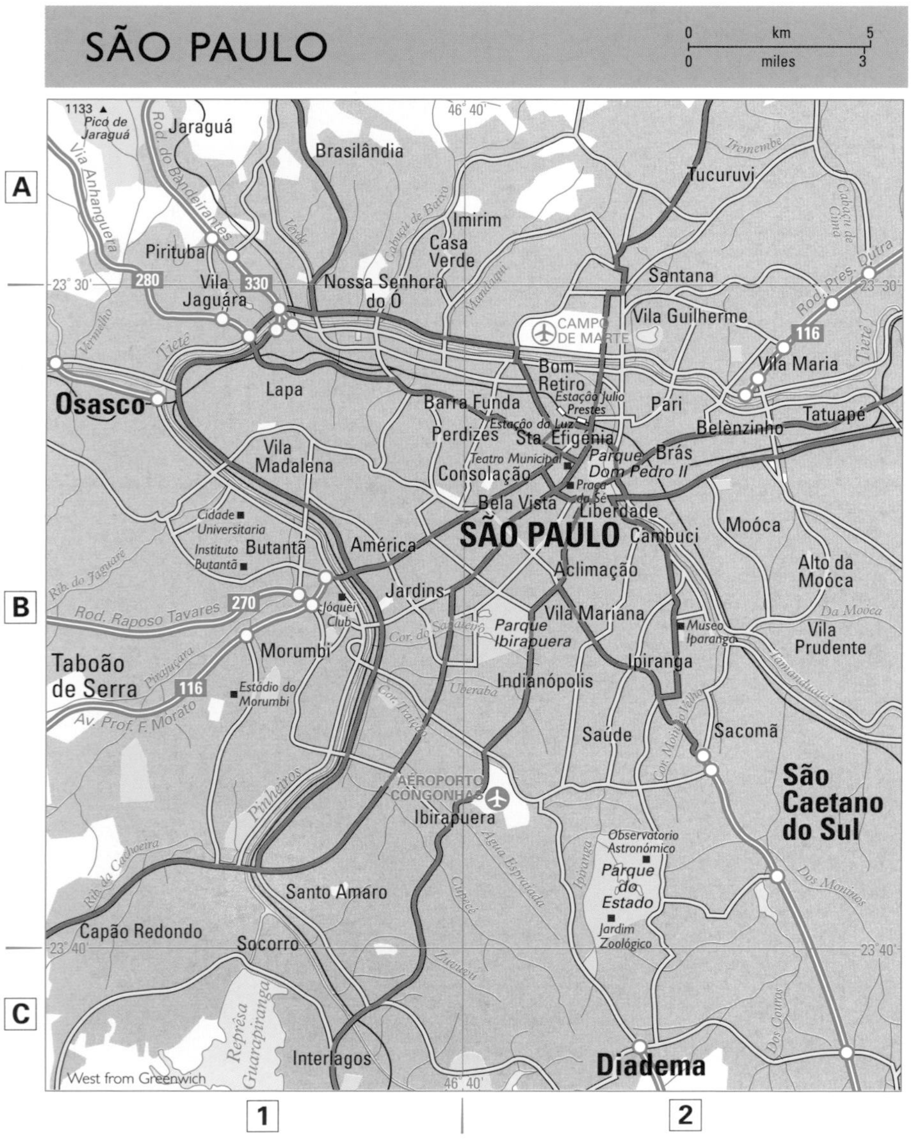
0 km 5
0 miles 3
A
B
C
1
2
1133 Pico de Jaraguá
Jaraguá
46° 40'
23° 30'
23° 40'
Brasilândia
Tucuruvi
Via Anhanguera
Rod. dos Bandeirantes
Imirim
Casa Verde
Pirituba
280
Vila Jaguára
330
Nossa Senhora do O
Santana
Vila Guilherme
CAMPO DE MARTE
116
Vila Maria
Osasco
Lapa
Bom Retiro
Barra Funda
Estação Júlio Prestes
Estação da Luz
Pari
Tatuapé
Belènzinho
Perdizes
Sta. Efigênia
Brás
Vila Madalena
Teatro Municipal
Consolação
Parque Dom Pedro II
Bela Vista
Praça da Sé
Liberdade
Cidade Universitaria
Instituto Butantã
Butantã
América
SÃO PAULO
Cambuci
Moóca
Alto da Moóca
Aclimação
270
Jóquei Club
Jardins
Vila Mariana
Museu Ipiranga
Vila Prudente
Rod. Raposo Tavares
Parque Ibirapuera
Morumbi
Ipiranga
Taboão de Serra
116
Estádio do Morumbi
Indianópolis
Av. Prof. F. Morato
Saúde
Sacomã
AEROPORTO CONGONHAS
São Caetano do Sul
Ibirapuera
Observatorio Astronómico
Parque do Estado
Jardim Zoológico
Santo Amaro
Capão Redondo
Socorro
Represa Guarapiranga
Interlagos
Diadema
West from Greenwich

SEOUL

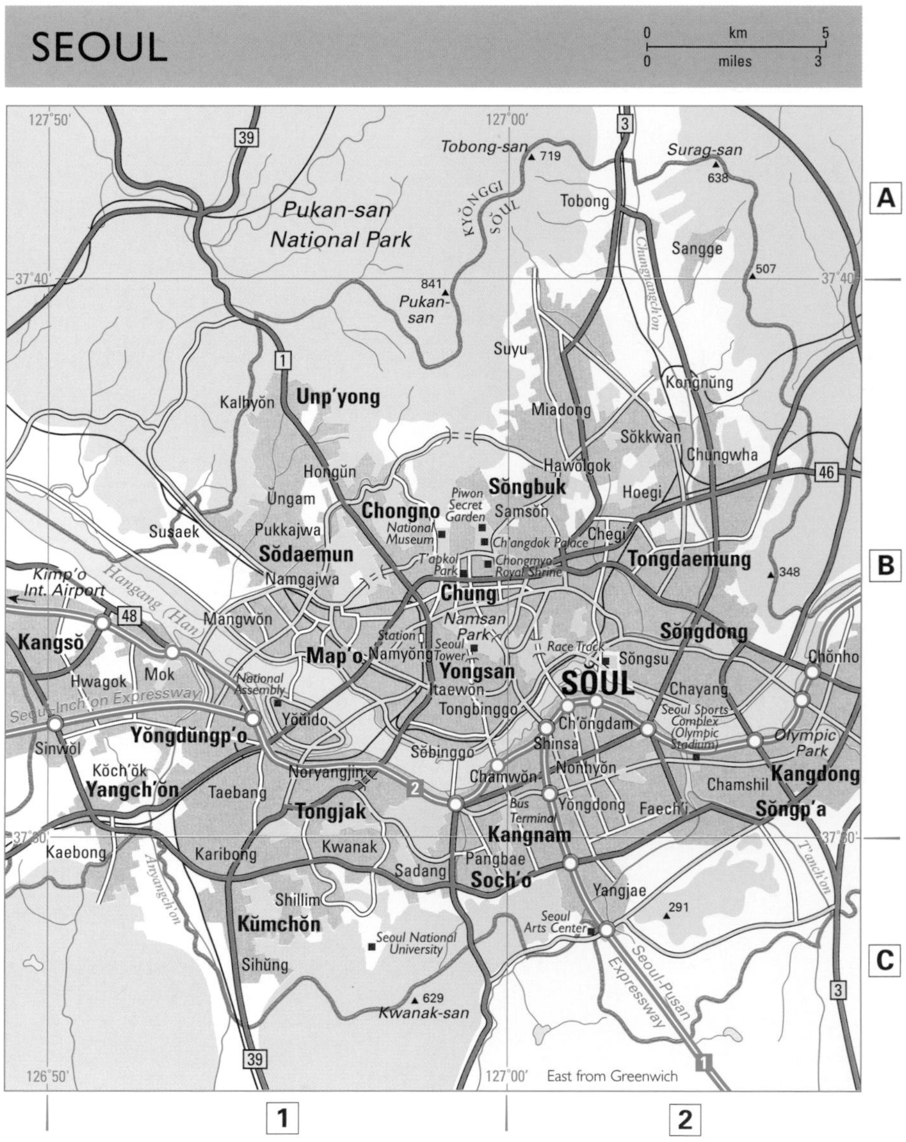
0 km 5
0 miles 3
A
B
C
1
2
127° 50'
127° 00'
37° 40'
37° 30'
126° 50'
39
3
Tobong-san 719
Surag-san 638
Pukan-san National Park
Tobong
KYŎNGGI SŎUL
Sangge
507
841 Pukan-san
Suyu
1
Kongnŭng
Kalhyŏn
Unp'yong
Miadong
Sŏkkwan
Hawŏlgok
Chungwha
Hongŭn
46
Ŭngam
Pirwon Secret Garden
Sŏngbuk
Hoegi
Pukkajwa
Chongno
Samsŏn
Susaek
National Museum
Ch'angdok Palace
Chegi
Sŏdaemun
Tapkol Park
Chongmyo Royal Shrine
Tongdaemung
348
Namgajwa
Chung
Kimp'o Int. Airport
Hangang (Han)
48
Mangwŏn
Namsan Park
Sŏngdong
Kangsŏ
Seoul Station
Seoul Tower
Map'o
Namyong
Race Track
Sŏngsu
Chŏnho
Hwagok
Mok
Yongsan
SŎUL
National Assembly
Itaewon
Tongbinggo
Chayang
Seoul-Inch'on Expressway
Yŏido
Seoul Sports Complex (Olympic Stadium)
Yŏngdŭngp'o
Shinsa
Ch'ŏngdam
Olympic Park
Sinwŏl
Noryangjin
Sŏbinggo
Kangdong
Kŏch'ŏk
Nonhyŏn
Chamshil
Yangch'ŏn
Chamwŏn
Taebang
Tongjak
Bus Terminal
Yŏngdong
Faech'i
Sŏngp'a
2
Kaebong
Karibong
Kwanak
Kangnam
Sadang
Pangbae
Soch'o
Yangjae
Shillim
291
Kŭmchŏn
Seoul Arts Center
Seoul National University
Sihŭng
Seoul-Pusan Expressway
629 Kwanak-san
East from Greenwich

SHANGHAI

0 km 5
0 miles 3

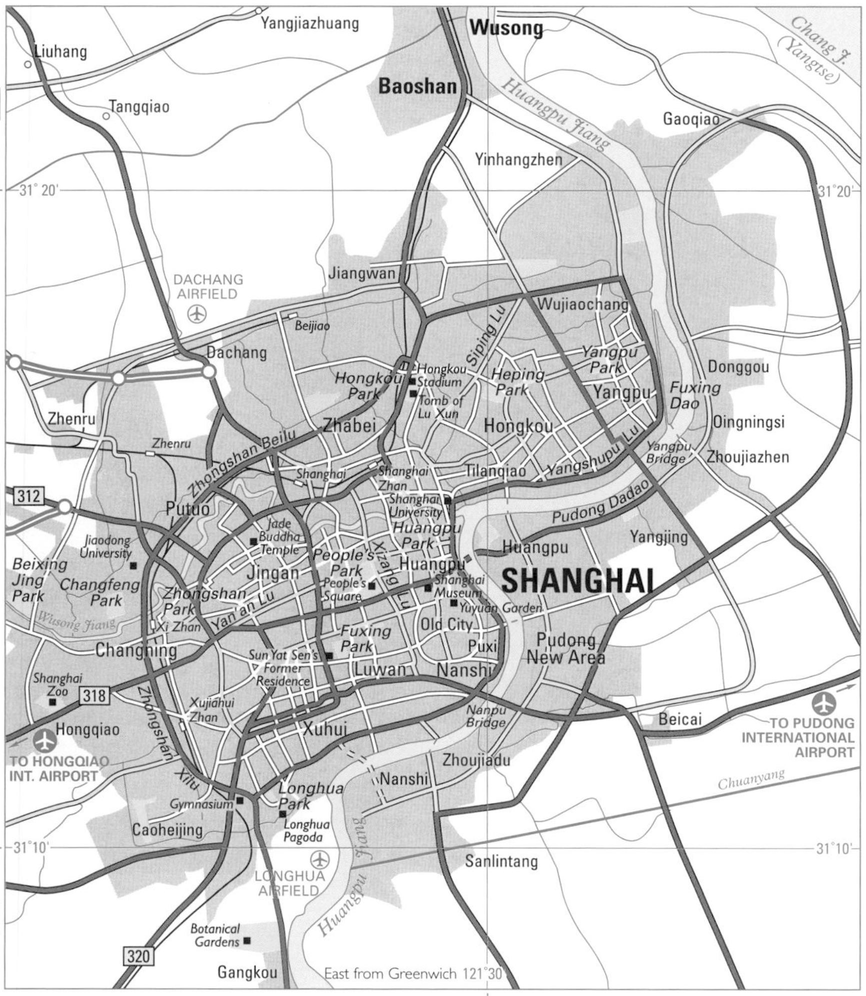

A B C
1 2

CENTRAL SINGAPORE

0 km 1
0 miles 0.5

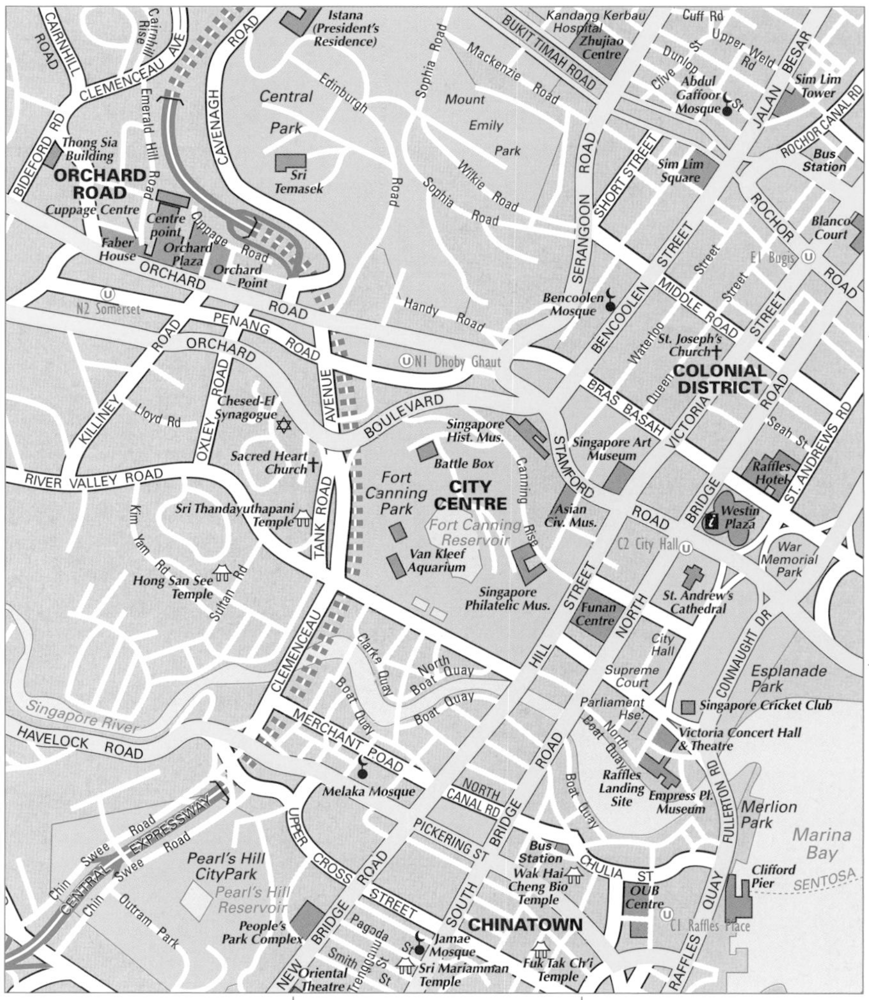

a b c
1 2 3

SINGAPORE

0 km 10
0 miles 6

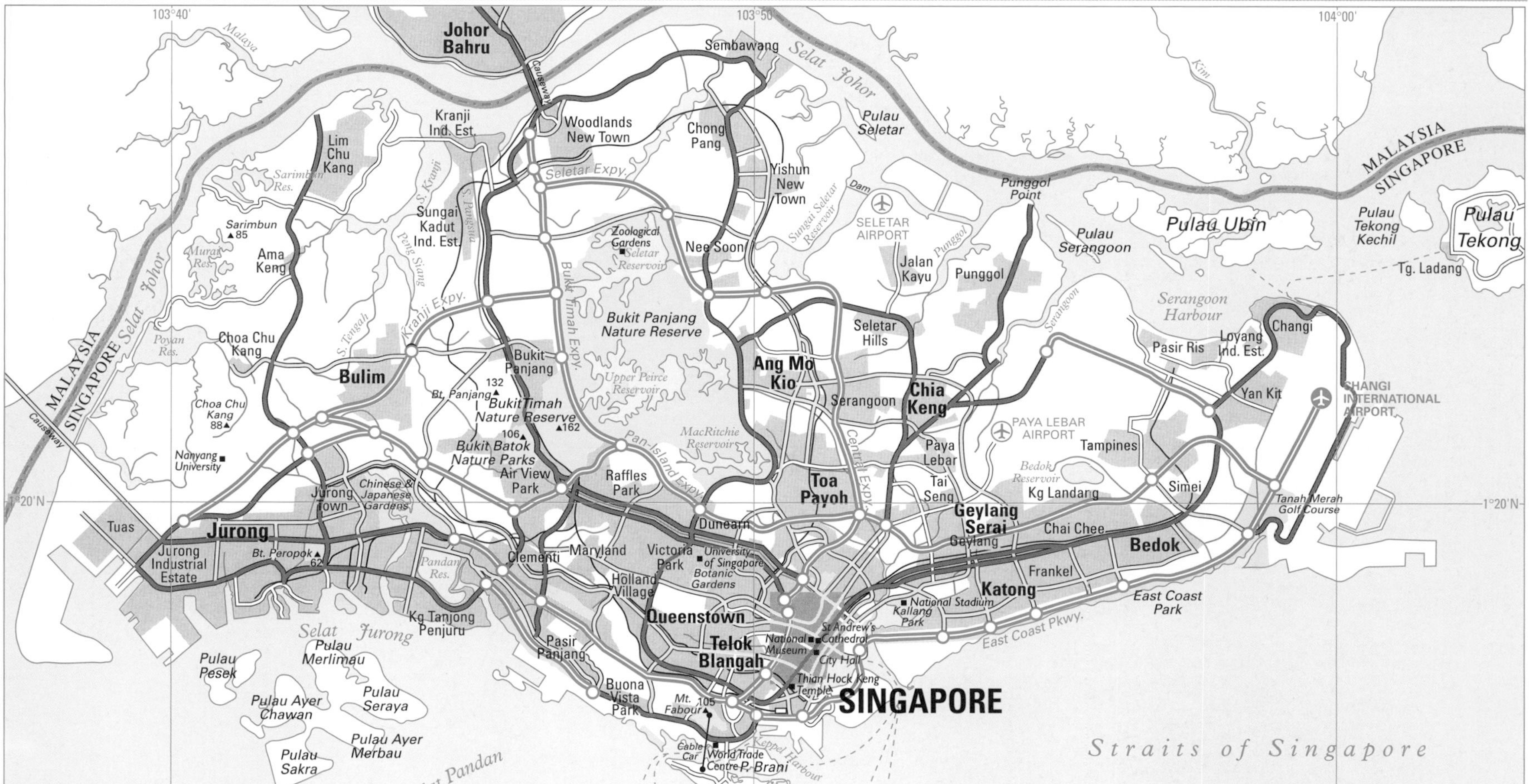

A B
1 2 3 4

STOCKHOLM

0 km 5
0 miles 3

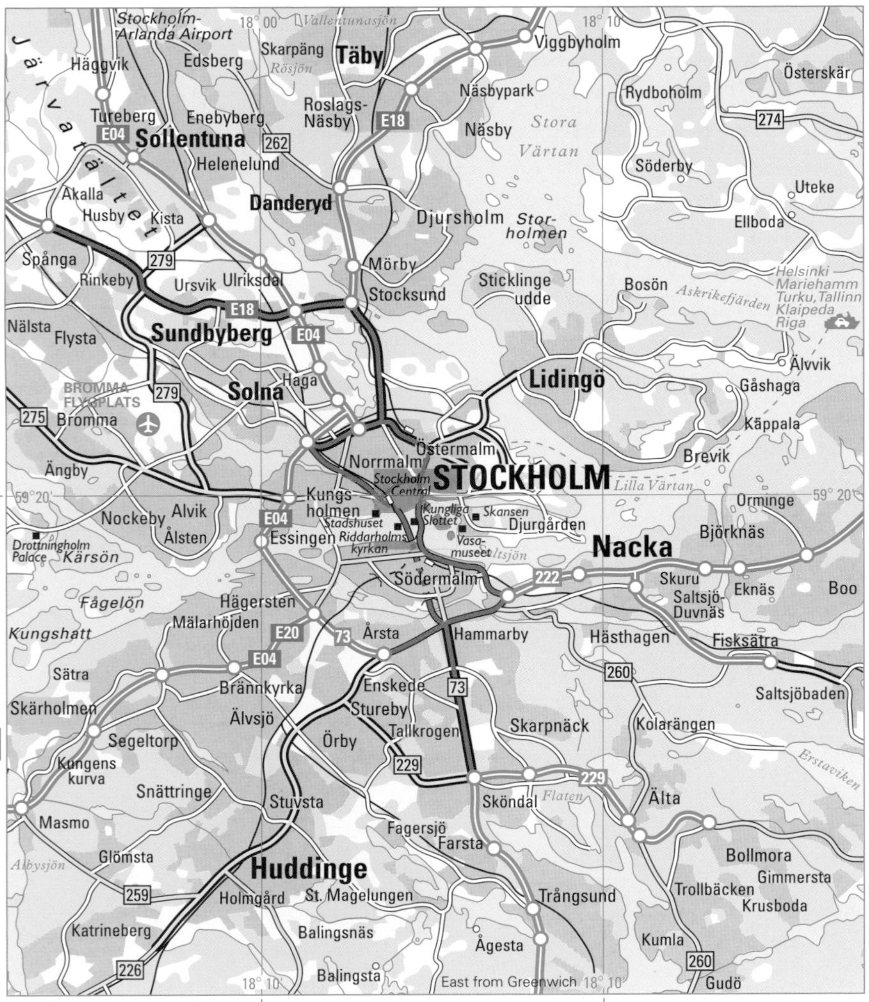

CENTRAL STOCKHOLM

0 km 0.5
0 miles 0.25

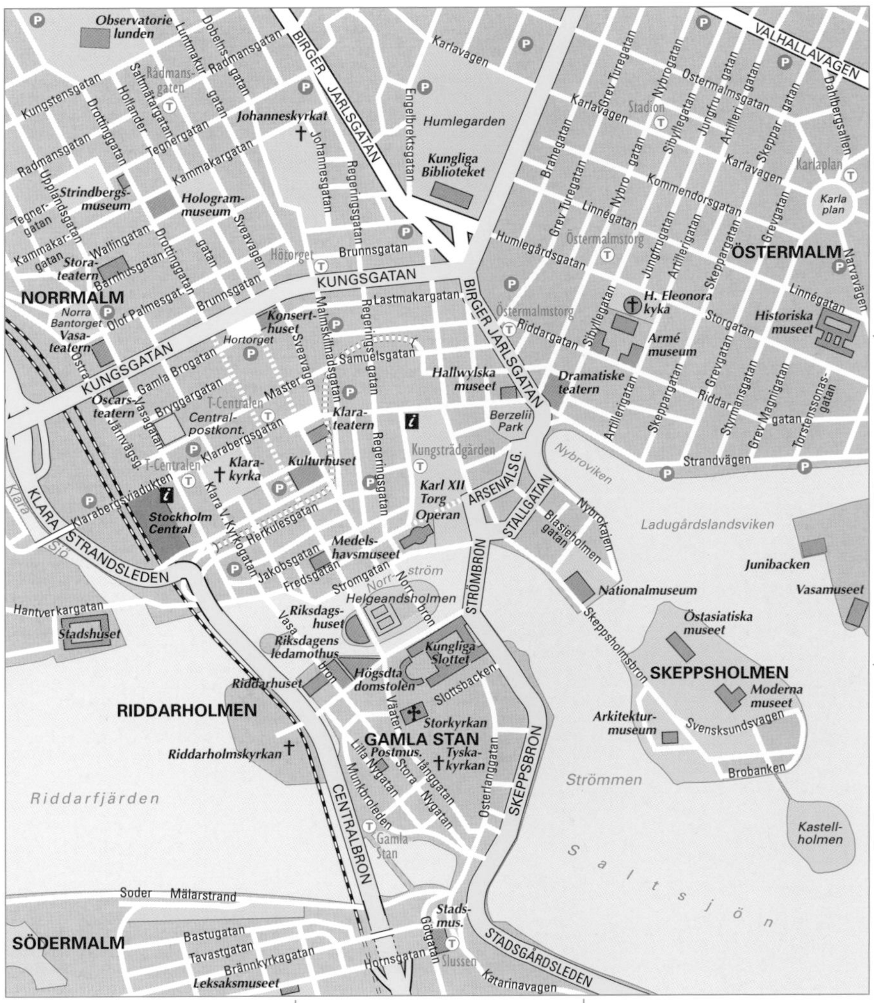

SYDNEY

0 km 5
0 miles 3

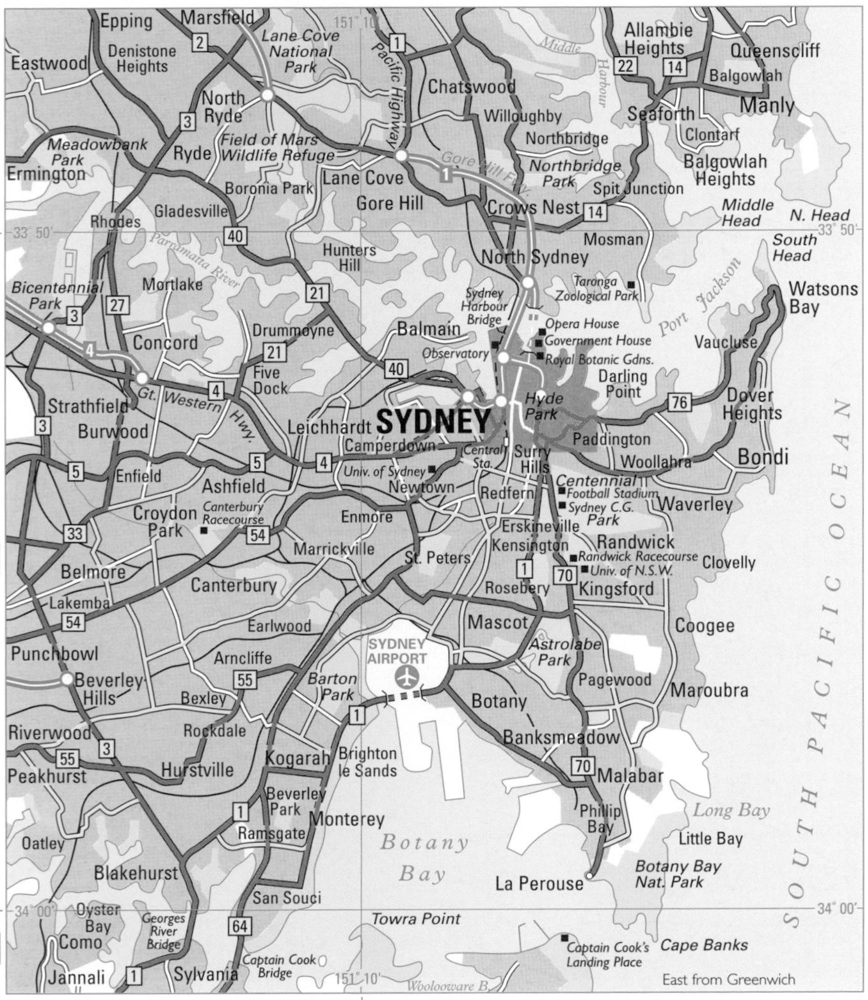

CENTRAL SYDNEY

0 km 2
0 miles 1

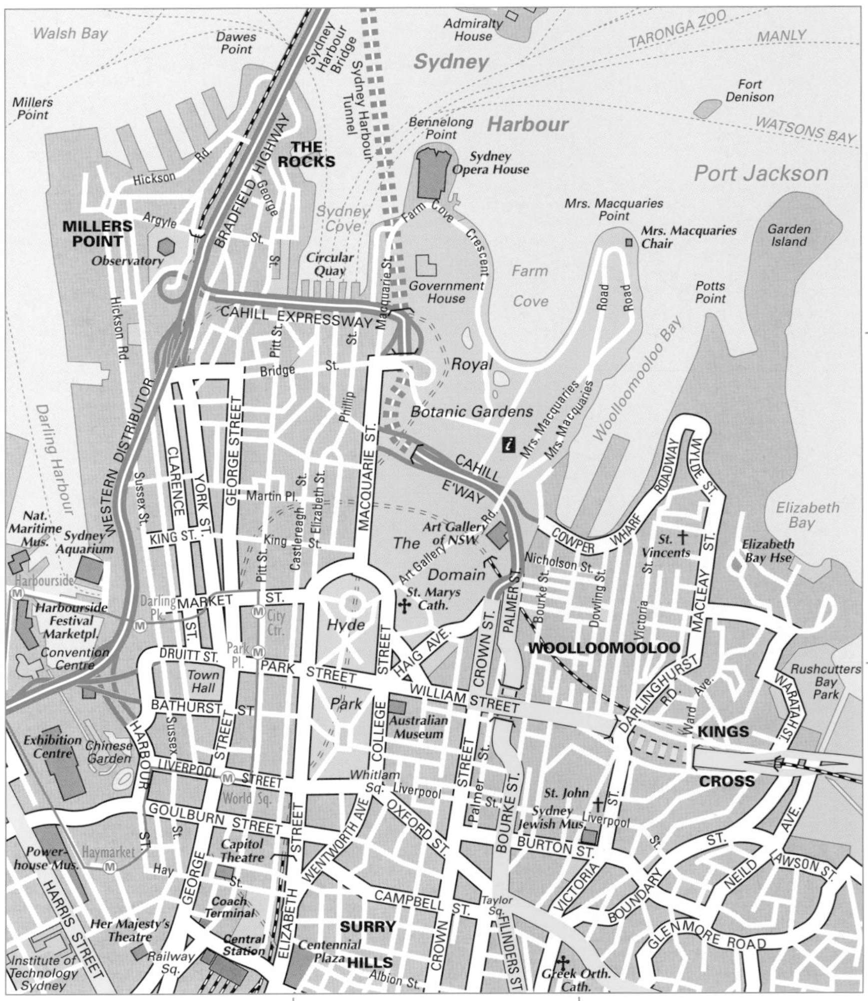

TOKYO

0 km 5
0 miles 3

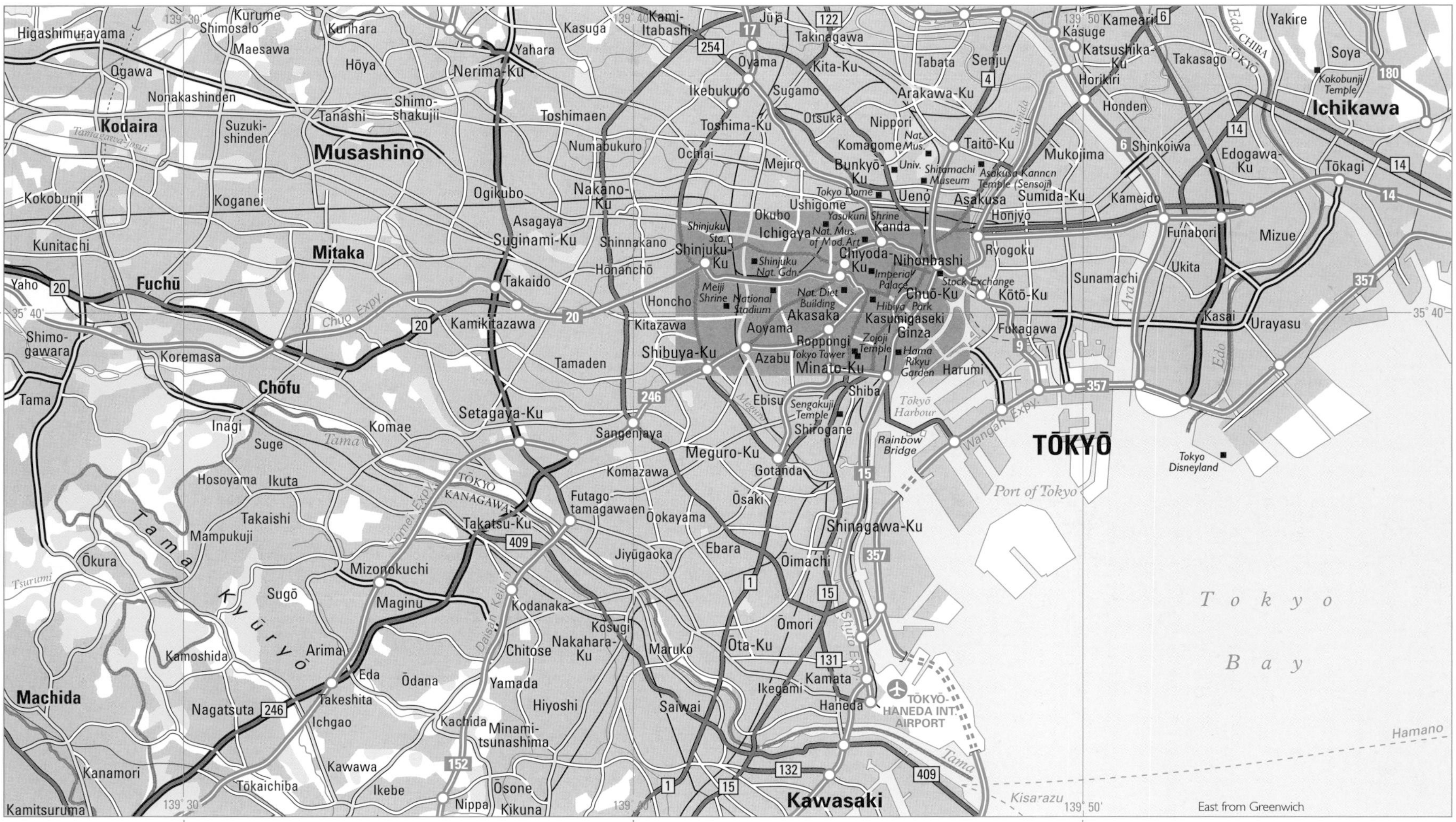

1 2 3 4

CENTRAL TOKYO

0 km 1
0 miles 0.5

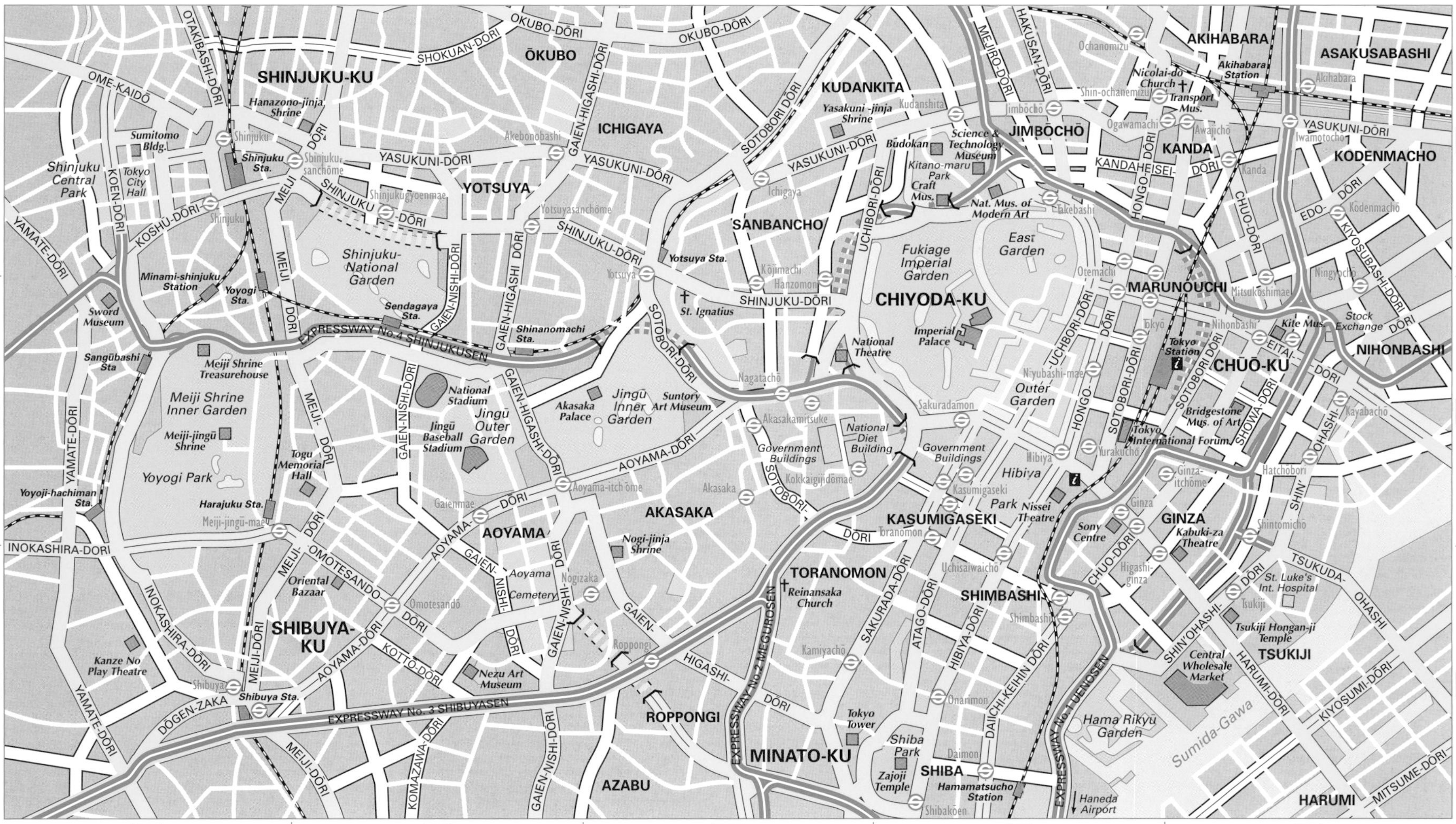

1 2 3 4 5

TEHRAN, TIANJIN, TORONTO

TEHRAN

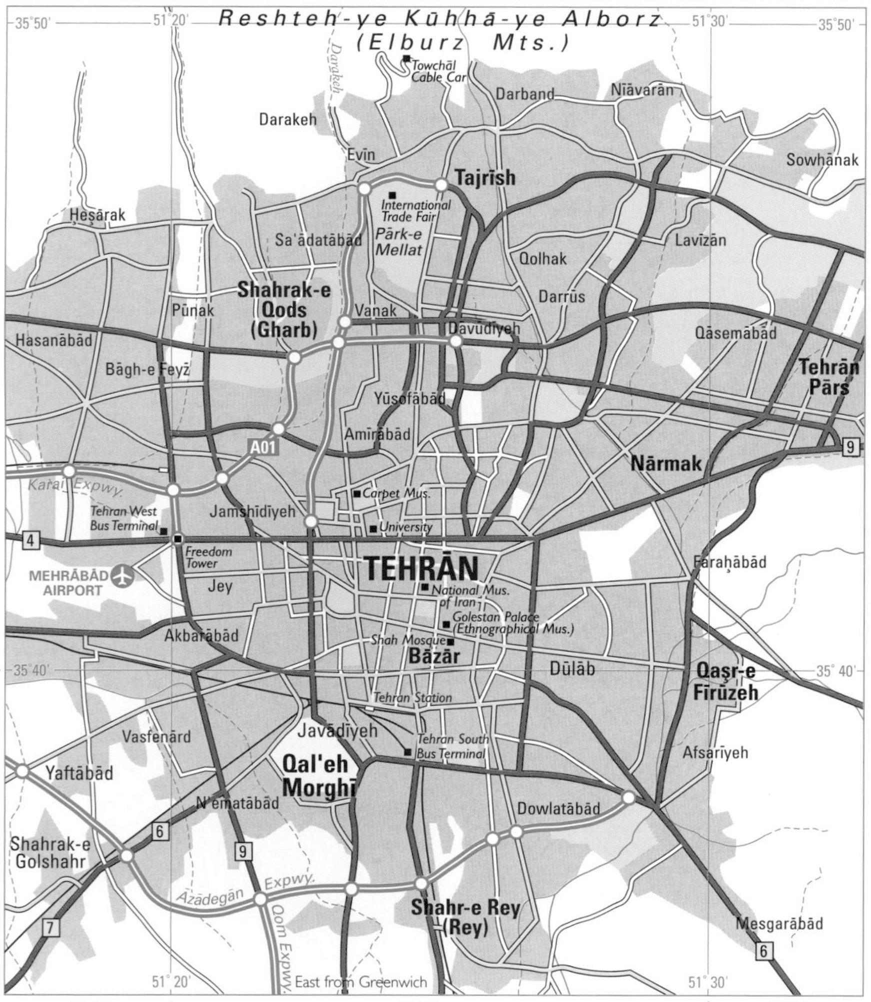
0 km 5
0 miles 3
Reshteh-ye Kūhhā-ye Alborz
(Elburz Mts.)
Towchāl Cable Car
Darband
Nīāvarān
Darakeh
Evin
Tajrīsh
Sowhānak
Hesārak
International Trade Fair
Pārk-e Mellat
Sa'ādatābād
Lavīzān
Qolhak
Pūnak
Shahrak-e Qods (Gharb)
Darrūs
Vanak
Dāvūdīyeh
Qāsemābād
Hasanābād
Bāgh-e Feyz
Tehrān Pārs
Yūsofābād
Amīrābād
Nārmak
Karaj Expwy.
Carpet Mus.
Tehran West Bus Terminal
Jamshīdīyeh
University
Freedom Tower
Farahābād
MEHRĀBĀD AIRPORT
Jey
TEHRĀN
National Mus. of Iran
Golestan Palace (Ethnographical Mus.)
Shah Mosque
Akbarābād
Bāzār
Dūlāb
Qasr-e Fīrūzeh
Tehran Station
Vasfenārd
Javādīyeh
Tehran South Bus Terminal
Qal'eh Morghī
Afsarīyeh
Yaftābād
N'ematābād
Dowlatābād
Shahrak-e Golshahr
Āzādegān Expwy.
Qom Expwy.
Shahr-e Rey (Rey)
Mesgarābād
East from Greenwich
35°50'
51°20'
51°30'
35°40'
A
B
1
2
3

TIANJIN

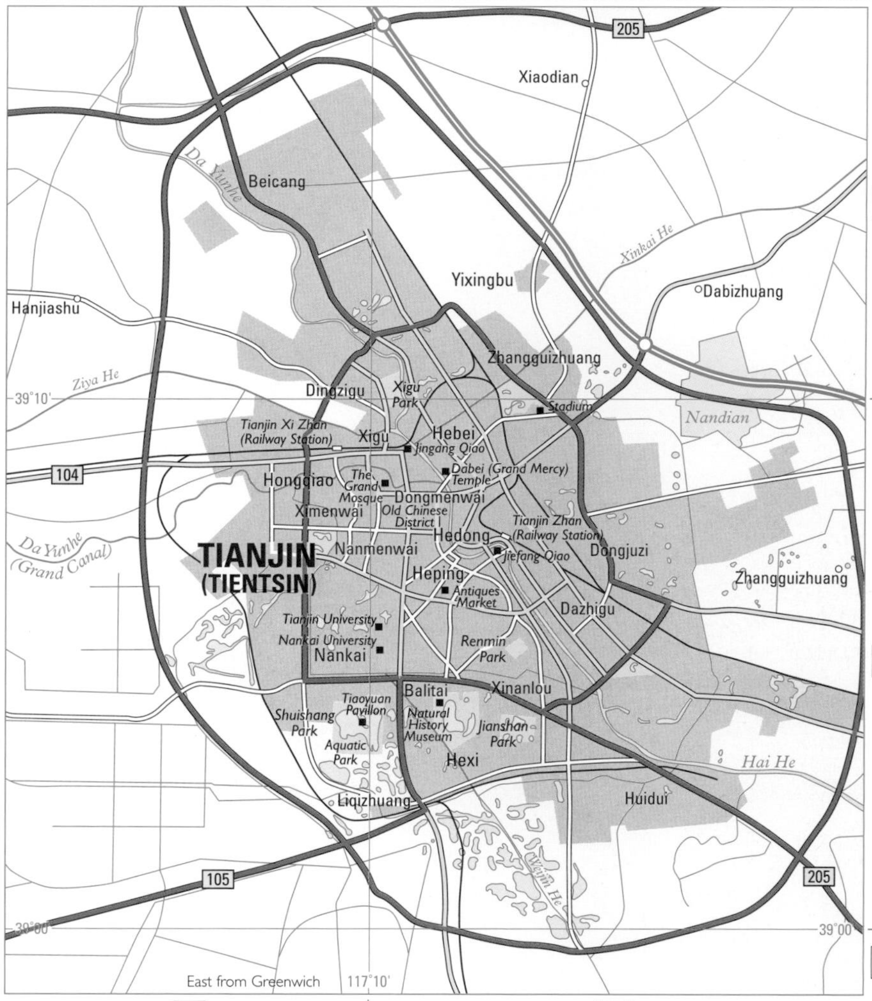
0 km 5
0 miles 3
205
Xiaodian
Da Yunhe
Beicang
A
Yixingbu
Ziya He
Xinkai He
Dabizhuang
Hanjiashu
Zhangguizhuang
39°10'
Dingzigu
Xigu Park
Stadium
Nandian
Tianjin Xi Zhan (Railway Station)
Xigu
Hebei
Jingang Qiao
104
Hongqiao
The Grand Mosque
Dabei (Grand Mercy) Temple
Xmenwai
Old Chinese District
Dongmenwai
Tianjin Zhan (Railway Station)
Da Yunhe (Grand Canal)
TIANJIN (TIENTSIN)
Nanmenwai
Hedong
Jiefang Qiao
Dongjuzi
Zhangguizhuang
Heping
Antiques Market
Dazhigu
Tianjin University
Nankai University
Nankai
Renmin Park
B
Balitai
Xinanlou
Tiaoyuan Pavilion
Shuishang Park
Natural History Museum
Jianshan Park
Aquatic Park
Hexi
Hai He
Huidui
Liqizhuang
105
205
39°00'
C
East from Greenwich
117°10'
1
2

TORONTO

0 km 5
0 miles 3
79°40'
79°30'
79°20'
79°10'
Markham
Metro Toronto Zoo
Fairport
407
Thornhill
East Don
401
Rouge Hill
Brown
Rouge
Little Rouge
West Rouge
27
Humber
Concord
48
Port Union
York
Pine Grove
Edgeley
Newtonbrook
Agincourt
Malvern
Highland Creek
Peel
Woodbridge
Fisherville
Willowdale
404
Black Creek Pioneer Village
York University
11
Northmount
Woburn
Humber Summit
Lansing
West Hill
Beaumonte Heights
North York
Bendale
Highland Creek
Armour Heights
York Mills
A
Wexford
Scarborough
Thistletown
400
DOWNSVIEW AIRPORT
Don Mills
407
Kipling Heights
427
Downsview
Lawrence Heights
Wilket Creek Park
Cliffside
Rexdale
Humberlea
Malton
Woodbine Race Track
Ontario Science Centre
Danforth
Thorncliffe
Weston
27
Leaside
Dentonia Park
409
Forest Hill
TORONTO INTERNATIONAL AIRPORT (LESTER B. PEARSON)
401
York
East York
Birch Cliff
Casa Loma
Don Valley Pkwy.
Humber Valley Village
Mount Dennis
Kew Gardens
43°40'
Riverdale Park
Parliament Buildings
University of Toronto
Swansea
Hanlon
Etobicoke
Lambton Mills
City Hall
CN Tower & SkyDome
Union Sta.
Gardiner Expy.
High Park
Islington
Kingsway
Old Fort York
TORONTO
Markland Wood
Parkdale
427
Humber Bay
Exhibition Place
TORONTO CITY CENTRE AIRPORT
Humber Bay
Ontario Place
Toronto Harbour
B
Burnhamthorpe
Summerville
Toronto Islands
Island Park
LAKE ONTARIO
Elizabeth Way
Queen
Mimico
Gibraltar Point
New Toronto
Cooksville
Mississauga
Long Branch
West from Greenwich
1
2
3
4

VIENNA

0 km 5
0 miles 3

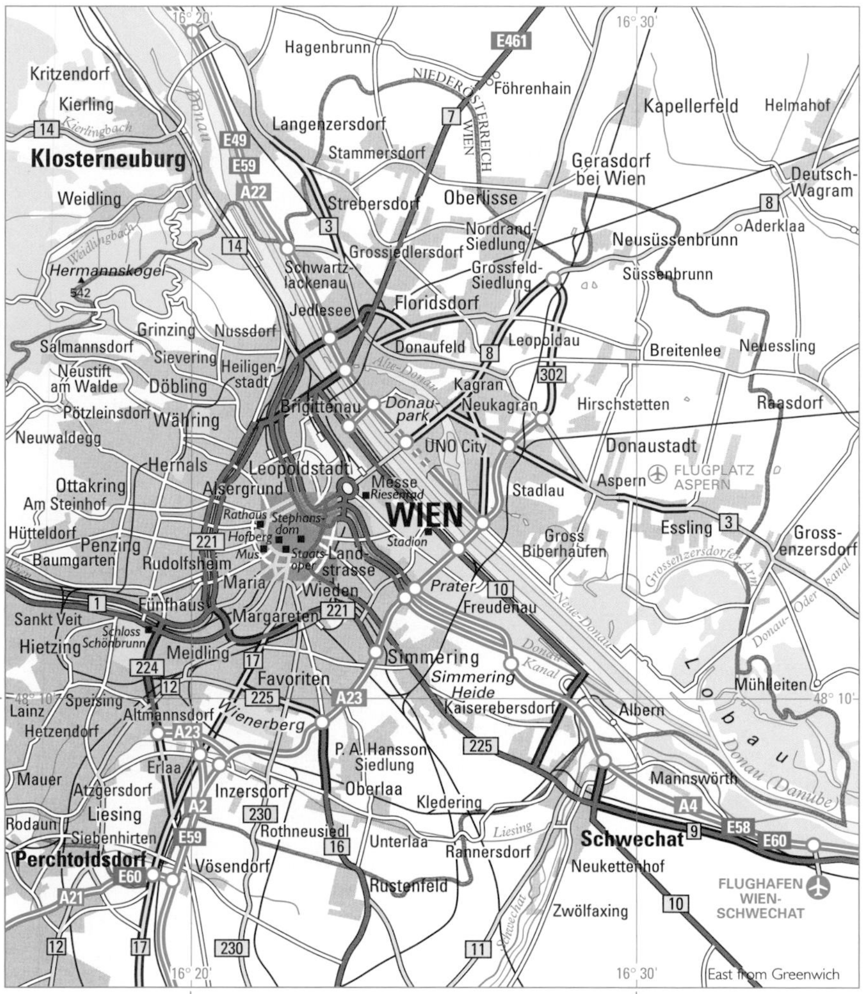

CENTRAL VIENNA

0 km 0.5
0 miles 0.25

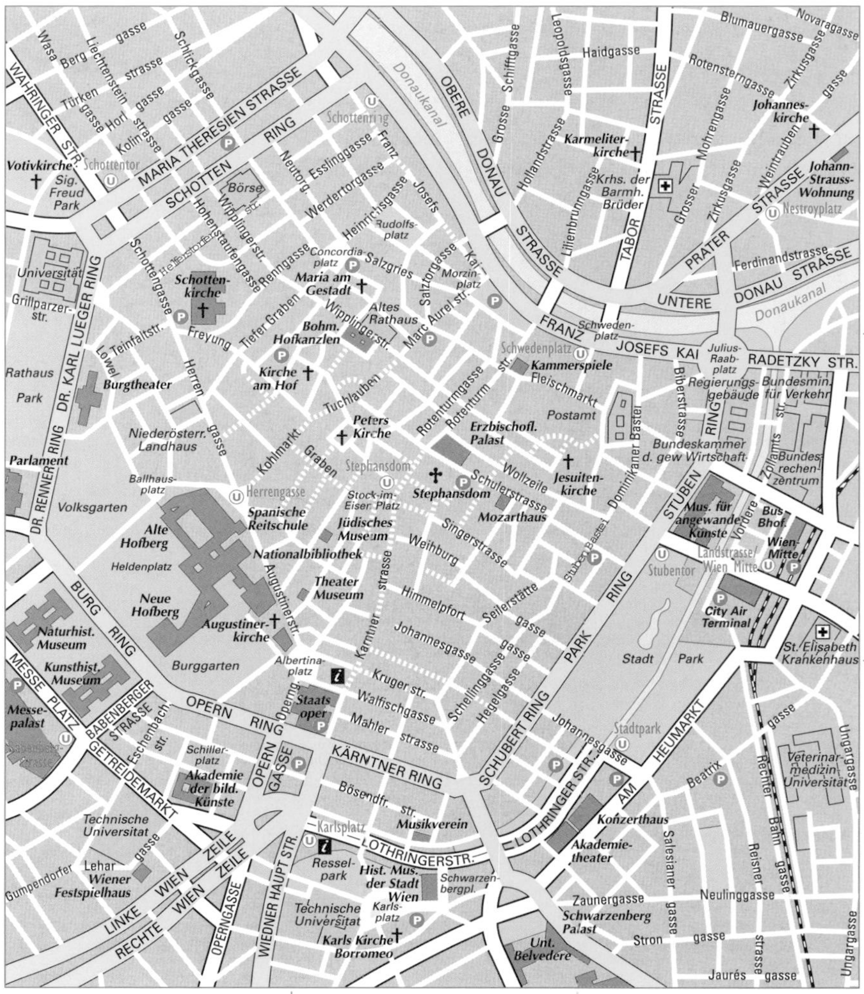

WARSAW

0 km 5
0 miles 3

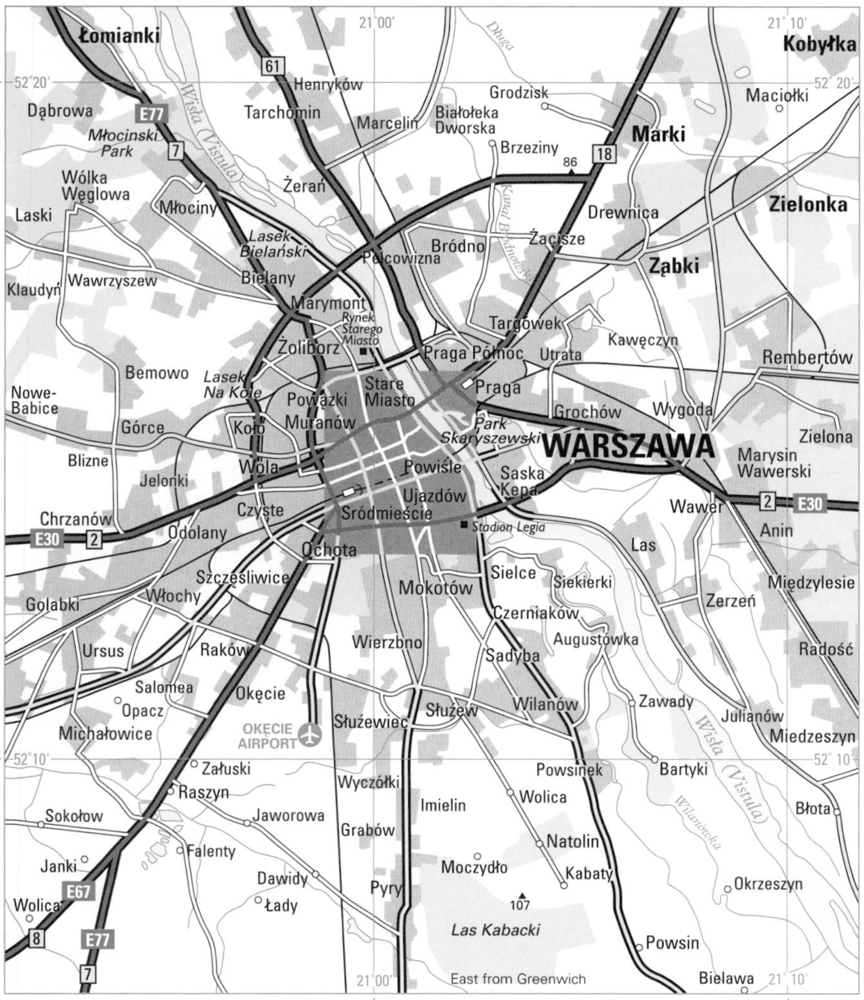

CENTRAL WARSAW

0 km 2
0 miles 1

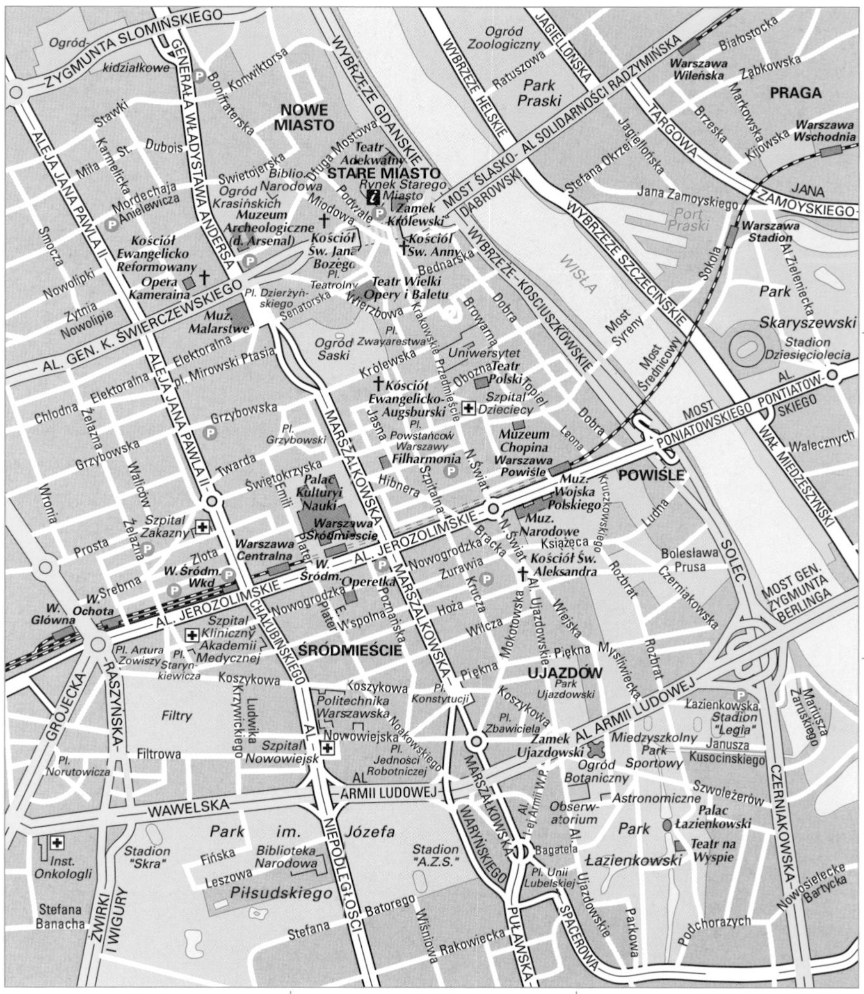

WASHINGTON

0 km 5
0 miles 3

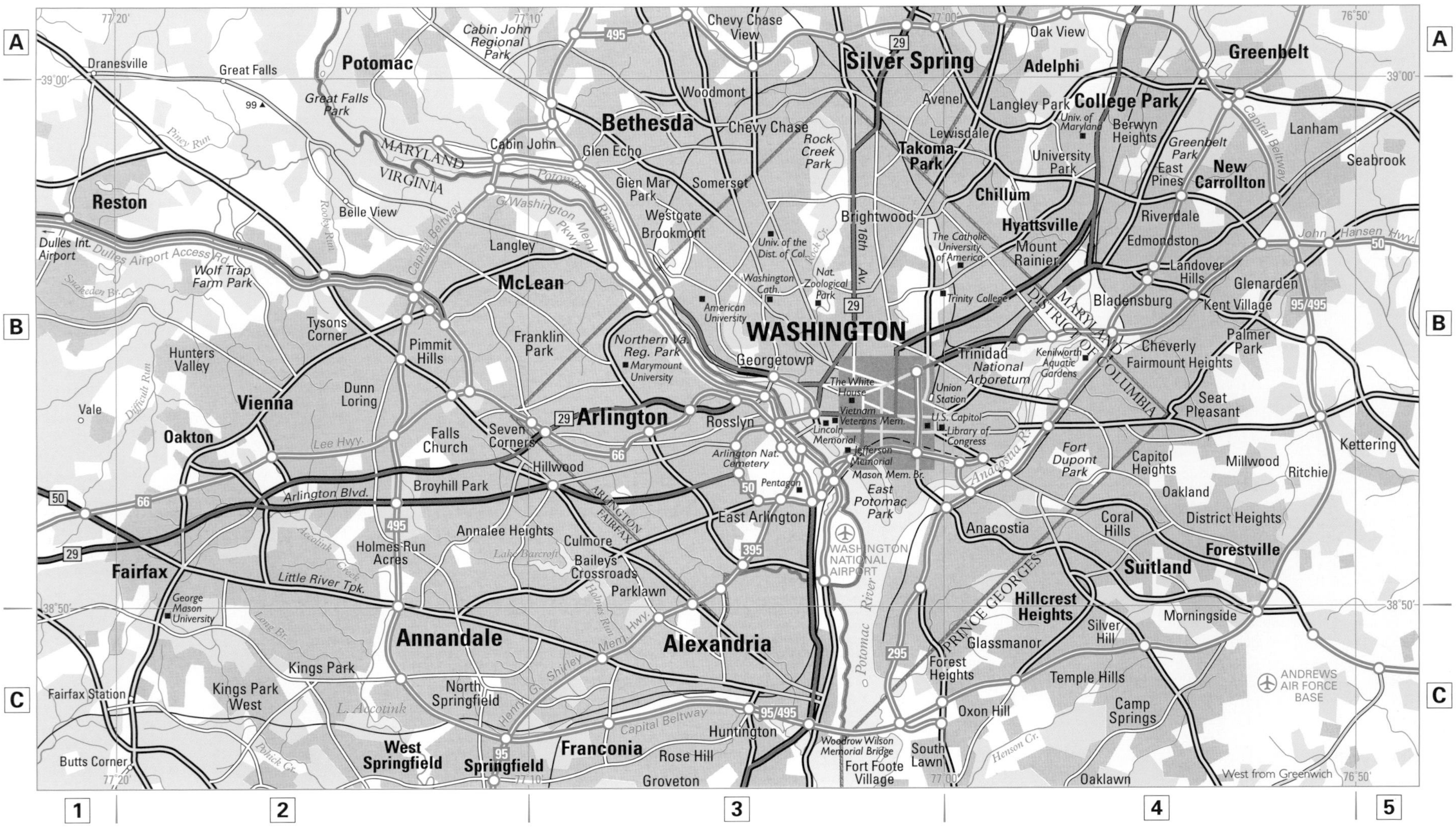

Chevy Chase View
Cabin John Regional Park
Dranesville
Great Falls
Potomac
Silver Spring
Oak View
Greenbelt
Adelphi
Woodmont
Avenel
Langley Park
College Park
Great Falls Park
Bethesda
Chevy Chase
Lewisdale
Univ. of Maryland
Berwyn Heights
Lanham
Cabin John
Glen Echo
Rock Creek Park
Takoma Park
University Park
Greenbelt Park
MARYLAND
VIRGINIA
Glen Mar Park
Somerset
East Pines
New Carrollton
Seabrook
Reston
Chillum
Belle View
Westgate
Brookmont
Brightwood
The Catholic University of America
Hyattsville
Riverdale
Dulles Int. Airport
Dulles Airport Access Rd.
Langley
Univ. of the Dist. of Col.
Mount Rainier
Edmondston
John Hansen Hwy.
Wolf Trap Farm Park
McLean
Washington Cath.
Nat. Zoological Park
Trinity College
Landover Hills
Glenarden
American University
Bladensburg
Kent Village
Tysons Corner
Pimmit Hills
Franklin Park
Northern Va. Reg. Park
Marymount University
WASHINGTON
Cheverly
Palmer Park
Hunters Valley
Georgetown
Trinidad
National Arboretum
Kenilworth Aquatic Gardens
Fairmount Heights
DISTRICT OF COLUMBIA
Vienna
Dunn Loring
The White House
Union Station
Seat Pleasant
Vale
Falls Church
Seven Corners
Arlington
Rosslyn
Vietnam Veterans Mem.
U.S. Capitol
Library of Congress
Oakton
Lincoln Memorial
Fort Dupont Park
Capitol Heights
Millwood
Kettering
Lee Hwy.
Hillwood
Arlington Nat. Cemetery
Jefferson Memorial
Mason Mem. Br.
Ritchie
Broyhill Park
Pentagon
East Potomac Park
Oakland
Arlington Blvd.
ARLINGTON
FAIRFAX
Anacostia
Coral Hills
District Heights
Annalee Heights
East Arlington
Holmes Run Acres
Culmore
WASHINGTON NATIONAL AIRPORT
Suitland
Forestville
Fairfax
Little River Tpk.
Baileys Crossroads
Parklawn
Hillcrest Heights
George Mason University
PRINCE GEORGES
Morningside
Annandale
Alexandria
Silver Hill
Glassmanor
Kings Park
Forest Heights
Temple Hills
ANDREWS AIR FORCE BASE
Fairfax Station
Kings Park West
L. Accotink
North Springfield
Huntington
Oxon Hill
Camp Springs
Capital Beltway
West Springfield
Springfield
Franconia
Rose Hill
Woodrow Wilson Memorial Bridge
South Lawn
Butts Corner
Groveton
Fort Foote Village
Oaklawn
West from Greenwich
Potomac River
A
B
C
1
2
3
4
5

CENTRAL WASHINGTON

0 km 1
0 miles 0.5

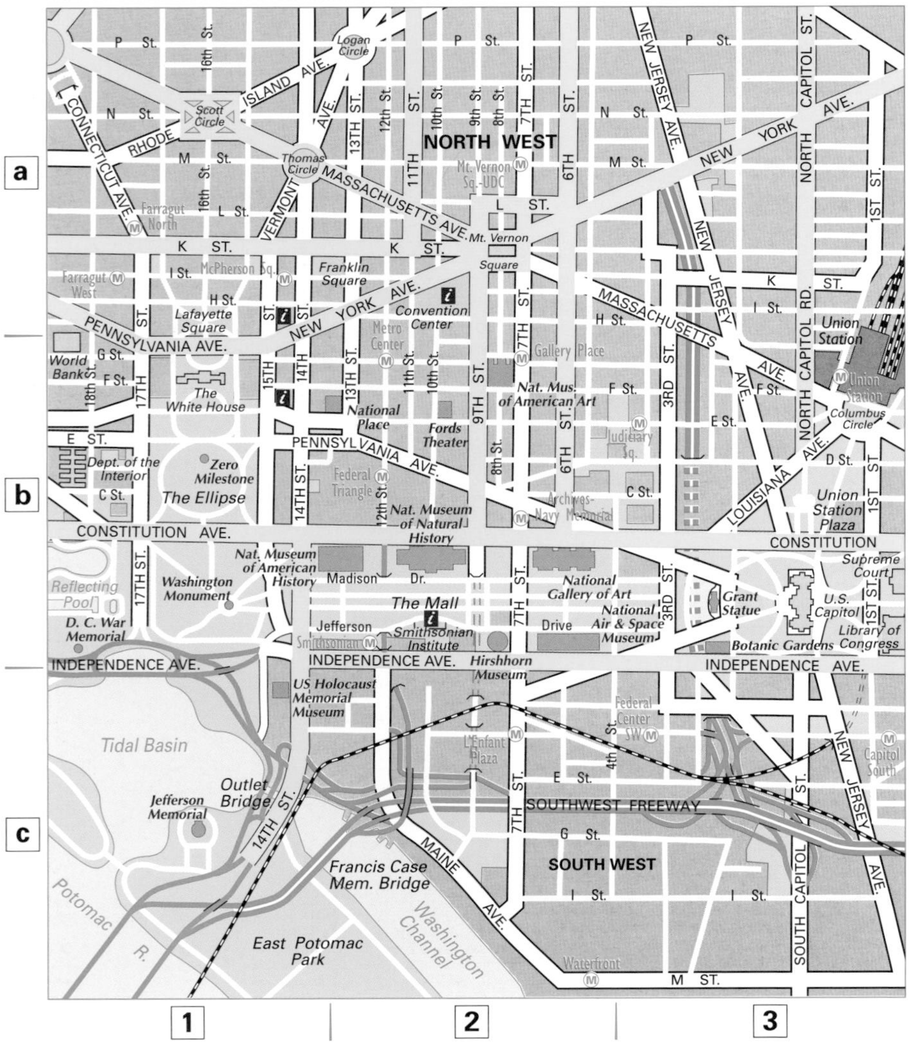

P St.
Logan Circle
NEW JERSEY AVE.
NORTH CAPITOL ST.
RHODE ISLAND AVE.
Scott Circle
CONNECTICUT AVE.
NORTH WEST
NEW YORK AVE.
Thomas Circle
MASSACHUSETTS AVE.
Mt. Vernon Sq.-UDC
Farragut North
Mt. Vernon Square
Farragut West
McPherson Sq.
Franklin Square
Convention Center
Lafayette Square
Union Station
PENNSYLVANIA AVE.
World Bank
Metro Center
Gallery Place
The White House
National Place
Nat. Mus. of American Art
Columbus Circle
Fords Theater
Judiciary Sq.
Dept. of the Interior
Zero Milestone
The Ellipse
Federal Triangle
Nat. Museum of Natural History
Archives-Navy Memorial
LOUISIANA AVE.
Union Station Plaza
CONSTITUTION AVE.
Supreme Court
Nat. Museum of American History
Reflecting Pool
Washington Monument
National Gallery of Art
Grant Statue
U.S. Capitol
Library of Congress
D. C. War Memorial
The Mall
Jefferson Drive
Smithsonian Institute
National Air & Space Museum
Botanic Gardens
INDEPENDENCE AVE.
Hirshhorn Museum
US Holocaust Memorial Museum
Federal Center SW
Tidal Basin
L'Enfant Plaza
Capitol South
Outlet Bridge
Jefferson Memorial
SOUTHWEST FREEWAY
14TH ST.
MAINE AVE.
SOUTH WEST
Francis Case Mem. Bridge
Potomac R.
East Potomac Park
Washington Channel
SOUTH CAPITOL ST.
Waterfront
M ST.
a
b
c
1
2
3

WELLINGTON

0 km 5
0 miles 3

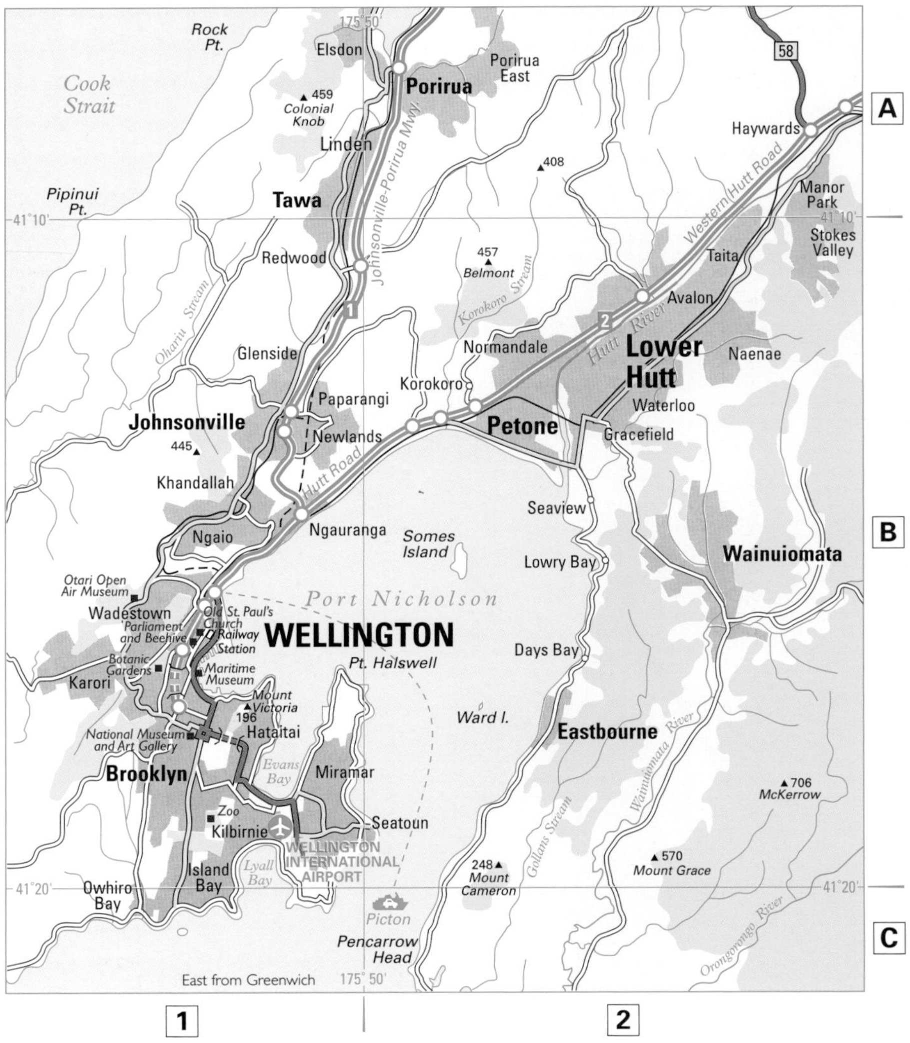

Rock Pt.
Elsdon
Porirua
Porirua East
Cook Strait
459 Colonial Knob
Linden
Haywards
Pipinui Pt.
Tawa
408
Manor Park
Stokes Valley
Redwood
457 Belmont
Taita
Western/Hutt Road
Johnsonville–Porirua Mwy.
Avalon
Glenside
Normandale
Lower Hutt
Naenae
Korokoro
Paparangi
Johnsonville
Newlands
Petone
Waterloo
Gracefield
445
Khandallah
Hutt Road
Seaview
Ngauranga
Somes Island
Ngaio
Lowry Bay
Wainuiomata
Port Nicholson
Otari Open Air Museum
Wadestown
Old St. Paul's Church
Railway Station
Parliament and Beehive
WELLINGTON
Botanic Gardens
Pt. Halswell
Days Bay
Karori
Maritime Museum
Mount Victoria
196
Ward I.
National Museum and Art Gallery
Hataitai
Eastbourne
Evans Bay
Brooklyn
Miramar
706 McKerrow
Zoo
Seatoun
Kilbirnie
WELLINGTON INTERNATIONAL AIRPORT
570 Mount Grace
Island Bay
Lyall Bay
248 Mount Cameron
Owhiro Bay
Picton
Pencarrow Head
East from Greenwich
A
B
C
1
2

INDEX TO CITY MAPS

The index contains the names of all the principal places and features shown on the City Maps. Each name is followed by an additional entry in italics giving the name of the City Map within which it is located.

The number in bold type which follows each name refers to the number of the City Map page where that feature or place will be found.

The letter and figure which are immediately after the page number give the grid square on the map within which the feature or place is situated. The letter represents the latitude and the figure the longitude. Upper case letters refer to the City Maps, lower case letters to the Central Area Maps. The full geographic reference is provided in the border of the City Maps.

The location given is the centre of the city, suburb or feature and is not necessarily the name. Rivers, canals and roads are indexed to their name. Rivers carry the symbol → after their name.

An explanation of the alphabetical order rules and a list of the abbreviations used are to be found at the beginning of the World Map Index.

A

Aalām, *Baghdad* **3** B2
Aalsmeer, *Amsterdam* **2** B1
Abbey Wood, *London* **15** B4
Abcoude, *Amsterdam* **2** B2
Âbdin, *Cairo* **7** A2
Abeno, *Osaka* **22** B4
Aberdeen, *Hong Kong* **12** B2
Aberdour, *Edinburgh* **11** A2
Aberdour Castle, *Edinburgh* **11** A2
Abfanggraben →, *Munich* **20** A3
Ablon-sur-Seine, *Paris* **23** B3
Abramtsevo, *Moscow* **19** B4
Abu Dis, *Jerusalem* **13** B2
Abû en Numrus, *Cairo* **7** B2
Abu Ghosh, *Jerusalem* **13** B1
Acacias, *Madrid* **17** c2
Acassuso, *Buenos Aires* **7** A1
Accotink Cr. →, *Washington* **32** B2
Acheres, *Paris* **23** A1
Acilia, *Rome* **25** C1
Aclimação, *São Paulo* **26** B2
Acton, *London* **15** A2
Açúcar, Pão de, *Rio de Janeiro* **24** B2
Ada Beja, *Lisbon* **14** A1
Adams Park, *Atlanta* **3** B2
Adams Shore, *Boston* **6** B4
Addiscombe, *London* **15** B3
Adelphi, *Washington* **32** A4
Aderklaa, *Vienna* **31** A3
Admiralteyskaya Storona, *St. Petersburg* **26** B2
Áffori, *Milan* **18** A2
Aflandshage, *Copenhagen* **10** B3
Afsarīyeh, *Tehran* **30** B2
Agboyi Cr. →, *Lagos* **14** A2
Ågerup, *Copenhagen* **10** A1
Ågesta, *Stockholm* **28** B2
Agincourt, *Toronto* **30** A3
Agora, Arhéa, *Athens* **2** c1
Agra Canal, *Delhi* **10** B2
Agricola Oriental, *Mexico City* **18** B2
Agua Espraiada →, *São Paulo* **26** B2
Agualva-Cacem, *Lisbon* **14** A1
Agustino, Cerro El, *Lima* **16** B2
Ahrensfelde, *Berlin* **5** A4
Ahuntsic, *Montreal* **19** A1
Ai →, *Osaka* **22** A4
Aigremont, *Paris* **23** A1
Air View Park, *Singapore* **27** A2
Airport West, *Melbourne* **17** A1
Aiyaleo, *Athens* **2** B2
Aiyáleos, Óros, *Athens* **2** B1
Ajegunle, *Lagos* **14** B2
Aji, *Osaka* **22** A3
Ajuda, *Lisbon* **14** A1
Akalla, *Stockholm* **28** A1
Akasaka, *Tokyo* **29** b3
Akbarābād, *Tehran* **30** A2
Akershus Slott, *Oslo* **22** A3
Akihabara, *Tokyo* **29** a5
Akrópolis, *Athens* **2** c2
Al 'Azamiyah, *Baghdad* **3** A2
Al Quds = Jerusalem, *Jerusalem* **13** B2
Alaguntan, *Lagos* **14** B2
Alameda, *San Francisco* **25** B3
Alameda, Parque, *Mexico City* **18** b2
Alameda Memorial State Beach Park, *San Francisco* **25** B3
Albern, *Vienna* **31** B2
Albert Park, *Melbourne* **17** B1
Alberton, *Johannesburg* **13** B2
Albertslund, *Copenhagen* **10** B2
Albysjön, *Stockholm* **28** B1
Alcantara, *Lisbon* **14** A1
Alcatraz I., *San Francisco* **25** B2
Alcobendas, *Madrid* **17** A2
Alcorcón, *Madrid* **17** B1
Aldershof, *Berlin* **5** B4
Aldo Bonzi, *Buenos Aires* **7** C1
Aleksandrovskoye, *St. Petersburg* **26** B2
Alexander Nevsky Abbey, *St. Petersburg* **26** B2
Alexander Soutzos Moussío, *Athens* **2** b3
Alexandra, *Johannesburg* **13** A2
Alexandra, *Singapore* **27** B2
Alexandria, *Washington* **32** C3
Alfama, *Lisbon* **14** c3
Alfortville, *Paris* **23** B3
Algés, *Lisbon* **14** A1
Alhambra, *Los Angeles* **16** B4
Alibey →, *Istanbul* **12** B1
Alibey Barajı, *Istanbul* **12** B1
Alibeyköy, *Istanbul* **12** B1
Alimos, *Athens* **2** B2
Alipur, *Calcutta* **8** B1
Allach, *Munich* **20** A1
Allambie Heights, *Sydney* **28** A2
Allard Pierson Museum, *Amsterdam* **2** b2
Allermuir Hill, *Edinburgh* **11** B2
Allerton, Pt., *Boston* **6** B4
Allston, *Boston* **6** A3
Almada, *Lisbon* **14** A2
Almagro, *Buenos Aires* **7** B2
Almargem do Bispo, *Lisbon* **14** A1
Almazovo, *Moscow* **19** A6
Almirante G. Brown, Parque, *Buenos Aires* **7** C2
Almon, *Jerusalem* **13** B2
Almond →, *Edinburgh* **11** B2
Alnabru, *Oslo* **22** A4
Alnsjøen, *Oslo* **22** A4
Alperton, *London* **15** A2
Alpine, *New York* **21** A2
Alrode, *Johannesburg* **13** B2
Alsemerg, *Brussels* **6** B1
Alsergrund, *Vienna* **31** A2
Alsip, *Chicago* **9** C2
Ålsten, *Stockholm* **28** B1
Älta, *Stockholm* **28** B3
Altadena, *Los Angeles* **16** A4
Alte-Donau →, *Vienna* **31** A2
Alte Hofburg, *Vienna* **31** b1
Alter Finkenkrug, *Berlin* **5** A1
Altes Rathaus, *Munich* **20** b3
Altglienicke, *Berlin* **5** B4
Altlandsberg, *Berlin* **5** A5
Altlandsberg Nord, *Berlin* **5** A5
Altmannsdorf, *Vienna* **31** B1
Alto da Moóca, *São Paulo* **26** B2
Alto do Pina, *Lisbon* **14** A2
Altona, *Melbourne* **17** B1
Alvaro Obregon, *Mexico City* **18** B1
Alvik, *Stockholm* **28** B1
Älvsjo, *Stockholm* **28** B2
Älvvik, *Stockholm* **28** A3
Am Hasenbergl, *Munich* **20** A2
Am Steinhof, *Vienna* **31** A1
Am Wald, *Munich* **20** B2
Ama Keng, *Singapore* **27** A2
Amadora, *Lisbon* **14** A1
Amagasaki, *Osaka* **22** A3
Amager, *Copenhagen* **10** B3
Amāl Qādisiya, *Baghdad* **3** B2
Amalienborg, *Copenhagen* **10** b3
Amata, *Milan* **18** A1
Ameixoeira, *Lisbon* **14** A2
América, *São Paulo* **26** B1
Amin, *Baghdad* **3** B2
Aminadov, *Jerusalem* **13** B1
Aminyevo, *Moscow* **19** B2
Amīrābād, *Tehran* **30** A2
Amora, *Lisbon* **14** B2
Amoreira, *Lisbon* **14** A1
Ampelokipi, *Athens* **2** B2
Amper →, *Munich* **20** A1
Amstel, *Amsterdam* **2** b2
Amstel →, *Amsterdam* **2** c2
Amstel-Drecht-Kanaal, *Amsterdam* **2** B2
Amstel Station, *Amsterdam* **2** c3
Amstelhof, *Amsterdam* **2** b2
Amstelveen, *Amsterdam* **2** B2
Amsterdam, *Amsterdam* **2** A2
Amsterdam-Rijnkanaal, *Amsterdam* **2** B3
Amsterdam Zoo, *Amsterdam* **2** b3
Amsterdam Zuidoost, *Amsterdam* **2** B2
Amsterdamse Bos, *Amsterdam* **2** B1
Anacostia, *Washington* **32** B4
Anadoluhisarı, *Istanbul* **12** B2
Anadolukavağı, *Istanbul* **12** A2
Anata, *Jerusalem* **13** B2
Ancol, *Jakarta* **13** A1
'Andalus, *Baghdad* **3** B1
Andarai, *Rio de Janeiro* **24** B1
Anderlecht, *Brussels* **6** A1
Anderson Park, *Atlanta* **3** B2
Andingmen, *Beijing* **4** B2
Andrews Air Force Base, *Washington* **32** C4
Ang Mo Kio, *Singapore* **27** A3
Ängby, *Stockholm* **28** A1
Angel I., *San Francisco* **25** A2
Angel Island State Park, *San Francisco* **25** A2
Angke, Kali →, *Jakarta* **13** A1
Angyalföld, *Budapest* **7** A2
Anik, *Mumbai* **20** A2
Anin, *Warsaw* **31** B2
Anjou, *Montreal* **19** A2
Annalee Heights, *Washington* **32** B2
Annandale, *Washington* **32** C2
Anne Frankhuis, *Amsterdam* **2** a1
Antony, *Paris* **23** B2
Anyangch'on, *Seoul* **26** C1
Aoyama, *Tokyo* **29** b2
Ap Lei Chau, *Hong Kong* **12** B1
Apapa, *Lagos* **14** B2
Apelacão, *Lisbon* **14** A2
Apterkarskiy Ostrov, *St. Petersburg* **26** B2
Ar Kazimiyah, *Baghdad* **3** B1
Ara →, *Tokyo* **29** A4
Arakawa-Ku, *Tokyo* **29** A3
Arany-hegyi-patak →, *Budapest* **7** A2
Aravaca, *Madrid* **17** B1
Arbataash, *Baghdad* **3** A1
Arc de Triomphe, *Paris* **23** a2
Arcadia, *Los Angeles* **16** B4
Arceuil, *Paris* **23** B2
Arco Plaza, *Los Angeles* **16** b1
Arese, *Milan* **18** A1
Arganzuela, *Madrid* **17** B1
Argenteuil, *Paris* **23** A2
Argonne Forest, *Chicago* **9** C1
Argüelles, *Madrid* **17** a1
Arima, *Osaka* **22** A2
Arima, *Tokyo* **29** B2
Ários Págos, *Athens* **2** c1
Arkhangelyskoye, *Moscow* **19** B1
Arlington, *Boston* **6** A2
Arlington, *Washington* **32** B3
Arlington Heights, *Boston* **6** A2
Arlington Nat. Cemetery, *Washington* **32** B3
Armação, *Rio de Janeiro* **24** B2
Armadale, *Melbourne* **17** B2
Armenian Quarter, *Jerusalem* **13** b3
Armour Heights, *Toronto* **30** A2
Arncliffe, *Sydney* **28** B1
Arnold Arboretum, *Boston* **6** B3
Árpádföld, *Budapest* **7** A3
Arrentela, *Lisbon* **14** B2
Årsta, *Stockholm* **28** B2
Art Institute, *Chicago* **9** c2
Artane, *Dublin* **11** A2
Artas, *Jerusalem* **13** B2
Arthur's Seat, *Edinburgh* **11** B3
Aryiróupolis, *Athens* **2** B2
Asagaya, *Tokyo* **29** A2
Asahi, *Osaka* **22** A4
Asakusa, *Tokyo* **29** A3
Asakusabashi, *Tokyo* **29** a5
Asati, *Calcutta* **8** C1
Aschheim, *Munich* **20** A3
Ascot Vale, *Melbourne* **17** A1
Ashburn, *Chicago* **9** C2
Ashburton, *Melbourne* **17** B2
Ashfield, *Sydney* **28** B1
Ashford, *London* **15** B1
Ashiya, *Osaka* **22** A2
Ashiya →, *Osaka* **22** A2
Ashtown, *Dublin* **11** A2
Askisto, *Helsinki* **12** B1
Askrikefjärden, *Stockholm* **28** A3
Asnières, *Paris* **23** A2
Aspern, *Vienna* **31** A2
Aspern, Flugplatz, *Vienna* **31** A3
Assago, *Milan* **18** B1
Assemblée Nationale, *Paris* **23** b3
Assendelft, *Amsterdam* **2** A1
Assiano, *Milan* **18** B1
Astoria, *New York* **21** B2
Astrolabe Park, *Sydney* **28** B2
Atarot Airport, *Jerusalem* **13** A2
Atghara, *Calcutta* **8** B2
Athens = Athínai, *Athens* **2** B2
Athínai, *Athens* **2** B2
Athis-Mons, *Paris* **23** B3
Athlone, *Cape Town* **8** A2
Atholl, *Johannesburg* **13** A2
Atīfīya, *Baghdad* **3** A2
Atişalen, *Istanbul* **12** B1
Atlanta, *Atlanta* **3** B2
Atlanta History Center, *Atlanta* **3** B2
Atomium, *Brussels* **6** A2
Attiki, *Athens* **2** A2
Atzgersdorf, *Vienna* **31** B1
Aubervilliers, *Paris* **23** A3
Aubing, *Munich* **20** B1
Auburndale, *Boston* **6** A2
Aucherdinny, *Edinburgh* **11** B2
Auckland Park, *Johannesburg* **13** B2
Auderghem, *Brussels* **6** B2
Augusta, Mausoleo di, *Rome* **25** b2
Augustówka, *Warsaw* **31** B2
Aulnay-sous-Bois, *Paris* **23** A3
Aurelio, *Rome* **25** B1
Ausîm, *Cairo* **7** A1
Austerlitz, Gare d', *Paris* **23** A3
Austin, *Chicago* **9** B2
Avalon, *Wellington* **32** B2
Avedøre, *Copenhagen* **10** B2
Avellaneda, *Buenos Aires* **7** C2
Avenel, *Washington* **32** B4
Avondale, *Chicago* **9** B2
Avondale Heights, *Melbourne* **17** A1
Avtovo, *St. Petersburg* **26** B1
Ayazağa, *Istanbul* **12** B1
Ayer Chawan, P., *Singapore* **27** B2
Ayer Merbau, P., *Singapore* **27** B2
Ayía Marina, *Athens* **2** C3
Ayía Paraskevi, *Athens* **2** A2
Áyios Dhimitrios, *Athens* **2** B2
Áyios Ioánnis Rendis, *Athens* **2** B1
Azabu, *Tokyo* **29** c3
Azcapotzalco, *Mexico City* **18** B1
Azteca, Estadia, *Mexico City* **18** C2
Azucar, Cerro Pan de, *Santiago* **26** A1

B

Baambrugge, *Amsterdam* **2** B2
Baba I., *Karachi* **14** B1
Babarpur, *Delhi* **10** A2
Babushkin, *Moscow* **19** A4
Back B., *Mumbai* **20** B1
Baclaran, *Manila* **17** B2
Bacoor, *Manila* **17** C1
Bacoor B., *Manila* **17** C1
Badalona, *Barcelona* **4** A2
Badhoevedorp, *Amsterdam* **2** A1
Badli, *Delhi* **10** A1
Bærum, *Oslo* **22** A2
Bağcılar, *Istanbul* **12** B1
Bággio, *Milan* **18** B1
Bāgh-e-Feyz, *Tehran* **30** A1
Baghdād, *Baghdad* **3** A2
Bagmari, *Calcutta* **8** B2
Bagneux, *Paris* **23** B2
Bagnolet, *Paris* **23** A3
Bagsværd, *Copenhagen* **10** A2
Bagsværd Sø, *Copenhagen* **10** A2
Baguiati, *Calcutta* **8** B2
Bagumbayan, *Manila* **17** C2
Bahçeköy, *Istanbul* **12** A1
Bahtîm, *Cairo* **7** A2
Baileys Crossroads, *Washington* **32** B3
Bailly, *Paris* **23** A1
Bairro Alto, *Lisbon* **14** c1
Bairro Lopes, *Lisbon* **14** b3
Baisha, *Canton* **8** B2
Baisha →, *Canton* **8** B2
Baixa, *Lisbon* **14** c2
Baiyun Airport, *Canton* **8** A2
Baiyun Hill Scenic Spot, *Canton* **8** B2
Bakırköy, *Istanbul* **12** C1
Bakovka, *Moscow* **19** B2
Bal Harbor, *Miami* **18** A2
Balara, *Manila* **17** B2
Balashikha, *Moscow* **19** B5
Baldia, *Karachi* **14** A1
Baldoyle, *Dublin* **11** A3
Baldwin Hills, *Los Angeles* **16** B2
Baldwin Hills Res., *Los Angeles* **16** B2
Balgowlah, *Sydney* **28** A2
Balgowlah Heights, *Sydney* **28** A2
Balham, *London* **15** B3
Bali, *Calcutta* **8** B1
Baliganja, *Calcutta* **8** B2
Balingsnäs, *Stockholm* **28** B2
Balingsta, *Stockholm* **28** B2
Balintawak, *Manila* **17** B1
Balitai, *Tianjin* **30** B2
Ballerup, *Copenhagen* **10** A2
Ballinteer, *Dublin* **11** B2
Ballyboden, *Dublin* **11** B2
Ballybrack, *Dublin* **11** B3
Ballyfermot, *Dublin* **11** A1
Ballymorefinn Hill, *Dublin* **11** B1
Ballymun, *Dublin* **11** A2
Balmain, *Sydney* **28** B2
Baluhati, *Calcutta* **8** B1
Balvanera, *Buenos Aires* **7** B2
Balwyn, *Melbourne* **17** A2
Balwyn North, *Melbourne* **17** A2
Banática, *Lisbon* **14** A1
Banco do Brasil, Centro Cultural, *Rio de Janeiro* **24** a2
Bandra, *Mumbai* **20** A1
Bandra Pt., *Mumbai* **20** A1
Bang Kapi, *Bangkok* **3** B2
Bang Kholaem, *Bangkok* **3** A2
Bang Na, *Bangkok* **3** B2
Bang Phlad, *Bangkok* **3** a1
Bangkhen, *Bangkok* **3** A2
Bangkok = Krung Thep, *Bangkok* **3** B2
Bangkok Noi, *Bangkok* **3** B1
Bangkok Yai, *Bangkok* **3** B1
Banglamphoo, *Bangkok* **3** b2
Banglo, *Calcutta* **8** B1
Bangrak, *Bangkok* **3** B2
Bangsu, *Bangkok* **3** B2
Bank, *London* **15** b5
Bank of America, *San Francisco* **25** b2
Bank of China Tower, *Hong Kong* **12** c1
Banks, C., *Sydney* **28** C2
Banksmeadow, *Sydney* **28** B2
Banstala, *Calcutta* **8** B2
Bantra, *Calcutta* **8** B1
Baoshan, *Shanghai* **27** A1
Bar Giyora, *Jerusalem* **13** B1
Barahanagar, *Calcutta* **8** B2
Barajas, *Madrid* **17** B2
Barajas, Aeropuerto Transoceanico de, *Madrid* **17** B2
Barakpur, *Calcutta* **8** A2
Barberini, Palazzo, *Rome* **25** b3
Barbican, *London* **15** a4
Barcarena, *Lisbon* **14** A1
Barcarena, Rib. de →, *Lisbon* **14** A1
Barcelona, *Barcelona* **4** A2
Barcelona-Prat, Aeropuerta de, *Barcelona* **4** B1
Barceloneta, *Barcelona* **4** A2
Barking, *London* **15** A4
Barkingside, *London* **15** A4
Barnes, *London* **15** B2
Barnet, *London* **15** A2
Barra Andai, *Karachi* **14** B2
Barra Funda, *São Paulo* **26** B2
Barracas, *Buenos Aires* **7** B2
Barranco, *Lima* **16** B2
Barreiro, *Lisbon* **14** B2
Barreto, *Rio de Janeiro* **24** B2
Bartala, *Calcutta* **8** B1
Barton Park, *Sydney* **28** B1
Bartyki, *Warsaw* **31** C2
Barvikha, *Moscow* **19** B1
Bastille, Place de la, *Paris* **23** c5
Basus, *Cairo* **7** A2
Batanagar, *Calcutta* **8** B1
Bath Beach, *New York* **21** C1
Bath I., *Karachi* **14** B2
Batir, *Jerusalem* **13** B1
Batok, Bukit, *Singapore* **27** A2
Battersea, *London* **15** B3
Battery Park, *New York* **21** f1
Bauman, *Moscow* **19** B4
Baumgarten, *Vienna* **31** A1
Bay Harbour Islands, *Miami* **18** A2
Bay Ridge, *New York* **21** C1
Bayonne, *New York* **21** B1
Bayshore, *San Francisco* **25** B3
Bayswater, *London* **15** b2
Bayt Lahm = Bethlehem, *Jerusalem* **13** B2
Bayview, *San Francisco* **25** B2
Bāzār, *Tehran* **30** A2
Beachmont, *Boston* **6** A4
Beacon Hill, *Hong Kong* **12** A2
Beato, *Lisbon* **14** A2
Beaumont, *Dublin* **11** A2
Beaumonte Heights, *Toronto* **30** A1
Bebek, *Istanbul* **12** B2
Běchovice, *Prague* **24** B3
Beck L., *Chicago* **9** A1
Beckenham, *London* **15** B3
Beckton, *London* **15** A4
Becontree, *London* **15** A4
Beddington Corner, *London* **15** B3
Bedford, *Boston* **6** A2
Bedford Park, *Chicago* **9** C2
Bedford Park, *New York* **21** A2
Bedford Stuyvesant, *New York* **21** B2
Bedford View, *Johannesburg* **13** B2
Bedok, *Singapore* **27** B3
Bedok, Res., *Singapore* **27** A3
Beersel, *Brussels* **6** B1
Behala, *Calcutta* **8** B1
Bei Hai, *Beijing* **4** B2
Beicai, *Shanghai* **27** B2
Beicang, *Tianjin* **30** A1
Beihai Park, *Beijing* **4** b2
Beijing, *Beijing* **4** B1
Beit Ghur el-Fawqa, *Jerusalem* **13** A1
Beit Hanina, *Jerusalem* **13** B2
Beit Iksa, *Jerusalem* **13** B2
Beit I'nan, *Jerusalem* **13** A1
Beit Jala, *Jerusalem* **13** B2
Beit Lekhem = Bethlehem, *Jerusalem* **13** B2
Beit Nekofa, *Jerusalem* **13** B1
Beit Sahur, *Jerusalem* **13** B2
Beit Surik, *Jerusalem* **13** B1
Beit Zayit, *Jerusalem* **13** B1
Beitaipingzhuan, *Beijing* **4** B1
Beitar Ilit, *Jerusalem* **13** B1
Beitsun, *Canton* **8** B2
Beitunya, *Jerusalem* **13** A2
Beixing Jing Park, *Shanghai* **27** B1
Békásmegyer, *Budapest* **7** A2
Bekkelaget, *Oslo* **22** A3
Bel Air, *Los Angeles* **16** B2
Bela Vista, *São Paulo* **26** B2
Bélanger, *Montreal* **19** A1
Belas, *Lisbon* **14** A1
Belas Artes, Museu Nacionale de, *Rio de Janeiro* **24** b2
Beleghata, *Calcutta* **8** B2
Belém, *Lisbon* **14** A1
Belém, Torre de, *Lisbon* **14** A1
Belènzinho, *São Paulo* **26** B2
Belgachiya, *Calcutta* **8** B2
Belgharia, *Calcutta* **8** B2
Belgrano, *Buenos Aires* **7** B2
Belgravia, *London* **15** c3
Bell, *Los Angeles* **16** C3
Bell Gardens, *Los Angeles* **16** C4
Bell Tower, *Beijing* **4** a2
Bellavista, *Lima* **16** B2
Bellavista, *Santiago* **26** C2
Belle Harbor, *New York* **21** C2
Belle View, *Washington* **32** B2
Bellevue, Schloss, *Berlin* **5** a2
Bellingham, *London* **15** B3
Bellwood, *Chicago* **9** B1
Belmont, *Boston* **6** A2
Belmont, *London* **15** A2
Belmont, *Wellington* **32** B2
Belmont Harbor, *Chicago* **9** B3
Belmore, *Sydney* **28** B1
Belur, *Calcutta* **8** B2
Belvedere, *Atlanta* **3** B3
Belvedere, *London* **15** B4
Belvedere, *San Francisco* **25** A2
Belyayevo Bogorodskoye, *Moscow* **19** C3
Bemowo, *Warsaw* **31** B1
Benaki, Moussío, *Athens* **2** b3
Bendale, *Toronto* **30** A3
Bendkhal, *Mumbai* **20** B2
Benefica, *Rio de Janeiro* **24** B1
Benfica, *Lisbon* **14** A1
Benito Juárez, *Mexico City* **18** B2
Benito Juárez, Aeropuerto Int., *Mexico City* **18** B2
Bensonhurst, *New York* **21** C2
Berchem-Sainte-Agathe, *Brussels* **6** A1
Berg am Laim, *Munich* **20** B2
Bergenfield, *New York* **21** A2
Bergham, *Munich* **20** B2
Bergvliet, *Cape Town* **8** B1
Beri, *Barcelona* **4** A1
Berkeley, *San Francisco* **25** A3
Berlin, *Berlin* **5** A3
Bermondsey, *London* **15** B3
Bernabeu, Estadio, *Madrid* **17** B1
Bernal Heights, *San Francisco* **25** B2
Berwyn, *Chicago* **9** B2
Berwyn Heights, *Washington* **32** B4
Besiktas, *Istanbul* **12** B2
Besós →, *Barcelona* **4** A2
Bethesda, *Washington* **32** B3
Bethlehem, *Jerusalem* **13** B2
Bethnal Green, *London* **15** A3
Betor, *Calcutta* **8** B1
Beurs, *Amsterdam* **2** b2
Beverley Hills, *Sydney* **28** B1
Beverley Park, *Sydney* **28** B1
Beverly, *Chicago* **9** C3
Beverly Glen, *Los Angeles* **16** B2
Beverly Hills, *Los Angeles* **16** B2
Bexley, *London* **15** B4
Bexley, *Sydney* **28** B1
Bexleyheath, *London* **15** B4
Beykoz, *Istanbul* **12** B2
Beylerbeyi, *Istanbul* **12** B2
Beyoğlu, *Istanbul* **12** B1
Bezons, *Paris* **23** A2
Bezuidenhout Park, *Johannesburg* **13** B2
Bhadrakali, *Calcutta* **8** A2
Bhalswa, *Delhi* **10** A2
Bhambo Khan Qarmati, *Karachi* **14** B2
Bhatsala, *Calcutta* **8** B1
Bhawanipur, *Calcutta* **8** B2
Bhuleshwar, *Mumbai* **20** b2
Białołeka Dworska, *Warsaw* **31** B2
Biblioteca Nacional, *Rio de Janeiro* **24** c2
Bicentennial Park, *Sydney* **28** B1
Bickley, *London* **15** B4
Bidu, *Jerusalem* **13** B1
Bielany, *Warsaw* **31** B1
Bielawa, *Warsaw* **31** C2
Biesdorf, *Berlin* **5** A4
Bièvre →, *Paris* **23** B1
Bièvres, *Paris* **23** B2
Bilston, *Edinburgh* **11** B2
Binacayan, *Manila* **17** C1
Binondo, *Manila* **17** B1
Birak el Kiyam, *Cairo* **7** A1
Birch Cliff, *Toronto* **30** A3
Birkenstein, *Berlin* **5** A5
Birkholz, *Berlin* **5** A4
Birkholzaue, *Berlin* **5** A4
Birrarrung Park, *Melbourne* **17** A2
Biscayne Bay, *Miami* **18** B2
Biscayne Park, *Miami* **18** A2
Bishop Lavis, *Cape Town* **8** A2
Bishopscourt, *Cape Town* **8** A1
Bispebjerg, *Copenhagen* **10** A3
Biwon Secret Garden, *Seoul* **26** B1
Björknas, *Stockholm* **28** B3
Black Cr. →, *Toronto* **30** A2
Blackfen, *London* **15** B4
Blackheath, *London* **15** B4
Blackrock, *Dublin* **11** B2
Bladensburg, *Washington* **32** B4
Blair Village, *Atlanta* **3** C2
Blairgowrie, *Johannesburg* **13** A2
Blakehurst, *Sydney* **28** B1
Blakstad, *Oslo* **22** B1
Blankenburg, *Berlin* **5** A3
Blankenfelde, *Berlin* **5** A3
Blizne, *Warsaw* **31** B1
Bloomsbury, *London* **15** a3
Błota, *Warsaw* **31** C3
Blue Island, *Chicago* **9** C2
Bluebell, *Dublin* **11** B1
Bluff Hd., *Hong Kong* **12** B2
Blumberg, *Berlin* **5** A4
Blunt Pt., *San Francisco* **25** A2
Blutenberg, *Munich* **20** B1
Blylaget, *Oslo* **22** B3
Bo-Kaap Museum, *Cape Town* **8** c2
Boa Vista, Alto do, *Rio de Janeiro* **24** B1
Boardwalk, *New York* **21** C3
Boavista, *Lisbon* **14** A2
Bobigny, *Paris* **23** A3
Bocanegra, *Lima* **16** A2
Boedo, *Buenos Aires* **7** B2
Bogenhausen, *Munich* **20** B2
Bogorodskoye, *Moscow* **19** B4
Bogota, *New York* **21** A1
Bogstadvatnet, *Oslo* **22** A2
Bohnsdorf, *Berlin* **5** B4
Bois-Colombes, *Paris* **23** A2
Bois-d'Arcy, *Paris* **23** B1
Boissy-St.-Léger, *Paris* **23** B4
Boldinasco, *Milan* **18** B1
Bøler, *Oslo* **22** A4
Bollate, *Milan* **18** A1
Bollebeek, *Brussels* **6** A1
Bollensdorf, *Berlin* **5** A5
Bollmora, *Stockholm* **28** B3
Bolshaya-Okhta, *St. Petersburg* **26** B2
Bolton, *Atlanta* **3** B2
Bom Retiro, *São Paulo* **26** B2
Bombay = Mumbai, *Mumbai* **20** B2
Bondi, *Sydney* **28** B2
Bondy, *Paris* **23** A3
Bondy, Forêt de, *Paris* **23** A4
Bonifacio Monument, *Manila* **17** B1
Bonneuil-sur-Marne, *Paris* **23** B4
Bonnington, *Edinburgh* **11** B1
Bonnyrig and Lasswade, *Edinburgh* **11** B3
Bonsucesso, *Rio de Janeiro* **24** B1
Bonteheuwel, *Cape Town* **8** A2
Boo, *Stockholm* **28** A3
Booterstown, *Dublin* **11** B2
Borisovo, *Moscow* **19** C4
Borle, *Mumbai* **20** A2
Boronia Park, *Sydney* **28** A1
Borough Park, *New York* **21** C2
Bosmont, *Johannesburg* **13** B1
Bosön, *Stockholm* **28** A3
Bosporus = Istanbul Boğazi, *Istanbul* **12** B2
Bostancı, *Istanbul* **12** C2
Boston Harbor, *Boston* **6** A4
Boston Harbor Islands, *Boston* **6** A4
Botafogo, *Rio de Janeiro* **24** B1
Botanisk Have, *Copenhagen* **10** b2
Botany, *Sydney* **28** B2
Botany B., *Sydney* **28** B2
Botany Bay Nat. Park, *Sydney* **28** B2
Botič →, *Prague* **24** B3
Botica Sete, *Lisbon* **14** A1
Boucherville, *Montreal* **19** A3
Boucherville, Îs. de, *Montreal* **19** A3
Bougival, *Paris* **23** A1
Boulder Pt., *Hong Kong* **12** B1
Boulogne, Bois de, *Paris* **23** A2
Boulogne-Billancourt, *Paris* **23** A2
Bourg-la-Reine, *Paris* **23** B2
Bouviers, *Paris* **23** B1
Bovenkerk, *Amsterdam* **2** B2
Bovenkerker Polder, *Amsterdam* **2** B2
Bovisa, *Milan* **18** A2
Bow, *London* **15** A3
Bowery, *New York* **21** e2
Boyacıköy, *Istanbul* **12** B2
Boyle Heights, *Los Angeles* **16** B3
Bradbury Building, *Los Angeles* **16** b2
Braepark, *Edinburgh* **11** B2
Braid, *Edinburgh* **11** B2
Bramley, *Johannesburg* **13** A2
Brandenburger Tor, *Berlin* **5** A3
Brani, P., *Singapore* **27** B3
Branik, *Prague* **24** B2
Brännkyrka, *Stockholm* **28** B2
Brás, *São Paulo* **26** B2
Brasilândia, *São Paulo* **26** A1
Brateyevo, *Moscow* **19** C4
Bratsevo, *Moscow* **19** A2
Bray, *Dublin* **11** B3
Braybrook, *Melbourne* **17** A1
Brázdim, *Prague* **24** A3
Breach Candy, *Mumbai* **20** a1
Breakheart Reservation, *Boston* **6** A3
Brede, *Copenhagen* **10** A3
Breeds Pond, *Boston* **6** A4
Breezy Point, *New York* **21** C2
Breitenlee, *Vienna* **31** A3
Breña, *Lima* **16** B2
Brent, *London* **15** A2
Brent Res., *London* **15** A2
Brentford, *London* **15** B2
Brentwood Park, *Los Angeles* **16** B2
Brera, *Milan* **18** B2
Bresso, *Milan* **18** A2
Brevik, *Stockholm* **28** A3
Břevnov, *Prague* **24** B2
Brewster Is., *Boston* **6** A4
Bridgeport, *Chicago* **9** B3
Bridgetown, *Cape Town* **8** A2
Bridgeview, *Chicago* **9** C2
Brighton, *Boston* **6** A3
Brighton, *Melbourne* **17** B1
Brighton le Sands, *Sydney* **28** B1
Brighton Park, *Chicago* **9** C2
Brightwood, *Washington* **32** B3
Brigittenau, *Vienna* **31** A2
Brimbank Park, *Melbourne* **17** A1
Brisbane, *San Francisco* **25** B2
British Museum, *London* **15** a3
Britz, *Berlin* **5** B3
Brixton, *London* **15** B3
Broad Sd., *Boston* **6** A4
Broadmeadows, *Melbourne* **17** A1
Broadmoor, *San Francisco* **25** B2
Broadview, *Chicago* **9** B1
Broadway, *New York* **21** e1
Brockley, *London* **15** B3
Bródno, *Warsaw* **31** B2
Bródnowski, Kanal, *Warsaw* **31** B2
Broek in Waterland, *Amsterdam* **2** A2
Bromley, *London* **15** B4
Bromley Common, *London* **15** B4
Bromma, *Stockholm* **28** A1
Bromma flygplats, *Stockholm* **28** A1
Brompton, *London* **15** c2
Brøndby Strand, *Copenhagen* **10** B2
Brøndbyøster, *Copenhagen* **10** B2
Brøndbyvester, *Copenhagen* **10** B2

Brondesbury, *London* 15 A2
Brønnøya, *Oslo* 22 A2
Brønshøj, *Copenhagen* 10 A2
Bronxville, *New York* 21 A3
Brookfield, *Chicago* 9 C1
Brookhaven, *Atlanta* 3 A2
Brookline, *Boston* 6 B3
Brooklyn, *Cape Town* 8 A1
Brooklyn, *New York* 21 C2
Brooklyn, *Wellington* 32 B1
Brooklyn Bridge, *New York* 21 f2
Brookmont, *Washington* 32 B3
Brossard, *Montreal* 19 B3
Brou-sur-Chantereine, *Paris* 23 A4
Brown, *Toronto* 30 A3
Broyhill Park, *Washington* 32 B2
Brughério, *Milan* 18 A2
Brunswick, *Melbourne* 17 A1
Brush Hill, *Boston* 6 B1
Brussegem, *Brussels* 6 A1
Brussel Nat. Luchthaven, *Brussels* 6 A2
Brussels = Bruxelles, *Brussels* 6 A2
Bruxelles, *Brussels* 6 A2
Bruzzano, *Milan* 18 A2
Bry-sur-Marne, *Paris* 23 A4
Bryanston, *Johannesburg* 13 A1
Bryn, *Oslo* 22 A1
Brzeziny, *Warsaw* 31 B2
Bubeneč, *Prague* 24 B2
Buc, *Paris* 23 B1
Buchenhain, *Munich* 20 B1
Buchholz, *Berlin* 5 A3
Buckhead, *Atlanta* 3 A2
Buckingham Palace, *London* 15 b3
Buckow, *Berlin* 5 B3
Buda, *Budapest* 7 A2
Budafok, *Budapest* 7 B2
Budaörs, *Budapest* 7 B1
Budapest, *Budapest* 7 B2
Budatétény, *Budapest* 7 B2
Budavaripalota, *Budapest* 7 b2
Buddinge, *Copenhagen* 10 A3
Budokan, *Tokyo* 29 a4
Buena Vista, *San Francisco* 25 B2
Buenos Aires, *Buenos Aires* 7 B2
Bufalotta, *Rome* 25 B2
Bugio, *Lisbon* 14 B1
Buiksloot, *Amsterdam* 2 A2
Buitenveldert, *Amsterdam* 2 B2
Buizingen, *Brussels* 6 B1
Bukit Panjang Nature Reserve, *Singapore* 27 A2
Bukit Timah Nature Reserve, *Singapore* 27 A2
Bukum, P., *Singapore* 27 B2
Bûlâq, *Cairo* 7 A2
Bule, *Manila* 17 C2
Bulim, *Singapore* 27 A2
Bullen Park, *Melbourne* 17 A2
Bundoora North, *Melbourne* 17 A2
Bundoora Park, *Melbourne* 17 A2
Bunker I., *Karachi* 14 B1
Bunkyo-Ku, *Tokyo* 29 A3
Bunnefjorden, *Oslo* 22 A3
Buona Vista Park, *Singapore* 27 B2
Burbank, *Chicago* 9 C2
Burbank, *Los Angeles* 16 A3
Burlington, *Boston* 6 A2
Burnham Park, *Chicago* 9 c2
Burnham Park Harbor, *Chicago* 9 B3
Burnhamthorpe, *Toronto* 30 B1
Burnt Oak, *London* 15 A2
Burntisland, *Edinburgh* 11 A2
Burnwynd, *Edinburgh* 11 B1
Burqa, *Jerusalem* 13 A2
Burtus, *Cairo* 7 A1
Burudvatn, *Oslo* 22 A2
Burwood, *Sydney* 28 B1
Bushwick, *New York* 21 B2
Bushy Park, *London* 15 B1
Butantã, *São Paulo* 26 B1
Butcher I., *Mumbai* 20 B2
Butts Corner, *Washington* 32 C2
Büyükdere, *Istanbul* 12 B2
Byculla, *Mumbai* 20 B2
Bygdøy, *Oslo* 22 A3

C

C.N. Tower, *Toronto* 30 B2
Cabaçu de Cima →, *São Paulo* 26 A2
Caballito, *Buenos Aires* 7 B2
Cabin John, *Washington* 32 B2
Cabin John Regional Park, *Washington* 32 A2
Cabinteely, *Dublin* 11 B3
Cabra, *Dublin* 11 A2
Cabuçú de Baixo →, *São Paulo* 26 A1
Cachan, *Paris* 23 B2
Cachenka →, *Moscow* 19 B1
Cachoeira, Rib. da →, *São Paulo* 26 B1
Cacilhas, *Lisbon* 14 A2
Cahuenga Pk., *Los Angeles* 16 B3
Cairo = El Qâhira, *Cairo* 7 A2
Caju, *Rio de Janeiro* 24 B1
Čakovice, *Prague* 24 B3
Calcutta = Kolkata, *Calcutta* 8 B2
California Inst. of Tech., *Los Angeles* 16 B4
California Plaza, *Los Angeles* 16 b1
California State Univ., *Los Angeles* 16 B3
Callao, *Lima* 16 B2
Caloocan, *Manila* 17 B1
Calumet Park, *Chicago* 9 C3
Calumet Sag Channel →, *Chicago* 9 C2
Calumpang, *Manila* 17 B2
Calvairate, *Milan* 18 B2
Camarate, *Lisbon* 14 A2
Camaroes, *Lisbon* 14 A1
Camberwell, *London* 15 B3
Camberwell, *Melbourne* 17 B2
Cambridge, *Boston* 6 A3
Cambridge Res., *Boston* 6 A2
Cambuci, *São Paulo* 26 B2
Camden, *London* 15 A3
Cameron, Mt., *Wellington* 32 B2
Çamlıca, *Istanbul* 12 B2
Camp Springs, *Washington* 32 C4
Campamento, *Madrid* 17 B1
Campbellfield, *Melbourne* 17 A1
Camperdown, *Sydney* 28 B2
Campidoglio, *Rome* 25 c3
Campo, Casa de, *Madrid* 17 B1
Campo F.C. Barcelona, *Barcelona* 4 A1
Campo Grando, *Lisbon* 14 A2
Campo Pequeño, *Lisbon* 14 A2
Campolide, *Lisbon* 14 A2
Camps Bay, *Cape Town* 8 A1
C'an San Joan, *Barcelona* 4 A2
Cañacao B., *Manila* 17 C1
Canarsie, *New York* 21 C2
Cancelleria, Palazzo dei, *Rome* 25 c2
Candiac, *Montreal* 19 B3
Caneças, *Lisbon* 14 A1
Canillas, *Madrid* 17 B2
Canillejas, *Madrid* 17 B2
Canning Town, *London* 15 A4
Canteras de Vallecas, *Madrid* 17 B2
Canterbury, *Melbourne* 17 A2
Canterbury, *Sydney* 28 B1
Canton = Guangzhou, *Canton* 8 B2
Caoheijing, *Shanghai* 27 B1
Capão Redondo, *São Paulo* 26 B1
Caparica, *Lisbon* 14 A2
Caparica, Costa da, *Lisbon* 14 B1
Cape Flats, *Cape Town* 8 B2
Cape Town, *Cape Town* 8 A1
Cape Town International Airport, *Cape Town* 8 A2
Capitol Heights, *Washington* 32 B4
Capitol Hill, *Washington* 32 B4
Capitolini, Musei, *Rome* 25 c3
Captain Cook Bridge, *Sydney* 28 C1
Captain Cook Landing Place Park, *Sydney* 28 C2
Capuchos, *Lisbon* 14 B1
Carabanchel Alto, *Madrid* 17 B1
Carabanchel Bajo, *Madrid* 17 B1
Carapachay, *Buenos Aires* 7 B1
Caraza, *Buenos Aires* 7 C2
Caridad, *Manila* 17 C1
Carioca, Sa. da, *Rio de Janeiro* 24 B1
Carlstadt, *New York* 21 A1
Carlton, *Melbourne* 17 A1
Carmen de Huechuraba, *Santiago* 26 B1
Carmen de la Legua, *Lima* 16 B2
Carnaxide, *Lisbon* 14 A1
Carnegie, *Melbourne* 17 B2
Carnegie Hall, *New York* 21 c2
Carnide, *Lisbon* 14 A1
Carol City, *Miami* 18 A1
Carrascal, *Santiago* 26 B1
Carrickmines, *Dublin* 11 B3
Carrières-sous-Bois, *Paris* 23 A1
Carrières-sous-Poissy, *Paris* 23 A1
Carrières-sur-Seine, *Paris* 23 A2
Carrigeen Bay, *Dublin* 11 A3
Cartierville, *Montreal* 19 A1
Casa Verde, *São Paulo* 26 A1
Casál Morena, *Rome* 25 C2
Casalotti, *Rome* 25 B1
Cascade Heights, *Atlanta* 3 B2
Castél di Leva, *Rome* 25 C2
Castel Sant'Angelo, *Rome* 25 B1
Castle, *Dublin* 11 c2
Castle, *Edinburgh* 11 b2
Castle of Good Hope, *Cape Town* 8 c3
Castleknock, *Dublin* 11 A1
Castleton Corners, *New York* 21 C1
Catedral Metropolitana, *Mexico City* 18 b3
Catedral Metropolitana, *Rio de Janeiro* 24 c1
Catete, *Rio de Janeiro* 24 B1
Catford, *London* 15 B3
Caulfield, *Melbourne* 17 B2
Causeway Bay, *Hong Kong* 12 c3
Cavite, *Manila* 17 C1
Caxias, *Lisbon* 14 A1
Cebeccı, *Istanbul* 12 B1
Cecchignola, *Rome* 25 C2
Cecilienhof, Schloss, *Berlin* 5 B1
Cedar Grove, *Atlanta* 3 C3
Cempaka Putih, *Jakarta* 13 B2
Çengelköy, *Istanbul* 12 B2
Cengkareng, *Jakarta* 13 A1
Centennial Park, *Sydney* 28 B2
Center Hill, *Atlanta* 3 B2
Centocelle, *Rome* 25 B2
Centraal Station, *Amsterdam* 2 a2
Central Park, *New York* 21 B2
Cerillos, *Santiago* 26 B1
Cerro de la Estrella, *Mexico City* 18 B2
Cerro de los Angeles, *Madrid* 17 C1
Cerro Navia, *Santiago* 26 B1
Certanovka →, *Moscow* 19 C3
Certanovo, *Moscow* 19 C3
Cesano Boscone, *Milan* 18 B1
Cesate, *Milan* 18 A1
Cha Kwo Ling, *Hong Kong* 12 B2
Chacarrita, *Buenos Aires* 7 B2
Chadwell Heath, *London* 15 A4
Chai Chee, *Singapore* 27 B3
Chai Wan, *Hong Kong* 12 B2
Chai Wan Kok, *Hong Kong* 12 A1
Chaillot, Palais de, *Paris* 23 b2
Chakdaha, *Calcutta* 8 C1
Chamartin, *Madrid* 17 B1
Chamberi, *Madrid* 17 B1
Chambourcy, *Paris* 23 A1
Champ de Mars, Parc du, *Paris* 23 c2
Champigny-sur-Marne, *Paris* 23 B4
Champlain, Pont, *Montreal* 19 B2
Champs Elysées, Avenue des, *Paris* 23 b2
Champs-sur-Marne, *Paris* 23 A4
Chamrail, *Calcutta* 8 B1
Chamshil, *Seoul* 26 B2
Chamwŏn, *Seoul* 26 B2
Chanakyapuri, *Delhi* 10 B2
Chanditala, *Calcutta* 8 A1
Changfeng Park, *Shanghai* 27 B1
Changi, *Singapore* 27 A3
Changi Int. Airport, *Singapore* 27 A3
Changning, *Shanghai* 27 B1
Chantereine, *Paris* 23 A4
Chantian, *Canton* 8 A2
Chao Phraya →, *Bangkok* 3 B2
Chaoyang, *Beijing* 4 B2
Chaoyangmen, *Beijing* 4 B2
Chapelizod, *Dublin* 11 A1
Chapultepec, Bosque de, *Mexico City* 18 B1
Chapultepec, Castillo de, *Mexico City* 18 B1
Charenton-le-Pont, *Paris* 23 B3
Charing Cross, *London* 15 b4
Charleroi, Kanal de →, *Brussels* 6 B1
Charles Bridge, *Prague* 24 b1
Charles Square, *Prague* 24 c1
Charlestown, *Boston* 6 A3
Charlottenburg, *Berlin* 5 A2
Charlottenburg, Schloss, *Berlin* 5 A2
Charlottenlund, *Copenhagen* 10 A3
Charlton, *London* 15 B4
Charneca, *Lisbon* 14 A2
Charneca, *Lisbon* 14 B1
Châteaufort, *Paris* 23 B1
Châtenay-Malabry, *Paris* 23 B2
Chatham, *Chicago* 9 C3
Châtillon, *Paris* 23 B2
Chatou, *Paris* 23 A1
Chatpur, *Calcutta* 8 B2
Chatswood, *Sydney* 28 A2
Chatuchak, *Bangkok* 3 B2
Chatuchak Park, *Bangkok* 3 B2
Chauki, *Karachi* 14 A1
Chavarria, *Lima* 16 B2
Chaville, *Paris* 23 B2
Chayang, *Seoul* 26 B2
Chegi, *Seoul* 26 B2
Chelles, *Paris* 23 A4
Chelles, Canal de, *Paris* 23 A4
Chells-le-Pin, Aérodrome, *Paris* 23 A4
Chelsea, *Boston* 6 A3
Chelsea, *London* 15 B2
Chelsea, *New York* 21 c1
Chembur, *Mumbai* 20 A2
Chennevières-sur-Marne, *Paris* 23 B4
Cheops, *Cairo* 7 B1
Cherepkovo, *Moscow* 19 B2
Chernyovo, *Moscow* 19 A1
Cheryomushki, *Moscow* 19 B3
Chestnut Hill, *Boston* 6 B2
Cheung Sha Wan, *Hong Kong* 12 A1
Cheverly, *Washington* 32 B4
Chevilly-Larue, *Paris* 23 B3
Chevry-Cossigny, *Paris* 23 B4
Chevy Chase, *Washington* 32 B3
Chevy Chase View, *Washington* 32 A3
Chia Keng, *Singapore* 27 A3
Chiaravalle Milanese, *Milan* 18 B2
Chicago, *Chicago* 9 B3
Chicago Harbor, *Chicago* 9 B3
Chicago Lawn, *Chicago* 9 C2
Chicago-Midway Airport, *Chicago* 9 C2
Chicago-O'Hare Int. Airport, *Chicago* 9 B1
Chicago Ridge, *Chicago* 9 C2
Chicago Sanitary and Ship Canal, *Chicago* 9 C2
Chienzui, *Canton* 8 A3
Chik Sha, *Hong Kong* 12 B2
Child's Hill, *London* 15 A2
Chilla Saroda, *Delhi* 10 B2
Chillum, *Washington* 32 B4
Chilly-Mazarin, *Paris* 23 B2
Chinatown, *Los Angeles* 16 a3
Chinatown, *New York* 21 e2
Chinatown, *San Francisco* 25 b2
Chinatown, *Singapore* 27 c2
Chingupota, *Calcutta* 8 C1
Chislehurst, *London* 15 B4
Chiswick, *London* 15 B2
Chiswick House, *London* 15 B2
Chitose, *Tokyo* 29 B2
Chitralada Palace, *Bangkok* 3 B2
Chiyoda-Ku, *Tokyo* 29 b4
Chkalova, *Moscow* 19 C5
Choa Chu Kang, *Singapore* 27 A2
Choboty, *Moscow* 19 C2
Chodov u Prahy, *Prague* 24 B3
Chōfu, *Tokyo* 29 B2
Choisy-le-Roi, *Paris* 23 B3
Cholupice, *Prague* 24 C2
Chom Thong, *Bangkok* 3 B1
Chong Pang, *Singapore* 27 A2
Ch'ŏngdam, *Seoul* 26 B2
Chongmyo Royal Shrine, *Seoul* 26 B1
Chongno, *Seoul* 26 B1
Chongwen, *Beijing* 4 B2
Chŏnho, *Seoul* 26 B2
Chopin, Muzeum, *Warsaw* 31 b2
Chornaya →, *Moscow* 19 B6
Chorrillos, *Lima* 16 C2
Chowpatty Beach, *Mumbai* 20 b1
Christian Quarter, *Jerusalem* 13 b3
Christiansborg, *Copenhagen* 10 c2
Christianshavn, *Copenhagen* 10 A3
Chrysler Building, *New York* 21 c2
Chrzanów, *Warsaw* 31 B1
Chuen Lung, *Hong Kong* 12 A1
Chuk Kok, *Hong Kong* 12 A2
Chulalongkom Univ., *Bangkok* 3 B2
Chung, *Seoul* 26 B1
Chunghwa, *Seoul* 26 B2
Chungnangch'on →, *Seoul* 26 B1
Chūō-Ku, *Tokyo* 29 b5
Church End, *London* 15 A2
Churchtown, *Dublin* 11 B2
Ciampino, *Rome* 25 C2
Ciampino, Aeroporto di, *Rome* 25 C2
Cicero, *Chicago* 9 B2
Cilandak, *Jakarta* 13 B1
Cilincing, *Jakarta* 13 A2
Ciliwung →, *Jakarta* 13 B2
Čimice, *Prague* 24 B2
Cinecittà, *Rome* 25 B2
Cinisello Bálsamo, *Milan* 18 A2
Cinkota, *Budapest* 7 A3
Cipete, *Jakarta* 13 B1
Citadella, *Budapest* 7 c2
Citta degli Studi, *Milan* 18 B2
Città del Vaticano, *Rome* 25 B1
City, *London* 15 A3
City Hall, *New York* 21 e1
Ciudad Deportiva, *Mexico City* 18 B2
Ciudad Fin de Semana, *Madrid* 17 B2
Ciudad General Belgrano, *Buenos Aires* 7 C1
Ciudad Lineál, *Madrid* 17 B2
Ciudad Satélite, *Mexico City* 18 A1
Ciudad Universitaria, *Buenos Aires* 7 B2
Ciudad Universitaria, *Mexico City* 18 C1
Ciutadella, Parc de la, *Barcelona* 4 b3
Civic Center, *Los Angeles* 16 b2
Clamart, *Paris* 23 B2
Clapham, *London* 15 B3
Clapton, *London* 15 A3
Claremont, *Cape Town* 8 A1
Clayhall, *London* 15 A4
Clerkenwell, *London* 15 a4
Clermiston, *Edinburgh* 11 B2
Clichy, *Paris* 23 A2
Clichy-sous-Bois, *Paris* 23 A4
Cliffside, *Toronto* 30 A3
Cliffside Park, *New York* 21 B2
Clifton, *Boston* 6 A4
Clifton, *Karachi* 14 B2
Clifton, *New York* 21 C1
Cliftondale, *Boston* 6 A3
Cloghran, *Dublin* 11 A2
Clonskeagh, *Dublin* 11 B2
Clontarf, *Dublin* 11 A2
Clontarf, *Sydney* 28 A2
Clovelly, *Sydney* 28 B2
Cobras, I. das, *Rio de Janeiro* 24 B2
Coburg, *Melbourne* 17 A1
Cochituate, *Boston* 6 A1
Cochituate, L., *Boston* 6 B1
Cocotá, *Rio de Janeiro* 24 A1
Cœuilly, *Paris* 23 B4
Coina, *Lisbon* 14 B2
Coit Tower, *San Francisco* 25 a2
Coker, *Lagos* 14 B2
Colaba, *Mumbai* 20 B1
Colaba Pt., *Mumbai* 20 B1
Colegiales, *Buenos Aires* 7 B2
Colindale, *London* 15 A2
Colinton, *Edinburgh* 11 B2
College Park, *Atlanta* 3 C2
College Park, *Washington* 32 B4
College Point, *New York* 21 B2
Collégien, *Paris* 23 A4
Collier Row, *London* 15 A4
Colliers Wood, *London* 15 B2
Colma, *San Francisco* 25 B2
Colney Hatch, *London* 15 A3
Cologno Monzese, *Milan* 18 A2
Colombes, *Paris* 23 A2
Colón, Monumente, *Barcelona* 4 c3
Colon, Plaza de, *Madrid* 17 a3
Colonia Güell, *Barcelona* 4 A1
Colonial Knob, *Wellington* 32 A1
Colosseo, *Rome* 25 c3
Columbus Circus, *New York* 21 b2
Combault, *Paris* 23 B4
Comércio, Praça do, *Lisbon* 14 A2
Commerce, *Los Angeles* 16 B4
Como, *Sydney* 28 C1
Company's Gardens, *Cape Town* 8 c2
Conceição, I. da, *Rio de Janeiro* 24 B2
Concertgebouw, *Amsterdam* 2 c1
Conchali, *Santiago* 26 B2
Concord, *Boston* 6 A1
Concord, *Sydney* 28 B1
Concord, *Toronto* 30 A2
Concorde, Place de la, *Paris* 23 b3
Concorezzo, *Milan* 18 A2
Coney Island, *New York* 21 C2
Congonhas, Aéroporto, *São Paulo* 26 B2
Connaught Place, *Delhi* 10 B2
Conservatori, Palazzo dei, *Rome* 25 c3
Consolação, *São Paulo* 26 B2
Constantia, *Cape Town* 8 B1
Constitución, *Buenos Aires* 7 B2
Constitution, *Atlanta* 3 B2
Convention and Exhibition Centre, *Hong Kong* 12 b2
Coogee, *Sydney* 28 B2
Cook Str., *Wellington* 32 A1
Cooksville, *Toronto* 30 B1
Coolock, *Dublin* 11 A2
Copacabana, *Rio de Janeiro* 24 B1
Copenhagen = København, *Copenhagen* 10 A2
Coral Gables, *Miami* 18 B2
Coral Hills, *Washington* 32 B4
Corcovado, Morro do, *Rio de Janeiro* 24 B1
Corduff, *Dublin* 11 A1
Cormano, *Milan* 18 A2
Cornaredo, *Milan* 18 A1
Córsico, *Milan* 18 B1
Corsini, Palazzo, *Rome* 25 c1
Corviale, *Rome* 25 B1
Coslada, *Madrid* 17 B2
Cossigny, *Paris* 23 B4
Cossipore, *Calcutta* 8 B2
Costantino, Arco di, *Rome* 25 c3
Costorphine, *Edinburgh* 11 B2
Cotao, *Lisbon* 14 A1
Côte St.-Luc, *Montreal* 19 B2
Cotunduba, I. de, *Rio de Janeiro* 24 B2
Coubron, *Paris* 23 A4
Countryside, *Chicago* 9 C1
Courbevoie, *Paris* 23 A2
Courtry, *Paris* 23 A4
Covent Garden, *London* 15 b4
Cowgate, *Edinburgh* 11 b3
Cowley, *London* 15 A1
Coyoacán, *Mexico City* 18 B2
Cragin, *Chicago* 9 B2
Craighall Park, *Johannesburg* 13 A2
Craiglockhart, *Edinburgh* 11 B2
Craigmillar, *Edinburgh* 11 B3
Cramond, *Edinburgh* 11 B2
Cramond Bridge, *Edinburgh* 11 B1
Cramond I., *Edinburgh* 11 B2
Cranford, *London* 15 B1
Crawford, *Cape Town* 8 A2
Crayford, *London* 15 B5
Creekmouth, *London* 15 A4
Crescenzago, *Milan* 18 A2
Cressely, *Paris* 23 B1
Cresskill, *New York* 21 A2
Creteil, *Paris* 23 B3
Cricklewood, *London* 15 A2
Cristo Redentor, Estatua do, *Rio de Janeiro* 24 B1
Crockenhill, *London* 15 B4
Croissy-Beaubourg, *Paris* 23 B4
Croissy-sur-Seine, *Paris* 23 A1
Crosby, *Johannesburg* 13 B1
Crosne, *Paris* 23 B3
Cross I., *Mumbai* 20 B2
Crouch End, *London* 15 A3
Crown Mine, *Johannesburg* 13 B1
Crows Nest, *Sydney* 28 A2
Croydon, *London* 15 B3
Croydon Park, *Sydney* 28 B1
Cruagh Mt., *Dublin* 11 B2
Crumlin, *Dublin* 11 B2
Cruz de Pau, *Lisbon* 14 B2
Crystal Palace, *London* 15 B3
Csepel, *Budapest* 7 B2
Csepelsziget, *Budapest* 7 B2
Csillaghegy, *Budapest* 7 A2
Csillagtelep, *Budapest* 7 B2
Csömör, *Budapest* 7 A3
Csömöri-patak →, *Budapest* 7 A3
Cuatro Vientos, *Madrid* 17 B1
Cuauhtémoc, *Mexico City* 18 B2
Cubao, *Manila* 17 B2
Çubuklu, *Istanbul* 12 B2
Cudahy, *Los Angeles* 16 C3
Cuicuilco, Pirámido de, *Mexico City* 18 C1
Culver City, *Los Angeles* 16 B2
Cumballa Hill, *Mumbai* 20 a1
Cumbres de Vallecas, *Madrid* 17 B2
Cupecé, *São Paulo* 26 B1
Currie, *Edinburgh* 11 B2
Cusago, *Milan* 18 B1
Cusano Milanino, *Milan* 18 A2
Custom House, *Dublin* 11 b3
Çuvuşabaşi →, *Istanbul* 12 B1
Czernriaków, *Warsaw* 31 B2
Czyste, *Warsaw* 31 B1

D

Da Moóca →, *São Paulo* 26 B2
Da Yunhe →, *Tianjin* 30 A1
Dabizhuang, *Tianjin* 30 A2
Ďablice, *Prague* 24 B2
Dąbrowa, *Warsaw* 31 B1
Dachang, *Shanghai* 27 B1
Dachang Airfield, *Shanghai* 27 B1
Dachau-Ost, *Munich* 20 A1
Dachauer Moos, *Munich* 20 A1
Dadar, *Mumbai* 20 A1
Dagenham, *London* 15 A4
Daglfing, *Munich* 20 B2
Daheisha, *Jerusalem* 13 B2
Dahlem, *Berlin* 5 B2
Dahlwitz-Hoppegarten, *Berlin* 5 A5
Dahongmen, *Beijing* 4 C2
Daitō, *Osaka* 22 A4
Dajiaoting, *Beijing* 4 B2
Dakhnoye, *St. Petersburg* 26 C1
Dalejsky potok →, *Prague* 24 B2
Dalgety Bay, *Edinburgh* 11 A1
Dalkeith, *Edinburgh* 11 B3
Dalkey, *Dublin* 11 B3
Dalkey Island, *Dublin* 11 B3
Dallgow, *Berlin* 5 A1
Dalmeny, *Edinburgh* 11 B1
Dalston, *London* 15 A3
Daly City, *San Francisco* 25 B2
Dam, *Amsterdam* 2 b2
Dam Rak, *Amsterdam* 2 a2
Damaia, *Lisbon* 14 A1
Dämeritzsee, *Berlin* 5 B5
Dan Ryan Woods, *Chicago* 9 C2
Danderhall, *Edinburgh* 11 B3
Danderyd, *Stockholm* 28 A2
Danforth, *Toronto* 30 A3
Darakeh, *Tehran* 30 A2
Darband, *Tehran* 30 A2
Darling Harbour, *Sydney* 28 b1
Darling Point, *Sydney* 28 B2
Darndale, *Dublin* 11 A2
Darrūs, *Tehran* 30 A2
Dartford, *London* 15 B5
Darya Ganj, *Delhi* 1 a3
Dashi, *Canton* 8 B2
Datansha, *Canton* 8 B2
Datun, *Beijing* 4 B2
Daulatpur, *Delhi* 10 A1
David's Citadel, *Jerusalem* 13 b3
David's Tomb, *Jerusalem* 13 b3
Davidson, Mt., *San Francisco* 25 B2
Davidson's Mains, *Edinburgh* 11 B2
Dāvūdiyeh, *Tehran* 30 A2
Davydkovo, *Moscow* 19 B2
Dawidy, *Warsaw* 31 C1
Days Bay, *Wellington* 32 B2
Dazhigu, *Tianjin* 30 B2
De Waag, *Amsterdam* 2 b2
Decatur, *Atlanta* 3 B3
Dedham, *Boston* 6 B2
Deer I., *Boston* 6 A4
Degunino, *Moscow* 19 A3
Deir Dibwan, *Jerusalem* 13 A2
Deir Ibzi'e, *Jerusalem* 13 A1
Dejvice, *Prague* 24 B2
Dekabristov, Ostrov, *St. Petersburg* 26 B1
Delhi, *Delhi* 10 B2
Delhi Gate, *Delhi* 1 b3
Demarest, *New York* 21 A2
Den Ilp, *Amsterdam* 2 A2
Denistone Heights, *Sydney* 28 A1
Dentonia Park, *Toronto* 30 A3
Deptford, *London* 15 B3
Deputati, Camera dei, *Rome* 25 b2
Des Plaines, *Chicago* 9 A1
Des Plaines →, *Chicago* 9 B1
Deshengmen, *Beijing* 4 B2
Deutsch-Wagram, *Vienna* 31 A3
Deutsche Oper, *Berlin* 5 A2
Deutscher Museum, *Munich* 20 B2
Devil's Peak, *Cape Town* 8 A1
Dháfni, *Athens* 2 B2
Dhakuria, *Calcutta* 8 B2
Dhamarakia, *Athens* 2 B1
Dharavi, *Mumbai* 20 A2
Dhrapersón, *Athens* 2 B1
Diadema, *São Paulo* 26 C2
Diegen, *Brussels* 6 A2
Diemen, *Amsterdam* 2 A2
Diepkloof, *Johannesburg* 13 B1
Dieprivier, *Cape Town* 8 B1
Difficult Run →, *Washington* 32 B2
Dilbeek, *Brussels* 6 A1
Dinzigu, *Tianjin* 30 A1
Dirnismaning, *Munich* 20 A2
District Heights, *Washington* 32 B4
Ditan Park, *Beijing* 4 a2
Diyāla →, *Baghdad* 3 B3
Djursholm, *Stockholm* 28 A2
Döberitz, *Berlin* 5 A1
Döbling, *Vienna* 31 A2
Docklands, *London* 15 A3
Dodder, R. →, *Dublin* 11 B1
Dodger Stadium, *Los Angeles* 16 B3
Dolgoe Ozero, *St. Petersburg* 26 A1
Doll Museum, *Delhi* 1 b3
Dollis Hill, *London* 15 A2
Dollymount, *Dublin* 11 A2
Dolni, *Prague* 24 B3
Dolni Chabry, *Prague* 24 B2
Dolni Počernice, *Prague* 24 B3
Dolphins Barn, *Dublin* 11 B2
Dom Pedro II, Parque, *São Paulo* 26 B2
Domain, The, *Sydney* 28 b2
Dome of the Rock, *Jerusalem* 13 b3
Don Mills, *Toronto* 30 A2
Don Muang Int. Airport, *Bangkok* 3 A2
Donaghmede, *Dublin* 11 A3
Donau-Oder Kanal, *Vienna* 31 A3
Donaufeld, *Vienna* 31 A2
Donaupark, *Vienna* 31 A2
Donaustadt, *Vienna* 31 A2
Dongan Hills, *New York* 21 C1
Dongcheng, *Beijing* 4 B2
Donggou, *Shanghai* 27 B2
Dongjiao, *Canton* 8 B2
Dongjuzi, *Tianjin* 30 B2
Dongmenwai, *Tianjin* 30 B2
Dongri, *Mumbai* 20 B2
Dongshanhu Park, *Canton* 8 B2
Dongzhimen, *Beijing* 4 B2
Donnybrook, *Dublin* 11 B2
Doornfontein, *Johannesburg* 13 B2
Dorchester, *Boston* 6 B3
Dorchester B., *Boston* 6 B3
Dornach, *Munich* 20 B3
Dorval, Aéroport de, *Montreal* 19 B1
Dos Couros →, *São Paulo* 26 C2
Dos Moninos →, *São Paulo* 26 C2
Douglas Park, *Chicago* 9 B2
Dover Heights, *Sydney* 28 B2
Dowlatābād, *Tehran* 30 B2
Downey, *Los Angeles* 16 C4
Downsview, *Toronto* 30 A1
Dragør, *Copenhagen* 10 B3
Drancy, *Paris* 23 A3
Dranesville, *Washington* 32 A1
Dreilinden, *Berlin* 5 B2
Drewnica, *Warsaw* 31 B2
Drigh Road, *Karachi* 14 A2
Drimnagh, *Dublin* 11 B2
Drogenbos, *Brussels* 6 B1
Druid Hills, *Atlanta* 3 B2
Drum Towwer, *Beijing* 4 a2
Drumcondra, *Dublin* 11 A2
Drummoyne, *Sydney* 28 B1
Drylaw, *Edinburgh* 11 B2
Dubeč, *Prague* 24 B3
Dublin, *Dublin* 11 A2
Dublin Airport, *Dublin* 11 A2
Dublin Bay, *Dublin* 11 B3
Dublin Harbour, *Dublin* 11 A2
Duddingston, *Edinburgh* 11 B3
Dugnano, *Milan* 18 A2
Dūlāb, *Tehran* 30 B2
Dulwich, *London* 15 B3
Dum Dum, *Calcutta* 8 B2
Dum Dum Int. Airport, *Calcutta* 8 B2
Dumont, *New York* 21 A2
Dún Laoghaire, *Dublin* 11 B3
Duna →, *Budapest* 7 A2
Duncan Dock, *Cape Town* 8 a3
Dundrum, *Dublin* 11 B2
Dunearn, *Singapore* 27 B2
Dunfermline, *Edinburgh* 11 A1
Dunn Loring, *Washington* 32 B2
Dunning, *Chicago* 9 B2
Dunvegan, *Johannesburg* 13 A2
Duomo, *Milan* 18 B2
Duque de Caxias, *Rio de Janeiro* 24 A1
Dusit, *Bangkok* 3 B2
Dusit Zoo, *Bangkok* 3 a2
Dworp, *Brussels* 6 B1
Dyakovo, *Moscow* 19 B3
Dzerzhinskiy, *Moscow* 19 C5
Dzerzhinskiy, *Moscow* 19 B3
Dzerzhinskiy Park, *Moscow* 19 B3

E

Eagle Rock, *Los Angeles* 16 B3
Ealing, *London* 15 A2
Earl's Court, *London* 15 c1
Earlsfield, *London* 15 B2
Earlwood, *Sydney* 28 B1
East Acton, *Boston* 6 A1
East Arlington, *Boston* 6 A3
East Arlington, *Washington* 32 B3
East Bedfont, *London* 15 B1
East Boston, *Boston* 6 A3
East Don →, *Toronto* 30 A2
East Elmhurst, *New York* 21 B2
East Finchley, *London* 15 A2
East Ham, *London* 15 A4
East Humber →, *Toronto* 30 A1
East Lamma Channel, *Hong Kong* 12 B1
East Lexington, *Boston* 6 A2
East Los Angeles, *Los Angeles* 16 B3
East Molesey, *London* 15 B1
East New York, *New York* 21 B2
East Pines, *Washington* 32 B4
East Point, *Atlanta* 3 B2
East Potomac Park, *Washington* 32 B3
East Pt., *Boston* 6 A4
East River →, *New York* 21 B2
East Rutherford, *New York* 21 A1
East Sheen, *London* 15 B2
East Village, *New York* 21 e2
East Wickham, *London* 15 B4
East York, *Toronto* 30 A2
Eastbourne, *Wellington* 32 B2
Eastcote, *London* 15 A1
Easter Howgate, *Edinburgh* 11 B2
Eastwood, *Sydney* 28 A1
Ebara, *Tokyo* 29 B3
Ebisu, *Tokyo* 29 B3
Ebute-Ikorodu, *Lagos* 14 A2
Ebute-Metta, *Lagos* 14 B2
Echo Park, *Los Angeles* 16 a1
Eda, *Tokyo* 29 B2
Edendale, *Johannesburg* 13 A2
Edenmore, *Dublin* 11 A2
Edgars Cr. →, *Melbourne* 17 A1
Edgeley, *Toronto* 30 A1
Edgemar, *San Francisco* 25 C2
Edinburgh, *Edinburgh* 11 B2
Edison Park, *Chicago* 9 A2
Edmondston, *Washington* 32 B4
Edmondstown, *Dublin* 11 B2
Edo →, *Tokyo* 29 B4
Edogawa-Ku, *Tokyo* 29 A4
Edsberg, *Stockholm* 28 A1
Edwards L., *Melbourne* 17 A1
Eiche, *Berlin* 5 A4
Eiche Sud, *Berlin* 5 A4
Eiffel, Tour, *Paris* 23 A2
Ein Arik, *Jerusalem* 13 A1
Ein Naquba, *Jerusalem* 13 B1
Ein Rafa, *Jerusalem* 13 B1
Eizariya, *Jerusalem* 13 B2
Ejby, *Copenhagen* 10 A2
Ejigbo, *Lagos* 14 A1
Ekeberg, *Oslo* 22 A3
Eknäs, *Stockholm* 28 B3
El 'Abbasiya, *Cairo* 7 A2
El Agustino, *Lima* 16 B2
El Baragil, *Cairo* 7 A1
El Basâlîn, *Cairo* 7 B2
El-Bira, *Jerusalem* 13 A2
El Bosque, *Santiago* 26 C2
El Carmen, *Santiago* 26 B1
El Cortijo, *Santiago* 26 B1
El Duqqi, *Cairo* 7 A2
El Encinar de los Reyes, *Madrid* 17 A2
El Ghurîya, *Cairo* 7 A2
El Gîza, *Cairo* 7 A2
El-Khadr, *Jerusalem* 13 B1
El Khalîfa, *Cairo* 7 A2
El Kôm el Ahmar, *Cairo* 7 A2
El Ma'âdi, *Cairo* 7 B2
El Matarîya, *Cairo* 7 A2
El Mohandessin, *Cairo* 7 A2
El Monte, *Los Angeles* 16 B4
El Mûskî, *Cairo* 7 A2
El Pardo, *Madrid* 17 A1
El Portal, *Miami* 18 A2
El Prat de Llobregat, *Barcelona* 4 B1
El Pueblo de L.A. Historic Park, *Los Angeles* 16 b2
El Qâhira, *Cairo* 7 A2
El Qubba, *Cairo* 7 A2
El Reloj, *Mexico City* 18 C2
El Retiro, *Madrid* 17 B1
El Salto, *Santiago* 26 B2
El Sereno, *Los Angeles* 16 B3
El Talibîya, *Cairo* 7 B2
El Vergel, *Mexico City* 18 C2
El Wâhli, *Cairo* 7 A2
El Zamâlik, *Cairo* 7 A2
El Zeitûn, *Cairo* 7 A2
Elephanta Caves, *Mumbai* 20 B2
Elephanta I., *Mumbai* 20 B2
Ellboda, *Stockholm* 28 A3
Ellinikón, *Athens* 2 B2
Ellinikón Olympic Complex, *Athens* 2 B2
Ellis I., *New York* 21 B1
Elm Park, *London* 15 A5
Elmers End, *London* 15 B3
Elmhurst, *New York* 21 B2
Elmstead, *London* 15 B4
Elmwood Park, *Chicago* 9 B2
Elmwood Park, *New York* 21 A1
Elsdon, *Wellington* 32 A1
Elsiesrivier, *Cape Town* 8 A2
Elsternwick, *Melbourne* 17 B2
Eltham, *London* 15 B4
Elwood, *Melbourne* 17 B1
Élysée, *Paris* 23 A2
Elysian Park, *Los Angeles* 16 a3
Embajadores, *Madrid* 17 c2
Embarcadero Center, *San Francisco* 25 b3
Emek Refa'im, *Jerusalem* 13 c2
Émerainville, *Paris* 23 B4
Emeryville, *San Francisco* 25 A3
Eminönü, *Istanbul* 12 B1
Emmarentia, *Johannesburg* 13 A2
Empire State Building, *New York* 21 c2
Encantado, *Rio de Janeiro* 24 B1
Encino, *Los Angeles* 16 B2
Encino Res., *Los Angeles* 16 B1
Enebyberg, *Stockholm* 28 A1
Enfield, *Sydney* 28 B1
Engenho, I. do, *Rio de Janeiro* 24 B2
Englewood, *Chicago* 9 C3
Englewood, *New York* 21 A2
Englewood Cliffs, *New York* 21 A2
Enmore, *Sydney* 28 B2
Enskede, *Stockholm* 28 B2
Entrevias, *Madrid* 17 B1
Epping, *Sydney* 28 A1
Erawan Shrine, *Bangkok* 3 c3
Eregun, *Lagos* 14 A2
Erenköy, *Istanbul* 12 C2
Erith, *London* 15 B5
Erlaa, *Vienna* 31 B1
Ermington, *Sydney* 28 A1
Ermita, *Manila* 17 B1
Ershatou, *Canton* 8 B2
Erskineville, *Sydney* 28 B2
Erunkan, *Lagos* 14 A2
Erzsébet-Telep, *Budapest* 7 B3
Eschenried, *Munich* 20 A1
Esenler, *Istanbul* 12 B1
Esher, *London* 15 B1
Eskbank, *Edinburgh* 11 B3
Esperanza, *Mexico City* 18 c3
Esplanade Park, *Singapore* 27 c3
Esplugas, *Barcelona* 4 A1
Esposizione Univ. di Roma (E.U.R.), *Rome* 25 C1
Essendon, *Melbourne* 17 A1
Essendon Airport, *Melbourne* 17 A1
Essingen, *Stockholm* 28 B1
Essling, *Vienna* 31 A3
Est, Gare de l', *Paris* 23 a5
Estadio Maracanã, *Rio de Janeiro* 24 B1
Estado, Parque do, *São Paulo* 26 B2
Estefânia, *Lisbon* 14 a2
Estrela, Basilica da, *Lisbon* 14 A2
Ethnikó Arheologiko Moussío, *Athens* 2 a2
Etobicoke, *Toronto* 30 B1
Etobicoke Cr. →, *Toronto* 30 B1
Etterbeek, *Brussels* 6 B2
Euston, *London* 15 a3
Evanston, *Chicago* 9 A2
Even Sapir, *Jerusalem* 13 B1
Evere, *Brussels* 6 A2
Everett, *Boston* 6 A3
Evergreen Park, *Chicago* 9 C2
Evīn, *Tehran* 30 A2
Évzonos, *Athens* 2 B2
Ewu, *Lagos* 14 A1
Exchange Square, *Hong Kong* 12 c1
Exposições, Palácio das, *Rio de Janeiro* 24 B1
Eyüp, *Istanbul* 12 B1

F

Fabour, Mt., *Singapore* 27 B2
Faechi, *Seoul* 26 B2
Fælledparken, *Copenhagen* 10 A3
Fågelön, *Stockholm* 28 B1
Fagersjö, *Stockholm* 28 B2
Fair Lawn, *New York* 21 A1
Fairfax, *Washington* 32 B2
Fairfax Station, *Washington* 32 C2
Fairhaven Bay, *Boston* 6 A1
Fairhaven Hill, *Boston* 6 A1
Fairland, *Johannesburg* 13 A1
Fairmilehead, *Edinburgh* 11 B2
Fairmount Heights, *Washington* 32 B4
Fairport, *Toronto* 30 A4
Fairview, *New York* 21 B2
Falenty, *Warsaw* 31 C1
Fálirou, Órmos, *Athens* 2 B2
Falkenburg, *Berlin* 5 A4
Falkenhagen, *Berlin* 5 A1
Falkensee, *Berlin* 5 A1
Falls Church, *Washington* 32 B2
Falomo, *Lagos* 14 B2
False Bay, *Cape Town* 8 B2
Fangcun, *Canton* 8 B2
Faraḥābād, *Tehran* 30 A2
Farforovskaya, *St. Petersburg* 26 B2
Farningham, *London* 15 B5
Farrar Pond, *Boston* 6 A1
Farsta, *Stockholm* 28 B2
Fasanerie-Nord, *Munich* 20 A2
Fasangarten, *Munich* 20 B2
Fasting Palace, *Beijing* 4 c2
Fatih, *Istanbul* 12 B1
Favoriten, *Vienna* 31 B2

Fawkner, *Melbourne* 17 A1
Fawkner Park, *Melbourne* 17 B1
Feijó, *Lisbon* 14 B2
Feldkirchen, *Munich* 20 B3
Feldmoching, *Munich* 20 A2
Feltham, *London* 15 B1
Fener, *Istanbul* 12 B1
Fenerbahçe, *Istanbul* 12 C2
Fengtai, *Beijing* 4 C1
Fenino, *Moscow* 19 B5
Ferencváros, *Budapest* 7 B2
Ferihegyi Airport, *Budapest* 7 B3
Ferndale, *Johannesburg* 13 A2
Férolles-Attilly, *Paris* 23 B4
Fichtenau, *Berlin* 5 B5
Fields Corner, *Boston* 6 B3
Fiera Camp, *Milan* 18 B1
Fifth Avenue, *New York* 21 b3
Figino, *Milan* 18 B1
Fijir, *Baghdad* 3 A2
Filadhélfia, *Athens* 2 A2
Fili-Mazilovo, *Moscow* 19 B2
Filothei, *Athens* 2 A2
Finchley, *London* 15 A2
Finglas, *Dublin* 11 A2
Finsbury, *London* 15 A3
Finsbury Park, *London* 15 A3
Fiorito, *Buenos Aires* 7 C2
Firhouse, *Dublin* 11 B2
Fischerhäuser, *Munich* 20 A3
Fisher Island, *Miami* 18 B2
Fishermans Bend, *Melbourne* 17 A1
Fisherman's Wharf, *San Francisco* 25 a1
Fisherville, *Toronto* 30 A2
Fisksätra, *Stockholm* 28 B3
Fitzroy Gardens, *Melbourne* 17 A1
Five Dock, *Sydney* 28 B1
Fjellstrand, *Oslo* 22 B2
Flamengo, *Rio de Janeiro* 24 B1
Flaminio, *Rome* 25 B1
Flaskebekk, *Oslo* 22 A2
Flatbush, *New York* 21 C2
Flaten, *Stockholm* 28 B2
Flemington Racecourse, *Melbourne* 17 A1
Flint Pk., *Los Angeles* 16 B3
Florence, *Los Angeles* 16 C3
Florence Bloom Bird Sanctuary, *Johannesburg* 13 A2
Florentia, *Johannesburg* 13 B2
Flores, *Buenos Aires* 7 B2
Floresta, *Buenos Aires* 7 B2
Florida, *Buenos Aires* 7 B2
Florida, *Johannesburg* 13 B1
Floridsdorf, *Vienna* 31 A2
Flushing, *New York* 21 B3
Flushing Meadows Corona Park, *New York* 21 B2
Flysta, *Stockholm* 28 A1
Fo Tan, *Hong Kong* 12 A2
Föhrenhain, *Vienna* 31 A2
Fontainebleau, *Johannesburg* 13 A1
Fontenay-aux-Roses, *Paris* 23 B2
Fontenay-le-Fleury, *Paris* 23 B1
Fontenay-sous-Bois, *Paris* 23 A3
Foots Cray, *London* 15 B4
Footscray, *Melbourne* 17 A1
Foreshore, *Cape Town* 8 a3
Forest, *Brussels* 6 B1
Forest Gate, *London* 15 A4
Forest Heights, *Washington* 32 C3
Forest Hill, *London* 15 B3
Forest Hill, *Toronto* 30 A2
Forest Hills, *New York* 21 B2
Forest Park, *Chicago* 9 B2
Forest View, *Chicago* 9 C2
Forestville, *Washington* 32 B4
Fornebu, *Oslo* 22 A2
Fornebu Airport, *Oslo* 22 A2
Foro Romano, *Rome* 25 c3
Forstenried, *Munich* 20 B1
Forstenrieder Park, *Munich* 20 B1
Fort, *Mumbai* 20 c2
Fort Canning Park, *Singapore* 27 b2
Fort Dupont Park, *Washington* 32 B4
Fort Foote Village, *Washington* 32 C3
Fort Lee, *New York* 21 A2
Fort Mason Center, *San Francisco* 25 a1
Forth, Firth of, *Edinburgh* 11 A2
Forth Rail Bridge, *Edinburgh* 11 A1
Forth Road Bridge, *Edinburgh* 11 A1
Fót, *Budapest* 7 A3
Fourqueux, *Paris* 23 A1
Foxrock, *Dublin* 11 B2
Framingham, *Boston* 6 B1
Franconia, *Washington* 32 C3
Frankel, *Singapore* 27 B3
Franklin Park, *Boston* 6 B3
Franklin Park, *Chicago* 9 B1
Franklin Park, *Washington* 32 B3
Franklin Res., *Los Angeles* 16 B2
Frauenkirche, *Munich* 20 b2
Frederiksberg, *Copenhagen* 10 A3
Frederiksdal, *Copenhagen* 10 A2
Fredersdorf, *Berlin* 5 A5
Freguesia, *Rio de Janeiro* 24 A1
Freidrichshain, Volkspark, *Berlin* 5 A3
Freiham, *Munich* 20 B1
Freimann, *Munich* 20 A2
Fresh Pond, *Boston* 6 A3
Fresnes, *Paris* 23 B2
Freudenau, *Vienna* 31 A2
Friarstown, *Dublin* 11 B1
Frick Collection, *New York* 21 b3
Friedenau, *Berlin* 5 B3
Friedrichsfelde, *Berlin* 5 B4
Friedrichshagen, *Berlin* 5 B4
Friedrichshain, *Berlin* 5 A3
Friedrichslust, *Berlin* 5 A5
Friherrs, *Helsinki* 12 B1
Frontón, I., *Lima* 16 B1
Frunze, *Moscow* 19 B3
Fuchū, *Tokyo* 29 A1
Fuencarral, *Madrid* 17 B1
Fuenlabrada, *Madrid* 17 C1
Fujidera, *Osaka* 22 B4
Fukagawa, *Tokyo* 29 B3
Fukiage Imperial Garden, *Tokyo* 29 a4
Fukiai, *Osaka* 22 A2
Fukushima, *Osaka* 22 A3
Fulham, *London* 15 B2
Funabori, *Tokyo* 29 A4
Funasaka, *Osaka* 22 A2
Fundão, I. do, *Rio de Janeiro* 24 B1
Fünfhaus, *Vienna* 31 A2
Furesø, *Copenhagen* 10 A2
Furth, *Munich* 20 B2
Futago-tamagawaen, *Tokyo* 29 B2
Fuxing Dao, *Shanghai* 27 B2
Fuxing Park, *Shanghai* 27 B1
Fuxinglu, *Beijing* 4 B1

G

Gage Park, *Chicago* 9 C2
Gagny, *Paris* 23 A4
Galata, *Istanbul* 12 B1
Galátsion, *Athens* 2 A2
Galeão, Aéroporto Int. de, *Rio de Janeiro* 24 A1
Galyanovo, *Moscow* 19 B4
Gambir, *Jakarta* 13 A1
Gamboa, *Rio de Janeiro* 24 B1
Gambolóita, *Milan* 18 B2
Gamla Stan , *Stockholm* 28 c2
Gamlebyen, *Oslo* 22 A3
Gangtou, *Canton* 8 A1
Gangwei, *Canton* 8 B2
Ganjiakou, *Beijing* 4 B1
Ganshoren, *Brussels* 6 A1
Gants Hill, *London* 15 A4
Gaoqiao, *Shanghai* 27 A2
Garbagnate Milanese, *Milan* 18 A1
Garbatella, *Rome* 25 B2
Garches, *Paris* 23 A2
Garching, *Munich* 20 A3
Garden City, *Cairo* 7 A2
Garden Reach, *Calcutta* 8 B1
Garder, *Oslo* 22 B2
Garfield, *New York* 21 A1
Garfield Park, *Chicago* 9 B2
Gargareta, *Athens* 2 B2
Garvanza, *Los Angeles* 16 B3
Gåshaga, *Stockholm* 28 A3
Gateway National Recreation Area, *New York* 21 C2
Gateway of India, *Mumbai* 20 B2
Gatow, *Berlin* 5 B1
Gávea, *Rio de Janeiro* 24 B1
Gávea, Pedra da, *Rio de Janeiro* 24 B1
Gazdagrét, *Budapest* 7 B1
Gebel el Ahmar, *Cairo* 7 A2
Gebel el Muqattam, *Cairo* 7 A2
Gebel el Tura, *Cairo* 7 B2
Geiselgasteig, *Munich* 20 B2
General San Martin, *Buenos Aires* 7 B1
Gennevilliers, *Paris* 23 A2
Gentilly, *Paris* 23 B3
Gentofte, *Copenhagen* 10 A3
Genval, *Brussels* 6 B2
George I., *Hong Kong* 12 B1
Georges I., *Boston* 6 B4
Georges River Bridge, *Sydney* 28 C1
Georgetown, *Washington* 32 B3
Georgia Dome, *Atlanta* 3 B2
Gerasdorf bei Wien, *Vienna* 31 A2
Gerberau, *Munich* 20 A1
Gerli, *Buenos Aires* 7 C2
Germiston, *Johannesburg* 13 B2
Gern, *Munich* 20 B2
Gesîrat el Rauda, *Cairo* 7 A2
Getafe, *Madrid* 17 C1
Geva Binyamin, *Jerusalem* 13 A2
Geylang Serai, *Singapore* 27 B3
Gezîrat el Dhahab, *Cairo* 7 B2
Gharapuri, *Mumbai* 20 B2
Ghatkopar, *Mumbai* 20 A2
Ghazipur, *Delhi* 10 B2
Ghizri, *Karachi* 14 B2
Ghizri Cr. →, *Karachi* 14 B2
Ghonda, *Delhi* 10 A2
Ghusuri, *Calcutta* 8 B2
Gianicolense, *Rome* 25 B1
Gianicolo, *Rome* 25 c1
Gibraltar Pt., *Toronto* 30 B2
Gidea Park, *London* 15 A5
Giesing, *Munich* 20 B2
Gilmerton, *Edinburgh* 11 B3
Gilo, *Jerusalem* 13 B2
Gimmersta, *Stockholm* 28 B3
Ginza, *Tokyo* 29 b5
Girgaum, *Mumbai* 20 b2
Giv'at Ye'arim, *Jerusalem* 13 B1
Giv'at Ze'ev, *Jerusalem* 13 A2
Giza Pyramids = Pyramids, *Cairo* 7 B1
Gjersjøen, *Oslo* 22 B3
Gladesville, *Sydney* 28 B1
Gladsakse, *Copenhagen* 10 A2
Glasnevin, *Dublin* 11 A2
Glassmanor, *Washington* 32 C3
Glasthule, *Dublin* 11 B3
Glen Iris, *Melbourne* 17 B2
Glen Mar Park, *Washington* 32 B3
Glen Rock, *New York* 21 A1
Glenarden, *Washington* 32 B4
Glenasmole Reservoirs, *Dublin* 11 B1
Glencorse Res., *Edinburgh* 11 B2
Glencullen, *Dublin* 11 B2
Glendale, *Los Angeles* 16 B3
Glendoo Mt., *Dublin* 11 B2
Glenhuntly, *Melbourne* 17 B2
Glenside, *Wellington* 32 B1
Glenview, *Chicago* 9 A2
Glenview Countryside, *Chicago* 9 A2
Glenvista, *Johannesburg* 13 B2
Glifádha, *Athens* 2 B2
Glömsta, *Stockholm* 28 B1
Glostrup, *Copenhagen* 10 B2
Gogar, *Edinburgh* 11 B2
Göktürk, *Istanbul* 12 A1
Golabari, *Calcutta* 8 B2
Golabki, *Warsaw* 31 B1
Gold Coast, *Chicago* 9 a2
Golden Gate, *San Francisco* 25 B2
Golden Gate Bridge, *San Francisco* 25 B2
Golden Gate Park, *San Francisco* 25 B2
Golden Horn, *Istanbul* 12 B1
Golders Green, *London* 15 A2
Gollans Stream →, *Wellington* 32 B2
Golyevo, *Moscow* 19 B1
Goodman Hill, *Boston* 6 A1
Goodmayes, *London* 15 A4
Goodwood, *Cape Town* 8 A2
Gopalpur, *Calcutta* 8 B2
Górce, *Warsaw* 31 B1
Gore Hill, *Sydney* 28 A2
Gorelyy →, *St. Petersburg* 26 A3
Gorenki, *Moscow* 19 B5
Gorgie, *Edinburgh* 11 B2
Gorky Park, *Moscow* 19 B3
Gosen, *Berlin* 5 B5
Gosener kanal, *Berlin* 5 B5
Gospel Oak, *London* 15 A3
Gotanda, *Tokyo* 29 B3
Goth Goli Mar, *Karachi* 14 A2
Goth Sher Shah, *Karachi* 14 A1
Gournay-sur-Marne, *Paris* 23 A4
Governador, I. do, *Rio de Janeiro* 24 A1
Governor's I., *New York* 21 B1
Graben, *Vienna* 31 b2
Grabów, *Warsaw* 31 C1
Graça, *Lisbon* 14 b3
Grace, Mt., *Wellington* 32 B2
Grace Cathedral, *San Francisco* 25 b1
Gracefield, *Wellington* 32 B2
Gracia, *Barcelona* 4 A2
Gräfelfing, *Munich* 20 B1
Gragoatá, *Rio de Janeiro* 24 B2
Grand Central Station, *New York* 21 c2
Grand Union Canal, *London* 15 A2
Grande Place, *Brussels* 6 b2
Grant Park, *Atlanta* 3 B2
Grant Park, *Chicago* 9 c2
Granton, *Edinburgh* 11 B2
Grape I., *Boston* 6 B4
Grassy Park, *Cape Town* 8 B2
Gratosóglio, *Milan* 18 B2
Gratzwalde, *Berlin* 5 B5
Gravesend, *New York* 21 C2
Grazhdanka, *St. Petersburg* 26 B2
Great Falls, *Washington* 32 B2
Great Falls Park, *Washington* 32 B2
Great Hall of the People, *Beijing* 4 b2
Great Meadows National Wildlife Refuge, *Boston* 6 A1
Greco, *Milan* 18 A2
Green I., *Hong Kong* 12 B1
Green Point, *Cape Town* 8 A1
Greenbelt, *Washington* 32 A4
Greenbelt Park, *Washington* 32 B4
Greenfield Park, *Montreal* 19 B3
Greenford, *London* 15 A1
Greenhill, *London* 15 A2
Greenhills, *Dublin* 11 B1
Greenmarket Square, *Cape Town* 8 c2
Greenpoint, *New York* 21 B2
Greenwich, *London* 15 B3
Greenwich Observatory, *London* 15 B3
Greenwich Village, *New York* 21 B2
Greenwood, *Boston* 6 A3
Grefsen, *Oslo* 22 A3
Gresham Park, *Atlanta* 3 B2
Greve Strand, *Copenhagen* 10 B1
Greyfriars Kirk, *Edinburgh* 11 c2
Griebnitzsee, *Berlin* 5 B1
Griffen Park, *Los Angeles* 16 B3
Grimbergen, *Brussels* 6 A2
Grinzing, *Vienna* 31 A2
Gröbenried, *Munich* 20 A1
Grochów, *Warsaw* 31 B2
Grodzisk, *Warsaw* 31 B2
Groenendaal, *Brussels* 6 B2
Grogol Petamburin, *Jakarta* 13 A1
Gronsdorf, *Munich* 20 B3
Grorud, *Oslo* 22 A4
Gross Glienicke, *Berlin* 5 B1
Gross-Hadern, *Munich* 20 B1
Gross-Lappen, *Munich* 20 A2
Grosse Krampe, *Berlin* 5 B5
Grosse Müggelsee, *Berlin* 5 B4
Grossenzersdorf, *Vienna* 31 A3
Grossenzersdorfer Arm →, *Vienna* 31 A3
Grosser Biberhaufen, *Vienna* 31 A2
Grosser Wannsee, *Berlin* 5 B2
Grossfeld-Siedlung, *Vienna* 31 A2
Grosshesselohe, *Munich* 20 B2
Grossjedlersdorf, *Vienna* 31 A2
Grossziethen, *Berlin* 5 B3
Grove Hall, *Boston* 6 B3
Grove Park, *Atlanta* 3 B2
Grove Park, *London* 15 B4
Grove Park, *London* 15 B2
Groveton, *Washington* 32 C3
Grünau, *Berlin* 5 B4
Grunewald, *Berlin* 5 B2
Grünwald, *Munich* 20 B2
Grünwalder Forst, *Munich* 20 B2
Grymes Hill, *New York* 21 C1
Guadalupe, *Manila* 17 B2
Guadalupe, Basilica de, *Mexico City* 18 B2
Guanabara, B. de, *Rio de Janeiro* 24 B1
Guanabara, Jardim, *Rio de Janeiro* 24 A1
Guanabara, Palácio da, *Rio de Janeiro* 24 B1
Guang'anmen, *Beijing* 4 B1
Guangqumen, *Beijing* 4 B2
Guangzhou, *Canton* 8 B2
Guanshuo, *Canton* 8 B3
Gudö, *Stockholm* 28 B3
Güell, Parque de, *Barcelona* 4 A2
Guerrero, *Mexico City* 18 a1
Guggenheim Museum, *New York* 21 b3
Guinardó, *Barcelona* 4 A2
Gulbai, *Karachi* 14 A1
Güngören, *Istanbul* 12 B1
Gunnersbury, *London* 15 B2
Gustavo A. Madero, *Mexico City* 18 B2
Guttenberg, *New York* 21 B1
Gutuyevskiy, Ostrov, *St. Petersburg* 26 B1
Guyancourt, *Paris* 23 B1
Gyál, *Budapest* 7 B3
Gyáli-patak →, *Budapest* 7 B2

H

Haaga, *Helsinki* 12 B2
Haar, *Munich* 20 B3
Hackbridge, *London* 15 B3
Hackensack, *New York* 21 A1
Hackensack →, *New York* 21 B1
Hackney, *London* 15 A3
Hackney Wick, *London* 15 A3
Haga, *Stockholm* 28 A2
Hagenbrunn, *Vienna* 31 A2
Hägersten, *Stockholm* 28 B1
Häggvik, *Stockholm* 28 A1
Hai He →, *Tianjin* 30 B2
Haidan, *Beijing* 4 B1
Haidarpur, *Delhi* 10 A1
Haidhausen, *Munich* 20 B2
Haight-Ashbury, *San Francisco* 25 B2
Hainault, *London* 15 A4
Haizhu Guangchang, *Canton* 8 B2
Hakunila, *Helsinki* 12 B3
Halásztelek, *Budapest* 7 B1
Haliç = Golden Horn, *Istanbul* 12 B1
Halim Perdanakusuma International Airport, *Jakarta* 13 B2
Halle, *Brussels* 6 B1
Haltiala, *Helsinki* 12 B2
Haltiavuori, *Helsinki* 12 B2
Ham, *London* 15 B2
Hämeenkylä, *Helsinki* 12 B1
Hammarby, *Stockholm* 28 B2
Hamme, *Brussels* 6 A1
Hammersmith, *London* 15 B2
Hampstead, *London* 15 A2
Hampstead, *Montreal* 19 B2
Hampstead Garden Suburb, *London* 15 A2
Hampstead Heath, *London* 15 A2
Hampton, *London* 15 B1
Hampton Court Palace, *London* 15 B1
Hampton Wick, *London* 15 B2
Hamrā', *Baghdad* 3 B1
Hanala, *Helsinki* 12 A3
Haneda, *Tokyo* 29 B3
Hang Hau, *Hong Kong* 12 B2
Hanging Gardens, *Mumbai* 20 b1
Hanjiashu, *Tianjin* 30 A1
Hanlon, *Toronto* 30 B1
Hanwell, *London* 15 A1
Hanworth, *London* 15 B1
Haora, *Calcutta* 8 B1
Hapeville, *Atlanta* 3 C2
Happy Valley, *Hong Kong* 12 B2
Har Adar, *Jerusalem* 13 B1
Haren, *Brussels* 6 A2
Hareskovby, *Copenhagen* 10 A2
Haringey, *London* 15 A3
Harjusuo, *Helsinki* 12 B3
Harlaching, *Munich* 20 B2
Harlaw Res., *Edinburgh* 11 B2
Harlem, *New York* 21 B2
Harlesden, *London* 15 A2
Harlington, *London* 15 B1
Harmaja, *Helsinki* 12 C2
Harmashatar hegy, *Budapest* 7 A2
Harolds Cross, *Dublin* 11 B2
Háros, *Budapest* 7 B2
Harperrig Reservoir, *Edinburgh* 11 B1
Harrow, *London* 15 A1
Harrow on the Hill, *London* 15 A1
Harrow School, *London* 15 A1
Harrow Weald, *London* 15 A1
Hartsfield-Atlanta International Airport, *Atlanta* 3 C2
Harumi, *Tokyo* 29 c5
Harvard Univ., *Boston* 6 A3
Harwood Heights, *Chicago* 9 B2
Hasanābād, *Tehran* 30 A1
Hasbrouck Heights, *New York* 21 A1
Haselhorst, *Berlin* 5 A2
Hasköy, *Istanbul* 12 B1
Hasle, *Oslo* 22 B2
Haslum, *Oslo* 22 A2
Hästhagen, *Stockholm* 28 B2
Hataitai, *Wellington* 32 B1
Hatch End, *London* 15 A1
Hatiara, *Calcutta* 8 B2
Hauketo, *Oslo* 22 A3
Havel →, *Berlin* 5 A2
Havelkanal, *Berlin* 5 A2
Havering, *London* 15 A5
Havering-atte-Bower, *London* 15 A5
Hawŏlgok, *Seoul* 26 B2
Haworth, *New York* 21 A2
Hayes, *London* 15 B4
Hayes, *London* 15 A1
Hayes End, *London* 15 A1
Hayford, *Chicago* 9 C2
Haywards, *Wellington* 32 A2
Heard Pond, *Boston* 6 A1
Heathfield, *Cape Town* 8 B1
Heathrow Airport, *London* 15 B1
Hebe Haven, *Hong Kong* 12 A2
Hebei, *Tianjin* 30 B2
Hedong, *Canton* 8 B2
Hedong, *Tianjin* 30 B2
Heidelberg Heights, *Melbourne* 17 A2
Heidelberg West, *Melbourne* 17 A2
Heidemühle, *Berlin* 5 B5
Heideveld, *Cape Town* 8 A2
Heiligensee, *Berlin* 5 A2
Heiligenstadt, *Vienna* 31 A2
Heinersdorf, *Berlin* 5 A3
Heldenplatz, *Vienna* 31 b1
Hélène Champlain, Parc, *Montreal* 19 A2
Helenelund, *Stockholm* 28 A1
Heliopolis = Masr el Gedida, *Cairo* 7 A2
Hellersdorf, *Berlin* 5 A4
Hellerup, *Copenhagen* 10 A3
Helmahof, *Vienna* 31 A3
Helsingfors = Helsinki, *Helsinki* 12 B2
Helsinki, *Helsinki* 12 B2
Helsinki Airport, *Helsinki* 12 B2
Hendon, *London* 15 A2
Hengsha, *Canton* 8 B2
Hennigsdorf, *Berlin* 5 A2
Henryków, *Warsaw* 31 B1
Henson Cr. →, *Washington* 32 C4
Henttaa, *Helsinki* 12 B1
Heping, *Tianjin* 30 B2
Heping Park, *Shanghai* 27 B2
Hepingli, *Beijing* 4 B2
Herlev, *Copenhagen* 10 A2
Herman Eckstein Park, *Johannesburg* 13 A2
Hermannskogel, *Vienna* 31 A1
Hermiston, *Edinburgh* 11 B2
Hermitage and Winter Palace, *St. Petersburg* 26 B1
Hermsdorf, *Berlin* 5 A2
Hernals, *Vienna* 31 A2
Herne Hill, *London* 15 B3
Héroes de Churubusco, *Mexico City* 18 B2
Herons, Î. aux, *Montreal* 19 B2
Herstedøster, *Copenhagen* 10 A2
Herttoniemi, *Helsinki* 12 B3
Ḥeşārak, *Tehran* 30 A1
Heston, *London* 15 B1
Hetzendorf, *Vienna* 31 B1
Hexi, *Tianjin* 30 B2
Hextable, *London* 15 B5
Hialeah, *Miami* 18 A1
Hickory Hills, *Chicago* 9 C2
Hiekkaharju, *Helsinki* 12 B3
Hietaniemi, *Helsinki* 12 B2
Hietzing, *Vienna* 31 A1
Higashi, *Osaka* 22 A4
Higashimurayama, *Tokyo* 29 A1
Higashinada, *Osaka* 22 A2
Higashinari, *Osaka* 22 A4
Higashiōsaka, *Osaka* 22 B4
Higashisumiyoshi, *Osaka* 22 B4
Higashiyodogawa, *Osaka* 22 A3
High Park, *Toronto* 30 B2
Highbury, *London* 15 A3
Highgate, *London* 15 A3
Highland Cr. →, *Toronto* 30 A3
Highland Creek, *Toronto* 30 A3
Highland Park, *Los Angeles* 16 B3
Highlands North, *Johannesburg* 13 A2
Hillcrest Heights, *Washington* 32 C4
Hillend, *Edinburgh* 11 A1
Hillingdon, *London* 15 A1
Hillwood, *Washington* 32 B3
Hilmîya, *Cairo* 7 A2
Hin Keng, *Hong Kong* 12 A2
Hingham, *Boston* 6 B4
Hingham B., *Boston* 6 B4
Hingham Harbor, *Boston* 6 B4
Hirakata, *Osaka* 22 A4
Hirota, *Osaka* 22 A3
Hirschstetten, *Vienna* 31 A2
Histórico Nacional, Museu, *Rio de Janeiro* 24 b3
Hither Green, *London* 15 B3
Hiyoshi, *Tokyo* 29 B2
Hizma, *Jerusalem* 13 B2
Hjortekær, *Copenhagen* 10 A3
Hjortespring, *Copenhagen* 10 A2
Hlubočepy, *Prague* 24 B2
Ho Chung, *Hong Kong* 12 A2
Ho Man Tin, *Hong Kong* 12 B2
Hoboken, *New York* 21 B1
Hobsons B., *Melbourne* 17 B1
Hochbrück, *Munich* 20 A2
Hochelaga, *Montreal* 19 A2
Hodgkins, *Chicago* 9 C1
Hoegi, *Seoul* 26 B2
Hoeilaart, *Brussels* 6 B2
Hofberg, *Vienna* 31 A2
Hoffman I., *New York* 21 C1
Hofgarten, *Munich* 20 a3
Högsdtadomstolen, *Stockholm* 28 c2
Hohenbrunn, *Munich* 20 B3
Hohenschönhausen, *Berlin* 5 A4
Holborn, *London* 15 a4
Holešovice, *Prague* 24 B2
Holland Village, *Singapore* 27 B2
Höllriegelskreuth, *Munich* 20 B1
Hollywood, *Los Angeles* 16 B3
Holmenkollen, *Oslo* 22 A3
Holmes Run Acres, *Washington* 32 B2
Holmgård, *Stockholm* 28 B1
Holysloot, *Amsterdam* 2 A3
Homerton, *London* 15 A3
Hometown, *Chicago* 9 C2
Hōnanchō, *Tokyo* 29 A2
Honcho, *Tokyo* 29 A3
Honden, *Tokyo* 29 A4
Hondo, Rio →, *Los Angeles* 16 B4
Hong Kong, *Hong Kong* 12 B1
Hong Kong, Univ. of, *Hong Kong* 12 B1
Hong Kong I., *Hong Kong* 12 B2
Hong Kong Park, *Hong Kong* 12 c1
Hongkou, *Shanghai* 27 B1
Hongkou Park, *Shanghai* 27 B1
Hongmiao, *Beijing* 4 B2
Hongqiao, *Shanghai* 27 B1
Hongqiao, *Tianjin* 30 B1
Hongqiao Airport, *Shanghai* 27 B1
Hongŭn, *Seoul* 26 B1
Honjyo, *Tokyo* 29 A3
Honoré Mercier, Pont, *Montreal* 19 B1
Hönow, *Berlin* 5 A4
Hooghly = Hugli →, *Calcutta* 8 A2
Hook, *London* 15 B2
Horikiri, *Tokyo* 29 A4
Horn Pond, *Boston* 6 A2
Hornchurch, *London* 15 A5
Horni, *Prague* 24 B3
Horni Počernice, *Prague* 24 B3
Hornsey, *London* 15 A3
Horoměřice, *Prague* 24 B1
Hortaleza, *Madrid* 17 B2
Hosoyama, *Tokyo* 29 B2
Hostafranchs, *Barcelona* 4 A1
Hostivař, *Prague* 24 B3
Hôtel des Invalides, *Paris* 23 c2
Houbětin, *Prague* 24 B3
Houghs Neck, *Boston* 6 B4
Houghton, *Johannesburg* 13 B2
Houilles, *Paris* 23 A2
Hounslow, *London* 15 B1
Houses of Parliament, *London* 15 c3
Hout Bay, *Cape Town* 8 B1
Hove Å →, *Copenhagen* 10 A1
Hovedøya, *Oslo* 22 A3
Høvik, *Oslo* 22 A2
Hovorčovice, *Prague* 24 A3
Howard Beach, *New York* 21 C2
Howth, *Dublin* 11 A3
Howth Head, *Dublin* 11 A3
Hoxton, *London* 15 a5
Hōya, *Tokyo* 29 A2
Hradčany, *Prague* 24 B2
Huanghuagang Mausoleum of the 72 Martyrs, *Canton* 8 B2
Huangpu, *Shanghai* 27 B2
Huangpu Jiang →, *Shanghai* 27 B1
Huangpu Park, *Shanghai* 27 B1
Huangtugang, *Beijing* 4 C1
Huascar, *Lima* 16 A2
Huay Khwang, *Bangkok* 3 B2
Huddinge, *Stockholm* 28 B2
Hudson →, *New York* 21 A2
Huechuraba, *Santiago* 26 B1
Huertas de San Beltran, *Barcelona* 4 A1
Hugli →, *Calcutta* 8 A2
Huidui, *Tianjin* 30 B2
Huizingen, *Brussels* 6 B1
Hull, *Boston* 6 B4
Humber →, *Toronto* 30 A1
Humber B., *Toronto* 30 B2
Humber Bay, *Toronto* 30 B2
Humber Summit, *Toronto* 30 A1
Humber Valley Village, *Toronto* 30 A1
Humberlea, *Toronto* 30 A1
Humboldt Park, *Chicago* 9 B2
Humera, *Madrid* 17 B1
Hunaydī, *Baghdad* 3 B2
Hundige, *Copenhagen* 10 B1
Hundige Strand, *Copenhagen* 10 B2
Hung Hom, *Hong Kong* 12 B2
Hunters Hill, *Sydney* 28 B1
Hunters Pt., *San Francisco* 25 B2
Hunters Valley, *Washington* 32 B2
Huntington, *Washington* 32 C3
Huntington Park, *Los Angeles* 16 C3
Hurīya, *Baghdad* 3 A1
Hurstville, *Sydney* 28 B1
Husby, *Stockholm* 28 A1
Husum, *Copenhagen* 10 A2
Hutt R. →, *Wellington* 32 B2
Hütteldorf, *Vienna* 31 A1
Hüvösvölgy, *Budapest* 7 A2
Hvalstad, *Oslo* 22 A1
Hvalstrand, *Oslo* 22 A2
Hvidovre, *Copenhagen* 10 B2
Hwagok, *Seoul* 26 B1
Hyattsville, *Washington* 32 B4
Hyde Park, *Boston* 6 B3
Hyde Park, *Chicago* 9 C3
Hyde Park, *Johannesburg* 13 A2
Hyde Park, *London* 15 A2
Hyde Park, *Sydney* 28 B2

I

Ibese, *Lagos* 14 A2
Ibirapuera, *São Paulo* 26 B1
Ibirapuera, Parque, *São Paulo* 26 B2
Icarai, *Rio de Janeiro* 24 B2
Içerenköy, *Istanbul* 12 C2
Ichgao, *Tokyo* 29 B2
Ichigaya, *Tokyo* 29 a3
Ichikawa, *Tokyo* 29 A4
Ickenham, *London* 15 A1
Iddo, *Lagos* 14 B2
Idi-Oro, *Lagos* 14 A2
Iganmu, *Lagos* 14 B2
Igbobi, *Lagos* 14 A2
Igbologun, *Lagos* 14 B1
Igny, *Paris* 23 B2
IJ, Het →, *Amsterdam* 2 A2
IJ-meer, *Amsterdam* 2 A3
Ijesa-Tedo, *Lagos* 14 B1
Ijora, *Lagos* 14 B2
IJtunnel, *Amsterdam* 2 a3
Ikebe, *Tokyo* 29 B2
Ikebukuro, *Tokyo* 29 A3
Ikegami, *Tokyo* 29 B3
Ikeja, *Lagos* 14 A2
Ikeuchi, *Osaka* 22 B4
Ikoyi, *Lagos* 14 B2
Ikuata, *Lagos* 14 B2
Ikuno, *Osaka* 22 A4
Ikuta, *Osaka* 22 A2
Ikuta, *Tokyo* 29 B2
Ila, *Oslo* 22 A2
Ilford, *London* 15 A4
Ilioúpolis, *Athens* 2 B2
Ilpendam, *Amsterdam* 2 A2
Ilsós →, *Athens* 2 B2
Imagem e do Som, Museu da, *Rio de Janeiro* 24 b3
Imbâbah, *Cairo* 7 A2
Imielin, *Warsaw* 31 C2
Imirim, *São Paulo* 26 A2
Imittós, *Athens* 2 B2
Imittoś, Óros, *Athens* 2 B2
Imperial Palace Museum, *Beijing* 4 b2
Inagi, *Tokyo* 29 B2
Inchcolm, *Edinburgh* 11 A2
Inchicore, *Dublin* 11 A1
Inchkeith, *Edinburgh* 11 A3
Inchmickery, *Edinburgh* 11 A2
Incirano, *Milan* 18 A1
Independencia, *Lima* 16 A2
Independencia, *Santiago* 26 B2
India Gate, *Delhi* 1 c2
Indian Creek Village, *Miami* 18 A2
Indian Head Park, *Chicago* 9 C1
Indianópolis, *São Paulo* 26 B2
Indios Verdes, *Mexico City* 18 B2
Indira Gandhi International Airport, *Delhi* 10 B1
Industria, *Johannesburg* 13 B1
Ingierstrand, *Oslo* 22 B3
Inglewood, *Los Angeles* 16 C3
Ingliston, *Edinburgh* 11 B1
Inhaúme, *Rio de Janeiro* 24 B1
Inner Port Shelter, *Hong Kong* 12 A2
Interlagos, *São Paulo* 26 C1
Intramuros, *Manila* 17 B1
Invalides, *Paris* 23 A2
Inverkeithing, *Edinburgh* 11 A1
Inzersdorf, *Vienna* 31 B2
Ipanema, *Rio de Janeiro* 24 B1
Ipiranga, *São Paulo* 26 B2
Ipiranga →, *São Paulo* 26 B2
Iponri, *Lagos* 14 B2
Ireland's Eye, *Dublin* 11 A3
Irving Park, *Chicago* 9 B2
Isabel, *Rio de Janeiro* 24 B1
Isagatedo, *Lagos* 14 A1
Isar →, *Munich* 20 A3
Ishbīlīya, *Baghdad* 3 A2
Ishikiri, *Osaka* 22 A4
Ishøj Strand, *Copenhagen* 10 B2
Island Bay, *Wellington* 32 B1
Island Park, *Toronto* 30 B2
Isle of Dogs, *London* 15 B3
Islev, *Copenhagen* 10 A2
Isleworth, *London* 15 B2
Islington, *London* 15 A3
Islington, *Toronto* 30 B1
Ismaning, *Munich* 20 A3
Ismayloskiy Park, *Moscow* 19 B4
Isolo, *Lagos* 14 A1
Issy-les-Moulineaux, *Paris* 23 B2
Istanbul, *Istanbul* 12 C1
Istanbul Boğazi, *Istanbul* 12 B2
Istinye, *Istanbul* 12 B2
Itä Hakkila, *Helsinki* 12 B3
Itaewŏn, *Seoul* 26 B1
Itahanga, *Rio de Janeiro* 24 B1
Itami, *Osaka* 22 A3
Ivanhoe, *Melbourne* 17 A2
Ivry-sur-Seine, *Paris* 23 B3
Iwazono, *Osaka* 22 A2
Ixelles, *Brussels* 6 B2
Izmaylovo, *Moscow* 19 B4
Iztacalco, *Mexico City* 18 B2
Iztapalapa, *Mexico City* 18 B2

J

Jaba, *Jerusalem* 13 A2
Jababpur, *Calcutta* 8 C2
Jacaré, *Rio de Janeiro* 24 B1
Jackson Heights, *New York* 21 B2
Jackson Park, *Chicago* 9 C3
Jacques Cartier, *Montreal* 19 A3
Jacques Cartier, Pont, *Montreal* 19 A2
Jade Buddha Temple, *Shanghai* 27 B1
Jægersborg, *Copenhagen* 10 A3
Jægersborg Dyrehave, *Copenhagen* 10 A3
Jagadishpur, *Calcutta* 8 B1
Jagatpur, *Delhi* 10 A2
Jaguaré, Rib. do →, *São Paulo* 26 B1
Jahangirpur, *Delhi* 10 A2
Jakarta, *Jakarta* 13 A2
Jakarta, Teluk, *Jakarta* 13 A1
Jalan Kayu, *Singapore* 27 A3
Jamaica B., *New York* 21 C3
Jamaica Plain, *Boston* 6 B3
Jamakpuri, *Delhi* 10 B1
Jamshīdīyeh, *Tehran* 30 A2
Janki, *Warsaw* 31 C1
Jannali, *Sydney* 28 C1
Japan Center, *San Francisco* 25 c1
Jaraguá, *São Paulo* 26 A1
Jaraguá, Pico de, *São Paulo* 26 A1
Jardim Paulista, *São Paulo* 26 B1
Jardin Botanique, *Brussels* 6 a3
Järvatältet, *Stockholm* 28 A1
Jaskhar, *Mumbai* 20 B2
Jatinegara, *Jakarta* 13 B2
Javādīyeh, *Tehran* 30 B2
Jaworowa, *Warsaw* 31 C1
Jedlesee, *Vienna* 31 A2
Jefferson Memorial, *Washington* 32 c1
Jefferson Park, *Chicago* 9 B2
Jelonki, *Warsaw* 31 B1
Jerónimos, Mosteiro dos, *Lisbon* 14 A1
Jersey City, *New York* 21 B1
Jerusalem, *Jerusalem* 13 B2
Jésus, Î., *Montreal* 19 A1
Jesús Maria, *Lima* 16 B2
Jette, *Brussels* 6 A1
Jewish Quarter, *Jerusalem* 13 b3
Jey, *Tehran* 30 B2
Jianguomen, *Beijing* 4 B2
Jiangwan, *Shanghai* 27 B1
Jianshan Park, *Tianjin* 30 B2
Jihād, *Baghdad* 3 B1
Jim Thompson's House, *Bangkok* 3 b3
Jimbōchō, *Tokyo* 29 a4
Jingan, *Shanghai* 27 B1
Jingu Outer Garden, *Tokyo* 29 b2
Jinočany, *Prague* 24 B1
Jinonice, *Prague* 24 B2
Jiyūgaoka, *Tokyo* 29 B3
Jizā'ir, *Baghdad* 3 B2
Jizīra, *Baghdad* 3 B2
Johannesburg, *Johannesburg* 13 B2
Johanneskirchen, *Munich* 20 A2
Johannesstift, *Berlin* 5 A2
Johannisthal, *Berlin* 5 B4
John Hancock Center, *Chicago* 9 a2
John McLaren Park, *San Francisco* 25 B2
Johnsonville, *Wellington* 32 B1
Joinville-le-Pont, *Paris* 23 B3
Joli-Bois, *Brussels* 6 B2
Jollas, *Helsinki* 12 B3
Jonstrup, *Copenhagen* 10 A2
Joppa, *Edinburgh* 11 B3
Jorge Chavez, Aeropuerto Int., *Lima* 16 B2
Jorge Newbury, Aeroparque, *Buenos Aires* 7 B2
Jósefa Piłsudskiego Park, *Warsaw* 31 B1
Jōtō, *Osaka* 22 A4
Jouy-en-Josas, *Paris* 23 B2
Juan Anchorena, *Buenos Aires* 7 A2
Juan González Romero, *Mexico City* 18 A2
Judeira, *Jerusalem* 13 A2
Juhu, *Mumbai* 20 A2
Jūjā, *Tokyo* 29 A3
Jukskeirivier →, *Johannesburg* 13 A2
Julianów, *Warsaw* 31 B2
Jungfernheide, Volkspark, *Berlin* 5 A2
Jungfernsee, *Berlin* 5 B1
Juniper Green, *Edinburgh* 11 B2
Junk B., *Hong Kong* 12 B2
Jurong, *Singapore* 27 B2
Jurong, Selat, *Singapore* 27 B2
Jurong Industrial Estate, *Singapore* 27 B1
Jurujuba, Enseada de, *Rio de Janeiro* 24 B2
Jūsō, *Osaka* 22 A3
Justice, *Chicago* 9 C2
Justicia, *Madrid* 17 a3
Jwalahari, *Delhi* 10 B1

K

Kabaty, *Warsaw* 31 C2
Kadıköy, *Istanbul* 12 C2
Kadoma, *Osaka* 22 A4
Kaebong, *Seoul* 26 C1
Kafr 'Aqab, *Jerusalem* 13 A2
Kâğıthane, *Istanbul* 12 B1
Kâğıthane →, *Istanbul* 12 B1
Kagran, *Vienna* 31 A2
Kahnawake, *Montreal* 19 B1
Kaimes, *Edinburgh* 11 B2
Kaisariani, *Athens* 2 B2
Kaiser Wilhelm Kirche, *Berlin* 5 b2
Kaiserebersdorf, *Vienna* 31 B2
Kaivoksela, *Helsinki* 12 B2
Kalamákion, *Athens* 2 B2
Kalbadevi, *Mumbai* 20 b2
Kalhyŏn, *Seoul* 26 B1
Kalipur, *Calcutta* 8 A1
Kalkaji, *Delhi* 10 B2
Kallithéa, *Athens* 2 B2
Kalveboderne, *Copenhagen* 10 B3
Kamarhati, *Calcutta* 8 A2
Kamata, *Tokyo* 29 B3
Kameari, *Tokyo* 29 A4
Kameido, *Tokyo* 29 A4
Kami-Itabashi, *Tokyo* 29 A3
Kamikitazawa, *Tokyo* 29 B2
Kamitsuruma, *Tokyo* 29 B1
Kamoshida, *Tokyo* 29 B2
Kampong Landang, *Singapore* 27 A3
Kampong Tanjong Penjuru, *Singapore* 27 B2
Kampung Bali, *Jakarta* 13 B1
Kanamori, *Tokyo* 29 B1
Kanda, *Tokyo* 29 a5
Kandilli, *Istanbul* 12 B2
Kangdong, *Seoul* 26 B2
Kangnam, *Seoul* 26 B1
Kangsŏ, *Seoul* 26 B1
Kankurgachi, *Calcutta* 8 B2
Kanlıca, *Istanbul* 12 B2
Kanonerskiy, Ostrov, *St. Petersburg* 26 B1
Kanzaki →, *Osaka* 22 A3

Kapellerfeld, *Vienna* 31 A2
Káposztásmegyer, *Budapest* 7 A2
Kapotnya, *Moscow* 19 C4
Käppala, *Stockholm* 28 A3
Käpylä, *Helsinki* 12 B2
Karachi, *Karachi* 14 A2
Karachi Int. Airport, *Karachi* 14 A2
Karato, *Osaka* 22 A2
Karibong, *Seoul* 26 C1
Karkh, *Baghdad* 3 A2
Karlin, *Prague* 24 B2
Karlsfeld, *Munich* 20 A1
Karlshorst, *Berlin* 5 B4
Karlsplatz, *Munich* 20 b1
Karntner Strasse, *Vienna* 31 b2
Karol Bagh, *Delhi* 10 B2
Karolinenhof, *Berlin* 5 B4
Karori, *Wellington* 32 B1
Karow, *Berlin* 5 A3
Karrādah, *Baghdad* 3 B2
Kärsön, *Stockholm* 28 B1
Kasai, *Tokyo* 29 B4
Kashiwara, *Osaka* 22 B4
Kastellet, *Copenhagen* 10 a3
Kastrup, *Copenhagen* 10 B3
Kastrup Lufthavn, *Copenhagen* 10 B3
Kasuga, *Tokyo* 29 A2
Kasuge, *Tokyo* 29 A3
Kasumigaseki, *Tokyo* 29 b4
Katong, *Singapore* 27 B3
Katrineberg, *Stockholm* 28 B1
Katsushika-Ku, *Tokyo* 29 A4
Kau Pei Chau, *Hong Kong* 12 B2
Kau Yi Chau, *Hong Kong* 12 B1
Kaulsdorf, *Berlin* 5 B4
Kauniainen, *Helsinki* 12 B1
Kawasaki, *Tokyo* 29 B3
Kawawa, *Tokyo* 29 B2
Kawęczyn, *Warsaw* 31 B2
Kayu Putih, *Jakarta* 13 B2
Kbely, *Prague* 24 B3
Kebayoran Baru, *Jakarta* 13 B1
Kebayoran Lama, *Jakarta* 13 B1
Kebon Jeruk, *Jakarta* 13 B1
Kedar, *Jerusalem* 13 B2
Keilor, *Melbourne* 17 A1
Keilor North, *Melbourne* 17 A1
Keimola, *Helsinki* 12 A1
Kelenföld, *Budapest* 7 B2
Kelvin, *Johannesburg* 13 A2
Kemang, *Jakarta* 13 B1
Kemayoran, *Jakarta* 13 B2
Kemerburgaz, *Istanbul* 12 B1
Kempton Park Races, *London* 15 B1
Kendall Green, *Boston* 6 A2
Kenilworth, *Cape Town* 8 A1
Kennedy Town, *Hong Kong* 12 B1
Kennington, *London* 15 c4
Kensal Green, *London* 15 A2
Kensal Rise, *London* 15 a1
Kensington, *Johannesburg* 13 B2
Kensington, *London* 15 B2
Kensington, *New York* 21 C2
Kensington, *Sydney* 28 B2
Kensington Palace, *London* 15 A2
Kent Village, *Washington* 32 B4
Kentish Town, *London* 15 A3
Kenton, *London* 15 A2
Kenwood House, *London* 15 A3
Kepa, *Warsaw* 31 B2
Keppel Harbour, *Singapore* 27 B2
Keramikos, *Athens* 2 b1
Kettering, *Washington* 32 B5
Kew, *London* 15 B2
Kew, *Melbourne* 17 A2
Kew Gardens, *London* 15 B2
Kew Gardens, *Toronto* 30 B3
Key Biscayne, *Miami* 18 B2
Khaidhárion, *Athens* 2 A1
Khalándrion, *Athens* 2 A2
Khalīj, *Baghdad* 3 B2
Khandallah, *Wellington* 32 B1
Khansā', *Baghdad* 3 A2
Kharavli, *Mumbai* 20 B2
Khefren, *Cairo* 7 B1
Khichripur, *Delhi* 10 B2
Khidirpur, *Calcutta* 8 B1
Khimki-Khovrino, *Moscow* 19 A3
Khirbet Jub e-Rum, *Jerusalem* 13 B2
Khlong San, *Bangkok* 3 B2
Khlong Toey, *Bangkok* 3 B2
Kholargós, *Athens* 2 B2
Khorel, *Calcutta* 8 A1
Khorosovo, *Moscow* 19 B2
Kiamari, *Karachi* 14 B1
Kierling, *Vienna* 31 A1
Kierlingbach →, *Vienna* 31 A1
Kifisós →, *Athens* 2 B2
Kikuna, *Tokyo* 29 B2
Kilbarrack, *Dublin* 11 A3
Kilbirnie, *Wellington* 32 B1
Kilburn, *London* 15 A2
Killakee, *Dublin* 11 B2
Killester, *Dublin* 11 A2
Killiney, *Dublin* 11 B3
Killiney Bay, *Dublin* 11 B3
Kilmacud, *Dublin* 11 B2
Kilmainham, *Dublin* 11 A2
Kilmashogue Mt., *Dublin* 11 B2
Kilmore, *Dublin* 11 A2
Kilnamanagh, *Dublin* 11 B1
Kilo, *Helsinki* 12 B1
Kilokri, *Delhi* 10 B2
Kiltiernan, *Dublin* 11 B2
Kimmage, *Dublin* 11 B2
Kindi, *Baghdad* 3 B2
Kinghorn, *Edinburgh* 11 A2
King's Cross, *London* 15 a4
Kings Cross, *Sydney* 28 c3
Kings Domain, *Melbourne* 17 A1
Kings Park, *Washington* 32 C2
Kings Park West, *Washington* 32 C2
Kingsbury, *London* 15 A2
Kingsbury, *Melbourne* 17 A2
Kingsford, *Sydney* 28 B2
Kingston upon Thames, *London* 15 B2
Kingston Vale, *London* 15 B2
Kingsway, *Toronto* 30 B1
Kinsaley, *Dublin* 11 A2
Kipling Heights, *Toronto* 30 A1
Kipséli, *Athens* 2 B2
Kirchstockbach, *Munich* 20 B3
Kirchtrudering, *Munich* 20 B3
Kirikiri, *Lagos* 14 B1
Kirke Værløse, *Copenhagen* 10 A1
Kirkhill, *Edinburgh* 11 B2
Kirkliston, *Edinburgh* 11 B1
Kirknewton, *Edinburgh* 11 B1
Kirov Palace of Culture, *St. Petersburg* 26 B1
Kısıklı, *Istanbul* 12 B2
Kispest, *Budapest* 7 B2
Kista, *Stockholm* 28 A1
Kita, *Osaka* 22 A4
Kita-Ku, *Tokyo* 29 A3
Kitazawa, *Tokyo* 29 B3
Kiu Tsiu, *Hong Kong* 12 A2
Kivistö, *Helsinki* 12 B2
Kızıltoprak, *Istanbul* 12 C2
Kizu →, *Osaka* 22 B3
Kizuri, *Osaka* 22 B4
Kjelsås, *Oslo* 22 A3
Kladow, *Berlin* 5 B1
Klampenborg, *Copenhagen* 10 A3
Klaudyn, *Warsaw* 31 B1
Klecany, *Prague* 24 A2
Kledering, *Vienna* 31 B2
Klein Jukskei →, *Johannesburg* 13 A1
Kleinmachnow, *Berlin* 5 B2
Kleinschönebeck, *Berlin* 5 B5
Klemetsrud, *Oslo* 22 A4
Kličany, *Prague* 24 A2
Kliprviersberg Nature Reserve, *Johannesburg* 13 B2
Klosterneuburg, *Vienna* 31 A1
Knesset, *Jerusalem* 13 b1
Knightsbridge, *London* 15 c2
Kőbánya, *Budapest* 7 B2
Kobbegem, *Brussels* 6 A1
Kōbe, *Osaka* 22 A2
Kōbe Harbour, *Osaka* 22 B2
København, *Copenhagen* 10 A2
Kobylisy, *Prague* 24 B2
Kobyłka, *Warsaw* 31 A3
Kŏch'ŏk, *Seoul* 26 B1
Kodaira, *Tokyo* 29 A1
Kodanaka, *Tokyo* 29 B2
Kodenmacho, *Tokyo* 29 a5
Koekelberg, *Brussels* 6 A1
Koganei, *Tokyo* 29 A2
Kogarah, *Sydney* 28 B1
Køge Bugt, *Copenhagen* 10 B2
Koivupää, *Helsinki* 12 B2
Koja, *Jakarta* 13 A2
Koja Utara, *Jakarta* 13 A2
Kokobunji, *Tokyo* 29 A1
Kokobunji-Temple, *Tokyo* 29 A4
Kolarängen, *Stockholm* 28 B3
Kolbotn, *Oslo* 22 B3
Kolkata, *Calcutta* 8 B2
Koło, *Warsaw* 31 B1
Kolokinthóu, *Athens* 2 B2
Kolomyagi, *St. Petersburg* 26 A1
Kolónos, *Athens* 2 B2
Kolsås, *Oslo* 22 A2
Komae, *Tokyo* 29 B2
Komagome, *Tokyo* 29 A3
Komazawa, *Tokyo* 29 B3
Kona, *Calcutta* 8 B1
Konala, *Helsinki* 12 B1
Kondli, *Delhi* 10 B2
Kongelige Slottet, *Oslo* 22 a1
Kongelunden, *Copenhagen* 10 B3
Kongens Lyngby, *Copenhagen* 10 A3
Kongnŭng, *Seoul* 26 B2
Kongo, *Helsinki* 12 A1
Koninklijk Paleis, *Amsterdam* 2 b2
Konnagar, *Calcutta* 8 A2
Konohana, *Osaka* 22 A3
Kōnoike, *Osaka* 22 A4
Konradshöhe, *Berlin* 5 A2
Konstancin, *Warsaw* 31 C2
Kopanina, *Prague* 24 B1
Koparkhairna, *Mumbai* 20 A2
Köpenick, *Berlin* 5 B4
Korangi, *Karachi* 14 B2
Koremasa, *Tokyo* 29 B1
Korenevo, *Moscow* 19 B6
Kori, *Osaka* 22 A4
Koridhallós, *Athens* 2 B1
Korokoro, *Wellington* 32 B2
Korokoro Stream →, *Wellington* 32 B2
Kosino, *Moscow* 19 B5
Kosugi, *Tokyo* 29 B2
Kota, *Jakarta* 13 A1
Kotelyniki, *Moscow* 19 C5
Kōtō-Ku, *Tokyo* 29 A3
Kotrung, *Calcutta* 8 A2
Kouponia, *Athens* 2 B2
Kowloon, *Hong Kong* 12 B1
Kowloon Park, *Hong Kong* 12 a2
Kowloon Peak, *Hong Kong* 12 A2
Kowloon Res., *Hong Kong* 12 A1
Kowloon Tong, *Hong Kong* 12 A2
Kozhukhovo, *Moscow* 19 B5
Kraainem, *Brussels* 6 A2
Krailling, *Munich* 20 B1
Krampnitz, *Berlin* 5 B1
Krampnitzsee, *Berlin* 5 B1
Kranji, Sungei →, *Singapore* 27 A2
Kranji Industrial Estate, *Singapore* 27 A2
Kraskovo, *Moscow* 19 C5
Krasnaya Presnenskaya, *Moscow* 19 B3
Krasnogorsk, *Moscow* 19 B1
Krč, *Prague* 24 B2
Krestovskiye, Ostrov, *St. Petersburg* 26 B1
Kreuzberg, *Berlin* 5 A3
Kritzendorf, *Vienna* 31 A1
Krumme Lanke, *Berlin* 5 B2
Krummensee, *Berlin* 5 A5
Krung Thep, *Bangkok* 3 B2
Krusboda, *Stockholm* 28 B3
Krylatskoye, *Moscow* 19 B2
Küçükköy, *Istanbul* 12 B1
Kudankita, *Tokyo* 29 a3
Kudrovo, *St. Petersburg* 26 B3
Kulosaari, *Helsinki* 12 B3
Kulturforum, *Berlin* 5 b3
Kultury i Nauki, Palac, *Warsaw* 31 b2
Kŭmch'ŏn, *Seoul* 26 C1
Kumla, *Stockholm* 28 B3
Kungens kurva, *Stockholm* 28 B1
Kungliga Slottet, *Stockholm* 28 b2
Kungshatt, *Stockholm* 28 B1
Kungsholmen, *Stockholm* 28 A2
Kuningan, *Jakarta* 13 B1
Kunitachi, *Tokyo* 29 A1
Kunming Hu, *Beijing* 4 B1
Kuntratice, *Prague* 24 B2
Kunsthistorischesmuseum, *Vienna* 31 b1
Kuntsevo, *Moscow* 19 B2
Kupchino, *St. Petersburg* 26 B2
Kurbağalı →, *Istanbul* 12 C2
Kurihara, *Tokyo* 29 A2
Kurla, *Mumbai* 20 A2
Kurmuri, *Mumbai* 20 A2
Kurume, *Tokyo* 29 A2
Kuryanovo, *Moscow* 19 C4
Kuskovo, *Moscow* 19 B4
Kustia, *Calcutta* 8 B2
Kutsino, *Moscow* 19 B5
Kuzguncuk, *Istanbul* 12 B2
Kuzyminki, *Moscow* 19 B4
Kwai Chung, *Hong Kong* 12 A1
Kwanak, *Seoul* 26 C1
Kwanak-san, *Seoul* 26 C1
Kyje, *Prague* 24 B3
Kyūhōji, *Osaka* 22 B4

L

La Blanca, *Santiago* 26 C2
La Boca, *Buenos Aires* 7 B2
La Bretèche, *Paris* 23 A1
La Campiña, *Lima* 16 C2
La Celle-St.-Cloud, *Paris* 23 A1
La Ciudadela, *Mexico City* 18 c2
La Courneuve, *Paris* 23 A3
La Dehesa, *Santiago* 26 B2
La Encantada, *Lima* 16 C2
La Estación, *Madrid* 17 B1
La Floresta, *Barcelona* 4 A1
La Fortuna, *Madrid* 17 B1
La Fransa, *Barcelona* 4 A1
La Garenne-Colombes, *Paris* 23 A2
La Giustiniana, *Rome* 25 B1
La Grange, *Chicago* 9 C1
La Grange Park, *Chicago* 9 C1
La Granja, *Santiago* 26 C2
La Guardia Airport, *New York* 21 B2
La Hulpe, *Brussels* 6 B2
La Llacuna, *Barcelona* 4 A2
La Loma, *Mexico City* 18 A1
La Lucila, *Buenos Aires* 7 B2
La Maladrerie, *Paris* 23 A1
La Milla, Cerro, *Lima* 16 B2
La Monachina, *Rome* 25 B1
La Moraleja, *Madrid* 17 A2
La Nopalera, *Mexico City* 18 C2
La Paternal, *Buenos Aires* 7 B2
La Perla, *Lima* 16 B2
La Perouse, *Sydney* 28 B2
La Pineda, *Barcelona* 4 B1
La Pisana, *Rome* 25 B1
La Prairie, *Montreal* 19 B3
La Punta, *Lima* 16 B1
La Puntigala, *Barcelona* 4 A2
La Queue-en-Brie, *Paris* 23 B4
La Reina, *Santiago* 26 B2
La Ribera, *Barcelona* 4 A1
La Sagrera, *Barcelona* 4 A2
La Salada, *Buenos Aires* 7 C2
La Scala, *Milan* 18 B2
La Storta, *Rome* 25 A1
La Taxonera, *Barcelona* 4 A2
La Victoria, *Lima* 16 B2
Laajalahti, *Helsinki* 12 B1
Laajasalo, *Helsinki* 12 B3
Laaksolahti, *Helsinki* 12 B1
Lablâba, W. el →, *Cairo* 7 A2
Lac Cisterna, *Santiago* 26 C2
Lachine, *Montreal* 19 B1
Lad Phrao, *Bangkok* 3 B2
Ladera Heights, *Los Angeles* 16 C2
Ládví, *Prague* 24 B2
Lady, *Warsaw* 31 C1
Lafontaine, Parc, *Montreal* 19 A2
Lagoa, *Rio de Janeiro* 24 B1
Lagos, *Lagos* 14 B2
Lagos Harbour, *Lagos* 14 B2
Lagos-Ikeja Airport, *Lagos* 14 A1
Lagos Island, *Lagos* 14 B2
Lagos Lagoon, *Lagos* 14 B2
Laguna de B., *Manila* 17 C2
Laim, *Munich* 20 B2
Lainate, *Milan* 18 A1
Lainz, *Vienna* 31 B1
Lakemba, *Sydney* 28 B1
Lakeside, *Cape Town* 8 B1
Lakeside, *Johannesburg* 13 A2
Lakeview, *Chicago* 9 B3
Lakewood Park, *Atlanta* 3 B2
Lakhtinskiy, *St. Petersburg* 26 B1
Lakhtinskiy Razliv, Oz., *St. Petersburg* 26 B1
Lakshmanpur, *Calcutta* 8 B1
Lal Qila, *Delhi* 1 a3
Lam Tin, *Hong Kong* 12 B2
Lambert, *Oslo* 22 A3
Lambeth, *London* 15 B3
Lambrate, *Milan* 18 B2
Lambro, Parco, *Milan* 18 B2
Lambton Mills, *Toronto* 30 B1
Lamma I., *Hong Kong* 12 B1
Landover Hills, *Washington* 32 B4
Landsmeer, *Amsterdam* 2 A2
Landstrasse, *Vienna* 31 A2
Landwehr kanal, *Berlin* 5 B3
Lane Cove, *Sydney* 28 A1
Lane Cove National Park, *Sydney* 28 A1
Langa, *Cape Town* 8 A2
Langenzersdorf, *Vienna* 31 A2
Langer See, *Berlin* 5 B4
Langley, *Washington* 32 B2
Langley Park, *Washington* 32 B4
Langwald, *Munich* 20 A1
Lanham, *Washington* 32 B4
Lankwitz, *Berlin* 5 B3
L'Annunziatella, *Rome* 25 C2
Lansdowne, *Cape Town* 8 A2
Lansing, *Toronto* 30 A2
Lanús, *Buenos Aires* 7 C2
Lapa, *Rio de Janeiro* 24 B1
Laranjeiras, *Rio de Janeiro* 24 B1
Larisa Sta., *Athens* 2 a1
Las, *Warsaw* 31 B2
Las Corts, *Barcelona* 4 A1
Las Kabacki, *Warsaw* 31 C2
Las Pinas, *Manila* 17 C1
Las Rejas, *Santiago* 26 B1
Lasalle, *Montreal* 19 B2
Lasek Bielański, *Warsaw* 31 B1
Lasek Na Kole, *Warsaw* 31 B1
Laski, *Warsaw* 31 B1
Latina, *Madrid* 17 B1
Laurence G. Hanscom Field, *Boston* 6 A2
Lauttasaari, *Helsinki* 12 C2
Laval, *Montreal* 19 A1
Lavīzān, *Tehran* 30 A2
Lavradio, *Lisbon* 14 A2
Lawndale, *Chicago* 9 B2
Lawrence Heights, *Toronto* 30 A2
Layari, *Karachi* 14 A2
Layari →, *Karachi* 14 A1
Lazare, Gare St., *Paris* 23 a3
Łazienkowski, Palac, *Warsaw* 31 c3
Łazienkowski Park, *Warsaw* 31 B2
Le Blanc-Mesnil, *Paris* 23 A3
Le Bourget, *Paris* 23 A3
Le Chenoi, *Brussels* 6 B2
Le Chesnay, *Paris* 23 B1
Le Christ de Saclay, *Paris* 23 B2
Le Kremlin-Bicêtre, *Paris* 23 B3
Le Mesnil-le-Roi, *Paris* 23 A1
Le Pecq, *Paris* 23 A1
Le Perreux, *Paris* 23 A4
Le Pin, *Paris* 23 A4
Le Plessis-Robinson, *Paris* 23 B2
Le Plessis-Trévise, *Paris* 23 B4
Le Port-Marly, *Paris* 23 A1
Le Pré-St.-Gervais, *Paris* 23 A3
Le Raincy, *Paris* 23 A4
Le Vésinet, *Paris* 23 A1
Lea Bridge, *London* 15 A3
Leaside, *Toronto* 30 A2
Leblon, *Rio de Janeiro* 24 B1
Lee, *London* 15 B4
Leganés, *Madrid* 17 C1
Legazpi, *Madrid* 17 B1
Lehtisaari, *Helsinki* 12 B2
Lei Yue Mun, *Hong Kong* 12 B2
Leião, *Lisbon* 14 A1
Leicester Square, *London* 15 b3
Leichhardt, *Sydney* 28 B1
Leith, *Edinburgh* 11 B3
Lemoyne, *Montreal* 19 B3
Lenin, *Moscow* 19 B3
Lenino, *Moscow* 19 C3
Leninskiye Gory, *Moscow* 19 B3
Lennox, *Los Angeles* 16 C2
Leonia, *New York* 21 A2
Leopardstown, *Dublin* 11 B2
Leopoldau, *Vienna* 31 A2
Leopoldstadt, *Vienna* 31 A2
Leportovo, *Moscow* 19 B4
Leppävaara, *Helsinki* 12 B1
Les Lilas, *Paris* 23 A3
Les Loges-en-Josas, *Paris* 23 B1
Les Pavillons-sous-Bois, *Paris* 23 A4
Lésigny, *Paris* 23 B4
Lesnozavodskaya, *St. Petersburg* 26 B2
L'Étang-la-Ville, *Paris* 23 A1
Letná, *Prague* 24 a1
Letňany, *Prague* 24 B3
Levallois-Perret, *Paris* 23 A2
Levent, *Istanbul* 12 B2
Lewisdale, *Washington* 32 B4
Lewisham, *London* 15 B3
Lexington, *Boston* 6 A2
Leyton, *London* 15 A3
Leytonstone, *London* 15 A4
L'Hay-les-Roses, *Paris* 23 B3
L'Hospitalet de Llobregat, *Barcelona* 4 A1
Lhotka, *Prague* 24 B2
Liangshui He →, *Beijing* 4 C2
Lianhua Chi, *Beijing* 4 B1
Lianhua He →, *Beijing* 4 B1
Libčice nad Vltavou, *Prague* 24 A2
Libeň, *Prague* 24 B2
Liberdade, *São Paulo* 26 B2
Liberdade, Ave da, *Lisbon* 14 b1
Liberton, *Edinburgh* 11 B3
Liberty I., *New York* 21 B1
Liberty State Park, *New York* 21 B1
Libeznice, *Prague* 24 A2
Library of Congress, *Washington* 32 c3
Libuš, *Prague* 24 B2
Lichiao, *Canton* 8 B2
Lichtenburg, *Berlin* 5 A4
Lichterfelde, *Berlin* 5 B3
Lidingö, *Stockholm* 28 A2
Lieshi Lingyuan, *Canton* 8 B2
Liesing, *Vienna* 31 B1
Liesing →, *Vienna* 31 B2
Liffey, R. →, *Dublin* 11 A1
Ligovo, *St. Petersburg* 26 C1
Lijordet, *Oslo* 22 A2
Likavitos, *Athens* 2 b3
Likhoborka →, *Moscow* 19 A3
Lilla Värtan, *Stockholm* 28 A3
Lille Værløse, *Copenhagen* 10 A2
Liluah, *Calcutta* 8 B1
Lim Chu Kang, *Singapore* 27 A2
Lima, *Lima* 16 B2
Limbiate, *Milan* 18 A1
Limehouse, *London* 15 A3
Limeil-Brévannes, *Paris* 23 B3
Linate, Aeroporto Internazionale di, *Milan* 18 B2
Linbropark, *Johannesburg* 13 A2
Lincoln, *Boston* 6 A2
Lincoln Center, *New York* 21 b2
Lincoln Heights, *Los Angeles* 16 B3
Lincoln Park, *Chicago* 9 B3
Lincoln Park, *New York* 21 B1
Lincoln Park, *San Francisco* 25 B1
Lincolnwood, *Chicago* 9 A2
Linda-a-Pastora, *Lisbon* 14 A1
Linden, *Johannesburg* 13 A2
Linden, *Wellington* 32 A1
Lindenberg, *Berlin* 5 A4
Lindøya, *Oslo* 22 A3
Liniers, *Buenos Aires* 7 B1
Linkebeek, *Brussels* 6 B2
Linksfield, *Johannesburg* 13 A2
Linmeyer, *Johannesburg* 13 B2
Linna, *Helsinki* 12 A2
Lintuvaara, *Helsinki* 12 B1
Lion Rock Country Park, *Hong Kong* 12 A2
Lioúmi, *Athens* 2 B2
Liqizhuang, *Tianjin* 30 B2
Lisboa, *Lisbon* 14 A2
Lisbon = Lisboa, *Lisbon* 14 A2
Lishui, *Canton* 8 A1
Little B., *Sydney* 28 B2
Little Calumet →, *Chicago* 9 D3
Little Ferry, *New York* 21 A1
Little Italy, *New York* 21 e2
Little Mermaid, *Copenhagen* 10 a3
Little Rouge →, *Toronto* 30 A4
Little Tokyo, *Los Angeles* 16 c2
Liuhang, *Shanghai* 27 A1
Liurong Temple, *Canton* 8 B2
Liuxi →, *Canton* 8 B2
Liverpool Street, *London* 15 a5
Livry-Gargan, *Paris* 23 A4
Ljan, *Oslo* 22 A3
Llano de Can Gineu, *Barcelona* 4 A2
Llobregat →, *Barcelona* 4 A1
Lo Aranguiz, *Santiago* 26 B2
Lo Boza, *Santiago* 26 B1
Lo Chau, *Hong Kong* 12 B2
Lo Espejo, *Santiago* 26 C1
Lo Hermida, *Santiago* 26 B2
Lo Prado, *Santiago* 26 B1
Lo So Shing, *Hong Kong* 12 B1
Lo Wai, *Hong Kong* 12 A1
Loanhead, *Edinburgh* 11 B3
Lobau, *Vienna* 31 A3
Lobos, Pt., *San Francisco* 25 B1
Locham, *Munich* 20 B1
Lochino, *Moscow* 19 B1
Lochkov, *Prague* 24 B2
Lockhausen, *Munich* 20 A1
Lodi, *New York* 21 A1
Lodi Estate, *Delhi* 10 B2
Logan Int. Airport, *Boston* 6 A4
Logan Square, *Chicago* 9 B2
Lognes-Émerainville, Aérodrome de, *Paris* 23 B4
Löhme, *Berlin* 5 A5
Lolokhet, *Karachi* 14 A2
Lomas Chapultepec, *Mexico City* 18 B1
Lomas de San Angel Inn, *Mexico City* 18 B1
Lomas de Zamora, *Buenos Aires* 7 C2
Lombardy East, *Johannesburg* 13 A2
Łomianki, *Warsaw* 31 A1
Lomus Reforma, *Mexico City* 18 B1
London, *London* 15 A3
London Bridge, *London* 15 b5
London City Airport, *London* 15 A4
London Zoo, *London* 15 A3
Long B., *Sydney* 28 B2
Long Branch, *Toronto* 30 B1
Long Brook →, *Washington* 32 C2
Long Ditton, *London* 15 B2
Long I., *Boston* 6 B4
Long Island City, *New York* 21 B2
Long Street, *Cape Town* 8 c2
Longchamp, Hippodrôme de, *Paris* 23 A2
Longhua Pagoda, *Shanghai* 27 B1
Longhua Park, *Shanghai* 27 B1
Longjohn Slough, *Chicago* 9 C1
Longtan Hu →, *Beijing* 4 B2
Longue-Pointe, *Montreal* 19 A2
Longueuil, *Montreal* 19 A3
Loni, *Delhi* 10 A2
Loop, The, *Chicago* 9 c1
Lord's Cricket Ground, *London* 15 A2
Loreto, *Milan* 18 B2
Los Angeles Int. Airport, *Los Angeles* 16 C2
Los Cerrillos, Aeropuerto, *Santiago* 26 B1
Los Nietos, *Los Angeles* 16 C4
Los Olivos, *Lima* 16 A2
Los Reyes, *Mexico City* 18 B2
Lot, *Brussels* 6 B1
Loughlinstown, *Dublin* 11 B3
Loures, *Lisbon* 14 A1
Louveciennes, *Paris* 23 A1
Louvre, Musée du, *Paris* 23 b4
Louvre, Palais du, *Paris* 23 b4
Lower East Side, *New York* 21 e2
Lower Hutt, *Wellington* 32 B2
Lower Manhattan, *New York* 21 e1
Lower New York B., *New York* 21 C1
Lower Shing Mun Res., *Hong Kong* 12 A1
Lowry Bay, *Wellington* 32 B2
Lu Xun Museum, *Beijing* 4 b1
Lübars, *Berlin* 5 A3
Ludwigsfeld, *Munich* 20 A1
Luhu, *Canton* 8 B2
Lumiar, *Lisbon* 14 A2
Lumphini Park, *Bangkok* 3 B2
Lundtofte, *Copenhagen* 10 A3
Lung Mei, *Hong Kong* 12 A2
Luojiang, *Canton* 8 B2
Lustheim, *Munich* 20 A2
Luwan, *Shanghai* 27 B1
Luxembourg, Palais du, *Paris* 23 c4
Luzhniki Sports Centre, *Moscow* 19 B3
Lyndhurst, *New York* 21 B1
Lynn, *Boston* 6 A4
Lynn Harbor, *Boston* 6 A4
Lynn Woods Res., *Boston* 6 A3
Lyon, Gare de, *Paris* 23 c5
Lyons, *Chicago* 9 C2
Lysaker, *Oslo* 22 A2
Lysakerselva →, *Oslo* 22 A2
Lysolaje, *Prague* 24 B2
Lyubertsy, *Moscow* 19 B5
Lyublino, *Moscow* 19 B4

M

Ma Nam Wat, *Hong Kong* 12 A2
Ma On Shan Country Park, *Hong Kong* 12 A2
Ma'ale Adumim, *Jerusalem* 13 B2
Ma'ale Ha Khamisha, *Jerusalem* 13 B1
Ma'ale Mikhmas, *Jerusalem* 13 A2
Maantiekylä, *Helsinki* 12 A3
Maarifa, *Baghdad* 3 B2
Mabato Pt., *Manila* 17 C2
Macaco, Morro do, *Rio de Janeiro* 24 B2
McCook, *Chicago* 9 C2
Machelen, *Brussels* 6 A2
Machida, *Tokyo* 29 B1
Maciołki, *Warsaw* 31 B2
McKerrow, *Wellington* 32 B2
McKinley Park, *Chicago* 9 C2
Mclean, *Washington* 32 B2
Macopocho, R. →, *Santiago* 26 B1
MacRitchie Res., *Singapore* 27 A2
Macul, *Santiago* 26 C2
Madame Tussaud's, *London* 15 a3
Madhudaha, *Calcutta* 8 B2
Madhyamgram, *Calcutta* 8 A2
Madinah Al Mansūr, *Baghdad* 3 B2
Madīnet Nasr, *Cairo* 7 A2
Madison Avenue, *New York* 21 c2
Madison Square, *New York* 21 d2
Madrid, *Madrid* 17 B1
Madrona, *Barcelona* 4 A1
Maesawa, *Tokyo* 29 A2
Magdalena, *Lima* 16 B2
Magdalena Contreras, *Mexico City* 18 C1
Maghreb, *Baghdad* 3 A2
Maginu, *Tokyo* 29 B2
Magliana, *Rome* 25 B1
Magny-les-Hameaux, *Paris* 23 B1
Magonoy, *Manila* 17 B2
Mahalaxmi, *Mumbai* 20 a1
Maheshtala, *Calcutta* 8 C1
Mahim, *Mumbai* 20 A1
Mahim B., *Mumbai* 20 A1
Mahlsdorf, *Berlin* 5 A4
Mahmoodabad, *Karachi* 14 B2
Mahrauli, *Delhi* 10 B1
Mahul, *Mumbai* 20 A2
Maida Vale, *London* 15 a1
Maidstone, *Melbourne* 17 A1
Maipú, *Santiago* 26 C1
Maisonneuve, Parc, *Montreal* 19 A2
Maisons-Alfort, *Paris* 23 B3
Maisons-Laffitte, *Paris* 23 A1
Maissoneuve, *Montreal* 19 A2
Maitland, *Cape Town* 8 A1
Makati, *Manila* 17 B2
Mäkiniitty, *Helsinki* 12 A2
Mala Straná, *Prague* 24 B2
Malabar, *Mumbai* 20 B1
Malabar, *Sydney* 28 B2
Malabar Hill, *Mumbai* 20 B1
Malabar Pt., *Mumbai* 20 B1
Malabon, *Manila* 17 B1
Malacañang Palace, *Manila* 17 B1
Malahide, *Dublin* 11 A3
Malakhovka, *Moscow* 19 C6
Malakoff, *Paris* 23 B2
Mälarhöjaen, *Stockholm* 28 B1
Malate, *Manila* 17 B1
Malay Quarter, *Cape Town* 8 c2
Malaya Neva, *St. Petersburg* 26 B1
Malaya-Okhta, *St. Petersburg* 26 B2
Malchow, *Berlin* 5 A3
Malden, *Boston* 6 A3
Malden, *London* 15 B2
Maleizen, *Brussels* 6 B3
Malešice, *Prague* 24 B3
Malir →, *Karachi* 14 B2
Mall, The, *Washington* 32 b2
Malleny Mills, *Edinburgh* 11 B2
Malmi, *Helsinki* 12 B3
Malmøya, *Oslo* 22 A3
Måløv, *Copenhagen* 10 A2
Malpasso, Ost., *Rome* 25 C1
Malton, *Toronto* 30 A1
Malvern, *Johannesburg* 13 B2
Malvern, *Melbourne* 17 B2
Malvern, *Toronto* 30 A3
Mamonovo, *Moscow* 19 B2
Mampang Prapatan, *Jakarta* 13 B1
Mampukuji, *Tokyo* 29 B2
Man Budrukh, *Mumbai* 20 A2
Man Khurd, *Mumbai* 20 A2
Mandaluyong, *Manila* 17 B2
Mandaoli, *Delhi* 10 B2
Mandaqui →, *São Paulo* 26 A2
Mandoli, *Delhi* 10 A2
Mandvi, *Mumbai* 20 B2
Manenberg, *Cape Town* 8 A2
Mang Kung Uk, *Hong Kong* 12 B2
Mangolpuri, *Delhi* 10 A1
Manguinhos, Aéroporto, *Rio de Janeiro* 24 B1
Mangwŏn, *Seoul* 26 B1
Manhattan, *New York* 21 B2
Manhattan Beach, *New York* 21 C2
Manila, *Manila* 17 B1
Manila B., *Manila* 17 B1
Manila Int. Airport, *Manila* 17 B2
Mankkaa, *Helsinki* 12 B1
Manly, *Sydney* 28 A2
Mannswörth, *Vienna* 31 B3
Manor Park, *London* 15 A4
Manor Park, *Wellington* 32 A2
Manora, *Karachi* 14 B1
Manquehue, Cerro, *Santiago* 26 B2
Manzanares, Canal de, *Madrid* 17 C2
Mao Mausoleum, *Beijing* 4 c2
Map'o, *Seoul* 26 B1
Maracanã, *Rio de Janeiro* 24 B1
Maraoli, *Mumbai* 20 A2
Marblehead, *Boston* 6 A4
Marcelin, *Warsaw* 31 B1
Mareil-Marly, *Paris* 23 A1
Margareten, *Vienna* 31 A2
Maria, *Vienna* 31 A2
Maridalen, *Oslo* 22 A3
Maridalsvatnet, *Oslo* 22 A3
Mariendorf, *Berlin* 5 B3
Marienfelde, *Berlin* 5 B3
Marienplatz, *Munich* 20 b2
Marikina →, *Manila* 17 B2
Marin City, *San Francisco* 25 A1
Marin Headlands State Park, *San Francisco* 25 A2
Marin Pen., *San Francisco* 25 A1
Marina del Rey, *Los Angeles* 16 C2
Marine Drive, *Mumbai* 20 b1
Marino, *Dublin* 11 A2
Maritim, Museu, *Barcelona* 4 c2
Markham, *Toronto* 30 A2
Marki, *Warsaw* 31 A2
Markland Wood, *Toronto* 30 B1
Marly, Forêt de, *Paris* 23 A1
Marly-le-Roi, *Paris* 23 A1
Marne →, *Paris* 23 B3
Marne-la-Vallée, *Paris* 23 A4
Marolles-en-Brie, *Paris* 23 B4
Maroubra, *Sydney* 28 B2
Marquette Park, *Chicago* 9 C2
Marrickville, *Sydney* 28 B1
Marsfield, *Sydney* 28 A1
Marshall Field's, *Chicago* 9 c2
Marte, Campo de, *São Paulo* 26 B2
Martesana, Navíglio della, *Milan* 18 A2
Martin Luther King National Historic Site, *Atlanta* 3 B2
Martinez, *Buenos Aires* 7 A1
Martinkylä, *Helsinki* 12 B2
Martinsried, *Munich* 20 B1
Maruko, *Tokyo* 29 B3
Marunouchi, *Tokyo* 29 b4
Marusino, *Moscow* 19 B5
Maryino, *Moscow* 19 B4
Maryland, *Singapore* 27 B2
Marylebone, *London* 15 A2
Marymont, *Warsaw* 31 B1
Marysin Wawerski, *Warsaw* 31 B2
Marzahn, *Berlin* 5 A4
Mascot, *Sydney* 28 B2
Masmo, *Stockholm* 28 B1
Maspeth, *New York* 21 B2
Masr el Gedida, *Cairo* 7 A2
Masr el Qadîma, *Cairo* 7 A2
Massachusetts B., *Boston* 6 A4
Massachusett's Inst. of Tech., *Boston* 6 A3
Massamá, *Lisbon* 14 A1
Massey →, *Toronto* 30 A3
Massy, *Paris* 23 B2
Matihutong, *Beijing* 4 B1
Matinha, *Lisbon* 14 A2
Matraman, *Jakarta* 13 B2
Matsubara, *Osaka* 22 B4
Mattapan, *Boston* 6 B3
Mátyásföld, *Budapest* 7 A3
Mátyástemplom, *Budapest* 7 b2
Mau Tso Ngam, *Hong Kong* 12 A2
Mauer, *Vienna* 31 B1
Mauripur, *Karachi* 14 A1
Maxhof, *Munich* 20 B1
Maya-San, *Osaka* 22 A2
Mayfair, *Johannesburg* 13 B2
Mayfair, *London* 15 b3
Mayor, Plaza, *Madrid* 17 b2
Maywood, *Chicago* 9 B1
Maywood, *Los Angeles* 16 C3
Maywood, *New York* 21 A1
Mazagaon, *Mumbai* 20 a2
Me'a She' Arim, *Jerusalem* 13 a2
Meadowbank Park, *Sydney* 28 A1
Měcholupy, *Prague* 24 B3
Měčice, *Prague* 24 A3
Mecidiyeköy, *Istanbul* 12 B2
Medford, *Boston* 6 A3
Mediodia, *Madrid* 17 B2
Medvezhiy Ozyora, *Moscow* 19 A5
Meguro →, *Tokyo* 29 B3
Meguro-Ku, *Tokyo* 29 B3
Mehpalpur, *Delhi* 10 B1
Mehrābād Airport, *Tehran* 30 A1
Mehram Nagar, *Delhi* 10 B1
Mehrow, *Berlin* 5 A4
Mei Lanfang, *Beijing* 4 a2
Meidling, *Vienna* 31 A2
Méier, *Rio de Janeiro* 24 B1
Meiji Shrine, *Tokyo* 29 b1
Meise, *Brussels* 6 A1
Mejiro, *Tokyo* 29 A3
Melbourne, *Melbourne* 17 A1
Melbourne Airport, *Melbourne* 17 A1
Melkki, *Helsinki* 12 C2
Mellunkylä, *Helsinki* 12 B3
Mellunmäki, *Helsinki* 12 B3
Melrose, *Boston* 6 A3
Melrose, *New York* 21 B2
Melrose Park, *Chicago* 9 B1
Melsbroek, *Brussels* 6 A2
Menteng, *Jakarta* 13 B1
Mérantaise →, *Paris* 23 B1
Mercamadrid, *Madrid* 17 B2
Merced, L., *San Francisco* 25 B2
Meredale, *Johannesburg* 13 B1
Merlimau, P., *Singapore* 27 B2
Merri Cr. →, *Melbourne* 17 A1
Merrion, *Dublin* 11 B2
Merrionette Park, *Chicago* 9 C2
Merton, *London* 15 B2
Mesgarābād, *Tehran* 30 B3
Meshcherskiy, *Moscow* 19 B2
Messe, *Vienna* 31 A2
Messe-palast, *Vienna* 31 c1
Metanópoli, *Milan* 18 B2
Metropolitan Museum of Art, *New York* 21 b3
Meudon, *Paris* 23 B2
Mevaseret Tsiyon, *Jerusalem* 13 B1
Mevo Beitar, *Jerusalem* 13 B1
México, Ciudad de, *Mexico City* 18 B1
Meyersdal, *Johannesburg* 13 B2
Mezzano, *Milan* 18 B2
Mezzate, *Milan* 18 B2
Miadong, *Seoul* 26 B2
Miami, *Miami* 18 B2
Miami Beach, *Miami* 18 B2
Miami Canal →, *Miami* 18 A1
Miami Int. Airport, *Miami* 18 B1
Miami Shores, *Miami* 18 A2
Miami Springs, *Miami* 18 B1
Miasto, *Warsaw* 31 B2
Michałowice, *Warsaw* 31 B1
Michigan Avenue, *Chicago* 9 b2
Michle, *Prague* 24 B2
Middle Harbour, *Sydney* 28 A2
Middle Hd., *Sydney* 28 A2
Middle Park, *Melbourne* 17 B1
Middle Village, *New York* 21 B2
Middlesex Fells Reservation, *Boston* 6 A3
Midi, Gare du, *Brussels* 6 c1
Midland Beach, *New York* 21 C1
Miedzeszyn, *Warsaw* 31 B3
Międzylesie, *Warsaw* 31 B3
Miessaari, *Helsinki* 12 C1
Miguel Hidalgo, *Mexico City* 18 B1
Mikhelysona, *Moscow* 19 B5
Milano, *Milan* 18 B1
Milano Due, *Milan* 18 B2
Milano San Felice, *Milan* 18 B2
Milbertshofen, *Munich* 20 A2
Mill Hill, *London* 15 A2
Millennium Dome, *London* 15 A4
Miller Meadow, *Chicago* 9 B1
Millerhill, *Edinburgh* 11 B3
Millers Point, *Sydney* 28 a1
Milltown, *Dublin* 11 B2
Millwood, *Washington* 32 B4
Milnerton, *Cape Town* 8 A1
Milon-la-Chapelle, *Paris* 23 B1
Milton, *Boston* 6 B3
Milton Bridge, *Edinburgh* 11 B2
Mimico, *Toronto* 30 B2
Minami, *Osaka* 22 A4
Minamitsunashima, *Tokyo* 29 B2
Minato, *Osaka* 22 B3
Minato-Ku, *Tokyo* 29 c3
Minshât el Bekkarî, *Cairo* 7 A1
Minute Man Nat. Hist. Park, *Boston* 6 A2
Miraflores, *Lima* 16 B2
Miramar, *Wellington* 32 B1
Misericordia, Sa. da, *Rio de Janeiro* 24 B1
Mission, *San Francisco* 25 B2
Mississauga, *Toronto* 30 B1
Mitaka, *Tokyo* 29 A2
Mitcham, *London* 15 B2
Mitcham Common, *London* 15 B3
Mitchell's Plain, *Cape Town* 8 B2
Mitino, *Moscow* 19 A2
Mitte, *Berlin* 5 A3
Mittel Isarkanal →, *Munich* 20 A3
Mixcoac, *Mexico City* 18 B1
Mixcoac, Presa de, *Mexico City* 18 B1
Miyakojima, *Osaka* 22 A4
Mizonokuchi, *Tokyo* 29 B2
Mizue, *Tokyo* 29 A4
Młociński Park, *Warsaw* 31 B1
Młociny, *Warsaw* 31 B1
Mnevniki, *Moscow* 19 B2
Moba, *Lagos* 14 B2
Moczydło, *Warsaw* 31 C2
Modderfontein, *Johannesburg* 13 A2
Modřany, *Prague* 24 B2
Mogyoród, *Budapest* 7 A3
Moinho Velho, Cor. →, *São Paulo* 26 B2
Mok, *Seoul* 26 B1
Mokotów, *Warsaw* 31 B2
Molenbeek-Saint-Jean, *Brussels* 6 A1
Molino de Rosas, *Mexico City* 18 B1
Mollem, *Brussels* 6 A1
Mollins de Rey, *Barcelona* 4 A1
Mondeor, *Johannesburg* 13 B2
Moneda, Palacio de la, *Santiago* 26 B2
Moneró, *Rio de Janeiro* 24 A1
Mong Kok, *Hong Kong* 12 B2
Monkstown, *Dublin* 11 B3
Monnickendam, *Amsterdam* 2 A3
Monrovia, *Los Angeles* 16 B4
Monsanto, *Lisbon* 14 A1
Monsanto, Parque Florestal de, *Lisbon* 14 A1
Mont Royal, *Montreal* 19 A1
Mont-Royal, Parc, *Montreal* 19 A2
Montana de Montjuïch, *Barcelona* 4 A1
Monte Chingolo, *Buenos Aires* 7 C2
Monte Palatino, *Rome* 25 c3
Montebello, *Los Angeles* 16 B4
Montemor, *Lisbon* 14 A1
Monterey Park, *Los Angeles* 16 B4
Montespaccato, *Rome* 25 B1
Montesson, *Paris* 23 A1

Monteverde Nuovo, *Rome* 25 B1
Montfermeil, *Paris* 23 A4
Montigny-le-Bretonneux, *Paris* 23 B1
Montjay-la-Tour, *Paris* 23 A4
Montjuic, Parc de, *Barcelona* 4 c1
Montparnasse, Gare, *Paris* 23 A2
Montréal, *Montreal* 19 A2
Montréal, Î. de, *Montreal* 19 A2
Montréal, Univ. de, *Montreal* 19 B2
Montréal Est, *Montreal* 19 A2
Montréal Nord, *Montreal* 19 A2
Montréal Ouest, *Montreal* 19 B1
Montreuil, *Paris* 23 A3
Montrouge, *Paris* 23 B2
Montserrat, *Buenos Aires* 7 B2
Monza, *Milan* 18 A2
Monzoro, *Milan* 18 B1
Moóca, *São Paulo* 26 B2
Moonachie, *New York* 21 B1
Moonee Ponds, *Melbourne* 17 A1
Moonee Valley Racecourse, *Melbourne* 17 A1
Moosach, *Munich* 20 A2
Mora, *Mumbai* 20 B2
Moratalaz, *Madrid* 17 B2
Mörby, *Stockholm* 28 A2
Morden, *London* 15 B2
Morée →, *Paris* 23 A3
Morgan Park, *Chicago* 9 C3
Moriguchi, *Osaka* 22 A4
Morivione, *Milan* 18 B2
Morningside, *Edinburgh* 11 B2
Morningside, *Johannesburg* 13 A2
Morningside, *Washington* 32 C4
Morro Solar, Cerro, *Lima* 16 C2
Mortlake, *London* 15 B2
Mortlake, *Sydney* 28 B1
Morton Grove, *Chicago* 9 A2
Morumbi, *São Paulo* 26 B1
Moscavide, *Lisbon* 14 A2
Moscow = Moskva, *Moscow* 19 B3
Moskhaton, *Athens* 2 B2
Moskva, *Moscow* 19 B3
Moskva →, *Moscow* 19 B2
Moskvoretskiy, *Moscow* 19 B3
Mosman, *Sydney* 28 A2
Móstoles, *Madrid* 17 C1
Moti Bagh, *Delhi* 10 B2
Motol, *Prague* 24 B1
Motsa, *Jerusalem* 13 B2
Motsa Ilit, *Jerusalem* 13 B1
Motspur Park, *London* 15 B2
Mottingham, *London* 15 B4
Moulin Rouge, *Paris* 23 a3
Mount Dennis, *Toronto* 30 A2
Mount Greenwood, *Chicago* 9 C2
Mount Hood Memorial Park, *Boston* 6 A3
Mount Merrion, *Dublin* 11 B2
Mount Rainier, *Washington* 32 B4
Mount Vernon, *New York* 21 A3
Mount Vernon Square, *Washington* 32 a2
Mount Zion, *Jerusalem* 13 b3
Mozarthaus, *Vienna* 31 b2
Müggelberge, *Berlin* 5 B4
Müggelheim, *Berlin* 5 B5
Muggiò, *Milan* 18 A2
Mughal Gardens, *Delhi* 1 c1
Mühleiten, *Vienna* 31 A3
Mühlenfliess →, *Berlin* 5 A5
Muiden, *Amsterdam* 2 A3
Muiderpoort Station, *Amsterdam* 2 b3
Muizenberg, *Cape Town* 8 B1
Mujahidpur, *Delhi* 10 B2
Mukandpur, *Delhi* 10 A2
Mukhmas, *Jerusalem* 13 A2
Muko →, *Osaka* 22 A3
Mukojima, *Tokyo* 29 A3
Mulbarton, *Johannesburg* 13 B2
Mumbai, *Mumbai* 20 B2
Mumbai Harbour, *Mumbai* 20 B2
Münchehofe, *Berlin* 5 B5
München, *Munich* 20 B2
Munich = München, *Munich* 20 B2
Munkkiniemi, *Helsinki* 12 B2
Munro, *Buenos Aires* 7 B1
Murai Res., *Singapore* 27 A2
Muranów, *Warsaw* 31 B1
Murino, *St. Petersburg* 26 B2
Murrayfield, *Edinburgh* 11 B2
Musashino, *Tokyo* 29 A2
Museu Nacional, *Rio de Janeiro* 24 B1
Mushin, *Lagos* 14 A2
Musiektheater, *Amsterdam* 2 b2
Muslim Quarter, *Jerusalem* 13 a3
Musocco, *Milan* 18 B1
Mustansiriya, *Baghdad* 3 A2
Musturud, *Cairo* 7 A2
Muswell Hill, *London* 15 A3
Mutanabi, *Baghdad* 3 B2
Muthana, *Baghdad* 3 B2
Myakinino, *Moscow* 19 B2
Mykerinos, *Cairo* 7 B1
Myllypuro, *Helsinki* 12 B3

N

Nacka, *Stockholm* 28 B3
Nada, *Osaka* 22 A2
Naenae, *Wellington* 32 B2
Nærsnes, *Oslo* 22 B1
Nagata, *Osaka* 22 B1
Nagatsuta, *Tokyo* 29 B2
Nagytétény, *Budapest* 7 B1
Nahant, *Boston* 6 A4
Nahant B., *Boston* 6 A4
Nahant Harbor, *Boston* 6 A4
Nahr Dijlah →, *Baghdad* 3 B2
Najafgarh Drain →, *Delhi* 10 B1
Nakahara-Ku, *Tokyo* 29 B2
Nakano-Ku, *Tokyo* 29 A2
Namgajwa, *Seoul* 26 B1
Namsan Park, *Seoul* 26 B1
Namyŏng, *Seoul* 26 B1
Nanbiancun, *Canton* 8 B1
Nanchang He →, *Beijing* 4 B1
Nandang, *Canton* 8 B2
Nandian, *Tianjin* 30 A2
Nangal Dewat, *Delhi* 10 B1
Naniwa, *Osaka* 22 B3
Nankai, *Tianjin* 30 B1
Nanmenwai, *Tianjin* 30 B2
Nanole, *Mumbai* 20 A2
Nanpu Bridge, *Shanghai* 27 B2
Nanshi, *Shanghai* 27 B1
Nantasket Beach, *Boston* 6 B4
Nanterre, *Paris* 23 A2
Naoabad, *Calcutta* 8 C2
Napier Mole, *Karachi* 14 B1
Naraina, *Delhi* 10 B1
Nariman Point, *Mumbai* 20 c1
Nariman Pt., *Mumbai* 20 B1
Närmak, *Tehran* 30 A2
Naruo, *Osaka* 22 A3
Näsby, *Stockholm* 28 A2
Näsbypark, *Stockholm* 28 A2
Nathan Road, *Hong Kong* 12 a2
Natick, *Boston* 6 B2
National Maritime Museum, *San Francisco* 25 a1
National Museum, *Bangkok* 3 b1
Nationalmuseum, *Stockholm* 28 b2
Natolin, *Warsaw* 31 C2
Naturhistorischesmuseum, *Vienna* 31 b1
Naucalpan de Juárez, *Mexico City* 18 B1
Naupada, *Mumbai* 20 A2
Naviglio di Pavia, *Milan* 18 B1
Naviglio Grande, *Milan* 18 B1
Navona, Piazza, *Rome* 25 b2
Navotas, *Manila* 17 B1
Navy Pier, *Chicago* 9 b3
Nazal Hikmat Beg, *Baghdad* 3 A2
Nazimabad, *Karachi* 14 A2
Nazlet el Simmân, *Cairo* 7 B1
Néa Alexandhria, *Athens* 2 B2
Néa Faliron, *Athens* 2 B1
Néa Ionía, *Athens* 2 A2
Néa Liósia, *Athens* 2 A2
Néa Smírni, *Athens* 2 B2
Neapolis, *Athens* 2 B2
Near North, *Chicago* 9 b2
Nebušice, *Prague* 24 B1
Nederhorst, *Amsterdam* 2 B3
Nedlitz, *Berlin* 5 B1
Nee Soon, *Singapore* 27 A2
Needham Heights, *Boston* 6 B2
Nekrasovka, *Moscow* 19 B5
N'ematābād, *Tehran* 30 B2
Nemchinovka, *Moscow* 19 B1
Nemzeti Muz, *Budapest* 7 c3
Neponsit, *New York* 21 C2
Nerima-Ku, *Tokyo* 29 A3
Nesodden, *Oslo* 22 B3
Nesoddtangen, *Oslo* 22 A3
Nesøya, *Oslo* 22 A2
Neu Aubing, *Munich* 20 B1
Neu Buch, *Berlin* 5 A4
Neu Buchhorst, *Berlin* 5 B5
Neu Fahrland, *Berlin* 5 B1
Neu Lindenberg, *Berlin* 5 A4
Neubiberg, *Munich* 20 B3
Neue Hofburg, *Vienna* 31 b1
Neuenhagen, *Berlin* 5 A4
Neuessling, *Vienna* 31 A3
Neuhausen, *Munich* 20 B2
Neuherberg, *Munich* 20 A2
Neuhönow, *Berlin* 5 A5
Neuilly-Plaisance, *Paris* 23 A4
Neuilly-sur-Marne, *Paris* 23 A4
Neuilly-sur-Seine, *Paris* 23 A2
Neukagran, *Vienna* 31 A2
Neukettenhof, *Vienna* 31 B2
Neukölln, *Berlin* 5 B3
Neuperlach, *Munich* 20 B2
Neuried, *Munich* 20 B1
Neustift am Walde, *Vienna* 31 A1
Neusüssenbrunn, *Vienna* 31 A2
Neuwaldegg, *Vienna* 31 A1
Neva →, *St. Petersburg* 26 B2
Neves, *Rio de Janeiro* 24 B2
New Baghdād, *Baghdad* 3 B2
New Barakpur, *Calcutta* 8 A2
New Brighton, *New York* 21 C1
New Canada, *Johannesburg* 13 B1
New Canada Dam, *Johannesburg* 13 B1
New Carrollton, *Washington* 32 B4
New Cross, *London* 15 B3
New Delhi, *Delhi* 10 B2
New Dorp, *New York* 21 C1
New Dorp Beach, *New York* 21 C1
New Malden, *London* 15 B2
New Milford, *New York* 21 A1
New Territories, *Hong Kong* 12 A1
New Toronto, *Toronto* 30 B1
New Town, *Edinburgh* 11 B2
New Utrecht, *New York* 21 C2
Newark B., *New York* 21 B1
Newbattle, *Edinburgh* 11 B3
Newbury Park, *London* 15 A4
Newcraighall, *Edinburgh* 11 B3
Newham, *London* 15 A4
Newhaven, *Edinburgh* 11 B2
Newington, *Edinburgh* 11 B2
Newington, *London* 15 c5
Newlands, *Johannesburg* 13 B1
Newlands, *Wellington* 32 B1
Newport, *Melbourne* 17 B1
Newton, *Boston* 6 A2
Newtonbrook, *Toronto* 30 A2
Newtongrange, *Edinburgh* 11 B3
Newtonville, *Boston* 6 A2
Newtown, *Sydney* 28 B2
Neyagawa, *Osaka* 22 A4
Ngaio, *Wellington* 32 B1
Ngau Chi Wan, *Hong Kong* 12 A2
Ngau Tau Kok, *Hong Kong* 12 B2
Ngauranga, *Wellington* 32 B1
Ngong Shuen Chau, *Hong Kong* 12 B1
Ngua Kok Wan, *Hong Kong* 12 A1
Niāvarān, *Tehran* 30 A2
Nibra, *Calcutta* 8 B1
Nidāl, *Baghdad* 3 B2
Niddrie, *Edinburgh* 11 B3
Niddrie, *Melbourne* 17 A1
Nieder Neuendorf, *Berlin* 5 A2
Niederschöneweide, *Berlin* 5 B3
Niederschönhausen, *Berlin* 5 A3
Niemeyer, *Rio de Janeiro* 24 B1
Nieuw Zuid, *Amsterdam* 2 c2
Nieuwe Kerk, *Amsterdam* 2 b2
Nieuwendam, *Amsterdam* 2 A2
Nihonbashi, *Tokyo* 29 b5
Niipperi, *Helsinki* 12 B1
Níkaia, *Athens* 2 B1
Nikolassee, *Berlin* 5 B2
Nikolskiy, *Moscow* 19 B2
Nikolyskoye, *Moscow* 19 B5
Nikulino, *Moscow* 19 B2
Nil, Nahr en →, *Cairo* 7 B2
Nile = Nil, Nahr en →, *Cairo* 7 B2
Niles, *Chicago* 9 A2
Nimta, *Calcutta* 8 A2
Ningyuan, *Tianjin* 30 B2
Nippa, *Tokyo* 29 B2
Nippori, *Tokyo* 29 A3
Nishi, *Osaka* 22 A3
Nishinari, *Osaka* 22 B3
Nishiyodogawa, *Osaka* 22 A3
Niterói, *Rio de Janeiro* 24 B2
Nob Hill, *San Francisco* 25 b1
Nockeby, *Stockholm* 28 B1
Noel Park, *London* 15 A3
Nogatino, *Moscow* 19 B4
Nogent-sur-Marne, *Paris* 23 A3
Noida, *Delhi* 10 B2
Noiseau, *Paris* 23 B4
Noisiel, *Paris* 23 A4
Noisy-le-Grand, *Paris* 23 A4
Noisy-le-Roi, *Paris* 23 A1
Noisy-le-Sec, *Paris* 23 A3
Nokkala, *Helsinki* 12 C1
Nomentano, *Rome* 25 B2
Nonakashinden, *Tokyo* 29 A2
Nongminyundong Jiangxisuo, *Canton* 8 B2
Nonhyŏn, *Seoul* 26 B2
Nonthaburi, *Bangkok* 3 A1
Noon Gun, *Cape Town* 8 b1
Noorder Kerk, *Amsterdam* 2 a1
Noordgesig, *Johannesburg* 13 B1
Noordzeekanaal, *Amsterdam* 2 A1
Nord, Gare du, *Paris* 23 a4
Nordrand-Siedlung, *Vienna* 31 A2
Nordstrand, *Oslo* 22 A3
Normandale, *Wellington* 32 B2
Nørrebro, *Copenhagen* 10 a1
Norridge, *Chicago* 9 B2
Norrmalm, *Stockholm* 28 a1
North Arlington, *New York* 21 B1
North Bay Village, *Miami* 18 A2
North Bergen, *New York* 21 B1
North Branch Chicago River →, *Chicago* 9 B2
North Bull Island, *Dublin* 11 A3
North Cambridge, *Boston* 6 A3
North Cheam, *London* 15 B2
North Cohasset, *Boston* 6 B4
North Cray, *London* 15 B4
North Decatur, *Atlanta* 3 B3
North Druid Hills, *Atlanta* 3 B3
North Esk →, *Edinburgh* 11 B2
North Gyle, *Edinburgh* 11 B2
North Hackensack, *New York* 21 A1
North Harbor, *Manila* 17 B1
North Hd., *Sydney* 28 A2
North Hollywood, *Los Angeles* 16 B2
North Lexington, *Boston* 6 A2
North Miami, *Miami* 18 A2
North Miami Beach, *Miami* 18 A2
North Nazimabad, *Karachi* 14 A2
North Pt., *Hong Kong* 12 B2
North Queensferry, *Edinburgh* 11 A1
North Quincy, *Boston* 6 B3
North Res., *Boston* 6 A3
North Riverside, *Chicago* 9 B2
North Saugus, *Boston* 6 A3
North Shore Channel →, *Chicago* 9 B2
North Springfield, *Washington* 32 C2
North Sudbury, *Boston* 6 A1
North Sydney, *Sydney* 28 B2
North Woolwich, *London* 15 A4
North York, *Toronto* 30 A2
Northbridge, *Sydney* 28 A2
Northbridge Park, *Sydney* 28 A2
Northcliff, *Johannesburg* 13 A1
Northcote, *Melbourne* 17 A2
Northlake, *Chicago* 9 B1
Northmount, *Toronto* 30 A2
Northolt, *London* 15 A1
Northumberland Heath, *London* 15 B5
Northwood, *London* 15 A1
Norumbega Res., *Boston* 6 B2
Norwood, *Johannesburg* 13 A2
Norwood Park, *Chicago* 9 B2
Noryangjin, *Seoul* 26 B1
Nossa Senhora de Candelária, *Rio de Janeiro* 24 a2
Nossa Senhora do Ó, *São Paulo* 26 B1
Nossegem, *Brussels* 6 A3
Notre-Dame, *Paris* 23 c4
Notre-Dame, Bois, *Paris* 23 B4
Notre-Dame-de-Grace, *Montreal* 19 B2
Notting Hill, *London* 15 b1
Nova Milanese, *Milan* 18 A2
Novate Milanese, *Milan* 18 A1
Novaya Derevnya, *St. Petersburg* 26 A1
Nové Město, *Prague* 24 B2
Novoaleksandrovskoye, *St. Petersburg* 26 B2
Novogireyevo, *Moscow* 19 B4
Novoivanovskoye, *Moscow* 19 B1
Novonikolyskoye, *Moscow* 19 A1
Novosaratovka, *St. Petersburg* 26 B3
Nowe-Babice, *Warsaw* 31 B1
Nöykkiö, *Helsinki* 12 B1
Nueva Atzacoalco, *Mexico City* 18 B2
Nueva Pompeya, *Buenos Aires* 7 C2
Nueva Tenochtitlán, *Mexico City* 18 B2
Nuijala, *Helsinki* 12 B1
Numabukuro, *Tokyo* 29 A2
Nunez, *Buenos Aires* 7 B2
Nunhead, *London* 15 B3
Nuñoa, *Santiago* 26 B2
Nusle, *Prague* 24 B2
Nussdorf, *Vienna* 31 A2
Nyanga, *Cape Town* 8 A2
Nymphenburg, *Munich* 20 B2
Nymphenburg, Schloss, *Munich* 20 B2

O

Oak Grove, *Atlanta* 3 A3
Oak Island, *Boston* 6 A4
Oak Lawn, *Chicago* 9 C2
Oak Park, *Chicago* 9 B2
Oak View, *Washington* 32 A4
Oakdale, *Atlanta* 3 A2
Oakland, *San Francisco* 25 B3
Oakland, *Washington* 32 B4
Oaklawn, *Washington* 32 C4
Oakleigh, *Melbourne* 17 B2
Oakton, *Washington* 32 B2
Oakwood Beach, *New York* 21 C1
Oatley, *Sydney* 28 B1
Obalende, *Lagos* 14 B2
Oba's Palace, *Lagos* 14 B2
Oberföhring, *Munich* 20 B2
Oberhaching, *Munich* 20 B2
Oberlaa, *Vienna* 31 B2
Oberlisse, *Vienna* 31 A2
Obermenzing, *Munich* 20 A1
Obermoos Schwaige, *Munich* 20 A1
Oberschleissheim, *Munich* 20 A2
Oberschöneweide, *Berlin* 5 B4
Observatory, *Johannesburg* 13 B2
Observatory, *Sydney* 28 a1
Ōbu, *Osaka* 22 A1
Ōbu-tōge, *Osaka* 22 A1
Óbuda, *Budapest* 7 A2
Obukhovo, *St. Petersburg* 26 B2
Obvodnyy Kanal, *St. Petersburg* 26 B1
Ocean Park, *Hong Kong* 12 B2
Ochakovo, *Moscow* 19 B2
Ochota, *Warsaw* 31 B1
O'Connell Street, *Dublin* 11 b2
Ōdana, *Tokyo* 29 B2
Oden-Stockach, *Munich* 20 B3
Odilampi, *Helsinki* 12 B1
Odintsovo, *Moscow* 19 B1
Odivelas, *Lisbon* 14 A1
Odolany, *Warsaw* 31 B1
Oeiras, *Lisbon* 14 A1
Ofin, *Lagos* 14 A3
Ogawa, *Tokyo* 29 A1
Ogden Park, *Chicago* 9 C2
Ogikubo, *Tokyo* 29 A2
Ogogoro, *Lagos* 14 B2
Ogoyo, *Lagos* 14 B2
Ogudu, *Lagos* 14 A2
Ohariu Stream →, *Wellington* 32 B1
O'Higgins, Parque, *Santiago* 26 B2
Ōimachi, *Tokyo* 29 B3
Ojota, *Lagos* 14 A2
Okamoto, *Osaka* 22 A2
Okęcie, *Warsaw* 31 B1
Okęcie Airport, *Warsaw* 31 B1
Okelra, *Lagos* 14 B2
Okeogbe, *Lagos* 14 B2
Okha, *Delhi* 10 B2
Okhta →, *St. Petersburg* 26 B2
Okkervil →, *St. Petersburg* 26 B2
Okrzeszyn, *Warsaw* 31 C2
Oksval, *Oslo* 22 A3
Oktyabrskiy, *Moscow* 19 B3
Ōkubo, *Tokyo* 29 a2
Ōkura, *Tokyo* 29 B1
Olari, *Helsinki* 12 B1
Olaria, *Rio de Janeiro* 24 B1
Old Admiralty, *St. Petersburg* 26 B1
Old City, *Delhi* 1 a3
Old City, *Jerusalem* 13 b3
Old City, *Shanghai* 27 B1
Old Fort = Purana Qila, *Delhi* 1 c3
Old Harbor, *Boston* 6 B3
Old Town, *Chicago* 9 B3
Old Town, *Edinburgh* 11 B2
Oldbawn, *Dublin* 11 B1
Olgino, *St. Petersburg* 26 A1
Olimpico, Estadio, *Mexico City* 18 C1
Olivais, *Lisbon* 14 A2
Olivar de los Padres, *Mexico City* 18 B1
Olivar del Conde, *Mexico City* 18 B1
Olivos, *Buenos Aires* 7 B2
Olona →, *Milan* 18 B1
Olympia, *London* 15 B2
Olympic Stadium, *Helsinki* 12 B2
Olympique, Stade, *Montreal* 19 A2
Omonias, Pl., *Athens* 2 b1
Ōmori, *Tokyo* 29 B3
Onchi, *Osaka* 22 B4
Onchi →, *Osaka* 22 B4
Onisigun, *Lagos* 14 A2
Ōokayama, *Tokyo* 29 B3
Oosterpark, *Amsterdam* 2 b3
Oostzaan, *Amsterdam* 2 A2
Opa-Locka, *Miami* 18 A1
Opa-Locka Airport, *Miami* 18 A1
Opacz, *Warsaw* 31 B1
Opera House, *Sydney* 28 a2
Ophirton, *Johannesburg* 13 B2
Oppegård, *Oslo* 22 B3
Oppem, *Brussels* 6 A1
Oppsal, *Oslo* 22 A4
Ora, *Jerusalem* 13 B1
Oradell, *New York* 21 A1
Orange Bowl Stadium, *Miami* 18 B2
Orangi, *Karachi* 14 A2
Orchard Road, *Singapore* 27 a1
Ordrup, *Copenhagen* 10 A3
Orech, *Prague* 24 B1
Øresund, *Copenhagen* 10 A3
Orient Heights, *Boston* 6 A4
Orlando Dam, *Johannesburg* 13 B1
Orlando East, *Johannesburg* 13 B1
Orlovo, *Moscow* 19 C2
Orly, *Paris* 23 B3
Ormesson-sur-Marne, *Paris* 23 B4
Ormond, *Melbourne* 17 B2
Ormøya, *Oslo* 22 A3
Orpington, *London* 15 B4
Orsay, Musée d', *Paris* 23 b3
Országház, *Budapest* 7 b1
Országos Levetár, *Budapest* 7 b1
Ortaköy, *Istanbul* 12 B2
Ortica, *Milan* 18 B2
Oruba, *Lagos* 14 A2
Orvostörteneti Múz., *Budapest* 7 c2
Ōsaka, *Osaka* 22 B4
Ōsaka B., *Osaka* 22 B2
Osaka Castle, *Osaka* 22 A4
Osaka Harbour, *Osaka* 22 B3
Osaka International Airport, *Osaka* 22 A3
Osaki, *Tokyo* 29 B3
Osasco, *São Paulo* 26 B1
Osdorf, *Berlin* 5 B3
Osdorp, *Amsterdam* 2 A1
Oshodi, *Lagos* 14 A2
Oslo, *Oslo* 22 A3
Oslofjorden, *Oslo* 22 B2
Ōsone, *Tokyo* 29 B2
Osorun, *Lagos* 14 A2
Ospiate, *Milan* 18 A1
Ostankino, *Moscow* 19 B3
Östasiatiskamuséet, *Stockholm* 28 b3
Österalm, *Stockholm* 28 a3
Østerbro, *Copenhagen* 10 a1
Osterley, *London* 15 B1
Osterley Park, *London* 15 B1
Östermalm, *Stockholm* 28 A2
Österskär, *Stockholm* 28 A3
Ostiense, *Rome* 25 B1
Østmarkkapellet, *Oslo* 22 A4
Ostøya, *Oslo* 22 A2
Østre Aker, *Oslo* 22 A3
Ōta-Ku, *Tokyo* 29 B3
Otaniemi, *Helsinki* 12 B1
Otari Open Air Museum, *Wellington* 32 B1
Otsuka, *Tokyo* 29 A3
Ottakring, *Vienna* 31 A1
Ottávia, *Rome* 25 B1
Ottery, *Cape Town* 8 B1
Ottobrunn, *Munich* 20 B3
Oud Zuid, *Amsterdam* 2 b1
Oude Kerk, *Amsterdam* 2 b2
Ouderkerk, *Amsterdam* 2 B2
Oulunkylä, *Helsinki* 12 B2
Ourcq, Canal de l', *Paris* 23 A3
Outer Mission, *San Francisco* 25 B2
Outremont, *Montreal* 19 A2
Overijse, *Brussels* 6 B3
Owhiro Bay, *Wellington* 32 C1
Oworonsoki, *Lagos* 14 A2
Oxford Street, *London* 15 b3
Oxgangs, *Edinburgh* 11 B2
Oxon Hill, *Washington* 32 C4
Oyodo, *Osaka* 22 A3
Oyster B., *Sydney* 28 C1
Oyster Rock, *Mumbai* 20 B1
Oyster Rocks, *Karachi* 14 B2
Ozoir-la-Ferrière, *Paris* 23 B4
Ozone Park, *New York* 21 B2

P

Pacific Heights, *San Francisco* 25 B2
Pacific Manor, *San Francisco* 25 C2
Pacific Palisades, *Los Angeles* 16 B1
Pacifica, *San Francisco* 25 C2
Paco, *Manila* 17 B1
Paco de Arcos, *Lisbon* 14 A1
Paco Imperial, *Rio de Janeiro* 24 a2
Paddington, *London* 15 b2
Paddington, *Sydney* 28 B2
Paderno, *Milan* 18 A1
Pagewood, *Sydney* 28 B2
Pagote, *Mumbai* 20 B2
Pai, I. do, *Rio de Janeiro* 24 B2
Pak Kong, *Hong Kong* 12 A2
Pakila, *Helsinki* 12 B2
Palacio de Bellas Artes, *Mexico City* 18 b2
Palacio de Communicaciones, *Madrid* 17 a3
Palacio Nacional, *Mexico City* 18 b3
Palacio Real, *Barcelona* 4 b3
Palacio Real, *Madrid* 17 b1
Palaión Fáliron, *Athens* 2 B2
Palais de Justice, *Brussels* 6 c2
Palais Royal, *Paris* 23 b4
Palais Royale, *Brussels* 6 b3
Palaiseau, *Paris* 23 B2
Palau Nacional Museu d'Art, *Barcelona* 4 c1
Palazzolo, *Milan* 18 A1
Palermo, *Buenos Aires* 7 B2
Palhais, *Lisbon* 14 B2
Palisades Park, *New York* 21 A1
Palmer Park, *Washington* 32 B4
Palmerston, *Dublin* 11 A1
Paloheinä, *Helsinki* 12 B2
Palomeras, *Madrid* 17 B2
Palos Heights, *Chicago* 9 D2
Palos Hills, *Chicago* 9 C2
Palos Hills Forest, *Chicago* 9 C1
Palos Park, *Chicago* 9 C1
Palpara, *Calcutta* 8 B2
Panchur, *Calcutta* 8 B1
Pandacan, *Manila* 17 B2
Pandan, Selat, *Singapore* 27 B2
Pandan Res., *Singapore* 27 B2
Panepistimio, *Athens* 2 b2
Pangbae, *Seoul* 26 C1
Pangrati, *Athens* 2 B2
Pangsua, Sungei →, *Singapore* 27 A2
Panihati, *Calcutta* 8 A2
Panjang, Bukit, *Singapore* 27 A2
Panje, *Mumbai* 20 B2
Panke →, *Berlin* 5 A3
Pankow, *Berlin* 5 A3
Panthéon, *Paris* 23 c4
Pantheon, *Rome* 25 b2
Pantin, *Paris* 23 A3
Pantitlán, *Mexico City* 18 B2
Panvel Cr. →, *Mumbai* 20 B2
Paparangi, *Wellington* 32 B1
Papiol, *Barcelona* 4 A1
Paramus, *New York* 21 A1
Paranaque, *Manila* 17 B1
Paray-Vieille-Poste, *Paris* 23 B3
Parco Regionale, *Milan* 18 A1
Parel, *Mumbai* 20 B1
Pari, *São Paulo* 26 B2
Parioli, *Rome* 25 B1
Paris, *Paris* 23 A3
Paris-Orly, Aéroport de, *Paris* 23 B3
Pārk-e Mellat, *Tehran* 30 A2
Park Ridge, *Chicago* 9 A1
Park Royal, *London* 15 A2
Parkchester, *New York* 21 B2
Parkdale, *Toronto* 30 B2
Parkhurst, *Johannesburg* 13 A2
Parklawn, *Washington* 32 B3
Parkmore, *Johannesburg* 13 A2
Parkside, *San Francisco* 25 B2
Parktown, *Johannesburg* 13 B2
Parktown North, *Johannesburg* 13 A2
Parkview, *Johannesburg* 13 A2
Parkville, *New York* 21 C2
Parkwood, *Cape Town* 8 B1
Parkwood, *Johannesburg* 13 A2
Parow, *Cape Town* 8 A2
Parque Chabuco, *Buenos Aires* 7 B2
Parque Patricios, *Buenos Aires* 7 B2
Parramatta →, *Sydney* 28 A1
Parthenon, *Athens* 2 c2
Paşabahçe, *Istanbul* 12 B2
Pasadena, *Los Angeles* 16 B4
Pasar Minggu, *Jakarta* 13 B1
Pasay, *Manila* 17 B1
Pascoe Vale, *Melbourne* 17 A1
Paseo de la Reforma, *Mexico City* 18 b1
Pasig, *Manila* 17 B2
Pasig →, *Manila* 17 B1
Pasila, *Helsinki* 12 B2
Pasing, *Munich* 20 B1
Pasir Panjang, *Singapore* 27 B2
Pasir Ris, *Singapore* 27 A3
Passaic →, *New York* 21 B1
Passirana, *Milan* 18 A1
Patel Nagar, *Delhi* 10 B1
Pateros, *Manila* 17 B2
Pathersville, *Atlanta* 3 B3
Pathumwan, *Bangkok* 3 B2
Patipukur, *Calcutta* 8 B2
Patisia, *Athens* 2 A2
Paulo E. Virginia, Gruta, *Rio de Janeiro* 24 B1
Paulshof, *Berlin* 5 A5
Pavshino, *Moscow* 19 B1
Paya Lebar, *Singapore* 27 A3
Peachtree →, *Atlanta* 3 B2
Peakhurst, *Sydney* 28 B1
Peania, *Athens* 2 B3
Peckham, *London* 15 B3
Peddocks I., *Boston* 6 B4
Pederstrup, *Copenhagen* 10 A2
Pedralbes, *Barcelona* 4 A1
Pedregal de San Angel, Jardines del, *Mexico City* 18 C1
Pekhorka →, *Moscow* 19 C6
Pekhra-Pokrovskoye, *Moscow* 19 A5
Pekhra-Yakovlevskaya, *Moscow* 19 B5
Peking = Beijing, *Beijing* 4 B1
Pelcowizna, *Warsaw* 31 B2
Pelopónnisos Sta., *Athens* 2 a1
Penalolén, *Santiago* 26 B2
Pencarrow Hd., *Wellington* 32 C2
Peng Siang →, *Singapore* 27 A2
Penge, *London* 15 B3
Penha, *Rio de Janeiro* 24 A1
Penicuik, *Edinburgh* 11 B2
Penjaringan, *Jakarta* 13 A1
Penn Station, *New York* 21 c2
Pennsylvania Avenue, *Washington* 32 b1
Pentland Hills, *Edinburgh* 11 B1
Penyagino, *Moscow* 19 A2
Penzing, *Vienna* 31 A1
People's Park, *Shanghai* 27 B1
People's Square, *Shanghai* 27 B1
Perales del Rio, *Madrid* 17 C2
Peravillo, *Mexico City* 18 a3
Perchtoldsdorf, *Vienna* 31 B1
Perdizes, *São Paulo* 26 B2
Peredelkino, *Moscow* 19 C2
Pergamon Museum, *Berlin* 5 a4
Peristérion, *Athens* 2 A2
Perivale, *London* 15 A2
Perk, *Brussels* 6 A2
Perlach, *Munich* 20 B2
Perlacher Forst, *Munich* 20 B2
Pero, *Milan* 18 A1
Peropok, Bukit, *Singapore* 27 B2
Perovo, *Moscow* 19 B4
Pershing Square, *Los Angeles* 16 c1
Pertusella, *Milan* 18 A1
Pesagot, *Jerusalem* 13 A2
Pesanggrahag, Kali →, *Jakarta* 13 B1
Peschiera Borromeo, *Milan* 18 B2
Pesek, P., *Singapore* 27 B2
Pest, *Budapest* 7 B2
Pesterzsébet, *Budapest* 7 B2
Pesthidegkút, *Budapest* 7 A1
Pestimre, *Budapest* 7 B3
Pestlörinc, *Budapest* 7 B3
Pestújhely, *Budapest* 7 A2
Petas, *Helsinki* 12 B2
Petone, *Wellington* 32 B2
Petrogradskaya Storona, *St. Petersburg* 26 B2
Petroúpolis, *Athens* 2 A2
Petrovice, *Prague* 24 B3
Petrovskiy Park, *Moscow* 19 B3
Petrovsko-Razumovskoye, *Moscow* 19 B3
Pettycur, *Edinburgh* 11 A2
Peutie, *Brussels* 6 A2
Pfaueninsel, *Berlin* 5 B1
Phaya Thai, *Bangkok* 3 B2
Phihai, *Karachi* 14 A2
Phillip B., *Sydney* 28 B2
Phoenix Park, *Dublin* 11 A2
Phra Khanong, *Bangkok* 3 B2
Phra Pradaeng, *Bangkok* 3 C2
Phranakhon, *Bangkok* 3 B1
Picasso, Museu, *Barcelona* 4 c2
Piccadilly, *London* 15 b3
Pico Rivera, *Los Angeles* 16 C4
Piedade, *Lisbon* 14 A1
Piedade, *Rio de Janeiro* 24 B1
Piedade, Cova da, *Lisbon* 14 A2
Piedmont Park, *Atlanta* 3 B2
Pietralata, *Rome* 25 B2
Pihlajamäki, *Helsinki* 12 B3
Pihlajasaari, *Helsinki* 12 C2
Pilares, *Rio de Janeiro* 24 B1
Pilton, *Edinburgh* 11 B2
Pimlico, *London* 15 c3
Pimmit Hills, *Washington* 32 B2
Pine Grove, *Toronto* 30 A1
Pinewood, *Miami* 18 A2
Piney Run →, *Washington* 32 B2
Pinganli, *Beijing* 4 B2
Pingzhou, *Canton* 8 B2
Pinheiros →, *São Paulo* 26 B1
Pinjrapur, *Karachi* 14 A2
Pinner, *London* 15 A1
Pinner Green, *London* 15 A1
Pioltello, *Milan* 18 A2
Pipinui Pt., *Wellington* 32 A1
Piraévs, *Athens* 2 B1
Pirajuçara →, *São Paulo* 26 B1
Pirinçi, *Istanbul* 12 B1
Pirituba, *São Paulo* 26 A1
Pirkkola, *Helsinki* 12 B2
Písnice, *Prague* 24 C2
Pitampura, *Delhi* 10 A1
Pitkäjärvi, *Helsinki* 12 B1
Planegg, *Munich* 20 B1
Plumstead, *Cape Town* 8 B1
Plumstead, *London* 15 B4
Plyushchevo, *Moscow* 19 B4
Pnika, *Athens* 2 c1
Po Toi I., *Hong Kong* 12 C2
Po Toi O, *Hong Kong* 12 B2
Poasco, *Milan* 18 B2
Podbaba, *Prague* 24 B2
Podoli, *Prague* 24 B2
Poduskino, *Moscow* 19 B1
Pointe-Aux-Trembles, *Montreal* 19 A2
Poissy, *Paris* 23 A1
Pok Fu Lam, *Hong Kong* 12 B1
Pokrovsko-Sresnevo, *Moscow* 19 B2
Polton, *Edinburgh* 11 B3
Polyustrovo, *St. Petersburg* 26 B2
Pompidou, Centre, *Paris* 23 b4
Pomprap, *Bangkok* 3 b2
Pondok Indah, *Jakarta* 13 B1
Ponta do Marisco, *Rio de Janeiro* 24 C1
Pontault-Combault, *Paris* 23 B4
Pontinha, *Lisbon* 14 A1
Poplar, *London* 15 A3
Popolo, Porta del, *Rome* 25 a2
Poppintree, *Dublin* 11 A2
Porirua, *Wellington* 32 A2
Porirua East, *Wellington* 32 A2
Port I., *Osaka* 22 B2
Port Melbourne, *Melbourne* 17 A1
Port Nicholson, *Wellington* 32 B2
Port Philip Bay, *Melbourne* 17 B1
Port Richmond, *New York* 21 C1
Port Shelter, *Hong Kong* 12 A2
Port Union, *Toronto* 30 A4
Portage Park, *Chicago* 9 B2
Portal de la Pau, Pl., *Barcelona* 4 c2
Portela, Aeroporto da, *Lisbon* 14 A2
Portmarnock, *Dublin* 11 A3
Porto Brandão, *Lisbon* 14 A1
Porto Novo, *Rio de Janeiro* 24 A2
Porto Novo Cr. →, *Lagos* 14 B2
Portobello, *Edinburgh* 11 B3
Portrero, *San Francisco* 25 B3
Potomac, *Washington* 32 A2
Potomac →, *Washington* 32 B3
Potrero Pt., *San Francisco* 25 B2
Potsdam, *Berlin* 5 B1
Potsdamer Platz, *Berlin* 5 b3
Potzham, *Munich* 20 B2
Pötzleinsdorf, *Vienna* 31 A1
Povoa de Santo Adriao, *Lisbon* 14 A2
Powązki, *Warsaw* 31 B1
Powiśle, *Warsaw* 31 B2
Powsin, *Warsaw* 31 C2
Powsinek, *Warsaw* 31 C2
Poyan Res., *Singapore* 27 A2
Pozuelo de Alarcon, *Madrid* 17 B1
Prado, Museo del, *Madrid* 17 b3
Prado Churubusco, *Mexico City* 18 B2
Praga, *Warsaw* 31 B2
Prague = Praha, *Prague* 24 B2
Praha, *Prague* 24 B2
Praha-Ruzyně Airport, *Prague* 24 B1
Praires, R. des →, *Montreal* 19 A2
Prater, *Vienna* 31 A2
Precotto, *Milan* 18 A2
Prenestino Labicano, *Rome* 25 B2
Prenzlauerberg, *Berlin* 5 A3
Preston, *Melbourne* 17 A1
Pretos Forros, Sa. dos, *Rio de Janeiro* 24 B1
Préville, *Montreal* 19 B3
Přezletice, *Prague* 24 B3
Prima Porta, *Rome* 25 B1
Primavalle, *Rome* 25 B1
Primrose, *Johannesburg* 13 B2
Princes Street, *Edinburgh* 11 b2
Printer's Row, *Chicago* 9 d2
Progreso Nacional, *Mexico City* 18 A2
Prosek, *Prague* 24 B3
Prospect Hill Park, *Boston* 6 A2
Providencia, *Santiago* 26 B2
Prudential Building, *Chicago* 9 c2
Průhonice, *Prague* 24 C3
Psikhikón, *Athens* 2 A2
Pudong New Area, *Shanghai* 27 B2
Pueblo Libre, *Lima* 16 B2
Pueblo Nuevo, *Barcelona* 4 A2
Pueblo Nuevo, *Madrid* 17 B2
Puerta del Sol, Plaza, *Madrid* 17 b2
Puerto Madero, *Buenos Aires* 7 B2
Puerto Retiro, *Buenos Aires* 7 B2
Puhuangyu, *Beijing* 4 B2
Puistola, *Helsinki* 12 B3
Pukan-san, *Seoul* 26 B1
Pukinmäki, *Helsinki* 12 B2
Pukkajwa, *Seoul* 26 B1
Pulkovo Int. Airport, *St. Petersburg* 26 C1
Pullach, *Munich* 20 B1
Pulo Gadung, *Jakarta* 13 B2
Pūnak, *Tehran* 30 A2
Punchbowl, *Sydney* 28 B1
Punde, *Mumbai* 20 B2
Punggol, *Singapore* 27 A3
Punggol, Sungei →, *Singapore* 27 A3
Punggol Pt., *Singapore* 27 A3
Punjabi Bagh, *Delhi* 10 A1
Puotila, *Helsinki* 12 B3
Purana Qila, *Delhi* 1 c3
Puteaux, *Paris* 23 A2
Putilkovo, *Moscow* 19 A2
Putney, *London* 15 B2
Putuo, *Shanghai* 27 B1
Putxet, *Barcelona* 4 A1
Puxi, *Shanghai* 27 B1
Pydhuni, *Mumbai* 20 b2
Pyramids, *Cairo* 7 B1
Pyry, *Warsaw* 31 C1

Q

Qalandya, *Jerusalem* 13 A2
Qal'eh Morghī, *Tehran* 30 B2
Qanâ el Ismâ'iliya, *Cairo* 7 A2
Qāsemābād, *Tehran* 30 A3
Qasr-e Firūzeh, *Tehran* 30 B3
Qatane, *Jerusalem* 13 B1
Qianmen, *Beijing* 4 B2
Qinghuayuan, *Beijing* 4 B1
Qingningsi, *Shanghai* 27 B2
Qolhak, *Tehran* 30 A2
Quadraro, *Rome* 25 B2
Quaid-i-Azam, *Karachi* 14 A1
Quartiere Zingone, *Milan* 18 B1
Quds, *Baghdad* 3 A2
Queen Mary Res., *London* 15 B1
Queen Street, *Edinburgh* 11 a1
Queensbury, *London* 15 A2
Queenscliffe, *Sydney* 28 A2
Queensferry, *Edinburgh* 11 B1
Queenstown, *Singapore* 27 B2
Quellerina, *Johannesburg* 13 A1
Queluz, *Lisbon* 14 A1
Quezon City, *Manila* 17 B2
Quezon Memorial Circle, *Manila* 17 B2
Quilicura, *Santiago* 26 B1
Quincy, *Boston* 6 B3
Quincy B., *Boston* 6 B4
Quinta Normal, *Santiago* 26 B1
Quinto de Stampi, *Milan* 18 B2
Quinto Romano, *Milan* 18 B1
Quirinale, *Rome* 25 b1
Quirinale, Palazzo dei, *Rome* 25 b3

R

Raasdorf, *Vienna* 31 A3
Rådhuset, *Oslo* 22 A3
Radlice, *Prague* 24 B2
Radość, *Warsaw* 31 B3
Radotín, *Prague* 24 C2
Rafat, *Jerusalem* 13 A2
Raffles Hotel, *Singapore* 27 b3
Raffles Park, *Singapore* 27 B2
Raheny, *Dublin* 11 A3
Rahnsdorf, *Berlin* 5 B5
Rainham, *London* 15 A5
Raj Ghat, *Delhi* 1 b3
Rajakylä, *Helsinki* 12 B3
Rajpath, *Delhi* 1 c2
Rajpura, *Delhi* 10 A2
Rákos-patak →, *Budapest* 7 B3
Rákoshegy, *Budapest* 7 B3
Rákoskeresztúr, *Budapest* 7 B3

Rákoskert, Budapest 7 B3
Rákosliget, Budapest 7 B3
Rákospalota, Budapest 7 A2
Rákosszentmihály, Budapest 7 A2
Raków, Warsaw 31 B1
Ram, Jerusalem 13 A2
Rām Allāh, Jerusalem 13 A2
Ramadān, Baghdad 3 B2
Ramakrishna Puram, Delhi 10 B1
Ramanathpur, Calcutta 8 A1
Rambla, La, Barcelona 4 b2
Rambler Channel, Hong Kong 12 A1
Ramenki, Moscow 19 B2
Ramersdorf, Munich 20 B2
Ramos, Rio de Janeiro 24 B1
Ramos Mejia, Buenos Aires 7 B1
Ramot, Jerusalem 13 B2
Rampur, Delhi 10 A2
Ramsgate, Sydney 28 B1
Rand Afrikaans Univ., Johannesburg 13 B2
Rand Airport, Johannesburg 13 B2
Randburg, Johannesburg 13 A1
Randhart, Johannesburg 13 B2
Randpark Ridge, Johannesburg 13 A1
Randwick, Sydney 28 B2
Ranelagh, Dublin 11 A2
Rannersdorf, Vienna 31 B2
Ransbèche, Brussels 6 B2
Ransdorp, Amsterdam 2 A2
Ranvad, Mumbai 20 B2
Raposo, Lisbon 14 A1
Rashtrapati Bhawan, Delhi 1 c1
Rasskazovka, Moscow 19 C2
Rastaala, Helsinki 12 B1
Rastila, Helsinki 12 B3
Raszyn, Warsaw 31 C1
Ratcha Thewi, Bangkok 3 b3
Rathfarnham, Dublin 11 B2
Ratho, Edinburgh 11 B1
Ratho Station, Edinburgh 11 B1
Rato, Lisbon 14 A2
Ravelston, Edinburgh 11 B2
Rawamangun, Jakarta 13 B2
Rayners Lane, London 15 A1
Raynes Park, London 15 B2
Raypur, Calcutta 8 C2
Razdory, Moscow 19 B1
Real Felipe, Fuerte, Lima 16 B2
Recoleta, Buenos Aires 7 B2
Recoleta, Santiago 26 B2
Red Fort = Lal Qila, Delhi 1 a3
Redbridge, London 15 A4
Redfern, Sydney 28 B2
Redwood, Wellington 32 B1
Reeves Hill, Boston 6 A1
Refshaleøen, Copenhagen 10 A3
Regents Park, Johannesburg 13 B2
Regent's Park, London 15 a2
Rego Park, New York 21 B2
Reichstag, Berlin 5 a3
Reina Sofia, Centro de Arte, Madrid 17 c3
Reinickendorf, Berlin 5 A3
Rekola, Helsinki 12 B3
Rembertów, Warsaw 31 B2
Rembrandthuis, Amsterdam 2 b2
Rembrandtpark, Amsterdam 2 A2
Rembrandtsplein, Amsterdam 2 b2
Remedios, Parque Nacional de los, Mexico City 18 B1
Remedios de Escalada, Buenos Aires 7 C2
Rémola, Laguna del, Barcelona 4 B1
Renca, Santiago 26 B1
Renmin Park, Tianjin 30 B2
Rennemoulin, Paris 23 A1
Řeporyje, Prague 24 B1
Republica, Plaza de la, Mexico City 18 b1
République, Place de la, Paris 23 b5
Repulse Bay, Hong Kong 12 B2
Repy, Prague 24 B1
Residenz, Munich 20 B2
Residenzmuseum, Munich 20 b3
Reston, Washington 32 B2
Retiro, Buenos Aires 7 B2
Retiro, Madrid 17 B1
Retreat, Cape Town 8 B1
Reutov, Moscow 19 B5
Réveillon →, Paris 23 B4
Revere, Boston 6 A3
Rexdale, Toronto 30 A1
Reynosa Tamaulipas, Mexico City 18 A1
Rho, Milan 18 A1
Rhodes, Sydney 28 A1
Rhodon, Paris 23 B1
Rhodon →, Paris 23 B1
Ribeira, Rio de Janeiro 24 A1
Ricarda, Laguna de la, Barcelona 4 B1
Richmond, Melbourne 17 A2
Richmond, San Francisco 25 B2
Richmond Hill, New York 21 B2
Richmond Park, London 15 B2
Richmond upon Thames, London 15 B2
Riddarholmen, Stockholm 28 c1
Riddarhuset, Stockholm 28 c2
Ridgefield, New York 21 B1
Ridgefield Park, New York 21 A1
Ridgewood, New York 21 B2
Riem, Munich 20 B3
Rijksmuseum, Amsterdam 2 b1
Rikers I., New York 21 B2
Riksdagensledamothus, Stockholm 28 b2
Riksdagshuset, Stockholm 28 b2
Rimac, Lima 16 B2
Ringsend, Dublin 11 A2
Rinkeby, Stockholm 28 A1
Rio Compride, Rio de Janeiro 24 B1
Rio de Janeiro, Rio de Janeiro 24 B1
Rio de la Plata, Buenos Aires 7 B2
Rio de Mouro, Lisbon 14 A1
Ripollet, Barcelona 4 A1
Ris, Oslo 22 A3
Risby, Copenhagen 10 A1
Rishra, Calcutta 8 A2
Ritchie, Washington 32 B4
Rithala, Delhi 10 A1
Rive Sud, Canal de la, Montreal 19 B2
River Edge, New York 21 A1
River Forest, Chicago 9 B2
River Grove, Chicago 9 B1
Riverdale, New York 21 A2
Riverdale, Washington 32 B4
Riverdale Park, Toronto 30 A2
Riverlea, Johannesburg 13 B1
Riverside, Chicago 9 C2
Riverwood, Sydney 28 B1
Rivière-des-Praires, Montreal 19 A2
Rixensart, Brussels 6 B3
Riyad, Baghdad 3 B2
Rizal Park, Manila 17 B1
Rizal Stadium, Manila 17 B1
Røa, Oslo 22 A2
Robbins, Chicago 9 D2
Robertsham, Johannesburg 13 B2
Rochelle Park, New York 21 A1
Rock Cr. →, Washington 32 B3
Rock Creek Park, Washington 32 B3
Rock Pt., Wellington 32 A1
Rockaway Pt., New York 21 C2
Rockdale, Sydney 28 B1
Rockefeller Center, New York 21 c2
Rodaon, Vienna 31 B1
Rødovre, Copenhagen 10 A2
Rodrigo de Freitas, L., Rio de Janeiro 24 B1
Roehampton, London 15 B2
Rogers Park, Chicago 9 A2
Roihuvuori, Helsinki 12 B3
Roissy-en-Brie, Paris 23 B4
Rokin, Amsterdam 2 b2
Rokkō I., Osaka 22 A2
Rokkō Sanchi, Osaka 22 A2
Rokkō-Zan, Osaka 22 A2
Rokytka →, Prague 24 B3
Roma, Rome 25 B1
Római-Fürdö, Budapest 7 A2
Romainville, Paris 23 A3
Romano Banco, Milan 18 B1
Romashkovo, Moscow 19 B1
Rome = Roma, Rome 25 B1
Romford, London 15 A5
Rondebosch, Cape Town 8 A1
Roppongi, Tokyo 29 c3
Rose Hill, Washington 32 C3
Rosebank, New York 21 C1
Rosebery, Sydney 28 B2
Rosedal La Candelaria, Mexico City 18 B2
Roseland, Chicago 9 C3
Rosemead, Los Angeles 16 B4
Rosemont, Montreal 19 A2
Rosenborg Have, Copenhagen 10 A3
Rosenthal, Berlin 5 A3
Rosettenville, Johannesburg 13 B2
Rosewell, Edinburgh 11 B3
Rosherville Dam, Johannesburg 13 B2
Rösjön, Stockholm 28 A2
Roslags-Näsby, Stockholm 28 A2
Roslin, Edinburgh 11 B3
Roslindale, Boston 6 B3
Rosny-sous-Bois, Paris 23 A4
Rosslyn, Washington 32 B3
Rosyth, Edinburgh 11 A1
Rotherhithe, London 15 B3
Rothneusiedl, Vienna 31 B2
Rothschmaige, Munich 20 A1
Rouge Hill, Toronto 30 A4
Round I., Hong Kong 12 B2
Roxbury, Boston 6 B3
Roxeth, London 15 A1
Royal Botanic Garden, Edinburgh 11 B2
Royal Botanic Gardens, Sydney 28 b2
Royal Grand Palace, Bangkok 3 b1
Royal Observatory, Edinburgh 11 B2
Royal Park, Melbourne 17 A1
Royal Turf Club, Bangkok 3 b2
Röylä, Helsinki 12 B1
Rozas, Portilleros de las, Madrid 17 B1
Roztoky, Prague 24 B2
Rozzano, Milan 18 B1
Rubi →, Barcelona 4 A1
Rublovo, Moscow 19 B2
Rudnevka →, Moscow 19 B5
Rudolfsheim, Vienna 31 A2
Rudolfshöhe, Berlin 5 A5
Rudow, Berlin 5 B3
Rueil-Malmaison, Paris 23 A2
Ruisbroek, Brussels 6 B1
Ruislip, London 15 A1
Rumelihisarı, Istanbul 12 B2
Rumyantsevo, Moscow 19 C2
Rungis, Paris 23 B3
Rusāfa, Baghdad 3 A2
Rush Green, London 15 A5
Russa, Calcutta 8 C2
Russian Hill, San Francisco 25 a1
Rustenfeld, Vienna 31 B2
Rutherford, New York 21 B1
Ruzyně, Prague 24 B1
Rybatskaya, St. Petersburg 26 B2
Rydboholm, Stockholm 28 A3
Ryde, Sydney 28 A1
Rynek, Warsaw 31 a2
Ryogoku, Tokyo 29 A3
Rzhevka, St. Petersburg 26 B3

S

Sa'ādatābād, Tehran 30 A2
Saadūn, Baghdad 3 B2
Saavedra, Buenos Aires 7 B2
Saboli, Delhi 10 A2
Sabugo, Lisbon 14 A1
Sabzi Mand, Delhi 10 A2
Sacavém, Lisbon 14 A2
Saclay, Paris 23 B2
Saclay, Étang de, Paris 23 B1
Sacomã, São Paulo 26 B2
Sacré Cœur, Paris 23 a4
Sacrow, Berlin 5 B1
Sacrower See, Berlin 5 B1
Sadang, Seoul 26 C1
Sadar Bazar, Delhi 1 a1
Saddle Brook, New York 21 A1
Sadr, Karachi 14 A2
Sadr City, Baghdad 3 A2
Sadyba, Warsaw 31 B2
Saft el Laban, Cairo 7 A2
Saganashkee Slough, Chicago 9 C1
Sagene, Oslo 22 A3
Sagrada Família, Templo de, Barcelona 4 A2
Sagrado Familia, Templo de, Barcelona 4 a2
Sahar Int. Airport, Mumbai 20 A2
Sai Kung, Hong Kong 12 A2
Sai Wan Ho, Hong Kong 12 B2
Sai Ying Pun, Hong Kong 12 B1
St.-Aubin, Paris 23 B1
St.-Cloud, Paris 23 A2
St.-Cyr-l'École, Paris 23 B1
St.-Cyr-l'École, Aérodrome de, Paris 23 B1
St.-Denis, Paris 23 A3
St.-Germain, Forêt de, Paris 23 A1
St.-Germain-en-Laye, Paris 23 A1
St. Giles Cathedral, Edinburgh 11 b2
St-Gilles, Brussels 6 B2
St. Helier, London 15 B2
St.-Hubert, Montreal 19 B3
St. Hubert, Galerie, Brussels 6 b2
St. Isaac's Cathedral, St. Petersburg 26 B1
St. Jacques →, Montreal 19 B3
St. James's, London 15 b3
St. John's Cathedral, Hong Kong 12 c1
St-Joose-Ten-Noode, Brussels 6 A2
St. Kilda, Melbourne 17 B1
St. Lambert, Montreal 19 A3
St.-Lambert, Paris 23 B1
St.-Laurent, Montreal 19 A1
St. Lawrence →, Montreal 19 B2
St.-Lazare, Gare, Paris 23 A2
St.-Léonard, Montreal 19 A2
St. Magelungen, Stockholm 28 B2
St.-Mandé, Paris 23 A3
St. Margaret's, Dublin 11 A2
St.-Martin, Bois, Paris 23 B4
St. Mary Cray, London 15 B4
St.-Maur-des-Fossés, Paris 23 B3
St.-Maurice, Paris 23 B3
St.-Michel, Montreal 19 A2
St. Nikolaus-Kirken, Prague 24 B2
St.-Ouen, Paris 23 A3
St. Patrick's Cathedral, Dublin 11 c1
St. Patrick's Cathedral, New York 21 c2
St. Paul's Cathedral, London 15 b4
St. Paul's Cray, London 15 B4
St. Peters, Sydney 28 B2
St. Petersburg = Sankt Peterburg, St. Petersburg 26 B1
St.-Pierre, Montreal 19 B2
St-Pieters-Leeuw, Brussels 6 B1
St.-Quentin, Étang de, Paris 23 B1
St. Stephen's Green, Dublin 11 c3
St-Stevens-Woluwe, Brussels 6 A2
St.-Vincent-de-Paul, Montreal 19 A2
Ste.-Catherine, Montreal 19 B2
Ste.-Hélène, Î., Montreal 19 A2
Saiwai, Tokyo 29 B3
Sakai, Osaka 22 B3
Sakai Harbour, Osaka 22 B3
Sakra, P., Singapore 27 B2
Salam, Baghdad 3 A2
Salamanca, Madrid 17 B1
Sâllynoggin, Dublin 11 B3
Salmannsdorf, Vienna 31 A1
Salmedina, Madrid 17 C2
Salomea, Warsaw 31 B1
Salsette I., Mumbai 20 A2
Salt Lake City, Calcutta 8 B2
Salt River, Cape Town 8 A1
Salt Water L., Calcutta 8 B2
Saltsjö-Duvnäs, Stockholm 28 B3
Saltykovka, Moscow 19 B5
Samatya, Istanbul 12 C1
Sampaloc, Manila 17 B1
Samphan Thawong, Bangkok 3 B2
Samsŏn, Seoul 26 B2
San Andrés, Barcelona 4 A2
San Angel, Mexico City 18 B1
San Angelo, Castel, Rome 25 b1
San Basilio, Rome 25 B2
San Borja, Lima 16 B3
San Bóvio, Milan 18 B2
San Bruno, Pt., San Francisco 25 C2
San Bruno Mt., San Francisco 25 B2
San Cristobal, Buenos Aires 7 B2
San Cristobal, Madrid 17 B2
San Cristóbal, Cerro, Santiago 26 B2
San Cristoforo, Milan 18 B1
San Donato Milanese, Milan 18 B2
San Francisco, San Francisco 25 B2
San Francisco B., San Francisco 25 B3
San Francisco Culhuacán, Mexico City 18 C2
San Fruttuoso, Milan 18 A2
San Gabriel, Los Angeles 16 B4
San Giuliano Milanese, Milan 18 B2
San Isidro, Lima 16 B2
San Jerónimo Lidice, Mexico City 18 C1
San Joaquin, Santiago 26 B2
San José Rio Hondo, Mexico City 18 B1
San Juan →, Manila 17 B2
San Juan de Aragón, Mexico City 18 B2
San Juan de Aragón, Parque, Mexico City 18 B2
San Juan de Lurigancho, Lima 16 A2
San Juan del Monte, Manila 17 B2
San Juan Ixtacala, Mexico City 18 A1
San Juan Toltotepec, Mexico City 18 B1
San Just Desvern, Barcelona 4 A1
San Justo, Buenos Aires 7 C1
San Lorenzo Tezonco, Mexico City 18 C2
San Luis, Lima 16 B2
San Marino, Los Angeles 16 B4
San Martin, Barcelona 4 A2
San Martin de Porras, Lima 16 B2
San Miguel, Lima 16 B2
San Miguel, Santiago 26 B2
San Nicolas, Buenos Aires 7 B2
San Onófrio, Rome 25 B1
San Pedro Martir, Barcelona 4 A1
San Pedro Zacatenco, Mexico City 18 A2
San Pietro, Piazza, Rome 25 b1
San Po Kong, Hong Kong 12 A2
San Rafael Chamapa, Mexico City 18 B1
San Rafael Hills, Los Angeles 16 A3
San Roque, Manila 17 B2
San Siro, Milan 18 B1
San Souci, Sydney 28 B1
San Telmo, Buenos Aires 7 B2
San Vicenc dels Horts, Barcelona 4 A1
Sanbancho, Tokyo 29 a3
Sandown, Johannesburg 13 A2
Sandown Park Races, London 15 B1
Sandton, Johannesburg 13 A2
Sandvika, Oslo 22 A2
Sandy Pond, Boston 6 A2
Sandyford, Dublin 11 B2
Sandymount, Dublin 11 B2
Sangenjaya, Tokyo 29 B2
Sangge, Seoul 26 B2
Sangley Pt., Manila 17 C1
Sankrail, Calcutta 8 B1
Sankt Peterburg, St. Petersburg 26 B1
Sankt Veit, Vienna 31 A1
Sanlihe, Beijing 4 B1
Sanlintang, Shanghai 27 C1
Sans, Barcelona 4 A1
Sant Agusti, Barcelona 4 c2
Sant Ambrogio, Basilica di, Milan 18 B2
Sant Boi de Llobregat, Barcelona 4 A1
Sant Cugat, Barcelona 4 A1
Sant Feliu de Llobregat, Barcelona 4 A1
Sant Joan Despi, Barcelona 4 A1
Sant Maria del Mar, Barcelona 4 b3
Sant Pau del Camp, Barcelona 4 c2
Santa Ana, Manila 17 B2
Santa Coloma de Gramanet, Barcelona 4 A2
Santa Cruz, Manila 17 B1
Santa Cruz, Mumbai 20 A1
Santa Cruz, I. de, Rio de Janeiro 24 B2
Santa Cruz de Olorde, Barcelona 4 A1
Santa Efigénia, São Paulo 26 B2
Santa Elena, Manila 17 B2
Santa Elena del Gomero, Santiago 26 B1
Santa Eulalia, Barcelona 4 A2
Santa Fe Springs, Los Angeles 16 C4
Santa Iria da Azóia, Lisbon 14 A2
Santa Julia, Santiago 26 C2
Santa Maria, Mexico City 18 a1
Santa Monica, Los Angeles 16 B2
Santa Monica Mts., Los Angeles 16 B2
Santa Rosa De Locobe, Santiago 26 B2
Santa Teresa de la Ovalle, Santiago 26 B1
Santahamina, Helsinki 12 C3
Santana, São Paulo 26 A2
Santeny, Paris 23 B4
Santiago, Santiago 26 B2
Santiago de Surco, Lima 16 B2
Santo Amaro, Lisbon 14 A1
Santo Amaro, São Paulo 26 B1
Santo Andre, Lisbon 14 B2
Santo Antão do Tojal, Lisbon 14 A2
Santo António, Qta. de, Lisbon 14 B1
Santo Tomas, Univ. of, Manila 17 B1
Santos Dumont, Aéroport, Rio de Janeiro 24 B2
Santoshpur, Calcutta 8 B1
Santragachi, Calcutta 8 B1
Santry, Dublin 11 A2
Sanyuanli, Canton 8 B2
São Caetano do Sul, São Paulo 26 B2
São Conrado, Rio de Janeiro 24 C1
São Cristovão, Rio de Janeiro 24 B1
São Francisco Penitência, Rio de Janeiro 24 b1
São Jorge, Castelo de, Lisbon 14 A2
São Juliao do Tojal, Lisbon 14 A2
São Paulo, São Paulo 26 B2
Sapa, Calcutta 8 B1
Sapateiro, Cor. do →, São Paulo 26 B1
Sarandi, Buenos Aires 7 C2
Saraswati →, Calcutta 8 A1
Sarecky potok →, Prague 24 B2
Sarimbun, Singapore 27 A2
Sarimbun Res., Singapore 27 A2
Sarıyer, Istanbul 12 A2
Saronikós Kólpos, Athens 2 B1
Sarriá, Barcelona 4 A1
Sarsuna, Calcutta 8 C1
Sartrouville, Paris 23 A2
Sasad, Budapest 7 B2
Sashalom, Budapest 7 A3
Saska, Warsaw 31 B2
Satalice, Prague 24 B3
Satgachi, Calcutta 8 B2
Sathorn, Bangkok 3 B2
Satpukur, Calcutta 8 B2
Sätra, Stockholm 28 B1
Sattru Pha, Bangkok 3 b2
Saúde, São Paulo 26 B2
Saugus, Boston 6 A3
Saugus →, Boston 6 A3
Sault-au-Récollet, Montreal 19 A2
Sausalito, San Francisco 25 A2
Sawah Besar, Jakarta 13 A1
Saxonville, Boston 6 B1
Scald Law, Edinburgh 11 B2
Scarborough, Toronto 30 A3
Sceaux, Paris 23 B2
Schaerbeek, Brussels 6 A2
Scharfenberg, Berlin 5 A2
Scheepvartmuseum, Amsterdam 2 b3
Schiller Park, Chicago 9 B1
Schiller Woods, Chicago 9 B1
Schiphol, Luchthaven, Amsterdam 2 B1
Schlachtensee, Berlin 5 B2
Schlossgarten, Berlin 5 A2
Schmargendorf, Berlin 5 B2
Schönblick, Berlin 5 B5
Schönbrunn, Schloss, Vienna 31 A1
Schöneberg, Berlin 5 B3
Schöneiche, Berlin 5 B5
Schönwalde, Berlin 5 A1
Schotschekloof, Cape Town 8 b1
Schulzendorf, Berlin 5 A2
Schwabing, Munich 20 B2
Schwanebeck, Berlin 5 A4
Schwanenwerder, Berlin 5 B2
Schwarzlackenau, Vienna 31 A2
Schwechat, Vienna 31 B2
Scitrek Museum, Atlanta 3 B2
Scott Monument, Edinburgh 11 b2
Scottdale, Atlanta 3 B3
Sea Point, Cape Town 8 A1
Seabrook, Washington 32 B5
Seacliff, San Francisco 25 B2
Seaforth, Sydney 28 A2
Seagate, New York 21 C1
Sears Tower, Chicago 9 c1
Seat Pleasant, Washington 32 B4
Seaview, Wellington 32 B2
Šeberov, Prague 24 B3
Secaucus, New York 21 B1
Seddinsee, Berlin 5 B5
Seeberg, Berlin 5 A5
Seeburg, Berlin 5 A1
Seefeld, Berlin 5 A5
Seegefeld, Berlin 5 A1
Seehof, Berlin 5 B2
Segeltorp, Stockholm 28 B1
Segrate, Milan 18 B2
Seguro, Milan 18 B1
Seine →, Paris 23 B3
Seixal, Lisbon 14 B2
Selby, Johannesburg 13 B2
Seletar, P., Singapore 27 A3
Seletar Hills, Singapore 27 A3
Seletar Res., Singapore 27 A2
Selhurst, London 15 B3
Sembawang, Singapore 27 A2
Senago, Milan 18 A1
Sendinger Tor Platz, Munich 20 c1
Sendling, Munich 20 B2
Senju, Tokyo 29 A3
Senriyama, Osaka 22 A4
Sentosa, P., Singapore 27 B2
Seoul = Sŏul, Seoul 26 B2
Seoul National Univ., Seoul 26 C1
Seoul Tower, Seoul 26 B1
Sepolia, Athens 2 A2
Sepulveda Flood Control Basin, Los Angeles 16 A2
Serangoon, Singapore 27 A3
Serangoon, P., Singapore 27 A3
Serangoon, Sungei →, Singapore 27 A3
Serangoon Harbour, Singapore 27 A3
Seraya, P., Singapore 27 B2
Serebryanka, Moscow 19 B5
Serebryanka →, Moscow 19 B4
Serramonte, San Francisco 25 C2
Sesto San Giovanni, Milan 18 A2
Sesto Ulteriano, Milan 18 B2
Setagaya-Ku, Tokyo 29 B2
Seter, Oslo 22 A3
Setia Budi, Jakarta 13 B1
Settebagni, Rome 25 A2
Settecamini, Rome 25 B2
Séttimo Milanese, Milan 18 B1
Settsu, Osaka 22 A4
Setuny →, Moscow 19 B2
Seutula, Helsinki 12 A2
Seven Corners, Washington 32 B3
Seven Kings, London 15 A4
Sévesco →, Milan 18 A1
Sevran, Paris 23 A4
Sewri, Mumbai 20 B2
Sforzesso, Castello, Milan 18 B2
Sha Kok Mei, Hong Kong 12 A2
Sha Tin, Hong Kong 12 A2
Sha Tin Wai, Hong Kong 12 A2
Shabrâmant, Cairo 7 B2
Shahdara, Delhi 10 A2
Shahe, Canton 8 B2
Shahr-e Rey, Tehran 30 B2
Shahrak-e Golshahr, Tehran 30 B1
Shahrak-e Qods, Tehran 30 A2
Shaikh Aomar, Baghdad 3 A2
Shakurbasti, Delhi 10 A1
Shalkiya, Calcutta 8 B2
Sham Shui Po, Hong Kong 12 B1
Shamapur, Delhi 10 A1
Shamian, Canton 8 B2
Shan Mei, Hong Kong 12 A2
Shanghai, Shanghai 27 B2
Shankill, Dublin 11 B3
Sharp I., Hong Kong 12 A2
Shastrinagar, Delhi 10 A2
Shau Kei Wan, Hong Kong 12 B2
Shawocun, Beijing 4 B1
Shayuan, Canton 8 B2
Sheepshead Bay, New York 21 C2
Shek O, Hong Kong 12 B2
Shelter I., Hong Kong 12 B2
Sheng Fa Shan, Hong Kong 12 A1
Shepherds Bush, London 15 A2
Shepperton, London 15 B1
Sherman Oaks, Los Angeles 16 B2
Sherman Park, Chicago 9 C2
Shet Bandar, Mumbai 20 B2
Sheung Lau Wan, Hong Kong 12 B2
Sheung Wan, Hong Kong 12 B1
Sheva, Mumbai 20 B2
Sheva Nhava, Mumbai 20 B2
Shiba, Tokyo 29 c4
Shibpur, Calcutta 8 B1
Shibuya-Ku, Tokyo 29 c1
Shijōnawate, Osaka 22 A4
Shillim, Seoul 26 C1
Shimogawara, Tokyo 29 B1
Shimosalo, Tokyo 29 A2
Shimoshakujii, Tokyo 29 A2
Shinagawa-Ku, Tokyo 29 B3
Shing Mun Res., Hong Kong 12 A1
Shinjuku-Ku, Tokyo 29 a1
Shinjuku National Garden, Tokyo 29 a2
Shinkoiwa, Tokyo 29 A4
Shinnakano, Tokyo 29 A3
Shinsa, Seoul 26 B2
Shipai, Canton 8 B3
Shirinashi →, Osaka 22 B3
Shirogane, Tokyo 29 B3
Shiweitang, Canton 8 B2
Shogunle, Lagos 14 A2
Shomolu, Lagos 14 A2
Shooters Hill, London 15 B4
Shoreditch, London 15 a5
Shortlands, London 15 B4
Shu' afat, Jerusalem 13 B2
Shubrâ, Cairo 7 A2
Shubrâ el Kheima, Cairo 7 A2
Shuikuo, Canton 8 A2
Shuishang Park, Tianjin 30 B1
Sidcup, London 15 B4
Siebenhirten, Vienna 31 B1
Siedlung, Berlin 5 A1
Siekierki, Warsaw 31 B2
Sielce, Warsaw 31 B2
Siemensstadt, Berlin 5 A2
Sierra Madre, Los Angeles 16 B4
Sievering, Vienna 31 A2
Sighthill, Edinburgh 11 B2
Signal Hill, Cape Town 8 A1
Sihŭng, Seoul 26 C1
Sikátorpuszta, Budapest 7 A3
Silampur, Delhi 10 B2
Silver Hill, Boston 6 A2
Silver Hill, Washington 32 C4
Silver Spring, Washington 32 A3
Silvermine Nature Reserve, Cape Town 8 B1
Silvolantekojärvi, Helsinki 12 B2
Simei, Singapore 27 A3
Simla, Calcutta 8 B2
Simmering, Vienna 31 A2
Simmering Heide, Vienna 31 A2
Simonkylä, Helsinki 12 B3
Singapore, Singapore 27 B3
Singapore, Univ. of, Singapore 27 B2
Sinicka →, Moscow 19 A1
Sinki, Selat, Singapore 27 B2
Sint-Genesius-Rode, Brussels 6 B2
Sinwŏl, Seoul 26 B1
Sion, Mumbai 20 A2
Sipson, London 15 B1
Siqeil, Cairo 7 A1
Şişli, Istanbul 12 B1
Skansen, Stockholm 28 B2
Skärholmen, Stockholm 28 B1
Skarpäng, Stockholm 28 A2
Skarpnäck, Stockholm 28 B2
Skaryszewski Park, Warsaw 31 B2
Skeppsholmen, Stockholm 28 c3
Skokie, Chicago 9 A2
Skokie →, Chicago 9 A2
Skoklefall, Oslo 22 A3
Sköndal, Stockholm 28 B2
Skovlunde, Copenhagen 10 A2
Skovshoved, Copenhagen 10 A3
Skuru, Stockholm 28 B3
Skyland, Atlanta 3 A3
Slade Green, London 15 B5
Slemmestad, Oslo 22 B1
Slependen, Oslo 22 A2
Slipi, Jakarta 13 B1
Slivenec, Prague 24 B2
Sloten, Amsterdam 2 A1
Sloterpark, Amsterdam 2 A1
Sluhy, Prague 24 A3
Służew, Warsaw 31 B2
Służewiec, Warsaw 31 B2
Smíchov, Prague 24 B2
Smith Forest Preserve, Chicago 9 B2
Smithsonian Institute, Washington 32 b2
Smolny, St. Petersburg 26 B2
Snake Creek Canal →, Miami 18 A2
Snarøya, Oslo 22 A2
Snättringe, Stockholm 28 B1
Sŏbinggo, Seoul 26 B1
Søborg, Copenhagen 10 A2
Sobreda, Lisbon 14 B1
Soch'o, Seoul 26 C1
Sŏdaemun, Seoul 26 B1
Söderby, Stockholm 28 A3
Södermalm, Stockholm 28 B2
Sodpur, Calcutta 8 A2
Soeurs, Î. des, Montreal 19 B2
Sognsvatn, Oslo 22 A3
Soho, London 15 b3
Soho, New York 21 e1
Soignes, Forêt de, Brussels 6 B2
Sok Kwu Wan, Hong Kong 12 B1
Sŏkkwan, Seoul 26 B2
Sokolniki, Moscow 19 B4
Sokolniki Park, Moscow 19 B4
Sokołów, Warsaw 31 C1
Solalinden, Munich 20 B3
Soldier Field, Chicago 9 e3
Sollentuna, Stockholm 28 A1
Solln, Munich 20 B2
Solna, Stockholm 28 A1
Solntsevo, Moscow 19 C2
Somerset, Washington 32 B3
Somerville, Boston 6 A3
Somes Is., Wellington 32 B2
Sonari, Mumbai 20 B2
Søndersø, Copenhagen 10 A2
Sŏngbuk, Seoul 26 B2
Sŏngdong, Seoul 26 B2
Sŏngp'a, Seoul 26 B2
Sŏngsu, Seoul 26 B2
Soong Qingling, Former Res. of, Beijing 4 a2
Soroksár, Budapest 7 B2
Soroksari Duna →, Budapest 7 B2
Sosenka →, Moscow 19 B4
Sosnovka, St. Petersburg 26 B2
Sŏul, Seoul 26 B2
Soundview, New York 21 B2
South Beach, New York 21 C1
South Beach Harbor, San Francisco 25 c3
South Bend Park, Atlanta 3 B2
South Boston, Boston 6 A3
South Brooklyn, New York 21 B2
South Decatur, Atlanta 3 B3
South Deering, Chicago 9 C3
South El Monte, Los Angeles 16 B4
South Gate, Los Angeles 16 C3
South Harbor, Manila 17 B1
South Harrow, London 15 A1
South Hd., Sydney 28 B2
South Hills, Johannesburg 13 B2
South Hornchurch, London 15 A5
South Kensington, London 15 c2
South Lawn, Washington 32 C3
South Lincoln, Boston 6 A2
South Miami, Miami 18 B1
South Norwood, London 15 B3
South of Market, San Francisco 25 B2
South Ozone Park, New York 21 B3
South Pasadena, Los Angeles 16 B4
South Res., Boston 6 A3
South Ruislip, London 15 A1
South San Francisco, San Francisco 25 C2
South San Gabriel, Los Angeles 16 B4
South Shore, Chicago 9 C3
South Sudbury, Boston 6 A1
Southall, London 15 A1
Southborough, London 15 B4
Southend, London 15 B3
Southfields, London 15 B2
Southwark, London 15 B3
Søvang, Copenhagen 10 B3
Soweto, Johannesburg 13 B1
Sowhānak, Tehran 30 A3
Soya, Tokyo 29 A4
Spandau, Berlin 5 A1
Spånga, Stockholm 28 A1
Spanische Reitschule, Vienna 31 b1
Spectacle I., Boston 6 A4
Speicher-See, Munich 20 A3
Speising, Vienna 31 B1
Sphinx, Cairo 7 B1
Spinaceto, Rome 25 C1
Spit Junction, Sydney 28 A2
Spořilov, Prague 24 B3
Spot Pond, Boston 6 A3
Spotswood, Melbourne 17 B1
Spree →, Berlin 5 A2
Spring Pond, Boston 6 A4
Springeberg, Berlin 5 B5
Springfield, Washington 32 C2
Squantum, Boston 6 B3
Srednaya Rogatka, St. Petersburg 26 C2
Śródmieście, Warsaw 31 B2
Staaken, Berlin 5 A1
Stabekk, Oslo 22 A2
Stadhion, Athens 2 c3
Stadhuis, Amsterdam 2 b2
Stadlau, Vienna 31 A2
Stadshuset, Stockholm 28 b1
Stains, Paris 23 A3
Stamford Hill, London 15 A3
Stammersdorf, Vienna 31 A2
Stanley, Hong Kong 12 B2
Stanley Mound, Hong Kong 12 B2
Stanley Pen., Hong Kong 12 B2
Stanmore, London 15 A2
Stapleton, New York 21 C1
Star Ferry, Hong Kong 12 a2
Staraya Derevnya, St. Petersburg 26 B1
Stare, Warsaw 31 B2
Staré Město, Prague 24 B2
Starego Miasto, Warsaw 31 a2
Staten Island Zoo, New York 21 C1
Statenice, Prague 24 B1
Statue Square, Hong Kong 12 c1
Stedelijk Museum, Amsterdam 2 c1
Steele Creek, Melbourne 17 A1
Steenokkerzeel, Brussels 6 A2
Steglitz, Berlin 5 B2
Stepaside, Dublin 11 B2
Stephansdom, Vienna 31 b2
Stepney, London 15 A3
Sterling Park, San Francisco 25 B2
Sticklinge udde, Stockholm 28 A2
Stickney, Chicago 9 C2
Stillorgan, Dublin 11 B2
Stockholm, Stockholm 28 B2
Stocksund, Stockholm 28 A2
Stodůlky, Prague 24 B1
Stoke Newington, London 15 A3
Stokes Valley, Wellington 32 B2
Stone Canyon Res., Los Angeles 16 B2
Stone Park, Chicago 9 B1
Stonebridge, London 15 A2
Stoneham, Boston 6 A3
Stony Brook Res., Boston 6 B3
Stora Värtan, Stockholm 28 A2
Store Hareskov, Copenhagen 10 A2
Store Magleby, Copenhagen 10 B3
Storholmen, Stockholm 28 A2
Stoyka, St. Petersburg 26 B2
Straiton, Edinburgh 11 B3
Strand, London 15 b4
Strandfontein, Cape Town 8 B2
Strašnice, Prague 24 B2
Strasstrudering, Munich 20 B3
Stratford, London 15 A4
Strathfield, Sydney 28 B1
Streatham, London 15 B3
Streatham Vale, London 15 B3
Strebersdorf, Vienna 31 A2
Střešovice, Prague 24 B2
Stŕížkov, Prague 24 B2
Strogino, Moscow 19 B2
Strombeek-Bever, Brussels 6 A2
Stromovka, Prague 24 B2
Studio City, Los Angeles 16 B2
Stureby, Stockholm 28 B2
Stuvsta, Stockholm 28 B2
Subhepur, Delhi 10 A2
Sucat, Manila 17 C2
Suchdol, Prague 24 B2
Sucy-en-Brie, Paris 23 B4
Sudbury, Boston 6 A1
Sugamo, Tokyo 29 A3
Sugar Loaf Mt. = Açúcar, Pão de, Rio de Janeiro 24 B2
Suge, Tokyo 29 B2
Suginami-Ku, Tokyo 29 A2
Sugō, Tokyo 29 B2
Suita, Osaka 22 A4
Suitland, Washington 32 B4
Sukchar, Calcutta 8 A2
Suma, Osaka 22 B1
Sumida →, Tokyo 29 A3
Sumida-Ku, Tokyo 29 A3
Sumiyoshi, Osaka 22 B4
Summerville, Toronto 30 B1
Summit, Chicago 9 C2
Sunamachi, Tokyo 29 A4
Sunbury-on-Thames, London 15 B1
Sundbyberg, Stockholm 28 A1
Sundbyerne, Copenhagen 10 B3
Sung Kong, Hong Kong 12 B2
Sungei Kadut Industrial Estate, Singapore 27 A2
Sungei Selatar Res., Singapore 27 A3
Sunter, Jakarta 13 A2
Sunter, Kali →, Jakarta 13 B2
Suomenlinna, Helsinki 12 C2
Supreme Court, Washington 32 b3
Sura, Calcutta 8 B2
Surag-san, Seoul 26 A2
Surbiton, London 15 B2
Suresnes, Paris 23 A2
Surfside, Miami 18 A2
Surquillo, Lima 16 B2
Surrey Hills, Sydney 28 B2
Susaek, Seoul 26 B1
Süssenbrunn, Vienna 31 A2
Sutton, Dublin 11 A3
Sutton, London 15 B2
Suyu, Seoul 26 B2
Suzukishinden, Tokyo 29 A2
Svanemøllen, Copenhagen 10 A3
Sverdlov, Moscow 19 B3
Svestad, Oslo 22 B2
Svinö, Helsinki 12 C1
Swampscott, Boston 6 A4
Swanley, London 15 B4
Swansea, Toronto 30 B2
Swinburne I., New York 21 C1
Swords, Dublin 11 A2
Sydenham, Johannesburg 13 A2
Sydney, Sydney 28 B2
Sydney, Univ. of, Sydney 28 B2
Sydney Airport, Sydney 28 B2
Sydney Harbour Bridge, Sydney 28 B2
Sydstranden, Copenhagen 10 B3
Sylvania, Sydney 28 C1
Syntagma, Pl., Athens 2 b3
Syon Park, London 15 B2
Szczęśliwice, Warsaw 31 B1
Széchnenyi-hegy, Budapest 7 B1
Szent Istvánbaz, Budapest 7 b2
Széphalom, Budapest 7 A1

T

Tabata, Tokyo 29 A3
Tablada, Buenos Aires 7 C1
Table Bay, Cape Town 8 A1
Table Mountain, Cape Town 8 A1
Taboão da Serra, São Paulo 26 B1
Täby, Stockholm 28 A2
Tacuba, Mexico City 18 B1
Tacubaya, Mexico City 18 B1
Taebang, Seoul 26 B1
Tagig, Manila 17 B2
Tagig →, Manila 17 B2
Tai Hang, Hong Kong 12 B2
Tai Lo Shan, Hong Kong 12 A2
Tai Po Tsai, Hong Kong 12 A2
Tai Seng, Singapore 27 A3
Tai Shui Hang, Hong Kong 12 A2
Tai Tam B., Hong Kong 12 B2
Tai Tam Tuk Res., Hong Kong 12 B2

Tai Wai, Hong Kong 12 A1
Tai Wan Tau, Hong Kong 12 B2
Tai Wo Hau, Hong Kong 12 A1
Tainaka, Osaka 22 B4
Taishō, Osaka 22 B3
Taita, Wellington 32 B2
Tajrīsh, Tehran 30 A2
Takaido, Tokyo 29 A2
Takaishi, Tokyo 29 B2
Takarazuka, Osaka 22 A2
Takasago, Tokyo 29 A4
Takatsu-Ku, Tokyo 29 B2
Takeshita, Tokyo 29 B2
Takinegawa, Tokyo 29 A3
Takoma Park, Washington 32 B3
Taksim, Istanbul 12 B1
Talaide, Lisbon 14 A1
Taliganga, Calcutta 8 B2
Talipapa, Manila 17 A2
Tallaght, Dublin 11 B1
Tallkrogen, Stockholm 28 B2
Tama, Tokyo 29 B1
Tama ✈, Tokyo 29 B2
Tama Kyūryō, Tokyo 29 B2
Tamaden, Tokyo 29 B2
Tamagawa-josui ✈, Tokyo 29 A1
Taman Sari, Jakarta 13 A1
Tamanduateí ✈, São Paulo 26 B2
Tamboerskloof, Cape Town 8 A1
Tambora, Jakarta 13 A1
Tammisalo, Helsinki 12 B3
Tammūh, Cairo 7 B2
Tampines, Singapore 27 A3
Tanah Abang, Jakarta 13 B1
Tanigami, Osaka 22 A2
Tanjung Duren, Jakarta 13 B1
Tanjung Priok, Jakarta 13 A2
Tanum, Oslo 22 A1
Taoranting Park, Beijing 4 c2
Tapada, Lisbon 14 A1
Tapanila, Helsinki 12 B3
Tapiales, Buenos Aires 7 C1
Tapiola, Helsinki 12 B1
Tapsia, Calcutta 8 B2
Tara, Mumbai 20 A1
Tarabya, Istanbul 12 B2
Tarango, Presa, Mexico City 18 B1
Tårbæk, Copenhagen 10 A3
Tarchomin, Warsaw 31 B1
Tardeo, Mumbai 20 B1
Targówek, Warsaw 31 B2
Tårnby, Copenhagen 10 B3
Tarqua Bay, Lagos 14 B2
Tåstrup, Copenhagen 10 B1
Tatarovo, Moscow 19 B2
Tathong Channel, Hong Kong 12 B2
Tathong Pt., Hong Kong 12 B2
Tatuapé, São Paulo 26 B2
Taufkirchen, Munich 20 B2
Tavares, I. dos, Rio de Janeiro 24 A2
Távros, Athens 2 B2
Tawa, Wellington 32 A1
Teaneck, New York 21 A1
Teatro Municipal, Rio de Janeiro 24 c2
Tebet, Jakarta 13 B2
Tecamachaleo, Mexico City 18 B1
Teddington, London 15 B1
Tegel, Berlin 5 A2
Tegel, Flughafen, Berlin 5 A2
Tegeler See, Berlin 5 A2
Tegelort, Berlin 5 A2
Tehrān, Tehran 30 A2
Tehrān Pārs, Tehran 30 A3
Tei Tong Tsui, Hong Kong 12 B2
Tejo, Rio ✈, Lisbon 14 A2
Tekstilyshchik, Moscow 19 B4
Telegraph hill, San Francisco 25 a2
Telhal, Lisbon 14 A1
Telok Blangah, Singapore 27 B2
Teltow, Berlin 5 B2
Teltow kanal, Berlin 5 B3
Temnikovo, Moscow 19 B6
Tempelhof, Berlin 5 B3
Tempelhof, Flughafen, Berlin 5 B3
Temple City, Los Angeles 16 B4
Temple Hills Park, Washington 32 C4
Temple Mount, Jerusalem 13 b3
Templeogue, Dublin 11 B2
Templo Mayor, Mexico City 18 b3
Tenafly, New York 21 A2
Tenayuca, Piramide de, Mexico City 18 A1
Tengah ✈, Singapore 27 A2
Tennoji, Osaka 22 B4
Tepalcates, Mexico City 18 B2
Terrazzano, Milan 18 A1
Terrugem, Lisbon 14 A1
Tervuren, Brussels 6 B3
Tervuren, Park van, Brussels 6 B3
Tetuán, Madrid 17 B1
Teufelsberg, Berlin 5 B2
Tévere ✈, Rome 25 B1
Thalkirchen, Munich 20 B2
Thames ✈, London 15 A4
Thames Ditton, London 15 B1
Thamesmead, London 15 A4
Thana Cr. ✈, Mumbai 20 A2
The Loop, Chicago 9 B3
The Ridge, Delhi 10 B2
The Wilds, Johannesburg 13 B2
Theater Carré, Amsterdam 2 b2
Théatro Dionissou, Athens 2 c2
Thiais, Paris 23 B3
Thissío, Athens 2 c1
Thistletown, Toronto 30 A1
Thomastown, Melbourne 17 A2
Thompson I., Boston 6 B4
Thon Buri, Bangkok 3 B1
Thornbury, Melbourne 17 A2
Thorncliffe, Toronto 30 A2
Thornhill, Toronto 30 A2
Thornton, Cape Town 8 A2
Thornton Heath, London 15 B3
Threipmuir Res., Edinburgh 11 B2
Throgs Neck, New York 21 B3
Thyssen Bornemisza, Museo, Madrid 17 b3
Tian'anmen Square, Beijing 4 B2
Tiancun, Beijing 4 B1
Tianjin, Tianjin 30 B1
Tiantan Park, Beijing 4 c2
Tibidabo, Barcelona 4 A1
Tibradden Mt., Dublin 11 B2
Tiburon, San Francisco 25 A2
Tiburtino, Rome 25 B2
Ticomán, Mexico City 18 A2
Tiefersee, Berlin 5 B1
Tiejiangyin, Beijing 4 C2
Tientsin = Tianjin, Tianjin 30 B1
Tiergarten, Berlin 5 A3
Tietê ✈, São Paulo 26 B2
Tigerhof, Cape Town 8 A2
Tigris = Nahr Dijlah ✈, Baghdad 3 B2
Tijuca, Rio de Janeiro 24 B1
Tijuca, Parque Nacional da, Rio de Janeiro 24 B1
Tijuca, Pico da, Rio de Janeiro 24 B1
Tikkurila, Helsinki 12 B3
Tilak Nagar, Delhi 10 B1
Tilanqiao, Shanghai 27 B1
Timah, Bukit, Singapore 27 A2
Times Square, New York 21 c2
Timiryazev Park, Moscow 19 B3
Ting Kau, Hong Kong 12 A1
Tira, Jerusalem 13 A1
Tirsa, Cairo 7 B2
Tishrīyaa, Baghdad 3 B2
Tiu Keng Leng, Hong Kong 12 B2
Tivoli, Copenhagen 10 a3
Tizapán, Mexico City 18 C1
Tlalnepantla ✈, Mexico City 18 A1
To Kwai Wan, Hong Kong 12 B2
Toa Payoh, Singapore 27 A3
Tobong, Seoul 26 B2
Tobong-san, Seoul 26 A2
Točná, Prague 24 C2
Toco Hills, Atlanta 3 B2
Todt Hill, New York 21 C1
Tōkagi, Tokyo 29 A4
Tokai Plantation, Cape Town 8 B1
Tōkaichiba, Tokyo 29 B2
Tokarevo, Moscow 19 C5
Tōkyō, Tokyo 29 B3
Tokyo B., Tokyo 29 B4
Tokyo-Haneda Int. Airport, Tokyo 29 B3
Tokyo Harbour, Tokyo 29 B3
Tolka R. ✈, Dublin 11 A1
Tolworth, London 15 B2
Tomb of Lu Xun, Shanghai 27 B1
Tomb of the Kings, Jerusalem 13 a2
Tomba di Nerone, Rome 25 B1
Tomilino, Moscow 19 C5
Tondo, Manila 17 B1
Tongbinggo, Seoul 26 B1
Tongjak, Seoul 26 B1
Tongmaemung, Seoul 26 B2
Tongqiao, Shanghai 27 A1
Toorak, Melbourne 17 B2
Topkapı, Istanbul 12 B1
Tor di Quinto, Rome 25 B1
Tor Pignattara, Rome 25 B2
Tor Sapienza, Rome 25 B2
Toranomon, Tokyo 29 c3
Torcy, Paris 23 A4
Toronto, Toronto 30 B2
Toronto, Univ. of, Toronto 30 B2
Toronto Harbour, Toronto 30 B2
Toronto I., Toronto 30 B2
Toronto Int. Airport, Toronto 30 A1
Toros Las Arenas, Pl. de, Barcelona 4 c1
Toros Monumental, Templo de, Barcelona 4 a3
Torre Latino-americana, Mexico City 18 b2
Torre Lupara, Rome 25 B2
Torre Nova, Rome 25 B2
Torrellas ✈, Barcelona 4 A1
Torrevécchia, Rome 25 B1
Toshima-Ku, Tokyo 29 A3
Toshimaen, Tokyo 29 A2
Tottenham, London 15 A3
Tottenham, Melbourne 17 A1
Tour Eiffel, Paris 23 c2
Toussus-le-Noble, Paris 23 B1
Toussus-le-Noble, Aérodrome de, Paris 23 B1
Tower Bridge, London 15 b5
Tower Hamlets, London 15 A3
Tower of London, London 15 A3
Towra Pt., Sydney 28 C2
Tøyen, Oslo 22 A3
Toyonaka, Osaka 22 A3
Trafalgar Square, London 15 b3
Trafaria, Lisbon 14 A1
Traição, Cor. ✈, São Paulo 26 B2
Tranegilde, Copenhagen 10 B2
Trångsund, Stockholm 28 B2
Transamerica Pyramid, San Francisco 25 b2
Transbay Terminal, San Francisco 25 b3
Trappenfelde, Berlin 5 A4
Trastévere, Rome 25 B1
Treasure I., San Francisco 25 B2
Třeboradice, Prague 24 B3
Třebotov, Prague 24 C1
Tremblay-en-France, Paris 23 A4
Tremembe ✈, São Paulo 26 A2
Tremont, New York 21 A2
Trenno, Milan 18 B1
Treptow, Berlin 5 B3
Três Rios, Sa. dos, Rio de Janeiro 24 B1
Trevi, Fontana di, Rome 25 b3
Trezzano sul Navíglio, Milan 18 B1
Tribune Tower, Chicago 9 b2
Trieste, Rome 25 B2
Trinidad, Washington 32 B4
Trinity, Edinburgh 11 B2
Trinity College, Dublin 11 c3
Trionfale, Rome 25 B1
Triulzo, Milan 18 B2
Trocadero, Paris 23 b1
Troitse-Lykovo, Moscow 19 B2
Troja, Prague 24 B2
Trollbäcken, Stockholm 28 B3
Trombay, Mumbai 20 A2
Troparevo, Moscow 19 C2
Tropenmuseum, Amsterdam 2 b3
Trudyashchikhsya, Ostrov, St. Petersburg 26 B1
Tryvasshøgda, Oslo 22 A3
Tseng Lan Shue, Hong Kong 12 A2
Tsim Sha Tsui, Hong Kong 12 a2
Tsing Yi, Hong Kong 12 A1
Tsova, Jerusalem 13 B1
Tsuen Wan, Hong Kong 12 A1
Tsukiji, Tokyo 29 c5
Tsur Hadassa, Jerusalem 13 B1
Tsurumi ✈, Tokyo 29 B3
Tsz Wan Shan, Hong Kong 12 A2
Tuas, Singapore 27 B1
Tuchoměřice, Prague 24 B1
Tuckahoe, New York 21 A3
Tucuruvi, São Paulo 26 A2
Tufello, Rome 25 B2
Tufnell Park, London 15 A3
Tughlakabad, Delhi 10 B2
Tuileries, Jardin des, Paris 23 b3
Tuindorp Oostzaan, Amsterdam 2 A2
Tullamarine, Melbourne 17 A1
Tulse Hill, London 15 B3
Tung Lung I., Hong Kong 12 B2
Tung O, Hong Kong 12 B1
Tunis, Baghdad 3 A2
Tuomarila, Helsinki 12 B1
Tureberg, Stockholm 28 A1
Turffontein, Johannesburg 13 B2
Turkso, Prague 24 A1
Turnham Green, London 15 B2
Turnhouse, Edinburgh 11 B1
Tuscolana, Via, Rome 25 B2
Tushino, Moscow 19 A2
Twelve Apostles, Cape Town 8 A1
Twickenham, London 15 B1
Twickenham Rugby Ground, London 15 B1
Twin Peaks, San Francisco 25 B2
Two Rock Mt., Dublin 11 B2
Tymon North, Dublin 11 B1
Tysons Corner, Washington 32 B2

U

U.S. Capitol, Washington 32 b3
Ubeidiya, Jerusalem 13 B2
Uberaba ✈, São Paulo 26 B2
Ubin, P., Singapore 27 A3
Uccle, Brussels 6 B2
Udelnaya, St. Petersburg 26 A2
Udelnoe, St. Petersburg 26 B1
Udlding, Munich 20 A1
Ueno, Tokyo 29 A3
Úholičky, Prague 24 B1
Uhříněves, Prague 24 B3
Uithoorn, Amsterdam 2 B1
Újpalota, Budapest 7 A2
Újpest, Budapest 7 A2
Ukita, Tokyo 29 A4
Ullerup, Copenhagen 10 B3
Ullevål, Oslo 22 A3
Ulriksdal, Stockholm 28 A1
Ulyanka, St. Petersburg 26 B1
Um Al-Khanazir Island, Baghdad 3 B2
Umeda, Osaka 22 A3
Umerkhadi, Mumbai 20 b2
Ümraniye, Istanbul 12 B2
Underground Atlanta, Atlanta 3 B2
Unětický potok ✈, Prague 24 B2
Ŭngam, Seoul 26 B1
Unhos, Lisbon 14 A2
Unidad Santa Fe, Mexico City 18 B1
Union City, New York 21 B1
Union Port, New York 21 B2
Union Square, New York 21 d2
Union Square, San Francisco 25 b2
Union Station, Washington 32 b3
United Nations H.Q., New York 21 c3
Universidad, Madrid 17 B1
Universidad de Chile, Santiago 26 B2
University Park, Washington 32 B4
Unp'yong, Seoul 26 B1
Unter den Linden, Berlin 5 a4
Unterbiberg, Munich 20 B2
Unterföhring, Munich 20 A3
Unterhaching, Munich 20 B2
Unterlaa, Vienna 31 B2
Untermenzing, Munich 20 A1
Upper East Side, New York 21 b3
Upper Elmers End, London 15 B3
Upper New York B., New York 21 C1
Upper Norwood, London 15 B3
Upper Peirce Res., Singapore 27 A2
Upper Sydenham, London 15 B3
Upper Tooting, London 15 B3
Upper West Side, New York 21 a2
Upton, London 15 A4
Uptown, Chicago 9 B2
Uran, Mumbai 20 B2
Urayasu, Tokyo 29 B4
Urbe, Aeroporto d', Rome 25 B2
Urca, Rio de Janeiro 24 B2
Uritsk, St. Petersburg 26 C1
Üröm, Budapest 7 A2
Ursus, Warsaw 31 B1
Ursvik, Stockholm 28 A1
Usera, Madrid 17 B1
Ushigome, Tokyo 29 A3
Usina, Rio de Janeiro 24 B1
Üsküdar, Istanbul 12 B2
Ust-Slavyanka, St. Petersburg 26 C3
Uteke, Stockholm 28 A3
Utrata, Warsaw 31 B2
Uttarpara, Calcutta 8 B1
Utterslev Mose, Copenhagen 10 A2

V

Vadaul, Mumbai 20 A2
Vaires-sur-Marne, Paris 23 A4
Valby, Copenhagen 10 B2
Valcannuta, Rome 25 B1
Valdelatas, Madrid 17 A1
Vale, Washington 32 B1
Valenton, Paris 23 B3
Valera, Milan 18 A1
Vallcarca, Barcelona 4 A1
Valldoreix, Barcelona 4 A1
Vallecas, Madrid 17 B2
Vallensbæk, Copenhagen 10 B2
Vallensbæk Strand, Copenhagen 10 B2
Vallentunasjön, Stockholm 28 A2
Valleranello, Rome 25 C1
Vallisaari, Helsinki 12 C3
Vallvidrera, Barcelona 4 A1
Valvidrera ✈, Barcelona 4 A1
Van Goghmuseum, Amsterdam 2 c1
Vanak, Tehran 30 A2
Vangede, Copenhagen 10 A3
Vaniköy, Istanbul 12 B2
Vanløse, Copenhagen 10 A2
Vantaa, Helsinki 12 B2
Vantaa ✈, Helsinki 12 B2
Vantaankoski, Helsinki 12 B2
Vantaanpuisto, Helsinki 12 B2
Vanves, Paris 23 B2
Varedo, Milan 18 A1
Varkiza, Athens 2 C2
Varszínház, Budapest 7 b2
Vartiokylä, Helsinki 12 B3
Vartiosaari, Helsinki 12 B3
Vasamuseet, Stockholm 28 b3
Vasco, Cape Town 8 A2
Vasfanārd, Tehran 30 B2
Vashi, Mumbai 20 A2
Vasilyevskiy, Ostrov, St. Petersburg 26 B1
Vaso Regulador El Cristo, Mexico City 18 B1
Vaucluse, Sydney 28 B2
Vaucresson, Paris 23 A1
Vauhallan, Paris 23 B2
Vaujours, Paris 23 A4
Vauxhall, London 15 c4
Vecsés, Budapest 7 B3
Veleň, Prague 24 A3
Veleslavín, Prague 24 B2
Vélizy-Villacoublay, Paris 23 B2
Velka-Chuchle, Prague 24 B2
Velké Přílepy, Prague 24 B1
Venda Seca, Lisbon 14 A1
Venetian Islands, Miami 18 B2
Venezia, Palazzo, Rome 25 c2
Venice, Los Angeles 16 C2
Ventas, Madrid 17 B1
Ventorro del Cano, Madrid 17 B1
Venustiano Carranza, Mexico City 18 B2
Verde ✈, São Paulo 26 A1
Verdi, Athens 2 A2
Verdun, Montreal 19 B2
Vérhalom, Budapest 7 A2
Vermelho ✈, São Paulo 26 B1
Vernon, Los Angeles 16 B3
Verrières-le-Buisson, Paris 23 B2
Versailles, Buenos Aires 7 B1
Versailles, Paris 23 B1
Veshnyaki, Moscow 19 B4
Vesolyy Posolok, St. Petersburg 26 B2
Vestra, Helsinki 12 B1
Vestskoven, Copenhagen 10 A2
Vicálvaro, Madrid 17 B2
Vicente Lopez, Buenos Aires 7 B2
Victoria, Hong Kong 12 B1
Victoria, London 15 c3
Victoria, Mt., Wellington 32 B1
Victoria, Pont, Montreal 19 a3
Victoria and Albert Waterfront, Cape Town 8 a1
Victoria Gardens, Mumbai 20 B2
Victoria Harbour, Hong Kong 12 B1
Victoria Island, Lagos 14 B2
Victoria L., Johannesburg 13 B2
Victoria Lawn Tennis Courts, Melbourne 17 B2
Victoria Park, Singapore 27 B2
Victoria Peak, Hong Kong 12 B1
Victoria Wharf, Cape Town 8 a2
Vienna = Wien, Vienna 31 A2
Vienna, Washington 32 B1
View Park, Los Angeles 16 B3
Vigário Geral, Rio de Janeiro 24 A1
Vigentino, Milan 18 B2
Viggbyholm, Stockholm 28 A2
Vighignolo, Milan 18 B1
Viikki, Helsinki 12 B3
Vikhroli, Mumbai 20 A2
Vila Guilherme, São Paulo 26 B2
Vila Isabel, Rio de Janeiro 24 B1
Vila Jaguára, São Paulo 26 B1
Vila Madalena, São Paulo 26 B1
Vila Maria, São Paulo 26 B2
Vila Mariana, São Paulo 26 B2
Vila Prudente, São Paulo 26 B2
Viladecans, Barcelona 4 B1
Vile Parle, Mumbai 20 A2
Villa Adelina, Buenos Aires 7 B1
Villa Ballester, Buenos Aires 7 B1
Villa Barilari, Buenos Aires 7 C2
Villa Borghese, Rome 25 a3
Villa Bosch, Buenos Aires 7 B1
Villa C. Colon, Buenos Aires 7 C2
Villa Ciudadela, Buenos Aires 7 B1
Villa de Guadalupe, Mexico City 18 B2
Villa Devoto, Buenos Aires 7 B1
Villa Diamante, Buenos Aires 7 C2
Villa Dominico, Buenos Aires 7 C3
Villa Lugano, Buenos Aires 7 C2
Villa Lynch, Buenos Aires 7 B1
Villa Madero, Buenos Aires 7 C1
Villa Sáenz Pena, Buenos Aires 7 B1
Villa Urquiza, Buenos Aires 7 B2
Villaverde, Madrid 17 B1
Villaverde Bajo, Madrid 17 B1
Ville-d'Avray, Paris 23 B1
Villecresnes, Paris 23 B4
Villejuif, Paris 23 B3
Villemomble, Paris 23 A4
Villeneuve-la-Garenne, Paris 23 A2
Villeneuve-le-Roi, Paris 23 B3
Villeneuve-St.-Georges, Paris 23 B3
Villeparisis, Paris 23 A4
Villevaudé, Paris 23 A4
Villiers-le-Bâcle, Paris 23 B1
Villiers-sur-Marne, Paris 23 B4
Villinki, Helsinki 12 C3
Viloresi, Canale, Milan 18 A1
Vilvoorde, Brussels 6 A2
Vimodrone, Milan 18 A2
Vimont, Montreal 19 A1
Vinanmek Palace, Bangkok 3 a2
Vincennes, Paris 23 A3
Vincennes, Bois de, Paris 23 B3
Vinings, Atlanta 3 A2
Vinohrady, Prague 24 c3
Vinoř, Prague 24 B3
Violet Hill, Hong Kong 12 B2
Virányos, Budapest 7 A1
Virgen del San Cristóbal, Santiago 26 B2
Virginia Gardens, Miami 18 B1
Virginia Key, Miami 18 B2
Viroflay, Paris 23 B2
Víron, Athens 2 B2
Virum, Copenhagen 10 A2
Vishnyaki, Moscow 19 B5
Visitacion Valley, San Francisco 25 B2
Vista Alegre, Lima 16 B3
Vista Alegre, Santiago 26 C1
Vista Grove, Atlanta 3 A3
Vitacura, Santiago 26 B2
Vitinia, Rome 25 C1
Vitry-sur-Seine, Paris 23 B3
Vizandinó, Moussio, Athens 2 b3
Vladykino, Moscow 19 A3
Vlezenbeek, Brussels 6 B1
Vltava ✈, Prague 24 A2
Vnukovo, Moscow 19 C1
Vokovice, Prague 24 B2
Volgelsdorf, Berlin 5 B5
Volkhonka-Zil, Moscow 19 C3
Vollen, Oslo 22 B1
Volodarskoye, St. Petersburg 26 B2
Volynkina-Derevnya, St. Petersburg 26 B1
Vondelpark, Amsterdam 2 A2
Vösendorf, Vienna 31 B2
Vostochnyy, Moscow 19 B5
Voula, Athens 2 C2
Vouliagmeni, Athens 2 C2
Vredehoek, Cape Town 8 A1
Vršovice, Prague 24 B2
Vyborgskaya Storona, St. Petersburg 26 B2
Vykhino, Moscow 19 B4
Vyšehrad, Prague 24 B2

W

Wachterhof, Munich 20 B3
Wadala, Mumbai 20 A2
Wadestown, Wellington 32 B1
Wadi Fukin, Jerusalem 13 B1
Wah Fu, Hong Kong 12 B1
Wahda, Baghdad 3 B2
Währing, Vienna 31 A2
Waidmannslust, Berlin 5 A3
Wainuiomata, Wellington 32 B2
Wainuiomata R. ✈, Wellington 32 B2
Wakefield, Boston 6 A3
Waldesruh, Berlin 5 B4
Waldperlach, Munich 20 B3
Waldtrudering, Munich 20 B3
Walkinstown, Dublin 11 B1
Wall Street, New York 21 f1
Walt Disney Concert Hall, Los Angeles 16 b1
Waltham, Boston 6 A2
Waltham Forest, London 15 A3
Walthamstow, London 15 A3
Walton on Thames, London 15 B1
Wambeek, Brussels 6 A3
Wan Chai, Hong Kong 12 B2
Wan Chai Lanes, Hong Kong 12 c2
Wandsworth, London 15 B2
Wankhede Stadium, Mumbai 20 c2
Wannsee, Berlin 5 B1
Wansdorf, Berlin 5 A1
Wanstead, London 15 A4
Wapping, London 15 A3
Ward, Dublin 11 A1
Ward I., Wellington 32 B2
Warnberg, Munich 20 B2
Warrāq el 'Arab, Cairo 7 A2
Warrāq el Hadr, Cairo 7 A2
Warringen Park, Melbourne 17 A2
Warriston, Edinburgh 11 B2
Warsaw = Warszawa, Warsaw 31 B2
Warszawa, Warsaw 31 B2
Wartenberg, Berlin 5 A4
Washington, Washington 32 B3
Washington Heights, New York 21 A2
Washington Monument, Washington 32 b1
Washington Nat. Airport, Washington 32 B3
Washington Park, Chicago 9 C3
Wat Arun, Bangkok 3 b1
Wat Pho, Bangkok 3 b1
Wat Phra Keo, Bangkok 3 b1
Wat Traimit, Bangkok 3 c2
Water of Leith, Edinburgh 11 B1
Water Tower Place, Chicago 9 a2
Watergraafsmeer, Amsterdam 2 A2
Waterland, Amsterdam 2 A2
Waterloo, Brussels 6 B2
Waterloo, Wellington 32 B2
Waterloo International, London 15 b4
Watermael-Boitsfort, Brussels 6 B2
Watertown, Boston 6 A2
Watsonia, Melbourne 17 A2
Waverley, Boston 6 A2
Waverley, Johannesburg 13 A2
Waverley, Sydney 28 B2
Waverley Station, Edinburgh 11 b3
Wawer, Warsaw 31 B2
Wawrzyszew, Warsaw 31 B1
Wayland, Boston 6 A1
Wazirabad, Delhi 10 A2
Wazīrīya, Baghdad 3 A2
Wazirpur, Delhi 10 A2
Wedding, Berlin 5 A3
Weehawken, New York 21 B1
Weesp, Amsterdam 2 B3
Weidling, Vienna 31 A1
Weidlingbach, Vienna 31 A1
Weigongcun, Beijing 4 B1
Weijin He ✈, Tianjin 30 B2
Weissensee, Berlin 5 A3
Wellesley, Boston 6 B2
Wellesley Falls, Boston 6 B2
Wellesley Hills, Boston 6 A1
Welling, London 15 B4
Wellington, Boston 6 A3
Wellington, Wellington 32 B1
Wells Fargo Center, Los Angeles 16 b1
Weltevreden Park, Johannesburg 13 A1
Wembley, London 15 A2
Wemmel, Brussels 6 A1
Wemmer Pan, Johannesburg 13 B2
Wenceslas Square, Prague 24 b2
Wendenschloss, Berlin 5 B4
Wenhuagong, Tianjin 30 B2
Wennington, London 15 A5
Werneuchen, Berlin 5 A5
West Bedford, Boston 6 A2
West Concord, Boston 6 A1
West Don ✈, Toronto 30 A2
West Drayton, London 15 A1
West Ham, London 15 A4
West Harrow, London 15 A1
West Heath, London 15 B4
West Hill, Toronto 30 A3
West Hollywood, Los Angeles 16 B2
West Kensington, London 15 c1
West Kilburn, London 15 a1
West Lamma Channel, Hong Kong 12 B1
West Lynn, Boston 6 A4
West Medford, Boston 6 A3
West Miami, Miami 18 B1
West Molesey, London 15 B1
West New York, New York 21 B1
West of Twin Peaks, San Francisco 25 B2
West Park, Johannesburg 13 A1
West Rouge, Toronto 30 A4
West Roxbury, Boston 6 B3
West Springfield, Washington 32 C2
West Town, Chicago 9 B2
West Wharf, Karachi 14 B1
Westbourne Green, London 15 a1
Westchester, Chicago 9 B1
Westchester, Los Angeles 16 C2
Westchester, New York 21 A2
Westcliff, Johannesburg 13 B2
Westdene, Johannesburg 13 B1
Westend, Helsinki 12 C1
Wester Hailes, Edinburgh 11 B3
Westerham, Munich 20 B2
Western Addition, San Francisco 25 B2
Western Wall, Jerusalem 13 b3
Westgate, Washington 32 B3
Westlake, Cape Town 8 B1
Westlake, San Francisco 25 B2
Westminster, London 15 A3
Westmount, Montreal 19 B2
Weston, Boston 6 A2
Weston, Toronto 30 A1
Weston Res., Boston 6 A2
Westwood Village, Los Angeles 16 B2
Westzaan, Amsterdam 2 A1
Wetton, Cape Town 8 B2
Wexford, Toronto 30 A3
Weybridge, London 15 B1
Wezembeek-Oppem, Brussels 6 A2
White House, The, Washington 32 b1
Whitechapel, London 15 A3
Whitehall, Dublin 11 A2
Whitehall, London 15 b3
Whittier, Los Angeles 16 C4
Whitton, London 15 B1
Wieden, Vienna 31 A2
Wien, Vienna 31 A2
Wien-Schwechat, Flughafen, Vienna 31 B3
Wienerberg, Vienna 31 B2
Wierzbno, Warsaw 31 B2
Wijde Wormer, Amsterdam 2 A2
Wilanów, Warsaw 31 B2
Wilanówka ✈, Warsaw 31 C2
Wilhelmshagen, Berlin 5 B5
Wilket Creek Park, Toronto 30 A2
Wilkieston, Edinburgh 11 B1
Willbrook, Dublin 11 B2
Willesden, London 15 A2
Willesden Green, London 15 A2
Williamsbridge, New York 21 A2
Williamsburg, New York 21 B2
Williamstown, Melbourne 17 B1
Willoughby, Sydney 28 A2
Willow Springs, Chicago 9 C1
Willowdale, Toronto 30 A2
Wilmersdorf, Berlin 5 c1
Wilmette, Chicago 9 A2
Wilmington, London 15 B5
Wilshire Boulevard, Los Angeles 16 c1
Wimbledon, London 15 B2
Wimbledon Common, London 15 B2
Wimbledon Park, London 15 B2
Wimbledon Tennis Ground, London 15 B2
Winchester, Boston 6 A3
Windermere, Cape Town 8 A2
Windsor, Johannesburg 13 A1
Windsor Hills, Los Angeles 16 C2
Windy Arbour, Dublin 11 B2
Winning, Munich 20 B2
Winthrop, Boston 6 A4
Wissous, Paris 23 B2
Wittenau, Berlin 5 A2
Witwatersrand, Univ. of, Johannesburg 13 B2
Włochy, Warsaw 31 B1
Wo Mei, Hong Kong 12 A2
Wo Yi Hop, Hong Kong 12 A1
Woburn, Boston 6 A3
Woburn, Toronto 30 A3
Woduk Pluit, Jakarta 13 A1
Wola, Warsaw 31 B1
Wolf Trap Farm Park, Washington 32 B2
Wolica, Warsaw 31 C2
Wolica, Warsaw 31 C1
Wólka Węglowa, Warsaw 31 B1
Wollaston, Boston 6 B3
Woltersdorf, Berlin 5 B5
Woluwe-Saint-Lambert, Brussels 6 A2
Woluwe-Saint-Pierre, Brussels 6 A2
Wong Chuk Hang, Hong Kong 12 B2
Wong Chuk Wan, Hong Kong 12 A2
Wong Chuk Yeung, Hong Kong 12 A2
Wong Tai Sin, Hong Kong 12 A2
Wood Green, London 15 A3
Wood Ridge, New York 21 A1
Woodbridge, Toronto 30 A1
Woodford, London 15 A4
Woodford Bridge, London 15 A4
Woodford Green, London 15 A4
Woodhaven, New York 21 B2
Woodhouselee, Edinburgh 11 B2
Woodlands New Town, Singapore 27 A2
Woodmont, Washington 32 B3
Woodside, London 15 B3
Woodside, New York 21 B2
Woodstock, Cape Town 8 A1
Woollahra, Sydney 28 B2
Woolloomooloo, Sydney 28 b2
Woolooware B., Sydney 28 C1
Woolwich, London 15 B4
Woolworth Building, New York 21 e1
World Trade Center, site of former, New York 21 B1
World's End, Boston 6 B4
Worli, Mumbai 20 A1
Worth, Chicago 9 C2
Wren's Nest, Atlanta 3 B2
Wrigley Building, Chicago 9 b2
Wuhlgarten, Berlin 5 A4
Wujiaochang, Shanghai 27 B2
Würm ✈, Munich 20 B1
Würm-kanal, Munich 20 A1
Wusong, Shanghai 27 A1
Wyczółki, Warsaw 31 C1
Wygoda, Warsaw 31 B2
Wynberg, Cape Town 8 B1

X

Xabregas, Lisbon 14 A2
Xianggang = Hong Kong, Hong Kong 12 B1
Xiaodian, Tianjin 30 A2
Xiaogang Park, Canton 8 B2
Xiaoping, Canton 8 A2
Xiasha chong, Canton 8 B1
Xichang, Canton 8 B2
Xicheng, Beijing 4 B1
Xidan, Beijing 4 B2
Xigu Park, Tianjin 30 A2
Xigucun, Tianjin 30 A1
Ximenwai, Tianjin 30 B2
Xinanlou, Tianjin 30 B2
Xinkai He ✈, Tianjin 30 A2
Xizhimen, Beijing 4 B1
Xu Beihong Mem. Hall, Beijing 4 a1
Xuanwu, Beijing 4 B2
Xuhui, Shanghai 27 B1

Y

Yaba, Lagos 14 A2
Yaftābād, Tehran 30 B1
Yahara, Tokyo 29 A2
Yaho, Tokyo 29 A1
Yakire, Tokyo 29 A4
Yamada, Osaka 22 A4
Yamada, Tokyo 29 B2
Yamamoto, Osaka 22 B4
Yamato ✈, Osaka 22 B3
Yamuna ✈, Delhi 10 B2
Yan Kit, Singapore 27 A3
Yanbu, Canton 8 B1
Yangch'ŏn, Seoul 26 B1
Yanghuayuan, Beijing 4 C1
Yangjae, Seoul 26 C2
Yangjiazhuang, Shanghai 27 A1
Yangpu, Shanghai 27 B2
Yangpu Park, Shanghai 27 B2
Yao, Osaka 22 B4
Yao Airport, Osaka 22 B4
Yarmūk, Baghdad 3 B1
Yarra ✈, Melbourne 17 A1
Yarra Bend Park, Melbourne 17 A2
Yarraville, Melbourne 17 A1
Yau Tong, Hong Kong 12 B2
Yauza ✈, Moscow 19 A4
Yeading, London 15 A1
Yedikule, Istanbul 12 C1
Yemin Moshe, Jerusalem 13 b2
Yenikapı, Istanbul 12 B1
Yeniköy, Istanbul 12 B2
Yerba Buena Gardens, San Francisco 25 c2
Yerba Buena I., San Francisco 25 B2
Yerres, Paris 23 B4
Yerushalayim = Jerusalem, Jerusalem 13 B2
Yiheyuan, Beijing 4 A1
Yinhangzhen, Shanghai 27 A2
Yishun New Town, Singapore 27 A3
Yixingbu, Tianjin 30 A2
Ylästö, Helsinki 12 B2
Yodo ✈, Osaka 22 A4
Yongdingman, Beijing 4 B2
Yŏngdong, Seoul 26 B2
Yŏngdŭngp'o, Seoul 26 B1
Yongfucun, Canton 8 B2
Yongjing, Shanghai 27 B2
Yongsan, Seoul 26 B1
Yonkers, New York 21 A2
York, Toronto 30 A2
York Mills, Toronto 30 A2
Yotsuya, Tokyo 29 a2
You'anmen, Beijing 4 B1
Yŏŭido, Seoul 26 B1
Youndsfield, Cape Town 8 B1
Yuanxiatian, Canton 8 A2
Yugo-Zarad, Moscow 19 B3
Yung Shue Wan, Hong Kong 12 B1
Yūsofābād, Tehran 30 A2
Yuyuantan Park, Beijing 4 b2

Z

Zaandam, Amsterdam 2 A1
Zaandijk, Amsterdam 2 A1
Zaanstad, Amsterdam 2 A1
Záběhlice, Prague 24 B2
Ząbki, Warsaw 31 B2
Zacisze, Warsaw 31 B2
Zahrā, Baghdad 3 A1
Zakharkovo, Moscow 19 B1
Žalov, Prague 24 A2
Załuski, Warsaw 31 C1
Zamdorf, Munich 20 B2
Zamek Królewski, Warsaw 31 a2
Zamek Ujazdowski, Warsaw 31 c3
Zanevka, St. Petersburg 26 B3
Zapote, Manila 17 C1
Záppeio, Athens 2 c2
Zarechye, Moscow 19 B2
Zaventem, Brussels 6 A2
Zawady, Warsaw 31 B2
Zāwiyet Abū Musallam, Cairo 7 B1
Zawrā' Park, Baghdad 3 B2
Zbraslav, Prague 24 C2
Zbuzany, Prague 24 B1
Zdiby, Prague 24 B2
Zeekoevlei, Cape Town 8 B2
Zehlendorf, Berlin 5 B2
Zenne ✈, Brussels 6 B1
Żerań, Warsaw 31 B1
Zerzeń, Warsaw 31 B2
Zeytinburnu, Istanbul 12 C1
Zhabei, Shanghai 27 B1
Zhangguizhuang, Tianjin 30 B2
Zhdanov, Moscow 19 B4
Zheleznodorozhnyy, Moscow 19 B6
Zhenru, Shanghai 27 B1
Zhernovka, St. Petersburg 26 B2
Zhicun, Canton 8 B2
Zhongshan Park, Beijing 4 b2
Zhongshan Park, Shanghai 27 B1
Zhoucun, Canton 8 A2
Zhoujiadu, Shanghai 27 B1
Zhoujiazhen, Shanghai 27 A2
Zhu Jiang ✈, Canton 8 B3
Zhulebino, Moscow 19 B5
Zhushadi, Canton 8 B2
Zielona, Warsaw 31 B3
Zielonka, Warsaw 31 B2
Ziya He ✈, Tianjin 30 A1
Žižkov, Prague 24 B2
Žličín, Prague 24 B1
Zócalo, Mexico City 18 b3
Zografos, Athens 2 B2
Zoliborz, Warsaw 31 B1
Zonnenbloem, Cape Town 8 A1
Zoo, Beijing 4 a1
Zugliget, Budapest 7 B1
Zugló, Budapest 7 A2
Zuiderwoude, Amsterdam 2 A3
Zumbi, Rio de Janeiro 24 A1
Zunderdorp, Amsterdam 2 A2
Zuvuvu ✈, São Paulo 26 C1
Zwanenburg, Amsterdam 2 A1
Zwölfaxing, Vienna 31 B2
Zyuzino, Moscow 19 C3

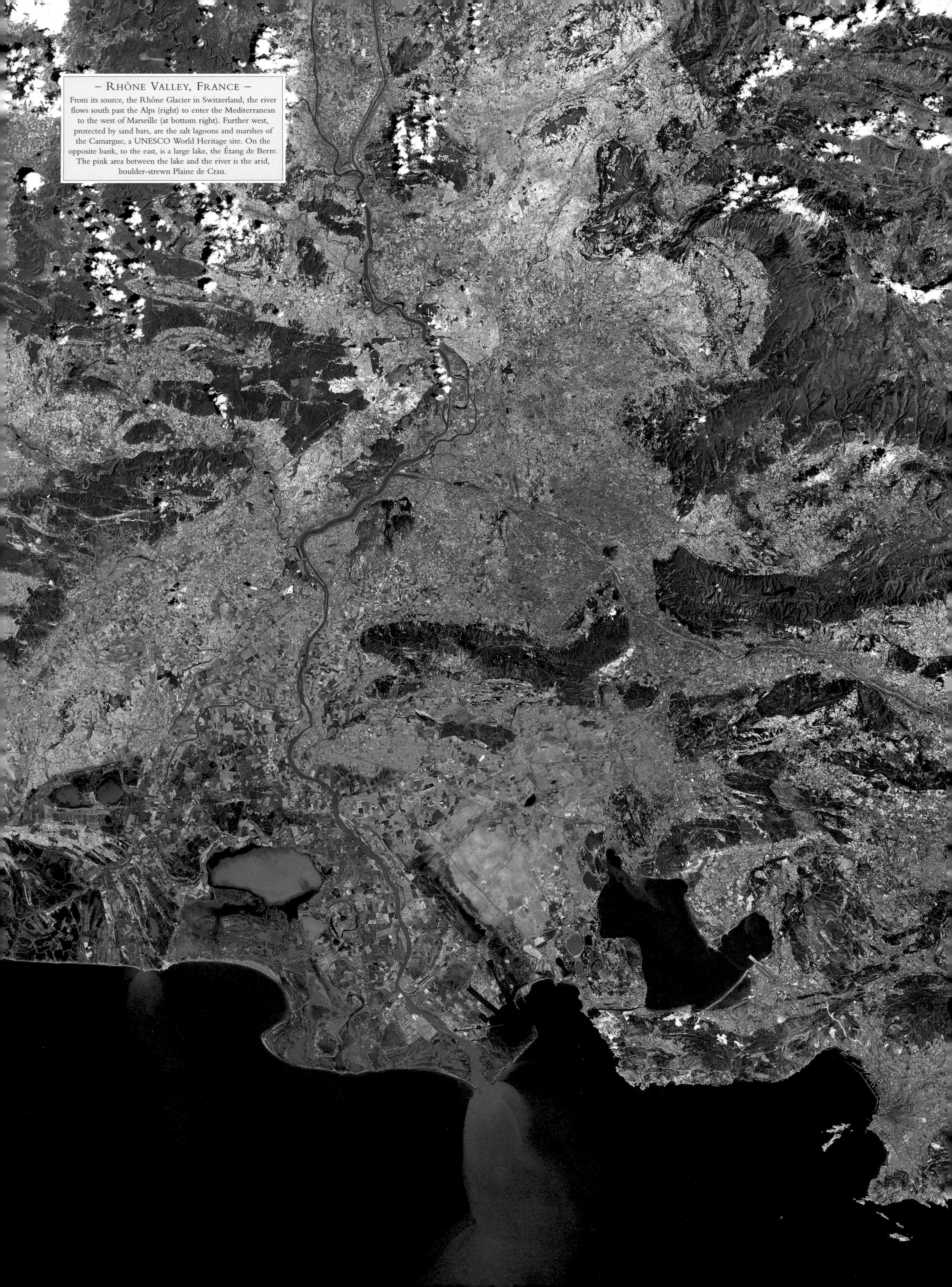

– Rhône Valley, France –

From its source, the Rhône Glacier in Switzerland, the river flows south past the Alps (right) to enter the Mediterranean to the west of Marseille (at bottom right). Further west, protected by sand bars, are the salt lagoons and marshes of the Camargue, a UNESCO World Heritage site. On the opposite bank, to the east, is a large lake, the Étang de Berre. The pink area between the lake and the river is the arid, boulder-strewn Plaine de Crau.

WORLD MAPS

SETTLEMENTS

PARIS · **Rotterdam** · **Livorno** · **Brugge** · Exeter · *Torremolinos* · *Oberammergau* · *Thira*

Settlement symbols and type styles vary according to the scale of each map and indicate the importance of towns on the map rather than specific population figures

Vaduz Capital cities have red infills

Urban agglomerations

Ruins or archaeological sites

Wells in desert

ADMINISTRATION

International boundaries

International boundaries (undefined or disputed)

Internal boundaries

National parks (*SNOWDONIA*)

PERU Country names

KENT Administrative area names

International boundaries show the *de facto* situation where there are rival claims to territory

COMMUNICATIONS

Motorways, freeways and expressways

Principal roads

Other roads

Road tunnels

Principal railways

Railways under construction

Other railways

Railway tunnels

LHR Principal airports (and location identifier)

Other airports

Principal canals

Passes

PHYSICAL FEATURES

Perennial streams

Intermittent streams

Perennial lakes

Intermittent lakes

Swamps and marshes

Permanent ice and glaciers

▲ 8850 Elevations in metres

▼ 8500 Sea depths in metres

1134 Height of lake surface above sea level in metres

ELEVATION AND DEPTH TINTS

Height of land above sea level

in metres	6000	4000	3000	2000	1500	1000	400	200	0
in feet	18 000	12 000	9000	6000	4500	3000	1200	600	

Land below sea level

Depth of sea

in feet		6000	12 000	15 000	18 000	24 000
in metres	0 / 200	2000	4000	5000	6000	8000

Some of the maps have different contours to highlight and clarify the principal relief features

Equatorial Scale 1:76 000 000

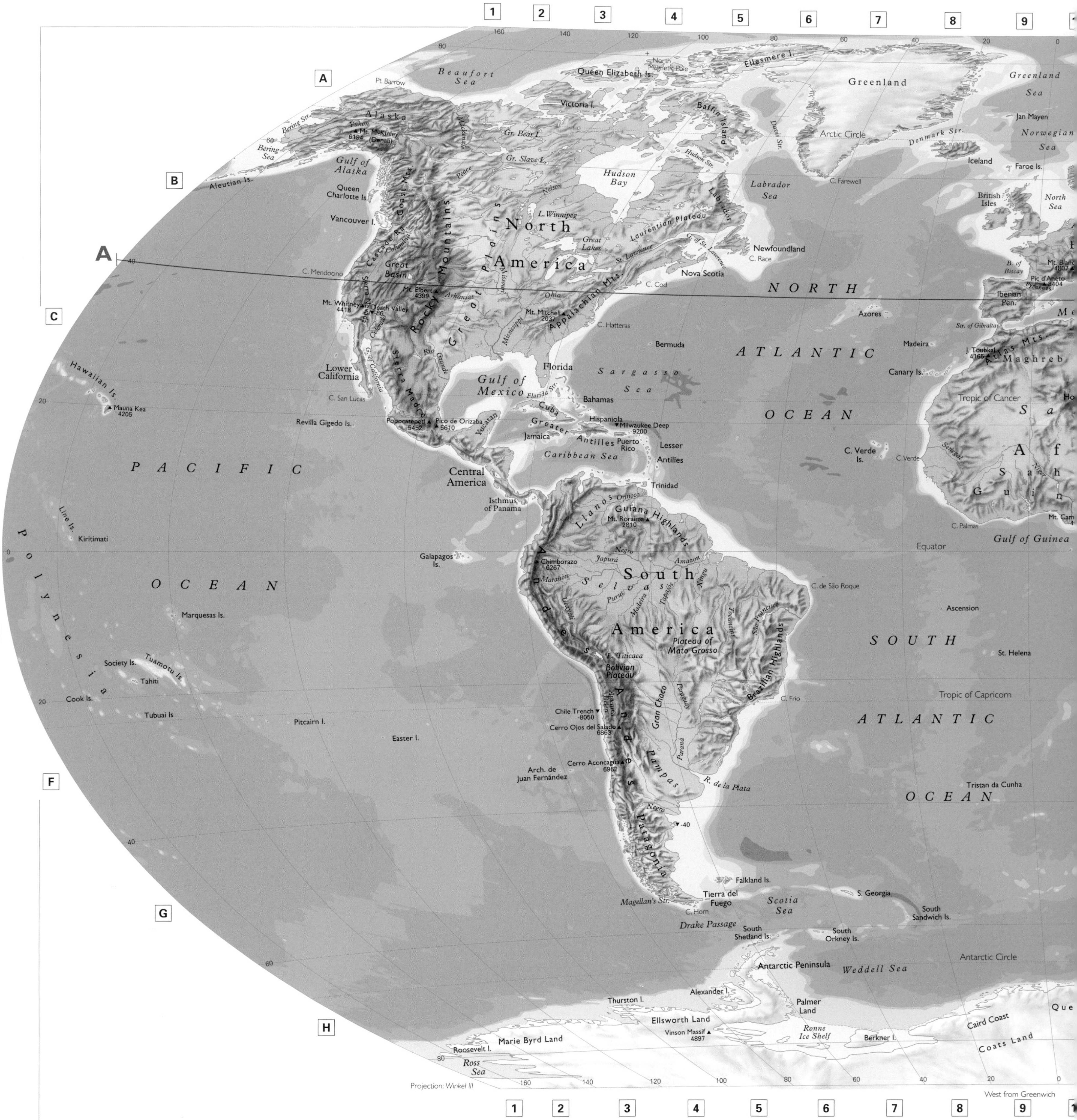
Beaufort Sea
Queen Elizabeth Is.
North Magnetic Pole
Ellesmere I.
Greenland
Greenland Sea
Pt. Barrow
Victoria I.
Baffin Island
Jan Mayen
Norwegian Sea
Bering Str.
Alaska
Mt. McKinley (Denali) 6194
Gr. Bear L.
Gr. Slave L.
Davis Str.
Arctic Circle
Denmark Str.
Iceland
Faroe Is.
Bering Sea
Gulf of Alaska
Aleutian Is.
Hudson Bay
Hudson Str.
Labrador Sea
C. Farewell
British Isles
North Sea
Queen Charlotte Is.
Labrador
L. Winnipeg
Vancouver I.
North America
Great Lakes
Laurentian Plateau
Newfoundland
C. Race
Rocky Mountains
Great Plains
Great Basin
Cascade Ra.
Coast Mts.
Sierra Nevada
C. Mendocino
St. Lawrence
Nova Scotia
C. Cod
Mt. Elbert 4399
Mt. Whitney 4418
Death Valley -86
Appalachian Mts.
Mt. Mitchell 2037
NORTH ATLANTIC OCEAN
B. of Biscay
Mt. Blanc 4807
Pic d'Aneto 3404
Pyrenees
Iberian Pen.
Azores
C. Hatteras
Str. of Gibraltar
Bermuda
Madeira
J. Toubkal 4165
Atlas Mts.
Maghreb
Canary Is.
Hawaiian Is.
Mauna Kea 4205
Lower California
G. of California
Sierra Madre
Rio Grande
Florida
Gulf of Mexico
Sargasso Sea
Bahamas
Cuba
C. San Lucas
Revilla Gigedo Is.
Popocatepetl 5452
Pico de Orizaba 5610
Yucatan
Greater Antilles
Hispaniola
Milwaukee Deep -9200
Puerto Rico
Jamaica
Caribbean Sea
Lesser Antilles
Tropic of Cancer
C. Verde Is.
C. Verde
Sahara
Africa
Guinea
Central America
Trinidad
Isthmus of Panama
PACIFIC OCEAN
Llanos
Orinoco
Guiana Highlands
Mt. Roraima 2810
Line Is.
Kiritimati
Polynesia
Galapagos Is.
Chimborazo 6267
Amazon
Negro
Japurá
South America
Selvas
Equator
Gulf of Guinea
C. Palmas
Mt. Cam
C. de São Roque
Ascension
Marquesas Is.
Madeira
Tapajós
Xingu
Purus
Tocantins
São Francisco
Plateau of Mato Grosso
Bolivian Plateau
L. Titicaca
Brazilian Highlands
SOUTH ATLANTIC OCEAN
St. Helena
Society Is.
Tuamotu Is.
Tahiti
Cook Is.
Tubuai Is.
Pitcairn I.
Easter I.
Chile Trench -8050
Cerro Ojos del Salado 6863
Gran Chaco
Paraná
C. Frio
Tropic of Capricorn
Andes
Pampas
Cerro Aconcagua 6962
Arch. de Juan Fernández
R. de la Plata
Tristan da Cunha
Patagonia
-40
Falkland Is.
Tierra del Fuego
Magellan's Str.
C. Horn
Scotia Sea
S. Georgia
South Sandwich Is.
Drake Passage
South Shetland Is.
South Orkney Is.
Antarctic Peninsula
Weddell Sea
Antarctic Circle
Alexander I.
Thurston I.
Palmer Land
Ellsworth Land
Vinson Massif 4897
Ronne Ice Shelf
Berkner I.
Caird Coast
Coats Land
Marie Byrd Land
Roosevelt I.
Ross Sea
Projection: Winkel III
West from Greenwich

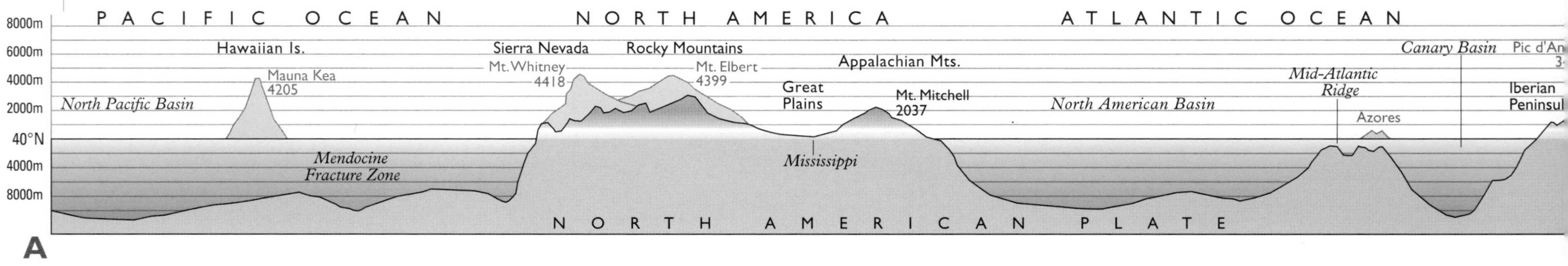
8000m
6000m
4000m
2000m
40°N
4000m
8000m
PACIFIC OCEAN
NORTH AMERICA
ATLANTIC OCEAN
Hawaiian Is.
Mauna Kea 4205
North Pacific Basin
Sierra Nevada
Mt. Whitney 4418
Rocky Mountains
Mt. Elbert 4399
Great Plains
Appalachian Mts.
Mt. Mitchell 2037
Mississippi
North American Basin
Mid-Atlantic Ridge
Azores
Canary Basin
Iberian Peninsul
Mendocino Fracture Zone
NORTH AMERICAN PLATE
A

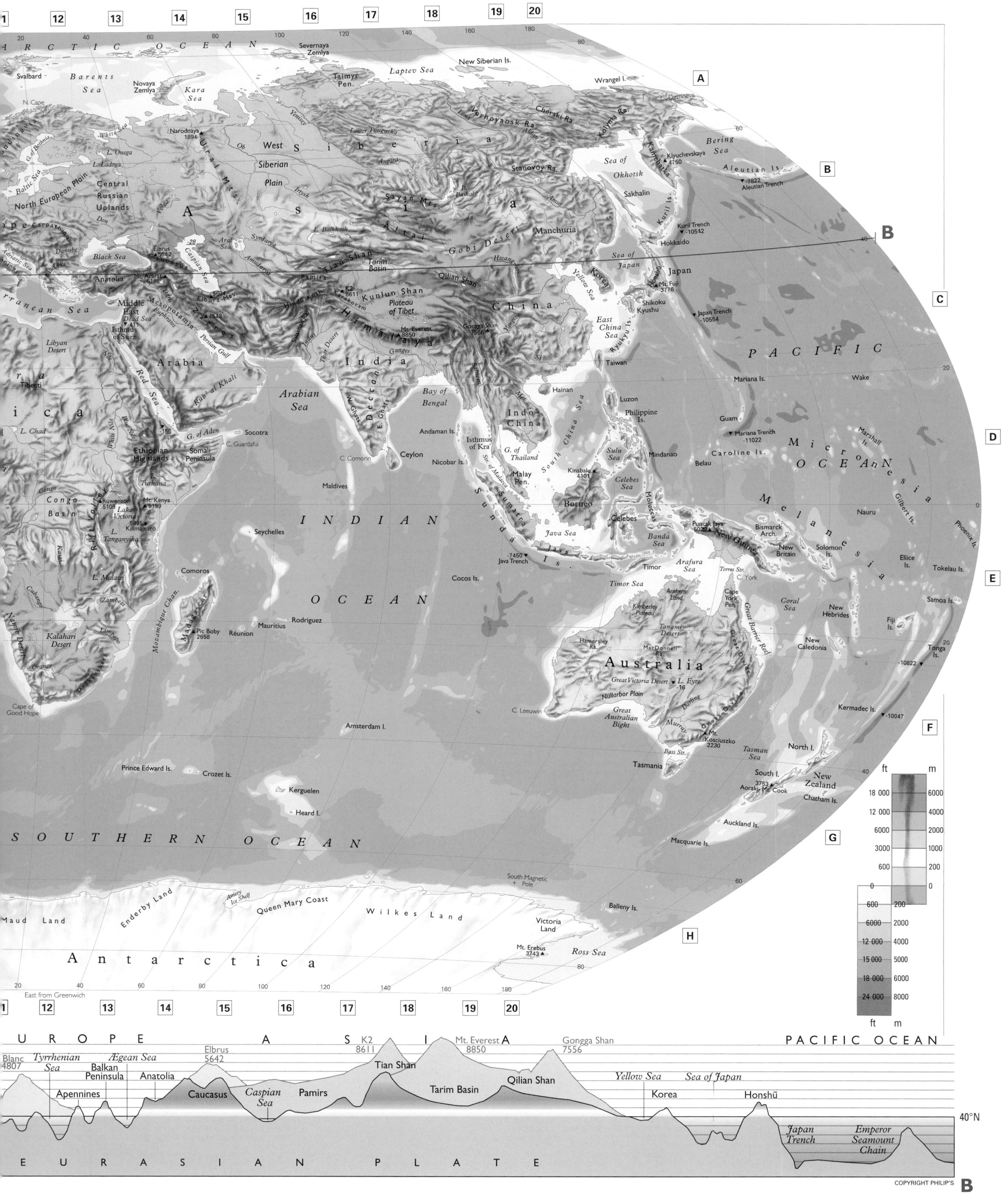

11
12
13
14
15
16
17
18
19
20
A
B
C
D
E
F
G
H
A R C T I C O C E A N
Svalbard
Barents Sea
Novaya Zemlya
Kara Sea
Severnaya Zemlya
Taimyr Pen.
Laptev Sea
New Siberian Is.
Wrangel I.
C. Dezhneva
N. Cape
White Sea
G. of Bothnia
L. Onega
L. Ladoga
Baltic Sea
North European Plain
Central Russian Uplands
Narodnaya 1894
Ural Mts.
West Siberian Plain
Ob
Yenisey
Lower Tunguska
Angara
Irtysh
S i b e r i a
A s i a
Verkhoyansk Ra.
Cherski Ra.
Kolyma Ra.
Lena
Aldan
Stanovoy Ra.
Sea of Okhotsk
Kamchatka
Klyuchevskaya 4750
Bering Sea
Aleutian Is.
-7822 Aleutian Trench
Sakhalin
Kuril Is.
Kuril Trench -10542
Hokkaido
Sayan Mts.
L. Baikal
Amur
Altai
Gobi Desert
Manchuria
L. Balkhash
Aral Sea
Syrdarya
Amudarya
Caspian Sea
-28
Black Sea
Carpathians
Danube
Adriatic Sea
Balkans
Elbrus 5642
Caucasus
Anatolia
Mt. Ararat 5165
Elburz Mts.
5604
Tian Shan
Tarim Basin
Pamirs
Hindu Kush
K2 8611
Karakoram
Kunlun Shan
Plateau of Tibet
Qilian Shan
Hwang Ho
Sea of Japan
Korea
Yellow Sea
Honshu
Japan
Mt. Fuji 3776
Shikoku
Kyushu
Japan Trench -10554
Middle East
Dead Sea -411
Isthmus of Suez
Mesopotamia
Euphrates
Tigris
Zagros
4548
Persian Gulf
Himalaya
Mt. Everest 8850
Gongga Shan 7556
China
Yangtze
East China Sea
Ryukyu Is.
Taiwan
Indus
Thar Desert
Ganges
India
Arabia
Rub' al Khali
Red Sea
Arabian Sea
Bay of Bengal
Deccan
W. Ghats
E. Ghats
Ceylon
C. Comorin
Maldives
Andaman Is.
Nicobar Is.
Isthmus of Kra
G. of Thailand
Malay Pen.
Indo-China
Mekong
Salween
Hainan
South China Sea
Luzon
Philippine Is.
Sulu Sea
Mindanao
Kinabalu 4101
Borneo
Celebes Sea
Celebes
Moluccas
Sumatra
Str. of Malacca
Java Sea
Banda Sea
Sunda Is.
-7450 Java Trench
Timor
Arafura Sea
Puncak Jaya 5029
New Guinea
Bismarck Arch.
New Britain
Solomon Is.
Nauru
P A C I F I C O C E A N
Mariana Is.
Guam
Mariana Trench -11022
Wake
Micronesia
Marshall Is.
Caroline Is.
Belau
Melanesia
Gilbert Is.
Phoenix Is.
Ellice Is.
Tokelau Is.
Samoa Is.
Fiji Is.
Tonga Is.
-10822
Libyan Desert
Tibesti
Sahara
Africa
L. Chad
Nile
White Nile
Blue Nile
Ethiopian Highlands
-156
G. of Aden
Socotra
C. Guardafui
Somali Peninsula
L. Turkana
Congo
Congo Basin
Ruwenzori 5109
Lake Victoria
Mt. Kenya 5199
Kilimanjaro 5895
L. Tanganyika
Rift Valley
Kasai
L. Malawi
Zambezi
Cubango
Kalahari Desert
Limpopo
Namib Desert
Orange
Drakensberg
Cape of Good Hope
Mozambique Chan.
Madagascar
Pic Boby 2658
Comoros
Seychelles
Réunion
Mauritius
Rodriguez
I N D I A N O C E A N
Cocos Is.
Amsterdam I.
Prince Edward Is.
Crozet Is.
Kerguelen
Heard I.
Timor Sea
Torres Str.
C. York
Cape York Pen.
Arnhem Land
Kimberley Plateau
Tanami Desert
Hamersley Ra.
MacDonnell Ra.
Australia
Great Victoria Desert
L. Eyre -16
Nullarbor Plain
Great Australian Bight
Darling
Murray
Great Dividing Range
Great Barrier Reef
Mt. Kosciuszko 2230
Bass Str.
Tasmania
Tasman Sea
C. Leeuwin
Coral Sea
New Hebrides
New Caledonia
Kermadec Is.
-10047
North I.
South I.
New Zealand
Aoraki Mt. Cook 3753
Chatham Is.
Auckland Is.
Macquarie Is.
S O U T H E R N O C E A N
South Magnetic Pole
Maud Land
Enderby Land
Amery Ice Shelf
Queen Mary Coast
Wilkes Land
Victoria Land
Balleny Is.
Mt. Erebus 3743
Ross Sea
Antarctica
East from Greenwich
ft
m
18 000
12 000
6000
3000
600
0
6000
4000
2000
1000
200
0
600
6000
12 000
15 000
18 000
24 000
200
2000
4000
5000
6000
8000
EUROPE
ASIA
PACIFIC OCEAN
Blanc 4807
Tyrrhenian Sea
Ægean Sea
Balkan Peninsula
Apennines
Anatolia
Elbrus 5642
Caucasus
Caspian Sea
Pamirs
K2 8611
Tian Shan
Tarim Basin
Mt. Everest 8850
Qilian Shan
Gongga Shan 7556
Yellow Sea
Korea
Sea of Japan
Honshū
Japan Trench
Emperor Seamount Chain
40°N
E U R A S I A N P L A T E
B

THE WORLD : Political

Equatorial Scale 1·76 000 000

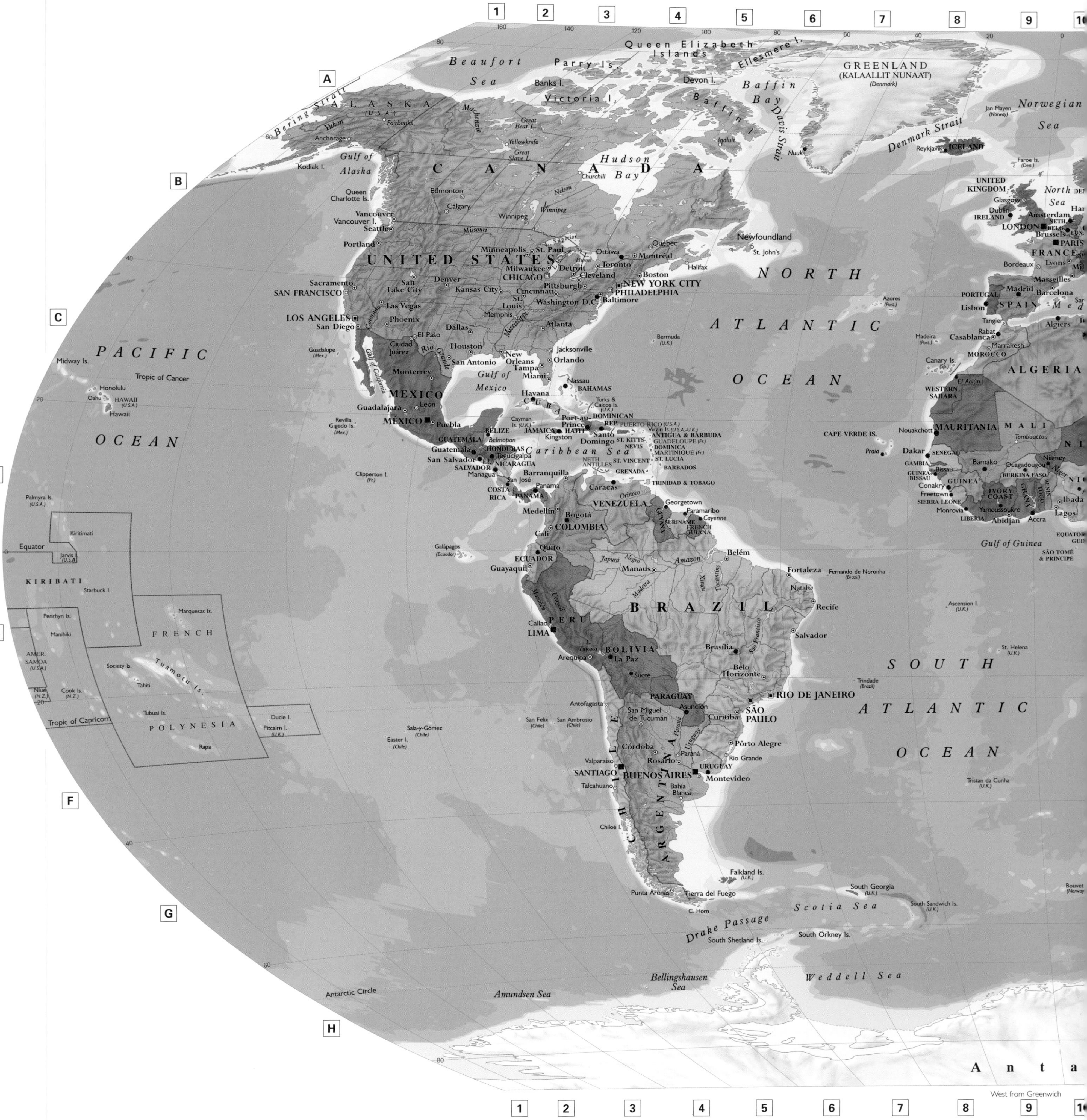

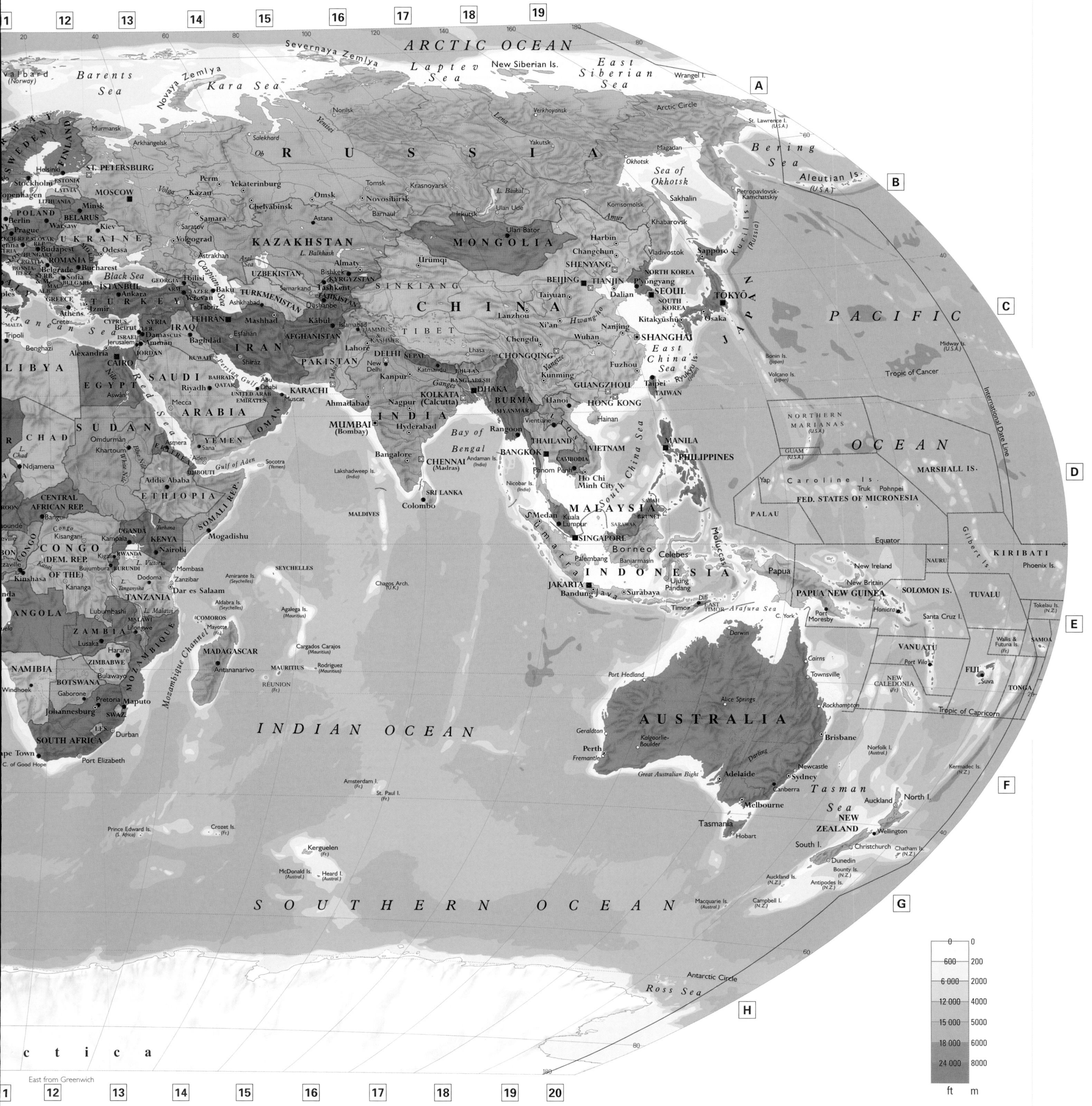
ARCTIC OCEAN
Severnaya Zemlya
Laptev Sea
New Siberian Is.
East Siberian Sea
Wrangel I.
Barents Sea
Novaya Zemlya
Kara Sea
Svalbard (Norway)
R U S S I A
Arctic Circle
Bering Sea
Aleutian Is. (U.S.A.)
Sea of Okhotsk
Sakhalin
Kuril Is. (Russia)
KAZAKHSTAN
MONGOLIA
C H I N A
SINKIANG
TIBET
ST. PETERSBURG
MOSCOW
Helsinki
Stockholm
Copenhagen
Berlin
Prague
Warsaw
Minsk
Kiev
UKRAINE
POLAND
BELARUS
Budapest
Bucharest
Belgrade
Sofia
Athens
ISTANBUL
Ankara
TURKEY
Black Sea
Caspian Sea
Aral Sea
UZBEKISTAN
TURKMENISTAN
TEHRAN
IRAN
IRAQ
Baghdad
SYRIA
Damascus
Beirut
Jerusalem
Amman
CAIRO
EGYPT
LIBYA
SAUDI ARABIA
Riyadh
Mecca
Persian Gulf
OMAN
YEMEN
Red Sea
SUDAN
Khartoum
CHAD
ETHIOPIA
Addis Ababa
SOMALI REP.
Mogadishu
KENYA
Nairobi
TANZANIA
Dar es Salaam
CONGO (DEM. REP. OF THE)
Kinshasa
ANGOLA
ZAMBIA
Lusaka
ZIMBABWE
Harare
MOZAMBIQUE
Maputo
BOTSWANA
NAMIBIA
Windhoek
SOUTH AFRICA
Pretoria
Johannesburg
Durban
Cape Town
Port Elizabeth
C. of Good Hope
MADAGASCAR
Antananarivo
Mozambique Channel
AFGHANISTAN
Kabul
PAKISTAN
Karachi
DELHI
INDIA
MUMBAI (Bombay)
KOLKATA (Calcutta)
CHENNAI (Madras)
Bangalore
Hyderabad
SRI LANKA
Colombo
Bay of Bengal
BURMA (MYANMAR)
Rangoon
DHAKA
THAILAND
BANGKOK
VIETNAM
Hanoi
Ho Chi Minh City
CAMBODIA
MALAYSIA
Kuala Lumpur
SINGAPORE
INDONESIA
JAKARTA
Borneo
Celebes
PHILIPPINES
MANILA
South China Sea
HONG KONG
GUANGZHOU
TAIWAN
Taipei
SHANGHAI
BEIJING
TIANJIN
NORTH KOREA
P'yongyang
SEOUL
SOUTH KOREA
JAPAN
TOKYO
Osaka
Sapporo
PACIFIC OCEAN
Tropic of Cancer
International Date Line
NORTHERN MARIANAS (U.S.A.)
GUAM (U.S.A.)
MARSHALL IS.
FED. STATES OF MICRONESIA
Caroline Is.
PALAU
Equator
NAURU
KIRIBATI
Phoenix Is.
PAPUA NEW GUINEA
Port Moresby
SOLOMON IS.
Honiara
TUVALU
VANUATU
Port Vila
NEW CALEDONIA (Fr.)
FIJI
Suva
TONGA
SAMOA
Tropic of Capricorn
AUSTRALIA
Darwin
Cairns
Townsville
Alice Springs
Rockhampton
Brisbane
Perth
Great Australian Bight
Adelaide
Newcastle
Sydney
Canberra
Melbourne
Tasmania
Hobart
Tasman Sea
NEW ZEALAND
Auckland
Wellington
Christchurch
Dunedin
North I.
South I.
INDIAN OCEAN
SEYCHELLES
MALDIVES
MAURITIUS
RÉUNION (Fr.)
Kerguelen (Fr.)
SOUTHERN OCEAN
Ross Sea
Antarctic Circle
A
B
C
D
E
F
G
H
11 12 13 14 15 16 17 18 19 20
East from Greenwich
0 0
600 200
6 000 2000
12 000 4000
15 000 5000
18 000 6000
24 000 8000
ft m

100 0 200 400 600 800 1000 1200 1400 km

100 0 200 400 600 800 1000 miles

1:28 000 000

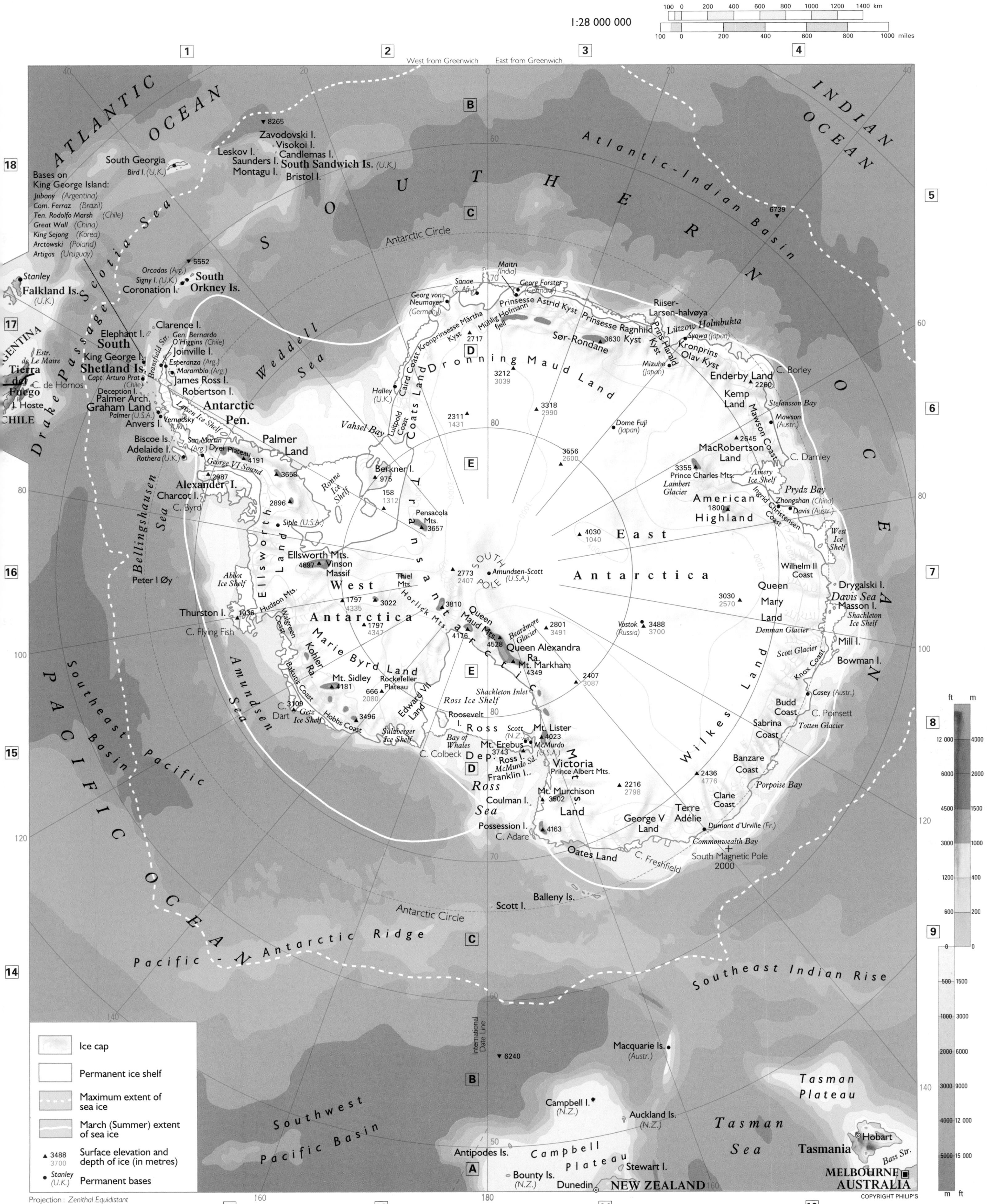

The Antarctic Treaty was signed in Washington in 1959 so that scientific and technical research could continue unhampered by international politics.

All territorial claims covering land areas south of latitude 60°S have been suspended. Those claims were:

Norwegian claim (Dronning Maud Land)	45°E - 20°W	French claim (Terre Adélie)	136°E - 142°E	British claim	80°W - 20°W
Australian claims	45°E - 136°E 142°E - 160°E	New Zealand claim (Ross Dependency)	160°E - 150°W	Argentine claim	74°W - 53°W
				Chilean claim	90°W - 53°W

Equatorial Scale 1:41 000 000

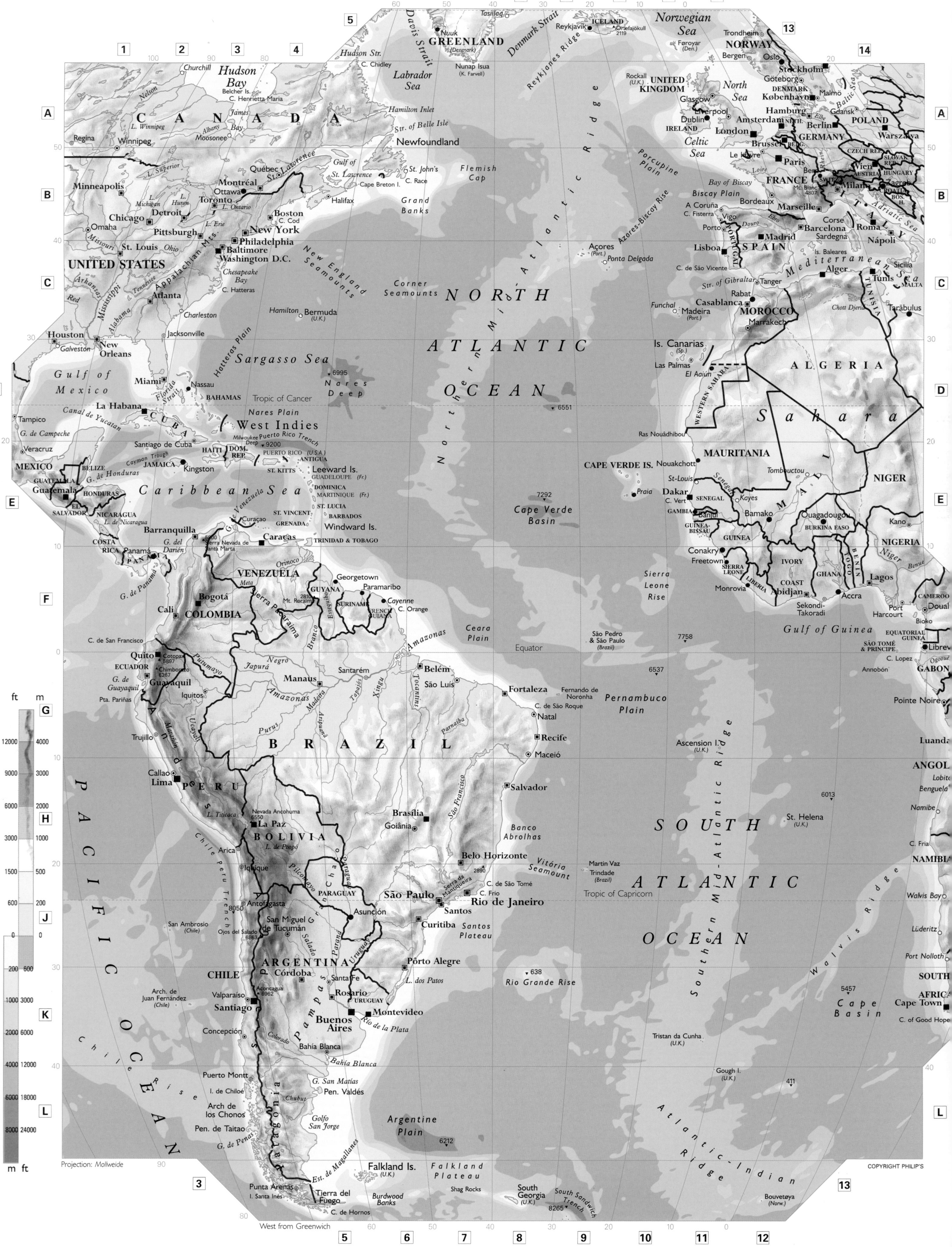

GREENLAND
Nuuk
Tasiilaq
Davis Strait
Denmark Strait
ICELAND
Reykjavík
Norwegian Sea
Labrador Sea
Hudson Bay
Hudson Str.
C A N A D A
Winnipeg
Regina
Churchill
Moosonee
Hamilton Inlet
Str. of Belle Isle
Newfoundland
St. John's
C. Race
Gulf of St. Lawrence
Halifax
Québec
Montréal
Ottawa
Toronto
Flemish Cap
Grand Banks
Reykjanes Ridge
North Atlantic Ridge
NORWAY
Oslo
Bergen
Trondheim
Stockholm
Göteborg
København
Malmö
Føroyar (Den.)
Rockall (U.K.)
UNITED KINGDOM
North Sea
Baltic Sea
Glasgow
Liverpool
Dublin
IRELAND
London
Amsterdam
Hamburg
Berlin
Gdansk
POLAND
Warszawa
GERMANY
Brussel
Celtic Sea
Le Havre
Paris
FRANCE
Porcupine Plain
Bay of Biscay
Biscay Plain
Bordeaux
Marseille
Milano
Roma
Nápoli
Corse
Sardegna
Sicilia
Barcelona
Madrid
SPAIN
PORTUGAL
Lisboa
Porto
Vigo
A Coruña
C. Fisterra
Azores-Biscay Rise
Açores (Port.)
Ponta Delgada
Mediterranean Sea
Alger
Tunis
Tarābulus
TUNISIA
ALGERIA
Str. of Gibraltar
Tanger
Rabat
Casablanca
MOROCCO
Marrakech
Funchal
Madeira (Port.)
Is. Canarias (Sp.)
Las Palmas
El Aaiún
WESTERN SAHARA
Sahara
Minneapolis
Chicago
Detroit
Omaha
Pittsburgh
Boston
C. Cod
New York
Philadelphia
Baltimore
Washington D.C.
St. Louis
UNITED STATES
Chesapeake Bay
C. Hatteras
Atlanta
Charleston
Jacksonville
Houston
Galveston
New Orleans
Miami
Nassau
BAHAMAS
Hamilton
Bermuda (U.K.)
New England Seamounts
Corner Seamounts
NORTH ATLANTIC OCEAN
Sargasso Sea
Hatteras Plain
Nares Deep
Tropic of Cancer
Nares Plain
Gulf of Mexico
Tampico
G. de Campeche
Veracruz
MEXICO
La Habana
CUBA
Canal de Yucatan
Santiago de Cuba
Cayman Trough
JAMAICA
Kingston
HAITI
DOM. REP.
PUERTO RICO (U.S.A.)
Puerto Rico Trench
West Indies
Leeward Is.
Windward Is.
BARBADOS
TRINIDAD & TOBAGO
Caribbean Sea
BELIZE
G. de Honduras
GUATEMALA
Guatemala
HONDURAS
EL SALVADOR
NICARAGUA
L. de Nicaragua
COSTA RICA
Panamá
PANAMA
Barranquilla
Curaçao
Caracas
VENEZUELA
Orinoco
Georgetown
Paramaribo
Cayenne
GUYANA
SURINAME
FRENCH GUIANA
C. Orange
Bogotá
Cali
COLOMBIA
Quito
ECUADOR
Guayaquil
G. de Guayaquil
Pta. Pariñas
Iquitos
Manaus
Santarém
Belém
São Luís
Amazonas
Fortaleza
Fernando de Noronha
C. de São Roque
Natal
Recife
Maceió
Salvador
B R A Z I L
Brasília
Goiânia
Belo Horizonte
Vitória Seamount
Martin Vaz
Trindade (Brazil)
Rio de Janeiro
C. Frio
São Paulo
Santos
Curitiba
Santos Plateau
Pôrto Alegre
L. dos Patos
Montevideo
URUGUAY
Río de la Plata
Buenos Aires
Rosario
Santa Fe
Córdoba
ARGENTINA
Pampas
Asunción
PARAGUAY
San Miguel de Tucumán
Bahía Blanca
G. San Matías
Pen. Valdés
Golfo San Jorge
Argentine Plain
Falkland Is. (U.K.)
Falkland Plateau
Shag Rocks
Burdwood Banks
South Georgia (U.K.)
South Sandwich Trench
Tierra del Fuego
C. de Hornos
Punta Arenas
Est. de Magallanes
Patagonia
Puerto Montt
I. de Chiloé
Arch de los Chonos
Pen. de Taitao
G. de Penas
Concepción
Santiago
Valparaíso
CHILE
Arch. de Juan Fernández (Chile)
San Ambrosio (Chile)
Antofagasta
Iquique
Arica
Chile Peru Trench
Chile Rise
BOLIVIA
La Paz
L. Titicaca
PERU
Lima
Callao
Trujillo
PACIFIC OCEAN
Equator
Tropic of Capricorn
Ceara Plain
Pernambuco Plain
São Pedro & São Paulo (Brazil)
Sierra Leone Rise
Gulf of Guinea
CAPE VERDE IS.
Praia
Cape Verde Basin
MAURITANIA
Nouakchott
Ras Nouâdhibou
Dakar
C. Vert
SENEGAL
GAMBIA
Banjul
GUINEA-BISSAU
GUINEA
Conakry
Freetown
SIERRA LEONE
LIBERIA
Monrovia
IVORY COAST
Abidjan
GHANA
Accra
TOGO
BENIN
Lagos
NIGERIA
Kano
NIGER
MALI
Tombouctou
Bamako
Kayes
BURKINA FASO
Ouagadougou
Sekondi-Takoradi
Port Harcourt
EQUATORIAL GUINEA
SÃO TOMÉ & PRÍNCIPE
Annobón
C. Lopez
GABON
Libreville
Pointe Noire
Luanda
ANGOLA
Lobito
Benguela
Namibe
C. Fria
NAMIBIA
Walvis Bay
Walvis Ridge
Lüderitz
Port Nolloth
SOUTH AFRICA
Cape Town
C. of Good Hope
Cape Basin
Ascension I. (U.K.)
St. Helena (U.K.)
SOUTH ATLANTIC OCEAN
Southern Mid-Atlantic Ridge
Banco Abrolhas
Rio Grande Rise
Tristan da Cunha (U.K.)
Gough I. (U.K.)
Atlantic-Indian Ridge
Bouvetøya (Norw.)
Projection: Mollweide
West from Greenwich
COPYRIGHT PHILIP'S

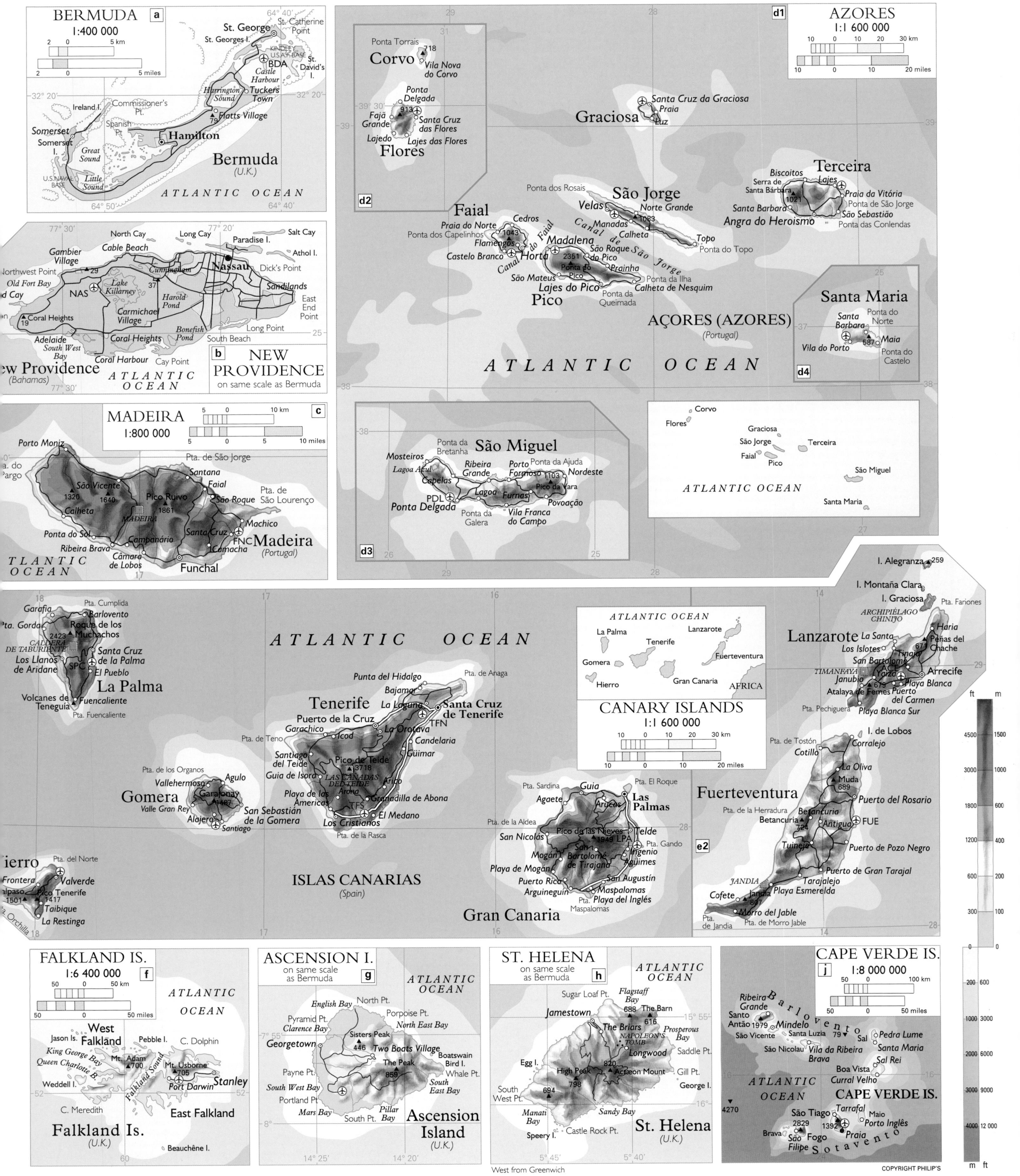
BERMUDA a
1:400 000
St. George
St. Georges I.
St. Catherine Point
KINDLEY USAF BASE
BDA
St. David's I.
Castle Harbour
Harrington Sound
Tuckers Town
Flatts Village
Ireland I.
Commissioner's Pt.
Spanish Pt.
Somerset
Somerset I.
Hamilton
Great Sound
Little Sound
U.S. NAVAL BASE
Bermuda
(U.K.)
ATLANTIC OCEAN
NEW PROVIDENCE b
on same scale as Bermuda
North Cay
Long Cay
Salt Cay
Paradise I.
Athol I.
Cable Beach
Gambier Village
Cunningham
Nassau
Dick's Point
Northwest Point
Old Fort Bay
Lake Killarney
NAS
Sandilands
East End Point
Coral Heights
Harold Pond
Carmichael Village
Long Point
Adelaide
South West Bay
Coral Harbour
Cay Point
Bonefish Pond
South Beach
New Providence
(Bahamas)
ATLANTIC OCEAN
MADEIRA c
1:800 000
Porto Moniz
Pta. de São Jorge
Santana
Faial
São Vicente
Pico Ruivo
1861
São Roque
Pta. de São Lourenço
Calheta
Machico
Ponta do Sol
Campanário
Santa Cruz
FNC
Madeira
(Portugal)
Ribeira Brava
Câmara de Lobos
Camacha
Funchal
ATLANTIC OCEAN
AZORES d1
1:1 600 000
Corvo
Ponta Torrais
Vila Nova do Corvo
Ponta Delgada
Fajã Grande
Santa Cruz das Flores
Lajedo
Lajes das Flores
Flores
d2
Graciosa
Santa Cruz da Graciosa
Praia
Luz
Terceira
Biscoitos
Serra de Santa Bárbara
Lajes
Praia da Vitória
Ponta de São Jorge
Santa Barbara
São Sebastião
Angra do Heroísmo
Ponta das Contendas
Ponta dos Rosais
São Jorge
Velas
Norte Grande
Manadas
Calheta
Topo
Ponta do Topo
Canal de São Jorge
Faial
Praia do Norte
Cedros
Ponta dos Capelinhos
Flamengos
Castelo Branco
Horta
Canal do Faial
Madalena
São Roque do Pico
Prainha
Ponta do Pico
2351
São Mateus
Lajes do Pico
Ponta da Ilha
Calheta de Nesquim
Ponta da Queimada
Pico
AÇORES (AZORES)
(Portugal)
Santa Maria
Santa Barbara
Ponta do Norte
Vila do Porto
Maia
Ponta do Castelo
d4
ATLANTIC OCEAN
São Miguel
Ponta da Bretanha
Mosteiros
Lagoa Azul
Ribeira Grande
Porto Formoso
Ponta da Ajuda
Nordeste
Capelas
Pico da Vara
PDL
Ponta Delgada
Lagoa
Furnas
Povoação
Ponta da Galera
Vila Franca do Campo
d3
ATLANTIC OCEAN
CANARY ISLANDS
1:1 600 000
La Palma
Lanzarote
Tenerife
Gomera
Fuerteventura
Hierro
Gran Canaria
AFRICA
I. Alegranza
I. Montaña Clara
I. Graciosa
ARCHIPIÉLAGO CHINIJO
Pta. Fariones
Haria
Peñas del Chache
La Santa
Los Islotes
Tinajo
San Bartolomé
TIMANFAYA
Janubio
Arrecife
Yaiza
ACE
Playa Blanca
Atalaya de Femes
Puerto del Carmen
Pta. Pechiguera
Playa Blanca Sur
Garafía
Pta. Cumplida
Barlovento
Pta. Gorda
Roque de los Muchachos
CALDERA DE TABURIENTE
Santa Cruz de la Palma
Los Llanos de Aridane
SPC
El Pueblo
La Palma
Volcanes de Teneguía
Fuencaliente
Pta. Fuencaliente
ATLANTIC OCEAN
Punta del Hidalgo
Bajamar
Pta. de Anaga
La Laguna
Santa Cruz de Tenerife
Tenerife
Puerto de la Cruz
Garachico
La Orotava
TFN
Icod
Candelaria
Pta. de Teno
Santiago del Teide
Güímar
Pico de Teide
3718
Guía de Isora
LAS CAÑADAS DEL TEIDE
Playa de las Americas
Arico
Arona
Granadilla de Abona
TFS
Los Cristianos
El Medano
Pta. de la Rasca
Pta. de los Organos
Agulo
Vallehermoso
Garajonay
1487
Gomera
Valle Gran Rey
Alajeró
San Sebastián de la Gomera
Santiago
Pta. Sardina
Guía
Pta. El Roque
Agaete
Arucas
Las Palmas
Pta. de la Aldea
San Nicolás
Pico de las Nieves
1949
LPA
Telde
Pta. Gando
Mogán
San Bartolomé de Tirajana
Ingenio
Agüimes
Playa de Mogán
San Agustín
Puerto Rico
Arguineguín
Maspalomas
Playa del Inglés
Pta. Maspalomas
Gran Canaria
ISLAS CANARIAS
(Spain)
Hierro
Pta. del Norte
Frontera
Valverde
Pico Tenerife
1501
1417
Taibique
La Restinga
Pta. Orchilla
I. de Lobos
Corralejo
Pta. de Tostón
Cotillo
La Oliva
Muda
689
Fuerteventura
Puerto del Rosario
Pta. de la Herradura
Betancuria
Antigua
FUE
Tuineje
Puerto de Pozo Negro
Puerto de Gran Tarajal
Tarajalejo
JANDIA
Playa Esmerelda
Cofete
Jandia
Morro del Jable
Pta. de Jandia
Pta. de Morro Jable
e2
FALKLAND IS. f
1:6 400 000
ATLANTIC OCEAN
West Falkland
Jason Is.
Pebble I.
C. Dolphin
King George Bay
Queen Charlotte B.
Mt. Adam
700
Mt. Usborne
705
Falkland Sound
Weddell I.
Port Darwin
Stanley
C. Meredith
East Falkland
Falkland Is.
(U.K.)
Beauchêne I.
ASCENSION I. g
on same scale as Bermuda
ATLANTIC OCEAN
English Bay
North Pt.
Porpoise Pt.
Pyramid Pt.
Clarence Bay
North East Bay
Sisters Peak
446
Georgetown
Two Boats Village
Boatswain Bird I.
The Peak
859
Payne Pt.
Whale Pt.
South West Bay
South East Bay
Portland Pt.
Mars Bay
Pillar Bay
South Pt.
Ascension Island
(U.K.)
ST. HELENA h
on same scale as Bermuda
ATLANTIC OCEAN
Sugar Loaf Pt.
Flagstaff Bay
688
The Barn
616
Jamestown
The Briars
NAPOLEON'S TOMB
Prosperous Bay
Longwood
Saddle Pt.
Egg I.
820
High Peak
Actæon Mount
798
Gill Pt.
George I.
694
South West Pt.
Sandy Bay
Manati Bay
Speery I.
Castle Rock Pt.
St. Helena
(U.K.)
West from Greenwich
CAPE VERDE IS. j
1:8 000 000
Ribeira Grande
Santo Antão
1979
Mindelo
Barlovento
São Vicente
Santa Luzia
Sal
Pedra Lume
São Nicolau
Vila da Ribeira Brava
Santa Maria
Sal Rei
Boa Vista
ATLANTIC OCEAN
Curral Velho
CAPE VERDE IS.
4270
Tarrafal
São Tiago
2829
Maio
1392
Porto Inglês
Brava
São Filipe
Fogo
Praia
Sotavento
COPYRIGHT PHILIP'S
ft m
4500 1500
3000 1000
1800 600
1200 400
600 200
300 100
0 0
200 600
1000 3000
2000 6000
3000 9000
4000 12 000
m ft

GREENLAND

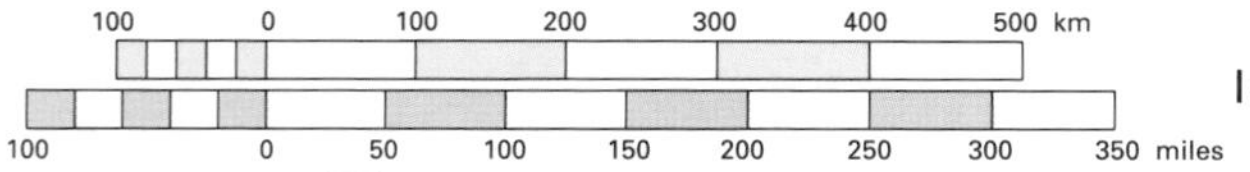
100 0 100 200 300 400 500 km
100 0 50 100 150 200 250 300 350 miles

1:10 000 000

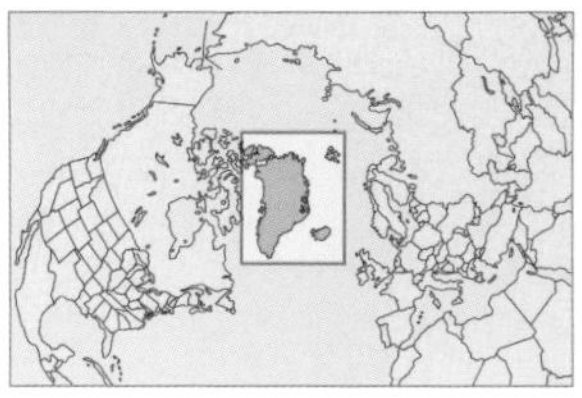

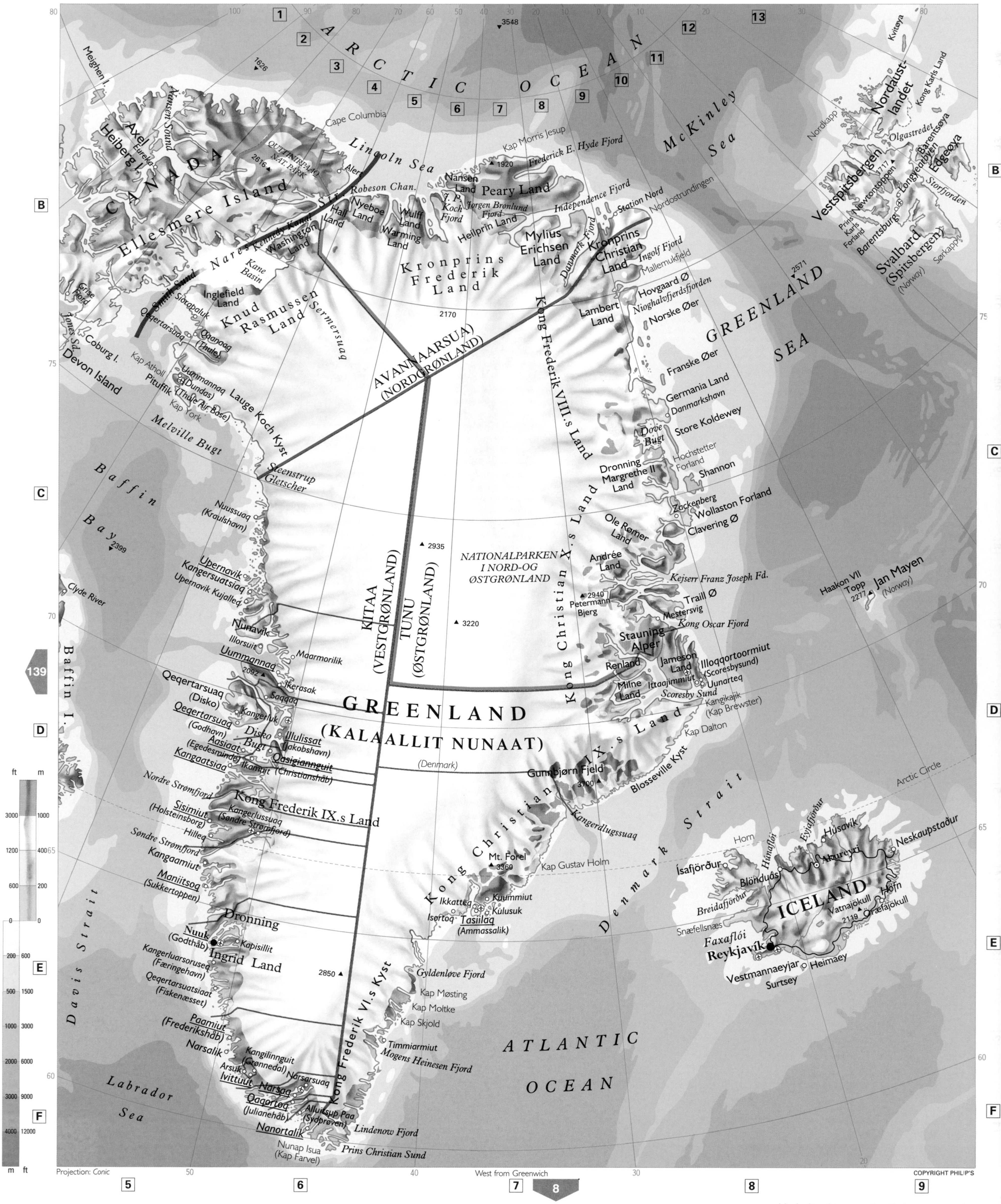
A
6
ARCTIC OCEAN
McKinley Sea
GREENLAND SEA
Lincoln Sea
Cape Columbia
Kap Morris Jesup
Frederick E. Hyde Fjord
Peary Land
Nansen Land
J. P. Koch Fjord
Jørgen Brønlund Fjord
Heilprin Land
Independence Fjord
Station Nord
Nordostrundingen
Mylius Erichsen Land
Danmark Fjord
Kronprins Christian Land
Ingolf Fjord
Mallemukfjeld
Kronprins Frederik Land
Wulff Land
Warming Land
Nyeboe Land
Hall Land
Washington Land
Robeson Chan.
Kennedy Kanal
Nares Strait
Kane Basin
Smith Sund
Inglefield Land
Knud Rasmussen Land
Sermersuaq
Siorapaluk
Qeqertarsuaq
Qaanaaq (Thule)
Kap Atholl
Uummannaq (Dundas)
Pituffik (Thule Air Base)
Kap York
Lauge Koch Kyst
Melville Bugt
Steenstrup Gletscher
AVANNAARSUA (NORDGRØNLAND)
Kong Frederik VIII.s Land
Lambert Land
Hovgaard Ø
Nioghalvfjerdsfjorden
Norske Øer
Franske Øer
Germania Land
Danmarkshavn
Store Koldewey
Dove Bugt
Hochstetter Forland
Shannon
Dronning Margrethe II Land
Zackenberg
Wollaston Forland
Clavering Ø
Ole Rømer Land
Andrée Land
Kejserr Franz Joseph Fd.
NATIONALPARKEN I NORD-OG ØSTGRØNLAND
Kong Christian X.s Land
Petermann Bjerg
Traill Ø
Mestersvig
Kong Oscar Fjord
Stauning Alper
Renland
Jameson Land
Milne Land
Illoqqortoormiut (Scoresbysund)
Ittaajimmiut
Uunarteq
Scoresby Sund
Kangikajik (Kap Brewster)
Kap Dalton
Kong Christian IX.s Land
Gunnbjørn Fjeld
Blosseville Kyst
Kangerdlugssuaq
Mt. Forel
Kap Gustav Holm
Kuummiut
Kulusuk
Ikkatteq
Isortoq
Tasiilaq (Ammassalik)
Denmark Strait
Arctic Circle
KITAA (VESTGRØNLAND)
TUNU (ØSTGRØNLAND)
GREENLAND (KALAALLIT NUNAAT)
(Denmark)
Nuussuaq (Kraulshavn)
Upernavik
Kangersuatsiaq
Upernavik Kujalleq
Nuugaatsiaq
Illorsuit
Maarmorilik
Uummannaq
Ikerasak
Saqqaq
Qeqertarsuaq (Disko)
Kangerluk
Disko Bugt
Qeqertarsuaq (Godhavn)
Ilulissat (Jakobshavn)
Aasiaat (Egedesminde)
Qasigiannguit (Christianshåb)
Ikamiut
Kangaatsiaq
Nordre Strømfjord
Kong Frederik IX.s Land
Sisimiut (Holsteinsborg)
Kangerlussuaq (Søndre Strømfjord)
Hilleq
Søndre Strømfjord
Kangaamiut
Maniitsoq (Sukkertoppen)
Dronning Ingrid Land
Nuuk (Godthåb)
Kapisillit
Kangerluarsoruseq (Færingehavn)
Qeqertarsuatsiaat (Fiskenæsset)
Paamiut (Frederikshåb)
Narsalik
Arsuk
Kangilinnguit (Grønnedal)
Ivittuut
Narsarsuaq
Narsaq
Qaqortoq (Julianehåb)
Alluitsup Paa (Sydprøven)
Nanortalik
Nunap Isua (Kap Farvel)
Prins Christian Sund
Lindenow Fjord
Kong Frederik VI.s Kyst
Gyldenløve Fjord
Kap Møsting
Kap Moltke
Kap Skjold
Timmiarmiut
Mogens Heinesen Fjord
ATLANTIC OCEAN
Labrador Sea
Davis Strait
Baffin Bay
Baffin I.
Clyde River
Devon Island
Coburg I.
Jones Sd.
Grise Fiord
Ellesmere Island
CANADA
Axel Heiberg I.
Eureka
Nansen Sund
Meighen I.
Alert
QUTTINIRPAAQ NAT. PARK
ICELAND
Reykjavík
Ísafjörður
Blönduós
Akureyri
Húsavík
Neskaupstaður
Höfn
Vatnajökull
Öræfajökull
Húnaflói
Eyjafjörður
Horn
Breidafjörður
Snæfellsnæs
Faxaflói
Vestmannaeyjar
Heimaey
Surtsey
Jan Mayen (Norway)
Haakon VII Topp
Svalbard (Spitsbergen) (Norway)
Vestspitsbergen
Nordaustlandet
Kong Karls Land
Kvitøya
Barentsøya
Edgeøya
Olgastredet
Storfjorden
Longyearbyen
Barentsburg
Newtontoppen
Prins Karls Forland
Nordkapp
Sørkapp
3548 1626 2616 1920 2571 2170 2935 3220 2940 3700 3360 2850 2399 2092 2277 2119 1717
80 75 70 65 60
Projection: Conic
West from Greenwich
COPYRIGHT PHILIP'S
ft m
3000 1000
1200 400
600 200
0 0
200 600
500 1500
1000 3000
2000 6000
3000 9000
4000 12000
m ft
139
8
5 6 7 8 9
B C D E F

Underlined towns give their name to the administrative area in which they stand.

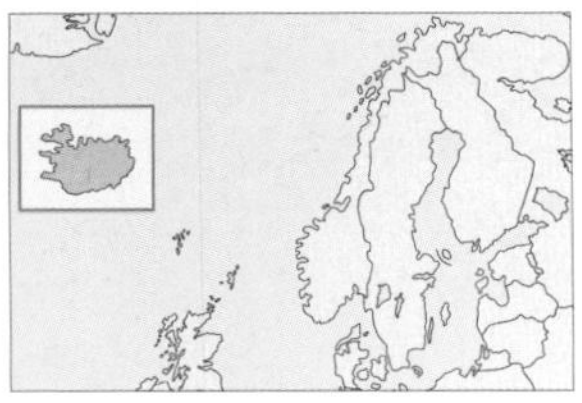

ICELAND 11

1:2 000 000

10 0 10 20 30 40 50 60 70 80 100 km

10 0 10 20 30 40 50 60 miles

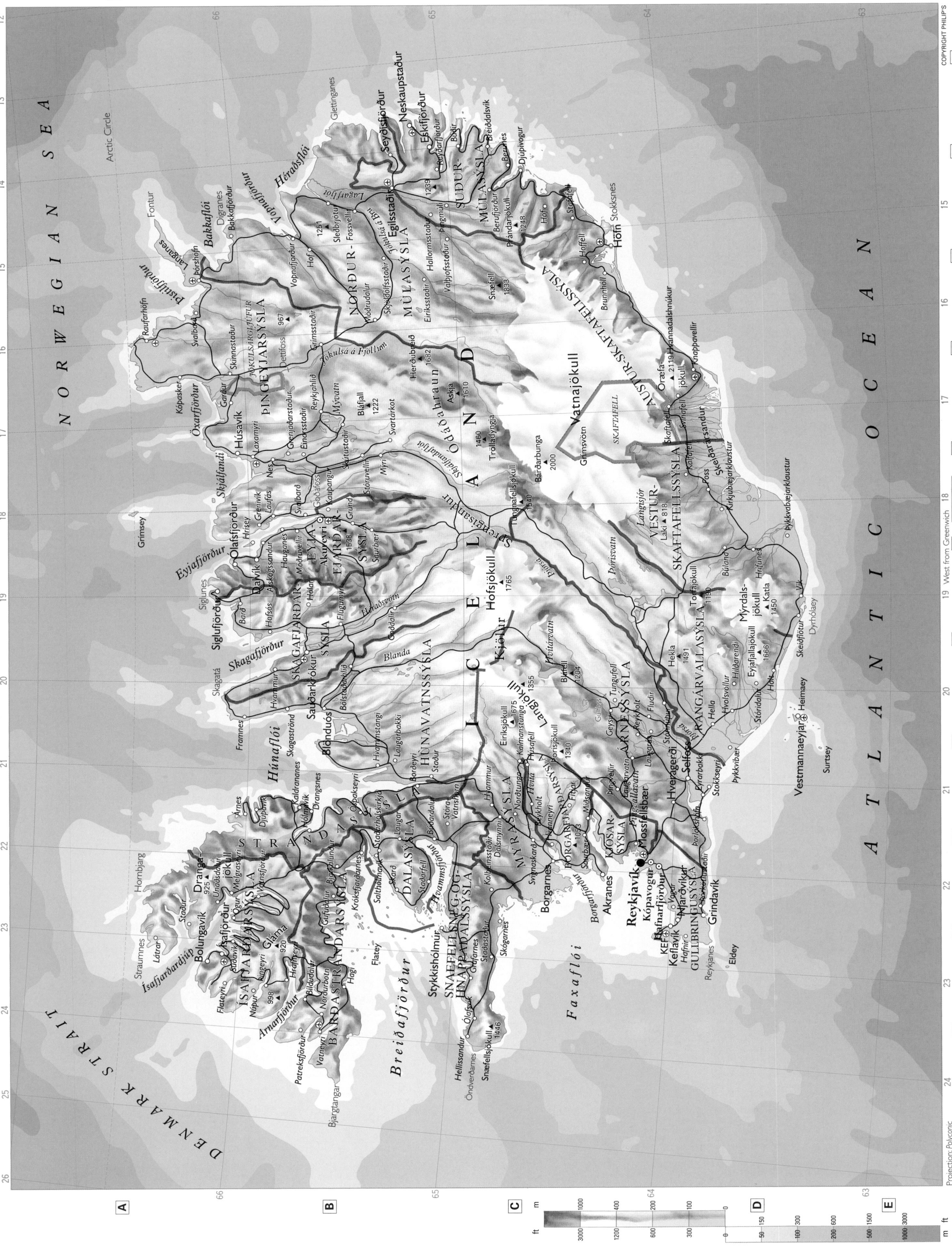

1:16 000 000

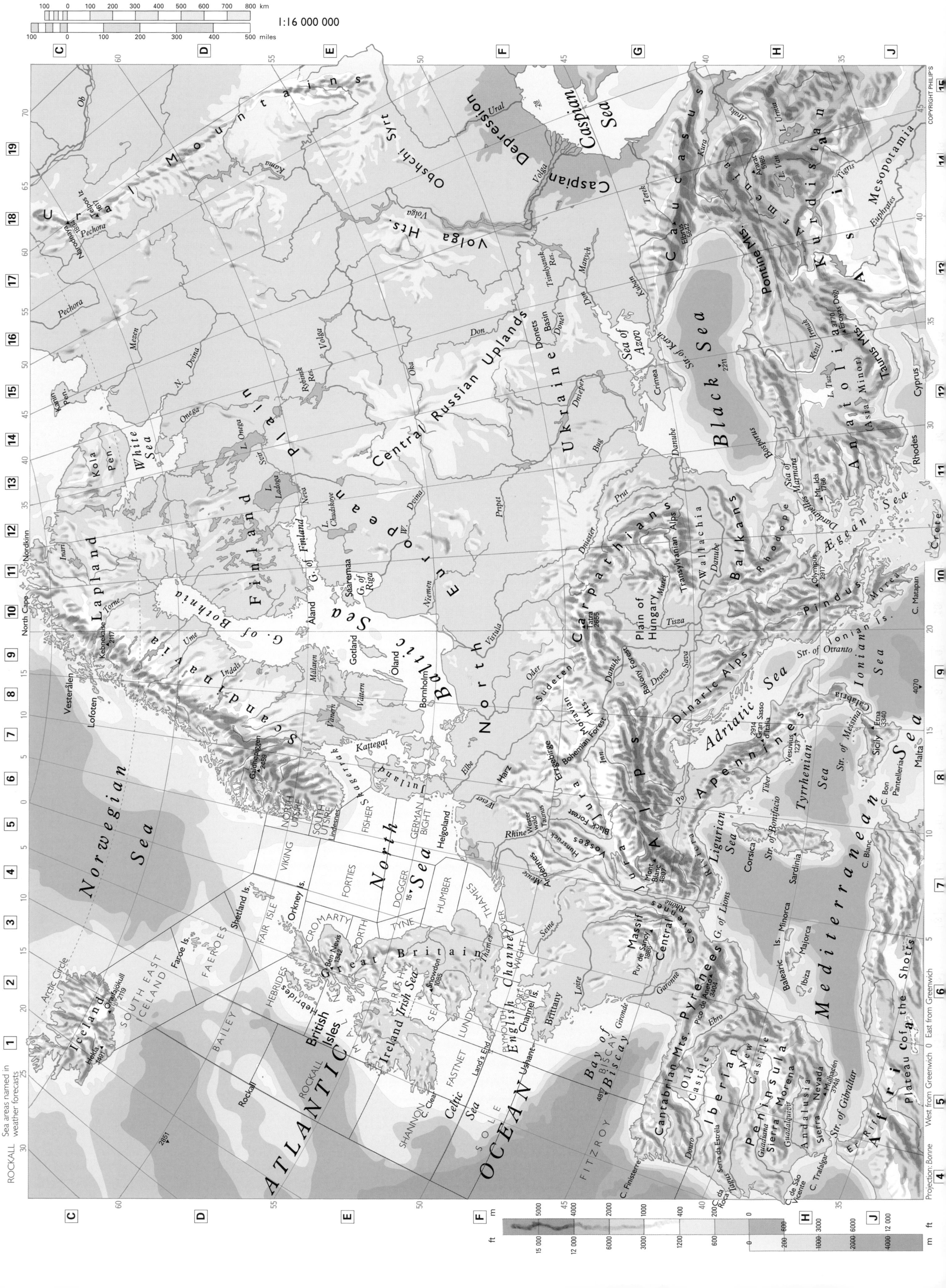
km 100 0 100 200 300 400 500 600 700 800
miles 100 0 100 200 300 400 500
Ural Mountains
Caspian Depression
Caspian Sea
Obshchi Syrt
Volga Hts.
Central Russian Uplands
Donets Basin
Ukraine
European Plain
Finland
Lapland
Kola Pen.
White Sea
Kanin Pen.
L. Ladoga
L. Onega
G. of Bothnia
G. of Finland
G. of Riga
Baltic Sea
North Sea
Norwegian Sea
Scandinavia
Galdhøpiggen 2469
Kebnekaise 2117
North Cape
Nordkinn
Lofoten
Vesterålen
Iceland
Hvannadalshnúkur 2119
Hekla 1491
Faroe Is.
Shetland Is.
Orkney Is.
British Isles
Great Britain
Ireland
Irish Sea
English Channel
Ben Nevis 1342
Snowdon 1085
Hebrides
ATLANTIC OCEAN
Bay of Biscay
Celtic Sea
Iberian Peninsula
Cantabrian Mts.
Sierra Morena
Sierra Nevada
Mulhacén 3478
Pyrenees
Pico de Aneto 3404
Massif Central
Puy de Sancy 1885
Alps
Mont Blanc 4807
Jura
Vosges
Black Forest
Bohemian Forest
Erzgebirge
Harz
Sudeten
Carpathians
Tatra 2655
Transylvanian Alps
Plain of Hungary
Wallachia
Balkans
Rhodope
Dinaric Alps
Pindus
Olympus 2917
Apennines
Gran Sasso d'Italia 2914
Vesuvius 1277
Etna 3340
Adriatic Sea
Tyrrhenian Sea
Ligurian Sea
Ionian Sea
Aegean Sea
Mediterranean Sea
Black Sea
Sea of Azov
Sea of Marmara
Bosporus
Dardanelles
Crimea
Caucasus
Elbrus 5642
Pontine Mts.
Anatolia (Asia Minor)
Taurus Mts.
Kurdistan
Mesopotamia
Ararat 5165
Cyprus
Rhodes
Crete
Sicily
Malta
Sardinia
Corsica
Balearic Is.
Majorca
Minorca
Ibiza
Atlas
Plateau of the Shotts
Africa
Volga
Don
Danube
Dnieper
Dniester
Vistula
Oder
Elbe
Rhine
Rhône
Loire
Seine
Garonne
Ebro
Tagus
Po
Sava
Tisza
Pechora
Kama
Ural
North Sea forecast areas: VIKING, NORTH UTSIRE, SOUTH UTSIRE, FORTIES, CROMARTY, FORTH, TYNE, DOGGER, FISHER, GERMAN BIGHT, HUMBER, THAMES, DOVER, WIGHT, PORTLAND, PLYMOUTH, LUNDY, FASTNET, IRISH SEA, SOLE, FITZROY, SHANNON, ROCKALL, MALIN, HEBRIDES, BAILEY, FAIR ISLE, FAEROES, SOUTH EAST ICELAND
Sea areas named in weather forecasts
Projection: Bonne
West from Greenwich 0 East from Greenwich
COPYRIGHT PHILIP'S
m 5000 4000 2000 1000 400 200 0 200 2000 4000
ft 15 000 12 000 6000 3000 1200 600 0 600 3000 6000 12 000

1:16 000 000

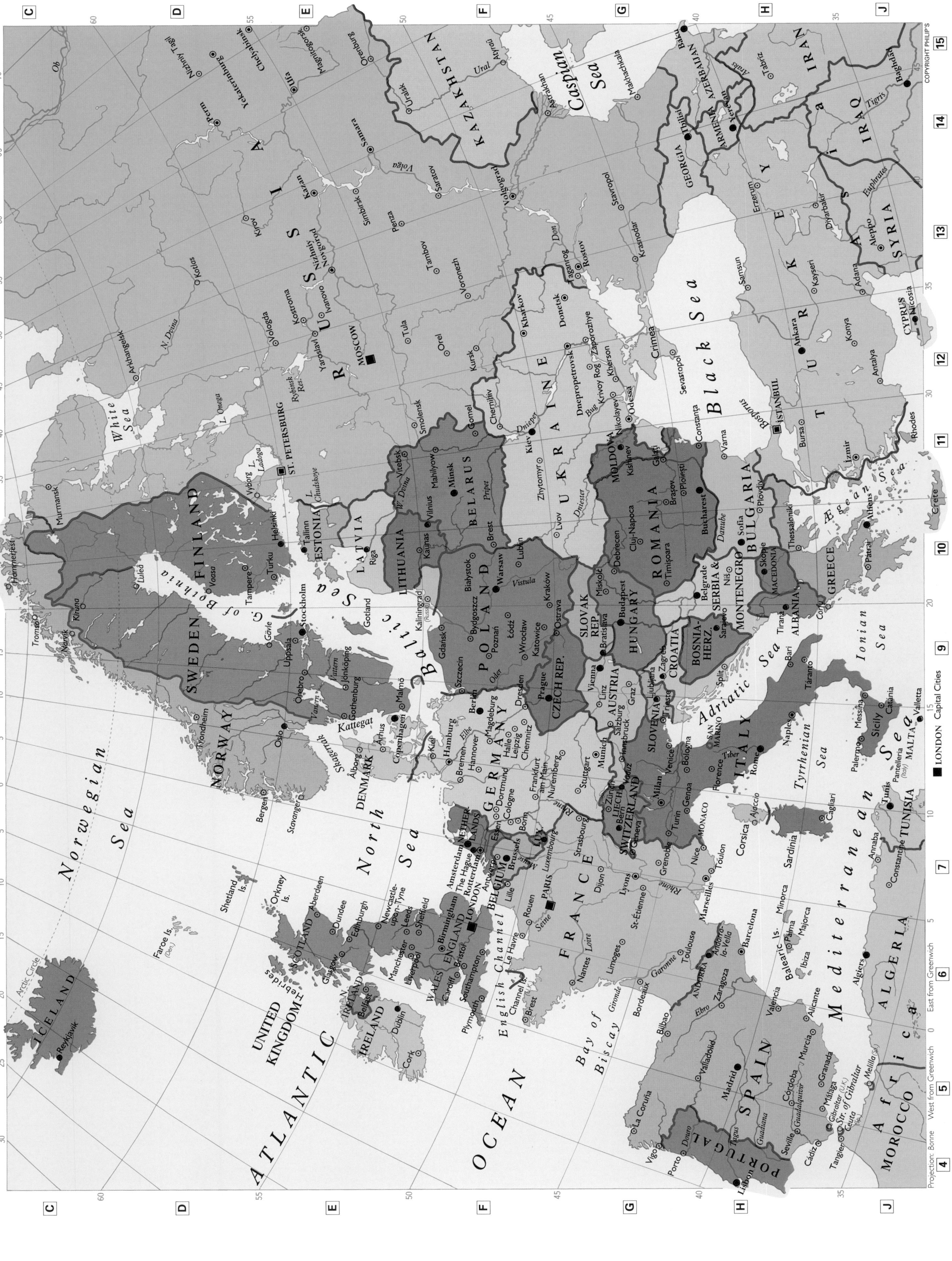
ICELAND
Reykjavik
Norwegian Sea
ATLANTIC OCEAN
North Sea
UNITED KINGDOM
IRELAND
NORWAY
SWEDEN
FINLAND
DENMARK
ESTONIA
LATVIA
LITHUANIA
BELARUS
POLAND
GERMANY
NETHERLANDS
BELGIUM
FRANCE
SWITZERLAND
AUSTRIA
CZECH REP.
SLOVAK REP.
HUNGARY
SLOVENIA
CROATIA
BOSNIA-HERZ.
SERBIA & MONTENEGRO
ALBANIA
MACEDONIA
GREECE
BULGARIA
ROMANIA
MOLDOVA
UKRAINE
RUSSIA
KAZAKHSTAN
GEORGIA
ARMENIA
AZERBAIJAN
TURKEY
CYPRUS
SYRIA
IRAQ
IRAN
ITALY
SPAIN
PORTUGAL
ANDORRA
MONACO
SAN MARINO
MALTA
MOROCCO
ALGERIA
TUNISIA
Baltic Sea
Black Sea
Caspian Sea
Mediterranean Sea
Adriatic Sea
Tyrrhenian Sea
Ionian Sea
Ægean Sea
White Sea
Bay of Biscay
English Channel
LONDON
PARIS
MOSCOW
ST. PETERSBURG
ISTANBUL
LONDON Capital Cities
COPYRIGHT PHILIP'S
Projection: Bonne

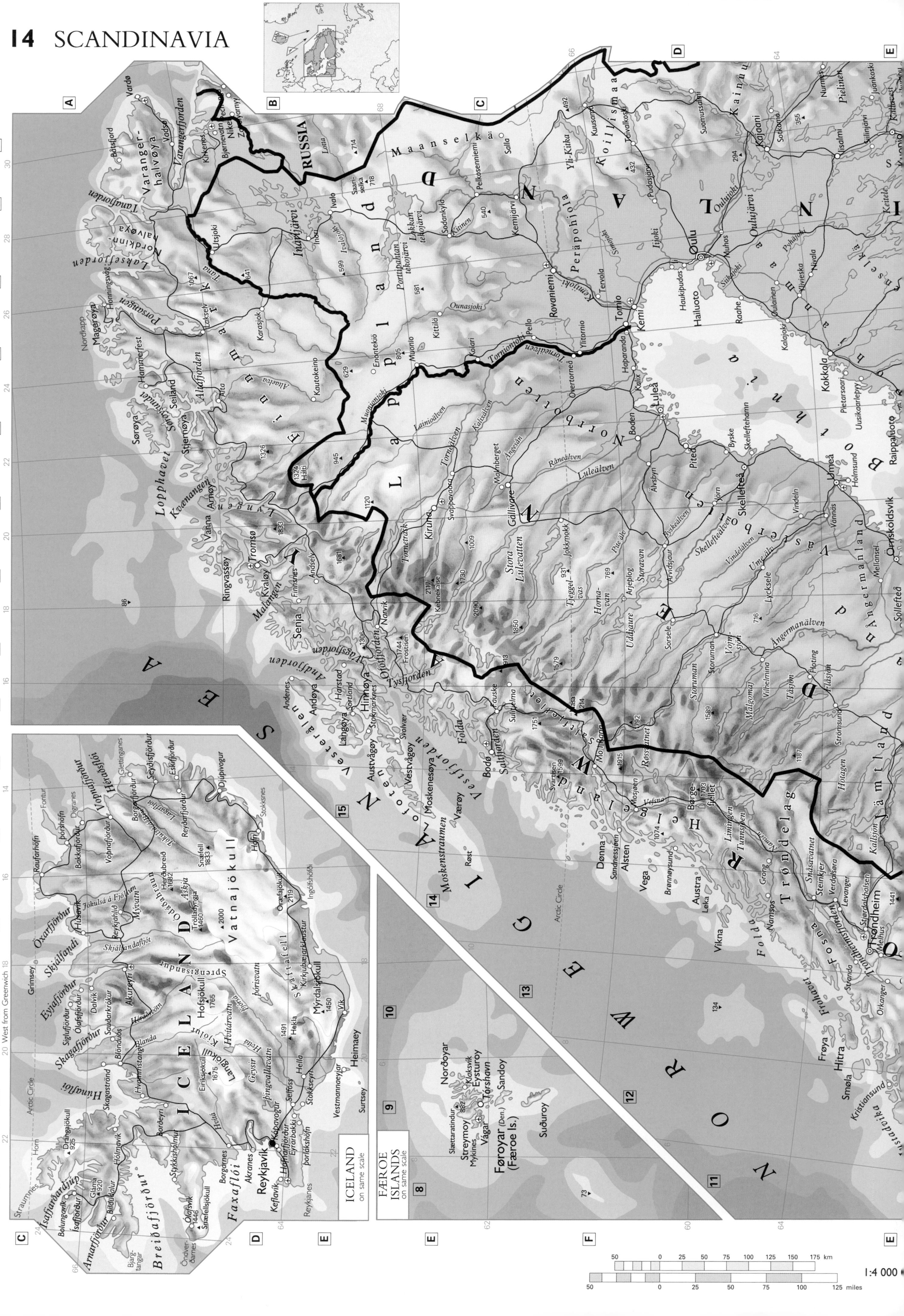
RUSSIA
Lapland
Finnmark
Norrbotten
Västerbotten
Ångermanland
Jämtland
Trøndelag
Helgeland
Lofoten
Vesterålen
NORWEGIAN SEA
Gulf of Bothnia
Pohjanmaa
Kainuu
Maanselkä
Koillismaa
Peräpohjola
Tromsø
Narvik
Kiruna
Gällivare
Luleå
Oulu
Umeå
Skellefteå
Piteå
Kemi
Tornio
Haparanda
Kokkola
Bodø
Trondheim
Hammerfest
Vardø
Vadsø
Kirkenes
Alta
Karasjok
Kautokeino
Ivalo
Inarijärvi
Rovaniemi
Stora Lulevatten
Kebnekaise
Mageroya
Nordkapp
Sørøya
Ringvassøy
Senja
Hinnøya
Andøya
Moskenesøya
Røst
Værøy
Vestvågøy
Austvågøy
Vestfjorden
Lofoten
Arctic Circle
ICELAND
on same scale
Reykjavík
Akureyri
Vatnajökull
Hofsjökull
Langjökull
Mýrdalsjökull
Hekla
Askja
Faxaflói
Breiðafjörður
Húnaflói
Skjálfandi
Vestmannaeyjar
Heimaey
Surtsey
West from Greenwich
FÆROE ISLANDS
on same scale
Føroyar (Færoe Is.)
Tórshavn
Streymoy
Eysturoy
Vagar
Sandoy
Suðuroy
Norðoyar
1:4 000

Gulf of Finland
Gulf of Riga
Gulf of Bothnia
BALTIC SEA
Ålands hav
Skagerrak
Kattegat
STOCKHOLM
Helsinki (Helsingfors)
Tallinn
Riga
Vilnius
Oslo
KØBENHAVN (Copenhagen)
ESTONIA
LATVIA
LITHUANIA
DENMARK
POLAND
GERMANY
Gotland
Öland
Bornholm
Saaremaa (Ösel)
Hiiumaa (Dagö)
Åland (Ahvenanmaa)
Göteborg (Gothenburg)
Kaliningrad (Russia)
Projection: Conical with two standard parallels
East from Greenwich
COPYRIGHT PHILIP'S

10 0 10 20 30 40 50 60 70 80 90 km

1:2 000 000

10 0 10 20 30 40 50 60 miles

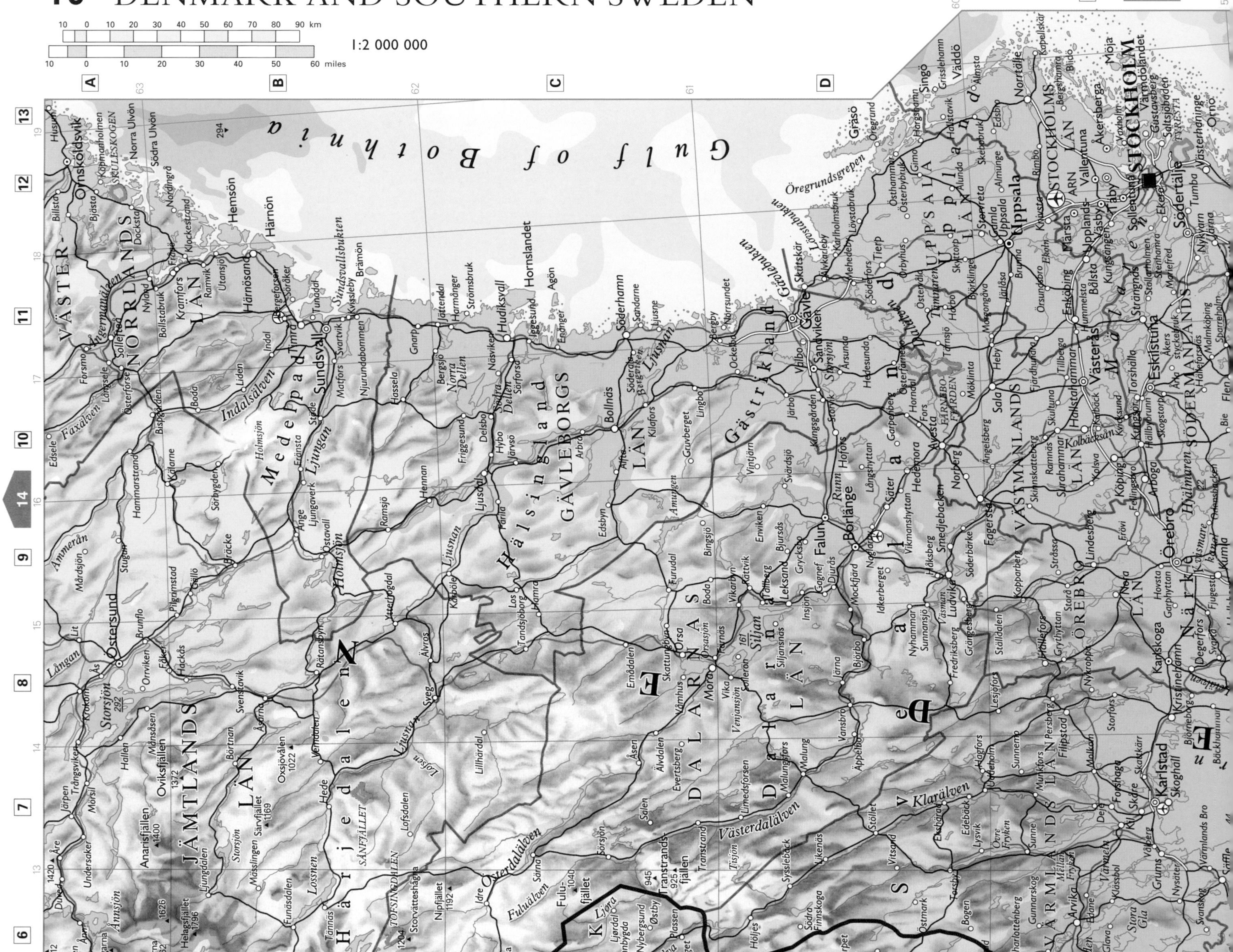

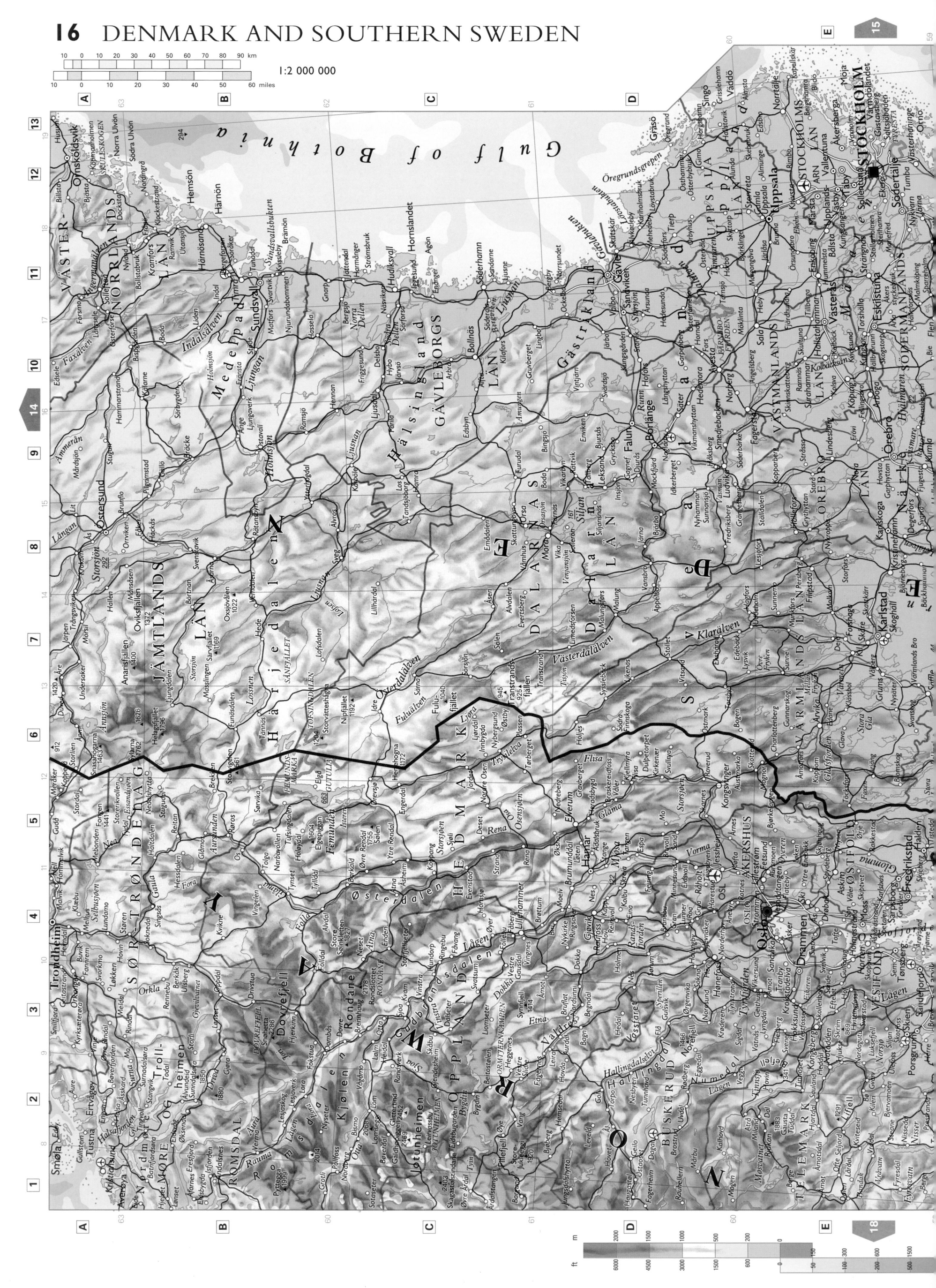

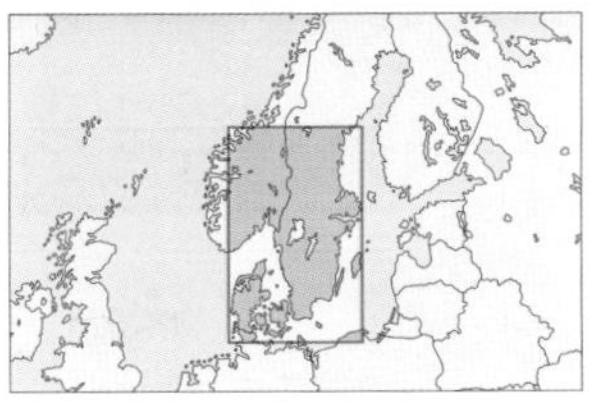

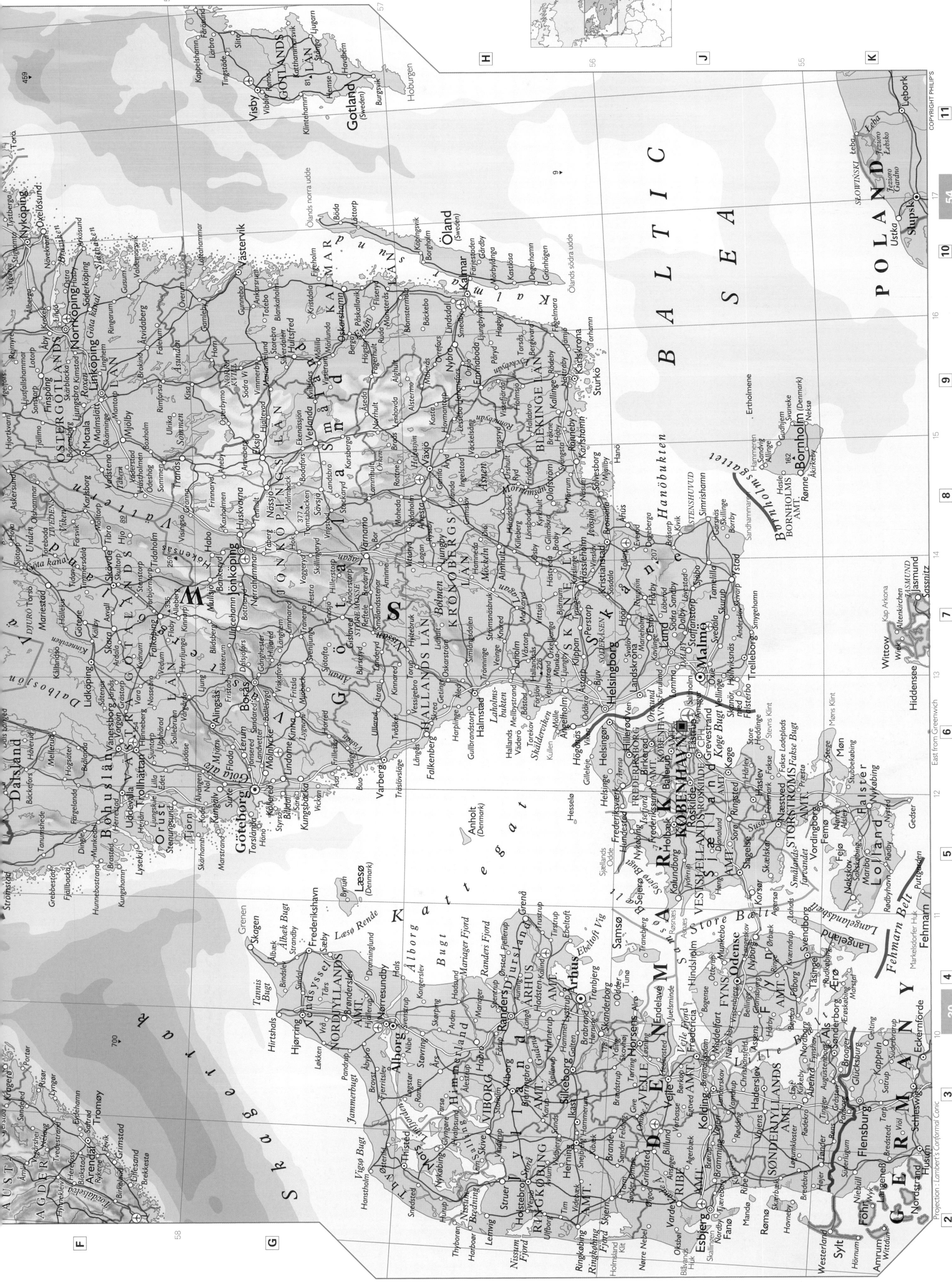
SKAGERRAK
KATTEGAT
BALTIC SEA
DENMARK
GERMANY
POLAND
Göteborg
KØBENHAVN
Malmö
Helsingborg
Jönköping
Linköping
Norrköping
Kalmar
Århus
Ålborg
Odense
Esbjerg
Kolding
Flensburg
Öland (Sweden)
Gotland (Sweden)
Bornholm (Denmark)
Anholt (Denmark)
Læsø (Denmark)
Sjælland
Fyn
Lolland
Hanöbukten
Store Bælt
Fehmarn Belt
Øresund
Projection : Lambert's Conformal Conic
East from Greenwich
COPYRIGHT PHILIP'S

National Parks

1:2 000 000

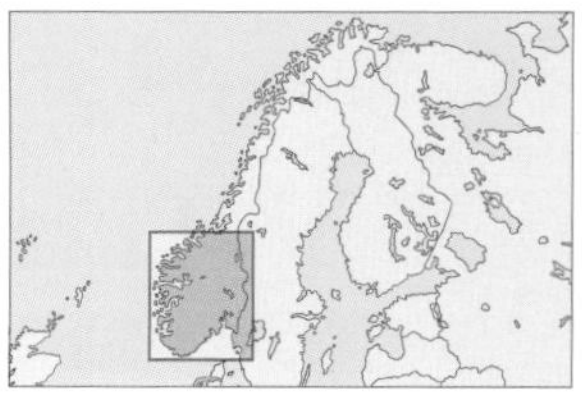

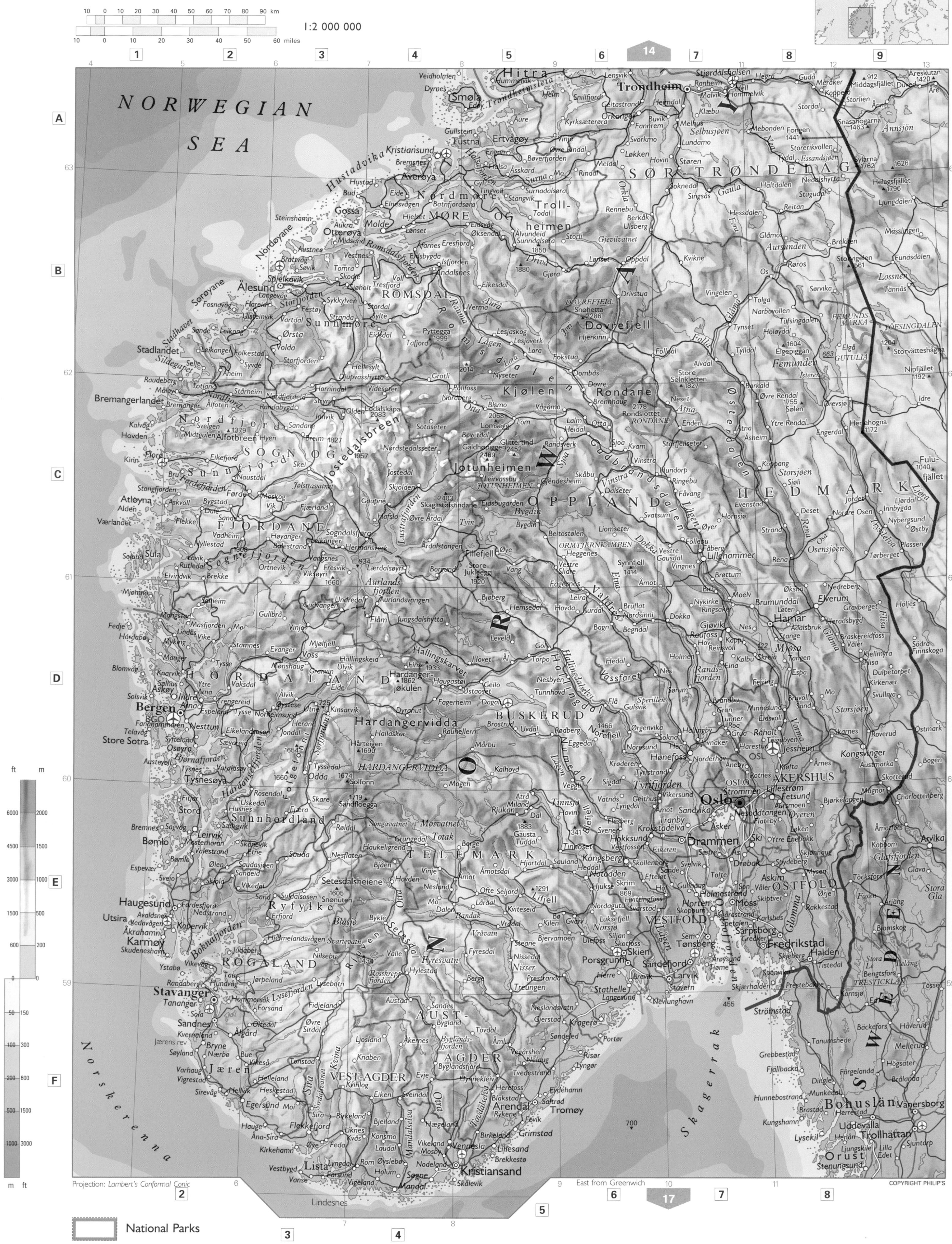
NORWEGIAN SEA
Hustadvika
Norskerenna
Skagerrak
SØR-TRØNDELAG
MØRE OG ROMSDAL
SOGN OG FJORDANE
HORDALAND
ROGALAND
VEST-AGDER
AUST-AGDER
TELEMARK
BUSKERUD
OPPLAND
HEDMARK
AKERSHUS
VESTFOLD
ØSTFOLD
SWEDEN
Bohuslän
Trondheim
Kristiansund
Molde
Ålesund
Bergen
Haugesund
Stavanger
Kristiansand
Arendal
Skien
Drammen
Oslo
Lillehammer
Hamar
Fredrikstad
Jotunheimen
Jostedalsbreen
Hardangervidda
Dovrefjell
Rondane
Sognefjorden
Hardangerfjorden
Mjøsa
Lindesnes
Projection: Lambert's Conformal Conic
East from Greenwich
COPYRIGHT PHILIP'S
National Parks

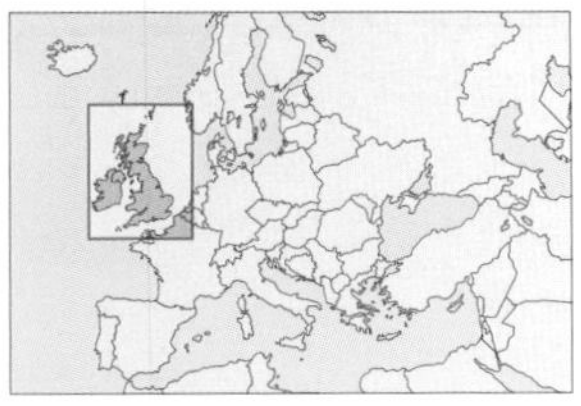

1:4 000 000
50 0 25 50 75 100 125 150 175 km
50 0 25 50 75 100 125 miles
ATLANTIC OCEAN
NORTH SEA
IRISH SEA
CELTIC SEA
English Channel
Shetland Is.
Orkney Is.
Pentland Firth
Moray Firth
Outer Hebrides
Inner Hebrides
Sea of the Hebrides
North Minch
North West Highlands
SCOTLAND
Grampian Mts.
Southern Uplands
North Channel
Firth of Clyde
UNITED KINGDOM
NORTHERN IRELAND
IRELAND
ENGLAND
WALES
Pennines
Cumbrian Mts.
Cambrian Mts.
Cheviot Hills
Cotswold Hills
Cardigan Bay
Bristol Channel
St. George's Channel
Str. of Dover
The Wash
Exmoor
Dartmoor
Isle of Wight
Channel Is. (U.K.)
NORWAY
NETHERLANDS
BELGIUM
FRANCE
Lewis
Harris
North Uist
South Uist
Skye
Mull
Islay
Jura
Arran
I. of Man
Anglesey
Isles of Scilly
Land's End
Edinburgh
Glasgow
Aberdeen
Dundee
Inverness
Belfast
Dublin
Cork
Limerick
Galway
Waterford
Londonderry
Newcastle-upon-Tyne
Middlesbrough
Leeds
Bradford
Sheffield
Manchester
Liverpool
Kingston upon Hull
Nottingham
Leicester
BIRMINGHAM
Coventry
Norwich
Cambridge
Oxford
LONDON
Southampton
Portsmouth
Brighton
Plymouth
Bristol
Cardiff
Swansea
Newport
Bergen
Stavanger
Haugesund
's-Gravenhage (Den Haag)
ROTTERDAM
Antwerpen
Brussel (Bruxelles)
Lille
Calais
Dunkerque
Boulogne-sur-Mer
Amiens
Rouen
Le Havre
Caen
Cherbourg
18
36
25
Projection: Conical with two standard parallels
East from Greenwich
West from Greenwich
COPYRIGHT PHILIP'S

 ENGLAND AND WALES

10 0 10 20 30 40 50 60 70 80 km
10 0 10 20 30 40 50 miles

1:1 600 000

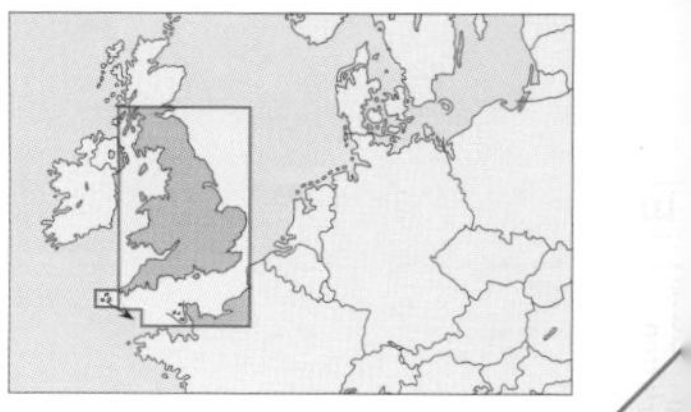

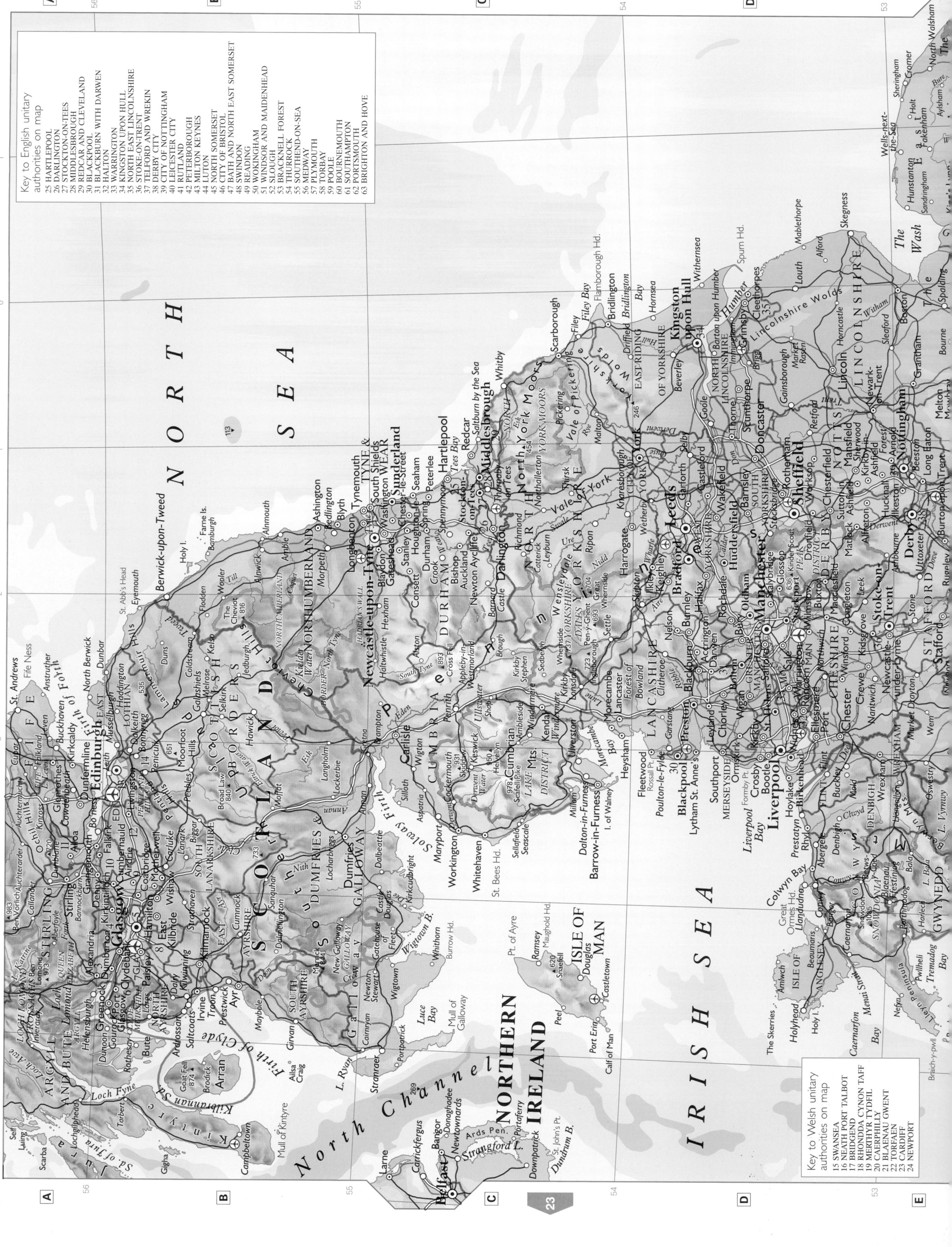

ENGLAND
WALES
FRANCE
ENGLISH CHANNEL
Bristol Channel
Cardigan Bay
Strait of Dover
CHANNEL ISLANDS (U.K.)
ISLES OF SCILLY on same scale
LONDON
BIRMINGHAM
Bristol
Cardiff
Southampton
Portsmouth
Plymouth
Brighton
Bournemouth
Le Havre
Cherbourg
National Parks in England and Wales
Forest Parks in Scotland
Projection : Lambert's Conformal Conic
COPYRIGHT PHILIP'S
West from Greenwich
East from Greenwich
m ft
1000 3000
500 1500
200 600
100 300
0
50 150
100 300
200 600

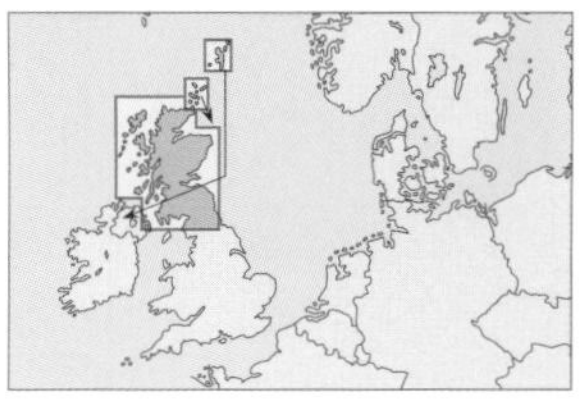

10 0 10 20 30 40 50 60 70 80 km
1:1 600 000
10 0 10 20 30 40 50 miles
Key to Scottish unitary authorities on map
1 CITY OF ABERDEEN
2 DUNDEE CITY
3 WEST DUNBARTONSHIRE
4 EAST DUNBARTONSHIRE
5 CITY OF GLASGOW
6 INVERCLYDE
7 RENFREWSHIRE
8 EAST RENFREWSHIRE
9 NORTH LANARKSHIRE
10 FALKIRK
11 CLACKMANNANSHIRE
12 WEST LOTHIAN
13 CITY OF EDINBURGH
14 MIDLOTHIAN
ORKNEY IS.
on same scale
ORKNEY
Mainland
Kirkwall
Stromness
Hoy
Scapa Flow
South Ronaldsay
Pentland Firth
Duncansby Head
John o' Groats
Thurso
Sinclair's Bay
SHETLAND IS.
on same scale
SHETLAND
Lerwick
Unst
Yell
Fetlar
Whalsay
Foula
Mainland
Sumburgh Hd.
Muckle Flugga
Papa Stour
St. Magnus Bay
West Burra
SCOTLAND
HIGHLAND
Sutherland
Caithness
Northwest Highlands
North Minch
Little Minch
The Minch
Lewis
Stornoway
Butt of Lewis
Harris
North Uist
Benbecula
South Uist
Barra
Outer Hebrides
Inner Hebrides
WESTERN ISLES
Sea of the Hebrides
Skye
Cuillin Hills
Rhum (Rùm)
Eigg
Mull
Iona
Tiree
Coll
Colonsay
Jura
Islay
Bowmore
Port Ellen
Kintyre
Campbeltown
Mull of Kintyre
Arran
Bute
ATLANTIC OCEAN
NORTH SEA
North Channel
Firth of Clyde
Firth of Lorn
Pentland Firth
Moray Firth
Dornoch Firth
Firth of Tay
Firth of Forth
Solway Firth
C. Wrath
Thurso
Wick
Helmsdale
Golspie
Ullapool
Inverness
Nairn
Elgin
Lossiemouth
Fort William
Ben Nevis
1342
Grampian Mountains
Cairngorm Mts.
CAIRNGORMS
Monadhliath Mts.
Glen More
Loch Ness
Oban
Aberdeen
ABERDEENSHIRE
Fraserburgh
Peterhead
Buchan
MORAY
Stonehaven
Montrose
Arbroath
ANGUS
Forfar
Dundee
Perth
PERTH AND KINROSS
St. Andrews
FIFE
Kirkcaldy
Dunfermline
Edinburgh
Leith
Musselburgh
Dunbar
North Berwick
EAST LOTHIAN
Stirling
STIRLING
Falkirk
Alloa
Glasgow
Paisley
Clydebank
Greenock
Dumbarton
Hamilton
Motherwell
Coatbridge
Airdrie
East Kilbride
Kilmarnock
Ayr
Irvine
Troon
Prestwick
SOUTH AYRSHIRE
EAST AYRSHIRE
NORTH AYRSHIRE
SOUTH LANARKSHIRE
ARGYLL AND BUTE
LOCH LOMOND & TROSSACHS
Loch Lomond
Southern Uplands
Lammermuir Hills
Pentland Hills
SCOTTISH BORDERS
Cheviot Hills
Galashiels
Hawick
Jedburgh
Kelso
Berwick-upon-Tweed
DUMFRIES & GALLOWAY
Dumfries
Galloway
Stranraer
Mull of Galloway
Kirkcudbright
Gretna
Carlisle
CUMBRIA
Workington
Whitehaven
Keswick
Penrith
NORTHUMBERLAND
ENGLAND
Newcastle-upon-Tyne
Gateshead
DURHAM
NORTHERN IRELAND
Larne
Belfast
Bangor
Carrickfergus
Projection : Lambert's Conformal Conic
West from Greenwich
COPYRIGHT PHILIP'S

23
20

Forest Parks in Scotland

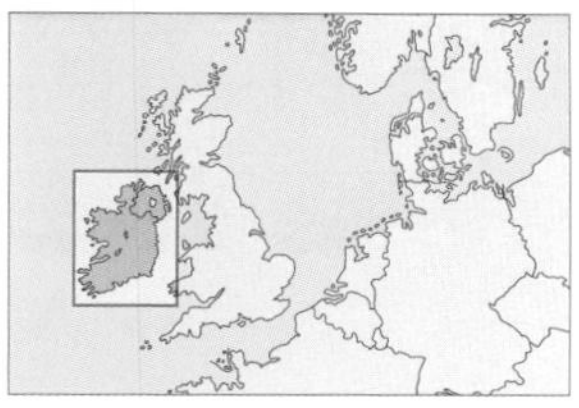

1:1 600 000

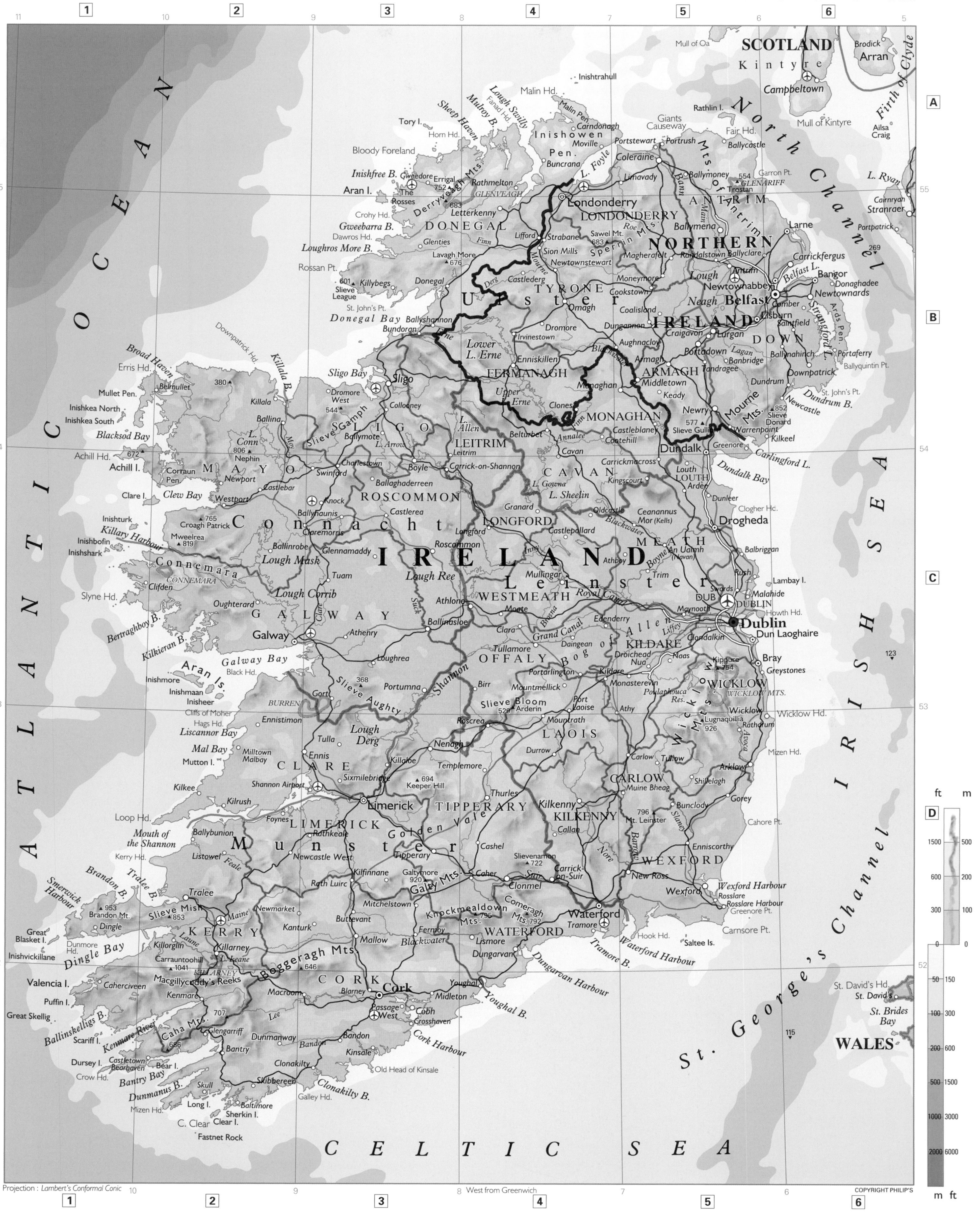

Projection: *Lambert's Conformal Conic*

West from Greenwich

National Parks

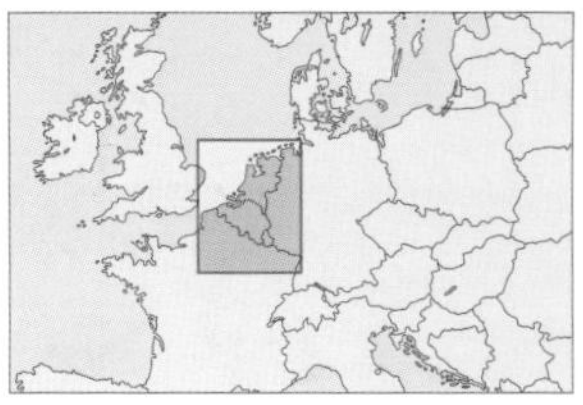

10 0 10 20 30 40 50 60 70 80 90 km

10 0 10 20 30 40 50 60 miles

1:2 000 000

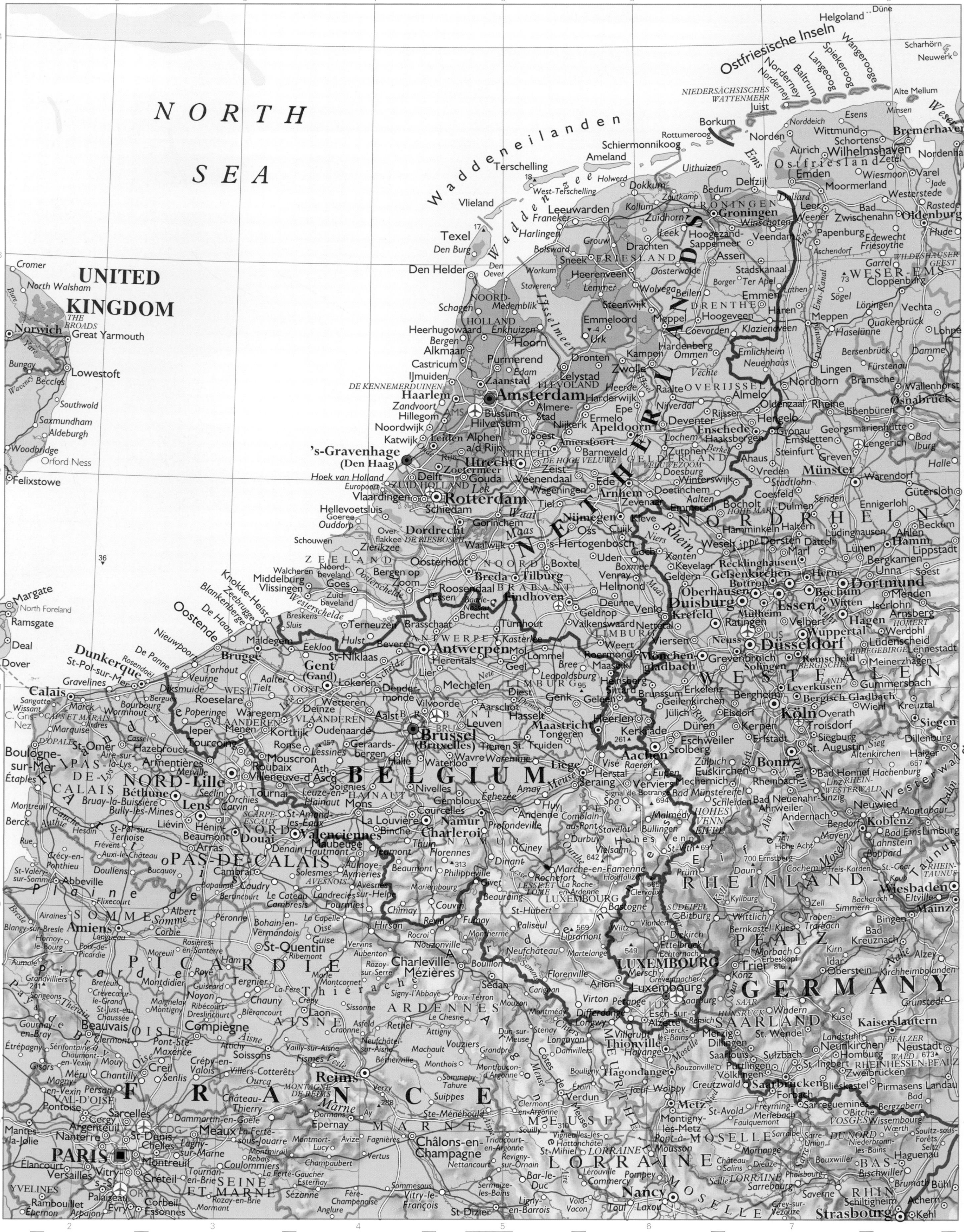

21
26
30
27

National Parks

Underlined towns give their name to the administrative area in which they stand.

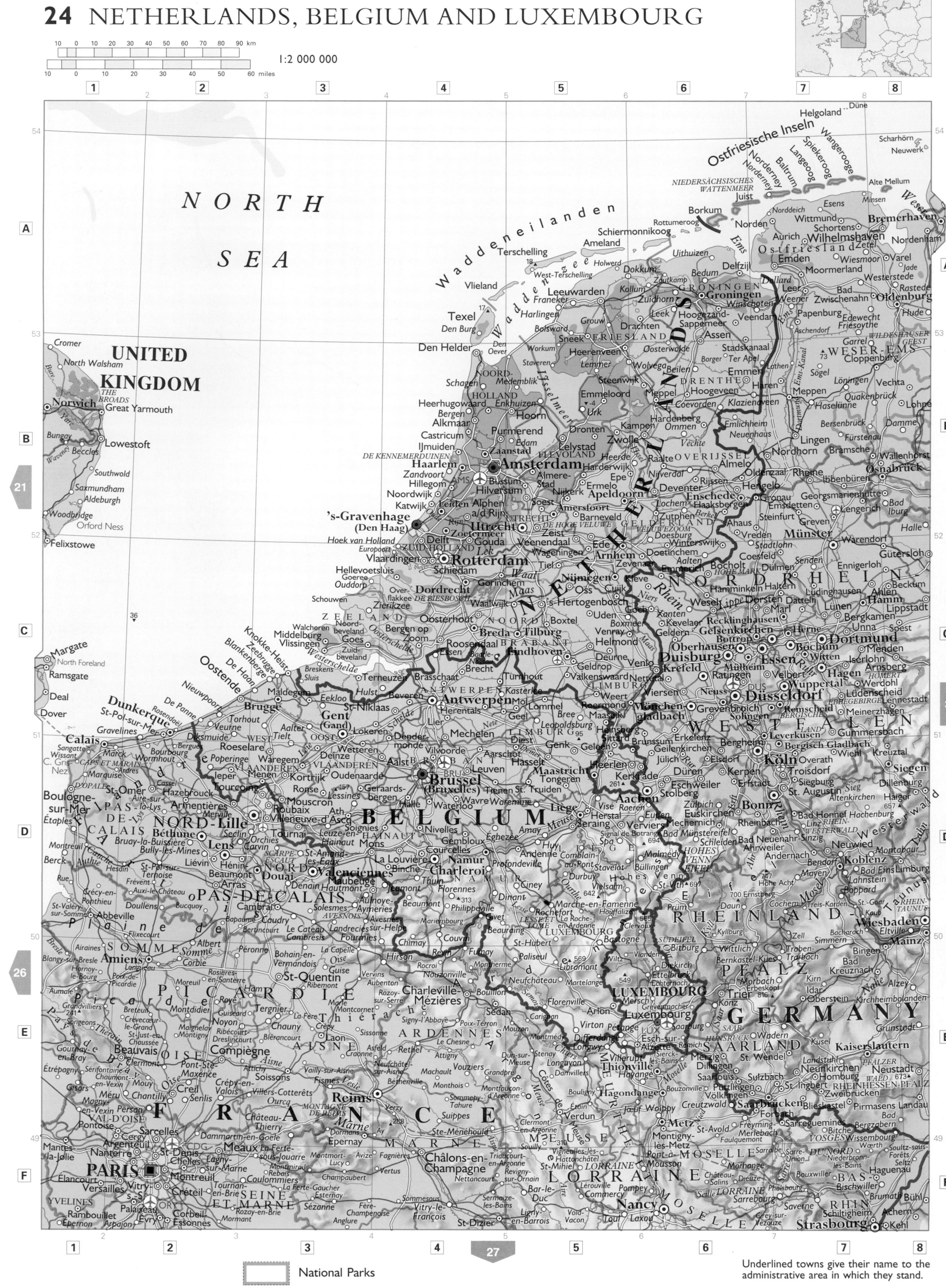

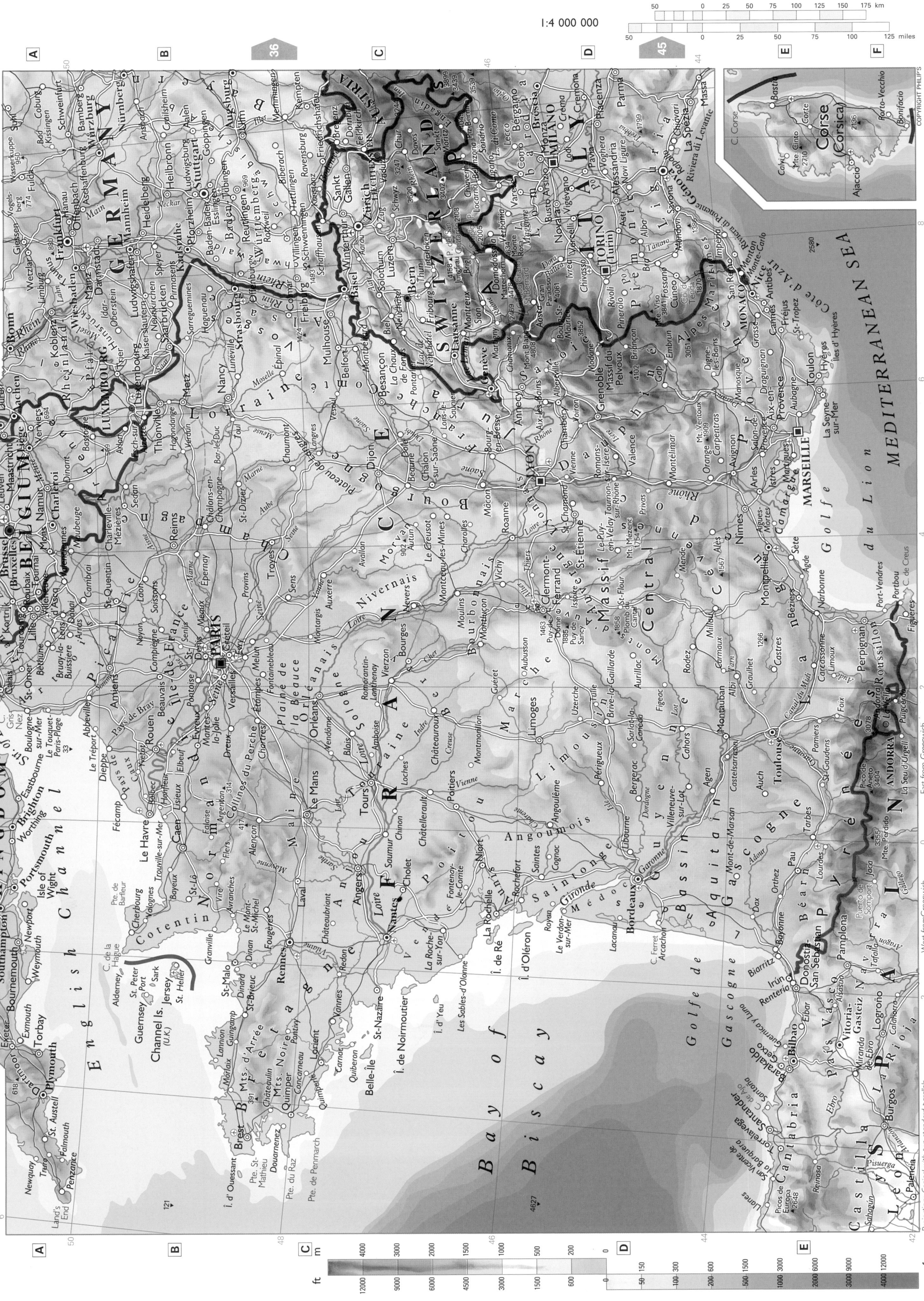
1:4 000 000
FRANCE
UNITED KINGDOM
BELGIUM
LUXEMBOURG
GERMANY
SWITZERLAND
AUSTRIA
ITALY
MONACO
ANDORRA
SPAIN
English Channel
Bay of Biscay
Golfe de Gascogne
Golfe du Lion
MEDITERRANEAN SEA
PARIS
MARSEILLE
LYON
Corse (Corsica)
Massif Central
Pyrénées
Projection: Conical with two standard parallels
COPYRIGHT PHILIP'S

1:2 000 000

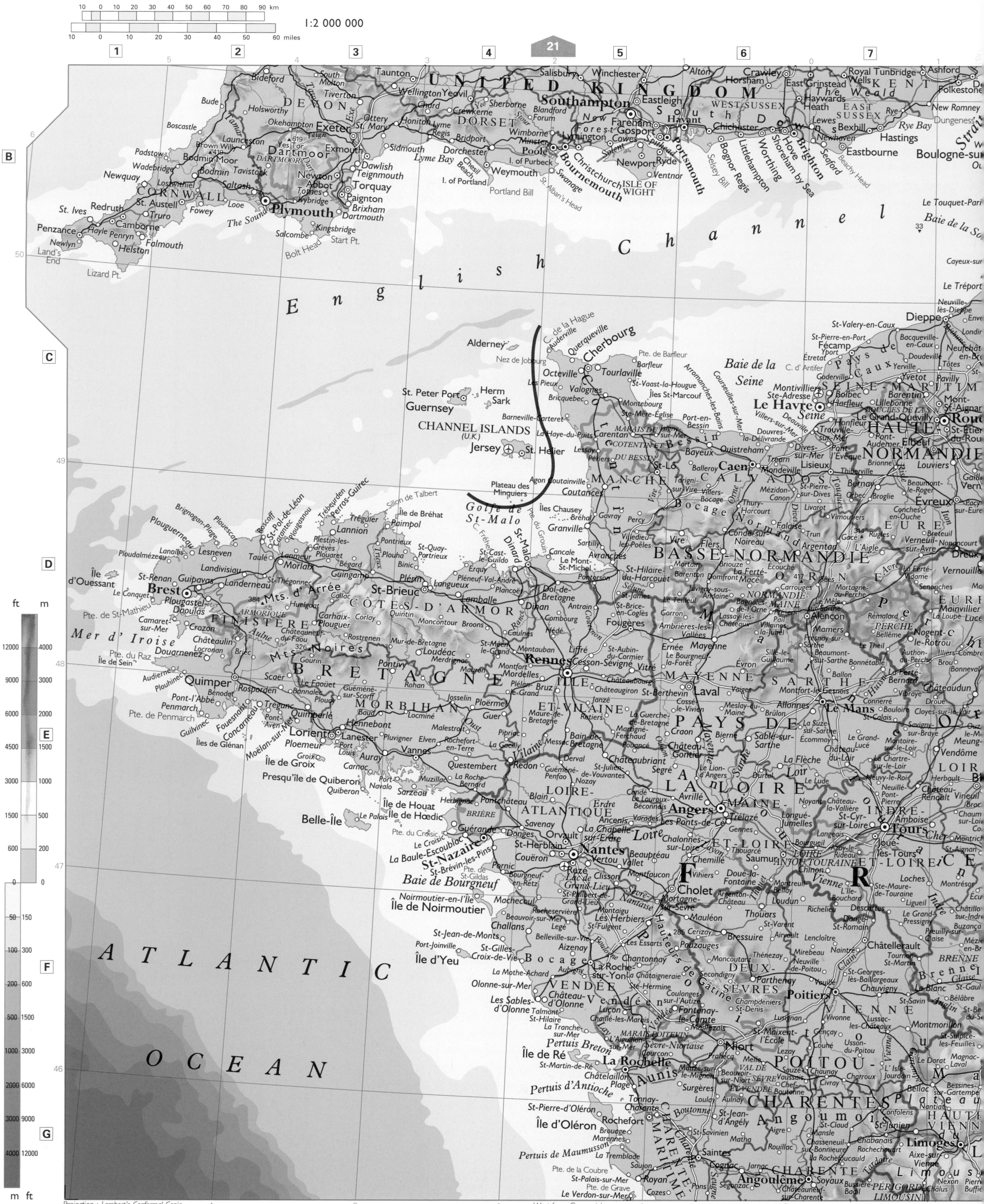

DÉPARTEMENTS IN THE PARIS AREA

1 Ville de Paris
2 Seine-St-Denis
3 Val-de-Marne
4 Hauts-de-Seine

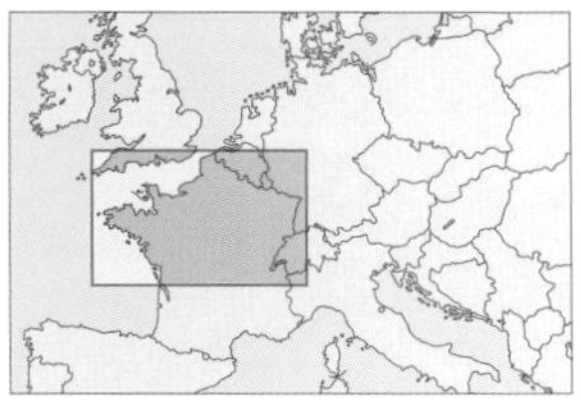

24
30
31
44
29

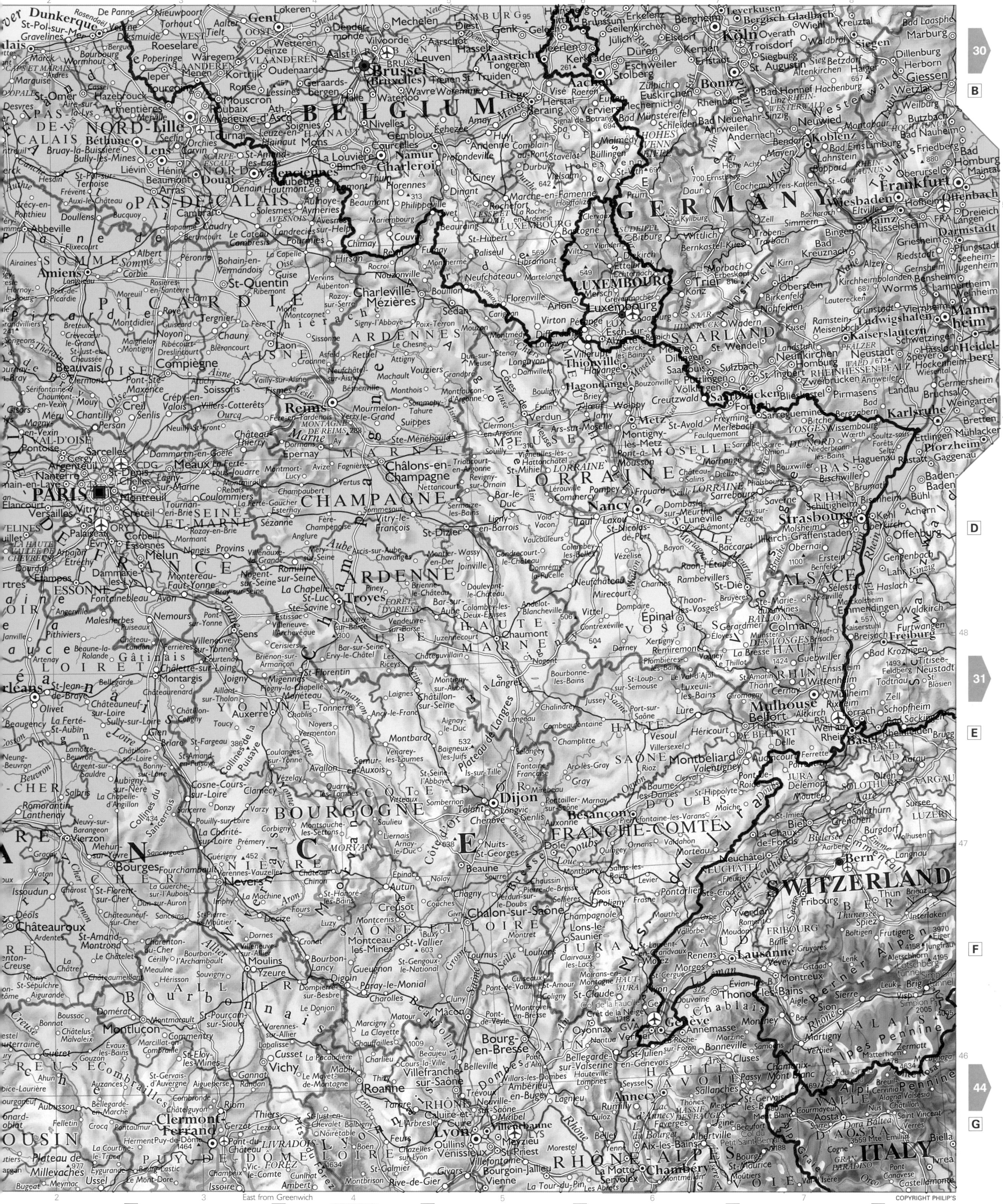

Underlined towns give their name to the administrative area in which they stand.

National Parks

Regional Nature Parks in France

1:2 000 000
km
miles
ATLANTIC
OCEAN
Golfe de Gascogne
FRANCE
SPAIN
ANDORRA
Bordeaux
Toulouse
Limoges
Poitiers
Clermont-Ferrand
Perpignan
Bayonne
Pau
Pamplona
Zaragoza
Lleida
BARCELONA
Montauban
Agen
Périgueux
Angoulême
La Rochelle
Niort
Brive-la-Gaillarde
Carcassonne
Béziers
Rodez
Albi
Tarbes
Dax
Mont-de-Marsan
Auch
Cahors
Aurillac
Montluçon
Châteauroux
Bourges
Nevers
Moulins
Vichy
Cholet
Donostia-San Sebastián
Irún
Huesca
Andorra La Vella
Figueres
Girona
AQUITAINE
POITOU-CHARENTES
LIMOUSIN
AUVERGNE
MIDI-PYRÉNÉES
LANGUEDOC-ROUSSILLON
NAVARRA
ARAGÓN
CATALUÑA
PYRÉNÉES
Costa Brava
Île d'Oléron
Île de Ré
Île d'Yeu
Projection : Lambert's Conformal Conic
West from Greenwich
East from Greenwich

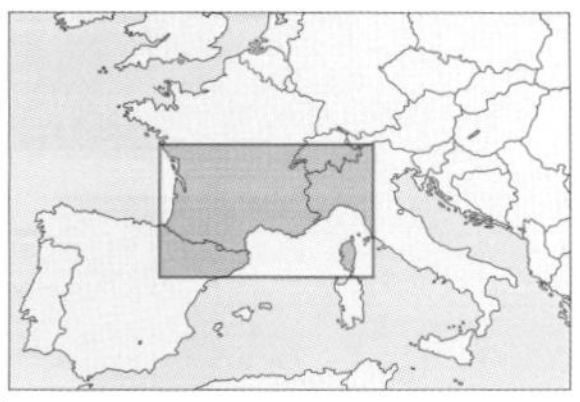

SWITZERLAND
ITALY
FRANCE
MEDITERRANEAN SEA
LIGURIAN SEA
Golfo di Génova
Riviera di Ponente
Riviera di Levante
Côte d'Azur
CORSE
Arcipelago Toscano
RHÔNE-ALPES
PROVENCE-ALPES-CÔTE D'AZUR
PIEMONTE
LOMBARDIA
LIGURIA
VALLE D'AOSTA
Lyon
Genève
Grenoble
Marseille
Toulon
Nice
MONACO
Torino
Milano
Genova
Bern
Lausanne
Avignon
Ajaccio
Bastia
Livorno
Parma
27
44

National Parks   Regional Nature Parks in France

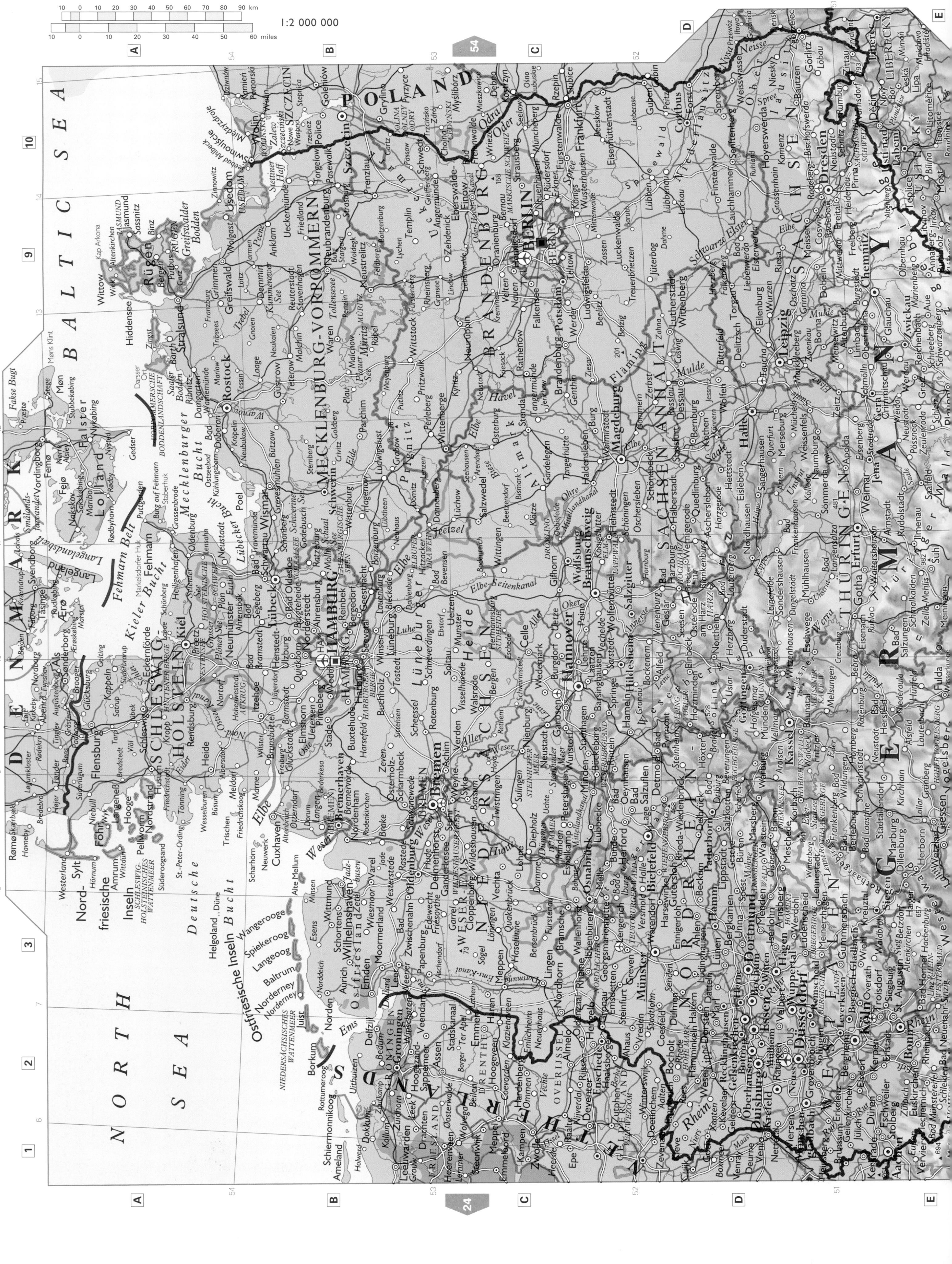
1:2 000 000
km
miles
POLAND
BALTIC SEA
NORTH SEA
DENMARK
GERMANY
BERLIN
HAMBURG
Bremen
Hannover
Dresden
Leipzig
Magdeburg
Kiel
Rostock
Szczecin
54
24
17

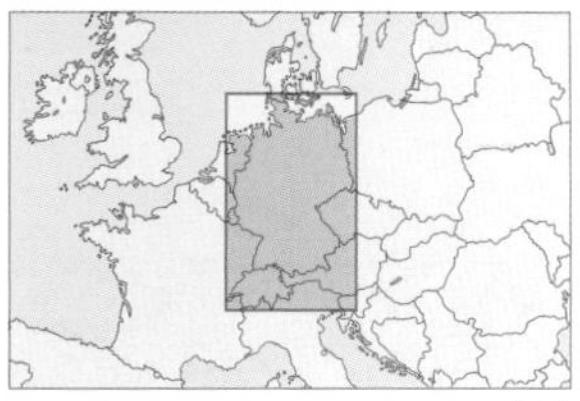

Underlined towns give their name to the administrative area in which they stand.
National Parks
Nature Parks in Germany
Projection: Lambert's Conformal Conic
East from Greenwich
COPYRIGHT PHILIP'S
m 4000 3000 2000 1500 1000 500 200 0
ft 12000 9000 6000 4500 3000 1500 600 0
50 150

1:800 000

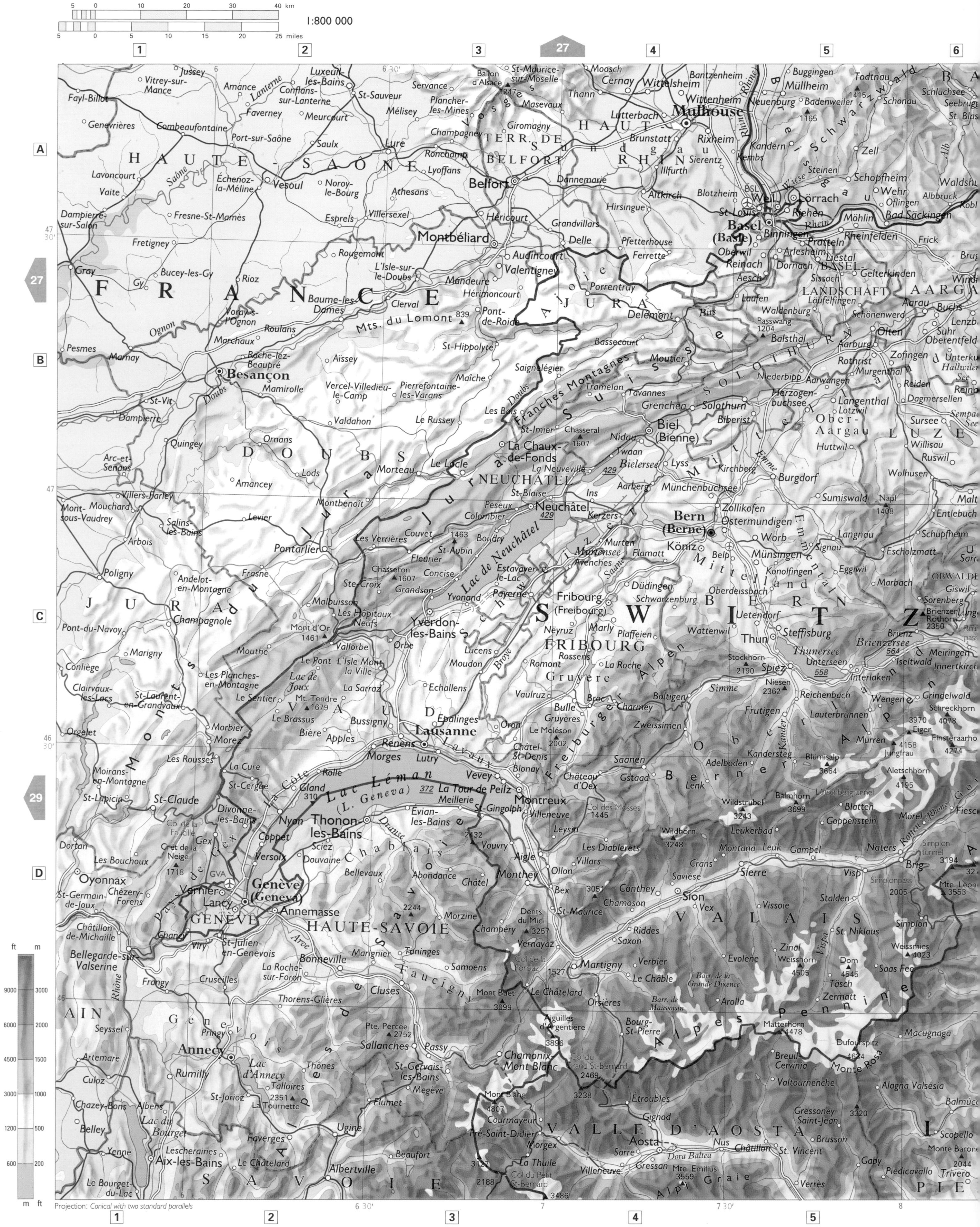

Projection: *Conical with two standard parallels*

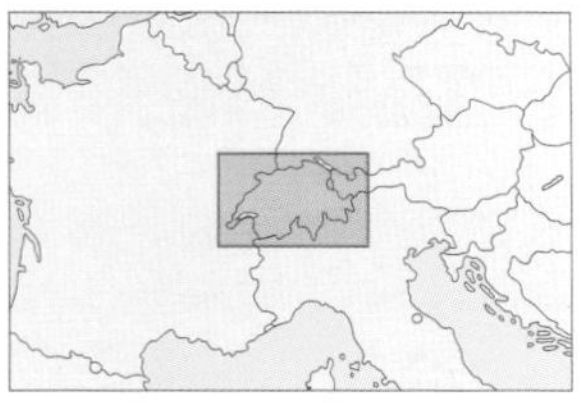

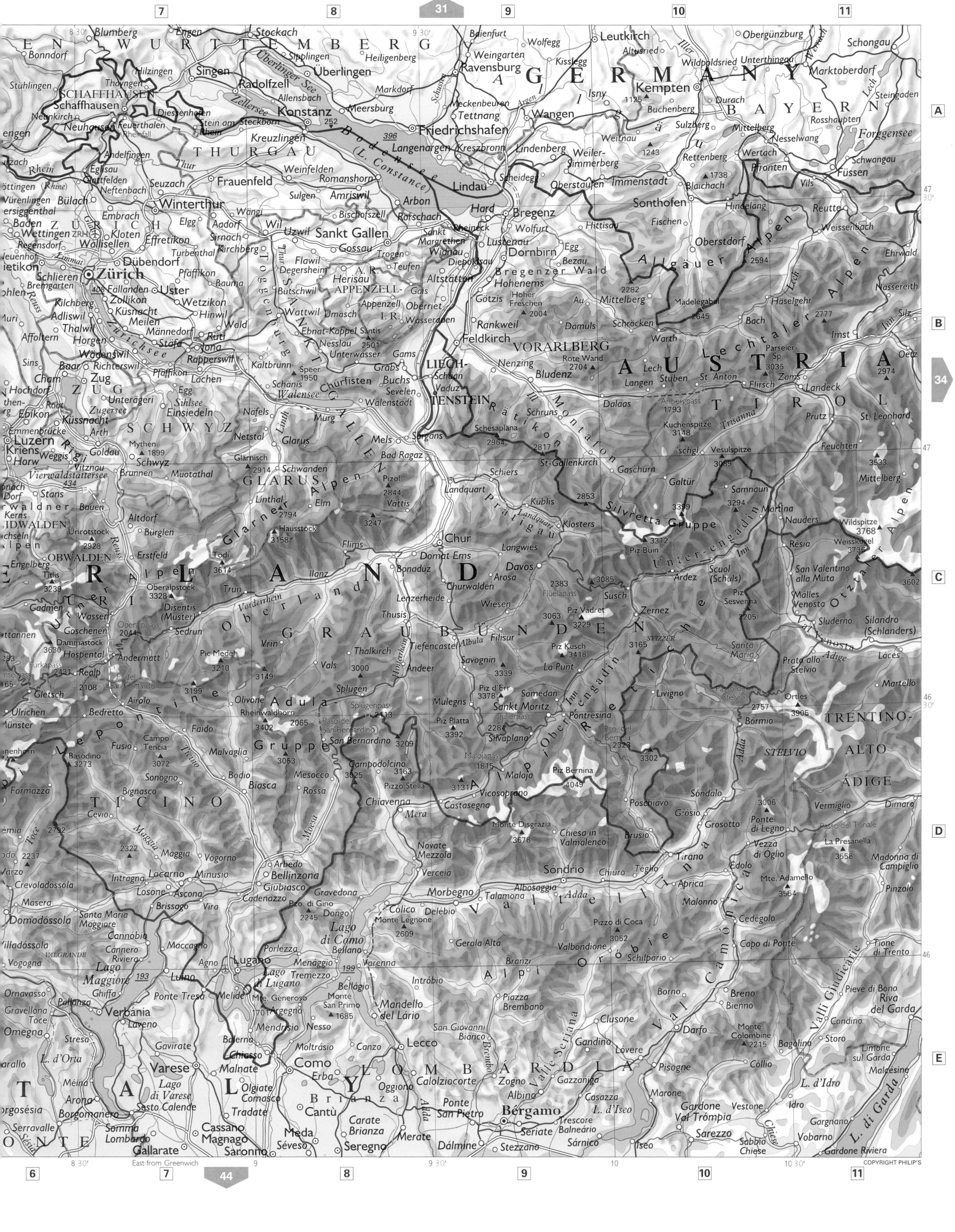
7
8
31
9
10
11
A
B
C
D
E
34
6
44
WÜRTTEMBERG
GERMANY
BAYERN
AUSTRIA
TIROL
VORARLBERG
LIECHTENSTEIN
SWITZERLAND
ITALY
LOMBARDIA
TRENTINO-ALTO ÁDIGE
SCHAFFHAUSEN
THURGAU
ZÜRICH
ZUG
SCHWYZ
GLARUS
SANKT GALLEN
APPENZELL-A.R.
APPENZELL-I.R.
OBWALDEN
NIDWALDEN
GRAUBÜNDEN
TICINO
Blumberg
Engen
Stockach
Bonndorf
Sipplingen
Überlingen
Heiligenberg
Baienfurt
Wolfegg
Leutkirch
Obergünzburg
Schongau
Weingarten
Ravensburg
Kisslegg
Altusried
Wildpoldsried
Unterthingau
Marktoberdorf
Hilzingen
Singen
Radolfzell
Allensbach
Markdorf
Isny
Kempten
Steingaden
Stühlingen
Thayngen
Schaffhausen
Neunkirch
Neuhausen
Feuerthalen
Rheinfall
Diessenhofen
Stein am Rhein
Steckborn
Konstanz
Meersburg
Meckenbeuren
Tettnang
Friedrichshafen
Wangen
Buchenberg
Durach
Rosshaupten
Forggensee
Sulzberg
Mittelberg
Nesselwang
Kreuzlingen
Bodensee (L. Constance)
Langenargen
Kreszbronn
Lindenberg
Weiler-Simmerberg
Weitnau
Rettenberg
Wertach
Pfronten
Schwangau
Füssen
Andelfingen
Eglisau
Glattfelden
Neftenbach
Seuzach
Frauenfeld
Weinfelden
Romanshorn
Scheidegg
Lindau
Oberstaufen
Immenstadt
Blaichach
Vils
Sulgen
Amriswil
Arbon
Bülach
Winterthur
Wängi
Bischofszell
Rorschach
Hard
Bregenz
Sonthofen
Hindelang
Reutte
Embrach
Elgg
Aadorf
Wil
Uzwil
Sankt Gallen
Rheineck
Wolfurt
Hittisau
Fischen
Weissenbach
Baden
Wettingen
Kloten
Wallisellen
Effretikon
Sirnach
Kirchberg
Gossau
Sankt Margrethen
Lustenau
Dornbirn
Egg
Oberstdorf
Ehrwald
Regensdorf
Turbenthal
Trogen
Widnau
Diepoldsau
Bezau
Dübendorf
Flawil
Degersheim
Herisau
Teufen
Altstätten
Bregenzer Wald
Hohenems
Allgäuer Alpen
Zürich
Schlieren
Bremgarten
Fällanden
Zollikon
Pfäffikon
Uster
Bauma
Bütschwil
Gais
Götzis
Hoher Freschen
Mittelberg
Mädelegabel
Nassereith
Kilchberg
Küsnacht
Wetzikon
Hinwil
Wattwil
Urnäsch
Appenzell
Oberriet
Au
Häselgehr
Adliswil
Meilen
Männedorf
Wald
Ebnat-Kappel
Säntis
Wasserauen
Rankweil
Damüls
Schröcken
Warth
Bach
Silz
Thalwil
Horgen
Rüti
Stäfa
Jona
Rapperswil
Nesslau
Unterwasser
Feldkirch
Imst
Affoltern
Wädenswil
Zürichsee
Gams
Lechtaler Alpen
Parseier-Sp.
Sins
Baar
Richterswil
Kaltbrunn
Speer
Grabs
Nenzing
Rote Wand
Oetz
Cham
Zug
Pfäffikon
Lachen
Schänis
Buchs
Schaan
Bludenz
Lech
Stuben
St. Anton
Zams
Landeck
Hochdorf
Unterägeri
Egg
Sihlsee
Walensee
Churfisten
Sevelen
Vaduz
Dalaas
Flirsch
Arlbergpass
Root
Ebikon
Zugersee
Einsiedeln
Näfels
Walenstadt
Rätikon
Schruns
Montafon
Trisanna
Prutz
St. Leonhard
Küssnacht
Emmenbrücke
Arth
Murg
Kuchenspitze
Luzern
Kriens
Horw
Rigi
Goldau
Netstal
Glarus
Mels
Sargans
Schesaplana
Ischgl
Vesulspitze
Feuchten
Vitznau
Weggis
Mythen
Schwyz
Glärnisch
Schwanden
Bad Ragaz
St-Gallenkirch
Gaschurn
Mittelberg
Vierwaldstättersee
Brunnen
Muotathal
Pizol
Schiers
Galtür
Samnaun
Stans
Glarner Alpen
Vättis
Landquart
Küblis
Prätigau
Silvretta Gruppe
Martina
Nauders
Wildspitze
Ötztaler Alpen
Kerns
Bauen
Linthal
Elm
Altdorf
Bürglen
Uri-Rotstock
Hausstock
Chur
Klosters
Piz Buin
Résia
Weisskugel
Flims
Domat Ems
Langwies
Erstfeld
Engelberg
Titlis
Tödi
Rhein
Bonaduz
Davos
Arosa
Unter-engadin
Scuol (Schuls)
Ardez
San Valentino alla Muta
Oberalpstock
Trun
Ilanz
Churwalden
Flüelapass
Susch
Malles Venosta
Urner Alpen
Gadmen
Wassen
Disentis (Muster)
Vorderrhein
Oberland
Lenzerheide
Wiesen
Piz Vadret
Zernez
Piz Sesvenna
Göschenen
Oberalppass
Sedrun
Thusis
Sluderno
Silandro (Schlanders)
Dammastock
Hospental
Andermatt
Vrin
Hinterrhein
Tiefencastel
Albula
Filisur
Piz Kesch
Santa Maria
Val Venosta
Furkapass
Realp
Pic Medel
Thalkirch
Vals
Savognin
La Punt
Prato allo Stelvio
Láces
St. Gotthard
Gletsch
Andeer
Piz d'Err
Samedan
Livigno
Passo dello Stelvio
Martello
Ulrichen
Bedretto
Airolo
Olivone
Adula-Gruppe
Rheinwaldhorn
Splügen
Splügenpass
Mulegns
Sankt Moritz
Pontresina
Julierpass
Ortles
Bórmio
Münster
Faido
Lepontine Alpen
Paso del San Bernardino
San Bernardino
Piz Platta
Silvaplana
Passo del Bernina
Basodino
Fusio
Campo Tencia
Malvaglia
Campodolcino
Malojapass
Maloja
Piz Bernina
Alpi Retiche
Stelvio
Formazza
Sonogno
Bodio
Biasca
Mesocco
Pizzo Stella
Vicosoprano
Rossa
Chiavenna
Castasegna
Poschiavo
Sóndalo
Vermiglio
Dimaro
Cevio
Maggia
Mera
Monte Disgrazia
Chiesa in Valmalenco
Grosio
Grosotto
Ponte di Legno
Passo del Tonale
La Presanella
Toce
Vogorno
Novate Mezzola
Brusio
Tirano
Vezza di Oglio
Madonna di Campiglio
Varzo
Arbedo
Bellinzona
Verceia
Sóndrio
Chiuro
Téglio
Edolo
Crevoladóssola
Intragna
Locarno
Minusio
Giubiasco
Gravedona
Morbegno
Albosaggia
Aprica
Mte. Adamello
Pinzolo
Masera
Losone
Ascona
Cadenazzo
Talamona
Adda
Valtellina
Malonno
Domodóssola
Brissago
Vira
Pzo. di Gino
Cólico
Delébio
Santa Maria Maggiore
Dongo
Monte Legnone
Cedégolo
Cannóbio
Lago di Como
Pizzo di Coca
Villadóssola
Cannero Riviera
Maccagno
Porlezza
Bellano
Gerola Alta
Valbondione
Capo di Ponte
Tione di Trento
Vogogna
Lago Maggiore
Agno
Lugano
Menaggio
Varenna
Branzi
Alpi Orobie
Schilpário
Val Camónica
Valli Giudicarie
Luino
Lago di Lugano
Tremezzo
Intróbio
Ornavasso
Ghiffa
Ponte Tresa
Melide
Mte. Generoso
Bellágio
Piazza Brembano
Borno
Breno
Bienno
Pieve di Bono
Riva del Garda
Gravellona Toce
Pallanza
Verbania
Laveno
Argegno
Mendrisio
Monte San Primo
Mandello del Lário
Valle Seriana
Clusone
Omegna
Nesso
San Giovanni Bianco
Brembo
Monte Colombine
Condino
Stresa
Gavirate
Balerna
Chiasso
Molrásio
Canzo
Lecco
Gandino
Darfo
Bagolino
Storo
L. d'Orta
Varese
Malnate
Como
Erba
Lovere
Pisogne
Cóllio
Limone sul Garda
Malcesine
Lago di Varese
Olgiate Comasco
Oggiono
Calolziocorte
Zogno
Albino
Gazzaniga
Marone
L. d'Idro
Méina
Arona
Borgomanero
Sesto Calende
Tradate
Cantù
Brianza
Ponte San Pietro
Bérgamo
Casazza
L. d'Iseo
Gardone Val Trómpia
Vestone
Idro
L. di Garda
Serravalle
Somma Lombardo
Cassano Magnago
Carate Brianza
Trescore Balneário
Sesia
Chiese
Gargnano
Meda
Séveso
Merate
Seriate
Sarezzo
Sabbio Chiese
Vobarno
Gallarate
Saronno
Seregno
Dálmine
Stezzano
Sárnico
Iseo
Gardone Riviera
East from Greenwich
COPYRIGHT PHILIP'S

1:2 000 000

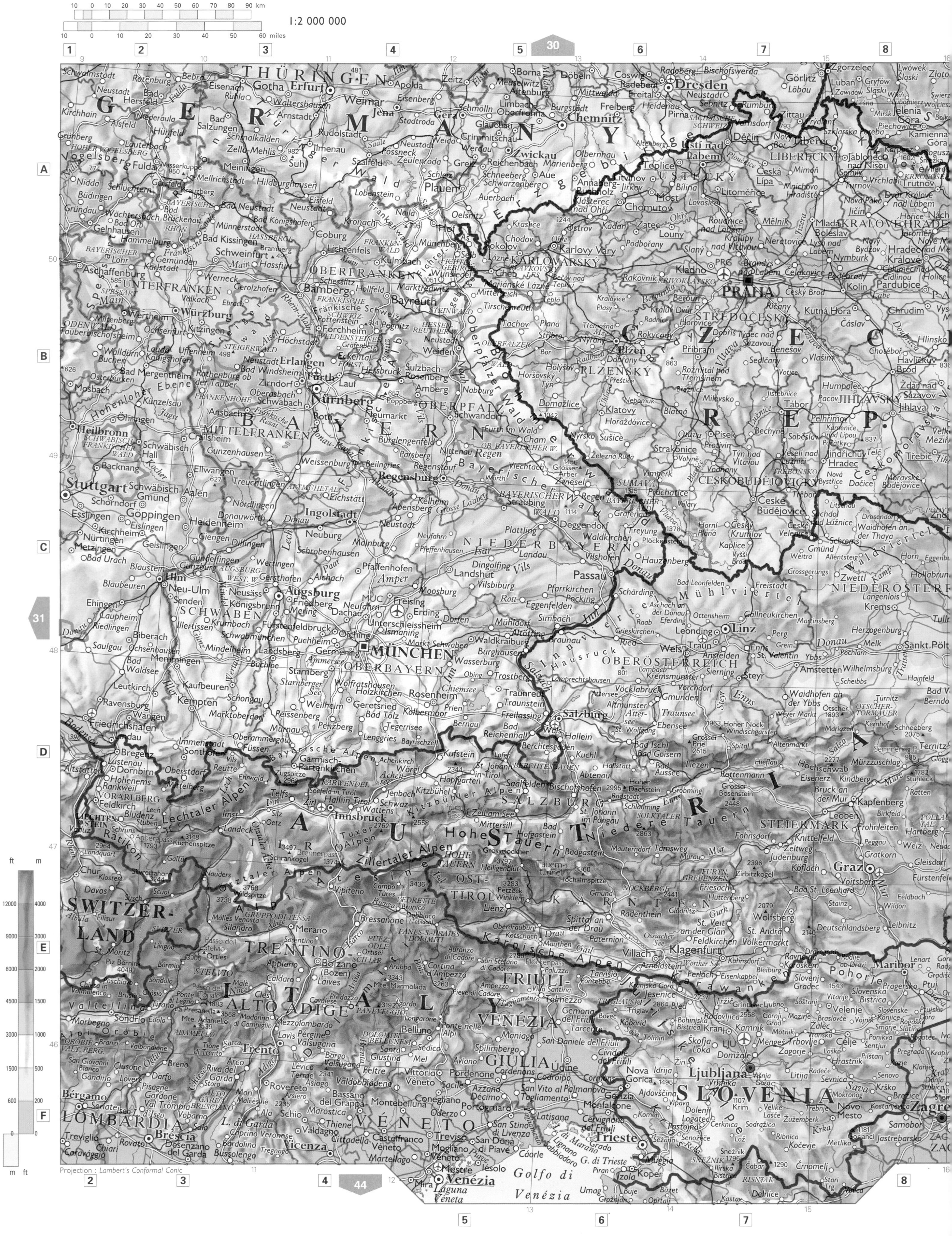
GERMANY
CZECH REP.
AUSTRIA
ITALY
SWITZERLAND
SLOVENIA
THÜRINGEN
BAYERN
OBERBAYERN
NIEDERBAYERN
OBERPFALZ
MITTELFRANKEN
OBERFRANKEN
UNTERFRANKEN
SCHWABEN
NIEDERÖSTERREICH
OBERÖSTERREICH
SALZBURG
STEIERMARK
KÄRNTEN
TIROL
VORARLBERG
TRENTINO-ALTO ADIGE
FRIULI-VENEZIA GIULIA
VENETO
LOMBARDIA
PLZEŇSKÝ
KARLOVARSKÝ
ÚSTECKÝ
LIBERECKÝ
STŘEDOČESKÝ
JIHOČESKÝ
ČESKOBUDĚJOVICKÝ
PRAHA
MÜNCHEN
Dresden
Nürnberg
Regensburg
Augsburg
Stuttgart
Würzburg
Ingolstadt
Linz
Salzburg
Innsbruck
Graz
Klagenfurt
Ljubljana
Venézia
Trieste
Plzeň
Chemnitz
Erfurt
Passau
Golfo di Venézia
Projection: Lambert's Conformal Conic

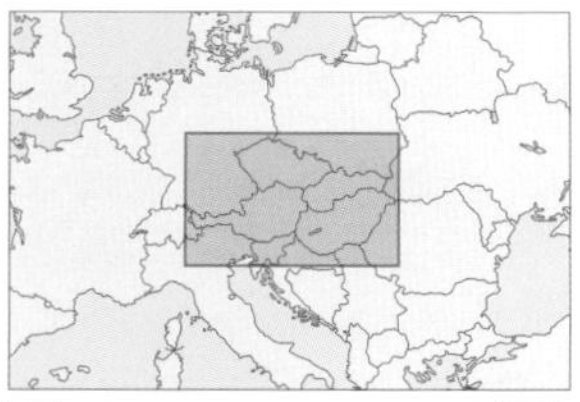

National Parks

Underlined towns give their name to the administrative area in which they stand.

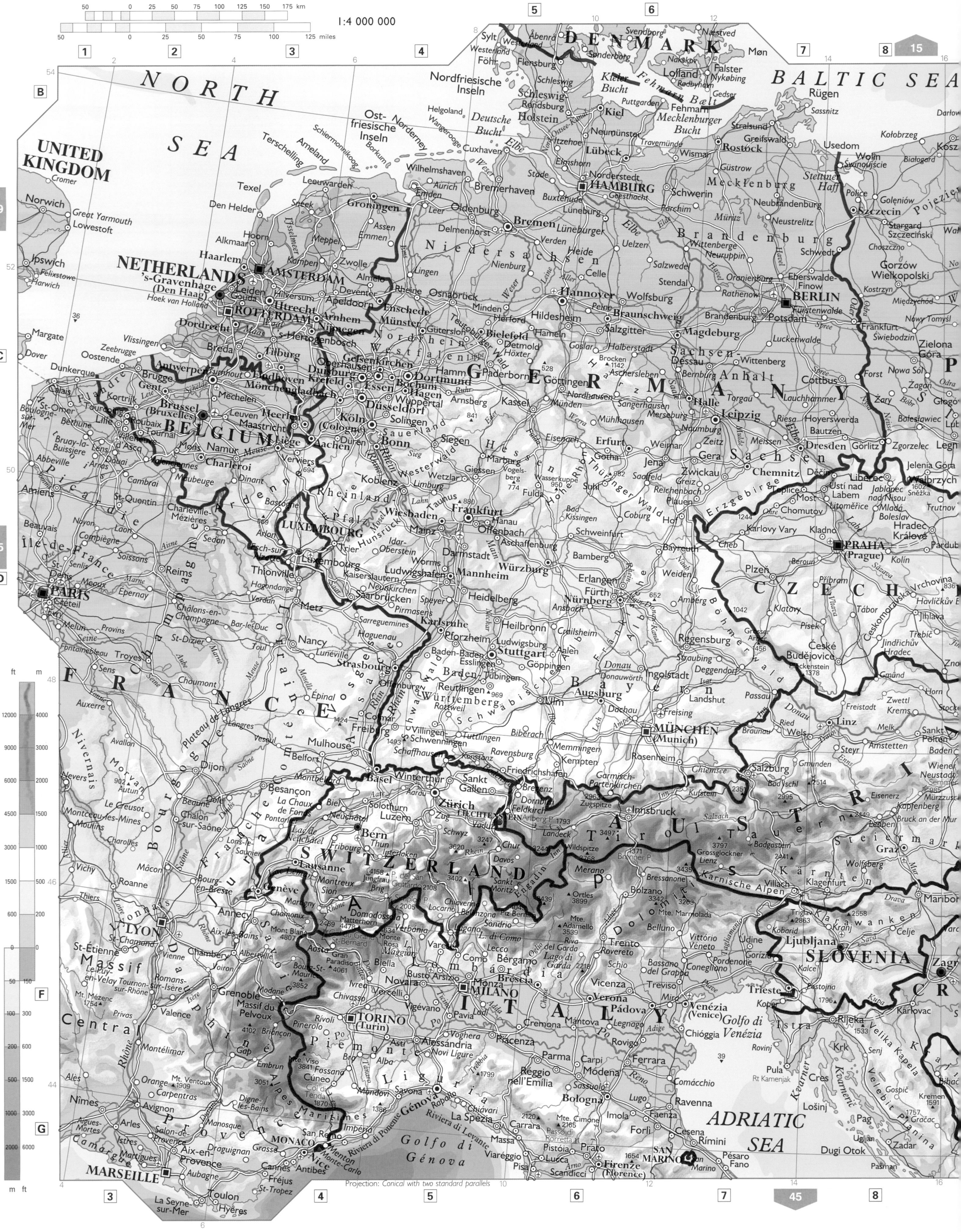
1:4 000 000
Projection: Conical with two standard parallels
NORTH SEA
BALTIC SEA
ADRIATIC SEA
UNITED KINGDOM
DENMARK
NETHERLANDS
BELGIUM
LUXEMBOURG
GERMANY
FRANCE
SWITZERLAND
LIECHTENSTEIN
AUSTRIA
CZECH
ITALY
SLOVENIA
MONACO
SAN MARINO
AMSTERDAM
's-Gravenhage (Den Haag)
ROTTERDAM
Utrecht
Brussel (Bruxelles)
Antwerpen
Gent
Brugge
Liège
LUXEMBOURG
Luxembourg
PARIS
Reims
Metz
Nancy
Strasbourg
Dijon
Besançon
Lyon
Grenoble
MARSEILLE
Toulon
Nice
Genève
Lausanne
Bern
Basel
Zürich
HAMBURG
Bremen
Hannover
BERLIN
Potsdam
Magdeburg
Leipzig
Dresden
Halle
Köln (Cologne)
Düsseldorf
Dortmund
Essen
Duisburg
Bonn
Frankfurt
Wiesbaden
Mainz
Mannheim
Stuttgart
Karlsruhe
Nürnberg
Würzburg
MÜNCHEN (Munich)
Augsburg
Kiel
Lübeck
Rostock
Schwerin
Szczecin
PRAHA (Prague)
Plzeň
Salzburg
Linz
Innsbruck
Graz
Klagenfurt
Ljubljana
Trieste
MILANO
TORINO (Turin)
Génova
Venézia (Venice)
Pádova
Verona
Bologna
Firenze (Florence)
Parma
Modena
Golfo di Génova
Golfo di Venézia
Deutsche Bucht
Kieler Bucht
Mecklenburger Bucht
Nordfriesische Inseln
Ostfriesische Inseln
Niedersachsen
Nordrhein-Westfalen
Mecklenburg
Brandenburg
Sachsen-Anhalt
Sachsen
Hessen
Thüringer Wald
Rheinland-Pfalz
Baden-Württemberg
Bayern
Schwäbische Alb
Schwarzwald
Erzgebirge
Böhmerwald
Ardennes
Lorraine
Vosges
Champagne
Picardie
Île-de-France
Bourgogne
Franche-Comté
Jura
Massif Central
Provence
Savoie
Dauphiné
Alpes Maritimes
Alpi
Tirol
Hohe Tauern
Dolomiti
Piemonte
Lombardia
Liguria
Istra
Karawanken
Mont Blanc 4807
Matterhorn 4478
Zugspitze 2963
Grossglockner 3797
Brocken 1142

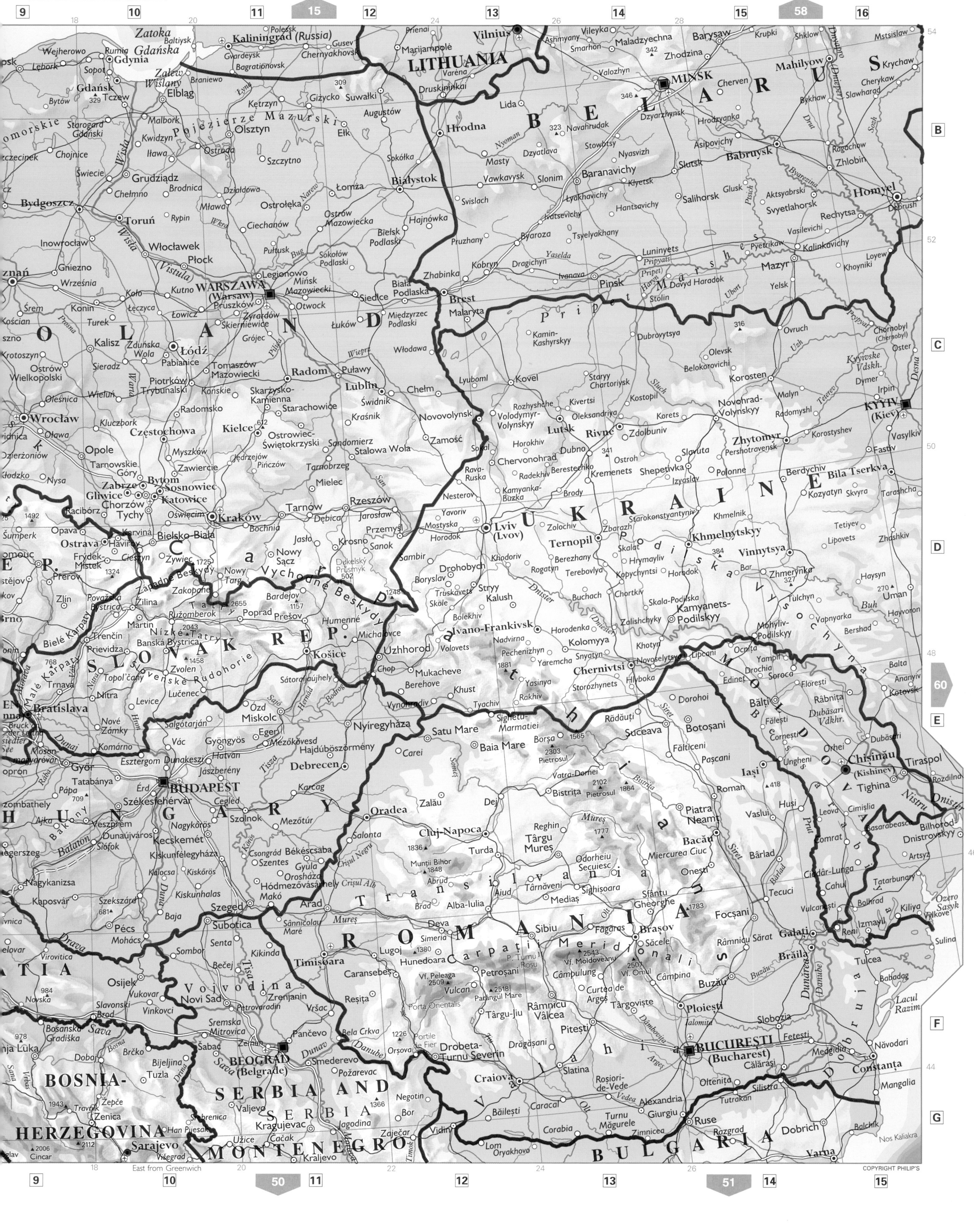

LITHUANIA
BELARUS
POLAND
UKRAINE
SLOVAK REP.
HUNGARY
ROMANIA
MOLDOVA
SERBIA AND MONTENEGRO
SERBIA
BOSNIA-HERZEGOVINA
BULGARIA
Vilnius
MINSK
Kaliningrad (Russia)
Zatoka Gdańska
Gdynia
Gdańsk
Elbląg
Olsztyn
Pojezierze Mazurski
Suwałki
Hrodna
Białystok
Bydgoszcz
Toruń
Włocławek
Płock
WARSZAWA (Warsaw)
Łódź
Radom
Lublin
Kielce
Częstochowa
Wrocław
Opole
Katowice
Kraków
Tarnów
Rzeszów
Przemyśl
Brest
Pinsk
Baranavichy
Babruysk
Mahilyow
Homyel
Mazyr
Pripyat
Kovel
Lutsk
Rivne
Zhytomyr
KYYIV (Kiev)
Bila Tserkva
Lviv (Lvov)
Ternopil
Khmelnytskyy
Vinnytsya
Ivano-Frankivsk
Chernivtsi
Uzhhorod
Košice
Prešov
Žilina
Bratislava
Ostrava
Miskolc
Debrecen
Nyíregyháza
BUDAPEST
Székesfehérvár
Kecskemét
Szeged
Pécs
Balaton
Oradea
Cluj-Napoca
Satu Mare
Baia Mare
Suceava
Iaşi
Bacău
Chişinău (Kishinev)
Tiraspol
Transilvania
Carpaţii Meridionali
Braşov
Sibiu
Timişoara
Arad
Craiova
Piteşti
Ploieşti
BUCUREŞTI (Bucharest)
Constanţa
Galaţi
Brăila
Novi Sad
BEOGRAD (Belgrade)
Osijek
Sarajevo
Tuzla
Zenica
Ruse
Varna
Dobrich
Dunav
Vojvodina
Dobrogea
East from Greenwich
COPYRIGHT PHILIP'S

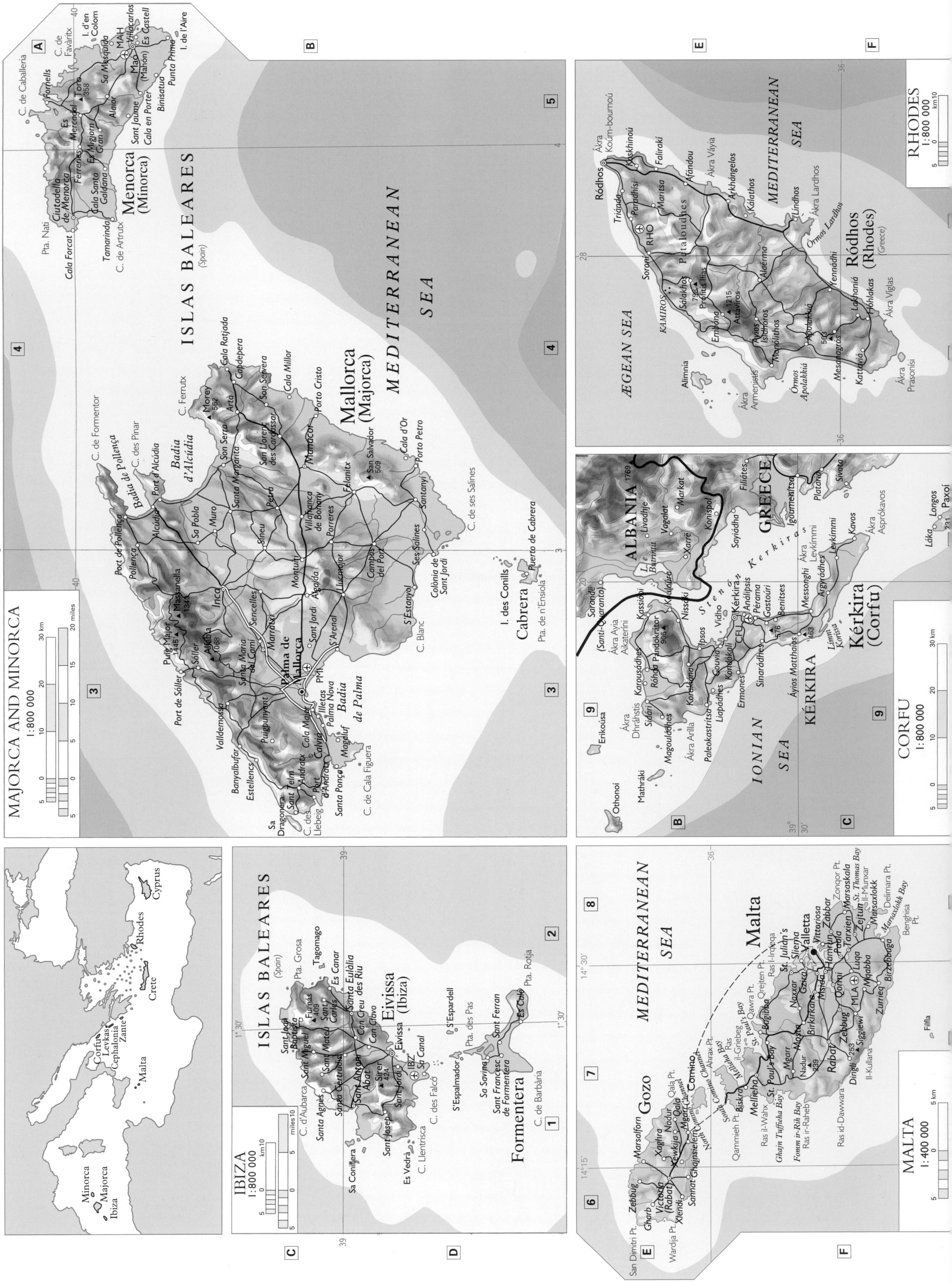
MAJORCA AND MINORCA
1:800 000
ISLAS BALEARES
(Spain)
MEDITERRANEAN
SEA
Mallorca
(Majorca)
Menorca
(Minorca)
Palma de Mallorca
Badia de Palma
Badia d'Alcúdia
Cabrera
IBIZA
1:800 000
Eivissa
(Ibiza)
Formentera
RHODES
1:800 000
Ródhos
(Rhodes)
(Greece)
ÆGEAN SEA
CORFU
1:800 000
Kérkira
(Corfu)
KÉRKIRA
IONIAN
SEA
ALBANIA
GREECE
MALTA
1:400 000
Malta
Gozo
Comino
Valletta
Minorca
Majorca
Ibiza
Corfu
Levkas
Cephalonia
Zante
Malta
Crete
Rhodes
Cyprus

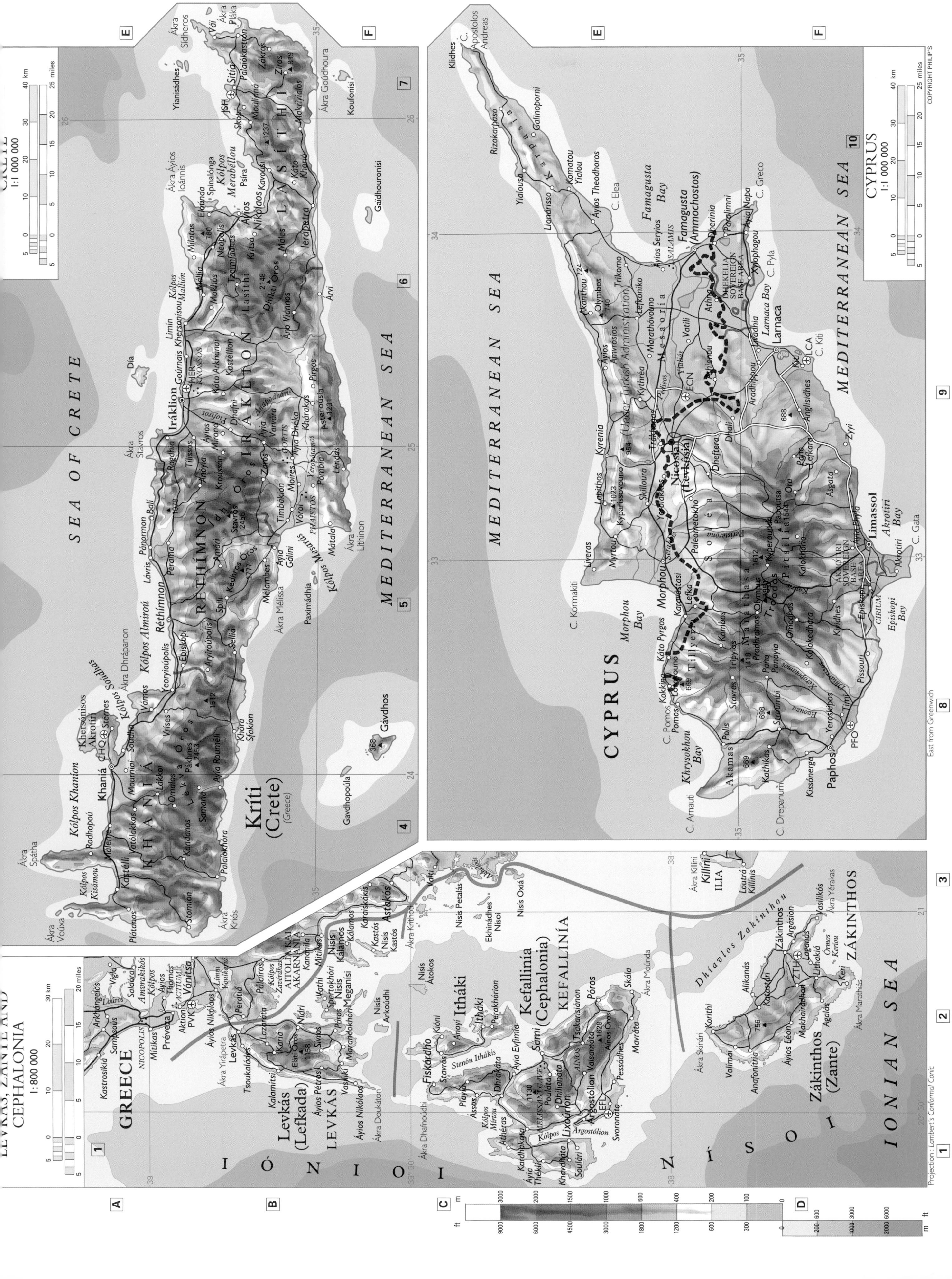

CRETE
1:1 000 000
SEA OF CRETE
MEDITERRANEAN SEA
Kríti
(Crete)
(Greece)
KHANIÁ
RÉTHIMNON
IRÁKLION
LASÍTHI
Khaniá
Réthimnon
Iráklion
Áyios Nikólaos
Sitía
Ierápetra
Gávdhos
CYPRUS
1:1 000 000
CYPRUS
MEDITERRANEAN SEA
Nicosia
(Lefkosia)
Limassol
Larnaca
Paphos
Famagusta
(Ammochostos)
Famagusta Bay
Morphou Bay
Kyrenia
Troodos
(Under Turkish Administration)
AKROTIRI SOVEREIGN BASE AREA
DHEKELIA SOVEREIGN BASE AREA
CEPHALONIA
1:800 000
GREECE
IÓNIOI NÍSOI
IONIAN SEA
Levkas
(Lefkada)
LEVKÁS
Itháki
Kefallinía
(Cephalonia)
KEFALLINÍA
Zákinthos
(Zante)
ZÁKINTHOS
Préveza
Argostólion
East from Greenwich
Projection : Lambert's Conformal Conic
COPYRIGHT PHILIP'S

1:2 000 000
km
miles
FRANCE
ESPAÑA
ANDORRA
BALEARES
MENORCA
MALLORCA
CATALUÑA
ARAGÓN
NAVARRA
LA RIOJA
PAÍS VASCO
CASTILLA Y LEÓN
LANGUEDOC
ROUSSILLON
MIDI-PYRÉNÉES
PYRÉNÉES
Golfe de Gascogne
Costa Brava
Costa Dorada
Costa del Azahar
BARCELONA
Zaragoza
Toulouse
Bilbao
Vitoria-Gasteiz
Pamplona
Donostia-San Sebastián
Logroño
Burgos
Soria
Huesca
Lleida
Tarragona
Girona
Perpignan
Bayonne
Pau
Tarbes
Carcassonne
Narbonne
Béziers
Santander
MADRID
Guadalajara
Teruel
Cuenca
Castelló de la Plana
Ebro
Segre
Cinca
Montes Universales
Sierra de Albarracín
Sistema Ibérico
Picos de Urbión
Sierra de la Demanda
Delta del Ebro

28
42

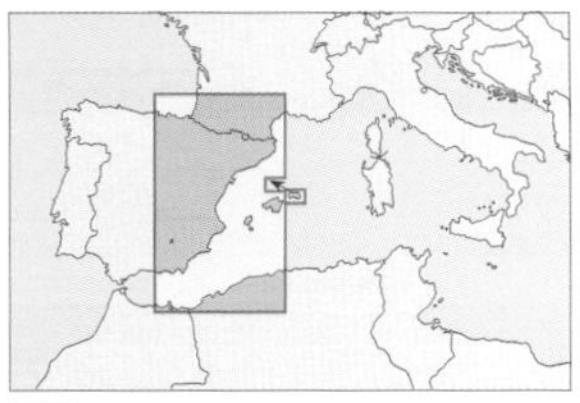

MEDITERRANEAN SEA
Golfo de Valencia
Costa Blanca
Costa del Sol
CASTILLA-LA MANCHA
VALENCIA
ALICANTE
MURCIA
ALMERÍA
GRANADA
JAÉN
ALBACETE
CIUDAD REAL
Valencia
Alicante
Murcia
Cartagena
Almería
Granada
Albacete
Lorca
Elche
Benidorm
Denia
Gandia
Eivissa (Ibiza)
Formentera
Cabrera
Palma
Alborán (Sp.)
Melilla (Sp.)
Nador
ALGER (Algiers)
Blida
Médéa
Oran
Mostaganem
Sidi-bel-Abbès
Mascara
Tiaret
Relizane
Ech Cheliff
G. de Almería
G. de Mazarrón
Golfe d'Arzew
National Parks
Nature Parks in Spain
Projection : Lambert's Conformal Conic
COPYRIGHT PHILIP'S
West from Greenwich
East from Greenwich
m
ft

10 0 10 20 30 40 50 60 70 80 90 km

1:2 000 000

10 0 10 20 30 40 50 60 miles

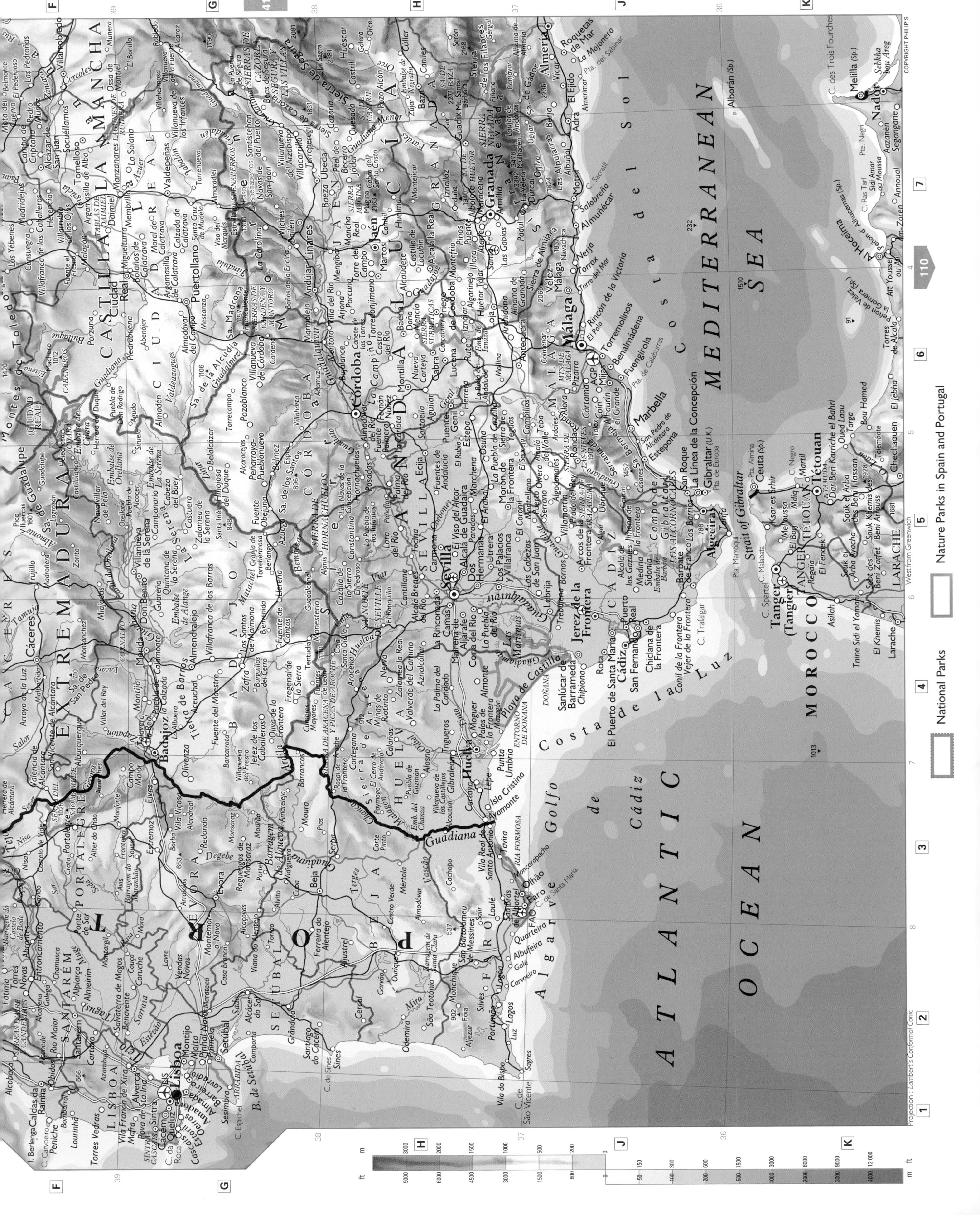
ATLANTIC OCEAN
MEDITERRANEAN SEA
MOROCCO
Golfo de Cádiz
Costa de la Luz
Costa del Sol
Strait of Gibraltar
EXTREMADURA
CASTILLA-LA MANCHA
ANDALUCÍA
Lisboa
Sevilla
Córdoba
Granada
Málaga
Cádiz
Gibraltar (U.K.)
Tanger (Tangier)
Tétouan
Ceuta (Sp.)
Melilla (Sp.)
National Parks
Nature Parks in Spain and Portugal
Projection : Lambert's Conformal Conic
West from Greenwich
COPYRIGHT PHILIP'S

1:2 000 000

10 0 10 20 30 40 50 60 70 80 90 km

10 0 10 20 30 40 50 60 miles

Projection : Lambert's Conformal Conic

East from Greenwich

m	4000	3000	2000	1500	1000	500	200	0
ft	12 000	9000	6000	4500	3000	1500	600	

ft	150	300	600	1500	3000	6000
m	0 50	100	200	500	1000	2000

National Parks

Underlined towns give their name to t administrative area in which they stand

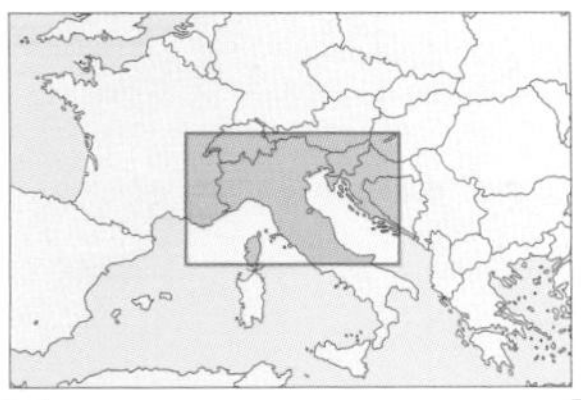

Administrative divisions in Croatia:
Brodsko-Posavska   4 Medimurska   8 Virovitičko-Podravska
Koprivničko-Križevačka   6 Požeško-Slavonska   10 Zagreba čka
Krapinsko-Zagorska   7 Varaždinska

Nature Parks in Italy

Inter-entity boundaries as agreed
at the 1995 Dayton Peace Agreement

COPYRIGHT PHILIP'S

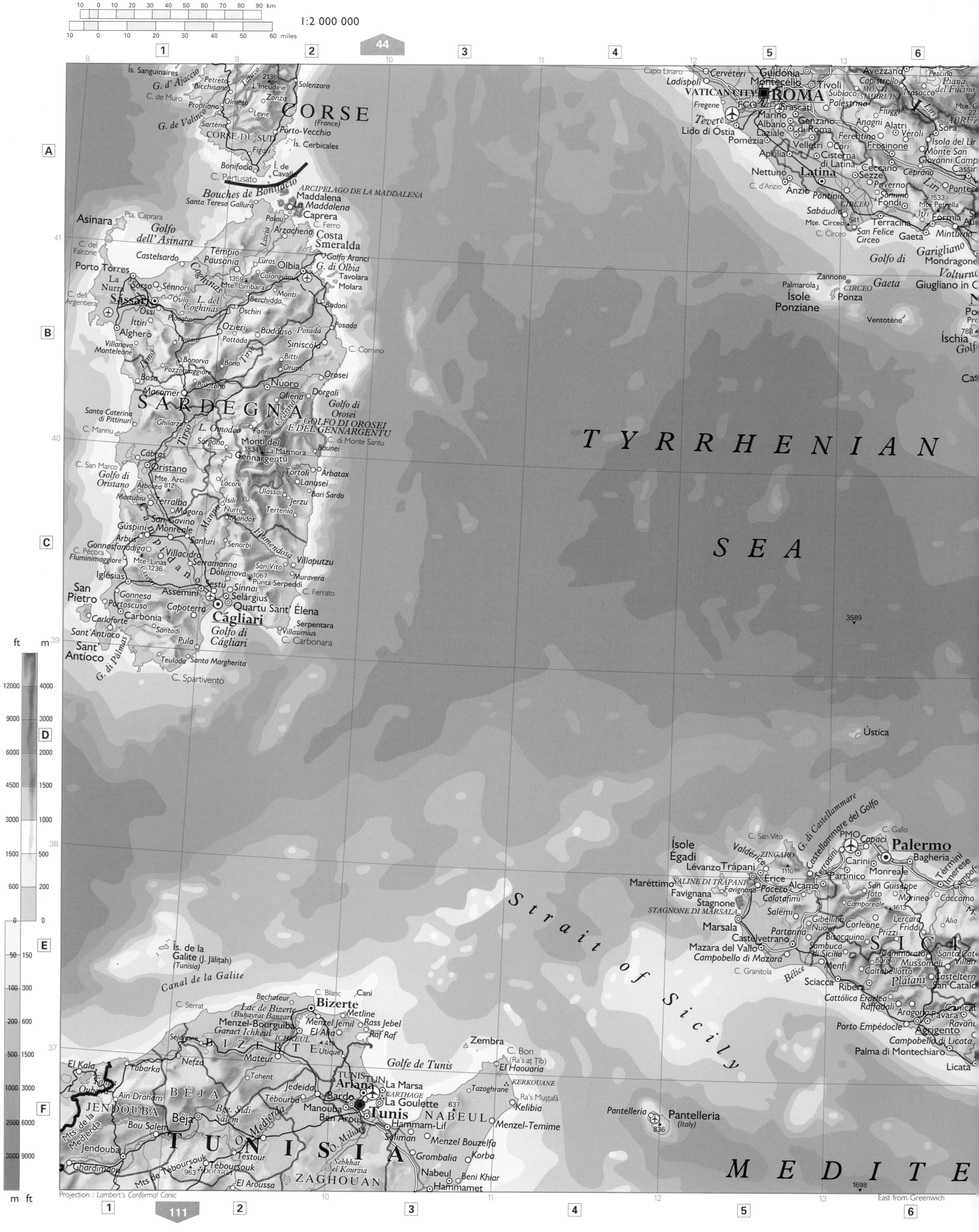
1:2 000 000
km
miles
44
111
CORSE
(France)
CORSE-DU-SUD
Îs. Sanguinaires
G. d' Ajaccio
Petreto-Bicchisano
C. de Muro
Propriano
G. de Valinco
Sartène
Olmeto
L'Incudine
2136
Zonza
Levie
Solenzara
Porto-Vecchio
Îs. Cerbicales
Figari
Bonifacio
Î. de Cavallo
C. Pertusato
Bouches de Bonifacio
ARCIPELAGO DE LA MADDALENA
Maddalena
La Maddalena
Caprera
Santa Teresa Gallura
Palau
Arzachena
Costa Smeralda
C. Ferro
Asinara
Pta. Caprara
Golfo dell' Asinara
C. del Falcone
Castelsardo
Tempio Pausania
Porto Torres
Golfo Aranci
G. di Ólbia
Ólbia
Luras
Calangianus
Tavolara
Molara
Sorso
Sénnori
Sássari
Osilo
L. del Coghinas
Mte. Limbara
1359
Berchidda
Monti
C. dell' Argentiera
Ossi
Íttiri
Ploaghe
Óschiri
Budoni
Alghero
Ozieri
Pattada
Buddusò
Posada
Villanova Monteleone
Thiesi
Siniscola
C. Comino
Bonorva
Bono
Bitti
Pozzomaggiore
Orune
Bosa
Orosei
Macomer
Bolotana
Núoro
Oliena
Dorgali
SARDEGNA
Golfo di Orosei
GOLFO DI OROSEI E DEL GENNARGENTU
Santa Caterina di Pittinuri
Ghilarza
C. Mannu
L. Omodeo
Fonni
Sórgono
Monti del Gennargentu
1834
La Mármora
C. di Monte Santu
Baunei
C. San Marco
Cábras
Oristano
Golfo di Oristano
Tortolì
Árbatax
Mte. Arci
812
Arborea
Lanusei
Láconi
Ulássai
Bari Sardo
Marrúbiu
Terralba
Jerzu
Ísili
Nurri
Tertenia
Mogoro
Mandas
San Gavino Monreale
Flumendosa
Gúspini
Arbus
Sanluri
Gonnosfanadiga
C. Pécora
Fluminimaggiore
Villacidro
Senorbì
Mte. Linas
1236
Villaputzu
Serramanna
Dolignova
San Vito
1067
Muravera
Iglésias
Punta Serpeddì
Sestu
Sinnai
C. Ferrato
Assémini
San Pietro
Gonnesa
Portoscuso
Selárgius
Quartu Sant' Élena
Capoterra
Carloforte
Carbónia
Cágliari
Serpentara
Golfo di Cágliari
Sant' Antioco
Santadi
Villasimius
C. Carbonara
Pula
Sant' Antíoco
G. di Palmas
Teulada
Santa Margherita
C. Spartivento
Capo Linaro
Ladispoli
Cerveteri
Guidonia-Montecelio
Tívoli
VATICAN CITY
ROMA
Subiaco
Fregene
Frascati
Palestrina
FCO
Tevere
Marino
Albano Laziale
Genzano di Roma
Lido di Ostia
Pomezia
Velletri
Cori
Aprilia
Cisterna di Latina
Anzio
Nettuno
C. d'Anzio
Latina
Pontinia
Sabáudia
Mte. Circeo
541
C. Circeo
San Felice Circeo
Terracina
Fondi
Priverno
Sezze
Ceccano
Frosinone
Ferentino
Anagni
Alatri
Veroli
Fiuggi
Avezzano
Capistrello
Trasacco
Pescina
Piana del Fucino
MONTI SIMBRUINI
Sora
Isola del Liri
Monte San Giovanni Campano
Cassino
Ceprano
Pontecorvo
Sonnino
Itri
1533
Mte. Petrella
Fórmia
Gaeta
Minturno
Golfo di Gaeta
Garigliano
Mondragone
Volturno
Giugliano in Campania
Palmarola
Zannone
Ísole Ponziane
CIRCEO
Ponza
Ventoténe
Íschia
788
TYRRHENIAN SEA
3589
Ústica
C. San Vito
G. di Castellammare
Castellammare del Golfo
C. Gallo
Capaci
PMO
Palermo
Bagheria
Carini
Ísole Égadi
Valdérice
ZINGARO
Lévanzo
Trápani
1110
Érice
Partinico
Monreale
Termini Imerese
Maréttimo
SALINE DI TRAPANI
Favignana
Paceco
Alcamo
San Giuseppe Jato
Calatafimi
Marineo
Stagnone
STAGNONE DI MARSALA
Salemi
Camporeale
1613
Cáccamo
Marsala
Gibellina Nuova
Corleone
Lercara Friddi
Partanna
Castelvetrano
Bisacquino
Prizzi
Mazara del Vallo
Sambuca di Sicilia
Cammarata
Campobello di Mazara
Menfi
Bivona
Mussomeli
Bélice
C. Granitola
Caltabellotta
Plátani
Sciacca
Ribera
Cattólica Eraclea
Raffadali
Aragona
Favara
Porto Empédocle
Agrigento
Campobello di Licata
Palma di Montechiaro
Licata
Strait of Sicily
Pantelleria
836
(Italy)
MEDITE
1698
Îs. de la Galite (J. Jâlitah)
(Tunisia)
Canal de la Galite
C. Serrat
Bechateur
C. Blanc
Cani
Lac de Bizerte
(Buhayrat Banzart)
Bizerte
Metline
Menzel-Bourguiba
Menzel Jemil
Rass Jebel
Garaet Ichkeul
El Alia
Raf Raf
Sejenane
ICHKEUL
BIZERTE
419
Utique
Zembra
C. Bon
(Ra's at Tib)
El Haouaria
Mateur
Golfe de Tunis
El Kala
Nefza
Tabarka
Tahent
KERKOUANE
Jedeida
TUNIS
La Marsa
CARTHAGE
Tazoghrane
Ain Draham
BÉJA
Tébourba
Ariana
Bardo
La Goulette
637
Ra's Muştafá
Kelibia
JENDOUBA
Béja
Bge. Sidi Salem
Medjerda
Manouba
Tunis
Ben Arous
NABEUL
Menzel-Temime
Bou Salem
Hammam-Lif
Mts. de la Medjerda
Jendouba
TUNISIA
O. Miliane
Soliman
Menzel Bouzelfa
Grombalia
Korba
Ghardimaou
Mts de Téboursouk
963
Téboursouk
Testour
DOUGGA
Sebkhat el Kourzia
Nabeul
Beni Khiar
El Aroussa
ZAGHOUAN
Hammamet
Projection : Lambert's Conformal Conic
East from Greenwich
ft
m
12000
9000
6000
4500
3000
1500
600
4000
3000
2000
1500
1000
500
200
0
50
100
200
500
1000
2000
3000
150
300
600
1500
3000
6000
9000

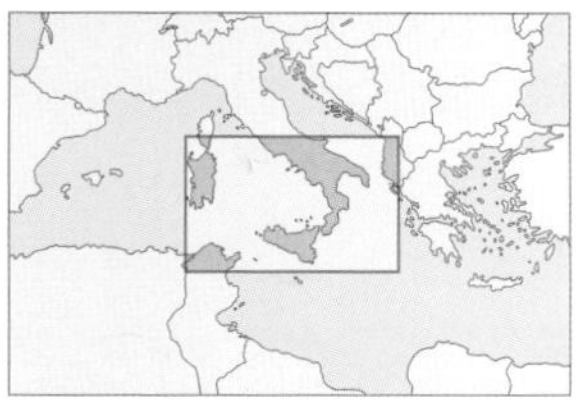

Nature Parks in Italy

National Parks

Underlined towns give their name to the administrative area in which they stand.

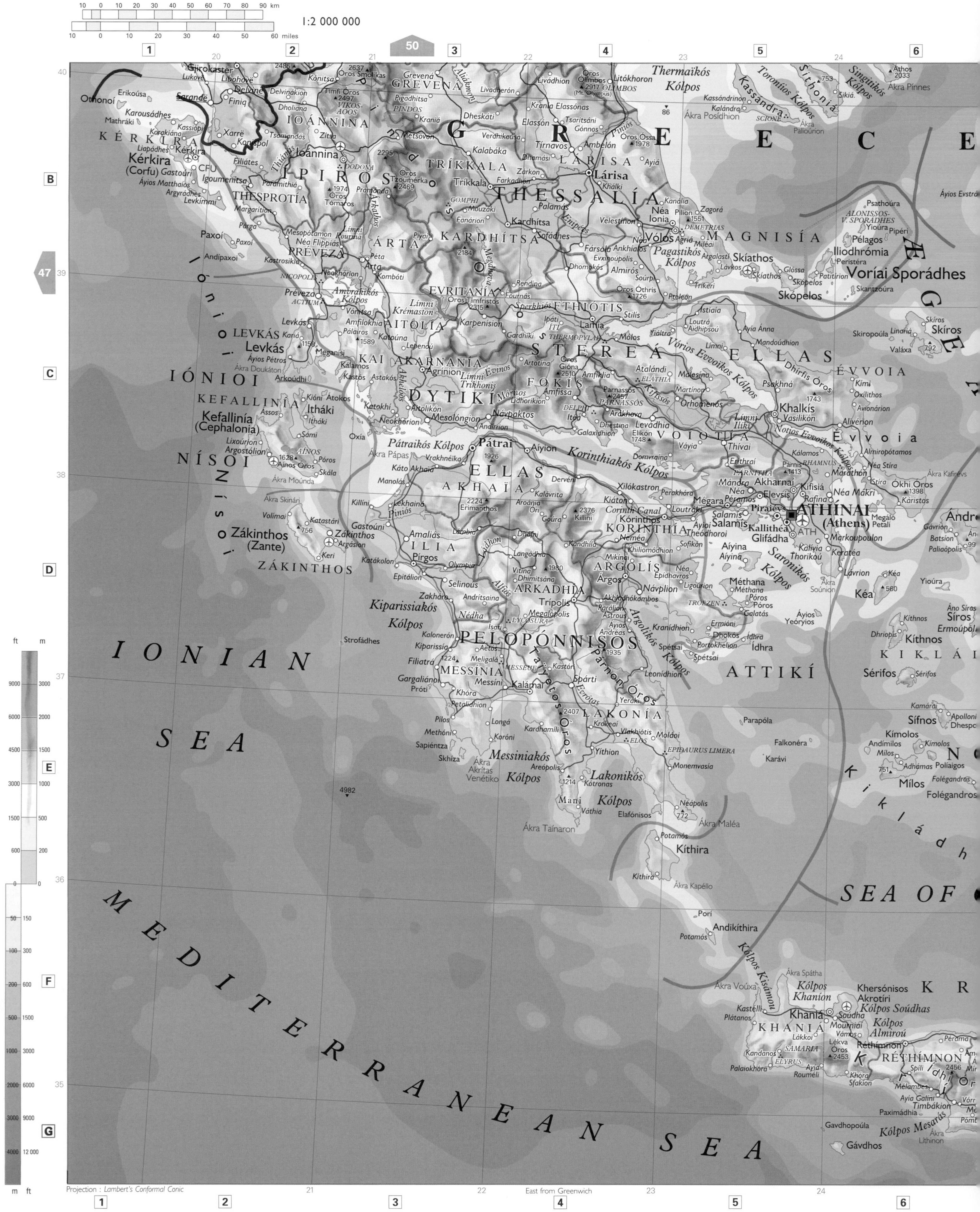
1:2 000 000
km
miles
IONIAN SEA
MEDITERRANEAN SEA
SEA OF
GREECE
IÓNIOI NÍSOI
Kérkira (Corfu)
Kefallinía (Cephalonia)
Zákinthos (Zante)
Levkás
Itháki
Ioánnina
IPIROS
THESSALÍA
Lárisa
Vólos
Tríkkala
Kardhítsa
MAGNISÍA
Vóriai Sporádhes
STERÉA ELLAS
ÉVVOIA
Khalkís
Athínai (Athens)
Piraiévs
ATTIKÍ
Pátrai
PELOPÓNNISOS
Kórinthos
Tripolis
Kalámai
Spárti
Kíthira
Khaniá
Réthimnon
Gávdhos
Thermaïkós Kólpos
Korinthiakós Kólpos
Saronikós Kólpos
Argolikós Kólpos
Lakonikós Kólpos
Messiniakós Kólpos
Kiparissiakós Kólpos
Pátraikós Kólpos
Projection : Lambert's Conformal Conic
East from Greenwich

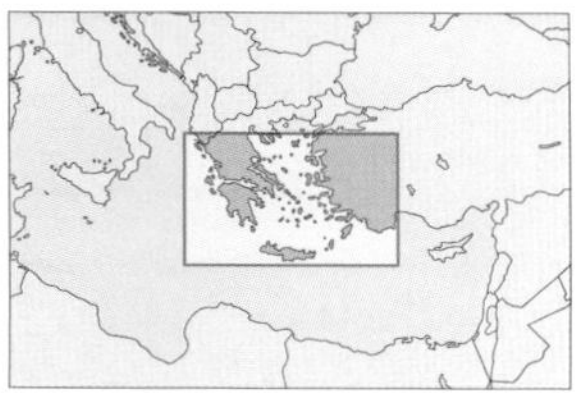

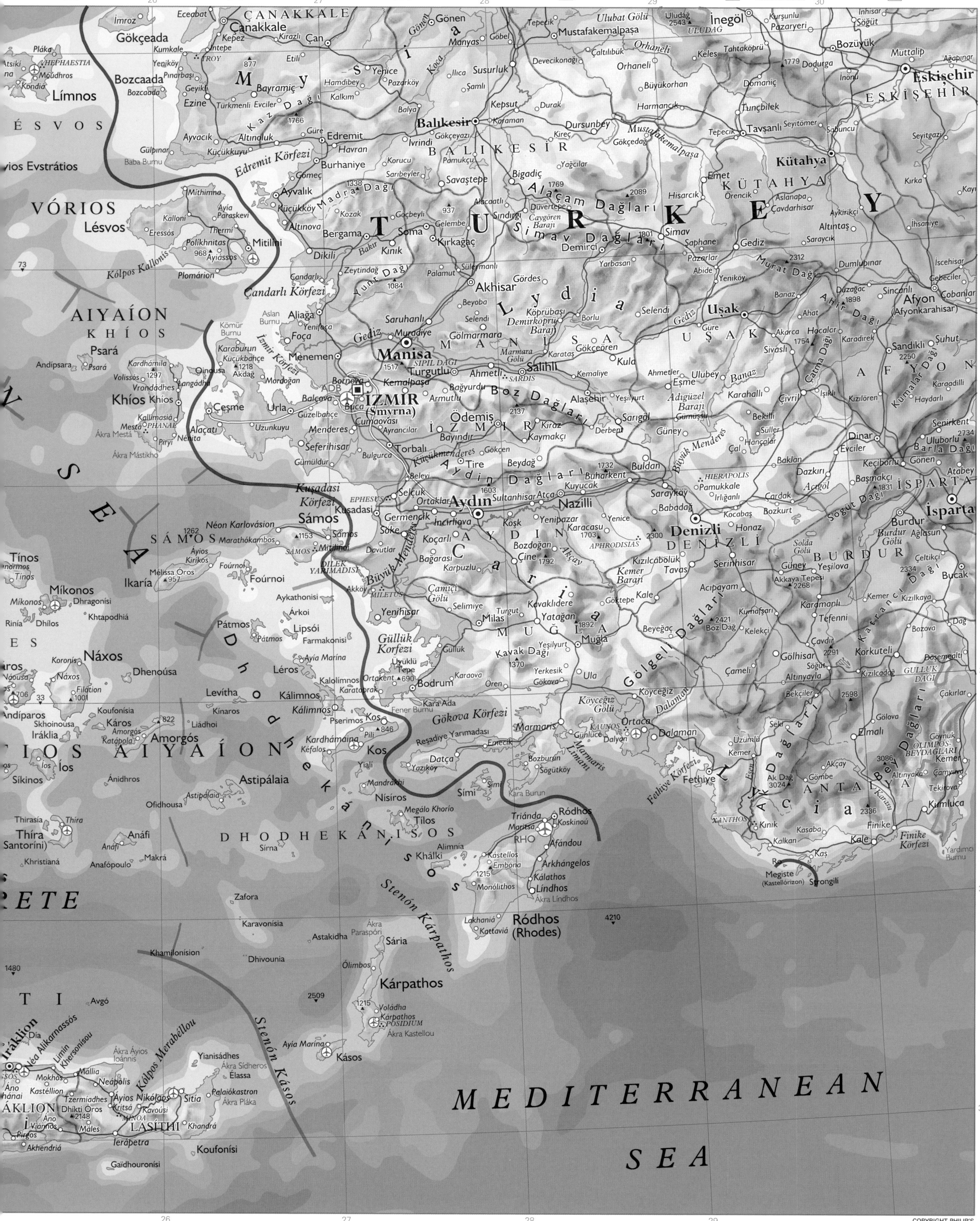

7
8
9
10
11
12
51
100
B
C
D
E
F
G
26
27
28
29
30
40
39
38
37
36
35
ÇANAKKALE
Çanakkale
Gökçeada
İmroz
Eceabat
Kepez
Kumkale
Intepe
TROY
Kirazlı
Çan
Etili
Gönen
Manyas
Gölcük
Mustafakemalpaşa
Ulubat Gölü
Uludağ 2543
ULUDAG
İnegöl
Kurşunlu
Pazaryeri
İnhisar
Söğüt
Bozüyük
Muttalip
Eskişehir
ESKİŞEHİR
Plaka
HEPHAESTIA
Moúdhros
Límnos
Bozcaada
Yeniköy
Pınarbaşı
Geyikli
Ezine
Bayramiç
Türkmenli
Evciler
Kaz Dağı
1766
Ayvacık
Altınoluk
Küçükkuyu
Gülpınar
Baba Burnu
Edremit
Havran
Edremit Körfezi
Burhaniye
Gömeç
Ayvalık
Küçükköy
Madra Dağı
1338
Altınova
Bergama
Kozak
Yenice
Pazarköy
Hamdibey
Kalkım
Balya
Ilıca
Susurluk
Şamlı
Kepsut
Balıkesir
Koraman
Gökçeyazı
İvrindi
BALIKESİR
Korucu
Pamukçu
Savaştepe
Sarıbeyler
Bigadiç
Dursunbey
Kireç
Yağcılar
Alaçam Dağları
1769
Düvertepe
Sındırgı
Çaygören Barajı
Devecikonağı
Çaltılıbük
Orhaneli
Keles
Tahtaköprü
Büyükorhan
Harmancık
Domaniç
Dodurga
İnönü
Tunçbilek
Tavşanlı
Seyitömer
Tepecik
Mustafakemalpaşa
Gökçedağ
Kütahya
KÜTAHYA
Emet
Örencik
Aslanapa
Çavdarhisar
Hisarcık
2089
Simav
Simav Dağları
1801
Demirci
Şaphane
Gediz
Saraycık
Altıntaş
Aykırıkçı
İhsaniye
Kırka
Seyitgazi
TURKEY
LESVOS
Áyios Evstrátios
VÓRIOS
Lésvos
Míthimna
Kalloní
Eressós
Thermí
Polikhnítas
Ayiássos
968
Mitilíni
Kólpos Kallonís
Plomárion
Dikili
Bakır
Soma
Kınık
Kırkağaç
Gelembe
Göçbeyli
Zeytindağ
Yunt Dağı
1084
Çandarlı
Çandarlı Körfezi
Palamut
Akhisar
Gördes
Süleymanlı
Yarbasan
Pazarlar
Abide
Yeniköy
Murat Dağı
2312
Dumlupınar
İscehisar
AIYAÍON
KHÍOS
Psará
Andipsara
Kómür Burnu
Aslan Burnu
Aliağa
Yenifoça
Foça
Menemen
Karaburun
Küçükbahçe
1218
Akdağ
Kardhámila
Volissós
1297
Vrondádhes
Langádha
Khíos
Mordoğan
Oinoúsa
Çeşme
Urla
İzmir Körfezi
Kallimasiá
Mestá
OPHANAI
Pirgi
Néna
Ákra Mestá
Ákra Mástikho
Alaçatı
Uzunkuyu
Güzelbahçe
Seferihisar
Gümüldür
Menderes
Cumaovası
Buca
Balçova
Bornova
ADB
İZMİR (Smyrna)
Manisa
SİPİL DAĞI
1517
Muradiye
Saruhanlı
Gediz
Turgutlu
Kemalpaşa
Armutlu
Ahmetli
Salihli
SARDIS
MANİSA
Gölmarmara
Marmara Gölü
Selendi
Beyoba
Köprübaşı
Demirköprü Barajı
Lydia
Borlu
Karataş
Gökçeören
Kula
Kemaliye
Uşak
UŞAK
Gure
Banaz
Ahat
Ahır Dağı
1898
Düzağaç
Sincanlı
Afyon (Afyonkarahisar)
Çobanlar
Gebeciler
Hocalar
Akarca
1754
Sivaslı
Karadirek
Sandıklı
2250
Suhut
AFYON
Kumalar Dağı
Karaadilli
Haydarlı
Kızılören
Işıklı
Çivril
Çatma Dağı
Ahmetler
Ulubey
Eşme
Adıgüzel Barajı
Güney
Gümüşsu
Karahallı
Bekilli
Süller
Hançalar
Çal
Sarıgöl
Derbent
Alaşehir
Yeşilyurt
Boz Dağları
2137
Ödemiş
Bağyurdu
Bayındır
Kiraz
Kaymakçı
İZMİR
Torbalı
Ayrancılar
Bulgurca
Küçükmenderes
Tire
Gökçen
Beydağ
Aydın Dağları
1732
Buharkent
Kuyucak
Buldan
Büyük Menderes
HIERAPOLIS
Pamukkale
Sarayköy
Irlıganlı
Babadağ
Denizli
DENİZLİ
Kocabaş
Honaz
Bozkurt
Çardak
Baklan
Dazkırı
Acıgöl
Dinar
Evciler
Keçiborlu
Gönen
Başmakçı
1831
Isparta
ISPARTA
Senirkent
Uluborlu
Barla Dağı
2734
Atabey
Söğüt Dağı
Burdur
BURDUR
Ağlasun
Burdur Gölü
Çeltikçi
Yeşilova
Salda Gölü
Bucak
Akkaya Tepesi
2268
2334
Kuşadası Körfezi
Kuşadası
Selçuk
EPHESUS
Belevi
Ortaklar
Aydın
Germencik
1603
Sultanhisar
Atça
Nazilli
Köşk
Yenipazar
Yenice
Karacasu
1703
APHRODISIAS
2300
İncirliova
Koçarlı
Söke
Davutlar
AYDIN
Bozdoğan
Çine
1792
Akçay
Kızılcabölük
Tavas
Kemer Barajı
Serinhisar
Acıpayam
Kale
Göktepe
Güney
Bağarası
Karpuzlu
Caria
Büyük Menderes
DİLEK YARIMADISI
Akköy
MILETUS
Bafa Gölü
Selimiye
Yenihisar
Milas
Turgut
Kavaklıdere
Yatağan
1892
MUĞLA
Muğla
Boz Dağ
2421
Kumafşarı
Kelekçi
Beyağaç
Karamanlı
Tefenni
Kemer
Kızılkaya
Katrancı Dağı
Bozova
Dağ
Çavdır
Gölhisar
2291
Korkuteli
Döşemealtı
GÜLLÜK DAĞI
Kızılcadağ
Altınyayla
Söğüt
Çameli
Gölgeli Dağları
Yeşilyurt
Kavak Dağı
1370
Yerkesik
Gökova
Ula
Güllük
Güllük Körfezi
Üyüklü Tepe
690
Ortakent
Karatoprak
Bodrum
Karaova
Ören
Kara Ada
Fener Burnu
Gökova Körfezi
Reşadiye Yarımadası
Datça
Yazıköy
Emecik
Marmaris
Bozburun
Söğütköy
Marmaris Limanı
Köyceğiz
Köyceğiz Gölü
KAUNOS
Gülüce
Dalyan
Ortaca
Dalaman
Fethiye
Fethiye Körfezi
Bekçiler
2598
Çakırlar
Seki
Elmalı
Gölova
Üzümlü
Kemer
Ak Dağ
3024
Akçay
Gömbe
OLIMPOS BEYDAĞLARI
Beydağları
3086
Kemer
Çamyuva
Altınyaka
Tekirova
ANTALYA
Lycia
2336
Kumluca
Finike
Finike Körfezi
Yardımcı Burnu
XANTHOS
Kınık
Kasaba
Kalkan
Kaş
Kale
Megiste (Kastellórizon)
Strongili
Tínos
Mikonos
Dhragonísi
Khtapodhiá
Rinía
Dhílos
Náxos
Koronis
Filotion
1001
Dhenoúsa
Andíparos
Koufonísia
Skhoinousa
Iráklia
Káros
Amorgós
Katápola
Íos
Síkinos
Ánidhros
Thira
Thíra (Santoríni)
Anáfi
Makrá
Anafópoulo
Khristianá
Ofidhousa
Astipálaia
SÁMOS
1262
Néon Karlovásion
Marathókambos
Sámos
1153
Mitilíni
Áyios Kírikos
Ikaría
Mélissa Oros 957
Fournoi
Fourni
Aykathonisi
Arkoi
Lipsói
Farmakonisi
Pátmos
Ayía Marína
Léros
Levítha
Kinaros
Kálimnos
Kalolímnos
Pserimos
Kos
846
Píli
Kardhámaina
Kéfalos
Yiali
Mandráki
Nísiros
Megálo Khorío
Tílos
Sími
Kara Burun
Alimnia
Khálki
Ródhos
Triánda
Maritsa
Koskinoú
RHO
Afándou
Kastellos
Émbona
1215
Arkhángelos
Kálathos
Líndhos
Ákra Líndhos
Monólithos
Lakhaniá
Kattaviá
Ródhos (Rhodes)
4210
DHODHEKÁNISOS
Dhodhekánisos
AIYAÍON
Sírna
Zafora
Karavonisia
Astakidha
Ákra Paraspóri
Sária
Khamilonísion
Dhívounia
Ólimbos
Kárpathos
2509
Voládha
POSIDIUM
Ákra Kastellou
Ayía Marína
Kásos
Stenón Kárpathos
Stenón Kásos
1480
KRÍTI
CRETE
Avgó
Iráklion
Día
Néa Alikarnassós
Límin Khersonísou
Mália
Mokhós
Neápolis
Kastéllion
Tzermiádhes
Áyios Nikólaos
Kritsá
Dhikti Oros
2148
Káto
Máles
Kavoúsi
Sitía
Palaiókastron
Ákra Pláka
Ákra Sídheros
Élassa
Yianisádhes
Ákra Áyios Ioannis
Kólpos Merabéllou
LASÍTHI
Ierápetra
Khandrá
Koufonísi
Gaïdhouronísi
Pírgos
Akhendriá
73
706
33
822
Liádhoi
Myssia
MEDITERRANEAN SEA
AEGEAN SEA
COPYRIGHT PHILIP'S

National Parks

1:2 000 000

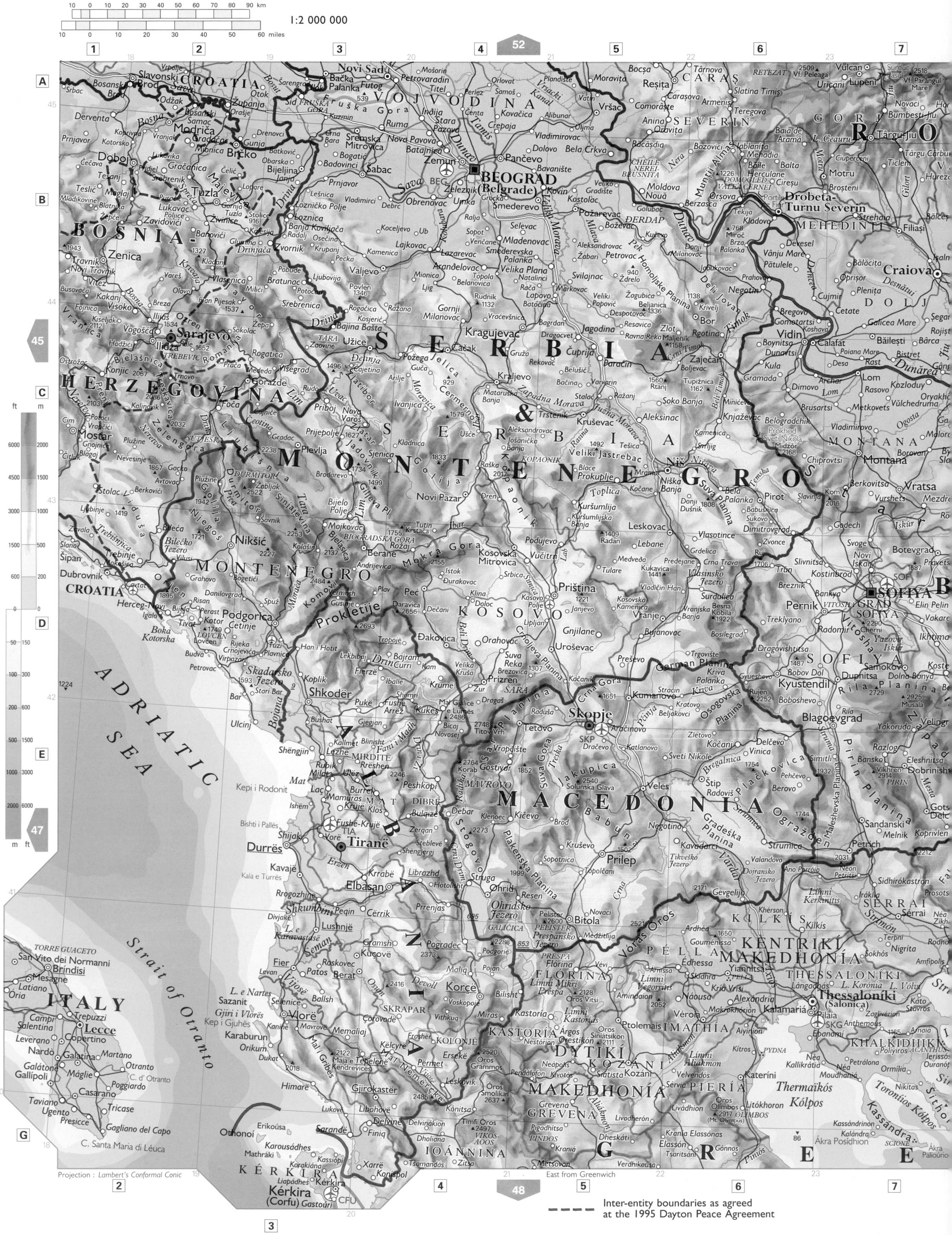

52
45
47
48

Inter-entity boundaries as agreed at the 1995 Dayton Peace Agreement

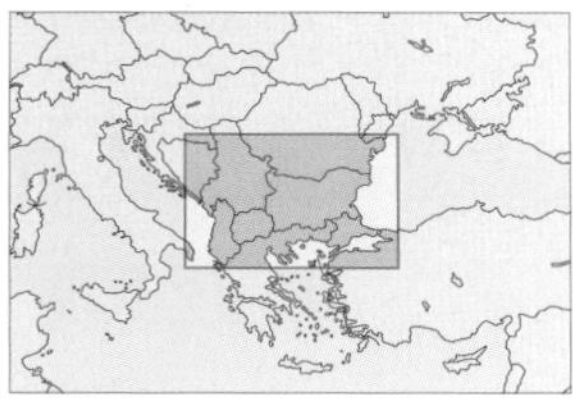

Underlined towns give their name to the administrative area in which they stand.

1:2 000 000

55

34
45

Projection : Lambert's Conformal Conic

East from Greenwich

50

Administrative divisions in Croatia:
1 Brodsko-Posavska
2 Koprivničko-Križevačka
4 Medimurska
5 Osječko-Baranjska
6 Požeško-Slavonska
8 Virovitičko-Podravska
9 Vukovarsko-Srijemska

Inter-entity boundaries as agreed at the 1995 Dayton Peace Agreement

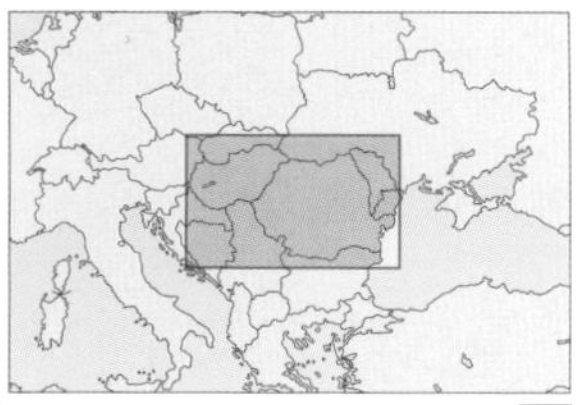

National Parks

Underlined towns give their name to the administrative area in which they stand.

1:2 000 000
km
miles
BALTIC SEA
Gulf of Riga
LATVIA
LITHUANIA
SWEDEN
KALININGRAD (Russia)
Riga
Jūrmala
Jelgava
Ventspils
Liepāja
Klaipėda
Šiauliai
Kaunas
Palanga
Neringa
Kaliningrad
Sovetsk
Chernyakhovsk
Baltiysk
Zelenogradsk
Gdańsk
Gdynia
Sopot
Elbląg
Olsztyn
Słupsk
Koszalin
Kołobrzeg
Szczecin
Świnoujście
Grudziądz
Malbork
Tczew
Hrodna
Suwałki
Ełk
Giżycko
Marijampolė
Alytus
Gotland (Sweden)
Visby
Öland (Sweden)
Kalmar
Karlskrona
Växjö
Västervik
Jönköping
Bornholm (Denmark)
Rønne
POMORSKIE
WARMIŃSKO-MAZURSKIE
ZACHODNIO-POMORSKIE
Zatoka Gdańska
Kurshskiy Zaliv
Vistula
Nemunas
Wisła
Hanöbukten
Irbes šaurums
Pojezierze Mazurskie
58
30
17

National Parks

Underlined towns give their name to the administrative area in which they stand.

50 0 100 200 300 400 km

1:8 000 000

50 0 50 100 150 200 250 miles

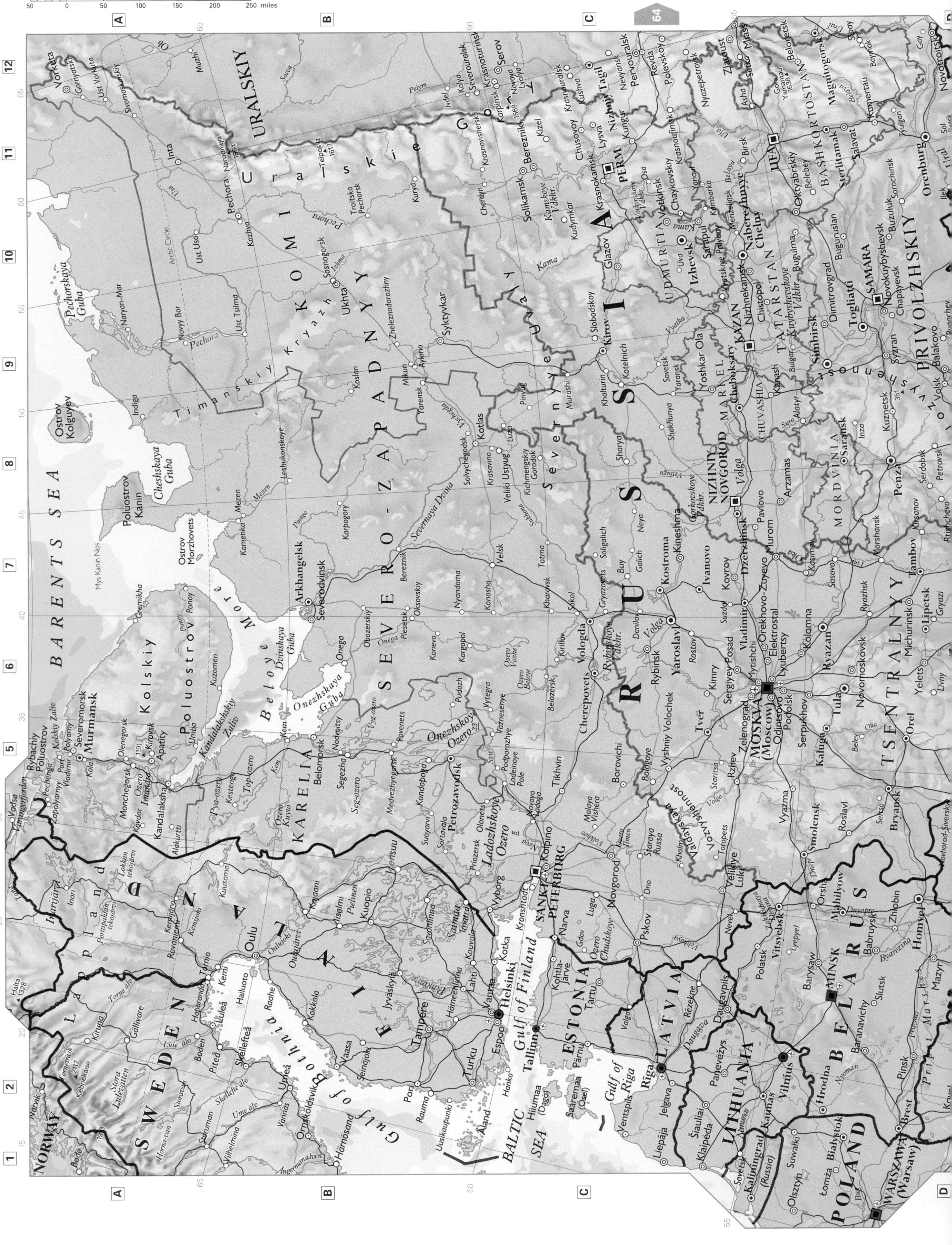

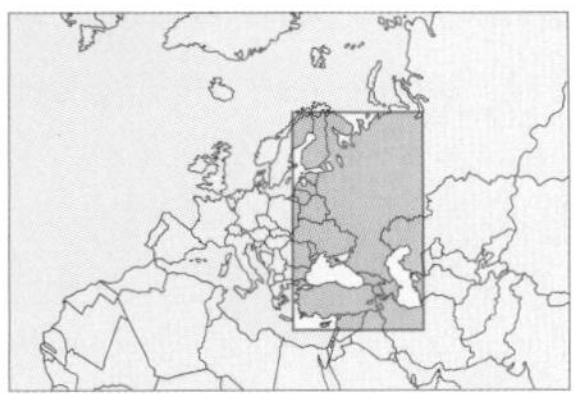

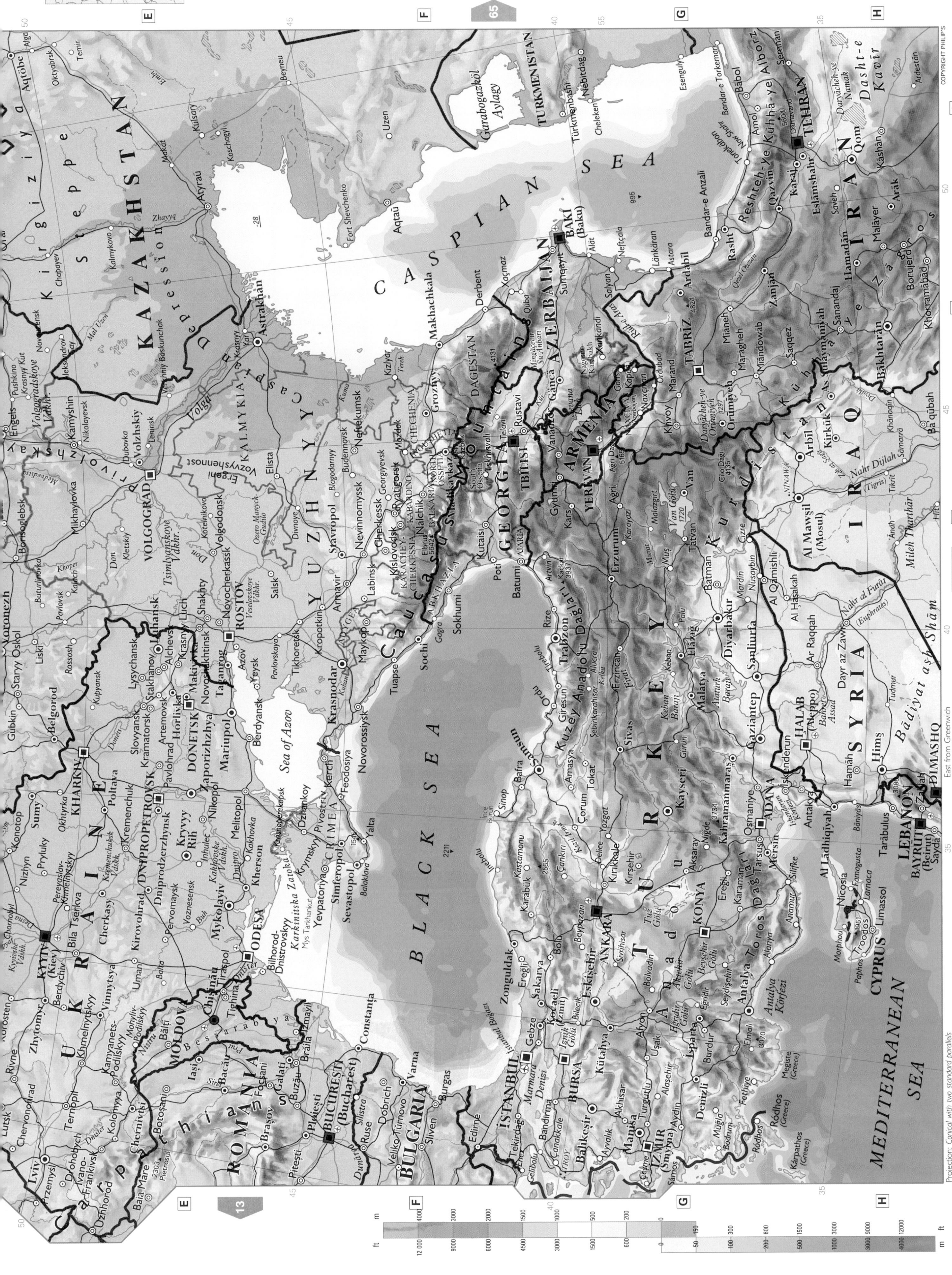

KAZAKHSTAN
UKRAINE
MOLDOVA
ROMANIA
BULGARIA
GEORGIA
ARMENIA
AZERBAIJAN
TURKMENISTAN
TURKEY
SYRIA
IRAQ
IRAN
LEBANON
CYPRUS
CASPIAN SEA
BLACK SEA
Sea of Azov
MEDITERRANEAN SEA
CRIMEA
KALMYKIA
DAGESTAN
CHECHENIA
ABKHAZIA
ADJARIA
KYYIV (Kiev)
CHIŞINĂU
BUCUREŞTI (Bucharest)
TBILISI
YEREVAN
BAKI (Baku)
TEHRĀN
ANKARA
DIMASHQ
BAYRUT (Beirut)
ISTANBUL
VOLGOGRAD
ROSTOV
DONETSK
KHARKIV
DNIPROPETROVSK
ODESA
KONYA
ADANA
HALAB (Aleppo)
TABRĪZ
Projection: Conical with two standard parallels
East from Greenwich
m
ft

50 0 25 50 75 100 125 150 175 km

1:4 000 000

50 0 25 50 75 100 125 miles

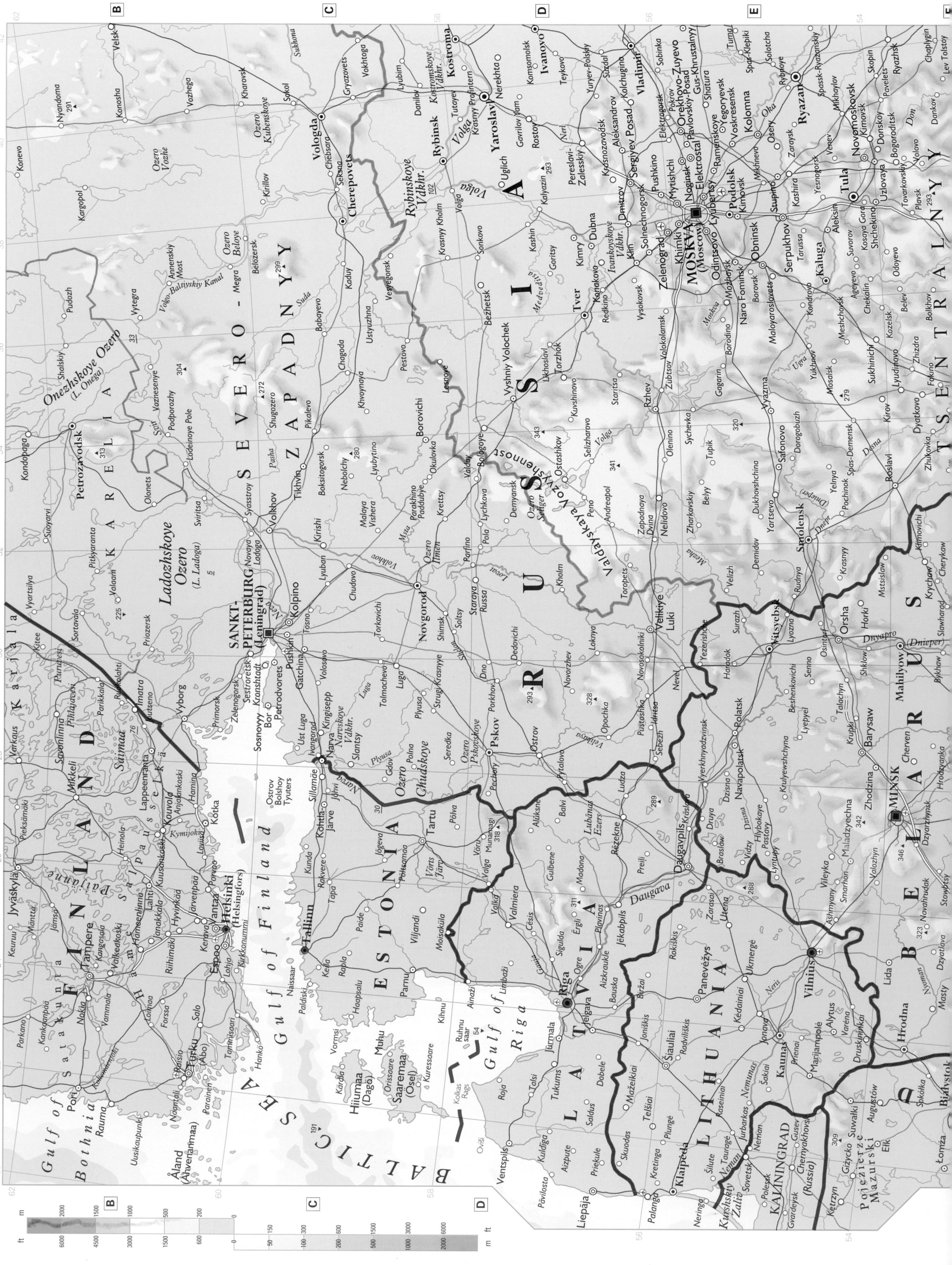

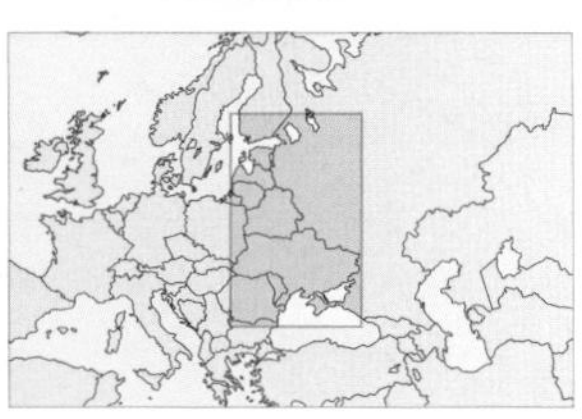

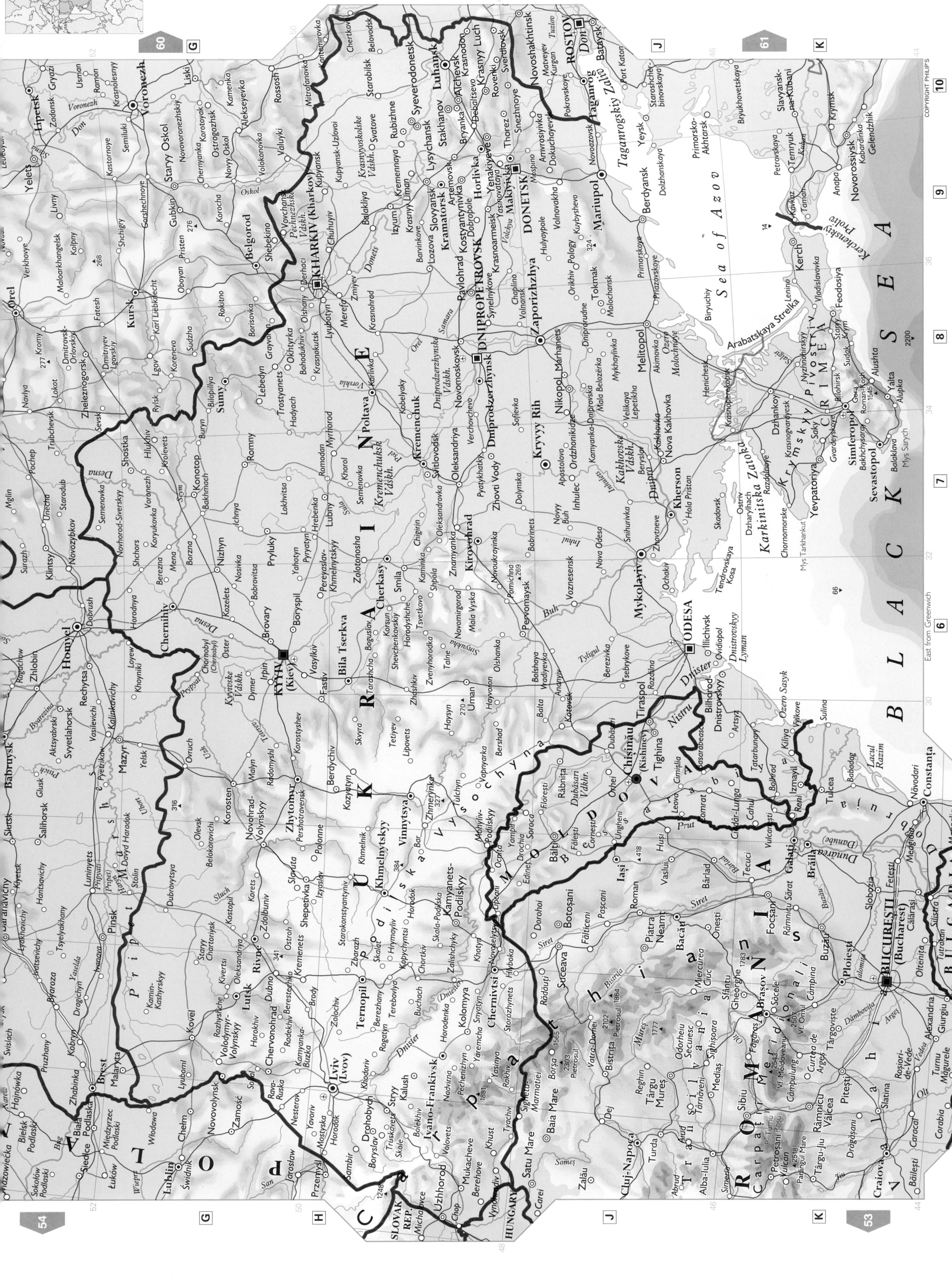
BLACK SEA
Sea of Azov
UKRAINE
MOLDOVA
ROMANIA
BULGARIA
HUNGARY
SLOVAK REP.
CRIMEA
KYIV (Kiev)
KHARKIV (Kharkov)
DNIPROPETROVSK
DONETSK
ODESA
ROSTOV
CHIŞINĂU (Kishinev)
BUCUREŞTI (Bucharest)
Lviv (Lvov)
Zaporizhzhya
Kryvyy Rih
Mykolayiv
Kherson
Sevastopol
Simferopol
Kerch
Mariupol
Luhansk
Poltava
Kremenchuk
Cherkasy
Vinnytsya
Zhytomyr
Chernihiv
Homyel
Sumy
Kursk
Belgorod
Voronezh
Orel
Constanţa
Galaţi
Brăila
Iaşi
Braşov
Ploieşti
Craiova
Cluj-Napoca
Lublin
Brest
Pinsk
Mazyr
Rivne
Lutsk
Ternopil
Chernivtsi
Ivano-Frankivsk
Uzhhorod
Khmelnytskyy
Kirovohrad
Melitopol
Berdyansk
Taganrog
Novorossiysk
Yalta
Feodosiya
Yevpatoriya
Tiraspol
Tulcea
Dnister
Dnipro
Prut
Desna
Don
Pripet
Carpathian Mountains
Transylvania
Moldova
Podolsk
Volhynia
Pripet Marshes
Kerchenskiy Proliv
Arabatskaya Strelka
Taganrogskiy Zaliv
Karkinitska Zatoka
East from Greenwich
Projection: Conical with two standard parallels
COPYRIGHT PHILIP'S
60
61
54
53

50 0 25 50 75 100 125 150 175 km

1:4 000 000

50 0 25 50 75 100 125 miles

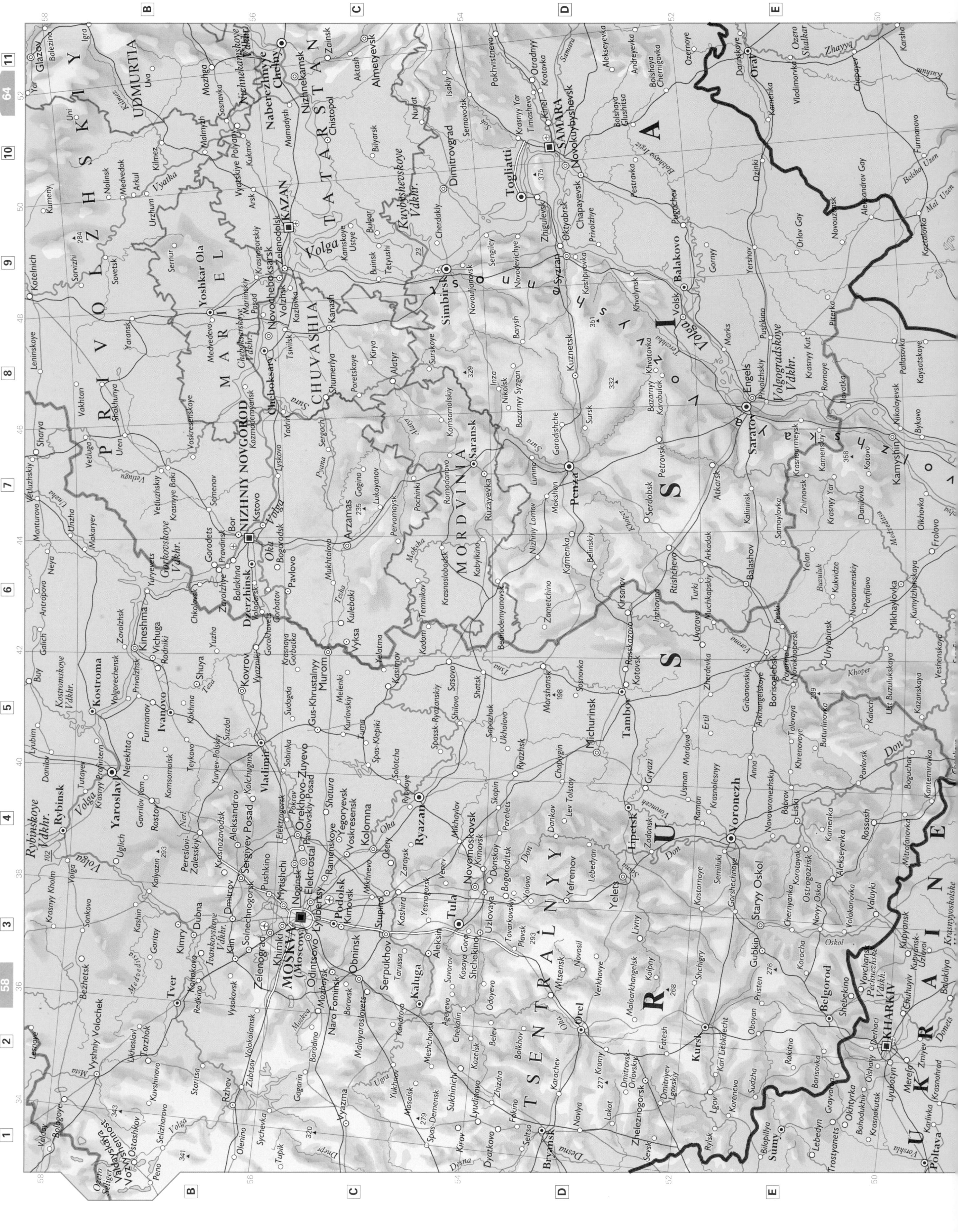

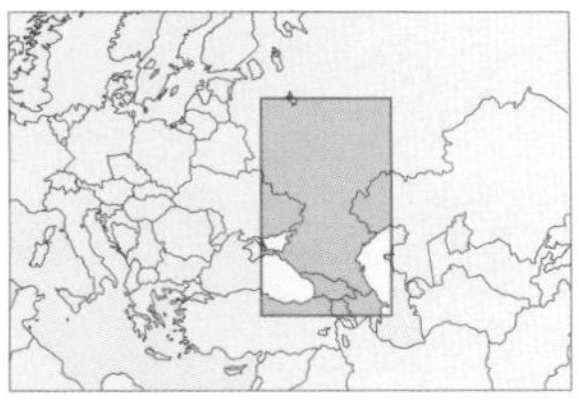

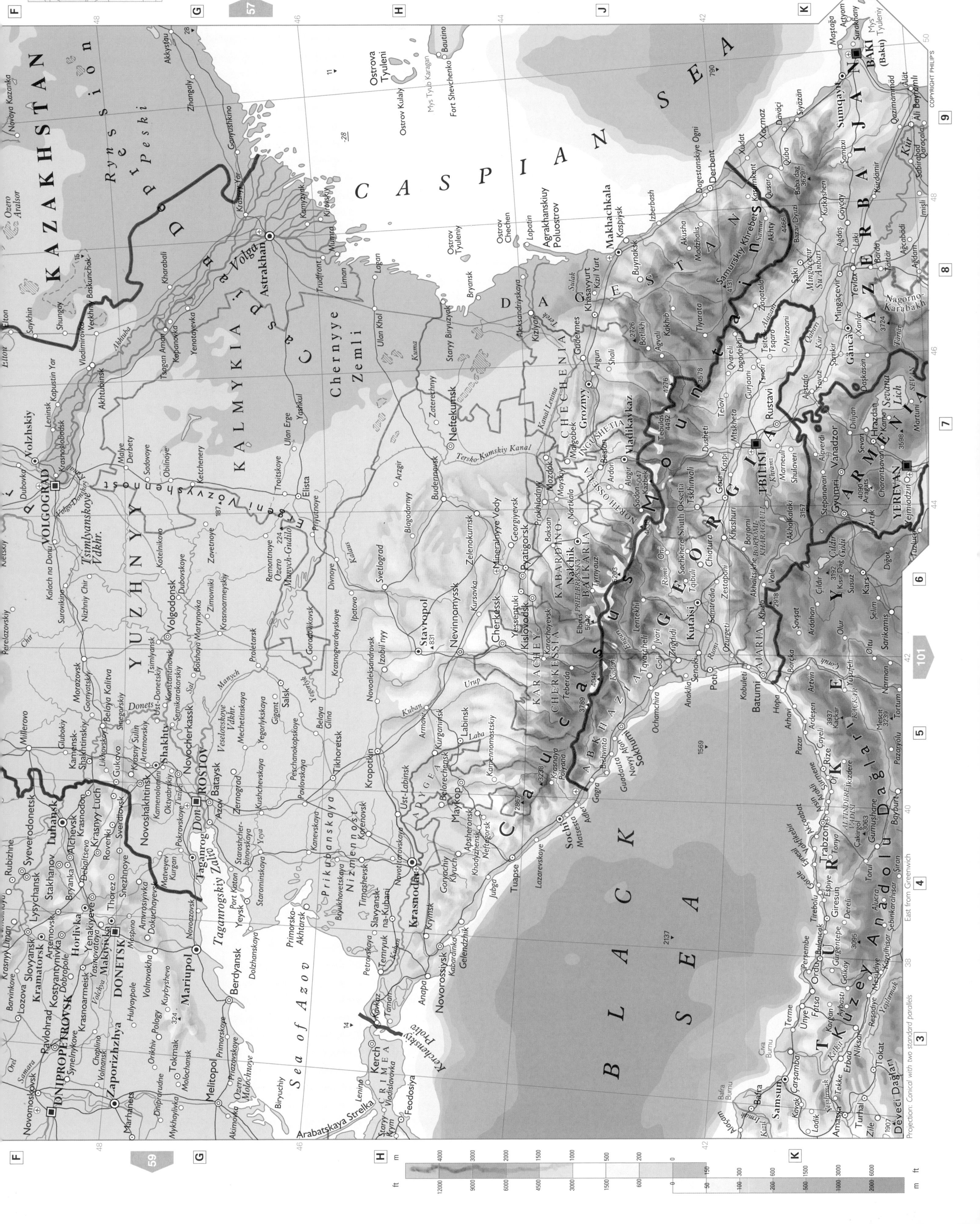
KAZAKHSTAN
CASPIAN SEA
BLACK SEA
Sea of Azov
KALMYKIA
DAGESTAN
CHECHENIA
INGUSHETIA
NORTH OSSETIA
KABARDINO-BALKARIA
KARACHAY-CHERKESSIA
ADYGEA
GEORGIA
ABKHAZIA
AJARIA
South Ossetia
ARMENIA
AZERBAIJAN
Nagorno-Karabakh
TURKEY
CRIMEA
Caucasus Mountains
Ryn Peski
Chernyye Zemli
Volgograd
Astrakhan
Elista
Makhachkala
Grozny
Vladikavkaz
Nalchik
Stavropol
Krasnodar
Rostov
Donetsk
Luhansk
Dnipropetrovsk
Zaporizhzhya
Mariupol
Taganrog
Novorossiysk
Sochi
Sokhumi
Batumi
Kutaisi
Tbilisi
Rustavi
Yerevan
Gyumri
Baki (Baku)
Sumqayit
Ganca
Derbent
Trabzon
Samsun
Kerch
Elbrus 5642
Kazbek 5047
Volga
Don
Kuban
Terek
Kura
Projection: Conical with two standard parallels
East from Greenwich
COPYRIGHT PHILIP'S
m
ft
4000
3000
2000
1500
1000
500
200
0
50
100
200
500
1000
2000
12000
9000
6000
4500
3000
1500
600
0
150
300
600
1500
3000
6000
57
59
101

500 0 250 500 750 1000 1250 1500 1750 km

500 0 250 500 750 1000 1250 miles

1:40 000 000

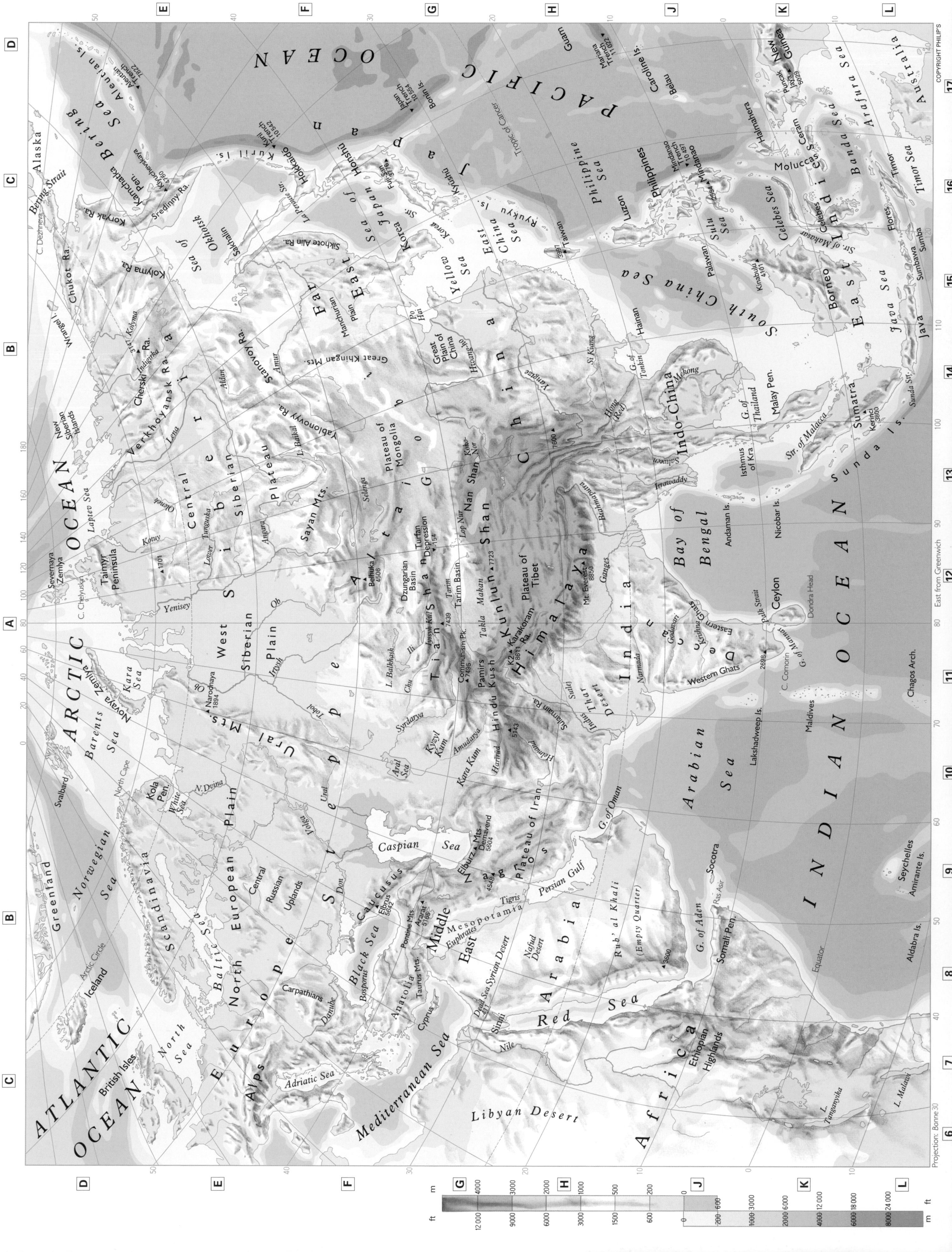

1:40 000 000

500 0 250 500 750 1000 1250 1500 1750 km

500 0 250 500 750 1000 1250 miles

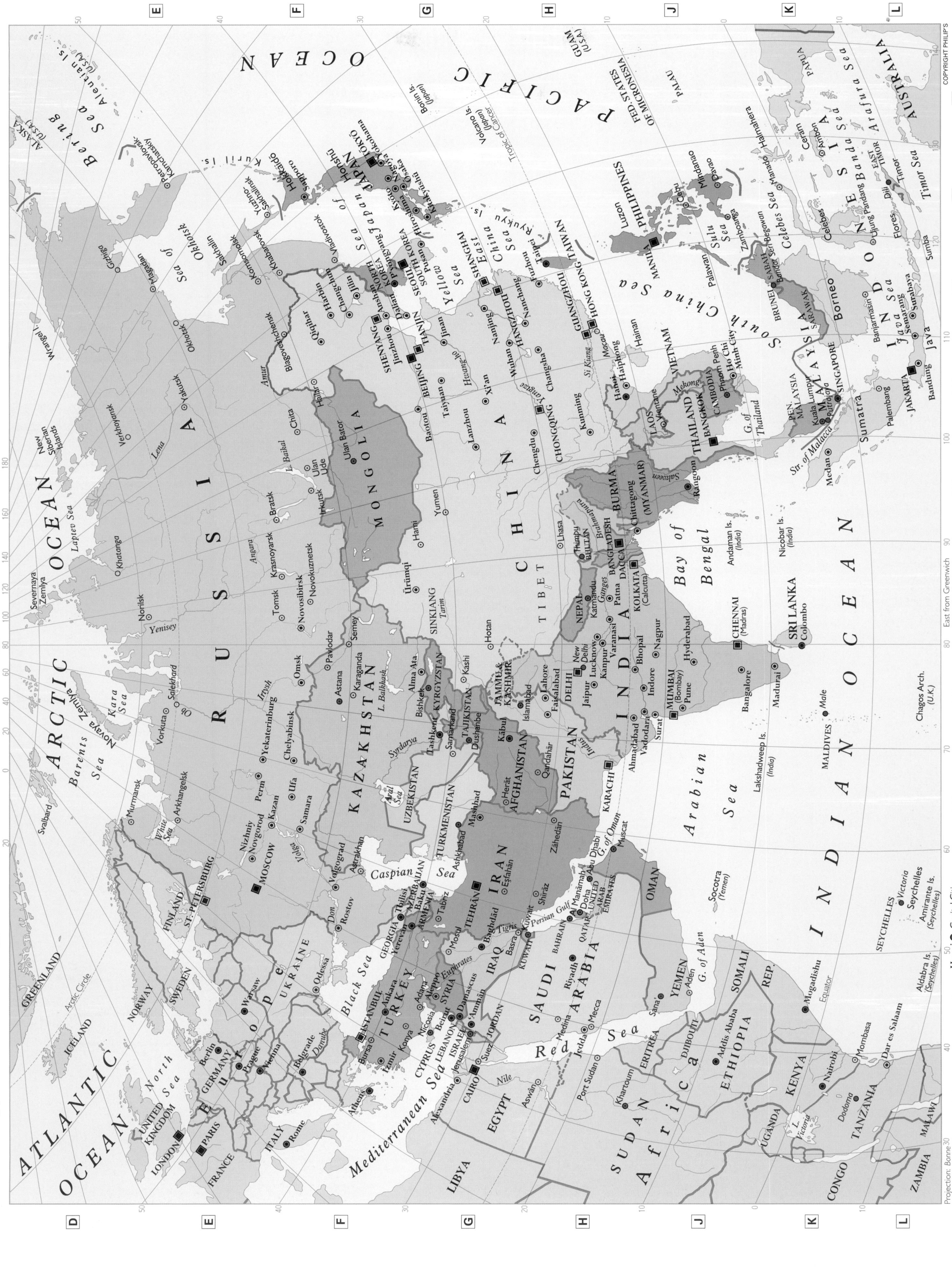

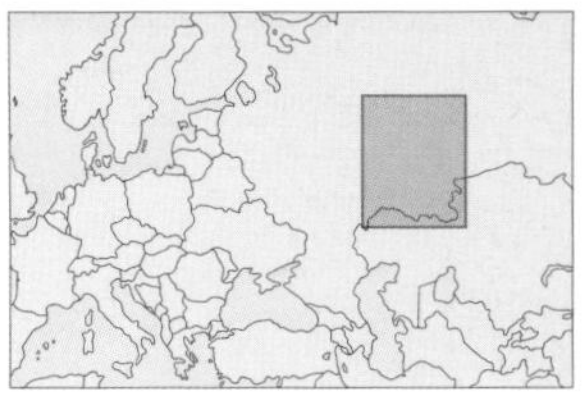

1:4 000 000

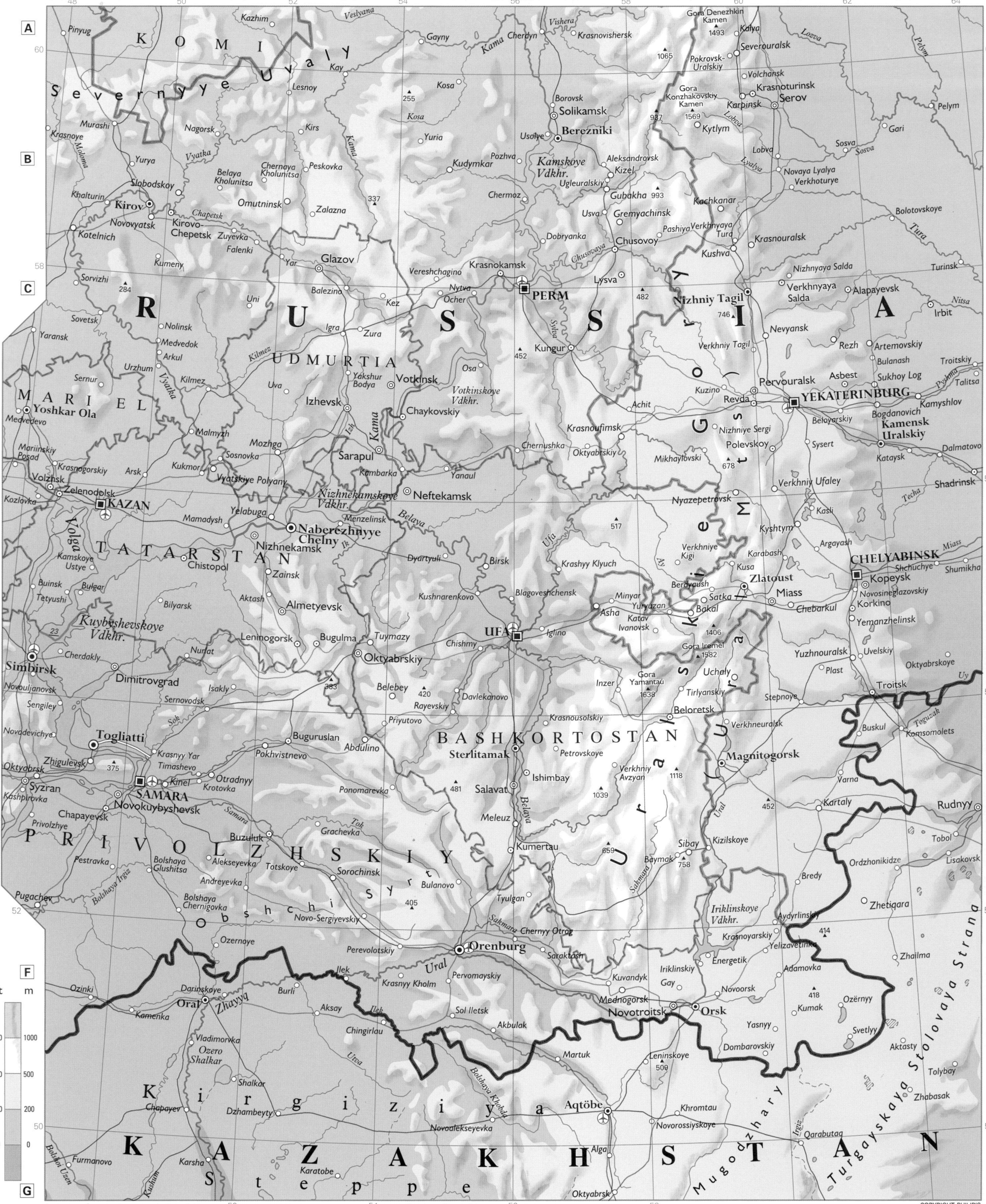

KOMI
Severnyye Uvaly
UDMURTIA
MARI EL
TATARSTAN
BASHKORTOSTAN
PRIVOLZHSKIY
Obshchi Syrt
RUSSIA
Ural'skiye Gory
KAZAKHSTAN
Kirgiziya Steppe
Mugodzhary
Turgayskaya Stolovaya Strana
Kazhim
Pinyug
Vesljana
Gayny
Kama
Cherdyn
Vishera
Krasnovishersk
Gora Denezhkin Kamen
1493
Kalya
Severouralsk
Lozva
Pelym
1065
Pokrovsk-Uralskiy
Volchansk
Krasnoturinsk
Serov
Kay
Lesnoy
Kosa
255
Borovsk
Solikamsk
Gora Konzhakovskiy Kamen
1569
Karpinsk
Murashi
Krasnoye
Molomа
Nagorsk
Kirs
Yuria
Usolye
Berezniki
937
Kytlym
Gari
Sosva
Yurya
Vyatka
Belaya Kholunitsa
Chernaya Kholunitsa
Peskovka
Kudymkar
Pozhva
Kamskoye Vdkhr.
Aleksandrovsk
Kizel
Lobva
Lyalya
Novaya Lyalya
Verkhoturye
Slobodskoy
Khalturin
Kirov
Omutninsk
337
Zalazna
Chermoz
Ugleuralskiy
Gubakha
993
Kachkanar
Novovyatsk
Kotelnich
Kirovo-Chepetsk
Chapetsk
Zuyevka
Falenki
Usva
Gremyachinsk
Pashiya
Verkhnyaya Tura
Dobryanka
Chusovoy
Krasnouralsk
Bolotovskoye
Tura
Kumeny
Yar
Glazov
Kushva
Chusovaya
Sorvizhi
284
Vereshchagino
Krasnokamsk
PERM
Lysva
482
Nizhnyaya Salda
Turinsk
Verkhnyaya Salda
Alapayevsk
Nitsa
Irbit
Balezino
Nytva
Ocher
Nizhniy Tagil
746
Uni
Kez
Sovetsk
Nolinsk
Igra
Zura
Sylva
Nevyansk
Rezh
Artemovskiy
Yaransk
Medvedok
Arkul
Kilmez
452
Kungur
Verkhniy Tagil
Bulanash
Troitskiy
Urzhum
Yakshur Bodya
Votkinsk
Osa
Pyshma
Talitsa
Sernur
Kilmez
Uva
Votkinskoye Vdkhr.
Asbest
Sukhoy Log
Pervouralsk
Kuzino
Revda
YEKATERINBURG
Kamyshlov
Yoshkar Ola
Medvedevo
Izhevsk
Chaykovskiy
Achit
Bogdanovich
Beloyarskiy
Kamensk Uralskiy
Malmyzh
Krasnoufimsk
Nizhniye Sergi
Polevskoy
Sysert
Dalmatovo
Mariinskiy Posad
Mozhga
Izh
Sosnovka
Sarapul
Chernushka
Oktyabrskiy
Mikhaylovski
678
Kataysk
Krasnogorskiy
Arsk
Kukmor
Vyatskiye Polyany
Kambarka
Yanaul
Volzhsk
Zelenodolsk
Nizhnekamskoye Vdkhr.
Neftekamsk
Verkhniy Ufaley
Shadrinsk
Techa
Kozlovka
KAZAN
Nyazepetrovsk
Kasli
Volga
Mamadysh
Yelabuga
Menzelinsk
Belaya
Naberezhnyye Chelny
517
Ufa
Kyshtym
Nizhnekamsk
Ik
Verkhniye Kigi
Argayash
Miass
Kamskoye Ustye
Chistopol
Dyurtyuli
Birsk
Krasnyy Klyuch
Ay
Karabash
CHELYABINSK
Shchuchye
Shumikha
Buinsk
Bulgar
Zainsk
Kusa
Berdyaush
Zlatoust
Tetyushi
Aktash
Kushnarenkovo
Blagoveshchensk
Minyar
Yuryuzan
Satka
Miass
Kopeysk
Novosineglazovskiy
Korkino
Bilyarsk
Almetyevsk
Asha
Katav Ivanovsk
Bakal
Chebarkul
Kuybyshevskoye Vdkhr.
23
Leninogorsk
Bugulma
Tuymazy
UFA
Iglino
1406
Yemanzhelinsk
Cherdakly
Nurlat
Oktyabrskiy
Chishmy
Gora Iremel
1582
Yuzhnouralsk
Uvelskiy
Simbirsk
Dimitrovgrad
383
Belebey
420
Uchaly
Plast
Oktyabrskoye
Novoulyanovsk
Isakly
Rayevskiy
Davlekanovo
Inzer
Gora Yamantau
1638
Tirlyanskiy
Troitsk
Uy
Sengiley
Sernovodsk
Priyutovo
Beloretsk
Stepnoye
Sok
Krasnousolskiy
Verkhneuralsk
Buskul
Toguzak
Novodevichye
Togliatti
Buguruslan
Abdulino
Komsomolets
Zhigulevsk
375
Krasnyy Yar
Timashevo
Pokhvistnevo
Sterlitamak
Petrovskoye
Magnitogorsk
Oktyabrsk
Syzran
SAMARA
Kinel
Otradnyy
Krotovka
Ishimbay
Verkhniy Avzyan
1118
Varna
Kashpirovka
Novokuybyshevsk
Ponomarevka
481
Salavat
1039
Ural
Kartaly
Rudnyy
Chapayevsk
Samara
Meleuz
452
Privolzhye
Buzuluk
Tok
Grachevka
Tobol
Kumertau
Sibay
Kizilskoye
Pestravka
Bolshaya Glushitsa
Alekseyevka
Totskoye
Sorochinsk
659
Baymak
758
Ordzhonikidze
Lisakovsk
Andreyevka
Bolshaya Irgiz
Bulanovo
Sakmara
Bredy
Pugachev
Bolshaya Chernigovka
405
Tyulgan
Iriklinskoye Vdkhr.
Zhetiqara
Novo-Sergiyevskiy
Sakmara
Chernyy Otrog
Aydyrlinskiy
414
Ozernoye
Perevolotskiy
Orenburg
Saraktash
Krasnoyarskiy
Yelizavetinka
Zhailma
Ilek
Ural
Pervomayskiy
Energetik
Iriklinskiy
Adamovka
Ozinki
Darinskoye
Burli
Krasnyy Kholm
Kuvandyk
Gay
Novoorsk
418
Oral
Zhayyq
Aksay
Ilek
Sol Iletsk
Mednogorsk
Novotroitsk
Orsk
Kumak
Ozërnyy
Kamenka
Chingirlau
Akbulak
Yasnyy
Svetlyy
Vladimorvka
Ozero Shalkar
Utva
Martuk
Dombarovskiy
Aktasty
Leninskoye
509
Tolybay
Shalkar
Bolshaya Khobda
Zhabasak
Chapayev
Dzhambeyty
Aqtöbe
Khromtau
Novoalekseyevka
Novorossiyskoye
Irgiz
Qarabutaq
Bolshoi Uzen
Furmanovo
Karsha
Kushum
Karatobe
Alga
Oktyabrsk
60
61
66
ft
m
3000
1000
1500
500
600
200
0
0

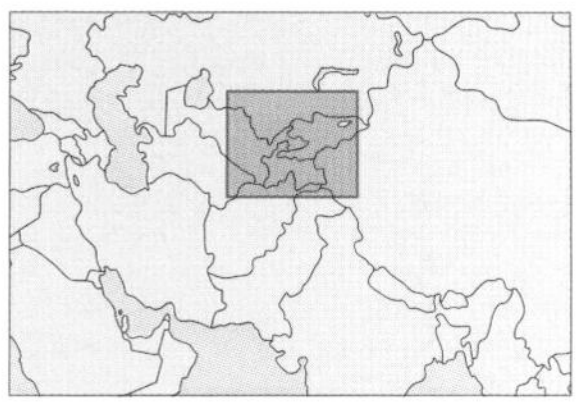

1:4 000 000

50 0 25 50 75 100 125 150 175 km

50 0 25 50 75 100 125 miles

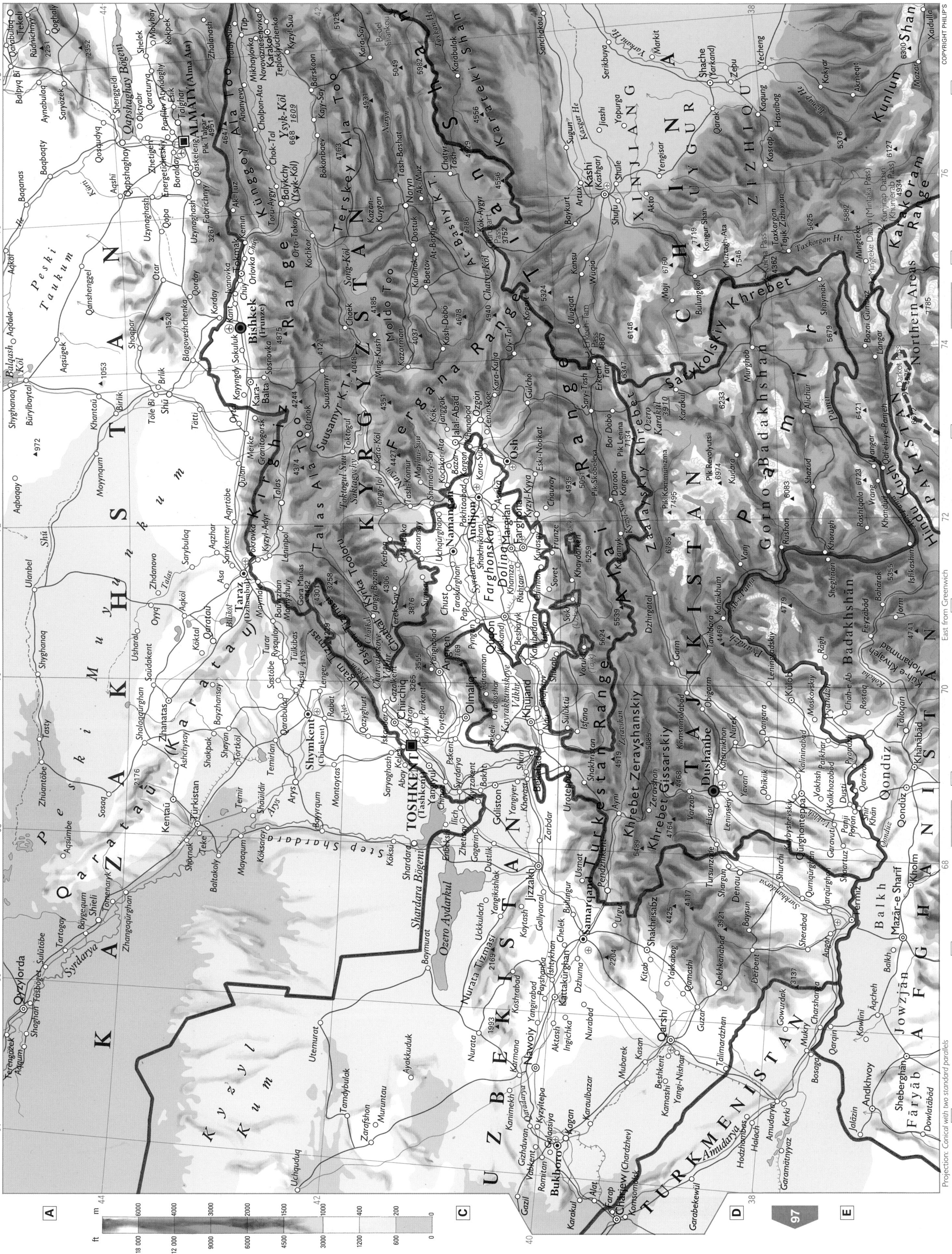

m 6000 4000 3000 2000 1500 1000 400 200 0
ft 18 000 12 000 9000 6000 4500 3000 1200 600 0

68 66 93 91 97

100 0 100 200 300 400 500 600 700 800 km

1:16 000 000

100 0 100 200 300 400 500 miles

D C B

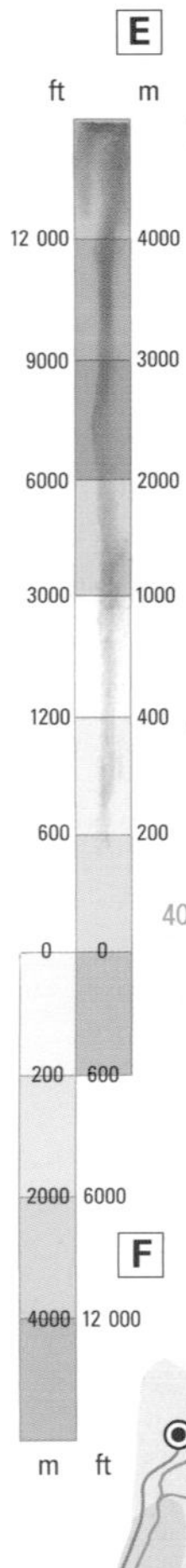

Projection: *Conical Orthomorphic with two standard parallels*

6 7 8 9

East from Greenwich

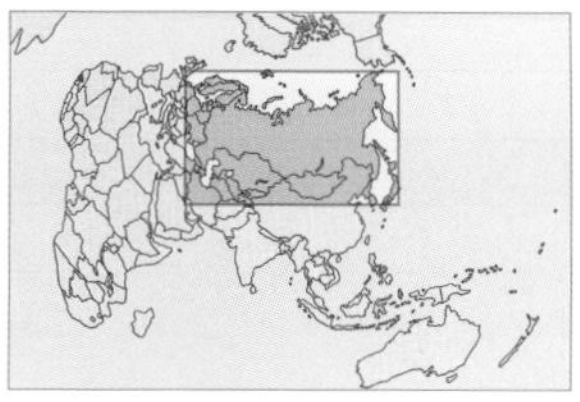

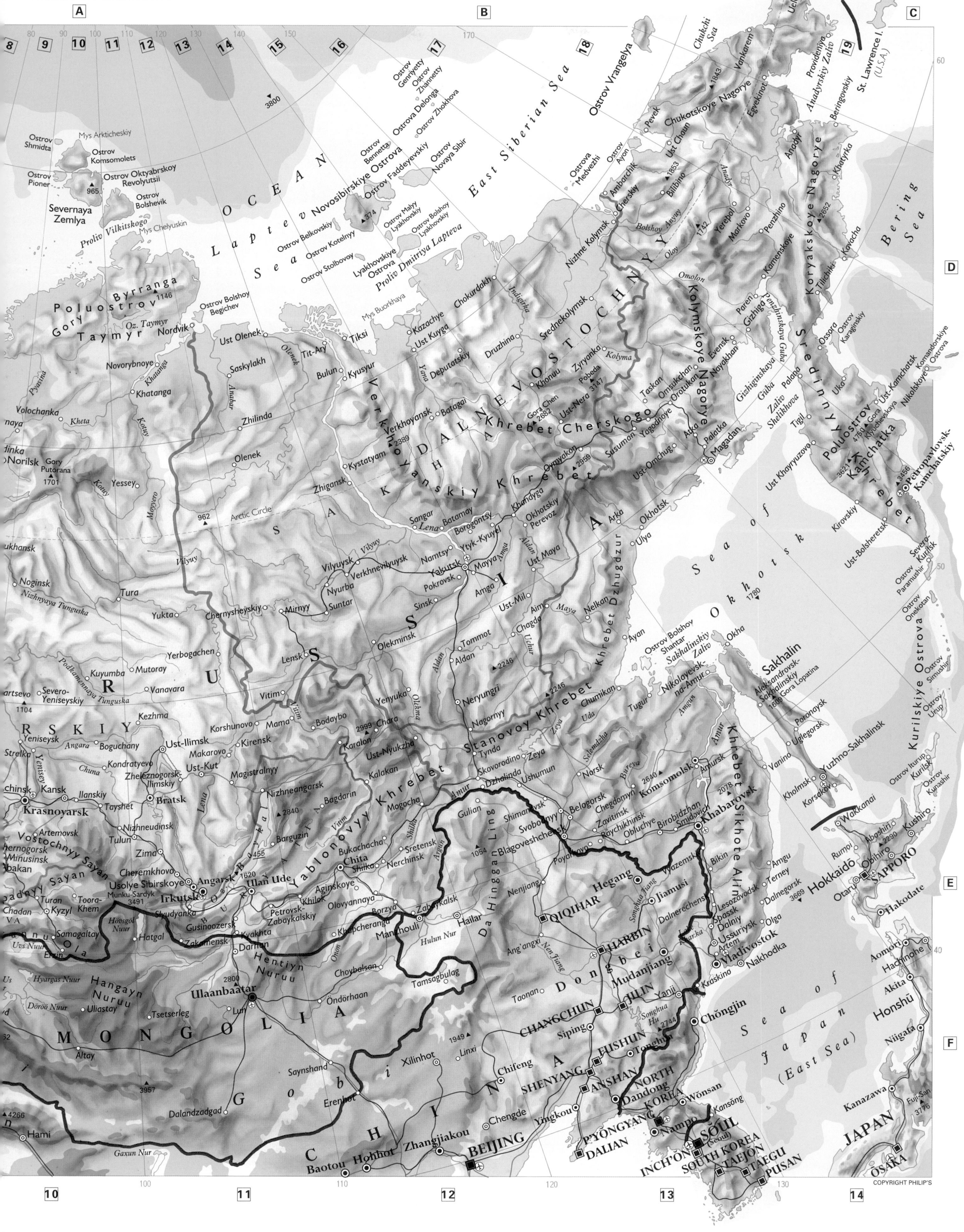
A
B
C
D
E
F
Mys Dezhneva (East C.)
Chukchi Sea
St. Lawrence I. (U.S.A.)
Ostrov Vrangelya
East Siberian Sea
Laptev Sea
OCEAN
Ostrov Shmidta
Mys Arkticheskiy
Ostrov Komsomolets
Ostrov Oktyabrskoy Revolyutsii
Ostrov Pioner
Ostrov Bolshevik
Severnaya Zemlya
Proliv Vilkitskogo
Mys Chelyuskin
Novosibirskiye Ostrova
Ostrov Kotelnyy
Ostrov Belkovskiy
Ostrov Faddeyevskiy
Ostrov Novaya Sibir
Ostrova Delonga
Ostrov Bennetta
Ostrov Zhokhova
Lyakhovskiye Ostrova
Proliv Dmitriya Lapteva
Ostrova Medvezhi
Poluostrov Taymyr
Gory Byrranga
Oz. Taymyr
Ostrov Bolshoy Begichev
Nordvik
Khatanga
Norilsk
Gory Putorana
Tiksi
Verkhoyanskiy Khrebet
Verkhoyansk
Khrebet Cherskogo
Kolymskoye Nagorye
Chukotskoye Nagorye
Koryakskoye Nagorye
Sredinnyy Khrebet
Poluostrov Kamchatka
Petropavlovsk-Kamchatskiy
Bering Sea
Anadyr
Magadan
Sea of Okhotsk
Okhotsk
Yakutsk
Arctic Circle
Lena
Vilyuy
Aldan
Khrebet Dzhugdzhur
Stanovoy Khrebet
Sakhalin
Yuzhno-Sakhalinsk
Kurilskiye Ostrova
Nikolayevsk-na-Amur
Komsomolsk
Khabarovsk
Khrebet Sikhote Alin
Vladivostok
Nakhodka
Hokkaidō
SAPPORO
Hakodate
Aomori
Honshū
Niigata
Sea of Japan (East Sea)
JAPAN
ŌSAKA
Kanazawa
Fuji-San 3776
RUSSIA
SIBERIA
Krasnoyarsk
Bratsk
Irkutsk
Angarsk
Ulan Ude
Chita
Ozero Baykal
Yablonovyy Khrebet
Vostochnyy Sayan
Zapadnyy Sayan
Kyzyl
Ulaanbaatar
Hentiyn Nuruu
Hangayn Nuruu
MONGOLIA
Gobi
Saynshand
Dalandzadgad
Erenhot
Hami
Gaxun Nur
Hulun Nur
Hailar
Manzhouli
Da Hinggan Ling
Dongbei
QIQIHAR
HARBIN
CHANGCHUN
JILIN
SHENYANG
FUSHUN
ANSHAN
DALIAN
BEIJING
Baotou
Hohhot
Zhangjiakou
Chengde
Chifeng
CHINA
NORTH KOREA
P'YONGYANG
Nampo
Chŏngjin
Wŏnsan
SOUTH KOREA
SŎUL (Seoul)
INCH'ŎN
TAEJŎN
TAEGU
PUSAN
Blagoveshchensk
Amur
COPYRIGHT PHILIP'S

CHINA AND THE FAR EAST

1:12 000 000

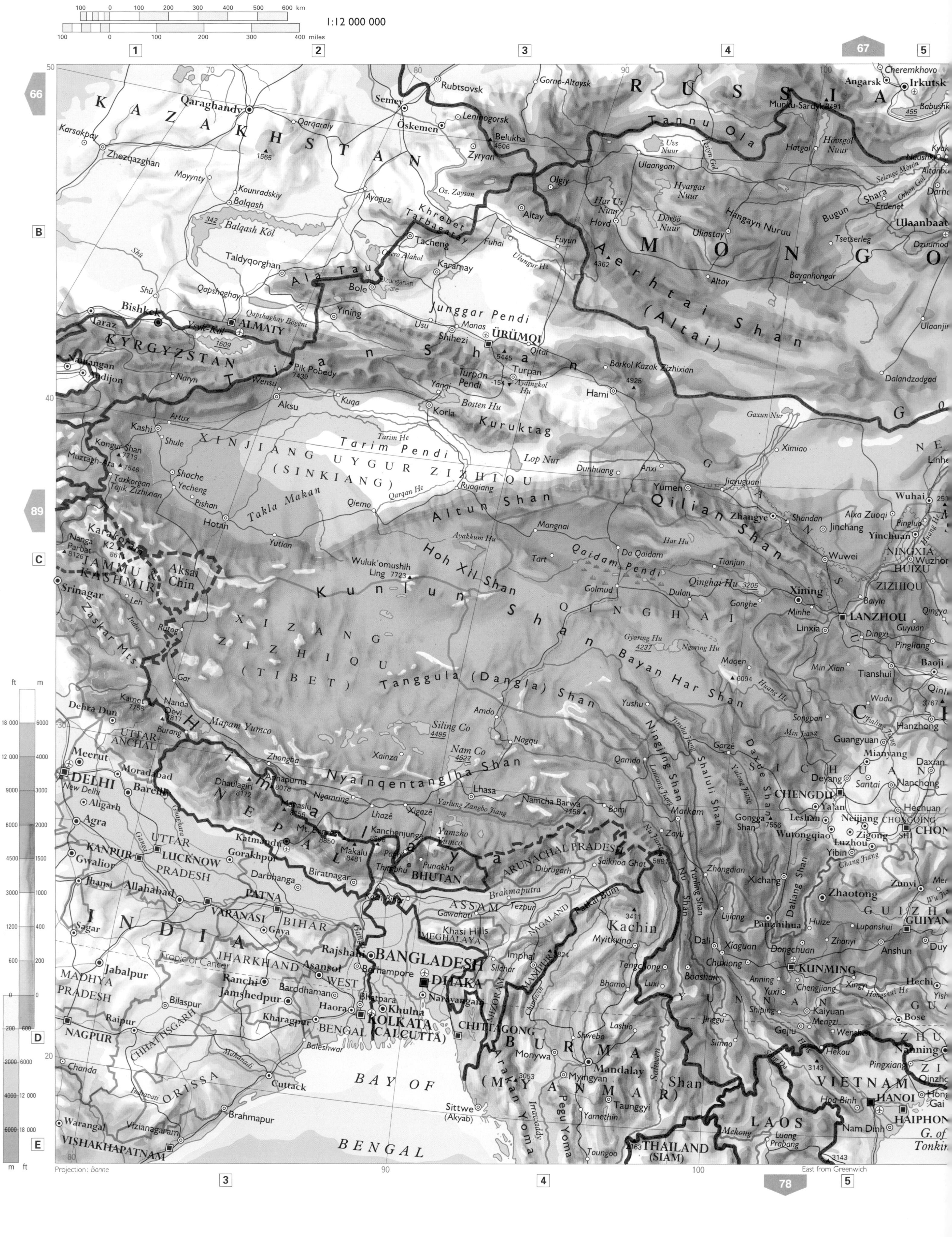
100 0 100 200 300 400 500 600 km
100 0 100 200 300 400 miles
1 2 3 4 5
67 66 89 78
B C D E
RUSSIA
KAZAKHSTAN
KYRGYZSTAN
MONGOLIA
XINJIANG UYGUR ZIZHIQU (SINKIANG)
XIZANG ZIZHIQU (TIBET)
QINGHAI
GANSU
NINGXIA HUIZU ZIZHIQU
SICHUAN
YUNNAN
GUIZHOU
JAMMU & KASHMIR
Aksai Chin
NEPAL
BHUTAN
BANGLADESH
INDIA
BURMA (MYANMAR)
LAOS
THAILAND (SIAM)
VIETNAM
Tannu Ola
Aerhtai Shan (Altai)
Hangayn Nuruu
Tian Shan
Junggar Pendi
Tarim Pendi
Takla Makan
Kuruktag
Altun Shan
Qilian Shan
Kunlun Shan
Hoh Xil Shan
Qaidam Pendi
Tanggula (Dangla) Shan
Bayan Har Shan
Nyainqentanglha Shan
Himalaya
Karakoram
Zaskar Mts.
Ala Tau
Khrebet Tarbagatay
Balqash Köl
Lop Nur
Qinghai Hu 3205
Siling Co 4495
Nam Co 4627
Ningjing Shan
Shaluli Shan
Daxue Shan
Daliang Shan
Arakan Yoma
Pegu Yoma
Shan
Kachin
Khasi Hills
ASSAM
MEGHALAYA
NAGALAND
MANIPUR
MIZORAM
ARUNACHAL PRADESH
UTTAR PRADESH
UTTARANCHAL
BIHAR
JHARKHAND
WEST BENGAL
ORISSA
CHHATTISGARH
MADHYA PRADESH
BAY OF BENGAL
Tropic of Cancer
Qaraghandy
Semey
Öskemen
Rubtsovsk
Leninogorsk
Zyryan
Belukha 4506
Gorno-Altaysk
Zhezqazghan
Karsakpay
Balqash
Taldyqorghan
Bishkek
ALMATY
Taraz
Namangan
Andijon
Naryn
Pik Pobedy 7439
ÜRÜMQI
Shihezi
Karamay
Tacheng
Yining
Turpan
Hami
Korla
Aksu
Kuqa
Kashi
Shache
Yecheng
Hotan
Qiemo
Ruoqiang
Golmud
Xining
LANZHOU
Yinchuan
Wuhai
Zhangye
Jiayuguan
Yumen
Dunhuang
Ulaanbaatar
Ulaangom
Hovd
Ölgiy
Uliastay
Bayanhongor
Dalandzadgad
Irkutsk
Angarsk
Cheremkhovo
Munku-Sardyk 3491
Hövsgöl Nuur
Uvs Nuur
Hyargas Nuur
Srinagar
Leh
Nanga Parbat 8126
K2 8611
Muztagh Ata 7546
Kongur Shan 7719
Dehra Dun
Kamet 7756
Nanda Devi 7817
DELHI
New Delhi
Meerut
Moradabad
Bareilly
Aligarh
Agra
KANPUR
LUCKNOW
Gwalior
Jhansi
Allahabad
VARANASI
PATNA
Gaya
Sagar
Jabalpur
NAGPUR
Raipur
Bilaspur
Ranchi
Jamshedpur
Asansol
Barddhaman
Kharagpur
Cuttack
Brahmapur
Vizianagaram
VISHAKHAPATNAM
Warangal
Chanda
Katmandu
Dhaulagiri 8172
Annapurna 8078
Manaslu 8156
Mt. Everest 8850
Makalu 8481
Kanchenjunga 8598
Thimphu
Punakha
Lhasa
Xigazê
Namcha Barwa 7756
Nagqu
Qamdo
Gongga Shan 7556
CHENGDU
CHONGQING
Zigong
Yibin
KUNMING
GUIYANG
Dali
Lijiang
Panzhihua
Xichang
Zhaotong
Rajshahi
DHAKA
Narayanganj
Khulna
KOLKATA (CALCUTTA)
CHITTAGONG
Sittwe (Akyab)
Imphal
Myitkyina
Bhamo
Lashio
Mandalay
Monywa
Taunggyi
HANOI
HAIPHONG
Nam Dinh
Luang Prabang
Nanning
Projection: Bonne
East from Greenwich
m ft
6000 18 000
4000 12 000
2000 6000
1000 3000
400 1200
200 600
0
200 600
2000 6000
4000 12 000
6000 18 000

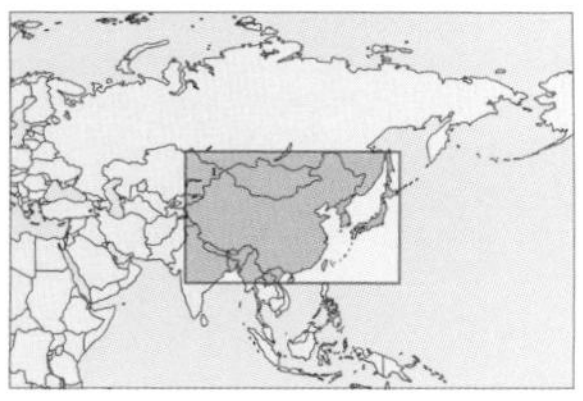

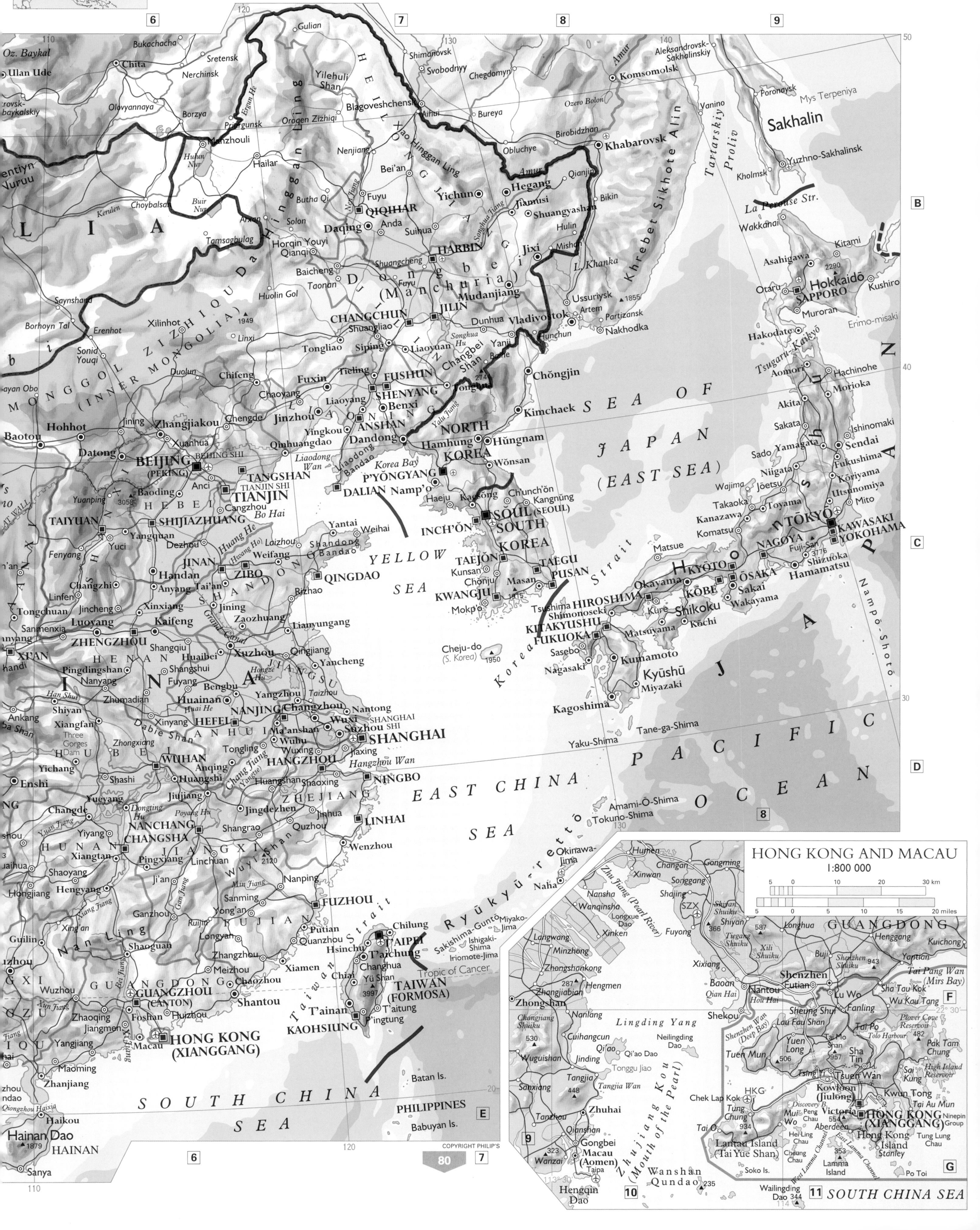
6
7
8
9
B
C
D
E
F
G
10
11
Oz. Baykal
Ulan Ude
Chita
Bukachacha
Sretensk
Nerchinsk
Olovyannaya
Borzya
Priargunsk
Manzhouli
Hulun Nur
Buir Nur
Choybalsan
Kerulen
Hailar
Gulian
Shimanovsk
Svobodnyy
Chegdomyn
Yilehuli Shan
Blagoveshchensk
Aihui
Bureya
Oroqen Zizhiqi
Komsomolsk
Aleksandrovsk-Sakhalinskiy
Amur
Ozero Bolon
Vanino
Poronaysk
Mys Terpeniya
Sakhalin
Yuzhno-Sakhalinsk
Kholmsk
La Perouse Str.
Tartarskiy Proliv
Birobidzhan
Obluchye
Khabarovsk
Khrebet Sikhote Alin
Nenjiang
Bei'an
Xiao Hinggan Ling
HEILONGJIANG
Yichun
Hegang
Jiamusi
Qianjin
Bikin
Shuangyashan
Fuyu
Nen Jiang
QIQIHAR
Butha Qi
Arxan
Solon
Daqing
Anda
Suihua
Songhua Jiang
Hulin
Mishan
L. Khanka
Tamsagbulag
Horqin Youyi Qianqi
HARBIN
Shuangcheng
Baicheng
Taonan
Dongbei (Manchuria)
Jixi
Mudanjiang
Ussuriysk
Artem
Partizansk
Nakhodka
Vladivostok
Hunchun
1855
Huolin Gol
Saynshand
Da Hinggan Ling
CHANGCHUN
JILIN
Shuangliao
Dunhua
Songhua Hu
Yanji
Baihe
Changbei Shan
2744
Xilinhot
1949
Linxi
Erenhot
Borhoyn Tal
Sonid Youqi
NEI MONGGOL ZIZHIQU (INNER MONGOLIA)
Tongliao
Siping
Liaoyuan
Tieling
FUSHUN
SHENYANG
Benxi
LIAONING
Fuxin
Liaoyang
Duolun
Chifeng
Chaoyang
Jinzhou
ANSHAN
Yingkou
Dandong
Chŏngjin
Kimchaek
Hamhung
Hŭngnam
NORTH KOREA
Wŏnsan
Yalu Jiang
Hohhot
Baotou
Jining
Zhangjiakou
Chengde
Qinhuangdao
Liaodong Wan
Liaodong Bandao
Korea Bay
P'YŎNGYANG
Namp'o
DALIAN
Datong
Xuanhua
BEIJING (PEKING)
BEIJING SHI
TANGSHAN
TIANJIN SHI
TIANJIN
Anci
Baoding
3058
Yuanping
HEBEI
Cangzhou
Bo Hai
SHIJIAZHUANG
TAIYUAN
Yangquan
Dezhou
Yuci
Fenyang
Huang He
Laizhou
Weifang
JINAN
ZIBO
Yantai
Weihai
Shandong Bandao
SHANDONG
QINGDAO
Handan
Anyang
Tai'an
Changzhi
Linfen
Jincheng
Xinxiang
Rizhao
Tongchuan
Luoyang
Kaifeng
Jining
Zaozhuang
Sanmenxia
ZHENGZHOU
XI'AN
Shangqiu
Huaibei
Xuzhou
Grand Canal
Lianyungang
Qingjiang
Yancheng
Pingdingshan
HENAN
Shangshui
Nanyang
Fuyang
Hongze Hu
JIANGSU
Bengbu
Han Shui
Zhumadian
Huainan
Huai He
Yangzhou
Taizhou
Nantong
Shiyan
Ankang
Xiangfan
HEFEI
NANJING
Changzhou
Wuxi
Suzhou
SHANGHAI SHI
SHANGHAI
Dabie Shan
ANHUI
Ma'anshan
Wuhu
Three Gorges Dam
Zhongxiang
HUBEI
Tongling
Wuxing
Jiaxing
HANGZHOU
Hangzhou Wan
Yichang
WUHAN
Anqing
Enshi
Shashi
Huangshi
Chang Jiang (Yangtze)
Huangshan
Shaoxing
NINGBO
Yueyang
Jiujiang
ZHEJIANG
Changde
Dongting Hu
Poyang Hu
Jingdezhen
Jinhua
LINHAI
NANCHANG
CHANGSHA
Yiyang
Shangrao
Quzhou
HUNAN
JIANGXI
Xiangtan
Pingxiang
Linchuan
Wuyi Shan
2120
Wenzhou
Shaoyang
Hengyang
Ji'an
Gan Jiang
Min Jiang
Nanping
Hongjiang
Sanming
FUZHOU
Xiang Jiang
Ganzhou
Yong'an
Xing'an
Ruijin
FUJIAN
Putian
Guilin
Nan Ling
Shaoguan
Longyan
Quanzhou
Zhangzhou
Xiamen
Meizhou
GUANGDONG
Chaozhou
Wuzhou
Bei Jiang
GUANGZHOU (CANTON)
Shantou
Xi Jiang
Zhaoqing
Foshan
Huizhou
Jiangmen
Yangjiang
Macau
HONG KONG (XIANGGANG)
Maoming
Zhanjiang
Haikou
Hainan Dao
HAINAN
1879
Sanya
Qiongzhou Haixia
SOUTH CHINA SEA
Batan Is.
PHILIPPINES
Babuyan Is.
Taiwan Strait
Chilung
T'AIPEI
Hsinchu
T'aichung
Changhua
Chiai
Yü Shan
3997
TAIWAN (FORMOSA)
T'ainan
T'aitung
P'ingtung
KAOHSIUNG
Tropic of Cancer
Ryūkyū-rettō
Sakishima-Guntō
Miyako-Jima
Ishigaki-Shima
Iriomote-Jima
Okinawa-Jima
Naha
Amami-Ō-Shima
Tokuno-Shima
EAST CHINA SEA
YELLOW SEA
Haeju
Kaesŏng
Ch'unch'ŏn
Kangnŭng
INCH'ŎN
SŎUL (SEOUL)
SOUTH KOREA
TAEJŎN
TAEGU
Kunsan
Chŏnju
KWANGJU
Masan
PUSAN
Mokp'o
1915
Cheju-do (S. Korea)
1950
Korea Strait
Tsushima
SEA OF JAPAN (EAST SEA)
Shimonoseki
KITAKYUSHU
FUKUOKA
Sasebo
Nagasaki
Kumamoto
Kyūshū
Miyazaki
Kagoshima
Yaku-Shima
Tane-ga-Shima
HIROSHIMA
Kure
Matsuyama
Shikoku
Kōchi
Okayama
KŌBE
KYOTO
ŌSAKA
Sakai
Wakayama
Matsue
Komatsu
Kanazawa
Takaoka
Toyama
Wajima
NAGOYA
Fuji-San
3776
Shizuoka
Hamamatsu
TŌKYŌ
KAWASAKI
YOKOHAMA
Niigata
Jōetsu
Utsunomiya
Mito
Kōriyama
Fukushima
Sado
Yamagata
Sendai
Ishinomaki
Sakata
Akita
Morioka
Aomori
Hachinohe
Tsugaru-Kaikyō
Hakodate
Honshu
JAPAN
Nampō-Shotō
Hokkaidō
SAPPORO
Otaru
Asahigawa
2290
Kitami
Kushiro
Muroran
Erimo-misaki
Wakkanai
PACIFIC OCEAN
COPYRIGHT PHILIP'S
80
HONG KONG AND MACAU
1:800 000
5 0 10 20 30 km
5 0 5 10 15 20 miles
Humen
Changan
Gongming
Xinwan
Songgang
Zhu Jiang (Pearl River)
Nansha
Wanqinsha
Longxue Dao
Xinken
Shajing
Fuyong
SZX
Shiyan Shuiku
366
Shiyan
Tiegang Shuiku
Xili Shuiku
587
Longhua
GUANGDONG
Henggang
Kuichong
Langwang
Minzhong
Zhongshankong
Xixiang
Buji
Shenzhen Shuiku
943
Yantian
Tai Pang Wan (Mirs Bay)
Shenzhen
Futian
287
Hengmen
Zhangjiabian
Zhongshan
Baoan
Nantou
Qian Hai
Hou Hai
Lu Wo
Sha Tau Kok
Wu Kau Tang
Changjiang Shuiku
Nanlang
530
Lingding Yang
Shekou
Sheung Shui
Fanling
Plover Cove Reservoir
Shenzhen Wan (Deep Bay)
Lau Fau Shan
Tai Po
Tolo Harbour
482
Cuihangcun
Neilingding Dao
Yuen Long
Tai Mo Shan
957
Sha Tin
Pak Tam Chung
Wuguishan
Qi'ao
Qi'ao Dao
Tuen Mun
506
Sai Kung
High Island Reservoir
Jinding
Tonggu Jiao
Tsing Yi
Tsuen Wan
Sanxiang
Tangjia
448
Tangjia Wan
HKG
Kowloon (Jiulong)
Kwun Tong
Tai Au Mun
Zhujiang Kou (Mouth of the Pearl)
Chek Lap Kok
Discovery B.
Peng Chau
Victoria
HONG KONG (XIANGGANG)
Ninepin Group
Tanzhou
Zhuhai
Tung Chung
934
Mui Wo
554
Qianshan
Tai O
Hei Ling Chau
Aberdeen
Hong Kong Island
Tung Lung Chau
Gongbei
Macau (Aomen)
Lantau Island (Tai Yue Shan)
Cheung Chau
East Lamma Channel
West Lamma Channel
353
Stanley
323
Wanzai
Taipa
Lamma Island
Soko Is.
Po Toi
Wanshan Qundao
235
Hengqin Dao
Wailingding Dao
344
SOUTH CHINA SEA

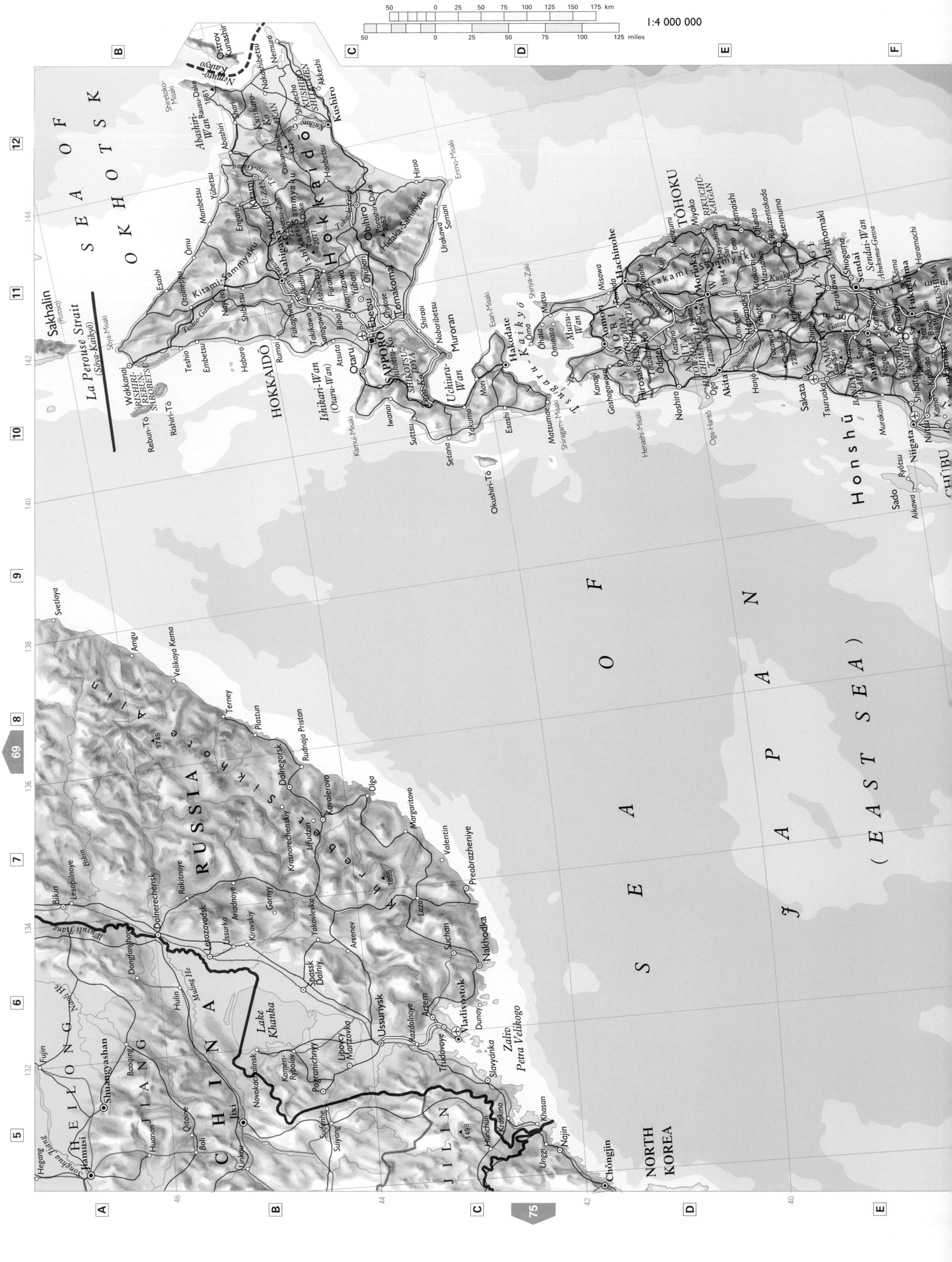
1:4 000 000
km
miles
SEA OF OKHOTSK
SEA OF JAPAN
(EAST SEA)
HOKKAIDŌ
RUSSIA
CHINA
NORTH KOREA
HEILONGJIANG
JILIN
TŌHOKU
Honshū
Sakhalin
(Russia)
La Perouse Strait
(Sōya-Kaikyō)
Tsugaru-Kaikyō
Ishikari-Wan
(Otaru-Wan)
Uchiura-Wan
Mutsu-Wan
Sendai-Wan
Abashiri-Wan
Nemuro-Kaikyō
Ostrov Kunashir
Zaliv Petra Velikogo
Lake Khanka
SAPPORO
Hakodate
Asahikawa
Kushiro
Obihiro
Otaru
Muroran
Wakkanai
Aomori
Akita
Morioka
Sendai
Hachinohe
Niigata
Yamagata
Vladivostok
Nakhodka
Ussuriysk
Dalnerechensk
Chŏngjin
Jixi
69
75

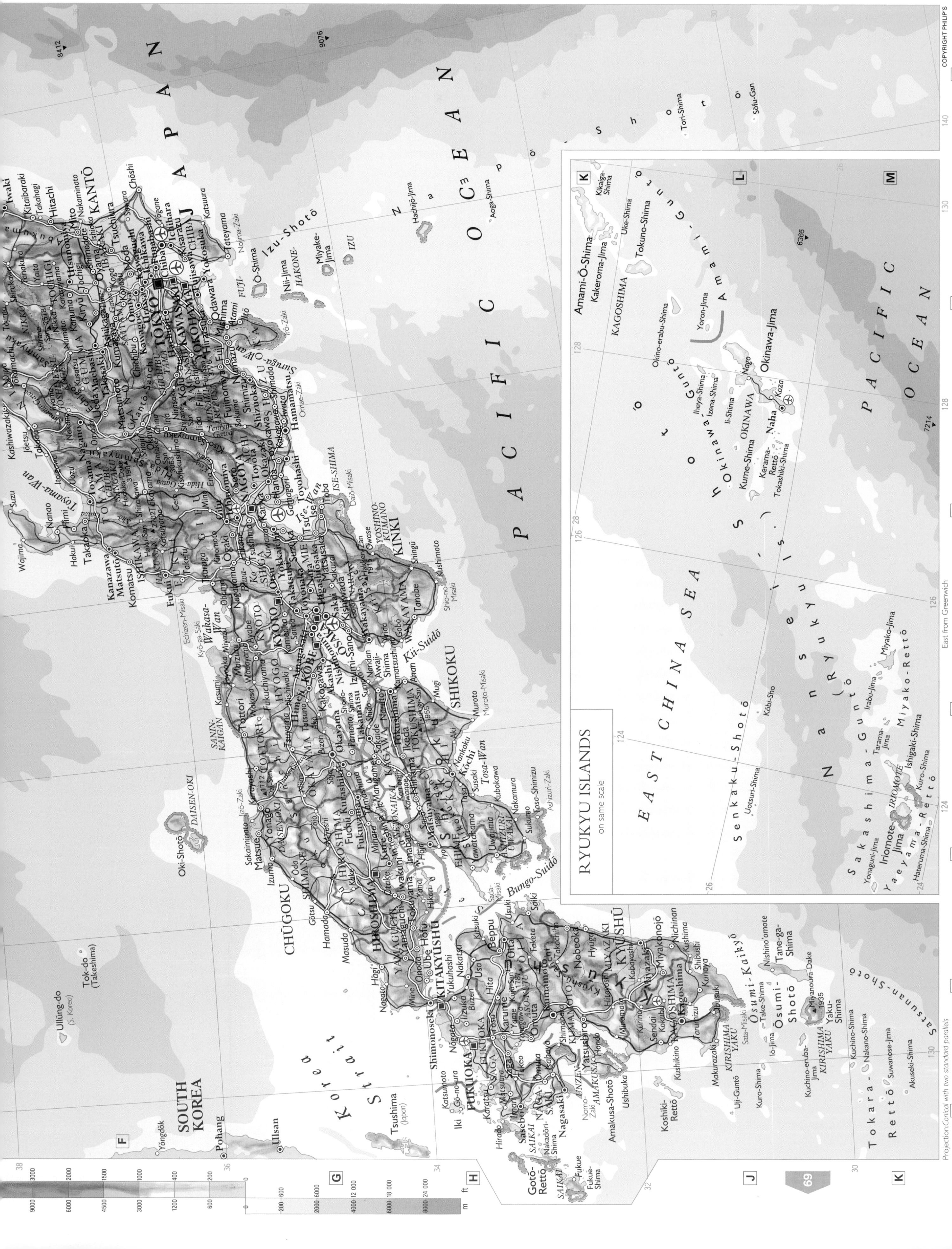
SOUTH KOREA
JAPAN
PACIFIC OCEAN
EAST CHINA SEA
Korea Strait
CHŪGOKU
SHIKOKU
KINKI
KANTŌ
KYŪSHŪ
TOKYO
NAGOYA
ŌSAKA
KŌBE
KYŌTO
HIROSHIMA
FUKUOKA
KITAKYŪSHŪ
Nagasaki
Kagoshima
Tsushima (Japan)
Oki-Shotō
Izu-Shotō
Ōsumi-Shotō
Satsunan-Shotō
Tokara-Rettō
Gotō-Rettō
Koshiki-Rettō
Amakusa-Shotō
Bungo-Suidō
Kii-Suidō
Tosa-Wan
Ullŭng-do (S. Korea)
Tok-do (Takeshima)
Pohang
Ulsan
RYUKYU ISLANDS
on same scale
Nansei-shotō (Ryukyu-rettō)
Okinawa-Jima
Naha
Amami-Ō-Shima
Sakashima-Guntō
Miyako-Rettō
Yaeyama-Rettō
Senkaku-Shotō
East from Greenwich
Projection: Conical with two standard parallels
COPYRIGHT PHILIP'S

1:2 000 000

S E A O F J A P A N
(E A S T S E A)
SOUTH KOREA
Yŏngdŏk
Chŏngha
Changgi-Ap
P'ohang
Oki-Shotō
Dōgo
Dōzen
Daimanji-San 608
Saigō
DAISEN-OKI
H o n s
Korea Strait
CHŪGOKU-DISTRICT
Shimane-Hantō
Jizō-Zaki
Matsue
Sakaiminato
Yonago
Hirata
Taisha
Izumo
Hi-no-Misaki
TOTTORI
Tottori
Kurayoshi
Dai-Sen 1729
Iwami
Kasumi
Toyooka
Hidaka
SANIN-KAIGAN
Oda
Sanbe-San 1126
Gōtsu
Hamada
SHIMANE
Dōgo-San 1269
Niimi
Tsuyama
OKAYAMA
Okayama
Kurashiki
Himeji
Kakogawa
Akashi
HYŌGO
Tsushima
Mitsushima
Izuhara
Kamiagata
Kamitsushima
Kara-Saki
Kō-Saki
Mi-Shima
Masuda
HIROSHIMA
Hiroshima
Miyoshi
Shōbara
Fukuyama
Onomichi
Mihara
Kure
Iwakuni
Hagi
Ōmi-Shima
Tsuno-Shima
Nagato
YAMAGUCHI
Yamaguchi
Ube
Hōfu
Tokuyama
Shimonoseki
KITAKYŪSHŪ
Hibiki-Nada
Genkai-Nada
Suō-Nada
Iki
Iki-Kaikyō
FUKUOKA
Fukuoka
Kurume
Saga
SAGA
Karatsu
Imari
Sasebo
Hirado
Hirado-Shima
Ikitsuki-Shima
Ō-Shima
NAGASAKI
Nagasaki
Ōmura
Isahaya
Unzen-Dake 1360
Shimabara
Kumamoto
KUMAMOTO
Ōmuta
Aso
Aso-Zan 1592
Kujū-San 1787
ŌITA
Ōita
Beppu
Beppu-Wan
Nakatsu
Kunisaki
Saiki
Sobo-Yama 1758
Nobeoka
Hyūga
Kunimi-Dake 1739
MIYAZAKI
Miyazaki
Amakusa-Shotō
Amakusa-Nada
Yatsushiro
Hitoyoshi
Minamata
Izumi
Sendai
Kirishima-Yama 1700
Kagoshima
KAGOSHIMA
Kagoshima-Wan
Miyakonojō
Nichinan
Kushima
Makurazaki
Kaimon-Dake 924
Sata-Misaki
Koshiki-Rettō
Kyūshū
KYŪSHŪ-DISTRICT
Matsuyama
EHIME
Imabari
Niihama
Uwajima
Iyo-Nada
Bungo-Suidō
Hōgo-Kaikyō
Sada-Misaki-Hantō
Takamatsu
KAGAWA
Marugame
Tokushima
TOKUSHIMA
Tsurugi-San 1955
Ishizuchi-Yama 1981
Kōchi
KŌCHI
Tosa-Wan
Muroto
Muroto-Misaki
Anan
Awaji-Shima
Naruto
Nakamura
Sukumo
Tosa-Shimizu
Ashizuri-Zaki
Oki-no-Shima
Shikoku
SHIKOKU-DISTRICT
SETO-NAIKAI
Harima-Nada
Shōdo-Shima
Projection: Lambert's Conformal Conic
Shinkansen line
National Parks

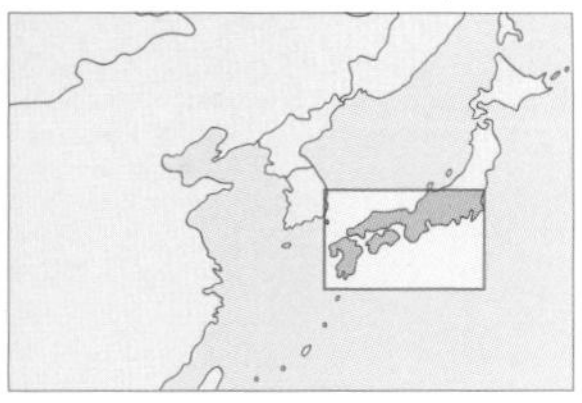

7
8
9
10
70
11
12
A
B
C
D
E
F
CHŪBU-DISTRICT
KINKI-DISTRICT
KANTŌ-DISTRICT
P A C I F I C O C E A N
Enshū-Nada
Kumano-Nada
Sagami-Nada
Kashima-Nada
Ise-Wan
Wakasa-Wan
Suruga-Wan
Sagami-Wan
Tōkyō-Wan
Izu-Hantō
Kii-Hantō
Izu-Shotō
Nampō-Shotō
TŌKYŌ
YOKOHAMA
KAWASAKI
NAGOYA
ŌSAKA
KYŌTO
KOBE
Chiba
Funabashi
Sakai
Higashiōsaka
Shizuoka
Hamamatsu
Toyohashi
Okazaki
Toyota
Gifu
Nagano
Matsumoto
Kōfu
Maebashi
Utsunomiya
Mito
Tsu
Nara
Wakayama
Fukui
Kanazawa
Toyama
Ōtsu
Yokosuka
Odawara
Numazu
Fuji
Shimizu
Hachiōji
Sagamihara
Fujisawa
Kamakura
Atami
Shimoda
Ise
Toba
Shingū
Tanabe
Kushimoto
Shio-no-Misaki
Irō-Zaki
Omae-Zaki
Inubō-Zaki
Nojima-Zaki
Ō-Shima
To-Shima
Nii-Jima
Shikine-Jima
Kōzu-Shima
Miyake-Jima
Mikura-Jima
Hachijō-Jima
Aoga-Shima
Sumisu-Jima
NRT
HND
NGO
KIX
CJI
136
137
138
139
140
East from Greenwich
34
33
32
ft
m
9000
3000
6000
2000
4500
1500
3000
1000
1200
400
600
200
0
0
200
600
2000
6000
4000
12 000
m
ft

1:4 800 000

50 0 50 100 150 200 km

50 0 50 100 150 miles

69

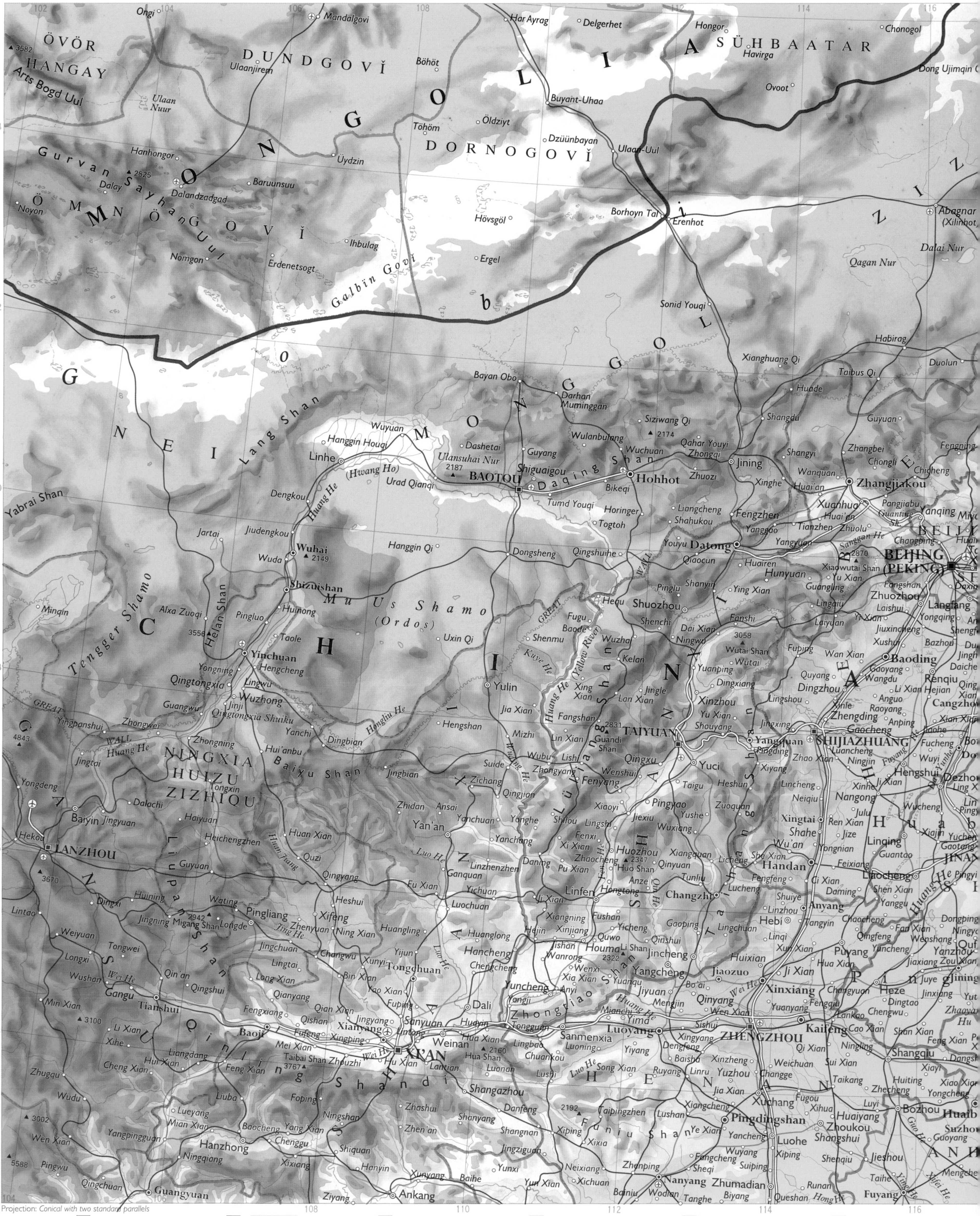

68

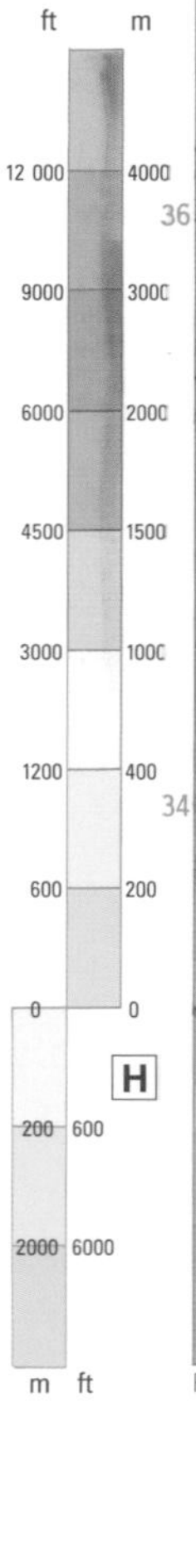

Projection: *Conical with two standard parallels*

76

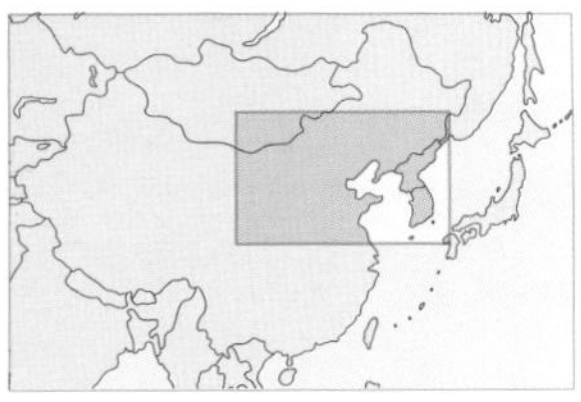

69
70
77
HARBIN
CHANGCHUN
JILIN
SHENYANG
FUSHUN
ANSHAN
DALIAN
TIANJIN
QINGDAO
ZIBO
P'YŎNGYANG
SŎUL
INCH'ON
TAEJŎN
TAEGU
KWANGJU
PUSAN
Vladivostok
NORTH KOREA
SOUTH KOREA
JAPAN
RUSSIA
HEILONGJIANG
JILIN
LIAONING
SHANDONG
JIANGSU
Bo Hai
Liaodong Wan
Korea Bay
YELLOW SEA
(Huang Hai)
SEA OF JAPAN
(EAST SEA)
Tongjosŏn Man
Korea Strait
Shandong Bandao
Liaodong Bandao
Changbai Shan
Dongbei
Cheju-do (S. Korea)
Tsushima
Lake Khanka
East from Greenwich
COPYRIGHT PHILIP'S

50 0 50 100 150 200 km

50 0 50 100 150 miles

1:4 800 000

74

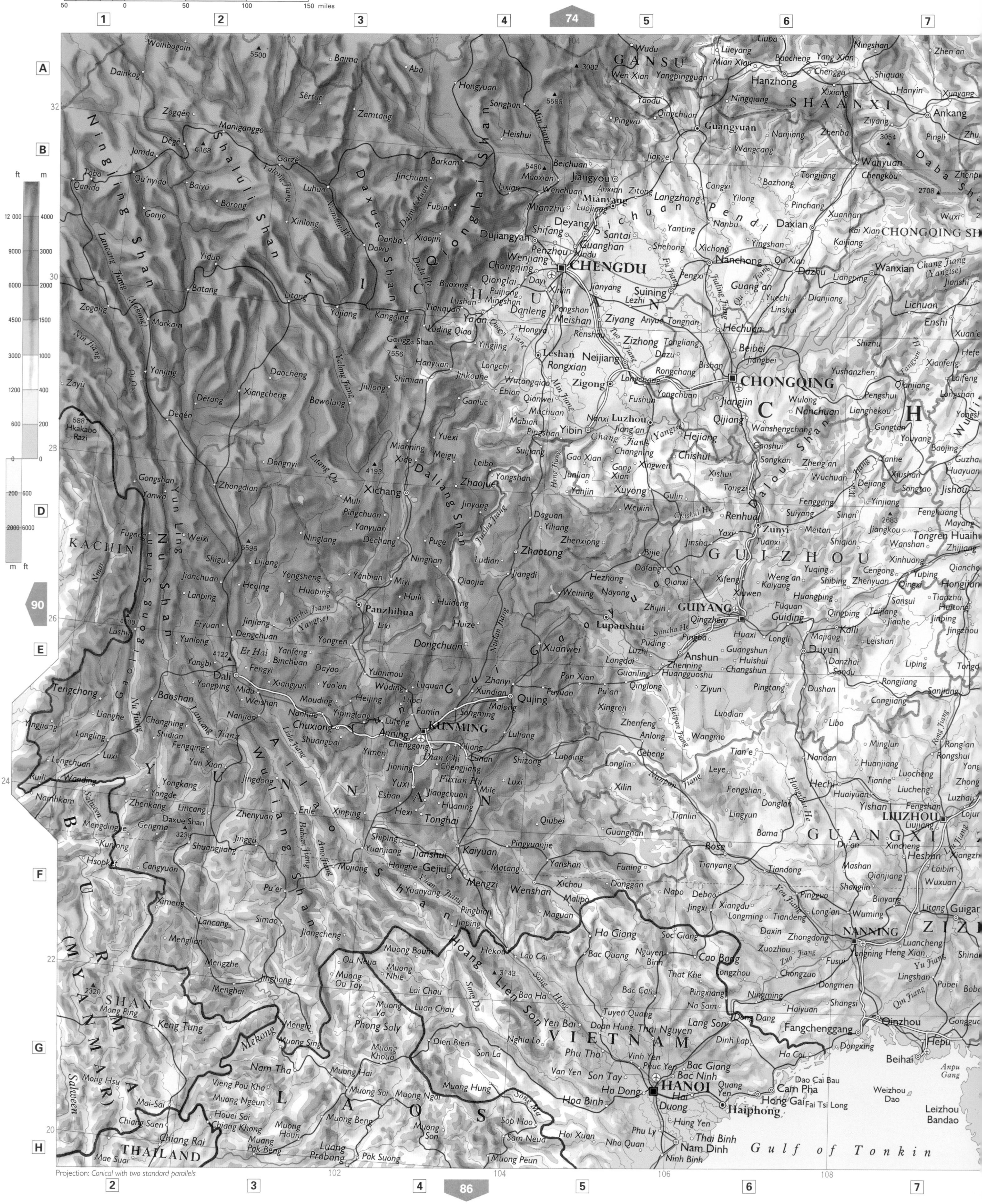

90

86

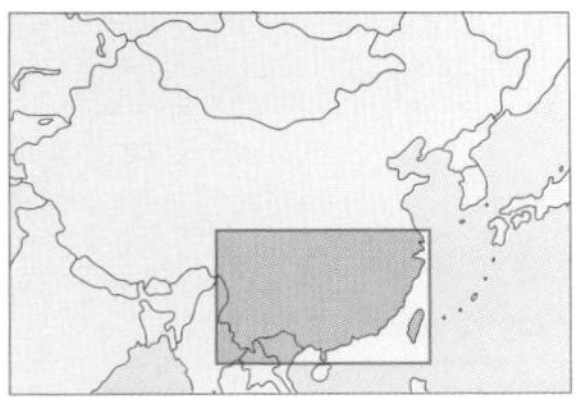

75
80
8
9
10
11
12
13
14
A
B
C
D
E
F
G
H
32
30
28
26
24
22
20
112
114
116
118
120
122
East from Greenwich
HENAN
ANHUI
JIANGSU
HUBEI
HUNAN
JIANGXI
ZHEJIANG
FUJIAN
GUANGDONG
TAIWAN
SHANGHAI SHI
NANJING
SHANGHAI
HANGZHOU
WUHAN
CHANGSHA
NANCHANG
GUANGZHOU
HONG KONG (XIANGGANG)
T'AIPEI
KAOHSIUNG
Hefei
Fuzhou
Xiamen
Shantou
Shenzhen
Kowloon
Macau
Zhuhai
Ningbo
Wenzhou
Suzhou
Wuxi
Changzhou
Zhenjiang
Yangzhou
Nantong
Huainan
Bengbu
Anqing
Jiujiang
Yichang
Shashi
Xiangtan
Zhuzhou
Hengyang
Ganzhou
Shaoguan
Chenzhou
Quanzhou
Putian
Nanping
Jingdezhen
Shangrao
Quzhou
Jinhua
Changde
Yueyang
Xiangfan
Shiyan
Nanyang
Xinyang
Zhanjiang
Maoming
Wuzhou
Foshan
Jiangmen
Huizhou
Meizhou
Chaozhou
T'aichung
T'ainan
Hualien
Chilung
Hsinchu
Dongting Hu
Poyang Hu
Tai Hu
Chang Jiang (Yangtze)
Dabie Shan
Wuyi Shan
Nan Ling
Luoxiao Shan
Jiuling Shan
Mufu Shan
Chungyang Shanmo
Taiwan Strait
Luzon Strait
SOUTH CHINA SEA
Tropic of Cancer
Dongsha Dao (Pratas I.) (China)
Matsu Tao (Taiwan)
Chinmen (Quemoy) Chinmen Tao (Taiwan)
Makung P'enghu Ch'üntou (Pescadores) (Taiwan)
Zhoushan
Chongming Dao
Honghai Wan
Leizhou Wan
Three Gorges Dam
3997
3931
2120
1810
1794
1725
1703
1636
1629
1596
1510
1474
1963
2393

INDONESIA AND THE PHILIPPINES

1:10 000 000
Projection: Mercator
East from Greenwich
86
68
BURMA (MYANMAR)
RANGOON (YANGON)
G. of Martaban
THAILAND
BANGKOK
LAOS
Vientiane (Viangchan)
VIETNAM
Da Nang
Hue
Quang Ngai
Qui Nhon
Nha Trang
Cam Ranh
Da Lat
Buon Ma Thuot
THANH PHO HO CHI MINH
Vung Tau
Can Tho
CAMBODIA
Phnom Penh (Phnum Penh)
Tonle Sap
Gulf of Thailand
ANDAMAN SEA
Mergui Arch.
Kho Khot Kra (Isthmus of Kra)
Malay Pen.
Straits of Malacca
MALAYSIA
PENINSULAR MALAYSIA
KUALA LUMPUR
SINGAPORE
Johor Bahru
Kota Bharu
Kuala Terengganu
George Town
Ipoh
Kuantan
Melaka
SOUTH CHINA SEA
Paracel Is.
Spratly Is.
Kepulauan Natuna
Kepulauan Anambas
BRUNEI
Bandar Seri Begawan
SABAH
Kota Kinabalu
SARAWAK
Kuching
Sibu
KALIMANTAN (BORNEO)
Pontianak
Banjarmasin
Balikpapan
Selat Karimata
INDONESIA
Sumatera
MEDAN
ACEH
Banda Aceh
Padang
Pekanbaru
Jambi
PALEMBANG
Bengkulu
Bangka
Belitung
Kepulauan Riau
Lingga
Greater Sunda Islands
JAVA SEA
JAKARTA
Bogor
BANDUNG
Cirebon
SEMARANG
Yogyakarta
Surakarta
SURABAYA
Malang
Madura
BALI
Denpasar
Lombok
Jawa (Java)
Java Trench
INDIAN OCEAN
Kepulauan Mentawai
Siberut
Nias
Simeulue
Enggano
NUSA TENGGARA BARAT

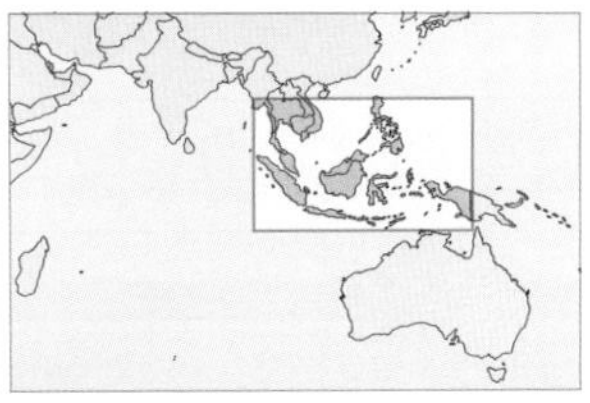

JAVA AND MADURA
1:6 000 000
BALI
1:1 600 000
JAKARTA
Bogor
BANDUNG
SEMARANG
Yogyakarta
Surakarta
SURABAYA
Malang
Madura
Cirebon
Kediri
Denpasar
Singaraja
Kuta
Nusa Penida
Lombok
Mataram
Jawa
Bali
INDIAN OCEAN
PACIFIC OCEAN
CELEBES SEA
SULU SEA
BANDA SEA
FLORES SEA
ARAFURA SEA
Luzon
MANILA
Quezon City
Mindanao
Zamboanga
Davao
Cebu
Iloilo
Bacolod
Samar
Leyte
Mindoro
Halmahera
Manado
Sulawesi (Celebes)
Seram
Ambon
Buru
Flores
Sumba
Alor
EAST TIMOR
Dili
Kupang
Kepulauan Aru
Kepulauan Tanimbar
Jazirah Doberai
Sorong
Manokwari
Pegunungan Maoke
PAPUA
Jayapura
Merauke
PAPUA NEW GUINEA
Equator
COPYRIGHT PHILIP'S

69
132
124
126

1:3 200 000

0 20 40 60 80 100 120 140 160 km

0 20 40 60 80 100 miles

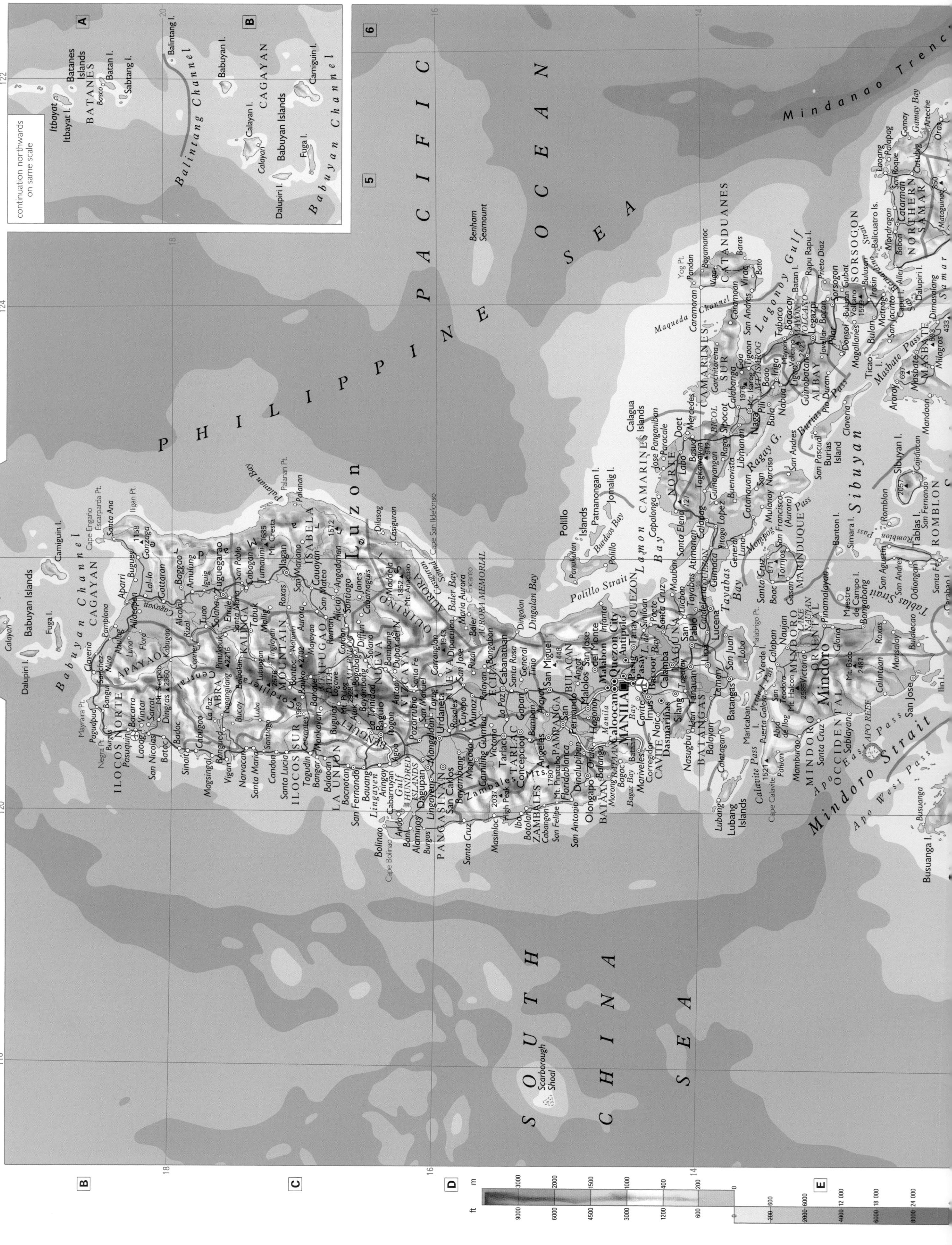

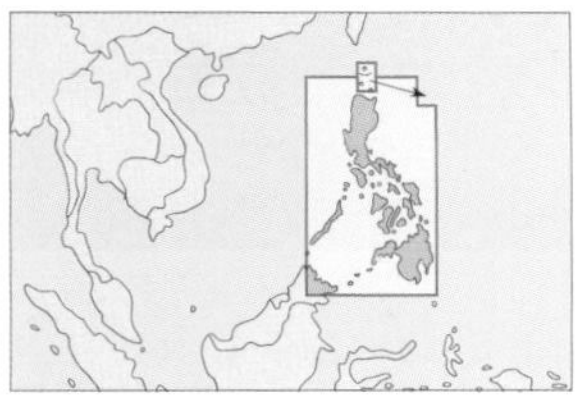

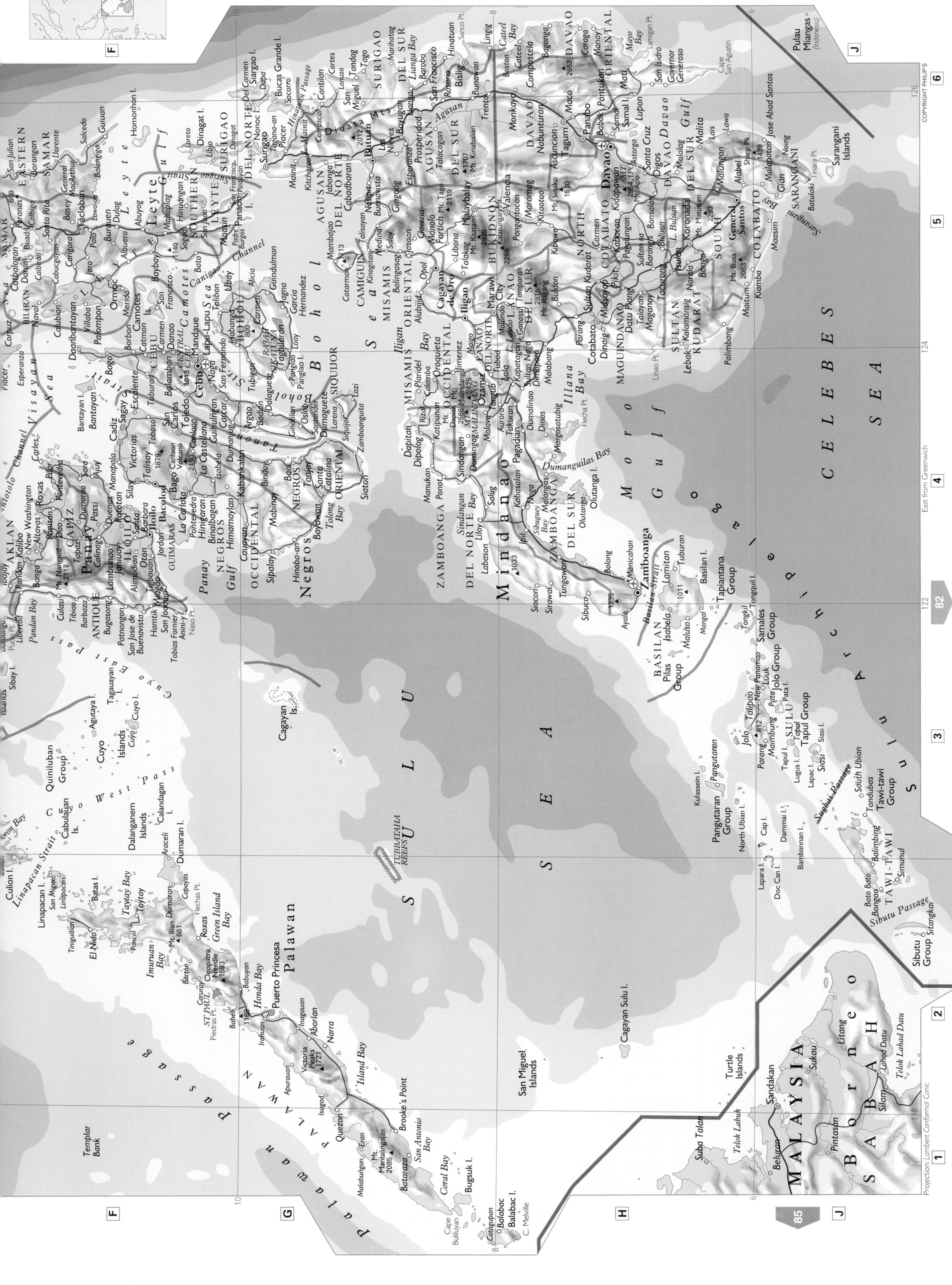
SULU SEA
CELEBES SEA
Moro Gulf
Sulu Archipelago
Palawan Passage
Bohol Sea
Visayan Sea
Camotes Sea
Leyte Gulf
Davao Gulf
Illana Bay
Cuyo West Pass
Cuyo East Pass
Mindanao
Negros
Panay
Palawan
Bohol
Leyte
Cebu
SIQUIJOR
CAMIGUIN
Dinagat I.
Siargao I.
Basilan Strait
BASILAN
SULU
TAWI-TAWI
Tawi-tawi Group
Jolo
Zamboanga
Davao
Cebu
Iloilo
Bacolod
Puerto Princesa
Cagayan de Oro
Iligan
Butuan
Surigao
Tacloban
Ormoc
Dumaguete
Dipolog
Pagadian
Cotabato
General Santos
Tagbilaran
Roxas
Quezon
Cagayan Is.
Cagayan Sulu I.
TUBBATAHA REEFS
Turtle Islands
San Miguel Islands
Sarangani Islands
Balabac I.
Bugsuk I.
Culion I.
Templar Bank
MALAYSIA
SABAH
Borneo
Sandakan
Pulau Miangas (Indonesia)
East from Greenwich
Projection: Lambert Conformal Conic
COPYRIGHT PHILIP'S
82
85

1:5 600 000

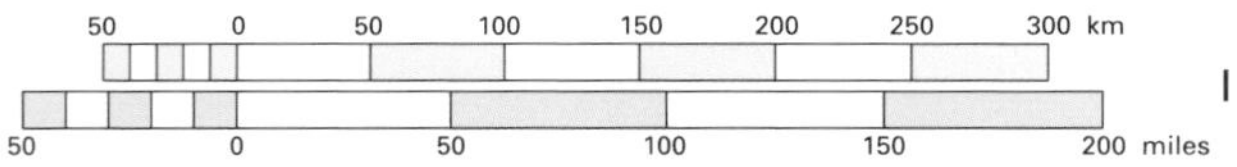

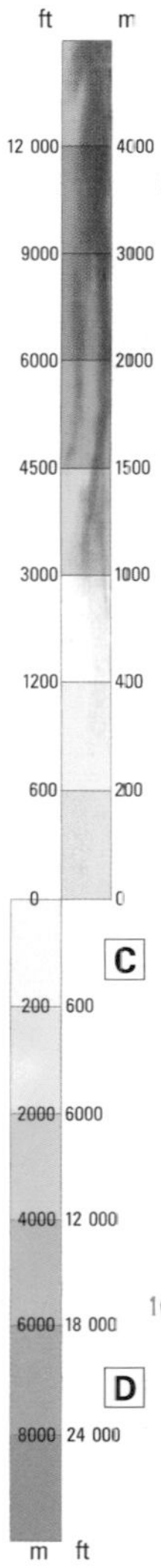

Projection: Mercator

East from Greenwich

PACIFIC OCEAN
Tobi
(Palau)
Helen Atoll
Kepulauan Asia
Kepulauan Mapia
Kepulauan Ayu
Waigeo
Kabarai
Wakre
Gebe
Saonek
Gam
Batanta
Selat Dampier
Sausapor
Warmandi
Waibeem
Peg. Tamrau
Kwoka
2452
4625
Makbon
Sorong
Samate
Salawati
Sailolof
Seget
Kofiau
Klamono
Jazirah Doberai (Vogelkop)
3100
2926
Kaironi
Manokwari
Warkopi
Ransiki
Wariap
Teminabuan
Konda
Misool
Lenmalu
Adua
Kepulauan Segaf
Inanwatan
Mogoi
Wasian
Bintuni
Kamundan
Rumberpon
Waar
Selat Aruri
Selat Woinui
Namber
Numfoor
Num
Supiori
Sansundi
Biak
Korim
Wardo
Bosnik
Kepulauan Padaido
Selat Yapen
Yapen
Ansus
Serui
Kepulauan Ambai
Nuboai
Waren
Barapasi
Teluk Cenderawasih
Wendesi
Roon
Wasior
Wosimi
Bawe
Kepulauan Moor
Napanwainami
Nabire
Kwatisore
Teluk Bintuni
Teluk Berau
Tanjung Fatagar
Kokas
Saga
Babo
Peg. Fakfak
Fakfak
Semenanjung
Susunu
Teluk Arguni
Bomberai
Wenut
Weri
Karas
Ibonma
Kaimana
Lobo
Karufa
Teluk Kamrau
Aiduma
Modowi
Manggawitu
Adi
Wahai
Hoti
Bula
Binaiya
3019
Sawai
Masohi
Tehoru
Haya
Waru
Seram (Ceram)
Geser
Kepulauan Gorong
Bandanaira
Kepulauan Banda
Kepulauan Watubela
Kur
Kepulauan Kai
Har
Tual
Kai Besar
Kai Kecil
Banda Elat
Kepulauan Tayandu
7440
Gumzai
Kola
Dobo
Sewer
Wokam
Wangal
Maikoor
Kobroor
Kepulauan Aru
Rebi
Koba
Penambulai
Trangan
Tafermaar
Gomogomo
Workai
Tanjung Ngabordamlu
Kepulauan Jin
Serua
Nila
Teun
Molu
Fordate
Larat
Wuliaru
Watmuri
Yamdena
Selu
Bukrane
Alusi
Sera
Saumlaki
Tepa
Babar
Adaut
Kepulauan Tanimbar
Kepulauan Babar
Masela
Eliase
Selaru
ARAFURA SEA
Tanjung D'Urville
Bonoi
Mataboor
Apauwar
Kepulauan Kumamba
Danau Rombebai
Sarmi
Saberania
Mamberamo
Teluk Walckenaer
Demta
Ansudu
Jayapura
Teluk Yos Sudarso
Genyem
Danau Sentani
Vanimo
Bewani
Pegunungan Van Rees
New Guinea
Tariku
Taritatu
Krau
PAPUA
Enarotali
Waghete
Puncak Jaya
5029
Wamena
Puncak Trikora
4730
Pegunungan Sudirman
Pegunungan Jayawijaya
Peg. Tiyo
Maoke
Puncak Mandala
4702
Sobger
Sepik
Aiduma
Wanapiri
Uta
Tembagapura
Timika
Kokonau
Amamapare
Yapero
Teluk Flamingo
Agats
Kaima
Baliem
Atsy
Pulau
Mindiptana
Tanahmerah
Mapi
Pirimapun
Kepi
Digul
Asike
Tg. De Jongs
Odammun
Kassue
Bade
Abemarre
Muli
Muting
Pulau Dolak
Kimaam
Okaba
Kurik
Kumbe
Merauke
Tanjung Vals
Pulau Komoran
PAPUA NEW GUINEA
Fly
Equator
132
A
B
C
D
4
5
6
130
135
140
0
5
10

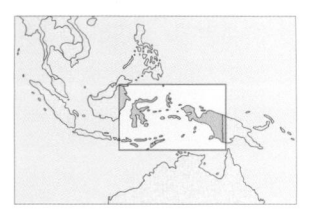

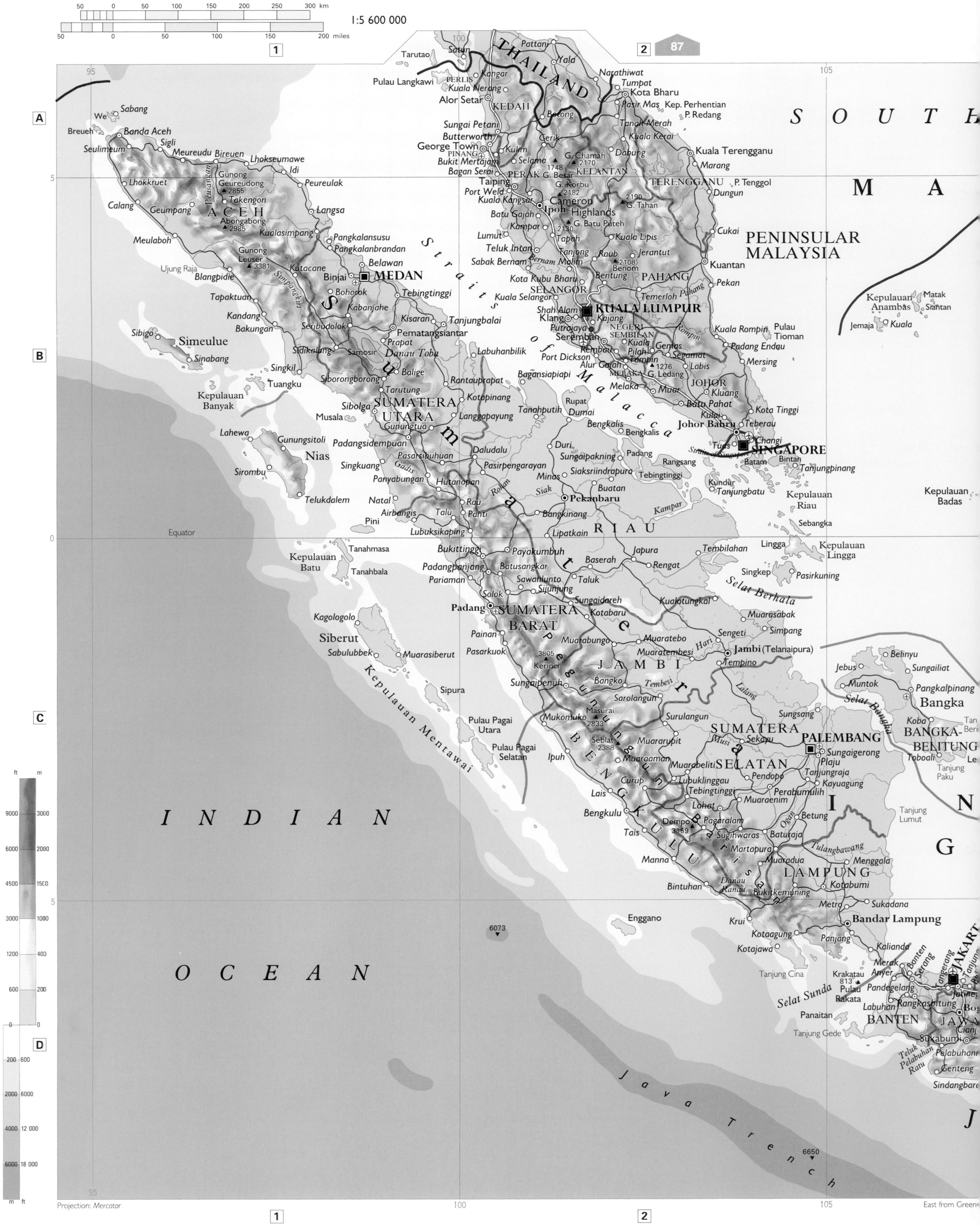
1:5 600 000
Projection: Mercator
East from Greenwich
THAILAND
PENINSULAR MALAYSIA
SINGAPORE
KUALA LUMPUR
MEDAN
PALEMBANG
ACEH
SUMATERA UTARA
SUMATERA BARAT
RIAU
JAMBI
BENGKULU
SUMATERA SELATAN
LAMPUNG
BANGKA-BELITUNG
BANTEN
KEDAH
PERAK
KELANTAN
TERENGGANU
PAHANG
SELANGOR
NEGERI SEMBILAN
MELAKA
JOHOR
Sumatera
Straits of Malacca
Pegunungan Barisan
Kepulauan Mentawai
Java Trench
INDIAN OCEAN
SOUTH
Selat Sunda
Selat Berhala
Selat Bangka
Equator
Simeulue
Nias
Siberut
Enggano
Bangka
Kepulauan Riau
Kepulauan Lingga
Kepulauan Batu
Kepulauan Banyak
Kepulauan Anambas
Kepulauan Badas
Pulau Pagai Utara
Pulau Pagai Selatan
Sipura
Danau Toba
Banda Aceh
Sabang
Lhokseumawe
Takengon
Meulaboh
Kutacane
Binjai
Belawan
Tebingtinggi
Pematangsiantar
Sibolga
Padangsidempuan
Gunungsitoli
Bukittinggi
Padang
Pekanbaru
Dumai
Jambi (Telanaipura)
Bengkulu
Lubuklinggau
Lahat
Pagaralam
Baturaja
Kotabumi
Bandar Lampung
Krakatau 813
Pangkalpinang
Sungailiat
Muntok
Tanjungpinang
Batam
Johor Bahru
Kuantan
Kuala Terengganu
Kota Bharu
Ipoh
Cameron Highlands
Seremban
Melaka
George Town
Alor Setar
Pulau Langkawi
Tarutao
Satun
Pattani
Yala
Narathiwat
Sukabumi
Cianjur
Merak
Serang
Rangkasbitung
Pandeglang
Tanjung Cina
Tanjung Gede
Abongabong 2985
Gunong Leuser 3381
Kerinci 3805
Masurai 2833
Seblat 2388
Dempo 3159
G. Tahan
6073
6650

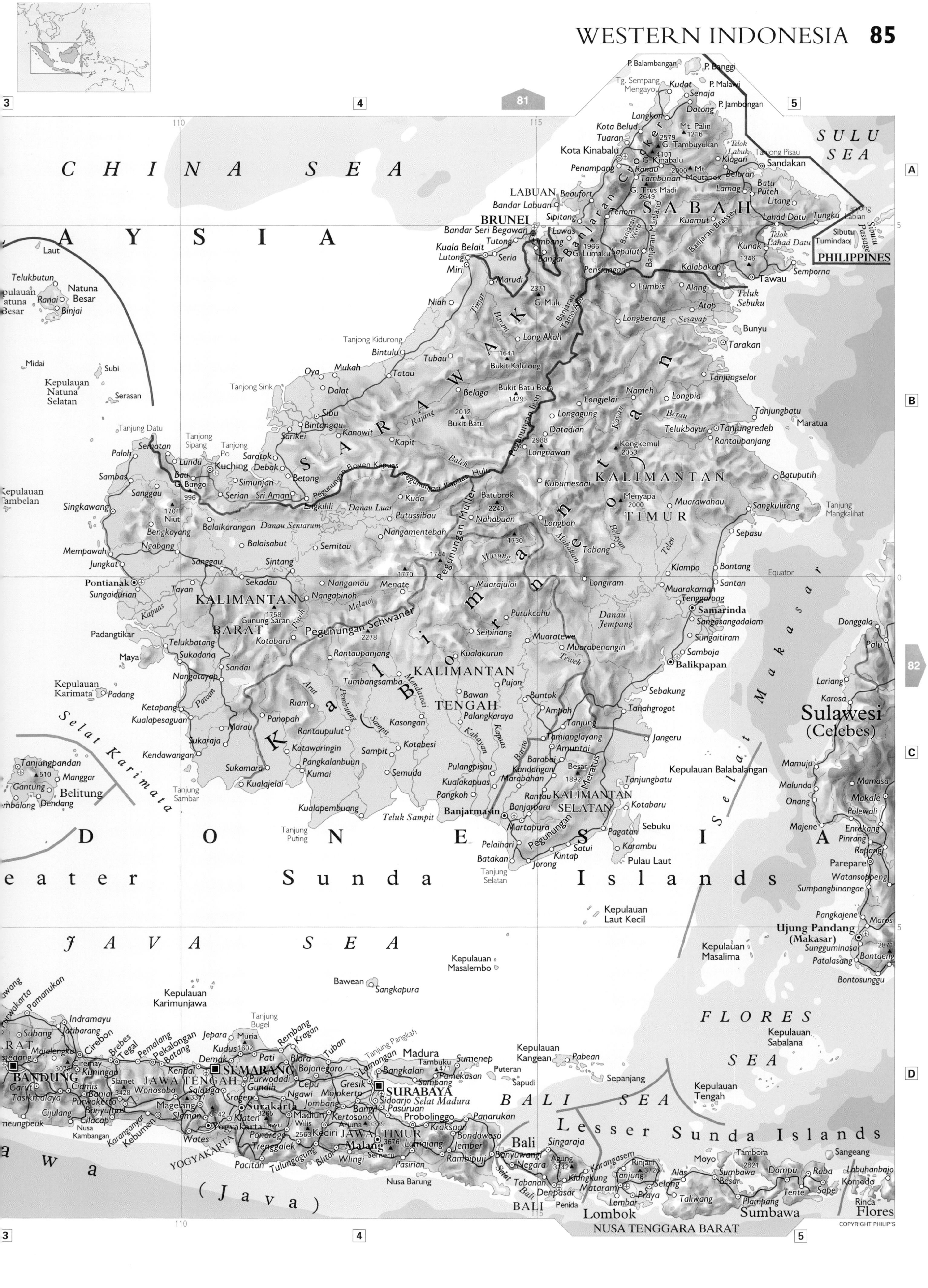

SULU SEA

CHINA SEA

AYSIA

P. Balambangan
P. Banggi
Tg. Sempang Mengayou
Kudat
P. Malawi
Senaja
P. Jambongan
Langkon
Datong
Kota Belud
Tuaran
Mt. Palin
G. Tambuyukan ▲1216
2579
Kota Kinabalu
Penampang
G. Kinabalu
Ranau
▲4101
Tambunan
Mt. Meutapek ▲2000
Klagan
Sandakan
Batu Puteh
Lamag
Litang
Beluran
LABUAN
Beaufort
G. Trus Madi 2649
Tenom
Kuamut
Banjaran Brassey
Tungku
Lahad Datu
Bandar Labuan
Sipitang
1966
Lumaku
Sapulut
Telok Lahad Datu
Kunak
1346
Tawau
BRUNEI
Bandar Seri Begawan
Lawas
Limbang
Bangar
Pensiangan
Lumbis
Alang
Kalabakan
Semporna
Kuala Belait
Tutong
Seria
Lutong
Miri
Marudi
2371
G. Mulu
Long Akah
Longberang
Sesayap
Atap
Bunyu
Tarakan

Niah
Tubau
1641
Bukit Kalulong
Longjelai
Nameh
Longbia
Tanjungselor
Tanjong Kidurong
Bintulu
Belaga
Bukit Batu Bora
1429
Longagung
Berau
Tanjungbatu
Oya
Mukah
Tatau
2012
Bukit Batu
Datadian
Kayan
Telukbayur
Tanjungredep
Maratua
Tanjong Sirik
Dalat
SARAWAK
Rajang
Baleh
2988
Longnawan
Kongkemul 2053
Batuputih
Sibu
Kanowit
Kapit
Hulu
KALIMANTAN
Tanjung Mangkalihat
Bintangau
Sarikei
Pegunungan Boven Kapuas
Kubumesaai
Betong
Sri Aman
Pegunungan Kapuas Hulu
TIMUR
Menyapa 2000
Muarawahau
Sangkulirang
Saratok
Tanjong Sipang
Tanjong Po
Kuching
Simunjan
Engkilili
Putussibau
Batubrok
Longboh
Tabang
Sepasu
Sematan
Lundu
Batu
Bungo
Serian
Danau Luar
Kuda
2240
Nahabuan
Telen
Paloh
996
1701 Niut
Balaikarangan
Danau Sentarum
1730
Melikium
Klampo
Bontang
Sambas
Bengkayang
Balaisabut
Semitau
Nangamentebah
Murung
Longiram
Santan
Singkawang
Ngabang
1744
Pegunungan Muller
Muarajuloi
Muarabenangin
Muarakaman
Tenggarong
Equator
Mempawah
Sintang
1770
Menate
Purukcahu
Teweh
Samarinda
Jungkat
Sekadau
Nangamau
Seipinang
Muaratewe
Sangasangadalam
Pontianak
Tayan
Nangapinoh
Danau Jempang
Sungaitiram
Sungaidurian
Melawi
KALIMANTAN
Purukcahu
Samboja
Donggala
Padangtikar
KALIMANTAN
1758
Gunung Saran
Balikpapan
BARAT
Pinoh
Pegunungan Schwaner
Kalahan
Buntok
Palu
Maya
2278
Rantaupanjang
Sebakung
Lariang
Telukbatang
Kotabaru
Kualakurun
Tanahgrogot
Karosa
Sukadana
Sandai
Bawan
Pujon
Tanjung
Sulawesi
Nangatayap
Riam
Tumbangsamba
Palangkaraya
Tamianglayang
(Celebes)
Kepulauan Karimata
Ketapang
Panopah
Kasongan
Amuntai
Padang
Marau
Kahayan
Jangeru
Mamuju
Rantaupulut
Kotawaringin
Sampit
Kotabesi
Barabai
Kepulauan Balabalangan
Malunda
Sukaraja
Kotawaringin
Pulangpisau
Kandangan
1892
Onang
Mamasa
Sukamara
Pangkalanbuun
Semuda
Kualakapuas
Marabahan
Besar
Tanjungbatu
Makale
Kendawangan
Kumai
Kualajelai
Pangkoh
Rantau
KALIMANTAN
Majene
Polewali
Kualapembuang
Teluk Sampit
Banjarmasin
Banjarbaru
SELATAN
Kotabaru
Enrekang
Pinrang
Tanjung Sambar
Martapura
Pegunungan
Sebuku
Ratang
Tanjung Puting
Satui
Pagatan
Parepare
Selat Makasar
Selat Karimata
Pelaihari
Karambu
Watansoppeng
Tanjungpandan
510
Batakan
Kintap
Pulau Laut
Sumpangbinangae
Manggar
Jorong
Pangkajene
Gantung
Belitung
Tanjung Selatan
Maros
Dendang
mbalong
Kepulauan Laut Kecil
Kepulauan Masalima
Ujung Pandang (Makasar)
2871
eater
Sunda
Islands
Sungguminasa
Patalasang
Bantaeng
JAVA SEA
Kepulauan Masalembo
Bawean
Sangkapura
Bontosunggu
Kepulauan Karimunjawa
FLORES
Kepulauan Sabalana
uwang
Pamanukan
Tanjung Bugel
Tuban
Sumenep
Kepulauan Kangean
Pabean
SEA
Indramayu
Jepara
Muria
Rembang
Kragan
Lamongan
Madura
Tambuku
Puteran
Subang
Pekalongan
Batang
Kudus
1602
Pati
Bojonegoro
Cepu
Gresik
Pamekasan
Sapudi
Sepanjang
Kepulauan Tengah
RAT
Majalengka
Cirebon
Brebes
Tegal
Pemalang
Demak
Blora
Bangkalan
Sampang
BANDUNG
302
Cikampek
Kuningan
SEMARANG
Gundih
Ngawi
Jombang
Mojokerto
SURABAYA
Sidoarjo
Selat Madura
BALI SEA
Garut
Ciamis
Kendal
JAWA TENGAH
Salatiga
3265
Madiun
Kertosono
Pasuruan
Singaraja
Lesser Sunda Islands
Taskmalaya
Purwokerto
Banyumas
Slamet
Wonosobo
3371
SURAKARTA
Sragen
Wilis
Probolinggo
Panarukan
Bali
Moyo
Tambora
Sangeang
neungpuk
Nusa Kambangan
Cilacap
Magelang
Sleman
3742
Klaten
Lawu
Kediri
Bangil
Bondowoso
Jember
Bali
Karangasem
Rinjani
Alas
Sumbawa
2821
Dompu
Raba
Labuhanbajo
Cijulang
Kebumen
Karanganyar
YOGYAKARTA
3265
Ponorogo
Kraksaan
Agung
Negara
3742
Sumbawa Besar
Tente
Sape
Wates
3339
Trenggalek
Tulungagung
Blitar
Wlingi
2563
JAWA TIMUR
Malang
3676
Semeru
Lumajang
Rambipuji
Banyuwangi
3728
Selong
Taliwang
Plampang
Rinca
Flores
wa
Pacitan
Arjuna 3339
Pasirian
Singaraja
Kalungkung
Karangasem
Matarm
Praya
(Java)
Nusa Barung
Tabanan
Denpasar
Penida
Lembar
Lombok
Sumbawa
NUSA TENGGARA BARAT

1:4 800 000

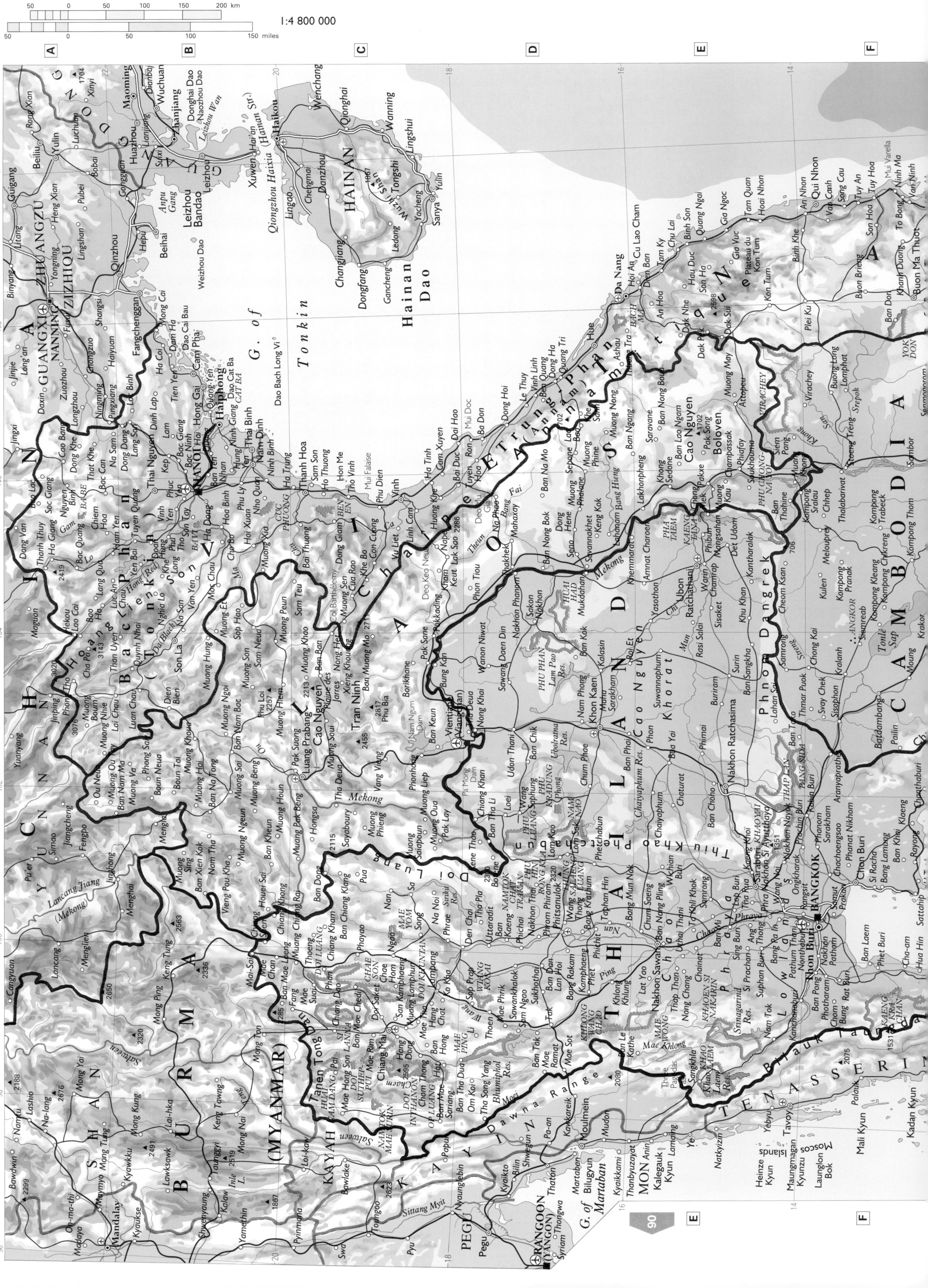

1:4 800 000
HAINAN
Hainan Dao
G. of Tonkin
CAMBODIA
THAILAND
BURMA (MYANMAR)
YUNNAN
LAOS
Mekong
BANGKOK
RANGOON (YANGON)
HANOI
Vientiane (Viangchan)
G. of Martaban

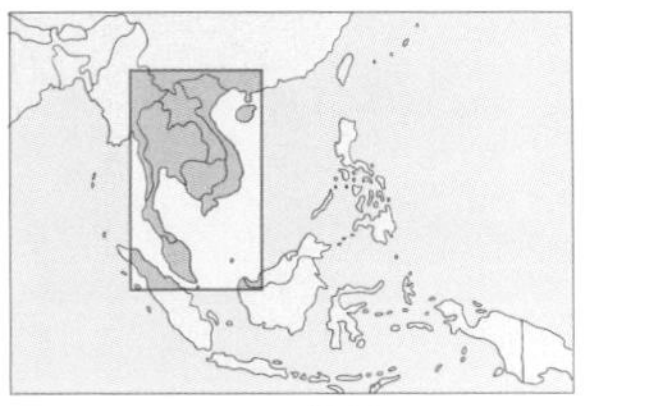

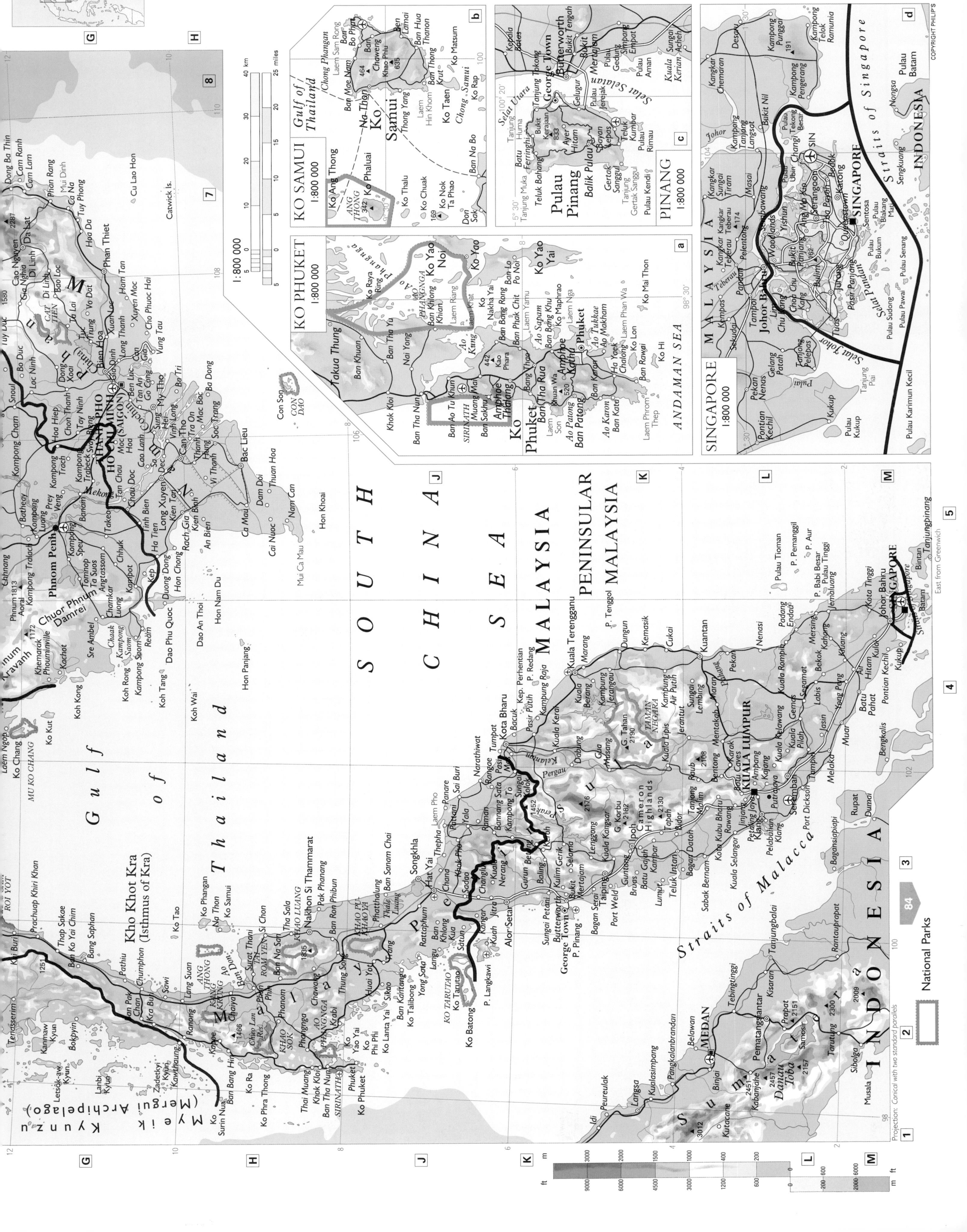

KO PHUKET 1:800 000
KO SAMUI 1:800 000
PINANG 1:800 000
SINGAPORE 1:800 000
1:800 000
SOUTH CHINA SEA
Gulf of Thailand
MALAYSIA
PENINSULAR MALAYSIA
INDONESIA
Straits of Malacca
ANDAMAN SEA
Kho Khot Kra (Isthmus of Kra)
KUALA LUMPUR
SINGAPORE
Phnom Penh
HO CHI MINH (SAIGON)
MEDAN
George Town
Phuket
Ko Samui
Pulau Pinang
National Parks
Projection: Conical with two standard parallels
East from Greenwich

50 0 100 200 300 400 500 600 km

1:14 000 000

50 0 100 200 300 400 miles

1 2 57 3 4 5 66

B C D E 106 107 30 20 10

Projection: Alber's Equal Area with two standard Parallels

East from Greenwich

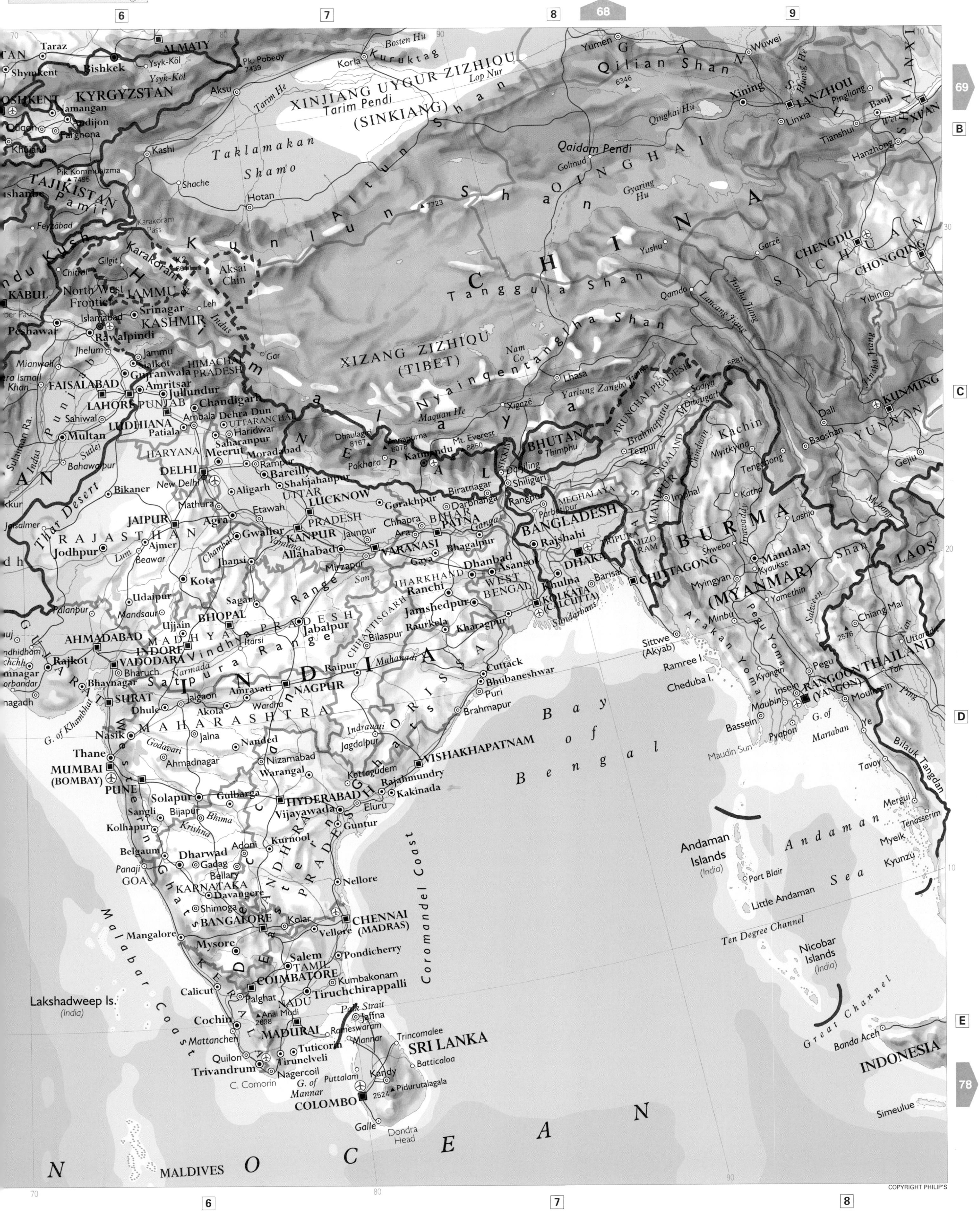
6
7
8
68
9
69
B
C
D
E
78
Taraz
ALMATY
Shymkent
Bishkek
Ysyk-Köl
Pk. Pobedy 7439
KYRGYZSTAN
Namangan
Andijon
Farghona
Kashi
Pik Kommunizma 7495
TAJIKISTAN
Pamir
Feyzābād
Karakoram Pass
KĀBUL
Gilgit
Chitral
Karakoram
K2 8611
Aksai Chin
North West Frontier
JAMMU &
KASHMIR
Srinagar
Leh
Islamabad
Rawalpindi
Peshawar
Jhelum
Jammu
Sialkot
Gujranwala
Mianwali
FAISALABAD
Amritsar
LAHORE
Jullundur
Chandigarh
PUNJAB
Sahiwal
Multan
LUDHIANA
Patiala
Ambala
Dehra Dun
Haridwar
Saharanpur
UTTARANCHAL
HIMACHAL PRADESH
Sulaiman Ra.
Indus
Sutlej
Bahawalpur
HARYANA
Meerut
Moradabad
Rampur
Bareilly
Shahjahanpur
DELHI
New Delhi
Aligarh
Bikaner
Thar Desert
Mathura
Agra
Etawah
JAIPUR
RAJASTHAN
Ajmer
Jodhpur
Beawar
Luni
Gwalior
Jhansi
Kota
Udaipur
Palanpur
Mandsaur
Ujjain
BHOPAL
Sagar
AHMADABAD
Rajkot
VADODARA
INDORE
Itarsi
Jabalpur
Bharuch
Narmada
Bhavnagar
SURAT
Dhule
Jalgaon
Amravati
NAGPUR
Wardha
G. of Khambhat
Nasik
Thane
MUMBAI (BOMBAY)
PUNE
Jalna
Nanded
Godavari
Ahmadnagar
Nizamabad
Warangal
Solapur
Gulbarga
HYDERABAD
Vijayawada
Sangli
Bijapur
Bhima
Kolhapur
Krishna
Belgaum
Dharwad
Gadag
Adoni
Kurnool
Guntur
Eluru
Panaji
GOA
Bellary
KARNATAKA
Davangere
Shimoga
BANGALORE
Kolar
Nellore
CHENNAI (MADRAS)
Vellore
Mangalore
Mysore
Salem
Pondicherry
TAMIL NADU
COIMBATORE
Kumbakonam
Tiruchchirappalli
Calicut
Palghat
Anai Mudi 2698
KERALA
Cochin
MADURAI
Mattancheri
Quilon
Trivandrum
Tirunelveli
Tuticorin
Nagercoil
C. Comorin
Lakshadweep Is. (India)
Malabar Coast
Coromandel Coast
Palk Strait
Jaffna
Rameswaram
Mannar
Trincomalee
SRI LANKA
Batticaloa
Kandy
Puttalam
G. of Mannar
Pidurutalagala 2524
COLOMBO
Galle
Dondra Head
MALDIVES
INDIAN OCEAN
LUCKNOW
UTTAR PRADESH
Gorakhpur
KANPUR
Allahabad
VARANASI
Jaunpur
Mirzapur
Son
Chhapra
BIHAR
PATNA
Ganga
Ara
Bhagalpur
Gaya
JHARKHAND
Ranchi
Dhanbad
Asansol
WEST BENGAL
Jamshedpur
KOLKATA (CALCUTTA)
Sundarbans
Kharagpur
Raurkela
CHHATTISGARH
Bilaspur
Raipur
Mahanadi
ORISSA
Cuttack
Bhubaneshwar
Puri
Brahmapur
Indravati
Jagdalpur
VISHAKHAPATNAM
Kottagudem
Rajahmundry
Kakinada
ANDHRA PRADESH
MADHYA PRADESH
MAHARASHTRA
Vindhya Range
Satpura Range
Western Ghats
Eastern Ghats
Deccan
INDIA
Bay of Bengal
NEPAL
Dhaulagiri 8167
Annapurna 8078
Kathmandu
Mt. Everest 8850
Pokhara
Biratnagar
Darbhanga
SIKKIM
Darjiling
Shiliguri
BHUTAN
Thimphu
Rangpur
Parbatipur
MEGHALAYA
BANGLADESH
Rajshahi
DHAKA
Khulna
Barisal
TRIPURA
MIZORAM
CHITTAGONG
ASSAM
NAGALAND
MANIPUR
Imphal
Tezpur
Brahmaputra
ARUNACHAL PRADESH
Sadiya
Dibrugarh
Himalaya
Xinjiang Uygur Zizhiqu (Sinkiang)
Tarim Pendi
Tarim He
Taklamakan Shamo
Aksu
Korla
Kuruktag
Bosten Hu
Lop Nur
Shache
Hotan
Kunlun Shan
Altun Shan
7723
Qilian Shan
6346
Yumen
Wuwei
GANSU
Xining
LANZHOU
Linxia
Huang He
Pingliang
Baoji
Wei
XI'AN
Tianshui
Hanzhong
SHAANXI
Qinghai Hu
Qaidam Pendi
Golmud
QINGHAI
Gyaring Hu
Yushu
CHINA
Tanggula Shan
Qamdo
Lancang Jiang
Jinsha Jiang
Garzê
CHENGDU
SICHUAN
CHONGQING
Yibin
Xizang Zizhiqu (Tibet)
Nam Co
Nyainqentanglha Shan
Gar
Lhasa
Yarlung Zangbo Jiang
Xigazê
Maquan He
5881
Yalong Jiang
KUNMING
Dali
YUNNAN
Baoshan
Gejiu
Mekong
Kachin
Myitkyina
Tengchong
Chindwin
Katha
Lashio
Irrawaddy
BURMA (MYANMAR)
Shwebo
Mandalay
Kyaukse
Myingyan
Shan
Yamethin
Minbu
Pegu Yoma
Arakan Yoma
Salween
LAOS
Chiang Mai
2576
Nan
Uttaradit
THAILAND
Tak
Ping
Sittwe (Akyab)
Ramree I.
Cheduba I.
Kyangin
Pegu
Insein
RANGOON (YANGON)
Moulmein
Maubin
Bassein
Pyapon
G. of Martaban
Ye
Maudin Sun
Tavoy
Bilauk Taungdan
Mergui
Tenasserim
Myeik
Kyunzu
Andaman Sea
Andaman Islands (India)
Port Blair
Little Andaman
Ten Degree Channel
Nicobar Islands (India)
Great Channel
Banda Aceh
INDONESIA
Simeulue
70
80
90
30
20
10
COPYRIGHT PHILIP'S

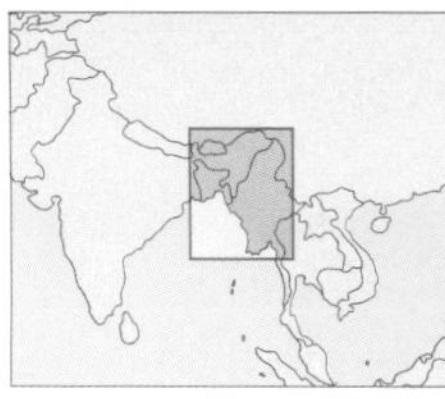

50 0 50 100 150 200 km

1:4 800 000

50 0 50 100 150 miles

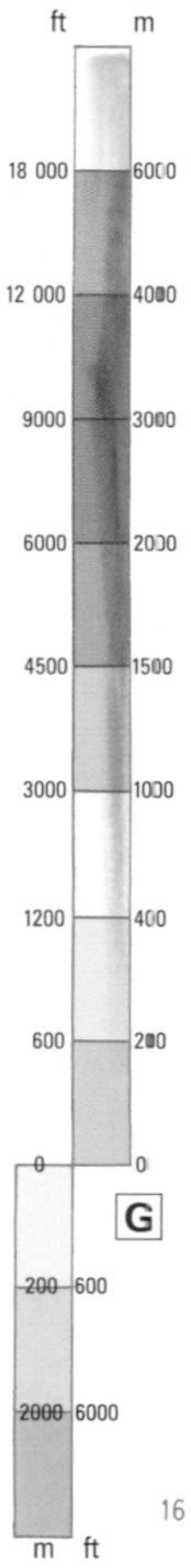

Projection: Conical with two standard parallels

East from Greenwich

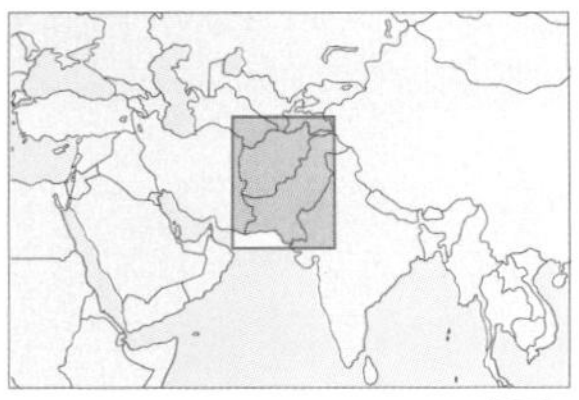

1:5 600 000

50 0 50 100 150 200 250 300 km

50 0 50 100 150 200 miles

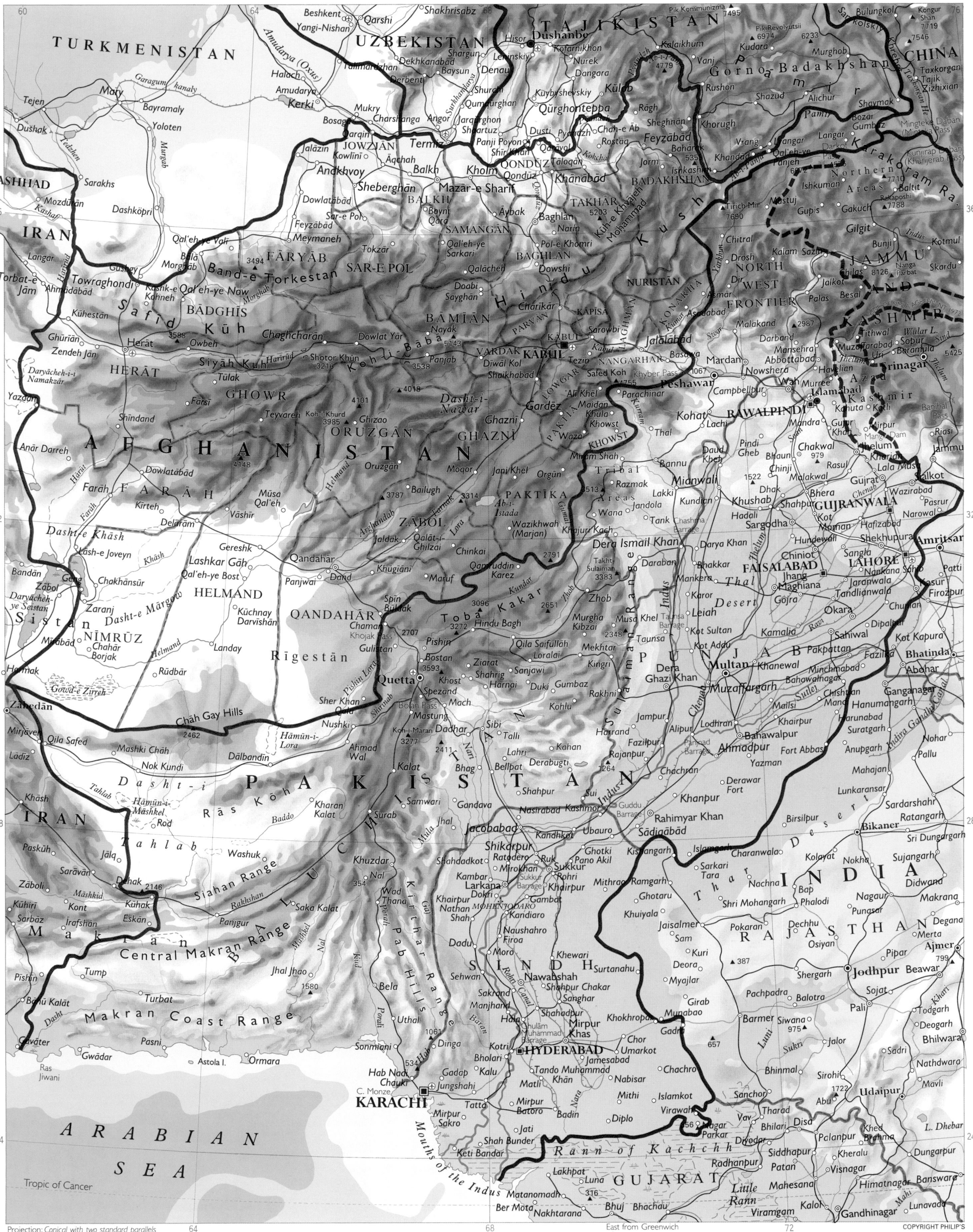

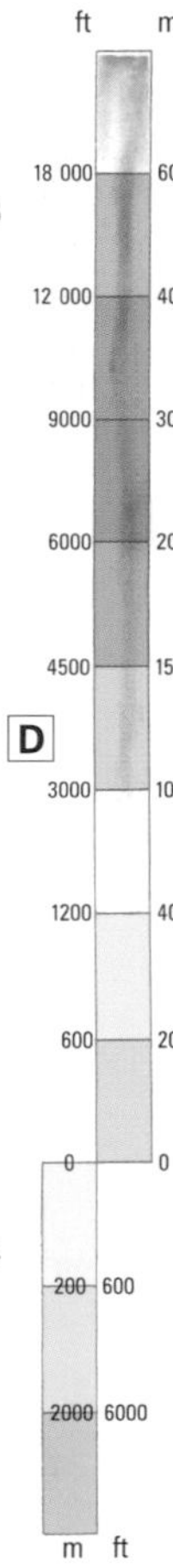

50 0 50 100 150 200 km

1:4 800 000

50 0 50 100 150 miles

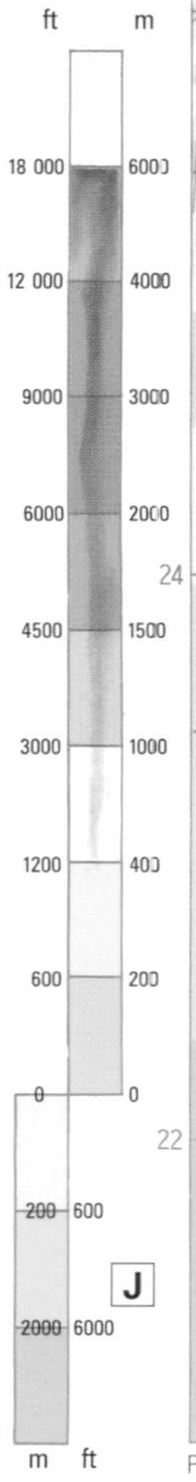

Projection: Conical with two standard parallels

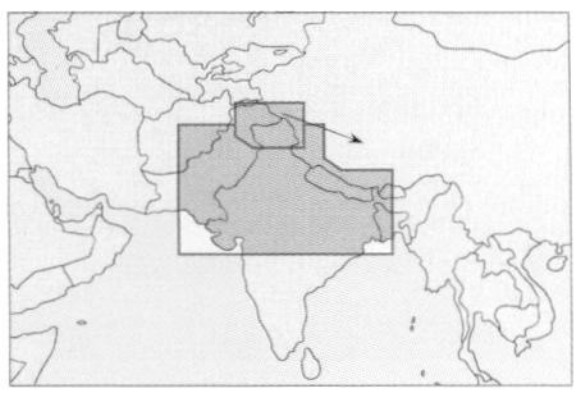

JAMMU AND KASHMIR
on same scale
AFGHANISTAN
CHINA
NORTH WEST FRONTIER
Northern Areas
Azad Kashmir
PUNJAB
JAMMU & KASHMIR
HIMACHAL PRADESH
Karakoram Range
Kunlun Shan
Zaskar Mountains
Ladakh Range
Pir Panjal Range
Deosai Mts.
Aksai Chin
Soda Plains
Siachen Glacier
Gasherbrum
Nanga Parbat
Islamabad
RAWALPINDI
Srinagar
Gilgit
Leh
Kargil
Jammu
Sialkot
Jhelum
Gujrat
Wazirabad
Karakoram Pass
Khunjerab Pass
CHINA
Ngangl ong Kangri
Gangdisê Shan
Xiangquan He (Sutlej)
Shiquan He (Indus)
Mt. Everest (Chomolungma or Sagarmatha)
Makalu
Kanchenjunga
Annapurna
Dhaulagiri
Manaslu
Himalchuli
XIZANG ZIZHIQU (TIBET)
Yarlung Zangbo Jiang (Brahmaputra)
Maquan He (Brahmaputra)
NEPAL
Mahabharat Lekh
Siwalik Range
Katmandu
Pokhara
Biratnagar
Birganj
Lhazê
Xigazê
Gyangzê
Saga
Zhongba
SIKKIM
Gangtok
Darjeeling
BHUTAN
Thimphu
ASSAM
Garo Hills
BANGLADESH
DHAKA
Rajshahi
Khulna
Jessore
Narayanganj
UTTARANCHAL
UTTAR PRADESH
BIHAR
JHARKHAND
WEST BENGAL
CHHATTISGARH
MADHYA PRADESH
LUCKNOW
Kanpur
Allahabad
Varanasi
Gorakhpur
Bareilly
Moradabad
Shahjahanpur
Faizabad
Rae Bareli
Fatehpur
Jhansi
Rewa
Satna
Jabalpur
Bilaspur
Korba
PATNA
Gaya
Bhagalpur
Muzaffarpur
Darbhanga
Dhanbad
Ranchi
Jamshedpur
Asansol
Durgapur
Bardhaman
KOLKATA
Haora
Kharagpur
Medinipur
Raurkela
Sambalpur
Kaimur Hills
Rajmahal Hills
Panna Hills
Ganga
Son
Gandak
Ghaghara
Kosi
Damodar
Mahanadi
Sundarbans
Mouths of the Ganges
The Sandheads
Bangaduni I.
East from Greenwich
A
B
C
E
F
G
H
J
5
6
7
8
9
10
11
12
13
68
90
94

50 0 50 100 150 200 km

1:4 800 000

50 0 50 100 150 miles

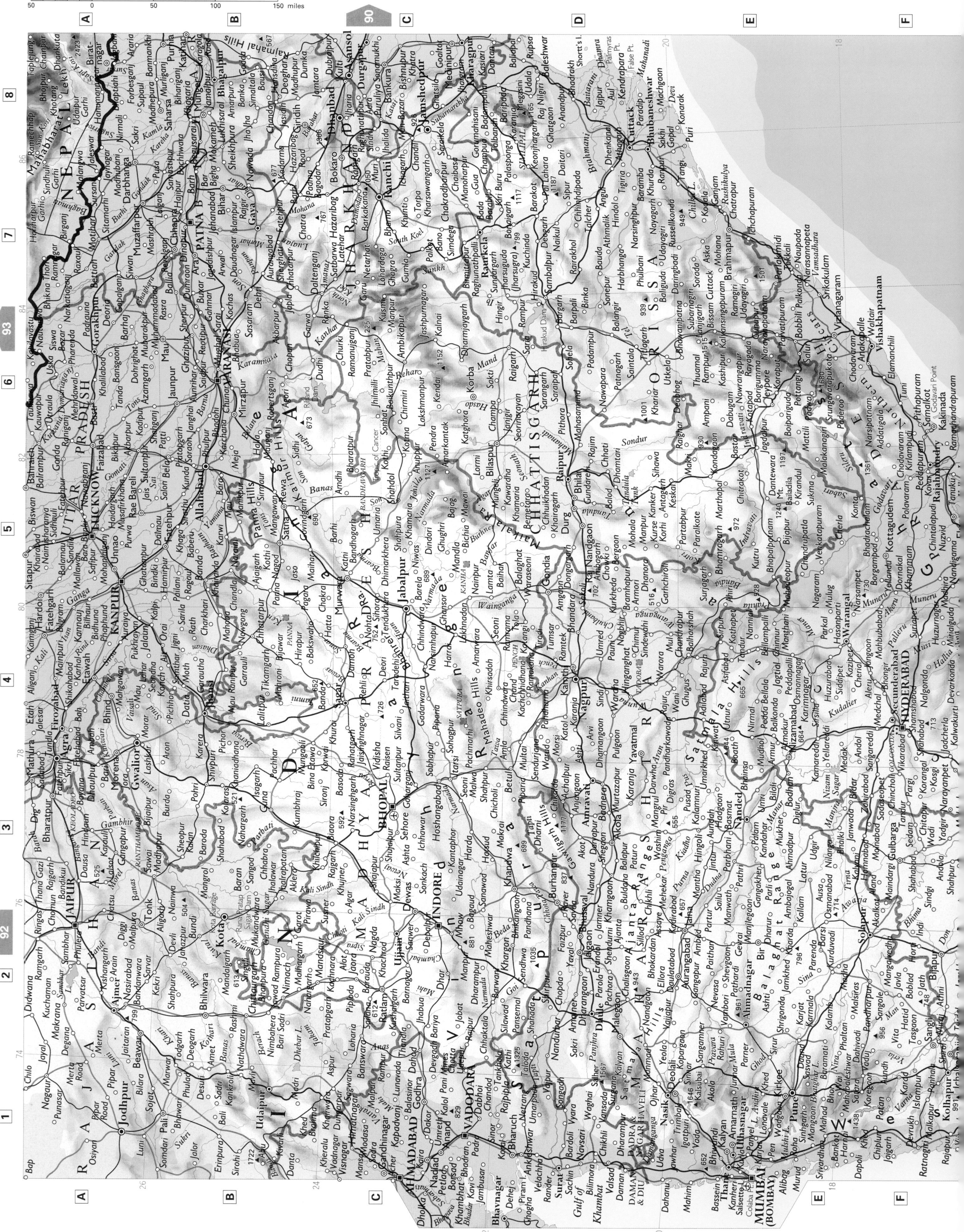

NEPAL
UTTAR PRADESH
JHARKHAND
MADHYA PRADESH
CHHATTISGARH
ORISSA
RAJASTHAN
MAHARASHTRA
LUCKNOW
KANPUR
PATNA
VARANASI
ALLAHABAD
JAIPUR
AGRA
GWALIOR
BHOPAL
INDORE
JABALPUR
NAGPUR
HYDERABAD
AHMADABAD
VADODARA
MUMBAI (BOMBAY)
Pune
Raipur
Ranchi
Jamshedpur
Cuttack
Bhubaneshwar
Vishakhapatnam
Aurangabad
Nasik
Kota
Udaipur
Jodhpur
Ajmer
Surat
Gulf of Khambhat
DAMAN & DIU
DADRA & NAGAR HAVELI
Satpura Range
Vindhya Range
Mahadeo Hills
Ajanta Range
Kaimur Hills
Chota Nagpur

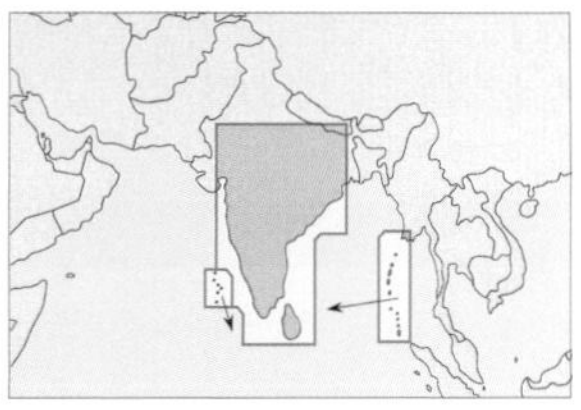

Projection: Conical with two standard parallels

50 0 50 100 150 200 250 300 km

1:5 600 000

50 0 50 100 150 200 miles

61

100

106

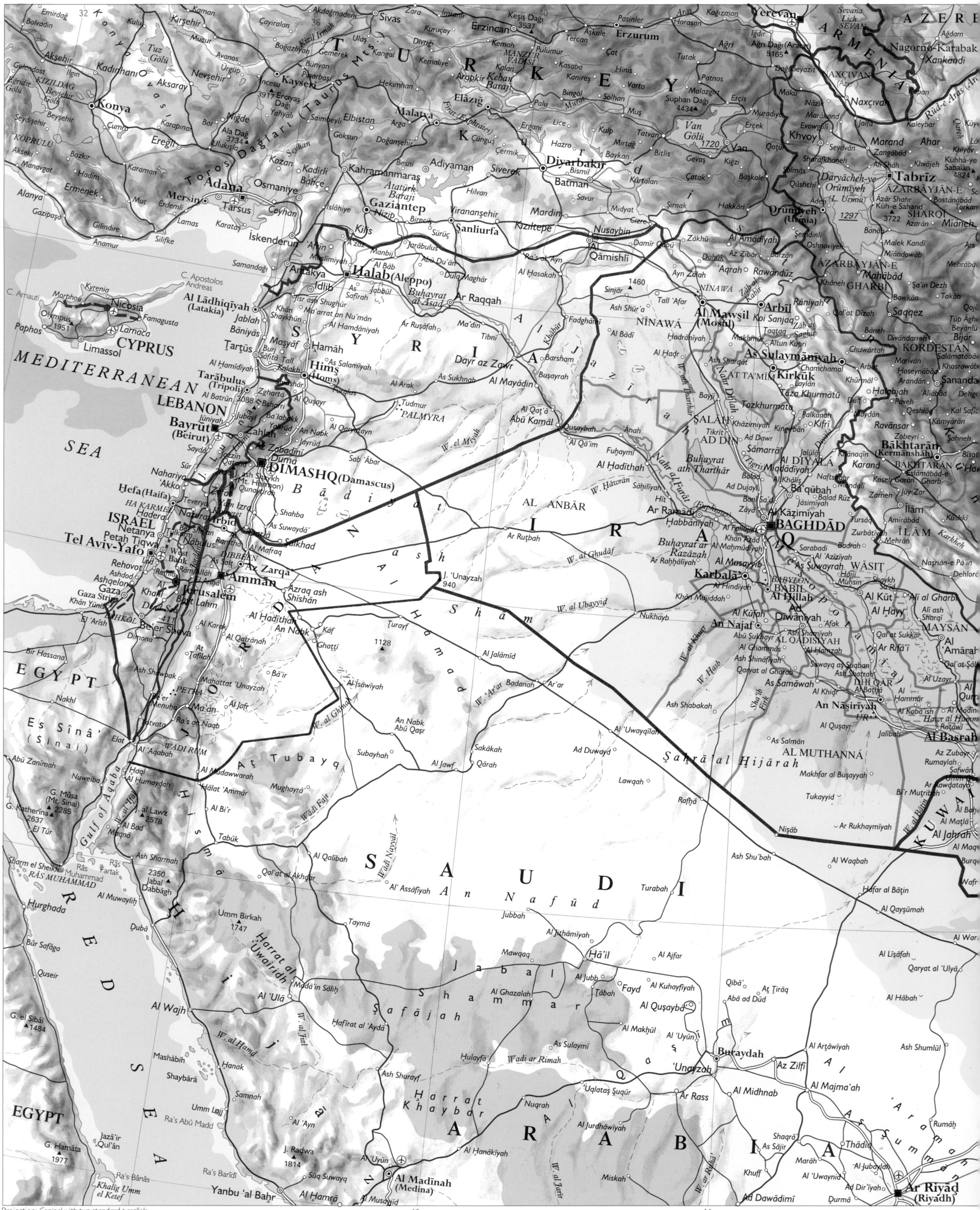

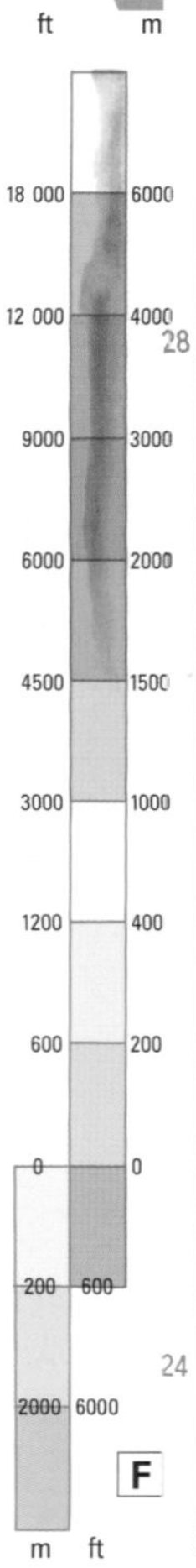

Projection: Conical with two standard parallels

98

Underlined towns in Iraq give their name to the administrative area in which they stand

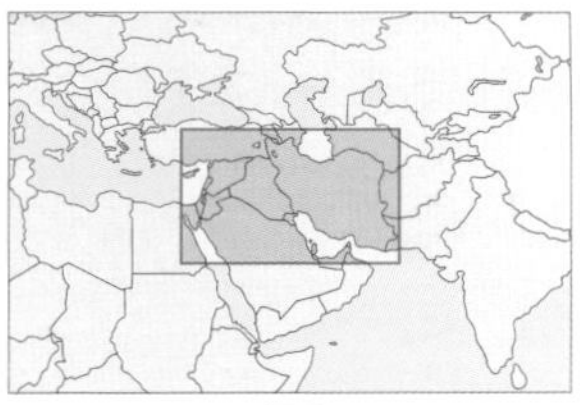

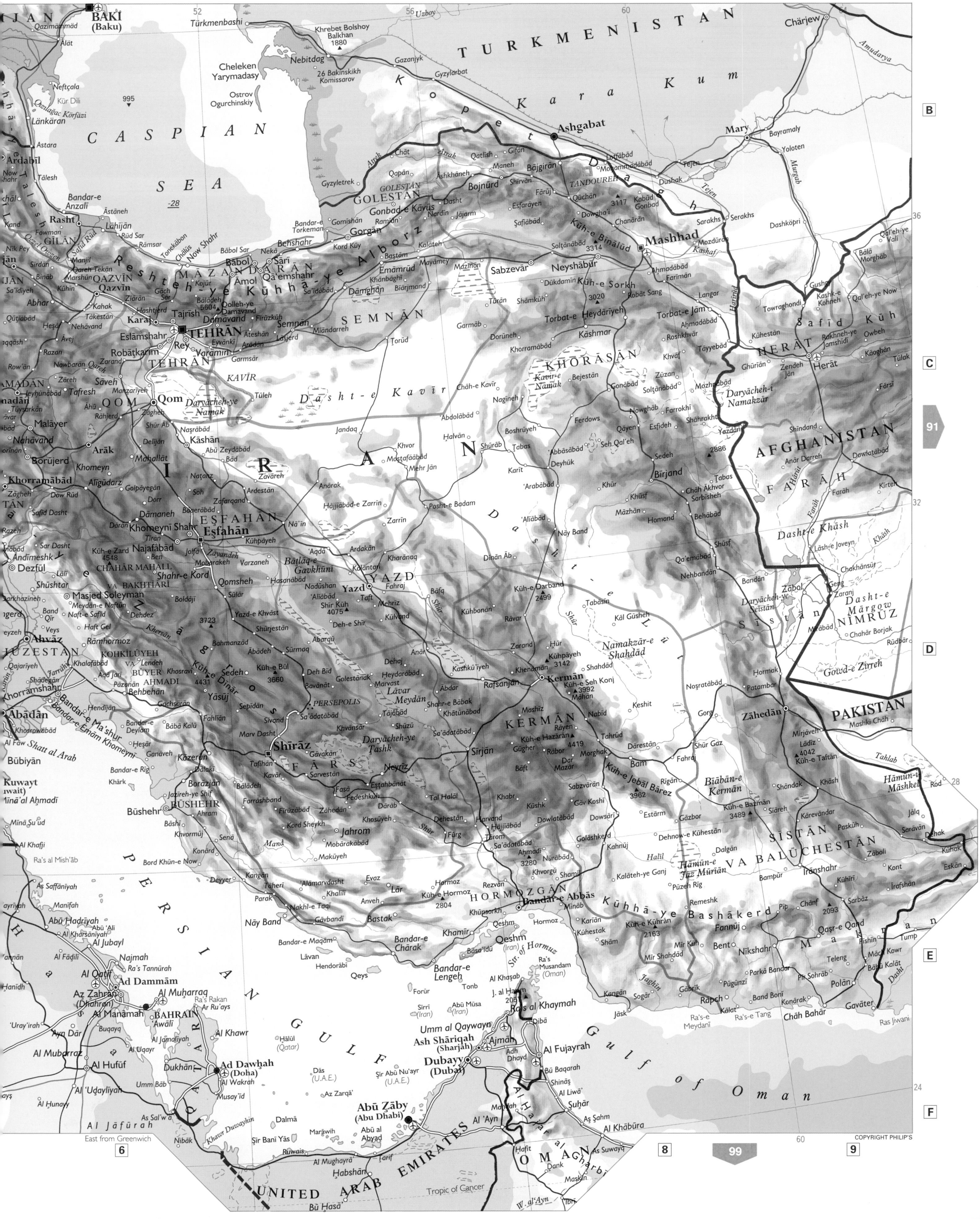

6
7
8
9
10
B
C
D
E
F
91
99
TURKMENISTAN
Kara Kum
Kopet Dagh
CASPIAN SEA
BAKI (Baku)
Türkmenbashi
Cheleken Yarymadasy
Ostrov Ogurchinskiy
Nebitdag
Khrebet Bolshoy Balkhan 1880
Gazanjyk
Gyzylarbat
Ashgabat
Mary
Bayramaly
Yoloten
Chärjew
Amudarya
Tejen
Sarakhs
Dashköpri
Länkäran
Astara
Ardabīl
Bandar-e Anzalī
Rasht
Lāhījān
Gīlān
Qazvīn
Karaj
Tajrīsh
TEHRĀN
Rey
Varāmīn
Damāvand
5604
Reshteh-ye Kūhhā-ye Alborz
MĀZANDARĀN
Āmol
Bābol
Sārī
Qā'emshahr
Behshahr
Gorgān
Gonbad-e Kāvūs
GOLESTĀN
Bojnūrd
Shīrvān
Qūchān
Mashhad
Kūh-e Bīnālūd
3314
Neyshābūr
Sabzevār
Semnān
SEMNĀN
Dāmghān
Shāhrūd
Torbat-e Heydarīyeh
Torbat-e Jām
Kāshmar
KHORĀSĀN
Dasht-e Kavīr
Qom
Daryācheh-ye Namak
Kāshān
Arāk
Malāyer
Borūjerd
Khorramābād
IRAN
Eşfahān
ESFAHĀN
Najafābād
Khomeynī Shahr
Yazd
YAZD
Dasht-e Lūt
Kermān
KERMĀN
Rafsanjān
Sīrjān
Bam
Zāhedān
SĪSTĀN VA BALŪCHESTĀN
Zābol
Shīrāz
FĀRS
PERSEPOLIS
Kāzerūn
Būshehr
BŪSHEHR
Bandar-e 'Abbās
HORMOZGĀN
Qeshm
Str. of Hormuz
Kūhhā-ye Bashākerd
Chāh Bahār
Gulf of Oman
PERSIAN GULF
Ahvāz
KHUZESTĀN
Ābādān
Khorramshahr
Dezfūl
Shūshtar
Masjed Soleyman
Kuwayt
Shatt al Arab
Būbiyān
Ad Dammām
Az Zahrān (Dhahran)
Al Manāmah
BAHRAIN
Al Muharraq
Ad Dawhah (Doha)
QATAR
Al Hufūf
Al Mubarraz
Abū Zāby (Abu Dhabi)
Dubayy (Dubai)
Ash Shāriqah (Sharjah)
Ajmān
Ras al Khaymah
Al Fujayrah
UNITED ARAB EMIRATES
OMAN
AFGHANISTAN
Herāt
HERĀT
Safīd Kūh
FARĀH
Farāh
NĪMRŪZ
Dasht-e Mārgow
Gowd-e Zirreh
PAKISTAN
Hāmūn-i Māshkel
Kūh-e Taftān 4042
Tropic of Cancer
East from Greenwich
COPYRIGHT PHILIP'S

50 0 50 100 150 200 250 300 km

1:5 600 000

50 0 50 100 150 200 miles

1 2 96 3 4

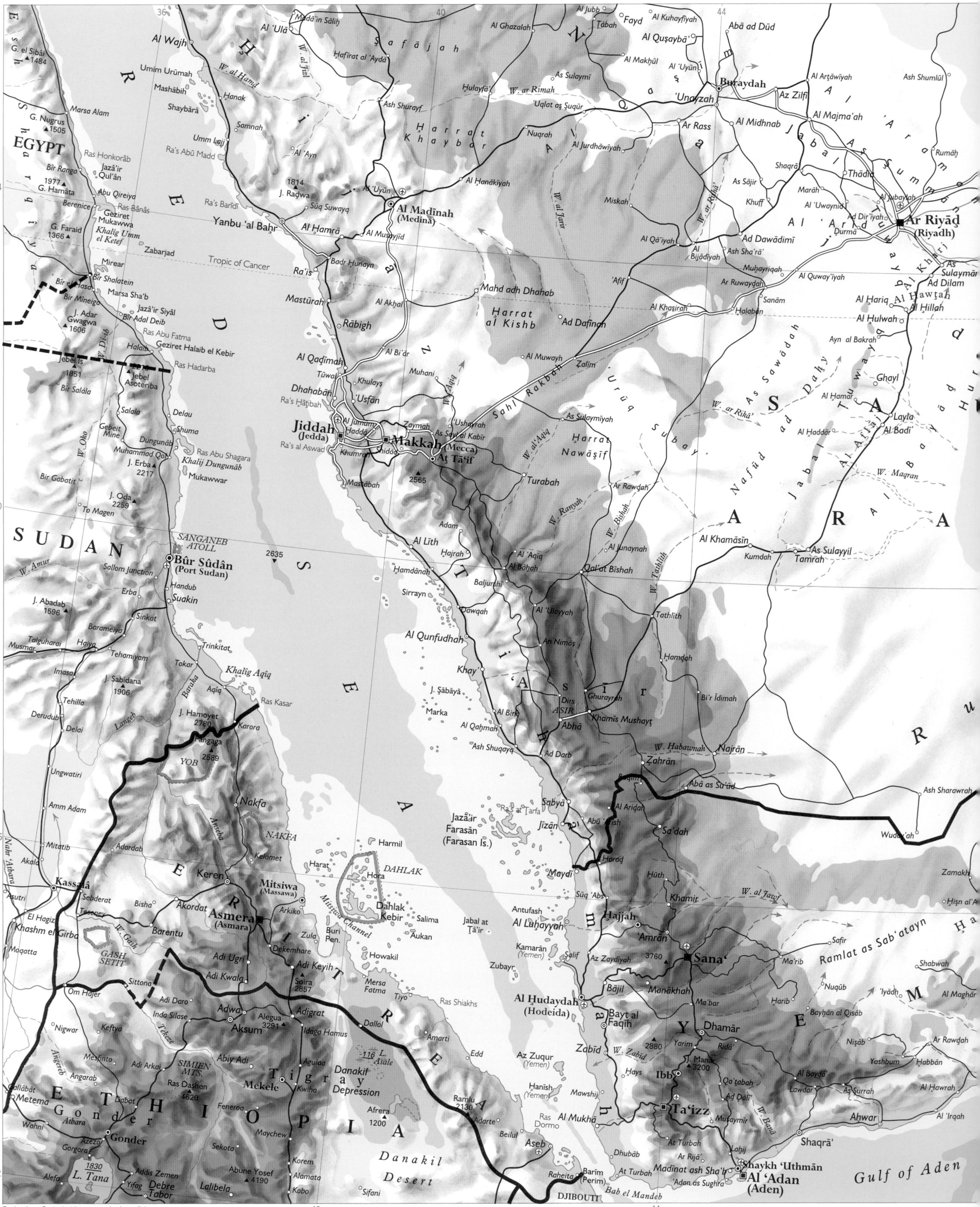

Projection: Conical with two standard parallels

2 120 3 4

107

ft m
12 000 4000
9000 3000
6000 2000
4500 1500
3000 1000
1200 400
600 200
0 0
200 600
2000 6000
4000 12 000
m ft

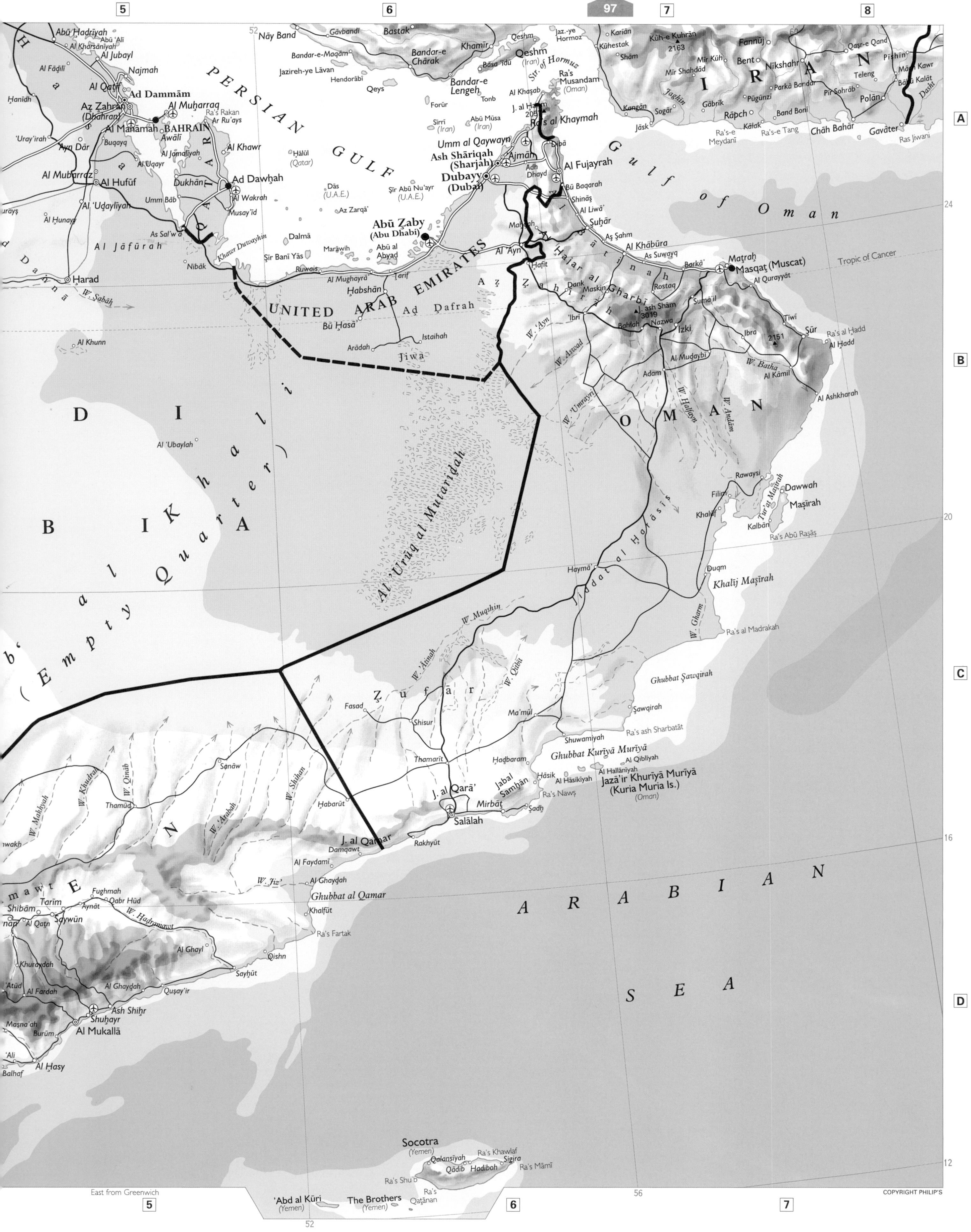
PERSIAN GULF
Gulf of Oman
ARABIAN SEA
UNITED ARAB EMIRATES
OMAN
IRAN
BAHRAIN
QATAR
Rub' al Khali (Empty Quarter)
Tropic of Cancer
Ad Dammām
Az Zahran (Dhahran)
Al Muharraq
Al Manāmah
Awālī
Al Hufūf
Al Mubarraz
Al Qatīf
Al Jubayl
Najmah
Abū Hadrīyah
Ad Dawhah
Al Wakrah
Musay'īd
Dukhān
Umm Bāb
Al Khawr
Harad
Al Khunn
Al 'Ubaylah
Abū Zaby (Abu Dhabi)
Dubayy (Dubai)
Ash Shāriqah (Sharjah)
'Ajmān
Umm al Qaywayn
Ra's al Khaymah
Al Fujayrah
Musandam (Oman)
Str. of Hormuz
Qeshm
Bandar-e Lengeh
Bandar-e Chārak
Bastak
Nāy Band
Gāvbandī
Khamīr
Kangān
Jāsk
Chāh Bahār
Gavāter
Ras Jiwani
Sohār
Al Khābūra
As Suwayq
Barkā'
Maṭraḥ
Masqaṭ (Muscat)
Al Qurayyāt
Şūr
Ra's al Hadd
Al Ashkharah
Al Kāmil
Ibra
Nazwa
Izki
Bahlah
'Ibrī
Rostaq
J. ash Sham 3019
Adam
Al Hajar al Gharbī
Az Zāhirah
Al Bāţinah
Jiwa
Liwa
Ḥabshān
Arādah
Bū Hasā
Aḍ Ḍafrah
Al 'Urūq al Mu'tariḍah
Jiddat al Ḥarāsīs
Haymā'
Duqm
Khalīj Maşīrah
Maşīrah
Dawwah
Rawaysī
Filim
Khalūf
Ra's al Madrakah
Ghubbat Şawqirah
Şawqirah
Shuwamiyah
Ma'mūl
Ẓufār
Fasad
Shisur
Thamarīt
Salālah
Mirbāţ
J. al Qarā'
Hadbaram
Ghubbat Kurīyā Murīyā
Jazā'ir Khurīyā Murīyā (Kuria Muria Is.)
Jabal Samhān
Sadh
Rakhyūt
J. al Qamar
Damqawt
Ḥabarūt
Thamūd
Sanāw
Al Ghaydah
Ghubbat al Qamar
Khalfūt
Ra's Fartak
Qishn
Sayḥūt
Al Ghayl
Quşay'ir
Ash Shiḥr
Shuḥayr
Al Mukallā
Burūm
Al Hasy
Balhaf
Tarīm
Shibām
Say'ūn
Al Qaṭn
W. Hadramawt
Socotra (Yemen)
Qalansīyah
Ḥadibōh
Ra's Mōmi
'Abd al Kūrī (Yemen)
The Brothers (Yemen)
East from Greenwich
COPYRIGHT PHILIP'S

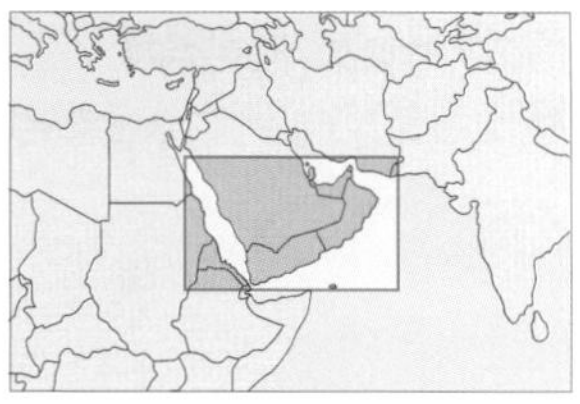

1: 4 000 000

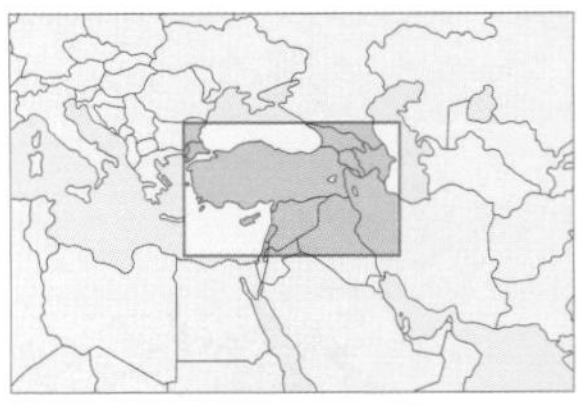

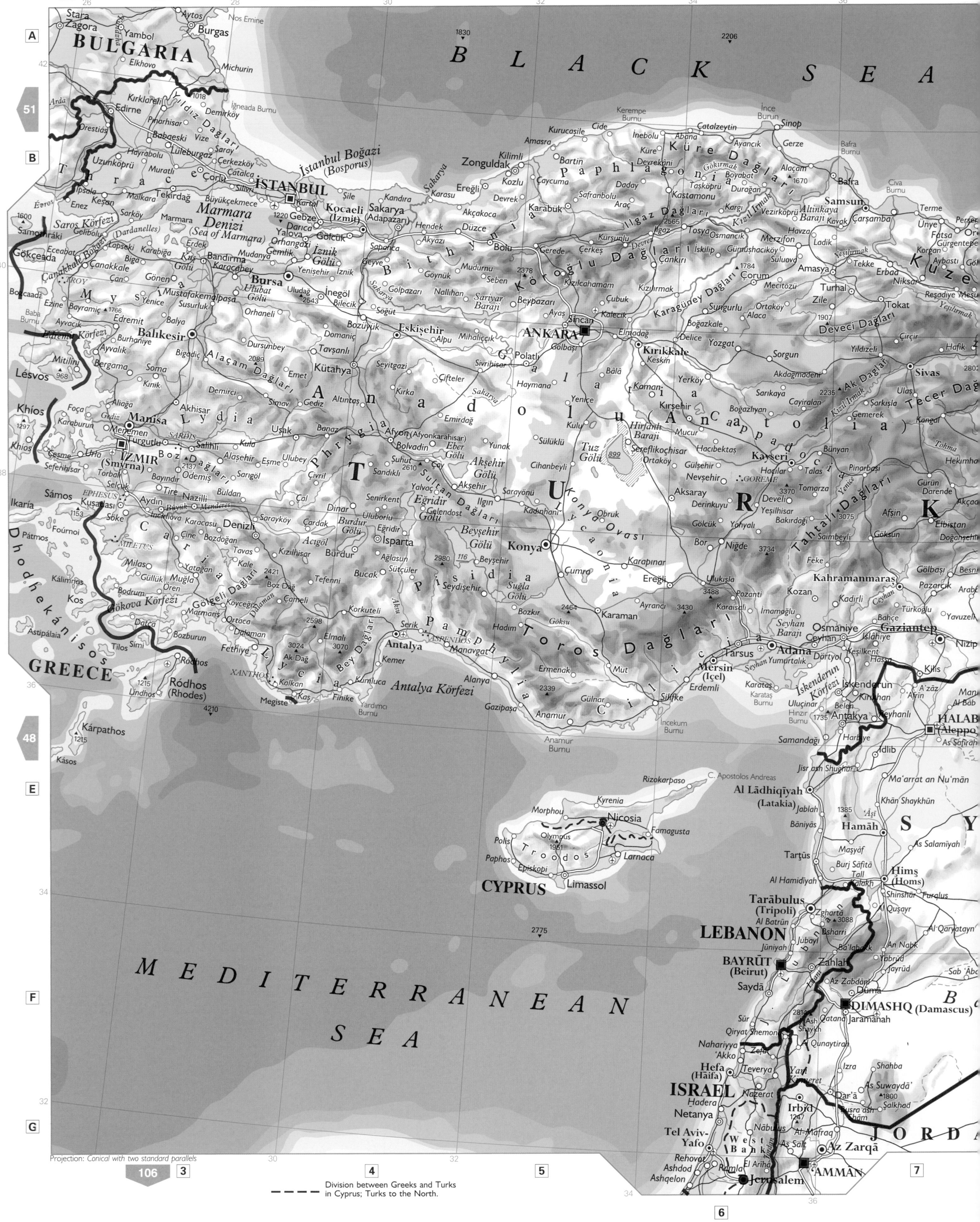

Projection: Conical with two standard parallels

Division between Greeks and Turks in Cyprus; Turks to the North.

59 51 48 106

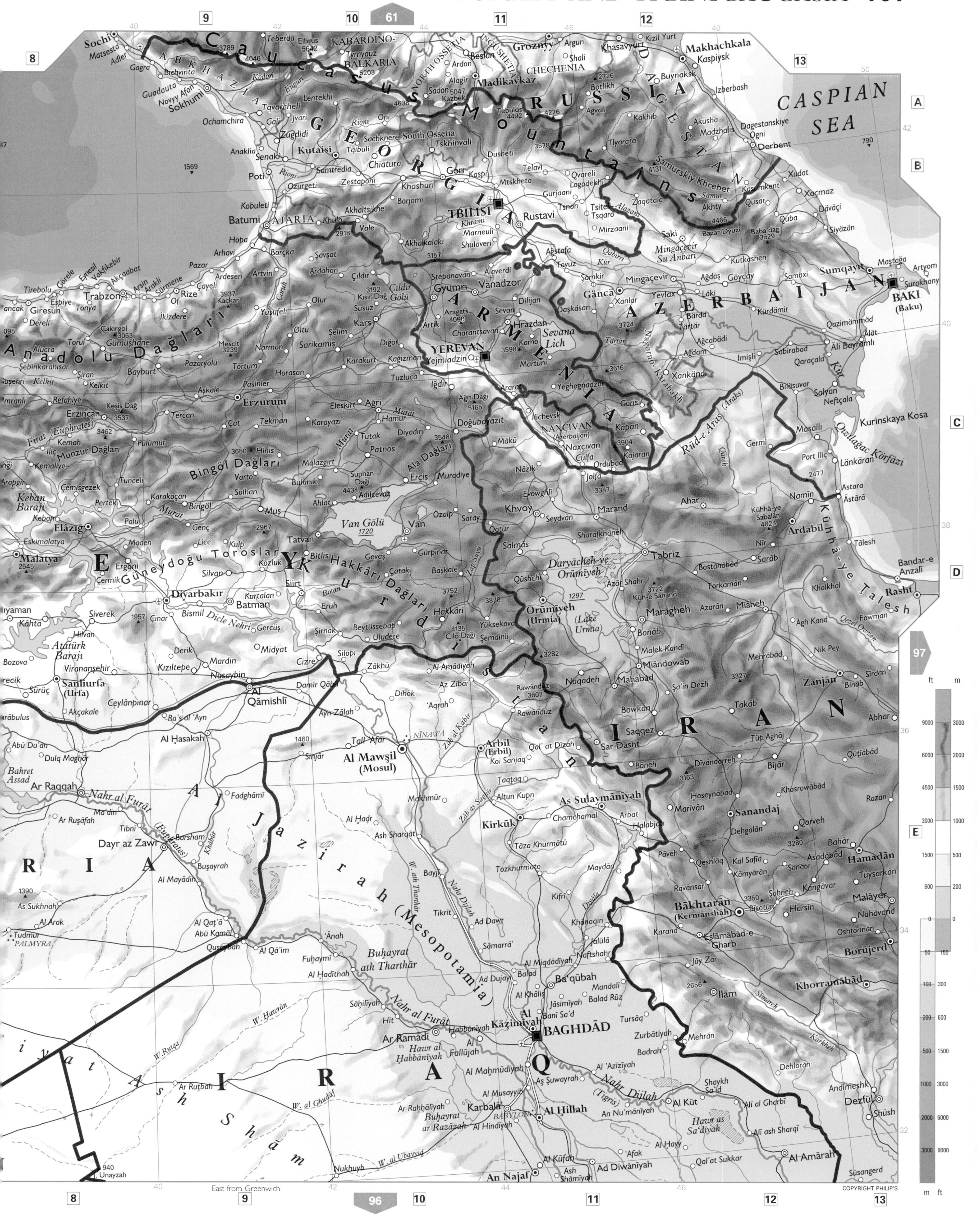
9
10
61
11
12
8
13
A
B
C
D
E
97
96
CASPIAN SEA
Caucasus Mountains
RUSSIA
DAGESTAN
GEORGIA
ARMENIA
AZERBAIJAN
IRAN
IRAQ
SYRIA
TURKEY
Anadolu Dağları
Güneydoğu Toroslar
Hakkâri Dağları
Kurdistan
Bingöl Dağları
Munzur Dağları
Al Jazīrah (Mesopotamia)
Bādiyat ash Shām
Kūhhā-ye Talesh
Sochi
Matsesta
Adler
Gagra
Bichvinta
Gudauta
Novyy Afon
Sokhumi
ABKHAZIA
Ochamchira
Tqvarcheli
Gali
Zugdidi
Anaklia
Senaki
Poti
Kutaisi
Samtredia
Ozurgeti
Kobuleti
Batumi
AJARIA
Khulo
Vale
Akhaltsikhe
Borjomi
Khashuri
Zestaponi
Chiatura
Tqibuli
Sachkhere
South Ossetia
Tskhinvali
Gori
Kaspi
Mtskheta
TBILISI
Rustavi
Marneuli
Shulaveri
Akhalkalaki
Dusheti
Telavi
Gurjaani
Tsnori
Tsiteli Tsqaro
Qvareli
Lagodekhi
Mirzaani
Teberda
Elbrus 5642
KABARDINO-BALKARIA
Tyrnyauz
5203
NORTH OSSETIA
INGUSHETIA
CHECHENIA
Beslan
Ardon
Alagir
Sadon
Kazbek 5047
Vladikavkaz
Grozny
Argun
Shali
Khasavyurt
Kizil Yurt
Makhachkala
Kaspiysk
Buynaksk
Botlikh
Izberbash
Agvali
Kakhib
Akusha
Madzhalis
Dagestanskiye Ogni
Derbent
Tlyarata
Samurskiy Khrebet
Akhty
Xudat
Qusar
Xaçmaz
Dävägi
Quba
Siyäzän
Zaqatala
Şäki
Mingäçevir Su Anbari
Kutkashen
Şamaxi
Sumqayit
Mastağa
Artyom
BAKI (Baku)
Surakhany
Gänca
Xanlar
Daşkäsän
Mingäçevir
Yevlax
Läki
Ağdaş
Göyçay
Kürdämir
Bärdä
Tärtär
Ağcabädi
Ağdam
Xankändi
Nagorno Karabakh
Qazimämmäd
Älät
Äli Bayramli
Sabirabad
Imişli
Qaraçala
Bilāsuvar
Salyan
Neftçala
Kurinskaya Kosa
Masalli
Port Iliç
Länkäran
Qızılağac Körfäzi
Astara
Āstārā
Gyumri
Vanadzor
Stepanavan
Alaverdi
Ağstafa
Tovuz
Şamkir
Dilijan
Sevan
Hrazdan
Aragats 4090
Artik
Charentsavan
Sevana Lich
Kamo
Martuni
YEREVAN
Yejmiadzin
Ararat
Yeghegnadzor
Goris
Kapan
Kajaran
NAXÇIVAN (Azerbaijan)
Naxçıvan
Ilichevsk
Culfa
Ordubad
Pazar
Arhavi
Hopa
Borçka
Şavşat
Ardahan
Artvin
Ardeşen
Çayeli
Rize
Of
Sürmene
Trabzon
Akçaabat
Arsin
Araklı
Vakfıkebir
Görele
Eynesil
Tirebolu
Giresun
Espiye
Tonya
Dereli
Çakırgöl 3063
Gümüşhane
Torul
Alucra
Şebinkarahisar
Kelkit
Şiran
Bayburt
Kaçkar 3937
İkizdere
Yusufeli
Mescit 3239
Narman
Oltu
Olur
Çıldır
Çıldır Gölü
Kısır Dağ 3192
Susuz
Kars
Şelim
Sarıkamış
Digor
Kağızman
Karakurt
Tuzluca
Iğdır
Ağrı Dağı 5165
Doğubayazıt
Horasan
Pazaryolu
Tortum
Erzurum
Pasinler
Aşkale
Tercan
Erzincan
Refahiye
Keşiş Dağ 3537
Fırat (Euphrates)
Çat
Tekman
Karayazı
Eleşkirt
Ağrı
Hamur
Murat
Tutak
Diyadin
Patnos
Ala Dağları
3548
Hınıs 3650
Pülümür
Kemaliye
İliç
Tunceli
Çemişgezek
Keban Barajı
Keban
Elazığ
Pertek
Karakoçan
Bingöl
Solhan
Varto
Malazgirt
Bulanık
Suphan Dağı 4434
Adilcevaz
Erciş
Muradiye
Ahlat
Muş
Palu
Genç
Van Gölü 1720
Van
Özalp
Saray
Tatvan
Bitlis
Maden
Lice
Kulp
Kozluk
Silvan
Ergani
Malatya
Eskimalatya
Gevaş
Gürpınar
Çatak
Başkale
Zap Suyu
Hakkâri
Yüksekova
Şemdinli
Cilo Dağı 4135
Beytüşşebap
Uludere
Şırnak
Eruh
Siirt
Botan
Batman
Kurtalan
Diyarbakır
Bismil
Dicle Nehri
Gercüş
Midyat
Mardin
Kızıltepe
Nusaybin
Cizre
Silopi
Derik
Çınar
Siverek
Hilvan
Atatürk Barajı
Viranşehir
Şanlıurfa (Urfa)
Ceylânpınar
Akçakale
Suruç
Bozova
Kâhta
Çermik
Mākū
Nāzīk
Jolfā
Marand
Ahar
Evowghlī
Khvoy
Seydvān
Qoţūr
Salmās
Sharafkhāneh
Tabrīz
Daryācheh-ye Orūmīyeh (Lake Urmia)
Qūshchī
Orūmīyeh (Urmia)
Āzar Shahr
Kūh-e Sahand
Marāgheh
Bonāb
Malek Kandī
Miāndowāb
Naqadeh
Mahābād
Bowkān
Saqqez
Sar Dasht
Bāneh
Dīvāndarreh
Bījār
Sanandaj
Marīvān
Hoseynābād
Khosrowābād
Qorveh
Dehgolān
Bahār
Hamadān
Asadābād
Sonqor
Kangāvar
Tūysarkān
Malāyer
Nahāvand
Bākhtarān (Kermānshāh)
Bīsotūn
Harsīn
Şahneh
Kāmyārān
Ravānsar
Pāveh
Karand
Eslāmābād-e Gharb
Oshtorīnān
Borūjerd
Khorramābād
Jūy Zar
Īlām
Mehrān
Dehlorān
Andīmeshk
Dezfūl
Shūsh
Sūsangerd
Ardabīl
Sabalān 4824
Kūhhā-ye Sabalān
Namīn
Nīr
Sarāb
Bostānābād
Torkamān
Mīāneh
Khalkhāl
Ágh Kand
Fowman
Rasht
Bandar-e Anzalī
Tālesh
Qezel Owzen
Zanjān
Bīnāb
Sīrdān
Abhar
Nīk Pey
Mehrābād
Takāb
Şā'īn Dezh
Tūp Āghāj
Qūtābād
Razan
Zākhū
Al Amādīyah
Dihōk
'Aqrah
Az Zībar
Rawāndūz
Arbīl (Erbil)
Koi Sanjaq
Qol' at Dizah
Tall 'Afar
NINAWA
Al Mawşil (Mosul)
Sinjār
Makhmūr
Altun Kupri
Taqtaq
As Sulaymānīyah
Chamchamal
Arbat
Halabjah
Kirkūk
Ţāza Khurmātū
Tozkhurmato
Maydān
Kifrī
Diyālā
Khānaqīn
Jalūlā
Naftshahr
Al Hadr
Ash Sharqāţ
Bayjī
Tikrīt
Ad Dawr
Sāmarrā'
Al Miqdādīyah
Ba'qūbah
Balad
Ad Dujayl
Al Khāliş
Mandalī
Balad Rūz
Jāsimīyah
Banī Sa'd
Al Kāzimīyah
BAGHDĀD
Turşāq
Zurbātīyah
Badrah
Al 'Azīzīyah
Aş Şuwayrah
Nahr Dijlah (Tigris)
Al Kūt
Shaykh Sa'd
'Alī al Gharbī
Hawr as Sa'dīyah
'Alī ash Sharqī
Al 'Amārah
Qal'at Sukkar
Al Hayy
'Afak
Ad Dīwānīyah
Al Kūfah
An Najaf
Ash Shāmīyah
Al Hillah
BABYLON
Karbalā'
Al Musayyib
Al Hindīyah
Al Mahmūdīyah
Buhayrat ar Razāzah
Ar Rahhālīyah
Al Fallūjah
Hawr al Habbānīyah
Habbānīyah
Ar Ramādī
Hīt
Nahr al Furāt
Şāhilīyah
Al Hadīthah
Fuhaymī
Buhayrat ath Tharthār
W. ath Tharthār
Nahr Dijlah
'Ānah
Al Qā'im
Al Qā'im
Ar Rutbah
W. Rutga
W. Hawrān
W. al Ghadaf
W. al Ubayyid
Nukhayb
Unayzah
Al Qāmishlī
Damir Qābū
Ayn Zālah
Ra's al 'Ayn
Al Hasakah
Dulq Maghār
Abū Du'ān
Bahret Assad
Ar Raqqah
Fadghāmī
Ma'dīn
Ar Ruşāfah
Tibnī
Barsham
Khābūr
Dayr az Zawr
Al Mayādīn
Buşayrah
As Sukhnah
Al Arak
Al Qaţ'ā
Abū Kamāl
Tudmur
PALMYRA
Qusaybah
Zāb al Kabīr
Zāb aş Şaghīr
East from Greenwich
COPYRIGHT PHILIP'S
ft
m
9000
3000
6000
2000
4500
1500
1000
1500
500
600
200
0
50
150
100
300
200
600
500
1500
1000
3000
2000
6000
3000
9000

1:12 000 000

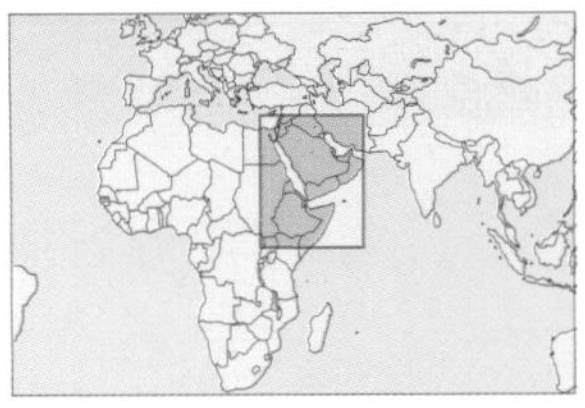

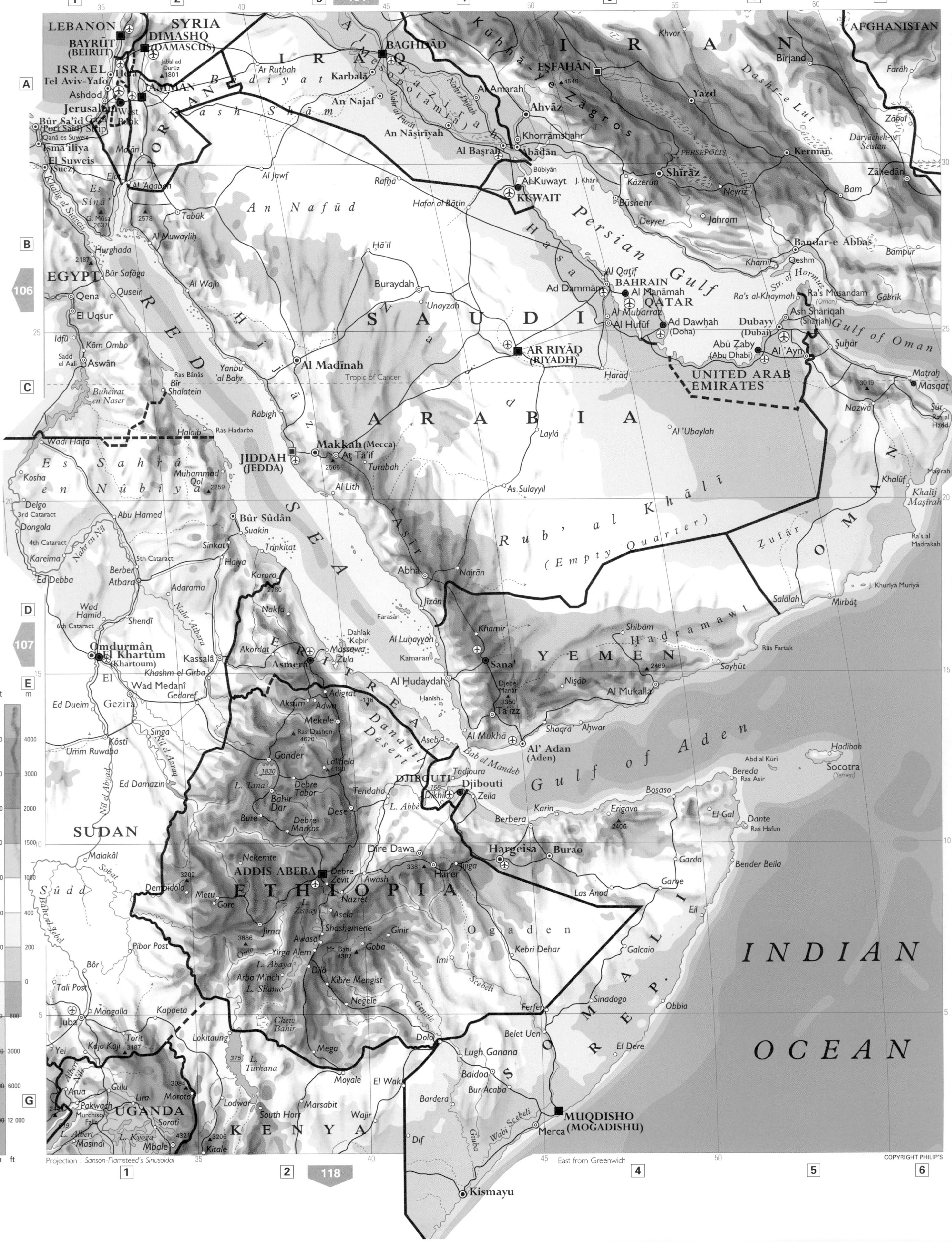

100 0 100 200 300 400 500 600 km
100 0 100 200 300 400 miles
101
91
106
107
118
LEBANON
SYRIA
DIMASHQ (DAMASCUS)
BAYRŪT (BEIRUT)
ISRAEL
Tel Aviv-Yafo
Ashdod
Jerusalem
West Bank
'AMMĀN
JORDAN
BAGHDĀD
IRAQ
Karbalā
An Najaf
An Nāṣirīyah
Al Baṣrah
Al 'Amārah
Ahvāz
Khorramshahr
Ābādān
IRAN
Eṣfahān
Kūhhā-ye Zāgros
Yazd
Dasht-e Lut
Kermān
Shīrāz
Būshehr
Bīrjand
AFGHANISTAN
Farāh
Zābol
Zāhedān
Bam
Bandar-e Abbās
Bampūr
Al Kuwayt
KUWAIT
Ar Ruṭbah
Al Jawf
Rafḥā
Ḥafar al Bāṭin
An Nafūd
Ḥā'il
Buraydah
'Unayzah
SAUDI ARABIA
Persian Gulf
Al Qaṭīf
Ad Dammām
BAHRAIN
Al Manāmah
QATAR
Ad Dawḥah (Doha)
Al Hufūf
Al Mubarraz
AR RIYĀḌ (RIYADH)
Ḥaraḍ
Al Madīnah
Tropic of Cancer
Yanbu 'al Baḥr
Rābigh
Makkah (Mecca)
JIDDAH (JEDDA)
Aṭ Ṭā'if
Turabah
Al Līth
Laylá
As Sulayyil
Rub' al Khālī (Empty Quarter)
UNITED ARAB EMIRATES
Abū Ẓaby (Abu Dhabi)
Dubayy (Dubai)
Ash Shāriqah (Sharjah)
Ra's al-Khaymah
Ra's Musandam
Str. of Hormuz
Gulf of Oman
Ṣuḥār
Masqaṭ
Maṭraḥ
Nazwā
Ra's al Ḥadd
OMAN
Khalūf
Maṣīrah
Khalīj Maṣīrah
Ra's al Madrakah
Ẓufār
Ṣalālah
Mirbāṭ
J. Khurīyā Murīyā
Abhā
Najrān
Jīzān
YEMEN
Ṣan'ā'
Ḥaḍramawt
Shibām
Al Ḥudaydah
Ta'izz
Al Mukhā
Al 'Adan (Aden)
Al Mukallā
Sayḥūt
Rās Fartak
Gulf of Aden
Socotra (Yemen)
Hadiboh
Abd al Kūrī
Bab el Mandeb
EGYPT
Bûr Sa'îd (Port Said)
Ismâ'ilîya
El Suweis (Suez)
Sinai
G. Mûsa 2637
Hurghada
Bûr Safâga
Qena
El Uqsur
Aswân
Buheirat en Naser
RED SEA
Ras Banâs
Halaib
SUDAN
Wadi Halfa
Es Sahrâ en Nûbîya
Dongola
Abu Hamed
Bûr Sûdân
Suakin
Atbara
Kassalâ
Omdurmân
El Khartûm (Khartoum)
Wad Medanî
Gedaref
Gezira
Kôstî
Ed Damazin
Malakâl
Sudd
Juba
ERITREA
Asmera
Massawa
Aseb
Danakil Desert
DJIBOUTI
Djibouti
ETHIOPIA
ADDIS ABEBA
Aksum
Mekele
Ras Dashen 4620
Gonder
L. Tana
Bahir Dar
Dese
Dire Dawa
Harer
Jima
Awasa
Goba
Negele
Ogaden
Hargeisa
Berbera
Burao
Zeila
Bosaso
Erigavo
SOMALI REP.
Garoe
Galcaio
Eil
Obbia
MUQDISHO (MOGADISHU)
Merca
Kismayu
Baidoa
Belet Uen
Lugh Ganana
KENYA
Moyale
L. Turkana
UGANDA
Gulu
L. Albert
L. Kyoga
INDIAN OCEAN
Projection : Sanson-Flamsteed's Sinusoidal
East from Greenwich

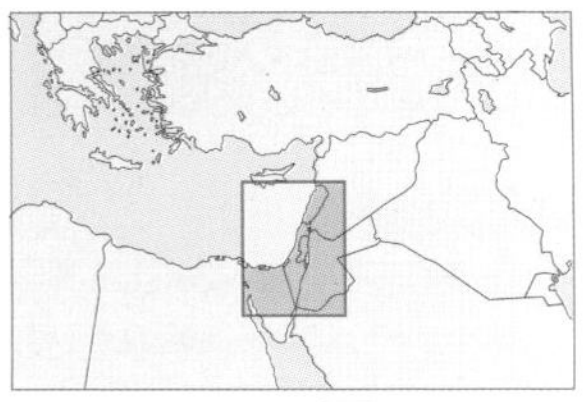

1:2 000 000

10 0 10 20 30 40 50 60 70 80 100 km

10 0 10 20 30 40 50 60 miles

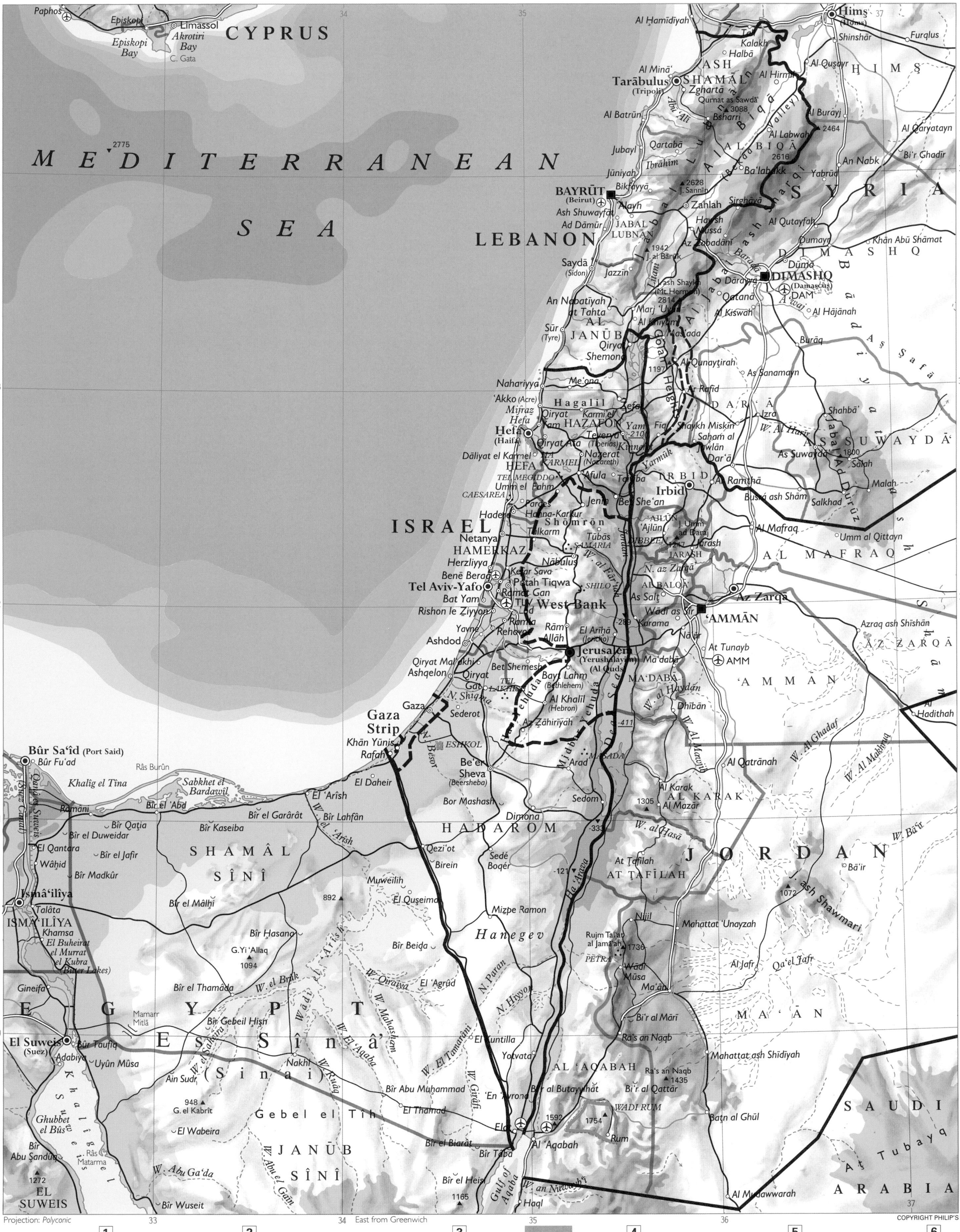

Projection: Polyconic   East from Greenwich

1974 Cease Fire Lines

National Parks

ft / m: 3000 – 3000; 6000 – 2000; 4500 – 1500; 3000 – 1000; 1200 – 400; 600 – 200; 0 – 0; 100 – 300; 200 – 600; 500 – 1500; 1000 – 3000; 2000 – 6000

101 96 106

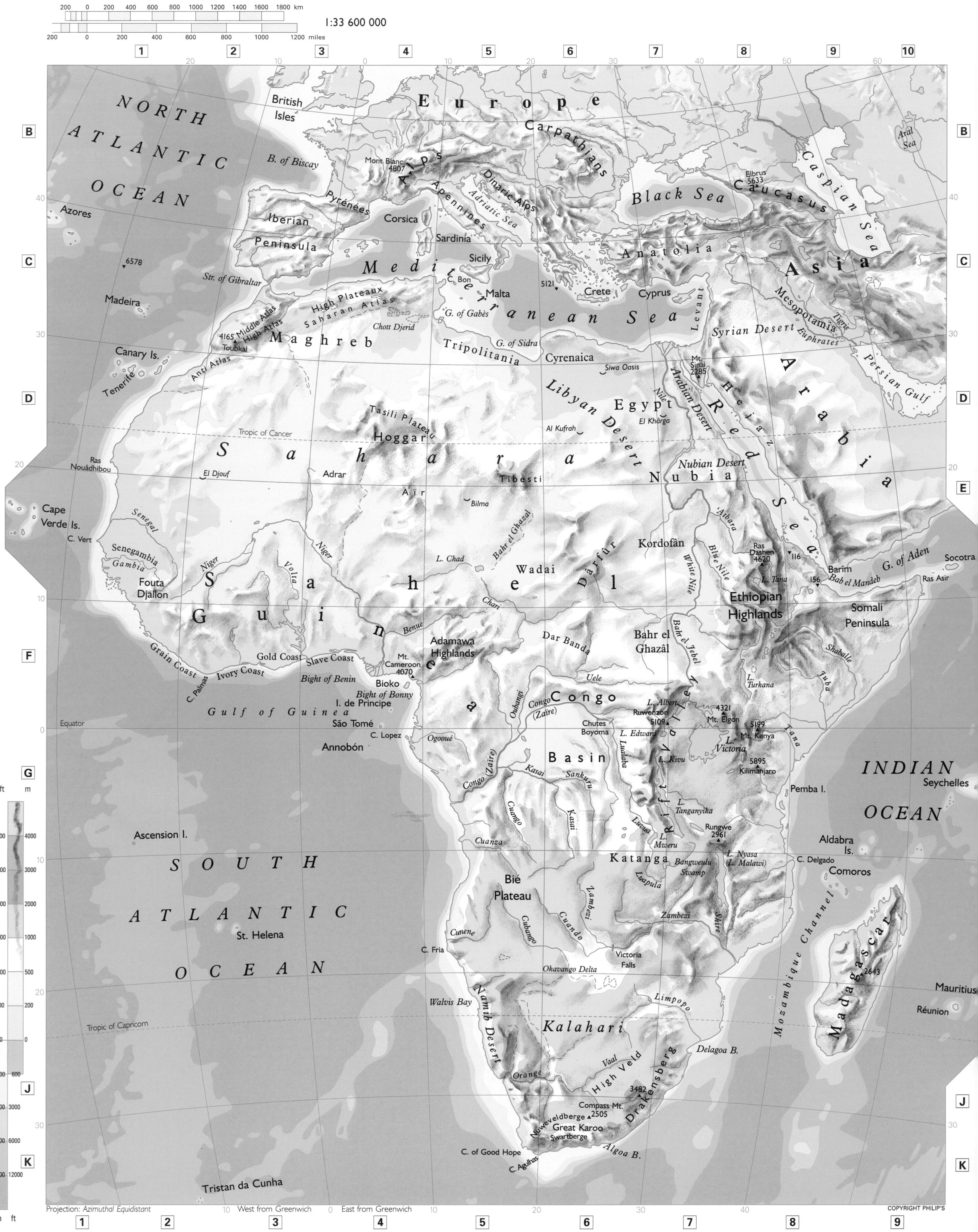

1:33 600 000
km
miles
NORTH ATLANTIC OCEAN
British Isles
Europe
Carpathians
Aral Sea
B. of Biscay
Mont Blanc 4807
Alps
Dinaric Alps
Apennines
Adriatic Sea
Black Sea
Elbrus 5633
Caucasus
Caspian Sea
Azores
Pyrénées
Iberian Peninsula
Corsica
Sardinia
Sicily
Anatolia
Asia
6578
Str. of Gibraltar
Mediterranean Sea
C. Bon
Malta
5121
Crete
Cyprus
Madeira
High Plateaux
Saharan Atlas
Middle Atlas
High Atlas
4165 Toubkal
G. of Gabès
Chott Djerid
Levant
Mesopotamia
Tigris
Euphrates
Syrian Desert
Maghreb
Tripolitania
G. of Sidra
Cyrenaica
Canary Is.
Tenerife
Anti Atlas
Siwa Oasis
Mt. Sinai 2285
Persian Gulf
Arabia
Libyan Desert
Egypt
Nile
Arabian Desert
Red Sea
Hejaz
El Khârga
Al Kufrah
Tasili Plateau
Hoggar
Tropic of Cancer
Sahara
Ras Nouâdhibou
El Djouf
Adrar
Tibesti
Nubian Desert
Nubia
Aïr
Bilma
Cape Verde Is.
C. Vert
Senegal
Niger
Bahr el Ghazal
'Atbara
Kordofân
L. Chad
Wadai
Darfur
White Nile
Blue Nile
Ras Dashen 4620
116
Barim
G. of Aden
Socotra
Senegambia
Gambia
Fouta Djallon
Volta
Sahel
L. Tana
156
Bab el Mandeb
Ras Asir
Ethiopian Highlands
Somali Peninsula
Chari
Guinea
Benue
Adamawa Highlands
Dar Banda
Bahr el Ghazâl
Bahr el Jebel
Shaballe
Grain Coast
Gold Coast
Slave Coast
Ivory Coast
C. Palmas
Bight of Benin
Mt. Cameroon 4070
Bioko
Bight of Bonny
I. de Principe
Uele
L. Turkana
Juba
Gulf of Guinea
Oubangi
Congo (Zaïre)
Congo Basin
L. Albert
Ruwenzori 5109
4321 Mt. Elgon
5199 Mt. Kenya
Tana
Equator
São Tomé
C. Lopez
Annobón
Ogooué
Chutes Boyoma
L. Edward
Lualaba
L. Victoria
L. Kivu
5895 Kilimanjaro
Rift Valley
INDIAN OCEAN
Seychelles
Pemba I.
Kasai
Sankuru
Cuango
L. Tanganyika
Rungwe 2961
Ascension I.
Lueya
L. Mweru
Cuanza
Aldabra Is.
SOUTH ATLANTIC OCEAN
Katanga
Bangweulu Swamp
L. Nyasa (L. Malawi)
C. Delgado
Comoros
Luapula
Bié Plateau
Zambezi
Shire
Mozambique Channel
Madagascar
Cunene
Cubango
Cuando
St. Helena
C. Fria
Victoria Falls
Okavango Delta
2643
Walvis Bay
Namib Desert
Limpopo
Mauritius
Réunion
Tropic of Capricorn
Kalahari
Vaal
Delagoa B.
Orange
High Veld
Drakensberg
3482
Compass Mt. 2505
Nuweveldberge
Great Karoo
Swartberge
C. of Good Hope
Algoa B.
C. Agulhas
Tristan da Cunha
Projection: Azimuthal Equidistant
West from Greenwich
East from Greenwich
ft
m

1:33 600 000

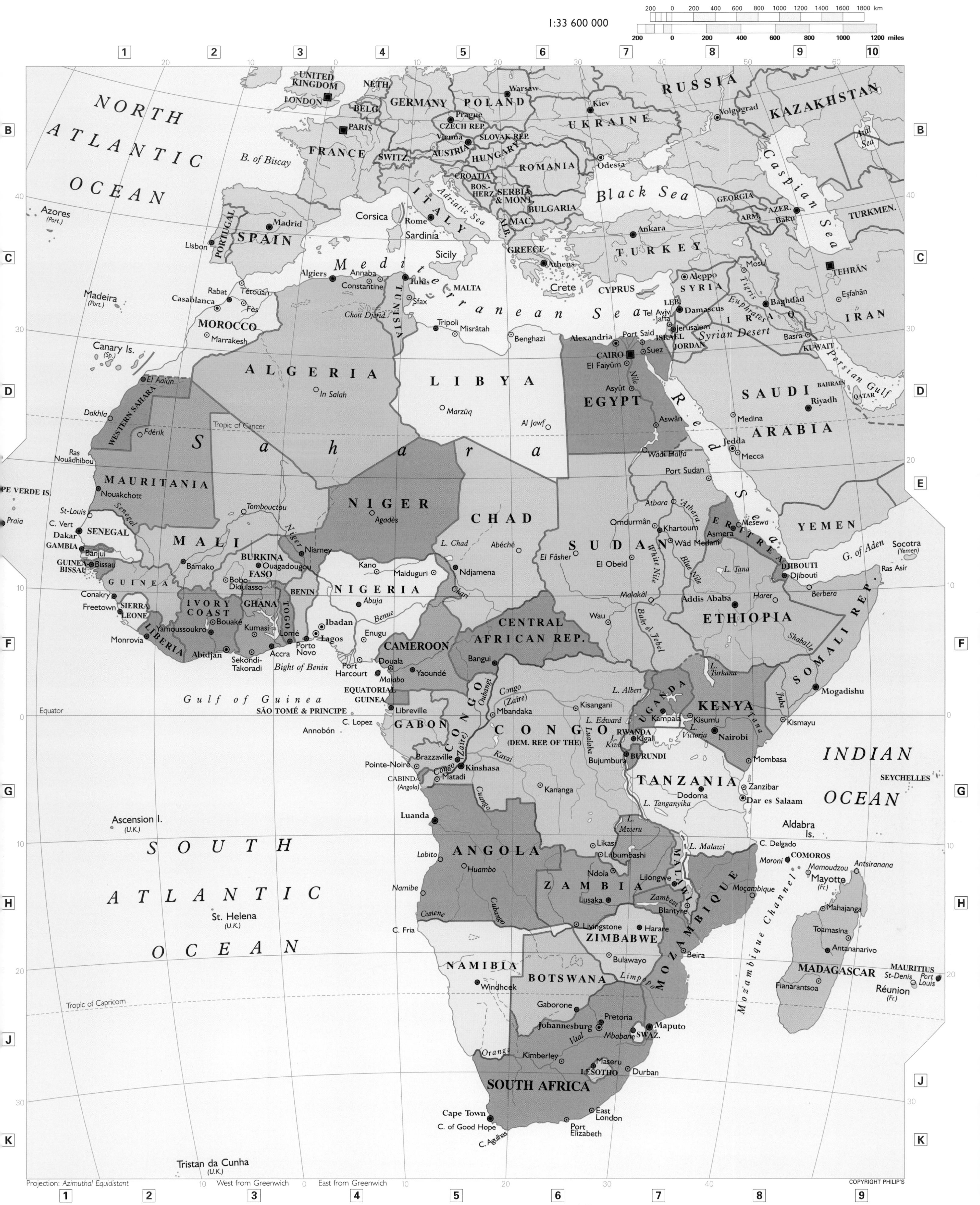

NORTH ATLANTIC OCEAN
B. of Biscay
Azores (Port.)
Madeira (Port.)
Canary Is. (Sp.)
CAPE VERDE IS.
Praia
UNITED KINGDOM
LONDON
NETH.
BELG.
PARIS
FRANCE
SWITZ.
GERMANY
POLAND
Warsaw
Prague
CZECH REP.
SLOVAK REP.
Vienna
AUSTRIA
HUNGARY
CROATIA
BOS.-HERZ.
SERBIA & MONT.
ALB.
MAC.
ROMANIA
BULGARIA
UKRAINE
Kiev
Odessa
RUSSIA
Volgograd
KAZAKHSTAN
Aral Sea
Caspian Sea
Black Sea
GEORGIA
ARM.
AZER.
Baku
TURKMEN.
TURKEY
Ankara
GREECE
Athens
Crete
CYPRUS
ITALY
Rome
Corsica
Sardinia
Sicily
MALTA
Adriatic Sea
PORTUGAL
Lisbon
SPAIN
Madrid
Mediterranean Sea
SYRIA
Aleppo
Damascus
LEB.
Tel Aviv-Jaffa
Jerusalem
ISRAEL
JORDAN
Syrian Desert
IRAQ
Mosul
Baghdad
Tigris
Euphrates
Basra
KUWAIT
IRAN
TEHRĀN
Eşfahān
Persian Gulf
BAHRAIN
QATAR
SAUDI ARABIA
Riyadh
Medina
Jedda
Mecca
YEMEN
G. of Aden
Socotra (Yemen)
Ras Asir
Red Sea
MOROCCO
Rabat
Casablanca
Tétouan
Fès
Marrakesh
ALGERIA
Algiers
Annaba
Constantine
In Salah
TUNISIA
Tunis
Sfax
Chott Djerid
LIBYA
Tripoli
Misrātah
Benghazi
Marzūq
Al Jawf
EGYPT
CAIRO
Alexandria
Port Said
Suez
El Faiyûm
Asyût
Aswân
Nile
WESTERN SAHARA
El Aaiún
Dakhla
Fdérik
Tropic of Cancer
Sahara
MAURITANIA
Nouakchott
Nouâdhibou
Ras Nouâdhibou
SENEGAL
St-Louis
Dakar
C. Vert
Senegal
GAMBIA
Banjul
GUINEA-BISSAU
Bissau
GUINEA
Conakry
SIERRA LEONE
Freetown
LIBERIA
Monrovia
IVORY COAST
Yamoussoukro
Bouaké
Abidjan
MALI
Bamako
Tombouctou
Niger
BURKINA FASO
Ouagadougou
Bobo-Dioulasso
GHANA
Kumasi
Accra
Sekondi-Takoradi
TOGO
Lomé
BENIN
Porto Novo
NIGER
Niamey
Agadès
NIGERIA
Abuja
Kano
Maiduguri
Ibadan
Lagos
Enugu
Port Harcourt
Benue
Bight of Benin
Gulf of Guinea
CHAD
Ndjamena
L. Chad
Abéché
Chari
SUDAN
Wadi Halfa
Port Sudan
Atbara
Omdurmân
Khartoum
Wad Medani
El Fâsher
El Obeid
Malakâl
Wau
White Nile
Blue Nile
Bahr el Jebel
ERITREA
Asmera
Mesewa
DJIBOUTI
Djibouti
ETHIOPIA
Addis Ababa
Harer
L. Tana
Shaballe
SOMALI REP.
Berbera
Mogadishu
Kismayu
Juba
CENTRAL AFRICAN REP.
Bangui
CAMEROON
Douala
Yaoundé
Malabo
EQUATORIAL GUINEA
SÃO TOMÉ & PRINCIPE
Annobón
C. Lopez
Equator
GABON
Libreville
CONGO
Brazzaville
Pointe-Noire
Oubangi
Congo (Zaïre)
CONGO (DEM. REP. OF THE)
Kinshasa
Mbandaka
Kisangani
Kananga
Kasai
Cuango
Lualaba
Matadi
CABINDA (Angola)
L. Albert
L. Edward
L. Kivu
UGANDA
Kampala
L. Turkana
KENYA
Kisumu
Nairobi
Mombasa
Tana
L. Victoria
RWANDA
Kigali
BURUNDI
Bujumbura
TANZANIA
Dodoma
Zanzibar
Dar es Salaam
L. Tanganyika
L. Mweru
INDIAN OCEAN
SEYCHELLES
Aldabra Is.
C. Delgado
COMOROS
Moroni
Mamoudzou
Mayotte (Fr.)
Antsiranana
ANGOLA
Luanda
Lobito
Huambo
Namibe
Cunene
Cubango
C. Fria
Likasi
Lubumbashi
ZAMBIA
Ndola
Lusaka
Zambezi
L. Malawi
MALAWI
Lilongwe
Blantyre
MOZAMBIQUE
Moçambique
Beira
Maputo
Mozambique Channel
ZIMBABWE
Harare
Bulawayo
Livingstone
Limpopo
NAMIBIA
Windhoek
BOTSWANA
Gaborone
Pretoria
Johannesburg
Mbabane
SWAZ.
Vaal
Orange
Kimberley
Maseru
LESOTHO
Durban
SOUTH AFRICA
Cape Town
C. of Good Hope
C. Agulhas
Port Elizabeth
East London
MADAGASCAR
Mahajanga
Toamasina
Antananarivo
Fianarantsoa
MAURITIUS
Port Louis
St-Denis
Réunion (Fr.)
Tropic of Capricorn
SOUTH ATLANTIC OCEAN
Ascension I. (U.K.)
St. Helena (U.K.)
Tristan da Cunha (U.K.)
Projection: Azimuthal Equidistant
West from Greenwich
East from Greenwich
COPYRIGHT PHILIP'S

● Dakar Capital Cities

1:6 400 000

50 0 50 100 150 200 250 300 km

50 0 50 100 150 200 miles

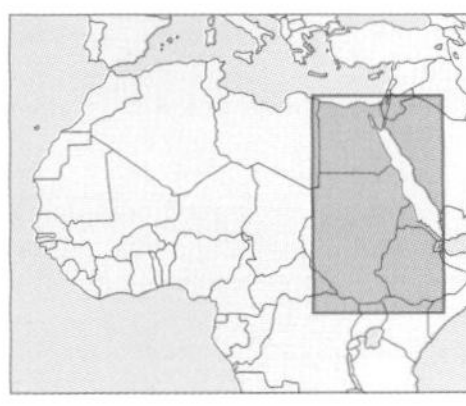

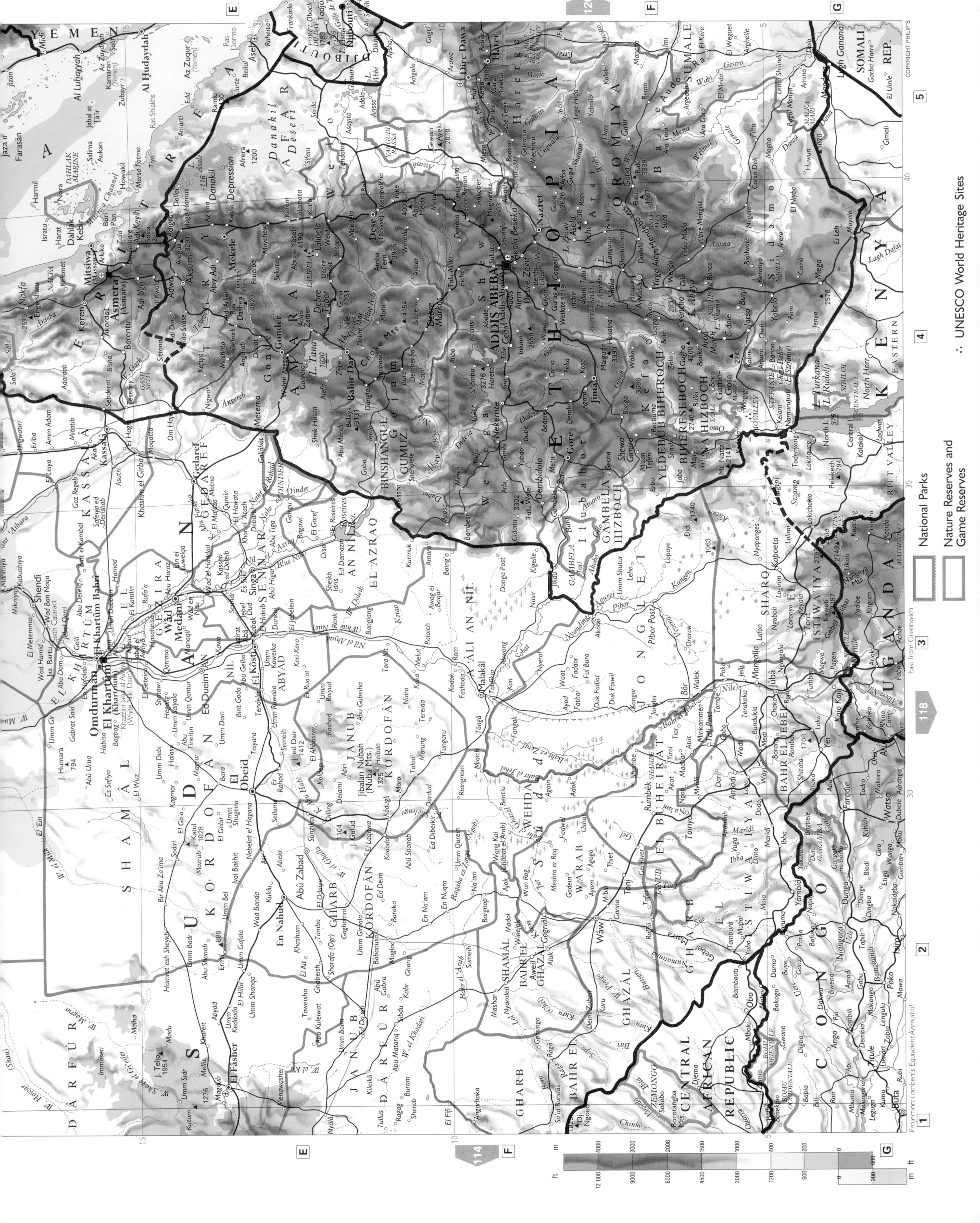
National Parks
Nature Reserves and Game Reserves
UNESCO World Heritage Sites
Projection: Lambert's Equivalent Azimuthal
East from Greenwich
COPYRIGHT PHILIP'S
YEMEN
ERITREA
DJIBOUTI
ETHIOPIA
SUDAN
KENYA
UGANDA
CONGO
CENTRAL AFRICAN REPUBLIC
SOMALI REP.
ADDIS ABEBA
El Khartûm (Khartoum)
Omdurman
Asmera (Asmara)
Djibouti

50 0 50 100 150 200 250 300 km

1:6 400 000

50 0 50 100 150 200 miles

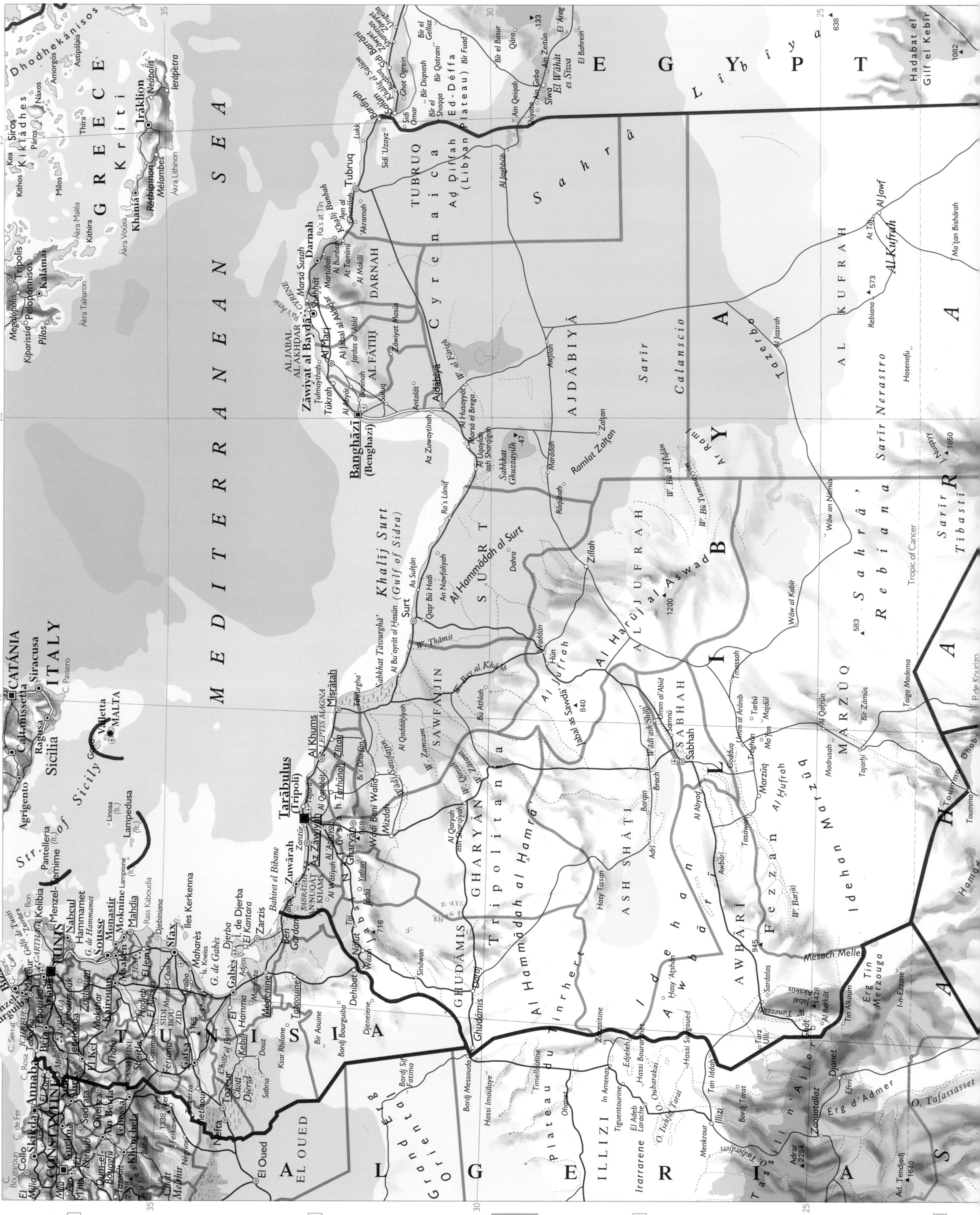

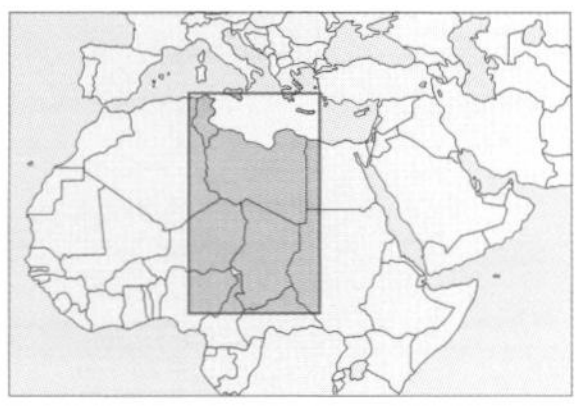

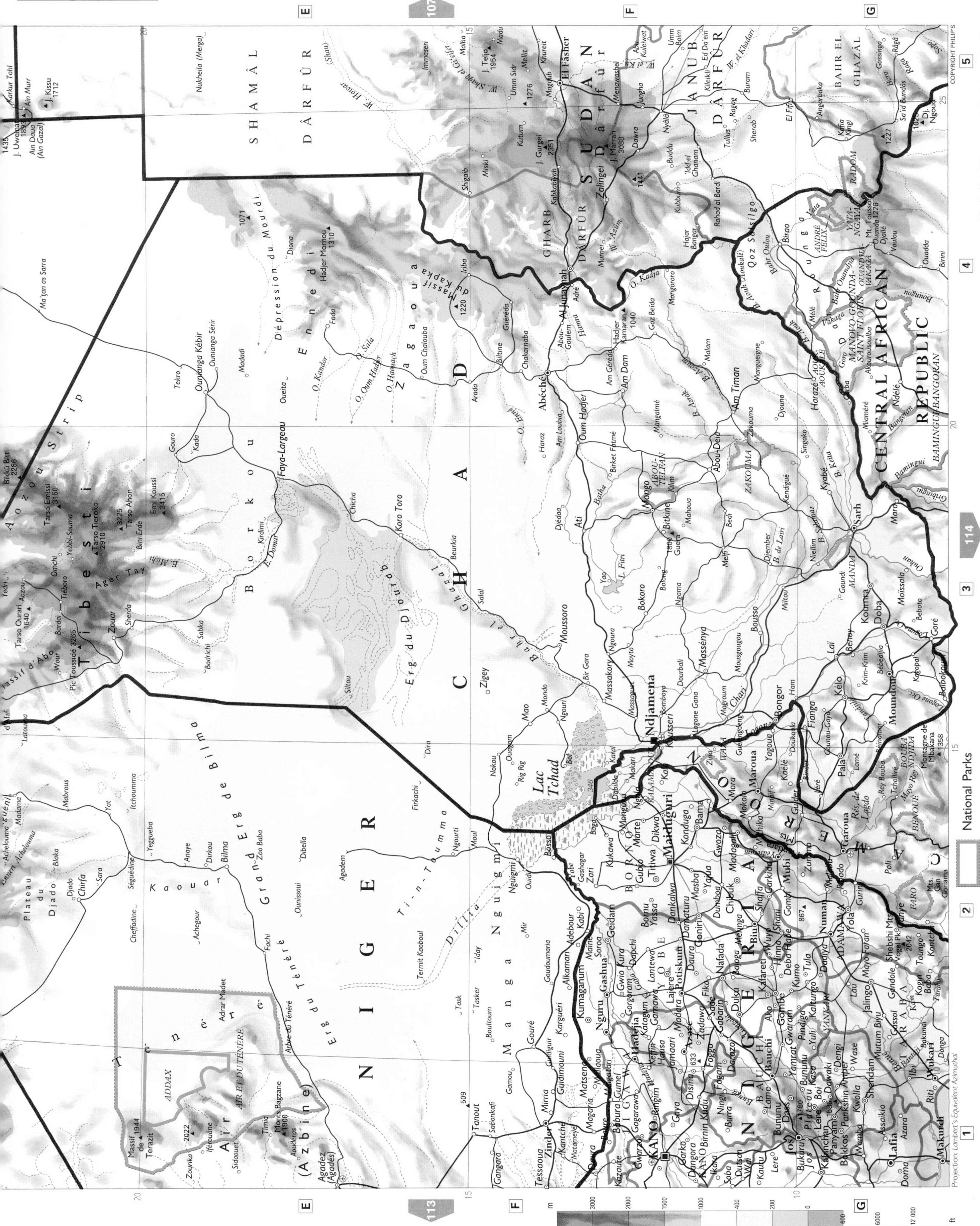
107
113
114
C H A D
N I G E R
S U D A N
N I G E R I A
CENTRAL AFRICAN REPUBLIC
Lac Tchad
Ndjamena
Abéché
Faya-Largeau
Tibesti
B o r k o u
E n n e d i
Grand Erg de Bilma
T é n é r é
Maiduguri
Kano
Zinder
Sarh
Moundou
Al Junaynah
El Fasher
Zalingei
Agadez (Agadés)
Emi Koussi 3415
National Parks
Nature Reserves and Game Reserves
UNESCO World Heritage Sites
Underlined towns give their name to the administrative area in which they stand.
Projection: Lambert's Equivalent Azimuthal
COPYRIGHT PHILIP'S

50 0 50 100 150 200 250 300 km

50 0 50 100 150 200 miles

1:6 400 000

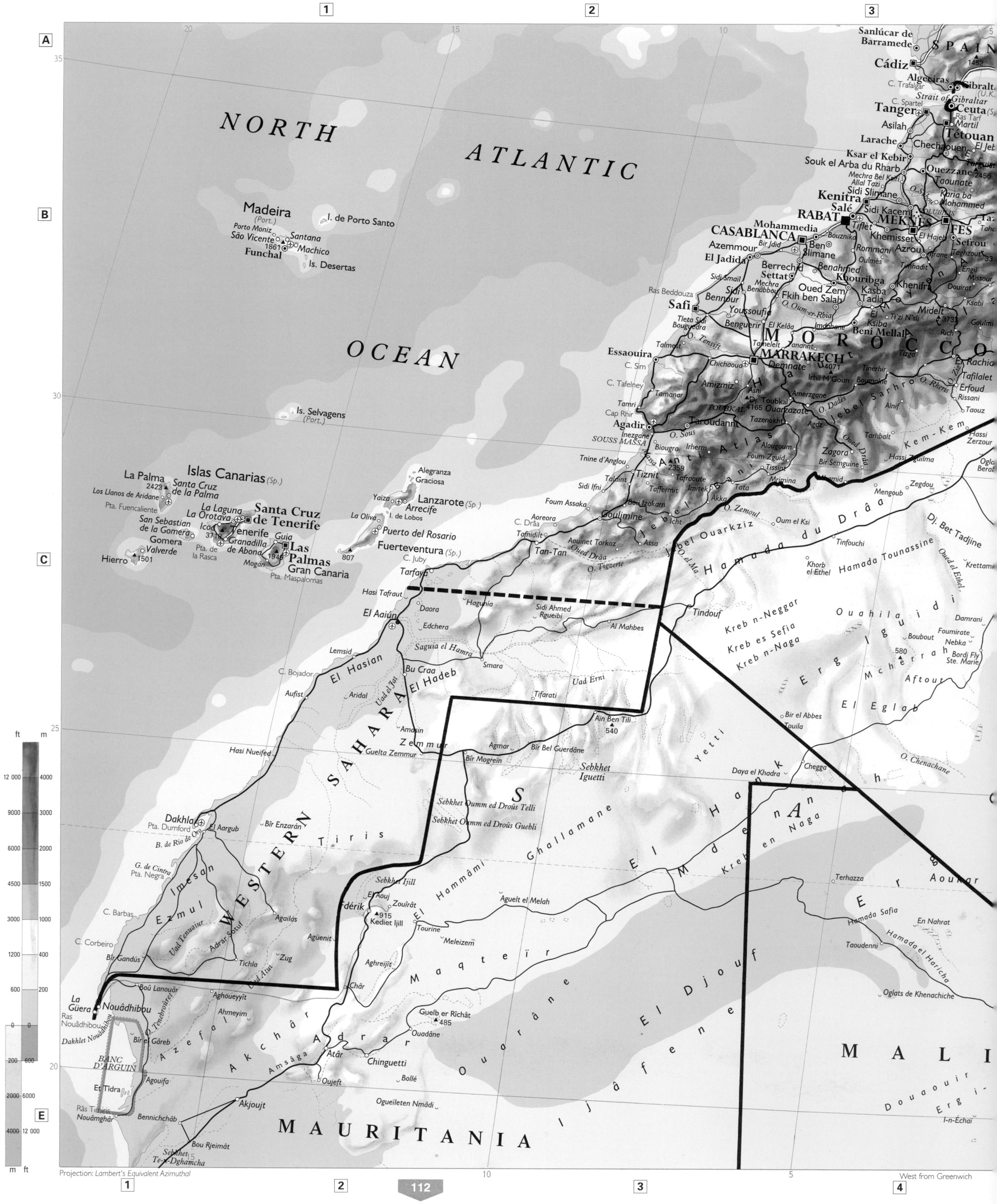

Projection: Lambert's Equivalent Azimuthal

West from Greenwich

112

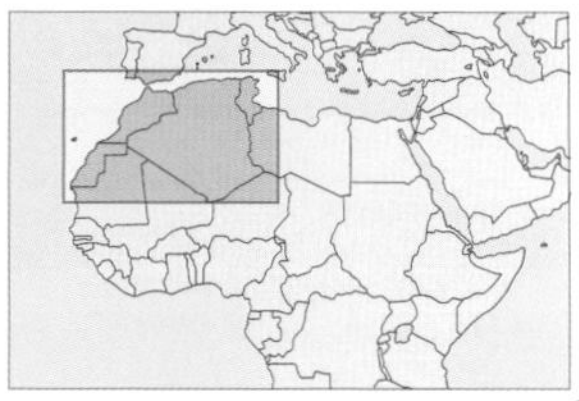

36

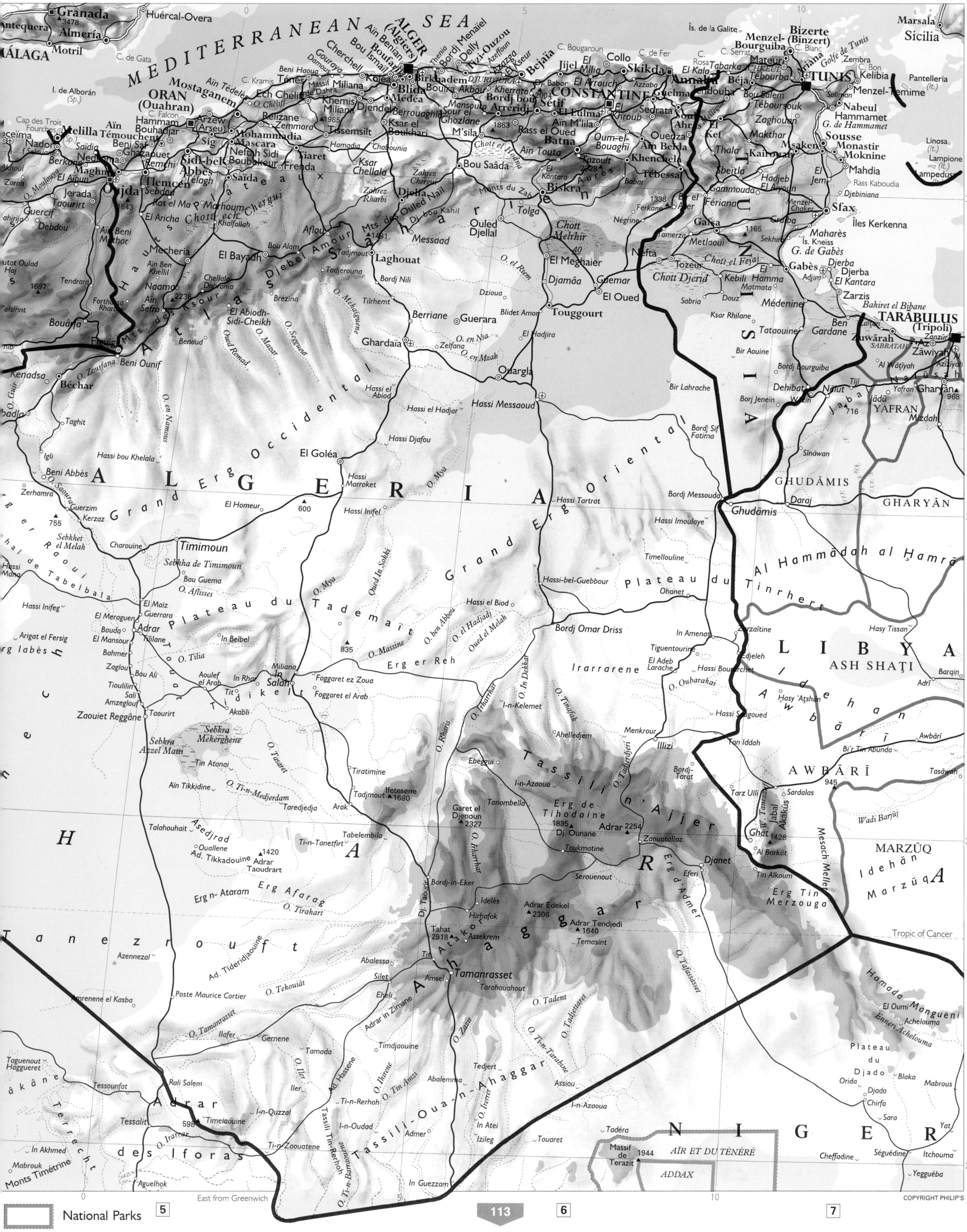

108

113

National Parks

Nature Reserves and Game Reserves

∴ UNESCO World Heritage Sites

1:6 400 000

Projection : Lambert's Equivalent Azimuthal

West from Greenwich

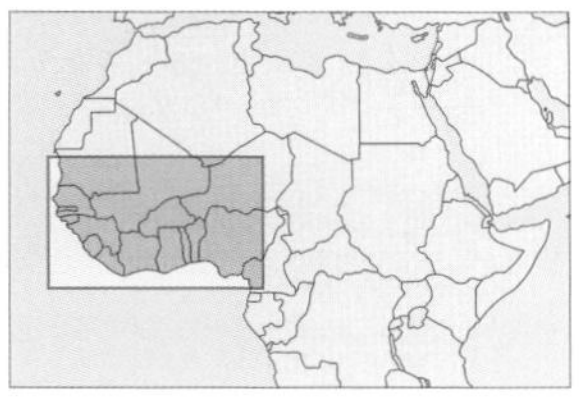

National Parks

Nature Reserves and Game Reserves

∴ UNESCO World Heritage Sites

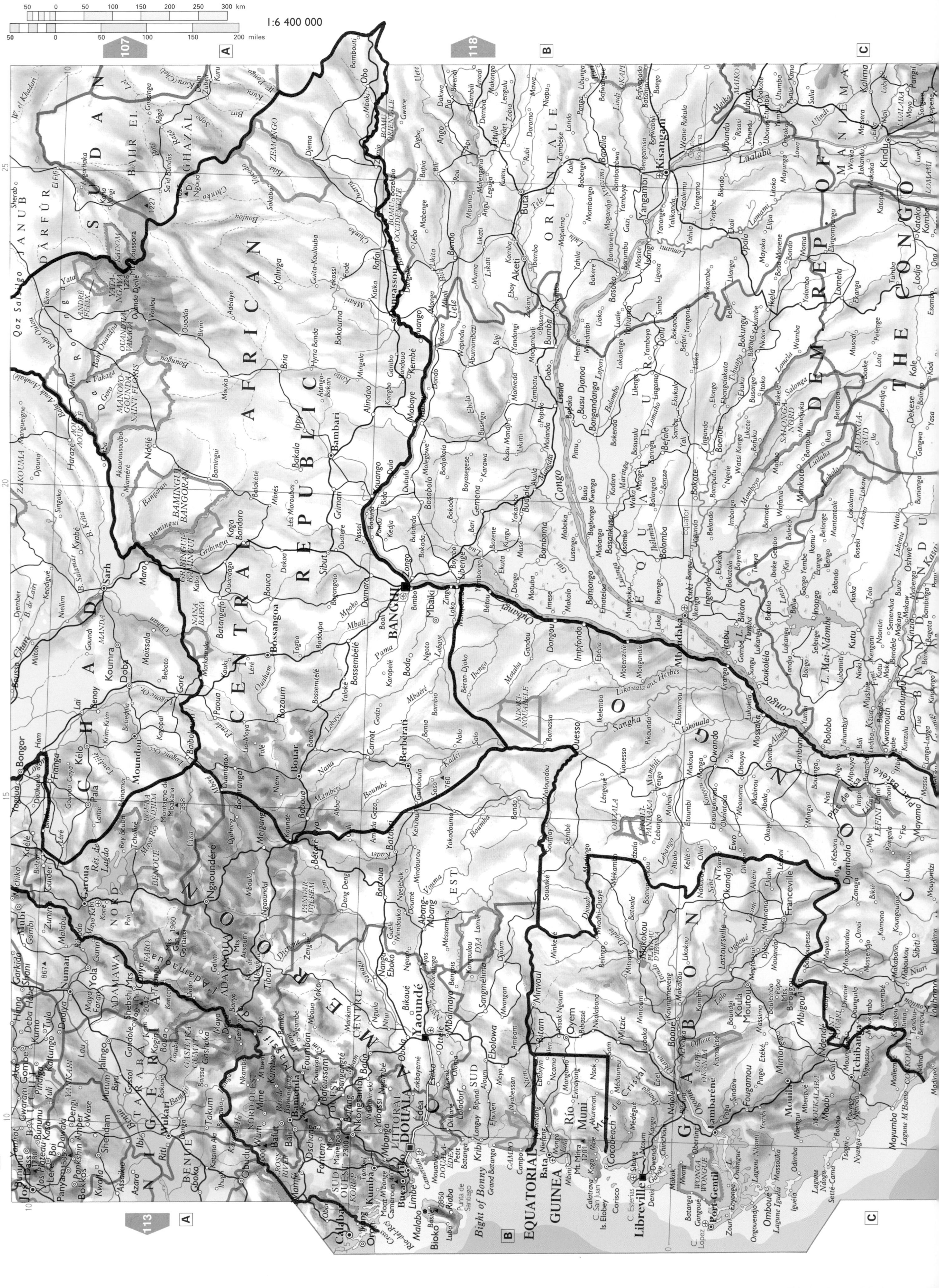
50 0 50 100 150 200 250 300 km
1:6 400 000
50 0 50 100 150 200 miles
107
118
109
113
A
B
C
1
2
3
4
5
CENTRAL AFRICAN REPUBLIC
CHAD
SUDAN
CAMEROON
NIGERIA
CONGO
GABON
EQUATORIAL GUINEA
DEM. REP. OF THE CONGO
BANGUI
YAOUNDÉ
Libreville
Malabo
DOUALA
Kisangani
Mbandaka
Bambari
Berbérati
Bouar
Bossangoa
Sarh
Moundou
Doba
Garoua
Ngaoundéré
Bertoua
Ouesso
Franceville
Port-Gentil
Lambaréné
Bangassou
Bumba
Lisala
Buta
Kindu
Bandundu
Bight of Bonny
Equator
Oubangui
Sangha
Congo
Lualaba
Logone
Chari

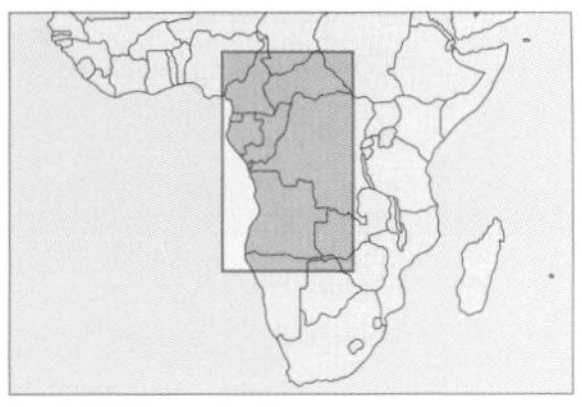

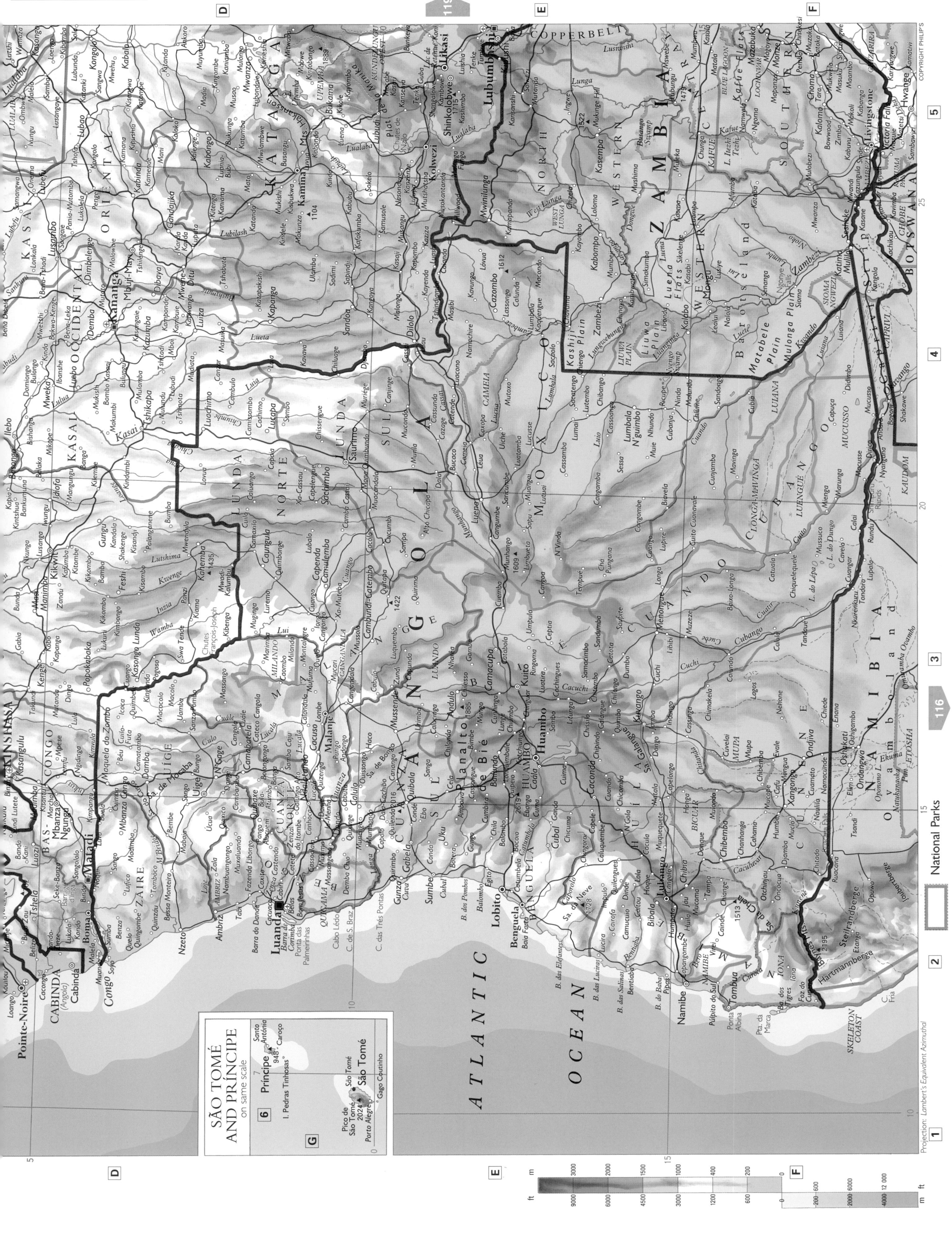
ATLANTIC
OCEAN
ANGOLA
ZAMBIA
NAMIBIA
BOTSWANA
KATANGA
COPPERBELT
Luanda
Lobito
Benguela
Huambo
Lubumbashi
Likasi
Kolwezi
Kananga
Matadi
Boma
Cabinda
Pointe-Noire
Livingstone
Namibe
Lubango
Menongue
Saurimo
Malanje
Kuito
SÃO TOMÉ AND PRÍNCIPE
on same scale
Príncipe
São Tomé
National Parks
Nature Reserves and Game Reserves
UNESCO World Heritage Sites
Projection: Lambert's Equivalent Azimuthal
COPYRIGHT PHILIP'S

50 0 50 100 150 200 250 300 km

1:6 400 000

50 0 50 100 150 200 miles

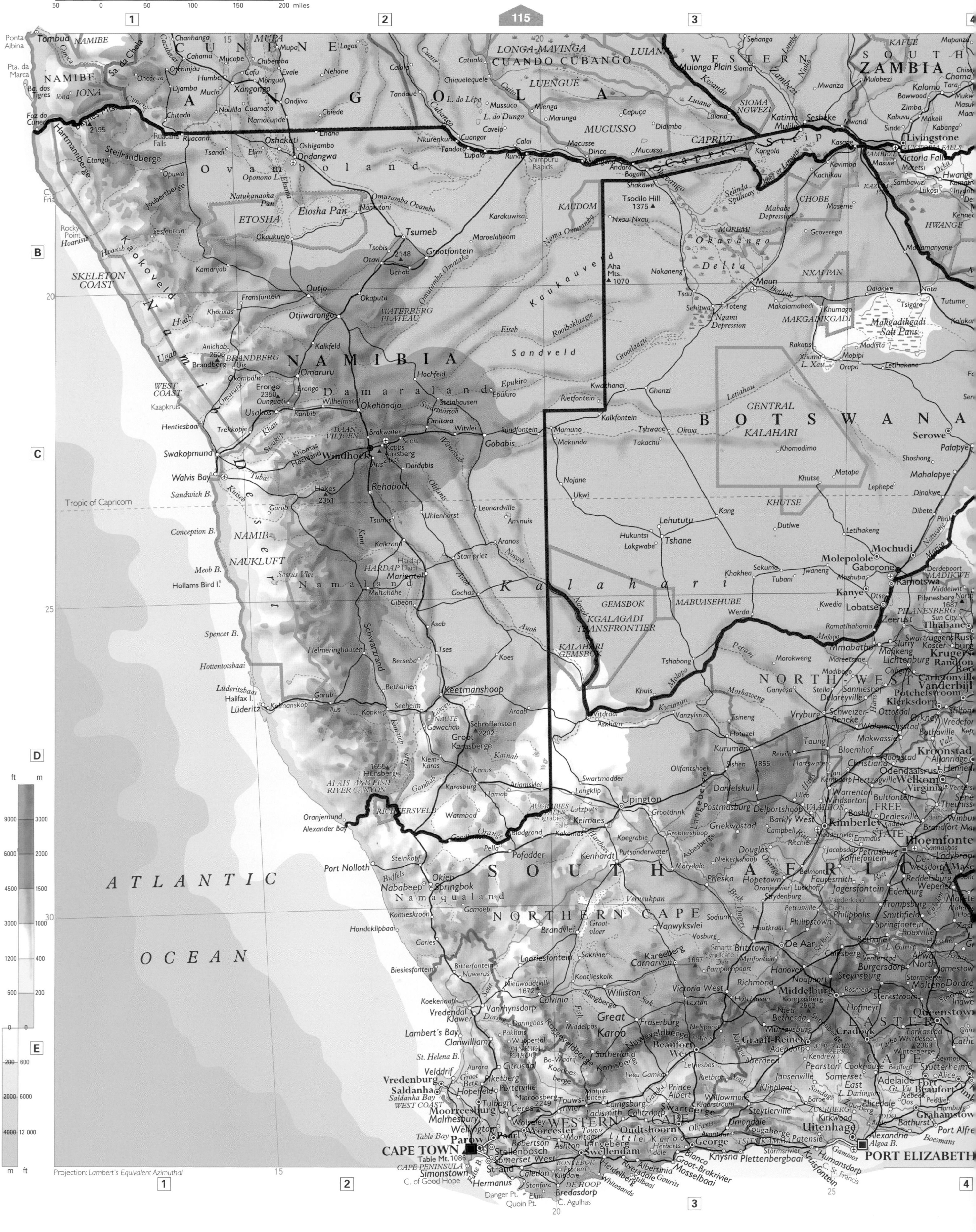

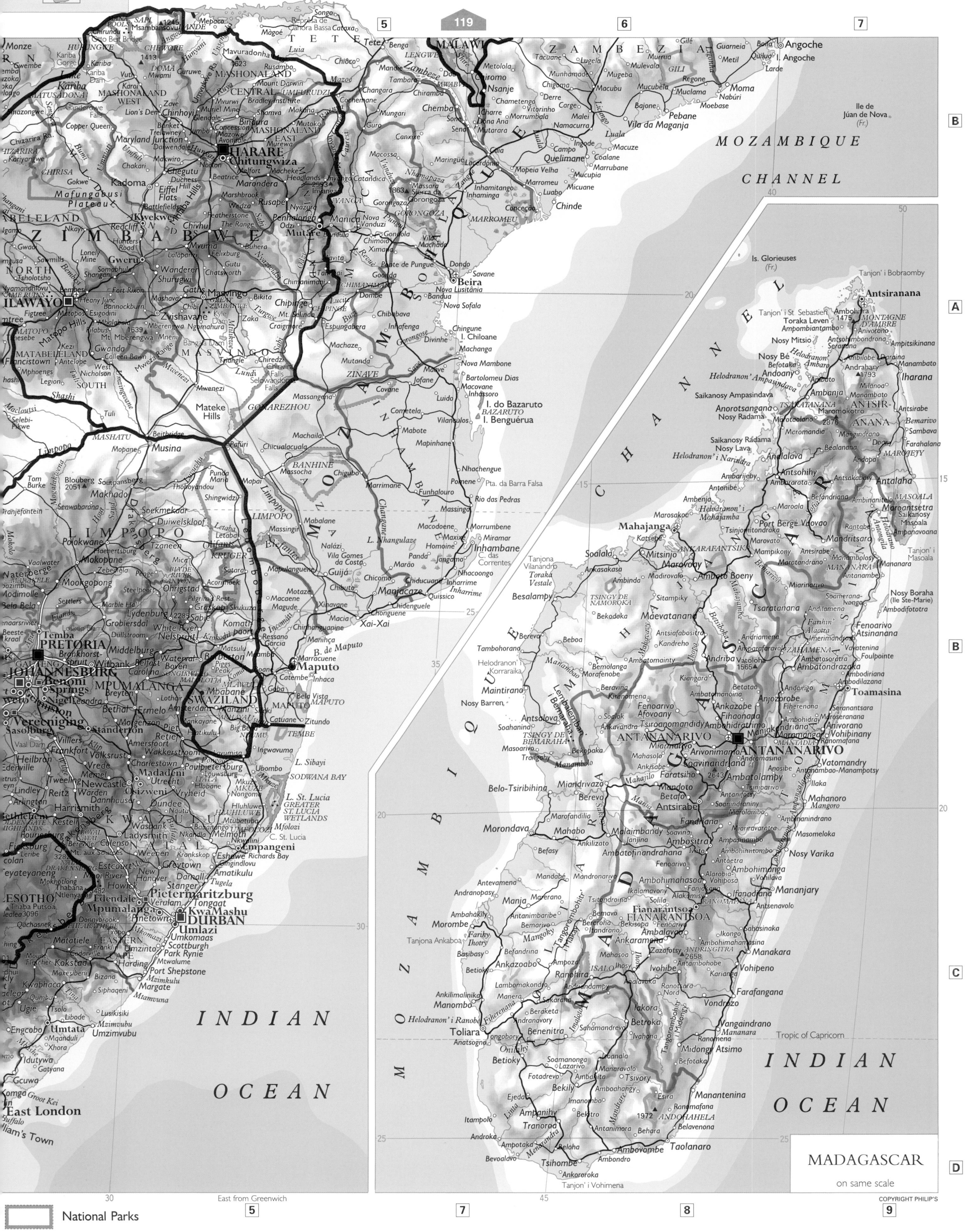

National Parks

Nature Reserves and Game Reserves

∴ UNESCO World Heritage Sites

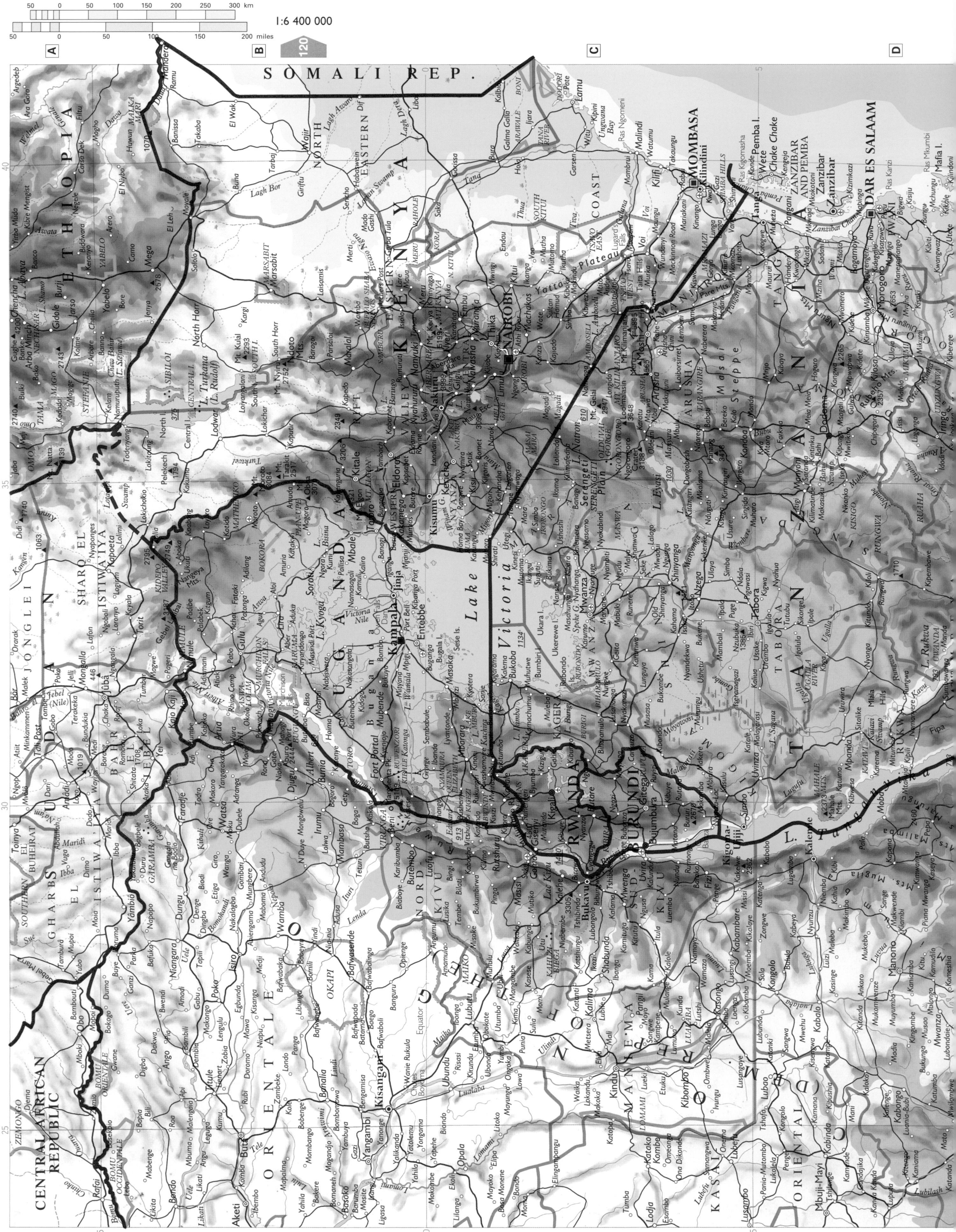

1:6 400 000
km 50 0 50 100 150 200 250 300
miles 50 0 50 100 150 200
SOMALI REP.
ETHIOPIA
KENYA
UGANDA
RWANDA
BURUNDI
TANZANIA
SUDAN
CENTRAL AFRICAN REPUBLIC
NAIROBI
MOMBASA
DAR ES SALAAM
Zanzibar
Kampala
Entebbe
Jinja
Kisumu
Nakuru
Eldoret
Kitale
Juba
Kisangani
Bukavu
Bujumbura
Kigoma-Ujiji
Tabora
Dodoma
Arusha
Moshi
Mwanza
Lake Victoria
L. Turkana (L. Rudolf)
L. Albert
L. Kyoga
L. Kivu
L. Tanganyika
Equator
120
107
114

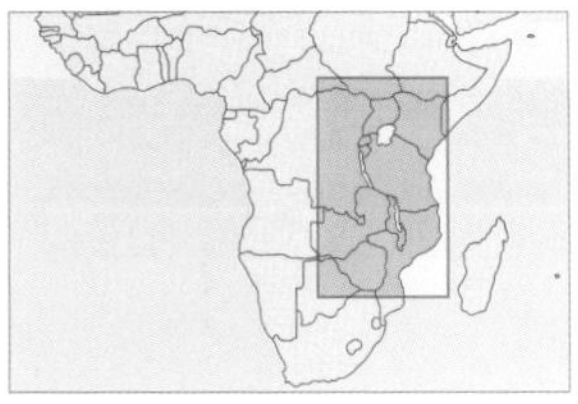

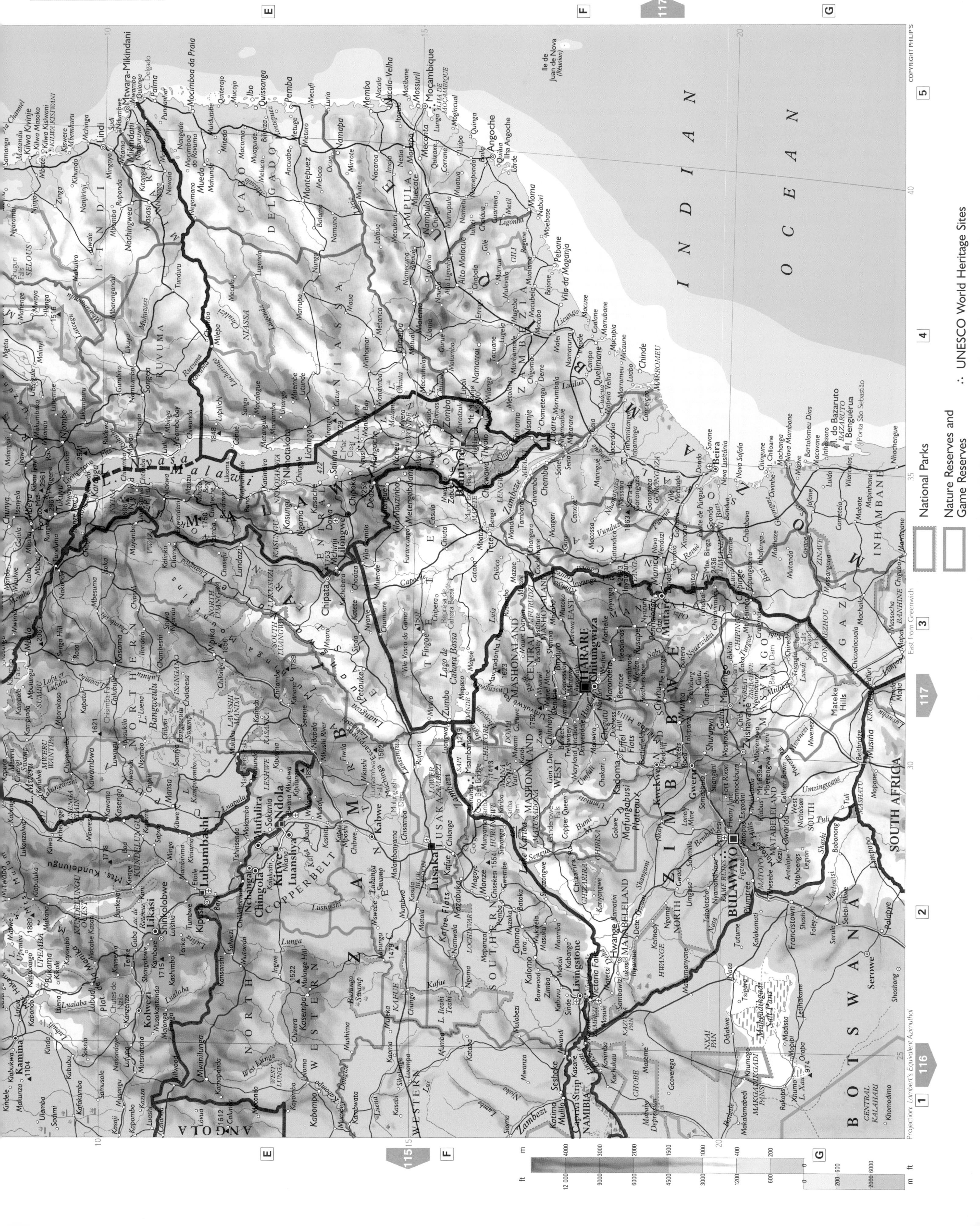
National Parks
Nature Reserves and Game Reserves
∴ UNESCO World Heritage Sites
INDIAN OCEAN
ZAMBIA
ZIMBABWE
MOZAMBIQUE
MALAWI
BOTSWANA
SOUTH AFRICA
NAMIBIA
ANGOLA
HARARE
LUSAKA
Lubumbashi
Bulawayo
Beira
East from Greenwich
Projection: Lambert's Equivalent Azimuthal
COPYRIGHT PHILIP'S
ft 12 000 9000 6000 4500 3000 1200 600 0
m 4000 3000 2000 1500 1000 400 200 0
0 200 600 2000 6000 ft
0 200 600 2000 m

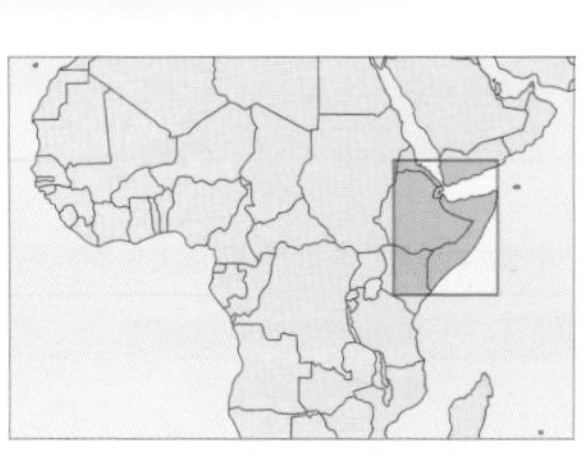

50 0 50 100 150 200 250 300 km

50 0 50 100 150 200 miles

1:6 400 000

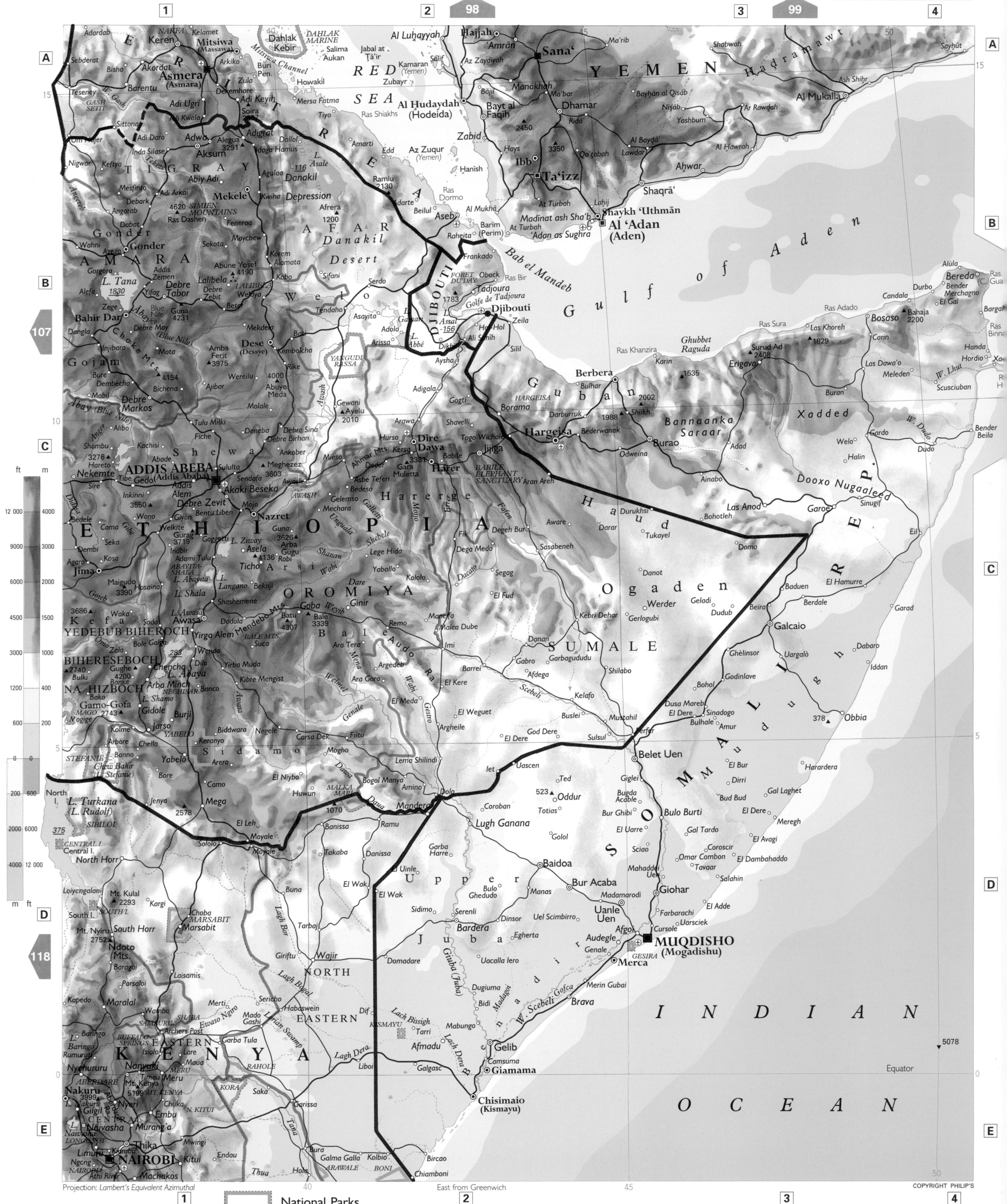

National Parks

Nature Reserves and Game Reserves

∴ UNESCO World Heritage Sites

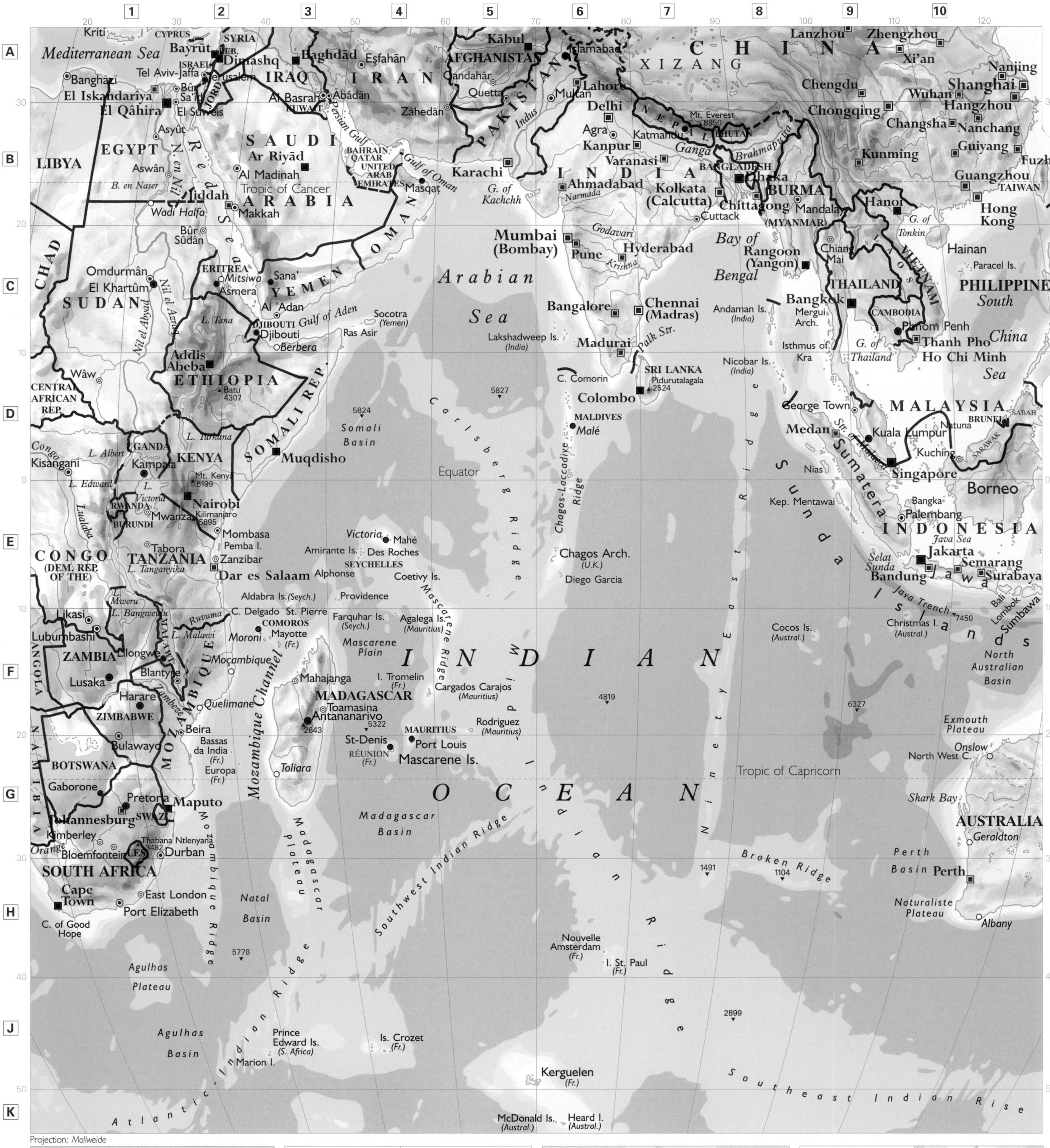

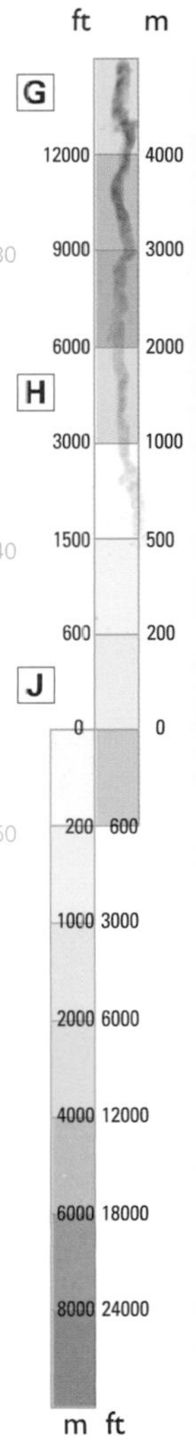

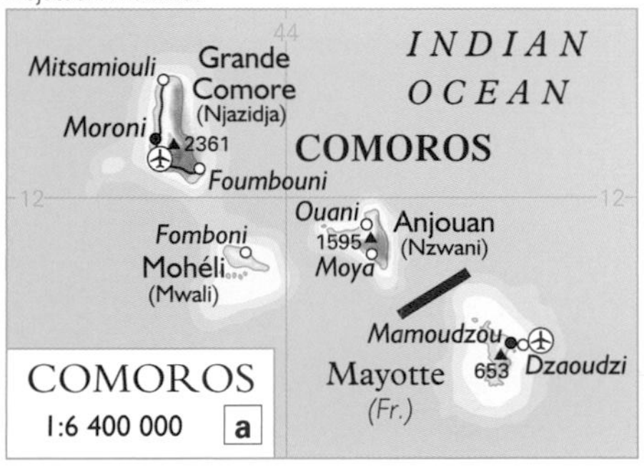

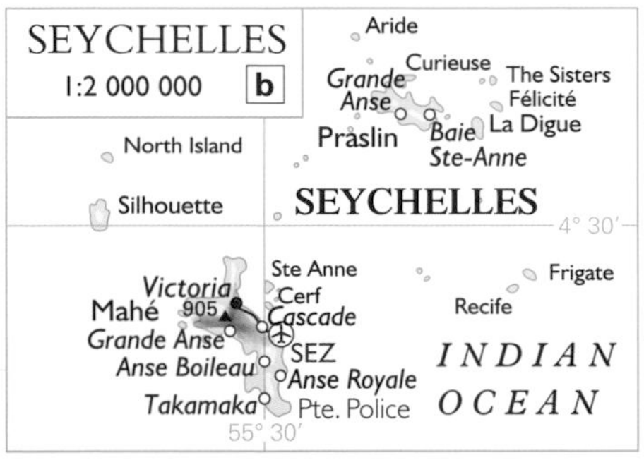

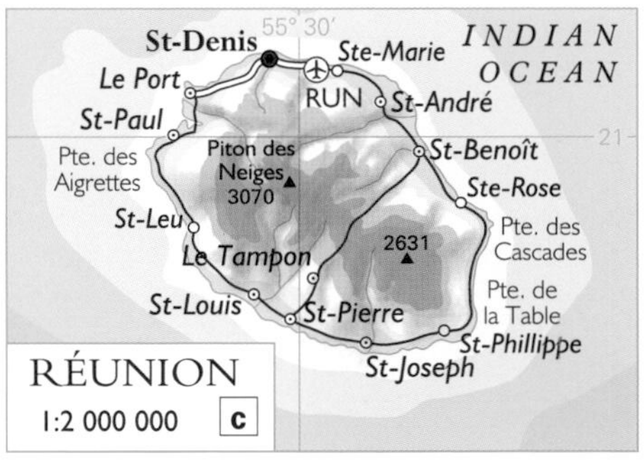

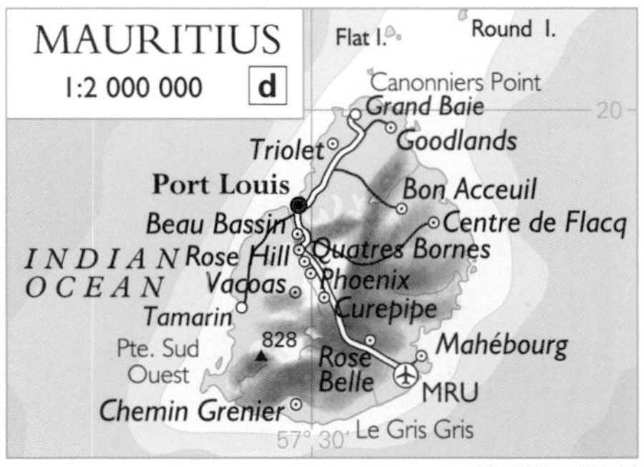

East from Greenwich

1: 6 400 000 (scale bar: 50 0 50 km; 50 0 50 miles)

1: 2 000 000 (scale bar: 10 0 10 20 km; 10 0 10 20 miles)

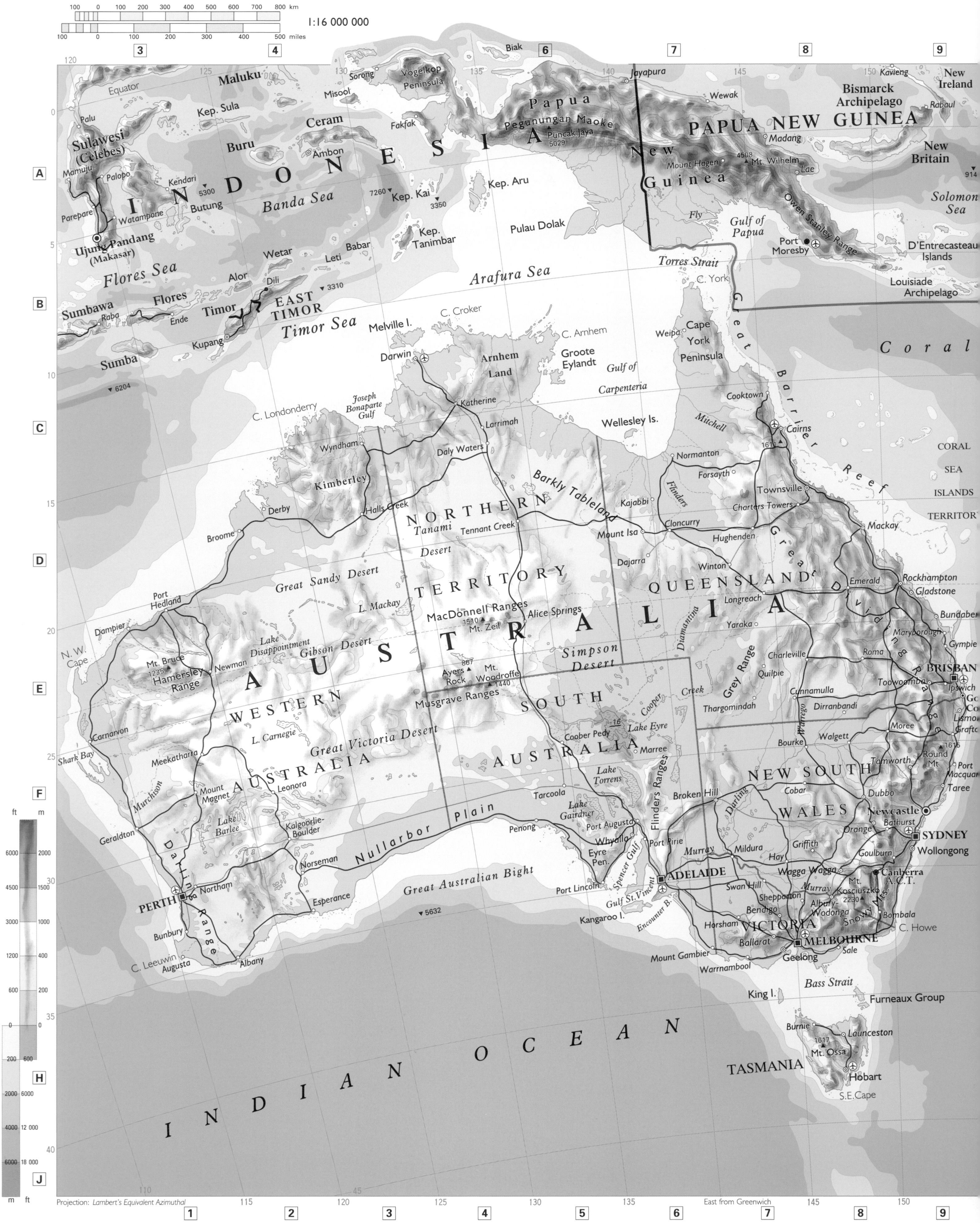

1:16 000 000
km
miles
Projection: Lambert's Equivalent Azimuthal
East from Greenwich
Equator
Maluku
Kep. Sula
Sulawesi (Celebes)
Palu
Mamuju
Palopo
Kendari
Parepare
Watampone
Ujung Pandang (Makasar)
Butung
Buru
Ceram
Ambon
Misool
Sorong
Vogelkop Peninsula
Fakfak
Biak
Jayapura
Papua
Pegunungan Maoke
Puncak Jaya
I N D O N E S I A
Banda Sea
Kep. Kai
Kep. Aru
Kep. Tanimbar
Pulau Dolak
Flores Sea
Wetar
Leti
Babar
Alor
Dili
EAST TIMOR
Timor
Flores
Ende
Sumbawa
Raba
Sumba
Kupang
Timor Sea
Arafura Sea
Wewak
PAPUA NEW GUINEA
Madang
Mount Hagen
Mt. Wilhelm
Lae
New Guinea
Fly
Gulf of Papua
Port Moresby
Owen Stanley Range
Bismarck Archipelago
Kavieng
New Ireland
Rabaul
New Britain
Solomon Sea
D'Entrecasteaux Islands
Louisiade Archipelago
Torres Strait
C. York
Cape York Peninsula
Weipa
Melville I.
C. Croker
C. Arnhem
Darwin
Arnhem Land
Groote Eylandt
Gulf of Carpentaria
Katherine
Larrimah
Joseph Bonaparte Gulf
C. Londonderry
Wyndham
Daly Waters
Wellesley Is.
Cooktown
Mitchell
Cairns
Normanton
Forsayth
Coral
Great Barrier Reef
CORAL SEA ISLANDS TERRITORY
Kimberley
Derby
Halls Creek
Broome
Barkly Tableland
NORTHERN TERRITORY
Tanami Desert
Tennant Creek
Kajabbi
Flinders
Townsville
Charters Towers
Cloncurry
Mount Isa
Hughenden
Mackay
Dajarra
Winton
Great Dividing Range
QUEENSLAND
Emerald
Rockhampton
Gladstone
Longreach
Bundaberg
Maryborough
Gympie
Yaraka
Diamantina
Great Sandy Desert
Port Hedland
L. Mackay
MacDonnell Ranges
Mt. Zeil
Alice Springs
Dampier
Lake Disappointment
Gibson Desert
N. W. Cape
Mt. Bruce
Hamersley Range
Newman
A U S T R A L I A
Ayers Rock
Mt. Woodroffe
Simpson Desert
Charleville
Roma
BRISBANE
Ipswich
Toowoomba
Grey Range
Quilpie
Cooper Creek
Cunnamulla
Dirranbandi
Thargomindah
Warrego
Musgrave Ranges
WESTERN AUSTRALIA
SOUTH AUSTRALIA
Lake Eyre
Carnarvon
L. Carnegie
Great Victoria Desert
Coober Pedy
Marree
Moree
Shark Bay
Meekatharra
Bourke
Walgett
Tamworth
Round Mt.
Port Macquarie
Lake Torrens
Flinders Ranges
NEW SOUTH WALES
Murchison
Mount Magnet
Leonora
Tarcoola
Broken Hill
Darling
Cobar
Dubbo
Taree
Lake Gairdner
Newcastle
Lake Barlee
Kalgoorlie-Boulder
Nullarbor Plain
Penong
Port Augusta
Whyalla
Port Pirie
Mildura
Orange
Bathurst
SYDNEY
Wollongong
Geraldton
Darling Range
Norseman
Eyre Pen.
Spencer Gulf
Murray
Hay
Griffith
Goulburn
Wagga Wagga
Great Australian Bight
ADELAIDE
Canberra
A.C.T.
Northam
PERTH
Esperance
Port Lincoln
Gulf St. Vincent
Swan Hill
Shepparton
Mt. Kosciuszko
Albury-Wodonga
Snowy Mts.
Bombala
Bendigo
Kangaroo I.
Encounter B.
Horsham
VICTORIA
C. Howe
Bunbury
Ballarat
MELBOURNE
Sale
C. Leeuwin
Augusta
Albany
Mount Gambier
Geelong
Warrnambool
Bass Strait
King I.
Furneaux Group
INDIAN OCEAN
Burnie
Launceston
Mt. Ossa
TASMANIA
Hobart
S.E.Cape

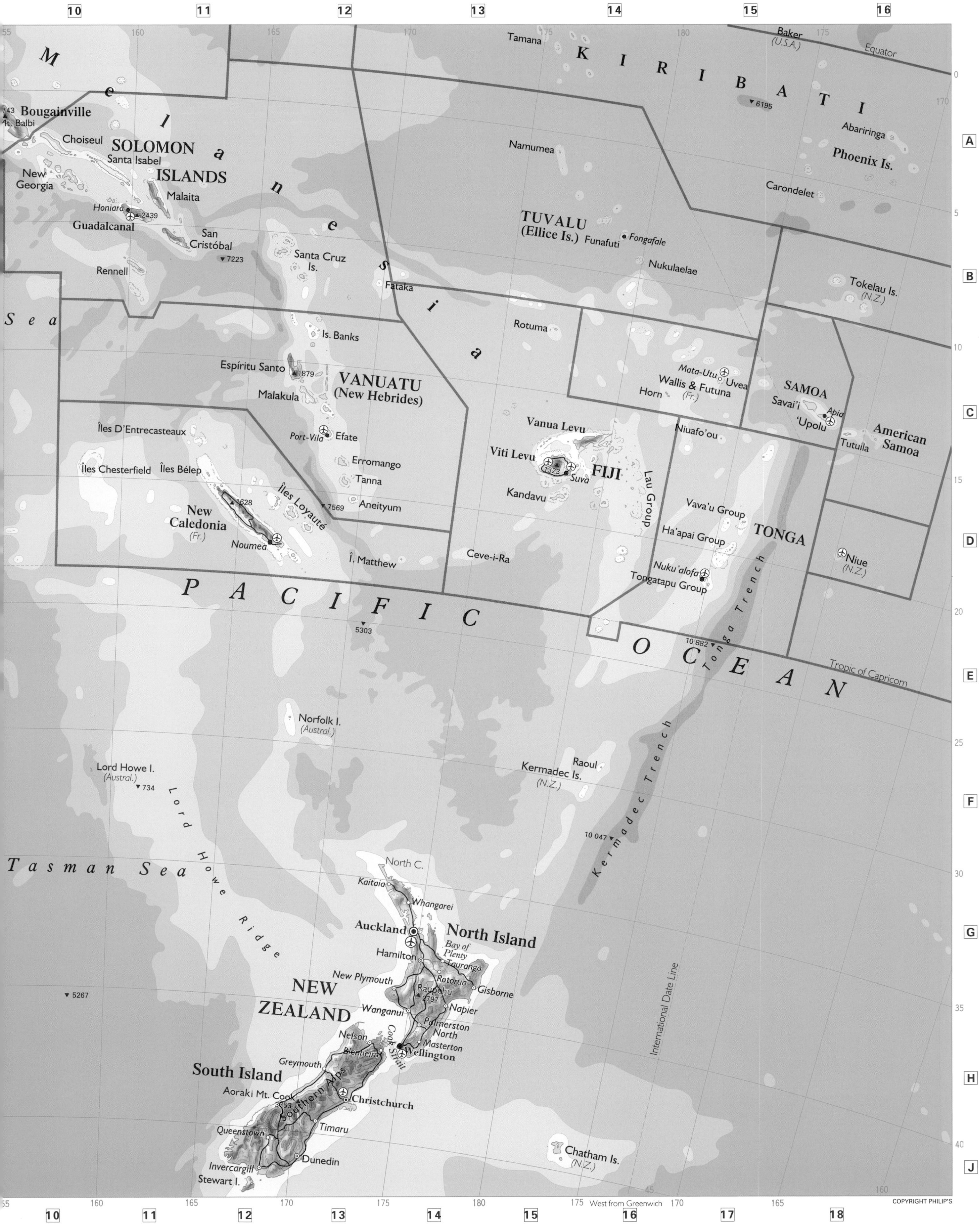

KIRIBATI
Tamana
Baker (U.S.A.)
Equator
Melanesia
Bougainville
Mt. Balbi
Choiseul
SOLOMON ISLANDS
Santa Isabel
New Georgia
Malaita
Honiara
2439
Guadalcanal
San Cristóbal
7223
Rennell
Santa Cruz Is.
Fataka
Namumea
6195
Abariringa
Phoenix Is.
Carondelet
TUVALU (Ellice Is.)
Funafuti
Fongafale
Nukulaelae
Tokelau Is. (N.Z.)
Rotuma
Is. Banks
Espíritu Santo
1879
VANUATU (New Hebrides)
Malakula
Port-Vila
Efate
Erromango
Tanna
Aneityum
7569
Îles D'Entrecasteaux
Îles Chesterfield
Îles Bélep
Îles Loyauté
1628
New Caledonia (Fr.)
Noumea
Î. Matthew
Mata-Utu
Uvea
Wallis & Futuna (Fr.)
Horn
SAMOA
Savai'i
Apia
'Upolu
American Samoa
Tutuila
Niuafo'ou
Vanua Levu
Viti Levu
1323
Suva
FIJI
Kandavu
Lau Group
Vava'u Group
Ha'apai Group
TONGA
Niue (N.Z.)
Ceve-i-Ra
Nuku'alofa
Tongatapu Group
Tonga Trench
10 882
Tropic of Capricorn
PACIFIC OCEAN
5303
Norfolk I. (Austral.)
Raoul
Kermadec Is. (N.Z.)
Lord Howe I. (Austral.)
734
Lord Howe Ridge
Kermadec Trench
10 047
Tasman Sea
North C.
Kaitaia
Whangarei
Auckland
North Island
Hamilton
Bay of Plenty
Tauranga
New Plymouth
Rotorua
Gisborne
Ruapehu
2797
NEW ZEALAND
Wanganui
Napier
Palmerston North
Masterton
Nelson
Blenheim
Cook Strait
Wellington
5267
Greymouth
South Island
Southern Alps
Aoraki Mt. Cook
3753
Christchurch
Timaru
Queenstown
Dunedin
Invercargill
Stewart I.
Chatham Is. (N.Z.)
International Date Line
West from Greenwich
COPYRIGHT PHILIP'S

50 0 50 100 150 200 250 300 km

1:6 400 000

50 0 50 100 150 200 miles

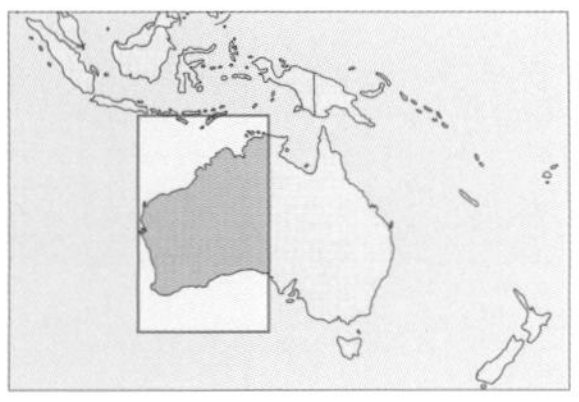

127

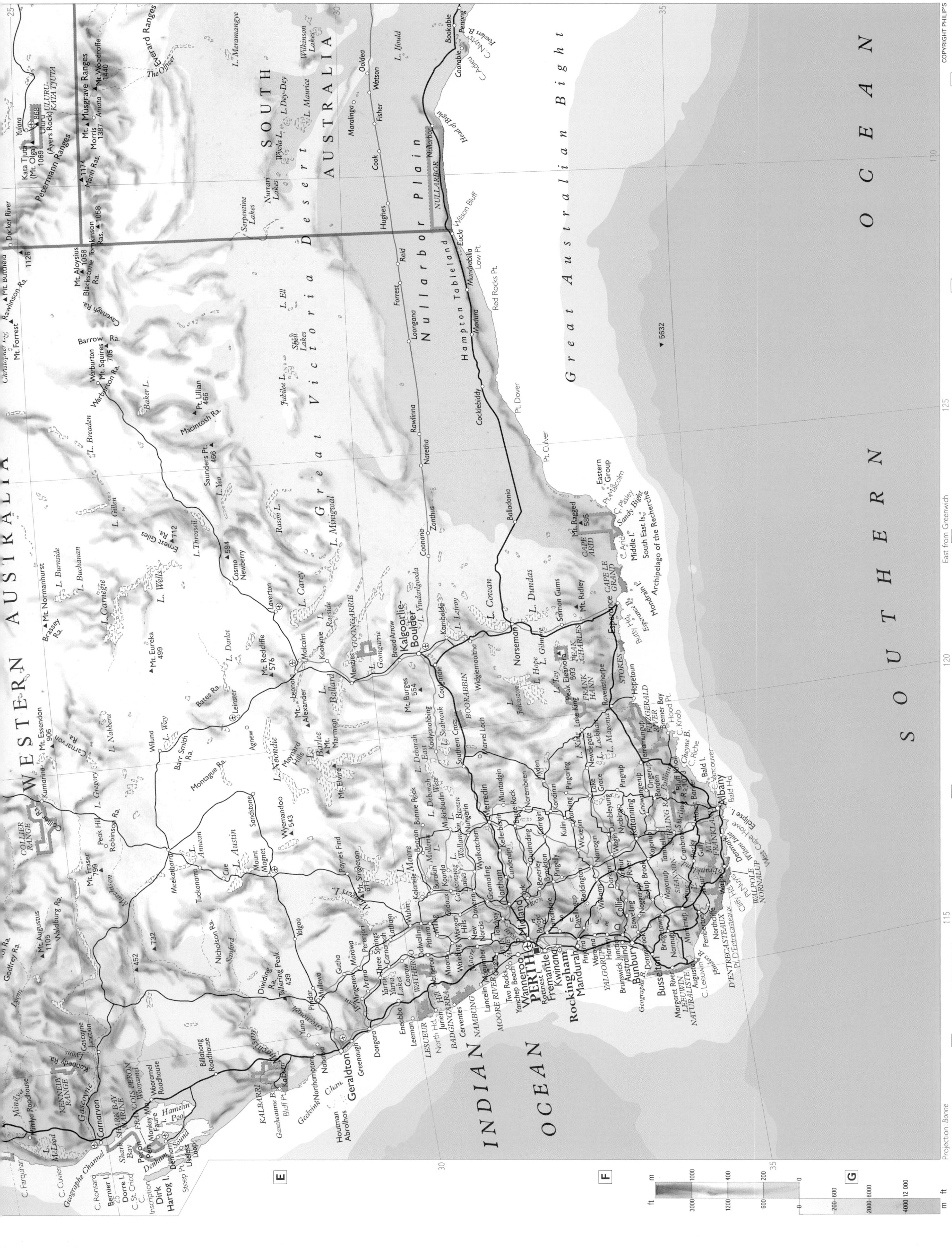
WESTERN AUSTRALIA
SOUTH AUSTRALIA
INDIAN OCEAN
SOUTHERN OCEAN
Great Australian Bight
Great Victoria Desert
Nullarbor Plain
Hampton Tableland
Petermann Ranges
Musgrave Ranges
Everard Ranges
PERTH
Fremantle
Rockingham
Mandurah
Bunbury
Busselton
Albany
Geraldton
Carnarvon
Kalgoorlie-Boulder
Norseman
Esperance
Hopetoun
Eucla
Cocklebiddy
Madura
Nullarbor
Penong
Kata Tjuta (Mt. Olga) 1069
Uluru (Ayers Rock) 863
Warburton
Laverton
Leonora
Menzies
Southern Cross
Merredin
Northam
Narrogin
Katanning
Kalbarri
Denham
Shark Bay
L. Carnegie
L. Wells
L. Barlee
L. Moore
L. Cowan
L. Dundas
Archipelago of the Recherche
Projection: Bonne
East from Greenwich
COPYRIGHT PHILIP'S
National Parks
m
ft
1000
400
200
0
3000
1200
600
0
200
2000
4000
600
6000
12 000

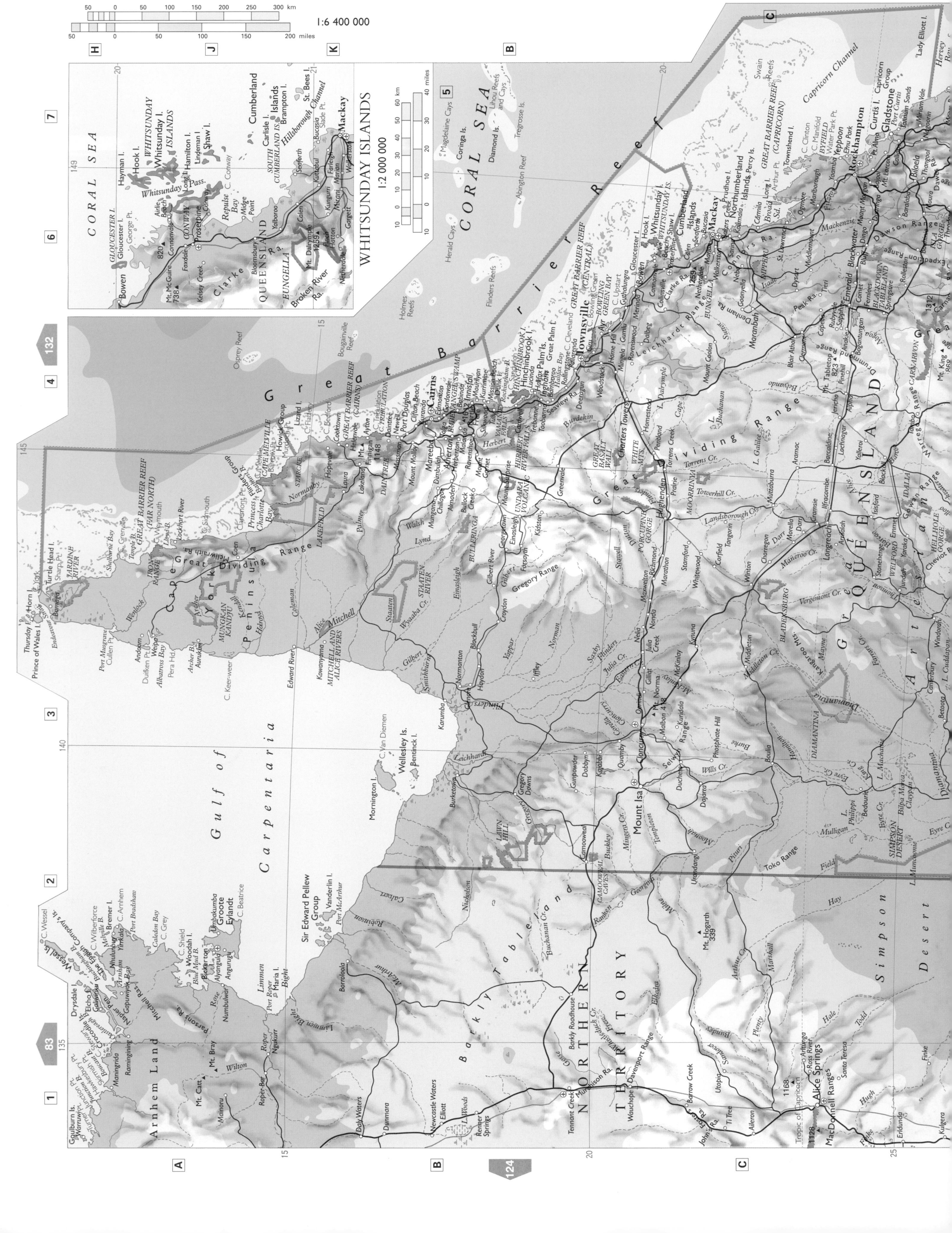
1:6 400 000
50 0 50 100 150 200 250 300 km
50 0 50 100 150 200 miles
WHITSUNDAY ISLANDS
1:2 000 000
CORAL SEA
Whitsunday I.
WHITSUNDAY ISLANDS
Hook I.
Hayman I.
Cumberland Islands
Brampton I.
Carlisle I.
Mackay
Proserpine
Bowen
Gloucester I.
Conway
Airlie Beach
Cannonvale
Shaw I.
Lindeman I.
Hamilton I.
Long I.
Repulse Bay
Mt. Dalrymple 1259
Eungella
Broken River Ra.
Nebo
St. Bees I.
Slade Pt.
Bucasia
Seaforth
Great Barrier Reef
GREAT BARRIER REEF (CAIRNS)
GREAT BARRIER REEF (CENTRAL)
GREAT BARRIER REEF (CAPRICORN)
GREAT BARRIER REEF (FAR NORTH)
Capricorn Channel
Swain Reefs
Magdelaine Cays
Coringa Is.
Lihou Reefs and Cays
Tregrosse Is.
Diamond Is.
Willis Is.
Abington Reef
Herald Cays
Flinders Reefs
Holmes Reefs
Bougainville Reef
Osprey Reef
Townsville
Cairns
Mackay
Rockhampton
Gladstone
Yeppoon
Emerald
Bowen
Ayr
Home Hill
Charters Towers
Hughenden
Innisfail
Tully
Cardwell
Ingham
Hinchinbrook I.
Palm Is.
Magnetic I.
Port Douglas
Mossman
Cooktown
Mareeba
Atherton
Herberton
Ravenshoe
Lizard I.
C. Melville
Princess Charlotte Bay
Cape York Peninsula
Great Dividing Range
Turtle Head I.
Thursday I.
Horn I.
Prince of Wales I.
Bamaga
Weipa
Aurukun
Coen
Laura
Lakeland
Gulf of Carpentaria
Wellesley Is.
Mornington I.
Bentinck I.
Sir Edward Pellew Group
Vanderlin I.
Groote Eylandt
Karumba
Normanton
Croydon
Burketown
Mount Isa
Cloncurry
Julia Creek
Richmond
Winton
Longreach
Barcaldine
Blackall
Jericho
Alpha
Clermont
Moranbah
Dysart
Middlemount
Blackwater
Biloela
Springsure
Boulia
Bedourie
Camooweal
Doomadgee
Borroloola
Roper Bar
Ngukurr
Numbulwar
Nhulunbuy
Arnhem Land
Wessel Is.
Elcho I.
Drysdale I.
Maningrida
Ramingining
Mainoru
Daly Waters
Dunmarra
Newcastle Waters
Elliott
Renner Springs
Tennant Creek
Barrow Creek
Ti Tree
Alice Springs
MacDonnell Ranges
Tropic of Capricorn
Barkly Tableland
Barkly Roadhouse
NORTHERN TERRITORY
QUEENSLAND
Simpson Desert
Mt. Hogarth 339
Davenport Range
Mitchell
Staaten
Gilbert
Flinders
Diamantina
Georgina
Gregory Range
Selwyn Range
Leichhardt Range
Drummond Range
Dawson Range
Great Artesian Basin
Lake Eyre
Hay
Plenty
Sandover
Todd
Finke
Kulgera
Erldunda
Curtis I.
Heron I.
Lady Elliott I.
Hervey Bay
Fraser I.
A B C
1 2 3 4 5 6 7
H J K
83 124 132
135 140 145 15 20 25

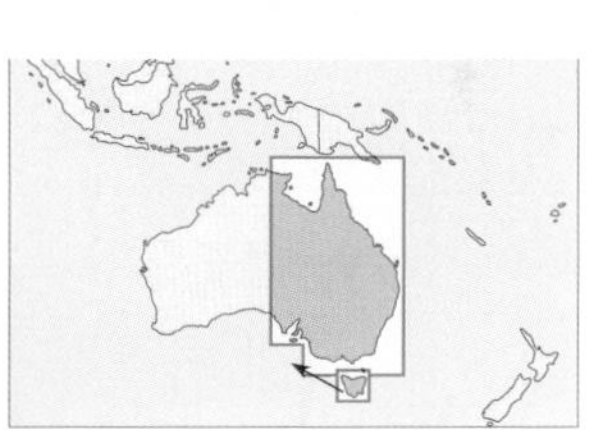

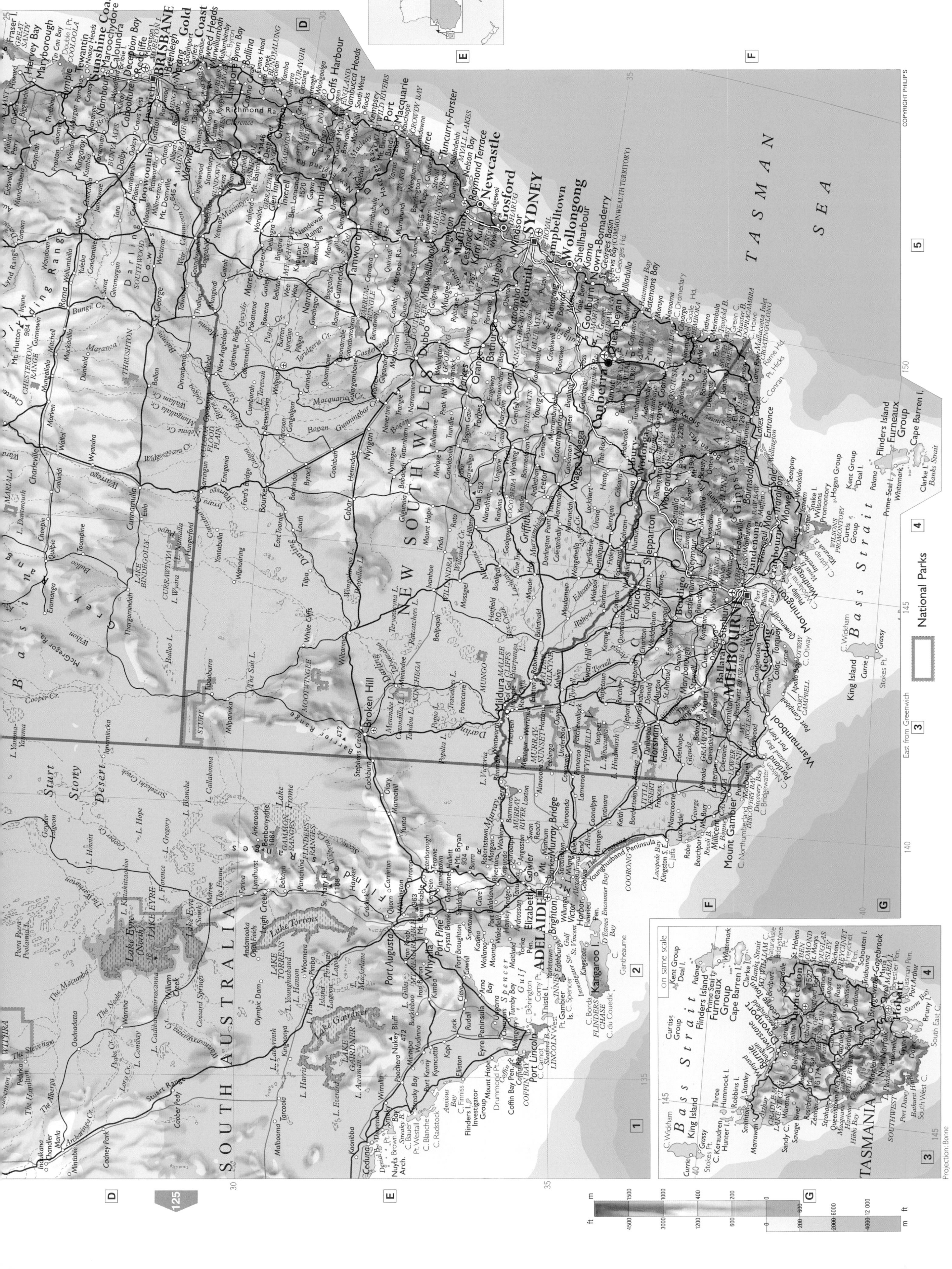
SOUTH AUSTRALIA
NEW SOUTH WALES
VICTORIA
TASMANIA
TASMAN SEA
Bass Strait
BRISBANE
SYDNEY
Canberra
MELBOURNE
ADELAIDE
Hobart
Newcastle
Wollongong
Gold Coast
Sunshine Coast
Toowoomba
Geelong
Ballarat
Bendigo
Wagga Wagga
Broken Hill
Mildura
Port Augusta
Port Pirie
Whyalla
Port Lincoln
Mount Gambier
Launceston
Devonport
Burnie
Kangaroo I.
King Island
Flinders Island
Furneaux Group
Cape Barren I.
Lake Eyre (North)
Lake Eyre (South)
Lake Torrens
Lake Frome
Lake Gairdner
Spencer Gulf
Sturt Stony Desert
Great Dividing Range
Grey Range
Darling
Murray
AUSTRALIAN CAPITAL TERRITORY
National Parks
on same scale
COPYRIGHT PHILIP'S
East from Greenwich
Projection: Bonne
125
m
ft
1500
1000
400
200
0
200
2000
4000
4500
3000
1200
600
0
600
6000
12 000

20 0 20 40 60 80 100 120 140 160 km

1:3 200 000

20 0 20 40 60 80 100 miles

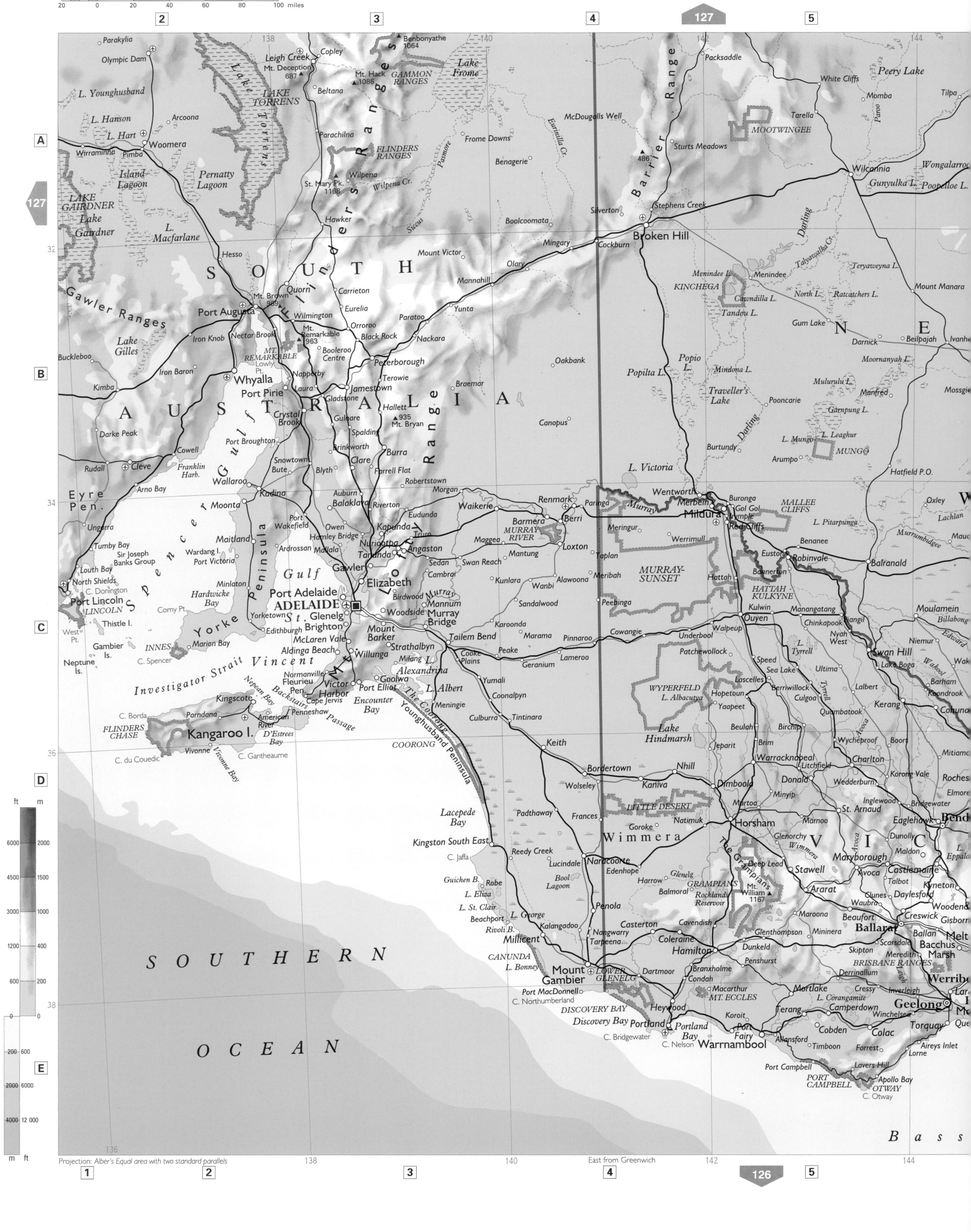

Projection: Alber's Equal area with two standard parallels

East from Greenwich

6 7 8 9 10

A
B
C
D
E
146
148
150
152
32
34
36
38
East from Greenwich
Louth
Darling
Curraweena
Byrock
Carinda
Bogan
Marra Cr.
Marthaguy Creek
Macquarie
Quambone
Teridgerie Cr.
Gwabegar
Bohena Cr.
Turrawan
Barraba
Black Mountain
Coffs Harbour
Dorrigo
Sawtell
Round Mt. 1610
Kingstown
Uralla
Armidale
Bellingen
NEW ENGLAND
Urunga
Nambucca Heads
Macksville
Scotts Head
Upper Manilla
Manilla
Boggabri
L. Keepit
Namoi
Bendemeer
OXLEY WILD RIVERS
Gunnedah
Peel
Attunga
Woolbrook
Walcha
South West Rocks
Coolabah
Girilambone
Coonamble
Baradine
Combara
WARRUMBUNGLE
Curlewis
Kootingal
Tamworth
Liverpool Plains
Hastings Range
Mt. Banda Banda 1263
WERRIKIMBEE
Kempsey
Crescent Head
Cobar
Hermidale
Nyngan
Canbelego
Barnato
Gulargambone
Coonabarabran
Ulamambri
Currabubula
Werris Creek
Armatree
Binnaway
Castlereagh
Premer
Caroona
Quirindi
Nowendoc
Wauchope
Yarras
Port Macquarie
Collie
Warren
Gilgandra
Willow Tree
Comboyne
Elands
Kendall
Bonny Hills
Crowl Creek
Nevertire
Mendooran
Merrygoen
Coolah
Liverpool Range
Murrurundi
WOKO
Barnard
Eumungerie
Dunedoo
Barrington Tops 1555
Manning
Wingham
Lansdowne
CROWDY BAY
Taree
Harrington
Nymagee
Trangie
Brocklehurst
Talbragar
GOULBURN RIVER
Cassilis
Merriwa
Scone
Aberdeen
Gloucester
Old Bar
Tottenham
Bobadah
Narromine
Minore
Dubbo
Geurie
Gungal
Muswellbrook
BARRINGTON TOPS
Stratford
Stroud Road
Tuncurry
Forster
Gilgunnia
Tomingley
Gulgong
Denman
Baerami
Ravensworth
Yathong
Tullamore
Wellington
Mudgee
Lue
Singleton
Paterson
Dungog
Bulahdelah
MYALL LAKES
Melrose
Mount Hope
Peak Hill
Trundle
GOOBANG
Lake Burrendong
L. Windamere
Rylstone
Hunter Range
Branxton
Karuah
Raymond Terrace
Hawks Nest
Conoble
Trida
Matakana
Gunebang
Condobolin
Cumnock
Coricudgy 1257
Kandos
Cessnock
Maitland
Nelson Bay
Thornton-Beresfield
Roto
Willandra Creek
WILLANDRA
Ootha
Bogan Gate
Parkes
Molong
Eurchareena
Capertree
Putty
Kurri Kurri
Wallsend
Newcastle
Toronto
WOLLEMI
Lake Cargelligo
Lachlan
Manildra
Orange
Cullen Bullen
Portland
YENGO
Morisset
Belmont
Swansea
552 Ural
Hillston
Burcher
Forbes
Eugowra
Bathurst
Millthorpe
Lithgow
Blue Mts.
Colo
Wyong
DHARUG
Budgewoi
Gosford
The Entrance
Marrowie Cr.
Naradhan
L. Cowal
Ungarie
Canowindra
Blayney
Wallerawang
Kurrajong
Woy Woy
Kikoira
Marsden
Carcoar
Oberon
Richmond
Windsor
MARRA MARRA
KU-RING-GAI CHASE
Merriwagga
Rankins Springs
Caragabal
Cowra
Woodstock
KANANGRA-BOYD
Katoomba
Penrith
Hornsby
Booligal
Goolgowi
West Wyalong
Grenfell
L. Wyangala
Parramatta
Fairfield
Manly
Quandialla
WEDDIN MTS.
Lake Burragorang
BLUE MTS.
Liverpool
SYDNEY
COCOPARRA
Barellan
Barmedman
Koorawatha
Camden
Sutherland
The Oaks
Campbelltown
Griffith
Hanwood
Yenda
Mirrool
Ardlethan
Young
NATTAI
Picton
ROYAL
Helensburgh
Willbriggie
Leeton
Yanco
Temora
Boorowa
Crookwell
Taralga
Mittagong
Bargo
Bulli
Wollongong
Darlington Point
Cootamundra
Murrumburrah
Harden
Galong
Binalong
Cullarin Range
Great Dividing Range
Moss Vale
Bowral
Port Kembla
Shellharbour
Narrandera
Ganmain
Bethungra
TARLO RIVER
Goulburn
Bundanoon
Kiama
Coleambally
Morundah
Coolamon
Junee
Yass
Burrinjuck Res.
Murrumbateman
Marulan
Berry
BUDDEROO
Gerringong
Kywong
Wagga Wagga
Murrumbidgee
MORTON
Nowra
Bomaderry
Culburra
Wanganella
Yanco Cr.
Bundure
L. Urana
Urana
Lockhart
Gundagai
L. George
Shoalhaven
St. Georges Basin
Huskisson
Conargo
The Rock
Tarcutta
Adelong
Tumut
AUSTRALIAN CAPITAL TERRITORY
Bungendore
Sussex Inlet
Jervis Bay (Commonwealth Territory)
BUDAWANG
Deniliquin
Jerilderie
Humula
Canberra
Queanbeyan
Milton
St. Georges Hd.
Ulladulla
Finley
Berrigan
Oaklands
Rand
Henty
Culcairn
Batlow
Royalla
Braidwood
Tocumwal
Walla Walla
Holbrook
Tumbarumba
Bimberi Pk. 1910
Captains Flat
NAMADGI
Majors Creek
Mathoura
Cobram
Batemans Bay
Nathalia
Mulwala
Yarrawonga
Corowa
Howlong
Gerogery
BURROWA PINE MT.
Walwa
KOSCIUSKO
Adaminaby
Gourock Ra
Mossy Point
DEUA
Barnes
Echuca
Numurkah
Katamatite
Rutherglen
Chiltern
Albury-Wodonga
L. Hume
Cudgewa
Bredbo
Moruya
Kyabram
Dookie
Wangaratta
Yackandandah
Tallangatta
Corryong
Mt. Jagungal 2060
L. Eucumbene
Tuross Head
Dalmeny
Tatura
Shepparton
Mooroopna
Beechworth
Everton
Mt. Benambra 1476
Cooma
Berridale
Rock Flat
Narooma
WADBILLIGA
Montague I.
C. Dromedary
TASMAN SEA
Mokoan
Glenrowan
Myrtleford
Perisher Valley
Jindabyne
Snowy
Cobargo
Bermagui
Violet Town
Benalla
MT. BUFFALO
Dartmouth Res.
Mt. Kosciuszko 2230
Thredbo
Nimmitabel
Goalen Hd.
Euroa
Bright
Mt. Bogong 1986
ALPINE
BIMBOKA
Bega
Nagambie
Whitfield
Mount Beauty
Snowy Mts.
SOUTH EAST FORESTS
Tathra
Heathcote
Seymour
Bonnie Doon
Mansfield
1836 Mt. Cobberas
Cathcart
Candelo
Merimbula
Tallarook
FRASER
L. Eildon
Mt. Buller 1804
Omeo
Bowen Mts.
Bombala
Alexandra
Delegate
Eden
Twofold Bay
BEN BOYD
Yea
Eildon
Swifts Creek
Bonang
Green C.
Disaster B.
KINGLAKE
Glenburn
YARRA RANGES
ALPINE
Mt. Tambontha 1640
MITCHELL RIVER
SNOWY RIVER
Mt. Ellery 1291
ERRINUNDRA
COOPRACAMBRA
Craigieburn
Great Dividing Range
Buchan
Club Terrace
Genoa
C. Howe
Healesville
Warburton
Cobbannah
Bruthen
Nowa Nowa
Orbost
Cann River
Mallacoota
Mallacoota Inlet
BAW BAW
Gippsland
Bairnsdale
CROAJINGOLONG
MELBOURNE
Dandenong
Walhalla
Maffra
Heyfield
Stratford
THE LAKES
Lakes Entrance
C. Conran
Pt. Hicks
Rame Hd.
Port Phillip Bay
Chelsea
Pakenham
Drouin
Moe
Sale
L. Wellington
Koo-wee-rup
Warragul
Trafalgar
Traralgon
Morwell
Seaspray
The Ninety Mile Beach
Hastings
French I.
Mirboo North
Churchill
Korumburra
San Remo
Cowes
Phillip I.
C. Woolamai
Leongatha
Meeniyan
Woodside
Wonthaggi
Inverloch
Foster
Toora
Yarram
Port Albert
Welshpool
Venus B.
Corner Inlet
Snake I.
C. Liptrap
Waratah B.
Wilsons Promontory
WILSONS PROMONTORY
Strait
South East Pt.
Hogan Group

6 7 8 9 10

National Parks

1:2 800 000

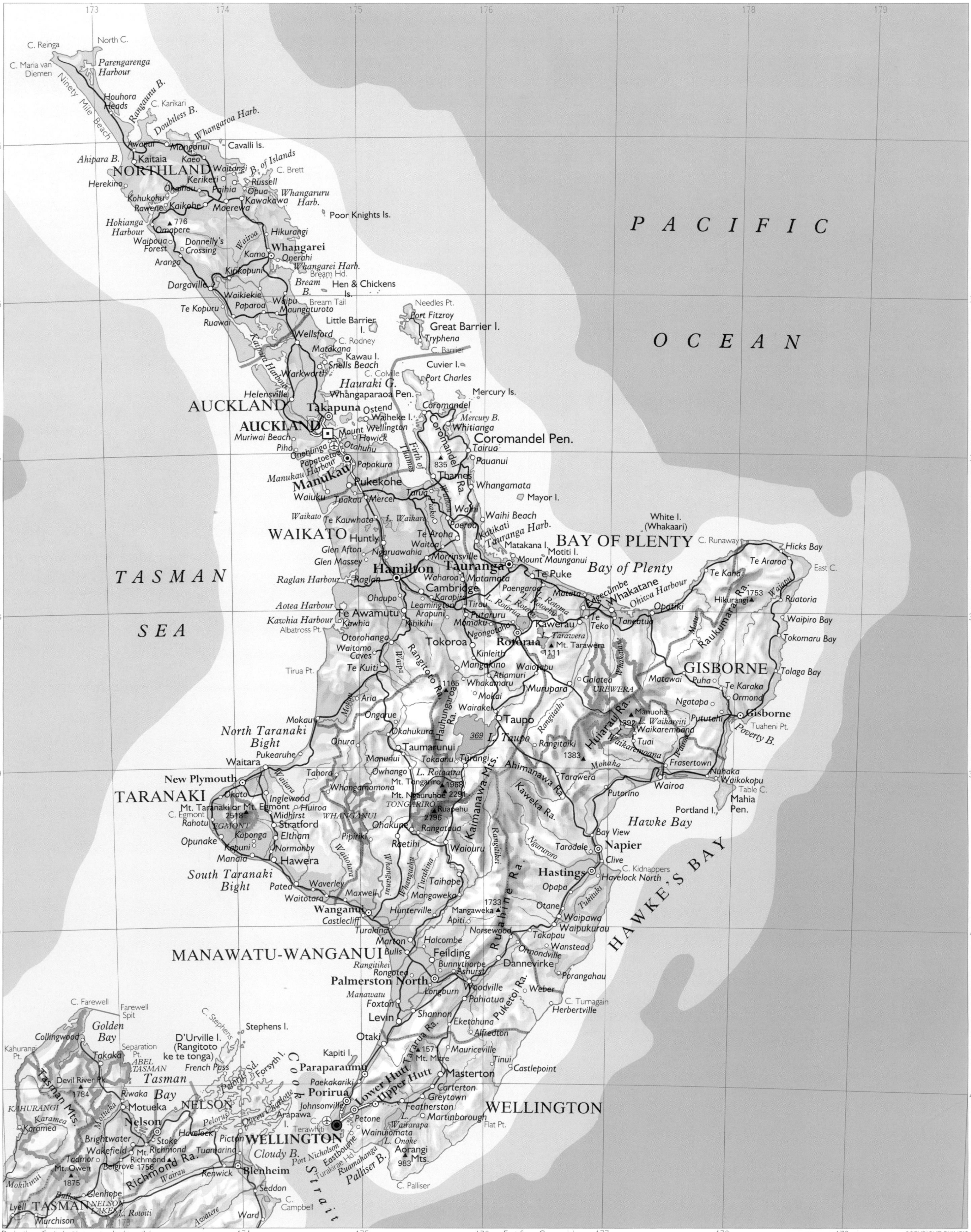

Projection: Conical with two standard parallels

COPYRIGHT PHILIP'S

131

National Parks

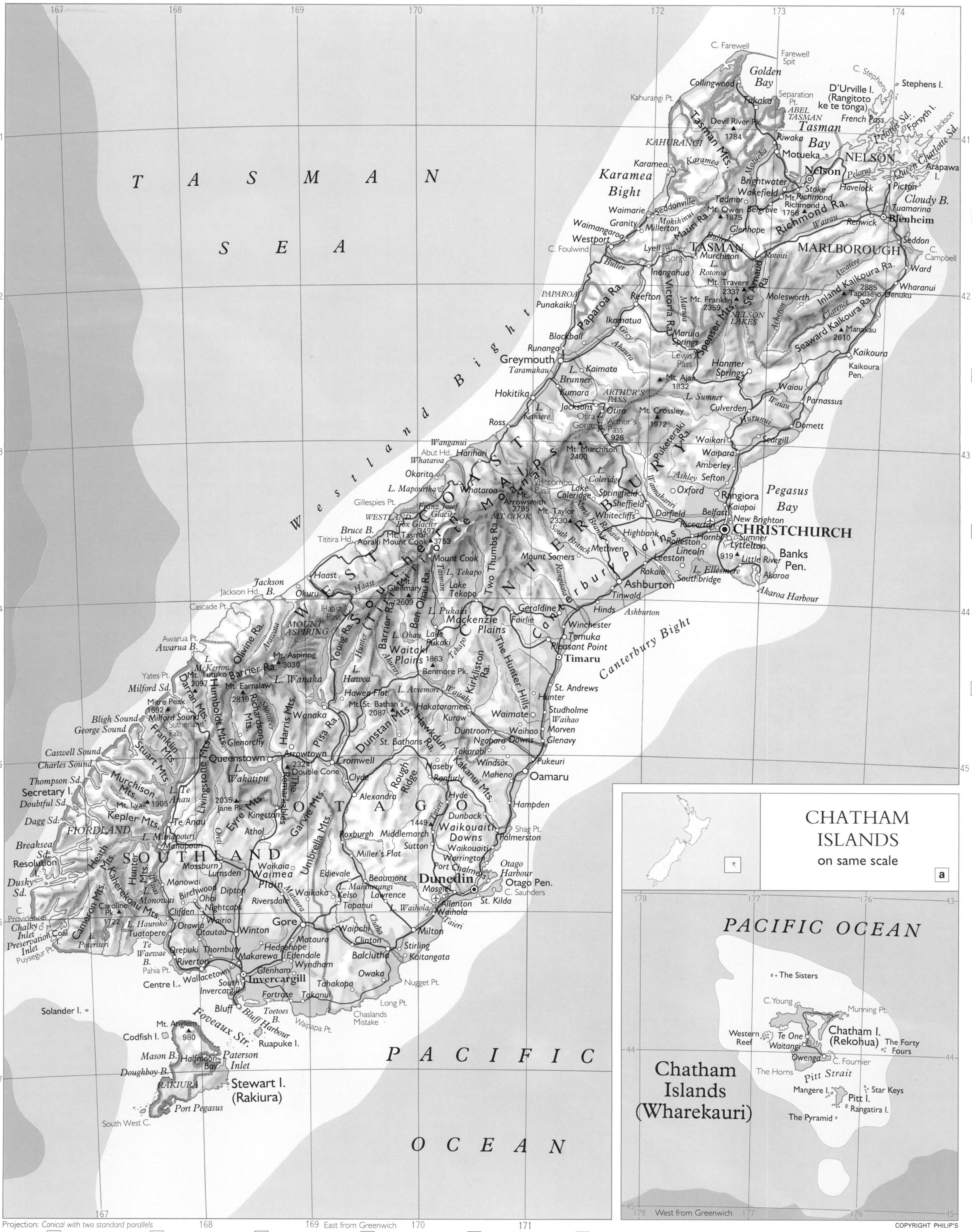
1:2 800 000
0 20 40 60 80 100 120 140 km
10 0 20 40 60 80 100 miles
130
1 2 3 4 5 6 7 8 9
A B C D E F G H
TASMAN SEA
Westland Bight
Karamea Bight
C. Farewell
Farewell Spit
Golden Bay
Collingwood
Kahurangi Pt.
Takaka
Separation Pt.
ABEL TASMAN
Tasman Bay
Devil River Pk. 1784
KAHURANGI
Tasman Mts.
Karamea
Riwaka
Motueka
Nelson
NELSON
C. Stephens
Stephens I.
D'Urville I. (Rangitoto ke te tonga)
French Pass
Pelorus Sd.
Forsyth I.
C. Jackson
Queen Charlotte Sd.
Arapawa I.
Picton
Havelock
Cloudy B.
Tuamarina
Blenheim
Renwick
Brightwater
Wakefield
Stoke
Mt. Richmond
Richmond 1756
Richmond Ra.
Tadmor
Belgrove
Mt. Owen 1875
Glenhope
Seddonville
Mokihinui
Millerton
Granity
Waimarie
Waimangaroa
Westport
C. Foulwind
Lyell
Buller Gorge
Matiri Ra.
TASMAN
Murchison
MARLBOROUGH
Rotoiti
Seddon
C. Campbell
Ward
Inangahua
L. Rotoroa
Mt. Travers 2337
Mt. Franklin 2359
NELSON LAKES
St. Arnaud Ra.
Molesworth
Inland Kaikoura Ra.
2885 Tapuae-o-Uenuku
Wharanui
Seaward Kaikoura Ra.
Manakau 2610
Kaikoura
Kaikoura Pen.
PAPAROA
Punakaiki
Paparoa Ra.
Reefton
Victoria Ra.
Spenser Mts.
Ikamatua
Blackball
Runanga
Greymouth
Maruia Springs
Lewis Pass
Hanmer Springs
Taramakau
L. Brunner
Kaimata
Kumara
Mt. Ajax 1832
Hokitika
ARTHUR'S PASS
Jacksons
Otira
Otira Gorge
Arthur's Pass 926
Mt. Crossley 1972
L. Sumner
Culverden
Waiau
Parnassus
Hurunui
Domett
Ross
L. Kaniere
Puketeraki Ra.
Waikari
Scargill
Wanganui
Abut Hd.
Harihari
Whataroa
Mt. Murchison 2400
Waipara
Amberley
Okarito
Ashley
Sefton
L. Mapourika
Whitcombe Pass
L. Coleridge
Lake Coleridge
Springfield
Oxford
Rangiora
Kaiapoi
Pegasus Bay
Gillespies Pt.
Franz Josef Glacier
Fox Glacier
WESTLAND
Mt. Arrowsmith 2795
Sheffield
Whitecliffs
Darfield
Belfast
New Brighton
CHRISTCHURCH
Bruce B.
Titira Hd.
Mt. Tasman 3497
Aoraki Mount Cook 3753
MT. COOK
Mt. Taylor 2330
Highbank
Riccarton
Hornby
Sumner
Lyttelton
Banks Pen.
Methven
Rolleston
Lincoln
919
Little River
Akaroa
Mount Cook
Mount Somers
Leeston
L. Ellesmere
Southbridge
Haast
L. Tekapo
Lake Tekapo
Two Thumbs Ra.
Rakaia
Ashburton
Tinwald
Akaroa Harbour
Jackson B.
Jackson Hd.
Okuru
Mt. Glenmary 2609
Ben Ohau Ra.
L. Pukaki
Mackenzie Plains
Geraldine
Fairlie
Hinds
Ashburton
Cascade Pt.
Haast Pass
MOUNT ASPIRING
Southern Alps
Winchester
Temuka
Pleasant Point
Timaru
Canterbury Plains
Canterbury Bight
CANTERBURY
WEST COAST
Awarua Pt.
Awarua B.
Olivine Ra.
Mt. Aspiring 3030
L. Ohau
Lake Pukaki
Waitaki Plains
1863
Benmore Pk.
Kirkliston Ra.
The Hunter Hills
Yates Pt.
Milford Sd.
L. McKerrow
Mt. Tutuko 2097
Barrier Ra.
Mt. Earnslaw 2819
L. Wanaka
L. Hawea
Hawea Flat
L. Aviemore
Waitaki
St. Andrews
Hunter
Darran Mts.
Humboldt Mts.
Richardson Mts.
Mitre Peak 1692
Milford Sound
Sutherland Falls
Bligh Sound
George Sound
Franklin Mts.
Harris Mts.
Wanaka
Mt. St. Bathan's 2087
Hakataramea
Kurow
Waimate
Studholme
Waihao
Morven
Glenavy
Duntroon
Ngapara
Glenorchy
Pisa Ra.
Dunstan Mts.
Hawkdun Ra.
St. Bathans
Tokarahi
Caswell Sound
Charles Sound
Stuart Mts.
Queenstown
Arrowtown
2324
Cromwell
Windsor
Maheno
Pukeuri
Oamaru
Thompson Sd.
Secretary I.
Doubtful Sd.
Murchison Mts.
Mt. Lyall 1905
L. Te Anau
Livingstone Mts.
L. Wakatipu
Double Cone
The Remarkables
Clyde
Rough Ridge
Naseby
Ranfurly
Kakanui Mts.
Alexandra
Hyde
Hampden
Dagg Sd.
Kepler Mts.
Te Anau
2035 Jane Pk.
Eyre Mts.
Kingston
Garvie Mts.
OTAGO
1449
Dunback
Shag Pt.
Palmerston
FIORDLAND
L. Manapouri
Oreti
Athol
Umbrella Mts.
Roxburgh
Middlemarch
Waikouaiti Downs
Waikouaiti
Breaksea Sd.
Resolution I.
Dusky Sd.
Heath Mts.
Hunter Mts.
SOUTHLAND
Manapouri
Mossburn
Lumsden
Waikaia
Waimea Plain
Miller's Flat
Sutton
Warrington
Port Chalmers
Otago Harbour
Otago Pen.
C. Saunders
Kaherekoau Mts.
Monowai
Birchwood
Dipton
Edievale
Beaumont
Dunedin
Mosgiel
St. Kilda
Caroline Pk. 1722
Ohai
Nightcaps
Riversdale
Waikaka
L. Mahinerangi
Kelso
Lawrence
Tapanui
L. Waihola
Allanton
Waihola
C. Providence
Chalky Inlet
Preservation Inlet
Coal I.
Puysegur Pt.
Cameron Mts.
L. Hauroko
Clifden
Orawia
Wairio
Otautau
Winton
Gore
Waipahi
Clutha
Clinton
Milton
Taieri
L. Poteriteri
Tuatapere
Te Waewae B.
Orepuki
Thornbury
Riverton
Hedgehope
Makarewa
Mataura
Edendale
Wyndham
Stirling
Kaitangata
Balclutha
Pahia Pt.
Centre I.
Wallacetown
South Invercargill
Invercargill
Glenham
Tahakopa
Owaka
Nugget Pt.
Fortrose
Tokanui
Long Pt.
Chaslands Mistake
Solander I.
Bluff
Bluff Harbour
Toetoes B.
Waipapa Pt.
Foveaux Str.
Ruapuke I.
Mt. Anglem 980
Codfish I.
Mason B.
Halfmoon Bay
Paterson Inlet
Doughboy B.
RAKIURA
Stewart I. (Rakiura)
Port Pegasus
South West C.
PACIFIC OCEAN
Projection: Conical with two standard parallels
East from Greenwich
CHATHAM ISLANDS on same scale
a
PACIFIC OCEAN
The Sisters
C. Young
Murning Pt.
Western Reef
Te One
Waitangi
Chatham I. (Rekohua)
The Forty Fours
Owenga
C. Fournier
The Horns
Pitt Strait
Mangere I.
Star Keys
Pitt I.
Rangatira I.
The Pyramid
Chatham Islands (Wharekauri)
West from Greenwich
COPYRIGHT PHILIP'S

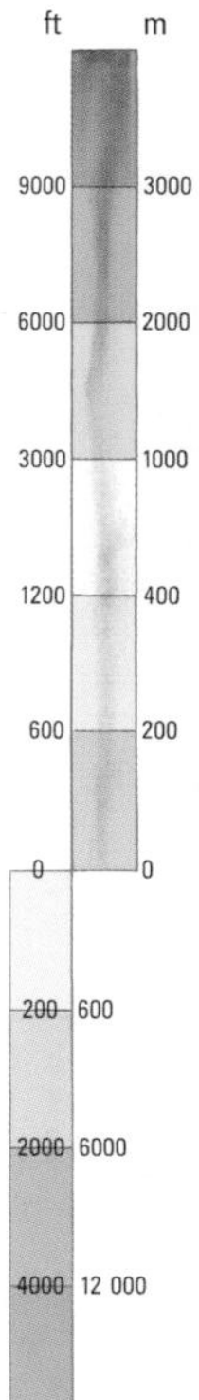
ft m
9000 3000
6000 2000
3000 1000
1200 400
600 200
0 0
200 600
2000 6000
4000 12 000
m ft

National Parks

50 0 50 100 150 200 km

1:5 200 000

50 0 50 100 150 miles

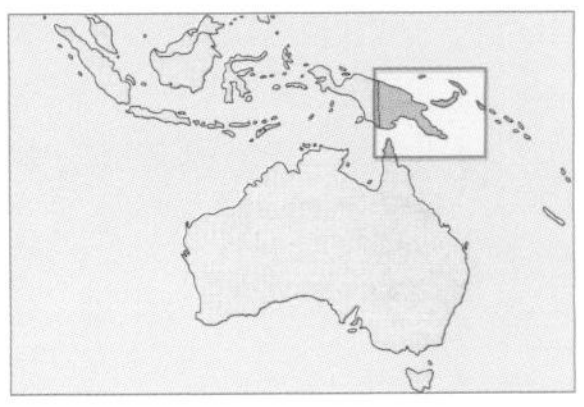

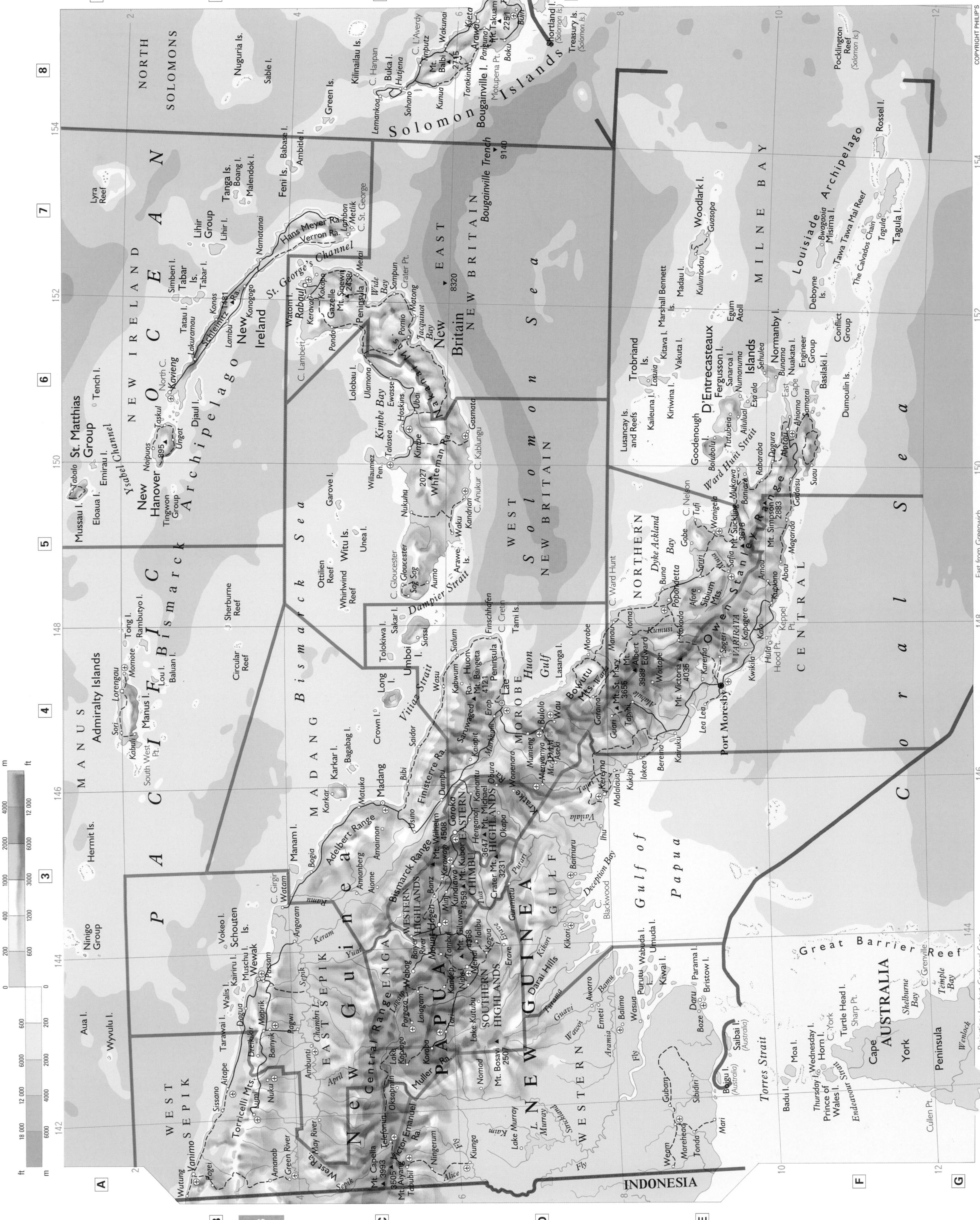

83

126

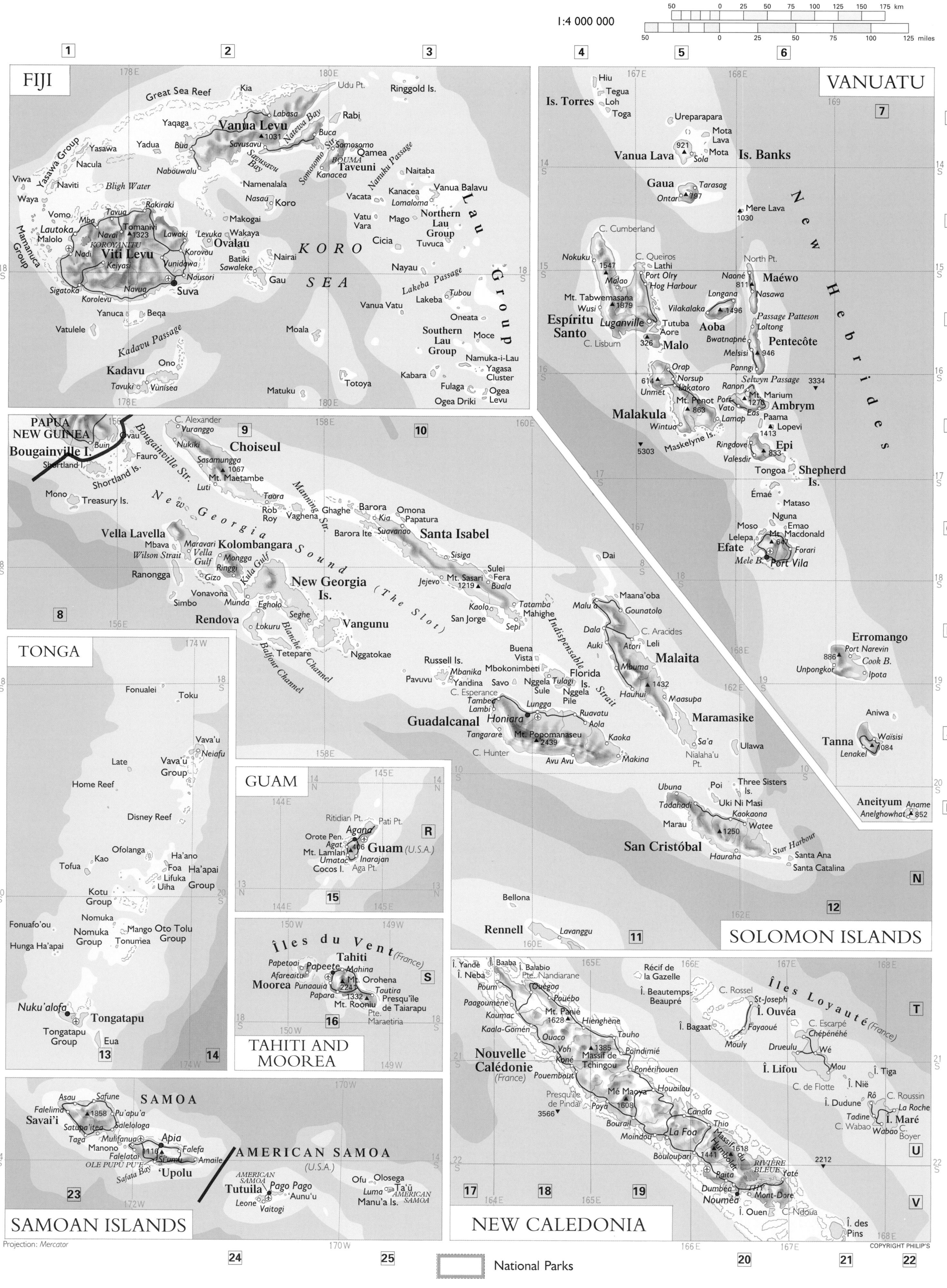
1:4 000 000
km
miles
FIJI
Great Sea Reef
Vanua Levu
Taveuni
Viti Levu
Suva
Lautoka
Nadi
Ovalau
Koro
KORO SEA
Lau Group
Northern Lau Group
Southern Lau Group
Kadavu
Kadavu Passage
Yasawa Group
Mamanuca Group
Bligh Water
Nanuku Passage
Lakeba Passage
VANUATU
Is. Torres
Is. Banks
Vanua Lava
Gaua
Espíritu Santo
Luganville
Maéwo
Aoba
Pentecôte
Malakula
Ambrym
Epi
Shepherd Is.
Efate
Port Vila
Erromango
Tanna
Aneityum
New Hebrides
PAPUA NEW GUINEA
Bougainville I.
Choiseul
Shortland Is.
Treasury Is.
Vella Lavella
Kolombangara
New Georgia Is.
Rendova
Vangunu
New Georgia Sound (The Slot)
Santa Isabel
Malaita
Florida Is.
Guadalcanal
Honiara
Mt. Popomanaseu 2439
Indispensable Strait
Maramasike
San Cristóbal
Rennell
Bellona
SOLOMON ISLANDS
TONGA
Vava'u Group
Ha'apai Group
Nuku'alofa
Tongatapu
Tongatapu Group
GUAM
Agana
Guam (U.S.A.)
TAHITI AND MOOREA
Îles du Vent (France)
Tahiti
Papeete
Moorea
SAMOAN ISLANDS
SAMOA
Savai'i
Apia
'Upolu
AMERICAN SAMOA (U.S.A.)
Tutuila
Pago Pago
Manu'a Is.
NEW CALEDONIA
Nouvelle Calédonie (France)
Nouméa
Îles Loyauté (France)
Î. Ouvéa
Î. Lifou
Î. Maré
Î. des Pins
Projection: Mercator
COPYRIGHT PHILIP'S
National Parks

 Equatorial Scale 1:43 200 000

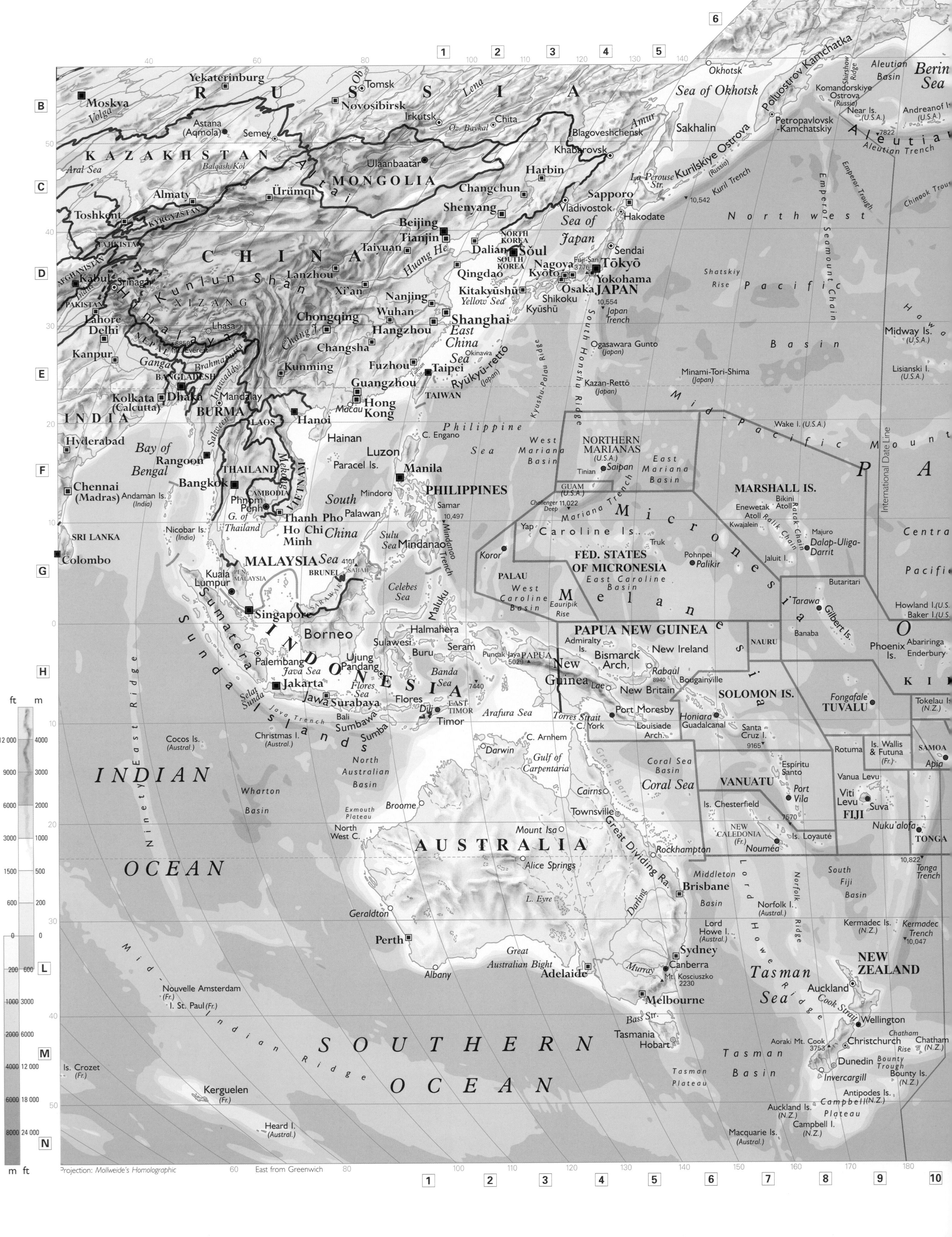
RUSSIA
Yekaterinburg
Moskva
Volga
Tomsk
Ob
Novosibirsk
Lena
Irkutsk
Oz. Baykal
Chita
Astana (Aqmola)
Semey
KAZAKHSTAN
Aral Sea
Balqash Köl
Altai
Ulaanbaatar
MONGOLIA
Blagoveshchensk
Amur
Khabarovsk
Harbin
Changchun
Almaty
Ürümqi
KYRGYZSTAN
Toshkent
TAJIKISTAN
AFGHANISTAN
Kabul
Srinagar
Indus
PAKISTAN
Lahore
Delhi
Kanpur
CHINA
Kunlun Shan
XIZANG
Himalaya
Lhasa
8850 Mt. Everest
NEPAL
Brahmaputra
Ganga
BANGLADESH
Dhaka
Kolkata (Calcutta)
INDIA
Irrawaddy
Mandalay
BURMA
Beijing
Tianjin
Taiyuan
Huang He
Lanzhou
Xi'an
Shenyang
Dalian
Qingdao
Yellow Sea
NORTH KOREA
SOUTH KOREA
Sŏul
Kitakyūshū
Nanjing
Wuhan
Shanghai
Chongqing
Chang Jiang
Hangzhou
Changsha
East China Sea
Okinawa
Ryūkyū-rettō (Japan)
Kunming
Fuzhou
Taipei
TAIWAN
Guangzhou
Hong Kong
Macau
Hanoi
LAOS
Salween
Mekong
Hainan
Sea of Okhotsk
Okhotsk
Sakhalin
Poluostrov Kamchatka
Petropavlovsk-Kamchatskiy
Kurilskiye Ostrova (Russia)
La Perouse Str.
Kuril Trench
10,542
Sapporo
Vladivostok
Sea of Japan
Hakodate
Sendai
Tōkyō
Fuji-San 3776
Yokohama
JAPAN
Nagoya
Kyōto
Osaka
Shikoku
Kyūshū
10,554
Japan Trench
South Honshu Ridge
Kyushu-Palau Ridge
Ogasawara Gunto (Japan)
Kazan-Rettō (Japan)
Minami-Tori-Shima (Japan)
Shatskiy Rise
Northwest Pacific Basin
Emperor Seamount Chain
Emperor Trough
Shirshov Ridge
Komandorskiye Ostrova (Russia)
Aleutian Basin
Bering Sea
Near Is. (U.S.A.)
Andreanof Is. (U.S.A.)
Aleutian Is.
7822
Aleutian Trench
Chinook Trough
Midway Is. (U.S.A.)
Hawaiian Ridge
Lisianski I. (U.S.A.)
Mid-Pacific Mountains
Wake I. (U.S.A.)
International Date Line
Philippine Sea
C. Engano
Luzon
Paracel Is.
Manila
PHILIPPINES
Mindoro
Samar
10,497
Palawan
Sulu Sea
Mindanao
Mindanao Trench
West Mariana Basin
NORTHERN MARIANAS (U.S.A.)
Tinian
Saipan
East Mariana Basin
GUAM (U.S.A.)
Challenger Deep 11,022
Mariana Trench
Micronesia
Caroline Is.
Yap
Truk
Koror
PALAU
West Caroline Basin
FED. STATES OF MICRONESIA
East Caroline Basin
Pohnpei
Palikir
Eauripik Rise
MARSHALL IS.
Bikini Atoll
Enewetak Atoll
Ratak Chain
Ralik Chain
Kwajalein
Majuro
Dalap-Uliga-Darrit
Jaluit I.
Butaritari
Tarawa
Gilbert Is.
Banaba
NAURU
Howland I. (U.S.A.)
Baker I. (U.S.A.)
Phoenix Is.
Abariringa
Enderbury
KIRIBATI
Central Pacific
PACIFIC OCEAN
Bay of Bengal
Rangoon
THAILAND
Bangkok
CAMBODIA
Phnom Penh
VIETNAM
G. of Thailand
Thanh Pho Ho Chi Minh
South China Sea
Hyderabad
Chennai (Madras)
Andaman Is. (India)
Nicobar Is. (India)
SRI LANKA
Colombo
MALAYSIA
Kuala Lumpur
PEN. MALAYSIA
BRUNEI
SABAH
4101
SARAWAK
Singapore
Celebes Sea
Maluku
Halmahera
Sumatera
Borneo
INDONESIA
Sulawesi
Seram
Buru
Palembang
Ujung Pandang
Java Sea
Banda Sea
7440
Jakarta
Jawa
Surabaya
Flores Sea
Flores
Selat Sunda
Java Trench
Bali
Sumbawa
Sumba
Dili
EAST TIMOR
Timor
Sunda Islands
Puncak Jaya 5029
PAPUA
New Guinea
PAPUA NEW GUINEA
Admiralty Is.
Bismarck Arch.
New Ireland
Rabaul
8940
Lae
New Britain
Bougainville
SOLOMON IS.
Port Moresby
Torres Strait
C. York
Louisiade Arch.
Honiara
Guadalcanal
Santa Cruz I.
9165
Arafura Sea
Melanesia
TUVALU
Fongafale
Tokelau Is. (N.Z.)
Rotuma
Is. Wallis & Futuna (Fr.)
SAMOA
Apia
Vanua Levu
Viti Levu
Suva
FIJI
Nuku'alofa
TONGA
10,822
Tonga Trench
Espíritu Santo
VANUATU
Port Vila
Coral Sea Basin
Coral Sea
Is. Chesterfield
7570
NEW CALEDONIA (Fr.)
Nouméa
Is. Loyauté
Christmas I. (Austral.)
Cocos Is. (Austral.)
Ninety East Ridge
INDIAN OCEAN
Wharton Basin
North Australian Basin
Exmouth Plateau
Broome
North West C.
C. Arnhem
Darwin
Gulf of Carpentaria
Cairns
Great Barrier Reef
Townsville
Mount Isa
AUSTRALIA
Great Dividing Ra.
Rockhampton
Alice Springs
Middleton Basin
Brisbane
Darling
L. Eyre
Geraldton
Perth
Albany
Great Australian Bight
Adelaide
Murray
Sydney
Canberra
Mt. Kosciuszko 2230
Melbourne
Bass Str.
Tasmania
Hobart
Lord Howe I. (Austral.)
Lord Howe Rise
Norfolk I. (Austral.)
Norfolk Ridge
South Fiji Basin
Kermadec Is. (N.Z.)
Kermadec Trench
10,047
NEW ZEALAND
Tasman Sea
Auckland
Cook Strait
Wellington
Chatham Rise
Chatham Is. (N.Z.)
Aoraki Mt. Cook 3753
Christchurch
Dunedin
Bounty Trough
Bounty Is. (N.Z.)
Invercargill
Antipodes Is. (N.Z.)
Campbell Plateau
Auckland Is. (N.Z.)
Campbell I. (N.Z.)
Macquarie Is. (Austral.)
Tasman Basin
Tasman Plateau
Nouvelle Amsterdam (Fr.)
I. St. Paul (Fr.)
Mid-Indian Ridge
SOUTHERN OCEAN
Is. Crozet (Fr.)
Kerguelen (Fr.)
Heard I. (Austral.)
ft m
12 000 4000
9000 3000
6000 2000
3000 1000
1500 500
600 200
0 0
200 600
1000 3000
2000 6000
4000 12 000
6000 18 000
8000 24 000
m ft
Projection: Mollweide's Homolographic
East from Greenwich

ALASKA
(U.S.A.)
Anchorage
Arctic Circle
Bristol Bay
Gulf of Alaska
Juneau
Prince of Wales I.
(U.S.A.)
Prince Rupert
Queen Charlotte Is.
(Canada)
Rocky Mts.
CANADA
Edmonton
Calgary
L. Winnipeg
Winnipeg
Regina
Vancouver
Victoria
Vancouver I.
Seattle
Portland
Snake
Boise
Minneapolis
Missouri
L. Superior
Newfoundland
St. Lawrence
Québec
St. John's
NORTH
Montréal
Ottawa
L. Huron
L. Michigan
Toronto
L. Ontario
Detroit
Buffalo
L. Erie
Boston
Chicago
Salt Lake City
Denver
Kansas City
Pittsburgh
New York
Philadelphia
Baltimore
Washington D.C.
Cincinnati
St. Louis
Appalachian Mts.
Northeast
Mendocino Fracture Zone
C. Mendocino
Sacramento
San Francisco
Colorado
4418
UNITED STATES
ATLANTIC
Oklahoma City
Memphis
Mississippi
Atlanta
C. Hatteras
6741
Murray Fracture Zone
Los Angeles
San Diego
Phoenix
Dallas
Bermuda
(U.K.)
Pacific
Ciudad Juárez
Houston
Jacksonville
Baja California
Golfo de California
Guadalupe
(Mex.)
San Antonio
New Orleans
Sargasso Sea
Tampa
Molokai Fracture Zone
MEXICO
Gulf of Mexico
Monterrey
Miami
Florida Str.
BAHAMAS
OCEAN
Tropic of Cancer
La Habana
CUBA
West Indies
Basin
C. San Lucas
Canal de Yucatán
Honolulu
Kauai
Maui
Oahu
HAWAIIAN IS.
(U.S.A.)
4205
Hilo
Hawaii
Guadalajara
Mexico
Mérida
5610
Puebla
7680
9200
HAITI
DOMINICAN REP.
JAMAICA
Kingston
Leeward Is.
Clarion Fracture Zone
Is. Revilla Gigedo
(Mex.)
BELIZE
PUERTO RICO
(U.S.A.)
Johnston I.
(U.S.A.)
Acapulco
GUATEMALA
HONDURAS
6662
Guatemala
Caribbean Sea
BARBADOS
PACIFIC
Middle America Trench
San Salvador
EL SALVADOR
NICARAGUA
Windward Is.
Managua
Barranquilla
Maracaibo
Caracas
I. Clipperton
(Fr.)
Guatemala Basin
San José
COSTA RICA
Colón
Panamá
PANAMA
Orinoco
Clipperton Fracture Zone
Cocos Ridge
VENEZUELA
North West Christmas I. Ridge
Palmyra Is.
(U.S.A.)
Teraina
Tabuaeran
Kiritimati
I. del Coco
(Costa Rica)
Medellín
Bogotá
Cali
I. de Malpelo
(Colombia)
COLOMBIA
Galápagos Fracture Zone
Equator
Galápagos
(Ecuador)
Carnegie Ridge
Quito
ECUADOR
Jarvis I.
(U.S.A.)
OCEAN
Line Islands
Malden I.
Starbuck I.
Guayaquil
Iquitos
Amazonas
C. Pariñas
BRAZIL
KIRIBATI
East Pacific Ridge
Galápagos Rise
Penrhyn
(Tongareva)
Manihiki
Pukapuka
Manihiki Plateau
Nuku Hiva
Is. Marquises
Hiva Oa
Marquesas Fracture Zone
Vostok I.
Caroline I.
(Millennium I.)
Flint I.
Trujillo
6369
PERU
Lima
Suwarrow Is.
Is. de la Société
Bora Bora
Huahine
Raiatea
Papeete
Tahiti
Rangiroa
Is. Tuamotu
Tuamotu Ridge
Peru Basin
Cuzco
L. Titicaca
Nevada Ancohuma
6550
Arequipa
La Paz
BOLIVIA
6866
Cook Is.
(N.Z.)
Aitutaki
Austral Seamount Chain
FRENCH POLYNESIA
Peru-Chile Trench
Arica
Atiu
Rarotonga
Mangaia
Gambier Is.
Mururoa
Nazca Ridge
Iquique
Andes
Is. Tubuai
Tropic of Capricorn
Antofagasta
PARAGUAY
Asunción
Oeno I.
Henderson I.
Pitcairn I.
(U.K.)
Ducie I.
Easter Fracture Zone
Sala-y-Gómez
(Chile)
Sala y Gómez Ridge
8050
San Felix
(Chile)
San Ambrosio
(Chile)
San Miguel de Tucumán
I. de Pascua
(Chile)
Rapa
Porto Alegre
Córdoba
Aconcagua
6962
Arch. de Juan Fernández
(Chile)
Valparaíso
Rosario
URUGUAY
Santiago
Buenos Aires
Montevideo
Río de la Plata
Challenger Fracture Zone
Chile Rise
Concepción
ARGENTINA
Southwest
Pacific
Basin
SOUTH ATLANTIC OCEAN
PATAGONIA
Menard Fracture Zone
6212
Pacific-Antarctic Ridge
Falkland Is.
(U.K.)
Punta Arenas
Est. de Magallanes
South Georgia
(U.K.)
Southeast Pacific Basin
C. de Hornos
Tierra del Fuego
Drake Passage
West from Greenwich

1:28 000 000
100 0 200 400 600 800 1000 1200 1400 km
100 0 200 400 600 800 1000 miles
ARCTIC OCEAN
Beaufort Sea
Greenland
Asia
Bering Sea
Bering Strait
St. Lawrence I.
C. Dezhneva
Nunivak I.
Barrow Pt.
C. Prince of Wales
Brooks Ra.
Yukon
Porcupine
Alaska
Mt. McKinley 6194
Alaska Range
Alaska Peninsula
Kodiak I.
Gulf of Alaska
Mt. St. Elias 5489
Mt. Logan 5959
Mackenzie Mts.
Mackenzie
Arctic Circle
Great Bear L.
Great Slave L.
Back
Liard
Dubawnt
Axel Heiberg I.
Ellesmere I.
Kane Basin
Nares Str.
Sverdrup Is.
Parry Is.
Queen Elizabeth Is.
Melville I.
Bathurst I.
Devon I.
M'Clure Strait
Viscount Melville Sd.
Lancaster Sd.
Bylot I.
Banks I.
Prince of Wales I.
Somerset I.
C. Bathurst
Victoria I.
Gulf of Boothia
Boothia Pen.
Baffin Bay
Baffin Island
Melville Pen.
Foxe Basin
Foxe Channel
Southampton I.
Cumberland Sd.
Frobisher B.
Hudson Strait
C. Chidley
C. Wolstenholme
Ungava Peninsula
Disko I.
Davis Strait
Peterman's Peak 2940
Mt. Forel 3360
Denmark Strait
Iceland
2119
Cape Farewell
Labrador Sea
Hamilton Inlet
Coast of Labrador
Str. of Belle Isle
Newfoundland
C. Race
Hudson Bay
Belcher Is.
C. Henrietta Maria
James Bay
Eastmain
Laurentian Plateau
St. Lawrence
Gulf of St. Lawrence
Pr. Edward I.
Cape Breton I.
Nova Scotia
Sable I.
C. Sable
B. of Fundy
Mt. Washington 1917
C. Cod
Nantucket I.
Long I.
Hudson
Alexander Archipelago
Stikine
Coast Mountains
Rocky Mountains
Queen Charlotte Islands
Skeena
Queen Charlotte Str.
Mt. Waddington 3994
Fraser
Mt. Robson 3954
Peace
Athabasca
L. Athabasca
Reindeer L.
Churchill
Nelson
L. Winnipeg
Great Plains
Saskatchewan
Selkirk Mts.
Vancouver I.
Juan de Fuca Str.
C. Flattery
Mt. Rainier 4392
Cascade Range
Columbia
C. Blanco
C. Mendocino
Coast Ranges
Mt. Shasta 4317
Sacramento
Sierra Nevada
San Joaquin
Mt. Whitney 4418
Death Valley -86
Snake
Great Salt Lake
Great Basin
Wasatch Ra.
Mt. Elbert 4399
Blanca Peak 4378
Grand Canyon
Colorado Plateau
Colorado
Gila
Missouri
Platte
Arkansas
Red
Mississippi
Ozark Plateau
Great Lakes
L. Superior
L. Michigan
L. Huron
L. Erie
L. Ontario
Niagara Falls
Ohio
Cumberland Plateau
Tennessee
Allegheny Mts.
Appalachian Mts.
Blue Ridge Mts.
Alabama
C. Charles
Chesapeake B.
C. Hatteras
Bermuda
NORTH ATLANTIC OCEAN
Sargasso Sea
Bahamas
Florida
Florida Strait
Mississippi River Delta
Gulf of Mexico
Rio Grande
Eastern Sierra Madre
Mexican Plateau
Western Sierra Madre
Santiago
Lower California
Gulf of California
Guadalupe
C. San Lucas
C. Corrientes
Revilla Gigedo Is.
Popocatepetl 5452
5610 Pico de Orizaba
Balsas
Isthmus of Tehuantepec
G. de Tehuantepec
Gulf of Campeche
Yucatán Peninsula
Yucatan Channel
Yucatan Basin
Cuba
Greater Antilles
Cayman Trough
Jamaica
Hispaniola
9200
Puerto Rico
G. of Honduras
C. Gracias a Dios
Coco
Caribbean Sea
Colombian Basin
Sierra Nevada de Santa Marta 5800
G. de Venezuela
L. Maracaibo
Cord. de Merida
Magdalena
Andes
G. of Darién
G. of Panamá
Guatemala Trench
Central America
PACIFIC OCEAN
Tropic of Cancer
Clarion Fracture Zone
Projection: Bonne
West from Greenwich
COPYRIGHT PHILIP'S
ft m
9000 3000
6000 2000
3000 1000
1500 500
600 200
0 0
200 600
1000 3000
2000 6000
4000 12000
6000 18000
8000 24000
m ft

1:28 000 000

100 0 200 400 600 800 1000 1200 1400 km

100 0 200 400 600 800 1000 miles

MÉXICO Capital Cities

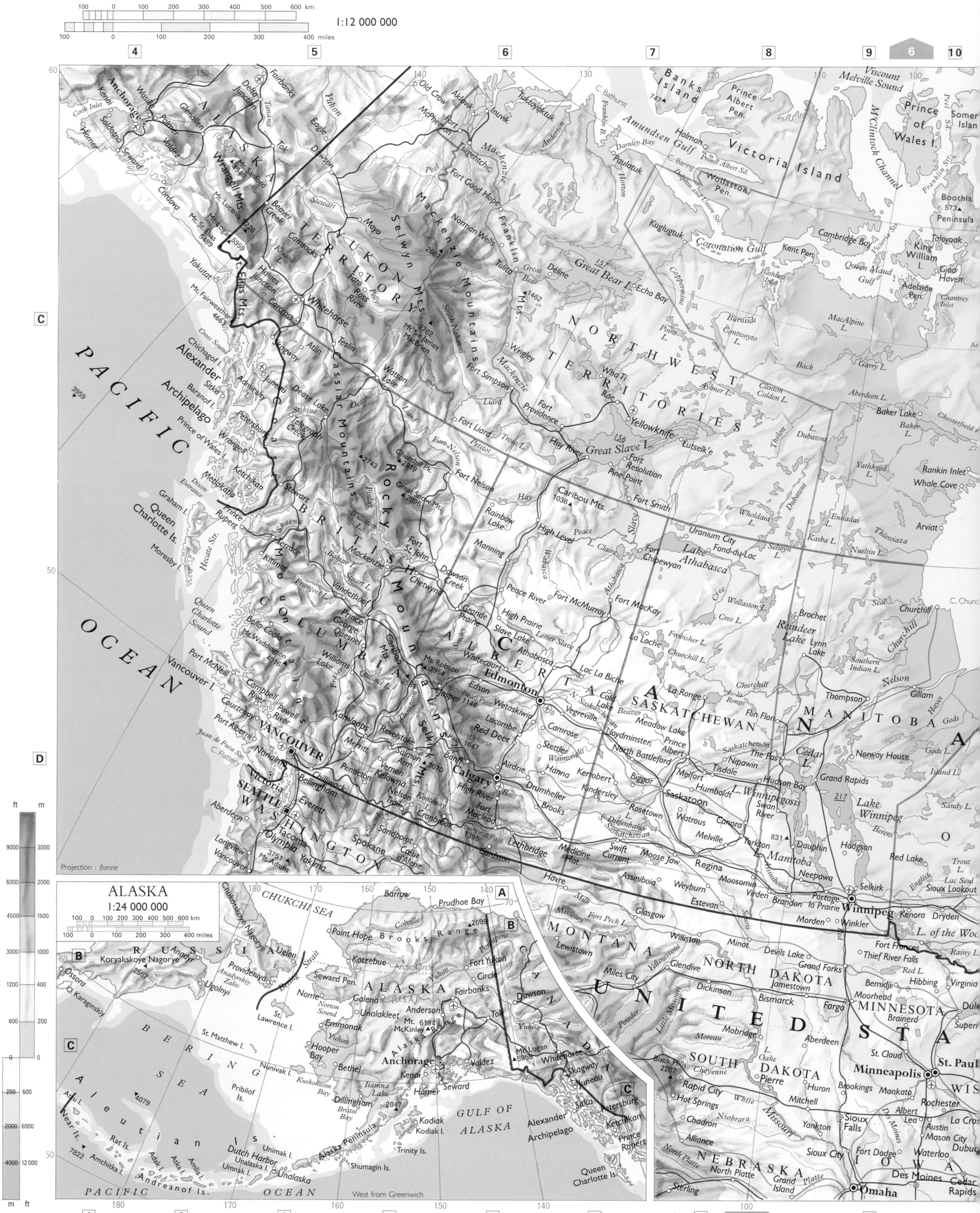
1:12 000 000
km
miles
Projection : Bonne
ALASKA
1:24 000 000
West from Greenwich
PACIFIC OCEAN
ALASKA
YUKON TERRITORY
NORTHWEST TERRITORIES
BRITISH COLUMBIA
ALBERTA
SASKATCHEWAN
MANITOBA
CANADA
UNITED STATES
WASHINGTON
MONTANA
NORTH DAKOTA
SOUTH DAKOTA
NEBRASKA
MINNESOTA
IOWA
RUSSIA
BERING SEA
CHUKCHI SEA
GULF OF ALASKA
Aleutian Is.
Anchorage
Fairbanks
Whitehorse
Yellowknife
Edmonton
Calgary
VANCOUVER
Victoria
SEATTLE
Regina
Saskatoon
Winnipeg
Minneapolis
St. Paul
Omaha
Juneau
Prince Rupert
Prince George
Kamloops
Dawson
Inuvik
Tuktoyaktuk
Great Bear L.
Great Slave L.
Lake Athabasca
Lake Winnipeg
L. Winnipegosis
L. Manitoba
Victoria Island
Banks Island
Prince of Wales I.
Amundsen Gulf
Coronation Gulf
Mackenzie Mountains
Rocky Mountains
Cassiar Mountains
Coast Mountains
Selwyn Mts.
St. Elias Mts.
Wrangell Mts.
Mt. Logan 5959
Mt. Robson 3954
Mt. McKinley 6194
Alexander Archipelago
Queen Charlotte Is.
Vancouver I.
Brooks Range
Alaska Range
Bering Strait
Kodiak I.
Alaska Peninsula

6
146

11
12
13
14
15
16
B
C
D
E
Devon I.
Lancaster Sound
Bylot I.
Arctic Bay
Nanisivik
Pond Inlet
Brodeur Peninsula
Borden Pen.
Baffin Bay
Nunavik
Uummannaq
Qeqertarsuaq
Ilulissat
Qasigiannguit
Ammassalik
GREENLAND
(KALAALLIT NUNAAT)
(Denmark)
Clyde River
C. Adair
C. Raper
Baffin Island
Davis Strait
Kangerlussuaq
Sisimiut
Maniitsoq
Kong Frederik VI's Kyst
Home B.
Qikiqtarjuaq
C. Dyer
Fury and Hecla Str.
Igloolik
Hall Beach
Simpson Pen.
Kugaaruk
Melville Peninsula
Foxe Basin
Prince Charles I.
Air Force I.
Cumberland Peninsula
Pangnirtung
Hoare B.
C. Mercy
Cumberland Sd.
Nuuk
Qeqertarsuatsiaat
Paamiut
Arsuk
Qaqortoq
Alluitsup Paa
Nanortalik
Nunap Isua
ATLANTIC OCEAN
Rae Isthmus
Repulse Bay
NUNAVUT
Nettilling L.
C. Dorchester
Amadjuak L.
Foxe Pen.
Iqaluit
Hall Peninsula
Meta Incognita Peninsula
Kimmirut
Frobisher Bay
Resolution I.
Foxe Channel
Cape Dorset
Southampton I.
Coral Harbour
Bell Pen.
Salisbury I.
Nottingham I.
Hudson Strait
Chesterfield Inlet
Coats I.
Mansel I.
Ivujivik
Salluit
Kangiqsujuaq
Quaqtaq
Akpatok I.
C. Chidley
Labrador Sea
Péninsule d'Ungava
Kangirsuk
Ungava Bay
Arnaud
Kangiqsualujjuaq
Hebron
Puvirnituq
L. Payne
Kuujjuaq
Hudson Bay
Ottawa Is.
Nain
Hopedale
C. Harrison
Rigolet
Cartwright
Inukjuak
L. Minto
Caniapiscau
Sleeper Is.
King George Is.
Baker's Dozen Is.
Sanikiluaq
Belcher Is.
C. Tatnam
Smallwood Res.
Labrador
North West River
Happy Valley-Goose Bay
NEWFOUNDLAND & LABRADOR
Port Hope Simpson
Belle Isle
C. Bauld
St. Anthony
Schefferville
Churchill Falls
Esker
L. à l'Eau Claire
L. Bienville
Kuujjuarapik
Grande Baleine
C. Henrietta Maria
Peawanuck
Winisk
Severn
Labrador City
Fermont
Caniapiscau
La Grande
Chisasibi
James Bay
St-Augustin
Natashquan
Lewisporte
Gander
Bonavista
Deer Lake
Grand Falls
Windsor
Corner Brook
Newfoundland
Carbonear
St. John's
Placentia
C. Race
Marystown
Stephenville
Channel-Port aux Basques
Gagnon
Rés. Manicouagan
QUÉBEC
Havre-St-Pierre
Î. d'Anticosti
Sept-Îles
Port-Cartier
Big Trout L.
Attawapiskat
Akimiski I.
Wemindji
Eastmain
Charlton I.
Fort Albany
Waskaganish
Rupert
L. Mistassini
L. Albanel
ONTARIO
Moosonee
Gulf of St. Lawrence
Cabot Str.
ST-PIERRE et MIQUELON (Fr.)
Baie-Comeau
Matane
Gaspé
Pén. de la Gaspésie
Chibougamau
Rimouski
Campbellton
Bathurst
Îs. de la Madeleine
C. North
Cape Breton I.
Glace Bay
Sydney
L. St. Joseph
Nakina
Matagami
Dolbeau-Mistassini
Chicoutimi
Jonquière
Roberval
Rivière-du-Loup
Edmundston
Chatham
PR. EDWARD I.
Summerside
Charlottetown
Port Hawkesbury
Antigonish
New Glasgow
Hearst
Cochrane
Greenstone
Nipigon
Kapuskasing
Marathon
Timmins
Amos
Rés. Gouin
NEW BRUNSWICK
Moncton
Amherst
Truro
NOVA SCOTIA
Dartmouth
Halifax
Sable I.
(Nova Scotia)
Thunder Bay
Kirkland Lake
Rouyn-Noranda
Val-d'Or
La Tuque
Québec
Lévis
Grand Falls
Woodstock
Fredericton
Saint John
Kentville
Digby
Bridgewater
Liverpool
Yarmouth
C. Sable
Lake Superior
Wawa
Chapleau
New Liskeard
Mont-Laurier
Shawinigan
Trois-Rivières
Thetford Mines
B. of Fundy
Houghton
Sault Ste. Marie
Elliot Lake
Sudbury
Joliette
St-Hyacinthe
Sherbrooke
MAINE
Bangor
Augusta
Lewiston
Portland
Ironwood
Marquette
North Bay
Parry Sound
Pembroke
MONTREAL
Hull
Ottawa
Cornwall
Burlington
Montpelier
Manistique
Escanaba
Menominee
Manitoulin I.
Lake Huron
Georgian Bay
Huntsville
VERMONT
NEW HAMPSHIRE
Concord
Manchester
Rhinelander
Petoskey
Traverse City
Cadillac
Peterborough
Kingston
Belleville
MICHIGAN
Wausau
Green Bay
Owen Sound
Barrie
Oshawa
TORONTO
L. Ontario
Syracuse
MASS.
BOSTON
C. Cod
Appleton
Sheboygan
WISCONSIN
Saginaw
Kitchener
Hamilton
Rochester
Albany
Springfield
Providence
Grand Rapids
Flint
London
Niagara Falls
Buffalo
NEW YORK
Hartford
CONN.
R.I.
Milwaukee
L. Michigan
Sarnia
Elmira
Binghamton
New Haven
Madison
Racine
Kenosha
Lansing
DETROIT
Windsor
L. Erie
Erie
Jamestown
Scranton
Bridgeport
NEW YORK
Rockford
CHICAGO
Gary
South Bend
Toledo
CLEVELAND
PENNSYLVANIA
Newark
N.J.
Allentown
Trenton
ILLINOIS
INDIANA
OHIO
West from Greenwich

50 0 50 100 150 200 250 300 km

1:5 600 000

50 0 50 100 150 200 miles

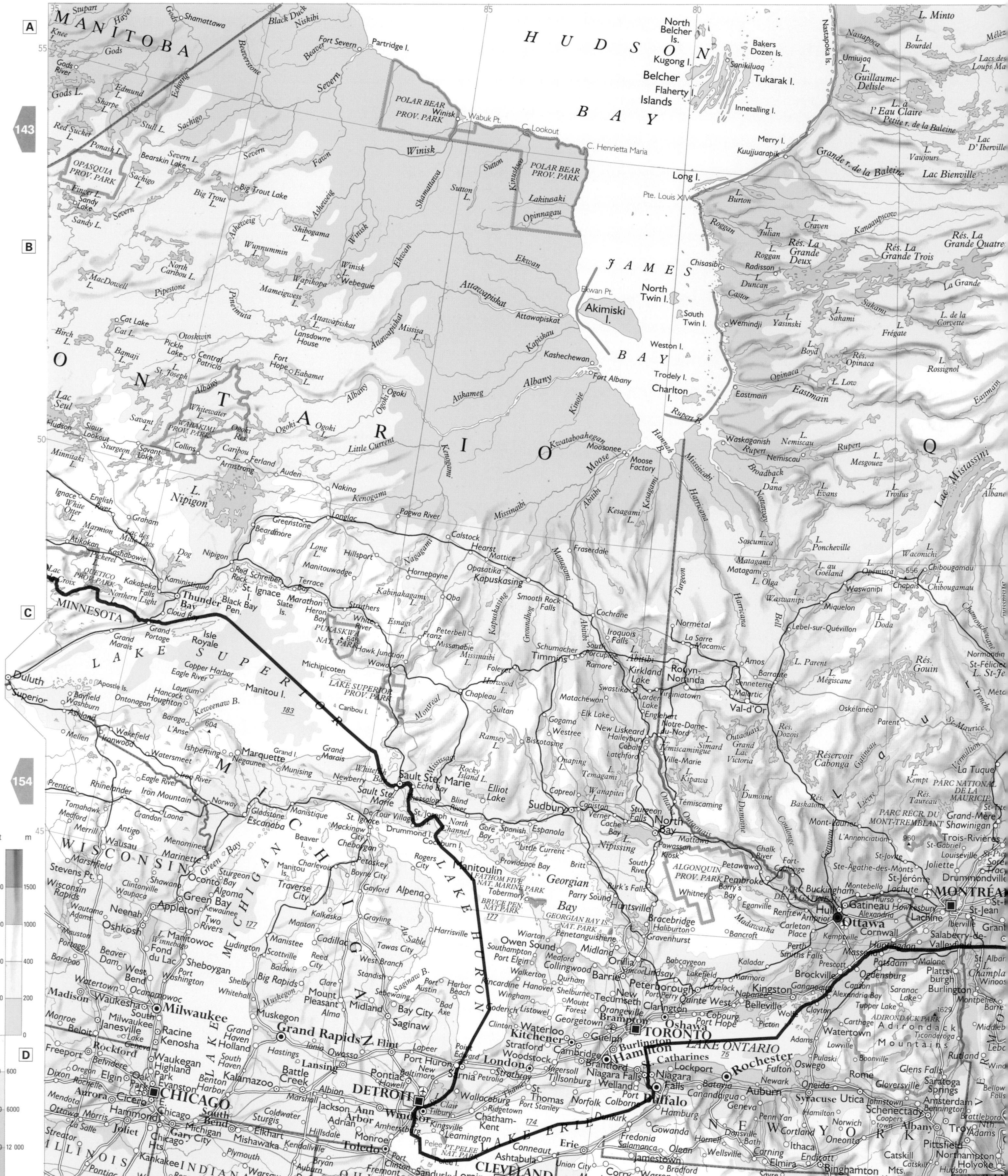

143
154
148

National Parks

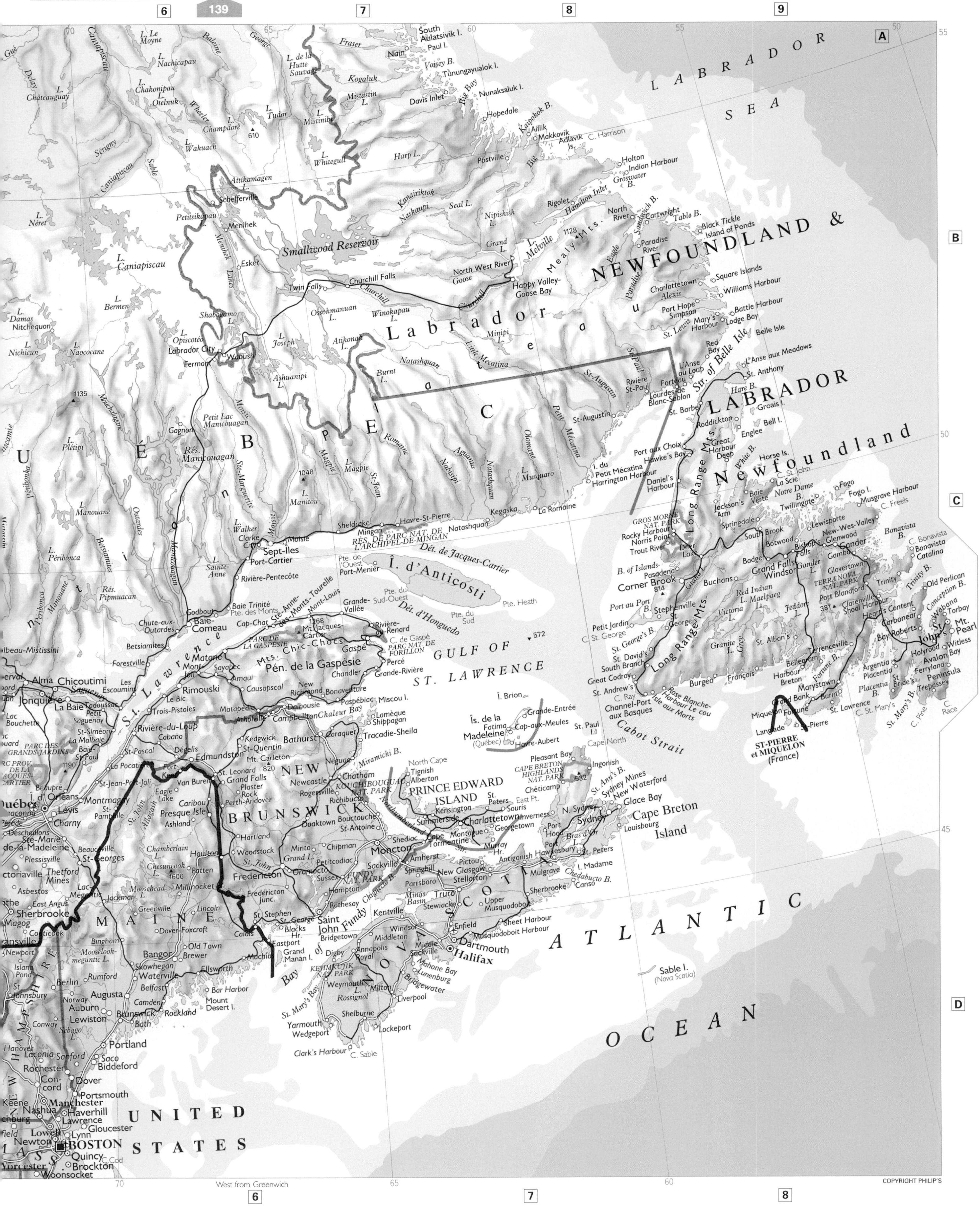
139
LABRADOR SEA
NEWFOUNDLAND & LABRADOR
Labrador
Newfoundland
QUÉBEC
GULF OF ST. LAWRENCE
ATLANTIC OCEAN
UNITED STATES
MAINE
NEW BRUNSWICK
NOVA SCOTIA
PRINCE EDWARD ISLAND
Cape Breton Island
ST-PIERRE et MIQUELON (France)
Smallwood Reservoir
Î. d'Anticosti
Îs. de la Madeleine (Québec)
Sable I. (Nova Scotia)
Cabot Strait
Str. of Belle Isle
Bay of Fundy
Long Range Mts.
Mealy Mts.
Mts. Chic-Chocs
Pén. de la Gaspésie
St. Lawrence
Schefferville
Labrador City
Wabush
Fermont
Churchill Falls
Happy Valley-Goose Bay
North West River
Nain
Hopedale
Makkovik
Postville
Cartwright
Sept-Îles
Port-Cartier
Baie-Comeau
Gaspé
Rimouski
Chicoutimi
Jonquière
Québec
Lévis
Sherbrooke
Edmundston
Fredericton
Saint John
Moncton
Bathurst
Charlottetown
Summerside
Truro
Halifax
Dartmouth
Sydney
Glace Bay
Yarmouth
Corner Brook
Stephenville
Grand Falls
Windsor
Gander
Deer Lake
St. John's
Mt. Pearl
Channel-Port aux Basques
Miquelon
St-Pierre
Bangor
Augusta
Portland
Lewiston
Manchester
Concord
Portsmouth
Nashua
Lowell
BOSTON
Woonsocket
West from Greenwich
6
7
8
9
A
B
C
D
55
50
45
70
65
60

1:5 600 000

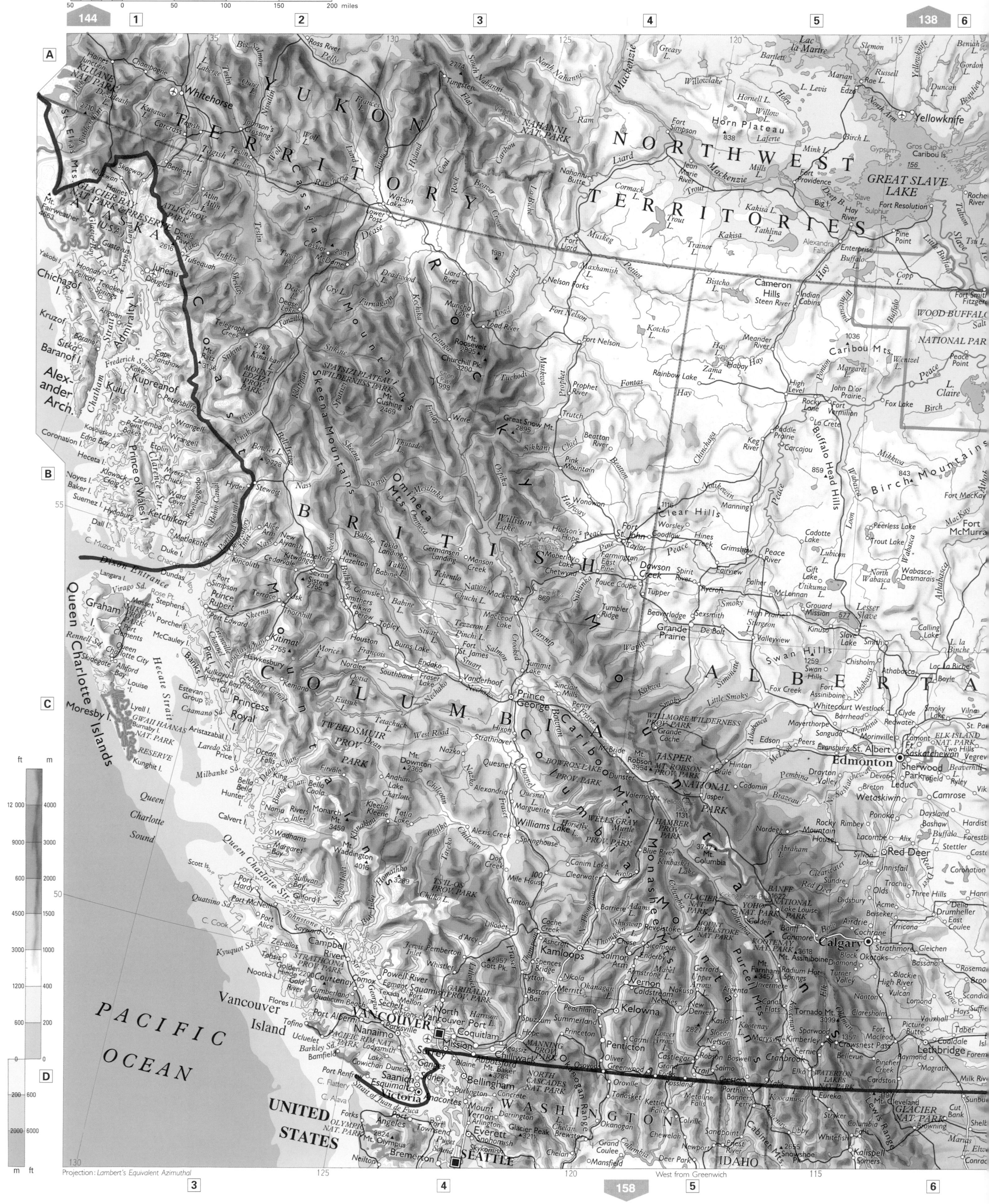
YUKON TERRITORY
NORTHWEST TERRITORIES
BRITISH COLUMBIA
ALBERTA
ALASKA (USA)
UNITED STATES
WASHINGTON
IDAHO
PACIFIC OCEAN
GREAT SLAVE LAKE
Whitehorse
Yellowknife
Juneau
Prince Rupert
Prince George
Edmonton
Calgary
Red Deer
Kamloops
Kelowna
VANCOUVER
Victoria
SEATTLE
Bellingham
Lethbridge
Grande Prairie
Dawson Creek
Fort St. John
Fort Nelson
Watson Lake
Queen Charlotte Islands
Queen Charlotte Sound
Vancouver Island
Hecate Strait
Dixon Entrance
Coast Mountains
Skeena Mountains
Cassiar Mountains
Rocky Mountains
Cariboo Mts
Columbia Mts
Monashee Mts
Purcell Mts
Birch Mountains
Caribou Mts
Swan Hills
Clear Hills
Horn Plateau
Mackenzie
Liard
Peace
Athabasca
Fraser
Skeena
Stikine
JASPER NATIONAL PARK
BANFF NATIONAL PARK
WOOD BUFFALO NATIONAL PARK
KLUANE NAT. PARK
NAHANNI NAT. PARK
TWEEDSMUIR PROV. PARK
Projection: Lambert's Equivalent Azimuthal
West from Greenwich

144 138 158

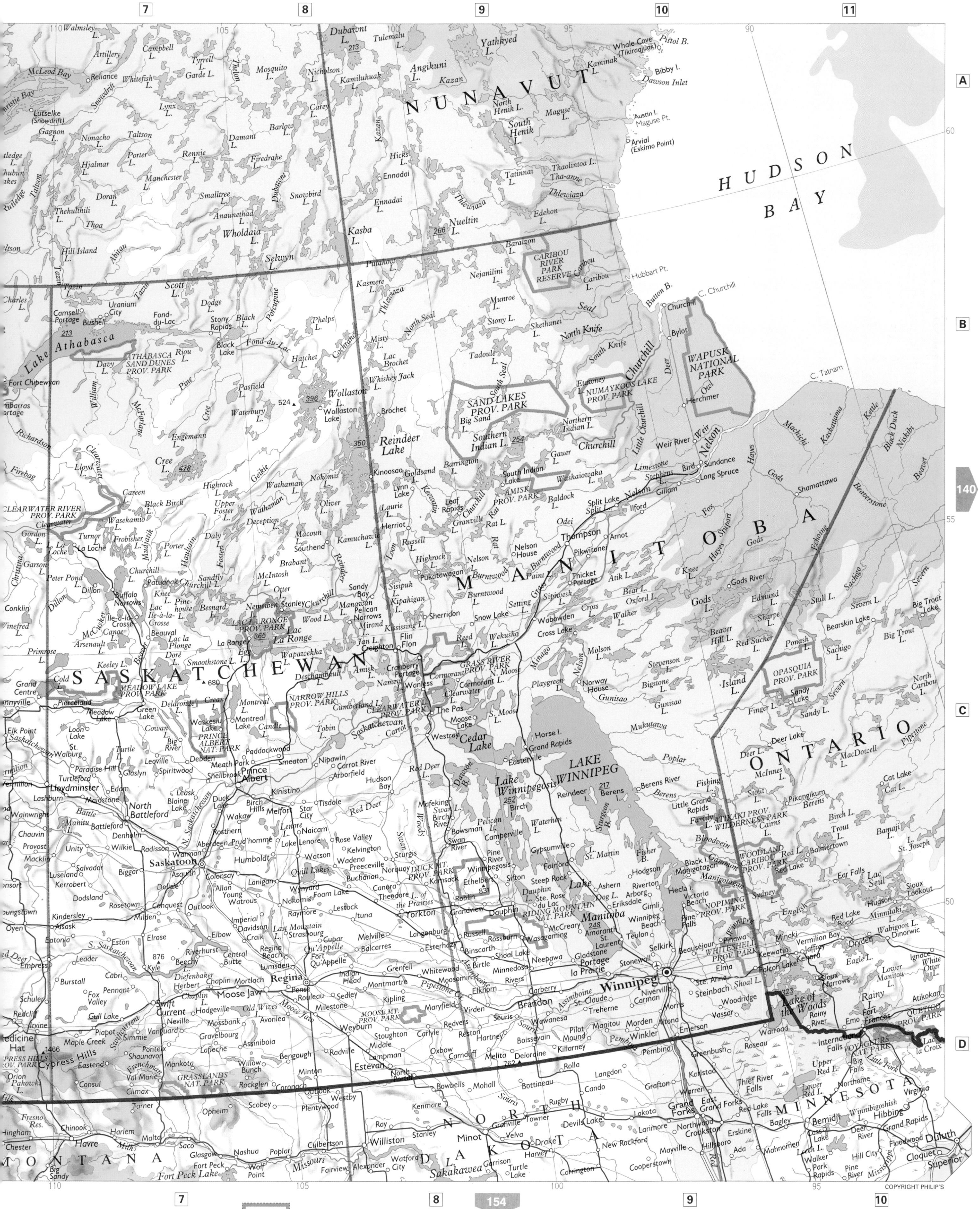

7
8
9
10
11
A
B
C
D
NUNAVUT
HUDSON BAY
MANITOBA
SASKATCHEWAN
ONTARIO
MONTANA
NORTH DAKOTA
MINNESOTA
LAKE WINNIPEG
Lake Winnipegosis
Lake Manitoba
Lake Athabasca
Reindeer Lake
Wollaston L.
Southern Indian L.
Cedar Lake
Lake of the Woods
Churchill
Thompson
The Pas
Flin Flon
Prince Albert
Saskatoon
Regina
Moose Jaw
Swift Current
Brandon
Winnipeg
Yorkton
North Battleford
Lloydminster
Medicine Hat
Kenora
Dryden
Minot
Grand Forks
Bemidji
Duluth
Kasba L.
Nueltin L.
Dubawnt L.
WAPUSK NATIONAL PARK
PRINCE ALBERT NAT. PARK
RIDING MOUNTAIN NAT. PARK
GRASSLANDS NAT. PARK
Cypress Hills
CARIBOU RIVER PARK RESERVE
SAND LAKES PROV. PARK
NUMAYKOOS LAKE PROV. PARK
LAC LA RONGE PROV. PARK
MEADOW LAKE PROV. PARK
NARROW HILLS PROV. PARK
CLEARWATER PROV. PARK
GRASS RIVER PROV. PARK
OPASQUIA PROV. PARK
ATIKAKI PROV. WILDERNESS PARK
WOODLAND CARIBOU PROV. PARK
NOPIMING PROV. PARK
WHITESHELL PROV. PARK
DUCK MT. PROV. PARK
MOOSE MT. PROV. PARK
QUETICO
VOYAGEURS
7
8
9
10
110
105
100
95
90
60
55
50
COPYRIGHT PHILIP'S

National Parks

140

154

50 0 100 200 300 400 km

1:8 000 000

50 0 50 100 150 200 250 miles

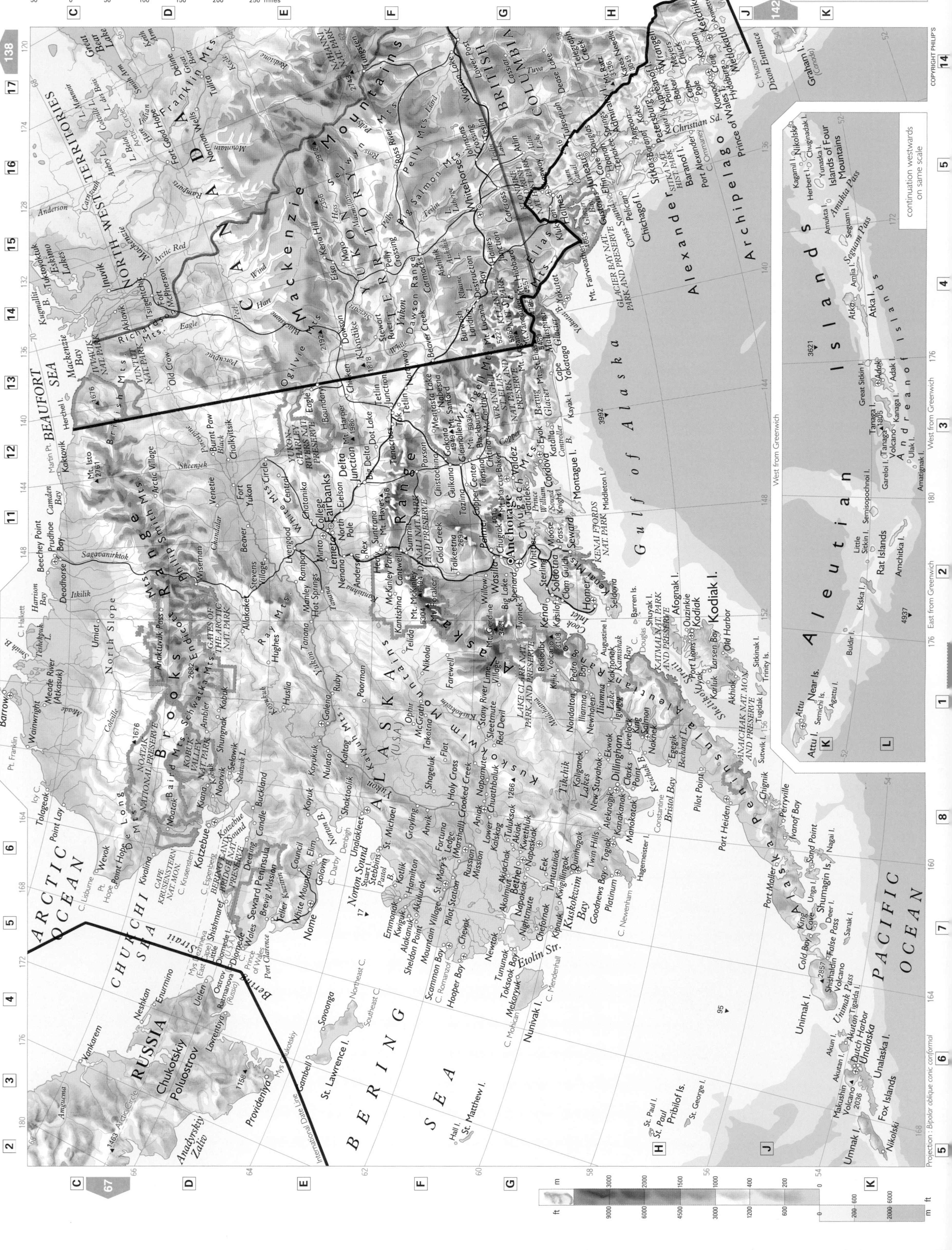

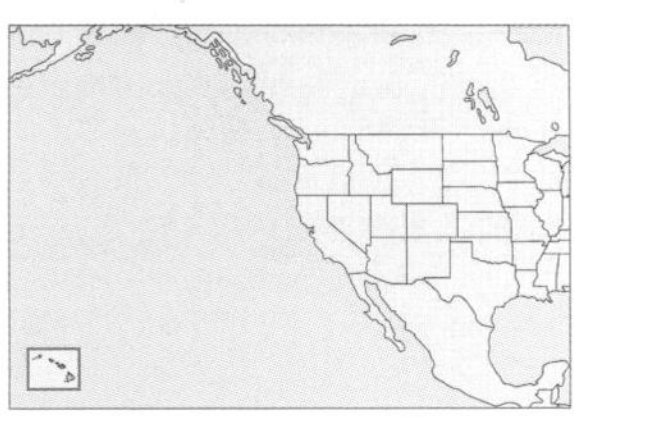

1:2 000 000

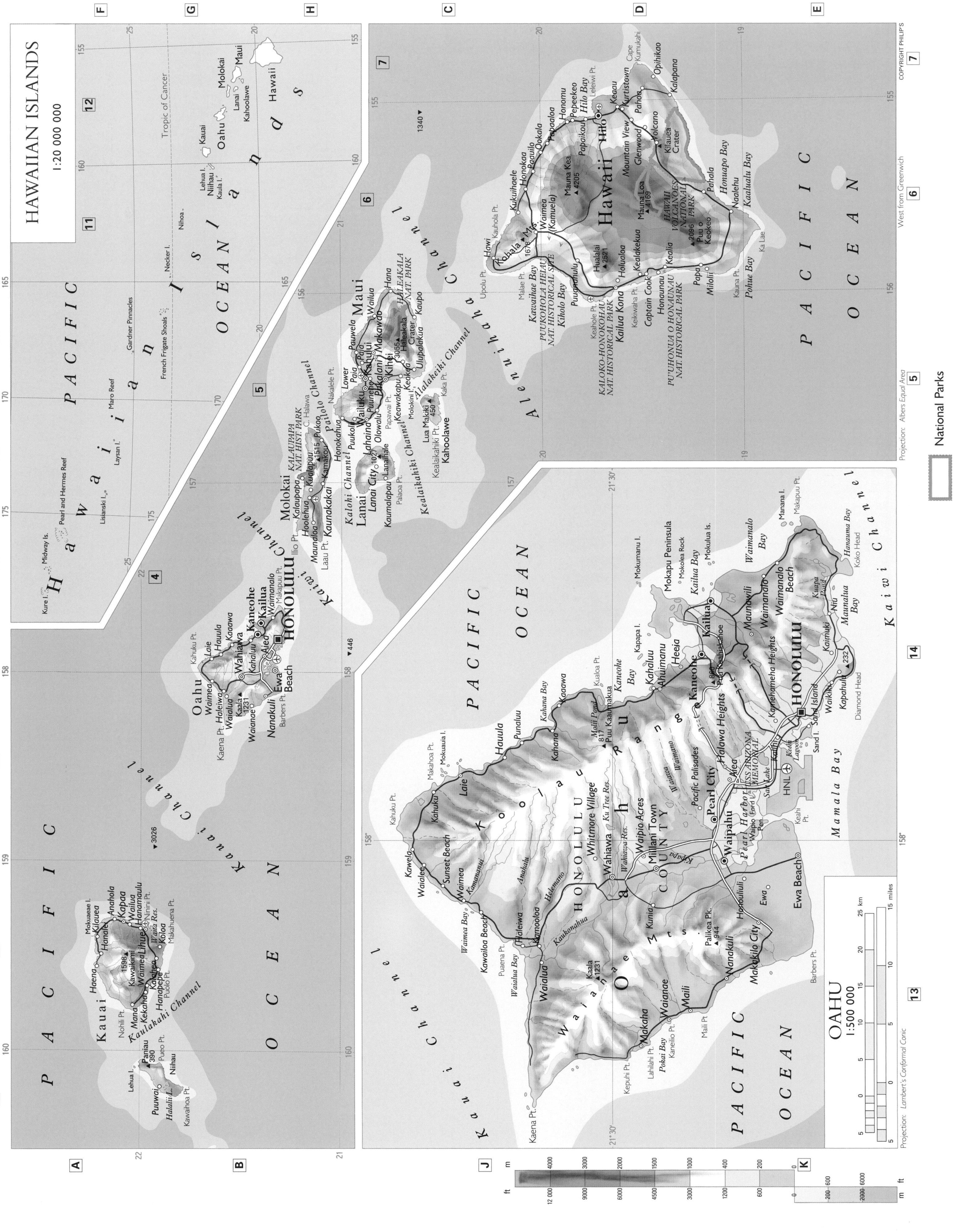
HAWAIIAN ISLANDS
1:20 000 000
PACIFIC OCEAN
Hawaiian Islands
Tropic of Cancer
Kauai
Oahu
Molokai
Maui
Lanai
Kahoolawe
Hawaii
Niihau
Nihoa
Necker I.
French Frigate Shoals
Gardner Pinnacles
Maro Reef
Laysan I.
Lisianski I.
Pearl and Hermes Reef
Midway Is.
Kure I.
Kauai Channel
Kaulakahi Channel
Kaiwi Channel
Pailolo Channel
Kalohi Channel
Kealaikahiki Channel
Alalakeiki Channel
Alenuihaha Channel
HONOLULU
Hilo
Mauna Kea 4205
Mauna Loa 4169
Kilauea Crater
HAWAII VOLCANOES NATIONAL PARK
HALEAKALA NAT. PARK
KALAUPAPA NAT. HIST. PARK
PUUKOHOLA HEIAU NAT. HISTORICAL SITE
KALOKO-HONOKOHAU NAT. HISTORICAL PARK
PU'UHONUA O HONAUNAU NAT. HISTORICAL PARK
OAHU
1:500 000
Koolau Range
Waianae Mts
Pearl Harbor
Mamala Bay
Kaneohe Bay
Kailua Bay
Waimanalo Bay
Diamond Head
Pearl City
Kaneohe
Kailua
Waipahu
Wahiawa
Ewa Beach
Projection: Albers Equal Area
Projection: Lambert's Conformal Conic
West from Greenwich
COPYRIGHT PHILIP'S
National Parks

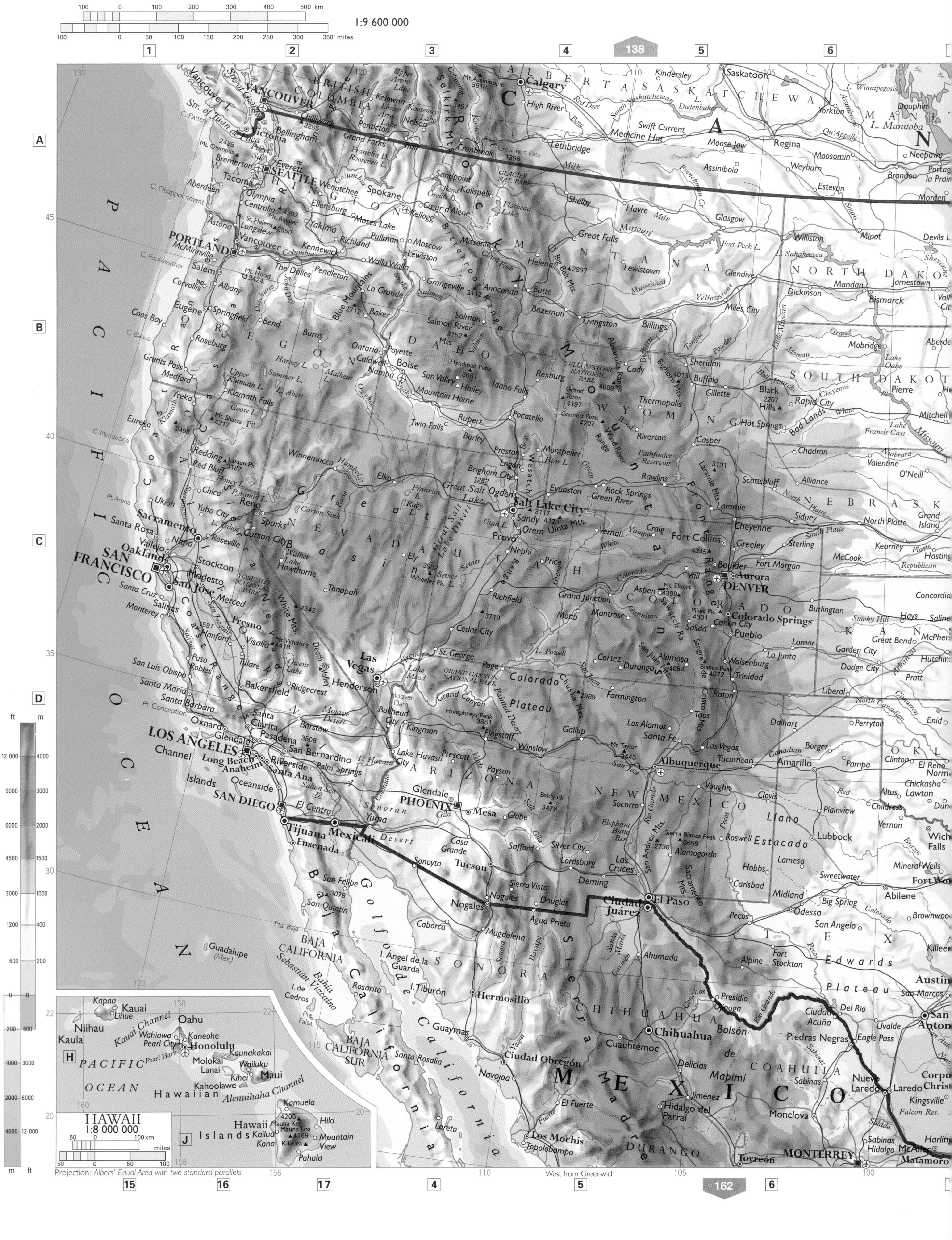
1:9 600 000
138
162
PACIFIC OCEAN
BRITISH COLUMBIA
ALBERTA
SASKATCHEWAN
MANITOBA
CANADA
WASHINGTON
OREGON
IDAHO
MONTANA
WYOMING
NORTH DAKOTA
SOUTH DAKOTA
NEBRASKA
KANSAS
COLORADO
UTAH
NEVADA
CALIFORNIA
ARIZONA
NEW MEXICO
TEXAS
OKLAHOMA
MEXICO
BAJA CALIFORNIA
BAJA CALIFORNIA SUR
SONORA
CHIHUAHUA
COAHUILA
DURANGO
Golfo de California
ROCKY MOUNTAINS
Great Basin
Colorado Plateau
Llano Estacado
Edwards Plateau
Bolsón de Mapimí
Sierra Madre
VANCOUVER
Victoria
SEATTLE
Calgary
Spokane
PORTLAND
Salt Lake City
Boise
Reno
Sacramento
SAN FRANCISCO
San Jose
Fresno
Las Vegas
LOS ANGELES
SAN DIEGO
Tijuana
Mexicali
PHOENIX
Tucson
Albuquerque
DENVER
Colorado Springs
El Paso
Ciudad Juárez
Chihuahua
Hermosillo
MONTERREY
Regina
Saskatoon
Bismarck
Cheyenne
Amarillo
Lubbock
HAWAII
1:8 000 000
Kauai
Oahu
Honolulu
Molokai
Lanai
Maui
Hawaii
Hawaiian Islands
PACIFIC OCEAN
Projection: Albers' Equal Area with two standard parallels
West from Greenwich

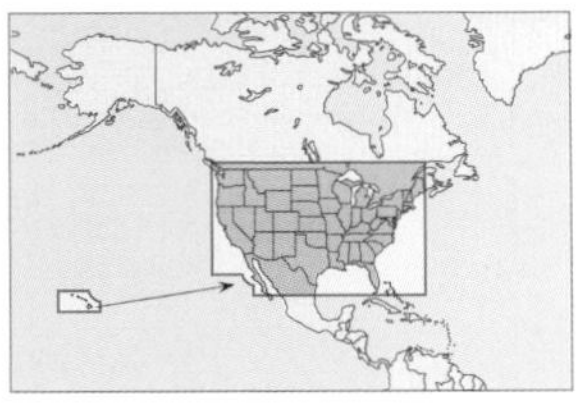

8 9 10 11 12 139 13

A
B
C
D
E
F
CANADA
Lake Winnipeg
Winnipeg
Kenora
Dryden
Lake of the Woods
Sioux Lookout
Nakina
Hearst
Moosonee
Albany
Chibougamau
Baie-Comeau
Matane
Rimouski
Rivière-du-Loup
Edmundston
NEW BRUNSWICK
Lake Nipigon
Nipigon
Greenstone
Marathon
Thunder Bay
Lake Superior
Wawa
Timmins
Cochrane
Kirkland Lake
Rouyn-Noranda
Amos
Roberval
Jonquière
Chicoutimi
Alma
St. Lawrence
La Tuque
Québec
Shawinigan
Trois-Rivières
Drummondville
Sherbrooke
MONTREAL
Ottawa
Hull
Pembroke
North Bay
Sudbury
Sault Ste. Marie
Huntsville
Orillia
Peterborough
Kingston
Barrie
Owen Sound
TORONTO
Oshawa
Kitchener
Hamilton
London
Lake Huron
Lake Ontario
Lake Erie
Lake Michigan
Fort Frances
International Falls
Thief River Falls
Grand Forks
Bemidji
Hibbing
Virginia
Two Harbors
Duluth
Superior
Houghton
Marquette
Ishpeming
Iron Mountain
Escanaba
Manistique
Petoskey
Alpena
MINNESOTA
Moorhead
Fargo
Fergus Falls
Brainerd
St. Cloud
Minneapolis
St. Paul
Rochester
Mankato
Owatonna
Winona
La Crosse
Eau Claire
Wausau
Stevens Point
Rhinelander
Green Bay
Appleton
Oshkosh
Manitowoc
Sheboygan
WISCONSIN
Madison
Milwaukee
Racine
Kenosha
Janesville
Rockford
Dubuque
Waterloo
Cedar Rapids
Iowa City
Davenport
IOWA
Des Moines
Ames
Fort Dodge
Mason City
Sioux City
Omaha
Council Bluffs
Lincoln
CHICAGO
Joliet
Aurora
Gary
South Bend
Elkhart
Fort Wayne
Kalamazoo
Grand Rapids
Muskegon
Lansing
Jackson
Ann Arbor
Flint
Saginaw
Midland
Bay City
Port Huron
DETROIT
Windsor
Toledo
Sandusky
CLEVELAND
Akron
Youngstown
Erie
Buffalo
Niagara Falls
Rochester
Syracuse
Utica
Schenectady
Albany
Troy
Oswego
Watertown
Ogdensburg
Plattsburgh
Burlington
Montpelier
VERMONT
NEW HAMPSHIRE
Concord
Manchester
Nashua
Lowell
Lawrence
BOSTON
Worcester
Springfield
Hartford
Providence
New Haven
Fall River
New Bedford
C. Cod
Nantucket I.
Martha's Vineyard
Portland
Lewiston
Augusta
Bangor
Waterville
Belfast
Penobscot Bay
MAINE
Presque Isle
Caribou
Houlton
Millinocket
Saint John
Calais
New England
NEW YORK
Yonkers
Paterson
Newark
Jersey City
Trenton
Allentown
Reading
Lancaster
Harrisburg
Scranton
Wilkes-Barre
Williamsport
Binghamton
Elmira
Ithaca
Poughkeepsie
Bridgeport
PENNSYLVANIA
PHILADELPHIA
Wilmington
Atlantic City
BALTIMORE
Dover
Annapolis
WASHINGTON D.C.
Frederick
PITTSBURGH
Johnstown
Altoona
Oil City
Canton
Mansfield
Columbus
Zanesville
Wheeling
Morgantown
Clarksburg
Parkersburg
Huntington
Charleston
WEST VIRGINIA
Dayton
Springfield
Cincinnati
Richmond
Muncie
Kokomo
Marion
Lima
Findlay
Indianapolis
INDIANA
Terre Haute
Bloomington
Columbus
Lafayette
Danville
Champaign
Decatur
Springfield
Peoria
Bloomington
Galesburg
Rock Island
Quincy
Hannibal
ILLINOIS
Mattoon
Effingham
Alton
East St. Louis
ST. LOUIS
Columbia
Jefferson City
MISSOURI
Kansas City
Lawrence
Topeka
Leavenworth
St. Joseph
Maryville
Kirksville
Chillicothe
Sedalia
Emporia
Wichita
Joplin
Springfield
Rolla
Lebanon
Cape Girardeau
Carbondale
Paducah
Evansville
Owensboro
Henderson
Vincennes
Louisville
Frankfort
Lexington
Richmond
KENTUCKY
Hazard
Bowling Green
Clarksville
Hopkinsville
Nashville
Murfreesboro
TENNESSEE
Knoxville
Oak Ridge
Johnson City
Kingsport
Chattanooga
Jackson
Memphis
Dyersburg
Athens
Huntsville
Florence
Decatur
Corinth
Tupelo
Columbus
Oxford
Clarksdale
Greenwood
Cleveland
Greenville
MISSISSIPPI
Yazoo City
Jackson
Vicksburg
Meridian
Laurel
Hattiesburg
McComb
Natchez
Biloxi
Gulfport
Mobile
Pensacola
ALABAMA
Tuscaloosa
Birmingham
Anniston
Gadsden
Montgomery
Selma
Demopolis
Auburn
Dothan
Troy
Andalusia
ATLANTA
Athens
Rome
Roswell
Gainesville
Macon
Columbus
Dublin
Albany
Valdosta
Tifton
Waycross
Douglas
Brunswick
Savannah
Statesboro
Augusta
GEORGIA
Greenville
Spartanburg
Anderson
Columbia
Rock Hill
SOUTH CAROLINA
Sumter
Florence
Myrtle Beach
Georgetown
Charleston
Orangeburg
Charlotte
Asheville
Hickory
Winston-Salem
Greensboro
Raleigh
Durham
Rocky Mount
Greenville
Goldsboro
New Bern
Fayetteville
Jacksonville
Wilmington
NORTH CAROLINA
C. Hatteras
Pamlico Sd.
Albemarle Sd.
Norfolk
Virginia Beach
Newport News
Elizabeth City
Richmond
Petersburg
Lynchburg
Roanoke
Danville
Charlottesville
Harrisonburg
Bluefield
Beckley
Radford
Pulaski
VIRGINIA
Chesapeake Bay
Salisbury
Delaware B.
C. May
Jacksonville
St. Augustine
Daytona Beach
Deltona
Gainesville
Ocala
Orlando
Lakeland
TAMPA
Clearwater
St. Petersburg
Tampa B.
Sarasota
Melbourne
Palm Bay
Fort Pierce
West Palm Beach
Fort Lauderdale
MIAMI
Naples
Fort Myers
Cape Coral
Charlotte Harbor
L. Okeechobee
Key West
Florida Bay
Florida Keys
C. Sable
Straits of Florida
Tallahassee
Lake City
Thomasville
Panama City
Apalachicola
Apalachee B.
C. San Blas
C. Canaveral
BAHAMAS
Grand Bahama I.
Freeport
Little Abaco I.
Great Abaco I.
N.E. Providence Channel
N.W. Providence Channel
Nassau
New Providence I.
Eleuthera I.
Cat I.
Exuma Sound
Great Exuma
Long I.
Andros I.
ATLANTIC OCEAN
GULF OF MEXICO
Mississippi River Delta
Breton Sd.
New Orleans
Baton Rouge
Lafayette
New Iberia
Houma
Morgan City
Lake Charles
L. Pontchartrain
LOUISIANA
Alexandria
Natchitoches
Shreveport
Monroe
De Ridder
Beaumont
Port Arthur
HOUSTON
Pasadena
Galveston
Freeport
Port Lavaca
Matagorda I.
Victoria
Aransas Pass
Brownsville
Rio Grande
Laguna Madre
Bryan
Huntsville
Lufkin
Nacogdoches
Palestine
Tyler
Longview
Marshall
Corsicana
Waco
Temple
DALLAS
Arlington
Sherman
Paris
Texarkana
Hope
Camden
El Dorado
Pine Bluff
Little Rock
Hot Springs
Stuttgart
ARKANSAS
Russellville
Conway
Fort Smith
Fayetteville
Boston Mts.
Jonesboro
Blytheville
Newport
Ouachita Mts.
Oklahoma City
Shawnee
Tulsa
Muskogee
Bartlesville
Ponca City
Fort Scott
Pittsburg
Parsons
Arkansas City
Ozark Plateau
Poplar Bluff
West Plains
Paragould
Midwest
Appalachian Mts.
Cumberland Plateau
Blue Ridge
Allegheny Mts.
95
90
85
80
75
65
45
40
35
30
25

163 8 9 10 11 164 12

1:4 800 000

50 0 50 100 150 200 km
50 0 50 100 150 miles
QUEBEC
ONTARIO
NEW YORK
PENNSYLVANIA
OHIO
INDIANA
MICHIGAN
WISCONSIN
KENTUCKY
WEST VIRGINIA
VIRGINIA
MARYLAND
DELAWARE
NEW JERSEY
VERMONT
NEW HAMPSHIRE
MASS.
CONN.
R.I.
WASHINGTON D.C.
MONTREAL
OTTAWA
TORONTO
BOSTON
PHILADELPHIA
PITTSBURGH
BALTIMORE
CLEVELAND
COLUMBUS
CINCINNATI
INDIANAPOLIS
DETROIT
CHICAGO
MILWAUKEE
LAKE SUPERIOR
LAKE HURON
LAKE ERIE
LAKE ONTARIO
Georgian Bay
Chesapeake Bay
Delaware Bay
141
140
154
A B C D E F G
1 2 3 4 5 6 7 8 9 10

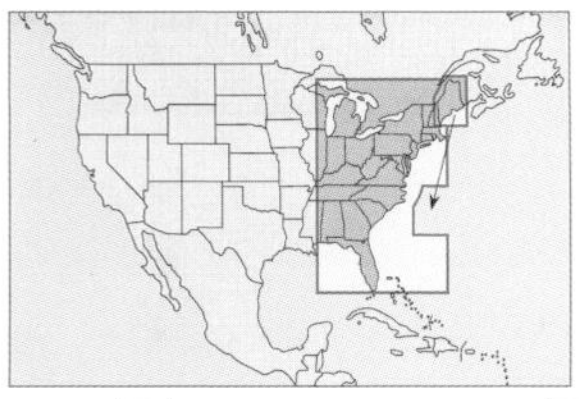

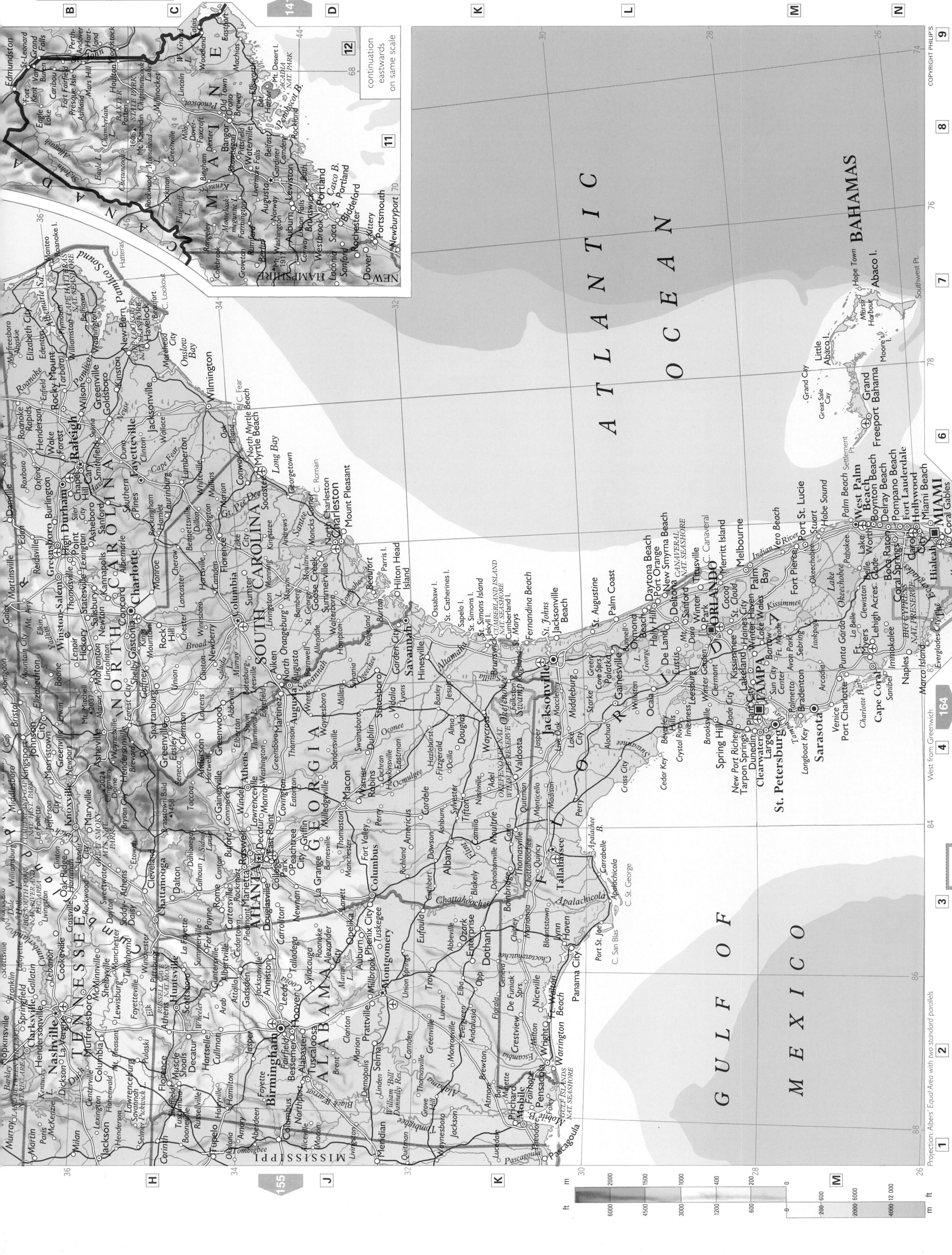
ATLANTIC OCEAN
GULF OF MEXICO
BAHAMAS
TENNESSEE
NORTH CAROLINA
SOUTH CAROLINA
GEORGIA
ALABAMA
FLORIDA
MISSISSIPPI
MAINE
CANADA
NEW HAMPSHIRE
Nashville
Raleigh
Columbia
ATLANTA
Montgomery
Tallahassee
MIAMI
TAMPA
ORLANDO
Jacksonville
Charlotte
Birmingham
Savannah
Charleston
Augusta
Portland
continuation eastwards on same scale
State Capitals
National Parks
Projection: Albers' Equal Area with two standard parallels
West from Greenwich
COPYRIGHT PHILIP'S
141
155
164

1:2 000 000

10 0 10 20 30 40 50 60 70 80 90 km

10 0 10 20 30 40 50 60 miles

National Parks

140
148
ATLANTIC OCEAN
MONTREAL
Ottawa
QUÉBEC
VERMONT
NEW HAMPSHIRE
MAINE
MASSACHUSETTS
RHODE ISLAND
CONNECTICUT
NEW JERSEY
NEW YORK
BOSTON
Providence
HARTFORD
Albany
Springfield
Worcester
New Haven
Bridgeport
Newark
Jersey City
PHILADELPHIA
Long Island
Adirondack Mountains
ADIRONDACK PARK
Green Mountains
White Mountains
Catskill Mts.
L. Champlain
St. Lawrence
Syracuse
Utica
Schenectady
Binghamton
Scranton
Allentown
Manchester
Concord
Burlington
Montpelier
Mt. Marcy 1629
Mt. Washington 1917
Block Island Sound
Long Island Sound
Martha's Vineyard
Nantucket
West from Greenwich

10 0 10 20 30 40 50 60 70 80 90 km

1:2 000 000

10 0 10 20 30 40 50 60 miles

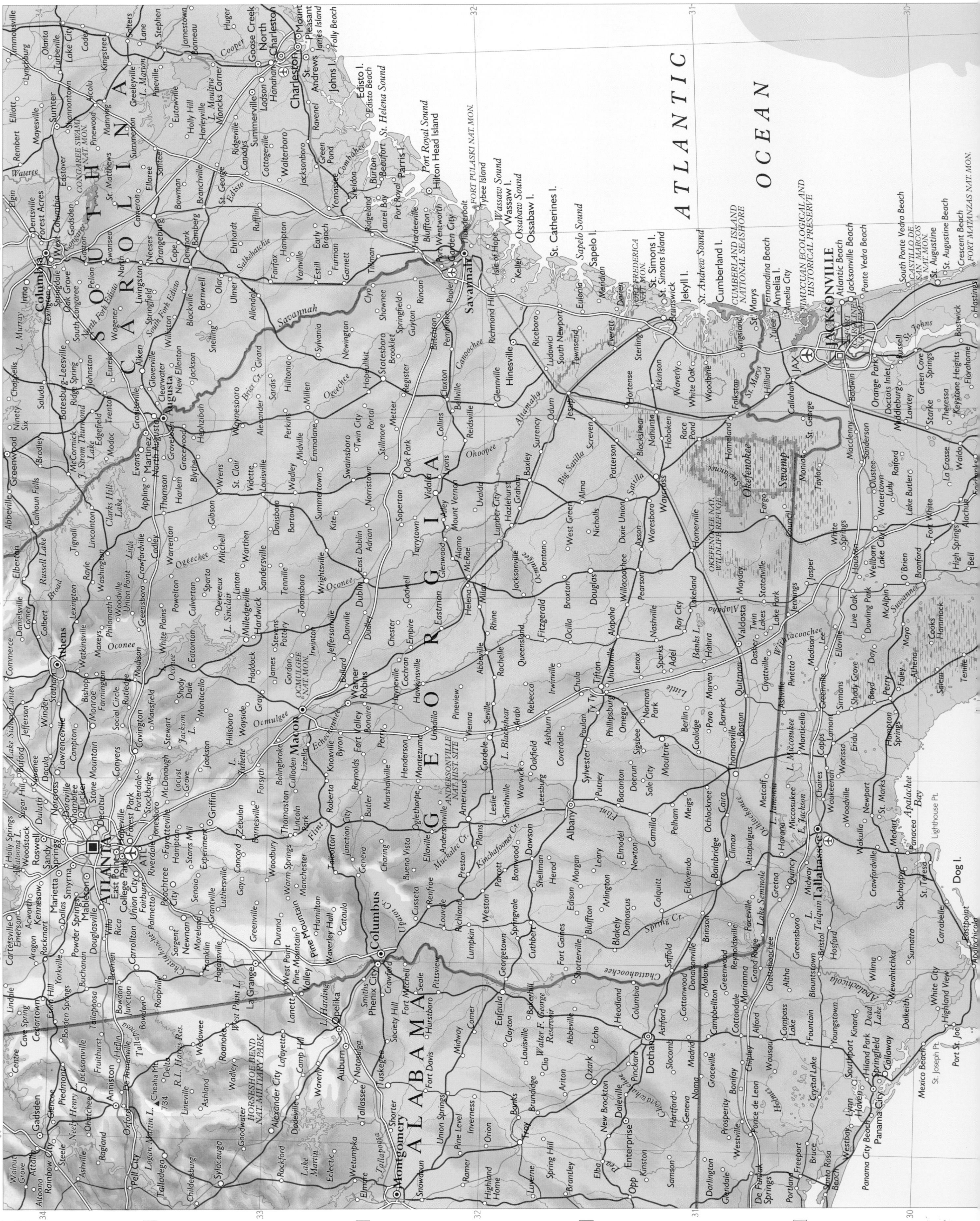

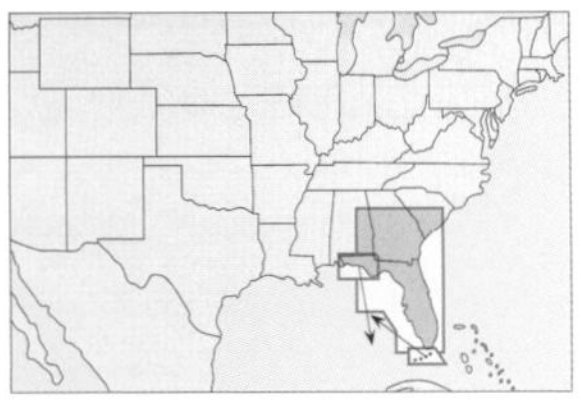

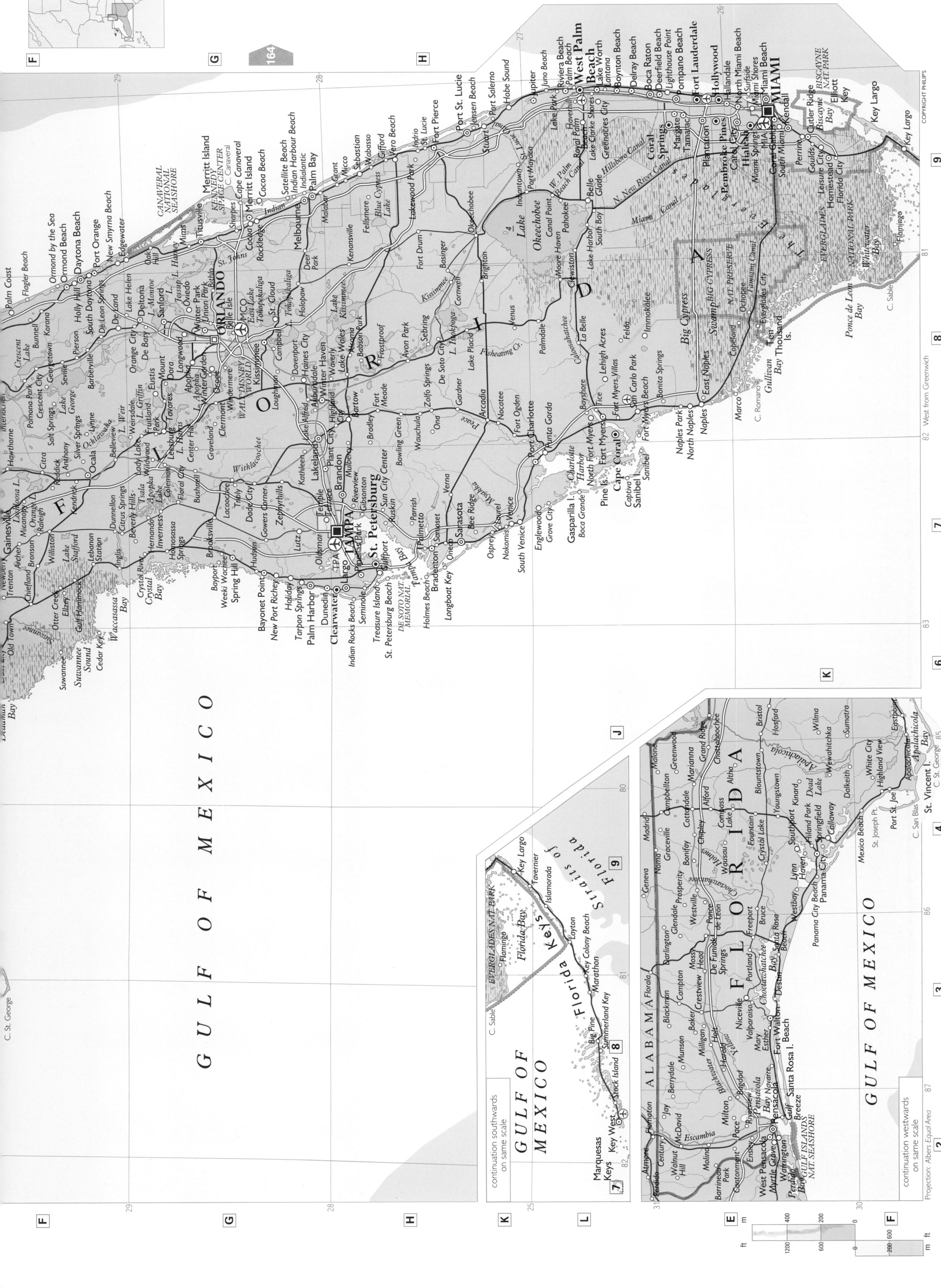
GULF OF MEXICO
FLORIDA
ALABAMA
Lake Okeechobee
MIAMI
ORLANDO
TAMPA
St. Petersburg
West Palm Beach
Fort Lauderdale
Florida Keys
Straits of Florida
EVERGLADES NATIONAL PARK
BISCAYNE NAT. PARK
BIG CYPRESS NAT. PRESERVE
CANAVERAL NATIONAL SEASHORE
GULF ISLANDS NAT. SEASHORE
DE SOTO NAT. MEMORIAL
National Parks
continuation southwards on same scale
continuation westwards on same scale
West from Greenwich
Projection: Albers Equal Area
COPYRIGHT PHILIPS
164

50 0 50 100 150 200 km

50 0 50 100 150 miles

1:4 800 000

C A N A D A
LAKE SUPERIOR
LAKE MICHIGAN
MICHIGAN
WISCONSIN
MINNESOTA
NORTH DAKOTA
SOUTH DAKOTA
IOWA
ILLINOIS
MISSOURI
NEBRASKA
KANSAS
COLORADO
WYOMING
MONTANA
CHICAGO
MILWAUKEE
MINNEAPOLIS
ST. PAUL
ST. LOUIS
KANSAS CITY
DENVER
Omaha
Des Moines
Madison
Bismarck
Pierre
Lincoln
Topeka
Jefferson City
Cheyenne
Colorado Springs
Sioux Falls
Fargo
Duluth
Rapid City
Sand Hills
Black Hills
Laramie Mountains
Lake of the Woods
Rainy Lake
Mississippi
Missouri
Platte
143
148
158
159

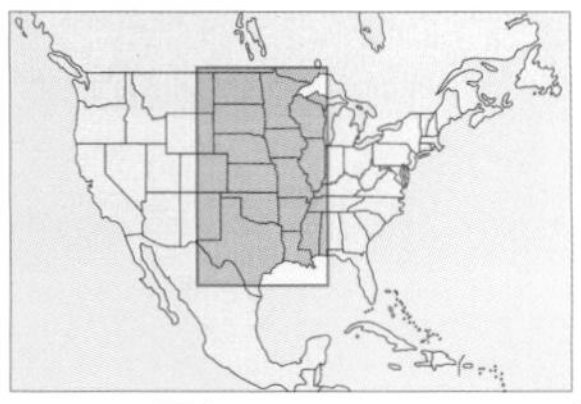

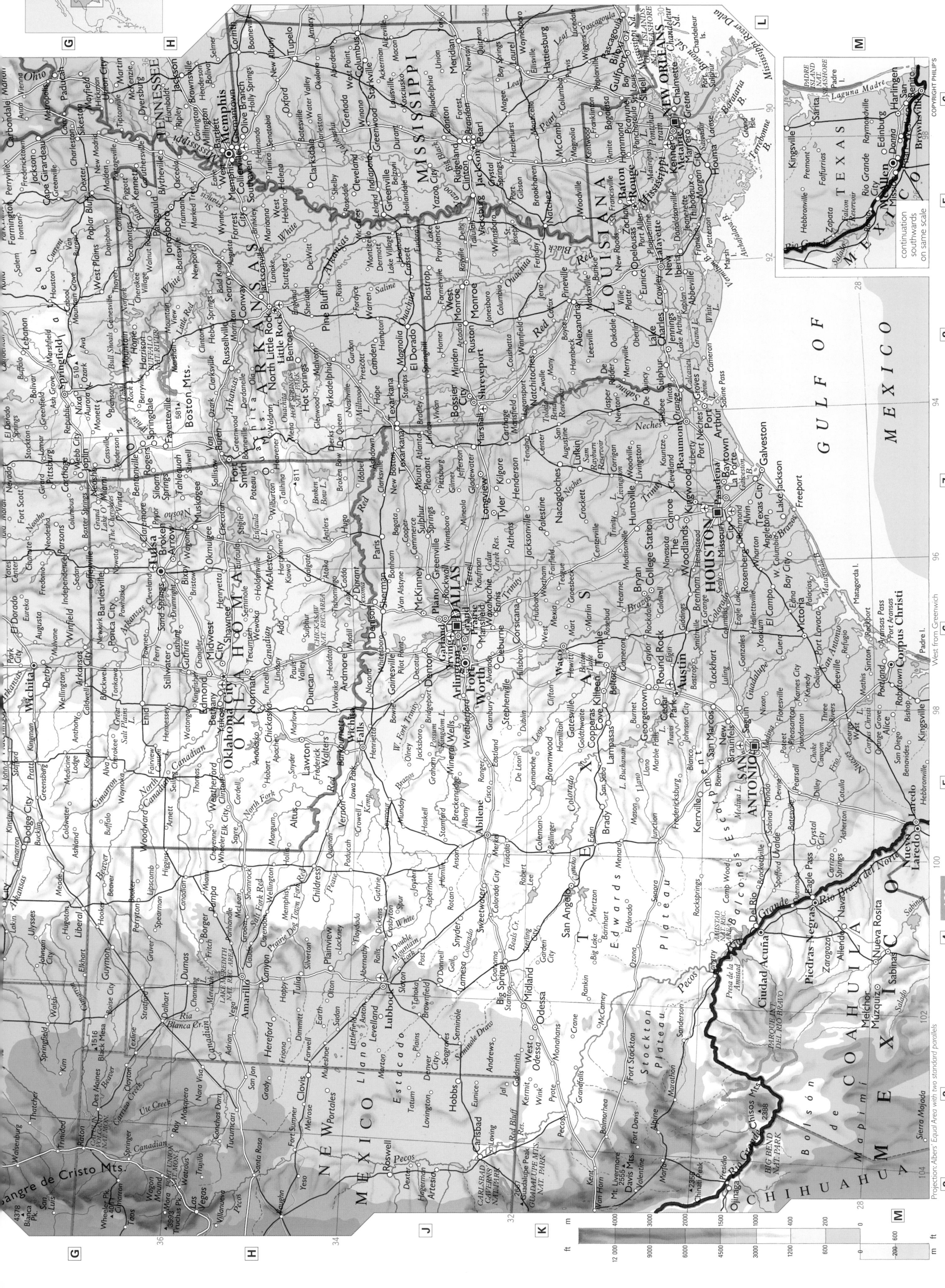
GULF OF MEXICO
OKLAHOMA
ARKANSAS
MISSISSIPPI
LOUISIANA
TEXAS
NEW MEXICO
MEXICO
COAHUILA
CHIHUAHUA
HOUSTON
DALLAS
SAN ANTONIO
NEW ORLEANS
Memphis
Oklahoma City
Little Rock
Jackson
Baton Rouge
Austin
Fort Worth
Tulsa
Shreveport
Amarillo
Lubbock
El Paso
continuation southwards on same scale
National Parks
State Capitals
Projection: Albers' Equal Area with two standard parallels
West from Greenwich
COPYRIGHT PHILIP'S
149
162

10 0 10 20 30 40 50 60 70 80 90 km

1:2 000 000

10 0 10 20 30 40 50 60 miles

National Parks

154
155

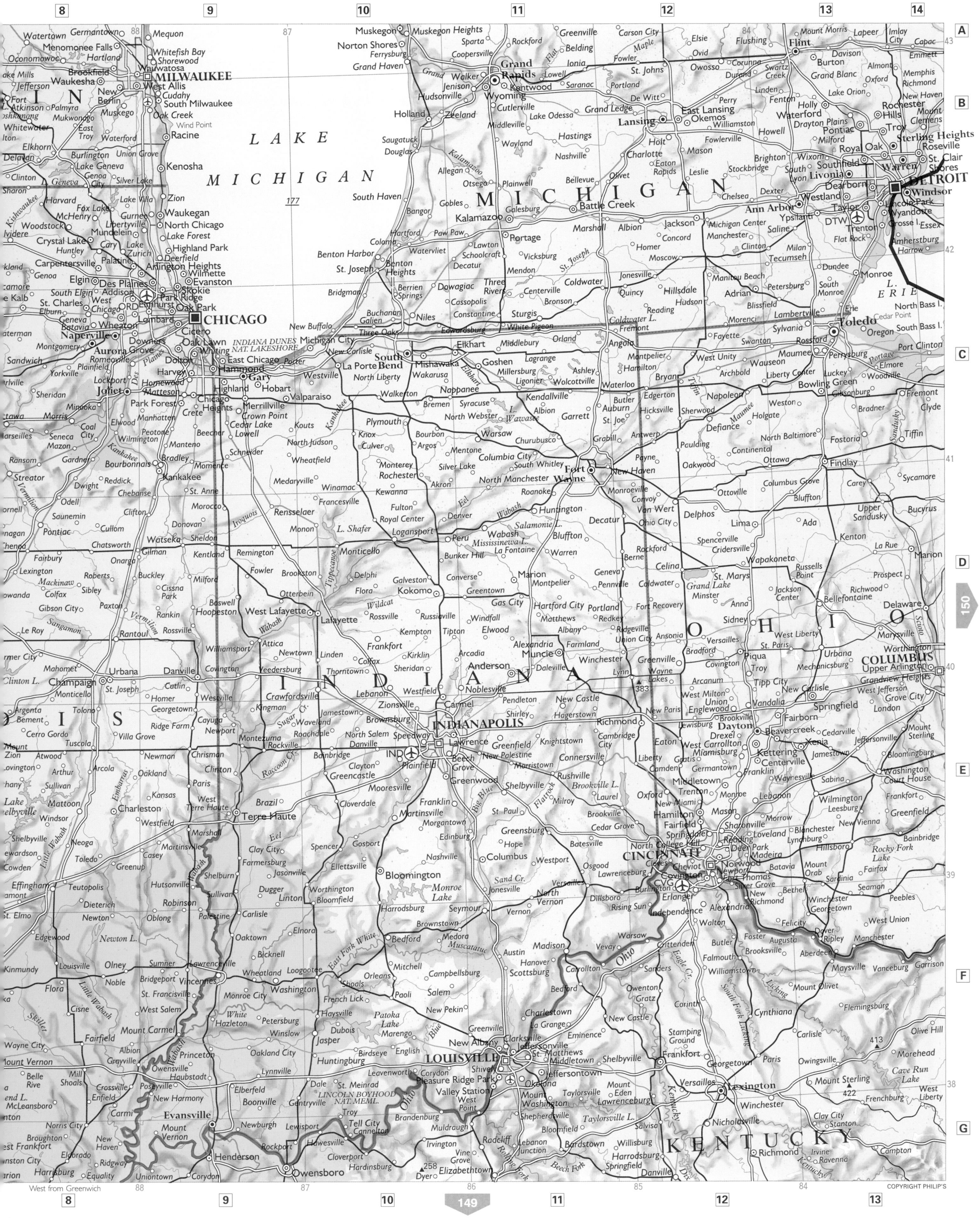
8
9
10
11
12
13
14
A
B
C
D
E
F
G
LAKE MICHIGAN
177
LAKE ERIE
MICHIGAN
INDIANA
OHIO
KENTUCKY
MILWAUKEE
CHICAGO
DETROIT
INDIANAPOLIS
COLUMBUS
CINCINNATI
LOUISVILLE
Grand Rapids
Lansing
Flint
Toledo
Fort Wayne
South Bend
Gary
Hammond
Kalamazoo
Ann Arbor
Dayton
Lexington
Frankfort
Evansville
Terre Haute
Lafayette
Muncie
Anderson
Kokomo
Bloomington
Springfield
Lima
Champaign
Urbana
Danville
Kankakee
Joliet
Aurora
Naperville
Elgin
Waukegan
Kenosha
Racine
Owensboro
Henderson
Windsor
Indiana Dunes Nat. Lakeshore
Lincoln Boyhood Nat. Meml.
Ohio
Wabash
Kankakee
Tippecanoe
Monroe Lake
Patoka Lake
Brookville L.
Grand Lake
383
413
422
258
43
42
41
40
39
38
88
87
86
85
84
150

50 0 50 100 150 200 km

1:4 800 000

50 0 50 100 150 miles

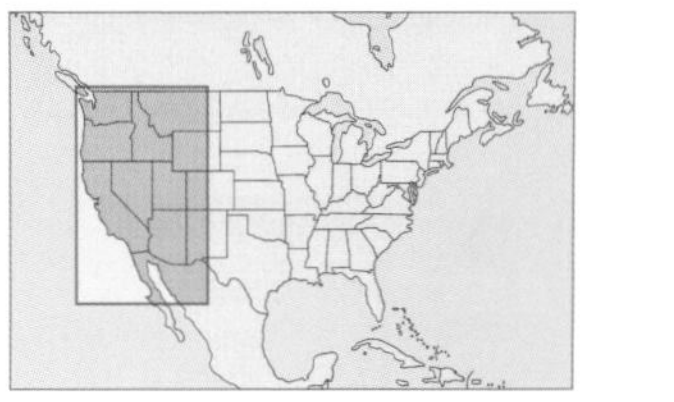

A
B
C
D
E
F
154
142
1
2
3
4
5
6
7
8
9
10
SASKATCHEWAN
ALBERTA
BRITISH COLUMBIA
CANADA
MONTANA
WYOMING
IDAHO
WASHINGTON
OREGON
NEVADA
UTAH
Bighorn Mountains
Absaroka Range
Wind River Range
Rocky Mts.
Uinta Mountains
Medicine Bow Mts.
Bitterroot Range
Lemhi Range
Salmon River Mountains
Sawtooth Range
Clearwater Mountains
Cabinet Mountains
Swan Range
Lewis Range
Little Belt Mts.
Big Belt Mts.
Crazy Mts.
Blue Mountains
Wallowa Mts.
Cascade Range
Olympic Mts.
Klamath Mts.
Coast Ranges
Columbia Basin
Snake River Plain
Great Salt Lake
Great Salt Lake Desert
Steens Mountain
Warner Mts.
Ruby Mts.
Independence Mts.
Santa Rosa Range
Trinity Range
Shoshone Mountains
Stillwater Ra.
Toiyabe Ra.
Roan Plateau
VANCOUVER
SEATTLE
PORTLAND
SACRAMENTO
Spokane
Boise
Salt Lake City
Billings
Great Falls
Helena
Missoula
Butte
Bozeman
Pocatello
Idaho Falls
Ogden
Provo
Reno
Carson City
Eugene
Salem
Medford
Redding
Casper
Laramie
Victoria
Tacoma
Olympia
Yakima
Walla Walla
Lewiston
Twin Falls
Elko
Klamath Falls
Bend
Eureka

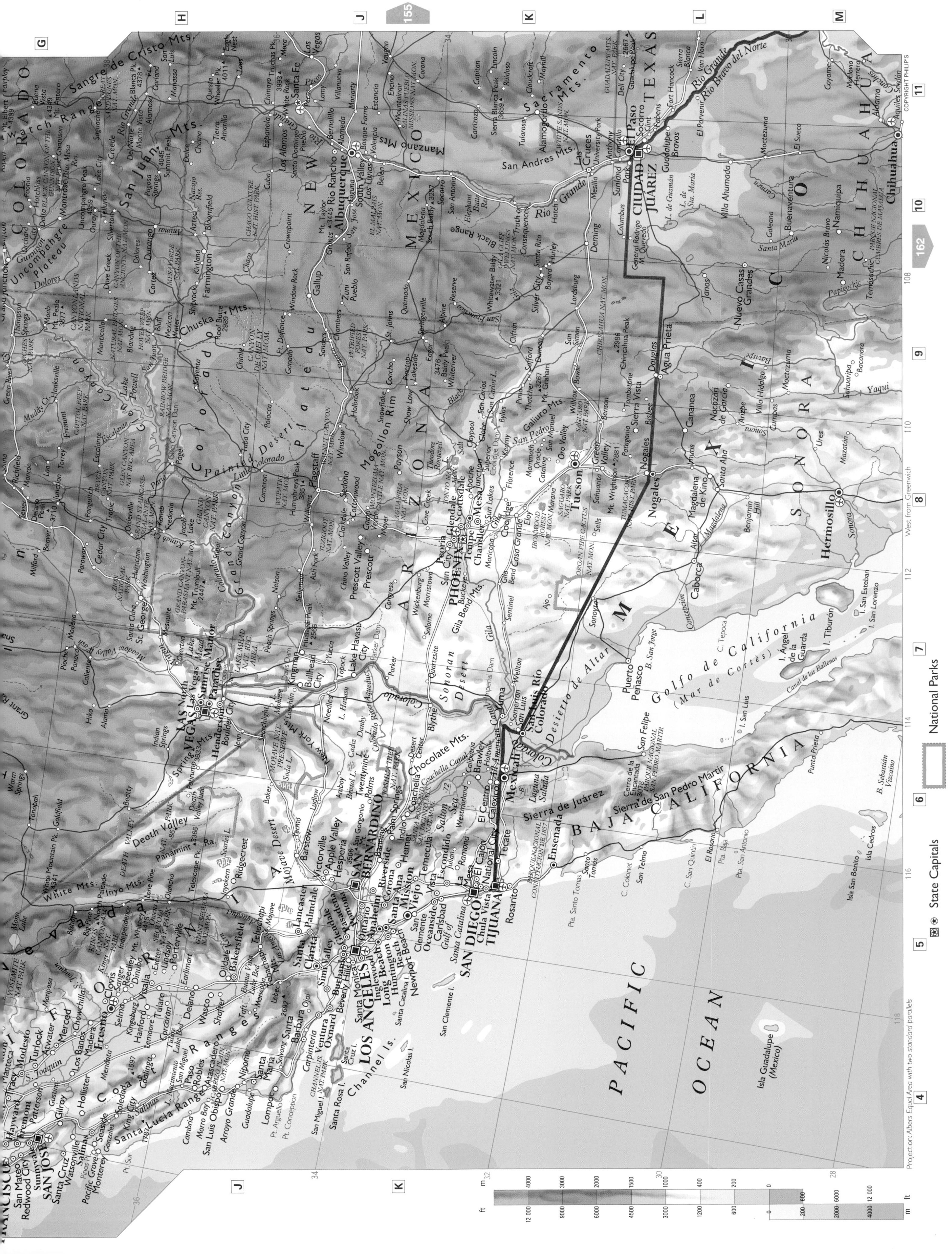

155
162
State Capitals
National Parks
Projection: Albers Equal Area with two standard parallels
COPYRIGHT PHILIP'S
West from Greenwich
m
4000
3000
2000
1500
1000
400
200
0
200
2000
4000
ft
12 000
9000
6000
4500
3000
1200
600
0
600
6000
12 000
PACIFIC
OCEAN
COLORADO
NEW MEXICO
ARIZONA
TEXAS
BAJA CALIFORNIA
SONORA
CHIHUAHUA
MEXICO
Colorado Plateau
Sangre de Cristo Mts.
San Juan Mts.
Uncompahgre Plateau
Chuska Mts.
Painted Desert
Grand Canyon
Mogollon Rim
Sacramento Mts.
San Andres Mts.
Black Range
Sonoran Desert
Mojave Desert
Death Valley
Chocolate Mts.
Sierra de Juárez
Sierra de San Pedro Mártir
Desierto de Altar
Golfo de California
(Mar de Cortés)
Channel Is.
Santa Lucia Range
Coast Ranges
Santa Fe
Albuquerque
El Paso
Ciudad Juárez
Chihuahua
Phoenix
Tucson
Flagstaff
Hermosillo
Las Vegas
Los Angeles
San Diego
Tijuana
Mexicali
San Bernardino
Fresno
San Jose
Las Cruces
Nogales
Yuma
Rio Grande
Río Bravo del Norte

1:2 000 000

159

WESTERN WASHINGTON REGION
on same scale
PACIFIC OCEAN
BRITISH COLUMBIA
CANADA
Vancouver Island
Strait of Georgia
Strait of Juan de Fuca
WASHINGTON
OREGON
Olympic Mountains
Cascade Range
VANCOUVER
Victoria
Bellingham
Everett
SEATTLE
Tacoma
Olympia
Aberdeen
Hoquiam
Longview
Astoria
Vancouver
PORTLAND
Mt. Rainier
4392
Mt. St. Helens
2550
Mt. Adams
3751
Sierra Nevada
Lake Tahoe
Reno
Sparks
Carson City
Mono Lake
White Mts.
Inyo Mts.
YOSEMITE NATIONAL PARK
KINGS CANYON NATIONAL PARK
SEQUOIA NATIONAL PARK
Mt. Whitney
4419
Sacramento Valley
San Joaquin Valley
SACRAMENTO
Stockton
Modesto
Merced
Fresno
Visalia
Madera
Chico
Yuba City
Marysville
SAN FRANCISCO
Oakland
San Jose
Santa Rosa
Napa
Vallejo
Santa Cruz
Salinas
Monterey
Santa Lucia Range
Diablo Range
Coast Ranges
Pahute Mesa

158

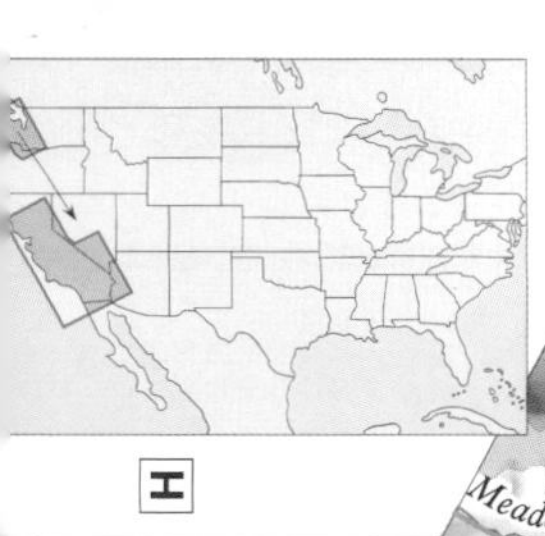

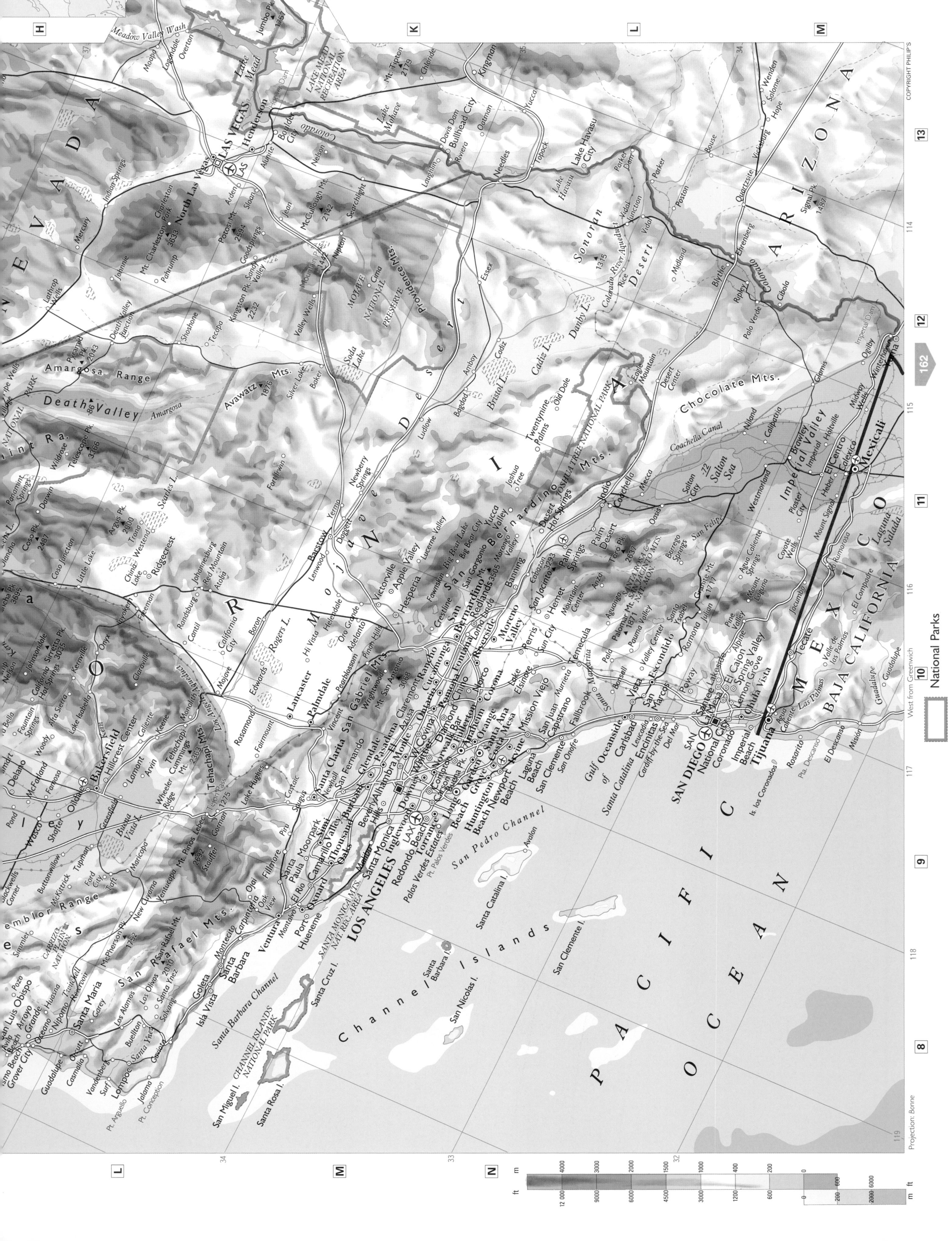

NEVADA
ARIZONA
CALIFORNIA
MEXICO
BAJA CALIFORNIA
PACIFIC OCEAN
Mojave Desert
Sonoran Desert
Channel Islands
LAS VEGAS
North Las Vegas
Henderson
Boulder City
Lake Mead
Bullhead City
Kingman
Needles
Lake Havasu City
Parker
Blythe
Barstow
Victorville
Lancaster
Palmdale
Bakersfield
Santa Clarita
Glendale
Pasadena
LOS ANGELES
Long Beach
Anaheim
Santa Ana
San Bernardino
Riverside
Palm Springs
Indio
Salton Sea
El Centro
Mexicali
Calexico
Yuma
Oceanside
Escondido
SAN DIEGO
Tijuana
Tecate
Oxnard
Ventura
Santa Barbara
Santa Maria
San Luis Obispo
Lompoc
Death Valley
Chocolate Mts.
Santa Catalina I.
San Clemente I.
San Nicolas I.
Santa Cruz I.
Santa Rosa I.
San Miguel I.
Gulf of Santa Catalina
San Pedro Channel
Santa Barbara Channel
CHANNEL ISLANDS NATIONAL PARK
JOSHUA TREE NATIONAL PARK
MOJAVE NATIONAL PRESERVE
LAKE MEAD NATIONAL RECREATION AREA
West from Greenwich
National Parks
Projection: Bonne
COPYRIGHT PHILIP'S
162
m
ft

50 0 50 100 150 200 250 300 km

1:6 400 000

50 0 50 100 150 200 miles

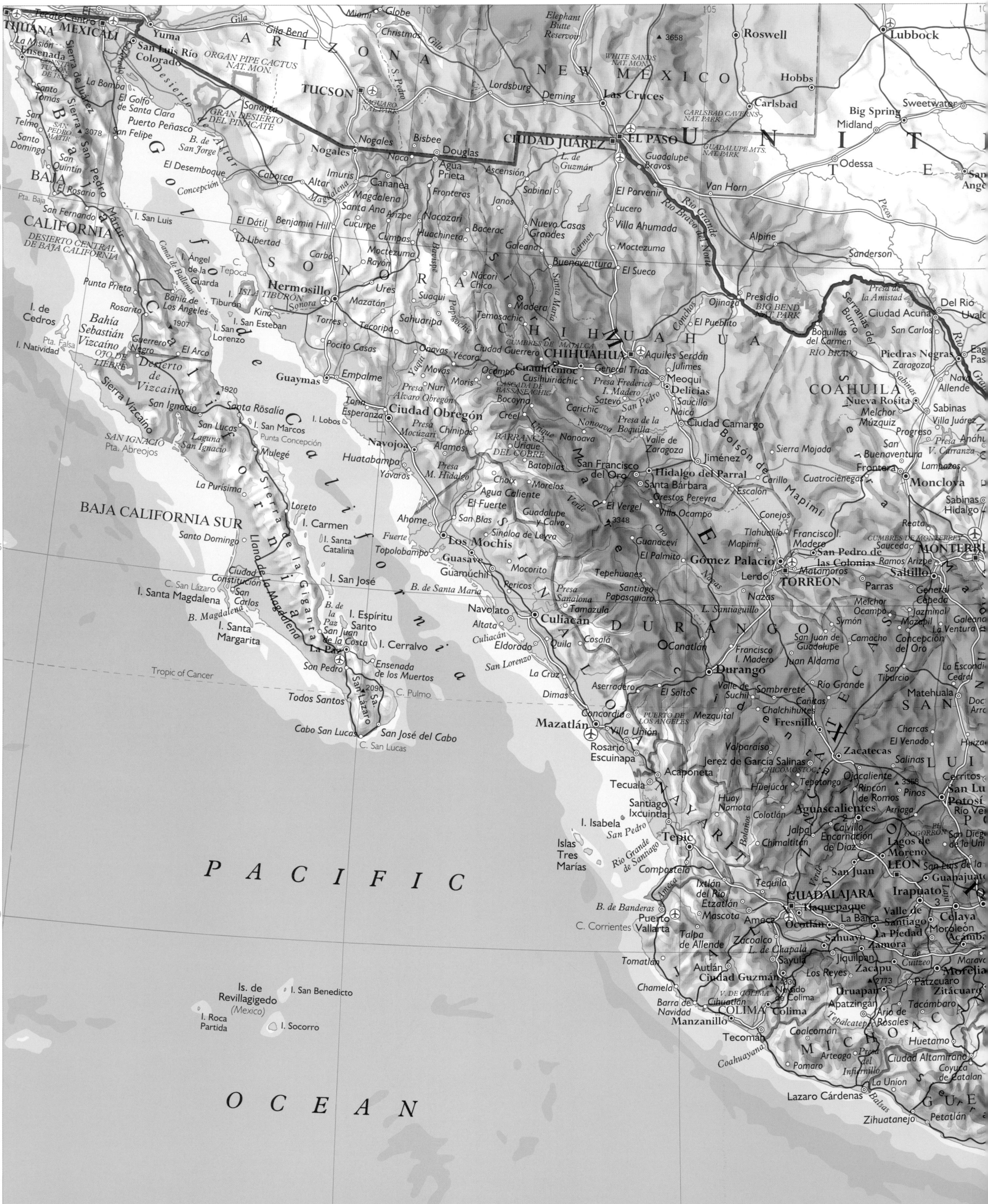

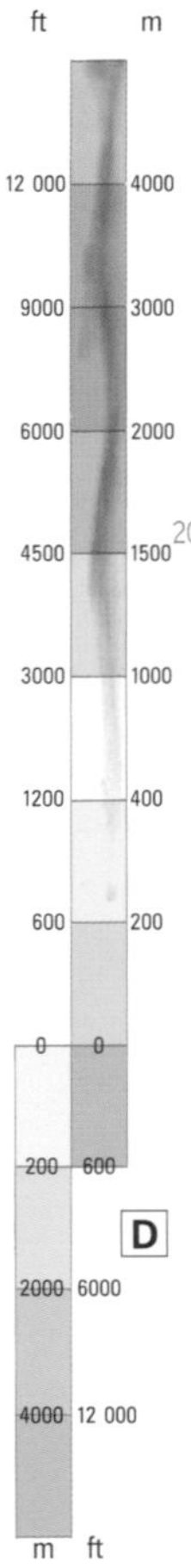

Projection: *Bi-polar oblique Conical Orthomorphic*

West from Greenwich

National Parks

State names in Central Mexico

1 DISTRITO FEDERAL	5 MÉXICO
2 AGUASCALIENTES	6 MORELOS
3 GUANAJUATO	7 QUERÉTARO
4 HIDALGO	8 TLAXCALA

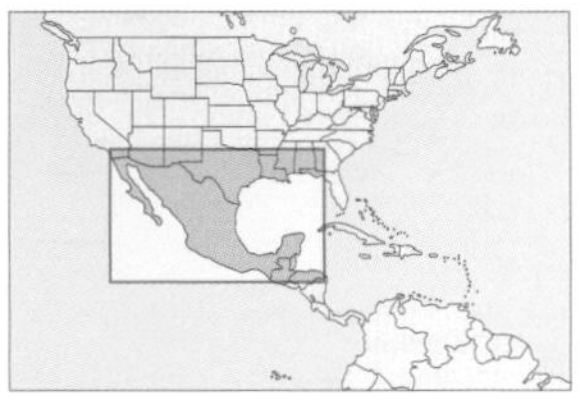

149

5
6
7
8
A
B
C
D
E
GULF OF MEXICO
Golfo de Campeche
Golfo de Tehuantepec
Golfo de Honduras
Canal de Yucatán
Tropic of Cancer
UNITED STATES
TEXAS
ARKANSAS
LOUISIANA
MISSISSIPPI
ALABAMA
GEORGIA
FLORIDA
CUBA
MEXICO
TAMAULIPAS
VERACRUZ
PUEBLA
OAXACA
CHIAPAS
TABASCO
CAMPECHE
YUCATÁN
QUINTANA ROO
GUATEMALA
BELIZE
HONDURAS
Wichita Falls
Denison
Sherman
Paris
Hope
Camden
Texarkana
El Dorado
Greenville
Tuscaloosa
Opelika
Columbus
McRae
Denton
Greenville
Possum Kingdom Res.
FORT WORTH
DALLAS
Marshall
Monroe
Vicksburg
Meridian
Selma
Montgomery
Phenix City
Americus
Cordele
Ranger
Longview
Shreveport
Tallulah
Jackson
Troy
Albany
Tifton
Abilene
Cleburne
Tyler
Waycross
Hillsboro
Corsicana
Toledo Bend Res.
Natchez
Laurel
Hattiesburg
Dothan
Valdosta
Brownwood
Palestine
Nacogdoches
Alexandria
McComb
Flomaton
Jim Woodruff Res.
Chattahoochee
Tallahassee
Waco
Lufkin
Sam Rayburn Reservoir
Jewett
Bogalusa
MOBILE
Pensacola
Panama City
Lake City
Temple
Baton Rouge
Hammond
Biloxi
Gulfport
Apalachee Bay
Bryan
Huntsville
College Station
L. Pontchartrain
Mobile Bay
C. San Blas
Austin
Navasota
Lake Charles
Lafayette
NEW ORLEANS
Breton Sd.
Suwannee
Beaumont
HOUSTON
Port Arthur
Atchafalaya Bay
Terrebonne Bay
Mississippi River Delta
Rosenberg
Galveston
Clearwater
SAN ANTONIO
Victoria
Dilley
Nueces
Alice
Corpus Christi
Laredo
Kingsville
Nuevo Laredo
PADRE ISLAND NAT. SEASHORE
Zapata
Laguna Madre
Camargo
McAllen
Harlingen
Brownsville
Reynosa
Matamoros
Valle Hermoso
Santa Teresa
Laguna Madre
China
Montemorelos
Mendez
San Fernando
Linares
Villagrán
Hidalgo
Santander Jiménez
La Pesca
Soto la Marina
Zaragoza
Ciudad Victoria
Sierra de Tamaulipas
Aldama
Pta. Jerez
Llera
Ocampo
Ciudad Mante
Ciudad Madero
Tampico
Altamira
Ciudad Valles
Cárdenas
Pánuco
L. de Tamiahua
Ozuluama
Tempoal
Naranjos
Tantoyuca
C. Rojo
Tamazunchale
Chicontepec
Tuxpan
Zimapán
Zacualtipán
Poza Rica
Papantla
San Juan del Río
Huichapan
Nautla
Pachuca
Huauchinango
Misantla
Tula
Zumpango
Tulancingo
Teziutlán
MEXICO
Xalapa
Apizaco
ZEMPOALA
Tlaxcala
4282
Coatepec
Veracruz
Amecameca
PUEBLA
Pico de Orizaba
5452
5610
Córdoba
Alvarado
Popocatépetl
Tlacotalpan
Orizaba
Cuernavaca
Tehuacán
Cosamaloapan
San Andrés Tuxtla
Jojutla
1879
Izúcar de Matamoros
Tierra Blanca
Tres Valles
Coatzacoalcos
Iguala
Huajuapan de León
Tuxtepec
Acayucan
Minatitlán
Cárdenas
Villahermosa
Asunción Nochixtlán
Juan Bautista Valle Nacional
Jesús Carranza
Chilapa
Tlaxiaco
Chilpancingo
Tierra Colorada
Oaxaca
Tlacolula
Istmo de Tehuantepec
Matías Romero
Tehuantepec
Juchitán
Salina Cruz
Ayutla
Ometepec
Ocotlán
San Jerónimo Taviche
Ixtepec
Acapulco
Pinotepa Nacional
Jamiltepec
Ejutla
Miahuatlán
Tututepec
3139
Punta Maldonado
San Pedro Mixtepec
Pochutla
Bahías de Huatulco
Puerto Escondido
Puerto Ángel
Puerto Arista
Arriaga
Tonalá
Pijijiapan
Mapastepec
Tuxtla Gutiérrez
Chiapa de Corzo
San Cristóbal de las Casas
Comitán
La Concordia
La Independencia
Ocosingo
Simojovel
Palenque
Tenosique
Balancán
Emiliano Zapata
Frontera
Paraíso
Comalcalco
Ciudad del Carmen
L. de Términos
Palizada
Escárcega
Champotón
Chenkán
Campeche
Tenabo
Hopelchén
Bolonchenticul
XOCHOB
EDZNÁ
Maxcanú
Mérida
Progreso
Dzilam de Bravo
Motul
Temax
Izamal
Espita
Tizimín
El Cuyo
Río Lagartos
Pta. Yalkubul
C. Catoche
Isla Mujeres
Cancún
Puerto Morelos
Valladolid
Sotuta
Ticul
Tekax
Peto
COBA
TULUM
Cozumel
Isla Cozumel
Vigia Chico
Felipe Carrillo Puerto
B. de la Ascensión
SIAN KA'AN
B. del Espíritu Santo
Banco Chinchorro
Bacalar
Chetumal
B. de Chetumal
CALAKMUL
BECAN
Orange Walk
Corozal
Ambergris Cay
San Pedro
Belize City
Turneffe Is.
Belmopan
Dangriga
Benque Viejo
1120
Maya Mts.
Monkey River
San Antonio
Punta Gorda
Puerto Barrios
Livingston
Is. de la Bahía
Roatán
Puerto Castilla
Trujillo
La Ceiba
Tela
Puerto Cortés
San Pedro Sula
Balfate
Iriona
Olanchito
El Progreso
Yoro
Santa Bárbara
Catacamas
Juticalpa
Comayagua
Tegucigalpa
Danlí
Santa Rosa de Copán
La Esperanza
La Paz
Yuscarán
Flores
San Luis
La Libertad
L. Petén Itzá
Uaxactún
TIKAL
San Ignacio
CHIQUIBUL
Sebol
L. de Izabal
Cobán
Huehuetenango
Cuchumatanes
3993
4220
Totonicapán
San Marcos
Sololá
Antigua
GUATEMALA
Jalapa
Zacapa
Chiquimula
Mazatenango
Retalhuleu
Coatepeque
Tapachula
Huixtla
Motozintla
Puerto Madero
Amatitlán
I. Desterrada
I. Pérez (Mexico)
La Esperanza
Guane
La Fe
C. San Antonio
C. Corrientes
95
90
85
30
25
20
15

164

50 0 50 100 150 200 250 300 km
1:6 400 000
50 0 50 100 150 200 miles

Projection: *Bi-polar oblique Conical Orthomorphic*

5

PUERTO RICO
1:2 400 000
d
ATLANTIC OCEAN
PUERTO RICO
(U.S.A.)
Pta. Agujereada
Isabela
Aguadilla
Arecibo
Barceloneta
SAN JUAN
Manatí
Vega Baja
Bayamón
Carolina
Rio Grande
Fajardo
Dewey
Culebra
Pta. Puerca
Vieques
Esperanza
San Sebastián
Mayagüez
Adjuntas
Utuado
Cordillera Central
Cerro de Punta
1338
Caguas
Cayey
Humacao
Naguabo
Yabucoa
Coamo
San Germán
Yauco
Ponce
Guayama
Guanica
Pta. Aguila
I. Caja de Muertos
VIRGIN ISLANDS
1:1 600 000
e
The Settlement
Rufling Pt.
Anegada
East Pt.
Virgin Islands
(U.K.)
Great Camanoe
Virgin Is.
(U.S.A.)
Jost Van Dyke I.
Guana I.
Tortola
Beef I.
Virgin Gorda
Spanish Town
Road Town
Cruz Bay
Peter I.
Charlotte Amalie
St. Thomas I.
St. John I.
ST. LUCIA
1:800 000
f
Cap Point
Pte. Hardy
Gros Islet
Esperance Bay
Castries
Marquis
Babonneau
L'Anse la Raye
Canaries
Dennery
Millet
Soufrière
Soufrière Bay
Mt. Gimie
950
Trou Gras Pt.
Micoud
Petit Piton
Gros Piton
Gros Piton Pt.
Vierge Pt.
Choiseul
ST. LUCIA
Laborie
Vieux Fort
C. Moule à Chique
ATLANTIC OCEAN
Crabhill
North Point
Spring Hall
Boscobelle
Fustic
Portland
Belleplaine
Speightstown
Westmoreland
Bathsheba
Hillcrest
BARBADOS
Alleynes Bay
Mt. Hillaby
Martin's Bay
Holetown
Jackson
Bridgefield
Massiah Street
Ragged Pt.
Black Rock
Ellerton
Six Cross Roads
The Crane
Bridgetown
Edey
Carlisle Bay
Worthing
Oistins
St. Martins
BGI
Chancery Lane
Oistins Bay
South Point
BARBADOS
1:800 000
g
MAS
ATLANTIC OCEAN
Arthur's Town
The Bight
Cat I.
San Salvador I.
Conception I.
Rum Cay
Tropic of Cancer
Long I.
Clarence Town
Samana Cay
Crooked I. Passage
Crooked I.
Plana Cays
Albert Town
Snug Corner
Mayaguana I.
Acklins I.
Cay Verde
Mira por vos Cay
Caicos Passage
Turks & Caicos
(U.K.)
Caicos Is.
Hogsty Reef
Cockburn Town
Turks Is.
Turks Island Passage
Little Inagua I.
INAGUA
Lake Rose
Great Inagua I.
Matthew Town
Moa
Baracoa
Pta. de Maisi
Paso de los Vientos (Windward Passage)
Î. de la Tortue
Monte Cristi
Cap-Haïtien
GUANTANAMO BAY (U.S.A.)
Jean Rabel
Port-de-Paix
Santiago de los Caballeros
San Francisco de Macorís
Puerto Plata
Puerto Rico Trench
Milwaukee Deep
9200
Gonaïves
Hinche
St-Marc
La Vega
Pico Duarte
3175
Nagua
Samana
Sanchez
Sabana de la Mar
HAITI
DOMINICAN REP.
Hato Mayor
Jérémie
Î. de la Gonâve
PORT-AU-PRINCE
San Juan
L. Enriquillo
San Pedro de Macorís
Higüey
C. Engaño
Dame Marie
Massif de la Hotte
SANTO DOMINGO
La Romana
Les Cayes
Aquin
Petit Goâve
Jacmel
Barahona
Azua de Compostela
Bani
San Cristóbal
Isla Mona
(U.S.A.)
I. Saona
Pedernales
Î. à Vache
Hispaniola
I. Beata
C. Beata
Antilles
Aguadilla
Arecibo
Bayamón
SAN JUAN
Carolina
Fajardo
Mayagüez
Ponce
Caguas
Guayama
PUERTO RICO
(U.S.A.)
Virgin Gorda
Tortola
Anegada
Virgin Is. (U.K.)
Road Town
Charlotte Amalie
Virgin Is. (U.S.A.)
Anegada Passage
Sombrero (U.K.)
Anguilla (U.K.)
St.-Martin (Fr.)
St.-Barthélemy (Fr.)
St. Maarten (Neth.)
Christiansted
Frederiksted
St. Croix (U.S.A.)
St. Eustatius (Neth.)
Saba (Neth.)
Barbuda
ANTIGUA & BARBUDA
ST. KITTS & NEVIS
Basseterre
Nevis
St. John's
Antigua
Redonda
Montserrat (U.K.)
Guadeloupe Passage
Leeward Islands
Lesser Antilles
Moule
La Désirade
Ste-Rose
GUADELOUPE (Fr.)
Pointe-à-Pitre
Basse-Terre
Marie-Galante (Fr.)
Grand-Bourg
I. des Saintes (Fr.)
Dominica Passage
Portsmouth
DOMINICA
Roseau
MORNE TROIS PITONS
Martinique Passage
I. de Aves (Venezuela)
BEAN SEA
Mt. Pelée
Ste-Marie
Le François
Fort-de-France
Rivière-Pilote
MARTINIQUE (Fr.)
St. Lucia Channel
Castries
ST. LUCIA
Soufrière
St. Vincent Passage
Soufrière
St. Vincent
Speightstown
Bridgetown
BARBADOS
Kingstown
Windward Islands
ST. VINCENT & THE GRENADINES
Hillsborough
Grenadines
St. George's
GRENADA
Lesser Antilles
Aruba (Neth.)
Oranjestad
Curaçao
Bonaire
Willemstad
NETH. ANTILLES
Pta. Gallinas
MACURIA
C. San Román
Pen. de Paraguaná
Punto Fijo
Is. Las Aves (Ven.)
ARC. LOS ROQUES
Is. Los Roques (Ven.)
I. Orchila (Ven.)
I. Blanquilla (Ven.)
Is. Los Hermanos (Ven.)
Is. Los Testigos (Ven.)
Tobago
Scarborough
COLOMBIA
Pen. de la Guajira
Pta. Espada
Ríohacha
Uribia
Santa Marta
TAYRONA
GUAJIRA
Golfo de Venezuela
Punta Cardón
Puerto Cumarebo
La Vela de Coro
Coro
NUEVA ESPARTA
I. de Margarita
La Asunción
Porlamar
I. La Tortuga
Pen. de Paria
Port of Spain
Arima
Trinidad
Galera Point
Rio Claro
San Fernando
TRINIDAD & TOBAGO
Serpent's Mouth
Dragon's Mouth
Ciénaga
S. NEVADA DE STA. MARTA
Sierra Nevada de Santa Marta
5800
Barranquilla
Soledad
Sabanalarga
San Rafael
MARACAIBO
Altagracia
Mene de Mauroa
FALCÓN
Tucacas
Puerto Cabello
Maracay
Maiquetía
La Guaira
CARACAS
VARGAS
C. Codera
Higuerote
Puerto La Cruz
Cumaná
Carúpano
Güiria
Río Caribe
G. de Paria
SUCRE
Caripito
Caicara
Maturín
MONAGAS
DELTA AMACURO
Tucupita
Barcelona
Anaco
Cantaura
El Tigre
Pariaguán
ANZOÁTEGUI
Los Barrancos
Ciudad Guayana
Sierra Imataca
Soledad
El Pao
Upata
Ciudad Bolívar
Guasipati
El Callao
Tumeremo
Embalse de Guri
La Concepción
Cabimas
Santa Rita
LARA
San Felipe
YARACUY
CARABOBO
Valencia
Los Teques
MIRANDA
Ocumare del Tuy
Altagracia de Orituco
Aragua de Barcelona
Valle de la Pascua
Río Chico
Villa del Rosario
Ciudad Ojeda
Lago de Maracaibo
Carora
BARQUISIMETO
Yaritagua
Acarigua
Villa de Cura
San Juan de los Morros
El Sombrero
San Carlos
COJEDES
Calabozo
GUÁRICO
Santa María de Ipire
Valledupar
Agustín Codazzi
CÉSAR
Machiques
ZULIA
Mene Grande
TRUJILLO
El Tocuyo
Trujillo
Valera
Betijoque
PORTUGUESA
Guanare
El Baúl
MAGDALENA
Plato
Zambrano
Calamar
Fundación
Mompós
Magangué
Sincé
Sahagún
El Banco
Encontrados
San Carlos del Zulia
CATATUMBO-BARI
MÉRIDA
Cord. de Mérida
Barinas
BARINAS
Libertad
Ciudad Bolívia
Bruzual
Puerto de Nutrias
San Fernando de Apure
Apure
Orinoco
Mapire
Calcara
VENEZUELA
NORTE DE SANTANDER
Ocaña
Cúcuta
TÁCHIRA
Santa Bárbara
Achaguas
BOLÍVAR
Simití
Caucasia
West from Greenwich
5
6
7
124
COPYRIGHT PHILIP'S
National Parks
ft
m

1:28 000 000

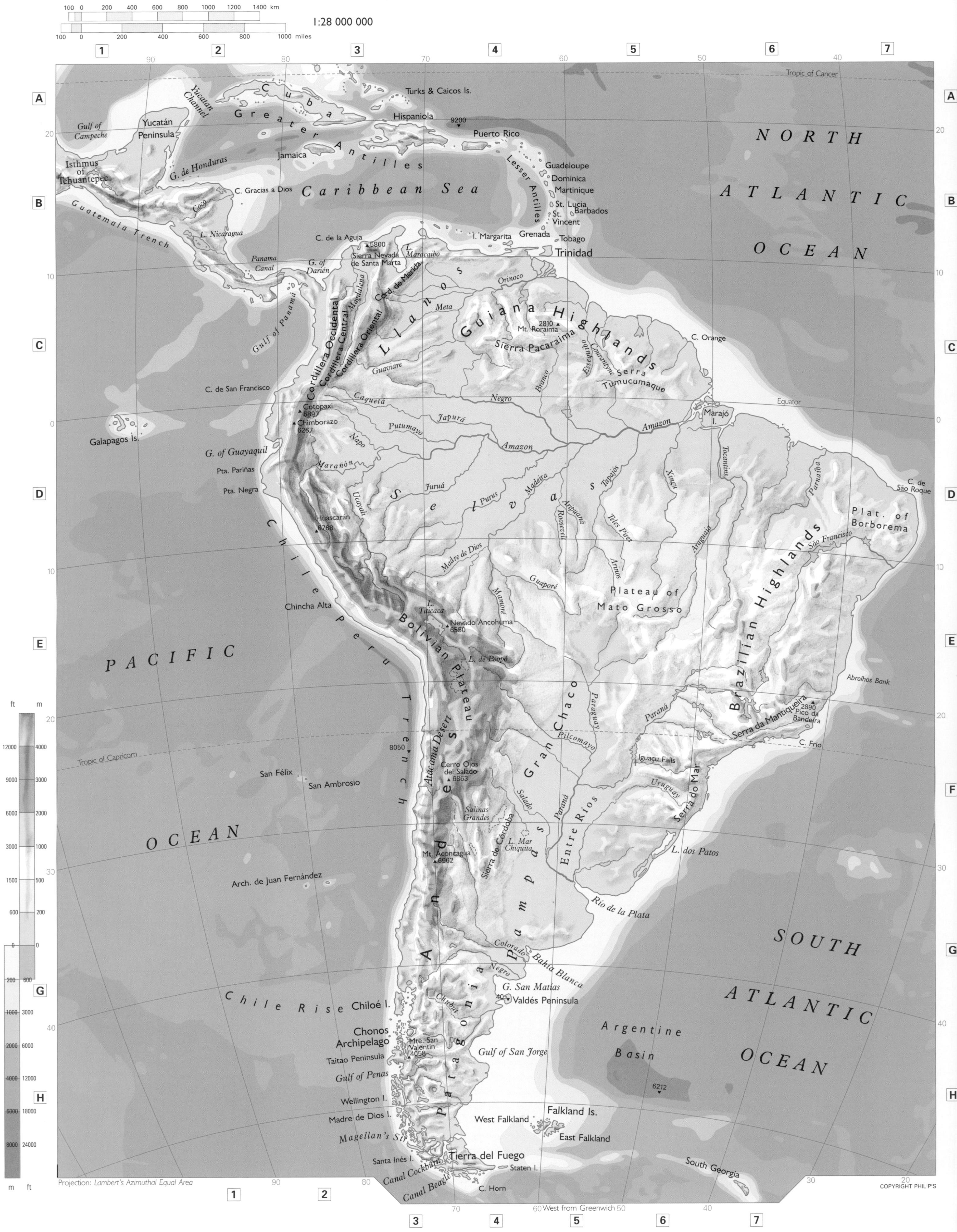

Projection: Lambert's Azimuthal Equal Area

1:28 000 000
100 0 200 400 600 800 1000 1200 1400 km
100 0 200 400 600 800 1000 miles
NORTH ATLANTIC OCEAN
Caribbean Sea
PACIFIC OCEAN
SOUTH ATLANTIC OCEAN
Tropic of Cancer
Equator
Tropic of Capricorn
Havana
CUBA
BAHAMAS
Turks & Caicos Is. (U.K.)
HAITI
Port-au-Prince
DOMINICAN REP.
San Juan
PUERTO RICO (U.S.A.)
Virgin Is. (U.K.)
JAMAICA
Kingston
ST. KITTS & NEVIS
ANTIGUA & BARBUDA
Basse-Terre
GUADELOUPE (Fr.)
DOMINICA
Fort-de-France
MARTINIQUE (Fr.)
Castries
ST. LUCIA
ST. VINCENT
Kingstown
BARBADOS
Bridgetown
GRENADA
St. George's
Port of Spain
TRINIDAD & TOBAGO
Aruba
Curaçao
MEXICO
BELIZE
GUATEMALA
Guatemala
HONDURAS
Tegucigalpa
San Salvador
EL SALVADOR
NICARAGUA
Managua
COSTA RICA
San José
Panamá
PANAMA
G. of Darién
Gulf of Panamá
Barranquilla
C. de la Aguja
Cartagena
Maracaibo
Barquisimeto
Caracas
Valencia
Cúcuta
San Cristóbal
Orinoco
Ciudad Guayana
Medellín
Bucaramanga
VENEZUELA
Georgetown
Paramaribo
Cayenne
C. Orange
GUYANA
SURINAME
FRENCH GUIANA
Bogotá
Magdalena
Cali
COLOMBIA
RORAIMA
Essequibo
Branco
AMAPÁ
Galapagos Is. (Ecuador)
Quito
ECUADOR
Guayaquil
G. of Guayaquil
Napo
Putumayo
Japurá
Amazon
Marajó I.
Belém
Manaus
Santarém
São Luís
Iquitos
Marañón
AMAZONAS
PARÁ
Xingu
Tapajós
Tocantins
Fortaleza
C. de São Roque
Teresina
MARANHÃO
CEARÁ
RIO G. DO NORTE
Natal
PARAÍBA
Juruá
Purus
Madeira
Chiclayo
Trujillo
Chimbote
Ucayali
ACRE
Pôrto Velho
Parnaíba
PIAUÍ
Campina Grande
PERNAMBUCO
Recife
ALAGOAS
Maceió
SERGIPE
Aracaju
PERU
Madre de Dios
RONDÔNIA
BRAZIL
Araguaia
TOCANTINS
Callao
LIMA
Cuzco
L. Titicaca
Mamoré
MATO GROSSO
BAHÍA
Salvador
Arequipa
La Paz
BOLIVIA
Cochabamba
Santa Cruz
Sucre
Cuiabá
GOIÁS
DIS. FED.
Brasília
Goiânia
São Francisco
MINAS GERAIS
Paraguay
MATO GROSSO DO SUL
Iquique
Belo Horizonte
ESPÍRITO SANTO
Vitória
Ribeirão Prêto
Juiz de Fora
Campinas
Paraná
SÃO PAULO
R. DE J.
Campos
PARAGUAY
Pilcomayo
Antofagasta
Salta
Asunción
PARANÁ
SÃO PAULO
Niterói
RIO DE JANEIRO
Curitiba
San Félix (Chile)
San Ambrosio (Chile)
San Miguel de Tucumán
Resistencia
Corrientes
SANTA CATARINA
Salado
Uruguay
RIO GRANDE DO SUL
Pôrto Alegre
Córdoba
Santa Fe
San Juan
Paraná
Pelotas
Viña del Mar
Valparaíso
SANTIAGO
Mendoza
Rosario
URUGUAY
Arch. de Juan Fernández (Chile)
BUENOS AIRES
Montevideo
La Plata
Río de la Plata
Talca
Concepción
Bahía Blanca
Mar del Plata
Colorado
CHILE
ARGENTINA
Valdivia
Negro
Viedma
Puerto Montt
Chubut
Comodoro Rivadavia
Gulf of San Jorge
Gulf of Penas
West Falkland
FALKLAND IS. (U.K.)
Stanley
East Falkland
Magellan's Str.
Punta Arenas
Tierra del Fuego
C. Horn
South Georgia (U.K.)
West from Greenwich
Projection: Lambert's Azimuthal Equal Area
LIMA Capital Cities
COPYRIGHT PHILIP'S

1:6 400 000
50 0 50 100 150 200 250 300 km
50 0 50 100 150 200 miles
165
172
164
CARIBBEAN SEA
PACIFIC OCEAN
Pta. Gallinas
Cabo de la Vela
Peninsula de la Guajira
Aruba (Neth.)
NETH. ANTILLES
Curaçao
Bonaire
Willemstad
Pen. de Paraguaná
Punto Fijo
Punta Cardón
Is. de Aves (Ven.)
Is. Los Roques (Ven.)
Ríohacha
Santa Marta
BARRANQUILLA
Ciénaga
Sierra Nevada de Santa Marta
Pico Cristóbal Colón
5800
Valledupar
CARTAGENA
Golfo de Venezuela
MARACAIBO
Cabimas
Lago de Maracaibo
Coro
FALCÓN
DISTRITO FEDERAL
CARACAS
Maracay
Valencia
BARQUISIMETO
LARA
ZULIA
TRUJILLO
MÉRIDA
Mérida
BARINAS
Barinas
PORTUGUESA
COJEDES
GUÁRICO
APURE
San Fernando de Apure
San Cristóbal
TÁCHIRA
Cúcuta
Colón
PANAMÁ
PANAMA
Golfo de Panamá
Arch. de las Perlas
Golfo del Darién
Golfo de Urabá
Montería
Sincelejo
SUCRE
CÓRDOBA
BOLÍVAR
MAGDALENA
CESAR
ANTIOQUIA
MEDELLÍN
BUCARAMANGA
SANTANDER
NORTE DE SANTANDER
ARAUCA
Arauca
CASANARE
BOYACÁ
Tunja
CHOCÓ
Quibdó
MANIZALES
Pereira
Armenia
Ibagué
BOGOTÁ
CUNDINAMARCA
TOLIMA
VALLE
Buenaventura
CALI
CAUCA
Popayán
HUILA
Neiva
NARIÑO
Pasto
Tumaco
Ipiales
Tulcán
META
Villavicencio
VICHADA
GUAINÍA
GUAVIARE
VAUPÉS
CAQUETÁ
Florencia
PUTUMAYO
AMAZONAS
COLOMBIA
VENEZUELA
ECUADOR
QUITO
ESMERALDAS
Esmeraldas
Ibarra
MANABÍ
Manta
Portoviejo
Latacunga
Ambato
Riobamba
GUAYAQUIL
GUAYAS
Golfo de Guayaquil
Cuenca
AZUAY
Machala
Loja
PERU
LORETO
Iquitos
Amazonas
Leticia
Tabatinga
Puerto Ayacucho
Puerto Carreño
Orinoco
Meta
Putumayo
Caquetá
Japurá
PICO DA NEBLINA
Projection: Lamberts Equivalent Azimuthal

5
6
7
A
B
C
D
E
F
G
TRINIDAD AND TOBAGO
1:2 000 000
10 0 10 20 30 40 50 km
10 0 10 20 30 miles
9
10
8
Tobago
Charlotteville
North Pt.
Little Tobago
Castara
Main Ridge
565
Roxborough
Plymouth
Buccoo Reef
Crown Pt.
Scarborough
Rockly Bay
VENEZUELA
Pen. de Paria
Macuro
Güiria
Corozal Pt.
Monos I.
Dragon's Mouth
Chacachacare
Maracas Bay Village
La Vache Pt.
Chupara Pt.
Blanchisseuse
Matelot
Sans Souci
Toco
Galera Pt.
Redhead
Salibea
Northern Range
936
940
Mt. Aripo
Maraval
Port of Spain
Tunapuna
Valencia
San Juan
Caroni
Arima
Guaico
Matura Bay
Sangre Grande
ATLANTIC OCEAN
Golfo de Paria
Chaguanas
Talparo
Upper Manzanilla
Nariva Swamp
Couva
Cocos Bay
Trinidad
Point Lisas
Otaheite Bay
San Fernando
Gasparillo
Rio Claro
Guatuaro Pt.
Brighton
Guapo Bay
La Brea
Princes Town
Pierreville
Mayaro Bay
Point Fortin
Pitch Lake
Penal
Basse Terre
Guayaguayare
Cedros Bay
Palo Seco
Siparia
304
Trinity Hills
Galeota Pt.
Bonasse
Icacos Pt.
Erin Pt.
La Lune
Moruga
Serpent's Mouth
VENEZUELA
Pta. Bombedor
West from Greenwich
I. Blanquilla (Ven.)
Is Los Hermanos (Ven.)
St. George's
GRENADA
Is. Los Testigos (Ven.)
NUEVA ESPARTA
I. de Margarita
La Asunción
Porlamar
Tortuga (Ven.)
Boca del Rio
Pen. de Araya
Carúpano
Rio Caribe
Pen. de Paria
Port of Spain
Arima
TRINIDAD AND TOBAGO
Tobago
Scarborough
Cumaná
Cariaco
El Pilar
Irapa
Güiria
San Fernando
Trinidad
Rio Claro
Galeota Pt.
Guayaguayare
Puerto La Cruz
Barcelona
Guanta
SUCRE
Golfo de Paria
La Brea
Serpent's Mouth
Caripito
Maturín
MARIUSA
Aragua de Barcelona
Cantaura
Anaco
MONAGAS
Zaraza
ANZOÁTEGUI
DELTA
El Tigre
Tucupita
Santa María de Ipire
Pariaguán
Barrancas
Orinoco
Boca Grande
I. Corocoro
Soledad
Pto. Ordaz
Ciudad Guayana
Curiapo
AMACURO
Morawhanna
Mabaruma
Upata
El Palmar
El Miamo
La Horqueta
Port Kaituma
Ciudad Bolívar
El Callao
Guasipati
Tumeremo
Matthew's Ridge
Kokerite
Charity
Anna Regina
Suddie
Embalse de Guri
El Dorado
Cuyuni
Spring Garden
Parika
Georgetown
Mahaicony
Bartica
GUYANA
Sand Hills
Rosignol
New Amsterdam
Port Mourant
Peter's Mine
Mazaruni
Issano
Rockstone
Mackenzie
Skeldon
Mara
Curatabaca
Salto del Angel (Angel Falls)
2560
CANAIMA
Luepa
Equeipa
La Gran Sabana
Mt. Roraima 2772
Imbaimadai
Tumatumari
Pakaraima Mts.
Kaieteur Falls
Mahdia
Itunì
Kwakwani
Guaina
Arabelo
Aparurén
Sta. Elena de Uairén
Orinduik
Icabarú
Sierra del Zamuro
Motocurunya
Catisimiña
Sierra Pacaraima
Sa. Tepequem
Owenteik
Apoteri
Annai
Conceição do Maú
Uraricoera
Pirara
Lethem
Bonfim
Alto Alegre
Boa Vista
Wichabai
Dadanawa
Shea
Isherton
Serra do Apiaú
Serra do Mucajaí
Serra Parima
PARIMA-TAPIRAPECÓ
Missão Catrimani
Caracaraí
RORAIMA
SERRA DA MOCIDADE
San José do Anauá
Novo Paraíso
São João da Baliza
Uberlândia
Kamoa Mts.
Biloku
Serra Acaraí
734
Catrimani
Santa Maria do Boiaçu
Tapurucuará
Sta. Isabel do Rio Negro
Barcelos
Represa de Balbina
Carvoeiro
Moura
Agua Preta
JAÚ
Mucura
Presidente Figueiredo
Balbina
Santo Antonio
Novo Airão
Arquipélago das Anavilhanas
Rio Preto da Eva
Itapiranga
Silves
Urucara
Manacapuru
MANAUS
Careiro da Várzea
Itaquatiara
Barreirinha
Parintins
Tabocal
Codajás
Anamã
Caapiranga
Tefé
Foz do Copeá
Autazes
Nova Olinda do Norte
Maués
Beruri
Coari
Careiro
Osório da Fonseca
Canumã
Paricatuba
Borba
Arumã
Nova Aripuanã
Hevelândia
BRAZIL
AMAZONAS
Nieuw Nickerie
Paramaribo
Alliance
Totness
Groningen
Nieuw Amsterdam
Onverwacht
Moengo
Wageningen
Tapoeripa
Lelydorp
Zanderij
Albina
Mana
Iracoubo
Sinnamary
I. du Diable
Iles du Salut
Kourou
St-Laurent
Oreala
Wakai
Apoera
Epira
Kwakoegron
Brokopondo
Brownsweg
Apatou
Gare Tigre
Tonate
Cayenne
Rémire
Roura
Avanavero
W. J. Van Blommestein Meer
Pokigron
Langatabbetje
Paul Isnard
Citron
St.-Élie
Kabalebo-stuwmeer
SURINAME
Bottopassi
Grand Santi
FRENCH GUIANA
Cacao
Kaw
Cabo Orange
Régina
Wilhelmina Geb.
Julianatop 1280
Papaichton
Benzdorp
Maripasoula
Saül
St-Georges
Oiapoque
Ouanary
Clevelândia do Norte
Peleloetepu
Antécume Pata
Bienvenue
Camopi
Vila Velha
CABO ORANGE
Kwamala-samutu
Serra Tumucumaque
690
Lourenço
Calçoene
I. de Maracá
Amapá
Sucuriju
AMAPÁ
Aporema
Serra do Navio
Pedra Branca
Pôrto Grande
Meirurnã
Maloca
Macapá
Pôrto Santana
Mazagão
Arere
Chaves
Afuá
Ilha de Marajó
Anajás
Monte Dourado
Bôca do Jari
Almeirim
Gurupá
I. Grande de Gurupá
Porteira
Cuminá
Oriximina
Óbidos
Alenquer
Prainha
Faro
Monte Alegre
Juruti
Curuai
Pacoval
Pôrto de Móz
Breves
Oeiras do Pará
Portel
Nhamundá
Alter do Chão
Santarém
Belterra
Mujuí dos Campos
Boim
Senador José Porfirio
Vitória
Altamira
Belo Monte
Brasil Novo
Fávânia
Medicilândia
Uruará
Aveiro
Brasília Legal
Itaituba
Rurópolis
São Luís do Tapajós
AMAZÔNIA
PARÁ
ATLANTIC OCEAN
Amazonas
West from Greenwich
COPYRIGHT PHILIP'S

50 0 50 100 150 200 250 300 km

1:6 400 000

50 0 50 100 150 200 miles

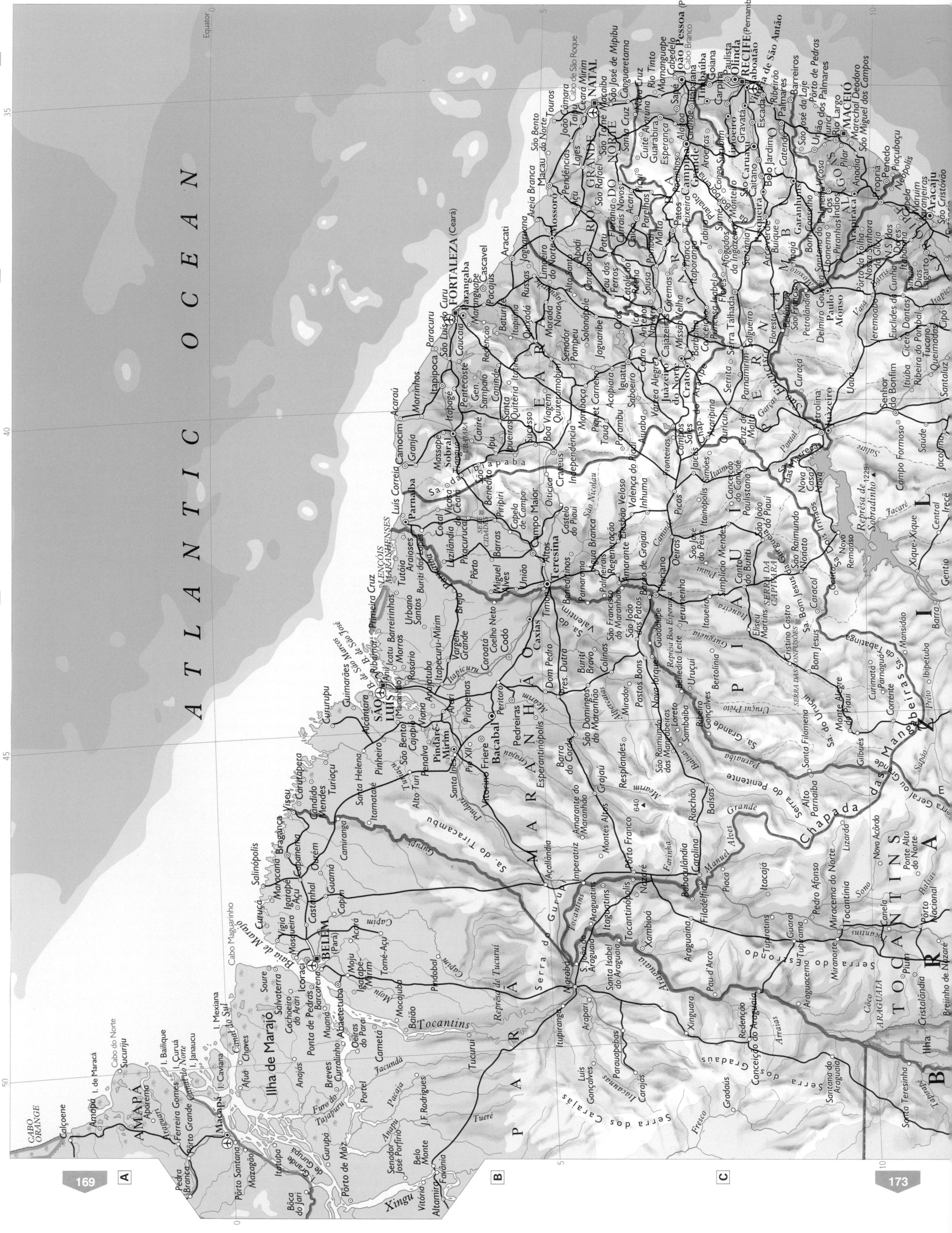

169

173

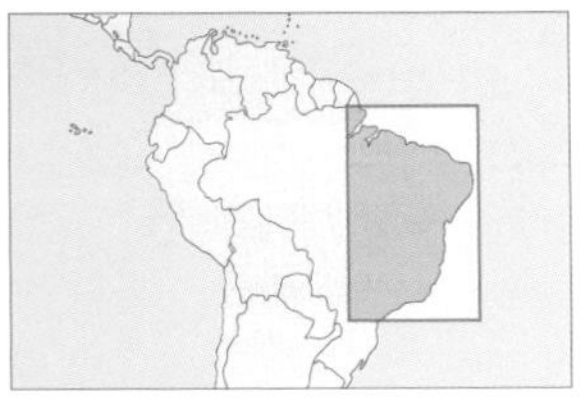

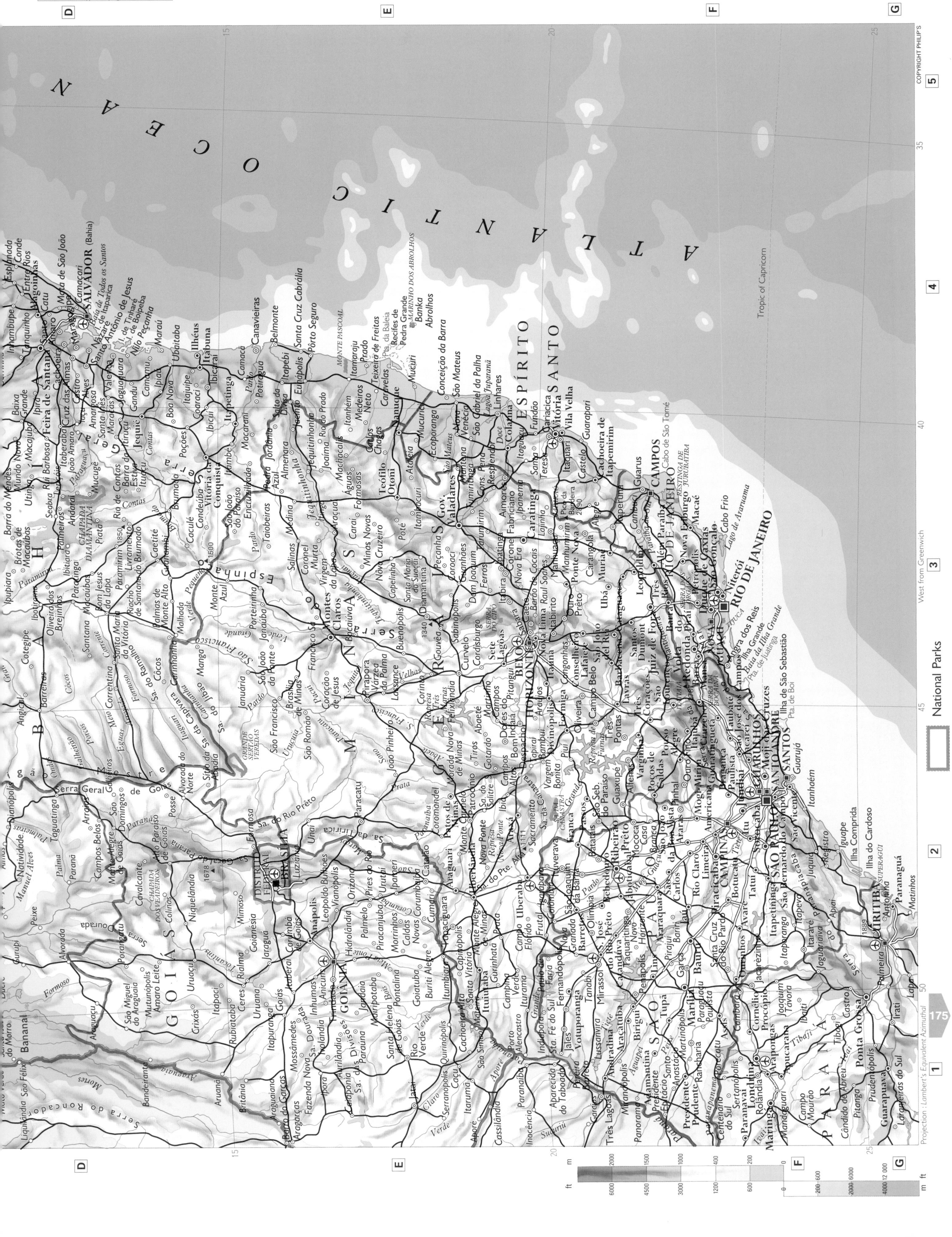

ATLANTIC OCEAN
SALVADOR (Bahia)
RIO DE JANEIRO
SÃO PAULO
BELO HORIZONTE
BRASÍLIA
DISTRITO FEDERAL
GOIÂNIA
CURITIBA
SANTOS
VITÓRIA
CAMPOS
BAHIA
MINAS GERAIS
GOIÁS
ESPÍRITO SANTO
PARANÁ
Tropic of Capricorn
West from Greenwich
National Parks
Projection : Lambert's Equivalent Azimuthal
COPYRIGHT PHILIP'S
175

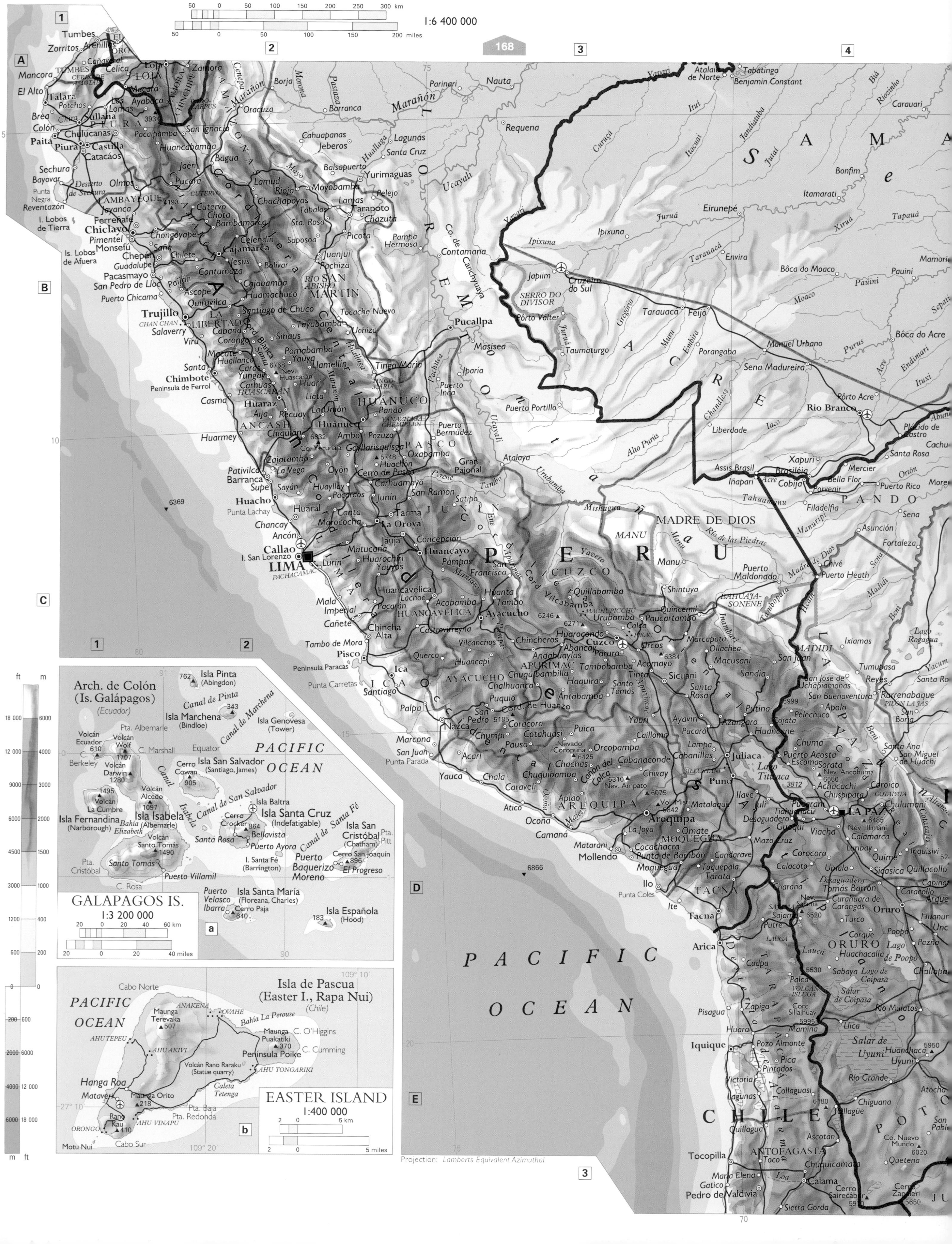

1:6 400 000
168
PACIFIC OCEAN
PERU
CHILE
A M A Z O N A S
A C R E
MADRE DE DIOS
PANDO
LA PAZ
ORURO
LIMA
Callao
Arequipa
Cuzco
Trujillo
Chiclayo
Piura
Iquitos
Pucallpa
Huancayo
Ayacucho
Puno
Juliaca
Lago Titicaca
Tacna
Arica
Iquique
Antofagasta
Rio Branco
Cruzeiro do Sul
Salar de Uyuni
Arch. de Colón (Is. Galápagos) (Ecuador)
GALAPAGOS IS.
1:3 200 000
Isla Pinta (Abingdon)
Isla Marchena (Bindloe)
Isla Genovesa (Tower)
Isla San Salvador (Santiago, James)
Isla Isabela (Albemarle)
Isla Fernandina (Narborough)
Isla Santa Cruz (Indefatigable)
Isla San Cristóbal (Chatham)
Isla Santa María (Floreana, Charles)
Isla Española (Hood)
Isla de Pascua (Easter I., Rapa Nui) (Chile)
EASTER ISLAND
1:400 000
Hanga Roa
Cabo Norte
Cabo Sur
Motu Nui
Península Poike
Volcán Rano Raraku (Statue quarry)
Projection: Lamberts Equivalent Azimuthal

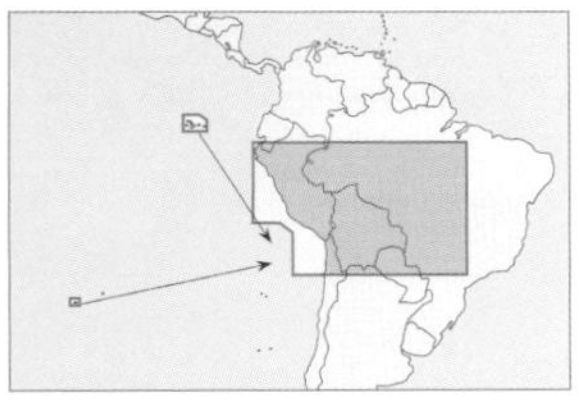

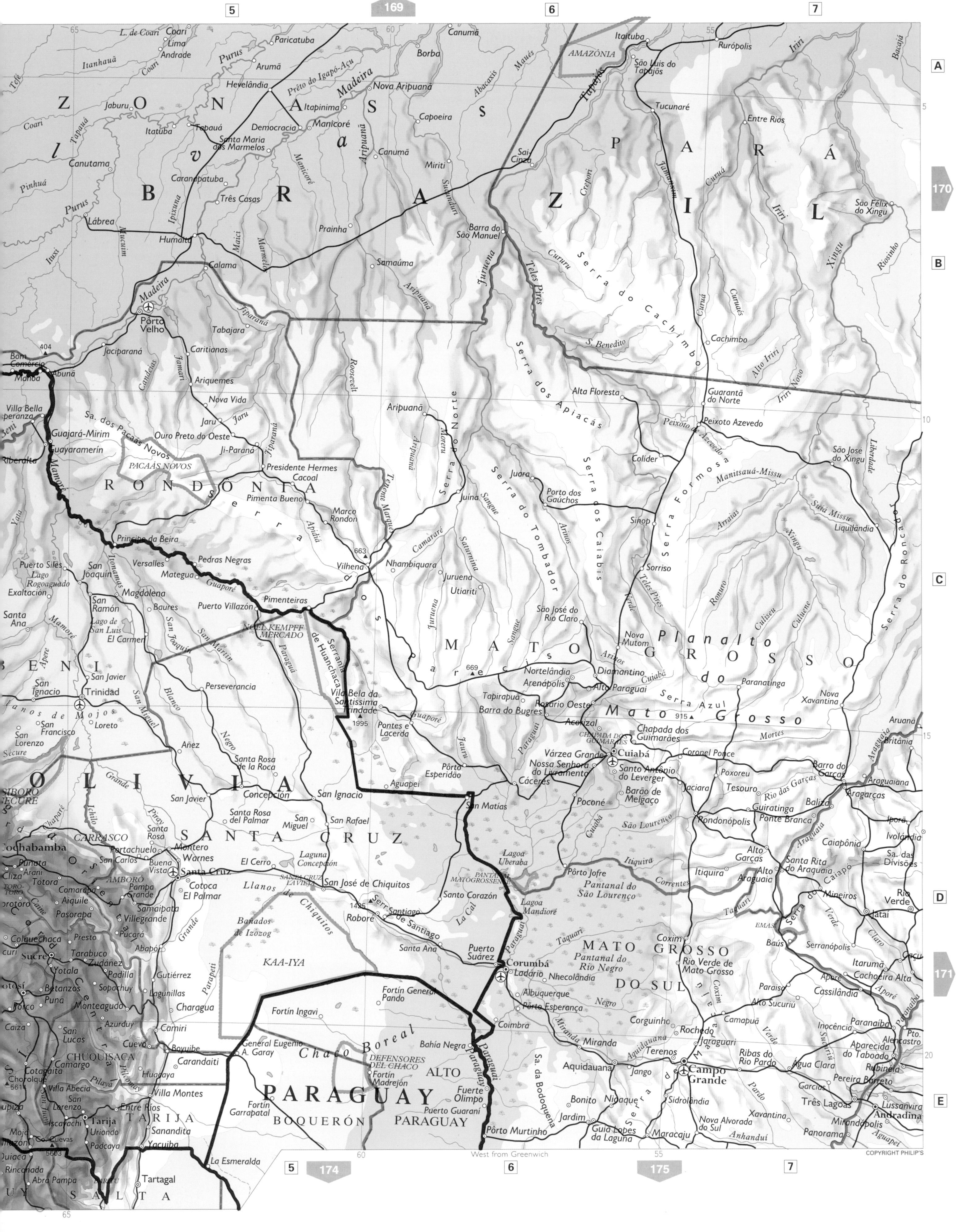

5
169
6
7
A
B
C
D
E
170
171
174
175
BRAZIL
PARÁ
BOLIVIA
PARAGUAY
RONDÔNIA
MATO GROSSO
MATO GROSSO DO SUL
SANTA CRUZ
CHUQUISACA
TARIJA
SALTA
Planalto do Mato Grosso
Serra do Cachimbo
Serra dos Apiacás
Serra do Tombador
Serra dos Caiabis
Serra Formosa
Serra do Roncador
Serra dos Parecis
Serra Azul
Serra de Maracaju
Sa. da Bodoquena
Serranía de Huanchaca
Llanos de Mojos
Llanos de Chiquitos
Chaco Boreal
Pantanal do São Lourenço
Pantanal do Rio Negro
Bañados de Izozog
Madeira
Purus
Tapajós
Juruena
Teles Pires
Xingu
Iriri
Araguaia
Paraguai
Paraná
Guaporé
Mamoré
Aripuanã
Porto Velho
Humaitá
Lábrea
Manicoré
Borba
Itaituba
Ariquemes
Ji-Paraná
Cacoal
Pimenta Bueno
Vilhena
Guajará-Mirim
Guayaramerín
Trinidad
Santa Cruz
Sucre
Potosí
Tarija
Cuiabá
Rondonópolis
Sinop
Sorriso
Cáceres
Corumbá
Campo Grande
Três Lagoas
Andradina
Dourados
Ponta Porã
Pôrto Murtinho
Aquidauana
Fuerte Olimpo
Bahía Negra
Puerto Suárez
Roboré
San José de Chiquitos
San Ignacio
Concepción
Camiri
Yacuiba
Villa Montes
Tartagal
West from Greenwich

1:6 400 000

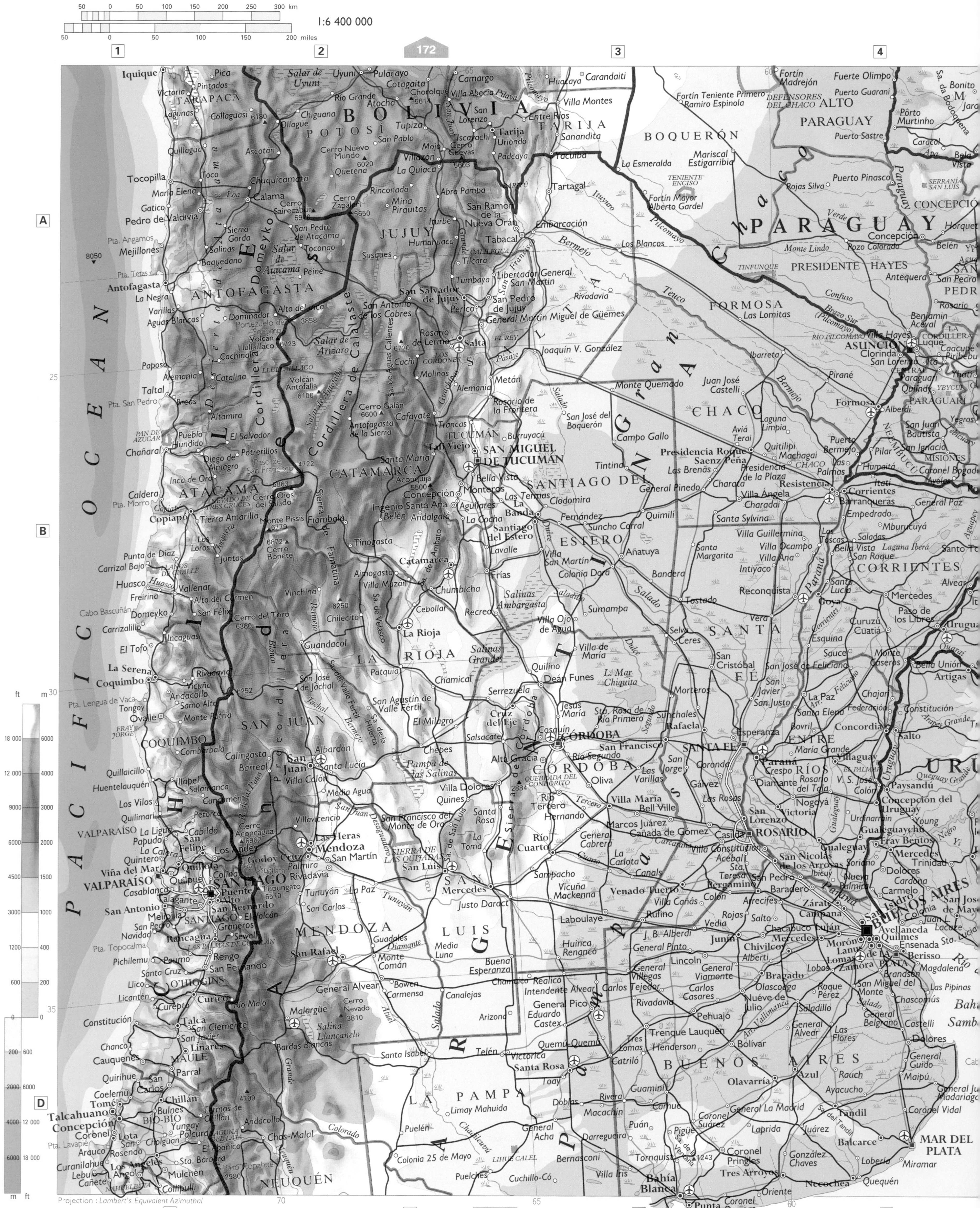
50 0 50 100 150 200 250 300 km
50 0 50 100 150 200 miles
1 2 3 4
A B C D
172
176
PACIFIC OCEAN
BOLIVIA
PARAGUAY
ARGENTINA
Gran Chaco
TARAPACÁ
ANTOFAGASTA
ATACAMA
COQUIMBO
VALPARAÍSO
SANTIAGO
O'HIGGINS
MAULE
BÍO-BÍO
POTOSÍ
TARIJA
JUJUY
SALTA
TUCUMÁN
CATAMARCA
SANTIAGO DEL ESTERO
LA RIOJA
SAN JUAN
CÓRDOBA
SANTA FE
CHACO
FORMOSA
CORRIENTES
ENTRE RÍOS
MENDOZA
SAN LUIS
LA PAMPA
NEUQUÉN
BUENOS AIRES
BOQUERÓN
ALTO PARAGUAY
PRESIDENTE HAYES
Cordillera Domeyko
Cordillera de Calalaste
Iquique
Antofagasta
Copiapó
Coquimbo
Valparaíso
SANTIAGO
Concepción
Talcahuano
ASUNCIÓN
SAN MIGUEL DE TUCUMÁN
CÓRDOBA
ROSARIO
Mendoza
BUENOS AIRES
LA PLATA
MAR DEL PLATA
Bahía Blanca
ft m
18 000 6000
12 000 4000
9000 3000
6000 2000
4500 1500
3000 1000
1200 400
600 200
0 0
200 600
2000 6000
4000 12 000
6000 18 000
m ft
Projection : Lambert's Equivalent Azimuthal

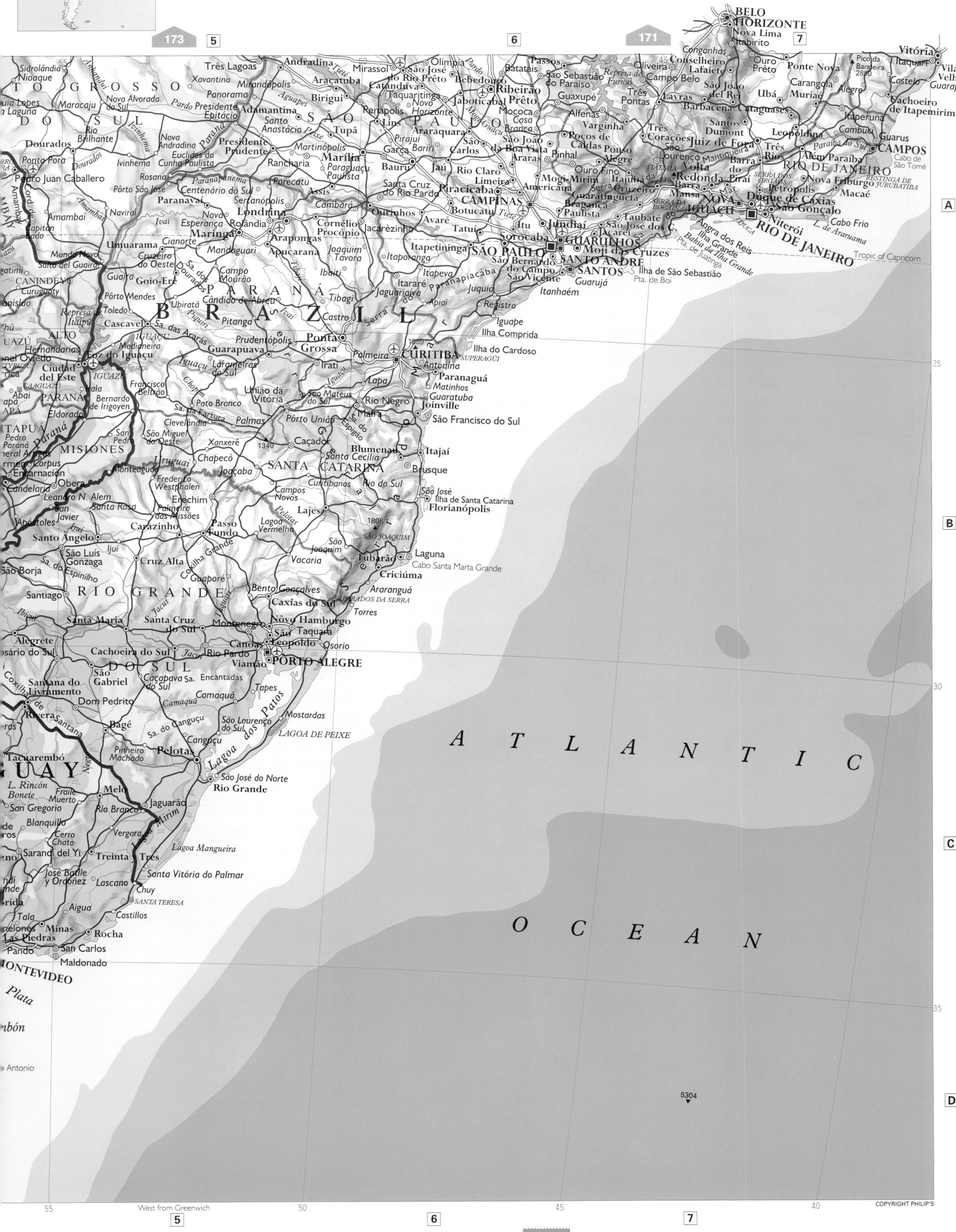

173
171
5
6
7
A
B
C
D
55
50
45
40
25
30
35
West from Greenwich
COPYRIGHT PHILIP'S
BELO HORIZONTE
Nova Lima
Itabirito
Vitória
Vila Velha
Guarapari
Cachoeiro de Itapemirim
CAMPOS
Cabo de São Tomé
RIO DE JANEIRO
Nova Friburgo
Macaé
Petrópolis
Duque de Caxias
NOVA IGUAÇU
São Gonçalo
Niterói
Cabo Frio
Tropic of Capricorn
Ilha Grande
Ilha de São Sebastião
SÃO PAULO
GUARULHOS
SANTO ANDRÉ
SANTOS
Guarujá
CAMPINAS
Sorocaba
Jundiaí
Ribeirão Prêto
Juiz de Fora
Volta Redonda
Taubaté
São José dos Campos
Três Lagoas
Andradina
Araçatuba
Presidente Prudente
Marília
Bauru
Londrina
Maringá
Apucarana
Ponta Grossa
CURITIBA
Paranaguá
Joinville
São Francisco do Sul
Itajaí
Blumenau
Brusque
Ilha de Santa Catarina
Florianópolis
Laguna
Cabo Santa Marta Grande
Tubarão
Criciúma
Araranguá
Torres
Caxias do Sul
Nôvo Hamburgo
PÔRTO ALEGRE
Pelotas
Rio Grande
Lagoa dos Patos
Lagoa Mirim
Lagoa Mangueira
Santa Vitória do Palmar
Chuy
Foz do Iguaçu
Ciudad del Este
Cascavel
Encarnación
Posadas
Santa Maria
Passo Fundo
Lajes
Bagé
Santana do Livramento
Rivera
Tacuarembó
Melo
Treinta y Tres
Rocha
Maldonado
MONTEVIDEO
Plata
Pedro Juan Caballero
Ponta Porã
Dourados
Umuarama
B R A Z I L
P A R A N Á
SANTA CATARINA
R I O G R A N D E D O S U L
S Ã O P A U L O
RIO DE JANEIRO
MISIONES
U R U G U A Y
A T L A N T I C
O C E A N
5304
1808
1899
Ilha do Cardoso
Iguape
Ilha Comprida
Itanhaém
Registro

National Parks

50 0 50 100 150 200 250 300 km

50 0 50 100 150 200 miles

1:6 400 000

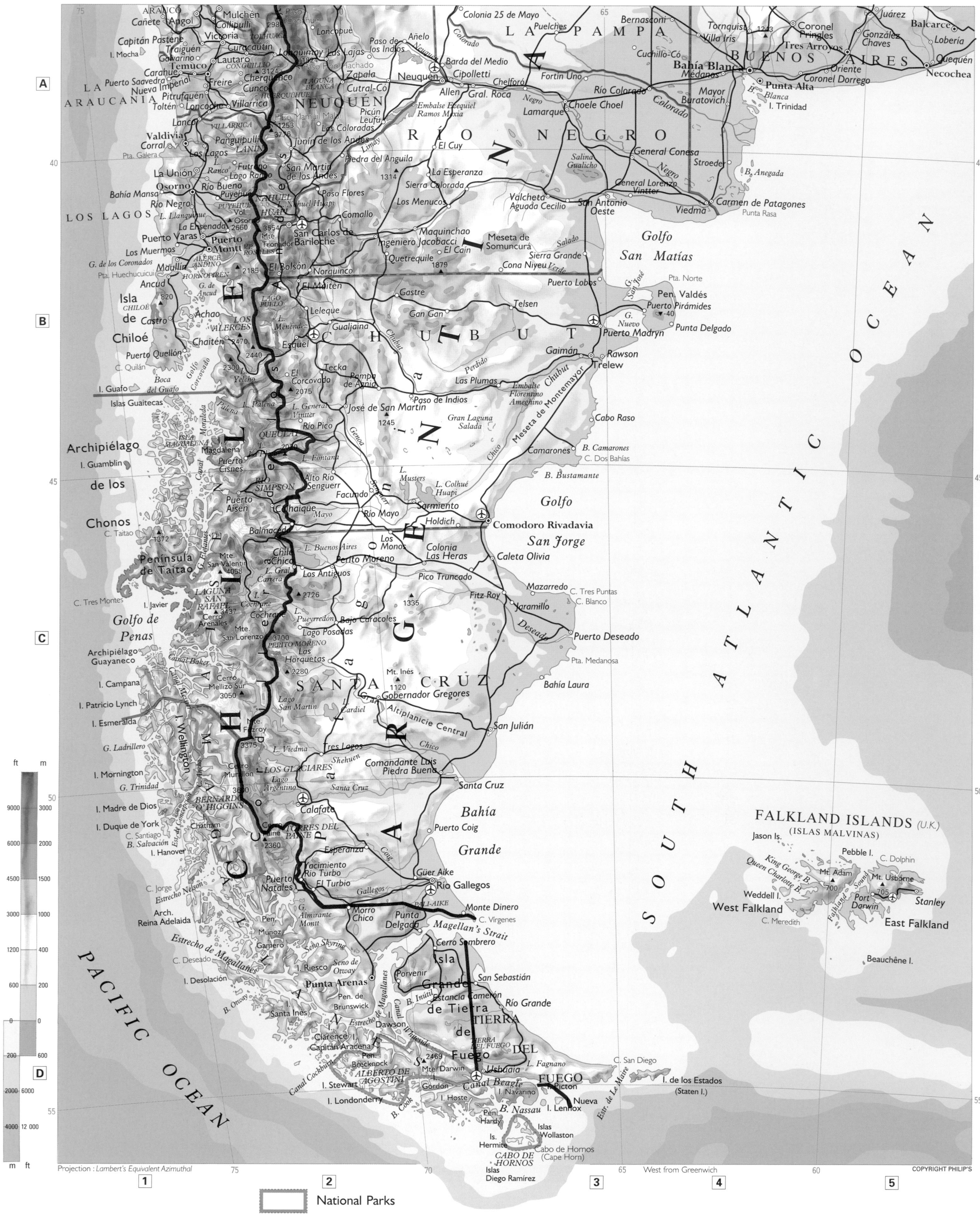

National Parks

Projection : Lambert's Equivalent Azimuthal

West from Greenwich

GEOGRAPHICAL GLOSSARY

This is a list of the geographical terms from various foreign languages that are found in the place names on the maps and in the index. Each is followed by the language and its English meaning.

Afr. Afrikaans
Alb. Albanian
Amh. Amharic
Ar. Arabic
Belo. Belorussian
Berb. Berber
Bulg. Bulgarian
Burm. Burmese
Cat. Catalan
Chin. Chinese
Czec. Czech
Dan. Danish
Dut. Dutch
Est. Estonian
Fr. French
Gae. Gaelic
Ger. German
Gr. Greek
Heb. Hebrew
Hin. Hindi
Hung. Hungarian
I.-C. Indo-Chinese
Ice. Icelandic
It. Italian
Indo. Indonesian
Jap. Japanese
Kaz. Kazakh
Kor. Korean
Kyrg. Kyrgyz
Lapp. Lapp (Sami)
Lat. Latvian
Lith. Lithuanian
Malag. Malagasy
Mong. Mongolian
Nor. Norway
Pash. Pashto
Per. Persian
Pol. Polish
Port. Portuguese
Rom. Romanian
Russ. Russian
Sin. Sinhalese
Ser.-Cr. Serbo-Croat
Slov. Slovene
Som. Somali
Sp. Spanish
Swe. Swedish
Tib. Tibetan
Turk. Turkish
Ukr. Ukrainian
Viet. Vietnamese

-á *Ice.* river
-å *Dan., Nor., Swe.* stream
-abad *Farsi, Russ.* town
Abyad *Ar.* white mountain
Ada, Adasi *Turk.* island
Addis *Amh.* new
Adrar *Ar., Ber.* mountains
Aiguille *Fr.* peak
Aïn, Aîn (A.) *Ar.* spring
Ákra *Gr.* cape, point
Akrotíri *Gr.* cape, point
Alb *Ger.* mountains
Albufera *Span.* lagoon
-ålen *Nor.* islands
Alpen *Ger.* mountain ranges
Alpes *Fr.* mountains
Alpi *It.* mountains
Alt *Ger.* old
Alta, Alto *Port.* high, upper
Altos *Span.* mountains
-älv, -älven *Swe.* stream, river
Amtskommune (Amt.) *Dan.* first-order administrative division
-ån *Swe.* river
Anse *Fr.* bay
Ao *Thai* bay
Appennino *It.* mountain range
Archipel *Fr.* archipelago
Archipiélago (Arch.) *Span.* archipelago
Arcipélago *It.* archipelago
Arquipélago (Arq.) *Port.* archipelago
Arrecife *Span.* reef
Arroyo (Arr.) *Span.* stream
-ås, -åsen *Nor., Swe.* hill
Ayios *Gr.* island
Ayn *Ar.* well, waterhole

Baai, -baai *Afr., Dut.* bay
Bāb *Ar.* gate, strait
Bäck, -bäcken *Swe.* stream
Back, -backen, *Swe.* hill
Bad, -baden *Ger.* spa
Badia *Cat.* bay
Bādiyah, Bādiyat *Ar.* desert
Bæk *Dan.* stream
Bælt *Dan.* strait
Baharu *Malay* new
Bahía (B.) *Span.* bay
Bahiret *Ar.* lagoon
Bahr *Ar.* sea, lake, river
Bahra Bahrat *Ar.* lake
Baia (B.) *Port.* bay
Baie (B.) *Fr.* bay
Baixa, Baixo *Port.* lower
Baja, Bajo *Span.* lower
Bakke *Nor.* hill
Bala *Farsi* upper
Ballon *Fr.* dome
Baltă *Rom.* marsh, lake
Ban *Lao, Thai* village
-Bana *Jap.* cape
Banc *Fr.* bank
Banco *Span.* bank
Bandao *Chin.* peninsula
Bandar *Ar., Malay* port, harbour
Bandar *Farsi* bay
Banja *Ser.-Cr.* spa, resort
Banjaran *Malay* mountain range
Baraji *Turk.* dam
Barat *Indo., Malay* western
Barrage (Barr.) *Fr.* dam
Barragem (Barr.) *Port.* dam, reservoir
Bas, basse *Fr.* lower
Bassin *Fr.* basin
-batang *Indo.* river
Baţlaq *Farsi* marsh
Batu *Malay* mountain
Bayt *Heb.* house, village
Bazar *Hin.* market, bazaar
-beek *Afr., Dut.* river
Be'er *Heb.* well
Bei *Chin.* north, northern
Beinn, Ben *Gae.* mountain
Beit *Heb.* village
Belaya, Belo, Beloye, Belyy *Russ.* white
Belogorye *Russ.* hills, mountain range
Bender *Som.* harbour
Berg(e), -berg(e) *Afr., Ger.* mountain(s)
-berg, -en, -et *Nor., Swe.* hill, mountain, rock
Besar *Indo., Malay* big
Bet *Heb.* house, village
Bir, Bîr, Bi'r *Ar.* well
Birkat, Birket *Ar.* lake, marsh, well
Bishti *Alb.* cape
-bjerg *Dan.* hill, point
Blaenau *Welsh* upland
-bo *Chin.* lake
Boca *Port., Span.* river mouth, inlet
Bodden *Ger.* bay, inlet
Bogaz, Boğazı *Turk.* channel, strait
Bogd *Mong.* mountain range
Bois *Fr.* woods
Boka *Ser.-Cr.* gulf, inlet
Bolshoi, Bolshaya, Bolshoye (Bol.) *Russ.* great, large
Bordj (Bj.) *Ar.* fort
-borg *Dan., Nor., Swe.* castle, fort
Bory *Pol.* woods
Bosque *Span.* woods
-botn *Nor.* valley floor
Bouche(s) *Fr.* mouth(s)
Braţul *Rom.* distributary stream, branch
-bre, -breen *Nor.* glacier
Bredning *Dan.* bay
Brücke *Ger.* bridge
-brug *Dut.* bridge
-brunn *Swe.* well, spring
Bucht *Ger.* bay
Bugt *Dan.* bay
-bugten *Dan.* bay
Buheirat *Ar.* lake, reservoir
Bukit *Malay* hill
-bukt, -a *Nor.* bay
-bukten *Swe.* bay
-bulag *Mong.* spring
Bulag *Chin.* lake
Bulu *Malay* mountain
Bum *Burm.* mountain
Bûr *Ar.* port
Burg. *Ar.* fort
Burg, -burg *Ger.* castle
Burnu, Burun *Turk.* cape
Butt *Gae.* promontory
Büyük *Turk.* big
-by *Dan., Nor., Swe.* town
-byen *Nor., Swe.* town

Cabeza *Span.* peak, hill
Cabo (C.) *Port., Span.* headland, cape
Cachoeira *Port.* waterfall
Cala Cat. *It.* bay
Camp Port. *Span.* land, field
Câmpia *Rom.* plain
Campo *It., Port., Span.* plain
Campos *Span.* upland
Canal (Can.) *Fr., Port., Span.* canal, channel
Canale (Can.) *It.* channel
Canalul (Can.) *Ser.-Cr.* canal
Cao Nguyen *Thai* plateau, tableland
Cap (C.) *Cat., Fr.* cape
Capo (C) *It.* cape
Carn *Gae.* hill
Carse *Gae.* valley
Catarata *Port., Span.* cataract
Cauce *Span.* intermittent stream
Causse *Fr.* limestone plateau
Cay, Cayi, -cay, -cayi *Turk.* river
Cayo(s) *Span.* rock(s), islet(s)
Cefn *Welsh* hill
Cerro *Span.* hill, peak
Česká, Český, České *Czec.* Czech
Chaco *Span.* jungle
Chaîne(s) *Fr.* mountain range(s)
Chang *Chin.* mountain
Chapa *Span.* hills, upland
Chapada *Port.* hills, upland
Chaung *Burm.* stream, river
Chi *Chin.* small lake
-ch'ŏn *Kor.* river
-chŏsuji *Kor.* reservoir
Chott *Ar.* salt lake, depression
Chu *Tib.* river
Chute *Fr.* waterfall
Città *It.* city
Ciudad *Span.* city
Co *Tib.* lake
Cochilla (Coch.) *Port.* hills
Col *Fr., It.* pass
Colina(s) *Span.* hill(s)
Colle *It.* pass
Colline(s) *Fr.* hill(s)
Conca *It.* plain, basin
Cordillera (Cord.) *Span.* mountain range
Costa *It., Port., Span.* coast
Côte *Fr.* coast, slope, hill
Coteaux *Fr.* hills
Cuchilla *Span.* hills
Cuenca *Span.* river basin
Cu-Lao *Viet.* island

Da *Chin.* big
Da *Viet.* river
Daban *Mong.* pass
Dağ(ı) *Turk.* mountain(s)
Dāgh *Farsi* mountain
Dağları *Turk.* mountain range
-dai, -daichi *Jap.* plateau
-Dake *Jap.* mountain
-dal, -e *Dan., Swe.* valley
-dal, -en *Swe., Nor.* valley, stream
Dalay Mong. large lake
-ðalir, -ðalur *Ice.* valley
-damm, -en *Swe.* lake
Danau *Malay* lake
Dao *Chin., Viet.* island
Dar *Ar.* region
Darya *Russ.* river
Daryācheh *Farsi* marshy lake, lake
Dasht *Farsi* desert, steppe
Daung *Burm.* mountain, hill
Dayr *Ar.* monastery
Debre *Amh.* hill
Deli *Ser.-Cr.* mountain
Deniz, -i *Turk.* sea
Département (Dépt.) *Fr.* first-order administrative division
Dere *Turk.* stream
Desierto (Des.) *Span.* desert
Détroit *Fr.* strait
Dhar *Ar.* region, mountain range
Diep *Dut.* channel
Dijk *Dut.* dyke
Ding *Chin.* mountain
Dingzi *Chin.* hill, mountain
Djebel (Dj.) *Ar.* mountain
-djúp *Ice.* fjord
-djupet *Swe.* channel, sound
-Do *Jap., Kor.* island
Dolina *Russ.* valley
Dolna, Dolni *Bulg.* lower
Dolna, Dolne, Dolny *Russ.* lower
Dolní *Czec.* lower
Dolok (D.) *Malay* mountain
-dong *Kor.* village, town
Dong *Chin.* east, eastern
Donja, Donji *Ser.-Cr.* lower
-dorf *Ger.* village
-dorp *Afr.* village
-drif *Afr.* ford
-dybet *Dan.* marine channel
Dzong *Tib.* town, settlement
Dzüün *Mong.* east, eastern

-egga *Nor.* peak
-eiland, -en (eil.) *Afr., Dut.* island(s)
Eilean *Gae.* island
-elv, -a *Nor.* river
Embalse *Span.* reservoir
'Emeq *Heb.* plain, valley
Ensenada *Span.* bay
Erg *Ar.* sand desert
Estero *Span.* estuary
Estrada *Span.* bay
Estrecho *Span.* strait
Estuaire *Fr.* estuary
Estuario *Span.* estuary
Étang *Fr.* lagoon, lake
-ey, -jar *Ice.* island(s)
-ežeras *Lith.* lake
-ezers *Lat.* lake

Falaise *Fr.* cliff
-fallet *Swe.* waterfall
Farihy *Malag.* lake
Faro *Span.* lighthouse
-feld *Ger.* field
-fell *Ice.* mountain, hill
Feng *Chin.* mountain range
Fiume (F.) *It.* river
-fjäll, -en, -et *Swe.* hill(s), mountain(s), ridge
-fjärden *Swe.* fjord
Fjeld *Dan.* mountain
-fjell, -et *Nor.* mountain range
-fjord, -en *Dan., Nor., Swe.* fjord
-fjorður *Ice.* fjord, bay, inlet
Fleuve (Fl.) *Fr.* river
-flói *Ice.* bay, marshy country
Fluss (F.) *Ger.* river
Foce, Foci *It.* mouth(s)
Folyó (F.) *Hung.* river
-fonn *Nor.* glacier
-fontein *Afr.* fountain, spring
Forêt *Fr.* forest
-fors, -en *Swe.* waterfall, rapids
-foss, -en *Ice., Nor.* waterfall
Forst *Ger.* forest
Foum *Ar.* pass
Fuente *Span.* source
-furt *Ger.* ford
Fylke *Nor.* first-order administrative division

-gang *Chin.* bay, harbour
-gang *Kor.* river
Ganga *Hin., Sin.* river
Gangri *Tib.* mountain
Gaoyuan *Chin.* plateau
-gat *Dan.* sound
-Gata *Jap.* lake
-gau *Ger.* district
-Gawa *Jap.* river
Gebel (G.) *Ar.* mountain
Gebirge (Geb.) *Ger.* hills, mountains
Gezirat, Geziret *Ar.* island
Ghat *Hin.* range of hills
Ghiol *Rom.* lake
Ghubbat *Ar.* bay, inlet
Gjiri *Alb.* bay
Gjol *Alb.* lagoon, lake
Glava (Gl.) *Ser.-Cr.* mountain, peak
Glen *Gae.* valley
Gletscher (Gl.) *Ger.* glacier
Gobi *Mong.* desert
Gol *Mong.* river
Göl *Azeri, Turk.* lake
Golfe (G.) *Fr.* gulf
Golfo (G.) *It., Span.* gulf
Gölü *Turk.* lake
Gomba *Tib.* settlement
Gora, Góra *Bulg., Russ., Ser.-Cr., Pol.* mountain
Gorje *Ser.-Cr.* hills, mountains
Gorno *Russ.* mountainous
-gorod *Russ.* small town
Gory, Góry *Pol., Russ.* mountain
-grad *Bulg. Russ., Ser.-Cr.* town, city
-grada *Russ.* ridge
Gran *It., Span.* big, great
Grand, -e *Fr.* big, great
Groot (Gt.) *Afr., Dut.* big, great
Gross, -e, -en, -er *Ger.* big, great(er)
Grupo *Span.* group
Gruppo *It.* group
Guan *Chin.* pass
Guba (G.) *Russ.* bay
-Guntō *Jap.* island group
Gunong, Gunung (G.) *Indo., Malay* mountain
Gurā *Rom.* passage

Hadabat *Ar.* plateau
Hadjer *Ar.* mountain
-hafen *Ger.* harbour, port
Haff *Ger.* bay, lagoon
Hai *Chin.* lake, sea
Haixia *Chin.* channel, strait
Halbinsel *Ger.* peninsula
Halvø *Dan.* peninsula
Halvøya *Nor.* peninsula
Hāmad, Hamada, Hammādah, Hammādat *Ar.* stony desert, plateau
-hamn *Swe., Nor.* harbour, anchorage
Hāmūn *Farsi* marsh, lake
-Hantō *Jap.* peninsula
Har(e) *Heb.* hill(s), mountain(s)
Hassi (Hi.) *Ar.* well
-haug *Nor.* hill
Hav, Havet *Nor., Swe.* sea
-havn *Dan., Nor.* bay, harbour
Havre *Fr.* harbour
Hawd *Ar.* oasis
Hawr *Ar.* lake, marsh
He *Chin.* river
-hegység *Hung.* hills, forest
Heide *Ger.* heath, moor
Helodranon' *Malag.* bay
Higashi *Jap.* east, eastern
-ho *Kor.* lake
-hø *Nor.* peak
Hoch *Ger.* high
Hochland *Afr.* highland
Hoek, -hoek *Afr., Dut.* cape, point
-höfn *Ice.* harbour, port
-hög, -en, -högar, -högarna *Swe.* hill(s), peak, mountain
Höhe *Ger.* height
Hohen *Ger.* high, upper
-hoi *Chin.* bay
-høj, -e *Dan.* hills
-holm, -holme, -holmen *Dan., Nor., Swe.* island
Hon *Viet.* island
Hoog *Dut.* high
Hora *Czec., Ukr.* mountain
-horn *Ger.* peak
Hory *Czec.* mountains, hills
-hot *Mong.* town
-hoved *Dan.* point, headland, peninsula
-hrad *Czec.* town
Hráun *Ice.* lava
-hsi *Chin.* river
-hsia *Chin.* gorge, strait
-hsien *Chin.* district
Hu *Chin.* lake, reservoir
Huk *Dan., Ger.* cape
-huk *Swe.* cape
Huken *Nor.* cape

Idd *Ar.* well
Idehan *Ar., Ber.* sandy plain, dunes
-ike *Jap.* lake
Île(s) (I(s).) *Fr.* island(s)
Ilha(s) (I(s).) *Port.* island(s)
imeni *Russ.* 'in the name of'
Inish *Gae.* island
Insel(n) (I.) *Ger.* island(s)
Irmak *Turk.* river
'Irq *Ar.* dunes
Isla(s) (I(s).) *Span.* island(s)
Iso *Fin.* big, great
Isol, -a, -e (I.) *It.* island(s)
Isthme *Fr.* isthmus
Istmo *Span.* isthmus
-iwa *Jap.* island

Jabal *Ar.* mountain range
Järv *Est.* lake
järvi *Fin.* lake, bay, pond
-jaur, -javre *Lap.* lake
Jazā'ir *Ar.* islands
Jazīra, jazīrat *Ar.* island
Jazireh *Farsi* island
Jebel *Ar.* mountain
Jezero *Ser.-Cr.* lake
Jezioro *Pol.* lake
Jiang *Chin.* river
Jiao *Chin.* cape
-Jima *Jap.* island
Jøkulen *Nor.* glacier, ice cap
-joki *Fin.* river
-jökull *Ice.* glacier, ice cap
Jūras Līcis *Lat.* bay, gulf

Kaap (K.) *Afr.* cape
-kai *Jap.* bay, channel, sea
-kaikyō *Jap.* strait
-kaise *Lap.* mountain
kalnas *Lith.* hill
Kamennyy *Russ.* stony
Kampong *Cam.* village
Kampung *Malay* village
-kanaal *Dut.* canal
Kanal *Dan.* channel, gulf
Kanal *Ger., Swe.* canal
-kanal *Ser.-Cr.* channel, canal
Kanava *Fin.* canal
Kang *Kor.* river, bay
Kap (K.) *Dan., Ger.* cape, point
-kapp *Nor.* cape, point
-kaupstaður *Ice.* market town
-kaupunki *Fin.* town
Kavīr *Farsi* salt desert
Kébir *Ar.* great
Kecil *Malay* lesser, little
Kefar *Heb.* village, hamlet
-Ken *Jap.* first-order administrative division
Kep, -i (K.) *Alb.* cape
Kepulauan (Kep.) *Indo., Malay* archipelago
Keski- *Fin.* middle, central
Khalīg, Khalīj *Ar.* gulf
-khamba *Tib.* source, spring
Khawr *Ar.* bay, channel, wadi
Khlong *Thai* river
Kho Khot *Thai* isthmus
Khōr *Farsi* bay, estuary
Khrebet *Russ.* mountain range
Kita- *Jap.* north
Klein,-e, -er *Ger.* small
-klint *Dan.* cliff
Klintar *Swe.* hills
-kloof *Afr.* gorge, pass
Knude *Dan.* point
-Ko *Jap.* lake
Ko *Thai* island
-kōchi *Jap.* mountainous region
-kōgen *Jap.* plateau
Kohi *Pash.* mountains
Kol *Kaz., Kyrg.* lake
Kólpos *Gr., Turk.* gulf, bay
Kolymskoye *Russ.* mountain range
Kompong *Malay* landing place
-kop *Afr.* hill
-kopf *Ger.* hill
-köping *Swe.* market town
Körfäzi *Azer.* gulf
Körfezi *Turk.* gulf
Kosa *Russ., Ukr.* spit
-koski *Fin.* rapids
-kraal *Afr.* native village
-kraj *Czec., Pol., Ser.-Cr.* region
Krasnyy *Russ.* red
Kryazh *Russ.* ridge, hills
Kuala *Malay* bay
-kuan *Chin.* pass
Kūh(ha) *Farsi* mountain(s)
Kul *Russ.* lake
-kulle *Swe.* hill
Kum *Russ.* sandy desert
Kumpu *Fin.* hill
Kwe *Burm.* bay, gulf
-kylä *Fin.* village
Kyst, -en *Dan., Nor.* coast
Kyun(zu) *Burm.* island(s)

La *Tib.* pass
-laagte *Afr.* watercourse

Lääni *Fin.* first-order administrative division
Lac (L.) *Fr.* lake
Lacul (L.) *Rom.* lake, lagoon
Lago (L.) *It., Port., Span.* lake, lagoon
Lagoa (L.) *Port.* lagoon
Lagos *Port., Span.* lakes
Laguna (L.) *It., Span.* lagoon, lake
Lagune (L.) *Fr.* lake
-laht *Est.* bay
Lahti *Fin.* bay, gulf, cove
Lakhti *Russ.* bay, gulf
Lam *Thai* river
Lampi *Fin.* lake
Län *Swe.* first-order administrative division
Land *Ger.* first-order administrative division
-land *Dan.* region
-land *Afr., Nor.* land, province
Lande *Fr.* heath
Laut *Indo.* sea
Law *Gae.* hill, mountain
Licis *Lat.* gulf
Lido *It.* beach, shore
Liedao *Chin.* islands
Lilla *Swe.* small
Lille *Dan., Nor.* small
Liman *Russ.* bay, gulf
Limni (L.) *Gr.* lake
Ling *Chin.* mountain range
-linna *Fin.* fort
Llano *Span.* prairie, plain
Llyn *Welsh* lake
Loch (L.) *Gae.* lake, inlet
Lough (L.) *Gae.* lake, inlet
Lum *Alb.* river
Lund *Dan.* forest
-lund, -en *Swe.* wood(s)
-luoto *Fin.* island

-maa *Est.* island
Madīnat *Ar.* town, city
Madiq *Ar.* strait
Maja *Alb.* mountains
-mäki *Fin.* hill, hillside
Mal *Alb.* mountain
Maloye, Malyy, Malyya *Russ.* little, small
Mala, Mali, Malo *Ser.-Cr.* little, small
Malaya *Belo.* small
Malé *Czec., Slovak* small
Mali *Alb.* mountain
-man *Kor.* bay
Mar *Span.* lagoon, sea
Marais *Fr.* marsh
Mare *It.* sea
Mare *Rom.* great
Marisma *Span.* marsh
-mark *Dan., Nor.* land
Marsā *Ar.* anchorage, bay, inlet
Masabb *Ar.* river mouth, estuary
Massif *Fr.* upland, mountains
Mato *Port.* forest
Mazar *Farsi* shrine, tomb
Meer, -meer *Afr., Dut., Ger.* lake, sea
-men *Chin.* bay, gorge, channel
Mesto *Ser.-Cr., Czec.* town
Mezzo *It.* middle
Midbar *Heb.* wilderness
Mierzeja *Pol.* spit
Mifraz *Heb.* bay
Mina *Ar.* port
Minami *Jap.* south, southern
-misaki *Jap.* cape, point
Mittel *Ger.* central, middle
-mo *Nor., Swe.* heath, island
-mon *Swe.* heath
Mong *Burm.* town
Mont(s) (Mt(s).) *Fr.* hill(s), mountain(s)
Montagna (Mt.) *It.* mountain
Montagne(s) (Mt(s).) *Fr.* hill(s), mountain(s)
Montaña(s) (Mt(s).) *Span.* mountain(s)
Montanyes *Cat.* mountains
Monte(s) (Mte(s).) *It., Port., Span.* mountain(s)
Monti (Mti.) *It.* mountains
More *Russ.* sea
Mörön *Mong.* river
Moyen *Fr.* central, middle
Muang *Malay* town
Mui *Viet.* cape
Mull *Gae.* promontory
Mund, -mund *Afr.* mouth
Munkhafed *Ar.* depression
Munte (Mte.) *Rom.* mount
Munţi(i) (Mti.) *Rom.* mountain(s)
Muong *Malay* village
Myit *Burm.* river
Myitwanya *Burm.* mouths of river
Mynydd *Welsh* mountain
-myr *Nor., Swe.* swamp
-mýri *Ice.* swamp
Mys (M.) *Russ.* cape

-Nada *Jap.* bay, gulf
-næs *Dan.* point, cape
Nafūd *Ar.* sandy desert
Nagorye *Russ.* hills, mountains
Nagy *Hung.* big
Nahal (N.) *Heb.* river
Nahr (N.) *Ar.* river, stream
Najd *Ar.* plateau, pass
Nakhon *Thai* town
Nam *Kor., Viet.* river
-nam *Kor.* south
Namakzār *Per.* salt flat
Nan *Chin.* south, southern
-nao *Chin.* lake
-näs *Swe.* cape
Neder *Dut.* lower
Nedre *Nor.* lower
Nei *Chin.* inner
Nek *Afr.* pass
-nes *Ice., Nor.* cape
Ness, -ness *Gae.* promontory, cape
Nevada, Nevado *Span.* snow-capped mountain
Nez *Fr.* cape
Nieder *Ger.* lower
-niemi *Fin.* cape, point, peninsula, island
Nieuw, -e *Dut.* new
Nishi *Jap.* west, western
Nisos, Nisoi *Gr.* island(s)
Nizhneye, Nizhniy *Russ.* lower
Nizina *Belo., Pol.* lowland
Nizmennost *Russ.* plain, lowland
Nizní *Czec.* lower
Noord *Dut.* north, northern
Nord *Fr.* north, northern
Norra *Swe.* north, northern
Nørre *Dan.* north, northern
Norte *Port., Span.* north, northern
Nos *Bulg., Russ.* cape, point
Nosy *Malag.* island
Nouveau, Nouvelle *Fr.* new
Nova, Novi *Bulg., Port., Serb.-Cr.* new
Novaya, Novo, Novoye, Novyy *Russ.* new
Nové, Novy *Czec., Slovak* new
Novo *Port.* new
Nowa, Nowe, Nowy *Pol.* new
Nudo *Span.* mountain
Nueva, Nuevo *Span.* new
Nur *Chin.* lake
Nur *Tib.* peak
Nuruu *Mong.* mountain range
Nusa *Indo.* island
Nuur *Mong.* lake
Ny *Dan., Nor., Swe.* new

-ø *Dan., Nor.* island
-ö *Swe.* island,
-öar, -na *Swe.* islands
Ober *Ger., Ukr.* upper
Oblast *Russ.* administrative division
Öbor *Mong.* inner
Occidental *Fr., Span.* western
-odde *Dan., Nor.* point, peninsula, cape
Oeste *Span.* west, western
Oglat *Ar.* well
Oji *Alb.* bay
Ojo *Span.* spring
-Oki *Jap.* bay
-ön *Swe.* island
Ondör *Mong.* upper
Oost(er) *Dut.* east(ern)
Oraşu *Rom.* city
Ord *Gae.* point
Óri *Gr.* mountains
Oriental, -e *Fr., Span.* east, eastern
Órmos *Gr.* bay
Óros *Gr.* mountain(s)
Ort *Ger.* point, cape
Ost *Ger.* east
Øst(er) *Den., Nor.* east(ern)
Öst(ra) *Swe.* east(ern)
Ostriv *Ukr.* island
Ostrov(a) *Russ.* island(s)
Otok(i) *Ser.-Cr.* island(s)
Ouabi, Ouadi (O.) *Ar.* dry watercourse, wadi
Oud, -e *Dut.* old
Oued, -i (O.) *Ar.* watercourse
Ouest *Fr.* west, western
Ouzan *Farsi* river
Ova, -si *Turk.* plains, lowlands
Over- *Dan., Dut.* upper
Över-, Övre *Nor., Swe.* upper
-øy, -a *Nor.* island(s)
Oya *Hin.* point
Oya *Sin.* river
Ozero, Ozera (Oz.) *Russ., Ukr.* lake(s)

-pää *Fin.* hill(s), mountain
Pahta *Lapp.* hill
Pampa(s) *Span.* plain(s)
Pantanal *Port.* marsh
Pantano *Span.* reservoir
Pantao *Chin.* peninsula
Parbat *Urdu* mountain
Pas *Fr.* strait
Paso (P.) *Span.* pass
Passage *Fr.* channel
Passe *Fr.* channel
Passo (P.) *It.* pass
Pasul (P.) *Rom.* pass
Patam *Hin.* small village
Patna, -patnam *Hin.* small village
Pegunungan *Indo., Malay* mountain range
Pei, -pei *Chin.* north
Pélagos *Gr.* sea
Pen *Welsh* hill
Peña *Span.* rock, peak
Pendi *Chin.* basin, depression
Péninsule *Fr.* peninsula
Penisola (Pen.) *It.* peninsula
Pereval (Per.) *Russ.* pass
Pervo-, Pervyy- *Russ.* first
Pertuis *Fr.* channel, strait
Peski *Russ.* sand desert
Petit, -e *Fr.* small
Phanom *Thai* mountain
Phnum *Cam.* mountain
Phou *Lao.* mountain
Phu *Thai, Viet.* mountain
Piano *It.* plain
Pic *Cat., Fr.* peak
Pico(s) *Span.* peak(s)
-piggen *Dan.* peak
Pik *Russ.* peak
Pingyuan *Chin.* plain
Pique *Fr.* peak
Piton *Fr.* peak
Pivostriv *Ukr.* peninsula
Piz, Pizzo *It.* peak
Plage *Fr.* beach
Plaine *Fr.* plain
Planalto *Port.* plateau
Planina (Pl.) *Bulg., Ser.-Cr.* mountain range
Plato *Russ., Bulg.* plateau
Playa *Span.* beach
-po *Chin.* lake, wetland
Pointe (Pte.) *Fr.* point, cape
Pojezierze *Pol.* lakes
Polder *Dut.* reclaimed farmland
-pólis *Gr.* city, town
Poluostrov (Pov.) *Russ.* peninsula
Półwysep *Pol.* peninsula
Pont *Fr.* bridge
Ponta (Pta.) *Port.* point, cape
Ponte *Port.* bridge
Poort *Afr.* passage, gate
-poort *Dut.* port
Porta *Port.* pass
Porţile *Rom.* gate
Portillo *Span.* pass
Porto *It., Port., Span.* port
Potámi, Potamós *Gr.* river
Pradesh *Hin.* state
Praia *Port.* beach, shore
Presa *Span.* reservoir
Presqu'île *Fr.* peninsula
Prokhod *Bulg.* pass
Proliv *Russ.* strait
Promontorio *Span.* promontory
Průsmyk (Pr.) *Czec.* pass
Pueblo *Span.* village
Puerto (Pto.) *Span.* port
Puig *Cat.* peak
Pulau (P.) *Indo., Malay* island
Puna *Span.* desert plateau
Puncak *Indo.* peak
Punta (Pta.) *It., Span.* point, peak
Puy *Fr.* peak

Qal'at *Ar.* fort
Qanat *Ar.* canal
Qasr *Ar.* fort
Qiryat *Heb.* town
Qiuling *Chin.* plateau
Qolleh *Farsi* mountain
-qundao *Chin.* islands

Rach *Viet.* river
Rags *Lat.* cape
Rambla *Cat.* river
Ramlat *Ar.* sandy desert
Rão (R.) *Port.* river
Rann *Hin.* swampy region
Rao *I.-C.* river
Ras *Amh., Ar., Farsi* cape, point
Récif(s) *Fr.* reef(s)
Recife(s) *Port.* reef(s)
Reka *Bulg.* river
Repede *Rom.* rapids
Represa *Port.* reservoir
Reshteh *Farsi* mountain range
-rettō *Jap.* group of islands, chain
Ria *Port., Span.* estuary, bay
Ribeirão (R.) *Port.* river
Ribera (R.) *Span.* river bank
Rijeka *Ser.-Cr.* river
Rio (R.) *Port., Span.* river
Rivier (R.) *Afr., Dut.* river
Riviera *It.* coastal plain, coast
Rivière (R.) *Fr.* river
Roca *Span.* rock
Rocca *It.* rock, peak
Roche *Fr.* rock
Rt *Ser.-Cr.* cape, point
Rubh', Rubha *Gae.* cape, point
-rück *Ger.* ridge
Rūd *Farsi* stream, river
Rudohorie *Slovak* mountains
Rzeka (R.) *Pol.* river

-saar *Est.* island
-saari *Fin.* island
Sabkhat, Sabkhet *Ar.* salt flats
Sadd *Ar.* dam
Sagar,-a *Hin., Urdu* lake
Sahrâ *Ar.* desert
-Saki *Jap.* cape, point
Salar *Span.* salt flat
Salina(s) *Span.* salt marsh(es)
-salmi *Fin.* strait, sound, lake, channel
Saltsjöbad *Swe.* resort
-Sammyaku *Jap.* mountain range
Samut *Thai* gulf
San (S.) *It., Port., Span.* saint
-San *Jap., Kor.* hill, mountain
-Sanchi *Jap.* mountain range
Sankt (St.) *Ger., Russ.* saint
-sanmaek *Kor.* mountain range
-sanmyaku *Jap.* mountain range
Santa (Sta.) *It., Port., Span.* saint
Santo (Sto.) *It. Port., Span.* saint
São (S.) *Port.* saint
Sarīr *Ar.* desert
Sasso *It.* mountain
Satu *Rom.* village
Saurums *Lat.* strait
Sebkha, Sebkhet *Ar.* salt flat
See, -see *Ger.* lake
-şehir *Turk.* town
Selat *Indo., Malay* strait
Selatan *Indo.* southern
-selkä *Fin.* bay, lake, ridge, hills
Selo *Ser.-Cr., Russ.* village
Selva *Port., Span.* forest, wood
Seno *Span.* bay, sound
Serir *Ar.* stony desert
Serra (Sa.) *Cat., Port.* range of hills
Serranía *Span.* mountain ridge
Severo, Severnaya, Severnoye, Severnyy (Sev.) *Russ.* north, northern
Sfântu *Rom.* saint
Shahr, -shahr *Farsi* city, town
Shamo *Chin.* desert
Shan *Chin.* hills, mountains
Shankou *Chin.* pass
Shanmo *Chin.* mountain range
Sharm *Ar.* bay
Shatt *Ar.* river mouth, estuary
-Shima *Jap.* island
Shimāli *Ar.* northern
-Shotō *Jap.* group of islands
-shui *Chin.* river
-shuiku *Chin.* reservoir
Sierra (Sa.) *Span.* mountain range
-sjö, -sjön, -sjø *Swe., Nor.* lake
-sjøen *Dan.* sea
-sjór *Ice.* lake
-sker *Ice.* island
-skär *Swe.* island, rock, cape
-skog, -skogen *Nor., Swe.* wood(s)
-skov *Dan.* forest
Slieve *Gae.* hill, mountain
Sø *Dan., Nor.* lake
Söder, Södra *Swe.* south, southern
Sør *Nor.* south, southern
Solonchak *Russ.* salt lake, marsh
Sønder, Søndra *Dan.* south, southern
Song *Viet.* river
Souk *Ar.* market
-spitze *Ger.* peak, mountain
-spruit *Afr.* stream
Sredna, Sredno *Bulg.* middle, central
Sredne, Sredneye *Russ.* middle, central
Srednja *Ser.-Cr.* middle, central
-stad *Afr., Nor., Swe.* town
-stadt *Ger.* town
-staður *Ice.* town
Stara, Stari *Ser.-Cr.* old
Stará, Staré, Stary *Czec.* old
Staraya, Staroye, Staryy *Russ.* old
Stare, Staro, Stary *Ukr.* old
Stausee *Ger.* reservoir
Stenón *Gr.* strait, pass
Step *Russ.* steppe
Stor, -a *Swe.* big
Store *Dan.* big
-strand *Dan., Ger., Nor., Swe.* beach
-strede *Nor.* straits
Strelka *Russ.* spit
-strete *Nor.* straits
Stretto (Str.) *It.* strait
Strædet (Str.) *Dan.* strait
-ström, -strömmen *Swe.* stream(s)
-stroom *Afr.* large river
Sud *Fr.* south, southern
Süd, -er *Ger.* south, southern
Suid *Afr.* south, southern
-Suidō *Jap.* strait, channel
Sul *Port.* south, southern
Sûn *Burm.* cape
-sund, -et *Swe., Nor.* sound, estuary, inlet
Sungai *Indo., Malay* river
Sur *Span.* south, southern
Sveti *Bulg.* saint
Syd *Dan., Swe.* south, southern
Sýsla *Ice.* first-order administrative division

-tag *Uighur* mountain
Tai -tai *Chin.* tower
-Take *Jap.* mountain
Tal *Mong.* plain, steppe
-tal *Ger.* valley
Tall *Ar.* hills
Tanjona *Malag.* cape, point
Tanjung, Tanjong (Tg.) *Indo., Malay.* cape, point
Tao *Chin.* island
Tasik *Malay* lake
Tassili *Ar.* rocky plateau
Tau *Russ.* mountain range
Taung *Burm.* mountain
Taungdan. *Burm.* mountain range
Taunggya *Burm.* pass
-tekojärvi *Fin.* reservoir
Teluk *Indo., Malay* bay, gulf
Ténéré *Berb.* desert
Tengah *Indo.* middle, central
-thal *Ger.* valley
Thok *Tib.* town
Tien *Chin.* lake, marsh
Tierra *Span.* land, country
Timur *Indo.* eastern
-tind *Nor.* peak
-ting *Chin.* mountain
Tjärn, -en, -et *Swe.* lake
-Tō *Jap.* island
Tong *Kor.* village, town
Tong *Burm., Thai, Kor.* mountain range
Tonlé *Cam.* lake
Top *Dut.* peak
-topp, -en *Nor.* peak
-träsk *Swe.* lake, swamp
Tsangpo *Tib.* large river
Tso *Tib.* lake
Tsu *Jap.* entrance, bay
Tsui *Chin.* cape, point
Tulur *Ar.* hill
-tunturi *Fin.* hill(s), mountain(s), ridge

Uad *Ar.* dry watercourse, wadi
Über *Ger.* upper
-udde, -udden *Swe.* point, cape
Uebi *Som.* river
Ujung *Indo., Malay* cape
Unter- *Ger.* lower
Us *Mong.* water
Ust, Ustye *Russ.* river mouth
Utara *Indo.* north, northern
Uttar *Hin.* north, northern
Uul *Mong., Russ.* mountain range

-vaara *Fin.* hill, mountain ridge, peak
Vaart *Dut.* canal
-våg *Nor.* bay
Val *Fr., Port., Span.* valley
Valea *Rom.* valley
-vall, -en *Swe.* mountain
Valle *It., Span.* valley
Vallée *Fr.* valley
Valli *It.* lake, lagoon
-város *Hung.* town
-varre *Nor.* mountain
Väst, Västra *Swe.* west, western
-vatn *Ice., Nor.* lake
-vatnet *Nor.* lake
-vatten, vattnet *Swe.* lake
-vecchio *It.* old
Vechi *Rom.* old
-ved, -veden *Swe.* hills
Veld, -veld *Afr.* field
Velha, Velho *Port.* old
Velika, Velike, Veliki, Veliko *Ser.-Cr., Slov.* big, large
Velikaya, Velikiy *Russ.* big, large
Velká, Velké, Velký *Czec.* big, large
Verkhne, Verkhniy *Russ.* upper
-vesi *Fin.* water, lake, bay, sound, strait
Vest, Vester, Vestre *Dan., Nor.* west, western
-vidda *Nor.* plateau
Vieille, Vieux *Fr.* old
Vieja, Vejo *Span.* old
Vig *Dan.* bay, inlet, cove, lagoon, lake
-vík *Ice.* bay
-vik, -a, -en *Nor., Swe.* bay, gulf, inlet, lake
Vila *Port.* small town
Villa *Span.* town
Ville *Fr.* town
Vinh *Viet.* bay
Virful (Vf.) *Rom.* peak, mountain
-viz *Hung.* river
-víztároló *Hung.* reservoir
-vlei *Afr.* lake, salt pan
-vliet *Dut.* canal
-vloer *Afr.* salt pan
Vodokhranilishche (Vdkhr.) *Russ.* reservoir
Vodoskovyshche (Vdskh.) *Ukr.* reservoir
Volcán (Vol.) *Span.* volcano, mountain
Vorota *Russ.* pass, channel, strait
Vostochno, Vostochnyy *Russ.* east, eastern
-vötn *Ice.* lakes
Vozvyshennost *Russ.* heights, uplands
Vozyera *Belo.* lake
Vrata *Bulg.* gate, pass
Vrchovina *Czec.* mountainous country
Vrch(y) *Czec.* mountain (range)
Vung *Viet.* bay, gulf
-vuori *Fin.* mountain, hill
Vychodné *Slovak* east, eastern
Vysochyna *Ukr.* upland

-waard *Dut.* polder
Wadi (W.) *Ar.* dry watercourse
Wâhât *Ar.* oasis
Wald *Ger.* forest, mountains
-Wan *Chin., Jap.* bay, harbour
Wāw *Ar.* well
Webi *Amh.* river
Wes *Afr.* west, western
Wielka, Wielki, Wielko *Pol.* big, large
Woestyn *Afr.* desert
Wysoka, Wysoki *Pol.* upper
Wyżyna *Pol.* plateau

Xi *Chin.* river
Xia *Chin.* gorge, strait
Xiao *Chin.* small

Yam *Heb.* sea
-Yama *Jap.* mountain
-yan *Chin.* gorge, island
Yang *Chin.* bay, sea, sound
Yangi *Russ.* new
Yazovir *Bulg.* reservoir
Yeni *Turk.* new
Yli *Fin.* upper
Ynys *Welsh* island
Yoma *Burm.* mountain range
Ytre-, Ytter- *Nor., Swe.* outer
-yuan *Chin.* stream
Yugo- *Ser.-Cr.* south, southern
Yunhe *Chin.* canal
Yuzhni, Yuzhno *Russ.* south, southern

-Zaki *Jap.* point
Zalew *Pol.* lagoon, swamp
Zaliv *Russ.* bay, gulf
-Zan *Jap.* mountain
Zangbo *Tib.* stream, river
Zapadnaya, Zapadno, Zapadnyi (Zap.) *Russ.* west, western
Zatoka *Pol., Ukr.* bay, gulf
-zee *Dut.* lake, sea
Zemlya *Russ.* land, island(s)
Zhang *Chin.* mountain
-zhou *Chin.* island
Zhong *Chin.* middle, central
Zhou *Chin.* island
Zizhiqu *Chin.* autonomous region
Zuid, Zuider *Dut.* south, southern

INDEX TO WORLD MAPS

How to use the index

The index contains the names of all the principal places and features shown on the World Maps. Each name is followed by an additional entry in italics giving the country or region within which it is located. The alphabetical order of names composed of two or more words is governed primarily by the first word and then by the second. This is an example of the rule:

Mīr Kūh, *Iran*	**97 E8**	26 22N 58 55 E
Mīr Shahdād, *Iran*	**97 E8**	26 15N 58 29 E
Mira, *Italy*	**45 C9**	45 26N 12 8 E
Mira por vos Cay, *Bahamas*	**165 B5**	22 9N 74 30W
Miraj, *India*	**94 F2**	16 50N 74 45 E

Physical features composed of a proper name (Erie) and a description (Lake) are positioned alphabetically by the proper name. The description is positioned after the proper name and is usually abbreviated:

Erie, L., *N. Amer.*	**150 D4**	42 15N 81 0W

Where a description forms part of a settlement or administrative name however, it is always written in full and put in its true alphabetic position:

Mount Olive, *U.S.A.*	**156 E7**	39 4N 89 44W

Names beginning with M' and Mc are indexed as if they were spelled Mac. Names beginning St. are alphabetized under Saint, but Sankt, Sint, Sant', Santa and San are all spelt in full and are alphabetized accordingly. If the same place name occurs two or more times in the index and all are in the same country, each is followed by the name of the administrative subdivision in which it is located.

The number in bold type which follows each name in the index refers to the number of the map page where that feature or place will be found. This is usually the largest scale at which the place or feature appears.

The letter and figure which are in bold type immediately after the page number give the grid square on the map page, within which the feature is situated. The letter represents the latitude and the figure the longitude. A lower case letter immediately after the page number refers to an inset map on that page.

In some cases the feature itself may fall within the specified square, while the name is outside. This is usually the case only with features which are larger than a grid square.

The geographical co-ordinates which follow the letter-figure references give the latitude and longitude of each place. The first co-ordinate indicates latitude – the distance north or south of the Equator. The second co-ordinate indicates longitude – the distance east or west of the Greenwich Meridian. Both latitude and longitude are measured in degrees and minutes (there are 60 minutes in a degree).

The latitude is followed by N(orth) or S(outh) and the longitude by E(ast) or W(est).

Rivers are indexed to their mouths or confluences, and carry the symbol ➔ after their names. The following symbols are also used in the index: ■ country, ☒ overseas territory or dependency, □ first order administrative area, △ national park, ⌓ other park (provincial park, nature reserve or game reserve), ✈ (LHR) principal airport (and location identifier).

How to pronounce place names

English-speaking people usually have no difficulty in reading and pronouncing correctly English place names. However, foreign place name pronunciations may present many problems. Such problems can be minimised by following some simple rules. However, these rules cannot be applied to all situations, and there will be many exceptions.

1. In general, stress each syllable equally, unless your experience suggests otherwise.
2. Pronounce the letter 'a' as a broad 'a' as in 'arm'.
3. Pronounce the letter 'e' as a short 'e' as in 'elm'.
4. Pronounce the letter 'i' as a cross between a short 'i' and long 'e', as the two 'i's in 'California'.
5. Pronounce the letter 'o' as an intermediate 'o' as in 'soft'.
6. Pronounce the letter 'u' as an intermediate 'u' as in 'sure'.
7. Pronounce consonants hard, except in the Romance-language areas where 'g's are likely to be pronounced softly like 'j' in 'jam'; 'j' itself may be pronounced as 'y'; and 'x's may be pronounced as 'h'.
8. For names in mainland China, pronounce 'q' like the 'ch' in 'chin', 'x' like the 'sh' in 'she', 'zh' like the 'j' in 'jam', and 'z' as if it were spelled 'dz'. In general pronounce 'a' as in 'father', 'e' as in 'but', 'i' as in 'keep', 'o' as in 'or', and 'u' as in 'rule'.

Moreover, English has no diacritical marks (accent and pronunciation signs), although some languages do. The following is a brief and general guide to the pronunciation of those most frequently used in the principal Western European languages.

		Pronunciation as in
French	é	day and shows that the e is to be pronounced; e.g. Orléans.
	è	mare
	î	used over any vowel and does not affect pronunciation; shows contraction of the name, usually omission of 's' following a vowel.
	ç	's' before 'a', 'o' and 'u'.
	ë, ï, ü	over 'e', 'i' and 'u' when they are used with another vowel and shows that each is to be pronounced.
German	ä	fate
	ö	fur
	ü	no English equivalent; like French 'tu'
Italian	à, é	over vowels and indicates stress.
Portuguese	ã, õ	vowels pronounced nasally.
	ç	boss
	á	shows stress
	ô	shows that a vowel has an 'i' or 'u' sound combined with it.
Spanish	ñ	canyon
	ü	pronounced as w and separately from adjoining vowels.
	á	usually indicates that this is a stressed vowel.

Abbreviations

A.C.T. – Australian Capital Territory
A.R. – Autonomous Region
Afghan. – Afghanistan
Afr. – Africa
Ala. – Alabama
Alta. – Alberta
Amer. – America(n)
Arch. – Archipelago
Ariz. – Arizona
Ark. – Arkansas
Atl. Oc. – Atlantic Ocean
B. – Baie, Bahía, Bay, Bucht, Bugt
B.C. – British Columbia
Bangla. – Bangladesh
Barr. – Barrage
Bos.-H. – Bosnia-Herzegovina
C. – Cabo, Cap, Cape, Coast
C.A.R. – Central African Republic
C. Prov. – Cape Province
Calif. – California
Cat. – Catarata
Cent. – Central
Chan. – Channel
Colo. – Colorado
Conn. – Connecticut
Cord. – Cordillera
Cr. – Creek
Czech. – Czech Republic
D.C. – District of Columbia
Del. – Delaware
Dem. – Democratic
Dep. – Dependency
Des. – Desert
Dét. – Détroit
Dist. – District
Dj. – Djebel
Domin. – Dominica
Dom. Rep. – Dominican Republic
E. – East
E. Salv. – El Salvador
Eq. Guin. – Equatorial Guinea
Est. – Estrecho
Falk. Is. – Falkland Is.
Fd. – Fjord
Fla. – Florida
Fr. – French
G. – Golfe, Golfo, Gulf, Guba, Gebel
Ga. – Georgia
Gt. – Great, Greater
Guinea-Biss. – Guinea-Bissau
H.K. – Hong Kong
H.P. – Himachal Pradesh
Hants. – Hampshire
Harb. – Harbor, Harbour
Hd. – Head
Hts. – Heights
I.(s). – Île, Ilha, Insel, Isla, Island, Isle
Ill. – Illinois
Ind. – Indiana
Ind. Oc. – Indian Ocean
Ivory C. – Ivory Coast
J. – Jabal, Jebel
Jaz. – Jazīrah
Junc. – Junction
K. – Kap, Kapp
Kans. – Kansas
Kep. – Kepulauan
Ky. – Kentucky
L. – Lac, Lacul, Lago, Lagoa, Lake, Limni, Loch, Lough
La. – Louisiana
Ld. – Land
Liech. – Liechtenstein
Lux. – Luxembourg
Mad. P. – Madhya Pradesh
Madag. – Madagascar
Man. – Manitoba
Mass. – Massachusetts
Md. – Maryland
Me. – Maine
Medit. S. – Mediterranean Sea
Mich. – Michigan
Minn. – Minnesota
Miss. – Mississippi
Mo. – Missouri
Mont. – Montana
Mozam. – Mozambique
Mt.(s) – Mont, Montaña, Mountain
Mte. – Monte
Mti. – Monti
N. – Nord, Norte, North, Northern, Nouveau
N.B. – New Brunswick
N.C. – North Carolina
N. Cal. – New Caledonia
N. Dak. – North Dakota
N.H. – New Hampshire
N.I. – North Island
N.J. – New Jersey
N. Mex. – New Mexico
N.S. – Nova Scotia
N.S.W. – New South Wales
N.W.T. – North West Territory
N.Y. – New York
N.Z. – New Zealand
Nac. – Nacional
Nat. – National
Nebr. – Nebraska
Neths. – Netherlands
Nev. – Nevada
Nfld & L.. – Newfoundland and Labrador
Nic. – Nicaragua
O. – Oued, Ouadi
Occ. – Occidentale
Okla. – Oklahoma
Ont. – Ontario
Or. – Orientale
Oreg. – Oregon
Os. – Ostrov
Oz. – Ozero
P. – Pass, Passo, Pasul, Pulau
P.E.I. – Prince Edward Island
Pa. – Pennsylvania
Pac. Oc. – Pacific Ocean
Papua N.G. – Papua New Guinea
Pass. – Passage
Peg. – Pegunungan
Pen. – Peninsula, Péninsule
Phil. – Philippines
Pk. – Peak
Plat. – Plateau
Prov. – Province, Provincial
Pt. – Point
Pta. – Ponta, Punta
Pte. – Pointe
Qué. – Québec
Queens. – Queensland
R. – Rio, River
R.I. – Rhode Island
Ra. – Range
Raj. – Rajasthan
Recr. – Recreational, Récréatif
Reg. – Region
Rep. – Republic
Res. – Reserve, Reservoir
Rhld-Pfz. – Rheinland-Pfalz
S. – South, Southern, Sur
Si. Arabia – Saudi Arabia
S.C. – South Carolina
S. Dak. – South Dakota
S.I. – South Island
S. Leone – Sierra Leone
Sa. – Serra, Sierra
Sask. – Saskatchewan
Scot. – Scotland
Sd. – Sound
Serbia & M. – Serbia & Montenegro
Sev. – Severnaya
Sib. – Siberia
Sprs. – Springs
St. – Saint
Sta. – Santa
Ste. – Sainte
Sto. – Santo
Str. – Strait, Stretto
Switz. – Switzerland
Tas. – Tasmania
Tenn. – Tennessee
Terr. – Territory, Territoire
Tex. – Texas
Tg. – Tanjung
Trin. & Tob. – Trinidad & Tobago
U.A.E. – United Arab Emirates
U.K. – United Kingdom
U.S.A. – United States of America
Ut. P. – Uttar Pradesh
Va. – Virginia
Vdkhr. – Vodokhranilishche
Vdskh. – Vodoskhovyshche
Vf. – Vírful
Vic. – Victoria
Vol. – Volcano
Vt. – Vermont
W. – Wadi, West
W. Va. – West Virginia
Wall. & F. Is. – Wallis and Futuna Is.
Wash. – Washington
Wis. – Wisconsin
Wlkp. – Wielkopolski
Wyo. – Wyoming
Yorks. – Yorkshire

A

A 'Âli an Nîl □, Sudan 107 F3 9 30N 33 0 E
A Baña, Spain 42 C2 42 58N 8 46W
A Cañiza, Spain 42 C2 42 13N 8 16W
A Coruña, Spain 42 B2 43 20N 8 25W
A Estrada, Spain 42 C2 42 43N 8 27W
A Fonsagrada, Spain 42 B3 43 8N 7 4W
A Guarda, Spain 42 D2 41 56N 8 52W
A Gudiña, Spain 42 C3 42 4N 7 8W
A Rúa, Spain 42 C3 42 24N 7 6W
Aachen, Germany 30 E2 50 45N 6 6 E
Aadorf, Switz. 33 B7 47 30N 8 55 E
Aalborg = Ålborg, Denmark 17 G3 57 2N 9 54 E
Aalen, Germany 31 G6 48 51N 10 6 E
Aalst, Belgium 24 D4 50 56N 4 2 E
Aalten, Neths. 24 C6 51 56N 6 35 E
Aalter, Belgium 24 C3 51 5N 3 28 E
Äänekoski, Finland 15 E21 62 36N 25 44 E
Aarau, Switz. 32 B6 47 23N 8 4 E
Aarberg, Switz. 32 B4 47 2N 7 16 E
Aarburg, Switz. 32 B5 47 19N 7 54 E
Aare →, Switz. 32 A6 47 33N 8 14 E
Aargau □, Switz. 32 B6 47 26N 8 10 E
Aarhus = Århus, Denmark 17 H4 56 8N 10 11 E
Aarlen = Arlon, Belgium 24 E5 49 42N 5 49 E
Aarschot, Belgium 24 D4 50 59N 4 49 E
Aarwangen, Switz. 32 B5 47 15N 7 46 E
Aasiaat, Greenland 10 D5 68 43N 52 56W
Ab-i-Istada, Afghan. 91 B2 32 29N 67 55 E
Ab-i-Panja = Pyandzh →, Asia 65 E4 37 6N 68 20 E
Aba, China 76 A3 32 59N 101 42 E
Aba, Dem. Rep. of the Congo 118 B3 3 58N 30 17 E
Aba, Nigeria 113 D6 5 10N 7 19 E
Âbâ, Jazîrat, Sudan 107 E3 13 30N 32 31 E
Abacaxis →, Brazil 169 D6 3 54 S 58 47W
Abaco I., Bahamas 164 A4 26 25N 77 10W
Abadab, J., Sudan 106 D4 18 54N 35 56 E
Ābādān, Iran 97 D6 30 22N 48 20 E
Abade, Ethiopia 107 F4 9 22N 38 3 E
Ābādeh, Iran 97 D7 31 8N 52 40 E
Abadin, Spain 42 B3 43 21N 7 29W
Abadla, Algeria 111 B4 31 2N 2 45W
Abaeté, Brazil 171 E2 19 9 S 45 27W
Abaeté →, Brazil 171 E2 18 2 S 45 12W
Abaetetuba, Brazil 170 B2 1 40 S 48 50W
Abagnar Qi, China 74 C9 43 52N 116 2 E
Abah, Tanjung, Indonesia 79 K18 8 46 S 115 38 E
Abai, Paraguay 175 B4 25 58 S 55 54W
Abak, Nigeria 113 E6 4 58N 7 50 E
Abakaliki, Nigeria 113 D6 6 22N 8 2 E
Abakan, Russia 67 D10 53 40N 91 10 E
Abala, Congo 114 C3 1 17 S 15 35 E
Abala, Niger 113 C5 14 56N 3 22 E
Abalak, Niger 113 B6 15 22N 6 21 E
Abalemma, Algeria 111 D6 20 51N 5 59 E
Abalemma, Niger 113 B6 16 12N 7 50 E
Abalessa, Algeria 111 D5 22 58N 4 47 E
Abana, Turkey 100 B6 41 59N 34 1 E
Abancay, Peru 172 C3 13 35 S 72 55W
Abanga →, Gabon 114 C2 0 20 S 10 30 E
Abano Terme, Italy 45 C8 45 22N 11 46 E
Abapó, Bolivia 173 D5 18 48 S 63 25W
Abarán, Spain 41 G3 38 12N 1 23W
Abariringa, Kiribati 134 H10 2 50 S 171 40W
Abarqū, Iran 97 D7 31 10N 53 20 E
Abashiri, Japan 70 B12 44 0N 144 15 E
Abashiri-Wan, Japan 70 C12 44 0N 144 30 E
Abau, Papua N. G. 132 F5 10 11 S 148 46 E
Abaújszántó, Hungary 52 B6 48 16N 21 12 E
Abava →, Latvia 54 A8 57 6N 21 54 E
Ābay = Nîl el Azraq →, Sudan 107 D3 15 38N 32 31 E
Abay, Kazakhstan 66 E8 49 38N 72 53 E
Abaya, L., Ethiopia 107 F4 6 30N 37 50 E
Abayita-Shala Lakes △, Ethiopia 107 F4 7 40N 38 37 E
Abaza, Russia 66 D9 52 39N 90 6 E
Abba, C.A.R. 114 A3 5 20N 15 11 E
Abbadia di Fiastra ⌂, Italy 45 E10 43 12N 13 24 E
Abbadia San Salvatore, Italy 45 F8 42 53N 11 41 E
'Abbāsābād, Iran 97 C8 33 34N 58 23 E
Abbay = Nîl el Azraq →, Sudan 107 D3 15 38N 32 31 E
Abbaye, Pt., U.S.A. 148 B1 46 58N 88 8W
Abbazia = Opatija, Croatia 45 C11 45 21N 14 17 E
Abbé, L., Ethiopia 107 E5 11 8N 41 47 E
Abbeville, France 27 B8 50 6N 1 49 E
Abbeville, Ala., U.S.A. 152 D4 31 34N 85 15W
Abbeville, Ga., U.S.A. 152 D6 31 59N 83 18W
Abbeville, La., U.S.A. 155 L8 29 58N 92 8W
Abbeville, S.C., U.S.A. 152 A7 34 11N 82 23W
Abbiategrasso, Italy 44 C5 45 24N 8 54 E
Abbot Ice Shelf, Antarctica 7 D16 73 0 S 92 0W
Abbottabad, Pakistan 92 B5 34 10N 73 15 E
Abbou, O. ben →, Algeria 111 C5 28 32N 5 14 E
ABC Islands = Netherlands Antilles ☒, W. Indies 168 A4 12 15N 69 0W
Abd al Kūrī, Yemen 99 D6 12 5N 52 20 E
Ābdar, Iran 97 D7 30 16N 55 19 E
'Abdolābād, Iran 97 C8 34 12N 56 30 E
Abdulino, Russia 64 E4 53 42N 53 40 E
Abdulpur, Bangla. 90 C2 24 15N 88 59 E
Abéché, Chad 109 F4 13 50N 20 35 E
Abejar, Spain 40 D2 41 48N 2 47W
Abekr, Sudan 107 E2 12 45N 28 50 E
Abel Tasman △, N.Z. 131 A8 40 59 S 173 3 E
Abemarre, Indonesia 83 C6 7 1 S 140 9 E
Abengourou, Ivory C. 112 D4 6 42N 3 27W
Abenójar, Spain 43 G6 38 53N 4 21W
Åbenrå, Denmark 17 J3 55 3N 9 25 E
Abensberg, Germany 31 G7 48 48N 11 51 E
Abeokuta, Nigeria 113 D5 7 3N 3 19 E
Aber, Uganda 118 B3 2 12N 32 25 E
Aberaeron, U.K. 21 E3 52 15N 4 15W
Aberayron = Aberaeron, U.K. 21 E3 52 15N 4 15W
Aberchirder, U.K. 22 D6 57 34N 2 37W
Abercorn = Mbala, Zambia 119 D3 8 46 S 31 24 E
Abercorn, Australia 127 D5 25 12 S 151 5 E
Aberdare, U.K. 21 F4 51 43N 3 27W
Aberdare △, Kenya 118 C4 0 22 S 36 44 E
Aberdare Ra., Kenya 118 C4 0 15 S 36 50 E
Aberdeen, Australia 129 B9 32 9 S 150 56 E
Aberdeen, Canada 143 C7 52 20N 106 8W
Aberdeen, China 69 G11 22 15N 114 9 E
Aberdeen, S. Africa 116 E3 32 28 S 24 2 E
Aberdeen, U.K. 22 D6 57 9N 2 5W
Aberdeen, Ala., U.S.A. 149 J1 33 49N 88 33W
Aberdeen, Idaho, U.S.A. 158 E7 42 57N 112 50W
Aberdeen, Md., U.S.A. 148 F7 39 31N 76 10W
Aberdeen, Ohio, U.S.A. 157 F13 38 39N 83 46W
Aberdeen, S. Dak., U.S.A. 154 C5 45 28N 98 29W
Aberdeen, Wash., U.S.A. 160 D3 46 59N 123 50W
Aberdeen, City of □, U.K. 22 D6 57 10N 2 10W
Aberdeenshire □, U.K. 22 D6 57 17N 2 36W
Aberdovey = Aberdyfi, U.K. 21 E3 52 33N 4 3W
Aberdyfi, U.K. 21 E3 52 33N 4 3W
Aberfeldy, U.K. 22 E5 56 37N 3 51W
Aberfoyle, U.K. 22 E4 56 11N 4 23W
Abergavenny, U.K. 21 F4 51 49N 3 1W
Abergele, U.K. 20 D4 53 17N 3 35W
Abernathy, U.S.A. 155 J4 33 50N 101 51W
Abert, L., U.S.A. 158 E3 42 38N 120 14W
Aberystwyth, U.K. 21 E3 52 25N 4 5W
Abhā, Si. Arabia 98 C3 18 0N 42 34 E
Abhar, Iran 97 B6 36 9N 49 13 E
Abhayapuri, India 90 B3 26 24N 90 38 E
Abia □, Nigeria 113 D6 5 30N 7 35 E
Abide, Turkey 49 C11 38 55N 29 20 E
Abidiya, Sudan 106 D3 18 18N 34 3 E
Abidjan, Ivory C. 112 D4 5 26N 3 58W
Abilene, Kans., U.S.A. 154 F6 38 55N 97 13W
Abilene, Tex., U.S.A. 155 J5 32 28N 99 43W
Abingdon, U.K. 21 F6 51 40N 1 17W
Abingdon, Ill., U.S.A. 156 D6 40 48N 90 24W
Abingdon, Va., U.S.A. 149 G5 36 43N 81 59W
Abingdon, I. = Pinta, I., Ecuador 172 a 0 35N 90 44W
Abington Reef, Australia 126 B4 18 0 S 149 35 E
Abitau →, Canada 143 B7 59 53N 109 3W
Abitibi →, Canada 140 B3 51 3N 80 55W
Abitibi, L., Canada 140 C4 48 40N 79 40W
Abiy Adi, Ethiopia 107 E4 13 39N 39 3 E
Abkhaz Republic = Abkhazia □, Georgia 61 J5 43 12N 41 5 E
Abkhazia □, Georgia 61 J5 43 12N 41 5 E
Abminga, Australia 127 D1 26 8 S 134 51 E
Abnûb, Egypt 106 B3 27 18N 31 4 E
Åbo = Turku, Finland 15 F20 60 30N 22 19 E
Abo, Massif d', Chad 109 D3 21 41N 16 8 E
Abocho, Nigeria 113 D6 7 35N 6 56 E
Abohar, India 92 D6 30 10N 74 10 E
Aboisso, Ivory C. 112 D4 5 30N 3 5W
Abolo, Congo 114 B2 0 8N 14 16 E
Abomey, Benin 113 D5 7 10N 2 5 E
Abong-Mbang, Cameroon 114 B2 4 0N 13 8 E
Abongabong, Indonesia 84 B1 4 15N 96 48 E
Abonnema, Nigeria 113 E6 4 41N 6 49 E
Abony, Hungary 52 C5 47 12N 20 3 E
Abor Hills, India 90 A5 28 25N 94 46 E
Aborlan, Phil. 81 G2 9 26N 118 33 E
Aboso, Ghana 112 D4 5 23N 1 57W
Abou-Deïa, Chad 109 F3 11 20N 19 20 E
Abou-Goulem, Chad 109 F4 13 37N 21 38 E
Abou-Telfan ⌂, Chad 109 F3 12 2N 18 58 E
Aboyne, U.K. 22 D6 57 4N 2 47W
Abra □, Phil. 80 C3 17 35N 120 45 E
Abra de Ilog, Phil. 80 E3 13 27N 120 44 E
Abra Pampa, Argentina 174 A2 22 43 S 65 42W
Abraham L., Canada 142 C5 52 15N 116 35W
Abrantes, Portugal 43 F2 39 24N 8 7W
Abreojos, Pta., Mexico 162 B2 26 50N 113 40W
Abri, Esh Shamâliya, Sudan 106 C3 20 50N 30 27 E
Abri, Janub Kordofân, Sudan 107 E3 11 40N 30 21 E
Abrolhos, Banco, Brazil 171 E4 18 0 S 38 0W
Abrud, Romania 52 D8 46 19N 23 5 E
Abruzzo □, Italy 45 F10 42 15N 14 0 E
Absaroka Range, U.S.A. 158 D9 44 45N 109 50W
Abtenau, Austria 34 D6 47 33N 13 21 E
Abu, India 92 G5 24 41N 72 50 E
Abū al Abyad, U.A.E. 97 E7 24 11N 53 50 E
Abū al Khaşīb, Iraq 97 D6 30 25N 48 0 E
Abū 'Alī, Si. Arabia 97 E6 27 20N 49 27 E
Abū 'Alī →, Lebanon 103 A4 34 25N 35 50 E
Abū 'Arīsh, Si. Arabia 98 C3 16 53N 42 48 E
Abu Ballas, Egypt 106 C2 24 26N 27 36 E
Abu Deleiq, Sudan 107 D3 15 57N 33 48 E
Abu Dhabi = Abū Ẓāby, U.A.E. 97 E7 24 28N 54 22 E
Abu Dis, Sudan 106 D3 19 12N 33 38 E
Abu Dom, Sudan 107 D3 16 18N 32 25 E
Abū Du'ān, Syria 101 D8 36 25N 38 15 E
Abu el Gairi, W. →, Egypt 103 F2 29 35N 33 30 E
Abu Fatma, Ras, Sudan 106 C4 22 25N 36 25 E
Abu Gabra, Sudan 107 E2 11 2N 26 50 E
Abu Ga'da, W. →, Egypt 103 F1 29 15N 32 53 E
Abu Gelba, Sudan 107 E3 13 11N 31 52 E
Abu Gubeiha, Sudan 107 E3 11 30N 31 15 E
Abu Habl, Khawr →, Sudan 107 E3 12 37N 31 0 E
Abū Ḩadrīyah, Si. Arabia 97 E6 27 20N 48 58 E
Abu Hamed, Sudan 106 D3 19 32N 33 13 E
Abu Haraz, An Nîl el Azraq, Sudan 106 D3 18 1N 33 58 E
Abu Haraz, El Gezira, Sudan 107 E3 14 35N 33 30 E
Abu Haraz, Esh Shamâliya, Sudan 106 D3 19 8N 32 18 E
Abu Higar, Sudan 107 E3 12 50N 33 59 E
Abū Kamāl, Syria 101 E9 34 30N 41 0 E
Abu Kuleiwat, Sudan 107 E2 12 20N 26 0 E
Abū Madd, Ra's, Si. Arabia 96 E3 24 50N 37 7 E
Abu Matariq, Sudan 107 E2 10 59N 26 9 E
Abu Mendi, Ethiopia 107 E4 11 48N 35 42 E
Abū Mūsā, U.A.E. 97 E7 25 52N 55 3 E
Abū Qaşr, Si. Arabia 96 D3 30 21N 38 34 E
Abu Qir, Egypt 106 H7 31 18N 30 0 E
Abu Qireiya, Egypt 106 C4 24 5N 35 28 E
Abu Qurqâs, Egypt 106 B3 28 1N 30 44 E
Abū Raşāş, Ra's, Oman 99 B7 20 10N 58 38 E
Abu Shagara, Ras, Sudan 106 C4 21 4N 37 19 E
Abu Shanab, Sudan 107 E2 13 58N 27 49 E
Abu Simbel, Egypt 106 C3 22 18N 31 40 E
Abū Şukhayr, Iraq 101 G11 31 54N 44 30 E
Abu Sultân, Egypt 106 H8 30 24N 32 21 E
Abu Tabari, Sudan 106 D2 17 32N 28 32 E
Abu Tig, Egypt 106 B3 27 4N 31 15 E
Abu Tiga, Sudan 107 E3 12 47N 34 12 E
Abu Tineitin, Sudan 107 E3 14 24N 31 1 E
Abu Uruq, Sudan 107 D3 15 52N 30 25 E
Abu Zabad, Sudan 107 E2 12 25N 29 10 E
Abū Ẓāby, U.A.E. 97 E7 24 28N 54 22 E
Abū Zeydābād, Iran 97 C6 33 54N 51 45 E
Abufari, Brazil 173 B5 5 25 S 62 59W
Abuja, Nigeria 113 D6 9 5N 7 32 E
Abukuma-Gawa →, Japan 70 E10 38 6N 140 52 E
Abukuma-Sammyaku, Japan 70 F10 37 30N 140 45 E
Abulug, Phil. 80 B3 18 27N 121 27 E
Abumombazi, Dem. Rep. of the Congo 114 B4 3 42N 22 10 E
Abunã, Brazil 173 B4 9 40 S 65 20W
Abunã →, Brazil 173 B4 9 41 S 65 20W
Abune Yosef, Ethiopia 107 E4 12 5N 39 12 E
Aburatsu, Japan 72 F3 31 34N 131 24 E
Aburo, Dem. Rep. of the Congo 118 B3 2 4N 30 53 E
Abut Hd., N.Z. 131 D5 43 7 S 170 15 E
Abuye Meda, Ethiopia 107 E4 10 30N 39 49 E
Abuyog, Phil. 81 F5 10 45N 125 0 E
Abwong, Sudan 107 F3 9 2N 32 14 E
Åby, Sweden 17 F10 58 40N 16 10 E
Aby, Lagune, Ivory C. 112 D4 5 15N 3 14W
Abyad, Sudan 107 E2 13 47N 26 24 E
Åbybro, Denmark 17 G3 57 10N 9 44 E
Acacías, Colombia 168 C3 3 59N 73 46W
Acadia △, U.S.A. 149 C11 44 20N 68 13W
Acajutla, El Salv. 164 D2 13 36N 89 50W
Açallândia, Brazil 170 C2 5 0 S 47 30W
Acámbaro, Mexico 162 D4 20 0N 100 40W
Acanthus, Greece 50 F7 40 27N 23 47 E
Acaponeta, Mexico 162 C3 22 30N 105 20W
Acapulco, Mexico 163 D5 16 51N 99 56W
Acará, Brazil 170 B2 1 57 S 48 11W
Acarai, Serra, Brazil 169 C6 1 50N 57 50W
Acaraú, Brazil 170 B3 2 53 S 40 7W
Acari, Brazil 170 C4 6 31 S 36 38W
Acarí, Peru 172 D3 15 25 S 74 36W
Acarigua, Venezuela 168 B4 9 33N 69 12W
Acatlán, Mexico 163 D5 18 10N 98 3W
Acayucan, Mexico 163 D6 17 59N 94 58W
Accéglio, Italy 44 D4 44 28N 7 0 E
Accomac, U.S.A. 148 G8 37 43N 75 40W
Accous, France 28 E3 43 0N 0 36W
Accra, Ghana 113 D4 5 35N 0 6W
Accrington, U.K. 20 D5 53 45N 2 22W
Acebal, Argentina 174 C3 33 20 S 60 50W
Aceh □, Indonesia 84 B1 4 15N 97 30 E
Acerra, Italy 47 B7 40 57N 14 22 E
Aceuchal, Spain 43 G4 38 39N 6 30W
Achacachi, Bolivia 172 D4 16 3 S 68 43W
Achaguas, Venezuela 168 B4 7 46N 68 14W
Achalpur, India 94 D3 21 22N 77 32 E
Achao, Chile 176 B2 42 28 S 73 30W
Acharnes = Akharnaí, Greece 48 C5 38 5N 23 44 E
Achegour, Niger 109 E2 19 10N 11 54 E
Acheloos = Akhelóös →, Greece 48 C3 38 19N 21 7 E
Achelouma, Niger 109 D2 22 12N 12 50 E
Achelouma, E. →, Niger 109 D2 21 55N 13 35 E
Acheng, China 75 B14 45 30N 126 58 E
Achenkirch, Austria 34 D4 47 32N 11 45 E
Achensee, Austria 34 D4 47 26N 11 45 E
Acher, India 92 H5 23 10N 72 32 E
Achern, Germany 31 G4 48 37N 8 4 E
Acheron →, N.Z. 131 C8 42 16 S 173 4 E
Achill Hd., Ireland 23 C1 53 58N 10 15W
Achill I., Ireland 23 C1 53 58N 10 1W
Achim, Germany 30 B5 53 1N 9 3 E
Achinsk, Russia 67 D10 56 20N 90 20 E
Achisay = Ashchysay, Kazakhstan 65 B4 43 35N 68 53 E
Achit, Russia 64 C6 56 48N 57 54 E
Achouka, Gabon 114 C2 0 52 S 9 45 E
Acıgöl, Turkey 49 D11 37 50N 29 50 E
Acıpayam, Turkey 49 D11 37 26N 29 22 E
Acireale, Italy 47 E8 37 37N 15 10 E
Ackerman, U.S.A. 155 J10 33 19N 89 11W
Ackley, U.S.A. 156 B3 42 33N 93 3W
Acklins I., Bahamas 165 B5 22 30N 74 0W
Acme, Canada 142 C6 51 33N 113 30W
Acme, U.S.A. 150 F5 40 8N 79 26W
Acobamba, Peru 172 C3 12 52 S 74 35W
Acomayo, Peru 172 C3 13 55 S 71 38W
Aconcagua, Cerro, Argentina 174 C2 32 39 S 70 0W
Aconquija, Mt., Argentina 174 B2 27 0 S 66 0W
Acopiara, Brazil 170 C4 6 6 S 39 27W
Açores, Is. dos, Atl. Oc. 8 C9 38 0N 27 0W
Acorizal, Brazil 173 D6 15 12 S 56 22W
Acornhoek, S. Africa 117 C5 24 37 S 31 2 E
Acquapendente, Italy 45 F8 42 44N 11 52 E
Acquasanta Terme, Italy 45 F10 42 46N 13 24 E
Acquasparta, Italy 45 F9 42 41N 12 33 E
Acquaviva delle Fonti, Italy 47 B9 40 54N 16 50 E
Ácqui Terme, Italy 44 D5 44 41N 8 28 E
Acraman, L., Australia 127 E2 32 2 S 135 23 E
Acre = 'Akko, Israel 103 C4 32 55N 35 4 E
Acre □, Brazil 172 B3 9 1 S 71 0W
Acre →, Brazil 172 B4 8 45 S 67 22W
Acri, Italy 47 C9 39 29N 16 23 E
Acs, Hungary 52 C3 47 42N 18 2 E
Actæon Mt., St. Helena 9 h 15 58 S 5 42W
Actium, Greece 39 B2 38 57N 20 45 E
Acton, Canada 150 C4 43 38N 80 3W
Açu, Brazil 170 C4 5 34 S 36 54W
Acul = Vidin, Bulgaria 50 C6 43 59N 22 50 E
Acuña, Mexico 162 B4 29 18N 100 55W
Acworth, U.S.A. 152 A5 34 4N 84 41W
Ad Dafinah, Si. Arabia 98 B3 23 18N 41 58 E
Aḑ Ḑafrah, U.A.E. 99 B6 23 30N 54 30 E
Ad Dahnā, Si. Arabia 99 A5 24 30N 48 10 E
Aḑ Ḑālī', Yemen 98 D4 13 42N 44 44 E
Ad Dammām, Si. Arabia 97 E6 26 20N 50 5 E
Ad Dāmūr, Lebanon 103 B4 33 44N 35 27 E
Ad Darb, Si. Arabia 98 C3 18 2N 43 7 E
Ad Dawādimī, Si. Arabia 96 E5 24 35N 44 15 E
Ad Dawḩah, Qatar 97 E6 25 15N 51 35 E
Ad Dawr, Iraq 101 E10 34 27N 43 47 E
Aḑ Ḑiffah, Libya 108 B4 30 30N 24 30 E
Ad Dilam, Si. Arabia 98 B4 23 55N 47 10 E
Ad Dir'īyah, Si. Arabia 96 E5 24 44N 46 35 E
Ad Dīwānīyah, Iraq 101 F11 32 0N 45 0 E
Ad Dujayl, Iraq 101 F11 33 51N 44 14 E
Ad Duwayd, Si. Arabia 96 D4 30 15N 42 17 E
Ada, Ghana 113 D5 5 44N 0 40 E
Ada, Serbia & M. 52 E5 45 49N 20 9 E
Ada, Minn., U.S.A. 154 B6 47 18N 96 31W
Ada, Ohio, U.S.A. 157 D13 40 46N 83 49W
Ada, Okla., U.S.A. 155 H6 34 46N 96 41W
Adabiya, Egypt 103 F1 29 53N 32 28 E
Adad, Somali Rep. 120 C3 9 27N 46 49 E
Adair, C., Canada 139 A12 71 30N 71 34W
Adaja →, Spain 42 D6 41 32N 4 52W
Adak, U.S.A. 144 L3 51 45N 176 45W
Adak I., U.S.A. 144 L3 51 45N 176 45W
Ådalsbruk, Norway 18 D8 60 43N 11 19 E
Adam, Oman 99 B7 22 15N 57 28 E
Adam, Mt., Falk. Is. 9 f 51 34 S 60 4W
Adamantina, Brazil 171 F1 21 42 S 51 4W
Adamaoua, Massif de l', Cameroon 113 D7 7 20N 12 20 E
Adamawa □, Nigeria 113 D7 9 20N 12 30 E
Adamawa Highlands = Adamaoua, Massif de l', Cameroon 113 D7 7 20N 12 20 E
Adamello ⌂, Italy 44 B7 46 4N 10 28 E
Adamello, Mte., Italy 44 B7 46 9N 10 30 E
Adami Tulu, Ethiopia 107 F4 7 53N 38 41 E
Adaminaby, Australia 129 D8 36 0 S 148 45 E
Adamovka, Russia 64 F7 51 32N 59 56 E
Adams, Mass., U.S.A. 151 D11 42 38N 73 7W
Adams, N.Y., U.S.A. 151 C8 43 49N 76 1W
Adams, Wis., U.S.A. 154 D10 43 57N 89 49W
Adams, Mt., U.S.A. 160 D5 46 12N 121 30W
Adam's Bridge, Sri Lanka 95 K4 9 15N 79 40 E
Adams L., Canada 142 C5 51 10N 119 40W
Adam's Peak, Sri Lanka 95 L5 6 48N 80 30 E
Adamuz, Spain 43 G6 38 2N 4 32W
Adana, Turkey 100 D6 37 0N 35 16 E
Adanero, Spain 42 E6 40 56N 4 36W
Adapazarı = Sakarya, Turkey 100 B4 40 48N 30 25 E
Adar Gwagwa, J., Sudan 106 C4 22 15N 35 20 E
Adarama, Sudan 107 D3 17 10N 34 52 E
Adare, C., Antarctica 7 D11 71 0 S 171 0 E
Adarte, Eritrea 107 E5 13 18N 42 8 E
Adaut, Indonesia 83 C4 8 8 S 131 7 E
Adavale, Australia 127 D3 25 52 S 144 32 E
Adda →, Italy 44 C6 45 8N 9 53 E
Addatigala, India 94 F6 17 31N 82 3 E
Addax ⌂, Niger 109 E1 19 17N 9 22 E
Addis Ababa = Addis Abeba, Ethiopia 107 F4 9 2N 38 42 E
Addis Abeba, Ethiopia 107 F4 9 2N 38 42 E
Addis Alem, Ethiopia 107 F4 9 0N 38 17 E
Addis Zemen, Ethiopia 107 E4 12 7N 37 47 E
Addison, Ill., U.S.A. 157 C8 41 55N 88 0W
Addison, N.Y., U.S.A. 150 D7 42 1N 77 14W
Addo, S. Africa 116 E4 33 32 S 25 45 E
Addo △, S. Africa 116 E4 33 30 S 25 50 E
Adebour, Niger 113 C7 13 17N 11 50 E
Ādeh, Iran 96 B5 37 42N 45 11 E
Adel, Ga., U.S.A. 152 D6 31 8N 83 25W
Adel, Iowa, U.S.A. 156 C2 41 37N 94 1W
Adelaide, Australia 128 C3 34 52 S 138 30 E
Adelaide, S. Africa 116 E4 32 42 S 26 20 E
Adelaide I., Antarctica 7 C17 67 15 S 68 30W
Adelaide Pen., Canada 138 B10 68 15N 97 30W
Adelaide River, Australia 124 B5 13 15 S 131 7 E
Adelaide Village, Bahamas 9 b 25 0N 77 31W
Adelanto, U.S.A. 161 L9 34 35N 117 22W
Adelaye, C.A.R. 114 A4 7 7N 22 49 E
Adelboden, Switz. 32 D5 46 29N 7 33 E
Adele I., Australia 124 C3 15 32 S 123 9 E
Adélie, Terre, Antarctica 7 C10 68 0 S 140 0 E
Adelie Land = Adélie, Terre, Antarctica 7 C10 68 0 S 140 0 E
Adelong, Australia 129 C8 35 16 S 148 4 E
Adelsk, Belarus 54 E10 53 24N 23 47 E
Ademuz, Spain 40 E3 40 5N 1 13W
Aden = Al 'Adan, Yemen 98 D4 12 45N 45 0 E
Aden, G. of, Asia 88 D3 12 30N 47 30 E
Adendorp, S. Africa 116 E3 32 15 S 24 30 E
Aderbissinat, Niger 113 B6 15 34N 7 54 E
Adh Dhayd, U.A.E. 97 E7 25 17N 55 53 E
Adhoi, India 92 H4 23 26N 70 32 E
Adi, Indonesia 83 B4 4 15 S 133 30 E
Adi Arkai, Ethiopia 107 E4 13 35N 37 57 E
Adi Daro, Ethiopia 107 E4 14 20N 38 14 E
Adi Keyih, Eritrea 107 E4 14 51N 39 22 E
Adi Kwala, Eritrea 107 E4 14 38N 38 48 E
Adi Ugri, Eritrea 107 E4 14 58N 38 48 E
Adieu, C., Australia 125 F5 32 0 S 132 10 E
Adieu Pt., Australia 124 C3 15 14 S 124 35 E
Adigala, Ethiopia 107 E5 10 24N 42 15 E
Adige →, Italy 45 C9 45 9N 12 20 E
Adigrat, Ethiopia 107 E4 14 20N 39 26 E
Adıgüzel Barajı, Turkey 49 C11 38 13N 29 14 E
Adilabad, India 94 E4 19 33N 78 20 E
Adilcevaz, Turkey 101 C10 38 47N 42 43 E
Adirondack ⌂, U.S.A. 151 C10 44 0N 74 20W
Adirondack Mts., U.S.A. 151 C10 44 0N 74 0W
Adis Abeba = Addis Abeba, Ethiopia 107 F4 9 2N 38 42 E
Adıyaman, Turkey 101 D8 37 45N 38 16 E
Adjim, Tunisia 108 B2 33 47N 10 50 E
Adjohon, Benin 113 D5 6 41N 2 32 E
Adjud, Romania 53 D12 46 7N 27 10 E
Adjumani, Uganda 118 B3 3 20N 31 50 E
Adjuntas, Puerto Rico 165 d 18 10N 66 43W
Adlavik Is., Canada 141 B8 55 0N 58 40W
Adler, Russia 61 J4 43 28N 39 52 E
Adliswil, Switz. 33 B7 47 19N 8 32 E
Admer, Algeria 111 D6 20 21N 5 27 E
Admer, Erg d', Algeria 111 D6 24 0N 9 5 E
Admiralty G., Australia 124 B4 14 20 S 125 55 E
Admiralty I., U.S.A. 142 B2 57 30N 134 30W
Admiralty Is., Papua N. G. 132 B4 2 0 S 147 0 E
Adnan Menderes, İzmir ✈ (ADB), Turkey 49 C9 38 23N 27 6 E
Ado, Nigeria 113 D5 6 36N 2 56 E
Ado-Ekiti, Nigeria 113 D6 7 38N 5 12 E
Adok, Sudan 107 F3 8 10N 30 20 E
Adola, Ethiopia 107 E5 11 14N 41 44 E
Adonara, Indonesia 82 C2 8 15 S 123 5 E
Adoni, India 95 G3 15 33N 77 18 E
Adony, Hungary 52 C3 47 6N 18 52 E
Adour →, France 28 E2 43 32N 1 32W
Adra, India 93 H12 23 30N 86 42 E
Adra, Spain 43 J7 36 43N 3 3W
Adrano, Italy 47 E7 37 40N 14 50 E
Adrar des Iforas, Algeria 111 C4 27 51N 0 11 E
Adrar Madet, Niger 109 E2 18 54N 10 35 E
Adrasman, Tajikistan 65 C4 40 38N 69 58 E
Adré, Chad 109 F4 13 40N 22 20 E
Adrī, Libya 108 C2 27 32N 13 2 E
Ádria, Italy 45 C9 45 3N 12 3 E
Adrian, Ga., U.S.A. 152 C7 32 33N 82 35W
Adrian, Mich., U.S.A. 157 C12 41 54N 84 2W
Adrian, Mo., U.S.A. 156 F2 38 24N 94 21W
Adrian, Tex., U.S.A. 155 H3 35 16N 102 40W
Adrianople = Edirne, Turkey 51 E10 41 40N 26 34 E
Adriatic Sea, Medit. S. 12 G9 43 0N 16 0 E
Adua, Indonesia 83 B3 1 45 S 129 50 E
Adula-Gruppe, Switz. 33 D8 46 30N 9 3 E
Adung Long, Burma 90 A6 28 7N 97 42 E
Adur, India 95 K3 9 8N 76 40 E
Adwa, Ethiopia 107 E4 14 15N 38 52 E
Adygea □, Russia 61 H5 45 0N 40 0 E
Adzhar Republic = Ajaria □, Georgia 61 K6 41 30N 42 0 E
Adzhibakul = Qazimämmäd, Azerbaijan 61 K9 40 3N 49 0 E
Adzopé, Ivory C. 112 D4 6 7N 3 49W
Ægean Sea, Medit. S. 49 C7 38 30N 25 0 E
Aerhtai Shan, Mongolia 68 B4 46 40N 92 45 E
Ærø, Denmark 17 K4 54 52N 10 25 E
Ærøskøbing, Denmark 17 K4 54 53N 10 24 E
Aesch, Switz. 32 B5 47 28N 7 36 E
Aëtós, Greece 48 D3 37 15N 21 50 E
Afafi, Massif d', Niger 109 D3 22 11N 15 10 E
'Afak, Iraq 101 F11 32 4N 45 15 E
Afándou, Greece 38 E12 36 18N 28 12 E
Afar □, Ethiopia 107 E5 12 0N 41 0 E
Afarag, Erg, Algeria 111 D5 23 50N 2 47 E
Afareaitu, Tahiti 133 S16 17 33 S 149 47W
Åfarnes, Norway 18 B4 62 40N 7 32 E
Afdega, Ethiopia 120 C2 6 4N 43 30 E
Affoltern, Switz. 33 B6 47 17N 8 27 E
Affreville = Khemis Miliana, Algeria 111 A5 36 11N 2 14 E
Affton, U.S.A. 156 F6 38 33N 90 20W
Afghanistan ■, Asia 91 B2 33 0N 65 0 E
Afgoi, Somali Rep. 120 D2 2 7N 44 59 E
'Afif, Si. Arabia 98 B3 23 53N 42 56 E
Afikpo, Nigeria 113 D6 5 53N 7 54 E
Aflisses, O. →, Algeria 111 C5 28 40N 0 50 E
Aflou, Algeria 111 B5 34 7N 2 3 E
Afmadu, Somali Rep. 120 D2 0 31N 42 4 E
Afogados da Ingàzeira, Brazil 170 C4 7 45 S 37 39W
Afognak I., U.S.A. 144 G9 58 15N 152 30W
Afore, Papua N. G. 132 E5 9 9 S 148 23 E
Afragóla, Italy 47 B7 40 55N 14 18 E
Afram →, Ghana 113 D4 7 0N 0 52W
Afrera, Ethiopia 107 E5 13 16N 41 5 E
Africa 104 E6 10 0N 20 0 E
'Afrīn, Syria 100 D7 36 32N 36 50 E
Afşin, Turkey 100 C7 38 14N 36 55 E
Afton, Iowa, U.S.A. 156 C2 41 2N 94 12W
Afton, N.Y., U.S.A. 151 D9 42 14N 75 32W
Afton, Wyo., U.S.A. 158 E8 42 44N 110 56W
Aftout, Algeria 110 C4 26 50N 3 45W
Afuá, Brazil 169 D7 0 15 S 50 20W
'Afula, Israel 103 C4 32 37N 35 17 E
Afumba, Zambia 115 F4 15 38 S 24 56 E
Afyon, Turkey 49 C12 38 45N 30 33 E
Afyon □, Turkey 49 C12 38 25N 30 30 E
Afyonkarahisar = Afyon, Turkey 49 C12 38 45N 30 33 E
Aga, Egypt 106 H7 30 55N 31 10 E
Aga Pt., Guam 133 R15 13 15N 144 43 E
Agadem, Niger 109 E2 16 50N 13 11 E
Agadès = Agadez, Niger 113 B6 16 58N 7 59 E
Agadez, Niger 113 B6 16 58N 7 59 E
Agadir, Morocco 110 B3 30 28N 9 55W
Agaete, Canary Is. 9 e1 28 6N 15 43W
Agaie, Nigeria 113 D6 9 1N 6 18 E
Agailás, Mauritania 110 D2 22 37N 14 22W
Again, Sudan 107 F2 8 28N 29 55 E
Agalás, Greece 39 D2 37 43N 20 47 E
Agalega Is., Mauritius 121 F4 11 0 S 57 0 E
Agana, Guam 133 R15 13 28N 144 45 E
Ağapınar, Turkey 49 B12 39 48N 30 47 E
Agar, India 92 H7 23 40N 76 2 E
Agar →, India 94 D6 21 0N 82 57 E
Agaro, Ethiopia 107 F4 7 50N 36 38 E
Agartala, India 90 D3 23 50N 91 23 E
Agăş, Romania 53 D11 46 28N 26 15 E
Agassiz, Canada 142 D4 49 14N 121 46W
Agat, Guam 133 R15 13 25N 144 40 E
Agats, Indonesia 83 C5 5 33 S 138 0 E
Agatti I., India 95 J1 10 50N 72 12 E
Agattu I., U.S.A. 144 K4 52 25N 173 35 E
Agawam, U.S.A. 151 D12 42 5N 72 37W
Agbélouvé, Togo 113 D5 6 35N 1 14 E
Agboville, Ivory C. 112 D4 5 55N 4 15W
Ağcabädi, Azerbaijan 61 K8 40 5N 47 27 E
Ağdam, Azerbaijan 61 L8 40 0N 46 58 E
Ağdaş, Azerbaijan 61 K8 40 44N 47 22 E
Agde, France 28 E7 43 19N 3 28 E
Agde, C. d', France 28 E7 43 16N 3 28 E
Agdz, Morocco 110 B3 30 47N 6 30W
Agdzhabedi = Ağcabädi, Azerbaijan 61 K8 40 5N 47 27 E
Agen, France 28 D4 44 12N 0 38 E
Ageo, Japan 73 B11 35 58N 139 36 E
Ager Tay, Chad 109 E3 20 0N 17 41 E
Agerbæk, Denmark 17 J2 55 36N 8 48 E
Agersø, Denmark 17 J5 55 13N 11 12 E
Ageyevo, Russia 58 E9 54 10N 36 27 E
Aggteleki △, Hungary 52 B5 48 27N 20 36 E
Āgh Kand, Iran 97 B6 37 15N 48 4 E
Aghios Efstratios = Áyios Evstrátios, Greece 48 B6 39 34N 24 58 E
Aghios Oros = Áthos, Greece 51 F8 40 9N 24 22 E
Aghireşu, Romania 53 D8 46 53N 23 15 E
Aghoueyyît, Mauritania 110 D1 21 10N 15 6W
Aghreïjît, Mauritania 110 D2 21 58N 12 11W
Aginskoye, Russia 67 D12 51 6N 114 32 E
Ağlasun, Turkey 49 D12 37 39N 30 31 E
Agly →, France 28 F7 42 46N 3 3 E
Agmar, Mauritania 110 C2 25 18N 10 50W
Agnew, Australia 125 E3 28 1 S 120 31 E
Agnibilékrou, Ivory C. 112 D4 7 10N 3 11W
Agnita, Romania 53 E9 45 59N 24 40 E
Agno, Switz. 33 E7 45 59N 8 53 E
Agnone, Italy 45 G11 41 48N 14 22 E
Ago, Japan 73 C8 34 20N 136 51 E
Agofie, Ghana 113 D5 8 27N 0 15 E
Agogna →, Italy 44 C5 45 4N 8 54 E
Agogo, Sudan 107 F2 7 50N 28 45 E
Agön, Sweden 16 C11 61 34N 17 23 E
Agon Coutainville, France 26 C5 49 2N 1 34W
Agoo, Phil. 80 C3 16 20N 120 22 E
Ágordo, Italy 45 B9 46 18N 12 2 E
Agori, India 93 G10 24 33N 82 57 E
Agouna, Benin 113 D5 7 39N 1 47 E
Agout →, France 28 E5 43 47N 1 41 E
Agra, India 92 F7 27 17N 77 58 E
Agrakhanskiuy Poluostrov, Russia 61 J8 43 42N 47 36 E
Agram = Zagreb, Croatia 45 C12 45 50N 15 58 E
Agramunt, Spain 40 D6 41 48N 1 6 E
Agreda, Spain 40 D3 41 51N 1 55W
Ağri, Turkey 101 C10 39 44N 43 3 E
Agri →, Italy 47 B9 40 13N 16 44 E
Ağrı Dağı, Turkey 101 C11 39 50N 44 15 E
Ağri Karakose = Ağri, Turkey 101 C10 39 44N 43 3 E
Agriá, Greece 48 B5 39 20N 23 1 E
Agrigento, Italy 46 E6 37 19N 13 34 E
Agrinio = Agrínion, Greece 48 C3 38 37N 21 27 E
Agrínion, Greece 48 C3 38 37N 21 27 E
Agrópoli, Italy 47 B7 40 21N 14 59 E
Ağstafa, Azerbaijan 61 K7 41 7N 45 27 E

Água Branca, Brazil 170 C3 5 50 S 42 40W
Agua Caliente, Baja Calif., Mexico 161 N10 32 29N 116 59W
Agua Caliente, Sinaloa, Mexico 162 B3 26 30N 108 20W
Agua Caliente Springs, U.S.A. 161 N10 32 56N 116 19W
Água Clara, Brazil 173 E7 20 25 S 52 45W
Agua Fria ⌓, U.S.A. 159 J8 34 14N 112 0W
Agua Hechicero, Mexico 161 N10 32 26N 116 14W
Água Preta →, Brazil 169 D5 1 41 S 63 48W
Agua Prieta, Mexico 162 A3 31 20N 109 32W
Aguachica, Colombia 168 B3 8 19N 73 38W
Aguada Cecilio, Argentina 176 B3 40 51 S 65 51W
Aguadas, Colombia 168 B2 5 40N 75 38W
Aguadilla, Puerto Rico 165 d 18 26N 67 10W
Aguadulce, Panama 164 E3 8 15N 80 32W
Aguanga, U.S.A. 161 M10 33 27N 116 51W
Aguanish, Canada 141 B7 50 14N 62 2W
Aguanus →, Canada 141 B7 50 13N 62 5W
Aguapeí, Brazil 173 D6 16 12 S 59 43W
Aguapeí →, Brazil 171 F1 21 0 S 51 0W
Aguapey →, Argentina 174 B4 29 7 S 56 36W
Aguaray Guazú →, Paraguay 174 A4 24 47 S 57 19W
Aguarico →, Ecuador 168 D2 0 59 S 75 11W
Aguaro-Guariquito △, Venezuela 165 E6 8 20N 66 35W
Aguas →, Spain 40 D4 41 20N 0 30W
Aguas Blancas, Chile 174 A2 24 15 S 69 55W
Aguas Calientes, Sierra de, Argentina 174 B2 25 26 S 66 40W
Águas Formosas, Brazil 171 E3 17 5 S 40 57W
Aguascalientes, Mexico 162 C4 21 53N 102 12W
Aguascalientes □, Mexico 162 C4 22 0N 102 20W
Agudo, Spain 43 G6 38 59N 4 52W
Águeda, Portugal 42 E2 40 34N 8 27W
Agueda →, Spain 42 D4 41 2N 6 56W
Aguelhok, Mali 113 B5 19 29N 0 52 E
Aguelt el Melah, Mauritania 110 D2 23 3N 8 28W
Agüenit, W. Sahara 110 D2 22 11N 13 8W
Aguié, Niger 113 C6 13 31N 7 46 E
Aguila, Punta, Puerto Rico 165 d 17 57N 67 13W
Aguilafuente, Spain 42 D6 41 13N 4 7W
Aguilar, Spain 43 H6 37 31N 4 40W
Aguilar de Campóo, Spain 42 C6 42 47N 4 15W
Aguilares, Argentina 174 B2 27 26 S 65 35W
Aguilas, Spain 41 H3 37 23N 1 35W
Agüimes, Canary Is. 9 e1 27 58N 15 27W
Aguja, C. de la, Colombia 168 A3 11 18N 74 12W
Agujereada, Pta., Puerto Rico 165 d 18 30N 67 8W
Agulaa, Ethiopia 107 E4 13 40N 39 40 E
Agulhas, C., S. Africa 116 E3 34 52 S 20 0 E
Agulhas Basin, Ind. Oc. 121 J1 46 0 S 26 0 E
Agulhas Plateau, Ind. Oc. 121 H1 40 0 S 26 0 E
Agulo, Canary Is. 9 e1 28 11N 17 12W
Agung, Gunung, Indonesia 85 D5 8 20 S 115 28 E
Agur, Uganda 118 B3 2 28N 32 55 E
Agusan →, Phil. 81 G5 9 0N 125 30 E
Agusan del Norte □, Phil. 81 G5 9 20N 125 10 E
Agusan del Sur □, Phil. 81 G5 8 30N 125 30 E
Agustín Codazzi, Colombia 168 A3 10 2N 73 14W
Agutaya I., Phil. 81 F3 11 9N 120 58 E
Ağva, Turkey 51 E13 41 8N 29 51 E
Agvali, Russia 61 J8 42 36N 46 8 E
Aha Mts., Botswana 116 B3 19 45 S 21 0 E
Ahaggar, Algeria 111 D6 23 0N 6 30 E
Ahamansu, Ghana 113 D5 7 38N 0 35 E
Ahar, Iran 101 C12 38 35N 47 0 E
Ahat, Turkey 49 C11 38 39N 29 47 E
Ahaura →, N.Z. 131 C6 42 21 S 171 34 E
Ahaus, Germany 30 C2 52 4N 7 0 E
Åheim, Norway 18 B2 62 2N 5 13 E
Ahelledjem, Algeria 111 C6 26 37N 6 58 E
Ahimanawa Ra., N.Z. 130 F5 39 3 S 176 30 E
Ahioma, Papua N. G. 132 F6 10 20 S 150 33 E
Ahipara B., N.Z. 130 B2 35 5 S 173 5 E
Ahir Dağı, Turkey 49 C12 38 45N 30 10 E
Ahiri, India 94 E5 19 30N 80 0 E
Ahlat, Turkey 101 C10 38 45N 42 29 E
Ahlen, Germany 30 D3 51 45N 7 53 E
Ahmad Wal, Pakistan 92 E1 29 18N 65 58 E
Ahmadabad, India 92 H5 23 0N 72 40 E
Aḥmadābād, Khorāsān, Iran 97 C9 35 3N 60 50 E
Aḥmadābād, Khorāsān, Iran 97 C8 35 49N 59 42 E
Aḥmadī, Iran 97 E8 27 56N 56 42 E
Ahmadnagar, India 94 E2 19 7N 74 46 E
Ahmadpur, India 94 E3 18 40N 76 57 E
Ahmadpur, Pakistan 92 E4 29 12N 71 10 E
Ahmadpur Lamma, Pakistan 92 E4 28 19N 70 3 E
Ahmar, Ethiopia 107 F5 9 20N 41 15 E
Ahmedabad = Ahmadabad, India 92 H5 23 0N 72 40 E
Ahmednagar = Ahmadnagar, India 94 E2 19 7N 74 46 E
Ahmetbey, Turkey 51 E11 41 26N 27 34 E
Ahmetler, Turkey 49 C11 38 28N 29 5 E
Ahmetli, Turkey 49 C9 38 32N 27 57 E
Ahmeyim, Mauritania 110 D2 20 51N 14 25W
Ahoada, Nigeria 113 D6 5 8N 6 36 E
Ahome, Mexico 162 B3 25 55N 109 11W
Ahon, Tarso, Chad 109 D3 20 23N 18 18 E
Ahoskie, U.S.A. 149 G7 36 17N 76 59W
Ahr →, Germany 30 E3 50 32N 7 16 E
Ahram, Iran 97 D6 28 52N 51 16 E
Ahrax Pt., Malta 38 F7 36 0N 14 22 E
Ahrensbök, Germany 30 A6 54 2N 10 35 E
Ahrensburg, Germany 30 B6 53 40N 10 13 E
Āhū, Iran 97 C6 34 33N 50 2 E
Ahu Akivi, Chile 172 b 27 7 S 109 24W
Ahu Tepeu, Chile 172 b 27 6 S 109 25W
Ahu Tongariki, Chile 172 b 27 8 S 109 17W
Ahu Vinapu, Chile 172 b 27 10 S 109 25W
Ahuachapán, El Salv. 164 D2 13 54N 89 52W
Ahun, France 27 F9 46 4N 2 5 E
Ahuriri →, N.Z. 131 E5 44 31 S 170 12 E
Åhus, Sweden 17 J8 55 56N 14 18 E
Ahvāz, Iran 97 D6 31 20N 48 40 E
Ahvenanmaa, Finland 15 F19 60 15N 20 0 E
Aḥwar, Yemen 98 D4 13 30N 46 40 E
Ahzar →, Mali 113 B5 15 30N 3 20 E
Ai →, India 90 B3 26 26N 90 44 E
Ai-Ais, Namibia 116 D2 27 54 S 17 59 E
Ai-Ais and Fish River Canyon △, Namibia 116 C2 24 45 S 17 15 E
Aiari →, Brazil 168 C4 1 22N 68 36W
Aichach, Germany 31 G7 48 27N 11 8 E
Aichi □, Japan 73 C9 35 0N 137 15 E
Aiduma, Indonesia 83 B4 4 0 S 134 6 E
Aiduna, Indonesia 83 B5 4 27 S 135 15 E
Aiea, U.S.A. 145 K14 21 23N 157 56W
Aigle, Switz. 32 D3 46 18N 6 58 E
Aignay-le-Duc, France 27 E11 47 40N 4 43 E
Aigoual, Mt., France 28 D7 44 8N 3 35 E
Aigre, France 28 C4 45 54N 0 1 E
Aigrettes, Pte. des, Réunion 121 c 21 3 S 55 13 E
Aigua, Uruguay 175 C5 34 13 S 54 46W
Aigueperse, France 27 F10 46 3N 3 13 E
Aigues →, France 29 D8 44 7N 4 43 E
Aigues-Mortes, France 29 E8 43 35N 4 12 E
Aigues-Mortes, G. d', France 29 E8 43 31N 4 3 E
Aigües Tortes y Lago San Mauricio △, Spain 40 C4 42 38N 0 31W
Aiguilles, France 29 D10 44 47N 6 51 E
Aiguillon, France 28 D4 44 18N 0 21 E
Aigurande, France 27 F8 46 27N 1 49 E
Aihui, China 69 A7 50 10N 127 30 E
Aija, Peru 172 B2 9 50 S 77 45W
Aikawa, Japan 70 E9 38 2N 138 15 E
Aiken, U.S.A. 152 B8 33 34N 81 43W
Ailao Shan, China 76 F3 24 0N 101 20 E
Aileron, Australia 126 C1 22 39 S 133 20 E
Ailey, U.S.A. 152 C7 32 11N 82 34W
Ailigandí, Panama 168 B2 9 14N 78 1W
Aillant-sur-Tholon, France 27 E10 47 52N 3 20 E
Aillik, Canada 141 A8 55 11N 59 18W
Ailsa Craig, U.K. 22 F3 55 15N 5 6W
Ailuluai, Papua N. G. 132 E6 9 38 S 150 35 E
Aim, Russia 67 D14 59 0N 133 55 E
Aimere, Indonesia 79 F6 8 45 S 121 3 E
Aimogasta, Argentina 174 B2 28 33 S 66 50W
Aimorés, Brazil 171 E3 19 30 S 41 4W
Ain □, France 27 F12 46 5N 5 20 E
Ain →, France 29 C9 45 45N 5 11 E
Aïn Beïda, Algeria 111 A6 35 50N 7 29 E
Aïn Ben Khellil, Algeria 111 B4 33 15N 0 49W
Aïn Ben Tili, Mauritania 110 C3 25 59N 9 27W
Aïn Beni Mathar, Morocco 111 B4 34 1N 2 0W
Aïn Benian, Algeria 111 A5 36 48N 2 55 E
Ain Dalla, Egypt 106 B2 27 20N 27 23 E
Ain el Mafki, Egypt 106 B2 27 30N 28 15 E
Ain Girba, Egypt 106 B2 29 20N 25 14 E
Aïn M'lila, Algeria 111 A6 36 2N 6 35 E
Aïn Mokra = Berrahal, Algeria 111 A6 36 54N 7 33 E
Ain Murr, Sudan 106 C2 21 50N 25 9 E
Ain Qeiqab, Egypt 106 B1 29 42N 24 55 E
Aïn Salah = In Salah, Algeria 111 C5 27 10N 2 32 E
Aïn Sefra, Algeria 111 B4 32 47N 0 37W
Ain Sheikh Murzûk, Egypt 106 B2 26 47N 27 45 E
Ain Sudr, Egypt 103 F2 29 50N 33 6 E
Ain Sukhna, Egypt 106 J8 29 32N 32 20 E
Aïn Tédelès, Algeria 111 A5 36 0N 0 21 E
Aïn Témouchent, Algeria 111 A4 35 16N 1 8W
Aïn Tikkidine, Algeria 111 C5 25 33N 1 24 E
Aïn Touta, Algeria 111 A6 35 26N 5 54 E
Ain Zeitûn, Egypt 106 B2 29 10N 25 48 E
Aïn Zorah, Morocco 111 B4 34 37N 3 32W
Ainabo, Somali Rep. 120 C3 9 0N 46 25 E
Ainaži, Latvia 15 H21 57 50N 24 24 E
Aínos Óros, Greece 39 C2 38 9N 20 40 E
Ainsworth, U.S.A. 154 D5 42 33N 99 52W
Aintab = Gaziantep, Turkey 100 D7 37 6N 37 23 E
Aioi, Japan 72 C6 34 48N 134 28 E
Aiome, Papua N. G. 132 C3 5 8 S 144 44 E
Aipe, Colombia 168 C2 3 13N 75 15W
Aiquile, Bolivia 173 D4 18 10 S 65 10W
Aïr, Niger 113 B6 18 30N 8 0 E
Aïr et du Ténéré ⌓, Niger 109 E1 18 12N 9 56 E
Air Force I., Canada 139 B12 67 58N 74 5W
Air Hitam, Malaysia 87 M4 1 55N 103 11 E
Aira, Japan 72 F2 31 43N 130 43 E
Airaines, France 27 C8 49 58N 1 55 E
Airão, Brazil 169 D5 1 56 S 61 22W
Airdrie, Canada 142 C6 51 18N 114 2W
Airdrie, U.K. 22 F5 55 52N 3 57W
Aire →, France 27 C11 49 18N 4 49 E
Aire →, U.K. 20 D7 53 43N 0 55W
Aire, I. de l', Spain 38 B5 39 48N 4 16 E
Aire-sur-la-Lys, France 27 B9 50 37N 2 22 E
Aire-sur-l'Adour, France 28 E3 43 42N 0 15W
Aireys Inlet, Australia 128 E6 38 29 S 144 5 E
Airlie Beach, Australia 126 J6 20 16 S 148 43 E
Airmadidi, Indonesia 82 A3 1 25N 125 0 E
Airolo, Switz. 33 C7 46 32N 8 37 E
Airvault, France 26 F6 46 50N 0 8W
Aisch →, Germany 31 F6 49 46N 10 58 E
Aisen □, Chile 176 C2 46 30 S 73 0W
Aisne □, France 27 C10 49 42N 3 40 E
Aisne →, France 27 C9 49 26N 2 50 E
Ait, India 93 G8 25 54N 79 14 E
Aitana, Sierra de, Spain 41 G4 38 35N 0 24W
Aitape, Papua N. G. 132 B2 3 11 S 142 22 E
Aitkin, U.S.A. 154 B8 46 32N 93 42W
Aitolía kai Akarnanía □, Greece 48 C3 38 45N 21 18 E
Aitolikón, Greece 48 C3 38 26N 21 21 E
Aitutaki, Cook Is. 135 J12 18 52 S 159 45 E
Aiuaba, Brazil 170 C3 6 38 S 40 7W
Aiud, Romania 53 D8 46 19N 23 44 E
Aix-en-Provence, France 29 E9 43 32N 5 27 E
Aix-la-Chapelle = Aachen, Germany 30 E2 50 45N 6 6 E
Aix-les-Bains, France 29 C9 45 41N 5 53 E
Aixe-sur-Vienne, France 28 C5 45 47N 1 9 E
Aiyang, Mt., Papua N. G. 132 C1 5 10 S 141 20 E
Aíyina, Greece 48 D5 37 45N 23 26 E
Aiyínion, Greece 50 F6 40 28N 22 28 E
Aíyion, Greece 48 C4 38 15N 22 5 E
Aizawl, India 90 D4 23 40N 92 44 E
Aizenay, France 26 F5 46 44N 1 38W
Aizkraukle, Latvia 15 H21 56 36N 25 11 E
Aizpute, Latvia 15 H19 56 43N 21 40 E
Aizuwakamatsu, Japan 70 F9 37 30N 139 56 E
Ajaccio, France 29 G12 41 55N 8 40 E
Ajaccio, G. d', France 29 G12 41 52N 8 40 E
Ajai ⌓, Uganda 118 B3 2 52N 31 16 E
Ajaigarh, India 93 G9 24 52N 80 16 E
Ajaju →, Colombia 168 C3 0 59N 72 20W
Ajalpan, Mexico 163 D5 18 22N 97 15W
Ajanta, India 94 D2 20 30N 75 48 E
Ajanta Ra., India 94 D2 20 28N 75 50 E
Ajari Rep. = Ajaria □, Georgia 61 K6 41 30N 42 0 E
Ajaria □, Georgia 61 K6 41 30N 42 0 E
Ajax, Canada 150 C5 43 50N 79 1W
Ajax, Mt., N.Z. 131 C7 42 35 S 172 5 E
Ajdābiyā, Libya 108 B4 30 54N 20 4 E
Ajdovščina, Slovenia 45 C10 45 54N 13 54 E
Ajibar, Ethiopia 107 E4 10 35N 38 36 E
Ajka, Hungary 52 C2 47 4N 17 31 E
'Ajlūn, Jordan 103 C4 32 18N 35 47 E
'Ajlūn □, Jordan 103 C4 32 18N 35 47 E
'Ajmān, U.A.E. 97 E7 25 25N 55 30 E
Ajmer, India 92 F6 26 28N 74 37 E
Ajnala, India 92 D6 31 50N 74 48 E
Ajo, U.S.A. 159 K7 32 22N 112 52W
Ajo, C. de, Spain 42 B7 43 31N 3 35W
Ajoie, Switz. 32 B4 47 22N 7 0 E
Ajok, Sudan 107 F2 9 15N 28 28 E
Ajuda, Pta. da, Azores 9 d3 37 52N 25 19W
Ajuy, Phil. 81 F4 11 10N 123 1 E
Ak Dağ, Turkey 49 E11 36 30N 29 32 E
Ak Dağları, Muğla, Turkey 49 E11 36 30N 29 30 E
Ak Dağları, Sivas, Turkey 100 C7 39 32N 36 12 E
Ak-Mechet = Qyzylorda, Kazakhstan 65 A2 44 48N 65 28 E
Ak-Mednet = Chornomorske, Ukraine 59 K7 45 31N 32 40 E
Ak-Muz, Kyrgyzstan 65 C8 41 15N 76 10 E
Ak-Sheikh = Razdolnoye, Ukraine 59 K7 45 46N 33 29 E
Ak-Tüz, Kyrgyzstan 65 B8 42 54N 76 7 E
Akaba, Togo 113 D5 8 10N 1 2 E
Akabira, Japan 70 C11 43 33N 142 5 E
Akabli, Algeria 111 C5 26 49N 1 31 E
Akagera △, Rwanda 118 C3 1 31 S 30 33 E
Akaishi-Dake, Japan 73 B10 35 27N 138 9 E
Akaishi-Sammyaku, Japan 73 B10 35 25N 138 10 E
Akaki Beseka, Ethiopia 107 F4 8 55N 38 45 E
Akākūs, Jabal, Libya 111 C7 25 20N 10 30 E
Akala, Sudan 107 D4 15 39N 36 13 E
Akalkot, India 94 F3 17 32N 76 13 E
Akamas, Cyprus 39 E8 35 3N 32 18 E
Akan △, Japan 70 C12 43 20N 144 20 E
Akanthou, Cyprus 39 E9 35 22N 33 45 E
Akarca, Turkey 49 C11 38 35N 29 35 E
Akaroa, N.Z. 131 D7 43 49 S 172 59 E
Akaroa Harbour, N.Z. 131 D7 43 50 S 172 55 E
Akasha, Sudan 106 C3 21 10N 30 32 E
Akashi, Japan 72 C6 34 45N 134 58 E
Akbarpur, Bihar, India 93 G10 24 39N 83 58 E
Akbarpur, Ut. P., India 93 F10 26 25N 82 32 E
Akbou, Algeria 111 A5 36 31N 4 31 E
Akbulak, Russia 64 F5 51 1N 55 37 E
Akçaabat, Turkey 101 B8 41 1N 39 34 E
Akçadağ, Turkey 100 C7 38 27N 37 43 E
Akçakale, Turkey 101 D8 36 41N 38 56 E
Akçakoca, Turkey 100 B4 41 5N 31 8 E
Akçaova, Turkey 51 E13 41 3N 29 57 E
Akçay, Turkey 49 E11 36 36N 29 45 E
Akçay →, Turkey 49 D10 37 50N 28 15 E
Akchâr, Mauritania 110 D2 20 20N 14 28W
Akchi-Karasu = Toktogul, Kyrgyzstan 65 C6 41 50N 72 50 E
Akdağ, Turkey 49 C8 38 33N 26 30 E
Akdağmadeni, Turkey 100 C6 39 39N 35 53 E
Akechi, Japan 73 B9 35 18N 137 23 E
Akelamo, Indonesia 82 A3 1 35N 129 40 E
Åkers styckebruk, Sweden 16 E11 59 15N 17 5 E
Åkersberga, Sweden 16 E12 59 29N 18 18 E
Akershus □, Norway 18 D8 60 0N 11 10 E
Akeru →, India 94 F5 17 25N 80 5 E
Aketi, Dem. Rep. of the Congo 114 B4 2 38N 23 47 E
Akhaïa □, Greece 48 C3 38 5N 21 45 E
Akhalkalaki, Georgia 61 K6 41 27N 43 25 E
Akhaltsikhe, Georgia 61 K6 41 40N 43 0 E
Akharnaí, Greece 48 C5 38 5N 23 44 E
Akhelóös →, Greece 48 C3 38 19N 21 7 E
Akhendriá, Greece 49 G7 34 59N 25 13 E
Akhiok, U.S.A. 144 H9 56 57N 154 10W
Akhisar, Turkey 49 C9 38 56N 27 48 E
Akhladhókambos, Greece 48 D4 37 31N 22 35 E
Akhmîm, Egypt 106 B3 26 31N 31 47 E
Akhnur, India 93 C6 32 52N 74 45 E
Akhtopol, Bulgaria 51 D11 42 6N 27 56 E
Akhtuba →, Russia 61 G8 47 41N 46 55 E
Akhtubinsk, Russia 61 F8 48 13N 46 7 E
Akhty, Russia 61 K8 41 30N 47 45 E
Akhtyrka = Okhtyrka, Ukraine 59 G8 50 25N 35 0 E
Aki, Japan 72 D5 33 30N 133 54 E
Aki-Nada, Japan 72 C4 34 5N 132 40 E
Akiachak, U.S.A. 144 F7 60 55N 161 26W
Akiak, U.S.A. 144 F7 60 55N 161 13W
Akiéni, Gabon 114 C2 1 11 S 13 53 E
Akimiski I., Canada 140 B3 52 50N 81 30W
Akimovka, Ukraine 59 J8 46 44N 35 0 E
Åkirkeby, Denmark 17 J8 55 4N 14 55 E
Akita, Japan 70 E10 39 45N 140 7 E
Akita □, Japan 70 E10 39 40N 140 30 E
Akjoujt, Mauritania 112 B2 19 45N 14 15W
Akka, Mali 112 B4 15 24N 4 11W
Akka, Morocco 110 C3 29 22N 8 9W
Akkaraipattu, Sri Lanka 95 L5 7 13N 81 51 E
Akkaya Tepesi, Turkey 49 D11 37 25N 29 38 E
Akkerman = Bilhorod-Dnistrovskyy, Ukraine 59 J6 46 11N 30 23 E
Akkeshi, Japan 70 C12 43 2N 144 51 E
'Akko, Israel 103 C4 32 55N 35 4 E
Akkol = Aqköl, Kazakhstan 65 A7 45 0N 75 39 E
Akkol = Aqköl, Kazakhstan 65 B5 43 36N 70 45 E
Akköy, Turkey 49 D9 37 29N 27 15 E
Aklampa, Benin 113 D5 8 15N 2 10 E
Aklan □, Phil. 81 F4 11 50N 122 30 E
Aklavik, Canada 138 B6 68 12N 135 0W
Aklera, India 92 G7 24 26N 76 32 E
Akmal-Abad = Gizhduvan, Uzbekistan 65 C2 40 6N 64 41 E
Akmenė, Lithuania 54 B9 56 15N 22 45 E
Akmenrags, Latvia 54 B8 56 50N 21 4 E
Akmeqit, China 65 E8 37 5N 76 55 E
Akmolinsk = Astana, Kazakhstan 66 D8 51 10N 71 30 E
Akmonte = Almonte, Spain 43 H4 37 13N 6 38W
Aknoul, Morocco 111 B4 34 40N 3 55W
Akō, Japan 72 C6 34 45N 134 24 E
Ako, Nigeria 113 C7 10 19N 10 48 E
Akôbô, Sudan 107 F3 7 47N 33 1 E
Akobo →, Ethiopia 107 F3 7 48N 33 3 E
Akola, Maharashtra, India 94 D3 20 42N 77 2 E
Akola, Maharashtra, India 94 E2 19 32N 74 3 E
Akolmiut, U.S.A. 144 F7 60 55N 162 20W
Akonolinga, Cameroon 113 E7 3 50N 12 18 E
Akor, Mali 112 C3 14 59N 6 58W
Akordat, Eritrea 107 D4 15 30N 37 40 E
Akosombo Dam, Ghana 113 D5 6 20N 0 5 E
Akot, India 94 D3 21 10N 77 10 E
Akot, Sudan 107 F3 6 31N 30 9 E
Akoupé, Ivory C. 112 D4 6 23N 3 54W
Akourousoulba, C.A.R. 114 A4 8 58N 20 46 E
Akpatok I., Canada 139 B13 60 25N 68 8W
Åkrahamn, Norway 18 E2 59 15N 5 10 E
'Akramah, Libya 108 B4 32 2N 23 41 E
Akranes, Iceland 11 C4 64 19N 22 5W
Akreïjit, Mauritania 112 B3 18 19N 9 11W
Akrítas Venétiko, Ákra, Greece 48 E3 36 43N 21 54 E
Akron, Colo., U.S.A. 154 E3 40 10N 103 13W
Akron, Ind., U.S.A. 157 C10 41 2N 86 1W
Akron, Ohio, U.S.A. 150 E3 41 5N 81 31W
Akrotiri, Cyprus 39 F8 34 36N 32 57 E
Akrotíri, Ákra, Greece 51 F9 40 26N 25 27 E
Akrotiri Bay, Cyprus 39 F9 34 35N 33 10 E
Aksai Chin, China 93 B8 35 15N 79 55 E
Aksaray, Turkey 100 C6 38 25N 34 2 E
Aksay, Kazakhstan 57 D9 51 11N 53 0 E
Akşehir, Turkey 100 C4 38 18N 31 30 E
Akşehir Gölü, Turkey 100 C4 38 30N 31 25 E
Akstafa = Ağstafa, Azerbaijan 61 K7 41 7N 45 27 E
Aksu, China 68 B3 41 5N 80 10 E
Aksu →, Turkey 100 D4 36 52N 30 57 E
Aksum, Ethiopia 107 E4 14 5N 38 40 E
Aktash, Russia 60 C11 55 2N 52 3 E
Aktash, Uzbekistan 65 D2 39 55N 65 55 E
Aktasty, Kazakhstan 64 F8 50 42N 61 42 E
Aktion, Greece 39 B2 38 57N 20 46 E
Akto, China 65 D7 39 5N 75 59 E
Aktogay, Kazakhstan 66 E8 46 57N 79 40 E
Aktsyabrski, Belarus 59 F5 52 38N 28 53 E
Aktyubinsk = Aqtöbe, Kazakhstan 57 D10 50 17N 57 10 E
Aktyuz = Ak-Tüz, Kyrgyzstan 65 B8 42 54N 76 7 E
Aku, Nigeria 113 D6 6 40N 7 18 E
Akula, Dem. Rep. of the Congo 114 B4 2 22N 20 12 E
Akulurak, U.S.A. 144 E6 63 33N 164 33W
Akun I., U.S.A. 144 J6 54 11N 165 32W
Akune, Japan 72 E2 32 1N 130 12 E
Akure, Nigeria 113 D6 7 15N 5 5 E
Akurenan, Eq. Guin. 114 B2 1 2N 10 40 E
Akuressa, Sri Lanka 95 L5 6 5N 80 29 E
Akureyri, Iceland 11 B8 65 40N 18 6W
Akuseki-Shima, Japan 71 K4 29 27N 129 37 E
Akusha, Russia 61 J8 42 18N 47 30 E
Akutan, U.S.A. 144 J6 54 8N 165 46W
Akutan I., U.S.A. 144 J6 54 7N 165 55W
Akwa-Ibom □, Nigeria 113 E6 4 30N 7 30 E
Akyab = Sittwe, Burma 90 E4 20 18N 92 45 E
Akyazı, Turkey 100 B4 40 40N 30 38 E
Ål, Norway 18 D5 60 38N 8 33 E
Al Abyaḍ, Libya 108 C2 26 49N 14 1 E
Al Abyār, Libya 108 B4 32 9N 20 29 E
Al 'Adan, Yemen 98 D4 12 45N 45 0 E
Al Aḥsā = Hasa □, Si. Arabia 97 E6 25 50N 49 0 E
Al Ajfar, Si. Arabia 96 E4 27 26N 43 0 E
Al Amādīyah, Iraq 101 D10 37 5N 43 30 E
Al 'Amārah, Iraq 101 G12 31 55N 47 15 E
Al 'Aqabah, Jordan 103 F4 29 31N 35 0 E
Al 'Aqabah □, Jordan 103 F4 29 30N 35 0 E
Al 'Aqīq, Si. Arabia 98 B3 20 39N 41 25 E
Al Arak, Syria 101 E8 34 38N 38 35 E
Al 'Aramah, Si. Arabia 96 E5 25 30N 46 0 E
Al 'Arīḍah, Si. Arabia 98 C3 17 3N 43 5 E
Al 'Arṭāwīyah, Si. Arabia 96 E5 26 31N 45 20 E
Al 'Āshkhara, Oman 99 B7 21 50N 59 30 E
Al 'Āṣimah = 'Ammān □, Jordan 103 D5 31 40N 36 30 E
Al 'Assāfīyah, Si. Arabia 96 D3 28 17N 38 59 E
Al 'Ayn, Si. Arabia 96 E3 25 4N 38 6 E
Al 'Ayn, U.A.E. 97 E7 24 15N 55 45 E
Al 'Azīzīyah, Iraq 101 F11 32 54N 45 4 E
Al 'Azīzīyah, Libya 108 B2 32 30N 13 1 E
Al Bāb, Syria 100 D7 36 23N 37 29 E
Al Bad', Si. Arabia 96 D2 28 28N 35 1 E
Al Bādī, Iraq 96 C4 35 56N 41 32 E
Al Badī', Si. Arabia 98 B4 22 0N 46 35 E
Al Baḥrah, Kuwait 96 D5 29 40N 47 52 E
Al Baḥral Mayyit = Dead Sea, Asia 103 D4 31 30N 35 30 E
Al Balqā' □, Jordan 103 C4 32 5N 35 45 E
Al Barkāt, Libya 108 D2 24 56N 10 14 E
Al Bārūk, J., Lebanon 103 B4 33 39N 35 40 E
Al Baṣrah, Iraq 96 D5 30 30N 47 50 E
Al Baṭḥā, Iraq 96 D5 31 6N 45 53 E
Al Batinah, Oman 99 A7 24 10N 56 50 E
Al Batrūn, Lebanon 103 A4 34 15N 35 40 E
Al Bayāḍ, Si. Arabia 98 B4 22 0N 47 0 E
Al Bayḍā, Libya 108 B4 32 50N 21 44 E
Al Bayḍā', Yemen 98 D4 14 5N 45 42 E
Al Bi'ār, Si. Arabia 98 B2 22 39N 39 40 E
Al Biqā, Lebanon 103 A5 34 10N 36 10 E
Al Bi'r, Si. Arabia 96 D3 28 51N 36 16 E
Al Birk, Si. Arabia 98 C3 18 13N 41 33 E
Al Bu'ayrāt al Ḥasūn, Libya 108 B3 31 24N 15 44 E
Al Bunbah, Libya 108 B4 32 24N 23 8 E
Al Burayj, Syria 103 A5 34 15N 36 46 E
Al Faḍilī, Si. Arabia 97 E6 26 58N 49 10 E
Al Fallūjah, Iraq 101 F10 33 20N 43 55 E
Al Fātiḥ □, Libya 108 B4 32 0N 21 0 E
Al Fāw, Iraq 97 D6 30 0N 48 30 E
Al Faydamī, Yemen 99 C6 16 25N 52 26 E
Al Fujayrah, U.A.E. 97 E8 25 7N 56 18 E
Al Ghadaf, W. →, Jordan 103 D5 31 26N 36 43 E
Al Ghammās, Iraq 96 D5 31 45N 44 37 E
Al Gharib, Libya 108 B4 32 35N 21 11 E
Al Ghayḍah, Yemen 99 C6 16 13N 52 11 E
Al Ghayḍah, Yemen 99 D5 14 55N 50 0 E
Al Ghayl, Yemen 99 D5 15 30N 50 54 E
Al Ghazālah, Si. Arabia 96 E4 26 48N 41 19 E
Al Ḥadd, Oman 99 B7 22 32N 59 48 E
Al Ḥaddār, Si. Arabia 98 B4 21 58N 45 57 E
Al Ḥadīthah, Iraq 101 E10 34 0N 41 13 E
Al Ḥadīthah, Si. Arabia 103 D6 31 28N 37 8 E
Al Ḥaḍr, Iraq 101 E10 35 35N 42 44 E
Al Ḥājānah, Syria 103 B5 33 20N 36 33 E
Al Ḥajar al Gharbī, Oman 97 E8 24 10N 56 15 E
Al Hallānīyah, Oman 99 C7 17 30N 56 1 E
Al Ḥāmad, Si. Arabia 96 D3 31 30N 39 30 E
Al Ḥamar, Si. Arabia 98 B4 22 26N 46 12 E
Al Ḥamdānīyah, Syria 96 C3 35 25N 36 50 E
Al Ḥamīdīyah, Syria 103 A4 34 42N 35 57 E
Al Ḥammādah al Ḥamrā', Libya 108 C2 29 30N 12 0 E
Al Ḥammār, Iraq 96 D5 30 57N 46 51 E
Al Ḥamrā', Si. Arabia 96 E3 24 2N 38 55 E
Al Ḥamzah, Iraq 96 D5 31 43N 44 58 E
Al Ḥanākīyah, Si. Arabia 96 E4 24 51N 40 31 E
Al Ḥarīq, Si. Arabia 98 B4 23 29N 46 27 E
Al Ḥarīr, W. →, Syria 103 C4 32 44N 35 59 E
Al Ḥarūj al Aswad, Libya 108 C3 27 0N 17 10 E
Al Ḥasā, W. →, Jordan 103 D4 31 4N 35 29 E
Al Ḥasakah, Syria 101 D9 36 35N 40 45 E
Al Hāsikīyah, Oman 99 C6 17 28N 55 36 E
Al Ḥasy, Yemen 99 D5 14 3N 48 40 E
Al Ḥawrah, Yemen 98 D4 13 50N 47 35 E
Al Hawtah = Laḥij, Yemen 98 D4 13 4N 44 53 E
Al Ḥawṭah, Si. Arabia 98 B4 23 30N 47 0 E
Al Haydān, W. →, Jordan 103 D4 31 29N 35 34 E
Al Ḥayy, Iraq 101 F12 32 5N 46 5 E
Al Ḥijarah, Asia 96 D4 30 0N 44 0 E
Al Ḥillah, Iraq 101 F11 32 30N 44 25 E
Al Ḥillah, Si. Arabia 98 B4 23 35N 46 50 E
Al Hindīyah, Iraq 101 F11 32 30N 44 10 E
Al Hirmil, Lebanon 103 A5 34 26N 36 24 E
Al Hoceïma, Morocco 110 A4 35 8N 3 58W
Al Ḥudaydah, Yemen 98 D3 14 50N 43 0 E
Al Ḥufrah, Libya 108 C2 25 32N 14 1 E
Al Hufūf, Si. Arabia 97 E6 25 25N 49 45 E
Al Ḥulwah, Si. Arabia 98 B4 23 24N 46 48 E
Al Ḥumayḍah, Si. Arabia 96 D2 29 14N 34 56 E
Al Ḥunayy, Si. Arabia 97 E6 25 58N 48 45 E
Al Husayyāt, Libya 108 B4 30 24N 20 37 E
Al 'Irqah, Yemen 98 D4 13 39N 47 22 E
Al Īsāwīyah, Si. Arabia 96 D3 30 43N 37 59 E
Al Ittihad = Madīnat ash Sha'b, Yemen 98 D4 12 50N 45 0 E
Al Jabal al Akhḍar, Libya 108 B4 32 30N 21 30 E
Al Jabal al Akhḍar □, Libya 108 B4 32 30N 21 41 E
Al Jafr, Jordan 103 E5 30 18N 36 14 E
Al Jāfūrah, Si. Arabia 97 E7 25 0N 50 15 E
Al Jaghbūb, Libya 108 C4 29 42N 24 38 E
Al Jahrah, Kuwait 96 D5 29 25N 47 40 E
Al Jalāmīd, Si. Arabia 96 D3 31 20N 40 6 E
Al Jamalīyah, Qatar 97 E6 25 37N 51 5 E
Al Janūb □, Lebanon 103 B4 33 20N 35 20 E
Al Jawf, Libya 108 D4 24 10N 23 24 E
Al Jawf, Si. Arabia 96 D3 29 55N 39 40 E
Al Jazair = Algeria ■, Africa 111 C5 28 30N 2 0 E
Al Jazirah, Iraq 101 E10 33 30N 44 0 E
Al Jazirah, Libya 108 C4 26 10N 21 20 E
Al Jithāmīyah, Si. Arabia 96 E4 27 41N 41 43 E
Al Jubayl, Si. Arabia 97 E6 27 0N 49 50 E
Al Jubaylah, Si. Arabia 96 E5 24 55N 46 25 E
Al Jubb, Si. Arabia 96 E4 27 11N 42 17 E
Al Jufrah, Libya 108 C3 29 10N 16 0 E
Al Jufrah □, Libya 108 C3 27 30N 17 30 E
Al Jumūm, Si. Arabia 98 B2 21 37N 39 42 E
Al Junaynah, Sudan 109 F4 13 27N 22 45 E
Al Kabā'ish, Iraq 96 D5 30 58N 47 0 E
Al Kāmil, Oman 99 B7 22 13N 59 12 E
Al Karak, Jordan 103 D4 31 11N 35 42 E
Al Karak □, Jordan 103 E5 31 0N 36 0 E
Al Kāẓimīyah, Iraq 101 F11 33 22N 44 18 E
Al Khābūra, Oman 97 F8 23 57N 57 5 E
Al Khafji, Si. Arabia 97 E6 28 24N 48 29 E
Al Khalīl, West Bank 103 D4 31 32N 35 6 E
Al Khāliṣ, Iraq 101 F11 33 49N 44 32 E
Al Khamāsīn, Si. Arabia 98 B4 20 29N 44 46 E
Al Kharj, Si. Arabia 98 B4 24 0N 47 0 E
Al Kharsānīyah, Si. Arabia 97 E6 27 13N 49 18 E
Al Khaṣab, Oman 97 E8 26 14N 56 15 E
Al Khāşirah, Si. Arabia 98 B3 23 30N 43 47 E
Al Khawr, Qatar 97 E6 25 41N 51 30 E
Al Khiḍr, Iraq 96 D5 31 12N 45 33 E
Al Khiyām, Lebanon 103 B4 33 20N 35 36 E
Al Khums, Libya 108 B2 32 40N 14 17 E
Al Khums □, Libya 108 B2 31 20N 14 10 E
Al Kiswah, Syria 103 B5 33 23N 36 14 E
Al Kūfah, Iraq 101 F11 32 2N 44 24 E
Al Kufrah, Libya 108 D4 24 17N 23 15 E
Al Kuhayfīyah, Si. Arabia 96 E4 27 12N 43 3 E
Al Kūt, Iraq 101 F11 32 30N 46 0 E
Al Kuwayt, Kuwait 96 D5 29 30N 48 0 E
Al Labwah, Lebanon 103 A5 34 11N 36 20 E
Al Lādhiqīyah, Syria 100 E6 35 30N 35 45 E
Al Līth, Si. Arabia 98 B3 20 9N 40 15 E
Al Liwā', Oman 97 E8 24 31N 56 36 E
Al Luḥayyah, Yemen 98 D3 15 45N 42 40 E
Al Madīnah, Iraq 96 D5 30 57N 47 16 E
Al Madīnah, Si. Arabia 96 E3 24 35N 39 52 E
Al Mafraq, Jordan 103 C5 32 17N 36 14 E
Al Mafraq □, Jordan 103 C5 32 17N 36 15 E
Al Maghārīm, Yemen 98 D4 15 1N 47 49 E
Al Maghreb = Morocco ■, N. Afr. 110 B3 32 0N 5 50W
Al Mahbes, W. Sahara 110 C3 27 10N 9 50W
Al Maḥmūdīyah, Iraq 101 F11 33 3N 44 21 E
Al Majma'ah, Si. Arabia 96 E5 25 57N 45 22 E
Al Makhruq, W. →, Jordan 103 D6 31 28N 37 0 E
Al Makḥūl, Si. Arabia 96 E4 26 37N 42 39 E
Al Makīlī, Libya 108 B4 32 10N 22 17 E
Al Manāmah, Bahrain 97 E6 26 10N 50 30 E
Al Maqwa', Kuwait 96 D5 29 10N 47 59 E
Al Marj, Libya 108 B4 32 25N 20 30 E
Al Maṭlā, Kuwait 96 D5 29 24N 47 40 E
Al Mawjib, W. →, Jordan 103 D4 31 28N 35 36 E
Al Mawṣil, Iraq 101 D10 36 15N 43 5 E
Al Mayādin, Syria 101 E9 35 1N 40 27 E
Al Mazār, Jordan 103 D4 31 4N 35 41 E
Al Midhnab, Si. Arabia 96 E5 25 50N 44 18 E
Al Minā', Lebanon 103 A4 34 24N 35 49 E
Al Miqdādīyah, Iraq 101 E11 34 0N 45 0 E
Al Mubarraz, Si. Arabia 97 E6 25 30N 49 40 E
Al Mudawwarah, Jordan 103 F5 29 19N 36 0 E
Al Muḍaybī, Oman 99 B7 22 34N 58 7 E
Al Mughayrā', U.A.E. 97 E7 24 5N 53 32 E
Al Muḥarraq, Bahrain 97 E6 26 15N 50 40 E
Al Mukallā, Yemen 99 D5 14 33N 49 2 E
Al Mukhā, Yemen 98 D3 13 18N 43 15 E
Al Musayjid, Si. Arabia 96 E3 24 5N 39 5 E
Al Musayyib, Iraq 101 F11 32 49N 44 20 E
Al Muthanná □, Iraq 96 D5 30 30N 45 15 E
Al Muwayh, Si. Arabia 106 C5 22 41N 41 37 E
Al Muwayliḥ, Si. Arabia 96 E2 27 40N 35 30 E
Al Owuho = Otukpa, Nigeria 113 D6 7 9N 7 41 E
Al Qaddāḥīyah, Libya 108 B3 31 15N 15 9 E
Al Qaḍīmah, Si. Arabia 98 B2 22 20N 39 13 E
Al Qādisīyah □, Iraq 96 D5 32 0N 45 0 E
Al Qaḥmah, Si. Arabia 98 C3 18 0N 41 41 E
Al Qā'im, Iraq 101 E9 34 21N 41 7 E
Al Qalībah, Si. Arabia 96 D3 28 24N 37 42 E
Al Qāmishlī, Syria 101 D9 37 2N 41 14 E
Al Qaryah ash Sharqīyah, Libya 108 B2 30 28N 13 40 E

Al Qaryatayn, *Syria* **103 A6** 34 12N 37 13 E
Al Qaşabát, *Libya* **108 B2** 32 39N 14 1 E
Al Qaşīm, *Si. Arabia* **96 E4** 26 0N 43 0 E
Al Qaṭ'ā, *Syria* **101 E9** 34 40N 40 48 E
Al Qaṭīf, *Si. Arabia* **97 E6** 26 35N 50 0 E
Al Qaṭn, *Yemen* **99 D5** 15 51N 48 26 E
Al Qatrānah, *Jordan* **103 D5** 31 12N 36 6 E
Al Qaṭrūn, *Libya* **108 D3** 24 56N 15 3 E
Al Qayşūmah, *Si. Arabia* **96 D5** 28 20N 46 7 E
Al Qiblīyah, *Oman* **99 C7** 17 30N 56 20 E
Al Quds = Jerusalem, *Israel* **103 D4** 31 47N 35 10 E
Al Qunayṭirah, *Syria* **103 C4** 32 55N 35 45 E
Al Qunfudhah, *Si. Arabia* **98 C3** 19 3N 41 4 E
Al Qurḥ, *Yemen* **99 C5** 16 44N 51 29 E
Al Qurnah, *Iraq* **96 D5** 31 1N 47 25 E
Al Quşayr, *Iraq* **96 D5** 30 39N 45 50 E
Al Quşayr, *Syria* **103 A5** 34 31N 36 34 E
Al Quṭayfah, *Syria* **103 B5** 33 44N 36 36 E
Al Quway'īyah, *Si. Arabia* **98 A4** 24 3N 45 15 E
Al 'Ubaylah, *Si. Arabia* **99 B5** 21 59N 50 57 E
Al 'Uḍaylīyah, *Si. Arabia* **97 E6** 25 8N 49 18 E
Al 'Ulā, *Si. Arabia* **96 E3** 26 35N 38 0 E
Al 'Ulayyah, *Si. Arabia* **98 C3** 19 39N 41 54 E
Al Uqaylah ash Sharqīgah, *Libya* **108 B3** 30 12N 19 10 E
Al 'Uqayr, *Si. Arabia* **97 E6** 25 40N 50 15 E
Al 'Urūq al Mutariḍah, *Si. Arabia* **99 B6** 21 0N 53 30 E
Al 'Uwaynid, *Si. Arabia* **96 E5** 24 50N 46 0 E
Al 'Uwayqīlah, *Si. Arabia* **96 D4** 30 30N 42 10 E
Al 'Uyūn, *Ḥijāz, Si. Arabia* **96 E3** 24 33N 39 35 E
Al 'Uyūn, *Najd, Si. Arabia* **96 E4** 26 30N 43 50 E
Al 'Uzayr, *Iraq* **96 D5** 31 19N 47 25 E
Al Wajh, *Si. Arabia* **96 E3** 26 10N 36 30 E
Al Wakrah, *Qatar* **97 E6** 25 10N 51 40 E
Al Waqbah, *Si. Arabia* **96 D5** 28 48N 45 33 E
Al Wari'āh, *Si. Arabia* **96 E5** 27 51N 47 25 E
Al Wāṭīyah, *Libya* **108 B2** 32 28N 11 57 E
Al Yaman = Yemen ■, *Asia* **98 D4** 15 0N 44 0 E
Ala, *Italy* **44 C8** 45 45N 11 0 E
Ala-Buka, *Kyrgyzstan* **65 C5** 41 23N 71 30 E
Ala Dağ, *Turkey* **96 B2** 37 44N 35 9 E
Ala Dağları, *Turkey* **101 C10** 39 15N 43 33 E
Ala Tau Shankou = Dzungarian Gates, *Asia* **68 B3** 45 0N 82 0 E
Alabama □, *U.S.A.* **149 J2** 33 0N 87 0W
Alabama →, *U.S.A.* **149 K2** 31 8N 87 57W
Alabaster, *U.S.A.* **149 J2** 33 15N 86 49W
Alabat I., *Phil.* **80 D4** 14 7N 122 3 E
Alabel, *Phil.* **81 H5** 6 4N 125 16 E
Alabule →, *Papua N. G.* **132 E4** 8 31 S 146 56 E
Alaca, *Turkey* **100 B6** 40 10N 34 51 E
Alacaatlı, *Turkey* **49 B10** 39 15N 28 3 E
Alaçam, *Turkey* **100 B6** 41 36N 35 36 E
Alaçam Dağları, *Turkey* **49 B10** 39 18N 28 49 E
Alacant = Alicante, *Spain* **41 G4** 38 23N 0 30W
Alaçatı, *Turkey* **49 C8** 38 15N 26 22 E
Alachua, *U.S.A.* **152 F7** 29 47N 82 30W
Alaejos, *Spain* **42 D5** 41 18N 5 13W
Alaérma, *Greece* **38 E11** 36 9N 27 57 E
Alagir, *Russia* **61 J7** 43 3N 44 14 E
Alagna Valsésia, *Italy* **44 C4** 45 51N 7 56 E
Alagoa de Baixo = Sertânia, *Brazil* **170 C4** 8 5 S 37 20W
Alagoa Grande, *Brazil* **170 C4** 7 3 S 35 35W
Alagoas = Marechal Deodoro, *Brazil* **170 C4** 9 43 S 35 54W
Alagoas □, *Brazil* **170 C4** 9 0 S 36 0W
Alagoinhas, *Brazil* **171 D4** 12 7 S 38 20W
Alagón, *Spain* **40 D3** 41 46N 1 12W
Alagón →, *Spain* **42 F4** 39 44N 6 53W
Alagyoz = Aragats, *Armenia* **61 K7** 40 30N 44 15 E
Alai Range, *Asia* **65 D5** 39 45N 72 0 E
Alaior, *Spain* **38 B5** 39 57N 4 8 E
Alajero, *Canary Is.* **9 e1** 28 3N 17 13W
Alajuela, *Costa Rica* **164 D3** 10 2N 84 8W
Alakamisy, *Madag.* **117 C8** 21 19 S 47 14 E
Alakanuk, *U.S.A.* **144 E6** 62 41N 164 37W
Alaknanda →, *India* **93 D8** 30 8N 78 36 E
Alakurtti, *Russia* **56 A5** 66 58N 30 25 E
Alalakeiki Channel, *U.S.A.* **145 C5** 20 30N 156 30W
Alalapura, *Suriname* **169 C6** 2 20N 56 25W
Alalaú →, *Brazil* **169 D5** 0 30 S 61 9W
Alamarvdasht, *Iran* **97 E7** 27 37N 52 59 E
Alamata, *Ethiopia* **107 E4** 12 25N 39 33 E
Alameda, *Calif., U.S.A.* **160 H4** 37 46N 122 15W
Alameda, *N. Mex., U.S.A.* **159 J10** 35 11N 106 37W
Alaminos, *Phil.* **80 C2** 16 10N 119 59 E
Alamo, *Ga., U.S.A.* **152 C7** 32 9N 82 47W
Alamo, *Nev., U.S.A.* **161 H11** 37 22N 115 10W
Alamo Crossing, *U.S.A.* **161 L13** 34 16N 113 33W
Alamogordo, *U.S.A.* **159 K11** 32 54N 105 57W
Alamos, *Mexico* **162 B3** 27 0N 109 0W
Alamosa, *U.S.A.* **159 H11** 37 28N 105 52W
Alampur, *India* **95 G4** 15 55N 78 6 E
Åland = Ahvenanmaa, *Finland* **15 F19** 60 15N 20 0 E
Aland, *India* **94 F3** 17 36N 76 35 E
Alandroal, *Portugal* **43 G3** 38 41N 7 24W
Ålands hav, *Europe* **15 F18** 60 0N 19 30 E
Alandur, *India* **95 H5** 13 0N 80 15 E
Alange, Embalse d', *Spain* **43 G4** 38 45N 6 18W
Alania = North Ossetia □, *Russia* **61 J7** 43 30N 44 30 E
Alanís, *Spain* **43 G5** 38 3N 5 43W
Alanya, *Turkey* **100 D5** 36 38N 32 0 E
Alaotra, Farihin', *Madag.* **117 B8** 17 30 S 48 30 E
Alapaha, *U.S.A.* **152 D6** 31 23N 83 13W
Alapayevsk, *Russia* **64 C8** 57 52N 61 42 E
Alappuzha = Alleppey, *India* **95 K3** 9 30N 76 28 E
Alar del Rey, *Spain* **42 C6** 42 38N 4 20W
Alaraz, *Spain* **42 E5** 40 45N 5 17W
Alarcón, Embalse de, *Spain* **40 F2** 39 36N 2 10W
Alarobia-Vohiposa, *Madag.* **117 C8** 20 59 S 47 9 E
Alaşehir, *Turkey* **49 C10** 38 23N 28 30 E
Alaska □, *U.S.A.* **144 E9** 64 0N 154 0W
Alaska, G. of, *Pac. Oc.* **144 G11** 58 0N 145 0W
Alaska Peninsula, *U.S.A.* **144 J8** 56 0N 159 0W
Alaska Range, *U.S.A.* **144 F10** 62 50N 151 0W
Alássio, *Italy* **44 E5** 44 0N 8 10 E
Ālāt, *Azerbaijan* **61 L9** 39 58N 49 25 E
Alat, *Uzbekistan* **65 D1** 39 24N 63 47 E
Alatri, *Italy* **45 G10** 41 43N 13 21 E
Alatyr, *Russia* **60 C8** 54 55N 46 35 E
Alatyr →, *Russia* **60 C8** 54 52N 46 36 E
Alausi, *Ecuador* **168 D2** 2 0 S 78 50W
Álava □, *Spain* **40 C2** 42 48N 2 28W
Alava, C., *U.S.A.* **158 B1** 48 10N 124 44W
Alaverdi, *Armenia* **61 K7** 41 15N 44 37 E
Alavo = Alavus, *Finland* **15 E20** 62 35N 23 36 E
Alavus, *Finland* **15 E20** 62 35N 23 36 E
Alawoona, *Australia* **128 C4** 34 45 S 140 30 E
'Alayh, *Lebanon* **103 B4** 33 46N 35 33 E
Alaykuu = Kögart, *Kyrgyzstan* **65 C7** 40 15N 74 25 E
Alazani →, *Azerbaijan* **61 K8** 41 5N 46 40 E
Alba, *Italy* **44 D5** 44 42N 8 2 E
Alba □, *Romania* **53 D8** 46 10N 23 30 E
Alba Adriática, *Italy* **45 F10** 42 50N 13 56 E
Alba de Tormes, *Spain* **42 E5** 40 50N 5 30W
Alba-Iulia, *Romania* **53 D8** 46 8N 23 39 E
Albac, *Romania* **52 D7** 46 28N 22 58 E
Albacete, *Spain* **41 F3** 39 0N 1 50W
Albacete □, *Spain* **41 G3** 38 50N 2 0W
Albacutya, L., *Australia* **128 C4** 35 45 S 141 58 E
Ålbæk, *Denmark* **17 G4** 57 36N 10 25 E
Ålbæk Bugt, *Denmark* **17 G4** 57 35N 10 40 E
Albaida, *Spain* **41 G4** 38 51N 0 31W
Albalate de las Nogueras, *Spain* **40 E2** 40 22N 2 18W
Albalate del Arzobispo, *Spain* **40 D4** 41 6N 0 31W
Alban, *France* **28 E6** 43 53N 2 28 E
Albanel, L., *Canada* **140 B5** 50 55N 73 12W
Albania ■, *Europe* **50 E4** 41 0N 20 0 E
Albano Laziale, *Italy* **45 G9** 41 44N 12 39 E
Albany, *Australia* **125 G2** 35 1 S 117 58 E
Albany, *Ga., U.S.A.* **152 D5** 31 35N 84 10W
Albany, *Ind., U.S.A.* **157 D11** 40 18N 85 14W
Albany, *Mo., U.S.A.* **156 D2** 40 15N 94 20W
Albany, *N.Y., U.S.A.* **151 D11** 42 39N 73 45W
Albany, *Oreg., U.S.A.* **158 D2** 44 38N 123 6W
Albany, *Tex., U.S.A.* **155 J5** 32 44N 99 18W
Albany, *Wis., U.S.A.* **156 B7** 42 43N 89 26W
Albany →, *Canada* **140 B3** 52 17N 81 31W
Albardón, *Argentina* **174 C2** 31 20 S 68 30W
Albarracín, *Spain* **40 E3** 40 25N 1 26W
Albarracín, Sierra de, *Spain* **40 E3** 40 30N 1 30W
Albatera, *Spain* **41 G4** 38 11N 0 52W
Albatross B., *Australia* **126 A3** 12 45 S 141 30 E
Albatross Pt., *N.Z.* **130 E3** 38 7 S 174 44 E
Albay □, *Phil.* **80 E4** 13 13N 123 33 E
Albegna →, *Italy* **45 F8** 42 30N 11 11 E
Albemarle, *U.S.A.* **149 H5** 35 21N 80 11W
Albemarle, I. = Isabela, I., *Ecuador* **172 a** 0 30 S 91 4W
Albemarle, Pta., *Ecuador* **172 a** 0 11N 91 21W
Albemarle Sd., *U.S.A.* **149 H7** 36 5N 76 0W
Albenga, *Italy* **44 D5** 44 3N 8 13 E
Alberche →, *Spain* **42 F6** 39 58N 4 46W
Alberdi, *Paraguay* **174 B4** 26 14 S 58 20W
Albères, Mts., *France* **28 F6** 42 28N 2 56 E
Ålberga, *Sweden* **17 F10** 58 44N 16 35 E
Alberga, The →, *Australia* **127 D2** 27 6 S 135 33 E
Albersdorf, *Germany* **30 A5** 54 8N 9 17 E
Albert, *France* **27 C9** 50 0N 2 38 E
Albert, L., *Africa* **118 B3** 1 30N 31 0 E
Albert, L., *Australia* **128 C3** 35 30 S 139 10 E
Albert Edward, Mt., *Papua N. G.* **132 E4** 8 20 S 147 24 E
Albert Edward Ra., *Australia* **124 C4** 18 17 S 127 57 E
Albert Lea, *U.S.A.* **154 D8** 43 39N 93 22W
Albert National Park = Virunga △, *Dem. Rep. of the Congo* **118 B2** 0 5N 29 38 E
Albert Nile →, *Uganda* **118 B3** 3 36N 32 2 E
Albert Town, *Bahamas* **165 B5** 22 37N 74 33W
Alberta □, *Canada* **142 C6** 54 40N 115 0W
Alberti, *Argentina* **174 D3** 35 1 S 60 16W
Albertinia, *S. Africa* **116 E3** 34 11 S 21 34 E
Albertirsa, *Hungary* **52 C4** 47 14N 19 37 E
Alberto de Agostini △, *Chile* **176 D2** 54 38 S 71 37W
Alberton, *Canada* **141 C7** 46 50N 64 0W
Albertville = Kalemie, *Dem. Rep. of the Congo* **118 D2** 5 55 S 29 9 E
Albertville, *France* **29 C10** 45 40N 6 22 E
Albertville, *U.S.A.* **149 H2** 34 16N 86 13W
Albi, *France* **28 E6** 43 56N 2 9 E
Albia, *U.S.A.* **156 C4** 41 2N 92 48W
Albina, *Suriname* **169 B7** 5 37N 54 15W
Albina, Ponta, *Angola* **116 B1** 15 52 S 11 44 E
Albino, *Italy* **44 C6** 45 46N 9 47 E
Albion, *Ill., U.S.A.* **157 F8** 38 23N 88 4W
Albion, *Ind., U.S.A.* **157 C11** 41 24N 85 25W
Albion, *Mich., U.S.A.* **157 B12** 42 15N 84 45W
Albion, *Nebr., U.S.A.* **154 E6** 41 42N 98 0W
Albion, *Pa., U.S.A.* **150 E4** 41 53N 80 22W
Albocácer, *Spain* **40 E5** 40 21N 0 1 E
Albolote, *Spain* **43 H7** 37 14N 3 39W
Alborán, *Medit. S.* **43 K7** 35 57N 3 0W
Alborea, *Spain* **41 F3** 39 17N 1 24W
Ålborg, *Denmark* **17 G3** 57 2N 9 54 E
Ålborg Bugt, *Denmark* **17 H4** 56 50N 10 35 E
Alborz, Reshteh-ye Kūhhā-ye, *Iran* **97 C7** 36 0N 52 0 E
Albosaggia, *Italy* **33 D9** 46 8N 9 51 E
Albox, *Spain* **41 H2** 37 23N 2 8W
Albuera, *Phil.* **81 F5** 10 55N 124 42 E
Albufeira, *Portugal* **43 H2** 37 5N 8 15W
Albula →, *Switz.* **33 C8** 46 38N 9 28 E
Albuñol, *Spain* **43 J7** 36 48N 3 11W
Albuquerque, *Brazil* **173 D6** 19 23 S 57 26W
Albuquerque, *U.S.A.* **159 J10** 35 5N 106 39W
Albuquerque, Cayos de, *Caribbean* **164 D3** 12 10N 81 50W
Alburg, *U.S.A.* **151 B11** 44 59N 73 18W
Alburno, Mte., *Italy* **47 B8** 40 33N 15 17 E
Alburquerque, *Spain* **43 F4** 39 15N 6 59W
Albury = Albury-Wodonga, *Australia* **129 D7** 36 3 S 146 56 E
Albury-Wodonga, *Australia* **129 D7** 36 3 S 146 56 E
Alcácer do Sal, *Portugal* **43 G2** 38 22N 8 33W
Alcáçovas, *Portugal* **43 G2** 38 23N 8 9W
Alcala, *Phil.* **80 C3** 17 54N 121 39 E
Alcalá de Chivert, *Spain* **40 E5** 40 19N 0 13 E
Alcalá de Guadaira, *Spain* **43 H5** 37 20N 5 50W
Alcalá de Henares, *Spain* **42 E7** 40 28N 3 22W
Alcalá de los Gazules, *Spain* **43 J5** 36 29N 5 43W
Alcalá del Júcar, *Spain* **41 F3** 39 12N 1 26W
Alcalá del Río, *Spain* **43 H5** 37 31N 5 59W
Alcalá del Valle, *Spain* **43 J5** 36 54N 5 10W
Alcalá la Real, *Spain* **43 H7** 37 27N 3 57W
Álcamo, *Italy* **46 E5** 37 59N 12 55 E
Alcanadre, *Spain* **40 C2** 42 24N 2 7W
Alcanadre →, *Spain* **40 D4** 41 43N 0 12W
Alcanar, *Spain* **40 E5** 40 33N 0 28 E
Alcanede, *Portugal* **43 F2** 39 25N 8 49W
Alcanena, *Portugal* **43 F2** 39 27N 8 40W
Alcañices, *Spain* **42 D4** 41 41N 6 21W
Alcaníz, *Spain* **40 D4** 41 2N 0 8W
Alcântara, *Brazil* **170 B3** 2 20 S 44 30W
Alcántara, *Spain* **42 F4** 39 41N 6 57W
Alcántara, Embalse de, *Spain* **42 F4** 39 44N 6 50W
Alcantarilla, *Spain* **41 H3** 37 59N 1 12W
Alcaracejos, *Spain* **43 G6** 38 24N 4 58W
Alcaraz, *Spain* **41 G2** 38 40N 2 29W
Alcaraz, Sierra de, *Spain* **41 G2** 38 40N 2 20W
Alcaudete, *Spain* **43 H6** 37 35N 4 5W
Alcázar de San Juan, *Spain* **43 F7** 39 24N 3 12W
Alcazarquivir = Ksar el Kebir, *Morocco* **110 B3** 35 0N 6 0W
Alcedo, Volcán, *Ecuador* **172 a** 0 24 S 91 6W
Alchevsk, *Ukraine* **59 H10** 48 30N 38 45 E
Alcira = Alzira, *Spain* **41 F4** 39 9N 0 30W
Alcobaça = Tucuruí, *Brazil* **170 B2** 3 42 S 49 44W
Alcobaça, *Portugal* **43 F2** 39 32N 8 58W
Alcobendas, *Spain* **42 E7** 40 32N 3 38W
Alcolea del Pinar, *Spain* **40 D2** 41 2N 2 28W
Alcoma, *U.S.A.* **153 H8** 27 54N 81 29W
Alcora, *Spain* **40 E4** 40 5N 0 14W
Alcorcón, *Spain* **42 E7** 40 20N 3 50W
Alcoutim, *Portugal* **43 H3** 37 25N 7 28W
Alcova, *U.S.A.* **158 E10** 42 34N 106 43W
Alcoy, *Spain* **41 G4** 38 43N 0 30W
Alcubierre, Sierra de, *Spain* **40 D4** 41 45N 0 22W
Alcublas, *Spain* **40 F4** 39 48N 0 43W
Alcúdia, *Spain* **38 B4** 39 51N 3 7 E
Alcúdia, B. d', *Spain* **38 B4** 39 47N 3 15 E
Alcudia, Sierra de la, *Spain* **43 G6** 38 34N 4 30W
Aldabra Is., *Seychelles* **121 E3** 9 22 S 46 28 E
Aldama, *Mexico* **163 C5** 23 0N 98 4W
Aldan, *Russia* **67 D13** 58 40N 125 30 E
Aldan →, *Russia* **67 C13** 63 28N 129 35 E
Aldea, Pta. de la, *Canary Is.* **9 e1** 28 0N 15 50W
Aldeburgh, *U.K.* **21 E9** 52 10N 1 37 E
Alden, *Norway* **18 C1** 61 19N 4 45 E
Alder Pk., *U.S.A.* **160 K5** 35 53N 121 22W
Alderney, *U.K.* **21 H5** 49 42N 2 11W
Aldershot, *U.K.* **21 F7** 51 15N 0 44W
Aldinga Beach, *Australia* **128 C3** 35 17 S 138 27 E
Åled, *Sweden* **17 H6** 56 44N 12 57 E
Aledo, *U.S.A.* **156 C6** 41 12N 90 45W
Alefa, *Ethiopia* **107 E4** 11 55N 36 55 E
Aleg, *Mauritania* **112 B2** 17 3N 13 55W
Alegranza, *Canary Is.* **110 C2** 29 23N 13 32W
Alegranza, I., *Canary Is.* **9 e2** 29 23N 13 32W
Alegre, *Brazil* **171 F3** 20 50 S 41 30W
Alegrete, *Brazil* **175 B4** 29 40 S 56 0W
Aleisk, *Russia* **66 D9** 52 40N 83 0 E
Aleknagik, *U.S.A.* **144 G8** 59 17N 158 36W
Aleksandriya = Oleksandriya, *Kirovohrad, Ukraine* **59 H7** 48 42N 33 3 E
Aleksandriya = Oleksandriya, *Rivne, Ukraine* **59 G4** 50 37N 26 19 E
Aleksandriyskaya, *Russia* **61 J8** 43 58N 47 14 E
Aleksandropol = Gyumri, *Armenia* **61 K6** 40 47N 43 50 E
Aleksandrov, *Russia* **58 D10** 56 23N 38 44 E
Aleksandrov Gay, *Russia* **60 E9** 50 9N 48 34 E
Aleksandrovac, *Serbia & M.* **50 C5** 43 28N 21 3 E
Aleksandrovac, *Serbia & M.* **50 B5** 44 28N 21 13 E
Aleksandrovka = Oleksandrovka, *Ukraine* **59 H7** 48 55N 32 20 E
Aleksandrovka = Ordzhonikidze, *Ukraine* **59 J8** 47 39N 34 3 E
Aleksandrovo, *Bulgaria* **51 C8** 43 14N 24 51 E
Aleksandrovsk = Belogorsk, *Russia* **67 D13** 51 0N 128 20 E
Aleksandrovsk = Polyarny, *Russia* **56 A5** 69 8N 33 20 E
Aleksandrovsk = Zaporizhzhya, *Ukraine* **59 J8** 47 50N 35 10 E
Aleksandrovsk, *Russia* **64 B6** 59 9N 57 33 E
Aleksandrovsk-Grushevsky = Shakhty, *Russia* **61 G5** 47 40N 40 16 E
Aleksandrovsk-Sakhalinskiy, *Russia* **67 D15** 50 50N 142 20 E
Aleksandrów Kujawski, *Poland* **55 F5** 52 53N 18 43 E
Aleksandrów Łódźki, *Poland* **55 G6** 51 49N 19 17 E
Aleksandry, Z., *Russia* **6 A10** 80 25N 48 0 E
Alekseyevka, *Samara, Russia* **60 D10** 52 35N 51 17 E
Alekseyevka, *Voronezh, Russia* **59 G10** 50 43N 38 40 E
Alekseyevsk = Svobodnyy, *Russia* **67 D13** 51 20N 128 0 E
Alekseyevskoye = Qazyghurt, *Kazakhstan* **65 C4** 41 45N 69 23 E
Aleksin, *Russia* **58 E9** 54 31N 37 9 E
Aleksinac, *Serbia & M.* **50 C5** 43 31N 21 42 E
Além Paraíba, *Brazil* **171 F3** 21 52 S 42 41W
Alemania, *Argentina* **174 B2** 25 40 S 65 30W
Alemania, *Chile* **174 B2** 25 10 S 69 55W
Alen, *Eq. Guin.* **114 B2** 1 58N 11 19 E
Alençon, *France* **26 D7** 48 27N 0 4 E
Alenuihaha Channel, *U.S.A.* **145 C6** 20 30N 156 0W
Alépé, *Ivory C.* **112 D4** 5 29N 3 40W
Aleppo = Ḥalab, *Syria* **100 D7** 36 10N 37 15 E
Alerce Andino △, *Chile* **176 B2** 41 33 S 72 29W
Aléria, *France* **29 F13** 42 5N 9 26 E
Alert, *Canada* **6 A4** 83 2N 60 0W
Aleru, *India* **94 F4** 17 39N 79 3 E
Alès, *France* **29 D8** 44 9N 4 5 E
Aleşd, *Romania* **52 C7** 47 3N 22 22 E
Alessándria, *Italy* **44 D5** 44 54N 8 37 E
Ålestrup, *Denmark* **17 H3** 56 42N 9 29 E
Ålesund, *Norway* **18 B3** 62 28N 6 12 E
Alet-les-Bains, *France* **28 F6** 42 59N 2 14 E
Aletschhorn, *Switz.* **32 D6** 46 28N 8 0 E
Aleutian Is., *Pac. Oc.* **138 C2** 52 0N 175 0W
Aleutian Range, *U.S.A.* **144 G9** 60 0N 154 0W
Aleutian Trench, *Pac. Oc.* **134 C10** 48 0N 180 0 E
Alexander, *Ga., U.S.A.* **152 B8** 33 1N 81 53W
Alexander, *N. Dak., U.S.A.* **154 B3** 47 51N 103 39W
Alexander, C., *Solomon Is.* **133 L9** 6 34 S 156 32 E
Alexander, Mt., *Australia* **125 E3** 28 58 S 120 16 E
Alexander Arch., *U.S.A.* **144 J14** 56 0N 136 0W
Alexander Bay, *S. Africa* **116 D2** 28 40 S 16 30 E
Alexander City, *U.S.A.* **152 C4** 32 56N 85 58W
Alexander I., *Antarctica* **7 C17** 69 0 S 70 0W
Alexandra, *Australia* **129 D6** 37 8 S 145 40 E
Alexandra, *N.Z.* **131 F4** 45 14 S 169 25 E
Alexandra Channel, *Burma* **95 G11** 14 7N 93 13 E
Alexandra Falls, *Canada* **142 A5** 60 29N 116 18W
Alexandretta = İskenderun, *Turkey* **100 D7** 36 32N 36 10 E
Alexandria = El Iskandarîya, *Egypt* **106 H7** 31 13N 29 58 E
Alexandria, *B.C., Canada* **142 C4** 52 35N 122 27W
Alexandria, *Ont., Canada* **140 C5** 45 19N 74 38W
Alexandria, *Romania* **53 G10** 43 57N 25 24 E
Alexandria, *S. Africa* **116 E4** 33 38 S 26 28 E
Alexandria, *U.K.* **22 F4** 55 59N 4 35W
Alexandria, *Ind., U.S.A.* **157 D11** 40 16N 85 41W
Alexandria, *Ky., U.S.A.* **157 F12** 38 58N 84 23W
Alexandria, *La., U.S.A.* **155 K8** 31 18N 92 27W
Alexandria, *Minn., U.S.A.* **154 C7** 45 53N 95 22W
Alexandria, *Mo., U.S.A.* **156 D5** 40 27N 91 28W
Alexandria, *S. Dak., U.S.A.* **154 D6** 43 39N 97 47W
Alexandria, *Va., U.S.A.* **148 F7** 38 48N 77 3W
Alexandria Bay, *U.S.A.* **151 B9** 44 20N 75 55W
Alexandrina, L., *Australia* **128 C3** 35 25 S 139 10 E
Alexandroupoli = Alexandroúpolis, *Greece* **51 F9** 40 50N 25 54 E
Alexandroúpolis, *Greece* **51 F9** 40 50N 25 54 E
Alexis, *U.S.A.* **156 C6** 41 4N 90 33W
Alexis →, *Canada* **141 B8** 52 33N 56 8W
Alexis Creek, *Canada* **142 C4** 52 10N 123 20W
Alfabia, *Spain* **38 B3** 39 44N 2 44 E
Alfambra, *Spain* **40 E3** 40 33N 1 5W
Alfândega da Fé, *Portugal* **42 D4** 41 20N 6 59W
Alfaro, *Spain* **40 C3** 42 10N 1 50W
Alfatar, *Bulgaria* **51 C11** 43 59N 27 13 E
Alfaz del Pi, *Spain* **41 G4** 38 35N 0 5W
Alfeld, *Germany* **30 D5** 51 59N 9 50 E
Alfenas, *Brazil* **175 A6** 21 20 S 46 10W
Alfiós →, *Greece* **48 D3** 37 40N 21 33 E
Alföld, *Hungary* **52 D5** 46 30N 20 0 E
Alfonsine, *Italy* **45 D9** 44 30N 12 3 E
Alford, *Aberds., U.K.* **22 D6** 57 14N 2 41W
Alford, *Lincs., U.K.* **20 D8** 53 15N 0 10 E
Alford, *U.S.A.* **152 E4** 30 42N 85 24W
Ålfotbreen, *Norway* **18 C2** 61 45N 5 39 E
Ålfoten, *Norway* **18 C2** 61 51N 5 41 E
Alfred, *Maine, U.S.A.* **151 C14** 43 29N 70 43W
Alfred, *N.Y., U.S.A.* **150 D7** 42 16N 77 48W
Alfredton, *N.Z.* **130 G4** 40 41 S 175 54 E
Alfreton, *U.K.* **20 D6** 53 6N 1 24W
Alfta, *Sweden* **16 C10** 61 21N 16 4 E
Alga, *Kazakhstan* **57 E10** 49 53N 57 20 E
Algaida, *Spain* **38 B3** 39 33N 2 53 E
Algar, *Spain* **43 J5** 36 40N 5 39W
Ålgård, *Norway* **18 F2** 58 46N 5 53 E
Algarinejo, *Spain* **43 H6** 37 19N 4 9W
Algarve, *Portugal* **43 J2** 36 58N 8 20W
Algeciras, *Spain* **43 J5** 36 9N 5 28W
Algemesí, *Spain* **41 F4** 39 11N 0 27W
Alger, *Algeria* **111 A5** 36 42N 3 8 E
Alger ✈ (ALG), *Algeria* **41 J8** 36 39N 3 13 E
Algeria ■, *Africa* **111 C5** 28 30N 2 0 E
Alghero, *Italy* **46 B1** 40 33N 8 19 E
Älghult, *Sweden* **17 G9** 57 0N 15 35 E
Algiers = Alger, *Algeria* **111 A5** 36 42N 3 8 E
Algoa B., *S. Africa* **116 E4** 33 50 S 25 45 E
Algodonales, *Spain* **43 J5** 36 54N 5 24W
Algodor →, *Spain* **42 F7** 39 55N 3 53W
Algoma, *U.S.A.* **148 C2** 44 36N 87 26W
Algona, *U.S.A.* **156 A2** 43 4N 94 14W
Algonac, *U.S.A.* **150 D2** 42 37N 82 32W
Algonquin ⌓, *Canada* **140 C4** 45 50N 78 30W
Alhama de Almería, *Spain* **43 J8** 36 57N 2 34W
Alhama de Aragón, *Spain* **40 D3** 41 18N 1 54W
Alhama de Granada, *Spain* **43 H7** 37 0N 3 59W
Alhama de Murcia, *Spain* **41 H3** 37 51N 1 25W
Alhambra, *U.S.A.* **161 L8** 34 8N 118 6W
Alhaurín el Grande, *Spain* **43 J6** 36 39N 4 41W
Alhucemas = Al Hoceïma, *Morocco* **110 A4** 35 8N 3 58W
'Alī al Gharbī, *Iraq* **101 F12** 32 30N 46 45 E
'Alī ash Sharqī, *Iraq* **101 F12** 32 7N 46 44 E
Äli Bayramlı, *Azerbaijan* **61 L9** 39 59N 48 52 E
'Alī Khēl, *Afghan.* **91 B3** 33 57N 69 43 E
Ali Sahîh, *Djibouti* **107 E5** 11 10N 42 44 E
Alī Shāh, *Iran* **96 B5** 38 9N 45 50 E
Ália, *Italy* **46 E6** 37 47N 13 43 E
'Alīābād, *Khorāsān, Iran* **97 C8** 32 30N 57 30 E
'Alīābād, *Kordestān, Iran* **96 C5** 35 4N 46 58 E
'Alīābād, *Yazd, Iran* **97 D7** 31 41N 53 49 E
Aliaga, *Spain* **40 E4** 40 40N 0 42W
Aliağa, *Turkey* **49 C8** 38 47N 26 59 E
Aliákmon →, *Greece* **50 F6** 40 30N 22 36 E
Aliakmonas = Aliákmon →, *Greece* **50 F6** 40 30N 22 36 E
Alibag, *India* **94 E1** 18 38N 72 56 E
Alibo, *Ethiopia* **107 F4** 9 52N 37 5 E
Alibori →, *Benin* **113 C5** 11 56N 3 17 E
Alibunar, *Serbia & M.* **52 E5** 45 5N 20 57 E
Alicante, *Spain* **41 G4** 38 23N 0 30W
Alicante □, *Spain* **41 G4** 38 30N 0 37W
Alicante ✈ (ALC), *Spain* **41 G4** 38 14N 0 36W
Alice, *S. Africa* **116 E4** 32 48 S 26 55 E
Alice, *U.S.A.* **155 M5** 27 45N 98 5W
Alice →, *Queens., Australia* **126 C3** 24 2 S 144 50 E
Alice →, *Queens., Australia* **126 B3** 15 35 S 142 20 E
Alice →, *Papua N. G.* **132 D1** 6 10 S 141 8 E
Alice, Punta, *Italy* **47 C10** 39 24N 17 9 E
Alice Arm, *Canada* **142 B3** 55 29N 129 31W
Alice Springs, *Australia* **126 C1** 23 40 S 133 50 E
Alicedale, *S. Africa* **116 E4** 33 15 S 26 4 E
Aliceville, *U.S.A.* **149 J1** 33 8N 88 9W
Alichur, *Tajikistan* **65 E6** 37 45N 73 33 E
Alicia, *Bohol, Phil.* **81 G5** 9 54N 124 26 E
Alicia, *Isabela, Phil.* **80 C3** 16 46N 121 42 E
Alicudi, *Italy* **47 D7** 38 33N 14 20 E
Aliganj, *India* **93 F8** 27 30N 79 10 E
Aligarh, *Raj., India* **92 G7** 25 55N 76 15 E
Aligarh, *Ut. P., India* **92 F8** 27 55N 78 10 E
Alīgūdarz, *Iran* **97 C6** 33 25N 49 45 E
Alijó, *Portugal* **42 D3** 41 16N 7 27W
Alikanás, *Greece* **39 D2** 37 51N 20 47 E
Alima →, *Congo* **114 C3** 1 35 S 16 37 E
Alimnía, *Greece* **38 E11** 36 16N 27 43 E
Alimodian, *Phil.* **81 F4** 10 49N 122 26 E
Alindao, *C.A.R.* **114 A4** 5 2N 21 13 E
Alingsås, *Sweden* **17 G6** 57 56N 12 31 E
Alipur, *Pakistan* **92 E4** 29 25N 70 55 E
Alipur Duar, *India* **90 B2** 26 30N 89 35 E
Aliquippa, *U.S.A.* **150 F4** 40 37N 80 15W
Alishan, *Taiwan* **77 F13** 23 31N 120 48 E
Aliste →, *Spain* **42 D5** 41 34N 5 58W
Alitus = Alytus, *Lithuania* **15 J21** 54 24N 24 3 E
Alivérion, *Greece* **48 C6** 38 24N 24 2 E
Aliwal North, *S. Africa* **116 E4** 30 45 S 26 45 E
Alix, *Canada* **142 C6** 52 24N 113 11W
Aljezur, *Portugal* **43 H2** 37 18N 8 49W
Aljustrel, *Portugal* **43 H2** 37 55N 8 10W
Alkamari, *Niger* **113 C7** 13 27N 11 10 E
Alkmaar, *Neths.* **24 B4** 52 37N 4 45 E
All American Canal, *U.S.A.* **159 K6** 32 45N 115 15W
Allacapan, *Phil.* **80 B3** 18 15N 121 35 E
Allada, *Benin* **113 D5** 6 41N 2 9 E
Allagadda, *India* **95 G4** 15 8N 78 30 E
Allagash →, *U.S.A.* **149 B11** 47 5N 69 3W
Allah Dad, *Pakistan* **92 G2** 25 38N 67 34 E
Allahabad, *India* **93 G9** 25 25N 81 58 E
Allakaket, *U.S.A.* **144 C9** 66 34N 152 39W
Allal Tazi, *Morocco* **110 B3** 34 30N 6 20W
Allan, *Canada* **143 C7** 51 53N 106 4W
Allanche, *France* **28 C6** 45 14N 2 57 E
Allanmyo, *Burma* **90 F5** 19 30N 95 17 E
Allanridge, *S. Africa* **116 D4** 27 45 S 26 40 E
Allansford, *Australia* **128 E5** 38 26 S 142 39 E
Allanton, *N.Z.* **131 F5** 45 55 S 170 15 E
Allaqi, Wadi →, *Egypt* **106 C3** 23 7N 32 47 E
Allariz, *Spain* **42 C3** 42 11N 7 50W
Allassac, *France* **28 C5** 45 15N 1 29 E
Allatoona L., *U.S.A.* **152 A5** 34 10N 84 44W
Ålleberg, *Sweden* **17 F7** 58 8N 13 36 E
Allegan, *U.S.A.* **157 B11** 42 32N 85 51W
Allegany, *U.S.A.* **150 D6** 42 6N 78 30W
Allegheny →, *U.S.A.* **150 F5** 40 27N 80 1W
Allegheny Mts., *U.S.A.* **148 G6** 38 15N 80 10W
Allegheny Plateau, *U.S.A.* **148 E6** 41 30N 78 30W
Allegheny Reservoir, *U.S.A.* **150 E6** 41 50N 79 0W
Allègre, *France* **28 C7** 45 12N 3 41 E
Allègre, Pte., *Guadeloupe* **164 b** 16 22N 61 46W
Allen, *Argentina* **176 A3** 38 58 S 67 50W
Allen, *Phil.* **80 E5** 12 30N 124 17 E
Allen, Bog of, *Ireland* **23 C5** 53 15N 7 0W
Allen, L., *Ireland* **23 B3** 54 8N 8 4W
Allendale, *U.S.A.* **152 B8** 33 1N 81 18W
Allende, *Mexico* **162 B4** 28 20N 100 50W
Allensbach, *Germany* **33 A8** 47 43N 9 4 E
Allenstein = Olsztyn, *Poland* **54 E7** 53 48N 20 29 E
Allentown, *U.S.A.* **151 F9** 40 37N 75 29W
Allentsteig, *Austria* **34 C8** 48 41N 15 20 E
Alleppey, *India* **95 K3** 9 30N 76 28 E
Allepuz, *Spain* **40 E4** 40 29N 0 44W
Aller →, *Germany* **30 C5** 52 56N 9 12 E
Alleynes B., *Barbados* **165 g** 13 13N 59 39W
Alliance, *Suriname* **169 B7** 5 50N 54 50W
Alliance, *Nebr., U.S.A.* **154 D3** 42 6N 102 52W
Alliance, *Ohio, U.S.A.* **150 F3** 40 55N 81 6W
Allier □, *France* **27 F9** 46 25N 2 40 E
Allier →, *France* **27 F10** 46 57N 3 4 E
Alliford Bay, *Canada* **142 C2** 53 12N 131 58W
Alligator Pond, *Jamaica* **164 a** 17 52N 77 34W
Allinagaram, *India* **95 J3** 10 2N 77 30 E
Allinge, *Denmark* **17 J8** 55 17N 14 50 E
Allison, *U.S.A.* **156 B4** 42 45N 92 48W
Alliston = New Tecumseth, *Canada* **140 D4** 44 9N 79 52W
Alloa, *U.K.* **22 E5** 56 7N 3 47W
Allones, *France* **26 D8** 48 20N 1 40 E
Allora, *Australia* **127 D5** 28 2 S 152 0 E
Allos, *France* **29 D10** 44 15N 6 38 E
Alluitsup Paa, *Greenland* **10 E6** 60 30N 45 35W
Allur, *India* **95 G5** 14 40N 80 4 E
Alluru Kottapatnam, *India* **95 G5** 15 24N 80 7 E
Alma, *Canada* **141 C5** 48 35N 71 40W
Alma, *Ga., U.S.A.* **152 D7** 31 33N 82 28W
Alma, *Kans., U.S.A.* **154 F6** 39 1N 96 17W
Alma, *Mich., U.S.A.* **148 D3** 43 23N 84 39W
Alma, *Nebr., U.S.A.* **154 E5** 40 6N 99 22W
Alma, *Wis., U.S.A.* **154 C9** 44 20N 91 55W
Alma Ata = Almaty, *Kazakhstan* **65 B8** 43 15N 76 57 E
Almacelles, *Spain* **40 D5** 41 43N 0 27 E
Almada, *Portugal* **43 G1** 38 40N 9 9W
Almaden, *Australia* **126 B3** 17 22 S 144 40 E
Almadén, *Spain* **43 G6** 38 49N 4 52W
Almalyk = Olmaliq, *Uzbekistan* **65 C4** 40 50N 69 35 E
Almanor, L., *U.S.A.* **158 F3** 40 14N 121 9W
Almansa, *Spain* **41 G3** 38 51N 1 5W
Almanza, *Spain* **42 C5** 42 39N 5 3W
Almanzor, Pico, *Spain* **42 E5** 40 15N 5 18W
Almanzora →, *Spain* **41 H3** 37 14N 1 46W
Almas, *Brazil* **171 D2** 11 33 S 47 9W
Almaş, Munţii, *Romania* **52 F7** 44 49N 22 12 E
Almassora, *Spain* **40 F4** 39 57N 0 3W
Almaty, *Kazakhstan* **65 B8** 43 15N 76 57 E
Almazán, *Spain* **40 D2** 41 30N 2 30W
Almeirim, *Brazil* **169 D7** 1 30 S 52 34W
Almeirim, *Portugal* **43 F2** 39 12N 8 37W
Almelo, *Neths.* **24 B6** 52 22N 6 42 E
Almenar de Soria, *Spain* **40 D2** 41 43N 2 12W
Almenara, *Brazil* **171 E3** 16 11 S 40 42W
Almenara, *Spain* **40 F4** 39 46N 0 14W
Almenara, Sierra de la, *Spain* **41 H3** 37 34N 1 32W
Almendra, Embalse de, *Spain* **42 D4** 41 10N 6 5W
Almendralejo, *Spain* **43 G4** 38 41N 6 26W
Almere-Stad, *Neths.* **24 B5** 52 20N 5 15 E
Almería, *Spain* **43 J8** 36 52N 2 27W
Almería □, *Spain* **41 H2** 37 20N 2 20W
Almería, G. de, *Spain* **41 J2** 36 41N 2 28W
Almetyevsk, *Russia* **60 C11** 54 53N 52 20 E
Älmhult, *Sweden* **17 H8** 56 33N 14 8 E
Almirante, *Panama* **164 E3** 9 10N 82 30W
Almirante Montt, G., *Chile* **176 D2** 51 52 S 72 50W

Almiropótamos, *Greece* 48 C6 38 16N 24 11 E
Almirós, *Greece* 48 B4 39 11N 22 45 E
Almiroú, Kólpos, *Greece* 39 E5 35 23N 24 20 E
Almodôvar, *Portugal* 43 H2 37 31N 8 2W
Almodóvar del Campo, *Spain* 43 G6 38 43N 4 10W
Almodóvar del Río, *Spain* 43 H5 37 48N 5 1W
Almond, *U.S.A.* 150 D7 42 19N 77 44W
Almont, *U.S.A.* 150 D1 42 55N 83 3W
Almonte, *Canada* 151 A8 45 14N 76 12W
Almonte, *Spain* 43 H4 37 13N 6 38W
Almora, *India* 93 E8 29 38N 79 40 E
Almoradí, *Spain* 41 G4 38 7N 0 46W
Almorox, *Spain* 42 E6 40 14N 4 24W
Almoustarat, *Mali* 113 B5 17 35N 0 8 E
Älmsta, *Sweden* 16 E12 59 58N 18 50 E
Almudévar, *Spain* 40 C4 42 3N 0 35W
Almuñécar, *Spain* 43 J7 36 43N 3 41W
Almunge, *Sweden* 16 E12 59 53N 18 3 E
Almuradiel, *Spain* 43 G7 38 32N 3 28W
Alness, *U.K.* 22 D4 57 41N 4 16W
Alnif, *Morocco* 110 B3 31 10N 5 8W
Alnmouth, *U.K.* 20 B6 55 24N 1 37W
Alnwick, *U.K.* 20 B6 55 24N 1 42W
Aloi, *Uganda* 118 B3 2 16N 33 10 E
Alon, *Burma* 90 D5 22 12N 95 5 E
Along, *India* 90 A5 28 10N 94 46 E
Alonissos-Vorίai Sporades △, *Greece* 48 B6 39 15N 24 5 E
Alor, *Indonesia* 82 C2 8 15 S 124 30 E
Alor Setar, *Malaysia* 87 J3 6 7N 100 22 E
Álora, *Spain* 43 J6 36 49N 4 46W
Alosno, *Spain* 43 H3 37 33N 7 7W
Alost = Aalst, *Belgium* 24 D4 50 56N 4 2 E
Alot, *India* 92 H6 23 56N 75 40 E
Alotau, *Papua N. G.* 132 F6 10 16 S 150 30 E
Alougoum, *Morocco* 110 B3 30 17N 6 56W
Aloum, *Cameroon* 114 B2 2 16N 10 34 E
Aloysius, Mt., *Australia* 125 E4 26 0 S 128 38 E
Alpaugh, *U.S.A.* 160 K7 35 53N 119 29W
Alpe Apuane ⌂, *Italy* 44 D7 44 4N 10 15 E
Alpedrinha, *Portugal* 42 E3 40 6N 7 27W
Alpena, *U.S.A.* 148 C4 45 4N 83 27W
Alpercatas →, *Brazil* 170 C3 6 2 S 44 19W
Alpes-de-Haute-Provence □, *France* 29 D10 44 8N 6 10 E
Alpes-Maritimes □, *France* 29 E11 43 55N 7 10 E
Alpha, *Australia* 126 C4 23 39 S 146 37 E
Alpha, *U.S.A.* 156 C6 41 12N 90 23W
Alpha Cordillera, *Arctic* 6 A2 84 0N 118 0W
Alphen aan den Rijn, *Neths.* 24 B4 52 7N 4 40 E
Alphonse, *Seychelles* 121 E4 7 0 S 52 45 E
Alpiarça, *Portugal* 43 F2 39 15N 8 35W
Alpine, *Ariz., U.S.A.* 159 K9 33 51N 109 9W
Alpine, *Calif., U.S.A.* 161 N10 32 50N 116 46W
Alpine, *Tex., U.S.A.* 155 K3 30 22N 103 40W
Alpine △, *Australia* 129 D7 37 15 S 146 45 E
Alpnach Dorf, *Switz.* 33 C6 46 57N 8 17 E
Alps, *Europe* 25 C8 46 30N 9 30 E
Alpu, *Turkey* 100 C4 39 46N 30 58 E
Alqueta, Barragem do, *Portugal* 43 G3 38 20N 7 25W
Alrø, *Denmark* 17 J4 55 52N 10 5 E
Als, *Denmark* 17 K3 54 59N 9 55 E
Alsace □, *France* 27 D14 48 15N 7 25 E
Alsask, *Canada* 143 C7 51 21N 109 59W
Alsasua, *Spain* 40 C2 42 54N 2 10W
Alsek →, *U.S.A.* 142 B1 59 10N 138 12W
Alsfeld, *Germany* 30 E5 50 44N 9 16 E
Alsten, *Norway* 14 D15 65 58N 12 40 E
Alstermo, *Sweden* 17 H9 56 58N 15 38 E
Alston, *U.K.* 20 C5 54 49N 2 25W
Alta, *Norway* 14 B20 69 57N 23 10 E
Alta, Sierra, *Spain* 40 E3 40 31N 1 30W
Alta Floresta, *Brazil* 173 B6 9 57 S 55 58W
Alta Gracia, *Argentina* 174 C3 31 40 S 64 30W
Alta Sierra, *U.S.A.* 161 K8 35 42N 118 33W
Altaelva →, *Norway* 14 B20 69 54N 23 17 E
Altafjorden, *Norway* 14 A20 70 5N 23 5 E
Altagracia, *Venezuela* 168 A3 10 45N 71 30W
Altagracia de Orituco, *Venezuela* 168 B4 9 52N 66 23W
Altai = Aerhtai Shan, *Mongolia* 68 B4 46 40N 92 45 E
Altamachi →, *Bolivia* 172 D4 16 8 S 66 50W
Altamaha →, *U.S.A.* 152 D8 31 20N 81 20W
Altamira, *Brazil* 169 D7 3 12 S 52 10W
Altamira, *Chile* 174 B2 25 47 S 69 51W
Altamira, *Colombia* 168 C2 2 3N 75 47W
Altamira, *Mexico* 163 C5 22 24N 97 55W
Altamira, Cuevas de, *Spain* 42 B6 43 20N 4 5W
Altamont, *Ill., U.S.A.* 157 E8 39 4N 88 45W
Altamont, *N.Y., U.S.A.* 151 D10 42 43N 74 3W
Altamont, *Oreg., U.S.A.* 158 E3 42 12N 121 44W
Altamura, *Italy* 47 B9 40 49N 16 33 E
Altanbulag, *Mongolia* 68 A5 50 16N 106 30 E
Altar, *Mexico* 162 A2 30 40N 111 50W
Altar, Desierto de, *Mexico* 162 B2 30 10N 112 0W
Altata, *Mexico* 162 C3 24 30N 108 0W
Altavas, *Phil.* 81 F4 11 32N 122 29 E
Altavista, *U.S.A.* 148 G6 37 6N 79 17W
Altay, *China* 68 B3 47 48N 88 10 E
Altdorf, *Switz.* 33 C7 46 52N 8 36 E
Alte Mellum, *Germany* 30 B4 53 43N 8 10 E
Altea, *Spain* 41 G4 38 38N 0 2W
Altenberg, *Germany* 30 E9 50 45N 13 45 E
Altenbruch, *Germany* 30 B4 53 49N 8 46 E
Altenburg, *Germany* 30 E8 50 59N 12 25 E
Altenkirchen, *Mecklenburg-Vorpommern, Germany* 30 A9 54 38N 13 22 E
Altenkirchen, *Rhld-Pfz., Germany* 30 E3 50 41N 7 39 E
Altenmarkt, *Austria* 34 D7 47 43N 14 39 E
Alter do Chão, *Brazil* 169 D6 2 31 S 54 57W
Alter do Chão, *Portugal* 43 F3 39 12N 7 40W
Altha, *U.S.A.* 152 E4 30 34N 85 8W
Altınoluk, *Turkey* 49 B8 39 34N 26 45 E
Altınova, *Turkey* 49 B8 39 12N 26 47 E
Altıntaş, *Turkey* 49 B12 39 4N 30 7 E
Altınyaka, *Turkey* 49 E12 36 33N 30 20 E
Altınyayla, *Turkey* 49 D11 37 0N 29 33 E
Altiplano, *Bolivia* 172 D4 17 0 S 68 0W
Altkirch, *France* 27 E14 47 37N 7 15 E
Altmark, *Germany* 30 C7 52 45N 11 30 E
Altmühl →, *Germany* 31 G7 48 54N 11 52 E
Altmühltal ⌂, *Germany* 31 G7 48 55N 11 15 E
Altmunster, *Austria* 34 D6 47 54N 13 45 E
Alto Adige = Trentino-Alto Adige □, *Italy* 45 B8 46 30N 11 20 E
Alto Alegre, *Brazil* 169 C5 2 50N 61 20W
Alto Araguaia, *Brazil* 173 D7 17 15 S 53 20W
Alto Chicapa, *Angola* 115 E3 10 52 S 19 17 E
Alto Cuchumatanes = Cuchumatanes, Sierra de los, *Guatemala* 164 C1 15 35N 91 25W
Alto Cuito = Tempué, *Angola* 115 E3 13 27 S 18 49 E
Alto del Carmen, *Chile* 174 B1 28 46 S 70 30W
Alto del Inca, *Chile* 174 A2 24 10 S 68 10W
Alto Garças, *Brazil* 173 D7 16 56 S 53 32W
Alto Garda Bresciano ⌂, *Italy* 44 C7 45 42N 10 38 E
Alto Iriri →, *Brazil* 173 B7 8 50 S 53 25W
Alto Ligonha, *Mozam.* 119 F4 15 30 S 38 11 E
Alto Molocue, *Mozam.* 119 F4 15 50 S 37 35 E
Alto Paraguai, *Brazil* 173 C6 14 30 S 56 31W
Alto Paraguay □, *Paraguay* 174 A4 21 0 S 58 30W
Alto Paraíso de Goiás, *Brazil* 171 D2 14 7 S 47 31W
Alto Paraná □, *Paraguay* 175 B5 25 30 S 54 50W
Alto Parnaíba, *Brazil* 170 C2 9 6 S 45 57W
Alto Purús →, *Peru* 172 B3 9 12 S 70 28W
Alto Río Senguerr, *Argentina* 176 C2 45 2 S 70 50W
Alto Santo, *Brazil* 170 C4 5 31 S 38 15W
Alto Sucuriú, *Brazil* 173 D7 19 19 S 52 47W
Alto Turi, *Brazil* 170 B2 2 54 S 45 38W
Alton, *Canada* 150 C4 43 54N 80 5W
Alton, *U.K.* 21 F7 51 9N 0 59W
Alton, *Ill., U.S.A.* 156 F6 38 53N 90 11W
Alton, *N.H., U.S.A.* 151 C13 43 27N 71 13W
Altona, *Canada* 143 D9 49 6N 97 33W
Altoona, *Ala., U.S.A.* 152 A3 34 2N 86 20W
Altoona, *Iowa, U.S.A.* 156 C3 41 39N 93 28W
Altoona, *Pa., U.S.A.* 150 F6 40 31N 78 24W
Altos, *Brazil* 170 C3 5 3 S 42 28W
Altötting, *Germany* 31 G8 48 12N 12 39 E
Altstätten, *Switz.* 33 B9 47 22N 9 33 E
Altun Kupri, *Iraq* 101 E11 35 45N 44 9 E
Altun Shan, *China* 68 C3 38 30N 88 0 E
Alturas, *U.S.A.* 158 F3 41 29N 120 32W
Altus, *U.S.A.* 155 H5 34 38N 99 20W
Alubijid, *Phil.* 81 G5 8 35N 124 29 E
Alucra, *Turkey* 101 B8 40 22N 38 47 E
Aluk, *Sudan* 107 F2 8 25N 27 30 E
Alūksne, *Latvia* 15 H22 57 24N 27 3 E
Alula, *Somali Rep.* 120 B4 11 50N 50 45 E
Alunda, *Sweden* 16 D12 60 4N 18 5 E
Alunite, *U.S.A.* 161 K12 35 59N 114 55W
Aluoro →, *Ethiopia* 107 F3 8 26N 33 24 E
Alupka, *Ukraine* 59 K8 44 23N 34 2 E
Alur, *India* 95 E3 15 24N 77 15 E
Alushta, *Ukraine* 59 K8 44 40N 34 25 E
Alusi, *Indonesia* 83 C4 7 35 S 131 40 E
Alustante, *Spain* 40 E3 40 36N 1 40W
Alutgama, *Sri Lanka* 95 L4 6 26N 79 59 E
Alutnuwara, *Sri Lanka* 95 L5 7 19N 80 59 E
Alva, *U.S.A.* 155 G5 36 48N 98 40W
Alvaiázere, *Portugal* 42 F2 39 49N 8 23W
Älvängen, *Sweden* 17 G6 57 58N 12 8 E
Alvão ⌂, *Portugal* 42 D3 41 22N 7 48W
Alvarado, *Mexico* 163 D5 18 40N 95 50W
Alvarado, *U.S.A.* 155 J6 32 24N 97 13W
Alvarães, *Brazil* 169 D5 3 12 S 64 50W
Alvaro Obregón, Presa, *Mexico* 162 B3 27 55N 109 52W
Alvdal, *Norway* 18 B7 62 6N 10 37 E
Älvdalen, *Sweden* 16 C8 61 13N 14 4 E
Alvear, *Argentina* 174 B4 29 5 S 56 30W
Alverca, *Portugal* 43 G1 38 56N 9 1W
Alvesta, *Sweden* 17 H8 56 54N 14 35 E
Ålvik, *Norway* 18 D3 60 26N 6 26 E
Alvin, *U.S.A.* 155 L7 29 26N 95 15W
Alvinston, *Canada* 150 D3 42 49N 81 52W
Alvito, *Portugal* 43 G3 38 15N 7 58W
Älvkarleby, *Sweden* 16 D11 60 34N 17 26 E
Alvorado, *Brazil* 171 D2 12 28 S 49 6W
Alvord Desert, *U.S.A.* 158 E4 42 30N 118 25W
Älvros, *Sweden* 16 B8 62 3N 14 38 E
Älvsbyn, *Sweden* 14 D19 65 40N 21 0 E
Ålvundeid, *Norway* 18 B5 62 45N 8 33 E
Alwar, *India* 92 F7 27 38N 76 34 E
Alwaye, *India* 95 J3 10 8N 76 24 E
Alxa Zuoqi, *China* 74 E3 38 50N 105 40 E
Alyangula, *Australia* 126 A2 13 55 S 136 30 E
Alyata = Älät, *Azerbaijan* 61 L9 39 58N 49 25 E
Alyth, *U.K.* 22 E5 56 38N 3 13W
Alytus, *Lithuania* 15 J21 54 24N 24 3 E
Alzada, *U.S.A.* 154 C2 45 2N 104 25W
Alzey, *Germany* 31 F4 49 45N 8 7 E
Alzira, *Spain* 41 F4 39 9N 0 30W
Am Dam, *Chad* 109 F4 12 40N 20 35 E
Am Géréda, *Chad* 109 F4 12 53N 21 14 E
Am Loubia, *Chad* 109 F4 13 39N 20 8 E
Am Timan, *Chad* 109 F4 11 0N 20 10 E
Amacayacu △, *Colombia* 168 D3 3 21 S 70 8W
Amada Gaza, *C.A.R.* 114 B3 4 46N 15 9 E
Amadeus, L., *Australia* 125 D5 24 54 S 131 0 E
Amadi, *Dem. Rep. of the Congo* 118 B2 3 40N 26 40 E
Amâdi, *Sudan* 107 F3 5 29N 30 25 E
Amadjuak L., *Canada* 139 B12 65 0N 71 8W
Amadora, *Portugal* 43 G1 38 45N 9 13W
Amagansett, *U.S.A.* 151 F12 40 59N 72 9W
Amagasaki, *Japan* 73 C7 34 42N 135 20 E
Amager, *Denmark* 17 J6 55 37N 12 35 E
Amagi, *Japan* 72 D2 33 25N 130 39 E
Amagunze, *Nigeria* 113 D6 6 20N 7 40 E
Amahai, *Indonesia* 83 C3 3 20 S 128 55 E
Amaile, *Samoa* 133 W24 13 59 S 171 22W
Amaimon, *Papua N. G.* 132 C3 5 12 S 145 30 E
Amakusa-Nada, *Japan* 72 E2 32 35N 130 5 E
Amakusa-Shotō, *Japan* 72 E2 32 15N 130 10 E
Åmål, *Sweden* 16 E6 59 3N 12 42 E
Amalapuram, *India* 95 F5 16 35N 81 55 E
Amalfi, *Colombia* 168 B2 6 55N 75 4W
Amalfi, *Italy* 47 B7 40 38N 14 36 E
Amaliás, *Greece* 48 D3 37 47N 21 22 E
Amalner, *India* 94 D2 21 5N 75 5 E
Amamapare, *Indonesia* 83 B5 4 53 S 136 38 E
Amambaí, *Brazil* 175 A4 23 5 S 55 13W
Amambaí →, *Brazil* 175 A5 23 22 S 53 56W
Amambay □, *Paraguay* 175 A4 23 0 S 56 0W
Amambay, Cordillera de, *S. Amer.* 175 A4 23 0 S 55 45W
Amami-Guntō, *Japan* 71 L4 27 16N 129 21 E
Amami-Ō-Shima, *Japan* 71 L4 28 0N 129 0 E
Aman, Pulau, *Malaysia* 87 c 5 16N 100 24 E
Amana →, *Venezuela* 169 B5 9 45N 62 39W
Amaná, L., *Brazil* 169 D5 2 35 S 64 40W
Amanab, *Papua N. G.* 132 B1 3 40 S 141 14 E
Amanat →, *India* 93 G11 24 7N 84 4 E
Amanda Park, *U.S.A.* 160 C3 47 28N 123 55W
Amangeldy, *Kazakhstan* 66 D7 50 10N 65 10 E
Amantea, *Italy* 47 C9 39 8N 16 4 E
Amapá, *Brazil* 169 C7 2 5N 50 50W
Amapá □, *Brazil* 169 C7 1 40N 52 0W
Amapari = Ferreira Gomes, *Brazil* 170 A1 0 48N 51 8W
Amapari, *Brazil* 169 C7 0 37N 51 39W
Amara, *Sudan* 107 E3 10 25N 34 10 E
Amara □, *Ethiopia* 107 E4 12 30N 37 30 E
Amaração = Luís Correia, *Brazil* 170 B3 3 0 S 41 35W
Amarante, *Brazil* 170 C3 6 14 S 42 50W
Amarante, *Portugal* 42 D2 41 16N 8 5W
Amarante do Maranhão, *Brazil* 170 C2 5 36 S 46 45W
Amaranth, *Canada* 143 C9 50 36N 98 43W
Amarapura, *Burma* 90 E6 21 54N 96 3 E
Amaravati →, *India* 95 J4 11 0N 78 15 E
Amareleja, *Portugal* 43 G3 38 12N 7 13W
Amargosa, *Brazil* 171 D4 13 2 S 39 36W
Amargosa →, *U.S.A.* 161 J10 36 14N 116 51W
Amargosa Range, *U.S.A.* 161 J10 36 20N 116 45W
Amári, *Greece* 39 E5 35 13N 24 40 E
Amarillo, *U.S.A.* 155 H4 35 13N 101 50W
Amarkantak, *India* 93 H9 22 40N 81 45 E
Amârna, Tell el', *Sudan* 106 B3 27 38N 30 52 E
Amarnath, *India* 94 E1 19 12N 73 22 E
Amaro, Mte., *Italy* 45 F11 42 5N 14 5 E
Amaro Leite, *Brazil* 171 D2 13 58 S 49 9W
Amarpur, *Bihar, India* 93 G12 25 5N 87 0 E
Amarpur, *Tripura, India* 90 D3 23 31N 91 39 E
Amarti, *Eritrea* 107 E5 14 17N 41 6 E
Amarwara, *India* 93 H8 22 18N 79 10 E
Amasin, *W. Sahara* 110 C2 25 45N 13 20W
Amasra, *Turkey* 100 B5 41 45N 32 23 E
Amassama, *Nigeria* 113 D6 5 1N 6 2 E
Amasya, *Turkey* 100 B6 40 40N 35 50 E
Amata, *Australia* 125 E5 26 9 S 131 9 E
Amataurá, *Brazil* 168 D4 3 29 S 68 6W
Amatignak I., *U.S.A.* 144 L3 51 16N 179 6W
Amatikulu, *S. Africa* 117 D5 29 3 S 31 33 E
Amatitlán, *Guatemala* 164 D1 14 29N 90 38W
Amatrice, *Italy* 45 F10 42 38N 13 17 E
Amau, *Papua N. G.* 132 F5 10 2 S 148 34 E
Amay, *Belgium* 24 D5 50 33N 5 19 E
Amazon = Amazonas →, *S. Amer.* 169 D7 0 5 S 50 0W
Amazonas □, *Brazil* 173 B5 5 0 S 65 0W
Amazonas □, *Peru* 172 B2 5 0 S 78 0W
Amazonas □, *Venezuela* 168 C4 3 30N 66 0W
Amazonas →, *S. Amer.* 169 D7 0 5 S 50 0W
Amba Ferit, *Ethiopia* 107 E4 10 55N 38 50 E
Ambad, *India* 94 E2 19 38N 75 50 E
Ambagarh Chowki, *India* 94 D5 20 47N 80 43 E
Ambah, *India* 92 F8 26 43N 78 13 E
Ambahakily, *Madag.* 117 C7 21 36 S 43 41 E
Ambahita, *Madag.* 117 C8 24 1 S 45 16 E
Ambajogal, *India* 94 E3 18 44N 76 23 E
Ambala, *India* 92 D7 30 23N 76 56 E
Ambalangoda, *Sri Lanka* 95 L5 6 15N 80 5 E
Ambalapulai, *India* 95 K3 9 25N 76 25 E
Ambalavao, *Madag.* 117 C8 21 50 S 46 56 E
Ambam, *Cameroon* 114 B2 2 20N 11 15 E
Ambanja, *Madag.* 117 A8 13 40 S 48 27 E
Ambararata, *Madag.* 117 B8 15 3 S 48 33 E
Ambarchik, *Russia* 67 C17 69 40N 162 20 E
Ambarijeby, *Madag.* 117 A8 14 56 S 47 41 E
Ambaro, Helodranon', *Madag.* 117 A8 13 23 S 48 38 E
Ambasamudram, *India* 95 K3 8 43N 77 25 E
Ambato, *Ecuador* 168 D2 1 5 S 78 42W
Ambato, *Madag.* 117 A8 13 24 S 48 29 E
Ambato, Sierra de, *Argentina* 174 B2 28 25 S 66 10W
Ambato Boeny, *Madag.* 117 B8 16 28 S 46 43 E
Ambatofinandrahana, *Madag.* 117 C8 20 33 S 46 48 E
Ambatolampy, *Madag.* 117 B8 19 20 S 47 35 E
Ambatomainty, *Madag.* 117 B8 17 41 S 45 40 E
Ambatomanoina, *Madag.* 117 B8 18 18 S 47 37 E
Ambatondrazaka, *Madag.* 117 B8 17 55 S 48 28 E
Ambatosoratra, *Madag.* 117 B8 17 37 S 48 31 E
Ambelau, *Indonesia* 82 B3 3 51 S 127 12 E
Ambelón, *Greece* 48 B4 39 45N 22 22 E
Ambenja, *Madag.* 117 B8 15 17 S 46 58 E
Amberg, *Germany* 31 F7 49 26N 11 52 E
Ambergris Cay, *Belize* 163 D7 18 0N 87 55W
Ambérieu-en-Bugey, *France* 29 C9 45 57N 5 20 E
Amberley, *N.Z.* 131 D7 43 9 S 172 44 E
Ambert, *France* 28 C7 45 33N 3 44 E
Ambidédi, *Mali* 112 C2 14 35N 11 47W
Ambikapur, *India* 93 H10 23 15N 83 15 E
Ambikol, *Sudan* 106 C3 21 20N 30 50 E
Ambilobé, *Madag.* 117 A8 13 10 S 49 3 E
Ambinanindrano, *Madag.* 117 C8 20 5 S 48 23 E
Ambinanitelo, *Madag.* 117 B8 15 21 S 49 35 E
Ambinda, *Madag.* 117 B8 16 25 S 45 52 E
Ambitle I., *Papua N. G.* 132 C7 4 5 S 153 37 E
Amble, *U.K.* 20 B6 55 20N 1 36W
Ambler, *U.S.A.* 144 C8 67 5N 157 52W
Ambleside, *U.K.* 20 C5 54 26N 2 58W
Ambo, *Peru* 172 C2 10 5 S 76 10W
Amboahangy, *Madag.* 117 C8 24 15 S 46 22 E
Ambodifototra, *Madag.* 117 B8 16 59 S 49 52 E
Ambodilazana, *Madag.* 117 B8 18 6 S 49 10 E
Ambodiriana, *Madag.* 117 B8 17 55 S 49 18 E
Ambohidratrimo, *Madag.* 117 B8 18 50 S 47 26 E
Ambohidray, *Madag.* 117 B8 18 36 S 48 18 E
Ambohimahamasina, *Madag.* 117 C8 21 56 S 47 11 E
Ambohimahasoa, *Madag.* 117 C8 21 7 S 47 13 E
Ambohimanga, *Madag.* 117 C8 20 52 S 47 36 E
Ambohimitombo, *Madag.* 117 C8 20 43 S 47 26 E
Ambohitra, *Madag.* 117 A8 12 30 S 49 10 E
Amboise, *France* 26 E8 47 24N 1 2 E
Amboiva, *Angola* 115 E2 11 33 S 14 43 E
Ambon, *Indonesia* 82 B3 3 43 S 128 12 E
Ambondro, *Madag.* 117 D8 25 13 S 45 44 E
Amboró △, *Bolivia* 173 D5 17 39 S 64 3W
Amboseli △, *Kenya* 118 C4 2 37 S 37 13 E
Amboseli, L., *Kenya* 118 C4 2 40 S 37 10 E
Ambositra, *Madag.* 117 C8 20 31 S 47 25 E
Ambovombe, *Madag.* 117 D8 25 11 S 46 5 E
Amboy, *Calif., U.S.A.* 161 L11 34 33N 115 45W
Amboy, *Ill., U.S.A.* 156 C7 41 44N 89 20W
Amboyna Cay, *S. China Sea* 78 C4 7 50N 112 50 E
Ambridge, *U.S.A.* 150 F4 40 36N 80 14W
Ambriz, *Angola* 115 D2 7 48 S 13 8 E
Ambriz ⌂, *Angola* 115 D2 7 56 S 10 27 E
Ambrym, *Vanuatu* 133 F6 16 15 S 168 10 E
Ambunti, *Papua N. G.* 132 C2 4 13 S 142 52 E
Ambur, *India* 95 H4 12 48N 78 43 E
Amchitka I., *U.S.A.* 144 L2 51 32N 179 0 E
Amderma, *Russia* 66 C7 69 45N 61 30 E
Amdhi, *India* 93 H9 23 51N 81 27 E
Ameca, *Mexico* 162 C4 20 30N 104 0W
Ameca →, *Mexico* 162 C3 20 40N 105 15W
Amecameca, *Mexico* 163 D5 19 7N 98 46W
Ameland, *Neths.* 24 A5 53 27N 5 45 E
Amélia, *Italy* 45 F9 42 33N 12 25 E
Amelia City, *U.S.A.* 152 E8 30 35N 81 28W
Amelia I., *U.S.A.* 152 E8 30 40N 81 25W
Amendolara, *Italy* 47 C9 39 57N 16 35 E
Amenia, *U.S.A.* 151 E11 41 51N 73 33W
American Falls, *U.S.A.* 158 E7 42 47N 112 51W
American Falls Reservoir, *U.S.A.* 158 E7 42 47N 112 52W
American Fork, *U.S.A.* 158 F8 40 23N 111 48W
American Highland, *Antarctica* 7 D6 73 0 S 75 0 E
American River, *Australia* 128 C2 35 47 S 137 46 E
American Samoa △, *Amer. Samoa* 133 X24 14 15 S 170 28W
American Samoa ☒, *Pac. Oc.* 133 X24 14 20 S 170 40W
Americana, *Brazil* 175 A6 22 45 S 47 20W
Americus, *U.S.A.* 152 C5 32 4N 84 14W
Amerigo Vespucci, Firenze ✈ (FLR), *Italy* 44 E8 43 49N 11 13 E
Amerika = Nakhodka, *Russia* 67 E14 42 53N 132 54 E
Amersfoort, *Neths.* 24 B5 52 9N 5 23 E
Amersfoort, *S. Africa* 117 D4 26 59 S 29 53 E
Amery Ice Shelf, *Antarctica* 7 C6 69 30 S 72 0 E
Amerzgane, *Morocco* 110 B3 31 4N 7 14W
Ames, *Spain* 42 C2 42 54N 8 38W
Ames, *U.S.A.* 156 C3 42 2N 93 37W
Amesbury, *U.S.A.* 151 D14 42 51N 70 56W
Amet, *India* 92 G5 25 18N 73 56 E
Amfíklia, *Greece* 48 C4 38 38N 22 35 E
Amfilokhía, *Greece* 48 C3 38 52N 21 9 E
Amfípolis, *Greece* 50 F7 40 48N 23 52 E
Ámfissa, *Greece* 48 C4 38 32N 22 22 E
Amga, *Russia* 67 C14 60 50N 132 0 E
Amga →, *Russia* 67 C14 62 38N 134 32 E
Amgaon, *India* 94 D5 21 22N 80 22 E
Amgu, *Russia* 67 E14 45 45N 137 15 E
Amgun →, *Russia* 67 D14 52 56N 139 38 E
Amherst = Kyaikkami, *Burma* 90 G6 16 4N 97 34 E
Amherst, *Canada* 141 C7 45 48N 64 8W
Amherst, *Mass., U.S.A.* 151 D12 42 23N 72 31W
Amherst, *N.Y., U.S.A.* 150 D6 42 59N 78 48W
Amherst, *Ohio, U.S.A.* 150 E2 41 24N 82 14W
Amherst I., *Canada* 151 B8 44 8N 76 43W
Amherstburg, *Canada* 140 D3 42 6N 83 6W
Amiata, Mte., *Italy* 45 F8 42 53N 11 37 E
Amidon, *U.S.A.* 154 B3 46 29N 103 19W
Amiens, *France* 27 C9 49 54N 2 16 E
Amili, *India* 90 A5 28 25N 95 52 E
Amindaion, *Greece* 50 F5 40 42N 21 42 E
Amindivi Is., *India* 95 J1 11 23N 72 23 E
Amingaon, *India* 90 B3 26 11N 91 40 E
Amini I., *India* 95 J1 11 6N 72 45 E
Åminne, *Sweden* 17 G7 57 7N 14 0 E
Amino, *Ethiopia* 107 G5 4 25N 41 52 E
Aminuis, *Namibia* 116 C2 23 43 S 19 21 E
Amîr, Ra's, *Libya* 108 B4 32 57N 21 43 E
Amīrābād, *Iran* 96 C5 33 20N 46 16 E
Amirante Is., *Seychelles* 121 E4 6 0 S 53 0 E
Amisk ⌂, *Canada* 143 B9 56 43N 98 0W
Amisk L., *Canada* 143 C8 54 35N 102 15W
Amistad ⌂, *U.S.A.* 155 L4 29 32N 101 12W
Amistad, Presa de la, *Mexico* 162 B4 29 24N 101 0W
Amite, *U.S.A.* 155 K9 30 44N 90 30W
Amizmiz, *Morocco* 110 B3 31 12N 8 15W
Amla, *India* 92 J8 21 56N 78 7 E
Amlapura = Karangasem, *Indonesia* 79 J18 8 27 S 115 37 E
Åmli, *Norway* 18 F5 58 45N 8 32 E
Amlia I., *U.S.A.* 144 K4 52 4N 173 30W
Amlwch, *U.K.* 20 D3 53 24N 4 20W
Amm Adam, *Sudan* 107 D4 16 20N 36 1 E
'Ammān, *Jordan* 103 D4 31 57N 35 52 E
'Ammān □, *Jordan* 103 D5 31 40N 36 30 E
'Ammān ✈ (AMM), *Jordan* 103 D5 31 45N 36 2 E
Ammanford, *U.K.* 21 F4 51 48N 3 59W
Ammassalik = Tasiilaq, *Greenland* 10 D7 65 40N 37 20W
Ammerån →, *Sweden* 16 A10 63 9N 16 13 E
Ammersee, *Germany* 31 G7 48 0N 11 7 E
Ammochostos = Famagusta, *Cyprus* 39 E9 35 8N 33 55 E
Ammon, *U.S.A.* 158 E8 43 28N 111 58W
Amnat Charoen, *Thailand* 86 E5 15 51N 104 38 E
Amnura, *Bangla.* 93 G13 24 37N 88 25 E
Amo Jiang →, *China* 76 F3 23 0N 101 50 E
Āmol, *Iran* 97 B7 36 23N 52 20 E
Amoret, *U.S.A.* 156 F2 38 15N 94 35W
Amorgós, *Greece* 49 E7 36 50N 25 57 E
Amory, *U.S.A.* 149 J1 33 59N 88 29W
Amos, *Canada* 140 C4 48 35N 78 5W
Åmot, *Buskerud, Norway* 18 E6 59 57N 9 54 E
Åmot, *Oppland, Norway* 18 D7 61 0N 10 2 E
Åmot, *Telemark, Norway* 18 E5 59 34N 8 0 E
Åmotfors, *Sweden* 16 E6 59 47N 12 22 E
Åmotsdal, *Norway* 18 E5 59 37N 8 26 E
Amour, Djebel, *Algeria* 111 B5 33 42N 1 37 E
Amoy = Xiamen, *China* 77 E12 24 25N 118 4 E
Ampanavoana, *Madag.* 117 B9 15 41 S 50 22 E
Ampang, *Malaysia* 87 L3 3 8N 101 45 E
Ampangalana, Lakandranon', *Madag.* 117 C8 22 48 S 47 50 E
Ampani, *India* 94 E6 19 35N 82 38 E
Ampanihy, *Madag.* 117 C7 24 40 S 44 45 E
Amparafaravola, *Madag.* 117 B8 17 35 S 48 13 E
Ampasinambo, *Madag.* 117 C8 20 31 S 48 0 E
Ampasindava, Helodranon', *Madag.* 117 A8 13 40 S 48 15 E
Ampasindava, Saikanosy, *Madag.* 117 A8 13 42 S 47 55 E
Ampato, Nevado, *Peru* 172 D3 15 40 S 71 56W
Ampenan, *Indonesia* 85 D5 8 34 S 116 4 E
Amper, *Nigeria* 113 D6 9 25N 9 40 E
Amper →, *Germany* 31 G7 48 29N 11 55 E
Ampezzo, *Italy* 45 B9 46 25N 12 48 E
Amphoe Kathu, *Thailand* 87 a 7 55N 98 21 E
Amphoe Thalang, *Thailand* 87 a 8 1N 98 20 E
Ampitsikinana, *Réunion* 117 A8 12 57 S 49 49 E
Ampombiantambo, *Madag.* 117 A8 12 42 S 48 57 E
Amposta, *Spain* 40 E5 40 43N 0 34 E
Ampotaka, *Madag.* 117 D7 25 3 S 44 41 E
Ampoza, *Madag.* 117 C7 22 20 S 44 44 E
Amqui, *Canada* 141 C6 48 28N 67 27W
Amrabad, *India* 95 F4 16 23N 78 50 E
'Amrān, *Yemen* 98 D3 15 41N 43 55 E
Amraoti = Amravati, *India* 94 D3 20 55N 77 45 E
Amravati, *India* 94 D3 20 55N 77 45 E
Amreli, *India* 92 J4 21 35N 71 17 E
Amrenene el Kasba, *Algeria* 111 D5 22 10N 0 30 E
Amriswil, *Switz.* 33 A8 47 33N 9 18 E
Amritsar, *India* 92 D6 31 35N 74 57 E
Amroha, *India* 93 E8 28 53N 78 30 E
Amrum, *Germany* 30 A4 54 38N 8 22 E
Amsâga, *Mauritania* 110 D2 20 7N 14 10W
Amsel, *Algeria* 111 D6 22 47N 5 29 E
Amsterdam, *Neths.* 24 B4 52 23N 4 54 E
Amsterdam, *U.S.A.* 151 D10 42 56N 74 11W
Amsterdam ✈ (AMS), *Neths.* 24 B4 52 18N 4 45 E
Amsterdam, I. = Nouvelle-Amsterdam, Î., *Ind. Oc.* 121 H6 38 30 S 77 30 E
Amstetten, *Austria* 34 C7 48 7N 14 51 E
Amudarya, *Turkmenistan* 65 E2 37 53N 65 15 E
Amudarya →, *Uzbekistan* 66 E6 43 58N 59 34 E
Amukta I., *U.S.A.* 144 K5 52 30N 171 16W
Amukta Pass, *U.S.A.* 144 L5 52 0N 171 0W
Amulung, *Phil.* 80 C3 17 50N 121 43 E
Amundsen Gulf, *Canada* 138 A7 71 0N 124 0W
Amundsen-Scott, *Antarctica* 7 E 90 0 S 166 0 E
Amundsen Sea, *Antarctica* 7 D15 72 0 S 115 0W
Amungen, *Sweden* 16 C9 61 10N 15 40 E
Amuntai, *Indonesia* 85 C5 2 28 S 115 25 E
Amur, *Somali Rep.* 120 C3 5 16N 46 30 E
Amur →, *Russia* 67 D15 52 56N 141 10 E
Amur, W. →, *Sudan* 106 D3 18 56N 33 34 E
Amurang, *Indonesia* 82 A2 1 5N 124 40 E
Amurrio, *Spain* 40 B1 43 3N 3 0W
Amursk, *Russia* 67 D14 50 14N 136 54 E
Amusco, *Spain* 42 C6 42 10N 4 28W
Amvrakikós Kólpos, *Greece* 48 C2 39 0N 20 55 E
Amvrosiyivka, *Ukraine* 59 J10 47 43N 38 30 E
Amyderya = Amudarya →, *Uzbekistan* 66 E6 43 58N 59 34 E
Amzeglouf, *Algeria* 111 C5 26 50N 0 1 E
An, *Burma* 90 F5 19 48N 94 0 E
An Anbār □, *Iraq* 96 C4 33 25N 42 0 E
An Bien, *Vietnam* 87 H5 9 45N 105 0 E
An Hoa, *Vietnam* 86 E7 15 40N 108 5 E
An Nabatīyah at Tahta, *Lebanon* 103 B4 33 23N 35 27 E
An Nabk, *Si. Arabia* 96 D3 31 20N 37 20 E
An Nabk, *Syria* 103 A5 34 2N 36 44 E
An Nafūd, *Si. Arabia* 96 D4 28 15N 41 0 E
An Najaf, *Iraq* 101 G11 32 3N 44 15 E
An Nāṣirīyah, *Iraq* 96 D5 31 0N 46 15 E
An Nawfaliyah, *Libya* 108 B3 30 54N 17 58 E
An Nhon, *Vietnam* 86 F7 13 55N 109 7 E
An Nîl □, *Sudan* 106 D3 19 30N 33 0 E
An Nîl el Abyad □, *Sudan* 107 E3 14 0N 32 15 E
An Nîl el Azraq □, *Sudan* 107 E3 11 30N 34 30 E
An Nimāş, *Si. Arabia* 98 C3 19 7N 42 8 E
An Nu'ayrīyah, *Si. Arabia* 97 E6 27 30N 48 30 E
An Nu'māniyah, *Iraq* 101 F11 32 32N 45 25 E
An Nuwayb'ī, W. →, *Si. Arabia* 103 F3 29 18N 34 57 E
An Thoi, Dao, *Vietnam* 87 H4 9 58N 104 0 E
An Uaimh, *Ireland* 23 C5 53 39N 6 41W
Åna-Sira, *Norway* 18 F3 58 17N 6 25 E
Anabanua, *Indonesia* 82 B2 3 57 S 120 4 E
Anabar →, *Russia* 67 B12 73 8N 113 36 E
'Anabtā, *West Bank* 103 C4 32 19N 35 7 E
Anaco, *Venezuela* 169 B5 9 27N 64 28W
Anaconda, *U.S.A.* 158 C7 46 8N 112 57W
Anacortes, *U.S.A.* 160 B4 48 30N 122 37W
Anacuao, Mt., *Phil.* 80 C3 16 16N 121 53 E
Anadarko, *U.S.A.* 155 H5 35 4N 98 15W
Anadia, *Brazil* 170 C4 9 42 S 36 18W
Anadia, *Portugal* 42 E2 40 26N 8 27W
Anadolu, *Turkey* 100 C5 39 0N 30 0 E
Anadyr, *Russia* 67 C18 64 35N 177 20 E
Anadyr →, *Russia* 67 C18 64 55N 176 5 E
Anadyrskiy Zaliv, *Russia* 67 C19 64 0N 180 0 E
Anáfi, *Greece* 49 E7 36 22N 25 48 E
Anafonítria, *Greece* 39 D2 37 51N 20 39 E
Anafópoulo, *Greece* 49 E7 36 17N 25 50 E
Anaga, Pta. de, *Canary Is.* 9 e1 28 34N 16 9W
Anagni, *Italy* 45 G10 41 44N 13 9 E
'Ānah, *Iraq* 101 E10 34 25N 42 0 E
Anahalu →, *U.S.A.* 145 J13 21 37N 158 6W
Anaheim, *U.S.A.* 161 M9 33 50N 117 55W
Anahim Lake, *Canada* 142 C3 52 28N 125 18W
Anahola, *U.S.A.* 145 A2 22 9N 159 19W
Anáhuac, *Mexico* 162 B4 27 14N 100 9W
Anai Mudi, *India* 95 J3 10 12N 77 4 E
Anaichak ⌂, *U.S.A.* 144 H8 56 50N 157 50W
Anaimalai Hills, *India* 95 J3 10 20N 76 40 E
Anajás, *Brazil* 170 B2 0 59 S 49 57W
Anajatuba, *Brazil* 170 B3 3 16 S 44 37W
Anakapalle, *India* 94 F6 17 42N 83 6 E
Anakena, *Chile* 172 b 27 5 S 109 20W
Anakie, *Australia* 126 C4 23 32 S 147 45 E
Anaklia, *Georgia* 61 J5 42 22N 41 35 E
Anaktuvuk Pass, *U.S.A.* 144 B10 68 8N 151 45W
Analalava, *Madag.* 117 A8 14 35 S 48 0 E
Analavoka, *Madag.* 117 C8 22 23 S 46 30 E
Análipsis, *Greece* 38 B9 39 36N 19 55 E
Anamã, *Brazil* 169 D5 3 35 S 61 22W
Anambar →, *Pakistan* 92 D3 30 15N 68 50 E
Anambas, Kepulauan, *Indonesia* 84 B3 3 20N 106 30 E
Anambas Is. = Anambas, Kepulauan, *Indonesia* 84 B3 3 20N 106 30 E
Anambra □, *Nigeria* 113 D6 6 20N 7 0 E
Aname, *Vanuatu* 133 K7 20 8 S 169 47 E
Anamosa, *U.S.A.* 156 B5 42 7N 91 17W
Anamur, *Turkey* 100 D5 36 8N 32 58 E
Anamur Burnu, *Turkey* 100 D5 36 2N 32 47 E
Anan, *Japan* 72 D6 33 54N 134 40 E
Anand, *India* 92 H5 22 32N 72 59 E
Anandapuram, *India* 95 G2 14 5N 75 12 E
Anandpur, *India* 94 D8 21 16N 86 13 E
Anánes, *Greece* 48 E6 36 33N 24 9 E
Anantapur, *India* 95 G3 14 39N 77 42 E
Anantnag, *India* 93 C6 33 45N 75 10 E
Ananyevo, *Kyrgyzstan* 65 B8 42 45N 77 40 E
Ananyiv, *Ukraine* 53 C14 47 44N 29 58 E
Anapa, *Russia* 59 K9 44 55N 37 25 E
Anapodháris →, *Greece* 39 F6 34 59N 25 20 E
Anápolis = Simão Dias, *Brazil* 170 D4 10 44 S 37 49W
Anápolis, *Brazil* 171 E2 16 15 S 48 50W
Anapu →, *Brazil* 169 D7 1 53 S 50 53W
Anār, *Iran* 97 D7 30 55N 55 13 E

Anār Darreh, Afghan. 91 B1 32 46N 61 39 E
Anārak, Iran 97 C7 33 25N 53 40 E
Anarisfjällen, Sweden 16 A7 63 6N 13 10 E
Anas →, India 92 H5 23 26N 74 0 E
Anatolia = Anadolu, Turkey 100 C5 39 0N 30 0 E
Anatsogno, Madag. 117 C7 23 33 S 43 46 E
Añatuya, Argentina 174 B3 28 20 S 62 50W
Anauá →, Brazil 169 C5 0 58N 61 21W
Anaunethad L., Canada 143 A8 60 55N 104 25W
Anavilhanas, Arquipélago das, Brazil 169 D5 2 42 S 60 45W
Anaye, Niger 109 E2 19 15N 12 50 E
Anbyŏn, N. Korea 75 E14 39 1N 127 35 E
Ancares ⌓, Spain 42 C4 42 50N 6 40W
Ancares, Sierra de, Spain 42 C4 42 51N 6 52W
Ancash □, Peru 172 B2 9 30 S 77 45W
Ancaster, Canada 150 C5 43 13N 79 59W
Ancenis, France 26 E5 47 21N 1 10W
Anchieta = Piatã, Brazil 171 D3 13 9 S 41 48W
Anch'ing = Anqing, China 77 B11 30 30N 117 3 E
Ancho, Canal, Chile 176 D2 50 0 S 74 20W
Anchor Bay, U.S.A. 160 G3 38 48N 123 34W
Anchorage, U.S.A. 144 F10 61 13N 149 54W
Anci, China 74 E9 39 20N 116 40 E
Ancohuma, Nevado, Bolivia 172 D4 16 0 S 68 50W
Ancón, Peru 172 C2 11 50 S 77 10W
Ancona, Italy 45 E10 43 38N 13 30 E
Ancud, Chile 176 B2 42 0 S 73 50W
Ancud, G. de, Chile 176 B2 42 0 S 73 0W
Ancy-le-Franc, France 27 E11 47 46N 4 10 E
Anda, China 69 B7 46 24N 125 19 E
Anda, Phil. 80 C2 16 17N 119 57 E
Andacollo, Argentina 174 D1 37 10 S 70 42W
Andacollo, Chile 174 C1 30 14 S 71 6W
Andahuaylas, Peru 172 C3 13 40 S 73 25W
Andaingo, Madag. 117 B8 18 12 S 48 17 E
Andalgalá, Argentina 174 B2 27 40 S 66 30W
Åndalsnes, Norway 18 B4 62 35N 7 43 E
Andalucía □, Spain 43 H6 37 35N 5 0W
Andalusia = Andalucía □, Spain 43 H6 37 35N 5 0W
Andalusia, U.S.A. 149 K2 31 18N 86 29W
Andaman & Nicobar Is. □, India 95 K11 10 0N 93 0 E
Andaman Is., Ind. Oc. 95 H11 12 30N 92 45 E
Andaman Sea, Ind. Oc. 78 B1 13 0N 96 0 E
Andamooka Opal Fields, Australia 127 E2 30 27 S 137 9 E
Andapa, Madag. 117 A8 14 39 S 49 39 E
Andara, Namibia 116 B3 18 2 S 21 9 E
Andaraí, Brazil 171 D3 12 48 S 41 20W
Andeer, Switz. 33 C8 46 36N 9 26 E
Andelfingen, Switz. 33 A7 47 36N 8 41 E
Andelot-Blancheville, France 27 D12 48 15N 5 18 E
Andenes, Norway 14 B17 69 19N 16 18 E
Andenne, Belgium 24 D5 50 28N 5 5 E
Andéranboukane, Mali 113 B5 15 26N 3 2 E
Andermatt, Switz. 33 C7 46 38N 8 35 E
Andernach, Germany 30 E3 50 26N 7 24 E
Andernos-les-Bains, France 28 D2 44 44N 1 6W
Anderslöv, Sweden 17 J7 55 26N 13 19 E
Anderson, Alaska, U.S.A. 144 D10 64 25N 149 15W
Anderson, Calif., U.S.A. 158 F2 40 27N 122 18W
Anderson, Ind., U.S.A. 157 D11 40 10N 85 41W
Anderson, Mo., U.S.A. 155 G7 36 39N 94 27W
Anderson, S.C., U.S.A. 149 H4 34 31N 82 39W
Anderson →, Canada 138 B7 69 42N 129 0W
Anderson I., India 95 H11 12 46N 92 43 E
Andersonville, U.S.A. 152 C5 32 12N 84 9W
Andersonville ⌓, U.S.A. 152 C5 32 12N 84 8W
Anderstorp, Sweden 17 G7 57 19N 13 39 E
Andes, Colombia 168 B2 5 39N 75 54W
Andes, U.S.A. 151 D10 42 12N 74 47W
Andes, Cord. de los, S. Amer. 172 C3 20 0 S 68 0W
Andfjorden, Norway 14 B17 69 10N 16 20 E
Andhra, L., India 94 E1 18 54N 73 32 E
Andhra Pradesh □, India 94 F4 18 0N 79 0 E
Andijon, Uzbekistan 65 C6 41 10N 72 15 E
Andikíthira, Greece 48 F5 35 52N 23 15 E
Andilamena, Madag. 117 B8 17 1 S 48 35 E
Andīmeshk, Iran 97 C6 32 27N 48 21 E
Andímilos, Greece 48 E6 36 47N 24 12 E
Andíparos, Greece 49 D7 37 0N 25 3 E
Andípaxoi, Greece 48 B2 39 9N 20 13 E
Andípsara, Greece 49 C7 38 30N 25 29 E
Andírrion, Greece 48 C3 38 20N 21 46 E
Andizhan = Andijon, Uzbekistan 65 C6 41 10N 72 15 E
Andkhvoy, Afghan. 65 E2 36 52N 65 8 E
Andoain, Spain 40 B2 43 13N 2 1W
Andoany, Madag. 117 A8 13 25 S 48 16 E
Andoas, Peru 168 D2 2 55 S 76 25W
Andohahela ⌓, Madag. 117 C8 24 4 S 46 44 E
Andol, India 94 F4 17 51N 78 4 E
Andola, India 94 F3 16 57N 76 50 E
Andong, S. Korea 75 F15 36 40N 128 43 E
Andongwei, China 75 G10 35 6N 119 20 E
Andoom, Australia 126 A3 12 25 S 141 53 E
Andorra, Spain 40 E4 40 59N 0 28W
Andorra ■, Europe 28 F5 42 30N 1 30 E
Andorra La Vella, Andorra 28 F5 42 31N 1 32 E
Andover, U.K. 21 F6 51 12N 1 29W
Andover, Maine, U.S.A. 151 B14 44 38N 70 45W
Andover, Mass., U.S.A. 151 D13 42 40N 71 8W
Andover, N.J., U.S.A. 151 F10 40 59N 74 45W
Andover, N.Y., U.S.A. 150 D7 42 10N 77 48W
Andover, Ohio, U.S.A. 150 E4 41 36N 80 34W
Andøya, Norway 14 B16 69 10N 15 50 E
Andrade, Brazil 169 D5 4 40 S 63 45W
Andradina, Brazil 171 F1 20 54 S 51 23W
Andrahary, Mt., Madag. 117 A8 13 37 S 49 17 E
Andramasina, Madag. 117 B8 19 11 S 47 35 E
Andranopasy, Madag. 117 C7 21 17 S 43 44 E
Andranovory, Madag. 117 C7 23 8 S 44 10 E
Andratx, Spain 38 B3 39 39N 2 25 E
André Félix △, C.A.R. 114 A4 9 29N 23 18 E
Andreanof Is., U.S.A. 144 L4 51 30N 176 0W
Andreapol, Russia 58 D7 56 40N 32 17 E
Andrée Land, Greenland 10 C8 73 40N 26 0W
Andrews, S.C., U.S.A. 149 J6 33 27N 79 34W
Andrews, Tex., U.S.A. 155 J3 32 19N 102 33W
Andreyev = Jędrzejów, Poland 55 H7 50 35N 20 15 E
Andreyevka, Russia 60 D10 52 19N 51 55 E
Ándria, Italy 47 A9 41 13N 16 17 E
Andriamena, Madag. 117 B8 17 26 S 47 30 E
Andriandampy, Madag. 117 C8 22 45 S 45 41 E
Andriba, Madag. 117 B8 17 30 S 46 58 E
Andrijevica, Serbia & M. 50 D3 42 45N 19 48 E
Andringitra ⌓, Madag. 117 C8 22 13 S 46 5 E
Andrítsaina, Greece 48 D3 37 29N 21 52 E
Androka, Madag. 117 C7 24 58 S 44 2 E
Andropov = Rybinsk, Russia 58 C10 58 5N 38 50 E
Ándros, Greece 48 D6 37 50N 24 57 E
Andros I., Bahamas 164 B4 24 30N 78 0W
Andros Town, Bahamas 164 B4 24 43N 77 47W
Androscoggin →, U.S.A. 151 C14 43 58N 70 0W
Androth I., India 95 J1 10 50N 73 41 E
Andrychów, Poland 55 J6 49 51N 19 18 E
Andselv, Norway 14 B18 69 4N 18 34 E
Andújar, Spain 43 G6 38 3N 4 5W
Andulo, Angola 115 E3 11 25 S 16 45 E
Åneby, Norway 18 D7 60 5N 10 51 E
Aneby, Sweden 17 G8 57 48N 14 49 E
Anegada, Br. Virgin Is. 165 e 18 45N 64 20W
Anegada, B., Argentina 176 B4 40 20 S 62 20W
Anegada Passage, W. Indies 165 C7 18 15N 63 45W
Aného, Togo 113 D5 6 12N 1 34 E
Aneityum, Vanuatu 133 K7 20 12 S 169 45 E
Anelghowhat, Vanuatu 133 K7 20 19 S 169 43 E
Añelo, Argentina 176 A3 38 20 S 68 45W
Anenni-Noi, Moldova 53 D14 46 53N 29 15 E
Aneto, Pico de, Spain 40 C5 42 37N 0 40 E
Añez, Bolivia 173 D5 15 40 S 63 10W
Anfu, China 77 D10 27 21N 114 40 E
Ang Mo Kio, Singapore 87 d 1 23N 103 50 E
Ang Thong, Thailand 86 E3 14 35N 100 31 E
Ang Thong △, Thailand 87 H2 9 40N 99 43 E
Ang Thong, Ko, Thailand 87 b 9 37N 99 41 E
Angadanan, Phil. 80 C3 16 45N 121 45 E
Angamos, Punta, Chile 174 A1 23 1 S 70 32W
Angara →, Russia 67 D10 58 5N 94 20 E
Angara-Débou, Benin 113 C5 11 19N 3 3 E
Angarab, Ethiopia 107 E4 13 11N 37 7 E
Angarbaka, Sudan 107 F1 9 44N 24 44 E
Angarsk, Russia 67 D11 52 30N 104 0 E
Angas Hills, Australia 124 D4 23 0 S 127 50 E
Angaston, Australia 128 C3 34 30 S 139 8 E
Angat, Phil. 80 D3 14 56N 121 2 E
Ånge, Sweden 16 B9 62 31N 15 35 E
Ángel, Salto = Angel Falls, Venezuela 169 B5 5 57N 62 30W
Ángel de la Guarda, I., Mexico 162 B2 29 30N 113 30W
Angel Falls, Venezuela 169 B5 5 57N 62 30W
Angeles, Phil. 80 D3 15 9N 120 33 E
Ängelholm, Sweden 17 H6 56 15N 12 58 E
Angels Camp, U.S.A. 160 G6 38 4N 120 32W
Ängelsberg, Sweden 16 E10 59 58N 16 0 E
Anger →, Ethiopia 107 F4 9 37N 36 6 E
Angerburg = Węgorzewo, Poland 54 D8 54 13N 21 43 E
Angereb →, Ethiopia 107 E4 13 45N 36 40 E
Ångermanälven →, Sweden 16 B11 62 40N 18 0 E
Ångermanland, Sweden 14 E18 63 36N 17 45 E
Angermünde, Germany 30 B9 53 0N 14 0 E
Angers, Canada 151 A9 45 31N 75 29W
Angers, France 26 E6 47 30N 0 35W
Angerville, France 27 D9 48 19N 2 0 E
Ängesån →, Sweden 14 C20 66 16N 22 47 E
Angical, Brazil 171 D3 12 0 S 44 42W
Angikuni L., Canada 143 A9 62 12N 99 59W
Angkor, Cambodia 86 F4 13 22N 103 50 E
Anglem, Mt., N.Z. 131 G2 46 45 S 167 53 E
Anglès, Spain 40 D7 41 57N 2 38 E
Anglesey, Isle of □, U.K. 20 D3 53 16N 4 18W
Anglet, France 28 E2 43 29N 1 31W
Angleton, U.S.A. 155 L7 29 10N 95 26W
Anglin →, France 28 B4 46 42N 0 52 E
Anglisidhes, Cyprus 39 F9 34 51N 33 27 E
Anglure, France 27 D10 48 35N 3 50 E
Angmagssalik = Tasiilaq, Greenland 10 D7 65 40N 37 20W
Ango, Dem. Rep. of the Congo 118 B2 4 10N 26 5 E
Angoche, Mozam. 119 F4 16 8 S 39 55 E
Angoche, I., Mozam. 119 F4 16 20 S 39 50 E
Angol, Chile 174 D1 37 56 S 72 45W
Angola, Ind., U.S.A. 157 C12 41 38N 85 0W
Angola, N.Y., U.S.A. 150 D5 42 38N 79 2W
Angola ■, Africa 115 E3 12 0 S 18 0 E
Angoon, U.S.A. 144 H14 57 30N 134 35W
Angor, Uzbekistan 65 E3 37 27N 67 9 E
Angora = Ankara, Turkey 100 C5 39 57N 32 54 E
Angoram, Papua N. G. 132 C3 4 4 S 144 4 E
Angoulême, France 28 C4 45 39N 0 10 E
Angoumois, France 28 C4 45 50N 0 25 E
Angra do Heroismo, Azores 9 d1 38 39N 27 13W
Angra dos Reis, Brazil 175 A7 23 0 S 44 10W
Angrapa →, Russia 54 D8 54 37N 21 54 E
Angren, Uzbekistan 65 C5 41 1N 70 12 E
Angtassom, Cambodia 87 G5 11 1N 104 41 E
Angu, Dem. Rep. of the Congo 118 B1 3 23N 24 30 E
Anguang, China 75 B12 45 15N 123 45 E
Anguilla ☒, W. Indies 165 C7 18 14N 63 5W
Angul, India 94 D7 20 51N 85 6 E
Anguo, China 74 E8 38 28N 115 15 E
Angurugu, Australia 126 A2 14 0 S 136 25 E
Angus □, U.K. 22 E6 56 46N 2 56W
Angwa →, Zimbabwe 117 B5 16 0 S 30 23 E
Anhanduí →, Brazil 175 A5 21 46 S 52 9W
Anholt, Denmark 17 H5 56 42N 11 33 E
Anhua, China 77 C8 28 23N 111 12 E
Anhui □, China 77 B11 32 0N 117 0 E
Anhwei = Anhui □, China 77 B11 32 0N 117 0 E
Aniak, U.S.A. 144 F8 61 35N 159 32W
Anichab, Namibia 116 C1 21 0 S 14 46 E
Anicuns, Brazil 171 E2 16 28 S 49 58W
Ánidhros, Greece 49 E7 36 38N 25 43 E
Anié, Togo 113 D5 7 42N 1 8 E
Anil, Brazil 170 B3 2 32 S 44 14W
Animas →, U.S.A. 159 H9 36 43N 108 13W
Anina, Romania 52 E6 45 6N 21 51 E
Anini-y, Phil. 81 F3 10 25N 121 55 E
Aninoasa, Romania 53 F9 44 47N 24 10 E
Anita, U.S.A. 156 C2 41 27N 94 46W
Anivorano, Madag. 117 B8 18 44 S 48 58 E
Aniwa, Vanuatu 133 J7 19 17 S 169 35 E
Anjalankoski, Finland 15 F22 60 45N 26 51 E
Anjangaon, India 94 D3 21 10N 77 20 E
Anjar, India 92 H4 23 6N 70 10 E
Anjengo, India 95 K3 8 40N 76 46 E
Anji, China 77 B12 30 46N 119 40 E
Anjidiv I., India 95 G2 14 40N 74 10 E
Anjō, Japan 73 C9 34 57N 137 5 E
Anjou, France 26 E6 47 20N 0 15W
Anjouan, Comoros Is. 121 a 12 15 S 44 20 E
Anjozorobe, Madag. 117 B8 18 22 S 47 52 E
Anju, N. Korea 75 E13 39 36N 125 40 E
Anka, Nigeria 113 C6 12 13N 5 58 E
Ankaboa, Tanjona, Madag. 117 C7 21 58 S 43 20 E
Ankang, China 74 H5 32 40N 109 1 E
Ankara, Turkey 100 C5 39 57N 32 54 E
Ankarafantsika ⌓, Madag. 117 B8 16 8 S 47 5 E
Ankaramena, Madag. 117 C8 21 57 S 46 39 E
Ankarsrum, Sweden 17 G10 57 41N 16 20 E
Ankasakasa, Madag. 117 B7 16 21 S 44 52 E
Ankavandra, Madag. 117 B8 18 46 S 45 18 E
Ankazoabo, Madag. 117 C7 22 18 S 44 31 E
Ankazobe, Madag. 117 B8 18 20 S 47 10 E
Ankeny, U.S.A. 156 C3 41 44N 93 36W
Ankhialo = Pomorie, Bulgaria 51 D11 42 32N 27 41 E
Ankilimalinika, Madag. 117 C7 22 58 S 43 45 E
Ankilizato, Madag. 117 C8 20 25 S 45 1 E
Anking = Anqing, China 77 B11 30 30N 117 3 E
Ankisabe, Madag. 117 B8 19 17 S 46 29 E
Anklam, Germany 30 B9 53 51N 13 41 E
Ankleshwar, India 94 D1 21 38N 73 3 E
Ankober, Ethiopia 107 F4 9 35N 39 40 E
Ankola, India 95 G2 14 40N 74 18 E
Ankoro, Dem. Rep. of the Congo 118 D2 6 45 S 26 55 E
Ankororoka, Madag. 117 D8 25 30 S 45 11 E
Anlong, China 76 E5 25 2N 105 27 E
Anlu, China 77 B9 31 15N 113 45 E
Anmyŏn-do, S. Korea 75 F14 36 25N 126 25 E
Ånn, Sweden 16 A6 63 19N 12 33 E
Ann, C., U.S.A. 151 D14 42 38N 70 35W
Ann Arbor, U.S.A. 157 B13 42 17N 83 45W
Anna, Russia 60 E5 51 28N 40 23 E
Anna, Ill., U.S.A. 155 G10 37 28N 89 15W
Anna, Ohio, U.S.A. 157 D12 40 24N 84 11W
Anna Regina, Guyana 169 B6 7 10N 58 30W
Annaba, Algeria 111 A6 36 50N 7 46 E
Annaberg-Buchholz, Germany 30 E9 50 34N 13 0 E
Annai, Guyana 169 C6 3 57N 59 8W
Annaka, Japan 73 A10 36 19N 138 54 E
Annalee →, Ireland 23 B4 54 2N 7 24W
Annam, Vietnam 86 E7 16 0N 108 0 E
Annamitique, Chaîne, Asia 86 D6 17 0N 106 0 E
Annan, U.K. 22 G5 54 59N 3 16W
Annan →, U.K. 22 G5 54 58N 3 16W
Annanberg, Papua N. G. 132 C3 4 52 S 144 42 E
Annapolis, U.S.A. 148 F7 38 59N 76 30W
Annapolis Royal, Canada 141 D6 44 44N 65 32W
Annapurna, Nepal 93 E10 28 34N 83 50 E
Annean, L., Australia 125 E2 26 54 S 118 14 E
Anneberg, Sweden 17 G8 57 44N 14 49 E
Annecy, France 29 C10 45 55N 6 8 E
Annecy, Lac d', France 29 C10 45 52N 6 10 E
Annemasse, France 27 F13 46 12N 6 16 E
Annenfeld = Şämkir, Azerbaijan 61 K8 40 50N 46 0 E
Annenskiy Most, Russia 58 B9 60 45N 37 10 E
Annette I., U.S.A. 144 J15 55 9N 131 28W
Annigeri, India 95 G2 15 26N 75 26 E
Anning, China 76 E4 24 55N 102 26 E
Anniston, U.S.A. 152 B4 33 39N 85 50W
Annobón, Atl. Oc. 105 G4 1 25 S 5 36 E
Annonay, France 29 C8 45 15N 4 40 E
Annot, France 29 E10 43 58N 6 38 E
Annotto B., Jamaica 164 a 18 17N 76 45W
Ånnsjön, Sweden 16 A6 63 19N 12 34 E
Annville, U.S.A. 151 F8 40 20N 76 31W
Annweiler, Germany 31 F3 49 12N 7 57 E
Áno Arkhánai, Greece 49 F7 35 16N 25 11 E
Áno Porróia, Greece 50 E7 41 17N 23 2 E
Áno Síros, Greece 48 D6 37 29N 24 56 E
Áno Viánnos, Greece 39 E6 35 2N 25 21 E
Anorotsangana, Madag. 117 A8 13 56 S 47 55 E
Anosibe, Madag. 117 B8 19 26 S 48 13 E
Anou Mellene, Mali 113 B5 17 29N 0 33 E
Anoumaba, Ivory C. 112 D4 6 23N 4 38W
Anoyí, Greece 39 C2 38 25N 20 40 E
Anóyia, Greece 39 E5 35 16N 24 52 E
Anping, Hebei, China 74 E8 38 15N 115 30 E
Anping, Liaoning, China 75 D12 41 5N 123 30 E
Anpu Gang, China 76 G7 21 25N 109 50 E
Anqing, China 77 B11 30 30N 117 3 E
Anqiu, China 75 F10 36 25N 119 10 E
Anren, China 77 D9 26 43N 113 18 E
Ansager, Denmark 17 J2 55 43N 8 45 E
Ansai, China 74 F5 36 50N 109 20 E
Ansbach, Germany 31 F6 49 28N 10 34 E
Anse Boileau, Seychelles 121 b 4 43 S 55 29 E
Anse la Raye, St. Lucia 165 f 13 55N 61 3W
Anse Royale, Seychelles 121 b 4 44 S 55 31 E
Anseba →, Eritrea 107 D4 16 0N 38 30 E
Anserma, Colombia 168 B2 5 13N 75 48W
Ansfelden, Austria 34 C7 48 12N 14 17 E
Anshan, China 75 D12 41 5N 122 58 E
Anshun, China 76 D5 26 18N 105 57 E
Ansião, Portugal 42 F2 39 56N 8 27W
Ansley, U.S.A. 154 E5 41 18N 99 23W
Ansó, Spain 40 C4 42 51N 0 48W
Ansoain, Spain 40 C3 42 50N 1 38W
Anson, U.S.A. 155 J5 32 45N 99 54W
Anson B., Australia 124 B5 13 20 S 130 6 E
Ansongo, Mali 113 B5 15 25N 0 35 E
Ansongo-Ménaka ⌓, Mali 113 B5 15 3N 1 37 E
Ansonia, Conn., U.S.A. 151 E11 41 21N 73 5W
Ansonia, Ohio, U.S.A. 157 D12 40 13N 84 38W
Anstruther, U.K. 22 E6 56 14N 2 41W
Ansudu, Indonesia 83 B5 2 11 S 139 22 E
Ansus, Indonesia 83 B5 1 44 S 135 49 E
Antabamba, Peru 172 C3 14 40 S 73 0W
Antagarh, India 94 D5 20 6N 81 9 E
Antakya, Turkey 100 D7 36 14N 36 10 E
Antalaha, Madag. 117 A9 14 57 S 50 20 E
Antalāt, Libya 108 B4 31 8N 20 42 E
Antalya, Turkey 100 D4 36 52N 30 45 E
Antalya □, Turkey 49 E12 36 30N 30 0 E
Antalya Körfezi, Turkey 100 D4 36 15N 31 30 E
Antambohobe, Madag. 117 C8 22 20 S 46 47 E
Antanambao-Manampotsy, Madag. 117 B8 19 29 S 48 34 E
Antanambe, Madag. 117 B8 16 26 S 49 52 E
Antananarivo, Madag. 117 B8 18 55 S 47 31 E
Antananarivo □, Madag. 117 B8 19 0 S 47 0 E
Antanifotsy, Madag. 117 B8 19 39 S 47 19 E
Antanimbaribe, Madag. 117 C7 21 30 S 44 48 E
Antanimora, Madag. 117 C8 24 49 S 45 40 E
Antarctic Pen., Antarctica 7 C18 67 0 S 60 0W
Antarctica 7 E3 90 0 S 0 0W
Antécume Pata, Fr. Guiana 169 C7 3 17N 54 4W
Antelope, Zimbabwe 119 G2 21 2 S 28 31 E
Antenor Navarro, Brazil 170 C4 6 44 S 38 27W
Antequera, Paraguay 174 A4 24 8 S 57 7W
Antequera, Spain 43 H6 37 5N 4 33W
Antero, Mt., U.S.A. 159 G10 38 41N 106 15W
Antevamena, Madag. 117 C7 21 2 S 44 8 E
Anthemoús, Greece 50 F7 40 31N 23 15 E
Anthony, Fla., U.S.A. 153 F7 29 18N 82 7W
Anthony, Kans., U.S.A. 155 G5 37 9N 98 2W
Anthony, N. Mex., U.S.A. 159 K10 32 0N 106 36W
Anti Atlas, Morocco 110 C3 30 0N 8 30W
Anti-Lebanon = Ash Sharqi, Al Jabal, Lebanon 103 B5 33 40N 36 10 E
Antibes, France 29 E11 43 34N 7 6 E
Antibes, C. d', France 29 E11 43 31N 7 7 E
Anticosti, Î. d', Canada 141 C7 49 30N 63 0W
Antifer, C. d', France 26 C7 49 41N 0 10 E
Antigo, U.S.A. 154 C10 45 9N 89 9W
Antigonish, Canada 141 C7 45 38N 61 58W
Antigua, Canary Is. 9 e2 28 24N 14 1W
Antigua, Guatemala 164 D1 14 34N 90 41W
Antigua, W. Indies 165 C7 17 0N 61 50W
Antigua & Barbuda ■, W. Indies 165 C7 17 20N 61 48W
Antikythira = Andikíthira, Greece 48 F5 35 52N 23 15 E
Antilla, Cuba 164 B4 20 40N 75 50W
Antilles = West Indies, Cent. Amer. 165 D7 15 0N 65 0W
Antioch = Antakya, Turkey 100 D7 36 14N 36 10 E
Antioch, U.S.A. 160 G5 38 1N 121 48W
Antioche, Pertuis d', France 28 B2 46 6N 1 20W
Antioquia, Colombia 168 B2 6 40N 75 55W
Antioquia □, Colombia 168 B2 7 0N 75 30W
Antipodes Is., Pac. Oc. 134 M9 49 45 S 178 40 E
Antipolo, Phil. 80 D3 14 35N 121 10 E
Antique □, Phil. 81 F4 11 10N 122 5 E
Antlers, U.S.A. 155 H7 34 14N 95 37W
Antoetra, Madag. 117 C8 20 46 S 47 20 E
Antofagasta, Chile 174 A1 23 50 S 70 30W
Antofagasta □, Chile 174 A2 24 0 S 69 0W
Antofagasta de la Sierra, Argentina 174 B2 26 5 S 67 20W
Antofalla, Argentina 174 B2 25 30 S 68 5W
Antofalla, Salar de, Argentina 174 B2 25 40 S 67 45W
Anton, U.S.A. 155 J3 33 49N 102 10W
Antongila, Helodrano, Madag. 117 B8 15 30 S 49 50 E
Antonibé, Madag. 117 B8 15 7 S 47 24 E
Antonibé, Presqu'île d', Madag. 117 A8 14 55 S 47 20 E
Antonina, Brazil 175 B6 25 26 S 48 42W
António Enes = Angoche, Mozam. 119 F4 16 8 S 39 55 E
Antrain, France 26 D5 48 28N 1 30W
Antrim, U.K. 23 B5 54 43N 6 14W
Antrim, U.S.A. 150 F3 40 7N 81 21W
Antrim □, U.K. 23 B5 54 56N 6 25W
Antrim, Mts. of, U.K. 23 A5 55 3N 6 14W
Antrim Plateau, Australia 124 C4 18 8 S 128 20 E
Antrodoco, Italy 45 F10 42 25N 13 5 E
Antropovo, Russia 60 A6 58 24N 43 6 E
Antsakabary, Madag. 117 B8 15 3 S 48 56 E
Antsalova, Madag. 117 B7 18 40 S 44 37 E
Antsenavolo, Madag. 117 C8 21 24 S 48 3 E
Antsiafabositra, Madag. 117 B8 17 18 S 46 57 E
Antsirabe, Antananarivo, Madag. 117 B8 19 55 S 47 2 E
Antsirabe, Antsiranana, Madag. 117 A8 14 0 S 49 59 E
Antsirabe, Mahajanga, Madag. 117 B8 15 57 S 48 58 E
Antsiranana, Madag. 117 A8 12 25 S 49 20 E
Antsiranana □, Madag. 117 A8 12 16 S 49 17 E
Antsohihy, Madag. 117 A8 14 50 S 47 59 E
Antsohimbondrona Seranana, Madag. 117 A8 13 7 S 48 48 E
Antu, China 75 C15 42 30N 128 20 E
Antufash, Yemen 98 D3 15 42N 42 25 E
Antwerp = Antwerpen, Belgium 24 C4 51 13N 4 25 E
Antwerp, N.Y., U.S.A. 151 B9 44 12N 75 37W
Antwerp, Ohio, U.S.A. 157 C12 41 11N 84 45W
Antwerpen, Belgium 24 C4 51 13N 4 25 E
Antwerpen □, Belgium 24 C4 51 15N 4 40 E
Anukur, C., Papua N. G. 132 D5 6 18 S 149 37 E
Anupgarh, India 92 E5 29 10N 73 10 E
Anuppur, India 93 H9 23 6N 81 41 E
Anuradhapura, Sri Lanka 95 K5 8 22N 80 28 E
Anveh, Iran 97 E7 27 23N 54 11 E
Anvers = Antwerpen, Belgium 24 C4 51 13N 4 25 E
Anvers I., Antarctica 7 C17 64 30 S 63 40W
Anvik, U.S.A. 144 E7 62 39N 160 13W
Anwen, China 77 C13 29 4N 120 26 E
Anxi, Fujian, China 77 E12 25 2N 118 12 E
Anxi, Gansu, China 68 B4 40 30N 95 43 E
Anxian, China 76 B5 31 40N 104 25 E
Anxiang, China 77 C9 29 27N 112 11 E
Anxious B., Australia 127 E1 33 24 S 134 45 E
Anyama, Ivory C. 112 D4 5 30N 4 3W
Anyang, China 74 F8 36 5N 114 21 E
Anyer, Indonesia 84 D3 6 4 S 105 53 E
Anyer-Kidul, Indonesia 79 G11 6 4 S 105 53 E
Anyi, Jiangxi, China 77 C10 28 49N 115 25 E
Anyi, Shanxi, China 74 G6 35 2N 111 2 E
Anyuan, China 77 E10 25 9N 115 21 E
Anyue, China 76 B5 30 9N 105 50 E
Anza, U.S.A. 161 M10 33 35N 116 39W
Anze, China 74 F7 36 10N 112 12 E
Anzhero-Sudzhensk, Russia 66 D9 56 10N 86 0 E
Ánzio, Italy 46 A5 41 27N 12 37 E
Anzoátegui □, Venezuela 169 B5 9 0N 64 30W
Ao Makham, Thailand 87 a 7 50N 98 24 E
Ao Phangnga △, Thailand 87 a 8 10N 98 32 E
Aoba, Vanuatu 133 E5 15 25 S 167 50 E
Aoga-Shima, Japan 73 E11 32 28N 139 46 E
Aoiz, Spain 40 C3 42 46N 1 22W
Aola, Solomon Is. 133 M11 9 30 S 160 30 E
Aomen = Macau, China 77 F9 22 12N 113 33 E
Aomori, Japan 70 D10 40 45N 140 45 E
Aomori □, Japan 70 D10 40 45N 140 40 E
Aonla, India 93 E8 28 16N 79 11 E
Aono-Yama, Japan 72 C3 34 28N 131 48 E
Aoraki Mount Cook, N.Z. 131 D5 43 36 S 170 9 E
Aoral, Phnum, Cambodia 87 G5 12 0N 104 15 E
Aorangi Mts., N.Z. 130 H4 41 28 S 175 22 E
Aore, Vanuatu 133 E5 15 35 S 167 10 E
Aoreora, Morocco 110 C2 28 51N 10 53W
Aosta, Italy 44 C4 45 45N 7 20 E
Aotea Harbour, N.Z. 130 D3 38 0 S 174 50 E
Aotearoa = New Zealand ■, Oceania 130 G5 40 0 S 176 0 E
Aoudéras, Niger 113 B6 17 45N 8 20 E
Aouinet Torkoz, Morocco 110 C3 28 31N 9 46W
Aouk, Bahr →, Africa 109 G3 8 51N 18 53 E
Aouk-Aoukalé ⌓, C.A.R. 114 A4 9 52N 21 25 E
Aoukar, Mali 110 D4 23 50N 2 45W
Aoukâr, Mauritania 112 B3 17 40N 10 0W
Aoulef el Arab, Algeria 111 C5 26 55N 1 2 E
Aozou, Chad 109 D3 21 45N 17 28 E
Aozou, Couloir d', Chad 109 D3 22 0N 19 0 E
Apa →, S. Amer. 174 A4 22 6 S 58 2W
Apache, U.S.A. 155 H5 34 54N 98 22W
Apache Junction, U.S.A. 159 K8 33 25N 111 33W
Apalachee B., U.S.A. 152 E5 30 0N 84 0W
Apalachicola, U.S.A. 152 F5 29 43N 84 59W
Apalachicola →, U.S.A. 152 F5 29 43N 84 58W
Apalachicola B., U.S.A. 152 F3 29 40N 85 0W
Apam, Ghana 113 D4 5 19N 0 42W
Apapa, Nigeria 113 D5 6 25N 3 25 E
Apaporis →, Colombia 168 D4 1 23 S 69 25W
Aparados da Serra △, Brazil 175 B5 29 10 S 50 8W
Aparecida = Bertolínia, Brazil 170 C3 7 38 S 43 57W
Aparecida do Taboado, Brazil 171 F1 20 5 S 51 5W
Aparri, Phil. 80 B3 18 22N 121 38 E
Aparurén, Venezuela 169 B5 5 6N 62 8W
Apateu, Romania 52 D6 46 36N 21 47 E
Apatin, Serbia & M. 52 E4 45 40N 19 0 E
Apatity, Russia 56 A5 67 34N 33 22 E
Apatou, Fr. Guiana 169 B7 5 9N 54 20W
Apatzingán, Mexico 162 D4 19 0N 102 20W
Apauwar, Indonesia 83 B5 1 39 S 138 11 E
Apayao □, Phil. 80 B3 18 10N 121 10 E
Apeldoorn, Neths. 24 B5 52 13N 5 57 E
Apen, Germany 30 B3 53 13N 7 48 E
Apennines = Appennini, Italy 44 D7 44 30N 10 0 E
Apenrade = Åbenrå, Denmark 17 J3 55 3N 9 25 E
Apere →, Bolivia 173 C4 13 44 S 65 18W
Aphrodisias, Turkey 49 D10 37 42N 28 46 E
Apia, Samoa 133 W24 13 50 S 171 50W
Apiacás, Serra dos, Brazil 173 B6 9 50 S 57 0W
Apiaí, Brazil 171 F2 24 31 S 48 50W
Apiaú →, Brazil 169 C5 2 39N 61 12W
Apiaú, Serra do, Brazil 169 C5 2 30N 62 0W
Apidiá →, Brazil 173 C5 11 39 S 61 11W
Apies →, S. Africa 117 D4 25 15 S 28 8 E
Apinajé, Brazil 171 D2 11 31 S 48 18W
Apiti, N.Z. 130 F4 39 58 S 175 54 E
Apizaco, Mexico 163 D5 19 26N 98 9W
Aplao, Peru 172 D3 16 0 S 72 40W
Apo, Mt., Phil. 81 H5 6 53N 125 14 E
Apo East Pass, Phil. 80 E3 12 40N 120 40 E
Apo Reef △, Phil. 80 E3 12 50N 120 50 E
Apo West Pass, Phil. 80 E3 12 31N 120 22 E
Apodi, Brazil 170 C4 5 39 S 37 48W
Apoera, Suriname 169 B6 5 12N 57 10W
Apolakkiá, Greece 38 E11 36 5N 27 48 E
Apolakkiá, Órmos, Greece 38 E11 36 5N 27 45 E
Apolda, Germany 30 D7 51 2N 11 32 E
Apollo Bay, Australia 128 E5 38 45 S 143 40 E
Apollonia = Marsá Susah, Libya 108 B4 32 52N 21 59 E
Apollonia, Greece 48 E6 36 58N 24 43 E
Apolo, Bolivia 172 C4 14 30 S 68 30W
Apónguao →, Venezuela 169 C5 4 48N 61 36W
Apopka, U.S.A. 153 G8 28 40N 81 31W
Apopka L., U.S.A. 153 G8 28 38N 81 38W
Aporé, Brazil 173 D7 18 58 S 52 1W
Aporé →, Brazil 171 E1 19 27 S 50 57W
Aporema, Brazil 170 A1 1 14N 50 49W
Apostle Is., U.S.A. 154 B9 47 0N 90 40W
Apostle Islands ⌓, U.S.A. 154 B9 46 57N 90 53W
Apóstoles, Argentina 175 B4 28 0 S 56 0W
Apostolos Andreas, C., Cyprus 39 E10 35 42N 34 35 E
Apostolovo, Ukraine 59 J7 47 39N 33 39 E
Apoteri, Guyana 169 C6 4 2N 58 32W
Appalachian Mts., U.S.A. 148 G6 38 0N 80 0W
Äppelbo, Sweden 16 D8 60 29N 14 1 E
Appennini, Italy 44 D7 44 30N 10 0 E
Appennino Ligure, Italy 44 D6 44 30N 9 0 E
Appenzell, Switz. 33 B8 47 20N 9 25 E
Appenzell-Ausser Rhoden □, Switz. 33 B8 47 23N 9 23 E
Appenzell-Inner Rhoden □, Switz. 33 B8 47 20N 9 25 E
Appiano, Italy 45 B8 46 28N 11 15 E
Apple Hill, Canada 151 A10 45 13N 74 46W
Apple Valley, U.S.A. 161 L9 34 32N 117 14W
Appleby-in-Westmorland, U.K. 20 C5 54 35N 2 29W
Appledore, U.K. 21 F3 51 3N 4 13W
Apples, Switz. 32 C2 46 33N 6 26 E
Appleton, U.S.A. 148 C1 44 16N 88 25W
Appleton City, U.S.A. 156 F2 38 11N 94 2W
Appling, U.S.A. 152 B7 33 33N 82 19W
Approuague, Fr. Guiana 169 C7 4 20N 52 0W
Aprica, Italy 33 D10 46 9N 10 6 E
Apricena, Italy 45 G12 41 47N 15 27 E
April →, Papua N. G. 132 C2 4 18 S 142 26 E
Aprília, Italy 46 A5 41 36N 12 39 E
Apsheronsk, Russia 61 H4 44 28N 39 42 E
Apsley, Canada 150 B6 44 45N 78 6W
Apt, France 29 E9 43 53N 5 24 E
Apuane, Alpi, Italy 44 D7 44 7N 10 14 E
Apuaú, Brazil 169 D5 2 25 S 60 53W
Apucarana, Brazil 175 A5 23 55 S 51 33W
Apulia = Púglia □, Italy 47 A9 41 15N 16 15 E
Apurauan, Phil. 81 G2 9 35N 118 20 E
Apure □, Venezuela 168 B4 7 10N 68 50W
Apure →, Venezuela 168 B4 7 37N 66 25W
Apurímac □, Peru 172 C3 14 0 S 73 0W
Apurimac →, Peru 172 C3 12 17 S 73 56W
Apuseni, Munţii, Romania 52 D7 46 30N 22 45 E
Āqā Jarī, Iran 97 D6 30 42N 49 50 E
Aqaba = Al 'Aqabah, Jordan 103 F4 29 31N 35 0 E
Aqaba, G. of, Red Sea 96 D2 28 15N 33 20 E
'Aqabah, Khalīj al = Aqaba, G. of, Red Sea 96 D2 28 15N 33 20 E
Aqbaqay, Kazakhstan 65 A6 45 0N 72 47 E
Āqchah, Afghan. 91 A2 37 0N 66 5 E
Āqcheh, Afghan. 65 E3 36 56N 66 11 E
'Aqdā, Iran 97 C7 32 26N 53 37 E
Aqîq, Sudan 106 D4 18 14N 38 12 E
Aqîq, Khalîg, Sudan 106 D4 18 20N 38 10 E
'Aqīq, W. al →, Si. Arabia 98 B3 20 16N 41 40 E

Aqköl, Kazakhstan 65 A7 45 0N 75 39 E
Aqköl, Kazakhstan 65 B5 43 36N 70 45 E
Aqmola = Astana, Kazakhstan 66 D8 51 10N 71 30 E
Aqqum, Kazakhstan 65 A2 44 50N 65 8 E
'Aqrah, Iraq 101 D10 36 46N 43 45 E
Aqshī, Kazakhstan 65 B8 43 59N 76 19 E
Aqsū, Kazakhstan 65 B4 42 25N 69 50 E
Aqsūgek, Kazakhstan 65 A7 44 37N 74 30 E
Aqsūmbe, Kazakhstan 65 A3 44 26N 67 33 E
Aqtaū, Kazakhstan 66 E6 43 39N 51 12 E
Aqtöbe, Kazakhstan 57 D10 50 17N 57 10 E
Aquidauana, Brazil 173 E6 20 30 S 55 50W
Aquidauana →, Brazil 173 D6 19 44 S 56 50W
Aquiles Serdán, Mexico 162 B3 28 37N 105 54W
Aquin, Haiti 165 C5 18 16N 73 24W
Aquitain, Bassin, France 25 D3 44 0N 0 30W
Aquitaine □, France 28 D3 44 25N 0 30W
Aqyrtöbe, Kazakhstan 65 B6 42 59N 72 7 E
Aqzhar, Kazakhstan 65 B5 43 8N 71 37 E
Ar Rachidiya = Er Rachidia, Morocco 110 B4 31 58N 4 20W
Ar Rafīd, Syria 103 C4 32 57N 35 52 E
Ar Raḩḩālīyah, Iraq 101 F10 32 44N 43 23 E
Ar Ramādī, Iraq 101 F10 33 25N 43 20 E
Ar Raml, Libya 108 C3 26 45N 19 40 E
Ar Ramthā, Jordan 103 C5 32 34N 36 0 E
Ar Raqqah, Syria 101 E8 35 59N 39 8 E
Ar Rass, Si. Arabia 96 E4 25 50N 43 40 E
Ar Rawḑah, Si. Arabia 98 B3 21 16N 42 50 E
Ar Rawḑah, Yemen 98 D4 14 28N 47 17 E
Ar Rawshān, Si. Arabia 106 C5 20 2N 42 36 E
Ar Rifā'ī, Iraq 96 D5 31 50N 46 10 E
Ar Rijā', Yemen 98 D4 13 1N 44 35 E
Ar Riyāḑ, Si. Arabia 96 E5 24 41N 46 42 E
Ar Ru'ays, Qatar 97 E6 26 8N 51 12 E
Ar Rukhaymīyah, Iraq 96 D5 29 22N 45 38 E
Ar Ruşāfah, Syria 101 E8 35 45N 38 49 E
Ar Rutbah, Iraq 101 F9 33 0N 40 15 E
Ar Ruwayḑah, Si. Arabia 98 B4 23 40N 44 40 E
Ara, India 93 G11 25 35N 84 32 E
Ara Goro, Ethiopia 107 F5 5 48N 41 18 E
Ara Tera, Ethiopia 107 F5 6 38N 40 57 E
Arab, U.S.A. 149 H2 34 19N 86 30W
'Arab, Bahr el →, Sudan 107 F2 9 0N 29 30 E
Arab, Khalîg el, Egypt 106 A2 30 55N 29 0 E
Arab, Shatt al →, Asia 97 D6 30 0N 48 31 E
'Araba, W. →, Egypt 106 J8 28 19N 33 31 E
'Arabābād, Iran 97 C8 33 2N 57 41 E
'Arabah, W. →, Yemen 99 C5 18 5N 51 26 E
Araban, Turkey 100 D7 37 28N 37 44 E
Arabatskaya Strelka, Ukraine 59 K8 45 40N 35 0 E
Arabba, Italy 45 B8 46 30N 11 52 E
Arabelo, Venezuela 169 C5 4 55N 64 13W
Arabi, U.S.A. 152 D6 31 50N 83 44W
Arabia, Asia 62 G8 25 0N 45 0 E
Arabian Desert = Es Sahrâ' Esh Sharqîya, Egypt 106 B3 27 30N 32 30 E
Arabian Gulf = Persian Gulf, Asia 97 E6 27 0N 50 0 E
Arabian Sea, Ind. Oc. 88 D5 16 0N 65 0 E
Arabistan = Khūzestān □, Iran 97 D6 31 0N 49 0 E
Araç, Turkey 100 B5 41 15N 33 21 E
Aracaju, Brazil 170 D4 10 55 S 37 4W
Aracataca, Colombia 168 A3 10 38N 74 9W
Aracati, Brazil 170 B4 4 30 S 37 44W
Araçatuba, Brazil 175 A5 21 10 S 50 30W
Araceli, Phil. 81 F2 10 33N 119 59 E
Aracena, Spain 43 H4 37 53N 6 38W
Aracena, Sierra de, Spain 43 H4 37 50N 6 50W
Aracides, C., Solomon Is. 133 M11 8 21 S 161 0 E
Aračinovo, Macedonia 50 D5 42 1N 21 34 E
Araçuaí, Brazil 171 E3 16 52 S 42 4W
Araçuaí →, Brazil 171 E3 16 46 S 42 2W
'Arad, Israel 103 D4 31 15N 35 12 E
Arad, Romania 52 D6 46 10N 21 20 E
Arad □, Romania 52 D6 46 20N 22 0 E
Arada, Chad 109 F4 15 0N 20 20 E
Arādān, Iran 97 C7 35 21N 52 30 E
Aradhippou, Cyprus 39 F9 34 57N 33 36 E
Arafura Sea, E. Indies 83 C5 9 0 S 135 0 E
Aragarças, Brazil 173 D7 15 55 S 52 15W
Aragats, Armenia 61 K7 40 30N 44 15 E
Aragon, U.S.A. 152 A4 34 2N 85 3W
Aragón □, Spain 40 D4 41 25N 0 40W
Aragón →, Spain 40 C3 42 13N 1 44W
Aragona, Italy 46 E6 37 24N 13 27 E
Aragua □, Venezuela 168 B4 10 0N 67 10W
Aragua de Barcelona, Venezuela 169 B5 9 28N 64 49W
Araguacema, Brazil 170 C2 8 50 S 49 20W
Araguaçu = Paraguaçu Paulista, Brazil 175 A5 22 22 S 50 35W
Araguaçu, Brazil 171 D2 12 49 S 49 51W
Araguaia △, Brazil 170 D2 10 30 S 50 0W
Araguaia →, Brazil 170 C2 5 21 S 48 41W
Araguaiana, Brazil 173 D7 15 43 S 51 51W
Araguaína, Brazil 170 C2 7 12 S 48 12W
Araguari, Brazil 171 E2 18 38 S 48 11W
Araguari →, Brazil 169 C8 1 15N 49 55W
Araguatins, Brazil 170 C2 5 38 S 48 7W
Arain, India 92 F6 26 27N 75 2 E
Araioses, Brazil 170 B3 2 53 S 41 55W
Arak, Algeria 111 C5 25 20N 3 45 E
Arāk, Iran 97 C6 34 0N 49 40 E
Araka, Sudan 107 G3 4 20N 30 23 E
Arakan □, Burma 90 F5 19 0N 94 15 E
Arakan Yoma, Burma 90 F5 20 0N 94 40 E
Arákhova, Greece 48 C4 38 28N 22 35 E
Arakkonam, India 95 H4 13 7N 79 43 E
Arakli, Turkey 101 B8 41 6N 40 2 E
Araks = Aras, Rūd-e →, Asia 61 K9 40 5N 48 29 E
Aral, Kazakhstan 66 E7 46 41N 61 45 E
Aral Sea, Asia 66 E7 44 30N 60 0 E
Aral Tengizi = Aral Sea, Asia 66 E7 44 30N 60 0 E
Aralsk = Aral, Kazakhstan 66 E7 46 41N 61 45 E
Aralskoye More = Aral Sea, Asia 66 E7 44 30N 60 0 E
Aralsor, Ozero, Kazakhstan 61 F9 49 5N 48 12 E
Aramac, Australia 126 C4 22 58 S 145 14 E
Aramia →, Papua N. G. 132 D2 7 55 S 143 22 E
Aran →, India 94 E4 19 55N 78 12 E
Aran Areh, Ethiopia 120 C2 9 2N 43 54 E
Aran I., Ireland 23 A3 55 0N 8 30W
Aran Is., Ireland 23 C2 53 6N 9 38W
Aranda de Duero, Spain 42 D7 41 39N 3 42W
Arandān, Iran 96 C5 35 23N 46 55 E
Aranđelovac, Serbia & M. 50 B4 44 18N 20 34 E
Aranga, N.Z. 130 B2 35 44 S 173 40 E
Arani, Bolivia 173 D4 17 34 S 65 46W
Arani, India 95 H4 12 43N 79 19 E
Aranjuez, Spain 42 E7 40 1N 3 40W
Aranos, Namibia 116 C2 24 9 S 19 7 E
Aransas Pass, U.S.A. 155 M6 27 55N 97 9W
Aranyaprathet, Thailand 86 F4 13 41N 102 30 E
Arao, Japan 72 E2 32 59N 130 25 E
Araouane, Mali 112 B4 18 55N 3 30W
Arapahoe, U.S.A. 154 E5 40 18N 99 54W
Arapari, Brazil 170 C2 5 34 S 49 15W
Arapawa I., N.Z. 131 B9 41 11 S 174 17 E
Arapey Grande →, Uruguay 174 C4 30 55 S 57 49W
Arapgir, Turkey 101 C8 39 5N 38 30 E
Arapiraca, Brazil 170 C4 9 45 S 36 39W
Arapongas, Brazil 175 A5 23 29 S 51 28W
Arapuni, N.Z. 130 D4 38 4 S 175 39 E
Ar'ar, Si. Arabia 96 D4 30 59N 41 2 E
Araracuara, Colombia 168 D3 0 24 S 72 17W
Araranguá, Brazil 175 B6 29 0 S 49 30W
Araraquara, Brazil 171 F2 21 50 S 48 0W
Araras, Brazil 171 F2 22 22 S 47 23W
Ararás, Serra das, Brazil 175 B5 25 0 S 53 10W
Ararat, Armenia 101 C11 39 48N 44 50 E
Ararat, Australia 128 D5 37 16 S 143 0 E
Ararat, Mt. = Ağrı Dağı, Turkey 101 C11 39 50N 44 15 E
Arari, Brazil 170 B3 3 28 S 44 47W
Araria, India 93 F12 26 9N 87 33 E
Araripe, Chapada do, Brazil 170 C3 7 20 S 40 0W
Araripina, Brazil 170 C3 7 33 S 40 34W
Araruama, L. de, Brazil 171 F3 22 53 S 42 12W
Araruna, Brazil 170 C4 6 52 S 35 44W
Aras, Rūd-e →, Asia 61 K9 40 5N 48 29 E
Aratâne, Mauritania 112 B3 18 24N 8 32W
Araticu, Brazil 170 B2 1 58 S 49 51W
Arauca, Colombia 168 B3 7 0N 70 40W
Arauca □, Colombia 168 B3 6 40N 71 0W
Arauca →, Venezuela 168 B4 7 24N 66 35W
Arauco, Chile 174 D1 37 16 S 73 25W
Araújos, Brazil 171 E2 19 56 S 45 14W
Arauquita, Colombia 168 B3 7 2N 71 25W
Araure, Venezuela 168 B4 9 34N 69 13W
Arawa, Ethiopia 107 F5 9 57N 41 58 E
Arawale △, Kenya 118 C5 1 24 S 40 9 E
Arawata →, N.Z. 131 E3 44 0 S 168 40 E
Arawe Is., Papua N. G. 132 D5 6 6 S 149 0 E
Araxá, Brazil 171 E2 19 35 S 46 55W
Araya, Pen. de, Venezuela 169 A5 10 40N 64 0W
Arayat, Phil. 80 D3 15 10N 120 46 E
Arba Gugu, Ethiopia 107 F5 8 40N 40 15 E
Arba Minch, Ethiopia 107 F4 6 0N 37 30 E
Arbat, Iraq 101 E11 35 25N 45 35 E
Árbatax, Italy 46 C2 39 56N 9 42 E
Arbedo, Switz. 33 D8 46 12N 9 3 E
Arbi, Ethiopia 107 F4 9 4N 35 7 E
Arbīl, Iraq 101 D11 36 15N 44 5 E
Arboga, Sweden 16 E9 59 24N 15 52 E
Arbois, France 27 F12 46 55N 5 46 E
Arboletes, Colombia 168 B2 8 51N 76 26W
Arbon, Switz. 33 A8 47 31N 9 26 E
Arbore, Ethiopia 107 F4 5 3N 36 50 E
Arborëa, Italy 46 C1 39 46N 8 35 E
Arborfield, Canada 143 C8 53 6N 103 39W
Arborg, Canada 143 C9 50 54N 97 13W
Arbre du Ténéré, Niger 113 B7 17 50N 10 4 E
Arbroath, U.K. 22 E6 56 34N 2 35W
Arbuckle, U.S.A. 160 F4 39 1N 122 3W
Arbus, Italy 46 C1 39 30N 8 33 E
Arc →, France 29 C10 45 34N 6 12 E
Arc-lès-Gray, France 27 E12 47 28N 5 34 E
Arcachon, France 28 D2 44 40N 1 10W
Arcachon, Bassin d', France 28 D2 44 42N 1 10W
Arcade, Calif., U.S.A. 161 L8 34 2N 118 15W
Arcade, N.Y., U.S.A. 156 D6 42 32N 78 25W
Arcadia, Fla., U.S.A. 153 H8 27 13N 81 52W
Arcadia, Ind., U.S.A. 157 D10 40 11N 86 1W
Arcadia, Iowa, U.S.A. 156 B1 42 5N 95 3W
Arcadia, La., U.S.A. 155 J8 32 33N 92 55W
Arcadia, Pa., U.S.A. 150 F6 40 47N 78 51W
Arcanum, U.S.A. 157 E12 39 59N 84 33W
Arcata, U.S.A. 158 F1 40 52N 124 5W
Arcévia, Italy 45 E9 43 30N 12 56 E
Archangel = Arkhangelsk, Russia 56 B7 64 38N 40 36 E
Archar, Bulgaria 50 C6 43 50N 22 54 E
Archbald, U.S.A. 151 E9 41 30N 75 32W
Archbold, U.S.A. 157 C12 41 31N 84 18W
Archena, Spain 41 G3 38 9N 1 16W
Archenu, J., Chad 109 D4 22 15N 24 45 E
Archer, U.S.A. 153 F7 29 32N 82 32W
Archer →, Australia 126 A3 13 28 S 141 41 E
Archer B., Australia 126 A3 13 20 S 141 30 E
Archer Bend = Mungkan Kandju △, Australia 126 A3 13 35 S 142 52 E
Archers Post, Kenya 118 B4 0 35N 37 35 E
Arches △, U.S.A. 159 G9 38 45N 109 25W
Archidona, Spain 43 H6 37 6N 4 22W
Archipel-de-Mingan △, Canada 141 B7 50 13N 63 10W
Archipiélago Chinijo △, Canary Is. 9 e2 29 20N 13 30W
Archipiélago Los Roques △, Venezuela 165 D6 11 50N 66 44W
Arci, Mte., Italy 46 C1 39 47N 8 45 E
Arcidosso, Italy 45 F8 42 52N 11 33 E
Arcila = Asilah, Morocco 110 A3 35 29N 6 0W
Arcipelago de la Maddalena △, Italy 46 A2 41 14N 9 24 E
Arcipelago Toscano △, Italy 44 F7 42 45N 10 15 E
Arcis-sur-Aube, France 27 D11 48 32N 4 10 E
Arckaringa Cr. →, Australia 127 D2 28 10 S 135 22 E
Arco, Italy 44 C7 45 55N 10 53 E
Arco, U.S.A. 158 E7 43 38N 113 18W
Arcola, U.S.A. 157 E8 39 41N 88 19W
Arcoona, Australia 128 A2 31 2 S 137 1 E
Arcos de Jalón, Spain 40 D2 41 12N 2 16W
Arcos de la Frontera, Spain 43 J5 36 45N 5 49W
Arcos de Valdevez, Portugal 42 D2 41 55N 8 22W
Arcot, India 95 H4 12 53N 79 20 E
Arcoverde, Brazil 170 C4 8 25 S 37 4W
Arcozelo, Portugal 42 E3 40 32N 7 47W
Arctic Bay, Canada 139 A11 73 1N 85 7W
Arctic Ocean, Arctic 6 B18 78 0N 160 0W
Arctic Red River = Tsiigehtchic, Canada 138 B6 67 15N 134 0W
Arctic Village, U.S.A. 144 B11 68 8N 145 32W
Arctowski, Antarctica 7 C18 62 30 S 58 0W
Arda →, Bulgaria 51 E10 41 40N 26 30 E
Arda →, Italy 44 C7 45 2N 10 2 E
Ardabīl, Iran 97 B6 38 15N 48 18 E
Ardabīl □, Iran 97 B6 38 15N 48 20 E
Ardahan, Turkey 101 B10 41 7N 42 41 E
Ardakān = Sepīdān, Iran 97 D7 30 20N 52 5 E
Ardakān, Iran 97 C7 32 19N 53 59 E
Ardala, Sweden 17 F7 58 22N 13 19 E
Ardales, Spain 43 J6 36 53N 4 51W
Årdalstangen, Norway 18 C4 61 14N 7 43 E
Ardèche □, France 29 D8 44 42N 4 16 E
Ardèche →, France 29 D8 44 16N 4 39 E
Ardee, Ireland 23 C5 53 52N 6 33W
Arden, Canada 150 B8 44 43N 76 56W
Arden, Denmark 17 H3 56 46N 9 52 E
Arden, Calif., U.S.A. 160 G5 38 36N 121 33W
Arden, Nev., U.S.A. 161 J11 36 1N 115 14W
Ardenne, Belgium 24 E5 49 50N 5 5 E
Ardennes = Ardenne, Belgium 24 E5 49 50N 5 5 E
Ardennes □, France 27 C11 49 35N 4 40 E
Ardentes, France 27 F8 46 45N 1 50 E
Arderin, Ireland 23 C4 53 2N 7 39W
Ardeşen, Turkey 101 B9 41 12N 41 2 E
Ardestān, Iran 97 C7 33 20N 52 25 E
Ardez, Switz. 33 C10 46 47N 10 12 E
Árdhas →, Greece 51 E10 41 40N 26 30 E
Ardhéa, Greece 50 F6 40 58N 22 3 E
Ardila →, Portugal 43 G3 38 12N 7 28W
Ardino, Bulgaria 51 E9 41 34N 25 9 E
Ardivachar Pt., U.K. 22 D1 57 23N 7 26W
Ardlethan, Australia 129 C7 34 22 S 146 53 E
Ardmore, Okla., U.S.A. 155 H6 34 10N 97 8W
Ardmore, Pa., U.S.A. 151 G9 39 58N 75 18W
Ardnamurchan, Pt. of, U.K. 22 E2 56 43N 6 14W
Ardnave Pt., U.K. 22 F2 55 53N 6 20W
Ardon, Russia 61 J7 43 10N 44 18 E
Ardore, Italy 47 D9 38 11N 16 10 E
Ardres, France 27 B8 50 50N 1 59 E
Ardrossan, Australia 128 C2 34 26 S 137 53 E
Ardrossan, U.K. 22 F4 55 39N 4 49W
Ards Pen., U.K. 23 B6 54 33N 5 34W
Arduan, Sudan 106 D3 19 54N 30 20 E
Ardud, Romania 52 C7 47 37N 22 52 E
Åre, Sweden 16 A7 63 22N 13 15 E
Arecibo, Puerto Rico 165 d 18 29N 66 43W
Areia Branca, Brazil 170 B4 5 0 S 37 0W
Arena, Pt., U.S.A. 160 G3 38 57N 123 44W
Arenal, Honduras 164 C2 15 21N 86 50W
Arenales, Cerro, Chile 176 C2 47 5 S 73 40W
Arenápolis, Brazil 173 C6 14 26 S 56 49W
Arenas = Las Arenas, Spain 42 B6 43 17N 4 50W
Arenas, Pta., Venezuela 169 A5 10 31N 64 14W
Arenas de San Pedro, Spain 42 E5 40 12N 5 5W
Arendal, Norway 18 F5 58 28N 8 46 E
Arendsee, Germany 30 C7 52 52N 11 27 E
Arenillas, Ecuador 168 D1 3 33 S 80 10W
Arensburg = Kuressaare, Estonia 15 G20 58 15N 22 30 E
Arenys de Mar, Spain 40 D7 41 35N 2 33 E
Arenzano, Italy 44 D5 44 24N 8 41 E
Arenzville, U.S.A. 156 E6 39 53N 90 22W
Areópolis, Greece 48 E4 36 40N 22 22 E
Arequipa, Peru 172 D3 16 20 S 71 30W
Arequipa □, Peru 172 D3 16 0 S 72 50W
Arere, Brazil 169 D7 0 16 S 53 52W
Arero, Ethiopia 107 G4 4 41N 38 50 E
Arès, France 28 D2 44 47N 1 8W
Arévalo, Spain 42 D6 41 3N 4 43W
Arezzo, Italy 45 E8 43 25N 11 53 E
Arga, Turkey 96 B3 38 21N 37 59 E
Arga →, Spain 40 C3 42 18N 1 47W
Argalastí, Greece 48 B5 39 13N 23 13 E
Argamakmur, Indonesia 84 C2 3 35 S 102 0 E
Argamasilla de Alba, Spain 43 F7 39 8N 3 5W
Argamasilla de Calatrava, Spain 43 G6 38 44N 4 4W
Arganda, Spain 42 E7 40 19N 3 26W
Arganil, Portugal 42 E2 40 13N 8 3W
Argao, Phil. 81 G4 9 52N 123 36 E
Argásion 39 D2 37 45N 20 56 E
Argayash, Russia 64 D8 55 29N 60 52 E
Argedeb, Ethiopia 107 F5 6 11N 41 13 E
Argelès-Gazost, France 28 E3 43 0N 0 6W
Argelès-sur-Mer, France 28 F7 42 34N 3 1 E
Argens →, France 29 E10 43 24N 6 44 E
Argent-sur-Sauldre, France 27 E9 47 33N 2 25 E
Argenta = North Little Rock, U.S.A. 155 H8 34 45N 92 16W
Argenta, Canada 142 C5 50 11N 116 56W
Argenta, Italy 45 D8 44 37N 11 50 E
Argenta, U.S.A. 157 E8 39 59N 88 49W
Argentan, France 26 D6 48 45N 0 1W
Argentário, Mte., Italy 45 F8 42 24N 11 9 E
Argentat, France 28 C5 45 6N 1 56 E
Argentera, Italy 44 D4 44 12N 7 5 E
Argenteuil, France 27 D9 48 57N 2 14 E
Argentia, Canada 141 C9 47 18N 53 58W
Argentiera, C. dell', Italy 46 B1 40 44N 8 8 E
Argentière, Aiguilles d', Switz. 32 E4 45 58N 7 2 E
Argentina ■, S. Amer. 176 B3 35 0 S 66 0W
Argentine Basin, S. Amer. 166 H5 45 0 S 58 0W
Argentine Plain, Atl. Oc. 8 L6 46 0 S 52 0W
Argentino, L., Argentina 176 D2 50 10 S 73 0W
Argenton-Château, France 26 F6 46 59N 0 27W
Argenton-sur-Creuse, France 27 F8 46 36N 1 30 E
Argeş □, Romania 53 F9 45 0N 24 45 E
Argeş →, Romania 53 F11 44 5N 26 38 E
Arghandab →, Afghan. 91 C2 31 30N 64 15 E
Argheile, Ethiopia 107 F5 5 19N 42 4 E
Argo, Sudan 106 D3 19 28N 30 30 E
Argolikós Kólpos, Greece 48 D4 37 20N 22 52 E
Argolís □, Greece 48 D4 37 38N 22 50 E
Argonne, France 27 C12 49 10N 5 0 E
Árgos, Greece 48 D4 37 40N 22 43 E
Argos, U.S.A. 157 C10 41 14N 86 15W
Árgos Orestikón, Greece 50 F5 40 27N 21 18 E
Argostoli = Argostólion, Greece 39 C2 38 11N 20 29 E
Argostólion, Greece 39 C2 38 11N 20 29 E
Argostólion, Kólpos, Greece 39 C1 38 10N 20 27 E
Arguedas, Spain 40 C3 42 11N 1 36W
Arguello, Pt., U.S.A. 161 L6 34 35N 120 39W
Arguineguín, Canary Is. 9 e1 27 46N 15 41W
Argun, Russia 61 J7 43 18N 45 52 E
Argun →, Russia 67 D13 53 20N 121 28 E
Argungu, Nigeria 113 C5 12 40N 4 31 E
Arguni, T., Indonesia 83 B4 3 6 S 133 42 E
Argus Pk., U.S.A. 161 K9 35 52N 117 26W
Argyle, L., Australia 124 C4 16 20 S 128 40 E
Argyll △, U.K. 22 E4 56 6N 5 0W
Argyll & Bute □, U.K. 22 E3 56 13N 5 28W
Arhavi, Turkey 101 B9 41 21N 41 18 E
Århus, Denmark 17 H4 56 8N 10 11 E
Århus Amtskommune □, Denmark 17 H4 56 15N 10 15 E
Aria, N.Z. 130 E4 38 33 S 175 0 E
Ariadnoye, Russia 70 B7 45 8N 134 25 E
Ariamsvlei, Namibia 116 D2 28 9 S 19 51 E
Ariana, Tunisia 108 A2 36 52N 10 12 E
Ariano Irpino, Italy 47 A8 41 9N 15 5 E
Ariari →, Colombia 168 C3 2 35N 72 47W
Aribinda, Burkina Faso 113 C4 14 17N 0 52W
Arica, Chile 172 D3 18 32 S 70 20W
Arica, Colombia 168 D3 2 0 S 71 50W
Arico, Canary Is. 9 e1 28 9N 16 29W
Arid, C., Australia 125 F3 34 1 S 123 10 E
Arida, Japan 73 C7 34 5N 135 8 E
Aridal, W. Sahara 110 C2 25 59N 13 54W
Aride, Seychelles 121 b 4 13 S 55 40 E
Ariège □, France 28 F5 42 56N 1 30 E
Ariège →, France 28 E5 43 30N 1 25 E
Arieş →, Romania 53 D8 46 24N 23 20 E
Arigat el Fersig, Algeria 111 C4 27 35N 2 7W
Arīḩā, Israel 106 A4 31 51N 35 27 E
Arilje, Serbia & M. 50 C4 43 44N 20 7 E
Arilla, Ákra, Greece 38 B9 39 43N 19 39 E
Arima, Trin. & Tob. 169 F9 10 38N 61 17W
Aringay, Phil. 80 C3 16 26N 120 21 E
Arinos →, Brazil 173 C6 10 25 S 58 20W
Ario de Rosales, Mexico 162 D4 19 12N 102 0W
Ariogala, Lithuania 54 C10 55 16N 23 28 E
Aripo, Mt., Trin. & Tob. 169 F9 10 45N 61 15W
Aripuanã, Brazil 173 B5 9 25 S 60 30W
Aripuanã →, Brazil 173 B5 5 7 S 60 25W
Ariquemes, Brazil 173 B5 9 55 S 63 6W
Arisaig, U.K. 22 E3 56 55N 5 51W
Arîsh, W. el →, Egypt 106 A3 31 9N 33 49 E
Arissa, Ethiopia 107 E5 11 10N 41 35 E
Aristazabal I., Canada 142 C3 52 40N 129 10W
Arita, Japan 72 D1 33 11N 129 54 E
Aritao, Phil. 80 C3 16 18N 121 2 E
Ariton, U.S.A. 152 D4 31 36N 85 43W
Arivonimamo, Madag. 117 B8 19 1 S 47 11 E
Ariyalur, India 95 J4 11 8N 79 8 E
Ariza, Spain 40 D2 41 19N 2 3W
Arizaro, Salar de, Argentina 174 A2 24 40 S 67 50W
Arizona, Argentina 174 D2 35 45 S 65 25W
Arizona □, U.S.A. 159 J8 34 0N 112 0W
Arizpe, Mexico 162 A2 30 20N 110 11W
Årjäng, Sweden 16 E6 59 24N 12 8 E
Arjeplog, Sweden 14 D18 66 3N 17 54 E
Arjepluovve = Arjeplog, Sweden 14 D18 66 3N 17 54 E
Arjona, Colombia 168 A2 10 14N 75 22W
Arjona, Spain 43 H6 37 56N 4 4W
Arjuna, Indonesia 85 D4 7 49 S 112 34 E
Arka, Russia 67 C15 60 15N 142 0 E
Arkadak, Russia 60 E6 51 58N 43 30 E
Arkadelphia, U.S.A. 155 H8 34 7N 93 4W
Arkadhía □, Greece 48 D4 37 30N 22 20 E
Arkaig, L., U.K. 22 E3 56 59N 5 10W
Arkalgud, India 95 H3 12 46N 76 3 E
Arkalyk = Arqalyk, Kazakhstan 66 D7 50 13N 66 50 E
Arkansas □, U.S.A. 155 H8 35 0N 92 30W
Arkansas →, U.S.A. 155 J9 33 47N 91 4W
Arkansas City, U.S.A. 155 G6 37 4N 97 2W
Arkaroola, Australia 127 E2 30 20 S 139 22 E
Árkathos →, Greece 48 B3 39 20N 21 4 E
Arkhangelo-Pashiskiy Zavod = Pashiya, Russia 64 B7 58 33N 58 26 E
Arkhángelos, Préveza, Greece 39 A2 39 6N 20 42 E
Arkhángelos, Ródhos, Greece 38 E12 36 13N 28 7 E
Arkhangelsk, Russia 56 B7 64 38N 40 36 E
Arkhangelskoye, Russia 60 E5 51 32N 40 58 E
Arki, India 92 D7 31 9N 76 58 E
Arkiko, Eritrea 107 D4 15 33N 39 30 E
Arklow, Ireland 23 D5 52 48N 6 10W
Árkoi, Greece 49 D8 37 24N 26 44 E
Arkona, Kap, Germany 30 A9 54 42N 13 26 E
Arkösund, Sweden 17 F10 58 29N 16 56 E
Arkoúdhi Nisís, Greece 39 B2 38 33N 20 43 E
Arkport, U.S.A. 150 D7 42 24N 77 42W
Arkticheskiy, Mys, Russia 67 A10 81 10N 95 0 E
Arkul, Russia 60 B10 57 17N 50 3 E
Arkville, U.S.A. 151 D10 42 9N 74 37W
Arla, Sweden 16 E10 59 17N 16 40 E
Arlanda, Stockholm ✈ (ARN), Sweden 16 E11 59 41N 17 56 E
Arlanza →, Spain 42 C6 42 6N 4 9W
Arlanzón →, Spain 42 C6 42 3N 4 17W
Arlberg pass, Austria 34 D3 47 9N 10 12 E
Arles, France 29 E8 43 41N 4 40 E
Arlesheim, Switz. 32 B5 47 30N 7 37 E
Arli, Burkina Faso 113 C5 11 35N 1 28 E
Arli △, Burkina Faso 113 C5 11 35N 1 28 E
Arlington, S. Africa 117 D4 28 1 S 27 53 E
Arlington, Ga., U.S.A. 152 D5 31 26N 84 44W
Arlington, N.Y., U.S.A. 151 E11 41 42N 73 54W
Arlington, Oreg., U.S.A. 158 D3 45 43N 120 12W
Arlington, S. Dak., U.S.A. 154 C6 44 22N 97 8W
Arlington, Tex., U.S.A. 155 J6 32 44N 97 7W
Arlington, Va., U.S.A. 148 F7 38 53N 77 7W
Arlington, Vt., U.S.A. 151 C11 43 5N 73 9W
Arlington, Wash., U.S.A. 160 B4 48 12N 122 8W
Arlington Heights, U.S.A. 157 B9 42 5N 87 59W
Arlon, Belgium 24 E5 49 42N 5 49 E
Arltunga, Australia 126 C1 23 26 S 134 41 E
Armagh, U.K. 23 B5 54 21N 6 39W
Armagh □, U.K. 23 B5 54 18N 6 37W
Armagnac, France 28 E4 43 50N 0 10 E
Armançon →, France 27 E10 47 59N 3 30 E
Armando Bermudez △, Dom. Rep. 165 C5 19 3N 71 0W
Armatree, Australia 129 A8 31 26 S 148 28 E
Armavir, Russia 61 H5 45 2N 41 7 E
Armenia, Colombia 168 C2 4 35N 75 45W
Armenia ■, Asia 61 K7 40 20N 45 0 E
Armeniş, Romania 52 E7 45 13N 22 17 E
Armenistís, Ákra, Greece 38 E11 36 8N 27 42 E
Armentières, France 27 B9 50 40N 2 50 E
Armero, Colombia 168 C3 4 58N 74 54W
Armidale, Australia 129 A9 30 30 S 151 40 E
Armilla, Spain 43 H7 37 9N 3 37W
Armori, India 94 D4 20 28N 79 59 E
Armorique △, France 26 D3 48 22N 3 50W
Armour, U.S.A. 154 D5 43 19N 98 21W
Armstrong, B.C., Canada 142 C5 50 25N 119 10W
Armstrong, Ont., Canada 140 B2 50 18N 89 4W
Armur, India 94 E4 18 48N 78 16 E
Armutlu, Bursa, Turkey 51 F12 40 31N 28 50 E
Armutlu, İzmir, Turkey 49 C9 38 24N 27 34 E
Arnaía, Greece 50 F7 40 30N 23 38 E
Arnarfjörður, Iceland 11 B3 65 48N 23 40W
Arnaud →, Canada 139 B12 59 59N 69 46W
Arnauti, C., Cyprus 39 E8 35 6N 32 17 E
Arnay-le-Duc, France 27 E11 47 10N 4 27 E
Arnedillo, Spain 40 C2 42 13N 2 14W
Arnedo, Spain 40 C2 42 12N 2 5W
Árnes, Iceland 11 A5 66 1N 21 31W
Årnes, Norway 18 D8 60 7N 11 28 E
Árnessýsla □, Iceland 11 C6 64 15N 20 30W
Arnett, U.S.A. 155 G5 36 8N 99 46W
Arnhem, Neths. 24 C5 51 58N 5 55 E
Arnhem, C., Australia 126 A2 12 20 S 137 30 E
Arnhem B., Australia 126 A2 12 20 S 136 10 E
Arnhem Land, Australia 126 A1 13 10 S 134 30 E
Árnissa, Greece 50 F5 40 47N 21 49 E
Arno →, Italy 44 E7 43 41N 10 17 E
Arno Bay, Australia 128 B2 33 54 S 136 34 E
Arnold, U.K. 20 D6 53 1N 1 7W
Arnold, U.S.A. 160 G6 38 15N 120 20W
Arnoldstein, Austria 34 E6 46 33N 13 43 E
Arnon →, France 27 E9 47 13N 2 1 E
Arnot, Canada 143 B9 55 56N 96 41W
Arnøy, Norway 14 A19 70 9N 20 40 E
Arnprior, Canada 140 C4 45 26N 76 21W
Arnsberg, Germany 30 D4 51 24N 8 5 E
Arnsberger Wald △, Germany 30 D4 51 25N 8 20 E
Arnstadt, Germany 30 E6 50 50N 10 56 E
Arnswalde = Choszczno, Poland 55 E2 53 7N 15 25 E
Aro →, Venezuela 169 B5 8 1N 64 11W
Aroab, Namibia 116 D2 26 41 S 19 39 E
Aroánia Óri, Greece 48 D4 37 56N 22 12 E
Aroche, Spain 43 H4 37 56N 6 57W
Arochuku, Nigeria 113 D6 5 21N 7 54 E
Aroeiras, Brazil 170 C4 7 31 S 35 41W
Arolla, Switz. 32 D4 46 2N 7 29 E
Arolsen, Germany 30 D5 51 23N 9 2 E
Aron, India 92 G6 25 57N 77 56 E
Aron →, France 27 F10 46 50N 3 28 E
Arona, Canary Is. 9 e1 28 6N 16 40W
Arona, Italy 44 C5 45 46N 8 34 E
Aroroy, Phil. 80 E4 12 31N 123 24 E
Arosa, Switz. 33 C9 46 47N 9 41 E
Arosa, Ría de, Spain 42 C2 42 28N 8 57W
Årøysund, Norway 18 E7 59 10N 10 27 E
Arpajon, France 27 D9 48 36N 2 15 E
Arpajon-sur-Cère, France 28 D6 44 53N 2 28 E
Arpaşu de Jos, Romania 53 E9 45 47N 24 37 E
Arqalyk, Kazakhstan 66 D7 50 13N 66 50 E
Arque, Bolivia 172 D4 17 48 S 66 23W
Arrah = Ara, India 93 G11 25 35N 84 32 E
Arrah, Ivory C. 112 D4 6 40N 3 58W
Arraias, Brazil 171 D2 12 56 S 46 57W
Arraias →, Mato Grosso, Brazil 173 C7 11 10 S 53 35W
Arraias →, Pará, Brazil 170 C2 7 30 S 49 20W
Arraiolos, Portugal 43 G3 38 44N 7 59W
Arran, U.K. 22 F3 55 34N 5 12W
Arras, France 27 B9 50 17N 2 46 E
Arrasate, Spain 40 B2 43 4N 2 30W
Arrats →, France 28 D4 44 6N 0 52 E
Arreau, France 28 F4 42 54N 0 22 E
Arrecife, Canary Is. 9 e2 28 57N 13 37W
Arrecifes, Argentina 174 C3 34 6 S 60 9W
Arrée, Mts. d', France 26 D3 48 26N 3 55W
Arresø, Denmark 17 J6 55 58N 12 6 E
Arriaga, Chiapas, Mexico 163 D6 16 15N 93 52W
Arriaga, San Luis Potosí, Mexico 162 C4 21 55N 101 23W
Arribes del Duero △, Spain 42 D4 41 11N 6 39W
Arrilalah, Australia 126 C3 23 43 S 143 54 E
Arrino, Australia 125 E2 29 30 S 115 40 E
Arriondas, Spain 42 B5 43 23N 5 11W
Arrojado →, Brazil 171 D3 13 24 S 44 20W
Arromanches-les-Bains, France 26 C6 49 20N 0 38W
Arronches, Portugal 43 F3 39 8N 7 16W
Arros →, France 28 E3 43 40N 0 2W
Arrow, L., Ireland 23 B3 54 3N 8 19W
Arrowhead, L., U.S.A. 161 L9 34 16N 117 10W
Arrowsmith, Mt., N.Z. 131 D5 43 20 S 170 55 E
Arrowtown, N.Z. 131 E3 44 57 S 168 50 E
Arroyo de la Luz, Spain 43 F4 39 30N 6 38W
Arroyo del Puerco = Arroyo de la Luz, Spain 43 F4 39 30N 6 38W
Arroyo Grande, U.S.A. 161 K6 35 7N 120 35W
Års, Denmark 17 H3 56 48N 9 30 E
Ars, Iran 96 B5 37 9N 47 46 E
Ars-sur-Moselle, France 27 C13 49 5N 6 4 E
Arsenault L., Canada 143 B7 55 6N 108 32W
Arsenev, Russia 70 B6 44 10N 133 15 E
Arsi, Ethiopia 107 F4 7 45N 39 0 E
Arsiero, Italy 45 C8 45 48N 11 21 E
Arsikere, India 95 H3 13 15N 76 15 E
Arsin, Turkey 101 B8 41 8N 39 55 E
Arsk, Russia 60 B9 56 10N 49 50 E
Árskógssandur, Iceland 11 B8 65 56N 18 27W
Årsunda, Sweden 16 D10 60 31N 16 45 E
Árta, Greece 48 B3 39 8N 21 2 E
Artà, Spain 38 B4 39 41N 3 21 E
Árta □, Greece 48 B3 39 15N 21 5 E
Arteaga, Mexico 162 D4 18 50N 102 20W
Arteche, Phil. 80 E5 12 17N 125 22 E
Arteijo = Arteixo, Spain 42 B2 43 19N 8 29W
Arteixo, Spain 42 B2 43 19N 8 29W
Artem = Artyom, Azerbaijan 61 K10 40 28N 50 20 E
Artem, Russia 70 C6 43 22N 132 13 E
Artemovsk, Russia 67 D10 54 45N 93 35 E
Artemovsk, Ukraine 59 H9 48 35N 38 0 E
Artemovskiy, Rostov, Russia 61 G5 47 45N 40 16 E
Artemovskiy, Yekaterinburg, Russia 64 C8 57 21N 61 54 E
Artenay, France 27 D8 48 5N 1 50 E
Artern, Germany 30 D7 51 22N 11 18 E
Artesa de Segre, Spain 40 D6 41 54N 1 3 E
Artesia = Mosomane, Botswana 116 C4 24 2 S 26 19 E
Artesia, U.S.A. 155 J2 32 51N 104 24W
Arth, Switz. 33 B7 47 4N 8 31 E
Arthington, Liberia 112 D2 6 35N 10 45W
Arthur, Canada 150 C4 43 50N 80 32W
Arthur, U.S.A. 157 E8 39 43N 88 28W
Arthur →, Australia 127 G3 41 2 S 144 40 E
Arthur Cr. →, Australia 126 C2 22 30 S 136 25 E
Arthur Pt., Australia 126 C5 22 7 S 150 3 E
Arthur River, Australia 125 F2 33 20 S 117 2 E
Arthur's Pass, N.Z. 131 C6 42 54 S 171 35 E
Arthur's Pass △, N.Z. 131 C6 42 53 S 171 42 E

Arthur's Town, *Bahamas* **165 B4** 24 38N 75 42W
Artigas = Río Branco, *Uruguay* **175 C5** 32 40 S 53 40W
Artigas, *Antarctica* **7 C18** 62 30 S 58 0W
Artigas, *Uruguay* **174 C4** 30 20 S 56 30W
Artik, *Armenia* **61 K6** 40 38N 43 58 E
Artillery L., *Canada* **143 A7** 63 9N 107 52W
Artois, *France* **27 B9** 50 20N 2 30 E
Artotína, *Greece* **48 C4** 38 42N 22 2 E
Artrutx, C. de, *Spain* **38 B4** 39 55N 3 49 E
Artsyz, *Ukraine* **53 D14** 46 4N 29 26 E
Artux, *China* **65 D8** 39 40N 76 10 E
Artvin, *Turkey* **101 B9** 41 14N 41 44 E
Artyom, *Azerbaijan* **61 K10** 40 28N 50 20 E
Aru, Kepulauan, *Indonesia* **83 C4** 6 0 S 134 30 E
Aru Is. = Aru, Kepulauan, *Indonesia* **83 C4** 6 0 S 134 30 E
Arua, *Uganda* **118 B3** 3 1N 30 58 E
Aruanã, *Brazil* **171 D1** 14 54 S 51 10W
Aruba ☒, *W. Indies* **165 D6** 12 30N 70 0W
Arudy, *France* **28 E3** 43 7N 0 28W
Arumã, *Brazil* **169 D5** 4 44 S 62 8W
Arumpo, *Australia* **128 B5** 33 48 S 142 55 E
Arun →, *Nepal* **93 F12** 26 55N 87 10 E
Arun →, *U.K.* **21 G7** 50 49N 0 33W
Arunachal Pradesh □, *India* **90 A5** 28 0N 95 0 E
Aruppukkottai, *India* **95 K4** 9 31N 78 8 E
Aruri, Selat, *Indonesia* **83 B5** 0 50 S 135 15 E
Arusha, *Tanzania* **118 C4** 3 20 S 36 40 E
Arusha □, *Tanzania* **118 C4** 4 0 S 36 30 E
Arusha △, *Tanzania* **118 C4** 3 16 S 36 47 E
Arusha Chini, *Tanzania* **118 C4** 3 32 S 37 20 E
Arut →, *Indonesia* **85 C4** 2 42 S 111 34 E
Aruvi →, *Sri Lanka* **95 K4** 8 48N 79 53 E
Aruwimi →, *Dem. Rep. of the Congo* **118 B1** 1 13N 23 36 E
Arvada, *Colo., U.S.A.* **154 F2** 39 48N 105 5W
Arvada, *Wyo., U.S.A.* **158 D10** 44 39N 106 8W
Arvakalu, *Sri Lanka* **95 K4** 8 20N 79 58 E
Arve →, *France* **27 F13** 46 11N 6 8 E
Árvi, *Greece* **39 F6** 34 59N 25 28 E
Arvi, *India* **94 D4** 20 59N 78 16 E
Arviat, *Canada* **143 A10** 61 6N 93 59W
Arvidsjaur, *Sweden* **14 D18** 65 35N 19 10 E
Arvika, *Sweden* **16 E6** 59 40N 12 36 E
Arvin, *U.S.A.* **161 K8** 35 12N 118 50W
Arwal, *India* **93 G11** 25 15N 84 41 E
Arxan, *China* **69 B6** 47 11N 119 57 E
Åryd, *Sweden* **17 H8** 56 49N 14 59 E
Aryirádhes, *Greece* **38 C9** 39 27N 19 58 E
Aryiroúpolis, *Greece* **39 E5** 35 17N 24 20 E
Arys, *Kazakhstan* **65 B4** 42 26N 68 48 E
Arys →, *Kazakhstan* **65 B4** 42 45N 68 15 E
Arzachena, *Italy* **46 A2** 41 5N 9 23 E
Arzamas, *Russia* **60 C6** 55 27N 43 55 E
Arzew, *Algeria* **111 A4** 35 50N 0 23W
Arzgir, *Russia* **61 H7** 45 18N 44 23 E
Arzignano, *Italy* **45 C8** 45 31N 11 20 E
Arzúa, *Spain* **42 C2** 42 56N 8 9W
Aš, *Czech Rep.* **34 A5** 50 13N 12 12 E
Ås, *Norway* **18 E7** 59 40N 10 48 E
Ås, *Sweden* **16 A8** 63 15N 14 34 E
As Pontes de García Rodríguez, *Spain* **42 B3** 43 27N 7 50W
Aş Şafā, *Syria* **103 B6** 33 10N 37 0 E
As Saffānīyah, *Si. Arabia* **97 E6** 27 55N 48 50 E
As Safīrah, *Syria* **100 D7** 36 5N 37 21 E
Aş Şahm, *Oman* **97 E8** 24 10N 56 53 E
As Sājir, *Si. Arabia* **96 E5** 25 11N 44 36 E
As Salamīyah, *Syria* **100 E7** 35 1N 37 2 E
As Salmān, *Iraq* **96 D5** 30 30N 44 32 E
As Salţ, *Jordan* **103 C4** 32 2N 35 43 E
As Sal'w'a, *Qatar* **97 E6** 24 23N 50 50 E
As Samāwah, *Iraq* **96 D5** 31 15N 45 15 E
As Sanamayn, *Syria* **103 B5** 33 3N 36 10 E
As Sawādah, *Si. Arabia* **98 B4** 22 24N 44 28 E
As Sayl al Kabīr, *Si. Arabia* **98 B3** 21 38N 40 25 E
As Sohar = Şuḩār, *Oman* **97 E8** 24 20N 56 40 E
As Sukhnah, *Syria* **101 E8** 34 52N 38 52 E
As Sulaymānīyah, *Iraq* **101 E11** 35 35N 45 29 E
As Sulaymānīyah, *Si. Arabia* **98 A4** 24 9N 47 18 E
As Sulaymī, *Si. Arabia* **96 E4** 26 17N 41 21 E
As Sulayyil, *Si. Arabia* **98 B4** 20 27N 45 34 E
As Sulţān, *Libya* **108 B3** 31 4N 17 8 E
As Summān, *Si. Arabia* **96 E5** 25 0N 47 0 E
Aş Şurrah, *Yemen* **98 D4** 13 57N 46 14 E
As Suwaydā', *Syria* **103 C5** 32 40N 36 30 E
As Suwaydā' □, *Syria* **103 C5** 32 45N 36 45 E
As Suwayq, *Oman* **97 F8** 23 51N 57 26 E
Aş Şuwayrah, *Iraq* **101 F11** 32 55N 45 0 E
Asa, *Kazakhstan* **65 B5** 43 2N 71 10 E
Åsa, *Sweden* **17 G6** 57 21N 12 8 E
Asab, *Namibia* **116 D2** 25 30 S 18 0 E
Asaba, *Nigeria* **113 D6** 6 12N 6 38 E
Asad, Buḩayrat al, *Syria* **101 D8** 36 0N 38 15 E
Asadābād, *Iran* **101 E13** 34 47N 48 7 E
Asafo, *Ghana* **112 D4** 6 20N 2 40W
Asahi, *Japan* **73 B12** 35 43N 140 39 E
Asahi-Gawa →, *Japan* **72 C5** 34 36N 133 58 E
Asahigawa, *Japan* **70 C11** 43 46N 142 22 E
Asaka, *Uzbekistan* **65 C6** 40 38N 72 15 E
Asale, L., *Ethiopia* **107 E5** 14 0N 40 20 E
Asama-Yama, *Japan* **73 A10** 36 24N 138 31 E
Asamankese, *Ghana* **113 D4** 5 50N 0 40W
Asan →, *India* **93 F8** 26 37N 78 24 E
Asansol, *India* **93 H12** 23 40N 87 1 E
Åsarna, *Sweden* **16 B8** 62 39N 14 22 E
Asau, *Samoa* **133 W23** 13 27 S 172 33W
Asayita, *Ethiopia* **107 E5** 11 35N 41 23 E
Asba Littoria = Asbe Teferi, *Ethiopia* **107 F5** 9 4N 40 49 E
Asbe Teferi, *Ethiopia* **107 F5** 9 4N 40 49 E
Asbesberge, *S. Africa* **116 D3** 29 0 S 23 0 E
Asbest, *Russia* **64 C8** 57 0N 61 30 E
Asbestos, *Canada* **141 C5** 45 47N 71 58W
Asbestovye Rudniki = Asbest, *Russia* **64 C8** 57 0N 61 30 E
Asbury Park, *U.S.A.* **151 F10** 40 13N 74 1W
Ascea, *Italy* **47 B8** 40 8N 15 11 E
Ascensión, *Mexico* **162 A3** 31 6N 107 59W
Ascensión, B. de la, *Mexico* **163 D7** 19 50N 87 20W
Ascension I., *Atl. Oc.* **9 g** 7 57 S 14 23W
Aschach an der Donau, *Austria* **34 C7** 48 22N 14 2 E
Aschaffenburg, *Germany* **31 F5** 49 58N 9 6 E
Aschendorf, *Germany* **30 B3** 53 3N 7 19 E
Aschersleben, *Germany* **30 D7** 51 45N 11 29 E
Asciano, *Italy* **45 E8** 43 14N 11 33 E
Áscoli Piceno, *Italy* **45 F10** 42 51N 13 34 E
Áscoli Satriano, *Italy* **47 A8** 41 11N 15 32 E
Ascona, *Switz.* **33 D7** 46 9N 8 46 E
Ascope, *Peru* **172 B2** 7 46 S 79 8W
Ascotán, *Chile* **174 A2** 21 45 S 68 17W
Ascuncion, *Phil.* **81 H5** 7 35N 125 45 E
Aseb, *Eritrea* **107 E5** 13 0N 42 40 E
Åseda, *Sweden* **17 G9** 57 10N 15 20 E
Asedjrad, *Algeria* **111 D5** 24 51N 1 29 E
Aseki, *Papua N. G.* **132 D4** 7 21 S 146 12 E
Asela, *Ethiopia* **107 F4** 8 0N 39 0 E
Åsen, *Sweden* **16 C7** 61 17N 13 50 E
Asenovgrad, *Bulgaria* **51 D8** 42 1N 24 51 E
Aserradero, *Mexico* **162 C3** 23 40N 105 43W
Asfeld, *France* **27 C11** 49 27N 4 5 E
Asfûn el Matâ'na, *Egypt* **106 B3** 25 26N 32 30 E
Åsgårdstrand, *Norway* **18 E7** 59 22N 10 27 E
Asgata, *Cyprus* **39 F9** 34 46N 33 15 E
Ash Fork, *U.S.A.* **159 J7** 35 13N 112 29W
Ash Grove, *U.S.A.* **155 G8** 37 19N 93 35W
Ash Shabakah, *Iraq* **96 D4** 30 49N 43 39 E
Ash Shamāl □, *Lebanon* **103 A5** 34 25N 36 0 E
Ash Shāmīyah, *Iraq* **101 G11** 31 55N 44 35 E
Ash Sha'rā', *Si. Arabia* **98 A4** 24 16N 44 11 E
Ash Shāriqah, *U.A.E.* **97 E7** 25 23N 55 26 E
Ash Sharmah, *Si. Arabia* **96 D2** 28 1N 35 16 E
Ash Sharqāt, *Iraq* **101 E10** 35 27N 43 16 E
Ash Sharqi, Al Jabal, *Lebanon* **103 B5** 33 40N 36 10 E
Ash Shāţi, *Libya* **108 C2** 27 30N 12 30 E
Ash Shaţi □, *Libya* **111 C7** 27 27N 13 37 E
Ash Shaţrah, *Iraq* **96 D5** 31 30N 46 10 E
Ash Shawbak, *Jordan* **96 D2** 30 32N 35 34 E
Ash Shawmari, J., *Jordan* **103 E5** 30 35N 36 35 E
Ash Shiḩr, *Yemen* **99 D5** 14 45N 49 36 E
Ash Shināfīyah, *Iraq* **96 D5** 31 35N 44 39 E
Ash Shu'bah, *Si. Arabia* **96 D5** 28 54N 44 44 E
Ash Shumlūl, *Si. Arabia* **96 E5** 26 31N 47 20 E
Ash Shuqayq, *Si. Arabia* **98 C3** 17 44N 42 1 E
Ash Shūr'a, *Iraq* **96 C4** 35 58N 43 13 E
Ash Shurayf, *Si. Arabia* **96 E3** 25 43N 39 14 E
Ash Shuwayfāt, *Lebanon* **103 B4** 33 45N 35 30 E
Asha, *Russia* **64 D6** 55 0N 57 16 E
Ashanti □, *Ghana* **113 D4** 7 30N 1 30W
Ashau, *Vietnam* **86 D6** 16 6N 107 22 E
Ashbourne, *U.K.* **20 D6** 53 2N 1 43W
Ashburn, *U.S.A.* **152 D6** 31 43N 83 39W
Ashburton, *N.Z.* **131 D6** 43 53 S 171 48 E
Ashburton →, *Australia* **124 D1** 21 40 S 114 56 E
Ashburton, North Branch →, *N.Z.* **131 D6** 43 54 S 171 44 E
Ashburton, South Branch →, *N.Z.* **131 D6** 43 54 S 171 44 E
Ashchysay, *Kazakhstan* **65 B4** 43 35N 68 53 E
Ashcroft, *Canada* **142 C4** 50 40N 121 20W
Ashdod, *Israel* **103 D3** 31 49N 34 35 E
Ashdown, *U.S.A.* **155 J7** 33 40N 94 8W
Asheboro, *U.S.A.* **149 H6** 35 43N 79 49W
Åsheim, *Norway* **18 C8** 61 42N 11 11 E
Ashern, *Canada* **143 C9** 51 11N 98 21W
Asherton, *U.S.A.* **155 L5** 28 27N 99 46W
Asheville, *U.S.A.* **149 H4** 35 36N 82 33W
Ashewat, *Pakistan* **92 D3** 31 22N 68 32 E
Asheweig →, *Canada* **140 B2** 54 17N 87 12W
Ashford, *Australia* **127 D5** 29 15 S 151 3 E
Ashford, *U.K.* **21 F8** 51 8N 0 53 E
Ashford, *U.S.A.* **152 D4** 31 11N 85 14W
Ashgabat, *Turkmenistan* **66 F6** 38 0N 57 50 E
Ashibetsu, *Japan* **70 C11** 43 31N 142 11 E
Ashikaga, *Japan* **73 A11** 36 28N 139 29 E
Ashington, *U.K.* **20 B6** 55 11N 1 33W
Ashio, *Japan* **73 A11** 36 38N 139 27 E
Ashizuri-Uwakai △, *Japan* **72 E4** 32 56N 132 32 E
Ashizuri-Zaki, *Japan* **72 E5** 32 44N 133 0 E
Ashkarkot, *Afghan.* **92 C2** 33 3N 67 58 E
Ashkhabad = Ashgabat, *Turkmenistan* **66 F6** 38 0N 57 50 E
Āshkhāneh, *Iran* **97 B8** 37 26N 56 55 E
Ashland, *Ala., U.S.A.* **152 B4** 33 16N 85 50W
Ashland, *Ill., U.S.A.* **156 E7** 39 53N 90 1W
Ashland, *Kans., U.S.A.* **155 G5** 37 11N 99 46W
Ashland, *Ky., U.S.A.* **148 F4** 38 28N 82 38W
Ashland, *Maine, U.S.A.* **149 B11** 46 38N 68 24W
Ashland, *Mont., U.S.A.* **158 D10** 45 36N 106 16W
Ashland, *Ohio, U.S.A.* **150 F2** 40 52N 82 19W
Ashland, *Oreg., U.S.A.* **158 E2** 42 12N 122 43W
Ashland, *Pa., U.S.A.* **151 F8** 40 45N 76 22W
Ashland, *Va., U.S.A.* **148 G7** 37 46N 77 29W
Ashland, *Wis., U.S.A.* **154 B9** 46 35N 90 53W
Ashley, *Ill., U.S.A.* **156 F7** 38 20N 89 11W
Ashley, *Ind., U.S.A.* **157 C11** 41 32N 85 4W
Ashley, *N. Dak., U.S.A.* **154 B5** 46 2N 99 22W
Ashley, *Pa., U.S.A.* **151 E9** 41 12N 75 55W
Ashley →, *N.Z.* **131 D7** 43 17 S 172 44 E
Ashmore and Cartier Is., *Ind. Oc.* **124 B3** 12 15 S 123 0 E
Ashmore Reef, *Australia* **124 B3** 12 14 S 123 5 E
Ashmûn, *Egypt* **106 H7** 30 18N 30 55 E
Ashmyany, *Belarus* **15 J21** 54 26N 25 52 E
Ashokan Reservoir, *U.S.A.* **151 E10** 41 56N 74 13W
Ashqelon, *Israel* **103 D3** 31 42N 34 35 E
Ashraf = Behshahr, *Iran* **97 B7** 36 45N 53 35 E
Ashta, *India* **92 H7** 23 1N 76 43 E
Ashtabula, *U.S.A.* **150 E4** 41 52N 80 47W
Ashti, *Maharashtra, India* **94 D4** 21 12N 78 11 E
Ashti, *Maharashtra, India* **94 E2** 18 50N 75 15 E
Ashton, *S. Africa* **116 E3** 33 50 S 20 5 E
Ashton, *U.S.A.* **158 D8** 44 4N 111 27W
Ashuanipi, L., *Canada* **141 B6** 52 45N 66 15W
Ashuapmushuan →, *Canada* **140 C5** 48 37N 72 20W
Ashurst, *N.Z.* **130 G4** 40 16 S 175 45 E
Ashville, *Ala., U.S.A.* **152 B3** 33 50N 86 15W
Ashville, *Fla., U.S.A.* **152 E6** 30 37N 83 39W
Ashville, *Pa., U.S.A.* **150 F6** 40 34N 78 33W
'Āşī →, *Asia* **100 D6** 36 1N 35 59 E
Asia **62 E11** 45 0N 75 0 E
Asia, Kepulauan, *Indonesia* **83 A4** 1 0N 131 13 E
Asiago, *Italy* **45 C8** 45 52N 11 30 E
Asidonhoppo, *Suriname* **169 C6** 3 50N 55 30W
Asifabad, *India* **94 E4** 19 20N 79 24 E
Asike, *Indonesia* **83 C6** 6 39 S 140 24 E
Asilah, *Morocco* **110 A3** 35 29N 6 0W
Asinara, *Italy* **46 A1** 41 4N 8 16 E
Asinara, G. dell', *Italy* **46 A1** 41 0N 8 30 E
Asino, *Russia* **66 D9** 57 0N 86 0 E
Asipovichy, *Belarus* **58 F5** 53 19N 28 33 E
'Asīr □, *Si. Arabia* **98 C3** 18 40N 42 30 E
Asir, Ras, *Somali Rep.* **120 B4** 11 55N 51 10 E
Aska, *India* **94 E7** 19 2N 84 42 E
Aşkale, *Turkey* **101 C9** 39 55N 40 41 E
Asker, *Norway* **18 E7** 59 50N 10 29 E
Askersund, *Sweden* **17 F8** 58 53N 14 55 E
Askham, *S. Africa* **116 D3** 26 59 S 20 47 E
Askim, *Norway* **18 E8** 59 35N 11 10 E
Askja, *Iceland* **11 B10** 65 3N 16 48W
Askøy, *Norway* **18 D2** 60 29N 5 10 E
Askvoll, *Norway* **18 C2** 61 21N 5 4 E
Asl, *Egypt* **106 B3** 29 33N 32 44 E
Aslan Burnu, *Turkey* **49 C8** 38 44N 26 45 E
Aslanapa, *Turkey* **49 B11** 39 13N 29 52 E
Āsmār, *Afghan.* **91 B3** 35 10N 71 27 E
Asmara = Asmera, *Eritrea* **107 D4** 15 19N 38 55 E
Asmera, *Eritrea* **107 D4** 15 19N 38 55 E
Asnæs, *Denmark* **17 J4** 55 40N 11 0 E
Åsnen, *Sweden* **17 H8** 56 37N 14 45 E
Asni, *Morocco* **110 B3** 31 17N 7 58W
Aso, *Japan* **72 E3** 32 55N 131 5 E
Aso Kuju △, *Japan* **72 E3** 32 53N 131 6 E
Aso-Zan, *Japan* **72 E3** 32 53N 131 6 E
Ásola, *Italy* **44 C7** 45 13N 10 24 E
Asosa, *Ethiopia* **107 E3** 10 3N 34 32 E
Asoteriba, Jebel, *Sudan* **106 C4** 21 51N 36 30 E
Aspatria, *U.K.* **20 C4** 54 47N 3 19W
Aspe, *Spain* **41 G4** 38 20N 0 40W
Aspen, *U.S.A.* **159 G10** 39 11N 106 49W
Aspendos, *Turkey* **100 D4** 36 54N 31 7 E
Aspermont, *U.S.A.* **155 J4** 33 8N 100 14W
Aspet, *France* **28 E4** 43 1N 0 48 E
Aspiring, Mt., *N.Z.* **131 E3** 44 23 S 168 46 E
Aspres-sur-Buëch, *France* **29 D9** 44 32N 5 44 E
Asprókavos, Ákra, *Greece* **38 C10** 39 21N 20 6 E
Aspromonte △, *Italy* **47 D8** 38 9N 15 58 E
Aspur, *India* **92 H6** 23 58N 74 7 E
Asquith, *Canada* **143 C7** 52 8N 107 13W
Assa, *Morocco* **110 C3** 28 35N 9 6W
Assab = Aseb, *Eritrea* **107 E5** 13 0N 42 40 E
Assâba, Massif de l', *Mauritania* **112 B2** 16 10N 11 45W
Assagny △, *Ivory C.* **112 D4** 5 10N 4 48W
Assaikio, *Nigeria* **113 D6** 8 34N 8 55 E
Assake = Asaka, *Uzbekistan* **65 C6** 40 38N 72 15 E
Assal, L., *Djibouti* **107 E5** 11 40N 42 26 E
Assam □, *India* **90 B4** 26 0N 93 0 E
Assamakka, *Niger* **113 B6** 19 21N 5 38 E
Assateague Island ⌓, *U.S.A.* **148 F8** 38 15N 75 10W
Assaye, *India* **94 D2** 20 15N 75 53 E
Asse, *Belgium* **24 D4** 50 24N 4 10 E
Assekrem, *Algeria* **111 D6** 23 16N 5 49 E
Assémini, *Italy* **46 C1** 39 17N 9 0 E
Assen, *Neths.* **24 A6** 53 0N 6 35 E
Assens, *Denmark* **17 J3** 55 16N 9 55 E
Assini, *Ivory C.* **112 D4** 5 9N 3 17W
Assiniboia, *Canada* **143 D7** 49 40N 105 59W
Assiniboine →, *Canada* **143 D9** 49 53N 97 8W
Assiniboine, Mt., *Canada* **142 C5** 50 52N 115 39W
Assiou, *Algeria* **111 D6** 21 7N 7 36 E
Assis, *Brazil* **175 A5** 22 40 S 50 20W
Assis Brasil, *Brazil* **172 C4** 10 55 S 69 32W
Assisi, *Italy* **45 E9** 43 4N 12 37 E
Åsskard, *Norway* **18 A5** 63 1N 8 30 E
Assok Ngoum, *Gabon* **114 B2** 1 45N 11 39 E
Ássos, *Greece* **39 C2** 38 22N 20 33 E
Assumption, *U.S.A.* **156 E7** 39 31N 89 3W
Assynt, L., *U.K.* **22 C3** 58 10N 5 3W
Astaffort, *France* **28 D4** 44 4N 0 40 E
Astakidha, *Greece* **49 F8** 35 53N 26 50 E
Astakós, *Greece* **39 B3** 38 32N 21 5 E
Astana, *Kazakhstan* **66 D8** 51 10N 71 30 E
Āstāneh, *Iran* **97 B6** 37 17N 49 59 E
Astapovo = Lev Tolstoy, *Russia* **58 F10** 53 13N 39 29 E
Astara, *Azerbaijan* **97 B6** 38 30N 48 50 E
Āstārā, *Iran* **101 C13** 38 20N 48 52 E
Astarabad = Gorgān, *Iran* **97 B7** 36 55N 54 30 E
Asteroúsia, *Greece* **39 F6** 34 59N 25 3 E
Asti, *Italy* **44 D5** 44 54N 8 12 E
Astipálaia, *Greece* **49 E8** 36 32N 26 22 E
Astipalea = Astipálaia, *Greece* **49 E8** 36 32N 26 22 E
Astola I., *Pakistan* **91 D1** 25 7N 63 51 E
Astorga, *Phil.* **81 H5** 6 54N 125 27 E
Astorga, *Spain* **42 C4** 42 29N 6 8W
Astoria, *Ill., U.S.A.* **156 D6** 40 14N 90 21W
Astoria, *Oreg., U.S.A.* **160 D3** 46 11N 123 50W
Åstorp, *Sweden* **17 H6** 56 6N 12 55 E
Astrakhan, *Russia* **61 G9** 46 25N 48 5 E
Astudillo, *Spain* **42 C6** 42 12N 4 22W
Asturias □, *Spain* **42 B5** 43 15N 6 0W
Asturias ✈ (OVD), *Spain* **42 B4** 43 33N 6 3W
Asunción, *Bolivia* **172 C4** 11 46 S 67 50W
Asunción, *Paraguay* **174 B4** 25 10 S 57 30W
Asunción Nochixtlán, *Mexico* **163 D5** 17 28N 97 14W
Åsunden, *Sweden* **17 F9** 58 0N 15 51 E
Asutri, *Sudan* **107 D4** 15 25N 35 45 E
Aswa →, *Uganda* **118 B3** 3 43N 31 55 E
Aswa-Lolim ⌓, *Uganda* **118 B3** 2 43N 31 35 E
Aswad, Ra's al, *Si. Arabia* **98 B2** 21 20N 39 0 E
Aswân, *Egypt* **106 C3** 24 4N 32 57 E
Aswan Dam = Sadd el Aali, *Egypt* **106 C3** 23 54N 32 54 E
Asyût, *Egypt* **106 B3** 27 11N 31 4 E
Asyûti, Wadi →, *Egypt* **106 B3** 27 11N 31 16 E
Aszód, *Hungary* **52 C4** 47 39N 19 28 E
At-Bashy, *Kyrgyzstan* **65 C7** 41 10N 75 48 E
At-Bashy Kyrka Tooloru, *Kyrgyzstan* **65 C7** 40 50N 75 30 E
At Ţafīlah, *Jordan* **103 E4** 30 45N 35 30 E
At Ţafīlah □, *Jordan* **103 E4** 30 45N 35 30 E
Aţ Ţā'if, *Si. Arabia* **98 B3** 21 5N 40 27 E
At Tāj, *Libya* **108 D4** 24 13N 23 18 E
At Ta'mīm □, *Iraq* **96 C5** 35 30N 44 20 E
At Tamīmī, *Libya* **108 B4** 32 20N 23 4 E
Aţ Ţirāq, *Si. Arabia* **96 E5** 27 19N 44 33 E
Aţ Tubayq, *Si. Arabia* **96 D3** 29 30N 37 0 E
At Turbah, *Yemen* **98 D4** 13 13N 44 7 E
At Turbah, *Yemen* **98 D3** 12 40N 43 30 E
Atabey, *Turkey* **49 D12** 37 57N 30 39 E
Atacama □, *Chile* **174 B2** 27 30 S 70 0W
Atacama, Desierto de, *Chile* **174 A2** 24 0 S 69 20W
Atacama, Salar de, *Chile* **174 A2** 23 30 S 68 20W
Ataco, *Colombia* **168 C2** 3 35N 75 23W
Atakor, *Algeria* **111 D6** 23 27N 5 31 E
Atakpamé, *Togo* **113 D5** 7 31N 1 13 E
Atalaia do Norte, *Brazil* **168 D3** 4 20 S 70 12W
Atalándi, *Greece* **48 C4** 38 39N 22 58 E
Atalaya, *Peru* **172 C3** 10 45 S 73 50W
Atalaya de Femes, *Canary Is.* **9 e2** 28 56N 13 47W
Ataléia, *Brazil* **171 E3** 18 3 S 41 6W
Atambua, *Indonesia* **82 C2** 9 7 S 124 54 E
Atami, *Japan* **73 B11** 35 5N 139 4 E
Atankawng, *Burma* **90 C6** 25 50N 97 47 E
Atapupu, *E. Timor* **82 C2** 9 0 S 124 51 E
Atâr, *Mauritania* **110 D2** 20 30N 13 5W
Ataram, Erg n-, *Algeria* **111 D5** 23 57N 2 0 E
Atarfe, *Spain* **43 H7** 37 13N 3 40W
Atari, *Pakistan* **92 D6** 30 56N 74 2 E
Atascadero, *U.S.A.* **160 K6** 35 29N 120 40W
Atasu, *Kazakhstan* **66 E8** 48 30N 71 0 E
Ataturk, Istanbul ✈ (IST), *Turkey* **51 F12** 40 59N 28 49 E
Atatürk Barajı, *Turkey* **101 D8** 37 28N 38 30 E
Atauro, *E. Timor* **82 C3** 8 10 S 125 30 E
'Atbara, *Sudan* **106 D3** 17 42N 33 59 E
'Atbara, Nahr →, *Sudan* **106 D3** 17 40N 33 56 E
Atbasar, *Kazakhstan* **66 D7** 51 48N 68 20 E
Atbashi = At-Bashy, *Kyrgyzstan* **65 C7** 41 10N 75 48 E
Atça, *Turkey* **49 D10** 37 53N 28 13 E
Atchafalaya B., *U.S.A.* **155 L9** 29 25N 91 25W
Atchison, *U.S.A.* **154 F7** 39 34N 95 7W
Atebubu, *Ghana* **113 D4** 7 47N 1 0W
Ateca, *Spain* **40 D3** 41 20N 1 49W
Aterno →, *Italy* **45 F10** 42 11N 13 51 E
Āteshān, *Iran* **97 C7** 35 35N 52 37 E
Atesine, Alpi, *Italy* **45 B8** 46 55N 11 30 E
Atessa, *Italy* **45 F11** 42 4N 14 27 E
Atfîh, *Egypt* **106 J7** 29 25N 31 15 E
Ath, *Belgium* **24 D3** 50 38N 3 47 E
Athabasca, *Canada* **142 C6** 54 45N 113 20W
Athabasca →, *Canada* **143 B6** 58 40N 110 50W
Athabasca, L., *Canada* **143 B7** 59 15N 109 15W
Athabasca Sand Dunes ⌓, *Canada* **143 B7** 59 4N 108 43W
Athagarh, *India* **94 D7** 20 32N 85 37 E
Athboy, *Ireland* **23 C5** 53 37N 6 56W
Athena, *U.S.A.* **152 F6** 29 59N 83 30W
Athenry, *Ireland* **23 C3** 53 18N 8 44W
Athens = Athínai, *Greece* **48 D5** 37 58N 23 46 E
Athens, *Ala., U.S.A.* **149 H2** 34 48N 86 58W
Athens, *Ga., U.S.A.* **152 B6** 33 57N 83 23W
Athens, *N.Y., U.S.A.* **151 D11** 42 16N 73 49W
Athens, *Ohio, U.S.A.* **148 F4** 39 20N 82 6W
Athens, *Pa., U.S.A.* **151 E8** 41 57N 76 31W
Athens, *Tenn., U.S.A.* **149 H3** 35 27N 84 36W
Athens, *Tex., U.S.A.* **155 J7** 32 12N 95 51W
Athéras, *Greece* **39 C1** 38 19N 20 25 E
Atherley, *Canada* **150 B5** 44 37N 79 20W
Atherton, *Australia* **126 B4** 17 17 S 145 30 E
Athiéme, *Benin* **113 D5** 6 37N 1 40 E
Athienou, *Cyprus* **39 E9** 35 3N 33 32 E
Athina = Athínai, *Greece* **48 D5** 37 58N 23 46 E
Athínai, *Greece* **48 D5** 37 58N 23 46 E
Athínai ✈ (ATH), *Greece* **48 D5** 37 55N 23 50 E
Athlone, *Ireland* **23 C4** 53 25N 7 56W
Athmalik, *India* **94 D7** 20 43N 84 32 E
Athna, *Cyprus* **39 E9** 35 3N 33 47 E
Athni, *India* **94 F2** 16 44N 75 6 E
Athol, *N.Z.* **131 F3** 45 30 S 168 35 E
Athol, *U.S.A.* **151 D12** 42 36N 72 14W
Athol Is., *Bahamas* **9 b** 25 5N 77 16W
Atholl, Forest of, *U.K.* **22 E5** 56 51N 3 50W
Atholl, Kap, *Greenland* **10 B4** 76 25N 69 30W
Atholville, *Canada* **141 C6** 47 59N 66 43W
Áthos, *Greece* **51 F8** 40 9N 24 22 E
Athy, *Ireland* **23 C5** 53 0N 7 0W
Ati, *Chad* **109 F3** 13 13N 18 20 E
Ati, *Sudan* **107 E2** 13 5N 29 2 E
Atiak, *Uganda* **118 B3** 3 12N 32 2 E
Atiamuri, *N.Z.* **130 E5** 38 24 S 176 5 E
Atico, *Peru* **172 D3** 16 14 S 73 40W
Atienza, *Spain* **40 D2** 41 12N 2 52W
Atiit, *Sudan* **107 F3** 6 10N 30 35 E
Atik L., *Canada* **143 B9** 55 15N 96 0W
Atikaki ⌓, *Canada* **143 C9** 51 30N 95 31W
Atikameg →, *Canada* **140 B3** 52 30N 82 46W
Atikokan, *Canada* **140 C1** 48 45N 91 37W
Atikonak L., *Canada* **141 B7** 52 40N 64 32W
Atimonan, *Phil.* **80 D3** 14 0N 121 55 E
'Ātinah, W. →, *Oman* **99 C6** 18 23N 53 28 E
Atirampattinam, *India* **95 J4** 10 28N 79 20 E
Atitlán △, *Cent. Amer.* **163 E6** 14 38N 91 10W
Atiu, *Cook Is.* **135 J12** 20 0 S 158 10W
Atka, *Russia* **67 C16** 60 50N 151 48 E
Atka, *U.S.A.* **144 K4** 52 12N 174 12W
Atka I., *U.S.A.* **144 K4** 52 7N 174 30W
Atkarsk, *Russia* **60 E7** 51 55N 45 2 E
Atkasuk = Meade River, *U.S.A.* **144 A8** 70 28N 157 24W
Atkinson, *Ga., U.S.A.* **152 D8** 31 13N 81 47W
Atkinson, *Ill., U.S.A.* **156 C6** 41 25N 90 1W
Atkinson, *Nebr., U.S.A.* **154 D5** 42 32N 98 59W
Atlanta, *Ga., U.S.A.* **152 B5** 33 45N 84 23W
Atlanta, *Ill., U.S.A.* **156 D7** 40 16N 89 14W
Atlanta, *Mo., U.S.A.* **156 E4** 39 54N 92 29W
Atlanta, *Tex., U.S.A.* **155 J7** 33 7N 94 10W
Atlanta Hartsfield International ✈ (ATL), *U.S.A.* **152 B5** 33 38N 84 26W
Atlantic, *U.S.A.* **156 C2** 41 24N 95 1W
Atlantic Beach, *U.S.A.* **152 E8** 30 20N 81 24W
Atlantic City, *U.S.A.* **148 F8** 39 21N 74 27W
Atlantic-Indian Basin, *Antarctica* **7 B4** 60 0 S 30 0 E
Atlantic-Indian Ridge, *Atl. Oc.* **8 M11** 53 0 S 5 0W
Atlantic Ocean **8 F8** 0 0 20 0W
Atlántico □, *Colombia* **168 A2** 10 45N 75 0W
Atlas Mts. = Haut Atlas, *Morocco* **110 B4** 32 30N 5 0W
Atlin, *Canada* **142 B2** 59 31N 133 41W
Atlin ⌓, *Canada* **142 B2** 59 10N 134 30W
Atlin, L., *Canada* **142 B2** 59 26N 133 45W
Atløyna, *Norway* **18 C1** 61 21N 4 58 E
Atmakur, *Andhra Pradesh, India* **94 E4** 18 45N 78 39 E
Atmakur, *Andhra Pradesh, India* **95 G4** 14 37N 79 40 E
Atmakur, *Andhra Pradesh, India* **95 G4** 15 53N 78 35 E
Atmore, *U.S.A.* **149 K2** 31 2N 87 29W
Atna, *Norway* **18 C7** 61 44N 10 49 E
Atna →, *Norway* **18 C7** 61 44N 10 49 E
Atō, *Japan* **72 C3** 34 25N 131 40 E
Atocha, *Bolivia* **172 E4** 20 56 S 66 14W
Atok, *Phil.* **80 C3** 16 35N 120 41 E
Atoka, *U.S.A.* **155 H6** 34 23N 96 8W
Átokos Nisís, *Greece* **39 C2** 38 28N 20 49 E
Atolia, *U.S.A.* **161 K9** 35 19N 117 37W
Atongo-Bakari, *C.A.R.* **114 A4** 5 49N 21 35 E
Atori, *Solomon Is.* **133 M11** 8 42 S 160 59 E
Atrå, *Norway* **18 E5** 59 59N 8 45 E
Atrai →, *Bangla.* **90 C2** 24 7N 89 22 E
Atrak = Atrek →, *Turkmenistan* **97 B8** 37 35N 53 58 E
Ätran, *Sweden* **17 G6** 57 7N 12 57 E
Ätran →, *Sweden* **17 H6** 56 53N 12 30 E
Atrato →, *Colombia* **168 B2** 8 17N 76 58W
Atrauli, *India* **92 E8** 28 2N 78 20 E
Atrek →, *Turkmenistan* **97 B8** 37 35N 53 58 E
Atri, *Italy* **45 F10** 42 35N 13 58 E
Atsikí, *Greece* **49 B7** 39 56N 25 13 E
Atsoum, Mts., *Cameroon* **113 D7** 6 41N 12 57 E
Atsugi, *Japan* **73 B11** 35 25N 139 21 E
Atsumi, *Japan* **73 C9** 34 35N 137 4 E
Atsumi-Wan, *Japan* **73 C9** 34 44N 137 13 E
Atsuta, *Japan* **70 C10** 43 24N 141 26 E
Atsy, *Indonesia* **83 C5** 5 48 S 138 20 E
Attalla, *U.S.A.* **152 A3** 34 1N 86 6W
Attapu, *Laos* **86 E6** 14 48N 106 50 E
Attapulgus, *U.S.A.* **152 E5** 30 45N 84 29W
Attáviros, *Greece* **38 E11** 36 12N 27 50 E
Attawapiskat, *Canada* **140 B3** 52 56N 82 24W
Attawapiskat →, *Canada* **140 B3** 52 57N 82 18W
Attawapiskat L., *Canada* **140 B2** 52 18N 87 54W
Attersee, *Austria* **34 D6** 47 55N 13 32 E
Attica, *Ind., U.S.A.* **157 D9** 40 18N 87 15W
Attica, *Ohio, U.S.A.* **150 E2** 41 4N 82 53W
Attichy, *France* **27 C10** 49 25N 3 3 E
Attigny, *France* **27 C11** 49 28N 4 35 E
Attika = Attikí □, *Greece* **48 D5** 37 10N 23 40 E
Attikamagen L., *Canada* **141 B6** 55 0N 66 30W
Attikí □, *Greece* **48 D5** 37 10N 23 40 E
Attleboro, *U.S.A.* **151 E13** 41 57N 71 17W
Attock = Campbellpur, *Pakistan* **92 C5** 33 46N 72 26 E
Attock, *Pakistan* **92 C5** 33 52N 72 20 E
Attopeu = Attapu, *Laos* **86 E6** 14 48N 106 50 E
Attu, *U.S.A.* **144 K1** 52 56N 173 15 E
Attu I., *U.S.A.* **144 K1** 52 55N 172 55 E
Attunga, *Australia* **129 A9** 30 55 S 150 50 E
Attur, *India* **95 J4** 11 35N 78 30 E
'Atūd, *Yemen* **99 D5** 14 53N 48 10 E
Atuel →, *Argentina* **174 D2** 36 17 S 66 50W
Åtvidaberg, *Sweden* **17 F10** 58 12N 16 0 E
Atwater, *U.S.A.* **160 H6** 37 21N 120 37W
Atwood, *Canada* **150 C3** 43 40N 81 1W
Atwood, *Ill., U.S.A.* **157 E8** 39 48N 88 28W
Atwood, *Kans., U.S.A.* **154 F4** 39 48N 101 3W
Atyraū, *Kazakhstan* **57 E9** 47 5N 52 0 E
Au, *Austria* **33 B9** 47 19N 9 59 E
Au Sable, *U.S.A.* **150 B1** 44 25N 83 20W
Au Sable →, *U.S.A.* **148 C4** 44 25N 83 20W
Au Sable Forks, *U.S.A.* **151 B11** 44 27N 73 41W
Au Sable Pt., *U.S.A.* **150 B1** 44 20N 83 20W
Aubagne, *France* **29 E9** 43 17N 5 37 E
Aubarca, C. d', *Spain* **38 C1** 39 4N 1 22 E
Aube □, *France* **27 D11** 48 15N 4 10 E
Aube →, *France* **27 D10** 48 34N 3 43 E
Aubenas, *France* **29 D8** 44 37N 4 24 E
Aubenton, *France* **27 C11** 49 50N 4 12 E
Auberry, *U.S.A.* **160 H7** 37 7N 119 29W
Aubigny-sur-Nère, *France* **27 E9** 47 30N 2 24 E
Aubin, *France* **28 D6** 44 33N 2 15 E
Aubrac, Mts. d', *France* **28 D7** 44 40N 3 2 E
Auburn, *Australia* **128 C3** 34 1 S 138 42 E
Auburn, *Ala., U.S.A.* **152 C4** 32 36N 85 29W
Auburn, *Calif., U.S.A.* **160 G5** 38 54N 121 4W
Auburn, *Ill., U.S.A.* **156 E7** 39 36N 89 45W
Auburn, *Ind., U.S.A.* **157 C11** 41 22N 85 4W
Auburn, *Maine, U.S.A.* **149 C10** 44 6N 70 14W
Auburn, *N.Y., U.S.A.* **151 D8** 42 56N 76 34W
Auburn, *Nebr., U.S.A.* **154 E7** 40 23N 95 51W
Auburn, *Pa., U.S.A.* **151 F8** 40 36N 76 6W
Auburn, *Wash., U.S.A.* **160 C4** 47 18N 122 14W
Auburn Ra., *Australia* **127 D5** 25 15 S 150 30 E
Auburndale, *U.S.A.* **153 G8** 28 4N 81 48W
Aubusson, *France* **28 C6** 45 57N 2 11 E
Auce, *Latvia* **54 B9** 56 28N 22 53 E
Auch, *France* **28 E4** 43 39N 0 36 E
Auchi, *Nigeria* **113 D6** 7 6N 6 13 E
Auchterarder, *U.K.* **22 E5** 56 18N 3 41W
Auchtermuchty, *U.K.* **22 E5** 56 18N 3 13W
Auckland, *N.Z.* **130 C3** 36 52 S 174 46 E
Auckland □, *N.Z.* **130 E6** 36 50 S 175 0 E
Auckland Is., *Pac. Oc.* **134 N8** 50 40 S 166 5 E
Aude □, *France* **28 E6** 43 8N 2 28 E
Aude →, *France* **28 E7** 43 13N 3 14 E
Audegle, *Somali Rep.* **120 D2** 1 59N 44 50 E
Auden, *Canada* **140 B2** 50 14N 87 53W
Auderville, *France* **26 C5** 49 43N 1 57W
Audierne, *France* **26 D2** 48 1N 4 34W
Audincourt, *France* **27 E13** 47 30N 6 50 E
Audo Ra., *Ethiopia* **107 F5** 6 20N 41 50 E
Audubon, *U.S.A.* **156 C2** 41 43N 94 56W
Aue, *Germany* **30 E8** 50 35N 12 41 E
Auerbach, *Germany* **30 E8** 50 30N 12 24 E
Aueti Paraná →, *Brazil* **168 D4** 1 51 S 65 37W
Aufist, *W. Sahara* **110 C2** 25 44N 14 39W
Augathella, *Australia* **127 D4** 25 48 S 146 35 E
Aughnacloy, *U.K.* **23 B5** 54 25N 6 59W
Augrabies Falls, *S. Africa* **116 D3** 28 35 S 20 20 E
Augrabies Falls △, *S. Africa* **116 D3** 28 40 S 20 22 E
Augsburg, *Germany* **31 G6** 48 25N 10 52 E
Augsburg-Westliche Wälder ⌓, *Germany* **31 G6** 48 22N 10 40 E
Augusta, *Australia* **125 F2** 34 19 S 115 9 E
Augusta, *Italy* **47 E8** 37 13N 15 13 E
Augusta, *Ark., U.S.A.* **155 H9** 35 17N 91 22W
Augusta, *Ga., U.S.A.* **152 B8** 33 28N 81 58W
Augusta, *Ill., U.S.A.* **156 D6** 40 14N 90 57W
Augusta, *Kans., U.S.A.* **155 G6** 37 41N 96 59W
Augusta, *Ky., U.S.A.* **157 F12** 38 47N 84 0W
Augusta, *Maine, U.S.A.* **139 D13** 44 19N 69 47W
Augusta, *Mont., U.S.A.* **158 C7** 47 30N 112 24W
Augustenborg, *Denmark* **17 K3** 54 57N 9 53 E
Augustine I., *U.S.A.* **144 G9** 59 22N 153 26W
Augusto Cardosa = Metangula, *Mozam.* **119 E3** 12 40 S 34 50 E
Augustów, *Poland* **54 E9** 53 51N 23 0 E
Augustus, Mt., *Australia* **125 D2** 24 20 S 116 50 E
Augustus I., *Australia* **124 C3** 15 20 S 124 30 E
Aukan, *Eritrea* **107 D5** 15 29N 40 50 E
Auki, *Solomon Is.* **133 M11** 8 45 S 160 42 E
Aukra, *Norway* **18 B3** 62 47N 6 55 E
Aukrug ⌓, *Germany* **30 A5** 54 5N 9 45 E
Aukum, *U.S.A.* **160 G6** 38 34N 120 43W
Aul, *India* **94 D8** 20 41N 86 39 E
Auld, L., *Australia* **124 D3** 22 25 S 123 50 E
Auliye-Ata = Taraz, *Kazakhstan* **65 B5** 42 54N 71 22 E
Aulla, *Italy* **44 D6** 44 12N 9 58 E
Aulnay, *France* **28 B3** 46 2N 0 22W
Aulne →, *France* **26 D2** 48 17N 4 16W
Aulnoye-Aymeries, *France* **27 B10** 50 12N 3 50 E
Ault, *France* **26 B8** 50 8N 1 26 E
Ault, *U.S.A.* **154 E2** 40 35N 104 44W
Aulus-les-Bains, *France* **28 F5** 42 49N 1 19 E
Aumale = Sour el Ghozlane, *Algeria* **111 A5** 36 10N 3 45 E
Aumale, *France* **27 C8** 49 46N 1 46 E
Aumo, *Papua N. G.* **132 C5** 5 44 S 148 30 E

Aumont-Aubrac, *France* 28 D7 44 43N 3 17 E
Auna, *Nigeria* 113 C5 10 9N 4 42 E
Aundah, *India* 94 E3 19 32N 77 3 E
Aundh, *India* 94 F2 17 33N 74 23 E
Auning, *Denmark* 17 H4 56 26N 10 22 E
Aunis, *France* 28 B3 46 5N 0 50W
'Aunu'u, *Amer. Samoa* 133 X24 14 20 S 170 31W
Auponhia, *Indonesia* 82 B3 1 58 S 125 27 E
Aups, *France* 29 E10 43 37N 6 15 E
Aur, Pulau, *Malaysia* 87 L5 2 35N 104 10 E
Aura, *Burma* 90 B6 26 59N 97 57 E
Auraiya, *India* 93 F8 26 28N 79 33 E
Aurangabad, *Bihar, India* 93 G11 24 45N 84 18 E
Aurangabad, *Maharashtra, India* 94 E2 19 50N 75 23 E
Auray, *France* 26 E4 47 40N 2 59W
Aurdal, *Norway* 18 D6 60 55N 9 26 E
Aure, *Norway* 18 A5 63 16N 8 33 E
Aurès, *Algeria* 111 A6 35 8N 6 30 E
Aurich, *Germany* 30 B3 53 28N 7 28 E
Aurilândia, *Brazil* 171 E1 16 44 S 50 28W
Aurillac, *France* 28 D6 44 55N 2 26 E
Aurlandsfjorden, *Norway* 18 C4 61 3N 7 1 E
Aurlandsvangen, *Norway* 18 D4 60 55N 7 12 E
Auronzo di Cadore, *Italy* 45 B9 46 33N 12 26 E
Aurora = Maéwo, *Vanuatu* 133 E6 15 10 S 168 10 E
Aurora = San Francisco, *Phil.* 80 E4 13 21N 122 31 E
Aurora, *Canada* 150 C5 44 0N 79 28W
Aurora, *Isabela, Phil.* 80 C3 16 59N 121 38 E
Aurora, *Zamboanga del S., Phil.* 81 H4 7 57N 123 36 E
Aurora, *S. Africa* 116 E2 32 40 S 18 29 E
Aurora, *Colo., U.S.A.* 154 F2 39 44N 104 52W
Aurora, *Ill., U.S.A.* 157 C8 41 45N 88 19W
Aurora, *Mo., U.S.A.* 155 G8 36 58N 93 43W
Aurora, *N.Y., U.S.A.* 151 D8 42 45N 76 42W
Aurora, *Nebr., U.S.A.* 154 E6 40 52N 98 0W
Aurora, *Ohio, U.S.A.* 150 E3 41 21N 81 20W
Aurora □, *Phil.* 80 D3 15 30N 121 30 E
Aurora ∆, *Phil.* 80 D3 15 40N 121 20 E
Aursmoen, *Norway* 18 E8 59 55N 11 26 E
Aursunden, *Norway* 18 B8 62 40N 11 40 E
Aurukun, *Australia* 126 A3 13 20 S 141 45 E
Aus, *Namibia* 116 D2 26 35 S 16 12 E
Ausa, *India* 94 E3 18 15N 76 30 E
Ausable →, *Canada* 150 C3 43 19N 81 46W
Auschwitz = Oświęcim, *Poland* 55 H6 50 2N 19 11 E
Auspitz = Hustopeče, *Czech Rep.* 35 C9 48 57N 16 43 E
Aussig = Ústí nad Labem, *Czech Rep.* 34 A7 50 41N 14 3 E
Aust-Agder □, *Norway* 18 F4 58 45N 8 0 E
Austad, *Norway* 18 F4 58 58N 7 37 E
Austen Harbour, *India* 95 H11 12 55N 92 45 E
Austerlitz = Slavkov u Brna, *Czech Rep.* 35 B9 49 10N 16 52 E
Austevoll, *Norway* 18 D2 60 5N 5 13 E
Austin, *Ind., U.S.A.* 157 F11 38 45N 85 49W
Austin, *Minn., U.S.A.* 154 D8 43 40N 92 58W
Austin, *Nev., U.S.A.* 158 G5 39 30N 117 4W
Austin, *Pa., U.S.A.* 150 E6 41 38N 78 6W
Austin, *Tex., U.S.A.* 155 K6 30 17N 97 45W
Austin, L., *Australia* 125 E2 27 40 S 118 0 E
Austin I., *Canada* 143 A10 61 10N 94 0W
Austmarka, *Norway* 18 D9 60 6N 12 21 E
Austnes, *Norway* 18 B3 62 38N 6 16 E
Austra, *Norway* 14 D14 65 8N 11 55 E
Austral Is. = Tubuai Is., *French Polynesia* 135 K13 25 0 S 150 0W
Austral Seamount Chain, *Pac. Oc.* 135 K13 24 0 S 150 0W
Australia ■, *Oceania* 134 K5 23 0 S 135 0 E
Australian Capital Territory □, *Australia* 129 C8 35 30 S 149 0 E
Australind, *Australia* 125 F2 33 17 S 115 42 E
Austria ■, *Europe* 34 E7 47 0N 14 0 E
Austur-Skaftafellssýsla □, *Iceland* 11 C10 64 15N 16 0W
Austvågøy, *Norway* 14 B16 68 20N 14 40 E
Autazes, *Brazil* 169 D6 3 35 S 59 8W
Auterive, *France* 28 E5 43 21N 1 29 E
Authie →, *France* 27 B8 50 22N 1 38 E
Authon-du-Perche, *France* 26 D7 48 12N 0 54 E
Autlán, *Mexico* 162 D4 19 40N 104 30W
Autun, *France* 27 F11 46 58N 4 17 E
Auvergne □, *France* 28 C7 45 20N 3 15 E
Auvergne, Mts. d', *France* 28 C6 45 20N 2 55 E
Auvézère →, *France* 28 C4 45 12N 0 50 E
Auxerre, *France* 27 E10 47 48N 3 32 E
Auxi-le-Château, *France* 27 B9 50 15N 2 8 E
Auxonne, *France* 27 E12 47 10N 5 20 E
Auxvasse, *U.S.A.* 156 E5 39 1N 91 54W
Auzances, *France* 27 F9 46 2N 2 30 E
Ava, *Ill., U.S.A.* 156 G7 37 53N 89 30W
Ava, *Mo., U.S.A.* 155 G8 36 57N 92 40W
Avaldsnes, *Norway* 18 E2 59 21N 5 20 E
Avallon, *France* 27 E10 47 30N 3 53 E
Avalon, *U.S.A.* 161 M8 33 21N 118 20W
Avalon Pen., *Canada* 141 C9 47 30N 53 20W
Avanavero, *Suriname* 169 C6 4 51N 57 22W
Avanigadda, *India* 95 G5 16 0N 80 56 E
Avannaarsua □, *Greenland* 10 B5 80 0N 55 0W
Avanos, *Turkey* 100 C6 38 43N 34 51 E
Avaré, *Brazil* 175 A6 23 4 S 48 58W
Ávas, *Greece* 51 F9 40 57N 25 56 E
Avawatz Mts., *U.S.A.* 161 K10 35 40N 116 30W
Avdan Dağı, *Turkey* 51 F13 40 23N 29 46 E
Aveiro, *Brazil* 169 D6 3 10 S 55 5W
Aveiro, *Portugal* 42 E2 40 37N 8 38W
Aveiro □, *Portugal* 42 E2 40 40N 8 35W
Āvej, *Iran* 97 C6 35 40N 49 15 E
Avellaneda, *Argentina* 174 C4 34 50 S 58 10W
Avellino, *Italy* 47 B7 40 54N 14 47 E
Avenal, *U.S.A.* 160 K6 36 0N 120 8W
Avenches, *Switz.* 32 C4 46 53N 7 2 E
Averøya, *Norway* 18 A4 63 0N 7 35 E
Aversa, *Italy* 47 B7 40 58N 14 12 E
Avery, *U.S.A.* 158 C6 47 15N 115 49W
Aves, I. de, *W. Indies* 165 C7 15 45N 63 55W
Aves, Is. las, *Venezuela* 165 D6 12 0N 67 30W
Avesnes-sur-Helpe, *France* 27 B10 50 8N 3 55 E
Avesnois ⌂, *France* 27 B10 50 10N 3 45 E
Avesta, *Sweden* 16 D10 60 9N 16 10 E
Aveyron □, *France* 28 D6 44 22N 2 45 E
Aveyron →, *France* 28 D5 44 5N 1 16 E
Avezzano, *Italy* 45 F10 42 2N 13 25 E
Avgó, *Greece* 49 F7 35 33N 25 37 E
Aviá Terai, *Argentina* 174 B3 26 45 S 60 50W
Aviano, *Italy* 45 B9 46 4N 12 36 E
Aviemore, *U.K.* 22 D5 57 12N 3 50W
Aviemore, L., *N.Z.* 131 E5 44 37 S 170 18 E
Avigliana, *Italy* 44 C4 45 5N 7 23 E
Avigliano, *Italy* 47 B8 40 44N 15 43 E
Avignon, *France* 29 E8 43 57N 4 50 E
Ávila, *Spain* 42 E6 40 39N 4 43W
Ávila □, *Spain* 42 E6 40 30N 5 0W
Ávila, Sierra de, *Spain* 42 E5 40 40N 5 15W
Avila Beach, *U.S.A.* 161 K6 35 11N 120 44W
Avilés, *Spain* 42 B5 43 35N 5 57W
Avintes, *Portugal* 42 D2 41 7N 8 33W
Avionárion, *Greece* 48 C6 38 31N 24 8 E
Avis, *Portugal* 43 F3 39 4N 7 53W
Avis, *U.S.A.* 150 E7 41 11N 77 19W
Avísio →, *Italy* 44 B8 46 7N 11 5 E
Avissawella, *Sri Lanka* 95 L5 6 56N 80 11 E
Aviston, *U.S.A.* 156 F7 38 36N 89 36W
Aviz = Avis, *Portugal* 43 F3 39 4N 7 53W
Avize, *France* 27 D11 48 59N 4 1 E
Avlona = Vlorë, *Albania* 50 F3 40 32N 19 28 E
Avlum, *Denmark* 17 H2 56 16N 8 47 E
Avoca, *Australia* 128 D5 37 5 S 143 26 E
Avoca, *U.S.A.* 150 D7 42 25N 77 25W
Avoca →, *Australia* 128 C5 35 40 S 143 43 E
Avoca →, *Ireland* 23 D5 52 48N 6 10W
Avola, *Canada* 142 C5 51 45N 119 19W
Avola, *Italy* 47 F8 36 56N 15 7 E
Avon, *Ill., U.S.A.* 156 D6 40 40N 90 26W
Avon, *N.Y., U.S.A.* 150 D7 42 55N 77 45W
Avon, *S. Dak., U.S.A.* 154 D5 43 0N 98 4W
Avon →, *Australia* 125 F2 31 40 S 116 7 E
Avon →, *Bristol, U.K.* 21 F5 51 29N 2 41W
Avon →, *Dorset, U.K.* 21 G6 50 44N 1 46W
Avon →, *Warks., U.K.* 21 E5 52 0N 2 8W
Avon Park, *U.S.A.* 153 H8 27 36N 81 31W
Avondale, *Zimbabwe* 119 F3 17 43 S 30 58 E
Avonlea, *Canada* 143 D8 50 0N 105 0W
Avonmore, *Canada* 151 A10 45 10N 74 58W
Avonmouth, *U.K.* 21 F5 51 30N 2 42W
Avramov, *Bulgaria* 51 D10 42 45N 26 38 E
Avranches, *France* 26 D5 48 40N 1 20W
Avre →, *France* 26 D8 48 47N 1 22 E
Avrig, *Romania* 53 E9 45 43N 24 21 E
Avrillé, *France* 26 E6 47 30N 0 35W
Avtovac, *Bos.-H.* 50 C2 43 9N 18 35 E
Avu Avu, *Solomon Is.* 133 M11 9 50 S 160 22 E
Awag el Baqar, *Sudan* 107 E3 10 10N 33 10 E
Awaji, *Japan* 73 C7 34 32N 135 1 E
Awaji-Shima, *Japan* 72 C6 34 30N 134 50 E
'Awālī, *Bahrain* 97 E6 26 0N 50 30 E
Awantipur, *India* 93 C6 33 55N 75 3 E
Awanui, *N.Z.* 130 B2 35 4 S 173 17 E
Awarja →, *India* 94 F3 17 5N 76 15 E
Awarua B., *N.Z.* 131 E3 44 28 S 168 4 E
Awarua Pt., *N.Z.* 131 E3 44 15 S 168 5 E
Awasa, *Ethiopia* 107 F4 7 2N 38 28 E
Awasa, L., *Ethiopia* 107 F4 7 0N 38 30 E
Awash, *Ethiopia* 107 F5 9 1N 40 10 E
Awash ∆, *Ethiopia* 107 F5 9 8N 40 0 E
Awash →, *Ethiopia* 107 E5 11 45N 41 5 E
Awaso, *Ghana* 112 D4 6 15N 2 22W
Awatere →, *N.Z.* 131 B9 41 37 S 174 10 E
Awbārī, *Libya* 108 C2 26 46N 12 57 E
Awbārī □, *Libya* 108 C2 26 35N 12 46 E
Awbārī, Idehan, *Libya* 108 C2 27 10N 11 30 E
Awe, L., *U.K.* 22 E3 56 17N 5 16W
Aweil, *Sudan* 107 F2 8 42N 27 20 E
Awgu, *Nigeria* 113 D6 6 4N 7 24 E
Awjilah, *Libya* 108 C4 29 8N 21 7 E
Awka, *Nigeria* 113 D6 6 12N 7 5 E
Aworro, *Papua N. G.* 132 D2 7 43 S 143 11 E
Ax-les-Thermes, *France* 28 F5 42 44N 1 50 E
Axat, *France* 28 F6 42 48N 2 13 E
Axe →, *U.K.* 21 F5 50 42N 3 4W
Axel Heiberg I., *Canada* 6 B3 80 0N 90 0W
Axim, *Ghana* 112 E4 4 51N 2 15W
Axinim, *Brazil* 169 D6 4 2 S 59 22W
Axintele, *Romania* 53 F11 44 37N 26 47 E
Axioma, *Brazil* 173 B5 6 45 S 64 31W
Axiós →, *Greece* 50 F6 40 57N 22 35 E
Axminster, *U.K.* 21 G4 50 46N 3 0W
Axson, *U.S.A.* 152 D7 31 17N 82 44W
Axvall, *Sweden* 17 F7 58 23N 13 34 E
Ay, *France* 27 C11 49 3N 4 1 E
Ay →, *Russia* 64 C6 56 8N 57 40 E
Ayaantang, *Eq. Guin.* 114 B2 1 58N 10 24 E
Ayabaca, *Peru* 172 A2 4 40 S 79 53W
Ayabe, *Japan* 73 B7 35 20N 135 20 E
Ayacucho, *Argentina* 174 D4 37 5 S 58 20W
Ayacucho, *Peru* 172 C3 13 0 S 74 0W
Ayacucho □, *Peru* 172 C3 14 0 S 74 0W
Ayaguz, *Kazakhstan* 66 E9 48 10N 80 10 E
Ayakkuduk, *Uzbekistan* 65 C2 41 12N 65 12 E
Ayakudi, *India* 95 J3 10 28N 77 56 E
Ayala, *Phil.* 81 H3 6 57N 121 57 E
Ayamé, *Ivory C.* 112 D4 5 35N 3 9W
Ayamonte, *Spain* 43 H3 37 12N 7 24W
Ayan, *Russia* 67 D14 56 30N 138 16 E
Ayancık, *Turkey* 100 B6 41 57N 34 35 E
Ayapel, *Colombia* 168 B2 8 19N 75 9W
Ayas, *Turkey* 100 B5 40 2N 32 21 E
Ayaviri, *Peru* 172 C3 14 50 S 70 35W
Āybak, *Afghan.* 91 A3 36 15N 68 5 E
Aybastı, *Turkey* 100 B7 40 41N 37 23 E
Aydarkul Ozero, *Uzbekistan* 65 C3 40 50N 67 10 E
Aydın, *Turkey* 100 D2 37 51N 27 51 E
Aydın □, *Turkey* 49 D9 37 50N 28 0 E
Aydin Dağları, *Turkey* 49 D10 38 0N 28 0 E
Aydyrlinskiy, *Russia* 64 E7 52 3N 59 50 E
Ayelu, *Ethiopia* 107 E5 10 5N 40 42 E
Ayenngré, *Togo* 113 D5 8 40N 1 1 E
Ayer, *U.S.A.* 151 D13 42 34N 71 35W
Ayer Hitam, *Malaysia* 87 c 5 24N 100 16 E
Ayerbe, *Spain* 40 C4 42 17N 0 41W
Ayer's Cliff, *Canada* 151 A12 45 10N 72 3W
Ayers Rock, *Australia* 125 E5 25 23 S 131 5 E
Ayiá, *Greece* 48 B4 39 43N 22 45 E
Ayia Aikaterini, Ákra, *Greece* 38 B9 39 50N 19 50 E
Ayia Ánna, *Greece* 48 C5 38 52N 23 24 E
Ayia Dhéka, *Greece* 39 E5 35 3N 24 58 E
Ayia Gálini, *Greece* 39 E5 35 6N 24 41 E
Ayia Marína, *Kásos, Greece* 49 F8 35 27N 26 53 E
Ayia Marína, *Léros, Greece* 49 D8 37 11N 26 48 E
Ayia Napa, *Cyprus* 39 F10 34 59N 34 0 E
Ayia Paraskeví, *Greece* 49 B8 39 14N 26 21 E
Ayia Phyla, *Cyprus* 39 F9 34 43N 33 1 E
Ayia Rouméli, *Greece* 39 E4 35 14N 23 58 E
Ayia Varvára, *Greece* 39 E6 35 8N 25 1 E
Ayiássos, *Greece* 49 B8 39 5N 26 23 E
Ayioi Theódhoroi, *Greece* 48 D5 37 55N 23 9 E
Áyion Óros □, *Greece* 51 F8 40 25N 24 6 E
Áyios Amvrósios, *Cyprus* 39 E9 35 20N 33 35 E
Áyios Andréas, *Greece* 48 D4 37 21N 22 45 E
Áyios Evstrátios, *Greece* 48 B6 39 34N 24 58 E
Áyios Ioánnis, Ákra, *Greece* 39 E6 35 20N 25 40 E
Áyios Isidhoros, *Greece* 38 E11 36 9N 27 51 E
Áyios Kiríkos, *Greece* 49 D8 37 34N 26 17 E
Áyios Léon, *Greece* 39 D2 37 47N 20 43 E
Áyios Matthaíos, *Greece* 38 C9 39 30N 19 47 E
Áyios Mírono, *Greece* 39 E6 35 15N 25 1 E
Áyios Nikólaos, *Aitolía kai Akarnanía, Greece* 39 B2 38 52N 20 48 E
Áyios Nikólaos, *Kríti, Greece* 39 E6 35 11N 25 41 E
Áyios Nikólaos, *Levkás, Greece* 39 B2 38 36N 20 34 E
Áyios Pétros, *Greece* 39 B2 38 40N 20 36 E
Áyios Seryios, *Cyprus* 39 E9 35 12N 33 53 E
Áyios Theodhoros, *Cyprus* 39 E10 35 22N 34 1 E
Áyios Thomás, *Greece* 39 B2 38 58N 20 47 E
Áyios Yeóryios, *Greece* 48 D5 37 28N 23 57 E
Aykathonisi, *Greece* 49 D8 37 28N 27 0 E
Aykino, *Russia* 56 B8 62 15N 49 56 E
Aykirikçi, *Turkey* 49 B12 39 8N 30 9 E
Aylesbury, *U.K.* 21 F7 51 49N 0 49W
Aylmer, *Canada* 150 D4 42 46N 80 59W
Aylmer, L., *Canada* 138 B8 64 0N 110 8W
'Ayn, Wādī al, *Oman* 97 F7 22 15N 55 28 E
'Ayn al Ghazālah, *Libya* 108 B4 32 10N 23 20 E
Ayn Dār, *Si. Arabia* 97 E7 25 55N 49 10 E
Ayn Zālah, *Iraq* 101 D10 36 45N 42 35 E
Ayna, *Spain* 41 G2 38 34N 2 3W
Aynabulaq, *Kazakhstan* 65 A8 44 36N 77 56 E
Aynāt, *Yemen* 99 C5 16 4N 49 9 E
Ayni, *Tajikistan* 65 D4 39 23N 68 32 E
Ayod, *Sudan* 107 F3 8 7N 31 26 E
Ayolas, *Paraguay* 174 B4 27 10 S 56 59W
Ayom, *Sudan* 107 F2 7 49N 28 23 E
Ayon, Ostrov, *Russia* 67 C17 69 50N 169 0 E
Ayora, *Spain* 41 F3 39 3N 1 3W
Ayorou, *Niger* 113 C5 14 53N 1 0 E
Ayos, *Cameroon* 114 B2 3 53N 12 31 E
'Ayoûn el 'Atroûs, *Mauritania* 112 B3 16 38N 9 37W
Ayr, *Australia* 126 B4 19 35 S 147 25 E
Ayr, *Canada* 150 C4 43 17N 80 27W
Ayr, *U.K.* 22 F4 55 28N 4 38W
Ayr →, *U.K.* 22 F4 55 28N 4 38W
Ayrancı, *Turkey* 100 D5 37 21N 33 41 E
Ayrancılar, *Turkey* 49 C9 38 15N 27 18 E
Ayre, Pt. of, *I. of Man* 20 C3 54 25N 4 21W
Aysha, *Ethiopia* 107 E5 10 50N 42 23 E
Ayton, *Australia* 126 B4 15 56 S 145 22 E
Aytos, *Bulgaria* 51 D11 42 42N 27 16 E
Aytoska Planina, *Bulgaria* 51 D11 42 45N 27 30 E
Ayu, Kepulauan, *Indonesia* 83 A4 0 35N 131 5 E
Ayutla, *Guatemala* 164 D1 14 40N 92 10W
Ayutla, *Mexico* 163 D5 16 58N 99 17W
Ayvacık, *Turkey* 100 C2 39 36N 26 24 E
Ayvalık, *Turkey* 49 B8 39 20N 26 46 E
Az Zabadānī, *Syria* 103 B5 33 43N 36 5 E
Az Ẓāhirīyah, *West Bank* 103 D3 31 25N 34 58 E
Az Ẓahrān, *Si. Arabia* 97 E6 26 10N 50 7 E
Az Zarqā, *Jordan* 103 C5 32 5N 36 4 E
Az Zarqā', *U.A.E.* 97 E7 24 53N 53 4 E
Az Zarqā □, *Jordan* 103 C5 32 5N 36 4 E
Az Zāwiyah, *Libya* 108 B2 32 52N 12 56 E
Az Zaydīyah, *Yemen* 98 D3 15 20N 43 1 E
Az Zībār, *Iraq* 101 D11 36 52N 44 4 E
Az Zilfī, *Si. Arabia* 96 E5 26 12N 44 52 E
Az Zubayr, *Iraq* 96 D5 30 26N 47 40 E
Az Zuqur, *Yemen* 98 D3 14 0N 42 45 E
Az Zuwaytīnah, *Libya* 108 B4 30 58N 20 7 E
Azad Kashmir □, *Pakistan* 93 C5 33 50N 73 50 E
Azambuja, *Portugal* 43 F2 39 4N 8 51W
Azamgarh, *India* 93 F10 26 5N 83 13 E
Azangaro, *Peru* 172 C3 14 55 S 70 13W
Azaoua, *Niger* 113 B5 15 50N 4 0 E
Azaouad, *Mali* 112 B4 19 0N 3 0W
Azaouak, Vallée de l', *Mali* 113 B5 15 50N 3 20 E
Āzār Shahr, *Iran* 101 D11 37 45N 45 59 E
Azara, *Nigeria* 113 D6 8 22N 9 12 E
Azarān, *Iran* 101 D12 37 25N 47 16 E
Āzarbayjan = Azerbaijan ■, *Asia* 61 K9 40 20N 48 0 E
Āzarbāyjān-e Gharbī □, *Iran* 96 B5 37 0N 44 30 E
Āzarbāyjān-e Sharqī □, *Iran* 96 B5 37 20N 47 0 E
Azare, *Nigeria* 113 C7 11 55N 10 10 E
Azay-le-Rideau, *France* 26 E7 47 16N 0 30 E
A'zāz, *Syria* 100 D7 36 36N 37 4 E
Azazga, *Algeria* 111 A5 36 48N 4 22 E
Azbine = Aïr, *Niger* 113 B6 18 30N 8 0 E
Azefal, *Mauritania* 110 D2 21 0N 14 45W
Azeffoun, *Algeria* 111 A5 36 51N 4 26 E
Azemmour, *Morocco* 110 B3 33 20N 9 20W
Azennezal, *Algeria* 111 D5 22 58N 0 43 E
Azerbaijan ■, *Asia* 61 K9 40 20N 48 0 E
Azerbaijchan = Azerbaijan ■, *Asia* 61 K9 40 20N 48 0 E
Azezo, *Ethiopia* 107 E4 12 28N 37 15 E
Azimganj, *India* 93 G13 24 14N 88 16 E
Aznalcóllar, *Spain* 43 H4 37 32N 6 17W
Azogues, *Ecuador* 168 D2 2 35 S 78 0W
Azores = Açores, Is. dos, *Atl. Oc.* 8 C9 38 0N 27 0W
Azores-Biscay Rise, *Atl. Oc.* 8 B9 42 0N 20 0W
Azoum, B. →, *Chad* 109 F4 10 53N 20 15 E
Azov, *Russia* 61 G4 47 3N 39 25 E
Azov, Sea of, *Europe* 59 J9 46 0N 36 30 E
Azovskoye More = Azov, Sea of, *Europe* 59 J9 46 0N 36 30 E
Azpeitia, *Spain* 40 B2 43 12N 2 19W
Azraq, B. →, *Chad* 109 F4 10 52N 20 35 E
Azraq ash Shīshān, *Jordan* 103 D5 31 50N 36 49 E
Azrou, *Morocco* 110 B3 33 28N 5 19W
Aztec, *U.S.A.* 159 H10 36 49N 107 59W
Azúa de Compostela, *Dom. Rep.* 165 C5 18 25N 70 44W
Azuaga, *Spain* 43 G5 38 16N 5 39W
Azuara, *Spain* 40 D4 41 15N 0 53W
Azuay □, *Ecuador* 168 D2 2 55 S 79 0W
Azuer →, *Spain* 43 F7 39 8N 3 36W
Azuero, Pen. de, *Panama* 164 E3 7 30N 80 30W
Azuga, *Romania* 53 E10 45 27N 25 33 E
Azul, *Argentina* 174 D4 36 42 S 59 43W
Azul, Lagoa, *Azores* 9 d3 37 52N 25 47W
Azul, Serra, *Brazil* 173 C7 14 50 S 54 50W
Azurduy, *Bolivia* 173 D5 19 59 S 64 29W
Azusa, *U.S.A.* 161 L9 34 8N 117 52W
Azzaba, *Algeria* 111 A6 36 48N 7 6 E
Azzano Décimo, *Italy* 45 C9 45 52N 12 56 E
Azzel Mati, Sebkra, *Algeria* 111 C5 26 10N 0 43 E

B

Ba Be ∆, *Vietnam* 86 A5 22 25N 105 37 E
Ba Don, *Vietnam* 86 D6 17 45N 106 26 E
Ba Dong, *Vietnam* 87 H6 9 40N 106 33 E
Ba Ngoi = Cam Lam, *Vietnam* 87 G7 11 54N 109 10 E
Ba Tri, *Vietnam* 87 G6 10 2N 106 36 E
Ba Vi ∆, *Vietnam* 86 B5 21 1N 105 22 E
Ba Xian = Bazhou, *China* 74 E9 39 8N 116 22 E
Baa, *Indonesia* 82 D2 10 50 S 123 0 E
Baaba, Î., *N. Cal.* 133 T18 20 3 S 163 59 E
Baamonde, *Spain* 42 B3 43 7N 7 44W
Baao, *Phil.* 80 E4 13 27N 123 22 E
Baar, *Switz.* 33 B7 47 12N 8 32 E
Baardeere = Bardera, *Somali Rep.* 120 D2 2 20N 42 27 E
Baarle-Nassau, *Belgium* 24 C4 51 27N 4 56 E
Bab el Mandeb, *Red Sea* 98 D3 12 35N 43 25 E
Baba, *Bulgaria* 50 D7 42 44N 23 59 E
Baba, B. do, *Angola* 115 E2 14 50 S 12 14 E
Bābā, Koh-i-, *Afghan.* 91 B2 34 30N 67 0 E
Baba Budan Hills, *India* 95 H2 13 30N 75 44 E
Baba Burnu, *Turkey* 49 B8 39 29N 26 2 E
Baba dag, *Azerbaijan* 61 K9 41 0N 48 19 E
Bābā Kalū, *Iran* 97 D6 30 7N 50 49 E
Babaçulândia, *Brazil* 170 C2 7 13 S 47 46W
Babadag, *Romania* 53 F13 44 53N 28 44 E
Babadağ, *Turkey* 49 D10 37 49N 28 52 E
Babaeski, *Turkey* 51 E11 41 26N 27 6 E
Babahoyo, *Ecuador* 168 D2 1 40 S 79 30W
Babai = Sarju →, *India* 93 F9 27 21N 81 23 E
Babak, *Phil.* 81 H5 7 8N 125 41 E
Babana, *Nigeria* 113 C5 10 31N 3 46 E
Babanusa, *Sudan* 107 E2 11 20N 27 48 E
Babar, *Algeria* 111 A6 35 10N 7 6 E
Babar, *Indonesia* 83 C3 8 0 S 129 30 E
Babar, *Pakistan* 92 D3 31 7N 69 32 E
Babar, Kepulauan, *Indonesia* 83 C4 8 0 S 131 30 E
Babarkach, *Pakistan* 92 E2 29 45N 68 0 E
Babase I., *Papua N. G.* 132 B7 4 0 S 153 42 E
Babayevo, *Russia* 58 C8 59 24N 35 55 E
Babb, *U.S.A.* 158 B7 48 51N 113 27W
Babenhausen, *Germany* 31 F4 49 57N 8 57 E
Băbeni, *Romania* 53 F9 44 59N 24 11 E
Baberu, *India* 93 G9 25 33N 80 43 E
Babi Besar, Pulau, *Malaysia* 87 L4 2 25N 103 59 E
Babia Gora, *Europe* 55 J6 49 38N 19 38 E
Babian Jiang →, *China* 76 F3 22 55N 101 47 E
Babīl □, *Iraq* 96 C5 32 30N 44 30 E
Babile, *Ethiopia* 107 F5 9 16N 42 11 E
Babile ⌂, *Ethiopia* 120 C2 8 45N 42 20 E
Babimost, *Poland* 55 F2 52 10N 15 49 E
Babinda, *Australia* 126 B4 17 20 S 145 56 E
Babine, *Canada* 142 B3 55 22N 126 37W
Babine →, *Canada* 142 B3 55 45N 127 44W
Babine L., *Canada* 142 C3 54 48N 126 0W
Babiogórski ∆, *Poland* 55 J6 49 38N 19 39 E
Babo, *Indonesia* 83 B4 2 30 S 133 30 E
Babócsa, *Hungary* 52 D2 46 2N 17 21 E
Bābol, *Iran* 97 B7 36 40N 52 50 E
Bābol Sar, *Iran* 97 B7 36 45N 52 45 E
Babor, Dj., *Algeria* 111 A6 36 31N 5 25 E
Baborów, *Poland* 55 H5 50 7N 18 1 E
Baboua, *C.A.R.* 114 A2 5 49N 14 58 E
Babruysk, *Belarus* 59 F5 53 10N 29 15 E
Babson Park, *U.S.A.* 153 H8 27 49N 81 32W
Babuhri, *India* 92 F3 26 49N 69 43 E
Babuna, *Macedonia* 50 E5 41 30N 21 40 E
Babura, *Nigeria* 113 C6 12 51N 8 59 E
Babusar Pass, *Pakistan* 93 B5 35 12N 73 59 E
Babušnica, *Serbia & M.* 50 C6 43 7N 22 27 E
Babuyan, *Phil.* 81 F2 10 0N 118 54 E
Babuyan Chan., *Phil.* 80 B3 18 40N 121 30 E
Babuyan I., *Phil.* 80 B3 19 32N 121 57 E
Babuyan Is., *Phil.* 80 B3 19 10N 121 40 E
Babylon, *Iraq* 101 F11 32 34N 44 22 E
Bač, *Serbia & M.* 52 E4 45 29N 19 17 E
Bâc →, *Moldova* 53 D14 46 55N 29 26 E
Bac Can, *Vietnam* 76 F5 22 8N 105 49 E
Bac Giang, *Vietnam* 76 G6 21 16N 106 11 E
Bac Lieu, *Vietnam* 87 H5 9 17N 105 43 E
Bac Ninh, *Vietnam* 76 G6 21 13N 106 4 E
Bac Phan, *Vietnam* 86 B5 22 0N 105 0 E
Bac Quang, *Vietnam* 76 F5 22 30N 104 48 E
Bacabal, *Brazil* 170 B3 4 15 S 44 45W
Bacacay, *Phil.* 80 E4 13 18N 123 47 E
Bacajá →, *Brazil* 169 D7 3 25 S 51 50W
Bacalar, *Mexico* 163 D7 18 50N 87 27W
Bacan, *Indonesia* 82 B3 0 50 S 127 30 E
Bacan, Kepulauan, *Indonesia* 82 B3 0 35 S 127 30 E
Bacarra, *Phil.* 80 B3 18 15N 120 37 E
Bacău, *Romania* 53 D11 46 35N 26 55 E
Bacău □, *Romania* 53 D11 46 30N 26 45 E
Baccarat, *France* 27 D13 48 28N 6 42 E
Bacchus Marsh, *Australia* 128 D6 37 43 S 144 27 E
Bacerac, *Mexico* 162 A3 30 18N 108 50W
Băceşti, *Romania* 53 D12 46 50N 27 11 E
Bach, *Austria* 33 B10 47 16N 10 25 E
Bach Long Vi, Dao, *Vietnam* 86 B6 20 10N 107 40 E
Bach Ma ∆, *Vietnam* 86 D6 16 11N 107 49 E
Bachaquero, *Venezuela* 168 B3 9 56N 71 8W
Bacharach, *Germany* 31 E3 50 3N 7 44 E
Bachhwara, *India* 93 G11 25 35N 85 54 E
Bachuma, *Ethiopia* 107 F4 6 48N 35 53 E
Bačina, *Serbia & M.* 50 C5 43 42N 21 23 E
Back →, *Canada* 138 B9 65 10N 104 0W
Bačka Palanka, *Serbia & M.* 52 E4 45 17N 19 27 E
Bačka Topola, *Serbia & M.* 52 E4 45 49N 19 39 E
Bäckebo, *Sweden* 17 H10 56 53N 16 4 E
Bäckefors, *Sweden* 17 F6 58 48N 12 9 E
Bäckhammar, *Sweden* 16 E8 59 10N 14 11 E
Bački Petrovac, *Serbia & M.* 52 E4 45 29N 19 32 E
Backnang, *Germany* 31 G5 48 56N 9 26 E
Backstairs Passage, *Australia* 128 C3 35 40 S 138 5 E
Baco, Mt., *Phil.* 80 E3 12 49N 121 10 E
Bacolod, *Phil.* 81 F4 10 40N 122 57 E
Bacon, *Phil.* 80 E5 13 3N 124 3 E
Baconton, *U.S.A.* 152 D5 31 23N 84 10W
Bacoor, *Phil.* 80 D3 14 28N 120 56 E
Bacqueville-en-Caux, *France* 26 C8 49 47N 1 0 E
Bács-Kiskun □, *Hungary* 52 D4 46 43N 19 30 E
Bácsalmás, *Hungary* 52 D4 46 8N 19 17 E
Bacuag = Placer, *Phil.* 81 G5 9 36N 125 38 E
Bacuit = El Nido, *Phil.* 81 F2 11 10N 119 25 E
Bacuk, *Malaysia* 87 J4 6 4N 102 25 E
Bād, *Iran* 97 C7 33 41N 52 1 E
Bad →, *U.S.A.* 154 C4 44 21N 100 22W
Bad Aussee, *Austria* 34 D6 47 43N 13 45 E
Bad Axe, *U.S.A.* 150 C2 43 48N 83 0W
Bad Bergzabern, *Germany* 31 F3 49 6N 7 59 E
Bad Berleburg, *Germany* 30 D4 51 2N 8 26 E
Bad Bevensen, *Germany* 30 B6 53 5N 10 35 E
Bad Bramstedt, *Germany* 30 B5 53 55N 9 53 E
Bad Brückenau, *Germany* 31 E5 50 18N 9 47 E
Bad Doberan, *Germany* 30 A7 54 6N 11 53 E
Bad Driburg, *Germany* 30 D5 51 43N 9 1 E
Bad Ems, *Germany* 31 E3 50 20N 7 43 E
Bad Frankenhausen, *Germany* 30 D7 51 21N 11 5 E
Bad Freienwalde, *Germany* 30 C10 52 46N 14 1 E
Bad Goisern, *Austria* 34 D6 47 38N 13 38 E
Bad Harzburg, *Germany* 30 D6 51 52N 10 34 E
Bad Hersfeld, *Germany* 30 E5 50 52N 9 42 E
Bad Hofgastein, *Austria* 34 D6 47 17N 13 6 E
Bad Homburg, *Germany* 31 E4 50 13N 8 38 E
Bad Honnef, *Germany* 30 E3 50 38N 7 13 E
Bad Iburg, *Germany* 30 C4 52 10N 8 3 E
Bad Ischl, *Austria* 34 D6 47 44N 13 38 E
Bad Kissingen, *Germany* 31 E6 50 11N 10 4 E
Bad Königshofen, *Germany* 31 E6 50 17N 10 28 E
Bad Kreuznach, *Germany* 31 F3 49 50N 7 51 E
Bad Krozingen, *Germany* 31 H3 47 54N 7 42 E
Bad Kudowa = Kudowa-Zdrój, *Poland* 55 H3 50 27N 16 15 E
Bad Laasphe, *Germany* 30 E4 50 56N 8 25 E
Bad Landeck = Lądek-Zdrój, *Poland* 55 H3 50 21N 16 53 E
Bad Langensalza, *Germany* 30 D6 51 5N 10 38 E
Bad Lauterberg, *Germany* 30 D6 51 38N 10 28 E
Bad Leonfelden, *Austria* 34 C7 48 31N 14 18 E
Bad Liebenwerda, *Germany* 30 D9 51 31N 13 24 E
Bad Mergentheim, *Germany* 31 F5 49 28N 9 42 E
Bad Münstereifel, *Germany* 30 E2 50 33N 6 46 E
Bad Nauheim, *Germany* 31 E4 50 21N 8 43 E
Bad Neuenahr-Ahrweiler, *Germany* 30 E3 50 32N 7 5 E
Bad Neustadt, *Germany* 31 E6 50 18N 10 13 E
Bad Oeynhausen, *Germany* 30 C4 52 12N 8 46 E
Bad Oldesloe, *Germany* 30 B6 53 48N 10 22 E
Bad Orb, *Germany* 31 E5 50 12N 9 22 E
Bad Polzin = Polanica-Zdrój, *Poland* 55 H3 50 24N 16 32 E
Bad Pyrmont, *Germany* 30 D5 51 59N 9 16 E
Bad Ragaz, *Switz.* 33 C9 47 0N 9 30 E
Bad Reichenhall, *Germany* 31 H8 47 43N 12 54 E
Bad Reinerz = Duszniki-Zdrój, *Poland* 55 H3 50 24N 16 24 E
Bad Säckingen, *Germany* 31 H3 47 33N 7 56 E
Bad Salzuflen, *Germany* 30 C4 52 5N 8 45 E
Bad Salzungen, *Germany* 30 E6 50 48N 10 14 E
Bad Schönfliess = Trzcińsko Zdrój, *Poland* 55 F1 52 58N 14 35 E
Bad Schwartau, *Germany* 30 B6 53 55N 10 41 E
Bad Segeberg, *Germany* 30 B6 53 56N 10 17 E
Bad St. Leonhard, *Austria* 34 E7 46 58N 14 47 E
Bad Tölz, *Germany* 31 H7 47 45N 11 34 E
Bad Urach, *Germany* 31 G5 48 29N 9 23 E
Bad Vöslau, *Austria* 35 D9 47 58N 16 12 E
Bad Waldsee, *Germany* 31 H5 47 55N 9 45 E
Bad Wildungen, *Germany* 30 D5 51 6N 9 7 E
Bad Wimpfen, *Germany* 31 F5 49 13N 9 11 E
Bad Windsheim, *Germany* 31 F6 49 36N 10 25 E
Bad Zwischenahn, *Germany* 30 B4 53 12N 8 1 E
Bada Barabil, *India* 93 H11 22 7N 85 24 E
Badagara, *India* 95 J2 11 35N 75 40 E
Badagri, *Nigeria* 113 D5 6 25N 2 55 E
Badajós, L., *Brazil* 169 D5 3 15 S 62 50W
Badajoz, *Spain* 43 G4 38 50N 6 59W
Badajoz □, *Spain* 43 G4 38 40N 6 30W
Badakhshān □, *Afghan.* 91 A4 36 30N 71 0 E
Badalona, *Spain* 40 D7 41 26N 2 15 E
Badalzai, *Afghan.* 92 E1 29 50N 65 35 E
Badami, *India* 95 G2 15 55N 75 41 E
Badampahar, *India* 94 C8 22 10N 86 10 E
Badanah, *Si. Arabia* 96 D4 30 58N 41 30 E
Badarinath, *India* 93 D8 30 45N 79 30 E
Badarpur, *India* 90 C4 24 54N 92 36 E
Badas, Kepulauan, *Indonesia* 84 B3 0 45N 107 5 E
Baddo →, *Pakistan* 91 D2 28 0N 64 20 E
Bade, *Indonesia* 83 C5 7 10 S 139 35 E
Badeggi, *Nigeria* 113 D6 9 1N 6 8 E
Badéguichéri, *Niger* 113 C6 14 30N 5 22 E
Baden, *Austria* 35 C9 48 1N 16 13 E
Baden, *Switz.* 33 B6 47 28N 8 18 E
Baden, *U.S.A.* 150 F4 40 38N 80 14W
Baden-Baden, *Germany* 31 G4 48 44N 8 13 E
Baden-Württemberg □, *Germany* 31 G4 48 20N 8 40 E
Badgastein, *Austria* 34 D6 47 7N 13 9 E
Badger, *Canada* 141 C8 49 0N 56 4W
Badger, *U.S.A.* 160 J7 36 38N 119 1W
Bādghīs □, *Afghan.* 91 B1 35 0N 63 0 E
Badgingarra ∆, *Australia* 125 F2 30 23 S 115 22 E
Badgom, *India* 93 B6 34 1N 74 45 E
Badia Polésine, *Italy* 45 C8 45 5N 11 29 E
Badian, *Phil.* 81 G4 9 55N 123 24 E
Badiar ∆, *Guinea* 112 C2 13 37N 13 11W
Badin, *Pakistan* 91 D3 24 38N 68 54 E
Badinka ⌂, *Mali* 112 C3 13 31N 9 28W
Badjokola, *Dem. Rep. of the Congo* 114 B4 3 54N 20 17 E
Badlands, *U.S.A.* 153 D3 43 40N 102 10W
Badlands ∆, *U.S.A.* 154 D3 43 38N 102 56W

Badnera, *India* **94 D3** 20 48N 77 44 E
Badoc, *Phil.* **80 C3** 17 56N 120 28 E
Badogo, *Mali* **112 C3** 11 2N 8 13W
Badoumbé, *Mali* **112 C2** 13 42N 10 15W
Badr Ḥunayn, *Si. Arabia* **98 B2** 23 44N 38 46 E
Badrah, *Iraq* **101 F11** 33 6N 45 58 E
Badrinath, *India* **93 D8** 30 44N 79 29 E
Badu I., *Papua N. G.* **132 F2** 10 5 S 142 10 E
Baduen, *Somali Rep.* **120 C3** 7 15N 47 40 E
Badulla, *Sri Lanka* **95 L5** 7 1N 81 7 E
Badung, Selat, *Indonesia* **79 K18** 8 40 S 115 22 E
Badupi, *Burma* **90 E4** 21 36N 93 27 E
Badvel, *India* **95 G4** 14 45N 79 3 E
Baena, *Spain* **43 H6** 37 37N 4 20W
Baerami, *Australia* **129 B9** 32 27 S 150 27 E
Baetov, *Kyrgyzstan* **65 C7** 41 13N 74 54 E
Baeza, *Ecuador* **168 D2** 0 25 S 77 53W
Baeza, *Spain* **43 H7** 37 57N 3 25W
Bafang, *Cameroon* **113 D7** 5 9N 10 11 E
Bafatá, *Guinea-Biss.* **112 C2** 12 8N 14 40W
Baffin B., *Canada* **139 A13** 72 0N 64 0W
Baffin I., *Canada* **139 B12** 68 0N 75 0W
Bafia, *Cameroon* **113 E7** 4 40N 11 10 E
Bafilo, *Togo* **113 D5** 9 22N 1 22 E
Bafing △, *Mali* **112 C2** 12 38N 10 28W
Bafing →, *Mali* **112 C2** 13 49N 10 50W
Bafliyūn, *Syria* **96 B3** 36 37N 36 59 E
Bafoulabé, *Mali* **112 C2** 13 50N 10 55W
Bafoussam, *Cameroon* **113 D7** 5 28N 10 25 E
Bāfq, *Iran* **97 D7** 31 40N 55 25 E
Bafra, *Turkey* **100 B6** 41 34N 35 54 E
Bafra Burnu, *Turkey* **100 B7** 41 45N 36 2 E
Bāft, *Iran* **97 D8** 29 15N 56 38 E
Bafut, *Cameroon* **113 D7** 6 6N 10 2 E
Bafwasende, *Dem. Rep. of the Congo* **118 B2** 1 3N 27 5 E
Bagaat, Î., *N. Cal.* **133 K4** 20 40 S 166 15 E
Bagabag, *Phil.* **80 C3** 16 30N 121 15 E
Bagabag I., *Papua N. G.* **132 C4** 4 48 S 146 14 E
Bagac, *Phil.* **80 D3** 14 36N 120 23 E
Bagac Bay, *Phil.* **80 D3** 14 36N 120 20 E
Bagalkot, *India* **95 F2** 16 10N 75 40 E
Bagam, *Niger* **113 B6** 15 43N 6 35 E
Bagamanoc, *Phil.* **80 E5** 13 57N 124 17 E
Bagamoyo, *Tanzania* **118 D4** 6 28 S 38 55 E
Bagan Datoh, *Malaysia* **87 L3** 3 59N 100 47 E
Bagan Serai, *Malaysia* **87 K3** 5 1N 100 32 E
Baganga, *Phil.* **81 H6** 7 34N 126 33 E
Bagani, *Namibia* **116 B3** 18 7 S 21 41 E
Bagansiapiapi, *Indonesia* **84 B2** 2 12N 100 50 E
Bagasra, *India* **92 J4** 21 30N 71 0 E
Bagata, *Dem. Rep. of the Congo* **114 C3** 3 44 S 17 57 E
Bagaud, *India* **92 H6** 22 19N 75 53 E
Bagawi, *Sudan* **107 E3** 12 20N 34 18 E
Bagbag, *Sudan* **107 D3** 15 23N 31 30 E
Bagdad, *Calif., U.S.A.* **161 L11** 34 35N 115 53W
Bagdad, *Fla., U.S.A.* **153 E2** 30 36N 87 2W
Bagdarin, *Russia* **67 D12** 54 26N 113 36 E
Bagé, *Brazil* **175 C5** 31 20 S 54 15W
Bagenalstown = Muine Bheag, *Ireland* **23 D5** 52 42N 6 58W
Bagepalli, *India* **95 H3** 13 47N 77 47 E
Bagevadi, *India* **94 F2** 16 35N 75 58 E
Baggao, *Phil.* **80 C3** 17 56N 121 46 E
Baggs, *U.S.A.* **158 F10** 41 2N 107 39W
Bagh, *Pakistan* **93 C5** 33 59N 73 45 E
Baghain →, *India* **93 G9** 25 32N 81 1 E
Baghdād, *Iraq* **101 F11** 33 20N 44 30 E
Bagherhat, *Bangla.* **90 D2** 22 40N 89 47 E
Bagheria, *Italy* **46 D6** 38 5N 13 30 E
Baghlān, *Afghan.* **91 A3** 32 12N 68 46 E
Baghlān □, *Afghan.* **91 B3** 36 0N 68 30 E
Bagley, *U.S.A.* **154 B7** 47 32N 95 24W
Bagn, *Norway* **18 D6** 60 49N 9 34 E
Bagnara Cálabra, *Italy* **47 D8** 38 17N 15 48 E
Bagnasco, *Italy* **44 D5** 44 18N 8 2 E
Bagnell Dam, *U.S.A.* **156 F4** 38 14N 92 36W
Bagnères-de-Bigorre, *France* **28 E4** 43 5N 0 9 E
Bagnères-de-Luchon, *France* **28 F4** 42 47N 0 38 E
Bagni di Lucca, *Italy* **44 D7** 44 1N 10 35 E
Bagno di Romagna, *Italy* **45 E8** 43 50N 11 57 E
Bagnoles-de-l'Orne, *France* **26 D6** 48 32N 0 25W
Bagnols-sur-Cèze, *France* **29 D8** 44 10N 4 36 E
Bagnorea = Bagnorégio, *Italy* **45 F9** 42 37N 12 5 E
Bagnorégio, *Italy* **45 F9** 42 37N 12 5 E
Bago = Pegu, *Burma* **90 G6** 17 20N 96 29 E
Bago, *Phil.* **81 F4** 10 32N 122 50 E
Bagodar, *India* **93 G11** 24 5N 85 52 E
Bagrationovsk, *Russia* **15 J19** 54 23N 20 39 E
Bagrdan, *Serbia & M.* **50 B5** 44 5N 21 11 E
Bagua, *Peru* **172 B2** 5 35 S 78 22W
Baguio, *Phil.* **80 C3** 16 26N 120 34 E
Bağyurdu, *Turkey* **49 C9** 38 25N 27 41 E
Bagzane, Monts, *Niger* **113 B6** 17 43N 8 45 E
Bah, *India* **93 F8** 26 53N 78 36 E
Bahabón de Esgueva, *Spain* **42 D7** 41 52N 3 43W
Bahadurabad Ghat, *Bangla.* **90 C2** 25 11N 89 44 E
Bahadurganj, *India* **93 F12** 26 16N 87 49 E
Bahadurgarh, *India* **92 E7** 28 40N 76 57 E
Bahama, Canal Viejo de, *W. Indies* **164 B4** 22 10N 77 30W
Bahamas ■, *N. Amer.* **165 B5** 24 0N 75 0W
Bahār, *Iran* **101 E13** 34 54N 48 26 E
Bahārak, *Afghan.* **65 E5** 37 0N 70 53 E
Baharampur, *India* **93 G13** 24 2N 88 27 E
Baharîya, El Wâhât al, *Egypt* **106 B2** 28 0N 28 50 E
Baharu Pandan = Pandan, *Malaysia* **87 d** 1 32N 103 46 E
Bahawalnagar, *Pakistan* **91 C4** 30 0N 73 15 E
Bahawalpur, *Pakistan* **91 C3** 29 24N 71 40 E
Bahçe, *Turkey* **100 D7** 37 13N 36 34 E
Bahçecik, *Turkey* **51 F13** 40 41N 29 44 E
Baheli, *Phil.* **81 F2** 10 0N 118 47 E
Baheri, *India* **93 E8** 28 45N 79 34 E
Bahgul →, *India* **93 F8** 27 45N 79 36 E
Bahi, *Tanzania* **118 D4** 5 58 S 35 21 E
Bahi Swamp, *Tanzania* **118 D4** 6 10 S 35 0 E
Bahía = Salvador, *Brazil* **171 D4** 13 0 S 38 30W
Bahía □, *Brazil* **171 D3** 12 0 S 42 0W
Bahía, Is. de la, *Honduras* **164 C2** 16 45N 86 15W
Bahía Blanca, *Argentina* **174 D3** 38 35 S 62 13W
Bahía de Caráquez, *Ecuador* **168 D1** 0 40 S 80 27W
Bahía Honda, *Cuba* **164 B3** 22 54N 83 10W
Bahía Laura, *Argentina* **176 C3** 48 10 S 66 30W
Bahía Mansa, *Chile* **176 B2** 40 33 S 73 46W
Bahía Negra, *Paraguay* **173 E6** 20 5 S 58 5W
Bahir Dar, *Ethiopia* **107 E4** 11 37N 37 10 E
Bahlah, *Oman* **99 B7** 22 58N 57 18 E
Bahmanzād, *Iran* **97 D6** 31 15N 51 47 E
Bahmer, *Algeria* **111 C4** 27 32N 0 10W
Bahr el Ahmar □, *Sudan* **106 D4** 20 0N 35 0 E
Bahr el Ghazâl □, *Sudan* **107 F2** 7 0N 28 0 E
Bahr el Jabal □, *Sudan* **107 G3** 4 0N 31 0 E
Bahraich, *India* **93 F9** 27 38N 81 37 E
Bahrain ■, *Asia* **97 E6** 26 0N 50 35 E
Bahror, *India* **92 F7** 27 51N 76 20 E
Bāhū Kalāt, *Iran* **97 E9** 25 43N 61 25 E
Bai, *Mali* **112 C4** 13 35N 3 28W
Bai Bung, Mui = Ca Mau, Mui, *Vietnam* **87 H5** 8 38N 104 44 E
Bai Duc, *Vietnam* **86 C5** 18 3N 105 49 E
Bai Thuong, *Vietnam* **86 C5** 19 54N 105 23 E
Baia de Aramă, *Romania* **52 E7** 45 0N 22 50 E
Baía dos Tigres, *Angola* **115 F2** 16 40 S 11 47 E
Baia Farta, *Angola* **115 E2** 12 40 S 13 11 E
Baia Mare, *Romania* **53 C8** 47 40N 23 35 E
Baia-Sprie, *Romania* **53 C8** 47 41N 23 43 E
Baião, *Brazil* **170 B2** 2 40 S 49 40W
Baïbokoum, *Chad* **109 G3** 7 46N 15 43 E
Baicheng, *China* **75 B12** 45 38N 122 42 E
Băicoi, *Romania* **53 E10** 45 3N 25 52 E
Baidoa, *Somali Rep.* **120 D2** 3 8N 43 30 E
Baie-Comeau, *Canada* **141 C6** 49 12N 68 10W
Baie-St-Paul, *Canada* **141 C5** 47 28N 70 32W
Baie Ste-Anne, *Seychelles* **121 b** 4 18 S 55 45 E
Baie-Trinité, *Canada* **141 C6** 49 25N 67 20W
Baie Verte, *Canada* **141 C8** 49 55N 56 12W
Baignes-Ste-Radegonde, *France* **28 C3** 45 23N 0 25W
Baigneux-les-Juifs, *France* **27 E11** 47 31N 4 39 E
Baihar, *India* **93 H9** 22 6N 80 33 E
Baihe, *China* **74 H6** 32 50N 110 5 E
Baijnath, *India* **93 E8** 29 55N 79 37 E
Baikal, L. = Baykal, Oz., *Russia* **67 D11** 53 0N 108 0 E
Baikunthpur, *India* **93 H10** 23 15N 82 33 E
Bailadila, Mt., *India* **94 E5** 18 43N 81 15 E
Baile Atha Cliath = Dublin, *Ireland* **23 C5** 53 21N 6 15W
Băile Govora, *Romania* **53 E9** 45 5N 24 11 E
Băile Herculane, *Romania* **52 F7** 44 53N 22 26 E
Băile Olăneşti, *Romania* **53 E9** 45 12N 24 14 E
Băile Tuşnad, *Romania* **53 D10** 46 9N 25 51 E
Bailén, *Spain* **43 G7** 38 8N 3 48W
Băileşti, *Romania* **53 F8** 44 1N 23 20 E
Bailhongal, *India* **95 G2** 15 55N 74 53 E
Bailique, Ilha, *Brazil* **170 A2** 1 2N 49 58W
Bailugh, *Afghan.* **91 B2** 32 40N 66 47 E
Bailundo = Luau, *Angola* **115 E4** 10 40 S 22 10 E
Bailundo, *Angola* **115 E3** 12 10 S 15 50 E
Baima, *China* **76 A3** 33 0N 100 26 E
Baimuru, *Papua N. G.* **132 D3** 7 35 S 144 51 E
Bain-de-Bretagne, *France* **26 E5** 47 50N 1 40W
Bainbridge, *Ga., U.S.A.* **152 E5** 30 55N 84 35W
Bainbridge, *Ind., U.S.A.* **157 E10** 39 46N 86 49W
Bainbridge, *N.Y., U.S.A.* **151 D9** 42 18N 75 29W
Bainbridge, *Ohio, U.S.A.* **157 E13** 39 14N 83 16W
Baing, *Indonesia* **82 D2** 10 14 S 120 34 E
Bainiu, *China* **74 H7** 32 50N 112 15 E
Bainyik, *Papua N. G.* **132 B2** 3 40 S 143 4 E
Baiona, *Spain* **42 C2** 42 6N 8 52W
Bā'ir, *Jordan* **103 E5** 30 45N 36 55 E
Baird Mts., *U.S.A.* **144 C8** 67 0N 160 0W
Bairiki = Tarawa, *Kiribati* **134 G9** 1 30N 173 0 E
Bairin Youqi, *China* **75 C10** 43 30N 118 35 E
Bairin Zuoqi, *China* **75 C10** 43 58N 119 15 E
Bairnsdale, *Australia* **129 D7** 37 48 S 147 36 E
Bais, *Phil.* **81 G4** 9 35N 123 7 E
Baisha, *China* **74 G7** 34 20N 112 32 E
Baissa, *Nigeria* **113 D7** 7 14N 10 38 E
Baitadi, *Nepal* **93 E9** 29 35N 80 25 E
Baitarani →, *India* **94 D8** 20 45N 86 48 E
Baixa Grande, *Brazil* **171 D3** 11 57 S 40 11W
Baixa Limia-Sierra do Xurés ⌂, *Spain* **42 D2** 41 59N 8 2W
Baixo-Longa, *Angola* **115 F3** 15 41 S 18 45 E
Baiyer River, *Papua N. G.* **132 C3** 5 32 S 144 9 E
Baiyin, *China* **74 F3** 36 45N 104 14 E
Baiyü, *China* **76 B2** 31 16N 98 50 E
Baiyu Shan, *China* **74 F4** 37 15N 107 30 E
Baiyuda, *Sudan* **106 D3** 17 35N 32 7 E
Baj Baj, *India* **93 H13** 22 30N 88 5 E
Baja, *Hungary* **52 D3** 46 12N 18 59 E
Baja, Pta., *Chile* **172 b** 27 10 S 109 22W
Baja, Pta., *Mexico* **162 B1** 29 50N 116 0W
Baja California, *Mexico* **162 A1** 31 10N 115 12W
Baja California □, *Mexico* **162 B2** 30 0N 115 0W
Baja California Sur □, *Mexico* **162 B2** 25 50N 111 50W
Bajag, *India* **93 H9** 22 40N 81 21 E
Bajamar, *Canary Is.* **9 e1** 28 33N 16 20W
Bajana, *India* **92 H4** 23 7N 71 49 E
Bajatrejo, *Indonesia* **79 J17** 8 29 S 114 19 E
Bajawa, *Indonesia* **82 C2** 8 47 S 120 59 E
Bajera, *Indonesia* **79 J18** 8 31 S 115 2 E
Bājgīrān, *Iran* **97 B8** 37 36N 58 24 E
Bājil, *Yemen* **98 D3** 15 4N 43 17 E
Bajimba, Mt., *Australia* **127 D5** 29 17 S 152 6 E
Bajina Bašta, *Serbia & M.* **50 C3** 43 58N 19 35 E
Bajmok, *Serbia & M.* **52 E4** 45 57N 19 24 E
Bajo Caracoles, *Argentina* **176 C2** 47 27 S 70 56W
Bajo Nuevo, *Caribbean* **164 C4** 15 40N 78 50W
Bajoga, *Nigeria* **113 C7** 10 57N 11 20 E
Bajool, *Australia* **126 C5** 23 40 S 150 35 E
Bak, *Hungary* **52 D1** 46 43N 16 51 E
Bakal, *Russia* **64 D7** 54 56N 58 48 E
Bakala, *C.A.R.* **114 A4** 6 15N 20 20 E
Bakalsky Zavod = Bakal, *Russia* **64 D7** 54 56N 58 48 E
Bakanas = Baqanas, *Kazakhstan* **65 A8** 44 50N 76 15 E
Bakar, *Croatia* **45 C11** 45 18N 14 32 E
Bakassi Pen., *Cameroon* **113 E6** 4 42N 8 20 E
Bakel, *Senegal* **112 C2** 14 56N 12 20W
Baker, *Calif., U.S.A.* **161 K10** 35 16N 116 4W
Baker, *Fla., U.S.A.* **153 E3** 30 48N 86 41W
Baker, *Mont., U.S.A.* **154 B2** 46 22N 104 17W
Baker, Canal, *Chile* **176 C2** 47 45 S 74 45W
Baker, L., *Canada* **138 B10** 64 0N 96 0W
Baker, Mt., *U.S.A.* **158 B3** 48 50N 121 49W
Baker City, *U.S.A.* **158 D5** 44 47N 117 50W
Baker I., *Pac. Oc.* **134 G10** 0 10N 176 35W
Baker I., *U.S.A.* **142 B2** 55 20N 133 40W
Baker L., *Australia* **125 E4** 26 54 S 126 5 E
Baker Lake, *Canada* **138 B10** 64 20N 96 3W
Bakere, *Dem. Rep. of the Congo* **114 B4** 1 36N 23 50 E
Bakerhill, *U.S.A.* **152 D4** 31 47N 85 18W
Bakers Creek, *Australia* **126 C4** 21 13 S 149 7 E
Bakers Dozen Is., *Canada* **140 A4** 56 45N 78 45W
Bakersfield, *Calif., U.S.A.* **161 K8** 35 23N 119 1W
Bakersfield, *Vt., U.S.A.* **151 B12** 44 45N 72 48W
Bakhchysaray, *Ukraine* **59 K7** 44 40N 33 45 E
Bakhmach, *Ukraine* **59 G7** 51 10N 32 45 E
Bakhmut = Artemovsk, *Ukraine* **59 H9** 48 35N 38 0 E
Bakht, *Uzbekistan* **65 C4** 40 43N 68 42 E
Bākhtarān, *Iran* **101 E12** 34 23N 47 0 E
Bākhtarān □, *Iran* **96 C5** 34 0N 46 30 E
Baki = Krasnyye Baki, *Russia* **60 B7** 57 8N 45 10 E
Bakı, *Azerbaijan* **61 K9** 40 29N 49 56 E
Bakır →, *Turkey* **49 C9** 38 55N 27 0 E
Bakırdaği, *Turkey* **100 C6** 38 13N 35 46 E
Bakkafjörður, *Iceland* **11 A12** 66 2N 14 48W
Bakkaflói, *Iceland* **11 A12** 66 10N 14 45W
Baklan, *Turkey* **49 C11** 38 0N 29 36 E
Bako, *Ethiopia* **107 F4** 5 51N 36 23 E
Bako, *Ivory C.* **112 D3** 9 8N 7 40W
Bakony, *Hungary* **52 C2** 47 10N 17 30 E
Bakony Forest = Bakony, *Hungary* **52 C2** 47 10N 17 30 E
Bakori, *Nigeria* **113 C6** 11 34N 7 25 E
Bakouma, *C.A.R.* **114 A4** 5 40N 22 56 E
Bakpakty = Baqbaqty, *Kazakhstan* **65 A8** 44 35N 76 40 E
Baksan, *Russia* **61 J6** 43 42N 43 32 E
Bakswaho, *India* **93 G8** 24 15N 79 18 E
Baku = Bakı, *Azerbaijan* **61 K9** 40 29N 49 56 E
Bakundi, *Nigeria* **113 D7** 8 2N 10 45 E
Bakutis Coast, *Antarctica* **7 D15** 74 0 S 120 0W
Bakwa-Kenge, *Dem. Rep. of the Congo* **115 C4** 4 51 S 22 4 E
Bakwanga = Mbuji-Mayi, *Dem. Rep. of the Congo* **118 D1** 6 9 S 23 40 E
Baky = Bakı, *Azerbaijan* **61 K9** 40 29N 49 56 E
Bala, *Canada* **150 A5** 45 1N 79 37W
Bala, *Senegal* **112 C2** 14 1N 13 8W
Bâlâ, *Turkey* **100 C5** 39 32N 33 6 E
Bala, *U.K.* **20 E4** 52 54N 3 36W
Bala, L., *U.K.* **20 E4** 52 53N 3 37W
Bālā Morghāb, *Afghan.* **91 B1** 35 35N 63 20 E
Balabac, *Phil.* **81 H1** 7 59N 117 4 E
Balabac I., *Phil.* **81 G1** 8 0N 117 0 E
Balabac Str., *E. Indies* **78 C5** 7 53N 117 5 E
Balabagh, *Afghan.* **92 B4** 34 25N 70 12 E
Ba'labakk, *Lebanon* **103 B5** 34 0N 36 10 E
Balabalangan, Kepulauan, *Indonesia* **85 C5** 2 20 S 117 30 E
Balabio, Î., *N. Cal.* **133 T18** 20 7 S 164 11 E
Bălăciţa, *Romania* **53 F8** 44 23N 23 8 E
Balad, *Iraq* **101 F11** 34 1N 44 9 E
Balad Rūz, *Iraq* **101 F11** 33 42N 45 5 E
Bālādeh, *Fārs, Iran* **97 D6** 29 17N 51 56 E
Bālādeh, *Māzandaran, Iran* **97 B6** 36 12N 51 48 E
Balaghat, *India* **94 D5** 21 49N 80 12 E
Balaghat Ra., *India* **94 E3** 18 50N 76 30 E
Balaguer, *Spain* **40 D5** 41 50N 0 50 E
Balaka, *Dem. Rep. of the Congo* **115 C3** 4 52 S 19 57 E
Balakété, *C.A.R.* **114 A3** 6 56N 19 54 E
Balakhna, *Russia* **60 B6** 56 25N 43 32 E
Balaklava, *Australia* **128 C3** 34 7 S 138 22 E
Balaklava, *Ukraine* **59 K7** 44 30N 33 30 E
Balakliya, *Ukraine* **59 H9** 49 28N 36 55 E
Balakovo, *Russia* **60 D8** 52 4N 47 55 E
Balamau, *India* **93 F9** 27 10N 80 21 E
Balamban, *Phil.* **81 F4** 10 30N 123 43 E
Balambangan, *Malaysia* **85 A5** 7 17N 116 55 E
Bălan, *Romania* **53 D10** 46 39N 25 49 E
Balancán, *Mexico* **163 D6** 17 48N 91 32W
Balanda = Kalininsk, *Russia* **60 E7** 51 30N 44 40 E
Balanga, *Phil.* **80 D3** 14 41N 120 32 E
Balangala, *Dem. Rep. of the Congo* **114 B3** 0 30N 19 56 E
Balangiga, *Phil.* **81 F5** 11 7N 125 23 E
Balangir, *India* **94 D6** 20 43N 83 35 E
Balanivka, *Ukraine* **53 B14** 48 24N 29 24 E
Balaoan, *Phil.* **80 C3** 16 49N 120 24 E
Balapur, *India* **94 D3** 20 40N 76 45 E
Balashov, *Russia* **60 E6** 51 30N 43 10 E
Balasinor, *India* **92 H5** 22 57N 73 23 E
Balasore = Baleshwar, *India* **94 D8** 21 35N 87 3 E
Balassagyarmat, *Hungary* **52 B4** 48 4N 19 15 E
Balât, *Egypt* **106 B2** 25 36N 29 19 E
Balaton, *Hungary* **52 D2** 46 50N 17 40 E
Balaton-Felvidéki △, *Hungary* **52 D2** 46 52N 17 30 E
Balatonboglár, *Hungary* **52 D2** 46 46N 17 40 E
Balatonfüred, *Hungary* **52 D2** 46 58N 17 54 E
Balatonszentgyörgy, *Hungary* **52 D2** 46 41N 17 19 E
Balayan, *Phil.* **80 E3** 13 57N 120 44 E
Balazote, *Spain* **41 G2** 38 54N 2 9W
Balbalan, *Phil.* **80 C3** 17 27N 121 12 E
Balbi, Mt., *Papua N. G.* **132 C8** 5 55 S 154 58 E
Balbieriškis, *Lithuania* **54 D10** 54 32N 23 53 E
Balbigny, *France* **29 C8** 45 49N 4 11 E
Balbina, *Brazil* **169 D6** 1 58 S 59 29W
Balbina, Reprêsa de, *Brazil* **169 D6** 2 0 S 59 30W
Balboa, *Panama* **164 E4** 8 57N 79 34W
Balbriggan, *Ireland* **23 C5** 53 37N 6 11W
Balcarce, *Argentina* **174 D4** 38 0 S 58 10W
Balcarres, *Canada* **143 C8** 50 50N 103 35W
Bălceşti, *Romania* **53 F8** 44 37N 23 57 E
Balchik, *Bulgaria* **51 C12** 43 28N 28 11 E
Balclutha, *N.Z.* **131 G4** 46 15 S 169 45 E
Balcones Escarpment, *U.S.A.* **155 L5** 29 30N 99 15W
Balçova, *Turkey* **49 C9** 38 22N 27 4 E
Bald Hd., *Australia* **125 G2** 35 6 S 118 1 E
Bald I., *Australia* **125 F2** 34 57 S 118 27 E
Bald Knob, *U.S.A.* **155 H9** 35 19N 91 34W
Baldenburg = Biały Bór, *Poland* **54 E3** 53 53N 16 51 E
Baldock L., *Canada* **143 B9** 56 33N 97 57W
Baldwin, *Fla., U.S.A.* **152 E8** 30 18N 81 59W
Baldwin, *Mich., U.S.A.* **148 D3** 43 54N 85 51W
Baldwin, *Pa., U.S.A.* **150 F5** 40 23N 79 59W
Baldwinsville, *U.S.A.* **151 C8** 43 10N 76 20W
Baldy Mt., *U.S.A.* **158 B9** 48 9N 109 39W
Baldy Peak, *U.S.A.* **159 K9** 33 54N 109 34W
Bale, *Croatia* **45 C10** 45 4N 13 46 E
Bale, *Ethiopia* **107 F5** 6 57N 40 8 E
Bale, *Ethiopia* **107 F5** 6 20N 41 30 E
Bale Mts. △, *Ethiopia* **107 F4** 6 59N 39 52 E
Baleares, Is., *Spain* **38 B4** 39 30N 3 0 E
Balearic Is. = Baleares, Is., *Spain* **38 B4** 39 30N 3 0 E
Balease, *Indonesia* **82 B2** 2 24 S 120 33 E
Baleia, Pta. da, *Brazil* **171 E4** 17 40 S 39 7W
Baleine = Whale →, *Canada* **141 A6** 58 15N 67 40W
Baleine, Petite R. de la →, *Canada* **140 A4** 56 0N 76 45W
Băleni, *Romania* **53 E12** 45 48N 27 51 E
Baler, *Phil.* **80 D3** 15 46N 121 34 E
Baler Bay, *Phil.* **80 D3** 15 50N 121 35 E
Balerna, *Switz.* **33 E8** 45 52N 9 0 E
Baleshare, *U.K.* **22 D1** 57 31N 7 22W
Baleshwar, *India* **94 D8** 21 35N 87 3 E
Balestrand, *Norway* **18 C3** 61 11N 6 31 E
Balezino, *Russia* **60 B11** 58 2N 53 6 E
Balfate, *Honduras* **164 C2** 15 48N 86 25W
Balfour Channel, *Solomon Is.* **133 M9** 8 43 S 157 27 E
Balharshah, *India* **94 E4** 19 50N 79 23 E
Bali, *Cameroon* **113 D7** 5 54N 10 0 E
Bali, *Dem. Rep. of the Congo* **114 C3** 2 50 S 16 12 E
Balí, *Greece* **39 E5** 35 25N 24 47 E
Bali, *India* **92 G5** 25 11N 73 17 E
Bali, *Indonesia* **85 D4** 8 20 S 115 0 E
Bali □, *Indonesia* **85 D4** 8 20 S 115 0 E
Bali, Selat, *Indonesia* **85 D4** 8 18 S 114 25 E
Bali Sea, *Indonesia* **85 D5** 8 0 S 115 0 E
Balia, *S. Leone* **112 D2** 9 22N 11 1W
Baliapal, *India* **93 J12** 21 40N 87 17 E
Balicuatro Is., *Phil.* **80 E5** 12 39N 124 24 E
Baliem →, *Indonesia* **83 C5** 5 44 S 138 8 E
Baligród, *Poland* **55 J9** 49 20N 22 17 E
Baliguda, *India* **94 D6** 20 12N 83 55 E
Balik Pulau, *Malaysia* **87 c** 5 21N 100 14 E
Balikeşir, *Turkey* **49 B9** 39 39N 27 53 E
Balikeşir □, *Turkey* **49 B9** 39 45N 28 0 E
Balıklıçeşme, *Turkey* **51 F11** 40 18N 27 5 E
Balikpapan, *Indonesia* **85 C5** 1 10 S 116 55 E
Balimbing, *Phil.* **81 J2** 5 5N 119 58 E
Balimo, *Papua N. G.* **132 E2** 8 6 S 142 57 E
Baling, *Malaysia* **87 K3** 5 41N 100 55 E
Balingasag, *Phil.* **81 G5** 8 45N 124 47 E
Balingen, *Germany* **31 G4** 48 16N 8 51 E
Balinţ, *Romania* **52 E6** 45 48N 21 54 E
Balintang Channel, *Phil.* **80 B3** 19 49N 121 40 E
Balintang I., *Phil.* **80 B4** 19 58N 122 9 E
Baliza, *Brazil* **173 D7** 16 0 S 52 20W
Baljurshī, *Si. Arabia* **98 C3** 19 51N 41 33 E
Balkan Mts. = Stara Planina, *Bulgaria* **50 C7** 43 15N 23 0 E
Balkh, *Afghan.* **65 E3** 36 44N 66 47 E
Balkh □, *Afghan.* **65 E3** 36 50N 67 0 E
Balkhash = Balqash, *Kazakhstan* **66 E8** 46 50N 74 50 E
Balkhash, Ozero = Balqash Köl, *Kazakhstan* **66 E8** 46 0N 74 50 E
Balkonda, *India* **94 E4** 18 52N 78 21 E
Ballachulish, *U.K.* **22 E3** 56 41N 5 8W
Balladonia, *Australia* **125 F3** 32 27 S 123 51 E
Ballaghaderreen, *Ireland* **23 C3** 53 55N 8 34W
Ballan, *Australia* **128 D6** 37 35 S 144 13 E
Ballarat, *Australia* **128 D5** 37 33 S 143 50 E
Ballard, L., *Australia* **125 E3** 29 20 S 120 40 E
Ballater, *U.K.* **22 D5** 57 3N 3 3W
Ballé, *Mali* **112 B3** 15 18N 8 33W
Ballena Gris = Ojo de Liebre ⌂, *Mexico* **162 B2** 27 50N 114 0W
Ballenas, Canal de, *Mexico* **162 B2** 29 10N 113 45W
Balleny Is., *Antarctica* **7 C11** 66 30 S 163 0 E
Balleroy, *France* **26 C6** 49 11N 0 50W
Ballerup, *Denmark* **17 J6** 55 44N 12 21 E
Ballı, *Turkey* **51 F11** 40 50N 27 3 E
Ballia, *India* **93 G11** 25 46N 84 12 E
Ballina, *Australia* **127 D5** 28 50 S 153 31 E
Ballina, *Ireland* **23 B2** 54 7N 9 9W
Ballinasloe, *Ireland* **23 C3** 53 20N 8 13W
Ballinger, *U.S.A.* **155 K5** 31 45N 99 57W
Ballinrobe, *Ireland* **23 C2** 53 38N 9 13W
Ballinskelligs B., *Ireland* **23 E1** 51 48N 10 13W
Ballon, *France* **26 D7** 48 10N 0 14 E
Ballons des Vosges ⌂, *France* **27 E14** 48 0N 7 0 E
Ballsh, *Albania* **50 F3** 40 36N 19 44 E
Ballston Spa, *U.S.A.* **151 D11** 43 0N 73 51W
Ballybunion, *Ireland* **23 D2** 52 31N 9 40W
Ballycastle, *U.K.* **23 A5** 55 12N 6 15W
Ballyclare, *U.K.* **23 B5** 54 46N 6 0W
Ballyhaunis, *Ireland* **23 C3** 53 46N 8 46W
Ballymena, *U.K.* **23 B5** 54 52N 6 17W
Ballymoney, *U.K.* **23 A5** 55 5N 6 31W
Ballymote, *Ireland* **23 B3** 54 5N 8 31W
Ballynahinch, *U.K.* **23 B6** 54 24N 5 54W
Ballyquintin Pt., *U.K.* **23 B6** 54 20N 5 30W
Ballyshannon, *Ireland* **23 B3** 54 30N 8 11W
Balmaceda, *Chile* **176 C2** 46 0 S 71 50W
Balmaseda, *Spain* **40 B1** 43 11N 3 12W
Balmazújváros, *Hungary* **52 C6** 47 37N 21 21 E
Balmertown, *Canada* **143 C10** 51 4N 93 41W
Balmhorn, *Switz.* **32 D5** 46 26N 7 42 E
Balmoral, *Australia* **128 D4** 37 15 S 141 48 E
Balmorhea, *U.S.A.* **155 K3** 30 59N 103 45W
Balochistan = Baluchistan □, *Pakistan* **91 D2** 27 30N 65 0 E
Balod, *India* **94 D5** 20 44N 81 13 E
Balombo, *Angola* **115 E2** 12 21 S 14 46 E
Balombo →, *Angola* **115 E2** 11 57 S 13 46 E
Balonne →, *Australia* **127 D4** 28 47 S 147 56 E
Balotra, *India* **92 G5** 25 50N 72 14 E
Balpyq Bī, *Kazakhstan* **65 A9** 44 52N 78 12 E
Balqash, *Kazakhstan* **66 E8** 46 50N 74 50 E
Balqash Köl, *Kazakhstan* **66 E8** 46 0N 74 50 E
Balrampur, *India* **93 F10** 27 30N 82 20 E
Balranald, *Australia* **128 C5** 34 38 S 143 33 E
Balş, *Romania* **53 F9** 44 22N 24 5 E
Balsapuerto, *Peru* **172 B2** 5 48 S 76 33W
Balsas, *Mexico* **163 D5** 18 0N 99 40W
Balsas →, *Maranhão, Brazil* **170 C3** 7 15 S 44 35W
Balsas →, *Tocantins, Brazil* **170 C2** 9 58 S 47 52W
Balsas →, *Mexico* **162 D4** 17 55N 102 10W
Bålsta, *Sweden* **16 E11** 59 35N 17 30 E
Balsthal, *Switz.* **32 B5** 47 19N 7 41 E
Balston Spa, *U.S.A.* **151 D11** 43 0N 73 52W
Balta, *Romania* **52 F7** 44 54N 22 38 E
Balta, *Ukraine* **53 B14** 48 2N 29 45 E
Baltanás, *Spain* **42 D6** 41 56N 4 15W
Bălţi, *Moldova* **53 C12** 47 48N 27 58 E
Baltic Sea, *Europe* **15 H18** 57 0N 19 0 E
Baltîm, *Egypt* **106 H7** 31 35N 31 10 E
Baltimore, *Ireland* **23 E2** 51 29N 9 22W
Baltimore, *Md., U.S.A.* **148 F7** 39 17N 76 37W
Baltimore, *Ohio, U.S.A.* **150 G2** 39 51N 82 36W
Baltit, *Pakistan* **93 A6** 36 15N 74 40 E
Baltiysk, *Russia* **15 J18** 54 41N 19 58 E
Baltiyskiy = Paldiski, *Estonia* **15 G21** 59 23N 24 9 E
Baltra, I., *Ecuador* **172 a** 0 26 S 90 16W
Baltrum, *Germany* **30 B3** 53 43N 7 24 E
Baluan I., *Papua N. G.* **132 B4** 2 33 S 147 17 E
Baluchistan □, *Pakistan* **91 D2** 27 30N 65 0 E
Balud, *Phil.* **80 E4** 12 2N 123 12 E
Balurghat, *India* **90 C2** 25 15N 88 44 E
Balvi, *Latvia* **15 H22** 57 8N 27 15 E
Balya, *Turkey* **49 B9** 39 44N 27 35 E
Balykchy, *Kyrgyzstan* **65 B8** 42 26N 76 12 E
Balzar, *Ecuador* **168 D2** 2 2 S 79 54W
Bam, *Iran* **97 D8** 29 7N 58 14 E
Bama, *China* **76 E6** 24 8N 107 12 E
Bama, *Nigeria* **113 C7** 11 33N 13 41 E
Bamaga, *Australia* **126 A3** 10 50 S 142 25 E
Bamaji L., *Canada* **140 B1** 51 9N 91 25W
Bamako, *Mali* **112 C3** 12 34N 7 55W
Bamba, *Dem. Rep. of the Congo* **115 D3** 5 45 S 18 23 E
Bamba, *Mali* **113 B4** 17 5N 1 24W
Bambamarca, *Peru* **172 B2** 6 36 S 78 32W
Bambang, *Phil.* **80 C3** 16 23N 121 6 E
Bambannan I., *Phil.* **81 J3** 5 37N 120 17 E
Bambara Maoundé, *Mali* **112 B4** 13 26N 4 3W
Bambari, *C.A.R.* **114 A4** 5 40N 20 35 E
Bambaroo, *Australia* **126 B4** 18 50 S 146 10 E
Bambaya, *Guinea* **112 D2** 10 55N 13 38W
Bamberg, *Germany* **31 F6** 49 54N 10 54 E
Bamberg, *U.S.A.* **152 B8** 33 18N 81 2W
Bambesi, *Ethiopia* **107 F3** 9 45N 34 40 E
Bambey, *Senegal* **112 C1** 14 42N 16 28W
Bambili, *Dem. Rep. of the Congo* **118 B2** 3 40N 26 0 E
Bambinga, *Dem. Rep. of the Congo* **114 C3** 3 43 S 18 53 E
Bambio, *C.A.R.* **114 B3** 3 55N 16 57 E
Bamboi, *Ghana* **112 D4** 8 13N 2 1W
Bambouti, *C.A.R.* **114 A5** 5 24N 27 12 E
Bambuí, *Brazil* **171 F2** 20 1 S 45 58W
Bamburgh, *U.K.* **20 B6** 55 37N 1 43W
Bamenda, *Cameroon* **113 D7** 5 57N 10 11 E
Bamfield, *Canada* **142 D3** 48 45N 125 10W
Bāmīān □, *Afghan.* **91 B2** 35 0N 67 0 E
Bamiancheng, *China* **75 C13** 43 15N 124 2 E
Bamingui, *C.A.R.* **114 A4** 7 34N 20 11 E
Bamingui →, *C.A.R.* **114 A3** 8 33N 19 5 E
Bamingui-Bangoran △, *C.A.R.* **114 A3** 8 30N 19 46 E
Bamkin, *Cameroon* **113 D7** 6 3N 11 27 E
Bampan, *Phil.* **80 D3** 15 40N 120 20 E
Bampūr, *Iran* **97 E9** 27 15N 60 21 E
Bamu →, *Papua N. G.* **132 E2** 8 1 S 143 33 E
Ban, *Burkina Faso* **112 C4** 14 5N 2 27W
Ban Ao Tu Khun, *Thailand* **87 a** 8 9N 98 20 E
Ban Ban, *Laos* **86 C4** 19 31N 103 30 E
Ban Bang Hin, *Thailand* **87 H2** 9 32N 98 35 E
Ban Bang Khu, *Thailand* **87 a** 7 57N 98 23 E
Ban Bang Rong, *Thailand* **87 a** 8 3N 98 25 E
Ban Bo Phut, *Thailand* **87 b** 9 33N 100 2 E
Ban Chaweng, *Thailand* **87 b** 9 32N 100 3 E
Ban Chiang Klang, *Thailand* **86 C3** 19 25N 100 55 E
Ban Chik, *Laos* **86 D4** 17 15N 102 22 E
Ban Choho, *Thailand* **86 E4** 15 2N 102 9 E
Ban Dan Lan Hoi, *Thailand* **86 D2** 17 0N 99 35 E
Ban Don = Surat Thani, *Thailand* **87 H2** 9 6N 99 20 E
Ban Don, *Vietnam* **86 F6** 12 53N 107 48 E
Ban Don, Ao →, *Thailand* **87 H2** 9 20N 99 25 E
Ban Dong, *Thailand* **86 C3** 19 30N 100 59 E
Ban Hong, *Thailand* **86 C2** 18 18N 98 50 E
Ban Hua Thanon, *Thailand* **87 b** 9 26N 100 1 E
Ban Kaeng, *Thailand* **86 D3** 17 29N 100 7 E
Ban Kantang, *Thailand* **87 J2** 7 25N 99 31 E
Ban Karon, *Thailand* **87 a** 7 51N 98 18 E
Ban Kata, *Thailand* **87 a** 7 50N 98 18 E
Ban Keun, *Laos* **86 C4** 18 22N 102 35 E
Ban Khai, *Thailand* **86 F3** 12 46N 101 18 E
Ban Kheun, *Laos* **86 B3** 20 13N 101 7 E
Ban Khlong Khian, *Thailand* **87 a** 8 10N 98 26 E
Ban Khlong Kua, *Thailand* **87 J3** 6 57N 100 8 E
Ban Khuan, *Thailand* **87 a** 8 20N 98 25 E
Ban Khuan Mao, *Thailand* **87 J2** 7 50N 99 37 E
Ban Ko Yai Chim, *Thailand* **87 G2** 11 17N 99 26 E
Ban Kok, *Thailand* **86 D4** 16 40N 103 40 E
Ban Laem, *Thailand* **86 F2** 13 13N 99 59 E
Ban Lamai, *Thailand* **87 b** 9 28N 100 3 E
Ban Lao Ngam, *Laos* **86 E6** 15 28N 106 10 E
Ban Le Kathe, *Thailand* **86 E2** 15 49N 98 53 E
Ban Lo Po Noi, *Thailand* **87 a** 8 1N 98 34 E
Ban Mae Chedi, *Thailand* **86 C2** 19 11N 99 31 E
Ban Mae Laeng, *Thailand* **86 B2** 20 1N 99 17 E
Ban Mae Nam, *Thailand* **87 b** 9 34N 100 0 E
Ban Mae Sariang, *Thailand* **86 C1** 18 10N 97 56 E
Ban Mê Thuôt = Buon Ma Thuot, *Vietnam* **86 F7** 12 40N 108 3 E
Ban Mi, *Thailand* **86 E3** 15 3N 100 32 E
Ban Muong Mo, *Laos* **86 C4** 19 4N 103 58 E
Ban Na Bo, *Thailand* **87 b** 9 19N 99 41 E
Ban Na Mo, *Laos* **86 D5** 17 7N 105 40 E
Ban Na San, *Thailand* **87 H2** 8 53N 99 52 E
Ban Na Tong, *Laos* **86 B3** 20 56N 101 47 E
Ban Nam Bac, *Laos* **86 B4** 20 38N 102 20 E
Ban Nam Ma, *Laos* **86 A3** 22 2N 101 37 E
Ban Ngang, *Laos* **86 E6** 15 59N 106 11 E
Ban Nong Bok, *Laos* **86 D5** 17 5N 104 48 E
Ban Nong Boua, *Laos* **86 E6** 15 40N 106 33 E
Ban Nong Pling, *Thailand* **86 E3** 15 40N 100 10 E
Ban Pak Chan, *Thailand* **87 G2** 10 32N 98 51 E
Ban Patong, *Thailand* **87 a** 7 54N 98 18 E
Ban Phai, *Thailand* **86 D4** 16 4N 102 44 E
Ban Phak Chit, *Thailand* **87 a** 8 0N 98 24 E
Ban Pong, *Thailand* **86 F2** 13 50N 99 55 E
Ban Rawai, *Thailand* **87 a** 7 47N 98 20 E
Ban Ron Phibun, *Thailand* **87 H2** 8 9N 99 51 E
Ban Sakhu, *Thailand* **87 a** 8 4N 98 18 E
Ban Sanam Chai, *Thailand* **87 J3** 7 33N 100 25 E

Ban Sangkha, *Thailand* **86 E4** 14 37N 103 52 E
Ban Tak, *Thailand* **86 D2** 17 2N 99 4 E
Ban Tako, *Thailand* **86 E4** 14 5N 102 40 E
Ban Tha Dua, *Thailand* **86 D2** 17 59N 98 39 E
Ban Tha Li, *Thailand* **86 D3** 17 37N 101 25 E
Ban Tha Nun, *Thailand* **87 a** 8 12N 98 18 E
Ban Tha Rua, *Thailand* **87 a** 7 59N 98 22 E
Ban Tha Yu, *Thailand* **87 a** 8 17N 98 22 E
Ban Thahine, *Laos* **86 E5** 14 12N 105 33 E
Ban Thong Krut, *Thailand* **87 b** 9 25N 99 57 E
Ban Xien Kok, *Laos* **86 B3** 20 54N 100 39 E
Ban Yen Nhan, *Vietnam* **86 B6** 20 57N 106 2 E
Banā, W. →, *Yemen* **98 D4** 13 3N 45 24 E
Banaba, *Kiribati* **134 H8** 0 45 S 169 50 E
Banalia, *Dem. Rep. of the Congo* **118 B2** 1 32N 25 5 E
Banam, *Cambodia* **87 G5** 11 20N 105 17 E
Banamba, *Mali* **112 C3** 13 29N 7 22W
Banana Is., *S. Leone* **112 D2** 8 7N 13 15W
Bananal, I. do, *Brazil* **171 D1** 11 30 S 50 30W
Bananga, *India* **95 L11** 6 57N 93 54 E
Banaras = Varanasi, *India* **93 G10** 25 22N 83 0 E
Banas →, *Gujarat, India* **92 H4** 23 45N 71 25 E
Banas →, *Mad. P., India* **93 G9** 24 15N 81 30 E
Bânâs, Ras, *Egypt* **106 C4** 23 57N 35 59 E
Banaue, *Phil.* **80 C3** 16 55N 121 4 E
Banaz, *Turkey* **49 C11** 38 46N 29 46 E
Banaz →, *Turkey* **49 C11** 38 12N 29 14 E
Banbridge, *U.K.* **23 B5** 54 22N 6 16W
Banbury, *U.K.* **21 E6** 52 4N 1 20W
Banc d'Arguin △, *Mauritania* **110 D1** 20 10N 16 20W
Banchory, *U.K.* **22 D6** 57 3N 2 29W
Banco, *Ethiopia* **107 F4** 6 12N 38 13 E
Bancroft = Chililabombwe, *Zambia* **119 E2** 12 18 S 27 43 E
Bancroft, *Canada* **140 C4** 45 3N 77 51W
Band, *Romania* **53 D9** 46 30N 24 25 E
Band Bonī, *Iran* **97 E8** 25 30N 59 33 E
Band-e Torkestan, *Afghan.* **91 B2** 35 30N 64 0 E
Band Qīr, *Iran* **97 D6** 31 39N 48 53 E
Banda, *Cameroon* **114 B2** 3 58N 14 32 E
Banda, *Mad. P., India* **93 G8** 24 3N 78 57 E
Banda, *Maharashtra, India* **95 G1** 15 49N 73 52 E
Banda, *Ut. P., India* **93 G9** 25 30N 80 26 E
Banda, Kepulauan, *Indonesia* **83 B3** 4 37 S 129 50 E
Banda Aceh, *Indonesia* **84 A1** 5 35N 95 20 E
Banda Banda, Mt., *Australia* **129 A10** 31 10 S 152 28 E
Banda Elat, *Indonesia* **83 C4** 5 40 S 133 5 E
Banda Is. = Banda, Kepulauan, *Indonesia* **83 B3** 4 37 S 129 50 E
Banda Kani, *Dem. Rep. of the Congo* **115 C2** 4 48 S 13 52 E
Banda Sea, *Indonesia* **82 C3** 6 0 S 130 0 E
Bandai-Asahi △, *Japan* **70 F10** 37 38N 140 5 E
Bandai-San, *Japan* **70 F10** 37 36N 140 4 E
Bandak, *Norway* **18 E5** 59 23N 8 29 E
Bandama →, *Ivory C.* **112 D3** 6 32N 4 30W
Bandama Blanc →, *Ivory C.* **112 D3** 6 55N 5 30W
Bandama Rouge →, *Ivory C.* **112 D4** 6 55N 5 30W
Bandān, *Iran* **97 D9** 31 23N 60 44 E
Bandanaira, *Indonesia* **83 B3** 4 32 S 129 54 E
Bandanwara, *India* **92 F6** 26 9N 74 38 E
Bandar = Machilipatnam, *India* **95 F5** 16 12N 81 8 E
Bandar-e Abbās, *Iran* **97 E8** 27 15N 56 15 E
Bandar-e Anzalī, *Iran* **97 B6** 37 30N 49 30 E
Bandar-e Bushehr = Būshehr, *Iran* **97 D6** 28 55N 50 55 E
Bandar-e Chārak, *Iran* **97 E7** 26 45N 54 20 E
Bandar-e Deylam, *Iran* **97 D6** 30 5N 50 10 E
Bandar-e Emām Khomeyni, *Iran* **97 D6** 30 30N 49 5 E
Bandar-e Lengeh, *Iran* **97 E7** 26 35N 54 58 E
Bandar-e Maqām, *Iran* **97 E7** 26 56N 53 29 E
Bandar-e Ma'shur, *Iran* **97 D6** 30 35N 49 10 E
Bandar-e Rīg, *Iran* **97 D6** 29 29N 50 38 E
Bandar-e Torkeman, *Iran* **97 B7** 37 0N 54 10 E
Bandar Lampung = Tanjungkarang Telukbetung, *Indonesia* **84 D3** 5 20 S 105 10 E
Bandar Maharani = Muar, *Malaysia* **87 L4** 2 3N 102 34 E
Bandar Penggaram = Batu Pahat, *Malaysia* **87 M4** 1 50N 102 56 E
Bandar Seri Begawan, *Brunei* **85 B4** 4 52N 115 0 E
Bandar Sri Aman = Sri Aman, *Malaysia* **85 B4** 1 15N 111 32 E
Bandawe, *Malawi* **119 E3** 11 58 S 34 5 E
Bande, *Spain* **42 C3** 42 3N 7 58W
Bandeira, Pico da, *Brazil* **171 F3** 20 26 S 41 47W
Bandeirante, *Brazil* **171 D1** 13 41 S 50 48W
Bandera, *Argentina* **174 B3** 28 55 S 62 20W
Banderas, B. de, *Mexico* **162 C3** 20 40N 105 30W
Bandhavgarh △, *India* **94 C5** 23 45N 81 10 E
Bandhogarh, *India* **93 H9** 23 40N 81 2 E
Bandi →, *India* **92 F6** 26 12N 75 47 E
Bandia →, *India* **94 E5** 19 2N 80 28 E
Bandiagara, *Mali* **112 C4** 14 12N 3 29W
Bandikui, *India* **92 F7** 27 3N 76 34 E
Bandipur △, *India* **95 J3** 11 45N 76 30 E
Bandırma, *Turkey* **51 F11** 40 20N 28 0 E
Bandjarmasin = Banjarmasin, *Indonesia* **85 C4** 3 20 S 114 35 E
Bandol, *France* **29 E9** 43 8N 5 46 E
Bandon, *Ireland* **23 E3** 51 44N 8 44W
Bandon →, *Ireland* **23 E3** 51 43N 8 37W
Bandoua, *C.A.R.* **114 B4** 4 39N 21 42 E
Bandula, *Mozam.* **119 F3** 19 0 S 33 7 E
Bandundu, *Dem. Rep. of the Congo* **114 C3** 3 15 S 17 22 E
Bandundu □, *Dem. Rep. of the Congo* **114 C3** 3 30 S 17 30 E
Bandung, *Indonesia* **85 D3** 6 54 S 107 36 E
Bané, *Burkina Faso* **113 C4** 11 42N 0 15W
Băneasa, *Romania* **53 E12** 45 56N 27 55 E
Bāneh, *Iran* **101 E11** 35 59N 45 53 E
Bañeres, *Spain* **41 G4** 38 44N 0 38W
Banes, *Cuba* **165 B4** 21 0N 75 42W
Banff, *Canada* **142 C5** 51 10N 115 34W
Banff, *U.K.* **22 D6** 57 40N 2 33W
Banff △, *Canada* **142 C5** 51 30N 116 15W
Banfora, *Burkina Faso* **112 C4** 10 40N 4 40W
Bang Fai →, *Laos* **86 D5** 16 57N 104 45 E
Bang Hieng →, *Laos* **86 D5** 16 10N 105 10 E
Bang Krathum, *Thailand* **86 D3** 16 34N 100 18 E
Bang Lamung, *Thailand* **86 F3** 13 3N 100 56 E
Bang Mun Nak, *Thailand* **86 D3** 16 2N 100 23 E
Bang Pa In, *Thailand* **86 E3** 14 14N 100 35 E
Bang Rakam, *Thailand* **86 D3** 16 45N 100 7 E
Bang Saphan, *Thailand* **87 G2** 11 14N 99 28 E
Bang Thao, *Thailand* **87 a** 7 59N 98 18 E
Banga, *Angola* **115 D3** 8 43 S 15 13 E
Banga, *Dem. Rep. of the Congo* **115 D4** 5 25 S 20 28 E
Banga, *Aklan, Phil.* **81 F4** 11 38N 122 20 E
Banga, *S. Cotabato, Phil.* **81 H5** 6 21N 124 47 E
Bangaduni I., *India* **90 E2** 21 34N 88 52 E
Bangala Dam, *Zimbabwe* **119 G3** 21 7 S 31 25 E
Bangalore, *India* **95 H3** 12 59N 77 40 E
Banganapalle, *India* **95 G4** 15 19N 78 14 E
Banganga →, *India* **92 F6** 27 6N 77 25 E
Bangangté, *Cameroon* **113 D7** 5 8N 10 32 E
Bangaon, *India* **93 H13** 23 0N 88 47 E
Bangar, *Phil.* **80 C3** 16 54N 120 25 E
Bangassou, *C.A.R.* **114 B4** 4 55N 23 7 E
Bangeta, Mt., *Papua N. G.* **132 D4** 6 21 S 147 3 E
Banggai, *Indonesia* **82 B2** 1 34 S 123 30 E
Banggai, Kepulauan, *Indonesia* **82 B2** 1 40 S 123 30 E
Banggai Arch. = Banggai, Kepulauan, *Indonesia* **82 B2** 1 40 S 123 30 E
Banggi, Pulau, *Malaysia* **85 A5** 7 17N 117 12 E
Banghāzī, *Libya* **108 B4** 32 11N 20 3 E
Banghāzī □, *Libya* **108 B4** 32 7N 20 4 E
Bangil, *Indonesia* **85 D4** 7 36 S 112 50 E
Bangjang, *Sudan* **107 E3** 11 23N 32 41 E
Bangka, *Sulawesi, Indonesia* **82 A3** 1 50N 125 5 E
Bangka, *Sumatera, Indonesia* **84 C3** 2 0 S 105 50 E
Bangka, Selat, *Indonesia* **84 C3** 2 30 S 105 30 E
Bangka-Belitung □, *Indonesia* **78 E3** 2 30 S 107 0 E
Bangkalan, *Indonesia* **85 D4** 7 2 S 112 46 E
Bangkinang, *Indonesia* **84 B2** 0 18N 101 5 E
Bangko, *Indonesia* **84 C2** 2 5 S 102 9 E
Bangkok, *Thailand* **86 F3** 13 45N 100 35 E
Bangladesh ■, *Asia* **90 C3** 24 0N 90 0 E
Bangli, *Indonesia* **79 J18** 8 27 S 115 21 E
Bangolo, *Ivory C.* **112 D3** 7 1N 7 29W
Bangong Co, *India* **93 B8** 35 50N 79 20 E
Bangor, *Down, U.K.* **23 B6** 54 40N 5 40W
Bangor, *Gwynedd, U.K.* **20 D3** 53 14N 4 8W
Bangor, *Maine, U.S.A.* **139 D13** 44 48N 68 46W
Bangor, *Mich., U.S.A.* **157 B10** 42 18N 86 7W
Bangor, *Pa., U.S.A.* **151 F9** 40 52N 75 13W
Bangoran →, *C.A.R.* **114 A3** 8 42N 19 6 E
Bangu, *Dem. Rep. of the Congo* **114 C3** 0 3N 19 12 E
Bangued, *Phil.* **80 C3** 17 40N 120 37 E
Bangui, *C.A.R.* **114 B3** 4 23N 18 35 E
Bangui, *Phil.* **80 B3** 18 32N 120 46 E
Banguru, *Dem. Rep. of the Congo* **118 B2** 0 30N 27 10 E
Bangweulu, L., *Zambia* **119 E3** 11 0 S 30 0 E
Bangweulu Swamp, *Zambia* **119 E3** 11 20 S 30 15 E
Banhine △, *Mozam.* **117 C5** 22 49 S 32 55 E
Baní, *Dom. Rep.* **165 C5** 18 16N 70 22W
Bani, *Phil.* **80 C2** 16 11N 119 52 E
Bani →, *Mali* **112 C4** 14 30N 4 12W
Bani, Jebel, *Morocco* **110 C3** 29 16N 8 0W
Bani Bangou, *Niger* **113 B5** 15 3N 2 42 E
Banī Sa'd, *Iraq* **101 F11** 33 34N 44 32 E
Bania, *C.A.R.* **114 B3** 4 1N 16 7 E
Bania, *Ivory C.* **112 D4** 9 4N 3 6W
Baniara, *Papua N. G.* **132 E5** 9 44 S 149 54 E
Banihal Pass, *India* **93 C6** 33 30N 75 12 E
Banikoara, *Benin* **113 C5** 11 18N 2 26 E
Banīnah, *Libya* **108 B4** 32 0N 20 12 E
Bāniyās, *Syria* **100 E6** 35 10N 36 0 E
Banja Luka, *Bos.-H.* **52 F2** 44 49N 17 11 E
Banjar, *India* **92 D7** 31 38N 77 21 E
Banjar, *Indonesia* **85 D3** 7 24 S 108 30 E
Banjar →, *India* **93 H9** 22 36N 80 22 E
Banjarmasin, *Indonesia* **85 C4** 3 20 S 114 35 E
Banjarnegara, *Indonesia* **85 D3** 7 24 S 109 42 E
Banjul, *Gambia* **112 C1** 13 28N 16 40W
Banka, *India* **93 G12** 24 53N 86 55 E
Bankas, *Mali* **112 C4** 14 4N 3 31W
Bankeryd, *Sweden* **17 G8** 57 53N 14 6 E
Banket, *Zimbabwe* **119 F3** 17 27 S 30 19 E
Bankilaré, *Niger* **113 C5** 14 35N 0 44 E
Bankot, *India* **94 F1** 17 58N 73 2 E
Banks, *U.S.A.* **152 D4** 31 49N 85 51W
Banks I. = Moa, I., *Papua N. G.* **132 F2** 10 10 S 142 15 E
Banks I., *B.C., Canada* **142 C3** 53 20N 130 0W
Banks I., *N.W.T., Canada* **138 A7** 73 15N 121 30W
Banks Is., *Vanuatu* **133 C5** 13 50 S 167 30 E
Banks L., *U.S.A.* **152 D6** 31 2N 83 6W
Banks Pen., *N.Z.* **131 D8** 43 45 S 173 15 E
Banks Str., *Australia* **127 G4** 40 40 S 148 10 E
Bankumuna, *Dem. Rep. of the Congo* **115 C3** 4 28 S 19 57 E
Bankura, *India* **93 H12** 23 11N 87 18 E
Bankya, *Bulgaria* **50 D7** 42 43N 23 8 E
Banmankhi, *India* **93 G12** 25 53N 87 11 E
Banmauk, *Burma* **90 C5** 24 24N 95 51 E
Bann →, *Arm., U.K.* **23 B5** 54 30N 6 31W
Bann →, *L'derry., U.K.* **23 A5** 55 8N 6 41W
Bannaanka Saraar, *Somali Rep.* **120 C3** 9 25N 46 17 E
Bannalec, *France* **26 E3** 47 57N 3 42W
Bannang Sata, *Thailand* **87 J3** 6 16N 101 16 E
Bannerton, *Australia* **128 C5** 34 42 S 142 47 E
Banning, *U.S.A.* **161 M10** 33 56N 116 53W
Banningville = Bandundu, *Dem. Rep. of the Congo* **114 C3** 3 15 S 17 22 E
Banno, *Ethiopia* **107 G4** 4 51N 37 24 E
Bannockburn, *Canada* **150 B7** 44 39N 77 33W
Bannockburn, *U.K.* **22 E5** 56 5N 3 55W
Bannockburn, *Zimbabwe* **119 G2** 20 17 S 29 48 E
Bannu, *Pakistan* **91 B3** 33 0N 70 18 E
Bano, *India* **93 H11** 22 40N 84 55 E
Bañolas = Banyoles, *Spain* **40 C7** 42 16N 2 44 E
Banon, *France* **29 D9** 44 2N 5 38 E
Baños de la Encina, *Spain* **43 G7** 38 10N 3 46W
Baños de Molgas, *Spain* **42 C3** 42 15N 7 40W
Bánovce nad Bebravou, *Slovak Rep.* **35 C11** 48 44N 18 16 E
Banovići, *Bos.-H.* **52 F3** 44 25N 18 32 E
Bansalan, *Phil.* **81 H5** 6 55N 125 13 E
Bansgaon, *India* **93 F10** 26 33N 83 21 E
Banská Bystrica, *Slovak Rep.* **35 C12** 48 46N 19 14 E
Banská Štiavnica, *Slovak Rep.* **35 C11** 48 25N 18 55 E
Bansko, *Bulgaria* **50 E7** 41 52N 23 28 E
Banskobystrický □, *Slovak Rep.* **35 C12** 48 20N 19 0 E
Banswara, *India* **92 H6** 23 32N 74 24 E
Bantaeng, *Indonesia* **82 C1** 5 32 S 119 56 E
Bantaji, *Nigeria* **113 D7** 8 6N 10 5 E
Bantayan, *Phil.* **81 F4** 11 10N 123 43 E
Bantayan I., *Phil.* **81 F4** 11 13N 123 44 E
Banten, *Indonesia* **84 D3** 6 5 S 106 8 E
Banten □, *Indonesia* **79 G11** 6 30 S 106 0 E
Banton I., *Phil.* **80 E4** 12 56N 122 4 E
Bantry, *Ireland* **23 E2** 51 41N 9 27W
Bantry B., *Ireland* **23 E2** 51 37N 9 44W
Bantul, *Indonesia* **85 D4** 7 55 S 110 19 E
Bantva, *India* **92 J4** 21 29N 70 12 E
Bantval, *India* **95 H2** 12 55N 75 0 E
Banya, *Bulgaria* **51 D8** 42 33N 24 50 E
Banyak, Kepulauan, *Indonesia* **84 B1** 2 10N 97 10 E
Banyalbufar, *Spain* **38 B3** 39 42N 2 31 E
Banyo, *Cameroon* **113 D7** 6 52N 11 45 E
Banyoles, *Spain* **40 C7** 42 16N 2 44 E
Banyuls-sur-Mer, *France* **28 F7** 42 28N 3 8 E
Banyumas, *Indonesia* **85 D3** 7 32 S 109 18 E
Banyuwangi, *Indonesia* **85 D4** 8 13 S 114 21 E
Banz, *Papua N. G.* **132 C3** 5 47 S 144 37 E
Banzare Coast, *Antarctica* **7 C9** 68 0 S 125 0 E
Banzyville = Mobayi, *Dem. Rep. of the Congo* **114 B4** 4 15N 21 8 E
Bao Ha, *Vietnam* **76 F5** 22 11N 104 21 E
Bao Lac, *Vietnam* **86 A5** 22 57N 105 40 E
Bao Loc, *Vietnam* **87 G6** 11 32N 107 48 E
Bao'an = Shenzhen, *China* **77 F10** 22 32N 114 5 E
Baocheng, *China* **74 H4** 33 12N 106 56 E
Baode, *China* **74 E6** 39 1N 111 5 E
Baodi, *China* **75 E9** 39 38N 117 20 E
Baoding, *China* **74 E8** 38 50N 115 28 E
Baoji, *China* **74 G4** 34 20N 107 5 E
Baojing, *China* **76 C7** 28 45N 109 41 E
Baokang, *China* **77 B8** 31 54N 111 12 E
Baoro, *C.A.R.* **114 A3** 5 40N 15 58 E
Baoshan, *Shanghai, China* **77 B13** 31 27N 121 26 E
Baoshan, *Yunnan, China* **76 E2** 25 10N 99 5 E
Baotou, *China* **74 D6** 40 32N 110 2 E
Baotow = Baotou, *China* **74 D6** 40 32N 110 2 E
Baoxing, *China* **76 B4** 30 24N 102 50 E
Baoying, *China* **75 H10** 33 17N 119 20 E
Baoyou = Ledong, *China* **86 C7** 18 41N 109 5 E
Bap, *India* **92 F5** 27 23N 72 18 E
Bapatla, *India* **95 G5** 15 55N 80 30 E
Bapaume, *France* **27 B9** 50 7N 2 50 E
Baqanas, *Kazakhstan* **65 A8** 44 50N 76 15 E
Baqbaqty, *Kazakhstan* **65 A8** 44 35N 76 40 E
Bāqerābād, *Iran* **97 C6** 33 2N 51 58 E
Ba'qūbah, *Iraq* **101 F11** 33 45N 44 50 E
Baquedano, *Chile* **174 A2** 23 20 S 69 52W
Bar, *Serbia & M.* **50 D3** 42 8N 19 6 E
Bar, *Ukraine* **59 H4** 49 4N 27 40 E
Bar Bigha, *India* **93 G11** 25 21N 85 47 E
Bar Harbor, *U.S.A.* **149 C11** 44 23N 68 13W
Bar-le-Duc, *France* **27 D12** 48 47N 5 10 E
Bar-sur-Aube, *France* **27 D11** 48 14N 4 40 E
Bar-sur-Seine, *France* **27 D11** 48 7N 4 20 E
Bara, *India* **93 G9** 25 16N 81 43 E
Bara, *Indonesia* **82 B3** 3 8 S 126 11 E
Bâra, *Romania* **53 C12** 47 2N 27 3 E
Bara Banki, *India* **93 F9** 26 55N 81 12 E
Barabai, *Indonesia* **85 C5** 2 32 S 115 34 E
Baraboo, *U.S.A.* **154 D10** 43 28N 89 45W
Baracoa, *Cuba* **165 B5** 20 20N 74 30W
Baradā →, *Syria* **103 B5** 33 33N 36 34 E
Baradero, *Argentina* **174 C4** 33 52 S 59 29W
Baradine, *Australia* **129 A8** 30 56 S 149 4 E
Baraga, *U.S.A.* **154 B10** 46 47N 88 30W
Bărăganul, *Romania* **53 F12** 44 49N 27 31 E
Barah →, *India* **92 F6** 27 42N 77 5 E
Barahona, *Dom. Rep.* **165 C5** 18 13N 71 7W
Barahona, *Spain* **40 D2** 41 17N 2 39W
Barail Range, *India* **90 C4** 25 15N 93 20 E
Barajas, Madrid ✕ (MAD), *Spain* **42 E7** 40 26N 3 34W
Barak →, *India* **90 C4** 24 52N 92 30 E
Baraka, *Sudan* **107 E2** 10 59N 27 59 E
Baraka →, *Sudan* **106 D4** 18 13N 37 35 E
Barakaldo, *Spain* **40 B2** 43 18N 2 59W
Barakar →, *India* **93 G12** 24 7N 86 14 E
Barakot, *India* **93 J11** 21 33N 84 59 E
Barakpur, *India* **93 H13** 22 44N 88 30 E
Baralaba, *Australia* **126 C4** 24 13 S 149 50 E
Baralla, *Spain* **42 C3** 42 53N 7 15W
Baralzon L., *Canada* **143 B9** 60 0N 98 3W
Baram →, *Malaysia* **84 B4** 4 35N 113 58 E
Baramati, *India* **94 E2** 18 11N 74 33 E
Baramba, *India* **94 D7** 20 25N 85 23 E
Barameiya, *Sudan* **106 D4** 18 32N 36 38 E
Baramula, *India* **93 B6** 34 15N 74 20 E
Baran, *India* **92 G7** 25 9N 76 40 E
Baran →, *Pakistan* **92 G3** 25 13N 68 17 E
Barañain, *Spain* **40 C3** 42 48N 1 40W
Baranavichy, *Belarus* **59 F4** 53 10N 26 0 E
Barani, *Burkina Faso* **112 C4** 13 10N 3 51W
Baranoa, *Colombia* **168 A3** 10 48N 74 55W
Baranof, *U.S.A.* **142 B2** 57 5N 134 50W
Baranof I., *U.S.A.* **144 H14** 57 0N 135 0W
Baranów Sandomierski, *Poland* **55 H8** 50 29N 21 30 E
Baranowicze = Baranavichy, *Belarus* **59 F4** 53 10N 26 0 E
Baranya □, *Hungary* **52 E3** 46 0N 18 15 E
Barão de Cocais, *Brazil* **171 E3** 19 56 S 43 28W
Barão de Grajaú, *Brazil* **170 C3** 6 45 S 43 1W
Barão de Melgaço, *Mato Grosso, Brazil* **173 D6** 16 14 S 55 52W
Barão de Melgaço, *Rondônia, Brazil* **173 C5** 11 50 S 60 45W
Baraolt, *Romania* **53 D10** 46 5N 25 34 E
Barapasi, *Indonesia* **83 B5** 2 15 S 137 5 E
Barapina = Panguna, *Papua N. G.* **132 D8** 6 21 S 155 25 E
Baras, *Phil.* **80 E5** 13 40N 124 22 E
Barasat, *India* **93 H13** 22 46N 88 31 E
Barat Daya, Kepulauan, *Indonesia* **82 C3** 7 30 S 128 0 E
Baratang I., *India* **95 H11** 12 13N 92 45 E
Barataria B., *U.S.A.* **155 L10** 29 20N 89 55W
Barauda, *India* **92 H6** 23 33N 75 15 E
Baraut, *India* **92 E7** 29 13N 77 7 E
Baraya, *Colombia* **168 C2** 3 10N 75 4W
Barbacan = Roxas, *Phil.* **81 F2** 10 20N 119 21 E
Barbacena, *Brazil* **171 F3** 21 15 S 43 56W
Barbacoas, *Colombia* **168 C2** 1 45N 78 0W
Barbados ■, *W. Indies* **165 g** 13 10N 59 30W
Barbalha, *Brazil* **170 C4** 7 19 S 39 17W
Barban, *Croatia* **45 C11** 45 5N 14 2 E
Barbària, C. de, *Spain* **38 D1** 38 39N 1 24 E
Barbaros, *Turkey* **51 F11** 40 54N 27 27 E
Barbas, C., *W. Sahara* **110 D1** 22 20N 16 42W
Barbastro, *Spain* **40 C5** 42 2N 0 5 E
Barbate de Franco, *Spain* **43 J5** 36 13N 5 56W
Barbaza, *Phil.* **81 F4** 11 12N 122 2 E
Barberino di Mugello, *Italy* **45 E8** 44 0N 11 15 E
Barbers Pt., *U.S.A.* **145 K13** 21 18N 158 7W
Barberton, *S. Africa* **117 D5** 25 42 S 31 2 E
Barberton, *U.S.A.* **150 E3** 41 0N 81 39W
Barberville, *U.S.A.* **153 F8** 29 11N 81 26W
Barbezieux-St-Hilaire, *France* **28 C3** 45 28N 0 9W
Barbosa, *Colombia* **168 B3** 5 57N 73 37W
Barbourville, *U.S.A.* **149 G4** 36 52N 83 53W
Barbuda, *W. Indies* **165 C7** 17 30N 61 40W
Bârca, *Romania* **53 G8** 43 59N 23 36 E
Barcaldine, *Australia* **126 C4** 23 43 S 145 6 E
Barcarena, *Brazil* **170 B2** 1 30 S 48 40W
Barcarrota, *Spain* **43 G4** 38 31N 6 51W
Barce = Al Marj, *Libya* **108 B4** 32 25N 20 30 E
Barcellona Pozzo di Gotto, *Italy* **47 D8** 38 9N 15 13 E
Barcelona, *Spain* **40 D7** 41 21N 2 10 E
Barcelona, *Venezuela* **169 A5** 10 10N 64 40W
Barcelona □, *Spain* **40 D7** 41 30N 2 0 E
Barcelona ✕ (BCN), *Spain* **40 D7** 41 18N 2 5 E
Barceloneta, *Puerto Rico* **165 d** 18 27N 66 32W
Barcelonette, *France* **29 D10** 44 23N 6 40 E
Barcelos, *Brazil* **169 D5** 1 0 S 63 0W
Barcin, *Poland* **55 F4** 52 52N 17 55 E
Barclayville, *Liberia* **112 E3** 4 48N 8 10W
Barcoo →, *Australia* **126 D3** 25 30 S 142 50 E
Barcs, *Hungary* **52 E2** 45 58N 17 28 E
Barczewo, *Poland* **54 E7** 53 50N 20 42 E
Bärdä, *Azerbaijan* **61 K8** 40 25N 47 10 E
Barda del Medio, *Argentina* **176 A3** 38 45 S 68 11W
Bardaï, *Chad* **109 D3** 21 25N 17 0 E
Bardas Blancas, *Argentina* **174 D2** 35 49 S 69 45W
Bardawīl, Sabkhet el, *Egypt* **103 D2** 31 10N 33 15 E
Barddhaman, *India* **93 H12** 23 14N 87 39 E
Bardejov, *Slovak Rep.* **35 B14** 49 18N 21 15 E
Bardera, *Somali Rep.* **120 D2** 2 20N 42 27 E
Barð, *Iceland* **11 A7** 66 3N 19 8W
Bárðarbunga, *Iceland* **11 C9** 64 38N 17 32W
Barðastrandarsýsla □, *Iceland* **11 B3** 65 40N 23 0W
Bardi, *Italy* **44 D6** 44 38N 9 44 E
Bardīyah, *Libya* **108 B5** 31 45N 25 5 E
Bardoli, *India* **94 D1** 21 12N 73 5 E
Bardolino, *Italy* **44 C7** 45 33N 10 43 E
Bardonécchia, *Italy* **44 C3** 45 5N 6 42 E
Bardsey I., *U.K.* **20 E3** 52 45N 4 47W
Bardstown, *U.S.A.* **157 G11** 37 49N 85 28W
Bareilly, *India* **93 E8** 28 22N 79 27 E
Barela, *India* **93 H9** 23 6N 80 3 E
Barellan, *Australia* **129 C7** 34 16 S 146 24 E
Barentin, *France* **26 C7** 49 33N 0 58 E
Barenton, *France* **26 D6** 48 38N 0 50W
Barents Sea, *Arctic* **6 B9** 73 0N 39 0 E
Barentsøya, *Svalbard* **10 B13** 78 25N 21 20 E
Barentu, *Eritrea* **107 D4** 15 2N 37 35 E
Barfleur, *France* **26 C5** 49 40N 1 17W
Barfleur, Pte. de, *France* **26 C5** 49 42N 1 16W
Barfurush = Bābol, *Iran* **97 B7** 36 40N 52 50 E
Barga, *Italy* **44 D7** 44 4N 10 29 E
Bargal, *Somali Rep.* **120 B4** 11 25N 51 0 E
Bargara, *Australia* **126 C5** 24 50 S 152 25 E
Bargarh, *India* **94 D6** 21 20N 83 37 E
Bargas, *Spain* **42 F6** 39 56N 4 3W
Bârgăului Bistrița, *Romania* **53 C9** 47 13N 24 46 E
Barge, *Italy* **44 D4** 44 43N 7 20 E
Bargnop, *Sudan* **107 F2** 9 32N 28 25 E
Bargo, *Australia* **129 C9** 34 18 S 150 35 E
Bargteheide, *Germany* **36 B6** 53 44N 10 14 E
Barguzin, *Russia* **67 D11** 53 37N 109 37 E
Barh, *India* **93 G11** 25 29N 85 46 E
Barhaj, *India* **93 F10** 26 18N 83 44 E
Barham, *Australia* **128 C6** 35 36 S 144 8 E
Barharwa, *India* **93 G12** 24 52N 87 47 E
Barhi, *India* **93 G11** 24 15N 85 25 E
Bari, *Dem. Rep. of the Congo* **114 B3** 3 20N 19 25 E
Bari, *India* **92 F7** 26 39N 77 39 E
Bari, *Italy* **47 A9** 41 8N 16 51 E
Bari Doab, *Pakistan* **92 D5** 30 20N 73 0 E
Bari Sadri, *India* **92 G6** 24 28N 74 30 E
Bari Sardo, *Italy* **46 C2** 39 50N 9 38 E
Barīdī, Ra's, *Si. Arabia* **96 E3** 24 17N 37 31 E
Barīm, *Yemen* **98 D3** 12 39N 43 25 E
Barima →, *Guyana* **169 B5** 8 33N 60 25W
Barinas, *Venezuela* **168 B3** 8 36N 70 15W
Barinas □, *Venezuela* **168 B4** 8 10N 69 50W
Baring, *U.S.A.* **156 D4** 40 15N 92 12W
Baring, C., *Canada* **138 B8** 70 0N 117 30W
Baringa, *Dem. Rep. of the Congo* **114 B4** 0 45N 20 52 E
Baringo, L., *Kenya* **118 B4** 0 47N 36 16 E
Barinitas, *Venezuela* **168 B3** 8 45N 70 25W
Baripada, *India* **94 D8** 21 57N 86 45 E
Bariri, *Brazil* **171 F2** 22 4 S 48 44W
Bârîs, *Egypt* **106 C3** 24 42N 30 31 E
Barisal, *Bangla.* **90 D3** 22 45N 90 20 E
Barisal □, *Bangla.* **90 D3** 22 45N 90 20 E
Barisan, Bukit, *Indonesia* **78 E2** 3 30 S 102 15 E
Barito →, *Indonesia* **85 C4** 4 0 S 114 50 E
Baritú △, *Argentina* **174 A3** 23 43 S 64 40W
Barjac, *France* **29 D8** 44 20N 4 22 E
Barjols, *France* **29 E10** 43 34N 6 2 E
Barjūj, Wadi →, *Libya* **108 C2** 25 26N 12 12 E
Bark L., *Canada* **150 A7** 45 27N 77 51W
Barka = Baraka →, *Sudan* **106 D4** 18 13N 37 35 E
Barkakana, *India* **93 H11** 23 37N 85 29 E
Barkald, *Norway* **16 C7** 61 59N 10 53 E
Barkam, *China* **76 B4** 31 51N 102 28 E
Barker, *U.S.A.* **150 C6** 43 20N 78 33W
Barkley, L., *U.S.A.* **149 G2** 37 1N 88 14W
Barkley Sound, *Canada* **142 D3** 48 50N 125 10W
Barkly East, *S. Africa* **116 E4** 30 58 S 27 33 E
Barkly Roadhouse, *Australia* **126 B2** 19 52 S 135 50 E
Barkly Tableland, *Australia* **126 B2** 17 50 S 136 40 E
Barkly West, *S. Africa* **116 D3** 28 5 S 24 31 E
Barkol, Wadi →, *Sudan* **106 D3** 17 40N 32 0 E
Barkol Kazak Zizhixian, *China* **66 E8** 43 37N 93 2 E
Barla Dağı, *Turkey* **49 C12** 38 5N 30 40 E
Bârlad, *Romania* **53 D12** 46 15N 27 38 E
Bârlad →, *Romania* **53 E12** 45 38N 27 32 E
Barlee, L., *Australia* **125 E2** 29 15 S 119 30 E
Barlee, Mt., *Australia* **125 D4** 24 38 S 128 13 E
Barletta, *Italy* **47 A9** 41 19N 16 17 E
Barlinek, *Poland* **55 F2** 53 0N 15 15 E
Barlovento, *Canary Is.* **9 e1** 28 48N 17 48W
Barlovento, *C. Verde Is.* **9 j** 17 0N 25 0W
Barlow L., *Canada* **143 A8** 62 0N 103 0W
Barmedman, *Australia* **129 C7** 34 9 S 147 21 E
Barmer, *India* **92 G4** 25 45N 71 20 E
Barmera, *Australia* **128 C4** 34 15 S 140 28 E
Barmouth, *U.K.* **20 E3** 52 44N 4 4W
Barmstedt, *Germany* **30 B5** 53 47N 9 46 E
Barn, The, *St. Helena* **9 h** 15 55 S 5 40W
Barna →, *India* **93 G10** 25 21N 83 3 E
Barnagar, *India* **92 H6** 23 7N 75 19 E
Barnala, *India* **92 D6** 30 23N 75 33 E
Barnard →, *Australia* **129 A9** 31 34 S 151 25 E
Barnard Castle, *U.K.* **20 C6** 54 33N 1 55W
Barnato, *Australia* **129 A6** 31 38 S 145 0 E
Barnaul, *Russia* **66 D9** 53 20N 83 40 E
Barnes, *Australia* **128 D6** 36 2 S 144 49 E
Barnesville, *U.S.A.* **152 B5** 33 3N 84 9W
Barnet □, *U.K.* **21 F7** 51 38N 0 9W
Barneveld, *Neths.* **24 B5** 52 7N 5 36 E
Barneveld, *U.S.A.* **151 C9** 43 16N 75 14W
Barneville-Cartevert, *France* **26 C5** 49 23N 1 46W
Barnhart, *U.S.A.* **155 K4** 31 8N 101 10W
Barnsley, *U.K.* **20 D6** 53 34N 1 27W
Barnstaple, *U.K.* **21 F3** 51 5N 4 4W
Barnstaple Bay = Bideford Bay, *U.K.* **21 F3** 51 5N 4 20W
Barnsville, *U.S.A.* **154 B6** 46 43N 96 28W
Barnwell, *U.S.A.* **152 B8** 33 15N 81 23W
Baro, *Nigeria* **113 D6** 8 35N 6 18 E
Baro →, *Ethiopia* **107 F3** 8 26N 33 13 E
Barobo, *Phil.* **81 G6** 8 33N 126 7 E
Baroda = Vadodara, *India* **92 H5** 22 20N 73 10 E
Baroda, *India* **92 G7** 25 29N 76 35 E
Baroe, *S. Africa* **116 E3** 33 13 S 24 33 E
Baron Ra., *Australia* **124 D4** 23 30 S 127 45 E
Barong, *China* **76 B2** 31 3N 99 20 E
Barora, *Solomon Is.* **133 L10** 7 30 S 158 20 E
Barora Ite, *Solomon Is.* **133 L10** 7 36 S 158 24 E
Barotse = Western □, *Zambia* **119 F1** 15 0 S 24 4 E
Barotseland, *Zambia* **115 F4** 15 0 S 24 0 E
Barouéli, *Mali* **112 C3** 13 4N 6 50W
Barpali, *India* **94 D6** 21 11N 83 35 E
Barpathar, *India* **90 B4** 26 17N 93 53 E
Barpeta, *India* **90 B3** 26 20N 91 10 E
Barqin, *Libya* **108 C2** 27 33N 13 34 E
Barques, Pt. Aux, *U.S.A.* **150 B2** 44 4N 82 58W
Barquísimeto, *Venezuela* **168 A4** 10 4N 69 19W
Barr, Ras el, *Egypt* **106 H7** 31 32N 31 50 E
Barr Smith Range, *Australia* **125 E3** 27 4 S 120 20 E
Barra, *Brazil* **170 D3** 11 5 S 43 10W
Barra, *U.K.* **22 E1** 57 0N 7 29W
Barra, Sd. of, *U.K.* **22 D1** 57 4N 7 25W
Barra Bonita = Ibaiti, *Brazil* **171 F1** 23 50 S 50 10W
Barra da Estiva, *Brazil* **171 D3** 13 38 S 41 19W
Barra de Navidad, *Mexico* **162 D4** 19 12N 104 41W
Barra do Bugres, *Brazil* **173 C6** 15 0 S 57 11W
Barra do Corda, *Brazil* **170 C2** 5 30 S 45 10W
Barra do Dande, *Angola* **115 D2** 8 28 S 13 22 E
Barra do Mendes, *Brazil* **171 D3** 11 43 S 42 4W
Barra do Piraí, *Brazil* **171 F3** 22 30 S 43 50W
Barra Falsa, Pta. da, *Mozam.* **117 C6** 22 58 S 35 37 E
Barra Hd., *U.K.* **22 E1** 56 47N 7 40W
Barra Mansa, *Brazil* **171 F3** 22 35 S 44 12W
Barraba, *Australia* **129 A9** 30 21 S 150 35 E
Barracão do Barreto, *Brazil* **173 B6** 8 48 S 58 24W
Barracas al Sur = Avellaneda, *Argentina* **174 C4** 34 50 S 58 10W
Barrackpur = Barakpur, *India* **93 H13** 22 44N 88 30 E
Barradale Roadhouse, *Australia* **124 D1** 22 42 S 114 58 E
Barrafranca, *Italy* **47 E7** 37 22N 14 12 E
Barraigh = Barra, *U.K.* **22 E1** 57 0N 7 29W
Barranca, *Lima, Peru* **172 C2** 10 45 S 77 50W
Barranca, *Loreto, Peru* **168 D2** 4 50 S 76 50W
Barranca del Cobre ⌓, *Mexico* **162 B3** 27 18N 107 40W
Barrancabermeja, *Colombia* **168 B3** 7 0N 73 50W
Barrancas, *Colombia* **168 A3** 10 57N 72 50W
Barrancas, *Venezuela* **169 B5** 8 55N 62 5W
Barrancos, *Portugal* **43 G4** 38 10N 6 58W
Barranqueras, *Argentina* **174 B4** 27 30 S 59 0W
Barranquilla, *Colombia* **168 A3** 11 0N 74 50W
Barras, *Brazil* **170 B3** 4 15 S 42 18W
Barras, *Colombia* **168 D3** 1 45 S 73 13W
Barraute, *Canada* **140 C4** 48 26N 77 38W
Barre, *Mass., U.S.A.* **151 D12** 42 25N 72 6W
Barre, *Vt., U.S.A.* **151 B12** 44 12N 72 30W
Barreal, *Argentina* **174 C2** 31 33 S 69 28W
Barrei, *Ethiopia* **120 C2** 6 10N 42 49 E
Barreiras, *Brazil* **171 D3** 12 8 S 45 0W
Barreirinha, *Brazil* **169 D6** 2 47 S 57 3W
Barreirinhas, *Brazil* **170 B3** 2 30 S 42 50W
Barreiro, *Portugal* **43 G1** 38 40N 9 6W
Barreiros, *Brazil* **170 C4** 8 49 S 35 12W
Barrême, *France* **29 E10** 43 57N 6 23 E
Barren, Nosy, *Madag.* **117 B7** 18 25 S 43 40 E
Barren I., *India* **95 H11** 12 16N 93 51 E
Barren Is., *U.S.A.* **144 G9** 58 55N 152 15W
Barretos, *Brazil* **171 F2** 20 30 S 48 35W
Barrhead, *Canada* **142 C6** 54 10N 114 24W
Barrie, *Canada* **140 D4** 44 24N 79 40W
Barrier, C., *N.Z.* **130 C4** 36 25 S 175 32 E
Barrier Ra., *Australia* **128 A4** 31 0 S 141 30 E
Barrier Ra., *Otago, N.Z.* **131 E4** 44 15 S 169 32 E
Barrier Ra., *W. Coast, N.Z.* **131 E3** 44 30 S 168 30 E
Barrière, *Canada* **142 C4** 51 12N 120 7W
Barrineau Park, *U.S.A.* **153 E2** 30 42N 87 26W
Barrington, *U.S.A.* **151 E13** 41 44N 71 18W
Barrington, I. = Santa Fé, I., *Ecuador* **172 a** 0 49 S 90 5W
Barrington L., *Canada* **143 B8** 56 55N 100 15W
Barrington Tops, *Australia* **129 B9** 32 6 S 151 28 E
Barrington Tops △, *Australia* **129 B9** 32 4 S 151 25 E
Barringun, *Australia* **127 D4** 29 1 S 145 41 E
Barrit-Luluno = Luba, *Phil.* **80 C3** 17 19N 120 42 E
Barro do Garças, *Brazil* **173 D7** 15 54 S 52 16W

Barron, *U.S.A.* **154 C9** 45 24N 91 51W
Barrow, *U.S.A.* **144 A8** 71 18N 156 47W
Barrow →, *Ireland* **23 D5** 52 25N 6 58W
Barrow Creek, *Australia* **126 C1** 21 30 S 133 55 E
Barrow I., *Australia* **124 D2** 20 45 S 115 20 E
Barrow-in-Furness, *U.K.* **20 C4** 54 7N 3 14W
Barrow Pt., *Australia* **126 A3** 14 20 S 144 40 E
Barrow Pt., *U.S.A.* **144 A8** 71 10N 156 20W
Barrow Ra., *Australia* **125 E4** 26 0 S 127 40 E
Barrow Str., *Canada* **6 B3** 74 20N 95 0W
Barruecopardo, *Spain* **42 D4** 41 4N 6 40W
Barruelo de Santullán, *Spain* **42 C6** 42 54N 4 17W
Barry, *U.K.* **21 F4** 51 24N 3 16W
Barry, *U.S.A.* **156 E5** 39 42N 91 2W
Barry's Bay, *Canada* **140 C4** 45 29N 77 41W
Barsalogho, *Burkina Faso* **113 C4** 13 25N 1 3W
Barsat, *Pakistan* **93 A5** 36 10N 72 45 E
Barsham, *Syria* **101 E9** 35 21N 40 33 E
Barsi, *India* **94 E2** 18 10N 75 50 E
Barsinghausen, *Germany* **30 C5** 52 18N 9 28 E
Barskoon, *Kyrgyzstan* **65 B8** 42 10N 77 37 E
Barstow, *U.S.A.* **161 L9** 34 54N 117 1W
Bartenstein = Bartoszyce, *Poland* **54 D7** 54 15N 20 55 E
Bartfeld = Bardejov, *Slovak Rep.* **35 B14** 49 18N 21 15 E
Barth, *Germany* **30 A8** 54 22N 12 42 E
Barthélemy, Col, *Vietnam* **86 C5** 19 26N 104 6 E
Bartica, *Guyana* **169 B6** 6 25N 58 40W
Bartin, *Turkey* **100 B5** 41 38N 32 21 E
Bartle Frere, *Australia* **126 B4** 17 27 S 145 50 E
Bartlesville, *U.S.A.* **155 G7** 36 45N 95 59W
Bartlett, *Calif., U.S.A.* **160 J8** 36 29N 118 2W
Bartlett, *Tenn., U.S.A.* **155 H10** 35 12N 89 52W
Bartlett, L., *Canada* **142 A5** 63 5N 118 20W
Bartolo = Betanzos, *Bolivia* **173 D4** 19 34 S 65 27W
Bartolomeu Dias, *Mozam.* **119 G4** 21 10 S 35 8 E
Barton, *Phil.* **81 F2** 10 24N 119 8 E
Barton, *U.S.A.* **151 B12** 44 45N 72 11W
Barton upon Humber, *U.K.* **20 D7** 53 41N 0 25W
Bartonville, *U.S.A.* **156 D7** 40 39N 89 39W
Bartoszyce, *Poland* **54 D7** 54 15N 20 55 E
Bartow, *Fla., U.S.A.* **153 H8** 27 54N 81 50W
Bartow, *Ga., U.S.A.* **152 C7** 32 53N 82 29W
Barú, I. de, *Colombia* **168 A2** 10 15N 75 35W
Barú, Volcan, *Panama* **164 E3** 8 55N 82 35W
Barumba, *Dem. Rep. of the Congo* **118 B1** 1 3N 23 37 E
Barumbu, *Dem. Rep. of the Congo* **114 B4** 1 14N 23 31 E
Baruth, *Germany* **30 C9** 52 4N 13 30 E
Baruunsuu, *Mongolia* **74 C3** 43 43N 105 35 E
Barvinkove, *Ukraine* **59 H9** 48 57N 37 0 E
Bärwalde = Barwice, *Poland* **54 E3** 53 44N 16 21 E
Barwani, *India* **92 H6** 22 2N 74 57 E
Barwice, *Poland* **54 E3** 53 44N 16 21 E
Barwick, *U.S.A.* **152 E6** 30 54N 83 44W
Barycz →, *Poland* **55 G3** 51 42N 16 15 E
Barysaw, *Belarus* **58 E5** 54 17N 28 28 E
Barysh, *Russia* **60 D8** 53 39N 47 8 E
Barzān, *Iraq* **96 B5** 36 55N 44 3 E
Bârzava, *Romania* **52 D6** 46 7N 21 59 E
Bas-Congo □, *Dem. Rep. of the Congo* **115 D2** 5 0 S 15 0 E
Bas-Kouilou, *Congo* **115 C2** 4 28 S 11 42 E
Bas-Rhin □, *France* **27 D14** 48 40N 7 30 E
Bašaid, *Serbia & M.* **52 E5** 45 38N 20 25 E
Bāsa'idū, *Iran* **97 E7** 26 35N 55 20 E
Basal, *Pakistan* **92 C5** 33 33N 72 13 E
Basankusa, *Dem. Rep. of the Congo* **114 B3** 1 5N 19 50 E
Basarabeasca, *Moldova* **53 D13** 46 21N 28 58 E
Basarabi, *Romania* **53 F13** 44 10N 28 26 E
Basarabia = Bessarabiya, *Moldova* **59 J5** 47 0N 28 10 E
Basauri, *Spain* **40 B2** 43 13N 2 53W
Basawa, *Afghan.* **91 B3** 34 15N 70 50 E
Basco, *Phil.* **80 A3** 20 27N 121 58 E
Bascuñán, C., *Chile* **174 B1** 28 52 S 71 35W
Basekpio, *Dem. Rep. of the Congo* **114 B4** 4 43N 24 36 E
Basel, *Switz.* **32 A5** 47 35N 7 35 E
Basel, Euroairport ✈ (BSL), *Europe* **27 E14** 47 36N 7 33 E
Basel-Landschaft □, *Switz.* **32 B5** 47 26N 7 45 E
Basel-Stadt □, *Switz.* **32 A5** 47 35N 7 35 E
Basento →, *Italy* **47 B9** 40 20N 16 49 E
Basey, *Phil.* **81 F5** 11 17N 125 4 E
Bashākerd, Kūhhā-ye, *Iran* **97 E8** 26 42N 58 35 E
Bashanta = Gorodovikovsk, *Russia* **61 G5** 46 8N 41 58 E
Bashaw, *Canada* **142 C6** 52 35N 112 58W
Bāshī, *Iran* **97 D6** 28 41N 51 4 E
Bashkir Republic = Bashkortostan □, *Russia* **64 E6** 54 0N 57 0 E
Bashkortostan □, *Russia* **64 E6** 54 0N 57 0 E
Bashtanivka, *Ukraine* **53 E14** 45 46N 29 29 E
Basibasy, *Madag.* **117 C7** 22 10 S 43 40 E
Basilaki I., *Papua N. G.* **132 F6** 10 35 S 151 0 E
Basilan □, *Phil.* **81 H4** 6 33N 122 4 E
Basilan I., *Phil.* **81 H4** 6 35N 122 0 E
Basilan Str., *Phil.* **81 H4** 6 50N 122 0 E
Basildon, *U.K.* **21 F8** 51 34N 0 28 E
Basile, *Eq. Guin.* **113 E6** 3 42N 8 48 E
Basilicata □, *Italy* **47 B9** 40 30N 16 30 E
Basim = Washim, *India* **94 D3** 20 3N 77 0 E
Basin, *U.S.A.* **158 D9** 44 23N 108 2W
Basinger, *U.S.A.* **153 H8** 27 23N 81 2W
Basingstoke, *U.K.* **21 F6** 51 15N 1 5W
Basirhat, *Bangla.* **90 D2** 22 40N 88 54 E
Baška, *Croatia* **45 D11** 44 58N 14 45 E
Başkale, *Turkey* **101 C10** 38 2N 43 59 E
Baskatong, Rés., *Canada* **140 C4** 46 46N 75 50W
Basle = Basel, *Switz.* **32 A5** 47 35N 7 35 E
Başmakçı, *Turkey* **49 D12** 37 54N 30 1 E
Basmat, *India* **94 E3** 19 15N 77 12 E
Basoda, *India* **92 H7** 23 52N 77 54 E
Basodino, *Switz.* **33 D6** 46 25N 8 28 E
Basoko, *Dem. Rep. of the Congo* **118 B1** 1 16N 23 40 E
Basongo, *Dem. Rep. of the Congo* **115 C4** 4 15 S 20 20 E
Basque, Pays, *France* **28 E2** 43 15N 1 20W
Basque Provinces = País Vasco □, *Spain* **40 C2** 42 50N 2 45W
Basra = Al Başrah, *Iraq* **96 D5** 30 30N 47 50 E
Bass Str., *Australia* **127 F4** 39 15 S 146 30 E
Bassano, *Canada* **142 C6** 50 48N 112 20W
Bassano del Grappa, *Italy* **45 C8** 45 46N 11 44 E
Bassar, *Togo* **113 D5** 9 19N 0 57 E
Bassas da India, *Ind. Oc.* **121 G2** 22 0 S 39 0 E
Basse-Normandie □, *France* **26 D6** 48 45N 0 30W
Basse-Pointe, *Martinique* **164 c** 14 52N 61 8W
Basse Santa-Su, *Gambia* **112 C2** 13 13N 14 15W
Basse-Terre, *Guadeloupe* **164 b** 16 0N 61 44W
Basse Terre, *Trin. & Tob.* **169 F9** 10 7N 61 19W
Bassecourt, *Switz.* **32 B4** 47 20N 7 15 E
Bassein, *Burma* **90 G5** 16 45N 94 30 E
Bassein, *India* **94 E1** 19 26N 72 48 E
Basses, Pte. des, *Guadeloupe* **164 b** 15 52N 61 17W
Basses-Alpes = Alpes-de-Haute-Provence □, *France* **29 D10** 44 8N 6 10 E
Basses-Pyrénées = Pyrénées-Atlantiques □, *France* **28 E3** 43 10N 0 50W
Basseterre, *St. Kitts & Nevis* **165 C7** 17 17N 62 43W
Bassett, *U.S.A.* **154 D5** 42 35N 99 32W
Bassi, *India* **92 D7** 30 44N 76 21 E
Bassigny, *France* **27 E12** 48 0N 5 30 E
Bassikounou, *Mauritania* **112 B3** 15 55N 6 1W
Bassila, *Benin* **113 D5** 9 1N 1 46 E
Bassum, *Germany* **30 C4** 52 50N 8 40 E
Båstad, *Sweden* **17 H6** 56 25N 12 51 E
Bastak, *Iran* **97 E7** 27 15N 54 25 E
Baştām, *Iran* **97 B7** 36 29N 55 4 E
Bastar, *India* **94 E5** 19 15N 81 40 E
Bastelica, *France* **29 F13** 42 1N 9 3 E
Basti, *India* **93 F10** 26 52N 82 55 E
Bastia, *France* **29 F13** 42 40N 9 30 E
Bastogne, *Belgium* **24 D5** 50 1N 5 43 E
Bastrop, *La., U.S.A.* **155 J9** 32 47N 91 55W
Bastrop, *Tex., U.S.A.* **155 K6** 30 7N 97 19W
Basud, *Phil.* **80 D4** 14 4N 122 58 E
Basuo = Dongfang, *China* **86 C7** 18 50N 108 33 E
Basutoland = Lesotho ■, *Africa* **117 D4** 29 40 S 28 0 E
Bat Yam, *Israel* **103 C3** 32 2N 34 44 E
Bata, *Eq. Guin.* **114 B1** 1 57N 9 50 E
Bata, *Romania* **52 D7** 46 1N 22 4 E
Bataan □, *Phil.* **80 D3** 14 40N 120 25 E
Bataan △, *Phil.* **80 D3** 14 45N 120 27 E
Batabanó, *Cuba* **164 B3** 22 41N 82 18W
Batabanó, G. de, *Cuba* **164 B3** 22 30N 82 30W
Batac, *Phil.* **80 B3** 18 3N 120 34 E
Batagai, *Russia* **67 C14** 67 38N 134 38 E
Batajnica, *Serbia & M.* **50 B4** 44 54N 20 17 E
Batak, *Bulgaria* **51 E8** 41 57N 24 12 E
Batala, *India* **92 D6** 31 48N 75 12 E
Batalha, *Portugal* **42 F2** 39 40N 8 50W
Batalpashinsk = Cherkessk, *Russia* **61 H6** 44 15N 42 5 E
Batam, *Indonesia* **84 B2** 1 5N 104 3 E
Batama, *Dem. Rep. of the Congo* **118 B2** 0 58N 26 33 E
Batamay, *Russia* **67 C13** 63 30N 129 15 E
Batan I., *Albay, Phil.* **80 E4** 13 15N 124 0 E
Batan I., *Batanes, Phil.* **80 A3** 20 26N 121 58 E
Batanes □, *Phil.* **80 A3** 20 40N 121 55 E
Batanes Is., *Phil.* **80 A3** 20 30N 122 0 E
Batang, *China* **76 B2** 30 1N 99 0 E
Batang, *Indonesia* **85 D3** 6 55 S 109 45 E
Batanga, *Gabon* **114 C1** 0 21 S 9 18 E
Batangafo, *C.A.R.* **114 A3** 7 25N 18 20 E
Batangas, *Phil.* **80 E3** 13 35N 121 10 E
Batangas □, *Phil.* **80 E3** 13 40N 121 5 E
Batanghari, *Indonesia* **84 C2** 1 36 S 103 37 E
Batanta, *Indonesia* **83 B4** 0 55 S 130 40 E
Bataraza, *Phil.* **81 G1** 8 40N 117 37 E
Batas I., *Phil.* **81 F2** 11 10N 119 36 E
Batatais, *Brazil* **175 A6** 20 54 S 47 37W
Batavia = Jakarta, *Indonesia* **84 D3** 6 9 S 106 49 E
Batavia, *Ill., U.S.A.* **157 C8** 41 51N 88 19W
Batavia, *N.Y., U.S.A.* **150 D6** 43 0N 78 11W
Batavia, *Ohio, U.S.A.* **157 E12** 39 5N 84 11W
Bataysk, *Russia* **59 J10** 47 3N 39 45 E
Batbakara = Amangeldy, *Kazakhstan* **66 D7** 50 10N 65 10 E
Batchelor, *Australia* **124 B5** 13 4 S 131 1 E
Batdambang, *Cambodia* **86 F4** 13 7N 103 12 E
Batéké, Plateau, *Congo* **114 C3** 3 30 S 15 45 E
Batemans B., *Australia* **129 C9** 35 40 S 150 12 E
Batemans Bay, *Australia* **129 C9** 35 44 S 150 11 E
Bates Ra., *Australia* **125 E3** 27 27 S 121 5 E
Batesburg-Leesville, *U.S.A.* **152 B8** 33 54N 81 33W
Batesville, *Ark., U.S.A.* **155 H9** 35 46N 91 39W
Batesville, *Ind., U.S.A.* **157 E11** 39 18N 85 13W
Batesville, *Miss., U.S.A.* **155 H10** 34 19N 89 57W
Batesville, *Tex., U.S.A.* **155 L5** 28 58N 99 37W
Bath, *Canada* **151 B8** 44 11N 76 47W
Bath, *U.K.* **21 F5** 51 23N 2 22W
Bath, *Maine, U.S.A.* **149 D11** 43 55N 69 49W
Bath, *N.Y., U.S.A.* **150 D7** 42 20N 77 19W
Bath, *S.C., U.S.A.* **152 B8** 33 31N 81 51W
Bath & North East Somerset □, *U.K.* **21 F5** 51 21N 2 27W
Batha →, *Chad* **109 F3** 12 47N 17 34 E
Batheay, *Cambodia* **87 G5** 11 59N 104 57 E
Bathsheba, *Barbados* **165 g** 13 13N 59 32W
Bathurst = Banjul, *Gambia* **112 C1** 13 28N 16 40W
Bathurst, *Australia* **129 B8** 33 25 S 149 31 E
Bathurst, *Canada* **141 C6** 47 37N 65 43W
Bathurst, *S. Africa* **116 E4** 33 30 S 26 50 E
Bathurst, C., *Canada* **138 A7** 70 34N 128 0W
Bathurst B., *Australia* **126 A3** 14 16 S 144 25 E
Bathurst Harb., *Australia* **127 G4** 43 15 S 146 10 E
Bathurst I., *Australia* **124 B5** 11 30 S 130 10 E
Bathurst I., *Canada* **6 B2** 76 0N 100 30W
Bathurst Inlet, *Canada* **138 B9** 66 50N 108 1W
Bati, *Ethiopia* **107 E5** 11 10N 40 0 E
Batie, *Burkina Faso* **112 D4** 9 53N 2 53W
Batiki, *Fiji* **133 A2** 17 48 S 179 10 E
Batlow, *Australia* **129 C8** 35 31 S 148 9 E
Batman, *Turkey* **101 D9** 37 55N 41 5 E
Baţn al Ghūl, *Jordan* **103 F4** 29 36N 35 56 E
Batna, *Algeria* **111 A6** 35 34N 6 15 E
Batnfjordsøra, *Norway* **18 B4** 62 53N 7 42 E
Bato, *Catanduanes, Phil.* **80 E5** 13 36N 124 18 E
Bato, *Leyte, Phil.* **81 F5** 10 13N 124 48 E
Bato Bato, *Phil.* **81 J2** 5 6N 119 49 E
Batoala, *Gabon* **114 B2** 0 48N 13 27 E
Batobato = San Isidro, *Phil.* **81 H6** 6 50N 126 5 E
Batočina, *Serbia & M.* **50 B5** 44 7N 21 5 E
Batoka, *Zambia* **119 F2** 16 45 S 27 15 E
Baton Rouge, *U.S.A.* **155 K9** 30 27N 91 11W
Batong, Ko, *Thailand* **87 J2** 6 32N 99 12 E
Bátonyterenye, *Hungary* **52 C4** 47 59N 19 50 E
Batopilas, *Mexico* **162 B3** 27 0N 107 45W
Batouri, *Cameroon* **114 B2** 4 30N 14 25 E
Batovany = Partizánske, *Slovak Rep.* **35 C11** 48 38N 18 23 E
Båtsfjord, *Norway* **14 A23** 70 38N 29 39 E
Battambang = Batdambang, *Cambodia* **86 F4** 13 7N 103 12 E
Batti Malv, *India* **95 K11** 8 50N 92 51 E
Batticaloa, *Sri Lanka* **95 L5** 7 43N 81 45 E
Battipáglia, *Italy* **47 B7** 40 37N 14 58 E
Battle, *U.K.* **21 G8** 50 55N 0 30 E
Battle →, *Canada* **143 C7** 52 43N 108 15W
Battle Creek, *U.S.A.* **157 B11** 42 19N 85 11W
Battle Ground, *U.S.A.* **160 E4** 45 47N 122 32W
Battle Harbour, *Canada* **141 B8** 52 16N 55 35W
Battle Lake, *U.S.A.* **154 B7** 46 17N 95 43W
Battle Mountain, *U.S.A.* **158 F5** 40 38N 116 56W
Battlefields, *Zimbabwe* **119 F2** 18 37 S 29 47 E
Battleford, *Canada* **143 C7** 52 45N 108 15W
Battonya, *Hungary* **52 D6** 46 16N 21 3 E
Batu, *Ethiopia* **107 F4** 6 55N 39 45 E
Batu, Bukit, *Malaysia* **85 B4** 2 16N 113 43 E
Batu, Kepulauan, *Indonesia* **84 C1** 0 30 S 98 25 E
Batu Bora, Bukit, *Malaysia* **85 B4** 2 43N 114 43 E
Batu Caves, *Malaysia* **87 L3** 3 15N 101 40 E
Batu Ferringhi, *Malaysia* **87 c** 5 28N 100 15 E
Batu Gajah, *Malaysia* **87 K3** 4 28N 101 3 E
Batu Is. = Batu, Kepulauan, *Indonesia* **84 C1** 0 30 S 98 25 E
Batu Pahat, *Malaysia* **87 M4** 1 50N 102 56 E
Batu Puteh, Gunung, *Malaysia* **84 B2** 4 15N 101 31 E
Batuata, *Indonesia* **82 C2** 6 12 S 122 42 E
Batugondang, Tanjung, *Indonesia* **79 J17** 8 6 S 114 29 E
Batui, *Indonesia* **82 B2** 1 17 S 122 33 E
Batukau, Gunung, *Indonesia* **79 J18** 8 20 S 115 5 E
Batulaki, *Phil.* **81 J5** 5 34N 125 19 E
Batuli = San Isidro, *Phil.* **81 H6** 6 50N 126 5 E
Batumi, *Georgia* **61 K5** 41 39N 41 44 E
Batur, *Indonesia* **79 J18** 8 15 S 115 20 E
Batur, Gunung, *Indonesia* **79 J18** 8 14 S 115 23 E
Baturaja, *Indonesia* **84 C2** 4 11 S 104 15 E
Baturité, *Brazil* **170 B4** 4 28 S 38 45W
Baturiti, *Indonesia* **79 J18** 8 19 S 115 11 E
Batusangkar, *Indonesia* **84 C2** 0 27 S 100 35 E
Bau, *Malaysia* **85 B4** 1 25N 110 9 E
Bauang, *Phil.* **80 C3** 16 31N 120 20 E
Baubau, *Indonesia* **82 C2** 5 25 S 122 38 E
Baucau, *E. Timor* **82 C3** 8 27 S 126 27 E
Bauchi, *Nigeria* **113 C6** 10 22N 9 48 E
Bauchi □, *Nigeria* **113 C7** 10 30N 10 0 E
Baud, *France* **26 E3** 47 52N 3 1W
Bauda, *India* **94 D7** 20 50N 84 25 E
Baudette, *U.S.A.* **154 A7** 48 43N 94 36W
Bauen, *Switz.* **33 C7** 46 56N 8 35 E
Bauer, C., *Australia* **127 E1** 32 44 S 134 4 E
Bauerwitz = Baborów, *Poland* **55 H5** 50 7N 18 1 E
Bauguen = Salcedo, *Phil.* **81 F5** 11 9N 125 40 E
Bauhinia, *Australia* **126 C4** 24 35 S 149 18 E
Baukau = Baucau, *E. Timor* **82 C3** 8 27 S 126 27 E
Bauko, *Phil.* **80 C3** 17 0N 120 52 E
Baulai →, *Bangla.* **90 C3** 24 22N 91 1 E
Bauld, C., *Canada* **139 C14** 51 38N 55 26W
Bauma, *Switz.* **33 B7** 47 23N 8 53 E
Baumanabad = Pyandzh, *Tajikistan* **65 E4** 37 14N 69 6 E
Baume-les-Dames, *France* **27 E13** 47 22N 6 22 E
Baunatal, *Germany* **30 D5** 51 14N 9 24 E
Baunei, *Italy* **46 B2** 40 2N 9 40 E
Baure, *Nigeria* **113 C6** 12 52N 8 50 E
Baures, *Bolivia* **173 C5** 13 35 S 63 35W
Bauru, *Brazil* **175 A6** 22 10 S 49 0W
Baús, *Brazil* **173 D7** 18 22 S 52 47W
Bausi, *India* **93 G12** 24 48N 87 1 E
Bauska, *Latvia* **15 H21** 56 24N 24 15 E
Bautino, *Kazakhstan* **61 H10** 44 35N 50 14 E
Bautzen, *Germany* **30 D10** 51 10N 14 26 E
Bauya, *S. Leone* **112 D2** 8 12N 12 38W
Baūyrzhan Momyshuly, *Kazakhstan* **65 B5** 42 36N 70 47 E
Bavānāt, *Iran* **97 D7** 30 28N 53 27 E
Bavanište, *Serbia & M.* **52 F5** 44 49N 20 55 E
Bavaria = Bayern □, *Germany* **31 G7** 48 50N 12 0 E
Båven, *Sweden* **16 E10** 59 0N 16 56 E
Bavispe →, *Mexico* **162 B3** 29 30N 109 11W
Baw Baw △, *Australia* **129 D7** 37 50 S 146 17 E
Bawdwin, *Burma* **90 D6** 23 5N 97 20 E
Bawe, *Indonesia* **83 B4** 2 59 S 134 43 E
Bawean, *Indonesia* **85 D4** 5 46 S 112 35 E
Bawku, *Ghana* **113 C4** 11 3N 0 19W
Bawlake, *Burma* **90 F6** 19 11N 97 21 E
Bawolung, *China* **76 C3** 28 50N 101 16 E
Baxley, *U.S.A.* **152 D7** 31 47N 82 21W
Baxoi, *China* **76 B1** 30 1N 96 50 E
Baxter, *Iowa, U.S.A.* **156 C3** 41 49N 93 9W
Baxter, *Minn., U.S.A.* **154 B7** 46 21N 94 17W
Baxter Springs, *U.S.A.* **155 G7** 37 2N 94 44W
Baxter State ◠, *U.S.A.* **149 B11** 46 5N 68 57W
Bay, L. de, *Phil.* **80 D3** 14 20N 121 11 E
Bay al Khā'ib, Wādī →, *Libya* **108 B3** 30 55N 15 29 E
Bay City, *Mich., U.S.A.* **148 D4** 43 36N 83 54W
Bay City, *Tex., U.S.A.* **155 L7** 28 59N 95 58W
Bay Minette, *U.S.A.* **149 K2** 30 53N 87 46W
Bay of Plenty □, *N.Z.* **130 D5** 38 0 S 177 0 E
Bay Roberts, *Canada* **141 C9** 47 36N 53 16W
Bay St. Louis, *U.S.A.* **155 K10** 30 19N 89 20W
Bay Springs, *U.S.A.* **155 K10** 31 59N 89 17W
Bay View, *N.Z.* **130 F5** 39 25 S 176 50 E
Baya, *Dem. Rep. of the Congo* **119 E2** 11 53 S 27 25 E
Bayambang, *Phil.* **80 D3** 15 49N 120 27 E
Bayamo, *Cuba* **164 B4** 20 20N 76 40W
Bayamón, *Puerto Rico* **165 d** 18 24N 66 9W
Bayan Har Shan, *China* **68 C4** 34 0N 98 0 E
Bayan Hot = Alxa Zuoqi, *China* **74 E3** 38 50N 105 40 E
Bayan Lepas, *Malaysia* **87 c** 5 17N 100 16 E
Bayan Obo, *China* **74 D5** 41 52N 109 59 E
Bayan-Ovoo = Erdenetsogt, *Mongolia* **74 C4** 42 55N 106 5 E
Bayan-Tumen = Choybalsan, *Mongolia* **69 B6** 48 4N 114 30 E
Bayana, *India* **92 F7** 26 55N 77 18 E
Bayanaūyl, *Kazakhstan* **66 D8** 50 45N 75 45 E
Bayandalay, *Mongolia* **74 C2** 43 30N 103 29 E
Bayanhongor, *Mongolia* **68 B5** 46 8N 102 43 E
Bayard, *N. Mex., U.S.A.* **159 K9** 32 46N 108 8W
Bayard, *Nebr., U.S.A.* **154 E3** 41 45N 103 20W
Bayawan, *Phil.* **81 G4** 9 46N 122 45 E
Baybay, *Phil.* **81 F5** 10 40N 124 55 E
Bayburt, *Turkey* **101 B9** 40 15N 40 20 E
Baydhabo = Baidoa, *Somali Rep.* **120 D2** 3 8N 43 30 E
Bayelsa □, *Nigeria* **113 E6** 4 30N 6 0 E
Bayerische Alpen, *Germany* **31 H7** 47 35N 11 30 E
Bayerische Rhön ◠, *Germany* **31 E6** 50 15N 10 5 E
Bayerischer Spessart ◠, *Germany* **31 F6** 49 58N 10 15 E
Bayerischer Wald, *Germany* **31 G8** 48 56N 12 50 E
Bayern □, *Germany* **31 G7** 48 50N 12 0 E
Bayeux, *France* **26 C6** 49 17N 0 42W
Bayfield, *Canada* **150 C3** 43 34N 81 42W
Bayfield, *U.S.A.* **154 B9** 46 49N 90 49W
Bäygequm, *Kazakhstan* **65 A3** 44 19N 66 27 E
Bayḩān al Qisāb, *Yemen* **98 D4** 15 48N 45 44 E
Bayındır, *Turkey* **49 C9** 38 13N 27 39 E
Bayjī, *Iraq* **101 E10** 35 0N 43 30 E
Baykal, Oz., *Russia* **67 D11** 53 0N 108 0 E
Baykan, *Turkey* **96 B4** 38 7N 41 44 E
Baykonur = Bayqongyr, *Kazakhstan* **66 E7** 47 48N 65 50 E
Baykurt, *China* **65 D7** 39 56N 75 33 E
Baymak, *Russia* **64 E7** 52 36N 58 19 E
Baymurat, *Uzbekistan* **65 C3** 41 8N 66 25 E
Baynes Mts., *Namibia* **116 B1** 17 15 S 13 0 E
Bayombong, *Phil.* **80 C3** 16 30N 121 10 E
Bayon, *France* **27 D13** 48 30N 6 20 E
Bayona = Baiona, *Spain* **42 C2** 42 6N 8 52W
Bayonet Point, *U.S.A.* **153 G7** 28 20N 82 42W
Bayonne, *France* **28 E2** 43 30N 1 28W
Bayonne, *U.S.A.* **151 F10** 40 40N 74 7W
Bayovar, *Peru* **172 B1** 5 50 S 81 0W
Bayport, *U.S.A.* **153 G7** 28 32N 82 39W
Bayqongyr, *Kazakhstan* **66 E7** 47 48N 65 50 E
Bayram-Ali = Bayramaly, *Turkmenistan* **66 F7** 37 37N 62 10 E
Bayramaly, *Turkmenistan* **66 F7** 37 37N 62 10 E
Bayramiç, *Turkey* **49 B8** 39 48N 26 36 E
Bayreuth, *Germany* **31 F7** 49 56N 11 35 E
Bayrischzell, *Germany* **31 H8** 47 41N 12 0 E
Bayrūt, *Lebanon* **103 B4** 33 53N 35 31 E
Bays, L. of, *Canada* **150 A5** 45 15N 79 4W
Bayshore, *U.S.A.* **153 J8** 26 43N 81 50W
Baysun, *Uzbekistan* **65 D3** 38 12N 67 12 E
Baysville, *Canada* **150 A5** 45 9N 79 7W
Bayt al Faqīh, *Yemen* **98 D3** 14 31N 43 19 E
Bayt Lahm, *West Bank* **103 D4** 31 43N 35 12 E
Baytown, *U.S.A.* **155 L7** 29 43N 94 59W
Bayugan, *Phil.* **81 G5** 8 43N 125 42 E
Bayun, *Indonesia* **79 J18** 8 11 S 115 16 E
Bayville = Kirkwood, *S. Africa* **116 E4** 33 22 S 25 15 E
Bayyrqum, *Kazakhstan* **65 B4** 42 7N 68 3 E
Bayzhansay, *Kazakhstan* **65 B4** 43 14N 69 54 E
Bayzo, *Niger* **113 C5** 13 52N 4 35 E
Baza, *Spain* **43 H8** 37 30N 2 47W
Bazar Dyuzi, *Russia* **61 K8** 41 12N 47 50 E
Bazar-Korgon, *Kyrgyzstan* **65 C6** 41 0N 72 43 E
Bazardüzü = Bazar Dyuzi, *Russia* **61 K8** 41 12N 47 50 E
Bazargic = Dobrich, *Bulgaria* **51 C11** 43 37N 27 49 E
Bazarny Karabulak, *Russia* **60 D8** 52 20N 46 29 E
Bazarnyy Syzgan, *Russia* **60 D8** 53 45N 46 40 E
Bazaruto △, *Mozam.* **117 C6** 21 42 S 35 26 E
Bazaruto, I. do, *Mozam.* **117 C6** 21 40 S 35 28 E
Bazas, *France* **28 D3** 44 27N 0 13W
Bazhong, *China* **76 B6** 31 52N 106 46 E
Bazhou, *China* **74 E9** 39 8N 116 22 E
Bazmān, Kūh-e, *Iran* **97 D9** 28 4N 60 1 E
Beach, *U.S.A.* **154 B3** 46 58N 104 0W
Beach City, *U.S.A.* **150 F3** 40 39N 81 35W
Beachport, *Australia* **128 D4** 37 29 S 140 0 E
Beachy Hd., *U.K.* **21 G8** 50 44N 0 15 E
Beacon, *Australia* **125 F2** 30 26 S 117 52 E
Beacon, *U.S.A.* **151 E11** 41 30N 73 58W
Beaconsfield, *Australia* **127 G4** 41 11 S 146 48 E
Beagle, Canal, *S. Amer.* **176 E3** 55 0 S 68 30W
Beagle Bay, *Australia* **124 C3** 16 58 S 122 40 E
Bealanana, *Madag.* **117 A8** 14 33 S 48 44 E
Beals Cr. →, *U.S.A.* **155 J4** 32 10N 100 51W
Beamsville, *Canada* **150 C5** 43 12N 79 28W
Bear →, *Calif., U.S.A.* **160 G5** 38 56N 121 36W
Bear →, *Utah, U.S.A.* **146 B4** 41 30N 112 8W
Béar, C., *France* **28 F7** 42 31N 3 8 E
Bear I., *Ireland* **23 E2** 51 38N 9 50W
Bear L., *Canada* **143 B9** 55 8N 96 0W
Bear L., *U.S.A.* **158 F8** 41 59N 111 21W
Beardmore, *Canada* **140 C2** 49 36N 87 57W
Beardmore Glacier, *Antarctica* **7 E11** 84 30 S 170 0 E
Beardstown, *U.S.A.* **156 E6** 40 1N 90 26W
Bearma →, *India* **93 G8** 24 20N 79 51 E
Béarn, *France* **28 E3** 43 20N 0 30W
Bearpaw Mts., *U.S.A.* **158 B9** 48 12N 109 30W
Bearskin Lake, *Canada* **140 B1** 53 58N 91 2W
Beas →, *India* **92 D6** 31 10N 74 59 E
Beas de Segura, *Spain* **43 G8** 38 15N 2 53W
Beasain, *Spain* **40 B2** 43 3N 2 11W
Beata, C., *Dom. Rep.* **165 C5** 17 40N 71 30W
Beata, I., *Dom. Rep.* **165 C5** 17 34N 71 31W
Beatrice, *U.S.A.* **154 E6** 40 16N 96 45W
Beatrice, *Zimbabwe* **119 F3** 18 15 S 30 55 E
Beatrice, C., *Australia* **126 A2** 14 20 S 136 55 E
Beatton →, *Canada* **142 B4** 56 15N 120 45W
Beatton River, *Canada* **142 B4** 57 26N 121 20W
Beatty, *U.S.A.* **160 J10** 36 54N 116 46W
Beau Bassin, *Mauritius* **121 d** 20 13 S 57 27 E
Beauaraba = Pittsworth, *Australia* **127 D5** 27 41 S 151 37 E
Beaucaire, *France* **29 E8** 43 48N 4 39 E
Beauce, Plaine de la, *France* **27 D8** 48 10N 1 45 E
Beauceville, *Canada* **141 C5** 46 13N 70 46W
Beauchêne, I., *Falk. Is.* **9 f** 52 55 S 59 15W
Beaudesert, *Australia* **127 D5** 27 59 S 153 0 E
Beaufort, *Australia* **128 D5** 37 25 S 143 25 E
Beaufort, *France* **29 C10** 45 44N 6 34 E
Beaufort, *Malaysia* **85 A5** 5 30N 115 40 E
Beaufort, *N.C., U.S.A.* **149 H7** 34 43N 76 40W
Beaufort, *S.C., U.S.A.* **152 C9** 32 26N 80 40W
Beaufort Sea, *Arctic* **6 B1** 72 0N 140 0W
Beaufort West, *S. Africa* **116 E3** 32 18 S 22 36 E
Beaugency, *France* **27 E8** 47 47N 1 38 E
Beauharnois, *Canada* **151 A11** 45 20N 73 52W
Beaujeu, *France* **27 F11** 46 10N 4 35 E
Beaujolais, *France* **27 F11** 46 0N 4 22 E
Beaulieu →, *Canada* **142 A6** 62 3N 113 11W
Beaulieu-sur-Dordogne, *France* **28 D5** 44 58N 1 50 E
Beaulieu-sur-Mer, *France* **29 E11** 43 42N 7 20 E
Beauly, *U.K.* **22 D4** 57 30N 4 28W
Beauly →, *U.K.* **22 D4** 57 29N 4 27W
Beaumaris, *U.K.* **20 D3** 53 16N 4 6W
Beaumont, *Belgium* **24 D4** 50 15N 4 14 E
Beaumont, *France* **28 D4** 44 45N 0 46 E
Beaumont, *N.Z.* **131 F4** 45 50 S 169 33 E
Beaumont, *U.S.A.* **155 K7** 30 5N 94 6W
Beaumont-de-Lomagne, *France* **28 E5** 43 53N 1 0 E
Beaumont-le-Roger, *France* **26 C7** 49 4N 0 47 E
Beaumont-sur-Sarthe, *France* **26 D7** 48 13N 0 8 E
Beaune, *France* **27 E11** 47 2N 4 50 E
Beaune-la-Rolande, *France* **27 D9** 48 4N 2 25 E
Beaupré, *Canada* **141 C5** 47 3N 70 54W
Beaupréau, *France* **26 E6** 47 12N 1 0W
Beauraing, *Belgium* **24 D4** 50 7N 4 57 E
Beaurepaire, *France* **29 C9** 45 22N 5 1 E
Beausejour, *Canada* **143 C9** 50 5N 96 35W
Beautemps-Beaupré, Î., *N. Cal.* **133 K4** 20 24 S 166 9 E
Beauvais, *France* **27 C9** 49 25N 2 8 E
Beauval, *Canada* **143 B7** 55 9N 107 37W
Beauvoir-sur-Mer, *France* **26 F4** 46 55N 2 2W
Beauvoir-sur-Niort, *France* **28 B3** 46 12N 0 30W
Beaver, *Alaska, U.S.A.* **144 C11** 66 22N 147 24W
Beaver, *Okla., U.S.A.* **155 G4** 36 49N 100 31W
Beaver, *Pa., U.S.A.* **150 F4** 40 42N 80 19W
Beaver, *Utah, U.S.A.* **159 G7** 38 17N 112 38W
Beaver →, *B.C., Canada* **142 B4** 59 52N 124 20W
Beaver →, *Ont., Canada* **140 A2** 55 55N 87 48W
Beaver →, *Sask., Canada* **143 B7** 55 26N 107 45W
Beaver →, *U.S.A.* **155 G5** 36 35N 99 30W
Beaver City, *U.S.A.* **154 E5** 40 8N 99 50W
Beaver Creek, *Canada* **138 B5** 63 0N 141 0W
Beaver Dam, *U.S.A.* **154 D10** 43 28N 88 50W
Beaver Falls, *U.S.A.* **150 F4** 40 46N 80 20W
Beaver Hill L., *Canada* **143 C10** 54 5N 94 50W
Beaver I., *U.S.A.* **148 C3** 45 40N 85 33W
Beavercreek, *U.S.A.* **157 E12** 39 43N 84 11W
Beaverhill L., *Canada* **142 C6** 53 27N 112 32W
Beaverlodge, *Canada* **142 B5** 55 11N 119 29W
Beaverstone →, *Canada* **140 B2** 54 59N 89 25W
Beaverton, *Canada* **150 B5** 44 26N 79 9W
Beaverton, *U.S.A.* **160 E4** 45 29N 122 48W
Beawar, *India* **92 F6** 26 3N 74 18 E
Bebedouro, *Brazil* **175 A6** 21 0 S 48 25W
Bebera, Tanjung, *Indonesia* **79 K18** 8 44 S 115 51 E
Beboa, *Madag.* **117 B7** 17 22 S 44 33 E
Beboto, *Chad* **109 G3** 8 16N 16 56 E
Bebra, *Germany* **30 E5** 50 58N 9 48 E
Becan, *Mexico* **163 D7** 18 31N 89 28W
Bécancour, *Canada* **148 B9** 46 20N 72 26W
Beccles, *U.K.* **21 E9** 52 27N 1 35 E
Bečej, *Serbia & M.* **52 E5** 45 36N 20 3 E
Beceni, *Romania* **53 E11** 45 23N 26 48 E
Becerreá, *Spain* **42 C3** 42 51N 7 10W
Béchar, *Algeria* **111 B4** 31 38N 2 18W
Becharof L., *U.S.A.* **144 H8** 57 56N 156 23W
Bechuanaland = Botswana ■, *Africa* **116 C3** 22 0 S 24 0 E
Bechyně, *Czech Rep.* **34 B7** 49 17N 14 29 E
Bečkerek = Zrenjanin, *Serbia & M.* **52 E5** 45 22N 20 23 E
Beckley, *U.S.A.* **148 G5** 37 47N 81 11W
Beckum, *Germany* **30 D4** 51 45N 8 3 E
Beclean, *Romania* **53 C9** 47 11N 24 11 E
Bečov nad Teplou, *Czech Rep.* **34 A5** 50 5N 12 49 E
Bečva →, *Czech Rep.* **35 B10** 49 31N 17 20 E
Bédar, *Spain* **41 H3** 37 11N 1 59W
Bédarieux, *France* **28 E7** 43 37N 3 10 E
Beddouza, Ras, *Morocco* **110 B3** 32 33N 9 9W
Bedeau = Ras el Ma, *Algeria* **111 B4** 34 26N 0 50W
Bedele, *Ethiopia* **107 F4** 8 31N 36 23 E
Bederkesa, *Germany* **30 B4** 53 37N 8 50 E
Bederwanak, *Somali Rep.* **120 C2** 9 34N 44 23 E
Bedeso, *Ethiopia* **107 F5** 9 58N 40 52 E
Bedford, *Canada* **151 A12** 45 7N 72 59W
Bedford, *S. Africa* **116 E4** 32 40 S 26 10 E
Bedford, *U.K.* **21 E7** 52 8N 0 28W
Bedford, *Ind., U.S.A.* **157 F10** 38 52N 86 29W
Bedford, *Iowa, U.S.A.* **156 D2** 40 40N 94 44W
Bedford, *Ky., U.S.A.* **157 F11** 38 36N 85 19W
Bedford, *Ohio, U.S.A.* **150 E3** 41 23N 81 32W
Bedford, *Pa., U.S.A.* **150 F6** 40 1N 78 30W
Bedford, *Va., U.S.A.* **148 G6** 37 20N 79 31W
Bedford, C., *Australia* **126 B4** 15 14 S 145 21 E
Bedfordshire □, *U.K.* **21 E7** 52 4N 0 28W
Bedi, *Chad* **109 F3** 11 6N 18 33 E
Będków, *Poland* **55 G6** 51 36N 19 44 E
Bednja →, *Croatia* **45 B13** 46 20N 16 52 E
Bednodemyanovsk, *Russia* **60 D6** 53 55N 43 15 E
Bedok, *Singapore* **87 d** 1 19N 103 56 E
Bedónia, *Italy* **44 D6** 44 30N 9 38 E
Bedourie, *Australia* **126 C2** 24 30 S 139 30 E
Bedretto, *Switz.* **33 C7** 46 31N 8 31 E
Bedti →, *India* **95 G2** 14 50N 74 44 E
Bedum, *Neths.* **24 A6** 53 18N 6 36 E
Będzin, *Poland* **55 H6** 50 19N 19 7 E
Bee Ridge, *U.S.A.* **153 H7** 27 17N 82 29W
Beebe Plain, *Canada* **151 A12** 45 1N 72 9W
Beech Creek, *U.S.A.* **150 E7** 41 5N 77 36W
Beech Fork →, *U.S.A.* **157 G11** 37 46N 85 41W
Beech Grove, *U.S.A.* **157 E10** 39 44N 86 3W
Beecher, *U.S.A.* **157 C9** 41 21N 87 38W
Beechey Point, *U.S.A.* **144 A10** 70 29N 149 9W
Beechworth, *Australia* **129 D7** 36 22 S 146 43 E
Beef I., *Br. Virgin Is.* **165 e** 18 26N 64 30W
Beelitz, *Germany* **30 C8** 52 14N 12 58 E
Beenleigh, *Australia* **127 D5** 27 43 S 153 10 E
Be'er Menuḥa, *Israel* **96 D2** 30 19N 35 8 E
Be'er Sheva, *Israel* **103 D3** 31 15N 34 48 E
Beersheba = Be'er Sheva, *Israel* **103 D3** 31 15N 34 48 E
Beeskow, *Germany* **30 C10** 52 10N 14 15 E

Beestekraal, *S. Africa* **117 D4** 25 23 S 27 38 E
Beeston, *U.K.* **20 E6** 52 56N 1 14W
Beetzendorf, *Germany* **30 C7** 52 42N 11 6 E
Beeville, *U.S.A.* **155 L6** 28 24N 97 45W
Befale, *Dem. Rep. of the Congo* **114 B4** 0 25N 20 45 E
Befandriana, *Mahajanga, Madag.* **117 B8** 15 16 S 48 32 E
Befandriana, *Toliara, Madag.* **117 C7** 21 55 S 44 0 E
Befasy, *Madag.* **117 C7** 20 33 S 44 23 E
Befori, *Dem. Rep. of the Congo* **114 B4** 0 8N 22 22 E
Befotaka, *Antsiranana, Madag.* **117 A8** 13 15 S 48 16 E
Befotaka, *Fianarantsoa, Madag.* **117 C8** 23 49 S 47 0 E
Bega, *Australia* **129 D8** 36 41 S 149 51 E
Bega, Canalul, *Romania* **52 E5** 45 37N 20 46 E
Bégard, *France* **26 D3** 48 38N 3 18W
Beğendik, *Turkey* **51 F10** 40 55N 26 34 E
Begndal, *Norway* **18 D6** 60 49N 9 46 E
Begoro, *Ghana* **113 D4** 6 23N 0 23W
Begovat = Bekabad, *Uzbekistan* **65 C4** 40 13N 69 14 E
Begusarai, *India* **93 G12** 25 24N 86 9 E
Behābād, *Iran* **97 C8** 32 24N 59 47 E
Behala, *India* **93 H13** 22 30N 88 20 E
Behara, *Madag.* **117 C8** 24 55 S 46 20 E
Behbehān, *Iran* **97 D6** 30 30N 50 15 E
Behm Canal, *U.S.A.* **142 B2** 55 10N 131 0W
Behshahr, *Iran* **97 B7** 36 45N 53 35 E
Bei Jiang →, *China* **77 F9** 23 2N 112 58 E
Bei'an, *China* **69 B7** 48 10N 126 20 E
Beibei, *China* **76 C6** 29 47N 106 22 E
Beichuan, *China* **76 B5** 31 55N 104 39 E
Beihai, *China* **76 G7** 21 28N 109 6 E
Beijing, *China* **74 E9** 39 55N 116 20 E
Beijing □, *China* **74 E9** 39 55N 116 20 E
Beilau = Pilawa, *Poland* **55 G8** 51 57N 21 32 E
Beilen, *Neths.* **24 B6** 52 52N 6 27 E
Beiliu, *China* **77 F8** 22 41N 110 21 E
Beilngries, *Germany* **31 F7** 49 2N 11 28 E
Beilpajah, *Australia* **128 B5** 32 54 S 143 52 E
Beilul, *Eritrea* **107 E5** 13 2N 42 20 E
Béinamar, *Chad* **109 G3** 8 40N 15 23 E
Beinn na Faoghla = Benbecula, *U.K.* **22 D1** 57 26N 7 21W
Beipan Jiang, *China* **76 E5** 25 7N 106 1 E
Beipiao, *China* **75 D11** 41 52N 120 32 E
Beira, *Mozam.* **119 F3** 19 50 S 34 52 E
Beira, *Somali Rep.* **120 C3** 6 57N 47 19 E
Beirut = Bayrūt, *Lebanon* **103 B4** 33 53N 35 31 E
Beiseker, *Canada* **142 C6** 51 23N 113 32W
Beitaolaizhao, *China* **75 B13** 44 58N 125 58 E
Beitbridge, *Zimbabwe* **119 G3** 22 12 S 30 0 E
Beiuş, *Romania* **52 D7** 46 40N 22 21 E
Beizhen = Binzhou, *China* **75 F10** 37 20N 118 2 E
Beizhen, *China* **75 D11** 41 38N 121 54 E
Beizhengzhen, *China* **75 B12** 44 31N 123 30 E
Beja, *Portugal* **43 G3** 38 2N 7 53W
Béja, *Tunisia* **108 A1** 36 43N 9 12 E
Beja □, *Portugal* **43 H3** 37 55N 7 55W
Bejaïa, *Algeria* **111 A6** 36 42N 5 2 E
Béjar, *Spain* **42 E5** 40 23N 5 46W
Bejestān, *Iran* **97 C8** 34 30N 58 5 E
Bek-Budi = Qarshi, *Uzbekistan* **65 D2** 38 53N 65 48 E
Bekaa Valley = Al Biqā, *Lebanon* **103 A5** 34 10N 36 10 E
Bekabad, *Uzbekistan* **65 C4** 40 13N 69 14 E
Bekasi, *Indonesia* **84 D3** 6 14 S 106 59 E
Bekçiler, *Turkey* **49 E11** 36 56N 29 44 E
Békés, *Hungary* **52 D6** 46 47N 21 9 E
Békés □, *Hungary* **52 D6** 46 45N 21 0 E
Békéscsaba, *Hungary* **52 D6** 46 40N 21 5 E
Bekilli, *Turkey* **49 C11** 38 17N 29 27 E
Bekily, *Madag.* **117 C8** 24 13 S 45 19 E
Bekisopa, *Madag.* **117 C8** 21 40 S 45 54 E
Bekitro, *Madag.* **117 C8** 24 33 S 45 18 E
Bekodoka, *Madag.* **117 B8** 16 58 S 45 7 E
Bekoji, *Ethiopia* **107 F4** 7 40N 39 17 E
Bekok, *Malaysia* **87 L4** 2 20N 103 7 E
Bekopaka, *Madag.* **117 B7** 19 9 S 44 48 E
Bekuli, *Indonesia* **79 J17** 8 22 S 114 13 E
Bekwai, *Ghana* **113 D4** 6 30N 1 34W
Bela, *India* **93 G10** 25 50N 82 0 E
Bela, *Pakistan* **91 D2** 26 12N 66 20 E
Bela Aliança = Rio do Sul, *Brazil* **175 B6** 27 13 S 49 37W
Bela Bela, *S. Africa* **117 C4** 24 51 S 28 19 E
Bela Crkva, *Serbia & M.* **52 F6** 44 55N 21 27 E
Bela Palanka, *Serbia & M.* **50 C6** 43 13N 22 17 E
Bela Vista, *Brazil* **174 A4** 22 12 S 56 20W
Bela Vista, *Mozam.* **117 D5** 26 10 S 32 44 E
Bélâbre, *France* **28 B5** 46 34N 1 8 E
Belaga, *Malaysia* **85 B4** 2 42N 113 47 E
Belalcázar, *Spain* **43 G5** 38 35N 5 10W
Belan →, *India* **93 G9** 24 2N 81 45 E
Belang, *Indonesia* **82 A2** 0 57N 124 47 E
Belanovica, *Serbia & M.* **50 B4** 44 15N 20 23 E
Belarus ■, *Europe* **58 F4** 53 30N 27 0 E
Belas, *Angola* **115 D2** 8 55 S 13 9 E
Belau = Palau ■, *Pac. Oc.* **62 J17** 7 30N 134 30 E
Belavenona, *Madag.* **117 C8** 24 50 S 47 4 E
Belawan, *Indonesia* **84 B1** 3 33N 98 32 E
Belaya, *Ethiopia* **107 E4** 11 25N 36 8 E
Belaya →, *Russia* **64 D6** 54 40N 56 0 E
Belaya Glina, *Russia* **61 G5** 46 5N 40 48 E
Belaya Kalitva, *Russia* **61 F5** 48 13N 40 50 E
Belaya Kholunitsa, *Russia* **64 B3** 58 51N 50 53 E
Belaya Tserkov = Bila Tserkva, *Ukraine* **59 H6** 49 45N 30 10 E
Belayan →, *Indonesia* **85 C5** 0 14 S 116 36 E
Belceşti, *Romania* **53 C12** 47 19N 27 7 E
Bełchatów, *Poland* **55 G6** 51 21N 19 22 E
Belcher Is., *Canada* **140 A3** 56 15N 78 45W
Belchite, *Spain* **40 D4** 41 18N 0 43W
Belden, *U.S.A.* **160 E5** 40 2N 121 17W
Belding, *U.S.A.* **157 A11** 43 6N 85 14W
Belebey, *Russia* **64 D5** 54 7N 54 7 E
Beled Weyne = Belet Uen, *Somali Rep.* **120 D3** 4 30N 45 5 E
Belém = Palmeirais, *Brazil* **170 C3** 6 0 S 43 0W
Belém, *Brazil* **170 B2** 1 20 S 48 30W
Belém de São Francisco, *Brazil* **170 C4** 8 46 S 38 58W
Belén, *Argentina* **174 B2** 27 40 S 67 5W
Belén, *Colombia* **168 C2** 1 26N 75 56W
Belén, *Paraguay* **174 A4** 23 30 S 57 6W
Belen, *U.S.A.* **159 J10** 34 40N 106 46W
Belene, *Bulgaria* **51 C9** 43 39N 25 10 E
Beleni, *Turkey* **100 D7** 36 31N 36 10 E
Belep, Îs., *N. Cal.* **123 D11** 19 45 S 163 40 E
Bélesta, *France* **28 F5** 42 55N 1 56 E
Belet Uen, *Somali Rep.* **120 D3** 4 30N 45 5 E
Belev, *Russia* **58 F9** 53 50N 36 5 E
Belevi, *Turkey* **49 C9** 38 0N 27 28 E
Belfair, *U.S.A.* **160 C4** 47 27N 122 50W
Belfast, *N.Z.* **131 D7** 43 27 S 172 39 E
Belfast, *S. Africa* **117 D5** 25 42 S 30 2 E
Belfast, *U.K.* **23 B6** 54 37N 5 56W
Belfast, *Maine, U.S.A.* **149 C11** 44 26N 69 1W
Belfast, *N.Y., U.S.A.* **150 D6** 42 21N 78 7W
Belfast L., *U.K.* **23 B6** 54 40N 5 50W
Belfield, *U.S.A.* **154 B3** 46 53N 103 12W
Belfort, *France* **27 E13** 47 38N 6 50 E
Belfort, Territoire de □, *France* **27 E13** 47 40N 6 55 E
Belfry, *U.S.A.* **158 D9** 45 9N 109 1W
Belgard = Białogard, *Poland* **54 D2** 54 2N 15 58 E
Belgaum, *India* **95 G2** 15 55N 74 35 E
Belgian Congo = Congo, Dem. Rep. of the ■, *Africa* **115 C4** 3 0 S 23 0 E
Belgioioso, *Italy* **44 C6** 45 10N 9 19 E
Belgium ■, *Europe* **24 D4** 50 30N 5 0 E
Belgodère, *France* **29 F13** 42 35N 9 1 E
Belgorod, *Russia* **59 G9** 50 35N 36 35 E
Belgorod-Dnestrovskiy = Bilhorod-Dnistrovskyy, *Ukraine* **59 J6** 46 11N 30 23 E
Belgrade = Beograd, *Serbia & M.* **50 B4** 44 50N 20 37 E
Belgrade, *U.S.A.* **158 D8** 45 47N 111 11W
Belgrove, *N.Z.* **131 B7** 41 27 S 172 59 E
Belhaven, *U.S.A.* **149 H7** 35 33N 76 37W
Beli Drim →, *Europe* **50 D4** 42 6N 20 25 E
Beli Manastir, *Croatia* **52 E3** 45 45N 18 36 E
Beli Timok →, *Serbia & M.* **50 C6** 43 53N 22 14 E
Bélice →, *Italy* **46 E5** 37 35N 12 55 E
Belimbing, *Indonesia* **79 J18** 8 24 S 115 2 E
Belinga, *Gabon* **114 B2** 1 10N 13 2 E
Belinskiy, *Russia* **60 D6** 53 0N 43 25 E
Belinyu, *Indonesia* **84 C3** 1 35 S 105 50 E
Beliton Is. = Belitung, *Indonesia* **85 C3** 3 10 S 107 50 E
Belitung, *Indonesia* **85 C3** 3 10 S 107 50 E
Beliu, *Romania* **52 D6** 46 30N 22 0 E
Belize, *Angola* **115 C2** 4 39 S 12 46 E
Belize ■, *Cent. Amer.* **163 D7** 17 0N 88 30W
Belize City, *Belize* **163 D7** 17 25N 88 10W
Beljakovci, *Macedonia* **50 D5** 42 6N 21 59 E
Beljanica, *Serbia & M.* **50 B5** 44 8N 21 43 E
Belkovskiy, Ostrov, *Russia* **67 B14** 75 32N 135 44 E
Bell, *U.S.A.* **152 F7** 29 45N 82 52W
Bell →, *Canada* **140 C4** 49 48N 77 38W
Bell I., *Canada* **141 B8** 50 46N 55 35W
Bell-Irving →, *Canada* **142 B3** 56 12N 129 5W
Bell Peninsula, *Canada* **139 B11** 63 50N 82 0W
Bell Ville, *Argentina* **174 C3** 32 40 S 62 40W
Bella, *Italy* **47 B8** 40 45N 15 32 E
Bella Bella, *Canada* **142 C3** 52 10N 128 10W
Bella Coola, *Canada* **142 C3** 52 25N 126 40W
Bella Flor, *Bolivia* **172 C4** 11 9 S 67 49W
Bella Unión, *Uruguay* **174 C4** 30 15 S 57 40W
Bella Vista, *Corrientes, Argentina* **174 B4** 28 33 S 59 0W
Bella Vista, *Tucuman, Argentina* **174 B2** 27 10 S 65 25W
Bellac, *France* **28 B5** 46 7N 1 3 E
Bellágio, *Italy* **44 C6** 45 59N 9 15 E
Bellaire, *U.S.A.* **150 F4** 40 1N 80 45W
Bellária, *Italy* **45 D9** 44 9N 12 28 E
Bellary, *India* **95 G3** 15 10N 76 56 E
Bellata, *Australia* **127 D4** 29 53 S 149 46 E
Bellavista, *Ecuador* **172 a** 0 41 S 90 18W
Belle, *U.S.A.* **156 F5** 38 17N 91 43W
Belle Fourche, *U.S.A.* **154 C3** 44 40N 103 51W
Belle Fourche →, *U.S.A.* **154 C3** 44 26N 102 18W
Belle Glade, *U.S.A.* **153 J9** 26 41N 80 40W
Belle-Île, *France* **26 E3** 47 20N 3 10W
Belle Isle, *Canada* **141 B8** 51 57N 55 25W
Belle Isle, *U.S.A.* **153 G8** 28 27N 81 21W
Belle Isle, Str. of, *Canada* **141 B8** 51 30N 56 30W
Belle Plaine, *U.S.A.* **156 C4** 41 54N 92 17W
Belle Rive, *U.S.A.* **157 F8** 38 14N 88 45W
Belle Yella, *Liberia* **112 D3** 7 24N 10 0W
Belledonne, *France* **29 C10** 45 20N 6 10 E
Bellefontaine, *U.S.A.* **157 D13** 40 22N 83 46W
Bellefonte, *U.S.A.* **150 F7** 40 55N 77 47W
Bellegarde, *France* **27 E9** 47 59N 2 26 E
Bellegarde-en-Marche, *France* **28 C6** 45 59N 2 18 E
Bellegarde-sur-Valserine, *France* **27 F12** 46 4N 5 50 E
Bellême, *France* **26 D7** 48 22N 0 34 E
Belleoram, *Canada* **141 C8** 47 31N 55 25W
Belleplaine, *Barbados* **165 g** 13 15N 59 34W
Belleview, *U.S.A.* **153 F7** 29 4N 82 3W
Belleville, *Canada* **140 D4** 44 10N 77 23W
Belleville, *France* **27 F11** 46 7N 4 45 E
Belleville, *Ill., U.S.A.* **156 F7** 38 31N 89 59W
Belleville, *Kans., U.S.A.* **154 F6** 39 50N 97 38W
Belleville, *N.Y., U.S.A.* **151 C8** 43 46N 76 10W
Belleville-sur-Vie, *France* **26 F5** 46 46N 1 25W
Bellevue, *Canada* **142 D6** 49 35N 114 22W
Bellevue, *Idaho, U.S.A.* **158 E6** 43 28N 114 16W
Bellevue, *Iowa, U.S.A.* **156 B6** 42 16N 90 26W
Bellevue, *Mich., U.S.A.* **157 B11** 42 27N 85 1W
Bellevue, *Nebr., U.S.A.* **154 E7** 41 8N 95 53W
Bellevue, *Ohio, U.S.A.* **150 E2** 41 17N 82 51W
Bellevue, *Wash., U.S.A.* **160 C4** 47 37N 122 12W
Belley, *France* **29 C9** 45 46N 5 41 E
Bellin = Kangirsuk, *Canada* **139 B13** 60 0N 70 0W
Bellinge, *Denmark* **17 J4** 55 20N 10 20 E
Bellingen, *Australia* **129 A10** 30 25 S 152 50 E
Bellingham, *U.S.A.* **160 B4** 48 46N 122 29W
Bellingshausen Sea, *Antarctica* **7 C17** 66 0 S 80 0W
Bellinzona, *Switz.* **33 D8** 46 11N 9 1 E
Bello, *Colombia* **168 B2** 6 20N 75 33W
Bellona, *Solomon Is.* **133 N10** 11 17 S 159 47 E
Bellows Falls, *U.S.A.* **151 C12** 43 8N 72 27W
Bellpat, *Pakistan* **92 E3** 29 0N 68 5 E
Bellpuig d'Urgell, *Spain* **40 D6** 41 37N 1 1 E
Belluno, *Italy* **45 B9** 46 9N 12 13 E
Bellville, *U.S.A.* **152 C8** 32 9N 81 59W
Bellwood, *U.S.A.* **150 F6** 40 36N 78 20W
Bélmez, *Spain* **43 G5** 38 17N 5 17W
Belmond, *U.S.A.* **156 B3** 42 51N 93 37W
Belmont, *Australia* **129 B9** 33 4 S 151 42 E
Belmont, *Canada* **150 D3** 42 53N 81 5W
Belmont, *S. Africa* **116 D3** 29 28 S 24 22 E
Belmont, *U.S.A.* **150 D6** 42 14N 78 2W
Belmonte, *Brazil* **171 E4** 16 0 S 39 0W
Belmonte, *Portugal* **42 E3** 40 21N 7 20W
Belmonte, *Spain* **41 F2** 39 34N 2 43W
Belmopan, *Belize* **163 D7** 17 18N 88 30W
Belmullet, *Ireland* **23 B2** 54 14N 9 58W
Belo, *Dem. Rep. of the Congo* **114 C4** 0 32 S 23 13 E
Belo Horizonte, *Brazil* **171 E3** 19 55 S 43 56W
Belo Jardim, *Brazil* **170 C4** 8 20 S 36 26W
Belo Monte, *Brazil* **169 D7** 3 5 S 51 46W
Belo-sur-Mer, *Madag.* **117 C7** 20 42 S 44 0 E
Belo-Tsiribihina, *Madag.* **117 B7** 19 40 S 44 30 E
Belogorsk = Bilohirsk, *Ukraine* **59 K8** 45 3N 34 35 E
Belogorsk, *Russia* **67 D13** 51 0N 128 20 E
Belogradchik, *Bulgaria* **50 C6** 43 53N 22 42 E
Belogradets, *Bulgaria* **51 C11** 43 22N 27 18 E
Beloha, *Madag.* **117 D8** 25 10 S 45 3 E
Beloit, *Kans., U.S.A.* **154 F5** 39 28N 98 6W
Beloit, *Wis., U.S.A.* **156 B7** 42 31N 89 2W
Belokalitvenskaya = Belaya Kalitva, *Russia* **61 F5** 48 13N 40 50 E
Belokorovichi, *Ukraine* **59 G5** 51 7N 28 2 E
Belomorsk, *Russia* **56 B5** 64 35N 34 54 E
Belondo, *Dem. Rep. of the Congo* **114 C3** 0 19 S 19 31 E
Belonge, *Dem. Rep. of the Congo* **114 C3** 2 7 S 19 33 E
Belonia, *India* **90 D3** 23 15N 91 30 E
Belopolye = Bilopillya, *Ukraine* **59 G8** 51 14N 34 20 E
Belorechensk, *Russia* **61 H4** 44 46N 39 52 E
Beloretsk, *Russia* **64 E7** 53 58N 58 24 E
Belorussia = Belarus ■, *Europe* **58 F4** 53 30N 27 0 E
Beloshchelye = Naryan-Mar, *Russia* **56 A9** 67 42N 53 12 E
Beloslav, *Bulgaria* **51 C11** 43 11N 27 42 E
Belotsarsk = Kyzyl, *Russia* **67 D10** 51 50N 94 30 E
Belovo, *Bulgaria* **51 D8** 42 13N 24 1 E
Belovo, *Russia* **66 D9** 54 30N 86 0 E
Belovodsk, *Ukraine* **59 H10** 49 13N 39 36 E
Beloyarskiy, *Russia* **64 C8** 56 45N 61 24 E
Beloye, Ozero, *Russia* **58 B9** 60 10N 37 35 E
Beloye More, *Russia* **56 A6** 66 30N 38 0 E
Belozem, *Bulgaria* **51 D9** 42 12N 25 2 E
Belozersk, *Russia* **58 B9** 60 1N 37 45 E
Belp, *Switz.* **32 C5** 46 53N 7 30 E
Belpasso, *Italy* **47 E7** 37 35N 14 58 E
Belpre, *U.S.A.* **148 F5** 39 17N 81 34W
Belrain, *India* **93 E9** 28 23N 80 55 E
Belt, *U.S.A.* **158 C8** 47 23N 110 55W
Beltana, *Australia* **128 A3** 30 48 S 138 25 E
Belterra, *Brazil* **169 D7** 2 45 S 55 0W
Beltinci, *Slovenia* **45 B13** 46 37N 16 20 E
Belton, *Mo., U.S.A.* **156 F2** 38 49N 94 32W
Belton, *Tex., U.S.A.* **155 K6** 31 3N 97 28W
Belton L., *U.S.A.* **155 K6** 31 8N 97 32W
Beltsy = Bălţi, *Moldova* **53 C12** 47 48N 27 58 E
Belturbet, *Ireland* **23 B4** 54 6N 7 26W
Belukha, *Russia* **66 E9** 49 50N 86 50 E
Beluran, *Malaysia* **78 C5** 5 48N 117 35 E
Beluša, *Slovak Rep.* **35 B11** 49 5N 18 17 E
Belušić, *Serbia & M.* **50 C5** 43 50N 21 10 E
Belvedere Maríttimo, *Italy* **47 C8** 39 37N 15 52 E
Belvès, *France* **28 D5** 44 46N 1 0 E
Belvidere, *Ill., U.S.A.* **154 D10** 42 15N 88 50W
Belvidere, *N.J., U.S.A.* **151 F9** 40 50N 75 5W
Belvis de la Jara, *Spain* **42 F6** 39 45N 4 57W
Bely Bychek = Chagoda, *Russia* **58 C8** 59 10N 35 15 E
Belyando →, *Australia* **126 C4** 21 38 S 146 50 E
Belyy, *Russia* **58 E7** 55 49N 33 3 E
Belyy, Ostrov, *Russia* **66 B8** 73 30N 71 0 E
Belyy Yar, *Russia* **66 D9** 58 26N 84 39 E
Belyye Vody = Aqsū, *Kazakhstan* **65 B4** 42 25N 69 50 E
Belz, *Ukraine* **55 H11** 50 23N 24 1 E
Bełżec, *Poland* **55 H10** 50 23N 23 26 E
Belzig, *Germany* **30 C8** 52 8N 12 35 E
Belzoni, *U.S.A.* **155 J9** 33 11N 90 29W
Bełżyce, *Poland* **55 G9** 51 11N 22 17 E
Bemaraha, Lembalemban' i, *Madag.* **117 B7** 18 40 S 44 45 E
Bemarivo, *Madag.* **117 C7** 21 45 S 44 45 E
Bemarivo →, *Antsiranana, Madag.* **117 A9** 14 9 S 50 9 E
Bemarivo →, *Mahajanga, Madag.* **117 B8** 15 27 S 47 40 E
Bemavo, *Madag.* **117 C8** 21 33 S 45 25 E
Bembe, *Angola* **115 D2** 7 3 S 14 25 E
Bembéréke, *Benin* **113 C5** 10 11N 2 43 E
Bembesi, *Zimbabwe* **119 G2** 20 0 S 28 58 E
Bembesi →, *Zimbabwe* **119 F2** 18 57 S 27 47 E
Bembézar →, *Spain* **43 H5** 37 45N 5 13W
Bembibre, *Spain* **42 C4** 42 37N 6 25W
Bemboka △, *Australia* **129 D8** 36 35 S 149 41 E
Bement, *U.S.A.* **157 E8** 39 55N 88 34W
Bemetara, *India* **93 J9** 21 42N 81 32 E
Bemidji, *U.S.A.* **154 B7** 47 28N 94 53W
Bemolanga, *Madag.* **117 B8** 17 44 S 45 6 E
Ben, *Iran* **97 C6** 32 32N 50 45 E
Ben Boyd △, *Australia* **129 D8** 37 0 S 149 55 E
Ben Cruachan, *U.K.* **22 E3** 56 26N 5 8W
Ben Dearg, *U.K.* **22 D4** 57 47N 4 56W
Ben En △, *Vietnam* **86 C5** 19 37N 105 30 E
Ben Gardane, *Tunisia* **108 B2** 33 11N 11 11 E
Ben Hope, *U.K.* **22 C4** 58 25N 4 36W
Ben Lawers, *U.K.* **22 E4** 56 32N 4 14W
Ben Lomond, *N.S.W., Australia* **127 E5** 30 1 S 151 43 E
Ben Lomond, *Tas., Australia* **127 G4** 41 38 S 147 42 E
Ben Lomond, *U.K.* **22 E4** 56 11N 4 38W
Ben Lomond △, *Australia* **127 G4** 41 33 S 147 39 E
Ben Luc, *Vietnam* **87 G6** 10 39N 106 29 E
Ben Macdhui, *U.K.* **22 D5** 57 4N 3 40W
Ben Mhor, *U.K.* **22 D1** 57 15N 7 18W
Ben More, *Arg. & Bute, U.K.* **22 E2** 56 26N 6 1W
Ben More, *Stirl., U.K.* **22 E4** 56 23N 4 32W
Ben More Assynt, *U.K.* **22 C4** 58 8N 4 52W
Ben Nevis, *U.K.* **22 E3** 56 48N 5 1W
Ben Ohau Ra., *N.Z.* **131 E5** 44 1 S 170 4 E
Ben Quang, *Vietnam* **86 D6** 17 3N 106 55 E
Ben Slimane, *Morocco* **110 B3** 33 38N 7 7W
Ben Vorlich, *U.K.* **22 E4** 56 21N 4 14W
Ben Wyvis, *U.K.* **22 D4** 57 40N 4 35W
Bena, *Nigeria* **113 C6** 11 20N 5 50 E
Bena-Dibele, *Dem. Rep. of the Congo* **115 C4** 4 4 S 22 50 E
Bena-Leka, *Dem. Rep. of the Congo* **115 D4** 5 8 S 22 10 E
Bena-Tshadi, *Dem. Rep. of the Congo* **115 C4** 4 40 S 22 49 E
Benadir, *Somali Rep.* **120 D2** 1 30N 44 30 E
Benagerie, *Australia* **128 A4** 31 25 S 140 22 E
Benahmed, *Morocco* **110 B3** 33 4N 7 9W
Benalla, *Australia* **129 D7** 36 30 S 146 0 E
Benalmádena, *Spain* **43 J6** 36 36N 4 34W
Benambra, Mt., *Australia* **129 D7** 36 31 S 147 34 E
Benanee, *Australia* **128 C5** 34 31 S 142 52 E
Benares = Varanasi, *India* **93 G10** 25 22N 83 0 E
Bénat, C., *France* **29 E10** 43 5N 6 22 E
Benavente, *Portugal* **43 G2** 38 59N 8 49W
Benavente, *Spain* **42 C5** 42 2N 5 43W
Benavides, *U.S.A.* **155 M5** 27 36N 98 25W
Benavides de Órbigo, *Spain* **42 C5** 42 30N 5 54W
Benbecula, *U.K.* **22 D1** 57 26N 7 21W
Benbonyathe, *Australia* **128 A3** 30 25 S 139 11 E
Bend, *U.S.A.* **158 D3** 44 4N 121 19W
Bendela, *Dem. Rep. of the Congo* **114 C3** 3 18 S 17 36 E
Bendemeer, *Australia* **129 A9** 30 53 S 151 8 E
Bender Beila, *Somali Rep.* **120 C4** 9 30N 50 48 E
Bender Merchagno, *Somali Rep.* **120 B4** 11 41N 50 34 E
Bendery = Tighina, *Moldova* **53 D14** 46 50N 29 30 E
Bendigo, *Australia* **128 D6** 36 40 S 144 15 E
Bendin = Będzin, *Poland* **55 H6** 50 19N 19 7 E
Bendorf, *Germany* **30 E3** 50 25N 7 35 E
Bendsburg = Będzin, *Poland* **55 H6** 50 19N 19 7 E
Benē Beraq, *Israel* **103 C3** 32 6N 34 51 E
Beneditinos, *Brazil* **170 C3** 5 27 S 42 22W
Benedito Leite, *Brazil* **170 C3** 7 13 S 44 34W
Bénéna, *Mali* **112 C4** 13 9N 4 17W
Benenitra, *Madag.* **117 C8** 23 27 S 45 5 E
Benešov, *Czech Rep.* **34 B7** 49 46N 14 41 E
Benevento, *Italy* **47 A7** 41 8N 14 45 E
Benfeld, *France* **27 D14** 48 22N 7 34 E
Benga, *Mozam.* **119 F3** 16 11 S 33 40 E
Bengal = West Bengal □, *India* **93 H13** 23 0N 88 0 E
Bengal, Bay of, *Ind. Oc.* **89 D7** 15 0N 90 0 E
Bengalûru = Bangalore, *India* **95 H3** 12 59N 77 40 E
Bengbis, *Cameroon* **113 E7** 3 27N 12 36 E
Bengbu, *China* **75 H9** 32 58N 117 20 E
Benghazi = Banghāzī, *Libya* **108 B4** 32 11N 20 3 E
Benghisa Point, *Malta* **38 F8** 35 49N 14 33 E
Bengkalis, *Indonesia* **84 B2** 1 30N 102 10 E
Bengkulu, *Indonesia* **84 C2** 3 50 S 102 12 E
Bengkulu □, *Indonesia* **84 C2** 3 48 S 102 16 E
Bengo, *Dem. Rep. of the Congo* **114 C3** 2 11 S 19 5 E
Bengo □, *Angola* **115 D2** 9 0 S 13 10 E
Bengough, *Canada* **143 D7** 49 25N 105 10W
Bengtsfors, *Sweden* **16 E6** 59 2N 12 14 E
Benguela, *Angola* **115 E2** 12 37 S 13 25 E
Benguela □, *Angola* **115 E2** 13 0 S 13 30 E
Benguerir, *Morocco* **110 B3** 32 16N 7 56W
Benguérua, I., *Mozam.* **117 C6** 21 58 S 35 28 E
Benguet □, *Phil.* **80 C3** 16 30N 120 40 E
Benha, *Egypt* **106 H7** 30 26N 31 8 E
Benham Seamount, *Pac. Oc.* **80 D5** 15 40N 124 30 E
Beni, *Dem. Rep. of the Congo* **118 B2** 0 30N 29 27 E
Beni □, *Bolivia* **173 C4** 14 0 S 65 0W
Beni →, *Bolivia* **173 C4** 10 23 S 65 24W
Beni Abbès, *Algeria* **111 B4** 30 5N 2 5W
Beni Haoua, *Algeria* **111 A5** 36 30N 1 30 E
Beni Mazâr, *Egypt* **106 B3** 28 32N 30 44 E
Beni Mellal, *Morocco* **110 B3** 32 21N 6 21W
Beni Ounif, *Algeria* **111 B4** 32 0N 1 10W
Beni Saf, *Algeria* **111 A4** 35 17N 1 15W
Beni Suef, *Egypt* **106 J7** 29 5N 31 6 E
Beniah L., *Canada* **142 A6** 63 23N 112 17W
Benicarló, *Spain* **40 E5** 40 23N 0 23 E
Benicássim, *Spain* **40 E5** 40 3N 0 4 E
Benicia, *U.S.A.* **160 G4** 38 3N 122 9W
Benidorm, *Spain* **41 G4** 38 33N 0 9W
Benin ■, *Africa* **113 D5** 10 0N 2 0 E
Benin →, *Nigeria* **113 D6** 5 45N 5 4 E
Benin, Bight of, *W. Afr.* **113 E5** 5 0N 3 0 E
Benin City, *Nigeria* **113 D6** 6 20N 5 31 E
Benisa, *Spain* **41 G5** 38 43N 0 3 E
Benitses, *Greece* **38 B9** 39 32N 19 55 E
Benjamin Aceval, *Paraguay* **174 A4** 24 58 S 57 34W
Benjamin Constant, *Brazil* **168 D3** 4 40 S 70 15W
Benjamin Hill, *Mexico* **162 A2** 30 10N 111 10W
Benkelman, *U.S.A.* **154 E4** 40 3N 101 32W
Benkovac, *Croatia* **45 D12** 44 2N 15 37 E
Benmore Pk., *N.Z.* **131 E5** 44 25 S 170 8 E
Bennett, *Canada* **142 B2** 59 56N 134 53W
Bennett, L., *Australia* **124 D5** 22 50 S 131 2 E
Bennetta, Ostrov, *Russia* **67 B15** 76 21N 148 56 E
Bennettsville, *U.S.A.* **149 H6** 34 37N 79 41W
Bennichchāb, *Mauritania* **112 B1** 19 32N 15 12W
Bennington, *N.H., U.S.A.* **151 D11** 43 0N 71 55W
Bennington, *Vt., U.S.A.* **151 D11** 42 53N 73 12W
Beno, *Dem. Rep. of the Congo* **114 C3** 3 41 S 17 49 E
Bénodet, *France* **26 E2** 47 53N 4 7W
Benoni, *S. Africa* **117 D4** 26 11 S 28 18 E
Benoud, *Algeria* **111 B5** 32 20N 0 16 E
Bénoué △, *Cameroon* **114 A2** 8 30N 13 55 E
Benoy, *Chad* **109 G3** 8 59N 16 19 E
Benque Viejo del Carmen, *Belize* **163 D7** 17 5N 89 8W
Bensheim, *Germany* **31 F4** 49 40N 8 38 E
Benson, *Ariz., U.S.A.* **159 L8** 31 58N 110 18W
Benson, *Minn., U.S.A.* **154 C7** 45 19N 95 36W
Bent, *Iran* **97 E8** 26 20N 59 31 E
Benteng, *Indonesia* **82 C2** 6 10 S 120 30 E
Bentiaba, *Angola* **115 E2** 14 15 S 12 21 E
Bentinck I., *Australia* **126 B2** 17 3 S 139 35 E
Bentiu, *Sudan* **107 F2** 9 10N 29 55 E
Bento Gonçalves, *Brazil* **175 B5** 29 10 S 51 31W
Benton, *Ark., U.S.A.* **155 H8** 34 34N 92 35W
Benton, *Calif., U.S.A.* **160 H8** 37 48N 118 32W
Benton, *Ill., U.S.A.* **156 G8** 38 0N 88 55W
Benton, *Pa., U.S.A.* **151 E8** 41 12N 76 23W
Benton Harbor, *U.S.A.* **157 B10** 42 6N 86 27W
Benton Heights, *U.S.A.* **157 B10** 42 7N 86 24W
Bentong, *Malaysia* **87 L3** 3 31N 101 55 E
Bentonville, *U.S.A.* **155 G7** 36 22N 94 13W
Bentu Liben, *Ethiopia* **107 F4** 8 32N 38 21 E
Benue □, *Nigeria* **113 D6** 7 20N 8 45 E
Benue →, *Nigeria* **113 D6** 7 48N 6 46 E
Benxi, *China* **75 D12** 41 20N 123 48 E
Benza, *Dem. Rep. of the Congo* **115 D2** 4 49 S 13 17 E
Benzdorp, *Suriname* **169 C7** 3 44N 54 5W
Beo, *Indonesia* **82 A3** 4 25N 126 50 E
Beograd, *Serbia & M.* **50 B4** 44 50N 20 37 E
Beograd ✈ (BEG), *Serbia & M.* **50 C4** 43 49N 20 17 E
Beoumi, *Ivory C.* **112 D3** 7 45N 5 23W
Bepan Jiang →, *China* **76 E6** 24 55N 106 5 E
Beppu, *Japan* **72 D3** 33 15N 131 30 E
Beppu-Wan, *Japan* **72 D3** 33 18N 131 34 E
Beqa, *Fiji* **133 B2** 18 23 S 178 8 E
Beqaa Valley = Al Biqā, *Lebanon* **103 A5** 34 10N 36 10 E
Ber Mota, *India* **92 H3** 23 27N 68 34 E
Bera, *Bangla.* **90 C2** 24 5N 89 37 E
Berach →, *India* **92 G6** 25 15N 75 2 E
Beraketa, *Madag.* **117 C7** 23 7 S 44 25 E
Béran-Djoko, *Congo* **114 B3** 3 15N 17 0 E
Berane, *Serbia & M.* **50 D3** 42 51N 19 52 E
Berat, *Albania* **50 F3** 40 43N 19 59 E
Berau →, *Indonesia* **85 B5** 2 10N 117 42 E
Berau, Teluk, *Indonesia* **83 B4** 2 30 S 132 30 E
Beravina, *Madag.* **117 B8** 18 10 S 45 14 E
Berber, *Sudan* **106 D3** 18 0N 34 0 E
Berbera, *Somali Rep.* **120 B3** 10 30N 45 2 E
Berbérati, *C.A.R.* **114 B3** 4 15N 15 40 E
Berbice →, *Guyana* **169 B6** 6 20N 57 32W
Berceto, *Italy* **44 D6** 44 31N 9 51 E
Berchidda, *Italy* **46 B2** 40 47N 9 10 E
Berchtesgaden, *Germany* **31 H8** 47 38N 13 0 E
Berchtesgaden △, *Germany* **31 H8** 47 34N 12 55 E
Berck, *France* **27 B8** 50 25N 1 36 E
Berdale, *Somali Rep.* **120 C3** 7 4N 47 51 E
Berdichev = Berdychiv, *Ukraine* **59 H5** 49 57N 28 30 E
Berdsk, *Russia* **66 D9** 54 47N 83 2 E
Berdyansk, *Ukraine* **59 J9** 46 45N 36 50 E
Berdyaush, *Russia* **64 D7** 55 9N 59 9 E
Berdychiv, *Ukraine* **59 H5** 49 57N 28 30 E
Berea, *U.S.A.* **148 G3** 37 34N 84 17W
Berebere, *Indonesia* **82 A3** 2 25N 128 45 E
Bereda, *Somali Rep.* **120 B4** 11 45N 51 0 E
Berehomet, *Ukraine* **53 B10** 48 10N 25 19 E
Berehove, *Ukraine* **52 B7** 48 15N 22 35 E
Bereina, *Papua N. G.* **132 E4** 8 39 S 146 30 E
Berekum, *Ghana* **112 D4** 7 29N 2 34W
Berenice, *Egypt* **106 C4** 24 2N 35 25 E
Berens →, *Canada* **143 C9** 52 25N 97 2W
Berens I., *Canada* **143 C9** 52 18N 97 18W
Berens River, *Canada* **143 C9** 52 25N 97 0W
Beresford, *U.S.A.* **154 D6** 43 5N 96 47W
Berestechko, *Ukraine* **59 G3** 50 22N 25 5 E
Bereşti, *Romania* **53 D12** 46 6N 27 50 E
Beretău →, *Romania* **52 C6** 47 10N 21 50 E
Berettyó →, *Hungary* **52 D6** 46 59N 21 7 E
Berettyóújfalu, *Hungary* **52 C6** 47 13N 21 33 E
Berevo, *Mahajanga, Madag.* **117 B7** 17 14 S 44 17 E
Berevo, *Toliara, Madag.* **117 B7** 19 44 S 44 58 E
Bereza = Byaroza, *Belarus* **59 F3** 52 31N 24 51 E
Berezhany, *Ukraine* **59 H3** 49 26N 24 58 E
Berezina = Byarezina →, *Belarus* **59 F6** 52 33N 30 14 E
Berezivka, *Ukraine* **59 J6** 47 14N 30 55 E
Berezna, *Ukraine* **59 G6** 51 35N 31 46 E
Bereznik, *Russia* **56 B7** 62 51N 42 40 E
Berezniki, *Russia* **64 B6** 59 24N 56 46 E
Berezovo, *Russia* **66 C7** 64 0N 65 0 E
Berezyne, *Ukraine* **53 D14** 46 14N 29 12 E
Berga, *Spain* **40 C6** 42 6N 1 48 E
Berga, *Sweden* **17 G10** 57 14N 16 3 E
Bergama, *Turkey* **49 B9** 39 8N 27 11 E
Bérgamo, *Italy* **44 C6** 45 41N 9 43 E
Bergaon, *India* **94 D5** 20 41N 80 27 E
Bergara, *Spain* **40 B2** 43 9N 2 28W
Bergby, *Sweden* **16 D11** 60 57N 17 2 E
Bergedorf, *Germany* **30 B6** 53 28N 10 6 E
Bergeforsen, *Sweden* **16 B11** 62 32N 17 23 E
Bergen, *Mecklenburg-Vorpommern, Germany* **30 A9** 54 25N 13 25 E
Bergen, *Niedersachsen, Germany* **30 C5** 52 49N 9 57 E
Bergen, *Neths.* **24 B4** 52 40N 4 43 E
Bergen, *Norway* **18 D2** 60 20N 5 20 E
Bergen, *U.S.A.* **150 C7** 43 5N 77 57W
Bergen ✈ (BGO), *Norway* **18 D2** 60 17N 5 19 E
Bergen op Zoom, *Neths.* **24 C4** 51 28N 4 18 E
Bergerac, *France* **28 D4** 44 51N 0 30 E
Bergheim, *Germany* **30 E2** 50 57N 6 38 E
Bergholz, *U.S.A.* **150 F4** 40 31N 80 53W
Bergisch Gladbach, *Germany* **24 D7** 50 59N 7 8 E
Bergisches Land ⌓, *Germany* **30 E3** 51 0N 7 30 E
Bergkamen, *Germany* **30 D3** 51 37N 7 38 E
Bergkvara, *Sweden* **17 H10** 56 23N 16 5 E
Bergshamra, *Sweden* **16 E12** 59 38N 18 37 E
Bergsjö, *Sweden* **16 C11** 61 59N 17 3 E
Bergstadt = Leśnica, *Poland* **55 H5** 50 26N 18 11 E
Bergstrasse-Odenwald ⌓, *Germany* **31 F1** 49 45N 5 55 E
Bergues, *France* **27 B9** 50 58N 2 24 E
Bergviken, *Sweden* **16 C10** 61 15N 16 40 E
Bergville, *S. Africa* **117 D4** 28 52 S 29 18 E
Berhala, Selat, *Indonesia* **84 C2** 1 0 S 104 15 E
Berhampore = Baharampur, *India* **93 G13** 24 2N 88 27 E
Berhampur = Brahmapur, *India* **94 E7** 19 15N 84 54 E
Berheci →, *Romania* **53 E12** 45 58N 27 28 E
Bering Glacier, *U.S.A.* **144 F12** 60 20N 143 30W
Bering Land Bridge ⌓, *U.S.A.* **144 C6** 66 20N 165 0W
Bering Sea, *Pac. Oc.* **138 C1** 58 0N 171 0W
Bering Strait, *Pac. Oc.* **144 D5** 65 30N 169 0W
Beringen, *Switz.* **33 A7** 47 38N 8 34 E
Beringovskiy, *Russia* **67 C18** 63 3N 179 19 E
Berisso, *Argentina* **174 C4** 34 56 S 57 50W
Berja, *Spain* **43 J8** 36 50N 2 56W
Berkåk, *Norway* **18 B6** 62 50N 10 0 E
Berkane, *Morocco* **111 B4** 34 52N 2 20W
Berkeley, *U.S.A.* **160 H4** 37 52N 122 16W
Berkeley, C., *Ecuador* **172 a** 0 1N 91 35W
Berkner I., *Antarctica* **7 D18** 79 30 S 50 0W
Berkovitsa, *Bulgaria* **50 C7** 43 16N 23 8 E
Berkshire, *U.S.A.* **151 D8** 42 19N 76 11W
Berkshire Downs, *U.K.* **21 F6** 51 33N 1 29W
Berlanga, *Spain* **43 G5** 38 17N 5 50W
Berlenga, I., *Portugal* **43 F1** 39 25N 9 30W
Berlengas = Valença do Piauí, *Brazil* **170 C3** 6 20 S 41 45W
Berlin = Kitchener, *Canada* **140 D3** 43 27N 80 29W
Berlin, *Germany* **30 C9** 52 30N 13 25 E
Berlin, *Ga., U.S.A.* **152 D6** 31 4N 83 37W
Berlin, *Md., U.S.A.* **148 F8** 38 20N 75 13W
Berlin, *N.H., U.S.A.* **151 B13** 44 28N 71 11W
Berlin, *N.Y., U.S.A.* **151 D11** 42 42N 73 23W
Berlin, *Wis., U.S.A.* **148 D1** 43 58N 88 57W
Berlin □, *Germany* **30 C9** 52 30N 13 20 E
Berlin L., *U.S.A.* **150 E4** 41 3N 81 0W
Berlin Tegel ✈ (TXL), *Germany* **30 C9** 52 35N 13 14 E

Berlinchen = Barlinek, Poland 55 F2 53 0N 15 15 E
Bermagui, Australia 129 D9 36 25 S 150 4 E
Bermeja, Sierra, Spain 43 J5 36 30N 5 11W
Bermejo →, Formosa, Argentina 174 B4 26 51 S 58 23W
Bermejo →, San Juan, Argentina 174 C2 32 30 S 67 30W
Bermen, L., Canada 141 B6 53 35N 68 55W
Bermeo, Spain 40 B2 43 25N 2 47W
Bermillo de Sayago, Spain 42 D4 41 22N 6 8W
Bermuda ☒, Atl. Oc. 9 a 32 45N 65 0W
Bermuda International ✕ (BDA), Bermuda 9 a 32 22N 64 41W
Bern, Switz. 32 C4 46 57N 7 28 E
Bern □, Switz. 32 C5 46 45N 7 40 E
Bernalda, Italy 47 B9 40 24N 16 41 E
Bernalillo, U.S.A. 159 J10 35 18N 106 33W
Bernam →, Malaysia 84 B2 3 45N 101 5 E
Bernardo de Irigoyen, Argentina 175 B5 26 15 S 53 40W
Bernardo O'Higgins □, Chile 174 C1 34 15 S 70 45W
Bernardo O'Higgins △, Chile 176 C1 48 50 S 75 36W
Bernardsville, U.S.A. 151 F10 40 43N 74 34W
Bernasconi, Argentina 174 D3 37 55 S 63 44W
Bernau, Bayern, Germany 31 H8 47 47N 12 22 E
Bernau, Brandenburg, Germany 30 C9 52 40N 13 35 E
Bernay, France 26 C7 49 5N 0 35 E
Bernburg, Germany 30 D7 51 47N 11 44 E
Berndorf, Austria 34 D9 47 59N 16 1 E
Berne = Bern, Switz. 32 C4 46 57N 7 28 E
Berne = Bern □, Switz. 32 C5 46 45N 7 40 E
Berne, U.S.A. 157 D12 40 39N 84 57W
Berner Alpen, Switz. 32 D5 46 27N 7 35 E
Berneray, U.K. 22 D1 57 43N 7 11W
Bernese Oberland = Oberland, Switz. 32 C5 46 35N 7 38 E
Bernier I., Australia 125 D1 24 50 S 113 12 E
Bernina, Passo del, Switz. 33 D10 46 25N 10 2 E
Bernina, Piz, Switz. 33 D9 46 20N 9 54 E
Bernkastel-Kues, Germany 31 F3 49 55N 7 3 E
Bernstadt = Bierutów, Poland 55 G4 51 7N 17 32 E
Bernstein = Pełczyce, Poland 55 E2 53 3N 15 16 E
Bero →, Angola 115 F2 15 10 S 12 9 E
Beroroha, Madag. 117 C8 21 40 S 45 10 E
Béroubouay, Benin 113 C5 10 34N 2 46 E
Beroun, Czech Rep. 34 B7 49 57N 14 5 E
Berounka →, Czech Rep. 34 B7 50 0N 14 22 E
Berovo, Macedonia 50 E6 41 38N 22 51 E
Berrahal, Algeria 111 A6 36 54N 7 33 E
Berre, Étang de, France 29 E9 43 27N 5 5 E
Berre-l'Étang, France 29 E9 43 27N 5 10 E
Berrechid, Morocco 110 B3 33 18N 7 36W
Berri, Australia 128 C4 34 14 S 140 35 E
Berriane, Algeria 111 B5 32 50N 3 46 E
Berridale, Australia 129 D8 36 22 S 148 48 E
Berrien Springs, U.S.A. 157 C10 41 57N 86 20W
Berrigan, Australia 129 C6 35 38 S 145 49 E
Berriwillock, Australia 128 C5 35 36 S 142 59 E
Berrouaghia, Algeria 111 A5 36 10N 2 53 E
Berry, Australia 129 C9 34 46 S 150 43 E
Berry, France 27 F8 46 50N 2 0 E
Berry Is., Bahamas 164 A4 25 40N 77 50W
Berrydale, U.S.A. 153 E2 30 53N 87 3W
Berryessa L., U.S.A. 160 G4 38 31N 122 6W
Berryville, U.S.A. 155 G8 36 22N 93 34W
Berseba, Namibia 116 D2 26 0 S 17 46 E
Bersenbrück, Germany 30 C3 52 34N 7 56 E
Bershad, Ukraine 53 B14 48 22N 29 31 E
Berthold, U.S.A. 154 A4 48 19N 101 44W
Berthoud, U.S.A. 154 E2 40 19N 105 5W
Bertincourt, France 27 B9 50 5N 2 58 E
Bertolínia, Brazil 170 C3 7 38 S 43 57W
Bertoua, Cameroon 114 B2 4 30N 13 45 E
Bertraghboy B., Ireland 23 C2 53 22N 9 54W
Bertys = Balqash, Kazakhstan 66 E8 46 50N 74 50 E
Berufjörður, Iceland 11 C12 64 48N 14 29W
Berunes, Iceland 11 C12 64 42N 14 16W
Beruri, Brazil 169 D5 3 54 S 61 22W
Berwick, U.S.A. 151 E8 41 3N 76 14W
Berwick-upon-Tweed, U.K. 20 B6 55 46N 2 0W
Berwyn Mts., U.K. 20 E4 52 54N 3 26W
Beryslav, Ukraine 59 J7 46 50N 33 30 E
Berzasca, Romania 52 F6 44 39N 21 58 E
Berzence, Hungary 52 D2 46 12N 17 11 E
Besal, Pakistan 93 B5 35 4N 73 56 E
Besalampy, Madag. 117 B7 16 43 S 44 29 E
Besançon, France 27 E13 47 15N 6 2 E
Besar, Indonesia 85 C5 2 40 S 116 0 E
Besar, Gunong, Malaysia 84 A2 5 10N 101 18 E
Besharyk, Uzbekistan 65 C5 40 26N 70 36 E
Beshenkovichi, Belarus 58 E5 55 2N 29 29 E
Beshkent, Uzbekistan 65 D2 38 49N 65 39 E
Beška, Serbia & M. 52 E5 45 8N 20 6 E
Beslan, Russia 61 J7 43 15N 44 28 E
Besna Kobila, Serbia & M. 50 D6 42 31N 22 10 E
Besnard L., Canada 143 B7 55 25N 106 0W
Besni, Turkey 100 D7 37 41N 37 52 E
Besor, N. →, Egypt 103 D3 31 28N 34 22 E
Bessa Monteiro, Angola 115 D2 7 7 S 13 44 E
Bessarabiya, Moldova 59 J5 47 0N 28 10 E
Bessarabka = Basarabeasca, Moldova 53 D13 46 21N 28 58 E
Bességès, France 29 D8 44 18N 4 8 E
Bessemer, Ala., U.S.A. 149 J2 33 24N 86 58W
Bessemer, Mich., U.S.A. 154 B9 46 29N 90 3W
Bessemer, Pa., U.S.A. 150 F4 40 59N 80 30W
Bessin, France 26 C6 49 18N 1 0W
Bessines-sur-Gartempe, France 28 B5 46 6N 1 22 E
Beswick, Australia 124 B5 14 34 S 132 53 E
Bet She'an, Israel 103 C4 32 30N 35 30 E
Bet Shemesh, Israel 103 D4 31 44N 35 0 E
Bet Tadjine, Djebel, Algeria 110 C4 29 0N 3 30W
Betafo, Madag. 117 B8 19 50 S 46 51 E
Betamba, Dem. Rep. of the Congo 114 C4 2 17 S 21 24 E
Betancuria, Canary Is. 9 e2 28 25N 14 3W
Betancuria, Mt., Canary Is. 9 e2 28 25N 14 6W
Betania, Colombia 168 C3 4 22N 72 54W
Betanzos, Bolivia 173 D4 19 34 S 65 27W
Betanzos, Spain 42 B2 43 15N 8 12W
Bétaré Oya, Cameroon 114 A2 5 40N 14 5 E
Betatao, Madag. 117 B8 18 11 S 47 52 E
Bétera, Spain 41 F4 39 35N 0 28W
Bétérou, Benin 113 D5 9 12N 2 16 E
Bethal, S. Africa 117 D4 26 27 S 29 28 E
Bethalto, U.S.A. 156 F6 38 55N 90 2W
Bethanien, Namibia 116 D2 26 31 S 17 8 E
Bethany, Canada 150 B6 44 11N 78 34W
Bethany, Ill., U.S.A. 157 E8 39 39N 88 45W
Bethany, Mo., U.S.A. 156 D2 40 16N 94 2W
Bethany, Okla., U.S.A. 155 H6 35 31N 97 38W
Bethel, Alaska, U.S.A. 144 F7 60 48N 161 45W
Bethel, Conn., U.S.A. 151 E11 41 22N 73 25W
Bethel, Maine, U.S.A. 151 B14 44 25N 70 47W
Bethel, Ohio, U.S.A. 157 F12 38 58N 84 5W
Bethel, Vt., U.S.A. 151 C12 43 50N 72 38W
Bethel Park, U.S.A. 150 F4 40 20N 80 1W
Béthenville, France 27 C11 49 18N 4 23 E
Bethlehem = Bayt Lahm, West Bank 103 D4 31 43N 35 12 E
Bethlehem, S. Africa 117 D4 28 14 S 28 18 E
Bethlehem, U.S.A. 151 F9 40 37N 75 23W
Bethulie, S. Africa 116 E4 30 30 S 25 59 E
Béthune, France 27 B9 50 30N 2 38 E
Béthune →, France 26 C8 49 53N 1 4 E
Bethungra, Australia 129 C7 34 45 S 147 51 E
Betijoque, Venezuela 168 B3 9 23N 70 44W
Betioky, Madag. 117 C7 23 48 S 44 20 E
Betong, Malaysia 84 B4 1 24N 111 31 E
Betong, Thailand 87 K3 5 45N 101 5 E
Betoota, Australia 126 D3 25 45 S 140 42 E
Betor, Ethiopia 107 E4 11 37N 39 2 E
Bétou, Congo 114 B3 3 2N 18 32 E
Betroka, Madag. 117 C8 23 16 S 46 0 E
Betsiamites, Canada 141 C6 48 56N 68 40W
Betsiamites →, Canada 141 C6 48 56N 68 38W
Betsiboka →, Madag. 117 B8 16 3 S 46 36 E
Bettendorf, U.S.A. 156 C6 41 32N 90 30W
Bettiah, India 93 F11 26 48N 84 33 E
Bettna, Sweden 17 F10 58 55N 16 38 E
Bèttola, Italy 44 D6 44 47N 9 36 E
Betul, India 94 D3 21 58N 77 59 E
Betws-y-Coed, U.K. 20 D4 53 5N 3 48W
Betxi, Spain 40 F4 39 56N 0 12W
Betzdorf, Germany 30 E3 50 46N 7 52 E
Béu, Angola 115 D3 6 15 S 15 32 E
Beuil, France 29 D10 44 6N 6 59 E
Beulah, Australia 128 C5 35 58 S 142 29 E
Beulah, Mich., U.S.A. 148 C2 44 38N 86 6W
Beulah, N. Dak., U.S.A. 154 B4 47 16N 101 47W
Beurkia, Chad 109 E3 15 20N 17 56 E
Beuthen = Bytom, Poland 55 H5 50 25N 18 54 E
Beuthen an der Oder = Bytom Odrzański, Poland 55 G2 51 44N 15 48 E
Beuvron →, France 26 E8 47 29N 1 15 E
Beveren, Belgium 24 C4 51 12N 4 16 E
Beverley, Australia 125 F2 32 9 S 116 56 E
Beverley, U.K. 20 D7 53 51N 0 26W
Beverley Hills, U.S.A. 153 G7 28 56N 82 28W
Beverly, U.S.A. 151 D14 42 33N 70 53W
Beverly Hills, U.S.A. 161 L8 34 4N 118 25W
Beverungen, Germany 30 D5 51 39N 9 22 E
Bevoalavo, Madag. 117 D7 25 13 S 45 26 E
Bewani, Papua N. G. 83 B6 3 2 S 141 10 E
Bewas →, India 93 H8 23 59N 79 21 E
Bex, Switz. 32 D4 46 15N 7 1 E
Bexhill, U.K. 21 G8 50 51N 0 29 E
Bey Dağları, Turkey 49 E12 36 38N 30 29 E
Beyānlū, Iran 96 C5 36 0N 47 51 E
Beyazköy, Turkey 51 E11 41 21N 27 42 E
Beyçayırı, Turkey 51 F10 40 15N 26 55 E
Beydağ, Turkey 49 C10 38 5N 28 13 E
Beyeğaç, Turkey 49 D10 37 14N 28 53 E
Beyin, Ghana 112 D4 5 1N 2 41W
Beykoz, Turkey 51 E13 41 8N 29 7 E
Beyla, Guinea 112 D3 8 30N 8 38W
Beynat, France 28 C5 45 8N 1 44 E
Beyneu, Kazakhstan 57 E10 45 18N 55 9 E
Beyoba, Turkey 49 C9 38 48N 27 47 E
Beyoğlu, Turkey 51 E12 41 2N 29 0 E
Beypazarı, Turkey 100 B4 40 10N 31 56 E
Beypore →, India 95 J2 11 10N 75 47 E
Beyşehir, Turkey 100 D4 37 41N 31 43 E
Beyşehir Gölü, Turkey 100 D4 37 41N 31 33 E
Beytüşşebap, Turkey 101 D10 37 35N 43 10 E
Bezdan, Serbia & M. 52 E3 45 50N 18 57 E
Bezhetsk, Russia 58 D9 57 47N 36 39 E
Béziers, France 28 E7 43 20N 3 12 E
Bezwada = Vijayawada, India 94 F5 16 31N 80 39 E
Bhabua, India 93 G10 25 3N 83 37 E
Bhadar →, Gujarat, India 92 H5 22 17N 72 20 E
Bhadar →, Gujarat, India 92 J3 21 27N 69 47 E
Bhadarwah, India 93 C6 32 58N 75 46 E
Bhadgaon = Bhaktapur, Nepal 93 F11 27 38N 85 24 E
Bhadohi, India 93 G10 25 25N 82 34 E
Bhadra, India 92 E6 29 8N 75 14 E
Bhadra →, India 95 H2 14 0N 75 20 E
Bhadrachalam, India 94 F5 17 40N 80 53 E
Bhadrakh, India 94 D8 21 10N 86 30 E
Bhadran, India 92 H5 22 19N 72 6 E
Bhadravati, India 95 H2 13 49N 75 40 E
Bhag, Pakistan 92 E2 29 2N 67 49 E
Bhagalpur, India 93 G12 25 10N 87 0 E
Bhagirathi →, Uttaranchal, India 93 D8 30 8N 78 35 E
Bhagirathi →, W. Bengal, India 93 H13 23 25N 88 23 E
Bhainsa, India 94 E3 19 10N 77 58 E
Bhairab →, Bangla. 90 D2 22 51N 89 34 E
Bhairab Bazar, Bangla. 90 C3 24 4N 90 58 E
Bhakkar, Pakistan 91 C3 31 40N 71 5 E
Bhakra Dam, India 92 D7 31 30N 76 45 E
Bhaktapur, Nepal 93 F11 27 38N 85 24 E
Bhalki, India 94 E3 18 2N 77 13 E
Bhamo, Burma 90 C6 24 15N 97 15 E
Bhamragarh, India 94 E5 19 30N 80 40 E
Bhandara, India 94 D4 21 5N 79 42 E
Bhanpura, India 92 G6 24 31N 75 44 E
Bhanrer Ra., India 93 H8 23 40N 79 45 E
Bhaptiahi, India 93 F12 26 19N 86 44 E
Bharat = India ■, Asia 89 C6 20 0N 78 0 E
Bharatpur, Chhattisgarh, India 93 H9 23 44N 81 46 E
Bharatpur, Raj., India 92 F7 27 15N 77 30 E
Bharno, India 93 H11 23 14N 84 53 E
Bharuch, India 94 D1 21 47N 73 0 E
Bhatghar L., India 94 E1 18 10N 73 48 E
Bhatiapara Ghat, Bangla. 90 D2 23 13N 89 42 E
Bhatinda, India 92 D6 30 15N 74 57 E
Bhatkal, India 95 H2 13 58N 74 35 E
Bhatpara, India 93 H13 22 50N 88 25 E
Bhattu, India 92 E6 29 36N 75 19 E
Bhaun, Pakistan 92 C5 32 55N 72 40 E
Bhaunagar = Bhavnagar, India 94 D1 21 45N 72 10 E
Bhavani, India 95 J3 11 27N 77 43 E
Bhavnagar, India 94 D1 21 45N 72 10 E
Bhawanipatna, India 94 E5 19 55N 83 10 E
Bhawari, India 92 G5 25 42N 73 4 E
Bhayavadar, India 92 J4 21 51N 70 15 E
Bhera, Pakistan 92 C5 32 29N 72 57 E
Bhikangaon, India 92 J6 21 52N 75 57 E
Bhilai, India 94 D5 21 13N 81 26 E
Bhilainagar = Bhilai, India 94 D5 21 13N 81 26 E
Bhilsa = Vidisha, India 92 H7 23 28N 77 53 E
Bhilwara, India 92 G6 25 25N 74 38 E
Bhima →, India 94 F3 16 25N 77 17 E
Bhimavaram, India 95 F5 16 30N 81 30 E
Bhimbar, Pakistan 93 C6 32 59N 74 3 E
Bhind, India 93 F8 26 30N 78 46 E
Bhinga, India 93 F9 27 43N 81 56 E
Bhinmal, India 92 G5 25 0N 72 15 E
Bhiwandi, India 94 E1 19 20N 73 0 E
Bhiwani, India 92 E7 28 50N 76 9 E
Bhogava →, India 92 H5 22 26N 72 20 E
Bhokardan, India 94 D2 20 16N 75 46 E
Bhola, Bangla. 90 D3 22 45N 90 35 E
Bholari, Pakistan 92 G3 25 19N 68 13 E
Bhongir, India 94 F4 17 30N 78 56 E
Bhopal, India 92 H7 23 20N 77 30 E
Bhopalpatnam, India 94 E5 18 52N 80 23 E
Bhor, India 94 E1 18 12N 73 53 E
Bhubaneshwar, India 94 D7 20 15N 85 50 E
Bhuj, India 92 H3 23 15N 69 49 E
Bhumiphol Res., Thailand 86 D2 17 20N 98 40 E
Bhusawal, India 94 D2 21 3N 75 46 E
Bhutan ■, Asia 90 B3 27 25N 90 30 E
Biá →, Brazil 168 D4 3 28 S 67 23W
Biafra, B. of = Bonny, Bight of, Africa 113 E6 3 30N 9 20 E
Biak, Indonesia 83 B5 1 10 S 136 6 E
Biała, Poland 55 H4 50 24N 17 40 E
Biała →, Poland 55 H7 50 3N 20 55 E
Biała Piska, Poland 54 E9 53 37N 22 5 E
Biała Podlaska, Poland 55 F10 52 4N 23 6 E
Biała Rawska, Poland 55 G7 51 48N 20 29 E
Białobrzegi, Poland 55 G7 51 39N 20 57 E
Białogard, Poland 54 D2 54 2N 15 58 E
Białowieski △, Poland 55 F10 52 43N 23 50 E
Białowieża, Poland 55 F10 52 41N 23 49 E
Biały Bór, Poland 54 E3 53 53N 16 51 E
Białystok, Poland 55 E10 53 10N 23 10 E
Bian →, Indonesia 83 C5 8 6 S 139 58 E
Biancavilla, Italy 47 E7 37 38N 14 52 E
Bianco, Italy 47 D9 38 5N 16 9 E
Biankouma, Ivory C. 112 D3 7 50N 7 40W
Biaora, India 92 H7 23 56N 76 56 E
Bīārjmand, Iran 97 B7 36 6N 55 53 E
Biaro, Indonesia 82 A3 2 5N 125 26 E
Biarritz, France 28 E2 43 29N 1 33W
Bias, Indonesia 79 J18 8 24 S 115 36 E
Biasca, Switz. 33 D7 46 22N 8 58 E
Biavela, Angola 115 E3 14 43 S 19 47 E
Biba, Egypt 106 J7 28 55N 31 0 E
Bibai, Japan 70 C10 43 19N 141 52 E
Bibala, Angola 115 E2 14 44 S 13 24 E
Bibane, Bahiret el, Tunisia 108 B2 33 16N 11 13 E
Bibassé, Gabon 114 B2 1 27N 11 37 E
Bibbiena, Italy 45 E8 43 42N 11 49 E
Bibby I., Canada 143 A10 61 55N 93 0W
Bibel →, Spain 42 C3 42 24N 7 13W
Biberach, Germany 31 G5 48 5N 9 47 E
Biberist, Switz. 32 B5 47 11N 7 34 E
Bibi, Papua N. G. 132 C4 5 30 S 146 2 E
Bibiani, Ghana 112 D4 6 30N 2 8W
Bibile, Sri Lanka 95 L5 7 10N 81 25 E
Bibungwa, Dem. Rep. of the Congo 118 C2 2 40 S 28 15 E
Bicaj, Albania 50 E4 41 58N 20 25 E
Bicaz, Romania 53 D11 46 53N 26 5 E
Bicazu Ardelean, Romania 53 D10 46 51N 25 56 E
Biccari, Italy 47 A8 41 23N 15 12 E
Bicester, U.K. 21 F6 51 54N 1 9W
Bichena, Ethiopia 107 E4 10 28N 38 10 E
Bicheno, Australia 127 G4 41 52 S 148 18 E
Bichia, India 93 H9 22 27N 80 42 E
Bichvinta, Georgia 61 J5 43 9N 40 21 E
Bickerton I., Australia 126 A2 13 45 S 136 10 E
Bicknell, U.S.A. 157 F9 38 47N 87 19W
Bicske, Hungary 52 C3 47 29N 18 38 E
Bicuar △, Angola 115 F2 15 14 S 14 45 E
Bida, Dem. Rep. of the Congo 114 B3 4 55N 19 56 E
Bida, Nigeria 113 D6 9 3N 5 58 E
Bidar, India 94 F3 17 55N 77 35 E
Biddeford, U.S.A. 149 D10 43 30N 70 28W
Biddwara, Ethiopia 107 F4 5 11N 38 34 E
Bideford, U.K. 21 F3 51 1N 4 13W
Bideford Bay, U.K. 21 F3 51 5N 4 20W
Bidhuna, India 93 F8 26 49N 79 31 E
Bidon 5 = Poste Maurice Cortier, Algeria 111 D5 22 14N 1 2 E
Bidor, Malaysia 87 K3 4 6N 101 15 E
Bidzar, Cameroon 114 A2 9 54N 14 7 E
Bie, Sweden 16 E10 59 5N 16 12 E
Bié □, Angola 115 E3 12 30 S 17 0 E
Bié, Planalto de, Angola 115 E3 12 0 S 16 0 E
Bieber, U.S.A. 158 F3 41 7N 121 8W
Biebrza →, Poland 55 E9 53 13N 22 25 E
Biebrzański △, Poland 54 E9 53 36N 22 45 E
Biecz, Poland 55 J8 49 44N 21 15 E
Biel, Switz. 32 B4 47 8N 7 14 E
Bielawa, Poland 55 H3 50 43N 16 37 E
Bielefeld, Germany 30 C4 52 1N 8 33 E
Bielersee, Switz. 32 B4 47 6N 7 5 E
Bielitz = Bielsko-Biała, Poland 55 J6 49 50N 19 2 E
Biella, Italy 44 C5 45 34N 8 3 E
Bielsk Podlaski, Poland 55 F10 52 47N 23 12 E
Bielsko-Biała, Poland 55 J6 49 50N 19 2 E
Bien Hoa, Vietnam 87 G6 10 57N 106 49 E
Bienne = Biel, Switz. 32 B4 47 8N 7 14 E
Bienno, Italy 33 E10 45 56N 10 18 E
Bienvenida, Spain 43 G4 38 18N 6 12W
Bienvenue, Fr. Guiana 169 C7 3 0N 52 30W
Bienville, L., Canada 140 A5 55 5N 72 40W
Bière, Switz. 32 C2 46 33N 6 20 E
Bierné, France 26 E6 47 48N 0 33W
Bierun, Poland 55 H6 50 6N 19 6 E
Bierutów, Poland 55 G4 51 7N 17 32 E
Biescas, Spain 40 C4 42 37N 0 20W
Biese →, Germany 30 C7 52 53N 11 46 E
Biesiesfontein, S. Africa 116 E2 30 57 S 17 58 E
Bieszczadzki △, Poland 55 J9 49 5N 22 43 E
Bietigheim-Bissingen, Germany 31 G5 48 58N 9 8 E
Bieżuń, Poland 55 F6 52 58N 19 55 E
Biferno →, Italy 45 G12 41 59N 15 2 E
Bifoum, Gabon 114 C2 0 20 S 10 23 E
Big →, Canada 141 B8 54 50N 58 55W
Big →, U.S.A. 156 F6 38 28N 90 37W
Big B., Canada 141 A7 55 43N 60 35W
Big Bear City, U.S.A. 161 L10 34 16N 116 51W
Big Bear Lake, U.S.A. 161 L10 34 15N 116 56W
Big Belt Mts., U.S.A. 158 C8 46 30N 111 25W
Big Bend, Swaziland 117 D5 26 50 S 31 58 E
Big Bend △, U.S.A. 155 L3 29 20N 103 5W
Big Black →, U.S.A. 155 K9 32 3N 91 4W
Big Blue →, Ind., U.S.A. 157 E11 39 12N 85 56W
Big Blue →, Kans., U.S.A. 154 F6 39 35N 96 34W
Big Creek, U.S.A. 160 H7 37 11N 119 14W
Big Cypress ⌂, U.S.A. 153 J8 26 0N 81 10W
Big Cypress Swamp, U.S.A. 153 J8 26 15N 81 30W
Big Delta, U.S.A. 144 D11 64 10N 145 51W
Big Falls, U.S.A. 154 A8 48 12N 93 48W
Big Fork →, U.S.A. 154 A8 48 31N 93 43W
Big Horn Mts. = Bighorn Mts., U.S.A. 158 D10 44 30N 107 30W
Big I., Canada 142 A5 61 7N 116 45W
Big Lake, Alaska, U.S.A. 144 F10 61 20N 150 20W
Big Lake, Tex., U.S.A. 155 K4 31 12N 101 28W
Big Moose, U.S.A. 151 C10 43 49N 74 58W
Big Muddy →, U.S.A. 156 G8 38 0N 89 0W
Big Muddy Cr. →, U.S.A. 154 A2 48 8N 104 36W
Big Pine, Calif., U.S.A. 160 H8 37 10N 118 17W
Big Pine, Fla., U.S.A. 153 L8 24 40N 81 21W
Big Piney, U.S.A. 158 E8 42 32N 110 7W
Big Rapids, U.S.A. 148 D3 43 42N 85 29W
Big Rideau L., Canada 151 B8 44 40N 76 15W
Big River, Canada 143 C7 53 50N 107 0W
Big Run, U.S.A. 150 F6 40 57N 78 55W
Big Sable Pt., U.S.A. 148 C2 44 3N 86 1W
Big Salmon →, Canada 142 A2 61 52N 134 55W
Big Sand L., Canada 143 B9 57 45N 99 45W
Big Sandy, U.S.A. 158 B8 48 11N 110 7W
Big Sandy →, U.S.A. 148 F4 38 25N 82 36W
Big Sandy Cr. →, U.S.A. 154 F3 38 7N 102 29W
Big Satilla →, U.S.A. 152 D7 31 27N 82 3W
Big Sioux →, U.S.A. 154 D6 42 29N 96 27W
Big South Fork △, U.S.A. 149 G3 36 27N 84 47W
Big Spring, U.S.A. 155 J4 32 15N 101 28W
Big Stone City, U.S.A. 154 C6 45 18N 96 28W
Big Stone Gap, U.S.A. 149 G4 36 52N 82 47W
Big Stone L., U.S.A. 154 C6 45 30N 96 35W
Big Sur, U.S.A. 160 J5 36 15N 121 48W
Big Timber, U.S.A. 158 D9 45 50N 109 57W
Big Trout L., Canada 140 B2 53 40N 90 0W
Big Trout Lake, Canada 140 B2 53 45N 90 0W
Biğa, Turkey 51 F11 40 13N 27 14 E
Biga →, Turkey 51 F11 40 20N 27 14 E
Bigadiç, Turkey 49 B10 39 22N 28 7 E
Biganos, France 28 D3 44 39N 0 59W
Biggar, Canada 143 C7 52 4N 108 0W
Biggar, U.K. 22 F5 55 38N 3 32W
Bigge I., Australia 124 B4 14 35 S 125 10 E
Biggenden, Australia 127 D5 25 31 S 152 4 E
Biggleswade, U.K. 21 E7 52 5N 0 14W
Biggs, U.S.A. 160 F5 39 25N 121 43W
Bighorn, U.S.A. 158 C10 46 10N 107 27W
Bighorn →, U.S.A. 158 C10 46 10N 107 28W
Bighorn Canyon ⌂, U.S.A. 158 D9 45 10N 108 0W
Bighorn L., U.S.A. 158 D9 44 55N 108 15W
Bighorn Mts., U.S.A. 158 D10 44 30N 107 30W
Bigi, Dem. Rep. of the Congo 114 B4 3 2N 22 25 E
Bignasco, Switz. 33 D7 46 21N 8 37 E
Bignona, Senegal 112 C1 12 52N 16 14W
Bigorre, France 28 E4 43 10N 0 5 E
Bigstone L., Canada 143 C9 53 42N 95 44W
Biguglia, Étang de, France 29 F13 42 36N 9 29 E
Bigwa, Tanzania 118 D4 7 10 S 39 10 E
Bihać, Bos.-H. 45 D12 44 49N 15 57 E
Bihar, India 93 G11 25 5N 85 40 E
Bihar □, India 93 G12 25 0N 86 0 E
Biharamulo, Tanzania 118 C3 2 25 S 31 25 E
Biharamulo ⌂, Tanzania 118 C3 2 24 S 31 26 E
Bihariganj, India 93 G12 25 44N 86 59 E
Biharkeresztes, Hungary 52 C6 47 8N 21 44 E
Bihor □, Romania 52 D7 47 0N 22 10 E
Bihor, Munţii, Romania 52 D7 46 29N 22 47 E
Bijagós, Arquipélago dos, Guinea-Biss. 112 C1 11 15N 16 10W
Bijaipur, India 92 F7 26 2N 77 20 E
Bijapur, Chhattisgarh, India 94 E5 18 50N 80 50 E
Bijapur, Karnataka, India 94 F2 16 50N 75 55 E
Bījār, Iran 101 E12 35 52N 47 35 E
Bijawar, India 93 G8 24 38N 79 30 E
Bijeljina, Bos.-H. 52 F4 44 46N 19 14 E
Bijelo Polje, Serbia & M. 50 C3 43 1N 19 45 E
Bijie, China 76 D5 27 20N 105 16 E
Bijnor, India 92 E8 29 27N 78 11 E
Bikaner, India 92 E5 28 2N 73 18 E
Bikapur, India 93 F10 26 30N 82 7 E
Bikeqi, China 74 D6 40 43N 111 20 E
Bikfayyā, Lebanon 103 B4 33 55N 35 41 E
Bikié, Congo 114 C2 3 7 S 13 52 E
Bikin, Russia 67 E14 46 50N 134 20 E
Bikin →, Russia 70 A7 46 51N 134 2 E
Bikini Atoll, Marshall Is. 134 F8 12 0N 167 30 E
Bikita, Zimbabwe 117 C5 20 6 S 31 41 E
Bîkkû Bîttî, Libya 109 D3 22 0N 19 12 E
Bikoro, Dem. Rep. of the Congo 114 C3 0 48 S 18 15 E
Bikoué, Cameroon 113 E7 3 55N 11 50 E
Bila Tserkva, Ukraine 59 H6 49 45N 30 10 E
Bilanga, Burkina Faso 113 C4 12 40N 0 1W
Bilara, India 92 F5 26 14N 73 53 E
Bilasipara, India 90 B3 26 13N 90 14 E
Bilaspur, Chhattisgarh, India 93 H10 22 2N 82 15 E
Bilaspur, Punjab, India 92 D7 31 19N 76 50 E
Biläsuvar, Azerbaijan 101 C13 39 27N 48 32 E
Bilauk Taungdan, Thailand 86 F2 13 0N 99 0 E
Bilbao, Spain 40 B2 43 16N 2 56W
Bilbao ✕ (BIO), Spain 42 B8 43 18N 2 57W
Bilbeis, Egypt 106 H7 30 25N 31 34 E
Bilbo = Bilbao, Spain 40 B2 43 16N 2 56W
Bilbor, Romania 53 C10 47 6N 25 30 E
Bilche-Zolote, Ukraine 53 B10 48 47N 25 53 E
Bilciureşti, Romania 53 F10 44 44N 25 48 E
Bíldudalur, Iceland 11 B3 65 41N 23 36W
Bílé Karpaty, Europe 35 B11 49 5N 18 0 E
Bileća, Bos.-H. 50 D2 42 53N 18 27 E
Bilecik, Turkey 100 B4 40 5N 30 5 E
Biłgoraj, Poland 55 H9 50 33N 22 42 E
Bilgram, India 93 F9 27 11N 80 2 E
Bilhaur, India 93 F9 26 51N 80 5 E
Bilhorod-Dnistrovskyy, Ukraine 59 J6 46 11N 30 23 E
Bili →, Dem. Rep. of the Congo 114 B4 4 9N 22 29 E
Bilibino, Russia 67 C17 68 3N 166 20 E
Bilibiza, Mozam. 119 E5 12 30 S 40 20 E
Biliköl, Kazakhstan 65 B5 43 5N 70 45 E
Bilimora, India 94 D1 20 45N 72 57 E
Bilin, Burma 90 G6 17 14N 97 15 E
Biliran □, Phil. 81 F5 11 35N 124 28 E
Bilisht, Albania 50 F5 40 37N 21 2 E
Billabong Cr. →, Australia 128 C6 35 5 S 144 2 E
Billabong Roadhouse, Australia 125 E2 27 25 S 115 49 E
Billdal, Sweden 17 G5 57 35N 11 57 E
Billiluna, Australia 124 C4 19 37 S 127 41 E
Billings, U.S.A. 158 D9 45 47N 108 30W
Billiton Is. = Belitung, Indonesia 85 C3 3 10 S 107 50 E
Billsta, Sweden 16 A12 63 20N 18 28 E
Billund, Denmark 17 J3 55 44N 9 6 E
Bilma, Niger 109 E2 18 50N 13 30 E
Bilo Gora, Croatia 52 E2 45 53N 17 15 E
Biloela, Australia 126 C5 24 24 S 150 31 E
Bilohirsk, Ukraine 59 K8 45 3N 34 35 E
Biloku, Guyana 169 C6 1 50N 58 25W
Biloli, India 94 E3 18 46N 77 44 E
Bilopillya, Ukraine 59 G8 51 14N 34 20 E
Biloxi, U.S.A. 155 K10 30 24N 88 53W
Bilpa Morea Claypan, Australia 126 D3 25 0 S 140 0 E
Biltine, Chad 109 F4 14 40N 20 50 E
Bilugyun, Burma 90 G6 16 24N 97 32 E
Bilyarsk, Russia 60 C10 54 58N 50 22 E
Bima, Indonesia 85 D5 8 22 S 118 49 E
Bimban, Egypt 106 C3 24 24N 32 54 E
Bimbe, Angola 115 E3 11 50 S 15 50 E
Bimberi Pk., Australia 129 C8 35 44 S 148 51 E
Bimbila, Ghana 113 D5 8 54N 0 5 E
Bimbo, C.A.R. 114 B3 4 15N 18 33 E
Bimini Is., Bahamas 164 A4 25 42N 79 25W
Bin Xian, Heilongjiang, China 75 B14 45 42N 127 32 E
Bin Xian, Shaanxi, China 74 G5 35 2N 108 4 E
Bin Yauri, Nigeria 113 C5 10 46N 4 45 E
Bina-Etawah, India 92 G8 24 13N 78 14 E
Bināb, Iran 97 B6 36 35N 48 41 E
Binaiya, Indonesia 83 B3 3 11 S 129 26 E
Binalbagan, Phil. 81 F4 10 12N 122 50 E
Binalong, Australia 129 C8 34 40 S 148 39 E
Bīnālūd, Kūh-e, Iran 97 B8 36 30N 58 30 E
Binangonan de Lampon = Infanta, Phil. 80 D3 14 45N 121 39 E
Binatang = Bintangau, Malaysia 85 B4 2 10N 111 40 E
Binche, Belgium 24 D4 50 26N 4 10 E
Binchuan, China 76 E3 25 42N 100 38 E
Binda, Dem. Rep. of the Congo 115 D2 5 52 S 13 14 E
Binder, Chad 113 D7 9 56N 14 27 E
Bindki, India 93 F9 26 2N 80 36 E
Bindloe, I. = Marchena, I., Ecuador 172 a 0 19N 90 29W
Bindoy, Phil. 81 G4 9 48N 123 5 E
Bindslev, Denmark 17 G4 57 33N 10 11 E
Bindura, Zimbabwe 119 F3 17 18 S 31 18 E
Binefar, Spain 40 D5 41 51N 0 18 E
Bingara, Australia 127 D5 29 52 S 150 36 E
Bingaram I., India 95 J1 10 56N 72 17 E
Bingen, Germany 31 F3 49 57N 7 55 E
Bingerau = Węgrów, Poland 55 F9 52 24N 22 0 E
Bingerville, Ivory C. 112 D4 5 18N 3 49W
Bingham, U.S.A. 149 C11 45 3N 69 53W
Binghamton, U.S.A. 151 D9 42 6N 75 55W
Bingo-Ochiai, Japan 72 C4 34 59N 133 8 E
Bingöl, Turkey 101 C9 38 53N 40 29 E
Bingöl Dağları, Turkey 101 C9 39 16N 41 9 E
Bingsjö, Sweden 16 C9 61 1N 15 39 E
Binh Dinh = An Nhon, Vietnam 86 F7 13 55N 109 7 E
Binh Khe, Vietnam 86 F7 13 57N 108 51 E
Binh Son, Vietnam 86 E7 15 20N 108 40 E
Binhai, China 75 G10 34 2N 119 49 E
Bini Erde, Chad 109 D3 20 6N 18 1 E
Binic, France 26 D4 48 36N 2 50W
Binisatua, Spain 38 B5 39 50N 4 11 E
Binjai, Indonesia 84 B1 3 20N 98 30 E
Binji, Nigeria 113 C5 13 10N 4 55 E
Binka, India 94 D6 21 2N 83 48 E
Binnaway, Australia 129 A8 31 28 S 149 24 E
Binningen, Switz. 32 A5 47 32N 7 34 E
Binongko, Indonesia 82 C2 5 57 S 124 2 E
Binscarth, Canada 143 C8 50 37N 101 17W
Binshangul Gumuz □, Ethiopia 107 E4 11 0N 35 30 E
Bint Goda, Sudan 107 E3 13 17N 31 33 E
Bintan, Indonesia 84 B2 1 0N 104 0 E
Bintangau, Malaysia 85 B4 2 10N 111 40 E
Bintulu, Malaysia 78 D4 3 10N 113 0 E
Bintuni, Indonesia 83 B4 2 7 S 133 32 E
Bintuni, Teluk, Indonesia 83 B4 2 20 S 133 30 E
Binyang, China 76 F7 23 12N 108 47 E
Binz, Germany 30 A9 54 24N 13 35 E
Binza, Dem. Rep. of the Congo 115 C3 4 21 S 15 14 E
Binzert = Bizerte, Tunisia 108 A1 37 15N 9 50 E
Binzhou, China 75 F10 37 20N 118 2 E
Bío Bío □, Chile 174 D1 37 35 S 72 0W
Biograd na Moru, Croatia 45 E12 43 56N 15 29 E
Biogradska Gora △, Serbia & M. 50 D3 42 55N 19 40 E
Bioko, Eq. Guin. 113 E6 3 30N 8 40 E
Biokovo, Croatia 45 E14 43 23N 17 0 E
Biougra, Morocco 110 B3 30 15N 9 14W
Bipindi, Cameroon 113 E7 3 6N 10 30 E
Bir, India 94 E2 19 4N 75 46 E
Bir, Ras, Djibouti 107 E5 12 0N 43 20 E
Bîr Abu Hashim, Egypt 106 C3 23 42N 34 6 E
Bîr Abu Minqar, Egypt 106 B2 26 33N 27 33 E
Bîr Abu Muḥammad, Egypt 103 F3 29 44N 34 14 E
Bi'r ad Dabbāghāt, Jordan 103 E4 30 26N 35 32 E
Bîr Adal Deib, Sudan 106 C4 22 35N 36 10 E
Bi'r al Butayyihāt, Jordan 103 F4 29 47N 35 20 E
Bi'r al Mārī, Jordan 103 E4 30 4N 35 33 E
Bi'r al Qattār, Jordan 103 F4 29 47N 35 32 E
Bir 'Ali, Yemen 99 D5 14 1N 48 20 E
Bir Aouine, Tunisia 108 B1 32 25N 9 18 E
Bîr 'Asal, Egypt 106 B3 25 55N 34 20 E
Bir Atrun, Sudan 106 D2 18 15N 26 40 E
Bîr Beiḍa, Egypt 103 E3 30 25N 34 29 E
Bir Bel Guerdâne, Mauritania 110 C2 25 24N 10 31W
Bi'r Dhu'fān, Libya 108 B2 31 59N 14 32 E
Bîr Diqnash, Egypt 106 A2 31 3N 25 23 E
Bir el Abbes, Algeria 110 C3 26 7N 6 9W
Bîr el 'Abd, Egypt 103 D2 31 2N 33 0 E
Bir el Ater, Algeria 111 B6 34 46N 8 3 E
Bîr el Basur, Egypt 106 B2 29 51N 25 49 E
Bîr el Biarât, Egypt 103 F3 29 30N 34 43 E
Bîr el Duweidar, Egypt 103 E1 30 56N 32 32 E

Bîr el Garârât, *Egypt* **103 D2** 31 3N 33 34 E
Bîr el Gâreb, *Mauritania* **110 D1** 20 33N 16 12W
Bîr el Gellaz, *Egypt* **106 A2** 30 50N 26 40 E
Bîr el Heisi, *Egypt* **103 F3** 29 22N 34 36 E
Bîr el Jafir, *Egypt* **103 E1** 30 50N 32 41 E
Bîr el Mâlḥi, *Egypt* **103 E2** 30 38N 33 19 E
Bîr el Shaqqa, *Egypt* **106 A2** 30 54N 25 1 E
Bîr el Thamâda, *Egypt* **103 E2** 30 12N 33 27 E
Bîr Enzarán, *W. Sahara* **110 D2** 23 53N 14 32W
Bîr Fuad, *Egypt* **106 A2** 30 35N 26 28 E
Bîr Gandús, *W. Sahara* **110 D1** 21 36N 16 30W
Bir Gara, *Chad* **109 F3** 13 11N 15 58 E
Bîr Gebeil Ḥiṣn, *Egypt* **103 E2** 30 2N 33 18 E
Bi'r Ghadīr, *Syria* **103 A6** 34 6N 37 3 E
Bîr Haimur, *Egypt* **106 C3** 22 45N 33 40 E
Bîr Ḥasana, *Egypt* **103 E2** 30 29N 33 46 E
Bîr Hōōker, *Egypt* **106 H7** 30 22N 30 21 E
Bi'r Īdimah, *Si. Arabia* **98 C4** 18 31N 44 12 E
Bir Jdid, *Morocco* **110 B3** 33 26N 8 0W
Bîr Kanayis, *Egypt* **106 C3** 24 59N 33 15 E
Bîr Kaseiba, *Egypt* **103 E2** 31 0N 33 17 E
Bîr Kerawein, *Egypt* **106 B2** 27 10N 28 25 E
Bîr Lahfân, *Egypt* **103 E2** 31 0N 33 51 E
Bir Lahrache, *Algeria* **111 B6** 32 1N 8 12 E
Bîr Madkûr, *Egypt* **103 E1** 30 44N 32 33 E
Bîr Maql, *Egypt* **106 C3** 23 7N 33 40 E
Bîr Mîneiga, *Sudan* **106 C4** 22 47N 35 12 E
Bîr Misaha, *Egypt* **106 C2** 22 13N 27 59 E
Bîr Mogreïn, *Mauritania* **110 C2** 25 10N 11 25W
Bîr Murr, *Egypt* **106 C3** 23 28N 30 10 E
Bi'r Muṭribah, *Kuwait* **96 D5** 29 54N 47 17 E
Bîr Nakheila, *Egypt* **106 C3** 24 1N 30 50 E
Bîr Qaṭia, *Egypt* **103 E1** 30 58N 32 45 E
Bîr Qatrani, *Egypt* **106 A2** 30 55N 26 10 E
Bîr Ranga, *Egypt* **106 C4** 24 25N 35 15 E
Bîr Sahara, *Egypt* **106 C2** 22 54N 28 40 E
Bîr Seiyâla, *Egypt* **106 B3** 26 10N 33 50 E
Bir Semguine, *Morocco* **110 B3** 30 1N 5 39W
Bîr Shalatein, *Egypt* **106 C4** 23 5N 35 25 E
Bîr Shebb, *Egypt* **106 C2** 22 25N 29 40 E
Bîr Shût, *Egypt* **106 C4** 23 50N 35 15 E
Bîr Terfawi, *Egypt* **106 C2** 22 57N 28 55 E
Bi'r Tin Abunda, *Libya* **111 C7** 26 28N 12 27 E
Bîr Umm Qubûr, *Egypt* **106 C3** 24 35N 34 2 E
Bîr Ungât, *Egypt* **106 C3** 22 8N 33 48 E
Bîr Za'farâna, *Egypt* **106 J8** 29 10N 32 40 E
Bîr Zāmūs, *Libya* **108 D3** 24 16N 15 6 E
Bîr Zeidûn, *Egypt* **106 B3** 25 45N 33 40 E
Bira, *Indonesia* **83 B4** 2 3 S 132 2 E
Biramféro, *Guinea* **112 C3** 11 40N 9 10W
Birao, *C.A.R.* **114 A4** 10 20N 22 47 E
Biratnagar, *Nepal* **93 F12** 26 27N 87 17 E
Birawa, *Dem. Rep. of the Congo* **118 C2** 2 20 S 28 48 E
Birch →, *Canada* **142 B6** 58 28N 112 17W
Birch Hills, *Canada* **143 C7** 52 59N 105 25W
Birch I., *Canada* **143 C9** 52 26N 99 54W
Birch L., *N.W.T., Canada* **142 A5** 62 4N 116 33W
Birch L., *Ont., Canada* **140 B1** 51 23N 92 18W
Birch Mts., *Canada* **142 B6** 57 30N 113 10W
Birch River, *Canada* **143 C8** 52 24N 101 6W
Birchip, *Australia* **128 C5** 35 56 S 142 55 E
Birchiş, *Romania* **52 E7** 45 58N 22 9 E
Birchwood, *N.Z.* **131 F2** 45 55 S 167 53 E
Bird, *Canada* **143 B10** 56 30N 94 13W
Bird I. = Aves, I. de, *W. Indies* **165 C7** 15 45N 63 55W
Bird I., *Antarctica* **7 B1** 54 0 S 38 0W
Birdseye, *U.S.A.* **157 F10** 38 19N 86 42W
Birdsville, *Australia* **126 D2** 25 51 S 139 20 E
Birdum Cr. →, *Australia* **124 C5** 15 14 S 133 0 E
Birdwood, *Australia* **128 C3** 34 51 S 138 58 E
Birecik, *Turkey* **101 D8** 37 2N 38 0 E
Birein, *Israel* **103 E3** 30 50N 34 28 E
Bireuen, *Indonesia* **84 A1** 5 14N 96 39 E
Birgu = Vittoriosa, *Malta* **38 F8** 35 54N 14 31 E
Biri, *Norway* **18 D7** 60 58N 10 35 E
Biri →, *Sudan* **107 F2** 7 56N 26 33 E
Birifo, *Gambia* **112 C2** 13 30N 14 0W
Birigui, *Brazil* **175 A5** 21 18 S 50 16W
Birini, *C.A.R.* **114 A4** 7 51N 22 24 E
Birjand, *Iran* **97 C8** 32 53N 59 13 E
Birkeland, *Norway* **18 F4** 58 24N 7 12 E
Birkenfeld, *Germany* **31 F3** 49 38N 7 9 E
Birkenhead, *U.K.* **20 D4** 53 23N 3 2W
Birkerød, *Denmark* **17 J6** 55 50N 12 25 E
Birket Fatmé, *Chad* **109 F3** 12 55N 19 7 E
Birket Qârûn, *Egypt* **106 J7** 29 30N 30 40 E
Birkfeld, *Austria* **34 D8** 47 21N 15 45 E
Birkhadem, *Algeria* **111 A5** 36 43N 3 3 E
Birkirkara, *Malta* **38 F7** 35 54N 14 28 E
Bîrlad = Bârlad, *Romania* **53 D12** 46 15N 27 38 E
Birlik, *Kazakhstan* **65 B6** 43 40N 73 49 E
Birlik, *Kazakhstan* **65 A6** 44 5N 73 31 E
Birmingham, *U.K.* **21 E6** 52 29N 1 52W
Birmingham, *Ala., U.S.A.* **149 J2** 33 31N 86 48W
Birmingham, *Iowa, U.S.A.* **156 D5** 40 53N 91 57W
Birmingham International ✈ (BHX), *U.K.* **21 E6** 52 26N 1 45W
Birmitrapur, *India* **94 C7** 22 24N 84 46 E
Birni Ngaouré, *Niger* **113 C5** 13 5N 2 51 E
Birni Nkonni, *Niger* **113 C6** 13 55N 5 15 E
Birnin Gwari, *Nigeria* **113 C6** 11 0N 6 45 E
Birnin Kebbi, *Nigeria* **113 C5** 12 32N 4 12 E
Birnin Kudu, *Nigeria* **113 C6** 11 30N 9 29 E
Birobidzhan, *Russia* **67 E14** 48 50N 132 50 E
Birougou, Mts., *Gabon* **114 C2** 1 51 S 12 20 E
Birr, *Ireland* **23 C4** 53 6N 7 54W
Birrie →, *Australia* **127 D4** 29 43 S 146 37 E
Birs →, *Switz.* **32 B5** 47 24N 7 32 E
Birsilpur, *India* **92 E5** 28 11N 72 15 E
Birsk, *Russia* **64 D5** 55 25N 55 30 E
Birštonas, *Lithuania* **54 D11** 54 37N 24 2 E
Birtle, *Canada* **143 C8** 50 30N 101 5W
Biryuchiy, *Ukraine* **59 J8** 46 10N 35 0 E
Biržai, *Lithuania* **15 H21** 56 11N 24 45 E
Birzebbugga, *Malta* **38 F8** 35 50N 14 32 E
Birzhi = Madona, *Latvia* **15 H22** 56 53N 26 5 E
Birzula = Kotovsk, *Ukraine* **59 J5** 47 45N 29 35 E
Bisa, *Indonesia* **82 B3** 1 15 S 127 28 E
Bisáccia, *Italy* **47 A8** 41 1N 15 22 E
Bisacquino, *Italy* **46 E6** 37 42N 13 15 E
Bisai, *Japan* **73 B8** 35 16N 136 44 E
Bisalpur, *India* **93 E8** 28 14N 79 48 E
Bisbee, *U.S.A.* **159 L9** 31 27N 109 55W
Biscarrosse, *France* **28 D2** 44 22N 1 20W
Biscarrosse et de Parentis, Étang de, *France* **28 D2** 44 21N 1 10W
Biscay, B. of, *Atl. Oc.* **8 B11** 45 0N 2 0W
Biscay Plain, *Atl. Oc.* **8 B11** 45 0N 8 0W
Biscayne △, *U.S.A.* **153 K9** 25 25N 80 12W
Biscayne B., *U.S.A.* **153 K9** 25 40N 80 12W
Biscéglie, *Italy* **47 A9** 41 14N 16 30 E
Bischheim, *France* **27 D14** 48 37N 7 46 E
Bischoflack = Škofja Loka, *Slovenia* **45 B11** 46 9N 14 19 E
Bischofsburg = Biskupiec, *Poland* **54 E7** 53 53N 20 58 E
Bischofshofen, *Austria* **34 D6** 47 26N 13 14 E
Bischofstal = Ujazd, *Poland* **55 H5** 50 23N 18 21 E
Bischofstein = Bisztynek, *Poland* **54 D7** 54 8N 20 53 E
Bischofswerda, *Germany* **30 D10** 51 7N 14 10 E
Bischofszell, *Switz.* **33 B8** 47 29N 9 15 E
Bischwiller, *France* **27 D14** 48 46N 7 50 E
Biscoe Is., *Antarctica* **7 C17** 66 0 S 67 0W
Biscoitos, *Azores* **9 d1** 38 47N 27 15W
Biscotasing, *Canada* **140 C3** 47 18N 82 9W
Biševo, *Croatia* **45 F13** 42 57N 16 3 E
Bisha, *Eritrea* **107 D4** 15 30N 37 31 E
Bishah, W. →, *Si. Arabia* **98 B3** 21 24N 43 26 E
Bishan, *China* **76 C6** 29 33N 106 12 E
Bishanga, *Dem. Rep. of the Congo* **115 C4** 4 31 S 21 2 E
Bishkek, *Kyrgyzstan* **65 B7** 42 54N 74 46 E
Bishnath, *India* **90 B4** 26 40N 93 10 E
Bishnupur, *India* **93 H12** 23 8N 87 20 E
Bisho, *S. Africa* **117 E4** 32 50 S 27 23 E
Bishop, *Calif., U.S.A.* **160 H8** 37 22N 118 24W
Bishop, *Ga., U.S.A.* **152 B6** 33 49N 83 26W
Bishop, *Tex., U.S.A.* **155 M6** 27 35N 97 48W
Bishop Auckland, *U.K.* **20 C6** 54 39N 1 40W
Bishop's Falls, *Canada* **141 C8** 49 2N 55 30W
Bishop's Stortford, *U.K.* **21 F8** 51 52N 0 10 E
Bisignano, *Italy* **47 C9** 39 31N 16 17 E
Bisina, L., *Uganda* **118 B3** 1 38N 33 56 E
Biskra, *Algeria* **111 B6** 34 50N 5 44 E
Biskra, *Malta* **38 F7** 35 58N 14 21 E
Biskupiec, *Poland* **54 E7** 53 53N 20 58 E
Bismarck, *Mo., U.S.A.* **156 G6** 37 46N 90 38W
Bismarck, *N. Dak., U.S.A.* **154 B4** 46 48N 100 47W
Bismarck Arch., *Papua N. G.* **132 B5** 2 30 S 150 0 E
Bismarck Ra., *Papua N. G.* **132 C3** 5 35 S 145 0 E
Bismarck Sea, *Papua N. G.* **132 C4** 4 10 S 146 50 E
Bismarckburg = Kasanga, *Tanzania* **119 D3** 8 30 S 31 10 E
Bismark, *Germany* **30 C7** 52 40N 11 33 E
Bismil, *Turkey* **101 D9** 37 51N 40 40 E
Bismo, *Norway* **18 C5** 61 54N 8 15 E
Biso, *Uganda* **118 B3** 1 44N 31 26 E
Bison, *U.S.A.* **154 C3** 45 31N 102 28W
Bīsotūn, *Iran* **101 E12** 34 23N 47 26 E
Bispgården, *Sweden* **16 A10** 63 2N 16 40 E
Bissagos = Bijagós, Arquipélago dos, *Guinea-Biss.* **112 C1** 11 15N 16 10W
Bissam Cuttack, *India* **94 E6** 19 31N 83 31 E
Bissau, *Guinea-Biss.* **112 C1** 11 45N 15 45W
Bissaula, *Nigeria* **113 D7** 7 0N 10 27 E
Bissikrima, *Guinea* **112 C2** 10 50N 10 58W
Bissorã, *Guinea-Biss.* **112 C1** 12 16N 15 35W
Bistcho L., *Canada* **142 B5** 59 45N 118 50W
Bistreţ, *Romania* **53 G8** 43 54N 23 23 E
Bistrica = Ilirska-Bistrica, *Slovenia* **45 C11** 45 34N 14 14 E
Bistriţa, *Romania* **53 C9** 47 9N 24 35 E
Bistriţa →, *Romania* **53 D11** 46 30N 26 57 E
Bistriţa Năsăud □, *Romania* **53 C9** 47 15N 24 30 E
Bistriţei, Munţii, *Romania* **53 C10** 47 15N 25 40 E
Biswan, *India* **93 F9** 27 29N 81 2 E
Bisztynek, *Poland* **54 D7** 54 8N 20 53 E
Bita →, *C.A.R.* **114 A4** 6 26N 24 43 E
Bitam, *Gabon* **114 B2** 2 5N 11 25 E
Bitburg, *Germany* **31 F2** 49 58N 6 31 E
Bitche, *France* **27 C14** 49 2N 7 25 E
Bithlo, *U.S.A.* **153 G8** 28 33N 81 6W
Bithynia, *Turkey* **100 B4** 40 40N 31 0 E
Bitkine, *Chad* **109 F3** 11 59N 18 13 E
Bitlis, *Turkey* **101 C10** 38 20N 42 3 E
Bitola, *Macedonia* **50 E5** 41 1N 21 20 E
Bitolj = Bitola, *Macedonia* **50 E5** 41 1N 21 20 E
Bitonto, *Italy* **47 A9** 41 6N 16 41 E
Bitra I., *India* **95 J1** 11 33N 72 9 E
Bitter Creek, *U.S.A.* **158 F9** 41 33N 108 33W
Bitter L. = Buheirat-Murrat-el-Kubra, *Egypt* **106 H8** 30 18N 32 26 E
Bitterfeld, *Germany* **30 D8** 51 37N 12 20 E
Bitterfontein, *S. Africa* **116 E2** 31 1 S 18 32 E
Bitterroot →, *U.S.A.* **158 C6** 46 52N 114 7W
Bitterroot Range, *U.S.A.* **158 D6** 46 0N 114 20W
Bitterwater, *U.S.A.* **160 J6** 36 23N 121 0W
Bitti, *Italy* **46 B2** 40 29N 9 23 E
Bittou, *Burkina Faso* **113 C4** 11 17N 0 18W
Bitung, *Indonesia* **82 A3** 1 27N 125 11 E
Biu, *Nigeria* **113 C7** 10 40N 12 3 E
Bivolari, *Romania* **53 C12** 47 31N 27 27 E
Bivolu, Vf., *Romania* **53 C10** 47 16N 25 58 E
Biwa-Ko, *Japan* **73 B8** 35 15N 136 10 E
Biwabik, *U.S.A.* **154 B8** 47 32N 92 21W
Bixad, *Romania* **53 C8** 47 56N 23 28 E
Bixby, *U.S.A.* **155 H7** 35 57N 95 53W
Biyang, *China* **74 H7** 32 38N 113 21 E
Biysk, *Russia* **66 D9** 52 40N 85 0 E
Bizana, *S. Africa* **117 E4** 30 50 S 29 52 E
Bizen, *Japan* **72 C6** 34 43N 134 8 E
Bizerte, *Tunisia* **108 A1** 37 15N 9 50 E
Bjåen, *Norway* **18 E4** 59 37N 7 26 E
Bjargtangar, *Iceland* **11 B2** 65 30N 24 30W
Bjarkalundur, *Iceland* **11 B4** 65 33N 22 9W
Bjärnum, *Sweden* **17 H7** 56 17N 13 43 E
Bjästa, *Sweden* **16 A12** 63 12N 18 29 E
Bjelasica, *Serbia & M.* **50 D3** 42 50N 19 40 E
Bjelašnica, *Bos.-H.* **52 G3** 43 43N 18 9 E
Bjelland, *Norway* **18 F4** 58 23N 7 32 E
Bjelovar, *Croatia* **45 C13** 45 56N 16 49 E
Bjerringbro, *Denmark* **17 H3** 56 23N 9 39 E
Bjervamoen, *Norway* **18 E6** 59 17N 9 5 E
Bjøberg, *Norway* **18 D5** 60 56N 8 13 E
Björbo, *Sweden* **16 D8** 60 27N 14 44 E
Bjørkelangen, *Norway* **18 E8** 59 53N 11 34 E
Björklinge, *Sweden* **16 D11** 60 2N 17 33 E
Bjørnafjorden, *Norway* **18 D2** 60 7N 5 28 E
Björneborg = Pori, *Finland* **15 F19** 61 29N 21 48 E
Björneborg, *Sweden* **16 E8** 59 14N 14 16 E
Bjørnevatn, *Norway* **14 B23** 69 40N 30 0 E
Bjørnøya, *Arctic* **6 B8** 74 30N 19 0 E
Bjursås, *Sweden* **16 D9** 60 44N 15 25 E
Bjuv, *Sweden* **17 H6** 56 5N 12 55 E
Bla, *Mali* **112 C3** 12 56N 5 47W
Blace, *Serbia & M.* **50 C5** 43 18N 21 17 E
Blachownia, *Poland* **55 H5** 50 49N 18 56 E
Black = Da →, *Vietnam* **76 G5** 21 15N 105 20 E
Black →, *Canada* **150 B5** 44 42N 79 19W
Black →, *Alaska, U.S.A.* **144 C11** 66 42N 144 42W
Black →, *Ariz., U.S.A.* **159 K8** 33 44N 110 13W
Black →, *Ark., U.S.A.* **155 H9** 35 38N 91 20W
Black →, *La., U.S.A.* **155 K9** 31 16N 91 50W
Black →, *Mich., U.S.A.* **150 D2** 42 59N 82 27W
Black →, *N.Y., U.S.A.* **151 C8** 43 59N 76 4W
Black →, *Wis., U.S.A.* **154 D9** 43 57N 91 22W
Black Bay Pen., *Canada* **140 C2** 48 38N 88 21W
Black Birch L., *Canada* **143 B7** 56 53N 107 45W
Black Canyon of the Gunnison ⌓, *U.S.A.* **159 G10** 38 40N 107 35W
Black Diamond = Pittsburg, *U.S.A.* **160 G5** 38 2N 121 53W
Black Diamond, *Canada* **142 C6** 50 45N 114 14W
Black Duck →, *Canada* **140 A2** 56 51N 89 2W
Black Forest = Schwarzwald, *Germany* **31 G4** 48 30N 8 20 E
Black Forest, *U.S.A.* **154 F2** 39 0N 104 43W
Black Hd., *Ireland* **23 C2** 53 9N 9 16W
Black Hills, *U.S.A.* **154 D3** 44 0N 103 45W
Black I., *Canada* **143 C9** 51 12N 96 30W
Black L., *Canada* **143 B7** 59 12N 105 15W
Black L., *Mich., U.S.A.* **148 C3** 45 28N 84 16W
Black L., *N.Y., U.S.A.* **151 B9** 44 31N 75 36W
Black Lake, *Canada* **143 B7** 59 11N 105 20W
Black Mesa, *U.S.A.* **155 G3** 36 58N 102 58W
Black Mountain, *Australia* **129 A9** 30 18 S 151 39 E
Black Mt. = Mynydd Du, *U.K.* **21 F4** 51 52N 3 50W
Black Mts., *U.K.* **21 F4** 51 55N 3 7W
Black Range, *U.S.A.* **159 K10** 33 15N 107 50W
Black River, *Jamaica* **164 a** 18 0N 77 50W
Black River Falls, *U.S.A.* **154 C9** 44 18N 90 51W
Black Rock, *Australia* **128 B3** 32 50 S 138 44 E
Black Rock, *Barbados* **165 g** 13 7N 59 37W
Black Sea, *Eurasia* **57 F6** 43 30N 35 0 E
Black Tickle, *Canada* **141 B8** 53 28N 55 45W
Black Volta →, *Africa* **112 D4** 8 41N 1 33W
Black Warrior →, *U.S.A.* **149 J2** 32 32N 87 51W
Blackall, *Australia* **126 C4** 24 25 S 145 45 E
Blackball, *N.Z.* **131 C6** 42 22 S 171 26 E
Blackbull, *Australia* **126 B3** 17 55 S 141 45 E
Blackburn, *U.K.* **20 D5** 53 45N 2 29W
Blackburn, Mt., *U.S.A.* **144 F12** 61 44N 143 26W
Blackburn with Darwen □, *U.K.* **20 D5** 53 45N 2 29W
Blackdown Tableland △, *Australia* **126 C4** 23 52 S 149 8 E
Blackfoot, *U.S.A.* **158 E7** 43 11N 112 21W
Blackfoot →, *U.S.A.* **158 C7** 46 52N 113 53W
Blackfoot River Reservoir, *U.S.A.* **158 E8** 43 0N 111 43W
Blackman, *U.S.A.* **153 E3** 30 56N 86 38W
Blackpool, *U.K.* **20 D4** 53 49N 3 3W
Blackpool □, *U.K.* **20 D4** 53 49N 3 3W
Blackriver, *U.S.A.* **150 B1** 44 46N 83 17W
Blacks Harbour, *Canada* **141 C6** 45 3N 66 49W
Blacksburg, *U.S.A.* **148 G5** 37 14N 80 25W
Blackshear, *U.S.A.* **152 D7** 31 18N 82 14W
Blackshear, L., *U.S.A.* **152 D6** 31 51N 83 56W
Blacksod B., *Ireland* **23 B1** 54 6N 10 0W
Blackstone, *U.S.A.* **148 G7** 37 4N 78 0W
Blackstone Ra., *Australia* **125 E4** 26 0 S 128 30 E
Blackville, *U.S.A.* **152 B8** 33 22N 81 16W
Blackwater = West Road →, *Canada* **142 C4** 53 18N 122 53W
Blackwater, *Australia* **126 C4** 23 35 S 148 53 E
Blackwater →, *Meath, Ireland* **23 C4** 53 39N 6 41W
Blackwater →, *Waterford, Ireland* **23 D4** 52 4N 7 52W
Blackwater →, *U.K.* **23 B5** 54 31N 6 35W
Blackwater →, *Fla., U.S.A.* **153 E2** 30 36N 87 2W
Blackwater →, *Mo., U.S.A.* **156 F4** 38 59N 92 59W
Blackwell, *U.S.A.* **155 G6** 36 48N 97 17W
Blackwells Corner, *U.S.A.* **161 K7** 35 37N 119 47W
Blackwood, C., *Papua N. G.* **132 D3** 7 49 S 144 31 E
Bladensburg △, *Australia* **126 C3** 22 30 S 142 59 E
Blaenau Ffestiniog, *U.K.* **20 E4** 53 0N 3 56W
Blaenau Gwent □, *U.K.* **21 F4** 51 48N 3 12W
Bláfell, *Iceland* **11 C7** 64 30N 19 51W
Bláfjall, *Iceland* **11 B10** 65 26N 16 50W
Blagaj, *Bos.-H.* **50 C1** 43 16N 17 55 E
Blagnac, *France* **28 E5** 43 37N 1 23 E
Blagnac, Toulouse ✈ (TLS), *France* **28 E5** 43 37N 1 22 E
Blagodarnoye = Blagodarnyy, *Russia* **61 H6** 45 7N 43 37 E
Blagodarnyy, *Russia* **61 H6** 45 7N 43 37 E
Blagoevgrad, *Bulgaria* **50 D7** 42 2N 23 5 E
Blagoveshchenka, *Kazakhstan* **65 B7** 43 18N 74 12 E
Blagoveshchensk, *Amur, Russia* **67 D13** 50 20N 127 30 E
Blagoveshchensk, *Bashkortostan, Russia* **64 D5** 55 1N 55 59 E
Blahkiuh, *Indonesia* **79 J18** 8 31 S 115 12 E
Blain, *France* **26 E5** 47 29N 1 45W
Blain, *U.S.A.* **150 F7** 40 20N 77 31W
Blaine, *Minn., U.S.A.* **154 C8** 45 10N 93 13W
Blaine, *Wash., U.S.A.* **160 B4** 48 59N 122 45W
Blaine Lake, *Canada* **143 C7** 52 51N 106 52W
Blair, *U.S.A.* **154 E6** 41 33N 96 8W
Blair Athol, *Australia* **126 C4** 22 42 S 147 31 E
Blair Atholl, *U.K.* **22 E5** 56 46N 3 50W
Blairgowrie, *U.K.* **22 E5** 56 35N 3 21W
Blairsden, *U.S.A.* **160 F6** 39 47N 120 37W
Blairsville, *U.S.A.* **150 F5** 40 26N 79 16W
Blaj, *Romania* **53 D8** 46 10N 23 57 E
Blaka, *Niger* **109 D2** 21 21N 12 47 E
Blakang Mati, Pulau, *Singapore* **87 d** 1 15N 103 50 E
Blake Pt., *U.S.A.* **154 A10** 48 11N 88 25W
Blakely, *Ga., U.S.A.* **152 D5** 31 23N 84 56W
Blakely, *Pa., U.S.A.* **151 E9** 41 28N 75 37W
Blakeng Mati, Pulau = Sentosa, *Singapore* **87 d** 1 15N 103 50 E
Blakesburg, *U.S.A.* **156 D4** 40 58N 92 38W
Blakstad, *Norway* **18 F5** 58 30N 8 39 E
Blâmont, *France* **27 D13** 48 35N 6 50 E
Blanc, C., *Spain* **38 B3** 39 21N 2 51 E
Blanc, C., *Tunisia* **108 A1** 37 15N 9 56 E
Blanc, Mont, *Europe* **29 C10** 45 48N 6 50 E
Blanc-Sablon, *Canada* **141 B8** 51 24N 57 12W
Blanca, B., *Argentina* **176 A4** 39 10 S 61 30W
Blanca Peak, *U.S.A.* **159 H11** 37 35N 105 29W
Blanchardville, *U.S.A.* **156 B7** 42 49N 89 52W
Blanche, C., *Australia* **127 E1** 33 1 S 134 9 E
Blanche, L., *S. Austral., Australia* **127 D2** 29 15 S 139 40 E
Blanche, L., *W. Austral., Australia* **124 D3** 22 25 S 123 17 E
Blanche Channel, *Solomon Is.* **133 M9** 8 30 S 157 30 E
Blanchester, *U.S.A.* **157 E13** 39 17N 83 59W
Blanchisseuse, *Trin. & Tob.* **169 F9** 10 48N 61 18W
Blanco, *S. Africa* **116 E3** 33 55 S 22 23 E
Blanco, *U.S.A.* **155 K5** 30 6N 98 25W
Blanco →, *Argentina* **174 C2** 30 20 S 68 42W
Blanco →, *Bolivia* **173 C5** 12 30 S 64 18W
Blanco, C., *Costa Rica* **164 E2** 9 34N 85 8W
Blanco, C., *U.S.A.* **158 E1** 42 51N 124 34W
Blanda →, *Iceland* **11 B6** 65 37N 20 9W
Blandford Forum, *U.K.* **21 G5** 50 51N 2 9W
Blanding, *U.S.A.* **159 H9** 37 37N 109 29W
Blandinsville, *U.S.A.* **156 D6** 40 33N 90 52W
Blanes, *Spain* **40 D7** 41 40N 2 48 E
Blangy-sur-Bresle, *France* **27 C8** 49 55N 1 37 E
Blanice →, *Czech Rep.* **34 B7** 49 10N 14 5 E
Blankaholm, *Sweden* **17 G10** 57 36N 16 31 E
Blankenberge, *Belgium* **24 C3** 51 20N 3 9 E
Blankenburg, *Germany* **30 D6** 51 47N 10 57 E
Blanquefort, *France* **28 D3** 44 55N 0 38W
Blanquillo, *Uruguay* **175 C4** 32 53 S 55 37W
Blansko, *Czech Rep.* **35 B9** 49 22N 16 40 E
Blantyre, *Malawi* **119 F4** 15 45 S 35 0 E
Blarney, *Ireland* **23 E3** 51 56N 8 33W
Blasdell, *U.S.A.* **150 D6** 42 48N 78 50W
Blåsjø, *Norway* **18 E3** 59 20N 6 50 E
Błaszki, *Poland* **55 G5** 51 38N 18 30 E
Blatná, *Czech Rep.* **34 B6** 49 25N 13 52 E
Blato, *Croatia* **45 F13** 42 56N 16 48 E
Blatten, *Switz.* **32 D5** 46 20N 7 50 E
Blaubeuren, *Germany* **31 G5** 48 24N 9 46 E
Blaustein, *Germany* **31 G5** 48 25N 9 53 E
Blåvands Huk, *Denmark* **17 J2** 55 33N 8 4 E
Blaydon, *U.K.* **20 C6** 54 58N 1 42W
Blaye, *France* **28 C3** 45 8N 0 40W
Blaye-les-Mines, *France* **28 D6** 44 1N 2 8 E
Blayney, *Australia* **129 B8** 33 32 S 149 14 E
Blaze, Pt., *Australia* **124 B5** 12 56 S 130 11 E
Błażowa, *Poland* **55 J9** 49 53N 22 7 E
Blechhammer = Blachownia, *Poland* **55 H5** 50 49N 18 56 E
Bleckede, *Germany* **30 B6** 53 17N 10 43 E
Bled, *Slovenia* **45 B11** 46 27N 14 7 E
Blefjell, *Norway* **18 E6** 59 48N 9 10 E
Bleiburg, *Austria* **34 E7** 46 35N 14 49 E
Blejeşti, *Romania* **53 F10** 44 19N 25 27 E
Blekinge, *Sweden* **15 H16** 56 25N 15 20 E
Blekinge län □, *Sweden* **17 H9** 56 20N 15 20 E
Blenheim, *Canada* **150 D3** 42 20N 82 0W
Blenheim, *N.Z.* **131 B8** 41 38 S 173 57 E
Bléone →, *France* **29 D10** 44 5N 6 0 E
Blérancourt, *France* **27 C10** 49 31N 3 9 E
Bletchley, *U.K.* **21 F7** 51 59N 0 44W
Blida, *Algeria* **111 A5** 36 30N 2 49 E
Blidet Amor, *Algeria* **111 B6** 32 59N 5 58 E
Blidö, *Sweden* **16 E12** 59 37N 18 53 E
Blidsberg, *Sweden* **17 G7** 57 56N 13 30 E
Blieskastel, *Germany* **31 F3** 49 14N 7 12 E
Bligh Sound, *N.Z.* **131 E2** 44 47 S 167 32 E
Bligh Water, *Fiji* **133 A2** 17 0 S 178 0 E
Blind River, *Canada* **140 C3** 46 10N 82 58W
Blinisht, *Albania* **50 E3** 41 52N 19 59 E
Blinnenhorn, *Switz.* **33 D6** 46 26N 8 19 E
Bliss, *Idaho, U.S.A.* **158 E6** 42 56N 114 57W
Bliss, *N.Y., U.S.A.* **150 D6** 42 34N 78 15W
Blissfield, *Mich., U.S.A.* **157 C13** 41 50N 83 52W
Blissfield, *Ohio, U.S.A.* **150 F3** 40 24N 81 58W
Blitar, *Indonesia* **85 D4** 8 5 S 112 11 E
Blitchton, *U.S.A.* **152 C8** 32 12N 81 26W
Blitta, *Togo* **113 D5** 8 23N 1 6 E
Block I., *U.S.A.* **151 E13** 41 11N 71 35W
Block Island Sd., *U.S.A.* **151 E13** 41 15N 71 40W
Bloemfontein, *S. Africa* **116 D4** 29 6 S 26 7 E
Bloemhof, *S. Africa* **116 D4** 27 38 S 25 32 E
Blois, *France* **26 E8** 47 35N 1 20 E
Blomskog, *Sweden* **16 E6** 59 16N 12 2 E
Blomstermåla, *Sweden* **17 H10** 56 59N 16 21 E
Blomvåg, *Norway* **18 D1** 60 32N 4 50 E
Blonay, *Switz.* **32 D3** 46 28N 6 54 E
Blönduós, *Iceland* **11 B6** 65 40N 20 12W
Blongas, *Indonesia* **79 K19** 8 53 S 116 2 E
Błonie, *Poland* **55 F7** 52 12N 20 37 E
Bloodvein →, *Canada* **143 C9** 51 47N 96 43W
Bloody Foreland, *Ireland* **23 A3** 55 10N 8 17W
Bloom = Chicago Heights, *U.S.A.* **157 C9** 41 30N 87 38W
Bloomer, *U.S.A.* **154 C9** 45 6N 91 29W
Bloomfield, *Canada* **150 C7** 43 59N 77 14W
Bloomfield, *Ind., U.S.A.* **157 E10** 39 1N 86 57W
Bloomfield, *Iowa, U.S.A.* **156 D4** 40 45N 92 25W
Bloomfield, *Ky., U.S.A.* **157 G11** 37 55N 85 19W
Bloomfield, *N. Mex., U.S.A.* **159 H10** 36 43N 107 59W
Bloomfield, *Nebr., U.S.A.* **154 D6** 42 36N 97 39W
Bloomingburg, *U.S.A.* **157 E13** 39 36N 83 24W
Bloomington, *Ill., U.S.A.* **156 D8** 40 28N 89 0W
Bloomington, *Ind., U.S.A.* **157 E10** 39 10N 86 32W
Bloomington, *Minn., U.S.A.* **154 C8** 44 50N 93 17W
Bloomington, *Wis., U.S.A.* **156 B6** 42 53N 90 55W
Bloomsburg, *U.S.A.* **151 F8** 41 0N 76 27W
Bloomsbury, *Australia* **126 J6** 20 48 S 148 38 E
Blora, *Indonesia* **85 D4** 6 57 S 111 25 E
Blossburg, *U.S.A.* **150 E7** 41 41N 77 4W
Blosseville Kyst, *Greenland* **10 D8** 68 50N 26 30W
Blotzheim, *France* **32 A4** 47 36N 7 29 E
Blouberg, *S. Africa* **117 C4** 23 8 S 28 59 E
Blountstown, *U.S.A.* **152 E4** 30 27N 85 3W
Bludenz, *Austria* **34 D2** 47 10N 9 50 E
Blue →, *U.S.A.* **157 F10** 38 11N 86 19W
Blue Cypress L., *U.S.A.* **153 H9** 27 44N 80 45W
Blue Earth, *U.S.A.* **154 D8** 43 38N 94 6W
Blue Hole △, *Belize* **164 C2** 17 24N 88 30W
Blue Lagoon △, *Zambia* **119 F2** 15 28 S 27 26 E
Blue Mesa Reservoir, *U.S.A.* **159 G10** 38 28N 107 20W
Blue Mound, *U.S.A.* **156 E7** 39 42N 89 7W
Blue Mountain Lake, *U.S.A.* **151 C10** 43 52N 74 30W
Blue Mountain Pk., *Jamaica* **164 a** 18 3N 76 36W
Blue Mts., *Australia* **129 B9** 33 40 S 150 15 E
Blue Mts., *Jamaica* **164 a** 18 3N 76 36W
Blue Mts., *Maine, U.S.A.* **151 B14** 44 50N 70 35W
Blue Mts., *Oreg., U.S.A.* **158 D4** 45 15N 119 0W
Blue Mts., *Pa., U.S.A.* **151 F8** 40 30N 76 30W
Blue Mts. △, *Australia* **129 C9** 34 2 S 150 15 E
Blue Mud B., *Australia* **126 A2** 13 30 S 136 0 E
Blue Nile = Nîl el Azraq →, *Sudan* **107 D3** 15 38N 32 31 E
Blue Nile Falls, *Ethiopia* **107 E4** 11 25N 37 45 E
Blue Rapids, *U.S.A.* **154 F6** 39 41N 96 39W
Blue Ridge Mts., *U.S.A.* **149 G5** 36 30N 80 15W
Blue River, *Canada* **142 C5** 52 6N 119 18W
Blue Springs, *U.S.A.* **156 E2** 39 1N 94 17W
Bluefield, *U.S.A.* **148 G5** 37 15N 81 17W
Bluefields, *Nic.* **164 D3** 12 20N 83 50W
Bluff, *Australia* **126 C4** 23 35 S 149 4 E
Bluff, *N.Z.* **131 G3** 46 37 S 168 20 E
Bluff, *U.S.A.* **159 H9** 37 17N 109 33W
Bluff Harbour, *N.Z.* **131 G3** 46 36 S 168 21 E
Bluff Knoll, *Australia* **125 F2** 34 24 S 118 15 E
Bluff Pt., *Australia* **125 E1** 27 50 S 114 5 E
Bluffs, *U.S.A.* **156 E6** 39 45N 90 32W
Bluffton, *Ga., U.S.A.* **152 D5** 31 31N 84 52W
Bluffton, *Ind., U.S.A.* **157 D11** 40 44N 85 11W
Bluffton, *Ohio, U.S.A.* **157 D13** 40 54N 83 54W
Bluffton, *S.C., U.S.A.* **152 C9** 32 14N 80 52W
Blumenau = Stettler, *Canada* **142 C6** 52 19N 112 40W
Blumenau, *Brazil* **175 B6** 27 0 S 49 0W
Blümisalphorn, *Switz.* **32 D5** 46 28N 7 47 E
Blunt, *U.S.A.* **154 C5** 44 31N 99 59W
Bly, *U.S.A.* **158 E3** 42 24N 121 3W
Blyde River Canyon ⌓, *S. Africa* **117 C5** 24 37 S 31 2 E
Blyth, *Australia* **128 B3** 33 49 S 138 28 E
Blyth, *Canada* **150 C3** 43 44N 81 26W
Blyth, *U.K.* **20 B6** 55 8N 1 31W
Blythe, *Calif., U.S.A.* **161 M12** 33 37N 114 36W
Blythe, *Ga., U.S.A.* **152 B7** 33 17N 82 12W
Blytheville, *U.S.A.* **155 H10** 35 56N 89 55W
Bø, *Norway* **18 E6** 59 25N 9 3 E
Bo, *S. Leone* **112 D2** 7 55N 11 50W
Bo Duc, *Vietnam* **87 G6** 11 58N 106 50 E
Bo Hai, *China* **75 E10** 39 0N 119 0 E
Bō-no-Misaki, *Japan* **72 F2** 31 15N 130 13 E
Bo Xian = Bozhou, *China* **74 H8** 33 55N 115 41 E
Boa Esperança, *Brazil* **169 C5** 3 21N 61 23W
Boa Esperança, Represa, *Brazil* **170 C3** 6 50 S 43 50W
Boa Nova, *Brazil* **171 D3** 14 22 S 40 10W
Boa Viagem, *Brazil* **170 C4** 5 7 S 39 44W
Boa Vista = Tocantinópolis, *Brazil* **170 C2** 6 20 S 47 25W
Boa Vista, *Brazil* **169 C5** 2 48N 60 30W
Boa Vista, *C. Verde Is.* **9 j** 16 0N 22 49W
Boa Vista do Erechim = Erechim, *Brazil* **175 B5** 27 35 S 52 15W
Boac, *Phil.* **80 E3** 13 27N 121 50 E
Boaco, *Nic.* **164 D2** 12 29N 85 35W
Bo'ai, *China* **74 G7** 35 10N 113 3 E
Boal, *Spain* **42 B4** 43 25N 6 49W
Boali, *C.A.R.* **114 B3** 4 48N 18 7 E
Boalsburg, *U.S.A.* **150 F7** 40 46N 77 47W
Boane, *Mozam.* **117 D5** 26 6 S 32 19 E
Boang I., *Papua N. G.* **132 B7** 3 23 S 153 18 E
Boano, *Indonesia* **82 B3** 3 0 S 127 56 E
Boardman, *U.S.A.* **150 E4** 41 2N 80 40W
Boath, *India* **94 E4** 19 20N 78 20 E
Boatswain Bird I., *Ascension I.* **9 g** 7 56 S 14 18W
Bobadah, *Australia* **129 B7** 32 19 S 146 41 E
Bobai, *China* **76 F7** 22 17N 109 59 E
Bobbili, *India* **94 E6** 18 35N 83 30 E
Bóbbio, *Italy* **44 D6** 44 46N 9 23 E
Bobcaygeon, *Canada* **140 D4** 44 33N 78 33W
Boblad, *India* **94 F2** 17 13N 75 26 E
Böblingen, *Germany* **31 G5** 48 40N 9 1 E
Bobo-Dioulasso, *Burkina Faso* **112 C4** 11 8N 4 13W
Bobolice, *Poland* **54 E3** 53 58N 16 37 E
Bobon, *Phil.* **80 E5** 12 32N 124 34 E
Bobonaro, *E. Timor* **82 C3** 9 2 S 125 22 E
Bobonaza →, *Ecuador* **168 D2** 2 36 S 76 38W
Boboshevo, *Bulgaria* **50 D7** 42 9N 23 0 E
Bobov Dol, *Bulgaria* **50 D6** 42 20N 23 0 E
Bóbr →, *Poland* **55 F2** 52 4N 15 4 E
Bobraomby, Tanjon' i, *Madag.* **117 A8** 12 40 S 49 10 E
Bobrinets, *Ukraine* **59 H7** 48 4N 32 5 E
Bobrov, *Russia* **60 E5** 51 5N 40 2 E
Bobrovitsa, *Ukraine* **59 G6** 50 45N 31 23 E
Bobruysk = Babruysk, *Belarus* **59 F5** 53 10N 29 15 E
Bobures, *Venezuela* **168 B3** 9 15N 71 11W
Boca de Drago, *Venezuela* **169 F9** 11 0N 61 50W
Bôca do Acre, *Brazil* **172 B4** 8 50 S 67 27W
Bôca do Jari, *Brazil* **169 D7** 1 7 S 51 58W
Bôca do Moaco, *Brazil* **172 B4** 7 41 S 68 17W
Boca Grande, *U.S.A.* **153 J7** 26 45N 82 16W
Boca Grande, *Venezuela* **169 B5** 8 40N 60 40W
Boca Raton, *U.S.A.* **153 J9** 26 21N 80 5W
Bocaiúva, *Brazil* **171 E3** 17 7 S 43 49W
Bocanda, *Ivory C.* **112 D4** 7 5N 4 31W
Bocaranga, *C.A.R.* **114 A3** 7 0N 15 35 E
Bocas del Toro, *Panama* **164 E3** 9 15N 82 20W
Boceguillas, *Spain* **42 D7** 41 20N 3 39W
Bochkarevo = Belogorsk, *Russia* **67 D13** 51 0N 128 20 E
Bochmanivka, *Ukraine* **53 C14** 47 40N 29 34 E
Bochnia, *Poland* **55 J7** 49 58N 20 27 E
Bocholt, *Germany* **30 D2** 51 50N 6 36 E
Bochum, *Germany* **30 D3** 51 28N 7 13 E
Bockenem, *Germany* **30 C6** 52 1N 10 8 E
Boćki, *Poland* **55 F10** 52 39N 23 3 E
Bocognano, *France* **29 F13** 42 5N 9 4 E
Bocoio, *Angola* **115 E2** 12 28 S 14 10 E
Boconó, *Venezuela* **168 B3** 9 15N 70 16W
Boconó →, *Venezuela* **168 B4** 8 43N 69 34W
Bocoyna, *Mexico* **162 B3** 27 52N 107 35W
Bocşa, *Romania* **52 E6** 45 21N 21 47 E
Boda, *C.A.R.* **114 B3** 4 19N 17 26 E
Boda, *Dalarna, Sweden* **16 C9** 61 1N 15 13 E
Böda, *Kalmar, Sweden* **17 G11** 57 15N 17 3 E
Boda, *Västernorrland, Sweden* **16 B10** 62 52N 16 39 E
Bodafors, *Sweden* **17 G8** 57 48N 14 23 E
Bodaybo, *Russia* **67 D12** 57 50N 114 0 E
Boddam, *U.K.* **22 B7** 59 56N 1 17W
Boddington, *Australia* **125 F2** 32 50 S 116 30 E
Bode Sadu, *Nigeria* **113 D5** 9 0N 4 47 E
Bodega Bay, *U.S.A.* **160 G3** 38 20N 123 3W
Boden, *Sweden* **14 D19** 65 50N 21 42 E
Bodensee, *Europe* **33 A8** 47 35N 9 25 E
Bodenteich, *Germany* **30 C6** 52 50N 10 42 E
Bodhan, *India* **94 E3** 18 40N 77 44 E
Bodinayakkanur, *India* **95 J3** 10 2N 77 10 E
Bodinga, *Nigeria* **113 C6** 12 58N 5 10 E
Bodio, *Switz.* **33 D7** 46 23N 8 55 E
Bodmin, *U.K.* **21 G3** 50 28N 4 43W
Bodmin Moor, *U.K.* **21 G3** 50 33N 4 36W
Bodø, *Norway* **14 C16** 67 17N 14 24 E
Bodoquena, Serra da, *Brazil* **173 E6** 21 0 S 56 50W

Bodoupa, *C.A.R.* **114 A3** 5 43N 17 36 E
Bodrichi, *Chad* **109 E3** 19 11N 15 54 E
Bodrog →, *Hungary* **52 B6** 48 11N 21 22 E
Bodrum, *Turkey* **49 D9** 37 3N 27 30 E
Boduna, *Dem. Rep. of the Congo* **114 A3** 5 5N 19 44 E
Bódva →, *Hungary* **52 B5** 48 19N 20 45 E
Boembé, *Congo* **114 C3** 2 54 S 15 39 E
Boën, *France* **29 C8** 45 44N 4 1 E
Boende, *Dem. Rep. of the Congo* **114 C4** 0 24 S 21 12 E
Boerne, *U.S.A.* **155 L5** 29 47N 98 44W
Boesmans →, *S. Africa* **116 E4** 33 42 S 26 39 E
Boffa, *Guinea* **112 C2** 10 16N 14 3W
Bofuku, *Dem. Rep. of the Congo* **114 C4** 0 57 S 20 53 E
Bogale, *Burma* **90 G5** 16 17N 95 24 E
Bogalusa, *U.S.A.* **155 K10** 30 47N 89 52W
Bogan →, *Australia* **129 A7** 30 20 S 146 55 E
Bogan Gate, *Australia* **129 B7** 33 7 S 147 49 E
Bogandé, *Burkina Faso* **113 C4** 13 2N 0 8W
Bogangolo, *C.A.R.* **114 A3** 5 34N 18 15 E
Bogantungan, *Australia* **126 C4** 23 41 S 147 17 E
Bogata, *U.S.A.* **155 J7** 33 28N 95 13W
Bogatić, *Serbia & M.* **50 B3** 44 51N 19 30 E
Boğazkale, *Turkey* **100 B6** 40 2N 34 37 E
Boğazlıyan, *Turkey* **100 C6** 39 11N 35 14 E
Bogbonga, *Dem. Rep. of the Congo* **114 B3** 1 36N 19 24 E
Bogdanovich, *Russia* **64 C9** 56 47N 62 1 E
Bogen, *Sweden* **16 D6** 60 4N 12 33 E
Bogense, *Denmark* **17 J4** 55 34N 10 5 E
Bogetići, *Serbia & M.* **50 D2** 42 41N 18 58 E
Boggabilla, *Australia* **127 D5** 28 36 S 150 24 E
Boggabri, *Australia* **129 A9** 30 45 S 150 5 E
Boggeragh Mts., *Ireland* **23 D3** 52 2N 8 55W
Boghari = Ksar el Boukhari, *Algeria* **111 A5** 35 51N 2 52 E
Bogia, *Papua N. G.* **132 C3** 4 9 S 145 0 E
Boglan = Solhan, *Turkey* **101 C9** 38 57N 41 3 E
Bognor Regis, *U.K.* **21 G7** 50 47N 0 40W
Bogo, *Phil.* **81 F4** 11 3N 124 0 E
Bogodukhov = Bohodukhiv, *Ukraine* **59 G8** 50 9N 35 33 E
Bogol Manya, *Ethiopia* **107 G5** 4 34N 41 29 E
Bogong, Mt., *Australia* **129 D7** 36 47 S 147 17 E
Bogor, *Indonesia* **84 D3** 6 36 S 106 48 E
Bogoroditsk, *Russia* **58 F10** 53 47N 38 8 E
Bogorodsk = Noginsk, *Russia* **58 E10** 55 50N 38 25 E
Bogorodsk, *Russia* **60 B6** 56 4N 43 30 E
Bogorodskoye = Kamskoye Ustye, *Russia* **60 C9** 55 10N 49 20 E
Bogorodskoye = Leninskoye, *Russia* **60 A8** 58 23N 47 3 E
Bogoslovsky = Karpinsk, *Russia* **64 B8** 59 45N 60 1 E
Bogoso, *Ghana* **112 D4** 5 38N 2 3W
Bogotá, *Colombia* **168 C3** 4 34N 74 0W
Bogotol, *Russia* **66 D9** 56 15N 89 50 E
Bogou, *Togo* **113 C5** 10 40N 0 12 E
Bogra, *Bangla.* **90 C2** 24 51N 89 22 E
Boguchany, *Russia* **67 D10** 58 40N 97 30 E
Boguchar, *Russia* **60 F5** 49 55N 40 32 E
Bogué, *Mauritania* **112 B2** 16 45N 14 10W
Boguslav, *Ukraine* **59 H6** 49 33N 30 56 E
Boguszów-Gorce, *Poland* **55 H3** 50 45N 16 12 E
Bohain-en-Vermandois, *France* **27 C10** 49 59N 3 28 E
Bohdan, *Ukraine* **53 B9** 48 2N 24 22 E
Bohemian Forest = Böhmerwald, *Germany* **31 F9** 49 8N 13 14 E
Bohena Cr. →, *Australia* **129 A8** 30 17 S 149 42 E
Bohinjska Bistrica, *Slovenia* **45 B11** 46 17N 14 1 E
Böhmerwald, *Germany* **31 F9** 49 8N 13 14 E
Böhmisch-Brod = Český Brod, *Czech Rep.* **34 A7** 50 4N 14 52 E
Böhmisch-Leipa = Česká Lípa, *Czech Rep.* **34 A7** 50 45N 14 30 E
Böhmisch-Trübau = Česká Třebová, *Czech Rep.* **35 B9** 49 54N 16 27 E
Bohmte, *Germany* **30 C4** 52 22N 8 19 E
Bohodukhiv, *Ukraine* **59 G8** 50 9N 35 33 E
Bohol, *Somali Rep.* **120 C3** 5 45N 46 9 E
Bohol □, *Phil.* **81 G5** 9 50N 124 10 E
Bohol Sea, *Phil.* **81 G5** 9 0N 124 0 E
Bohol Str., *Phil.* **81 G4** 9 45N 123 40 E
Bohongou, *Burkina Faso* **113 C5** 12 30N 0 40 E
Böhönye, *Hungary* **52 D2** 46 25N 17 28 E
Bohorodchany, *Ukraine* **53 B9** 48 48N 24 32 E
Bohotleh, *Somali Rep.* **120 C3** 8 20N 46 25 E
Bohuslän, *Sweden* **17 F5** 58 25N 12 0 E
Boi, *Nigeria* **113 D6** 9 35N 9 27 E
Boi, Pta. de, *Brazil* **175 A6** 23 55 S 45 15W
Boiaçu, *Brazil* **169 D5** 0 27 S 61 46W
Boigu I., *Australia* **132 E2** 9 15 S 142 14 E
Boileau, C., *Australia* **124 C3** 17 40 S 122 7 E
Boim, *Brazil* **169 D6** 2 49 S 55 10W
Boing'o, *Sudan* **107 F3** 9 58N 33 44 E
Boipariguda, *India* **94 E6** 18 46N 82 26 E
Boipeba, I. de, *Brazil* **171 D4** 13 39 S 38 55W
Boiro, *Spain* **42 C2** 42 39N 8 54W
Bois →, *Brazil* **171 E1** 18 35 S 50 2W
Boise, *U.S.A.* **158 E5** 43 37N 116 13W
Boise City, *U.S.A.* **155 G3** 36 44N 102 31W
Boissevain, *Canada* **143 D8** 49 15N 100 5W
Bóite →, *Italy* **45 B9** 46 5N 12 5 E
Boitzenburg, *Germany* **30 B9** 53 16N 13 35 E
Boizenburg, *Germany* **30 B6** 53 23N 10 43 E
Bojador, C., *W. Sahara* **110 C2** 26 0N 14 30W
Bojana →, *Albania* **50 E3** 41 52N 19 22 E
Bojano, *Italy* **47 A7** 41 29N 14 29 E
Bojanowo, *Poland* **55 G3** 51 43N 16 42 E
Bøjden, *Denmark* **17 J4** 55 6N 10 7 E
Bojnūrd, *Iran* **97 B8** 37 30N 57 20 E
Bojonegoro, *Indonesia* **85 D4** 7 11 S 111 54 E
Boju, *Nigeria* **113 D6** 7 22N 7 55 E
Boka, *Serbia & M.* **52 E5** 45 22N 20 52 E
Boka Kotorska, *Serbia & M.* **50 D2** 42 23N 18 32 E
Bokada, *Dem. Rep. of the Congo* **114 B3** 4 8N 19 23 E
Bokala, *Dem. Rep. of the Congo* **114 C3** 3 8 S 17 4 E
Bokala, *Ivory C.* **112 D4** 8 31N 4 33W
Bokani, *Nigeria* **113 D6** 9 28N 5 10 E
Bokaro, *India* **93 H11** 23 46N 85 55 E
Bokatola, *Dem. Rep. of the Congo* **114 C3** 0 38 S 18 46 E
Boké, *Guinea* **112 C2** 10 56N 14 17W
Bokela, *Dem. Rep. of the Congo* **114 C4** 1 10 S 21 59 E
Bokenda, *Dem. Rep. of the Congo* **114 B4** 1 16N 21 22 E
Bokhara →, *Australia* **127 D4** 29 55 S 146 42 E
Bokkos, *Nigeria* **113 D6** 9 17N 9 1 E
Boknafjorden, *Norway* **18 E2** 59 14N 5 40 E
Bokode, *Dem. Rep. of the Congo* **114 B3** 3 55N 19 30 E
Bokolo, *Gabon* **114 C2** 2 40 S 10 10 E
Bökönbaev, *Kyrgyzstan* **65 B8** 42 10N 76 55 E
Bokondo, *Dem. Rep. of the Congo* **114 B4** 0 15N 22 32 E
Bokora ⌓, *Uganda* **118 B3** 2 12N 31 32 E
Bokoro, *Chad* **109 F3** 12 25N 17 14 E
Bokota, *Dem. Rep. of the Congo* **114 C4** 0 56 S 22 24 E
Bokote, *Dem. Rep. of the Congo* **114 C4** 0 12 S 21 8 E
Bokpyin, *Burma* **87 G2** 11 18N 98 42 E
Boksitogorsk, *Russia* **58 C7** 59 22N 33 50 E
Boku, *Papua N. G.* **132 D8** 6 34 S 155 21 E
Bokungu, *Dem. Rep. of the Congo* **114 C4** 0 35 S 22 50 E
Bol, *Chad* **109 F2** 13 30N 14 40 E
Bol, *Croatia* **45 E13** 43 18N 16 38 E
Bolama, *Guinea-Biss.* **112 C1** 11 30N 15 30W
Bolan →, *Pakistan* **92 E2** 28 38N 67 42 E
Bolan Pass, *Pakistan* **91 C2** 29 50N 67 20 E
Bolaños →, *Mexico* **162 C4** 21 14N 104 8W
Bolaños de Calatrava, *Spain* **43 G7** 38 54N 3 40W
Bolayır, *Turkey* **51 F10** 40 31N 26 45 E
Bolbec, *France* **26 C7** 49 30N 0 30 E
Boldājī, *Iran* **97 D6** 31 56N 51 3 E
Boldeşti-Scăeni, *Romania* **53 E11** 45 3N 26 2 E
Bole, *China* **68 B3** 45 11N 81 37 E
Bole, *Ethiopia* **107 F4** 6 36N 37 20 E
Bole, *Ghana* **112 D4** 9 3N 2 23W
Bolekhiv, *Ukraine* **59 H2** 49 0N 23 57 E
Boleko, *Dem. Rep. of the Congo* **114 C3** 1 35 S 19 50 E
Bolesławiec, *Poland* **55 G2** 51 17N 15 37 E
Bolgatanga, *Ghana* **113 C4** 10 44N 0 53W
Bolgrad = Bolhrad, *Ukraine* **53 E13** 45 40N 28 32 E
Bolhrad, *Ukraine* **53 E13** 45 40N 28 32 E
Bolia, *Dem. Rep. of the Congo* **114 C3** 1 36 S 18 22 E
Bolinao, *Phil.* **80 C2** 16 23N 119 54 E
Bolinao, C., *Phil.* **80 C2** 16 23N 119 55 E
Bolingbroke, *U.S.A.* **152 C6** 32 57N 83 48W
Bolingo, *Dem. Rep. of the Congo* **114 C4** 3 31 S 21 43 E
Bolintin-Vale, *Romania* **53 F10** 44 27N 25 46 E
Bolívar, *Argentina* **174 D3** 36 15 S 60 53W
Bolívar, *Antioquía, Colombia* **168 B2** 5 50N 76 1W
Bolívar, *Cauca, Colombia* **168 C2** 2 0N 77 0W
Bolívar, *Peru* **172 B2** 7 18 S 77 48W
Bolivar, *Mo., U.S.A.* **155 G8** 37 37N 93 25W
Bolivar, *N.Y., U.S.A.* **150 D6** 42 4N 78 10W
Bolivar, *Tenn., U.S.A.* **155 H10** 35 12N 89 0W
Bolívar □, *Colombia* **168 B3** 9 0N 74 40W
Bolívar □, *Ecuador* **168 D2** 1 15 S 79 5W
Bolívar □, *Venezuela* **169 B5** 6 20N 63 30W
Bolivia ■, *S. Amer.* **173 D5** 17 6 S 64 0W
Bolivian Plateau = Altiplano, *Bolivia* **172 D4** 17 0 S 68 0W
Boljevac, *Serbia & M.* **50 C5** 43 51N 21 58 E
Bolkhov, *Russia* **58 F9** 53 25N 36 0 E
Bolków, *Poland* **55 H3** 50 55N 16 6 E
Bollé, *Mauritania* **110 D2** 20 8N 11 40W
Bollebygd, *Sweden* **17 G6** 57 40N 12 35 E
Bollène, *France* **29 D8** 44 18N 4 45 E
Bollnäs, *Sweden* **16 C10** 61 21N 16 24 E
Bollon, *Australia* **127 D4** 28 2 S 147 29 E
Bollstabruk, *Sweden* **16 B11** 62 59N 17 40 E
Bolmen, *Sweden* **17 H7** 56 55N 13 40 E
Bolobo, *Dem. Rep. of the Congo* **114 C3** 2 6 S 16 20 E
Bologna, *Italy* **45 D8** 44 29N 11 20 E
Bologna ✕ (BLQ), *Italy* **45 D8** 44 34N 11 16 E
Bologoye, *Russia* **58 D8** 57 55N 34 5 E
Bolomba, *Dem. Rep. of the Congo* **114 B3** 0 35N 19 0 E
Bolombo →, *Dem. Rep. of the Congo* **114 B4** 1 32N 21 14 E
Bolonchenticul, *Mexico* **163 D7** 20 0N 89 49W
Bolondo, *Dem. Rep. of the Congo* **114 C3** 2 12 S 18 42 E
Bolong, *Chad* **109 F3** 12 3N 17 45 E
Bolong, *Phil.* **81 H4** 7 6N 122 14 E
Bolongongo, *Angola* **115 D3** 8 28 S 15 16 E
Bolótana, *Italy* **46 B1** 40 20N 8 52 E
Bolotovskoye, *Russia* **64 B9** 58 31N 62 28 E
Boloven, Cao Nguyen, *Laos* **86 E6** 15 10N 106 30 E
Bolpur, *India* **93 H12** 23 40N 87 45 E
Bolsena, *Italy* **45 F8** 42 39N 11 59 E
Bolsena, L. di, *Italy* **45 F8** 42 36N 11 56 E
Bolshakovo, *Russia* **54 D8** 54 53N 21 40 E
Bolshaya Chernigovka, *Russia* **60 D10** 52 6N 50 52 E
Bolshaya Garmanda = Evensk, *Russia* **67 C16** 62 12N 159 30 E
Bolshaya Glushitsa, *Russia* **60 D10** 52 28N 50 30 E
Bolshaya Khobda →, *Kazakhstan* **64 F5** 50 56N 54 34 E
Bolshaya Martynovka, *Russia* **61 G5** 47 19N 41 37 E
Bolshaya Tsaryovshchina = Volzhskiy, *Russia* **61 F7** 48 56N 44 46 E
Bolshaya Vradiyevka, *Ukraine* **59 J6** 47 50N 30 40 E
Bolshevik, Ostrov, *Russia* **67 B11** 78 30N 102 0 E
Bolshoy Anyuy →, *Russia* **67 C17** 68 30N 160 49 E
Bolshoy Begichev, Ostrov, *Russia* **67 B12** 74 20N 112 30 E
Bolshoy Kavkas = Caucasus Mountains, *Eurasia* **61 J7** 42 50N 44 0 E
Bolshoy Lyakhovskiy, Ostrov, *Russia* **67 B15** 73 35N 142 0 E
Bolshoy Tokmak = Tokmak, *Kyrgyzstan* **65 B7** 42 49N 75 15 E
Bolshoy Tyuters, Ostrov, *Russia* **15 G22** 59 51N 27 13 E
Bólstaðarhlíð, *Iceland* **11 B7** 65 31N 19 49W
Bolsward, *Neths.* **24 A5** 53 3N 5 32 E
Bolt Head, *U.K.* **21 G4** 50 12N 3 48W
Boltaña, *Spain* **40 C5** 42 28N 0 4 E
Boltigen, *Switz.* **32 C4** 46 38N 7 24 E
Bolton, *Canada* **150 C5** 43 54N 79 45W
Bolton, *U.K.* **20 D5** 53 35N 2 26W
Bolton Landing, *U.S.A.* **151 C11** 43 32N 73 35W
Bolu, *Turkey* **100 B4** 40 45N 31 35 E
Bolubolu, *Papua N. G.* **132 E6** 9 21 S 150 20 E
Bolungavík, *Iceland* **11 A3** 66 9N 23 15W
Boluo, *China* **77 F10** 23 3N 114 21 E
Bolvadin, *Turkey* **100 C4** 38 45N 31 4 E
Bolzano, *Italy* **45 B8** 46 31N 11 22 E
Bom Comércio, *Brazil* **173 B4** 9 45 S 65 54W
Bom Conselho, *Brazil* **170 C4** 9 10 S 36 41W
Bom Despacho, *Brazil* **171 E2** 19 43 S 45 15W
Bom Jesus, *Angola* **115 D2** 9 11 S 13 34 E
Bom Jesus, *Brazil* **170 C3** 9 4 S 44 22W
Bom Jesus da Gurguéia, Serra, *Brazil* **170 C3** 9 0 S 43 0W
Bom Jesus da Lapa, *Brazil* **171 D3** 13 15 S 43 25W
Boma, *Dem. Rep. of the Congo* **115 D2** 5 50 S 13 4 E
Bomaderry, *Australia* **129 C9** 34 52 S 150 37 E
Bomandjokou, *Congo* **114 B2** 0 34N 14 23 E
Bomaneh, *Dem. Rep. of the Congo* **114 B4** 1 18N 23 47 E
Bomassa, *Congo* **114 B3** 2 12N 16 12 E
Bomate, *Dem. Rep. of the Congo* **114 C3** 2 14N 25 15 E
Bombala, *Australia* **129 D8** 36 56 S 149 15 E
Bombarral, *Portugal* **43 F1** 39 15N 9 9W
Bombay = Mumbai, *India* **94 E1** 18 55N 72 50 E
Bombedor, Pta., *Venezuela* **169 G9** 9 53N 61 37W
Bomberai, Semenanjung, *Indonesia* **83 B4** 3 0 S 133 0 E
Bombo Kasani, *Dem. Rep. of the Congo* **115 D4** 5 51 S 21 54 E
Bomboma, *Dem. Rep. of the Congo* **114 B3** 2 25N 18 55 E
Bombombwa, *Dem. Rep. of the Congo* **118 B2** 1 40N 25 40 E
Bomboyo, *Chad* **109 F3** 12 1N 15 28 E
Bomdila, *India* **90 B4** 27 18N 92 22 E
Bomdo, *India* **90 A5** 28 44N 94 54 E
Bomi Hills, *Liberia* **112 D2** 7 1N 10 38W
Bomili, *Dem. Rep. of the Congo* **118 B2** 1 45N 27 5 E
Bømlo, *Norway* **18 E2** 59 37N 5 13 E
Bomokandi →, *Dem. Rep. of the Congo* **118 B2** 3 39N 26 8 E
Bomongo, *Dem. Rep. of the Congo* **114 B3** 1 27N 18 21 E
Bompoka, *India* **95 K11** 8 15N 93 13 E
Bomputu, *Dem. Rep. of the Congo* **114 C4** 0 23 S 20 6 E
Bomst = Babimost, *Poland* **55 F2** 52 10N 15 49 E
Bomu →, *C.A.R.* **114 B4** 4 40N 22 30 E
Bomu Occidentale ⌓, *Dem. Rep. of the Congo* **114 B4** 4 48N 24 17 E
Bomu Orientale ⌓, *Dem. Rep. of the Congo* **114 B2** 5 0N 25 50 E
Bon, C., *Tunisia* **108 A2** 37 1N 11 2 E
Bon Acceuil, *Mauritius* **121 d** 20 10 S 57 39 E
Bon Sar Pa, *Vietnam* **86 F6** 12 24N 107 35 E
Bonāb, *Iran* **101 D12** 37 20N 46 4 E
Bonaduz, *Switz.* **33 C8** 46 49N 9 25 E
Bonaigarh, *India* **93 J11** 21 50N 84 57 E
Bonaire, *Neth. Ant.* **165 D6** 12 10N 68 15W
Bonaire, *U.S.A.* **152 C6** 32 33N 83 36W
Bonampak, *Mexico* **163 D6** 16 44N 91 5W
Bonang, *Australia* **129 D8** 37 11 S 148 41 E
Bonanza, *Nic.* **164 D3** 13 54N 84 35W
Bonaparte Arch., *Australia* **124 B3** 14 0 S 124 30 E
Boñar, *Spain* **42 C5** 42 52N 5 19W
Bonar Bridge, *U.K.* **22 D4** 57 54N 4 20W
Bonasse, *Trin. & Tob.* **169 F9** 10 5N 61 54W
Bonaventure, *Canada* **141 C6** 48 5N 65 32W
Bonavista, *Canada* **141 C9** 48 40N 53 5W
Bonavista, C., *Canada* **141 C9** 48 42N 53 5W
Bonavista B., *Canada* **141 C9** 48 45N 53 25W
Bondeno, *Italy* **45 D8** 44 53N 11 25 E
Bondo, *Équateur, Dem. Rep. of the Congo* **114 C4** 1 22 S 23 54 E
Bondo, *Orientale, Dem. Rep. of the Congo* **118 B1** 3 55N 23 53 E
Bondoukou, *Ivory C.* **112 D4** 8 2N 2 47W
Bondowoso, *Indonesia* **85 D4** 7 55 S 113 49 E
Bône = Annaba, *Algeria* **111 A6** 36 50N 7 46 E
Bone, Teluk, *Indonesia* **82 B2** 4 10 S 120 50 E
Bonefish Pond, *Bahamas* **9 b** 25 59N 77 23W
Bonerate, *Indonesia* **82 C2** 7 25 S 121 5 E
Bonerate, Kepulauan, *Indonesia* **82 C2** 6 30 S 121 10 E
Bo'ness, *U.K.* **22 E5** 56 1N 3 37W
Bonete, Cerro, *Argentina* **174 B2** 27 55 S 68 40W
Bonfim = Senhor-do-Bonfim, *Brazil* **170 D3** 10 30 S 40 10W
Bonfim, *Brazil* **169 C6** 3 33N 59 25W
Bong Son = Hoai Nhon, *Vietnam* **86 E7** 14 28N 109 1 E
Bonga, *Ethiopia* **107 F4** 7 15N 36 14 E
Bongabon, *Phil.* **80 D3** 15 38N 121 8 E
Bongabong, *Phil.* **80 E3** 12 45N 121 29 E
Bongaigon, *India* **90 B3** 26 28N 90 34 E
Bongandanga, *Dem. Rep. of the Congo* **114 B4** 1 24N 21 3 E
Bongao, *Phil.* **81 J2** 5 2N 119 46 E
Bongka, *Indonesia* **82 B2** 0 58 S 121 27 E
Bongo, *Dem. Rep. of the Congo* **114 C3** 1 47 S 17 41 E
Bongo, Sa. de, *Angola* **115 E3** 10 3 S 15 15 E
Bongor, *Chad* **109 F3** 10 35N 15 20 E
Bongouanou, *Ivory C.* **112 D4** 6 42N 4 15W
Bonham, *U.S.A.* **155 J6** 33 35N 96 11W
Boni, *Mali* **112 B4** 15 3N 2 10W
Boni ⌓, *Kenya* **118 C5** 1 35 S 41 18 E
Bonifacio, *France* **29 G13** 41 24N 9 10 E
Bonifacio, Bouches de, *Medit. S.* **46 A2** 41 12N 9 15 E
Bonifay, *U.S.A.* **152 E4** 30 47N 85 41W
Bonin Is. = Ogasawara Gunto, *Pac. Oc.* **62 G18** 27 0N 142 0 E
Bonita Springs, *U.S.A.* **153 J8** 26 21N 81 47W
Bonito, *Brazil* **173** 21 8 S 56 28W
Bonke, *Ethiopia* **107 F4** 6 5N 37 16 E
Bonkoukou, *Niger* **113 C5** 14 0N 3 15 E
Bonn, *Germany* **30 E3** 50 46N 7 6 E
Bonnat, *France* **27 F8** 46 20N 1 54 E
Bonne Terre, *U.S.A.* **155 G9** 37 55N 90 33W
Bonneau, *U.S.A.* **152 B10** 33 16N 79 58W
Bonners Ferry, *U.S.A.* **158 B5** 48 42N 116 19W
Bonnétable, *France* **26 D7** 48 11N 0 25 E
Bonneval, *France* **29 C11** 45 22N 7 3 E
Bonneval-sur-Arc, *France* **26 D8** 48 11N 1 24 E
Bonneville, *France* **27 F13** 46 4N 6 24 E
Bonney, L., *Australia* **128 D4** 37 50 S 140 20 E
Bonnie Doon, *Australia* **129 D6** 37 2 S 145 53 E
Bonnie Rock, *Australia* **125 F2** 30 29 S 118 22 E
Bonny, *Nigeria* **113 E6** 4 25N 7 13 E
Bonny →, *Nigeria* **113 E6** 4 20N 7 10 E
Bonny, Bight of, *Africa* **113 E6** 3 30N 9 20 E
Bonny Hills, *Australia* **129 A10** 31 36 S 152 51 E
Bonny-sur-Loire, *France* **27 E9** 47 33N 2 50 E
Bonnyrigg, *U.K.* **22 F5** 55 53N 3 6W
Bonnyville, *Canada* **143 C6** 54 20N 110 45W
Bono, *Italy* **46 B2** 40 25N 9 2 E
Bonoi, *Indonesia* **83 B5** 1 45 S 137 41 E
Bonorva, *Italy* **46 B1** 40 25N 8 46 E
Bonsall, *U.S.A.* **161 M9** 33 16N 117 14W
Bontang, *Indonesia* **85 B5** 0 10N 117 30 E
Bontebok △, *S. Africa* **116 E3** 34 5 S 20 28 E
Bonthe, *S. Leone* **112 D2** 7 30N 12 33W
Bontoc, *Phil.* **80 C3** 17 7N 120 58 E
Bontosunggu, *Indonesia* **82 C1** 5 41 S 119 42 E
Bonyeri, *Ghana* **112 D4** 5 1N 2 46W
Bonyhád, *Hungary* **52 D3** 46 18N 18 32 E
Bonython Ra., *Australia* **124 D4** 23 40 S 128 45 E
Boo, Kepulauan, *Indonesia* **83 B3** 1 12 S 129 24 E
Bookabie, *Australia* **125 F5** 31 50 S 132 41 E
Booke, *Dem. Rep. of the Congo* **114 C4** 2 34 S 22 3 E
Booker, *U.S.A.* **155 G4** 36 27N 100 32W
Bool Lagoon, *Australia* **128 D4** 37 7 S 140 40 E
Boola, *Guinea* **112 D3** 8 22N 8 41 E
Boolcoomata, *Australia* **128 A4** 31 57 S 140 33 E
Booleroo Centre, *Australia* **128 B3** 32 53 S 138 21 E
Booligal, *Australia* **129 B6** 33 58 S 144 53 E
Boonah, *Australia* **127 D5** 27 58 S 152 41 E
Boone, *Iowa, U.S.A.* **156 B3** 42 4N 93 53W
Boone, *N.C., U.S.A.* **149 G5** 36 13N 81 41W
Booneville, *Ark., U.S.A.* **155 H8** 35 8N 93 55W
Booneville, *Miss., U.S.A.* **149 H1** 34 39N 88 34W
Boonville, *Calif., U.S.A.* **160 F3** 39 1N 123 22W
Boonville, *Ind., U.S.A.* **157 F9** 38 3N 87 16W
Boonville, *Mo., U.S.A.* **156 F4** 38 58N 92 44W
Boonville, *N.Y., U.S.A.* **151 C9** 43 29N 75 20W
Boorabbin △, *Australia* **125 F4** 31 30 S 129 57 E
Boorindal, *Australia* **127 E4** 30 22 S 146 11 E
Boorowa, *Australia* **129 C8** 34 28 S 148 44 E
Boort, *Australia* **128 D5** 36 7 S 143 46 E
Boosaaso = Bosaso, *Somali Rep.* **120 B3** 11 12N 49 18 E
Boothia, Gulf of, *Canada* **139 A11** 71 0N 90 0W
Boothia Pen., *Canada* **138 A10** 71 0N 94 0W
Bootle, *U.K.* **20 D4** 53 28N 3 1W
Booué, *Gabon* **114 C2** 0 5 S 11 55 E
Bopako, *Dem. Rep. of the Congo* **114 B4** 1 53N 21 13 E
Boppard, *Germany* **31 E3** 50 13N 7 35 E
Boquerón □, *Paraguay* **173 E5** 23 0 S 60 0W
Boquete, *Panama* **164 E3** 8 46N 82 27W
Boquilla, Presa de la, *Mexico* **162 B3** 27 40N 105 30W
Boquillas del Carmen, *Mexico* **162 B4** 29 17N 102 53W
Bor, *Czech Rep.* **34 B5** 49 41N 12 45 E
Bor, *Russia* **60 B7** 56 28N 43 59 E
Bor, *Serbia & M.* **50 B6** 44 5N 22 7 E
Bôr, *Sudan* **107 F3** 6 10N 31 40 E
Bor, *Sweden* **17 G8** 57 9N 14 10 E
Bor, *Turkey* **100 D6** 37 54N 34 32 E
Bor Döbö, *Kyrgyzstan* **65 D6** 39 31N 73 16 E
Bor Mashash, *Israel* **103 D3** 31 7N 34 50 E
Bor u Ceske Lipy = Nový Bor, *Czech Rep.* **34 A7** 50 46N 14 35 E
Bora-Bora, *French Polynesia* **135 J12** 16 30 S 151 45W
Borah Peak, *U.S.A.* **158 D7** 44 8N 113 47W
Boralday, *Kazakhstan* **65 B8** 43 20N 76 51 E
Borama, *Somali Rep.* **120 C2** 9 55N 43 7 E
Borang, *Sudan* **107 G3** 4 50N 30 59 E
Borangapara, *India* **90 C3** 25 14N 90 14 E
Borås, *Sweden* **17 G6** 57 43N 12 56 E
Borāzjān, *Iran* **97 D6** 29 22N 51 10 E
Borba, *Brazil* **169 D6** 4 12 S 59 34W
Borba, *Portugal* **43 G3** 38 50N 7 26W
Borbon, *Phil.* **81 F5** 10 50N 124 2 E
Borborema, Planalto da, *Brazil* **170 C4** 7 0 S 37 0W
Borcea, *Romania* **53 F12** 44 20N 27 45 E
Borchalo = Marneuli, *Georgia* **61 K7** 41 30N 44 48 E
Borçka, *Turkey* **101 B9** 41 25N 41 41 E
Bord Khūn-e Now, *Iran* **97 D6** 28 3N 51 28 E
Borda, C., *Australia* **128 C2** 35 45 S 136 34 E
Bordeaux, *France* **28 D3** 44 50N 0 36W
Bordeaux ✕ (BOD), *France* **28 D3** 44 50N 0 35W
Borden, *Australia* **125 F2** 34 3 S 118 12 E
Borden-Carleton, *Canada* **141 C7** 46 18N 63 47W
Borden I., *Canada* **6 B2** 78 30N 111 30W
Borden Pen., *Canada* **139 A11** 73 0N 83 0W
Borden Springs, *U.S.A.* **152 B4** 33 56N 85 28W
Border Ranges △, *Australia* **127 D5** 28 24 S 152 56 E
Borders = Scottish Borders □, *U.K.* **22 F6** 55 35N 2 50W
Bordertown, *Australia* **128 D4** 36 19 S 140 45 E
Borðeyri, *Iceland* **11 B5** 65 12N 21 6W
Bordighera, *Italy* **44 E4** 43 46N 7 39 E
Bordj bou Arreridj, *Algeria* **111 A5** 36 4N 4 45 E
Bordj Bourguiba, *Tunisia* **108 B2** 32 12N 10 2 E
Bordj Fly Ste. Marie, *Algeria* **110 C4** 27 19N 2 32W
Bordj-in-Eker, *Algeria* **111 D6** 24 9N 5 3 E
Bordj Menaïel, *Algeria* **111 A5** 36 46N 3 43 E
Bordj Messouda, *Algeria* **111 B6** 30 12N 9 25 E
Bordj Nili, *Algeria* **111 B5** 33 28N 3 2 E
Bordj Omar Driss, *Algeria* **111 C6** 28 10N 6 40 E
Bordj Sif Fatima, *Algeria* **111 B6** 31 6N 8 41 E
Bordj Tarat, *Algeria* **111 C6** 25 55N 9 3 E
Borduttighat, *India* **90 B4** 26 57N 93 58 E
Bore, *Ethiopia* **107 G4** 4 39N 37 39 E
Borehamwood, *U.K.* **21 F7** 51 40N 0 15W
Borek Wielkopolski, *Poland* **55 G4** 51 54N 17 11 E
Borensberg, *Sweden* **17 F9** 58 34N 15 17 E
Borgå = Porvoo, *Finland* **15 F21** 60 24N 25 40 E
Borgampad, *India* **94 F5** 17 39N 80 52 E
Borgarfjarðarsýsla □, *Iceland* **11 C5** 64 30N 21 30W
Borgarfjörður, *Borgarfjarðarsýsla, Iceland* **11 C4** 64 30N 22 0W
Borgarfjörður, *Norður-Múlasýsla, Iceland* **14 D7** 65 31N 13 49W
Borgarnes, *Iceland* **11 C5** 64 32N 21 55W
Børgefjellet, *Norway* **14 D15** 65 20N 13 45 E
Borger, *Neths.* **24 B6** 52 54N 6 44 E
Borger, *U.S.A.* **155 H4** 35 39N 101 24W
Borgholm, *Sweden* **17 H10** 56 52N 16 39 E
Bórgia, *Italy* **47 D9** 38 49N 16 30 E
Borgo San Dalmazzo, *Italy* **44 D4** 44 20N 7 30 E
Borgo San Donnino = Fidenza, *Italy* **44 D7** 44 52N 10 3 E
Borgo San Lorenzo, *Italy* **45 E8** 43 57N 11 23 E
Borgo Val di Taro, *Italy* **44 D6** 44 29N 9 46 E
Borgo Valsugana, *Italy* **45 B8** 46 3N 11 27 E
Borgomanero, *Italy* **44 C5** 45 42N 8 28 E
Borgorose, *Italy* **45 F10** 42 11N 13 13 E
Borgosésia, *Italy* **44 C5** 45 43N 8 16 E
Borgotaro = Borgo Val di Taro, *Italy* **44 D6** 44 29N 9 46 E
Borgund, *Norway* **18 C4** 61 3N 7 48 E
Borhoyn Tal, *Mongolia* **74 C6** 43 50N 111 58 E
Bori, *Nigeria* **113 E6** 4 42N 7 21 E
Borigumma, *India* **94 E6** 19 3N 82 33 E
Borikhane, *Laos* **86 C4** 18 33N 103 43 E
Borisoglebsk, *Russia* **60 E6** 51 27N 42 5 E
Borisov = Barysaw, *Belarus* **58 E5** 54 17N 28 28 E
Borisovgrad = Pŭrvomay, *Bulgaria* **51 D9** 42 8N 25 17 E
Borisovka, *Russia* **59 G9** 50 36N 36 1 E
Borja, *Peru* **168 D2** 4 20 S 77 40W
Borja, *Spain* **40 D3** 41 48N 1 34W
Borjas Blancas = Les Borges Blanques, *Spain* **40 D5** 41 31N 0 52 E
Borjomi, *Georgia* **61 K6** 41 48N 43 28 E
Børkop, *Denmark* **17 J3** 55 39N 9 39 E
Borkou, *Chad* **109 E3** 18 15N 18 50 E
Borkum, *Germany* **30 B2** 53 34N 6 40 E
Borlänge, *Sweden* **16 D9** 60 29N 15 26 E
Borley, C., *Antarctica* **7 C5** 66 15 S 52 30 E
Borlu, *Turkey* **49 C10** 38 44N 28 27 E
Bormida →, *Italy* **44 D5** 44 23N 8 13 E
Bórmio, *Italy* **44 B7** 46 28N 10 22 E
Borna, *Germany* **30 D8** 51 7N 12 29 E
Borne Sulinowo, *Poland* **54 E3** 53 32N 16 36 E
Borneo, *E. Indies* **85 B4** 1 0N 115 0 E
Bornholm, *Denmark* **17 J8** 55 10N 15 0 E
Bornholms Amtskommune □, *Denmark* **17 J8** 55 5N 15 0 E
Bornholmsgattet, *Europe* **17 J8** 55 15N 14 20 E
Borno, *Italy* **33 E10** 45 56N 10 12 E
Borno □, *Nigeria* **113 C7** 11 30N 13 0 E
Bornos, *Spain* **43 J5** 36 48N 5 42W
Bornova, *Turkey* **49 C9** 38 27N 27 14 E
Bornu Yassa, *Nigeria* **113 C7** 12 14N 12 25 E
Boro →, *Sudan* **107 F2** 8 52N 26 11 E
Borobudur, *Indonesia* **85 D4** 7 36 S 110 13 E
Borodino, *Russia* **58 E8** 55 31N 35 40 E
Borodino, *Ukraine* **53 D14** 46 18N 29 15 E
Borogontsy, *Russia* **67 C14** 62 42N 131 8 E
Boromo, *Burkina Faso* **112 C4** 11 45N 2 58W
Boron, *U.S.A.* **161 L9** 35 0N 117 39W
Boronga Is., *Burma* **90 F4** 19 58N 93 6 E
Borongan, *Phil.* **81 F5** 11 37N 125 26 E
Borotangba Mts., *C.A.R.* **107 F2** 6 30N 25 0 E
Borotou, *Ivory C.* **112 D3** 8 46N 7 30W
Borovan, *Bulgaria* **50 C7** 43 27N 23 45 E
Borovichi, *Russia* **58 C7** 58 25N 33 55 E
Borovsk, *Berezniki, Russia* **64 B6** 59 43N 56 40 E
Borovsk, *Moskva, Russia* **58 E9** 55 12N 36 24 E
Borrby, *Sweden* **17 J8** 55 27N 14 10 E
Borrego Springs, *U.S.A.* **161 M10** 33 15N 116 23W
Borriol, *Spain* **40 E4** 40 4N 0 4W
Borroloola, *Australia* **126 B2** 16 4 S 136 17 E
Borşa, *Cluj, Romania* **53 D8** 46 56N 23 40 E
Borşa, *Maramureş, Romania* **53 C9** 47 41N 24 50 E
Borsad, *India* **92 H5** 22 25N 72 54 E
Borsec, *Romania* **53 D10** 46 57N 25 34 E
Borshchiv, *Ukraine* **53 B11** 48 48N 26 3 E
Borsod-Abaúj-Zemplén □, *Hungary* **52 B6** 48 20N 21 0 E
Bort-les-Orgues, *France* **28 C6** 45 24N 2 29 E
Borth, *U.K.* **21 E3** 52 29N 4 2W
Börtnan, *Sweden* **16 B7** 62 45N 13 50 E
Borūjerd, *Iran* **97 C6** 33 55N 48 50 E
Borynya, *Ukraine* **55 J10** 49 4N 23 0 E
Boryslav, *Ukraine* **55 J10** 49 18N 23 28 E
Boryspil, *Ukraine* **59 G6** 50 21N 30 59 E
Borzhomi = Borjomi, *Georgia* **61 K6** 41 48N 43 28 E
Borzna, *Ukraine* **59 G7** 51 18N 32 26 E
Borzya, *Russia* **67 D12** 50 24N 116 31 E
Bosa, *Italy* **46 B1** 40 18N 8 30 E
Bosa Monene, *Dem. Rep. of the Congo* **114 C4** 1 16 S 23 40 E
Bosaga, *Turkmenistan* **65 E2** 37 33N 65 41 E
Bosambi, *Dem. Rep. of the Congo* **114 B4** 2 24N 22 39 E
Bosanska Dubica, *Bos.-H.* **45 C13** 45 10N 16 50 E
Bosanska Gradiška, *Bos.-H.* **52 E2** 45 10N 17 15 E
Bosanska Kostajnica, *Bos.-H.* **45 C13** 45 11N 16 33 E
Bosanska Krupa, *Bos.-H.* **45 D13** 44 53N 16 10 E
Bosanski Brod, *Bos.-H.* **52 E2** 45 10N 18 0 E
Bosanski Novi, *Bos.-H.* **45 C13** 45 2N 16 22 E
Bosanski Petrovac, *Bos.-H.* **45 D13** 44 35N 16 21 E
Bosanski Šamac, *Bos.-H.* **52 E3** 45 3N 18 29 E
Bosansko Grahovo, *Bos.-H.* **45 D13** 44 12N 16 26 E
Bosaso, *Somali Rep.* **120 B3** 11 12N 49 18 E
Bosavi, Mt., *Papua N. G.* **132 D2** 6 30 S 142 49 E
Boscastle, *U.K.* **21 G3** 50 41N 4 42W
Boscobel, *U.S.A.* **156 A6** 43 8N 90 42W
Boscobelle, *Barbados* **165 g** 13 17N 59 35W
Bose, *China* **76 F6** 23 53N 106 35 E
Boseki, *Dem. Rep. of the Congo* **114 C3** 2 34 S 19 38 E
Boshan, *China* **75 F9** 36 28N 117 49 E
Boshof, *S. Africa* **116 D4** 28 31 S 25 13 E
Boshrūyeh, *Iran* **97 C8** 33 50N 57 30 E
Bosilegrad, *Serbia & M.* **50 D6** 42 30N 22 27 E
Boskovice, *Czech Rep.* **35 B9** 49 29N 16 40 E
Bosna →, *Bos.-H.* **52 E3** 45 4N 18 29 E
Bosna i Hercegovina = Bosnia-Herzegovina ■, *Europe* **52 G2** 44 0N 18 0 E
Bosnia-Herzegovina ■, *Europe* **52 G2** 44 0N 18 0 E

Bosnik, *Indonesia* **83 B5** 1 5S 136 10 E
Bōsō-Hantō, *Japan* **73 B12** 35 20N 140 20 E
Bosobolo, *Dem. Rep. of the Congo* **114 B3** 4 15N 19 50 E
Bosporus = İstanbul Boğazı, *Turkey* **51 E13** 41 10N 29 10 E
Bosque Farms, *U.S.A.* **159 J10** 34 53N 106 40W
Bossangoa, *C.A.R.* **114 A3** 6 35N 17 30 E
Bossé Bangou, *Niger* **113 C5** 13 20N 1 18 E
Bossembélé, *C.A.R.* **114 A3** 5 25N 17 40 E
Bossemtélé, *C.A.R.* **114 A3** 5 41N 16 38 E
Bossier City, *U.S.A.* **155 J8** 32 31N 93 44W
Bosso, *Niger* **113 C7** 13 43N 13 19 E
Bosso, Dallol →, *Niger* **113 C5** 12 25N 2 50 E
Bostan, *Pakistan* **92 D2** 30 26N 67 2 E
Bostānābād, *Iran* **101 D12** 37 50N 46 50 E
Bosten Hu, *China* **68 B3** 41 55N 87 40 E
Boston, *Phil.* **81 H6** 7 52N 126 22 E
Boston, *U.K.* **20 E7** 52 59N 0 2W
Boston, *Ga., U.S.A.* **152 E6** 30 47N 83 47W
Boston, *Mass., U.S.A.* **151 D13** 42 22N 71 4W
Boston Bar, *Canada* **142 D4** 49 52N 121 30W
Boston Mts., *U.S.A.* **155 H8** 35 42N 93 15W
Bostwick, *U.S.A.* **152 F8** 29 46N 81 38W
Bosumtwi, L., *Ghana* **113 D4** 6 30N 1 25W
Bosusulu, *Dem. Rep. of the Congo* **114 B4** 0 50N 20 45 E
Bosut →, *Croatia* **52 E3** 45 20N 18 45 E
Boswell, *Canada* **142 D5** 49 28N 116 45W
Boswell, *Ind., U.S.A.* **157 D9** 40 31N 87 23W
Boswell, *Pa., U.S.A.* **150 F5** 40 10N 79 2W
Bosworth, *U.S.A.* **156 E3** 39 28N 93 20W
Botad, *India* **92 H4** 22 15N 71 40 E
Botan →, *Turkey* **101 D10** 37 57N 42 2 E
Botene, *Laos* **86 D3** 17 35N 101 12 E
Botera, *Angola* **115 E2** 11 37S 14 16 E
Botev, *Bulgaria* **51 D8** 42 44N 24 52 E
Botevgrad, *Bulgaria* **50 D7** 42 55N 23 47 E
Bothaville, *S. Africa* **116 D4** 27 23S 26 34 E
Bothnia, G. of, *Europe* **14 E19** 62 0N 20 0 E
Bothwell, *Australia* **127 G4** 42 20S 147 1 E
Bothwell, *Canada* **150 D3** 42 38N 81 52W
Boticas, *Portugal* **42 D3** 41 41N 7 40W
Botletle →, *Botswana* **116 C3** 20 10S 23 15 E
Botlikh, *Russia* **61 J8** 42 39N 46 11 E
Botna →, *Moldova* **53 D14** 46 45N 29 34 E
Botola, *Dem. Rep. of the Congo* **114 C3** 1 17S 18 13 E
Botolan, *Phil.* **80 D3** 15 17N 120 1 E
Botoroaga, *Romania* **53 F10** 44 8N 25 32 E
Botoșani, *Romania* **53 C11** 47 42N 26 41 E
Botoșani □, *Romania* **53 C11** 47 50N 26 50 E
Botou, *Burkina Faso* **113 C5** 12 42N 1 59 E
Botricello, *Italy* **47 D9** 38 56N 16 51 E
Botro, *Ivory C.* **112 D3** 7 51N 5 19W
Botswana ■, *Africa* **116 C3** 22 0S 24 0 E
Bottineau, *U.S.A.* **154 A4** 48 50N 100 27W
Bottnaryd, *Sweden* **17 G7** 57 47N 13 50 E
Bottopassi, *Suriname* **169 C6** 4 14N 55 27W
Bottrop, *Germany* **24 C6** 51 31N 6 58 E
Botucatu, *Brazil* **175 A6** 22 55S 48 30W
Botwood, *Canada* **141 C8** 49 6N 55 23W
Bou Alam, *Algeria* **111 B5** 33 50N 1 26 E
Bou Ali, *Algeria* **111 C4** 27 11N 0 4W
Bou Djébéha, *Mali* **112 B4** 18 25N 2 45W
Bou Guema, *Algeria* **111 C5** 28 49N 0 19 E
Bou Ismaïl, *Algeria* **111 A5** 36 38N 2 42 E
Bou Izakarn, *Morocco* **110 C3** 29 12N 9 46W
Boû Lanouâr, *Mauritania* **110 D1** 21 12N 16 34W
Boû Rjeïmât, *Mauritania* **112 B1** 19 4N 15 3W
Bou Saâda, *Algeria* **111 A5** 35 11N 4 9 E
Bou Salem, *Tunisia* **108 A1** 36 45N 9 2 E
Bouaflé, *Ivory C.* **112 D3** 7 1N 5 47W
Bouaké, *Ivory C.* **112 D3** 7 40N 5 2W
Bouanga, *Congo* **114 C3** 2 7S 16 8 E
Bouar, *C.A.R.* **114 A3** 6 0N 15 40 E
Bouârfa, *Morocco* **111 B4** 32 32N 1 58W
Bouba Ndjida △, *Cameroon* **114 A2** 8 50N 14 45 E
Boubout, *Algeria* **110 C4** 27 26N 4 30W
Bouca, *C.A.R.* **114 A3** 6 45N 18 25 E
Boucaut B., *Australia* **126 A1** 12 0S 134 25 E
Bouches-du-Rhône □, *France* **29 E9** 43 37N 5 2 E
Boucle de Baoule △, *Mali* **112 C3** 13 53N 9 0W
Boucles de la Seine Normande ⌂, *France* **26 C7** 49 32N 0 35 E
Bouctouche, *Canada* **141 C7** 46 30N 64 45W
Bouda, *Algeria* **111 C4** 27 50N 0 27W
Boudenib, *Morocco* **110 B4** 31 59N 3 31W
Boudry, *Switz.* **32 C3** 46 57N 6 50 E
Boufarik, *Algeria* **111 A5** 36 34N 2 58 E
Bougainville, C., *Australia* **124 B4** 13 57S 126 4 E
Bougainville I., *Papua N. G.* **133 L8** 6 0S 155 0 E
Bougainville Reef, *Australia* **126 B4** 15 30S 147 5 E
Bougainville Str., *Solomon Is.* **133 L9** 6 40S 156 10 E
Bougaroun, C., *Algeria* **111 A6** 37 6N 6 30 E
Bougie = Bejaïa, *Algeria* **111 A6** 36 42N 5 2 E
Bougouni, *Mali* **112 C3** 11 30N 7 20W
Bouillon, *Belgium* **24 E5** 49 44N 5 3 E
Bouïra, *Algeria* **111 A5** 36 20N 3 59 E
Boukombé, *Benin* **113 C5** 10 13N 1 9 E
Boulal, *Mali* **112 B3** 15 8N 8 21W
Boulazac, *France* **28 C4** 45 10N 0 47 E
Boulder, *Colo., U.S.A.* **154 E2** 40 1N 105 17W
Boulder, *Mont., U.S.A.* **158 C7** 46 14N 112 7W
Boulder City, *U.S.A.* **161 K12** 35 59N 114 50W
Boulder Creek, *U.S.A.* **160 H4** 37 7N 122 7W
Boulder Dam = Hoover Dam, *U.S.A.* **161 K12** 36 1N 114 44W
Boulembo, *Gabon* **114 C2** 1 26S 12 0 E
Bouli, *Mauritania* **112 B2** 15 17N 12 18W
Boulia, *Australia* **126 C2** 22 52S 139 51 E
Bouligny, *France* **27 C12** 49 17N 5 45 E
Boulogne →, *France* **26 E5** 47 12N 1 47W
Boulogne-sur-Gesse, *France* **28 E4** 43 18N 0 38 E
Boulogne-sur-Mer, *France* **27 B8** 50 42N 1 36 E
Bouloire, *France* **26 E7** 47 59N 0 45 E
Boulou →, *C.A.R.* **114 A4** 6 45N 24 16 E
Boulouli, *Mali* **112 B3** 15 30N 9 25W
Bouloupari, *N. Cal.* **133 U20** 21 52S 166 4 E
Bouloupesse, *Congo* **114 C2** 1 58S 12 40 E
Boulsa, *Burkina Faso* **113 C4** 12 39N 0 34W
Boultoum, *Niger* **113 C7** 14 45N 10 25 E
Bouma △, *Fiji* **133 A2** 16 50S 179 52 E
Boumalne, *Morocco* **110 B3** 31 25N 6 0W
Boumba →, *Cameroon* **114 B2** 2 2N 15 12 E
Boumbé →, *C.A.R.* **114 B3** 4 4N 15 23 E
Boûmdeïd, *Mauritania* **112 B2** 17 25N 9 50W
Boun Neua, *Laos* **86 B3** 21 38N 101 54 E
Boun Tai, *Laos* **86 B3** 21 23N 101 58 E
Bouna, *Ivory C.* **112 D4** 9 10N 3 0W
Boundary, *U.S.A.* **144 D12** 64 4N 141 6W
Boundary Peak, *U.S.A.* **160 H8** 37 51N 118 21W
Boundgi, *Gabon* **114 C2** 1 0S 11 51 E
Boundiali, *Ivory C.* **112 D3** 9 30N 6 20W
Boungou →, *C.A.R.* **114 A4** 8 21N 23 48 E
Bountiful, *U.S.A.* **158 F8** 40 53N 111 53W
Bounty Is., *Pac. Oc.* **134 M9** 48 0S 178 30 E
Boura, *Mali* **112 C4** 12 25N 4 33W
Bourail, *N. Cal.* **133 U19** 21 34S 165 30 E
Bourbeuse →, *U.S.A.* **156 F6** 38 24N 90 53W
Bourbon, *U.S.A.* **157 C10** 41 18N 86 7W
Bourbon-Lancy, *France* **27 F10** 46 37N 3 45 E
Bourbon-l'Archambault, *France* **27 F10** 46 36N 3 4 E
Bourbonnais, *France* **27 F10** 46 28N 3 0 E
Bourbonnais, *U.S.A.* **157 C9** 41 9N 87 52W
Bourbonne-les-Bains, *France* **27 E12** 47 54N 5 45 E
Bourbourg, *France* **27 B9** 50 56N 2 12 E
Bourdel L., *Canada* **140 A5** 56 43N 74 10W
Bourem, *Mali* **113 B4** 17 0N 0 24W
Bourg, *France* **28 C3** 45 3N 0 34W
Bourg-Argental, *France* **29 C8** 45 18N 4 32 E
Bourg-de-Péage, *France* **29 C9** 45 2N 5 3 E
Bourg-en-Bresse, *France* **27 F12** 46 13N 5 12 E
Bourg-Lastic, *France* **28 C6** 45 39N 2 35 E
Bourg-Madame, *France* **28 F5** 42 26N 1 55 E
Bourg-St-Andéol, *France* **29 D8** 44 23N 4 39 E
Bourg-St-Maurice, *France* **29 C10** 45 35N 6 46 E
Bourg-St. Pierre, *Switz.* **32 E4** 45 57N 7 12 E
Bourganeuf, *France* **28 C5** 45 57N 1 45 E
Bourgas = Burgas, *Bulgaria* **51 D11** 42 33N 27 29 E
Bourges, *France* **27 E9** 47 9N 2 25 E
Bourget, *Canada* **151 A9** 45 26N 75 9W
Bourget, Lac du, *France* **29 C9** 45 44N 5 52 E
Bourgneuf, B. de, *France* **26 E4** 47 3N 2 10W
Bourgneuf-en-Retz, *France* **26 E5** 47 2N 1 58W
Bourgogne □, *France* **27 F11** 47 0N 4 50 E
Bourgoin-Jallieu, *France* **29 C9** 45 36N 5 17 E
Bourgueil, *France* **26 E7** 47 17N 0 10 E
Bourke, *Australia* **127 E4** 30 8S 145 55 E
Bourne, *U.K.* **20 E7** 52 47N 0 22W
Bournemouth, *U.K.* **21 G6** 50 43N 1 52W
Bournemouth □, *U.K.* **21 G6** 50 43N 1 52W
Bouroum, *Burkina Faso* **113 C4** 13 37N 0 39W
Bouse, *U.S.A.* **161 M13** 33 56N 114 0W
Boussac, *France* **27 F9** 46 22N 2 13 E
Boussé, *Burkina Faso* **113 C4** 12 39N 1 53W
Bousso, *Chad* **109 F3** 10 34N 16 52 E
Boussouma, *Burkina Faso* **113 C4** 12 52N 1 13W
Boutilimit, *Mauritania* **112 B2** 17 45N 14 40W
Boutonne →, *France* **28 C3** 45 55N 0 50W
Bouvet I. = Bouvetøya, *Antarctica* **8 M12** 54 26S 3 24 E
Bouvetøya, *Antarctica* **8 M12** 54 26S 3 24 E
Bouxwiller, *France* **27 D14** 48 49N 7 27 E
Bouza, *Niger* **113 C6** 14 29N 6 2 E
Bouznika, *Morocco* **110 B3** 33 46N 7 6W
Bouzonville, *France* **27 C13** 49 17N 6 32 E
Bova Marina, *Italy* **47 E8** 37 56N 15 55 E
Bovalino Marina, *Italy* **47 D9** 38 10N 16 10 E
Bovec, *Slovenia* **45 B10** 46 20N 13 33 E
Boven Kapuas, Pegunungan, *Malaysia* **85 B4** 1 25N 113 15 E
Bøverdal, *Norway* **18 C5** 61 44N 8 20 E
Bøverfjorden, *Norway* **18 A5** 63 1N 8 32 E
Bovill, *U.S.A.* **158 C5** 46 51N 116 24W
Bovino, *Italy* **47 A8** 41 15N 15 20 E
Bovril, *Argentina* **174 C4** 31 21S 59 26W
Bow →, *Canada* **142 C6** 49 57N 111 41W
Bow Island, *Canada* **158 B8** 49 50N 111 23W
Bowbells, *U.S.A.* **154 A3** 48 48N 102 15W
Bowdle, *U.S.A.* **154 C5** 45 27N 99 39W
Bowdon, *U.S.A.* **152 B4** 33 32N 85 15W
Bowdon Junction, *U.S.A.* **152 B4** 33 40N 85 9W
Bowelling, *Australia* **125 F2** 33 25S 116 30 E
Bowen, *Argentina* **174 D2** 35 0S 67 31W
Bowen, *Australia* **126 J6** 20 0S 148 16 E
Bowen Mts., *Australia* **129 D7** 37 0S 147 50 E
Bowie, *Ariz., U.S.A.* **159 K9** 32 19N 109 29W
Bowie, *Tex., U.S.A.* **155 J6** 33 34N 97 51W
Bowkān, *Iran* **101 D12** 36 31N 46 12 E
Bowland, Forest of, *U.K.* **20 D5** 54 0N 2 30W
Bowling Green, *Fla., U.S.A.* **153 H8** 27 38N 81 50W
Bowling Green, *Ky., U.S.A.* **148 G2** 36 59N 86 27W
Bowling Green, *Mo., U.S.A.* **156 E5** 39 21N 91 12W
Bowling Green, *Ohio, U.S.A.* **157 C13** 41 23N 83 39W
Bowling Green, C., *Australia* **126 B4** 19 19S 147 25 E
Bowling Green Bay △, *Australia* **126 B4** 19 26S 146 57 E
Bowman, *N. Dak., U.S.A.* **154 B3** 46 11N 103 24W
Bowman, *S.C., U.S.A.* **152 B9** 33 21N 80 41W
Bowman I., *Antarctica* **7 C8** 65 0S 104 0 E
Bowmanville = Clarington, *Canada* **150 C6** 43 55N 78 41W
Bowmore, *U.K.* **22 F2** 55 45N 6 17W
Bowral, *Australia* **129 C9** 34 26S 150 27 E
Bowraville, *Australia* **127 E5** 30 37S 152 52 E
Bowron →, *Canada* **142 C4** 54 3N 121 50W
Bowron Lake ⌂, *Canada* **142 C4** 53 10N 121 5W
Bowser L., *Canada* **142 B3** 56 30N 129 30W
Bowsman, *Canada* **143 C8** 52 14N 101 12W
Bowutu Mts., *Papua N. G.* **132 D4** 7 45S 147 10 E
Bowwood, *Zambia* **119 F2** 17 5S 26 20 E
Box Cr. →, *Australia* **127 E3** 34 10S 143 50 E
Boxholm, *Sweden* **17 F9** 58 12N 15 3 E
Boxmeer, *Neths.* **24 C5** 51 38N 5 56 E
Boxtel, *Neths.* **24 C5** 51 36N 5 20 E
Boyabat, *Turkey* **100 B6** 41 28N 34 47 E
Boyabo, *Dem. Rep. of the Congo* **114 B3** 3 43N 18 46 E
Boyaca □, *Colombia* **168 B3** 5 30N 73 20W
Boyalıca, *Turkey* **51 F13** 40 29N 29 33 E
Boyang, *China* **77 C11** 29 0N 116 38 E
Boyanovo, *Ukraine* **53 B11** 48 17N 26 8 E
Boyasegese, *Dem. Rep. of the Congo* **114 B4** 3 29N 20 33 E
Boyce, *U.S.A.* **155 K8** 31 23N 92 40W
Boyd, *U.S.A.* **152 E6** 30 11N 83 37W
Boyd L., *Canada* **140 B4** 52 46N 76 42W
Boyenge, *Dem. Rep. of the Congo* **114 B3** 0 14N 18 55 E
Boyer, C., *N. Cal.* **133 U22** 21 37S 168 6 E
Boyera, *Dem. Rep. of the Congo* **114 C3** 0 40S 19 23 E
Boyle, *Canada* **142 C6** 54 35N 112 49W
Boyle, *Ireland* **23 C3** 53 59N 8 18W
Boyne →, *Ireland* **23 C5** 53 43N 6 15W
Boyne City, *U.S.A.* **148 C3** 45 13N 85 1W
Boyni Qara, *Afghan.* **91 A2** 36 20N 67 0 E
Boynitsa, *Bulgaria* **50 C6** 43 58N 22 32 E
Boynton Beach, *U.S.A.* **153 J9** 26 32N 80 4W
Boyolali, *Indonesia* **85 D4** 7 32S 110 35 E
Boyoma, Chutes, *Dem. Rep. of the Congo* **118 B2** 0 35N 25 23 E
Boysen Reservoir, *U.S.A.* **158 E9** 43 25N 108 11W
Boyup Brook, *Australia* **125 F2** 33 50S 116 23 E
Boz Burun, *Turkey* **51 F12** 40 32N 28 46 E
Boz Dağ, *Turkey* **49 D11** 37 18N 29 11 E
Boz Dağları, *Turkey* **49 C10** 38 20N 28 0 E
Bozai Gumbaz, *Afghan.* **65 E7** 37 8N 74 0 E
Bozburun, *Turkey* **49 E10** 36 43N 28 4 E
Bozcaada, *Turkey* **100 C2** 39 49N 26 3 E
Bozdoğan, *Turkey* **49 D10** 37 40N 28 17 E
Boze, *Papua N. G.* **132 E2** 9 3S 143 3 E
Bozeman, *U.S.A.* **158 D8** 45 41N 111 2W
Bozen = Bolzano, *Italy* **45 B8** 46 31N 11 22 E
Bozene, *Dem. Rep. of the Congo* **114 B3** 2 56N 19 12 E
Boževac, *Serbia & M.* **50 B5** 44 32N 21 24 E
Bozhou, *China* **74 H8** 33 55N 115 41 E
Bozkır, *Turkey* **100 D5** 37 11N 32 14 E
Bozkurt, *Turkey* **49 D11** 37 50N 29 37 E
Bozouls, *France* **28 D6** 44 28N 2 43 E
Bozoum, *C.A.R.* **114 A3** 6 25N 16 35 E
Bozova, *Antalya, Turkey* **49 D12** 37 13N 30 18 E
Bozova, *Sanliurfa, Turkey* **101 D8** 37 21N 38 32 E
Bozovici, *Romania* **52 F7** 44 56N 22 0 E
Bozüyük, *Turkey* **49 B12** 39 54N 30 3 E
Bra, *Italy* **44 D4** 44 42N 7 51 E
Braås, *Sweden* **17 G9** 57 4N 15 3 E
Brabant □, *Belgium* **24 D4** 50 46N 4 30 E
Brabant L., *Canada* **143 B8** 55 58N 103 43W
Brabrand, *Denmark* **17 H4** 56 9N 10 7 E
Brač, *Croatia* **45 E13** 43 20N 16 40 E
Bracadale, L., *U.K.* **22 D2** 57 20N 6 30W
Bracciano, *Italy* **45 F9** 42 6N 12 10 E
Bracciano, L. di, *Italy* **45 F9** 42 7N 12 14 E
Bracebridge, *Canada* **140 C4** 45 2N 79 19W
Brach, *Libya* **108 C2** 27 31N 14 20 E
Bracieux, *France* **26 E8** 47 30N 1 30 E
Bräcke, *Sweden* **16 B9** 62 45N 15 26 E
Brackettville, *U.S.A.* **155 L4** 29 19N 100 25W
Brački Kanal, *Croatia* **45 E13** 43 24N 16 40 E
Bracknell, *U.K.* **21 F7** 51 25N 0 43W
Bracknell Forest □, *U.K.* **21 F7** 51 25N 0 44W
Brad, *Romania* **52 D7** 46 10N 22 50 E
Brádano →, *Italy* **47 B9** 40 23N 16 51 E
Bradenton, *U.S.A.* **153 H7** 27 30N 82 34W
Bradford, *Canada* **150 B5** 44 7N 79 34W
Bradford, *U.K.* **20 D6** 53 47N 1 45W
Bradford, *Ill., U.S.A.* **156 C7** 41 11N 89 39W
Bradford, *Ohio, U.S.A.* **157 D12** 40 8N 84 27W
Bradford, *Pa., U.S.A.* **150 E6** 41 58N 78 38W
Bradford, *Vt., U.S.A.* **151 C12** 43 59N 72 9W
Bradley, *Ark., U.S.A.* **155 J8** 33 6N 93 39W
Bradley, *Calif., U.S.A.* **160 K6** 35 52N 120 48W
Bradley, *Fla., U.S.A.* **153 H8** 27 48N 81 59W
Bradley, *Ill., U.S.A.* **157 C9** 41 9N 87 52W
Bradley Institute, *Zimbabwe* **119 F3** 17 7S 31 25 E
Bradner, *U.S.A.* **157 C13** 41 20N 83 26W
Brady, *U.S.A.* **155 K5** 31 9N 99 20W
Brædstrup, *Denmark* **17 J3** 55 58N 9 37 E
Braemar, *Australia* **128 B3** 33 12S 139 35 E
Braeside, *Canada* **151 A8** 45 28N 76 24W
Braga, *Portugal* **42 D2** 41 35N 8 25W
Braga □, *Portugal* **42 D2** 41 30N 8 30W
Bragadiru, *Romania* **53 G10** 43 46N 25 31 E
Bragado, *Argentina* **174 D3** 35 2S 60 27W
Bragança, *Brazil* **170 B2** 1 0S 47 2W
Bragança, *Portugal* **42 D4** 41 48N 6 50W
Bragança □, *Portugal* **42 D4** 41 30N 6 45W
Bragança Paulista, *Brazil* **175 A6** 22 55S 46 32W
Bragg's Spur = West Memphis, *U.S.A.* **155 H9** 35 9N 90 11W
Brahestad = Raahe, *Finland* **14 D21** 64 40N 24 28 E
Brahmakund, *India* **90 B6** 27 52N 96 22 E
Brahmanbaria, *Bangla.* **90 D3** 23 58N 91 15 E
Brahmani →, *India* **94 D8** 20 39N 86 46 E
Brahmapur, *India* **94 E7** 19 15N 84 54 E
Brahmaputra →, *Asia* **68 D3** 23 40N 90 35 E
Braich-y-pwll, *U.K.* **20 E3** 52 47N 4 46W
Braidwood, *Australia* **129 C8** 35 27S 149 49 E
Brăila, *Romania* **53 E12** 45 19N 27 59 E
Brăila □, *Romania* **53 E12** 45 5N 27 30 E
Brainerd, *U.S.A.* **154 B7** 46 22N 94 12W
Braintree, *U.K.* **21 F8** 51 53N 0 34 E
Braintree, *U.S.A.* **151 D14** 42 13N 71 0W
Brak →, *S. Africa* **116 D3** 29 35S 22 55 E
Brake, *Germany* **30 B4** 53 20N 8 28 E
Brakel, *Germany* **30 D5** 51 42N 9 11 E
Bräkne-Hoby, *Sweden* **17 H9** 56 14N 15 6 E
Brakwater, *Namibia* **116 C2** 22 28S 17 3 E
Brålanda, *Sweden* **17 F6** 58 34N 12 21 E
Bramberg, *Germany* **31 E6** 50 6N 10 40 E
Bramdrupdam, *Denmark* **17 J3** 55 31N 9 28 E
Bramhapuri, *India* **94 D4** 20 36N 79 52 E
Bramming, *Denmark* **17 J2** 55 28N 8 42 E
Brämön, *Sweden* **16 B11** 62 14N 17 40 E
Brampton, *Canada* **140 D4** 43 45N 79 45W
Brampton, *U.K.* **20 C5** 54 57N 2 44W
Bramsche, *Germany* **30 C3** 52 24N 7 59 E
Branton I., *Australia* **126 J7** 20 50S 149 17 E
Branchville, *U.S.A.* **152 B9** 33 15N 80 49W
Branco →, *Brazil* **169 D5** 1 20S 61 50W
Branco, C., *Brazil* **170 C5** 7 9S 34 47W
Brandberg, *Namibia* **116 C1** 21 10S 14 33 E
Brandberg ⌂, *Namibia* **116 C1** 21 10S 14 30 E
Brandbu, *Norway* **18 D7** 60 26N 10 28 E
Brande, *Denmark* **17 J3** 55 57N 9 8 E
Brandenburg = Neubrandenburg, *Germany* **30 B9** 53 33N 13 15 E
Brandenburg, *Germany* **30 C8** 52 25N 12 33 E
Brandenburg, *U.S.A.* **157 G10** 38 0N 86 10W
Brandenburg □, *Germany* **30 C9** 52 50N 13 0 E
Brandfort, *S. Africa* **116 D4** 28 40S 26 30 E
Brando, *France* **29 F13** 42 47N 9 27 E
Brandon, *Canada* **143 D9** 49 50N 99 57W
Brandon, *Fla., U.S.A.* **153 H7** 27 56N 82 17W
Brandon, *Vt., U.S.A.* **151 C11** 43 48N 73 4W
Brandon B., *Ireland* **23 D1** 52 17N 10 8W
Brandon Mt., *Ireland* **23 D1** 52 15N 10 15W
Brandsen, *Argentina* **174 D4** 35 10S 58 15W
Brandvlei, *S. Africa* **116 E3** 30 25S 20 30 E
Brandýs nad Labem, *Czech Rep.* **34 A7** 50 10N 14 40 E
Brănești, *Romania* **53 F11** 44 27N 26 20 E
Branford, *Conn., U.S.A.* **151 E12** 41 17N 72 49W
Branford, *Fla., U.S.A.* **152 F7** 29 58N 82 56W
Braniewo, *Poland* **54 D6** 54 25N 19 50 E
Bransfield Str., *Antarctica* **7 C18** 63 0S 59 0W
Brańsk, *Poland* **55 F9** 52 45N 22 50 E
Branson, *U.S.A.* **155 G8** 36 39N 93 13W
Brantford, *Canada* **140 D3** 43 10N 80 15W
Brantley, *U.S.A.* **152 D3** 31 35N 86 16W
Brantôme, *France* **28 C4** 45 22N 0 39 E
Branxholme, *Australia* **128 D4** 37 52S 141 49 E
Branxton, *Australia* **129 B9** 32 38S 151 21 E
Branzi, *Italy* **44 B6** 46 1N 9 46 E
Brás, *Brazil* **169 D6** 2 5S 58 10W
Bras d'Or L., *Canada* **141 C7** 45 50N 60 50W
Brasher Falls, *U.S.A.* **151 B10** 44 49N 74 47W
Brasil = Brazil ■, *S. Amer.* **171 D2** 12 0S 50 0W
Brasil, Planalto, *Brazil* **166 E6** 18 0S 46 30W
Brasil Novo, *Brazil* **169 D7** 3 19S 52 38W
Brasiléia, *Brazil* **172 C4** 11 0S 68 45W
Brasília, *Distrito Federal, Brazil* **171 E2** 15 47S 47 55W
Brasília, *Minas Gerais, Brazil* **171 E3** 16 12S 44 26W
Brasília △, *Brazil* **171 E2** 15 41S 48 8W
Brasília Legal, *Brazil* **169 D6** 3 49S 55 36W
Braskereidfoss, *Norway* **18 D8** 60 44N 11 46 E
Braslaw, *Belarus* **15 J22** 55 38N 27 0 E
Braslovče, *Slovenia* **45 B12** 46 21N 15 3 E
Brașov, *Romania* **53 E10** 45 38N 25 35 E
Brașov □, *Romania* **53 E10** 45 45N 25 15 E
Brass, *Nigeria* **113 E6** 4 35N 6 14 E
Brass →, *Nigeria* **113 E6** 4 15N 6 13 E
Brassac-les-Mines, *France* **28 C7** 45 24N 3 20 E
Brasschaat, *Belgium* **24 C4** 51 19N 4 27 E
Brassey, Banjaran, *Malaysia* **85 B5** 5 0N 117 15 E
Brassey Ra., *Australia* **125 E3** 25 8S 122 15 E
Brasstown Bald, *U.S.A.* **149 H4** 34 53N 83 49W
Brastad, *Sweden* **17 F5** 58 23N 11 30 E
Brastavățu, *Romania* **53 G9** 43 55N 24 24 E
Bratan = Morozov, *Bulgaria* **51 D9** 42 30N 25 10 E
Brateș, *Romania* **53 E11** 45 50N 26 4 E
Bratislava, *Slovak Rep.* **35 C10** 48 10N 17 7 E
Bratislava M.R. Stefanik ✕ (BTS), *Slovak Rep.* **35 C10** 48 11N 17 9 E
Bratislavský □, *Slovak Rep.* **35 C10** 48 15N 17 20 E
Bratsberg = Telemark □, *Norway* **18 E5** 59 25N 8 30 E
Bratsigovo, *Bulgaria* **51 D8** 42 1N 24 22 E
Bratsk, *Russia* **67 D11** 56 10N 101 30 E
Brattleboro, *U.S.A.* **151 D12** 42 51N 72 34W
Brattvåg, *Norway* **18 B3** 62 37N 6 25 E
Bratunac, *Bos.-H.* **52 F4** 44 13N 19 21 E
Braunau, *Austria* **34 C6** 48 15N 13 3 E
Braunsberg = Braniewo, *Poland* **54 D6** 54 25N 19 50 E
Braunschweig, *Germany* **30 C6** 52 15N 10 31 E
Braunton, *U.K.* **21 F3** 51 7N 4 10W
Brava, *C. Verde Is.* **9 j** 15 0N 24 40W
Brava, *Somali Rep.* **120 D2** 1 20N 44 8 E
Bravicea, *Moldova* **53 C13** 47 22N 28 27 E
Bråviken, *Sweden* **17 F10** 58 38N 16 32 E
Bravo del Norte, Rio = Grande, Rio →, *U.S.A.* **155 N6** 25 58N 97 9W
Brawley, *U.S.A.* **161 N11** 32 59N 115 31W
Bray, *Ireland* **23 C5** 53 13N 6 7W
Bray, Mt., *Australia* **126 A1** 14 0S 134 30 E
Bray, Pays de, *France* **25 B4** 49 46N 1 26 E
Bray-sur-Seine, *France* **27 D10** 48 25N 3 14 E
Braymer, *U.S.A.* **156 E3** 39 35N 93 48W
Brazeau →, *Canada* **142 C5** 52 55N 115 14W
Brazil, *U.S.A.* **157 E9** 39 32N 87 8W
Brazil ■, *S. Amer.* **171 D2** 12 0S 50 0W
Brazilian Highlands = Brasil, Planalto, *Brazil* **166 E6** 18 0S 46 30W
Brazo Sur →, *S. Amer.* **174 B4** 25 21S 57 42W
Brazos →, *U.S.A.* **155 L7** 28 53N 95 23W
Brazzaville, *Congo* **115 C3** 4 9S 15 12 E
Brčko, *Bos.-H.* **52 F3** 44 54N 18 46 E
Brda →, *Poland* **55 E5** 53 8N 18 8 E
Brdy, *Czech Rep.* **34 B6** 49 43N 13 55 E
Brea, *Peru* **172 A1** 4 40S 81 7W
Breaden, L., *Australia* **125 E4** 25 51S 125 28 E
Breaksea Sd., *N.Z.* **131 F1** 45 35S 166 35 E
Bream B., *N.Z.* **130 B3** 35 56S 174 28 E
Bream Hd., *N.Z.* **130 B3** 35 51S 174 36 E
Bream Tail, *N.Z.* **130 C3** 36 3S 174 36 E
Breas, *Chile* **174 B1** 25 29S 70 24W
Breaza, *Romania* **53 E10** 45 11N 25 40 E
Brebes, *Indonesia* **85 D3** 6 52S 109 3 E
Brechin, *Canada* **150 B5** 44 32N 79 10W
Brechin, *U.K.* **22 E6** 56 44N 2 39W
Brecht, *Belgium* **24 C4** 51 21N 4 38 E
Breckenridge, *Colo., U.S.A.* **158 G10** 39 29N 106 3W
Breckenridge, *Minn., U.S.A.* **154 B6** 46 16N 96 35W
Breckenridge, *Tex., U.S.A.* **155 J5** 32 45N 98 54W
Breckland, *U.K.* **21 E8** 52 30N 0 40 E
Brecknock, Pen., *Chile* **176 D2** 54 35S 71 30W
Břeclav, *Czech Rep.* **35 C9** 48 46N 16 53 E
Brecon, *U.K.* **21 F4** 51 57N 3 23W
Brecon Beacons, *U.K.* **21 F4** 51 53N 3 26W
Brecon Beacons △, *U.K.* **21 F4** 51 50N 3 30W
Breda, *Neths.* **24 C4** 51 35N 4 45 E
Bredaryd, *Sweden* **17 G7** 57 10N 13 45 E
Bredasdorp, *S. Africa* **116 E3** 34 33S 20 2 E
Bredbo, *Australia* **129 C8** 35 58S 149 10 E
Bredebro, *Denmark* **17 J2** 55 4N 8 50 E
Bredstedt, *Germany* **30 A4** 54 37N 8 55 E
Bredy, *Russia* **64 E8** 52 26N 60 21 E
Bree, *Belgium* **24 C5** 51 8N 5 35 E
Bregalnica →, *Macedonia* **50 E6** 41 43N 22 9 E
Bregenz, *Austria* **34 D2** 47 30N 9 45 E
Bregenzer Wald, *Austria* **33 B9** 47 20N 10 0 E
Bregovo, *Bulgaria* **50 B6** 44 9N 22 39 E
Bréhal, *France* **26 D5** 48 53N 1 30W
Bréhat, Î. de, *France* **26 D4** 48 51N 3 0W
Breiðafjörður, *Iceland* **11 B3** 65 15N 23 15W
Breiðdalsvík, *Iceland* **11 C13** 64 44N 14 0W
Breil-sur-Roya, *France* **29 E11** 43 56N 7 31 E
Breim, *Norway* **18 C3** 61 44N 6 25 E
Breisach, *Germany* **31 G3** 48 1N 7 36 E
Brejinho de Nazaré, *Brazil* **170 D2** 11 1S 48 34W
Brejo, *Brazil* **170 B3** 3 41S 42 47W
Brekke, *Norway* **18 C2** 61 1N 5 26 E
Brekken, *Norway* **18 B8** 62 40N 11 51 E
Brekkestø, *Norway* **18 F5** 58 11N 8 22 E
Bremanger, *Norway* **18 C1** 61 51N 4 58 E
Bremangerlandet, *Norway* **18 C1** 61 51N 5 0 E
Bremen, *Germany* **30 B4** 53 4N 8 47 E
Bremen, *Ga., U.S.A.* **152 B4** 33 43N 85 9W
Bremen, *Ind., U.S.A.* **157 C10** 41 27N 86 9W
Bremen □, *Germany* **30 B4** 53 4N 8 50 E
Bremer Bay, *Australia* **125 F2** 34 21S 119 20 E
Bremer I., *Australia* **126 A2** 12 5S 136 45 E
Bremerhaven, *Germany* **30 B4** 53 33N 8 36 E
Bremersdorp = Manzini, *Swaziland* **117 D5** 26 30S 31 25 E
Bremerton, *U.S.A.* **160 C4** 47 34N 122 38W
Bremervörde, *Germany* **30 B5** 53 29N 9 8 E
Bremgarten, *Switz.* **33 B6** 47 22N 8 20 E
Bremnes, *Norway* **18 E2** 59 47N 5 8 E
Bremsnes, *Norway* **18 A4** 63 6N 7 40 E
Brenes, *Spain* **43 H5** 37 32N 5 54W
Brenham, *U.S.A.* **155 K6** 30 10N 96 24W
Brenne, *France* **28 B5** 46 44N 1 14 E
Brenne ⌂, *France* **28 B5** 46 40N 1 15 E
Brennerpass, *Austria* **34 D4** 47 2N 11 30 E
Brennhaug, *Norway* **18 C6** 61 54N 9 21 E
Breno, *Italy* **44 C7** 45 57N 10 18 E
Brent, *U.S.A.* **149 J2** 32 56N 87 10W
Brenta →, *Italy* **45 C9** 45 11N 12 18 E
Brentwood, *U.K.* **21 F8** 51 37N 0 19 E
Brentwood, *Calif., U.S.A.* **160 H5** 37 56N 121 42W
Brentwood, *N.Y., U.S.A.* **151 F11** 40 47N 73 15W
Bréscia, *Italy* **44 C7** 45 33N 10 15 E
Breskens, *Neths.* **24 C3** 51 23N 3 33 E
Breslau = Wrocław, *Poland* **55 G4** 51 5N 17 5 E
Bresle →, *France* **26 B8** 50 4N 1 22 E
Bressanone, *Italy* **45 B8** 46 43N 11 39 E
Bressay, *U.K.* **22 A7** 60 9N 1 6W
Bresse, *France* **27 F12** 46 50N 5 10 E
Bressuire, *France* **26 F6** 46 51N 0 30W
Brest, *Belarus* **59 F2** 52 10N 23 40 E
Brest, *France* **26 D2** 48 24N 4 31W
Brest-Litovsk = Brest, *Belarus* **59 F2** 52 10N 23 40 E
Bretagne □, *France* **26 D3** 48 10N 3 0W
Bretanha, Pta. da, *Azores* **9 d3** 37 54N 25 47W
Bretçu, *Romania* **53 D11** 46 7N 26 18 E
Bretenoux, *France* **28 D5** 44 54N 1 51 E
Breteuil, *Eure, France* **26 D7** 48 50N 0 57 E
Breteuil, *Oise, France* **27 C9** 49 38N 2 18 E
Breton, *Canada* **142 C6** 53 7N 114 28W
Breton, Pertuis, *France* **28 B2** 46 17N 1 25W
Breton Sd., *U.S.A.* **155 L10** 29 35N 89 15W
Brett, C., *N.Z.* **130 B3** 35 10S 174 20 E
Bretten, *Germany* **31 F4** 49 2N 8 42 E
Breuil-Cervínia, *Italy* **44 C4** 45 56N 7 38 E
Brevard, *U.S.A.* **149 H4** 35 14N 82 44W
Breves, *Brazil* **170 B1** 1 40S 50 29W
Brevig Mission, *U.S.A.* **144 D6** 65 20N 166 29W
Brevik, *Norway* **18 E6** 59 4N 9 42 E
Brewarrina, *Australia* **127 E4** 30 0S 146 51 E
Brewer, *U.S.A.* **149 C11** 44 48N 68 46W
Brewer, Mt., *U.S.A.* **160 J8** 36 44N 118 28W
Brewerville, *Liberia* **112 D2** 6 26N 10 47W
Brewster, *N.Y., U.S.A.* **151 E11** 41 23N 73 37W
Brewster, *Ohio, U.S.A.* **150 F3** 40 43N 81 36W
Brewster, *Wash., U.S.A.* **158 B4** 48 6N 119 47W
Brewster, Kap = Kangikajik, *Greenland* **10 C8** 70 7N 22 0W
Brewton, *U.S.A.* **149 K2** 31 7N 87 4W
Breyten, *S. Africa* **117 D5** 26 16S 30 0 E
Breza, *Bos.-H.* **52 F3** 44 2N 18 16 E
Brežice, *Slovenia* **45 C12** 45 54N 15 35 E
Brézina, *Algeria* **111 B5** 33 4N 1 14 E
Březnice, *Czech Rep.* **34 B6** 49 32N 13 57 E
Breznik, *Bulgaria* **50 D6** 42 44N 22 55 E
Brezno, *Slovak Rep.* **35 C12** 48 50N 19 40 E
Brezoi, *Romania* **53 E9** 45 21N 24 15 E
Brezovica, *Serbia & M.* **50 D5** 42 15N 21 3 E
Brezovo, *Bulgaria* **51 D9** 42 21N 25 5 E
Bria, *C.A.R.* **114 A4** 6 30N 21 58 E
Briançon, *France* **29 D10** 44 54N 6 39 E
Briare, *France* **27 E9** 47 38N 2 45 E
Briático, *Italy* **47 D9** 38 43N 16 2 E
Bribie I., *Australia* **127 D5** 27 0S 153 10 E
Bribri, *Costa Rica* **164 E3** 9 38N 82 50W
Briceni, *Moldova* **53 B12** 48 22N 27 6 E
Bricquebec, *France* **26 C5** 49 28N 1 38W
Bridgefield, *Barbados* **165 g** 13 9N 59 36W
Bridgehampton, *U.S.A.* **151 F12** 40 56N 72 19W
Bridgend, *U.K.* **21 F4** 51 30N 3 34W
Bridgend □, *U.K.* **21 F4** 51 36N 3 36W
Bridgeport, *Calif., U.S.A.* **160 G7** 38 15N 119 14W
Bridgeport, *Conn., U.S.A.* **151 E11** 41 11N 73 12W
Bridgeport, *Ill., U.S.A.* **157 F9** 38 43N 87 46W
Bridgeport, *Nebr., U.S.A.* **154 E3** 41 40N 103 6W
Bridgeport, *Tex., U.S.A.* **155 J6** 33 13N 97 45W
Bridger, *U.S.A.* **158 D9** 45 18N 108 55W
Bridgeton, *U.S.A.* **148 F8** 39 26N 75 14W
Bridgetown, *Australia* **125 F2** 33 58S 116 7 E
Bridgetown, *Barbados* **165 g** 13 6N 59 37W
Bridgetown, *Canada* **141 D6** 44 55N 65 18W
Bridgewater, *Australia* **128 D5** 36 36S 143 59 E
Bridgewater, *Canada* **141 D7** 44 25N 64 31W
Bridgewater, *Mass., U.S.A.* **151 E14** 41 59N 70 58W
Bridgewater, *N.Y., U.S.A.* **151 D9** 42 53N 75 15W
Bridgewater, C., *Australia* **128 E4** 38 23S 141 23 E
Bridgewater-Gagebrook, *Australia* **127 G4** 42 44S 147 14 E
Bridgman, *U.S.A.* **157 C10** 41 57N 86 33W
Bridgnorth, *U.K.* **21 E5** 52 32N 2 25W
Bridgton, *U.S.A.* **151 B14** 44 3N 70 42W
Bridgwater, *U.K.* **21 F5** 51 8N 2 59W
Bridgwater B., *U.K.* **21 F4** 51 15N 3 15W
Bridlington, *U.K.* **20 C7** 54 5N 0 12W
Bridlington B., *U.K.* **20 C7** 54 4N 0 10W
Bridport, *Australia* **127 G4** 40 59S 147 23 E
Bridport, *U.K.* **21 G5** 50 44N 2 45W
Briec, *France* **26 D2** 48 6N 4 0W
Brieg = Brzeg, *Poland* **55 H4** 50 52N 17 30 E
Brienne-le-Château, *France* **27 D11** 48 24N 4 30 E
Brienon-sur-Armançon, *France* **27 E10** 47 59N 3 38 E
Brienz, *Switz.* **32 C5** 46 46N 8 2 E
Brienzer Rothorn, *Switz.* **32 C6** 46 48N 8 2 E
Brienzersee, *Switz.* **32 C5** 46 44N 7 53 E
Brier Cr. →, *U.S.A.* **152 C8** 32 44N 81 26W
Brière ⌂, *France* **26 E4** 47 22N 2 13W
Brig, *Switz.* **32 D5** 46 18N 7 59 E
Brigg, *U.K.* **20 D7** 53 34N 0 28W
Brigham City, *U.S.A.* **158 F7** 41 31N 112 1W
Bright, *Australia* **129 D7** 36 42S 146 56 E
Brighton, *Australia* **128 C3** 35 5S 138 30 E
Brighton, *Canada* **150 B7** 44 2N 77 44W
Brighton, *Trin. & Tob.* **169 F9** 10 13N 61 39W
Brighton, *U.K.* **21 G7** 50 49N 0 7W
Brighton, *Fla., U.S.A.* **153 H8** 27 14N 81 6W

Brighton, *Ill., U.S.A.* **156 E6** 39 2N 90 8W
Brighton, *Iowa, U.S.A.* **156 C5** 41 10N 91 49W
Brighton, *Mich., U.S.A.* **157 B13** 42 32N 83 47W
Brighton, *N.Y., U.S.A.* **150 C7** 43 8N 77 34W
Brightwater, *N.Z.* **131 B8** 41 22 S 173 9 E
Brignogan-Plage, *France* **26 D2** 48 40N 4 20W
Brignoles, *France* **29 E10** 43 25N 6 5 E
Brihuega, *Spain* **40 E2** 40 45N 2 52W
Brikama, *Gambia* **112 C1** 13 15N 16 45W
Brilliant, *U.S.A.* **150 F4** 40 15N 80 39W
Brilon, *Germany* **30 D4** 51 23N 8 35 E
Brim, *Australia* **128 D5** 36 3 S 142 27 E
Brimfield, *U.S.A.* **156 D7** 40 50N 89 53W
Bríndisi, *Italy* **47 B10** 40 39N 17 55 E
Brinje, *Croatia* **45 D12** 44 59N 15 9 E
Brinkley, *U.S.A.* **155 H9** 34 53N 91 12W
Brinkworth, *Australia* **128 B3** 33 42 S 138 26 E
Brinnon, *U.S.A.* **160 C4** 47 41N 122 54W
Brinson, *U.S.A.* **152 E5** 30 59N 84 44W
Brion, Î., *Canada* **141 C7** 47 46N 61 26W
Brionne, *France* **26 C7** 49 11N 0 43 E
Brionski, *Croatia* **45 D10** 44 55N 13 45 E
Brioude, *France* **28 C7** 45 18N 3 24 E
Briouze, *France* **26 D6** 48 42N 0 23W
Brisbane, *Australia* **127 D5** 27 25 S 153 2 E
Brisbane →, *Australia* **127 D5** 27 24 S 153 9 E
Brisbane Ranges △, *Australia* **128 D6** 37 47 S 144 16 E
Brisighella, *Italy* **45 D8** 44 13N 11 46 E
Brissago, *Switz.* **33 D7** 46 7N 8 43 E
Bristol, *U.K.* **21 F5** 51 26N 2 35W
Bristol, *Conn., U.S.A.* **151 E12** 41 40N 72 57W
Bristol, *Fla., U.S.A.* **152 E5** 30 26N 84 59W
Bristol, *Pa., U.S.A.* **151 F10** 40 6N 74 51W
Bristol, *R.I., U.S.A.* **151 E13** 41 40N 71 16W
Bristol, *Tenn., U.S.A.* **149 G4** 36 36N 82 11W
Bristol, City of □, *U.K.* **21 F5** 51 27N 2 36W
Bristol B., *U.S.A.* **144 H8** 58 0N 160 0W
Bristol Channel, *U.K.* **21 F3** 51 18N 4 30W
Bristol I., *Antarctica* **7 B1** 58 45 S 28 0W
Bristol L., *U.S.A.* **159 J5** 34 23N 116 50W
Bristow, *U.S.A.* **155 H6** 35 50N 96 23W
Bristow I., *Papua N. G.* **132 E2** 9 8 S 143 14 E
Britain = Great Britain, *Europe* **12 E5** 54 0N 2 15W
Britânia, *Brazil* **173 D7** 15 14 S 51 9W
British Central Africa = Malawi ■, *Africa* **119 E3** 11 55 S 34 0 E
British Columbia □, *Canada* **142 C3** 55 0N 125 15W
British East Africa = Kenya ■, *Africa* **118 B4** 1 0N 38 0 E
British Guiana = Guyana ■, *S. Amer.* **169 B6** 5 0N 59 0W
British Honduras = Belize ■, *Cent. Amer.* **163 D7** 17 0N 88 30W
British Indian Ocean Terr. = Chagos Arch. ☒, *Ind. Oc.* **121 E6** 6 0 S 72 0 E
British Isles, *Europe* **19 D5** 54 0N 4 0W
British Virgin Is. ☒, *W. Indies* **165 e** 18 30N 64 30W
Brits, *S. Africa* **117 D4** 25 37 S 27 48 E
Britstown, *S. Africa* **116 E3** 30 37 S 23 30 E
Britt, *Canada* **140 C3** 45 46N 80 34W
Britt, *U.S.A.* **156 A3** 43 6N 93 48W
Brittany = Bretagne □, *France* **26 D3** 48 10N 3 0W
Britton, *U.S.A.* **154 C6** 45 48N 97 45W
Brive-la-Gaillarde, *France* **28 C5** 45 10N 1 32 E
Briviesca, *Spain* **42 C7** 42 32N 3 19W
Brixen = Bressanone, *Italy* **45 B8** 46 43N 11 39 E
Brixham, *U.K.* **21 G4** 50 23N 3 31W
Brlik = Birlik, *Kazakhstan* **65 B6** 43 40N 73 49 E
Brlik = Birlik, *Kazakhstan* **65 A6** 44 5N 73 31 E
Brnaze, *Croatia* **45 E13** 43 41N 16 40 E
Brnenský □, *Czech Rep.* **35 B9** 49 10N 16 40 E
Brno, *Czech Rep.* **35 B9** 49 10N 16 35 E
Broach = Bharuch, *India* **94 D1** 21 47N 73 0 E
Broad →, *Ga., U.S.A.* **152 B7** 33 59N 82 39W
Broad →, *S.C., U.S.A.* **149 J5** 34 1N 81 4W
Broad Arrow, *Australia* **125 F3** 30 23 S 121 15 E
Broad B., *U.K.* **22 C2** 58 14N 6 18W
Broad Haven, *Ireland* **23 B2** 54 20N 9 55W
Broad Law, *U.K.* **22 F5** 55 30N 3 21W
Broad Sd., *Australia* **126 C4** 22 0 S 149 45 E
Broadalbin, *U.S.A.* **151 C10** 43 4N 74 12W
Broadback →, *Canada* **140 B4** 51 21N 78 52W
Broadford, *Australia* **129 D6** 37 14 S 145 4 E
Broadhurst Ra., *Australia* **124 D3** 22 30 S 122 30 E
Broads △, *U.K.* **21 E9** 52 45N 1 30 E
Broads, The, *U.K.* **20 E9** 52 45N 1 30 E
Broadus, *U.S.A.* **154 C2** 45 27N 105 25W
Broager, *Denmark* **17 K3** 54 53N 9 40 E
Broby, *Sweden* **17 H8** 56 15N 14 4 E
Broc, *Switz.* **32 C4** 46 37N 7 6 E
Brocēni, *Latvia* **54 B9** 56 42N 22 32 E
Brochet, *Canada* **143 B8** 57 53N 101 40W
Brochet, L., *Canada* **143 B8** 58 36N 101 35W
Brocken, *Germany* **30 D6** 51 47N 10 37 E
Brocklehurst, *Australia* **129 B8** 32 9 S 148 38 E
Brockport, *U.S.A.* **150 C7** 43 13N 77 56W
Brockton, *U.S.A.* **151 D13** 42 5N 71 1W
Brockville, *Canada* **140 D4** 44 35N 75 41W
Brockway, *Mont., U.S.A.* **154 B2** 47 18N 105 45W
Brockway, *Pa., U.S.A.* **150 E6** 41 15N 78 47W
Brocton, *U.S.A.* **150 D5** 42 23N 79 26W
Brod, *Macedonia* **50 E5** 41 32N 21 17 E
Brodarevo, *Serbia & M.* **50 C3** 43 14N 19 44 E
Brodeur Pen., *Canada* **139 A11** 72 30N 88 10W
Brodhead, *U.S.A.* **156 B7** 42 37N 89 22W
Brodhead, Mt., *U.S.A.* **150 E7** 41 39N 77 47W
Brodick, *U.K.* **22 F3** 55 35N 5 9W
Brodnica, *Poland* **55 E6** 53 15N 19 25 E
Brody, *Ukraine* **59 G3** 50 5N 25 10 E
Brogan, *U.S.A.* **158 D5** 44 15N 117 31W
Broglie, *France* **26 C7** 49 2N 0 30 E
Brok, *Poland* **55 F8** 52 43N 21 52 E
Broken Arrow, *U.S.A.* **155 G7** 36 3N 95 48W
Broken Bow, *Nebr., U.S.A.* **154 E5** 41 24N 99 38W
Broken Bow, *Okla., U.S.A.* **155 H7** 34 2N 94 44W
Broken Bow Lake, *U.S.A.* **155 H7** 34 9N 94 40W
Broken Hill = Kabwe, *Zambia* **119 E2** 14 30 S 28 29 E
Broken Hill, *Australia* **128 A4** 31 58 S 141 29 E
Broken Ridge, *Ind. Oc.* **121 H8** 30 0 S 94 0 E
Broken River Ra., *Australia* **126 K6** 21 0 S 148 22 E
Brokind, *Sweden* **17 F9** 58 13N 15 42 E
Brokopondo, *Suriname* **169 B7** 5 3N 54 59W
Bromberg = Bydgoszcz, *Poland* **55 E5** 53 10N 18 0 E
Bromley □, *U.K.* **21 F8** 51 24N 0 2 E
Bromo, *Indonesia* **79 G15** 7 55 S 112 55 E
Bromölla, *Sweden* **17 H8** 56 5N 14 28 E
Bromsgrove, *U.K.* **21 E5** 52 21N 2 2W
Bronaugh, *U.S.A.* **156 G2** 37 41N 94 28W
Brønderslev, *Denmark* **17 G3** 57 16N 9 57 E
Brong-Ahafo □, *Ghana* **112 D4** 7 50N 2 0W
Broni, *Italy* **44 C6** 45 4N 9 16 E
Bronkhorstspruit, *S. Africa* **117 D4** 25 46 S 28 45 E
Brønnøysund, *Norway* **14 D15** 65 28N 12 14 E
Bronson, *Fla., U.S.A.* **153 F7** 29 27N 82 39W
Bronson, *Mich., U.S.A.* **157 C11** 41 52N 85 12W
Bronte, *Italy* **47 E7** 37 47N 14 50 E
Bronwood, *U.S.A.* **152 D5** 31 50N 84 22W
Brook Park, *U.S.A.* **150 E4** 41 24N 81 51W
Brooke's Point, *Phil.* **81 G1** 8 47N 117 50 E
Brookfield, *Mo., U.S.A.* **156 E3** 39 47N 93 4W
Brookfield, *Wis., U.S.A.* **157 A8** 43 4N 88 9W
Brookhaven, *U.S.A.* **155 K9** 31 35N 90 26W
Brookings, *Oreg., U.S.A.* **158 E1** 42 3N 124 17W
Brookings, *S. Dak., U.S.A.* **154 C6** 44 19N 96 48W
Brookland = West Columbia, *U.S.A.* **152 B8** 33 59N 81 4W
Brooklet, *U.S.A.* **152 C8** 32 23N 81 40W
Brooklin, *Canada* **150 C6** 43 55N 78 55W
Brooklyn, *U.S.A.* **156 C4** 41 44N 92 27W
Brooklyn Park, *U.S.A.* **154 C8** 45 6N 93 23W
Brooks, *Canada* **142 C6** 50 35N 111 55W
Brooks Range, *U.S.A.* **144 C10** 68 0N 152 0W
Brookston, *U.S.A.* **157 D10** 40 36N 86 52W
Brooksville, *Fla., U.S.A.* **153 G7** 28 33N 82 23W
Brooksville, *Ky., U.S.A.* **157 F12** 38 41N 84 4W
Brookton, *Australia* **125 F2** 32 22 S 117 0 E
Brookville, *Ind., U.S.A.* **157 E12** 39 25N 85 1W
Brookville, *Ohio, U.S.A.* **157 E12** 39 50N 84 27W
Brookville, *Pa., U.S.A.* **150 E5** 41 10N 79 5W
Brookville L., *U.S.A.* **157 E11** 39 28N 85 0W
Broom, L., *U.K.* **22 D3** 57 55N 5 15W
Broome, *Australia* **124 C3** 18 0 S 122 15 E
Broons, *France* **26 D4** 48 20N 2 16W
Brora, *U.K.* **22 C5** 58 0N 3 52W
Brora →, *U.K.* **22 C5** 58 0N 3 51W
Brørup, *Denmark* **17 J2** 55 29N 9 1 E
Brösarp, *Sweden* **17 J8** 55 43N 14 6 E
Brosna →, *Ireland* **23 C4** 53 14N 7 58W
Broşteni, *Mehedinţi, Romania* **52 F7** 44 45N 22 59 E
Broşteni, *Suceava, Romania* **53 C10** 47 14N 25 43 E
Brostrud, *Norway* **18 D5** 60 18N 8 34 E
Brotas de Macaúbas, *Brazil* **171 D3** 12 0 S 42 38W
Brothers, *U.S.A.* **158 E3** 43 49N 120 36W
Brothers, The, *Yemen* **99 D6** 12 8N 53 10 E
Brøttum, *Norway* **18 C7** 61 2N 10 34 E
Brou, *France* **26 D8** 48 13N 1 11 E
Brouage, *France* **28 C2** 45 52N 1 4W
Brough, *U.K.* **20 C5** 54 32N 2 18W
Brough Hd., *U.K.* **22 B5** 59 8N 3 20W
Broughton, *U.S.A.* **157 G8** 37 56N 88 27W
Broughton Island = Qikiqtarjuaq, *Canada* **139 B13** 67 33N 63 0W
Broumov, *Czech Rep.* **35 A9** 50 35N 16 20 E
Brovary, *Ukraine* **59 G6** 50 34N 30 48 E
Brovst, *Denmark* **17 G3** 57 6N 9 31 E
Brown, L., *Australia* **125 F2** 31 5 S 118 15 E
Brown, Mt., *Australia* **128 B3** 32 30 S 138 0 E
Brown, Pt., *Australia* **127 E1** 32 32 S 133 50 E
Brown City, *U.S.A.* **150 C2** 43 13N 82 59W
Brown Willy, *U.K.* **21 G3** 50 35N 4 37W
Brownfield, *U.S.A.* **155 J3** 33 11N 102 17W
Browning, *Ill., U.S.A.* **156 D6** 40 8N 90 22W
Browning, *Mo., U.S.A.* **156 D3** 40 3N 93 12W
Browning, *Mont., U.S.A.* **158 B7** 48 34N 113 1W
Brownsburg, *U.S.A.* **157 E10** 39 51N 86 24W
Brownstown, *U.S.A.* **157 F10** 38 53N 86 3W
Brownsville, *Oreg., U.S.A.* **158 D2** 44 24N 122 59W
Brownsville, *Pa., U.S.A.* **150 F5** 40 1N 79 53W
Brownsville, *Tenn., U.S.A.* **155 H10** 35 36N 89 16W
Brownsville, *Tex., U.S.A.* **155 N6** 25 54N 97 30W
Brownsweg, *Suriname* **169 B6** 5 5N 55 15W
Brownville, *U.S.A.* **151 C9** 44 0N 75 59W
Brownwood, *U.S.A.* **155 K5** 31 43N 98 59W
Browse I., *Australia* **124 B3** 14 7 S 123 33 E
Broxton, *U.S.A.* **152 D7** 31 38N 82 53W
Broye →, *Switz.* **32 C3** 46 52N 6 58 E
Bru, *Norway* **18 C2** 61 32N 5 11 E
Bruas, *Malaysia* **87 K3** 4 30N 100 47 E
Bruay-la-Buissière, *France* **27 B9** 50 29N 2 33 E
Bruce, *U.S.A.* **152 E4** 30 28N 85 58W
Bruce, Mt., *Australia* **124 D2** 22 37 S 118 8 E
Bruce B., *N.Z.* **131 D4** 43 35 S 169 42 E
Bruce Pen., *Canada* **150 B3** 45 0N 81 30W
Bruce Peninsula △, *Canada* **140 C3** 45 14N 81 36W
Bruce Rock, *Australia* **125 F2** 31 52 S 118 8 E
Bruche →, *France* **27 D14** 48 34N 7 43 E
Bruchsal, *Germany* **31 F4** 49 7N 8 35 E
Bruck an der Leitha, *Austria* **35 C9** 48 1N 16 47 E
Bruck an der Mur, *Austria* **34 D8** 47 24N 15 16 E
Brue →, *U.K.* **21 F5** 51 13N 2 59W
Bruflat, *Norway* **18 D6** 60 53N 9 37 E
Bruges = Brugge, *Belgium* **24 C3** 51 13N 3 13 E
Brugg, *Switz.* **32 B6** 47 29N 8 11 E
Brugge, *Belgium* **24 C3** 51 13N 3 13 E
Bruin, *U.S.A.* **150 E5** 41 3N 79 43W
Bruini, *India* **90 A6** 29 10N 96 11 E
Brûlé, *Canada* **142 C5** 53 15N 117 58W
Brûlon, *France* **26 E6** 47 58N 0 15W
Brumado, *Brazil* **171 D3** 14 14 S 41 40W
Brumado →, *Brazil* **171 D3** 14 13 S 41 40W
Brumath, *France* **27 D14** 48 43N 7 40 E
Brumunddal, *Norway* **18 D7** 60 53N 10 56 E
Brundidge, *U.S.A.* **152 D4** 31 43N 85 49W
Bruneau, *U.S.A.* **158 E6** 42 53N 115 48W
Bruneau →, *U.S.A.* **158 E6** 42 56N 115 57W
Bruneck = Brunico, *Italy* **45 B8** 46 48N 11 56 E
Brunei = Bandar Seri Begawan, *Brunei* **85 B4** 4 52N 115 0 E
Brunei ■, *Asia* **85 B4** 4 50N 115 0 E
Brunflo, *Sweden* **16 A8** 63 5N 14 50 E
Brunico, *Italy* **45 B8** 46 48N 11 56 E
Brünigpass, *Switz.* **32 C6** 46 46N 8 8 E
Brünn = Brno, *Czech Rep.* **35 B9** 49 10N 16 35 E
Brunna, *Sweden* **16 E11** 59 52N 17 25 E
Brunnen, *Switz.* **33 C7** 46 59N 8 37 E
Brunner, L., *N.Z.* **131 C6** 42 37 S 171 27 E
Brunnhóll, *Iceland* **11 C11** 64 17N 15 26W
Brunsbüttel, *Germany* **30 B5** 53 53N 9 6 E
Brunssum, *Neths.* **24 D5** 50 57N 5 59 E
Brunswick = Braunschweig, *Germany* **30 C6** 52 15N 10 31 E
Brunswick, *Ga., U.S.A.* **152 D8** 31 10N 81 30W
Brunswick, *Maine, U.S.A.* **149 D11** 43 55N 69 58W
Brunswick, *Mo., U.S.A.* **156 E3** 39 26N 93 8W
Brunswick, *Ohio, U.S.A.* **150 E3** 41 14N 81 51W
Brunswick, Pen. de, *Chile* **176 D2** 53 30 S 71 30W
Brunswick B., *Australia* **124 C3** 15 15 S 124 50 E
Brunswick Junction, *Australia* **125 F2** 33 15 S 115 50 E
Bruntál, *Czech Rep.* **35 B10** 49 59N 17 27 E
Bruny I., *Australia* **127 G4** 43 20 S 147 15 E
Brus Laguna, *Honduras* **164 C3** 15 47N 84 35W
Brusa = Bursa, *Turkey* **51 F13** 40 15N 29 5 E
Brusartsi, *Bulgaria* **50 C7** 43 40N 23 5 E
Brush, *U.S.A.* **154 E3** 40 15N 103 37W
Brushton, *U.S.A.* **151 B10** 44 50N 74 31W
Brusio, *Switz.* **33 D10** 46 14N 10 8 E
Brusque, *Brazil* **175 B6** 27 5 S 49 0W
Brussel, *Belgium* **24 D4** 50 51N 4 21 E
Brussel ✈ (BRU), *Belgium* **24 D5** 50 54N 5 41 E
Brussels = Brussel, *Belgium* **24 D4** 50 51N 4 21 E
Brussels, *Canada* **150 C3** 43 44N 81 15W
Brusy, *Poland* **54 E4** 53 53N 17 43 E
Bruthen, *Australia* **129 D7** 37 42 S 147 50 E
Bruvoll, *Norway* **18 D8** 60 27N 11 29 E
Bruxelles = Brussel, *Belgium* **24 D4** 50 51N 4 21 E
Bruyères, *France* **27 D13** 48 10N 6 40 E
Bruz, *France* **26 D5** 48 1N 1 46W
Brwinów, *Poland* **55 F7** 52 9N 20 40 E
Bryagovo, *Bulgaria* **51 E9** 41 58N 25 8 E
Bryan, *Ohio, U.S.A.* **157 C12** 41 28N 84 33W
Bryan, *Tex., U.S.A.* **155 K6** 30 40N 96 22W
Bryan, Mt., *Australia* **128 B3** 33 30 S 139 0 E
Bryanka, *Ukraine* **59 H10** 48 32N 38 45 E
Bryansk, *Bryansk, Russia* **59 F8** 53 13N 34 25 E
Bryansk, *Dagestan, Russia* **61 H8** 44 20N 47 10 E
Bryanskoye = Bryansk, *Russia* **61 H8** 44 20N 47 10 E
Bryce Canyon △, *U.S.A.* **159 H7** 37 30N 112 10W
Bryne, *Norway* **18 F2** 58 44N 5 38 E
Bryson City, *U.S.A.* **149 H4** 35 26N 83 27W
Bryukhovetskaya, *Russia* **59 K10** 45 48N 39 0 E
Brza Palanka, *Serbia & M.* **50 B6** 44 28N 22 27 E
Brzeg, *Poland* **55 H4** 50 52N 17 30 E
Brzeg Dolny, *Poland* **55 G3** 51 16N 16 41 E
Brześć Kujawski, *Poland* **55 F5** 52 36N 18 55 E
Brzešč nad Bugiem = Brest, *Belarus* **59 F2** 52 10N 23 40 E
Brzesko, *Poland* **55 J7** 49 59N 20 34 E
Brzeziny, *Poland* **55 G6** 51 49N 19 42 E
Brzozów, *Poland* **55 J9** 49 41N 22 3 E
Bsharri, *Lebanon* **103 A5** 34 15N 36 0 E
Bū al Ḩīḑān, W. →, *Libya* **108 C3** 27 25N 19 22 E
Bū Athlah, *Libya* **108 B3** 30 9N 15 39 E
Bū Baqarah, *U.A.E.* **97 E8** 25 35N 56 25 E
Bu Craa, *W. Sahara* **110 C2** 26 45N 12 50W
Bū Ḩasā, *U.A.E.* **97 F7** 23 30N 53 20 E
Bū Tummayyim, W. →, *Libya* **108 C3** 26 56N 19 13 E
Bua, *Fiji* **133 A2** 16 48 S 178 37 E
Bua, *Sweden* **17 G6** 57 14N 12 7 E
Bua Yai, *Thailand* **86 E4** 15 33N 102 26 E
Buad I., *Phil.* **81 F5** 11 40N 124 51 E
Buala, *Solomon Is.* **133 M10** 8 10 S 159 35 E
Buapinang, *Indonesia* **82 B2** 4 40 S 121 30 E
Buayan = General Santos, *Phil.* **81 H5** 6 5N 125 14 E
Buba, *Guinea-Biss.* **112 C2** 11 40N 14 59W
Bubanda, *Dem. Rep. of the Congo* **114 B3** 4 14N 19 38 E
Bubanza, *Burundi* **118 C2** 3 6 S 29 23 E
Bubaque, *Guinea-Biss.* **112 C1** 11 16N 15 51W
Bube, *Ethiopia* **107 F4** 8 46N 35 48 E
Būbiyān, *Kuwait* **97 D6** 29 45N 48 15 E
Buca, *Fiji* **133 A2** 16 38 S 179 52 E
Buca, *Turkey* **49 C9** 38 22N 27 11 E
Bucaco, *Angola* **115 E4** 11 26 S 20 10 E
Bucak, *Turkey* **49 D12** 37 28N 30 36 E
Bucaramanga, *Colombia* **168 B3** 7 0N 73 0W
Bucas Grande I., *Phil.* **81 G5** 9 40N 125 57 E
Bucasia, *Australia* **126 K7** 21 2 S 149 10 E
Bucay, *Phil.* **80 C3** 17 32N 120 43 E
Buccaneer Arch., *Australia* **124 C3** 16 7 S 123 20 E
Buccino, *Italy* **47 B8** 40 38N 15 22 E
Buccoo Reef, *Trin. & Tob.* **169 E10** 11 10N 60 51W
Bucecea, *Romania* **53 C11** 47 47N 26 28 E
Bucegi △, *Romania* **53 E10** 45 25N 25 25 E
Bucey-lès-Gy, *France* **32 B1** 47 25N 5 51 E
Buchach, *Ukraine* **59 H3** 49 5N 25 25 E
Buchan, *Australia* **129 D8** 37 30 S 148 12 E
Buchan, *U.K.* **22 D6** 57 32N 2 21W
Buchan Ness, *U.K.* **22 D7** 57 29N 1 46W
Buchanan, *Canada* **143 C8** 51 40N 102 45W
Buchanan, *Liberia* **112 D2** 5 57N 10 2W
Buchanan, *Ga., U.S.A.* **152 B4** 33 48N 85 11W
Buchanan, *Mich., U.S.A.* **157 C10** 41 50N 86 22W
Buchanan, L., *Queens., Australia* **126 C4** 21 35 S 145 52 E
Buchanan, L., *W. Austral., Australia* **125 E3** 25 33 S 123 2 E
Buchanan, L., *U.S.A.* **155 K5** 30 45N 98 25W
Buchanan Cr. →, *Australia* **126 B2** 19 13 S 136 33 E
Buchans, *Canada* **141 C8** 48 50N 56 52W
Bucharest = Bucureşti, *Romania* **53 F11** 44 27N 26 10 E
Buchen, *Germany* **31 F5** 49 32N 9 20 E
Bucheon = Puch'ŏn, *S. Korea* **57 F14** 37 30N 126 50 E
Buchholz, *Germany* **30 B5** 53 19N 9 52 E
Buchloe, *Germany* **31 G6** 48 1N 10 44 E
Buchon, Pt., *U.S.A.* **160 K6** 35 15N 120 54W
Buchs, *Aargau, Switz.* **32 B6** 47 23N 8 4 E
Buchs, *St. Galen, Switz.* **33 B8** 47 10N 9 28 E
Buciumi, *Romania* **52 C8** 47 3N 23 1 E
Buck Hill Falls, *U.S.A.* **151 E9** 41 11N 75 16W
Bückeburg, *Germany* **30 C5** 52 16N 9 7 E
Buckeye Lake, *U.S.A.* **150 G2** 39 55N 82 29W
Buckhannon, *U.S.A.* **148 F5** 39 0N 80 8W
Buckhaven, *U.K.* **22 E5** 56 11N 3 3W
Buckhorn L., *Canada* **150 B6** 44 29N 78 23W
Buckie, *U.K.* **22 D6** 57 41N 2 58W
Buckingham, *Canada* **140 C4** 45 37N 75 24W
Buckingham, *U.K.* **21 F7** 51 59N 0 57W
Buckingham B., *Australia* **126 A2** 12 10 S 135 40 E
Buckingham Canal, *India* **95 H5** 14 0N 80 5 E
Buckinghamshire □, *U.K.* **21 F7** 51 53N 0 55W
Buckland, *U.S.A.* **144 D7** 65 59N 161 8W
Buckle Hd., *Australia* **124 B4** 14 26 S 127 52 E
Buckleboo, *Australia* **128 B2** 32 54 S 136 12 E
Buckley, *U.K.* **20 D4** 53 10N 3 5W
Buckley, *U.S.A.* **157 D8** 40 36N 88 2W
Buckley →, *Australia* **126 C2** 20 10 S 138 49 E
Bucklin, *Kans., U.S.A.* **155 G5** 37 33N 99 38W
Bucklin, *Mo., U.S.A.* **156 E4** 39 47N 92 53W
Bucks L., *U.S.A.* **160 F5** 39 54N 121 12W
Buco Zau, *Angola* **115 C2** 4 46 S 12 33 E
Bucquoy, *France* **27 B9** 50 9N 2 43 E
Bucureşti, *Romania* **53 F11** 44 27N 26 10 E
Bucureşti Otopeni ✈ (OTP), *Romania* **53 F11** 44 30N 26 11 E
Bucyrus, *U.S.A.* **157 D14** 40 48N 82 59W
Bud, *Norway* **18 B3** 62 55N 6 55 E
Budacu, Vf., *Romania* **53 C10** 47 7N 25 41 E
Budalin, *Burma* **90 D5** 22 20N 95 10 E
Budaörs, *Hungary* **52 C3** 47 27N 18 58 E
Budapest, *Hungary* **52 C4** 47 29N 19 5 E
Budapest □, *Hungary* **52 C4** 47 29N 19 5 E
Budapest ✈ (BUD), *Hungary* **52 C4** 47 25N 19 12 E
Budaun, *India* **93 E8** 28 5N 79 10 E
Budawang △, *Australia* **129 C9** 35 10 S 150 12 E
Budd Coast, *Antarctica* **7 C8** 68 0 S 112 0 E
Buddenbrock = Brodnica, *Poland* **55 E6** 53 15N 19 25 E
Budderoo △, *Australia* **129 C9** 35 40 S 150 41 E
Buddusò, *Italy* **46 B2** 40 35N 9 15 E
Bude, *U.K.* **21 G3** 50 49N 4 34W
Budennovsk, *Russia* **61 H7** 44 50N 44 10 E
Budeşti, *Romania* **53 F11** 44 13N 26 30 E
Budeyi, *Ukraine* **53 B14** 48 3N 29 16 E
Budge Budge = Baj Baj, *India* **93 H13** 22 30N 88 5 E
Budgewoi, *Australia* **129 B9** 33 13 S 151 34 E
Búðardalur, *Iceland* **11 B5** 65 7N 21 46W
Búðir, *Iceland* **11 C12** 64 56N 14 1W
Budia, *Spain* **40 E2** 40 38N 2 46W
Büdingen, *Germany* **31 E5** 50 16N 9 7 E
Budjala, *Dem. Rep. of the Congo* **114 B3** 2 50N 19 40 E
Budoni, *Italy* **46 B2** 40 40N 9 45 E
Búdrio, *Italy* **45 D8** 44 32N 11 32 E
Bűdszentmihály = Tiszavasvári, *Hungary* **52 C6** 47 58N 21 18 E
Budungbudung, *Indonesia* **82 B1** 2 6 S 119 13 E
Budva, *Serbia & M.* **50 D2** 42 17N 18 50 E
Budweis = České Budějovice, *Czech Rep.* **34 C7** 48 55N 14 25 E
Budyonnovka = Novoazovsk, *Ukraine* **59 J10** 47 15N 38 4 E
Budzyń, *Poland* **55 F3** 52 54N 16 59 E
Bue, *Norway* **18 F2** 58 40N 5 58 E
Buea, *Cameroon* **113 E6** 4 10N 9 9 E
Buela, *Angola* **115 D2** 5 54 S 14 40 E
Buellton, *U.S.A.* **161 L6** 34 37N 120 12W
Buena Esperanza, *Argentina* **174 C2** 34 45 S 65 15W
Buena Park, *U.S.A.* **161 M9** 33 52N 117 59W
Buena Vista, *Bolivia* **173 D5** 17 27 S 63 40W
Buena Vista, *Solomon Is.* **133 M11** 8 52 S 160 3 E
Buena Vista, *Colo., U.S.A.* **159 G10** 38 51N 106 8W
Buena Vista, *Ga., U.S.A.* **152 C5** 32 19N 84 31W
Buena Vista, *Va., U.S.A.* **148 G6** 37 44N 79 21W
Buena Vista Lake Bed, *U.S.A.* **161 K7** 35 12N 119 18W
Buenaventura, *Colombia* **168 C2** 3 53N 77 4W
Buenaventura, *Mexico* **162 B3** 29 50N 107 30W
Buenaventura, B. de, *Colombia* **168 C2** 3 48N 77 17W
Buenavista, *Agusan del N., Phil.* **81 G5** 8 59N 125 24 E
Buenavista, *Quezon, Phil.* **80 E4** 13 35N 122 34 E
Buendía, Embalse de, *Spain* **40 E2** 40 25N 2 43W
Buenópolis, *Brazil* **171 E3** 17 54 S 44 11W
Buenos Aires, *Argentina* **174 C4** 34 30 S 58 20W
Buenos Aires, *Colombia* **168 C3** 1 36N 73 18W
Buenos Aires, *Costa Rica* **164 E3** 9 10N 83 20W
Buenos Aires □, *Argentina* **174 D4** 36 30 S 60 0W
Buenos Aires, L., *Chile* **176 C2** 46 35 S 72 30W
Buesaco, *Colombia* **168 C2** 1 23N 77 9W
Buet, Mont, *France* **32 D3** 46 2N 6 52 E
Buffalo, *Mo., U.S.A.* **155 G8** 37 39N 93 6W
Buffalo, *N.Y., U.S.A.* **150 D6** 42 53N 78 53W
Buffalo, *Okla., U.S.A.* **155 G5** 36 50N 99 38W
Buffalo, *S. Dak., U.S.A.* **154 C3** 45 35N 103 33W
Buffalo, *Wyo., U.S.A.* **158 D10** 44 21N 106 42W
Buffalo △, *U.S.A.* **155 G8** 36 14N 92 36W
Buffalo →, *Canada* **142 A5** 60 5N 115 5W
Buffalo →, *S. Africa* **117 D5** 28 43 S 30 37 E
Buffalo Head Hills, *Canada* **142 B5** 57 25N 115 55W
Buffalo L., *Alta., Canada* **142 C6** 52 27N 112 54W
Buffalo L., *N.W.T., Canada* **142 A5** 60 12N 115 25W
Buffalo Narrows, *Canada* **143 B7** 55 51N 108 29W
Buffalo Springs ⌓, *Kenya* **118 B4** 0 32N 37 35 E
Buffels →, *S. Africa* **116 D2** 29 36 S 17 3 E
Buford, *U.S.A.* **149 H4** 34 10N 84 0W
Bug = Buh →, *Ukraine* **59 J6** 46 59N 31 58 E
Bug →, *Poland* **55 F8** 52 31N 21 5 E
Buga, *Colombia* **168 C2** 4 0N 76 15W
Bugala I., *Uganda* **118 C3** 0 40 S 32 20 E
Buganda, *Uganda* **118 C3** 0 0 31 30 E
Buganga, *Uganda* **118 C3** 0 3 S 32 0 E
Bugasong, *Phil.* **81 F4** 11 3N 122 4 E
Bugeat, *France* **28 C5** 45 36N 1 55 E
Bugel, Tanjung, *Indonesia* **85 D4** 6 26 S 111 3 E
Buggingen, *Germany* **32 A5** 47 51N 7 38 E
Bugibba, *Malta* **38 F7** 35 57N 14 25 E
Bugojno, *Bos.-H.* **52 F2** 44 2N 17 25 E
Bugsuk, *Phil.* **78 C5** 8 15N 117 15 E
Bugsuk I., *Phil.* **81 G1** 8 12N 117 18 E
Buguey, *Phil.* **80 B3** 18 17N 121 50 E
Buguias, *Phil.* **80 C3** 16 43N 120 50 E
Bugulma, *Russia* **64 D4** 54 33N 52 48 E
Buguma, *Nigeria* **113 E6** 4 42N 6 55 E
Bugun Shara, *Mongolia* **68 B5** 49 0N 104 0 E
Bugungu ⌓, *Uganda* **118 B3** 2 17N 31 50 E
Buguruslan, *Russia* **64 E4** 53 39N 52 26 E
Buh →, *Ukraine* **59 J6** 46 59N 31 58 E
Buharkent, *Turkey* **49 D10** 37 58N 28 44 E
Buheirat-Murrat-el-Kubra, *Egypt* **106 H8** 30 18N 32 26 E
Buhera, *Zimbabwe* **117 B5** 19 18 S 31 29 E
Bühl, *Germany* **31 G4** 48 40N 8 8 E
Buhl, *U.S.A.* **158 E6** 42 36N 114 46W
Buhuşi, *Romania* **53 D11** 46 41N 26 45 E
Bui △, *Ghana* **112 D4** 8 21N 2 21W
Builth Wells, *U.K.* **21 E4** 52 9N 3 25W
Buin, *Papua N. G.* **133 L8** 6 48 S 155 42 E
Buin, Piz, *Switz.* **33 C10** 46 51N 10 7 E
Buinsk, *Russia* **60 C9** 55 0N 48 18 E
Buíque, *Brazil* **170 C4** 8 37 S 37 9W
Buir Nur, *Mongolia* **69 B6** 47 50N 117 42 E
Buis-les-Baronnies, *France* **29 D9** 44 17N 5 16 E
Buitenzorg = Bogor, *Indonesia* **84 D3** 6 36 S 106 48 E
Buitrago del Lozoya, *Spain* **42 E7** 40 58N 3 38W
Bujalance, *Spain* **43 H6** 37 54N 4 23W
Bujanovac, *Serbia & M.* **50 D5** 42 28N 21 44 E
Bujaraloz, *Spain* **40 D4** 41 29N 0 10W
Buje, *Croatia* **45 C10** 45 24N 13 39 E
Buji, *China* **69 F11** 22 37N 114 5 E
Bujumbura, *Burundi* **118 C2** 3 16 S 29 18 E
Bük, *Hungary* **52 C1** 47 22N 16 45 E
Buk, *Poland* **55 F3** 52 21N 16 30 E
Buka I., *Papua N. G.* **132 C8** 5 10 S 154 35 E
Bukachacha, *Russia* **67 D12** 52 55N 116 50 E
Bukama, *Dem. Rep. of the Congo* **119 D2** 9 10 S 25 50 E
Bukavu, *Dem. Rep. of the Congo* **118 C2** 2 20 S 28 52 E
Bukene, *Tanzania* **118 C3** 4 15 S 32 48 E
Bukhara = Bukhoro, *Uzbekistan* **65 D2** 39 48N 64 25 E
Bukhoro, *Uzbekistan* **65 D2** 39 48N 64 25 E
Bukidnon □, *Phil.* **81 H5** 8 0N 125 0 E
Bukima, *Tanzania* **118 C3** 1 50 S 33 25 E
Bukit Badung, *Indonesia* **79 K18** 8 49 S 115 10 E
Bukit Kerajaan, *Malaysia* **87 c** 5 25N 100 15 E
Bukit Mertajam, *Malaysia* **87 c** 5 22N 100 28 E
Bukit Ni, *Malaysia* **87 d** 1 22N 104 12 E
Bukit Panjang, *Singapore* **87 d** 1 23N 103 46 E
Bukit Tengah, *Malaysia* **87 c** 5 22N 100 25 E
Bukittinggi, *Indonesia* **84 C2** 0 20 S 100 20 E
Bükk, *Hungary* **52 B5** 48 0N 20 30 E
Bukkapatnam, *India* **95 G3** 14 14N 77 46 E
Bükki △, *Hungary* **52 B5** 48 3N 20 30 E
Bukoba, *Tanzania* **118 C3** 1 20 S 31 49 E
Bukrane, *Indonesia* **83 C4** 7 43 S 131 9 E
Bukum, Pulau, *Singapore* **87 d** 1 14N 103 46 E
Bukuru, *Nigeria* **113 D6** 9 42N 8 48 E
Bukuya, *Uganda* **118 B3** 0 40N 31 52 E
Būl, Kuh-e, *Iran* **97 D7** 30 48N 52 45 E
Bula, *Guinea-Biss.* **112 C1** 12 7N 15 43W
Bula, *Indonesia* **83 B4** 3 6 S 130 30 E
Bula, *Phil.* **80 E4** 13 28N 123 16 E
Bula-Atumba, *Angola* **115 D2** 8 41 S 14 52 E
Bulacan □, *Phil.* **80 D3** 15 0N 121 5 E
Bülach, *Switz.* **33 A7** 47 31N 8 32 E
Bulahdelah, *Australia* **129 B10** 32 23 S 152 13 E
Bulalacao, *Phil.* **80 E3** 12 31N 121 26 E
Bulan, *Phil.* **80 E4** 12 40N 123 52 E
Bulanash, *Russia* **64 C9** 57 16N 62 0 E
Bulancak, *Turkey* **101 B8** 40 56N 38 14 E
Búland, *Iceland* **11 D8** 63 46N 18 30W
Bulandshahr, *India* **92 E7** 28 28N 77 51 E
Bulanık, *Turkey* **101 C10** 39 4N 42 14 E
Bulanovo, *Russia* **64 E5** 52 27N 55 10 E
Bûlâq, *Egypt* **106 B3** 25 10N 30 38 E
Bulawayo, *Zimbabwe* **119 G2** 20 7 S 28 32 E
Buldan, *Turkey* **49 C10** 38 2N 28 50 E
Buldana, *India* **94 D3** 20 30N 76 18 E
Buldir I., *U.S.A.* **144 K1** 52 21N 175 56 E
Buldon, *Phil.* **81 H5** 7 33N 124 25 E
Bulgar, *Russia* **60 C9** 54 57N 49 4 E
Bulgaria ■, *Europe* **51 D9** 42 35N 25 30 E
Bulgheria, Monte, *Italy* **47 B8** 40 4N 15 26 E
Bulgurca, *Turkey* **49 C9** 38 9N 27 9 E
Bulhale, *Somali Rep.* **120 C3** 5 20N 46 29 E
Bulhar, *Somali Rep.* **120 B2** 10 25N 44 30 E
Buli, *Indonesia* **82 A3** 0 53N 128 18 E
Buli, Teluk, *Indonesia* **82 A3** 0 48N 128 25 E
Buliluyan, C., *Phil.* **81 G1** 8 20N 117 15 E
Bulim, *Singapore* **87 d** 1 22N 103 43 E
Bulki, *Ethiopia* **107 F4** 6 11N 36 31 E
Bulkley →, *Canada* **142 B3** 55 15N 127 40W
Bull Shoals L., *U.S.A.* **155 G8** 36 22N 92 35W
Bullaque →, *Spain* **43 G6** 38 59N 4 17W
Bullard, *U.S.A.* **152 C6** 32 38N 83 30W
Bullas, *Spain* **41 G3** 38 2N 1 40W
Bulle, *Switz.* **32 C4** 46 37N 7 3 E
Buller →, *N.Z.* **131 B6** 41 44 S 171 36 E
Buller, Mt., *Australia* **129 D7** 37 10 S 146 28 E
Buller Gorge, *N.Z.* **131 B7** 41 40 S 172 10 E
Bulleringa △, *Australia* **126 B3** 17 39 S 143 56 E
Bullhead City, *U.S.A.* **161 K12** 35 8N 114 32W
Bulli, *Australia* **129 C9** 34 15 S 150 57 E
Büllingen, *Belgium* **24 D6** 50 25N 6 16 E
Bullock Creek, *Australia* **126 B3** 17 43 S 144 31 E
Bulloo →, *Australia* **127 D3** 28 43 S 142 30 E
Bulloo L., *Australia* **127 D3** 28 43 S 142 25 E
Bulls, *N.Z.* **130 G4** 40 10 S 175 24 E
Bully-les-Mines, *France* **27 B9** 50 27N 2 44 E
Bulnes, *Chile* **174 D1** 36 42 S 72 19W
Bulo Burti, *Somali Rep.* **120 D3** 3 50N 45 33 E
Bulo Ghedudo, *Somali Rep.* **120 D2** 2 52N 43 1 E
Bulolo, *Papua N. G.* **132 D4** 7 10 S 146 40 E
Bulongo, *Dem. Rep. of the Congo* **115 C4** 4 45 S 21 30 E
Bulqizë, *Albania* **50 E4** 41 30N 20 21 E
Bulsar = Valsad, *India* **94 D1** 20 40N 72 58 E
Bultfontein, *S. Africa* **116 D4** 28 18 S 26 10 E
Buluan, *Phil.* **81 H5** 6 44N 124 47 E
Buluan, L., *Phil.* **81 H5** 6 40N 124 49 E
Bulukumba, *Indonesia* **82 C2** 5 33 S 120 11 E
Bulun, *Russia* **67 B13** 70 37N 127 30 E
Bulungkol, *China* **65 D7** 38 36N 74 58 E
Bulungu, *Dem. Rep. of the Congo* **115 D4** 6 4 S 21 54 E
Bulungur, *Uzbekistan* **65 D3** 39 46N 67 16 E
Bulusan, *Phil.* **80 E5** 12 45N 124 8 E
Bulusan Vol., *Phil.* **80 E5** 12 46N 124 3 E
Bumba, *Bandundu, Dem. Rep. of the Congo* **115 D3** 6 58 S 19 19 E
Bumba, *Équateur, Dem. Rep. of the Congo* **114 B4** 2 13N 22 30 E
Bumbeşti-Jiu, *Romania* **53 E8** 45 10N 23 24 E
Bumbiri I., *Tanzania* **118 C3** 1 40 S 31 55 E
Bumbuna, *S. Leone* **112 D2** 9 2N 11 49W
Bumhkang, *Burma* **90 B6** 26 51N 97 40 E
Bumhpa Bum, *Burma* **90 B6** 26 51N 97 14 E

Bumi →, Zimbabwe 119 F2 17 0S 28 20 E
Bumtang →, Bhutan 90 B3 26 56N 90 53 E
Buna, Dem. Rep. of the Congo 114 C3 3 14 S 18 59 E
Buna, Kenya 118 B4 2 58N 39 30 E
Buna, Papua N. G. 132 E5 8 42 S 148 27 E
Bunama, Papua N. G. 132 F6 10 9 S 151 9 E
Bunawan, Phil. 81 G5 8 12N 125 57 E
Bunazi, Tanzania 118 C3 1 3 S 31 23 E
Bunbah, Khalīj, Libya 108 B4 32 20N 23 15 E
Bunbury, Australia 125 F2 33 20 S 115 35 E
Bunclody, Ireland 23 D5 52 39N 6 40W
Buncrana, Ireland 23 A4 55 8N 7 27W
Bunda, Dem. Rep. of the Congo 115 C3 4 58 S 14 29 E
Bundaberg, Australia 127 C5 24 54 S 152 22 E
Bundanoon, Australia 129 C9 34 40 S 150 16 E
Bünde, Germany 30 C4 52 11N 8 35 E
Bundey →, Australia 126 C2 21 46 S 135 37 E
Bundi, India 92 G6 25 30N 75 35 E
Bundjalung △, Australia 127 D5 29 16 S 153 21 E
Bundoran, Ireland 23 B3 54 28N 8 16W
Bundukia, Sudan 107 F3 5 14N 30 55 E
Bundure, Australia 129 C7 35 10 S 146 1 E
Bung Kan, Thailand 86 C4 18 23N 103 37 E
Bunga →, Nigeria 113 C6 11 23N 9 56 E
Bungay, U.K. 21 E9 52 27N 1 28 E
Bungendore, Australia 129 C8 35 14 S 149 30 E
Bungil Cr. →, Australia 127 D4 27 5 S 149 5 E
Bungle Bungle = Purnululu Nat. Park △, Australia 124 C4 17 20 S 128 20 E
Bungo, Angola 115 D3 7 26 S 15 33 E
Bungo, Gunung, Malaysia 85 B4 1 16N 110 9 E
Bungo-Suidō, Japan 72 E4 33 0N 132 15 E
Bungoma, Kenya 118 B3 0 34N 34 34 E
Bungotakada, Japan 72 D3 33 35N 131 25 E
Bungu, Tanzania 118 D4 7 35 S 39 0 E
Bunia, Dem. Rep. of the Congo 118 B3 1 35N 30 20 E
Bunianga, Dem. Rep. of the Congo 114 C4 3 28 S 20 11 E
Bunji, Pakistan 93 B6 35 45N 74 40 E
Bunker Hill, Ill., U.S.A. 156 E7 39 3N 89 57W
Bunker Hill, Ind., U.S.A. 157 D10 40 40N 86 6W
Bunkie, U.S.A. 155 K8 30 57N 92 11W
Bunnell, U.S.A. 153 F8 29 28N 81 16W
Bunnythorpe, N.Z. 130 G4 40 16 S 175 39 E
Buñol, Spain 41 F4 39 25N 0 47W
Bunsuru, Nigeria 113 C5 13 21N 6 23 E
Bunta, Indonesia 82 B2 0 48 S 122 10 E
Buntok, Indonesia 85 C4 1 40 S 114 58 E
Bununu Dass, Nigeria 113 C6 10 5N 9 31 E
Bununu Kasa, Nigeria 113 D6 9 51N 9 32 E
Bunya Mts. △, Australia 127 D5 26 51 S 151 34 E
Bünyan, Turkey 100 C6 38 51N 35 51 E
Bunyu, Indonesia 85 B5 3 35N 117 50 E
Bunza, Nigeria 113 C5 12 8N 4 0 E
Bunzlau = Bolesławiec, Poland 55 G2 51 17N 15 37 E
Buol, Indonesia 82 A2 1 15N 121 32 E
Buon Brieng, Vietnam 86 F7 13 9N 108 12 E
Buon Ma Thuot, Vietnam 86 F7 12 40N 108 3 E
Buong Long, Cambodia 86 F6 13 44N 106 59 E
Buorkhaya, Mys, Russia 67 B14 71 50N 132 40 E
Buqayq, Si. Arabia 97 E6 26 0N 49 45 E
Buqbuq, Egypt 106 A2 31 29N 25 29 E
Bur Acaba, Somali Rep. 120 D2 3 12N 44 20 E
Bûr Fuad, Egypt 106 H8 31 15N 32 20 E
Bur Ghibi, Somali Rep. 120 D3 3 56N 45 7 E
Bûr Safâga, Egypt 96 E2 26 43N 33 57 E
Bûr Sa'îd, Egypt 106 H8 31 16N 32 18 E
Bûr Sûdân, Sudan 106 D4 19 32N 37 9 E
Bûr Taufiq, Egypt 106 J8 29 54N 32 32 E
Bura, Kenya 118 C4 1 4 S 39 58 E
Burakin, Australia 125 F2 30 31 S 117 10 E
Buram, Sudan 107 E2 10 51N 25 9 E
Buran, Somali Rep. 120 B3 10 14N 48 44 E
Burao, Somali Rep. 120 C3 9 32N 45 32 E
Burâq, Syria 103 B5 33 11N 36 29 E
Burauen, Phil. 81 F5 10 58N 124 53 E
Buraydah, Si. Arabia 96 E4 26 20N 43 59 E
Burbank, U.S.A. 161 L8 34 11N 118 19W
Burcher, Australia 129 B7 33 30 S 147 16 E
Burda, India 92 G6 25 50N 77 35 E
Burdekin →, Australia 126 B4 19 38 S 147 25 E
Burdeos Bay, Phil. 80 D4 14 44N 122 6 E
Burdur, Turkey 49 D12 37 45N 30 17 E
Burdur □, Turkey 49 D12 37 45N 30 0 E
Burdur Gölü, Turkey 49 D12 37 44N 30 10 E
Burdwan = Barddhaman, India 93 H12 23 14N 87 39 E
Burdwood Banks, Atl. Oc. 8 M6 54 0 S 59 0W
Bure, Gojam, Ethiopia 107 E4 10 40N 37 4 E
Bure, Ilubabor, Ethiopia 107 F4 8 19N 35 8 E
Bure →, U.K. 20 E9 52 38N 1 43 E
Büren, Germany 30 D4 51 33N 8 35 E
Bureya →, Russia 67 E13 49 27N 129 30 E
Burford, Canada 150 C4 43 7N 80 27W
Burg, Germany 30 C7 52 16N 11 51 E
Burg auf Fehmarn, Germany 30 A7 54 28N 11 9 E
Burg el Arab, Egypt 106 H6 30 54N 29 32 E
Burg et Tuyur, Sudan 106 C2 20 55N 27 56 E
Burg Stargard, Germany 30 B9 53 29N 13 18 E
Burgas, Bulgaria 51 D11 42 33N 27 29 E
Burgas □, Bulgaria 51 D10 42 30N 26 50 E
Burgaski Zaliv, Bulgaria 51 D11 42 30N 27 39 E
Burgdorf, Germany 30 C6 52 27N 10 1 E
Burgdorf, Switz. 32 B5 47 3N 7 37 E
Burgenland □, Austria 35 D9 47 20N 16 20 E
Burgeo, Canada 141 C8 47 37N 57 38W
Burgersdorp, S. Africa 116 E4 31 0 S 26 20 E
Burges, Mt., Australia 125 F3 30 50 S 121 5 E
Burghausen, Germany 31 G8 48 9N 12 49 E
Burghead, U.K. 22 D5 57 43N 3 30W
Búrgio, Italy 46 E6 37 36N 13 17 E
Bürglen, Switz. 33 C7 46 53N 8 40 E
Burglengenfeld, Germany 31 F8 49 12N 12 2 E
Burgohondo, Spain 42 E6 40 26N 4 47W
Burgos, Ilocos N., Phil. 80 B3 18 31N 120 39 E
Burgos, Pangasinan, Phil. 80 C2 16 4N 119 52 E
Burgos, Spain 42 C7 42 21N 3 41W
Burgos □, Spain 42 C7 42 21N 3 42W
Burgstädt, Germany 30 E8 50 54N 12 49 E
Burgsvik, Sweden 17 G12 57 3N 18 19 E
Burguillos del Cerro, Spain 43 G4 38 23N 6 35W
Burgundy = Bourgogne □, France 27 F11 47 0N 4 50 E
Burhaniye, Turkey 49 B8 39 30N 26 58 E
Burhanpur, India 94 J3 21 18N 76 14 E
Burhi Gandak →, India 93 G12 25 20N 86 37 E
Burhner →, India 93 H9 22 43N 80 31 E
Buri Pen., Eritrea 107 D4 15 25N 39 55 E
Burias I., Phil. 80 E4 12 55N 123 5 E
Burias Pass, Phil. 80 E4 13 0N 123 15 E
Burica, Pta., Costa Rica 164 E3 8 3N 82 51W
Burien, U.S.A. 160 C4 47 28N 122 21W
Burigi ⌓, Tanzania 118 C3 2 20 S 31 6 E
Burigi, L., Tanzania 118 C3 2 2 S 31 22 E
Burin, Canada 141 C8 47 1N 55 14W
Buriram, Thailand 86 E4 15 0N 103 0 E
Buriti Alegre, Brazil 171 E2 18 9 S 49 3W
Buriti Bravo, Brazil 170 C3 5 50 S 43 50W
Buriti dos Lopes, Brazil 170 B3 3 10 S 41 52W
Burj Sāfitā, Syria 100 E7 34 48N 36 7 E
Burji, Ethiopia 107 F4 5 29N 37 51 E
Burkburnett, U.S.A. 155 H5 34 6N 98 34W
Burke →, Australia 126 C2 23 12 S 139 33 E
Burke Chan., Canada 142 C3 52 10N 127 30W
Burketown, Australia 126 B2 17 45 S 139 33 E
Burkina Faso ■, Africa 112 C4 12 0N 1 0W
Burk's Falls, Canada 140 C4 45 37N 79 24W
Burlada, Spain 40 C3 42 49N 1 36W
Burleigh Falls, Canada 150 B6 44 33N 78 12W
Burley, U.S.A. 158 E7 42 32N 113 48W
Burli, Kazakhstan 64 F4 51 25N 52 40 E
Burlingame, U.S.A. 160 H4 37 35N 122 21W
Burlington, Canada 140 D4 43 18N 79 45W
Burlington, Colo., U.S.A. 154 F3 39 18N 102 16W
Burlington, Iowa, U.S.A. 156 D5 40 49N 91 14W
Burlington, Kans., U.S.A. 154 F7 38 12N 95 45W
Burlington, Ky., U.S.A. 157 E12 39 2N 84 43W
Burlington, N.C., U.S.A. 149 G6 36 6N 79 26W
Burlington, N.J., U.S.A. 151 F10 40 4N 74 51W
Burlington, Vt., U.S.A. 151 B11 44 29N 73 12W
Burlington, Wash., U.S.A. 160 B4 48 28N 122 20W
Burlington, Wis., U.S.A. 157 B8 42 41N 88 17W
Burlyu-Tyube, Kazakhstan 66 E8 46 30N 79 10 E
Burma ■, Asia 90 E6 21 0N 96 30 E
Burnaby I., Canada 142 C2 52 25N 131 19W
Burnet, U.S.A. 155 K5 30 45N 98 14W
Burney, U.S.A. 158 F3 40 53N 121 40W
Burnham, U.S.A. 150 F7 40 38N 77 34W
Burnham-on-Sea, U.K. 21 F5 51 14N 3 0W
Burnie, Australia 127 G4 41 4 S 145 56 E
Burnley, U.K. 20 D5 53 47N 2 14W
Burns, U.S.A. 158 E4 43 35N 119 3W
Burns Junction, U.S.A. 158 E5 42 47N 117 51W
Burns Lake, Canada 142 C3 54 20N 125 45W
Burnside →, Canada 138 B9 66 51N 108 4W
Burnside, L., Australia 125 E3 25 22 S 123 0 E
Burnsville, U.S.A. 154 C8 44 47N 93 17W
Burnt, L., Canada 141 B7 53 35N 64 4W
Burnt Paw, U.S.A. 144 C12 66 54N 143 44W
Burnt River, Canada 150 B6 44 41N 78 42W
Burntwood →, Canada 143 B9 56 8N 96 34W
Burntwood L., Canada 143 B8 55 22N 100 26W
Buronga, Australia 128 C5 34 18 S 142 20 E
Burqān, Kuwait 96 D5 29 0N 47 57 E
Burra, Australia 128 B3 33 40 S 138 55 E
Burra, Nigeria 113 C6 11 0N 8 56 E
Burragorang, L., Australia 129 B9 33 52 S 150 37 E
Burray, U.K. 22 C6 58 51N 2 54W
Burrel, Albania 50 E4 41 36N 20 1 E
Burren △, Ireland 23 C3 53 1N 8 58W
Burren Junction, Australia 127 E4 30 7 S 148 59 E
Burrendong, L., Australia 129 B8 32 45 S 149 10 E
Burriana, Spain 40 F4 39 50N 0 4W
Burrinjuck Res., Australia 129 C8 35 0 S 148 36 E
Burro, Serranías del, Mexico 162 B4 29 0N 102 0W
Burrow Hd., U.K. 22 G4 54 41N 4 24W
Burrowa Pine Mountain △, Australia 129 D7 36 6 S 147 45 E
Burrum Coast △, Australia 127 D5 25 13 S 152 36 E
Burruyacú, Argentina 174 B3 26 30 S 64 40W
Burry Port, U.K. 21 F3 51 41N 4 15W
Bursa, Turkey 51 F13 40 15N 29 5 E
Burseryd, Sweden 17 G7 57 12N 13 17 E
Burstall, Canada 143 C7 50 39N 109 54W
Burton, Mich., U.S.A. 157 B13 43 0N 83 40W
Burton, Ohio, U.S.A. 150 E3 41 28N 81 8W
Burton, S.C., U.S.A. 149 J5 32 25N 80 45W
Burton, L., Canada 140 B4 54 45N 78 20W
Burton upon Trent, U.K. 20 E6 52 48N 1 38W
Burtundy, Australia 128 B5 33 45 S 142 15 E
Buru, Indonesia 82 B3 3 30 S 126 30 E
Buruanga, Phil. 81 F3 11 51N 121 53 E
Burullus, Bahra el, Egypt 106 H7 31 25N 31 0 E
Burûm, Yemen 99 D5 14 22N 48 59 E
Burûn, Râs, Egypt 103 D2 31 14N 33 7 E
Burunday = Boralday, Kazakhstan 65 B8 43 20N 76 51 E
Burundi ■, Africa 118 C3 3 15 S 30 0 E
Burunny = Tsagan Aman, Russia 61 G8 47 34N 46 43 E
Bururi, Burundi 118 C2 3 57 S 29 37 E
Burutu, Nigeria 113 D6 5 20N 5 29 E
Burwell, U.S.A. 154 E5 41 47N 99 8W
Burwick, U.K. 22 C5 58 45N 2 58W
Bury, U.K. 20 D5 53 35N 2 17W
Bury St. Edmunds, U.K. 21 E8 52 15N 0 43 E
Buryatia □, Russia 67 D11 53 0N 110 0 E
Bûrylbaytal, Kazakhstan 65 A7 45 5N 74 1 E
Buryn, Ukraine 59 G7 51 13N 33 50 E
Burzenin, Poland 55 G5 51 28N 18 47 E
Busa, Mt., Phil. 81 H5 6 8N 124 39 E
Busalla, Italy 44 D5 44 34N 8 57 E
Busan = Pusan, S. Korea 75 G15 35 5N 129 0 E
Busanga, Dem. Rep. of the Congo 114 C4 0 53 S 22 7 E
Busango Swamp, Zambia 119 E2 14 15 S 25 45 E
Buşayrah, Syria 101 E9 35 9N 40 26 E
Busca, Italy 44 D4 44 31N 7 29 E
Bushat, Albania 50 E3 41 58N 19 34 E
Būshehr, Iran 97 D6 28 55N 50 55 E
Būshehr □, Iran 97 D6 28 20N 51 45 E
Bushell, Canada 143 B7 59 31N 108 45W
Bushenyi, Uganda 118 C3 0 35 S 30 10 E
Bushimaie →, Dem. Rep. of the Congo 115 D4 6 2 S 23 45 E
Bushire = Būshehr, Iran 97 D6 28 55N 50 55 E
Bushnell, Fla., U.S.A. 153 G7 28 40N 82 7W
Bushnell, Ill., U.S.A. 156 D6 40 33N 90 31W
Bushtyna, Ukraine 53 B8 48 3N 23 28 E
Busie, Ghana 112 C4 10 29N 2 22W
Businga, Dem. Rep. of the Congo 114 B4 3 16N 20 59 E
Buskerud □, Norway 18 D5 60 20N 9 0 E
Busko-Zdrój, Poland 55 H7 50 28N 20 42 E
Buskul, Kazakhstan 64 E8 53 45N 61 12 E
Buslei, Ethiopia 120 C2 5 28N 44 25 E
Busovača, Bos.-H. 52 F2 44 6N 17 53 E
Buşra ash Shām, Syria 103 C5 32 30N 36 25 E
Busselton, Australia 125 F2 33 42 S 115 15 E
Busseri →, Sudan 107 F2 7 41N 28 3 E
Busseto, Italy 44 D7 44 59N 10 2 E
Bussière-Badil, France 28 C4 45 39N 0 36 E
Bussigny, Switz. 32 C3 46 33N 6 33 E
Bussolengo, Italy 44 C7 45 28N 10 51 E
Bussum, Neths. 24 B5 52 16N 5 10 E
Bustamante, B., Argentina 176 C3 45 5 S 66 18W
Buşteni, Romania 53 E10 45 24N 25 32 E
Busto, C., Spain 42 B4 43 34N 6 28W
Busto Arsízio, Italy 44 C5 45 37N 8 51 E
Busu Djanoa, Dem. Rep. of the Congo 114 B4 1 43N 21 23 E
Busu Kwanga, Dem. Rep. of the Congo 114 B4 1 48N 20 21 E
Busu Mandji, Dem. Rep. of the Congo 114 B4 2 52N 21 14 E
Busuanga, Phil. 80 E2 12 14N 119 52 E
Busuanga I., Phil. 80 E2 12 10N 120 0 E
Büsum, Germany 30 A4 54 7N 8 51 E
Busungbiu, Indonesia 79 J17 8 16 S 114 58 E
Buta, Dem. Rep. of the Congo 118 B1 2 50N 24 53 E
Butare, Rwanda 118 C2 2 31 S 29 52 E
Butaritari, Kiribati 134 G9 3 30N 174 0 E
Bute, Australia 128 B3 33 51 S 138 2 E
Bute, U.K. 22 F3 55 48N 5 2W
Bute Inlet, Canada 142 C4 50 40N 124 53W
Butemba, Uganda 118 B3 1 9N 31 37 E
Butembo, Dem. Rep. of the Congo 118 B2 0 9N 29 18 E
Buteni, Romania 52 D7 46 19N 22 7 E
Butera, Italy 47 E7 37 11N 14 11 E
Butha Qi, China 69 B7 48 0N 122 32 E
Buthidaung, Burma 90 E4 20 52N 92 32 E
Butiaba, Uganda 118 B3 1 50N 31 20 E
Butler, Ga., U.S.A. 152 C5 32 33N 84 14W
Butler, Ind., U.S.A. 157 C12 41 26N 84 52W
Butler, Ky., U.S.A. 157 F12 38 47N 84 22W
Butler, Mo., U.S.A. 156 F2 38 16N 94 20W
Butler, Pa., U.S.A. 150 F5 40 52N 79 54W
Buton, Indonesia 82 C2 5 0 S 122 45 E
Bütow = Bytów, Poland 54 D4 54 10N 17 30 E
Butrintit, L. e, Albania 38 B10 39 43N 20 5 E
Bütschwil, Switz. 33 B8 47 23N 9 5 E
Butte, Mont., U.S.A. 158 C7 46 0N 112 32W
Butte, Nebr., U.S.A. 154 D5 42 58N 98 51W
Butte Creek →, U.S.A. 160 F5 39 12N 121 56W
Butterworth = Gcuwa, S. Africa 117 E4 32 20 S 28 11 E
Butterworth, Malaysia 87 c 5 24N 100 23 E
Buttevant, Ireland 23 D3 52 14N 8 40W
Buttfield, Mt., Australia 125 D4 24 45 S 128 9 E
Button B., Canada 143 B10 58 45N 94 23W
Buttonwillow, U.S.A. 161 K7 35 24N 119 28W
Butty Hd., Australia 125 F3 33 54 S 121 39 E
Butuan, Phil. 81 G5 8 57N 125 33 E
Butuku-Luba, Eq. Guin. 113 E6 3 29N 8 33 E
Butung = Buton, Indonesia 82 C2 5 0 S 122 45 E
Buturlinovka, Russia 60 E5 50 50N 40 35 E
Butzbach, Germany 31 E4 50 25N 8 40 E
Bützow, Germany 30 B7 53 50N 11 58 E
Buulobarde = Bulo Burti, Somali Rep. 120 D3 3 50N 45 33 E
Buur Hakaba = Bur Acaba, Somali Rep. 120 D2 3 12N 44 20 E
Buvik, Norway 18 A7 63 18N 10 11 E
Buxa Duar, India 93 F13 27 45N 89 35 E
Buxar, India 93 G10 25 34N 83 58 E
Buxtehude, Germany 30 B5 53 28N 9 39 E
Buxton, Guyana 169 B6 6 48N 58 2W
Buxton, U.K. 20 D6 53 16N 1 54W
Buxy, France 27 F11 46 44N 4 40 E
Buy, Russia 60 A5 58 28N 41 28 E
Buynaksk, Russia 61 J8 42 48N 47 7 E
Buyo, Ivory C. 112 D3 6 21N 7 5W
Buyo, L. de, Ivory C. 112 D3 6 16N 7 10W
Büyük Menderes →, Turkey 49 D9 37 28N 27 11 E
Büyükçekmece, Turkey 51 E12 41 2N 28 35 E
Büyükkarıştıran, Turkey 51 E11 41 18N 27 33 E
Büyükkemikli Burnu, Turkey 51 F10 40 18N 26 14 E
Büyükorhan, Turkey 49 B10 39 46N 28 56 E
Büyükyoncalı, Turkey 51 E11 41 20N 27 55 E
Buzançais, France 26 F8 46 54N 1 25 E
Buzău, Romania 53 E11 45 10N 26 50 E
Buzău □, Romania 53 E11 45 20N 26 30 E
Buzău →, Romania 53 E12 45 26N 27 44 E
Buzău, Pasul, Romania 53 E11 45 35N 26 12 E
Buzen, Japan 72 D3 33 35N 131 5 E
Buzet, Croatia 45 C10 45 24N 13 58 E
Buzi →, Mozam. 119 F3 19 50 S 34 43 E
Buziaş, Romania 52 E6 45 38N 21 36 E
Buzuluk, Russia 64 E4 52 48N 52 12 E
Buzuluk →, Russia 60 E6 50 15N 42 7 E
Buzzards B., U.S.A. 151 E14 41 45N 70 37W
Buzzards Bay, U.S.A. 151 E14 41 44N 70 37W
Bwagaoia, Papua N. G. 132 F7 10 40 S 152 52 E
Bwana Mkubwe, Dem. Rep. of the Congo 119 E2 13 8 S 28 38 E
Bwasa, Dem. Rep. of the Congo 114 C3 3 55 S 18 24 E
Bwatnapné, Vanuatu 133 E6 15 41 S 168 9 E
Bwindi △, Uganda 118 C2 1 2 S 29 42 E
Byala, Ruse, Bulgaria 51 C9 43 28N 25 44 E
Byala, Varna, Bulgaria 51 D11 42 53N 27 55 E
Byala Slatina, Bulgaria 50 C7 43 26N 23 55 E
Byarezina →, Belarus 59 F6 52 33N 30 14 E
Byaroza, Belarus 59 F3 52 31N 24 51 E
Bychawa, Poland 55 G9 51 1N 22 36 E
Byczyna, Poland 55 G5 51 7N 18 12 E
Bydgoszcz, Poland 55 E5 53 10N 18 0 E
Byelarus = Belarus ■, Europe 58 F4 53 30N 27 0 E
Byelorussia = Belarus ■, Europe 58 F4 53 30N 27 0 E
Byers, U.S.A. 154 F2 39 43N 104 14W
Byesville, U.S.A. 150 G3 39 58N 81 32W
Byfield △, Australia 126 C5 22 52 S 150 45 E
Byford, Australia 125 F2 32 15 S 116 0 E
Bygdin, Norway 18 C5 61 21N 8 32 E
Bygland, Norway 18 F4 58 50N 7 48 E
Byglandsfjorden, Norway 18 F4 58 44N 7 50 E
Bygstad, Norway 18 C2 61 23N 5 40 E
Bykhaw, Belarus 58 F6 53 31N 30 14 E
Bykhov = Bykhaw, Belarus 58 F6 53 31N 30 14 E
Bykle, Norway 18 E4 59 20N 7 22 E
Bykovo, Russia 60 F7 49 50N 45 25 E
Bylas, U.S.A. 159 K8 33 8N 110 7W
Bylot, Canada 143 B10 58 25N 94 8W
Bylot I., Canada 139 A12 73 13N 78 34W
Byrd, C., Antarctica 7 C17 69 38 S 76 7W
Byrock, Australia 129 A7 30 40 S 146 27 E
Byron, Ga., U.S.A. 152 C6 32 39N 83 46W
Byron, Ill., U.S.A. 156 B7 42 8N 89 15W
Byron, C., Australia 127 D5 28 43 S 153 38 E
Byron Bay, Australia 127 D5 28 43 S 153 37 E
Byrranga, Gory, Russia 67 B11 75 0N 100 0 E
Byrranga Mts. = Byrranga, Gory, Russia 67 B11 75 0N 100 0 E
Byrum, Denmark 17 G5 57 16N 11 0 E
Byske, Sweden 14 D19 64 57N 21 11 E
Byskeälven →, Sweden 14 D19 64 57N 21 13 E
Bystrovka = Kemin, Kyrgyzstan 65 B7 42 47N 75 42 E
Bystrytsya, Ukraine 53 B9 48 27N 24 14 E
Bystrzyca →, Dolnośląskie, Poland 55 G3 51 12N 16 55 E
Bystrzyca →, Lubelskie, Poland 55 G9 51 21N 22 46 E
Bystrzyca Kłodzka, Poland 55 H3 50 19N 16 39 E
Bytča, Slovak Rep. 35 B11 49 13N 18 34 E
Bytkiv, Ukraine 53 B9 48 38N 24 28 E
Bytom, Poland 55 H5 50 25N 18 54 E
Bytom Odrzański, Poland 55 G2 51 44N 15 48 E
Bytów, Poland 54 D4 54 10N 17 30 E
Byumba, Rwanda 118 C3 1 35 S 30 4 E
Bzenec, Czech Rep. 35 C10 48 58N 17 18 E
Bzura →, Poland 55 F7 52 25N 20 15 E

C

C.W. McConaughy, L., U.S.A. 154 E4 41 14N 101 40W
Ca →, Vietnam 86 C5 18 45N 105 45 E
Ca Mau, Vietnam 87 H5 9 7N 105 8 E
Ca Mau, Mui, Vietnam 87 H5 8 38N 104 44 E
Ca Na, Vietnam 87 G7 11 20N 108 54 E
Caacupé, Paraguay 174 B4 25 23 S 57 5W
Caaguazú △, Paraguay 175 B4 26 5 S 55 31W
Caála, Angola 115 E3 12 46 S 15 30 E
Caamaño Sd., Canada 142 C3 52 55N 129 25W
Caapiranga, Brazil 169 D5 3 18 S 61 13W
Caazapá, Paraguay 174 B4 26 8 S 56 19W
Caazapá □, Paraguay 175 B4 26 10 S 56 0W
Cabadbaran, Phil. 81 G5 9 10N 125 38 E
Cabagan, Phil. 80 C3 17 26N 121 46 E
Cabalian = San Juan, Phil. 81 F5 10 16N 125 10 E
Caballeria, C. de, Spain 38 A5 40 5N 4 5 E
Cabana, Peru 172 B2 8 25 S 78 5W
Cabana, Spain 42 B2 43 13N 8 54W
Cabanaconde, Peru 172 D3 15 38 S 71 58W
Cabañaquinta, Spain 42 B5 43 10N 5 38W
Cabanatuan, Phil. 80 D3 15 30N 120 58 E
Cabañeros ⌓, Spain 43 F6 39 18N 4 35W
Cabanes, Spain 40 E5 40 9N 0 2 E
Cabangan, Phil. 80 D3 15 10N 120 3 E
Cabanillas, Peru 172 D3 15 36 S 70 28W
Cabano, Canada 141 C6 47 40N 68 56W
Čabar, Croatia 45 C11 45 36N 14 39 E
Cabarroguis, Phil. 80 C3 16 50N 121 30 E
Cabarruyan I., Phil. 80 C2 16 18N 119 59 E
Cabazon, U.S.A. 161 M10 33 55N 116 47W
Cabedelo, Brazil 170 C5 7 0 S 34 50W
Cabeza del Buey, Spain 43 G5 38 44N 5 13W
Cabezón de la Sal, Spain 42 B6 43 18N 4 14W
Cabildo, Chile 174 C1 32 30 S 71 5W
Cabimas, Venezuela 168 A3 10 23N 71 25W
Cabinda, Angola 115 D2 5 33 S 12 11 E
Cabinda □, Angola 115 D2 5 0 S 12 30 E
Cabinet Mts., U.S.A. 158 C6 48 0N 115 30W
Cabiri, Angola 115 D2 8 52 S 13 39 E
Cable Beach, Bahamas 9 b 25 4N 77 24W
Cabo Blanco, Argentina 176 C3 47 15 S 65 47W
Cabo de Gata-Níjar ⌓, Spain 41 J2 36 51N 2 6W
Cabo de Hornos △, Chile 176 E3 55 42 S 67 20W
Cabo Frio, Brazil 171 F3 22 51 S 42 3W
Cabo Pantoja, Peru 168 D2 1 0 S 75 10W
Cabo Raso, Argentina 176 B3 44 20 S 65 15W
Cabo Verde = Cape Verde Is. ■, Atl. Oc. 8 E9 16 0N 24 0W
Cabo Yubi = Tarfaya, Morocco 110 C2 27 55N 12 55W
Cabonga, Réservoir, Canada 140 C4 47 20N 76 40W
Cabool, U.S.A. 155 G8 37 7N 92 6W
Caboolture, Australia 127 D5 27 5 S 152 58 E
Cabora Bassa Dam = Cahora Bassa, Represa de, Mozam. 119 F3 15 20 S 32 50 E
Caborca, Mexico 162 A2 30 40N 112 10W
Cabot, Mt., U.S.A. 151 B13 44 30N 71 25W
Cabot Hd., Canada 150 A3 45 14N 81 17W
Cabot Str., Canada 141 C8 47 15N 59 40W
Cabra, Spain 43 H6 37 30N 4 28W
Cabra del Santo Cristo, Spain 43 H7 37 42N 3 16W
Cabra I., India 95 L11 7 18N 93 50 E
Cábras, Italy 46 C1 39 56N 8 32 E
Cabrera, Spain 38 B3 39 8N 2 57 E
Cabrera △, Spain 41 F7 39 13N 2 53 E
Cabrera, Sierra, Spain 42 C4 42 12N 6 40W
Cabri, Canada 143 C7 50 35N 108 25W
Cabriel →, Spain 41 F3 39 14N 1 3W
Cabruta, Venezuela 168 B4 7 50N 66 10W
Cabucgayan, Phil. 81 F5 11 29N 124 34 E
Cabugao, Phil. 80 C3 17 48N 120 27 E
Cabulauan Is., Phil. 81 F3 11 25N 120 8 E
Cabulo, Angola 115 E3 10 18 S 16 22 E
Caburan = Jose Abad Santos, Phil. 81 J5 5 55N 125 39 E
Cabuta, Angola 115 D2 9 48 S 14 58 E
Cabuyaro, Colombia 168 C3 4 18N 72 49W
Cacabelos, Spain 42 C4 42 36N 6 44W
Caçador, Brazil 175 B5 26 47 S 51 0W
Čačak, Serbia & M. 50 C4 43 54N 20 20 E
Cacao, Fr. Guiana 169 C7 4 33N 52 26W
Caçapava do Sul, Brazil 175 C5 30 30 S 53 30W
Cáccamo, Italy 46 E6 37 56N 13 40 E
Cacém, Portugal 43 G1 38 46N 9 18W
Cáceres, Brazil 173 D6 16 5 S 57 40W
Cáceres, Colombia 168 B2 7 35N 75 20W
Cáceres, Spain 43 F4 39 26N 6 23W
Cáceres □, Spain 42 F5 39 45N 6 0W
Cache Bay, Canada 140 C4 46 22N 80 0W
Cache Cr. →, U.S.A. 160 G5 38 42N 121 42W
Cache Creek, Canada 142 C4 50 48N 121 19W
Cacheu, Guinea-Biss. 112 C1 12 14N 16 8W
Cachi, Argentina 174 B2 25 5 S 66 10W
Cachimbo, Brazil 173 B7 8 57 S 54 54W
Cachimbo, Serra do, Brazil 173 B6 9 30 S 55 30W
Cachimo, Angola 115 D4 8 21 S 21 24 E
Cachinal de la Sierra, Chile 174 A2 24 58 S 69 32W
Cachingues, Angola 115 E3 13 5 S 16 43 E
Cachoeira = Solonópole, Brazil 170 C4 5 44 S 39 1W
Cachoeira, Brazil 171 D4 12 30 S 39 0W
Cachoeira Alta, Brazil 171 E1 18 48 S 50 58W
Cachoeira do Sul, Brazil 175 C5 30 3 S 52 53W
Cachoeiro de Itapemirim, Brazil 171 F3 20 51 S 41 7W
Cachoeiro do Arari, Brazil 170 B2 1 1 S 48 58W
Cachopo, Portugal 43 H3 37 20N 7 49W
Cachuela Esperanza, Bolivia 173 C4 10 32 S 65 38W
Cacine, Guinea-Biss. 112 C1 11 8N 14 57W
Cacoal, Brazil 173 C5 11 30 S 61 25W
Cacólo, Angola 115 E3 10 9 S 19 21 E
Caconda, Angola 115 E3 13 48 S 15 8 E
Cacongo, Angola 115 D2 5 11 S 12 5 E
Caçu, Brazil 171 E1 18 37 S 51 4W
Cacuaco, Angola 115 D2 8 47 S 13 21 E
Cacuchi →, Angola 115 E3 14 26 S 16 46 E
Cacula, Angola 115 E2 14 29 S 14 10 E
Caculé, Brazil 171 D3 14 30 S 42 13W
Caculuvar →, Angola 115 F2 16 47 S 14 56 E
Cacuso, Angola 115 D3 9 25 S 15 45 E
Čadca, Slovak Rep. 35 B11 49 26N 18 45 E
Caddo, U.S.A. 155 H6 34 7N 96 16W
Cadenazzo, Switz. 33 D7 46 9N 8 57 E
Cader Idris, U.K. 21 E4 52 42N 3 53W
Cadereyta, Mexico 162 B5 25 36N 100 0W
Cades, U.S.A. 152 B10 33 47N 79 47W
Cadí, Sierra del, Spain 40 C6 42 17N 1 42 E
Cadí-Moixeró ⌓, Spain 40 C3 42 17N 1 44W
Cadibarrawirracanna, L., Australia 127 D2 28 52 S 135 27 E
Cadillac, France 28 D3 44 38N 0 20W
Cadillac, U.S.A. 148 C3 44 15N 85 24W
Cadiz, Phil. 81 F4 10 57N 123 15 E
Cádiz, Spain 43 J4 36 30N 6 20W
Cadiz, Calif., U.S.A. 161 L11 34 30N 115 28W
Cadiz, Ohio, U.S.A. 150 F4 40 22N 81 0W
Cádiz □, Spain 43 J5 36 36N 5 45W
Cádiz, G. de, Spain 43 J3 36 40N 7 0W
Cadiz L., U.S.A. 159 J6 34 18N 115 24W
Cadley, U.S.A. 152 B7 33 32N 82 40W
Cadney Park, Australia 127 D1 27 55 S 134 3 E
Cadomin, Canada 142 C5 53 2N 117 20W
Cadotte Lake, Canada 142 B5 56 26N 116 23W
Cadours, France 28 E5 43 44N 1 2 E
Cadoux, Australia 125 F2 30 46 S 117 7 E
Cadwell, U.S.A. 152 C6 32 20N 83 3W
Caen, France 26 C6 49 10N 0 22W
Caernarfon, U.K. 20 D3 53 8N 4 16W
Caernarfon B., U.K. 20 D3 53 4N 4 40W
Caernarvon = Caernarfon, U.K. 20 D3 53 8N 4 16W
Caerphilly, U.K. 21 F4 51 35N 3 13W
Caerphilly □, U.K. 21 F4 51 37N 3 12W
Caesarea, Israel 103 C3 32 30N 34 53 E
Caeté, Brazil 171 E3 19 55 S 43 40W
Caetité, Brazil 171 D3 13 50 S 42 32W
Cafayate, Argentina 174 B2 26 2 S 66 0W
Cafu, Angola 116 B2 16 30 S 15 8 E
Cagayan □, Phil. 80 C3 18 0N 121 50 E
Cagayan →, Phil. 80 B3 18 25N 121 42 E
Cagayan de Oro, Phil. 81 G5 8 30N 124 40 E
Cagayan Is., Phil. 81 G3 9 40N 121 16 E
Cagayan Sulu I., Phil. 81 H2 7 1N 118 30 E
Cagli, Italy 45 E9 43 33N 12 39 E
Cágliari, Italy 46 C2 39 13N 9 7 E
Cágliari, G. di, Italy 46 C2 39 8N 9 11 E
Cagnano Varano, Italy 45 G12 41 49N 15 47 E
Cagnes-sur-Mer, France 29 E11 43 40N 7 9 E
Caguán →, Colombia 168 D3 0 8 S 74 18W
Caguas, Puerto Rico 165 d 18 14N 66 2W
Caha Mts., Ireland 23 E2 51 45N 9 40W
Cahama, Angola 116 B1 16 17 S 14 19 E
Caher, Ireland 23 D4 52 22N 7 56W
Caherciveen, Ireland 23 E1 51 56N 10 14W
Cahora Bassa, L. de, Mozam. 119 F3 15 35 S 32 0 E
Cahora Bassa, Represa de, Mozam. 119 F3 15 20 S 32 50 E
Cahore Pt., Ireland 23 D5 52 33N 6 12W
Cahors, France 28 D5 44 27N 1 27 E
Cahuapanas, Peru 172 B2 5 15 S 77 0W
Cahuinari △, Colombia 168 D3 1 20 S 71 10W
Cahuinari →, Colombia 168 D3 1 21 S 70 44W
Cahul, Moldova 53 E13 45 50N 28 15 E
Cai Bau, Dao, Vietnam 76 G6 21 10N 107 27 E
Cai Nuoc, Vietnam 87 H5 8 56N 105 1 E
Caia, Mozam. 119 F4 17 51 S 35 24 E
Caiabis, Serra dos, Brazil 173 C6 11 30 S 56 30W
Caianda, Angola 119 E1 11 2 S 23 31 E
Caiapó, Serra do, Brazil 173 D7 17 0 S 52 0W
Caiapônia, Brazil 173 D7 16 57 S 51 49W
Caibarién, Cuba 164 B4 22 30N 79 30W
Caibiran, Phil. 81 F5 11 34N 124 35 E
Caiçara = Alvarães, Brazil 169 D5 3 12 S 64 50W
Caicara, Bolívar, Venezuela 168 B4 7 38N 66 10W
Caicara, Monagas, Venezuela 169 B5 9 52N 63 38W
Caicó, Brazil 170 C4 6 20 S 37 0W
Caicos Is., Turks & Caicos 165 B5 21 40N 71 40W
Caicos Passage, W. Indies 165 B5 22 45N 72 45W
Caidian, China 77 B10 30 35N 114 2 E
Cailloma, Peru 172 D3 15 9 S 71 45W
Căinari, Moldova 53 D14 46 41N 29 3 E
Cainde, Angola 115 F2 15 29 S 13 24 E
Caine →, Bolivia 173 D4 18 23 S 65 21W
Caird Coast, Antarctica 7 D1 75 0 S 25 0W
Cairn Gorm, U.K. 22 D5 57 7N 3 39W
Cairngorm Mts., U.K. 22 D5 57 6N 3 42W
Cairngorms △, U.K. 22 D5 57 10N 3 50W
Cairnryan, U.K. 22 G3 54 59N 5 1W
Cairns, Australia 126 B4 16 57 S 145 45 E
Cairns L., Canada 143 C10 51 42N 94 30W
Cairo = El Qâhira, Egypt 106 H7 30 1N 31 14 E
Cairo, Ga., U.S.A. 152 E5 30 52N 84 13W
Cairo, Ill., U.S.A. 155 G10 37 0N 89 11W
Cairo, N.Y., U.S.A. 151 D11 42 18N 74 0W
Cairo Montenotte, Italy 44 D5 44 23N 8 16 E
Cairofa, Angola 115 E2 14 3 S 12 54 E
Caithness, U.K. 22 C5 58 25N 3 35W
Caithness, Ord of, U.K. 22 C5 58 8N 3 36W
Caitou, Angola 115 E2 14 28 S 13 7 E
Caiuás = Rio Brilhante, Brazil 175 A5 21 48 S 54 33W
Caiundo, Angola 115 F3 15 50 S 17 28 E
Caiza, Bolivia 173 E4 20 2 S 65 40W

Caja de Muertos, I., *Puerto Rico* **165 d** 17 54N 66 32W
Cajabamba, *Peru* **172 B2** 7 38 S 78 4W
Cajamarca, *Peru* **172 B2** 7 5 S 78 28W
Cajamarca □, *Peru* **172 B2** 6 15 S 78 50W
Cajamarquilla = Bolívar, *Peru* **172 B2** 7 18 S 77 48W
Cajapió, *Brazil* **170 B3** 2 58 S 44 48W
Cajarc, *France* **28 D5** 44 29N 1 50 E
Cajas △, *Ecuador* **168 D2** 2 48 S 79 15W
Cajatambo, *Peru* **172 C2** 10 30 S 77 2W
Cajàzeiras, *Brazil* **170 C4** 6 52 S 38 30W
Cajetina, *Serbia & M.* **50 C3** 43 47N 19 42 E
Cajidiocan, *Phil.* **80 E4** 12 22N 122 41 E
Çakirgol, *Turkey* **101 B8** 40 33N 39 40 E
Çakırlar, *Turkey* **49 E12** 36 52N 30 33 E
Čakovec, *Croatia* **45 B13** 46 23N 16 26 E
Çal, *Turkey* **49 C11** 38 4N 29 23 E
Cala, *Spain* **43 H4** 37 59N 6 21W
Cala →, *Spain* **43 H4** 37 38N 6 5W
Cala Cadolar, Punta de = Rotja, Pta., *Spain* **38 D2** 38 38N 1 35 E
Cala d'Or, *Spain* **38 B4** 39 23N 3 14 E
Cala en Porter, *Spain* **38 B5** 39 52N 4 8 E
Cala Figuera, C. de, *Spain* **38 B3** 39 27N 2 31 E
Cala Forcat, *Spain* **38 B4** 40 0N 3 47 E
Cala Major, *Spain* **38 B3** 39 33N 2 37 E
Cala Mezquida = Sa Mesquida, *Spain* **38 B5** 39 55N 4 16 E
Cala Millor, *Spain* **38 B4** 39 35N 3 22 E
Cala Ratjada, *Spain* **38 B4** 39 43N 3 27 E
Cala Santa Galdana, *Spain* **38 B4** 39 56N 3 58 E
Calabanga, *Phil.* **80 E4** 13 42N 123 17 E
Calabar, *Nigeria* **113 E6** 4 57N 8 20 E
Calabogie, *Canada* **151 A8** 45 18N 76 43W
Calabozo, *Venezuela* **168 B4** 9 0N 67 28W
Calábria □, *Italy* **47 C9** 39 0N 16 30 E
Calábria △, *Italy* **47 C9** 39 6N 16 35 E
Calaburras, Pta. de, *Spain* **43 J6** 36 30N 4 38W
Calaceite, *Spain* **40 D5** 41 1N 0 11 E
Calacoto, *Bolivia* **172 D4** 17 16 S 68 38W
Calacuccia, *France* **29 F13** 42 21N 9 1 E
Calafat, *Romania* **52 G7** 43 58N 22 59 E
Calafate, *Argentina* **176 D2** 50 19 S 72 15W
Calafell, *Spain* **40 D6** 41 11N 1 34 E
Calagua Is., *Phil.* **80 D4** 14 30N 122 55 E
Calahorra, *Spain* **40 C3** 42 18N 1 59W
Calai, *Angola* **115 F3** 17 47 S 19 41 E
Calais, *France* **27 B8** 50 57N 1 56 E
Calais, *U.S.A.* **149 C12** 45 11N 67 17W
Calakmul △, *Mexico* **163 D7** 18 14N 89 48W
Calalaste, Cord. de, *Argentina* **174 B2** 25 0 S 67 0W
Calama, *Brazil* **173 B5** 8 0 S 62 50W
Calama, *Chile* **174 A2** 22 30 S 68 55W
Calamar, *Bolívar, Colombia* **168 A3** 10 15N 74 55W
Calamar, *Vaupés, Colombia* **168 C3** 1 58N 72 32W
Calamarca, *Bolivia* **172 D4** 16 55 S 68 9W
Calamba, *Cavite, Phil.* **80 D3** 14 13N 121 10 E
Calamba, *Mis. Occ., Phil.* **81 G4** 8 35N 123 39 E
Calamian Group, *Phil.* **81 F2** 11 50N 119 55 E
Calamocha, *Spain* **40 E3** 40 50N 1 17W
Calamonte, *Spain* **43 G4** 38 53N 6 23W
Călan, *Romania* **52 E7** 45 44N 22 59 E
Calañas, *Spain* **43 H4** 37 40N 6 53W
Calanda, *Spain* **40 E4** 40 56N 0 15W
Calandagan I., *Phil.* **81 F3** 10 39N 120 15 E
Calandula, *Angola* **115 D3** 9 6 S 15 57 E
Calang, *Indonesia* **84 B1** 4 37N 95 37 E
Calangiánus, *Italy* **46 B2** 40 56N 9 11 E
Calanscio, Sarīr, *Libya* **108 C4** 27 30N 21 30 E
Calapan, *Phil.* **80 E3** 13 25N 121 7 E
Călărasi, *Moldova* **53 C13** 47 16N 28 19 E
Călăraşi, *Romania* **53 F12** 44 12N 27 20 E
Călăraşi □, *Romania* **53 F12** 44 10N 27 0 E
Calasparra, *Spain* **41 G3** 38 14N 1 41W
Calatafimi, *Italy* **46 E5** 37 55N 12 52 E
Calatagan, *Phil.* **80 E3** 13 50N 120 38 E
Calatayud, *Spain* **40 D3** 41 20N 1 40W
Călăţele, *Romania* **52 D8** 46 46N 23 1 E
Calato = Kálathos, *Greece* **38 E12** 36 9N 28 8 E
Calatrava, *Eq. Guin.* **114 B1** 1 6N 9 25 E
Calauag, *Phil.* **80 E4** 13 55N 122 15 E
Calavà, C., *Italy* **47 D7** 38 11N 14 55 E
Calavite, C., *Phil.* **80 E3** 13 26N 120 20 E
Calavite Pass, *Phil.* **80 E3** 13 36N 120 25 E
Calayan, *Phil.* **80 B3** 19 16N 121 28 E
Calayan I., *Phil.* **80 B3** 19 20N 121 27 E
Calbayog, *Phil.* **80 E5** 12 4N 124 38 E
Calbiga, *Phil.* **81 F5** 11 38N 125 0 E
Calca, *Peru* **172 C3** 13 22 S 72 0W
Calcasieu L., *U.S.A.* **155 L8** 29 55N 93 18W
Calcutta = Kolkata, *India* **93 H13** 22 36N 88 24 E
Calcutta, *U.S.A.* **150 F4** 40 40N 80 34W
Caldaro, *Italy* **45 B8** 46 25N 11 14 E
Caldas □, *Colombia* **168 B2** 5 15N 75 30W
Caldas da Rainha, *Portugal* **43 F1** 39 24N 9 8W
Caldas de Reis, *Spain* **42 C2** 42 36N 8 39W
Caldas Novas, *Brazil* **171 E2** 17 45 S 48 38W
Calder →, *U.K.* **20 D6** 53 44N 1 22W
Caldera, *Chile* **174 B1** 27 5 S 70 55W
Caldera de Taburiente △, *Canary Is.* **9 e1** 28 43N 17 52W
Caldwell, *Idaho, U.S.A.* **158 E5** 43 40N 116 41W
Caldwell, *Kans., U.S.A.* **155 G6** 37 2N 97 37W
Caldwell, *Tex., U.S.A.* **155 K6** 30 32N 96 42W
Caledon, *S. Africa* **116 E2** 34 14 S 19 26 E
Caledon →, *S. Africa* **116 E4** 30 31 S 26 5 E
Caledon B., *Australia* **126 A2** 12 45 S 137 0 E
Caledonia, *Canada* **150 C5** 43 7N 79 58W
Caledonia, *Mo., U.S.A.* **156 G6** 37 45N 90 46W
Caledonia, *N.Y., U.S.A.* **150 D7** 42 58N 77 51W
Calella, *Spain* **40 D7** 41 37N 2 40 E
Calemba, *Angola* **116 B2** 16 0 S 15 44 E
Calen, *Australia* **126 J6** 20 56 S 148 48 E
Calenzana, *France* **29 F12** 42 31N 8 51 E
Caleta Olivia, *Argentina* **176 C3** 46 25 S 67 25W
Caletones, *Chile* **174 C1** 34 6 S 70 27W
Calexico, *U.S.A.* **161 N11** 32 40N 115 30W
Calf of Man, *I. of Man* **20 C3** 54 3N 4 48W
Calgary, *Canada* **142 C6** 51 0N 114 10W
Calheta, *Azores* **9 d1** 38 36N 28 1W
Calheta, *Madeira* **9 c** 32 44N 17 11W
Calheta de Nesquim, *Azores* **9 d1** 38 24N 28 5W
Calhoun, *U.S.A.* **149 H3** 34 30N 84 57W
Calhoun Falls, *U.S.A.* **152 A7** 34 6N 82 36W
Cali, *Colombia* **168 C2** 3 25N 76 35W
Calicut, *India* **95 J2** 11 15N 75 43 E
Caliente, *U.S.A.* **159 H6** 37 37N 114 31W
California, *Mo., U.S.A.* **156 F4** 38 38N 92 34W
California, *Pa., U.S.A.* **150 F5** 40 4N 79 54W
California □, *U.S.A.* **160 H7** 37 30N 119 30W
California, Baja, *Mexico* **162 A1** 32 10N 115 12W
California, Baja, T.N. = Baja California □, *Mexico* **162 B2** 30 0N 115 0W
California, Baja, T.S. = Baja California Sur □, *Mexico* **162 B2** 25 50N 111 50W
California, G. de, *Mexico* **162 B2** 27 0N 111 0W
California City, *U.S.A.* **161 K9** 35 10N 117 55W
California Hot Springs, *U.S.A.* **161 K8** 35 51N 118 41W
Calilegua △, *Argentina* **174 B3** 25 36 S 64 50W
Călimăneşti, *Romania* **53 E9** 45 14N 24 20 E
Călimani, Munţii, *Romania* **53 C10** 47 12N 25 0 E
Calingasta, *Argentina* **174 C2** 31 15 S 69 30W
Calinog, *Phil.* **81 F4** 11 7N 122 32 E
Calintaan, *Phil.* **80 E3** 12 35N 120 57 E
Calipatria, *U.S.A.* **161 M11** 33 8N 115 31W
Calistoga, *U.S.A.* **160 G4** 38 35N 122 35W
Calitri, *Italy* **47 B8** 40 54N 15 26 E
Calitzdorp, *S. Africa* **116 E3** 33 33 S 21 42 E
Callabonna, L., *Australia* **127 D3** 29 40 S 140 5 E
Callac, *France* **26 D3** 48 25N 3 27W
Callahan, *U.S.A.* **152 E8** 30 34N 81 50W
Callan, *Ireland* **23 D4** 52 32N 7 24W
Callander, *U.K.* **22 E4** 56 15N 4 13W
Callang = San Manuel, *Phil.* **80 C3** 16 4N 120 40 E
Callao, *Peru* **172 C2** 12 0 S 77 0W
Callaway, *U.S.A.* **152 E4** 30 8N 85 36W
Calles, *Mexico* **163 C5** 23 2N 98 42W
Callicoon, *U.S.A.* **151 E9** 41 46N 75 3W
Calling Lake, *Canada* **142 B6** 55 15N 113 12W
Calliope, *Australia* **126 C5** 24 0 S 151 16 E
Callosa de Ensarriá, *Spain* **41 G4** 38 40N 0 8W
Callosa de Segura, *Spain* **41 G4** 38 7N 0 53W
Calmar, *U.S.A.* **156 A5** 43 11N 91 52W
Calne, *U.K.* **21 F6** 51 26N 2 0W
Calola, *Angola* **116 B2** 16 25 S 17 48 E
Calolbon = San Andres, *Phil.* **80 E5** 13 36N 124 6 E
Calonge, *Spain* **40 D8** 41 52N 3 5 E
Caloocan, *Phil.* **80 D3** 14 39N 120 58 E
Caloosahatchee →, *U.S.A.* **153 J7** 26 31N 82 1W
Calore →, *Italy* **47 A7** 41 11N 14 28 E
Caloundra, *Australia* **127 D5** 26 45 S 153 10 E
Calpe, *Spain* **41 G5** 38 39N 0 3 E
Calpella, *U.S.A.* **160 F3** 39 14N 123 12W
Calpine, *U.S.A.* **160 F6** 39 40N 120 27W
Calstock, *Canada* **140 C3** 49 47N 84 9W
Caltabellotta, *Italy* **46 E6** 37 34N 13 13 E
Caltagirone, *Italy* **47 E7** 37 14N 14 31 E
Caltanissetta, *Italy* **47 E7** 37 29N 14 4 E
Çaltılıbük, *Turkey* **51 G12** 39 57N 28 36 E
Caluango, *Angola* **115 D3** 8 20 S 19 39 E
Calubian, *Phil.* **81 F5** 11 27N 124 26 E
Calucinga, *Angola* **115 E3** 11 18 S 16 12 E
Caluire-et-Cuire, *France* **27 G11** 45 48N 4 52 E
Calulo, *Angola* **115 E2** 10 1 S 14 56 E
Calunda, *Angola* **115 E4** 12 7 S 23 36 E
Caluquembe, *Angola* **115 E2** 13 47 S 14 44 E
Caluso, *Italy* **44 C4** 45 18N 7 53 E
Caluya I., *Phil.* **81 F3** 11 55N 121 34 E
Calvados □, *France* **26 C6** 49 5N 0 15W
Calvados Chain, The, *Papua N. G.* **132 F7** 11 10 S 152 45 E
Calvert →, *Australia* **126 B2** 16 17 S 137 44 E
Calvert I., *Canada* **142 C3** 51 30N 128 0W
Calvert Ra., *Australia* **124 D3** 24 0 S 122 30 E
Calvi, *France* **29 F12** 42 34N 8 45 E
Calviá, *Spain* **38 B3** 39 34N 2 31 E
Calvillo, *Mexico* **162 C4** 21 51N 102 43W
Calvinia, *S. Africa* **116 E2** 31 28 S 19 45 E
Calvo, Mte., *Italy* **45 G12** 41 44N 15 46 E
Calwa, *U.S.A.* **160 J7** 36 42N 119 46W
Calzada Almuradiel = Almuradiel, *Spain* **43 G7** 38 32N 3 28W
Calzada de Calatrava, *Spain* **43 G7** 38 42N 3 46W
Cam →, *U.K.* **21 E8** 52 21N 0 16 E
Cam Lam, *Vietnam* **87 G7** 11 54N 109 10 E
Cam Pha, *Vietnam* **76 G6** 21 7N 107 18 E
Cam Ranh, *Vietnam* **87 G7** 11 54N 109 12 E
Cam Xuyen, *Vietnam* **86 C6** 18 15N 106 0 E
Camabatela, *Angola* **115 D3** 8 20 S 15 26 E
Camacã, *Brazil* **171 E4** 15 24 S 39 30W
Camaçari, *Brazil* **171 D4** 12 41 S 38 18W
Camacha, *Madeira* **9 c** 32 41N 16 49W
Camacho, *Mexico* **162 C4** 24 25N 102 18W
Camacupa, *Angola* **115 E3** 11 58 S 17 22 E
Camaguán, *Venezuela* **168 B4** 8 6N 67 36W
Camagüey, *Cuba* **164 B4** 21 20N 77 55W
Camaiore, *Italy* **44 E7** 43 56N 10 18 E
Camamu, *Brazil* **171 D4** 13 57 S 39 7W
Camaná, *Peru* **172 D3** 16 30 S 72 50W
Camanche, *U.S.A.* **156 C6** 41 47N 90 15W
Camanche Reservoir, *U.S.A.* **160 G6** 38 14N 121 1W
Camapuã, *Brazil* **173 D7** 19 30 S 54 5W
Camaquã, *Brazil* **175 C5** 30 51 S 51 49W
Camaquã →, *Brazil* **175 C5** 31 17 S 51 47W
Câmara de Lobos, *Madeira* **9 c** 32 39N 16 59W
Camararé →, *Brazil* **173 C6** 12 15 S 58 55W
Camarat, C., *France* **29 E10** 43 12N 6 41 E
Camarès, *France* **28 E6** 43 49N 2 53 E
Camaret-sur-Mer, *France* **26 D2** 48 16N 4 37W
Camargo, *Bolivia* **173 E4** 20 38 S 65 15W
Camargo, *Mexico* **163 B5** 26 19N 98 50W
Camargue, *France* **29 E8** 43 34N 4 34 E
Camargue △, *France* **29 E8** 43 30N 4 40 E
Camarillo, *U.S.A.* **161 L7** 34 13N 119 2W
Camariñas, *Spain* **42 B1** 43 8N 9 12W
Camarines Norte □, *Phil.* **80 D4** 14 10N 122 45 E
Camarines Sur □, *Phil.* **80 E4** 13 40N 123 20 E
Camarón, C., *Honduras* **164 C2** 16 0N 85 5W
Camarones, *Argentina* **176 B3** 44 50 S 65 40W
Camarones, B., *Argentina* **176 B3** 44 45 S 65 35W
Camas, *Spain* **43 H4** 37 24N 6 2W
Camas, *U.S.A.* **160 E4** 45 35N 122 24W
Camas Valley, *U.S.A.* **158 E2** 43 2N 123 40W
Camatambo, *Angola* **115 D3** 6 31 S 15 21 E
Camataquí = Villa Abecia, *Bolivia* **174 A2** 21 0 S 68 18W
Camaxilo, *Angola* **115 D3** 8 21 S 18 56 E
Camba Cassai, *Angola* **115 D3** 9 47 S 19 9 E
Camballin, *Australia* **124 C3** 17 59 S 124 12 E
Cambamba, *Angola* **115 D2** 8 53 S 14 44 E
Cambará, *Brazil* **175 A5** 23 2 S 50 5W
Cambay = Khambhat, *India* **92 H5** 22 23N 72 33 E
Cambay, G. of = Khambhat, G. of, *India* **89 C6** 20 45N 72 30 E
Cambil, *Spain* **43 H7** 37 40N 3 33W
Cambo, *Angola* **115 D3** 10 55 S 20 6 E
Cambo-les-Bains, *France* **28 E2** 43 22N 1 23W
Cambodia ■, *Asia* **86 F5** 12 15N 105 0 E
Camborne, *U.K.* **21 G2** 50 12N 5 19W
Cambrai, *Australia* **128 C3** 34 40 S 139 16 E
Cambrai, *France* **27 B10** 50 11N 3 14 E
Cambre, *Spain* **42 B2** 43 17N 8 20W
Cambria, *U.S.A.* **160 K5** 35 34N 121 5W
Cambrian Mts., *U.K.* **21 E4** 52 3N 3 57W
Cambridge, *Canada* **140 D3** 43 23N 80 15W
Cambridge, *Jamaica* **164 a** 18 18N 77 54W
Cambridge, *N.Z.* **130 D4** 37 54 S 175 29 E
Cambridge, *U.K.* **21 E8** 52 12N 0 8 E
Cambridge, *Ill., U.S.A.* **156 C6** 41 18N 90 12W
Cambridge, *Iowa, U.S.A.* **156 C3** 41 54N 93 32W
Cambridge, *Mass., U.S.A.* **151 D13** 42 22N 71 6W
Cambridge, *Md., U.S.A.* **148 F7** 38 34N 76 5W
Cambridge, *Minn., U.S.A.* **154 C8** 45 34N 93 13W
Cambridge, *N.Y., U.S.A.* **151 C11** 43 2N 73 22W
Cambridge, *Nebr., U.S.A.* **154 E4** 40 17N 100 10W
Cambridge, *Ohio, U.S.A.* **150 F3** 40 2N 81 35W
Cambridge Bay = Ikaluktutiak, *Canada* **138 B9** 69 10N 105 0W
Cambridge City, *U.S.A.* **157 E11** 39 49N 85 10W
Cambridge G., *Australia* **124 B4** 14 55 S 128 15 E
Cambridge Springs, *U.S.A.* **150 E4** 41 48N 80 4W
Cambridgeshire □, *U.K.* **21 E7** 52 25N 0 7W
Cambrils, *Spain* **40 D6** 41 8N 1 3 E
Cambuci, *Brazil* **171 F3** 21 35 S 41 55W
Cambulo, *Angola* **115 D4** 7 49 S 21 15 E
Cambundi-Catembo, *Angola* **115 E3** 10 10 S 17 35 E
Camden, *Australia* **129 C9** 34 1 S 150 43 E
Camden, *Ala., U.S.A.* **149 K2** 31 59N 87 17W
Camden, *Ark., U.S.A.* **155 J8** 33 35N 92 50W
Camden, *Maine, U.S.A.* **149 C11** 44 13N 69 4W
Camden, *N.J., U.S.A.* **151 G9** 39 56N 75 7W
Camden, *N.Y., U.S.A.* **151 C9** 43 20N 75 45W
Camden, *Ohio, U.S.A.* **157 E12** 39 38N 84 39W
Camden, *S.C., U.S.A.* **149 H5** 34 16N 80 36W
Camden Bay, *U.S.A.* **144 A11** 70 10N 145 15W
Camden Sd., *Australia* **124 C3** 15 27 S 124 25 E
Camdenton, *U.S.A.* **155 F8** 38 1N 92 45W
Cameia △, *Angola* **115 E4** 12 5 S 21 40 E
Camelford, *U.K.* **21 G3** 50 37N 4 42W
Çameli, *Turkey* **49 D11** 37 5N 29 24 E
Camenca, *Moldova* **53 B13** 48 3N 28 42 E
Camerino, *Italy* **45 E10** 43 8N 13 4 E
Cameron, *Ariz., U.S.A.* **159 J8** 35 53N 111 25W
Cameron, *La., U.S.A.* **155 L8** 29 48N 93 20W
Cameron, *Mo., U.S.A.* **156 E2** 39 44N 94 14W
Cameron, *S.C., U.S.A.* **152 B9** 33 34N 80 43W
Cameron, *Tex., U.S.A.* **155 K6** 30 51N 96 59W
Cameron Highlands, *Malaysia* **87 K3** 4 27N 101 22 E
Cameron Hills, *Canada* **142 B5** 59 48N 118 0W
Cameron Mts., *N.Z.* **131 G1** 46 1 S 167 0 E
Cameroon ■, *Africa* **114 A2** 6 0N 12 30 E
Camerota, *Italy* **47 B8** 40 2N 15 22 E
Cameroun →, *Cameroon* **113 E6** 4 0N 9 35 E
Cameroun, Mt., *Cameroon* **113 E6** 4 13N 9 10 E
Cametá, *Brazil* **170 B2** 2 12 S 49 30W
Çamiçi Gölü, *Turkey* **49 D9** 37 29N 27 28 E
Camiguin □, *Phil.* **81 G5** 9 11N 124 42 E
Camiguin I., *Phil.* **80 B3** 18 56N 121 55 E
Camiling, *Phil.* **80 D3** 15 42N 120 24 E
Camilla, *U.S.A.* **152 D5** 31 14N 84 12W
Caminha, *Portugal* **42 D2** 41 50N 8 50W
Camino, *U.S.A.* **160 G6** 38 44N 120 41W
Camira Creek, *Australia* **127 D5** 29 15 S 152 58 E
Camiranga, *Brazil* **170 B2** 1 48 S 46 17W
Camiri, *Bolivia* **173 E5** 20 3 S 63 31W
Camissombo, *Angola* **115 D4** 8 7 S 20 38 E
Cammal, *U.S.A.* **150 E7** 41 24N 77 28W
Cammarata, *Italy* **46 E6** 37 38N 13 38 E
Cammin = Kamień Pomorski, *Poland* **54 E1** 53 57N 14 43 E
Camocim, *Brazil* **170 B3** 2 55 S 40 50W
Camooweal, *Australia* **126 B2** 19 56 S 138 7 E
Camooweal Caves △, *Australia* **126 C2** 20 1 S 138 11 E
Camopi, *Fr. Guiana* **169 C7** 3 12N 52 17W
Camopi →, *Fr. Guiana* **169 C7** 3 10N 52 20W
Camorta, *India* **95 K11** 8 8N 93 30 E
Camotes Is., *Phil.* **81 F5** 10 40N 124 24 E
Camotes Sea, *Phil.* **81 F5** 10 30N 124 15 E
Camp Borden, *Canada* **150 B5** 44 18N 79 56W
Camp Coulter = Powell, *U.S.A.* **158 D9** 44 45N 108 46W
Camp Hill, *Ala., U.S.A.* **152 C4** 32 48N 85 39W
Camp Hill, *Pa., U.S.A.* **150 F8** 40 14N 76 55W
Camp Nelson, *U.S.A.* **161 J8** 36 8N 118 39W
Camp Pendleton, *U.S.A.* **161 M9** 33 16N 117 23W
Camp Point, *U.S.A.* **156 D5** 40 3N 91 4W
Camp Verde, *U.S.A.* **159 J8** 34 34N 111 51W
Camp Wood, *U.S.A.* **155 L5** 29 40N 100 1W
Campagna, *Italy* **47 B8** 40 40N 15 6 E
Campana, *Argentina* **174 C4** 34 10 S 58 55W
Campana, I., *Chile* **176 C1** 48 20 S 75 20W
Campanário, *Madeira* **9 c** 32 39N 17 2W
Campanario, *Spain* **43 G5** 38 52N 5 36W
Campânia □, *Italy* **47 B7** 41 0N 14 30 E
Campbell, *S. Africa* **116 D3** 28 48 S 23 44 E
Campbell, *Calif., U.S.A.* **160 H5** 37 17N 121 57W
Campbell, *Fla., U.S.A.* **153 G8** 28 16N 81 27W
Campbell, *Ohio, U.S.A.* **150 E4** 41 5N 80 37W
Campbell I., *Pac. Oc.* **134 N8** 52 30 S 169 0 E
Campbell L., *Canada* **143 A7** 63 14N 106 55W
Campbell River, *Canada* **142 C3** 50 5N 125 20W
Campbell Town, *Australia* **127 G4** 41 52 S 147 30 E
Campbellford, *Canada* **150 B7** 44 18N 77 48W
Campbellpur, *Pakistan* **92 C5** 33 46N 72 26 E
Campbellsburg, *U.S.A.* **157 F10** 38 39N 86 16W
Campbellsville, *U.S.A.* **148 G3** 37 21N 85 20W
Campbellton, *Canada* **141 C6** 47 57N 66 43W
Campbellton, *U.S.A.* **152 E4** 30 57N 85 24W
Campbelltown = Bluff, *N.Z.* **131 G3** 46 37 S 168 20 E
Campbelltown, *Australia* **129 C9** 34 4 S 150 49 E
Campbeltown, *U.K.* **22 F3** 55 26N 5 36W
Campeche, *Mexico* **163 D6** 19 50N 90 32W
Campeche □, *Mexico* **163 D6** 19 50N 90 32W
Campeche, Golfo de, *Mexico* **163 D6** 19 30N 93 0W
Campello, *Spain* **41 G4** 38 26N 0 24W
Câmpeni, *Romania* **52 D8** 46 22N 23 3 E
Camperdown, *Australia* **128 E5** 38 14 S 143 9 E
Camperville, *Canada* **143 C8** 51 59N 100 9W
Campi Salentina, *Italy* **47 B11** 40 24N 18 1 E
Câmpia Turzii, *Romania* **53 D8** 46 34N 23 53 E
Campidano, *Italy* **46 C1** 39 30N 8 47 E
Campíglia Maríttima, *Italy* **44 E7** 43 4N 10 37 E
Campillo de Altobuey, *Spain* **41 F3** 39 36N 1 49W
Campillos, *Spain* **43 H6** 37 4N 4 51W
Câmpina, *Romania* **53 E10** 45 10N 25 45 E
Campina Grande, *Brazil* **170 C4** 7 20 S 35 47W
Campina Verde, *Brazil* **171 E2** 19 31 S 49 28W
Campinas, *Brazil* **175 A6** 22 50 S 47 0W
Campli, *Italy* **45 F10** 42 43N 13 41 E
Campo = Ntem →, *Cameroon* **114 B2** 2 21N 9 49 E
Campo, *Cameroon* **114 B1** 2 22N 9 50 E
Campo, *Spain* **40 C5** 42 25N 0 24 E
Campo △, *Cameroon* **114 B2** 2 23N 10 5 E
Campo Belo, *Brazil* **171 F2** 20 52 S 45 16W
Campo de Criptana, *Spain* **43 F7** 39 24N 3 7W
Campo de Diauarum, *Brazil* **173 C7** 11 12 S 53 14W
Campo de Gibraltar, *Spain* **43 J5** 36 15N 5 25W
Campo Flórido, *Brazil* **171 E2** 19 47 S 48 35W
Campo Formoso = Campo Flórido, *Brazil* **171 E2** 19 47 S 48 35W
Campo Formoso, *Brazil* **170 D3** 10 30 S 40 20W
Campo Grande, *Brazil* **173 E7** 20 25 S 54 40W
Campo Maior, *Brazil* **170 B3** 4 50 S 42 12W
Campo Maior, *Portugal* **43 F3** 39 2N 7 7W
Campo Mourão, *Brazil* **175 A5** 24 3 S 52 22W
Campo Tencia, *Switz.* **33 D7** 46 26N 8 43 E
Campo Túres, *Italy* **45 B8** 46 53N 11 55 E
Campoalegre, *Colombia* **168 C2** 2 41N 75 20W
Campobasso, *Italy* **47 A7** 41 34N 14 39 E
Campobello di Licata, *Italy* **46 E6** 37 15N 13 55 E
Campobello di Mazara, *Italy* **46 E5** 37 38N 12 45 E
Campofelice di Roccella, *Italy* **46 E6** 37 59N 13 53 E
Campomarino, *Italy* **45 G12** 41 57N 15 2 E
Camporeale, *Italy* **46 E6** 37 54N 13 6 E
Camporrobles, *Spain* **40 F3** 39 39N 1 24W
Campos, *Brazil* **171 F3** 21 50 S 41 20W
Campos Altos, *Brazil* **171 E2** 19 47 S 46 10W
Campos Belos, *Brazil* **171 D2** 13 10 S 47 3W
Campos del Port, *Spain* **38 B4** 39 26N 3 1 E
Campos Novos, *Brazil* **175 B5** 27 21 S 51 50W
Campos Sales, *Brazil* **170 C3** 7 4 S 40 23W
Camprodón, *Spain* **40 C7** 42 19N 2 23 E
Campton, *Fla., U.S.A.* **153 E3** 30 53N 86 31W
Campton, *Ga., U.S.A.* **152 B6** 33 52N 83 43W
Campton, *Ky., U.S.A.* **157 G13** 37 44N 83 33W
Camptonville, *U.S.A.* **160 F5** 39 27N 121 3W
Camptown, *U.S.A.* **151 E8** 41 44N 76 14W
Câmpulung, *Argeş, Romania* **53 E10** 45 17N 25 3 E
Câmpulung, *Suceava, Romania* **53 C10** 47 32N 25 30 E
Câmpuri, *Romania* **53 D11** 46 0N 26 50 E
Campuya →, *Peru* **168 D3** 1 40 S 73 30W
Campville, *U.S.A.* **152 F7** 29 40N 82 7W
Camrose, *Canada* **142 C6** 53 0N 112 50W
Camsell Portage, *Canada* **143 B7** 59 37N 109 15W
Camucuio, *Angola* **115 E2** 14 7 S 13 15 E
Çamyuva, *Turkey* **49 E12** 36 30N 30 30 E
Çan, *Turkey* **51 F11** 40 2N 27 3 E
Can Clavo, *Spain* **38 D1** 38 57N 1 27 E
Can Creu, *Spain* **38 D1** 38 58N 1 28 E
Can Gio, *Vietnam* **87 G6** 10 25N 106 58 E
Can Tho, *Vietnam* **87 G5** 10 2N 105 46 E
Canaan, *U.S.A.* **151 D11** 42 2N 73 20W
Canacona, *India* **95 G2** 15 1N 74 4 E
Canada ■, *N. Amer.* **138 C10** 60 0N 100 0W
Canada Basin, *Arctic* **6 B18** 80 0N 145 0W
Cañada de Gómez, *Argentina* **174 C3** 32 40 S 61 30W
Canadian, *U.S.A.* **155 H4** 35 55N 100 23W
Canadian →, *U.S.A.* **155 H7** 35 28N 95 3W
Canadys, *U.S.A.* **152 B9** 33 3N 80 37W
Canajoharie, *U.S.A.* **151 D10** 42 54N 74 35W
Çanakkale, *Turkey* **51 F10** 40 8N 26 24 E
Çanakkale □, *Turkey* **51 F10** 40 10N 26 25 E
Çanakkale Boğazı, *Turkey* **51 F10** 40 17N 26 32 E
Canal Flats, *Canada* **142 C5** 50 10N 115 48W
Canal Point, *U.S.A.* **153 J9** 26 52N 80 38W
Canala, *N. Cal.* **133 U19** 21 32 S 165 57 E
Canalejas, *Argentina* **174 D2** 35 15 S 66 34W
Canals, *Argentina* **174 C3** 33 35 S 62 53W
Canals, *Spain* **41 G4** 38 58N 0 35W
Canandaigua, *U.S.A.* **150 D7** 42 54N 77 17W
Canandaigua L., *U.S.A.* **150 D7** 42 47N 77 19W
Cananea, *Mexico* **162 A2** 31 0N 110 20W
Cañar, *Ecuador* **168 D2** 2 33 S 78 56W
Cañar □, *Ecuador* **168 D2** 2 30 S 79 0W
Canarias, Is., *Atl. Oc.* **9 e1** 28 30N 16 0W
Canaries, *St. Lucia* **165 f** 13 55N 61 4W
Canarreos, Arch. de los, *Cuba* **164 B3** 21 35N 81 40W
Canary Is. = Canarias, Is., *Atl. Oc.* **9 e1** 28 30N 16 0W
Canaseraga, *U.S.A.* **150 D7** 42 27N 77 45W
Canastra, Serra da, *Brazil* **171 F2** 20 0 S 46 20W
Canatlán, *Mexico* **162 C4** 24 31N 104 47W
Cañaveral, *Peru* **168 D1** 3 56 S 80 39W
Canaveral △, *U.S.A.* **153 G9** 28 28N 80 34W
Canaveral, C., *U.S.A.* **153 G9** 28 27N 80 32W
Cañaveruelas, *Spain* **40 E2** 40 24N 2 38W
Canavieiras, *Brazil* **171 E4** 15 39 S 39 0W
Canbelego, *Australia* **129 A7** 31 32 S 146 18 E
Canberra, *Australia* **129 C8** 35 15 S 149 8 E
Canby, *Calif., U.S.A.* **158 F3** 41 27N 120 52W
Canby, *Minn., U.S.A.* **154 C6** 44 43N 96 16W
Canby, *Oreg., U.S.A.* **160 E4** 45 16N 122 42W
Cancale, *France* **26 D5** 48 40N 1 50W
Canche →, *France* **27 B8** 50 31N 1 39 E
Canchungo = Teixeira Pinto, *Guinea-Biss.* **112 C1** 12 3N 16 0W
Canchyuaya, Cordillera de, *Peru* **172 B3** 7 30 S 74 0W
Cancún, *Mexico* **163 C7** 21 8N 86 44W
Candala, *Somali Rep.* **120 B3** 11 30N 49 58 E
Candanchu, *Spain* **40 C4** 42 47N 0 32W
Candarave, *Peru* **172 D3** 17 15 S 70 13W
Çandarlı, *Turkey* **49 C8** 38 56N 26 56 E
Çandarlı Körfezi, *Turkey* **49 C8** 38 52N 26 55 E
Candas, *Spain* **42 B5** 43 35N 5 45W
Candé, *France* **26 E5** 47 34N 1 2W
Candeias →, *Brazil* **173 B5** 8 39 S 63 31W
Candela, *Italy* **47 A8** 41 8N 15 31 E
Candelaria, *Argentina* **175 B4** 27 29 S 55 44W
Candelaria, *Canary Is.* **9 e1** 28 22N 16 22W
Candelaria, *Phil.* **80 E3** 13 56N 121 25 E
Candelario △, *Spain* **42 E5** 40 20N 5 46W
Candeleda, *Spain* **42 E5** 40 10N 5 14W
Candelo, *Australia* **129 D8** 36 47 S 149 43 E
Candi Dasa, *Indonesia* **79 J18** 8 30 S 115 34 E
Candia = Iráklion, *Greece* **39 E6** 35 20N 25 12 E
Candia, Sea of = Crete, Sea of, *Greece* **49 E7** 36 0N 25 0 E
Cândido de Abreu, *Brazil* **171 F1** 24 35 S 51 20W
Cândido Mendes, *Brazil* **170 B2** 1 27 S 45 43W
Candle, *U.S.A.* **144 D7** 65 55N 161 56W
Candle L., *Canada* **143 C7** 53 50N 105 18W
Candlemas I., *Antarctica* **7 B1** 57 3 S 26 40W
Cando, *U.S.A.* **154 A5** 48 32N 99 12W
Candon, *Phil.* **80 C3** 17 12N 120 27 E
Canea = Khaniá, *Greece* **39 E5** 35 30N 24 4 E
Canela, *Brazil* **170 D2** 10 15 S 48 25W
Canelli, *Italy* **44 D5** 44 43N 8 17 E
Canelones, *Uruguay* **175 C4** 34 32 S 56 17W
Canet-Plage, *France* **28 F7** 42 41N 3 2 E
Cañete, *Chile* **174 D1** 37 50 S 73 30W
Cañete, *Peru* **172 C2** 13 8 S 76 30W
Cañete, *Spain* **40 E3** 40 3N 1 54W
Cañete de las Torres, *Spain* **43 H6** 37 53N 4 19W
Cangamba, *Angola* **115 E3** 13 40 S 19 54 E
Cangandala, *Angola* **115 D3** 9 45 S 16 33 E
Cangandala △, *Angola* **115 D3** 9 53 S 16 42 E
Cangas, *Spain* **42 C2** 42 16N 8 47W
Cangas de Narcea, *Spain* **42 B4** 43 10N 6 32W
Cangas de Onís, *Spain* **42 B5** 43 21N 5 8W
Cangas de Tineo = Cangas de Narcea, *Spain* **42 B4** 43 10N 6 32W
Cangnan, *China* **77 D13** 27 30N 120 23 E
Cangoa, *Angola* **115 E3** 13 8 S 18 30 E
Cangola, *Angola* **115 D3** 7 58 S 15 53 E
Cangolo, *Angola* **115 E2** 15 0 S 13 52 E
Cangombe, *Angola* **115 E3** 14 24 S 19 59 E
Cangongo, *Angola* **115 D3** 9 24 S 17 30 E
Canguaretama, *Brazil* **170 C4** 6 20 S 35 5W
Canguçu, *Brazil* **175 C5** 31 22 S 52 43W
Canguçu, Serra do, *Brazil* **175 C5** 31 20 S 52 40W
Cangumbe, *Angola* **115 E3** 11 58 S 19 12 E
Cangwu, *China* **77 F8** 23 25N 111 17 E
Cangxi, *China* **76 B5** 31 47N 105 59 E
Cangyuan, *China* **76 F2** 23 12N 99 14 E
Cangzhou, *China* **74 E9** 38 19N 116 52 E
Canhoca, *Angola* **115 D2** 9 15 S 14 41 E
Cani, I., *Tunisia* **108 A2** 36 21N 10 5 E
Caniapiscau →, *Canada* **141 A6** 56 40N 69 30W
Caniapiscau, L. de, *Canada* **141 B6** 54 10N 69 55W
Canicattì, *Italy* **46 E6** 37 21N 13 51 E
Canicattini Bagni, *Italy* **47 E8** 37 2N 15 4 E
Canigao Channel, *Phil.* **81 F5** 10 15N 124 42 E
Caniles, *Spain* **43 H8** 37 26N 2 43W
Canim Lake, *Canada* **142 C4** 51 47N 120 54W
Canindé, *Brazil* **170 B4** 4 22 S 39 19W
Canindé →, *Brazil* **170 C3** 6 15 S 42 52W
Canindeyu □, *Paraguay* **175 A5** 24 10 S 55 0W
Canino, *Italy* **45 F8** 42 28N 11 45 E
Canisteo, *U.S.A.* **150 D7** 42 16N 77 36W
Canisteo →, *U.S.A.* **150 D7** 42 7N 77 8W
Cañitas, *Mexico* **162 C4** 23 36N 102 43W
Cañizal, *Spain* **42 D5** 41 12N 5 22W
Canjáyar, *Spain* **43 H8** 37 1N 2 44W
Canjinge, *Angola* **115 E4** 10 12 S 21 17 E
Çankırı, *Turkey* **100 B5** 40 40N 33 37 E
Cankuzo, *Burundi* **118 C3** 3 10 S 30 31 E
Canlaon, *Phil.* **81 F4** 10 22N 123 12 E
Canlaon Volcano, *Phil.* **81 F4** 10 25N 123 8 E
Canmore, *Canada* **142 C5** 51 7N 115 18W
Cann River, *Australia* **129 D8** 37 35 S 149 7 E
Canna, *U.K.* **22 D2** 57 3N 6 33W
Cannanore, *India* **95 J2** 11 53N 75 27 E
Cannanore Is., *India* **95 J1** 10 30N 72 30 E
Cannelton, *U.S.A.* **157 G10** 37 55N 86 45W
Cannes, *France* **29 E11** 43 32N 7 1 E
Canning Town = Port Canning, *India* **93 H13** 22 23N 88 40 E
Cannington, *Canada* **150 B5** 44 20N 79 2W
Cannóbio, *Italy* **44 B5** 46 4N 8 42 E
Cannock, *U.K.* **21 E5** 52 41N 2 1W
Cannonball →, *U.S.A.* **154 B4** 46 20N 100 38W
Cannondale Mt., *Australia* **126 D4** 25 13 S 148 57 E
Cannonsville Reservoir, *U.S.A.* **151 D9** 42 4N 75 22W
Cannonvale, *Australia* **126 J6** 20 17 S 148 43 E
Caño Colorado, *Colombia* **168 C4** 2 18N 68 22W
Canoas, *Brazil* **175 B5** 29 56 S 51 11W
Canoe L., *Canada* **143 B7** 55 10N 108 15W
Cañon City, *U.S.A.* **154 F2** 38 27N 105 14W
Cañon de Rio Blanco △, *Mexico* **163 D5** 18 43N 97 15W
Cañon del Río Lobos △, *Spain* **42 D7** 41 46N 3 28W
Cañon del Sumidero △, *Mexico* **163 D5** 19 22N 96 24W
Canonniers Pt., *Mauritius* **121 d** 20 2 S 57 32 E
Canoochee →, *U.S.A.* **152 D8** 31 59N 81 19W
Canopus, *Australia* **128 B4** 33 29 S 140 42 E
Canora, *Canada* **143 C8** 51 40N 102 30W
Canosa di Púglia, *Italy* **47 A9** 41 13N 16 4 E
Canowindra, *Australia* **129 B8** 33 35 S 148 38 E
Canso, *Canada* **141 C7** 45 20N 61 0W
Canta, *Peru* **172 C2** 11 29 S 76 37W
Cantabria □, *Spain* **42 B7** 43 10N 4 0W
Cantabria, Sierra de, *Spain* **40 C2** 42 40N 2 30W
Cantabrian Mts. = Cantábrica, Cordillera, *Spain* **42 C5** 43 0N 5 10W
Cantábrica, Cordillera, *Spain* **42 C5** 43 0N 5 10W
Cantal □, *France* **28 C6** 45 5N 2 45 E
Cantal, Plomb du, *France* **28 C6** 45 3N 2 45 E
Cantanhede, *Portugal* **42 E2** 40 20N 8 36W
Cantaura, *Venezuela* **169 B5** 9 19N 64 21W
Cantavieja, *Spain* **40 E4** 40 31N 0 25W
Čantavir, *Serbia & M.* **52 E4** 45 55N 19 46 E
Cantemir, *Moldova* **53 D13** 46 17N 28 14 E
Canterbury = Invermere, *Canada* **142 C5** 50 30N 116 2W
Canterbury, *Australia* **126 D3** 25 23 S 141 53 E
Canterbury, *U.K.* **21 F9** 51 16N 1 6 E
Canterbury □, *N.Z.* **131 D6** 43 45 S 171 19 E
Canterbury Bight, *N.Z.* **131 E6** 44 16 S 171 55 E
Canterbury Plains, *N.Z.* **131 D6** 43 55 S 171 22 E
Cantil, *U.S.A.* **161 K9** 35 18N 117 58W

Cantilan, Phil. 81 G5 9 20N 125 58 E
Cantillana, Spain 43 H5 37 36N 5 50W
Canto do Buriti, Brazil 170 C3 8 7 S 42 58W
Canton = Guangzhou, China 77 F9 23 5N 113 10 E
Canton, Ga., U.S.A. 149 H3 34 14N 84 29W
Canton, Ill., U.S.A. 156 D6 40 33N 90 2W
Canton, Miss., U.S.A. 155 J9 32 37N 90 2W
Canton, Mo., U.S.A. 156 D5 40 8N 91 32W
Canton, N.Y., U.S.A. 151 B9 44 36N 75 10W
Canton, Ohio, U.S.A. 150 F3 40 48N 81 23W
Canton, Pa., U.S.A. 150 E8 41 39N 76 51W
Canton, S. Dak., U.S.A. 154 D6 43 18N 96 35W
Canton L., U.S.A. 155 G5 36 6N 98 35W
Cantonment, U.S.A. 153 E2 30 37N 87 20W
Cantù, Italy 44 C6 45 44N 9 8 E
Cantwell, U.S.A. 144 E10 63 24N 148 57W
Canudos, Brazil 173 B6 7 13 S 58 5W
Canumã, Amazonas, Brazil 169 D6 4 2 S 59 4W
Canumã, Amazonas, Brazil 173 B5 6 8 S 60 10W
Canumã →, Brazil 173 A6 3 55 S 59 10W
Canunda △, Australia 128 D4 37 42 S 140 16 E
Canutama, Brazil 173 B5 6 30 S 64 20W
Canutillo, U.S.A. 159 L10 31 55N 106 36W
Canvey, U.K. 21 F8 51 31N 0 37 E
Canyon, U.S.A. 155 H4 34 59N 101 55W
Canyon De Chelly ⌓, U.S.A. 159 H9 36 10N 109 20W
Canyon of the Ancients ⌓, U.S.A. 159 H9 37 30N 108 50W
Canyonlands △, U.S.A. 159 G9 38 15N 110 0W
Canyonville, U.S.A. 158 E2 42 56N 123 17W
Canzar, Angola 115 D4 7 35 S 21 34 E
Cao Bang, Vietnam 76 F6 22 40N 106 15 E
Cao He →, China 75 D13 40 10N 124 32 E
Cao Lanh, Vietnam 87 G5 10 27N 105 38 E
Cao Xian, China 74 G8 34 50N 115 35 E
Caombo, Angola 115 D3 8 42 S 16 33 E
Cáorle, Italy 45 C9 45 36N 12 53 E
Cap-aux-Meules, Canada 141 C7 47 23N 61 52W
Cap-Chat, Canada 141 C6 49 6N 66 40W
Cap-de-la-Madeleine, Canada 140 C5 46 22N 72 31W
Cap-Haïtien, Haiti 165 C5 19 40N 72 20W
Cap I., Phil. 81 J3 5 57N 120 6 E
Cap Pt., St. Lucia 165 f 14 7N 60 57W
Capac, U.S.A. 150 C2 43 1N 82 56W
Capáccio, Italy 47 B8 40 25N 15 5 E
Capaci, Italy 46 D6 38 10N 13 14 E
Capaia, Angola 115 D4 8 27 S 20 13 E
Capalonga, Phil. 80 D4 14 20N 122 30 E
Capanaparo →, Venezuela 168 B4 7 1N 67 7W
Capanema, Brazil 170 B2 1 12 S 47 11W
Capangombe, Angola 115 F2 15 6 S 13 8 E
Capánnori, Italy 44 E7 43 50N 10 34 E
Caparaó △, Brazil 171 F3 20 25 S 41 46W
Caparo →, Barinas, Venezuela 168 B3 7 46N 70 23W
Caparo →, Bolívar, Venezuela 169 B5 7 30N 64 0W
Capatárida, Venezuela 168 A3 11 11N 70 37W
Capayas, Phil. 81 F2 10 28N 119 39 E
Capbreton, France 28 E2 43 39N 1 26W
Capdenac, France 28 D6 44 34N 2 5 E
Capdepera, Spain 38 B4 39 42N 3 26 E
Cape →, Australia 126 C4 20 59 S 146 51 E
Cape Arid △, Australia 125 F3 33 58 S 123 13 E
Cape Barren I., Australia 127 G4 40 25 S 148 15 E
Cape Basin, Atl. Oc. 8 K12 34 0 S 7 0W
Cape Breton Highlands △, Canada 141 C7 46 50N 60 40W
Cape Breton I., Canada 141 C7 46 0N 60 30W
Cape Canaveral, U.S.A. 153 G9 28 24N 80 36W
Cape Charles, U.S.A. 148 G8 37 16N 76 1W
Cape Coast, Ghana 113 D4 5 5N 1 15W
Cape Cod ⌓, U.S.A. 148 E10 41 56N 70 6W
Cape Coral, U.S.A. 153 J8 26 33N 81 57W
Cape Dorset, Canada 139 B12 64 14N 76 32W
Cape Fear →, U.S.A. 149 H6 33 53N 78 1W
Cape Girardeau, U.S.A. 155 G10 37 19N 89 32W
Cape Hatteras ⌓, U.S.A. 149 H8 35 30N 75 28W
Cape Jervis, Australia 128 C3 35 40 S 138 5 E
Cape Krusenstern ⌓, U.S.A. 144 C7 67 30N 163 30W
Cape Lee △, Australia 125 F3 33 54 S 122 26 E
Cape Lisburne = Wevok, U.S.A. 144 B6 68 53N 166 13W
Cape Lookout ⌓, U.S.A. 149 H7 35 45N 76 25W
Cape May, U.S.A. 148 F8 38 56N 74 56W
Cape May Point, U.S.A. 147 C12 38 56N 74 58W
Cape Melville △, Australia 126 A3 14 26 S 144 28 E
Cape Mount △, Liberia 112 D2 6 44N 11 24W
Cape Peninsula △, S. Africa 116 E2 34 20 S 18 28 E
Cape Pole, U.S.A. 144 J14 55 58N 133 48W
Cape Range △, Australia 124 D1 22 3 S 114 0 E
Cape Tormentine, Canada 141 C7 46 8N 63 47W
Cape Town, S. Africa 116 E2 33 55 S 18 22 E
Cape Tribulation △, Australia 126 B4 16 5 S 145 25 E
Cape Verde Is. ■, Atl. Oc. 8 E9 16 0N 24 0W
Cape Vincent, U.S.A. 151 B8 44 8N 76 20W
Cape Yakataga, U.S.A. 144 F12 60 4N 142 26W
Cape York Peninsula, Australia 126 A3 12 0 S 142 30 E
Capela, Brazil 170 D4 10 30 S 37 0W
Capela de Campo, Brazil 170 B3 4 40 S 41 55W
Capelas, Azores 9 d3 37 50N 25 41W
Capele, Angola 115 E2 13 39 S 14 53 E
Capelengue, Angola 115 D3 8 53 S 19 42 E
Capelinha, Brazil 171 E3 17 42 S 42 31W
Capelinhos, Pta. dos, Azores 9 d1 38 36N 28 50W
Capella, Australia 126 C4 23 2 S 148 1 E
Capella, Mt., Papua N. G. 132 C1 5 4 S 141 8 E
Capelongo, Angola 115 E3 14 54 S 15 8 E
Capenda Camulemba, Angola 115 D3 9 24 S 18 27 E
Capendu, France 28 E6 43 11N 2 31 E
Capertree, Australia 129 B8 33 6 S 149 58 E
Capestang, France 28 E7 43 20N 3 2 E
Capesterre-Belle-Eau, Guadeloupe 164 b 16 4N 61 36W
Capesterre-de-Marie-Galante, Guadeloupe 164 b 15 53N 61 14W
Capim, Brazil 170 B2 1 41 S 47 47W
Capim →, Brazil 170 B2 1 40 S 47 47W
Capinópolis, Brazil 171 E2 18 41 S 49 35W
Capinota, Bolivia 172 D4 17 43 S 66 14W
Capira, Panama 168 B2 8 45N 79 53W
Capistrello, Italy 45 G10 41 57N 13 23 E
Capitan, U.S.A. 159 K11 33 35N 105 35W
Capitán Aracena, I., Chile 176 D2 54 10 S 71 20W
Capitán Arturo Prat, Antarctica 7 C17 63 0 S 61 0W
Capitán Pastene, Chile 176 A2 38 13 S 73 1W
Capitol Reef △, U.S.A. 159 G8 38 15N 111 10W
Capitola, U.S.A. 160 J5 36 59N 121 57W
Capivara, Serra da, Brazil 171 D3 14 35 S 45 0W
Capiz □, Phil. 81 F4 11 35N 122 30 E
Capizzi, Italy 47 E7 37 51N 14 29 E
Capoche →, Mozam. 119 F3 15 35 S 33 0 E
Capodichino, Nápoli ✈ (NAP), Italy 47 B7 40 53N 14 16 E
Capoeira, Brazil 173 B6 5 37 S 59 33W
Capolo, Angola 115 E2 10 22 S 14 7 E
Caporetto = Kobarid, Slovenia 45 B10 46 15N 13 30 E
Caporolo →, Angola 115 E2 12 56 S 12 58 E
Capoterra, Italy 46 C1 39 11N 8 58 E
Cappadocia, Turkey 100 C6 39 0N 35 0 E
Capps, U.S.A. 152 E6 30 24N 83 54W
Capraia, Italy 44 E6 43 2N 9 50 E
Caprara, Pta., Italy 46 A1 41 7N 8 19 E
Caprarola, Italy 45 F9 42 19N 12 14 E
Capreol, Canada 140 C3 46 43N 80 56W
Caprera, Italy 46 A2 41 12N 9 28 E
Capri, Italy 47 B7 40 33N 14 14 E
Capricorn Group, Australia 126 C5 23 30 S 151 55 E
Capricorn Ra., Australia 124 D2 23 20 S 116 50 E
Caprino Veronese, Italy 44 C7 45 36N 10 47 E
Caprivi Game ⌓, Namibia 116 B3 17 55 S 22 37 E
Caprivi Strip, Namibia 116 B3 18 0 S 23 0 E
Caps et Marais d'Opale ⌓, France 27 B9 50 40N 2 0 E
Captain Cook, U.S.A. 145 D6 19 30N 155 55W
Captain's Flat, Australia 129 C8 35 35 S 149 27 E
Captieux, France 28 D3 44 18N 0 16W
Captiva, U.S.A. 153 J7 26 31N 82 11W
Capuça, Angola 115 F4 17 22 S 21 18 E
Capul I., Phil. 80 E5 12 26N 124 10 E
Capulin Volcano ⌓, U.S.A. 155 G3 36 47N 103 58W
Capunda, Angola 115 E3 10 41 S 17 23 E
Caquetá □, Colombia 168 C3 1 0N 74 0W
Caquetá →, Colombia 168 D4 1 15 S 69 15W
Car Nicobar, India 95 K11 9 10N 92 47 E
Carabao I., Phil. 80 E3 12 4N 121 56 E
Carabobo □, Venezuela 168 A4 10 10N 68 5W
Caracal, Romania 53 F9 44 8N 24 22 E
Caracaraí, Brazil 169 C5 1 50N 61 8W
Caracas, Venezuela 168 A4 10 30N 66 55W
Caracol, Mato Grosso do Sul, Brazil 174 A4 22 18 S 57 1W
Caracol, Piauí, Brazil 170 C3 9 15 S 43 22W
Caracollo, Bolivia 172 D4 17 39 S 67 10W
Caraga, Phil. 81 H6 7 20N 126 34 E
Caragabal, Australia 129 B7 33 49 S 147 45 E
Caráglio, Italy 44 D4 44 25N 7 26 E
Carahue, Chile 176 A2 38 43 S 73 12W
Caraí, Brazil 171 E3 17 12 S 41 42W
Carajás, Brazil 170 C1 2 57 S 51 22W
Carajás, Serra dos, Brazil 170 C1 6 0 S 51 30W
Caramoan, Phil. 80 E4 13 46N 123 52 E
Caramoran, Phil. 80 D5 14 0N 124 8 E
Caranapatuba, Brazil 173 B5 6 38 S 62 34W
Carandaiti, Bolivia 173 E5 20 45 S 63 4W
Carangola, Brazil 171 F3 20 44 S 42 5W
Caransebeş, Romania 52 E7 45 28N 22 18 E
Carantec, France 26 D3 48 40N 3 55W
Caraparanã →, Colombia 168 D3 1 45 S 73 13W
Caraquet, Canada 141 C6 47 48N 64 57W
Caras, Peru 172 B2 9 3 S 77 47W
Caraş Severin □, Romania 52 E7 45 10N 22 10 E
Caraşova, Romania 52 E6 45 11N 21 51 E
Caratasca, L., Honduras 164 C3 15 20N 83 40W
Caratinga, Brazil 171 E3 19 50 S 42 10W
Caraúari, Brazil 168 D4 4 52 S 66 54W
Caraúbas, Brazil 170 C4 5 43 S 37 33W
Caravaca de la Cruz, Spain 41 G3 38 8N 1 52W
Caravággio, Italy 44 C6 45 30N 9 38 E
Caravela, Guinea-Biss. 112 C1 11 30N 16 30W
Caravelas, Brazil 171 E4 17 45 S 39 15W
Caraveli, Peru 172 D3 15 45 S 73 25W
Caravelle, Presqu'île de la, Martinique 164 c 14 46N 60 48W
Caràzinho, Brazil 175 B5 28 16 S 52 46W
Carballino = O Carballiño, Spain 42 C2 42 26N 8 5W
Carballo, Spain 42 B2 43 13N 8 41W
Carberry, Canada 143 D9 49 50N 99 25W
Carbó, Mexico 162 B2 29 42N 110 58W
Carbonara, C., Italy 46 C2 39 6N 9 31 E
Carbondale, Colo., U.S.A. 158 G10 39 24N 107 13W
Carbondale, Ill., U.S.A. 155 G10 37 44N 89 13W
Carbondale, Pa., U.S.A. 151 E9 41 35N 75 30W
Carbonear, Canada 141 C9 47 42N 53 13W
Carboneras, Spain 41 J3 36 59N 1 53W
Carboneras de Guadazaón, Spain 40 F3 39 54N 1 50W
Carbónia, Italy 46 C1 39 10N 8 30 E
Carcabuey, Spain 43 H6 37 27N 4 17W
Carcagente = Carcaixent, Spain 41 F4 39 8N 0 28W
Carcaixent, Spain 41 F4 39 8N 0 28W
Carcajou, Canada 142 B5 57 47N 117 6W
Carcar, Phil. 81 F4 10 6N 123 38 E
Carcarana →, Argentina 174 C3 32 27 S 60 48W
Carcasse, C., Haiti 165 C5 18 30N 74 28W
Carcassonne, France 28 E6 43 13N 2 20 E
Carchi □, Ecuador 168 C2 0 45N 78 0W
Carcoar, Australia 129 B8 33 36 S 149 8 E
Carcross, Canada 142 A2 60 13N 134 45W
Çardak, Çanakkale, Turkey 51 F10 40 22N 26 43 E
Çardak, Denizli, Turkey 49 D11 37 49N 29 39 E
Cardamon Hills, India 95 K3 9 30N 77 15 E
Cardeña, Spain 43 G6 38 16N 4 20W
Cárdenas, Cuba 164 B3 23 0N 81 30W
Cárdenas, San Luis Potosí, Mexico 163 C5 22 0N 99 41W
Cárdenas, Tabasco, Mexico 163 D6 17 59N 93 21W
Cardenete, Spain 40 F3 39 46N 1 41W
Cardiel, L., Argentina 176 C2 48 55 S 71 10W
Cardiff, U.K. 21 F4 51 29N 3 10W
Cardiff □, U.K. 21 F4 51 31N 3 12W
Cardiff-by-the-Sea, U.S.A. 161 M9 33 1N 117 17W
Cardigan, U.K. 21 E3 52 5N 4 40W
Cardigan B., U.K. 21 E3 52 30N 4 30W
Cardinal, Canada 151 B9 44 47N 75 23W
Cardón, Punta, Venezuela 168 A3 11 37N 70 14W
Cardona, Spain 40 D6 41 56N 1 40 E
Cardona, Uruguay 174 C4 33 53 S 57 18W
Cardoner →, Spain 40 D6 41 41N 1 51 E
Cardoso, Ilha do, Brazil 175 B5 25 8 S 47 58W
Cardston, Canada 142 D6 49 15N 113 20W
Cardwell, Australia 126 B4 18 14 S 146 2 E
Careen L., Canada 143 B7 57 0N 108 11W
Carei, Romania 52 C7 47 40N 22 29 E
Careiro, Brazil 169 D6 3 12 S 59 45W
Careme = Ciremay, Indonesia 85 D3 6 55 S 108 27 E
Carentan, France 26 C5 49 19N 1 15W
Carey, Idaho, U.S.A. 158 E7 43 19N 113 57W
Carey, Ohio, U.S.A. 157 D13 40 57N 83 23W
Carey, L., Australia 125 E3 29 0 S 122 15 E
Carey L., Canada 143 A8 62 12N 102 55W
Careysburg, Liberia 112 D2 6 34N 10 30W
Cargados Garajos, Ind. Oc. 121 F4 17 0 S 59 0 E
Cargèse, France 29 F12 42 7N 8 35 E
Carhaix-Plouguer, France 26 D3 48 18N 3 36W
Carhuamayo, Peru 172 C2 10 51 S 76 4W
Carhuas, Peru 172 B2 9 15 S 77 39W
Carhué, Argentina 174 D3 37 10 S 62 50W
Caria, Turkey 49 D10 37 20N 28 10 E
Cariacica, Brazil 171 F3 20 16 S 40 25W
Cariaco, Venezuela 169 A5 10 29N 63 33W
Cariango, Angola 115 E3 10 37 S 15 20 E
Cariati, Italy 47 C9 39 30N 16 57 E
Caribbean Sea, W. Indies 165 D5 15 0N 75 0W
Cariboo Mts., Canada 142 C4 53 0N 121 0W
Caribou, U.S.A. 149 B12 46 52N 68 1W
Caribou →, Man., Canada 143 B10 59 20N 94 44W
Caribou →, N.W.T., Canada 142 A3 61 27N 125 45W
Caribou I., Canada 140 C2 47 22N 85 49W
Caribou Is., Canada 142 A6 61 55N 113 15W
Caribou L., Man., Canada 143 B9 59 21N 96 10W
Caribou L., Ont., Canada 140 B2 50 25N 89 5W
Caribou Mts., Canada 142 B5 59 12N 115 40W
Caribou River ⌓, Canada 143 B9 59 35N 96 35W
Caribrod = Dimitrovgrad, Serbia & M. 50 C6 43 2N 22 48 E
Carichic, Mexico 162 B3 27 56N 107 3W
Carigara, Phil. 81 F5 11 18N 124 41 E
Carignan, France 27 C12 49 38N 5 10 E
Carignano, Italy 44 D4 44 55N 7 40 E
Carillo, Mexico 162 B4 26 50N 103 55W
Carin, Somali Rep. 120 B3 10 59N 49 13 E
Carinda, Australia 129 A7 30 28 S 147 41 E
Cariñena, Spain 40 D3 41 20N 1 13W
Carinhanha, Brazil 171 D3 14 15 S 44 46W
Carinhanha →, Brazil 171 D3 14 20 S 43 47W
Carini, Italy 46 D6 38 8N 13 11 E
Cariño, Spain 42 B3 43 45N 7 52W
Carínola, Italy 46 A6 41 11N 13 58 E
Carinthia = Kärnten □, Austria 34 E6 46 52N 13 30 E
Caripito, Venezuela 169 A5 10 8N 63 6W
Cariré, Brazil 170 B3 3 57 S 40 27W
Caritianas, Brazil 173 B5 9 20 S 63 6W
Carles, Phil. 81 F4 11 34N 123 8 E
Carlet, Spain 41 F4 39 14N 0 31W
Carleton, Mt., Canada 141 C6 47 23N 66 53W
Carleton Place, Canada 140 C4 45 8N 76 9W
Carletonville, S. Africa 116 D4 26 23 S 27 22 E
Cârlibaba, Romania 53 C10 47 35N 25 8 E
Carlin, U.S.A. 158 F5 40 43N 116 7W
Carlingford L., U.K. 23 B5 54 3N 6 9W
Carlinville, U.S.A. 156 E7 39 17N 89 53W
Carlisle, U.K. 20 C5 54 54N 2 56W
Carlisle, Ind., U.S.A. 157 F9 38 58N 87 24W
Carlisle, Ky., U.S.A. 157 F12 38 19N 84 1W
Carlisle, Pa., U.S.A. 150 F7 40 12N 77 12W
Carlisle B., Barbados 165 g 13 5N 59 37W
Carlisle I., Australia 126 J7 20 49 S 149 18 E
Carlit, Pic, France 28 F5 42 35N 1 55 E
Carloforte, Italy 46 C1 39 8N 8 18 E
Carlos Casares, Argentina 174 D3 35 32 S 61 20W
Carlos Chagas, Brazil 171 E3 17 43 S 40 45W
Carlos Tejedor, Argentina 174 D3 35 25 S 62 25W
Carlow, Ireland 23 D5 52 50N 6 56W
Carlow □, Ireland 23 D5 52 43N 6 50W
Carlsbad = Karlovy Vary, Czech Rep. 34 A5 50 13N 12 51 E
Carlsbad, Calif., U.S.A. 161 M9 33 10N 117 21W
Carlsbad, N. Mex., U.S.A. 155 J2 32 25N 104 14W
Carlsbad Caverns △, U.S.A. 155 J2 32 10N 104 35W
Carlsberg Ridge, Ind. Oc. 121 D5 1 0N 66 0 E
Carluke, U.K. 22 F5 55 45N 3 50W
Carlyle, Canada 143 D8 49 40N 102 20W
Carlyle, U.S.A. 156 F7 38 37N 89 22W
Carlyle L., U.S.A. 156 F7 38 37N 89 21W
Carmacks, Canada 138 B6 62 5N 136 16W
Carmagnola, Italy 44 D4 44 51N 7 43 E
Carman, Canada 143 D9 49 30N 98 0W
Carmarthen, U.K. 21 F3 51 52N 4 19W
Carmarthen B., U.K. 21 F3 51 40N 4 30W
Carmarthenshire □, U.K. 21 F3 51 55N 4 13W
Carmaux, France 28 D6 44 3N 2 10 E
Carmel, Ind., U.S.A. 157 E10 39 59N 86 8W
Carmel, N.Y., U.S.A. 151 E11 41 26N 73 41W
Carmel-by-the-Sea, U.S.A. 160 J5 36 33N 121 55W
Carmel Valley, U.S.A. 160 J5 36 29N 121 43W
Carmelo, Uruguay 174 C4 34 0 S 58 20W
Carmen, Bolivia 172 C4 11 40 S 67 51W
Carmen, Colombia 168 B2 9 43N 75 8W
Carmen, Paraguay 175 B4 27 13 S 56 12W
Carmen, Bohol, Phil. 81 G5 9 50N 124 12 E
Carmen, Cebu, Phil. 81 F5 10 35N 124 1 E
Carmen, Cotabato, Phil. 81 H5 7 13N 124 45 E
Carmen, Venezuela 168 C4 1 16N 66 52W
Carmen →, Mexico 162 A3 30 42N 106 29W
Carmen, I., Mexico 162 B2 26 0N 111 20W
Carmen de Patagones, Argentina 176 B4 40 50 S 63 0W
Cármenes, Spain 42 C5 42 58N 5 34W
Carmensa, Argentina 174 D2 35 15 S 67 40W
Carmi, Canada 142 D5 49 36N 119 8W
Carmi, U.S.A. 157 F8 38 5N 88 10W
Carmichael, U.S.A. 160 G5 38 38N 121 19W
Carmichael Village, Bahamas 9 b 25 0N 77 26W
Carmila, Australia 126 C4 21 55 S 149 24 E
Carmona, Costa Rica 164 E2 10 0N 85 15W
Carmona, Spain 43 H5 37 28N 5 42W
Carn Ban, U.K. 22 D4 57 7N 4 15W
Carn Eige, U.K. 22 D3 57 17N 5 8W
Carnac, France 25 C2 47 35N 3 6W
Carnamah, Australia 125 E2 29 41 S 115 53 E
Carnarvon, Australia 125 D1 24 51 S 113 42 E
Carnarvon, S. Africa 116 E3 30 56 S 22 8 E
Carnarvon △, Australia 126 C4 24 54 S 148 2 E
Carnarvon Ra., Queens., Australia 126 D4 25 15 S 148 30 E
Carnarvon Ra., W. Austral., Australia 125 E3 25 20 S 120 45 E
Carnatic, India 95 K3 9 40N 77 50 E
Carnation, U.S.A. 160 C5 47 39N 121 55W
Carndonagh, Ireland 23 A4 55 16N 7 15W
Carnduff, Canada 143 D8 49 10N 101 50W
Carnegie, U.S.A. 150 F4 40 24N 80 5W
Carnegie, L., Australia 125 E3 26 5 S 122 30 E
Carnegie Ridge, Pac. Oc. 135 H19 1 0 S 87 0W
Carnic Alps = Karnische Alpen, Europe 34 E6 46 36N 13 0 E
Carniche Alpi = Karnische Alpen, Europe 34 E6 46 36N 13 0 E
Carnot, C.A.R. 114 B3 4 59N 15 56 E
Carnot, C., Australia 127 E2 34 57 S 135 38 E
Carnot B., Australia 124 C3 17 20 S 122 15 E
Carnoustie, U.K. 22 E6 56 30N 2 42W
Carnsore Pt., Ireland 23 D5 52 10N 6 22W
Caro, U.S.A. 148 D4 43 29N 83 24W
Caroço, São Tomé & Príncipe 115 G6 1 32N 7 27 E
Carol City, U.S.A. 153 K9 25 56N 80 16W
Carolina, Brazil 170 C2 7 10 S 47 30W
Carolina, Puerto Rico 165 d 18 23N 65 58W
Carolina, S. Africa 117 D5 26 5 S 30 6 E
Caroline I., Kiribati 135 H12 9 58 S 150 13W
Caroline Is., Micronesia 62 J17 8 0N 150 0 E
Caroline Pk., N.Z. 131 F2 45 57 S 167 15 E
Carondelet, Kiribati 123 B16 5 33 S 173 50 E
Caroni, Trin. & Tob. 169 F9 10 34N 61 23W
Caroní →, Venezuela 169 B5 8 21N 62 43W
Caroníe = Nébrodi, Monti, Italy 47 E7 37 54N 14 35 E
Caroona, Australia 129 A9 31 24 S 150 26 E
Carora, Venezuela 168 A3 10 11N 70 5W
Carpathians, Europe 37 D11 49 30N 21 0 E
Carpaţii Meridionali, Romania 53 E9 45 30N 25 0 E
Carpentaria, G. of, Australia 126 A2 14 0 S 139 0 E
Carpentersville, U.S.A. 157 B8 42 6N 88 17W
Carpentras, France 29 D9 44 3N 5 2 E
Carpi, Italy 44 D7 44 47N 10 53 E
Carpina, Brazil 170 C4 7 51 S 35 15W
Cărpineni, Moldova 53 D13 46 46N 28 22 E
Carpinteria, U.S.A. 161 L7 34 24N 119 31W
Carpio, Spain 42 D5 41 13N 5 7W
Carr Boyd Ra., Australia 124 C4 16 15 S 128 35 E
Carrabelle, U.S.A. 152 F5 29 51N 84 40W
Carral, Spain 42 B2 43 14N 8 21W
Carranglan, Phil. 80 D3 15 58N 121 4 E
Carranza, Presa V., Mexico 162 B4 27 20N 100 50W
Carrara, Italy 44 D7 44 5N 10 6 E
Carrascal, Phil. 81 G5 9 22N 125 56 E
Carrasco △, Bolivia 173 D5 17 23 S 64 59W
Carrascosa del Campo, Spain 40 E2 40 2N 2 45W
Carrauntoohill, Ireland 23 D2 52 0N 9 45W
Carretas, Punta, Peru 172 C2 14 12 S 76 17W
Carrick-on-Shannon, Ireland 23 C3 53 57N 8 5W
Carrick-on-Suir, Ireland 23 D4 52 21N 7 24W
Carrickfergus, U.K. 23 B6 54 43N 5 49W
Carrickmacross, Ireland 23 C5 53 59N 6 43W
Carrieton, Australia 128 B3 32 25 S 138 31 E
Carrington, U.S.A. 154 B5 47 27N 99 8W
Carrión →, Spain 42 D6 41 53N 4 32W
Carrión de los Condes, Spain 42 C6 42 20N 4 37W
Carrizal Bajo, Chile 174 B1 28 5 S 71 20W
Carrizalillo, Chile 174 B1 29 5 S 71 30W
Carrizo Cr. →, U.S.A. 155 G3 36 55N 103 55W
Carrizo Plain ⌓, U.S.A. 160 K7 35 11N 119 47W
Carrizo Springs, U.S.A. 155 L5 28 31N 99 52W
Carrizozo, U.S.A. 159 K11 33 38N 105 53W
Carroll, U.S.A. 156 B2 42 4N 94 52W
Carrollton, Ga., U.S.A. 152 B4 33 35N 85 5W
Carrollton, Ill., U.S.A. 156 E6 39 18N 90 24W
Carrollton, Ky., U.S.A. 157 F11 38 41N 85 11W
Carrollton, Mo., U.S.A. 156 E3 39 22N 93 30W
Carrollton, Ohio, U.S.A. 150 F3 40 34N 81 5W
Carron →, U.K. 22 D4 57 53N 4 22W
Carron, L., U.K. 22 D3 57 22N 5 35W
Carrot →, Canada 143 C8 53 50N 101 17W
Carrot River, Canada 143 C8 53 17N 103 35W
Carrouges, France 26 D6 48 34N 0 10W
Carrù, Italy 44 D4 44 29N 7 52 E
Carruthers, Canada 143 C7 52 52N 109 16W
Carsa Dek, Ethiopia 107 F4 5 13N 39 50 E
Çarşamba, Turkey 100 B7 41 11N 36 44 E
Carsóli, Italy 45 F10 42 6N 13 5 E
Carson, Calif., U.S.A. 161 M8 33 48N 118 17W
Carson, N. Dak., U.S.A. 154 B4 46 25N 101 34W
Carson →, U.S.A. 160 F8 39 45N 118 40W
Carson City, Mich., U.S.A. 157 A12 43 11N 84 51W
Carson City, Nev., U.S.A. 160 F7 39 10N 119 46W
Carson Sink, U.S.A. 158 G4 39 50N 118 25W
Carstensz Pyramid = Jaya, Puncak, Indonesia 83 B5 3 57 S 137 17 E
Cartagena, Colombia 168 A2 10 25N 75 33W
Cartagena, Spain 41 H4 37 38N 0 59W
Cartago, Colombia 168 C2 4 45N 75 55W
Cartago, Costa Rica 164 E3 9 50N 83 55W
Cártama, Spain 43 J6 36 43N 4 39W
Cartaxo, Portugal 43 F2 39 10N 8 47W
Cartaya, Spain 43 H3 37 16N 7 9W
Cartersville, U.S.A. 152 A5 34 10N 84 48W
Carterton, N.Z. 130 H4 41 2 S 175 31 E
Carterville, U.S.A. 156 G7 37 46N 89 5W
Carthage, Tunisia 46 F3 36 50N 10 21 E
Carthage, Ill., U.S.A. 156 D5 40 25N 91 8W
Carthage, Mo., U.S.A. 155 G7 37 11N 94 19W
Carthage, N.Y., U.S.A. 148 D8 43 59N 75 37W
Carthage, Tex., U.S.A. 155 J7 32 9N 94 20W
Cartier I., Australia 124 B3 12 31 S 123 29 E
Cartwright, Canada 141 B8 53 41N 56 58W
Caruaru, Brazil 170 C4 8 15 S 35 55W
Carúpano, Venezuela 169 A5 10 39N 63 15W
Caruray, Phil. 81 F2 10 20N 119 0 E
Carutapera, Brazil 170 B2 1 13 S 46 1W
Caruthersville, U.S.A. 155 G10 36 11N 89 39W
Carvalho, Brazil 169 D7 2 16 S 51 29W
Carvin, France 27 B9 50 30N 2 57 E
Carvoeiro, Brazil 169 D5 1 30 S 61 59W
Carvoeiro, C., Portugal 43 F1 39 21N 9 24W
Cary, Ill., U.S.A. 157 B8 42 13N 88 14W
Cary, N.C., U.S.A. 149 H6 35 47N 78 46W
Casa, Pas de la = Envalira, Port d', Europe 40 C6 42 33N 1 43 E
Casa Branca, Brazil 171 F2 21 46 S 47 4W
Casa Branca, Portugal 43 G2 38 29N 8 12W
Casa Grande, U.S.A. 159 K8 32 53N 111 45W
Casablanca, Chile 174 C1 33 20 S 71 25W
Casablanca, Morocco 110 B3 33 36N 7 36W
Casacalenda, Italy 45 G11 41 44N 14 51 E
Casalbordino, Italy 45 F11 42 9N 14 35 E
Casale Monferrato, Italy 44 C5 45 8N 8 27 E
Casalmaggiore, Italy 44 D7 44 59N 10 26 E
Casalpusterlengo, Italy 44 C6 45 11N 9 39 E
Casamance →, Senegal 112 C1 12 33N 16 46W
Casanare □, Colombia 168 B3 5 30N 72 0W
Casanare →, Colombia 168 B4 6 2N 69 51W
Casarano, Italy 47 B11 40 0N 18 10 E
Casares, Spain 43 J5 36 27N 5 16W
Casas Ibáñez, Spain 41 F3 39 17N 1 30W
Casasimarro, Spain 41 F2 39 22N 2 3W
Casatejada, Spain 42 F5 39 54N 5 40W
Casavieja, Spain 42 E6 40 17N 4 46W
Cascada de Basaseachic △, Mexico 162 B3 28 9N 108 15W
Cascade, Seychelles 121 b 4 39 S 55 29 E
Cascade, Idaho, U.S.A. 158 D5 44 31N 116 2W
Cascade, Iowa, U.S.A. 156 B6 42 18N 91 0W
Cascade, Mont., U.S.A. 158 C8 47 16N 111 42W
Cascade Locks, U.S.A. 160 E5 45 40N 121 54W
Cascade Pt., N.Z. 131 E3 44 1 S 168 20 E
Cascade Ra., U.S.A. 160 D5 47 0N 121 30W
Cascade Reservoir, U.S.A. 158 D5 44 32N 116 3W
Cascades, Pte. des, Réunion 121 c 21 9 S 55 51 E
Cascais, Portugal 43 G1 38 41N 9 25W
Cascavel, Ceará, Brazil 170 B4 4 7 S 38 14W
Cascavel, Paraná, Brazil 175 A5 24 57 S 53 28W
Cáscina, Italy 44 E7 43 41N 10 33 E
Casco B., U.S.A. 149 D10 43 45N 70 0W
Caselle Torinese, Italy 44 C4 45 10N 7 39 E
Caserta, Italy 47 A7 41 4N 14 20 E
Casey, Antarctica 7 C8 66 0 S 76 0 E
Casey, U.S.A. 157 E9 39 18N 87 59W
Caseyr, Raas = Asir, Ras, Somali Rep. 120 B4 11 55N 51 10 E
Cashel, Ireland 23 D4 52 30N 7 53W
Casibare →, Colombia 168 C3 3 48N 72 18W
Casiguran, Phil. 80 C4 16 22N 122 7 E
Casiguran Sound, Phil. 80 C3 16 6N 121 58 E
Casilda, Argentina 174 C3 33 10 S 61 10W
Casim = General Toshevo, Bulgaria 51 C12 43 42N 28 6 E
Casimcea, Romania 53 F13 44 45N 28 23 E
Casino, Australia 127 D5 28 52 S 153 3 E
Casiquiare →, Venezuela 168 C4 2 1N 67 7W
Casitas, Peru 172 A1 3 54 S 80 39W
Čáslav, Czech Rep. 34 B8 49 54N 15 22 E
Casma, Peru 172 B2 9 30 S 78 20W
Casmalia, U.S.A. 161 L6 34 50N 120 32W
Cásola Valsénio, Italy 45 D8 44 12N 11 40 E
Cásoli, Italy 45 F11 42 7N 14 18 E
Caspe, Spain 40 D4 41 14N 0 1W
Casper, U.S.A. 158 E10 42 51N 106 19W
Caspian Depression, Eurasia 61 G9 47 0N 48 0 E
Caspian Sea, Eurasia 57 F9 43 0N 50 0 E
Cass Lake, U.S.A. 154 B7 47 23N 94 37W
Cassà de la Selva, Spain 40 D7 41 53N 2 52 E
Cassadaga, U.S.A. 150 D5 42 20N 79 19W
Cassai, Angola 115 E4 10 33 S 21 59 E
Cassai →, Angola 115 E4 3 2 S 16 57 E
Cassamba, Angola 115 E4 13 6 S 20 18 E
Cassano allo Iónio, Italy 47 C9 39 47N 16 20 E
Cassel, France 27 B9 50 48N 2 30 E
Casselman, Canada 151 A9 45 19N 75 5W
Casselton, U.S.A. 154 B6 46 54N 97 13W
Cassiar, Canada 142 B3 59 16N 129 40W
Cassiar Mts., Canada 142 B2 59 30N 130 30W
Cassilândia, Brazil 173 D7 19 9 S 51 45W
Cassilis, Australia 129 B8 32 3 S 149 58 E
Cassinga, Angola 115 F3 15 5 S 16 4 E
Cassino, Italy 46 A6 41 30N 13 49 E
Cassis, France 29 E9 43 14N 5 32 E
Cassoalala, Angola 115 D2 9 30 S 14 22 E
Cassoango, Angola 115 E4 13 42 S 20 56 E
Cassongue, Angola 115 E3 11 53 S 15 2 E
Cassopolis, U.S.A. 157 C10 41 55N 86 1W
Cassunda, Angola 115 E4 10 57 S 21 3 E
Cassville, Mo., U.S.A. 155 G8 36 41N 93 52W
Cassville, Wis., U.S.A. 156 B6 42 43N 90 59W
Castagneto Carducci, Italy 44 E7 43 9N 10 36 E
Castaic, U.S.A. 161 L8 34 30N 118 38W
Castalia, U.S.A. 150 E2 41 24N 82 49W
Castanhal, Brazil 170 B2 1 18 S 47 55W
Castara, Trin. & Tob. 169 E10 11 17N 60 42W
Castasegna, Switz. 33 D9 46 20N 9 31 E
Castéggio, Italy 44 C6 45 0N 9 7 E
Castejón de Monegros, Spain 40 D4 41 37N 0 15W
Castèl di Sangro, Italy 45 G11 41 47N 14 6 E
Castèl San Giovanni, Italy 44 C6 45 4N 9 26 E
Castèl San Pietro Terme, Italy 45 D8 44 24N 11 35 E
Castelbuono, Italy 47 E7 37 56N 14 5 E
Castelfidardo, Italy 45 E10 43 28N 13 33 E
Castelfiorentino, Italy 44 E7 43 36N 10 58 E
Castelfranco Emília, Italy 44 D8 44 37N 11 3 E
Castelfranco Véneto, Italy 45 C8 45 40N 11 55 E
Casteljaloux, France 28 D4 44 19N 0 6 E
Castellabate, Italy 47 B7 40 17N 14 57 E
Castellammare, G. di, Italy 46 D5 38 8N 12 54 E
Castellammare del Golfo, Italy 46 D5 38 1N 12 53 E
Castellammare di Stábia, Italy 47 B7 40 42N 14 29 E
Castellamonte, Italy 44 C4 45 23N 7 42 E
Castellane, France 29 E10 43 50N 6 31 E
Castellaneta, Italy 47 B9 40 38N 16 56 E
Castelli, Argentina 174 D4 36 7 S 57 47W
Castelló de la Plana, Spain 40 F4 39 58N 0 3W
Castellón de la Plana □, Spain 40 E4 40 15N 0 5W
Castellote, Spain 40 E4 40 48N 0 15W
Castelmáuro, Italy 45 G11 41 50N 14 43 E
Castelnau-de-Médoc, France 28 C3 45 2N 0 48W
Castelnau-Magnoac, France 28 E4 43 17N 0 31 E
Castelnaudary, France 28 E5 43 20N 1 58 E
Castelnovo ne' Monti, Italy 44 D7 44 26N 10 24 E
Castelnuovo di Val di Cécina, Italy 44 E7 43 12N 10 59 E

Castelo = Manuel Urbano, Brazil 172 B4 8 53 S 69 18W
Castelo, Brazil 171 F3 20 33 S 41 14W
Castelo, Pta. do, Azores 9 d4 36 56N 25 1W
Castelo Branco, Azores 9 d1 38 31N 28 44W
Castelo Branco, Portugal 42 F3 39 50N 7 31W
Castelo Branco □, Portugal 42 F3 39 52N 7 45W
Castelo de Paiva, Portugal 42 D2 41 2N 8 16W
Castelo de Vide, Portugal 43 F3 39 25N 7 27W
Castelo do Piauí, Brazil 170 C3 5 20 S 41 33W
Castelrosso = Megiste, Greece 49 E11 36 8N 29 34 E
Castelsardo, Italy 46 B1 40 55N 8 43 E
Castelsarrasin, France 28 D5 44 2N 1 7 E
Casteltérmini, Italy 46 E6 37 32N 13 39 E
Castelvetrano, Italy 46 E5 37 41N 12 47 E
Castendo, Angola 115 D2 8 39 S 14 10 E
Casterton, Australia 128 D4 37 30 S 141 30 E
Castets, France 28 E2 43 52N 1 6W
Castiglion Fiorentino, Italy 45 E8 43 20N 11 55 E
Castiglione = Bou Ismaïl, Algeria 111 A5 36 38N 2 42 E
Castiglione del Lago, Italy 45 E9 43 7N 12 3 E
Castiglione della Pescáia, Italy 44 F7 42 46N 10 53 E
Castiglione delle Stiviere, Italy 44 C7 45 23N 10 29 E
Castilblanco, Spain 43 F5 39 17N 5 5W
Castile, U.S.A. 150 D6 42 38N 78 3W
Castilla, Peru 172 B1 5 12 S 80 38W
Castilla, Playa de, Spain 43 J4 37 0N 6 33W
Castilla-La Mancha □, Spain 12 H5 39 30N 3 30W
Castilla y Leon □, Spain 42 D6 42 0N 5 0W
Castillo de Locubín, Spain 43 H7 37 32N 3 56W
Castillo de San Marcos ⌓, U.S.A. 152 F8 29 54N 81 19W
Castillon-en-Couserans, France 28 F5 42 56N 1 1 E
Castillonès, France 28 D4 44 39N 0 37 E
Castillos, Uruguay 175 C5 34 12 S 53 52W
Castle Dale, U.S.A. 158 G8 39 13N 111 1W
Castle Douglas, U.K. 22 G5 54 56N 3 56W
Castle Harbour, Bermuda 9 a 32 21N 64 40W
Castle Rock, Colo., U.S.A. 154 F2 39 22N 104 51W
Castle Rock, Wash., U.S.A. 160 D4 46 17N 122 54W
Castle Rock Pt., St. Helena 9 h 16 1 S 5 45W
Castlebar, Ireland 23 C2 53 52N 9 18W
Castlebay, U.K. 22 E1 56 57N 7 31W
Castleblaney, Ireland 23 B5 54 7N 6 44W
Castlecliff, N.Z. 130 F4 39 57 S 175 5 E
Castlederg, U.K. 23 B4 54 42N 7 35W
Castleford, U.K. 20 D6 53 43N 1 21W
Castlegar, Canada 142 D5 49 20N 117 40W
Castlemaine, Australia 128 D6 37 2 S 144 12 E
Castlepoint, N.Z. 130 G5 40 54 S 176 15 E
Castlepollard, Ireland 23 C4 53 41N 7 19W
Castlerea, Ireland 23 C3 53 46N 8 29W
Castlereagh →, Australia 129 A7 30 12 S 147 32 E
Castlereagh B., Australia 126 A2 12 10 S 135 10 E
Castleton, U.S.A. 151 C11 43 37N 73 11W
Castletown, I. of Man 20 C3 54 5N 4 38W
Castletown Bearhaven, Ireland 23 E2 51 39N 9 55W
Castor, Canada 142 C6 52 15N 111 50W
Castor →, Canada 140 B4 53 24N 78 58W
Castorland, U.S.A. 151 C9 43 53N 75 31W
Castres, France 28 E6 43 37N 2 13 E
Castricum, Neths. 24 B4 52 33N 4 40 E
Castries, St. Lucia 165 f 14 2N 60 58W
Castril, Spain 43 H8 37 48N 2 46W
Castro, Brazil 175 A6 24 45 S 50 0W
Castro, Chile 176 B2 42 30 S 73 50W
Castro Alves, Brazil 171 D4 12 46 S 39 33W
Castro del Río, Spain 43 H6 37 41N 4 29W
Castro-Urdiales, Spain 42 B7 43 23N 3 11W
Castro Verde, Portugal 43 H2 37 41N 8 4W
Castrogiovanni = Enna, Italy 47 E7 37 34N 14 16 E
Castrojeriz, Spain 42 C6 42 17N 4 9W
Castropol, Spain 42 B4 43 32N 7 0W
Castroreale, Italy 47 D8 38 6N 15 12 E
Castrovillari, Italy 47 C9 39 49N 16 12 E
Castroville, U.S.A. 160 J5 36 46N 121 45W
Castrovirreyna, Peru 172 C2 13 20 S 75 18W
Castuera, Spain 43 G5 38 43N 5 37W
Caswell Sound, N.Z. 131 E2 44 59 S 167 8 E
Çat, Turkey 101 C9 39 40N 41 3 E
Cat Ba △, Vietnam 86 B6 20 47N 107 3 E
Cat Ba, Dao, Vietnam 86 B6 20 50N 107 0 E
Cat I., Bahamas 165 B4 24 30N 75 30W
Cat L., Canada 140 B1 51 40N 91 50W
Cat Lake, Canada 140 B1 51 40N 91 50W
Cat Tien △, Vietnam 87 G6 11 25N 107 17 E
Čata, Slovak Rep. 35 D11 47 58N 18 38 E
Catabola, Angola 115 E3 12 9 S 17 16 E
Catacamas, Honduras 164 D2 14 54N 85 56W
Catacáos, Peru 172 B1 5 20 S 80 45W
Cataguases, Brazil 171 F3 21 23 S 42 39W
Catagupan, Phil. 81 G1 8 1N 116 58 E
Cataingan, Phil. 80 E4 12 0N 124 0 E
Çatak, Turkey 101 C10 38 1N 43 8 E
Catalão, Brazil 171 E2 18 10 S 47 57W
Çatalca, Turkey 51 E12 41 8N 28 27 E
Catalina, Canada 141 C9 48 31N 53 4W
Catalina, Chile 174 B2 25 13 S 69 43W
Catalina, U.S.A. 159 K8 32 30N 110 50W
Catalonia = Cataluña □, Spain 40 D6 41 40N 1 15 E
Cataluña □, Spain 40 D6 41 40N 1 15 E
Çatalzeytin, Turkey 100 B6 41 57N 34 12 E
Catamarca, Argentina 174 B2 28 30 S 65 50W
Catamarca □, Argentina 174 B2 27 0 S 65 50W
Catanauan, Phil. 80 E4 13 36N 122 19 E
Catanduanes □, Phil. 80 E5 13 50N 124 20 E
Catanduva, Brazil 175 A6 21 5 S 48 58W
Catánia, Italy 47 E8 37 30N 15 6 E
Catánia, G. di, Italy 47 E8 37 24N 15 9 E
Catanzaro, Italy 47 D9 38 54N 16 35 E
Catarman, Camiguin, Phil. 81 G5 9 8N 124 40 E
Catarman, N. Samar, Phil. 80 E5 12 28N 124 35 E
Catatumbo →, Venezuela 168 B3 9 21N 71 45W
Catatumbo-Bari △, Colombia 165 E5 9 3N 73 12W
Cataula, U.S.A. 152 C5 32 39N 84 52W
Catbalogan, Phil. 81 F5 11 46N 124 53 E
Cateco Cangola, Angola 115 D3 8 28 S 15 51 E
Cateel, Phil. 81 H6 7 47N 126 24 E
Cateel Bay, Phil. 81 H6 7 54N 126 25 E
Catembe, Mozam. 117 D5 26 0 S 32 33 E
Catende, Angola 115 E4 11 14 S 21 30 E
Catende, Brazil 170 C4 8 40 S 35 43W
Caterham, U.K. 21 F7 51 15N 0 4W
Catete, Angola 115 D2 9 6 S 13 43 E
Cathcart, Australia 129 D8 36 52 S 149 24 E
Cathcart, S. Africa 116 E4 32 18 S 27 10 E
Cathlamet, U.S.A. 160 D3 46 12N 123 23W
Catio, Guinea-Biss. 112 C1 11 17N 15 15W
Catismiña, Venezuela 169 C5 4 5N 63 40W
Catita, Brazil 170 C3 9 31 S 43 1W
Catlettsburg, U.S.A. 148 F4 38 25N 82 36W
Catlin, U.S.A. 157 D9 40 4N 87 42W
Çatma Dağı, Turkey 49 C11 38 25N 29 50 E
Catmon, Phil. 81 F5 10 43N 124 1 E
Catoche, C., Mexico 163 C7 21 40N 87 8W
Catolé do Rocha, Brazil 170 C4 6 21 S 37 45W
Catota, Angola 115 E3 13 57 S 17 30 E
Cátria, Mte., Italy 45 E9 43 28N 12 42 E
Catriló, Argentina 174 D3 36 26 S 63 24W
Catrimani, Brazil 169 C5 0 27N 61 41W
Catrimani →, Brazil 169 C5 0 28N 61 44W
Catskill, U.S.A. 151 D11 42 14N 73 52W
Catskill ⌓, U.S.A. 151 D10 42 7N 74 39W
Catskill Mts., U.S.A. 151 D10 42 10N 74 25W
Catt, Mt., Australia 126 A1 13 49 S 134 23 E
Cattaraugus, U.S.A. 150 D6 42 22N 78 52W
Cattaro = Kotor, Serbia & M. 50 D2 42 25N 18 47 E
Catterick, U.K. 20 C6 54 23N 1 37W
Cattólica, Italy 45 E9 43 58N 12 44 E
Cattólica Eraclea, Italy 46 E6 37 26N 13 24 E
Catu, Brazil 171 D4 12 21 S 38 23W
Catuala, Angola 116 B2 16 25 S 19 2 E
Catuane, Mozam. 117 D5 26 48 S 32 18 E
Catubig, Phil. 80 E5 12 24N 125 3 E
Catumbela, Angola 115 E2 12 25 S 13 34 E
Catumbela →, Angola 115 E2 12 29 S 13 28 E
Catur, Mozam. 119 E4 13 45 S 35 30 E
Catwick Is., Vietnam 87 G7 10 0N 109 0 E
Cauayan, Isabela, Phil. 80 C3 16 56N 121 46 E
Cauayan, Neg. Occ., Phil. 81 G4 9 58N 122 37 E
Cauca □, Colombia 168 C2 2 30N 76 50W
Cauca →, Colombia 168 B3 8 54N 74 28W
Caucaia, Brazil 170 B4 3 40 S 38 35W
Caucasia, Colombia 168 B2 8 0N 75 12W
Caucasus Mountains, Eurasia 61 J7 42 50N 44 0 E
Caudete, Spain 41 G3 38 42N 1 2W
Caudry, France 27 B10 50 7N 3 22 E
Caulnes, France 26 D4 48 18N 2 10W
Caulónia, Italy 47 D9 38 23N 16 24 E
Caungula, Angola 115 D3 8 26 S 18 38 E
Cauquenes, Chile 174 D1 36 0 S 72 22W
Caura →, Venezuela 169 B5 7 38N 64 53W
Caurés →, Brazil 169 D5 1 21 S 62 20W
Cauresi →, Mozam. 119 F3 17 8 S 33 0 E
Căuşani, Moldova 53 D14 46 38N 29 25 E
Causapscal, Canada 141 C6 48 19N 67 12W
Caussade, France 28 D5 44 10N 1 33 E
Causse-Méjean, France 28 D7 44 18N 3 42 E
Causses du Quercy ⌓, France 28 D5 44 35N 1 35 E
Cauterets, France 28 F3 42 52N 0 8W
Caux, Pays de, France 26 C7 49 38N 0 35 E
Cava de' Tirreni, Italy 47 B7 40 42N 14 42 E
Cávado →, Portugal 42 D2 41 32N 8 48W
Cavagrande del Cassibile ⌓, Italy 47 F8 36 58N 15 6 E
Cavaillon, France 29 E9 43 50N 5 2 E
Cavalaire-sur-Mer, France 29 E10 43 10N 6 33 E
Cavalcante, Brazil 171 D2 13 48 S 47 30W
Cavalese, Italy 45 B8 46 17N 11 27 E
Cavalier, U.S.A. 154 A6 48 48N 97 37W
Cavalla = Cavally →, Africa 112 E3 4 22N 7 32W
Cavalli Is., N.Z. 130 B2 35 0 S 173 58 E
Cavallo, Î. de, France 29 G13 41 22N 9 16 E
Cavally →, Africa 112 E3 4 22N 7 32W
Cavan, Ireland 23 B4 54 0N 7 22W
Cavan □, Ireland 23 C4 54 1N 7 16W
Cavárzere, Italy 45 C9 45 8N 12 5 E
Cavazzucherina = Iésolo, Italy 45 C9 45 32N 12 38 E
Çavdarhisar, Turkey 49 B11 39 12N 29 37 E
Çavdır, Turkey 49 D11 37 10N 29 42 E
Cave Creek, U.S.A. 159 K7 33 50N 111 57W
Cave Run L., U.S.A. 157 F13 38 5N 83 25W
Cave Spring, U.S.A. 152 A4 34 6N 85 20W
Cavenagh Ra., Australia 125 E4 26 12 S 127 55 E
Cavendish, Australia 128 D5 37 31 S 142 2 E
Caviana, I., Brazil 169 C7 0 10N 50 10W
Cavite, Phil. 80 D3 14 29N 120 55 E
Cavite □, Phil. 80 D3 14 15N 120 50 E
Caviúna = Rolândia, Brazil 175 A5 23 18 S 51 23W
Cavnic, Romania 53 C8 47 40N 23 52 E
Cavour, Italy 44 D4 44 47N 7 22 E
Cavtat, Croatia 50 D2 42 35N 18 13 E
Cawayan, Phil. 81 F4 11 56N 123 46 E
Cawayanon = Vintar, Phil. 80 B3 18 14N 120 39 E
Cawndilla L., Australia 128 B5 32 30 S 142 15 E
Cawnpore = Kanpur, India 93 F9 26 28N 80 20 E
Caxias, Brazil 170 B3 4 55 S 43 20W
Caxias do Sul, Brazil 175 B5 29 10 S 51 10W
Caxito, Angola 115 D2 8 30 S 13 30 E
Caxopa, Angola 115 E4 11 52 S 20 52 E
Çay, Turkey 100 C4 38 35N 31 1 E
Cay Pt., Bahamas 9 b 25 59N 77 25W
Cay Sal Bank, Bahamas 164 B4 23 45N 80 0W
Cayambe, Napo, Ecuador 168 C2 0 2N 77 59W
Cayambe, Quito, Ecuador 168 C2 0 3N 78 8W
Çaycuma, Turkey 100 B5 41 25N 32 4 E
Çayeli, Turkey 101 B9 41 5N 40 45 E
Cayenne, Fr. Guiana 169 B7 5 5N 52 18W
Cayenne □, Fr. Guiana 169 C7 5 0N 53 0W
Cayey, Puerto Rico 165 d 18 7N 66 10W
Caygören Barajı, Turkey 49 B10 39 15N 28 12 E
Cayiralan, Turkey 100 C6 39 17N 35 38 E
Caylus, France 28 D5 44 15N 1 47 E
Cayman Brac, Cayman Is. 164 C4 19 43N 79 49W
Cayman Is. ∅, W. Indies 164 C3 19 40N 80 30W
Cayman Trough, Caribbean 136 H11 19 0N 81 0W
Cayres, France 28 D7 44 55N 3 48 E
Cayuga, Ind., U.S.A. 157 E9 39 57N 87 28W
Cayuga, N.Y., U.S.A. 151 D8 42 54N 76 44W
Cayuga L., U.S.A. 151 D8 42 41N 76 41W
Cazage, Angola 115 E4 11 2 S 20 45 E
Cazalla de la Sierra, Spain 43 H5 37 56N 5 45W
Căzăneşti, Romania 53 F12 44 36N 27 3 E
Cazaubon, France 28 E3 43 56N 0 3W
Cazaux et de Sanguinet, Étang de, France 28 D2 44 29N 1 10W
Cazenovia, U.S.A. 151 D9 42 56N 75 51W
Cazères, France 28 E5 43 13N 1 5 E
Cazin, Bos.-H. 45 D12 44 57N 15 57 E
Čazma, Croatia 45 C13 45 45N 16 39 E
Cazombo, Angola 115 E4 11 54 S 22 56 E
Cazorla, Spain 43 H7 37 55N 3 2W
Cazorla, Sierra de, Spain 43 G8 38 5N 2 55W
Cea →, Spain 42 C5 42 0N 5 36W
Ceamurlia de Jos, Romania 53 F13 44 43N 28 47 E
Ceanannus Mor, Ireland 23 C5 53 44N 6 53W
Ceará = Fortaleza, Brazil 170 B4 3 45 S 38 35W
Ceará □, Brazil 170 C4 5 0 S 40 0W
Ceará Mirim, Brazil 170 C4 5 38 S 35 25W
Ceara Plain, Atl. Oc. 8 F7 2 0N 42 0W
Ceauru, L., Romania 53 F8 44 58N 23 11 E
Cebaco, I. de, Panama 164 E3 7 33N 81 9W
Cebollar, Argentina 174 B2 29 10 S 66 35W
Cebollera, Sierra de, Spain 40 D2 42 0N 2 30W
Cebreros, Spain 42 E6 40 27N 4 28W
Cebu, Phil. 81 F4 10 18N 123 54 E
Cebu □, Phil. 81 F4 10 20N 123 40 E
Čečava, Bos.-H. 52 F2 44 42N 17 44 E
Ceccano, Italy 46 A6 41 34N 13 20 E
Cece, Hungary 52 D3 46 46N 18 39 E
Cechi, Ivory C. 112 D4 6 15N 4 25W
Cecil Plains, Australia 127 D5 27 30 S 151 11 E
Cécina, Italy 44 E7 43 19N 10 31 E
Cécina →, Italy 44 E7 43 18N 10 29 E
Ceclavín, Spain 42 F4 39 50N 6 45W
Cedar →, U.S.A. 156 C5 41 17N 91 21W
Cedar City, U.S.A. 159 H7 37 41N 113 4W
Cedar Creek Reservoir, U.S.A. 155 J6 32 11N 96 4W
Cedar Falls, Iowa, U.S.A. 156 B4 42 32N 92 27W
Cedar Falls, Wash., U.S.A. 160 C5 47 25N 121 45W
Cedar Grove, U.S.A. 157 E12 39 22N 84 56W
Cedar Key, U.S.A. 153 F6 29 8N 83 2W
Cedar L., Canada 143 C9 53 10N 100 0W
Cedar Lake, U.S.A. 157 C9 41 22N 87 26W
Cedar Park, U.S.A. 155 K6 30 30N 97 49W
Cedar Point, U.S.A. 157 C13 41 44N 83 21W
Cedar Rapids, U.S.A. 156 C5 41 59N 91 40W
Cedartown, U.S.A. 152 A4 34 1N 85 15W
Cedarvale, Canada 142 B3 55 1N 128 22W
Cedarville, S. Africa 117 E4 30 23 S 29 3 E
Cedarville, Ill., U.S.A. 156 B7 42 23N 89 38W
Cedarville, Ohio, U.S.A. 157 E13 39 44N 83 49W
Cedeira, Spain 42 B2 43 39N 8 2W
Cedral, Mexico 162 C4 23 50N 100 42W
Cedrino →, Italy 46 B2 40 11N 9 24 E
Cedro, Brazil 170 C4 6 34 S 39 3W
Cedros, Azores 9 d1 38 38N 28 42W
Cedros, I. de, Mexico 162 B1 28 10N 115 20W
Cedros B., Trin. & Tob. 169 F9 10 16N 61 54W
Ceduna, Australia 127 E1 32 7 S 133 46 E
Cedynia, Poland 55 F1 52 53N 14 12 E
Cée, Spain 42 C1 42 57N 9 10W
Ceel Dheere = El Dere, Somali Rep. 120 C3 5 22N 46 11 E
Ceerigaabo = Erigavo, Somali Rep. 120 B3 10 35N 47 20 E
Cefalù, Italy 47 D7 38 2N 14 1 E
Cega →, Spain 42 D6 41 33N 4 46W
Cegléd, Hungary 52 C4 47 11N 19 47 E
Céglie Messápico, Italy 47 B10 40 39N 17 31 E
Cehegín, Spain 41 G3 38 6N 1 48W
Ceheng, China 76 E5 24 58N 105 48 E
Cehu-Silvaniei, Romania 53 C8 47 24N 23 9 E
Ceica, Romania 52 D7 46 53N 22 10 E
Ceira →, Portugal 42 E2 40 13N 8 16W
Cekik, Indonesia 79 J17 8 12 S 114 27 E
Cela, Angola 115 E3 11 25 S 15 7 E
Čelákovice, Czech Rep. 34 A7 50 10N 14 46 E
Celano, Italy 45 F10 42 5N 13 33 E
Celanova, Spain 42 C3 42 9N 7 58W
Celaque △, Honduras 164 D2 14 30N 88 43W
Celaya, Mexico 162 C4 20 31N 100 37W
Celebes = Sulawesi □, Indonesia 82 B2 2 0 S 120 0 E
Celebes Sea, Indonesia 82 A2 3 0N 123 0 E
Celendín, Peru 172 B2 6 52 S 78 10W
Čelić, Bos.-H. 52 F3 44 43N 18 49 E
Celica, Ecuador 168 D2 4 7 S 79 59W
Celina, U.S.A. 157 D12 40 33N 84 35W
Celinac, Bos.-H. 52 F2 44 44N 17 22 E
Celje, Slovenia 45 B12 46 16N 15 18 E
Celldömölk, Hungary 52 C2 47 16N 17 10 E
Celle, Germany 30 C6 52 37N 10 4 E
Celorico da Beira, Portugal 42 E3 40 38N 7 24W
Celtic Sea, Atl. Oc. 8 A11 50 9N 9 34W
Çeltikçi, Turkey 49 D12 37 32N 30 29 E
Çemişgezek, Turkey 101 C8 39 3N 38 56 E
Cenderwasih, Teluk, Indonesia 79 E9 3 0 S 135 20 E
Cenepa →, Peru 168 D2 4 40 S 78 10W
Cengong, China 76 D7 27 13N 108 44 E
Ceno →, Italy 44 D7 44 43N 10 5 E
Centallo, Italy 44 D4 44 30N 7 35 E
Centelles, Spain 40 D7 41 50N 2 14 E
Centenário do Sul, Brazil 171 F1 22 48 S 51 36W
Center, N. Dak., U.S.A. 154 B4 47 7N 101 18W
Center, Tex., U.S.A. 155 K7 31 48N 94 11W
Center Hill, U.S.A. 153 G7 28 38N 82 3W
Center Point, U.S.A. 156 B5 42 12N 91 46W
Centerburg, U.S.A. 150 F2 40 18N 82 42W
Centerville, Calif., U.S.A. 160 J7 36 44N 119 30W
Centerville, Iowa, U.S.A. 156 D4 40 44N 92 52W
Centerville, Mich., U.S.A. 157 C11 41 55N 85 32W
Centerville, Ohio, U.S.A. 157 E12 39 38N 84 8W
Centerville, Pa., U.S.A. 150 F5 40 3N 79 59W
Centerville, Tenn., U.S.A. 149 H2 35 47N 87 28W
Centerville, Tex., U.S.A. 155 K7 31 16N 95 59W
Cento, Italy 45 D8 44 43N 11 17 E
Central = Tsentralnyy □, Russia 60 D4 52 0N 40 0 E
Central, Brazil 170 D3 11 8 S 42 8W
Central, U.S.A. 144 D11 65 35N 144 48W
Central □, Ghana 113 D4 5 30N 1 0W
Central □, Kenya 118 C4 0 30 S 37 30 E
Central □, Malawi 119 E3 13 30 S 33 30 E
Central □, Papua N. G. 132 F5 10 0 S 148 0 E
Central □, Zambia 119 E2 14 25 S 28 50 E
Central, Cordillera, Bolivia 173 D5 18 30 S 64 55W
Central, Cordillera, Colombia 168 C2 5 0N 75 0W
Central, Cordillera, Costa Rica 164 D3 10 10N 84 5W
Central, Cordillera, Dom. Rep. 165 C5 19 15N 71 0W
Central, Cordillera, Peru 172 B2 7 0 S 77 30W
Central, Cordillera, Phil. 80 C3 17 20N 120 57 E
Central, Cordillera, Puerto Rico 165 d 18 8N 66 35W
Central African Empire = Central African Rep. ■, Africa 114 A4 7 0N 20 0 E
Central African Rep. ■, Africa 114 A4 7 0N 20 0 E
Central America, America 136 H11 12 0N 85 0W
Central Butte, Canada 143 C7 50 48N 106 31W
Central City, Colo., U.S.A. 158 G11 39 48N 105 31W
Central City, Iowa, U.S.A. 156 B5 42 12N 91 32W
Central City, Ky., U.S.A. 148 G2 37 18N 87 7W
Central City, Nebr., U.S.A. 154 E6 41 7N 98 0W
Central I., Kenya 118 B4 3 30N 36 0 E
Central Island △, Kenya 118 B4 2 33N 36 1 E
Central Japan International ✈ (CJI), Japan 73 C8 34 53N 136 45 E
Central Kalahari ⌓, Botswana 116 C3 22 36 S 23 58 E
Central Makran Range, Pakistan 91 D2 26 30N 64 15 E
Central Pacific Basin, Pac. Oc. 134 G10 8 0N 175 0W
Central Patricia, Canada 140 B1 51 30N 90 9W
Central Point, U.S.A. 158 E2 42 23N 122 55W
Central Provinces = Madhya Pradesh □, India 92 J8 22 50N 78 0 E
Central Ra., Papua N. G. 132 C2 5 0 S 143 0 E
Central Russian Uplands, Europe 12 E13 54 0N 36 0 E
Central Siberian Plateau, Russia 62 C14 65 0N 105 0 E
Central Square, U.S.A. 151 C8 43 17N 76 9W
Centralia, Ill., U.S.A. 156 F7 38 32N 89 8W
Centralia, Mo., U.S.A. 156 E4 39 13N 92 8W
Centralia, Wash., U.S.A. 160 D4 46 43N 122 58W
Centre, U.S.A. 152 A4 34 9N 85 41W
Centre de Flacq, Mauritius 121 d 20 12 S 57 43 E
Century, U.S.A. 153 E2 30 58N 87 16W
Cenxi, China 77 F8 22 57N 110 57 E
Čeotina →, Bos.-H. 50 C2 43 36N 18 50 E
Cephalonia = Kefallinía, Greece 39 C2 38 15N 20 30 E
Čepin, Croatia 52 E3 45 32N 18 34 E
Ceprano, Italy 46 A6 41 33N 13 31 E
Ceptura, Romania 53 E11 45 1N 26 21 E
Cepu, Indonesia 85 D4 7 9 S 111 35 E
Ceram = Seram, Indonesia 83 B3 3 10 S 129 0 E
Ceram Sea = Seram Sea, Indonesia 82 B3 2 30 S 128 30 E
Cerbère, France 28 F7 42 26N 3 10 E
Cerbicales, Îs., France 29 G13 41 33N 9 22 E
Cercal, Portugal 43 H2 37 48N 8 40W
Cerdaña, Spain 40 C6 42 22N 1 35 E
Cère →, France 28 D5 44 55N 1 49 E
Cerea, Italy 45 C8 45 12N 11 13 E
Ceredigion □, U.K. 21 E3 52 16N 4 15W
Ceres, Argentina 173 B3 29 55 S 61 55W
Ceres, Brazil 171 E2 15 17 S 49 35W
Ceres, S. Africa 116 E2 33 21 S 19 18 E
Ceres, U.S.A. 160 H6 37 35N 120 57W
Céret, France 28 F6 42 30N 2 42 E
Cereté, Colombia 168 B2 8 53N 75 48W
Cerf, Seychelles 121 b 4 38 S 55 40 E
Cergy, France 27 C9 49 2N 2 4 E
Cerignola, Italy 47 A8 41 17N 15 53 E
Cerigo = Kíthira, Greece 48 E5 36 8N 23 0 E
Cérilly, France 27 F9 46 37N 2 50 E
Cerisiers, France 27 D10 48 8N 3 30 E
Cerizay, France 26 F6 46 50N 0 40W
Çerkeş, Turkey 100 B5 40 49N 32 52 E
Çerkezköy, Turkey 51 E12 41 17N 28 0 E
Cerknica, Slovenia 45 C11 45 48N 14 21 E
Cerkovica, Bulgaria 51 C8 43 41N 24 50 E
Cermerno, Serbia & M. 50 C4 43 35N 20 25 E
Çermik, Turkey 101 C8 38 8N 39 26 E
Cerna, Romania 53 E13 45 4N 28 17 E
Cerna →, Romania 53 F8 44 38N 23 58 E
Cernauti = Chernivtsi, Ukraine 53 B10 48 15N 25 52 E
Cernavodă, Romania 53 F13 44 22N 28 3 E
Cernay, France 27 E14 47 44N 7 10 E
Černik, Croatia 52 E2 45 17N 17 22 E
Cerralvo, I., Mexico 162 C3 24 20N 109 45W
Cërrik, Albania 50 E3 41 2N 19 58 E
Cerritos, Mexico 162 C4 22 27N 100 20W
Cerro Chato, Uruguay 175 C4 33 6 S 55 8W
Cerro Corá △, Paraguay 175 A4 22 35 S 56 2W
Cerro el Copey △, Venezuela 165 D7 10 59N 63 53W
Cerro Gordo, U.S.A. 157 E8 39 53N 88 44W
Cerro Hoya △, Panama 164 E3 7 17N 80 45W
Cerro Saroche △, Venezuela 165 D6 10 8N 69 38W
Cerro Sombrero, Chile 176 D3 52 45 S 69 15W
Certaldo, Italy 44 E8 43 33N 11 2 E
Cervantes, Phil. 80 C3 17 0N 120 44 E
Cervaro →, Italy 47 A8 41 30N 15 52 E
Cervati, Monte, Italy 47 B8 40 17N 15 29 E
Cervera, Spain 40 D6 41 40N 1 16 E
Cervera de Pisuerga, Spain 42 C6 42 51N 4 30W
Cervera del Río Alhama, Spain 40 C3 42 2N 1 58W
Cervéteri, Italy 45 F9 42 0N 12 6 E
Cérvia, Italy 45 D9 44 15N 12 22 E
Cervignano del Friuli, Italy 45 C10 45 49N 13 20 E
Cervinara, Italy 47 A7 41 1N 14 37 E
Cervione, France 29 F13 42 20N 9 29 E
Cervo, Spain 42 B3 43 40N 7 24W
César □, Colombia 168 B3 9 0N 73 30W
Cesarò, Italy 47 E7 37 50N 14 38 E
Cesena, Italy 45 D9 44 8N 12 15 E
Cesenático, Italy 45 D9 44 12N 12 24 E
Cēsis, Latvia 15 H21 57 18N 25 15 E
Česká Lípa, Czech Rep. 34 A7 50 45N 14 30 E
Česká Rep. = Czech Rep. ■, Europe 34 B8 50 0N 15 0 E
Česká Třebová, Czech Rep. 35 B9 49 54N 16 27 E
České Budějovice, Czech Rep. 34 C7 48 55N 14 25 E
České Velenice, Czech Rep. 34 C7 48 45N 14 57 E
Českobudějovický □, Czech Rep. 34 B7 49 10N 14 30 E
Českomoravská Vrchovina, Czech Rep. 34 B8 49 30N 15 40 E
Český Brod, Czech Rep. 34 A7 50 4N 14 52 E
Český Krumlov, Czech Rep. 34 C7 48 43N 14 21 E
Český Těšín, Czech Rep. 35 B11 49 45N 18 39 E
Česma →, Croatia 45 C13 45 35N 16 29 E
Çeşme, Turkey 49 C8 38 20N 26 23 E
Cessnock, Australia 129 B9 32 50 S 151 21 E
Cesson-Sévigné, France 26 D5 48 7N 1 36W
Cestas, France 28 D3 44 44N 0 41W
Cestos →, Liberia 112 D3 5 40N 9 10W
Cestos Sehnkwehn △, Liberia 112 D3 5 40N 9 10W
Cetate, Romania 52 F8 44 7N 23 2 E
Cetatea-Albă = Bilhorod-Dnistrovskyy, Ukraine 59 J6 46 11N 30 23 E
Cetin Grad, Croatia 45 C12 45 9N 15 45 E
Cetina →, Croatia 45 E13 43 26N 16 42 E
Cetinje, Serbia & M. 50 D2 42 23N 18 59 E
Cetraro, Italy 47 C8 39 31N 15 55 E
Ceuta, N. Afr. 110 A3 35 52N 5 18W
Ceva, Italy 44 D5 44 23N 8 2 E
Ceve-i-Ra, Fiji 123 E13 21 46 S 174 31 E
Cévennes, France 28 D7 44 10N 3 50 E
Cévennes △, France 28 D7 44 15N 3 45 E
Cevio, Switz. 33 D7 46 19N 8 36 E
Ceyhan, Turkey 100 D6 37 4N 35 47 E
Ceyhan →, Turkey 100 D6 36 38N 35 40 E
Ceylânpınar, Turkey 101 D9 36 50N 40 2 E
Ceylon = Sri Lanka ■, Asia 95 L5 7 30N 80 50 E
Cèze →, France 29 D8 44 6N 4 43 E
Cha-am, Thailand 86 F2 12 48N 99 58 E
Cha Pa, Vietnam 86 A4 22 20N 103 47 E
Chá Pungana, Angola 115 E3 13 44 S 18 39 E
Chabanais, France 28 C4 45 52N 0 48 E
Chabeuil, France 29 D9 44 54N 5 3 E
Chablais, France 27 F13 46 20N 6 36 E
Chablis, France 27 E10 47 47N 3 48 E
Chabounia, Algeria 111 A5 35 30N 2 38 E
Chacabuco, Argentina 174 C3 34 40 S 60 27W
Chachapoyas, Peru 172 B2 6 15 S 77 50W
Chachasp, Peru 172 D3 15 30 S 72 15W
Chachoengsao, Thailand 86 F3 13 42N 101 5 E
Chachro, Pakistan 92 G4 25 5N 70 15 E
Chaco △, Argentina 174 B4 27 0 S 59 30W
Chaco □, Argentina 174 B3 26 30 S 61 0W
Chaco □, Paraguay 174 B4 26 0 S 60 0W
Chaco →, U.S.A. 159 H9 36 46N 108 39W
Chaco Culture △, U.S.A. 159 H10 36 3N 107 58W
Chacon, C., U.S.A. 142 C2 54 42N 132 0W
Chad = Oktyabrskiy, Russia 64 C6 56 31N 57 12 E
Chad ■, Africa 109 F3 15 0N 17 15 E
Chad, L. = Tchad, L., Chad 109 F2 13 30N 14 30 E
Chadan, Russia 67 D10 51 17N 91 35 E
Chadileuvú →, Argentina 174 D2 37 46 S 66 0W
Chadiza, Zambia 119 E3 14 45 S 32 27 E
Chadron, U.S.A. 154 D3 42 50N 103 0W
Chadyr-Lunga = Ciadâr-Lunga, Moldova 53 D13 46 3N 28 51 E
Chae Hom, Thailand 86 C2 18 43N 99 35 E
Chae Son △, Thailand 86 C2 18 42N 99 20 E
Chaek, Kyrgyzstan 65 C7 41 55N 74 30 E
Chaem →, Thailand 86 C2 18 11N 98 38 E
Chaeryŏng, N. Korea 75 E13 38 24N 125 36 E
Chagai Hills = Chāh Gay Hills, Afghan. 91 C1 29 30N 64 0 E
Chagda, Russia 67 D14 58 45N 130 38 E
Chaghcharān, Afghan. 91 B2 34 31N 65 15 E
Chagny, France 27 F11 46 57N 4 45 E
Chagoda, Russia 58 C8 59 10N 35 15 E
Chagos Arch. ∅, Ind. Oc. 121 E6 6 0 S 72 0 E
Chagres △, Panama 164 E4 9 33N 79 37W
Chagrin Falls, U.S.A. 150 E3 41 26N 81 24W
Chaguanas, Trin. & Tob. 169 F9 10 30N 61 26W
Chāh Ākhvor, Iran 97 C8 32 41N 59 40 E
Chāh Bahar, Iran 97 E9 25 20N 60 40 E
Chāh-e Āb, Afghan. 65 E4 37 23N 69 48 E
Chāh-e Kavīr, Iran 97 C8 34 29N 56 52 E
Chāh Gay Hills, Afghan. 91 C1 29 30N 64 0 E
Chahār Borjak, Afghan. 91 C1 30 17N 62 3 E
Chahār Mahāll va Bakhtīarī □, Iran 97 C6 32 0N 49 0 E
Chahtung, Burma 90 B7 26 41N 98 10 E
Chai Wan, China 69 G11 22 16N 114 14 E
Chaillé-les-Marais, France 28 B2 46 25N 1 2W
Chainat, Thailand 86 E3 15 11N 100 8 E
Chaires, U.S.A. 152 E5 30 26N 84 7W
Chaitén, Chile 176 B2 42 55 S 72 43W
Chaiya, Thailand 87 H2 9 23N 99 14 E
Chaiyaphum, Thailand 86 E4 15 48N 102 2 E
Chaj Doab, Pakistan 92 C5 32 15N 73 0 E
Chajari, Argentina 174 C4 30 42 S 58 0W
Chak Amru, Pakistan 92 C6 32 22N 75 11 E
Chaka, Sudan 107 G3 4 49N 31 14 E
Chakar →, Pakistan 92 E3 29 29N 68 2 E
Chakari, Zimbabwe 117 B4 18 5 S 29 51 E
Chakaria, Bangla. 90 E4 21 45N 92 5 E
Chakarnaba, Chad 109 F4 14 13N 20 51 E
Chake Chake, Tanzania 118 D4 5 15 S 39 45 E
Chakhānsūr, Afghan. 91 C1 31 10N 62 0 E
Chakonipau, L., Canada 141 A6 56 18N 68 30W
Chakradharpur, India 93 H11 22 45N 85 40 E
Chakrata, India 92 D7 30 42N 77 51 E
Chakwadam, Burma 90 B7 27 29N 98 31 E
Chakwal, Pakistan 91 B4 32 56N 72 53 E
Chala, Peru 172 D3 15 48 S 74 20W
Chalais, France 28 C4 45 16N 0 3 E
Chalakudi, India 95 J3 10 18N 76 20 E
Chalchihuites, Mexico 162 C4 23 29N 103 53W
Chalcis = Khalkís, Greece 48 C5 38 27N 23 42 E
Châlette-sur-Loing, France 27 D9 48 1N 2 44 E

Chaleur B., *Canada* 141 C6 47 55N 65 30W
Chalfant, *U.S.A.* 160 H8 37 32N 118 21W
Chalhuanca, *Peru* 172 C3 14 15 S 73 15W
Chalindrey, *France* 27 E12 47 43N 5 26 E
Chaling, *China* 77 D9 26 58N 113 30 E
Chalisgaon, *India* 94 D2 20 30N 75 10 E
Chalk River, *Canada* 140 C4 46 1N 77 27W
Chalkar = Shalkar, *Kazakhstan* 64 F3 50 40N 51 53 E
Chalkar, Ozero = Shalkar, Ozero, *Kazakhstan* 64 F3 50 35N 51 47 E
Chalky Inlet, *N.Z.* 131 G1 46 3 S 166 31 E
Chalkyitsik, *U.S.A.* 144 C12 66 39N 143 43W
Challakere, *India* 95 G3 14 19N 76 39 E
Challans, *France* 26 F5 46 50N 1 52W
Challapata, *Bolivia* 172 D4 18 53 S 66 50W
Challenger Deep, *Pac. Oc.* 134 F6 11 30N 142 0 E
Challenger Fracture Zone, *Pac. Oc.* 135 L17 35 0 S 105 0W
Challis, *U.S.A.* 158 D6 44 30N 114 14W
Chalmette, *U.S.A.* 155 L10 29 56N 89 58W
Chalon-sur-Saône, *France* 27 F11 46 48N 4 50 E
Chalonnes-sur-Loire, *France* 26 E6 47 20N 0 45W
Châlons-en-Champagne, *France* 27 D11 48 58N 4 20 E
Châlus, *France* 28 C4 45 39N 0 58 E
Châlūs, *Iran* 97 B6 36 38N 51 26 E
Cham, *Germany* 31 F8 49 13N 12 39 E
Cham, *Switz.* 33 B6 47 11N 8 28 E
Cham, Cu Lao, *Vietnam* 86 E7 15 57N 108 30 E
Chama, *U.S.A.* 159 H10 36 54N 106 35W
Chamah, Gunong, *Malaysia* 84 A2 5 13N 101 35 E
Chamaicó, *Argentina* 174 D3 35 3 S 64 58W
Chaman, *Pakistan* 91 C2 30 58N 66 25 E
Chamba, *India* 92 C7 32 35N 76 10 E
Chamba, *Tanzania* 119 E4 11 37 S 37 0 E
Chambal →, *India* 93 F8 26 29N 79 15 E
Chamberlain, *U.S.A.* 154 D5 43 49N 99 20W
Chamberlain →, *Australia* 124 C4 15 30 S 127 54 E
Chamberlain L., *U.S.A.* 149 B11 46 14N 69 19W
Chambers, *U.S.A.* 159 J9 35 11N 109 26W
Chambersburg, *U.S.A.* 148 F7 39 56N 77 40W
Chambéry, *France* 29 C9 45 34N 5 55 E
Chamblee, *U.S.A.* 152 B5 33 53N 84 18W
Chambly, *Canada* 151 A11 45 27N 73 17W
Chambord, *Canada* 141 C5 48 25N 72 6W
Chamboulive, *France* 28 C5 45 26N 1 42 E
Chambri L., *Papua N. G.* 132 C2 4 15 S 143 10 E
Chamchamal, *Iraq* 101 E11 35 32N 44 50 E
Chamela, *Mexico* 162 D3 19 32N 105 5W
Chamical, *Argentina* 174 C2 30 22 S 66 27W
Chamkar Luong, *Cambodia* 87 G4 11 0N 103 45 E
Chamois, *U.S.A.* 156 F5 38 41N 91 46W
Chamoli, *India* 93 D8 30 24N 79 21 E
Chamonix-Mont Blanc, *France* 29 C10 45 55N 6 51 E
Chamoson, *Switz.* 32 D4 46 12N 7 13 E
Champa, *India* 93 H10 22 2N 82 43 E
Champagne, *Canada* 142 A1 60 49N 136 30W
Champagne, *France* 27 D11 48 40N 4 20 E
Champagnole, *France* 27 F12 46 45N 5 55 E
Champaign, *U.S.A.* 157 D8 40 7N 88 15W
Champassak, *Laos* 86 E5 14 53N 105 52 E
Champaubert, *France* 27 D10 48 50N 3 45 E
Champawat, *India* 93 E9 29 20N 80 6 E
Champdeniers-St-Denis, *France* 28 B3 46 29N 0 25W
Champdoré, L., *Canada* 141 A6 55 55N 65 49W
Champeix, *France* 28 C7 45 37N 3 8 E
Champéry, *Switz.* 32 D3 46 11N 6 52 E
Champion, *U.S.A.* 150 E4 41 19N 80 51W
Champlain, *U.S.A.* 151 B11 44 59N 73 27W
Champlain, L., *U.S.A.* 151 B11 44 40N 73 20W
Champlitte, *France* 27 E12 47 32N 5 31 E
Champotón, *Mexico* 163 D6 19 20N 90 50W
Champua, *India* 93 H11 22 5N 85 40 E
Chamrajnagar, *India* 95 J3 11 52N 76 52 E
Chamusca, *Portugal* 43 F2 39 21N 8 29W
Chan Chan, *Peru* 172 B2 8 7 S 79 0W
Chana, *Thailand* 87 J3 6 55N 100 44 E
Chañaral, *Chile* 174 B1 26 23 S 70 40W
Chanārān, *Iran* 97 B8 36 39N 59 6 E
Chanasma, *India* 92 H5 23 44N 72 5 E
Chancay, *Peru* 172 C2 11 32 S 77 25W
Chancery Lane, *Barbados* 165 g 13 3N 59 30W
Chanchiang = Zhanjiang, *China* 77 G8 21 15N 110 20 E
Chanco, *Chile* 174 D1 35 44 S 72 32W
Chancy, *Switz.* 32 D1 46 8N 5 58 E
Chand, *India* 93 J8 21 57N 79 7 E
Chandalar →, *U.S.A.* 144 C11 66 37N 146 0W
Chandan, *India* 93 G12 24 38N 86 40 E
Chandan Chauki, *India* 93 E9 28 33N 80 47 E
Chandannagar, *India* 93 H13 22 52N 88 24 E
Chandausi, *India* 93 E8 28 27N 78 49 E
Chandeleur Is., *U.S.A.* 155 L10 29 55N 88 57W
Chandeleur Sd., *U.S.A.* 155 L10 29 55N 89 0W
Chandigarh, *India* 92 D7 30 43N 76 47 E
Chandil, *India* 93 H12 22 58N 86 3 E
Chandler, *Australia* 127 D1 27 0 S 133 19 E
Chandler, *Canada* 141 C7 48 18N 64 46W
Chandler, *Ariz., U.S.A.* 159 K8 33 18N 111 50W
Chandler, *Okla., U.S.A.* 155 H6 35 42N 96 53W
Chandless →, *Brazil* 172 B4 9 8 S 69 51W
Chandod, *India* 92 J5 21 59N 73 28 E
Chandpur, *Bangla.* 90 D3 23 8N 90 45 E
Chandragiri, *India* 95 H4 13 35N 79 19 E
Chandrapur, *India* 94 E4 19 57N 79 25 E
Chandrupatla, *India* 94 F5 18 33N 80 24 E
Chānf, *Iran* 97 E9 26 38N 60 29 E
Chang, *Pakistan* 92 F3 26 59N 68 30 E
Chang, Ko, *Thailand* 87 F4 12 0N 102 23 E
Ch'ang Chiang = Chang Jiang →, *China* 77 B13 31 48N 121 10 E
Chang Jiang →, *China* 77 B13 31 48N 121 10 E
Changa, *India* 93 C7 33 53N 77 35 E
Chang'an = Xi'an, *China* 74 G5 34 15N 109 0 E
Changan, *China* 69 F10 22 48N 113 48 E
Changanacheri, *India* 95 K3 9 25N 76 31 E
Changane →, *Mozam.* 117 C5 24 30 S 33 30 E
Changbai, *China* 75 D15 41 25N 128 5 E
Changbai Shan, *China* 75 C15 42 20N 129 0 E
Changchiak'ou = Zhangjiakou, *China* 74 D8 40 48N 114 55 E
Changchih = Changzhi, *China* 74 F7 36 10N 113 6 E
Ch'angchou = Changzhou, *China* 77 B12 31 47N 119 58 E
Changchow = Changzhou, *China* 77 B12 31 47N 119 58 E
Changchun, *China* 75 C13 43 57N 125 17 E
Changchunling, *China* 75 B13 45 18N 125 27 E
Changde, *China* 77 C8 29 4N 111 35 E
Changdo-ri, *N. Korea* 75 E14 38 30N 127 40 E
Changfeng, *China* 77 A11 32 28N 117 10 E
Changhai = Shanghai, *China* 77 B13 31 15N 121 26 E
Changhua, *China* 77 B12 30 12N 119 12 E
Changhua, *Taiwan* 77 E13 24 2N 120 30 E
Changhŭng, *S. Korea* 75 G14 34 41N 126 52 E
Changhŭngni, *N. Korea* 75 D15 40 24N 128 19 E
Changi, *Malaysia* 84 B2 1 23N 103 59 E
Changi, *Singapore* 87 d 1 23N 103 59 E
Changi, Singapore ✕ (SIN), *Singapore* 87 M4 1 23N 103 59 E
Changjiang, *China* 86 C7 19 20N 108 55 E
Changjiang Shuiku, *China* 69 G10 22 29N 113 27 E
Changjin, *N. Korea* 75 D14 40 23N 127 15 E
Changjin-chŏsuji, *N. Korea* 75 D14 40 30N 127 15 E
Changle, *China* 77 E12 25 59N 119 27 E
Changli, *China* 75 E10 39 40N 119 13 E
Changling, *China* 75 B12 44 20N 123 58 E
Changlun, *Malaysia* 87 J3 6 25N 100 26 E
Changning, *Hunan, China* 77 D9 26 28N 112 22 E
Changning, *Sichuan, China* 76 C5 28 40N 104 56 E
Changning, *Yunnan, China* 76 E2 24 45N 99 30 E
Changping, *China* 74 D9 40 14N 116 12 E
Changsha, *China* 77 C9 28 12N 113 0 E
Changshan, *China* 77 C12 28 55N 118 27 E
Changshu, *China* 77 B13 31 38N 120 43 E
Changshun, *China* 76 D6 26 3N 106 25 E
Changtai, *China* 77 E11 24 35N 117 42 E
Changt'e = Chongde, *China* 77 B13 30 32N 120 26 E
Changting, *China* 77 E11 25 50N 116 22 E
Changwu, *China* 74 G4 35 10N 107 45 E
Changxing, *China* 77 B12 31 0N 119 55 E
Changyang, *China* 77 B8 30 30N 111 10 E
Changyi, *China* 75 F10 36 40N 119 30 E
Changyŏn, *N. Korea* 75 E13 38 15N 125 6 E
Changyuan, *China* 74 G8 35 15N 114 42 E
Changzhi, *China* 74 F7 36 10N 113 6 E
Changzhou, *China* 77 B12 31 47N 119 58 E
Chanhanga, *Angola* 116 B1 16 0 S 14 8 E
Chania = Khaniá, *Greece* 39 E5 35 30N 24 4 E
Chanlar = Xanlar, *Azerbaijan* 61 K8 40 37N 46 12 E
Channagiri, *India* 95 G2 14 2N 75 56 E
Channapatna, *India* 95 H3 12 40N 77 15 E
Channel Is., *U.K.* 21 H5 49 19N 2 24W
Channel Is., *U.S.A.* 161 M7 33 40N 119 15W
Channel Islands △, *U.S.A.* 161 L7 34 0N 119 24W
Channel-Port aux Basques, *Canada* 141 C8 47 30N 59 9W
Channel Tunnel, *Europe* 21 F9 51 0N 1 30 E
Channing, *U.S.A.* 155 H3 35 41N 102 20W
Chantada, *Spain* 42 C3 42 36N 7 46W
Chanthaburi, *Thailand* 86 F4 12 38N 102 12 E
Chantilly, *France* 27 C9 49 12N 2 29 E
Chantonnay, *France* 26 F5 46 40N 1 3W
Chantrey Inlet, *Canada* 138 B10 67 48N 96 20W
Chanumla, *India* 95 K11 8 19N 93 5 E
Chanute, *U.S.A.* 155 G7 37 41N 95 27W
Chanza →, *Spain* 43 H3 37 32N 7 30W
Chao Hu, *China* 77 B11 31 30N 117 30 E
Chao Phraya →, *Thailand* 86 F3 13 32N 100 36 E
Chao Phraya Lowlands, *Thailand* 86 E3 15 30N 100 0 E
Chaocheng, *China* 74 F8 36 4N 115 37 E
Chaohu, *China* 77 B11 31 38N 117 50 E
Chaoyang, *Guangdong, China* 77 F11 23 17N 116 30 E
Chaoyang, *Liaoning, China* 75 D11 41 35N 120 22 E
Chaozhou, *China* 77 F11 23 42N 116 32 E
Chapada Diamantina △, *Brazil* 171 D3 12 52 S 41 30W
Chapada dos Guimarães, *Brazil* 173 D6 15 26 S 55 45W
Chapada dos Guimarães △, *Brazil* 173 D6 15 18 S 55 54W
Chapada dos Veadeiros △, *Brazil* 171 D2 14 0 S 47 30W
Chapais, *Canada* 140 C5 49 47N 74 51W
Chapala, *Mozam.* 119 F4 15 50 S 37 35 E
Chapala, L. de, *Mexico* 162 C4 20 10N 103 20W
Chaparé →, *Bolivia* 173 D5 15 58 S 64 42W
Chaparmukh, *India* 90 B4 26 12N 92 31 E
Chaparral, *Colombia* 168 C2 3 43N 75 28W
Chapayev, *Kazakhstan* 60 E10 50 25N 51 10 E
Chapayevsk, *Russia* 60 D9 53 0N 49 40 E
Chapecó, *Brazil* 175 B5 27 14 S 52 41W
Chapel Hill, *U.S.A.* 149 H6 35 55N 79 4W
Chapetsk →, *Russia* 64 B3 58 36N 50 4 E
Chapin = Edinburg, *U.S.A.* 155 M5 26 18N 98 10W
Chapin, *U.S.A.* 156 E6 39 46N 90 24W
Chapleau, *Canada* 140 C3 47 50N 83 24W
Chaplin, *Canada* 143 C7 50 28N 106 40W
Chaplin L., *Canada* 143 C7 50 22N 106 36W
Chaplino, *Ukraine* 59 H9 48 8N 36 15 E
Chaplygin, *Russia* 58 F11 53 15N 40 0 E
Chappell, *U.S.A.* 154 E3 41 6N 102 28W
Chappells, *U.S.A.* 152 A8 34 11N 81 52W
Chapra = Chhapra, *India* 93 G11 25 48N 84 44 E
Châr, *Mauritania* 110 D2 21 32N 12 45W
Chara, *Russia* 67 D12 56 54N 118 20 E
Charadai, *Argentina* 174 B4 27 35 S 59 55W
Charagua, *Bolivia* 173 D5 19 45 S 63 10W
Charalá, *Colombia* 168 B3 6 17N 73 10W
Charambirá, Punta, *Colombia* 168 C2 4 16N 77 32W
Charaña, *Bolivia* 172 D4 17 30 S 69 25W
Charantsavan, *Armenia* 61 K7 40 35N 44 41 E
Charanwala, *India* 92 F5 27 51N 72 10 E
Charapita, *Colombia* 168 D3 0 37 S 74 21W
Charata, *Argentina* 174 B3 27 13 S 61 14W
Charcas, *Mexico* 162 C4 23 10N 101 20W
Charcot I., *Antarctica* 7 C17 70 0 S 70 0W
Chard, *U.K.* 21 G5 50 52N 2 58W
Chardon, *U.S.A.* 150 E3 41 35N 81 12W
Charduar, *India* 90 B4 26 51N 92 46 E
Chardzhou = Chärjew, *Turkmenistan* 65 D1 39 6N 63 34 E
Charente □, *France* 28 C4 45 50N 0 16 E
Charente →, *France* 28 C2 45 57N 1 5W
Charente-Inférieure = Charente-Maritime □, *France* 28 C3 45 45N 0 45W
Charente-Maritime □, *France* 28 C3 45 45N 0 45W
Charenton-du-Cher, *France* 27 F9 46 44N 2 39 E
Chari →, *Chad* 109 F2 12 58N 14 31 E
Chārīkār, *Afghan.* 91 B3 35 0N 69 10 E
Charing, *U.S.A.* 152 C5 32 28N 84 22W
Chariton, *Iowa, U.S.A.* 154 E8 40 59N 93 20W
Chariton, *Iowa, U.S.A.* 156 C3 41 1N 93 19W
Chariton →, *U.S.A.* 156 E4 39 19N 92 58W
Charity, *Guyana* 169 B6 7 24N 58 36W
Chärjew, *Turkmenistan* 65 D1 39 6N 63 34 E
Charkhari, *India* 93 G8 25 24N 79 45 E
Charkhi Dadri, *India* 92 E7 28 37N 76 17 E
Charleroi, *Belgium* 24 D4 50 24N 4 27 E
Charleroi, *U.S.A.* 150 F5 40 9N 79 57W
Charles, C., *U.S.A.* 148 G8 37 7N 75 58W
Charles, I. = Santa María, I., *Ecuador* 172 a 1 17 S 90 26W
Charles City, *U.S.A.* 156 A4 43 4N 92 41W
Charles de Gaulle, Paris ✕ (CDG), *France* 27 D9 49 0N 2 32 E
Charles L., *Canada* 143 B6 59 50N 110 33W
Charles Sound, *N.Z.* 131 F2 45 2 S 167 4 E
Charles Town, *U.S.A.* 148 F7 39 17N 77 52W
Charlesbourg, *Canada* 148 B10 46 51N 71 16W
Charleston, *Ill., U.S.A.* 157 E8 39 30N 88 10W
Charleston, *Miss., U.S.A.* 155 H9 34 1N 90 4W
Charleston, *Mo., U.S.A.* 155 G10 36 55N 89 21W
Charleston, *S.C., U.S.A.* 152 C10 32 46N 79 56W
Charleston, *W. Va., U.S.A.* 148 F5 38 21N 81 38W
Charleston L., *Canada* 151 B9 44 32N 76 0W
Charleston Peak, *U.S.A.* 161 J11 36 16N 115 42W
Charlestown, *Ireland* 23 C3 53 58N 8 48W
Charlestown, *S. Africa* 117 D4 27 26 S 29 53 E
Charlestown, *Ind., U.S.A.* 157 F11 38 27N 85 40W
Charlestown, *N.H., U.S.A.* 151 C12 43 14N 72 25W
Charlestown of Aberlour, *U.K.* 22 D5 57 28N 3 14W
Charleville = Rath Luirc, *Ireland* 23 D3 52 21N 8 40W
Charleville, *Australia* 127 D4 26 24 S 146 15 E
Charleville-Mézières, *France* 27 C11 49 44N 4 40 E
Charlevoix, *U.S.A.* 148 C3 45 19N 85 16W
Charlieu, *France* 27 F11 46 10N 4 10 E
Charlotte, *Mich., U.S.A.* 157 B12 42 34N 84 50W
Charlotte, *N.C., U.S.A.* 149 H5 35 13N 80 51W
Charlotte, *Vt., U.S.A.* 151 B11 44 19N 73 14W
Charlotte Amalie, *U.S. Virgin Is.* 165 e 18 21N 64 56W
Charlotte Harbor, *U.S.A.* 153 J7 26 50N 82 10W
Charlotte L., *Canada* 142 C3 52 12N 125 19W
Charlottenberg, *Sweden* 16 E6 59 54N 12 17 E
Charlottesville, *U.S.A.* 148 F6 38 2N 78 30W
Charlottetown, *Nfld. & L., Canada* 141 B8 52 46N 56 7W
Charlottetown, *P.E.I., Canada* 141 C7 46 14N 63 8W
Charlotteville, *Trin. & Tob.* 169 E10 11 20N 60 33W
Charlton, *Australia* 128 D5 36 16 S 143 24 E
Charlton I., *Canada* 140 B4 52 0N 79 20W
Charmes, *France* 27 D13 48 22N 6 17 E
Charmey, *Switz.* 32 C4 46 37N 7 10 E
Charny, *Canada* 141 C5 46 43N 71 15W
Charnyany, *Belarus* 55 G11 51 59N 24 12 E
Charolles, *France* 27 F11 46 27N 4 16 E
Chârost, *France* 27 F9 47 0N 2 7 E
Charouine, *Algeria* 111 C4 29 0N 0 15W
Charre, *Mozam.* 119 F4 17 13 S 35 10 E
Charroux, *France* 28 B4 46 9N 0 25 E
Charsadda, *Pakistan* 92 B4 34 7N 71 45 E
Charshanga, *Turkmenistan* 65 E3 37 30N 66 1 E
Charters Towers, *Australia* 126 C4 20 5 S 146 13 E
Chartres, *France* 26 D8 48 29N 1 30 E
Chartreuse ⌂, *France* 29 C9 45 22N 5 42 E
Charvakskoye Vdkhr., *Uzbekistan* 65 C5 41 35N 70 0 E
Chascomús, *Argentina* 174 D4 35 30 S 58 0W
Chasefu, *Zambia* 119 E3 11 55 S 33 8 E
Chashma Barrage, *Pakistan* 91 B3 32 27N 71 20 E
Chaslands Mistake, *N.Z.* 131 G4 46 38 S 169 22 E
Chasseneuil-sur-Bonnieure, *France* 28 C4 45 52N 0 29 E
Chasseron, *Switz.* 32 C3 46 52N 6 32 E
Chāt, *Iran* 97 B7 37 59N 55 16 E
Chatal Balkan = Udvoy Balkan, *Bulgaria* 51 D10 42 50N 26 50 E
Chatanika, *U.S.A.* 144 D11 65 7N 147 28W
Château-Arnoux-St-Auban, *France* 29 D10 44 6N 6 0 E
Château-Chinon, *France* 27 E10 47 4N 3 56 E
Château d'Oex, *Switz.* 32 D4 46 28N 7 8 E
Château-d'Olonne, *France* 28 B2 46 30N 1 44W
Château-du-Loir, *France* 26 E7 47 40N 0 25 E
Château-Gontier, *France* 26 E6 47 50N 0 48W
Château-la-Vallière, *France* 26 E7 47 30N 0 20 E
Château-Landon, *France* 27 D9 48 8N 2 40 E
Château-Renard, *France* 27 E9 47 56N 2 55 E
Château-Renault, *France* 26 E7 47 36N 0 56 E
Château-Salins, *France* 27 D13 48 50N 6 30 E
Château-Thierry, *France* 27 C10 49 3N 3 20 E
Châteaubourg, *France* 26 D5 48 7N 1 25W
Châteaubriant, *France* 26 E5 47 43N 1 23W
Châteaudun, *France* 26 D8 48 3N 1 20 E
Chateaugay, *U.S.A.* 151 B10 44 56N 74 5W
Châteaugiron, *France* 26 D5 48 3N 1 30W
Châteauguay, L., *Canada* 141 A5 56 26N 70 3W
Châteaulin, *France* 26 D2 48 11N 4 8W
Châteaumeillant, *France* 27 F9 46 35N 2 12 E
Châteauneuf-du-Faou, *France* 26 D3 48 11N 3 50W
Châteauneuf-sur-Charente, *France* 28 C3 45 36N 0 3W
Châteauneuf-sur-Cher, *France* 27 F9 46 52N 2 18 E
Châteauneuf-sur-Loire, *France* 27 E9 47 52N 2 13 E
Châteaurenard, *France* 29 E8 43 53N 4 51 E
Châteauroux, *France* 27 F8 46 50N 1 40 E
Châteauvillain, *France* 27 D11 48 2N 4 55 E
Châteaux, Pte. des, *Guadeloupe* 164 b 16 15N 61 10W
Châtel-St.-Denis, *Switz.* 32 C3 46 32N 6 54 E
Châtelaillon-Plage, *France* 28 B2 46 5N 1 5W
Châtelguyon, *France* 28 C7 45 55N 3 4 E
Châtellerault, *France* 26 F7 46 50N 0 30 E
Châtelus-Malvaleix, *France* 27 F9 46 18N 2 1 E
Chatham = Chatham-Kent, *Canada* 140 D3 42 24N 82 11W
Chatham = Miramichi, *Canada* 141 C6 47 2N 65 28W
Chatham, *U.K.* 21 F8 51 22N 0 32 E
Chatham, *Ill., U.S.A.* 156 E7 39 40N 89 42W
Chatham, *N.Y., U.S.A.* 151 D11 42 21N 73 36W
Chatham, I. = San Cristóbal, I., *Ecuador* 172 a 0 50 S 89 26W
Chatham, I., *Chile* 176 D2 50 40 S 74 25W
Chatham I., *N.Z.* 131 a 43 50 S 176 20W
Chatham Is., *Pac. Oc.* 130 a 44 0 S 176 40W
Chatham-Kent, *Canada* 140 D3 42 24N 82 11W
Châtillon, *Italy* 44 C4 45 45N 7 37 E
Châtillon-Coligny, *France* 27 E9 47 50N 2 51 E
Châtillon-en-Diois, *France* 29 D9 44 41N 5 29 E
Châtillon-sur-Indre, *France* 26 F8 46 59N 1 10 E
Châtillon-sur-Loire, *France* 27 E9 47 35N 2 44 E
Châtillon-sur-Seine, *France* 27 E11 47 50N 4 33 E
Chatkal →, *Uzbekistan* 65 C5 41 38N 70 1 E
Chatkal Kyrka Tooloru, *Kyrgyzstan* 65 C5 41 30N 70 45 E
Chatmohar, *Bangla.* 93 G13 24 15N 89 15 E
Chatra, *India* 93 G11 24 12N 84 56 E
Chatrapur, *India* 94 E7 19 22N 85 2 E
Chats, L. des, *Canada* 151 A8 45 30N 76 20W
Chatsu, *India* 92 F6 26 36N 75 57 E
Chatsworth, *Canada* 150 B4 44 27N 80 54W
Chatsworth, *U.S.A.* 157 D8 40 45N 88 18W
Chatsworth, *Zimbabwe* 119 F3 19 38 S 31 13 E
Chatta-Hantō, *Japan* 73 C8 34 45N 136 55 E
Chāttāgām = Chittagong, *Bangla.* 90 D3 22 19N 91 48 E
Chattahoochee, *U.S.A.* 152 E5 30 42N 84 51W
Chattahoochee →, *U.S.A.* 152 E5 30 54N 84 57W
Chattanooga, *U.S.A.* 149 H3 35 3N 85 19W
Chatteris, *U.K.* 21 E8 52 28N 0 2 E
Chaturat, *Thailand* 86 E3 15 40N 101 51 E
Chatyr-Köl, *Kyrgyzstan* 65 C7 40 40N 75 18 E
Chatyr-Tash, *Kyrgyzstan* 65 C8 40 55N 76 25 E
Chau Doc, *Vietnam* 87 G5 10 42N 105 7 E
Chaudes-Aigues, *France* 28 D7 44 51N 3 1 E
Chauffailles, *France* 27 F11 46 13N 4 20 E
Chauk, *Burma* 90 E5 20 53N 94 49 E
Chaukan Pass, *Burma* 90 B6 27 8N 97 10 E
Chaumont, *France* 27 D12 48 7N 5 8 E
Chaumont, *U.S.A.* 151 B8 44 4N 76 8W
Chaumont-en-Vexin, *France* 27 C8 49 16N 1 53 E
Chaumont-sur-Loire, *France* 26 E8 47 29N 1 11 E
Chaunay, *France* 28 B4 46 13N 0 9 E
Chaunskaya G., *Russia* 6 C16 69 0N 169 0 E
Chauny, *France* 27 C10 49 37N 3 12 E
Chaura, *India* 95 K11 8 27N 93 2 E
Chausey, Îs., *France* 26 D5 48 52N 1 49W
Chaussin, *France* 27 F12 46 59N 5 22 E
Chautauqua L., *U.S.A.* 150 D5 42 10N 79 24W
Chauvigny, *France* 26 F7 46 34N 0 39 E
Chauvin, *Canada* 143 C6 52 45N 110 10W
Chavakachcheri, *Sri Lanka* 95 K5 9 39N 80 9 E
Chavanges, *France* 27 D11 48 30N 4 35 E
Chavantina, *Brazil* 173 C7 14 40 S 52 21W
Chaves, *Brazil* 170 B2 0 15 S 49 55W
Chaves, *Portugal* 42 D3 41 45N 7 32W
Chavuma, *Zambia* 115 E4 13 4 S 22 40 E
Chawang, *Thailand* 87 H2 8 25N 99 30 E
Chayan = Shayan, *Kazakhstan* 65 B4 43 5N 69 25 E
Chaykovskiy, *Russia* 64 C5 56 47N 54 9 E
Chazelles-sur-Lyon, *France* 29 C8 45 39N 4 22 E
Chazuta, *Peru* 172 B2 6 30 S 76 0W
Chazy, *U.S.A.* 151 B11 44 53N 73 26W
Cheaha Mt., *U.S.A.* 152 B4 33 29N 85 49W
Cheb, *Czech Rep.* 34 A5 50 9N 12 28 E
Chebanse, *U.S.A.* 157 D9 41 0N 87 54W
Chebarkul, *Russia* 64 D8 55 0N 60 25 E
Cheboksarskoye Vdkhr., *Russia* 60 B8 56 13N 46 58 E
Cheboksary, *Russia* 60 B8 56 8N 47 12 E
Cheboygan, *U.S.A.* 148 C3 45 39N 84 29W
Chebsara, *Russia* 58 C10 59 10N 38 59 E
Chech, Erg, *Africa* 110 D4 25 0N 2 15W
Chechaouen, *Morocco* 110 A3 35 9N 5 15W
Chechelnyk, *Ukraine* 53 B14 48 13N 29 22 E
Chechen, Ostrov, *Russia* 61 H8 43 59N 47 40 E
Chechenia □, *Russia* 61 J7 43 30N 45 29 E
Checheno-Ingush Republic = Chechenia □, *Russia* 61 J7 43 30N 45 29 E
Chechnya = Chechenia □, *Russia* 61 J7 43 30N 45 29 E
Chech'ŏn, *S. Korea* 75 F15 37 8N 128 12 E
Chęciny, *Poland* 55 H7 50 46N 20 28 E
Checotah, *U.S.A.* 155 H7 35 28N 95 31W
Chedabucto B., *Canada* 141 C7 45 25N 61 8W
Cheduba I., *Burma* 90 F4 18 45N 93 40 E
Cheepie, *Australia* 127 D4 26 33 S 145 1 E
Chef-Boutonne, *France* 28 B3 46 7N 0 4W
Cheffadine, *Niger* 109 D2 19 57N 12 11 E
Chefoo = Yantai, *China* 75 F11 37 34N 121 22 E
Chefornak, *U.S.A.* 144 F6 60 13N 164 12W
Chegdomyn, *Russia* 67 D14 51 7N 133 1 E
Chegga, *Mauritania* 110 C3 25 27N 5 40W
Chegutu, *Zimbabwe* 119 F3 18 10 S 30 14 E
Chehalis, *U.S.A.* 160 D4 46 40N 122 58W
Chehalis →, *U.S.A.* 160 D3 46 57N 123 50W
Cheile Nerei-Beusnita △, *Romania* 52 F6 44 56N 21 52 E
Cheiron, Mt., *France* 29 E10 43 49N 6 58 E
Cheju do, *S. Korea* 75 H14 33 29N 126 34 E
Chekalin, *Russia* 58 E9 54 10N 36 10 E
Chekhov, *Russia* 54 D7 54 33N 20 43 E
Chekiang = Zhejiang □, *China* 77 C13 29 0N 120 0 E
Chel = Kuru, Bahr el →, *Sudan* 107 F2 8 10N 26 50 E
Chela, Sa. da, *Angola* 116 B1 16 20 S 13 20 E
Chelan, *U.S.A.* 158 C4 47 51N 120 1W
Chelan, L., *U.S.A.* 158 B3 48 11N 120 30W
Chelek, *Uzbekistan* 65 D3 39 55N 66 51 E
Cheleken, *Turkmenistan* 57 G9 39 34N 53 16 E
Cheleken Yarymadasy, *Turkmenistan* 97 B7 39 30N 53 15 E
Chelforó, *Argentina* 176 A3 39 0 S 66 33W
Chéliff, O. →, *Algeria* 111 A5 36 0N 0 8 E
Chelkar = Shalqar, *Kazakhstan* 66 E6 47 48N 59 39 E
Chelkar Tengiz, Solonchak, *Kazakhstan* 66 E7 48 5N 63 7 E
Chella, *Ethiopia* 107 F4 5 0N 37 26 E
Chellala Dahrania, *Algeria* 111 B5 33 2N 0 1 E
Chelles, *France* 27 D9 48 52N 2 33 E
Chełm, *Poland* 55 G10 51 8N 23 30 E
Chełmno, *Poland* 55 E5 53 20N 18 30 E
Chelmsford, *U.K.* 21 F8 51 44N 0 29 E
Chełmża, *Poland* 55 E5 53 10N 18 39 E
Chelny = Naberezhnyye Chelny, *Russia* 60 C11 55 42N 52 19 E
Chelsea, *Australia* 129 E6 38 5 S 145 8 E
Chelsea, *Mich., U.S.A.* 157 B12 42 19N 84 1W
Chelsea, *Vt., U.S.A.* 151 C12 43 59N 72 27W
Cheltenham, *U.K.* 21 F5 51 54N 2 4W
Chelva, *Spain* 40 F4 39 45N 1 0W
Chelyabinsk, *Russia* 64 D8 55 10N 61 24 E
Chelyakobi = Kopeysk, *Russia* 64 D8 55 7N 61 37 E
Chelyuskin, C. = Chelyuskin, Mys, *Russia* 67 B11 77 30N 103 0 E
Chelyuskin, Mys, *Russia* 67 B11 77 30N 103 0 E
Chemainus, *Canada* 160 B3 48 55N 123 42W
Chembar = Belinskiy, *Russia* 60 D6 53 0N 43 25 E
Chemillé, *France* 26 E6 47 14N 0 45W
Chemin Grenier, *Mauritius* 121 d 20 29 S 57 28 E
Chemnitz, *Germany* 30 E8 50 51N 12 54 E
Chemulpo = Inch'ŏn, *S. Korea* 75 F14 37 27N 126 40 E
Chemult, *U.S.A.* 158 E3 43 14N 121 47W
Chen, Gora, *Russia* 67 C15 65 16N 141 50 E
Chenab →, *Pakistan* 91 C3 30 23N 71 2 E
Chenachane, O. →, *Algeria* 110 C4 25 20N 3 20W
Chenango Forks, *U.S.A.* 151 D9 42 15N 75 51W
Chencha, *Ethiopia* 107 F4 6 15N 37 32 E
Chenchiang = Zhenjiang, *China* 77 A12 32 11N 119 26 E
Cheney, *U.S.A.* 158 C5 47 30N 117 35W
Cheng Xian, *China* 74 H3 33 43N 105 42 E
Chengalpattu, *India* 95 H4 12 42N 79 58 E
Chengbu, *China* 77 D8 26 18N 110 16 E
Chengcheng, *China* 74 G5 35 8N 109 56 E
Chengchou = Zhengzhou, *China* 74 G7 34 45N 113 34 E
Chengde, *China* 75 D9 40 59N 117 58 E
Chengdong Hu, *China* 77 A11 32 15N 116 20 E
Chengdu, *China* 76 B5 30 38N 104 2 E
Chengele, *India* 90 A6 28 47N 96 16 E
Chenggong, *China* 76 E4 24 52N 102 56 E
Chenggu, *China* 74 H4 33 10N 107 21 E
Chenghai, *China* 77 F11 23 30N 116 42 E
Chengjiang, *China* 76 E4 24 39N 103 0 E
Chengkou, *China* 76 B7 31 54N 108 31 E
Chengmai, *China* 86 C7 19 50N 109 58 E
Chengteh = Chengde, *China* 75 D9 40 59N 117 58 E
Ch'engtu = Chengdu, *China* 76 B5 30 38N 104 2 E
Chengwu, *China* 74 G8 34 58N 115 50 E
Chengxi Hu, *China* 77 A11 32 15N 116 10 E
Chengyang, *China* 75 F11 36 18N 120 21 E
Chenjiagang, *China* 75 G10 34 23N 119 47 E
Chenkaladi, *Sri Lanka* 95 L5 7 47N 81 35 E
Chenkán, *Mexico* 163 D6 19 8N 90 58W
Chennai, *India* 95 H5 13 8N 80 19 E
Chenoa, *U.S.A.* 157 D8 40 45N 88 43W
Chenôve, *France* 27 E12 47 16N 5 1 E
Chenxi, *China* 77 C8 28 2N 110 12 E
Chenzhou, *China* 77 E9 25 47N 113 1 E
Cheo Reo, *Vietnam* 78 B3 13 25N 108 28 E
Cheom Ksan, *Cambodia* 86 E5 14 13N 104 56 E
Chepelare, *Bulgaria* 51 E8 41 44N 24 40 E
Chepén, *Peru* 172 B2 7 15 S 79 23W
Chépénéhé, *Vanuatu* 133 K5 20 47 S 167 9 E
Chepes, *Argentina* 174 C2 31 20 S 66 35W
Chepo, *Panama* 164 E4 9 10N 79 6W
Chepstow, *U.K.* 21 F5 51 38N 2 41W
Cheptsa = Chapetsk →, *Russia* 64 B3 58 36N 50 4 E
Chequamegon B., *U.S.A.* 154 B9 46 40N 90 30W
Cher □, *France* 27 E9 47 10N 2 30 E
Cher →, *France* 26 E7 47 21N 0 29 E
Chéradi, *Italy* 47 B10 40 27N 17 10 E
Cheran, *India* 90 C3 25 45N 90 44 E
Cherasco, *Italy* 44 D4 44 39N 7 51 E
Cheraw, *U.S.A.* 149 H6 34 42N 79 53W
Cherbourg, *France* 26 C5 49 39N 1 40W
Cherchell, *Algeria* 111 A5 36 35N 2 12 E
Cherdakly, *Russia* 60 C9 54 25N 48 50 E
Cherdyn, *Russia* 64 A6 60 24N 56 29 E
Cheremkhovo, *Russia* 67 D11 53 8N 103 1 E
Cherepanovo, *Russia* 66 D9 54 15N 83 30 E
Cherepovets, *Russia* 58 C9 59 5N 37 55 E
Chergui, Chott ech, *Algeria* 111 B5 34 21N 0 25 E
Chergui, Zahrez, *Algeria* 111 B5 35 11N 3 31 E
Cherial, *India* 94 F4 17 55N 78 59 E
Cheribon = Cirebon, *Indonesia* 85 D3 6 45 S 108 32 E
Cherikov = Cherykaw, *Belarus* 58 F6 53 32N 31 20 E
Cheriyam I., *India* 95 J1 10 9N 73 40 E
Cherkasy, *Ukraine* 59 H7 49 27N 32 4 E
Cherkessk, *Russia* 61 H6 44 15N 42 5 E
Cherla, *India* 94 E5 18 5N 80 49 E
Cherlak, *Russia* 66 D8 54 15N 74 55 E
Chermoz, *Russia* 64 B6 58 46N 56 10 E
Chernak = Shornak, *Kazakhstan* 65 B4 43 24N 68 2 E
Chernaya, *Russia* 67 B9 70 30N 89 10 E
Chernaya Kholunitsa, *Russia* 64 B3 58 57N 51 39 E
Chernelytsya, *Ukraine* 53 B10 48 49N 25 26 E
Cherni, *Bulgaria* 50 D7 42 35N 23 18 E
Chernigov = Chernihiv, *Ukraine* 59 G6 51 28N 31 20 E
Chernihiv, *Ukraine* 59 G6 51 28N 31 20 E
Chernivetska □, *Ukraine* 53 B10 48 20N 26 0 E
Chernivtsi, *Ukraine* 53 B13 48 32N 28 9 E
Chernivtsi, *Ukraine* 53 B10 48 15N 25 52 E
Chernobyl = Chornobyl, *Ukraine* 59 G6 51 20N 30 15 E
Chernogorsk, *Russia* 67 D10 53 49N 91 18 E
Chernomorskoye = Chornomorske, *Ukraine* 59 K7 45 31N 32 40 E
Chernorechye = Dzerzhinsk, *Russia* 60 B6 56 14N 43 30 E
Chernovtsy = Chernivtsi, *Ukraine* 53 B10 48 15N 25 52 E
Chernushka, *Russia* 64 C6 56 29N 56 3 E
Chernyakhovsk, *Russia* 15 J19 54 36N 21 48 E
Chernyanka, *Russia* 59 G9 50 56N 37 49 E
Chernyayevo = Yangiyer, *Uzbekistan* 65 C4 40 16N 68 49 E
Chernysheyskiy, *Russia* 67 C12 63 0N 112 30 E
Chernyy Otrog, *Russia* 64 D6 51 53N 56 0 E
Chernyye Zemli, *Russia* 61 H8 46 10N 46 0 E

Cherokee, Iowa, U.S.A. **154 D7** 42 45N 95 33W
Cherokee, Okla., U.S.A. **155 G5** 36 45N 98 21W
Cherokee Village, U.S.A. **155 G9** 36 17N 91 30W
Cherokees, Grand Lake O' The, U.S.A. **155 G7** 36 28N 95 2W
Cherquenco, Chile **176 A2** 38 35S 72 0W
Cherrapunji, India **90 C3** 25 17N 91 47 E
Cherry Valley, Calif., U.S.A. **161 M10** 33 59N 116 57W
Cherry Valley, N.Y., U.S.A. **151 D10** 42 48N 74 45W
Cherryville, U.S.A. **156 G5** 37 51N 91 16W
Cherskiy, Russia **67 C17** 68 45N 161 18 E
Cherskogo Khrebet, Russia **67 C15** 65 0N 143 0 E
Chertkov = Chortkiv, Ukraine **59 H3** 49 2N 25 46 E
Chertkovo, Russia **59 H11** 49 25N 40 19 E
Cherven, Belarus **58 F5** 53 45N 28 28 E
Cherven-Bryag, Bulgaria **51 C8** 43 17N 24 7 E
Chervonoarmeyskoye = Volnansk, Ukraine **59 H8** 48 2N 35 29 E
Chervonoarmiyske, Ukraine **53 E13** 45 47N 28 44 E
Chervonohrad, Ukraine **59 G3** 50 25N 24 10 E
Cherwell →, U.K. **21 F6** 51 44N 1 14W
Cherykaw, Belarus **58 F6** 53 32N 31 20 E
Chesapeake, U.S.A. **148 G7** 36 50N 76 17W
Chesapeake B., U.S.A. **148 G7** 38 0N 76 10W
Cheshire □, U.K. **20 D5** 53 14N 2 30W
Cheshskaya Guba, Russia **56 A8** 67 20N 47 0 E
Cheshunt, U.K. **21 F7** 51 43N 0 1W
Chesil Beach, U.K. **21 G5** 50 37N 2 33W
Chesley, Canada **150 B3** 44 17N 81 5W
Chesnokovka = Novoaltaysk, Russia **66 D9** 53 30N 84 0 E
Cheste, Spain **41 F4** 39 30N 0 41W
Chester, U.K. **20 D5** 53 12N 2 53W
Chester, Calif., U.S.A. **158 F3** 40 19N 121 14W
Chester, Ga., U.S.A. **152 C6** 32 24N 83 9W
Chester, Ill., U.S.A. **155 G10** 37 55N 89 49W
Chester, Mont., U.S.A. **158 B8** 48 31N 110 58W
Chester, Pa., U.S.A. **148 F8** 39 51N 75 22W
Chester, S.C., U.S.A. **149 H5** 34 43N 81 12W
Chester, Vt., U.S.A. **151 C12** 43 16N 72 36W
Chester, W. Va., U.S.A. **150 F4** 40 37N 80 34W
Chester-le-Street, U.K. **20 C6** 54 51N 1 34W
Chesterfield, U.K. **20 D6** 53 15N 1 25W
Chesterfield, Is., N. Cal. **134 J7** 19 52S 158 15 E
Chesterfield Inlet, Canada **138 B10** 63 30N 90 45W
Chesterton Ra., Australia **127 D4** 25 30S 147 27 E
Chesterton Range △, Australia **127 D4** 26 16S 147 22 E
Chestertown, U.S.A. **151 C11** 43 40N 73 48W
Chesterville, Canada **151 A9** 45 6N 75 14W
Chestnut Ridge, U.S.A. **150 F5** 40 20N 79 10W
Chesuncook L., U.S.A. **149 C11** 46 0N 69 21W
Chetamale, India **95 J11** 10 43N 92 33 E
Chéticamp, Canada **141 C7** 46 37N 60 59W
Chetlat I., India **95 J1** 11 42N 72 42 E
Chetrosu, Moldova **53 B12** 48 5N 27 54 E
Chetumal, Mexico **163 D7** 18 30N 88 20W
Chetumal, B. de, Mexico **163 D7** 18 40N 88 10W
Chetwynd, Canada **142 B4** 55 45N 121 36W
Chevak, U.S.A. **144 F6** 61 32N 165 35W
Chevanceaux, France **28 C3** 45 18N 0 14W
Cheviot, U.S.A. **157 E12** 39 10N 84 37W
Cheviot, The, U.K. **20 B5** 55 29N 2 9W
Cheviot Hills, U.K. **20 B5** 55 20N 2 30W
Cheviot Ra., Australia **126 D3** 25 20S 143 45 E
Chew Bahir, Ethiopia **107 G4** 4 40N 36 50 E
Chewelah, U.S.A. **158 B5** 48 17N 117 43W
Chewore ⌓, Zimbabwe **119 F2** 16 0S 29 52 E
Cheyenne, Okla., U.S.A. **155 H5** 35 37N 99 40W
Cheyenne, Wyo., U.S.A. **154 E2** 41 8N 104 49W
Cheyenne →, U.S.A. **154 C4** 44 41N 101 18W
Cheyenne Wells, U.S.A. **154 F3** 38 49N 102 21W
Cheyne B., Australia **125 F2** 34 35S 118 50 E
Cheyur, India **95 H5** 12 21N 80 0 E
Chhabra, India **92 G7** 24 40N 76 54 E
Chhaktala, India **92 H6** 22 6N 74 11 E
Chhapra, India **93 G11** 25 48N 84 44 E
Chhata, India **92 F7** 27 42N 77 30 E
Chhatak, Bangla. **90 C3** 25 5N 91 37 E
Chhatarpur, Jharkhand, India **93 G11** 24 23N 84 11 E
Chhatarpur, Mad. P., India **93 G8** 24 55N 79 35 E
Chhati, India **94 D5** 20 47N 81 40 E
Chhattisgarh □, India **93 J10** 22 0N 82 0 E
Chhaygaon, India **90 B3** 26 3N 91 24 E
Chhep, Cambodia **86 F5** 13 45N 105 24 E
Chhindwara, Mad. P., India **93 H8** 23 3N 79 29 E
Chhindwara, Mad. P., India **93 H8** 22 2N 78 59 E
Chhinhdipada, India **94 D7** 21 6N 84 52 E
Chhlong, Cambodia **87 F5** 12 15N 105 58 E
Chhota Tawa →, India **92 H7** 22 14N 76 36 E
Chhoti Kali Sindh →, India **92 G6** 24 2N 75 31 E
Chhuikhadan, India **93 J9** 21 32N 80 59 E
Chhuk, Cambodia **87 G5** 10 46N 104 28 E
Chi →, Thailand **86 E5** 15 11N 104 43 E
Chiai, Taiwan **77 F13** 23 29N 120 25 E
Chiali, Taiwan **77 F13** 23 10N 120 11 E
Chiamussu = Jiamusi, China **69 B8** 46 40N 130 26 E
Chianciano Terme, Italy **45 E8** 43 2N 11 49 E
Chiang Dao, Thailand **86 C2** 19 22N 98 58 E
Chiang Kham, Thailand **86 C3** 19 32N 100 18 E
Chiang Khan, Thailand **86 D3** 17 52N 101 36 E
Chiang Khong, Thailand **76 G3** 20 17N 100 24 E
Chiang Mai, Thailand **86 C2** 18 47N 98 59 E
Chiang Rai, Thailand **76 H2** 19 52N 99 50 E
Chiang Saen, Thailand **76 G3** 20 16N 100 5 E
Chiange, Angola **115 F2** 15 35S 13 40 E
Chianti, Italy **45 E8** 43 32N 11 25 E
Chiapa →, Mexico **163 D6** 16 42N 93 0W
Chiapa de Corzo, Mexico **163 D6** 16 42N 93 0W
Chiapas □, Mexico **163 D6** 17 0N 92 45W
Chiaramonte Gulfi, Italy **47 E7** 37 2N 14 42 E
Chiaravalle, Italy **45 E10** 43 36N 13 19 E
Chiaravalle Centrale, Italy **47 D9** 38 41N 16 25 E
Chiari, Italy **44 C6** 45 32N 9 56 E
Chiasso, Switz. **33 E8** 45 50N 9 2 E
Chiatura, Georgia **61 J6** 42 15N 43 17 E
Chiautla, Mexico **163 D5** 18 18N 98 34W
Chiávari, Italy **44 D6** 44 19N 9 19 E
Chiavenna, Italy **44 B6** 46 19N 9 24 E
Chiba, Japan **73 B12** 35 30N 140 7 E
Chiba □, Japan **73 B12** 35 30N 140 20 E
Chibabava, Mozam. **117 C5** 20 17S 33 35 E
Chibango, Angola **115 E4** 13 38S 21 56 E
Chibemba, Cunene, Angola **115 F2** 15 48S 14 8 E
Chibemba, Huila, Angola **116 B2** 16 20S 15 20 E
Chibi, Zimbabwe **117 C5** 20 18S 30 25 E
Chibia, Angola **115 F2** 15 10S 13 42 E
Chibizovka = Zherdevka, Russia **60 E5** 51 56N 41 29 E
Chibougamau, Canada **140 C5** 49 56N 74 24W
Chibougamau, L., Canada **140 C5** 49 50N 74 20W
Chibuk, Nigeria **113 C7** 10 52N 12 50 E
Chibuto, Mozam. **117 C5** 24 40S 33 33 E
Chibyu = Ukhta, Russia **56 B9** 63 34N 53 41 E
Chic-Chocs, Mts., Canada **141 C6** 48 55N 66 0W
Chicacole = Srikakulam, India **94 E6** 18 14N 83 58 E
Chicago, U.S.A. **157 C9** 41 53N 87 38W
Chicago Heights, U.S.A. **157 C9** 41 30N 87 38W
Chicago O'Hare International ✕ (ORD), U.S.A. **157 C9** 41 59N 87 54W
Chicapa →, Dem. Rep. of the Congo **115 D4** 6 25S 20 48 E
Chicha, Chad **109 E3** 16 57N 18 34 E
Chichagof I., U.S.A. **144 H14** 57 30N 135 30W
Chichaoua, Morocco **110 B3** 31 32N 8 44W
Chichén-Itzá, Mexico **163 C7** 20 40N 88 36W
Chicheng, China **74 D8** 40 55N 115 55 E
Chichester, U.K. **21 G7** 50 50N 0 47W
Chichester Ra., Australia **124 D2** 22 12S 119 15 E
Chichibu, Japan **73 A11** 35 59N 139 10 E
Chichibu-Tama △, Japan **73 B10** 35 52N 138 42 E
Ch'ich'ihaerh = Qiqihar, China **67 E13** 47 26N 124 0 E
Chicholi, India **92 H8** 22 1N 77 40 E
Chickasaw ⌓, U.S.A. **155 H6** 34 26N 97 0W
Chickasha, U.S.A. **155 H6** 35 3N 97 58W
Chicken, U.S.A. **144 D12** 64 5N 141 56W
Chiclana de la Frontera, Spain **43 J4** 36 26N 6 9W
Chiclayo, Peru **172 B2** 6 42S 79 50W
Chico, U.S.A. **160 F5** 39 44N 121 50W
Chico →, Chubut, Argentina **176 B3** 44 0S 67 0W
Chico →, Santa Cruz, Argentina **176 C3** 50 0S 68 30W
Chicomba, Angola **115 E2** 14 10S 14 52 E
Chicomo, Mozam. **117 C5** 24 31S 34 6 E
Chicomostoc, Mexico **162 C4** 22 28N 102 49W
Chicontepec, Mexico **163 C5** 20 58N 98 10W
Chicopee, U.S.A. **151 D12** 42 9N 72 37W
Chicoutimi, Canada **141 C5** 48 28N 71 5W
Chicualacuala, Mozam. **117 C5** 22 6S 31 42 E
Chicuma, Angola **115 E2** 13 26S 14 50 E
Chidambaram, India **95 J4** 11 20N 79 45 E
Chidenguele, Mozam. **117 C5** 24 55S 34 11 E
Chidley, C., Canada **139 B13** 60 23N 64 26W
Chiducuane, Mozam. **117 C5** 24 35S 34 25 E
Chiede, Angola **116 B2** 17 15S 16 22 E
Chiefland, U.S.A. **153 F7** 29 29N 82 52W
Chiefs Pt., Canada **150 B3** 44 41N 81 18W
Chiem Hoa, Vietnam **86 A5** 22 12N 105 17 E
Chiemsee, Germany **31 H8** 47 53N 12 28 E
Chiengi, Zambia **119 D2** 8 45S 29 10 E
Chiengmai = Chiang Mai, Thailand **86 C2** 18 47N 98 59 E
Chiengo, Angola **115 E4** 13 20S 21 55 E
Chienti →, Italy **45 E10** 43 18N 13 45 E
Chieri, Italy **44 C4** 45 1N 7 49 E
Chiers →, France **27 C11** 49 39N 4 59 E
Chiesa in Valmalenco, Italy **44 B6** 46 16N 9 51 E
Chiese →, Italy **44 C7** 45 8N 10 25 E
Chieti, Italy **45 F11** 42 21N 14 10 E
Chifeng, China **75 C10** 42 18N 118 58 E
Chigasaki, Japan **73 B11** 35 19N 139 24 E
Chigirin, Ukraine **59 H7** 49 4N 32 38 E
Chignecto B., Canada **141 C7** 45 30N 64 40W
Chignik, U.S.A. **144 H8** 56 18N 158 24W
Chigorodó, Colombia **168 B2** 7 41N 76 42W
Chiguana, Bolivia **174 A2** 21 0S 67 58W
Chigwell, U.K. **21 F8** 51 37N 0 5 E
Chiha-ri, N. Korea **75 E14** 38 40N 126 30 E
Chihli, G. of = Bo Hai, China **75 E10** 39 0N 119 0 E
Chihsi = Jixi, China **75 B16** 45 20N 130 50 E
Chihuahua, Mexico **162 B3** 28 40N 106 3W
Chihuahua □, Mexico **162 B3** 28 40N 106 3W
Chiili = Shīeli, Kazakhstan **65 A3** 44 20N 66 15 E
Chik Bollapur, India **95 H3** 13 25N 77 45 E
Chikalda, India **94 D3** 21 24N 77 19 E
Chikhli, Ahmadabad, India **94 D1** 20 45N 73 4 E
Chikhli, Maharashtra, India **94 D3** 20 20N 76 18 E
Chikmagalur, India **95 H2** 13 15N 75 45 E
Chiknayakanhalli, India **95 H3** 13 26N 76 37 E
Chikodi, India **95 F2** 16 26N 74 38 E
Chikugo, Japan **72 D2** 33 14N 130 28 E
Chikuma-Gawa →, Japan **73 A10** 36 59N 138 35 E
Chikushino, Japan **72 D2** 33 30N 130 30 E
Chikwawa, Malawi **119 F3** 16 2S 34 50 E
Chila, Angola **115 E2** 12 3S 14 29 E
Chilac, Mexico **163 D5** 18 20N 97 24W
Chilam Chavki, Pakistan **93 B6** 35 5N 75 5 E
Chilanga, Zambia **119 F2** 15 33S 28 16 E
Chilapa, Mexico **163 D5** 17 40N 99 11W
Chilas, Pakistan **93 B6** 35 25N 74 5 E
Chilaw, Sri Lanka **95 L4** 7 30N 79 50 E
Chilcotin →, Canada **142 C4** 51 44N 122 23W
Childers, Australia **127 D5** 25 15S 152 17 E
Childersburg, U.S.A. **152 B3** 33 16N 86 21W
Childress, U.S.A. **155 H4** 34 25N 100 13W
Chile ■, S. Amer. **176 B2** 35 0S 72 0W
Chile Chico, Chile **176 C2** 46 33S 71 44W
Chile Rise, Pac. Oc. **135 L18** 38 0S 92 0W
Chilecito, Argentina **174 B2** 29 10S 67 30W
Chilesso, Angola **115 E3** 11 35S 16 34 E
Chilete, Peru **172 B2** 7 10S 78 50W
Chilhowee, U.S.A. **156 F3** 38 36N 93 51W
Chilia, Braţul →, Romania **53 E14** 45 14N 29 42 E
Chilik = Shelek, Kazakhstan **65 B9** 43 33N 78 17 E
Chililabombwe, Zambia **119 E2** 12 18S 27 43 E
Chilin = Jilin, China **75 C14** 43 44N 126 30 E
Chilka L., India **94 E7** 19 40N 85 25 E
Chilko →, Canada **142 C4** 52 0N 123 40W
Chilko L., Canada **142 C4** 51 20N 124 10W
Chillagoe, Australia **126 B3** 17 7S 144 33 E
Chillán, Chile **174 D1** 36 40S 72 10W
Chillicothe, Ill., U.S.A. **156 D7** 40 55N 89 29W
Chillicothe, Mo., U.S.A. **156 E3** 39 48N 93 33W
Chillicothe, Ohio, U.S.A. **148 F4** 39 20N 82 59W
Chilliwack, Canada **142 D4** 49 10N 121 54W
Chilo, India **92 F5** 27 25N 73 32 E
Chiloane, I., Mozam. **117 C5** 20 40S 34 55 E
Chiloé △, Chile **176 B2** 42 11S 73 59W
Chiloé, I. de, Chile **176 B2** 42 30S 73 50W
Chilonda, Angola **115 E3** 11 19S 16 12 E
Chilongo, Angola **115 E3** 13 55S 16 35 E
Chilpancingo, Mexico **163 D5** 17 30N 99 30W
Chiltern, Australia **129 D7** 36 10S 146 36 E
Chiltern Hills, U.K. **21 F7** 51 40N 0 53W
Chilton, U.S.A. **148 C1** 44 2N 88 10W
Chiluage, Angola **115 D4** 9 30S 21 50 E
Chilubi, Zambia **119 E2** 11 5S 29 58 E
Chilubula, Zambia **119 E3** 10 14S 30 51 E
Chilumba, Malawi **119 E3** 10 28S 34 12 E
Chilung, Taiwan **77 E13** 25 3N 121 45 E
Chilwa, L., Malawi **119 F4** 15 15S 35 40 E
Chimakela, Angola **115 F3** 15 24S 16 58 E
Chimakudi, India **90 C4** 25 47N 93 48 E
Chimaltitán, Mexico **162 C4** 21 46N 103 50W
Chimán, Panama **164 E4** 8 45N 78 40W
Chimanimani, Zimbabwe **117 B5** 19 48S 32 52 E
Chimanimani △, Zimbabwe **119 F3** 19 48S 33 0 E
Chimay, Belgium **24 D4** 50 3N 4 20 E
Chimayo, U.S.A. **159 H11** 36 0N 105 56W
Chimbay, Uzbekistan **66 E6** 42 57N 59 47 E
Chimborazo, Ecuador **168 D2** 1 29S 78 55W
Chimborazo □, Ecuador **168 D2** 1 0S 78 40W
Chimbote, Peru **172 B2** 9 0S 78 35W
Chimbu □, Papua N. G. **132 D3** 6 15S 144 50 E
Chimichagua, Colombia **168 B3** 9 15N 73 49W
Chimion, Uzbekistan **65 C5** 40 15N 71 32 E
Chimkent = Shymkent, Kazakhstan **65 B4** 42 18N 69 36 E
Chimoio, Mozam. **119 F3** 19 4S 33 30 E
Chimpembe, Zambia **119 D2** 9 31S 29 33 E
Chimur, India **94 D4** 20 30N 79 23 E
Chin □, Burma **90 D4** 22 0N 93 0 E
Chin Hills, Burma **90 D4** 22 30N 93 30 E
Chin Ling Shan = Qinling Shandi, China **74 H5** 33 50N 108 10 E
China, Mexico **163 B5** 25 40N 99 20W
China ■, Asia **69 C6** 30 0N 110 0 E
China, Great Plain of, Asia **62 F15** 35 0N 115 0 E
China Lake, U.S.A. **161 K9** 35 44N 117 37W
Chinacota, Colombia **168 B3** 7 37N 72 36W
Chinan = Jinan, China **74 F9** 36 38N 117 1 E
Chinandega, Nic. **164 D2** 12 35N 87 12W
Chinati Peak, U.S.A. **155 L2** 29 57N 104 29W
Chinaz, Uzbekistan **65 C4** 40 56N 68 46 E
Chincha Alta, Peru **172 C2** 13 25S 76 7W
Chinchaga →, Canada **142 B5** 58 53N 118 20W
Chincheros, Peru **172 C3** 13 30S 73 44W
Chinchilla, Australia **127 D5** 26 45S 150 38 E
Chinchilla de Monte Aragón, Spain **41 G3** 38 53N 1 40W
Chincholi, India **94 E3** 17 28N 77 26 E
Chinchorro, Banco, Mexico **163 D7** 18 35N 87 20W
Chinchou = Jinzhou, China **75 D11** 41 5N 121 3 E
Chinchoua, Gabon **114 B1** 0 1N 9 48 E
Chincoteague, U.S.A. **148 G8** 37 56N 75 23W
Chinde, Mozam. **119 F4** 18 35S 36 30 E
Chindo, S. Korea **75 G14** 34 28N 126 15 E
Chindwin →, Burma **90 E5** 21 26N 95 15 E
Chineni, India **93 C6** 33 2N 75 15 E
Chinga, Mozam. **119 F4** 15 13S 38 35 E
Chingaza △, Colombia **168 C3** 4 30N 73 40W
Chingirlau, Kazakhstan **64 F5** 51 7N 54 7 E
Chingola, Zambia **119 E2** 12 31S 27 53 E
Chingole, Malawi **119 E3** 13 4S 34 17 E
Chingoroi, Angola **115 E2** 13 37S 14 1 E
Ch'ingtao = Qingdao, China **75 F11** 36 5N 120 20 E
Chinguar, Angola **115 E3** 12 25S 16 45 E
Chinguetti, Mauritania **110 D2** 20 25N 12 24W
Chingune, Mozam. **117 C5** 20 33S 34 58 E
Chinhae, S. Korea **75 G15** 35 9N 128 47 E
Chinhanguanine, Mozam. **117 D5** 25 21S 32 30 E
Chinhoyi, Zimbabwe **119 F3** 17 20S 30 8 E
Chinhsien = Jinxian, China **77 C11** 28 26N 116 17 E
Chini, India **92 D8** 31 32N 78 15 E
Chiniot, Pakistan **91 C4** 31 45N 73 0 E
Chínipas, Mexico **162 B3** 27 22N 108 32W
Chinji, Pakistan **92 C5** 32 42N 72 22 E
Chinju, S. Korea **75 G15** 35 12N 128 2 E
Chinkai, Afghan. **91 C2** 31 57N 67 26 E
Chinkapook, Australia **128 C5** 35 11S 142 57 E
Chinkiang = Zhenjiang, China **77 A12** 32 11N 119 26 E
Chinko →, C.A.R. **114 B4** 4 50N 23 53 E
Chinle, U.S.A. **159 H9** 36 9N 109 33W
Chinmen, Taiwan **77 E13** 24 26N 118 19 E
Chinmen Tao, Taiwan **77 E12** 24 27N 118 23 E
Chinnamanur, India **95 K3** 9 50N 77 24 E
Chinnampo = Namp'o, N. Korea **75 E13** 38 52N 125 10 E
Chinnur, India **94 E4** 18 57N 79 49 E
Chino, Japan **73 B10** 35 59N 138 9 E
Chino, U.S.A. **161 L9** 34 1N 117 41W
Chino Valley, U.S.A. **159 J7** 34 45N 112 27W
Chinon, France **26 E7** 47 10N 0 15 E
Chinook, U.S.A. **158 B9** 48 35N 109 14W
Chinook Trough, Pac. Oc. **134 C10** 44 0N 175 0W
Chinoya, Zambia **115 E4** 13 55S 23 16 E
Chinsali, Zambia **119 E3** 10 30S 32 2 E
Chintalapudi, India **94 F5** 17 4N 80 59 E
Chintamani, India **95 H4** 13 26N 78 3 E
Chinwangtao = Qinhuangdao, China **75 E10** 39 56N 119 30 E
Chióggia, Italy **45 C9** 45 13N 12 17 E
Chíos = Khíos, Greece **49 C8** 38 27N 26 9 E
Chipata, Zambia **119 E3** 13 38S 32 28 E
Chiperceni, Moldova **53 C13** 47 31N 28 50 E
Chipindo, Angola **115 E3** 13 49S 15 48 E
Chipinge, Zimbabwe **119 G3** 20 13S 32 28 E
Chipinge ⌓, Zimbabwe **119 G3** 20 14S 33 0 E
Chipiona, Spain **43 J4** 36 44N 6 26W
Chipley, U.S.A. **152 E4** 30 47N 85 32W
Chiplun, India **94 F1** 17 31N 73 34 E
Chipman, Canada **141 C6** 46 6N 65 53W
Chipoka, Malawi **119 E3** 13 57S 34 28 E
Chippenham, U.K. **21 F5** 51 27N 2 6W
Chippewa →, U.S.A. **154 C8** 44 25N 92 5W
Chippewa Falls, U.S.A. **154 C9** 44 56N 91 24W
Chipping Norton, U.K. **21 F6** 51 56N 1 32W
Chiprovtsi, Bulgaria **50 C6** 43 24N 22 52 E
Chiputneticook Lakes, U.S.A. **149 C11** 45 35N 67 35W
Chiputo = Vila Vasco da Gama, Mozam. **119 E3** 14 54S 32 14 E
Chiquelequele, Angola **115 F3** 16 44S 19 5 E
Chiquián, Peru **172 C2** 10 10S 77 0W
Chiquibul △, Belize **164 C2** 16 49N 88 52W
Chiquimula, Guatemala **164 D2** 14 51N 89 37W
Chiquinquira, Colombia **168 B3** 5 37N 73 50W
Chiquitos, Llanos de, Bolivia **173 D5** 18 0S 61 30W
Chir →, Russia **61 F6** 48 30N 43 0 E
Chira →, Peru **168 D1** 4 54S 81 8W
Chirala, India **95 G5** 15 50N 80 26 E
Chiramba, Mozam. **119 F3** 16 55S 34 39 E
Chirawa, India **92 E6** 28 14N 75 42 E
Chirayinkil, India **95 K3** 8 41N 76 49 E
Chirchiq, Uzbekistan **65 C4** 41 29N 69 35 E
Chiredzi, Zimbabwe **117 C5** 21 0S 31 38 E
Chirfa, Niger **109 D2** 20 55N 12 22 E
Chirgua →, Venezuela **168 B4** 8 54N 67 58W
Chiribiquete △, Colombia **168 C3** 0 31N 72 50W
Chiricahua ⌓, U.S.A. **159 K9** 32 0N 109 20W
Chiricahua Peak, U.S.A. **159 L9** 31 51N 109 18W
Chiriquí, G. de, Panama **164 E3** 8 0N 82 10W
Chiriquí, L. de, Panama **164 E3** 9 10N 82 0W
Chirisa ⌓, Zimbabwe **119 F2** 17 53S 28 15 E
Chirivira Falls, Zimbabwe **119 G3** 21 10S 32 12 E
Chirnogi, Romania **53 F11** 44 7N 26 32 E
Chirpan, Bulgaria **51 D9** 42 10N 25 19 E
Chirripó Grande, Cerro, Costa Rica **164 E3** 9 29N 83 29W
Chirundu, Zimbabwe **117 B4** 16 3S 28 50 E
Chisamba, Zambia **119 E2** 14 55S 28 20 E
Chisasibi, Canada **140 B4** 53 50N 79 0W
Ch'ishan, Taiwan **77 F13** 22 44N 120 31 E
Chishmy, Russia **64 D5** 54 35N 55 23 E
Chisholm, Canada **142 C6** 54 55N 114 10W
Chisholm, U.S.A. **154 B8** 47 29N 92 53W
Chishtian Mandi, Pakistan **92 E5** 29 50N 72 55 E
Chishui, China **76 C5** 28 30N 105 42 E
Chishui He →, China **76 C5** 28 49N 105 50 E
Chisimaio, Somali Rep. **120 E2** 0 22S 42 32 E
Chisimba Falls, Zambia **119 E3** 10 12S 30 56 E
Chişinău, Moldova **53 C13** 47 2N 28 50 E
Chişinău ✕ (KIV), Moldova **53 C13** 47 3N 28 46 E
Chişineu Criş, Romania **52 D6** 46 32N 21 37 E
Chisone →, Italy **44 D4** 44 49N 7 25 E
Chisos Mts., U.S.A. **155 L3** 29 5N 103 15W
Chissengue, Angola **115 D4** 9 13S 20 34 E
Chissilo, Angola **115 E3** 13 48S 16 31 E
Chistochina, U.S.A. **144 E11** 62 34N 144 40W
Chistopol, Russia **60 C10** 55 25N 50 38 E
Chita, Colombia **168 B3** 6 11N 72 28W
Chita, Russia **67 D12** 52 0N 113 35 E
Chitado, Angola **115 F2** 17 10S 14 8 E
Chitaldrug = Chitradurga, India **95 G3** 14 14N 76 24 E
Chitanda →, Angola **115 F3** 16 1S 15 12 E
Chitapur, India **94 F3** 17 10N 77 5 E
Chitembo, Angola **115 E3** 13 30S 16 50 E
Chitina, U.S.A. **144 F11** 61 31N 144 26W
Chitipa, Malawi **119 D3** 9 41S 33 19 E
Chitose, Japan **70 C10** 42 49N 141 39 E
Chitradurga, India **95 G3** 14 14N 76 24 E
Chitrakot, India **94 E5** 19 10N 81 40 E
Chitral, Pakistan **91 B3** 35 50N 71 56 E
Chitravati →, India **95 G4** 14 45N 78 15 E
Chitré, Panama **164 E3** 7 59N 80 27W
Chittagong, Bangla. **90 D3** 22 19N 91 48 E
Chittagong □, Bangla. **90 C3** 24 5N 91 0 E
Chittaurgarh, India **92 G6** 24 52N 74 38 E
Chittoor, India **95 H4** 13 15N 79 5 E
Chittur, India **95 J3** 10 40N 76 45 E
Chitungwiza, Zimbabwe **119 F3** 18 0S 31 6 E
Chiumbe →, Dem. Rep. of the Congo **115 D4** 6 59S 21 12 E
Chiumbo, Angola **115 E3** 12 29S 16 8 E
Chiume, Angola **115 F4** 15 3S 21 14 E
Chiuro, Italy **33 D9** 46 10N 9 59 E
Chiusi, Italy **45 E8** 43 1N 11 57 E
Chiva, Spain **41 F4** 39 27N 0 41W
Chivacoa, Venezuela **168 A4** 10 10N 68 54W
Chivasso, Italy **44 C4** 45 11N 7 53 E
Chivay, Peru **172 D3** 15 40S 71 35W
Chivé, Bolivia **172 C4** 12 23S 68 35W
Chivhu, Zimbabwe **119 F3** 19 2S 30 52 E
Chivilcoy, Argentina **174 C4** 34 55S 60 0W
Chiwanda, Tanzania **119 E3** 11 23S 34 55 E
Chixi, China **77 G9** 22 0N 112 58 E
Chizarira, Zimbabwe **119 F2** 17 36S 27 45 E
Chizarira △, Zimbabwe **119 F2** 17 44S 27 52 E
Chizela, Zambia **115 E4** 13 8S 25 0 E
Chizera, Zambia **119 E2** 13 10S 25 0 E
Chizu, Japan **72 B6** 35 16N 134 14 E
Chkalov = Orenburg, Russia **64 F5** 51 45N 55 6 E
Chkolovsk, Russia **60 B6** 56 50N 43 10 E
Chloride, U.S.A. **161 K12** 35 25N 114 12W
Chlumec nad Cidlinou, Czech Rep. **34 A8** 50 9N 15 29 E
Chmielnik, Poland **55 H7** 50 37N 20 43 E
Cho Bo, Vietnam **76 G5** 20 46N 105 10 E
Cho-do, N. Korea **75 E13** 38 30N 124 40 E
Cho Phuoc Hai, Vietnam **87 G6** 10 26N 107 18 E
Choa Chu Kang, Singapore **87 d** 1 22N 103 41 E
Choba, Kenya **118 B4** 2 30N 38 5 E
Chobe △, Botswana **116 B4** 18 37S 24 23 E
Choch'iwŏn, S. Korea **75 F14** 36 37N 127 18 E
Chocianów, Poland **55 G2** 51 27N 15 55 E
Chociwel, Poland **54 E2** 53 29N 15 21 E
Chocó □, Colombia **168 B2** 6 0N 77 0W
Chocolate Mts., U.S.A. **161 M11** 33 15N 115 15W
Chocontá, Colombia **168 B3** 5 9N 73 41W
Choctawhatchee →, U.S.A. **152 E3** 30 25N 86 8W
Choctawhatchee B., U.S.A. **153 E3** 30 20N 86 20W
Chodavaram, Andhra Pradesh, India **94 F6** 17 50N 82 57 E
Chodavaram, Andhra Pradesh, India **94 F5** 17 27N 81 46 E
Chodecz, Poland **55 F6** 52 24N 19 2 E
Chodov, Czech Rep. **34 A5** 50 15N 12 45 E
Chodziez, Poland **55 F3** 52 58N 16 58 E
Choele Choel, Argentina **176 A3** 39 11S 65 40W
Chōfu, Japan **73 B11** 35 39N 139 33 E
Choiseul, St. Lucia **165 f** 13 47N 61 3W
Choiseul, Solomon Is. **133 L9** 7 0S 156 40 E
Choix, Mexico **162 B3** 26 40N 108 23W
Chojna, Poland **55 F1** 52 58N 14 25 E
Chojnice, Poland **54 E4** 53 42N 17 32 E
Chojnów, Poland **55 G2** 51 18N 15 58 E
Chok-Tal, Kyrgyzstan **65 B8** 42 35N 76 45 E
Chōkai-San, Japan **70 E10** 39 6N 140 3 E
Choke Canyon Res., U.S.A. **155 L5** 28 30N 98 20W
Choke Mts., Ethiopia **107 E4** 11 18N 37 15 E
Chokurdakh, Russia **67 B15** 70 38N 147 55 E
Cholame, U.S.A. **160 K6** 35 44N 120 18W
Cholet, France **26 E6** 47 4N 0 52W
Cholguan, Chile **174 D1** 37 10S 72 3W
Cholpon-Ata, Kyrgyzstan **65 B8** 42 40N 77 6 E
Choluteca, Honduras **164 D2** 13 20N 87 14W
Choluteca →, Honduras **164 D2** 13 0N 87 20W
Chom Bung, Thailand **86 F2** 13 37N 99 36 E
Chom Thong, Thailand **86 C2** 18 25N 98 41 E
Choma, Zambia **119 F2** 16 48S 26 59 E
Chomolungma = Everest, Mt., Nepal **93 E12** 28 5N 86 58 E
Chomun, India **92 F6** 27 15N 75 40 E
Chomutov, Czech Rep. **34 A6** 50 28N 13 23 E
Chon Buri, Thailand **86 F3** 13 21N 101 1 E
Chon Thanh, Vietnam **87 G6** 11 24N 106 36 E
Ch'onan, S. Korea **75 F14** 36 48N 127 9 E
Chone, Ecuador **168 D2** 0 40S 80 0W
Chong Kai, Cambodia **86 F4** 13 57N 103 35 E
Chong Mek, Thailand **86 E5** 15 10N 105 27 E
Chong Phangan, Thailand **87 b** 9 39N 100 0 E
Chong Samui, Thailand **87 b** 9 21N 99 50 E
Chongde, China **77 B13** 30 32N 120 26 E
Chŏngdo, S. Korea **75 G15** 35 38N 128 42 E
Chŏngha, S. Korea **75 F15** 36 12N 129 21 E
Chŏngjin, N. Korea **75 D15** 41 47N 129 50 E
Chŏngju, N. Korea **75 E13** 39 40N 125 5 E
Chŏngju, S. Korea **75 F14** 36 39N 127 27 E
Chongli, China **74 D8** 40 58N 115 15 E
Chongming, China **77 B13** 31 38N 121 23 E
Chongming Dao, China **77 B13** 31 40N 121 30 E
Chongoyape, Peru **172 B2** 6 35S 79 25W
Chongqing, Chongqing, China **76 C6** 29 35N 106 25 E
Chongqing, Sichuan, China **76 B4** 30 38N 103 40 E
Chongqing Shi □, China **76 C6** 30 0N 108 0 E
Chongren, China **77 D11** 27 46N 116 3 E
Chonguene, Mozam. **117 D5** 25 3S 33 49 E
Chŏngŭp, S. Korea **75 G14** 35 35N 126 50 E
Chongyi, China **77 E10** 25 45N 114 29 E
Chongzuo, China **76 F6** 22 23N 107 20 E
Chŏnju, S. Korea **75 G14** 35 50N 127 4 E
Chonos, Arch. de los, Chile **176 C2** 45 0S 75 0W
Chop, Ukraine **52 B7** 48 26N 22 12 E
Chopda, India **94 D2** 21 20N 75 15 E
Chopim →, Brazil **175 B5** 25 35S 53 5W
Chor, Pakistan **92 G3** 25 31N 69 46 E
Chorbat La, India **93 B7** 34 42N 76 37 E
Chorley, U.K. **20 D5** 53 39N 2 38W
Chorna, Ukraine **53 C14** 47 36N 29 20 E
Chornobyl, Ukraine **59 G6** 51 20N 30 15 E
Chornomorske, Ukraine **59 K7** 45 31N 32 40 E
Chorolque, Cerro, Bolivia **174 A2** 20 59S 66 5W
Choroszcz, Poland **55 E9** 53 10N 22 59 E
Chorregon, Australia **126 C3** 22 40S 143 32 E
Chorro el Indio △, Venezuela **165 E5** 7 43N 72 9W
Chortkiv, Ukraine **59 H3** 49 2N 25 46 E
Ch'ŏrwŏn, S. Korea **75 E14** 38 15N 127 10 E
Chorzele, Poland **55 E7** 53 15N 20 55 E
Chorzów, Poland **55 H5** 50 18N 18 57 E
Chos-Malal, Argentina **174 D1** 37 20S 70 15W
Ch'osan, N. Korea **75 D13** 40 50N 125 47 E
Chōshi, Japan **73 B12** 35 45N 140 51 E
Choszczno, Poland **55 E2** 53 7N 15 25 E
Chota, Peru **172 B2** 6 33S 78 39W
Choteau, U.S.A. **158 C7** 47 49N 112 11W
Chotěboř, Czech Rep. **34 B8** 49 43N 15 40 E
Chotila, India **92 H4** 22 23N 71 15 E
Chotta Udepur, India **92 H6** 22 19N 74 1 E
Chowchilla, U.S.A. **160 H6** 37 7N 120 16W
Choybalsan, Mongolia **69 B6** 48 4N 114 30 E
Chrisman, U.S.A. **157 E9** 39 48N 87 41W
Christburg = Dzierzgoń, Poland **54 E6** 53 58N 19 20 E
Christchurch, N.Z. **131 D7** 43 33S 172 47 E
Christchurch, U.K. **21 G6** 50 44N 1 47W
Christian I., Canada **150 B4** 44 50N 80 12W
Christian Sd., U.S.A. **144 J14** 55 56N 134 40W
Christiana, S. Africa **116 D4** 27 52S 25 8 E
Christiansfeld, Denmark **17 J3** 55 21N 9 29 E
Christianshåb = Qasigiannguit, Greenland **10 D5** 68 50N 51 18W
Christiansted, U.S. Virgin Is. **165 C7** 17 45N 64 42W
Christie B., Canada **143 A6** 62 32N 111 10W
Christina →, Canada **143 B6** 56 40N 111 3W
Christmas Cr. →, Australia **124 C4** 18 29S 125 23 E
Christmas I. = Kiritimati, Kiribati **135 G12** 1 58N 157 27W
Christmas I., Ind. Oc. **121 F9** 10 30S 105 40 E
Christopher, U.S.A. **156 G7** 37 59N 89 3W
Christopher L., Australia **125 D4** 24 49S 127 42 E
Christyakovo = Thorez, Ukraine **59 H10** 48 4N 38 34 E
Chrudim, Czech Rep. **34 B8** 49 58N 15 43 E
Chrzanów, Poland **55 H6** 50 10N 19 21 E
Chtimba, Malawi **119 E3** 10 35S 34 13 E
Chū = Shū, Kazakhstan **65 B6** 43 36N 73 42 E
Chū = Shū →, Kazakhstan **65 A3** 45 0N 67 44 E
Chu →, Vietnam **86 C5** 19 53N 105 45 E
Chu Lai, Vietnam **86 E7** 15 28N 108 45 E
Chuadanga, Bangla. **90 D2** 23 38N 88 51 E
Chuak, Ko, Thailand **87 b** 9 28N 99 41 E
Ch'uanchou = Quanzhou, China **77 E12** 24 55N 118 34 E
Chüanchow = Quanzhou, China **77 E12** 24 55N 118 34 E
Chuankou, China **74 G6** 34 20N 110 59 E
Chuathbaluk, U.S.A. **144 F8** 61 40N 159 15W
Chubarovka = Pology, Ukraine **59 J9** 47 29N 36 15 E
Chubbuck, U.S.A. **158 E7** 42 55N 112 28W
Chubek = Moskovskiy, Tajikistan **65 E4** 37 37N 69 42 E
Chūbu □, Japan **73 A9** 36 45N 137 30 E
Chubu-Sangaku △, Japan **73 A9** 36 30N 137 40 E
Chubut □, Argentina **176 B3** 43 30S 69 0W
Chubut →, Argentina **176 B3** 43 20S 65 5W
Chuchi L., Canada **142 B4** 55 12N 124 30W
Chuchow = Zhuzhou, China **77 D9** 27 49N 113 12 E
Chuda, India **92 H4** 22 29N 71 41 E
Chudovo, Russia **58 C6** 59 10N 31 41 E
Chudskoye, Ozero, Russia **15 G22** 58 13N 27 30 E
Chugach Mts., U.S.A. **144 F11** 60 45N 147 0W
Chugiak, U.S.A. **144 F10** 61 24N 149 29W
Chuginadak I., U.S.A. **144 K5** 52 50N 169 45W

Chūgoku □, *Japan* **72 C5** 35 0N 133 0 E
Chūgoku-Sanchi, *Japan* **72 C5** 35 0N 133 0 E
Chuguyev = Chuhuyiv, *Ukraine* **59 H9** 49 55N 36 45 E
Chugwater, *U.S.A.* **154 E2** 41 46N 104 50W
Chuhuyiv, *Ukraine* **59 H9** 49 55N 36 45 E
Chukchi Sea, *Russia* **67 C19** 68 0N 175 0W
Chukotskoye Nagorye, *Russia* **67 C18** 68 0N 175 0 E
Chula, *U.S.A.* **152 D6** 31 33N 83 32W
Chula Vista, *U.S.A.* **161 N9** 32 39N 117 5W
Chulakkurgan = Sholaqqūrghan, *Kazakhstan* **65 B4** 43 46N 69 9 E
Chulband →, *India* **94 D4** 20 40N 79 54 E
Chulucanas, *Peru* **172 B1** 5 8 S 80 10W
Chulumani, *Bolivia* **172 D4** 16 24 S 67 31W
Chulym →, *Russia* **66 D9** 57 43N 83 51 E
Chum Phae, *Thailand* **86 D4** 16 40N 102 6 E
Chum Saeng, *Thailand* **86 E3** 15 55N 100 15 E
Chuma, *Bolivia* **172 D4** 15 24 S 68 56W
Chumar, *India* **93 C8** 32 40N 78 35 E
Chumbicha, *Argentina* **174 B2** 29 0 S 66 10W
Chumerna, *Bulgaria* **51 D9** 42 45N 25 55 E
Chumikan, *Russia* **67 D14** 54 40N 135 10 E
Chumphon, *Thailand* **87 G2** 10 35N 99 14 E
Chumpi, *Peru* **172 D3** 15 4 S 73 46W
Chumuare, *Mozam.* **119 E3** 14 31 S 31 50 E
Chumunjin, *S. Korea* **75 F15** 37 55N 128 54 E
Chuna →, *Russia* **67 D10** 57 47N 94 37 E
Chun'an, *China* **77 C12** 29 35N 119 3 E
Ch'unch'ŏn, *S. Korea* **75 F14** 37 58N 127 44 E
Chunchura, *India* **93 H13** 22 53N 88 27 E
Chunga, *Zambia* **119 F2** 15 0 S 26 2 E
Ch'ungch'ing = Chongqing, *China* **76 C6** 29 35N 106 25 E
Chunggang-ŭp, *N. Korea* **75 D14** 41 48N 126 48 E
Chunghwa, *N. Korea* **75 E13** 38 52N 125 47 E
Ch'ungju, *S. Korea* **75 F14** 36 58N 127 58 E
Chungking = Chongqing, *China* **76 C6** 29 35N 106 25 E
Chungli, *Taiwan* **77 E13** 24 57N 121 13 E
Ch'ungmu, *S. Korea* **75 G15** 34 50N 128 20 E
Chungt'iaoshan = Zhongtiao Shan, *China* **74 G6** 35 0N 111 10 E
Chungyang Shanmo, *Taiwan* **77 F13** 23 10N 121 0 E
Chunian, *Pakistan* **92 D6** 30 57N 74 0 E
Chunya, *Tanzania* **119 D3** 8 30 S 33 27 E
Chunyang, *China* **75 C15** 43 38N 129 23 E
Chupara Pt., *Trin. & Tob.* **169 F9** 10 49N 61 22W
Chuquibamba, *Peru* **172 D3** 15 47 S 72 44W
Chuquibambilla, *Peru* **172 C3** 14 7 S 72 41W
Chuquicamata, *Chile* **174 A2** 22 15 S 69 0W
Chuquisaca □, *Bolivia* **173 E5** 20 30 S 63 30W
Chur, *Switz.* **33 C9** 46 52N 9 32 E
Churachandpur, *India* **90 C4** 24 20N 93 40 E
Church Stretton, *U.K.* **21 E5** 52 32N 2 48W
Churchill, *Australia* **129 E7** 38 19 S 146 25 E
Churchill, *Canada* **143 B10** 58 47N 94 11W
Churchill →, *Man., Canada* **143 B10** 58 47N 94 12W
Churchill →, *Nfld. & L., Canada* **141 B7** 53 19N 60 10W
Churchill, C., *Canada* **143 B10** 58 46N 93 12W
Churchill Falls, *Canada* **141 B7** 53 36N 64 19W
Churchill L., *Canada* **143 B7** 55 55N 108 20W
Churchill Pk., *Canada* **142 B3** 58 10N 125 10W
Churdan, *U.S.A.* **156 B2** 42 9N 94 29W
Churfisten, *Switz.* **33 B8** 47 8N 9 17 E
Churki, *India* **93 H10** 23 50N 83 12 E
Churu, *India* **92 E6** 28 20N 74 50 E
Churubusco, *U.S.A.* **157 C11** 41 14N 85 19W
Churún Merú = Angel Falls, *Venezuela* **169 B5** 5 57N 62 30W
Churwalden, *Switz.* **33 C9** 46 47N 9 33 E
Chushal, *India* **93 C8** 33 40N 78 40 E
Chuska Mts., *U.S.A.* **159 H9** 36 15N 108 50W
Chusovaya →, *Russia* **64 B6** 58 12N 56 54 E
Chusovoy, *Russia* **64 B6** 58 22N 57 50 E
Chusovskoy Zavod = Chusovoy, *Russia* **64 B6** 58 22N 57 50 E
Chuspipata, *Bolivia* **172 D4** 16 18 S 67 48W
Chust = Khust, *Ukraine* **53 B8** 48 10N 23 18 E
Chust, *Uzbekistan* **65 C5** 41 0N 71 13 E
Chute-aux-Outardes, *Canada* **141 C6** 49 7N 68 24W
Chuuronjang, *N. Korea* **75 D15** 41 35N 129 40 E
Chuvash Republic = Chuvashia □, *Russia* **60 C8** 55 30N 47 0 E
Chuvashia □, *Russia* **60 C8** 55 30N 47 0 E
Chuwārtah, *Iraq* **96 C5** 35 43N 45 34 E
Chuxiong, *China* **76 E3** 25 2N 101 28 E
Chüy, *Kyrgyzstan* **65 B7** 42 55N 75 15 E
Chuy, *Uruguay* **175 C5** 33 41 S 53 27W
Chuzenji-Ko, *Japan* **73 A11** 36 44N 139 27 E
Chuzhou, *China* **77 A12** 32 19N 118 20 E
Chynadiyeve, *Ukraine* **52 B7** 48 29N 22 50 E
Ci Xian, *China* **74 F8** 36 20N 114 25 E
Ciacova, *Romania* **52 E6** 45 35N 21 10 E
Ciadâr-Lunga, *Moldova* **53 D13** 46 3N 28 51 E
Ciamis, *Indonesia* **85 D3** 7 20 S 108 21 E
Cianjur, *Indonesia* **84 D3** 6 49 S 107 8 E
Cianorte, *Brazil* **175 A5** 23 37 S 52 37W
Cibola, *U.S.A.* **161 M12** 33 17N 114 42W
Cicero, *U.S.A.* **157 C9** 41 51N 87 45W
Cícero Dantas, *Brazil* **170 D4** 10 36 S 38 23W
Cicia, *Fiji* **133 A3** 17 45 S 179 18W
Cidacos →, *Spain* **40 C3** 42 21N 1 38W
Cidade de Minas = Belo Horizonte, *Brazil* **171 E3** 19 55 S 43 56W
Cide, *Turkey* **100 B5** 41 53N 33 1 E
Ciéagas del Cataumbo △, *Venezuela* **165 E5** 9 25N 71 54W
Ciechanów, *Poland* **55 F7** 52 52N 20 38 E
Ciechanowiec, *Poland* **55 F9** 52 40N 22 31 E
Ciechocinek, *Poland* **55 F5** 52 53N 18 45 E
Ciego de Avila, *Cuba* **164 B4** 21 50N 78 50W
Ciénaga, *Colombia* **168 A3** 11 1N 74 15W
Ciénaga de Oro, *Colombia* **168 B2** 8 53N 75 37W
Ciénagas del Catatumbo △, *Venezuela* **168 B3** 9 26N 72 8W
Cienfuegos, *Cuba* **164 B3** 22 10N 80 30W
Cierp-Gaud, *France* **28 F4** 42 55N 0 40 E
Cíes, Is., *Spain* **42 C2** 42 12N 8 55W
Cieszanów, *Poland* **55 H10** 50 14N 23 8 E
Cieszyn, *Poland* **55 J5** 49 45N 18 35 E
Cieza, *Spain* **41 G3** 38 17N 1 23W
Çifteler, *Turkey* **100 C4** 39 22N 31 2 E
Cifuentes, *Spain* **40 E2** 40 47N 2 37W
Cihanbeyli, *Turkey* **100 C5** 38 40N 32 55 E
Cihuatlán, *Mexico* **162 D4** 19 14N 104 35W
Cijara ⌓, *Spain* **43 F6** 39 18N 4 35W
Cijara, Embalse de, *Spain* **43 F6** 39 18N 4 52W
Cijulang, *Indonesia* **79 G13** 7 42 S 108 27 E
Cilacap, *Indonesia* **85 D3** 7 43 S 109 0 E
Çıldır, *Turkey* **101 B10** 41 7N 43 8 E
Çıldır Gölü, *Turkey* **101 B10** 41 5N 43 15 E
Cilento e Vallo di Diano △, *Italy* **47 B8** 40 15N 15 20 E
Cili, *China* **77 C8** 29 30N 111 8 E
Cilibia, *Romania* **53 E12** 45 4N 27 4 E
Cilicia, *Turkey* **100 D5** 36 30N 33 40 E
Cill Chainnigh = Kilkenny, *Ireland* **23 D4** 52 39N 7 15W
Cilo Dağı, *Turkey* **101 D10** 37 28N 43 55 E
Cima, *U.S.A.* **161 K11** 35 14N 115 30W
Cimarron, *Kans., U.S.A.* **155 G4** 37 48N 100 21W
Cimarron, *N. Mex., U.S.A.* **155 G2** 36 31N 104 55W
Cimarron →, *U.S.A.* **155 G6** 36 10N 96 17W
Cimişlia, *Moldova* **53 D13** 46 34N 28 44 E
Cimone, Mte., *Italy* **44 D7** 44 12N 10 42 E
Cimpu, *Indonesia* **82 B2** 3 25 S 120 22 E
Çinar, *Turkey* **101 D9** 37 46N 40 19 E
Çınarcık, *Turkey* **51 F13** 40 38N 29 5 E
Cinaruco-Capanaparo △, *Venezuela* **168 B4** 6 51N 67 32W
Cinca →, *Spain* **40 D5** 41 26N 0 21 E
Cincar, *Bos.-H.* **52 G2** 43 55N 17 5 E
Cincinnati, *Iowa, U.S.A.* **156 D4** 40 38N 92 56W
Cincinnati, *Ohio, U.S.A.* **157 E12** 39 6N 84 31W
Cincinnati-Northern Kentucky International ✈ (CVG), *U.S.A.* **157 E12** 39 3N 84 40W
Cincinnatus, *U.S.A.* **151 D9** 42 33N 75 54W
Çine, *Turkey* **49 D10** 37 37N 28 2 E
Ciney, *Belgium* **24 D5** 50 18N 5 5 E
Cíngoli, *Italy* **45 E10** 43 23N 13 10 E
Cinigiano, *Italy* **45 F8** 42 53N 11 24 E
Cinque I., *India* **95 J11** 11 16N 92 42 E
Cinto, Mte., *France* **29 F12** 42 24N 8 54 E
Cintra, G. de, *W. Sahara* **110 D1** 23 0N 16 15W
Cintruénigo, *Spain* **40 C3** 42 5N 1 49W
Ciocile, *Romania* **53 F12** 44 49N 27 14 E
Ciolănești din Deal, *Romania* **53 F10** 44 19N 25 5 E
Ciorani, *Romania* **53 F11** 44 45N 26 25 E
Čiovo, *Croatia* **45 E13** 43 30N 16 17 E
Cipó, *Brazil* **170 D4** 11 6 S 38 31W
Cipolletti, *Argentina* **176 A3** 38 56 S 67 59W
Circeo, Mte., *Italy* **46 A6** 41 14N 13 3 E
Çirçir, *Turkey* **100 C7** 40 5N 36 47 E
Circle, *Alaska, U.S.A.* **144 D11** 65 50N 144 4W
Circle, *Mont., U.S.A.* **154 B2** 47 25N 105 35W
Circleville, *U.S.A.* **148 F4** 39 36N 82 57W
Circular Reef, *Papua N. G.* **132 B4** 3 25 S 147 47 E
Cirebon, *Indonesia* **85 D3** 6 45 S 108 32 E
Ciremay, *Indonesia* **85 D3** 6 55 S 108 27 E
Cirencester, *U.K.* **21 F6** 51 43N 1 57W
Cireşu, *Romania* **52 F7** 44 47N 22 31 E
Cirey-sur-Vezouze, *France* **27 D13** 48 35N 6 57 E
Ciriè, *Italy* **44 C4** 45 14N 7 36 E
Cirium, *Cyprus* **39 F8** 34 40N 32 53 E
Cirò, *Italy* **47 C10** 39 23N 17 4 E
Cirò Marina, *Italy* **47 C10** 39 22N 17 8 E
Ciron →, *France* **28 D3** 44 36N 0 18W
Cisco, *U.S.A.* **155 J5** 32 23N 98 59W
Cislău, *Romania* **53 E11** 45 14N 26 20 E
Cisna, *Poland* **55 J9** 49 12N 22 20 E
Cisnădie, *Romania* **53 E9** 45 42N 24 9 E
Cisne, *U.S.A.* **157 F8** 38 31N 88 26W
Cisneros, *Colombia* **168 B2** 6 33N 75 4W
Cissna Park, *U.S.A.* **157 D9** 40 34N 87 54W
Cisterna di Latina, *Italy* **46 A5** 41 35N 12 49 E
Cisternino, *Italy* **47 B10** 40 44N 17 25 E
Cistierna, *Spain* **42 C5** 42 48N 5 7W
Citaré →, *Brazil* **169 C7** 1 11N 54 41W
Citeli-Ckaro = Tsiteli-Tsqaro, *Georgia* **61 K8** 41 33N 46 0 E
Citlaltépetl = Orizaba, Pico de, *Mexico* **163 D5** 19 0N 97 20W
Citra, *U.S.A.* **153 F7** 29 25N 82 7W
Citron, *Fr. Guiana* **169 C7** 4 44N 53 57W
Citrus Heights, *U.S.A.* **160 G5** 38 42N 121 17W
Citrus Springs, *U.S.A.* **153 F7** 29 2N 82 27W
Citrusdal, *S. Africa* **116 E2** 32 35 S 19 0 E
Città della Pieve, *Italy* **45 F9** 42 57N 12 1 E
Città di Castello, *Italy* **45 E9** 43 27N 12 14 E
Città Sant' Angelo, *Italy* **45 F11** 42 32N 14 5 E
Cittadella, *Italy* **45 C8** 45 39N 11 47 E
Cittaducale, *Italy* **45 F9** 42 23N 12 57 E
Cittanova, *Italy* **47 D9** 38 21N 16 5 E
Ciuc, Munţii, *Romania* **53 D11** 46 25N 26 5 E
Ciucaş, Vf., *Romania* **53 E10** 45 31N 25 56 E
Ciucea, *Romania* **52 D7** 46 57N 22 49 E
Ciuciulea, *Moldova* **53 C12** 47 40N 27 29 E
Ciuciuleni, *Moldova* **53 C13** 47 2N 28 25 E
Ciudad Altamirano, *Mexico* **162 D4** 18 20N 100 40W
Ciudad Bolívar, *Venezuela* **169 B5** 8 5N 63 36W
Ciudad Camargo, *Mexico* **162 B3** 27 41N 105 10W
Ciudad de Valles, *Mexico* **163 C5** 22 0N 99 0W
Ciudad del Carmen, *Mexico* **163 D6** 18 38N 91 50W
Ciudad del Este, *Paraguay* **175 B5** 25 30 S 54 50W
Ciudad Delicias = Delicias, *Mexico* **162 B3** 28 10N 105 30W
Ciudad Guayana, *Venezuela* **169 B5** 8 0N 62 30W
Ciudad Guerrero, *Mexico* **162 B3** 28 33N 107 28W
Ciudad Guzmán, *Mexico* **162 D4** 19 40N 103 30W
Ciudad Juárez, *Mexico* **162 A3** 31 40N 106 28W
Ciudad Madero, *Mexico* **163 C5** 22 19N 97 50W
Ciudad Mante, *Mexico* **163 C5** 22 50N 99 0W
Ciudad Obregón, *Mexico* **162 B3** 27 28N 109 59W
Ciudad Ojeda, *Venezuela* **168 A3** 10 12N 71 19W
Ciudad Piar, *Venezuela* **169 B5** 7 27N 63 19W
Ciudad Porfirio Díaz = Piedras Negras, *Mexico* **162 B4** 28 42N 100 31W
Ciudad Real, *Spain* **43 G7** 38 59N 3 55W
Ciudad Real □, *Spain* **43 G7** 38 50N 4 0W
Ciudad Rodrigo, *Spain* **42 E4** 40 35N 6 32W
Ciudad Trujillo = Santo Domingo, *Dom. Rep.* **165 C6** 18 30N 69 59W
Ciudad Victoria, *Mexico* **163 C5** 23 41N 99 9W
Ciudadela, *Spain* **38 B4** 40 0N 3 50 E
Ciulniţa, *Romania* **53 F12** 44 26N 27 22 E
Ciumeghiu, *Romania* **52 D6** 46 44N 21 35 E
Ciuperceni, *Romania* **52 F8** 44 54N 23 4 E
Civa Burnu, *Turkey* **100 B7** 41 21N 36 38 E
Cividale del Friuli, *Italy* **45 B10** 46 6N 13 25 E
Civita Castellana, *Italy* **45 F9** 42 18N 12 24 E
Civitanova Marche, *Italy* **45 E10** 43 18N 13 44 E
Civitavécchia, *Italy* **45 F8** 42 6N 11 48 E
Civray, *France* **28 B4** 46 10N 0 17 E
Çivril, *Turkey* **49 C11** 38 20N 29 43 E
Cixerri →, *Italy* **46 C1** 39 17N 8 59 E
Cixi, *China* **77 B13** 30 17N 121 9 E
Cizre, *Turkey* **101 D10** 37 19N 42 10 E
Cizur Mayor, *Spain* **40 C3** 42 47N 1 41W
Clackmannanshire □, *U.K.* **22 E5** 56 10N 3 43W
Clacton-on-Sea, *U.K.* **21 F9** 51 47N 1 11 E
Clain →, *France* **26 F7** 46 47N 0 33 E
Claire, L., *Canada* **142 B6** 58 35N 112 5W
Clairton, *U.S.A.* **150 F5** 40 18N 79 53W
Clairvaux-les-Lacs, *France* **27 F12** 46 35N 5 45 E
Claise →, *France* **28 B5** 46 56N 0 42 E
Clallam Bay, *U.S.A.* **160 B2** 48 15N 124 16W
Clam Gulch, *U.S.A.* **144 F10** 60 15N 151 23W
Clamecy, *France* **27 E10** 47 28N 3 30 E
Clanton, *U.S.A.* **149 J2** 32 51N 86 38W
Clanwilliam, *S. Africa* **116 E2** 32 11 S 18 52 E
Clara, *Ireland* **23 C4** 53 21N 7 37W
Claraville, *U.S.A.* **161 K8** 35 24N 118 20W
Clare, *Australia* **128 B3** 33 50 S 138 37 E
Clare, *U.S.A.* **148 D3** 43 49N 84 46W
Clare □, *Ireland* **23 D3** 52 45N 9 0W
Clare →, *Ireland* **23 C2** 53 20N 9 2W
Clare I., *Ireland* **23 C1** 53 49N 10 0W
Claremont, *Calif., U.S.A.* **161 L9** 34 6N 117 43W
Claremont, *N.H., U.S.A.* **151 C12** 43 23N 72 20W
Claremont Pt., *Australia* **126 A3** 14 1 S 143 41 E
Claremore, *U.S.A.* **155 G7** 36 19N 95 36W
Claremorris, *Ireland* **23 C3** 53 45N 9 0W
Clarence, *U.S.A.* **156 E4** 39 45N 92 16W
Clarence →, *Australia* **127 D5** 29 25 S 153 22 E
Clarence →, *N.Z.* **131 C8** 42 10 S 173 56 E
Clarence, I., *Chile* **176 D2** 54 0 S 72 0W
Clarence, Port, *U.S.A.* **144 D6** 65 15N 166 40W
Clarence B., *Ascension I.* **9 g** 7 55 S 14 25W
Clarence I., *Antarctica* **7 C18** 61 10 S 54 0W
Clarence Str., *Australia* **124 B5** 12 0 S 131 0 E
Clarence Town, *Bahamas* **165 B5** 23 6N 74 59W
Clarendon, *Pa., U.S.A.* **150 E5** 41 47N 79 6W
Clarendon, *Tex., U.S.A.* **155 H4** 34 56N 100 53W
Clarenville-Shoal Harbour, *Canada* **141 C9** 48 10N 54 1W
Claresholm, *Canada* **142 D6** 50 2N 113 33W
Clarie Coast, *Antarctica* **7 C9** 68 0 S 135 0 E
Clarinda, *U.S.A.* **154 E7** 40 44N 95 2W
Clarington, *Canada* **150 C6** 43 55N 78 41W
Clarion, *Iowa, U.S.A.* **156 B3** 42 44N 93 44W
Clarion, *Pa., U.S.A.* **150 E5** 41 13N 79 23W
Clarion →, *U.S.A.* **150 E5** 41 7N 79 41W
Clarion Fracture Zone, *Pac. Oc.* **136 H7** 20 0N 120 0W
Clark, *Mo., U.S.A.* **156 E4** 39 17N 92 21W
Clark, *S. Dak., U.S.A.* **154 C6** 44 53N 97 44W
Clark, Pt., *Canada* **150 B3** 44 4N 81 45W
Clark Fork, *U.S.A.* **158 B5** 48 9N 116 11W
Clark Fork →, *U.S.A.* **158 B5** 48 9N 116 15W
Clarkdale, *U.S.A.* **159 J7** 34 46N 112 3W
Clarke City, *Canada* **141 B6** 50 12N 66 38W
Clarke I., *Australia* **127 G4** 40 32 S 148 10 E
Clarke Ra., *Australia* **126 J6** 20 40 S 148 30 E
Clark's Fork →, *U.S.A.* **158 D9** 45 39N 108 43W
Clark's Harbour, *Canada* **141 D6** 43 25N 65 38W
Clarks Hill L. = J. Strom Thurmond L., *U.S.A.* **152 B7** 33 40N 82 12W
Clarks Point, *U.S.A.* **144 G8** 58 51N 158 33W
Clarks Summit, *U.S.A.* **151 E9** 41 30N 75 42W
Clarksburg, *U.S.A.* **148 F5** 39 17N 80 30W
Clarksdale, *U.S.A.* **155 H9** 34 12N 90 35W
Clarkston, *U.S.A.* **158 C5** 46 25N 117 3W
Clarksville, *Ark., U.S.A.* **155 H8** 35 28N 93 28W
Clarksville, *Ind., U.S.A.* **157 F11** 38 17N 85 45W
Clarksville, *Iowa, U.S.A.* **156 B4** 42 47N 92 40W
Clarksville, *Mo., U.S.A.* **156 E6** 39 22N 90 54W
Clarksville, *Tenn., U.S.A.* **149 G2** 36 32N 87 21W
Clarksville, *Tex., U.S.A.* **155 J7** 33 37N 95 3W
Claro →, *Brazil* **171 E1** 19 8 S 50 40W
Clatskanie, *U.S.A.* **160 D3** 46 6N 123 12W
Claude, *U.S.A.* **155 H4** 35 7N 101 22W
Claveria, *Cagayan, Phil.* **80 B3** 18 37N 121 4 E
Claveria, *Masbate, Phil.* **80 E4** 12 54N 123 15 E
Claveria, *Mis. Or., Phil.* **81 G5** 8 38N 124 55 E
Clavering Ø, *Greenland* **10 C8** 74 15N 21 0W
Claxton, *U.S.A.* **152 C8** 32 10N 81 55W
Clay, *U.S.A.* **160 G5** 38 17N 121 10W
Clay Center, *U.S.A.* **154 F6** 39 23N 97 8W
Clay City, *Ind., U.S.A.* **157 E9** 39 17N 87 7W
Clay City, *Ky., U.S.A.* **157 G13** 37 52N 83 55W
Claypool, *U.S.A.* **159 K8** 33 25N 110 51W
Claysburg, *U.S.A.* **150 F6** 40 17N 78 27W
Claysville, *U.S.A.* **150 F4** 40 7N 80 25W
Clayton, *Ala., U.S.A.* **152 D4** 31 53N 85 27W
Clayton, *Ind., U.S.A.* **157 E10** 39 41N 86 31W
Clayton, *N. Mex., U.S.A.* **155 G3** 36 27N 103 11W
Clayton, *N.Y., U.S.A.* **151 B8** 44 14N 76 5W
Clear, C., *Ireland* **23 E2** 51 25N 9 32W
Clear, L., *Canada* **150 A7** 45 26N 77 12W
Clear Hills, *Canada* **142 B5** 56 40N 119 30W
Clear I., *Ireland* **23 E2** 51 26N 9 30W
Clear L., *U.S.A.* **160 F4** 39 2N 122 47W
Clear Lake, *Iowa, U.S.A.* **156 A3** 43 8N 93 23W
Clear Lake, *S. Dak., U.S.A.* **154 C6** 44 45N 96 41W
Clear Lake Reservoir, *U.S.A.* **158 F3** 41 56N 121 5W
Clearfield, *Pa., U.S.A.* **150 E6** 41 2N 78 27W
Clearfield, *Utah, U.S.A.* **158 F8** 41 7N 112 2W
Clearlake, *U.S.A.* **158 G2** 38 57N 122 38W
Clearlake Highlands, *U.S.A.* **160 G4** 38 57N 122 38W
Clearwater, *Canada* **142 C4** 51 38N 120 2W
Clearwater, *U.S.A.* **153 H7** 27 58N 82 48W
Clearwater →, *Alta., Canada* **142 C6** 52 22N 114 57W
Clearwater →, *Alta., Canada* **143 B6** 56 44N 111 23W
Clearwater L., *Canada* **143 C9** 53 34N 99 49W
Clearwater Lake ⌓, *Canada* **143 C8** 54 0N 101 0W
Clearwater Mts., *U.S.A.* **158 C6** 46 5N 115 20W
Clearwater River ⌓, *Canada* **143 B7** 56 55N 109 10W
Cleburne, *U.S.A.* **155 J6** 32 21N 97 23W
Clee Hills, *U.K.* **21 E5** 52 26N 2 35W
Cleethorpes, *U.K.* **20 D7** 53 33N 0 3W
Cleeve Cloud, *U.K.* **21 F6** 51 56N 2 0W
Clelles, *France* **29 D9** 44 50N 5 38 E
Clemson, *U.S.A.* **149 H4** 34 41N 82 50W
Cleopatra Needle, *Phil.* **81 F2** 10 7N 118 58 E
Clerke Reef, *Australia* **124 C2** 17 22 S 119 20 E
Clermont, *Australia* **126 C4** 22 49 S 147 39 E
Clermont, *France* **27 C9** 49 23N 2 24 E
Clermont, *U.S.A.* **153 G8** 28 33N 81 46W
Clermont-en-Argonne, *France* **27 C12** 49 5N 5 4 E
Clermont-Ferrand, *France* **28 C7** 45 46N 3 4 E
Clermont-l'Hérault, *France* **28 E7** 43 38N 3 26 E
Clerval, *France* **27 E13** 47 25N 6 30 E
Clervaux, *Lux.* **24 D6** 50 4N 6 2 E
Cles, *Italy* **44 B8** 46 22N 11 2 E
Cleve, *Australia* **128 B2** 33 43 S 136 30 E
Clevedon, *U.K.* **21 F5** 51 26N 2 52W
Cleveland, *Miss., U.S.A.* **155 J9** 33 45N 90 43W
Cleveland, *Ohio, U.S.A.* **150 E3** 41 30N 81 42W
Cleveland, *Okla., U.S.A.* **155 G6** 36 19N 96 28W
Cleveland, *Tenn., U.S.A.* **149 H3** 35 10N 84 53W
Cleveland, *Tex., U.S.A.* **155 K7** 30 21N 95 5W
Cleveland, C., *Australia* **126 B4** 19 11 S 147 1 E
Cleveland, Mt., *U.S.A.* **158 B7** 48 56N 113 51W
Cleveland Heights, *U.S.A.* **150 E3** 41 30N 81 34W
Clevelândia, *Brazil* **175 B5** 26 24 S 52 23W
Clevelândia do Norte, *Brazil* **169 C7** 3 49N 51 52W
Cleves, *U.S.A.* **157 E12** 39 10N 84 45W
Clew B., *Ireland* **23 C2** 53 50N 9 49W
Clewiston, *U.S.A.* **153 J9** 26 45N 80 56W
Clifden, *Ireland* **23 C1** 53 29N 10 1W
Clifden, *N.Z.* **131 G2** 46 1 S 167 42 E
Cliffdell, *U.S.A.* **160 D5** 46 56N 121 5W
Cliffy Hd., *Australia* **125 G2** 35 1 S 116 29 E
Clifton, *Australia* **127 D5** 27 59 S 151 53 E
Clifton, *Ariz., U.S.A.* **159 K9** 33 3N 109 18W
Clifton, *Colo., U.S.A.* **159 G9** 39 7N 108 25W
Clifton, *Ill., U.S.A.* **157 D9** 40 56N 87 56W
Clifton, *Tex., U.S.A.* **155 K6** 31 47N 97 35W
Clifton Beach, *Australia* **126 B4** 16 46 S 145 39 E
Clifton Pt., *Bahamas* **9 b** 25 1N 77 34W
Climax, *Canada* **143 D7** 49 10N 108 20W
Climax, *U.S.A.* **152 E5** 30 53N 84 26W
Clinch →, *U.S.A.* **149 H3** 35 53N 84 29W
Clingmans Dome, *U.S.A.* **149 H4** 35 34N 83 30W
Clint, *U.S.A.* **159 L10** 31 35N 106 14W
Clinton, *B.C., Canada* **142 C4** 51 6N 121 35W
Clinton, *Ont., Canada* **140 D3** 43 37N 81 32W
Clinton, *N.Z.* **131 G4** 46 12 S 169 23 E
Clinton, *Ark., U.S.A.* **155 H8** 35 36N 92 28W
Clinton, *Conn., U.S.A.* **151 E12** 41 17N 72 32W
Clinton, *Ill., U.S.A.* **156 D8** 40 9N 88 57W
Clinton, *Ind., U.S.A.* **157 E9** 39 40N 87 24W
Clinton, *Iowa, U.S.A.* **156 C6** 41 51N 90 12W
Clinton, *Mass., U.S.A.* **151 D13** 42 25N 71 41W
Clinton, *Mich., U.S.A.* **157 B13** 42 4N 83 58W
Clinton, *Miss., U.S.A.* **155 J9** 32 20N 90 20W
Clinton, *Mo., U.S.A.* **156 F3** 38 22N 93 46W
Clinton, *N.C., U.S.A.* **149 H6** 35 0N 78 22W
Clinton, *Okla., U.S.A.* **155 H5** 35 31N 98 58W
Clinton, *S.C., U.S.A.* **149 H5** 34 29N 81 53W
Clinton, *Tenn., U.S.A.* **149 G3** 36 6N 84 8W
Clinton, *Wash., U.S.A.* **160 C4** 47 59N 122 21W
Clinton, *Wis., U.S.A.* **157 B8** 42 34N 88 52W
Clinton C., *Australia* **126 C5** 22 30 S 150 45 E
Clinton Colden L., *Canada* **138 B9** 63 58N 107 27W
Clinton L., *U.S.A.* **157 D8** 40 15N 88 45W
Clintonville, *U.S.A.* **154 C10** 44 37N 88 46W
Clio, *U.S.A.* **152 D4** 31 43N 85 37W
Clipperton, I., *Pac. Oc.* **135 F17** 10 18N 109 13W
Clipperton Fracture Zone, *Pac. Oc.* **135 G16** 19 0N 122 0W
Clisham, *U.K.* **22 D2** 57 57N 6 49W
Clisson, *France* **26 E5** 47 5N 1 16W
Clitheroe, *U.K.* **20 D5** 53 53N 2 22W
Clive, *N.Z.* **130 F5** 39 36 S 176 58 E
Cliza, *Bolivia* **173 D4** 17 36 S 65 56W
Clo-oose, *Canada* **160 B2** 48 39N 124 49W
Cloates, Pt., *Australia* **124 D1** 22 43 S 113 40 E
Clocolan, *S. Africa* **117 D4** 28 55 S 27 34 E
Clodomira, *Argentina* **174 B3** 27 35 S 64 14W
Clogher Hd., *Ireland* **23 C5** 53 48N 6 14W
Clonakilty, *Ireland* **23 E3** 51 37N 8 53W
Clonakilty B., *Ireland* **23 E3** 51 35N 8 51W
Cloncurry, *Australia* **126 C3** 20 40 S 140 28 E
Cloncurry →, *Australia* **126 B3** 18 37 S 140 40 E
Clondalkin, *Ireland* **23 C5** 53 19N 6 25W
Clones, *Ireland* **23 B4** 54 11N 7 15W
Clonmel, *Ireland* **23 D4** 52 21N 7 42W
Cloppenburg, *Germany* **30 C4** 52 51N 8 1 E
Cloquet, *U.S.A.* **154 B8** 46 43N 92 28W
Clorinda, *Argentina* **174 B4** 25 16 S 57 45W
Cloud Bay, *Canada* **140 C2** 48 5N 89 26W
Cloud Peak, *U.S.A.* **158 D10** 44 23N 107 11W
Cloudcroft, *U.S.A.* **159 K11** 32 58N 105 45W
Cloudy B., *N.Z.* **131 B9** 41 25 S 174 10 E
Cloverdale, *Calif., U.S.A.* **160 G4** 38 48N 123 1W
Cloverdale, *Ind., U.S.A.* **157 E10** 39 31N 86 48W
Cloverport, *U.S.A.* **157 G10** 37 50N 86 38W
Clovis, *Calif., U.S.A.* **160 J7** 36 49N 119 42W
Clovis, *N. Mex., U.S.A.* **155 H3** 34 24N 103 12W
Cloyes-sur-le-Loir, *France* **26 E8** 48 0N 1 14 E
Cloyne, *Canada* **150 B7** 44 49N 77 11W
Club Terrace, *Australia* **129 D8** 37 35 S 148 58 E
Cluj □, *Romania* **53 D8** 46 45N 23 30 E
Cluj-Napoca, *Romania* **53 D8** 46 47N 23 38 E
Clunes, *Australia* **128 D5** 37 20 S 143 45 E
Cluny, *France* **27 F11** 46 26N 4 38 E
Cluses, *France* **27 F13** 46 5N 6 35 E
Clusone, *Italy* **44 C6** 45 53N 9 57 E
Clutha →, *N.Z.* **131 G4** 46 20 S 169 49 E
Clwyd →, *U.K.* **20 D4** 53 19N 3 31W
Clyattville, *U.S.A.* **152 E6** 30 42N 83 19W
Clyde, *Canada* **142 C6** 54 9N 113 39W
Clyde, *N.Z.* **131 F4** 45 12 S 169 20 E
Clyde, *N.Y., U.S.A.* **150 C8** 43 5N 76 52W
Clyde, *Ohio, U.S.A.* **157 C14** 41 18N 82 59W
Clyde →, *U.K.* **22 F4** 55 55N 4 30W
Clyde, Firth of, *U.K.* **22 F3** 55 22N 5 1W
Clyde Muirshiel ⌓, *U.K.* **22 F4** 55 50N 4 40W
Clyde River, *Canada* **139 A13** 70 30N 68 30W
Clydebank, *U.K.* **22 F4** 55 54N 4 23W
Clymer, *N.Y., U.S.A.* **150 D5** 42 1N 79 37W
Clymer, *Pa., U.S.A.* **150 D5** 40 40N 79 1W
Clyo, *U.S.A.* **152 C8** 32 29N 81 16W
Ćmielów, *Poland* **55 H8** 50 53N 21 31 E
Côa →, *Portugal* **42 D3** 41 5N 7 6W
Coachella, *U.S.A.* **161 M10** 33 41N 116 10W
Coachélla Canal, *U.S.A.* **161 N12** 32 43N 114 57W
Coahoma, *U.S.A.* **155 J4** 32 18N 101 18W
Coahuayana →, *Mexico* **162 D4** 18 41N 103 45W
Coahuila □, *Mexico* **162 B4** 27 0N 103 0W
Coal →, *Canada* **142 B3** 59 39N 126 57W
Coal City, *U.S.A.* **157 C8** 41 17N 88 17W
Coal I., *N.Z.* **131 G1** 46 8 S 166 40 E
Coalane, *Mozam.* **119 F4** 17 48 S 37 2 E
Coalcomán, *Mexico* **162 D4** 18 40N 103 10W
Coaldale, *Canada* **142 D6** 49 45N 112 35W
Coalgate, *U.S.A.* **155 H6** 34 32N 96 13W
Coalinga, *U.S.A.* **160 J6** 36 9N 120 21W
Coalisland, *U.K.* **23 B5** 54 33N 6 42W
Coalville, *U.K.* **20 E6** 52 44N 1 23W
Coalville, *U.S.A.* **158 F8** 40 55N 111 24W
Coamo, *Puerto Rico* **165 d** 18 5N 66 22W
Coaraci, *Brazil* **171 D4** 14 38 S 39 32W
Coari, *Brazil* **169 D5** 4 8 S 63 7W
Coari →, *Brazil* **169 D5** 4 30 S 63 33W
Coari, L. de, *Brazil* **169 D5** 4 15 S 63 22W
Coast □, *Kenya* **118 C4** 2 40 S 39 45 E
Coast Mts., *Canada* **142 C3** 55 0N 129 20W
Coast Ranges, *U.S.A.* **160 G4** 39 0N 123 0W
Coatbridge, *U.K.* **22 F4** 55 52N 4 6W
Coatepec, *Mexico* **163 D5** 19 27N 96 58W
Coatepeque, *Guatemala* **164 D1** 14 46N 91 55W
Coatesville, *U.S.A.* **148 F8** 39 59N 75 50W
Coaticook, *Canada* **141 C5** 45 10N 71 46W
Coats I., *Canada* **139 B11** 62 30N 83 0W
Coats Land, *Antarctica* **7 D1** 77 0 S 25 0W
Coatzacoalcos, *Mexico* **163 D6** 18 7N 94 25W
Coba, *Mexico* **163 C7** 20 31N 87 39W
Cobadin, *Romania* **53 F13** 44 5N 28 13 E
Cobalt, *Canada* **140 C4** 47 25N 79 42W
Cobán, *Guatemala* **164 C1** 15 30N 90 21W
Çobanlar, *Turkey* **49 C12** 38 41N 30 47 E
Cobar, *Australia* **129 A6** 31 27 S 145 48 E
Cobargo, *Australia* **129 D8** 36 20 S 149 55 E
Cobbannah, *Australia* **129 D7** 37 37 S 147 13 E
Cobberas, Mt., *Australia* **129 D8** 36 53 S 148 12 E
Cobden, *Australia* **128 E5** 38 20 S 143 3 E
Cóbh, *Ireland* **23 E3** 51 51N 8 17W
Cobija, *Bolivia* **172 C4** 11 0 S 68 50W
Cobleskill, *U.S.A.* **151 D10** 42 41N 74 29W
Coboconk, *Canada* **150 B6** 44 39N 78 48W
Cobourg, *Canada* **140 D4** 43 58N 78 10W
Cobourg ⌓, *Australia* **124 B5** 11 26 S 131 58 E
Cobourg Pen., *Australia* **124 B5** 11 20 S 132 15 E
Cobram, *Australia* **129 C6** 35 54 S 145 40 E
Cóbué, *Mozam.* **119 E3** 12 0 S 34 58 E
Coburg, *Germany* **31 E6** 50 15N 10 58 E
Coca, *Spain* **42 D6** 41 13N 4 32W
Coca →, *Ecuador* **168 D2** 0 29 S 76 58W
Cocachacra, *Peru* **172 D3** 17 5 S 71 45W
Cocal, *Brazil* **170 B3** 3 28 S 41 34W
Cocanada = Kakinada, *India* **94 F6** 16 57N 82 11 E
Cocentaina, *Spain* **41 G4** 38 45N 0 27W
Cochabamba, *Bolivia* **173 D4** 17 26 S 66 10W
Coche, I., *Venezuela* **169 A5** 10 47N 63 56W
Cochem, *Germany* **31 E3** 50 9N 7 9 E
Cochemane, *Mozam.* **119 F3** 17 0 S 32 54 E
Cochin, *India* **95 K3** 9 58N 76 20 E
Cochin China = Nam-Phan, *Vietnam* **87 G6** 10 30N 106 0 E
Cochran, *U.S.A.* **152 C6** 32 23N 83 21W
Cochrane, *Alta., Canada* **142 C6** 51 11N 114 30W
Cochrane, *Ont., Canada* **140 C3** 49 0N 81 0W
Cochrane, *Chile* **176 C2** 47 15 S 72 33W
Cochrane →, *Canada* **143 B8** 59 0N 103 40W
Cochrane, L., *Chile* **176 C2** 47 10 S 72 0W
Cochranton, *U.S.A.* **150 E4** 41 31N 80 3W
Cockburn, *Australia* **128 B4** 32 5 S 141 0 E
Cockburn, Canal, *Chile* **176 D2** 54 30 S 72 0W
Cockburn I., *Canada* **140 C3** 45 55N 83 22W
Cockburn Ra., *Australia* **124 C4** 15 46 S 128 0 E
Cockermouth, *U.K.* **20 C4** 54 40N 3 22W
Cocklebiddy, *Australia* **125 F4** 32 0 S 126 3 E
Cockpit Country, The, *Jamaica* **164 a** 18 15N 77 45W
Côco →, *Brazil* **170 C2** 9 27 S 50 2W
Coco →, *Cent. Amer.* **164 D3** 15 0N 83 8W
Coco, I. del, *Pac. Oc.* **135 G19** 5 25N 87 55W
Coco, Pta., *Colombia* **168 C2** 2 58N 77 43W
Coco Channel, *Asia* **95 H11** 13 45N 93 10 E
Cocoa, *U.S.A.* **153 G9** 28 21N 80 44W
Cocoa Beach, *U.S.A.* **153 G9** 28 19N 80 37W
Cocobeach, *Gabon* **114 B1** 0 59N 9 34 E
Cocoparra △, *Australia* **129 C7** 34 10 S 146 12 E
Cocora, *Romania* **53 F12** 44 45N 27 3 E
Côcos, *Brazil* **171 D3** 14 10 S 44 33W
Côcos →, *Brazil* **171 D3** 12 44 S 44 48W
Cocos B., *Trin. & Tob.* **169 F10** 10 25N 61 2W
Cocos I., *Guam* **133 R15** 13 14N 144 39 E
Cocos Is., *Ind. Oc.* **121 F8** 12 10 S 96 55 E
Cocos Ridge, *Pac. Oc.* **135 G19** 4 0N 88 0W
Cod, C., *U.S.A.* **148 D10** 42 5N 70 10W
Codajás, *Brazil* **169 D5** 3 55 S 62 0W
Codera, C., *Venezuela* **168 A4** 10 35N 66 4W
Codfish I., *N.Z.* **131 G2** 46 47 S 167 38 E
Codigoro, *Italy* **45 D9** 44 49N 12 8 E
Codlea, *Romania* **53 E10** 45 42N 25 27 E
Codó, *Brazil* **170 B3** 4 30 S 43 55W
Codogno, *Italy* **44 C6** 45 9N 9 42 E
Codpa, *Chile* **172 D4** 18 50 S 69 44W
Codróipo, *Italy* **45 C10** 45 58N 13 0 E
Codru, Munţii, *Romania* **52 D7** 46 30N 22 15 E
Cody, *U.S.A.* **158 D9** 44 32N 109 3W
Coe Hill, *Canada* **150 B7** 44 52N 77 50W
Coelemu, *Chile* **174 D1** 36 30 S 72 48W
Coelho Neto, *Brazil* **170 B3** 4 15 S 43 0W
Coen, *Australia* **126 A3** 13 52 S 143 12 E
Coeroeni →, *Suriname* **169 C6** 3 21N 57 31W
Coesfeld, *Germany* **30 D3** 51 56N 7 10 E
Coetivy Is., *Seychelles* **121 E4** 7 8 S 56 16 E
Cœur d'Alene, *U.S.A.* **158 C5** 47 45N 116 51W
Cœur d'Alene L., *U.S.A.* **158 C5** 47 32N 116 48W
Coevorden, *Neths.* **24 B6** 52 40N 6 44 E
Cofete, *Canary Is.* **9 e2** 28 6N 14 23W
Coffeyville, *U.S.A.* **155 G7** 37 2N 95 37W
Coffin B., *Australia* **127 E2** 34 38 S 135 28 E
Coffin Bay, *Australia* **127 E2** 34 37 S 135 29 E
Coffin Bay △, *Australia* **127 E2** 34 34 S 135 19 E
Coffin Bay Peninsula, *Australia* **127 E2** 34 32 S 135 15 E
Coffs Harbour, *Australia* **129 A10** 30 16 S 153 5 E
Cofre de Perote △, *Mexico* **163 D5** 19 29N 97 8W
Cofrentes, *Spain* **41 F3** 39 13N 1 5W
Cogalnic →, *Moldova* **53 E14** 45 49N 29 40 E
Cogealac, *Romania* **53 F13** 44 36N 28 36 E
Coghinas →, *Italy* **46 B1** 40 55N 8 48 E
Coghinas, L. del, *Italy* **46 B2** 40 46N 9 3 E
Cognac, *France* **28 C3** 45 41N 0 20W
Cogne, *Italy* **44 C4** 45 37N 7 21 E
Cogolin, *France* **29 E10** 43 15N 6 32 E
Cogolludo, *Spain* **40 E1** 40 59N 3 10W
Cohocton, *U.S.A.* **150 D7** 42 30N 77 30W
Cohocton →, *U.S.A.* **150 D7** 42 9N 77 6W
Cohoes, *U.S.A.* **151 D11** 42 46N 73 42W
Cohuna, *Australia* **128 C6** 35 45 S 144 15 E
Coiba, I., *Panama* **164 E3** 7 30N 81 40W
Coig →, *Argentina* **176 D3** 51 0 S 69 10W

Coigeach, Rubha, U.K. **22 C3** 58 6N 5 26W
Coihaique, Chile **176 C2** 45 30 S 71 45W
Coimbatore, India **95 J3** 11 2N 76 59 E
Coimbra, Brazil **173 D6** 19 55 S 57 48W
Coimbra, Portugal **42 E2** 40 15N 8 27W
Coimbra □, Portugal **42 E2** 40 12N 8 25W
Coín, Spain **43 J6** 36 40N 4 48W
Coipasa, L. de, Bolivia **172 D4** 19 12 S 68 7W
Coipasa, Salar de, Bolivia **172 D4** 19 26 S 68 9W
Cojata, Peru **172 D4** 15 2 S 69 25W
Cojedes □, Venezuela **168 B4** 9 20N 68 20W
Cojedes →, Venezuela **168 B4** 8 34N 68 5W
Cojimies, Ecuador **168 C1** 0 20N 80 0W
Cojocna, Romania **53 D8** 46 45N 23 50 E
Cojutepequé, El Salv. **164 D2** 13 41N 88 54W
Čoka, Serbia & M. **52 E5** 45 57N 20 12 E
Cokeville, U.S.A. **158 E8** 42 5N 110 57W
Colaba Pt., India **94 E1** 18 54N 72 47 E
Colac, Australia **128 E5** 38 21 S 143 35 E
Colachel = Kolachel, India **95 K3** 8 10N 77 15 E
Colatina, Brazil **171 E3** 19 32 S 40 37W
Colbeck, C., Antarctica **7 D13** 77 6 S 157 48W
Colbert, U.S.A. **152 A6** 34 2N 83 13W
Colborne, Canada **150 C7** 44 0N 77 53W
Colby, U.S.A. **154 F4** 39 24N 101 3W
Colca, Canon de, Peru **172 D3** 15 50 S 72 20W
Colchester, U.K. **21 F8** 51 54N 0 55 E
Cold Bay, U.S.A. **144 J7** 55 12N 162 42W
Cold L., Canada **143 C7** 54 33N 110 5W
Coldstream, Canada **142 C5** 50 13N 119 11W
Coldstream, U.K. **22 F6** 55 39N 2 15W
Coldwater, Canada **150 B5** 44 42N 79 40W
Coldwater, Kans., U.S.A. **155 G5** 37 16N 99 20W
Coldwater, Mich., U.S.A. **157 C11** 41 57N 85 0W
Coldwater, Ohio, U.S.A. **157 D12** 40 29N 84 38W
Coldwater, L., U.S.A. **157 C12** 41 48N 84 59W
Cole Camp, U.S.A. **156 F3** 38 28N 93 12W
Coleambally, Australia **129 C6** 34 49 S 145 52 E
Colebrook, U.S.A. **151 B13** 44 54N 71 30W
Coleman, Fla., U.S.A. **153 G7** 28 48N 82 4W
Coleman, Tex., U.S.A. **155 K5** 31 50N 99 26W
Coleman →, Australia **126 B3** 15 6 S 141 38 E
Colenso, S. Africa **117 D4** 28 44 S 29 50 E
Coleraine, Australia **128 D4** 37 36 S 141 40 E
Coleraine, U.K. **23 A5** 55 8N 6 41W
Coleridge, L., N.Z. **131 D6** 43 17 S 171 30 E
Coleroon →, India **95 J4** 11 25N 79 50 E
Colesberg, S. Africa **116 E4** 30 45 S 25 5 E
Coleville, U.S.A. **160 G7** 38 34N 119 30W
Colfax, Calif., U.S.A. **160 F6** 39 6N 120 57W
Colfax, Ill., U.S.A. **157 D8** 40 34N 88 37W
Colfax, Ind., U.S.A. **157 D10** 40 12N 86 40W
Colfax, Iowa, U.S.A. **156 C3** 41 41N 93 14W
Colfax, La., U.S.A. **155 K8** 31 31N 92 42W
Colfax, Wash., U.S.A. **158 C5** 46 53N 117 22W
Colhué Huapi, L., Argentina **176 C3** 45 30 S 69 0W
Colibaşi, Moldova **53 E13** 45 43N 28 11 E
Colibaşi, Romania **53 F9** 44 56N 24 54 E
Cólico, Italy **44 B6** 46 8N 9 22 E
Colíder, Brazil **173 C6** 10 45 S 55 25W
Coligny, France **27 F12** 46 23N 5 21 E
Coligny, S. Africa **117 D4** 26 17 S 26 15 E
Colima, Mexico **162 D4** 19 14N 103 43W
Colima □, Mexico **162 D4** 19 10N 103 40W
Colima, Nevado de, Mexico **162 D4** 19 35N 103 45W
Colina, Chile **174 C1** 33 13 S 70 45W
Colina do Norte, Guinea-Biss. **112 C2** 12 28N 15 0W
Colinas, Goiás, Brazil **171 D2** 14 15 S 48 2W
Colinas, Maranhão, Brazil **170 C3** 6 0 S 44 10W
Colindres, Spain **42 B7** 43 24N 3 27W
Coll, U.K. **22 E2** 56 39N 6 34W
Collaguasi, Chile **174 A2** 21 5 S 68 45W
Collarada, Peña, Spain **40 C4** 42 43N 0 29W
Collarenebri, Australia **127 D4** 29 33 S 148 34 E
Colle di Val d'Elsa, Italy **44 E8** 43 25N 11 7 E
Collécchio, Italy **44 D7** 44 45N 10 13 E
Colleen Bawn, Zimbabwe **119 G2** 21 0 S 29 12 E
College, U.S.A. **144 D11** 64 52N 147 49W
College Park, U.S.A. **152 B5** 33 40N 84 27W
College Station, U.S.A. **155 K6** 30 37N 96 21W
Collesalvetti, Italy **44 E7** 43 34N 10 27 E
Colli Euganei ⌓, Italy **45 C8** 45 18N 11 43 E
Collie, N.S.W., Australia **129 A8** 31 41 S 148 18 E
Collie, W. Austral., Australia **125 F2** 33 22 S 116 8 E
Collier B., Australia **124 C3** 16 10 S 124 15 E
Collier Ra., Australia **125 D2** 24 45 S 119 10 E
Collier Range △, Australia **125 D2** 24 39 S 119 7 E
Collierville, U.S.A. **155 H10** 35 3N 89 40W
Collina, Passo di, Italy **44 D7** 44 2N 10 56 E
Collingwood, Canada **140 D3** 44 29N 80 13W
Collingwood, N.Z. **131 A7** 40 41 S 172 40 E
Collins, Canada **140 B2** 50 17N 89 27W
Collins, Ga., U.S.A. **152 C7** 32 11N 82 7W
Collins, Mo., U.S.A. **156 G3** 37 54N 93 37W
Collinsville, Australia **126 C4** 20 30 S 147 56 E
Collinsville, U.S.A. **156 F7** 38 40N 89 59W
Collipulli, Chile **174 D1** 37 55 S 72 30W
Collo, Algeria **111 A6** 36 58N 6 37 E
Collooney, Ireland **23 B3** 54 11N 8 29W
Colmar, France **27 D14** 48 5N 7 20 E
Colmars, France **29 D10** 44 11N 6 39 E
Colmenar, Spain **43 J6** 36 54N 4 20W
Colmenar de Oreja, Spain **42 E7** 40 6N 3 25W
Colmenar Viejo, Spain **42 E7** 40 39N 3 47W
Colo →, Australia **129 B9** 33 25 S 150 52 E
Cologne = Köln, Germany **30 E2** 50 56N 6 57 E
Colom, I. d'en, Spain **38 B5** 39 58N 4 16 E
Coloma, Calif., U.S.A. **160 G6** 38 48N 120 53W
Coloma, Mich., U.S.A. **157 B10** 42 11N 86 19W
Colomb-Béchar = Béchar, Algeria **111 B4** 31 38N 2 18W
Colombey-les-Belles, France **27 D12** 48 32N 5 54 E
Colombey-les-Deux-Églises, France **27 D11** 48 13N 4 50 E
Colômbia, Brazil **171 F2** 20 10 S 48 40W
Colombia ■, S. Amer. **168 C3** 3 45N 73 0W
Colombian Basin, S. Amer. **136 H12** 14 0N 76 0W
Colombier, Switz. **32 C3** 46 58N 6 53 E
Colombo, Sri Lanka **95 L4** 6 56N 79 58 E
Colomiers, France **28 E5** 43 36N 1 21 E
Colón, Buenos Aires, Argentina **174 C3** 33 53 S 61 7W
Colón, Entre Ríos, Argentina **174 C4** 32 12 S 58 10W
Colón, Cuba **164 B3** 22 42N 80 54W
Colón, Panama **164 E4** 9 20N 79 54W
Colón, Peru **172 A1** 5 0 S 81 0W
Colón, Arch. de, Ecuador **172 a** 0 0 91 0W
Colonia 25 de Mayo, Argentina **176 A3** 37 48 S 67 41W
Colònia de Sant Jordi, Spain **38 B3** 39 19N 2 59 E
Colonia del Sacramento, Uruguay **174 C4** 34 25 S 57 50W
Colonia Dora, Argentina **174 B3** 28 34 S 62 59W
Colonia Las Heras, Argentina **176 C3** 46 33 S 68 57W
Colonial Beach, U.S.A. **148 F7** 38 15N 76 58W
Colonie, U.S.A. **151 D11** 42 43N 73 50W
Colonna, C., Italy **47 C10** 39 2N 17 12 E
Colonsay, Canada **143 C7** 51 59N 105 52W
Colonsay, U.K. **22 E2** 56 5N 6 12W
Colorado □, U.S.A. **159 G10** 39 30N 105 30W
Colorado →, Argentina **176 A4** 39 50 S 62 8W
Colorado →, N. Amer. **159 L6** 31 45N 114 40W
Colorado →, U.S.A. **155 L7** 28 36N 95 59W
Colorado City, U.S.A. **155 J4** 32 24N 100 52W
Colorado Plateau, U.S.A. **159 H8** 37 0N 111 0W
Colorado River Aqueduct, U.S.A. **161 L12** 34 17N 114 10W
Colorado Springs, U.S.A. **154 F2** 38 50N 104 49W
Colorno, Italy **44 D7** 44 56N 10 23 E
Colotlán, Mexico **162 C4** 22 6N 103 16W
Colquechaca, Bolivia **173 D4** 18 40 S 66 1W
Colquitt, U.S.A. **152 D5** 31 10N 84 44W
Colstrip, U.S.A. **158 D10** 45 53N 106 38W
Colton, U.S.A. **151 B10** 44 33N 74 56W
Columbia, Ala., U.S.A. **152 D4** 31 18N 85 7W
Columbia, Ill., U.S.A. **156 F6** 38 27N 90 12W
Columbia, Ky., U.S.A. **148 G3** 37 6N 85 18W
Columbia, La., U.S.A. **155 J8** 32 6N 92 5W
Columbia, Miss., U.S.A. **155 K10** 31 15N 89 50W
Columbia, Mo., U.S.A. **156 F4** 38 57N 92 20W
Columbia, Pa., U.S.A. **151 F8** 40 2N 76 30W
Columbia, S.C., U.S.A. **152 A8** 34 0N 81 2W
Columbia, Tenn., U.S.A. **149 H2** 35 37N 87 2W
Columbia →, N. Amer. **160 D2** 46 15N 124 5W
Columbia, C., Canada **6 A4** 83 6N 69 57W
Columbia, District of □, U.S.A. **148 F7** 38 55N 77 0W
Columbia, Mt., Canada **142 C5** 52 8N 117 20W
Columbia Basin, U.S.A. **158 C4** 46 45N 119 5W
Columbia City, U.S.A. **157 C11** 41 10N 85 29W
Columbia Falls, U.S.A. **158 B6** 48 23N 114 11W
Columbia Mts., Canada **142 C5** 52 0N 119 0W
Columbia Plateau, U.S.A. **158 D5** 44 0N 117 30W
Columbiana, U.S.A. **150 F4** 40 53N 80 42W
Columbretes, Is., Spain **40 F5** 39 50N 0 50 E
Columbus, Ga., U.S.A. **152 C5** 32 28N 84 59W
Columbus, Ind., U.S.A. **157 E11** 39 13N 85 55W
Columbus, Kans., U.S.A. **155 G7** 37 10N 94 50W
Columbus, Miss., U.S.A. **149 J1** 33 30N 88 25W
Columbus, Mont., U.S.A. **158 D9** 45 38N 109 15W
Columbus, N. Mex., U.S.A. **159 L10** 31 50N 107 38W
Columbus, Nebr., U.S.A. **154 E6** 41 26N 97 22W
Columbus, Ohio, U.S.A. **157 E13** 39 58N 83 0W
Columbus, Tex., U.S.A. **155 L6** 29 42N 96 33W
Columbus Grove, U.S.A. **157 D12** 40 55N 84 4W
Columbus Junction, U.S.A. **156 C5** 41 17N 91 22W
Colunga, Spain **42 B5** 43 29N 5 16W
Colusa, U.S.A. **160 F4** 39 13N 122 1W
Colville, U.S.A. **158 B5** 48 33N 117 54W
Colville →, U.S.A. **144 A10** 70 25N 150 30W
Colville, C., N.Z. **130 C4** 36 29 S 175 21 E
Colwood, Canada **160 B3** 48 26N 123 29W
Colwyn Bay, U.K. **20 D4** 53 18N 3 44W
Coma, Ethiopia **107 F4** 8 29N 36 53 E
Comácchio, Italy **45 D9** 44 42N 12 11 E
Comalcalco, Mexico **163 D6** 18 16N 93 13W
Comallo, Argentina **176 B2** 41 0 S 70 5W
Comana, Romania **53 F11** 44 10N 26 10 E
Comanche, U.S.A. **155 K5** 31 54N 98 36W
Comandante Arbues = Mirandópolis, Brazil **175 A5** 21 9 S 51 6W
Comandante Ferraz, Antarctica **7 C18** 62 30 S 58 0W
Comandante Luis Piedrabuena, Argentina **176 C3** 49 59 S 68 54W
Comăneşti, Romania **53 D11** 46 25N 26 26 E
Comarapa, Bolivia **173 D5** 17 54 S 64 29W
Comarnic, Romania **53 E10** 45 15N 25 38 E
Comayagua, Honduras **164 D2** 14 25N 87 37W
Combahee →, U.S.A. **149 J5** 32 30N 80 31W
Combara, Australia **129 A8** 31 10 S 148 22 E
Combarbalá, Chile **174 C1** 31 11 S 71 2W
Combe Martin, U.K. **21 F3** 51 12N 4 3W
Combeaufontaine, France **27 E12** 47 38N 5 54 E
Comber, Canada **150 D2** 42 14N 82 33W
Comber, U.K. **23 B6** 54 33N 5 45W
Combermere, Canada **150 A7** 45 22N 77 37W
Combermere Bay, Burma **90 F4** 19 37N 93 34 E
Comblain-au-Pont, Belgium **24 D5** 50 29N 5 35 E
Combourg, France **26 D5** 48 25N 1 46W
Comboyne, Australia **129 A10** 31 34 S 152 27 E
Combrailles, France **27 F9** 46 8N 2 8 E
Combronde, France **28 C7** 45 58N 3 5 E
Comer, Ala., U.S.A. **152 C4** 32 2N 85 23W
Comer, Ga., U.S.A. **152 A6** 34 4N 83 8W
Comeragh Mts., Ireland **23 D4** 52 18N 7 34W
Comet, Australia **126 C4** 23 36 S 148 38 E
Comilla, Bangla. **90 D3** 23 28N 91 10 E
Comino, Malta **38 E7** 36 1N 14 20 E
Comino, C., Italy **46 B2** 40 32N 9 49 E
Cómiso, Italy **47 F7** 36 56N 14 36 E
Comitán, Mexico **163 D6** 16 18N 92 9W
Commentry, France **27 F9** 46 20N 2 46 E
Commerce, Ga., U.S.A. **149 H4** 34 12N 83 28W
Commerce, Tex., U.S.A. **155 J7** 33 15N 95 54W
Commercy, France **27 D12** 48 43N 5 34 E
Commissioner's Pt., Bermuda **9 a** 32 19N 64 49W
Committee B., Canada **139 B11** 68 30N 86 30W
Commonwealth B., Antarctica **7 C10** 67 0 S 144 0 E
Commoron Cr. →, Australia **127 D5** 28 22 S 150 8 E
Communism Pk. = Kommunizma, Pik, Tajikistan **65 D6** 39 0N 72 2 E
Como, Italy **44 C6** 45 47N 9 5 E
Como, Lago di, Italy **44 B6** 46 0N 9 11 E
Comodoro Rivadavia, Argentina **176 C3** 45 50 S 67 40W
Comoé △, Ivory C. **112 D4** 9 0N 3 35W
Comorâşte, Romania **52 E6** 45 10N 21 35 E
Comorin, C., India **95 K3** 8 3N 77 40 E
Comoros ■, Ind. Oc. **121 a** 12 10 S 44 15 E
Comox, Canada **142 D4** 49 42N 124 55W
Compass Lake, U.S.A. **152 E4** 30 36N 85 24W
Compiègne, France **27 C9** 49 24N 2 50 E
Comporta, Portugal **43 G2** 38 22N 8 46W
Compostela, Mexico **162 C4** 21 15N 104 53W
Compostela, Phil. **81 H6** 7 40N 126 2 E
Comprida, I., Brazil **175 A6** 24 50 S 47 42W
Compton, Canada **151 A13** 45 14N 71 49W
Compton, U.S.A. **161 M8** 33 54N 118 13W
Comrat, Moldova **53 D13** 46 18N 28 40 E
Con Cuong, Vietnam **86 C5** 19 2N 104 54 E
Con Dao △, Vietnam **87 H6** 8 42N 106 35 E
Con Son, Vietnam **87 H6** 8 41N 106 37 E
Cona Niyeu, Argentina **176 B3** 41 58 S 67 0W
Conakry, Guinea **112 D2** 9 29N 13 49W
Conara, Australia **127 G4** 41 50 S 147 26 E
Conargo, Australia **129 C6** 35 16 S 145 10 E
Concarneau, France **26 E3** 47 52N 3 56W
Conceição, Brazil **170 C4** 7 33 S 38 31W
Conceição, Mozam. **119 F4** 18 47 S 36 7 E
Conceição da Barra, Brazil **171 E4** 18 35 S 39 45W
Conceição do Araguaia, Brazil **170 C2** 8 0 S 49 2W
Conceição do Canindé, Brazil **170 C3** 7 54 S 41 34W
Conceição do Maú, Brazil **169 C6** 3 35N 59 53W
Conçeicão do Paraíba = Capela, Brazil **170 D4** 10 30 S 37 0W
Concepción, Argentina **174 B2** 27 20 S 65 35W
Concepción, Bolivia **173 D5** 16 15 S 62 8W
Concepción, Chile **174 D1** 36 50 S 73 0W
Concepción, Mexico **163 D6** 18 15N 90 5W
Concepción, Paraguay **174 A4** 23 22 S 57 26W
Concepción, Peru **172 C2** 11 54 S 75 19W
Concepcion, Phil. **80 D3** 15 27N 120 47 E
Concepción □, Chile **174 D1** 37 0 S 72 30W
Concepción →, Mexico **162 A2** 30 32N 113 2W
Concepción, Est. de, Chile **176 D2** 50 30 S 74 55W
Concepción, L., Bolivia **173 D5** 17 20 S 61 20W
Concepción, Punta, Mexico **162 B2** 26 55N 111 59W
Concepción del Oro, Mexico **162 C4** 24 40N 101 30W
Concepción del Uruguay, Argentina **174 C4** 32 35 S 58 20W
Conception, Pt., U.S.A. **161 L6** 34 27N 120 28W
Conception B., Canada **141 C9** 47 45N 53 0W
Conception B., Namibia **116 C1** 23 55 S 14 22 E
Conception I., Bahamas **165 B4** 23 52N 75 9W
Concession, Zimbabwe **119 F3** 17 27 S 30 56 E
Conchas Dam, U.S.A. **155 H2** 35 22N 104 11W
Conches-en-Ouche, France **26 D7** 48 58N 0 56 E
Concho, U.S.A. **159 J9** 34 28N 109 36W
Concho →, U.S.A. **155 K5** 31 34N 99 43W
Conchos →, Chihuahua, Mexico **162 B4** 29 32N 105 0W
Conchos →, Tamaulipas, Mexico **163 B5** 25 9N 98 35W
Concise, Switz. **32 C3** 46 51N 6 43 E
Concord, Calif., U.S.A. **160 H4** 37 59N 122 2W
Concord, Ga., U.S.A. **152 B5** 33 5N 84 27W
Concord, Mich., U.S.A. **157 B12** 42 11N 84 38W
Concord, Mo., U.S.A. **156 F6** 38 32N 90 23W
Concord, N.C., U.S.A. **149 H5** 35 25N 80 35W
Concord, N.H., U.S.A. **151 C13** 43 12N 71 32W
Concordia, Argentina **174 C4** 31 20 S 58 2W
Concórdia, Brazil **168 D4** 4 36 S 66 36W
Concordia, Mexico **162 C3** 23 18N 106 2W
Concordia, Kans., U.S.A. **154 F6** 39 34N 97 40W
Concordia, Mo., U.S.A. **156 F3** 38 59N 93 34W
Concrete, U.S.A. **158 B3** 48 32N 121 45W
Conda, Angola **115 E2** 11 9 S 14 20 E
Condah, Australia **128 D4** 37 57 S 141 44 E
Condamine, Australia **127 D5** 26 56 S 150 9 E
Condat, France **28 C6** 45 21N 2 46 E
Condé, Angola **115 E2** 10 50 S 14 37 E
Conde, Brazil **171 D4** 11 49 S 37 37W
Conde, U.S.A. **154 C5** 45 9N 98 6W
Condé-sur-Noireau, France **26 D6** 48 51N 0 33W
Condeúba, Brazil **171 D3** 14 52 S 42 0W
Condobolin, Australia **129 B7** 33 4 S 147 6 E
Condom, France **28 E4** 43 57N 0 22 E
Condon, U.S.A. **158 D3** 45 14N 120 11W
Conegliano, Italy **45 C9** 45 53N 12 18 E
Conejera, I. = Conills, I. des, Spain **38 B3** 39 11N 2 58 E
Conejos, Mexico **162 B4** 26 14N 103 53W
Conemaugh →, U.S.A. **150 F5** 40 28N 79 19W
Conero ⌓, Italy **45 E10** 43 32N 13 35 E
Conflict Group, Papua N. G. **132 F6** 10 47 S 151 45 E
Confolens, France **28 B4** 46 2N 0 40 E
Confuso →, Paraguay **174 B4** 25 9 S 57 34W
Congaree →, U.S.A. **152 B9** 33 44N 80 38W
Congaree Swamp ⌓, U.S.A. **152 B9** 33 47N 80 47W
Congaz, Moldova **53 D13** 46 7N 28 36 E
Congerville, U.S.A. **156 D7** 40 38N 89 11W
Conghua, China **77 F9** 23 36N 113 31 E
Congjiang, China **76 E7** 25 43N 108 52 E
Congleton, U.K. **20 D5** 53 10N 2 13W
Congo, Brazil **170 C4** 7 48 S 36 40W
Congo (Brazzaville) = Congo ■, Africa **114 C3** 1 0 S 16 0 E
Congo (Kinshasa) = Congo, Dem. Rep. of the ■, Africa **115 C4** 3 0 S 23 0 E
Congo ■, Africa **114 C3** 1 0 S 16 0 E
Congo →, Africa **115 D2** 6 4 S 12 24 E
Congo, Dem. Rep. of the ■, Africa **115 C4** 3 0 S 23 0 E
Congo Basin, Africa **104 G6** 0 10 S 24 30 E
Congo Free State = Congo, Dem. Rep. of the ■, Africa **115 C4** 3 0 S 23 0 E
Congonhas, Brazil **171 F3** 20 30 S 43 52W
Congress, U.S.A. **159 J7** 34 9N 112 51W
Conguillio △, Chile **176 A2** 38 40 S 71 42W
Conil de la Frontera, Spain **43 J4** 36 17N 6 10W
Conills, I. des, Spain **38 B3** 39 11N 2 58 E
Coniston, Canada **140 C3** 46 29N 80 51W
Conjeeveram = Kanchipuram, India **95 H4** 12 52N 79 45 E
Conklin, Canada **143 B6** 55 38N 111 5W
Conklin, U.S.A. **151 D9** 42 2N 75 49W
Conkouati ⌓, Congo **114 C2** 3 50 S 11 28 E
Conlendas, Pta. das, Azores **9 d1** 38 38N 27 14W
Conn, L., Ireland **23 B2** 54 3N 9 15W
Connacht □, Ireland **23 C2** 53 43N 9 12W
Conneaut, U.S.A. **150 E4** 41 57N 80 34W
Connecticut □, U.S.A. **151 E12** 41 30N 72 45W
Connecticut →, U.S.A. **151 E12** 41 16N 72 20W
Connell, U.S.A. **158 C4** 46 40N 118 52W
Connellsville, U.S.A. **150 F5** 40 1N 79 35W
Connemara, Ireland **23 C2** 53 29N 9 45W
Connemara △, Ireland **23 C2** 53 32N 9 52W
Conner, Phil. **80 C3** 17 48N 121 19 E
Connerré, France **26 D7** 48 3N 0 30 E
Connersville, U.S.A. **157 E11** 39 39N 85 8W
Connors Ra., Australia **126 C4** 21 40 S 149 10 E
Conoble, Australia **129 B6** 32 55 S 144 33 E
Cononaco →, Ecuador **168 D2** 1 32 S 75 35W
Conques, France **28 D6** 44 36N 2 23 E
Conquest, Canada **143 C7** 51 32N 107 14W
Conquista = Vitória da Conquista, Brazil **171 D3** 14 51 S 40 51W
Conrad, Iowa, U.S.A. **156 B4** 42 14N 92 52W
Conrad, Mont., U.S.A. **158 B8** 48 10N 111 57W
Conran, C., Australia **129 D8** 37 49 S 148 44 E
Conroe, U.S.A. **155 K7** 30 19N 95 27W
Consecon, Canada **150 C7** 44 0N 77 31W
Conselheiro Lafaiete, Brazil **171 F3** 20 40 S 43 48W
Conselheiro Pena, Brazil **171 E3** 19 10 S 41 30W
Conselve, Italy **45 C8** 45 14N 11 52 E
Consett, U.K. **20 C6** 54 51N 1 50W
Consort, Canada **143 C6** 52 1N 110 46W
Constance = Konstanz, Germany **31 H5** 47 40N 9 10 E
Constance, L. = Bodensee, Europe **33 A8** 47 35N 9 25 E
Constanţa, Romania **53 F13** 44 14N 28 38 E
Constanţa □, Romania **53 F13** 44 15N 28 15 E
Constantia, U.S.A. **151 C8** 43 15N 76 1W
Constantina, Spain **43 H5** 37 51N 5 40W
Constantine, Algeria **111 A6** 36 25N 6 42 E
Constantine, U.S.A. **157 C11** 41 50N 85 40W
Constantine, C., U.S.A. **144 G8** 58 24N 158 54W
Constitución, Chile **174 D1** 35 20 S 72 30W
Constitución, Uruguay **174 C4** 31 0 S 57 50W
Constitucion de 1857 △, Mexico **162 A1** 32 4N 115 55W
Consuegra, Spain **43 F7** 39 28N 3 36W
Consul, Canada **143 D7** 49 20N 109 30W
Contact, U.S.A. **158 F6** 41 46N 114 45W
Contai, India **93 J12** 21 54N 87 46 E
Contamana, Peru **172 B3** 7 19 S 74 55W
Contarina, Italy **45 C9** 45 1N 12 13 E
Contas →, Brazil **171 D4** 14 17 S 39 1W
Contes, France **29 E11** 43 49N 7 19 E
Conthey, Switz. **32 D4** 46 14N 7 18 E
Continental, U.S.A. **157 C12** 41 6N 84 16W
Contoocook, U.S.A. **151 C13** 43 13N 71 45W
Contra Costa, Mozam. **117 D5** 25 9 S 33 30 E
Contres, France **26 E8** 47 24N 1 26 E
Contrexéville, France **27 D12** 48 10N 5 53 E
Controller B., U.S.A. **144 F11** 60 7N 144 15W
Contumaza, Peru **172 B2** 7 23 S 78 57W
Contwoyto L., Canada **138 B8** 65 42N 110 50W
Convención, Colombia **168 B3** 8 28N 73 21W
Conversano, Italy **47 B10** 40 58N 17 7 E
Converse, U.S.A. **157 D11** 40 35N 85 52W
Convoy, U.S.A. **157 D12** 40 55N 84 43W
Conway = Conwy, U.K. **20 D4** 53 17N 3 50W
Conway = Conwy →, U.K. **20 D4** 53 17N 3 50W
Conway, Australia **126 J6** 20 24 S 148 41 E
Conway, Ark., U.S.A. **155 H8** 35 5N 92 26W
Conway, N.H., U.S.A. **151 C13** 43 59N 71 7W
Conway, S.C., U.S.A. **149 J6** 33 51N 79 3W
Conway, C., Australia **126 J6** 20 34 S 148 46 E
Conway, L., Australia **127 D2** 28 17 S 135 35 E
Conwy, U.K. **20 D4** 53 17N 3 50W
Conwy □, U.K. **20 D4** 53 10N 3 44W
Conwy →, U.K. **20 D4** 53 17N 3 50W
Conyers, U.S.A. **152 B5** 33 40N 84 1W
Coober Pedy, Australia **127 D1** 29 1 S 134 43 E
Cooch Behar = Koch Bihar, India **90 B2** 26 22N 89 29 E
Cooinda, Australia **124 B5** 13 15 S 130 5 E
Cook, Australia **125 F5** 30 37 S 130 25 E
Cook, U.S.A. **154 B8** 47 49N 92 39W
Cook, B., Chile **176 E2** 55 10 S 70 0W
Cook, C., Canada **142 C3** 50 8N 127 55W
Cook, Mt. = Aoraki Mount Cook, N.Z. **131 D5** 43 36 S 170 9 E
Cook B., Vanuatu **133 H7** 18 46 S 169 15 E
Cook Inlet, U.S.A. **144 G10** 60 0N 152 0W
Cook Is., Pac. Oc. **135 J12** 17 0 S 160 0W
Cook Strait, N.Z. **130 H3** 41 15 S 174 29 E
Cooke Plains, Australia **128 C3** 35 23 S 139 34 E
Cookeville, U.S.A. **149 G3** 36 10N 85 30W
Cookhouse, S. Africa **116 E4** 32 44 S 25 47 E
Cooks Hammock, U.S.A. **152 F6** 29 56N 83 17W
Cookshire, Canada **151 A13** 45 25N 71 38W
Cookstown, U.K. **23 B5** 54 39N 6 45W
Cooksville, Canada **150 C5** 43 36N 79 35W
Cooktown, Australia **126 B4** 15 30 S 145 16 E
Coolabah, Australia **129 A7** 31 1 S 146 43 E
Cooladdi, Australia **127 D4** 26 37 S 145 23 E
Coolah, Australia **129 A8** 31 48 S 149 41 E
Coolamon, Australia **129 C7** 34 46 S 147 8 E
Coolgardie, Australia **125 F3** 30 55 S 121 8 E
Coolidge, Ariz., U.S.A. **159 K8** 32 59N 111 31W
Coolidge, Ga., U.S.A. **152 D6** 31 1N 83 52W
Coolidge Dam, U.S.A. **159 K8** 33 0N 110 20W
Cooloola △, Australia **127 D5** 26 13 S 153 2 E
Cooma, Australia **129 D8** 36 12 S 149 8 E
Coon Rapids, Iowa, U.S.A. **156 C2** 41 53N 94 41W
Coon Rapids, Minn., U.S.A. **154 C8** 45 9N 93 19W
Coonabarabran, Australia **129 A8** 31 14 S 149 18 E
Coonalpyn, Australia **128 C3** 35 43 S 139 52 E
Coonamble, Australia **129 A8** 30 56 S 148 27 E
Coonana, Australia **125 F3** 31 0 S 123 0 E
Coondapoor, India **95 H2** 13 42N 74 40 E
Cooninie, L., Australia **127 D2** 26 4 S 139 59 E
Coonoor, India **95 J3** 11 21N 76 45 E
Cooper, U.S.A. **155 J7** 33 23N 95 42W
Cooper →, U.S.A. **152 C10** 32 50N 79 56W
Cooper Cr. →, Australia **127 D2** 28 29 S 137 46 E
Cooperstown, N. Dak., U.S.A. **154 B5** 47 27N 98 8W
Cooperstown, N.Y., U.S.A. **151 D10** 42 42N 74 56W
Coopersville, U.S.A. **157 A11** 43 4N 85 57W
Coopracambra △, Australia **129 D8** 37 20 S 149 20 E
Coorabie, Australia **125 F5** 31 54 S 132 18 E
Coorong △, Australia **128 D3** 36 0 S 139 29 E
Coorong, The, Australia **128 C3** 35 50 S 139 20 E
Coorow, Australia **125 E2** 29 53 S 116 2 E
Cooroy, Australia **127 D5** 26 22 S 152 54 E
Coos Bay, U.S.A. **158 E1** 43 22N 124 13W
Coosa →, U.S.A. **149 J2** 32 30N 86 16W
Cootamundra, Australia **129 C8** 34 36 S 148 1 E
Cootehill, Ireland **23 B4** 54 4N 7 5W
Copahue Paso, Argentina **174 D1** 37 49 S 71 8W
Copainalá, Mexico **163 D6** 17 8N 93 11W
Copake Falls, U.S.A. **151 D11** 42 7N 73 31W
Copalnic Mănăştur, Romania **53 C8** 47 30N 23 41 E
Copán, Honduras **164 D2** 14 50N 89 9W
Copatana, Brazil **168 D4** 2 48 S 67 4W
Cope, Colo., U.S.A. **154 F3** 39 40N 102 51W
Cope, S.C., U.S.A. **152 B8** 33 23N 81 0W
Cope, C., Spain **41 H3** 37 26N 1 28W
Copeland, U.S.A. **153 K8** 25 57N 81 22W
Copenhagen = København, Denmark **17 J6** 55 41N 12 34 E
Copenhagen, U.S.A. **151 C9** 43 54N 75 41W
Copertino, Italy **47 B11** 40 16N 18 3 E
Copiapó, Chile **174 B1** 27 30 S 70 20W
Copiapó →, Chile **174 B1** 27 19 S 70 56W
Coplay, U.S.A. **151 F9** 40 44N 75 29W
Copley, Australia **128 A3** 30 36 S 138 26 E
Copp L., Canada **142 A6** 60 14N 114 40W
Copparo, Italy **45 D8** 44 54N 11 49 E
Coppename →, Suriname **169 B6** 5 48N 55 55W
Copper →, U.S.A. **144 F11** 60 18N 145 3W
Copper Center, U.S.A. **144 F11** 61 58N 145 18W
Copper City = Invermere, Canada **142 C5** 50 30N 116 2W
Copper Harbor, U.S.A. **148 B2** 47 28N 87 53W
Copper Queen, Zimbabwe **119 F2** 17 29 S 29 18 E
Copperas Cove, U.S.A. **155 K6** 31 8N 97 54W
Copperbelt □, Zambia **119 E2** 13 15 S 27 30 E
Coppermine = Kugluktuk, Canada **138 B8** 67 50N 115 5W
Coppermine →, Canada **138 B8** 67 49N 116 4W
Copperopolis, U.S.A. **160 H6** 37 58N 120 38W
Coppet, Switz. **32 D2** 46 19N 6 12 E
Copşa Mică, Romania **53 D9** 46 7N 24 15 E
Coquet →, U.K. **20 B6** 55 20N 1 32W
Coquilhatville = Mbandaka, Dem. Rep. of the Congo **114 B3** 0 1N 18 18 E
Coquille, U.S.A. **158 E1** 43 11N 124 11W
Coquimbo, Chile **174 C1** 30 0 S 71 20W
Coquimbo □, Chile **174 C1** 31 0 S 71 0W
Corabia, Romania **53 G9** 43 48N 24 30 E
Coração de Jesus, Brazil **171 E3** 16 43 S 44 22W
Coracora, Peru **172 D3** 15 5 S 73 45W
Coraki, Australia **127 D5** 28 59 S 153 17 E
Coral, U.S.A. **150 F5** 40 29N 79 10W
Coral Bay, Phil. **81 G1** 8 25N 117 20 E
Coral Gables, U.S.A. **153 K9** 25 45N 80 16W
Coral Harbour, Bahamas **9 b** 24 58N 77 28W
Coral Harbour, Canada **139 B11** 64 8N 83 10W
Coral Heights, Bahamas **9 b** 25 0N 77 27W
Coral Sea, Pac. Oc. **132 F3** 15 0 S 150 0 E
Coral Sea Islands Terr. □, Australia **122 D9** 20 0 S 155 0 E
Coral Springs, U.S.A. **153 J9** 26 16N 80 13W
Corales del Rosario △, Colombia **168 A2** 10 8N 75 46W
Coralville, U.S.A. **156 C5** 41 40N 91 35W
Coralville L., U.S.A. **156 C5** 41 50N 91 40W
Corangamite, L., Australia **128 E5** 38 5 S 143 30 E
Corantijn →, Suriname **169 B6** 5 50N 57 8W
Coraopolis, U.S.A. **150 F4** 40 31N 80 10W
Corato, Italy **47 A9** 41 9N 16 25 E
Corbeil-Essonnes, France **27 D9** 48 36N 2 26 E
Corbeiro, C., W. Sahara **110 D1** 21 50N 17 0W
Corbett △, India **93 E8** 29 20N 79 0 E
Corbie, France **27 C9** 49 54N 2 30 E
Corbières, France **28 F6** 42 55N 2 35 E
Corbigny, France **27 E10** 47 16N 3 40 E
Corbin, U.S.A. **148 G3** 36 57N 84 6W
Corbones →, Spain **43 H5** 37 36N 5 39W
Corbu, Romania **53 F13** 44 25N 28 39 E
Corby, U.K. **21 E7** 52 30N 0 41W
Corcaigh = Cork, Ireland **23 E3** 51 54N 8 29W
Corcoran, U.S.A. **160 J7** 36 6N 119 33W
Corcovado △, Costa Rica **164 E3** 8 33N 83 35W
Cordele, U.S.A. **152 D6** 31 58N 83 47W
Cordell, U.S.A. **155 H5** 35 17N 98 59W
Cordenòns, Italy **45 C9** 45 59N 12 42 E
Cordes-sur-Ciel, France **28 D5** 44 5N 1 57 E
Cordillera de los Picachos △, Colombia **168 C3** 2 39N 74 30W
Cordisburgo, Brazil **171 E3** 19 7 S 44 21W
Córdoba, Argentina **174 C3** 31 20 S 64 10W
Córdoba, Mexico **163 D5** 18 50N 97 0W
Córdoba, Spain **43 H6** 37 50N 4 50W
Córdoba □, Argentina **174 C3** 31 22 S 64 15W
Córdoba □, Colombia **168 B2** 8 20N 75 40W
Córdoba □, Spain **43 G6** 38 5N 5 0W
Córdoba, Sierra de, Argentina **174 C3** 31 10 S 64 25W
Cordon, Phil. **80 C3** 16 42N 121 32 E
Cordova, U.S.A. **144 F11** 60 33N 145 45W
Corella, Spain **40 C3** 42 7N 1 48W
Corella →, Australia **126 B3** 19 34 S 140 47 E
Coremas, Brazil **170 C4** 7 1 S 37 58W
Corentyne →, Guyana **169 B6** 5 50N 57 8W
Corfield, Australia **126 C3** 21 40 S 143 21 E
Corfu = Kérkira, Greece **38 B9** 39 38N 19 50 E
Corfu ✕ (CFU), Greece **48 B1** 39 35N 19 54 E
Corgo = O Corgo, Spain **42 C3** 42 56N 7 25W
Corguinho, Brazil **173 D7** 19 53 S 54 52W
Cori, Italy **46 A5** 41 39N 12 55 E
Coria, Spain **42 F4** 39 58N 6 33W
Coria del Río, Spain **43 H4** 37 16N 6 3W
Coricudgy, Australia **129 B9** 32 51 S 150 24 E
Corigliano Cálabro, Italy **47 C9** 39 36N 16 31 E
Corimba, Barra de, Angola **115 D2** 8 52 S 13 9 E
Coringa Is., Australia **126 B4** 16 58 S 149 58 E
Corinth = Kórinthos, Greece **48 D4** 37 56N 22 55 E
Corinth, Ky., U.S.A. **157 F12** 38 30N 84 34W
Corinth, Miss., U.S.A. **149 H1** 34 56N 88 31W
Corinth, N.Y., U.S.A. **151 C11** 43 15N 73 49W
Corinth, G. of = Korinthiakós Kólpos, Greece **48 C4** 38 16N 22 30 E
Corinth Canal, Greece **48 D4** 37 58N 23 0 E
Corinto, Brazil **171 E3** 18 20 S 44 30W
Corinto, Nic. **164 D2** 12 30N 87 10W
Corisco, Eq. Guin. **114 B1** 0 55N 9 18 E
Cork, Ireland **23 E3** 51 54N 8 29W
Cork □, Ireland **23 E3** 51 57N 8 40W
Cork Harbour, Ireland **23 E3** 51 47N 8 16W
Corlay, France **26 D3** 48 20N 3 5W
Corleone, Italy **46 E6** 37 49N 13 18 E
Corleto Perticara, Italy **47 B9** 40 23N 16 2 E
Çorlu, Turkey **51 E11** 41 11N 27 49 E

Cormack L., *Canada* **142 A4** 60 56N 121 37W
Cormòns, *Italy* **45 C10** 45 58N 13 28 E
Cormorant, *Canada* **143 C8** 54 14N 100 35W
Cormorant L., *Canada* **143 C8** 54 15N 100 50W
Corn Is. = Maiz, Is. del, *Nic.* **164 D3** 12 15N 83 4W
Cornalvo ⌓, *Spain* **43 F4** 39 1N 6 13W
Cornélio Procópio, *Brazil* **175 A5** 23 7 S 50 40W
Cornell, *U.S.A.* **157 D8** 41 0N 88 44W
Corner Brook, *Canada* **141 C8** 48 57N 57 58W
Corner Inlet, *Australia* **129 E7** 38 45 S 146 20 E
Corner Seamounts, *Atl. Oc.* **8 C6** 35 0N 52 0W
Corneşti, *Moldova* **53 C13** 47 21N 28 1 E
Corneto = Tarquínia, *Italy* **45 F8** 42 15N 11 45 E
Corníglio, *Italy* **44 D7** 44 29N 10 5 E
Corning, *Ark., U.S.A.* **155 G9** 36 25N 90 35W
Corning, *Calif., U.S.A.* **158 G2** 39 56N 122 11W
Corning, *Iowa, U.S.A.* **156 D2** 40 59N 94 44W
Corning, *N.Y., U.S.A.* **150 D7** 42 9N 77 3W
Corno Grande, *Italy* **45 F10** 42 28N 13 34 E
Cornwall, *Canada* **140 C5** 45 2N 74 44W
Cornwall, *U.S.A.* **151 F8** 40 17N 76 25W
Cornwall □, *U.K.* **21 G3** 50 26N 4 40W
Cornwell, *U.S.A.* **153 H8** 27 23N 81 6W
Corny Pt., *Australia* **128 C2** 34 55 S 137 0 E
Coro, *Venezuela* **168 A4** 11 25N 69 41W
Coroaci, *Brazil* **171 E3** 18 35 S 42 17W
Coroatá, *Brazil* **170 B3** 4 8 S 44 0W
Coroban, *Somali Rep.* **120 D2** 3 58N 42 44 E
Corocoro, *Bolivia* **172 D4** 17 15 S 68 28W
Corocoro, I., *Venezuela* **169 B5** 8 30N 60 10W
Coroico, *Bolivia* **172 D4** 16 0 S 67 50W
Coromandel, *Brazil* **171 E2** 18 28 S 47 13W
Coromandel, *N.Z.* **130 C4** 36 45 S 175 31 E
Coromandel Coast, *India* **95 H5** 12 30N 81 0 E
Coromandel Pen., *N.Z.* **130 C4** 37 0 S 175 45 E
Coromandel Ra., *N.Z.* **130 C4** 37 0 S 175 40 E
Coron, *Phil.* **80 E3** 12 1N 120 12 E
Coron Bay, *Phil.* **81 F3** 11 54N 120 8 E
Coron I., *Phil.* **81 F3** 11 55N 120 14 E
Corona, *Calif., U.S.A.* **161 M9** 33 53N 117 34W
Corona, *N. Mex., U.S.A.* **159 J11** 34 15N 105 36W
Coronach, *Canada* **143 D7** 49 7N 105 31W
Coronado, *U.S.A.* **161 N9** 32 41N 117 11W
Coronado, B. de, *Costa Rica* **164 E3** 9 0N 83 40W
Coronados, G. de los, *Chile* **176 B2** 41 40 S 74 0W
Coronados, Is. los, *U.S.A.* **161 N9** 32 25N 117 15W
Coronation, *Canada* **142 C6** 52 5N 111 27W
Coronation Gulf, *Canada* **138 B8** 68 25N 110 0W
Coronation I., *Antarctica* **7 C18** 60 45 S 46 0W
Coronation Is., *Australia* **124 B3** 14 57 S 124 55 E
Coronda, *Argentina* **174 C3** 31 58 S 60 56W
Coronel, *Chile* **174 D1** 37 0 S 73 10W
Coronel Bogado, *Paraguay* **174 B4** 27 11 S 56 18W
Coronel Dorrego, *Argentina* **174 D3** 38 40 S 61 10W
Coronel Fabriciano, *Brazil* **171 E3** 19 31 S 42 38W
Coronel Murta, *Brazil* **171 E3** 16 37 S 42 11W
Coronel Oviedo, *Paraguay* **174 B4** 25 24 S 56 30W
Coronel Ponce, *Brazil* **173 D6** 15 34 S 55 1W
Coronel Pringles, *Argentina* **174 D3** 38 0 S 61 30W
Coronel Suárez, *Argentina* **174 D3** 37 30 S 61 52W
Coronel Vidal, *Argentina* **174 D4** 37 28 S 57 45W
Corongo, *Peru* **172 B2** 8 30 S 77 53W
Coropuna, Nevado, *Peru* **172 D3** 15 30 S 72 41W
Çorovodë, *Albania* **50 F4** 40 31N 20 14 E
Corowa, *Australia* **129 C7** 35 58 S 146 21 E
Corozal, *Colombia* **168 B2** 9 19N 75 18W
Corozal □, *Belize* **163 D7** 18 23N 88 23W
Corozal Pt., *Trin. & Tob.* **169 F9** 10 45N 61 37W
Corps, *France* **29 D9** 44 50N 5 56 E
Corpus, *Argentina* **175 B4** 27 10 S 55 30W
Corpus Christi, *U.S.A.* **155 M6** 27 47N 97 24W
Corpus Christi, L., *U.S.A.* **155 L6** 28 2N 97 52W
Corque, *Bolivia* **172 D4** 18 20 S 67 41W
Corral, *Chile* **176 A2** 39 52 S 73 26W
Corral de Almaguer, *Spain* **42 F7** 39 45N 3 10W
Corralejo, *Canary Is.* **9 e2** 28 43N 13 53W
Corraun Pen., *Ireland* **23 C2** 53 54N 9 54W
Corréggio, *Italy* **44 D7** 44 46N 10 47 E
Corregidor, *Phil.* **80 D3** 14 23N 120 35 E
Corrente, *Brazil* **170 D2** 10 27 S 45 10W
Corrente →, *Brazil* **171 D3** 13 8 S 43 28W
Correntes →, *Brazil* **173 D6** 17 38 S 55 8W
Correntes, C. das, *Mozam.* **117 C6** 24 6 S 35 34 E
Correntina, *Brazil* **171 D3** 13 20 S 44 39W
Corrèze □, *France* **28 C5** 45 20N 1 45 E
Corrèze →, *France* **28 C5** 45 10N 1 28 E
Corrib, L., *Ireland* **23 C2** 53 27N 9 16W
Corridónia, *Italy* **45 E10** 43 15N 13 30 E
Corrientes, *Argentina* **174 B4** 27 30 S 58 45W
Corrientes □, *Argentina* **174 B4** 28 0 S 57 0W
Corrientes →, *Argentina* **174 C4** 30 42 S 59 38W
Corrientes →, *Peru* **168 D3** 3 43 S 74 35W
Corrientes, C., *Colombia* **168 B2** 5 30N 77 34W
Corrientes, C., *Cuba* **164 B3** 21 43N 84 30W
Corrientes, C., *Mexico* **162 C3** 20 25N 105 42W
Corrigan, *U.S.A.* **155 K7** 31 0N 94 52W
Corrigin, *Australia* **125 F2** 32 20 S 117 53 E
Corry, *U.S.A.* **150 E5** 41 55N 79 39W
Corryong, *Australia* **129 D7** 36 12 S 147 53 E
Corse ⌓, *France* **29 F13** 42 14N 9 10 E
Corse □, *France* **29 G13** 42 0N 9 0 E
Corse, C., *France* **29 E13** 43 1N 9 25 E
Corse-du-Sud □, *France* **29 G13** 41 45N 9 0 E
Corsica = Corse □, *France* **29 G13** 42 0N 9 0 E
Corsicana, *U.S.A.* **155 J6** 32 6N 96 28W
Corte, *France* **29 F13** 42 19N 9 11 E
Corte Pinto, *Portugal* **43 H3** 37 42N 7 29W
Cortegana, *Spain* **43 H4** 37 52N 6 49W
Cortes, *Phil.* **81 G6** 9 17N 126 11 E
Cortés, Mar de = California, G. de, *Mexico* **162 B2** 27 0N 111 0W
Cortez, *U.S.A.* **159 H9** 37 21N 108 35W
Cortina d'Ampezzo, *Italy* **45 B9** 46 32N 12 8 E
Cortland, *N.Y., U.S.A.* **151 D8** 42 36N 76 11W
Cortland, *Ohio, U.S.A.* **150 E4** 41 20N 80 44W
Cortona, *Italy* **45 E8** 43 16N 11 59 E
Corubal →, *Guinea-Biss.* **112 C2** 11 57N 15 5W
Coruche, *Portugal* **43 G2** 38 57N 8 30W
Çoruh →, *Turkey* **61 K5** 41 38N 41 38 E
Çorum, *Turkey* **100 B6** 40 30N 34 57 E
Corumbá, *Brazil* **173 D6** 19 0 S 57 30W
Corumbá →, *Brazil* **171 E2** 18 19 S 48 55W
Corumbá de Goiás, *Brazil* **171 E2** 16 0 S 48 50W
Corumbaíba, *Brazil* **171 E2** 18 9 S 48 34W
Corund, *Romania* **53 D10** 46 30N 25 13 E
Corunna = A Coruña, *Spain* **42 B2** 43 20N 8 25W
Corunna, *U.S.A.* **157 B12** 42 59N 84 7W
Corvallis, *U.S.A.* **158 D2** 44 34N 123 16W
Corvette, L. de la, *Canada* **140 B5** 53 25N 74 3W
Corvo, *Azores* **9 d2** 39 42N 31 6W
Corydon, *Ind., U.S.A.* **157 F10** 38 13N 86 7W
Corydon, *Iowa, U.S.A.* **156 D3** 40 46N 93 19W
Corydon, *Ky., U.S.A.* **157 G9** 37 44N 87 43W
Cosalá, *Mexico* **162 C3** 24 28N 106 40W
Cosamaloapan, *Mexico* **163 D5** 18 23N 95 50W
Cosenza, *Italy* **47 C9** 39 18N 16 15 E
Coşereni, *Romania* **53 F11** 44 38N 26 35 E
Coshocton, *U.S.A.* **150 F3** 40 16N 81 51W
Cosmo Newberry, *Australia* **125 E3** 28 0 S 122 54 E
Cosne-Cours-sur-Loire, *France* **27 E9** 47 24N 2 54 E
Coso Junction, *U.S.A.* **161 J9** 36 3N 117 57W
Coso Pk., *U.S.A.* **161 J9** 36 13N 117 44W
Cospeito, *Spain* **42 B3** 43 12N 7 34W
Cosquín, *Argentina* **174 C3** 31 15 S 64 30W
Cossato, *Italy* **44 C5** 45 34N 8 10 E
Cossé-le-Vivien, *France* **26 E6** 47 57N 0 54W
Cosson →, *France* **26 E8** 47 30N 1 15 E
Costa Blanca, *Spain* **41 G4** 38 25N 0 10W
Costa Brava, *Spain* **40 D8** 41 30N 3 0 E
Costa del Sol, *Spain* **43 J6** 36 30N 4 30W
Costa Dorada, *Spain* **40 D6** 41 12N 1 15 E
Costa Mesa, *U.S.A.* **161 M9** 33 38N 117 55W
Costa Rica ■, *Cent. Amer.* **164 E3** 10 0N 84 0W
Costa Smeralda, *Italy* **46 A2** 41 5N 9 35 E
Costermansville = Bukavu, *Dem. Rep. of the Congo* **118 C2** 2 20 S 28 52 E
Costeşti, *Romania* **53 F9** 44 40N 24 53 E
Costigliole d'Asti, *Italy* **44 D5** 44 47N 8 11 E
Cosumnes →, *U.S.A.* **160 G5** 38 16N 121 26W
Coswig, *Sachsen, Germany* **30 D9** 51 7N 13 34 E
Coswig, *Sachsen-Anhalt, Germany* **30 D8** 51 53N 12 27 E
Cotabato, *Phil.* **81 H5** 7 14N 124 15 E
Cotabato □, *Phil.* **81 H5** 7 10N 125 0 E
Cotacajes →, *Bolivia* **172 D4** 16 0 S 67 1W
Cotagaita, *Bolivia* **174 A2** 20 45 S 65 40W
Cotahuasi, *Peru* **172 D3** 15 12 S 72 50W
Côte d'Azur, *France* **29 E11** 43 25N 7 10 E
Côte-d'Ivoire = Ivory Coast ■, *Africa* **112 D4** 7 30N 5 0W
Côte d'Or, *France* **27 E11** 47 10N 4 50 E
Côte-d'Or □, *France* **27 E11** 47 30N 4 50 E
Coteau des Prairies, *U.S.A.* **154 C6** 45 20N 97 50W
Coteau du Missouri, *U.S.A.* **154 B4** 47 0N 100 0W
Cotegipe, *Brazil* **171 D3** 12 2 S 44 15W
Cotentin, *France* **26 C5** 49 15N 1 30W
Côtes-d'Armor □, *France* **26 D4** 48 25N 2 40W
Côtes de Meuse, *France* **27 C12** 49 15N 5 22 E
Côtes-du-Nord = Côtes-d'Armor □, *France* **26 D4** 48 25N 2 40W
Cotiella, *Spain* **40 C5** 42 31N 0 19 E
Cotillo, *Canary Is.* **9 e2** 28 41N 14 1W
Cotiujeni, *Moldova* **53 C13** 47 51N 28 33 E
Cotoca, *Bolivia* **173 D5** 17 49 S 63 3W
Cotonou, *Benin* **113 D5** 6 20N 2 25 E
Cotopaxi, *Ecuador* **168 D2** 0 40 S 78 30W
Cotopaxi △, *Ecuador* **168 D2** 0 39 S 78 24W
Cotopaxi □, *Ecuador* **168 D2** 0 5 S 78 55W
Cotronei, *Italy* **47 C9** 39 9N 16 47 E
Cotswold Hills, *U.K.* **21 F5** 51 42N 2 10W
Cottage Grove, *U.S.A.* **158 E2** 43 48N 123 3W
Cottageville, *U.S.A.* **152 C9** 32 56N 80 29W
Cottbus, *Germany* **30 D10** 51 45N 14 20 E
Cottondale, *U.S.A.* **152 E4** 30 48N 85 23W
Cottonwood, *Ala., U.S.A.* **152 D4** 31 3N 85 18W
Cottonwood, *Ariz., U.S.A.* **159 J7** 34 45N 112 1W
Cotulla, *U.S.A.* **155 L5** 28 26N 99 14W
Coubre, Pte. de la, *France* **28 C2** 45 42N 1 15W
Couches, *France* **27 F11** 46 53N 4 30 E
Couço, *Portugal* **43 G2** 38 59N 8 17W
Coudersport, *U.S.A.* **150 E6** 41 46N 78 1W
Couedic, C. du, *Australia* **128 D2** 36 5 S 136 40 E
Couëron, *France* **26 E5** 47 13N 1 44W
Couesnon →, *France* **26 D5** 48 38N 1 32W
Couhé, *France* **28 B4** 46 17N 0 11 E
Coulanges-sur-Yonne, *France* **27 E10** 47 31N 3 33 E
Coulee City, *U.S.A.* **158 C4** 47 37N 119 17W
Coulman I., *Antarctica* **7 D11** 73 35 S 170 0 E
Coulommiers, *France* **27 D10** 48 50N 3 3 E
Coulon →, *France* **29 E9** 43 51N 5 6 E
Coulonge →, *Canada* **140 C4** 45 52N 76 46W
Coulonges-sur-l'Autize, *France* **28 B3** 46 29N 0 36W
Coulounieix-Chamiers, *France* **28 C4** 45 11N 0 42 E
Coulterville, *Calif., U.S.A.* **160 H6** 37 43N 120 12W
Coulterville, *Ill., U.S.A.* **156 F7** 38 11N 89 36W
Council, *Alaska, U.S.A.* **144 D7** 64 53N 163 41W
Council, *Ga., U.S.A.* **152 E7** 30 37N 82 31W
Council, *Idaho, U.S.A.* **158 D5** 44 44N 116 26W
Council Bluffs, *U.S.A.* **154 E7** 41 16N 95 52W
Council Grove, *U.S.A.* **154 F6** 38 40N 96 29W
Coupeville, *U.S.A.* **160 B4** 48 13N 122 41W
Courantyne →, *S. Amer.* **169 B6** 5 55N 57 5W
Courcelles, *Belgium* **24 D4** 50 28N 4 22 E
Courchevel, *France* **29 C10** 45 25N 6 36 E
Courçon, *France* **28 B3** 46 15N 0 50W
Courmayeur, *Italy* **44 C3** 45 47N 6 58 E
Couronne, C., *France* **29 E9** 43 19N 5 3 E
Cours-la-Ville, *France* **27 F11** 46 7N 4 19 E
Coursan, *France* **28 E7** 43 14N 3 4 E
Courseulles-sur-Mer, *France* **26 C6** 49 20N 0 29W
Courtenay, *Canada* **142 D4** 49 45N 125 0W
Courtenay, *France* **27 D10** 48 2N 3 3 E
Courtland, *U.S.A.* **160 G5** 38 20N 121 34W
Courtrai = Kortrijk, *Belgium* **24 D3** 50 50N 3 17 E
Courtright, *Canada* **150 D2** 42 49N 82 28W
Coushatta, *U.S.A.* **155 J8** 32 1N 93 21W
Coutances, *France* **26 C5** 49 3N 1 28W
Coutras, *France* **28 C3** 45 3N 0 8W
Coutts Crossing, *Australia* **127 D5** 29 49 S 152 55 E
Couva, *Trin. & Tob.* **169 F9** 10 25N 61 27W
Couvet, *Switz.* **32 C3** 46 57N 6 38 E
Couvin, *Belgium* **24 D4** 50 3N 4 29 E
Covarrubias, *Spain* **42 C7** 42 4N 3 31W
Covasna, *Romania* **53 E11** 45 50N 26 10 E
Covasna □, *Romania* **53 E10** 45 50N 26 0 E
Cove I., *Canada* **150 A3** 45 17N 81 44W
Coveñas, *Colombia* **168 B2** 9 24N 75 44W
Coventry, *U.K.* **21 E6** 52 25N 1 28W
Coverdale, *U.S.A.* **152 D6** 31 38N 83 58W
Covilhã, *Portugal* **42 E3** 40 17N 7 31W
Covington, *Ga., U.S.A.* **152 B6** 33 36N 83 51W
Covington, *Ind., U.S.A.* **157 D9** 40 9N 87 24W
Covington, *Ky., U.S.A.* **157 E12** 39 5N 84 31W
Covington, *Ohio, U.S.A.* **157 D12** 40 7N 84 21W
Covington, *Tenn., U.S.A.* **155 H10** 35 34N 89 39W
Covington, *Va., U.S.A.* **148 G5** 37 47N 79 59W
Cowal, L., *Australia* **129 B7** 33 40 S 147 25 E
Cowan, Cerro, *Ecuador* **172 a** 0 12 S 90 48W
Cowan, L., *Australia* **125 F3** 31 45 S 121 45 E
Cowan L., *Canada* **143 C7** 54 0N 107 15W
Cowangie, *Australia* **128 C4** 35 12 S 141 26 E
Cowansville, *Canada* **140 C5** 45 14N 72 46W
Coward Springs, *Australia* **127 D2** 29 24 S 136 49 E
Cowcowing Lakes, *Australia* **125 F2** 30 55 S 117 20 E
Cowden, *U.S.A.* **157 E8** 39 15N 88 52W
Cowdenbeath, *U.K.* **22 E5** 56 7N 3 21W
Cowell, *Australia* **128 B2** 33 39 S 136 56 E
Cowes, *Australia* **129 E6** 38 28 S 145 14 E
Cowes, *U.K.* **21 G6** 50 45N 1 18W
Cowichan L., *Canada* **160 B2** 48 53N 124 17W
Cowlitz →, *U.S.A.* **160 D4** 46 6N 122 55W
Cowra, *Australia* **129 B8** 33 49 S 148 42 E
Cox, *Spain* **41 G4** 38 8N 0 53W
Coxilha Grande, *Brazil* **175 B5** 28 18 S 51 30W
Coxim, *Brazil* **173 D7** 18 30 S 54 55W
Coxim →, *Brazil* **173 D7** 18 34 S 54 46W
Cox's Bazar, *Bangla.* **90 E3** 21 26N 91 59 E
Coyote Wells, *U.S.A.* **161 N11** 32 44N 115 58W
Coyuca de Benítez, *Mexico* **163 D4** 17 1N 100 8W
Coyuca de Catalan, *Mexico* **162 D4** 18 18N 100 41W
Cozad, *U.S.A.* **154 E5** 40 52N 99 59W
Cozes, *France* **28 C3** 45 34N 0 49W
Cozumel, *Mexico* **163 C7** 20 31N 86 55W
Cozumel, Isla, *Mexico* **163 C7** 20 30N 86 40W
Crab Hill, *Barbados* **165 g** 13 19N 59 38W
Cracow = Kraków, *Poland* **55 H6** 50 4N 19 57 E
Cracow, *Australia* **127 D5** 25 17 S 150 17 E
Cradle Mt.-Lake St. Clair △, *Australia* **127 G4** 41 49 S 147 56 E
Cradock, *Australia* **127 E2** 32 6 S 138 31 E
Cradock, *S. Africa* **116 E4** 32 8 S 25 36 E
Craig, *Alaska, U.S.A.* **144 J14** 55 29N 133 9W
Craig, *Colo., U.S.A.* **158 F10** 40 31N 107 33W
Craigavon, *U.K.* **23 B5** 54 27N 6 23W
Craigieburn, *Australia* **129 D6** 37 36 S 144 56 E
Craigmore, *Zimbabwe* **119 G3** 20 28 S 32 50 E
Craik, *Canada* **143 C7** 51 3N 105 49W
Crailsheim, *Germany* **31 F6** 49 8N 10 5 E
Craiova, *Romania* **53 F8** 44 21N 23 48 E
Cramsie, *Australia* **126 C3** 23 20 S 144 15 E
Cranberry L., *U.S.A.* **151 B10** 44 11N 74 50W
Cranberry Portage, *Canada* **143 C8** 54 35N 101 23W
Cranbrook, *Australia* **125 F2** 34 18 S 117 33 E
Cranbrook, *Canada* **142 D5** 49 30N 115 46W
Crandon, *U.S.A.* **154 C10** 45 34N 88 54W
Crane, *Oreg., U.S.A.* **158 E4** 43 25N 118 35W
Crane, *Tex., U.S.A.* **155 K3** 31 24N 102 21W
Cranganore, *India* **95 J3** 10 13N 76 13 E
Cranston, *U.S.A.* **151 E13** 41 47N 71 26W
Craon, *France* **26 E6** 47 50N 0 58W
Craonne, *France* **27 C10** 49 27N 3 46 E
Craponne-sur-Arzon, *France* **28 C7** 45 19N 3 51 E
Crasna, *Romania* **53 D12** 46 32N 27 51 E
Crasna →, *Romania* **52 C7** 47 44N 22 35 E
Crasnei, Munţii, *Romania* **53 C8** 47 0N 23 20 E
Crater L., *U.S.A.* **158 E2** 42 56N 122 6W
Crater Lake △, *U.S.A.* **158 E2** 42 55N 122 10W
Crater Mt., *Papua N. G.* **132 D3** 6 37 S 145 7 E
Crater Pt., *Papua N. G.* **132 C7** 5 25 S 152 9 E
Craters of the Moon △, *U.S.A.* **158 E7** 43 25N 113 30W
Crateús, *Brazil* **170 C3** 5 10 S 40 39W
Crati →, *Italy* **47 C9** 39 43N 16 31 E
Crato, *Brazil* **170 C4** 7 10 S 39 25W
Crato, *Portugal* **43 F3** 39 16N 7 39W
Craven, L., *Canada* **140 B4** 54 20N 76 56W
Cravo Norte, *Colombia* **168 B3** 6 18N 70 12W
Cravo Norte →, *Colombia* **168 B3** 6 18N 70 12W
Crawford, *Ala., U.S.A.* **152 C4** 32 27N 85 11W
Crawford, *Nebr., U.S.A.* **154 D3** 42 41N 103 25W
Crawfordsville, *Ind., U.S.A.* **157 D10** 40 2N 86 54W
Crawfordsville, *Iowa, U.S.A.* **156 C5** 41 12N 91 32W
Crawfordville, *Fla., U.S.A.* **152 E5** 30 11N 84 23W
Crawfordville, *Ga., U.S.A.* **152 B7** 33 33N 82 54W
Crawley, *U.K.* **21 F7** 51 7N 0 11W
Crazy Mts., *U.S.A.* **158 C8** 46 12N 110 20W
Crean L., *Canada* **143 C7** 54 5N 106 9W
Crécy-en-Ponthieu, *France* **27 B8** 50 15N 1 53 E
Crediton, *Canada* **150 C3** 43 17N 81 33W
Crediton, *U.K.* **21 G4** 50 47N 3 40W
Cree →, *Canada* **143 B7** 58 57N 105 47W
Cree →, *U.K.* **22 G4** 54 55N 4 25W
Cree L., *Canada* **143 B7** 57 30N 106 30W
Creede, *U.S.A.* **159 H10** 37 51N 106 56W
Creekside, *U.S.A.* **150 F5** 40 40N 79 11W
Creel, *Mexico* **162 B3** 27 45N 107 38W
Creemore, *Canada* **150 B4** 44 19N 80 6W
Creighton, *Canada* **143 C8** 54 45N 101 54W
Creighton, *U.S.A.* **154 D6** 42 28N 97 54W
Creil, *France* **27 C9** 49 15N 2 29 E
Crema, *Italy* **44 C6** 45 22N 9 41 E
Cremona, *Italy* **44 C7** 45 7N 10 2 E
Crepaja, *Serbia & M.* **52 E5** 45 1N 20 38 E
Crepori →, *Brazil* **173 B6** 5 42 S 57 8W
Crépy, *France* **27 C10** 49 35N 3 32 E
Crépy-en-Valois, *France* **27 C9** 49 14N 2 54 E
Cres, *Croatia* **45 D11** 44 58N 14 25 E
Crescent Beach, *U.S.A.* **152 F8** 29 46N 81 15W
Crescent City, *Calif., U.S.A.* **158 F1** 41 45N 124 12W
Crescent City, *Fla., U.S.A.* **153 F8** 29 26N 81 31W
Crescent Hd., *Australia* **129 A10** 31 11 S 152 59 E
Crescent L., *U.S.A.* **153 F8** 29 28N 81 30W
Crescentino, *Italy* **44 C5** 45 11N 8 6 E
Crespo, *Argentina* **174 C3** 32 2 S 60 19W
Cresson, *U.S.A.* **150 F6** 40 28N 78 36W
Cressy, *Australia* **128 E5** 38 2 S 143 40 E
Crest, *France* **29 D9** 44 44N 5 2 E
Cresta, Mt., *Phil.* **80 C4** 17 17N 122 6 E
Crestline, *Calif., U.S.A.* **161 L9** 34 14N 117 18W
Crestline, *Ohio, U.S.A.* **150 F2** 40 47N 82 44W
Creston, *Canada* **142 D5** 49 10N 116 31W
Creston, *Calif., U.S.A.* **160 K6** 35 32N 120 33W
Creston, *Iowa, U.S.A.* **156 C2** 41 4N 94 22W
Crestview, *Calif., U.S.A.* **160 H8** 37 46N 118 58W
Crestview, *Fla., U.S.A.* **153 E3** 30 46N 86 34W
Creswick, *Australia* **128 D5** 37 25 S 143 58 E
Crêt de la Neige, *France* **27 F12** 46 16N 5 58 E
Crete = Kríti, *Greece* **39 E6** 35 15N 25 0 E
Crete, *Ill., U.S.A.* **157 C9** 41 27N 87 38W
Crete, *Nebr., U.S.A.* **154 E6** 40 38N 96 58W
Crete, Sea of, *Greece* **49 E7** 36 0N 25 0 E
Créteil, *France* **27 D9** 48 47N 2 28 E
Cretin, C., *Papua N. G.* **132 D4** 6 40 S 147 53 E
Creus, C. de, *Spain* **40 C8** 42 20N 3 19 E
Creuse □, *France* **27 F9** 46 10N 2 0 E
Creuse →, *France* **28 B4** 47 0N 0 34 E
Creutzwald, *France* **27 C13** 49 12N 6 42 E
Creuzburg, *Germany* **30 D6** 51 3N 10 14 E
Crèvecœur-le-Grand, *France* **27 C9** 49 37N 2 5 E
Crevillente, *Spain* **41 G4** 38 12N 0 48W
Crewe, *U.K.* **20 D5** 53 6N 2 26W
Crewkerne, *U.K.* **21 G5** 50 53N 2 48W
Crianlarich, *U.K.* **22 E4** 56 24N 4 37W
Criciúma, *Brazil* **175 B6** 28 40 S 49 23W
Cricova, *Moldova* **53 C13** 47 8N 28 52 E
Cridersville, *U.S.A.* **157 D12** 40 39N 84 9W
Crieff, *U.K.* **22 E5** 56 22N 3 50W
Crikvenica, *Croatia* **45 C11** 45 11N 14 40 E
Crimea □, *Ukraine* **59 K8** 45 30N 33 10 E
Crimean Pen. = Krymskyy Pivostriv, *Ukraine* **59 K8** 45 0N 34 0 E
Crimmitschau, *Germany* **30 E8** 50 48N 12 24 E
Cristal, Mts. de, *Gabon* **114 B2** 0 30N 10 30 E
Cristalândia, *Brazil* **170 D2** 10 36 S 49 11W
Cristino Castro, *Brazil* **170 C3** 8 49 S 44 13W
Cristóbal, Pta., *Ecuador* **172 a** 0 54 S 91 31W
Cristuru Secuiesc, *Romania* **53 D10** 46 17N 25 2 E
Crişul Alb →, *Romania* **52 D6** 46 42N 21 17 E
Crişul Negru →, *Romania* **52 D6** 46 42N 21 16 E
Crişul Repede →, *Romania* **52 D5** 46 55N 20 59 E
Crittenden, *U.S.A.* **157 F12** 38 47N 84 36W
Criuleni, *Moldova* **53 C14** 47 13N 29 10 E
Crivitz, *Germany* **30 B7** 53 34N 11 39 E
Crixás, *Brazil* **171 D2** 14 27 S 49 58W
Crna →, *Macedonia* **50 E5** 41 33N 21 59 E
Crna Gora = Montenegro □, *Serbia & M.* **50 D3** 42 40N 19 20 E
Crna Gora, *Macedonia* **50 D5** 42 10N 21 30 E
Crna Reka = Crna →, *Macedonia* **50 E5** 41 33N 21 59 E
Crna Trava, *Serbia & M.* **50 D6** 42 49N 22 19 E
Crni Drim →, *Macedonia* **50 E4** 41 17N 20 40 E
Crni Timok →, *Serbia & M.* **50 C6** 43 53N 22 15 E
Crnoljeva Planina, *Serbia & M.* **50 D5** 42 20N 21 0 E
Črnomelj, *Slovenia* **45 C12** 45 33N 15 10 E
Croagh Patrick, *Ireland* **23 C2** 53 46N 9 40W
Croajingolong △, *Australia* **129 D8** 37 45 S 149 26 E
Croatia ■, *Europe* **45 C13** 45 20N 16 0 E
Crocker, *U.S.A.* **156 G4** 37 57N 92 16W
Crocker, Banjaran, *Malaysia* **85 A5** 5 40N 116 30 E
Crocker, Cerro, *Ecuador* **172 a** 0 36 S 90 21W
Crockett, *U.S.A.* **155 K7** 31 19N 95 27W
Crocodile = Krokodil →, *Mozam.* **117 D5** 25 14 S 32 18 E
Crocodile Is., *Australia* **126 A1** 12 3 S 134 58 E
Crocq, *France* **28 C6** 45 52N 2 21 E
Crodo, *Italy* **44 B5** 46 13N 8 19 E
Crohy Hd., *Ireland* **23 B3** 54 55N 8 26W
Croisette, C., *France* **29 E9** 43 14N 5 22 E
Croisic, Pte. du, *France* **26 E4** 47 19N 2 31W
Croix, L. La, *Canada* **140 C1** 48 20N 92 15W
Croker, C., *Australia* **124 B5** 10 58 S 132 35 E
Croker, C., *Canada* **150 B4** 44 58N 80 59W
Croker I., *Australia* **124 B5** 11 12 S 132 32 E
Cromarty, *U.K.* **22 D4** 57 40N 4 2W
Cromer, *U.K.* **20 E9** 52 56N 1 17 E
Cromwell, *N.Z.* **131 F4** 45 3 S 169 14 E
Cromwell, *U.S.A.* **151 E12** 41 36N 72 39W
Cronat, *France* **27 F10** 46 43N 3 40 E
Crook, *U.K.* **20 C6** 54 43N 1 45W
Crooked →, *Canada* **142 C4** 54 50N 122 54W
Crooked →, *U.S.A.* **158 D3** 44 32N 121 16W
Crooked Creek, *U.S.A.* **144 F8** 61 52N 158 7W
Crooked I., *Bahamas* **165 B5** 22 50N 74 10W
Crooked Island Passage, *Bahamas* **165 B5** 22 55N 74 35W
Crookston, *Minn., U.S.A.* **154 B6** 47 47N 96 37W
Crookston, *Nebr., U.S.A.* **154 D4** 42 56N 100 45W
Crookwell, *Australia* **129 C8** 34 28 S 149 24 E
Cropane-Micone ⌓, *Italy* **47 D9** 38 31N 16 18 E
Crosby, *U.K.* **20 D4** 53 30N 3 3W
Crosby, *N. Dak., U.S.A.* **154 A3** 48 55N 103 18W
Crosby, *Pa., U.S.A.* **150 E6** 41 45N 78 23W
Crosbyton, *U.S.A.* **155 J4** 33 40N 101 14W
Crosía, *Italy* **47 C9** 39 35N 16 45 E
Cross →, *Nigeria* **113 E6** 4 42N 8 21 E
Cross City, *U.S.A.* **153 F6** 29 38N 83 7W
Cross Fell, *U.K.* **20 C5** 54 43N 2 28W
Cross L., *Canada* **143 C9** 54 45N 97 30W
Cross Lake, *Canada* **143 C9** 54 37N 97 47W
Cross River □, *Nigeria* **113 D6** 6 0N 8 0 E
Cross River △, *Nigeria* **113 D6** 5 50N 9 50 E
Cross Sound, *U.S.A.* **144 H14** 58 0N 135 0W
Cross Timbers, *U.S.A.* **156 F3** 38 1N 93 14W
Crossen = Krosno Odrzańskie, *Poland* **55 F2** 52 3N 15 7 E
Crossett, *U.S.A.* **155 J9** 33 8N 91 58W
Crosshaven, *Ireland* **23 E3** 51 47N 8 17W
Crossley, Mt., *N.Z.* **131 C7** 42 50 S 172 5 E
Crossville, *Ill., U.S.A.* **157 F8** 38 10N 88 4W
Crossville, *Tenn., U.S.A.* **149 G3** 35 57N 85 2W
Croswell, *U.S.A.* **150 C2** 43 16N 82 37W
Croton-on-Hudson, *U.S.A.* **151 E11** 41 12N 73 55W
Crotone, *Italy* **47 C10** 39 5N 17 8 E
Crow →, *Canada* **142 B4** 59 41N 124 20W
Crow Agency, *U.S.A.* **158 D10** 45 36N 107 28W
Crow Hd., *Ireland* **23 E1** 51 35N 10 9W
Crowdy Bay △, *Australia* **129 A10** 31 45 S 152 45 E
Crowell, *U.S.A.* **155 J5** 33 59N 99 43W
Crowl Cr. →, *Australia* **129 B6** 32 0 S 145 30 E
Crowley, *U.S.A.* **155 K8** 30 13N 92 22W
Crowley, L., *U.S.A.* **160 H8** 37 35N 118 42W
Crown I., *Papua N. G.* **132 C4** 5 7 S 146 58 E
Crown Point, *Ind., U.S.A.* **157 C9** 41 25N 87 22W
Crown Point, *N.Y., U.S.A.* **151 C11** 43 57N 73 26W
Crown Pt., *Trin. & Tob.* **169 E10** 11 18N 60 51W
Crownpoint, *U.S.A.* **159 J9** 35 41N 108 9W
Crows Landing, *U.S.A.* **160 H5** 37 23N 121 6W
Crows Nest, *Australia* **127 D5** 27 16 S 152 4 E
Crowsnest Pass, *Canada* **142 D6** 49 40N 114 40W
Croydon, *Australia* **126 B3** 18 13 S 142 14 E
Croydon □, *U.K.* **21 F7** 51 22N 0 5W
Crozet, Is., *Ind. Oc.* **121 J4** 46 27 S 52 0 E
Crozon, *France* **26 D2** 48 15N 4 30W
Cruces, Punta, *Colombia* **168 B2** 6 39N 77 32W
Cruz, C., *Cuba* **164 C4** 19 50N 77 50W
Cruz Alta, *Brazil* **175 B5** 28 45 S 53 40W
Cruz Bay, *U.S. Virgin Is.* **165 e** 18 20N 64 48W
Cruz das Almas, *Brazil* **171 D4** 12 0 S 39 6W
Cruz de Incio, *Spain* **42 C3** 42 39N 7 21W
Cruz de Malta, *Brazil* **170 C3** 8 15 S 40 20W
Cruz del Eje, *Argentina* **174 C3** 30 45 S 64 50W
Cruzeiro, *Brazil* **171 F2** 22 33 S 45 0W
Cruzeiro do Oeste, *Brazil* **175 A5** 23 46 S 53 4W
Cruzeiro do Sul = Joaçaba, *Brazil* **175 B5** 27 5 S 51 31W
Cruzeiro do Sul, *Brazil* **172 B3** 7 35 S 72 35W
Cry L., *Canada* **142 B3** 58 45N 129 0W
Crystal B., *U.S.A.* **153 G7** 28 50N 82 45W
Crystal Bay, *U.S.A.* **160 F7** 39 15N 120 0W
Crystal Brook, *Australia* **128 B3** 33 21 S 138 12 E
Crystal City, *Mo., U.S.A.* **156 F6** 38 13N 90 23W
Crystal City, *Tex., U.S.A.* **155 L5** 28 41N 99 50W
Crystal Falls, *U.S.A.* **148 B1** 46 5N 88 20W
Crystal Lake, *Fla., U.S.A.* **152 E4** 30 26N 85 42W
Crystal Lake, *Ill., U.S.A.* **157 B8** 42 14N 88 19W
Crystal River, *U.S.A.* **153 G7** 28 54N 82 35W
Crystal Springs, *U.S.A.* **155 K9** 31 59N 90 21W
Csenger, *Hungary* **52 C7** 47 50N 22 41 E
Csongrád, *Hungary* **52 D5** 46 43N 20 12 E
Csongrád □, *Hungary* **52 D5** 46 32N 20 15 E
Csorna, *Hungary* **52 C2** 47 38N 17 18 E
Csurgo, *Hungary* **52 D2** 46 16N 17 9 E
Cu Lao Hon, *Vietnam* **87 G7** 10 54N 108 18 E
Cua Rao, *Vietnam* **86 C5** 19 16N 104 27 E
Cuácua →, *Mozam.* **119 F4** 17 54 S 37 0 E
Cuále, *Angola* **115 D3** 8 22 S 16 10 E
Cuále →, *Angola* **115 D3** 8 29 S 15 1 E
Cuamato, *Angola* **116 B2** 17 2 S 15 7 E
Cuamba, *Mozam.* **119 E4** 14 45 S 36 22 E
Cuando, *Angola* **115 E3** 14 34 S 19 1 E
Cuando →, *Angola* **115 F4** 17 30 S 23 15 E
Cuando Cubango □, *Angola* **116 B3** 16 25 S 20 0 E
Cuangar, *Angola* **116 B2** 17 36 S 18 39 E
Cuango = Kwango →, *Dem. Rep. of the Congo* **114 C3** 3 14 S 17 22 E
Cuango, *Lunda Norte, Angola* **115 D3** 9 8 S 18 3 E
Cuango, *Moxico, Angola* **115 E3** 6 20 S 16 42 E
Cuango, *Uíge, Angola* **115 D3** 6 15 S 16 42 E
Cuanza →, *Angola* **115 D2** 9 21 S 13 9 E
Cuanza Norte □, *Angola* **115 D2** 8 50 S 14 30 E
Cuanza Sul □, *Angola* **115 E2** 10 50 S 14 50 E
Cuao →, *Venezuela* **168 C4** 4 55N 67 40W
Cuarto →, *Argentina* **174 C3** 33 25 S 63 2W
Cuatir →, *Angola* **115 F3** 17 1 S 18 9 E
Cuatrociénegas, *Mexico* **162 B4** 26 59N 102 5W
Cuauhtémoc, *Mexico* **162 B3** 28 25N 106 52W
Cuba, *Portugal* **43 G3** 38 10N 7 54W
Cuba, *Mo., U.S.A.* **156 F5** 38 4N 91 24W
Cuba, *N. Mex., U.S.A.* **159 J10** 36 1N 107 4W
Cuba, *N.Y., U.S.A.* **150 D6** 42 13N 78 17W
Cuba ■, *W. Indies* **164 B4** 22 0N 79 0W
Cuba City, *U.S.A.* **156 B6** 42 36N 90 26W
Cubal, *Angola* **115 E2** 12 26 S 14 3 E
Cubal →, *Angola* **115 E2** 12 13 S 13 39 E
Cubango →, *Africa* **116 B3** 18 50 S 22 25 E
Cubanja, *Angola* **115 E4** 14 49 S 21 20 E
Cubia, *Angola* **115 F4** 15 58 S 21 42 E
Çubuk, *Turkey* **100 B5** 40 14N 33 3 E
Cuc Phuong △, *Vietnam* **86 B5** 20 17N 105 38 E
Cuchi, *Angola* **115 E3** 14 37 S 16 58 E
Cuchi →, *Angola* **115 F3** 15 13 S 17 20 E
Cuchillo-Có, *Argentina* **176 A4** 38 20 S 64 37W
Cuchivero →, *Venezuela* **168 B4** 7 40N 65 57W
Cuchumatanes, Sierra de los, *Guatemala* **164 C1** 15 35N 91 25W
Cuckfield, *U.K.* **21 F7** 51 1N 0 8W
Cucuí, *Brazil* **168 C4** 1 12N 66 50W
Cucumbi, *Angola* **115 E3** 10 17 S 19 5 E
Cucurpe, *Mexico* **162 A2** 30 20N 110 43W
Cucurrupí, *Colombia* **168 C2** 4 23N 76 56W
Cúcuta, *Colombia* **168 B3** 7 54N 72 31W
Cudahy, *U.S.A.* **157 B9** 42 58N 87 52W
Cudalbi, *Romania* **53 E12** 45 46N 27 41 E
Cuddalore, *India* **95 J4** 11 46N 79 45 E
Cuddapah, *India* **95 G4** 14 30N 78 47 E
Cuddapan, L., *Australia* **126 D3** 25 45 S 141 26 E
Cudgewa, *Australia* **129 D7** 36 10 S 147 42 E
Cudillero, *Spain* **42 B4** 43 33N 6 9W
Cue, *Australia* **125 E2** 27 25 S 117 54 E
Cuebe →, *Angola* **115 F3** 15 46 S 17 32 E
Cuéllar, *Spain* **42 D6** 41 23N 4 21W
Cuemba, *Angola* **115 E3** 11 50 S 17 42 E
Cuenca, *Ecuador* **168 D2** 2 50 S 79 9W
Cuenca, *Spain* **40 E2** 40 5N 2 10W
Cuenca □, *Spain* **40 F3** 40 0N 2 0W
Cuenca, Serranía de, *Spain* **40 F3** 39 55N 1 50W
Cuenca Alta del Manzanares ⌓, *Spain* **42 E7** 40 40N 3 55W
Cuerdo del Pozo, Embalse de la, *Spain* **40 D2** 41 51N 2 44W
Cuernavaca, *Mexico* **163 D5** 18 55N 99 15W
Cuero, *U.S.A.* **155 L6** 29 6N 97 17W
Cuers, *France* **29 E10** 43 14N 6 5 E
Cueva de la Quebrada del Toro △, *Venezuela* **165 D6** 10 46N 69 3W

Cueva de los Guácharos △, *Colombia* **168 C2** 1 35N 76 1W
Cuevas, Cerro, *Bolivia* **173 E4** 22 0 S 65 12W
Cuevas de Vera = Cuevas del Almanzora, *Spain* **41 H3** 37 18N 1 58W
Cuevas del Almanzora, *Spain* **41 H3** 37 18N 1 58W
Cuevo, *Bolivia* **173 E5** 20 15 S 63 30W
Cugir, *Romania* **53 E8** 45 48N 23 25 E
Cugnaux, *France* **28 E5** 43 32N 1 20 E
Cuhai-Bakony →, *Hungary* **52 C2** 47 35N 17 54 E
Cuiabá, *Brazil* **173 D6** 15 30 S 56 0W
Cuiabá →, *Brazil* **173 D6** 17 5 S 56 36W
Cuihangcun, *China* **69 G10** 22 27N 113 32 E
Cuijk, *Neths.* **24 C5** 51 44N 5 50 E
Cuilco, *Guatemala* **164 C1** 15 24N 91 58W
Cuillin Hills, *U.K.* **22 D2** 57 13N 6 15W
Cuillin Sd., *U.K.* **22 D2** 57 4N 6 20W
Cuilo = Kwilu →, *Dem. Rep. of the Congo* **115 C3** 3 22 S 17 22 E
Cuilo, *Angola* **115 D3** 8 12 S 19 28 E
Cuilo-Futa, *Angola* **115 D3** 6 28 S 15 51 E
Cuima, *Angola* **115 E3** 13 25 S 15 45 E
Cuimba, *Angola* **115 D2** 6 10 S 14 41 E
Cuiseaux, *France* **27 F12** 46 30N 5 22 E
Cuité, *Brazil* **170 C4** 6 29 S 36 9W
Cuito →, *Angola* **116 B3** 18 1 S 20 48 E
Cuito Cuanavale, *Angola* **115 F3** 15 10 S 19 10 E
Cuitzeo, L. de, *Mexico* **162 D4** 19 55N 101 5W
Cuiuni →, *Brazil* **169 D5** 0 45 S 63 7W
Cuivre →, *U.S.A.* **156 F6** 38 55N 90 44W
Cuivre, West Fork →, *U.S.A.* **156 E6** 39 2N 90 58W
Cujmir, *Romania* **52 F7** 44 13N 22 57 E
Cukai, *Malaysia* **87 K4** 4 13N 103 25 E
Culasi, *Phil.* **81 F4** 11 26N 122 3 E
Culbertson, *U.S.A.* **154 A2** 48 9N 104 31W
Culburra, *N.S.W., Australia* **129 C9** 34 56 S 150 46 E
Culburra, *S. Austral., Australia* **128 C3** 35 50 S 139 58 E
Culcairn, *Australia* **129 C7** 35 41 S 147 3 E
Culebra = Dewey, *Puerto Rico* **165 d** 18 18N 65 18W
Culebra, Isla de, *Puerto Rico* **165 d** 18 19N 65 18W
Culebra, Sierra de la, *Spain* **42 D4** 41 55N 6 20W
Culfa, *Azerbaijan* **101 C11** 38 57N 45 38 E
Culgoa, *Australia* **128 C5** 35 44 S 143 6 E
Culgoa →, *Australia* **127 D4** 29 56 S 146 20 E
Culgoa Flood Plain △, *Australia* **127 D4** 28 58 S 147 5 E
Culiacán, *Mexico* **162 C3** 24 50N 107 23W
Culiacán →, *Mexico* **162 C3** 24 30N 107 42W
Culik, *Indonesia* **79 J18** 8 21 S 115 37 E
Culion, *Phil.* **81 F3** 11 54N 119 58 E
Culion I., *Phil.* **81 F2** 11 50N 120 0 E
Culiseu →, *Brazil* **173 C7** 12 14 S 53 17W
Cúllar, *Spain* **43 H8** 37 35N 2 34W
Cullarin Ra., *Australia* **129 C8** 34 30 S 149 30 E
Cullen, *U.K.* **22 D6** 57 42N 2 49W
Cullen Bullen, *Australia* **129 B9** 33 18 S 150 2 E
Cullen Pt., *Australia* **126 A3** 11 57 S 141 54 E
Cullera, *Spain* **41 F4** 39 9N 0 17W
Cullman, *U.S.A.* **149 H2** 34 11N 86 51W
Culloden, *U.S.A.* **152 C5** 32 52N 84 6W
Cullom, *U.S.A.* **157 D8** 40 53N 88 16W
Cullompton, *U.K.* **21 G4** 50 51N 3 24W
Culo →, *Angola* **115 D3** 6 13 S 15 34 E
Culoz, *France* **29 C9** 45 47N 5 46 E
Culpeper, *U.S.A.* **148 F7** 38 30N 78 0W
Culuene →, *Brazil* **173 C7** 12 56 S 52 51W
Culver, *U.S.A.* **157 C10** 41 13N 86 25W
Culver, Pt., *Australia* **125 F3** 32 54 S 124 43 E
Culverden, *N.Z.* **131 C7** 42 47 S 172 49 E
Culverton, *U.S.A.* **152 B7** 33 19N 82 54W
Cuma, *Angola* **115 E3** 12 52 S 15 5 E
Cumaná, *Venezuela* **169 A5** 10 30N 64 5W
Cumaovası, *Turkey* **49 C9** 38 15N 27 9 E
Cumare, *Colombia* **168 C3** 0 49N 72 32W
Cumari, *Brazil* **171 E2** 18 16 S 48 11W
Cumbe = Euclides da Cunha, *Brazil* **170 D4** 10 31 S 39 1W
Cumberland, *B.C., Canada* **142 D4** 49 40N 125 0W
Cumberland, *Ont., Canada* **151 A9** 45 29N 75 24W
Cumberland, *Iowa, U.S.A.* **156 C2** 41 16N 94 52W
Cumberland, *Md., U.S.A.* **148 F6** 39 39N 78 46W
Cumberland →, *U.S.A.* **149 G2** 36 15N 87 0W
Cumberland, C., *Vanuatu* **133 D4** 14 39 S 166 37 E
Cumberland, L., *U.S.A.* **149 G3** 36 57N 84 55W
Cumberland Gap △, *U.S.A.* **149 G4** 36 36N 83 40W
Cumberland I., *U.S.A.* **152 E8** 30 50N 81 25W
Cumberland Is., *Australia* **126 J7** 20 35 S 149 10 E
Cumberland Island ⌓, *U.S.A.* **152 E8** 30 12N 81 24W
Cumberland L., *Canada* **143 C8** 54 3N 102 18W
Cumberland Pen., *Canada* **139 B13** 67 0N 64 0W
Cumberland Plateau, *U.S.A.* **149 H3** 36 0N 85 0W
Cumberland Sd., *Canada* **139 B13** 65 30N 66 0W
Cumbernauld, *U.K.* **22 F5** 55 57N 3 58W
Cumbira, *Angola* **115 E3** 12 11 S 15 8 E
Cumborah, *Australia* **127 D4** 29 40 S 147 45 E
Cumbres de Majalca △, *Mexico* **162 B3** 28 52N 106 24W
Cumbres de Monterrey △, *Mexico* **162 B4** 25 40N 100 35W
Cumbres Mayores, *Spain* **43 G4** 38 4N 6 39W
Cumbria □, *U.K.* **20 C5** 54 42N 2 52W
Cumbrian Mts., *U.K.* **20 C5** 54 30N 3 0W
Cumbum, *India* **95 G4** 15 40N 79 10 E
Cuminá, *Brazil* **169 D6** 1 57 S 56 2W
Cuminá →, *Brazil* **169 D6** 1 30 S 56 0W
Cuminapanema →, *Brazil* **169 D7** 1 9 S 54 54W
Cumming, C., *Chile* **172 b** 27 6 S 109 14W
Cummings Mt., *U.S.A.* **161 K8** 35 2N 118 34W
Cummins, *Australia* **127 E2** 34 16 S 135 43 E
Cumnock, *Australia* **129 B8** 32 59 S 148 46 E
Cumnock, *U.K.* **22 F4** 55 28N 4 17W
Cumpas, *Mexico* **162 B3** 30 0N 109 48W
Cumplida, Pta., *Canary Is.* **9 e1** 28 50N 17 48W
Çumra, *Turkey* **100 D5** 37 34N 32 45 E
Cuncumén, *Chile* **174 C1** 31 53 S 70 38W
Cunderdin, *Australia* **125 F2** 31 37 S 117 12 E
Cundinamarca □, *Colombia* **168 C3** 5 0N 74 0W
Cunene □, *Angola* **115 F3** 16 30 S 15 0 E
Cunene →, *Angola* **116 B1** 17 20 S 11 50 E
Cúneo, *Italy* **44 D4** 44 23N 7 32 E
Çüngüş, *Turkey* **96 B3** 38 13N 39 17 E
Cunhinga, *Angola* **115 E3** 12 11 S 16 47 E
Cunillera, I. = Sa Conillera, *Spain* **38 D1** 38 59N 1 13 E
Cunjamba, *Angola* **115 F4** 15 27 S 20 10 E
Cunlhat, *France* **28 C7** 45 38N 3 32 E
Cunnamulla, *Australia* **127 D4** 28 2 S 145 38 E
Cunningham, *Bahamas* **9 b** 25 5N 77 26W
Cuorgnè, *Italy* **44 C4** 45 23N 7 39 E
Cupar, *Canada* **143 C8** 50 57N 104 10W
Cupar, *U.K.* **22 E5** 56 19N 3 1W
Cupcini, *Moldova* **53 B12** 48 6N 27 23 E
Cupica, G. de, *Colombia* **168 B2** 6 25N 77 30W
Ćuprija, *Serbia & M.* **50 C5** 43 57N 21 26 E
Curaçá, *Brazil* **170 C4** 8 59 S 39 54W
Curaçao, *Neth. Ant.* **165 D6** 12 10N 69 0W
Curacautín, *Chile* **176 A2** 38 26 S 71 53W
Curador = Presidente Dutra, *Brazil* **170 C3** 5 15 S 44 30W
Curahuara de Carangas, *Bolivia* **172 D4** 17 52 S 68 26W
Curalhinho = Coelho Neto, *Brazil* **170 B3** 4 15 S 43 0W
Curanilahue, *Chile* **174 D1** 37 29 S 73 28W
Curaray →, *Peru* **168 D3** 2 20 S 74 5W
Curatabaca, *Venezuela* **169 B5** 6 19N 62 51W
Cure →, *France* **27 E10** 47 40N 3 41 E
Curepipe, *Mauritius* **121 d** 20 19 S 57 31 E
Curepto, *Chile* **174 D1** 35 8 S 72 1W
Curiapo, *Venezuela* **169 B5** 8 33N 61 5W
Curicó, *Chile* **174 C1** 34 55 S 71 20W
Curicuriari →, *Brazil* **168 D4** 0 14 S 66 48W
Curieuse, *Seychelles* **121 b** 4 15 S 55 44 E
Curimatá, *Brazil* **170 D3** 10 2 S 44 17W
Curinga, *Italy* **47 D9** 38 49N 16 19 E
Curiplaya, *Colombia* **168 C3** 0 16N 74 52W
Curitiba, *Brazil* **175 B6** 25 20 S 49 10W
Curitibanos, *Brazil* **175 B5** 27 18 S 50 36W
Curlewis, *Australia* **129 A9** 31 7 S 150 16 E
Curoca →, *Angola* **115 F2** 15 43 S 11 55 E
Currabubula, *Australia* **129 A9** 31 16 S 150 44 E
Currais Novos, *Brazil* **170 C4** 6 13 S 36 30W
Curral Velho, *C. Verde Is.* **9 j** 16 8N 22 48W
Curralinho, *Brazil* **170 B2** 1 45 S 49 46W
Currant, *U.S.A.* **158 G6** 38 51N 115 32W
Curraweena, *Australia* **129 A6** 30 47 S 145 54 E
Currawinya △, *Australia* **127 D3** 28 55 S 144 27 E
Current →, *U.S.A.* **155 G9** 36 15N 90 55W
Currie, *Australia* **127 F3** 39 56 S 143 53 E
Currie, *U.S.A.* **158 F6** 40 16N 114 45W
Cursole, *Somali Rep.* **120 D3** 2 14N 45 25 E
Curt-Bunar = Tervel, *Bulgaria* **51 C11** 43 45N 27 28 E
Curtea de Argeş, *Romania* **53 E9** 45 12N 24 42 E
Curtici, *Romania* **52 D6** 46 21N 21 18 E
Curtis, *U.S.A.* **154 E4** 40 38N 100 31W
Curtis Group, *Australia* **127 F4** 39 30 S 146 37 E
Curtis I., *Australia* **126 C5** 23 35 S 151 10 E
Curuá →, *Pará, Brazil* **169 D7** 2 24 S 54 5W
Curuá →, *Pará, Brazil* **173 B7** 5 23 S 54 22W
Curuá, I., *Brazil* **170 A1** 0 48N 50 10W
Curuaés →, *Brazil* **173 B7** 7 30 S 54 45W
Curuaí, *Brazil* **169 D6** 2 17 S 55 29W
Curuápanema →, *Brazil* **169 D6** 2 25 S 55 2W
Curuçá, *Brazil* **170 B2** 0 43 S 47 50W
Curuçá →, *Brazil* **172 B3** 4 27 S 71 23W
Curuguaty, *Paraguay* **175 A4** 24 31 S 55 42W
Curup, *Indonesia* **84 C2** 4 26 S 102 13 E
Curupira, Serra, *S. Amer.* **169 C5** 1 25N 64 30W
Cururu →, *Brazil* **173 B6** 7 12 S 58 3W
Cururupu, *Brazil* **170 B3** 1 50 S 44 50W
Curuzú Cuatiá, *Argentina* **174 B4** 29 50 S 58 5W
Curvelo, *Brazil* **171 E3** 18 45 S 44 27W
Cushing, *U.S.A.* **155 H6** 35 59N 96 46W
Cushing, Mt., *Canada* **142 B3** 57 35N 126 57W
Cusihuiriáchic, *Mexico* **162 B3** 28 10N 106 50W
Cusna, Mte., *Italy* **44 D7** 44 17N 10 23 E
Cussabat = Al Qaşabát, *Libya* **108 B2** 32 39N 14 1 E
Cusset, *France* **27 F10** 46 8N 3 28 E
Cusseta, *U.S.A.* **152 C5** 32 18N 84 47W
Cusso, Sa. do, *Angola* **115 D2** 6 30 S 14 58 E
Custer, *U.S.A.* **154 D3** 43 46N 103 36W
Cut Bank, *U.S.A.* **158 B7** 48 38N 112 20W
Cutchogue, *U.S.A.* **151 E12** 41 1N 72 30W
Cutervo, *Peru* **172 B2** 6 25 S 78 55W
Cuthbert, *U.S.A.* **152 D5** 31 46N 84 48W
Cutler, *U.S.A.* **160 J7** 36 31N 119 17W
Cutler Ridge, *U.S.A.* **153 K9** 25 35N 80 20W
Cutlerville, *U.S.A.* **157 B11** 42 50N 85 40W
Cutral-Có, *Argentina* **176 A3** 38 58 S 69 15W
Cutro, *Italy* **47 C9** 39 2N 16 59 E
Cuttaburra →, *Australia* **127 D3** 29 43 S 144 22 E
Cuttack, *India* **94 D7** 20 25N 85 57 E
Cuva →, *Angola* **115 E2** 11 42 S 14 52 E
Cuvelai, *Angola* **115 F3** 15 44 S 15 50 E
Cuvier, C., *Australia* **125 D1** 23 14 S 113 22 E
Cuvier I., *N.Z.* **130 C4** 36 27 S 175 50 E
Cuxhaven, *Germany* **30 B4** 53 51N 8 41 E
Cuyabeno, *Ecuador* **168 D2** 0 16 S 75 53W
Cuyahoga Falls, *U.S.A.* **150 E3** 41 8N 81 29W
Cuyahoga Valley △, *U.S.A.* **150 E3** 41 15N 81 33W
Cuyapo, *Phil.* **80 D3** 15 46N 120 40 E
Cuyo, *Phil.* **81 F3** 10 50N 121 5 E
Cuyo East Pass, *Phil.* **81 F3** 11 0N 121 28 E
Cuyo I., *Phil.* **81 F3** 10 51N 121 2 E
Cuyo Islands, *Phil.* **81 F3** 11 4N 120 57 E
Cuyo West Pass, *Phil.* **81 F3** 11 0N 120 30 E
Cuyuni →, *Guyana* **169 B6** 6 23N 58 41W
Cuzco, *Bolivia* **172 E4** 20 0 S 66 50W
Cuzco, *Peru* **172 C3** 13 32 S 72 0W
Cuzco □, *Peru* **172 C3** 13 31 S 71 59W
Čvrsnica, *Bos.-H.* **52 G2** 43 36N 17 35 E
Cwmbran, *U.K.* **21 F4** 51 39N 3 2W
Cyangugu, *Rwanda* **118 C2** 2 29 S 28 54 E
Cybinka, *Poland* **55 F1** 52 12N 14 46 E
Cyclades = Kikládhes, *Greece* **48 E6** 37 0N 24 30 E
Cygnet, *Australia* **127 G4** 43 8 S 147 1 E
Cynthiana, *U.S.A.* **157 F12** 38 23N 84 18W
Cypress Hills, *Canada* **143 D7** 49 40N 109 30W
Cypress Hills ⌓, *Canada* **143 D7** 49 40N 109 30W
Cyprus ■, *Asia* **39 F9** 35 0N 33 0 E
Cyrenaica, *Libya* **108 B4** 27 0N 23 0 E
Cyrene = Shaḩḩāt, *Libya* **108 B4** 32 48N 21 54 E
Cyrene, *Libya* **108 B4** 32 53N 21 52 E
Czaplinek, *Poland* **54 E3** 53 34N 16 14 E
Czar, *Canada* **143 C6** 52 27N 110 50W
Czarna →, *Łódzkie, Poland* **55 G6** 51 18N 19 55 E
Czarna →, *Świętokrzyskie, Poland* **55 H8** 50 28N 21 21 E
Czarna Białostocka, *Poland* **55 E10** 53 18N 23 17 E
Czarna Woda, *Poland* **54 E5** 53 51N 18 6 E
Czarne, *Poland* **54 E3** 53 42N 16 58 E
Czarnków, *Poland* **55 F3** 52 55N 16 38 E
Czaslau = Čáslav, *Czech Rep.* **34 B8** 49 54N 15 22 E
Czech Rep. ■, *Europe* **34 B8** 50 0N 15 0 E
Czechowice-Dziedzice, *Poland* **55 J5** 49 54N 18 59 E
Czempiń, *Poland* **55 F3** 52 9N 16 43 E
Czeremcha, *Poland* **55 F10** 52 31N 23 21 E
Czerniejewo, *Poland* **55 F4** 52 26N 17 30 E
Czernowitz = Chernivtsi, *Ukraine* **53 B10** 48 15N 25 52 E
Czersk, *Poland* **54 E4** 53 46N 17 58 E
Czerwieńsk, *Poland* **55 F2** 52 1N 15 23 E
Czerwionka-Leszczyny, *Poland* **55 H5** 50 7N 18 37 E
Częstochowa, *Poland* **55 H6** 50 49N 19 7 E
Człopa, *Poland* **55 E3** 53 6N 16 6 E
Człuchów, *Poland* **54 E4** 53 41N 17 22 E
Czortków = Chortkiv, *Ukraine* **59 H3** 49 2N 25 46 E
Czyżew-Osada, *Poland* **55 F9** 52 48N 22 19 E

D

Da →, *Vietnam* **76 G5** 21 15N 105 20 E
Da Hinggan Ling, *China* **69 B7** 48 0N 121 0 E
Da Lat, *Vietnam* **87 G7** 11 56N 108 25 E
Da Nang, *Vietnam* **86 D7** 16 4N 108 13 E
Da Qaidam, *China* **68 C4** 37 50N 95 15 E
Da Yunhe →, *China* **75 G11** 34 25N 120 5 E
Da'an, *China* **75 B13** 45 30N 124 7 E
Daan Viljoen ⌓, *Namibia* **116 C2** 22 2 S 16 45 E
Daanbantayan, *Phil.* **81 F5** 11 17N 124 2 E
Dab'a, Ras el, *Egypt* **106 H6** 31 3N 28 31 E
Daba Shan, *China* **76 B7** 32 0N 109 0 E
Dabai, *Nigeria* **113 C6** 11 25N 5 15 E
Dabajuro, *Venezuela* **168 A3** 11 2N 70 40W
Dabakala, *Ivory C.* **112 D4** 8 15N 4 20W
Dabaro, *Somali Rep.* **120 C3** 6 21N 48 43 E
Dabas, *Hungary* **52 C4** 47 11N 19 19 E
Dabat, *Ethiopia* **107 E4** 12 58N 37 41 E
Dabbagh, Jabal, *Si. Arabia* **96 E2** 27 52N 35 45 E
Dabeiba, *Colombia* **168 B2** 7 1N 76 16W
Daber = Dobra, *Poland* **54 E2** 53 34N 15 20 E
Dabhoi, *India* **92 H5** 22 10N 73 20 E
Dąbie, *Poland* **55 F5** 52 5N 18 50 E
Dabie Shan, *China* **77 B10** 31 20N 115 20 E
Dabilda, *Cameroon* **109 F2** 12 14N 14 34 E
Dabilda, *Cameroon* **113 C7** 12 45N 14 35 E
Dabnou, *Niger* **113 C6** 14 10N 5 22 E
Dabo = Pasirkuning, *Indonesia* **84 C2** 0 30 S 104 33 E
Dabola, *Guinea* **112 C2** 10 50N 11 5W
Dabou, *Ivory C.* **112 D4** 5 20N 4 23W
Daboya, *Ghana* **113 D4** 9 30N 1 20W
Dabravolya, *Belarus* **55 F10** 52 55N 23 59 E
Dąbrowa Białostocka, *Poland* **54 E10** 53 40N 23 21 E
Dąbrowa Górnicza, *Poland* **55 H6** 50 15N 19 10 E
Dąbrowa Tarnowska, *Poland* **55 H7** 50 10N 20 59 E
Dabu, *China* **77 E11** 24 22N 116 41 E
Dabugam, *India* **94 E6** 19 27N 82 26 E
Dabung, *Malaysia* **87 K4** 5 23N 102 1 E
Dabus →, *Ethiopia* **107 E4** 10 48N 35 10 E
Dacato →, *Ethiopia* **107 F5** 7 25N 42 40 E
Dacca = Dhaka, *Bangla.* **90 D3** 23 43N 90 26 E
Dacca = Dhaka □, *Bangla.* **90 C3** 24 25N 90 25 E
Dachau, *Germany* **31 G7** 48 15N 11 26 E
Dachigam △, *India* **92 B6** 34 10N 75 0 E
Dachstein, Hoher, *Austria* **34 D6** 47 28N 13 35 E
Dačice, *Czech Rep.* **34 B8** 49 5N 15 26 E
Dacula, *U.S.A.* **152 B6** 33 59N 83 54W
Dadanawa, *Guyana* **169 C6** 2 50N 59 30W
Daday, *Turkey* **100 B5** 41 28N 33 27 E
Dade City, *U.S.A.* **153 G7** 28 22N 82 11W
Dadès, Oued →, *Morocco* **110 B3** 30 58N 6 44W
Dadeville, *U.S.A.* **152 C4** 32 50N 85 46W
Dadhar, *Pakistan* **92 E2** 29 28N 67 39 E
Dadiya, *Nigeria* **113 D7** 9 35N 11 24 E
Dadra = Achalpur, *India* **94 D3** 21 22N 77 32 E
Dadra & Nagar Haveli □, *India* **94 D1** 20 5N 73 0 E
Dadri = Charkhi Dadri, *India* **92 E7** 28 37N 76 17 E
Dadu, *Pakistan* **91 D2** 26 45N 67 45 E
Dadu He →, *China* **76 C4** 29 31N 103 46 E
Daegu = Taegu, *S. Korea* **75 G15** 35 50N 128 37 E
Daejeon = Taejŏn, *S. Korea* **75 F14** 36 20N 127 28 E
Daet, *Phil.* **80 D4** 14 2N 122 55 E
Dafang, *China* **76 D5** 27 9N 105 39 E
Dağ, *Turkey* **49 D12** 37 12N 30 31 E
Dagali, *Norway* **18 D5** 60 25N 8 28 E
Dagana, *Senegal* **112 B1** 16 30N 15 35W
Dagash, *Sudan* **106 D3** 19 19N 33 25 E
Dagestan □, *Russia* **61 J8** 42 30N 47 0 E
Dagestanskiye Ogni, *Russia* **61 J9** 42 6N 48 12 E
Dagg Sd., *N.Z.* **131 F1** 45 23 S 166 45 E
Daggett, *U.S.A.* **161 L10** 34 52N 116 52W
Daghestan Republic = Dagestan □, *Russia* **61 J8** 42 30N 47 0 E
Daghfeli, *Sudan* **106 D3** 19 18N 32 40 E
Dağlıq Qarabağ = Nagorno-Karabakh □, *Azerbaijan* **101 C12** 39 55N 46 45 E
Dagmersellen, *Switz.* **32 B5** 47 13N 7 59 E
Dagö = Hiiumaa, *Estonia* **15 G20** 58 50N 22 45 E
Dagu, *China* **75 E9** 38 59N 117 40 E
Dagua, *Papua N. G.* **132 B2** 3 27 S 143 20 E
Daguan, *China* **76 D4** 27 43N 103 56 E
Dagupan, *Phil.* **80 C3** 16 3N 120 20 E
Daguragu, *Australia* **124 C5** 17 33 S 130 30 E
Dahab, *Egypt* **106 B3** 28 31N 34 31 E
Dahanu, *India* **94 E1** 19 58N 72 44 E
Dahivadi, *India* **94 F2** 17 43N 74 33 E
Dahlak △, *Eritrea* **107 D5** 15 35N 40 1 E
Dahlak Kebir, *Eritrea* **107 D5** 15 50N 40 10 E
Dahlenburg, *Germany* **30 B6** 53 11N 10 44 E
Dahlonega, *U.S.A.* **149 H4** 34 32N 83 59W
Dahme, *Germany* **30 D9** 51 52N 13 25 E
Dahod, *India* **92 H6** 22 50N 74 15 E
Dahomey = Benin ■, *Africa* **113 D5** 10 0N 2 0 E
Dahong Shan, *China* **77 B9** 31 25N 113 0 E
Dahra, *Libya* **108 C3** 29 30N 17 50 E
Dahra, *Senegal* **112 B1** 15 22N 15 30W
Dahra, Massif de, *Algeria* **111 A5** 36 7N 1 21 E
Dahshûr, *Egypt* **106 J7** 29 45N 31 14 E
Dahūk, *Iraq* **101 D10** 36 50N 43 1 E
Daḩy, Nafūd ad, *Si. Arabia* **98 B4** 22 0N 45 25 E
Dai, *Solomon Is.* **133 L11** 7 54 S 160 40 E
Dai Hao, *Vietnam* **86 C6** 18 1N 106 25 E
Dai-Sen, *Japan* **72 B5** 35 22N 133 32 E
Dai Shan, *China* **77 B14** 30 25N 122 10 E
Dai Xian, *China* **74 E7** 39 4N 112 58 E
Daicheng, *China* **74 E9** 38 42N 116 38 E
Daigo, *Japan* **73 A12** 36 46N 140 21 E
Daik-u, *Burma* **90 G6** 17 47N 96 40 E
Daimanji-San, *Japan* **72 A5** 36 14N 133 20 E
Daimiel, *Spain* **43 F7** 39 5N 3 35W
Daingean, *Ireland* **23 C4** 53 18N 7 17W
Dainkog, *China* **76 A1** 32 30N 97 58 E
Daintree, *Australia* **126 B4** 16 20 S 145 20 E
Daintree △, *Australia* **126 B4** 16 8 S 145 2 E
Daiō-Misaki, *Japan* **73 C8** 34 15N 136 45 E
Dair, J. ed, *Sudan* **107 E3** 12 27N 30 42 E
Dairen = Dalian, *China* **75 E11** 38 50N 121 40 E
Dairût, *Egypt* **106 B3** 27 34N 30 43 E
Daisen-Oki △, *Japan* **72 B5** 35 23N 133 34 E
Daisetsu-Zan, *Japan* **70 C11** 43 30N 142 57 E
Daisetsu-Zan △, *Japan* **70 C11** 43 30N 142 55 E
Daitari, *India* **94 D7** 21 10N 85 46 E
Daito, *Japan* **72 B4** 35 19N 132 58 E
Dajarra, *Australia* **126 C2** 21 42 S 139 30 E
Dajin Chuan →, *China* **76 B3** 31 16N 101 59 E
Dak Dam, *Cambodia* **86 F6** 12 20N 107 21 E
Dak Nhe, *Vietnam* **86 E6** 15 28N 107 48 E
Dak Pek, *Vietnam* **86 E6** 15 4N 107 44 E
Dak Song, *Vietnam* **87 F6** 12 19N 107 35 E
Dak Sui, *Vietnam* **86 E6** 14 55N 107 43 E
Dakar, *Senegal* **112 C1** 14 34N 17 29W
Dakhin, *Bangla.* **90 D3** 22 30N 90 45 E
Dakhla, *W. Sahara* **110 D1** 23 50N 15 53W
Dakhla, El Wâhât el-, *Egypt* **106 B2** 25 30N 28 50 E
Dakingari, *Nigeria* **113 C5** 11 37N 4 1 E
Dakoank, *India* **95 L11** 7 2N 93 43 E
Dakor, *India* **92 H5** 22 45N 73 11 E
Dakoro, *Niger* **113 C6** 14 31N 6 46 E
Dakota City, *Iowa, U.S.A.* **156 B2** 42 43N 94 12W
Dakota City, *Nebr., U.S.A.* **154 D6** 42 25N 96 25W
Đakovica, *Serbia & M.* **50 D4** 42 22N 20 26 E
Đakovo, *Croatia* **52 E3** 45 19N 18 24 E
Dal, *Norway* **18 E5** 59 53N 8 40 E
Dala, *Lunda Sul, Angola* **115 E4** 11 3 S 20 17 E
Dala, *Uíge, Angola* **115 D3** 8 5 S 15 49 E
Dala, *Solomon Is.* **133 M11** 8 30 S 160 41 E
Dala-Cachibo, *Angola* **115 E2** 10 30 S 14 41 E
Dalaas, *Austria* **33 B10** 47 7N 10 0 E
Dalaba, *Guinea* **112 C2** 10 47N 12 12W
Dalachi, *China* **74 F3** 36 48N 105 0 E
Dalagan = San Antonio, *Phil.* **80 D3** 14 57N 120 5 E
Dalaguete, *Phil.* **81 G4** 9 46N 123 32 E
Dalai Nur, *China* **74 C9** 43 20N 116 45 E
Dālakī, *Iran* **97 D6** 29 26N 51 17 E
Dalälven →, *Sweden* **16 D10** 60 12N 16 43 E
Dalaman, *Turkey* **49 E10** 36 48N 28 47 E
Dalaman →, *Turkey* **49 E10** 36 41N 28 43 E
Dalandzadgad, *Mongolia* **74 C3** 43 27N 104 30 E
Dalanganem Is., *Phil.* **81 F3** 10 40N 120 17 E
Dalap-Uliga-Darrit, *Marshall Is.* **134 G9** 7 7N 171 24 E
Dalarna, *Sweden* **16 D8** 61 0N 14 0 E
Dalarnas län □, *Sweden* **16 C8** 61 0N 14 15 E
Dalasýsla □, *Iceland* **11 B4** 65 15N 22 0W
Dalat, *Malaysia* **85 B4** 2 44N 111 56 E
Dālbandīn, *Pakistan* **91 C2** 29 0N 64 23 E
Dalbeattie, *U.K.* **22 G5** 54 56N 3 50W
Dalbeg, *Australia* **126 C4** 20 16 S 147 18 E
Dalbosjön, *Sweden* **17 F6** 58 40N 12 45 E
Dalby, *Australia* **127 D5** 27 10 S 151 17 E
Dalby, *Sweden* **17 J7** 55 40N 13 22 E
Dalby Söderskog △, *Sweden* **17 J7** 55 41N 13 21 E
Dale, *Norway* **18 C2** 61 22N 5 23 E
Dale, *U.S.A.* **157 F10** 38 10N 86 59W
Dale City, *U.S.A.* **148 F7** 38 38N 77 18W
Dale Hollow L., *U.S.A.* **149 G3** 36 32N 85 27W
Dalen, *Norway* **18 E4** 59 26N 8 0 E
Dalet, *Burma* **90 F4** 19 59N 93 51 E
Daletme, *Burma* **90 E4** 21 36N 92 46 E
Daleville, *Ala., U.S.A.* **152 D4** 31 19N 85 43W
Daleville, *Ind., U.S.A.* **157 D11** 40 7N 85 33W
Dalga, *Egypt* **106 B3** 27 39N 30 41 E
Dalgān, *Iran* **97 E8** 27 31N 59 19 E
Dalhart, *U.S.A.* **155 G3** 36 4N 102 31W
Dalhousie, *Canada* **141 C6** 48 5N 66 26W
Dalhousie, *India* **92 C6** 32 38N 75 58 E
Dali, *Shaanxi, China* **74 G5** 34 48N 109 58 E
Dali, *Yunnan, China* **76 E3** 25 40N 100 10 E
Dalian, *China* **75 E11** 38 50N 121 40 E
Daliang Shan, *China* **76 D4** 28 0N 102 45 E
Daling He →, *China* **75 D11** 40 55N 121 40 E
Dāliyat el Karmel, *Israel* **103 C4** 32 43N 35 2 E
Dalj, *Croatia* **52 E3** 45 29N 18 59 E
Dalkeith, *U.K.* **22 F5** 55 54N 3 4W
Dalkeith, *U.S.A.* **152 E4** 30 0N 85 9W
Dallas, *Ga., U.S.A.* **152 B5** 33 55N 84 51W
Dallas, *Oreg., U.S.A.* **158 D2** 44 55N 123 19W
Dallas, *Tex., U.S.A.* **155 J6** 32 47N 96 49W
Dallas Center, *U.S.A.* **156 C3** 41 41N 93 58W
Dallas City, *U.S.A.* **156 D5** 40 38N 91 10W
Dalle = Yirga Alem, *Ethiopia* **107 F4** 6 48N 38 22 E
Dallol, *Ethiopia* **107 E5** 14 14N 40 17 E
Dalmā, *U.A.E.* **97 E7** 24 30N 52 20 E
Dalmacija, *Croatia* **45 E13** 43 20N 17 0 E
Dalmas, L., *Canada* **141 B5** 53 30N 71 50W
Dalmatia = Dalmacija, *Croatia* **45 E13** 43 20N 17 0 E
Dalmatovo, *Russia* **64 C9** 56 16N 62 56 E
Dalmau, *India* **93 F9** 26 4N 81 2 E
Dalmellington, *U.K.* **22 F4** 55 19N 4 23W
Dalmeny, *Australia* **129 D9** 36 10 S 150 8 E
Dalnegorsk, *Russia* **67 E14** 44 32N 135 33 E
Dalnerechensk, *Russia* **67 E14** 45 50N 133 40 E
Dalnevostochnyy □, *Russia* **67 C14** 67 0N 140 0 E
Dalny = Dalian, *China* **75 E11** 38 50N 121 40 E
Daloa, *Ivory C.* **112 D3** 7 0N 6 30W
Dalou Shan, *China* **76 C6** 28 15N 107 0 E
Dalry, *U.K.* **22 F4** 55 42N 4 43W
Dalrymple, L., *Australia* **126 C4** 20 40 S 147 0 E
Dalrymple, Mt., *Australia* **126 K6** 21 1 S 148 39 E
Dals Långed, *Sweden* **17 F6** 58 56N 12 18 E
Dalseter, *Norway* **18 C6** 61 28N 9 26 E
Dalsjöfors, *Sweden* **17 G7** 57 46N 13 5 E
Dalsland, *Sweden* **17 F6** 58 50N 12 15 E
Dalsmynni, *Iceland* **11 C5** 64 48N 21 29W
Daltenganj, *India* **93 H11** 24 0N 84 4 E
Dalton, *Ga., U.S.A.* **149 H3** 34 46N 84 58W
Dalton, *Mass., U.S.A.* **151 D11** 42 28N 73 11W
Dalton, *Nebr., U.S.A.* **154 E3** 41 25N 102 58W
Dalton, Kap, *Greenland* **10 D8** 69 25N 24 3W
Dalton-in-Furness, *U.K.* **20 C4** 54 10N 3 11W
Dalupiri I., *Cagayan, Phil.* **80 B3** 19 5N 121 12 E
Dalupiri I., *N. Samar, Phil.* **80 E5** 12 25N 124 16 E
Dalvík, *Iceland* **11 B8** 65 58N 18 32W
Dálvvadis = Jokkmokk, *Sweden* **14 C18** 66 35N 19 50 E
Dalwallinu, *Australia* **125 F2** 30 17 S 116 40 E
Daly →, *Australia* **124 B5** 13 35 S 130 19 E
Daly City, *U.S.A.* **160 H4** 37 42N 122 28W
Daly L., *Canada* **143 B7** 56 32N 105 39W
Daly River, *Australia* **124 B5** 13 46 S 130 42 E
Daly Waters, *Australia* **126 B1** 16 15 S 133 24 E
Dalyan, *Turkey* **49 E10** 36 50N 28 39 E
Dam Doi, *Vietnam* **87 H5** 8 50N 105 12 E
Dam Ha, *Vietnam* **86 B6** 21 21N 107 36 E
Damachova, *Belarus* **55 G10** 51 45N 23 36 E
Daman, *India* **94 D1** 20 25N 72 57 E
Daman & Diu □, *India* **94 D1** 20 25N 72 58 E
Dāmaneh, *Iran* **97 C6** 33 1N 50 29 E
Damanganga →, *India* **94 D1** 20 25N 72 56 E
Damanhûr, *Egypt* **106 H7** 31 0N 30 30 E
Damant L., *Canada* **143 A7** 61 45N 105 5W
Damanzhuang, *China* **74 E9** 38 5N 116 35 E
Damar, *Indonesia* **82 C3** 7 7 S 128 40 E
Damara, *C.A.R.* **114 B3** 4 58N 18 42 E
Damaraland, *Namibia* **116 C2** 20 0 S 15 0 E
Damascus = Dimashq, *Syria* **103 B5** 33 30N 36 18 E
Damascus, *U.S.A.* **152 D5** 31 18N 84 43W
Damaturu, *Nigeria* **113 C7** 11 45N 11 55 E
Damāvand, *Iran* **97 C7** 35 47N 52 0 E
Damāvand, Qolleh-ye, *Iran* **97 C7** 35 56N 52 10 E
Damba, *Angola* **115 D3** 6 44 S 15 20 E
Dâmboviţa □, *Romania* **53 F10** 45 0N 25 30 E
Dâmboviţa →, *Romania* **53 F11** 44 12N 26 26 E
Dâmbovnic →, *Romania* **53 F10** 44 28N 25 18 E
Dambrowica = Dubrovytsya, *Ukraine* **59 G4** 51 31N 26 35 E
Dambulla, *Sri Lanka* **95 L5** 7 51N 80 39 E
Dame Marie, *Haiti* **165 C5** 18 36N 74 26W
Dāmghān, *Iran* **97 B7** 36 10N 54 17 E
Dămienesti, *Romania* **53 D11** 46 44N 26 59 E
Damietta = Dumyât, *Egypt* **106 H7** 31 24N 31 48 E
Daming, *China* **74 F8** 36 15N 115 6 E
Damīr Qābū, *Syria* **96 B4** 36 58N 41 51 E
Dammai I., *Phil.* **81 J3** 5 47N 120 25 E
Dammam = Ad Dammām, *Si. Arabia* **97 E6** 26 20N 50 5 E
Dammarie-les-Lys, *France* **27 D9** 48 31N 2 39 E
Dammartin-en-Goële, *France* **27 C9** 49 3N 2 41 E
Dammastock, *Switz.* **33 C6** 46 38N 8 24 E
Damme, *Germany* **30 C4** 52 32N 8 11 E
Damodar →, *India* **93 H12** 23 17N 87 35 E
Damoh, *India* **93 H8** 23 50N 79 28 E
Damous, *Algeria* **111 A5** 36 31N 1 42 E
Dampier, *Australia* **124 D2** 20 41 S 116 42 E
Dampier, Selat, *Indonesia* **83 B4** 0 40 S 131 0 E
Dampier Arch., *Australia* **124 D2** 20 38 S 116 32 E
Dampier Str., *Papua N. G.* **132 C5** 5 50 S 148 0 E
Dampierre-sur-Salon, *France* **32 A1** 47 33N 5 41 E
Damqawt, *Yemen* **99 C6** 16 34N 52 50 E
Damrani, *Algeria* **110 C4** 27 45N 2 56W
Damrei, Chuor Phnum, *Cambodia* **87 G4** 11 30N 103 0 E
Damroh, *India* **90 A5** 28 26N 95 14 E
Damüls, *Austria* **33 B9** 47 17N 9 53 E
Damvillers, *France* **27 C12** 49 20N 5 21 E
Dan-Gulbi, *Nigeria* **113 C6** 11 40N 6 15 E
Dana, *Indonesia* **82 D2** 11 0 S 122 52 E
Dana, L., *Canada* **140 B4** 50 53N 77 20W
Dana, Mt., *U.S.A.* **160 H7** 37 54N 119 12W
Danakil Desert, *Ethiopia* **107 E5** 12 45N 41 0 E
Danané, *Ivory C.* **112 D3** 7 16N 8 9W
Danao, *Phil.* **81 F5** 10 31N 124 1 E
Danau Poso, *Indonesia* **79 E6** 1 52 S 120 35 E
Danba, *China* **76 B3** 30 54N 101 48 E
Danbury, *U.S.A.* **151 E11** 41 24N 73 28W
Danby L., *U.S.A.* **159 J6** 34 13N 115 5W
Dand, *Afghan.* **91 C2** 31 28N 65 32 E
Dande ⌓, *Zimbabwe* **119 F3** 15 56 S 30 16 E
Dande →, *Angola* **115 D2** 6 15 S 15 34 E
Dandeldhura, *Nepal* **93 E9** 29 20N 80 35 E
Dandeli, *India* **95 G2** 15 5N 74 30 E
Dandenong, *Australia* **129 E6** 38 0 S 145 15 E
Dandîl, *Egypt* **106 J7** 29 10N 31 2 E
Dandong, *China* **75 D13** 40 10N 124 20 E
Danfeng, *China* **74 H6** 33 45N 110 25 E
Dangan Liedao, *China* **77 F10** 22 2N 114 8 E
Dangara, *Tajikistan* **65 D4** 38 6N 69 22 E
Dange, *Angola* **115 D3** 7 56 S 15 3 E
Dangé-St-Romain, *France* **28 B4** 46 56N 0 36 E
Dângeni, *Romania* **53 C11** 47 51N 26 58 E
Danger Is. = Pukapuka, *Cook Is.* **135 J11** 10 53 S 165 49W
Danger Pt., *S. Africa* **116 E2** 34 40 S 19 17 E
Danginpuri, *Indonesia* **79 K18** 8 40 S 115 13 E
Dangla, *Ethiopia* **107 E4** 11 18N 36 56 E
Dangla Shan = Tanggula Shan, *China* **68 C4** 32 40N 92 10 E
Dangora, *Nigeria* **113 C6** 11 30N 8 7 E
Dangouadougou, *Burkina Faso* **112 D4** 10 9N 4 56W
Dangrek, Phnom, *Thailand* **86 E5** 14 15N 105 0 E
Dangriga, *Belize* **163 D7** 17 0N 88 13W
Dangshan, *China* **74 G9** 34 27N 116 22 E
Dangtu, *China* **77 B12** 31 32N 118 25 E
Dangyang, *China* **77 B8** 30 52N 111 44 E
Dani, *Burkina Faso* **113 C4** 13 43N 0 10W
Daniel, *U.S.A.* **158 E8** 42 52N 110 4W
Daniel's Harbour, *Canada* **141 B8** 50 13N 57 35W
Danielskuil, *S. Africa* **116 D3** 28 11 S 23 33 E
Danielson, *U.S.A.* **151 E13** 41 48N 71 53W
Danielsville, *U.S.A.* **152 A6** 34 8N 83 13W
Danilov, *Russia* **58 C11** 58 16N 40 13 E
Danilovgrad, *Serbia & M.* **50 D3** 42 38N 19 4 E

Danilovka, *Russia* **60 E7** 50 25N 44 12 E
Daning, *China* **74 F6** 36 28N 110 45 E
Danish West Indies = Virgin Is. (U.S.) ☒, *W. Indies* **165 e** 18 20N 65 0W
Danja, *Nigeria* **113 C6** 11 21N 7 30 E
Danje-la-Menha, *Angola* **115 D2** 9 32 S 14 39 E
Danjiangkou, *China* **77 A8** 32 31N 111 30 E
Danjiangkou Shuiku, *China* **77 A8** 32 37N 111 30 E
Ḑank, *Oman* **97 F8** 23 33N 56 16 E
Dankalwa, *Nigeria* **113 C7** 11 52N 12 12 E
Dankama, *Nigeria* **113 C6** 13 20N 7 44 E
Dankov, *Russia* **58 F10** 53 20N 39 5 E
Danleng, *China* **76 B4** 30 1N 103 31 E
Danlí, *Honduras* **164 D2** 14 4N 86 35W
Danmark = Denmark ■, *Europe* **17 J3** 55 45N 10 0 E
Danmark Fjord, *Greenland* **10 A8** 81 30N 22 0W
Danmarkshavn, *Greenland* **10 B9** 76 45N 18 50W
Dannemora, *U.S.A.* **151 B11** 44 43N 73 44W
Dannenberg, *Germany* **30 B7** 53 6N 11 5 E
Dannevirke, *N.Z.* **130 G5** 40 12 S 176 8 E
Dannhauser, *S. Africa* **117 D5** 28 0 S 30 3 E
Danot, *Ethiopia* **120 C3** 7 33N 45 17 E
Dansalan = Marawi City, *Phil.* **81 G5** 8 0N 124 21 E
Dansville, *U.S.A.* **150 D7** 42 34N 77 42W
Danta, *India* **92 G5** 24 11N 72 46 E
Dantan, *India* **93 J12** 21 57N 87 20 E
Dantewara, *India* **94 E5** 18 54N 81 21 E
Danube = Dunărea →, *Europe* **53 E14** 45 20N 29 40 E
Danubyu, *Burma* **90 G5** 17 15N 95 35 E
Danvers, *U.S.A.* **151 D14** 42 34N 70 56W
Danville, *Ga., U.S.A.* **152 C6** 32 37N 83 15W
Danville, *Ill., U.S.A.* **157 D9** 40 8N 87 37W
Danville, *Ind., U.S.A.* **157 E10** 39 46N 86 32W
Danville, *Ky., U.S.A.* **157 G12** 37 39N 84 46W
Danville, *Pa., U.S.A.* **151 F8** 40 58N 76 37W
Danville, *Va., U.S.A.* **149 G6** 36 36N 79 23W
Danville, *Vt., U.S.A.* **151 B12** 44 25N 72 9W
Danyang, *China* **77 B12** 32 0N 119 31 E
Danzhai, *China* **76 D6** 26 11N 107 48 E
Danzhou, *China* **86 C7** 19 31N 109 33 E
Danzig = Gdańsk, *Poland* **54 D5** 54 22N 18 40 E
Dao = Tobias Fornier, *Phil.* **81 F3** 10 30N 121 57 E
Dao, *Phil.* **81 F4** 11 24N 122 41 E
Dão →, *Portugal* **42 E2** 40 20N 8 11W
Dao Xian, *China* **77 E8** 25 36N 111 31 E
Daocheng, *China* **76 C3** 29 0N 100 10 E
Daora, *W. Sahara* **110 C2** 27 5N 12 59W
Daoud = Aïn Beïda, *Algeria* **111 A6** 35 50N 7 29 E
Daoukro, *Ivory C.* **112 D4** 7 10N 3 58W
Dapa, *Phil.* **81 G6** 9 46N 126 3 E
Dapaong, *Togo* **113 C5** 10 55N 0 16 E
Dapchi, *Nigeria* **113 C7** 12 32N 11 31 E
Dapiak, Mt., *Phil.* **81 G4** 8 15N 123 28 E
Dapitan, *Phil.* **81 G4** 8 39N 123 25 E
Dapoli, *India* **94 F1** 17 46N 73 11 E
Daqing Shan, *China* **74 D6** 40 40N 111 0 E
Daqu Shan, *China* **77 B14** 30 25N 122 20 E
Dar Banda, *Africa* **104 F6** 8 0N 23 0 E
Dar el Beida = Casablanca, *Morocco* **110 B3** 33 36N 7 36W
Dar es Salaam, *Tanzania* **118 D4** 6 50 S 39 12 E
Dar Mazār, *Iran* **97 D8** 29 14N 57 20 E
Dar Rounga, *C.A.R.* **114 A4** 0 45N 22 20 E
Dar'ā, *Syria* **103 C5** 32 36N 36 7 E
Dar'ā □, *Syria* **103 C5** 32 55N 36 10 E
Dara Dere = Zlatograd, *Bulgaria* **51 E9** 41 22N 25 7 E
Dārāb, *Iran* **97 D7** 28 50N 54 30 E
Daraban, *Pakistan* **92 D4** 31 44N 70 20 E
Darabani, *Romania* **53 B11** 48 10N 26 39 E
Darai Hills, *Papua N. G.* **132 D2** 7 8 S 143 33 E
Daraina, *Madag.* **117 A8** 13 12 S 49 40 E
Daraj, *Libya* **108 B2** 30 10N 10 28 E
Daram, *Phil.* **81 F5** 11 38N 124 48 E
Dārān, *Iran* **97 C6** 32 59N 50 24 E
Daraut Kurgan = Daroot-Korgan, *Kyrgyzstan* **65 D6** 39 33N 72 11 E
Daravica, *Serbia & M.* **50 D4** 42 32N 20 8 E
Daraw, *Egypt* **106 C3** 24 22N 32 51 E
Dārayyā, *Syria* **103 B5** 33 28N 36 15 E
Darazo, *Nigeria* **113 C7** 11 1N 10 24 E
Darband, *Pakistan* **92 B5** 34 20N 72 50 E
Darband, Kūh-e, *Iran* **97 D8** 31 34N 57 8 E
Darbhanga, *India* **93 F11** 26 15N 85 55 E
Darburruk, *Somali Rep.* **120 C2** 9 44N 44 31 E
Darby, C., *U.S.A.* **144 D7** 64 19N 162 47W
D'Arcy, *Canada* **142 C4** 50 27N 122 35W
Darda, *Croatia* **52 E3** 45 40N 18 41 E
Dardanelle, *Ark., U.S.A.* **155 H8** 35 13N 93 9W
Dardanelle, *Calif., U.S.A.* **160 G7** 38 20N 119 50W
Dardanelles = Çanakkale Boğazı, *Turkey* **51 F10** 40 17N 26 32 E
Dare →, *Ethiopia* **107 F5** 7 20N 42 11 E
Darende, *Turkey* **100 C7** 38 31N 37 30 E
Dārestān, *Iran* **97 D8** 29 9N 58 42 E
Darfield, *N.Z.* **131 D7** 43 29 S 172 7 E
Darfo, *Italy* **44 C7** 45 53N 10 11 E
Dârfûr, *Sudan* **104 E6** 13 40N 24 0 E
Dargai, *Pakistan* **92 B4** 34 25N 71 55 E
Dargan Ata, *Turkmenistan* **66 E7** 40 29N 62 10 E
Dargaville, *N.Z.* **130 B2** 35 57 S 173 52 E
Dargol, *Niger* **113 C5** 13 54N 1 22 E
Darhan, *Mongolia* **68 B5** 49 37N 106 21 E
Darhan Muminggan Lianheqi, *China* **74 D6** 41 40N 110 28 E
Dari, *Sudan* **107 F3** 5 48N 30 26 E
Darıca, *Turkey* **100 B3** 40 45N 29 23 E
Darien, *U.S.A.* **152 D8** 31 23N 81 26W
Darién △, *Panama* **164 E4** 7 36N 77 57W
Darién, G. del, *Colombia* **168 B2** 9 0N 77 0W
Dariganga = Ovoot, *Mongolia* **74 B7** 45 21N 113 45 E
Daringbadi, *India* **94 E7** 19 54N 84 8 E
Darinskoye, *Kazakhstan* **60 E10** 51 20N 51 44 E
Darjeeling = Darjiling, *India* **90 B2** 27 3N 88 18 E
Darjiling, *India* **90 B2** 27 3N 88 18 E
Darkan, *Australia* **125 F2** 33 20 S 116 43 E
Darke Peak, *Australia* **128 B2** 33 27 S 136 12 E
Darkhana, *Pakistan* **92 D5** 30 39N 72 11 E
Darkhazīneh, *Iran* **97 D6** 31 54N 48 39 E
Darkot Pass, *Pakistan* **65 E6** 36 45N 73 26 E
Darling →, *Australia* **128 C4** 34 4 S 141 54 E
Darling Downs, *Australia* **127 D5** 27 30 S 150 30 E
Darling Ra., *Australia* **125 F2** 32 30 S 116 0 E
Darlington, *U.K.* **20 C6** 54 32N 1 33W
Darlington, *Fla., U.S.A.* **152 E3** 30 57N 86 3W
Darlington, *S.C., U.S.A.* **149 H6** 34 18N 79 52W
Darlington, *Wis., U.S.A.* **156 B6** 42 41N 90 7W
Darlington □, *U.K.* **20 C6** 54 32N 1 33W
Darlington, L., *S. Africa* **116 E4** 33 10 S 25 9 E
Darlington Point, *Australia* **129 C7** 34 37 S 146 1 E
Darlot, L., *Australia* **125 E3** 27 48 S 121 35 E
Darłowo, *Poland* **54 D3** 54 25N 16 25 E
Dărmănești, *Bacău, Romania* **53 D11** 46 21N 26 33 E
Dărmănești, *Suceava, Romania* **53 C11** 47 44N 26 9 E
Darmstadt, *Germany* **31 F4** 49 51N 8 39 E
Darnah, *Libya* **108 B4** 32 45N 22 45 E
Darnah □, *Libya* **108 B4** 31 0N 23 40 E
Darnall, *S. Africa* **117 D5** 29 23 S 31 18 E
Darney, *France* **27 D13** 48 5N 6 2 E
Darnick, *Australia* **128 B5** 32 48 S 143 38 E
Darnley, C., *Antarctica* **7 C6** 68 0 S 69 0 E
Darnley B., *Canada* **138 B7** 69 30N 123 30W
Daroca, *Spain* **40 D3** 41 9N 1 25W
Daroot-Korgan, *Kyrgyzstan* **65 D6** 39 33N 72 11 E
Darou-Mousti, *Senegal* **112 B1** 15 3N 16 3W
Darr →, *Australia* **126 C3** 23 39 S 143 50 E
Darra Pezu, *Pakistan* **92 C4** 32 19N 70 44 E
Darran Mts., *N.Z.* **131 E2** 44 37 S 167 59 E
Darrequeira, *Argentina* **174 D3** 37 42 S 63 10W
Darrington, *U.S.A.* **158 B3** 48 15N 121 36W
Darsana, *Bangla.* **90 D2** 23 35N 88 48 E
Darsi, *India* **95 G4** 15 46N 79 44 E
Darsser Ort, *Germany* **30 A8** 54 28N 12 32 E
Dart →, *U.K.* **21 G4** 50 24N 3 39W
Dart, C., *Antarctica* **7 D14** 73 6 S 126 20W
Dartford, *U.K.* **21 F8** 51 26N 0 13 E
Dartmoor, *Australia* **128 D4** 37 56 S 141 19 E
Dartmoor, *U.K.* **21 G4** 50 38N 3 57W
Dartmoor △, *U.K.* **21 G4** 50 37N 3 59W
Dartmouth, *Canada* **141 D7** 44 40N 63 30W
Dartmouth, *U.K.* **21 G4** 50 21N 3 36W
Dartmouth, L., *Australia* **129 D7** 36 34 S 147 32 E
Dartmouth Res., *Australia* **127 D4** 26 4 S 145 18 E
Dartuch, C. = Artrutx, C. de, *Spain* **38 B4** 39 55N 3 49 E
Daru, *Papua N. G.* **132 E2** 9 3 S 143 13 E
Daruba, *Indonesia* **82 A3** 2 5N 128 14 E
Daruvar, *Croatia* **52 E2** 45 35N 17 14 E
Darvaza, *Turkmenistan* **66 E6** 40 11N 58 24 E
Darvel, Teluk = Lahad Datu, Telok, *Malaysia* **85 B5** 4 50N 118 20 E
Darwen, *U.K.* **20 D5** 53 42N 2 29W
Darwendale, *Zimbabwe* **117 B5** 17 41 S 30 33 E
Darwha, *India* **94 D3** 20 15N 77 45 E
Darwin, *Australia* **124 B5** 12 25 S 130 51 E
Darwin, *U.S.A.* **161 J9** 36 15N 117 35W
Darwin, Mt., *Chile* **176 D3** 54 47 S 69 55W
Darwin, Volcán, *Ecuador* **172 a** 0 10 S 91 18W
Darya Khan, *Pakistan* **92 D4** 31 48N 71 6 E
Daryapur, *India* **94 D3** 20 55N 77 20 E
Daryoi Amu = Amudarya →, *Uzbekistan* **66 E6** 43 58N 59 34 E
Dās, *U.A.E.* **97 E7** 25 20N 53 30 E
Dashen, Ras, *Ethiopia* **107 E4** 13 8N 38 26 E
Dasher, *U.S.A.* **152 E6** 30 45N 83 13W
Dashetai, *China* **74 D5** 41 0N 109 5 E
Dashhowuz, *Turkmenistan* **66 E6** 41 49N 59 58 E
Dashkesan = Daşkäsän, *Azerbaijan* **61 K7** 40 25N 46 0 E
Dashköpri, *Turkmenistan* **97 B9** 36 16N 62 8 E
Dasht, *Iran* **97 B8** 37 17N 56 7 E
Dasht →, *Pakistan* **91 D1** 25 10N 61 40 E
Dasht-i-Tahlab, *Pakistan* **91 C1** 28 40N 62 25 E
Daska, *Pakistan* **92 C6** 32 20N 74 20 E
Daşkäsän, *Azerbaijan* **61 K7** 40 25N 46 0 E
Dasmariñas, *Phil.* **80 D3** 14 20N 120 56 E
Dassa, *Benin* **113 D5** 7 46N 2 14 E
Dasuya, *India* **92 D6** 31 49N 75 38 E
Datça, *Turkey* **49 E9** 36 46N 27 40 E
Datia, *India* **93 G8** 25 39N 78 27 E
Datian, *China* **77 E11** 25 40N 117 50 E
Datong, *Anhui, China* **77 B11** 30 48N 117 44 E
Datong, *Shanxi, China* **74 D7** 40 6N 113 18 E
Dattakhel, *Pakistan* **92 C3** 32 54N 69 46 E
Dattapur = Dhamangaon, *India* **94 D4** 20 48N 78 9 E
Datteln, *Germany* **30 D3** 51 39N 7 21 E
Datu, Tanjung, *Indonesia* **85 B3** 2 5N 109 39 E
Datu Piang, *Phil.* **81 H5** 7 2N 124 30 E
Datuk, Tanjong = Datu, Tanjung, *Indonesia* **85 B3** 2 5N 109 39 E
Daua = Dawa →, *Africa* **107 G5** 4 11N 42 6 E
Daud Khel, *Pakistan* **92 C4** 32 53N 71 34 E
Daudnagar, *India* **93 G11** 25 2N 84 24 E
Daugava →, *Latvia* **15 H21** 57 4N 24 3 E
Daugavpils, *Latvia* **15 J22** 55 53N 26 32 E
Daulatabad, *India* **94 E2** 19 57N 75 15 E
Daule, *Ecuador* **168 D2** 1 56 S 79 56W
Daule →, *Ecuador* **168 D2** 2 10 S 79 52W
Daulpur, *India* **92 F7** 26 45N 77 59 E
Daun, *Germany* **31 E2** 50 11N 6 49 E
Daund, *India* **94 E2** 18 26N 74 40 E
Dauphin, *Canada* **143 C8** 51 9N 100 5W
Dauphin, *U.S.A.* **150 F8** 40 22N 76 56W
Dauphin L., *Canada* **143 C9** 51 20N 99 45W
Dauphiné, *France* **29 C9** 45 15N 5 25 E
Daura, *Borno, Nigeria* **113 C7** 11 31N 11 24 E
Daura, *Katsina, Nigeria* **113 C6** 13 2N 8 21 E
Dausa, *India* **92 F7** 26 52N 76 20 E
Däväçi, *Azerbaijan* **61 K9** 41 15N 48 57 E
Davangere, *India* **95 G2** 14 25N 75 55 E
Davao, *Phil.* **81 H5** 7 0N 125 40 E
Davao □, *Phil.* **81 H5** 7 0N 125 55 E
Davao del Sur □, *Phil.* **81 H5** 6 30N 125 25 E
Davao G., *Phil.* **81 H5** 6 30N 125 48 E
Davao Oriental □, *Phil.* **81 H6** 7 10N 126 30 E
Dāvar Panāh = Sarāvān, *Iran* **97 E9** 27 25N 62 15 E
Davenport, *Calif., U.S.A.* **160 H4** 37 1N 122 12W
Davenport, *Fla., U.S.A.* **153 G8** 28 10N 81 36W
Davenport, *Iowa, U.S.A.* **156 C6** 41 32N 90 35W
Davenport, *Wash., U.S.A.* **158 C4** 47 39N 118 9W
Davenport Ra., *Australia* **126 C1** 20 28 S 134 0 E
Daventry, *U.K.* **21 E6** 52 16N 1 10W
David, *Panama* **164 E3** 8 30N 82 30W
David City, *U.S.A.* **154 E6** 41 15N 97 8W
David Gorodok = Davyd Haradok, *Belarus* **59 F4** 52 4N 27 8 E
Davidson, *Canada* **143 C7** 51 16N 105 59W
Davis, *Antarctica* **7 C6** 68 34 S 77 55 E
Davis, *U.S.A.* **160 G5** 38 33N 121 44W
Davis Dam, *U.S.A.* **161 K12** 35 11N 114 34W
Davis Inlet, *Canada* **141 A7** 55 50N 60 59W
Davis Mts., *U.S.A.* **155 K2** 30 50N 103 55W
Davis Sea, *Antarctica* **7 C7** 66 0 S 92 0 E
Davis Str., *N. Amer.* **139 B14** 65 0N 58 0W
Davisboro, *U.S.A.* **152 C7** 32 59N 82 36W
Davison, *U.S.A.* **157 A13** 43 2N 83 31W
Davlekanovo, *Russia* **64 D5** 54 13N 55 3 E
Davo →, *Ivory C.* **112 D3** 5 0N 6 10W
Davos, *Switz.* **33 C9** 46 48N 9 49 E
Davutlar, *Turkey* **49 D9** 37 43N 27 17 E
Davy L., *Canada* **143 B7** 58 53N 108 18W
Davyd Haradok, *Belarus* **59 F4** 52 4N 27 8 E
Dawa →, *Africa* **107 G5** 4 11N 42 6 E
Dawaki, *Bauchi, Nigeria* **113 D6** 9 25N 9 33 E
Dawaki, *Kano, Nigeria* **113 C6** 12 5N 8 23 E
Dawei = Tavoy, *Burma* **86 E2** 14 2N 98 12 E
Dawes Ra., *Australia* **126 C5** 24 40 S 150 40 E
Dawley = Telford, *U.K.* **21 E5** 52 40N 2 27W
Dawlish, *U.K.* **21 G4** 50 35N 3 28W
Dawna Ra., *Burma* **86 D2** 16 30N 98 30 E
Dawnyein, *Burma* **90 G5** 15 54N 95 36 E
Dawqah, *Si. Arabia* **98 C3** 19 36N 40 54 E
Dawros Hd., *Ireland* **23 B3** 54 50N 8 33W
Dawson, *Canada* **138 B6** 64 10N 139 30W
Dawson, *U.S.A.* **152 D5** 31 46N 84 27W
Dawson, I., *Chile* **176 D2** 53 50 S 70 50W
Dawson B., *Canada* **143 C8** 52 53N 100 49W
Dawson Creek, *Canada* **142 B4** 55 45N 120 15W
Dawson Inlet, *Canada* **143 A10** 61 50N 93 25W
Dawson Ra., *Australia* **126 C4** 24 30 S 149 48 E
Dawu, *Hubei, China* **77 B9** 31 34N 114 7 E
Dawu, *Sichuan, China* **76 B3** 30 55N 101 10 E
Dawwah, *Oman* **99 B7** 20 33N 58 48 E
Dawwara, Ras id-, *Malta* **38 F7** 35 52N 14 21 E
Dax, *France* **28 E2** 43 44N 1 3W
Daxian, *China* **76 B6** 31 15N 107 23 E
Daxin, *China* **76 F6** 22 50N 107 11 E
Daxindian, *China* **75 F11** 37 30N 120 50 E
Daxinggou, *China* **75 C15** 43 25N 129 40 E
Daxue Shan, *Sichuan, China* **76 B3** 30 30N 101 30 E
Daxue Shan, *Yunnan, China* **76 F2** 23 42N 99 48 E
Day, *U.S.A.* **152 E6** 30 12N 83 17W
Daya el Khadra, *Mauritania* **110 C3** 25 14N 6 2W
Dayao, *China* **76 E3** 25 43N 101 20 E
Daye, *China* **77 B10** 30 6N 114 58 E
Dayet en Naharat, *Mali* **112 B4** 17 39N 3 10W
Dayi, *China* **76 B4** 30 41N 103 29 E
Daylesford, *Australia* **128 D6** 37 21 S 144 9 E
Dayong, *China* **77 C8** 29 11N 110 30 E
Dayr az Zawr, *Syria* **101 E9** 35 20N 40 5 E
Daysland, *Canada* **142 C6** 52 50N 112 20W
Dayton, *Iowa, U.S.A.* **156 B2** 42 14N 94 6W
Dayton, *Ky., U.S.A.* **157 E12** 39 47N 84 28W
Dayton, *Nev., U.S.A.* **160 F7** 39 14N 119 36W
Dayton, *Ohio, U.S.A.* **148 F3** 39 45N 84 12W
Dayton, *Pa., U.S.A.* **150 F5** 40 53N 79 15W
Dayton, *Tenn., U.S.A.* **149 H3** 35 30N 85 1W
Dayton, *Wash., U.S.A.* **158 C4** 46 19N 117 59W
Dayton, *Wyo., U.S.A.* **158 D10** 44 53N 107 16W
Daytona Beach, *U.S.A.* **153 F8** 29 13N 81 1W
Dayu, *China* **77 E10** 25 24N 114 22 E
Dayville, *U.S.A.* **158 D4** 44 28N 119 32W
Dazaifu, *Japan* **72 D2** 33 32N 130 32 E
Dazhu, *China* **76 B6** 30 41N 107 15 E
Dazkırı, *Turkey* **49 D11** 37 57N 29 52 E
Dazu, *China* **76 C5** 29 40N 105 42 E
De Aar, *S. Africa* **116 E3** 30 39 S 24 0 E
De Armanville, *U.S.A.* **152 B4** 33 38N 85 45W
De Bary, *U.S.A.* **153 G8** 28 54N 81 18W
De Biesbosch △, *Neths.* **24 C4** 51 45N 4 48 E
De Forest, *U.S.A.* **156 A7** 43 15N 89 20W
De Funiak Springs, *U.S.A.* **152 E3** 30 43N 86 7W
De Grey →, *Australia* **124 D2** 20 12 S 119 13 E
De Haan, *Belgium* **24 C3** 51 16N 3 2 E
De Hoge Veluwe △, *Neths.* **24 B5** 52 5N 5 46 E
De Hoop ⌓, *S. Africa* **116 E3** 34 30 S 20 28 E
De Jongs, Tg., *Indonesia* **83 C5** 6 55 S 138 30 E
De Kalb, *U.S.A.* **154 E10** 41 56N 88 46W
De Kennemerduinen △, *Neths.* **24 B4** 52 27N 4 33 E
De Land, *U.S.A.* **153 F8** 29 2N 81 18W
De Leon, *U.S.A.* **155 J5** 32 7N 98 32W
De Leon Springs, *U.S.A.* **153 F8** 29 7N 81 21W
De Long Mts., *U.S.A.* **144 B7** 68 30N 163 0W
De Panne, *Belgium* **24 C2** 51 6N 2 34 E
De Pere, *U.S.A.* **148 C1** 44 27N 88 4W
De Queen, *U.S.A.* **155 H7** 34 2N 94 21W
De Quincy, *U.S.A.* **155 K8** 30 27N 93 26W
De Ridder, *U.S.A.* **155 K8** 30 51N 93 17W
De Smet, *U.S.A.* **154 C6** 44 23N 97 33W
De Soto, *U.S.A.* **156 F6** 38 8N 90 34W
De Soto City, *U.S.A.* **153 H8** 27 27N 81 24W
De Tour Village, *U.S.A.* **148 C4** 46 0N 83 56W
De Witt, *Ark., U.S.A.* **155 H9** 34 18N 91 20W
De Witt, *Iowa, U.S.A.* **156 C6** 41 49N 90 33W
De Witt, *Mich., U.S.A.* **157 B12** 42 51N 84 34W
Dead L., *U.S.A.* **152 E4** 30 10N 85 10W
Dead Sea, *Asia* **103 D4** 31 30N 35 30 E
Deadhorse, *U.S.A.* **144 A10** 70 11N 148 27W
Deadman B., *U.S.A.* **153 F6** 29 30N 83 30W
Deadwood, *U.S.A.* **154 C3** 44 23N 103 44W
Deadwood L., *Canada* **142 B3** 59 10N 128 30W
Deal, *U.K.* **21 F9** 51 13N 1 25 E
Deal I., *Australia* **127 F4** 39 30 S 147 20 E
Dealesville, *S. Africa* **116 D4** 28 41 S 25 44 E
De'an, *China* **77 C10** 29 21N 115 46 E
Dean →, *Canada* **142 C3** 52 49N 126 58W
Dean, Forest of, *U.K.* **21 F5** 51 45N 2 33W
Dean Chan., *Canada* **142 C3** 52 30N 127 15W
Deán Funes, *Argentina* **174 C3** 30 20 S 64 20W
Dearborn, *Mich., U.S.A.* **157 B13** 42 19N 83 11W
Dearborn, *Mo., U.S.A.* **156 E2** 39 32N 94 46W
Dease →, *Canada* **142 B3** 59 56N 128 32W
Dease L., *Canada* **142 B2** 58 40N 130 5W
Dease Lake, *Canada* **142 B2** 58 25N 130 6W
Death Valley, *U.S.A.* **161 J10** 36 15N 116 50W
Death Valley △, *U.S.A.* **161 J10** 36 45N 117 15W
Death Valley Junction, *U.S.A.* **161 J10** 36 20N 116 25W
Deauville, *France* **26 C7** 49 23N 0 2 E
Deba, *Spain* **40 B2** 43 18N 2 21W
Deba Habe, *Nigeria* **113 C7** 10 14N 11 20 E
Debak, *Malaysia* **85 B4** 1 34N 111 25 E
Debaltsevo, *Ukraine* **59 H10** 48 22N 38 26 E
Debao, *China* **76 F6** 23 21N 106 46 E
Debar, *Macedonia* **50 E4** 41 31N 20 30 E
Debark, *Ethiopia* **107 E4** 13 1N 37 48 E
Debden, *Canada* **143 C7** 53 30N 106 50W
Debdou, *Morocco* **111 B4** 33 59N 3 0W
Dębica, *Poland* **55 H8** 50 2N 21 25 E
Dęblin, *Poland* **55 G8** 51 34N 21 50 E
Dębno, *Poland* **55 F1** 52 44N 14 41 E
Débo, L., *Mali* **112 B4** 15 14N 4 15W
DeBolt, *Canada* **142 B5** 55 12N 118 1W
Deborah East, L., *Australia* **125 F2** 30 45 S 119 0 E
Deborah West, L., *Australia* **125 F2** 30 45 S 118 50 E
Deboyne Is., *Papua N. G.* **132 F7** 10 43 S 152 22 E
Debrc, *Serbia & M.* **50 B3** 44 38N 19 53 E
Debre Birhan, *Ethiopia* **107 F4** 9 41N 39 31 E
Debre Markos, *Ethiopia* **107 E4** 10 20N 37 40 E
Debre May, *Ethiopia* **107 E4** 11 20N 37 25 E
Debre Sina, *Ethiopia* **107 F4** 9 51N 39 50 E
Debre Tabor, *Ethiopia* **107 E4** 11 50N 38 26 E
Debre Zebit, *Ethiopia* **107 E4** 11 48N 38 30 E
Debre Zevit, *Ethiopia* **107 F4** 8 50N 39 0 E
Debrecen, *Hungary* **52 C6** 47 33N 21 42 E
Debrzno, *Poland* **54 E4** 53 31N 17 14 E
Dečani, *Serbia & M.* **50 D4** 42 30N 20 18 E
Decatur, *Ala., U.S.A.* **149 H2** 34 36N 86 59W
Decatur, *Ga., U.S.A.* **152 B5** 33 47N 84 18W
Decatur, *Ill., U.S.A.* **156 E8** 39 51N 88 57W
Decatur, *Ind., U.S.A.* **157 D12** 40 50N 84 56W
Decatur, *Mich., U.S.A.* **157 B11** 42 7N 85 58W
Decatur, *Tex., U.S.A.* **155 J6** 33 14N 97 35W
Decazeville, *France* **28 D6** 44 34N 2 15 E
Deccan, *India* **94 F4** 18 0N 79 0 E
Deception, Mt., *Australia* **128 A3** 30 42 S 138 16 E
Deception B., *Papua N. G.* **132 D3** 7 45 S 144 40 E
Deception Bay, *Australia* **127 D5** 27 10 S 153 5 E
Deception I., *Antarctica* **7 C17** 63 0 S 60 15W
Deception L., *Canada* **143 B8** 56 33N 104 13W
Dechang, *China* **76 D4** 27 25N 102 11 E
Dechhu, *India* **92 F5** 26 46N 72 20 E
Děčín, *Czech Rep.* **34 A7** 50 47N 14 12 E
Decize, *France* **27 F10** 46 50N 3 28 E
Deckerville, *U.S.A.* **150 C2** 43 32N 82 44W
Decollatura, *Italy* **47 C9** 39 3N 16 21 E
Decorah, *U.S.A.* **154 D9** 43 18N 91 48W
Deda, *Romania* **53 D9** 46 56N 24 50 E
Dedaye, *Burma* **90 G5** 16 24N 95 53 E
Dedéagach = Alexandroúpolis, *Greece* **51 F9** 40 50N 25 54 E
Deder, *Ethiopia* **107 F5** 9 19N 41 27 E
Dedham, *U.S.A.* **151 D13** 42 15N 71 10W
Dédougou, *Burkina Faso* **112 C4** 12 30N 3 25W
Dedovichi, *Russia* **58 D5** 57 32N 29 56 E
Dedza, *Malawi* **119 E3** 14 20 S 34 20 E
Dee →, *Aberds., U.K.* **22 D6** 57 9N 2 5W
Dee →, *Dumf. & Gall., U.K.* **22 G4** 54 51N 4 3W
Dee →, *Wales, U.K.* **20 D4** 53 22N 3 17W
Deep B., *Canada* **142 A5** 61 15N 116 35W
Deep Bay = Chilumba, *Malawi* **119 E3** 10 28 S 34 12 E
Deep Bay = Shenzhen Wan, *China* **69 G10** 22 27N 113 55 E
Deep Lead, *Australia* **128 D5** 37 0 S 142 43 E
Deepwater, *Australia* **127 D5** 29 25 S 151 51 E
Deepwater, *U.S.A.* **156 F3** 38 16N 93 47W
Deer →, *Canada* **143 B10** 58 23N 94 13W
Deer I., *U.S.A.* **144 J7** 54 55N 162 18W
Deer L., *Canada* **143 C10** 52 40N 94 20W
Deer Lake, *Nfld. & L., Canada* **141 C8** 49 11N 57 27W
Deer Lake, *Ont., Canada* **143 C10** 52 36N 94 20W
Deer Lodge, *U.S.A.* **158 C7** 46 24N 112 44W
Deer Park, *Fla., U.S.A.* **153 G9** 28 6N 80 54W
Deer Park, *Ohio, U.S.A.* **157 E12** 39 13N 84 23W
Deer Park, *Wash., U.S.A.* **158 C5** 47 57N 117 28W
Deer River, *U.S.A.* **154 B8** 47 20N 93 48W
Deeragun, *Australia* **126 B4** 19 16 S 146 33 E
Deerdepoort, *S. Africa* **116 C4** 24 37 S 26 27 E
Deerfield, *Ill., U.S.A.* **157 B9** 42 10N 87 51W
Deerfield, *Mo., U.S.A.* **156 G2** 37 50N 94 30W
Deerfield Beach, *U.S.A.* **153 J9** 26 19N 80 6W
Deering, *U.S.A.* **144 C7** 66 4N 162 42W
Defensores del Chaco △, *Paraguay* **173 E5** 20 13 S 60 27W
Deferiet, *U.S.A.* **151 B9** 44 2N 75 41W
Defiance, *U.S.A.* **157 C12** 41 17N 84 22W
Degana, *India* **92 F6** 26 50N 74 20 E
Dêgê, *China* **76 B2** 31 44N 98 39 E
Degebe →, *Portugal* **43 G3** 38 13N 7 29W
Degeberga, *Sweden* **17 J8** 55 51N 14 5 E
Degeh Bur, *Ethiopia* **120 C2** 8 11N 43 31 E
Dégelis, *Canada* **141 C6** 47 30N 68 35W
Degema, *Nigeria* **113 E6** 4 50N 6 48 E
Degerfors, *Sweden* **16 E8** 59 15N 14 27 E
Degerhamn, *Sweden* **17 H10** 56 20N 16 24 E
Degersheim, *Switz.* **33 B8** 47 23N 9 12 E
Deggendorf, *Germany* **31 G8** 48 50N 12 57 E
Degh →, *Pakistan* **92 D5** 31 3N 73 21 E
Değirmendere, *Turkey* **51 F13** 40 42N 29 47 E
Deh Bīd, *Iran* **97 D7** 30 39N 53 11 E
Deh-e Shīr, *Iran* **97 D7** 31 29N 53 45 E
Deh Nugaled = Nugaaleed, Dooxo, *Somali Rep.* **120 C3** 8 35N 48 35 E
Dehaj, *Iran* **97 D7** 30 42N 54 53 E
Dehak, *Iran* **91 D1** 27 11N 62 37 E
Déhane, *Cameroon* **114 B2** 3 30N 10 5 E
Dehdez, *Iran* **97 D6** 31 43N 50 17 E
Dehej, *India* **92 J5** 21 44N 72 40 E
Dehestān, *Iran* **97 D7** 28 30N 55 35 E
Dehgolān, *Iran* **101 E12** 35 17N 47 25 E
Dehibat, *Tunisia* **108 B2** 32 0N 10 47 E
Dehiwala, *Sri Lanka* **95 L4** 6 50N 79 51 E
Dehlorān, *Iran* **101 F12** 32 41N 47 16 E
Dehnow-e Kūhestān, *Iran* **97 E8** 27 58N 58 32 E
Dehra Dun, *India* **92 D8** 30 20N 78 4 E
Dehri, *India* **93 G11** 24 50N 84 15 E
Dehua, *China* **77 E12** 25 26N 118 14 E
Dehui, *China* **75 B13** 44 30N 125 40 E
Deim Zubeir, *Sudan* **107 F2** 7 49N 26 16 E
Deinze, *Belgium* **24 D3** 50 59N 3 32 E
Dej, *Romania* **53 C8** 47 10N 23 52 E
Deje, *Sweden* **16 E7** 59 35N 13 29 E
Dejiang, *China* **76 C7** 28 18N 108 7 E
Deka →, *Zimbabwe* **116 B4** 18 4 S 26 42 E
Dekemhare, *Eritrea* **107 D4** 15 6N 39 0 E
Dekese, *Dem. Rep. of the Congo* **114 C4** 3 24 S 21 24 E
Dekhkanabad, *Uzbekistan* **65 D3** 38 21N 66 30 E
Dekoa, *C.A.R.* **114 A3** 6 19N 19 4 E
Del Carmen, *Phil.* **81 G6** 9 50N 126 0 E
Del Mar, *U.S.A.* **161 N9** 32 58N 117 16W
Del Norte, *U.S.A.* **159 H10** 37 41N 106 21W
Del Rio, *U.S.A.* **155 L4** 29 22N 100 54W
Delai, *Sudan* **106 D4** 17 21N 36 6 E
Delambre I., *Australia* **124 D2** 20 26 S 117 5 E
Delami, *Sudan* **107 E3** 11 38N 30 23 E
Delano, *U.S.A.* **161 K7** 35 46N 119 15W
Delano Peak, *U.S.A.* **159 G7** 38 22N 112 22W
Delārām, *Afghan.* **91 B1** 32 9N 63 25 E
Delareyville, *S. Africa* **116 D4** 26 41 S 25 26 E
Delaronde L., *Canada* **143 C7** 54 3N 107 3W
Delavan, *Ill., U.S.A.* **156 D7** 40 22N 89 33W
Delavan, *Wis., U.S.A.* **154 D10** 42 38N 88 39W
Delaware, *U.S.A.* **157 D13** 40 18N 83 4W
Delaware □, *U.S.A.* **148 F8** 39 0N 75 20W
Delaware →, *U.S.A.* **151 G9** 39 15N 75 20W
Delaware B., *U.S.A.* **148 F8** 39 0N 75 10W
Delaware Water Gap ⌓, *U.S.A.* **151 E10** 41 10N 74 55W
Delay →, *Canada* **141 A5** 56 56N 71 28W
Delbrück, *Germany* **30 D4** 51 46N 8 34 E
Delčevo, *Macedonia* **50 E6** 41 58N 22 46 E
Delébio, *Italy* **33 D8** 46 8N 9 27 E
Delegate, *Australia* **129 D8** 37 4 S 148 56 E
Delémont, *Switz.* **32 B4** 47 22N 7 20 E
Delevan, *U.S.A.* **150 D6** 42 29N 78 29W
Delft, *Neths.* **24 B4** 52 1N 4 22 E
Delft I., *Sri Lanka* **95 K4** 9 30N 79 40 E
Delfzijl, *Neths.* **24 A6** 53 20N 6 55 E
Delgada, Punta, *Chile* **176 D3** 52 28 S 69 32W
Delgado, C., *Mozam.* **119 E5** 10 45 S 40 40 E
Delgerhet, *Mongolia* **74 B6** 45 50N 110 30 E
Delgo, *Sudan* **106 C3** 20 6N 30 40 E
Delhi, *Canada* **150 D4** 42 51N 80 30W
Delhi, *India* **92 E7** 28 38N 77 17 E
Delhi, *La., U.S.A.* **155 J9** 32 28N 91 30W
Delhi, *N.Y., U.S.A.* **151 D10** 42 17N 74 55W
Deli Jovan, *Serbia & M.* **50 B6** 44 13N 22 9 E
Delia, *Canada* **142 C6** 51 38N 112 23W
Delice, *Turkey* **100 C6** 39 54N 34 2 E
Delicias, *Mexico* **162 B3** 28 10N 105 30W
Delījān, *Iran* **97 C6** 33 59N 50 40 E
Delimara Point, *Malta* **38 F8** 35 49N 14 34 E
Déline, *Canada* **138 B7** 65 11N 123 25W
Delisle, *Canada* **143 C7** 51 55N 107 8W
Delitzsch, *Germany* **30 D8** 51 31N 12 20 E
Dell City, *U.S.A.* **159 L11** 31 56N 105 12W
Dell Rapids, *U.S.A.* **154 D6** 43 50N 96 43W
Delle, *France* **27 E14** 47 30N 7 2 E
Dellys, *Algeria* **111 A5** 36 57N 3 57 E
Delmar, *Iowa, U.S.A.* **156 C6** 42 0N 90 37W
Delmar, *N.Y., U.S.A.* **151 D11** 42 37N 73 47W
Delmenhorst, *Germany* **30 B4** 53 3N 8 37 E
Delmiro Gouveia, *Brazil* **170 C4** 9 24 S 38 6W
Delnice, *Croatia* **45 C11** 45 23N 14 50 E
Delonga, Ostrova, *Russia* **67 B15** 76 40N 149 20 E
Deloraine, *Australia* **127 G4** 41 30 S 146 40 E
Deloraine, *Canada* **143 D8** 49 15N 100 29W
Delphi, *Greece* **48 C4** 38 28N 22 30 E
Delphi, *U.S.A.* **157 D10** 40 36N 86 41W
Delphos, *U.S.A.* **157 D12** 40 51N 84 21W
Delportshoop, *S. Africa* **116 D3** 28 22 S 24 20 E
Delray Beach, *U.S.A.* **153 J9** 26 28N 80 4W
Delsbo, *Sweden* **16 C10** 61 48N 16 32 E
Delta, *Ala., U.S.A.* **152 B4** 33 26N 85 42W
Delta, *Colo., U.S.A.* **159 G9** 38 44N 108 4W
Delta, *Utah, U.S.A.* **158 G7** 39 21N 112 35W
Delta □, *Nigeria* **113 D6** 5 30N 6 0 E
Delta Amacuro □, *Venezuela* **169 B5** 8 30N 61 30W
Delta del Ebro ⌓, *Spain* **40 E5** 40 43N 0 43 E
Delta del Po ⌓, *Italy* **45 D9** 44 50N 12 15 E
Delta du Saloum △, *Senegal* **112 C1** 13 42N 16 43W
Delta Dunărea ⌓, *Romania* **53 E14** 45 15N 29 25 E
Delta Junction, *U.S.A.* **144 D11** 64 2N 145 44W
Deltona, *U.S.A.* **153 G8** 28 54N 81 16W
Delungra, *Australia* **127 D5** 29 39 S 150 51 E
Delvada, *India* **92 J4** 20 46N 71 2 E
Delvinákion, *Greece* **48 B2** 39 57N 20 32 E
Delvinë, *Albania* **50 G4** 39 59N 20 6 E
Delyatyn, *Ukraine* **53 B9** 48 32N 24 38 E
Demagiri, *India* **90 D4** 22 55N 92 28 E
Demak, *Indonesia* **85 D4** 6 53 S 110 38 E
Demanda, Sierra de la, *Spain* **40 C2** 42 15N 3 0W
Demavend = Damāvand, Qolleh-ye, *Iran* **97 C7** 35 56N 52 10 E
Demba, *Dem. Rep. of the Congo* **115 D4** 5 28 S 22 15 E
Demba Chio, *Angola* **115 D2** 9 41 S 13 41 E
Dembecha, *Ethiopia* **107 E4** 10 32N 37 30 E
Dembi, *Ethiopia* **107 F4** 8 5N 36 25 E
Dembia, *Dem. Rep. of the Congo* **118 B2** 3 33N 25 48 E
Dembica = Dębica, *Poland* **55 H8** 50 2N 21 25 E
Dembidolo, *Ethiopia* **107 F3** 8 34N 34 50 E
Demchok, *India* **93 C8** 32 42N 79 29 E
Demer →, *Belgium* **24 D4** 50 57N 4 42 E
Demetrias, *Greece* **48 B5** 39 22N 23 1 E
Demidov, *Russia* **58 E6** 55 16N 31 30 E
Deming, *N. Mex., U.S.A.* **159 K10** 32 16N 107 46W
Deming, *Wash., U.S.A.* **160 B4** 48 50N 122 13W
Demini →, *Brazil* **169 D5** 0 46 S 62 56W
Demirci, *Turkey* **49 B10** 39 2N 28 38 E
Demirköprü Barajı, *Turkey* **49 C10** 38 42N 28 25 E
Demirköy, *Turkey* **51 E11** 41 49N 27 45 E
Demmin, *Germany* **30 B9** 53 54N 13 2 E
Demnate, *Morocco* **110 B3** 31 44N 6 59W
Democracia, *Brazil* **173 B5** 5 48 S 61 26W
Demonte, *Italy* **44 D4** 44 19N 7 17 E
Demopolis, *U.S.A.* **149 J2** 32 31N 87 50W
Dempo, *Indonesia* **84 C2** 4 2 S 103 15 E
Demta, *Indonesia* **83 B6** 2 20 S 140 8 E
Demyansk, *Russia* **58 D7** 57 40N 32 27 E
Den Burg, *Neths.* **24 A4** 53 3N 4 47 E
Den Chai, *Thailand* **86 D3** 17 59N 100 4 E
Den Haag = 's-Gravenhage, *Neths.* **24 B4** 52 7N 4 17 E
Den Helder, *Neths.* **24 B4** 52 57N 4 45 E
Den Oever, *Neths.* **24 B5** 52 56N 5 2 E
Denain, *France* **27 B10** 50 20N 3 22 E
Denair, *U.S.A.* **160 H6** 37 32N 120 48W
Denali △, *U.S.A.* **144 E10** 63 30N 152 0W
Denau, *Uzbekistan* **65 -** 38 16N 67 54 E
Denbigh, *Canada* **150 A7** 45 8N 77 15W
Denbigh, *U.K.* **20 D4** 53 12N 3 25W
Denbigh, C., *U.S.A.* **144 D7** 64 23N 161 32W
Denbighshire □, *U.K.* **20 D4** 53 8N 3 22W
Dendang, *Indonesia* **85 C3** 3 7 S 107 56 E
Dendé = Ndindi, *Gabon* **114 C2** 3 46 S 11 9 E
Dendermonde, *Belgium* **24 C4** 51 2N 4 5 E
Deneba, *Ethiopia* **107 F4** 9 47N 39 10 E
Denezhkin Kamen, Gora, *Russia* **64 A7** 60 25N 59 32 E
Deng Deng, *Cameroon* **114 A2** 5 12N 13 31 E
Dengchuan, *China* **76 E3** 25 59N 100 3 E
Denge, *Nigeria* **113 C6** 12 52N 5 21 E

Dengfeng, *China* **74 G7** 34 25N 113 2 E
Dengi, *Nigeria* **113 D6** 9 25N 9 55 E
Dengkou, *China* **74 D4** 40 18N 106 55 E
Dengzhou, *China* **77 A9** 32 34N 112 4 E
Denham, *Australia* **125 E1** 25 56 S 113 31 E
Denham, Mt., *Jamaica* **164 a** 18 13N 77 32W
Denham Ra., *Australia* **126 C4** 21 55 S 147 46 E
Denham Sd., *Australia* **125 E1** 25 45 S 113 15 E
Denholm, *Canada* **143 C7** 52 39N 108 1W
Denia, *Spain* **41 G5** 38 49N 0 8 E
Denial B., *Australia* **127 E1** 32 14 S 133 32 E
Deniliquin, *Australia* **129 C6** 35 30 S 144 58 E
Denis, *Gabon* **114 B1** 0 19N 9 22 E
Denison, *Iowa, U.S.A.* **154 E7** 42 1N 95 21W
Denison, *Tex., U.S.A.* **155 J6** 33 45N 96 33W
Denison Plains, *Australia* **124 C4** 18 35 S 128 0 E
Denisovka = Ordzhonikidze, *Kazakhstan* **64 E8** 52 27N 61 39 E
Deniyaya, *Sri Lanka* **95 L5** 6 21N 80 33 E
Denizli, *Turkey* **49 D11** 37 42N 29 2 E
Denizli □, *Turkey* **49 D11** 37 45N 29 5 E
Denman, *Australia* **129 B9** 32 24 S 150 42 E
Denman Glacier, *Antarctica* **7 C7** 66 45 S 99 25 E
Denmark, *Australia* **125 F2** 34 59 S 117 25 E
Denmark, *U.S.A.* **152 B8** 33 19N 81 9W
Denmark ■, *Europe* **17 J3** 55 45N 10 0 E
Denmark Str., *Atl. Oc.* **6 C6** 66 0N 30 0W
Dennery, *St. Lucia* **165 f** 13 55N 60 54W
Dennison, *U.S.A.* **150 F3** 40 24N 81 19W
Denny, *U.K.* **22 E5** 56 1N 3 55W
Denpasar, *Indonesia* **85 D5** 8 39 S 115 13 E
Denpasar ✈ (DPS), *Indonesia* **79 K18** 8 44 S 115 10 E
Denton, *Ga., U.S.A.* **152 D7** 31 44N 82 42W
Denton, *Mont., U.S.A.* **158 C9** 47 19N 109 57W
Denton, *Tex., U.S.A.* **155 J6** 33 13N 97 8W
D'Entrecasteaux △, *Australia* **125 F2** 34 20 S 115 33 E
D'Entrecasteaux, Pt., *Australia* **125 F2** 34 50 S 115 57 E
D'Entrecasteaux Is., *Papua N. G.* **132 E6** 9 0 S 151 0 E
Dents du Midi, *Switz.* **32 D3** 46 10N 6 56 E
Dentsville, *U.S.A.* **152 A9** 34 4N 80 58W
Denu, *Ghana* **113 D5** 6 4N 1 8 E
Denver, *Colo., U.S.A.* **154 F2** 39 44N 104 59W
Denver, *Ind., U.S.A.* **157 D10** 40 52N 86 5W
Denver, *Iowa, U.S.A.* **156 B4** 42 40N 92 20W
Denver, *Pa., U.S.A.* **151 F8** 40 14N 76 8W
Denver City, *U.S.A.* **155 J3** 32 58N 102 50W
Denwood = Wainwright, *Canada* **143 C6** 52 50N 110 50W
Deoband, *India* **92 E7** 29 42N 77 43 E
Deobhog, *India* **94 E6** 19 53N 82 44 E
Deodrug, *India* **95 F3** 16 26N 76 55 E
Deogarh, *Orissa, India* **94 D7** 21 32N 84 45 E
Deogarh, *Raj., India* **92 G5** 25 32N 73 54 E
Deoghar, *India* **93 G12** 24 30N 86 42 E
Deolali, *India* **94 E1** 19 58N 73 50 E
Deoli = Devli, *India* **92 G6** 25 50N 75 20 E
Déols, *France* **27 F8** 46 50N 1 43 E
Deora, *India* **92 F4** 26 22N 70 55 E
Deorha = Jubbal, *India* **92 D7** 31 5N 77 40 E
Deori, *India* **93 H8** 23 24N 79 1 E
Deoria, *India* **93 F10** 26 31N 83 48 E
Deosai Mts., *Pakistan* **93 B6** 35 40N 75 0 E
Deosri, *India* **90 B3** 26 46N 90 29 E
Depalpur, *India* **92 H6** 22 51N 75 33 E
Deping, *China* **75 F9** 37 25N 116 58 E
Deposit, *U.S.A.* **151 D9** 42 4N 75 25W
Depuch I., *Australia* **124 D2** 20 37 S 117 44 E
Deputatskiy, *Russia* **67 C14** 69 18N 139 54 E
Dêqên, *China* **76 C2** 28 34N 98 51 E
Deqing, *China* **77 F8** 23 8N 111 42 E
Dera Ghazi Khan, *Pakistan* **91 C3** 30 5N 70 43 E
Dera Ismail Khan, *Pakistan* **91 C3** 31 50N 70 50 E
Derabugti, *Pakistan* **92 E3** 29 2N 69 9 E
Derawar Fort, *Pakistan* **92 E4** 28 46N 71 20 E
Derbent, *Russia* **61 J9** 42 5N 48 15 E
Derbent, *Turkey* **49 C10** 38 11N 28 33 E
Derbent, *Uzbekistan* **65 D3** 38 13N 67 1 E
Derby, *Australia* **124 C3** 17 18 S 123 38 E
Derby, *U.K.* **20 E6** 52 56N 1 28W
Derby, *Conn., U.S.A.* **151 E11** 41 19N 73 5W
Derby, *Kans., U.S.A.* **155 G6** 37 33N 97 16W
Derby, *N.Y., U.S.A.* **150 D6** 42 41N 78 58W
Derby City □, *U.K.* **20 E6** 52 56N 1 28W
Derby Line, *U.S.A.* **151 B12** 45 0N 72 6W
Derbyshire □, *U.K.* **20 D6** 53 11N 1 38W
Đerdap △, *Serbia & M.* **50 B6** 44 40N 22 23 E
Derdepoort, *S. Africa* **116 C4** 24 38 S 26 24 E
Derecske, *Hungary* **52 C6** 47 20N 21 33 E
Dereham, *U.K.* **21 E8** 52 41N 0 57 E
Dereköy, *Turkey* **51 E11** 41 55N 27 21 E
Dereli, *Turkey* **101 B8** 40 44N 38 26 E
Derg →, *U.K.* **23 B4** 54 44N 7 26W
Derg, L., *Ireland* **23 D3** 53 0N 8 20W
Dergachi = Derhaci, *Ukraine* **59 G9** 50 9N 36 11 E
Derhaci, *Ukraine* **59 G9** 50 9N 36 11 E
Derik, *Turkey* **101 D9** 37 21N 40 18 E
Derinkuyu, *Turkey* **100 C6** 38 22N 34 45 E
Dermantsi, *Bulgaria* **51 C8** 43 8N 24 17 E
Dermott, *U.S.A.* **155 J9** 33 32N 91 26W
Dêrong, *China* **76 C2** 28 44N 99 9 E
Derrinallum, *Australia* **128 D5** 37 57 S 143 15 E
Derry = Londonderry, *U.K.* **23 B4** 55 0N 7 20W
Derry = Londonderry □, *U.K.* **23 B4** 55 0N 7 20W
Derry, *N.H., U.S.A.* **151 D13** 42 53N 71 19W
Derry, *Pa., U.S.A.* **150 F5** 40 20N 79 18W
Derryveagh Mts., *Ireland* **23 B3** 54 56N 8 11W
Derudub, *Sudan* **106 D4** 17 31N 36 7 E
Derval, *France* **26 E5** 47 40N 1 41W
Dervéni, *Greece* **48 C4** 38 8N 22 25 E
Derventa, *Bos.-H.* **52 F2** 44 59N 17 55 E
Derwent →, *Cumb., U.K.* **20 C4** 54 39N 3 33W
Derwent →, *Derby, U.K.* **20 E6** 52 57N 1 28W
Derwent →, *N. Yorks., U.K.* **20 D7** 53 45N 0 58W
Derwent Water, *U.K.* **20 C4** 54 35N 3 9W
Des Moines, *Iowa, U.S.A.* **156 C3** 41 35N 93 37W
Des Moines, *N. Mex., U.S.A.* **155 G3** 36 46N 103 50W
Des Moines →, *U.S.A.* **156 D5** 40 23N 91 25W
Des Plaines, *U.S.A.* **157 B9** 42 3N 87 52W
Des Plaines →, *U.S.A.* **157 C8** 41 23N 88 15W
Desa, *Romania* **52 G8** 43 52N 23 2 E
Desaguadero, *Peru* **172 D4** 16 34 S 69 3W
Desaguadero →, *Argentina* **174 C2** 34 30 S 66 46W
Desaguadero →, *Bolivia* **172 D4** 16 35 S 69 5W
Desantne, *Ukraine* **53 E14** 45 34N 29 32 E
Desar, *Malaysia* **87 d** 1 31N 104 17 E
Descanso, Pta., *Mexico* **161 N9** 32 21N 117 3W
Descartes, *France* **28 B4** 46 59N 0 42 E
Deschaillons-sur-St-Laurent, *Canada* **141 C5** 46 32N 72 7W
Deschambault L., *Canada* **143 C8** 54 50N 103 30W
Deschutes →, *U.S.A.* **158 D3** 45 38N 120 55W
Dese, *Ethiopia* **107 E4** 11 5N 39 40 E
Deseado, C., *Chile* **176 D2** 52 45 S 74 42W
Desenzano del Garda, *Italy* **44 C7** 45 28N 10 32 E
Desert Center, *U.S.A.* **161 M11** 33 43N 115 24W
Desert Hot Springs, *U.S.A.* **161 M10** 33 58N 116 30W
Desertas, Ilhas, *Madeira* **110 B1** 32 30N 16 30W
Deset, *Norway* **18 C8** 61 20N 11 26 E
Deshnok, *India* **92 F5** 27 48N 73 21 E
Desierto Central de Baja California ⌂, *Mexico* **162 B2** 29 40N 114 43W
Desna →, *Ukraine* **59 G6** 50 33N 30 32 E
Desnătui →, *Romania* **53 G8** 43 53N 23 35 E
Desolación, I., *Chile* **176 D2** 53 0 S 74 0W
Despeñaperros ⌂, *Spain* **43 G7** 38 23N 3 32W
Despeñaperros, Paso, *Spain* **43 G7** 38 24N 3 30W
Despotovac, *Serbia & M.* **50 B5** 44 6N 21 30 E
Dessau, *Germany* **30 D8** 51 51N 12 14 E
Dessye = Dese, *Ethiopia* **107 E4** 11 5N 39 40 E
Destin, *U.S.A.* **153 E3** 30 24N 86 30W
D'Estrees B., *Australia* **128 C2** 35 55 S 137 45 E
Desuri, *India* **92 G5** 25 18N 73 35 E
Desvres, *France* **27 B8** 50 40N 1 48 E
Det Udom, *Thailand* **86 E5** 14 54N 105 5 E
Deta, *Romania* **52 E6** 45 24N 21 13 E
Dete, *Zimbabwe* **116 B4** 18 38 S 26 50 E
Đetinja →, *Serbia & M.* **50 C4** 43 51N 20 5 E
Detmold, *Germany* **30 D4** 51 56N 8 52 E
Detour, Pt., *U.S.A.* **148 C2** 45 40N 86 40W
Detroit, *U.S.A.* **150 D1** 42 20N 83 3W
Detroit Lakes, *U.S.A.* **154 B7** 46 49N 95 51W
Detroit Wayne County ✈ (DTW), *U.S.A.* **157 B13** 42 13N 83 21W
Detskoye Selo = Pushkin, *Russia* **58 C6** 59 45N 30 25 E
Dettifoss, *Iceland* **11 B10** 65 48N 16 24W
Detva, *Slovak Rep.* **35 C12** 48 34N 19 25 E
Deurne, *Neths.* **24 C5** 51 27N 5 49 E
Deutsch = Przemyśl, *Poland* **55 J9** 49 50N 22 45 E
Deutsch Brod = Havlíčkův Brod, *Czech Rep.* **34 B8** 49 36N 15 33 E
Deutsch-Eylau = Iława, *Poland* **54 E6** 53 36N 19 34 E
Deutsch Krone = Wałcz, *Poland* **55 E3** 53 17N 16 27 E
Deutsch-Luxemburgischer ⌂, *Germany* **31 F2** 49 58N 6 12 E
Deutsche Bucht, *Germany* **30 A4** 54 15N 8 0 E
Deutschland = Germany ■, *Europe* **30 E6** 51 0N 10 0 E
Deutschlandsberg, *Austria* **34 E8** 46 49N 15 14 E
Deux-Sèvres □, *France* **26 F6** 46 35N 0 20W
Deva, *Romania* **52 E7** 45 53N 22 55 E
Deva △, *Australia* **129 C8** 35 55 S 149 48 E
Devakottai, *India* **95 K4** 9 55N 78 45 E
Devaprayag, *India* **93 D8** 30 13N 78 35 E
Devarkonda, *India* **94 F4** 16 42N 78 56 E
Dévaványa, *Hungary* **52 C5** 47 2N 20 59 E
Deveci Dağları, *Turkey* **100 B7** 40 6N 36 15 E
Devecikonağı, *Turkey* **51 G12** 39 55N 28 34 E
Devecser, *Hungary* **52 C2** 47 6N 17 26 E
Develi, *Turkey* **100 C6** 38 23N 35 29 E
Deventer, *Neths.* **24 B6** 52 15N 6 10 E
Devereux, *U.S.A.* **152 B6** 33 13N 83 5W
Deveron →, *U.K.* **22 D6** 57 41N 2 32W
Devesel, *Romania* **52 F7** 44 28N 22 41 E
Devgad I., *India* **95 G2** 14 48N 74 5 E
Devgadh Bariya, *India* **92 H5** 22 40N 73 55 E
Devgarh, *India* **95 F1** 16 23N 73 23 E
Devi →, *India* **94 E8** 19 59N 86 24 E
Devikot, *India* **92 F4** 26 42N 71 12 E
Devil River Pk., *N.Z.* **131 A7** 40 56 S 172 37 E
Devils Den, *U.S.A.* **160 K7** 35 46N 119 58W
Devils Island, I. = Diable, Île du, *Fr. Guiana* **169 B7** 5 16N 52 34W
Devils Lake, *U.S.A.* **154 A5** 48 7N 98 52W
Devils Paw, *Canada* **142 B2** 58 47N 134 0W
Devils Postpile ⌂, *U.S.A.* **160 H7** 37 37N 119 5W
Devil's Pt., *Sri Lanka* **95 K5** 9 26N 80 6 E
Devils Tower, *U.S.A.* **154 C2** 44 31N 104 57W
Devils Tower ⌂, *U.S.A.* **154 C2** 44 35N 104 43W
Devin, *Bulgaria* **51 E8** 41 44N 24 24 E
Devine, *U.S.A.* **155 L5** 29 8N 98 54W
Devipattinam, *India* **95 K4** 9 29N 78 54 E
Devizes, *U.K.* **21 F6** 51 22N 1 58W
Devli, *India* **92 G6** 25 50N 75 20 E
Devnya, *Bulgaria* **51 C11** 43 13N 27 33 E
Devoll →, *Albania* **50 F4** 40 57N 20 15 E
Devon, *Canada* **142 C6** 53 24N 113 44W
Devon □, *U.K.* **21 G4** 50 50N 3 40W
Devon I., *Canada* **6 B3** 75 10N 85 0W
Devonport, *Australia* **127 G4** 41 10 S 146 22 E
Devrek, *Turkey* **100 B4** 41 13N 31 57 E
Devrekâni, *Turkey* **100 B5** 41 36N 33 50 E
Devrez →, *Turkey* **100 B6** 41 6N 34 25 E
Devrukh, *India* **94 F1** 17 3N 73 37 E
Dewas, *India* **92 H7** 22 59N 76 3 E
Dewetsdorp, *S. Africa* **116 D4** 29 33 S 26 39 E
Dewey, *Puerto Rico* **165 d** 18 18N 65 18W
Dexing, *China* **77 C11** 28 46N 117 30 E
Dexter, *Maine, U.S.A.* **149 C11** 45 1N 69 18W
Dexter, *Mich., U.S.A.* **157 B13** 42 20N 83 53W
Dexter, *Mo., U.S.A.* **155 G10** 36 48N 89 57W
Dexter, *N. Mex., U.S.A.* **155 J2** 33 12N 104 22W
Dey-Dey, L., *Australia* **125 E5** 29 12 S 131 4 E
Deyang, *China* **76 B5** 31 3N 104 27 E
Deyhūk, *Iran* **97 C8** 33 15N 57 30 E
Deyyer, *Iran* **97 E6** 27 55N 51 55 E
Dezadeash L., *Canada* **142 A1** 60 28N 136 58W
Dezfūl, *Iran* **97 C6** 32 20N 48 30 E
Dezhneva, Mys, *Russia* **67 C19** 66 5N 169 40W
Dezhou, *China* **74 F9** 37 26N 116 18 E
Dhadhar →, *India* **93 G11** 24 56N 85 24 E
Dháfni, *Kríti, Greece* **39 E6** 35 13N 25 3 E
Dháfni, *Pelóponnisos, Greece* **48 D4** 37 48N 22 1 E
Dhafnoúdhi, Ákra, *Greece* **39 C2** 38 28N 20 33 E
Dhahabān, *Si. Arabia* **98 B2** 21 58N 39 3 E
Dhahiriya = Az Zāhirīyah, *West Bank* **103 D3** 31 25N 34 58 E
Dhahran = Az Zahrān, *Si. Arabia* **97 E6** 26 10N 50 7 E
Dhak, *Pakistan* **92 C5** 32 25N 72 33 E
Dhaka, *Bangla.* **90 D3** 23 43N 90 26 E
Dhaka □, *Bangla.* **90 C3** 24 25N 90 25 E
Dhali, *Cyprus* **39 E9** 35 1N 33 25 E
Dhamangaon, *India* **94 D4** 20 48N 78 9 E
Dhamār, *Yemen* **98 D4** 14 30N 44 20 E
Dhamási, *Greece* **48 B4** 39 43N 22 11 E
Dhampur, *India* **93 E8** 29 19N 78 33 E
Dhamra →, *India* **94 D8** 20 47N 86 58 E
Dhamtari, *India* **94 D5** 20 42N 81 35 E
Dhanbad, *India* **93 H12** 23 50N 86 30 E
Dhankuta, *Nepal* **93 F12** 26 55N 87 40 E
Dhanora, *India* **94 D5** 20 20N 80 22 E
Dhanushkodi, *India* **95 K4** 9 11N 79 24 E
Dhar, *India* **92 H6** 22 35N 75 26 E
Dharampur, *Gujarat, India* **94 D1** 20 32N 73 17 E
Dharampur, *Mad. P., India* **92 H6** 22 13N 75 18 E
Dharamsala = Dharmsala, *India* **92 C7** 32 16N 76 23 E
Dharangaon, *India* **94 D2** 21 1N 75 16 E
Dharapuram, *India* **95 J3** 10 45N 77 34 E
Dhariwal, *India* **92 D6** 31 57N 75 19 E
Dharla →, *Bangla.* **93 G13** 25 46N 89 42 E
Dharmapuri, *India* **95 H4** 12 10N 78 10 E
Dharmavaram, *India* **95 G3** 14 29N 77 44 E
Dharmjaygarh, *India* **93 H10** 22 28N 83 13 E
Dharmsala, *India* **92 C7** 32 16N 76 23 E
Dharni, *India* **92 J7** 21 33N 76 53 E
Dharug △, *Australia* **129 B9** 33 20 S 151 2 E
Dharur, *India* **94 E3** 18 3N 76 8 E
Dharwad, *India* **95 G2** 15 30N 75 4 E
Dhasan →, *India* **93 G8** 25 48N 79 24 E
Dhaulagiri, *Nepal* **93 E10** 28 39N 83 28 E
Dhebar, L., *India* **92 G6** 24 10N 74 0 E
Dheftera, *Cyprus* **39 E9** 35 5N 33 16 E
Dhenkanal, *India* **94 D7** 20 45N 85 35 E
Dhenoúsa, *Greece* **49 D7** 37 8N 25 48 E
Dherinia, *Cyprus* **39 E9** 35 3N 33 57 E
Dheskáti, *Greece* **50 G5** 39 55N 21 49 E
Dhespotikó, *Greece* **48 E6** 36 57N 24 58 E
Dhestina, *Greece* **48 C4** 38 25N 22 31 E
Dhī Qār □, *Iraq* **96 D5** 31 0N 46 15 E
Dhiarrizos →, *Cyprus* **39 F8** 34 41N 32 34 E
Dhíavlos Zakínthou, *Greece* **39 D2** 37 50N 21 0 E
Dhībān, *Jordan* **103 D4** 31 30N 35 46 E
Dhidhimótikhon, *Greece* **51 E10** 41 22N 26 29 E
Dhíkti Óros, *Greece* **39 E6** 35 8N 25 30 E
Dhilianáta, *Greece* **39 C2** 38 13N 20 31 E
Dhílos, *Greece* **49 D7** 37 23N 25 15 E
Dhilwan, *India* **92 D6** 31 31N 75 21 E
Dhimarkhera, *India* **93 H9** 23 28N 80 22 E
Dhimitsána, *Greece* **48 D4** 37 36N 22 3 E
Dhírfis Óros, *Greece* **48 C5** 38 40N 23 54 E
Dhodhekánisos, *Greece* **49 E8** 36 35N 27 0 E
Dhodhekánisos □, *Greece* **49 E8** 36 35N 27 0 E
Dhokós, *Greece* **48 D5** 37 20N 23 20 E
Dholiana, *Greece* **48 B2** 39 54N 20 32 E
Dholka, *India* **92 H5** 22 44N 72 29 E
Dhomokós, *Greece* **48 B4** 39 10N 22 18 E
Dhone, *India* **95 E3** 15 25N 77 53 E
Dhoraji, *India* **92 J4** 21 45N 70 37 E
Dhoxáton, *Greece* **51 E8** 41 9N 24 16 E
Dhragonísi, *Greece* **49 D7** 37 27N 25 29 E
Dhráhstis, Ákra, *Greece* **38 B9** 39 48N 19 40 E
Dhrakáta, *Greece* **39 C2** 38 20N 20 33 E
Dhrangadhra, *India* **92 H4** 22 59N 71 31 E
Dhrápanon, Ákra, *Greece* **39 E5** 35 28N 24 14 E
Dhriopís, *Greece* **48 D6** 37 25N 24 26 E
Dhrol, *India* **92 H4** 22 33N 70 25 E
Dhubāb, *Yemen* **98 D3** 12 56N 43 25 E
Dhuburi, *India* **90 B2** 26 2N 89 59 E
Dhulasar, *Bangla.* **90 E3** 21 52N 90 14 E
Dhule, *India* **94 D2** 20 58N 74 50 E
Dhupdhara, *India* **90 B3** 26 10N 91 4 E
Dhuusa Marreeb = Dusa Mareb, *Somali Rep.* **120 C3** 5 30N 46 15 E
Di-ib, W. →, *Sudan* **106 C4** 22 38N 36 6 E
Di Linh, *Vietnam* **87 G7** 11 35N 108 4 E
Di Linh, Cao Nguyen, *Vietnam* **87 G7** 11 30N 108 0 E
Día, *Greece* **39 E6** 35 28N 25 14 E
Diabakania, *Guinea* **112 C2** 10 38N 10 58W
Diable, Île du, *Fr. Guiana* **169 B7** 5 16N 52 34W
Diablo, Mt., *U.S.A.* **160 H5** 37 53N 121 56W
Diablo Range, *U.S.A.* **160 J5** 37 20N 121 25W
Diafarabé, *Mali* **112 C4** 14 9N 4 57W
Diala, *Mali* **112 C3** 14 10N 9 58W
Dialakoro, *Mali* **112 C3** 12 18N 7 54W
Dialakoto, *Senegal* **112 C2** 13 21N 13 19W
Diallassagou, *Mali* **112 C4** 13 47N 3 41W
Diamante, *Argentina* **174 C3** 32 5 S 60 40W
Diamante, *Italy* **47 C8** 39 41N 15 49 E
Diamante →, *Argentina* **174 C2** 34 30 S 66 46W
Diamantina, *Brazil* **171 E3** 18 17 S 43 40W
Diamantina △, *Australia* **126 C3** 23 33 S 141 23 E
Diamantina →, *Australia* **127 D2** 26 45 S 139 10 E
Diamantino, *Brazil* **173 C6** 14 30 S 56 30W
Diamond Bar, *U.S.A.* **161 L9** 34 1N 117 48W
Diamond Harbour, *India* **93 H13** 22 11N 88 14 E
Diamond Head, *U.S.A.* **145 K14** 21 16N 157 49W
Diamond Is., *Australia* **126 B5** 17 25 S 151 5 E
Diamond Mts., *U.S.A.* **158 G6** 39 50N 115 30W
Diamond Springs, *U.S.A.* **160 G6** 38 42N 120 49W
Dian Chi, *China* **76 E4** 24 50N 102 43 E
Dianalund, *Denmark* **17 J5** 55 32N 11 30 E
Dianbai, *China* **77 G8** 21 33N 111 0 E
Diancheng, *China* **77 G8** 21 30N 111 4 E
Dianjiang, *China* **76 B6** 30 24N 107 20 E
Diano Marina, *Italy* **44 E5** 43 54N 8 5 E
Dianópolis, *Brazil* **171 D2** 11 38 S 46 50W
Dianra, *Ivory C.* **112 D3** 8 45N 6 14W
Diapaga, *Burkina Faso* **113 C5** 12 5N 1 46 E
Diapangou, *Burkina Faso* **113 C5** 12 5N 0 10 E
Diariguila, *Guinea* **112 C2** 10 35N 10 2W
Diavolo, Mt., *India* **95 H11** 12 40N 92 56 E
Dībā, *U.A.E.* **97 E8** 25 45N 56 16 E
Dibai, *India* **92 E8** 28 13N 78 15 E
Dibaya, *Dem. Rep. of the Congo* **115 D4** 6 30 S 22 57 E
Dibaya-Lubue, *Dem. Rep. of the Congo* **115 C3** 4 12 S 19 54 E
Dibbeen △, *Jordan* **103 C4** 32 20N 35 45 E
Dibella, *Niger* **109 E2** 17 32N 13 6 E
Dibete, *Botswana* **116 C4** 23 45 S 26 32 E
Dibrugarh, *India* **90 B5** 27 29N 94 55 E
Dicioşănmartin = Târnăveni, *Romania* **53 D9** 46 19N 24 13 E
Dickens, *U.S.A.* **155 J4** 33 37N 100 50W
Dickeyville, *U.S.A.* **156 B6** 42 38N 90 36W
Dickinson, *U.S.A.* **154 B3** 46 53N 102 47W
Dick's Pt., *Bahamas* **9 b** 25 4N 77 18W
Dickson = Dikson, *Russia* **66 B9** 73 40N 80 5 E
Dickson, *U.S.A.* **149 G2** 36 5N 87 23W
Dickson City, *U.S.A.* **151 E9** 41 29N 75 40W
Dicle Nehri →, *Turkey* **101 D9** 37 44N 41 10 E
Dicomano, *Italy* **45 E8** 43 53N 11 31 E
Didesa, W. →, *Ethiopia* **107 E4** 10 2N 35 32 E
Didi, *Sudan* **107 F3** 6 18N 34 29 E
Didiéni, *Mali* **112 C3** 13 53N 8 6W
Didimbo, *Angola* **115 F4** 17 30 S 21 45 E
Didsbury, *Canada* **142 C6** 51 35N 114 10W
Didwana, *India* **92 F6** 27 23N 74 36 E
Die, *France* **29 D9** 44 47N 5 22 E
Diébougou, *Burkina Faso* **112 C4** 11 0N 3 15W
Diecke, *Guinea* **112 D3** 7 27N 8 54W
Diedenhofen = Thionville, *France* **27 C13** 49 20N 6 10 E
Diefenbaker, L., *Canada* **143 C7** 51 0N 106 55W
Diego de Almagro, *Chile* **174 B1** 26 22 S 70 3W
Diego Garcia, *Ind. Oc.* **121 E6** 7 50 S 72 50 E
Diego Ramírez, Islas, *Chile* **176 E3** 56 30 S 68 44W
Diekirch, *Lux.* **24 E6** 49 52N 6 10 E
Diéma, *Mali* **112 C3** 14 32N 9 12W
Diembéring, *Senegal* **112 C1** 12 29N 16 47W
Diemelsee ⌂, *Germany* **30 D4** 51 20N 8 40 E
Dien Ban, *Vietnam* **86 E7** 15 53N 108 16 E
Dien Bien, *Vietnam* **76 G4** 21 20N 103 0 E
Dien Khanh, *Vietnam* **87 F7** 12 15N 109 6 E
Diepholz, *Germany* **30 C4** 52 37N 8 22 E
Diepoldsau, *Switz.* **33 B9** 47 23N 9 40 E
Dieppe, *France* **26 C8** 49 54N 1 4 E
Dierks, *U.S.A.* **155 H8** 34 7N 94 1W
Diessenhofen, *Switz.* **33 A7** 47 42N 8 46 E
Diest, *Belgium* **24 D5** 50 58N 5 4 E
Dieterich, *U.S.A.* **157 E8** 39 4N 88 23W
Dietikon, *Switz.* **33 B6** 47 24N 8 24 E
Dieulefit, *France* **29 D9** 44 32N 5 4 E
Dieuze, *France* **27 D13** 48 49N 6 43 E
Dievenow = Dziwnów, *Poland* **54 D1** 54 2N 14 45 E
Dif, *Somali Rep.* **120 D2** 0 59N 40 58 E
Differdange, *Lux.* **24 E5** 49 31N 5 54 E
Diffun, *Phil.* **80 C3** 16 36N 121 33 E
Dig, *India* **92 F7** 27 28N 77 20 E
Digba, *Dem. Rep. of the Congo* **118 B2** 4 25N 25 48 E
Digboi, *India* **90 B5** 27 23N 95 38 E
Digby, *Canada* **141 D6** 44 38N 65 50W
Diggi, *India* **92 F6** 26 22N 75 26 E
Dighinala, *Bangla.* **90 D4** 23 15N 92 5 E
Dighton, *U.S.A.* **154 F4** 38 29N 100 28W
Diglur, *India* **94 E3** 18 34N 77 33 E
Digna, *Mali* **112 C3** 14 48N 8 10W
Digne-les-Bains, *France* **29 D10** 44 5N 6 12 E
Digoin, *France* **27 F11** 46 29N 4 1 E
Digor, *Turkey* **101 B10** 40 22N 43 25 E
Digos, *Phil.* **81 H5** 6 45N 125 20 E
Digranes, *Iceland* **11 A12** 66 4N 14 44W
Digras, *India* **94 D3** 20 6N 77 45 E
Digul →, *Indonesia* **83 C5** 7 7 S 138 42 E
Digya △, *Ghana* **113 D5** 7 15N 0 5 E
Dihang = Brahmaputra →, *Asia* **68 D3** 23 40N 90 35 E
Dijlah, Nahr →, *Asia* **96 D5** 31 0N 47 25 E
Dijon, *France* **27 E12** 47 20N 5 3 E
Dikhil, *Djibouti* **107 E5** 11 8N 42 20 E
Dikili, *Turkey* **49 B8** 39 4N 26 53 E
Dikirnis, *Egypt* **106 H7** 31 6N 31 35 E
Dikkil = Dikhil, *Djibouti* **107 E5** 11 8N 42 20 E
Dikodougou, *Ivory C.* **112 D3** 9 4N 5 45W
Diksmuide, *Belgium* **24 C2** 51 2N 2 52 E
Dikson, *Russia* **66 B9** 73 40N 80 5 E
Dikwa, *Nigeria* **113 C7** 12 4N 13 30 E
Dila, *Ethiopia* **107 F4** 6 21N 38 22 E
Dilasag, *Phil.* **80 C4** 16 25N 122 11 E
Dilek Yarimadisi △, *Turkey* **49 D9** 37 40N 27 10 E
Dili, *E. Timor* **82 C3** 8 39 S 125 34 E
Diligent Strait, *India* **95 H11** 12 11N 92 57 E
Dilijan, *Armenia* **61 K7** 40 46N 44 57 E
Dilizhan = Dilijan, *Armenia* **61 K7** 40 46N 44 57 E
Dilj, *Croatia* **52 E3** 45 29N 18 1 E
Dillenburg, *Germany* **30 E4** 50 43N 8 17 E
Dilley, *U.S.A.* **155 L5** 28 40N 99 10W
Dilli = Delhi, *India* **92 E7** 28 38N 77 17 E
Dillia →, *Niger* **109 F2** 14 9N 12 50 E
Dilling, *Sudan* **107 E2** 12 3N 29 35 E
Dillingen, *Bayern, Germany* **31 G6** 48 36N 10 30 E
Dillingen, *Saarland, Germany* **31 F2** 49 22N 6 43 E
Dillingham, *U.S.A.* **144 G8** 59 3N 158 28W
Dillon, *Canada* **143 B7** 55 56N 108 35W
Dillon, *Mont., U.S.A.* **158 D7** 45 13N 112 38W
Dillon, *S.C., U.S.A.* **149 H6** 34 25N 79 22W
Dillon →, *Canada* **143 B7** 55 56N 108 56W
Dillsboro, *U.S.A.* **157 E11** 39 1N 85 4W
Dillsburg, *U.S.A.* **150 F7** 40 7N 77 2W
Dilly, *Mali* **112 C3** 15 1N 7 40W
Dilolo, *Dem. Rep. of the Congo* **115 E4** 10 28 S 22 18 E
Dilove, *Ukraine* **53 C9** 47 56N 24 11 E
Dimapur, *India* **90 C4** 25 54N 93 45 E
Dimas, *Mexico* **162 C3** 23 43N 106 47W
Dimasalang, *Phil.* **80 E4** 12 12N 123 51 E
Dimashq, *Syria* **103 B5** 33 30N 36 18 E
Dimashq □, *Syria* **103 B5** 33 30N 36 30 E
Dimbaza, *S. Africa* **117 E4** 32 50 S 27 14 E
Dimbelenge, *Dem. Rep. of the Congo* **115 D4** 5 33 S 23 7 E
Dimbokro, *Ivory C.* **112 D4** 6 45N 4 46W
Dimboola, *Australia* **128 D5** 36 28 S 142 7 E
Dîmboviţa = Dâmboviţa →, *Romania* **53 F11** 44 12N 26 26 E
Dimbulah, *Australia* **126 B4** 17 8 S 145 4 E
Dimitrovgrad, *Bulgaria* **51 D9** 42 5N 25 35 E
Dimitrovgrad, *Russia* **60 C9** 54 14N 49 39 E
Dimitrovgrad, *Serbia & M.* **50 C6** 43 2N 22 48 E
Dimitrovo = Pernik, *Bulgaria* **50 D7** 42 35N 23 2 E
Dimmitt, *U.S.A.* **155 H3** 34 33N 102 19W
Dimo, *Sudan* **107 F2** 5 19N 29 10 E
Dimona, *Israel* **103 D4** 31 2N 35 1 E
Dimonika ⌂, *Congo* **114 C2** 4 13 S 12 21 E
Dimovo, *Bulgaria* **50 C6** 43 43N 22 50 E
Dinagat, *Phil.* **81 F5** 10 10N 125 40 E
Dinaig, *Phil.* **81 H5** 7 11N 124 10 E
Dinajpur, *Bangla.* **90 C2** 25 33N 88 43 E
Dinalupihan, *Phil.* **80 D3** 14 52N 120 28 E
Dinan, *France* **26 D4** 48 28N 2 2W
Dīnān Āb, *Iran* **97 C8** 32 4N 56 49 E
Dinant, *Belgium* **24 D4** 50 16N 4 55 E
Dinapur, *India* **93 G11** 25 38N 85 5 E
Dinar, *Turkey* **49 C12** 38 5N 30 10 E
Dīnār, Kūh-e, *Iran* **97 D6** 30 42N 51 46 E
Dinara Planina, *Croatia* **45 D13** 44 0N 16 30 E
Dinard, *France* **26 D4** 48 38N 2 6W
Dinaric Alps = Dinara Planina, *Croatia* **45 D13** 44 0N 16 30 E
Dinas, *Phil.* **81 H4** 7 38N 123 20 E
Dindanko, *Mali* **112 C3** 14 8N 9 30W
Dinde, *Angola* **115 E2** 14 17 S 13 42 E
Dinder △, *Sudan* **107 E4** 12 30N 35 10 E
Dinder, Nahr ed →, *Sudan* **107 E3** 14 6N 33 40 E
Dindi →, *India* **95 F4** 16 24N 78 15 E
Dindigul, *India* **95 J4** 10 25N 78 0 E
Dindori, *India* **93 H9** 22 57N 81 5 E
Ding Xian = Dingzhou, *China* **74 E8** 38 30N 114 59 E
Dinga, *Dem. Rep. of the Congo* **115 D3** 5 17 S 16 42 E
Dinga, *Pakistan* **92 G2** 25 26N 67 10 E
Dingalan, *Phil.* **80 D3** 15 18N 121 25 E
Dingalan Bay, *Phil.* **80 D3** 15 18N 121 25 E
Dingbian, *China* **74 F4** 37 35N 107 32 E
Dingelstädt, *Germany* **30 D6** 51 18N 10 19 E
Dingle, *Ireland* **23 D1** 52 9N 10 17W
Dingle, *Sweden* **17 F5** 58 32N 11 35 E
Dingle B., *Ireland* **23 D1** 52 3N 10 20W
Dingli, *Malta* **38 F7** 35 52N 14 23 E
Dingmans Ferry, *U.S.A.* **151 E10** 41 13N 74 55W
Dingnan, *China* **77 E10** 24 45N 115 0 E
Dingo, *Australia* **126 C4** 23 38 S 149 19 E
Dingolfing, *Germany* **31 G8** 48 37N 12 30 E
Dingras, *Phil.* **80 B3** 18 6N 120 42 E
Dingtao, *China* **74 G8** 35 5N 115 35 E
Dinguira, *Mali* **112 C2** 14 11N 11 16W
Dinguiraye, *Guinea* **112 C2** 11 18N 10 49W
Dingwall, *U.K.* **22 D4** 57 36N 4 26W
Dingxi, *China* **74 G3** 35 30N 104 33 E
Dingxiang, *China* **74 E7** 38 30N 112 58 E
Dingyuan, *China* **77 A11** 32 32N 117 41 E
Dingzhou, *China* **74 E8** 38 30N 114 59 E
Dinh, Mui, *Vietnam* **87 G7** 11 22N 109 1 E
Dinh Lap, *Vietnam* **76 G6** 21 33N 107 6 E
Dinhata, *India* **90 B2** 26 8N 89 27 E
Dinira △, *Venezuela* **165 E6** 9 57N 70 6W
Dinokwe, *Botswana* **116 C4** 23 29 S 26 37 E
Dinorwic, *Canada* **143 D10** 49 41N 92 30W
Dinosaur ⌂, *Canada* **142 C6** 50 47N 111 30W
Dinosaur ⌂, *U.S.A.* **158 F9** 40 30N 108 45W
Dinsor, *Somali Rep.* **120 D2** 2 24N 42 59 E
Dinuba, *U.S.A.* **160 J7** 36 32N 119 23W
Diö, *Sweden* **17 H8** 56 37N 14 15 E
Dioïla, *Mali* **112 C3** 12 23N 6 50W
Dioka, *Mali* **112 C2** 14 57N 10 4W
Diomede, *U.S.A.* **144 D5** 65 47N 169 0W
Diona, *Chad* **109 E4** 17 51N 22 36 E
Diongoï, *Mali* **112 C3** 14 38N 8 34W
Diósgyör, *Hungary* **52 B5** 48 7N 20 43 E
Diosig, *Romania* **52 C7** 47 18N 22 2 E
Diougani, *Mali* **112 C4** 14 19N 2 44W
Diouloulou, *Senegal* **112 C1** 13 5N 16 38W
Dioura, *Mali* **112 C3** 14 59N 5 12W
Diourbel, *Senegal* **112 C1** 14 39N 16 12W
Dipaculao, *Phil.* **80 D3** 15 51N 121 32 E
Dipalpur, *Pakistan* **92 D5** 30 40N 73 39 E
Diplo, *Pakistan* **92 G3** 24 35N 69 35 E
Dipolog, *Phil.* **81 G4** 8 36N 123 20 E
Dipperu △, *Australia* **126 C4** 21 56 S 148 42 E
Dipton, *N.Z.* **131 F3** 45 54 S 168 22 E
Dir, *Pakistan* **91 B3** 35 8N 71 59 E
Diré, *Mali* **112 B4** 16 20N 3 25W
Dire Dawa, *Ethiopia* **107 F5** 9 35N 41 45 E
Diriamba, *Nic.* **164 D2** 11 51N 86 19W
Dirico, *Angola* **115 F4** 17 50 S 20 42 E
Dirk Hartog I., *Australia* **125 E1** 25 50 S 113 5 E
Dirkou, *Niger* **109 E2** 19 1N 12 53 E
Dirranbandi, *Australia* **127 D4** 28 33 S 148 17 E
Dirs, *Si. Arabia* **98 C3** 18 32N 42 5 E
Dirschau = Tczew, *Poland* **54 D5** 54 8N 18 50 E
Disa, *India* **92 G5** 24 18N 72 10 E
Disa, *Sudan* **107 E3** 12 5N 34 15 E
Disappointment, C., *U.S.A.* **158 C2** 46 18N 124 5W
Disappointment, L., *Australia* **124 D3** 23 20 S 122 40 E
Disaster B., *Australia* **129 D8** 37 15 S 149 58 E
Discovery B., *Australia* **128 E4** 38 10 S 140 40 E
Discovery B., *China* **69 G11** 22 18N 114 1 E
Discovery Bay △, *Australia* **128 E4** 38 9 S 141 16 E
Disentis Muster, *Switz.* **33 C7** 46 42N 8 50 E
Dishna, *Egypt* **106 B3** 26 9N 32 32 E
Disina, *Nigeria* **113 C6** 11 35N 9 50 E
Disko = Qeqertarsuaq, *Greenland* **10 D5** 69 45N 53 30W
Disko Bugt, *Greenland* **10 D5** 69 10N 52 0W
Disna = Dzisna →, *Belarus* **58 E5** 55 34N 28 12 E
Disney Reef, *Tonga* **133 P13** 19 17 S 174 7W
Dispur, *India* **90 B3** 26 3N 91 52 E
Diss, *U.K.* **21 E9** 52 23N 1 7 E
Disteghil Sar, *Pakistan* **93 A6** 36 20N 75 12 E
Distrito Federal □, *Brazil* **171 E2** 15 45 S 47 45W
Distrito Federal □, *Mexico* **163 D5** 19 15N 99 10W
Distrito Federal □, *Venezuela* **168 A4** 10 30N 66 55W
Disûq, *Egypt* **106 H7** 31 8N 30 35 E
Diu, *India* **92 J4** 20 45N 70 58 E
Diuata Mts., *Phil.* **81 G5** 9 0N 125 50 E
Dīvāndarreh, *Iran* **101 E12** 35 55N 47 2 E
Divenié, *Congo* **114 C2** 2 43 S 12 1 E
Dives →, *France* **26 C6** 49 18N 0 7W
Dives-sur-Mer, *France* **26 C6** 49 18N 0 8W
Divi Pt., *India* **95 G5** 15 59N 81 9 E
Divichi = Däväçi, *Azerbaijan* **61 K9** 41 15N 48 57 E
Divide, *U.S.A.* **158 D7** 45 45N 112 45W
Dividing Ra., *Australia* **125 E2** 27 45 S 116 0 E
Divinópolis, *Brazil* **171 F3** 20 10 S 44 54W
Divisões, Serra dos, *Brazil* **171 E1** 17 0 S 51 0W
Divjake, *Albania* **50 F3** 41 0N 19 32 E
Divnoye, *Russia* **61 H6** 45 55N 43 21 E
Divo, *Ivory C.* **112 D3** 5 48N 5 15W
Divriği, *Turkey* **101 C8** 39 22N 38 7 E
Dīwāl Kol, *Afghan.* **91 B2** 34 23N 67 52 E
Dix →, *U.S.A.* **157 G12** 37 49N 84 43W
Dixie Mt., *U.S.A.* **160 F6** 39 55N 120 16W
Dixie Union, *U.S.A.* **152 D7** 31 20N 82 28W
Dixon, *Calif., U.S.A.* **160 G5** 38 27N 121 49W
Dixon, *Ill., U.S.A.* **156 C7** 41 50N 89 29W
Dixon, *Mo., U.S.A.* **156 G4** 37 59N 92 6W
Dixon Entrance, *U.S.A.* **138 C6** 54 30N 132 0W
Dixville, *Canada* **151 A13** 45 4N 71 46W
Diyadin, *Turkey* **101 C10** 39 33N 43 40 E
Diyālā □, *Iraq* **96 C5** 33 45N 44 50 E
Diyālā →, *Iraq* **101 F11** 33 14N 44 31 E
Diyarbakır, *Turkey* **101 D9** 37 55N 40 18 E

Diyodar, *India* **92 G4** 24 8N 71 50 E
Dja △, *Cameroon* **114 B2** 3 10N 12 58 E
Djadié →, *Gabon* **114 B2** 0 46N 12 58 E
Djado, *Niger* **109 D2** 21 4N 12 14 E
Djado, Plateau du, *Niger* **109 D2** 21 29N 12 21 E
Djakarta = Jakarta, *Indonesia* **84 D3** 6 9 S 106 49 E
Djalma Dutra = Miguel Calmon, *Brazil* **170 D3** 11 26 S 40 36W
Djalma Dutra = Poções, *Brazil* **171 D3** 14 31 S 40 21W
Djamâa, *Algeria* **111 B6** 33 32N 5 59 E
Djamba, *Angola* **116 B1** 16 45 S 13 58 E
Djambala, *Congo* **114 C2** 2 32 S 14 30 E
Djanet, *Algeria* **111 D6** 24 35N 9 32 E
Djaul I., *Papua N. G.* **132 B6** 2 58 S 150 57 E
Djawa = Jawa, *Indonesia* **85 D4** 7 0 S 110 0 E
Djebiniana, *Tunisia* **108 A2** 35 1N 11 0 E
Djédaa, *Chad* **109 F3** 13 31N 18 34 E
Djelfa, *Algeria* **111 B5** 34 40N 3 15 E
Djema, *C.A.R.* **118 A2** 6 3N 25 15 E
Djember, *Chad* **109 F3** 10 25N 17 50 E
Djembo, *Dem. Rep. of the Congo* **115 D4** 9 54 S 22 18 E
Djendel, *Algeria* **111 A5** 36 15N 2 25 E
Djeneïene, *Tunisia* **108 B2** 31 45N 10 9 E
Djenné, *Mali* **112 C4** 14 0N 4 30W
Djenoun, Garet el, *Algeria* **111 C6** 25 4N 5 31 E
Djerba, *Tunisia* **108 B2** 33 52N 10 51 E
Djerba, I. de, *Tunisia* **108 B2** 33 50N 10 48 E
Djerém →, *Cameroon* **114 A2** 5 20N 13 24 E
Djerid, Chott, *Tunisia* **108 B1** 33 42N 8 30 E
Djiba, *Gabon* **114 C2** 1 20 S 13 9 E
Djibo, *Burkina Faso* **113 C4** 14 9N 1 35W
Djibouti, *Djibouti* **107 E5** 11 30N 43 5 E
Djibouti ■, *Africa* **107 E5** 12 0N 43 0 E
Djohong, *Cameroon* **114 A2** 6 47N 14 20 E
Djolu, *Dem. Rep. of the Congo* **114 B4** 0 35N 22 5 E
Djouab →, *Gabon* **114 B2** 1 13N 13 12 E
Djougou, *Benin* **113 D5** 9 40N 1 45 E
Djoum, *Cameroon* **114 B2** 2 41N 12 35 E
Djouna, *Chad* **109 F4** 10 27N 20 4 E
Djourab, Erg du, *Chad* **109 E3** 16 40N 18 50 E
Djugu, *Dem. Rep. of the Congo* **118 B3** 1 55N 30 35 E
Djúpavík, *Iceland* **11 B5** 65 57N 21 34W
Djúpivogur, *Iceland* **11 C12** 64 39N 14 17W
Djupvasshytta, *Norway* **18 B4** 62 2N 7 16 E
Djurås, *Sweden* **16 D9** 60 34N 15 8 E
Djurdjura △, *Algeria* **111 A5** 35 20N 4 15 E
Djurö △, *Sweden* **17 F7** 58 52N 13 28 E
Djursland, *Denmark* **17 H4** 56 27N 10 45 E
Dmitriya Lapteva, Proliv, *Russia* **67 B15** 73 0N 140 0 E
Dmitriyev Lgovskiy, *Russia* **59 F8** 52 10N 35 0 E
Dmitriyevsk = Makiyivka, *Ukraine* **59 H9** 48 0N 38 0 E
Dmitriyevskoye = Talas, *Kyrgyzstan* **65 B6** 42 30N 72 13 E
Dmitrov, *Russia* **58 D9** 56 25N 37 32 E
Dmitrovsk-Orlovskiy, *Russia* **59 F8** 52 29N 35 10 E
Dnepr = Dnipro →, *Ukraine* **59 J7** 46 30N 32 18 E
Dneprodzerzhinsk = Dniprodzerzhynsk, *Ukraine* **59 H8** 48 32N 34 37 E
Dneprodzerzhinskoye Vdkhr. = Dniprodzerzhynske Vdskh., *Ukraine* **59 H8** 48 49N 34 8 E
Dnepropetrovsk = Dnipropetrovsk, *Ukraine* **59 H8** 48 30N 35 0 E
Dneprorudnoye = Dniprorudne, *Ukraine* **59 J8** 47 21N 34 58 E
Dnestr = Dnister →, *Europe* **59 J6** 46 18N 30 17 E
Dnestrovski = Belgorod, *Russia* **59 G9** 50 35N 36 35 E
Dnieper = Dnipro →, *Ukraine* **59 J7** 46 30N 32 18 E
Dniester = Dnister →, *Europe* **59 J6** 46 18N 30 17 E
Dnipro →, *Ukraine* **59 J7** 46 30N 32 18 E
Dniprodzerzhynsk, *Ukraine* **59 H8** 48 32N 34 37 E
Dniprodzerzhynske Vdskh., *Ukraine* **59 H8** 48 49N 34 8 E
Dnipropetrovsk, *Ukraine* **59 H8** 48 30N 35 0 E
Dniprorudne, *Ukraine* **59 J8** 47 21N 34 58 E
Dnister →, *Europe* **59 J6** 46 18N 30 17 E
Dnistrovskyy Lyman, *Ukraine* **59 J6** 46 15N 30 17 E
Dno, *Russia* **58 D5** 57 50N 29 58 E
Dnyapro = Dnipro →, *Ukraine* **59 J7** 46 30N 32 18 E
Doabi, *Afghan.* **91 A3** 36 1N 69 32 E
Doaktown, *Canada* **141 C6** 46 33N 66 8W
Doan Hung, *Vietnam* **76 G5** 21 30N 105 10 E
Doany, *Madag.* **117 A8** 14 21 S 49 30 E
Doba, *Chad* **109 G3** 8 40N 16 50 E
Dobandi, *Pakistan* **92 D2** 31 13N 66 50 E
Dobbiaco, *Italy* **45 B9** 46 44N 12 14 E
Dobbyn, *Australia* **126 B3** 19 44 S 140 2 E
Dobczyce, *Poland* **55 J7** 49 52N 20 5 E
Dobele, *Latvia* **15 H20** 56 37N 23 16 E
Dobele □, *Latvia* **54 B10** 56 35N 23 5 E
Döbeln, *Germany* **30 D9** 51 6N 13 7 E
Doberai, Jazirah, *Indonesia* **83 B4** 1 25 S 133 0 E
Dobiegniew, *Poland* **55 F2** 52 59N 15 45 E
Doblas, *Argentina* **174 D3** 37 5 S 64 0W
Dobo, *Dem. Rep. of the Congo* **114 B4** 2 20N 22 11 E
Dobo, *Indonesia* **83 C4** 5 45 S 134 15 E
Doboj, *Bos.-H.* **52 F3** 44 46N 18 4 E
Dobra, *Wielkopolskie, Poland* **55 G5** 51 55N 18 37 E
Dobra, *Zachodnio-Pomorskie, Poland* **54 E2** 53 34N 15 20 E
Dobra, *Dâmbovita, Romania* **53 F10** 44 52N 25 40 E
Dobra, *Hunedoara, Romania* **52 E7** 45 54N 22 36 E
Dobre Miasto, *Poland* **54 E7** 53 58N 20 26 E
Dobreşti, *Romania* **52 D7** 46 51N 22 18 E
Dobrich, *Bulgaria* **51 C11** 43 37N 27 49 E
Dobrinishta, *Bulgaria* **50 E7** 41 49N 23 34 E
Dobříš, *Czech Rep.* **34 B7** 49 46N 14 10 E
Dobrodzień, *Poland* **55 H5** 50 45N 18 25 E
Dobromyl, *Ukraine* **55 J9** 49 34N 22 46 E
Dobron, *Ukraine* **52 B7** 48 25N 22 23 E
Dobropole, *Ukraine* **59 H9** 48 25N 37 2 E
Dobrovolsk, *Russia* **54 D9** 54 46N 22 31 E
Dobruja, *Europe* **53 F13** 44 30N 28 15 E
Dobrush, *Belarus* **59 F6** 52 25N 31 22 E
Dobryanka, *Russia* **64 B6** 58 27N 56 25 E
Dobrzany, *Poland* **54 E2** 53 22N 15 25 E
Dobrzyń nad Wisłą, *Poland* **55 F6** 52 39N 19 22 E
Doc, Mui, *Vietnam* **86 D6** 17 58N 106 30 E
Doc Can I., *Phil.* **81 J2** 5 55N 119 56 E
Doce →, *Brazil* **171 E4** 19 37 S 39 49W
Docker River, *Australia* **125 D4** 24 52 S 129 5 E
Docksta, *Sweden* **16 A12** 63 3N 18 18 E
Doctor Arroyo, *Mexico* **162 C4** 23 40N 100 11W
Doctors Inlet, *U.S.A.* **152 E8** 30 6N 81 47W
Doda, *India* **93 C6** 33 10N 75 34 E
Doda, L., *Canada* **140 C4** 49 25N 75 13W
Doda Betta, *India* **95 J3** 11 24N 76 44 E
Dodaga, *Indonesia* **82 A3** 1 9N 128 11 E
Dodballapur, *India* **95 H3** 13 18N 77 32 E
Dodecanese = Dhodhekánisos, *Greece* **49 E8** 36 35N 27 0 E
Dodge City, *U.S.A.* **155 G5** 37 45N 100 1W
Dodge L., *Canada* **143 B7** 59 50N 105 36W
Dodgeville, *U.S.A.* **156 B6** 42 58N 90 8W
Dodo, *Cameroon* **113 D7** 7 30N 12 3 E
Dodo, *Sudan* **107 F2** 5 10N 29 57 E
Dodola, *Ethiopia* **107 F4** 6 59N 39 11 E
Dodoma, *Tanzania* **118 D4** 6 8 S 35 45 E
Dodoma □, *Tanzania* **118 D4** 6 0 S 36 0 E
Dodona, *Greece* **48 B2** 39 40N 20 46 E
Dodori △, *Kenya* **118 C5** 1 55 S 41 7 E
Dodsland, *Canada* **143 C7** 51 50N 108 45W
Dodson, *U.S.A.* **158 B9** 48 24N 108 15W
Dodurga, *Turkey* **49 B11** 39 49N 29 57 E
Doerun, *U.S.A.* **152 D6** 31 19N 83 55W
Doesburg, *Neths.* **24 B6** 52 1N 6 9 E
Doetinchem, *Neths.* **24 C6** 51 59N 6 18 E
Dog Creek, *Canada* **142 C4** 51 35N 122 14W
Dog I., *U.S.A.* **152 F5** 29 48N 84 36W
Dog L., *Man., Canada* **143 C9** 51 2N 98 31W
Dog L., *Ont., Canada* **140 C2** 48 48N 89 30W
Doğanşehir, *Turkey* **100 C7** 38 5N 37 53 E
Dogliani, *Italy* **44 D4** 44 32N 7 56 E
Dōgo, *Japan* **72 A5** 36 15N 133 16 E
Dōgo-San, *Japan* **72 B5** 35 2N 133 13 E
Dogondoutchi, *Niger* **113 C5** 13 38N 4 2 E
Dogran, *Pakistan* **92 D5** 31 48N 73 35 E
Doğubayazıt, *Turkey* **101 C11** 39 31N 44 5 E
Doguéraoua, *Niger* **113 C6** 14 0N 5 31 E
Dogura, *Papua N. G.* **132 F6** 10 6 S 150 5 E
Doha = Ad Dawḩah, *Qatar* **97 E6** 25 15N 51 35 E
Dohazari, *Bangla.* **90 D4** 22 10N 92 5 E
Dohinog = Manukan, *Phil.* **81 G4** 8 32N 123 12 E
Dohrighat, *India* **93 F10** 26 16N 83 31 E
Dohrn Banke, *Greenland* **10 D8** 65 55N 25 50W
Doi, *Indonesia* **82 A3** 2 14N 127 49 E
Doi Inthanon △, *Thailand* **86 C2** 18 33N 98 34 E
Doi Khuntan △, *Thailand* **86 C2** 18 33N 99 14 E
Doi Luang, *Thailand* **86 C3** 18 30N 101 0 E
Doi Luang △, *Thailand* **86 C2** 19 22N 99 35 E
Doi Saket, *Thailand* **86 C2** 18 52N 99 9 E
Doi Suthep △, *Thailand* **86 C2** 18 49N 98 53 E
Dois Irmãos, Sa., *Brazil* **170 C3** 9 0 S 42 30W
Dojransko Jezero, *Macedonia* **50 E6** 41 13N 22 44 E
Dokka, *Norway* **18 D7** 60 49N 10 7 E
Dokka →, *Norway* **18 D7** 60 49N 10 7 E
Dokkum, *Neths.* **24 A5** 53 20N 5 59 E
Dokri, *Pakistan* **92 F3** 27 25N 68 7 E
Dokshukino = Nartkala, *Russia* **61 J6** 43 33N 43 51 E
Dokuchayevsk, *Ukraine* **59 J9** 47 44N 37 40 E
Dol-de-Bretagne, *France* **26 D5** 48 34N 1 47W
Dolac, *Serbia & M.* **50 D4** 42 36N 20 36 E
Dolak, Pulau, *Indonesia* **83 C5** 8 0 S 138 30 E
Dolban = Liman, *Russia* **61 H8** 45 45N 47 12 E
Dolbeau-Mistassini, *Canada* **141 C5** 48 53N 72 14W
Dole, *France* **27 E12** 47 7N 5 31 E
Doleib, Wadi →, *Sudan* **107 E3** 12 10N 33 15 E
Dolenji Logatec, *Slovenia* **45 C11** 45 56N 14 15 E
Dolgellau, *U.K.* **20 E4** 52 45N 3 53W
Dolgelley = Dolgellau, *U.K.* **20 E4** 52 45N 3 53W
Dolhasca, *Romania* **53 C11** 47 26N 26 36 E
Dolianova, *Italy* **46 C2** 39 22N 9 10 E
Dolinskaya = Dolynska, *Ukraine* **59 H7** 48 6N 32 46 E
Dolj □, *Romania* **53 F8** 44 10N 23 30 E
Dollard, *Neths.* **24 A7** 53 20N 7 10 E
Dolna Banya, *Bulgaria* **50 D7** 42 18N 23 44 E
Dolni Chiflik, *Bulgaria* **51 D11** 42 59N 27 43 E
Dolni Dŭbnik, *Bulgaria* **51 C8** 43 24N 24 26 E
Dolnośląskie □, *Poland* **55 G3** 51 10N 16 30 E
Dolný Kubín, *Slovak Rep.* **35 B12** 49 12N 19 18 E
Dolo, *Ethiopia* **107 G5** 4 11N 42 3 E
Dolo, *Italy* **45 C9** 45 25N 12 5 E
Dolomites = Dolomiti, *Italy* **45 B8** 46 23N 11 51 E
Dolomiti, *Italy* **45 B8** 46 23N 11 51 E
Dolomiti Bellunesi △, *Italy* **45 B9** 46 10N 12 5 E
Dolores, *Argentina* **174 D4** 36 20 S 57 40W
Dolores, *Phil.* **80 E5** 12 2N 125 29 E
Dolores, *Uruguay* **174 C4** 33 34 S 58 15W
Dolores, *U.S.A.* **159 H9** 37 28N 108 30W
Dolores →, *U.S.A.* **159 G9** 38 49N 109 17W
Dolovo, *Serbia & M.* **52 F5** 44 55N 20 52 E
Dolphin, C., *Falk. Is.* **9 f** 51 10 S 59 0W
Dolphin and Union Str., *Canada* **138 B8** 69 5N 114 45W
Dolsk, *Poland* **55 G4** 51 59N 17 3 E
Dolton, *U.S.A.* **157 C9** 41 38N 87 36W
Dolungmukh, *India* **90 B5** 27 30N 94 18 E
Dolyna, *Ukraine* **53 B9** 48 58N 24 1 E
Dolynska, *Ukraine* **59 H7** 48 6N 32 46 E
Dolynske, *Ukraine* **53 C14** 47 32N 29 55 E
Dolzhanskaya, *Russia* **59 J9** 46 37N 37 48 E
Dom, *Switz.* **32 D5** 46 6N 7 50 E
Dom Joaquim, *Brazil* **171 E3** 18 57 S 43 16W
Dom Pedrito, *Brazil* **175 C5** 31 0 S 54 40W
Dom Pedro, *Brazil* **170 B3** 4 59 S 44 27W
Doma = Gombe, *Nigeria* **113 C7** 10 19N 11 2 E
Doma, *Nigeria* **113 D6** 8 25N 8 18 E
Doma →, *Zimbabwe* **119 F3** 16 28 S 30 12 E
Domaniç, *Turkey* **49 B11** 39 48N 29 36 E
Domar, E. →, *Chad* **109 E3** 18 11N 18 4 E
Domariaganj →, *India* **93 F10** 26 17N 83 44 E
Domasi, *Malawi* **119 F4** 15 15 S 35 22 E
Domat Ems, *Switz.* **33 C8** 46 50N 9 27 E
Domažlice, *Czech Rep.* **34 B5** 49 28N 12 58 E
Dombarovka = Dombarovskiy, *Russia* **64 F7** 50 46N 59 32 E
Dombarovskiy, *Russia* **64 F7** 50 46N 59 32 E
Dombås, *Norway* **18 B6** 62 4N 9 8 E
Dombasle-sur-Meurthe, *France* **27 D13** 48 38N 6 21 E
Dombes, *France* **29 C9** 45 58N 5 0 E
Dombóvár, *Hungary* **52 D3** 46 21N 18 9 E
Dombrád, *Hungary* **52 B6** 48 13N 21 54 E
Dombrova = Dąbrowa Górnicza, *Poland* **55 H6** 50 15N 19 10 E
Dombrowitsa = Dubrovytsya, *Ukraine* **59 G4** 51 31N 26 35 E
Dome Fuji, *Antarctica* **7 D5** 77 20 S 39 45 E
Domel I. = Letsôk-aw Kyun, *Burma* **87 G2** 11 30N 98 25 E
Domérat, *France* **27 F9** 46 21N 2 32 E
Domett, *N.Z.* **131 C8** 42 53 S 173 12 E
Domeyko, *Chile* **174 B1** 29 0 S 71 0W
Domeyko, Cordillera, *Chile* **174 A2** 24 30 S 69 0W
Domfront, *France* **26 D6** 48 37N 0 40W
Dominador, *Chile* **174 A2** 24 21 S 69 20W
Dominica ■, *W. Indies* **165 C7** 15 20N 61 20W
Dominica Passage, *W. Indies* **165 C7** 15 10N 61 20W
Dominican Rep. ■, *W. Indies* **165 C5** 19 0N 70 30W
Domiongo, *Dem. Rep. of the Congo* **115 C4** 4 37 S 21 15 E
Dömitz, *Germany* **30 B7** 53 8N 11 15 E
Domme, *France* **28 D5** 44 48N 1 12 E
Domneşti, *Romania* **53 E9** 45 12N 24 50 E
Domo, *Ethiopia* **120 C3** 7 50N 47 10 E
Domodóssola, *Italy* **44 B5** 46 7N 8 17 E
Domogled-Valea Cernei △, *Romania* **52 F7** 44 52N 22 27 E
Dompaire, *France* **27 D13** 48 14N 6 14 E
Dompierre-sur-Besbre, *France* **27 F10** 46 31N 3 41 E
Dompim, *Ghana* **112 D4** 5 10N 2 5W
Dompu, *Indonesia* **85 D5** 8 32 S 118 28 E
Domrémy-la-Pucelle, *France* **27 D12** 48 26N 5 40 E
Domville, Mt., *Australia* **127 D5** 28 1 S 151 15 E
Domvraína, *Greece* **48 C4** 38 15N 22 59 E
Domžale, *Slovenia* **45 B11** 46 9N 14 35 E
Don →, *India* **95 F3** 16 20N 76 15 E
Don →, *Russia* **59 J10** 47 4N 39 18 E
Don →, *Aberds., U.K.* **22 D6** 57 11N 2 5W
Don →, *S. Yorks., U.K.* **20 D7** 53 41N 0 52W
Don, C., *Australia* **124 B5** 11 18 S 131 46 E
Don Benito, *Spain* **43 G5** 38 53N 5 51W
Don Figuerero Mts., *Jamaica* **164 a** 18 5N 77 36W
Don Sak, *Thailand* **87 b** 9 18N 99 41 E
Dona Ana = Nhamaabué, *Mozam.* **119 F4** 17 25 S 35 5 E
Doña Mencía, *Spain* **43 H6** 37 33N 4 21W
Donaghadee, *U.K.* **23 B6** 54 39N 5 33W
Donald, *Australia* **128 D5** 36 23 S 143 0 E
Donaldsonville, *U.S.A.* **155 K9** 30 6N 90 59W
Donalsonville, *U.S.A.* **152 D5** 31 3N 84 53W
Doñana △, *Spain* **43 J4** 36 59N 6 23W
Donau = Dunărea →, *Europe* **53 E14** 45 20N 29 40 E
Donau →, *Austria* **35 C10** 48 10N 17 0 E
Donau Auen △, *Austria* **35 C9** 48 8N 16 44 E
Donaueschingen, *Germany* **31 H4** 47 56N 8 29 E
Donauwörth, *Germany* **31 G6** 48 43N 10 47 E
Doncaster, *U.K.* **20 D6** 53 32N 1 6W
Dondo, *Angola* **115 D2** 9 45 S 14 25 E
Dondo, *Dem. Rep. of the Congo* **114 B4** 4 11N 21 39 E
Dondo, *Mozam.* **119 F3** 19 33 S 34 46 E
Dondo, Teluk, *Indonesia* **82 A2** 0 50N 120 30 E
Dondra Head, *Sri Lanka* **95 M5** 5 55N 80 40 E
Donduşeni, *Moldova* **53 B12** 48 14N 27 36 E
Donegal, *Ireland* **23 B3** 54 39N 8 5W
Donegal □, *Ireland* **23 B4** 54 53N 8 0W
Donegal B., *Ireland* **23 B3** 54 31N 8 49W
Donets →, *Russia* **61 G5** 47 33N 40 55 E
Donets Basin, *Ukraine* **12 F13** 49 0N 38 0 E
Donetsk, *Ukraine* **59 J9** 48 0N 37 45 E
Dong Ba Thin, *Vietnam* **87 F7** 12 8N 109 13 E
Dong Dang, *Vietnam* **76 G6** 21 54N 106 42 E
Dong Giam, *Vietnam* **86 C5** 19 25N 105 31 E
Dong Ha, *Vietnam* **86 D6** 16 55N 107 8 E
Dong Hene, *Laos* **86 D5** 16 40N 105 18 E
Dong Hoi, *Vietnam* **86 D6** 17 29N 106 36 E
Dong Jiang →, *China* **77 F10** 23 6N 114 0 E
Dong Khe, *Vietnam* **86 A6** 22 26N 106 27 E
Dong Ujimqin Qi, *China* **74 B9** 45 32N 116 55 E
Dong Van, *Vietnam* **86 A5** 23 16N 105 22 E
Dong Xoai, *Vietnam* **87 G6** 11 32N 106 55 E
Donga, *Nigeria* **113 D7** 7 45N 10 2 E
Donga →, *Nigeria* **113 D7** 8 20N 9 58 E
Dong'an, *China* **77 D8** 26 23N 111 12 E
Dongara, *Australia* **125 E1** 29 14 S 114 57 E
Dongargarh, *India* **94 D5** 21 10N 80 40 E
Dongbei, *China* **67 E13** 45 0N 125 0 E
Dongchuan, *China* **76 D4** 26 8N 103 1 E
Donges, *France* **26 E4** 47 18N 2 4W
Dongfang, *China* **86 C7** 18 50N 108 33 E
Dongfeng, *China* **75 C13** 42 40N 125 34 E
Donggala, *Indonesia* **82 B1** 0 30 S 119 40 E
Donggan, *China* **76 F5** 23 22N 105 9 E
Donggou, *China* **75 E13** 39 52N 124 10 E
Dongguan, *China* **77 F9** 22 58N 113 44 E
Dongguang, *China* **74 F9** 37 50N 116 30 E
Donghai Dao, *China* **77 G8** 21 0N 110 15 E
Dongjingcheng, *China* **75 B15** 44 5N 129 10 E
Dongkou, *China* **77 D8** 27 6N 110 35 E
Donglan, *China* **76 E6** 24 30N 107 21 E
Dongliu, *China* **77 B11** 30 13N 116 55 E
Dongmen, *China* **76 F6** 22 20N 107 48 E
Dongning, *China* **75 B16** 44 2N 131 5 E
Dongnyi, *China* **76 C3** 28 3N 100 15 E
Dongo, *Angola* **115 E3** 14 36 S 15 48 E
Dongobe, *Dem. Rep. of the Congo* **114 B4** 4 35N 23 13 E
Dongola, *Sudan* **106 D3** 19 9N 30 22 E
Dongou, *Congo* **114 B3** 2 0N 18 5 E
Dongping, *China* **74 G9** 35 55N 116 20 E
Dongsha Dao, *China* **77 G11** 20 45N 116 43 E
Dongshan, *China* **77 F11** 23 43N 117 30 E
Dongsheng, *China* **74 E6** 39 50N 110 0 E
Dongtai, *China* **75 H11** 32 51N 120 21 E
Dongting Hu, *China* **77 C9** 29 18N 112 45 E
Dongtou, *China* **77 D13** 27 51N 121 10 E
Dongwe →, *Zambia* **115 E4** 13 59 S 23 53 E
Dongxiang, *China* **77 C11** 28 11N 116 34 E
Dongxing, *China* **76 G7** 21 34N 108 0 E
Dongyang, *China* **77 C13** 29 13N 120 15 E
Dongzhi, *China* **77 B11** 30 9N 117 0 E
Donington, C., *Australia* **128 C2** 34 45 S 136 0 E
Doniphan, *U.S.A.* **155 G9** 36 37N 90 50W
Donja Stubica, *Croatia* **45 C12** 45 59N 15 59 E
Donji Dušnik, *Serbia & M.* **50 C6** 43 12N 22 5 E
Donji Miholjac, *Croatia* **52 E3** 45 45N 18 10 E
Donji Milanovac, *Serbia & M.* **50 B6** 44 28N 22 6 E
Donji Vakuf, *Bos.-H.* **52 F2** 44 8N 17 24 E
Dønna, *Norway* **14 C15** 66 6N 12 30 E
Donna, *U.S.A.* **155 M5** 26 9N 98 4W
Donnacona, *Canada* **141 C5** 46 41N 71 41W
Donnelly's Crossing, *N.Z.* **130 B2** 35 42 S 173 38 E
Donnybrook, *Australia* **125 F2** 33 34 S 115 48 E
Donnybrook, *S. Africa* **117 D4** 29 59 S 29 48 E
Donora, *U.S.A.* **150 F5** 40 11N 79 52W
Donostia = Donostia-San Sebastián, *Spain* **40 B3** 43 17N 1 58W
Donostia-San Sebastián, *Spain* **40 B3** 43 17N 1 58W
Donovan, *U.S.A.* **157 D9** 40 53N 87 37W
Donque, *Angola* **115 F2** 15 28 S 14 6 E
Donskoy, *Russia* **58 F10** 53 55N 38 15 E
Donsol, *Phil.* **80 E4** 12 54N 123 36 E
Donzère, *France* **29 D8** 44 28N 4 43 E
Donzy, *France* **27 E10** 47 20N 3 6 E
Dookie, *Australia* **129 D6** 36 20 S 145 41 E
Doon →, *U.K.* **22 F4** 55 27N 4 39W
Doornik = Tournai, *Belgium* **24 D3** 50 35N 3 25 E
Dora, L., *Australia* **124 D3** 22 0 S 123 0 E
Dora Báltea →, *Italy* **44 C5** 45 11N 8 3 E
Dora Ripária →, *Italy* **44 C4** 45 5N 7 44 E
Doran L., *Canada* **143 A7** 61 13N 108 6W
Doraville, *U.S.A.* **152 B5** 33 54N 84 17W
Dorchester, *U.K.* **21 G5** 50 42N 2 27W
Dorchester, C., *Canada* **139 B12** 65 27N 77 27W
Dordabis, *Namibia* **116 C2** 22 52 S 17 38 E
Dordogne □, *France* **28 C4** 45 5N 0 40 E
Dordogne →, *France* **28 C3** 45 2N 0 36W
Dordrecht, *Neths.* **24 C4** 51 48N 4 39 E
Dordrecht, *S. Africa* **116 E4** 31 20 S 27 3 E
Dore →, *France* **28 C7** 45 50N 3 35 E
Dore, Mts., *France* **28 C6** 45 32N 2 50 E
Doré L., *Canada* **143 C7** 54 46N 107 17W
Doré Lake, *Canada* **143 C7** 54 38N 107 36W
Dores da Boa Esperança = Boa Esperança, *Brazil* **169 C5** 3 21N 61 23W
Dores do Indaiá, *Brazil* **171 E2** 19 27 S 45 36W
Dorfen, *Germany* **31 G8** 48 15N 12 8 E
Dorgali, *Italy* **46 B2** 40 17N 9 35 E
Dori, *Burkina Faso* **113 C4** 14 3N 0 2W
Doring →, *S. Africa* **116 E2** 31 54 S 18 39 E
Doringbos, *S. Africa* **116 E2** 31 59 S 19 16 E
Dorking, *U.K.* **21 F7** 51 14N 0 19W
Dormaa-Ahenkro, *Ghana* **112 D4** 7 15N 2 52W
Dormans, *France* **27 C10** 49 4N 3 38 E
Dormo, Ras, *Eritrea* **107 E5** 13 14N 42 35 E
Dornach, *Switz.* **32 B5** 47 29N 7 37 E
Dornakal, *India* **94 F5** 17 27N 80 10 E
Dornbirn, *Austria* **34 D2** 47 25N 9 45 E
Dornes, *France* **27 F10** 46 48N 3 18 E
Dorneşti, *Romania* **53 C11** 47 52N 26 1 E
Dornie, *U.K.* **22 D3** 57 17N 5 31W
Dornoch, *U.K.* **22 D4** 57 53N 4 2W
Dornoch Firth, *U.K.* **22 D4** 57 51N 4 4W
Dornogovĭ □, *Mongolia* **74 C6** 44 0N 110 0 E
Doro, *Mali* **113 B4** 16 9N 0 51W
Dorog, *Hungary* **52 C3** 47 42N 18 45 E
Dorogobuzh, *Russia* **58 E7** 54 50N 33 18 E
Dorohoi, *Romania* **53 C11** 47 56N 26 23 E
Döröö Nuur, *Mongolia* **68 B4** 48 0N 93 0 E
Dorpat = Tartu, *Estonia* **15 G22** 58 20N 26 44 E
Dorr, *Iran* **97 C6** 33 17N 50 38 E
Dorre I., *Australia* **125 E1** 25 13 S 113 12 E
Dorrigo, *Australia* **129 A10** 30 20 S 152 44 E
Dorrigo △, *Australia* **129 A10** 30 22 S 152 47 E
Dorris, *U.S.A.* **158 F3** 41 58N 121 55W
Dorset, *Canada* **150 A6** 45 14N 78 54W
Dorset, *U.S.A.* **150 E4** 41 40N 80 40W
Dorset □, *U.K.* **21 G5** 50 45N 2 26W
Dorsten, *Germany* **30 D2** 51 40N 6 58 E
Dortmund, *Germany* **30 D3** 51 30N 7 28 E
Dortmund-Ems-Kanal →, *Germany* **30 D3** 51 50N 7 26 E
Dörtyol, *Turkey* **100 D7** 36 50N 36 13 E
Dorum, *Germany* **30 B4** 53 41N 8 34 E
Doruma, *Dem. Rep. of the Congo* **118 B2** 4 42N 27 33 E
Dorüneh, *Iran* **97 C8** 35 10N 57 18 E
Dos Bahías, C., *Argentina* **176 B3** 44 58 S 65 32W
Dos Hermanas, *Spain* **43 H5** 37 16N 5 55W
Dos Palos, *U.S.A.* **160 J6** 36 59N 120 37W
Döşemealtı, *Turkey* **49 D12** 37 4N 30 36 E
Dosso, *Niger* **113 C5** 13 0N 3 13 E
Dosso △, *Niger* **113 C5** 12 36N 2 36 E
Dostuk, *Kyrgyzstan* **65 C7** 41 20N 75 30 E
Dot Lake, *U.S.A.* **144 E11** 63 40N 144 4W
Dothan, *U.S.A.* **152 D4** 31 13N 85 24W
Döttingen, *Switz.* **32 A6** 47 34N 8 15 E
Doty, *U.S.A.* **160 D3** 46 38N 123 17W
Douai, *France* **27 B10** 50 21N 3 4 E
Douako, *Guinea* **112 D2** 9 45N 10 8W
Douala, *Cameroon* **113 E6** 4 0N 9 45 E
Douala-Édéa △, *Cameroon* **114 B1** 3 20N 9 41 E
Douaouir, *Mali* **110 D4** 20 45N 3 0W
Douarnenez, *France* **26 D2** 48 6N 4 21W
Doubabougou, *Mali* **112 C3** 14 13N 7 59W
Double Cone, *N.Z.* **131 F3** 45 4 S 168 49 E
Double Island Pt., *Australia* **127 D5** 25 56 S 153 11 E
Double Mountain Fork →, *U.S.A.* **155 J4** 33 16N 100 0W
Doubrava →, *Czech Rep.* **34 A8** 50 2N 15 20 E
Doubs □, *France* **27 E13** 47 10N 6 20 E
Doubs →, *France* **27 F12** 46 53N 5 1 E
Doubtful Sd., *N.Z.* **131 F1** 45 20 S 166 49 E
Doubtless B., *N.Z.* **130 A2** 34 55 S 173 26 E
Doudeville, *France* **26 C7** 49 43N 0 47 E
Doué-la-Fontaine, *France* **26 E6** 47 11N 0 16W
Douentza, *Mali* **112 C4** 14 58N 2 48W
Douentza △, *Mali* **112 B4** 15 40N 2 25W
Dougga, *Tunisia* **108 A1** 36 30N 8 55 E
Doughboy B., *N.Z.* **131 H2** 47 2 S 167 40 E
Douglas, *I. of Man* **20 C3** 54 10N 4 28W
Douglas, *S. Africa* **116 D3** 29 4 S 23 46 E
Douglas, *Alaska, U.S.A.* **144 G14** 58 17N 134 24W
Douglas, *Ariz., U.S.A.* **159 L9** 31 21N 109 33W
Douglas, *Ga., U.S.A.* **152 D7** 31 31N 82 51W
Douglas, *Mich., U.S.A.* **157 B10** 42 39N 86 14W
Douglas, *Wyo., U.S.A.* **154 D2** 42 45N 105 24W
Douglas Apsley △, *Australia* **127 G4** 41 45 S 148 11 E
Douglas C., *U.S.A.* **144 G9** 58 51N 153 15W
Douglas Chan., *Canada* **142 C3** 53 40N 129 20W
Douglas Pt., *Canada* **150 B3** 44 19N 81 37W
Douglasville, *U.S.A.* **152 B5** 33 45N 84 45W
Douirat, *Morocco* **110 B4** 33 2N 4 11W
Doukáton, Ákra, *Greece* **39 B2** 38 34N 20 33 E
Doukoula, *Cameroon* **109 F2** 10 10N 15 0 E
Doukoula, *Cameroon* **114 A2** 10 0N 15 0 E
Doulevant-le-Château, *France* **27 D11** 48 23N 4 55 E
Doullens, *France* **27 B9** 50 10N 2 20 E
Doumé, *Cameroon* **114 B2** 4 15N 13 25 E
Doumen, *China* **77 F9** 22 10N 113 18 E
Douna, *Mali* **112 C3** 13 13N 6 0W
Dounguila, *Congo* **114 C2** 2 53 S 11 58 E
Dounreay, *U.K.* **22 C5** 58 35N 3 44W
Dourada, Serra, *Brazil* **171 D2** 13 10 S 48 45W
Dourados, *Brazil* **175 A5** 22 9 S 54 50W
Dourados →, *Brazil* **175 A5** 21 58 S 54 18W
Dourados, Serra dos, *Brazil* **175 A5** 23 30 S 53 30W
Dourbali, *Chad* **109 F3** 11 49N 15 52 E
Dourdan, *France* **27 D9** 48 30N 2 1 E
Douro →, *Europe* **42 D2** 41 8N 8 40W
Douvaine, *France* **27 F13** 46 19N 6 16 E
Douvres-la-Délivrande, *France* **26 C6** 49 17N 0 23W
Douz, *Tunisia* **108 B1** 33 25N 9 0 E
Douze →, *France* **28 E3** 43 54N 0 30W
Dove →, *U.K.* **20 E6** 52 51N 1 36W
Dove Creek, *U.S.A.* **159 H9** 37 46N 108 54W
Dover, *Australia* **127 G4** 43 18 S 147 2 E
Dover, *U.K.* **21 F9** 51 7N 1 19 E
Dover, *Del., U.S.A.* **148 F8** 39 10N 75 32W
Dover, *Ky., U.S.A.* **157 F13** 38 43N 83 52W
Dover, *N.H., U.S.A.* **151 C14** 43 12N 70 56W
Dover, *N.J., U.S.A.* **151 F10** 40 53N 74 34W
Dover, *Ohio, U.S.A.* **150 F3** 40 32N 81 29W
Dover, Pt., *Australia* **125 F4** 32 32 S 125 32 E
Dover, Str. of, *Europe* **21 G9** 51 0N 1 30 E
Dover-Foxcroft, *U.S.A.* **149 C11** 45 11N 69 13W
Dover Plains, *U.S.A.* **151 E11** 41 43N 73 35W
Dovey = Dyfi →, *U.K.* **21 E3** 52 32N 4 3W
Dovhe, *Ukraine* **53 B8** 48 22N 23 17 E
Dovlen = Devin, *Bulgaria* **51 E8** 41 44N 24 24 E
Dovre, *Norway* **18 C6** 61 58N 9 15 E
Dovrefjell, *Norway* **18 B6** 62 15N 9 33 E
Dovrefjell △, *Norway* **18 B6** 62 20N 9 25 E
Dow Rūd, *Iran* **97 C6** 33 28N 49 4 E
Dowa, *Malawi* **119 E3** 13 38 S 33 58 E
Dowagiac, *U.S.A.* **157 C10** 41 59N 86 6W
Dowerin, *Australia* **125 F2** 31 12 S 117 2 E
Dowgha'i, *Iran* **97 B8** 36 54N 58 32 E
Dowlat Yār, *Afghan.* **91 B2** 34 30N 65 45 E
Dowlatābād, *Farāh, Afghan.* **91 B1** 32 47N 62 40 E
Dowlatābād, *Fāryāb, Afghan.* **65 E2** 36 26N 64 55 E
Dowlatābād, *Iran* **97 D8** 28 20N 56 40 E
Dowling Park, *U.S.A.* **152 E6** 30 15N 83 15W
Down □, *U.K.* **23 B5** 54 23N 6 2W
Downers Grove, *U.S.A.* **157 C8** 41 48N 88 1W
Downey, *Calif., U.S.A.* **161 M8** 33 56N 118 7W
Downey, *Idaho, U.S.A.* **158 E7** 42 26N 112 7W
Downham Market, *U.K.* **21 E8** 52 37N 0 23 E
Downieville, *U.S.A.* **160 F6** 39 34N 120 50W
Downing, *U.S.A.* **156 D4** 40 29N 92 22W
Downpatrick, *U.K.* **23 B6** 54 20N 5 43W
Downpatrick Hd., *Ireland* **23 B2** 54 20N 9 21W
Downsville, *U.S.A.* **151 D10** 42 5N 74 50W
Downton, Mt., *Canada* **142 C4** 52 42N 124 52W
Dowsārī, *Iran* **97 D8** 28 25N 57 59 E
Dowshī, *Afghan.* **91 B3** 35 35N 68 43 E
Doyle, *U.S.A.* **160 E6** 40 2N 120 6W
Doylestown, *U.S.A.* **151 F9** 40 21N 75 10W
Dōzen, *Japan* **72 A5** 36 5N 133 5 E
Dozois, Rés., *Canada* **140 C4** 47 30N 77 5W
Dra Khel, *Pakistan* **92 F2** 27 58N 66 45 E
Drâa, C., *Morocco* **110 C2** 28 47N 11 0W
Drâa, Hamada du, *Algeria* **110 C3** 28 0N 7 0W
Drâa, Oued →, *Morocco* **110 C2** 28 40N 11 10W
Drac →, *France* **29 C9** 45 12N 5 42 E
Dračevo, *Macedonia* **50 E5** 41 56N 21 31 E
Drachten, *Neths.* **24 A6** 53 7N 6 5 E
Drăgăneşti, *Moldova* **53 C13** 47 43N 28 15 E
Drăgăneşti-Olt, *Romania* **53 F9** 44 9N 24 32 E
Drăgăneşti-Vlaşca, *Romania* **53 F10** 44 5N 25 33 E
Dragaš, *Serbia & M.* **50 D4** 42 5N 20 41 E
Drăgăşani, *Romania* **53 F9** 44 39N 24 17 E
Dragichyn, *Belarus* **59 F3** 52 15N 25 8 E
Dragocvet, *Serbia & M.* **50 C5** 43 58N 21 15 E
Dragon's Mouth = Boca de Drago, *Venezuela* **169 F9** 11 0N 61 50W
Dragovishtitsa, *Bulgaria* **50 D6** 42 22N 22 39 E
Draguignan, *France* **29 E10** 43 32N 6 27 E
Drahove, *Ukraine* **53 B8** 48 14N 23 33 E
Drain, *U.S.A.* **158 E2** 43 40N 123 19W
Drake, *U.S.A.* **154 B4** 47 55N 100 23W
Drake Passage, *S. Ocean* **7 B17** 58 0 S 68 0W
Drakensberg, *S. Africa* **117 D4** 31 0 S 28 0 E
Dráma, *Greece* **51 E8** 41 9N 24 10 E
Dráma □, *Greece* **51 E8** 41 20N 24 0 E
Dramburg = Drawsko Pomorskie, *Poland* **54 E2** 53 35N 15 50 E
Drammen, *Norway* **18 E7** 59 42N 10 12 E
Drangajökull, *Iceland* **11 A4** 66 9N 22 15W
Drangedal, *Norway* **18 E6** 59 6N 9 3 E
Drangsnes, *Iceland* **11 B5** 65 41N 21 27W
Dranov, Ostrov, *Romania* **53 F14** 44 55N 29 30 E
Dras, *India* **93 B6** 34 25N 75 48 E
Drau = Drava →, *Croatia* **52 E3** 45 33N 18 55 E
Drava →, *Croatia* **52 E3** 45 33N 18 55 E
Dravograd, *Slovenia* **45 B12** 46 36N 15 5 E
Drawa →, *Poland* **55 F2** 52 52N 15 59 E
Drawieński △, *Poland* **55 E2** 53 6N 15 58 E
Drawno, *Poland* **55 E2** 53 13N 15 46 E
Drawsko Pomorskie, *Poland* **54 E2** 53 35N 15 50 E
Drayton Plains, *U.S.A.* **157 B13** 42 42N 83 23W
Drayton Valley, *Canada* **142 C6** 53 12N 114 58W
Dreieich, *Germany* **31 E4** 50 1N 8 41 E
Dreikikir, *Papua N. G.* **132 B2** 3 35 S 142 46 E
Dren, *Serbia & M.* **50 C4** 43 8N 20 46 E
Drenthe □, *Neths.* **24 B6** 52 52N 6 40 E
Drepanum, C., *Cyprus* **39 F8** 34 54N 32 19 E
Dresden, *Canada* **150 D2** 42 35N 82 11W
Dresden, *Germany* **30 D9** 51 3N 13 44 E
Dresden, *U.S.A.* **150 D7** 42 41N 76 57W
Dreux, *France* **26 D8** 48 44N 1 23 E
Drevsjø, *Norway* **18 C9** 61 53N 12 1 E
Drexel, *U.S.A.* **157 E12** 39 45N 84 18W
Drezdenko, *Poland* **55 F2** 52 50N 15 49 E
Driesen = Drezdenko, *Poland* **55 F2** 52 50N 15 49 E
Driffield, *U.K.* **20 C7** 54 0N 0 26W
Driftwood, *U.S.A.* **150 E6** 41 20N 78 8W
Driggs, *U.S.A.* **158 E8** 43 44N 111 6W
Drin →, *Albania* **50 D3** 42 1N 19 38 E
Drin i Zi →, *Albania* **50 E4** 41 37N 20 28 E
Drina →, *Bos.-H.* **50 B3** 44 53N 19 21 E
Drincea →, *Romania* **52 F7** 44 20N 22 55 E

Drinjača →, Bos.-H. 52 F4 44 15N 19 8 E
Drissa = Vyerkhnyadzvinsk, Belarus 58 E4 55 45N 27 58 E
Driva →, Norway 18 B6 62 41N 9 31 E
Drivstua, Norway 18 B6 62 26N 9 47 E
Drniš, Croatia 45 E13 43 51N 16 10 E
Drøbak, Norway 18 E7 59 39N 10 39 E
Drobeta-Turnu Severin, Romania 52 F7 44 39N 22 41 E
Drobin, Poland 55 F6 52 42N 19 58 E
Drochia, Moldova 53 B12 48 2N 27 48 E
Drogheda, Ireland 23 C5 53 43N 6 22W
Drogichin = Dragichyn, Belarus 59 F3 52 15N 25 8 E
Drogobych = Drohobych, Ukraine 55 J10 49 20N 23 30 E
Drohiczyn, Poland 55 F9 52 24N 22 39 E
Drohobych, Ukraine 55 J10 49 20N 23 30 E
Droichead Atha = Drogheda, Ireland 23 C5 53 43N 6 22W
Droichead Nua, Ireland 23 C5 53 11N 6 48W
Droitwich, U.K. 21 E5 52 16N 2 8W
Drôme □, France 29 D9 44 38N 5 15 E
Drôme →, France 29 D8 44 46N 4 46 E
Dromedary, C., Australia 129 D9 36 17 S 150 10 E
Drömling ⌂, Germany 30 C7 52 29N 11 5 E
Dromore, U.K. 23 B4 54 31N 7 28W
Dromore West, Ireland 23 B3 54 15N 8 52W
Dronero, Italy 44 D4 44 28N 7 22 E
Dronfield, U.K. 20 D6 53 19N 1 27W
Dronne →, France 28 C3 45 2N 0 9W
Dronning Ingrid Land, Greenland 10 D5 66 25N 52 5W
Dronning Maud Land, Antarctica 7 D3 72 30 S 12 0 E
Dronninglund, Denmark 17 G4 57 10N 10 19 E
Dronten, Neths. 24 B5 52 32N 5 43 E
Dropt →, France 28 D3 44 35N 0 6W
Drosendorf, Austria 34 C8 48 52N 15 37 E
Drosh, Pakistan 91 B3 35 33N 71 48 E
Droué, France 26 D8 48 3N 1 6 E
Drouin, Australia 129 E6 38 10 S 145 53 E
Drueulu, N. Cal. 133 K5 20 56 S 167 5 E
Druk Yul = Bhutan ■, Asia 90 B3 27 25N 90 30 E
Drumbo, Canada 150 C4 43 16N 80 35W
Drumheller, Canada 142 C6 51 25N 112 40W
Drummond, U.S.A. 158 C7 46 40N 113 9W
Drummond I., U.S.A. 148 C4 46 1N 83 39W
Drummond Pt., Australia 127 E2 34 9 S 135 16 E
Drummond Ra., Australia 126 C4 23 45 S 147 10 E
Drummondville, Canada 140 C5 45 55N 72 25W
Drumright, U.S.A. 155 H6 35 59N 96 36W
Druskeniki = Druskininkai, Lithuania 15 J20 54 3N 23 58 E
Druskininkai, Lithuania 15 J20 54 3N 23 58 E
Drut →, Belarus 59 F6 53 8N 30 5 E
Druya, Belarus 58 E4 55 45N 27 28 E
Druzhba, Bulgaria 51 C12 43 15N 28 1 E
Druzhina, Russia 67 C15 68 14N 145 18 E
Drvar, Bos.-H. 45 D13 44 21N 16 23 E
Drvenik, Croatia 45 E13 43 27N 16 3 E
Drwęca →, Poland 55 E5 53 0N 18 42 E
Dry Harbour Mts., Jamaica 164 a 18 19N 77 24W
Dry Tortugas, U.S.A. 164 B3 24 38N 82 55W
Dryanovo, Bulgaria 51 D9 42 59N 25 28 E
Dryden, Canada 143 D10 49 47N 92 50W
Dryden, U.S.A. 151 D8 42 30N 76 18W
Drygalski I., Antarctica 7 C7 66 0 S 92 0 E
Drysdale →, Australia 124 B4 13 59 S 126 51 E
Drysdale I., Australia 126 A2 11 41 S 136 0 E
Drysdale River △, Australia 124 B4 14 56 S 127 2 E
Drzewica, Poland 55 G7 51 27N 20 29 E
Drzewiczka →, Poland 55 G7 51 36N 20 36 E
Dschang, Cameroon 113 D7 5 32N 10 3 E
Du Gué →, Canada 140 A5 57 21N 70 45W
Du He, China 77 A8 32 48N 110 40 E
Du Quoin, U.S.A. 156 G7 38 1N 89 14W
Du'an, China 76 F7 23 59N 108 3 E
Duanesburg, U.S.A. 151 D10 42 45N 74 11W
Duaringa, Australia 126 C4 23 42 S 149 42 E
Duarte, Pico, Dom. Rep. 165 D5 19 2N 70 59W
Ḑubā, Si. Arabia 96 E2 27 10N 35 40 E
Dubai = Dubayy, U.A.E. 97 E7 25 18N 55 20 E
Dubăsari, Moldova 53 C14 47 15N 29 10 E
Dubăsari Vdkhr., Moldova 53 C13 47 30N 29 0 E
Dubawnt →, Canada 143 A8 64 33N 100 6W
Dubawnt L., Canada 143 A8 63 8N 101 28W
Dubayy, U.A.E. 97 E7 25 18N 55 20 E
Dubbo, Australia 129 B8 32 11 S 148 35 E
Dubele, Dem. Rep. of the Congo 118 B2 2 56N 29 35 E
Dübendorf, Switz. 33 B7 47 24N 8 37 E
Dubica, Croatia 45 C13 45 11N 16 48 E
Dublin, Ireland 23 C5 53 21N 6 15W
Dublin, Ga., U.S.A. 152 C7 32 32N 82 54W
Dublin, Tex., U.S.A. 155 J5 32 5N 98 21W
Dublin □, Ireland 23 C5 53 24N 6 20W
Dublin ✈ (DUB), Ireland 23 C5 53 26N 6 15W
Dubna, Russia 58 D9 56 44N 37 10 E
Dubnica nad Váhom, Slovak Rep. 35 C11 48 58N 18 11 E
Dubno, Ukraine 59 G3 50 25N 25 45 E
Dubois, Idaho, U.S.A. 158 D7 44 10N 112 14W
Dubois, Ind., U.S.A. 157 F10 38 27N 86 48W
Dubois, Pa., U.S.A. 150 E6 41 8N 78 46W
Dubossary = Dubăsari, Moldova 53 C14 47 15N 29 10 E
Dubossary Vdkhr. = Dubăsari Vdkhr., Moldova 53 C13 47 30N 29 0 E
Dubove, Ukraine 53 B8 48 10N 23 53 E
Dubovka, Russia 61 F7 49 5N 44 50 E
Dubovskoye, Russia 61 G6 47 28N 42 46 E
Dubrajpur, India 93 H12 23 48N 87 25 E
Dubréka, Guinea 112 D2 9 46N 13 31W
Dubrovitsa = Dubrovytsya, Ukraine 59 G4 51 31N 26 35 E
Dubrovnik, Croatia 50 D2 42 39N 18 6 E
Dubrovytsya, Ukraine 59 G4 51 31N 26 35 E
Dubulu, Dem. Rep. of the Congo 114 B4 4 18N 20 16 E
Dubuque, U.S.A. 156 B6 42 30N 90 41W
Dubysa →, Lithuania 54 C10 55 5N 23 26 E
Duchang, China 77 C11 29 18N 116 12 E
Duchesne, U.S.A. 158 F8 40 10N 110 24W
Duchess, Australia 126 C2 21 20 S 139 50 E
Ducie I., Pac. Oc. 135 K15 24 40 S 124 48W
Duck →, U.S.A. 149 G2 36 2N 87 52W
Duck Cr. →, Australia 124 D2 22 37 S 116 53 E
Duck Lake, Canada 143 C7 52 50N 106 16W
Duck Mountain ⌂, Canada 143 C8 51 45N 101 0W
Duckwall, Mt., U.S.A. 160 H6 37 58N 120 7W
Duda →, Colombia 168 C3 2 34N 74 3W
Duderstadt, Germany 30 D6 51 31N 10 15 E
Dudhnai, India 90 C3 25 59N 90 47 E
Düdingen, Switz. 32 C4 46 52N 7 12 E
Dudinka, Russia 67 C9 69 30N 86 13 E
Dudley, U.K. 21 E5 52 31N 2 5W
Dudley, U.S.A. 152 C6 32 32N 83 5W
Dudna →, India 94 E3 19 17N 76 54 E
Dudo, Somali Rep. 120 C4 9 20N 50 12 E
Dudub, Ethiopia 120 C3 6 55N 46 43 E
Dudune, Î., N. Cal. 133 U21 21 21 S 167 46 E
Dudwa, India 93 E9 28 30N 80 41 E
Dudwa △, India 93 E9 28 30N 80 40 E
Duékoué, Ivory C. 112 D3 6 40N 7 15W
Duenas, Phil. 81 F4 11 4N 122 37 E
Dueñas, Spain 42 D6 41 52N 4 33W
Dueré, Brazil 171 D2 11 20 S 49 17W
Duero = Douro →, Europe 42 D2 41 8N 8 40W
Dufftown, U.K. 22 D5 57 27N 3 8W
Dufourspitz, Switz. 32 E5 45 56N 7 52 E
Dugger, U.S.A. 157 E9 39 4N 87 18W
Dugi Otok, Croatia 45 D11 44 0N 15 3 E
Dugiuma, Somali Rep. 120 D2 1 15N 42 34 E
Dugo Selo, Croatia 45 C13 45 51N 16 18 E
Duida-Marahuaca △, Venezuela 168 C4 3 33N 65 33W
Duifken Pt., Australia 126 A3 12 33 S 141 38 E
Duisburg, Germany 30 D2 51 26N 6 45 E
Duitama, Colombia 168 B3 5 50N 73 2W
Duiwelskloof, S. Africa 117 C5 23 42 S 30 10 E
Dujiangyan, China 76 B4 31 2N 103 38 E
Duk Fadiat, Sudan 107 F3 7 45N 31 25 E
Duk Faiwil, Sudan 107 F3 7 30N 31 29 E
Dukat, Albania 50 F3 40 16N 19 32 E
Dūkdamīn, Iran 97 C8 35 59N 57 43 E
Dukelský Průsmyk, Slovak Rep. 35 B14 49 25N 21 42 E
Dukhān, Qatar 97 E6 25 25N 50 50 E
Dukhovshchina, Russia 58 E7 55 15N 32 27 E
Duki, Pakistan 91 C3 30 14N 68 25 E
Dukla, Poland 55 J8 49 30N 21 35 E
Duku, Bauchi, Nigeria 113 C7 10 43N 10 43 E
Duku, Sokoto, Nigeria 113 C5 11 11N 4 55 E
Dula, Dem. Rep. of the Congo 114 B4 4 40N 20 21 E
Dulag, Phil. 81 F5 10 57N 125 2 E
Dulawan = Datu Piang, Phil. 81 H5 7 2N 124 30 E
Dulce, U.S.A. 159 H10 36 56N 107 0W
Dulce →, Argentina 174 C3 30 32 S 62 33W
Dulce, G., Costa Rica 164 E3 8 40N 83 20W
Dulf, Iraq 96 C5 35 7N 45 51 E
Dŭlgopol, Bulgaria 51 C11 43 3N 27 22 E
Duliu, China 74 E9 39 2N 116 55 E
Dullabchara, India 90 C4 24 30N 92 26 E
Dullewala, Pakistan 92 D4 31 50N 71 25 E
Dullstroom, S. Africa 117 D5 25 27 S 30 7 E
Dülmen, Germany 30 D3 51 49N 7 17 E
Dulovo, Bulgaria 51 C11 43 48N 27 9 E
Dulpetorpet, Norway 18 D9 60 34N 12 19 E
Dulq Maghār, Syria 101 D8 36 22N 38 39 E
Duluth, Ga., U.S.A. 152 A5 34 0N 84 9W
Duluth, Minn., U.S.A. 154 B8 46 47N 92 6W
Dum Dum, India 93 H13 22 39N 88 33 E
Dum Duma, India 90 B5 27 40N 95 40 E
Dūmā, Syria 103 B5 33 34N 36 24 E
Dumaguete, Phil. 81 G4 9 17N 123 15 E
Dumai, Indonesia 84 B2 1 35N 101 28 E
Dumalinao, Phil. 81 H4 7 49N 123 23 E
Dumanguilas Bay, Phil. 81 H4 7 34N 123 4 E
Dumanjug, Phil. 81 F4 10 4N 123 26 E
Dumaran = Araceli, Phil. 81 F2 10 33N 119 59 E
Dumaran, Phil. 81 F2 10 33N 119 50 E
Dumaran I., Phil. 81 F2 10 33N 119 51 E
Dumarao, Phil. 81 F4 11 16N 122 41 E
Dumas, Ark., U.S.A. 155 J9 33 53N 91 29W
Dumas, Tex., U.S.A. 155 H4 35 52N 101 58W
Ḑumayr, Syria 103 B5 33 39N 36 42 E
Dumbarton, U.K. 22 F4 55 57N 4 33W
Dumbéa, N. Cal. 133 V20 22 10 S 166 27 E
Ďumbier, Slovak Rep. 35 C12 48 56N 19 38 E
Dumbleyung, Australia 125 F2 33 17 S 117 42 E
Dumbo, Angola 115 E3 14 6 S 17 24 E
Dumboa, Nigeria 113 C7 11 15N 12 55 E
Dumbrăveni, Romania 53 D9 46 14N 24 34 E
Dumfries, U.K. 22 F5 55 4N 3 37W
Dumfries & Galloway □, U.K. 22 F5 55 9N 3 58W
Dumingag, Phil. 81 G4 8 20N 123 20 E
Dumitreşti, Romania 53 E11 45 33N 26 55 E
Dumka, India 93 G12 24 12N 87 15 E
Dumlupınar, Turkey 49 C12 38 53N 30 0 E
Dümmer, Germany 30 C4 52 31N 8 20 E
Dümmer ⌂, Germany 30 C4 52 31N 8 21 E
Dumoine →, Canada 140 C4 46 13N 77 51W
Dumoine, L., Canada 140 C4 46 55N 77 55W
Dumont d'Urville, Antarctica 7 C10 67 0 S 110 0 E
Dumoulin Is., Papua N. G. 132 F6 10 54 S 150 46 E
Dumpu, Papua N. G. 132 C3 5 53 S 145 44 E
Dumraon, India 93 G11 25 33N 84 8 E
Dumyât, Egypt 106 H7 31 24N 31 48 E
Dumyât, Masabb, Egypt 106 H7 31 28N 31 51 E
Dún Dealgan = Dundalk, Ireland 23 B5 54 1N 6 24W
Dún Laoghaire, Ireland 23 C5 53 17N 6 8W
Dun-le-Palestel, France 27 F8 46 18N 1 39 E
Dun-sur-Auron, France 27 F9 46 53N 2 33 E
Dun-sur-Meuse, France 27 C12 49 23N 5 11 E
Duna = Dunărea →, Europe 53 E14 45 20N 29 40 E
Duna →, Hungary 52 E3 45 51N 18 48 E
Duna-Drava △, Hungary 52 D3 46 15N 18 50 E
Duna-völgyi-főcsatorna, Hungary 52 D4 46 40N 19 14 E
Dünaburg = Daugavpils, Latvia 15 J22 55 53N 26 32 E
Dunaföldvár, Hungary 52 D3 46 50N 18 57 E
Dunagiri, India 93 D8 30 31N 79 52 E
Dunaj = Dunărea →, Europe 53 E14 45 20N 29 40 E
Dunaj →, Slovak Rep. 35 D11 47 50N 18 50 E
Dunajec →, Poland 55 H7 50 15N 20 44 E
Dunajská Streda, Slovak Rep. 35 C10 48 0N 17 37 E
Dunakeszi, Hungary 52 C4 47 37N 19 8 E
Dunapataj, Hungary 52 D4 46 39N 19 4 E
Dunărea →, Europe 53 E14 45 20N 29 40 E
Dunaszekcső, Hungary 52 D3 46 6N 18 45 E
Dunaújváros, Hungary 52 D3 46 58N 18 57 E
Dunav = Dunărea →, Europe 53 E14 45 20N 29 40 E
Dunavaţu de Jos, Romania 53 F14 44 59N 29 13 E
Dunavtsi, Bulgaria 50 C6 43 57N 22 53 E
Dunay, Russia 70 C6 42 52N 132 22 E
Dunayivtsi, Ukraine 53 B11 48 54N 26 50 E
Dunback, N.Z. 131 F5 45 23 S 170 36 E
Dunbar, U.K. 22 E6 56 0N 2 31W
Dunblane, U.K. 22 E5 56 11N 3 58W
Duncan, Canada 142 D4 48 45N 123 40W
Duncan, Ariz., U.S.A. 159 K9 32 43N 109 6W
Duncan, Okla., U.S.A. 155 H6 34 30N 97 57W
Duncan, L., Canada 140 B4 53 29N 77 58W
Duncan L., Canada 142 A6 62 51N 113 58W
Duncan Passage, India 95 J11 11 0N 92 0 E
Duncan Town, Bahamas 164 B4 22 15N 75 45W
Duncannon, U.S.A. 150 F7 40 23N 77 2W
Duncansby Head, U.K. 22 C5 58 38N 3 1W
Duncansville, U.S.A. 150 F6 40 25N 78 26W
Dundaga, Latvia 54 A9 57 31N 22 21 E
Dundalk, Canada 150 B4 44 10N 80 24W
Dundalk, Ireland 23 B5 54 1N 6 24W
Dundalk, U.S.A. 148 F7 39 16N 76 32W
Dundalk Bay, Ireland 23 C5 53 55N 6 15W
Dundas = Uummannaq, Greenland 10 B4 77 0N 69 0W
Dundas = Uummannaq, Greenland 6 B5 70 58N 52 0W
Dundas, Canada 150 C5 43 17N 79 59W
Dundas, L., Australia 125 F3 32 35 S 121 50 E
Dundas I., Canada 142 C2 54 30N 130 50W
Dundas Str., Australia 124 B5 11 15 S 131 35 E
Dundee, S. Africa 117 D5 28 11 S 30 15 E
Dundee, U.K. 22 E6 56 28N 2 59W
Dundee, Mich., U.S.A. 157 C13 41 57N 83 40W
Dundee, N.Y., U.S.A. 150 D8 42 32N 76 59W
Dundee City □, U.K. 22 E6 56 30N 2 58W
Dundgovĭ □, Mongolia 74 B4 45 10N 106 0 E
Dundrum, U.K. 23 B6 54 16N 5 52W
Dundrum B., U.K. 23 B6 54 13N 5 47W
Dunedin, N.Z. 131 F5 45 50 S 170 33 E
Dunedin, U.S.A. 153 G7 28 1N 82 47W
Dunedoo, Australia 129 A8 32 0 S 149 25 E
Dunfermline, U.K. 22 E5 56 5N 3 27W
Dungannon, Canada 150 C3 43 51N 81 36W
Dungannon, U.K. 23 B5 54 31N 6 46W
Dungarpur, India 92 H5 23 52N 73 45 E
Dungarvan, Ireland 23 D4 52 5N 7 37W
Dungarvan Harbour, Ireland 23 D4 52 4N 7 35W
Dungeness, U.K. 21 G8 50 54N 0 59 E
Dungo, L. do, Angola 116 B2 17 15 S 19 0 E
Dungog, Australia 129 B9 32 22 S 151 46 E
Dungu, Dem. Rep. of the Congo 118 B2 3 40N 28 32 E
Dungun, Malaysia 87 K4 4 45N 103 25 E
Dungunâb, Sudan 106 C4 21 10N 37 9 E
Dungunâb, Khalîg, Sudan 106 C4 21 5N 37 12 E
Dunhua, China 75 C15 43 20N 128 14 E
Dunhuang, China 68 B4 40 8N 94 36 E
Dunk I., Australia 126 B4 17 59 S 146 29 E
Dunkassa, Benin 113 C5 10 21N 3 10 E
Dunkeld, Queens., Australia 127 E4 33 25 S 149 29 E
Dunkeld, Vic., Australia 128 D5 37 40 S 142 22 E
Dunkeld, U.K. 22 E5 56 34N 3 35W
Dunkerque, France 27 A9 51 2N 2 20 E
Dunkery Beacon, U.K. 21 F4 51 9N 3 36W
Dunkirk = Dunkerque, France 27 A9 51 2N 2 20 E
Dunkirk, U.S.A. 150 D5 42 29N 79 20W
Dunkuj, Sudan 107 E3 12 50N 32 49 E
Dunkwa, Central, Ghana 112 D4 6 0N 1 47W
Dunkwa, Central, Ghana 113 D4 5 30N 1 0W
Dúnleary = Dún Laoghaire, Ireland 23 C5 53 17N 6 8W
Dunleer, Ireland 23 C5 53 50N 6 24W
Dunmanus B., Ireland 23 E2 51 31N 9 50W
Dunmanway, Ireland 23 E2 51 43N 9 6W
Dunmara, Australia 126 B1 16 42 S 133 25 E
Dunmore, U.S.A. 151 E9 41 25N 75 38W
Dunmore Hd., Ireland 23 D1 52 10N 10 35W
Dunmore Town, Bahamas 164 A4 25 30N 76 39W
Dunn, U.S.A. 149 H6 35 19N 78 37W
Dunnellon, U.S.A. 153 F7 29 3N 82 28W
Dunnet Hd., U.K. 22 C5 58 40N 3 21W
Dunning, U.S.A. 154 E4 41 50N 100 6W
Dunnville, Canada 150 D5 42 54N 79 36W
Dunolly, Australia 128 D5 36 51 S 143 44 E
Dunoon, U.K. 22 F4 55 57N 4 56W
Dunphy, U.S.A. 158 F5 40 42N 116 31W
Dunqul, Egypt 106 C3 23 26N 31 37 E
Duns, U.K. 22 F6 55 47N 2 20W
Dunseith, U.S.A. 154 A4 48 50N 100 3W
Dunsmuir, U.S.A. 158 F2 41 13N 122 16W
Dunstable, U.K. 21 F7 51 53N 0 32W
Dunstan Mts., N.Z. 131 E4 44 53 S 169 35 E
Dunster, Canada 142 C5 53 8N 119 50W
Duntroon, N.Z. 131 E5 44 51 S 170 40 E
Dunvegan, U.K. 22 D2 57 27N 6 35W
Dunvegan L., Canada 143 A7 60 8N 107 10W
Duolun, China 74 C9 42 12N 116 28 E
Duong Dong, Vietnam 87 G4 10 13N 103 58 E
Dupax, Phil. 80 C3 16 17N 121 5 E
Dupree, U.S.A. 154 C4 45 4N 101 35W
Dupuyer, U.S.A. 158 B7 48 13N 112 30W
Duqm, Oman 99 C7 19 39N 57 42 E
Duque de Caxias, Brazil 171 F3 22 45 S 43 19W
Duque de York, I., Chile 176 D1 50 37 S 75 25W
Durack →, Australia 124 C4 15 33 S 127 52 E
Durack Ra., Australia 124 C4 16 50 S 127 40 E
Durağan, Turkey 100 B6 41 25N 35 3 E
Durak, Turkey 49 B10 39 42N 28 17 E
Đurakovac, Serbia & M. 50 D4 42 43N 20 29 E
Durance →, France 29 E8 43 55N 4 45 E
Durand, Ga., U.S.A. 152 C5 32 54N 84 51W
Durand, Ill., U.S.A. 156 B7 42 26N 89 20W
Durand, Mich., U.S.A. 157 B13 42 55N 83 59W
Durand, Wis., U.S.A. 154 C9 44 38N 91 58W
Durango, Mexico 162 C4 24 3N 104 39W
Durango, U.S.A. 159 H10 37 16N 107 53W
Durango □, Mexico 162 C4 25 0N 105 0W
Durankulak, Bulgaria 51 C12 43 41N 28 32 E
Durant, Iowa, U.S.A. 156 C6 41 36N 90 54W
Durant, Miss., U.S.A. 155 J10 33 4N 89 51W
Durant, Okla., U.S.A. 155 J6 33 59N 96 25W
Duratón →, Spain 42 D6 41 37N 4 7W
Durazno, Uruguay 174 C4 33 25 S 56 31W
Durazzo = Durrës, Albania 50 E3 41 19N 19 28 E
Durban, France 28 F6 42 59N 2 49 E
Durban, S. Africa 117 D5 29 49 S 31 1 E
Durbo, Somali Rep. 120 B4 11 37N 50 20 E
Durbuy, Belgium 24 D5 50 21N 5 28 E
Dúrcal, Spain 43 J7 36 59N 3 34W
Đurđevac, Croatia 52 D2 46 2N 17 3 E
Düren, Germany 30 E2 50 48N 6 29 E
Durg, India 94 D5 21 15N 81 22 E
Durgapur, India 93 H12 23 30N 87 20 E
Durham, Canada 140 D3 44 10N 80 49W
Durham, U.K. 20 C6 54 47N 1 34W
Durham, Calif., U.S.A. 160 F5 39 39N 121 48W
Durham, N.C., U.S.A. 149 H6 35 59N 78 54W
Durham, N.H., U.S.A. 151 C14 43 8N 70 56W
Durham □, U.K. 20 C6 54 42N 1 45W
Durleşti, Moldova 53 C13 47 1N 28 46 E
Ḑurmā, Si. Arabia 96 E5 24 37N 46 8 E
Durmitor, Serbia & M. 50 C2 43 10N 19 0 E
Durmitor △, Serbia & M. 50 C3 43 15N 19 5 E
Durness, U.K. 22 C4 58 34N 4 45W
Durnford, Pta., W. Sahara 110 D1 23 37N 16 0W
Durrës, Albania 50 E3 41 19N 19 28 E
Durrow, Ireland 23 D4 52 51N 7 24W
Dursey I., Ireland 23 E1 51 36N 10 12W
Dursley, U.K. 21 F5 51 40N 2 21W
Dursunbey, Turkey 49 B10 39 35N 28 37 E
Durtal, France 26 E6 47 40N 0 18W
Duru, Dem. Rep. of the Congo 118 B2 4 14N 28 50 E
Duru Gölü, Turkey 51 E12 41 20N 28 35 E
Durusu, Turkey 51 E12 41 17N 28 41 E
Durūz, Jabal ad, Jordan 103 C5 32 35N 36 40 E
D'Urville, Tanjung, Indonesia 83 B5 1 28 S 137 54 E
D'Urville I., N.Z. 131 A8 40 50 S 173 55 E
Duryea, U.S.A. 151 E9 41 20N 75 45W
Dusa Mareb, Somali Rep. 120 C3 5 30N 46 15 E
Dûsh, Egypt 106 C3 24 35N 30 41 E
Dushak, Turkmenistan 66 F7 37 13N 60 1 E
Dushan, China 76 E6 25 48N 107 30 E
Dushanbe, Tajikistan 65 D4 38 33N 68 48 E
Dusheti, Georgia 61 J7 42 10N 44 42 E
Dushore, U.S.A. 151 E8 41 31N 76 24W
Dusky Sd., N.Z. 131 F1 45 47 S 166 30 E
Dussejour, C., Australia 124 B4 14 45 S 128 13 E
Düsseldorf, Germany 30 D2 51 14N 6 47 E
Düsseldorf Rhein-Ruhr ✈ (DUS), Germany 30 D2 51 17N 6 46 E
Dusti, Tajikistan 65 E4 37 20N 68 40 E
Dustlik, Uzbekistan 65 C4 40 31N 68 2 E
Duszniki-Zdrój, Poland 55 H3 50 24N 16 24 E
Dutch East Indies = Indonesia ■, Asia 85 C4 5 0 S 115 0 E
Dutch Guiana = Suriname ■, S. Amer. 169 C6 4 0N 56 0W
Dutch Harbor, U.S.A. 144 K6 53 53N 166 32W
Dutlwe, Botswana 116 C3 23 58 S 23 46 E
Dutsan Wai, Nigeria 113 C6 10 50N 8 10 E
Dutton, Canada 150 D3 42 39N 81 30W
Dutton →, Australia 126 C3 20 44 S 143 10 E
Duved, Sweden 16 A6 63 23N 12 55 E
Düvertepe, Turkey 49 B10 39 14N 28 27 E
Dúvida = Roosevelt →, Brazil 173 B5 7 35 S 60 20W
Duwayhin, Khawr, U.A.E. 97 E6 24 20N 51 25 E
Duyun, China 76 D6 26 18N 107 29 E
Düzağac, Turkey 49 C12 38 48N 30 10 E
Düzce, Turkey 100 B4 40 50N 31 10 E
Duzdab = Zāhedān, Iran 97 D9 29 30N 60 50 E
Dve Mogili, Bulgaria 51 C9 43 35N 25 55 E
Dvigatelstroy = Kaspiysk, Russia 61 J8 42 52N 47 40 E
Dvina, Severnaya →, Russia 56 B7 64 32N 40 30 E
Dvinsk = Daugavpils, Latvia 15 J22 55 53N 26 32 E
Dvinskaya Guba, Russia 56 B6 65 0N 39 0 E
Dvor, Croatia 45 C13 45 4N 16 22 E
Dvůr Králové nad Labem, Czech Rep. 34 A8 50 27N 15 50 E
Dwarka, India 92 H3 22 18N 69 8 E
Dwellingup, Australia 125 F2 32 43 S 116 4 E
Dwight, Canada 150 A5 45 20N 79 1W
Dwight, U.S.A. 157 C8 41 5N 88 26W
Dyakove, Ukraine 52 B7 48 1N 23 0 E
Dyatkovo, Russia 58 F8 53 40N 34 27 E
Dyatlovo = Dzyatlava, Belarus 58 F3 53 28N 25 28 E
Dyce, U.K. 22 D6 57 13N 2 12W
Dyer, U.S.A. 157 G10 37 24N 86 13W
Dyer, C., Canada 139 B13 66 37N 61 16W
Dyer Bay, Canada 150 A3 45 10N 81 20W
Dyer Plateau, Antarctica 7 D17 70 45 S 65 30W
Dyersburg, U.S.A. 155 G10 36 3N 89 23W
Dyersville, U.S.A. 156 B5 42 29N 91 8W
Dyfi →, U.K. 21 E3 52 32N 4 3W
Dyhernfurth = Brzeg Dolny, Poland 55 G3 51 16N 16 41 E
Dyje →, Czech Rep. 35 C9 48 37N 16 56 E
Dyke Ackland B., Papua N. G. 132 E5 9 0 S 148 45 E
Dymer, Ukraine 59 G6 50 47N 30 18 E
Dynów, Poland 55 J9 49 50N 22 11 E
Dyranut, Norway 18 D4 60 22N 7 31 E
Dyrhólaey, Iceland 11 D7 63 24N 19 8W
Dyrnes, Norway 18 A4 63 25N 7 52 E
Dysart, Australia 126 C4 22 32 S 148 23 E
Dysart, U.S.A. 156 B4 42 10N 92 18W
Dyurtyuli, Russia 64 D5 55 9N 54 40 E
Dyushambe = Dushanbe, Tajikistan 65 D4 38 33N 68 48 E
Dyviziya 53 E14 45 55N 29 59 E
Dzamin Üüd = Borhoyn Tal, Mongolia 74 C6 43 50N 111 58 E
Dzaoudzi, Mayotte 121 a 12 47 S 45 16 E
Dzaudzhikau = Vladikavkaz, Russia 61 J7 43 0N 44 35 E
Dzerzhinsk, Russia 60 B6 56 14N 43 30 E
Dzhalal-Abad = Jalal-Abad, Kyrgyzstan 65 C6 40 56N 73 0 E
Dzhalal-Ogly = Stepanavan, Armenia 61 K7 41 1N 44 23 E
Dzhalinda, Russia 67 D13 53 26N 124 0 E
Dzhambeyty, Kazakhstan 64 F4 50 16N 52 35 E
Dzhambul = Taraz, Kazakhstan 65 B5 42 54N 71 22 E
Dzhankoy, Ukraine 59 K8 45 40N 34 20 E
Dzhanybek, Kazakhstan 60 F8 49 25N 46 50 E
Dzhargalantu = Hovd, Mongolia 68 B4 48 2N 91 37 E
Dzharkent = Panfilov, Kazakhstan 66 E8 44 10N 80 0 E
Dzharkurgan = Jarqŭrghon, Uzbekistan 65 E3 37 31N 67 25 E
Dzharylhach, Ostriv, Ukraine 59 J7 46 2N 32 55 E
Dzhezkazgan = Zhezqazghan, Kazakhstan 66 E7 47 44N 67 40 E
Dzhibkhalantu = Uliastay, Mongolia 68 B4 47 56N 97 28 E
Dzhirgatal, Tajikistan 65 D5 39 13N 71 12 E
Dzhizak = Jizzakh, Uzbekistan 65 C3 40 6N 67 50 E
Dzhugdzur, Khrebet, Russia 67 D14 57 30N 138 0 E
Dzhulynk, Ukraine 53 B14 48 26N 29 45 E
Dzhuma, Uzbekistan 65 D3 39 42N 66 40 E
Dzhungarskiye Vorota = Dzungarian Gates, Asia 68 B3 45 0N 82 0 E
Dzhuryn, Ukraine 53 B13 48 41N 28 18 E
Dzhvari = Jvari, Georgia 61 J6 42 42N 42 4 E
Działdowo, Poland 55 E7 53 15N 20 15 E
Działoszyce, Poland 55 H7 50 22N 20 20 E
Działoszyn, Poland 55 G5 51 6N 18 50 E
Dzibilchaltún, Mexico 163 C7 21 5N 89 36W
Dzibilchaltun, Yucatán, Mexico 163 C7 21 5N 89 36W
Dzierzgoń, Poland 54 E6 53 58N 19 20 E
Dzierżoniów, Poland 55 H3 50 45N 16 39 E
Dzilam de Bravo, Mexico 163 C7 21 24N 88 53W
Dzioua, Algeria 111 B6 33 14N 5 14 E
Dzisna, Belarus 58 E5 55 34N 28 12 E
Dzisna →, Belarus 58 E5 55 34N 28 12 E
Dziwnów, Poland 54 D1 54 2N 14 45 E
Dzungaria = Junggar Pendi, China 68 B3 44 30N 86 0 E
Dzungarian Basin = Junggar Pendi, China 68 B3 44 30N 86 0 E
Dzungarian Gates, Asia 68 B3 45 0N 82 0 E
Dzuumod, Mongolia 68 B5 47 45N 106 58 E
Dzyarzhynsk, Belarus 58 F4 53 40N 27 1 E
Dzyatlava, Belarus 58 F3 53 28N 25 28 E

E

E.C. Manning ⌂, Canada 142 D4 49 5N 120 45W
Eabamet L., Canada 140 B2 51 30N 87 46W
Eads, U.S.A. 154 F3 38 29N 102 47W
Eagar, U.S.A. 159 J9 34 6N 109 17W
Eagle, Alaska, U.S.A. 144 D12 64 47N 141 12W
Eagle, Colo., U.S.A. 158 G10 39 39N 106 50W
Eagle, Idaho, U.S.A. 158 E5 43 42N 116 21W
Eagle →, Canada 141 B8 53 36N 57 26W
Eagle Butte, U.S.A. 154 C4 45 0N 101 10W
Eagle Cr. →, U.S.A. 157 F11 38 36N 85 4W
Eagle Grove, U.S.A. 156 B3 42 40N 93 54W
Eagle L., Canada 143 D10 49 42N 93 13W
Eagle L., Calif., U.S.A. 158 F3 40 39N 120 45W
Eagle L., Maine, U.S.A. 149 B11 46 20N 69 22W
Eagle Lake, Canada 150 A6 45 8N 78 29W
Eagle Lake, Maine, U.S.A. 149 B11 47 3N 68 36W
Eagle Lake, Tex., U.S.A. 155 L6 29 35N 96 20W
Eagle Mountain, U.S.A. 161 M11 33 49N 115 27W
Eagle Nest, U.S.A. 159 H11 36 33N 105 16W
Eagle Pass, U.S.A. 155 L4 28 43N 100 30W
Eagle Pk., U.S.A. 160 G7 38 10N 119 25W
Eagle Pt., Australia 124 C3 16 11 S 124 23 E
Eagle River, Mich., U.S.A. 148 B1 47 24N 88 18W
Eagle River, Wis., U.S.A. 154 C10 45 55N 89 15W
Eaglehawk, N.S.W., Australia 127 F3 36 44 S 144 15 E
Eaglehawk, Vic., Australia 128 D6 36 44 S 144 15 E
Eagles Mere, U.S.A. 151 E8 41 25N 76 33W
Eagleville, U.S.A. 156 D3 40 28N 93 59W
Ealing □, U.K. 21 F7 51 31N 0 20W
Ear Falls, Canada 143 C10 50 38N 93 13W
Earle, U.S.A. 155 H9 35 16N 90 28W
Earlimart, U.S.A. 161 K7 35 53N 119 16W
Earlville, U.S.A. 157 C8 41 35N 88 55W
Early Branch, U.S.A. 152 C9 32 45N 80 55W
Earn →, U.K. 22 E5 56 21N 3 18W
Earn, L., U.K. 22 E4 56 23N 4 13W
Earnslaw, Mt., N.Z. 131 E3 44 32 S 168 27 E
Earth, U.S.A. 155 H3 34 14N 102 24W
Eas, Vanuatu 133 F6 16 20 S 168 15 E
Easley, U.S.A. 149 H4 34 50N 82 36W
East Anglia, U.K. 20 E9 52 30N 1 0 E
East Angus, Canada 141 C5 45 30N 71 40W
East Antarctica, Antarctica 7 D7 80 0 S 90 0 E
East Aurora, U.S.A. 150 D6 42 46N 78 37W
East Ayrshire □, U.K. 22 F4 55 26N 4 11W
East Beskids = Vychodné Beskydy, Europe 35 B15 49 20N 22 0 E
East Brady, U.S.A. 150 F5 40 59N 79 36W
East C., N.Z. 130 D7 37 42 S 178 35 E
East C., Papua N. G. 132 F6 10 13 S 150 53 E
East Chicago, U.S.A. 157 C9 41 38N 87 27W
East China Sea, Asia 69 D7 30 0N 126 0 E
East Coulee, Canada 142 C6 51 23N 112 27W
East Dereham = Dereham, U.K. 21 E8 52 41N 0 57 E
East Dublin, U.S.A. 152 C7 32 32N 82 52W
East Dubuque, U.S.A. 156 B6 42 30N 90 39W
East Dunbartonshire □, U.K. 22 F4 55 57N 4 13W
East End Pt., Bahamas 9 b 25 3N 77 16W
East Falkland, Falk. Is. 9 f 51 30 S 58 30W
East Grand Forks, U.S.A. 154 B6 47 56N 97 1W
East Greenwich, U.S.A. 151 E13 41 40N 71 27W
East Grinstead, U.K. 21 F8 51 7N 0 0W
East Hartford, U.S.A. 151 E12 41 46N 72 39W
East Helena, U.S.A. 158 C8 46 35N 111 56W
East Indies, Asia 62 K15 0 0 120 0 E
East Kilbride, U.K. 22 F4 55 47N 4 11W
East Lamma Channel, China 69 G11 22 14N 114 9 E
East Lansing, U.S.A. 157 B12 42 44N 84 29W
East Livermore = Livermore Falls, U.S.A. 149 C11 44 29N 70 11W
East Liverpool, U.S.A. 150 F4 40 37N 80 35W
East London, S. Africa 117 E4 33 0 S 27 55 E
East Lothian □, U.K. 22 F6 55 58N 2 44W
East Main = Eastmain, Canada 140 B4 52 10N 78 30W
East Milwaukee = Shorewood, U.S.A. 157 A9 43 5N 87 54W
East Moline, U.S.A. 156 C6 41 32N 90 26W
East Naples, U.S.A. 153 J8 26 8N 81 46W
East New Britain □, Papua N. G. 132 D7 6 30 S 152 30 E
East Northport, U.S.A. 151 F11 40 53N 73 20W
East Orange, U.S.A. 151 F10 40 46N 74 13W
East Pacific Ridge, Pac. Oc. 135 J17 15 0 S 110 0W
East Pakistan = Bangladesh ■, Asia 90 C3 24 0N 90 0 E
East Palatka, U.S.A. 152 F8 29 39N 81 36W
East Palestine, U.S.A. 150 F4 40 50N 80 33W

East Peoria, *U.S.A.* **156 D7** 40 40N 89 34W
East Pine, *Canada* **142 B4** 55 48N 120 12W
East Point, *U.S.A.* **152 B5** 33 41N 84 27W
East Providence, *U.S.A.* **151 E13** 41 49N 71 23W
East Pt., *Br. Virgin Is.* **165 e** 18 40N 64 18W
East Pt., *Canada* **141 C7** 46 27N 61 58W
East Renfrewshire □, *U.K.* **22 F4** 55 46N 4 21W
East Retford = Retford, *U.K.* **20 D7** 53 19N 0 56W
East Riding of Yorkshire □, *U.K.* **20 D7** 53 55N 0 30W
East Rochester, *U.S.A.* **150 C7** 43 7N 77 29W
East St. Louis, *U.S.A.* **156 F6** 38 37N 90 9W
East Schelde = Oosterschelde →, *Neths.* **24 C4** 51 33N 4 0 E
East Sea = Japan, Sea of, *Asia* **70 E7** 40 0N 135 0 E
East Sepik □, *Papua N. G.* **132 C2** 4 0 S 143 45 E
East Siberian Sea, *Russia* **67 B17** 73 0N 160 0 E
East Stroudsburg, *U.S.A.* **151 E9** 41 1N 75 11W
East Sussex □, *U.K.* **21 G8** 50 56N 0 19 E
East Tawas, *U.S.A.* **148 C4** 44 17N 83 29W
East Timor ■, *Asia* **82 C3** 8 50 S 126 0 E
East Tohopekaliga, Lake, *U.S.A.* **153 G8** 28 18N 81 15W
East Toorale, *Australia* **127 E4** 30 27 S 145 28 E
East Troy, *U.S.A.* **157 B8** 42 47N 88 24W
East Walker →, *U.S.A.* **160 G7** 38 52N 119 10W
East Windsor, *U.S.A.* **151 F10** 40 17N 74 34W
East Youngstown = Campbell, *U.S.A.* **150 E4** 41 5N 80 37W
Eastbourne, *N.Z.* **130 H3** 41 19 S 174 55 E
Eastbourne, *U.K.* **21 G8** 50 46N 0 18 E
Eastend, *Canada* **143 D7** 49 32N 108 50W
Easter Fracture Zone, *Pac. Oc.* **135 K16** 25 0 S 115 0W
Easter I. = Pascua, I. de, *Chile* **172 b** 27 7 S 109 23W
Eastern □, *Ghana* **113 D4** 6 30N 0 30W
Eastern □, *Kenya* **118 C4** 0 0 38 30 E
Eastern □, *S. Leone* **112 D2** 8 15N 11 0W
Eastern Cape □, *S. Africa* **116 E4** 32 0 S 26 0 E
Eastern Cr. →, *Australia* **126 C3** 20 40 S 141 35 E
Eastern Ghats, *India* **95 H4** 14 0N 78 50 E
Eastern Group = Lau Group, *Fiji* **133 A3** 17 0 S 178 30W
Eastern Group, *Australia* **125 F3** 33 30 S 124 30 E
Eastern Highlands □, *Papua N. G.* **132 D3** 6 30 S 145 35 E
Eastern Samar □, *Phil.* **81 F5** 11 40N 125 40 E
Eastern Transvaal = Mpumalanga □, *S. Africa* **117 D5** 26 0 S 30 0 E
Easterville, *Canada* **143 C9** 53 8N 99 49W
Easthampton, *U.S.A.* **151 D12** 42 16N 72 40W
Eastlake, *U.S.A.* **150 E3** 41 40N 81 26W
Eastland, *U.S.A.* **155 J5** 32 24N 98 49W
Eastleigh, *U.K.* **21 G6** 50 58N 1 21W
Eastmain, *Canada* **140 B4** 52 10N 78 30W
Eastmain →, *Canada* **140 B4** 52 27N 78 26W
Eastman, *Canada* **151 A12** 45 18N 72 19W
Eastman, *Ga., U.S.A.* **152 C6** 32 12N 83 11W
Eastman, *Wis., U.S.A.* **156 A5** 43 10N 91 1W
Easton, *Md., U.S.A.* **148 F7** 38 47N 76 5W
Easton, *Pa., U.S.A.* **151 F9** 40 41N 75 13W
Easton, *Wash., U.S.A.* **160 C5** 47 14N 121 11W
Eastover, *U.S.A.* **152 B9** 33 52N 80 41W
Eastpoint, *U.S.A.* **152 F5** 29 44N 84 53W
Eastpointe, *U.S.A.* **150 D2** 42 27N 82 56W
Eastport, *U.S.A.* **149 C12** 44 56N 67 0W
Eastsound, *U.S.A.* **160 B4** 48 42N 122 55W
Eaton, *Colo., U.S.A.* **154 E2** 40 32N 104 42W
Eaton, *Ohio, U.S.A.* **157 E12** 39 45N 84 38W
Eaton Rapids, *U.S.A.* **157 B12** 42 31N 84 39W
Eatonia, *Canada* **143 C7** 51 13N 109 25W
Eatonton, *U.S.A.* **152 B6** 33 20N 83 23W
Eatontown, *U.S.A.* **151 F10** 40 19N 74 4W
Eatonville, *U.S.A.* **160 D4** 46 52N 122 16W
Eau Claire, *Fr. Guiana* **169 C7** 3 30N 53 40W
Eau Claire, *U.S.A.* **154 C9** 44 49N 91 30W
Eau Claire, L. à l', *Canada* **140 A5** 56 10N 74 25W
Eauze, *France* **28 E4** 43 53N 0 7 E
Eban, *Nigeria* **113 D5** 9 40N 4 50 E
Ebanga, *Angola* **115 E2** 12 45 S 14 45 E
Ebangalakata, *Dem. Rep. of the Congo* **114 C4** 0 29 S 21 29 E
Ebbegebirge ⌓, *Germany* **30 D3** 51 10N 7 55 E
Ebbw Vale, *U.K.* **21 F4** 51 46N 3 12W
Ebebiyín, *Eq. Guin.* **114 B2** 2 9N 11 20 E
Ebeggui, *Algeria* **111 C6** 26 2N 6 0 E
Ebel, *Gabon* **114 B2** 0 7N 11 5 E
Ebeltoft, *Denmark* **17 H4** 56 12N 10 41 E
Ebeltoft Vig, *Denmark* **17 H4** 56 10N 10 35 E
Ebensburg, *U.S.A.* **150 F6** 40 29N 78 44W
Ebensee, *Austria* **34 D6** 47 48N 13 46 E
Eber Gölü, *Turkey* **100 C4** 38 38N 31 11 E
Eberbach, *Germany* **31 F4** 49 28N 8 59 E
Eberswalde-Finow, *Germany* **30 C9** 52 50N 13 49 E
Ebetsu, *Japan* **70 C10** 43 7N 141 34 E
Ebey's Landing ⌓, *U.S.A.* **160 B4** 48 13N 122 41W
Ebian, *China* **76 C4** 29 11N 103 13 E
Ebikon, *Switz.* **33 B6** 47 5N 8 21 E
Ebingen, *Germany* **31 G5** 48 13N 9 1 E
Ebino, *Japan* **72 E2** 32 2N 130 48 E
Ebnat-Kappel, *Switz.* **33 B8** 47 16N 9 7 E
Ebo, *Angola* **115 E2** 11 40 S 14 40 E
Ebola →, *Dem. Rep. of the Congo* **114 B4** 3 20N 20 57 E
Éboli, *Italy* **47 B8** 40 39N 15 2 E
Ebolowa, *Cameroon* **113 E7** 2 55N 11 10 E
Ebonyi □, *Nigeria* **113 D6** 6 20N 8 0 E
Eboy, *Dem. Rep. of the Congo* **114 B4** 2 50N 23 11 E
Ebrach, *Germany* **31 F6** 49 51N 10 29 E
Ébrié, Lagune, *Ivory C.* **112 D4** 5 12N 4 26W
Ebro →, *Spain* **40 E5** 40 43N 0 54 E
Ebro, Embalse del, *Spain* **42 C7** 43 0N 3 58W
Ebstorf, *Germany* **30 B6** 53 2N 10 24 E
Eceabat, *Turkey* **51 F10** 40 11N 26 21 E
Ech Chéliff, *Algeria* **111 A5** 36 10N 1 20 E
Echallens, *Switz.* **32 C3** 46 38N 6 38 E
Echechonnee →, *U.S.A.* **152 C6** 32 39N 83 36W
Echigo-Sammyaku, *Japan* **71 F9** 36 50N 139 50 E
Échirolles, *France* **29 C9** 45 8N 5 44 E
Echizen-Misaki, *Japan* **73 B7** 35 59N 135 57 E
Echmiadzin = Yejmiadzin, *Armenia* **61 K7** 40 12N 44 19 E
Echo, *U.S.A.* **152 D4** 31 29N 85 28W
Echo Bay, *N.W.T., Canada* **138 B8** 66 5N 117 55W
Echo Bay, *Ont., Canada* **140 C3** 46 29N 84 4W
Echoing →, *Canada* **140 B1** 55 51N 92 5W
Echterdingen, Stuttgart ✈ (STR), *Germany* **31 G5** 48 42N 9 11 E
Echternach, *Lux.* **24 E6** 49 49N 6 25 E
Echuca, *Australia* **129 D6** 36 10 S 144 45 E
Ecija, *Spain* **43 H5** 37 30N 5 10W
Eckental, *Germany* **31 F7** 49 35N 11 12 E
Eckernförde, *Germany* **30 A5** 54 28N 9 50 E
Eclectic, *U.S.A.* **152 C3** 32 38N 86 2W
Eclipse I., *Australia* **125 G2** 35 5 S 117 58 E
Eclipse Is., *Australia* **124 B4** 13 54 S 126 19 E
Eclipse Sd., *Canada* **139 A11** 72 38N 79 0W
Écommoy, *France* **26 E7** 47 50N 0 17 E
Economy = Ambridge, *U.S.A.* **150 F4** 40 36N 80 14W
Ecoporanga, *Brazil* **171 E3** 18 23 S 40 50W
Écouché, *France* **26 D6** 48 42N 0 10W
Ecrins △, *France* **29 D10** 44 54N 6 18 E
Ecuador ■, *S. Amer.* **168 D2** 2 0 S 78 0W
Ecuador, Volcán, *Ecuador* **172 a** 1 1 S 91 32W
Écueillé, *France* **26 E8** 47 5N 1 21 E
Ed, *Sweden* **17 F5** 58 55N 11 55 E
Ed Dabbura, *Sudan* **106 D3** 17 40N 34 15 E
Ed Da'ein, *Sudan* **107 E2** 11 26N 26 9 E
Ed Dâmer, *Sudan* **106 D3** 17 27N 34 0 E
Ed Dar el Beida = Casablanca, *Morocco* **110 B3** 33 36N 7 36W
Ed Debba, *Sudan* **106 D3** 18 0N 30 51 E
Ed-Déffa, *Egypt* **106 A2** 30 40N 26 30 E
Ed Deim, *Sudan* **107 E2** 10 10N 28 20 E
Ed Dueim, *Sudan* **107 E3** 14 0N 32 10 E
Edam, *Canada* **143 C7** 53 11N 108 46W
Edam, *Neths.* **24 B5** 52 31N 5 3 E
Edane, *Sweden* **16 E6** 59 38N 12 49 E
Edapally, *India* **95 J4** 11 19N 78 3 E
Eday, *U.K.* **22 B6** 59 11N 2 47W
Edchera, *W. Sahara* **110 C2** 27 2N 13 4W
Edd, *Eritrea* **107 E5** 14 0N 41 38 E
Eddrachillis B., *U.K.* **22 C3** 58 17N 5 14W
Eddystone, *U.K.* **21 G3** 50 11N 4 16W
Eddystone Pt., *Australia* **127 G4** 40 59 S 148 20 E
Eddyville, *U.S.A.* **156 C4** 41 9N 92 38W
Ede, *Neths.* **24 B5** 52 4N 5 40 E
Ede, *Nigeria* **113 D5** 7 45N 4 29 E
Édéa, *Cameroon* **113 E7** 3 51N 10 9 E
Edebäck, *Sweden* **16 D7** 60 4N 13 32 E
Edehon L., *Canada* **143 A9** 60 25N 97 15W
Edekel, Adrar, *Algeria* **111 D6** 23 56N 6 47 E
Edelény, *Hungary* **52 B5** 48 18N 20 44 E
Eden = Bar Harbor, *U.S.A.* **149 C11** 44 23N 68 13W
Eden, *Australia* **129 D8** 37 3 S 149 55 E
Eden, *N.C., U.S.A.* **149 G6** 36 29N 79 53W
Eden, *N.Y., U.S.A.* **150 D6** 42 39N 78 55W
Eden, *Tex., U.S.A.* **155 K5** 31 13N 99 51W
Eden →, *U.K.* **20 C4** 54 57N 3 1W
Edenburg, *S. Africa* **116 D4** 29 43 S 25 58 E
Edendale, *N.Z.* **131 G3** 46 19 S 168 48 E
Edendale, *S. Africa* **117 D5** 29 39 S 30 18 E
Edenderry, *Ireland* **23 C4** 53 21N 7 4W
Edenhope, *Australia* **128 D4** 37 4 S 141 19 E
Edenton, *U.S.A.* **149 G7** 36 4N 76 39W
Edenville, *S. Africa* **117 D4** 27 37 S 27 34 E
Eder →, *Germany* **30 D5** 51 12N 9 28 E
Eder-Stausee, *Germany* **30 D4** 51 10N 8 57 E
Edessa = Édhessa, *Greece* **50 F6** 40 48N 22 5 E
Edewecht, *Germany* **30 B3** 53 8N 7 58 E
Edgar, *U.S.A.* **154 E6** 40 22N 97 58W
Edgartown, *U.S.A.* **151 E14** 41 23N 70 31W
Edge Hill, *U.K.* **21 E6** 52 8N 1 26W
Edgecumbe, *N.Z.* **130 D5** 37 59 S 176 47 E
Edgefield, *U.S.A.* **152 B8** 33 47N 81 56W
Edgeley, *U.S.A.* **154 B5** 46 22N 98 43W
Edgemont, *U.S.A.* **154 D3** 43 18N 103 50W
Edgeøya, *Svalbard* **6 B9** 77 45N 22 30 E
Edgerton, *Ohio, U.S.A.* **157 C12** 41 27N 84 45W
Edgerton, *Wis., U.S.A.* **156 B7** 42 50N 89 4W
Edgewater, *U.S.A.* **153 G9** 28 59N 80 54W
Edgewood, *U.S.A.* **157 F8** 38 55N 88 40W
Édhessa, *Greece* **50 F6** 40 48N 22 5 E
Edievale, *N.Z.* **131 F4** 45 49 S 169 22 E
Edina, *Liberia* **112 D2** 6 0N 10 10W
Edina, *U.S.A.* **156 D4** 40 10N 92 11W
Edinboro, *U.S.A.* **150 E4** 41 52N 80 8W
Edinburg, *Ill., U.S.A.* **156 E7** 39 39N 89 23W
Edinburg, *Ind., U.S.A.* **157 E11** 39 21N 85 58W
Edinburg, *Tex., U.S.A.* **155 M5** 26 18N 98 10W
Edinburgh, *U.K.* **22 F5** 55 57N 3 13W
Edinburgh ✈ (EDI), *U.K.* **22 F5** 55 54N 3 22W
Edinburgh, City of □, *U.K.* **22 F5** 55 57N 3 17W
Edineţ, *Moldova* **53 B12** 48 9N 27 18 E
Edirne, *Turkey* **51 E10** 41 40N 26 34 E
Edirne □, *Turkey* **51 E10** 41 12N 26 30 E
Edison, *Ga., U.S.A.* **152 D5** 31 34N 84 44W
Edison, *Wash., U.S.A.* **160 B4** 48 33N 122 27W
Edisto →, *U.S.A.* **152 C9** 32 29N 80 21W
Edisto Beach, *U.S.A.* **152 C9** 32 29N 80 20W
Edisto I., *U.S.A.* **152 C9** 32 35N 80 20W
Edithburgh, *Australia* **128 C2** 35 5 S 137 43 E
Edjeleh, *Algeria* **111 C6** 28 38N 9 50 E
Edmeston, *U.S.A.* **151 D9** 42 42N 75 15W
Edmond, *U.S.A.* **155 H6** 35 39N 97 29W
Edmonds, *U.S.A.* **160 C4** 47 49N 122 23W
Edmonton, *Australia* **126 B4** 17 2 S 145 46 E
Edmonton, *Canada* **142 C6** 53 30N 113 30W
Edmund L., *Canada* **140 B1** 54 45N 93 17W
Edmundston, *Canada* **141 C6** 47 23N 68 20W
Edna, *U.S.A.* **155 L6** 28 59N 96 39W
Edo □, *Nigeria* **113 D6** 6 30N 6 0 E
Edolo, *Italy* **44 B7** 46 10N 10 21 E
Edøy, *Norway* **18 A5** 63 18N 8 10 E
Edremit, *Turkey* **49 B9** 39 34N 27 0 E
Edremit Körfezi, *Turkey* **49 B8** 39 30N 26 45 E
Edsbro, *Sweden* **16 E12** 59 54N 18 29 E
Edsbyn, *Sweden* **16 C9** 61 23N 15 49 E
Edson, *Canada* **142 C5** 53 35N 116 28W
Eduardo Castex, *Argentina* **174 D3** 35 50 S 64 18W
Edward →, *Australia* **128 C5** 35 5 S 143 30 E
Edward, L., *Africa* **118 C2** 0 25 S 29 40 E
Edward River, *Australia* **126 A3** 14 59 S 141 26 E
Edward VII Land, *Antarctica* **7 E13** 80 0 S 150 0W
Edwardesabad = Bannu, *Pakistan* **91 B3** 33 0N 70 18 E
Edwards, *Calif., U.S.A.* **161 L9** 34 55N 117 51W
Edwards, *N.Y., U.S.A.* **151 B9** 44 20N 75 15W
Edwards →, *U.S.A.* **156 C6** 41 9N 90 59W
Edwards Air Force Base, *U.S.A.* **161 L9** 34 50N 117 40W
Edwards Plateau, *U.S.A.* **155 K4** 30 45N 101 20W
Edwardsburg, *U.S.A.* **157 C10** 41 48N 86 6W
Edwardsville, *Ill., U.S.A.* **156 F7** 38 49N 89 58W
Edwardsville, *Pa., U.S.A.* **151 E9** 41 15N 75 56W
Edxná, *Mexico* **163 D6** 19 35N 90 15W
Edzo, *Canada* **142 A5** 62 49N 116 4W
Eek, *U.S.A.* **144 F7** 60 14N 162 2W
Eeklo, *Belgium* **24 C3** 51 11N 3 33 E
Eel →, *Ind., U.S.A.* **157 E10** 39 7N 86 57W
Eel →, *Ind., U.S.A.* **157 D10** 40 45N 86 22W
Eesti = Estonia ■, *Europe* **15 G21** 58 30N 25 30 E
Efate, *Vanuatu* **133 G6** 17 40 S 168 25 E
Efate, I., *Vanuatu* **133 G6** 17 40 S 168 25 E
Eferding, *Austria* **34 C7** 48 18N 14 1 E
Eferi, *Algeria* **111 D6** 24 30N 9 28 E
Effigy Mounds ⌓, *U.S.A.* **156 A5** 43 5N 91 11W
Effingham, *U.S.A.* **157 E8** 39 7N 88 33W
Effretikon, *Switz.* **33 B7** 47 25N 8 42 E
Eforie, *Romania* **53 F13** 44 1N 28 37 E
Efoulen, *Cameroon* **114 B2** 2 46N 10 43 E
Efteløt, *Norway* **18 E6** 59 33N 9 49 E
Ega →, *Spain* **40 C3** 42 19N 1 55W
Égadi, Ísole, *Italy* **46 E5** 37 55N 12 16 E
Egan Range, *U.S.A.* **158 G6** 39 35N 114 55W
Eganville, *Canada* **140 C4** 45 32N 77 5W
Egedesminde = Aasiaat, *Greenland* **10 D5** 68 43N 52 56W
Egegik, *U.S.A.* **144 G8** 58 13N 157 22W
Eger = Cheb, *Czech Rep.* **34 A5** 50 9N 12 28 E
Eger, *Hungary* **52 C5** 47 53N 20 27 E
Eger →, *Hungary* **52 C5** 47 38N 20 50 E
Egersund, *Norway* **18 F3** 58 26N 6 1 E
Egg, *Austria* **33 B9** 47 26N 9 54 E
Egg, *Switz.* **33 B7** 47 18N 8 41 E
Egg I., *St. Helena* **9 h** 15 58 S 5 47W
Egg L., *Canada* **143 B7** 55 5N 105 30W
Eggedal, *Norway* **18 D6** 60 14N 9 22 E
Eggegebirge Südlicher Teutoburger Wald ⌓, *Germany* **30 D4** 51 40N 8 59 E
Eggenburg, *Austria* **34 C8** 48 38N 15 50 E
Eggenfelden, *Germany* **31 G8** 48 23N 12 46 E
Eggiwil, *Switz.* **32 C5** 46 52N 7 47 E
Egherta, *Somali Rep.* **120 D2** 2 4N 43 11 E
Éghezée, *Belgium* **24 D4** 50 35N 4 55 E
Egholo, *Solomon Is.* **133 M9** 8 25 S 157 25 E
Egilsstaðir, *Iceland* **11 B12** 65 16N 14 25W
Egio = Aíyion, *Greece* **48 C4** 38 15N 22 5 E
Egito, *Angola* **115 E2** 12 4 S 13 58 E
Égletons, *France* **28 C6** 45 24N 2 3 E
Eglisau, *Switz.* **33 A7** 47 35N 8 31 E
Egmont, *Canada* **142 D4** 49 45N 123 56W
Egmont △, *N.Z.* **130 F3** 39 17 S 174 4 E
Egmont, C., *N.Z.* **130 F2** 39 16 S 173 45 E
Egmont, Mt. = Taranaki, Mt., *N.Z.* **130 F3** 39 17 S 174 5 E
Egra, *India* **93 J12** 21 54N 87 32 E
Eğridir, *Turkey* **100 D4** 37 52N 30 51 E
Eğridir Gölü, *Turkey* **100 D4** 37 53N 30 50 E
Egtved, *Denmark* **17 J3** 55 38N 9 18 E
Éguas →, *Brazil* **171 D3** 13 26 S 44 14W
Egum Atoll, *Papua N. G.* **132 E7** 9 25 S 152 0 E
Egume, *Nigeria* **113 D6** 7 30N 7 14 E
Éguzon-Chantôme, *France* **27 F8** 46 27N 1 33 E
Egvekinot, *Russia* **67 C19** 66 19N 179 50W
Egyek, *Hungary* **52 C5** 47 39N 20 52 E
Egypt ■, *Africa* **106 B3** 28 0N 31 0 E
Eha Amufu, *Nigeria* **113 D6** 6 30N 7 46 E
Eheli, *Algeria* **111 D5** 22 26N 4 40 E
Ehime □, *Japan* **72 D4** 33 30N 132 40 E
Ehingen, *Germany* **31 G5** 48 16N 9 43 E
Ehrenberg, *U.S.A.* **161 M12** 33 36N 114 31W
Ehrhardt, *U.S.A.* **152 B8** 33 6N 81 1W
Ehrwald, *Austria* **34 D3** 47 24N 10 56 E
Eibar, *Spain* **40 B2** 43 11N 2 28W
Eibenschitz = Ivančice, *Czech Rep.* **35 B9** 49 6N 16 23 E
Eichstätt, *Germany* **31 G7** 48 54N 11 11 E
Eide, *Hordaland, Norway* **18 D3** 60 31N 6 44 E
Eide, *Møre og Romsdal, Norway* **18 B4** 62 55N 7 27 E
Eider →, *Germany* **30 A4** 54 19N 8 57 E
Eidsbugarden, *Norway* **18 C5** 61 23N 8 16 E
Eidsbygda, *Norway* **18 B4** 62 36N 7 30 E
Eidsdal, *Norway* **18 B4** 62 16N 7 10 E
Eidsvåg, *Norway* **18 B5** 62 46N 8 2 E
Eidsvold, *Australia* **127 D5** 25 25 S 151 12 E
Eidsvoll, *Norway* **18 D8** 60 19N 11 14 E
Eielson, *U.S.A.* **144 D11** 64 40N 147 4W
Eifel, *Germany* **31 E2** 50 15N 6 50 E
Eiffel Flats, *Zimbabwe* **119 F3** 18 20 S 30 0 E
Eiger, *Switz.* **32 C6** 46 34N 8 1 E
Eigg, *U.K.* **22 E2** 56 54N 6 10W
Eighty Mile Beach, *Australia* **124 C3** 19 30 S 120 40 E
Eikefjord, *Norway* **18 C2** 61 35N 5 27 E
Eikelandsosen, *Norway* **18 D2** 60 15N 5 43 E
Eiken, *Norway* **18 F4** 58 29N 7 14 E
Eikeren, *Norway* **18 E6** 59 38N 9 58 E
Eikesdal, *Norway* **18 B5** 62 28N 8 12 E
Eil, *Somali Rep.* **120 C3** 8 0N 49 50 E
Eil, L., *U.K.* **22 E3** 56 51N 5 16W
Eildon, *Australia* **129 D6** 37 14 S 145 55 E
Eildon, L., *Australia* **129 D7** 37 10 S 146 0 E
Eilean Sar = Western Isles □, *U.K.* **22 D1** 57 30N 7 10W
Eilenburg, *Germany* **30 D8** 51 27N 12 36 E
Ein el Luweiqa, *Sudan* **107 E3** 14 5N 33 50 E
Eina, *Norway* **18 D7** 60 38N 10 35 E
Einarsstaðir, *Iceland* **11 B9** 65 44N 17 24W
Einasleigh, *Australia* **126 B3** 18 32 S 144 5 E
Einasleigh →, *Australia* **126 B3** 17 30 S 142 17 E
Einbeck, *Germany* **30 D5** 51 49N 9 53 E
Eindhoven, *Neths.* **24 C5** 51 26N 5 28 E
Einsiedeln, *Switz.* **33 B7** 47 7N 8 46 E
Eire = Ireland ■, *Europe* **23 C4** 53 50N 7 52W
Eiríksjökull, *Iceland* **11 C6** 64 46N 20 24W
Eiríksstaðir, *Iceland* **11 B11** 65 7N 15 25W
Eirunepé, *Brazil* **172 B4** 6 35 S 69 53W
Eiseb →, *Namibia* **116 C2** 20 33 S 20 59 E
Eisenach, *Germany* **30 E6** 50 58N 10 19 E
Eisenberg, *Germany* **30 E7** 50 58N 11 54 E
Eisenerz, *Austria* **34 D7** 47 32N 14 54 E
Eisenhüttenstadt, *Germany* **30 C10** 52 9N 14 38 E
Eisenkappel, *Austria* **34 E7** 46 29N 14 36 E
Eisenstadt, *Austria* **35 D9** 47 51N 16 31 E
Eisenstein = Železná Ruda, *Czech Rep.* **34 B6** 49 8N 13 15 E
Eisfeld, *Germany* **31 E6** 50 25N 10 54 E
Eisleben, *Germany* **30 D7** 51 32N 11 32 E
Eislingen, *Germany* **31 G5** 48 41N 9 42 E
Eivindvik, *Norway* **18 D2** 60 59N 5 5 E
Eivissa, *Spain* **38 D1** 38 54N 1 26 E
Eixe, Serra do, *Spain* **42 C4** 42 24N 6 54W
Ejea de los Caballeros, *Spain* **40 C3** 42 7N 1 9W
Ejeda, *Madag.* **117 C7** 24 20 S 44 31 E
Ejura, *Ghana* **113 D4** 7 23N 1 15W
Ejutla, *Mexico* **163 D5** 16 34N 96 44W
Ekalaka, *U.S.A.* **154 C2** 45 53N 104 33W
Ekalla, *Gabon* **114 C2** 1 27 S 14 0 E
Ekanga, *Dem. Rep. of the Congo* **114 C4** 2 23 S 23 14 E
Ekenäs = Tammisaari, *Finland* **15 F20** 60 0N 23 26 E
Ekenässjön, *Sweden* **17 G9** 57 28N 15 1 E
Ekerö, *Sweden* **16 E11** 59 16N 17 45 E
Eket, *Nigeria* **113 E6** 4 38N 7 56 E
Eketahuna, *N.Z.* **130 G4** 40 38 S 175 43 E
Ekhinádhes Nísoi, *Greece* **39 C3** 38 25N 21 2 E
Ekhínos, *Greece* **51 E9** 41 16N 25 1 E
Ekibastuz, *Kazakhstan* **66 D8** 51 50N 75 10 E
Ekiti □, *Nigeria* **113 D6** 7 25N 5 20 E
Ekoli, *Dem. Rep. of the Congo* **118 C1** 0 23 S 24 13 E
Ekoln, *Sweden* **16 E11** 59 45N 17 37 E
Ekouamou, *Congo* **114 B3** 0 8N 16 31 E
Ekoungounou, *Congo* **114 C3** 1 10 S 15 52 E
Ekshärad, *Sweden* **16 D7** 60 10N 13 30 E
Eksjö, *Sweden* **17 G8** 57 40N 14 58 E
Ekukola, *Dem. Rep. of the Congo* **114 C3** 0 31 S 18 56 E
Ekuku, *Dem. Rep. of the Congo* **114 C4** 0 41 S 21 42 E
Ekukula, *Dem. Rep. of the Congo* **114 B4** 0 15N 21 30 E
Ekuma →, *Namibia* **116 B2** 18 40 S 16 2 E
Ekuta, *Dem. Rep. of the Congo* **114 B3** 3 0N 18 50 E
Ekwan →, *Canada* **140 B3** 53 12N 82 15W
Ekwan Pt., *Canada* **140 B3** 53 16N 82 7W
Ekwok, *U.S.A.* **144 G8** 59 22N 157 30W
El Aaiún, *W. Sahara* **110 C2** 27 9N 13 12W
El Aargub, *Mauritania* **110 D1** 23 37N 15 52W
El Abanico, *Chile* **174 D1** 37 20 S 71 31W
El Abbasiya, *Sudan* **107 E3** 12 10N 31 18 E
El Abiodh-Sidi-Cheikh, *Algeria* **111 B5** 32 53N 0 31 E
El Adde, *Somali Rep.* **120 D3** 2 35N 46 9 E
El 'Agrûd, *Egypt* **103 E3** 30 14N 34 24 E
El Aïoun, *Morocco* **111 B4** 34 33N 2 30W
El Ait, *Sudan* **107 E2** 12 22N 27 27 E
El 'Aiyat, *Egypt* **106 J7** 29 36N 31 15 E
El 'Alamein, *Egypt* **106 A2** 30 48N 28 58 E
El Alto, *Peru* **172 A1** 4 15 S 81 14W
El Aouj, *Mauritania* **110 D2** 22 53N 12 49W
El 'Aqaba, W. →, *Egypt* **103 E2** 30 7N 33 54 E
El 'Arag, *Egypt* **106 B2** 28 40N 26 20 E
El Arahal, *Spain* **43 H5** 37 15N 5 33W
El Aricha, *Algeria* **111 B4** 34 13N 1 10W
El Arīḥā, *West Bank* **103 D4** 31 52N 35 27 E
El 'Arîsh, *Egypt* **103 D2** 31 8N 33 50 E
El 'Arîsh, W. →, *Egypt* **103 D2** 31 8N 33 47 E
El Arrouch, *Algeria* **111 A6** 36 37N 6 53 E
El Asnam = Ech Chéliff, *Algeria* **111 A5** 36 10N 1 20 E
El Astillero, *Spain* **42 B7** 43 24N 3 49W
El Badâri, *Egypt* **106 B3** 27 4N 31 25 E
El Bahrein, *Egypt* **106 B2** 28 30N 26 25 E
El Ballâs, *Egypt* **106 B3** 26 2N 32 43 E
El Balyana, *Egypt* **106 B3** 26 10N 32 3 E
El Banco, *Colombia* **168 B3** 9 0N 73 58W
El Baqeir, *Sudan* **106 D3** 18 40N 33 40 E
El Barco de Ávila, *Spain* **42 E5** 40 21N 5 31W
El Barco de Valdeorras = O Barco, *Spain* **42 C4** 42 23N 6 58W
El Bauga, *Sudan* **106 D3** 18 18N 33 52 E
El Baúl, *Venezuela* **168 B4** 8 57N 68 17W
El Bawiti, *Egypt* **106 B2** 28 25N 28 45 E
El Bayadh, *Algeria* **111 B5** 33 40N 1 1 E
El Bierzo, *Spain* **42 C4** 42 45N 6 30W
El Bluff, *Nic.* **164 D3** 11 59N 83 40W
El Bolsón, *Argentina* **176 B2** 41 55 S 71 30W
El Bonillo, *Spain* **41 G2** 38 57N 2 35W
El Brûk, W. →, *Egypt* **103 E2** 30 15N 33 50 E
El Buheirat □, *Sudan* **107 F3** 7 0N 30 0 E
El Bur, *Somali Rep.* **120 D3** 4 40N 46 37 E
El Burgo de Osma, *Spain* **40 D1** 41 35N 3 4W
El Caín, *Argentina* **176 B3** 41 38 S 68 19W
El Cajon, *U.S.A.* **161 N10** 32 48N 116 58W
El Callao, *Venezuela* **169 B5** 7 18N 61 50W
El Campo, *U.S.A.* **155 L6** 29 12N 96 16W
El Carmen, *Bolivia* **173 C5** 13 40 S 63 55W
El Centro, *U.S.A.* **161 N11** 32 48N 115 34W
El Cerro, *Bolivia* **173 D5** 17 30 S 61 40W
El Cerro de Andévalo, *Spain* **43 H4** 37 45N 6 57W
El Cocuy, *Colombia* **168 B3** 6 25N 72 27W
El Cocuy △, *Colombia* **168 B3** 6 33N 72 5W
El Compadre, *Mexico* **161 N10** 32 20N 116 14W
El Corcovado, *Argentina* **176 B2** 43 25 S 71 35W
El Coronil, *Spain* **43 H5** 37 5N 5 38W
El Cuy, *Argentina* **176 A3** 39 55 S 68 25W
El Cuyo, *Mexico* **163 C7** 21 30N 87 40W
El Dab'a, *Egypt* **106 H6** 31 0N 28 27 E
El Daheir, *Egypt* **103 D3** 31 13N 34 10 E
El Dambahaddo, *Somali Rep.* **120 D3** 3 17N 46 40 E
El Dátil, *Mexico* **162 B2** 30 7N 112 15W
El Deir, *Egypt* **106 B3** 25 25N 32 20 E
El Dere, *Ethiopia* **120 C2** 5 6N 43 5 E
El Dere, *Somali Rep.* **120 D3** 3 50N 47 8 E
El Dere, *Somali Rep.* **120 C3** 5 22N 46 11 E
El Descanso, *Mexico* **161 N10** 32 12N 116 58W
El Desemboque, *Mexico* **162 A2** 30 30N 112 57W
El Dilingat, *Egypt* **106 H7** 30 50N 30 31 E
El Diviso, *Colombia* **168 C2** 1 22N 78 14W
El Djouf, *Mauritania* **104 D3** 20 0N 9 0W
El Dorado, *Ark., U.S.A.* **155 J8** 33 12N 92 40W
El Dorado, *Kans., U.S.A.* **155 G6** 37 49N 96 52W
El Dorado, *Venezuela* **169 B5** 6 55N 61 37W
El Dorado Springs, *U.S.A.* **155 G8** 37 52N 94 1W
El Eglab, *Algeria* **110 C4** 26 20N 4 30W
El 'Ein, *Sudan* **107 D2** 16 35N 29 22 E
El Ejido, *Spain* **43 J8** 36 47N 2 49W
El Escorial, *Spain* **42 E6** 40 35N 4 7W
El Espinar, *Spain* **42 D6** 41 43N 4 15W
El Eulma, *Algeria* **111 A6** 36 9N 5 42 E
El Faiyûm, *Egypt* **106 J7** 29 19N 30 50 E
El Fâsher, *Sudan* **107 E2** 13 33N 25 26 E
El Fashn, *Egypt* **106 J7** 28 50N 30 54 E
El Ferrol = Ferrol, *Spain* **42 B2** 43 29N 8 15W
El Fifi, *Sudan* **107 E2** 10 4N 25 0 E
El Fud, *Ethiopia* **120 C2** 7 15N 42 52 E
El Fuerte, *Mexico* **162 B3** 26 30N 108 40W
El Ga'a, *Sudan* **107 E2** 14 16N 29 59 E
El Gal, *Somali Rep.* **120 B4** 10 58N 50 20 E
El Garef, *Sudan* **107 E3** 12 3N 34 19 E
El Gebir, *Sudan* **107 E2** 13 40N 29 40 E
El Gedida, *Egypt* **106 B2** 25 40N 28 30 E
El Geneina = Al Junaynah, *Sudan* **109 F4** 13 27N 22 45 E
El Geteina, *Sudan* **107 E3** 14 50N 32 27 E
El Gezira □, *Sudan* **107 E3** 15 0N 33 0 E
El Gir, *Sudan* **106 D2** 19 50N 28 18 E
El Gîza, *Egypt* **106 J7** 30 0N 31 10 E
El Gogorron △, *Mexico* **162 C4** 21 50N 100 50W
El Goléa, *Algeria* **111 B5** 30 30N 2 50 E
El Grau, *Spain* **41 G4** 39 0N 0 7W
El Guácharo △, *Venezuela* **165 D7** 10 8N 63 21W
El Guache △, *Venezuela* **165 E6** 9 45N 69 30W
El Hadeb, *W. Sahara* **110 C2** 25 51N 13 0W
El Hadjira, *Algeria* **111 B6** 32 36N 5 30 E
El Hagiz, *Sudan* **107 D4** 15 15N 35 50 E
El Hâi, *Egypt* **106 J7** 29 39N 31 18 E
El Hajeb, *Morocco* **110 B3** 33 43N 5 13W
El Hamma, *Tunisia* **108 B1** 33 54N 9 48 E
El Hammam, *Egypt* **106 A2** 30 52N 29 25 E
El Hammâmi, *Mauritania* **110 D2** 23 3N 11 30W
El Hamurre, *Somali Rep.* **120 C3** 7 13N 48 54 E
El Hank, *Mauritania* **110 D3** 24 30N 7 0W
El Hasian, *W. Sahara* **110 C2** 26 20N 14 0W
El Hawata, *Sudan* **107 E3** 13 25N 34 42 E
El Heiz, *Egypt* **106 B2** 27 50N 28 40 E
El Hideib, *Sudan* **107 E3** 13 0N 32 50 E
El Hilla, *Sudan* **107 E2** 13 24N 27 2 E
El Homeur, *Algeria* **111 C5** 29 43N 1 45 E
El 'Idisât, *Egypt* **106 B3** 25 30N 32 35 E
El Iskandarîya, *Egypt* **106 H7** 31 13N 29 58 E
El Jadida, *Morocco* **110 B3** 33 11N 8 17W
El Jardal, *Honduras* **164 D2** 14 54N 88 50W
El Jebelein, *Sudan* **107 E3** 12 40N 32 55 E
El Jebha, *Morocco* **110 A4** 35 11N 4 43W
El Jem, *Tunisia* **108 A2** 35 18N 10 42 E
El Kab, *Sudan* **106 D3** 19 27N 32 46 E
El Kabrît, G., *Egypt* **103 F2** 29 42N 33 16 E
El Kafr el Sharqi, *Egypt* **106 H7** 31 16N 31 10 E
El Kala, *Algeria* **111 A6** 36 50N 8 30 E
El Kamlin, *Sudan* **107 D3** 15 3N 33 11 E
El Kantara, *Algeria* **111 A6** 35 14N 5 45 E
El Kantara, *Tunisia* **108 B2** 33 45N 10 58 E
El Karaba, *Sudan* **106 D3** 18 32N 33 41 E
El Kef, *Tunisia* **108 A1** 36 12N 8 47 E
El Kelâa, *Morocco* **110 B3** 32 4N 7 27W
El Kere, *Ethiopia* **107 F5** 5 50N 42 5 E
El Khandaq, *Sudan* **106 D3** 18 30N 30 30 E
El Khârga, *Egypt* **106 B3** 25 30N 30 33 E
El Khartûm, *Sudan* **107 D3** 15 31N 32 35 E
El Khartûm □, *Sudan* **107 D3** 16 0N 33 0 E
El Khartûm Bahrî, *Sudan* **107 D3** 15 40N 32 31 E
El Khroub, *Algeria* **111 A6** 36 10N 6 55 E
El Kseur, *Algeria* **111 A5** 36 46N 4 49 E
El Ksiba, *Morocco* **110 B3** 32 45N 6 1W
El Kuntilla, *Egypt* **103 E3** 30 1N 34 45 E
El Laqâwa, *Sudan* **107 E2** 11 25N 29 1 E
El Leh, *Ethiopia* **107 G4** 3 46N 39 13 E
El Leiya, *Sudan* **107 D4** 16 15N 35 28 E
El Maestrazgo, *Spain* **40 E4** 40 30N 0 25W
El Mafâza, *Sudan* **107 E3** 13 38N 34 30 E
El Maghra, *Egypt* **106 A2** 30 15N 28 55 E
El Mahalla el Kubra, *Egypt* **106 H7** 31 0N 31 0 E
El Mahârîq, *Egypt* **106 B3** 25 35N 30 35 E
El Maîmûn, *Egypt* **106 J7** 29 14N 31 12 E
El Maitén, *Argentina* **176 B2** 42 3 S 71 10W
El Maiz, *Algeria* **111 C4** 28 19N 0 9W
El Maks el Bahari, *Egypt* **106 C3** 24 30N 30 40 E
El Malpais ⌓, *U.S.A.* **159 J10** 34 53N 108 0W
El Manshâh, *Egypt* **106 B3** 26 26N 31 50 E
El Mansour, *Algeria* **111 C4** 27 47N 0 14W
El Mansûra, *Egypt* **106 H7** 31 0N 31 19 E
El Manteco, *Venezuela* **169 B5** 7 38N 62 45W
El Manzala, *Egypt* **106 H7** 31 10N 31 50 E
El Marâgha, *Egypt* **106 B3** 26 35N 31 10 E
El Masid, *Sudan* **107 D3** 15 15N 33 0 E
El Masnou, *Spain* **40 D7** 41 28N 2 20 E
El Matariya, *Egypt* **106 H8** 31 15N 32 0 E
El Meda, *Ethiopia* **107 F5** 5 39N 41 47 E
El Medano, *Canary Is.* **9 e1** 28 3N 16 32W
El Meghaier, *Algeria* **111 B6** 33 55N 5 58 E
El Meraguen, *Algeria* **111 C4** 28 0N 0 7W
El Metemma, *Sudan* **107 D3** 16 50N 33 10 E
El Miamo, *Venezuela* **169 B5** 7 39N 61 46W
El Milagro, *Argentina* **174 C2** 30 59 S 65 59W
El Milia, *Algeria* **111 A6** 36 51N 6 13 E
El Minyâ, *Egypt* **106 B3** 28 7N 30 33 E
El Monte, *U.S.A.* **161 L8** 34 4N 118 1W
El Montseny, *Spain* **40 D7** 41 55N 2 25 E
El Mreyye, *Mauritania* **112 B3** 18 0N 6 0W
El Nido, *Phil.* **81 F2** 11 10N 119 25 E
El Niybo, *Ethiopia* **107 G4** 4 40N 39 55 E
El Obeid, *Sudan* **107 E3** 13 8N 30 10 E
El Odaiya, *Sudan* **107 E2** 12 8N 28 12 E
El Oro, *Mexico* **163 D4** 19 48N 100 8W
El Oro □, *Ecuador* **168 D2** 3 30 S 79 50W
El Oued, *Algeria* **111 B6** 33 20N 6 58 E
El Oumi, *Niger* **111 D7** 20 11N 0 15 E
El Palmar, *Bolivia* **173 D5** 17 50 S 63 9W
El Palmar, *Venezuela* **169 B5** 7 58N 61 53W
El Palmar △, *Argentina* **174 C4** 32 10 S 58 31W
El Palmito, Presa, *Mexico* **162 B3** 25 40N 105 30W
El Paso = Derby, *U.S.A.* **155 G6** 37 33N 97 16W
El Paso, *Ill., U.S.A.* **156 D7** 40 44N 89 1W
El Paso, *Tex., U.S.A.* **159 L10** 31 45N 106 29W
El Paso Robles, *U.S.A.* **160 K6** 35 38N 120 41W
El Pedernoso, *Spain* **41 F2** 39 29N 2 45W
El Pedroso, *Spain* **43 H5** 37 51N 5 45W
El Pilar, *Venezuela* **169 A5** 10 32N 63 9W
El Pinacate y Gran Desierto de Altar = Gran Desierto del Pinacate ⌓, *Mexico* **162 A2** 31 51N 113 32W
El Pobo de Dueñas, *Spain* **40 E3** 40 46N 1 39W
El Portal, *U.S.A.* **160 H7** 37 41N 119 47W
El Porvenir, *Mexico* **162 A3** 31 15N 105 51W
El Prat de Llobregat, *Spain* **40 D7** 41 18N 2 3 E
El Progreso, *Ecuador* **172 a** 0 54 S 89 33W
El Progreso, *Honduras* **164 C2** 15 26N 87 51W
El Pueblito, *Mexico* **162 B3** 29 3N 105 4W
El Pueblo, *Canary Is.* **9 e1** 28 36N 17 47W
El Puente del Arzobispo, *Spain* **42 F5** 39 48N 5 10W
El Puerto de Santa María, *Spain* **43 J4** 36 36N 6 13W
El Qâhira, *Egypt* **106 H7** 30 1N 31 14 E
El Qantara, *Egypt* **103 E1** 30 51N 32 20 E
El Qasr, *Egypt* **106 B2** 25 44N 28 42 E
El Qubâbât, *Egypt* **106 J7** 29 28N 31 16 E
El Quseima, *Egypt* **103 E3** 30 40N 34 15 E
El Qusîya, *Egypt* **106 B3** 27 29N 30 44 E
El Râshda, *Egypt* **106 B2** 25 36N 28 57 E
El Reno, *U.S.A.* **146 C7** 35 32N 97 57W
El Rey △, *Argentina* **174 A3** 24 40 S 64 34W
El Rîdisiya, *Egypt* **106 C3** 24 56N 32 51 E

El Rio, *U.S.A.* **161 L7** 34 14N 119 10W
El Ronquillo, *Spain* **43 H4** 37 44N 6 10W
El Roque, Pta., *Canary Is.* **9 e1** 28 10N 15 25W
El Rosarito, *Mexico* **162 B2** 28 38N 114 4W
El Rubio, *Spain* **43 H5** 37 22N 5 0W
El Saff, *Egypt* **106 J7** 29 34N 31 16 E
El Saheira, W. →, *Egypt* **103 E2** 30 5N 33 25 E
El Salto, *Mexico* **162 C3** 23 47N 105 22W
El Salvador ■, *Cent. Amer.* **164 D2** 13 50N 89 0W
El Sauce, *Nic.* **164 D2** 13 0N 86 40W
El Saucejo, *Spain* **43 H5** 37 4N 5 6W
El Shallal, *Egypt* **106 C3** 24 0N 32 53 E
El Simbillawein, *Egypt* **106 H7** 30 48N 31 13 E
El Sombrero, *Venezuela* **168 B4** 9 23N 67 3W
El Sueco, *Mexico* **162 B3** 29 54N 106 24W
El Suweis, *Egypt* **106 J8** 29 58N 32 31 E
El Tabbîn, *Egypt* **106 J7** 29 47N 31 18 E
El Tamá △, *S. Amer.* **168 B3** 7 25N 72 25W
El Tamarâni, W. →, *Egypt* **103 E3** 30 7N 34 43 E
El Thamad, *Egypt* **103 F3** 29 40N 34 28 E
El Tigre, *Venezuela* **169 B5** 8 44N 64 15W
El Tîh, Gebal, *Egypt* **103 F2** 29 40N 33 50 E
El Tîna, *Egypt* **106 H8** 31 3N 32 22 E
El Tîna, Khalîg, *Egypt* **103 D1** 31 10N 32 40 E
El Tocuyo, *Venezuela* **168 B4** 9 47N 69 48W
El Tofo, *Chile* **174 B1** 29 22 S 71 18W
El Tránsito, *Chile* **174 B1** 28 52 S 70 17W
El Tuparro △, *Colombia* **168 B4** 5 19N 68 28W
El Tûr, *Egypt* **96 D2** 28 14N 33 36 E
El Turbio, *Argentina* **176 D2** 51 45 S 72 5W
El Uinle, *Somali Rep.* **120 D2** 3 4N 41 42 E
El Uqsur, *Egypt* **106 B3** 25 41N 32 38 E
El Valle ⌓, *Spain* **41 H3** 37 56N 1 6W
El Venado, *Mexico* **162 C4** 22 56N 101 10W
El Vendrell, *Spain* **40 D6** 41 10N 1 30 E
El Vergel, *Mexico* **162 B3** 26 28N 106 22W
El Vigía, *Venezuela* **168 B3** 8 38N 71 39W
El Viso del Alcor, *Spain* **43 H5** 37 23N 5 43W
El Wabeira, *Egypt* **103 F2** 29 34N 33 6 E
El Wak, *Kenya* **118 B5** 2 49N 40 56 E
El Wak, *Somali Rep.* **120 D2** 2 44N 41 1 E
El Waqf, *Egypt* **106 B3** 25 45N 32 15 E
El Weguet, *Ethiopia* **107 F5** 5 28N 42 17 E
El Wuz, *Sudan* **107 D3** 15 5N 30 7 E
Elafónisos, *Greece* **48 E4** 36 29N 22 56 E
Elamanchili, *India* **94 F6** 17 33N 82 50 E
Élancourt, *France* **27 D8** 48 47N 1 58 E
Elands, *Australia* **129 A10** 31 37 S 152 20 E
Elandsfontein Junc. = Germiston, *S. Africa* **117 D4** 26 15 S 28 10 E
Élassa, *Greece* **49 F8** 35 18N 26 21 E
Elassón, *Greece* **48 B4** 39 53N 22 12 E
Elat, *Israel* **103 F3** 29 30N 34 56 E
Eláthia, *Greece* **48 C4** 38 37N 22 46 E
Eláti Óros, *Greece* **39 B2** 38 43N 20 39 E
Elâzığ, *Turkey* **101 C8** 38 37N 39 14 E
Elba, *Italy* **44 F7** 42 46N 10 17 E
Elba, *U.S.A.* **152 D3** 31 25N 86 4W
Elbasan, *Albania* **50 E4** 41 9N 20 9 E
Elbe, *U.S.A.* **160 D4** 46 45N 122 10W
Elbe →, *Europe* **30 B4** 53 50N 9 0 E
Elbe-Seitenkanal, *Germany* **30 C6** 52 45N 10 32 E
Elberfeld, *U.S.A.* **157 F9** 38 10N 87 27W
Elbert, Mt., *U.S.A.* **159 G10** 39 7N 106 27W
Elberton, *U.S.A.* **152 A7** 34 7N 82 52W
Elbeuf, *France* **26 C8** 49 17N 1 2 E
Elbidtan, *Turkey* **96 B3** 38 13N 37 12 E
Elbing = Elbląg, *Poland* **54 D6** 54 10N 19 25 E
Elbistan, *Turkey* **100 C7** 38 13N 37 15 E
Elbląg, *Poland* **54 D6** 54 10N 19 25 E
Elbow, *Canada* **143 C7** 51 7N 106 35W
Elbow, Pta., *W. Sahara* **110 D1** 24 5N 15 35W
Elbrus, *Asia* **61 J6** 43 21N 42 30 E
Elbufer-Drawehn ⌓, *Germany* **30 B6** 53 8N 10 58 E
Elburn, *U.S.A.* **157 C8** 41 54N 88 28W
Elburz Mts. = Alborz, Reshteh-ye Kūhhā-ye, *Iran* **97 C7** 36 0N 52 0 E
Elche, *Spain* **41 G4** 38 15N 0 42W
Elche de la Sierra, *Spain* **41 G2** 38 27N 2 3W
Elcho I., *Australia* **126 A2** 11 55 S 135 45 E
Elda, *Spain* **41 G4** 38 29N 0 47W
Elde →, *Germany* **30 B7** 53 7N 11 15 E
Eldey, *Iceland* **11 D4** 63 45N 22 55W
Eldon, *Iowa, U.S.A.* **156 D4** 40 55N 92 13W
Eldon, *Mo., U.S.A.* **156 F4** 38 21N 92 35W
Eldon, *Wash., U.S.A.* **160 C3** 47 33N 123 3W
Eldora, *U.S.A.* **156 B3** 42 22N 93 5W
Eldorado = Echo Bay, *Canada* **138 B8** 66 5N 117 55W
Eldorado, *Argentina* **175 B5** 26 28 S 54 43W
Eldorado, *Canada* **150 B7** 44 35N 77 31W
Eldorado, *Mexico* **162 C3** 24 20N 107 22W
Eldorado, *Ill., U.S.A.* **157 G8** 37 49N 88 26W
Eldorado, *Tex., U.S.A.* **155 K4** 30 52N 100 36W
Eldorendo, *U.S.A.* **152 D5** 31 3N 84 39W
Eldoret, *Kenya* **118 B4** 0 30N 35 17 E
Eldred, *U.S.A.* **150 E6** 41 58N 78 23W
Eldridge, *U.S.A.* **156 C6** 41 39N 90 35W
Elea, C., *Cyprus* **39 E10** 35 19N 34 4 E
Eleanora, Pk., *Australia* **125 F3** 32 57 S 121 9 E
Elefantes →, *Africa* **117 C5** 24 10 S 32 40 E
Elefantes, B. das, *Angola* **115 E2** 13 13 S 12 44 E
Elefantes, G., *Chile* **176 C2** 46 28 S 73 49W
Eleftherios Venizelos Airport, ✕ (ATH), *Greece* **48 D5** 37 55N 23 50 E
Elektrogorsk, *Russia* **58 E10** 55 56N 38 50 E
Elektroperedacha = Elektrogorsk, *Russia* **58 E10** 55 56N 38 50 E
Elektrostal, *Russia* **58 E10** 55 41N 38 32 E
Elektrovoz = Stupino, *Russia* **58 E10** 54 57N 38 2 E
Elele, *Nigeria* **113 D6** 5 5N 6 50 E
Elena, *Bulgaria* **51 D9** 42 55N 25 53 E
Elephant Butte Reservoir, *U.S.A.* **159 K10** 33 9N 107 11W
Elephant I., *Antarctica* **7 C18** 61 0 S 55 0W
Elephant Pass, *Sri Lanka* **95 K5** 9 35N 80 25 E
Elesbão Veloso, *Brazil* **170 C3** 6 13 S 42 8W
Eleshnitsa, *Bulgaria* **50 E7** 41 52N 23 36 E
Eleşkirt, *Turkey* **101 C10** 39 50N 42 50 E
Eleuthera, *Bahamas* **164 B4** 25 0N 76 20W
Elevsís, *Greece* **48 C5** 38 4N 23 26 E
Elevtheroúpolis, *Greece* **51 F8** 40 52N 24 20 E
Elfin Cove, *U.S.A.* **144 G13** 58 12N 136 22W
Elgå, *Norway* **18 B8** 62 10N 11 56 E
Elgepiggen, *Norway* **18 B8** 62 10N 11 21 E
Elgg, *Switz.* **33 B7** 47 29N 8 52 E
Elgin, *Canada* **151 B8** 44 36N 76 13W
Elgin, *U.K.* **22 D5** 57 39N 3 19W
Elgin, *Ill., U.S.A.* **157 B8** 42 2N 88 17W
Elgin, *N. Dak., U.S.A.* **154 B4** 46 24N 101 51W
Elgin, *Oreg., U.S.A.* **158 D5** 45 34N 117 55W
Elgin, *S.C., U.S.A.* **152 A9** 34 10N 80 48W
Elgin, *Tex., U.S.A.* **155 K6** 30 21N 97 22W
Elgoibar, *Spain* **40 B2** 43 13N 2 24W
Elgon, Mt., *Africa* **118 B3** 1 10N 34 30 E
Eliase, *Indonesia* **83 C4** 8 21 S 130 48 E
Elikón, *Greece* **48 C4** 38 18N 22 45 E
Elim, *Namibia* **116 B2** 17 48 S 15 31 E
Elim, *S. Africa* **116 E2** 34 35 S 19 45 E
Elim, *U.S.A.* **144 D7** 64 37N 162 15W
Elin Pelin, *Bulgaria* **50 D7** 42 40N 23 36 E
Elingampangu, *Dem. Rep. of the Congo* **114 C4** 2 0 S 24 4 E
Elipa, *Dem. Rep. of the Congo* **114 C4** 1 3 S 24 20 E
Eliseu Martins, *Brazil* **170 C3** 8 13 S 43 42W
Elista, *Russia* **61 G7** 46 16N 44 14 E
Eliza, L., *Australia* **128 D3** 37 15 S 139 50 E
Elizabeth, *Australia* **128 C3** 34 42 S 138 41 E
Elizabeth, *Ill., U.S.A.* **156 B6** 42 19N 90 13W
Elizabeth, *N.J., U.S.A.* **151 F10** 40 40N 74 13W
Elizabeth, B., *Ecuador* **172 a** 0 36 S 91 12W
Elizabeth City, *U.S.A.* **149 G7** 36 18N 76 14W
Elizabethton, *U.S.A.* **149 G4** 36 21N 82 13W
Elizabethtown, *Ky., U.S.A.* **157 G11** 37 42N 85 52W
Elizabethtown, *N.Y., U.S.A.* **151 B11** 44 13N 73 36W
Elizabethtown, *Pa., U.S.A.* **151 F8** 40 9N 76 36W
Elizabethville = Lubumbashi, *Dem. Rep. of the Congo* **119 E2** 11 40 S 27 28 E
Elizondo, *Spain* **40 B3** 43 12N 1 30W
Ełk, *Poland* **54 E9** 53 50N 22 21 E
Elk →, *Canada* **142 C5** 49 11N 115 14W
Ełk →, *Poland* **54 E9** 53 41N 22 28 E
Elk →, *U.S.A.* **149 H2** 34 46N 87 16W
Elk City, *U.S.A.* **155 H5** 35 25N 99 25W
Elk Creek, *U.S.A.* **160 F4** 39 36N 122 32W
Elk Grove, *U.S.A.* **160 G5** 38 25N 121 22W
Elk Island △, *Canada* **142 C6** 53 35N 112 59W
Elk Lake, *Canada* **140 C3** 47 40N 80 25W
Elk Point, *Canada* **143 C6** 53 54N 110 55W
Elk River, *Idaho, U.S.A.* **158 C5** 46 47N 116 11W
Elk River, *Minn., U.S.A.* **154 C8** 45 18N 93 35W
Elkader, *U.S.A.* **156 B5** 42 51N 91 24W
Elkedra →, *Australia* **126 C2** 21 8 S 136 22 E
Elkhart, *Ind., U.S.A.* **157 C11** 41 41N 85 58W
Elkhart, *Kans., U.S.A.* **155 G4** 37 0N 101 54W
Elkhart →, *U.S.A.* **157 C11** 41 41N 85 58W
Elkhorn, *Canada* **143 D8** 49 59N 101 14W
Elkhorn, *U.S.A.* **157 B8** 42 40N 88 33W
Elkhorn →, *U.S.A.* **154 E6** 41 8N 96 19W
Elkhovo, *Bulgaria* **51 D10** 42 10N 26 35 E
Elkin, *U.S.A.* **149 G5** 36 15N 80 51W
Elkins, *U.S.A.* **148 F6** 38 55N 79 51W
Elkland, *U.S.A.* **150 E7** 41 59N 77 19W
Elko, *Canada* **142 D5** 49 20N 115 10W
Elko, *U.S.A.* **158 F6** 40 50N 115 46W
Elkton, *U.S.A.* **150 C1** 43 49N 83 11W
Ell, L., *Australia* **125 E4** 29 13 S 127 46 E
Ellas = Greece ■, *Europe* **48 B3** 40 0N 23 0 E
Ellaville, *Fla., U.S.A.* **152 E6** 30 23N 83 10W
Ellaville, *Ga., U.S.A.* **152 C5** 32 14N 84 19W
Ellef Ringnes I., *Canada* **6 B2** 78 30N 102 2W
Ellen, Mt., *U.S.A.* **151 B12** 44 9N 72 56W
Ellenburg, *U.S.A.* **151 B11** 44 54N 73 48W
Ellendale, *U.S.A.* **154 B5** 46 0N 98 32W
Ellensburg, *U.S.A.* **158 C3** 46 59N 120 34W
Ellenville, *U.S.A.* **151 E10** 41 43N 74 24W
Ellerton, *Barbados* **165 g** 13 7N 59 33W
Ellery, Mt., *Australia* **129 D8** 37 28 S 148 47 E
Ellesmere = Scottsdale, *Australia* **127 G4** 41 9 S 147 31 E
Ellesmere, L., *N.Z.* **131 H7** 43 47 S 172 28 E
Ellesmere I., *Canada* **6 B4** 79 30N 80 0W
Ellesmere Port, *U.K.* **20 D5** 53 17N 2 54W
Ellettsville, *U.S.A.* **157 E10** 39 14N 86 38W
Ellice Is. = Tuvalu ■, *Pac. Oc.* **134 H9** 8 0 S 178 0 E
Ellicottville, *U.S.A.* **150 D6** 42 17N 78 40W
Elliot, *Australia* **126 B1** 17 33 S 133 32 E
Elliot, *S. Africa* **117 E4** 31 22 S 27 48 E
Elliot Lake, *Canada* **140 C3** 46 25N 82 35W
Elliotdale = Xhora, *S. Africa* **117 E4** 31 55 S 28 38 E
Elliott, *U.S.A.* **152 A9** 34 6N 80 10W
Elliott Key, *U.S.A.* **153 K9** 25 27N 80 12W
Ellis, *U.S.A.* **154 F5** 38 56N 99 34W
Elliston, *Australia* **127 E1** 33 39 S 134 53 E
Ellisville, *U.S.A.* **155 K10** 31 36N 89 12W
Ellon, *U.K.* **22 D6** 57 22N 2 4W
Ellora, *India* **94 D2** 20 1N 75 10 E
Ellore = Eluru, *India* **94 F5** 16 48N 81 8 E
Elloree, *U.S.A.* **152 B9** 33 32N 80 34W
Ellsworth, *Kans., U.S.A.* **154 F5** 38 44N 98 14W
Ellsworth, *Maine, U.S.A.* **149 C11** 44 33N 68 25W
Ellsworth Land, *Antarctica* **7 D16** 76 0 S 89 0W
Ellsworth Mts., *Antarctica* **7 D16** 78 30 S 85 0W
Ellwangen, *Germany* **31 G6** 48 57N 10 8 E
Ellwood City, *U.S.A.* **150 F4** 40 52N 80 17W
Ellzey, *U.S.A.* **153 F7** 29 19N 82 48W
Elm, *Switz.* **33 C8** 46 54N 9 10 E
Elm-Lappwald ⌓, *Germany* **30 C6** 52 15N 10 50 E
Elma, *Canada* **143 D9** 49 52N 95 55W
Elma, *U.S.A.* **160 D3** 47 0N 123 25W
Elmadağ, *Turkey* **100 C5** 39 55N 33 14 E
Elmalı, *Turkey* **49 E11** 36 44N 29 56 E
Elmhurst, *U.S.A.* **157 C9** 41 53N 87 56W
Elmina, *Ghana* **113 D4** 5 5N 1 21W
Elmira, *Canada* **150 C4** 43 36N 80 33W
Elmira, *U.S.A.* **150 D8** 42 6N 76 48W
Elmira Heights, *U.S.A.* **150 D8** 42 8N 76 50W
Elmodel, *U.S.A.* **152 D5** 31 21N 84 29W
Elmore, *Australia* **128 D6** 36 30 S 144 37 E
Elmore, *Ala., U.S.A.* **152 C3** 32 32N 86 19W
Elmore, *Calif., U.S.A.* **161 M11** 33 7N 115 49W
Elmore, *Minn., U.S.A.* **157 C13** 41 29N 83 18W
Elmshorn, *Germany* **30 B5** 53 43N 9 40 E
Elmvale, *Canada* **150 B5** 44 35N 79 52W
Elmwood, *U.S.A.* **156 D7** 40 47N 89 58W
Elne, *France* **28 F6** 42 36N 2 58 E
Elnesvågen, *Norway* **18 B4** 62 52N 7 10 E
Elnora, *U.S.A.* **157 F9** 38 53N 87 5W
Eloaua I., *Papua N. G.* **132 A5** 1 38 S 149 40 E
Elobey, Is., *Eq. Guin.* **114 B1** 1 1N 9 29 E
Elongo, *Dem. Rep. of the Congo* **114 C4** 0 19 S 21 39 E
Elora, *Canada* **150 C4** 43 41N 80 26W
Elorza, *Venezuela* **168 B4** 7 3N 69 31W
Elos, *Greece* **48 E4** 36 46N 22 43 E
Eloúnda, *Greece* **39 E6** 35 16N 25 42 E
Eloy, *U.S.A.* **159 K8** 32 45N 111 33W
Éloyes, *France* **27 D13** 48 6N 6 36 E
Elpitiya, *Sri Lanka* **95 L5** 6 17N 80 10 E
Elrose, *Canada* **143 C7** 51 12N 108 0W
Elsberry, *U.S.A.* **156 E6** 39 10N 90 47W
Elsdorf, *Germany* **30 E2** 50 55N 6 34 E
Elsie, *Mich., U.S.A.* **157 A12** 43 5N 84 23W
Elsie, *Oreg., U.S.A.* **160 E3** 45 52N 123 36W
Elsinore = Helsingør, *Denmark* **17 H6** 56 2N 12 35 E
Elster →, *Germany* **30 D7** 51 25N 11 57 E
Elsterwerda, *Germany* **30 D9** 51 27N 13 31 E
Eltham, *N.Z.* **130 F3** 39 26 S 174 19 E
Elton, *Russia* **61 F8** 49 5N 46 52 E
Elton, Ozero, *Russia* **61 F8** 49 5N 46 42 E
Eltville, *Germany* **31 E4** 50 2N 8 7 E
Eluru, *India* **94 F5** 16 48N 81 8 E
Elvas, *Portugal* **43 G3** 38 50N 7 10W
Elven, *France* **26 E4** 47 44N 2 36W
Elverum, *Norway* **18 D8** 60 53N 11 34 E
Elvire →, *Australia* **124 C4** 17 51 S 128 11 E
Elvire, Mt., *Australia* **125 E2** 29 22 S 119 36 E
Elvo →, *Italy* **44 C5** 45 23N 8 21 E
Elwell, L., *U.S.A.* **158 B8** 48 22N 111 17W
Elwood, *Ill., U.S.A.* **157 C8** 41 24N 88 7W
Elwood, *Ind., U.S.A.* **157 D11** 40 17N 85 50W
Elwood, *Nebr., U.S.A.* **154 E5** 40 36N 99 52W
Elx = Elche, *Spain* **41 G4** 38 15N 0 42W
Ely, *U.K.* **21 E8** 52 24N 0 16 E
Ely, *Minn., U.S.A.* **154 B9** 47 55N 91 51W
Ely, *Nev., U.S.A.* **158 G6** 39 15N 114 54W
Elyria, *U.S.A.* **150 E2** 41 22N 82 7W
Elyrus, *Greece* **48 F5** 35 15N 23 45 E
Elz →, *Germany* **31 G3** 48 18N 7 44 E
Emådalen, *Sweden* **16 C8** 61 20N 14 44 E
Émaé, *Vanuatu* **133 G6** 17 4 S 168 24 E
Emāmrūd, *Iran* **97 B7** 36 30N 55 0 E
Emån →, *Sweden* **17 G10** 57 8N 16 30 E
Emao, *Vanuatu* **133 G6** 17 29 S 168 30 E
Emas △, *Brazil* **173 D7** 18 2 S 52 50W
Emateloa, *Dem. Rep. of the Congo* **114 B3** 1 16N 18 42 E
Emba, *Kazakhstan* **66 E6** 48 50N 58 8 E
Emba →, *Kazakhstan* **57 E9** 46 55N 53 28 E
Embarcación, *Argentina* **174 A3** 23 10 S 64 0W
Embarras →, *U.S.A.* **157 F9** 38 39N 87 37W
Embarras Portage, *Canada* **143 B6** 58 27N 111 28W
Embetsu, *Japan* **70 B10** 44 44N 141 47 E
Embi = Emba, *Kazakhstan* **66 E6** 48 50N 58 8 E
Embi = Emba →, *Kazakhstan* **57 E9** 46 55N 53 28 E
Embira →, *Brazil* **172 B3** 7 19 S 70 15W
Embóna, *Greece* **38 E11** 36 13N 27 51 E
Embrach, *Switz.* **33 B7** 47 30N 8 36 E
Embrun, *France* **29 D10** 44 34N 6 30 E
Embu, *Kenya* **118 C4** 0 32 S 37 38 E
Emden, *Germany* **30 B3** 53 21N 7 12 E
Emecik, *Turkey* **49 E9** 36 46N 27 49 E
Emerald, *Queens., Australia* **126 C4** 23 32 S 148 10 E
Emerald, *Vic., Australia* **122 E8** 37 56 S 145 29 E
Emerson, *Canada* **143 D9** 49 0N 97 10W
Emerson, *U.S.A.* **152 A5** 34 8N 84 45W
Emet, *Turkey* **49 B11** 39 20N 29 15 E
Emeti, *Papua N. G.* **132 D2** 7 53 S 143 15 E
Emi Koussi, *Chad* **109 E3** 19 45N 18 55 E
Emília-Romagna □, *Italy* **44 D8** 44 45N 11 0 E
Emilius, Mte., *Italy* **44 C4** 45 45N 7 20 E
Eminabad, *Pakistan* **92 C6** 32 2N 74 8 E
Emine, Nos, *Bulgaria* **51 D11** 42 40N 27 56 E
Eminence, *U.S.A.* **157 F11** 38 22N 85 11W
Emirau I., *Papua N. G.* **132 A6** 1 40 S 150 0 E
Emirdağ, *Turkey* **100 C4** 39 2N 31 8 E
Emissi, Tarso, *Chad* **109 D3** 21 27N 18 36 E
Emlenton, *U.S.A.* **150 E5** 41 11N 79 43W
Emlichheim, *Germany* **30 C2** 52 37N 6 51 E
Emmaboda, *Sweden* **17 H9** 56 37N 15 32 E
Emmalane, *U.S.A.* **152 C7** 32 46N 82 0W
Emmaus, *S. Africa* **116 D4** 29 2 S 25 15 E
Emmaus, *U.S.A.* **151 F9** 40 32N 75 30W
Emme →, *Switz.* **32 B5** 47 14N 7 32 E
Emmeloord, *Neths.* **24 B5** 52 44N 5 46 E
Emmen, *Neths.* **24 B6** 52 48N 6 57 E
Emmen, *Switz.* **31 H4** 47 5N 8 18 E
Emmenbrücke, *Switz.* **33 B6** 47 4N 8 16 E
Emmendingen, *Germany* **31 G3** 48 6N 7 51 E
Emmental, *Switz.* **32 C4** 46 55N 7 40 E
Emmerich, *Germany* **30 D2** 51 50N 6 14 E
Emmet, *Australia* **126 C3** 24 45 S 144 30 E
Emmetsburg, *U.S.A.* **156 A2** 43 7N 94 41W
Emmett, *U.S.A.* **150 D2** 42 59N 82 46W
Emmiganuru, *India* **95 G3** 15 44N 77 29 E
Emmonak, *U.S.A.* **144 E6** 62 46N 164 30W
Emo, *Canada* **143 D10** 48 38N 93 50W
Emőd, *Hungary* **52 C5** 47 57N 20 47 E
Emona, *Bulgaria* **51 D11** 42 43N 27 53 E
Empalme, *Mexico* **162 B2** 28 1N 110 49W
Empangeni, *S. Africa* **117 D5** 28 50 S 31 52 E
Empedrado, *Argentina* **174 B4** 28 0 S 58 46W
Emperor Seamount Chain, *Pac. Oc.* **134 D9** 40 0N 170 0 E
Empingham Res. = Rutland Water, *U.K.* **21 E7** 52 39N 0 38W
Empire, *U.S.A.* **152 C6** 32 21N 83 18W
Empoli, *Italy* **44 E7** 43 43N 10 57 E
Emporia, *Kans., U.S.A.* **154 F6** 38 25N 96 11W
Emporia, *Va., U.S.A.* **149 G7** 36 42N 77 32W
Emporium, *U.S.A.* **150 E6** 41 31N 78 14W
Empress, *Canada* **143 C7** 50 57N 110 0W
Empty Quarter = Rub' al Khālī, *Si. Arabia* **99 C5** 19 0N 48 0 E
Ems →, *Germany* **30 B3** 53 20N 7 12 E
Emsdale, *Canada* **150 A5** 45 32N 79 19W
Emsdetten, *Germany* **30 C3** 52 10N 7 32 E
Emu, *China* **75 C15** 43 40N 128 6 E
Emu Park, *Australia* **126 C5** 23 13 S 150 50 E
'En 'Avrona, *Israel* **103 F4** 29 43N 35 0 E
En Gannim = Ramat Gan, *Israel* **103 C3** 32 4N 34 48 E
En Nahrat, *Mali* **110 D4** 22 55N 3 36W
En Nahud, *Sudan* **107 E2** 12 45N 28 25 E
En Nofalab, *Sudan* **107 D3** 15 52N 32 32 E
Ena, *Japan* **73 B9** 35 25N 137 25 E
Ena-San, *Japan* **73 B9** 35 26N 137 36 E
Enambú, *Colombia* **168 C3** 1 1N 70 17W
Enana, *Namibia* **116 B2** 17 30 S 16 23 E
Enånger, *Sweden* **16 C11** 61 30N 17 9 E
Enard B., *U.K.* **22 C3** 58 5N 5 20W
Enare = Inarijärvi, *Finland* **14 B22** 69 0N 28 0 E
Enarotali, *Indonesia* **83 B5** 3 55 S 136 21 E
Enbekshi, *Kazakhstan* **65 C4** 41 22N 68 3 E
Encampment, *U.S.A.* **158 F10** 41 12N 106 47W
Encantadas, Serra, *Brazil* **175 C5** 30 40 S 53 0W
Encarnación, *Paraguay* **175 B4** 27 15 S 55 50W
Encarnación de Diaz, *Mexico* **162 C4** 21 30N 102 13W
Enchi, *Ghana* **112 D4** 5 53N 2 48W
Encinitas, *U.S.A.* **161 M9** 33 3N 117 17W
Encino, *U.S.A.* **159 J11** 34 39N 105 28W
Encontrados, *Venezuela* **168 B3** 9 3N 72 14W
Encounter B., *Australia* **128 C3** 35 45 S 138 45 E
Encruzilhada, *Brazil* **171 E3** 15 31 S 40 54W
Encs, *Hungary* **52 B6** 48 20N 21 8 E
Endako, *Canada* **142 C3** 54 6N 125 2W
Ende, *Indonesia* **82 C2** 8 45 S 121 40 E
Endeavour Str., *Australia* **126 A3** 10 45 S 142 0 E
Endelave, *Denmark* **17 J4** 55 46N 10 18 E
Enden, *Norway* **18 C7** 61 47N 10 15 E
Enderbury I., *Kiribati* **134 H10** 3 8 S 171 5W
Enderby, *Canada* **142 C5** 50 35N 119 10W
Enderby I., *Australia* **124 D2** 20 35 S 116 30 E
Enderby Land, *Antarctica* **7 C5** 66 0 S 53 0 E
Enderlin, *U.S.A.* **154 B6** 46 38N 97 36W
Endicott, *U.S.A.* **151 D8** 42 6N 76 4W
Endicott Mts., *U.S.A.* **144 C10** 68 0N 152 0W
Endimari →, *Brazil* **172 B4** 8 46 S 66 7W
Endwell, *U.S.A.* **151 D8** 42 6N 76 2W
Endyalgout I., *Australia* **124 B5** 11 40 S 132 35 E
Ene →, *Peru* **172 C3** 11 10 S 74 18W
Eneabba, *Australia* **125 E2** 29 49 S 115 16 E
Energetīcheskīy, *Kazakhstan* **65 B8** 43 25N 77 1 E
Energetik, *Russia* **64 F7** 51 45N 58 45 E
Enewetak Atoll, *Marshall Is.* **134 F8** 11 30N 162 15 E
Enez, *Turkey* **51 F10** 40 45N 26 5 E
Enfer, Pte. d', *Martinique* **164 c** 14 22N 60 54W
Enfield, *Canada* **141 D7** 44 56N 63 32W
Enfield, *Conn., U.S.A.* **151 E12** 41 58N 72 36W
Enfield, *Ill., U.S.A.* **157 F8** 38 6N 88 20W
Enfield, *N.C., U.S.A.* **149 G7** 36 11N 77 41W
Enfield, *N.H., U.S.A.* **151 C12** 43 39N 72 9W
Enga □, *Papua N. G.* **132 C2** 5 30 S 143 30 E
Engadin, *Switz.* **31 J6** 46 45N 10 10 E
Engan, *Norway* **18 A5** 63 8N 8 31 E
Engaño, C., *Dom. Rep.* **165 C6** 18 30N 68 20W
Engaño, C., *Phil.* **80 B4** 18 35N 122 23 E
Engaru, *Japan* **70 B11** 44 3N 143 31 E
Engcobo, *S. Africa* **117 E4** 31 37 S 28 0 E
Engelberg, *Switz.* **33 C6** 46 48N 8 26 E
Engels, *Russia* **60 E8** 51 28N 46 6 E
Engemann L., *Canada* **143 B7** 58 0N 106 55W
Engerdal, *Norway* **18 C8** 61 45N 11 58 E
Engershatu, *Eritrea* **107 D4** 16 7N 38 34 E
Enggano, *Indonesia* **84 D2** 5 20 S 102 40 E
Engil, *Morocco* **110 B4** 33 12N 4 32W
Engineer Group, *Papua N. G.* **132 F6** 10 35 S 151 20 E
Engkilili, *Malaysia* **85 B4** 1 3N 111 42 E
England, *U.S.A.* **155 H9** 34 33N 91 58W
England □, *U.K.* **21 E5** 53 0N 2 0W
Englee, *Canada* **141 B8** 50 45N 56 5W
Englehart, *Canada* **140 C4** 47 49N 79 52W
Englewood, *Colo., U.S.A.* **154 F2** 39 39N 104 59W
Englewood, *Fla., U.S.A.* **153 J7** 26 58N 82 21W
Englewood, *Ohio, U.S.A.* **157 E12** 39 53N 84 18W
English, *U.S.A.* **157 F10** 38 20N 86 28W
English →, *Canada* **143 C10** 49 12N 91 5W
English →, *U.S.A.* **156 C5** 41 29N 91 32W
English B., *Ascension I.* **9 g** 7 54 S 14 23W
English Bazar = Ingraj Bazar, *India* **93 G13** 24 58N 88 10 E
English Channel, *Europe* **21 G6** 50 0N 2 0W
English Company's Is., The, *Australia* **126 A2** 11 50 S 136 32 E
English River, *Canada* **140 C1** 49 14N 91 0W
Engures ezers, *Latvia* **54 A10** 57 16N 23 6 E
Enguri →, *Georgia* **61 J5** 42 27N 41 38 E
Enid, *U.S.A.* **155 G6** 36 24N 97 53W
Enipévs →, *Greece* **48 B4** 39 22N 22 17 E
Enkhuizen, *Neths.* **24 B5** 52 42N 5 17 E
Enköping, *Sweden* **16 E11** 59 37N 17 4 E
Enle, *China* **76 F3** 24 0N 101 9 E
Enna, *Italy* **47 E7** 37 34N 14 16 E
Ennadai, *Canada* **143 A8** 61 8N 100 53W
Ennadai L., *Canada* **143 A8** 60 58N 101 20W
Enné, O. →, *Chad* **109 F4** 14 24N 18 45 E
Ennedi, *Chad* **109 E4** 17 15N 22 0 E
Enneri Achelouma →, *Niger* **111 D7** 21 55N 13 35 E
Enngonia, *Australia* **127 D4** 29 21 S 145 50 E
Ennigerloh, *Germany* **30 D4** 51 50N 8 2 E
Ennis, *Ireland* **23 D3** 52 51N 8 59W
Ennis, *Mont., U.S.A.* **158 D8** 45 21N 111 44W
Ennis, *Tex., U.S.A.* **155 J6** 32 20N 96 38W
Enniscorthy, *Ireland* **23 D5** 52 30N 6 34W
Enniskillen, *U.K.* **23 B4** 54 21N 7 39W
Ennistimon, *Ireland* **23 D2** 52 57N 9 17W
Enns, *Austria* **34 C7** 48 12N 14 28 E
Enns →, *Austria* **34 C7** 48 14N 14 32 E
Enontekiö, *Finland* **14 B20** 68 23N 23 37 E
Enosburg Falls, *U.S.A.* **151 B12** 44 55N 72 48W
Enping, *China* **77 F9** 22 16N 112 21 E
Enrekang, *Indonesia* **82 B1** 3 34 S 119 47 E
Enrile, *Phil.* **80 C3** 17 34N 121 42 E
Enriquillo, L., *Dom. Rep.* **165 C5** 18 20N 72 5W
Enschede, *Neths.* **24 B6** 52 13N 6 53 E
Ensenada, *Argentina* **174 C4** 34 55 S 57 55W
Ensenada, *Mexico* **162 A1** 31 50N 116 50W
Ensenada de los Muertos, *Mexico* **162 C2** 23 59N 109 50W
Enshi, *China* **76 B7** 30 18N 109 29 E
Enshū-Nada, *Japan* **73 C9** 34 27N 137 38 E
Ensiola, Pta. de n', *Spain* **38 B3** 39 7N 2 55 E
Ensisheim, *France* **27 E14** 47 50N 7 20 E
Ensley, *U.S.A.* **153 E2** 30 31N 87 16W
Entebbe, *Uganda* **118 B3** 0 4N 32 28 E
Enterprise, *Canada* **142 A5** 60 47N 115 45W
Enterprise, *Ala., U.S.A.* **152 D4** 31 19N 85 51W
Enterprise, *Oreg., U.S.A.* **158 D5** 45 25N 117 17W
Entlebuch, *Switz.* **32 C6** 46 59N 8 4 E
Entorno de Doñana ⌓, *Spain* **43 J4** 37 0N 6 26W
Entraygues-sur-Truyère, *France* **28 D6** 44 38N 2 35 E
Entre Rios = Rio Brilhante, *Brazil* **175 A5** 21 48 S 54 33W
Entre Rios = Três Rios, *Brazil* **171 F3** 22 6 S 43 15W
Entre Ríos, *Bolivia* **174 A3** 21 30 S 64 25W
Entre Rios, *Bahia, Brazil* **171 D4** 11 56 S 38 5W
Entre Rios, *Pará, Brazil* **173 B7** 5 24 S 54 21W
Entre Ríos □, *Argentina* **174 C4** 30 30 S 58 30W
Entrepeñas, Embalse de, *Spain* **40 E2** 40 34N 2 42W
Entroncamento, *Portugal* **43 F2** 39 28N 8 28W
Enugu, *Nigeria* **113 D6** 6 30N 7 30 E
Enugu □, *Nigeria* **113 D6** 6 30N 7 45 E
Enugu Ezike, *Nigeria* **113 D6** 7 0N 7 29 E
Enumclaw, *U.S.A.* **160 C5** 47 12N 121 59W
Envalira, Port d', *Europe* **40 C6** 42 33N 1 43 E
Envermeu, *France* **26 C8** 49 53N 1 15 E
Envigado, *Colombia* **168 B2** 6 10N 75 35W
Enviken, *Sweden* **16 D9** 60 49N 15 46 E
Envira, *Brazil* **172 B3** 7 18 S 70 13W
Enying, *Hungary* **52 D3** 46 56N 18 15 E
Enyonga, *Gabon* **114 C1** 0 59 S 9 22 E
Enza →, *Italy* **44 D7** 44 54N 10 31 E
Enzan, *Japan* **73 B10** 35 42N 138 44 E
Eólie, Ís., *Italy* **47 D7** 38 30N 14 57 E
Epalinges, *Switz.* **32 C3** 46 33N 6 40 E
Epanomí, *Greece* **50 F6** 40 25N 22 59 E
Epe, *Neths.* **24 B5** 52 21N 5 59 E
Epe, *Nigeria* **113 D5** 6 36N 3 59 E
Epéna, *Congo* **114 B3** 1 22N 17 29 E
Épernay, *France* **27 C10** 49 3N 3 56 E
Épernon, *France* **27 D8** 48 35N 1 40 E
Ephesus, *Turkey* **49 D9** 37 55N 27 22 E
Ephraim, *U.S.A.* **158 G8** 39 22N 111 35W
Ephrata, *Pa., U.S.A.* **151 F8** 40 11N 76 11W
Ephrata, *Wash., U.S.A.* **158 C4** 47 19N 119 33W
Epi, *Vanuatu* **133 F6** 16 43 S 168 15 E
Epidaurus Limera, *Greece* **48 E5** 36 46N 23 0 E
Épila, *Spain* **40 D3** 41 36N 1 17W
Épinac, *France* **27 F11** 46 59N 4 31 E
Épinal, *France* **27 D13** 48 10N 6 27 E
Epira, *Guyana* **169 B6** 5 5N 57 20W
Episkopi, *Cyprus* **39 F8** 34 40N 32 54 E
Episkopí, *Greece* **39 E5** 35 20N 24 20 E
Episkopi Bay, *Cyprus* **39 F8** 34 35N 32 50 E
Epitálion, *Greece* **48 D3** 37 37N 21 30 E
Eppalock, L., *Australia* **128 D6** 36 52 S 144 34 E
Eppan = Appiano, *Italy* **45 B8** 46 28N 11 15 E
Eppingen, *Germany* **31 F4** 49 8N 8 53 E
Epsom, *U.K.* **21 F7** 51 19N 0 16W
Epukiro, *Namibia* **116 C2** 21 40 S 19 9 E
Equality, *U.S.A.* **157 G8** 37 44N 88 20W
Équateur □, *Dem. Rep. of the Congo* **114 B4** 2 0N 21 0 E
Equatorial Guinea ■, *Africa* **114 B1** 2 0N 8 0 E
Equeipa, *Venezuela* **169 B5** 5 22N 62 43W
Er Hai, *China* **76 E3** 25 48N 100 11 E
Er Rachidia, *Morocco* **110 B4** 31 58N 4 20W
Er Rahad, *Sudan* **107 E3** 12 45N 30 32 E
Er Rif, *Morocco* **111 A4** 35 1N 4 1W
Er Rogel, *Sudan* **106 D4** 18 10N 35 25 E
Er Roseires, *Sudan* **107 E3** 11 55N 34 30 E
Er Rua'at, *Sudan* **107 E3** 12 21N 32 17 E
Eraclea, *Italy* **45 C9** 45 35N 12 40 E
Eran, *Phil.* **81 G1** 9 4N 117 42 E
Erandol, *India* **94 D2** 20 56N 75 20 E
Eranga, *Dem. Rep. of the Congo* **114 C3** 1 52 S 18 56 E
Erap, *Papua N. G.* **132 D4** 6 37 S 146 51 E
Erasmus = Bronkhorstspruit, *S. Africa* **117 D4** 25 46 S 28 45 E
Erave, *Papua N. G.* **132 D2** 6 39 S 144 0 E
Erave →, *Papua N. G.* **132 D3** 6 54 S 144 47 E
Erāwadī Myit = Irrawaddy →, *Burma* **90 G5** 15 50N 95 6 E
Erāwadī Myitwanya = Irrawaddy, Mouths of the, *Burma* **90 H5** 15 30N 95 0 E
Erba, *Italy* **44 C6** 45 48N 9 15 E
Erba, *Sudan* **106 D4** 19 5N 36 51 E
Erba, J., *Sudan* **106 C4** 20 48N 36 47 E
Erbaa, *Turkey* **100 B7** 40 42N 36 36 E
Erbeskopf, *Germany* **31 F3** 49 44N 7 2 E
Erbil = Arbīl, *Iraq* **101 D11** 36 15N 44 5 E
Erbu, *Ethiopia* **107 E3** 6 44N 34 53 E
Ercan, Nicosia ✕ (ECN), *Cyprus* **39 E9** 35 10N 33 30 E
Erçek, *Turkey* **96 B4** 38 39N 43 36 E
Erçis, *Turkey* **101 C10** 39 2N 43 21 E
Erciyaş Dağı, *Turkey* **96 B2** 38 30N 35 30 E
Érd, *Hungary* **52 C3** 47 22N 18 56 E
Erdao Jiang →, *China* **75 C14** 43 0N 127 0 E
Erdek, *Turkey* **51 F11** 40 23N 27 47 E
Erdély = Transilvania, *Romania* **53 D9** 46 30N 24 0 E
Erdemli, *Turkey* **100 D6** 36 36N 34 19 E
Erdene = Ulaan-Uul, *Mongolia* **74 B6** 44 13N 111 10 E
Erdenet, *Mongolia* **68 B5** 49 2N 104 5 E
Erdenetsogt, *Mongolia* **74 C4** 42 55N 106 5 E
Erding, *Germany* **31 G7** 48 18N 11 54 E
Erdre →, *France* **26 E5** 47 13N 1 32W
Erebato →, *Venezuela* **169 B5** 5 54N 64 16W
Erebus, Mt., *Antarctica* **7 D11** 77 35 S 167 0 E
Erechim, *Brazil* **175 B5** 27 35 S 52 15W
Ereğli, *Konya, Turkey* **100 D6** 37 31N 34 4 E
Ereğli, *Zonguldak, Turkey* **100 B4** 41 15N 31 24 E
Erei, Monti, *Italy* **47 E7** 37 20N 14 20 E
Erenhot, *China* **74 C7** 43 48N 112 2 E
Erenköy = Kokkina, *Cyprus* **39 E8** 35 11N 32 36 E
Eresfjord, *Norway* **18 B5** 62 40N 8 8 E
Eresma →, *Spain* **42 D6** 41 26N 4 45W
Eressós, *Greece* **49 B7** 39 11N 25 57 E
Erfenisdam, *S. Africa* **116 D4** 28 30 S 26 50 E
Erfjord, *Norway* **18 E3** 59 20N 6 14 E
Erfoud, *Morocco* **110 B4** 31 30N 4 15W
Erfstadt, *Germany* **30 E2** 50 50N 6 50 E
Erft →, *Germany* **30 D2** 51 11N 6 44 E
Erfurt, *Germany* **30 E7** 50 58N 11 2 E
Ergani, *Turkey* **101 C8** 38 17N 39 49 E
Ergel, *Mongolia* **74 C5** 43 8N 109 5 E
Ergene →, *Turkey* **51 E10** 41 1N 26 22 E
Ergeni Vozvyshennost, *Russia* **61 G7** 47 0N 44 0 E
Ērgli, *Latvia* **15 H21** 56 54N 25 38 E
Erhlin, *Taiwan* **77 F13** 23 54N 120 22 E
Eria →, *Spain* **42 C5** 42 3N 5 44W
Eriba, *Sudan* **107 D4** 16 40N 36 10 E
Eriboll, L., *U.K.* **22 C4** 58 30N 4 42W
Érice, *Italy* **46 D5** 38 2N 12 35 E
Eridu, *U.S.A.* **152 E6** 30 18N 83 45W
Erie, *Mich., U.S.A.* **157 C13** 41 47N 83 31W
Erie, *Pa., U.S.A.* **150 D4** 42 8N 80 5W
Erie, L., *N. Amer.* **150 D4** 42 15N 81 0W
Erie Canal, *U.S.A.* **150 C7** 43 5N 78 43W
Erieau, *Canada* **150 D3** 42 16N 81 57W
Erigavo, *Somali Rep.* **120 B3** 10 35N 47 20 E
Erikoúsa, *Greece* **38 B9** 39 53N 19 34 E
Eriksdale, *Canada* **143 C9** 50 52N 98 7W
Erímanthos, *Greece* **48 D3** 37 57N 21 50 E
Erimo-misaki, *Japan* **70 D11** 41 50N 143 15 E
Erin Pt., *Trin. & Tob.* **169 F9** 10 3N 61 39W
Erinpura, *India* **92 G5** 25 9N 73 3 E
Eriskay, *U.K.* **22 D1** 57 4N 7 18W
Eriswil, *Switz.* **32 B5** 47 5N 7 46 E
Erithraí, *Greece* **48 C5** 38 13N 23 20 E
Eritrea ■, *Africa* **107 E4** 14 0N 38 30 E
Erivan = Yerevan, *Armenia* **61 K7** 40 10N 44 31 E
Erjas →, *Portugal* **42 F3** 39 40N 7 1W
Erkech-Tam, *Kyrgyzstan* **65 D6** 39 41N 73 55 E

Erkech-Tam Pass, *Asia* **65 D7** 39 46N 74 2 E
Erkelenz, *Germany* **30 D2** 51 4N 6 19 E
Erkner, *Germany* **30 C9** 52 25N 13 44 E
Erlangen, *Germany* **31 F6** 49 36N 11 0 E
Erlanger, *U.S.A.* **157 E12** 39 1N 84 36W
Erldunda, *Australia* **126 D1** 25 14 S 133 12 E
Ermelo, *Neths.* **24 B5** 52 18N 5 35 E
Ermelo, *S. Africa* **117 D4** 26 31 S 29 59 E
Ermenek, *Turkey* **100 D5** 36 38N 33 0 E
Ermil, *Sudan* **107 E2** 13 35N 27 40 E
Ermióni, *Greece* **48 D5** 37 23N 23 15 E
Ermones, *Greece* **38 B9** 39 37N 19 46 E
Erne →, *Ireland* **23 B3** 54 30N 8 16W
Erne, Lower L., *U.K.* **23 B4** 54 28N 7 47W
Erne, Upper L., *U.K.* **23 B4** 54 14N 7 32W
Ernée, *France* **26 D6** 48 18N 0 56W
Ernest Giles Ra., *Australia* **125 E3** 27 0 S 123 45 E
Ernstberg, *Germany* **31 E2** 50 13N 6 47 E
Erode, *India* **95 J3** 11 24N 77 45 E
Eromanga, *Australia* **127 D3** 26 40 S 143 11 E
Erongo, *Namibia* **116 C2** 21 39 S 15 58 E
Erquy, *France* **26 D4** 48 38N 2 29W
Err, Piz d', *Switz.* **33 C9** 46 34N 9 43 E
Erramala Hills, *India* **95 G4** 15 30N 78 15 E
Errer →, *Ethiopia* **107 F5** 7 32N 42 35 E
Errigal, *Ireland* **23 A3** 55 2N 8 6W
Errinundra △, *Australia* **129 D8** 37 20 S 148 47 E
Erris Hd., *Ireland* **23 B1** 54 19N 10 0W
Erromango, *Vanuatu* **133 H7** 18 45 S 169 5 E
Ersekë, *Albania* **50 F4** 40 22N 20 40 E
Érsekújvár = Nové Zámky, *Slovak Rep.* **35 C11** 48 2N 18 8 E
Erskine, *U.S.A.* **154 B7** 47 40N 96 0W
Erstein, *France* **27 D14** 48 25N 7 38 E
Erstfeld, *Switz.* **33 C7** 46 50N 8 38 E
Ertholmene, *Denmark* **17 J9** 55 19N 15 11 E
Ertil, *Russia* **60 E5** 51 55N 40 50 E
Ertis = Irtysh →, *Russia* **66 C7** 61 4N 68 52 E
Ertvågøy, *Norway* **18 A5** 63 13N 8 26 E
Eruh, *Turkey* **101 D10** 37 46N 42 13 E
Eruwa, *Nigeria* **113 D5** 7 33N 3 26 E
Ervy-le-Châtel, *France* **27 D10** 48 2N 3 55 E
Erwin, *U.S.A.* **149 G4** 36 9N 82 25W
Eryuan, *China* **76 D2** 26 7N 99 57 E
Erzgebirge, *Germany* **30 E8** 50 27N 12 55 E
Erzin, *Russia* **67 D10** 50 15N 95 10 E
Erzincan, *Turkey* **101 C8** 39 46N 39 30 E
Erzurum, *Turkey* **101 C9** 39 57N 41 15 E
Es Caló, *Spain* **38 D2** 38 40N 1 30 E
Es Canar, *Spain* **38 C2** 39 2N 1 36 E
Es Mercadal, *Spain* **38 B5** 39 59N 4 5 E
Es Migjorn Gran, *Spain* **38 B5** 39 57N 4 3 E
Es Safiya, *Sudan* **107 D3** 15 31N 30 7 E
Es Sahrâ' Esh Sharqîya, *Egypt* **106 B3** 27 30N 32 30 E
Es Sînâ', *Egypt* **103 F3** 29 0N 34 0 E
Es Sûkî, *Sudan* **107 E3** 13 20N 33 58 E
Es Vedrà, *Spain* **38 D1** 38 52N 1 12 E
Esa'ala, *Papua N. G.* **132 E6** 9 45 S 150 49 E
Esambo, *Dem. Rep. of the Congo* **118 C1** 3 48 S 23 30 E
Esan-Misaki, *Japan* **70 D10** 41 40N 141 10 E
Esashi, *Hokkaidō, Japan* **70 B11** 44 56N 142 35 E
Esashi, *Hokkaidō, Japan* **70 D10** 41 52N 140 7 E
Esbjerg, *Denmark* **17 J2** 55 29N 8 29 E
Esbo = Espoo, *Finland* **15 F21** 60 12N 24 40 E
Escada, *Brazil* **170 C4** 8 22 S 35 8W
Escalante, *U.S.A.* **159 H8** 37 47N 111 36W
Escalante →, *U.S.A.* **159 H8** 37 24N 110 57W
Escalente, *Phil.* **81 F4** 10 50N 123 33 E
Escalón, *Mexico* **162 B4** 26 46N 104 20W
Escambia →, *U.S.A.* **153 E2** 30 32N 87 11W
Escanaba, *U.S.A.* **148 C2** 45 45N 87 4W
Escarpada Pt., *Phil.* **80 B4** 18 31N 122 13 E
Escarpé, C., *Vanuatu* **133 K5** 20 41 S 167 13 E
Escaut = Schelde →, *Belgium* **24 C4** 51 15N 4 16 E
Esch-sur-Alzette, *Lux.* **24 E6** 49 32N 6 0 E
Eschede, *Germany* **30 C6** 52 44N 10 14 E
Escholzmatt, *Switz.* **32 C5** 46 55N 7 56 E
Eschwege, *Germany* **30 D6** 51 11N 10 2 E
Eschweiler, *Germany* **30 E2** 50 49N 6 15 E
Escoma, *Bolivia* **172 D4** 15 40 S 69 8W
Escondido, *U.S.A.* **161 M9** 33 7N 117 5W
Escravos →, *Nigeria* **113 D6** 5 35N 5 10 E
Escuinapa, *Mexico* **162 C3** 22 50N 105 50W
Escuintla, *Guatemala* **164 D1** 14 20N 90 48W
Eséka, *Cameroon* **113 E7** 3 41N 10 44 E
Eşen →, *Turkey* **49 E11** 36 27N 29 16 E
Esenguly, *Turkmenistan* **66 F6** 37 37N 53 59 E
Esens, *Germany* **30 B3** 53 38N 7 36 E
Esenyurt, *Turkey* **51 E12** 41 3N 28 48 E
Esera →, *Spain* **40 C5** 42 6N 0 15 E
Eşfahān, *Iran* **97 C6** 32 39N 51 43 E
Eşfahān □, *Iran* **97 C6** 32 50N 51 50 E
Esfarāyen, *Iran* **97 B8** 37 4N 57 30 E
Esfideh, *Iran* **97 C8** 33 39N 59 46 E
Esgueva →, *Spain* **42 D6** 41 40N 4 43W
Esh Sham = Dimashq, *Syria* **103 B5** 33 30N 36 18 E
Esh Shamâlîya □, *Sudan* **106 D2** 19 0N 29 0 E
Esha Ness, *U.K.* **22 A7** 60 29N 1 38W
Eshan, *China* **76 E4** 24 11N 102 24 E
Esher, *U.K.* **21 F7** 51 21N 0 20W
Eshkāshem = Ishkashim, *Tajikistan* **65 E5** 36 44N 71 37 E
Eshkol △, *Israel* **103 D3** 31 20N 34 30 E
Eshowe, *S. Africa* **117 D5** 28 50 S 31 30 E
Esiama, *Ghana* **112 E4** 4 56N 2 25W
Esigodini, *Zimbabwe* **117 C4** 20 18 S 28 56 E
Esik, *Kazakhstan* **65 B8** 43 21N 77 27 E
Esil = Ishim →, *Russia* **66 D8** 57 45N 71 10 E
Esino →, *Italy* **45 E10** 43 39N 13 22 E
Esira, *Madag.* **117 C8** 24 20 S 46 42 E
Esk →, *Cumb., U.K.* **22 G5** 54 58N 3 2W
Esk →, *N. Yorks., U.K.* **20 C7** 54 30N 0 37W
Eskān, *Iran* **91 D1** 26 48N 63 9 E
Esker, *Canada* **141 B6** 53 53N 66 25W
Eski-Nookat, *Kyrgyzstan* **65 C6** 40 16N 72 36 E
Eskifjörður, *Iceland* **11 B13** 65 3N 13 55W
Eskije = Xánthi, *Greece* **51 E8** 41 10N 24 58 E
Eskilsäter, *Sweden* **17 F7** 58 57N 13 10 E
Eskilstuna, *Sweden* **16 E10** 59 22N 16 32 E
Eskimalatya, *Turkey* **101 C8** 38 24N 38 22 E
Eskimo Point = Arviat, *Canada* **143 A10** 61 6N 93 59W
Eskişehir, *Turkey* **49 B12** 39 50N 30 30 E
Eskişehir □, *Turkey* **49 B12** 39 40N 31 0 E
Esla →, *Spain* **42 D4** 41 29N 6 3W
Eslāmābād-e Gharb, *Iran* **101 E12** 34 10N 46 30 E
Eslāmshahr, *Iran* **97 C6** 35 40N 51 10 E
Eslöv, *Sweden* **17 J7** 55 50N 13 20 E
Eşme, *Turkey* **49 C10** 38 23N 28 58 E
Esmeralda, I., *Chile* **176 C1** 48 55 S 75 25W
Esmeraldas, *Ecuador* **168 C2** 1 0N 79 40W
Esmeraldas □, *Ecuador* **168 C2** 0 40N 79 30W
Esmeraldas →, *Ecuador* **168 C2** 0 58N 79 38W
Esnagi L., *Canada* **140 C3** 48 36N 84 33W
Esom Hill, *U.S.A.* **152 B4** 33 57N 85 23W
Espa, *Norway* **18 D8** 60 34N 11 16 E
Espada, Pta., *Colombia* **168 A3** 12 5N 71 7W
Espalion, *France* **28 D6** 44 32N 2 47 E
España = Spain ■, *Europe* **13 H5** 39 0N 4 0W
Espanola, *Canada* **140 C3** 46 15N 81 46W
Espanola, *U.S.A.* **159 H10** 35 59N 106 5W
Española, I., *Ecuador* **172 a** 1 23 S 89 39W
Esparreguera, *Spain* **40 D6** 41 33N 1 52 E
Esparta, *Costa Rica* **164 E3** 9 59N 84 40W
Espeland, *Norway* **18 D2** 60 23N 5 28 E
Espelkamp, *Germany* **30 C4** 52 24N 8 36 E
Espenberg, C., *U.S.A.* **144 C7** 66 33N 163 36W
Esperança, *Amazonas, Brazil* **168 D4** 4 24 S 69 52W
Esperança, *Paraíba, Brazil* **170 C4** 7 1 S 35 51W
Esperance, *Australia* **125 F3** 33 45 S 121 55 E
Esperance, C., *Solomon Is.* **133 M10** 9 15 S 159 43 E
Esperance B., *Australia* **125 F3** 33 48 S 121 55 E
Esperance Harbour, *St. Lucia* **165 f** 14 4N 60 55W
Esperantinópolis, *Brazil* **170 B3** 4 53 S 44 53W
Esperanza, *Antarctica* **7 C18** 65 0 S 55 0W
Esperanza, *Santa Cruz, Argentina* **176 D2** 51 1 S 70 49W
Esperanza, *Santa Fe, Argentina* **174 C3** 31 29 S 61 3W
Esperanza, *Agusan del S., Phil.* **81 G5** 8 43N 125 36 E
Esperanza, *Masbate, Phil.* **81 F5** 11 45N 124 3 E
Esperanza, *Puerto Rico* **165 d** 18 6N 65 28W
Espéraza, *France* **28 F6** 42 56N 2 14 E
Espevær, *Norway* **18 E2** 59 35N 5 7 E
Espichel, C., *Portugal* **43 G1** 38 22N 9 16W
Espiel, *Spain* **43 G5** 38 11N 5 1W
Espigão, Serra do, *Brazil* **175 B5** 26 35 S 50 30W
Espinal, *Colombia* **168 C3** 4 9N 74 53W
Espinar, *Peru* **172 C3** 14 51 S 71 24W
Espinazo, Sierra del = Espinhaço, Serra do, *Brazil* **171 E3** 17 30 S 43 30W
Espinhaço, Serra do, *Brazil* **171 E3** 17 30 S 43 30W
Espinho, *Portugal* **42 D2** 41 1N 8 38W
Espinilho, Serra do, *Brazil* **175 B5** 28 30 S 55 0W
Espinosa de los Monteros, *Spain* **42 B7** 43 5N 3 34W
Espírito Santo □, *Brazil* **171 F3** 20 0 S 40 45W
Espíritu Santo, *Vanuatu* **133 E4** 15 15 S 166 50 E
Espíritu Santo, B. del, *Mexico* **163 D7** 19 15N 87 0W
Espíritu Santo, I., *Mexico* **162 C2** 24 30N 110 23W
Espita, *Mexico* **163 C7** 21 1N 88 19W
Espiye, *Turkey* **101 B8** 40 56N 38 43 E
Esplanada, *Brazil* **171 D4** 11 47 S 37 57W
Espluga de Francolí, *Spain* **40 D6** 41 24N 1 7 E
Espoo, *Finland* **15 F21** 60 12N 24 40 E
Esprels, *France* **32 A2** 47 32N 6 22 E
Espuña, Sierra de, *Spain* **41 H3** 37 51N 1 35W
Espungabera, *Mozam.* **117 C5** 20 29 S 32 45 E
Esquel, *Argentina* **176 B2** 42 55 S 71 20W
Esquimalt, *Canada* **142 D4** 48 26N 123 25W
Esquina, *Argentina* **174 C4** 30 0 S 59 30W
Essandsjøen, *Norway* **18 A8** 63 0N 12 0 E
Essaouira, *Morocco* **110 B3** 31 32N 9 42W
Essebie, *Dem. Rep. of the Congo* **118 B3** 2 58N 30 40 E
Essen, *Belgium* **24 C4** 51 28N 4 28 E
Essen, *Germany* **30 D3** 51 28N 7 2 E
Essendon, Mt., *Australia* **125 E3** 25 0 S 120 29 E
Essequibo →, *Guyana* **169 B6** 6 50N 58 30W
Essex, *Canada* **150 D2** 42 10N 82 49W
Essex, *Calif., U.S.A.* **161 L11** 34 44N 115 15W
Essex, *N.Y., U.S.A.* **151 B11** 44 19N 73 21W
Essex □, *U.K.* **21 F8** 51 54N 0 27 E
Essex Junction, *U.S.A.* **151 B11** 44 29N 73 7W
Esslingen, *Germany* **31 G5** 48 44N 9 18 E
Essonne □, *France* **27 D9** 48 30N 2 20 E
Estaca de Bares, C. de, *Spain* **42 B3** 43 46N 7 42W
Estadilla, *Spain* **40 C5** 42 4N 0 16 E
Estados, I. de Los, *Argentina* **176 D4** 54 40 S 64 30W
Estagel, *France* **28 F6** 42 47N 2 40 E
Eşţahbānāt, *Iran* **97 D7** 29 8N 54 4 E
Estância, *Brazil* **170 D4** 11 16 S 37 26W
Estancia, *U.S.A.* **159 J10** 34 46N 106 4W
Estancia Cameron, *Chile* **176 D3** 53 38 S 69 39W
Estārm, *Iran* **97 D8** 28 21N 58 21 E
Estarreja, *Portugal* **42 E2** 40 45N 8 35W
Estats, Pic d', *Spain* **40 C6** 42 40N 1 24 E
Estavayer-le-Lac, *Switz.* **32 C3** 46 51N 6 51 E
Estcourt, *S. Africa* **117 D4** 29 0 S 29 53 E
Este, *Italy* **45 C8** 45 14N 11 39 E
Este △, *Dom. Rep.* **165 C6** 18 14N 68 42W
Estelí, *Nic.* **164 D2** 13 9N 86 22W
Estella, *Spain* **40 C2** 42 40N 2 2W
Estellencs, *Spain* **38 B3** 39 39N 2 29 E
Estena →, *Spain* **43 F6** 39 23N 4 44W
Estepa, *Spain* **43 H6** 37 17N 4 52W
Estepona, *Spain* **43 J5** 36 24N 5 7W
Esterhazy, *Canada* **143 C8** 50 37N 102 5W
Esterias, C., *Gabon* **114 B1** 0 40N 9 20 E
Esternay, *France* **27 D10** 48 44N 3 33 E
Esterri d'Aneu, *Spain* **40 C6** 42 38N 1 5 E
Estevan, *Canada* **143 D8** 49 10N 102 59W
Estevan Group, *Canada* **142 C3** 53 3N 129 38W
Estherville, *U.S.A.* **154 D7** 43 24N 94 50W
Estill, *U.S.A.* **152 C8** 32 45N 81 15W
Estissac, *France* **27 D10** 48 16N 3 48 E
Eston, *Canada* **143 C7** 51 8N 108 40W
Estonia ■, *Europe* **15 G21** 58 30N 25 30 E
Estoril, *Portugal* **43 G1** 38 42N 9 23W
Estouk, *Mali* **113 B5** 18 14N 1 2 E
Estrela, Serra da, *Portugal* **42 E3** 40 10N 7 45W
Estrella, *Spain* **43 G7** 38 25N 3 35W
Estremoz, *Portugal* **43 G3** 38 51N 7 39W
Estrondo, Serra do, *Brazil* **170 C2** 7 20 S 48 0W
Esutoru = Uglegorsk, *Russia* **67 E15** 49 5N 142 2 E
Esztergom, *Hungary* **52 C3** 47 47N 18 44 E
Et Tîdra, *Mauritania* **112 B1** 19 45N 16 20W
Etah, *India* **93 F8** 27 35N 78 40 E
Étain, *France* **27 C12** 49 13N 5 38 E
Étampes, *France* **27 D9** 48 26N 2 10 E
Étaples, *France* **27 B8** 50 30N 1 39 E
Etawah, *India* **93 F8** 26 48N 79 6 E
Etawney L., *Canada* **143 B9** 57 50N 96 50W
Ete, *Nigeria* **113 D6** 7 2N 7 28 E
Etéké, *Gabon* **114 C2** 1 29 S 11 35 E
Ethel, *U.S.A.* **160 D4** 46 32N 122 46W
Ethel, Oued el →, *Algeria* **110 C4** 28 31N 3 37W
Ethelbert, *Canada* **143 C8** 51 32N 100 25W
Ethiopia ■, *Africa* **102 F3** 8 0N 40 0 E
Ethiopian Highlands, *Ethiopia* **62 J7** 10 0N 37 0 E
Etili, *Turkey* **51 G10** 39 59N 26 54 E
Etive, L., *U.K.* **22 E3** 56 29N 5 10W
Etna, *Italy* **47 E7** 37 50N 14 55 E
Etna →, *Norway* **18 C6** 60 49N 10 7 E
Etne, *Norway* **18 E2** 59 40N 5 58 E
Etoile, *Dem. Rep. of the Congo* **119 E2** 11 33 S 27 30 E
Etolin Strait, *U.S.A.* **144 F6** 60 20N 165 15W
Etosha △, *Namibia* **116 B2** 19 0 S 16 0 E
Etosha Pan, *Namibia* **116 B2** 18 40 S 16 30 E
Etoumbi, *Congo* **114 C2** 0 1 S 14 57 E
Etowah, *U.S.A.* **149 H3** 35 20N 84 32W
Étréchy, *France* **27 D9** 48 30N 2 12 E
Étrépagny, *France* **27 C8** 49 18N 1 36 E
Étretat, *France* **26 C7** 49 42N 0 12 E
Etropole, *Bulgaria* **51 D8** 42 50N 24 0 E
Ettelbruck, *Lux.* **24 E6** 49 51N 6 5 E
Ettlingen, *Germany* **31 G4** 48 56N 8 25 E
Ettrick Water →, *U.K.* **22 F6** 55 31N 2 55W
Etuku, *Dem. Rep. of the Congo* **118 C2** 3 42 S 25 45 E
Etulia, *Moldova* **53 E13** 45 32N 28 27 E
Etzatlán, *Mexico* **162 C4** 20 48N 104 5W
Etzná, *Mexico* **163 D6** 19 35N 90 15W
Etzná-Tixmucuy = Edzná, *Mexico* **163 D6** 19 35N 90 15W
Eu, *France* **26 B8** 50 3N 1 26 E
Eua, *Tonga* **133 Q13** 21 22 S 174 56W
Eubenangee Swamp △, *Australia* **126 B4** 16 25 S 146 1 E
Euboea = Évvoia, *Greece* **48 C6** 38 30N 24 0 E
Eucaliptus = Tomás Barrón, *Bolivia* **172 D4** 17 35 S 67 31W
Eucharenna, *Australia* **129 B8** 32 57 S 149 6 E
Eucla, *Australia* **125 F4** 31 41 S 128 52 E
Euclid, *U.S.A.* **150 E3** 41 34N 81 32W
Euclides da Cunha, *Brazil* **170 D4** 10 31 S 39 1W
Eucumbene, L., *Australia* **129 D8** 36 2 S 148 40 E
Eudora, *U.S.A.* **155 J9** 33 7N 91 16W
Eudunda, *Australia* **128 C3** 34 12 S 139 7 E
Eufaula, *Ala., U.S.A.* **152 D4** 31 54N 85 9W
Eufaula, *Okla., U.S.A.* **155 H7** 35 17N 95 35W
Eufaula L., *U.S.A.* **155 H7** 35 18N 95 21W
Eugene, *U.S.A.* **158 E2** 44 5N 123 4W
Eugowra, *Australia* **129 B8** 33 22 S 148 24 E
Eulo, *Australia* **127 D4** 28 10 S 145 3 E
Eulonia, *U.S.A.* **152 D8** 31 32N 81 26W
Eumungerie, *Australia* **129 A8** 31 56 S 148 36 E
Eungella △, *Australia* **126 C4** 20 57 S 148 40 E
Eunice, *La., U.S.A.* **155 K8** 30 30N 92 25W
Eunice, *N. Mex., U.S.A.* **155 J3** 32 26N 103 10W
Eupen, *Belgium* **24 D6** 50 37N 6 3 E
Euphrates = Furāt, Nahr al →, *Asia* **96 D5** 31 0N 47 25 E
Eurapik Rise, *Pac. Oc.* **134 G6** 2 0N 142 0 E
Eure □, *France* **26 C8** 49 10N 1 0 E
Eure →, *France* **26 C8** 49 18N 1 12 E
Eure-et-Loir □, *France* **26 D8** 48 22N 1 30 E
Eureka, *Canada* **6 B3** 80 0N 85 56W
Eureka, *Calif., U.S.A.* **158 F1** 40 47N 124 9W
Eureka, *Ill., U.S.A.* **156 D7** 40 43N 89 16W
Eureka, *Kans., U.S.A.* **155 G6** 37 49N 96 17W
Eureka, *Mo., U.S.A.* **156 F6** 38 30N 90 38W
Eureka, *Mont., U.S.A.* **158 B6** 48 53N 115 3W
Eureka, *Nev., U.S.A.* **158 G5** 39 31N 115 58W
Eureka, *S.C., U.S.A.* **152 B8** 33 42N 81 46W
Eureka, *S. Dak., U.S.A.* **154 C5** 45 46N 99 38W
Eureka, Mt., *Australia* **125 E3** 26 35 S 121 35 E
Eurelia, *Australia* **128 B3** 32 33 S 138 35 E
Eurinilla Cr. →, *Australia* **128 A4** 30 53 S 140 11 E
Euroa, *Australia* **129 D6** 36 44 S 145 35 E
Europa, Île, *Ind. Oc.* **121 G2** 22 20 S 40 22 E
Europa, Picos de, *Spain* **42 B6** 43 10N 4 49W
Europa, Pta. de, *Gib.* **43 J5** 36 3N 5 21W
Europe **12 E10** 50 0N 20 0 E
Europoort, *Neths.* **24 C4** 51 57N 4 10 E
Euskirchen, *Germany* **30 E2** 50 39N 6 48 E
Eustis, *U.S.A.* **153 G8** 28 51N 81 41W
Euston, *Australia* **128 C5** 34 30 S 142 46 E
Eutawville, *U.S.A.* **152 B9** 33 24N 80 21W
Eutin, *Germany* **30 A6** 54 8N 10 36 E
Eutsuk L., *Canada* **142 C3** 53 20N 126 45W
Eva, *Brazil* **169 D6** 3 9 S 59 56W
Eva Perón = La Pampa □, *Argentina* **174 D2** 36 50 S 66 0W
Eva Perón = La Plata, *Argentina* **174 D4** 35 0 S 57 55W
Evale, *Angola* **116 B2** 16 33 S 15 44 E
Evanger, *Norway* **18 D3** 60 39N 6 7 E
Evans, *U.S.A.* **154 E2** 40 23N 104 41W
Evans, L., *Canada* **140 B4** 50 50N 77 0W
Evans City, *U.S.A.* **150 F4** 40 46N 80 4W
Evans Head, *Australia* **127 D5** 29 7 S 153 27 E
Evans Mills, *U.S.A.* **151 B9** 44 6N 75 48W
Evansburg, *Canada* **142 C5** 53 36N 114 59W
Evansdale, *U.S.A.* **156 B4** 42 30N 92 17W
Evanston, *Ill., U.S.A.* **157 B9** 42 3N 87 41W
Evanston, *Wyo., U.S.A.* **158 F8** 41 16N 110 58W
Evansville, *Ill., U.S.A.* **156 F7** 38 5N 89 56W
Evansville, *Ind., U.S.A.* **157 G9** 37 58N 87 35W
Evansville, *Wis., U.S.A.* **156 B7** 42 47N 89 18W
Évaux-les-Bains, *France* **27 F9** 46 12N 2 29 E
Evaz, *Iran* **97 E7** 27 46N 53 59 E
Evciler, *Afyon, Turkey* **49 C11** 38 4N 29 54 E
Evciler, *Çanakkale, Turkey* **49 B8** 39 47N 26 44 E
Eveleth, *U.S.A.* **154 B8** 47 28N 92 32W
Evensk, *Russia* **67 C16** 62 12N 159 30 E
Evenstad, *Norway* **18 C8** 61 25N 11 7 E
Everard, L., *Australia* **127 E2** 31 30 S 135 0 E
Everard Ranges, *Australia* **125 E5** 27 5 S 132 28 E
Everest, Mt., *Nepal* **93 E12** 28 5N 86 58 E
Everett, *Ga., U.S.A.* **152 D8** 31 24N 81 38W
Everett, *Pa., U.S.A.* **150 F6** 40 1N 78 23W
Everett, *Wash., U.S.A.* **160 C4** 47 59N 122 12W
Everglades △, *U.S.A.* **153 K9** 25 30N 81 0W
Everglades, The, *U.S.A.* **153 K9** 25 50N 81 0W
Everglades City, *U.S.A.* **153 K8** 25 52N 81 23W
Evergreen, *Ala., U.S.A.* **152 D3** 31 26N 86 57W
Evergreen, *Mont., U.S.A.* **158 B6** 48 9N 114 13W
Everöd, *Sweden* **17 J8** 55 53N 14 5 E
Everton, *Australia* **129 D7** 36 25 S 146 33 E
Evertsberg, *Sweden* **16 C7** 61 8N 13 58 E
Evesham, *U.K.* **21 E6** 52 6N 1 56W
Evfimía, Ayía, *Greece* **39 C2** 38 18N 20 36 E
Evia = Évvoia, *Greece* **48 C6** 38 30N 24 0 E
Évian-les-Bains, *France* **27 F13** 46 24N 6 35 E
Evinayong, *Eq. Guin.* **114 B2** 1 26N 10 35 E
Évinos →, *Greece* **48 C3** 38 27N 21 40 E
Évisa, *France* **29 F12** 42 15N 8 48 E
Evje, *Norway* **18 F4** 58 36N 7 51 E
Evolène, *Switz.* **32 D4** 46 7N 7 30 E
Évora, *Portugal* **43 G3** 38 33N 7 57W
Évora □, *Portugal* **43 G3** 38 33N 7 50W
Evowghlī, *Iran* **101 C11** 38 43N 45 13 E
Évreux, *France* **26 C8** 49 3N 1 8 E
Evritania □, *Greece* **48 B3** 39 5N 21 30 E
Évron, *France* **26 D6** 48 10N 0 24W
Évros □, *Greece* **51 E10** 41 10N 26 0 E
Évros →, *Greece* **100 B2** 41 40N 26 34 E
Evrótas →, *Greece* **48 E4** 36 50N 22 40 E
Évry, *France* **27 D9** 48 38N 2 27 E
Évvoia, *Greece* **48 C6** 38 30N 24 0 E
Évvoia □, *Greece* **48 C5** 38 40N 23 40 E
Evxinoúpolis, *Greece* **48 B4** 39 12N 22 42 E
Ewa, *U.S.A.* **145 K13** 21 20N 158 3W
Ewa Beach, *U.S.A.* **145 K13** 21 19N 158 1W
Ewasse, *Papua N. G.* **132 C6** 5 19 S 151 1 E
Ewe, L., *U.K.* **22 D3** 57 49N 5 38W
Ewing, *Mo., U.S.A.* **156 E5** 40 6N 91 43W
Ewing, *Nebr., U.S.A.* **154 D5** 42 16N 98 21W
Ewo, *Congo* **114 C2** 0 48 S 14 45 E
Exaltación, *Bolivia* **173 C4** 13 10 S 65 20W
Excelsior Springs, *U.S.A.* **156 E2** 39 20N 94 13W
Excideuil, *France* **28 C5** 45 20N 1 4 E
Exe →, *U.K.* **21 G4** 50 41N 3 29W
Exeter, *Canada* **150 C3** 43 21N 81 29W
Exeter, *U.K.* **21 G4** 50 43N 3 31W
Exeter, *Calif., U.S.A.* **160 J7** 36 18N 119 9W
Exeter, *N.H., U.S.A.* **151 D14** 42 59N 70 57W
Exira, *U.S.A.* **156 C2** 41 35N 94 52W
Exmoor, *U.K.* **21 F4** 51 12N 3 45W
Exmoor △, *U.K.* **21 F4** 51 8N 3 42W
Exmouth, *Australia* **124 D1** 21 54 S 114 10 E
Exmouth, *U.K.* **21 G4** 50 37N 3 25W
Exmouth G., *Australia* **124 D1** 22 15 S 114 15 E
Expedition △, *Australia* **127 D4** 25 41 S 149 7 E
Expedition Ra., *Australia* **126 C4** 24 30 S 149 12 E
Experiment, *U.S.A.* **152 B5** 33 17N 84 17W
Extremadura □, *Spain* **43 F4** 39 30N 6 5W
Exuma Sound, *Bahamas* **164 B4** 24 30N 76 20W
Eyak, *U.S.A.* **144 F11** 60 32N 145 36W
Eyasi, L., *Tanzania* **118 C4** 3 30 S 35 0 E
Eydehamn, *Norway* **18 F5** 58 30N 8 53 E
Eye Pen., *U.K.* **22 C2** 58 13N 6 10W
Eyemouth, *U.K.* **22 F6** 55 52N 2 5W
Eygues = Aigues →, *France* **29 D8** 44 7N 4 43 E
Eygurande, *France* **27 G9** 45 40N 2 26 E
Eyjafjallajökull, *Iceland* **11 D7** 63 38N 19 36W
Eyjafjarðarsýsla □, *Iceland* **11 B8** 65 30N 18 30W
Eyjafjörður, *Iceland* **11 A8** 66 15N 18 30W
Eymet, *France* **28 D4** 44 40N 0 25 E
Eymoutiers, *France* **28 C5** 45 40N 1 45 E
Eynesil, *Turkey* **101 B8** 41 4N 39 9 E
Eyrarbakki, *Iceland* **11 D5** 63 52N 21 9W
Eyre (North), L., *Australia* **127 D2** 28 30 S 137 20 E
Eyre (South), L., *Australia* **127 D2** 29 18 S 137 25 E
Eyre, L., *Australia* **122 F6** 29 30 S 137 26 E
Eyre Mts., *N.Z.* **131 F3** 45 25 S 168 25 E
Eyre Pen., *Australia* **127 E2** 33 30 S 136 17 E
Eysturoy, *Færoe Is.* **14 E9** 62 13N 6 54W
Eyvānkī, *Iran* **97 C6** 35 24N 51 56 E
Ez Zeidab, *Sudan* **106 D3** 17 25N 33 55 E
Ezcaray, *Spain* **40 C1** 42 19N 3 0W
Ežerėlis, *Lithuania* **54 D10** 54 53N 23 37 E
Ezhou, *China* **77 B10** 30 23N 114 50 E
Ezine, *Turkey* **49 B8** 39 48N 26 20 E
Ezmul, *Mauritania* **110 D1** 22 15N 15 40W
Ezouza →, *Cyprus* **39 F8** 34 44N 32 27 E

F

F.Y.R.O.M. = Macedonia ■, *Europe* **50 E5** 41 53N 21 40 E
Fabala, *Guinea* **112 D3** 9 44N 9 5W
Fabens, *U.S.A.* **159 L10** 31 30N 106 10W
Fåberg, *Norway* **18 C7** 61 10N 10 25 E
Fabero, *Spain* **42 C4** 42 46N 6 37W
Fåborg, *Denmark* **17 J4** 55 6N 10 15 E
Fabriano, *Italy* **45 E9** 43 20N 12 54 E
Fabrīchnyy, *Kazakhstan* **65 B8** 43 9N 76 24 E
Făcăeni, *Romania* **53 F12** 44 32N 27 53 E
Facatativá, *Colombia* **168 C3** 4 49N 74 22W
Faceville, *U.S.A.* **152 E5** 30 45N 84 38W
Fachi, *Niger* **109 E2** 18 6N 11 34 E
Facundo, *Argentina* **176 C3** 45 18 S 69 58W
Fada, *Chad* **109 E4** 17 13N 21 34 E
Fada-n-Gourma, *Burkina Faso* **113 C5** 12 10N 0 30 E
Fadd, *Hungary* **52 D3** 46 28N 18 49 E
Faddeyevskiy, Ostrov, *Russia* **67 B15** 76 0N 144 0 E
Faddor, *Sudan* **107 F3** 8 7N 32 17 E
Fadghāmī, *Syria* **101 E9** 35 53N 40 52 E
Fadlab, *Sudan* **106 D3** 17 42N 34 2 E
Faenza, *Italy* **45 D8** 44 17N 11 53 E
Færingehavn = Kangerluarsoruseq, *Greenland* **10 E5** 63 45N 51 27W
Færoe Is. = Føroyar, *Atl. Oc.* **14 F9** 62 0N 7 0W
Fafa, *Mali* **113 B5** 15 22N 0 48 E
Fafe, *Portugal* **42 D2** 41 27N 8 11W
Fagam, *Nigeria* **113 C7** 11 1N 10 1 E
Făgăraş, *Romania* **53 E9** 45 48N 24 58 E
Făgăraş, Munţii, *Romania* **53 E9** 45 40N 24 40 E
Fågelmara, *Sweden* **17 H9** 56 16N 15 58 E
Fagerheim, *Norway* **18 D4** 60 26N 7 46 E
Fagerhult, *Sweden* **17 G9** 57 8N 15 40 E
Fagernes, *Norway* **18 D6** 60 59N 9 14 E
Fagersta, *Sweden* **16 D9** 60 1N 15 46 E
Făget, *Romania* **52 E7** 45 52N 22 10 E
Făget, Munţii, *Romania* **53 C8** 47 40N 23 10 E
Fagnano, L., *Argentina* **176 D3** 54 30 S 68 0W
Fagnières, *France* **27 D11** 48 58N 4 20 E
Faguibine, L., *Mali* **112 B4** 16 45N 4 0W
Fahlīān, *Iran* **97 D6** 30 11N 51 28 E
Fahraj, *Kermān, Iran* **97 D8** 29 0N 59 0 E
Fahraj, *Yazd, Iran* **97 D7** 31 46N 54 36 E
Fai Tsi Long, *Vietnam* **76 G6** 21 0N 107 30 E
Faial, *Azores* **9 d1** 38 34N 28 42W
Faial, *Madeira* **9 c** 32 47N 16 53W
Faial, Canal do, *Azores* **9 d1** 38 33N 28 35W
Faido, *Switz.* **33 D7** 46 29N 8 48 E
Fair Haven, *U.S.A.* **148 D9** 43 36N 73 16W
Fair Hd., *U.K.* **23 A5** 55 14N 6 9W
Fair Isle, *U.K.* **19 B6** 59 30N 1 40W
Fair Oaks, *U.S.A.* **160 G5** 38 39N 121 16W
Fairbank, *U.S.A.* **156 B4** 42 38N 92 3W
Fairbanks, *Alaska, U.S.A.* **144 D11** 64 51N 147 43W
Fairbanks, *Fla., U.S.A.* **152 F7** 29 44N 82 16W
Fairborn, *Ohio, U.S.A.* **157 E12** 39 49N 84 2W
Fairburn, *U.S.A.* **152 B5** 33 34N 84 35W
Fairbury, *Ill., U.S.A.* **157 D8** 40 45N 88 31W
Fairbury, *Nebr., U.S.A.* **154 E6** 40 8N 97 11W
Fairfax, *Ohio, U.S.A.* **157 E13** 39 5N 83 37W
Fairfax, *S.C., U.S.A.* **152 C8** 32 59N 81 15W
Fairfax, *Vt., U.S.A.* **151 B11** 44 40N 73 1W
Fairfield, *Australia* **129 B9** 33 53 S 150 57 E
Fairfield, *Ala., U.S.A.* **149 J2** 33 29N 86 55W
Fairfield, *Calif., U.S.A.* **160 G4** 38 15N 122 3W
Fairfield, *Conn., U.S.A.* **151 E11** 41 9N 73 16W
Fairfield, *Idaho, U.S.A.* **158 E6** 43 21N 114 44W
Fairfield, *Ill., U.S.A.* **157 F8** 38 23N 88 22W
Fairfield, *Iowa, U.S.A.* **156 D5** 40 56N 91 57W
Fairfield, *Ohio, U.S.A.* **157 E12** 39 21N 84 34W
Fairfield, *Tex., U.S.A.* **155 K7** 31 44N 96 10W
Fairford, *Canada* **143 C9** 51 37N 98 38W
Fairhope, *U.S.A.* **149 K2** 30 31N 87 54W
Fairlie, *N.Z.* **131 E5** 44 5 S 170 49 E
Fairmead, *U.S.A.* **160 H6** 37 5N 120 10W
Fairmont, *Minn., U.S.A.* **154 D7** 43 39N 94 28W
Fairmont, *W. Va., U.S.A.* **148 F5** 39 29N 80 9W
Fairmount, *Calif., U.S.A.* **161 L8** 34 45N 118 26W
Fairmount, *N.Y., U.S.A.* **151 C8** 43 5N 76 12W
Fairplay, *U.S.A.* **159 G11** 39 15N 106 2W
Fairport, *U.S.A.* **150 C7** 43 6N 77 27W
Fairport Harbor, *U.S.A.* **150 E3** 41 45N 81 17W
Fairview, *Canada* **142 B5** 56 5N 118 25W
Fairview, *Mont., U.S.A.* **154 B2** 47 51N 104 3W
Fairview, *Okla., U.S.A.* **155 G5** 36 16N 98 29W
Fairweather, Mt., *U.S.A.* **142 B1** 58 55N 137 32W
Faisalabad, *Pakistan* **91 C4** 31 30N 73 5 E
Faith, *U.S.A.* **154 C3** 45 2N 102 2W
Faizabad, *India* **93 F10** 26 45N 82 10 E
Faizpur, *India* **94 D2** 21 14N 75 49 E
Fajã Grande, *Azores* **9 d2** 39 27N 31 16W
Fajardo, *Puerto Rico* **165 d** 18 20N 65 39W
Fajr, W. →, *Si. Arabia* **96 D3** 29 10N 38 10 E
Fakenham, *U.K.* **20 E8** 52 51N 0 51 E
Fåker, *Sweden* **16 A8** 63 0N 14 34 E
Fakfak, *Indonesia* **83 B4** 2 55 S 132 18 E
Fakfak, Peg., *Indonesia* **83 B4** 2 50 S 132 20 E
Fakiya, *Bulgaria* **51 D11** 42 10N 27 6 E
Fakobli, *Ivory C.* **112 D3** 7 23N 7 23W
Fakse, *Denmark* **17 J6** 55 15N 12 8 E
Fakse Bugt, *Denmark* **17 J6** 55 11N 12 15 E
Fakse Ladeplads, *Denmark* **17 J6** 55 11N 12 9 E
Faku, *China* **75 C12** 42 32N 123 21 E
Falaba, *S. Leone* **112 D2** 9 54N 11 22W
Falaise, *France* **26 D6** 48 54N 0 12W
Falaise, Mui, *Vietnam* **86 C5** 19 6N 105 45 E
Falakrón Óros, *Greece* **50 E7** 41 15N 23 58 E
Falam, *Burma* **90 D4** 23 0N 93 45 E
Falces, *Spain* **40 C3** 42 24N 1 48W
Fălciu, *Romania* **53 D13** 46 17N 28 7 E
Falcó, C. des, *Spain* **38 D1** 38 50N 1 23 E
Falcón □, *Venezuela* **168 A4** 11 0N 69 50W
Falcon, C., *Algeria* **111 A4** 35 50N 0 50W
Falcón, Presa, *Mexico* **163 B5** 26 35N 99 10W
Falcon Lake, *Canada* **143 D9** 49 42N 95 15W
Falcon Reservoir, *U.S.A.* **155 M5** 26 34N 99 10W
Falconara Marittima, *Italy* **45 E10** 43 37N 13 24 E
Falcone, C. del, *Italy* **46 B1** 40 58N 8 12 E
Falconer, *U.S.A.* **150 D5** 42 7N 79 13W
Faléa, *Mali* **112 C2** 12 16N 11 17W
Falefa, *Samoa* **133 W24** 13 54 S 171 31W
Falelatai, *Samoa* **133 W24** 13 55 S 171 59W
Falelima, *Samoa* **133 W23** 13 32 S 172 41W
Falémé →, *Senegal* **112 C2** 14 46N 12 14W
Falenki, *Russia* **64 B3** 58 22N 51 35 E
Falerum, *Sweden* **17 F10** 58 8N 16 13 E
Faleshty = Făleşti, *Moldova* **53 C12** 47 32N 27 44 E
Făleşti, *Moldova* **53 C12** 47 32N 27 44 E
Falfurrias, *U.S.A.* **155 M5** 27 14N 98 9W
Falher, *Canada* **142 B5** 55 44N 117 15W
Faliraki, *Greece* **38 E12** 36 22N 28 12 E
Falkenberg, *Germany* **30 D9** 51 35N 13 14 E
Falkenberg, *Sweden* **17 H6** 56 54N 12 30 E
Falkenburg = Niemodlin, *Poland* **55 H4** 50 38N 17 38 E
Falkensee, *Germany* **30 C9** 52 34N 13 4 E
Falkirk, *U.K.* **22 F5** 56 0N 3 47W
Falkirk □, *U.K.* **22 F5** 55 58N 3 49W
Falkland, *U.K.* **22 E5** 56 16N 3 12W
Falkland, East, I., *Falk. Is.* **176 D5** 51 40 S 58 30W
Falkland, West, I., *Falk. Is.* **176 D4** 51 40 S 60 0W
Falkland Is. ☑, *Atl. Oc.* **9 f** 51 30 S 59 0W
Falkland Sd., *Falk. Is.* **9 f** 52 0 S 60 0W
Falknov nad Ohří = Sokolov, *Czech Rep.* **34 A5** 50 12N 12 40 E
Falkonéra, *Greece* **48 E5** 36 50N 23 52 E
Falköping, *Sweden* **17 F7** 58 12N 13 33 E
Fall River, *U.S.A.* **151 E13** 41 43N 71 10W
Fällanden, *Switz.* **33 B7** 47 22N 8 38 E
Fallbrook, *U.S.A.* **161 M9** 33 23N 117 15W
Fallon, *U.S.A.* **158 G4** 39 28N 118 47W
Falls City, *U.S.A.* **154 E7** 40 3N 95 36W
Falls Creek, *U.S.A.* **150 E6** 41 9N 78 48W
Falmouth, *Jamaica* **164 a** 18 30N 77 40W
Falmouth, *U.K.* **21 G2** 50 9N 5 5W
Falmouth, *Ky., U.S.A.* **157 F12** 38 41N 84 20W
Falmouth, *Mass., U.S.A.* **151 E14** 41 33N 70 37W
Falsa, Pta., *Mexico* **162 B1** 27 51N 115 3W
False B., *S. Africa* **116 E2** 34 15 S 18 40 E
False Divi Pt., *India* **95 G5** 15 43N 80 50 E
False Pass, *U.S.A.* **144 J7** 54 51N 163 25W
False Pt., *India* **94 D8** 20 18N 86 48 E
Falso, C., *Honduras* **164 C3** 15 12N 83 21W
Falster, *Denmark* **17 K5** 54 45N 11 55 E
Falsterbo, *Sweden* **15 J15** 55 23N 12 50 E
Fălticeni, *Romania* **53 C11** 47 21N 26 20 E
Falun, *Sweden* **16 D9** 60 37N 15 37 E
Famagusta, *Cyprus* **39 E9** 35 8N 33 55 E
Famagusta Bay, *Cyprus* **39 E10** 35 15N 34 0 E
Famatina, Sierra de, *Argentina* **174 B2** 27 30 S 68 0W
Family L., *Canada* **143 C9** 51 54N 95 27W
Famoso, *U.S.A.* **161 K7** 35 37N 119 12W
Fan Xian, *China* **74 G8** 35 55N 115 38 E
Fana, *Mali* **112 C3** 13 0N 6 56W
Fanad Hd., *Ireland* **23 A4** 55 17N 7 38W
Fanahammaren, *Norway* **18 D2** 60 16N 5 20 E
Fanárion, *Greece* **48 B3** 39 24N 21 47 E
Fandriana, *Madag.* **117 C8** 20 14 S 47 21 E
Fánes-Sénnes e Braies △, *Italy* **45 B9** 46 38N 12 4 E
Fang, *Thailand* **76 H2** 19 55N 99 13 E
Fang Xian, *China* **77 A8** 32 3N 110 40 E
Fangaga, *Sudan* **106 D4** 17 40N 37 50 E
Fangak, *Sudan* **107 F3** 9 4N 30 53 E
Fangchang, *China* **77 B12** 31 5N 118 4 E
Fangcheng, *China* **74 H7** 33 18N 112 59 E

Fangchenggang, *China* **76 G7** 21 42N 108 21 E
Fangliao, *Taiwan* **77 F13** 22 22N 120 38 E
Fangshan, *China* **74 E6** 38 3N 111 25 E
Fangzi, *China* **75 F10** 36 33N 119 10 E
Fani i Madh →, *Albania* **50 E4** 41 56N 20 16 E
Fanjakana, *Madag.* **117 C8** 21 10 S 46 53 E
Fanjiatun, *China* **75 C13** 43 40N 125 15 E
Fanling, *China* **69 F11** 22 30N 114 8 E
Fannich, L., *U.K.* **22 D4** 57 38N 4 59W
Fannrem, *Norway* **18 A6** 63 16N 9 50 E
Fannūj, *Iran* **97 E8** 26 35N 59 38 E
Fanø, *Denmark* **17 J2** 55 25N 8 25 E
Fano, *Italy* **45 E10** 43 50N 13 1 E
Fanshi, *China* **74 E7** 39 12N 113 20 E
Fao = Al Fāw, *Iraq* **97 D6** 30 0N 48 30 E
Faqirwali, *Pakistan* **92 E5** 29 27N 73 0 E
Fâqûs, *Egypt* **106 H7** 30 44N 31 47 E
Far East = Dalnevostochnyy □, *Russia* **67 C14** 67 0N 140 0 E
Far East, *Asia* **62 E16** 40 0N 130 0 E
Fara in Sabina, *Italy* **45 F9** 42 12N 12 43 E
Faradje, *Dem. Rep. of the Congo* **118 B2** 3 50N 29 45 E
Farafangana, *Madag.* **117 C8** 22 49 S 47 50 E
Farâfra, El Wâhât el-, *Egypt* **106 B2** 27 15N 28 20 E
Farāh, *Afghan.* **91 B1** 32 20N 62 7 E
Farāh □, *Afghan.* **91 B1** 32 25N 62 10 E
Farāh →, *Afghan.* **88 B5** 31 27N 61 28 E
Farahalana, *Madag.* **117 A9** 14 26 S 50 10 E
Faraid, Gebel, *Egypt* **106 C4** 23 33N 35 19 E
Farako, *Ivory C.* **112 D4** 10 45N 6 50W
Farallones de Cali △, *Colombia* **168 C2** 3 13N 76 46W
Faramana, *Burkina Faso* **112 C4** 11 56N 4 45W
Faranah, *Guinea* **112 C2** 10 3N 10 45W
Farap, *Turkmenistan* **65 D1** 39 9N 63 36 E
Farasān, Jazā'ir, *Si. Arabia* **98 C3** 16 45N 41 55 E
Farasan Is. = Farasān, Jazā'ir, *Si. Arabia* **98 C3** 16 45N 41 55 E
Faratsiho, *Madag.* **117 B8** 19 24 S 46 57 E
Farbarachi, *Somali Rep.* **120 D3** 2 30N 45 30 E
Fardes →, *Spain* **43 H7** 37 35N 3 0W
Fareham, *U.K.* **21 G6** 50 51N 1 11W
Farewell, *U.S.A.* **144 E9** 62 31N 153 54W
Farewell, C., *N.Z.* **131 A7** 40 29 S 172 43 E
Farewell C. = Nunap Isua, *Greenland* **10 F6** 59 48N 43 55W
Farewell Spit, *N.Z.* **131 A8** 40 35 S 173 0 E
Färgelanda, *Sweden* **17 F5** 58 34N 12 0 E
Farghona, *Uzbekistan* **65 C5** 40 23N 71 19 E
Farghonskaya Dolina, *Uzbekistan* **65 C5** 40 50N 71 30 E
Fargo, *Ga., U.S.A.* **152 E7** 30 41N 82 34W
Fargo, *N. Dak., U.S.A.* **154 B6** 46 53N 96 48W
Fār'iah, W. al →, *West Bank* **103 C4** 32 12N 35 27 E
Faribault, *U.S.A.* **154 C8** 44 18N 93 16W
Faridabad, *India* **92 E6** 28 26N 77 19 E
Faridkot, *India* **92 D6** 30 44N 74 45 E
Faridpur, *Bangla.* **90 D2** 23 15N 89 55 E
Faridpur, *India* **93 E8** 28 13N 79 33 E
Fārigh, W. al →, *Libya* **108 B3** 30 28N 20 44 E
Färila, *Sweden* **16 C9** 61 48N 15 50 E
Farim, *Guinea-Biss.* **112 C1** 12 27N 15 9W
Farīmān, *Iran* **97 C8** 35 40N 59 49 E
Farina, *Australia* **127 E2** 30 3 S 138 15 E
Farinha →, *Brazil* **170 C2** 6 51 S 47 30W
Fariones, Pta., *Canary Is.* **9 e2** 29 13N 13 28W
Fâriskûr, *Egypt* **106 H7** 31 20N 31 43 E
Färjestaden, *Sweden* **17 H10** 56 39N 16 27 E
Farkadhón, *Greece* **48 B4** 39 36N 22 4 E
Farkhor = Parkhar, *Tajikistan* **65 E4** 37 30N 69 34 E
Farleigh, *Australia* **126 K7** 21 4 S 149 8 E
Farley, *U.S.A.* **156 B6** 42 27N 91 0W
Farmakonisi, *Greece* **49 D9** 37 17N 27 5 E
Farmer City, *U.S.A.* **157 D8** 40 15N 88 39W
Farmersburg, *U.S.A.* **157 E9** 39 15N 87 23W
Farmerville, *U.S.A.* **155 J8** 32 47N 92 24W
Farmingdale, *U.S.A.* **151 F10** 40 12N 74 10W
Farmington, *Canada* **142 B4** 55 54N 120 30W
Farmington, *Calif., U.S.A.* **160 H6** 37 55N 120 59W
Farmington, *Ga., U.S.A.* **152 B6** 33 47N 83 26W
Farmington, *Ill., U.S.A.* **156 D7** 40 42N 90 0W
Farmington, *Iowa, U.S.A.* **156 D5** 40 38N 91 44W
Farmington, *Maine, U.S.A.* **149 C10** 44 40N 70 9W
Farmington, *Mo., U.S.A.* **155 G9** 37 47N 90 25W
Farmington, *N.H., U.S.A.* **151 C13** 43 24N 71 4W
Farmington, *N. Mex., U.S.A.* **159 H9** 36 44N 108 12W
Farmington, *Utah, U.S.A.* **158 F8** 41 0N 111 12W
Farmington →, *U.S.A.* **151 E12** 41 51N 72 38W
Farmland, *U.S.A.* **157 D11** 40 15N 85 5W
Farmville, *U.S.A.* **148 G6** 37 18N 78 24W
Färnäs, *Sweden* **16 D8** 61 0N 14 39 E
Farne Is., *U.K.* **20 B6** 55 38N 1 37W
Färnebofjärden △, *Sweden* **16 D10** 60 10N 16 48 E
Farnham, *Canada* **151 A12** 45 17N 72 59W
Farnham, Mt., *Canada* **142 C5** 50 29N 116 30W
Faro, *Brazil* **169 D6** 2 10 S 56 39W
Faro, *Canada* **138 B6** 62 11N 133 22W
Faro, *Portugal* **43 H3** 37 2N 7 55W
Fårö, *Sweden* **15 H18** 57 55N 19 5 E
Faro ⌓, *Cameroon* **114 A2** 8 15N 12 37 E
Faro □, *Portugal* **43 H2** 37 12N 8 10W
Faro ✈ (FAO), *Portugal* **43 H3** 37 2N 7 57W
Fårösund, *Sweden* **17 G13** 57 52N 19 2 E
Farquhar, C., *Australia* **125 D1** 23 50 S 113 36 E
Farquhar Is., *Seychelles* **121 F4** 11 0 S 52 0 E
Farrars Cr. →, *Australia* **126 D3** 25 35 S 140 43 E
Farrāshband, *Iran* **97 D7** 28 57N 52 5 E
Farrell, *U.S.A.* **150 E4** 41 13N 80 30W
Farrell Flat, *Australia* **128 B3** 33 48 S 138 48 E
Farrokhī, *Iran* **97 C8** 33 50N 59 31 E
Farruch, C. = Ferrutx, C., *Spain* **38 B4** 39 47N 3 21 E
Fārs □, *Iran* **97 D7** 29 30N 55 0 E
Fársala, *Greece* **48 B4** 39 17N 22 23 E
Fārsī, *Afghan.* **91 B1** 33 47N 63 15 E
Farsø, *Denmark* **17 H3** 56 46N 9 19 E
Farson, *U.S.A.* **158 E9** 42 6N 109 27W
Farsund, *Norway* **18 F3** 58 5N 6 55 E
Fartak, Râs, *Si. Arabia* **96 D2** 28 5N 34 34 E
Fartak, Ra's, *Yemen* **99 D6** 15 38N 52 15 E
Fârţăneşti, *Romania* **53 E12** 45 49N 27 59 E
Fartura, Serra da, *Brazil* **175 B5** 26 21 S 52 52W
Faru, *Nigeria* **113 C6** 12 48N 6 12 E
Fārūj, *Iran* **97 B8** 37 14N 58 14 E
Fårup, *Denmark* **17 H3** 56 33N 9 51 E
Farvel, Kap = Nunap Isua, *Greenland* **10 F6** 59 48N 43 55W
Farwell, *U.S.A.* **155 H3** 34 23N 103 2W
Fāryāb □, *Afghan.* **65 E2** 36 0N 65 0 E
Fasā, *Iran* **97 D7** 29 0N 53 39 E
Fasano, *Italy* **47 B10** 40 50N 17 22 E
Fashoda, *Sudan* **107 F3** 9 50N 32 2 E
Fassa, *Mali* **112 C3** 13 26N 8 15 E
Fastiv, *Ukraine* **59 G5** 50 7N 29 57 E
Fastnet Rock, *Ireland* **23 E2** 51 22N 9 37W
Fastov = Fastiv, *Ukraine* **59 G5** 50 7N 29 57 E
Fatagar, Tanjung, *Indonesia* **83 B4** 2 46 S 131 57 E
Fataka, *Solomon Is.* **123 C12** 11 55 S 170 12 E
Fatehabad, *Haryana, India* **92 E6** 29 31N 75 27 E
Fatehabad, *Ut. P., India* **92 F8** 27 1N 78 19 E
Fatehgarh, *India* **93 F8** 27 25N 79 35 E
Fatehpur, *Bihar, India* **93 G11** 24 38N 85 14 E
Fatehpur, *Raj., India* **92 F6** 28 0N 74 40 E
Fatehpur, *Ut. P., India* **93 G9** 25 56N 81 13 E
Fatehpur, *Ut. P., India* **93 F9** 27 10N 81 13 E
Fatehpur Sikri, *India* **92 F6** 27 6N 77 40 E
Fatesh, *Russia* **59 F8** 52 8N 35 57 E
Fathai, *Sudan* **107 F3** 8 5N 31 48 E
Fathom Five ⌓, *Canada* **140 C3** 45 17N 81 40W
Fatick, *Senegal* **112 C1** 14 19N 16 27W
Fatima, *Canada* **141 C7** 47 24N 61 53W
Fátima, *Portugal* **43 F2** 39 37N 8 39W
Fatoya, *Guinea* **112 C3** 11 37N 9 10W
Fatsa, *Turkey* **100 B7** 41 2N 37 31 E
Fatshan = Foshan, *China* **77 F9** 23 4N 113 5 E
Faucille, Col de la, *France* **27 F13** 46 22N 6 2 E
Faulkton, *U.S.A.* **154 C5** 45 2N 99 8W
Faulquemont, *France* **27 C13** 49 3N 6 36 E
Faure I., *Australia* **125 E1** 25 52 S 113 50 E
Făurei, *Romania* **53 E12** 45 6N 27 19 E
Fauresmith, *S. Africa* **116 D4** 29 44 S 25 17 E
Fauro, *Solomon Is.* **133 L9** 6 55 S 156 7 E
Fauske, *Norway* **14 C16** 67 17N 15 25 E
Fåvang, *Norway* **18 C7** 61 27N 10 11 E
Favânia, *Brazil* **169 D7** 3 7 S 51 48W
Favara, *Italy* **46 E6** 37 19N 13 39 E
Faváritx, C. de, *Spain* **38 B5** 40 0N 4 15 E
Faverges, *France* **29 C10** 45 45N 6 17 E
Favignana, *Italy* **46 E5** 37 56N 12 20 E
Favignana, I., *Italy* **46 E5** 37 56N 12 19 E
Fawcett, Pt., *Australia* **124 B5** 11 46 S 130 2 E
Fawn →, *Canada* **140 A2** 55 20N 87 35W
Fawnskin, *U.S.A.* **161 L10** 34 16N 116 56W
Faxaflói, *Iceland* **11 C3** 64 29N 23 0W
Faxälven →, *Sweden* **16 A10** 63 13N 17 13 E
Faya-Largeau, *Chad* **109 E3** 17 58N 19 6 E
Fayaoué, *Vanuatu* **133 K4** 20 38 S 166 33 E
Fayd, *Si. Arabia* **96 E4** 27 1N 42 52 E
Fayence, *France* **29 E10** 43 38N 6 42 E
Fayette, *Ala., U.S.A.* **149 J2** 33 41N 87 50W
Fayette, *Iowa, U.S.A.* **156 B5** 42 51N 91 48W
Fayette, *Mo., U.S.A.* **156 E4** 39 9N 92 41W
Fayette, *Ohio, U.S.A.* **157 C12** 41 40N 84 20W
Fayetteville, *Ark., U.S.A.* **155 G7** 36 4N 94 10W
Fayetteville, *Ga., U.S.A.* **152 B5** 33 27N 84 27W
Fayetteville, *N.C., U.S.A.* **149 H6** 35 3N 78 53W
Fayetteville, *Tenn., U.S.A.* **149 H2** 35 9N 86 34W
Fayied, *Egypt* **106 H8** 30 18N 32 16 E
Fayón, *Spain* **40 D5** 41 15N 0 20 E
Fazao-Malfakassa △, *Togo* **113 D5** 8 45N 0 50 E
Fazenda Libongo, *Angola* **115 D2** 8 24 S 13 24 E
Fazenda Nova, *Brazil* **171 E1** 16 11 S 50 48W
Fazilka, *India* **92 D6** 30 27N 74 2 E
Fazilpur, *Pakistan* **92 E4** 29 18N 70 29 E
Fdérik, *Mauritania* **110 D2** 22 40N 12 45W
Feale →, *Ireland* **23 D2** 52 27N 9 37W
Fear, C., *U.S.A.* **149 J7** 33 50N 77 58W
Feather →, *U.S.A.* **158 G3** 38 47N 121 36W
Feather Falls, *U.S.A.* **160 F5** 39 36N 121 16W
Featherston, *N.Z.* **130 H4** 41 6 S 175 20 E
Featherstone, *Zimbabwe* **119 F3** 18 42 S 30 55 E
Fécamp, *France* **26 C7** 49 45N 0 22 E
Feda, *Norway* **18 F3** 58 17N 6 50 E
Fedala = Mohammedia, *Morocco* **110 B3** 33 44N 7 21W
Federación, *Argentina* **174 C4** 31 0 S 57 55W
Federal Capital Terr. □, *Nigeria* **113 D6** 9 0N 7 10 E
Federal Way, *U.S.A.* **160 C4** 47 18N 122 19W
Fedeshkūh, *Iran* **97 D7** 28 49N 53 50 E
Fedje, *Norway* **18 D1** 60 47N 4 43 E
Fehérgyarmat, *Hungary* **52 C7** 47 58N 22 30 E
Fehmarn, *Germany* **30 A7** 54 27N 11 7 E
Fehmarn Bælt, *Europe* **17 K5** 54 35N 11 20 E
Fehmarn Belt = Fehmarn Bælt, *Europe* **17 K5** 54 35N 11 20 E
Fei Xian, *China* **75 G9** 35 18N 117 59 E
Feijó, *Brazil* **172 B3** 8 9 S 70 21W
Feilding, *N.Z.* **130 G4** 40 13 S 175 35 E
Feira de Santana, *Brazil* **171 D4** 12 15 S 38 57W
Feiring, *Norway* **18 D8** 60 30N 11 10 E
Feixi, *China* **77 B11** 31 43N 117 59 E
Feixiang, *China* **74 F8** 36 30N 114 45 E
Fejaj, Chott el, *Tunisia* **108 B1** 33 52N 9 14 E
Fejér □, *Hungary* **52 C3** 47 9N 18 30 E
Fejø, *Denmark* **17 K5** 54 55N 11 30 E
Feke, *Turkey* **100 D6** 37 48N 35 56 E
Fekete →, *Hungary* **52 E3** 45 47N 18 15 E
Felanitx, *Spain* **38 B4** 39 28N 3 9 E
Felda, *U.S.A.* **153 J8** 26 34N 81 26W
Feldbach, *Austria* **34 E8** 46 57N 15 52 E
Feldberg, *Baden-W., Germany* **31 H3** 47 52N 8 0 E
Feldberg, *Mecklenburg-Vorpommern, Germany* **30 B9** 53 20N 13 25 E
Feldkirch, *Austria* **34 D2** 47 15N 9 37 E
Feldkirchen, *Austria* **34 E7** 46 44N 14 6 E
Felicité, *Seychelles* **121 b** 4 19 S 55 52 E
Felicity, *U.S.A.* **157 F12** 38 51N 84 6W
Felipe Carrillo Puerto, *Mexico* **163 D7** 19 38N 88 3W
Felixburg, *Zimbabwe* **117 B5** 19 29 S 30 51 E
Felixlândia, *Brazil* **171 E3** 18 47 S 44 55W
Felixstowe, *U.K.* **21 F9** 51 58N 1 23 E
Felletin, *France* **28 C6** 45 53N 2 11 E
Fellingsbro, *Sweden* **16 E9** 59 26N 15 37 E
Fellsmere, *U.S.A.* **153 H9** 27 46N 80 36W
Felshtin = Gvardeyskoye, *Ukraine* **59 K8** 45 7N 34 1 E
Felsogalla = Tatabánya, *Hungary* **52 C3** 47 32N 18 25 E
Felton, *U.S.A.* **160 H4** 37 3N 122 4W
Feltre, *Italy* **45 B8** 46 1N 11 54 E
Femer Bælt = Fehmarn Bælt, *Europe* **17 K5** 54 35N 11 20 E
Femø, *Denmark* **17 K5** 54 58N 11 35 E
Femunden, *Norway* **18 B8** 62 10N 11 53 E
Femundsmarka △, *Norway* **18 B9** 62 18N 12 6 E
Fen He →, *China* **74 G6** 35 36N 110 42 E
Fene, *Spain* **42 B2** 43 27N 8 9W
Fenelon Falls, *Canada* **150 B6** 44 32N 78 45W
Fener Burnu, *Turkey* **49 E9** 36 58N 27 18 E
Feneroa, *Ethiopia* **107 E4** 13 5N 39 3 E
Feng Xian, *Jiangsu, China* **74 G9** 34 43N 116 35 E
Feng Xian, *Shaanxi, China* **74 H4** 33 54N 106 40 E
Fengári, *Greece* **51 F9** 40 25N 25 32 E
Fengcheng, *Jiangxi, China* **77 C10** 28 12N 115 48 E
Fengcheng, *Liaoning, China* **75 D13** 40 28N 124 5 E
Fengfeng, *China* **74 F8** 36 28N 114 8 E
Fenggang, *China* **76 D6** 27 57N 107 47 E
Fenghua, *China* **77 C13** 29 40N 121 25 E
Fenghuang, *China* **76 D7** 27 57N 109 29 E
Fengkai, *China* **77 F8** 23 24N 111 30 E
Fengkang, *Taiwan* **77 F13** 22 12N 120 41 E
Fengle, *China* **77 B9** 31 29N 112 29 E
Fenglin, *Taiwan* **77 F13** 23 45N 121 26 E
Fengning, *China* **74 D9** 41 10N 116 33 E
Fengqing, *China* **76 E2** 24 38N 99 55 E
Fengqiu, *China* **74 G8** 35 2N 114 25 E
Fengrun, *China* **75 E10** 39 48N 118 8 E
Fengshan, *Guangxi Zhuangzu, China* **76 E7** 24 39N 109 15 E
Fengshan, *Guangxi Zhuangzu, China* **76 E6** 24 31N 107 3 E
Fengshan, *Taiwan* **77 F13** 22 38N 120 21 E
Fengshun, *China* **77 F11** 23 46N 116 10 E
Fengtai, *Anhui, China* **77 A11** 32 50N 116 40 E
Fengtai, *Beijing, China* **74 E9** 39 50N 116 18 E
Fengxian, *China* **77 B13** 30 55N 121 26 E
Fengxiang, *China* **74 G4** 34 29N 107 25 E
Fengxin, *China* **77 C10** 28 41N 115 18 E
Fengyang, *China* **75 H9** 32 51N 117 29 E
Fengyi, *China* **76 E3** 25 37N 100 20 E
Fengyüan, *Taiwan* **77 E13** 24 15N 120 35 E
Fengzhen, *China* **74 D7** 40 25N 113 2 E
Feni Is., *Papua N. G.* **132 C7** 4 0 S 153 40 E
Fennimore, *U.S.A.* **156 B6** 42 59N 90 39W
Fenny, *Bangla.* **90 D3** 22 55N 91 32 E
Feno, C. de, *France* **29 G12** 41 58N 8 33 E
Fenoarivo, *Fianarantsoa, Madag.* **117 C8** 21 43 S 46 24 E
Fenoarivo, *Fianarantsoa, Madag.* **117 C8** 20 52 S 46 53 E
Fenoarivo Afovoany, *Madag.* **117 B8** 18 26 S 46 34 E
Fenoarivo Atsinanana, *Madag.* **117 B8** 17 22 S 49 25 E
Fens, The, *U.K.* **20 E7** 52 38N 0 2W
Fensmark, *Denmark* **17 J5** 55 17N 11 48 E
Fenton, *U.S.A.* **157 B13** 42 48N 83 42W
Fenxi, *China* **74 F6** 36 40N 111 31 E
Fenyang, *China* **74 F6** 37 18N 111 48 E
Fenyi, *China* **77 D10** 27 45N 114 47 E
Feodosiya, *Ukraine* **59 K8** 45 2N 35 16 E
Fer, C. de, *Algeria* **111 A6** 37 3N 7 10 E
Fera, *Solomon Is.* **133 M10** 8 6 S 159 37 E
Ferdows, *Iran* **97 C8** 33 58N 58 2 E
Fère-Champenoise, *France* **27 D10** 48 45N 3 59 E
Fère-en-Tardenois, *France* **27 C10** 49 10N 3 30 E
Ferentino, *Italy* **45 G10** 41 42N 13 15 E
Ferfer, *Somali Rep.* **120 C3** 5 4N 45 9 E
Fergana = Farghona, *Uzbekistan* **65 C5** 40 23N 71 19 E
Fergana Range, *Asia* **65 C6** 41 0N 73 50 E
Ferganskaya Dolina = Farghonskaya Dolina, *Uzbekistan* **65 C5** 40 50N 71 30 E
Fergus, *Canada* **150 C4** 43 43N 80 24W
Fergus Falls, *U.S.A.* **154 B6** 46 17N 96 4W
Ferguson, *U.S.A.* **156 F6** 38 45N 90 18W
Fergusson I., *Papua N. G.* **132 E6** 9 30 S 150 45 E
Fériana, *Tunisia* **108 B1** 34 59N 8 33 E
Feričanci, *Croatia* **52 E2** 45 32N 18 0 E
Ferihegy, Budapest ✈ (BUD), *Hungary* **52 C4** 47 25N 19 12 E
Ferkane, *Algeria* **111 B6** 34 37N 7 26 E
Ferkéssédougou, *Ivory C.* **112 D3** 9 35N 5 6W
Ferlach, *Austria* **34 E7** 46 32N 14 18 E
Ferland, *Canada* **140 B2** 50 19N 88 27W
Ferlo, Vallée du, *Senegal* **112 B2** 15 15N 14 15W
Ferlo-Nord ⌓, *Senegal* **112 B2** 15 43N 14 0W
Ferlo-Sud ⌓, *Senegal* **112 B2** 15 43N 14 0W
Fermanagh □, *U.K.* **23 B4** 54 21N 7 40W
Fermo, *Italy* **45 E10** 43 9N 13 43 E
Fermont, *Canada* **141 B6** 52 47N 67 5W
Fermoselle, *Spain* **42 D4** 41 19N 6 27W
Fermoy, *Ireland* **23 D3** 52 9N 8 16W
Fernán Nuñéz, *Spain* **43 H6** 37 40N 4 44W
Fernández, *Argentina* **174 B3** 27 55 S 63 50W
Fernandina, I., *Ecuador* **172 a** 0 25 S 91 30W
Fernandina Beach, *U.S.A.* **152 E8** 30 40N 81 27W
Fernando de Noronha, *Brazil* **8 G8** 4 0 S 33 10W
Fernando Póo = Bioko, *Eq. Guin.* **113 E6** 3 30N 8 40 E
Fernandópolis, *Brazil* **171 F1** 20 16 S 50 14W
Ferndale, *U.S.A.* **160 B4** 48 51N 122 36W
Fernie, *Canada* **142 D5** 49 30N 115 5W
Fernlees, *Australia* **126 C4** 23 51 S 148 7 E
Fernley, *U.S.A.* **158 G4** 39 36N 119 15W
Feroke, *India* **95 J2** 11 9N 75 46 E
Ferozepore = Firozpur, *India* **92 D6** 30 55N 74 40 E
Férrai, *Greece* **51 F10** 40 53N 26 10 E
Ferrandina, *Italy* **47 B9** 40 29N 16 27 E
Ferrara, *Italy* **45 D8** 44 50N 11 35 E
Ferrato, C., *Italy* **46 C2** 39 18N 9 38 E
Ferreira do Alentejo, *Portugal* **43 G2** 38 4N 8 6W
Ferreira Gomes, *Brazil* **170 A1** 0 48N 51 8W
Ferreñafe, *Peru* **172 B2** 6 42 S 79 50W
Ferrerías, *Spain* **38 B5** 39 59N 4 1 E
Ferret, C., *France* **28 D2** 44 38N 1 15W
Ferrette, *France* **27 E14** 47 30N 7 20 E
Ferriday, *U.S.A.* **155 K9** 31 38N 91 33W
Ferriere, *Italy* **44 D6** 44 40N 9 30 E
Ferrières, *France* **27 D9** 48 5N 2 48 E
Ferro, Capo, *Italy* **46 A2** 41 9N 9 31 E
Ferrol, *Spain* **42 B2** 43 29N 8 15W
Ferrol, Pen. de, *Peru* **172 B2** 9 10 S 78 35W
Ferron, *U.S.A.* **159 G8** 39 5N 111 8W
Ferros, *Brazil* **171 E3** 19 14 S 43 2W
Ferrutx, C., *Spain* **38 B4** 39 47N 3 21 E
Ferryland, *Canada* **141 C9** 47 2N 52 53W
Ferrysburg, *U.S.A.* **157 A10** 43 5N 86 13W
Ferryville = Menzel-Bourguiba, *Tunisia* **108 A1** 37 9N 9 49 E
Fertile, *U.S.A.* **154 B6** 47 32N 96 17W
Fertőszentmiklós, *Hungary* **52 C1** 47 35N 16 53 E
Fertotavi △, *Hungary* **52 C1** 47 25N 16 50 E
Fès, *Morocco* **110 B4** 34 0N 5 0W
Feshi, *Dem. Rep. of the Congo* **115 D3** 6 8 S 18 10 E
Fessenden, *U.S.A.* **154 B5** 47 39N 99 38W
Festenberg = Twardogóra, *Poland* **55 G4** 51 23N 17 28 E
Festøy, *Norway* **18 B3** 62 22N 6 19 E
Festus, *U.S.A.* **156 F6** 38 13N 90 24W
Feté Bowé, *Senegal* **112 C2** 14 56N 13 30W
Feteşti, *Romania* **53 F12** 44 22N 27 51 E
Fethiye, *Turkey* **49 E11** 36 36N 29 6 E
Fethiye Körfezi, *Turkey* **49 E10** 36 40N 28 50 E
Fetlar, *U.K.* **22 A8** 60 36N 0 52W
Fetsund, *Norway* **18 E8** 59 56N 11 10 E
Feuchten, *Austria* **33 B11** 47 2N 10 44 E
Feuerthalen, *Switz.* **33 A7** 47 37N 8 38 E
Feuilles →, *Canada* **139 C12** 58 47N 70 4W
Feurs, *France* **29 C8** 45 45N 4 13 E
Fevik, *Norway* **18 F5** 58 22N 8 39 E
Feyẕābād, *Badākhshān, Afghan.* **65 E5** 37 7N 70 33 E
Feyẕābād, *Fāryāb, Afghan.* **91 A2** 36 17N 64 52 E
Fez = Fès, *Morocco* **110 B4** 34 0N 5 0W
Fezzan, *Libya* **108 C2** 27 0N 13 0 E
Fia, *Congo* **114 C2** 3 25 S 14 49 E
Fiambalá, *Argentina* **174 B2** 27 45 S 67 37W
Fianarantsoa, *Madag.* **117 C8** 21 26 S 47 5 E
Fianarantsoa □, *Madag.* **117 B8** 19 30 S 47 0 E
Fianga, *Cameroon* **109 G3** 9 55N 15 9 E
Fiche, *Ethiopia* **107 F4** 9 50N 38 46 E
Fichtelgebirge, *Germany* **31 E7** 50 2N 11 55 E
Fichtelgebirge ⌓, *Germany* **31 E8** 50 8N 12 0 E
Ficksburg, *S. Africa* **117 D4** 28 51 S 27 53 E
Fidenza, *Italy* **44 D7** 44 52N 10 3 E
Fiditi, *Nigeria* **113 D5** 7 45N 3 53 E
Fidjeland, *Norway* **18 F3** 58 57N 6 56 E
Field →, *Australia* **126 C2** 23 48 S 138 0 E
Field I., *Australia* **124 B5** 12 5 S 132 23 E
Fieni, *Romania* **53 E10** 45 8N 25 25 E
Fier, *Albania* **50 F3** 40 43N 19 33 E
Fierzë, *Albania* **50 D4** 42 15N 20 1 E
Fiesch, *Switz.* **32 D6** 46 25N 8 12 E
Fife ⌓, *U.K.* **22 E5** 56 15N 3 15W
Fife □, *U.K.* **22 E5** 56 16N 3 1W
Fife Ness, *U.K.* **22 E6** 56 17N 2 35W
Fifth Cataract, *Sudan* **106 D3** 18 22N 33 50 E
Figari, *France* **29 G13** 41 29N 9 7 E
Figeac, *France* **28 D6** 44 37N 2 2 E
Figeholm, *Sweden* **17 G10** 57 22N 16 33 E
Figline Valdarno, *Italy* **45 E8** 43 37N 11 28 E
Figtree, *Zimbabwe* **119 G2** 20 22 S 28 20 E
Figueira = Governador Valadares, *Brazil* **171 E3** 18 15 S 41 57W
Figueira Castelo Rodrigo, *Portugal* **42 E4** 40 57N 6 58W
Figueira da Foz, *Portugal* **42 E2** 40 7N 8 54W
Figueiró dos Vinhos, *Portugal* **42 F2** 39 55N 8 16W
Figueres, *Spain* **40 C7** 42 18N 2 58 E
Figuig, *Morocco* **111 B4** 32 5N 1 11W
Fihaonana, *Madag.* **117 B8** 18 36 S 47 12 E
Fiherenana, *Madag.* **117 B8** 18 29 S 48 24 E
Fiherenana →, *Madag.* **117 C7** 23 19 S 43 37 E
Fiji ■, *Pac. Oc.* **133 A2** 17 20 S 179 0 E
Fik, *Ethiopia* **107 F5** 8 10N 42 19 E
Fika, *Nigeria* **113 C7** 11 15N 11 13 E
Filabres, Sierra de los, *Spain* **43 H8** 37 13N 2 20W
Filabusi, *Zimbabwe* **117 C4** 20 34 S 29 20 E
Filadelfia, *Bolivia* **172 C4** 11 20 S 68 46W
Filadélfia, *Brazil* **170 C2** 7 21 S 47 30W
Filadélfia, *Italy* **47 D9** 38 47N 16 17 E
Fil'akovo, *Slovak Rep.* **35 C12** 48 17N 19 50 E
Filey, *U.K.* **20 C7** 54 12N 0 18W
Filey B., *U.K.* **20 C7** 54 12N 0 15W
Filfla, *Malta* **38 F7** 35 47N 14 24 E
Filiaşi, *Romania* **53 F8** 44 32N 23 31 E
Filiátes, *Greece* **38 B10** 39 38N 20 16 E
Filiatrá, *Greece* **48 D3** 37 9N 21 35 E
Filicudi, *Italy* **47 D7** 38 35N 14 33 E
Filim, *Oman* **99 B7** 20 37N 58 12 E
Filingué, *Niger* **113 C5** 14 21N 3 22 E
Filiourí →, *Greece* **51 E9** 41 15N 25 40 E
Filipstad, *Sweden* **16 E8** 59 43N 14 9 E
Filisur, *Switz.* **33 C9** 46 41N 9 40 E
Fillefjell, *Norway* **18 C5** 61 8N 8 10 E
Fillmore, *Calif., U.S.A.* **161 L8** 34 24N 118 55W
Fillmore, *Utah, U.S.A.* **159 G7** 38 58N 112 20W
Filótion, *Greece* **49 D7** 37 3N 25 30 E
Filottrano, *Italy* **45 E10** 43 26N 13 21 E
Filtu, *Ethiopia* **107 F5** 5 8N 40 35 E
Fimi →, *Dem. Rep. of the Congo* **114 C3** 3 1 S 16 58 E
Fina ⌓, *Mali* **112 C3** 13 15N 8 46W
Finale Emília, *Italy* **45 D8** 44 50N 11 18 E
Finale Lígure, *Italy* **44 D5** 44 10N 8 20 E
Finalmarina = Finale Lígure, *Italy* **44 D5** 44 10N 8 20 E
Fiñana, *Spain* **43 H8** 37 10N 2 50W
Finch, *Canada* **151 A9** 45 11N 75 7W
Finch Hatton, *Australia* **126 K6** 20 25 S 148 39 E
Findhorn →, *U.K.* **22 D5** 57 38N 3 38W
Findlay, *U.S.A.* **157 C13** 41 2N 83 39W
Finger L., *Canada* **140 B1** 53 33N 93 30W
Finger Lakes, *U.S.A.* **151 D8** 42 40N 76 30W
Fíngoè, *Mozam.* **119 E3** 14 55 S 31 50 E
Finike, *Turkey* **49 E12** 36 21N 30 10 E
Finike Körfezi, *Turkey* **49 E12** 36 17N 30 16 E
Finiq, *Albania* **50 G4** 39 54N 20 3 E
Finistère □, *France* **26 D3** 48 20N 4 0W
Finisterre = Fisterra, *Spain* **42 C1** 42 54N 9 16W
Finisterre, C. = Fisterra, C., *Spain* **42 C1** 42 50N 9 19W
Finisterre Ra., *Papua N. G.* **132 D4** 6 0 S 146 30 E
Finke, *Australia* **126 D1** 25 34 S 134 35 E
Finke Gorge △, *Australia* **124 D5** 24 8 S 132 49 E
Finland ■, *Europe* **14 E22** 63 0N 27 0 E
Finland, G. of, *Europe* **15 G21** 60 0N 26 0 E
Finlay →, *Canada* **142 B3** 57 0N 125 10W
Finley, *Australia* **129 C6** 35 38 S 145 35 E
Finley, *U.S.A.* **154 B6** 47 31N 97 50W
Finn →, *Ireland* **23 B4** 54 51N 7 28W
Finnerödja, *Sweden* **17 F8** 58 57N 14 24 E
Finnigan, Mt., *Australia* **126 B4** 15 49 S 145 17 E
Finniss, C., *Australia* **127 E1** 33 8 S 134 51 E
Finnmark, *Norway* **14 B20** 69 37N 23 57 E
Finnsnes, *Norway* **14 B18** 69 14N 18 0 E
Finschhafen, *Papua N. G.* **132 D4** 6 33 S 147 50 E
Finse, *Norway* **18 D4** 60 36N 7 30 E
Finspång, *Sweden* **17 F9** 58 43N 15 47 E
Finsteraarhorn, *Switz.* **32 C6** 46 31N 8 10 E
Finsterwalde, *Germany* **30 D9** 51 37N 13 42 E
Fiora →, *Italy* **45 F8** 42 20N 11 34 E
Fiordland △, *N.Z.* **131 F2** 45 46 S 167 0 E
Fiorenzuola d'Arda, *Italy* **44 D6** 44 56N 9 55 E
Fīq, *Syria* **103 C4** 32 46N 35 41 E
Firat = Furāt, Nahr al →, *Asia* **96 D5** 31 0N 47 25 E
Fire Island ⌓, *U.S.A.* **151 F11** 40 38N 73 8W
Firebag →, *Canada* **143 B6** 57 45N 111 21W
Firebaugh, *U.S.A.* **160 J6** 36 52N 120 27W
Firedrake L., *Canada* **143 A8** 61 25N 104 30W
Firenze, *Italy* **45 E8** 43 46N 11 15 E
Firenze Amerigo Vespucci ✈ (FLR), *Italy* **44 E8** 43 49N 11 13 E
Firenze Pisa ✈ (PSA), *Italy* **44 E7** 43 40N 10 22 E
Firenzuola, *Italy* **45 D8** 44 7N 11 23 E
Firk, Sha'ib →, *Iraq* **96 D5** 30 59N 44 34 E
Firkachi, *Niger* **109 E2** 15 40N 14 20 E
Firmi, *France* **28 D6** 44 33N 2 19 E
Firminy, *France* **29 C8** 45 23N 4 18 E
Firozabad, *India* **93 F8** 27 10N 78 25 E
Firozpur, *India* **92 D6** 30 55N 74 40 E
Firozpur-Jhirka, *India* **92 F7** 27 48N 76 57 E
Fīrūzābād, *Iran* **97 D7** 28 52N 52 35 E
Fīrūzkūh, *Iran* **97 C7** 35 50N 52 50 E
Firvale, *Canada* **142 C3** 52 27N 126 13W
Fish →, *Namibia* **116 D2** 28 7 S 17 10 E
Fish →, *S. Africa* **116 E3** 31 30 S 20 16 E
Fish River Canyon, *Namibia* **116 D2** 27 40 S 17 35 E
Fisheating Cr. →, *U.S.A.* **153 J8** 26 57N 81 7W
Fisher, *Australia* **125 F5** 30 30 S 131 0 E
Fisher B., *Canada* **143 C9** 51 35N 97 13W
Fishers I., *U.S.A.* **151 E13** 41 15N 72 0W
Fishguard, *U.K.* **21 E3** 52 0N 4 58W
Fishing L., *Canada* **143 C9** 52 10N 95 24W
Fishkill, *U.S.A.* **151 E11** 41 32N 73 53W
Fiskárdho, *Greece* **39 C2** 38 28N 20 35 E
Fiskenæsset = Qeqertarsuatsiaat, *Greenland* **10 E5** 63 5N 50 45W
Fismes, *France* **27 C10** 49 20N 3 40 E
Fisterra, *Spain* **42 C1** 42 54N 9 16W
Fisterra, C., *Spain* **42 C1** 42 50N 9 19W
Fitchburg, *Mass., U.S.A.* **151 D13** 42 35N 71 48W
Fitchburg, *Wis., U.S.A.* **154 D10** 42 58N 89 28W
Fitjar, *Iceland* **11 C5** 64 28N 21 18W
Fitjar, *Norway* **18 E2** 59 55N 5 17 E
Fitri, L., *Chad* **109 F3** 12 50N 17 28 E
Fitz Roy, *Argentina* **176 C3** 47 0 S 67 0W
Fitzgerald, *Canada* **142 B6** 59 51N 111 36W
Fitzgerald, *U.S.A.* **152 D6** 31 43N 83 15W
Fitzgerald River △, *Australia* **125 F3** 33 53 S 120 3 E
Fitzmaurice →, *Australia* **124 B5** 14 45 S 130 5 E
Fitzroy →, *Queens., Australia* **126 C5** 23 32 S 150 52 E
Fitzroy →, *W. Austral., Australia* **124 C3** 17 31 S 123 35 E
Fitzroy Crossing, *Australia* **124 C4** 18 9 S 125 38 E
Fitzwilliam I., *Canada* **150 A3** 45 30N 81 45W
Fiuggi, *Italy* **45 G10** 41 48N 13 13 E
Fiume = Rijeka, *Croatia* **45 C11** 45 20N 14 21 E
Fiumicino, Roma ✈ (FCO), *Italy* **45 G9** 41 48N 12 15 E
Five Points, *U.S.A.* **160 J6** 36 26N 120 6W
Fivizzano, *Italy* **44 D7** 44 14N 10 8 E
Fizi, *Dem. Rep. of the Congo* **118 C2** 4 17 S 28 55 E
Fjæra, *Norway* **18 E3** 59 52N 6 22 E
Fjærland, *Norway* **18 C3** 61 24N 6 43 E
Fjällbacka, *Sweden* **17 F5** 58 36N 11 17 E
Fjärdhundra, *Sweden* **16 E10** 59 47N 16 56 E
Fjellerup, *Denmark* **17 H4** 56 29N 10 34 E
Fjerritslev, *Denmark* **17 G3** 57 5N 9 15 E
Fjugesta, *Sweden* **16 E8** 59 11N 14 52 E
Fkih ben Salah, *Morocco* **110 B3** 32 32N 6 45W
Flå, *Norway* **18 D6** 60 25N 9 28 E
Flagler Beach, *U.S.A.* **153 F8** 29 29N 81 8W
Flagstaff, *U.S.A.* **159 J8** 35 12N 111 39W
Flagstaff B., *St. Helena* **9 h** 15 54 S 5 41W
Flagstaff L., *U.S.A.* **149 C10** 45 12N 70 18W
Flaherty I., *Canada* **140 A4** 56 15N 79 15W
Flåm, *Norway* **18 D4** 60 50N 7 7 E
Flamatt, *Switz.* **32 C4** 46 53N 7 19 E
Flambeau →, *U.S.A.* **154 C9** 45 18N 91 14W
Flamborough Hd., *U.K.* **20 C7** 54 7N 0 5W
Flamengos, *Azores* **9 d1** 38 33N 28 39W
Fläming, *Germany* **30 C8** 52 6N 12 23 E
Flaming Gorge ⌓, *U.S.A.* **158 F9** 41 10N 109 25W
Flaming Gorge Reservoir, *U.S.A.* **158 F9** 41 10N 109 25W
Flamingo, *U.S.A.* **153 K9** 25 8N 80 57W
Flamingo, Teluk, *Indonesia* **83 C5** 5 30 S 138 0 E
Flanagan, *U.S.A.* **157 D8** 40 53N 88 52W
Flanders = Flandre, *Europe* **27 B9** 50 50N 2 30 E
Flandre, *Europe* **27 B9** 50 50N 2 30 E
Flandre-Occidentale = West-Vlaanderen □, *Belgium* **24 D2** 51 0N 3 0 E
Flandre-Orientale = Oost-Vlaanderen □, *Belgium* **24 C3** 51 5N 3 50 E
Flandreau, *U.S.A.* **154 C6** 44 3N 96 36W
Flanigan, *U.S.A.* **160 E7** 40 10N 119 53W
Flannan Is., *U.K.* **22 C1** 58 9N 7 52W
Flåsjön, *Sweden* **14 D16** 64 5N 15 40 E
Flat, *U.S.A.* **144 E8** 62 28N 158 1W
Flat →, *Canada* **142 A3** 61 33N 125 18W
Flat →, *U.S.A.* **157 B11** 42 56N 85 20W
Flat I., *Mauritius* **121 d** 19 53 S 57 35 E
Flat Pt., *N.Z.* **130 H4** 41 14 S 175 57 E
Flat Rock, *U.S.A.* **157 B13** 42 6N 83 17W
Flateby, *Norway* **18 E8** 59 50N 11 10 E
Flateyri, *Iceland* **11 A3** 66 3N 23 31W
Flathead L., *U.S.A.* **158 C7** 47 51N 114 8W
Flatow = Złotów, *Poland* **54 E4** 53 22N 17 2 E
Flatrock →, *U.S.A.* **157 F10** 39 12N 85 56W
Flattery, C., *Australia* **126 A4** 14 58 S 145 21 E
Flattery, C., *U.S.A.* **160 B2** 48 23N 124 29W
Flatts Village, *Bermuda* **9 a** 32 18N 64 43W
Flatwoods, *U.S.A.* **148 F4** 38 31N 82 43W
Flawil, *Switz.* **33 B8** 47 26N 9 11 E
Flecha Pt., *Phil.* **81 H4** 7 22N 123 24 E
Flechas Pt., *Phil.* **81 F2** 10 22N 119 34 E
Fleetwood, *U.K.* **20 D4** 53 55N 3 1W
Fleetwood, *U.S.A.* **151 F9** 40 27N 75 49W
Flekke, *Norway* **18 C2** 61 19N 5 20 E
Flekkefjord, *Norway* **18 F3** 58 18N 6 39 E

Flemingsburg, U.S.A. 157 F13 38 25N 83 45W
Flemington, U.S.A. 150 E7 41 7N 77 28W
Flemish Cap, Atl. Oc. 8 B7 47 0N 45 0W
Flen, Sweden 16 E10 59 4N 16 35 E
Flensburg, Germany 30 A5 54 47N 9 27 E
Flers, France 26 D6 48 47N 0 33W
Flesberg, Norway 18 E6 59 51N 9 27 E
Flesherton, Canada 150 B4 44 16N 80 33W
Flesko, Tanjung, Indonesia 82 A2 0 29N 124 30 E
Fletcher = Aurora, U.S.A. 154 F2 39 44N 104 52W
Fleurance, France 28 E4 43 52N 0 40 E
Fleurier, Switz. 32 C3 46 54N 6 35 E
Fleurieu Pen., Australia 128 C3 35 40 S 138 5 E
Flevoland □, Neths. 24 B5 52 30N 5 30 E
Flims, Switz. 33 C8 46 50N 9 17 E
Flin Flon, Canada 143 C8 54 46N 101 53W
Flinders →, Australia 126 B3 17 36 S 140 36 E
Flinders B., Australia 125 F2 34 19 S 115 19 E
Flinders Chase △, Australia 128 C2 35 50 S 136 42 E
Flinders Group, Australia 126 A3 14 11 S 144 15 E
Flinders I., S. Austral., Australia 127 E1 33 44 S 134 41 E
Flinders I., Tas., Australia 127 G4 40 0 S 148 0 E
Flinders Ranges, Australia 128 A3 31 30 S 138 30 E
Flinders Ranges △, Australia 128 A3 31 30 S 138 40 E
Flinders Reefs, Australia 126 B4 17 37 S 148 31 E
Flint, U.K. 20 D4 53 15N 3 8W
Flint, U.S.A. 157 A13 43 1N 83 41W
Flint →, U.S.A. 152 E5 30 57N 84 34W
Flint I., Kiribati 135 J12 11 26 S 151 48W
Flintshire □, U.K. 20 D4 53 17N 3 17W
Flirsch, Austria 33 B10 47 9N 10 24 E
Flisa, Norway 18 D9 60 37N 12 0 E
Flisa →, Norway 18 D9 60 37N 12 0 E
Fliseryd, Sweden 17 G10 57 6N 16 15 E
Flix, Spain 40 D5 41 14N 0 32 E
Flixecourt, France 27 B9 50 1N 2 5 E
Floby, Sweden 17 F7 58 8N 13 20 E
Floda, Sweden 17 G6 57 49N 12 22 E
Flodden, U.K. 20 B5 55 37N 2 8W
Flogny-la-Chapelle, France 27 E10 47 57N 3 57 E
Floodplains △, Sri Lanka 95 K5 8 10N 81 10 E
Floodwood, U.S.A. 154 B8 46 55N 92 55W
Flora, Phil. 80 B3 18 14N 121 5 E
Flora, Ill., U.S.A. 156 F8 38 40N 88 29W
Flora, Ind., U.S.A. 157 D10 40 33N 86 31W
Florac, France 28 D7 44 20N 3 37 E
Florahome, U.S.A. 152 F8 29 44N 81 54W
Floral City, U.S.A. 153 G7 28 45N 82 17W
Florala, U.S.A. 149 K2 31 0N 86 20W
Florânia, Brazil 170 C4 6 8 S 36 49W
Floreana, I. = Santa María, I., Ecuador 172 a 1 17 S 90 26W
Florence = Firenze, Italy 45 E8 43 46N 11 15 E
Florence, Ala., U.S.A. 149 H2 34 48N 87 41W
Florence, Ariz., U.S.A. 159 K8 33 2N 111 23W
Florence, Colo., U.S.A. 154 F2 38 23N 105 8W
Florence, Oreg., U.S.A. 158 E1 43 58N 124 7W
Florence, S.C., U.S.A. 149 H6 34 12N 79 46W
Florence, L., Australia 127 D2 28 53 S 138 9 E
Florence Bay = Chtimba, Malawi 119 E3 10 35 S 34 13 E
Florencia, Colombia 168 C2 1 36N 75 36W
Florennes, Belgium 24 D4 50 15N 4 35 E
Florensac, France 28 E7 43 23N 3 28 E
Florenville, Belgium 24 E5 49 40N 5 19 E
Flores = Florânia, Brazil 170 C4 6 8 S 36 49W
Flores = Timon, Brazil 170 C4 5 8 S 42 52W
Flores, Azores 9 d2 39 26N 31 13W
Flores, Brazil 170 C4 7 51 S 37 59W
Flores, Guatemala 164 C2 16 59N 89 50W
Flores, Indonesia 82 C2 8 35 S 121 0 E
Flores I., Canada 142 D3 49 20N 126 10W
Flores Sea, Indonesia 82 C2 6 30 S 120 0 E
Floresta, Brazil 170 C4 8 40 S 37 26W
Floreşti, Moldova 53 C13 47 53N 28 17 E
Floresville, U.S.A. 155 L5 29 8N 98 10W
Floriano, Brazil 170 C3 6 50 S 43 0W
Florianópolis, Brazil 175 B6 27 30 S 48 30W
Florida, Cuba 164 B4 21 32N 78 14W
Florida, Uruguay 175 C4 34 7 S 56 10W
Florida □, U.S.A. 149 L5 28 0N 82 0W
Florida, Straits of, U.S.A. 164 B4 25 0N 80 0W
Florida B., U.S.A. 164 B3 25 0N 80 45W
Florida City, U.S.A. 153 K9 25 27N 80 29W
Florida Is., Solomon Is. 133 M11 9 55 S 160 15 E
Florida Keys, U.S.A. 153 L8 24 40N 81 0W
Floridablanca, Phil. 80 D3 14 59N 120 31 E
Florídia, Italy 47 E8 37 5N 15 9 E
Flórina, Greece 50 F5 40 48N 21 26 E
Flórina □, Greece 50 F5 40 45N 21 20 E
Florissant, U.S.A. 156 F6 38 48N 90 20W
Florø, Norway 18 C2 61 35N 5 1 E
Flotte, C. de, N. Cal. 133 U21 21 10 S 167 25 E
Flower Station, Canada 151 A8 45 10N 76 41W
Flowerpot I., Canada 150 A3 45 18N 81 38W
Floydada, U.S.A. 155 J4 33 59N 101 20W
Fludir, Iceland 11 C6 64 7N 20 6W
Flüelapass, Switz. 33 C9 46 46N 9 56 E
Flugumyri, Iceland 11 B7 65 34N 19 19W
Fluk, Indonesia 82 B3 1 42 S 127 44 E
Flúmen →, Spain 40 D4 41 43N 0 9W
Flumendosa →, Italy 46 C2 39 26N 9 37 E
Fluminimaggiore, Italy 46 C1 39 26N 8 30 E
Flushing = Vlissingen, Neths. 24 C3 51 26N 3 34 E
Flushing, U.S.A. 157 A13 43 4N 83 51W
Fluviá →, Spain 40 C8 42 12N 3 7 E
Fly →, Papua N. G. 132 E2 8 25 S 143 0 E
Flying Fish, C., Antarctica 7 D15 72 6 S 102 29W
Foa, Tonga 133 P13 19 45 S 174 18W
Foam Lake, Canada 143 C8 51 40N 103 32W
Foča, Bos.-H. 50 C2 43 31N 18 47 E
Foça, Turkey 49 C8 38 39N 26 46 E
Fochabers, U.K. 22 D5 57 37N 3 6W
Focşani, Romania 53 E12 45 41N 27 15 E
Fodé, C.A.R. 114 A4 5 29N 23 18 E
Fodécontéa, Guinea 112 C2 10 50N 14 22W
Fogang, China 77 F9 23 52N 113 30 E
Foggaret el Arab, Algeria 111 C5 27 13N 2 49 E
Foggaret ez Zoua, Algeria 111 C5 27 20N 2 53 E
Fóggia, Italy 47 A8 41 27N 15 34 E
Foggo, Nigeria 113 C6 11 21N 9 57 E
Foglia →, Italy 45 E9 43 55N 12 54 E
Fogo, Canada 141 C9 49 43N 54 17W
Fogo, C. Verde Is. 9 j 15 5N 24 20W
Fogo I., Canada 141 C9 49 40N 54 5W
Fohnsdorf, Austria 34 D7 47 12N 14 40 E
Föhr, Germany 30 A4 54 43N 8 30 E
Foia, Portugal 43 H2 37 19N 8 37W
Foix, France 28 F5 42 58N 1 38 E
Fojnica, Bos.-H. 52 G2 43 59N 17 51 E
Fokino, Russia 58 F8 53 30N 34 22 E
Fokís □, Greece 48 C4 38 30N 22 15 E
Fokku, Nigeria 113 C5 11 36N 4 32 E
Fokstua, Norway 18 B6 62 7N 9 17 E
Folda, Nord-Trøndelag, Norway 14 D14 64 32N 10 30 E
Folda, Nordland, Norway 14 C16 67 38N 14 50 E
Földeák, Hungary 52 D5 46 19N 20 30 E
Folégandros, Greece 48 E6 36 40N 24 55 E
Foley, Botswana 116 C4 21 34 S 27 21 E
Foley, Ala., U.S.A. 149 K2 30 24N 87 41W
Foley, Fla., U.S.A. 152 E6 30 4N 83 32W
Foleyet, Canada 140 C3 48 15N 82 25W
Folgefonni, Norway 18 D3 60 3N 6 23 E
Foligno, Italy 45 F9 42 57N 12 42 E
Folkestad, Norway 18 B3 62 7N 6 1 E
Folkestone, U.K. 21 F9 51 5N 1 12 E
Folkston, U.S.A. 152 E7 30 50N 82 0W
Folla →, Norway 18 B7 62 7N 10 37 E
Follansbee, U.S.A. 150 F4 40 19N 80 35W
Folldal, Norway 18 B6 62 8N 10 0 E
Follebu, Norway 18 C7 61 13N 10 16 E
Follónica, Italy 44 F7 42 55N 10 45 E
Follónica, G. di, Italy 44 F7 42 54N 10 43 E
Folsom L., U.S.A. 160 G5 38 42N 121 9W
Folteşti, Romania 53 E13 45 45N 28 3 E
Fomboni, Comoros Is. 121 a 12 18 S 43 46 E
Fomm ir-Rih Bay, Malta 38 F7 35 54N 14 20 E
Fond-du-Lac, Canada 143 B7 59 19N 107 12W
Fond du Lac, U.S.A. 154 D10 43 47N 88 27W
Fond-du-Lac →, Canada 143 B7 59 17N 106 0W
Fonda, Iowa, U.S.A. 156 B2 42 35N 94 51W
Fonda, N.Y., U.S.A. 151 D10 42 57N 74 22W
Fondi, Italy 46 A6 41 21N 13 25 E
Fonfría, Spain 42 D4 41 37N 6 9W
Fongafale, Tuvalu 134 H9 8 31 S 179 13 E
Fongen, Norway 18 A8 63 11N 11 38 E
Fonni, Italy 46 B2 40 7N 9 15 E
Fonsagrada = A Fonsagrada, Spain 42 B3 43 8N 7 4W
Fonseca, G. de, Cent. Amer. 164 D2 13 10N 87 40W
Font-Romeu-Odeillo-Via, France 28 F5 42 31N 2 3 E
Fontaine-Française, France 27 E12 47 32N 5 21 E
Fontainebleau, France 27 D9 48 24N 2 40 E
Fontana, U.S.A. 161 L9 34 6N 117 26W
Fontana, L., Argentina 176 B2 44 55 S 71 30W
Fontas →, Canada 142 B4 58 14N 121 48W
Fonte Boa, Brazil 168 D4 2 33 S 66 0W
Fontem, Cameroon 113 D6 5 32N 9 52 E
Fontenay-le-Comte, France 28 B3 46 28N 0 48W
Fontenelle Reservoir, U.S.A. 158 E8 42 1N 110 3W
Fontur, Iceland 14 C6 66 23N 14 32W
Fonuafo'ou, Tonga 133 Q13 20 19 S 175 25W
Fonualei, Tonga 133 P13 18 1 S 174 19W
Fonyód, Hungary 52 D2 46 44N 17 33 E
Foochow = Fuzhou, China 77 D12 26 5N 119 16 E
Foping, China 74 H5 33 41N 108 0 E
Fora →, Norway 18 B7 62 57N 10 40 E
Foraker, Mt., U.S.A. 144 E10 62 58N 151 24W
Forari, Vanuatu 133 G6 17 40 S 168 31 E
Forbach, France 27 C13 49 10N 6 52 E
Forbes, Australia 129 B8 33 22 S 148 5 E
Forbesganj, India 93 F12 26 17N 87 18 E
Forcados, Nigeria 113 D6 5 26N 5 26 E
Forcados →, Nigeria 113 D6 5 25N 5 19 E
Forcalquier, France 29 E9 43 58N 5 47 E
Forchheim, Germany 31 F7 49 43N 11 2 E
Forclaz, Col de la, Switz. 32 D4 46 3N 7 1 E
Ford City, Calif., U.S.A. 161 K7 35 9N 119 27W
Ford City, Pa., U.S.A. 150 F5 40 46N 79 32W
Ford I., U.S.A. 145 K14 21 22N 157 58W
Fordate, Indonesia 83 C4 7 0 S 131 58 E
Førde, Hordaland, Norway 18 E2 59 36N 5 27 E
Førde, Sogn og Fjordane, Norway 18 C2 61 27N 5 53 E
Førdefjorden, Norway 18 C2 61 29N 5 18 E
Førdesfjord, Norway 18 E2 59 25N 5 20 E
Ford's Bridge, Australia 127 D4 29 41 S 145 29 E
Fordyce, U.S.A. 155 J8 33 49N 92 25W
Forécariah, Guinea 112 D2 9 28N 13 10W
Forel, Mt., Greenland 10 D7 66 52N 36 55W
Foremost, Canada 142 D6 49 26N 111 34W
Forest, Canada 150 C3 43 6N 82 0W
Forest, U.S.A. 155 J10 32 22N 89 29W
Forest Acres, U.S.A. 152 A9 34 1N 80 58W
Forest City, Iowa, U.S.A. 154 D8 43 16N 93 39W
Forest City, N.C., U.S.A. 149 H5 35 20N 81 52W
Forest City, Pa., U.S.A. 151 E9 41 39N 75 28W
Forest Grove, U.S.A. 160 E3 45 31N 123 7W
Forest Park, U.S.A. 152 B3 33 37N 84 22W
Forestburg, Canada 142 C6 52 35N 112 1W
Foreste Casentinesi-Monte Falterona-Campigna △, Italy 45 E8 43 50N 11 48 E
Foresthill, U.S.A. 160 F6 39 1N 120 49W
Forestier Pen., Australia 127 G4 43 0 S 148 0 E
Forestville, Canada 141 C6 48 48N 69 2W
Forestville, Calif., U.S.A. 160 G4 38 28N 122 54W
Forestville, N.Y., U.S.A. 150 D5 42 28N 79 10W
Forêt d'Orient ⌓, France 27 D11 48 16N 4 25 E
Forêt du Day △, Djibouti 120 B2 11 56N 42 40 E
Forez, Mts. du, France 28 C7 45 40N 3 50 E
Forfar, U.K. 22 E6 56 39N 2 53W
Forggensee, Germany 33 A11 47 35N 10 44 E
Forillon △, Canada 141 C7 48 46N 64 12W
Forks, U.S.A. 160 C2 47 57N 124 23W
Forksville, U.S.A. 151 E8 41 29N 76 35W
Forlì, Italy 45 D9 44 13N 12 3 E
Forman, U.S.A. 154 B6 46 7N 97 38W
Formazza, Italy 44 B5 46 22N 8 26 E
Formby Pt., U.K. 20 D4 53 33N 3 6W
Formentera, Spain 38 D1 38 43N 1 27 E
Formentor, C. de, Spain 38 B4 39 58N 3 13 E
Former Yugoslav Republic of Macedonia = Macedonia ■, Europe 50 E5 41 53N 21 40 E
Fórmia, Italy 46 A6 41 15N 13 37 E
Formiga, Brazil 171 F2 20 27 S 45 25W
Formigine, Italy 44 D7 44 37N 10 51 E
Formosa = Taiwan ■, Asia 77 F13 23 30N 121 0 E
Formosa, Argentina 174 B4 26 15 S 58 10W
Formosa, Brazil 171 E2 15 32 S 47 20W
Formosa □, Argentina 174 B4 25 0 S 60 0W
Formosa, Serra, Brazil 173 C6 12 0 S 55 0W
Formosa B. = Ungwana B., Kenya 118 C5 2 40 S 40 20 E
Formosa Strait = Taiwan Strait, Asia 77 E12 24 40N 120 0 E
Formoso →, Brazil 171 D2 10 34 S 49 56W
Fornells, Spain 38 A5 40 3N 4 7 E
Fornos de Algodres, Portugal 42 E3 40 38N 7 32W
Fornovo di Taro, Italy 44 D7 44 42N 10 6 E
Føroyar, Atl. Oc. 14 F9 62 0N 7 0W
Forres, U.K. 22 D5 57 37N 3 37W
Forrest, Vic., Australia 128 E5 38 33 S 143 47 E
Forrest, W. Austral., Australia 125 F4 30 51 S 128 6 E
Forrest, Mt., Australia 125 D4 24 48 S 127 45 E
Forrest City, U.S.A. 155 H9 35 1N 90 47W
Forreston, U.S.A. 156 B7 42 8N 89 35W
Fors, Sweden 16 D10 60 14N 16 20 E
Forsand, Norway 18 F3 58 54N 6 5 E
Forsayth, Australia 126 B3 18 33 S 143 34 E
Forshaga, Sweden 16 E7 59 33N 13 29 E
Förslöv, Sweden 17 H6 56 21N 12 48 E
Forsmo, Sweden 16 A11 63 16N 17 11 E
Forssa, Finland 15 F20 60 49N 23 38 E
Forst, Germany 30 D10 51 45N 14 37 E
Forster, Australia 129 B10 32 12 S 152 31 E
Forsvik, Sweden 17 F8 58 35N 14 26 E
Forsyth, Ga., U.S.A. 152 B6 33 2N 83 56W
Forsyth, Mont., U.S.A. 158 C10 46 16N 106 41W
Forsyth I., N.Z. 131 A9 40 58 S 174 5 E
Fort Abbas, Pakistan 92 E5 29 12N 72 52 E
Fort Albany, Canada 140 B3 52 15N 81 35W
Fort-Aleksandrovsky = Fort Shevchenko, Kazakhstan 61 H10 44 35N 50 23 E
Fort Ann, U.S.A. 151 C11 43 25N 73 30W
Fort Archambault = Sarh, Chad 109 G3 9 5N 18 23 E
Fort Assiniboine, Canada 142 C6 54 20N 114 45W
Fort Atkinson, U.S.A. 157 B8 42 56N 88 50W
Fort Augustus, U.K. 22 D4 57 9N 4 42W
Fort Bayard = Zhanjiang, China 77 G8 21 15N 110 20 E
Fort Beaufort, S. Africa 116 E4 32 46 S 26 40 E
Fort Benton, U.S.A. 158 C8 47 49N 110 40W
Fort Bragg, U.S.A. 158 G2 39 26N 123 48W
Fort Bridger, U.S.A. 158 F8 41 19N 110 23W
Fort Caroline ⌓, U.S.A. 152 E8 30 23N 81 30W
Fort Chipewyan, Canada 143 B6 58 42N 111 8W
Fort Clatsop ⌓, U.S.A. 160 D3 46 8N 123 53W
Fort Collins, U.S.A. 154 E2 40 35N 105 5W
Fort-Coulonge, Canada 140 C4 45 50N 76 45W
Fort Covington, U.S.A. 151 B10 44 59N 74 29W
Fort Davis, Ala., U.S.A. 152 C4 32 15N 85 43W
Fort Davis, Tex., U.S.A. 155 K3 30 35N 103 54W
Fort-de-France, Martinique 164 c 14 36N 61 2W
Fort de Kock = Bukittinggi, Indonesia 84 C2 0 20 S 100 20 E
Fort de Polignac = Illizi, Algeria 111 C6 26 31N 8 32 E
Fort de Possel = Possel, C.A.R. 114 A3 5 5N 19 10 E
Fort Defiance, U.S.A. 159 J9 35 45N 109 5W
Fort Dodge, U.S.A. 156 B2 42 30N 94 11W
Fort Drum, U.S.A. 153 H9 27 32N 80 48W
Fort Edward, U.S.A. 151 C11 43 16N 73 35W
Fort Erie, Canada 150 D6 42 54N 78 56W
Fort Fairfield, U.S.A. 149 B12 46 46N 67 50W
Fort Flatters = Bordj Omar Driss, Algeria 111 C6 28 10N 6 40 E
Fort-Foureau = Kousseri, Cameroon 109 F2 12 0N 14 55 E
Fort Frances, Canada 143 D10 48 36N 93 24W
Fort Franklin = Déline, Canada 138 B7 65 11N 123 25W
Fort Frederica ⌓, U.S.A. 152 D8 31 13N 81 23W
Fort Gaines, U.S.A. 152 D4 31 36N 85 3W
Fort Garland, U.S.A. 159 H11 37 26N 105 26W
Fort George = Chisasibi, Canada 140 B4 53 50N 79 0W
Fort George = Prince George, Canada 142 C4 53 55N 122 50W
Fort Good Hope, Canada 138 B7 66 14N 128 40W
Fort Gouraud = Fdérik, Mauritania 110 D2 22 40N 12 45W
Fort Hancock, U.S.A. 159 L11 31 18N 105 51W
Fort Hertz = Putao, Burma 90 B6 27 28N 97 30 E
Fort Hill = Chitipa, Malawi 119 D3 9 41 S 33 19 E
Fort Hope, Canada 140 B2 51 30N 88 0W
Fort Irwin, U.S.A. 161 K10 35 16N 116 34W
Fort Jameson = Chipata, Zambia 119 E3 13 38 S 32 28 E
Fort Johnston = Mangoche, Malawi 119 E4 14 25 S 35 16 E
Fort Kent, U.S.A. 149 B11 47 15N 68 36W
Fort Klamath, U.S.A. 158 E3 42 42N 122 0W
Fort Lamy = Ndjamena, Chad 109 F2 12 10N 14 59 E
Fort-Laperrine = Tamanrasset, Algeria 111 D6 22 50N 5 30 E
Fort Laramie, U.S.A. 154 D2 42 13N 104 31W
Fort Lauderdale, U.S.A. 153 J9 26 7N 80 8W
Fort Liard, Canada 142 A4 60 14N 123 30W
Fort Liberté, Haiti 165 C5 19 42N 71 51W
Fort Lupton, U.S.A. 154 E2 40 5N 104 49W
Fort MacKay, Canada 142 B6 57 12N 111 41W
Fort Macleod, Canada 142 D6 49 45N 113 30W
Fort MacMahon = El Homeur, Algeria 111 C5 29 43N 1 45 E
Fort McMurray, Canada 142 B6 56 44N 111 7W
Fort McPherson, Canada 138 B6 67 30N 134 55W
Fort Madison, U.S.A. 156 D5 40 38N 91 27W
Fort Manning = Mchinji, Malawi 119 E3 13 47 S 32 58 E
Fort Matanzas ⌓, U.S.A. 152 F8 29 43N 81 14W
Fort Meade, U.S.A. 153 H8 27 45N 81 48W
Fort Mitchell, U.S.A. 152 C4 32 20N 85 1W
Fort Morgan, U.S.A. 154 E3 40 15N 103 48W
Fort Myers, U.S.A. 153 J8 26 39N 81 52W
Fort Myers Beach, U.S.A. 153 J8 26 26N 81 52W
Fort Myers Villas, U.S.A. 153 J8 26 33N 81 52W
Fort Nelson, Canada 142 B4 58 50N 122 44W
Fort Nelson →, Canada 142 B4 59 32N 124 0W
Fort Norman = Tulita, Canada 138 B7 64 57N 125 30W
Fort Ogden, U.S.A. 153 H8 27 5N 81 57W
Fort Payne, U.S.A. 149 H3 34 26N 85 43W
Fort Peck, U.S.A. 158 B10 48 1N 106 27W
Fort Peck Dam, U.S.A. 158 C10 48 0N 106 26W
Fort Peck L., U.S.A. 158 C10 48 0N 106 26W
Fort Pierce, U.S.A. 153 H9 27 27N 80 20W
Fort Pierre, U.S.A. 154 C4 44 21N 100 22W
Fort Pierre Bordes = Ti-n-Zaouatene, Algeria 111 E5 19 55N 2 55 E
Fort Plain, U.S.A. 151 D10 42 56N 74 37W
Fort Portal, Uganda 118 B3 0 40N 30 20 E
Fort Providence, Canada 142 A5 61 3N 117 40W
Fort Pulaski ⌓, U.S.A. 152 C9 32 2N 80 56W
Fort Qu'Appelle, Canada 143 C8 50 45N 103 50W
Fort Recovery, U.S.A. 157 D12 40 25N 84 47W
Fort Resolution, Canada 142 A6 61 10N 113 40W
Fort Rixon, Zimbabwe 119 G2 20 2 S 29 17 E
Fort Rosebery = Mansa, Zambia 119 E2 11 13 S 28 55 E
Fort Ross, U.S.A. 160 G3 38 32N 123 13W
Fort-Rousset = Owando, Congo 114 C3 0 29 S 15 55 E
Fort Rupert = Waskaganish, Canada 140 B4 51 30N 78 40W
Fort St. James, Canada 142 C4 54 30N 124 10W
Fort St. John, Canada 142 B4 56 15N 120 50W
Fort Sandeman = Zhob, Pakistan 91 C3 31 20N 69 31 E
Fort Saskatchewan, Canada 142 C6 53 40N 113 15W
Fort Scott, U.S.A. 155 G7 37 50N 94 42W
Fort Severn, Canada 140 A2 56 0N 87 40W
Fort Shevchenko, Kazakhstan 61 H10 44 35N 50 23 E
Fort Simpson, Canada 142 A4 61 45N 121 15W
Fort Smith, Canada 142 B6 60 0N 111 51W
Fort Smith, U.S.A. 155 H7 35 23N 94 25W
Fort Stockton, U.S.A. 155 K3 30 53N 102 53W
Fort Sumner, U.S.A. 155 H2 34 28N 104 15W
Fort Thomas, U.S.A. 157 E12 39 5N 84 27W
Fort Thompson, U.S.A. 154 C5 44 3N 99 26W
Fort Trinquet = Bîr Mogreïn, Mauritania 110 C2 25 10N 11 25W
Fort Union ⌓, U.S.A. 155 H2 35 54N 105 1W
Fort Uritskogo = Fort Shevchenko, Kazakhstan 61 H10 44 35N 50 23 E
Fort Valley, U.S.A. 152 C6 32 33N 83 53W
Fort Vermilion, Canada 142 B5 58 24N 116 0W
Fort Walton Beach, U.S.A. 153 E3 30 25N 86 36W
Fort Wayne, U.S.A. 157 C11 41 4N 85 9W
Fort White, U.S.A. 152 F7 29 55N 82 43W
Fort William, U.K. 22 E3 56 49N 5 7W
Fort Worth, U.S.A. 155 J6 32 45N 97 18W
Fort Yates, U.S.A. 154 B4 46 5N 100 38W
Fort Yukon, U.S.A. 144 C11 66 34N 145 16W
Fortaleza = Pedra Azul, Brazil 171 E3 16 2 S 41 17W
Fortaleza, Bolivia 172 C4 12 6 S 66 49W
Fortaleza, Brazil 170 B4 3 45 S 38 35W
Forteau, Canada 141 B8 51 28N 56 58W
Fortescue →, Australia 124 D2 21 0 S 116 4 E
Forth →, U.K. 22 E5 56 9N 3 50W
Forth, Firth of, U.K. 22 E6 56 5N 2 55W
Forthassa Rharbia, Algeria 111 B4 32 52N 1 18W
Fortín Garrapatal, Paraguay 173 E5 21 27 S 61 30W
Fortín General Pando, Paraguay 173 D6 19 45 S 59 47W
Fortín Ingavi, Paraguay 173 D5 19 55 S 60 47W
Fortín Madrejón, Paraguay 173 E6 20 45 S 59 52W
Fortín Uno, Argentina 176 A3 38 50 S 65 18W
Fortore →, Italy 45 G12 41 55N 15 17 E
Fortrose, N.Z. 131 G3 46 38 S 168 45 E
Fortrose, U.K. 22 D4 57 35N 4 9W
Fortuna, Spain 41 G3 38 11N 1 7W
Fortuna, Calif., U.S.A. 158 F1 40 36N 124 9W
Fortuna, N. Dak., U.S.A. 154 A3 48 55N 103 47W
Fortuna Ledge, U.S.A. 144 F7 61 53N 162 5W
Fortune, Canada 141 C8 47 4N 55 50W
Fortune B., Canada 141 C8 47 30N 55 22W
Forūr, Iran 97 E7 26 17N 54 32 E
Fos-sur-Mer, France 29 E8 43 26N 4 56 E
Foshan, China 77 F9 23 4N 113 5 E
Fosna, Norway 14 E14 63 50N 10 20 E
Fosnavåg, Norway 18 B2 62 22N 5 38 E
Foso, Ghana 113 D4 5 43N 1 15W
Foss, Iceland 11 D9 63 51N 17 52W
Fossano, Italy 44 D4 44 33N 7 43 E
Fossil, U.S.A. 158 D3 45 0N 120 9W
Fossil Butte ⌓, U.S.A. 158 F8 41 50N 110 27W
Fossombrone, Italy 45 E9 43 41N 12 48 E
Fossvellir, Iceland 11 B12 65 27N 14 37W
Foster, Australia 129 E7 38 40 S 146 15 E
Foster, Canada 151 A12 45 17N 72 30W
Foster, U.S.A. 157 F12 38 48N 84 13W
Foster →, Canada 143 B7 55 47N 105 49W
Fosters Ra., Australia 126 C1 21 35 S 133 48 E
Fostoria, U.S.A. 157 C13 41 10N 83 25W
Fotadrevo, Madag. 117 C8 24 3 S 45 1 E
Fouesnant, France 26 E2 47 53N 4 1W
Fougamou, Gabon 114 C2 1 16 S 10 30 E
Fougères, France 26 D5 48 21N 1 14W
Foul Pt., Sri Lanka 95 K5 8 35N 81 18 E
Foula, U.K. 22 A6 60 10N 2 5W
Foulalaba, Mali 112 C3 10 40N 7 20W
Foulness I., U.K. 21 F8 51 36N 0 55 E
Foulpointe, Madag. 117 B8 17 41 S 49 31 E
Foulweather, C., U.S.A. 146 B2 44 50N 124 5W
Foulwind, C., N.Z. 131 B6 41 45 S 171 28 E
Foum Assaka, Morocco 110 C2 29 8N 10 24W
Foum Zguid, Morocco 110 B3 30 2N 6 59W
Foumban, Cameroon 113 D7 5 45N 10 50 E
Foumbot, Cameroon 113 D7 5 31N 10 28 E
Foumbouni, Comoros Is. 121 a 11 52 S 43 32 E
Foumirate, Algeria 110 C4 27 30N 3 12W
Foundiougne, Senegal 112 C1 14 5N 16 32W
Fountain, Colo., U.S.A. 154 F2 38 41N 104 42W
Fountain, Fla., U.S.A. 152 E4 30 29N 85 25W
Fountain Hill, U.S.A. 159 K8 33 37N 111 43W
Fountain Springs, U.S.A. 161 K8 35 54N 118 51W
Four Mountains, Is. of, U.S.A. 144 K5 53 0N 170 0W
Fourchambault, France 27 E10 47 2N 3 3 E
Fouriesburg, S. Africa 116 D4 28 38 S 28 14 E
Fourmies, France 27 B11 50 1N 4 2 E
Fournás, Greece 48 B3 39 3N 21 52 E
Fourni = Foúrnoi, Greece 49 D8 37 36N 26 32 E
Foúrnoi, Greece 49 D8 37 36N 26 32 E
Fours, France 27 F10 46 50N 3 42 E
Fourth Cataract, Sudan 106 D3 18 47N 32 3 E
Fousinshin = Fuxin, China 75 C11 42 5N 121 48 E
Fouta Djallon, Guinea 112 C2 11 20N 12 10W
Foux, Cap-à-, Haiti 165 C5 19 43N 73 27W
Foveaux Str., N.Z. 131 G3 46 42 S 168 10 E
Fowey, U.K. 21 G3 50 20N 4 39W
Fowler, Calif., U.S.A. 160 J7 36 38N 119 41W
Fowler, Colo., U.S.A. 154 F3 38 8N 104 2W
Fowler, Ind., U.S.A. 157 D9 40 37N 87 19W
Fowler, Mich., U.S.A. 157 B12 43 0N 84 45W
Fowlers B., Australia 125 F5 31 59 S 132 34 E
Fowlerville, U.S.A. 157 B12 42 40N 84 4W
Fowman, Iran 97 B6 37 13N 49 19 E
Fox →, Canada 143 B10 56 3N 93 18W
Fox Creek, Canada 142 C5 54 24N 116 48W
Fox Is., U.S.A. 144 K6 53 0N 168 0W
Fox Lake, Canada 142 B6 58 28N 114 31W
Fox Lake, U.S.A. 157 B8 42 24N 88 11W
Fox Valley, Canada 143 C7 50 30N 109 25W
Foxboro, U.S.A. 151 D13 42 4N 71 16W
Foxdale, Australia 126 J6 20 22 S 148 35 E
Foxe Basin, Canada 139 B12 66 0N 77 0W
Foxe Chan., Canada 139 B11 65 0N 80 0W
Foxe Pen., Canada 139 B12 65 0N 76 0W
Foxen, Sweden 16 E5 59 25N 11 55 E
Foxton, N.Z. 130 G4 40 29 S 175 18 E
Foyle, Lough, U.K. 23 A4 55 7N 7 4W
Foynes, Ireland 23 D2 52 37N 9 7W
Foz, Spain 42 B3 43 33N 7 20W
Foz do Copeá, Brazil 169 D5 3 52 S 63 19W
Foz do Cunene, Angola 116 B1 17 15 S 11 48 E
Foz do Gregório, Brazil 172 B3 6 47 S 70 44W
Foz do Iguaçu, Brazil 175 B5 25 30 S 54 30W
Foz do Mamoriá, Brazil 168 D4 2 27 S 66 32W
Foz do Riosinho, Brazil 172 B3 7 11 S 71 50W
Frackville, U.S.A. 151 F8 40 47N 76 14W
Fraga, Spain 40 D5 41 32N 0 21 E
Fraile Muerto, Uruguay 175 C5 32 31 S 54 32W
Fram Basin, Arctic 6 A 87 30N 80 0 E
Framingham, U.S.A. 151 D13 42 17N 71 25W
Framnes, Iceland 11 A6 66 1N 20 26W
Frampol, Poland 55 H9 50 41N 22 40 E
Franca, Brazil 171 F2 20 33 S 47 30W
Francavilla al Mare, Italy 45 F11 42 25N 14 17 E
Francavilla Fontana, Italy 47 B10 40 32N 17 35 E
France ■, Europe 25 C5 47 0N 3 0 E
Frances, Australia 128 D4 36 41 S 140 55 E
Frances →, Canada 142 A3 60 16N 129 10W
Frances L., Canada 142 A3 61 23N 129 30W
Francesville, U.S.A. 157 D10 40 59N 86 53W
Franceville, Gabon 114 C2 1 40 S 13 32 E
Franche-Comté □, France 27 F12 46 50N 5 55 E
Franches Montagnes, Switz. 32 B4 47 10N 7 0 E
Francis Case, L., U.S.A. 154 D5 43 4N 98 34W
Francisco Beltrão, Brazil 175 B5 26 5 S 53 4W
Francisco de Orellana, Ecuador 168 D2 0 28 S 76 58W
Francisco I. Madero, Coahuila, Mexico 162 B4 25 48N 103 18W
Francisco I. Madero, Durango, Mexico 162 C4 24 32N 104 22W
Francisco Sá, Brazil 171 E3 16 28 S 43 30W
Francistown, Botswana 117 C4 21 7 S 27 33 E
Francofonte, Italy 47 E7 37 14N 14 53 E
François, Canada 141 C8 47 35N 56 45W
François-Joseph, Chutes, Dem. Rep. of the Congo 115 D3 7 37 S 17 17 E
François L., Canada 142 C3 54 0N 125 30W
Francois Peron △, Australia 125 E1 25 42 S 113 33 E
Franeker, Neths. 24 A5 53 12N 5 33 E
Frank Hann △, Australia 125 F3 32 52 S 120 19 E
Frankado, Djibouti 107 E5 12 30N 43 12 E
Frankenberg, Germany 30 D4 51 3N 8 48 E
Frankenhöhe ⌓, Germany 31 F6 49 20N 10 25 E
Frankenstein = Ząbkowice Śląskie, Poland 55 H3 50 35N 16 50 E
Frankenwald, Germany 31 E7 50 20N 11 30 E
Frankenwald ⌓, Germany 31 E7 50 15N 11 30 E
Frankford, Canada 150 B7 44 12N 77 36W
Frankford, U.S.A. 156 E5 39 29N 91 19W
Frankfort, S. Africa 117 D4 27 17 S 28 30 E
Frankfort, Ind., U.S.A. 157 D10 40 17N 86 31W
Frankfort, Kans., U.S.A. 154 F6 39 42N 96 25W
Frankfort, Ky., U.S.A. 157 F12 38 12N 84 52W
Frankfort, N.Y., U.S.A. 151 C9 43 2N 75 4W
Frankfort, Ohio, U.S.A. 157 E13 39 24N 83 11W
Frankfurt, Brandenburg, Germany 30 C10 52 20N 14 32 E
Frankfurt, Hessen, Germany 31 E4 50 7N 8 41 E
Frankfurt ✕ (FRA), Germany 31 E4 50 1N 8 34 E
Fränkische Alb, Germany 31 F7 49 10N 11 23 E
Fränkische Rezat →, Germany 31 F7 49 11N 11 1 E
Fränkische Saale →, Germany 31 E5 50 3N 9 42 E
Fränkische Schweiz, Germany 31 F7 49 50N 11 16 E
Fränkische Schweiz-Veldensteiner Forst ⌓, Germany 31 F7 49 45N 11 22 E
Frankland →, Australia 125 G2 35 0 S 116 48 E
Franklin, Ga., U.S.A. 152 B4 33 17N 85 6W
Franklin, Ind., U.S.A. 157 E10 39 29N 86 3W
Franklin, Ky., U.S.A. 149 G2 36 43N 86 35W
Franklin, La., U.S.A. 155 L9 29 48N 91 30W
Franklin, Mass., U.S.A. 151 D13 42 5N 71 24W
Franklin, N.H., U.S.A. 151 C13 43 27N 71 39W
Franklin, Nebr., U.S.A. 154 E5 40 6N 98 57W
Franklin, Ohio, U.S.A. 157 E12 39 34N 84 18W
Franklin, Pa., U.S.A. 150 E5 41 24N 79 50W
Franklin, Va., U.S.A. 149 G7 36 41N 76 56W
Franklin, W. Va., U.S.A. 148 F6 38 39N 79 20W
Franklin, Pt., U.S.A. 144 A8 70 55N 158 48W
Franklin B., Canada 138 B7 69 45N 126 0W
Franklin D. Roosevelt L., U.S.A. 158 B4 48 18N 118 9W
Franklin-Gordon Wild Rivers △, Australia 127 G4 42 19 S 145 51 E
Franklin Harb., Australia 128 B2 33 43 S 136 55 E
Franklin I., Antarctica 7 D11 76 10 S 168 30 E
Franklin L., U.S.A. 158 F6 40 25N 115 22W
Franklin Mts., Canada 138 B7 65 0N 125 0W
Franklin Mts., N.Z. 131 E2 44 55 S 167 45 E
Franklin Str., Canada 138 A10 72 0N 96 0W
Franklinton, U.S.A. 155 K9 30 51N 90 9W
Franklinville, U.S.A. 150 D6 42 20N 78 27W
Franklyn Mt., N.Z. 131 C7 42 4 S 172 42 E
Franks Pk., U.S.A. 158 E9 43 58N 109 18W
Frankston, Australia 129 E6 38 8 S 145 8 E
Frånö, Sweden 16 B11 62 55N 17 50 E

Fransfontein, Namibia 116 C2 20 12 S 15 1 E
Fränsta, Sweden 16 B10 62 30N 16 11 E
Frantsa Iosifa, Zemlya, Russia 66 A6 82 0N 55 0 E
Franz, Canada 140 C3 48 25N 84 30W
Franz Josef Land = Frantsa Iosifa, Zemlya, Russia 66 A6 82 0N 55 0 E
Franz Josef Strauss, München ✕ (MUC), Germany 31 G7 48 20N 11 50 E
Franzburg, Germany 30 A8 54 11N 12 51 E
Frascati, Italy 45 G9 41 48N 12 41 E
Fraser, U.S.A. 150 D2 42 32N 82 57W
Fraser △, Australia 129 D6 37 9 S 145 51 E
Fraser →, B.C., Canada 142 D4 49 7N 123 11W
Fraser →, Nfld. & L., Canada 141 A7 56 39N 62 10W
Fraser, Mt., Australia 125 E2 25 35 S 118 20 E
Fraser I., Australia 127 D5 25 15 S 153 10 E
Fraser Lake, Canada 142 C4 54 0N 124 50W
Fraserburg, S. Africa 116 E3 31 55 S 21 30 E
Fraserburg Road = Leeu Gamka, S. Africa 116 E3 32 47 S 21 59 E
Fraserburgh, U.K. 22 D6 57 42N 2 1W
Fraserdale, Canada 140 C3 49 55N 81 37W
Fraserpet = Kushalnagar, India 95 H2 12 14N 75 57 E
Frasertown, N.Z. 130 E6 38 58 S 177 28 E
Fraserville = Rivière-du-Loup, Canada 141 C6 47 50N 69 30W
Frashër, Albania 50 F4 40 23N 20 30 E
Frasne, France 27 F13 46 50N 6 10 E
Frătești, Romania 53 G10 43 58N 25 58 E
Frauenfeld, Switz. 33 A7 47 34N 8 54 E
Frauenstadt = Wadowice, Poland 55 J6 49 52N 19 30 E
Fraustadt = Wschowa, Poland 55 G3 51 48N 16 20 E
Fray Bentos, Uruguay 174 C4 33 10 S 58 15W
Fray Jorge △, Chile 174 C1 30 42 S 71 40W
Frechilla, Spain 42 C6 42 8N 4 50W
Fredericia, Denmark 17 J3 55 34N 9 45 E
Frederick, Md., U.S.A. 148 F7 39 25N 77 25W
Frederick, Okla., U.S.A. 155 H5 34 23N 99 1W
Frederick, S. Dak., U.S.A. 154 C5 45 50N 98 31W
Frederick E. Hyde Fjord, Greenland 10 A8 83 25N 29 0W
Fredericksburg, Pa., U.S.A. 151 F8 40 27N 76 26W
Fredericksburg, Tex., U.S.A. 155 K5 30 16N 98 52W
Fredericksburg, Va., U.S.A. 148 F7 38 18N 77 28W
Fredericktown, Mo., U.S.A. 155 G9 37 34N 90 18W
Fredericktown, Ohio, U.S.A. 150 F2 40 29N 82 33W
Frederico I. Madero, Presa, Mexico 162 B3 28 7N 105 40W
Frederico Westphalen, Brazil 175 B5 27 22 S 53 24W
Fredericton, Canada 141 C6 45 57N 66 40W
Fredericton Junction, Canada 141 C6 45 41N 66 40W
Frederiksborg Amtskommune □, Denmark 17 J6 55 50N 12 10 E
Frederikshåb = Paamiut, Greenland 10 E6 62 0N 49 43W
Frederikshald = Halden, Norway 18 E8 59 9N 11 23 E
Frederikshamn = Hamina, Finland 15 F22 60 34N 27 12 E
Frederikshavn, Denmark 17 G4 57 28N 10 31 E
Frederikssund, Denmark 17 J6 55 50N 12 3 E
Frederiksted, U.S. Virgin Is. 165 C7 17 43N 64 53W
Frederiksværk, Denmark 17 J6 55 58N 12 4 E
Fredonia, Ariz., U.S.A. 159 H7 36 57N 112 32W
Fredonia, Kans., U.S.A. 155 G7 37 32N 95 49W
Fredonia, N.Y., U.S.A. 150 D5 42 26N 79 20W
Fredriksberg, Sweden 16 D8 60 8N 14 23 E
Fredrikstad, Norway 18 E7 59 13N 10 57 E
Fredriksvern = Stavern, Norway 18 F7 59 0N 10 1 E
Free State □, S. Africa 116 D4 28 30 S 27 0 E
Freeburg, U.S.A. 156 F5 38 19N 91 56W
Freehold, U.S.A. 151 F10 40 16N 74 17W
Freel Peak, U.S.A. 160 G7 38 52N 119 54W
Freeland, U.S.A. 151 E9 41 1N 75 54W
Freels, C., Canada 141 C9 49 15N 53 30W
Freeman, Calif., U.S.A. 161 K9 35 35N 117 53W
Freeman, Mo., U.S.A. 156 F2 38 37N 94 30W
Freeman, S. Dak., U.S.A. 154 D6 43 21N 97 26W
Freeport, Bahamas 164 A4 26 30N 78 47W
Freeport, Fla., U.S.A. 152 E3 30 30N 86 8W
Freeport, Ill., U.S.A. 156 B7 42 17N 89 36W
Freeport, N.Y., U.S.A. 151 F11 40 39N 73 35W
Freeport, Ohio, U.S.A. 150 F3 40 12N 81 15W
Freeport, Pa., U.S.A. 150 F5 40 41N 79 41W
Freeport, Tex., U.S.A. 155 L7 28 57N 95 21W
Freetown, S. Leone 112 D2 8 30N 13 17W
Frégate, L. de la, Canada 140 B5 53 15N 74 45W
Fregenal de la Sierra, Spain 43 G4 38 10N 6 39W
Fregene, Italy 45 G9 41 51N 12 12 E
Fréhel, C., France 26 D4 48 40N 2 20W
Freiberg, Germany 30 E9 50 55N 13 20 E
Freibourg = Fribourg, Switz. 32 C4 46 49N 7 9 E
Freiburg, Baden-W., Germany 31 H3 47 59N 7 51 E
Freiburg, Niedersachsen, Germany 30 B5 53 49N 9 16 E
Freiburg in Schlesien = Świebodzice, Poland 55 H3 50 51N 16 20 E
Freiburger Alpen, Switz. 32 C4 46 37N 7 10 E
Freienwalde = Chociwel, Poland 54 E2 53 29N 15 21 E
Freilassing, Germany 31 H8 47 50N 12 58 E
Freire, Chile 176 A2 38 54 S 72 38W
Freirina, Chile 174 B1 28 30 S 71 10W
Freising, Germany 31 G7 48 24N 11 45 E
Freistadt, Austria 34 C7 48 30N 14 30 E
Freital, Germany 30 D9 51 1N 13 39 E
Freiwaldau = Jeseník, Czech Rep. 35 A10 50 14N 17 8 E
Fréjus, France 29 E10 43 25N 6 44 E
Fremantle, Australia 125 F2 32 7 S 115 47 E
Fremont, Calif., U.S.A. 160 H4 37 32N 121 57W
Fremont, Ind., U.S.A. 157 C12 41 44N 84 56W
Fremont, Iowa, U.S.A. 156 C4 41 13N 92 26W
Fremont, Mich., U.S.A. 148 D3 43 28N 85 57W
Fremont, Nebr., U.S.A. 154 E6 41 26N 96 30W
Fremont, Ohio, U.S.A. 157 C13 41 21N 83 7W
Fremont →, U.S.A. 159 G8 38 24N 110 42W
French Camp, U.S.A. 160 H5 37 53N 121 16W
French Cays = Plana Cays, Bahamas 165 B5 22 38N 73 30W
French Creek →, U.S.A. 150 E5 41 24N 79 50W
French Frigate Shoals, U.S.A. 145 G10 23 45N 166 10W
French Guiana ☒, S. Amer. 169 C7 4 0N 53 0W
French Guinea = Guinea ■, W. Afr. 112 C2 10 20N 11 30W
French I., Australia 129 E6 38 20 S 145 22 E
French Lick, U.S.A. 157 F10 38 33N 86 37W
French Pass, N.Z. 131 A8 40 55 S 173 55 E
French Polynesia ☒, Pac. Oc. 135 K13 20 0 S 145 0W
French Sudan = Mali ■, Africa 112 B4 17 0N 3 0W
French Territory of the Afars and Issas = Djibouti ■, Africa 107 E5 12 0N 43 0 E
French Togoland = Togo ■, W. Afr. 113 D5 8 30N 1 35 E
Frenchburg, U.S.A. 157 G13 37 57N 83 38W
Frenchman Cr. →, N. Amer. 158 B10 48 31N 107 10W
Frenchman Cr. →, U.S.A. 154 E4 40 14N 100 50W
Frenda, Algeria 111 A5 35 2N 1 1 E
Frenštát pod Radhoštěm, Czech Rep. 35 B11 49 33N 18 13 E
Fresco, Ivory C. 112 D3 5 3N 5 31W
Fresco →, Brazil 173 B7 7 15 S 51 30W
Freshfield, C., Antarctica 7 C10 68 25 S 151 10 E
Fresnay-sur-Sarthe, France 26 D7 48 17N 0 1 E
Fresnillo, Mexico 162 C4 23 10N 103 0W
Fresno, U.S.A. 160 J7 36 44N 119 47W
Fresno Alhandiga, Spain 42 E5 40 42N 5 37W
Fresno Reservoir, U.S.A. 158 B9 48 36N 109 57W
Fresvik, Norway 18 C3 61 4N 6 55 E
Freudenstadt, Germany 31 G4 48 27N 8 24 E
Freudenthal = Bruntál, Czech Rep. 35 B10 49 59N 17 27 E
Frévent, France 27 B9 50 15N 2 17 E
Frew →, Australia 126 C2 20 0 S 135 38 E
Frewsburg, U.S.A. 150 D5 42 3N 79 10W
Freycinet △, Australia 127 G4 42 11 S 148 19 E
Freycinet Pen., Australia 127 G4 42 10 S 148 25 E
Freyming-Merlebach, France 27 C13 49 8N 6 48 E
Freystadt = Kisielice, Poland 54 E6 53 36N 19 16 E
Freystadt = Kożuchów, Poland 55 G2 51 45N 15 31 E
Freyung, Germany 31 G9 48 48N 13 31 E
Fria, Guinea 112 C2 10 27N 13 38W
Fria, C., Namibia 116 B1 18 0 S 12 0 E
Friant, U.S.A. 160 J7 36 59N 119 43W
Frías, Argentina 174 B2 28 40 S 65 5W
Fribourg, Switz. 32 C4 46 49N 7 9 E
Fribourg □, Switz. 32 C4 46 40N 7 0 E
Frick, Switz. 32 A6 47 31N 8 1 E
Fridafors, Sweden 17 H8 56 25N 14 39 E
Friday Harbor, U.S.A. 160 B3 48 32N 123 1W
Friedberg, Bayern, Germany 31 G6 48 21N 10 59 E
Friedberg, Hessen, Germany 31 E4 50 19N 8 45 E
Friedeberg = Mirsk, Poland 55 H2 50 58N 15 23 E
Friedeberg in Neumark = Strzelce Krajeńskie, Poland 55 F2 52 52N 15 33 E
Friedens, U.S.A. 150 F6 40 3N 78 59W
Friedland = Mieroszów, Poland 55 H3 50 40N 16 11 E
Friedland = Pravdinsk, Russia 60 B6 56 29N 43 28 E
Friedland, Germany 30 B9 53 40N 13 33 E
Friedrichshafen, Germany 31 H5 47 39N 9 30 E
Friedrichskoog, Germany 30 A4 54 1N 8 53 E
Friedrichstadt, Germany 30 A5 54 23N 9 6 E
Friendly Is. = Tonga ■, Pac. Oc. 133 P13 19 50 S 174 30W
Friendship, U.S.A. 150 D6 42 12N 78 8W
Friesach, Austria 34 E7 46 57N 14 24 E
Friesack, Germany 30 C8 52 44N 12 34 E
Friesland □, Neths. 24 A5 53 5N 5 50 E
Friesoythe, Germany 30 B3 53 1N 7 51 E
Frigate, Seychelles 121 b 4 35 S 55 56 E
Friggesund, Sweden 16 C10 61 54N 16 33 E
Frillesås, Sweden 17 G6 57 20N 12 12 E
Frinnaryd, Sweden 17 G8 57 55N 14 50 E
Frio →, U.S.A. 155 L5 28 26N 98 11W
Frio, C., Brazil 166 F6 22 50 S 41 50W
Friol, Spain 42 B3 43 2N 7 47W
Friona, U.S.A. 155 H3 34 38N 102 43W
Frisches Haff = Zalew Wiślany, Poland 54 D6 54 20N 19 50 E
Fristad, Sweden 17 G6 57 50N 13 0 E
Fritch, U.S.A. 155 H4 35 38N 101 36W
Fritsla, Sweden 17 G6 57 33N 12 47 E
Fritzlar, Germany 30 D5 51 7N 9 16 E
Friuli-Venézia Giulia □, Italy 45 B9 46 0N 13 0 E
Frobisher B., Canada 139 B13 62 30N 66 0W
Frobisher Bay = Iqaluit, Canada 139 B13 63 44N 68 31W
Frobisher L., Canada 143 B7 56 20N 108 15W
Frohavet, Norway 14 E13 64 0N 9 30 E
Frohenbruck = Veselí nad Lužnicí, Czech Rep. 34 B7 49 12N 14 43 E
Frohnleiten, Austria 34 D8 47 16N 15 19 E
Frolovo, Russia 60 F6 49 45N 43 40 E
Frombork, Poland 54 D6 54 21N 19 41 E
Frome, U.K. 21 F5 51 14N 2 19W
Frome →, U.K. 21 G5 50 41N 2 6W
Frome, L., Australia 128 A3 30 45 S 139 45 E
Frome, The →, Australia 127 D2 29 8 S 137 54 E
Frome Downs, Australia 128 A3 31 13 S 139 45 E
Frómista, Spain 42 C6 42 16N 4 25W
Front Range, U.S.A. 146 C5 40 25N 105 45W
Front Royal, U.S.A. 148 F6 38 55N 78 12W
Fronteira, Portugal 43 F3 39 3N 7 39W
Fronteiras, Brazil 170 C3 7 5 S 40 37W
Frontera, Canary Is. 9 e1 27 47N 17 59W
Frontera, Mexico 163 D6 18 30N 92 40W
Fronteras, Mexico 162 A3 30 56N 109 31W
Frontignan, France 28 E7 43 27N 3 45 E
Frosinone, Italy 46 A6 41 38N 13 19 E
Frostburg, U.S.A. 148 F6 39 39N 78 56W
Frostisen, Norway 14 B17 68 14N 17 10 E
Frostproof, U.S.A. 153 H8 27 45N 81 32W
Frouard, France 27 D13 48 47N 6 8 E
Frövi, Sweden 16 E9 59 28N 15 24 E
Frøya, Norway 14 E13 63 43N 8 40 E
Fruithurst, U.S.A. 152 B4 33 44N 85 26W
Fruitland Park, U.S.A. 153 G8 28 51N 81 54W
Frumoasa, Romania 53 D10 46 28N 25 48 E
Frunze = Bishkek, Kyrgyzstan 65 B7 42 54N 74 46 E
Frunze, Kyrgyzstan 65 C5 40 7N 71 44 E
Frunzivka, Ukraine 53 C14 47 20N 29 45 E
Fruška Gora, Serbia & M. 52 E4 45 7N 19 30 E
Fruška Gora △, Serbia & M. 50 A3 45 8N 19 40 E
Frutal, Brazil 171 F2 20 0 S 49 0W
Frutigen, Switz. 32 C5 46 35N 7 38 E
Frýdek-Místek, Czech Rep. 35 B11 49 40N 18 20 E
Frýdlant, Czech Rep. 34 A8 50 56N 15 9 E
Fryeburg, U.S.A. 151 B14 44 1N 70 59W
Fryvaldov = Jeseník, Czech Rep. 35 A10 50 14N 17 8 E
Fthiótis □, Greece 48 C4 38 50N 22 25 E
Fu Jiang →, China 76 C6 30 0N 106 16 E
Fu Xian = Wafangdian, China 75 E11 39 38N 121 58 E
Fu Xian, China 74 G5 36 0N 109 20 E
Fu'an, China 77 D12 27 11N 119 36 E
Fubian, China 76 B4 31 17N 102 22 E
Fucécchio, Italy 44 E7 43 44N 10 48 E
Fucheng, China 74 F9 37 50N 116 10 E
Fuchou = Fuzhou, China 77 D12 26 5N 119 16 E
Fuchū, Hiroshima, Japan 72 C5 34 34N 133 14 E
Fūchū, Tōkyō, Japan 73 B11 35 40N 139 29 E
Fuchuan, China 77 E8 24 50N 111 5 E
Fuchun Jiang →, China 77 B13 30 5N 120 5 E
Fúcino, Piana del, Italy 45 F10 42 1N 13 31 E
Fuding, China 77 D13 27 20N 120 12 E
Fuencaliente, Canary Is. 9 e1 28 28N 17 50W
Fuencaliente, Spain 43 G6 38 25N 4 18W
Fuencaliente, Pta., Canary Is. 9 e1 28 27N 17 51W
Fuengirola, Spain 43 J6 36 32N 4 41W
Fuenlabrada, Spain 42 E7 40 17N 3 48W
Fuensalida, Spain 42 E6 40 3N 4 12W
Fuente-Álamo, Spain 43 G3 38 44N 1 24W
Fuente-Álamo de Murcia, Spain 41 H3 37 42N 1 6W
Fuente de Cantos, Spain 43 G4 38 15N 6 18W
Fuente del Maestre, Spain 43 G4 38 31N 6 28W
Fuente el Fresno, Spain 43 F7 39 14N 3 46W
Fuente Obejuna, Spain 43 G5 38 15N 5 25W
Fuente Palmera, Spain 43 H5 37 42N 5 6W
Fuentes de Andalucía, Spain 43 H5 37 28N 5 20W
Fuentes de Ebro, Spain 40 D4 41 31N 0 38W
Fuentes de León, Spain 43 G4 38 5N 6 32W
Fuentes de Oñoro, Spain 42 E4 40 33N 6 52W
Fuentesaúco, Spain 42 D5 41 15N 5 30W
Fuerte →, Mexico 162 B3 25 50N 109 25W
Fuerte Olimpo, Paraguay 174 A4 21 0 S 57 51W
Fuerteventura, Canary Is. 9 e2 28 30N 14 0W
Fuerteventura ✕ (FUE), Canary Is. 9 e2 28 24N 13 52W
Fufeng, China 74 G5 34 22N 108 0 E
Fuga I., Phil. 80 B3 18 52N 121 20 E
Fughmah, Yemen 99 C5 16 9N 49 26 E
Fugong, China 76 D2 27 5N 98 47 E
Fugou, China 74 G8 34 3N 114 25 E
Fugu, China 74 E6 39 2N 111 3 E
Fuhai, China 68 B3 47 2N 87 25 E
Fuḩaymī, Iraq 101 E10 34 16N 42 10 E
Fuhlsbüttel, Hamburg ✕ (HAM), Germany 30 B5 53 35N 9 59 E
Fuhsien = Fu Xian, China 74 G5 36 0N 109 20 E
Fuji, Japan 73 B10 35 9N 138 39 E
Fuji-Hakone-Izu △, Japan 73 B10 35 15N 138 45 E
Fuji-San, Japan 73 B10 35 22N 138 44 E
Fuji-Yoshida, Japan 73 B10 35 30N 138 46 E
Fujian □, China 77 E12 26 0N 118 0 E
Fujieda, Japan 73 C10 34 52N 138 16 E
Fujinomiya, Japan 73 B10 35 10N 138 40 E
Fujioka, Japan 73 A11 36 15N 139 5 E
Fujisawa, Japan 73 B11 35 22N 139 29 E
Fujiyama, Mt. = Fuji-San, Japan 73 B10 35 22N 138 44 E
Fukagawa, Japan 70 C11 43 43N 142 2 E
Fukaya, Japan 73 A11 36 12N 139 12 E
Fukiage, Japan 72 F2 31 27N 130 17 E
Fukien = Fujian □, China 77 E12 26 0N 118 0 E
Fukuchiyama, Japan 73 B7 35 19N 135 9 E
Fukue-Shima, Japan 71 H4 32 40N 128 45 E
Fukui, Japan 73 A8 36 5N 136 10 E
Fukui □, Japan 73 B8 36 0N 136 12 E
Fukuma, Japan 72 D2 33 46N 130 28 E
Fukuoka, Japan 72 D2 33 39N 130 21 E
Fukuoka □, Japan 72 D3 33 30N 131 0 E
Fukuoka International ✕ (FUK), Japan 72 D2 33 34N 130 28 E
Fukuroi, Japan 73 C9 34 45N 137 55 E
Fukushima, Japan 70 F10 37 44N 140 28 E
Fukushima □, Japan 70 F10 37 30N 140 15 E
Fukuyama, Japan 72 C5 34 35N 133 20 E
Fulacunda, Guinea-Biss. 112 C1 11 44N 15 3W
Fulaga, Fiji 133 B3 19 8 S 178 33W
Fulda, Germany 30 E5 50 32N 9 40 E
Fulda →, Germany 30 D5 51 25N 9 39 E
Fulford = North Miami Beach, U.S.A. 153 K9 25 56N 80 10W
Fulford Harbour, Canada 160 B3 48 47N 123 27W
Fuliang, China 77 C11 29 23N 117 14 E
Fullerton, Calif., U.S.A. 161 M9 33 53N 117 56W
Fullerton, Nebr., U.S.A. 154 E6 41 22N 97 58W
Fulongquan, China 75 B13 44 20N 124 42 E
Fülöpszállás, Hungary 52 D4 46 49N 19 15 E
Fulton, Ill., U.S.A. 156 C6 41 52N 90 11W
Fulton, Ind., U.S.A. 157 D10 40 57N 86 16W
Fulton, Ky., U.S.A. 157 G8 36 30N 88 53W
Fulton, Mo., U.S.A. 156 F5 38 52N 91 57W
Fulton, N.Y., U.S.A. 151 C8 43 19N 76 25W
Fuluälven →, Sweden 16 C7 61 18N 13 4 E
Fulufjället, Sweden 16 C6 61 32N 12 41 E
Fumay, France 27 C11 49 58N 4 40 E
Fumel, France 28 D4 44 30N 0 58 E
Fumin, China 76 E4 25 10N 102 20 E
Funabashi, Japan 73 B12 35 45N 140 0 E
Funafuti = Fongafale, Tuvalu 134 H9 8 31 S 179 13 E
Funäsdalen, Sweden 16 B6 62 33N 12 32 E
Funchal, Madeira 9 c 32 38N 16 54W
Funchal ✕ (FNC), Madeira 9 c 32 42N 16 45W
Fundación, Colombia 168 A3 10 31N 74 11W
Fundão, Brazil 171 E3 19 55 S 40 24W
Fundão, Portugal 42 E3 40 8N 7 30W
Fundu Moldovei, Romania 53 C10 47 32N 25 24 E
Fundulea, Romania 53 F11 44 28N 26 31 E
Fundy △, Canada 141 C6 45 35N 65 10W
Fundy, B. of, Canada 141 D6 45 0N 66 0W
Fünfkirchen = Pécs, Hungary 52 D3 46 5N 18 15 E
Funhalouro, Mozam. 117 C5 23 3 S 34 25 E
Funing, Hebei, China 75 E10 39 53N 119 12 E
Funing, Jiangsu, China 75 H10 33 45N 119 50 E
Funing, Yunnan, China 76 F5 23 35N 105 45 E
Funiu Shan, China 74 H7 33 30N 112 20 E
Funsi, Ghana 112 C4 10 21N 1 54W
Funtua, Nigeria 113 C6 11 30N 7 18 E
Fuping, Hebei, China 74 E8 38 48N 114 12 E
Fuping, Shaanxi, China 74 G5 34 42N 109 10 E
Fuqing, China 77 E12 25 41N 119 21 E
Fuquan, China 76 D6 26 40N 107 27 E
Furano, Japan 70 C11 43 21N 142 23 E
Furāt, Nahr al →, Asia 96 D5 31 0N 47 25 E
Fūrg, Iran 97 D7 28 18N 55 13 E
Furkapass, Switz. 33 C7 46 34N 8 35 E
Furkating, India 90 B4 26 28N 93 59 E
Furman, U.S.A. 152 C8 32 41N 81 11W
Furmanov, Russia 60 B5 57 10N 41 9 E
Furmanovo, Kazakhstan 60 F9 49 42N 49 25 E
Furnas, Azores 9 d3 37 46N 25 19W
Furnás, Spain 38 C2 39 3N 1 32 E
Furnas, Reprêsa de, Brazil 171 F2 20 50 S 45 30W
Furneaux Group, Australia 127 G4 40 10 S 147 50 E
Furqlus, Syria 103 A6 34 36N 37 8 E
Fürstenau, Germany 30 C3 52 31N 7 40 E
Fürstenberg = Eisenhüttenstadt, Germany 30 C10 52 9N 14 38 E
Fürstenberg, Germany 30 B9 53 10N 13 8 E
Fürstenfeld, Austria 34 D9 47 3N 16 3 E
Fürstenfeldbruck, Germany 31 G7 48 11N 11 15 E
Fürstenwalde, Germany 30 C10 52 22N 14 3 E
Fürth, Germany 31 F6 49 28N 10 59 E
Furth im Wald, Germany 31 F8 49 18N 12 50 E
Furtwangen, Germany 31 G4 48 2N 8 12 E
Furudal, Sweden 16 C9 61 10N 15 11 E
Furukawa, Gifu, Japan 73 A9 36 14N 137 11 E
Furukawa, Miyagi, Japan 70 E10 38 34N 140 58 E
Furulund, Sweden 17 J7 55 46N 13 6 E
Fury and Hecla Str., Canada 139 B11 69 56N 84 0W
Fusagasuga, Colombia 168 C3 4 21N 74 22W
Fuscaldo, Italy 47 C9 39 25N 16 2 E
Fushan, Shandong, China 75 F11 37 30N 121 15 E
Fushan, Shanxi, China 74 G6 35 58N 111 51 E
Fushë Arrëz, Albania 50 D4 42 4N 20 2 E
Fushë Krujë, Albania 50 E3 41 29N 19 43 E
Fushun, Liaoning, China 75 D12 41 50N 123 56 E
Fushun, Sichuan, China 76 C5 29 13N 104 52 E
Fusio, Switz. 33 D7 46 27N 8 40 E
Fusong, China 75 C14 42 20N 127 15 E
Füssen, Germany 31 H6 47 34N 10 42 E
Fustic, Barbados 165 g 13 16N 59 38W
Fusui, China 76 F6 22 40N 107 56 E
Futago-Yama, Japan 72 D3 33 35N 131 36 E
Futian, China 69 F11 22 32N 114 4 E
Futog, Serbia & M. 52 E4 45 15N 19 42 E
Futrono, Chile 176 B2 40 8 S 72 24W
Futtsu, Japan 73 B11 35 13N 139 49 E
Futuna, Wall. & F. Is. 134 J9 14 25 S 178 20W
Fuwa, Egypt 106 H7 31 12N 30 33 E
Fuxian Hu, China 76 E4 24 30N 102 53 E
Fuxin, China 75 C11 42 5N 121 48 E
Fuyang, Anhui, China 74 H8 33 0N 115 48 E
Fuyang, Zhejiang, China 77 B12 30 5N 119 57 E
Fuyang He →, China 74 E9 38 12N 117 0 E
Fuying Dao, China 77 D13 26 34N 120 9 E
Fuyong, China 69 F10 22 40N 113 49 E
Fuyu, Heilongjiang, China 69 B7 47 49N 124 27 E
Fuyu, Jilin, China 75 B13 45 12N 124 43 E
Fuyuan, China 76 E5 25 40N 104 16 E
Füzesgyarmat, Hungary 52 C6 47 6N 21 14 E
Fuzhou, China 77 D12 26 5N 119 16 E
Fylde, U.K. 20 D5 53 50N 2 58W
Fyn, Denmark 17 J4 55 20N 10 30 E
Fyne, L., U.K. 22 F3 55 59N 5 23W
Fyns Amtskommune □, Denmark 17 J4 55 15N 10 30 E
Fynshav, Denmark 17 K3 54 59N 9 59 E
Fyresdal, Norway 18 E5 59 11N 8 5 E
Fyresvatn, Norway 18 E5 59 6N 8 10 E
Fyzabad = Faizabad, India 93 F10 26 45N 82 10 E

G

Ga, Ghana 112 D4 9 47N 2 30W
Gaanda, Nigeria 113 C7 10 10N 12 27 E
Gabarin, Nigeria 113 C7 11 8N 10 27 E
Gabas →, France 28 E3 43 46N 0 42W
Gabela, Angola 115 E2 11 0 S 14 24 E
Gaberones = Gaborone, Botswana 116 C4 24 45 S 25 57 E
Gabès, Tunisia 108 B2 33 53N 10 2 E
Gabès, G. de, Tunisia 108 B2 34 0N 10 30 E
Gabgaba, W. →, Egypt 106 C3 22 10N 33 5 E
Gabia, Dem. Rep. of the Congo 115 C3 4 37 S 17 14 E
Gąbin, Poland 55 F6 52 23N 19 41 E
Gablonz = Jablonec nad Nisou, Czech Rep. 34 A8 50 43N 15 10 E
Gabon ■, Africa 114 C2 0 10 S 10 0 E
Gabon →, Gabon 114 B1 0 25N 9 20 E
Gaborone, Botswana 116 C4 24 45 S 25 57 E
Gabriels, U.S.A. 151 B10 44 26N 74 12W
Gabrīk, Iran 97 E8 25 44N 58 28 E
Gabro, Ethiopia 120 C2 6 18N 43 16 E
Gabrovo, Bulgaria 51 D9 42 52N 25 19 E
Gabú = Nova Lamego, Guinea-Biss. 112 C2 12 19N 14 11W
Gacé, France 26 D7 48 49N 0 20 E
Gāch Sār, Iran 97 B6 36 7N 51 19 E
Gachsārān, Iran 97 D6 30 15N 50 45 E
Gacko, Bos.-H. 50 C2 43 10N 18 33 E
Gad Hinglaj, India 95 F2 16 14N 74 21 E
Gadag, India 95 G2 15 30N 75 45 E
Gadaisu, Papua N. G. 132 F5 10 22 S 149 46 E
Gadamai, Sudan 107 D4 17 11N 36 10 E
Gadap, Pakistan 92 G2 25 5N 67 28 E
Gadarwara, India 93 H8 22 50N 78 50 E
Gadebusch, Germany 30 B7 53 42N 11 7 E
Gadein, Sudan 107 F2 8 10N 28 45 E
Gadhada, India 92 J4 22 0N 71 35 E
Gadmen, Switz. 33 C6 46 45N 8 16 E
Gádor, Sierra de, Spain 43 J8 36 57N 2 45W
Gadra, Pakistan 92 G4 25 40N 70 38 E
Gadsden, Ala., U.S.A. 152 A3 34 1N 86 1W
Gadsden, S.C., U.S.A. 152 B9 33 51N 80 46W
Gadwal, India 95 F3 16 10N 77 50 E
Gadyach = Hadyach, Ukraine 59 G8 50 21N 34 0 E
Gadzi, C.A.R. 114 B3 4 47N 16 42 E
Găeşti, Romania 53 F10 44 48N 25 19 E
Gaeta, Italy 46 A6 41 12N 13 35 E
Gaeta, G. di, Italy 46 A6 41 6N 13 30 E
Gaffney, U.S.A. 149 H5 35 5N 81 39W
Gafsa, Tunisia 108 B1 34 24N 8 43 E
Gag, Indonesia 83 B3 0 27 S 129 52 E
Gagarawa, Nigeria 113 C6 12 25N 9 32 E
Gagaria, India 92 G4 25 43N 70 46 E
Gagarin, Russia 58 E8 55 38N 35 0 E
Gagarin, Uzbekistan 65 C4 40 39N 68 10 E
Găgăuzia □, Moldova 53 D13 46 10N 28 40 E
Gaggenau, Germany 31 G4 48 48N 8 18 E
Gaghamni, Sudan 107 E2 11 41N 28 19 E
Gagino, Russia 60 C7 55 15N 45 1 E
Gagliano del Capo, Italy 47 C11 39 50N 18 22 E
Gagnef, Sweden 16 D9 60 36N 15 5 E
Gagnoa, Ivory C. 112 D3 6 56N 5 16W
Gagnon, Canada 141 B6 51 50N 68 5W
Gagnon, L., Canada 143 A6 62 3N 110 27W
Gago Coutinho, São Tomé & Príncipe 115 G6 0 1 S 6 32 E
Gagra, Georgia 61 J5 43 20N 40 10 E
Gahini, Rwanda 118 C3 1 50 S 30 30 E
Gahmar, India 93 G10 25 27N 83 49 E
Gai Xian = Gaizhou, China 75 D12 40 22N 122 20 E
Gaibanda, Bangla. 90 C2 25 20N 89 36 E
Gaïdhouronísi, Greece 39 F6 34 53N 25 41 E
Gail, U.S.A. 155 J4 32 46N 101 27W
Gail →, Austria 34 E6 46 36N 13 53 E
Gaillac, France 28 E5 43 54N 1 54 E
Gaillimh = Galway, Ireland 23 C2 53 17N 9 3W
Gaillon, France 26 C8 49 10N 1 20 E
Gaimán, Argentina 176 B3 43 10 S 65 25W
Gaines, U.S.A. 150 E7 41 46N 77 35W
Gainesville, Fla., U.S.A. 153 F7 29 40N 82 20W
Gainesville, Ga., U.S.A. 149 H4 34 18N 83 50W
Gainesville, Mo., U.S.A. 155 G8 36 36N 92 26W
Gainesville, Tex., U.S.A. 155 J6 33 38N 97 8W
Gainsborough, U.K. 20 D7 53 24N 0 46W
Gairdner, L., Australia 128 A2 31 30 S 136 0 E
Gairloch, U.K. 22 D3 57 43N 5 41W
Gairloch, L., U.K. 22 D3 57 43N 5 45W
Gais, Switz. 33 B8 47 22N 9 27 E
Gaizhou, China 75 D12 40 22N 122 20 E
Gaj, Croatia 52 E2 45 28N 17 3 E
Gaj →, Pakistan 92 F2 26 26N 67 21 E
Gajendragarh, India 95 G2 15 44N 75 59 E
Gakona, U.S.A. 144 E11 62 18N 145 18W
Gakuch, Pakistan 93 A5 36 7N 73 45 E
Gal Laghet, Somali Rep. 120 D3 4 9N 47 10 E
Gal Oya △, Sri Lanka 95 L5 7 0N 81 20 E
Gal Oya Res., Sri Lanka 95 L5 7 5N 81 30 E
Gal Tardo, Somali Rep. 120 D3 3 34N 45 58 E
Galaasiya, Uzbekistan 65 D2 39 51N 64 26 E
Galachipa, Bangla. 90 D3 22 8N 90 26 E
Galala, Gebel el, Egypt 106 J8 29 21N 32 22 E
Galán, Cerro, Argentina 174 B2 25 55 S 66 52W
Galana →, Kenya 118 C5 3 9 S 40 8 E
Galangue, Angola 115 E3 13 42 S 16 9 E
Galangue, Serra, Angola 115 E3 14 18 S 15 52 E
Galanta, Slovak Rep. 35 C10 48 11N 17 45 E
Galapagar, Spain 42 E7 40 36N 3 58W
Galápagos = Colón, Arch. de, Ecuador 172 a 0 0 91 0W
Galapagos Fracture Zone, Pac. Oc. 135 G17 3 0N 110 0W
Galapagos Rise, Pac. Oc. 135 J18 15 0 S 95 0W
Galashiels, U.K. 22 F6 55 37N 2 49W
Galatás, Greece 48 D5 37 30N 23 26 E
Galatea, N.Z. 130 E5 38 24 S 176 45 E
Galaţi, Romania 53 E13 45 27N 28 2 E
Galaţi □, Romania 53 E12 45 45N 27 30 E
Galatia, Turkey 100 C5 39 30N 33 0 E
Galatina, Italy 47 B11 40 10N 18 10 E
Galátone, Italy 47 B11 40 9N 18 4 E
Galax, U.S.A. 149 G5 36 40N 80 56W
Galaxídhion, Greece 48 C4 38 22N 22 23 E
Galcaio, Somali Rep. 120 C3 6 30N 47 30 E
Galdhøpiggen, Norway 18 C5 61 38N 8 18 E
Galeana, Chihuahua, Mexico 162 A3 30 7N 107 38W
Galeana, Nuevo León, Mexico 162 A3 24 50N 100 4W
Galegu, Sudan 107 E4 12 36N 35 2 E
Galela, Indonesia 82 A3 1 50N 127 49 E
Galena, Alaska, U.S.A. 144 D8 64 44N 156 56W
Galena, Ill., U.S.A. 156 B6 42 25N 90 26W
Galeota Pt., Trin. & Tob. 169 F10 10 8N 60 59W
Galera, Spain 41 H2 37 45N 2 33W
Galera, Pta., Chile 176 A2 39 59 S 73 43W
Galera, Pta. da, Azores 9 d3 37 42N 25 30W
Galera Pt., Trin. & Tob. 169 F10 10 49N 60 54W
Galesburg, Ill., U.S.A. 156 D6 40 57N 90 22W
Galesburg, Mich., U.S.A. 157 B11 42 17N 85 26W
Galeton, U.S.A. 150 E7 41 44N 77 39W
Galga, Ethiopia 107 F4 6 39N 37 47 E
Galgasc, Somali Rep. 120 D2 0 11N 41 38 E
Galheirão →, Brazil 171 D2 12 23 S 45 5W
Galheiros, Brazil 171 D2 13 18 S 46 25W
Gali, Georgia 61 J5 42 37N 41 46 E
Galicea Mare, Romania 53 F8 44 4N 23 19 E
Galich, Russia 60 A6 58 22N 42 24 E
Galiche, Bulgaria 50 C7 43 34N 23 53 E
Galicia □, Spain 42 C3 42 43N 7 45W
Galičica △, Macedonia 50 E4 41 2N 20 55 E
Galien, U.S.A. 157 C10 41 48N 86 30W
Galilee = Hagalil, Israel 103 C4 32 53N 35 18 E
Galilee, L., Australia 126 C4 22 20 S 145 50 E
Galilee, Sea of = Yam Kinneret, Israel 103 C4 32 45N 35 35 E
Galim, Cameroon 113 D7 7 6N 12 25 E
Galina Pt., Jamaica 164 a 18 24N 76 58W
Galinoporni, Cyprus 39 E10 35 31N 34 18 E
Galion, U.S.A. 150 F2 40 44N 82 47W
Galite, Îs. de la, Tunisia 111 A6 37 30N 8 59 E
Galiuro Mts., U.S.A. 159 K8 32 30N 110 20W
Galiwinku, Australia 126 A2 12 2 S 135 34 E
Gallabat, Sudan 107 E4 12 58N 36 11 E

Gallan Hd., U.K. 22 C1 58 15N 7 2W
Gallarate, Italy 44 C5 45 40N 8 48 E
Gallatin, Mo., U.S.A. 156 E3 39 55N 93 58W
Gallatin, Tenn., U.S.A. 149 G2 36 24N 86 27W
Galle, Sri Lanka 95 L5 6 5N 80 10 E
Gállego →, Spain 40 D4 41 39N 0 51W
Gallegos →, Argentina 176 D3 51 35 S 69 0W
Galletti →, Ethiopia 107 F5 8 46N 41 10 E
Galley Hd., Ireland 23 E3 51 32N 8 55W
Galliate, Italy 44 C5 45 29N 8 42 E
Gallinas, Pta., Colombia 168 A3 12 28N 71 40W
Gallipoli = Gelibolu, Turkey 51 F10 40 28N 26 43 E
Gallípoli, Italy 47 B10 40 3N 17 58 E
Gallipolis, U.S.A. 148 F4 38 49N 82 12W
Gällivare, Sweden 14 C19 67 9N 20 40 E
Gallneukirchen, Austria 34 C7 48 21N 14 25 E
Gällö, Sweden 16 B9 62 55N 15 13 E
Gallo, C., Italy 46 D6 38 13N 13 19 E
Gallocanta, L. de, Spain 40 E3 40 58N 1 30W
Galloo I., U.S.A. 151 C8 43 55N 76 25W
Galloway, U.K. 22 F4 55 1N 4 29W
Galloway ⌓, U.K. 22 F4 55 3N 4 20W
Galloway, Mull of, U.K. 22 G4 54 39N 4 52W
Gallup, U.S.A. 159 J9 35 32N 108 45W
Gallur, Spain 40 D3 41 52N 1 19W
Gallyaaral, Uzbekistan 65 C3 40 2N 67 35 E
Galong, Australia 129 C8 34 37 S 148 34 E
Galoya, Sri Lanka 95 K5 8 10N 80 55 E
Galt, Calif., U.S.A. 160 G5 38 15N 121 18W
Galt, Mo., U.S.A. 156 D3 40 8N 93 23W
Galten, Denmark 17 H3 56 9N 9 54 E
Galtür, Austria 34 E3 46 58N 10 11 E
Galty Mts., Ireland 23 D3 52 22N 8 10W
Galtymore, Ireland 23 D3 52 21N 8 11W
Galva, U.S.A. 156 C6 41 10N 90 3W
Galvarino, Chile 176 A2 38 24 S 72 47W
Galve de Sorbe, Spain 40 D1 41 13N 3 10W
Galveston, Ind., U.S.A. 157 D10 40 35N 86 11W
Galveston, Tex., U.S.A. 155 L7 29 18N 94 48W
Galveston B., U.S.A. 155 L7 29 36N 94 50W
Gálvez, Argentina 174 C3 32 0 S 61 14W
Galway, Ireland 23 C2 53 17N 9 3W
Galway □, Ireland 23 C2 53 22N 9 1W
Galway B., Ireland 23 C2 53 13N 9 10W
Gam, Indonesia 83 B4 0 27 S 130 36 E
Gam →, Vietnam 86 B5 21 55N 105 12 E
Gamagōri, Japan 73 C9 34 50N 137 14 E
Gamari, L., Ethiopia 107 E5 11 32N 41 40 E
Gamawa, Nigeria 113 C7 12 10N 10 31 E
Gamay, Phil. 80 E5 12 23N 125 18 E
Gamay Bay, Phil. 80 E5 12 21N 125 21 E
Gamba, Angola 115 E3 11 42 S 17 14 E
Gambaga, Ghana 113 C4 10 30N 0 28W
Gambat, Pakistan 92 F3 27 17N 68 26 E
Gambela, Ethiopia 107 F3 8 14N 34 38 E
Gambela △, Ethiopia 107 F3 8 0N 34 0 E
Gambela-Hizboch □, Ethiopia 107 F3 8 0N 34 0 E
Gambell, U.S.A. 144 E5 63 47N 171 45W
Gambhir →, India 92 F6 26 58N 77 27 E
Gambia ■, W. Afr. 112 C1 13 25N 16 0W
Gambia →, W. Afr. 112 C1 13 28N 16 34W
Gambier, U.S.A. 150 F2 40 22N 82 23W
Gambier, C., Australia 124 B5 11 56 S 130 57 E
Gambier, Îs., French Polynesia 135 K14 23 8 S 134 58W
Gambier Is., Australia 128 C2 35 3 S 136 30 E
Gambier Village, Bahamas 9 b 25 4N 77 30W
Gambo, C.A.R. 114 B4 4 39N 22 16 E
Gambo, Canada 141 C9 48 47N 54 13W
Gamboli, Pakistan 92 E3 29 53N 68 24 E
Gamboma, Congo 114 C3 1 55 S 15 52 E
Gamboula, C.A.R. 114 B3 4 8N 15 9 E
Gambuta, Indonesia 82 A2 0 30N 123 20 E
Gamka →, S. Africa 116 E3 33 18 S 21 39 E
Gamkab →, Namibia 116 D2 28 4 S 17 54 E
Gamla Uppsala, Sweden 16 E11 59 54N 17 40 E
Gamlakarleby = Kokkola, Finland 14 E20 63 50N 23 8 E
Gamleby, Sweden 17 G10 57 54N 16 24 E
Gammon →, Canada 143 C9 51 24N 95 44W
Gammon Ranges △, Australia 127 E2 30 38 S 139 8 E
Gammouda, Tunisia 108 A1 35 3N 9 39 E
Gamo-Gofa, Ethiopia 107 F4 5 40N 36 40 E
Gamoda-Saki, Japan 72 D6 33 50N 134 45 E
Gamou, Niger 113 C6 14 20N 9 55 E
Gampaha, Sri Lanka 95 L4 7 5N 79 59 E
Gampel, Switz. 32 D5 46 19N 7 44 E
Gampola, Sri Lanka 95 L5 7 10N 80 34 E
Gams, Switz. 33 B8 47 12N 9 26 E
Gamtoos →, S. Africa 116 E4 33 58 S 25 1 E
Gan, France 28 E3 43 12N 0 27W
Gan Gan, Argentina 176 B3 42 30 S 68 10W
Gan Goriama, Mts., Cameroon 113 D7 7 44N 12 45 E
Gan Jiang →, China 77 C11 29 15N 116 0 E
Ganado, U.S.A. 159 J9 35 43N 109 33W
Gananita, Sudan 106 D3 18 22N 33 50 E
Gananoque, Canada 140 D4 44 20N 76 10W
Ganassi, Phil. 81 H5 7 49N 124 6 E
Ganāveh, Iran 97 D6 29 35N 50 35 E
Gäncä, Azerbaijan 61 K8 40 45N 46 20 E
Gancheng, China 86 C7 18 51N 108 37 E
Gand = Gent, Belgium 24 C3 51 2N 3 42 E
Ganda, Angola 115 E2 13 3 S 14 35 E
Gandajika, Dem. Rep. of the Congo 115 D4 6 46 S 23 58 E
Gandak →, India 93 G11 25 39N 85 13 E
Gandara, Phil. 80 E5 12 1N 124 49 E
Gandava, Pakistan 91 C2 28 32N 67 32 E
Gander, Canada 141 C9 48 58N 54 35W
Gander L., Canada 141 C9 48 58N 54 35W
Ganderkesee, Germany 30 B4 53 2N 8 32 E
Ganderowe Falls, Zimbabwe 119 F2 17 20 S 29 10 E
Gandesa, Spain 40 D5 41 3N 0 26 E
Gandhi Sagar, India 92 G6 24 40N 75 40 E
Gandhinagar, India 92 H5 23 15N 72 45 E
Gandi, Nigeria 113 C6 12 55N 5 49 E
Gandía, Spain 41 G4 38 58N 0 9W
Gandino, Italy 44 C6 45 49N 9 54 E
Gando, Pta., Canary Is. 9 e1 27 55N 15 22W
Gandole, Nigeria 113 D7 8 28N 11 35 E
Gandou, Congo 114 B3 2 25N 17 25 E
Gandu, Brazil 171 D4 13 45 S 39 30W
Gâneb, Mauritania 112 B2 18 29N 10 8W
Ganedidalem = Gani, Indonesia 82 B3 0 48 S 128 14 E
Ganetti, Sudan 106 D3 18 0N 31 10 E
Ganga →, India 93 H14 23 20N 90 30 E
Ganga Sagar, India 93 J13 21 38N 88 5 E
Gangafani, Mali 112 C4 14 20N 2 20W
Gangakher, India 94 E3 18 57N 76 45 E
Gangan →, India 93 E8 28 38N 78 58 E
Ganganagar, India 92 E5 29 56N 73 56 E
Gangapur, Maharashtra, India 94 E2 19 41N 75 1 E
Gangapur, Raj., India 92 F7 26 32N 76 49 E
Gangara, Niger 113 C6 14 35N 8 29 E
Gangaw, Burma 90 D5 22 5N 94 5 E
Gangaw Taungdan, Burma 90 C6 24 55N 96 35 E
Gangawati, India 95 G3 15 30N 76 36 E
Ganges = Ganga →, India 93 H14 23 20N 90 30 E
Ganges, Canada 142 D4 48 51N 123 31W
Ganges, France 28 E7 43 56N 3 42 E
Ganges, Mouths of the, India 90 E3 21 30N 90 0 E
Gånghester, Sweden 17 G7 57 42N 13 1 E
Gangi, Italy 47 E7 37 48N 14 12 E
Gângiova, Romania 53 G8 43 54N 23 50 E
Gangoh, India 92 E7 29 46N 77 18 E
Gangotri, India 93 D8 30 50N 79 10 E
Gangotri △, India 93 D8 30 50N 79 10 E
Gangtok, India 90 B2 27 20N 88 37 E
Gangu, China 74 G3 34 40N 105 15 E
Gangwa, Dem. Rep. of the Congo 114 C4 3 30 S 20 54 E
Gangyao, China 75 B14 44 12N 126 37 E
Gani, Indonesia 82 B3 0 48 S 128 14 E
Ganj, India 93 F8 27 45N 78 57 E
Ganjam, India 94 E7 19 23N 85 4 E
Ganluc, China 76 C4 28 58N 102 59 E
Ganmain, Australia 129 C7 34 47 S 147 1 E
Gannat, France 27 F10 46 7N 3 11 E
Gannett Peak, U.S.A. 158 E9 43 11N 109 39W
Ganquan, China 74 F5 36 20N 109 20 E
Gänserdorf, Austria 35 C9 48 20N 16 43 E
Ganshui, China 76 C6 28 40N 106 40 E
Gansu □, China 74 G3 36 0N 104 0 E
Ganta, Liberia 112 D3 7 15N 8 59W
Gantheaume, C., Australia 128 D2 36 4 S 137 32 E
Gantheaume B., Australia 125 E1 27 40 S 114 10 E
Gantsevichi = Hantsavichy, Belarus 59 F4 52 49N 26 30 E
Ganye, Nigeria 113 D7 8 25N 12 4 E
Ganyem = Genyem, Indonesia 83 B6 2 46 S 140 12 E
Ganyu, China 75 G10 34 50N 119 8 E
Ganyushkino, Kazakhstan 61 G9 46 35N 49 20 E
Ganzhou, China 77 E10 25 51N 114 56 E
Gao, Mali 113 B4 16 15N 0 5W
Gao Xian, China 76 C5 28 21N 104 32 E
Gao'an, China 77 C10 28 26N 115 17 E
Gaochun, China 77 B12 31 20N 118 49 E
Gaohe, China 77 F9 22 46N 112 57 E
Gaohebu, China 77 B11 30 43N 116 49 E
Gaokeng, China 77 D9 27 40N 113 58 E
Gaolan Dao, China 77 G9 21 55N 113 10 E
Gaoligong Shan, China 76 E2 24 45N 98 45 E
Gaomi, China 75 F10 36 20N 119 42 E
Gaoping, China 74 G7 35 45N 112 55 E
Gaotang, China 74 F9 36 50N 116 15 E
Gaoua, Burkina Faso 112 C4 10 20N 3 8W
Gaoual, Guinea 112 C2 11 45N 13 25W
Gaoxiong = Kaohsiung, Taiwan 77 F13 22 35N 120 16 E
Gaoyang, China 74 E8 38 40N 115 45 E
Gaoyao, China 77 F9 23 3N 112 27 E
Gaoyou, China 77 A12 32 47N 119 26 E
Gaoyou Hu, China 75 H10 32 45N 119 20 E
Gaoyuan, China 75 F9 37 8N 117 58 E
Gaozhou, China 77 G8 21 58N 110 50 E
Gap, France 29 D10 44 33N 6 5 E
Gapan, Phil. 80 D3 15 19N 120 57 E
Gapat →, India 93 G10 24 30N 82 28 E
Gapuwiyak, Australia 126 A2 12 25 S 135 43 E
Gar, China 68 C2 32 10N 79 58 E
Garabekewül, Turkmenistan 65 D2 38 30N 64 8 E
Garabogazköl Aylagy, Turkmenistan 57 F9 41 0N 53 30 E
Garachico, Canary Is. 9 e1 28 22N 16 46W
Garachiné, Panama 164 E4 8 0N 78 12W
Garad, Somali Rep. 120 C3 6 57N 49 24 E
Garafia, Canary Is. 9 e1 28 48N 17 57W
Garah, Australia 127 D4 29 5 S 149 38 E
Garaina, Papua N. G. 132 D4 7 53 S 147 8 E
Garajonay, Canary Is. 9 e1 28 7N 17 14W
Garamätnyyaz, Turkmenistan 65 E2 37 45N 64 34 E
Garamba △, Dem. Rep. of the Congo 118 B2 4 10N 29 40 E
Garango, Burkina Faso 113 C4 11 48N 0 34W
Garanhuns, Brazil 170 C4 8 50 S 36 30W
Garautha, India 93 G8 25 34N 79 18 E
Garavuti, Tajikistan 65 E4 37 34N 68 26 E
Garawe, Liberia 112 E3 4 35N 8 0W
Garba Harre, Somali Rep. 120 D2 3 19N 42 13 E
Garba Tula, Kenya 118 B4 0 30N 38 32 E
Garbagududu, Ethiopia 120 C2 6 12N 43 50 E
Garbahaarrey = Garba Harre, Somali Rep. 120 D2 3 19N 42 13 E
Garberville, U.S.A. 158 F2 40 6N 123 48W
Garbiyang, India 93 D9 30 8N 80 54 E
Garbsen, Germany 30 C5 52 26N 9 31 E
Garça, Brazil 171 F2 22 14 S 49 37W
Garças →, Mato Grosso, Brazil 173 D7 15 54 S 52 16W
Garças →, Pernambuco, Brazil 170 C4 8 43 S 39 41W
Garchitorena, Phil. 80 E4 13 52N 123 40 E
Garcia Hernandez, Phil. 81 G5 9 37N 124 18 E
Garcias, Brazil 173 E7 20 34 S 52 13W
Gard □, France 29 D8 44 2N 4 10 E
Gard →, France 29 E8 43 51N 4 37 E
Garda, L. di, Italy 44 C7 45 40N 10 41 E
Gardanne, France 29 E9 43 27N 5 27 E
Gårdby, Sweden 17 H10 56 36N 16 38 E
Garde L., Canada 143 A7 62 50N 106 13W
Gardelegen, Germany 30 C7 52 32N 11 24 E
Garden City, Ga., U.S.A. 152 C8 32 6N 81 9W
Garden City, Idaho, U.S.A. 158 E5 43 38N 116 16W
Garden City, Kans., U.S.A. 155 G4 37 58N 100 53W
Garden City, Mo., U.S.A. 156 F2 38 34N 94 12W
Garden City, Tex., U.S.A. 155 K4 31 52N 101 29W
Garden Grove, U.S.A. 161 M9 33 47N 117 55W
Gardēz, Afghan. 91 B3 33 37N 69 9 E
Gardhíki, Greece 48 C3 38 50N 21 55 E
Garður, Iceland 11 A10 66 4N 16 46W
Gardiner, Maine, U.S.A. 149 C11 44 14N 69 47W
Gardiner, Mont., U.S.A. 158 D8 45 2N 110 22W
Gardiners I., U.S.A. 151 E12 41 6N 72 6W
Gardner, Fla., U.S.A. 153 H8 27 21N 81 48W
Gardner, Ill., U.S.A. 157 C8 41 12N 88 17W
Gardner, Mass., U.S.A. 151 D13 42 34N 71 59W
Gardner Canal, Canada 142 C3 53 27N 128 8W
Gardner Pinnacles, U.S.A. 145 G10 25 0N 167 55W
Gardnerville, U.S.A. 160 G7 38 56N 119 45W
Gardno, Jezioro, Poland 54 D4 54 40N 17 7 E
Gardo, Somali Rep. 120 C3 9 30N 49 6 E
Gardone Val Trómpia, Italy 44 C7 45 41N 10 11 E
Gárdony, Hungary 52 C3 47 12N 18 39 E
Gare Tigre, Fr. Guiana 169 C7 4 58N 53 9W
Gareloi I., U.S.A. 144 L3 51 48N 178 48W
Garešnica, Croatia 45 C13 45 36N 16 56 E
Garéssio, Italy 44 D5 44 12N 8 2 E
Garey, U.S.A. 161 L6 34 53N 120 19W
Garfield, U.S.A. 158 C5 47 1N 117 9W
Garforth, U.K. 20 D6 53 47N 1 24W
Gargaliánoi, Greece 48 D3 37 4N 21 38 E
Gargan, Mt., France 28 C5 45 37N 1 39 E
Gargano △, Italy 45 G12 41 43N 15 52 E
Gargantua, C., Canada 148 B3 47 36N 85 2W
Gargett, Australia 126 K6 21 9 S 148 46 E
Gargouna, Mali 113 B5 15 56N 0 13 E
Gargždai, Lithuania 54 C8 55 43N 21 24 E
Garhchiroli, India 94 D5 20 10N 80 0 E
Gari, Russia 64 B9 59 26N 62 21 E
Garibaldi ⌓, Canada 142 D4 49 50N 122 40W
Gariep, L., S. Africa 116 E4 30 40 S 25 40 E
Garies, S. Africa 116 E2 30 32 S 17 59 E
Garigliano →, Italy 46 A6 41 13N 13 45 E
Garissa, Kenya 118 C4 0 25 S 39 40 E
Garkida, Nigeria 113 C7 10 27N 12 36 E
Garko, Nigeria 113 C6 11 45N 8 35 E
Garland, Tex., U.S.A. 155 J6 32 55N 96 38W
Garland, Utah, U.S.A. 158 F7 41 47N 112 10W
Garlasco, Italy 44 C5 45 12N 8 55 E
Garliava, Lithuania 54 D10 54 49N 23 52 E
Garlin, France 28 E3 43 33N 0 16W
Garm, Tajikistan 65 D5 39 0N 70 20 E
Garmāb, Iran 97 C8 35 25N 56 45 E
Garmisch-Partenkirchen, Germany 31 H7 47 30N 11 6 E
Garmo, Qullai = Kommunizma, Pik, Tajikistan 65 D6 39 0N 72 2 E
Garmsār, Iran 97 C7 35 20N 52 25 E
Garner, U.S.A. 156 A3 43 6N 93 36W
Garnett, U.S.A. 154 F7 38 17N 95 14W
Garnpung L., Australia 128 B5 33 25 S 143 10 E
Garo Hills, India 90 C3 25 30N 90 30 E
Garoe, Somali Rep. 120 C3 8 25N 48 33 E
Garonne →, France 28 C3 45 2N 0 36W
Garonne, Canal Latéral à la, France 28 D4 44 15N 0 18 E
Garoowe = Garoe, Somali Rep. 120 C3 8 25N 48 33 E
Garot, India 92 G6 24 19N 75 41 E
Garoua, Cameroon 113 D7 9 19N 13 21 E
Garove I., Papua N. G. 132 C5 4 42 S 149 30 E
Garpenberg, Sweden 16 D10 60 19N 16 12 E
Garphyttan, Sweden 16 E8 59 18N 14 56 E
Garrauli, India 93 G8 25 5N 79 22 E
Garrel, Germany 30 C4 52 57N 8 1 E
Garrett, U.S.A. 157 C11 41 21N 85 8W
Garrigues, France 28 E7 43 40N 3 55 E
Garrison, Ky., U.S.A. 157 F13 38 36N 83 10W
Garrison, Mont., U.S.A. 158 C7 46 31N 112 49W
Garrison, N. Dak., U.S.A. 154 B4 47 40N 101 25W
Garrison Res. = Sakakawea, L., U.S.A. 154 B4 47 30N 101 25W
Garron Pt., U.K. 23 A6 55 3N 5 59W
Garrovillas, Spain 43 F4 39 40N 6 33W
Garrucha, Spain 41 H3 37 11N 1 49W
Garry →, U.K. 22 E5 56 44N 3 47W
Garry, L., Canada 138 B9 65 58N 100 18W
Garsen, Kenya 118 C5 2 20 S 40 5 E
Gärsnäs, Sweden 17 J8 55 32N 14 10 E
Garson L., Canada 143 B6 56 19N 110 2W
Garstang, U.K. 20 D5 53 55N 2 46W
Gartempe →, France 28 B4 46 47N 0 49 E
Gartz, Germany 30 B10 53 13N 14 22 E
Garu, Ghana 113 C4 10 55N 0 11W
Garu, India 93 H11 23 40N 84 14 E
Garub, Namibia 116 D2 26 37 S 16 0 E
Garut, Indonesia 85 D3 7 14 S 107 53 E
Garvão, Portugal 43 H2 37 42N 8 21W
Garvie Mts., N.Z. 131 F3 45 30 S 168 50 E
Garwa = Garoua, Cameroon 113 D7 9 19N 13 21 E
Garwa, India 93 G10 24 11N 83 47 E
Garwolin, Poland 55 G8 51 55N 21 38 E
Gary, U.S.A. 157 C9 41 36N 87 20W
Garz, Germany 30 A9 54 19N 13 20 E
Garzê, China 76 B3 31 38N 100 1 E
Garzón, Colombia 168 C2 2 10N 75 40W
Gas City, U.S.A. 157 D11 40 29N 85 37W
Gas-San, Japan 70 E10 38 32N 140 1 E
Gasan, Phil. 80 E3 13 19N 121 51 E
Gasan Kuli = Esenguly, Turkmenistan 66 F6 37 37N 53 59 E
Gaschurn, Austria 33 C10 46 59N 10 2 E
Gascogne, France 28 E4 43 45N 0 20 E
Gascogne, G. de, Europe 28 E2 44 0N 2 0W
Gasconade, U.S.A. 156 F5 38 40N 91 34W
Gasconade →, U.S.A. 156 F5 38 41N 91 33W
Gascony = Gascogne, France 28 E4 43 45N 0 20 E
Gascoyne →, Australia 125 D1 24 52 S 113 37 E
Gascoyne Junction, Australia 125 E2 25 2 S 115 17 E
Gascueña, Spain 40 E2 40 18N 2 31W
Gash, Wadi →, Ethiopia 107 D4 16 48N 35 51 E
Gash-Setit ⌓, Eritrea 107 D4 15 12N 36 58 E
Gashagar, Nigeria 113 C7 13 22N 12 47 E
Gashaka, Nigeria 113 D7 7 20N 11 29 E
Gashaka-Gumti △, Nigeria 113 D7 7 23N 11 34 E
Gasherbrum, Pakistan 93 B7 35 40N 76 40 E
Gashua, Nigeria 113 C7 12 54N 11 0 E
Gasmata, Papua N. G. 132 D6 6 17 S 150 20 E
Gasparilla I., U.S.A. 153 J7 26 46N 82 16W
Gasparillo, Trin. & Tob. 169 F9 10 18N 61 26W
Gaspé, Canada 141 C7 48 52N 64 30W
Gaspé, C., Canada 141 C7 48 48N 64 7W
Gaspé Pen. = Gaspésie, Pén. de la, Canada 141 C6 48 45N 65 40W
Gaspésie ⌓, Canada 141 C6 48 55N 66 10W
Gaspésie, Pén. de la, Canada 141 C6 48 45N 65 40W
Gassan, Burkina Faso 112 C4 12 49N 3 12W
Gassen = Jasień, Poland 55 G2 51 46N 15 0 E
Gassol, Nigeria 113 D7 8 34N 10 25 E
Gasteiz = Vitoria-Gasteiz, Spain 40 C2 42 50N 2 41W
Gaston, U.S.A. 152 B8 33 49N 81 5W
Gastonia, U.S.A. 149 H5 35 16N 81 11W
Gastoúni, Greece 48 D3 37 51N 21 15 E
Gastoúri, Greece 38 B9 39 34N 19 54 E
Gastre, Argentina 176 B3 42 20 S 69 15W
Gästrikland, Sweden 16 D10 60 45N 16 40 E
Gata, C., Cyprus 39 F9 34 34N 33 2 E
Gata, C. de, Spain 41 J2 36 41N 2 13W
Gata, Sierra de, Spain 42 E4 40 20N 6 45W
Gataga →, Canada 142 B3 58 35N 126 59W
Gătaia, Romania 52 E6 45 26N 21 30 E
Gatchina, Russia 58 C6 59 35N 30 9 E
Gatehouse of Fleet, U.K. 22 G4 54 53N 4 12W
Gates, U.S.A. 150 C7 43 9N 77 42W
Gates of the Arctic △, U.S.A. 144 C10 67 20N 152 0W
Gateshead, U.K. 20 C6 54 57N 1 35W
Gatesville, U.S.A. 155 K6 31 26N 97 45W
Gateway ⌓, U.S.A. 151 F11 40 26N 73 59W
Gaths, Zimbabwe 119 G3 20 2 S 30 32 E
Gatico, Chile 174 A1 22 29 S 70 20W
Gâtinais, France 27 D9 48 5N 2 40 E
Gâtine, Hauteurs de, France 28 B3 46 35N 0 45W
Gatineau, Canada 151 A9 45 29N 75 38W
Gatineau △, Canada 140 C4 45 40N 76 0W
Gatineau →, Canada 140 C4 45 27N 75 42W
Gattaran, Phil. 80 B3 18 4N 121 38 E
Gattinara, Italy 44 C5 45 37N 8 22 E
Gatton, Australia 127 D5 27 32 S 152 17 E
Gatun, L., Panama 164 E4 9 7N 79 56W
Gatwick, London ✈ (LGW), U.K. 21 F7 51 10N 0 11W
Gatyana, S. Africa 117 E4 32 16 S 28 31 E
Gau, Fiji 133 B2 18 2 S 179 18 E
Gaua, Vanuatu 133 D5 14 15 S 167 30 E
Gaucín, Spain 43 J5 36 31N 5 19W
Gauer L., Canada 143 B9 57 0N 97 50W
Gauhati = Guwahati, India 90 B3 26 10N 91 45 E
Gauja →, Latvia 15 H21 57 10N 24 16 E
Gaula →, Norway 18 A7 63 21N 10 14 E
Gaupne, Norway 18 C4 61 25N 7 18 E
Gaurdak = Gowurdak, Turkmenistan 65 E3 37 50N 66 4 E
Gauri Phanta, India 93 E9 28 41N 80 36 E
Gauribidanur, India 95 H3 13 37N 77 32 E
Gausta, Norway 18 E5 59 48N 8 40 E
Gauteng □, S. Africa 117 D4 26 0 S 28 0 E
Gāv Koshī, Iran 97 D8 28 38N 57 12 E
Gāvakān, Iran 97 D7 29 37N 53 10 E
Gavallai △, Liberia 112 D3 5 8N 7 20W
Gavarnie, France 28 F3 42 44N 0 1W
Gavāter, Iran 97 E9 25 10N 61 31 E
Gāvbandī, Iran 97 E7 27 12N 53 4 E
Gavdhopoúla, Greece 39 F5 34 56N 24 0 E
Gávdhos, Greece 39 F5 34 50N 24 5 E
Gavdos = Gávdhos, Greece 39 F5 34 50N 24 5 E
Gavi, Italy 44 D5 44 41N 8 49 E
Gavião, Portugal 43 F3 39 28N 7 56W
Gaviota, U.S.A. 161 L6 34 29N 120 13W
Gāvkhūnī, Bāţlāq-e, Iran 97 C7 32 6N 52 52 E
Gävle, Sweden 16 D11 60 40N 17 9 E
Gävleborgs län □, Sweden 16 C10 61 30N 16 15 E
Gävlebukten, Sweden 16 D11 60 40N 17 20 E
Gavorrano, Italy 44 F7 42 55N 10 54 E
Gavray, France 26 D5 48 55N 1 20W
Gavrilov Yam, Russia 58 D10 57 18N 39 49 E
Gávrion, Greece 48 D6 37 54N 24 44 E
Gawachab, Namibia 116 D2 27 4 S 17 55 E
Gawai, Burma 90 B6 27 56N 97 30 E
Gawilgarh Hills, India 94 D3 21 15N 76 45 E
Gawler, Australia 128 C3 34 30 S 138 42 E
Gawler Ranges, Australia 128 B2 32 20 S 136 0 E
Gawu, Nigeria 113 D6 9 14N 6 52 E
Gaxun Nur, China 68 B5 42 22N 100 30 E
Gay, Russia 64 F7 51 27N 58 27 E
Gay, U.S.A. 152 B5 33 6N 84 35W
Gaya, India 93 G11 24 47N 85 4 E
Gaya, Niger 113 C5 11 52N 3 28 E
Gaya, Nigeria 113 C6 11 57N 9 0 E
Gayéri, Burkina Faso 113 C5 12 39N 0 29 E
Gaylord, U.S.A. 148 C3 45 2N 84 41W
Gayndah, Australia 127 D5 25 35 S 151 32 E
Gayny, Russia 64 A5 60 18N 54 19 E
Gaysin = Haysyn, Ukraine 53 B14 48 57N 29 25 E
Gayvoron = Hayvoron, Ukraine 53 B14 48 22N 29 52 E
Gaza, Gaza Strip 103 D3 31 30N 34 28 E
Gaza □, Mozam. 117 C5 23 10 S 32 45 E
Gaza Strip ⊠, Asia 103 D3 31 29N 34 25 E
Gazalkent, Uzbekistan 65 C4 41 33N 69 46 E
Gazanjyk, Turkmenistan 97 B7 39 16N 55 32 E
Gazaoua, Niger 113 C6 13 32N 7 55 E
Gāzbor, Iran 97 D8 28 5N 58 51 E
Gazelle, Récif de la, N. Cal. 133 T19 20 10 S 165 30 E
Gazelle Pen., Papua N. G. 132 C6 4 40 S 152 0 E
Gazi, Dem. Rep. of the Congo 118 B1 1 3N 24 30 E
Gaziantep, Turkey 100 D7 37 6N 37 23 E
Gazimağosa = Famagusta, Cyprus 39 E9 35 8N 33 55 E
Gazipaşa, Turkey 100 D5 36 16N 32 18 E
Gbarnga, Liberia 112 D3 7 19N 9 13W
Gbekebo, Nigeria 113 D5 6 20N 4 56 E
Gboko, Nigeria 113 D6 7 17N 9 4 E
Gbongan, Nigeria 113 D5 7 28N 4 20 E
Gcoverega, Botswana 116 B3 19 8 S 24 18 E
Gcuwa, S. Africa 117 E4 32 20 S 28 11 E
Gdańsk, Poland 54 D5 54 22N 18 40 E
Gdansk ✈ (GDN), Poland 54 D5 54 22N 18 30 E
Gdańska, Zatoka, Poland 54 D6 54 30N 19 20 E
Gdingen = Gdynia, Poland 54 D5 54 35N 18 33 E
Gdov, Russia 15 G22 58 48N 27 55 E
Gdynia, Poland 54 D5 54 35N 18 33 E
Geba →, Guinea-Biss. 112 C1 11 46N 15 36W
Gebe, Indonesia 83 A3 0 5N 129 25 E
Gebeciler, Turkey 49 C12 38 46N 30 46 E
Gebeit Mine, Sudan 106 C4 21 3N 36 29 E
Gebel Abyad, Sudan 106 D2 19 0N 28 0 E
Gebel Iweibid, Egypt 106 H8 30 8N 32 13 E
Gebze, Turkey 51 F13 40 47N 29 25 E
Gecha, Ethiopia 107 F4 7 30N 35 18 E
Gedaref, Sudan 107 E4 14 2N 35 28 E
Gedaref □, Sudan 107 E4 14 0N 35 0 E
Gede, Tanjung, Indonesia 84 D3 6 46 S 105 12 E
Gediz, Turkey 49 B11 39 1N 29 24 E
Gediz →, Turkey 49 C8 38 35N 26 48 E
Gedo, Ethiopia 107 F4 9 2N 37 25 E
Gèdre, France 28 F4 42 47N 0 2 E
Gedser, Denmark 17 K5 54 35N 11 55 E
Gedung, Pulau, Malaysia 87 c 5 17N 100 23 E
Geegully Cr. →, Australia 124 C3 18 32 S 123 41 E
Geel, Belgium 24 C4 51 10N 4 59 E
Geelong, Australia 128 E6 38 10 S 144 22 E
Geelvink B. = Cenderwasih, Teluk, Indonesia 79 E9 3 0 S 135 20 E
Geelvink Chan., Australia 125 E1 28 30 S 114 0 E
Geesthacht, Germany 30 B6 53 26N 10 22 E
Geidam, Nigeria 113 C7 12 57N 11 57 E
Geikie →, Canada 143 B8 57 45N 103 52W
Geikie Gorge △, Australia 124 C4 18 3 S 125 41 E
Geilenkirchen, Germany 30 E2 50 57N 6 8 E
Geili, Sudan 107 D3 16 1N 32 37 E
Geilo, Norway 18 D5 60 32N 8 14 E
Geisingen, Germany 31 H4 47 54N 8 38 E
Geislingen, Germany 31 G5 48 37N 9 50 E
Geistown, U.S.A. 150 F6 40 18N 78 52W
Geita, Tanzania 118 C3 2 48 S 32 12 E
Geitastrand, Norway 18 A6 63 22N 9 56 E
Geithus, Norway 18 E6 59 57N 9 59 E
Gejiu, China 76 F4 23 20N 103 10 E
Gel →, Sudan 107 F2 7 5N 29 10 E
Gel, Meydān-e, Iran 97 D7 29 4N 54 50 E
Gel River, Sudan 107 F2 7 5N 29 10 E
Gela, Italy 47 E7 37 4N 14 15 E
Gela, G. di, Italy 47 F7 37 0N 14 20 E
Geladi, Ethiopia 120 C3 6 59N 46 30 E
Gelahun, Liberia 112 D2 7 55N 10 28W
Gelang Patah, Malaysia 87 d 1 27N 103 35 E
Gelderland □, Neths. 24 B6 52 5N 6 10 E
Geldern, Germany 30 D2 51 31N 6 20 E
Geldrop, Neths. 24 C5 51 25N 5 32 E
Geleen, Neths. 24 D5 50 57N 5 49 E
Gelehun, S. Leone 112 D2 8 20N 11 40W
Gelembe, Turkey 49 B9 39 10N 27 50 E
Gelemso, Ethiopia 107 F5 8 49N 40 31 E
Gelendost, Turkey 100 C4 38 7N 31 1 E
Gelendzhik, Russia 59 K10 44 33N 38 10 E
Gelib, Somali Rep. 120 D2 0 29N 42 46 E
Gelibolu, Turkey 51 F10 40 28N 26 43 E
Gelibolu Yarımadası, Turkey 51 F10 40 20N 26 30 E
Gelidonya Burnu, Turkey 100 D4 36 12N 30 24 E
Gelnhausen, Germany 31 E5 50 11N 9 11 E
Gelnica, Slovak Rep. 35 C13 48 51N 20 55 E
Gelsenkirchen, Germany 30 D3 51 32N 7 6 E
Gelterkinden, Switz. 32 B5 47 28N 7 51 E
Gelting, Germany 30 A5 54 45N 9 53 E
Gelugur, Malaysia 87 c 5 22N 100 18 E
Gemas, Malaysia 87 L4 2 37N 102 36 E
Gembloux, Belgium 24 D4 50 34N 4 43 E
Gembu, Nigeria 113 D7 6 42N 11 10 E
Gemena, Dem. Rep. of the Congo 114 B3 3 13N 19 48 E
Gemerek, Turkey 100 C7 39 15N 36 10 E
Gemla, Sweden 17 H8 56 52N 14 39 E
Gemlik, Turkey 51 F13 40 26N 29 9 E
Gemlik Körfezi, Turkey 51 F12 40 25N 28 55 E
Gemona del Friuli, Italy 45 B10 46 16N 13 9 E
Gemsa, Egypt 106 B3 27 39N 33 35 E
Gemsbok △, Botswana 116 D3 25 5 S 21 1 E
Gemünden, Germany 31 E5 50 3N 9 42 E
Genale, Somali Rep. 120 D2 1 48N 44 42 E
Genale →, Ethiopia 107 F4 6 2N 39 1 E
Genç, Turkey 101 C9 38 44N 40 34 E
Gençay, France 28 B4 46 23N 0 23 E
Geneina, Gebel, Egypt 106 B3 29 2N 33 55 E
General Acha, Argentina 174 D3 37 20 S 64 38W
General Alvear, Buenos Aires, Argentina 174 D4 36 0 S 60 0W
General Alvear, Mendoza, Argentina 174 D2 35 0 S 67 40W
General Artigas, Paraguay 174 B4 26 52 S 56 16W
General Belgrano, Argentina 174 D4 36 35 S 58 47W
General Bernardo O'Higgins, Antarctica 7 C18 63 0 S 58 3W
General Cabrera, Argentina 174 C3 32 53 S 63 52W
General Carrera, L., Chile 176 C2 46 35 S 72 0W
General Cepeda, Mexico 162 B4 25 23N 101 27W
General Conesa, Argentina 176 B4 40 6 S 64 25W
General Eugenio A. Garay, Paraguay 173 E5 20 31 S 62 8W
General Germán Busch = Villa Abecia, Bolivia 174 A2 21 0 S 68 18W
General Guido, Argentina 174 D4 36 40 S 57 50W
General Juan Madariaga, Argentina 174 D4 37 0 S 57 0W
General La Madrid, Argentina 174 D3 37 17 S 61 20W
General Lorenzo Vintter, Argentina 176 B4 40 45 S 64 26W
General Luna, Phil. 80 E4 13 41N 122 10 E
General MacArthur, Phil. 81 F5 11 18N 125 28 E
General Martin Miguel de Güemes, Argentina 174 A3 24 50 S 65 0W
General Paz, Argentina 174 B4 27 45 S 57 36W
General Pico, Argentina 174 D3 35 45 S 63 50W
General Pinedo, Argentina 174 B3 27 15 S 61 20W
General Pinto, Argentina 174 C3 34 45 S 61 50W
General Sampaio, Brazil 170 B4 4 2 S 39 29W
General Santos, Phil. 81 H5 6 5N 125 14 E
General Tinio, Phil. 80 D3 15 39N 121 10 E
General Toshevo, Bulgaria 51 C12 43 42N 28 6 E
General Trevino, Mexico 163 B5 26 14N 99 29W
General Trías, Mexico 162 B3 28 21N 106 22W
General Uriburu = Zárate, Argentina 174 C4 34 7 S 59 0W
General Viamonte, Argentina 174 D3 35 1 S 61 3W
General Villegas, Argentina 174 D3 35 5 S 63 0W
General Vintter, L., Argentina 176 B2 43 55 S 71 40W
Generoso, Mte., Switz. 33 E8 45 56N 9 2 E
Generoso Ponce = Jaciparaná, Brazil 173 B5 9 15 S 64 23W
Genesee, Idaho, U.S.A. 158 C5 46 33N 116 56W
Genesee, Pa., U.S.A. 150 E7 41 59N 77 54W
Genesee →, U.S.A. 150 C7 43 16N 77 36W
Geneseo, Ill., U.S.A. 156 C6 41 27N 90 9W
Geneseo, N.Y., U.S.A. 150 D7 42 48N 77 49W
Geneva = Genève, Switz. 32 D2 46 12N 6 9 E
Geneva, Ala., U.S.A. 152 D4 31 2N 85 52W
Geneva, Ga., U.S.A. 152 C5 32 35N 84 33W
Geneva, Ill., U.S.A. 157 C8 41 53N 88 18W
Geneva, Ind., U.S.A. 157 D12 40 36N 84 58W
Geneva, N.Y., U.S.A. 150 D8 42 52N 76 59W

Geneva, Nebr., U.S.A. 154 E6 40 32N 97 36W
Geneva, Ohio, U.S.A. 150 E4 41 48N 80 57W
Geneva ✈ (GVA), Switz. 32 D2 46 14N 6 11 E
Geneva, L. = Léman, L., Europe 27 F13 46 26N 6 30 E
Geneva, L., U.S.A. 154 D10 42 38N 88 30W
Genève, Switz. 32 D2 46 12N 6 9 E
Genève □, Switz. 32 D2 46 10N 6 10 E
Geng, Afghan. 91 C1 31 22N 61 28 E
Gengenbach, Germany 31 G4 48 24N 8 1 E
Gengma, China 76 F2 23 32N 99 20 E
Genichesk = Henichesk, Ukraine 59 J8 46 12N 34 50 E
Genil →, Spain 43 H5 37 42N 5 19W
Genk, Belgium 24 D5 50 58N 5 32 E
Genkai-Nada, Japan 72 D2 34 0N 130 0 E
Genlis, France 27 E12 47 11N 5 12 E
Gennargentu, Mti. del, Italy 46 B2 40 1N 9 19 E
Gennes, France 26 E6 47 20N 0 17W
Genoa = Génova, Italy 44 D5 44 25N 8 57 E
Genoa, Australia 129 D8 37 29 S 149 35 E
Genoa, Ill., U.S.A. 157 B8 42 6N 88 42W
Genoa, N.Y., U.S.A. 151 D8 42 40N 76 32W
Genoa, Nebr., U.S.A. 154 E6 41 27N 97 44W
Genoa, Nev., U.S.A. 160 F7 39 2N 119 50W
Genoa →, Argentina 176 B2 44 55 S 70 5W
Genoa City, U.S.A. 157 B8 42 30N 88 20W
Génova, Italy 44 D5 44 25N 8 57 E
Genova ✈ (GOA), Italy 44 D5 44 25N 8 56 E
Génova, G. di, Italy 44 E6 44 0N 9 0 E
Genovesa, I., Ecuador 172 a 0 20N 89 58W
Genriyetty, Ostrov, Russia 67 B16 77 6N 156 30 E
Gent, Belgium 24 C3 51 2N 3 42 E
Genteng, Bali, Indonesia 79 J17 8 22 S 114 9 E
Genteng, Jawa, Indonesia 79 G12 7 22 S 106 24 E
Genthin, Germany 30 C8 52 25N 12 9 E
Gentio do Ouro, Brazil 170 D3 11 25 S 42 30W
Gentryville, U.S.A. 157 F9 38 6N 87 2W
Genyem, Indonesia 83 B6 2 46 S 140 12 E
Genzano di Lucánia, Italy 47 B9 40 51N 16 2 E
Genzano di Roma, Italy 45 G9 41 42N 12 41 E
Geoagiu, Romania 53 E8 45 55N 23 12 E
Geographe B., Australia 125 F2 33 30 S 115 15 E
Geographe Chan., Australia 125 D1 24 30 S 113 0 E
Geokchay = Göyçay, Azerbaijan 61 K8 40 42N 47 43 E
Georg Forster, Antarctica 7 D3 71 0 S 12 0 E
Georg von Neumayer, Antarctica 7 D17 71 0 S 68 30W
Georga, Zemlya, Russia 66 A5 80 30N 49 0 E
George, S. Africa 116 E3 33 58 S 22 29 E
George →, Canada 141 A6 58 49N 66 10W
George, L., N.S.W., Australia 129 C8 35 10 S 149 25 E
George, L., S. Austral., Australia 128 D4 37 25 S 140 0 E
George, L., W. Austral., Australia 124 D3 22 45 S 123 40 E
George, L., Uganda 118 B3 0 5N 30 10 E
George, L., Fla., U.S.A. 153 F8 29 17N 81 36W
George, L., N.Y., U.S.A. 151 C11 43 37N 73 33W
George Gill Ra., Australia 124 D5 24 22 S 131 45 E
George I., St. Helena 9 h 15 58 S 5 38W
George Pt., Australia 126 J6 20 6 S 148 36 E
George River = Kangiqsualujjuaq, Canada 139 C13 58 30N 65 59W
George Sound, N.Z. 131 E2 44 52 S 167 25 E
George Town, Australia 127 G4 41 6 S 146 49 E
George Town, Bahamas 164 B4 23 33N 75 47W
George Town, Cayman Is. 164 C3 19 20N 81 24W
George Town, Malaysia 87 c 5 25N 100 20 E
George V Land, Antarctica 7 C10 69 0 S 148 0 E
George VI Sound, Antarctica 7 D17 71 0 S 68 0W
George West, U.S.A. 155 L5 28 20N 98 7W
Georgetown = Janjanbureh, Gambia 112 C2 13 30N 14 47W
Georgetown, Ascension I. 9 g 7 56 S 14 25W
Georgetown, Australia 126 B3 18 17 S 143 33 E
Georgetown, Ont., Canada 140 D4 43 40N 79 56W
Georgetown, P.E.I., Canada 141 C7 46 13N 62 24W
Georgetown, Guyana 169 B6 6 50N 58 12W
Georgetown, Calif., U.S.A. 160 G6 38 54N 120 50W
Georgetown, Colo., U.S.A. 158 G11 39 42N 105 42W
Georgetown, Fla., U.S.A. 153 F8 29 23N 81 38W
Georgetown, Ga., U.S.A. 152 D4 31 53N 85 6W
Georgetown, Ill., U.S.A. 157 E9 39 59N 87 38W
Georgetown, Ky., U.S.A. 157 F12 38 13N 84 33W
Georgetown, N.Y., U.S.A. 151 D9 42 46N 75 44W
Georgetown, Ohio, U.S.A. 157 F13 38 52N 83 54W
Georgetown, S.C., U.S.A. 149 J6 33 23N 79 17W
Georgetown, Tex., U.S.A. 155 K6 30 38N 97 41W
Georgia □, U.S.A. 152 C6 32 50N 83 15W
Georgia ■, Asia 61 J6 42 0N 43 0 E
Georgia, Str. of, Canada 142 D4 49 25N 124 0W
Georgian B., Canada 140 C3 45 15N 81 0W
Georgian Bay Islands △, Canada 140 D4 44 53N 79 52W
Georgina →, Australia 126 C2 23 30 S 139 47 E
Georgina I., Canada 150 B5 44 22N 79 17W
Georgiu-Dezh = Liski, Russia 59 G10 51 3N 39 30 E
Georgiyevsk, Russia 61 H6 44 12N 43 28 E
Georgsmarienhütte, Germany 30 C4 52 13N 8 3 E
Gera, Germany 30 E8 50 53N 12 4 E
Geraardsbergen, Belgium 24 D3 50 45N 3 53 E
Geral, Serra, Bahia, Brazil 171 D3 14 0 S 41 0W
Geral, Serra, Goiás, Brazil 170 D2 11 15 S 46 30W
Geral, Serra, Sta. Catarina, Brazil 175 B6 26 25 S 50 0W
Geral de Goiás, Serra, Brazil 171 D2 12 0 S 46 0W
Geral do Paranã, Serra, Brazil 171 E2 15 0 S 47 30W
Gerald, U.S.A. 156 F5 38 24N 91 20W
Geraldine, N.Z. 131 E6 44 5 S 171 15 E
Geraldine, U.S.A. 158 C8 47 36N 110 16W
Geraldton = Innisfail, Australia 126 B4 17 33 S 146 5 E
Geraldton, Australia 125 E1 28 48 S 114 32 E
Geraldton, Canada 140 C2 49 44N 86 59W
Geranium, Australia 128 C4 35 23 S 140 11 E
Gérardmer, France 27 D13 48 3N 6 50 E
Gercüş, Turkey 101 D9 37 34N 41 23 E
Gerdine, Mt., U.S.A. 144 F9 61 35N 152 27W
Gerede, Turkey 100 B5 40 45N 32 10 E
Gerês, Sierra do, Portugal 42 D3 41 48N 8 0W
Gereshk, Afghan. 91 C2 31 47N 64 35 E
Geretsried, Germany 31 H7 47 51N 11 28 E
Gérgal, Spain 41 H2 37 7N 2 31W
Gerik, Malaysia 87 K3 5 50N 101 15 E
Gering, U.S.A. 154 E3 41 50N 103 40W
Gerlach, U.S.A. 158 F4 40 39N 119 21W
Gerlachovský štit, Slovak Rep. 35 B13 49 11N 20 7 E
Gerlogubi, Ethiopia 120 C3 6 53N 45 3 E
German East Africa = Tanzania ■, Africa 118 D3 6 0 S 34 0 E
German Planina, Macedonia 50 D6 42 20N 22 0 E
German South West Africa = Namibia ■, Africa 116 C2 22 0 S 18 9 E
Germania Land, Greenland 10 B9 77 5N 19 30W
Germansen Landing, Canada 142 B4 55 43N 124 40W
Germantown, Ohio, U.S.A. 157 E12 39 38N 84 22W
Germantown, Tenn., U.S.A. 155 M10 35 5N 89 49W
Germantown, Wis., U.S.A. 157 A8 43 14N 88 6W
Germany ■, Europe 30 E6 51 0N 10 0 E
Germencik, Turkey 49 D9 37 52N 27 37 E
Germering, Germany 31 G7 48 8N 11 22 E
Germersheim, Germany 31 F4 49 12N 8 22 E
Germī, Iran 97 B6 39 1N 48 3 E
Germiston, S. Africa 117 D4 26 15 S 28 10 E
Gernene, Algeria 111 D5 21 40N 2 24 E
Gernika-Lumo, Spain 40 B2 43 19N 2 40W
Gernsheim, Germany 31 F4 49 45N 8 30 E
Gero, Japan 73 B9 35 48N 137 14 E
Gerogery, Australia 129 C7 35 50 S 147 1 E
Gerokgak, Indonesia 79 J17 8 11 S 114 27 E
Gerolzhofen, Germany 31 F6 49 54N 10 21 E
Gerona = Girona, Spain 40 D7 41 58N 2 46 E
Gerrard, Canada 142 C5 50 30N 117 17W
Gerringong, Australia 129 C9 34 46 S 150 47 E
Gers □, France 28 E4 43 35N 0 30 E
Gers →, France 28 D4 44 9N 0 39 E
Gersfeld, Germany 30 E5 50 27N 9 56 E
Gersoppa Falls, India 95 G2 14 12N 74 46 E
Gersthofen, Germany 31 G6 48 25N 10 53 E
Gertak Sanggul, Malaysia 87 c 5 17N 100 12 E
Gertak Sanggul, Tanjung, Malaysia 87 c 5 16N 100 11 E
Gerung, Indonesia 79 K19 8 43 S 116 7 E
Géryville = El Bayadh, Algeria 111 B5 33 40N 1 1 E
Gerzat, France 28 C7 45 48N 3 8 E
Gerze, Turkey 100 B6 41 48N 35 12 E
Geseke, Germany 30 D4 51 38N 8 31 E
Geser, Indonesia 83 B4 3 50 S 130 54 E
Gesira △, Somali Rep. 120 D2 1 58N 44 59 E
Gesso →, Italy 44 D4 44 24N 7 33 E
Gestro, Wabi →, Ethiopia 107 G5 4 12N 42 2 E
Getafe, Spain 42 E7 40 18N 3 44W
Getinge, Sweden 17 H6 56 49N 12 44 E
Gettysburg, Pa., U.S.A. 148 F7 39 50N 77 14W
Gettysburg, S. Dak., U.S.A. 154 C5 45 1N 99 57W
Getxo, Spain 40 B2 43 21N 2 59W
Getz Ice Shelf, Antarctica 7 D14 75 0 S 130 0W
Geureudong, Gunong, Indonesia 84 B1 4 13N 96 42 E
Geurie, Australia 129 B8 32 22 S 148 50 E
Gevaş, Turkey 101 C10 38 15N 43 6 E
Gévaudan, France 28 D7 44 40N 3 40 E
Gevgelija, Macedonia 50 E6 41 9N 22 30 E
Gévora →, Spain 43 G4 38 53N 6 57W
Gevrai, India 94 E2 19 16N 75 45 E
Gewani, Ethiopia 107 E5 10 12N 40 40 E
Gex, France 27 F13 46 21N 6 3 E
Geyikli, Turkey 49 B8 39 48N 26 12 E
Geyser, U.S.A. 158 C8 47 16N 110 30W
Geyserville, U.S.A. 160 G4 38 42N 122 54W
Geysir, Iceland 11 C6 64 19N 20 18W
Geyve, Turkey 100 B4 40 30N 30 18 E
Ghâbat el Arab = Wang Kai, Sudan 107 F2 9 3N 29 23 E
Ghabeish, Sudan 107 E2 12 9N 27 21 E
Ghafurov, Tajikistan 65 C4 40 13N 69 43 E
Ghaggar →, India 92 E6 29 30N 74 53 E
Ghaghara →, India 93 G11 25 45N 84 40 E
Ghaghat →, Bangla. 90 C2 25 19N 89 38 E
Ghaghe, Solomon Is. 133 L10 7 24 S 158 15 E
Ghagra, India 93 H11 23 17N 84 33 E
Ghagra →, India 93 F9 27 29N 81 9 E
Ghajn Tuffieha Bay, Malta 38 F7 35 56N 14 21 E
Ghajnsielem, Malta 38 E7 36 2N 14 17 E
Ghalla, Wadi el →, Sudan 107 E2 10 25N 27 32 E
Ghana ■, W. Afr. 113 D4 8 0N 1 0W
Ghansor, India 93 H9 22 39N 80 1 E
Ghanzi, Botswana 116 C3 21 50 S 21 34 E
Gharb, Malta 38 E6 36 4N 14 13 E
Gharb el Istiwa'iya □, Sudan 107 G3 5 0N 30 0 E
Gharb Kordofân □, Sudan 107 E2 12 0N 28 0 E
Gharbîya, Es Sahrâ el, Egypt 106 B2 27 40N 26 30 E
Ghardaïa, Algeria 111 B5 32 20N 3 37 E
Ghârib, G., Egypt 106 B3 28 6N 32 54 E
Gharig, Sudan 107 E2 10 47N 27 33 E
Gharm, W. →, Oman 99 C7 19 57N 57 38 E
Gharyān, Libya 108 B2 32 10N 13 0 E
Gharyān □, Libya 108 B2 30 35N 13 0 E
Ghat, Libya 108 D2 24 59N 10 11 E
Ghatal, India 93 H12 22 40N 87 46 E
Ghatampur, India 93 F9 26 8N 80 13 E
Ghatgaon, India 94 D7 21 24N 85 53 E
Ghatprabha →, India 95 F2 16 15N 75 20 E
Ghats, Eastern, India 95 H4 14 0N 78 50 E
Ghats, Western, India 95 H2 14 0N 75 0 E
Ghatsila, India 93 H12 22 36N 86 29 E
Ghaţţī, Si. Arabia 96 D3 31 16N 37 31 E
Ghawdex = Gozo, Malta 38 E7 36 3N 14 15 E
Ghayl, Si. Arabia 98 B4 21 40N 46 20 E
Ghazal, Bahr el →, Chad 109 F3 13 0N 15 47 E
Ghazâl, Bahr el →, Sudan 107 F3 9 31N 30 25 E
Ghazaouet, Algeria 111 A4 35 8N 1 50W
Ghaziabad, India 92 E7 28 42N 77 26 E
Ghazipur, India 93 G10 25 38N 83 35 E
Ghaznī, Afghan. 91 B3 33 30N 68 28 E
Ghaznī □, Afghan. 91 B3 32 10N 68 20 E
Ghedi, Italy 44 C7 45 24N 10 16 E
Ghelari, Romania 52 E7 45 38N 22 45 E
Ghèlinsor, Somali Rep. 120 C3 6 28N 46 39 E
Ghent = Gent, Belgium 24 C3 51 2N 3 42 E
Gheorghe Gheorghiu-Dej = Oneşti, Romania 53 D11 46 17N 26 47 E
Gheorgheni, Romania 53 D10 46 43N 25 41 E
Gherla, Romania 53 C8 47 2N 23 57 E
Ghidigeni, Romania 53 D12 46 3N 27 30 E
Ghiffa, Italy 33 E7 45 58N 8 37 E
Ghilarza, Italy 46 B1 40 7N 8 50 E
Ghimeş-Făget, Romania 53 D11 46 35N 26 2 E
Ghīnah, Wādī al →, Si. Arabia 96 D3 30 27N 38 14 E
Ghisonaccia, France 29 F13 42 1N 9 26 E
Ghisoni, France 29 F13 42 7N 9 12 E
Ghizao, Afghan. 91 B2 33 20N 65 44 E
Ghizar →, Pakistan 93 A5 36 15N 73 43 E
Ghod →, India 94 E2 18 30N 74 35 E
Ghogha, India 94 D1 21 40N 72 20 E
Ghot Ogrein, Egypt 106 A2 31 10N 25 20 E
Ghotaru, India 92 F4 27 20N 70 1 E
Ghotki, Pakistan 92 E3 28 5N 69 21 E
Ghowr □, Afghan. 91 B2 34 0N 64 20 E
Ghudāf, W. al →, Iraq 101 F10 32 56N 43 30 E
Ghudāmis, Libya 108 B1 30 11N 9 29 E
Ghudāmis □, Libya 108 B2 30 25N 10 25 E
Ghughri, India 93 H9 22 39N 80 41 E
Ghugus, India 94 E4 19 58N 79 12 E
Ghulam Mohammad Barrage, Pakistan 92 G3 25 30N 68 20 E
Ghurayrah, Si. Arabia 98 C3 18 37N 42 41 E
Ghūrīān, Afghan. 91 B1 34 17N 61 25 E
Ghuzzayil, Sabkhat, Libya 108 C3 29 30N 19 30 E
Gia Dinh, Vietnam 87 G6 10 49N 106 42 E
Gia Lai = Plei Ku, Vietnam 86 F7 13 57N 108 0 E
Gia Nghia, Vietnam 87 G6 11 58N 107 42 E
Gia Ngoc, Vietnam 86 E7 14 50N 108 58 E
Gia Vuc, Vietnam 86 E7 14 42N 108 34 E
Giamama, Somali Rep. 120 D2 0 4N 42 44 E
Gianitsa = Yiannitsa, Greece 50 F6 40 46N 22 24 E
Giannutri, Italy 44 F8 42 15N 11 6 E
Giant Forest, U.S.A. 160 J8 36 36N 118 43W
Giant Mts. = Krkonoše, Czech Rep. 34 A8 50 50N 15 35 E
Giant Sequoia ⌓, U.S.A. 160 K8 36 0N 118 32W
Giants Causeway, U.K. 23 A5 55 16N 6 29W
Giant's Tank, Sri Lanka 95 K5 8 51N 80 2 E
Gianyar, Indonesia 79 K18 8 32 S 115 20 E
Giarabub = Al Jaghbūb, Libya 108 C4 29 42N 24 38 E
Giarre, Italy 47 E8 37 43N 15 11 E
Giaveno, Italy 44 C4 45 2N 7 21 E
Gibara, Cuba 164 B4 21 9N 76 11W
Gibb River, Australia 124 C4 16 26 S 126 26 E
Gibbon, U.S.A. 154 E5 40 45N 98 51W
Gibe →, Ethiopia 107 F4 7 20N 37 36 E
Gibellina Nuova, Italy 46 E5 37 47N 12 58 E
Gibeon, Namibia 116 D2 25 9 S 17 43 E
Gibraleón, Spain 43 H4 37 23N 6 58W
Gibraltar ☒, Europe 43 J5 36 7N 5 22W
Gibraltar, Str. of, Medit. S. 43 K5 35 55N 5 40W
Gibraltar Range △, Australia 127 D5 29 31 S 152 19 E
Gibson, U.S.A. 152 B7 33 14N 82 36W
Gibson City, U.S.A. 157 D8 40 28N 88 22W
Gibson Desert, Australia 124 D4 24 0 S 126 0 E
Gibsonburg, U.S.A. 157 C13 41 23N 83 19W
Gibsons, Canada 142 D4 49 24N 123 32W
Gibsonton, U.S.A. 153 H7 27 51N 82 23W
Gibsonville, U.S.A. 160 F6 39 46N 120 54W
Giddalur, India 95 G4 15 20N 78 57 E
Giddings, U.S.A. 155 K6 30 11N 96 56W
Gidole, Ethiopia 107 F4 5 40N 37 25 E
Giebnegáisi = Kebnekaise, Sweden 14 C18 67 53N 18 33 E
Gien, France 27 E9 47 40N 2 36 E
Giengen, Germany 31 G6 48 37N 10 14 E
Giessen, Germany 30 E4 50 34N 8 41 E
Gīfān, Iran 97 B8 37 54N 57 28 E
Gifatin, Geziret, Egypt 106 B3 27 10N 33 50 E
Gifford, U.S.A. 153 H9 27 40N 80 25W
Gifhorn, Germany 30 C6 52 30N 10 33 E
Gift Lake, Canada 142 B5 55 53N 115 49W
Gifu, Japan 73 B8 35 30N 136 45 E
Gifu □, Japan 73 B9 35 40N 137 0 E
Gigant, Russia 61 G5 46 28N 41 20 E
Giganta, Sa. de la, Mexico 162 B2 25 30N 111 30W
Gigen, Bulgaria 51 C8 43 40N 24 28 E
Gigha, U.K. 22 F3 55 42N 5 44W
Giglei, Somali Rep. 120 C3 5 25N 45 20 E
Gíglio, Italy 44 F7 42 20N 10 52 E
Gignac, France 28 E7 43 39N 3 32 E
Gignod, Italy 32 E4 45 47N 7 17 E
Gigüela →, Spain 43 F7 39 8N 3 44W
Gijón, Spain 42 B5 43 32N 5 42W
Gil I., Canada 142 C3 53 12N 129 15W
Gila →, U.S.A. 159 K6 32 43N 114 33W
Gila Bend, U.S.A. 159 K7 32 57N 112 43W
Gila Bend Mts., U.S.A. 159 K7 33 10N 113 0W
Gila Cliff Dwellings ⌓, U.S.A. 159 K9 33 2N 108 16W
Gīlān □, Iran 97 B6 37 0N 50 0 E
Gilău, Romania 53 D8 46 45N 23 23 E
Gilbert →, Australia 126 B3 16 35 S 141 15 E
Gilbert Is., Kiribati 134 G9 1 0N 172 0 E
Gilbert River, Australia 126 B3 18 9 S 142 52 E
Gilbués, Brazil 170 C2 9 50 S 45 21W
Gilead, U.S.A. 151 B14 44 24N 70 59W
Gilf el Kebîr, Hadabat el, Egypt 106 C2 23 50N 25 50 E
Gilford I., Canada 142 C3 50 40N 126 30W
Gilgandra, Australia 129 A8 31 43 S 148 39 E
Gilgil, Kenya 118 C4 0 30 S 36 20 E
Gilgit, India 93 B6 35 50N 74 15 E
Gilgit →, Pakistan 93 B6 35 44N 74 37 E
Gilgunnia, Australia 129 B7 32 26 S 146 2 E
Gili ⌓, Mozam. 119 F4 16 39 S 38 27 E
Gilimanuk, Indonesia 79 J17 8 10 S 114 26 E
Giljeva Planina, Serbia & M. 50 C3 43 9N 20 0 E
Gill Pt., St. Helena 9 h 15 58 S 5 38W
Gillam, Canada 143 B10 56 20N 94 40W
Gilleleje, Denmark 17 H6 56 8N 12 19 E
Gillen, L., Australia 125 E3 26 11 S 124 38 E
Gilles, L., Australia 128 B2 32 50 S 136 45 E
Gillespie, U.S.A. 156 E7 39 8N 89 49W
Gillespies Pt., N.Z. 131 D4 43 24 S 169 49 E
Gillette, U.S.A. 154 C2 44 18N 105 30W
Gilliat, Australia 126 C3 20 40 S 141 28 E
Gillingham, U.K. 21 F8 51 23N 0 33 E
Gilman, U.S.A. 157 D9 40 46N 88 0W
Gilman City, U.S.A. 156 D3 40 8N 93 53W
Gilmer, U.S.A. 155 J7 32 44N 94 57W
Gilmore, L., Australia 125 F3 32 29 S 121 37 E
Gilo →, Ethiopia 107 F3 8 10N 33 15 E
Gilort →, Romania 53 F8 44 38N 23 32 E
Gilroy, U.S.A. 160 H5 37 1N 121 34W
Giluwe, Mt., Papua N. G. 132 D2 6 8 S 143 52 E
Gimbi, Ethiopia 107 F4 9 3N 35 42 E
Gimie, Mt, St. Lucia 165 f 13 54N 61 0W
Gimli, Canada 143 C9 50 40N 97 0W
Gimo, Sweden 16 D12 60 11N 18 12 E
Gimone →, France 28 E5 44 0N 1 6 E
Gimont, France 28 E4 43 38N 0 52 E
Gimpu, Indonesia 82 B2 1 36 S 120 2 E
Gin →, Sri Lanka 95 L5 6 5N 80 7 E
Gin Gin, Australia 127 D5 25 0 S 151 58 E
Ginâh, Egypt 106 B3 25 21N 30 30 E
Ginatilan, Phil. 81 G4 9 34N 123 19 E
Gineifa, Egypt 106 H8 30 12N 32 25 E
Gingee, India 95 H4 12 15N 79 25 E
Gingin, Australia 125 F2 31 22 S 115 54 E
Gingindlovu, S. Africa 117 D5 29 2 S 31 30 E
Gingoog, Phil. 81 G5 8 50N 125 7 E
Ginir, Ethiopia 107 F5 7 6N 40 40 E
Gino, Pizzo di, Italy 33 D8 46 7N 9 10 E
Ginosa, Italy 47 B9 40 35N 16 45 E
Ginzo de Limia = Xinzo de Limia, Spain 42 C3 42 3N 7 47W
Giohar, Somali Rep. 120 D3 2 48N 45 30 E
Gióia, G. di, Italy 47 D8 38 30N 15 45 E
Gióia del Colle, Italy 47 B9 40 48N 16 55 E
Gióia Táuro, Italy 47 D8 38 25N 15 54 E
Gioiosa Iónica, Italy 47 D9 38 20N 16 18 E
Gioiosa Marea, Italy 47 D7 38 10N 14 54 E
Gióna, Óros, Greece 48 C4 38 38N 22 14 E
Giovi, Passo dei, Italy 44 D5 44 33N 8 57 E
Giovinazzo, Italy 47 A9 41 11N 16 40 E
Gippsland, Australia 129 D7 37 52 S 147 0 E
Gir △, India 92 J4 21 0N 71 0 E
Gir Hills, India 92 J4 21 0N 71 0 E
Girab, India 92 F4 26 2N 70 38 E
Girâfi, W. →, Egypt 103 F3 29 58N 34 39 E
Giraltovce, Slovak Rep. 35 B14 49 7N 21 32 E
Girard, Ga., U.S.A. 152 B8 33 3N 81 43W
Girard, Ill., U.S.A. 156 E7 39 27N 89 47W
Girard, Kans., U.S.A. 155 G7 37 31N 94 51W
Girard, Ohio, U.S.A. 150 E4 41 9N 80 42W
Girard, Pa., U.S.A. 150 E4 42 0N 80 19W
Girardot, Colombia 168 C3 4 18N 74 48W
Girdle Ness, U.K. 22 D6 57 9N 2 3W
Giresun, Turkey 101 B8 40 55N 38 30 E
Girga, Egypt 106 B3 26 17N 31 55 E
Girgenti = Agrigento, Italy 46 E6 37 19N 13 34 E
Girgir, C., Papua N. G. 132 B3 3 50 S 144 35 E
Giri →, Dem. Rep. of the Congo 114 B3 0 28N 17 59 E
Giri →, India 92 D7 30 28N 77 41 E
Giridih, India 93 G12 24 10N 86 21 E
Girifalco, Italy 47 D9 38 49N 16 25 E
Girilambone, Australia 129 A7 31 16 S 146 57 E
Girne = Kyrenia, Cyprus 39 E9 35 20N 33 20 E
Giro, Nigeria 113 C5 11 7N 4 42 E
Giromagny, France 27 E13 47 45N 6 50 E
Giron = Kiruna, Sweden 14 C19 67 52N 20 15 E
Girona, Spain 40 D7 41 58N 2 46 E
Girona □, Spain 40 C7 42 11N 2 30 E
Gironde □, France 28 D3 44 45N 0 30W
Gironde →, France 28 C2 45 32N 1 7W
Gironella, Spain 40 C6 42 2N 1 53 E
Girraween △, Australia 127 D5 28 46 S 151 54 E
Giru, Australia 126 B4 19 30 S 147 5 E
Girvan, U.K. 22 F4 55 14N 4 51W
Gisborne, Australia 128 D6 37 29 S 144 36 E
Gisborne, N.Z. 130 E7 38 39 S 178 5 E
Gisborne □, N.Z. 130 E6 38 30 S 178 0 E
Gisenyi, Rwanda 118 C2 1 41 S 29 15 E
Gislaved, Sweden 17 G7 57 19N 13 32 E
Gisors, France 27 C8 49 15N 1 47 E
Gissarskiy Khrebet, Tajikistan 65 D4 39 0N 69 0 E
Giswil, Switz. 32 C6 46 50N 8 11 E
Gitega, Burundi 118 C2 3 26 S 29 56 E
Githio = Yíthion, Greece 48 E4 36 46N 22 34 E
Gitschin = Jičín, Czech Rep. 34 A8 50 25N 15 28 E
Giuba →, Somali Rep. 120 D2 1 30N 42 35 E
Giubiasco, Switz. 33 D8 46 11N 9 1 E
Giugliano in Campania, Italy 47 B7 40 56N 14 12 E
Giulianova, Italy 45 F10 42 45N 13 57 E
Giurgeni, Romania 53 F12 44 45N 27 48 E
Giurgiu, Romania 53 G10 43 52N 25 57 E
Giurgiu □, Romania 53 F10 44 20N 26 0 E
Giurgiuleşti, Moldova 53 E13 45 29N 28 12 E
Give, Denmark 17 J3 55 51N 9 13 E
Givet, France 27 B11 50 8N 4 49 E
Givors, France 29 C8 45 35N 4 45 E
Givry, France 27 F11 46 41N 4 46 E
Giyon, Ethiopia 107 F4 8 33N 38 1 E
Giza = El Gîza, Egypt 106 J7 30 0N 31 10 E
Gizhduvan, Uzbekistan 65 C2 40 6N 64 41 E
Gizhiga, Russia 67 C17 62 3N 160 30 E
Gizhiginskaya Guba, Russia 67 C16 61 0N 158 0 E
Gizo, Solomon Is. 133 M9 8 7 S 156 50 E
Giżycko, Poland 54 D8 54 2N 21 48 E
Gizzeria, Italy 47 D9 38 59N 16 12 E
Gjalicë e Lumës, Mal., Albania 50 D4 42 2N 20 25 E
Gjegjan, Albania 50 E4 41 58N 20 3 E
Gjendesheim, Norway 18 C5 61 30N 8 48 E
Gjerstad, Norway 18 F6 58 54N 9 1 E
Gjevilvatnet, Norway 18 B6 62 43N 9 23 E
Gjirokastër, Albania 50 F4 40 7N 20 10 E
Gjoa Haven, Canada 138 B10 68 38N 95 53W
Gjøra, Norway 18 B6 62 33N 9 4 E
Gjøvik, Norway 18 D7 60 47N 10 43 E
Gjuhës, Kep i, Albania 50 F3 40 28N 19 15 E
Glace Bay, Canada 141 C8 46 11N 59 58W
Glacier △, Canada 142 C5 51 15N 117 30W
Glacier △, U.S.A. 158 B7 48 30N 113 18W
Glacier Bay, U.S.A. 144 G14 58 40N 136 0W
Glacier Bay △, U.S.A. 142 B1 58 45N 136 30W
Glacier Peak, U.S.A. 158 B3 48 7N 121 7W
Gladewater, U.S.A. 155 J7 32 33N 94 56W
Gladstone, Queens., Australia 126 C5 23 52 S 151 16 E
Gladstone, S. Austral., Australia 128 B3 33 15 S 138 22 E
Gladstone, Canada 143 C9 50 13N 98 57W
Gladstone, Ill., U.S.A. 156 D6 40 52N 90 57W
Gladstone, Mich., U.S.A. 148 C2 45 51N 87 1W
Gladstone, Mo., U.S.A. 156 E2 39 13N 94 35W
Gladwin, U.S.A. 148 D3 43 59N 84 29W
Glafsfjorden, Sweden 16 E6 59 30N 12 37 E
Glagah, Indonesia 79 J17 8 13 S 114 18 E
Głagów Małapolski, Poland 55 H8 50 10N 21 56 E
Glåma = Glomma →, Norway 18 E7 59 12N 10 57 E
Gláma, Iceland 11 B4 65 48N 23 0W
Glamis, U.S.A. 161 N11 32 55N 115 5W
Glamoč, Bos.-H. 45 D13 44 3N 16 51 E
Glamorgan, Vale of □, U.K. 21 F4 51 28N 3 25W
Glåmos, Norway 18 B8 62 41N 11 25 E
Glamsbjerg, Denmark 17 J4 55 17N 10 6 E
Gland, Switz. 32 D2 46 26N 6 16 E
Glarner Alpen, Switz. 33 C8 46 50N 9 0 E
Glärnisch, Switz. 33 C8 47 0N 9 0 E
Glarus, Switz. 33 B8 47 3N 9 4 E
Glarus □, Switz. 33 C8 47 0N 9 5 E
Glasco, Kans., U.S.A. 154 F6 39 22N 97 50W
Glasco, N.Y., U.S.A. 151 D11 42 3N 73 57W
Glasgow, U.K. 22 F4 55 51N 4 15W
Glasgow, Ky., U.S.A. 148 G3 37 0N 85 55W
Glasgow, Mo., U.S.A. 156 E4 39 14N 92 51W
Glasgow, Mont., U.S.A. 158 B10 48 12N 106 38W
Glasgow, City of □, U.K. 22 F4 55 51N 4 12W
Glasgow International ✈ (GLA), U.K. 22 F4 55 51N 4 21W
Glaslyn, Canada 143 C7 53 22N 108 21W
Glastonbury, U.K. 21 F5 51 9N 2 43W
Glastonbury, U.S.A. 151 E12 41 43N 72 37W
Glatt →, Switz. 33 B7 47 28N 8 32 E
Glattfelden, Switz. 33 A7 47 33N 8 30 E
Glatz = Kłodzko, Poland 55 H3 50 28N 16 38 E
Glauchau, Germany 30 E8 50 49N 12 31 E
Glava, Sweden 16 E6 59 33N 12 35 E
Glavice, Croatia 45 E13 43 43N 16 41 E
Glazov, Russia 60 A11 58 9N 52 40 E
Gleichen, Canada 142 C6 50 52N 113 3W
Gleisdorf, Austria 34 D8 47 6N 15 44 E
Gleiwitz = Gliwice, Poland 55 H5 50 22N 18 41 E
Glen, U.S.A. 151 B13 44 7N 71 11W
Glen Affric, U.K. 22 D3 57 17N 5 1W
Glen Afton, N.Z. 130 D4 37 37 S 175 4 E
Glen Canyon, U.S.A. 159 H8 37 30N 110 40W
Glen Canyon ⌓, U.S.A. 159 H8 37 15N 111 0W
Glen Canyon Dam, U.S.A. 159 H8 36 57N 111 29W
Glen Coe, U.K. 22 E3 56 40N 5 0W
Glen Cove, U.S.A. 151 F11 40 52N 73 38W
Glen Garry, U.K. 22 D3 57 3N 5 7W
Glen Innes, Australia 127 D5 29 44 S 151 44 E
Glen Lyon, U.S.A. 151 E8 41 10N 76 5W
Glen Massey, N.Z. 130 D4 37 38 S 175 2 E
Glen Mor, U.K. 22 D4 57 9N 4 37W
Glen More ⌓, U.K. 22 D5 57 8N 3 40W
Glen Moriston, U.K. 22 D4 57 11N 4 52W
Glen Robertson, Canada 151 A10 45 22N 74 30W
Glen Spean, U.K. 22 E4 56 53N 4 40W
Glen Ullin, U.S.A. 154 B4 46 49N 101 50W
Glénan, Îs. de, France 26 E3 47 42N 4 0W
Glenariff △, Ireland 23 A5 55 2N 6 10W
Glenavy, N.Z. 131 E6 44 54 S 171 7 E
Glenburn, Australia 129 D6 37 27 S 145 26 E
Glencoe, Canada 150 D3 42 45N 81 43W
Glencoe, S. Africa 117 D5 28 11 S 30 11 E
Glencoe, Ala., U.S.A. 152 B4 33 57N 85 56W
Glencoe, Minn., U.S.A. 154 C7 44 46N 94 9W
Glendale, Ariz., U.S.A. 159 K7 33 32N 112 11W
Glendale, Calif., U.S.A. 161 L8 34 9N 118 15W
Glendale, Fla., U.S.A. 152 E3 30 52N 86 7W
Glendale, Zimbabwe 119 F3 17 22 S 31 5 E
Glendive, U.S.A. 154 B2 47 7N 104 43W
Glendo, U.S.A. 154 D2 42 30N 105 2W
Glenelg, Australia 128 C3 34 58 S 138 31 E
Glenelg →, Australia 128 E4 38 4 S 140 59 E
Glenfield, U.S.A. 151 C9 43 43N 75 24W
Glengarriff, Ireland 23 E2 51 45N 9 34W
Glenham, N.Z. 131 G3 46 26 S 168 52 E
Glenhope, N.Z. 131 B7 41 40 S 172 39 E
Glenmary, Mt., N.Z. 131 D4 43 55 S 169 55 E
Glenmont, U.S.A. 150 F2 40 31N 82 6W
Glenmorgan, Australia 127 D4 27 14 S 149 42 E
Glenn, U.S.A. 160 F4 39 31N 122 1W
Glennallen, U.S.A. 144 E11 62 7N 145 33W
Glennamaddy, Ireland 23 C3 53 37N 8 33W
Glenns Ferry, U.S.A. 158 E6 42 57N 115 18W
Glennville, U.S.A. 152 D8 31 56N 81 56W
Glenorchy, Australia 128 D5 36 55 S 142 41 E
Glenorchy, N.Z. 131 E3 44 51 S 168 24 E
Glenore, Australia 126 B3 17 50 S 141 12 E
Glenreagh, Australia 127 E5 30 2 S 153 1 E
Glenrock, U.S.A. 158 E11 42 52N 105 52W
Glenrothes, U.K. 22 E5 56 12N 3 10W
Glenrowan, Australia 129 D7 36 29 S 146 13 E
Glens Falls, U.S.A. 151 C11 43 19N 73 39W
Glenside, U.S.A. 151 F9 40 6N 75 9W
Glenthompson, Australia 128 D5 37 38 S 142 38 E
Glenties, Ireland 23 B3 54 49N 8 16W
Glenveagh △, Ireland 23 A3 55 3N 8 1W
Glenville, U.S.A. 148 F5 38 56N 80 50W
Glenwood, Canada 141 C9 49 0N 54 58W
Glenwood, Ark., U.S.A. 155 H8 34 20N 93 33W
Glenwood, Ga., U.S.A. 152 C7 32 11N 82 40W
Glenwood, Hawaii, U.S.A. 145 D6 19 29N 155 9W
Glenwood, Iowa, U.S.A. 154 E7 41 3N 95 45W
Glenwood, Minn., U.S.A. 154 C7 45 39N 95 23W
Glenwood, Wash., U.S.A. 160 D5 46 1N 121 17W
Glenwood Springs, U.S.A. 158 G10 39 33N 107 19W
Gletsch, Switz. 33 C6 46 34N 8 22 E
Glettinganes, Iceland 11 B13 65 30N 13 37W
Glidden, U.S.A. 156 B2 42 4N 94 44W
Glifádha, Greece 48 D5 37 52N 23 45 E
Glimåkra, Sweden 17 H8 56 19N 14 7 E
Glina, Croatia 45 C13 45 20N 16 6 E
Glinojeck, Poland 55 F7 52 49N 20 21 E
Glittertind, Norway 18 C5 61 40N 8 32 E
Gliwice, Poland 55 H5 50 22N 18 41 E
Globe, U.S.A. 159 K8 33 24N 110 47W
Glodeanu Siliştea, Romania 53 F11 44 50N 26 48 E
Glodeni, Moldova 53 C12 47 45N 27 31 E
Glödnitz, Austria 34 E7 46 53N 14 7 E
Glogau = Głogów, Poland 55 G3 51 37N 16 5 E
Gloggnitz, Austria 34 D8 47 41N 15 56 E
Głogów, Poland 55 G3 51 37N 16 5 E
Głogówek, Poland 55 H4 50 21N 17 53 E
Glomma →, Norway 18 E7 59 12N 10 57 E
Gloria, Phil. 80 E3 12 59N 121 30 E
Glorieuses, Is., Ind. Oc. 117 A8 11 30 S 47 20 E
Glóssa, Greece 48 B5 39 10N 23 45 E

Glossop, *U.K.* **20 D6** 53 27N 1 56W
Gloucester, *Australia* **129 B9** 32 0 S 151 59 E
Gloucester, *Papua N. G.* **132 C5** 5 31 S 148 31 E
Gloucester, *U.K.* **21 F5** 51 53N 2 15W
Gloucester, *U.S.A.* **151 D14** 42 37N 70 40W
Gloucester, C., *Papua N. G.* **132 C5** 5 26 S 148 21 E
Gloucester I., *Australia* **126 J6** 20 0 S 148 30 E
Gloucester Island △, *Australia* **126 J6** 20 2 S 148 30 E
Gloucester Point, *U.S.A.* **148 G7** 37 15N 76 29W
Gloucestershire □, *U.K.* **21 F5** 51 46N 2 15W
Gloversville, *U.S.A.* **151 C10** 43 3N 74 21W
Glovertown, *Canada* **141 C9** 48 40N 54 3W
Gloverville, *U.S.A.* **152 B8** 33 32N 81 48W
Głowno, *Poland* **55 G6** 51 59N 19 42 E
Glubczyce, *Poland* **55 H4** 50 13N 17 52 E
Glubokiy, *Russia* **61 F5** 48 35N 40 25 E
Glubokoye = Hlybokaye, *Belarus* **58 E4** 55 10N 27 45 E
Głuchołazy, *Poland* **55 H4** 50 19N 17 24 E
Glücksburg, *Germany* **30 A5** 54 50N 9 33 E
Glückstadt, *Germany* **30 B5** 53 45N 9 25 E
Glukhov = Hlukhiv, *Ukraine* **59 G7** 51 40N 33 58 E
Glusk, *Belarus* **59 F5** 52 53N 28 41 E
Głuszyca, *Poland* **55 H3** 50 41N 16 23 E
Glyngøre, *Denmark* **17 H2** 56 46N 8 52 E
Gmünd, *Kärnten, Austria* **34 E6** 46 54N 13 31 E
Gmünd, *Niederösterreich, Austria* **34 C8** 48 45N 15 0 E
Gmunden, *Austria* **34 D6** 47 55N 13 48 E
Gnali, *Gabon* **114 C2** 2 34 S 11 18 E
Gnarp, *Sweden* **16 B11** 62 3N 17 16 E
Gnesen = Gniezno, *Poland* **55 F4** 52 30N 17 35 E
Gnesta, *Sweden* **16 E11** 59 3N 17 17 E
Gniew, *Poland* **54 E5** 53 50N 18 50 E
Gniewkowo, *Poland* **55 F5** 52 54N 18 25 E
Gniezno, *Poland* **55 F4** 52 30N 17 35 E
Gnjilane, *Serbia & M.* **50 D5** 42 28N 21 29 E
Gnoien, *Germany* **30 B8** 53 58N 12 41 E
Gnosjö, *Sweden* **17 G7** 57 22N 13 43 E
Gnowangerup, *Australia* **125 F2** 33 58 S 117 59 E
Go Cong, *Vietnam* **87 G6** 10 22N 106 40 E
Gō-Gawa →, *Japan* **72 B4** 35 2N 132 13 E
Gō-no-ura, *Japan* **72 D1** 33 44N 129 40 E
Goa, *India* **95 G1** 15 33N 73 59 E
Goa, *Phil.* **80 E4** 13 42N 123 29 E
Goa □, *India* **95 G1** 15 33N 73 59 E
Goalen Hd., *Australia* **129 D9** 36 33 S 150 4 E
Goalpara, *India* **90 B3** 26 10N 90 40 E
Goaltor, *India* **93 H12** 22 43N 87 10 E
Goalundo Ghat, *Bangla.* **93 H13** 23 50N 89 47 E
Goaso, *Ghana* **112 D4** 6 48N 2 30W
Goat Fell, *U.K.* **22 F3** 55 38N 5 11W
Goba, *Ethiopia* **107 F4** 7 1N 39 59 E
Goba, *Mozam.* **117 D5** 26 15 S 32 13 E
Gobabis, *Namibia* **116 C2** 22 30 S 19 0 E
Gobe, *Papua N. G.* **132 E5** 9 4 S 149 0 E
Göbel, *Turkey* **51 F12** 40 0N 28 9 E
Gobernador Gregores, *Argentina* **176 C2** 48 46 S 70 15W
Gobi, *Asia* **74 C6** 44 0N 110 0 E
Gobichettipalayam, *India* **95 J3** 11 31N 77 21 E
Gobles, *U.S.A.* **157 B11** 42 22N 85 53W
Gobō, *Japan* **73 D7** 33 53N 135 10 E
Gobo, *Sudan* **107 F3** 5 40N 31 10 E
Göçbeyli, *Turkey* **49 B9** 39 13N 27 25 E
Goch, *Germany* **30 D2** 51 41N 6 9 E
Gochas, *Namibia* **116 C2** 24 59 S 18 55 E
Godalming, *U.K.* **21 F7** 51 11N 0 36W
Godavari →, *India* **94 F6** 16 25N 82 18 E
Godavari Pt., *India* **94 F6** 17 0N 82 20 E
Godbout, *Canada* **141 C6** 49 20N 67 38W
Godda, *India* **93 G12** 24 50N 87 13 E
Goddua, *Libya* **108 C2** 26 26N 14 19 E
Godech, *Bulgaria* **50 C7** 43 1N 23 4 E
Goderich, *Canada* **140 D3** 43 45N 81 41W
Goderville, *France* **26 C7** 49 38N 0 22 E
Godfrey, *U.S.A.* **156 F6** 38 58N 90 11W
Godfrey Ra., *Australia* **125 D2** 24 0 S 117 0 E
Goðafoss, *Iceland* **11 B9** 65 41N 17 33W
Godhavn = Qeqertarsuaq, *Greenland* **10 D5** 69 15N 53 38W
Goðdalir, *Iceland* **11 B7** 65 20N 19 6W
Godhra, *India* **92 H5** 22 49N 73 40 E
Godinlave, *Somali Rep.* **120 C3** 5 54N 46 38 E
Gödöllő, *Hungary* **52 C4** 47 38N 19 25 E
Godoy Cruz, *Argentina* **174 C2** 32 56 S 68 52W
Gods →, *Canada* **140 A1** 56 22N 92 51W
Gods L., *Canada* **140 B1** 54 40N 94 15W
Gods River, *Canada* **143 C10** 54 50N 94 5W
Godthåb = Nuuk, *Greenland* **10 E5** 64 10N 51 35W
Godwin Austen = K2, *Pakistan* **93 B7** 35 58N 76 32 E
Goeie Hoop, Kaap die = Good Hope, C. of, *S. Africa* **116 E2** 34 24 S 18 30 E
Goéland, L. au, *Canada* **140 C4** 49 50N 76 48W
Goélands, L. aux, *Canada* **141 A7** 55 27N 64 17W
Goeree, *Neths.* **24 C3** 51 50N 4 0 E
Goes, *Neths.* **24 C3** 51 30N 3 55 E
Goffstown, *U.S.A.* **151 C13** 43 1N 71 36W
Gogama, *Canada* **140 C3** 47 35N 81 43W
Gogebic, L., *U.S.A.* **154 B10** 46 30N 89 35W
Goggetti, *Ethiopia* **107 F4** 8 11N 38 35 E
Gogolin, *Poland* **55 H5** 50 30N 18 0 E
Gogonou, *Benin* **113 C5** 10 50N 2 50 E
Gogra = Ghaghara →, *India* **93 G11** 25 45N 84 40 E
Gogriâl, *Sudan* **107 F2** 8 30N 28 8 E
Gogti, *Ethiopia* **107 E5** 10 7N 42 51 E
Gohana, *India* **92 E7** 29 8N 76 42 E
Goharganj, *India* **92 H7** 23 1N 77 41 E
Goi →, *India* **92 H6** 22 4N 74 46 E
Goiana, *Brazil* **170 C5** 7 33 S 34 59W
Goianésia, *Brazil* **171 E2** 15 18 S 49 7W
Goiânia, *Brazil* **171 E2** 16 43 S 49 20W
Goiás, *Brazil* **171 E1** 15 55 S 50 10W
Goiás □, *Brazil* **170 D2** 12 10 S 48 0W
Goiatuba, *Brazil* **171 E2** 18 1 S 49 23W
Goio-Erê, *Brazil* **175 A5** 24 12 S 53 1W
Góis, *Portugal* **42 E2** 40 10N 8 6W
Gojam, *Ethiopia* **107 E4** 10 55N 36 30 E
Gojeb, Wabi →, *Ethiopia* **107 F4** 7 12N 36 40 E
Gojō, *Japan* **73 C7** 34 21N 135 42 E
Gojra, *Pakistan* **92 D5** 31 10N 72 40 E
Gokak, *India* **95 F2** 16 11N 74 52 E
Gokarn, *India* **95 G2** 14 33N 74 17 E
Gökçe = Sevana Lich, *Armenia* **61 K7** 40 30N 45 20 E
Gökçeada, *Turkey* **51 F9** 40 10N 25 50 E
Gökçedağ, *Turkey* **49 B10** 39 33N 28 56 E
Gökçen, *Turkey* **49 C9** 38 7N 27 53 E
Gökçeören, *Turkey* **49 C10** 38 37N 28 35 E
Gökçeyazı, *Turkey* **49 B9** 39 40N 27 40 E
Gökırmak →, *Turkey* **100 B6** 41 25N 35 8 E
Gökova, *Turkey* **49 D10** 37 1N 28 17 E
Gökova Körfezi, *Turkey* **49 E9** 36 55N 27 50 E
Göksu →, *Turkey* **100 D6** 36 19N 34 5 E
Göksun, *Turkey* **100 C7** 38 2N 36 30 E
Gokteik, *Burma* **90 D6** 22 26N 97 0 E
Göktepe, *Turkey* **49 D10** 37 25N 28 34 E
Gokurt, *Pakistan* **92 E2** 29 40N 67 26 E
Gokwe, *Zimbabwe* **117 B4** 18 7 S 28 58 E
Gol, *Norway* **18 D5** 60 42N 8 55 E
Gol Gol, *Australia* **128 C5** 34 12 S 142 14 E
Gola, *India* **93 E9** 28 3N 80 32 E
Golaghat, *India* **90 B5** 26 30N 94 0 E
Golakganj, *India* **90 B2** 26 8N 89 52 E
Golan Heights = Hagolan, *Syria* **103 C4** 33 0N 35 45 E
Gołańcz, *Poland* **55 F4** 52 57N 17 18 E
Golāshkerd, *Iran* **97 E8** 27 59N 57 16 E
Golaya Pristen = Hola Pristan, *Ukraine* **59 J7** 46 29N 32 32 E
Gölbaşı, *Adiyaman, Turkey* **100 D7** 37 43N 37 25 E
Gölbaşı, *Ankara, Turkey* **100 C5** 39 47N 32 49 E
Golchikha, *Russia* **6 B12** 71 45N 83 30 E
Golconda, *India* **94 F4** 17 24N 78 23 E
Golconda, *U.S.A.* **158 F5** 40 58N 117 30W
Gölcük, *Kocaeli, Turkey* **51 F13** 40 42N 29 48 E
Gölcük, *Niğde, Turkey* **100 C6** 38 14N 34 47 E
Gold, *U.S.A.* **150 E7** 41 52N 77 50W
Gold Beach, *U.S.A.* **158 E1** 42 25N 124 25W
Gold Coast = Ghana ■, *W. Afr.* **113 D4** 8 0N 1 0W
Gold Coast, *Australia* **127 F9** 28 0 S 153 25 E
Gold Coast, *W. Afr.* **113 E4** 4 0N 1 40W
Gold Creek, *U.S.A.* **144 E10** 62 46N 149 41W
Gold Hill, *U.S.A.* **158 E2** 42 26N 123 3W
Gold River, *Canada* **142 D3** 49 46N 126 3W
Goldach, *Switz.* **33 B8** 47 28N 9 28 E
Gołdap, *Poland* **54 D9** 54 19N 22 18 E
Goldau, *Switz.* **33 B7** 47 3N 8 33 E
Goldberg = Złotoryja, *Poland* **55 G2** 51 8N 15 55 E
Goldberg, *Germany* **30 B8** 53 35N 12 4 E
Golden, *Canada* **142 C5** 51 20N 116 59W
Golden, *U.S.A.* **156 D5** 40 7N 91 1W
Golden B., *N.Z.* **131 A7** 40 40 S 172 50 E
Golden Gate, *U.S.A.* **158 H2** 37 54N 122 30W
Golden Gate Highlands △, *S. Africa* **117 D4** 28 40 S 28 40 E
Golden Hinde, *Canada* **142 D3** 49 40N 125 44W
Golden Lake, *Canada* **150 A7** 45 34N 77 21W
Golden Rock, *India* **95 J4** 10 45N 78 48 E
Golden Spike ⌂, *U.S.A.* **158 F7** 41 37N 112 33W
Golden Vale, *Ireland* **23 D3** 52 33N 8 17W
Goldendale, *U.S.A.* **158 D3** 45 49N 120 50W
Goldfield, *U.S.A.* **159 H5** 37 42N 117 14W
Goldingen = Kuldīga, *Latvia* **15 H19** 56 58N 21 59 E
Goldsand L., *Canada* **143 B8** 57 2N 101 8W
Goldsboro, *U.S.A.* **149 H7** 35 23N 77 59W
Goldsmith, *U.S.A.* **155 K3** 31 59N 102 37W
Goldsworthy, *Australia* **124 D2** 20 21 S 119 30 E
Goldthwaite, *U.S.A.* **155 K5** 31 27N 98 34W
Golegã, *Portugal* **43 F2** 39 24N 8 29W
Goleniów, *Poland* **54 E1** 53 35N 14 50 E
Golestān □, *Iran* **97 B7** 37 20N 55 25 E
Golestānak, *Iran* **97 D7** 30 36N 54 14 E
Goleta, *U.S.A.* **161 L7** 34 27N 119 50W
Golfito, *Costa Rica* **164 E3** 8 41N 83 5W
Golfo Aranci, *Italy* **46 B2** 40 59N 9 38 E
Golfo di Orosei e del Gennargentu △, *Italy* **46 B2** 40 5N 9 15 E
Gölgeli Dağları, *Turkey* **49 D10** 37 10N 28 55 E
Gölhisar, *Turkey* **49 D11** 37 8N 29 31 E
Goliad, *U.S.A.* **155 L6** 28 40N 97 23W
Golija, *Serbia & M.* **50 C2** 43 5N 18 45 E
Golija, *Serbia & M.* **50 C4** 43 22N 20 15 E
Golina, *Poland* **55 F5** 52 15N 18 4 E
Goljam Bratan = Morozov, *Bulgaria* **51 D9** 42 30N 25 10 E
Gölköy, *Turkey* **100 B7** 40 41N 37 37 E
Gollel = Lavumisa, *Swaziland* **117 D5** 27 20 S 31 55 E
Göllersdorf, *Austria* **34 C9** 48 29N 16 7 E
Gollnow = Goleniów, *Poland* **54 E1** 53 35N 14 50 E
Gölmarmara, *Turkey* **49 C9** 38 42N 27 55 E
Golo →, *France* **29 F13** 42 31N 9 32 E
Golol, *Somali Rep.* **120 D2** 3 38N 43 49 E
Gölova, *Turkey* **49 E12** 36 48N 30 5 E
Golovin, *U.S.A.* **144 D7** 64 33N 163 2W
Golpāyegān, *Iran* **97 C6** 33 27N 50 18 E
Gölpazarı, *Turkey* **100 B4** 40 16N 30 18 E
Golra, *Pakistan* **92 C5** 33 37N 72 56 E
Golspie, *U.K.* **22 D5** 57 58N 3 59W
Golub-Dobrzyń, *Poland* **55 E6** 53 7N 19 2 E
Golubac, *Serbia & M.* **50 B5** 44 38N 21 38 E
Golungo Alto, *Angola* **115 D2** 9 8 S 14 46 E
Golyam Perelik, *Bulgaria* **51 E8** 41 36N 24 33 E
Golyama Kamchiya →, *Bulgaria* **51 C11** 43 10N 27 55 E
Golyshi = Vetluzhskiy, *Russia* **60 A7** 58 23N 45 26 E
Goma, *Dem. Rep. of the Congo* **118 C2** 1 37 S 29 10 E
Gomal Pass, *Pakistan* **92 D3** 31 56N 69 20 E
Gomati →, *India* **93 G10** 25 32N 83 11 E
Gombari, *Dem. Rep. of the Congo* **118 B2** 2 45N 29 3 E
Gombe, *Dem. Rep. of the Congo* **114 C3** 0 45 S 17 36 E
Gombe, *Nigeria* **113 C7** 10 19N 11 2 E
Gömbe, *Turkey* **49 E11** 36 33N 29 38 E
Gombe □, *Nigeria* **113 C7** 10 0N 11 10 E
Gombe →, *Tanzania* **118 C3** 4 38 S 31 40 E
Gombi, *Nigeria* **113 C7** 10 12N 12 30 E
Gomel = Homyel, *Belarus* **59 F6** 52 28N 31 0 E
Gomera, *Canary Is.* **9 e1** 28 7N 17 14W
Gómez Palacio, *Mexico* **162 B4** 25 40N 104 0W
Gomīshān, *Iran* **97 B7** 37 4N 54 6 E
Gommern, *Germany* **30 C7** 52 4N 11 50 E
Gomogomo, *Indonesia* **83 C4** 6 39 S 134 43 E
Gomotartsi, *Bulgaria* **50 B6** 44 6N 22 57 E
Gompa = Ganta, *Liberia* **112 D3** 7 15N 8 59W
Gomphi, *Greece* **48 B3** 39 26N 21 36 E
Goms, *Switz.* **32 D6** 46 27N 8 15 E
Gonābād, *Iran* **97 C8** 34 15N 58 45 E
Gonaïves, *Haiti* **165 C5** 19 20N 72 42W
Gonarezhou △, *Zimbabwe* **119 G3** 21 32 S 31 55 E
Gonâve, G. de la, *Haiti* **165 C5** 19 29N 72 42W
Gonâve, Île de la, *Haiti* **165 C5** 18 51N 73 3W
Gonbad-e Kāvūs, *Iran* **97 B7** 37 20N 55 25 E
Gönc, *Hungary* **52 B6** 48 28N 21 14 E
Gonda, *India* **93 F9** 27 9N 81 58 E
Gondal, *India* **92 J4** 21 58N 70 52 E
Gonder, *Ethiopia* **107 E4** 12 39N 37 30 E
Gondia, *India* **94 D5** 21 23N 80 10 E
Gondola, *Mozam.* **119 F3** 19 10 S 33 37 E
Gondomar, *Portugal* **42 D2** 41 10N 8 35W
Gondrecourt-le-Château, *France* **27 D12** 48 31N 5 30 E
Gönen, *Balıkesir, Turkey* **51 F11** 40 6N 27 39 E
Gönen, *Isparta, Turkey* **49 D12** 37 57N 30 31 E
Gönen →, *Turkey* **51 F11** 40 6N 27 39 E
Gong Xian, *China* **76 C5** 28 23N 104 47 E
Gong'an, *China* **77 B9** 30 7N 112 12 E
Gongbei, *China* **69 G10** 22 12N 113 32 E
Gongcheng, *China* **77 E8** 24 50N 110 49 E
Gongga Shan, *China* **76 C3** 29 40N 101 55 E
Gongguan, *China* **76 G7** 21 48N 109 36 E
Gonghe, *China* **68 C5** 36 18N 100 32 E
Gongming, *China* **69 F10** 22 47N 113 53 E
Gongo Yembe, *Dem. Rep. of the Congo* **114 C3** 1 58 S 18 40 E
Gongola →, *Nigeria* **113 D7** 9 30N 12 4 E
Gongolgon, *Australia* **127 E4** 30 21 S 146 54 E
Gongoué, *Gabon* **114 C1** 0 31 S 9 13 E
Gongshan, *China* **76 D2** 27 43N 98 29 E
Gongtan, *China* **76 C7** 28 55N 108 20 E
Gongzhuling, *China* **75 C13** 43 30N 124 40 E
Goniadz, *Poland* **54 E9** 53 30N 22 44 E
Goniri, *Nigeria* **113 C7** 11 30N 12 15 E
Gonjo, *China* **76 B2** 30 52N 98 17 E
Gonnesa, *Italy* **46 C1** 39 16N 8 28 E
Gónnos, *Greece* **48 B4** 39 52N 22 29 E
Gonnosfanàdiga, *Italy* **46 C1** 39 29N 8 39 E
Gonzaga, *Phil.* **80 B4** 18 16N 122 0 E
Gonzales, *Calif., U.S.A.* **160 J5** 36 30N 121 26W
Gonzales, *Tex., U.S.A.* **155 L6** 29 30N 97 27W
González Chaves, *Argentina* **174 D3** 38 2 S 60 5W
Goobang △, *Australia* **129 B8** 33 0 S 148 32 E
Good Hope, C. of, *S. Africa* **116 E2** 34 24 S 18 30 E
Goodenough I., *Papua N. G.* **132 E6** 9 20 S 150 15 E
Gooderham, *Canada* **150 B6** 44 54N 78 21W
Goodhouse, *S. Africa* **116 D2** 28 57 S 18 13 E
Gooding, *U.S.A.* **158 E6** 42 56N 114 43W
Goodland, *U.S.A.* **154 F4** 39 21N 101 43W
Goodlands, *Mauritius* **121 d** 20 2 S 57 39 E
Goodlow, *Canada* **142 B4** 56 20N 120 8W
Goodnews Bay, *U.S.A.* **144 G7** 59 7N 161 35W
Goodooga, *Australia* **127 D4** 29 3 S 147 28 E
Goodsprings, *U.S.A.* **161 K11** 35 49N 115 27W
Goodwater, *U.S.A.* **152 B3** 33 4N 86 3W
Goole, *U.K.* **20 D7** 53 42N 0 53W
Goolgowi, *Australia* **129 B6** 33 58 S 145 41 E
Goolwa, *Australia* **128 C3** 35 30 S 138 47 E
Goomalling, *Australia* **125 F2** 31 15 S 116 49 E
Goomeri, *Australia* **127 D5** 26 12 S 152 6 E
Goonda, *Mozam.* **119 F3** 19 48 S 33 57 E
Goondiwindi, *Australia* **127 D5** 28 30 S 150 21 E
Goongarrie △, *Australia* **125 F3** 30 7 S 121 30 E
Goongarrie, L., *Australia* **125 F3** 30 3 S 121 9 E
Goonyella, *Australia* **126 C4** 21 47 S 147 58 E
Goose →, *Canada* **141 B7** 53 20N 60 35W
Goose Creek, *U.S.A.* **152 C9** 32 59N 80 2W
Goose L., *U.S.A.* **158 F3** 41 56N 120 26W
Gooty, *India* **95 G3** 15 7N 77 41 E
Gopalganj, *Bangla.* **90 D2** 23 1N 89 50 E
Gopalganj, *India* **93 F11** 26 28N 84 30 E
Goppenstein, *Switz.* **32 D5** 46 23N 7 46 E
Göppingen, *Germany* **31 G5** 48 42N 9 39 E
Gor, *Spain* **43 H8** 37 23N 2 58W
Góra, *Dolnośląskie, Poland* **55 G3** 51 40N 16 31 E
Góra, *Mazowieckie, Poland* **55 F7** 52 39N 20 6 E
Góra Kalwaria, *Poland* **55 G8** 51 59N 21 14 E
Gorakhpur, *India* **93 F10** 26 47N 83 23 E
Goražde, *Bos.-H.* **52 G3** 43 38N 18 58 E
Gorbatov, *Russia* **60 B6** 56 12N 43 2 E
Gorbea, Peña, *Spain* **40 B2** 43 1N 2 50W
Gorczański △, *Poland* **55 J7** 49 30N 20 10 E
Gorda, *U.S.A.* **160 K5** 35 53N 121 26W
Gorda, Pta., *Canary Is.* **9 e1** 28 45N 18 0W
Gorda, Pta., *Nic.* **164 D3** 14 20N 83 10W
Gordan B., *Australia* **124 B5** 11 35 S 130 10 E
Gördes, *Turkey* **49 C10** 38 54N 28 17 E
Gordon, *Ga., U.S.A.* **152 C6** 32 54N 83 20W
Gordon, *Nebr., U.S.A.* **154 D3** 42 48N 102 12W
Gordon →, *Australia* **127 G4** 42 27 S 145 30 E
Gordon, I., *Chile* **176 D3** 54 55 S 69 30W
Gordon L., *Alta., Canada* **143 B6** 56 30N 110 25W
Gordon L., *N.W.T., Canada* **142 A6** 63 5N 113 11W
Gordonvale, *Australia* **126 B4** 17 5 S 145 50 E
Goré, *Chad* **109 G3** 7 59N 16 31 E
Gore, *Ethiopia* **107 F4** 8 12N 35 32 E
Gore, *N.Z.* **131 G3** 46 5 S 168 58 E
Gore Bay, *Canada* **140 C3** 45 57N 82 28W
Görele, *Turkey* **101 B8** 41 2N 39 0 E
Goreme, *Turkey* **100 C6** 38 35N 34 52 E
Gorey, *Ireland* **23 D5** 52 41N 6 18W
Gorg, *Iran* **97 D8** 29 29N 59 43 E
Gorgān, *Iran* **97 B7** 36 55N 54 30 E
Gorgona, *Italy* **44 E6** 43 26N 9 54 E
Gorgora, *Ethiopia* **107 E4** 12 15N 37 17 E
Gorgoram, *Nigeria* **113 C7** 12 40N 10 45 E
Gorham, *U.S.A.* **151 B13** 44 23N 71 10W
Gori, *Georgia* **61 J7** 42 0N 44 7 E
Goribidnur = Gauribidanur, *India* **95 H3** 13 37N 77 32 E
Goriganga →, *India* **93 E9** 29 45N 80 23 E
Gorinchem, *Neths.* **24 C4** 51 50N 4 59 E
Gorinhatã, *Brazil* **171 E2** 19 15 S 49 45W
Goris, *Armenia* **101 C12** 39 31N 46 22 E
Goritsy, *Russia* **58 D9** 57 4N 36 43 E
Gorízia, *Italy* **45 C10** 45 56N 13 37 E
Gorj □, *Romania* **53 E8** 45 5N 23 25 E
Gorki = Horki, *Belarus* **58 E6** 54 17N 30 59 E
Gorki = Nizhniy Novgorod, *Russia* **60 B7** 56 20N 44 0 E
Gorkiy = Nizhniy Novgorod, *Russia* **60 B7** 56 20N 44 0 E
Gorkovskoye Vdkhr., *Russia* **60 B6** 57 2N 43 4 E
Gorleston, *U.K.* **21 E9** 52 35N 1 44 E
Gorlice, *Poland* **55 J8** 49 35N 21 11 E
Görlitz, *Germany* **30 D10** 51 9N 14 58 E
Gorlovka = Horlivka, *Ukraine* **59 H10** 48 19N 38 5 E
Gorman, *U.S.A.* **161 L8** 34 47N 118 51W
Gorna Djumaya = Blagoevgrad, *Bulgaria* **50 D7** 42 2N 23 5 E
Gorna Dzhumayo = Blagoevgrad, *Bulgaria* **50 D7** 42 2N 23 5 E
Gorna Oryakhovitsa, *Bulgaria* **51 C9** 43 7N 25 40 E
Gornja Radgona, *Slovenia* **45 B13** 46 40N 16 2 E
Gornja Tuzla, *Bos.-H.* **52 F3** 44 35N 18 46 E
Gornji Grad, *Slovenia* **45 B11** 46 20N 14 52 E
Gornji Milanovac, *Serbia & M.* **50 B4** 44 3N 20 29 E
Gornji Vakuf, *Bos.-H.* **52 G2** 43 57N 17 34 E
Gorno Ablanovo, *Bulgaria* **51 C9** 43 37N 25 43 E
Gorno-Altay □, *Russia* **66 D9** 51 0N 86 0 E
Gorno-Altaysk, *Russia* **66 D9** 51 50N 86 5 E
Gorno-Badakhshan □, *Tajikistan* **65 D6** 38 30N 73 0 E
Gornyatski, *Russia* **56 A11** 67 32N 64 3 E
Gornyatskiy, *Russia* **61 F5** 48 18N 40 56 E
Gornyy, *Saratov, Russia* **60 E9** 51 50N 48 30 E
Gornyy, *Sib., Russia* **70 B6** 44 57N 133 59 E
Goro →, *C.A.R.* **114 A4** 9 14N 21 16 E
Gorodenka = Horodenka, *Ukraine* **53 B10** 48 41N 25 29 E
Gorodets, *Russia* **60 B6** 56 38N 43 28 E
Gorodishche = Horodyshche, *Ukraine* **59 H6** 49 17N 31 27 E
Gorodishche, *Russia* **60 D7** 53 13N 45 40 E
Gorodnya = Horodnya, *Ukraine* **59 G6** 51 55N 31 33 E
Gorodok = Haradok, *Belarus* **58 E6** 55 30N 30 3 E
Gorodok = Horodok, *Ukraine* **59 H2** 49 46N 23 32 E
Gorodok = Zakamensk, *Russia* **67 D11** 50 23N 103 17 E
Gorodovikovsk, *Russia* **61 G5** 46 8N 41 58 E
Goroka, *Papua N. G.* **132 D3** 6 7 S 145 25 E
Goroke, *Australia* **128 D4** 36 43 S 141 29 E
Gorokhov = Horokhiv, *Ukraine* **59 G3** 50 30N 24 45 E
Gorokhovets, *Russia* **60 B6** 56 13N 42 39 E
Gorom Gorom, *Burkina Faso* **113 C4** 14 26N 0 14W
Goromonzi, *Zimbabwe* **119 F3** 17 52 S 31 22 E
Gorong, Kepulauan, *Indonesia* **83 B4** 3 59 S 131 25 E
Gorongosa △, *Mozam.* **117 B5** 18 50 S 34 29 E
Gorongose →, *Mozam.* **117 C5** 20 30 S 34 40 E
Gorongoza, *Mozam.* **119 F3** 18 44 S 34 2 E
Gorongoza, Sa. da, *Mozam.* **119 F3** 18 27 S 34 2 E
Gorontalo, *Indonesia* **82 A2** 0 35N 123 5 E
Gorontalo □, *Indonesia* **79 D6** 0 50N 122 20 E
Goronyo, *Nigeria* **113 C6** 13 29N 5 39 E
Górowo Iławeckie, *Poland* **54 D7** 54 17N 20 30 E
Gorron, *France* **26 D6** 48 25N 0 50W
Gorshechnoye, *Russia* **59 G10** 51 31N 38 2 E
Gort, *Ireland* **23 C3** 53 3N 8 49W
Gortis, *Greece* **39 E5** 35 4N 24 58 E
Gorumahisani, *India* **94 C8** 22 20N 86 24 E
Góry Bystrzyckie, *Poland* **55 H3** 50 16N 16 33 E
Goryachiy Klyuch, *Russia* **61 H4** 44 38N 39 8 E
Gorzkowice, *Poland* **55 G6** 51 13N 19 36 E
Górzno, *Poland* **55 E6** 53 12N 19 38 E
Gorzów Śląski, *Poland* **55 G5** 51 3N 18 22 E
Gorzów Wielkopolski, *Poland* **55 F2** 52 43N 15 15 E
Göschenen, *Switz.* **33 C7** 46 40N 8 36 E
Gose, *Japan* **73 C7** 34 27N 135 44 E
Gosford, *Australia* **129 B9** 33 23 S 151 18 E
Goshen, *Calif., U.S.A.* **160 J7** 36 21N 119 25W
Goshen, *Ind., U.S.A.* **157 C11** 41 35N 85 50W
Goshen, *N.Y., U.S.A.* **151 E10** 41 24N 74 20W
Goshogawara, *Japan* **70 D10** 40 48N 140 27 E
Goskopi = Kopeysk, *Russia* **64 D8** 55 7N 61 37 E
Goslar, *Germany* **30 D6** 51 54N 10 25 E
Gospić, *Croatia* **45 D12** 44 35N 15 23 E
Gosport, *U.K.* **21 G6** 50 48N 1 9W
Gosport, *U.S.A.* **157 E10** 39 21N 86 40W
Gossa, *Norway* **18 B3** 62 52N 6 50 E
Gossas, *Senegal* **112 C1** 14 28N 16 0W
Gossau, *Switz.* **33 B8** 47 25N 9 15 E
Gosse →, *Australia* **126 B1** 19 32 S 134 37 E
Gossi, *Mali* **113 B4** 15 48N 1 20W
Gossinga, *Sudan* **107 F2** 8 36N 25 59 E
Gostingen = Gostyń, *Poland* **55 G4** 51 50N 17 3 E
Gostinopolye = Volkhov, *Russia* **58 C7** 59 55N 32 15 E
Gostivar, *Macedonia* **50 E4** 41 48N 20 57 E
Gostyń, *Poland* **55 G4** 51 50N 17 3 E
Gostynin, *Poland* **55 F6** 52 26N 19 29 E
Göta älv →, *Sweden* **17 G5** 57 42N 11 54 E
Göta kanal, *Sweden* **17 F9** 58 30N 15 58 E
Götaland, *Sweden* **17 G8** 57 30N 14 30 E
Göteborg, *Sweden* **17 G5** 57 43N 11 59 E
Götemba, *Japan* **73 B10** 35 18N 138 56 E
Götene, *Sweden* **17 F7** 58 32N 13 30 E
Gotenhafen = Gdynia, *Poland* **54 D5** 54 35N 18 33 E
Gotești, *Moldova* **53 D13** 46 9N 28 10 E
Gotha, *Germany* **30 E6** 50 56N 10 42 E
Gothenburg = Göteborg, *Sweden* **17 G5** 57 43N 11 59 E
Gothenburg, *U.S.A.* **154 E4** 40 56N 100 10W
Gothèye, *Niger* **113 C5** 13 52N 1 34 E
Gotland, *Sweden* **17 G12** 57 30N 18 33 E
Gotlands län □, *Sweden* **17 G12** 57 15N 18 30 E
Gotō-Rettō, *Japan* **71 H4** 32 55N 129 5 E
Gotse Delchev, *Bulgaria* **50 E7** 41 36N 23 46 E
Gotska Sandön, *Sweden* **15 G18** 58 24N 19 15 E
Gōtsu, *Japan* **72 C4** 35 0N 132 14 E
Gott Pk., *Canada* **142 C4** 50 18N 122 16W
Göttero, Monte, *Italy* **44 D6** 44 22N 9 42 E
Gottesberg = Boguszów-Gorce, *Poland* **55 H3** 50 45N 16 12 E
Göttingen, *Germany* **30 D5** 51 31N 9 55 E
Gottschee = Kočevje, *Slovenia* **45 C11** 45 39N 14 50 E
Gottwald = Zmiyev, *Ukraine* **59 H9** 49 39N 36 27 E
Gottwaldov = Zlín, *Czech Rep.* **35 B10** 49 14N 17 40 E
Götzis, *Austria* **33 B9** 47 20N 9 38 E
Goubangzi, *China* **75 D11** 41 20N 121 52 E
Gouda, *Neths.* **24 B4** 52 1N 4 42 E
Goúdhoura, Ákra, *Greece* **39 F7** 34 59N 26 6 E
Goudiry, *Senegal* **112 C2** 14 15N 12 45W
Goudoumaria, *Niger* **113 C7** 13 40N 11 10 E
Gouéké, *Guinea* **112 D3** 8 2N 8 43W
Gough I., *Atl. Oc.* **8 L11** 40 10 S 9 45W
Gouin, Rés., *Canada* **140 C5** 48 35N 74 40W
Gouitafla, *Ivory C.* **112 D3** 7 30N 5 53W
Goulburn, *Australia* **129 C8** 34 44 S 149 44 E
Goulburn Is., *Australia* **126 A1** 11 40 S 133 20 E
Goulburn River △, *Australia* **129 B9** 32 19 S 150 10 E
Goulds, *U.S.A.* **153 K9** 25 33N 80 23W
Goulia, *Ivory C.* **112 C3** 10 1N 7 11W
Goulimine, *Morocco* **110 C3** 28 56N 10 0W
Goulmima, *Morocco* **110 B4** 31 41N 4 57W
Goumbou, *Mali* **112 B3** 15 2N 7 25W
Gouménissa, *Greece* **50 F6** 40 56N 22 37 E
Gounatolo, *Solomon Is.* **133 M11** 8 25 S 160 52 E
Goundam, *Mali* **112 B4** 16 27N 3 40W
Goundi, *Chad* **109 G3** 9 22N 17 21 E
Gounou-Gaya, *Chad* **109 G3** 9 38N 15 31 E
Goúra, *Greece* **48 D4** 37 56N 22 20 E
Gouraya, *Algeria* **111 A5** 36 31N 1 56 E
Gourbassi, *Mali* **112 C2** 13 24N 11 38W
Gourdon, *France* **28 D5** 44 44N 1 23 E
Gouré, *Niger* **113 C7** 14 0N 10 10 E
Gouri, *Chad* **109 E3** 18 50N 16 49 E
Gourin, *France* **26 D3** 48 8N 3 37W
Gourits →, *S. Africa* **116 E3** 34 21 S 21 52 E
Gourma-Rharous, *Mali* **113 B4** 16 55N 1 50W
Goúrnais, *Greece* **39 E6** 35 19N 25 16 E
Gournay-en-Bray, *France* **27 C8** 49 29N 1 44 E
Gouro, *Chad* **109 E3** 19 36N 19 36 E
Gourock, *U.K.* **22 F4** 55 57N 4 49W
Gourock Ra., *Australia* **129 D8** 36 0 S 149 25 E
Goursi, *Burkina Faso* **112 C4** 12 42N 2 37W
Gouvêa, *Brazil* **171 E3** 18 27 S 43 44W
Gouverneur, *U.S.A.* **151 B9** 44 20N 75 28W
Gouviá, *Greece* **38 B9** 39 39N 19 50 E
Gouzon, *France* **27 F9** 46 12N 2 14 E
Governador Valadares, *Brazil* **171 E3** 18 15 S 41 57W
Governor Generoso, *Phil.* **81 H6** 6 39N 126 5 E
Governor's Harbour, *Bahamas* **164 A4** 25 10N 76 14W
Govindgarh, *India* **93 G9** 24 23N 81 18 E
Gowan Ra., *Australia* **126 D4** 25 0 S 145 0 E
Gowanda, *U.S.A.* **150 D6** 42 28N 78 56W
Gower, *U.K.* **21 F3** 51 35N 4 10W
Gowers Corner, *U.S.A.* **153 G7** 28 20N 82 30W
Gowna, L., *Ireland* **23 C4** 53 51N 7 34W
Gowrie, *U.S.A.* **156 B2** 42 17N 94 17W
Gowurdak, *Turkmenistan* **65 E3** 37 50N 66 4 E
Goya, *Argentina* **174 B4** 29 10 S 59 10W
Göyçay, *Azerbaijan* **61 K8** 40 42N 47 43 E
Goyder Lagoon, *Australia* **127 D2** 27 3 S 138 58 E
Goyllarisquisga, *Peru* **172 C2** 10 31 S 76 24W
Göynük, *Antalya, Turkey* **49 E12** 36 41N 30 33 E
Göynük, *Bolu, Turkey* **100 B4** 40 24N 30 48 E
Goz Beïda, *Chad* **109 F4** 12 10N 21 20 E
Goz Regeb, *Sudan* **107 D4** 16 3N 35 33 E
Gozdnica, *Poland* **55 G2** 51 28N 15 4 E
Gozo, *Malta* **38 E7** 36 3N 14 15 E
Graaff-Reinet, *S. Africa* **116 E3** 32 13 S 24 32 E
Grabill, *U.S.A.* **157 C12** 41 13N 84 57W
Grabo, *Ivory C.* **112 D3** 4 57N 7 30W
Grabow, *Germany* **30 B7** 53 17N 11 34 E
Grabów nad Prosną, *Poland* **55 G5** 51 31N 18 7 E
Grabs, *Switz.* **33 B8** 47 11N 9 27 E
Gračac, *Croatia* **45 D12** 44 18N 15 57 E
Gračanica, *Bos.-H.* **52 F3** 44 43N 18 18 E
Graçay, *France* **27 E8** 47 10N 1 50 E
Graceville, *U.S.A.* **152 E4** 30 58N 85 31W
Gracewood, *U.S.A.* **152 B7** 33 22N 82 2W
Grachevka, *Russia* **64 E4** 52 55N 52 52 E
Gracias a Dios, C., *Honduras* **164 D3** 15 0N 83 10W
Graciosa, *Azores* **9 d1** 39 4N 28 0W
Graciosa, I., *Canary Is.* **9 e2** 29 15N 13 32W
Grad Sofiya □, *Bulgaria* **50 D7** 42 35N 23 20 E
Gradac, *Serbia & M.* **50 C3** 43 23N 19 9 E
Gradačac, *Bos.-H.* **52 F3** 44 52N 18 26 E
Gradaús, *Brazil* **170 C1** 7 43 S 51 11W
Gradaús, Serra dos, *Brazil* **170 C1** 8 0 S 50 45W
Gradeška Planina, *Macedonia* **50 E6** 41 30N 22 15 E
Gradets, *Bulgaria* **51 D10** 42 46N 26 30 E
Gradište, *Slovenia* **45 B12** 46 37N 15 50 E
Grădiștea de Munte, *Romania* **53 E8** 45 37N 23 13 E
Grado, *Italy* **45 C10** 45 40N 13 23 E
Grado, *Spain* **42 B4** 43 23N 6 4W
Grady, *U.S.A.* **155 H3** 34 49N 103 19W
Graeca, Lacul, *Romania* **53 F11** 44 5N 26 10 E
Grafarnes, *Iceland* **11 C3** 64 55N 23 16W
Grafenau, *Germany* **31 G9** 48 51N 13 22 E
Gräfenberg, *Germany* **31 F7** 49 39N 11 14 E
Grafham Water, *U.K.* **21 E7** 52 19N 0 18W
Grafton, *Australia* **127 D5** 29 38 S 152 58 E
Grafton, *Ill., U.S.A.* **156 F6** 38 58N 90 26W
Grafton, *N. Dak., U.S.A.* **154 A6** 48 25N 97 25W
Grafton, *W. Va., U.S.A.* **148 F5** 39 21N 80 2W
Graham, *Canada* **140 C1** 49 20N 90 30W
Graham, *Ga., U.S.A.* **152 D7** 31 50N 82 30W
Graham, *Tex., U.S.A.* **155 J5** 33 6N 98 35W
Graham, Mt., *U.S.A.* **159 K9** 32 42N 109 52W
Graham Bell, Ostrov = Greem-Bell, Ostrov, *Russia* **66 A7** 81 0N 62 0 E
Graham I., *Canada* **142 C2** 53 40N 132 30W
Graham Land, *Antarctica* **7 C17** 65 0 S 64 0W
Grahamstown, *S. Africa* **116 E4** 33 19 S 26 31 E
Grahamsville, *U.S.A.* **151 E10** 41 51N 74 33W
Grahovo, *Serbia & M.* **50 D2** 42 40N 18 40 E
Graïba, *Tunisia* **108 B2** 34 30N 10 13 E
Graie, Alpi, *Europe* **29 C11** 45 30N 7 10 E
Grain Coast, *W. Afr.* **112 E3** 4 20N 10 0W
Grajagan, *Indonesia* **79 K17** 8 35 S 114 13 E
Grajagan, Teluk, *Indonesia* **79 K17** 8 40 S 114 18 E
Grajaú, *Brazil* **170 C2** 5 50 S 46 4W
Grajaú →, *Brazil* **170 B3** 3 41 S 44 48W
Grajewo, *Poland* **54 E9** 53 39N 22 30 E
Gramada, *Bulgaria* **50 C6** 43 49N 22 39 E
Gramat, *France* **28 D5** 44 48N 1 43 E
Grammichele, *Italy* **47 E7** 37 13N 14 38 E
Grámmos, Óros, *Greece* **50 F4** 40 18N 20 47 E
Grampian, *U.S.A.* **150 F6** 40 58N 78 37W
Grampian Highlands = Grampian Mts., *U.K.* **22 E5** 56 50N 4 0W
Grampian Mts., *U.K.* **22 E5** 56 50N 4 0W
Grampians △, *Australia* **128 D5** 37 15 S 142 28 E
Grampians, The, *Australia* **128 D5** 37 0 S 142 20 E
Gramsh, *Albania* **50 F4** 40 52N 20 12 E
Gran, *Norway* **18 D7** 60 23N 10 31 E
Gran →, *Suriname* **169 C6** 4 1N 55 30W
Gran Altiplanicie Central, *Argentina* **176 C3** 49 0 S 69 30W
Gran Canaria, *Canary Is.* **9 e1** 27 55N 15 35W
Gran Chaco, *S. Amer.* **174 B3** 25 0 S 61 0W
Gran Desierto del Pinacate ⌂, *Mexico* **162 A2** 31 51N 113 32W

Gran Laguna Salada, *Argentina* **176 B3** 44 24 S 67 23W
Gran Pajonal, *Peru* **172 C3** 10 45 S 74 30W
Gran Paradiso, *Italy* **44 C4** 45 33N 7 17 E
Gran Sasso d'Itália, *Italy* **45 F10** 42 27N 13 42 E
Gran Sasso e Monti Della Laga △, *Italy* **45 F10** 42 32N 13 22 E
Granada, *Nic.* **164 D2** 11 58N 86 0W
Granada, *Spain* **43 H7** 37 10N 3 35W
Granada, *U.S.A.* **155 F3** 38 4N 102 19W
Granada □, *Spain* **43 H7** 37 18N 3 0W
Granadilla de Abona, *Canary Is.* **9 e1** 28 7N 16 33W
Granard, *Ireland* **23 C4** 53 47N 7 30W
Granbury, *U.S.A.* **155 J6** 32 27N 97 47W
Granby, *Canada* **140 C5** 45 25N 72 45W
Granby, *U.S.A.* **158 F11** 40 5N 105 56W
Grand →, *Canada* **150 D5** 42 51N 79 34W
Grand →, *Mich., U.S.A.* **157 A10** 43 4N 86 15W
Grand →, *Mo., U.S.A.* **156 E3** 39 23N 93 7W
Grand →, *S. Dak., U.S.A.* **154 C4** 45 40N 100 45W
Grand Anse, *Seychelles* **121 b** 4 18 S 55 45 E
Grand Bahama I., *Bahamas* **164 A4** 26 40N 78 30W
Grand Baie, *Mauritius* **121 d** 20 0 S 57 35 E
Grand Bank, *Canada* **141 C8** 47 6N 55 48W
Grand Banks, *Atl. Oc.* **8 B6** 45 0N 52 0W
Grand Bassam, *Ivory C.* **112 D4** 5 10N 3 49W
Grand Batanga, *Cameroon* **114 B1** 2 50N 9 55 E
Grand Béréby, *Ivory C.* **112 E3** 4 38N 6 55W
Grand Blanc, *U.S.A.* **157 B13** 42 56N 83 38W
Grand-Bourg, *Guadeloupe* **164 b** 15 53N 61 19W
Grand Canal = Yun Ho →, *China* **75 E9** 39 10N 117 10 E
Grand Canyon, *U.S.A.* **159 H7** 36 3N 112 9W
Grand Canyon △, *U.S.A.* **159 H7** 36 15N 112 30W
Grand Canyon-Parashant ⌓, *U.S.A.* **159 H7** 36 30N 113 20W
Grand Cayman, *Cayman Is.* **164 C3** 19 20N 81 20W
Grand Centre, *Canada* **143 C6** 54 25N 110 13W
Grand Cess, *Liberia* **112 E3** 4 40N 8 12W
Grand Coulee, *U.S.A.* **158 C4** 47 57N 119 0W
Grand Coulee Dam, *U.S.A.* **158 C4** 47 57N 118 59W
Grand Erg de Bilma, *Niger* **109 E2** 18 30N 14 0 E
Grand Falls, *Canada* **141 C6** 47 3N 67 44W
Grand Falls-Windsor, *Canada* **141 C8** 48 56N 55 40W
Grand Forks, *Canada* **142 D5** 49 0N 118 30W
Grand Forks, *U.S.A.* **154 B6** 47 55N 97 3W
Grand Gorge, *U.S.A.* **151 D10** 42 21N 74 29W
Grand Haven, *U.S.A.* **157 A10** 43 4N 86 13W
Grand I., *Mich., U.S.A.* **148 B2** 46 31N 86 40W
Grand I., *N.Y., U.S.A.* **150 D6** 43 0N 78 58W
Grand Island, *U.S.A.* **154 E5** 40 55N 98 21W
Grand Isle, *La., U.S.A.* **155 L9** 29 14N 90 0W
Grand Isle, *Vt., U.S.A.* **151 B11** 44 43N 73 18W
Grand Junction, *Colo., U.S.A.* **159 G9** 39 4N 108 33W
Grand Junction, *Iowa, U.S.A.* **156 B2** 42 2N 94 14W
Grand L., *N.B., Canada* **141 C6** 45 57N 66 7W
Grand L., *Nfld. & L., Canada* **141 C8** 49 0N 57 30W
Grand L., *Nfld. & L., Canada* **141 B7** 53 40N 60 30W
Grand L., *La., U.S.A.* **155 L8** 29 55N 92 47W
Grand L., *Ohio, U.S.A.* **157 D12** 40 32N 84 25W
Grand Lahou, *Ivory C.* **112 D3** 5 10N 5 5W
Grand Lake, *U.S.A.* **158 F11** 40 15N 105 49W
Grand Ledge, *U.S.A.* **157 B12** 42 45N 84 45W
Grand-Lieu, L. de, *France* **26 E5** 47 6N 1 40W
Grand Manan I., *Canada* **141 D6** 44 45N 66 52W
Grand Marais, *Canada* **154 B9** 47 45N 90 25W
Grand Marais, *U.S.A.* **148 B3** 46 40N 85 59W
Grand-Mère, *Canada* **140 C5** 46 36N 72 40W
Grand Popo, *Benin* **113 D5** 6 15N 1 57 E
Grand Portage, *U.S.A.* **154 B10** 47 58N 89 41W
Grand Prairie, *U.S.A.* **155 J6** 32 47N 97 0W
Grand Rapids = Wisconsin Rapids, *U.S.A.* **154 C10** 44 23N 89 49W
Grand Rapids, *Canada* **143 C9** 53 12N 99 19W
Grand Rapids, *Mich., U.S.A.* **157 B10** 42 58N 85 40W
Grand Rapids, *Minn., U.S.A.* **154 B8** 47 14N 93 31W
Grand Ridge, *U.S.A.* **152 E4** 30 43N 85 1W
Grand River, *U.S.A.* **156 D3** 40 49N 93 58W
Grand St-Bernard, Col du, *Europe* **32 E4** 45 50N 7 10 E
Grand Santi, *Fr. Guiana* **169 C7** 4 20N 54 24W
Grand Staircase-Escalante ⌓, *U.S.A.* **159 H8** 37 5N 112 0W
Grand Teton, *U.S.A.* **158 E8** 43 54N 111 50W
Grand Teton △, *U.S.A.* **158 D8** 43 50N 110 50W
Grand Union Canal, *U.K.* **21 E7** 52 7N 0 53W
Grand-Vigie, Pte. de la, *Guadeloupe* **164 b** 16 32N 61 27W
Grandas de Salime, *Spain* **42 B4** 43 13N 6 53W
Grande →, *Jujuy, Argentina* **174 A2** 24 20 S 65 2W
Grande →, *Mendoza, Argentina* **174 D2** 36 52 S 69 45W
Grande →, *Bolivia* **173 D5** 15 51 S 64 39W
Grande →, *Bahia, Brazil* **170 D3** 11 30 S 44 30W
Grande →, *Minas Gerais, Brazil* **171 F1** 20 6 S 51 4W
Grande →, *Venezuela* **169 B5** 8 36N 61 39W
Grande, B., *Argentina* **176 D3** 50 30 S 68 20W
Grande, I., *Brazil* **171 F3** 23 9 S 44 14W
Grande, Rio →, *U.S.A.* **155 N6** 25 58N 97 9W
Grande, Serra, *Piauí, Brazil* **170 C2** 8 0 S 45 10W
Grande, Serra, *Tocantins, Brazil* **170 D2** 11 15 S 46 30W
Grande Anse, *Seychelles* **121 b** 4 40 S 55 26 E
Grande Baleine, R. de la →, *Canada* **140 A4** 55 16N 77 47W
Grande Cache, *Canada* **142 C5** 53 53N 119 8W
Grande Casse, Pte. de la, *France* **29 C10** 45 24N 6 49 E
Grande Comore, *Comoros Is.* **121 a** 11 35 S 43 20 E
Grande Dixence, Barr. de la, *Switz.* **32 D4** 46 5N 7 23 E
Grande-Entrée, *Canada* **141 C7** 47 30N 61 40W
Grande Prairie, *Canada* **142 B5** 55 10N 118 50W
Grande-Rivière, *Canada* **141 C7** 48 26N 64 30W
Grande Sertão Veredas △, *Brazil* **171 E2** 15 10 S 45 40W
Grande-Terre, *Guadeloupe* **164 b** 16 20N 61 25W
Grande-Vallée, *Canada* **141 C6** 49 14N 65 8W
Grandfalls, *U.S.A.* **155 K3** 31 20N 102 51W
Grândola, *Portugal* **43 G2** 38 12N 8 35W
Grandpré, *France* **27 C11** 49 20N 4 50 E
Grands Causses ⌓, *France* **28 D6** 44 5N 2 58 E
Grands-Jardins ⌓, *Canada* **141 C5** 47 41N 70 51W
Grandson, *Switz.* **32 C3** 46 49N 6 39 E
Grandview, *Canada* **143 C8** 51 10N 100 42W
Grandview, *Mo., U.S.A.* **156 F2** 38 53N 94 32W
Grandview, *Wash., U.S.A.* **158 C4** 46 15N 119 54W
Grandview Heights, *U.S.A.* **157 E13** 39 58N 83 2W
Grandvilliers, *France* **27 C8** 49 40N 1 57 E
Graneros, *Chile* **174 C1** 34 5 S 70 45W
Grangemouth, *U.K.* **22 E5** 56 1N 3 42W
Granger, *U.S.A.* **158 F9** 41 35N 109 58W
Grängesberg, *Sweden* **16 D9** 60 6N 15 1 E
Grangeville, *U.S.A.* **158 D5** 45 56N 116 7W
Granisle, *Canada* **142 C3** 54 53N 126 13W
Granite City, *U.S.A.* **156 F6** 38 42N 90 9W
Granite Falls, *U.S.A.* **154 C7** 44 49N 95 33W
Granite L., *Canada* **141 C8** 48 8N 57 5W
Granite Mt., *U.S.A.* **161 M10** 33 5N 116 28W
Granite Pk., *U.S.A.* **158 D9** 45 10N 109 48W
Graniteville, *S.C., U.S.A.* **152 B8** 33 34N 81 49W
Graniteville, *Vt., U.S.A.* **151 B12** 44 8N 72 29W
Granītogorsk, *Kazakhstan* **65 B6** 42 44N 73 28 E
Granitola, C., *Italy* **46 E5** 37 34N 12 39 E
Granity, *N.Z.* **131 B6** 41 39 S 171 51 E
Granja, *Brazil* **170 B3** 3 7 S 40 50W
Granja de Moreruela, *Spain* **42 D5** 41 48N 5 44W
Granja de Torrehermosa, *Spain* **43 G5** 38 19N 5 35W
Gränna, *Sweden* **17 F8** 58 1N 14 28 E
Granollers, *Spain* **40 D7** 41 39N 2 18 E
Gransee, *Germany* **30 B9** 53 1N 13 8 E
Grant, *Fla., U.S.A.* **153 H9** 27 56N 80 32W
Grant, *Nebr., U.S.A.* **154 E4** 40 53N 101 42W
Grant, Mt., *U.S.A.* **158 G4** 38 34N 118 48W
Grant City, *U.S.A.* **156 D2** 40 29N 94 25W
Grant I., *Australia* **124 B5** 11 10 S 132 52 E
Grant Range, *U.S.A.* **159 G6** 38 30N 115 25W
Grantham, *U.K.* **20 E7** 52 55N 0 38W
Grantown-on-Spey, *U.K.* **22 D5** 57 20N 3 36W
Grants, *U.S.A.* **159 J10** 35 9N 107 52W
Grants Pass, *U.S.A.* **158 E2** 42 26N 123 19W
Grantsville, *U.S.A.* **158 F7** 40 36N 112 28W
Grantville, *U.S.A.* **152 B5** 33 14N 84 50W
Granville, *France* **26 D5** 48 50N 1 35W
Granville, *Ill., U.S.A.* **156 C7** 41 16N 89 14W
Granville, *N. Dak., U.S.A.* **154 A4** 48 16N 100 47W
Granville, *N.Y., U.S.A.* **151 C11** 43 24N 73 16W
Granville, *Ohio, U.S.A.* **150 F2** 40 4N 82 31W
Granville L., *Canada* **143 B8** 56 18N 100 30W
Granvin, *Norway* **18 D3** 60 33N 6 45 E
Graskop, *S. Africa* **117 C5** 24 56 S 30 49 E
Gräsö, *Sweden* **16 D12** 60 28N 18 35 E
Grass →, *Canada* **143 B9** 56 3N 96 33W
Grass Range, *U.S.A.* **158 C9** 47 0N 109 0W
Grass River ⌓, *Canada* **143 C8** 54 40N 100 50W
Grass Valley, *Calif., U.S.A.* **160 F6** 39 13N 121 4W
Grass Valley, *Oreg., U.S.A.* **158 D3** 45 22N 120 47W
Grassano, *Italy* **47 B9** 40 38N 16 17 E
Grasse, *France* **29 E10** 43 38N 6 56 E
Grassflat, *U.S.A.* **150 F6** 41 0N 78 6W
Grasslands △, *Canada* **143 D7** 49 11N 107 38W
Grassy, *Australia* **127 G3** 40 3 S 144 5 E
Gråsten, *Denmark* **17 K3** 54 55N 9 35 E
Grästorp, *Sweden* **17 F6** 58 20N 12 40 E
Gratis, *U.S.A.* **157 E12** 39 38N 84 32W
Gratkorn, *Austria* **34 D8** 47 8N 15 21 E
Gratz, *U.S.A.* **157 F12** 38 28N 84 57W
Graubünden □, *Switz.* **33 C9** 46 45N 9 30 E
Graudenz = Grudziądz, *Poland* **54 E5** 53 30N 18 47 E
Graulhet, *France* **28 E5** 43 45N 1 59 E
Graus, *Spain* **40 C5** 42 11N 0 20 E
Gravatá, *Brazil* **170 C4** 8 10 S 35 29W
Gravberget, *Norway* **18 D9** 60 53N 12 14 E
Grave, Pte. de, *France* **28 C2** 45 34N 1 4W
Gravelbourg, *Canada* **143 D7** 49 50N 106 35W
Gravelines, *France* **27 A9** 51 1N 2 10 E
's-Gravenhage, *Neths.* **24 B4** 52 7N 4 17 E
Gravenhurst, *Canada* **140 D4** 44 52N 79 20W
Gravesend, *Australia* **127 D5** 29 35 S 150 20 E
Gravesend, *U.K.* **21 F8** 51 26N 0 22 E
Gravina in Púglia, *Italy* **47 B9** 40 49N 16 25 E
Gravois, Pointe-à-, *Haiti* **165 C5** 18 15N 73 56W
Gravone →, *France* **29 G12** 41 58N 8 45 E
Gray, *France* **27 E12** 47 22N 5 35 E
Gray, *U.S.A.* **152 B6** 33 1N 83 32W
Grayling, *Alaska, U.S.A.* **144 E7** 62 57N 160 3W
Grayling, *Mich., U.S.A.* **148 C3** 44 40N 84 43W
Grays, *U.K.* **21 F8** 51 28N 0 21 E
Grays Harbor, *U.S.A.* **158 C1** 46 59N 124 1W
Grays L., *U.S.A.* **158 E8** 43 4N 111 26W
Grays River, *U.S.A.* **160 D3** 46 21N 123 37W
Grayville, *U.S.A.* **157 F9** 38 16N 88 0W
Grayvoron, *Russia* **59 G8** 50 29N 35 41 E
Graz, *Austria* **34 D8** 47 4N 15 27 E
Grdelica, *Serbia & M.* **50 D6** 42 55N 22 3 E
Greåker, *Norway* **18 E8** 59 16N 11 12 E
Greasy L., *Canada* **142 A4** 62 55N 122 12W
Great Abaco I. = Abaco I., *Bahamas* **164 A4** 26 25N 77 10W
Great Artesian Basin, *Australia* **126 C3** 23 0 S 144 0 E
Great Australian Bight, *Australia* **125 F5** 33 30 S 130 0 E
Great Bahama Bank, *Bahamas* **164 B4** 23 15N 78 0W
Great Barrier I., *N.Z.* **130 C4** 36 11 S 175 25 E
Great Barrier Reef, *Australia* **126 B4** 18 0 S 146 50 E
Great Barrier Reef ⌓, *Australia* **126 B4** 20 0 S 150 0 E
Great Barrington, *U.S.A.* **151 D11** 42 12N 73 22W
Great Basalt Wall △, *Australia* **126 B4** 19 52 S 145 43 E
Great Basin, *U.S.A.* **158 G5** 40 0N 117 0W
Great Basin △, *U.S.A.* **158 G6** 38 55N 114 14W
Great Basses, *Sri Lanka* **95 L5** 6 11N 81 29 E
Great Bear →, *Canada* **138 B7** 65 0N 124 0W
Great Bear L., *Canada* **138 B7** 65 30N 120 0W
Great Belt = Store Bælt, *Denmark* **17 J4** 55 20N 11 0 E
Great Bend, *Kans., U.S.A.* **154 F5** 38 22N 98 46W
Great Bend, *Pa., U.S.A.* **151 E9** 41 58N 75 45W
Great Blasket I., *Ireland* **23 D1** 52 6N 10 32W
Great Britain, *Europe* **12 E5** 54 0N 2 15W
Great Camanoe, *Br. Virgin Is.* **165 e** 18 30N 64 35W
Great Channel, *Asia* **95 L11** 6 0N 94 0 E
Great Coco I., *Burma* **95 G11** 14 7N 93 22 E
Great Codroy, *Canada* **141 C8** 47 51N 59 16W
Great Dividing Ra., *Australia* **126 C4** 23 0 S 146 0 E
Great Driffield = Driffield, *U.K.* **20 C7** 54 0N 0 26W
Great Exuma I., *Bahamas* **164 B4** 23 30N 75 50W
Great Falls, *U.S.A.* **158 C8** 47 30N 111 17W
Great Fish = Groot Vis →, *S. Africa* **116 E4** 33 28 S 27 5 E
Great Guana Cay, *Bahamas* **164 B4** 24 0N 76 20W
Great Himalayan △, *India* **92 D7** 31 30N 77 30 E
Great Inagua I., *Bahamas* **165 B5** 21 0N 73 20W
Great Indian Desert = Thar Desert, *India* **92 F5** 28 0N 72 0 E
Great Karoo, *S. Africa* **116 E3** 31 55 S 21 0 E
Great Khingan Mts. = Da Hinggan Ling, *China* **69 B7** 48 0N 121 0 E
Great Lake, *Australia* **127 G4** 41 50 S 146 40 E
Great Lakes, *N. Amer.* **136 E11** 46 0N 84 0W
Great Malvern, *U.K.* **21 E5** 52 7N 2 18W
Great Miami →, *U.S.A.* **148 F3** 39 20N 84 40W
Great Nicobar, *India* **95 L11** 7 0N 93 50 E
Great Ormes Head, *U.K.* **20 D4** 53 20N 3 52W
Great Ouse →, *U.K.* **20 E8** 52 48N 0 21 E
Great Palm I., *Australia* **126 B4** 18 45 S 146 40 E
Great Pedro Bluff, *Jamaica* **164 a** 17 51N 77 44W
Great Plains, *N. Amer.* **136 E9** 47 0N 105 0W
Great Ruaha →, *Tanzania* **118 D4** 7 56 S 37 52 E
Great Sacandaga L., *U.S.A.* **151 C10** 43 6N 74 16W
Great Saint Bernard Pass = Grand St-Bernard, Col du, *Europe* **32 E4** 45 50N 7 10 E
Great Salt L., *U.S.A.* **158 F7** 41 15N 112 40W
Great Salt Lake Desert, *U.S.A.* **158 F7** 40 50N 113 30W
Great Salt Plains L., *U.S.A.* **155 G5** 36 45N 98 8W
Great Sand Dunes ⌓, *U.S.A.* **159 H11** 37 48N 105 45W
Great Sandy △, *Australia* **127 D5** 26 13 S 153 2 E
Great Sandy Desert, *Australia* **124 D3** 21 0 S 124 0 E
Great Sangi = Sangihe, Pulau, *Indonesia* **82 A3** 3 35N 125 30 E
Great Scarcies →, *S. Leone* **112 D2** 9 0N 13 0W
Great Sd., *Bermuda* **9 a** 32 17N 64 51W
Great Sea Reef, *Fiji* **133 A2** 16 15 S 179 0 E
Great Sitkin I., *U.S.A.* **144 K3** 52 3N 176 6W
Great Skellig, *Ireland* **23 E1** 51 47N 10 33W
Great Slave L., *Canada* **142 A5** 61 23N 115 38W
Great Smoky Mts. △, *U.S.A.* **149 H4** 35 40N 83 40W
Great Snow Mt., *Canada* **142 B4** 57 26N 124 0W
Great Stour = Stour →, *U.K.* **21 F9** 51 18N 1 22 E
Great Victoria Desert, *Australia* **125 E4** 29 30 S 126 30 E
Great Wall, *Antarctica* **7 C18** 62 30 S 58 0W
Great Wall, *China* **74 E5** 38 30N 109 30 E
Great Whale River = Kuujjuarapik, *Canada* **140 A4** 55 20N 77 35W
Great Whernside, *U.K.* **20 C6** 54 10N 1 58W
Great Yarmouth, *U.K.* **21 E9** 52 37N 1 44 E
Great Zab = Zāb al Kabīr →, *Iraq* **101 D10** 36 1N 43 24 E
Great Zimbabwe, *Zimbabwe* **119 G3** 20 16 S 30 54 E
Greater Antilles, *W. Indies* **165 C5** 17 40N 74 0W
Greater London □, *U.K.* **21 F7** 51 31N 0 6W
Greater Manchester □, *U.K.* **20 D5** 53 30N 2 15W
Greater St. Lucia Wetlands ⌓, *S. Africa* **117 D5** 28 6 S 32 27 E
Greater Sudbury = Sudbury, *Canada* **140 C3** 46 30N 81 0W
Greater Sunda Is., *Indonesia* **78 F4** 7 0 S 112 0 E
Grebbestad, *Sweden* **17 F5** 58 42N 11 15 E
Grebenka = Hrebenka, *Ukraine* **59 G7** 50 9N 32 22 E
Greco, C., *Cyprus* **39 F10** 34 57N 34 5 E
Greco, Mte., *Italy* **45 G10** 41 48N 13 58 E
Gredos, Sierra de, *Spain* **42 E6** 40 20N 5 0W
Greece, *U.S.A.* **150 C7** 43 13N 77 41W
Greece ■, *Europe* **48 B3** 40 0N 23 0 E
Greeley, *Colo., U.S.A.* **154 E2** 40 25N 104 42W
Greeley, *Nebr., U.S.A.* **154 E5** 41 33N 98 32W
Greeleyville, *U.S.A.* **152 B10** 33 40N 79 59W
Greem-Bell, Ostrov, *Russia* **66 A7** 81 0N 62 0 E
Green, *U.S.A.* **158 E2** 43 9N 123 22W
Green →, *Ky., U.S.A.* **148 G2** 37 54N 87 30W
Green →, *Utah, U.S.A.* **159 G9** 38 11N 109 53W
Green B., *U.S.A.* **148 C2** 45 0N 87 30W
Green Bay, *U.S.A.* **148 C2** 44 31N 88 0W
Green C., *Australia* **129 D9** 37 13 S 150 1 E
Green City, *U.S.A.* **156 D4** 40 16N 92 57W
Green Cove Springs, *U.S.A.* **152 F8** 29 59N 81 42W
Green Is., *Papua N. G.* **132 C8** 4 35 S 154 10 E
Green Island Bay, *Phil.* **81 F2** 10 12N 119 22 E
Green Lake, *Canada* **143 C7** 54 17N 107 47W
Green Mts., *U.S.A.* **151 C12** 43 45N 72 45W
Green Pond, *U.S.A.* **152 C9** 32 44N 80 37W
Green River, *Papua N. G.* **132 B1** 3 54 S 141 11 E
Green River, *Utah, U.S.A.* **159 G8** 38 59N 110 10W
Green River, *Wyo., U.S.A.* **158 F9** 41 32N 109 28W
Green Valley, *U.S.A.* **159 L8** 31 52N 110 56W
Greenacres City, *U.S.A.* **153 J9** 26 38N 80 7W
Greenbank, *U.S.A.* **160 B4** 48 6N 122 34W
Greenbush, *Mich., U.S.A.* **150 B1** 44 35N 83 19W
Greenbush, *Minn., U.S.A.* **154 A6** 48 42N 96 11W
Greencastle, *U.S.A.* **157 E10** 39 38N 86 52W
Greene, *Iowa, U.S.A.* **156 B4** 42 54N 92 48W
Greene, *N.Y., U.S.A.* **151 D9** 42 20N 75 46W
Greenfield, *Calif., U.S.A.* **160 J5** 36 19N 121 15W
Greenfield, *Calif., U.S.A.* **161 K8** 35 15N 119 0W
Greenfield, *Ill., U.S.A.* **156 E6** 39 21N 90 12W
Greenfield, *Ind., U.S.A.* **157 E11** 39 47N 85 46W
Greenfield, *Iowa, U.S.A.* **156 C2** 41 18N 94 28W
Greenfield, *Mass., U.S.A.* **151 D12** 42 35N 72 36W
Greenfield, *Mo., U.S.A.* **155 G8** 37 25N 93 51W
Greenfield, *Ohio, U.S.A.* **157 E13** 39 21N 83 23W
Greenfield Park, *Canada* **151 A11** 45 29N 73 29W
Greenland ☒, *N. Amer.* **10 D6** 66 0N 45 0W
Greenland Sea, *Arctic* **10 B10** 73 0N 10 0W
Greenock, *U.K.* **22 F4** 55 57N 4 46W
Greenore, *Ireland* **23 B5** 54 2N 6 8W
Greenore Pt., *Ireland* **23 D5** 52 14N 6 19W
Greenough, *Australia* **125 E1** 28 58 S 114 43 E
Greenough →, *Australia* **125 E1** 28 51 S 114 38 E
Greenough Pt., *Canada* **150 B3** 44 58N 81 26W
Greenport, *U.S.A.* **151 E12** 41 6N 72 22W
Greensboro, *Fla., U.S.A.* **152 E5** 30 34N 84 45W
Greensboro, *Ga., U.S.A.* **152 B6** 33 35N 83 11W
Greensboro, *N.C., U.S.A.* **149 G6** 36 4N 79 48W
Greensboro, *Vt., U.S.A.* **151 B12** 44 36N 72 18W
Greensburg, *Ind., U.S.A.* **157 E11** 39 20N 85 29W
Greensburg, *Kans., U.S.A.* **155 G5** 37 36N 99 18W
Greensburg, *Pa., U.S.A.* **150 F5** 40 18N 79 33W
Greenstone Pt., *U.K.* **22 D3** 57 55N 5 37W
Greentown, *U.S.A.* **157 D11** 40 29N 85 58W
Greenup, *U.S.A.* **157 E8** 39 15N 88 10W
Greenvale, *Australia* **126 B4** 18 59 S 145 7 E
Greenville, *Liberia* **112 D3** 5 1N 9 6W
Greenville, *Ala., U.S.A.* **149 K2** 31 50N 86 38W
Greenville, *Calif., U.S.A.* **160 E6** 40 8N 120 57W
Greenville, *Fla., U.S.A.* **152 E6** 30 28N 83 38W
Greenville, *Ga., U.S.A.* **152 B5** 33 2N 84 43W
Greenville, *Ill., U.S.A.* **156 F7** 38 53N 89 25W
Greenville, *Ind., U.S.A.* **157 F11** 38 22N 85 59W
Greenville, *Maine, U.S.A.* **149 C11** 45 28N 69 35W
Greenville, *Mich., U.S.A.* **157 A11** 43 11N 85 15W
Greenville, *Miss., U.S.A.* **155 J9** 33 24N 91 4W
Greenville, *Mo., U.S.A.* **155 G9** 37 8N 90 27W
Greenville, *N.C., U.S.A.* **149 H7** 35 37N 77 23W
Greenville, *N.H., U.S.A.* **151 D13** 42 46N 71 49W
Greenville, *N.Y., U.S.A.* **151 D10** 42 25N 74 1W
Greenville, *Ohio, U.S.A.* **157 D12** 40 6N 84 38W
Greenville, *Pa., U.S.A.* **150 E4** 41 24N 80 23W
Greenville, *S.C., U.S.A.* **149 H4** 34 51N 82 24W
Greenville, *Tenn., U.S.A.* **149 G4** 36 13N 82 51W
Greenville, *Tex., U.S.A.* **155 J6** 33 8N 96 7W
Greenwater Lake ⌓, *Canada* **143 C8** 52 32N 103 30W
Greenwich, *Conn., U.S.A.* **151 E11** 41 2N 73 38W
Greenwich, *N.Y., U.S.A.* **151 C11** 43 5N 73 30W
Greenwich, *Ohio, U.S.A.* **150 E2** 41 2N 82 31W
Greenwich □, *U.K.* **21 F8** 51 29N 0 1 E
Greenwood, *Canada* **142 D5** 49 10N 118 40W
Greenwood, *Ark., U.S.A.* **155 H7** 35 13N 94 16W
Greenwood, *Fla., U.S.A.* **152 E4** 30 52N 85 10W
Greenwood, *Ind., U.S.A.* **157 E10** 39 37N 86 7W
Greenwood, *Miss., U.S.A.* **155 J9** 33 31N 90 11W
Greenwood, *S.C., U.S.A.* **149 H4** 34 12N 82 10W
Greenwood, Mt., *Australia* **124 B5** 13 48 S 130 4 E
Gregbe, *Ivory C.* **112 D3** 6 48N 6 43W
Gregório →, *Brazil* **172 B3** 6 50 S 70 46W
Gregory, *U.S.A.* **154 D5** 43 14N 99 20W
Gregory △, *Australia* **124 C5** 15 38 S 131 15 E
Gregory →, *Australia* **126 B2** 17 53 S 139 17 E
Gregory, L., *S. Austral., Australia* **127 D2** 28 55 S 139 0 E
Gregory, L., *W. Austral., Australia* **125 E2** 25 38 S 119 58 E
Gregory Downs, *Australia* **126 B2** 18 35 S 138 45 E
Gregory L., *Australia* **124 D4** 20 0 S 127 40 E
Gregory Ra., *Queens., Australia* **126 B3** 19 30 S 143 40 E
Gregory Ra., *W. Austral., Australia* **124 D3** 21 20 S 121 12 E
Greifenberg = Gryfice, *Poland* **54 E2** 53 55N 15 13 E
Greifenhagen = Gryfino, *Poland* **55 E1** 53 16N 14 29 E
Greiffenberg = Gryfów Śląski, *Poland* **55 G2** 51 2N 15 24 E
Greiffenberg, *Germany* **30 B9** 53 5N 13 57 E
Greifswald, *Germany* **30 A9** 54 5N 13 23 E
Greifswalder Bodden, *Germany* **30 A9** 54 12N 13 35 E
Grein, *Austria* **34 C7** 48 14N 14 51 E
Greiz, *Germany* **30 E8** 50 39N 12 10 E
Gremikha, *Russia* **56 A6** 67 59N 39 47 E
Gremyachinsk, *Russia* **64 B6** 58 34N 57 51 E
Grenå, *Denmark* **17 H4** 56 25N 10 53 E
Grenada, *U.S.A.* **155 J10** 33 47N 89 49W
Grenada ■, *W. Indies* **165 D7** 12 10N 61 40W
Grenade, *France* **28 E5** 43 47N 1 17 E
Grenadier I., *U.S.A.* **151 B8** 44 3N 76 22W
Grenadines, The, *St. Vincent* **165 D7** 12 40N 61 20W
Grenchen, *Switz.* **32 B4** 47 12N 7 24 E
Grenen, *Denmark* **17 G4** 57 44N 10 40 E
Grenfell, *Australia* **129 B8** 33 52 S 148 8 E
Grenfell, *Canada* **143 C8** 50 30N 102 56W
Grenivík, *Iceland* **11 B8** 65 57N 18 11W
Grenjaðarstaður, *Iceland* **11 B9** 65 49N 17 21W
Grenoble, *France* **29 C9** 45 12N 5 42 E
Grenville, C., *Australia* **126 A3** 12 0 S 143 13 E
Grenville Chan., *Canada* **142 C3** 53 40N 129 46W
Gréoux-les-Bains, *France* **29 E9** 43 45N 5 52 E
Gresham, *U.S.A.* **160 E4** 45 30N 122 26W
Gresik, *Indonesia* **85 D4** 7 13 S 112 38 E
Gressan, *Italy* **32 E4** 45 43N 7 17 E
Gretna, *U.K.* **22 F5** 55 0N 3 3W
Gretna, *Fla., U.S.A.* **152 E5** 30 37N 84 40W
Gretna, *La., U.S.A.* **155 L9** 29 55N 90 4W
Greven, *Germany* **30 C3** 52 6N 7 37 E
Grevená, *Greece* **50 F5** 40 4N 21 25 E
Grevená □, *Greece* **50 F5** 40 2N 21 25 E
Grevenbroich, *Germany* **30 D2** 51 5N 6 35 E
Grevenmacher, *Lux.* **24 E6** 49 41N 6 26 E
Grevesmühlen, *Germany* **30 B7** 53 52N 11 12 E
Grevestrand, *Denmark* **17 J6** 55 36N 12 19 E
Grey →, *Canada* **141 C8** 47 34N 57 6W
Grey →, *N.Z.* **131 C6** 42 27 S 171 12 E
Grey, C., *Australia* **126 A2** 13 0 S 136 35 E
Grey Ra., *Australia* **127 D3** 27 0 S 143 30 E
Greybull, *U.S.A.* **158 D9** 44 30N 108 3W
Greymouth, *N.Z.* **131 C6** 42 29 S 171 13 E
Greystones, *Ireland* **23 C5** 53 9N 6 5W
Greytown, *N.Z.* **130 H4** 41 5 S 175 29 E
Greytown, *S. Africa* **117 D5** 29 1 S 30 36 E
Gribanovskiy, *Russia* **60 E5** 51 28N 41 50 E
Gribbell I., *Canada* **142 C3** 53 23N 129 0W
Gribës, Mal i, *Albania* **50 F3** 40 17N 19 45 E
Gribingui →, *C.A.R.* **114 A3** 8 33N 19 5 E
Gribingui-Bamingui ⌓, *C.A.R.* **114 A3** 7 45N 19 17 E
Gridley, *U.S.A.* **160 F5** 39 22N 121 42W
Griebeg, Ras il-, *Malta* **38 F7** 35 58N 14 23 E
Griekwastad, *S. Africa* **116 D3** 28 49 S 23 15 E
Griesheim, *Germany* **31 F4** 49 51N 8 33 E
Grieskirchen, *Austria* **34 C6** 48 16N 13 48 E
Griffin, *U.S.A.* **152 B5** 33 15N 84 16W
Griffin, L., *U.S.A.* **153 G8** 28 52N 81 51W
Griffith, *Australia* **129 C7** 34 18 S 146 2 E
Griffith, *Canada* **150 A7** 45 15N 77 10W
Griffith I., *Canada* **150 B4** 44 50N 80 55W
Griggsville, *U.S.A.* **156 E6** 39 43N 90 43W
Grignols, *France* **28 D3** 44 23N 0 2W
Grigoriopol, *Moldova* **53 C14** 47 9N 29 18 E
Grimari, *C.A.R.* **114 A4** 5 43N 20 6 E
Grimaylov = Hrymayliv, *Ukraine* **59 H4** 49 20N 26 5 E
Grimes, *U.S.A.* **160 F5** 39 4N 121 54W
Grimm = Kamenskiy, *Russia* **60 E7** 50 48N 45 25 E
Grimma, *Germany* **30 D8** 51 14N 12 43 E
Grimmen, *Germany* **30 A9** 54 7N 13 3 E
Grimsay, *U.K.* **22 D1** 57 29N 7 14W
Grimsby, *Canada* **150 C5** 43 12N 79 34W
Grimsby, *U.K.* **20 D7** 53 34N 0 5W
Grimselpass, *Switz.* **33 C6** 46 34N 8 23 E
Grímsey, *Iceland* **11 A9** 66 33N 17 58W
Grimshaw, *Canada* **142 B5** 56 10N 117 40W
Grimslöv, *Sweden* **17 H8** 56 44N 14 34 E
Grímsstaðir, *Iceland* **11 B10** 65 39N 16 7W
Grimstad, *Norway* **18 F5** 58 20N 8 35 E
Grímsvötn, *Iceland* **11 C9** 64 26N 17 22W
Grindavík, *Iceland* **11 D4** 63 50N 22 26W
Grindelwald, *Switz.* **32 C6** 46 38N 8 2 E
Grindsted, *Denmark* **17 J2** 55 46N 8 55 E
Grindstone I., *Canada* **151 B8** 44 43N 76 14W
Grindu, *Romania* **53 F11** 44 44N 26 50 E
Grinnell, *U.S.A.* **156 C4** 41 45N 92 43W
Grintavec, *Slovenia* **45 B11** 46 22N 14 32 E
Gris-Nez, C., *France* **27 B8** 50 52N 1 35 E
Grishino = Krasnoarmeisk, *Ukraine* **59 H9** 48 18N 37 11 E
Grisolles, *France* **28 E5** 43 49N 1 19 E
Grisons = Graubünden □, *Switz.* **33 C9** 46 45N 9 30 E
Grisslehamn, *Sweden* **16 D12** 60 5N 18 49 E
Grmeč Planina, *Bos.-H.* **45 D13** 44 43N 16 16 E
Groais I., *Canada* **141 B8** 50 55N 55 35W
Grobiņa, *Latvia* **54 B8** 56 33N 21 10 E
Groblersdal, *S. Africa* **117 D4** 25 15 S 29 25 E
Grobming, *Austria* **34 D6** 47 27N 13 54 E
Grocka, *Serbia & M.* **50 B4** 44 40N 20 42 E
Gródek, *Poland* **55 E10** 53 6N 23 40 E
Gródek Tagiellońśki = Horodok, *Ukraine* **59 H2** 49 46N 23 32 E
Grodekovo = Pogranichnyy, *Russia* **70 B5** 44 25N 131 24 E
Grodków, *Poland* **55 H4** 50 43N 17 21 E
Grodno = Hrodna, *Belarus* **54 E10** 53 42N 23 52 E
Grodzisk Mazowiecki, *Poland* **55 F7** 52 7N 20 37 E
Grodzisk Wielkopolski, *Poland* **55 F3** 52 15N 16 22 E
Grodzyanka = Hrodzyanka, *Belarus* **58 F5** 53 31N 28 42 E
Groesbeck, *U.S.A.* **155 K6** 30 48N 96 31W
Groix, *France* **26 E3** 47 38N 3 29W
Groix, Î. de, *France* **26 E3** 47 38N 3 28W
Grójec, *Poland* **55 G7** 51 50N 20 58 E
Gronau, *Niedersachsen, Germany* **30 C5** 52 5N 9 47 E
Gronau, *Nordrhein-Westfalen, Germany* **30 C3** 52 12N 7 2 E
Grong, *Norway* **14 D15** 64 25N 12 8 E
Grönhögen, *Sweden* **17 H10** 56 16N 16 24 E
Groningen, *Neths.* **24 A6** 53 15N 6 35 E
Groningen, *Suriname* **169 B6** 5 48N 55 28W
Groningen □, *Neths.* **24 A6** 53 16N 6 40 E
Grønnedal = Kangilinnguit, *Greenland* **10 E6** 61 20N 47 57W
Groom, *U.S.A.* **155 H4** 35 12N 101 6W
Groot →, *S. Africa* **116 E3** 33 45 S 24 36 E
Groot Berg →, *S. Africa* **116 E2** 32 47 S 18 8 E
Groot-Brakrivier, *S. Africa* **116 E3** 34 2 S 22 18 E
Groot Karasberge, *Namibia* **116 D2** 27 20 S 18 40 E
Groot-Kei →, *S. Africa* **117 E4** 32 41 S 28 22 E
Groot Vis →, *S. Africa* **116 E4** 33 28 S 27 5 E
Grootdrink, *S. Africa* **116 D3** 28 33 S 21 42 E
Groote Eylandt, *Australia* **126 A2** 14 0 S 136 40 E
Grootfontein, *Namibia* **116 B2** 19 31 S 18 6 E
Grootlaagte →, *Africa* **116 C3** 20 55 S 21 27 E
Grootvloer →, *S. Africa* **116 E3** 30 0 S 20 40 E
Gros C., *Canada* **142 A6** 61 59N 113 32W
Gros Islet, *St. Lucia* **165 f** 14 5N 60 58W
Gros Morne △, *Canada* **141 C8** 49 40N 57 50W
Gros Piton, *St. Lucia* **165 f** 13 49N 61 5W
Gros Piton Pt., *St. Lucia* **165 f** 13 49N 61 5W
Grósio, *Italy* **44 B7** 46 18N 10 16 E
Grosne →, *France* **27 F11** 46 42N 4 56 E
Grosotto, *Italy* **33 D10** 46 17N 10 15 E
Gross-Meseritsch = Velké Meziříčí, *Czech Rep.* **34 B9** 49 21N 16 1 E
Gross Strehlitz = Strzelce Opolskie, *Poland* **55 H5** 50 31N 18 18 E
Gross Wartenberg = Syców, *Poland* **55 G4** 51 19N 17 40 E

Grossa, Pta., Spain **38 C2** 39 6N 1 36 E
Grosse I., U.S.A. **157 B13** 42 8N 83 9W
Grossenbrode, Germany **30 A7** 54 21N 11 4 E
Grossenhain, Germany **30 D9** 51 17N 13 32 E
Grosser Arber, Germany **31 F9** 49 6N 13 8 E
Grosser Plöner See, Germany **30 A6** 54 10N 10 22 E
Grosseto, Italy **45 F8** 42 46N 11 8 E
Grossgerungs, Austria **34 C7** 48 34N 14 57 E
Grossglockner, Austria **34 D5** 47 5N 12 40 E
Grosswardein = Oradea, Romania **52 C6** 47 2N 21 58 E
Groswater B., Canada **141 B8** 54 20N 57 40W
Grotli, Norway **18 B4** 62 2N 7 42 E
Groton, Conn., U.S.A. **151 E12** 41 21N 72 5W
Groton, N.Y., U.S.A. **151 D8** 42 36N 76 22W
Groton, S. Dak., U.S.A. **154 C5** 45 27N 98 6W
Grottáglie, Italy **47 B10** 40 32N 17 26 E
Grottaminarda, Italy **47 A8** 41 4N 15 2 E
Grottammare, Italy **45 F10** 42 59N 13 52 E
Grottkau = Grodków, Poland **55 H4** 50 43N 17 21 E
Grouard Mission, Canada **142 B5** 55 33N 116 9W
Grouin, Pte. du, France **26 D5** 48 43N 1 51W
Groundhog →, Canada **140 C3** 48 45N 82 58W
Grouw, Neths. **24 A5** 53 5N 5 51 E
Grove City, Fla., U.S.A. **153 J7** 26 56N 82 19W
Grove City, Ohio, U.S.A. **157 E13** 39 53N 83 6W
Grove City, Pa., U.S.A. **150 E4** 41 10N 80 5W
Grove Hill, U.S.A. **149 K2** 31 42N 87 47W
Groveland, Calif., U.S.A. **160 H6** 37 50N 120 14W
Groveland, Fla., U.S.A. **153 G8** 28 34N 81 51W
Grover = Tiltonsville, U.S.A. **150 F4** 40 10N 80 41W
Grover City, U.S.A. **161 K6** 35 7N 120 37W
Groves, U.S.A. **155 L8** 29 57N 93 54W
Groveton, U.S.A. **151 B13** 44 36N 71 31W
Grovetown, U.S.A. **152 B7** 33 27N 82 12W
Grožnjan, Croatia **45 C10** 45 22N 13 43 E
Groznyy, Russia **61 J7** 43 20N 45 45 E
Grua, Norway **18 D7** 60 16N 10 40 E
Grubišno Polje, Croatia **52 E2** 45 44N 17 12 E
Grudovo, Bulgaria **51 D11** 42 21N 27 10 E
Grudusk, Poland **55 E7** 53 3N 20 38 E
Grudziądz, Poland **54 E5** 53 30N 18 47 E
Gruinard B., U.K. **22 D3** 57 56N 5 35W
Gruissan, France **28 E7** 43 8N 3 7 E
Grukhi = Novovyatsk, Russia **64 B2** 58 24N 49 45 E
Grumo Áppula, Italy **47 A9** 41 1N 16 42 E
Grums, Sweden **16 E7** 59 22N 13 5 E
Grünberg, Germany **30 E4** 50 35N 8 58 E
Grünberg in Schlesien = Zielona Góra, Poland **55 G2** 51 57N 15 31 E
Grund, Iceland **11 B8** 65 31N 18 9W
Gründau, Germany **31 E5** 50 10N 9 9 E
Grundy Center, U.S.A. **156 B4** 42 22N 92 47W
Grungedal, Norway **18 E4** 59 44N 7 43 E
Grünstadt, Germany **31 F4** 49 34N 8 9 E
Gruppo di Tessa ⌓, Italy **44 B8** 46 47N 11 0 E
Gruvberget, Sweden **16 C10** 61 6N 16 10 E
Gruver, U.S.A. **155 G4** 36 16N 101 24W
Gruyères, Switz. **32 C4** 46 35N 7 4 E
Gruža, Serbia & M. **50 C4** 43 54N 20 46 E
Gryazi, Russia **59 F10** 52 30N 39 58 E
Gryazliv = Borovichi, Russia **58 C7** 58 25N 33 55 E
Gryazovets, Russia **58 C11** 58 50N 40 10 E
Grybów, Poland **55 J7** 49 36N 20 55 E
Grycksbo, Sweden **16 D9** 60 40N 15 29 E
Gryfice, Poland **54 E2** 53 55N 15 13 E
Gryfino, Poland **55 E1** 53 16N 14 29 E
Gryfów Śląski, Poland **55 G2** 51 2N 15 24 E
Grythyttan, Sweden **16 E8** 59 41N 14 32 E
Gstaad, Switz. **32 D4** 46 28N 7 18 E
Gua Musang, Malaysia **87 K3** 4 53N 101 58 E
Guacanayabo, G. de, Cuba **164 B4** 20 40N 77 20W
Guacara, Venezuela **168 A4** 10 14N 67 53W
Guachípas →, Argentina **174 B2** 25 40 S 65 30W
Guachiría →, Colombia **168 B3** 5 27N 70 36W
Guadajoz →, Spain **43 H6** 37 50N 4 51W
Guadalajara, Mexico **162 C4** 20 40N 103 20W
Guadalajara, Spain **40 E1** 40 37N 3 12W
Guadalajara □, Spain **40 E2** 40 47N 2 30W
Guadalcanal, Solomon Is. **133 M11** 9 32 S 160 12 E
Guadalcanal, Spain **43 G5** 38 5N 5 52W
Guadalén →, Spain **43 G7** 38 5N 3 32W
Guadales, Argentina **174 C2** 34 30 S 67 55W
Guadalete →, Spain **43 J4** 36 35N 6 13W
Guadalimar →, Spain **43 G7** 38 5N 3 28W
Guadalmena →, Spain **43 G8** 38 19N 2 56W
Guadalmez →, Spain **43 G5** 38 46N 5 4W
Guadalope →, Spain **40 D4** 41 15N 0 3W
Guadalquivir →, Spain **43 J4** 36 47N 6 22W
Guadalupe = Guadeloupe ⊠, W. Indies **164 b** 16 20N 61 40W
Guadalupe, Brazil **170 C3** 6 44 S 43 47W
Guadalupe, Mexico **161 N10** 32 4N 116 32W
Guadalupe, Spain **43 F5** 39 27N 5 17W
Guadalupe, U.S.A. **161 L6** 34 59N 120 33W
Guadalupe →, Mexico **161 N10** 32 6N 116 51W
Guadalupe →, U.S.A. **155 L6** 28 27N 96 47W
Guadalupe, Sierra de, Spain **43 F5** 39 28N 5 30W
Guadalupe Bravos, Mexico **162 A3** 31 20N 106 10W
Guadalupe I., Pac. Oc. **136 G8** 29 0N 118 50W
Guadalupe Mts. △, U.S.A. **155 K2** 31 40N 104 30W
Guadalupe Peak, U.S.A. **155 K2** 31 50N 104 52W
Guadalupe y Calvo, Mexico **162 B3** 26 6N 106 58W
Guadarrama, Sierra de, Spain **42 E7** 41 0N 4 0W
Guadauta, Georgia **61 J5** 43 7N 40 32 E
Guadeloupe △, Guadeloupe **164 b** 16 10N 61 40W
Guadeloupe ⊠, W. Indies **164 b** 16 20N 61 40W
Guadeloupe Passage, W. Indies **165 C7** 16 50N 62 15W
Guadelupe, Peru **172 B2** 7 15 S 79 29W
Guadiamar →, Spain **43 J4** 36 55N 6 24W
Guadiana →, Portugal **43 H3** 37 14N 7 22W
Guadiana Menor →, Spain **43 H7** 37 56N 3 15W
Guadiaro →, Spain **43 J5** 36 17N 5 17W
Guadiato →, Spain **43 H5** 37 48N 5 5W
Guadiela →, Spain **40 E2** 40 22N 2 49W
Guadix, Spain **43 H7** 37 18N 3 11W
Guafo, Boca del, Chile **176 B2** 43 35 S 74 0W
Guafo, I., Chile **176 B2** 43 35 S 74 50W
Guaico, Trin. & Tob. **169 F9** 10 35N 61 9W
Guainía □, Colombia **168 C4** 2 30N 69 0W
Guainía →, Colombia **168 C4** 2 1N 67 7W
Guaíra, Brazil **175 A5** 24 5 S 54 10W
Guaíra □, Paraguay **174 B4** 25 45 S 56 30W
Guaitecas, Is., Chile **176 B2** 44 0 S 74 30W
Guajará-Mirim, Brazil **173 C4** 10 50 S 65 20W
Guajira □, Colombia **168 A3** 11 30N 72 30W
Guajira, Pen. de la, Colombia **168 A3** 12 0N 72 0W
Gualaceo, Ecuador **168 D2** 2 54 S 78 47W
Gualán, Guatemala **164 C2** 15 8N 89 22W
Gualdo Tadino, Italy **45 E9** 43 14N 12 47 E
Gualeguay, Argentina **174 C4** 33 10 S 59 14W
Gualeguaychú, Argentina **174 C4** 33 3 S 59 31W
Gualequay →, Argentina **174 C4** 33 19 S 59 39W
Gualicho, Salina, Argentina **176 B3** 40 25 S 65 20W
Gualjaina, Argentina **176 B2** 42 45 S 70 30W
Guam ⊠, Pac. Oc. **133 R15** 13 27N 144 45 E
Guamá, Brazil **170 B2** 1 37 S 47 29W
Guamá →, Brazil **170 B2** 1 29 S 48 30W
Guamblin, I., Chile **176 B1** 44 50 S 75 0W
Guaminí, Argentina **174 D3** 37 1 S 62 28W
Guamote, Ecuador **168 D2** 1 56 S 78 43W
Guampí, Sierra de, Venezuela **169 B4** 6 0N 65 35W
Guamúchil, Mexico **162 B3** 25 25N 108 3W
Guana I., Br. Virgin Is. **165 e** 18 30N 64 30W
Guanabacoa, Cuba **164 B3** 23 8N 82 18W
Guanacaste △, Costa Rica **164 D2** 10 57N 85 30W
Guanacaste, Cordillera del, Costa Rica **164 D2** 10 40N 85 4W
Guanaceví, Mexico **162 B3** 25 40N 106 0W
Guanahani = San Salvador I., Bahamas **165 B5** 24 0N 74 40W
Guanajay, Cuba **164 B3** 22 56N 82 42W
Guanajuato, Mexico **162 C4** 21 0N 101 20W
Guanajuato □, Mexico **162 C4** 20 40N 101 20W
Guanambi, Brazil **171 D3** 14 13 S 42 47W
Guanare, Venezuela **168 B4** 8 42N 69 12W
Guanare →, Venezuela **168 B4** 8 13N 67 46W
Guandacol, Argentina **174 B2** 29 30 S 68 40W
Guane, Cuba **164 B3** 22 10N 84 7W
Guang'an, China **76 B6** 30 28N 106 35 E
Guangchang, China **77 D11** 26 50N 116 21 E
Guangde, China **77 B12** 30 54N 119 25 E
Guangdong □, China **77 F9** 23 0N 113 0 E
Guangfeng, China **77 C12** 28 20N 118 15 E
Guanghan, China **76 B5** 30 58N 104 17 E
Guangling, China **74 E8** 39 47N 114 22 E
Guangnan, China **76 E5** 24 5N 105 4 E
Guangning, China **77 F9** 23 40N 112 22 E
Guangrao, China **75 F10** 37 5N 118 25 E
Guangshui, China **77 B9** 31 37N 114 0 E
Guangshun, China **76 D6** 26 8N 106 21 E
Guangwu, China **74 F3** 37 48N 105 57 E
Guangxi Zhuangzu Zizhiqu □, China **76 F7** 24 0N 109 0 E
Guangyuan, China **76 A5** 32 26N 105 51 E
Guangze, China **77 D11** 27 30N 117 12 E
Guangzhou, China **77 F9** 23 5N 113 10 E
Guanhães, Brazil **171 E3** 18 47 S 42 57W
Guánica, Puerto Rico **165 d** 17 58N 66 55W
Guanipa →, Venezuela **169 B5** 9 56N 62 26W
Guanling, China **76 E5** 25 56N 105 35 E
Guannan, China **75 G10** 34 8N 119 21 E
Guanta, Venezuela **169 A5** 10 14N 64 36W
Guantánamo, Cuba **165 B4** 20 10N 75 14W
Guantánamo B., Cuba **165 C4** 19 59N 75 10W
Guantao, China **74 F8** 36 42N 115 25 E
Guanyang, China **77 E8** 25 30N 111 8 E
Guanyun, China **75 G10** 34 20N 119 18 E
Guapí, Colombia **168 C2** 2 36N 77 54W
Guápiles, Costa Rica **164 D3** 10 10N 83 46W
Guapo B., Trin. & Tob. **169 F9** 10 12N 61 41W
Guaporé = Rondônia, Brazil **173 C5** 10 52 S 61 57W
Guaporé, Brazil **175 B5** 28 51 S 51 54W
Guaporé →, Brazil **173 C4** 11 55 S 65 4W
Guaqui, Bolivia **172 D4** 16 41 S 68 54W
Guara, Sierra de, Spain **40 C4** 42 19N 0 15W
Guarabira, Brazil **170 C4** 6 51 S 35 29W
Guaramacal △, Venezuela **165 E5** 9 13N 70 12W
Guaranda, Ecuador **168 D2** 1 36 S 79 0W
Guarani = Pacajus, Brazil **170 B4** 4 10 S 38 31W
Guarapari, Brazil **171 F3** 20 40 S 40 30W
Guarapuava, Brazil **171 G1** 25 20 S 51 30W
Guaratinguetá, Brazil **175 A6** 22 49 S 45 9W
Guaratuba, Brazil **175 B6** 25 53 S 48 38W
Guarda, Portugal **42 E3** 40 32N 7 20W
Guarda □, Portugal **42 E3** 40 40N 7 20W
Guardafui, C. = Asir, Ras, Somali Rep. **120 B4** 11 55N 51 10 E
Guardamar del Segura, Spain **41 G4** 38 5N 0 39W
Guardavalle, Italy **47 D9** 38 30N 16 30 E
Guárdia Sanframondi, Italy **47 A7** 41 15N 14 36 E
Guardiagrele, Italy **45 F11** 42 11N 14 13 E
Guardo, Spain **42 C6** 42 47N 4 50W
Guareña, Spain **43 G4** 38 51N 6 6W
Guareña →, Spain **42 D5** 41 29N 5 23W
Guari, Papua N. G. **132 E4** 8 3 S 146 52 E
Guárico □, Venezuela **168 B4** 8 40N 66 35W
Guarrojo →, Colombia **168 C3** 4 6N 70 42W
Guarujá, Brazil **175 A6** 24 2 S 46 25W
Guarulhos = Guarus, Brazil **171 F3** 21 44 S 41 20W
Guarulhos, Brazil **175 A6** 23 29 S 46 33W
Guarus, Brazil **171 F3** 21 44 S 41 20W
Guasave, Mexico **162 B3** 25 34N 108 27W
Guascama, Pta., Colombia **168 C2** 2 32N 78 24W
Guasdualito, Venezuela **168 B3** 7 15N 70 44W
Guasipati, Venezuela **169 B5** 7 28N 61 54W
Guasopa, Papua N. G. **132 E7** 9 12 S 152 56 E
Guastalla, Italy **44 D7** 44 55N 10 39 E
Guatemala, Guatemala **164 D1** 14 40N 90 22W
Guatemala ■, Cent. Amer. **164 C1** 15 40N 90 30W
Guatemala Trench, Pac. Oc. **136 H10** 15 0N 95 0W
Guatire, Venezuela **168 A4** 10 28N 66 32W
Guatopo △, Venezuela **165 D6** 10 5N 66 30W
Guatuaro Pt., Trin. & Tob. **169 F10** 10 19N 60 59W
Guavi →, Papua N. G. **132 D2** 7 48 S 143 16 E
Guaviare □, Colombia **168 C3** 2 0N 72 30W
Guaviare →, Colombia **168 C4** 4 3N 67 44W
Guaxupé, Brazil **175 A6** 21 10 S 47 5W
Guayabero →, Colombia **168 C3** 2 36N 72 47W
Guayaguayare, Trin. & Tob. **169 F10** 10 8N 61 2W
Guayama, Puerto Rico **165 d** 17 59N 66 7W
Guayaneco, Arch., Chile **176 C1** 47 45 S 75 10W
Guayaquil, Ecuador **168 D2** 2 15 S 79 52W
Guayaquil, G. de, Ecuador **168 D1** 3 10 S 81 0W
Guayaramerín, Bolivia **173 C4** 10 48 S 65 23W
Guayas →, Ecuador **168 D2** 2 36 S 79 52W
Guaymas, Mexico **162 B2** 27 59N 110 54W
Guba, Dem. Rep. of the Congo **119 E2** 10 38 S 26 27 E
Guba, Ethiopia **107 E4** 11 17N 35 20 E
Gubakha, Russia **64 B6** 58 52N 57 36 E
Gûbâl, Madîq, Egypt **106 B3** 27 30N 34 0 E
Gubam, Papua N. G. **132 E1** 8 39 S 141 53 E
Guban, Somali Rep. **120 B1** 10 30N 44 0 E
Gubat, Phil. **80 E5** 12 55N 124 7 E
Gubbi, India **95 H3** 13 19N 76 56 E
Gúbbio, Italy **45 E9** 43 21N 12 35 E
Guben, Germany **30 D10** 51 57N 14 42 E
Gubin, Poland **55 G1** 51 57N 14 43 E
Gubio, Nigeria **113 C7** 12 30N 12 42 E
Gubkin, Russia **59 G9** 51 17N 37 32 E
Guča, Serbia & M. **50 C4** 43 46N 20 15 E
Gucheng, China **77 A8** 32 20N 111 30 E
Gudå, Norway **18 A8** 63 27N 11 36 E
Gudalur, India **95 J3** 11 30N 76 29 E
Gudata = Guadauta, Georgia **61 J5** 43 7N 40 32 E
Gudbrandsdalen, Norway **15 F14** 61 33N 10 10 E
Gudenå →, Denmark **17 H4** 56 29N 10 13 E
Gudermes, Russia **61 J8** 43 24N 46 5 E
Gudhjem, Denmark **17 J8** 55 12N 14 58 E
Gudivada, India **95 F5** 16 30N 81 3 E
Gudiyattam, India **95 H4** 12 57N 78 55 E
Gudur, India **95 G4** 14 12N 79 55 E
Gudvangen, Norway **18 D3** 60 52N 6 49 E
Guebwiller, France **27 E14** 47 55N 7 12 E
Guecho = Getxo, Spain **40 B2** 43 21N 2 59W
Guékédou, Guinea **112 D2** 8 40N 10 5W
Guelb er Richât, Mauritania **110 D2** 21 7N 11 24W
Guéle Mendouka, Cameroon **113 E7** 4 23N 12 55 E
Guélengdeng, Chad **109 F3** 10 55N 15 31 E
Guelma, Algeria **111 A6** 36 25N 7 29 E
Guelmine = Goulimine, Morocco **110 C3** 28 56N 10 0W
Guelph, Canada **140 D3** 43 35N 80 20W
Guelta Zemmur, W. Sahara **110 C2** 25 8N 12 22W
Guemar, Algeria **111 B6** 33 30N 6 49 E
Guéméné-Penfao, France **26 E5** 47 38N 1 50W
Guéméné-sur-Scorff, France **26 D3** 48 4N 3 13W
Guéné, Benin **113 C5** 11 44N 3 16 E
Güeppí, Peru **168 D2** 0 7 S 75 15W
Guer, France **26 E4** 47 54N 2 8W
Güer Aike, Argentina **176 D3** 51 39 S 69 35W
Guera, Chad **109 F3** 11 55N 18 12 E
Guérande, France **26 E4** 47 20N 2 26W
Guerara, Algeria **111 B5** 32 51N 4 22 E
Guercif, Morocco **111 B4** 34 14N 3 21W
Guéréda, Chad **109 F4** 14 31N 22 5 E
Guéret, France **27 F8** 46 11N 1 51 E
Guérigny, France **27 E10** 47 6N 3 10 E
Guerneville, U.S.A. **160 G4** 38 30N 123 0W
Guernica = Gernika-Lumo, Spain **40 B2** 43 19N 2 40W
Guernsey, U.K. **21 H5** 49 26N 2 35W
Guernsey, U.S.A. **154 D2** 42 19N 104 45W
Guerrara, Algeria **111 C4** 28 5N 0 8W
Guerrero □, Mexico **163 D5** 17 30N 100 0W
Guerzim, Algeria **111 C4** 29 39N 1 40W
Guessou-Sud, Benin **113 C5** 10 3N 2 38 E
Gueugnon, France **27 F11** 46 36N 4 4 E
Guéyo, Ivory C. **112 D3** 5 25N 6 5W
Gufuðalur, Iceland **11 B4** 65 34N 22 25W
Gughe, Ethiopia **107 F4** 6 12N 37 30 E
Gügher, Iran **97 D8** 29 28N 56 27 E
Guglionesi, Italy **45 G11** 41 55N 14 55 E
Guhakolak, Tanjung, Indonesia **79 G11** 6 50 S 105 14 E
Guhrau = Góra, Poland **55 G3** 51 40N 16 31 E
Gui Jiang →, China **77 F8** 23 30N 111 15 E
Guia, Canary Is. **9 e1** 28 8N 15 38W
Guia de Isora, Canary Is. **9 e1** 28 12N 16 46W
Guia Lopes da Laguna, Brazil **175 A4** 21 26 S 56 7W
Guiana, Venezuela **169 B5** 5 9N 63 36W
Guiana Highlands, S. Amer. **166 C4** 5 10N 60 40W
Guibéroua, Ivory C. **112 D3** 6 14N 6 10W
Guichen B., Australia **128 D3** 37 10 S 139 45 E
Guichi, China **77 B11** 30 39N 117 27 E
Guider, Cameroon **113 D7** 9 56N 13 57 E
Guidiguir, Niger **113 C6** 13 40N 9 50 E
Guidimouni, Niger **113 C6** 13 42N 9 31 E
Guiding, China **76 D6** 26 34N 107 11 E
Guidong, China **77 D9** 26 7N 113 57 E
Guidónia-Montecélio, Italy **45 F9** 42 1N 12 45 E
Guiers, L. de, Senegal **112 B1** 16 10N 15 50W
Guigang, China **76 F7** 23 8N 109 35 E
Guiglo, Ivory C. **112 D3** 6 45N 7 30W
Guihulñgan, Phil. **81 F4** 10 7N 123 16 E
Guijá, Mozam. **117 C5** 24 27 S 33 0 E
Guijuelo, Spain **42 E5** 40 33N 5 40W
Guildford, U.K. **21 F7** 51 14N 0 34W
Guilford, U.S.A. **151 E12** 41 17N 72 41W
Guilin, China **77 E8** 25 18N 110 15 E
Guillaume-Delisle, L., Canada **140 A4** 56 15N 76 17W
Guillaumes, France **29 D10** 44 5N 6 52 E
Guillestre, France **29 D10** 44 39N 6 40 E
Guilvinec, France **26 E2** 47 48N 4 17W
Güímar, Canary Is. **9 e1** 28 18N 16 24W
Guimarães, Brazil **170 B3** 2 9 S 44 42W
Guimarães, Portugal **42 D2** 41 28N 8 24W
Guimaras □, Phil. **81 F4** 10 35N 122 37 E
Guimba, Phil. **80 D3** 15 40N 120 46 E
Guinayangan, Phil. **80 E4** 13 54N 122 27 E
Guinda, U.S.A. **160 G4** 38 50N 122 12W
Guindulman, Phil. **81 G5** 9 46N 124 29 E
Guinea, Africa **104 F4** 8 0N 8 0 E
Guinea ■, W. Afr. **112 C2** 10 20N 11 30W
Guinea, Gulf of, Atl. Oc. **113 E5** 3 0N 2 30 E
Guinea-Bissau ■, Africa **112 C2** 12 0N 15 0W
Güines, Cuba **164 B3** 22 50N 82 0W
Guingamp, France **26 D3** 48 34N 3 10W
Guinguinéo, Senegal **112 C1** 14 20N 15 57W
Guinobatan, Phil. **80 E4** 13 11N 123 36 E
Guipavas, France **26 D2** 48 26N 4 29W
Guiping, China **77 F8** 23 21N 110 2 E
Guipúzcoa □, Spain **40 B2** 43 12N 2 15W
Guir, Mali **112 B4** 18 52N 2 52W
Guir, O. →, Algeria **111 B4** 31 29N 2 17W
Guiratinga, Brazil **173 D7** 16 21 S 53 45W
Guirel, Mauritania **112 B3** 15 30N 7 3W
Güiria, Venezuela **169 F8** 10 32N 62 18W
Guiscard, France **27 C10** 49 40N 3 1 E
Guise, France **27 C10** 49 52N 3 35 E
Guita-Koulouba, C.A.R. **114 A4** 5 58N 23 21 E
Guitiriz, Spain **42 B3** 43 11N 7 50W
Guitri, Ivory C. **112 D3** 5 30N 5 14W
Guiuan, Phil. **81 F5** 11 5N 125 55 E
Guixi, China **77 C11** 28 16N 117 15 E
Guiyang, Guizhou, China **76 D6** 26 32N 106 40 E
Guiyang, Hunan, China **77 E9** 25 46N 112 42 E
Guizhou □, China **76 D6** 27 0N 107 0 E
Gujan-Mestras, France **28 D2** 44 38N 1 4W
Gujar Khan, Pakistan **92 C5** 33 16N 73 19 E
Gujarat □, India **92 H4** 23 20N 71 0 E
Gujiang, China **77 D10** 27 11N 114 47 E
Gujranwala, Pakistan **91 B4** 32 10N 74 12 E
Gujrat, Pakistan **91 B4** 32 40N 74 2 E
Gukovo, Russia **61 F5** 48 1N 39 58 E
Gulargambone, Australia **129 A8** 31 20 S 148 30 E
Gulbarga, India **94 F3** 17 20N 76 50 E
Gulbene, Latvia **15 H22** 57 8N 26 52 E
Gülchö, Kyrgyzstan **65 C6** 40 19N 73 26 E
Guledagudda, India **95 F2** 16 3N 75 48 E
Gulf □, Papua N. G. **132 D3** 8 0 S 145 0 E
Gulf, The = Persian Gulf, Asia **97 E6** 27 0N 50 0 E
Gulf Breeze, U.S.A. **153 E2** 30 21N 87 9W
Gulf Hammock, U.S.A. **153 F7** 29 15N 82 43W
Gulf Islands ⌓, U.S.A. **153 K2** 30 10N 87 10W
Gulfport, Fla., U.S.A. **153 H7** 27 44N 82 43W
Gulfport, Miss., U.S.A. **155 K10** 30 22N 89 6W
Gulgong, Australia **129 B8** 32 20 S 149 49 E
Gulin, China **76 C5** 28 1N 105 50 E
Gulistan, Pakistan **92 D2** 30 30N 66 35 E
Guliston, Uzbekistan **65 C4** 40 29N 68 46 E
Gulkana, U.S.A. **144 E11** 62 16N 145 23W
Gull Lake, Canada **143 C7** 50 10N 108 29W
Gullbrå, Norway **18 D3** 60 50N 6 17 E
Gullbrandstorp, Sweden **17 H6** 56 42N 12 43 E
Gullbringusýsla □, Iceland **11 D4** 64 0N 22 0W
Gullfoss, Iceland **11 C6** 64 20N 20 8W
Gullhaug, Norway **18 E7** 59 30N 10 15 E
Gullivan B., U.S.A. **153 K8** 25 45N 81 40W
Gullspång, Sweden **17 F8** 58 59N 14 6 E
Gullstein, Norway **18 A5** 63 13N 8 9 E
Güllük, Turkey **49 D9** 37 14N 27 35 E
Güllük Daği △, Turkey **49 E12** 37 0N 30 30 E
Güllük Korfezi, Turkey **49 D9** 37 12N 27 30 E
Gulma, Nigeria **113 C5** 12 40N 4 23 E
Gulmarg, India **93 B6** 34 3N 74 25 E
Gülnar, Turkey **100 D5** 36 19N 33 24 E
Gulnare, Australia **128 B3** 33 27 S 138 27 E
Gülpınar, Turkey **49 B8** 39 32N 26 7 E
Gülşehir, Turkey **100 C6** 38 44N 34 37 E
Gulshad, Kazakhstan **66 E8** 46 45N 74 25 E
Gulsvik, Norway **18 D6** 60 24N 9 38 E
Gulu, Uganda **118 B3** 2 48N 32 17 E
Gŭlŭbovo, Bulgaria **51 D9** 42 8N 25 55 E
Gulud, J., Sudan **107 E2** 11 41N 29 31 E
Gulwe, Tanzania **118 D4** 6 30 S 36 25 E
Gulyaypole = Hulyaypole, Ukraine **59 J9** 47 45N 36 21 E
Gum Lake, Australia **128 B5** 32 42 S 143 9 E
Gumaca, Phil. **80 E4** 13 55N 122 6 E
Gumal →, Pakistan **92 D4** 31 40N 71 50 E
Gumbaz, Pakistan **92 D3** 30 2N 69 0 E
Gumbinnen = Gusev, Russia **15 J20** 54 35N 22 10 E
Gumel, Nigeria **113 C6** 12 39N 9 22 E
Gumiel de Hizán, Spain **42 D7** 41 46N 3 41W
Gumla, India **93 H11** 23 3N 84 33 E
Gumlu, Australia **126 B4** 19 53 S 147 41 E
Gumma □, Japan **73 A10** 36 30N 138 20 E
Gummersbach, Germany **30 D3** 51 1N 7 34 E
Gummi, Nigeria **113 C6** 12 4N 5 9 E
Gümüldür, Turkey **49 C9** 38 6N 27 0 E
Gumuljina = Komotini, Greece **51 E9** 41 9N 25 26 E
Gümüşçay, Turkey **51 F11** 40 16N 27 17 E
Gümüşhaciköy, Turkey **100 B6** 40 50N 35 18 E
Gümüşhane, Turkey **101 B8** 40 30N 39 30 E
Gümüşsu, Turkey **49 C11** 38 14N 29 1 E
Gumzai, Indonesia **83 C4** 5 28 S 134 42 E
Guna, Ethiopia **107 F4** 8 18N 39 52 E
Guna, India **92 G7** 24 40N 77 19 E
Gundagai, Australia **129 C8** 35 3 S 148 6 E
Gundarehi, India **94 D5** 20 57N 81 17 E
Gundelfingen, Germany **31 G6** 48 34N 10 22 E
Gundih, Indonesia **85 D4** 7 10 S 110 56 E
Gundlakamma →, India **95 G5** 15 30N 80 15 E
Gundlupet, India **95 J3** 11 48N 76 41 E
Gunebang, Australia **129 B7** 33 1 S 146 38 E
Güney, Burdur, Turkey **49 D11** 37 29N 29 34 E
Güney, Denizli, Turkey **49 C11** 38 10N 29 4 E
Güneydoğu Toroslar, Turkey **101 C9** 38 20N 40 30 E
Gungal, Australia **129 B9** 32 17 S 150 32 E
Gungo, Angola **115 E2** 10 58 S 15 30 E
Gungu, Dem. Rep. of the Congo **115 D3** 5 43 S 19 20 E
Gunisao →, Canada **143 C9** 53 56N 97 53W
Gunisao L., Canada **143 C9** 53 33N 96 15W
Gunjyal, Pakistan **92 C4** 32 20N 71 55 E
Günlüce, Turkey **49 E10** 36 50N 28 20 E
Gunnarskog, Sweden **16 E6** 59 49N 12 34 E
Gunnbjørn Fjeld, Greenland **10 D8** 68 55N 29 47W
Gunnebo, Sweden **17 G10** 57 44N 16 32 E
Gunnedah, Australia **129 A9** 30 59 S 150 15 E
Gunnewin, Australia **127 D4** 25 59 S 148 33 E
Gunningbar Cr. →, Australia **129 A7** 31 14 S 147 6 E
Gunnison, Colo., U.S.A. **159 G10** 38 33N 106 56W
Gunnison, Utah, U.S.A. **158 G8** 39 9N 111 49W
Gunnison →, U.S.A. **159 G9** 39 4N 108 35W
Gunpowder, Australia **126 B2** 19 42 S 139 22 E
Guntakal, India **95 G3** 15 11N 77 27 E
Guntersville, U.S.A. **149 H2** 34 21N 86 18W
Guntong, Malaysia **87 K3** 4 36N 101 3 E
Guntur, India **95 F5** 16 23N 80 30 E
Gunungapi, Indonesia **82 C3** 6 45 S 126 30 E
Gunungsitoli, Indonesia **84 B1** 1 15N 97 30 E
Gunupur, India **94 E6** 19 5N 83 50 E
Günz →, Germany **31 G6** 48 27N 10 16 E
Gunza, Angola **115 E2** 10 50 S 13 50 E
Günzburg, Germany **31 G6** 48 26N 10 17 E
Gunzenhausen, Germany **31 F6** 49 7N 10 44 E
Guo He →, China **75 H9** 32 59N 117 10 E
Guoyang, China **74 H9** 33 32N 116 12 E
Gupis, Pakistan **93 A5** 36 15N 73 20 E
Gura Humorului, Romania **53 C10** 47 35N 25 53 E
Gura-Teghii, Romania **53 E11** 45 30N 26 25 E
Gurag, Ethiopia **107 F4** 8 20N 38 20 E
Gurahonţ, Romania **52 D7** 46 16N 22 21 E
Gurdaspur, India **92 C6** 32 5N 75 31 E
Gurdon, U.S.A. **155 J8** 33 55N 93 9W
Güre, Balıkesir, Turkey **49 B8** 39 36N 26 54 E
Güre, Uşak, Turkey **49 C11** 38 39N 29 10 E
Gurgaon, India **92 E7** 28 27N 77 1 E
Gürgentepe, Turkey **100 B7** 40 51N 37 50 E
Gurghiu, Munţii, Romania **53 D10** 46 41N 25 15 E
Gurgueia →, Brazil **170 C3** 6 50 S 43 24W
Gurha, India **92 G4** 25 12N 71 39 E
Guri, Embalse de, Venezuela **169 B5** 7 50N 62 52W
Gurig △, Australia **124 B5** 11 36 S 132 7 E
Gurimatu, Papua N. G. **132 D3** 6 45 S 144 45 E
Gurin, Nigeria **113 D7** 9 5N 12 54 E
Gurinhatã, Brazil **171 E2** 19 14 S 49 48W
Gurjaani, Georgia **61 K7** 41 43N 45 52 E
Gurk →, Austria **34 E7** 46 35N 14 31 E
Gurkfeld = Krško, Slovenia **45 C12** 45 57N 15 30 E
Gurkha, Nepal **93 E11** 28 5N 84 40 E
Gurley, Australia **127 D4** 29 45 S 149 48 E
Gurnee, U.S.A. **157 B9** 42 22N 87 55W
Gurnet Point, U.S.A. **151 D14** 42 1N 70 34W
Guro, Mozam. **119 F3** 17 26 S 32 30 E
Gürpınar, İst., Turkey **51 F12** 40 59N 28 37 E
Gürpınar, Van, Turkey **101 C10** 38 18N 43 25 E
Gürsu, Turkey **51 F13** 40 13N 29 11 E
Gurué, Mozam. **119 F4** 15 25 S 36 58 E
Gurun, Malaysia **87 K3** 5 49N 100 27 E
Gürün, Turkey **100 C7** 38 43N 37 15 E
Gurupá, Brazil **169 D7** 1 25 S 51 35W
Gurupá, I. Grande de, Brazil **169 D7** 1 25 S 51 45W
Gurupi, Brazil **171 D2** 11 43 S 49 4W
Gurupi →, Brazil **170 B2** 1 13 S 46 6W
Gurupi, Serra do, Brazil **170 C2** 5 0 S 47 50W
Guruwe, Zimbabwe **117 B5** 16 40 S 30 42 E
Guryev = Atyraū, Kazakhstan **57 E9** 47 5N 52 0 E
Guryevsk, Russia **54 D7** 54 47N 20 38 E
Gus-Khrustalnyy, Russia **60 C5** 55 42N 40 44 E
Gusau, Nigeria **113 C6** 12 12N 6 40 E
Gusev, Russia **15 J20** 54 35N 22 10 E
Gushan, China **75 E12** 39 50N 123 35 E
Gushgy, Turkmenistan **66 F7** 35 20N 62 18 E
Gushi, China **77 A10** 32 11N 115 41 E
Gushiago, Ghana **113 D4** 9 55N 0 15W
Gusinje, Serbia & M. **50 D3** 42 35N 19 50 E
Gusinoozersk, Russia **67 D11** 51 16N 106 27 E
Gúspini, Italy **46 C1** 39 32N 8 37 E
Güssing, Austria **35 D9** 47 3N 16 20 E
Gustav Holm, Kap, Greenland **10 D7** 66 36N 34 15W
Gustavsberg, Sweden **16 E12** 59 19N 18 23 E
Gustavus, U.S.A. **142 B1** 58 25N 135 44W
Gustine, U.S.A. **160 H6** 37 16N 121 0W
Güstrow, Germany **30 B8** 53 47N 12 10 E
Gusum, Sweden **17 F10** 58 16N 16 30 E
Guta = Kolárovo, Slovak Rep. **35 D10** 47 54N 18 0 E
Gütersloh, Germany **30 D4** 51 54N 8 24 E
Gutha, Australia **125 E2** 28 58 S 115 55 E
Guthalungra, Australia **126 B4** 19 52 S 147 50 E
Guthrie, Okla., U.S.A. **155 H6** 35 53N 97 25W
Guthrie, Tex., U.S.A. **155 J4** 33 37N 100 19W
Guthrie Center, U.S.A. **156 C2** 41 41N 94 30W
Gutian, China **77 D12** 26 32N 118 43 E
Gutiérrez, Bolivia **173 D5** 19 25 S 63 34W
Guttannen, Switz. **33 C6** 46 38N 8 18 E
Guttenberg, U.S.A. **156 B5** 42 47N 91 6W
Guttentag = Dobrodzień, Poland **55 H5** 50 45N 18 25 E
Guttstadt = Dobre Miasto, Poland **54 E7** 53 58N 20 26 E
Gutu, Zimbabwe **117 B5** 19 41 S 31 9 E
Gutulia △, Norway **18 B9** 62 2N 12 11 E
Guwahati, India **90 B3** 26 10N 91 45 E
Guy Fawkes River △, Australia **127 D5** 30 0 S 152 20 E
Guyana ■, S. Amer. **169 B6** 5 0N 59 0W
Guyane française = French Guiana ⊠, S. Amer. **169 C7** 4 0N 53 0W
Guyang, China **74 D6** 41 0N 110 5 E
Guyenne, France **28 D4** 44 30N 0 40 E
Guymon, U.S.A. **155 G4** 36 41N 101 29W
Guyotville = Aïn Benian, Algeria **111 A5** 36 48N 2 55 E
Guyra, Australia **127 E5** 30 15 S 151 40 E
Guyton, U.S.A. **152 C8** 32 20N 81 24W
Guyuan, Hebei, China **74 D8** 41 37N 115 40 E
Guyuan, Ningxia Huizu, China **74 G4** 36 0N 106 20 E
Guzar, Uzbekistan **65 D3** 38 36N 66 15 E
Güzelbahçe, Turkey **49 C8** 38 21N 26 54 E
Güzelyurt = Morphou, Cyprus **39 E8** 35 12N 32 59 E
Guzhang, China **76 C7** 28 42N 109 58 E
Guzhen, China **75 H9** 33 22N 117 18 E
Guzmán, L. de, Mexico **162 A3** 31 25N 107 25W
Gvardeysk, Russia **15 J19** 54 39N 21 5 E
Gvardeyskoye, Ukraine **59 K8** 45 7N 34 1 E
Gvarv, Norway **18 E6** 59 23N 9 9 E
Gwa, Burma **90 G5** 17 36N 94 34 E
Gwaai, Zimbabwe **119 F2** 19 15 S 27 45 E
Gwaai →, Zimbabwe **119 F2** 17 59 S 26 52 E
Gwabegar, Australia **129 A8** 30 31 S 149 0 E
Gwadabawa, Nigeria **113 C6** 13 28N 5 15 E
Gwādar, Pakistan **91 D1** 25 10N 62 18 E
Gwagwada, Nigeria **113 C6** 10 15N 7 15 E
Gwaii Haanas △, Canada **142 C2** 52 21N 131 26W
Gwalior, India **92 F8** 26 12N 78 10 E
Gwanara, Nigeria **113 D5** 8 55N 3 9 E
Gwanda, Zimbabwe **119 G2** 20 55 S 29 0 E
Gwandu, Nigeria **113 C5** 12 30N 4 41 E
Gwane, Dem. Rep. of the Congo **118 B2** 4 45N 25 48 E
Gwanju = Kwangju, S. Korea **75 G14** 35 9N 126 54 E
Gwaram, Nigeria **113 C7** 10 15N 10 25 E
Gwarzo, Nigeria **113 C6** 12 20N 8 55 E
Gwasero, Nigeria **113 D5** 9 29N 3 30 E
Gwda →, Poland **55 E3** 53 3N 16 44 E
Gweebarra B., Ireland **23 B3** 54 51N 8 23W
Gweedore, Ireland **23 A3** 55 3N 8 13W
Gweru, Zimbabwe **119 F2** 19 28 S 29 45 E
Gwi, Nigeria **113 D6** 9 0N 7 10 E
Gwinn, U.S.A. **148 B2** 46 19N 87 27W
Gwio Kura, Nigeria **113 C7** 12 40N 11 2 E
Gwoza, Nigeria **113 C7** 11 5N 13 40 E
Gwydir →, Australia **127 D4** 29 27 S 149 48 E
Gwynedd □, U.K. **20 E3** 52 52N 4 10W
Gyandzha = Gäncä, Azerbaijan **61 K8** 40 45N 46 20 E
Gyaring Hu, China **68 C4** 34 50N 97 40 E
Gydanskiy Poluostrov, Russia **66 C8** 70 0N 78 0 E
Gyl, Norway **18 B5** 62 57N 8 7 E
Gyldenløve Fjord, Greenland **10 E6** 64 15N 40 30W
Gympie, Australia **127 D5** 26 11 S 152 38 E
Gyobingauk, Burma **90 F5** 18 13N 95 39 E
Gyōda, Japan **73 A11** 36 10N 139 30 E
Gyomaendrőd, Hungary **52 D5** 46 56N 20 50 E

Gyöngyös, *Hungary* **52 C4** 47 48N 19 56 E
Győr, *Hungary* **52 C2** 47 41N 17 40 E
Győr-Moson-Sopron □, *Hungary* **52 C2** 47 40N 17 20 E
Gypsum Pt., *Canada* **142 A6** 61 53N 114 35W
Gypsumville, *Canada* **143 C9** 51 45N 98 40W
Gyueshevo, *Bulgaria* **50 D6** 42 14N 22 28 E
Gyula, *Hungary* **52 D6** 46 38N 21 17 E
Gyumri, *Armenia* **61 K6** 40 47N 43 50 E
Gyzylarbat, *Turkmenistan* **66 F6** 39 4N 56 23 E
Gyzyletrek, *Turkmenistan* **97 B7** 37 36N 54 46 E
Gzhatsk = Gagarin, *Russia* **58 E8** 55 38N 35 0 E
Gzira, *Malta* **38 F7** 35 54N 14 29 E

H

Ha 'Arava →, *Israel* **103 E4** 30 50N 35 20 E
Ha Coi, *Vietnam* **76 G6** 21 26N 107 46 E
Ha Dong, *Vietnam* **76 G5** 20 58N 105 46 E
Ha Giang, *Vietnam* **76 F5** 22 50N 104 59 E
Ha Karmel △, *Israel* **103 C4** 32 45N 35 5 E
Ha Tien, *Vietnam* **87 G5** 10 23N 104 29 E
Ha Tinh, *Vietnam* **86 C5** 18 20N 105 54 E
Ha Trung, *Vietnam* **86 C5** 19 58N 105 50 E
Ha Yaek Chalong, *Thailand* **87 a** 7 50N 98 22 E
Haakon VII Topp, *Norway* **10 C10** 71 0N 8 20W
Haaksbergen, *Neths.* **24 B6** 52 9N 6 45 E
Ha'ano, *Tonga* **133 P13** 19 41 S 174 18W
Ha'apai Group, *Tonga* **133 P13** 19 47 S 174 27W
Haapsalu, *Estonia* **15 G20** 58 56N 23 30 E
Haarlem, *Neths.* **24 B4** 52 23N 4 39 E
Haast, *N.Z.* **131 D4** 43 51 S 169 1 E
Haast →, *N.Z.* **131 D4** 43 50 S 169 2 E
Haast Bluff, *Australia* **124 D5** 23 22 S 132 0 E
Haast Pass, *N.Z.* **131 E4** 44 6 S 169 21 E
Hab →, *Pakistan* **92 G3** 24 53N 66 41 E
Hab Nadi Chauki, *Pakistan* **92 G2** 25 0N 66 50 E
Ḩabarūt, *Yemen* **99 C6** 17 18N 52 44 E
Habaswein, *Kenya* **118 B4** 1 2N 39 30 E
Ḩabawnah, W. →, *Si. Arabia* **98 C4** 17 57N 44 58 E
Habay, *Canada* **142 B5** 58 50N 118 44W
Ḩabbān, *Yemen* **98 D4** 14 21N 47 5 E
Ḩabbānīyah, *Iraq* **101 F10** 33 17N 43 29 E
Ḩabbānīyah, Hawr al, *Iraq* **101 F10** 33 17N 43 29 E
Habelschwerdt = Bystrzyca Kłodzka, *Poland* **55 H3** 50 19N 16 39 E
Habichtswald ⌓, *Germany* **30 D5** 51 15N 9 15 E
Habiganj, *Bangla.* **90 C3** 24 24N 91 30 E
Habo, *Sweden* **17 G8** 57 55N 14 6 E
Haboro, *Japan* **70 B10** 44 22N 141 42 E
Ḩabshān, *U.A.E.* **97 F7** 23 50N 53 37 E
Hachenburg, *Germany* **30 E3** 50 40N 7 49 E
Hachi, *India* **90 B5** 27 48N 94 2 E
Hachijō-Jima, *Japan* **73 D11** 33 5N 139 45 E
Hachiman, *Japan* **73 B8** 35 45N 136 57 E
Hachinohe, *Japan* **70 D10** 40 30N 141 29 E
Hachiōji, *Japan* **73 B11** 35 40N 139 20 E
Hachŏn, *N. Korea* **75 D15** 41 29N 129 2 E
Hacıbektaş, *Turkey* **100 C6** 38 56N 34 33 E
Hacılar, *Turkey* **100 C6** 38 38N 35 26 E
Hack, Mt., *Australia* **128 A3** 30 45 S 138 55 E
Hackås, *Sweden* **16 B8** 62 56N 14 30 E
Hackensack, *U.S.A.* **151 F10** 40 53N 74 3W
Hackettstown, *U.S.A.* **151 F10** 40 51N 74 50W
Haco, *Angola* **115 E3** 10 15 S 15 44 E
Hadali, *Pakistan* **92 C5** 32 16N 72 11 E
Hadano, *Japan* **73 B11** 35 22N 139 14 E
Hadarba, Ras, *Sudan* **106 C4** 22 4N 36 51 E
Hadarom □, *Israel* **103 E4** 31 0N 35 0 E
Ḩadbaram, *Oman* **99 C6** 17 27N 55 15 E
Ḩadd, Ra's al, *Oman* **99 B7** 22 35N 59 50 E
Ḩaddā, *Si. Arabia* **98 B2** 21 27N 39 34 E
Haddington, *U.K.* **22 F6** 55 57N 2 47W
Haddock, *U.S.A.* **152 B6** 33 2N 83 26W
Haded Plain = Xadded, *Somali Rep.* **120 C3** 9 46N 48 2 E
Hadejia, *Nigeria* **113 C7** 12 30N 10 5 E
Hadejia →, *Nigeria* **113 C7** 12 50N 10 51 E
Ḫadera, *Israel* **103 C3** 32 27N 34 55 E
Ḫadera, N. →, *Israel* **103 C3** 32 28N 34 52 E
Hadersleben = Haderslev, *Denmark* **17 J3** 55 15N 9 30 E
Haderslev, *Denmark* **17 J3** 55 15N 9 30 E
Hadgaon, *India* **94 E3** 19 30N 77 40 E
Hadhramaut = Ḩaḑramawt, *Yemen* **99 D5** 15 30N 49 30 E
Hadiboh, *Yemen* **99 D6** 12 39N 54 2 E
Hadım, *Turkey* **100 D5** 36 58N 32 26 E
Hadjadj, O. el →, *Algeria* **111 C6** 28 18N 5 20 E
Hadjeb El Aïoun, *Tunisia* **108 A1** 35 21N 9 32 E
Hadjer Kamaran, *Chad* **109 F4** 12 41N 21 46 E
Hadjer Mornou, *Chad* **109 E4** 17 12N 23 8 E
Hadong, *S. Korea* **75 G14** 35 5N 127 44 E
Ḩaḑramawt, *Yemen* **99 D5** 15 30N 49 30 E
Ḩaḑramawt, W. →, *Yemen* **99 D5** 15 10N 51 8 E
Ḩadrānīyah, *Iraq* **96 C4** 35 38N 43 14 E
Hadrian's Wall, *U.K.* **20 B5** 55 0N 2 30W
Hadsten, *Denmark* **17 H4** 56 19N 10 3 E
Hadsund, *Denmark* **17 H4** 56 44N 10 8 E
Hadyach, *Ukraine* **59 G8** 50 21N 34 0 E
Hægeland, *Norway* **18 F4** 58 22N 7 45 E
Haeju, *N. Korea* **75 E13** 38 3N 125 45 E
Haena, *U.S.A.* **145 A2** 22 14N 159 34W
Haenam, *S. Korea* **75 G14** 34 34N 126 35 E
Haenertsburg, *S. Africa* **117 C4** 24 0 S 29 50 E
Haerhpin = Harbin, *China* **75 B14** 45 48N 126 40 E
Hafar al Bāţin, *Si. Arabia* **96 D5** 28 32N 45 52 E
Hafik, *Turkey* **100 C7** 39 51N 37 23 E
Ḩafīrat al 'Aydā, *Si. Arabia* **96 E3** 26 26N 39 12 E
Ḩafit, *Oman* **97 F7** 23 59N 55 49 E
Hafizabad, *Pakistan* **92 C5** 32 5N 73 40 E
Haflong, *India* **90 C4** 25 10N 93 5 E
Hafnarfjörður, *Iceland* **11 C5** 64 4N 21 57W
Hafnir, *Iceland* **11 D4** 63 56N 22 41W
Hafslo, *Norway* **18 C4** 61 19N 7 10 E
Haft Gel, *Iran* **97 D6** 31 30N 49 32 E
Hafun, Ras, *Somali Rep.* **102 E5** 10 29N 51 30 E
Hagalil, *Israel* **103 C4** 32 53N 35 18 E
Hagari →, *India* **95 G3** 15 40N 77 0 E
Hagby, *Sweden* **17 H10** 56 34N 16 11 E
Hagemeister I., *U.S.A.* **144 G7** 58 39N 160 54W
Hagen, *Germany* **30 D3** 51 21N 7 27 E
Hagenow, *Germany* **30 B7** 53 26N 11 12 E
Hagerman, *U.S.A.* **155 J2** 33 7N 104 20W
Hagerman Fossil Beds ⌓, *U.S.A.* **158 E6** 42 48N 114 57W
Hagerstown, *Ind., U.S.A.* **157 E11** 39 55N 85 10W
Hagerstown, *Md., U.S.A.* **148 F7** 39 39N 77 43W
Hagersville, *Canada* **150 D4** 42 58N 80 3W
Hagetmau, *France* **28 E3** 43 39N 0 37W
Hagfors, *Sweden* **16 D7** 60 3N 13 45 E
Hagi, *Iceland* **11 B3** 65 28N 23 25W
Hagi, *Japan* **72 C3** 34 30N 131 22 E
Hagolan, *Syria* **103 C4** 33 0N 35 45 E
Hagondange, *France* **27 C13** 49 16N 6 11 E
Hagonoy, *Phil.* **80 D3** 14 50N 120 44 E
Hags Hd., *Ireland* **23 D2** 52 57N 9 28W
Hague, C. de la, *France* **26 C5** 49 44N 1 56W
Hague, The = 's-Gravenhage, *Neths.* **24 B4** 52 7N 4 17 E
Haguenau, *France* **27 D14** 48 49N 7 47 E
Hagunía, *W. Sahara* **110 C2** 27 26N 12 24W
Hahira, *U.S.A.* **152 E6** 30 59N 83 22W
Hai Duong, *Vietnam* **76 G6** 20 56N 106 19 E
Hai'an, *Guangdong, China* **77 G8** 20 18N 110 11 E
Hai'an, *Jiangsu, China* **77 A13** 32 37N 120 27 E
Haicheng, *Fujian, China* **77 E11** 24 23N 117 48 E
Haicheng, *Liaoning, China* **75 D12** 40 50N 122 45 E
Haidar Khel, *Afghan.* **92 C3** 33 58N 68 38 E
Haidarâbâd = Hyderabad, *India* **94 F4** 17 22N 78 29 E
Haidargarh, *India* **93 F9** 26 37N 81 22 E
Haifa = Ḫefa, *Israel* **103 C4** 32 46N 35 0 E
Haifeng, *China* **77 F10** 22 58N 115 10 E
Haiger, *Germany* **30 E4** 50 43N 8 12 E
Haikou, *China* **69 D6** 20 1N 110 16 E
Ḩā'il, *Si. Arabia* **96 E4** 27 28N 41 45 E
Hailakandi, *India* **90 C4** 24 42N 92 34 E
Hailar, *China* **69 B6** 49 10N 119 38 E
Hailey, *U.S.A.* **158 E6** 43 31N 114 19W
Haileybury, *Canada* **140 C4** 47 30N 79 38W
Hailin, *China* **75 B15** 44 37N 129 30 E
Hailing Dao, *China* **77 G8** 21 35N 111 47 E
Hailong, *China* **75 C13** 42 32N 125 40 E
Hailuoto, *Finland* **14 D21** 65 3N 24 45 E
Haimen, *Guangdong, China* **77 F11** 23 15N 116 38 E
Haimen, *Jiangsu, China* **77 B13** 31 52N 121 10 E
Hainan □, *China* **69 E5** 19 0N 109 30 E
Hainan Dao, *China* **86 C7** 19 0N 109 30 E
Hainan Str. = Qiongzhou Haixia, *China* **86 B8** 20 10N 110 15 E
Hainaut □, *Belgium* **24 D4** 50 30N 4 0 E
Hainburg, *Austria* **35 C9** 48 9N 16 56 E
Haines, *Alaska, U.S.A.* **142 B1** 59 14N 135 26W
Haines, *Oreg., U.S.A.* **158 D5** 44 55N 117 56W
Haines City, *U.S.A.* **153 G8** 28 7N 81 38W
Haines Junction, *Canada* **142 A1** 60 45N 137 30W
Hainfeld, *Austria* **34 C8** 48 3N 15 48 E
Haining, *China* **77 B13** 30 28N 120 40 E
Haiphong, *Vietnam* **76 G6** 20 47N 106 41 E
Haitan Dao, *China* **77 E12** 25 30N 119 45 E
Haiti ■, *W. Indies* **165 C5** 19 0N 72 30W
Haiya, *Sudan* **106 D4** 18 20N 36 21 E
Haiyan, *China* **77 B13** 30 28N 120 58 E
Haiyang, *China* **75 F11** 36 47N 121 9 E
Haiyuan, *Guangxi Zhuangzu, China* **76 F6** 22 8N 107 35 E
Haiyuan, *Ningxia Huizu, China* **74 F3** 36 35N 105 52 E
Haizhou, *China* **75 G10** 34 37N 119 7 E
Haizhou Wan, *China* **75 G10** 34 50N 119 20 E
Hajar Bangar, *Sudan* **109 F4** 10 40N 22 45 E
Hajdú-Bihar □, *Hungary* **52 C6** 47 30N 21 30 E
Hajdúböszörmény, *Hungary* **52 C6** 47 40N 21 30 E
Hajdúdorog, *Hungary* **52 C6** 47 48N 21 30 E
Hajdúhadház, *Hungary* **52 C6** 47 40N 21 40 E
Hajdúnánás, *Hungary* **52 C6** 47 50N 21 26 E
Hajdúsámson, *Hungary* **52 C6** 47 37N 21 42 E
Hajdúszoboszló, *Hungary* **52 C6** 47 27N 21 22 E
Hajiganj, *Bangla.* **90 D3** 23 15N 90 50 E
Hajipur, *India* **93 G11** 25 45N 85 13 E
Ḩajjah, *Yemen* **98 D3** 15 42N 43 36 E
Ḩājjī Muḩsin, *Iraq* **96 C5** 32 35N 45 29 E
Ḩājjīābād, *Iran* **97 D7** 28 19N 55 55 E
Ḩājjīābād-e Zarrīn, *Iran* **97 C7** 33 9N 54 51 E
Hajnówka, *Poland* **55 F10** 52 47N 23 35 E
Ḩajrah, *Si. Arabia* **98 B3** 20 14N 41 3 E
Haka, *Burma* **90 D4** 22 39N 93 37 E
Hakansson, Mts., *Dem. Rep. of the Congo* **119 D2** 8 40 S 25 45 E
Hakataramea, *N.Z.* **131 E5** 44 43 S 170 30 E
Hakkâri, *Turkey* **101 D10** 37 34N 43 44 E
Hakkâri Dağları, *Turkey* **101 C10** 38 2N 42 58 E
Hakken-Zan, *Japan* **73 C7** 34 10N 135 54 E
Hakodate, *Japan* **70 D10** 41 45N 140 44 E
Hakos, *Namibia* **116 C2** 23 13 S 16 21 E
Hakota, *Japan* **73 A12** 36 5N 140 30 E
Håksberg, *Sweden* **16 D9** 60 11N 15 12 E
Haku-San, *Japan* **73 A8** 36 9N 136 46 E
Haku-San △, *Japan* **73 A8** 36 15N 136 45 E
Hakuba, *Japan* **73 A9** 36 42N 137 51 E
Hakui, *Japan* **71 F8** 36 53N 136 47 E
Hakun, *Burma* **90 B5** 26 46N 95 42 E
Hala, *Pakistan* **91 D3** 25 43N 68 20 E
Ḩalab, *Syria* **100 D7** 36 10N 37 15 E
Ḩalaban, *Si. Arabia* **98 B4** 23 29N 44 23 E
Ḩalabjah, *Iraq* **101 E11** 35 10N 45 58 E
Halach, *Turkmenistan* **65 D2** 38 4N 64 52 E
Halaib, *Sudan* **106 C4** 22 12N 36 30 E
Halalii L., *U.S.A.* **145 B1** 21 52N 160 11W
Halasa, *Sudan* **107 E3** 14 26N 30 39 E
Hālat 'Ammār, *Si. Arabia* **96 D3** 29 10N 36 4 E
Halawa, C., *U.S.A.* **145 B5** 21 10N 156 43W
Halawa Heights, *U.S.A.* **145 K14** 21 23N 157 55W
Halbā, *Lebanon* **103 A5** 34 34N 36 6 E
Halberstadt, *Germany* **30 D7** 51 54N 11 3 E
Halcombe, *N.Z.* **130 G4** 40 8 S 175 30 E
Halcon, *Phil.* **79 B6** 13 0N 121 30 E
Halcon, Mt., *Phil.* **80 E3** 13 16N 121 0 E
Halde Fjäll = Haltiatunturi, *Finland* **14 B19** 69 17N 21 18 E
Halden, *Norway* **18 E8** 59 9N 11 23 E
Haldensleben, *Germany* **30 C7** 52 17N 11 24 E
Haldimand, *Canada* **150 D5** 42 59N 79 52W
Haldwani, *India* **93 E8** 29 31N 79 30 E
Hale, *U.S.A.* **156 E3** 39 36N 93 20W
Hale →, *Australia* **126 C2** 24 56 S 135 53 E
Haleakala △, *U.S.A.* **145 C5** 20 40N 156 15W
Haleakala Crater, *U.S.A.* **145 C5** 20 43N 156 16W
Haleiwa, *U.S.A.* **145 J13** 21 36N 158 6W
Halesowen, *U.K.* **21 E5** 52 27N 2 3W
Halesworth, *U.K.* **21 E9** 52 20N 1 31 E
Haleyville, *U.S.A.* **149 H2** 34 14N 87 37W
Half Assini, *Ghana* **112 D4** 5 1N 2 50W
Halfmoon Bay, *N.Z.* **131 G3** 46 50 S 168 5 E
Halfway →, *Canada* **142 B4** 56 12N 121 32W
Halia, *India* **93 G10** 24 50N 82 19 E
Haliburton, *Canada* **140 C4** 45 3N 78 30W
Halifax, *Australia* **126 B4** 18 32 S 146 22 E
Halifax, *Canada* **141 D7** 44 38N 63 35W
Halifax, *U.K.* **20 D6** 53 43N 1 52W
Halifax, *U.S.A.* **150 F8** 40 25N 76 55W
Halifax B., *Australia* **126 B4** 18 50 S 147 0 E
Halifax I., *Namibia* **116 D2** 26 38 S 15 4 E
Halīl →, *Iran* **97 E8** 27 40N 58 30 E
Halin, *Somali Rep.* **120 C3** 9 6N 48 37 E
Halkett, C., *U.S.A.* **144 A9** 70 48N 152 11W
Halkida = Khalkís, *Greece* **48 C5** 38 27N 23 42 E
Halkidiki = Khalkidhikí □, *Greece* **50 F7** 40 25N 23 20 E
Halkirk, *U.K.* **22 C5** 58 30N 3 29W
Hall Beach = Sanirajak, *Canada* **139 B11** 68 46N 81 12W
Hall I., *U.S.A.* **144 F4** 60 40N 173 6W
Hall in Tirol, *Austria* **34 D4** 47 17N 11 30 E
Hall Pen., *Canada* **139 B13** 63 30N 66 0W
Hall Pt., *Australia* **124 C3** 15 40 S 124 23 E
Hallabro, *Sweden* **17 H9** 56 22N 15 5 E
Halland, *Sweden* **15 H15** 57 8N 12 47 E
Hallandale, *U.S.A.* **153 K9** 25 59N 80 8W
Hallands län □, *Sweden* **17 H6** 57 0N 12 40 E
Hallands Väderö, *Sweden* **17 H6** 56 27N 12 34 E
Hallandsås, *Sweden* **17 H7** 56 22N 13 0 E
Hallaskar, *Norway* **18 D4** 60 15N 7 9 E
Hällbybrunn, *Sweden* **16 E10** 59 24N 16 25 E
Halle, *Belgium* **24 D4** 50 44N 4 13 E
Halle, *Nordrhein-Westfalen, Germany* **30 C4** 52 3N 8 22 E
Halle, *Sachsen-Anhalt, Germany* **30 D7** 51 30N 11 56 E
Hällefors, *Sweden* **16 E8** 59 47N 14 31 E
Hälleforsnäs, *Sweden* **16 E10** 59 10N 16 30 E
Hallein, *Austria* **34 D6** 47 40N 13 5 E
Hällekis, *Sweden* **17 F7** 58 38N 13 27 E
Hallen, *Sweden* **16 A8** 63 11N 14 4 E
Hallett, *Australia* **128 B3** 33 25 S 138 55 E
Hallettsville, *U.S.A.* **155 L6** 29 27N 96 57W
Hallia →, *India* **94 F4** 16 55N 79 20 E
Hallim, *S. Korea* **75 H14** 33 24N 126 15 E
Hallingby, *Norway* **18 D7** 60 7N 10 10 E
Hallingdal, *Norway* **18 D6** 60 40N 9 8 E
Hallingdalselvi →, *Norway* **18 D6** 60 23N 9 35 E
Hallingskarvet, *Norway* **18 D4** 60 36N 7 47 E
Hallingskeid, *Norway* **18 D4** 60 40N 7 17 E
Hallock, *U.S.A.* **154 A6** 48 47N 96 57W
Hallormsstaður, *Iceland* **11 B12** 65 6N 14 45W
Halls Creek, *Australia* **124 C4** 18 16 S 127 38 E
Hallsberg, *Sweden* **16 E9** 59 5N 15 7 E
Hallstahammar, *Sweden* **16 E10** 59 38N 16 15 E
Hallstatt, *Austria* **34 D6** 47 33N 13 38 E
Hallstavik, *Sweden* **16 D12** 60 5N 18 37 E
Hallstead, *U.S.A.* **151 E9** 41 58N 75 45W
Halmahera, *Indonesia* **82 A3** 0 40N 128 0 E
Halmahera Sea, *Indonesia* **83 B3** 0 0 129 0 E
Halmeu, *Romania* **52 C8** 47 57N 23 2 E
Halmstad, *Sweden* **17 H6** 56 41N 12 52 E
Halq el Oued, *Tunisia* **108 A2** 36 53N 10 18 E
Hals, *Denmark* **17 H4** 57 0N 10 18 E
Halsa, *Norway* **18 A5** 63 3N 8 14 E
Halsafjorden, *Norway* **18 A5** 63 5N 8 10 E
Hälsingborg = Helsingborg, *Sweden* **17 H6** 56 3N 12 42 E
Hälsingland, *Sweden* **16 C10** 61 40N 16 5 E
Halstead, *U.K.* **21 F8** 51 57N 0 40 E
Haltdalen, *Norway* **18 B8** 62 56N 11 8 E
Haltern, *Germany* **30 D3** 51 44N 7 11 E
Haltiatunturi, *Finland* **14 B19** 69 17N 21 18 E
Halton □, *U.K.* **20 D5** 53 22N 2 45W
Haltwhistle, *U.K.* **20 C5** 54 58N 2 26W
Ḩālūl, *Qatar* **97 E7** 25 40N 52 40 E
Halvad, *India* **92 H4** 23 1N 71 11 E
Ḩalvān, *Iran* **97 C8** 33 57N 56 15 E
Ham, *Chad* **109 F3** 10 1N 15 35 E
Ham, *France* **27 C10** 49 45N 3 4 E
Ham Tan, *Vietnam* **87 G6** 10 40N 107 45 E
Ham Yen, *Vietnam* **86 A5** 22 4N 105 3 E
Hamab, *Namibia* **116 D2** 28 7 S 19 16 E
Hamad, *Sudan* **107 D3** 15 20N 33 32 E
Hamada, *Japan* **72 C4** 34 56N 132 4 E
Hamadān, *Iran* **97 C6** 34 52N 48 32 E
Hamadān □, *Iran* **97 C6** 35 0N 49 0 E
Hamadia, *Algeria* **111 A5** 35 28N 1 57 E
Hamāh, *Syria* **100 E7** 35 5N 36 40 E
Hamakita, *Japan* **73 C9** 34 45N 137 47 E
Hamamatsu, *Japan* **73 C9** 34 45N 137 45 E
Hamar, *Norway* **18 D8** 60 48N 11 7 E
Hamâta, Gebel, *Egypt* **96 E2** 24 17N 35 0 E
Hambantota, *Sri Lanka* **95 L5** 6 10N 81 10 E
Hamber ⌓, *Canada* **142 C5** 52 20N 118 0W
Hamburg, *Germany* **30 B5** 53 33N 9 59 E
Hamburg, *Ark., U.S.A.* **155 J9** 33 14N 91 48W
Hamburg, *N.Y., U.S.A.* **150 D6** 42 43N 78 50W
Hamburg, *Pa., U.S.A.* **151 F9** 40 33N 75 59W
Hamburg □, *Germany* **30 B5** 53 30N 10 0 E
Hamburg Fuhlsbüttel ✈ (HAM), *Germany* **30 B5** 53 35N 9 59 E
Ḩamḑ, W. al →, *Si. Arabia* **96 E3** 24 55N 36 20 E
Ḩamḑah, *Si. Arabia* **98 C3** 19 2N 43 36 E
Ḩamdānah, *Si. Arabia* **98 C3** 19 59N 40 34 E
Hamden, *U.S.A.* **151 E12** 41 23N 72 54W
Hamdibey, *Turkey* **49 B9** 39 50N 27 15 E
Häme, *Finland* **15 F20** 61 38N 25 10 E
Hämeenlinna, *Finland* **15 F21** 61 0N 24 28 E
Hamélé, *Ghana* **112 C4** 10 56N 2 45W
Hamelin Pool, *Australia* **125 E1** 26 22 S 114 20 E
Hameln, *Germany* **30 C5** 52 6N 9 21 E
Hamerkaz □, *Israel* **103 C3** 32 15N 34 55 E
Hamersley Ra., *Australia* **124 D2** 22 0 S 117 45 E
Hamhŭng, *N. Korea* **75 E14** 39 54N 127 30 E
Hami, *China* **68 B4** 42 55N 93 25 E
Hamilton = Churchill →, *Canada* **141 B7** 53 19N 60 10W
Hamilton, *Australia* **128 D5** 37 45 S 142 2 E
Hamilton, *Bermuda* **9 a** 32 17N 64 47W
Hamilton, *Canada* **140 D4** 43 15N 79 50W
Hamilton, *N.Z.* **130 D4** 37 47 S 175 19 E
Hamilton, *U.K.* **22 F4** 55 46N 4 2W
Hamilton, *Ala., U.S.A.* **149 H1** 34 9N 87 59W
Hamilton, *Alaska, U.S.A.* **144 E7** 62 54N 163 53W
Hamilton, *Ga., U.S.A.* **152 C5** 32 45N 84 53W
Hamilton, *Ill., U.S.A.* **156 D5** 40 24N 91 21W
Hamilton, *Ind., U.S.A.* **157 C12** 41 33N 84 56W
Hamilton, *Mo., U.S.A.* **156 E2** 39 45N 94 0W
Hamilton, *Mont., U.S.A.* **158 C6** 46 15N 114 10W
Hamilton, *N.Y., U.S.A.* **151 D9** 42 50N 75 33W
Hamilton, *Ohio, U.S.A.* **157 E12** 39 24N 84 34W
Hamilton, *Tex., U.S.A.* **155 K5** 31 42N 98 7W
Hamilton →, *Australia* **126 C2** 23 30 S 139 47 E
Hamilton, The →, *Australia* **127 D2** 26 40 S 135 19 E
Hamilton City, *U.S.A.* **160 F4** 39 45N 122 1W
Hamilton I., *Australia* **126 J6** 20 21 S 148 56 E
Hamilton Inlet, *Canada* **141 B8** 54 0N 57 30W
Hamilton Mt., *U.S.A.* **151 C10** 43 25N 74 22W
Hamina, *Finland* **15 F22** 60 34N 27 12 E
Hamirpur, *H.P., India* **92 D7** 31 41N 76 31 E
Hamirpur, *Ut. P., India* **93 G9** 25 57N 80 9 E
Hamitabat, *Turkey* **51 E11** 41 30N 27 17 E
Hamlet, *U.S.A.* **149 H6** 34 53N 79 42W
Hamley Bridge, *Australia* **128 C3** 34 17 S 138 35 E
Hamlin = Hameln, *Germany* **30 C5** 52 6N 9 21 E
Hamlin, *N.Y., U.S.A.* **150 C7** 43 17N 77 55W
Hamlin, *Tex., U.S.A.* **155 J4** 32 53N 100 8W
Hamm, *Germany* **30 D3** 51 40N 7 50 E
Hammam Bouhadjar, *Algeria* **111 A4** 35 23N 0 58W
Hammamet, *Tunisia* **108 A2** 36 24N 10 38 E
Hammamet, G. de, *Tunisia* **108 A2** 36 10N 10 48 E
Ḩammār, Hawr al, *Iraq* **96 D5** 30 50N 47 10 E
Hammarstrand, *Sweden* **16 A10** 63 7N 16 20 E
Hammelburg, *Germany* **31 E5** 50 6N 9 53 E
Hammeren, *Denmark* **17 J8** 55 18N 14 47 E
Hammerfest, *Norway* **14 A20** 70 39N 23 41 E
Hammerstein = Czarne, *Poland* **54 E3** 53 42N 16 58 E
Hammerum, *Denmark* **17 H3** 56 8N 9 3 E
Hamminkeln, *Germany* **30 D2** 51 43N 6 35 E
Hammond, *Ind., U.S.A.* **157 C9** 41 38N 87 30W
Hammond, *La., U.S.A.* **155 K9** 30 30N 90 28W
Hammond, *N.Y., U.S.A.* **151 B9** 44 27N 75 42W
Hammondsport, *U.S.A.* **150 D7** 42 25N 77 13W
Hammonton, *U.S.A.* **148 F8** 39 39N 74 48W
Hamneda, *Sweden* **17 H7** 56 41N 13 51 E
Hamoyet, Jebel, *Sudan* **106 D4** 17 33N 38 2 E
Hampden, *N.Z.* **131 F5** 45 18 S 170 50 E
Hampshire □, *U.K.* **21 F6** 51 7N 1 23W
Hampshire Downs, *U.K.* **21 F6** 51 15N 1 10W
Hampton, *N.B., Canada* **141 C6** 45 32N 65 51W
Hampton, *Ont., Canada* **150 C6** 43 58N 78 45W
Hampton, *Ark., U.S.A.* **155 J8** 33 32N 92 28W
Hampton, *Ga., U.S.A.* **152 B5** 33 23N 84 17W
Hampton, *Iowa, U.S.A.* **156 B3** 42 45N 93 13W
Hampton, *N.H., U.S.A.* **151 D14** 42 57N 70 50W
Hampton, *S.C., U.S.A.* **152 C8** 32 52N 81 7W
Hampton, *Va., U.S.A.* **148 G7** 37 2N 76 21W
Hampton Bays, *U.S.A.* **151 F12** 40 53N 72 30W
Hampton Springs, *U.S.A.* **152 E6** 30 5N 83 40W
Hampton Tableland, *Australia* **125 F4** 32 0 S 127 0 E
Hamra, *Sweden* **16 C8** 61 39N 14 59 E
Hamra →, *Chad* **109 F4** 12 52N 21 15 E
Hamrat esh Sheykh, *Sudan* **107 E2** 14 38N 27 55 E
Hamrun, *Malta* **38 F8** 35 53N 14 29 E
Hamtik, *Phil.* **81 F3** 10 42N 121 59 E
Hamur, *Turkey* **101 C10** 39 37N 43 3 E
Hamyang, *S. Korea* **75 G14** 35 32N 127 42 E
Han Jiang →, *China* **77 F11** 23 25N 116 40 E
Han Shui →, *China* **77 B10** 30 34N 114 17 E
Han Shui →, *Henan, China* **77 B10** 30 35N 114 18 E
Hana, *U.S.A.* **145 C6** 20 45N 155 59W
Hanahan, *U.S.A.* **152 C10** 32 55N 80 0W
Hanak, *Si. Arabia* **96 E3** 25 32N 37 0 E
Hanalei, *U.S.A.* **145 A2** 22 12N 159 30W
Hanamaki, *Japan* **70 E10** 39 23N 141 7 E
Hanamaulu, *U.S.A.* **145 B2** 21 59N 159 22W
Hanang, *Tanzania* **118 C4** 4 30 S 35 25 E
Hanapepe, *U.S.A.* **145 B2** 21 55N 159 35W
Hanau, *Germany* **31 E4** 50 7N 8 56 E
Hanauma B., *U.S.A.* **145 K14** 21 15N 157 40W
Hanbogd = Ihbulag, *Mongolia* **74 C4** 43 11N 107 10 E
Hançalar, *Turkey* **49 C11** 38 8N 29 24 E
Hânceşti, *Moldova* **53 D13** 46 50N 28 36 E
Hancheng, *China* **74 G6** 35 31N 110 25 E
Hanchuan, *China* **77 B9** 30 40N 113 50 E
Hanchung = Hanzhong, *China* **74 H4** 33 10N 107 1 E
Hancock, *Mich., U.S.A.* **154 B10** 47 8N 88 35W
Hancock, *N.Y., U.S.A.* **151 E9** 41 57N 75 17W
Handa, *Japan* **73 C8** 34 53N 136 55 E
Handa, *Somali Rep.* **120 B4** 10 37N 51 2 E
Handan, *China* **74 F8** 36 35N 114 28 E
Handeni, *Tanzania* **118 D4** 5 25 S 38 2 E
Handlová, *Slovak Rep.* **35 C11** 48 45N 18 35 E
Handub, *Sudan* **106 D4** 19 15N 37 16 E
Handwara, *India* **93 B6** 34 21N 74 20 E
Haneda, Tokyo ✈ (HND), *Japan* **73 B11** 35 33N 139 46 E
Hanegev, *Israel* **103 E4** 30 50N 35 0 E
Hanford, *U.S.A.* **160 J7** 36 20N 119 39W
Hanford Reach ⌓, *U.S.A.* **158 C4** 46 40N 119 28W
Hang Chat, *Thailand* **86 C2** 18 20N 99 21 E
Hang Dong, *Thailand* **86 C2** 18 41N 98 55 E
Hanga Roa, *Chile* **172 b** 27 8 S 109 26W
Hangang →, *S. Korea* **75 F14** 37 50N 126 30 E
Hangayn Nuruu, *Mongolia* **68 B4** 47 30N 99 0 E
Hangchou = Hangzhou, *China* **77 B13** 30 18N 120 11 E
Hanggin Houqi, *China* **74 D4** 40 58N 107 4 E
Hanggin Qi, *China* **74 E5** 39 52N 108 50 E
Hangkow = Wuhan, *China* **77 B10** 30 31N 114 18 E
Hangku = Hangu, *China* **75 E9** 39 18N 117 53 E
Hangu, *China* **75 E9** 39 18N 117 53 E
Hangzhou, *China* **77 B13** 30 18N 120 11 E
Hangzhou Wan, *China* **77 B13** 30 15N 120 45 E
Hanhongor, *Mongolia* **74 C3** 43 55N 104 28 E
Hania = Khaniá, *Greece* **39 E5** 35 30N 24 4 E
Ḩanīdh, *Si. Arabia* **97 E6** 26 35N 48 38 E
Ḩanīsh, *Yemen* **98 D3** 13 45N 42 46 E
Haniska, *Slovak Rep.* **35 C14** 48 37N 21 15 E
Hanjiang, *China* **77 E12** 25 26N 119 6 E
Hankinson, *U.S.A.* **154 B6** 46 4N 96 54W
Hankö, *Finland* **15 G20** 59 50N 22 57 E
Hankou, *China* **77 B10** 30 35N 114 30 E
Hanksville, *U.S.A.* **159 G8** 38 22N 110 43W
Hanle, *India* **93 C8** 32 42N 79 4 E
Hanmer Springs, *N.Z.* **131 C7** 42 32 S 172 50 E
Hann →, *Australia* **124 C4** 17 26 S 126 17 E
Hann, Mt., *Australia* **124 C4** 15 45 S 126 0 E
Hanna, *Canada* **142 C6** 51 40N 111 54W
Hanna, *U.S.A.* **158 F10** 41 52N 106 34W
Hannah B., *Canada* **140 B4** 51 40N 80 0W
Hannibal, *Mo., U.S.A.* **156 E5** 39 42N 91 22W
Hannibal, *N.Y., U.S.A.* **151 C8** 43 19N 76 35W
Hannik, *Sudan* **106 D3** 18 12N 32 20 E
Hannover, *Germany* **30 C5** 52 22N 9 46 E
Hanö, *Sweden* **17 H8** 56 1N 14 50 E
Hanöbukten, *Sweden* **17 J8** 55 35N 14 30 E
Hanoi, *Vietnam* **76 G5** 21 5N 105 55 E
Hanover = Hannover, *Germany* **30 C5** 52 22N 9 46 E
Hanover, *Canada* **140 D3** 44 9N 81 2W
Hanover, *S. Africa* **116 E3** 31 4 S 24 29 E
Hanover, *Ind., U.S.A.* **157 F11** 38 43N 85 28W
Hanover, *N.H., U.S.A.* **151 C12** 43 42N 72 17W
Hanover, *Ohio, U.S.A.* **150 F2** 40 4N 82 16W
Hanover, *Pa., U.S.A.* **148 F7** 39 48N 76 59W
Hanover, I., *Chile* **176 D2** 51 0 S 74 50W
Hanpan, C., *Papua N. G.* **132 C8** 5 0 S 154 35 E
Hans Lollik I., *U.S. Virgin Is.* **165 e** 18 24N 64 53W
Hans Meyer Ra., *Papua N. G.* **132 C7** 4 20 S 152 55 E
Hansdiha, *India* **93 G12** 24 36N 87 5 E
Hanshou, *China* **77 C8** 28 56N 111 50 E
Hansi, *India* **92 E6** 29 10N 75 57 E
Hanson, L., *Australia* **128 A2** 31 0 S 136 15 E
Hanstholm, *Denmark* **17 G2** 57 7N 8 36 E
Hantan = Handan, *China* **74 F8** 36 35N 114 28 E
Hantsavichy, *Belarus* **59 F4** 52 49N 26 30 E
Hanumangarh, *India* **92 E6** 29 35N 74 19 E
Hanyin, *China* **76 A7** 32 54N 108 28 E
Hanyū, *Japan* **73 A11** 36 10N 139 32 E
Hanyuan, *China* **76 C4** 29 21N 102 40 E
Hanzhong, *China* **74 H4** 33 10N 107 1 E
Hanzhuang, *China* **75 G9** 34 33N 117 23 E
Haora, *India* **93 H13** 22 37N 88 20 E
Haouach, O. →, *Chad* **109 E4** 16 45N 19 35 E
Haoxue, *China* **77 B9** 30 3N 112 24 E
Haparanda, *Sweden* **14 D21** 65 52N 24 8 E
Hapeville, *U.S.A.* **152 B5** 33 40N 84 25W
Happy, *U.S.A.* **155 H4** 34 45N 101 52W
Happy Camp, *U.S.A.* **158 F2** 41 48N 123 23W
Happy Valley-Goose Bay, *Canada* **141 B7** 53 15N 60 20W
Hapsu, *N. Korea* **75 D15** 41 13N 128 51 E
Hapur, *India* **92 E7** 28 45N 77 45 E
Ḩaql, *Si. Arabia* **103 F3** 29 10N 34 58 E
Haquira, *Peru* **172 C3** 14 14 S 72 12W
Har, *Indonesia* **83 C4** 5 16 S 133 14 E
Har-Ayrag, *Mongolia* **74 B5** 45 47N 109 16 E
Har Hu, *China* **68 C4** 38 20N 97 38 E
Har Us Nuur, *Mongolia* **68 B4** 48 0N 92 0 E
Har Yehuda, *Israel* **103 D3** 31 35N 34 57 E
Ḩaraḑ, *Si. Arabia* **99 A5** 24 22N 49 0 E
Ḩaraḑ, *Yemen* **98 C3** 16 26N 43 5 E
Haradok, *Belarus* **58 E6** 55 30N 30 3 E
Häradsbäck, *Sweden* **17 H8** 56 32N 14 26 E
Haranomachi, *Japan* **70 F10** 37 38N 140 58 E
Harardera, *Somali Rep.* **120 D3** 4 33N 47 38 E
Harare, *Zimbabwe* **119 F3** 17 43 S 31 2 E
Ḩarāsīs, Jiddat al, *Oman* **99 C7** 19 30N 56 0 E
Harat, *Eritrea* **107 D4** 16 5N 39 26 E
Haraz, *Chad* **109 F3** 14 20N 19 12 E
Harazé, *Chad* **109 G4** 9 57N 20 48 E
Harbhanga, *India* **94 D7** 20 38N 84 36 E
Harbin, *China* **75 B14** 45 48N 126 40 E
Harbiye, *Turkey* **100 D7** 36 10N 36 8 E
Harbo, *Sweden* **16 D11** 60 7N 17 12 E
Harboør, *Denmark* **17 H2** 56 38N 8 10 E
Harbor Beach, *U.S.A.* **150 C2** 43 51N 82 39W
Harbour Breton, *Canada* **141 C8** 47 29N 55 50W
Harbour Deep, *Canada* **141 B8** 50 25N 56 32W
Harburg, *Germany* **30 B5** 53 27N 9 58 E
Harburger Berge ⌓, *Germany* **30 B5** 53 26N 9 51 E
Hårby, *Denmark* **17 J4** 55 13N 10 7 E
Harda, *India* **92 H7** 22 27N 77 5 E
Hardangerfjorden, *Norway* **18 D3** 60 5N 6 0 E
Hardangerjøkulen, *Norway* **18 D4** 60 30N 7 27 E
Hardangervidda, *Norway* **18 D4** 60 7N 7 20 E
Hardangervidda △, *Norway* **18 D4** 60 10N 7 25 E
Hardap ⌓, *Namibia* **116 C2** 24 29 S 17 45 E
Hardap Dam, *Namibia* **116 C2** 24 32 S 17 50 E
Hardeeville, *U.S.A.* **152 C8** 32 17N 81 5W
Harden, *Australia* **129 C8** 34 32 S 148 24 E
Hardenberg, *Neths.* **24 B6** 52 34N 6 37 E
Harderwijk, *Neths.* **24 B5** 52 21N 5 38 E
Hardey →, *Australia* **124 D2** 22 45 S 116 8 E
Hardin, *Ill., U.S.A.* **156 E6** 39 10N 90 37W
Hardin, *Mont., U.S.A.* **158 D10** 45 44N 107 37W
Harding, *S. Africa* **117 E4** 30 35 S 29 55 E
Harding, L., *U.S.A.* **152 C4** 32 40N 85 5W
Harding Ra., *Australia* **124 C3** 16 17 S 124 55 E
Hardinsburg, *U.S.A.* **157 G10** 37 47N 86 28W
Hardisty, *Canada* **142 C6** 52 40N 111 18W
Hardoi, *India* **93 F9** 27 26N 80 6 E
Hardwar = Haridwar, *India* **92 E8** 29 58N 78 9 E
Hardwick, *Ga., U.S.A.* **152 B6** 33 4N 83 14W
Hardwick, *Vt., U.S.A.* **151 B12** 44 30N 72 22W
Hardwicke B., *Australia* **128 C2** 34 55 S 137 20 E
Hardy, Pen., *Chile* **176 E3** 55 30 S 68 20W
Hardy, Pte., *St. Lucia* **165 f** 14 6N 60 56W
Hare B., *Canada* **141 B8** 51 15N 55 45W
Hareid, *Norway* **18 B3** 62 22N 6 1 E
Haren, *Germany* **30 C3** 52 47N 7 13 E
Harer, *Ethiopia* **107 F5** 9 20N 42 8 E
Harerge, *Ethiopia* **107 F5** 7 12N 42 0 E
Harestua, *Norway* **18 D7** 60 11N 10 44 E
Hareto, *Ethiopia* **107 F4** 9 23N 37 6 E
Harfleur, *France* **26 C7** 49 30N 0 10 E
Hargeisa, *Somali Rep.* **120 C2** 9 30N 44 2 E
Hargeisa Game ⌓, *Somali Rep.* **120 B2** 10 2N 44 2 E
Harghita □, *Romania* **53 D10** 46 30N 25 30 E
Harghita, Munţii, *Romania* **53 D10** 46 25N 25 35 E
Hargshamn, *Sweden* **16 D12** 60 12N 18 30 E
Hari →, *Indonesia* **84 C2** 1 16 S 104 5 E
Haria, *Canary Is.* **9 e2** 29 8N 13 32W
Ḩarīb, *Yemen* **98 D4** 14 56N 45 30 E
Haricha, Hamada el, *Mali* **110 D4** 22 40N 3 15W
Haridwar, *India* **92 E8** 29 58N 78 9 E
Harihar, *India* **95 G2** 14 32N 75 44 E
Harihari, *N.Z.* **131 D5** 43 9 S 170 33 E
Harim, Jabal al, *Oman* **97 E8** 25 58N 56 14 E
Harima-Nada, *Japan* **72 C6** 34 30N 134 35 E
Haringhata →, *Bangla.* **90 E2** 22 0N 89 58 E
Haripad, *India* **95 K3** 9 14N 76 28 E
Harīrūd →, *Asia* **91 A1** 37 24N 60 38 E
Härjedalen, *Sweden* **16 B7** 62 22N 13 5 E
Harlan, *Iowa, U.S.A.* **154 E7** 41 39N 95 19W
Harlan, *Ky., U.S.A.* **149 G4** 36 51N 83 19W
Hârlău, *Romania* **53 C11** 47 23N 26 55 E
Harlech, *U.K.* **20 E3** 52 52N 4 6W
Harlem, *Ga., U.S.A.* **152 B7** 33 25N 82 19W
Harlem, *Mont., U.S.A.* **158 B9** 48 32N 108 47W
Hårlev, *Denmark* **17 J6** 55 21N 12 14 E
Harleyville, *U.S.A.* **152 B9** 33 13N 80 27W
Harlingen, *Neths.* **24 A5** 53 11N 5 25 E

Harlingen, *U.S.A.* **155 M6** 26 12N 97 42W
Harlow, *U.K.* **21 F8** 51 46N 0 8 E
Harlowton, *U.S.A.* **158 C9** 46 26N 109 50W
Harmancık, *Turkey* **49 B11** 39 41N 29 9 E
Harmånger, *Sweden* **16 C11** 61 55N 17 20 E
Harmil, *Eritrea* **107 D5** 16 30N 40 10 E
Harnai, *India* **94 F1** 17 48N 73 6 E
Harnai, *Pakistan* **92 D2** 30 6N 67 56 E
Harney, L., *U.S.A.* **153 G8** 28 45N 81 3W
Harney Basin, *U.S.A.* **158 E4** 43 30N 119 0W
Harney L., *U.S.A.* **158 E4** 43 14N 119 8W
Harney Peak, *U.S.A.* **154 D3** 43 52N 103 32W
Härnön, *Sweden* **16 B12** 62 36N 18 0 E
Härnösand, *Sweden* **16 B11** 62 38N 17 55 E
Haro, *Spain* **40 C2** 42 35N 2 55W
Harold, *U.S.A.* **153 E3** 30 40N 86 53W
Harold Pond, *Bahamas* **9 b** 25 2N 77 22W
Haroldswick, *U.K.* **22 A8** 60 48N 0 50W
Harp L., *Canada* **141 A7** 55 5N 61 50W
Harpanahalli, *India* **95 G3** 14 47N 76 2 E
Harper = Costa Mesa, *U.S.A.* **161 M9** 33 38N 117 55W
Harper, *Liberia* **112 E3** 4 25N 7 43W
Harper, Mt., *U.S.A.* **144 D12** 64 14N 143 51W
Harplinge, *Sweden* **17 H6** 56 45N 12 45 E
Harr, *Mauritania* **112 B2** 15 20N 12 28W
Harrai, *India* **93 H8** 22 37N 79 13 E
Harrand, *Pakistan* **92 E4** 29 28N 70 3 E
Ḥarrat Khaybar, *Si. Arabia* **106 B5** 25 30N 39 45 E
Ḥarrat Nawāṣīf, *Si. Arabia* **106 C5** 21 20N 42 10 E
Harricana →, *Canada* **140 B4** 50 56N 79 32W
Harriman, *U.S.A.* **149 H3** 35 56N 84 33W
Harrington, *Australia* **129 A10** 31 52 S 152 42 E
Harrington Harbour, *Canada* **141 B8** 50 31N 59 30W
Harrington Sd., *Bermuda* **9 a** 32 20N 64 44W
Harris, *U.K.* **22 D2** 57 50N 6 55W
Harris, L., *Australia* **127 E2** 31 10 S 135 10 E
Harris, L., *U.S.A.* **153 G8** 28 47N 81 49W
Harris, Sd. of, *U.K.* **22 D1** 57 44N 7 6W
Harris Mts., *N.Z.* **131 E3** 44 49 S 168 49 E
Harris Pt., *Canada* **150 C2** 43 6N 82 9W
Harrisburg, *Ill., U.S.A.* **155 G10** 37 44N 88 32W
Harrisburg, *Nebr., U.S.A.* **154 E3** 41 33N 103 44W
Harrisburg, *Pa., U.S.A.* **150 F8** 40 16N 76 53W
Harrismith, *S. Africa* **117 D4** 28 15 S 29 8 E
Harrison, *Ark., U.S.A.* **155 G8** 36 14N 93 7W
Harrison, *Maine, U.S.A.* **151 B14** 44 7N 70 39W
Harrison, *Nebr., U.S.A.* **154 D3** 42 41N 103 53W
Harrison, C., *Canada* **141 B8** 54 55N 57 55W
Harrison Bay, *U.S.A.* **144 A10** 70 40N 151 0W
Harrison L., *Canada* **142 D4** 49 33N 121 50W
Harrisonburg, *U.S.A.* **148 F6** 38 27N 78 52W
Harrisonville, *U.S.A.* **156 F2** 38 39N 94 21W
Harriston, *Canada* **150 C4** 43 57N 80 53W
Harrisville, *Mich., U.S.A.* **150 B1** 44 39N 83 17W
Harrisville, *N.Y., U.S.A.* **151 B9** 44 9N 75 19W
Harrisville, *Pa., U.S.A.* **150 E5** 41 8N 80 0W
Harrodsburg, *Ind., U.S.A.* **157 E10** 39 1N 86 33W
Harrodsburg, *Ky., U.S.A.* **157 G12** 37 46N 84 51W
Harrogate, *U.K.* **20 C6** 54 0N 1 33W
Harrow, *Australia* **128 D4** 37 9 S 141 35 E
Harrow, *Canada* **157 B14** 42 2N 82 55W
Harrow □, *U.K.* **21 F7** 51 35N 0 21W
Harrowsmith, *Canada* **151 B8** 44 24N 76 40W
Harry S. Truman Reservoir, *U.S.A.* **156 F3** 38 16N 93 24W
Harsefeld, *Germany* **30 B5** 53 27N 9 30 E
Harsewinkel, *Germany* **30 D4** 51 56N 8 14 E
Harsīn, *Iran* **101 E12** 34 18N 47 33 E
Hârşova, *Romania* **53 F12** 44 40N 27 59 E
Harstad, *Norway* **14 B17** 68 48N 16 30 E
Harsud, *India* **92 H7** 22 6N 76 44 E
Hart, *U.S.A.* **148 D2** 43 42N 86 22W
Hart, L., *Australia* **128 A2** 31 10 S 136 25 E
Hartbees →, *S. Africa* **116 D3** 28 45 S 20 32 E
Hartberg, *Austria* **34 D8** 47 17N 15 58 E
Hårteigen, *Norway* **18 D4** 60 11N 7 3 E
Hartford, *Ala., U.S.A.* **152 D4** 31 6N 85 42W
Hartford, *Conn., U.S.A.* **151 E12** 41 46N 72 41W
Hartford, *Ky., U.S.A.* **148 G2** 37 27N 86 55W
Hartford, *Mich., U.S.A.* **157 B10** 42 13N 86 10W
Hartford, *S. Dak., U.S.A.* **154 D6** 43 38N 96 57W
Hartford, *Wis., U.S.A.* **154 D10** 43 19N 88 22W
Hartford City, *U.S.A.* **157 D11** 40 27N 85 22W
Hartingsburg = Bela Bela, *S. Africa* **117 C4** 24 51 S 28 19 E
Hartland, *Canada* **141 C6** 46 20N 67 32W
Hartland, *U.S.A.* **157 A8** 43 6N 88 21W
Hartland Pt., *U.K.* **21 F3** 51 1N 4 32W
Hartlepool, *U.K.* **20 C6** 54 42N 1 13W
Hartlepool □, *U.K.* **20 C6** 54 42N 1 17W
Hartley Bay, *Canada* **142 C3** 53 25N 129 15W
Hartmannberge, *Namibia* **116 B1** 17 0 S 13 0 E
Hartney, *Canada* **143 D8** 49 30N 100 35W
Hârtop, *Moldova* **53 D13** 46 39N 28 40 E
Harts →, *S. Africa* **116 D3** 28 24 S 24 17 E
Hartselle, *U.S.A.* **149 H2** 34 27N 86 56W
Hartshorne, *U.S.A.* **155 H7** 34 51N 95 34W
Hartstown, *U.S.A.* **150 E4** 41 33N 80 23W
Hartsville, *U.S.A.* **149 H5** 34 23N 80 4W
Hartswater, *S. Africa* **116 D3** 27 34 S 24 43 E
Hartwell, *U.S.A.* **149 H4** 34 21N 82 56W
Haruku, *Indonesia* **82 B3** 3 34 S 128 29 E
Harunabad, *Pakistan* **92 E5** 29 35N 73 8 E
Harur, *India* **95 H4** 12 3N 78 29 E
Harūt →, *Afghan.* **91 C1** 31 29N 61 24 E
Harvand, *Iran* **97 D7** 28 25N 55 43 E
Harvard, *U.S.A.* **157 B8** 42 25N 88 37W
Harvey, *Australia* **125 F2** 33 5 S 115 54 E
Harvey, *Ill., U.S.A.* **157 C9** 41 36N 87 50W
Harvey, *N. Dak., U.S.A.* **154 B5** 47 47N 99 56W
Harwich, *U.K.* **21 F9** 51 56N 1 17 E
Haryana □, *India* **92 E7** 29 0N 76 10 E
Haryn →, *Belarus* **59 F4** 52 7N 27 17 E
Harz, *Germany* **30 D6** 51 38N 10 44 E
Harz △, *Germany* **30 D6** 51 40N 10 18 E
Harzgerode, *Germany* **30 D7** 51 38N 11 8 E
Hasa □, *Si. Arabia* **97 E6** 25 50N 49 0 E
Hasaheisa, *Sudan* **107 E3** 14 44N 33 20 E
Hasalbag, *China* **65 E8** 37 52N 76 42 E
Ḥasanābād, *Iran* **97 C7** 32 8N 52 44 E
Hasanparti, *India* **94 E4** 18 4N 79 32 E
Ḥasb, W. →, *Iraq* **96 D5** 31 45N 44 17 E
Hasdo →, *India* **93 J10** 21 44N 82 44 E
Häselgehr, *Austria* **33 B10** 47 19N 10 30 E
Haselünne, *Germany* **30 C3** 52 40N 7 29 E
Hashima, *Japan* **73 B8** 35 20N 136 40 E
Hashimoto, *Japan* **73 C7** 34 19N 135 37 E
Hashtjerd, *Iran* **97 C6** 35 52N 50 40 E
Hasi Nueifed, *W. Sahara* **110 D2** 24 54N 14 49W
Hasi Tafraut, *W. Sahara* **110 C2** 27 24N 13 15W
Ḥāsik, *Oman* **99 C6** 17 22N 55 17 E
Haskell, *U.S.A.* **155 J5** 33 10N 99 44W
Haskovo = Khaskovo, *Bulgaria* **51 E9** 41 56N 25 30 E
Hasköy, *Turkey* **51 E10** 41 38N 26 52 E
Haslach, *Germany* **31 G4** 48 16N 8 5 E
Hasle, *Denmark* **17 J8** 55 11N 14 44 E
Haslemere, *U.K.* **21 F7** 51 5N 0 43W
Haslev, *Denmark* **17 J5** 55 18N 11 57 E
Hasilpur, *Pakistan* **92 B5** 34 2N 73 10 E
Hasparren, *France* **28 E2** 43 24N 1 18W
Hassa, *Turkey* **100 D7** 36 48N 36 29 E
Hassan, *India* **95 H3** 13 0N 76 5 E
Hassberge △, *Germany* **31 E6** 50 8N 10 45 E
Hassela, *Sweden* **16 B10** 62 7N 16 42 E
Hasselt, *Belgium* **24 D5** 50 56N 5 21 E
Hassene, Adrar, *Algeria* **111 D5** 21 0N 4 0 E
Hassfurt, *Germany* **31 E6** 50 2N 10 30 E
Hassi bou Khelala, *Algeria* **111 B4** 30 17N 0 18W
Hassi Bourarchet, *Algeria* **111 C6** 27 26N 9 19 E
Hassi Djafou, *Algeria* **111 B5** 30 55N 3 35 E
Hassi el Abiod, *Algeria* **111 B5** 31 47N 3 37 E
Hassi el Biod, *Algeria* **111 C6** 28 30N 6 0 E
Hassi el Hadjar, *Algeria* **111 B5** 31 28N 4 45 E
Hassi Imoulaye, *Algeria* **111 C6** 29 54N 9 10 E
Hassi Inifeg, *Algeria* **111 C4** 28 15N 1 30W
Hassi Inifel, *Algeria* **111 C5** 29 50N 3 41 E
Hassi Mana, *Algeria* **111 C4** 28 48N 2 37W
Hassi Messaoud, *Algeria* **111 B6** 31 51N 6 1 E
Hassi Sougoued, *Algeria* **111 C6** 26 50N 9 28 E
Hassi Tartrat, *Algeria* **111 B6** 30 5N 6 28 E
Hassi Zerzour, *Morocco* **110 B4** 30 51N 3 56W
Hassi Zguilma, *Algeria* **111 B4** 30 12N 2 19W
Hässleholm, *Sweden* **17 H7** 56 10N 13 46 E
Hassloch, *Germany* **31 F4** 49 22N 8 16 E
Hästholmen, *Sweden* **17 F8** 58 17N 14 38 E
Hastings, *Australia* **129 E6** 38 18 S 145 12 E
Hastings, *N.Z.* **130 F5** 39 39 S 176 52 E
Hastings, *U.K.* **21 G8** 50 51N 0 35 E
Hastings, *Fla., U.S.A.* **152 F8** 29 43N 81 31W
Hastings, *Mich., U.S.A.* **157 B11** 42 39N 85 17W
Hastings, *Minn., U.S.A.* **154 C8** 44 44N 92 51W
Hastings, *Nebr., U.S.A.* **154 E5** 40 35N 98 23W
Hastings Ra., *Australia* **129 A10** 31 15 S 152 14 E
Hästveda, *Sweden* **17 H7** 56 17N 13 55 E
Ḥasy 'Aṭshān, *Libya* **108 C2** 27 20N 10 25 E
Ḥasy Tissan, *Libya* **111 C7** 28 14N 12 26 E
Hat, *Ukraine* **52 B7** 48 19N 22 38 E
Hat Yai, *Thailand* **87 J3** 7 1N 100 27 E
Hatanbulag = Ergel, *Mongolia* **74 C5** 43 8N 109 5 E
Hatay = Antalya, *Turkey* **100 D4** 36 52N 30 45 E
Hatch, *U.S.A.* **159 K10** 32 40N 107 9W
Hatchet L., *Canada* **143 B8** 58 36N 103 40W
Haţeg, *Romania* **52 E7** 45 36N 22 55 E
Hateruma-Shima, *Japan* **71 M1** 24 3N 123 47 E
Hatfield P.O., *Australia* **128 B5** 33 54 S 143 49 E
Hatgal, *Mongolia* **68 A5** 50 26N 100 9 E
Hathras, *India* **92 F8** 27 36N 78 6 E
Hatia, *Bangla.* **90 D3** 22 30N 91 5 E
Hatia Is., *Bangla.* **90 D3** 22 30N 91 0 E
Ḥāṭibah, Ra's, *Si. Arabia* **106 C4** 21 55N 38 57 E
Hatid, *India* **94 F2** 17 17N 75 3 E
Hato Corozal, *Colombia* **168 B3** 6 11N 71 45W
Hato Mayor, *Dom. Rep.* **165 C6** 18 46N 69 15W
Hatsukaichi, *Japan* **72 C4** 34 22N 132 22 E
Hatta, *India* **93 G8** 24 7N 79 36 E
Hattah, *Australia* **128 C5** 34 48 S 142 17 E
Hattah Kulkyne △, *Australia* **128 C5** 35 40 S 142 22 E
Hatteras, C., *U.S.A.* **149 H8** 35 14N 75 32W
Hatteras Plain, *Atl. Oc.* **8 D4** 28 0N 72 0W
Hattiesburg, *U.S.A.* **155 K10** 31 20N 89 17W
Hatvan, *Hungary* **52 C4** 47 40N 19 45 E
Hau Bon = Cheo Reo, *Vietnam* **78 B3** 13 25N 108 28 E
Hau Duc, *Vietnam* **86 E7** 15 20N 108 13 E
Haubstadt, *U.S.A.* **157 F9** 38 12N 87 34W
Haud, *Ethiopia* **120 C2** 8 0N 45 0 E
Hauganes, *Iceland* **11 B8** 65 55N 18 18W
Haugastøl, *Norway* **18 D4** 60 30N 7 50 E
Hauge, *Norway* **18 F3** 58 20N 6 15 E
Haugesund, *Norway* **18 E2** 59 23N 5 13 E
Hauhui, *Solomon Is.* **133 M11** 9 10 S 160 59 E
Hauhungaroa Ra., *N.Z.* **130 E4** 38 42 S 175 40 E
Haukeligrend, *Norway* **18 E4** 59 44N 7 33 E
Haukipudas, *Finland* **14 D21** 65 12N 25 20 E
Haultain →, *Canada* **143 B7** 55 51N 106 46W
Haungpa, *Burma* **90 C6** 25 29N 96 7 E
Hauraha, *Solomon Is.* **133 N11** 10 46 S 161 59 E
Hauraki G., *N.Z.* **130 C4** 36 35 S 175 5 E
Hauroko L., *N.Z.* **131 F2** 45 59 S 167 21 E
Hausruck, *Austria* **34 C6** 48 6N 13 30 E
Hausstock, *Switz.* **33 C8** 46 53N 9 3 E
Haut Atlas, *Morocco* **110 B4** 32 30N 5 0W
Haut-Jura △, *France* **29 F9** 46 23N 2 23 E
Haut-Languedoc △, *France* **28 E6** 43 30N 2 43 E
Haut Niger △, *Guinea* **112 C2** 10 20N 10 20W
Haut-Rhin □, *France* **27 E14** 48 0N 7 15 E
Haut-Zaïre = Orientale □, *Dem. Rep. of the Congo* **118 B2** 2 20N 26 0 E
Haute-Corse □, *France* **29 F13** 42 30N 9 30 E
Haute-Garonne □, *France* **28 E5** 43 30N 1 30 E
Haute-Loire □, *France* **28 C7** 45 5N 3 50 E
Haute-Marne □, *France* **27 D12** 48 10N 5 20 E
Haute-Normandie □, *France* **26 C7** 49 20N 1 0 E
Haute-Saône □, *France* **27 E13** 47 45N 6 10 E
Haute-Savoie □, *France* **29 C10** 46 0N 6 20 E
Haute-Vienne □, *France* **28 C5** 45 50N 1 10 E
Hautes-Alpes □, *France* **29 D10** 44 42N 6 20 E
Hautes Fagnes = Hohe Venn, *Belgium* **24 D6** 50 30N 6 5 E
Hautes Fagnes = Hohes Venn-Eifel △, *Europe* **30 E2** 50 30N 6 10 E
Hautes-Pyrénées □, *France* **28 F4** 43 0N 0 10 E
Hauteville-Lompnès, *France* **29 C9** 45 58N 5 36 E
Hautmont, *France* **27 B10** 50 15N 3 55 E
Hauts-de-Seine □, *France* **27 D9** 48 52N 2 15 E
Hauts Plateaux, *Algeria* **111 B5** 35 0N 1 0 E
Hauula, *U.S.A.* **145 J14** 21 37N 157 55W
Hauzenberg, *Germany* **31 G9** 48 40N 13 37 E
Havana = La Habana, *Cuba* **164 B3** 23 8N 82 22W
Havana, *Fla., U.S.A.* **152 E5** 30 37N 84 25W
Havana, *Ill., U.S.A.* **156 D6** 40 18N 90 4W
Havant, *U.K.* **21 G7** 50 51N 0 58W
Havârna, *Romania* **53 B11** 48 4N 26 43 E
Havasor = Kığızı, *Turkey* **96 B4** 38 18N 43 25 E
Havasu, L., *U.S.A.* **161 L12** 34 18N 114 28W
Havdhem, *Sweden* **17 G12** 57 10N 18 20 E
Havel →, *Germany* **30 C8** 52 50N 12 3 E
Havelian, *Pakistan* **92 B5** 34 2N 73 10 E
Havelock, *Canada* **140 D4** 44 26N 77 53W
Havelock, *N.Z.* **131 B8** 41 17 S 173 48 E
Havelock, *U.S.A.* **149 H7** 34 53N 76 54W
Havelock I., *India* **95 J11** 11 58N 93 0 E
Havelock North, *N.Z.* **130 F5** 39 40 S 176 53 E
Haverfordwest, *U.K.* **21 F3** 51 48N 4 58W
Haverhill, *U.K.* **21 E8** 52 5N 0 28 E
Haverhill, *Fla., U.S.A.* **153 J9** 26 42N 80 7W
Haverhill, *Mass., U.S.A.* **151 D13** 42 47N 71 5W
Haveri, *India* **95 G2** 14 53N 75 24 E
Haverstraw, *U.S.A.* **151 E11** 41 12N 73 58W
Håverud, *Sweden* **17 F6** 58 50N 12 28 E
Havirga, *Mongolia* **74 B7** 45 41N 113 5 E
Havířov, *Czech Rep.* **35 B11** 49 46N 18 20 E
Havlíčkův Brod, *Czech Rep.* **34 B8** 49 36N 15 33 E
Havneby, *Denmark* **17 J2** 55 5N 8 34 E
Havran, *Turkey* **49 B9** 39 33N 27 6 E
Havre, *U.S.A.* **158 B9** 48 33N 109 41W
Havre-Aubert, *Canada* **141 C7** 47 12N 61 56W
Havre-St.-Pierre, *Canada* **141 B7** 50 18N 63 33W
Havsa, *Turkey* **51 E10** 41 31N 26 48 E
Havza, *Turkey* **100 B6** 41 0N 35 35 E
Haw →, *U.S.A.* **149 H6** 35 36N 79 3W
Hawaii, *U.S.A.* **145 D6** 19 30N 155 30W
Hawaii □, *U.S.A.* **145 D5** 19 30N 156 30W
Hawaii I., *Pac. Oc.* **146 J17** 20 0N 155 0W
Hawaii Volcanoes △, *U.S.A.* **145 D6** 19 23N 155 17W
Hawaiian Is., *Pac. Oc.* **135 E12** 20 30N 156 0W
Hawaiian Ridge, *Pac. Oc.* **135 E11** 24 0N 165 0W
Hawarden, *U.S.A.* **154 D6** 43 0N 96 29W
Hawea, L., *N.Z.* **131 E4** 44 28 S 169 19 E
Hawea Flat, *N.Z.* **131 E4** 44 40 S 169 19 E
Hawera, *N.Z.* **130 F3** 39 35 S 174 19 E
Hawesville, *U.S.A.* **157 G10** 37 54N 86 45W
Hawi, *U.S.A.* **145 C6** 20 14N 155 50W
Hawick, *U.K.* **22 F6** 55 26N 2 47W
Hawk Junction, *Canada* **140 C3** 48 5N 84 38W
Hawk Point, *U.S.A.* **156 F5** 38 58N 91 8W
Hawkdun Ra., *N.Z.* **131 E5** 44 53 S 170 5 E
Hawke B., *N.Z.* **130 F6** 39 25 S 177 20 E
Hawker, *Australia* **128 A3** 31 59 S 138 22 E
Hawke's Bay □, *N.Z.* **130 F5** 39 45 S 176 35 E
Hawkesbury, *Canada* **140 C5** 45 37N 74 37W
Hawkesbury I., *Canada* **142 C3** 53 37N 129 3W
Hawkesbury Pt., *Australia* **126 A1** 11 55 S 134 5 E
Hawkinsville, *U.S.A.* **152 C6** 32 17N 83 28W
Hawks Nest, *Australia* **129 B10** 32 41 S 152 11 E
Hawley, *Minn., U.S.A.* **154 B6** 46 53N 96 19W
Hawley, *Pa., U.S.A.* **151 E9** 41 28N 75 11W
Ḥawrān, W. →, *Iraq* **101 F10** 33 58N 42 34 E
Hawsh Mūssá, *Lebanon* **103 B4** 33 45N 35 55 E
Hawthorne, *Fla., U.S.A.* **153 F7** 29 36N 82 5W
Hawthorne, *Nev., U.S.A.* **158 G4** 38 32N 118 38W
Hay, *Australia* **129 C6** 34 30 S 144 51 E
Hay →, *Australia* **126 C2** 24 50 S 138 0 E
Hay →, *Canada* **142 A5** 60 50N 116 26W
Hay, C., *Australia* **124 B4** 14 5 S 129 29 E
Hay I., *Canada* **150 B4** 44 53N 80 58W
Hay L., *Canada* **142 B5** 58 50N 118 50W
Hay-on-Wye, *U.K.* **21 E4** 52 5N 3 8W
Hay River, *Canada* **142 A5** 60 51N 115 44W
Hay Springs, *U.S.A.* **154 D3** 42 41N 102 41W
Haya = Tehoru, *Indonesia* **83 B3** 3 23 S 129 30 E
Hayachine-San, *Japan* **70 E10** 39 34N 141 29 E
Hayange, *France* **27 C13** 49 20N 6 2 E
Hayastan = Armenia ■, *Asia* **61 K7** 40 20N 45 0 E
Hayato, *Japan* **72 F2** 31 40N 130 43 E
Haydarlı, *Turkey* **49 C12** 38 16N 30 23 E
Hayden, *U.S.A.* **158 F10** 40 30N 107 16W
Haydon, *Australia* **126 B3** 18 0 S 141 30 E
Hayes, *U.S.A.* **154 C4** 44 23N 101 1W
Hayes →, *Canada* **140 A1** 57 3N 92 12W
Hayes, Mt., *U.S.A.* **144 E11** 63 37N 146 43W
Hayes Creek, *Australia* **124 B5** 13 43 S 131 22 E
Hayle, *U.K.* **21 G2** 50 11N 5 26W
Hayling I., *U.K.* **21 G7** 50 48N 0 59W
Haymana, *Turkey* **100 C5** 39 26N 32 31 E
Haymen I., *Australia* **126 J6** 20 3 S 148 52 E
Haynan, *Yemen* **99 D5** 15 50N 48 18 E
Haynau = Chojnów, *Poland* **55 G2** 51 18N 15 58 E
Hayneville, *U.S.A.* **152 C6** 32 23N 83 37W
Hayrabolu, *Turkey* **51 E11** 41 12N 27 5 E
Hays, *Canada* **142 C6** 50 6N 111 48W
Hays, *U.S.A.* **154 F5** 38 53N 99 20W
Ḥays, *Yemen* **98 D3** 13 56N 43 29 E
Haysville, *U.S.A.* **157 F10** 38 28N 86 55W
Haysyn, *Ukraine* **53 B14** 48 57N 29 25 E
Hayvoron, *Ukraine* **53 B14** 48 22N 29 52 E
Hayward, *Calif., U.S.A.* **160 H4** 37 40N 122 5W
Hayward, *Wis., U.S.A.* **154 B9** 46 1N 91 29W
Haywards Heath, *U.K.* **21 G7** 51 0N 0 5W
Haẕafon □, *Israel* **103 C4** 32 40N 35 20 E
Hazārān, Kūh-e, *Iran* **97 D8** 29 35N 57 20 E
Hazard, *U.S.A.* **148 G4** 37 15N 83 12W
Hazaribag, *India* **93 H11** 23 58N 85 26 E
Hazaribag Road, *India* **93 G11** 24 12N 85 57 E
Hazebrouck, *France* **27 B9** 50 42N 2 31 E
Hazelton, *Canada* **142 B3** 55 20N 127 42W
Hazelton, *U.S.A.* **154 B4** 46 29N 100 17W
Hazen, *U.S.A.* **154 B4** 47 18N 101 38W
Hazlehurst, *Ga., U.S.A.* **152 D7** 31 52N 82 36W
Hazlehurst, *Miss., U.S.A.* **155 K9** 31 52N 90 24W
Hazlet, *U.S.A.* **151 F10** 40 25N 74 12W
Hazleton, *Ind., U.S.A.* **157 F9** 38 29N 87 33W
Hazleton, *Pa., U.S.A.* **151 F9** 40 57N 75 59W
Hazlett, L., *Australia* **124 D4** 21 30 S 128 48 E
Hazro, *Turkey* **96 B4** 38 15N 40 47 E
He Xian, *Anhui, China* **77 B12** 31 45N 118 20 E
He Xian, *Guangxi Zhuangzu, China* **77 E8** 24 27N 111 30 E
Head of Bight, *Australia* **125 F5** 31 30 S 131 25 E
Headland, *U.S.A.* **152 D4** 31 21N 85 21W
Headlands, *Zimbabwe* **119 F3** 18 15 S 32 2 E
Healdsburg, *U.S.A.* **160 G4** 38 37N 122 52W
Healdton, *U.S.A.* **155 H6** 34 14N 97 29W
Healesville, *Australia* **129 D6** 37 35 S 145 30 E
Healy, *U.S.A.* **144 E10** 63 52N 148 58W
Heany Junction, *Zimbabwe* **117 C4** 20 6 S 28 54 E
Heard I., *Ind. Oc.* **121 K6** 53 0 S 74 0 E
Hearne, *U.S.A.* **155 K6** 30 53N 96 36W
Hearst, *Canada* **140 C3** 49 40N 83 41W
Heart →, *U.S.A.* **154 B4** 46 46N 100 50W
Heart's Content, *Canada* **141 C9** 47 54N 53 27W
Heath →, *Bolivia* **172 C4** 12 31 S 68 38W
Heath, Pte., *Canada* **141 C7** 49 8N 61 40W
Heath Mts., *N.Z.* **131 F2** 45 39 S 167 9 E
Heathcote, *Australia* **129 D6** 36 56 S 144 45 E
Heatherwood = Edson, *Canada* **142 C5** 53 35N 116 28W
Heathrow, London ✕ (LHR), *U.K.* **21 F7** 51 28N 0 27W
Heavener, *U.S.A.* **155 H7** 34 53N 94 36W
Hebbronville, *U.S.A.* **155 M5** 27 18N 98 41W
Hebei □, *China* **74 E9** 39 0N 116 0 E
Hebel, *Australia* **127 D4** 28 58 S 147 47 E
Heber, *U.S.A.* **161 N11** 32 44N 115 32W
Heber Springs, *U.S.A.* **155 H9** 35 30N 92 2W
Hebert, *Canada* **143 C7** 50 30N 107 10W
Hebgen L., *U.S.A.* **158 D8** 44 52N 111 20W
Hebi, *China* **74 G8** 35 57N 114 7 E
Hebrides, *U.K.* **12 D4** 57 30N 7 0W
Hebrides, Sea of the, *U.K.* **22 D2** 57 5N 7 0W
Hebron = Al Khalīl, *West Bank* **103 D4** 31 32N 35 6 E
Hebron, *Canada* **139 C13** 58 5N 62 30W
Hebron, *N. Dak., U.S.A.* **154 B3** 46 54N 102 3W
Hebron, *Nebr., U.S.A.* **154 E6** 40 10N 97 35W
Heby, *Sweden* **16 E10** 59 56N 16 53 E
Hecate Str., *Canada* **142 C2** 53 10N 130 30W
Heceta I., *U.S.A.* **142 B2** 55 46N 133 40W
Hechi, *China* **76 E7** 24 40N 108 2 E
Hechingen, *Germany* **31 G4** 48 21N 8 57 E
Hechuan, *China* **76 B6** 30 2N 106 12 E
Hecla, *U.S.A.* **154 C5** 45 53N 98 9W
Hecla I., *Canada* **143 C9** 51 10N 96 43W
Hedal, *Norway* **18 D6** 60 37N 9 41 E
Heddal, *Norway* **18 E6** 59 36N 9 9 E
Hédé, *France* **26 D5** 48 18N 1 49W
Hede, *Sweden* **16 B7** 62 23N 13 30 E
Hedemora, *Sweden* **16 D9** 60 18N 15 58 E
Hedensted, *Denmark* **17 J3** 55 46N 9 42 E
Hedesunda, *Sweden* **16 D10** 60 24N 17 0 E
Hedgehope, *N.Z.* **131 G3** 46 12 S 168 34 E
Hedmark □, *Norway* **18 C8** 61 17N 11 40 E
Hedrick, *U.S.A.* **156 C4** 41 11N 92 19W
Heerde, *Neths.* **24 B6** 52 24N 6 2 E
Heerenveen, *Neths.* **24 B5** 52 57N 5 55 E
Heerhugowaard, *Neths.* **24 B4** 52 40N 4 51 E
Heerlen, *Neths.* **24 D5** 50 55N 5 58 E
Heerwegen = Polkowice, *Poland* **55 G3** 51 29N 16 3 E
Ḥefa, *Israel* **103 C4** 32 46N 35 0 E
Ḥefa □, *Israel* **103 C4** 32 40N 35 0 E
Hefei, *China* **77 B11** 31 52N 117 18 E
Hefeng, *China* **77 C8** 29 55N 109 52 E
Heflin, *U.S.A.* **152 B4** 33 39N 85 35W
Hegalig, *Sudan* **107 E3** 14 36N 31 54 E
Hegang, *China* **69 B8** 47 20N 130 19 E
Heggenes, *Norway* **18 C6** 61 9N 9 4 E
Hegra, *Norway* **18 A8** 63 27N 11 8 E
Hei Ling Chau, *China* **69 G11** 22 15N 114 2 E
Heiban, *Sudan* **107 E3** 11 13N 30 31 E
Heichengzhen, *China* **74 F4** 36 24N 106 3 E
Heidal, *Norway* **18 C6** 61 45N 9 19 E
Heide, *Germany* **30 A5** 54 11N 9 6 E
Heidelberg, *Germany* **31 F4** 49 24N 8 42 E
Heidelberg, *S. Africa* **116 E3** 34 6 S 20 59 E
Heidenau, *Germany* **30 E9** 50 57N 13 52 E
Heidenheim, *Germany* **31 G6** 48 41N 10 9 E
Heigun-Tō, *Japan* **72 D4** 33 47N 132 14 E
Heijing, *China* **76 E3** 25 22N 101 44 E
Heijo = P'yŏngyang, *N. Korea* **75 E13** 39 0N 125 30 E
Heilbad Heiligenstadt, *Germany* **30 D6** 51 22N 10 8 E
Heilbron, *S. Africa* **117 D4** 27 16 S 27 59 E
Heilbronn, *Germany* **31 F5** 49 9N 9 13 E
Heiligenblut, *Austria* **34 D5** 47 2N 12 51 E
Heiligenhafen, *Germany* **30 A6** 54 22N 10 59 E
Heilongjiang □, *China* **69 B7** 48 0N 126 0 E
Heilprin Land, *Greenland* **10 A7** 82 5N 33 0W
Heilsberg = Lidzbark Warmiński, *Poland* **54 D7** 54 7N 20 34 E
Heilunkiang = Heilongjiang □, *China* **69 B7** 48 0N 126 0 E
Heim, *Norway* **18 A6** 63 26N 9 5 E
Heimaey, *Iceland* **11 D6** 63 26N 20 17W
Heimdal, *Norway* **18 A7** 63 21N 10 22 E
Heinola, *Finland* **15 F22** 61 13N 26 2 E
Heinsberg, *Germany* **30 D2** 51 3N 6 5 E
Heinsun, *Burma* **90 C5** 25 52N 95 35 E
Heinze Kyun, *Burma* **86 E1** 14 25N 97 45 E
Heirnkut, *Burma* **90 C5** 25 14N 94 44 E
Heishan, *China* **75 D12** 41 40N 122 5 E
Heishui, *Liaoning, China* **75 C10** 42 8N 119 30 E
Heishui, *Sichuan, China* **76 A4** 32 4N 103 2 E
Hejaz = Ḥijāz □, *Si. Arabia* **96 E3** 24 0N 40 0 E
Hejian, *China* **74 E9** 38 25N 116 5 E
Hejiang, *China* **76 C5** 28 43N 105 46 E
Hejin, *China* **74 G6** 35 35N 110 42 E
Hekimhan, *Turkey* **100 C7** 38 50N 37 55 E
Hekinan, *Japan* **73 C9** 34 52N 137 0 E
Hekla, *Iceland* **11 D7** 63 56N 19 35W
Hekou, *Guangdong, China* **77 F9** 23 13N 112 45 E
Hekou, *Yunnan, China* **76 F4** 22 30N 103 59 E
Hel, *Poland* **54 D5** 54 37N 18 47 E
Helagsfjället, *Sweden* **16 B6** 62 54N 12 25 E
Helan Shan, *China* **74 E3** 38 30N 105 55 E
Helechosa, *Spain* **43 F6** 39 22N 4 53W
Helemano →, *U.S.A.* **145 J13** 21 35N 158 7W
Helen Atoll, *Pac. Oc.* **83 A4** 2 40N 131 49 E
Helena, *Ark., U.S.A.* **155 H9** 34 32N 90 36W
Helena, *Ga., U.S.A.* **152 C7** 32 5N 82 55W
Helena, *Mont., U.S.A.* **158 C7** 46 36N 112 2W
Helendale, *U.S.A.* **161 L9** 34 44N 117 19W
Helensburgh, *Australia* **129 C9** 34 11 S 151 1 E
Helensburgh, *U.K.* **22 E4** 56 1N 4 43W
Helensville, *N.Z.* **130 C3** 36 41 S 174 29 E
Helenvale, *Australia* **126 B4** 15 43 S 145 14 E
Helgasjön, *Sweden* **17 H8** 56 55N 14 50 E
Helgeland, *Norway* **14 C15** 66 7N 13 29 E
Helgoland, *Germany* **30 A3** 54 10N 7 53 E
Heligoland = Helgoland, *Germany* **30 A3** 54 10N 7 53 E
Heligoland B. = Deutsche Bucht, *Germany* **30 A4** 54 15N 8 0 E
Heliopolis, *Egypt* **106 H7** 30 6N 31 17 E
Hell, *Norway* **18 A7** 63 26N 10 54 E
Hella, *Iceland* **11 D6** 63 50N 20 24W
Hellas = Greece ■, *Europe* **48 B3** 40 0N 23 0 E
Helleland, *Norway* **18 F3** 58 33N 6 7 E
Hellertown, *U.S.A.* **151 F9** 40 35N 75 21W
Hellespont = Çanakkale Boğazı, *Turkey* **51 F10** 40 17N 26 32 E
Hellesylt, *Norway* **18 B3** 62 6N 6 51 E
Hellevoetsluis, *Neths.* **24 C4** 51 50N 4 8 E
Hellhole Gorge △, *Australia* **126 D3** 25 31 S 144 12 E
Hellín, *Spain* **41 G3** 38 31N 1 40W
Hellissandur, *Iceland* **11 C3** 64 55N 23 54W
Hells Canyon △, *U.S.A.* **158 D5** 45 30N 117 45W
Hell's Gate △, *Kenya* **118 C4** 0 54 S 36 19 E
Hellvik, *Norway* **18 F2** 58 29N 5 52 E
Helmand □, *Afghan.* **91 C2** 31 20N 64 0 E
Helmand →, *Afghan.* **91 C1** 31 12N 61 34 E
Helme →, *Germany* **30 D7** 51 20N 11 21 E
Helmeringhausen, *Namibia* **116 D2** 25 54 S 16 57 E
Helmond, *Neths.* **24 C5** 51 29N 5 41 E
Helmsdale, *U.K.* **22 C5** 58 7N 3 39W
Helmsdale →, *U.K.* **22 C5** 58 7N 3 40W
Helmstedt, *Germany* **30 C7** 52 12N 11 0 E
Helong, *China* **75 C15** 42 40N 129 0 E
Helper, *U.S.A.* **158 G8** 39 41N 110 51W
Helsingborg, *Sweden* **17 H6** 56 3N 12 42 E
Helsinge, *Denmark* **17 H6** 56 2N 12 12 E
Helsingfors = Helsinki, *Finland* **15 F21** 60 15N 25 3 E
Helsingør, *Denmark* **17 H6** 56 2N 12 35 E
Helsinki, *Finland* **15 F21** 60 15N 25 3 E
Helska, Mierzeja, *Poland* **54 D5** 54 45N 18 40 E
Helston, *U.K.* **21 G2** 50 6N 5 17W
Helvellyn, *U.K.* **20 C4** 54 32N 3 1W
Helwân, *Egypt* **106 J7** 29 50N 31 20 E
Hemavati →, *India* **95 H3** 12 30N 76 20 E
Hemel Hempstead, *U.K.* **21 F7** 51 44N 0 28W
Hemet, *U.S.A.* **161 M10** 33 45N 116 58W
Hemingford, *U.S.A.* **154 D3** 42 19N 103 4W
Hemis △, *India* **92 B7** 34 10N 77 15 E
Hemmingford, *Canada* **151 A11** 45 3N 73 35W
Hempe, *Dem. Rep. of the Congo* **114 B4** 1 54N 22 42 E
Hempstead, *U.S.A.* **155 K6** 30 6N 96 5W
Hemse, *Sweden* **17 G12** 57 15N 18 22 E
Hemsedal, *Norway* **18 D5** 60 53N 8 30 E
Hemsön, *Sweden* **16 B12** 62 42N 18 5 E
Hen, *Norway* **18 D7** 60 13N 10 14 E
Hen and Chickens Is., *N.Z.* **130 B3** 35 58 S 174 45 E
Henån, *Sweden* **17 F5** 58 14N 11 40 E
Henan □, *China* **74 H8** 34 0N 114 0 E
Henares →, *Spain* **42 E7** 40 24N 3 30W
Henashi-Misaki, *Japan* **70 D9** 40 37N 139 51 E
Hendaye, *France* **28 E2** 43 23N 1 47W
Hendek, *Turkey* **100 B4** 40 48N 30 44 E
Henderson, *Argentina* **174 D3** 36 18 S 61 43W
Henderson, *Ga., U.S.A.* **152 C6** 32 21N 83 47W
Henderson, *Ky., U.S.A.* **157 G9** 37 50N 87 35W
Henderson, *N.C., U.S.A.* **149 G6** 36 20N 78 25W
Henderson, *Nev., U.S.A.* **161 J12** 36 2N 114 59W
Henderson, *Tenn., U.S.A.* **149 H1** 35 26N 88 38W
Henderson, *Tex., U.S.A.* **155 J7** 32 9N 94 48W
Henderson I., *Pac. Oc.* **135 K15** 24 22 S 128 19W
Hendersonville, *N.C., U.S.A.* **149 H4** 35 19N 82 28W
Hendersonville, *Tenn., U.S.A.* **149 G2** 36 18N 86 37W
Hendījān, *Iran* **97 D6** 30 14N 49 43 E
Hendorābī, *Iran* **97 E7** 26 40N 53 37 E
Heng Jiang, *China* **76 C5** 28 40N 104 25 E
Heng Xian, *China* **76 F7** 22 40N 109 17 E
Henganofi, *Papua N. G.* **132 D3** 6 15 S 145 38 E
Hengcheng, *China* **74 E4** 38 18N 106 28 E
Hengchun, *Taiwan* **77 F13** 22 0N 120 44 E
Hengdaohezi, *China* **75 B15** 44 52N 129 0 E
Hengelo, *Neths.* **24 B6** 52 16N 6 48 E
Hengfeng, *China* **77 C10** 28 12N 115 48 E
Henggang, *China* **69 F11** 22 39N 114 12 E
Hengmen, *China* **69 F10** 22 33N 113 35 E
Hengqin Dao, *China* **69 G10** 22 7N 113 34 E
Hengshan, *Hunan, China* **77 D9** 27 16N 112 45 E
Hengshan, *Shaanxi, China* **74 F5** 37 58N 109 5 E
Hengshui, *China* **74 F8** 37 41N 115 40 E
Hengyang, *China* **77 D9** 26 59N 112 22 E
Henichesk, *Ukraine* **59 J8** 46 12N 34 50 E
Henima, *India* **90 C4** 25 22N 93 36 E
Hénin-Beaumont, *France* **27 B9** 50 25N 2 58 E
Hénin-Liétard = Hénin-Beaumont, *France* **27 B9** 50 25N 2 58 E
Henley-on-Thames, *U.K.* **21 F7** 51 32N 0 54W
Henlopen, C., *U.S.A.* **148 F8** 38 48N 75 6W
Hennan, *Sweden* **16 B9** 62 2N 15 54 E
Hennebont, *France* **26 E3** 47 49N 3 19W
Hennenman, *S. Africa* **116 D4** 27 59 S 27 1 E
Hennepin, *U.S.A.* **156 C7** 41 15N 89 21W
Hennessey, *U.S.A.* **155 G6** 36 6N 97 54W
Hennigsdorf, *Germany* **30 C9** 52 38N 13 12 E
Henri Pittier △, *Venezuela* **165 D6** 10 26N 67 37W
Henrietta, *U.S.A.* **155 J5** 33 49N 98 12W
Henrietta, Ostrov = Genriyetty, Ostrov, *Russia* **67 B16** 77 6N 156 30 E
Henrietta Maria, C., *Canada* **140 A3** 55 9N 82 20W
Henry, *U.S.A.* **156 C7** 41 7N 89 22W
Henry Lawrence I., *India* **95 H11** 12 9N 93 5 E
Henryetta, *U.S.A.* **155 H7** 35 27N 95 59W
Henryville, *Canada* **151 A11** 45 8N 73 11W
Hensall, *Canada* **150 C3** 43 26N 81 30W
Henstedt-Ulzburg, *Germany* **30 B6** 53 47N 10 0 E
Hentiesbaai, *Namibia* **116 C1** 22 8 S 14 18 E
Hentiyn Nuruu, *Mongolia* **69 B5** 48 30N 108 30 E
Henty, *Australia* **129 C7** 35 30 S 147 0 E
Henzada, *Burma* **90 G5** 17 38N 95 26 E
Hephaestia, *Greece* **49 B7** 39 55N 25 14 E
Hephzibah, *U.S.A.* **152 B7** 33 19N 82 6W
Heping, *China* **77 E10** 24 29N 115 0 E
Heppner, *U.S.A.* **158 D4** 45 21N 119 33W
Hepu, *China* **76 G7** 21 40N 109 12 E
Hepworth, *Canada* **150 B3** 44 37N 81 9W
Heqing, *China* **76 D3** 26 37N 100 11 E
Hequ, *China* **74 E6** 39 20N 111 15 E
Héraðsflói, *Iceland* **11 B12** 65 42N 14 12W
Héraðsvötn →, *Iceland* **11 B7** 65 45N 19 25W
Heradsbygd, *Norway* **18 D8** 60 49N 11 39 E
Heraklion = Iráklion, *Greece* **39 E6** 35 20N 25 12 E
Herald Cays, *Australia* **126 B4** 16 58 S 149 9 E
Herand, *Norway* **18 D3** 60 20N 6 22 E
Herāt, *Afghan.* **91 B1** 34 20N 62 7 E
Herāt □, *Afghan.* **91 B1** 35 0N 62 0 E
Hérault □, *France* **28 E7** 43 34N 3 15 E
Hérault →, *France* **28 E7** 43 17N 3 26 E
Herbault, *France* **26 E8** 47 36N 1 8 E
Herbert →, *Australia* **126 B4** 18 31 S 146 17 E
Herbert I., *U.S.A.* **144 K5** 52 45N 170 7W

Herbert River Falls △, *Australia* .... **126 B4** 18 15 S 145 32 E
Herbertabad, *India* ... **95 J11** 11 43N 92 37 E
Herberton, *Australia* . **126 B4** 17 20 S 145 25 E
Herbertsdale, *S. Africa* **116 E3** 34 1 S 21 46 E
Herbertville, *N.Z.* .... **130 G5** 40 30 S 176 33 E
Herbignac, *France* **26 E4** 47 27N 2 18W
Herborn, *Germany* ... **30 E4** 50 40N 8 18 E
Herby, *Poland* .... **55 H5** 50 45N 18 50 E
Herceg-Novi, *Serbia & M.* .... **50 D2** 42 30N 18 33 E
Hercegfalva = Mezőfalva, *Hungary* **52 D3** 46 55N 18 49 E
Herchmer, *Canada* ... **143 B10** 57 22N 94 10W
Herculânia = Coxim, *Brazil* .... **173 D7** 18 30 S 54 55W
Herðubreið, *Iceland* .. **11 B10** 65 11N 16 21W
Hereford, *U.K.* **21 E5** 52 4N 2 43W
Hereford, *U.S.A.* **155 H3** 34 49N 102 24W
Herefordshire □, *U.K.* **21 E5** 52 8N 2 40W
Herefoss, *Norway* .... **18 F5** 58 32N 8 23 E
Herehogna, *Sweden* .. **18 C9** 61 44N 12 8 E
Hereke, *Turkey* ...... **51 F13** 40 47N 29 38 E
Herekino, *N.Z.* ...... **130 B2** 35 18 S 173 11 E
Herencia, *Spain* **43 F7** 39 21N 3 22W
Herentals, *Belgium* ... **24 C4** 51 12N 4 51 E
Herford, *Germany* ... **30 C4** 52 7N 8 39 E
Héricourt, *France* .... **27 E13** 47 32N 6 45 E
Herington, *U.S.A.* **154 F6** 38 40N 96 57W
Herisau, *Switz.* ...... **33 B8** 47 22N 9 17 E
Hérisson, *France* ..... **27 F9** 46 32N 2 42 E
Herkimer, *U.S.A.* **151 D10** 43 0N 74 59W
Herlong, *U.S.A.* **160 E6** 40 8N 120 8W
Herm, *U.K.* **21 H5** 49 30N 2 28W
Hermakivka, *Ukraine* . **53 B11** 48 42N 26 11 E
Hermann, *U.S.A.* **156 F5** 38 42N 91 27W
Hermannsbad = Ciechocinek, *Poland* **55 F5** 52 53N 18 45 E
Hermannsburg, *Australia* .... **124 D5** 23 57 S 132 45 E
Hermannsburg, *Germany* .... **30 C6** 52 50N 10 5 E
Hermannstadt = Sibiu, *Romania* .... **53 E9** 45 45N 24 9 E
Hermansverk, *Norway* **18 C3** 61 11N 6 52 E
Hermanus, *S. Africa* .. **116 E2** 34 27 S 19 12 E
Herment, *France* ..... **28 C6** 45 45N 2 24 E
Hermidale, *Australia* . **129 A7** 31 30 S 146 42 E
Hermiston, *U.S.A.* **158 D4** 45 51N 119 17W
Hermit Is., *Papua N. G.* **132 A3** 1 32 S 145 5 E
Hermitage, *U.S.A.* **156 G3** 37 56N 93 19W
Hermite, I., *Chile* .... **176 E3** 55 50 S 68 0W
Hermon, *U.S.A.* **151 B9** 44 28N 75 14W
Hermon, Mt. = Shaykh, J. ash, *Lebanon* ..... **103 B4** 33 25N 35 50 E
Hermosillo, *Mexico* .. **162 B2** 29 10N 111 0W
Hernád ⟶, *Hungary* . **52 C6** 47 56N 21 8 E
Hernandarias, *Paraguay* .... **175 B5** 25 20 S 54 40W
Hernandez, *U.S.A.* .. **160 J6** 36 24N 120 46W
Hernando, *Argentina* . **174 C3** 32 28 S 63 40W
Hernando, *Fla., U.S.A.* **153 G7** 28 54N 82 23W
Hernando, *Miss., U.S.A.* **155 H10** 34 50N 90 0W
Hernani, *Spain* **40 B3** 43 16N 1 58W
Herndon, *U.S.A.* **150 F8** 40 43N 76 51W
Herne, *Germany* ..... **24 C7** 51 32N 7 14 E
Herne Bay, *U.K.* ..... **21 F9** 51 21N 1 8 E
Herning, *Denmark* ... **17 H2** 56 8N 8 58 E
Herod, *U.S.A.* **152 D5** 31 42N 84 26W
Heroica = Caborca, *Mexico* **162 A2** 30 40N 112 10W
Heroica Nogales = Nogales, *Mexico* ... **162 A2** 31 20N 110 56W
Heron Bay, *Canada* .. **140 C2** 48 40N 86 25W
Herradura, Pta. de la, *Canary Is.* **9 e2** 28 26N 14 8W
Herre, *Norway* ...... **18 E6** 59 6N 9 34 E
Herreid, *U.S.A.* **154 C4** 45 50N 100 4W
Herrenberg, *Germany* **31 G4** 48 35N 8 52 E
Herrera, *Spain* **43 H6** 37 26N 4 55W
Herrera de Alcántara, *Spain* **43 F3** 39 39N 7 25W
Herrera de Pisuerga, *Spain* **42 C6** 42 35N 4 20W
Herrera del Duque, *Spain* **43 F5** 39 10N 5 3W
Herrestad, *Sweden* ... **17 F5** 58 21N 11 50 E
Herrin, *U.S.A.* **155 G10** 37 48N 89 2W
Herriot, *Canada* **143 B8** 56 22N 101 16W
Herrljunga, *Sweden* .. **17 F7** 58 5N 13 1 E
Hersbruck, *Germany* . **31 F7** 49 30N 11 26 E
Herschel I., *Canada* .. **6 C1** 69 35N 139 5W
Hershey, *U.S.A.* **151 F8** 40 17N 76 39W
Herstal, *Belgium* ..... **24 D5** 50 40N 5 38 E
Hertford, *U.K.* **21 F7** 51 48N 0 4W
Hertfordshire □, *U.K.* **21 F7** 51 51N 0 5W
's-Hertogenbosch, *Neths.* .... **24 C5** 51 42N 5 17 E
Hertsa, *Ukraine* ..... **53 B11** 48 9N 26 15 E
Hertzogville, *S. Africa* **116 D4** 28 9 S 25 30 E
Hervás, *Spain* **42 E5** 40 16N 5 52W
Hervey B., *Australia* .. **126 C5** 25 0 S 152 52 E
Herzberg, *Brandenburg, Germany* .... **30 D9** 51 41N 13 14 E
Herzberg, *Niedersachsen, Germany* .... **30 D6** 51 38N 10 20 E
Herzliyya, *Israel* ..... **103 C3** 32 10N 34 50 E
Herzogenbuchsee, *Switz.* .... **32 B5** 47 11N 7 42 E
Herzogenburg, *Austria* **34 C8** 48 17N 15 41 E
Ḩeşār, *Fārs, Iran* .... **97 D6** 29 52N 50 16 E
Ḩeşār, *Markazī, Iran* . **97 C6** 35 50N 49 12 E
Hesdin, *France* ...... **27 B9** 50 21N 2 2 E
Heshan, *China* ...... **76 F7** 23 50N 108 53 E
Heshui, *China* ...... **74 G5** 35 48N 108 0 E
Heshun, *China* ...... **74 F7** 37 22N 113 32 E
Heskestad, *Norway* .. **18 F3** 58 28N 6 22 E
Hesperia, *U.S.A.* **161 L9** 34 25N 117 18W
Hessdalen, *Norway* .. **18 B8** 62 48N 11 10 E
Hesse = Hessen □, *Germany* .... **30 E4** 50 30N 9 0 E
Hessen □, *Germany* .. **30 E4** 50 30N 9 0 E
Hessenreuther und Manteler Wald ⌓, *Germany* .... **31 F8** 49 45N 12 1 E
Hesso, *Australia* ..... **128 B2** 32 8 S 137 27 E
Hesteyri, *Iceland* **11 A4** 66 20N 22 53W
Hestra, *Sweden* ..... **17 G7** 57 26N 13 35 E
Hetch Hetchy Aqueduct, *U.S.A.* .. **160 H5** 37 29N 122 19W
Hettinger, *U.S.A.* **154 C3** 46 0N 102 42W
Hettstedt, *Germany* .. **30 D7** 51 39N 11 31 E
Heuvelton, *U.S.A.* **151 B9** 44 37N 75 25W
Hevelândia, *Brazil* ... **169 E5** 5 12 S 61 50W
Heves, *Hungary* ..... **52 C5** 47 36N 20 17 E
Heves □, *Hungary* ... **52 C5** 47 50N 20 0 E
Hewitt, *U.S.A.* **155 K6** 31 27N 97 11W
Hexham, *U.K.* **20 C5** 54 58N 2 4W
Hexi, *Yunnan, China* . **76 E4** 24 9N 102 38 E
Hexi, *Zhejiang, China* **77 D12** 27 58N 119 38 E
Hexigten Qi, *China* ... **75 C9** 43 18N 117 30 E
Ḩeydarābād, *Iran* .... **97 D7** 30 33N 55 38 E
Heydebreck = Kędzierzyn-Koźle, *Poland* .... **55 H5** 50 20N 18 12 E
Heyfield, *Australia* ... **129 D7** 37 59 S 146 47 E
Heysham, *U.K.* **20 C5** 54 3N 2 53W
Heyuan, *China* ...... **77 F10** 23 39N 114 40 E
Heywood, *Australia* .. **128 E4** 38 8 S 141 37 E
Heyworth, *U.S.A.* **156 D8** 40 19N 88 59W
Heze, *China* .... **74 G8** 35 14N 115 20 E
Hezhang, *China* ..... **76 D5** 27 8N 104 41 E
Hi, Ko, *Thailand* ..... **87 a** 7 44N 98 22 E
Hi-no-Misaki, *Japan* .. **72 B4** 35 26N 132 38 E
Hi Vista, *U.S.A.* **161 L9** 34 45N 117 46W
Hialeah, *U.S.A.* **153 K9** 25 50N 80 17W
Hiawatha, *U.S.A.* **154 F7** 39 51N 95 32W
Hibbing, *U.S.A.* **154 B8** 47 25N 92 56W
Hibbs B., *Australia* ... **127 G4** 42 35 S 145 15 E
Hibernia Reef, *Australia* .... **124 B3** 12 0 S 123 23 E
Hibiki-Nada, *Japan* ... **72 D2** 34 0N 130 0 E
Hickman, *U.S.A.* **155 G10** 36 34N 89 11W
Hickory, *U.S.A.* **149 H5** 35 44N 81 21W
Hicks, Pt., *Australia* .. **129 D8** 37 49 S 149 17 E
Hicks Bay, *N.Z.* ..... **130 D7** 37 34 S 178 21 E
Hicks L., *Canada* **143 A9** 61 25N 100 0W
Hicksville, *N.Y., U.S.A.* **151 F11** 40 46N 73 32W
Hicksville, *Ohio, U.S.A.* **157 C12** 41 18N 84 46W
Hida, *Romania* ...... **53 C8** 47 10N 23 19 E
Hida-Gawa ⟶, *Japan* **73 B9** 35 26N 137 3 E
Hida-Sammyaku, *Japan* **73 A9** 36 30N 137 40 E
Hida-Sanchi, *Japan* ... **73 A9** 36 10N 137 0 E
Hidaka, *Japan* .... **72 B6** 35 30N 134 44 E
Hidaka-Sammyaku, *Japan* .... **70 C11** 42 35N 142 45 E
Hidalgo, *Mexico* **163 C5** 24 15N 99 26W
Hidalgo □, *Mexico* ... **163 C5** 20 30N 99 10W
Hidalgo, Presa M., *Mexico* **162 B3** 26 30N 108 35W
Hidalgo del Parral, *Mexico* **162 B3** 26 58N 105 40W
Hiddensee, *Germany* . **30 A9** 54 32N 13 6 E
Hidrolândia, *Brazil* ... **171 E2** 17 0 S 49 15W
Hieflau, *Austria* ...... **34 D7** 47 36N 14 46 E
Hiendelaencina, *Spain* **40 D2** 41 5N 3 0W
Hienghène, *N. Cal.* ... **133 T18** 20 41 S 164 56 E
Hierro, *Canary Is.* **9 e1** 27 44N 18 0W
Higashi-Hiroshima, *Japan* .... **72 C4** 34 25N 132 45 E
Higashi-Matsuyama, *Japan* .... **73 A11** 36 2N 139 25 E
Higashiajima-San, *Japan* .... **70 F10** 37 40N 140 10 E
Higashiōsaka, *Japan* .. **73 C7** 34 40N 135 37 E
Higasi-Suidō, *Japan* .. **72 D1** 34 0N 129 30 E
Higbee, *U.S.A.* **156 E4** 39 19N 92 31W
Higgins, *U.S.A.* **155 G4** 36 7N 100 2W
Higgins Corner, *U.S.A.* **160 F5** 39 2N 121 5W
Higginsville, *U.S.A.* .. **156 E3** 39 4N 93 43W
High Bridge, *U.S.A.* .. **151 F10** 40 40N 74 54W
High Island Res., *China* **69 G11** 22 22N 114 21 E
High Level, *Canada* .. **142 B5** 58 31N 117 8W
High Peak, *Phil.* ..... **80 D3** 15 29N 120 7 E
High Pk., *St. Helena* .. **9 h** 15 58 S 5 44W
High Point, *U.S.A.* ... **149 H6** 35 57N 80 0W
High Prairie, *Canada* . **142 B5** 55 30N 116 30W
High River, *Canada* .. **142 C6** 50 30N 113 50W
High Springs, *U.S.A.* .. **152 F7** 29 50N 82 36W
High Tatra = Tatry, *Slovak Rep.* .... **35 B13** 49 20N 20 0 E
High Veld, *Africa* .... **104 J6** 27 0 S 27 0 E
High Wycombe, *U.K.* . **21 F7** 51 37N 0 45W
Highbank, *N.Z.* ..... **131 D6** 43 37 S 171 45 E
Highland, *Ill., U.S.A.* . **156 F7** 38 44N 89 41W
Highland, *Ind., U.S.A.* **157 C9** 41 33N 87 28W
Highland, *Wis., U.S.A.* **156 A6** 43 5N 90 22W
Highland □, *U.K.* **22 D4** 57 17N 4 21W
Highland City, *U.S.A.* . **153 H8** 27 58N 81 53W
Highland Home, *U.S.A.* **152 D3** 31 57N 86 19W
Highland Mills = Experiment, *U.S.A.* **152 B5** 33 17N 84 17W
Highland Park, *U.S.A.* **157 B9** 42 11N 87 48W
Highland View, *U.S.A.* **152 F4** 29 50N 85 19W
Highlands = Fort Thomas, *U.S.A.* **157 E12** 39 5N 84 27W
Highmore, *U.S.A.* **154 C5** 44 31N 99 27W
Highrock L., *Man., Canada* **143 B8** 55 45N 100 30W
Highrock L., *Sask., Canada* **143 B7** 57 5N 105 32W
Higüey, *Dom. Rep.* ... **165 C6** 18 37N 68 42W
Hihya, *Egypt* .... **106 H7** 30 40N 31 36 E
Hiiumaa, *Estonia* .... **15 G20** 58 50N 22 45 E
Híjar, *Spain* **40 D4** 41 10N 0 27W
Ḩijāz □, *Si. Arabia* ... **96 E3** 24 0N 40 0 E
Hiji, *Japan* .... **72 D3** 33 22N 131 32 E
Hijo = Tagum, *Phil.* .. **81 H5** 7 33N 125 53 E
Hikari, *Japan* .... **72 D3** 33 58N 131 58 E
Hiketa, *Japan* .... **72 C6** 34 13N 134 24 E
Hikkaduwa, *Sri Lanka* **95 L5** 6 8N 80 6 E
Hikmak, Ras el, *Egypt* **106 A2** 31 15N 27 51 E
Hiko, *U.S.A.* **160 H11** 37 32N 115 14W
Hikone, *Japan* ...... **73 B8** 35 15N 136 10 E
Hikurangi, *Gisborne, N.Z.* .... **130 E5** 37 55 S 178 4 E
Hikurangi, *Northland, N.Z.* .... **130 B3** 35 36 S 174 17 E
Hiland Park, *U.S.A.* .. **152 E4** 30 12N 85 33W
Hilawng, *Burma* ..... **90 E4** 21 23N 93 48 E
Hildburghausen, *Germany* .... **30 E6** 50 25N 10 42 E
Hildesheim, *Germany* **30 C5** 52 9N 9 56 E
Hildarendi, *Iceland* .. **11 D7** 63 44N 19 57W
Hill ⟶, *Australia* .... **125 F2** 30 23 S 115 3 E
Hill City, *Idaho, U.S.A.* **158 E6** 43 18N 115 3W
Hill City, *Kans., U.S.A.* **154 F5** 39 22N 99 51W
Hill City, *Minn., U.S.A.* **154 B8** 46 59N 93 36W
Hill City, *S. Dak., U.S.A.* **154 D3** 43 56N 103 35W
Hill Island L., *Canada* **143 A7** 60 30N 109 50W
Hillaby, Mt., *Barbados* **165 g** 13 12N 59 35W
Hillared, *Sweden* .... **17 G7** 57 37N 13 10 E
Hillcrest, *Barbados* ... **165 g** 13 13N 59 31W
Hillcrest Center, *U.S.A.* **161 K8** 35 23N 118 57W
Hillegom, *Neths.* .... **24 B4** 52 18N 4 35 E
Hillerød, *Denmark* ... **17 J6** 55 56N 12 19 E
Hillerstorp, *Sweden* .. **17 G7** 57 20N 13 52 E
Hillgrove, *Bangl.* .... **90 C2** 25 17N 89 1 E
Hilliard, *U.S.A.* **152 E8** 30 41N 81 55W
Hillsboro = Deerfield Beach, *U.S.A.* **153 J9** 26 19N 80 6W
Hillsboro, *Ga., U.S.A.* **152 B6** 33 11N 83 38W
Hillsboro, *Ill., U.S.A.* . **156 E7** 39 9N 89 29W
Hillsboro, *Kans., U.S.A.* **154 F6** 38 21N 97 12W
Hillsboro, *Mo., U.S.A.* **156 F6** 38 14N 90 34W
Hillsboro, *N. Dak., U.S.A.* **154 B6** 47 26N 97 3W
Hillsboro, *Ohio, U.S.A.* **157 E13** 39 12N 83 37W
Hillsboro, *Oreg., U.S.A.* **160 E4** 45 31N 122 59W
Hillsboro, *Tex., U.S.A.* **155 J6** 32 1N 97 8W
Hillsboro Canal, *U.S.A.* **153 J9** 26 30N 80 15W
Hillsborough, *Grenada* **165 D7** 12 28N 61 28W
Hillsborough, *U.S.A.* . **151 C13** 43 7N 71 54W
Hillsborough Channel, *Australia* .... **126 J7** 20 56 S 149 15 E
Hillsborough Land = Belle Glade, *U.S.A.* **153 J9** 26 41N 80 40W
Hillsdale, *Mich., U.S.A.* **157 C12** 41 56N 84 38W
Hillsdale, *N.Y., U.S.A.* **151 D11** 42 11N 73 30W
Hillsport, *Canada* **140 C2** 49 27N 85 34W
Hillston, *Australia* ... **129 B6** 33 30 S 145 31 E
Hilltonia, *U.S.A.* **152 C8** 32 53N 81 40W
Hilo, *U.S.A.* **145 D6** 19 44N 155 5W
Hilo B., *U.S.A.* **145 D6** 19 45N 155 5W
Hilton, *U.S.A.* **150 C7** 43 17N 77 48W
Hilton Head Island, *U.S.A.* **152 C9** 32 13N 80 45W
Hilvan, *Turkey* ...... **101 D8** 37 34N 38 58 E
Hilversum, *Neths.* .... **24 B5** 52 14N 5 10 E
Hilzingen, *Germany* .. **33 A7** 47 46N 8 47 E
Himachal Pradesh □, *India* .... **92 D7** 31 30N 77 0 E
Himalaya, *Asia* ...... **93 E11** 29 0N 84 0 E
Himamaylan, *Phil.* ... **81 F4** 10 6N 122 52 E
Himarë, *Albania* ..... **50 F3** 40 8N 19 43 E
Hime-Jima, *Japan* .... **72 D3** 33 43N 131 40 E
Himeji, *Japan* .... **72 C6** 34 50N 134 40 E
Himi, *Japan* .... **73 A8** 36 50N 136 55 E
Himmerland, *Denmark* **17 H3** 56 45N 9 30 E
Ḩimş, *Syria* .... **103 A5** 34 40N 36 45 E
Ḩimş □, *Syria* ...... **103 A6** 34 30N 37 0 E
Hinatuan, *Phil.* ..... **81 G6** 8 23N 126 20 E
Hinatuan Passage, *Phil.* **81 G5** 9 45N 125 47 E
Hinche, *Haiti* **165 C5** 19 9N 72 1W
Hinchinbrook I., *Australia* .... **126 B4** 18 20 S 146 15 E
Hinchinbrook Island △, *Australia* .... **126 B4** 18 14 S 146 6 E
Hinckley, *U.K.* **21 E6** 52 33N 1 22W
Hinckley, *U.S.A.* **154 B8** 46 1N 92 56W
Hindaun, *India* ...... **92 F7** 26 44N 77 5 E
Hindenburg = Zabrze, *Poland* .... **55 H5** 50 18N 18 50 E
Hindmarsh, L., *Australia* .... **128 D4** 36 5 S 141 55 E
Hindol, *India* .... **94 D7** 20 40N 85 10 E
Hinds, *N.Z.* .... **131 D6** 43 59 S 171 36 E
Hindsholm, *Denmark* . **17 J4** 55 30N 10 40 E
Hindu Bagh, *Pakistan* **92 C2** 30 56N 67 50 E
Hindu Kush, *Asia* .... **65 E5** 36 0N 71 0 E
Hindupur, *India* ..... **95 H3** 13 49N 77 32 E
Hines Creek, *Canada* . **142 B5** 56 20N 118 40W
Hinesville, *U.S.A.* **152 D8** 31 51N 81 36W
Hinganghat, *India* .... **94 D4** 20 30N 78 52 E
Hingham, *U.S.A.* **158 B8** 48 33N 110 25W
Hinghwa = Xinghua, *China* .... **75 H10** 32 58N 119 48 E
Hingir, *India* .... **93 J10** 21 57N 83 41 E
Hingoli, *India* ...... **94 E3** 19 41N 77 15 E
Hinigaran, *Phil.* ..... **81 F4** 10 16N 122 50 E
Hinis, *Turkey* .... **101 C9** 39 22N 41 43 E
Hinna = Imi, *Ethiopia* **107 F5** 6 28N 42 10 E
Hinna, *Nigeria* ...... **113 C7** 10 25N 11 35 E
Hinnerup, *Denmark* .. **17 H4** 56 16N 10 4 E
Hinnøya, *Norway* .... **14 B16** 68 35N 15 50 E
Hino, *Japan* .... **73 C8** 35 0N 136 15 E
Hinoba-an, *Phil.* .... **81 G4** 9 35N 122 28 E
Hinojosa del Duque, *Spain* **43 G5** 38 30N 5 9W
Hinokage, *Japan* .... **72 E3** 32 39N 131 24 E
Hinsdale, *U.S.A.* **151 D12** 42 47N 72 29W
Hinterrhein ⟶, *Switz.* **33 C8** 46 40N 9 25 E
Hinton, *Canada* **142 C5** 53 26N 117 34W
Hinton, *U.S.A.* **148 G5** 37 40N 80 54W
Hinuangan, *Phil.* .... **81 F5** 10 25N 125 12 E
Hinubuan = Antipolo, *Phil.* .... **80 D3** 14 35N 121 10 E
Hinwil, *Switz.* ...... **33 B7** 47 18N 8 51 E
Hınzır Burnu, *Turkey* . **100 D6** 36 19N 35 46 E
Hios = Khíos, *Greece* . **49 C8** 38 27N 26 9 E
Hirado, *Japan* ...... **72 D1** 33 22N 129 33 E
Hirado-Shima, *Japan* . **72 D1** 33 20N 129 30 E
Hirakata, *Japan* ..... **73 C7** 34 48N 135 40 E
Hirakud, *India* ...... **94 D6** 21 32N 83 51 E
Hirakud Dam, *India* .. **94 D6** 21 32N 83 45 E
Hiran ⟶, *India* ..... **93 H8** 23 6N 79 21 E
Hirapur, *India* ...... **93 G8** 24 22N 79 13 E
Hirata, *Japan* ...... **72 B4** 35 24N 132 49 E
Hiratsuka, *Japan* .... **73 B11** 35 19N 139 21 E
Hirekerur, *India* ..... **95 G2** 14 28N 75 23 E
Hirfanlı Barajı, *Turkey* **100 C5** 39 18N 33 31 E
Hirhafok, *Algeria* .... **111 D6** 23 49N 5 45 E
Hiromi, *Japan* ...... **72 D4** 33 13N 132 36 E
Hiroo, *Japan* .... **70 C11** 42 17N 143 19 E
Hirosaki, *Japan* ..... **70 D10** 40 34N 140 28 E
Hiroshima, *Japan* .... **72 C4** 34 24N 132 30 E
Hiroshima □, *Japan* .. **72 C5** 34 50N 133 0 E
Hiroshima-Wan, *Japan* **72 C4** 34 5N 132 20 E
Hirschberg = Jelenia Góra, *Poland* ...... **55 H2** 50 50N 15 45 E
Hirson, *France* ...... **27 C11** 49 55N 4 4 E
Hirtshals, *Denmark* .. **17 G3** 57 36N 9 57 E
Hisai, *Japan* .... **73 C8** 34 40N 136 28 E
Hisar, *India* .... **92 E6** 29 12N 75 45 E
Hisarcık, *Turkey* ..... **49 B11** 39 15N 29 14 E
Hisarya, *Bulgaria* .... **51 D8** 42 30N 24 44 E
Hisb, Sha'ib = Ḩasb, W. ⟶, *Iraq* .... **96 D5** 31 45N 44 17 E
Ḩismá, *Si. Arabia* .... **96 D3** 28 30N 36 0 E
Ḩişn al 'Abr, *Yemen* .. **98 C4** 16 8N 47 14 E
Hisor, *Tajikistan* ..... **65 D4** 38 31N 68 33 E
Hispaniola, *W. Indies* . **165 C5** 19 0N 71 0W
Hīt, *Iraq* .... **101 F10** 33 38N 42 49 E
Hita, *Japan* .... **72 D2** 33 20N 130 58 E
Hitachi, *Japan* ...... **73 A12** 36 36N 140 39 E
Hitachi-Ota, *Japan* ... **73 A12** 36 30N 140 30 E
Hitchin, *U.K.* **21 F7** 51 58N 0 16W
Hitoyoshi, *Japan* .... **72 E2** 32 13N 130 45 E
Hitra, *Norway* ...... **18 A5** 63 30N 8 45 E
Hittisau, *Austria* ..... **33 B9** 47 28N 9 58 E
Hitzacker, *Germany* .. **30 B7** 53 9N 11 2 E
Hiu, *Vanuatu* .... **133 C4** 13 10 S 166 35 E
Hiuchi-Nada, *Japan* .. **72 C5** 34 5N 133 20 E
Hiva-Oa, *French Polynesia* ... **135 H14** 9 45 S 139 0W
Hixon, *Canada* **142 C4** 53 25N 122 35W
Ḩiyyon, N. ⟶, *Israel* . **103 E4** 30 25N 35 10 E
Hjalmar L., *Canada* .. **143 A7** 61 33N 109 25W
Hjälmaren, *Sweden* ... **16 E9** 59 18N 15 40 E
Hjältevad, *Sweden* ... **17 G9** 57 38N 15 20 E
Hjartdal, *Norway* .... **18 E5** 59 37N 8 41 E
Hjelmelandsvågen, *Norway* .... **18 E3** 59 14N 6 10 E
Hjelset, *Norway* ..... **18 B4** 62 48N 7 30 E
Hjerkinn, *Norway* .... **18 B6** 62 13N 9 33 E
Hjo, *Sweden* .... **17 F8** 58 22N 14 17 E
Hjørring, *Denmark* ... **17 G3** 57 29N 9 59 E
Hjortkvarn, *Sweden* .. **17 F9** 58 54N 15 26 E
Hjukse, *Norway* ..... **18 E6** 59 31N 9 19 E
Hkakabo Razi, *Burma* **90 B6** 28 17N 97 46 E
Hko-lam, *Burma* ..... **90 E7** 21 7N 98 5 E
Hko-ut, *Burma* ...... **90 E7** 20 58N 98 2 E
Hkyenhpa, *Burma* .... **90 B6** 27 43N 97 25 E
Hlaingbwe, *Burma* ... **90 G6** 17 8N 97 50 E
Hlinsko, *Czech Rep.* .. **34 B8** 49 45N 15 54 E
Hlobane, *S. Africa* ... **117 D5** 27 42 S 31 0 E
Hlohovec, *Slovak Rep.* **35 C10** 48 26N 17 49 E
Hlučín, *Czech Rep.* ... **35 B11** 49 54N 18 11 E
Hluhluwe, *S. Africa* .. **117 D5** 28 1 S 32 15 E
Hluhluwe ⌓, *S. Africa* **117 C5** 22 10 S 32 5 E
Hlukhiv, *Ukraine* .... **59 G7** 51 40N 33 58 E
Hlwaze, *Burma* ...... **90 F6** 18 54N 96 37 E
Hlyboka, *Ukraine* .... **53 B10** 48 5N 25 56 E
Hlybokaye, *Belarus* .. **58 E4** 55 10N 27 45 E
Hnappadalssýsla □, *Iceland* **11 C4** 64 50N 22 30W
Hnífsdalur, *Iceland* ... **11 A3** 66 7N 23 8W
Hnúšťa, *Slovak Rep.* . **35 C12** 48 35N 19 58 E
Ho, *Ghana* .... **113 D5** 6 37N 0 27 E
Ho Chi Minh City = Thanh Pho Ho Chi Minh, *Vietnam* ..... **87 G6** 10 58N 106 40 E
Ho Thuong, *Vietnam* . **86 C5** 19 32N 105 48 E
Hoa Binh, *Vietnam* ... **76 G5** 20 50N 105 20 E
Hoa Da, *Vietnam* .... **87 G7** 11 16N 108 40 E
Hoa Hiep, *Vietnam* ... **87 G5** 11 34N 105 51 E
Hoai Nhon, *Vietnam* .. **86 E7** 14 28N 109 1 E
Hoang Lien Son, *Vietnam* .... **76 F4** 22 0N 104 0 E
Hoanib ⟶, *Namibia* .. **116 B2** 19 27 S 12 46 E
Hoare B., *Canada* **139 B13** 65 17N 62 30W
Hoarusib ⟶, *Namibia* **116 B2** 19 3 S 12 36 E
Hobart, *Australia* .... **127 G4** 42 50 S 147 21 E
Hobart, *Ind., U.S.A.* .. **157 C9** 41 32N 87 15W
Hobart, *Okla., U.S.A.* . **155 H5** 35 1N 99 6W
Hobbs, *U.S.A.* **155 J3** 32 42N 103 8W
Hobbs Coast, *Antarctica* .... **7 D14** 74 50 S 131 0W
Hobe Sound, *U.S.A.* .. **153 H9** 27 4N 80 8W
Hobo, *Colombia* **168 C2** 2 35N 75 30W
Hoboken, *Ga., U.S.A.* . **152 D7** 31 11N 82 8W
Hoboken, *N.J., U.S.A.* **151 F10** 40 45N 74 4W
Hobro, *Denmark* ..... **17 H3** 56 39N 9 46 E
Hoburgen, *Sweden* ... **17 H12** 56 55N 18 7 E
Hocalar, *Turkey* ..... **49 C11** 38 36N 30 0 E
Hochdorf, *Switz.* ..... **33 B6** 47 10N 8 17 E
Hochfeld, *Namibia* ... **116 C2** 21 28 S 17 58 E
Hochharz △, *Germany* **30 D6** 51 48N 10 38 E
Hochschwab, *Austria* . **34 D8** 47 35N 15 0 E
Höchstadt, *Germany* . **31 F6** 49 42N 10 47 E
Hochtaunus ⌓, *Germany* .... **31 E4** 50 20N 8 30 E
Hoch'uan = Hechuan, *China* .... **76 B6** 30 2N 106 12 E
Hochwan = Hechuan, *China* .... **76 B6** 30 2N 106 12 E
Hockenheim, *Germany* **31 F4** 49 19N 8 32 E
Hockley = Levelland, *U.S.A.* **155 J3** 33 35N 102 23W
Hodaka-Dake, *Japan* . **73 A9** 36 17N 137 39 E
Hodeida = Al Ḩudaydah, *Yemen* .. **98 D3** 14 50N 43 0 E
Hodgeville, *Canada* .. **143 C7** 50 7N 106 58W
Hodgson, *Canada* **143 C9** 51 13N 97 36W
Hódmezővásárhely, *Hungary* .... **52 D5** 46 28N 20 22 E
Hodna, Chott el, *Algeria* .... **111 A6** 35 26N 4 43 E
Hodonín, *Czech Rep.* . **35 C10** 48 50N 17 10 E
Hodzhambas, *Turkmenistan* ...... **65 D2** 38 7N 65 0 E
Hoeamdong, *N. Korea* **75 C16** 42 30N 130 16 E
Hœdic, Î. de, *France* .. **26 E4** 47 20N 2 53W
Hoek van Holland, *Neths.* .... **24 C4** 52 0N 4 7 E
Hoengsŏng, *S. Korea* . **75 F14** 37 29N 127 59 E
Hoeryong, *N. Korea* .. **75 C15** 42 30N 129 45 E
Hoeyang, *N. Korea* .. **75 E14** 38 43N 127 36 E
Hof, *Germany* ...... **31 E7** 50 19N 11 55 E
Hof, *Norður-Múlasýsla, Iceland* **11 B11** 65 39N 15 0W
Hof, *Suður-Múlasýsla, Iceland* **11 C12** 64 33N 14 40W
Hof, *Norway* .... **18 E7** 59 32N 10 5 E
Hofei = Hefei, *China* . **77 B11** 31 52N 117 18 E
Hoffell, *Iceland* **11 C11** 64 23N 15 20W
Hofgeismar, *Germany* **30 D5** 51 29N 9 23 E
Hofheim, *Germany* ... **31 E4** 50 5N 8 26 E
Hofmeyr, *S. Africa* ... **116 E4** 31 39 S 25 50 E
Höfn, *Iceland* **11 C11** 64 15N 15 13W
Hofors, *Sweden* ..... **16 D10** 60 31N 16 15 E
Hofsjökull, *Iceland* ... **11 C8** 64 49N 18 48W
Hofsós, *Iceland* **11 B7** 65 53N 19 26W
Hōfu, *Japan* .... **72 C3** 34 3N 131 34 E
Hog Harbour, *Vanuatu* **133 E5** 15 8 S 167 6 E
Hog I. = Paradise I., *Bahamas* .... **9 b** 25 6N 77 19W
Hogan Group, *Australia* .... **127 F4** 39 13 S 147 1 E
Höganäs, *Sweden* .... **17 H6** 56 12N 12 33 E
Hogansville, *U.S.A.* .. **152 B5** 33 10N 84 55W
Hogarth, Mt., *Australia* **126 C2** 21 48 S 136 58 E
Hogenakai Falls, *India* **95 H3** 12 6N 77 50 E
Hoggar = Ahaggar, *Algeria* .... **111 D6** 23 0N 6 30 E
Högsäter, *Sweden* .... **17 F6** 58 38N 12 5 E
Högsby, *Sweden* ..... **17 G10** 57 10N 16 1 E
Högsjö, *Sweden* ..... **16 E9** 59 4N 15 44 E
Hogsty Reef, *Bahamas* **165 B5** 21 41N 73 48W
Hoh ⟶, *U.S.A.* **160 C2** 47 45N 124 29W
Hohe Acht, *Germany* . **31 E3** 50 22N 7 0 E
Hohe Tauern, *Austria* **34 D5** 47 11N 12 40 E
Hohe Tauern △, *Austria* .... **34 D5** 47 5N 12 20 E
Hohe Venn, *Belgium* . **24 D6** 50 30N 6 5 E
Hohenau, *Austria* .... **35 C9** 48 36N 16 55 E
Hohenelbe = Vrchlabí, *Czech Rep.* .... **34 A8** 50 38N 15 37 E
Hohenems, *Austria* ... **34 D2** 47 22N 9 42 E
Hohenloher Ebene, *Germany* .... **31 F5** 49 14N 9 36 E
Hohenmauth = Vysoké Mýto, *Czech Rep.* .. **35 B9** 49 58N 16 10 E
Hohensalza = Inowrocław, *Poland* **55 F5** 52 50N 18 12 E
Hohensalzburg = Lunino, *Russia* ..... **60 D7** 53 38N 45 18 E
Hohenstadt = Zábřeh, *Czech Rep.* .... **35 B9** 49 53N 16 52 E
Hohenstein = Olsztynek, *Poland* .. **54 E7** 53 34N 20 19 E
Hohenwald, *U.S.A.* ... **149 H2** 35 33N 87 33W
Hohenwestedt, *Germany* .... **30 A5** 54 5N 9 40 E
Hoher Freschen, *Austria* .... **33 B9** 47 18N 9 46 E
Hoher Rhön = Rhön, *Germany* .... **30 E5** 50 24N 9 58 E
Hoher Vogelsberg ⌓, *Germany* .... **30 D5** 51 45N 9 35 E
Hohes Venn-Eifel ⌓, *Europe* .... **30 E2** 50 30N 6 10 E
Hohhot, *China* ...... **74 D6** 40 52N 111 40 E
Hóhlakas, *Greece* .... **38 F11** 35 57N 27 53 E
Hohoe, *Ghana* ...... **113 D5** 7 8N 0 32 E
Hoi An, *Vietnam* ..... **86 E7** 15 30N 108 19 E
Hoi Xuan, *Vietnam* ... **76 G5** 20 25N 105 9 E
Hoihow = Haikou, *China* .... **69 D6** 20 1N 110 16 E
Hoisington, *U.S.A.* ... **154 F5** 38 31N 98 47W
Hojai, *India* .... **90 B4** 26 2N 92 54 E
Højer, *Denmark* ..... **17 K2** 54 58N 8 42 E
Hōjō, *Japan* .... **72 D4** 33 58N 132 46 E
Hok, *Sweden* .... **17 G8** 57 31N 14 16 E
Hokang = Hegang, *China* .... **69 B8** 47 20N 130 19 E
Hökensås, *Sweden* ... **17 G8** 58 0N 14 5 E
Hökerum, *Sweden* ... **17 G7** 57 51N 13 16 E
Hokianga Harbour, *N.Z.* .... **130 B2** 35 31 S 173 22 E
Hokitika, *N.Z.* .... **131 C5** 42 42 S 171 0 E
Hokkaidō □, *Japan* .. **70 C11** 43 30N 143 0 E
Hokksund, *Norway* ... **18 E6** 59 48N 9 54 E
Hol-Hol, *Djibouti* .... **107 E5** 11 20N 42 50 E
Hola Pristan, *Ukraine* . **59 J7** 46 29N 32 32 E
Holalkere, *India* ..... **95 G3** 14 2N 76 11 E
Hólar, *Iceland* **11 B7** 65 44N 19 8W
Holbæk, *Denmark* .... **17 J5** 55 43N 11 43 E
Holbrook, *Australia* .. **129 C7** 35 42 S 147 18 E
Holbrook, *U.S.A.* **159 J8** 34 54N 110 10W
Holden, *Mo., U.S.A.* . **156 F3** 38 43N 94 0W
Holden, *Utah, U.S.A.* . **158 G7** 39 6N 112 16W
Holdenville, *U.S.A.* .. **155 H6** 35 5N 96 24W
Holdich, *Argentina* ... **176 C3** 45 57 S 68 13W
Holdrege, *U.S.A.* **154 E5** 40 26N 99 23W
Hole-Narsipur, *India* . **95 H3** 12 48N 76 16 E
Holešov, *Czech Rep.* .. **35 B10** 49 20N 17 35 E
Holetown, *Barbados* .. **165 g** 13 11N 59 38W
Holgate, *U.S.A.* **157 C12** 41 15N 84 8W
Holguín, *Cuba* **164 B4** 20 50N 76 20W
Holíč, *Slovak Rep.* ... **35 C10** 48 49N 17 10 E
Holice, *Czech Rep.* ... **34 A8** 50 5N 16 0 E
Holiday, *U.S.A.* **153 G7** 28 13N 82 43W
Höljes, *Sweden* ..... **16 D6** 60 50N 12 35 E
Hollabrunn, *Austria* .. **34 C9** 48 34N 16 5 E
Hollams Bird I., *Namibia* .... **116 C1** 24 40 S 14 30 E
Holland, *Mich., U.S.A.* **157 B10** 42 47N 86 7W
Holland, *N.Y., U.S.A.* . **150 D6** 42 38N 78 32W
Hollandale, *U.S.A.* ... **155 J9** 33 10N 90 51W
Hollandia = Jayapura, *Indonesia* .... **83 B6** 2 28 S 140 38 E
Holley, *U.S.A.* **150 C6** 43 14N 78 2W
Hollfeld, *Germany* ... **31 F7** 49 56N 11 18 E
Hollidaysburg, *U.S.A.* **150 F6** 40 26N 78 24W
Hollis, *U.S.A.* **155 H5** 34 41N 99 55W
Hollister, *Calif., U.S.A.* **160 J5** 36 51N 121 24W
Hollister, *Idaho, U.S.A.* **158 E6** 42 21N 114 35W
Höllviken = Höllviksnäs, *Sweden* **17 J6** 55 26N 12 58 E
Höllviksnäs, *Sweden* .. **17 J6** 55 26N 12 58 E
Holly, *U.S.A.* **157 B13** 42 48N 83 38W
Holly Hill, *Fla., U.S.A.* **153 F8** 29 16N 81 3W
Holly Hill, *S.C., U.S.A.* **152 B9** 33 19N 80 25W
Holly Springs, *Ga., U.S.A.* **152 A5** 34 10N 84 30W
Holly Springs, *Miss., U.S.A.* **155 H10** 34 46N 89 27W
Hollywood, *U.S.A.* **153 J9** 26 1N 80 9W
Holman, *Canada* **138 A8** 70 44N 117 44W
Hólmavík, *Iceland* **11 B5** 65 42N 21 40W
Holmen, *Norway* ..... **18 D7** 60 40N 10 22 E
Holmen, *U.S.A.* **154 D9** 43 58N 91 15W
Holmes ⟶, *U.S.A.* ... **152 E4** 30 30N 85 50W
Holmes Beach, *U.S.A.* **153 H7** 27 31N 82 43W
Holmes Reefs, *Australia* .... **126 B4** 16 27 S 148 0 E
Holmestrand, *Norway* **18 E7** 59 31N 10 14 E
Holmsjö, *Sweden* .... **17 H9** 56 25N 15 32 E
Holmsjön, *Västernorrland, Sweden* .... **16 B10** 62 41N 16 33 E
Holmsjön, *Västernorrland, Sweden* .... **16 B9** 62 26N 15 20 E
Holmsland Klit, *Denmark* .... **17 J2** 56 0N 8 5 E
Holmsund, *Sweden* ... **14 E19** 63 41N 20 20 E
Holod, *Romania* ..... **52 D7** 46 49N 22 8 E
Holopaw, *U.S.A.* **153 G8** 28 8N 81 5W
Holovne, *Ukraine* .... **55 G11** 51 20N 24 5 E
Holøydal, *Norway* .... **18 B8** 62 18N 11 27 E
Holozubyntsi, *Ukraine* **53 B11** 48 50N 26 55 E
Holroyd ⟶, *Australia* **126 A3** 14 10 S 141 36 E
Holstebro, *Denmark* .. **17 H2** 56 22N 8 37 E
Holsteinische Schweiz ⌓, *Germany* **30 A6** 54 8N 10 30 E
Holsteinsborg = Sisimiut, *Greenland* **10 D5** 66 40N 53 30W
Holsworthy, *U.K.* **21 G3** 50 48N 4 22W
Holt, *Iceland* **11 D7** 63 33N 19 48W
Holt, *Fla., U.S.A.* **153 E3** 30 43N 86 45W
Holt, *Mich., U.S.A.* .. **157 B12** 42 39N 84 31W
Holton, *Canada* **141 B8** 54 31N 57 12W
Holton, *U.S.A.* **154 F7** 39 28N 95 44W
Holts Summit, *U.S.A.* . **156 F4** 38 38N 92 7W
Holtville, *U.S.A.* **161 N11** 32 49N 115 23W
Holualoa, *U.S.A.* **145 D6** 19 37N 155 57W
Holum, *Norway* ..... **18 F4** 58 6N 7 32 E
Holwerd, *Neths.* .... **24 A5** 53 22N 5 54 E
Holy Cross, *U.S.A.* ... **144 E8** 62 12N 159 46W
Holy I., *Angl., U.K.* ... **20 D3** 53 17N 4 37W
Holy I., *Northumberland, U.K.* **20 B6** 55 40N 1 47W
Holyhead, *U.K.* **20 D3** 53 18N 4 38W
Holyoke, *Colo., U.S.A.* **154 E3** 40 35N 102 18W
Holyoke, *Mass., U.S.A.* **151 D12** 42 12N 72 37W
Holyrood, *Canada* ... **141 C9** 47 27N 53 8W
Holzkirchen, *Germany* **31 H7** 47 52N 11 42 E
Holzminden, *Germany* **30 D5** 51 50N 9 28 E
Homa Bay, *Kenya* .... **118 C3** 0 36 S 34 30 E
Homalin, *Burma* ..... **90 C5** 24 55N 95 0 E
Homand, *Iran* .... **97 C8** 32 28N 59 37 E
Homathko ⟶, *Canada* **142 C4** 51 0N 124 56W
Homberg, *Germany* .. **30 D5** 51 2N 9 25 E
Hombori, *Mali* **113 B4** 15 20N 1 38W
Homburg, *Germany* .. **31 F3** 49 28N 7 18 E
Home B., *Canada* **139 B13** 68 40N 67 10W
Home Hill, *Australia* . **126 B4** 19 43 S 147 25 E
Home Reef, *Tonga* ... **133 P13** 18 59 S 174 47W
Homedale, *U.S.A.* **158 E5** 43 37N 116 56W
Homeland, *U.S.A.* **152 E7** 30 51N 82 1W
Homer, *Alaska, U.S.A.* **144 G10** 59 39N 151 33W
Homer, *Ill., U.S.A.* ... **157 D9** 40 4N 87 57W
Homer, *La., U.S.A.* ... **155 J8** 32 48N 93 4W
Homer, *Mich., U.S.A.* . **157 B12** 42 9N 84 49W
Homer City, *U.S.A.* ... **150 F5** 40 32N 79 10W
Homert ⌓, *Germany* .. **30 D4** 51 15N 8 0 E
Homerville, *U.S.A.* ... **152 D7** 31 2N 82 45W
Homestead, *Australia* . **126 C4** 20 20 S 145 40 E
Homestead, *U.S.A.* ... **153 K9** 25 28N 80 29W
Homestead ⌓, *U.S.A.* . **154 E6** 40 17N 96 50W
Homewood, *Calif., U.S.A.* **160 F6** 39 4N 120 8W
Homewood, *Ill., U.S.A.* **157 C9** 41 34N 87 40W
Hommelvik, *Norway* .. **18 A7** 63 25N 10 48 E
Hommersåk, *Norway* .. **18 F2** 58 56N 5 50 E
Homnabad, *India* ..... **94 F3** 17 45N 77 11 E
Homoine, *Mozam.* .... **117 C6** 23 55 S 35 8 E
Homoljske Planina, *Serbia & M.* .... **50 B5** 44 10N 21 45 E
Homonhon I., *Phil.* ... **81 F5** 10 44N 125 43 E
Homorod, *Romania* ... **53 D10** 46 5N 25 15 E
Homosassa Springs, *U.S.A.* **153 G7** 28 48N 82 35W
Homs = Al Khums, *Libya* .... **108 B2** 32 40N 14 17 E

Homs = Ḩimş, *Syria* **103 A5** 34 40N 36 45 E
Homyel, *Belarus* **59 F6** 52 28N 31 0 E
Hon Chong, *Vietnam* **87 G5** 10 25N 104 30 E
Hon Me, *Vietnam* **86 C5** 19 23N 105 56 E
Honan = Henan □, *China* **74 H8** 34 0N 114 0 E
Honaunau, *U.S.A.* **145 D6** 19 26N 155 55W
Honavar, *India* **95 G2** 14 17N 74 27 E
Honaz, *Turkey* **49 D11** 37 46N 29 18 E
Honbetsu, *Japan* **70 C11** 43 7N 143 37 E
Honcut, *U.S.A.* **160 F5** 39 20N 121 32W
Honda, *Colombia* **168 B3** 5 12N 74 45W
Honda Bay, *Phil.* **81 G2** 9 53N 118 49 E
Hondarribia, *Spain* **40 B3** 43 22N 1 47W
Hondeklipbaai, *S. Africa* **116 E2** 30 19 S 17 17 E
Hondo, *Japan* **72 E2** 32 27N 130 12 E
Hondo, *U.S.A.* **155 L5** 29 21N 99 9W
Hondo, Rio →, *Belize* **163 D7** 18 25N 88 21W
Honduras ■, *Cent. Amer.* **164 D2** 14 40N 86 30W
Honduras, G. de, *Caribbean* **164 C2** 16 50N 87 0W
Hønefoss, *Norway* **18 D7** 60 10N 10 18 E
Honesdale, *U.S.A.* **151 E9** 41 34N 75 16W
Honey L., *U.S.A.* **160 E6** 40 15N 120 19W
Honfleur, *France* **26 C7** 49 25N 0 13 E
Høng, *Denmark* **17 J5** 55 31N 11 18 E
Hong →, *Vietnam* **76 F5** 22 0N 104 0 E
Hong Gai, *Vietnam* **76 G6** 20 57N 107 5 E
Hong He →, *China* **74 H8** 32 25N 115 35 E
Hong Hu, *China* **77 C9** 29 54N 113 24 E
Hong Kong □, *China* **77 F10** 22 11N 114 14 E
Hong Kong I., *China* **69 G11** 22 16N 114 12 E
Hong Kong International ✕ (HKG), *China* **69 G10** 22 19N 113 57 E
Honga, *Angola* **115 F3** 15 9 S 15 12 E
Hong'an, *China* **77 B10** 31 20N 114 40 E
Hongch'ŏn, *S. Korea* **75 F14** 37 44N 127 53 E
Honghai Wan, *China* **77 F10** 22 40N 115 0 E
Honghe, *China* **76 F4** 23 25N 102 25 E
Honghu, *China* **77 C9** 29 50N 113 30 E
Hongjiang, *China* **76 D7** 27 7N 109 59 E
Hongliu He →, *China* **74 F5** 38 0N 109 50 E
Hongor, *Mongolia* **74 B7** 45 45N 112 50 E
Hongsa, *Laos* **86 C3** 19 43N 101 20 E
Hongshui He →, *China* **76 F7** 23 48N 109 30 E
Hongsŏng, *S. Korea* **75 F14** 36 37N 126 38 E
Hongtong, *China* **74 F6** 36 16N 111 40 E
Honguedo, Détroit d', *Canada* **141 C7** 49 15N 64 0W
Hongwon, *N. Korea* **75 E14** 40 0N 127 56 E
Hongya, *China* **76 C4** 29 57N 103 22 E
Hongyuan, *China* **76 A4** 32 51N 102 40 E
Hongze Hu, *China* **75 H10** 33 15N 118 35 E
Honiara, *Solomon Is.* **133 M10** 9 27 S 159 57 E
Honiton, *U.K.* **21 G4** 50 47N 3 11W
Honjō, *Akita, Japan* **70 E10** 39 23N 140 3 E
Honjō, *Gumma, Japan* **73 A11** 36 14N 139 11 E
Honkawane, *Japan* **73 B10** 35 5N 138 5 E
Honkorâb, Ras, *Egypt* **106 C4** 24 35N 35 10 E
Honnali, *India* **95 G2** 14 15N 75 40 E
Honningsvåg, *Norway* **14 A21** 70 59N 25 59 E
Hönö, *Sweden* **17 G5** 57 41N 11 39 E
Honokaa, *U.S.A.* **145 C6** 20 5N 155 28W
Honokahua, *U.S.A.* **145 C5** 21 0N 156 40W
Honolulu, *U.S.A.* **145 K14** 21 19N 157 52W
Honolulu International ✕ (HNL), *U.S.A.* **145 B4** 21 19N 157 55W
Honomu, *U.S.A.* **145 D6** 19 52N 155 7W
Honouliuli, *U.S.A.* **145 K13** 21 22N 158 2W
Honshū, *Japan* **73 A8** 36 0N 138 0 E
Hontoria del Pinar, *Spain* **40 D1** 41 50N 3 10W
Honuapo B., *U.S.A.* **145 D6** 19 5N 155 33W
Hood, I. = Española, I., *Ecuador* **172 a** 1 23 S 89 39W
Hood, Mt., *U.S.A.* **158 D3** 45 23N 121 42W
Hood, Pt., *Australia* **125 F2** 34 23 S 119 34 E
Hood Pt., *Papua N. G.* **132 F4** 10 4 S 147 45 E
Hood River, *U.S.A.* **158 D3** 45 43N 121 31W
Hoodsport, *U.S.A.* **160 C3** 47 24N 123 9W
Hooge, *Germany* **30 A4** 54 34N 8 33 E
Hoogeveen, *Neths.* **24 B6** 52 44N 6 28 E
Hoogezand-Sappemeer, *Neths.* **24 A6** 53 9N 6 45 E
Hooghly = Hugli →, *India* **93 J13** 21 56N 88 4 E
Hooghly-Chinsura = Chunchura, *India* **93 H13** 22 53N 88 27 E
Hook Hd., *Ireland* **23 D5** 52 7N 6 56W
Hook I., *Australia* **126 J6** 20 4 S 149 0 E
Hook of Holland = Hoek van Holland, *Neths.* **24 C4** 52 0N 4 7 E
Hooker, *U.S.A.* **155 G4** 36 52N 101 13W
Hooker Creek, *Australia* **124 C5** 18 23 S 130 38 E
Hoolehua, *U.S.A.* **145 B4** 21 10N 157 5W
Hoonah, *U.S.A.* **142 B1** 58 7N 135 27W
Hooper Bay, *U.S.A.* **144 F6** 61 32N 166 6W
Hoopeston, *U.S.A.* **157 D9** 40 28N 87 40W
Hoopstad, *S. Africa* **116 D4** 27 50 S 25 55 E
Höör, *Sweden* **17 J7** 55 56N 13 33 E
Hoorn, *Neths.* **24 B5** 52 38N 5 4 E
Hoover, *U.S.A.* **149 J2** 33 20N 86 11W
Hoover Dam, *U.S.A.* **161 K12** 36 1N 114 44W
Hooversville, *U.S.A.* **150 F6** 40 9N 78 55W
Hop Bottom, *U.S.A.* **151 E9** 41 42N 75 46W
Hopa, *Turkey* **101 B9** 41 28N 41 30 E
Hope, *Canada* **142 D4** 49 25N 121 25W
Hope, *Ariz., U.S.A.* **161 M13** 33 43N 113 42W
Hope, *Ark., U.S.A.* **155 J8** 33 40N 93 36W
Hope, *Ind., U.S.A.* **157 E11** 39 18N 85 46W
Hope, L., *S. Austral., Australia* **127 D2** 28 24 S 139 18 E
Hope, L., *W. Austral., Australia* **125 F3** 32 35 S 120 15 E
Hope, Pt., *Alaska, U.S.A.* **144 B6** 68 21N 166 47W
Hope, Pt., *Alaska, U.S.A.* **6 C17** 68 20N 166 50W
Hope I., *Canada* **150 B4** 44 55N 80 11W
Hope Town, *Bahamas* **164 A4** 26 35N 76 57W
Hopedale, *Canada* **141 A7** 55 28N 60 13W
Hopedale, *U.S.A.* **151 D13** 42 8N 71 33W
Hopefield, *S. Africa* **116 E2** 33 3 S 18 22 E
Hopei = Hebei □, *China* **74 E9** 39 0N 116 0 E
Hopelchén, *Mexico* **163 D7** 19 46N 89 50W
Hopetoun, *Vic., Australia* **128 C5** 35 42 S 142 22 E
Hopetoun, *W. Austral., Australia* **125 F3** 33 57 S 120 7 E
Hopetown, *S. Africa* **116 D3** 29 34 S 24 3 E
Hopevale, *Australia* **126 B4** 15 16 S 145 20 E
Hopewell, *U.S.A.* **148 G7** 37 18N 77 17W
Hopfgarten, *Austria* **34 D5** 47 27N 12 10 E
Hopin, *Burma* **90 C6** 24 58N 96 30 E
Hopkins, *U.S.A.* **156 D2** 40 33N 94 49W
Hopkins, L., *Australia* **124 D4** 24 15 S 128 35 E
Hopkinsville, *U.S.A.* **149 G2** 36 52N 87 29W
Hopland, *U.S.A.* **160 G3** 38 58N 123 7W
Hopong, *Burma* **90 E6** 20 47N 97 11 E
Hopwood's Ferry = Echuca, *Australia* **129 D6** 36 10 S 144 45 E
Hoque, *Angola* **115 E2** 14 40 S 13 55 E
Hoquiam, *U.S.A.* **160 D3** 46 59N 123 53W
Hora Hoverla, *Ukraine* **53 B9** 48 7N 24 41 E
Hora Sfakion = Khóra Sfakíon, *Greece* **39 E5** 35 15N 24 9 E
Hōrai, *Japan* **73 C9** 34 58N 137 32 E
Horana, *Sri Lanka* **95 L5** 6 43N 80 4 E
Horasan, *Turkey* **101 B10** 40 3N 42 11 E
Horažďovice, *Czech Rep.* **34 B6** 49 19N 13 42 E
Horb, *Germany* **31 G4** 48 26N 8 47 E
Hörby, *Sweden* **17 J7** 55 51N 13 40 E
Horcajo de Santiago, *Spain* **40 F1** 39 50N 3 1W
Hordabø, *Norway* **18 D1** 60 42N 4 54 E
Hordaland □, *Norway* **18 D3** 60 25N 6 15 E
Horden Hills, *Australia* **124 D5** 20 15 S 130 0 E
Hordio, *Somali Rep.* **120 B4** 10 33N 51 6 E
Horezu, *Romania* **53 E8** 45 6N 24 0 E
Horgen, *Switz.* **33 B7** 47 15N 8 35 E
Horgoš, *Serbia & M.* **52 D4** 46 10N 20 0 E
Hořice, *Czech Rep.* **34 A8** 50 21N 15 39 E
Horinchove, *Ukraine* **53 B8** 48 16N 23 26 E
Horinger, *China* **74 D6** 40 28N 111 48 E
Horki, *Belarus* **58 E6** 54 17N 30 59 E
Horlick Mts., *Antarctica* **7 E15** 84 0 S 102 0W
Horlivka, *Ukraine* **59 H10** 48 19N 38 5 E
Hormak, *Iran* **97 D9** 29 58N 60 51 E
Hormoz, *Iran* **97 E7** 27 35N 55 0 E
Hormoz, Jaz.-ye, *Iran* **97 E8** 27 8N 56 28 E
Hormozgān □, *Iran* **97 E8** 27 30N 56 0 E
Hormuz, Kūh-e, *Iran* **97 E7** 27 27N 55 10 E
Hormuz, Str. of, *The Gulf* **97 E8** 26 30N 56 30 E
Horn, *Austria* **34 C8** 48 39N 15 40 E
Horn, *Iceland* **14 C2** 66 28N 22 28W
Horn, *Sweden* **17 G9** 57 54N 15 51 E
Horn →, *Canada* **142 A5** 61 30N 118 1W
Horn, Cape = Hornos, C. de, *Chile* **176 E3** 55 50 S 67 30W
Horn, Is., *Wall. & F. Is.* **123 C15** 14 16 S 178 6W
Horn Head, *Ireland* **23 A3** 55 14N 8 0W
Horn I., *Australia* **126 A3** 10 37 S 142 17 E
Horn Plateau, *Canada* **142 A5** 62 15N 119 15W
Hornachuelos, *Spain* **43 H5** 37 50N 5 14W
Hornavan, *Sweden* **14 C17** 66 15N 17 30 E
Hornbeck, *U.S.A.* **155 K8** 31 20N 93 24W
Hornbjarg, *Iceland* **11 A4** 66 28N 22 25W
Hornbrook, *U.S.A.* **158 F2** 41 55N 122 33W
Hornburg, *Germany* **30 C6** 52 2N 10 37 E
Hornby, *N.Z.* **131 D7** 43 33 S 172 33 E
Horncastle, *U.K.* **20 D7** 53 13N 0 7W
Horndal, *Sweden* **16 D10** 60 18N 16 23 E
Hornell, *U.S.A.* **150 D7** 42 20N 77 40W
Hornell L., *Canada* **142 A5** 62 20N 119 25W
Hornepayne, *Canada* **140 C3** 49 14N 84 48W
Horní Planá, *Czech Rep.* **34 C7** 48 46N 14 2 E
Hornindal, *Norway* **18 C3** 61 58N 6 30 E
Hornings Mills, *Canada* **150 B4** 44 9N 80 12W
Hornitos, *U.S.A.* **160 H6** 37 30N 120 14W
Hornopirén △, *Chile* **176 B2** 41 58 S 72 17W
Hornos, C. de, *Chile* **176 E3** 55 50 S 67 30W
Hornos Is., *Papua N. G.* **132 B4** 2 12 S 147 45 E
Hornoy-le-Bourg, *France* **27 C8** 49 50N 1 54 E
Hornsby, *Australia* **129 B9** 33 42 S 151 2 E
Hornsea, *U.K.* **20 D7** 53 55N 0 11W
Hornsjø, *Norway* **18 C7** 61 19N 10 38 E
Hornslandet, *Sweden* **16 C11** 61 35N 17 37 E
Hörnum, *Germany* **30 A4** 54 45N 8 17 E
Horobetsu = Noboribetsu, *Japan* **70 C10** 42 24N 141 6 E
Horodenka, *Ukraine* **53 B10** 48 41N 25 29 E
Horodnya, *Ukraine* **59 G6** 51 55N 31 33 E
Horodok, *Khmelnytskyy, Ukraine* **59 H4** 49 10N 26 34 E
Horodok, *Lviv, Ukraine* **59 H2** 49 46N 23 32 E
Horodyshche, *Ukraine* **59 H6** 49 17N 31 27 E
Horokhiv, *Ukraine* **59 G3** 50 30N 24 45 E
Horovice, *Czech Rep.* **34 B6** 49 48N 13 53 E
Horqin Youyi Qianqi, *China* **75 A12** 46 5N 122 3 E
Horqueta, *Paraguay* **174 A4** 23 15 S 56 55W
Horred, *Sweden* **17 G6** 57 22N 12 28 E
Horse Cr. →, *U.S.A.* **154 E3** 41 57N 105 10W
Horse I., *Canada* **143 C9** 53 20N 99 6W
Horse Is., *Canada* **141 B8** 50 15N 55 50W
Horsefly L., *Canada* **142 C4** 52 25N 121 0W
Horseheads, *U.S.A.* **150 D8** 42 10N 76 49W
Horsens, *Denmark* **17 J3** 55 52N 9 51 E
Horseshoe Bend △, *U.S.A.* **152 C4** 32 59N 85 44W
Horsham, *Australia* **128 D5** 36 44 S 142 13 E
Horsham, *U.K.* **21 F7** 51 4N 0 20W
Horšovský Týn, *Czech Rep.* **34 B5** 49 31N 12 58 E
Horta, *Azores* **9 d1** 38 32N 28 38W
Horten, *Norway* **18 E7** 59 25N 10 32 E
Hortense, *U.S.A.* **152 D8** 31 20N 81 57W
Horti, *India* **94 F2** 17 7N 75 47 E
Hortobágy →, *Hungary* **52 C6** 47 30N 21 6 E
Hortobágyi △, *Hungary* **52 C6** 47 36N 21 10 E
Horton, *Kans., U.S.A.* **154 F7** 39 40N 95 32W
Horton, *Mo., U.S.A.* **156 G2** 37 58N 94 22W
Horton →, *Canada* **138 B7** 69 56N 126 52W
Horw, *Switz.* **33 B6** 47 1N 8 19 E
Horwood L., *Canada* **140 C3** 48 5N 82 20W
Hosaina, *Ethiopia* **107 F4** 7 30N 37 47 E
Hosdurga, *India* **95 H3** 13 49N 76 17 E
Hosenofu, *Libya* **108 D4** 23 41N 21 4 E
Ḩoseynābād, *Khuzestān, Iran* **97 C6** 32 45N 48 20 E
Ḩoseynābād, *Kordestān, Iran* **101 E12** 35 33N 47 8 E
Hosford, *U.S.A.* **152 E5** 30 23N 84 48W
Hoshangabad, *India* **92 H7** 22 45N 77 45 E
Hoshiarpur, *India* **92 D6** 31 30N 75 58 E
Hoskins, *Papua N. G.* **132 C6** 5 29 S 150 27 E
Hoskote, *India* **95 H3** 13 4N 77 48 E
Hospental, *Switz.* **33 C7** 46 37N 8 34 E
Hospet, *India* **95 G3** 15 15N 76 20 E
Hoste, I., *Chile* **176 E3** 55 0 S 69 0W
Hostens, *France* **28 D3** 44 30N 0 40W
Hosur, *India* **95 H3** 12 43N 77 49 E
Hot, *Thailand* **86 C2** 18 8N 98 29 E
Hot Creek Range, *U.S.A.* **158 G6** 38 40N 116 20W
Hot Springs = Truth or Consequences, *U.S.A.* **159 K10** 33 8N 107 15W
Hot Springs, *Ark., U.S.A.* **155 H8** 34 31N 93 3W
Hot Springs, *S. Dak., U.S.A.* **154 D3** 43 26N 103 29W
Hot Springs △, *U.S.A.* **155 H8** 34 32N 93 4W
Hotagen, *Sweden* **14 E16** 63 59N 14 12 E
Hotan, *China* **68 C2** 37 25N 79 55 E
Hotazel, *S. Africa* **116 D3** 27 17 S 22 58 E
Hotchkiss, *U.S.A.* **159 G10** 38 48N 107 43W
Hotham, C., *Australia* **124 B5** 12 2 S 131 18 E
Hoti, *Indonesia* **83 B4** 3 0 S 130 22 E
Hoting, *Sweden* **14 D17** 64 8N 16 15 E
Hotolisht, *Albania* **50 E4** 41 10N 20 25 E
Hotte, Massif de la, *Haiti* **165 C5** 18 30N 73 45W
Hottentotsbaai, *Namibia* **116 D1** 26 8 S 14 59 E
Hou Hai, *China* **69 F10** 22 32N 113 56 E
Houailou, *N. Cal.* **133 U19** 21 17 S 165 38 E
Houat, Î. de, *France* **26 E4** 47 24N 2 58W
Houdan, *France* **27 D8** 48 48N 1 35 E
Houei Sai, *Laos* **76 G3** 20 18N 100 26 E
Houeillès, *France* **28 D4** 44 12N 0 2 E
Houffalize, *Belgium* **24 D5** 50 8N 5 48 E
Houghton, *Mich., U.S.A.* **154 B10** 47 7N 88 34W
Houghton, *N.Y., U.S.A.* **150 D6** 42 25N 78 10W
Houghton L., *U.S.A.* **148 C3** 44 21N 84 44W
Houghton-le-Spring, *U.K.* **20 C6** 54 51N 1 28W
Houhora Heads, *N.Z.* **130 A2** 34 49 S 173 9 E
Houlton, *U.S.A.* **149 B12** 46 8N 67 51W
Houma, *U.S.A.* **155 L9** 29 36N 90 43W
Houmt Souk = Djerba, *Tunisia* **108 B2** 33 52N 10 51 E
Houndé, *Burkina Faso* **112 C4** 11 34N 3 31W
Hourtin, *France* **28 C2** 45 11N 1 4W
Hourtin-Carcans, Étang d', *France* **28 C2** 45 10N 1 6W
Housatonic →, *U.S.A.* **151 E11** 41 10N 73 7W
Houston, *Canada* **142 C3** 54 25N 126 39W
Houston, *Fla., U.S.A.* **152 E7** 30 15N 82 54W
Houston, *Mo., U.S.A.* **155 G9** 37 22N 91 58W
Houston, *Tex., U.S.A.* **155 L7** 29 46N 95 22W
Hout →, *S. Africa* **117 C4** 23 4 S 29 36 E
Houtkraal, *S. Africa* **116 E3** 30 23 S 24 5 E
Houtman Abrolhos, *Australia* **125 E1** 28 43 S 113 48 E
Hov, *Norway* **18 D7** 60 42N 10 20 E
Hovd, *Mongolia* **68 B4** 48 2N 91 37 E
Hovda, *Norway* **18 D6** 60 53N 9 11 E
Hovden, *Aust-Agder, Norway* **18 E4** 59 33N 7 22 E
Hovden, *Sogn og Fjordane, Norway* **18 C1** 61 41N 4 52 E
Hove, *U.K.* **21 G7** 50 50N 0 10W
Hovenweep △, *U.S.A.* **159 H9** 37 20N 109 0W
Hovet, *Norway* **18 D5** 60 38N 8 8 E
Hoveyzeh, *Iran* **97 D6** 31 27N 48 4 E
Hovgaard Ø, *Greenland* **10 B9** 79 55N 18 50W
Hovin, *Norway* **18 E6** 59 51N 9 0 E
Hovmantorp, *Sweden* **17 H9** 56 47N 15 7 E
Hövsgöl, *Mongolia* **74 C5** 43 37N 109 39 E
Hövsgöl Nuur, *Mongolia* **68 A5** 51 0N 100 30 E
Hovsta, *Sweden* **16 E9** 59 22N 15 15 E
Howakil, *Eritrea* **107 D5** 15 10N 40 16 E
Howar, Wadi →, *Sudan* **107 D2** 17 30N 27 8 E
Howard, *Australia* **127 D5** 25 16 S 152 32 E
Howard, *Pa., U.S.A.* **150 F7** 41 1N 77 40W
Howard, *S. Dak., U.S.A.* **154 C6** 44 1N 97 32W
Howe, *U.S.A.* **158 E7** 43 48N 113 0W
Howe, C., *Australia* **129 D9** 37 30 S 150 0 E
Howe I., *Canada* **151 B8** 44 16N 76 17W
Howell, *U.S.A.* **157 B13** 42 36N 83 56W
Howick, *Canada* **151 A11** 45 11N 73 51W
Howick, *N.Z.* **130 C3** 36 54 S 174 56 E
Howick, *S. Africa* **117 D5** 29 28 S 30 14 E
Howick Group, *Australia* **126 A4** 14 20 S 145 30 E
Howitt, L., *Australia* **127 D2** 27 40 S 138 40 E
Howland I., *Pac. Oc.* **134 G10** 0 48N 176 38W
Howlong, *Australia* **129 C7** 35 59 S 146 38 E
Howrah = Haora, *India* **93 H13** 22 37N 88 20 E
Howth Hd., *Ireland* **23 C5** 53 22N 6 3W
Höxter, *Germany* **30 D5** 51 46N 9 22 E
Hoy, *U.K.* **22 C5** 58 50N 3 15W
Hoya, *Germany* **30 C5** 52 49N 9 8 E
Høyanger, *Norway* **18 C3** 61 13N 6 4 E
Hoyerswerda, *Germany* **30 D10** 51 26N 14 14 E
Hoylake, *U.K.* **20 D4** 53 24N 3 10W
Hōyo-Kaikyō, *Japan* **72 D3** 33 20N 131 58 E
Hoyos, *Spain* **42 E4** 40 9N 6 45W
Hpa-an = Pa-an, *Burma* **90 G6** 16 51N 97 40 E
Hpawlum, *Burma* **90 B7** 27 12N 98 12 E
Hpettintha, *Burma* **90 C5** 24 14N 95 23 E
Hpizow, *Burma* **90 B7** 26 57N 98 24 E
Hpunan Pass, *India* **90 A6** 28 9N 97 20 E
Hradec Králové, *Czech Rep.* **34 A8** 50 15N 15 50 E
Hrádek, *Czech Rep.* **35 C9** 48 46N 16 16 E
Hrafnseyri, *Iceland* **11 B3** 65 46N 23 28W
Hranice, *Czech Rep.* **35 B10** 49 34N 17 45 E
Hrazdan, *Armenia* **61 K7** 40 30N 44 46 E
Hrebenka, *Ukraine* **59 G7** 50 9N 32 22 E
Hrífunes, *Iceland* **11 D8** 63 38N 18 30W
Hrísey, *Iceland* **11 B8** 66 0N 18 23W
Hrodna, *Belarus* **54 E10** 53 42N 23 52 E
Hrodzyanka, *Belarus* **58 F5** 53 31N 28 42 E
Hron →, *Slovak Rep.* **35 D11** 47 49N 18 45 E
Hrubieszów, *Poland* **55 H10** 50 49N 23 51 E
Hrubý Jeseník, *Czech Rep.* **35 A10** 50 5N 17 10 E
Hrvatska = Croatia ■, *Europe* **45 C13** 45 20N 16 0 E
Hrymayliv, *Ukraine* **59 H4** 49 20N 26 5 E
Hrynyava, *Ukraine* **53 C9** 47 59N 24 53 E
Hsa-paw, *Burma* **90 F6** 19 1N 97 30 E
Hsenwi, *Burma* **90 D6** 23 22N 97 55 E
Hsi-hkip, *Burma* **90 E6** 20 25N 96 42 E
Hsiamen = Xiamen, *China* **77 E12** 24 25N 118 4 E
Hsian = Xi'an, *China* **74 G5** 34 15N 109 0 E
Hsinchu, *Taiwan* **77 E13** 24 48N 120 58 E
Hsinhailien = Lianyungang, *China* **75 G10** 34 40N 119 11 E
Hsinking = Changchun, *China* **75 C13** 43 57N 125 17 E
Hsinying, *Taiwan* **77 F13** 23 18N 120 19 E
Hsipaw, *Burma* **90 D6** 22 37N 97 18 E
Hsopket, *Burma* **76 F2** 23 11N 98 26 E
Hsüchou = Xuzhou, *China* **75 G9** 34 18N 117 10 E
Htawgaw, *Burma* **90 C7** 25 57N 98 23 E
Hu Xian, *China* **74 G5** 34 8N 108 42 E
Hua Hin, *Thailand* **86 F2** 12 34N 99 58 E
Hua Xian, *Henan, China* **74 G8** 35 30N 114 30 E
Hua Xian, *Shaanxi, China* **74 G5** 34 30N 109 48 E
Hua'an, *China* **77 E11** 25 1N 117 32 E
Huab →, *Namibia* **116 B2** 20 52 S 13 25 E
Huacaya, *Bolivia* **173 E5** 20 45 S 63 43W
Huachacalla, *Bolivia* **172 D4** 18 45 S 68 17W
Huacheng, *China* **77 E10** 24 4N 115 37 E
Huachinera, *Mexico* **162 A3** 30 9N 108 55W
Huacho, *Peru* **172 C2** 11 10 S 77 35W
Huachón, *Peru* **172 C2** 10 35 S 76 0W
Huade, *China* **74 D7** 41 55N 113 59 E
Huadian, *China* **75 C14** 43 0N 126 40 E
Huadu, *China* **77 F9** 23 22N 113 12 E
Huahine, I., *French Polynesia* **135 J12** 16 46 S 150 58W
Huai Had △, *Thailand* **86 D5** 16 52N 104 17 E
Huai He →, *China* **77 A12** 33 0N 118 30 E
Huai Nam Dang △, *Thailand* **86 C2** 19 30N 98 30 E
Huai Yot, *Thailand* **87 J2** 7 45N 99 37 E
Huai'an, *Hebei, China* **74 D8** 40 30N 114 20 E
Huai'an, *Jiangsu, China* **75 H10** 33 30N 119 10 E
Huaibei, *China* **74 G9** 34 0N 116 48 E
Huaibin, *China* **77 A10** 32 32N 115 27 E
Huaicho = Puerto Acosta, *Bolivia* **172 D4** 15 32 S 69 15W
Huaide = Gongzhuling, *China* **75 C13** 43 30N 124 40 E
Huaidezhen, *China* **75 C13** 43 48N 124 50 E
Huaihua, *China* **76 D7** 27 32N 109 57 E
Huaiji, *China* **77 F9** 23 55N 112 12 E
Huainan, *China* **77 A11** 32 38N 116 58 E
Huaining, *China* **77 B11** 30 24N 116 40 E
Huairen, *China* **74 E7** 39 48N 113 20 E
Huairou, *China* **74 D9** 40 20N 116 35 E
Huaiyang, *China* **74 H8** 33 40N 114 52 E
Huaiyin, *China* **75 H10** 33 30N 119 2 E
Huaiyuan, *Anhui, China* **75 H9** 32 55N 117 10 E
Huaiyuan, *Guangxi Zhuangzu, China* **76 E7** 24 31N 108 22 E
Huajianzi, *China* **75 D13** 41 23N 125 20 E
Huajuapan de Leon, *Mexico* **163 D5** 17 50N 97 48W
Hualalai, *U.S.A.* **145 D6** 19 42N 155 52W
Hualapai Peak, *U.S.A.* **159 J7** 35 5N 113 54W
Hualien, *Taiwan* **77 E13** 24 0N 121 30 E
Huallaga →, *Peru* **172 B2** 5 15 S 75 30W
Huallanca, *Peru* **172 B2** 8 50 S 77 56W
Huamachuco, *Peru* **172 B2** 7 50 S 78 5W
Huambo, *Angola* **115 E3** 12 42 S 15 54 E
Huambo □, *Angola* **115 E3** 13 0 S 16 0 E
Huan Jiang →, *China* **74 G5** 34 28N 109 0 E
Huan Xian, *China* **74 F4** 36 33N 107 7 E
Huancabamba, *Peru* **172 B2** 5 10 S 79 15W
Huancane, *Peru* **172 D4** 15 10 S 69 44W
Huancapi, *Peru* **172 C3** 13 40 S 74 0W
Huancavelica, *Peru* **172 C2** 12 50 S 75 5W
Huancavelica □, *Peru* **172 C3** 13 0 S 75 0W
Huancayo, *Peru* **172 C2** 12 5 S 75 12W
Huanchaca, *Bolivia* **172 E4** 20 15 S 66 40W
Huanchaca, Serranía de, *Bolivia* **173 C5** 14 30 S 60 39W
Huang Hai = Yellow Sea, *China* **75 G12** 35 0N 123 0 E
Huang He →, *China* **75 F10** 37 55N 118 50 E
Huang Xian, *China* **75 F11** 37 38N 120 30 E
Huangchuan, *China* **77 A10** 32 15N 115 10 E
Huanggang, *China* **77 B10** 30 29N 114 52 E
Huangguoshu, *China* **76 E5** 26 0N 105 40 E
Huangling, *China* **74 G5** 35 34N 109 15 E
Huanglong, *China* **74 G5** 35 30N 109 59 E
Huanglongtan, *China* **77 A8** 32 40N 110 33 E
Huangmei, *China* **77 B10** 30 5N 115 56 E
Huangpi, *China* **77 B10** 30 50N 114 22 E
Huangping, *China* **76 D6** 26 52N 107 54 E
Huangshan, *China* **77 C12** 29 42N 118 25 E
Huangshi, *China* **77 B10** 30 10N 115 3 E
Huangsongdian, *China* **75 C14** 43 45N 127 25 E
Huangyan, *China* **77 C13** 28 38N 121 19 E
Huangyangsi, *China* **77 D8** 26 33N 111 39 E
Huaning, *China* **76 E4** 24 17N 102 56 E
Huanjiang, *China* **76 E7** 24 50N 108 18 E
Huanta, *Peru* **172 C3** 12 55 S 74 20W
Huantai, *China* **75 F9** 36 58N 117 56 E
Huánuco, *Peru* **172 B2** 9 55 S 76 15W
Huánuco □, *Peru* **172 B2** 9 55 S 76 14W
Huanuni, *Bolivia* **172 D4** 18 16 S 66 51W
Huanzo, Cordillera de, *Peru* **172 C3** 14 35 S 73 20W
Huaping, *China* **76 D3** 26 46N 101 25 E
Huara, *Chile* **172 D4** 19 59 S 69 47W
Huaral, *Peru* **172 C2** 11 32 S 77 13W
Huaraz, *Peru* **172 B2** 9 30 S 77 32W
Huari, *Peru* **172 B2** 9 14 S 77 14W
Huarmey, *Peru* **172 C2** 10 5 S 78 5W
Huarochiri, *Peru* **172 C2** 12 9 S 76 15W
Huarocondo, *Peru* **172 C3** 13 26 S 72 14W
Huarong, *China* **77 C9** 29 29N 112 30 E
Huascarán, *Peru* **172 B2** 9 8 S 77 36W
Huascarán, Nevado, *Peru* **172 B2** 9 7 S 77 37W
Huasco, *Chile* **174 B1** 28 30 S 71 15W
Huasco →, *Chile* **174 B1** 28 27 S 71 13W
Huasna, *U.S.A.* **161 K6** 35 6N 120 24W
Huatabampo, *Mexico* **162 B3** 26 50N 109 50W
Huauchinango, *Mexico* **163 C5** 20 11N 98 3W
Huautla de Jiménez, *Mexico* **163 D5** 18 8N 96 51W
Huaxi, *China* **76 D6** 26 25N 106 40 E
Huay Namota, *Mexico* **162 C4** 21 56N 104 30W
Huayin, *China* **74 G6** 34 35N 110 5 E
Huayllay, *Peru* **172 C2** 11 3 S 76 21W
Huayuan, *China* **76 C7** 28 37N 109 29 E
Huayun, *China* **76 B6** 30 14N 106 40 E
Huazhou, *China* **77 G8** 21 33N 110 33 E
Hubbard, *Iowa, U.S.A.* **156 B3** 42 18N 93 18W
Hubbard, *Ohio, U.S.A.* **150 E4** 41 9N 80 34W
Hubbard, *Tex., U.S.A.* **155 K6** 31 51N 96 48W
Hubbart Pt., *Canada* **143 B10** 59 21N 94 41W
Hubei □, *China* **77 B9** 31 0N 112 0 E
Hubli, *India* **95 G2** 15 22N 75 15 E
Huch'ang, *N. Korea* **75 D14** 41 25N 127 2 E
Huchow = Huzhou, *China* **77 B13** 30 51N 120 8 E
Hucknall, *U.K.* **20 D6** 53 3N 1 13W
Huddersfield, *U.K.* **20 D6** 53 39N 1 47W
Hude, *Germany* **30 B4** 53 7N 8 26 E
Hudi, *Sudan* **106 D3** 17 43N 34 18 E
Hudiksvall, *Sweden* **16 C11** 61 43N 17 10 E
Hudson, *Canada* **140 B1** 50 6N 92 9W
Hudson, *Fla., U.S.A.* **153 G7** 28 22N 82 42W
Hudson, *Mass., U.S.A.* **151 D13** 42 23N 71 34W
Hudson, *Mich., U.S.A.* **157 C12** 41 51N 84 21W
Hudson, *N.Y., U.S.A.* **151 D11** 42 15N 73 46W
Hudson, *Wis., U.S.A.* **154 C8** 44 58N 92 45W
Hudson, *Wyo., U.S.A.* **158 E9** 42 54N 108 35W
Hudson →, *U.S.A.* **151 F10** 40 42N 74 2W
Hudson Bay, *Nunavut, Canada* **139 C11** 60 0N 86 0W
Hudson Bay, *Sask., Canada* **143 C8** 52 51N 102 23W
Hudson Falls, *U.S.A.* **151 C11** 43 18N 73 35W
Hudson Mts., *Antarctica* **7 D16** 74 32 S 99 20W
Hudson Str., *Canada* **139 B13** 62 0N 70 0W
Hudson's Hope, *Canada* **142 B4** 56 0N 121 54W
Hudsonville, *U.S.A.* **157 B11** 42 52N 85 52W
Hue, *Vietnam* **86 D6** 16 30N 107 35 E
Huebra →, *Spain* **42 D4** 41 2N 6 48W
Huechucuicui, Pta., *Chile* **176 B2** 41 48 S 74 2W
Huedin, *Romania* **52 D8** 46 52N 23 2 E
Huehuetenango, *Guatemala* **164 C1** 15 20N 91 28W
Huejúcar, *Mexico* **162 C4** 22 21N 103 13W
Huélamo, *Spain* **40 E3** 40 17N 1 48W
Huelgoat, *France* **26 D3** 48 22N 3 46W
Huelma, *Spain* **43 H7** 37 39N 3 28W
Huelva, *Spain* **43 H4** 37 18N 6 57W
Huelva □, *Spain* **43 H4** 37 40N 7 0W
Huelva →, *Spain* **43 H5** 37 27N 6 0W
Hueneme = Port Hueneme, *U.S.A.* **161 L7** 34 7N 119 12W
Huentelauquén, *Chile* **174 C1** 31 38 S 71 33W
Huércal-Overa, *Spain* **41 H3** 37 23N 1 57W
Huerquehue △, *Chile* **176 A2** 39 6 S 71 42W
Huerta, Sa. de la, *Argentina* **174 C2** 31 10 S 67 30W
Huertas, C. de las, *Spain* **41 G4** 38 21N 0 24W
Huerva →, *Spain* **40 D4** 41 39N 0 52W
Huesca, *Spain* **40 C4** 42 8N 0 25W
Huesca □, *Spain* **40 C5** 42 20N 0 1 E
Huéscar, *Spain* **41 H2** 37 44N 2 35W
Huetamo, *Mexico* **162 D4** 18 36N 100 54W
Huete, *Spain* **40 E2** 40 10N 2 43W
Huger, *U.S.A.* **152 B10** 33 6N 79 48W
Hugh →, *Australia* **126 D1** 25 1 S 134 1 E
Hughenden, *Australia* **126 C3** 20 52 S 144 10 E
Hughes, *Australia* **125 F4** 30 42 S 129 31 E
Hughes, *U.S.A.* **144 C9** 66 3N 154 15W
Hughesville, *U.S.A.* **151 E8** 41 14N 76 44W
Hugli →, *India* **93 J13** 21 56N 88 4 E
Hugo, *Colo., U.S.A.* **154 F3** 39 8N 103 28W
Hugo, *Okla., U.S.A.* **155 H7** 34 1N 95 31W
Hugoton, *U.S.A.* **155 G4** 37 11N 101 21W
Huhehaote = Hohhot, *China* **74 D6** 40 52N 111 40 E
Hui Xian = Huixian, *China* **74 G7** 35 27N 113 12 E
Hui Xian, *China* **74 H4** 33 50N 106 4 E
Hui'an, *China* **77 E12** 25 1N 118 43 E
Hui'anbu, *China* **74 F4** 37 28N 106 38 E
Huiarau Ra., *N.Z.* **130 E5** 38 45 S 176 55 E
Huichang, *China* **77 E10** 25 32N 115 45 E
Huichapán, *Mexico* **163 C5** 20 24N 99 40W
Huidong, *Guangdong, China* **77 F10** 22 58N 114 43 E
Huidong, *Sichuan, China* **76 D4** 26 34N 102 35 E
Huifa He →, *China* **75 C14** 43 0N 127 50 E
Huíla, *Angola* **115 F2** 15 4 S 13 32 E
Huíla □, *Angola* **115 E2** 14 0 S 15 0 E
Huila □, *Colombia* **168 C2** 2 30N 75 45W
Huila, Nevado del, *Colombia* **168 C2** 3 0N 76 0W
Huilai, *China* **77 F11** 23 0N 116 18 E
Huili, *China* **76 D4** 26 35N 102 17 E
Huimin, *China* **75 F9** 37 27N 117 28 E
Huinan, *China* **75 C14** 42 40N 126 2 E
Huinca Renancó, *Argentina* **174 C3** 34 51 S 64 22W
Huining, *China* **74 G3** 35 38N 105 0 E
Huinong, *China* **74 E4** 39 5N 106 35 E
Huiroa, *N.Z.* **130 F3** 39 15 S 174 30 E
Huisache, *Mexico* **162 C4** 22 55N 100 25W
Huishui, *China* **76 D6** 26 7N 106 38 E
Huisne →, *France* **26 E7** 47 59N 0 11 E
Huiting, *China* **74 G9** 34 5N 116 5 E
Huitong, *China* **76 D7** 26 51N 109 45 E
Huixian, *China* **74 G7** 35 27N 113 12 E
Huixtla, *Mexico* **163 D6** 15 9N 92 28W
Huize, *China* **76 D4** 26 24N 103 15 E
Huizhou, *China* **77 F10** 23 0N 114 23 E
Hukeri, *India* **95 F2** 16 14N 74 36 E
Hukou, *China* **77 C11** 29 45N 116 21 E
Hüksan-chedo, *S. Korea* **75 G13** 34 40N 125 30 E
Hukuntsi, *Botswana* **116 C3** 23 58 S 21 45 E
Hula, *Papua N. G.* **132 F4** 10 5 S 147 43 E
Ḩulayfā', *Si. Arabia* **96 E4** 25 58N 40 45 E
Huld = Ulaanjirem, *Mongolia* **74 B3** 45 5N 105 30 E
Hulin He →, *China* **75 B12** 45 0N 122 10 E
Hull = Kingston upon Hull, *U.K.* **20 D7** 53 45N 0 21W
Hull, *Canada* **140 C4** 45 25N 75 44W
Hull →, *U.K.* **20 D7** 53 44N 0 20W
Hulst, *Neths.* **24 C4** 51 17N 4 2 E
Hultschin = Hlučín, *Czech Rep.* **35 B11** 49 54N 18 11 E
Hultsfred, *Sweden* **17 G9** 57 30N 15 52 E
Hulun = Hailar, *China* **69 B6** 49 10N 119 38 E
Hulun Nur, *China* **69 B6** 49 0N 117 30 E
Hulyaypole, *Ukraine* **59 J9** 47 45N 36 21 E
Huma, Tanjung, *Malaysia* **87 c** 5 29N 100 16 E
Humacao, *Puerto Rico* **165 d** 18 9N 65 50W
Humahuaca, *Argentina* **174 A2** 23 10 S 65 25W
Humaita = Pôrto Válter, *Brazil* **172 B3** 8 15 S 72 40W
Humaitá, *Brazil* **173 B5** 7 35 S 63 1W
Humaitá, *Paraguay* **174 B4** 27 2 S 58 31W
Humansdorp, *S. Africa* **116 E3** 34 2 S 24 46 E
Humansville, *U.S.A.* **156 G3** 37 48N 93 35W
Humara, J., *Sudan* **107 D3** 16 16N 30 59 E
Humbe, *Angola* **116 B1** 16 40 S 14 55 E
Humber →, *U.K.* **20 D7** 53 42N 0 27W
Humboldt, *Canada* **143 C7** 52 15N 105 9W
Humboldt, *Iowa, U.S.A.* **156 B2** 42 44N 94 13W
Humboldt, *Tenn., U.S.A.* **155 H10** 35 50N 88 55W
Humboldt →, *U.S.A.* **158 F4** 39 59N 118 36W
Humboldt, Massif du, *N. Cal.* **133 U20** 21 53 S 166 25 E
Humboldt Gletscher = Sermersuaq, *Greenland* **10 B4** 79 30N 62 0W
Humboldt Mts., *N.Z.* **131 E3** 44 30 S 168 15 E
Hume, *U.S.A.* **160 J8** 36 48N 118 54W
Hume, L., *Australia* **129 D7** 36 0 S 147 5 E
Humen, *China* **69 F10** 22 50N 113 40 E
Humenné, *Slovak Rep.* **35 C14** 48 55N 21 50 E
Humeston, *U.S.A.* **156 D3** 40 52N 93 30W
Hummelsta, *Sweden* **16 E10** 59 34N 16 58 E
Hummelvik, *Norway* **18 A5** 63 29N 8 19 E
Hummock Hill = Whyalla, *Australia* **128 B2** 33 2 S 137 30 E
Humpata, *Angola* **115 F2** 15 2 S 13 24 E
Humphreys, Mt., *U.S.A.* **160 H8** 37 17N 118 40W
Humphreys Peak, *U.S.A.* **159 J8** 35 21N 111 41W
Humpolec, *Czech Rep.* **34 B8** 49 31N 15 20 E
Humptulips, *U.S.A.* **160 C3** 47 14N 123 57W
Humula, *Australia* **129 C7** 35 30 S 147 46 E
Hūn, *Libya* **108 C3** 29 2N 16 0 E
Hun Jiang →, *China* **75 D13** 40 50N 125 38 E
Húnaflói, *Iceland* **11 B6** 65 50N 20 50W
Hunan □, *China* **77 D9** 27 30N 112 0 E
Hunavatnssýsla □, *Iceland* **11 B6** 65 30N 20 25W
Hunchun, *China* **75 C16** 42 52N 130 28 E
Hundested, *Denmark* **17 J5** 55 58N 11 52 E
Hundewali, *Pakistan* **92 D5** 31 55N 72 38 E
Hundorp, *Norway* **18 C7** 61 33N 9 59 E
Hundred Islands △, *Phil.* **80 C3** 16 10N 120 2 E

Hundred Mile House, Canada 142 C4 51 38N 121 18W
Hundvåg, Norway 18 E2 59 0N 5 43 E
Hunedoara, Romania 52 E7 45 40N 22 50 E
Hunedoara □, Romania 52 E7 45 50N 22 54 E
Hünfeld, Germany 30 E5 50 39N 9 46 E
Hung Yen, Vietnam 76 G6 20 39N 106 4 E
Hunga Ha'apai, Tonga 133 Q13 20 41 S 175 7W
Hungary ■, Europe 35 D12 47 20N 19 20 E
Hungary, Plain of, Europe 12 F10 47 0N 20 0 E
Hungerford, Australia 127 D3 28 58 S 144 24 E
Hŭngnam, N. Korea 75 E14 39 49N 127 45 E
Hungt'ou Hsü, Taiwan 77 G13 22 0N 121 30 E
Hungund, India 95 F3 16 4N 76 3 E
Huni Valley, Ghana 112 D4 5 33N 1 56W
Hunjiang, China 75 D14 41 56N 126 29 E
Hunneberg, Sweden 17 F6 58 18N 12 30 E
Hunnebostrand, Sweden 17 F5 58 27N 11 18 E
Hunsberge, Namibia 116 D2 27 45 S 17 12 E
Hunsrück, Germany 31 F3 49 56N 7 27 E
Hunstanton, U.K. 20 E8 52 56N 0 29 E
Hunsur, India 95 H3 12 16N 76 16 E
Hunte →, Germany 30 B4 53 14N 8 28 E
Hunter, N.Z. 131 E6 44 36 S 171 2 E
Hunter, U.S.A. 151 D10 42 13N 74 13W
Hunter →, Australia 129 B9 32 52 S 151 46 E
Hunter →, N.Z. 131 E4 44 21 S 169 27 E
Hunter, C., Solomon Is. 133 M10 9 48 S 159 50 E
Hunter Hills, The, N.Z. 131 E5 44 26 S 170 46 E
Hunter I., Australia 127 G3 40 30 S 144 45 E
Hunter I., Canada 142 C3 51 55N 128 0W
Hunter Mts., N.Z. 131 F2 45 43 S 167 25 E
Hunter Ra., Australia 129 B9 32 45 S 150 15 E
Hunters Road, Zimbabwe 119 F2 19 9 S 29 49 E
Hunterville, N.Z. 130 F4 39 56 S 175 35 E
Huntingburg, U.S.A. 157 F10 38 18N 86 57W
Huntingdon, Canada 140 C5 45 6N 74 10W
Huntingdon, U.K. 21 E7 52 20N 0 11W
Huntingdon, U.S.A. 150 F6 40 30N 78 1W
Huntington = Shelton, U.S.A. 151 E11 41 19N 73 5W
Huntington, Ind., U.S.A. 157 D11 40 53N 85 30W
Huntington, N.Y., U.S.A. 151 F11 40 52N 73 26W
Huntington, Oreg., U.S.A. 158 D5 44 21N 117 16W
Huntington, Utah, U.S.A. 158 G8 39 20N 110 58W
Huntington, W. Va., U.S.A. 148 F4 38 25N 82 27W
Huntington Beach, U.S.A. 161 M9 33 40N 118 5W
Huntley, U.S.A. 157 B8 42 10N 88 26W
Huntly, N.Z. 130 D4 37 34 S 175 11 E
Huntly, U.K. 22 D6 57 27N 2 47W
Huntsville, Canada 140 C4 45 20N 79 14W
Huntsville, Ala., U.S.A. 149 H2 34 44N 86 35W
Huntsville, Mo., U.S.A. 156 E4 39 26N 92 33W
Huntsville, Tex., U.S.A. 155 K7 30 43N 95 33W
Hunyani →, Zimbabwe 119 F3 15 57 S 30 39 E
Hunyuan, China 74 E7 39 42N 113 42 E
Hunza →, India 93 B6 35 54N 74 20 E
Huo Xian = Huozhou, China 74 F6 36 36N 111 42 E
Huon G., Papua N. G. 132 D4 7 0 S 147 30 E
Huon Pen., Papua N. G. 132 D4 6 20 S 147 30 E
Huong Khe, Vietnam 86 C5 18 13N 105 41 E
Huonville, Australia 127 G4 43 0 S 147 5 E
Huoqiu, China 77 A11 32 20N 116 12 E
Huoshan, Anhui, China 77 A12 32 28N 118 30 E
Huoshan, Anhui, China 77 B11 31 25N 116 20 E
Huoshao Dao = Lü-Tao, Taiwan 77 F13 22 40N 121 30 E
Huozhou, China 74 F6 36 36N 111 42 E
Hupeh = Hubei □, China 77 B9 31 0N 112 0 E
Ḥūr, Iran 97 D8 30 50N 57 7 E
Hurbanovo, Slovak Rep. 35 D11 47 51N 18 11 E
Hurd, C., Canada 150 A3 45 13N 81 44W
Hure Qi, China 75 C11 42 45N 121 45 E
Hurezani, Romania 53 F8 44 49N 23 40 E
Hurghada, Egypt 106 B3 27 15N 33 50 E
Hurley, N. Mex., U.S.A. 159 K9 32 42N 108 8W
Hurley, Wis., U.S.A. 154 B9 46 27N 90 11W
Huron, Calif., U.S.A. 160 J6 36 12N 120 6W
Huron, Ohio, U.S.A. 150 E2 41 24N 82 33W
Huron, S. Dak., U.S.A. 154 C5 44 22N 98 13W
Huron, L., U.S.A. 150 B2 44 30N 82 40W
Huron East, Canada 150 C3 43 37N 81 18W
Hurricane, U.S.A. 159 H7 37 11N 113 17W
Hurso, Ethiopia 107 F5 9 35N 41 33 E
Hurstbridge, U.S.A. 152 C4 32 15N 85 25W
Hurungwe ⌂, Zimbabwe 119 F2 16 7 S 29 5 E
Hurunui →, N.Z. 131 C8 42 54 S 173 18 E
Hurup, Denmark 17 H2 56 46N 8 25 E
Húsafell, Iceland 11 C6 64 42N 20 53W
Húsavík, Iceland 11 A9 66 3N 17 21W
Huşi, Romania 53 D13 46 41N 28 7 E
Huskisson, Australia 129 C9 35 2 S 150 41 E
Huskvarna, Sweden 17 G8 57 47N 14 15 E
Huslia, U.S.A. 144 D8 65 41N 156 24W
Husnes, Norway 18 E2 59 52N 5 45 E
Hustad, Norway 18 B4 62 57N 7 6 E
Hustadvika, Norway 18 A3 63 0N 7 0 E
Hustontown, U.S.A. 150 F6 40 3N 78 2W
Hustopeče, Czech Rep. 35 C9 48 57N 16 43 E
Husum, Germany 30 A5 54 28N 9 4 E
Husum, Sweden 16 A13 63 21N 19 12 E
Huszt = Khust, Ukraine 53 B8 48 10N 23 18 E
Hutchinson, Kans., U.S.A. 155 F6 38 5N 97 56W
Hutchinson, Minn., U.S.A. 154 C7 44 54N 94 22W
Ḥūth, Yemen 98 C3 16 14N 43 58 E
Hutjena, Papua N. G. 132 C8 5 23 S 154 42 E
Hutsonville, U.S.A. 157 E9 39 7N 87 40W
Hutte Sauvage, L. de la, Canada 141 A7 56 15N 64 45W
Hüttenberg, Austria 34 E7 46 56N 14 33 E
Hüttener Berge ⌂, Germany 30 A5 54 24N 9 40 E
Hutton, Mt., Australia 127 D4 25 51 S 148 20 E
Huttwil, Switz. 32 B5 47 7N 7 50 E
Huwun, Ethiopia 107 G5 4 23N 40 6 E
Huy, Belgium 24 D5 50 31N 5 15 E
Huzhou, China 77 B13 30 51N 120 8 E
Huzurabad, India 94 E4 18 12N 79 25 E
Huzurnagar, India 94 F4 16 54N 79 53 E
Hvalpsund, Denmark 17 H3 56 42N 9 11 E
Hvammsfjörður, Iceland 11 B4 65 4N 22 5W
Hvammstangi, Iceland 11 B6 65 24N 20 57W
Hvammur, Mýrasýsla, Iceland 11 C5 64 50N 21 21W
Hvammur, Skagafjarðarsýsla, Iceland 11 B7 65 53N 19 51W
Hvannadalshnúkur, Iceland 11 C10 64 1N 16 41W
Hvanneyri, Iceland 11 C5 64 34N 21 36W
Hvar, Croatia 45 E13 43 11N 16 28 E
Hvarski Kanal, Croatia 45 E13 43 15N 16 35 E
Hveragerði, Iceland 11 C5 64 0N 21 12W
Hvítá →, Iceland 11 C5 64 30N 21 58W
Hvítárvatn, Iceland 11 C7 64 37N 19 50W
Hvittingfoss, Norway 18 E7 59 29N 10 0 E
Hvizdets, Ukraine 53 B10 48 35N 25 17 E
Hvolsvöllur, Iceland 11 D6 63 45N 20 14W
Hwachŏn-chŏsuji, S. Korea 75 E14 38 5N 127 50 E
Hwainan = Huainan, China 77 A11 32 38N 116 58 E
Hwaiyin = Huaiyin, China 75 H10 33 30N 119 2 E
Hwang Ho = Huang He →, China 75 F10 37 55N 118 50 E
Hwange, Zimbabwe 119 F2 18 18 S 26 30 E
Hwange △, Zimbabwe 116 B4 19 0 S 26 30 E
Hwangshih = Huangshi, China 77 B10 30 10N 115 3 E
Hwekum, Burma 90 B5 26 7N 95 22 E
Hyaing, Burma 90 D5 22 39N 94 44 E
Hyannis, Mass., U.S.A. 148 E10 41 39N 70 17W
Hyannis, Nebr., U.S.A. 154 E4 42 0N 101 46W
Hyargas Nuur, Mongolia 68 B4 49 0N 93 0 E
Hybo, Sweden 16 C10 61 49N 16 15 E
Hydaburg, U.S.A. 142 B2 55 15N 132 50W
Hyde, N.Z. 131 F5 45 18 S 170 16 E
Hyde Park, Guyana 169 B6 6 30N 58 16W
Hyde Park, U.S.A. 151 E11 41 47N 73 56W
Hyden, Australia 125 F2 32 24 S 118 53 E
Hyder, U.S.A. 142 B2 55 55N 130 5W
Hyderabad, India 94 F4 17 22N 78 29 E
Hyderabad, Pakistan 91 D3 25 23N 68 24 E
Hydra = Ídhra, Greece 48 D5 37 20N 23 28 E
Hyen, Norway 18 C2 61 44N 5 56 E
Hyères, France 29 E10 43 8N 6 9 E
Hyères, Îs. d', France 29 E10 43 0N 6 20 E
Hyesan, N. Korea 75 D15 41 20N 128 10 E
Hyland →, Canada 142 B3 59 52N 128 12W
Hylestad, Norway 18 E4 59 6N 7 29 E
Hyllestad, Norway 18 C2 61 10N 5 17 E
Hyltebruk, Sweden 17 H7 56 59N 13 15 E
Hymia, India 93 C8 33 40N 78 2 E
Hyndman Peak, U.S.A. 158 E6 43 45N 114 8W
Hynnekleiv, Norway 18 F5 58 36N 8 25 E
Hyōgo □, Japan 72 B6 35 15N 134 50 E
Hyrra Banda, C.A.R. 114 A4 5 58N 22 1 E
Hyrum, U.S.A. 158 F8 41 38N 111 51W
Hysham, U.S.A. 158 C10 46 18N 107 14W
Hythe, U.K. 21 F9 51 4N 1 5 E
Hyūga, Japan 72 E3 32 25N 131 35 E
Hyvinge = Hyvinkää, Finland 15 F21 60 38N 24 50 E
Hyvinkää, Finland 15 F21 60 38N 24 50 E

I

I-n-Azaoua, Illizi, Algeria 111 C6 25 42N 6 54 E
I-n-Azaoua, Tamanrasset, Algeria 111 D6 20 46N 7 32 E
I-n-Échaï, Mali 110 D4 20 10N 2 5W
I-n-Gall, Niger 113 B6 16 51N 7 1 E
I-n-Kelemet, Algeria 111 C6 26 57N 5 47 E
I-n-Oudad, Algeria 111 D5 20 17N 4 38 E
I-n-Ouzzal, Algeria 113 A5 20 40N 2 35 E
I-n-Ouzzal, Algeria 111 D5 20 41N 2 34 E
I-n-Tadreft, Niger 113 B6 19 5N 6 38 E
Iabès, Erg, Algeria 111 C4 27 30N 2 2W
Iablaniţa, Romania 52 F7 44 57N 22 19 E
Iaco →, Brazil 172 B4 9 3 S 68 34W
Iacobeni, Romania 53 C10 47 25N 25 20 E
Iaçu, Brazil 171 D3 12 45 S 40 13W
Iakora, Madag. 117 C8 23 6 S 46 40 E
Ialibu, Papua N. G. 132 D2 6 17 S 143 59 E
Ialomiţa □, Romania 53 F12 44 30N 27 30 E
Ialomiţa →, Romania 53 F12 44 42N 27 51 E
Ialoveni, Moldova 53 D13 46 56N 28 47 E
Ialpug →, Moldova 53 E13 45 41N 28 35 E
Iamonia L., U.S.A. 152 E5 30 38N 84 14W
Ianca, Romania 53 E12 45 6N 27 29 E
Iara, Romania 53 D8 46 31N 23 35 E
Iarda, Ethiopia 107 E4 11 9N 35 53 E
Iargara, Moldova 53 D13 46 24N 28 23 E
Iaşi, Romania 53 C12 47 10N 27 40 E
Iaşi □, Romania 53 C12 47 20N 27 0 E
Íasmos, Greece 51 E9 41 8N 25 11 E
Iauaretê, Colombia 168 C4 0 36N 69 12W
Ib →, India 93 J10 21 34N 83 48 E
Iba, Phil. 80 D2 15 22N 120 0 E
Ibadan, Nigeria 113 D5 7 22N 3 58 E
Ibagué, Colombia 168 C2 4 20N 75 20W
Ibaiti, Brazil 171 F1 23 50 S 50 10W
Ibajay, Phil. 81 F4 11 49N 122 10 E
Iballë, Albania 50 D4 42 12N 20 2 E
Ibăneşti, Botoşani, Romania 53 B11 48 4N 26 22 E
Ibăneşti, Mureş, Romania 53 D9 46 45N 24 57 E
Ibanshe, Dem. Rep. of the Congo 115 C4 4 58 S 21 30 E
Ibar →, Serbia & M. 50 C4 43 43N 20 45 E
Ibara, Japan 72 C5 34 36N 133 28 E
Ibaraki, Japan 73 C7 34 49N 135 34 E
Ibaraki □, Japan 73 A12 36 10N 140 10 E
Ibarra, Ecuador 168 C2 0 21N 78 7W
Ibb, Yemen 98 D4 14 2N 44 10 E
Ibba, Sudan 107 G2 4 49N 29 2 E
Ibba, Bahr el →, Sudan 107 F2 5 30N 28 55 E
Ibbenbüren, Germany 30 C3 52 16N 7 43 E
Ibeke Gembo, Dem. Rep. of the Congo 114 C3 1 24 S 18 51 E
Ibembo, Dem. Rep. of the Congo 118 B1 2 35N 23 35 E
Ibenga →, Congo 114 B3 2 19N 18 9 E
Ibera, L., Argentina 174 B4 28 30 S 57 9W
Iberia, U.S.A. 156 F4 38 5N 92 18W
Iberian Peninsula, Europe 12 H5 40 0N 5 0W
Iberville, Canada 140 C5 45 19N 73 17W
Iberville, Lac d', Canada 140 A5 55 55N 73 15W
Ibi, Nigeria 113 D6 8 15N 9 44 E
Ibi, Spain 41 G4 38 38N 0 34W
Ibiá, Brazil 171 E2 19 30 S 46 30W
Ibiapaba, Sa. da, Brazil 170 B3 4 0 S 41 30W
Ibicaraí, Brazil 171 D4 14 51 S 39 36W
Ibicuí, Brazil 171 D4 14 51 S 39 59W
Ibicuí →, Brazil 175 B4 29 25 S 56 47W
Ibicuy, Argentina 174 C4 33 55 S 59 10W
Ibipetuba, Brazil 170 D3 11 0 S 44 32W
Ibitiara, Brazil 171 D3 12 39 S 42 13W
Ibiza = Eivissa, Spain 38 D1 38 54N 1 26 E
Ibiza ✕ (IBZ), Spain 41 G6 38 53N 1 22 E
Íblei, Monti, Italy 47 E7 37 15N 14 45 E
Ibo, Mozam. 119 E5 12 22 S 40 40 E
Ibonma, Indonesia 83 B4 3 29 S 133 31 E
Ibotirama, Brazil 171 D3 12 13 S 43 12W
Ibrāhīm →, Lebanon 103 A4 34 4N 35 38 E
'Ibrī, Oman 97 F8 23 14N 56 30 E
İbriktepe, Turkey 51 E10 41 0N 26 30 E
Ibshawâi, Egypt 106 J7 29 21N 30 40 E
Ibu, Indonesia 82 A3 1 35N 127 33 E
Ibuki-Sanchi, Japan 73 B8 35 25N 136 18 E
Ibusuki, Japan 72 F2 31 12N 130 40 E
Ica, Peru 172 C2 14 0 S 75 48W
Ica □, Peru 172 C2 14 20 S 75 30W
Iça →, Brazil 172 A4 2 55 S 67 58W
Icabarú, Venezuela 169 C5 4 20N 61 45W
Icabarú →, Venezuela 169 C5 4 45N 62 15W
Icacos Pt., Trin. & Tob. 169 F9 10 3N 61 57W
Içana, Brazil 168 C4 0 21N 67 19W
Içana →, Brazil 168 C4 0 26N 67 19W
Icatu, Brazil 170 B3 2 46 S 44 4W
Icaturama = Santa Rosa de Viterbo, Colombia 168 B3 5 53N 72 59W
İçel = Mersin, Turkey 100 D6 36 51N 34 36 E
Iceland ■, Europe 11 C8 64 45N 19 0W
Iceland Plateau, Arctic 6 C7 64 0N 10 0W
Ichalkaranji, India 94 F2 16 40N 74 33 E
Ich'ang = Yichang, China 77 B8 30 40N 111 20 E
Ichchapuram, India 94 E7 19 10N 84 40 E
Ichhawar, India 92 H7 23 1N 77 1 E
Ichihara, Japan 73 B12 35 28N 140 5 E
Ichikawa, Japan 73 B11 35 44N 139 55 E
Ichilo →, Bolivia 173 D5 15 57 S 64 50W
Ichinohe, Japan 70 D10 40 13N 141 17 E
Ichinomiya, Gifu, Japan 73 B8 35 18N 136 48 E
Ichinomiya, Kumamoto, Japan 72 E3 32 58N 131 5 E
Ichinoseki, Japan 70 E10 38 55N 141 8 E
Ichkeul △, Tunisia 108 A1 37 5N 9 37 E
Ichnya, Ukraine 59 G7 50 52N 32 24 E
Icht, Morocco 110 C3 29 6N 8 54W
Ichun = Yichun, China 69 B7 47 44N 128 52 E
Icó, Brazil 170 C4 6 24 S 38 51W
Icoca, Angola 115 D3 6 12 S 16 20 E
Icod, Canary Is. 9 e1 28 22N 16 43W
Icoraci, Brazil 170 B2 1 18 S 48 28W
Icy C., U.S.A. 144 A7 70 20N 161 52W
Ida Grove, U.S.A. 154 D7 42 21N 95 28W
Idabel, U.S.A. 155 J7 33 54N 94 50W
Idaga Hamus, Ethiopia 107 E4 14 13N 39 48 E
Idah, Nigeria 113 D6 7 5N 6 40 E
Idaho □, U.S.A. 158 D7 45 0N 115 0W
Idaho City, U.S.A. 158 E6 43 50N 115 50W
Idaho Falls, U.S.A. 158 E7 43 30N 112 2W
Idalia △, Australia 126 C3 24 49 S 144 36 E
Idanha-a-Nova, Portugal 42 F3 39 50N 7 15W
Idar-Oberstein, Germany 31 F3 49 43N 7 16 E
Iday, Niger 109 F2 14 54N 11 33 E
'Idd el Ghanam, Sudan 109 F4 11 30N 24 19 E
Iddan, Somali Rep. 120 C3 6 10N 48 55 E
Idelès, Algeria 111 D6 23 50N 5 53 E
Idensalmi = Iisalmi, Finland 14 E22 63 32N 27 10 E
Idfû, Egypt 106 C3 24 55N 32 49 E
Ídhi Óros, Greece 39 E5 35 15N 24 45 E
Ídhra, Greece 48 D5 37 20N 23 28 E
Idi, Indonesia 84 A1 5 2N 97 37 E
Idi Amin Dada, L. = Edward, L., Africa 118 C2 0 25 S 29 40 E
Idiofa, Dem. Rep. of the Congo 115 C3 4 55 S 19 42 E
Idjil = Fdérik, Mauritania 110 D2 22 40N 12 45W
Idkerberget, Sweden 16 D9 60 22N 15 15 E
Idku, Bahra el, Egypt 106 H7 31 18N 30 18 E
Idlib, Syria 100 E7 35 55N 36 36 E
Idre, Sweden 16 C6 61 52N 12 42 E
Idria, U.S.A. 160 J6 36 25N 120 41W
Idrija, Slovenia 45 C11 46 0N 14 5 E
Idritsa, Russia 58 D5 56 17N 28 53 E
Idro, Italy 33 E10 45 44N 10 29 E
Idutywa, S. Africa 117 E4 32 8 S 28 18 E
Ieper, Belgium 24 D2 50 51N 2 53 E
Ierápetra, Greece 39 F6 35 1N 25 44 E
Ierissós, Greece 50 F7 40 22N 23 52 E
Ierissóu Kólpos, Greece 50 F7 40 27N 23 57 E
Iernut, Romania 53 D9 46 27N 24 15 E
Ieshima-Shotō, Japan 72 C6 34 40N 134 32 E
Iesi, Italy 45 E10 43 31N 13 14 E
Iésolo, Italy 45 C9 45 32N 12 38 E
Ifach, Peñón de, Spain 41 G5 38 38N 0 5 E
'Ifāl, W. al →, Si. Arabia 96 D2 28 7N 35 3 E
Ifanadiana, Madag. 117 C8 21 19 S 47 39 E
Ife, Nigeria 113 D5 7 30N 4 31 E
Iférouâne, Niger 113 B6 19 5N 8 24 E
Ifetesene, Algeria 111 C5 25 30N 4 33 E
Iffley, Australia 126 B3 18 53 S 141 12 E
Ifon, Nigeria 113 D6 6 58N 5 40 E
Iforas, Adrar des, Africa 111 D5 19 40N 1 40 E
Ifould, L., Australia 125 F5 30 52 S 132 6 E
Ifrane, Morocco 110 B3 33 33N 5 7W
Ifugao □, Phil. 80 C3 16 40N 121 10 E
Iga, Japan 73 C8 34 45N 136 10 E
Iganga, Uganda 118 B3 0 37N 33 28 E
Igara Paraná →, Colombia 168 D3 2 9 S 71 47W
Igarapava, Brazil 171 F2 20 3 S 47 47W
Igarapé Açu, Brazil 170 B2 1 4 S 47 33W
Igarapé-Mirim, Brazil 170 B2 1 59 S 48 58W
Igarka, Russia 66 C9 67 30N 86 33 E
Igatimi, Paraguay 175 A4 24 5 S 55 40W
Igatpuri, India 94 E1 19 40N 73 35 E
Igbetti, Nigeria 113 D5 8 44N 4 8 E
Igbo-Ora, Nigeria 113 D5 7 29N 3 15 E
Igboho, Nigeria 113 D5 8 53N 3 50 E
Igbor, Nigeria 113 D6 7 27N 8 34 E
Iğdır, Turkey 101 C11 39 55N 44 2 E
Igelfors, Sweden 17 F9 58 52N 15 41 E
Iggesund, Sweden 16 C11 61 39N 17 10 E
Ighil Izane = Relizane, Algeria 111 A5 35 44N 0 31 E
Igiugig, U.S.A. 144 G9 59 20N 155 55W
Iglau = Jihlava, Czech Rep. 34 B8 49 28N 15 35 E
Iglésias, Italy 46 C1 39 19N 8 32 E
Igli, Algeria 111 B4 30 25N 2 19W
Iglino, Russia 64 D6 54 50N 56 26 E
Igloolik, Canada 139 B11 69 20N 81 49W
Igluligaarjuk = Chesterfield Inlet, Canada 138 B10 63 30N 90 45W
Iglulik = Igloolik, Canada 139 B11 69 20N 81 49W
'Igma, Gebel el, Egypt 106 B3 28 55N 34 0 E
Ignace, Canada 140 C1 49 30N 91 40W
İğneada, Turkey 51 E11 41 52N 27 59 E
İğneada Burnu, Turkey 51 E12 41 53N 28 2 E
Igoumenítsa, Greece 50 G3 39 32N 20 18 E
Igra, Russia 60 B11 57 33N 53 7 E
Iguaçu △, Brazil 175 B5 25 30 S 54 0W
Iguaçu →, Brazil 175 B5 25 36 S 54 36W
Iguaçu, Cat. del, Brazil 175 B5 25 41 S 54 26W
Iguaçu Falls = Iguaçu, Cat. del, Brazil 175 B5 25 41 S 54 26W
Iguala, Mexico 163 D5 18 20N 99 40W
Igualada, Spain 40 D6 41 37N 1 37 E
Iguape, Brazil 171 F2 24 43 S 47 33W
Iguaratinga = São Francisco do Maranhão, Brazil 170 C3 6 15 S 42 52W
Iguassu = Iguaçu →, Brazil 175 B5 25 36 S 54 36W
Iguatu, Brazil 170 C4 6 20 S 39 18W
Iguazú △, Argentina 175 B5 25 42 S 54 22W
Iguéla, Gabon 114 C1 2 0 S 9 16 E
Iguéla, Lagune, Gabon 114 C2 1 48 S 9 16 E
Iguetti, Sebkhet, Mauritania 110 C3 25 5N 9 50W
Iguig, Phil. 80 C3 17 45N 121 44 E
Igumen = Cherven, Belarus 58 F5 53 45N 28 28 E
Iharana, Madag. 117 A9 13 25 S 50 0 E
Ihbulag, Mongolia 74 C4 43 11N 107 10 E
Iheya-Shima, Japan 71 L3 27 4N 127 58 E
Ihiala, Nigeria 113 D6 5 51N 6 55 E
Ihirene →, Algeria 111 D5 20 28N 4 37 E
Ihosy, Madag. 117 C8 22 24 S 46 8 E
Ihotry, Farihy, Madag. 117 C7 21 56 S 43 41 E
Ihu, Papua N. G. 132 D3 7 55 S 145 24 E
Ihugh, Nigeria 113 D6 7 2N 9 0 E
Ii, Finland 14 D21 65 19N 25 22 E
Ii-Shima, Japan 71 L3 26 43N 127 47 E
Iida, Japan 73 B9 35 35N 137 50 E
Iijoki →, Finland 14 D21 65 20N 25 20 E
Iisalmi, Finland 14 E22 63 32N 27 10 E
Iiyama, Japan 71 F9 36 51N 138 22 E
Iizuka, Japan 72 D2 33 38N 130 42 E
Ijâfene, Mauritania 110 D3 20 40N 8 0W
Ijebu-Igbo, Nigeria 113 D5 6 56N 4 1 E
Ijebu-Ode, Nigeria 113 D5 6 47N 3 58 E
Ijill, Sebkhet, Mauritania 110 D2 22 47N 12 53W
IJmuiden, Neths. 24 B4 52 28N 4 35 E
Ijo älv = Iijoki →, Finland 14 D21 65 20N 25 20 E
IJssel →, Neths. 24 B5 52 35N 5 50 E
IJsselmeer, Neths. 24 B5 52 45N 5 20 E
Ijuí, Brazil 175 B5 28 23 S 53 55W
Ijuí →, Brazil 175 B4 27 58 S 55 20W
Ijūin, Japan 72 F2 31 37N 130 24 E
Ik →, Russia 64 D4 55 41N 53 29 E
Ikalamavony, Madag. 117 C8 21 9 S 46 35 E
Ikale, Nigeria 113 D6 7 40N 5 37 E
Ikali, Dem. Rep. of the Congo 114 C4 2 2 S 21 4 E
Ikaluktutiak, Canada 138 B9 69 10N 105 0W
Ikamatua, N.Z. 131 C6 42 16 S 171 41 E
Ikang, Nigeria 113 E6 4 49N 8 30 E
Ikara, Nigeria 113 C6 11 12N 8 15 E
Ikare, Nigeria 113 D6 7 32N 5 40 E
Ikaría, Greece 49 D8 37 35N 26 10 E
Ikast, Denmark 17 H3 56 8N 9 10 E
Ikeda, Japan 72 C5 34 1N 133 48 E
Ikeja, Nigeria 113 D5 6 36N 3 23 E
Ikela, Dem. Rep. of the Congo 114 C4 1 6 S 23 6 E
Ikélemba, Congo 114 B3 1 12N 16 38 E
Ikélemba →, Dem. Rep. of the Congo 114 B3 0 7N 18 17 E
Ikengo, Dem. Rep. of the Congo 114 C3 0 8 S 18 8 E
Ikerre-Ekiti, Nigeria 113 D6 7 25N 5 19 E
Ikhtiman, Bulgaria 50 D7 42 27N 23 48 E
Iki, Japan 72 D1 33 45N 129 42 E
Iki-Kaikyō, Japan 72 D1 33 40N 129 45 E
Ikimba L., Tanzania 118 C3 1 30 S 31 20 E
Ikire, Nigeria 113 D5 7 23N 4 15 E
Ikitsuki-Shima, Japan 72 D1 33 23N 129 26 E
İkizdere, Turkey 101 B9 40 46N 40 32 E
Iko, Congo 114 C3 0 35 S 16 0 E
Ikom, Nigeria 113 D6 6 0N 8 42 E
Ikomu, Dem. Rep. of the Congo 114 C3 1 54 S 19 40 E
Ikongo, Madag. 117 C8 21 52 S 47 27 E
Ikopa →, Madag. 117 B8 16 45 S 46 40 E
Ikorongo ⌂, Tanzania 118 C3 1 50 S 34 53 E
Ikot Ekpene, Nigeria 113 D6 5 12N 7 40 E
Ikparjuk = Arctic Bay, Canada 139 A11 73 1N 85 7W
Ikramovo = Dzhuma, Uzbekistan 65 D3 39 42N 66 40 E
Ikungu, Tanzania 118 C3 1 33 S 33 42 E
Ikuno, Japan 72 B6 35 10N 134 48 E
Ikurun, Nigeria 113 D5 7 54N 4 40 E
Il-Kullana, Malta 38 F7 35 50N 14 24 E
Il-Munxar, Malta 38 F8 35 51N 14 34 E
Ila, Dem. Rep. of the Congo 114 C4 2 53 S 21 7 E
Ila, Nigeria 113 D5 8 0N 4 39 E
Ilafer, Algeria 111 D5 21 40N 1 58 E
Ilagan, Phil. 80 C3 17 7N 121 53 E
Ilaka, Madag. 117 B8 19 33 S 48 52 E
Īlām, Iran 101 F12 33 36N 46 36 E
Ilam, Nepal 93 F12 26 58N 87 58 E
Īlām □, Iran 96 C5 33 0N 47 0 E
Ilan, Taiwan 77 E13 24 45N 121 44 E
Ilanskiy, Russia 67 D10 56 14N 96 3 E
Ilanz, Switz. 33 C8 46 46N 9 12 E
Ilaro, Nigeria 113 D5 6 53N 3 3 E
Ilatane, Niger 113 B5 16 30N 4 45 E
Ilave, Peru 172 D4 16 5 S 69 40W
Iława, Poland 54 E6 53 36N 19 34 E
Ilayangudi, India 95 K4 9 34N 78 37 E
Ile →, Kazakhstan 66 E8 45 53N 77 10 E
Île-à-la-Crosse, Canada 143 B7 55 27N 107 53W
Île-à-la-Crosse, Lac, Canada 143 B7 55 40N 107 45W
Île-de-France □, France 27 D9 49 0N 2 20 E
Ileanda, Romania 53 C8 47 20N 23 38 E
Ilebo, Dem. Rep. of the Congo 115 C4 4 17 S 20 55 E
Ilek, Russia 64 F4 51 32N 53 21 E
Ilek →, Russia 64 F4 51 30N 53 22 E
Iler, Algeria 111 D5 20 57N 3 21 E
Iler, O. →, Algeria 111 D5 20 59N 3 14 E
Ilero, Nigeria 113 D5 8 0N 3 20 E
Ilesha, Kwara, Nigeria 113 D5 8 57N 3 28 E
Ilesha, Oyo, Nigeria 113 D5 7 37N 4 40 E
Ilet = Krasnogorskiy, Russia 60 B9 56 10N 48 28 E
Iletskaya = Sol Iletsk, Russia 64 F5 51 10N 55 0 E
Iletsky Gorodok = Ilek, Russia 64 F4 51 32N 53 21 E
Ilford, Canada 143 B9 56 4N 95 35W
Ilfracombe, Australia 126 C3 23 30 S 144 30 E
Ilfracombe, U.K. 21 F3 51 12N 4 8W
Ilgaz, Turkey 100 B5 40 55N 33 37 E
Ilgaz Dağları, Turkey 100 B5 41 10N 33 50 E
Ilgın, Turkey 100 C4 38 16N 31 55 E
Ilha, Pta. da, Azores 9 d1 38 25N 28 3W
Ilha de Moçambique, Mozam. 119 F5 15 4 S 40 52 E
Ilha Grande, Brazil 169 D4 0 27 S 65 2W
Ilha Grande, B. da, Brazil 171 F3 23 9 S 44 30W
Ílhavo, Portugal 42 E2 40 33N 8 43W
Ilhéus, Brazil 171 D4 14 49 S 39 2W
Ili = Ile →, Kazakhstan 66 E8 45 53N 77 10 E
Ilia, Romania 52 E7 45 57N 22 40 E
Ilia □, Greece 48 D3 37 45N 21 35 E
Iliamna, U.S.A. 144 G9 59 45N 154 55W
Iliamna L., U.S.A. 144 G9 59 30N 155 0W
Ilian, Mt., Phil. 81 F2 10 26N 119 33 E
Iliç, Turkey 101 C8 39 27N 38 33 E
Ilıca, Turkey 49 B9 39 52N 27 46 E
Ilich, Kazakhstan 65 C4 40 50N 68 27 E
Ilichevsk, Azerbaijan 101 C11 39 22N 45 5 E
Iligan, Phil. 81 G5 8 12N 124 13 E
Iligan Bay, Phil. 81 G5 8 25N 124 5 E
Iligan Pt., Phil. 80 B4 18 25N 122 25 E
Ilíki, L., Greece 48 C5 38 24N 23 15 E
Ilin I., Phil. 80 E3 12 14N 121 5 E
Ilio Pt., U.S.A. 145 B4 21 13N 157 16W
Iliodhrómia, Greece 48 B5 39 12N 23 50 E
Ilion, U.S.A. 151 D9 43 1N 75 2W
Ilirska-Bistrica, Slovenia 45 C11 45 34N 14 14 E
Iliysk = Qapshaghay, Kazakhstan 65 B8 43 51N 77 14 E
Ilkal, India 95 G3 15 57N 76 8 E
Ilkenau = Olkusz, Poland 55 H6 50 18N 19 33 E
Ilkeston, U.K. 20 E6 52 58N 1 19W
Ilkley, U.K. 20 D6 53 56N 1 48W
Illampu = Ancohuma, Nevado, Bolivia 172 D4 16 0 S 68 50W
Illana B., Phil. 81 H4 7 35N 123 45 E
Illapel, Chile 174 C1 32 0 S 71 10W
Ille-et-Vilaine □, France 26 D5 48 10N 1 30W
Ille-sur-Têt, France 28 F6 42 40N 2 38 E
Illéla, Niger 113 C6 14 32N 5 20 E
Iller →, Germany 31 G5 48 23N 9 58 E
Illertissen, Germany 31 G6 48 12N 10 7 E
Illescas, Spain 42 E7 40 8N 3 51W
Illetas, Spain 38 B3 39 32N 2 35 E
Illichivsk, Ukraine 59 J6 46 20N 30 35 E
Illiers-Combray, France 26 D8 48 18N 1 15 E
Illimani, Nevado, Bolivia 172 D4 16 30 S 67 50W
Illinois □, U.S.A. 156 D7 40 15N 89 30W
Illinois →, U.S.A. 156 F6 38 58N 90 28W
Illiopolis, U.S.A. 156 E7 39 51N 89 15W
Illium = Troy, Turkey 49 B8 39 57N 26 12 E
Illizi, Algeria 111 C6 26 31N 8 32 E
Illkirch-Graffenstaden, France 27 D14 48 34N 7 42 E
Íllora, Spain 43 H7 37 17N 3 53W
Ilulissat, Greenland 10 D5 69 12N 51 10W
Ilm →, Germany 30 D7 51 6N 11 40 E
Ilmajoki, Finland 15 E20 62 44N 22 34 E
Ilmen, Ozero, Russia 58 C6 58 15N 31 10 E
Ilmenau = Jordanów, Poland 55 J6 49 41N 19 49 E
Ilmenau = Limanowa, Poland 55 J7 49 42N 20 22 E
Ilmenau, Germany 30 E6 50 41N 10 54 E
Ilnytsya, Ukraine 52 B8 48 21N 23 5 E
Ilo, Peru 172 D3 17 40 S 71 20W
Ilobu, Nigeria 113 D5 7 45N 4 25 E
Ilocos Norte □, Phil. 80 B3 18 10N 120 45 E
Ilocos Sur □, Phil. 80 C3 17 20N 120 35 E
Iloilo, Phil. 81 F4 10 45N 122 33 E
Iloilo □, Phil. 81 F4 11 0N 122 40 E
Ilora, Nigeria 113 D5 7 45N 3 50 E
Ilorin, Nigeria 113 D5 8 30N 4 35 E
Ilovatka, Russia 60 E7 50 30N 45 50 E
Ilovlya, Russia 61 F7 49 15N 44 2 E
Ilovlya →, Russia 61 F7 49 14N 44 0 E
Iłowa, Poland 55 G2 51 30N 15 10 E
Ilubabor, Ethiopia 107 F4 7 25N 35 0 E
Ilva Mică, Romania 53 C9 47 17N 24 40 E
Ilwaco, U.S.A. 160 D2 46 19N 124 3W
Ilwaki, Indonesia 82 C3 7 55 S 126 30 E
Ilyichevsk = Illichivsk, Ukraine 59 J6 46 20N 30 35 E
Iłża, Poland 55 G8 51 10N 21 15 E
Iłżanka →, Poland 55 G8 51 14N 21 48 E
Imabari, Japan 72 C5 34 4N 133 0 E
Imaichi, Japan 73 A11 36 43N 139 46 E
Imaloto →, Madag. 117 C8 23 27 S 45 13 E
İmamoğlu, Turkey 100 D6 37 15N 35 38 E
Iman = Dalnerechensk, Russia 67 E14 45 50N 133 40 E
Imandra, Ozero, Russia 56 A5 67 30N 33 0 E
Imanombo, Madag. 117 C8 24 26 S 45 49 E
Imari, Japan 72 D1 33 15N 129 52 E
Imasa, Sudan 106 D4 18 0N 36 12 E
Imathía □, Greece 50 F6 40 30N 22 15 E
Imatra, Finland 58 B5 61 12N 28 48 E
Imazu, Japan 73 B8 35 24N 136 2 E
Imbabura □, Ecuador 168 C2 0 30N 78 45W
Imbaimadai, Guyana 169 B5 5 44N 60 17W
Imbonga, Dem. Rep. of the Congo 114 C3 0 43 S 19 44 E
Imdahane, Morocco 110 B3 32 8N 7 0W
Iménas, Mali 113 B5 16 20N 0 40 E
imeni 26 Bakinskikh Komissarov = Neftçala, Azerbaijan 97 B6 39 19N 49 12 E
imeni 26 Bakinskikh Komissarov, Turkmenistan 97 B7 39 22N 54 10 E
imeni Dvadtsati Shesti Bakinskikh Komissarov = Neftçala, Azerbaijan 97 B6 39 19N 49 12 E
imeni Dzerzhinskogo = Naryan-Mar, Russia 56 A9 67 42N 53 12 E
imeni Khamzy Khakimzade = Khamza, Uzbekistan 65 C5 40 25N 71 29 E
imeni Mikoyana = Kara-Balta, Kyrgyzstan 65 B6 42 50N 73 49 E
imeni Petrovskogo G.I. = Horodyshche, Ukraine 59 H6 49 17N 31 27 E
imeni Stalina = Shakhrikhan, Uzbekistan 65 C6 40 42N 72 3 E
imeni Sverdlova = Sverdlovsk, Ukraine 59 H10 48 5N 39 47 E
imeni Tovarishcha Khateyevicha = Synelnykove, Ukraine 59 H8 48 25N 35 30 E
imeni Tretyego Internatsionala = Novoshakhtinsk, Russia 59 J10 47 46N 39 58 E
Imeri, Serra, Brazil 168 C4 0 50N 65 25W
Imerimandroso, Madag. 117 B8 17 26 S 48 35 E
Imesan, Mauritania 110 D1 22 54N 15 30W
Imese, Dem. Rep. of the Congo 114 B3 2 6N 18 9 E

Imi, *Ethiopia* **107 F5** 6 28N 42 10 E
Imishly = Imişli, *Azerbaijan* **61 L9** 39 55N 48 4 E
Imişli, *Azerbaijan* **61 L9** 39 55N 48 4 E
Imitek, *Morocco* **110 C3** 29 43N 8 10W
Imlay, *U.S.A.* **158 F4** 40 40N 118 9W
Imlay City, *U.S.A.* **150 D1** 43 2N 83 5W
Immaseri, *Sudan* **107 D2** 15 40N 25 31 E
Immenstadt, *Germany* **31 H6** 47 33N 10 13 E
Immingham, *U.K.* **20 D7** 53 37N 0 13W
Immokalee, *U.S.A.* **153 J8** 26 25N 81 25W
Imo □, *Nigeria* **113 D6** 5 30N 7 10 E
Imo →, *Nigeria* **113 E6** 4 36N 7 35 E
Imola, *Italy* **45 D8** 44 20N 11 42 E
Imotski, *Croatia* **45 E14** 43 27N 17 12 E
Impé, *Congo* **114 C3** 2 45 S 15 16 E
Imperatorskaya Gavan = Vanino, *Russia* **67 E15** 48 50N 140 5 E
Imperatriz, *Amazonas, Brazil* **172 B4** 5 18 S 67 11W
Imperatriz, *Maranhão, Brazil* **170 C2** 5 30 S 47 29W
Impéria, *Italy* **44 E5** 43 53N 8 3 E
Imperial, *Canada* **143 C7** 51 21N 105 28W
Imperial, *Peru* **172 C2** 13 4 S 76 21W
Imperial, *Calif., U.S.A.* **161 N11** 32 51N 115 34W
Imperial, *Nebr., U.S.A.* **154 E4** 40 31N 101 39W
Imperial Beach, *U.S.A.* **161 N9** 32 35N 117 8W
Imperial Dam, *U.S.A.* **161 N12** 32 55N 114 25W
Imperial Reservoir, *U.S.A.* **161 N12** 32 53N 114 28W
Imperial Valley, *U.S.A.* **161 N11** 33 0N 115 30W
Imperieuse Reef, *Australia* **124 C2** 17 36 S 118 50 E
Impfondo, *Congo* **114 B3** 1 40N 18 0 E
Imphal, *India* **90 C4** 24 48N 93 56 E
Imphy, *France* **27 F10** 46 55N 3 16 E
Impulo, *Angola* **115 E2** 13 51 S 13 39 E
Imranlı, *Turkey* **101 C8** 39 54N 38 7 E
Imroz = Gökçeada, *Turkey* **51 F9** 40 10N 25 50 E
Imroz, *Turkey* **51 F9** 40 10N 25 55 E
Imst, *Austria* **34 D3** 47 15N 10 44 E
Imuris, *Mexico* **162 A2** 30 47N 110 52W
Imuruan B., *Phil.* **81 F2** 10 40N 119 10 E
Imus, *Phil.* **80 D3** 14 26N 120 56 E
In Akhmed, *Mali* **113 B4** 19 49N 0 56W
In Aleï, *Mali* **112 B4** 17 42N 2 30W
In Amenas, *Algeria* **111 C6** 28 5N 9 33 E
In Atei, *Algeria* **111 D6** 20 33N 6 4 E
In Belbel, *Algeria* **111 C5** 27 55N 1 12 E
In Dekkar, O. →, *Algeria* **111 C6** 27 12N 6 16 E
In Delimane, *Mali* **113 B5** 15 52N 1 31 E
In Guezzam, *Algeria* **111 E6** 19 37N 5 52 E
In Koufi, *Mali* **113 B5** 19 11N 1 25 E
In Rhar, *Algeria* **111 C5** 27 10N 1 59 E
In Salah, *Algeria* **111 C5** 27 10N 2 32 E
In Tallak, *Mali* **113 B5** 16 19N 3 15 E
In Tebezas, *Mali* **113 B5** 17 49N 1 53 E
Ina, *Japan* **73 B9** 35 50N 137 55 E
Ina, *U.S.A.* **157 F8** 38 9N 88 54W
Ina-Bonchi, *Japan* **73 B9** 35 45N 137 58 E
Inabanga, *Phil.* **81 F5** 10 2N 124 4 E
Inaguan, *Phil.* **81 G2** 9 33N 118 39 E
Inagua △, *Bahamas* **165 B5** 21 5N 73 24W
Inajá, *Brazil* **170 C4** 8 54 S 37 49W
Inambari →, *Peru* **172 C4** 12 41 S 69 44W
Inangahua, *N.Z.* **131 B6** 41 52 S 171 59 E
Inanwatan, *Indonesia* **83 B4** 2 8 S 132 10 E
Iñapari, *Peru* **172 C4** 11 0 S 69 40W
Inarajan, *Guam* **133 R15** 13 16N 144 45 E
Inari, *Finland* **14 B22** 68 54N 27 1 E
Inarijärvi, *Finland* **14 B22** 69 0N 28 0 E
Inawashiro-Ko, *Japan* **70 F10** 37 29N 140 6 E
Inazawa, *Japan* **73 B8** 35 15N 136 47 E
Inbin, *Burma* **90 F5** 18 6N 95 16 E
Inca, *Spain* **38 B3** 39 43N 2 54 E
Inca de Oro, *Chile* **174 B2** 26 45 S 69 54W
Incaguasi, *Chile* **174 B1** 29 12 S 71 5W
Ince Burun, *Turkey* **100 A6** 42 7N 34 56 E
Incekum Burnu, *Turkey* **100 D5** 36 13N 33 57 E
Incesu, *Turkey* **96 B2** 38 38N 35 11 E
Inch'ŏn, *S. Korea* **75 F14** 37 27N 126 40 E
Incio = Cruz de Incio, *Spain* **42 C3** 42 39N 7 21W
Incirliova, *Turkey* **49 D9** 37 50N 27 41 E
Incline Village, *U.S.A.* **158 G4** 39 10N 119 58W
Incomáti →, *Mozam.* **117 D5** 25 46 S 32 43 E
Incudine, Mte., *France* **29 G13** 41 50N 9 12 E
Inda Silase, *Ethiopia* **107 E4** 14 10N 38 15 E
Indal, *Sweden* **16 B11** 62 35N 17 5 E
Indalsälven →, *Sweden* **16 B11** 62 36N 17 30 E
Indaw, *Burma* **90 C6** 24 15N 96 5 E
Indawgyi In, *Burma* **90 C6** 25 8N 96 20 E
Indbir, *Ethiopia* **107 F4** 8 7N 37 52 E
Indefatigable, I. = Santa Cruz, I., *Ecuador* **172 a** 0 38 S 90 23W
Independence, *Calif., U.S.A.* **160 J8** 36 48N 118 12W
Independence, *Iowa, U.S.A.* **156 B5** 42 28N 91 54W
Independence, *Kans., U.S.A.* **155 G7** 37 14N 95 42W
Independence, *Ky., U.S.A.* **157 F12** 38 57N 84 33W
Independence, *Mo., U.S.A.* **156 E2** 39 6N 94 25W
Independence Fjord, *Greenland* **10 A8** 82 10N 29 0W
Independence Mts., *U.S.A.* **158 F5** 41 20N 116 0W
Independência, *Brazil* **170 C3** 5 23 S 40 19W
Independenţa, *Romania* **53 E12** 45 25N 27 42 E
Index, *U.S.A.* **160 C5** 47 50N 121 33W
Indi, *India* **94 F2** 17 10N 75 58 E
India ■, *Asia* **89 C6** 20 0N 78 0 E
Indialantic, *U.S.A.* **153 G9** 28 6N 80 34W
Indian →, *U.S.A.* **153 G9** 27 59N 80 34W
Indian Cabins, *Canada* **142 B5** 59 52N 117 40W
Indian Harbour, *Canada* **141 B8** 54 27N 57 13W
Indian Harbour Beach, *U.S.A.* **153 G9** 28 10N 80 35W
Indian Head, *Canada* **143 C8** 50 30N 103 41W
Indian Lake, *U.S.A.* **151 C10** 43 47N 74 16W
Indian Ocean **121 E6** 5 0 S 75 0 E
Indian Rocks Beach, *U.S.A.* **153 H7** 27 53N 82 51W
Indian Springs, *U.S.A.* **161 J11** 36 35N 115 40W
Indiana, *U.S.A.* **150 F5** 40 37N 79 9W
Indiana □, *U.S.A.* **157 E11** 40 0N 86 0W
Indiana Dunes ⌓, *U.S.A.* **157 C9** 41 40N 87 0W
Indianapolis, *U.S.A.* **157 E10** 39 46N 86 9W
Indianapolis International ✕ (IND), *U.S.A.* **157 E10** 39 43N 86 17W
Indianola, *Iowa, U.S.A.* **156 C3** 41 22N 93 34W
Indianola, *Miss., U.S.A.* **155 J9** 33 27N 90 39W
Indiantown, *U.S.A.* **153 H9** 27 1N 80 28W
Indiapora, *Brazil* **171 E1** 19 57 S 50 17W
Indiga, *Russia* **56 A8** 67 38N 49 9 E
Indigirka →, *Russia* **67 B15** 70 48N 148 54 E
Inđija, *Serbia & M.* **52 E5** 45 6N 20 7 E
Indio, *U.S.A.* **161 M10** 33 43N 116 13W
Indira Gandhi Canal, *India* **92 F5** 28 0N 72 0 E
Indira Pt., *India* **95 L11** 6 44N 93 49 E
Indispensable Strait, *Solomon Is.* **133 M11** 9 0 S 160 30 E
Indo-China, *Asia* **62 H14** 15 0N 102 0 E
Indonesia ■, *Asia* **85 C4** 5 0 S 115 0 E
Indore, *India* **92 H6** 22 42N 75 53 E
Indramayu, *Indonesia* **85 D3** 6 20 S 108 19 E
Indrapura = Kerinci, *Indonesia* **84 C2** 1 40 S 101 15 E
Indravati →, *India* **94 E5** 19 20N 80 20 E
Indre □, *France* **27 F8** 46 50N 1 39 E
Indre →, *France* **26 E7** 47 16N 0 11 E
Indre Arna, *Norway* **18 D2** 60 26N 5 30 E
Indre-et-Loire □, *France* **26 E7** 47 20N 0 40 E
Indrio, *U.S.A.* **153 H9** 27 31N 80 21W
Indulkana, *Australia* **127 D1** 26 58 S 133 5 E
Indungo, *Angola* **115 E3** 14 48 S 16 17 E
Indura, *Belarus* **54 E10** 53 26N 23 53 E
Indus →, *Pakistan* **91 D2** 24 20N 67 47 E
Indus, Mouths of the, *Pakistan* **91 E3** 24 0N 68 0 E
Industry, *U.S.A.* **156 D6** 40 20N 90 36W
Inebolu, *Turkey* **100 B5** 41 55N 33 40 E
Inecik, *Turkey* **51 F11** 40 56N 27 16 E
İnegöl, *Turkey* **51 F13** 40 5N 29 31 E
Inés, Mt., *Argentina* **176 C3** 48 30 S 69 40W
Ineu, *Romania* **52 D6** 46 26N 21 51 E
Inezgane, *Morocco* **110 B3** 30 25N 9 29W
Infanta, *Phil.* **80 D3** 14 45N 121 39 E
Infantes = Villanueva de los Infantes, *Spain* **43 G7** 38 43N 3 1W
Infiernillo, Presa del, *Mexico* **162 D4** 18 9N 102 0W
Infiesto, *Spain* **42 B5** 43 21N 5 21W
Inga, Barrage d', *Dem. Rep. of the Congo* **115 D2** 5 39 S 13 39 E
Ingabu, *Burma* **90 G5** 17 37N 95 20 E
Inganda, *Dem. Rep. of the Congo* **114 C4** 0 5 S 20 57 E
Ingapirca, *Ecuador* **168 D2** 2 38 S 78 56W
Ingelstad, *Sweden* **17 H8** 56 45N 14 56 E
Ingende, *Dem. Rep. of the Congo* **114 C3** 0 12 S 18 57 E
Ingeniero Jacobacci, *Argentina* **176 B3** 41 20 S 69 36W
Ingenio, *Canary Is.* **9 e1** 27 55N 15 26W
Ingenio Santa Ana, *Argentina* **174 B2** 27 25 S 65 40W
Ingersoll, *Canada* **140 D3** 43 4N 80 55W
Ingham, *Australia* **126 B4** 18 43 S 146 10 E
Ingichka, *Uzbekistan* **65 D2** 39 47N 65 58 E
Ingleborough, *U.K.* **20 C5** 54 10N 2 22W
Inglefield Land, *Greenland* **10 B4** 78 30N 70 0W
Inglewood, *Queens., Australia* **127 D5** 28 25 S 151 2 E
Inglewood, *Vic., Australia* **128 D5** 36 29 S 143 53 E
Inglewood, *N.Z.* **130 F3** 39 9 S 174 14 E
Inglewood, *U.S.A.* **161 M8** 33 58N 118 21W
Inglis, *U.S.A.* **153 F7** 29 2N 82 40W
Ingólf Fjord, *Greenland* **10 A9** 80 35N 17 30W
Ingólfshöfði, *Iceland* **14 E5** 63 48N 16 39W
Ingolstadt, *Germany* **31 G7** 48 46N 11 26 E
Ingomar, *U.S.A.* **158 C10** 46 35N 107 23W
Ingonish, *Canada* **141 C7** 46 42N 60 18W
Ingore, *Guinea-Biss.* **112 C1** 12 24N 15 48W
Ingraj Bazar, *India* **93 G13** 24 58N 88 10 E
Ingrid Christensen Coast, *Antarctica* **7 C6** 69 30 S 76 0 E
Ingul = Inhul →, *Ukraine* **59 J7** 46 50N 32 0 E
Ingulec = Inhulec, *Ukraine* **59 J7** 47 42N 33 14 E
Ingulets = Inhulets →, *Ukraine* **59 J7** 46 46N 32 47 E
Inguri = Enguri →, *Georgia* **61 J5** 42 27N 41 38 E
Ingushetia □, *Russia* **61 J7** 43 20N 44 50 E
Ingwavuma, *S. Africa* **117 D5** 27 9 S 31 59 E
Inhaca, *Mozam.* **117 D5** 26 1 S 32 57 E
Inhafenga, *Mozam.* **117 C5** 20 36 S 33 53 E
Inhambane, *Mozam.* **117 C6** 23 54 S 35 30 E
Inhambane □, *Mozam.* **117 C5** 22 30 S 34 20 E
Inhambupe, *Brazil* **171 D4** 11 47 S 38 21W
Inhaminga, *Mozam.* **119 F4** 18 26 S 35 0 E
Inharrime, *Mozam.* **117 C6** 24 30 S 35 0 E
Inharrime →, *Mozam.* **117 C6** 24 30 S 35 0 E
Inhisar, *Turkey* **49 A12** 40 3N 30 23 E
Inhul →, *Ukraine* **59 J7** 46 50N 32 0 E
Inhulec, *Ukraine* **59 J7** 47 42N 33 14 E
Inhulets →, *Ukraine* **59 J7** 46 46N 32 47 E
Inhuma, *Brazil* **170 C3** 6 40 S 41 42W
Inhumas, *Brazil* **171 E2** 16 22 S 49 30W
Iniesta, *Spain* **41 F3** 39 27N 1 45W
Ining = Yining, *China* **66 E9** 43 58N 81 10 E
Inini □, *Fr. Guiana* **169 C7** 4 0N 53 0W
Inírida →, *Colombia* **168 C4** 3 55N 67 52W
Inishbofin, *Ireland* **23 C1** 53 37N 10 13W
Inisheer, *Ireland* **23 C2** 53 3N 9 32W
Inishfree B., *Ireland* **23 A3** 55 4N 8 23W
Inishkea North, *Ireland* **23 B1** 54 9N 10 11W
Inishkea South, *Ireland* **23 B1** 54 7N 10 12W
Inishmaan, *Ireland* **23 C2** 53 5N 9 35W
Inishmore, *Ireland* **23 C2** 53 8N 9 45W
Inishowen Pen., *Ireland* **23 A4** 55 14N 7 15W
Inishshark, *Ireland* **23 C1** 53 37N 10 16W
Inishturk, *Ireland* **23 C1** 53 42N 10 7W
Inishvickillane, *Ireland* **23 D1** 52 3N 10 37W
Injibara, *Ethiopia* **107 E4** 10 59N 37 0 E
Injune, *Australia* **127 D4** 25 53 S 148 32 E
Inkisi →, *Dem. Rep. of the Congo* **115 D3** 4 46 S 14 52 E
Inklin →, *Canada* **142 B2** 58 50N 133 10W
Inland Kaikoura Ra., *N.Z.* **131 B8** 41 59 S 173 41 E
Inland Sea = Setonaikai, *Japan* **72 C5** 34 20N 133 30 E
Inle L., *Burma* **90 E6** 20 30N 96 58 E
Inlet, *U.S.A.* **151 C10** 43 45N 74 48W
Inn →, *Austria* **34 C6** 48 35N 13 28 E
Innamincka, *Australia* **127 D3** 27 44 S 140 46 E
Innbygda, *Norway* **18 C9** 61 19N 12 17 E
Inner Hebrides, *U.K.* **22 E2** 57 0N 6 30W
Inner Mongolia = Nei Monggol Zizhiqu □, *China* **74 D7** 42 0N 112 0 E
Inner Sound, *U.K.* **22 D3** 57 30N 5 55W
Innerkip, *Canada* **150 C4** 43 13N 80 42W
Innerkirchen, *Switz.* **32 C6** 46 43N 8 14 E
Innes △, *Australia* **128 C2** 35 52 S 136 53 E
Innetalling I., *Canada* **140 A4** 56 0N 79 0W
Innisfail, *Australia* **126 B4** 17 33 S 146 5 E
Innisfail, *Canada* **142 C6** 52 2N 113 57W
In'noshima, *Japan* **72 C5** 34 19N 133 10 E
Innsbruck, *Austria* **34 D4** 47 16N 11 23 E
Innviertel, *Austria* **34 C6** 48 15N 13 15 E
Innvik, *Norway* **18 C3** 61 51N 6 37 E
Inny →, *Ireland* **23 C4** 53 30N 7 50W
Ino, *Japan* **72 D5** 33 33N 133 26 E
Inobonto, *Indonesia* **82 A2** 0 52N 123 57 E
Inocência, *Brazil* **171 E1** 19 47 S 51 48W
Inongo, *Dem. Rep. of the Congo* **114 C3** 1 55 S 18 30 E
Inoni, *Congo* **114 C3** 3 4 S 15 39 E
İnönü, *Turkey* **49 B12** 39 48N 30 9 E
Inoucdjouac = Inukjuak, *Canada* **139 C12** 58 25N 78 15W
Inowrocław, *Poland* **55 F5** 52 50N 18 12 E
Inpundong, *N. Korea* **75 D14** 41 25N 126 34 E
Inquisivi, *Bolivia* **172 D4** 16 50 S 67 10W
Ins, *Switz.* **32 B4** 47 1N 7 7 E
Inscription, C., *Australia* **125 E1** 25 29 S 112 59 E
Insein, *Burma* **90 G6** 16 50N 96 5 E
Insjön, *Sweden* **16 D9** 60 41N 15 6 E
Ińsko, *Poland* **54 E2** 53 25N 15 32 E
Insterberg = Chernyakhovsk, *Russia* **15 J19** 54 36N 21 48 E
Însurăţei, *Romania* **53 F12** 44 50N 27 40 E
Inta, *Russia* **56 A11** 66 5N 60 8 E
Intendente Alvear, *Argentina* **174 D3** 35 12 S 63 32W
Intepe, *Turkey* **49 A8** 40 1N 26 20 E
Interlachen, *U.S.A.* **153 F8** 29 37N 81 53W
Interlaken, *Switz.* **32 C5** 46 41N 7 50 E
Interlaken, *U.S.A.* **151 D8** 42 37N 76 44W
International Falls, *U.S.A.* **154 A8** 48 36N 93 25W
Interview I., *India* **95 H11** 12 55N 92 43 E
Intiyaco, *Argentina* **174 B3** 28 43 S 60 5W
Întorsura Buzăului, *Romania* **53 E11** 45 41N 26 2 E
Intragna, *Switz.* **33 D7** 46 11N 8 42 E
Intutu, *Peru* **168 D3** 3 32 S 74 48W
Inubō-Zaki, *Japan* **73 B12** 35 42N 140 52 E
Inukjuak, *Canada* **139 C12** 58 25N 78 15W
Inútil, B., *Chile* **176 D2** 53 30 S 70 15W
Inuvik, *Canada* **138 B6** 68 16N 133 40W
Inuyama, *Japan* **73 B8** 35 23N 136 56 E
Inveraray, *U.K.* **22 E3** 56 14N 5 5W
Inverbervie, *U.K.* **22 E6** 56 51N 2 17W
Invercargill, *N.Z.* **131 G3** 46 24 S 168 24 E
Inverclyde □, *U.K.* **22 F4** 55 55N 4 49W
Inverell, *Australia* **127 D5** 29 45 S 151 8 E
Invergordon, *U.K.* **22 D4** 57 41N 4 10W
Inverleigh, *Australia* **128 E6** 38 6 S 144 3 E
Inverloch, *Australia* **127 F4** 38 38 S 145 45 E
Invermere, *Canada* **142 C5** 50 30N 116 2W
Inverness, *Canada* **141 C7** 46 15N 61 19W
Inverness, *U.K.* **22 D4** 57 29N 4 13W
Inverness, *Ala., U.S.A.* **152 C4** 32 1N 85 45W
Inverness, *Fla., U.S.A.* **153 G7** 28 50N 82 20W
Inverurie, *U.K.* **22 D6** 57 17N 2 23W
Investigator Group, *Australia* **127 E1** 34 45 S 134 20 E
Investigator Str., *Australia* **128 C2** 35 30 S 137 0 E
Inya, *Russia* **66 D9** 50 28N 86 37 E
Inyanga, *Zimbabwe* **119 F3** 18 12 S 32 40 E
Inyangani, *Zimbabwe* **119 F3** 18 5 S 32 50 E
Inyantue, *Zimbabwe* **116 B4** 18 33 S 26 39 E
Inyo Mts., *U.S.A.* **160 J9** 36 40N 118 0W
Inyokern, *U.S.A.* **161 K9** 35 39N 117 49W
Inywa, *Burma* **90 D6** 23 56N 96 17 E
Inza, *Russia* **60 D8** 53 55N 46 25 E
Inzer, *Russia* **64 D6** 54 14N 57 34 E
Inzhavino, *Russia* **60 D6** 52 22N 42 30 E
Inzia →, *Dem. Rep. of the Congo* **115 C3** 3 45 S 17 57 E
Iō-Jima, *Japan* **71 J5** 30 48N 130 18 E
Ioánnina, *Greece* **48 B2** 39 42N 20 47 E
Ioánnina □, *Greece* **48 B2** 39 39N 20 57 E
Iokea, *Papua N. G.* **132 E4** 8 25 S 146 16 E
Iola, *U.S.A.* **155 G7** 37 55N 95 24W
Ioma, *Papua N. G.* **132 E4** 8 19 S 147 52 E
Ion Corvin, *Romania* **53 F12** 44 7N 27 50 E
Iôna, *Angola* **115 F2** 16 54 S 12 34 E
Iona, *U.K.* **22 E2** 56 20N 6 25W
Iona △, *Angola* **115 F2** 16 47 S 12 20 E
Ione, *U.S.A.* **160 G6** 38 21N 120 56W
Iongo, *Angola* **115 D3** 9 11 S 17 45 E
Ionia, *U.S.A.* **157 B11** 42 59N 85 4W
Ionian Is. = Iónioi Nísoi, *Greece* **39 B1** 38 40N 20 0 E
Ionian Sea, *Medit. S.* **12 H9** 37 30N 17 30 E
Iónioi Nísoi, *Greece* **39 B1** 38 40N 20 0 E
Iónioi Nísoi □, *Greece* **39 B2** 38 40N 20 0 E
Íos, *Greece* **49 E7** 36 41N 25 20 E
Iowa □, *U.S.A.* **156 C3** 42 18N 93 30W
Iowa →, *U.S.A.* **156 C5** 41 10N 91 1W
Iowa City, *U.S.A.* **156 C5** 41 40N 91 32W
Iowa Falls, *U.S.A.* **156 B3** 42 31N 93 16W
Iowa Park, *U.S.A.* **155 J5** 33 57N 98 40W
Ipala, *Tanzania* **118 C3** 4 30 S 32 52 E
Ipameri, *Brazil* **171 E2** 17 44 S 48 9W
Ipanema, *Brazil* **171 E3** 19 47 S 41 44W
Iparía, *Peru* **172 B3** 9 17 S 74 29W
Ipáti, *Greece* **48 C4** 38 52N 22 14 E
Ipatinga, *Brazil* **171 E3** 19 32 S 42 30W
Ipatovo, *Russia* **61 H6** 45 45N 42 50 E
Ipek = Peć, *Serbia & M.* **50 D4** 42 40N 20 17 E
Ipel' →, *Europe* **35 D11** 47 48N 18 53 E
Ipiales, *Colombia* **168 C2** 0 50N 77 37W
Ipiaú, *Brazil* **171 D4** 14 8 S 39 44W
Ipil, *Phil.* **81 H4** 7 47N 122 35 E
Ipin = Yibin, *China* **76 C5** 28 45N 104 32 E
Ipirá, *Brazil* **171 D4** 12 10 S 39 44W
Ipiranga, *Brazil* **168 D4** 3 13 S 65 57W
Ípiros □, *Greece* **48 B2** 39 30N 20 30 E
Ipixuna, *Brazil* **172 B3** 7 0 S 71 40W
Ipixuna →, *Amazonas, Brazil* **172 B3** 7 11 S 71 51W
Ipixuna →, *Amazonas, Brazil* **173 B5** 5 45 S 63 2W
Ipoh, *Malaysia* **87 K3** 4 35N 101 5 E
Iporá, *Brazil* **173 D7** 16 28 S 51 7W
Ipota, *Vanuatu* **133 H7** 18 52 S 169 20 E
Ippy, *C.A.R.* **114 A4** 6 5N 21 7 E
Ipsala, *Turkey* **51 F10** 40 55N 26 23 E
Ipsário, Óros, *Greece* **51 F8** 40 40N 24 40 E
Ipsos, *Greece* **38 B9** 39 43N 19 48 E
Ipswich, *Australia* **127 D5** 27 35 S 152 40 E
Ipswich, *U.K.* **21 E9** 52 4N 1 10 E
Ipswich, *Mass., U.S.A.* **151 D14** 42 41N 70 50W
Ipswich, *S. Dak., U.S.A.* **154 C5** 45 27N 99 2W
Ipu, *Brazil* **170 B3** 4 23 S 40 44W
Ipueiras, *Brazil* **170 B3** 4 33 S 40 43W
Ipupiara, *Brazil* **171 D3** 11 49 S 42 37W
Iqaluit, *Canada* **139 B13** 63 44N 68 31W
Iquique, *Chile* **172 E3** 20 19 S 70 5W
Iquitos, *Peru* **168 D3** 3 45 S 73 10W
Ir Gannim = Bat Yam, *Israel* **103 C3** 32 2N 34 44 E
Irabu-Jima, *Japan* **71 M2** 24 50N 125 10 E
Iracoubo, *Fr. Guiana* **169 B7** 5 30N 53 10W
Īrafshān, *Iran* **97 E9** 26 42N 61 56 E
Irahuan, *Phil.* **81 G2** 9 48N 118 41 E
Iráklia, *Kikládhes, Greece* **49 E7** 36 50N 25 28 E
Iráklia, *Sérrai, Greece* **50 E7** 41 10N 23 16 E
Iraklio = Iráklion, *Greece* **39 E6** 35 20N 25 12 E
Iráklion, *Greece* **39 E6** 35 20N 25 12 E
Iráklion □, *Greece* **39 E6** 35 10N 25 10 E
Iraklion ✕ (HER), *Greece* **39 E6** 35 20N 25 15 E
Irako-Zaki, *Japan* **73 C9** 34 35N 137 1 E
Irala, *Paraguay* **175 B5** 25 55 S 54 35W
Iran ■, *Asia* **97 C7** 33 0N 53 0 E
Iran, Pegunungan, *Malaysia* **85 B4** 2 20N 114 50 E
Iran, Plateau of, *Asia* **62 F9** 32 0N 55 0 E
Iran Ra. = Iran, Pegunungan, *Malaysia* **85 B4** 2 20N 114 50 E
Iranamadu Tank, *Sri Lanka* **95 K5** 9 23N 80 29 E
Irānshahr, *Iran* **97 E9** 27 15N 60 40 E
Irapa, *Venezuela* **169 A5** 10 34N 62 35W
Irapuato, *Mexico* **162 C4** 20 40N 101 30W
Iraq ■, *Asia* **101 F10** 33 0N 44 0 E
Irarrar, O. →, *Mali* **111 E5** 20 0N 1 30 E
Irarrarene, *Algeria* **111 C6** 27 37N 7 30 E
Irati, *Brazil* **175 B5** 25 25 S 50 38W
Irbes saurums, *Latvia* **54 A9** 57 45N 22 5 E
Irbid, *Jordan* **103 C4** 32 35N 35 48 E
Irbid □, *Jordan* **103 C5** 32 15N 36 35 E
Irbit, *Russia* **64 C9** 57 41N 63 3 E
Irebu, *Dem. Rep. of the Congo* **114 C3** 0 40 S 17 46 E
Irecê, *Brazil* **170 D3** 11 18 S 41 52W
Iregua →, *Spain* **40 C7** 42 27N 2 24 E
Ireland ■, *Europe* **23 C4** 53 50N 7 52W
Ireland I., *Bermuda* **9 a** 32 19N 64 50W
Irele, *Nigeria* **113 D6** 7 40N 5 40 E
Iremel, Gora, *Russia* **64 D7** 54 33N 58 50 E
Ireng →, *Brazil* **169 C6** 3 33N 59 51W
Irerrer, O. →, *Algeria* **111 E6** 19 25N 5 47 E
Irgiz, Bolshaya →, *Russia* **60 D9** 52 10N 49 10 E
Irharrhar, O. →, *Algeria* **111 C6** 28 3N 6 15 E
Irherm, *Morocco* **110 B3** 30 7N 8 18W
Irhil M'Goun, *Morocco* **110 B3** 31 30N 6 28W
Irhyangdong, *N. Korea* **75 D15** 41 15N 129 30 E
Iri, *S. Korea* **75 G14** 35 59N 127 0 E
Irian Barat = Papua □, *Indonesia* **83 B5** 4 0 S 137 0 E
Irian Jaya = Papua □, *Indonesia* **83 B5** 4 0 S 137 0 E
Iriba, *Chad* **109 E4** 15 7N 22 15 E
Irié, *Guinea* **112 D3** 8 15N 9 10W
Iriga, *Phil.* **80 E4** 13 25N 123 25 E
Iriklinskiy, *Russia* **64 F7** 51 39N 58 38 E
Iriklinskoye Vdkhr., *Russia* **64 F7** 52 0N 59 0 E
Iringa, *Tanzania* **118 D4** 7 48 S 35 43 E
Iringa □, *Tanzania* **118 D4** 7 48 S 35 43 E
Irinjalakuda, *India* **95 J3** 10 21N 76 14 E
Iriomote △, *Japan* **71 M1** 24 29N 123 53 E
Iriomote-Jima, *Japan* **71 M1** 24 19N 123 48 E
Iriona, *Honduras* **164 C2** 15 57N 85 11W
Iriri →, *Brazil* **169 D7** 3 52 S 52 37W
Iriri Novo →, *Brazil* **173 B7** 8 46 S 53 22W
Irish Free State = Ireland ■, *Europe* **23 C4** 53 50N 7 52W
Irish Republic ■, *Europe* **23 C4** 53 50N 7 52W
Irish Sea, *Europe* **20 D3** 53 38N 4 48W
Irkeshtam = Erkech-Tam, *Kyrgyzstan* **65 D6** 39 41N 73 55 E
Irkutsk, *Russia* **67 D11** 52 18N 104 20 E
Irlığanlı, *Turkey* **49 D11** 37 53N 29 12 E
Irma, *Canada* **143 C6** 52 55N 111 14W
Irō-Zaki, *Japan* **73 C10** 34 36N 138 51 E
Iroise, Mer d', *France* **26 D2** 48 15N 4 45W
Iron Baron, *Australia* **128 B2** 32 58 S 137 11 E
Iron Gate = Portile de Fier, *Europe* **52 F7** 44 44N 22 30 E
Iron Knob, *Australia* **128 B2** 32 46 S 137 8 E
Iron Mountain, *U.S.A.* **148 C1** 45 49N 88 4W
Iron Range △, *Australia* **126 A3** 12 34 S 143 18 E
Iron River, *U.S.A.* **154 B10** 46 6N 88 39W
Irondequoit, *U.S.A.* **150 C7** 43 13N 77 35W
Ironton, *Mo., U.S.A.* **155 G9** 37 36N 90 38W
Ironton, *Ohio, U.S.A.* **148 F4** 38 32N 82 41W
Ironwood, *U.S.A.* **154 B9** 46 27N 90 9W
Ironwood Forest ⌓, *U.S.A.* **159 K8** 32 28N 111 36W
Iroquois, *Canada* **151 B9** 44 51N 75 19W
Iroquois →, *U.S.A.* **157 C9** 41 5N 87 49W
Iroquois Falls, *Canada* **140 C3** 48 46N 80 41W
Irosin, *Phil.* **80 E5** 12 42N 124 2 E
Irpin, *Ukraine* **59 G6** 50 30N 30 15 E
Irqieqa, Ras I-, *Malta* **38 F7** 35 56N 14 29 E
Irrara Cr. →, *Australia* **127 D4** 29 35 S 145 31 E
Irrawaddy □, *Burma* **90 G5** 17 0N 95 0 E
Irrawaddy →, *Burma* **90 G5** 15 50N 95 6 E
Irrawaddy, Mouths of the, *Burma* **90 H5** 15 30N 95 0 E
Irricana, *Canada* **142 C6** 51 19N 113 37W
Irshava, *Ukraine* **52 B8** 48 19N 23 3 E
Irsina, *Italy* **47 B9** 40 45N 16 14 E
Irtysh →, *Russia* **66 C7** 61 4N 68 52 E
Irumu, *Dem. Rep. of the Congo* **118 B2** 1 32N 29 53 E
Irún, *Spain* **40 B3** 43 20N 1 52W
Irunea = Pamplona, *Spain* **40 C3** 42 48N 1 38W
Iruzun, *Spain* **40 C3** 42 55N 1 50W
Irvine, *U.K.* **22 F4** 55 37N 4 41W
Irvine, *Calif., U.S.A.* **161 M9** 33 41N 117 46W
Irvine, *Ky., U.S.A.* **157 G13** 37 42N 83 58W
Irvinestown, *U.K.* **23 B4** 54 28N 7 39W
Irving, *U.S.A.* **155 J6** 32 49N 96 56W
Irvington, *U.S.A.* **157 G10** 37 53N 86 17W
Irvona, *U.S.A.* **150 F6** 40 46N 78 33W
Irwin →, *Australia* **125 E1** 29 15 S 114 54 E
Irwinton, *U.S.A.* **152 C6** 32 49N 83 10W
Irwinville, *U.S.A.* **152 D6** 31 39N 83 23W
Irymple, *Australia* **128 C5** 34 14 S 142 8 E
Is, Jebel, *Sudan* **106 C4** 22 3N 35 28 E
Is-sur-Tille, *France* **27 E12** 47 30N 5 8 E
Isa, *Nigeria* **113 C6** 13 14N 6 24 E
Isa Khel, *Pakistan* **92 C4** 32 41N 71 17 E
Isaac →, *Australia* **126 C4** 22 55 S 149 20 E
Isabel, *U.S.A.* **154 C4** 45 24N 101 26W
Isabela, *Basilan, Phil.* **81 H3** 6 40N 121 59 E
Isabela, *Negros, Phil.* **81 F4** 10 12N 122 59 E
Isabela, *Puerto Rico* **165 d** 18 30N 67 2W
Isabela □, *Phil.* **80 C4** 17 0N 122 0 E
Isabela, Canal, *Ecuador* **172 a** 0 20 S 90 55W
Isabela, I., *Ecuador* **172 a** 0 30 S 91 4W
Isabela, I., *Mexico* **162 C3** 21 51N 105 55W
Isabelia, Cord., *Nic.* **164 D2** 13 30N 85 25W
Isabella Ra., *Australia* **124 D3** 21 0 S 121 4 E
Isaccea, *Romania* **53 E13** 45 16N 28 28 E
Ísafjarðardjúp, *Iceland* **14 C2** 66 10N 23 0W
Ísafjarðarsýsla □, *Iceland* **11 B3** 66 0N 23 0W
Ísafjörður, *Iceland* **11 A3** 66 5N 23 9W
Isagarh, *India* **92 G7** 24 48N 77 51 E
Isahaya, *Japan* **72 E2** 32 52N 130 2 E
Isaka, *Dem. Rep. of the Congo* **114 C3** 2 33 S 18 54 E
Isaka, *Tanzania* **118 C3** 3 56 S 32 59 E
Işalniţa, *Romania* **53 F8** 44 24N 23 44 E
Isalo △, *Madag.* **117 C8** 22 23 S 45 16 E
Isan →, *India* **93 F9** 26 51N 80 7 E
Isana = Içana →, *Brazil* **168 C4** 0 26N 67 19W
Isandja, *Dem. Rep. of the Congo* **114 C4** 2 59 S 21 59 E
Isangano △, *Zambia* **119 E3** 11 8 S 30 35 E
Isangi, *Dem. Rep. of the Congo* **114 B4** 0 52N 24 10 E
Isanlu Makutu, *Nigeria* **113 D6** 8 20N 5 50 E
Isar →, *Germany* **31 G8** 48 48N 12 57 E
Isarco →, *Italy* **45 B8** 46 27N 11 18 E
Ísari, *Greece* **48 D3** 37 22N 22 0 E
Isarog, Mt., *Phil.* **80 E4** 13 39N 123 23 E
Íscar, *Spain* **42 D6** 41 22N 4 32W
Iscayachi, *Bolivia* **173 E4** 21 31 S 65 3W
İscehisar, *Turkey* **49 C12** 38 51N 30 45 E
Ischgl, *Austria* **33 B10** 47 1N 10 17 E
Íschia, *Italy* **46 B6** 40 44N 13 57 E
Iscuandé, *Colombia* **168 C2** 2 28N 77 59W
Isdell →, *Australia* **124 C3** 16 27 S 124 51 E
Ise, *Japan* **73 C8** 34 25N 136 45 E
Ise-Shima △, *Japan* **73 C8** 34 25N 136 48 E
Ise-Wan, *Japan* **73 C8** 34 43N 136 43 E
Isefjord, *Denmark* **17 J5** 55 53N 11 50 E
Isel →, *Austria* **34 E5** 46 50N 12 47 E
Iseltwald, *Switz.* **32 C5** 46 43N 7 58 E
Isenthal, *Switz.* **33 C7** 46 55N 8 34 E
Iseo, *Italy* **44 C7** 45 39N 10 3 E
Iseo, L. d', *Italy* **44 C7** 45 43N 10 4 E
Iseramagazi, *Tanzania* **118 C3** 4 37 S 32 10 E
Isère □, *France* **29 C9** 45 15N 5 40 E
Isère →, *France* **29 D8** 44 59N 4 51 E
Iserlohn, *Germany* **30 D3** 51 22N 7 41 E
Isérnia, *Italy* **47 A7** 41 36N 14 14 E
Isesaki, *Japan* **73 A11** 36 19N 139 12 E
Iseyin, *Nigeria* **113 D5** 8 0N 3 36 E
Isfahan = Eşfahān, *Iran* **97 C6** 32 39N 51 43 E
Isfana, *Kyrgyzstan* **65 D4** 39 50N 69 31 E
Isfara, *Tajikistan* **65 C5** 40 7N 70 38 E
Isfjorden, *Norway* **18 B4** 62 35N 7 49 E
Ishëm, *Albania* **50 E3** 41 33N 19 34 E
Ishenga Oshwe, *Dem. Rep. of the Congo* **114 C4** 3 57 S 22 33 E
Isherton, *Guyana* **169 C6** 2 20N 59 25W
Ishigaki-Shima, *Japan* **71 M2** 24 20N 124 10 E
Ishikari-Gawa →, *Japan* **70 C10** 43 15N 141 23 E
Ishikari-Sammyaku, *Japan* **70 C11** 43 30N 143 0 E
Ishikari-Wan, *Japan* **70 C10** 43 25N 141 1 E
Ishikawa □, *Japan* **73 A8** 36 30N 136 30 E
Ishim, *Russia* **66 D7** 56 10N 69 30 E
Ishim →, *Russia* **66 D8** 57 45N 71 10 E
Ishimbay, *Russia* **64 E6** 53 28N 56 2 E
Ishinomaki, *Japan* **70 E10** 38 32N 141 20 E
Ishioka, *Japan* **73 A12** 36 11N 140 16 E
Ishizuchi-Yama, *Japan* **72 D5** 33 45N 133 6 E
Ishkashim, *Tajikistan* **65 E5** 36 44N 71 37 E
Ishkuman, *Pakistan* **93 A5** 36 30N 73 50 E
Ishpeming, *U.S.A.* **148 B2** 46 29N 87 40W
Ishtykhan, *Uzbekistan* **65 D3** 39 58N 66 29 E
Ishurdi, *Bangla.* **90 C2** 24 9N 89 3 E
Isiboro Sécure △, *Bolivia* **173 D4** 16 15 S 65 50W
Isigny-sur-Mer, *France* **26 C5** 49 19N 1 6W
Isıklar Dağı, *Turkey* **51 F11** 40 45N 27 15 E
Işıklı, *Turkey* **49 C11** 38 19N 29 51 E
Isil Kul, *Russia* **66 D8** 54 55N 71 16 E
Ísili, *Italy* **46 C2** 39 44N 9 6 E
Isiolo, *Kenya* **118 B4** 0 24N 37 33 E
Isiro, *Dem. Rep. of the Congo* **118 B2** 2 53N 27 40 E
Isisford, *Australia* **126 C3** 24 15 S 144 21 E
Iskandar, *Uzbekistan* **65 C4** 41 36N 69 41 E
Iskenderun, *Turkey* **100 D7** 36 32N 36 10 E
Iskenderun Körfezi, *Turkey* **100 D6** 36 40N 35 50 E
Iski-Naukat = Eski-Nookat, *Kyrgyzstan* **65 C6** 40 16N 72 36 E
Iskilip, *Turkey* **100 B6** 40 45N 34 29 E
Iskŭr →, *Bulgaria* **51 C8** 43 45N 24 25 E
Iskŭr, Yazovir, *Bulgaria* **50 D7** 42 23N 23 30 E
Iskut →, *Canada* **142 B2** 56 45N 131 49W
Isla →, *U.K.* **22 E5** 56 32N 3 20W
Isla Coiba △, *Panama* **164 E3** 7 33N 81 36W
Isla Cristina, *Spain* **43 H3** 37 13N 7 17W
Isla de Salamanca △, *Colombia* **165 D5** 10 59N 74 40W
Isla Gorge △, *Australia* **126 D4** 25 10 S 149 57 E
Isla Gorgona △, *Colombia* **168 C2** 2 59N 78 10W
Isla Guamblin △, *Chile* **176 B1** 44 50 S 75 4W
Isla Magdalena △, *Chile* **176 B2** 44 20 S 73 13W
Isla Tiburón y San Esteban ⌓, *Mexico* **162 B2** 29 0N 112 27W
Isla Vista, *U.S.A.* **161 L7** 34 25N 119 53W
Islâhiye, *Turkey* **100 D7** 37 0N 36 35 E
Islam Headworks, *Pakistan* **92 E5** 29 49N 72 33 E
Islamabad, *Pakistan* **91 B4** 33 40N 73 10 E
Islamgarh, *Pakistan* **92 F4** 27 51N 70 48 E
Islamkot, *Pakistan* **92 G4** 24 42N 70 13 E
Islamorada, *U.S.A.* **153 L9** 24 56N 80 37W
Islampur, *Bihar, India* **93 G11** 25 9N 85 12 E
Islampur, *Maharashtra, India* **94 F2** 17 2N 74 20 E
Island = Iceland ■, *Europe* **11 C8** 64 45N 19 0W
Island Bay, *Phil.* **81 G2** 9 6N 118 10 E
Island L., *Canada* **143 C10** 53 47N 94 25W
Island Lagoon, *Australia* **128 A2** 31 30 S 136 40 E
Island Pond, *U.S.A.* **151 B13** 44 49N 71 53W
Islands, B. of, *Canada* **141 C8** 49 11N 58 15W
Islands, B. of, *N.Z.* **130 B3** 35 15 S 174 6 E
Islay, *U.K.* **22 F2** 55 46N 6 10W
Isle →, *France* **28 D3** 44 55N 0 15W
Isle aux Morts, *Canada* **141 C8** 47 35N 59 0W
Isle of Hope, *U.S.A.* **152 D8** 31 58N 81 5W
Isle of Wight □, *U.K.* **21 G6** 50 41N 1 17W
Isle Royale △, *U.S.A.* **148 B1** 48 0N 88 55W
Isleton, *U.S.A.* **160 G5** 38 10N 121 37W
Ismail = Izmayil, *Ukraine* **53 E13** 45 22N 28 46 E
Ismâ'ilîya, *Egypt* **106 H8** 30 37N 32 18 E
Ismaning, *Germany* **31 G7** 48 13N 11 40 E
Isna, *Egypt* **106 B3** 25 17N 32 30 E
Isoanala, *Madag.* **117 C8** 23 50 S 45 44 E
Isogstalo, *India* **93 B8** 34 15N 78 46 E
Ísola del Liri, *Italy* **45 G10** 41 41N 13 34 E
Ísola della Scala, *Italy* **44 C7** 45 16N 11 0 E
Ísola di Capo Rizzuto, *Italy* **47 D10** 38 58N 17 6 E
Isparta, *Turkey* **49 D12** 37 47N 30 30 E
Isperikh, *Bulgaria* **51 C10** 43 43N 26 50 E
Íspica, *Italy* **47 F7** 36 47N 14 55 E
Israel ■, *Asia* **103 D3** 32 0N 34 50 E
Isratu, *Eritrea* **107 D4** 16 20N 39 53 E
Issakly, *Russia* **60 C10** 54 8N 51 32 E

Issano, *Guyana* **169 B6** 5 49N 59 26W
Issia, *Ivory C.* **112 D3** 6 33N 6 33W
Issoire, *France* **28 C7** 45 32N 3 15 E
Issoudun, *France* **27 F8** 46 57N 1 59 E
Issyk-Kul = Balykchy, *Kyrgyzstan* **65 B8** 42 26N 76 12 E
Issyk-Kul, Ozero = Ysyk-Köl, *Kyrgyzstan* **65 B8** 42 25N 77 15 E
Ist, *Croatia* **45 D11** 44 17N 14 47 E
Istaihah, *U.A.E.* **99 B6** 23 19N 54 4 E
Istállós-kő, *Hungary* **52 B5** 48 4N 20 26 E
İstanbul, *Turkey* **51 E12** 41 0N 29 0 E
İstanbul □, *Turkey* **51 E12** 41 0N 29 0 E
Istanbul ✈ (IST), *Turkey* **51 F12** 40 59N 28 49 E
İstanbul Boğazı, *Turkey* **51 E13** 41 10N 29 10 E
Isteren, *Norway* **18 B8** 61 58N 11 47 E
Istiaía, *Greece* **48 C5** 38 57N 23 9 E
Istiea = Istiaía, *Greece* **48 C5** 38 57N 23 9 E
Istmina, *Colombia* **168 B2** 5 10N 76 39W
Isto, Mt., *U.S.A.* **144 B12** 69 12N 143 48W
Istok, *Serbia & M.* **50 D4** 42 45N 20 24 E
Istokpoga, L., *U.S.A.* **153 H8** 27 23N 81 17W
Istra, *Croatia* **45 C10** 45 10N 14 0 E
Istres, *France* **29 E8** 43 31N 4 59 E
Istria = Istra, *Croatia* **45 C10** 45 10N 14 0 E
Isugod, *Phil.* **81 G2** 9 19N 118 5 E
Isulan, *Phil.* **81 H5** 6 30N 124 29 E
Itá, *Paraguay* **174 B4** 25 29 S 57 21W
Itabaiana, *Paraíba, Brazil* **170 C4** 7 18 S 35 19W
Itabaiana, *Sergipe, Brazil* **170 D4** 10 41 S 37 37W
Itabaianinha, *Brazil* **170 D4** 11 16 S 37 47W
Itaberaba, *Brazil* **171 D3** 12 32 S 40 18W
Itaberaí, *Brazil* **171 E2** 16 2 S 49 48W
Itabira, *Brazil* **171 E3** 19 37 S 43 13W
Itabirito, *Brazil* **171 F3** 20 15 S 43 48W
Itaboca, *Brazil* **169 D5** 4 50 S 62 40W
Itabuna, *Brazil* **171 D4** 14 48 S 39 16W
Itacajá, *Brazil* **170 C2** 8 19 S 47 46W
Itacaunas →, *Brazil* **170 C2** 5 21 S 49 8W
Itacuaí →, *Brazil* **172 A3** 4 20 S 70 12W
Itaguaçu, *Brazil* **171 E3** 19 48 S 40 51W
Itaguari →, *Brazil* **171 D3** 14 11 S 44 40W
Itaguatins, *Brazil* **170 C2** 5 47 S 47 29W
Itaim →, *Brazil* **170 C3** 7 2 S 42 2W
Itainópolis, *Brazil* **170 C3** 7 24 S 41 31W
Itaipú, Represa de, *Brazil* **175 B5** 25 30 S 54 30W
Itaituba, *Brazil* **169 D6** 4 10 S 55 50W
Itajaí, *Brazil* **175 B6** 27 50 S 48 39W
Itajany do Sul = Rio do Sul, *Brazil* **175 B6** 27 13 S 49 37W
Itajubá, *Brazil* **171 F2** 22 24 S 45 30W
Itajuípe, *Brazil* **171 D4** 14 41 S 39 22W
Itaka, *Tanzania* **119 D3** 8 50 S 32 49 E
Itako, *Japan* **73 B12** 35 56N 140 33 E
Itala ⌂, *S. Africa* **117 D5** 27 30 S 31 7 E
Italy ■, *Europe* **13 G8** 42 0N 13 0 E
Itamaraju, *Brazil* **171 E4** 17 4 S 39 32W
Itamarati, *Brazil* **172 B4** 6 24 S 68 15W
Itamataré, *Brazil* **170 B2** 2 16 S 46 24W
Itambacuri, *Brazil* **171 E3** 18 1 S 41 42W
Itambé, *Brazil* **171 E3** 15 15 S 40 37W
Itami, *Japan* **73 C7** 34 46N 135 25 E
Itampolo, *Madag.* **117 C7** 24 41 S 43 57 E
Itandrano, *Madag.* **117 C8** 21 47 S 45 17 E
Itanhaém, *Brazil* **171 F2** 24 11 S 46 47W
Itanhauã →, *Brazil* **169 D5** 4 45 S 63 48W
Itanhém, *Brazil* **171 E3** 17 9 S 40 20W
Itano, *Japan* **72 C6** 34 7N 134 28 E
Itapaci, *Brazil* **171 D2** 14 57 S 49 34W
Itapagé, *Brazil* **170 B4** 3 41 S 39 34W
Itaparica = Petrolândia, *Brazil* **170 C4** 9 5 S 38 20W
Itaparica, I. de, *Brazil* **171 D4** 12 54 S 38 42W
Itapebi, *Brazil* **171 E4** 15 56 S 39 32W
Itapecuru-Mirim, *Brazil* **170 B3** 3 24 S 44 20W
Itaperuna, *Brazil* **171 F3** 21 10 S 41 54W
Itapetinga, *Brazil* **171 E3** 15 15 S 40 15W
Itapetininga, *Brazil* **175 A6** 23 36 S 48 7W
Itapeva, *Brazil* **175 A6** 23 59 S 48 59W
Itapicuru →, *Bahia, Brazil* **170 D4** 11 47 S 37 32W
Itapicuru →, *Maranhão, Brazil* **170 B3** 2 52 S 44 12W
Itapinima, *Brazil* **173 B5** 5 25 S 60 44W
Itapipoca, *Brazil* **170 B4** 3 30 S 39 35W
Itapira = Ubaitaba, *Brazil* **171 D4** 14 18 S 39 20W
Itapiranga, *Brazil* **169 D6** 2 45 S 58 1W
Itapiúna, *Brazil* **170 B4** 4 33 S 38 57W
Itaporanga, *Paraíba, Brazil* **170 C4** 7 18 S 38 0W
Itaporanga, *São Paulo, Brazil* **171 F2** 23 42 S 49 29W
Itapuá □, *Paraguay* **175 B4** 26 40 S 55 40W
Itapuranga, *Brazil* **171 E2** 15 40 S 49 59W
Itaquari, *Brazil* **171 F3** 20 20 S 40 25W
Itaquatiara, *Brazil* **169 D6** 2 58 S 58 30W
Itaquí, *Brazil* **174 B4** 29 8 S 56 30W
Itararé, *Brazil* **175 A6** 24 6 S 49 23W
Itarsi, *India* **92 H7** 22 36N 77 51 E
Itarumã, *Brazil* **171 E1** 18 42 S 51 25W
Itatí, *Argentina* **174 B4** 27 16 S 58 15W
Itatiaia △, *Brazil* **175 A7** 22 22 S 44 38W
Itatira, *Brazil* **170 B4** 4 30 S 39 37W
Itatuba, *Brazil* **173 B5** 5 46 S 63 20W
Itatupa, *Brazil* **169 D7** 0 37 S 51 12W
Itaueira, *Brazil* **170 C3** 7 36 S 43 2W
Itaueira →, *Brazil* **170 C3** 6 41 S 42 55W
Itaúna, *Brazil* **171 F3** 20 4 S 44 34W
Itbayat, *Phil.* **80 A3** 20 47N 121 51 E
Itbayat I., *Phil.* **80 A3** 20 45N 121 50 E
Itchen →, *U.K.* **21 G6** 50 55N 1 22W
Itchouma, *Niger* **111 D7** 20 14N 13 32 E
Ite, *Peru* **172 D3** 17 55 S 70 57W
Itéa, *Greece* **48 C4** 38 25N 22 25 E
Itezhi Tezhi, L., *Zambia* **119 F2** 15 30 S 25 30 E
Ithaca = Itháki, *Greece* **39 C2** 38 25N 20 40 E
Ithaca, *U.S.A.* **151 D8** 42 27N 76 30W
Itháki, *Greece* **39 C2** 38 25N 20 40 E
Íti △, *Greece* **48 C4** 38 50N 22 15 E
Itinga, *Brazil* **171 E3** 16 36 S 41 47W
Itiquira, *Brazil* **173 D7** 17 12 S 54 7W
Itiquira →, *Brazil* **173 D6** 17 18 S 56 44W
Itiruçu, *Brazil* **171 D3** 13 31 S 40 9W
Itiúba, *Brazil* **170 D4** 10 43 S 39 51W
Itkilik →, *U.S.A.* **144 A10** 70 9N 150 56W
Itō, *Japan* **73 C11** 34 58N 139 5 E
Itogon, *Phil.* **80 C3** 16 22N 120 41 E
Itoigawa, *Japan* **71 F8** 37 2N 137 51 E
Itoko, *Dem. Rep. of the Congo* **114 C4** 1 0 S 21 48 E
Iton →, *France* **26 C8** 49 9N 1 12 E
Itonamas →, *Bolivia* **173 C5** 12 28 S 64 24W
Itri, *Italy* **46 A6** 41 17N 13 32 E
Itsa, *Egypt* **106 J7** 29 15N 30 47 E
Itsuki, *Japan* **72 E2** 32 24N 130 50 E
Íttiri, *Italy* **46 B1** 40 36N 8 34 E
Ittoqqortoormiit, *Greenland* **10 C8** 70 20N 23 0W
Itu, *Brazil* **175 A6** 23 17 S 47 15W
Itu, *Nigeria* **113 D6** 5 10N 7 58 E
Itu Aba I., *S. China Sea* **78 B4** 10 23N 114 21 E
Ituaçu, *Brazil* **171 D3** 13 50 S 41 18W
Ituango, *Colombia* **168 B2** 7 4N 75 45W
Ituí →, *Brazil* **168 D3** 4 38 S 70 19W
Ituiutaba, *Brazil* **171 E2** 19 0 S 49 25W
Itumbiara, *Brazil* **171 E2** 18 20 S 49 10W
Ituna, *Canada* **143 C8** 51 10N 103 24W
Itunge Port, *Tanzania* **119 D3** 9 40 S 33 55 E
Ituni, *Guyana* **169 B6** 5 28N 58 15W
Itupiranga, *Brazil* **170 C2** 5 9 S 49 20W
Iturama, *Brazil* **171 E1** 19 44 S 50 11W
Iturbe, *Argentina* **174 A2** 23 0 S 65 25W
Ituri →, *Dem. Rep. of the Congo* **118 B2** 1 40N 27 1 E
Iturup, Ostrov, *Russia* **67 E15** 45 0N 148 0 E
Ituverava, *Brazil* **171 F2** 20 20 S 47 47W
Ituxi →, *Brazil* **173 B5** 7 18 S 64 51W
Ituyuro →, *Argentina* **174 A3** 22 40 S 63 50W
Itzehoe, *Germany* **30 B5** 53 55N 9 31 E
Iuka, *U.S.A.* **157 F8** 38 37N 88 47W
Ivahona, *Madag.* **117 C8** 23 27 S 46 10 E
Ivaí →, *Brazil* **175 A5** 23 18 S 53 42W
Ivalo, *Finland* **14 B22** 68 38N 27 35 E
Ivalojoki →, *Finland* **14 B22** 68 40N 27 40 E
Ivanava, *Belarus* **59 F3** 52 7N 25 29 E
Ivančice, *Czech Rep.* **35 B9** 49 6N 16 23 E
Ivane-Puste, *Ukraine* **53 B11** 48 39N 26 10 E
Ivăneşti, *Romania* **53 D12** 46 39N 27 27 E
Ivangorod = Dęblin, *Poland* **55 G8** 51 34N 21 50 E
Ivangorod, *Russia* **58 C5** 59 27N 28 13 E
Ivanhoe, *N.S.W., Australia* **128 B6** 32 56 S 144 20 E
Ivanhoe, *Vic., Australia* **129 D6** 37 46 S 145 2 E
Ivanhoe, *Calif., U.S.A.* **160 J7** 36 23N 119 13W
Ivanhoe, *Minn., U.S.A.* **154 C6** 44 28N 96 15W
Ivanhorod, *Ukraine* **53 B14** 48 48N 29 50 E
Ivanić Grad, *Croatia* **45 C13** 45 41N 16 25 E
Ivanjica, *Serbia & M.* **50 C4** 43 35N 20 12 E
Ivanjska, *Bos.-H.* **52 F2** 44 55N 17 4 E
Ivankoyskoye Vdkhr., *Russia* **58 D9** 56 37N 36 32 E
Ivano-Frankivsk, *Ukraine* **53 B9** 48 40N 24 40 E
Ivano-Frankivska □, *Ukraine* **53 B9** 48 45N 24 30 E
Ivanof Bay, *U.S.A.* **144 J8** 55 54N 159 29W
Ivanovka, *Kyrgyzstan* **65 B7** 42 53N 75 6 E
Ivanovo = Ivanava, *Belarus* **59 F3** 52 7N 25 29 E
Ivanovo, *Russia* **58 D11** 57 5N 41 0 E
Ivanšćica, *Croatia* **45 B13** 46 12N 16 13 E
Ivashchenkovo = Chapayevsk, *Russia* **60 D9** 53 0N 49 40 E
Ivato, *Madag.* **117 C8** 20 37 S 47 10 E
Ivatsevichy, *Belarus* **59 F3** 52 43N 25 21 E
Ivaylovgrad, *Bulgaria* **51 E10** 41 32N 26 8 E
Ivdel, *Russia* **56 B11** 60 42N 60 24 E
Ivgres = Komsomolsk, *Russia* **58 D11** 57 2N 40 20 E
Ivindo →, *Gabon* **114 C2** 0 9 S 12 9 E
Ivinheima →, *Brazil* **175 A5** 23 14 S 53 42W
Ivinhema, *Brazil* **175 A5** 22 10 S 53 37W
Ivittuut, *Greenland* **10 E6** 61 14N 48 12W
Iviza = Eivissa, *Spain* **38 D1** 38 54N 1 26 E
Ivohibe, *Madag.* **117 C8** 22 31 S 46 57 E
Ivolândia, *Brazil* **171 E1** 16 34 S 50 51W
Ivory Coast, *W. Afr.* **112 E4** 4 20N 5 0W
Ivory Coast ■, *Africa* **112 D4** 7 30N 5 0W
Ivösjön, *Sweden* **17 H8** 56 8N 14 25 E
Ivrea, *Italy* **44 C4** 45 28N 7 52 E
İvrindi, *Turkey* **49 B9** 39 34N 27 30 E
Ivujivik, *Canada* **139 B12** 62 24N 77 55W
Ivvavik △, *Canada* **144 B13** 69 6N 139 30W
Ivybridge, *U.K.* **21 G4** 50 23N 3 56W
Iwai-Jima, *Japan* **72 D3** 33 47N 131 58 E
Iwaizumi, *Japan* **70 E10** 39 50N 141 45 E
Iwaki, *Japan* **71 F10** 37 3N 140 55 E
Iwakuni, *Japan* **72 C4** 34 15N 132 8 E
Iwami, *Japan* **72 B6** 35 32N 134 15 E
Iwamizawa, *Japan* **70 C10** 43 12N 141 46 E
Iwanai, *Japan* **70 C10** 42 58N 140 30 E
Iwase, *Japan* **73 A12** 36 21N 140 6 E
Iwata, *Japan* **73 C9** 34 42N 137 51 E
Iwate □, *Japan* **70 E10** 39 30N 141 30 E
Iwate-San, *Japan* **70 E10** 39 51N 141 0 E
Iwo, *Nigeria* **113 D5** 7 39N 4 9 E
Iwonicz-Zdrój, *Poland* **55 J8** 49 37N 21 47 E
Iwungu, *Dem. Rep. of the Congo* **115 D3** 5 16 S 19 17 E
Ixiamas, *Bolivia* **172 C4** 13 50 S 68 5W
Ixopo, *S. Africa* **117 E5** 30 11 S 30 5 E
Ixtepec, *Mexico* **163 D5** 16 32N 95 10W
Ixtlán del Río, *Mexico* **162 C4** 21 5N 104 21W
'Iyādh, *Yemen* **98 D4** 14 59N 46 51 E
Iyal Bakhit, *Sudan* **107 E2** 13 20N 28 39 E
Iyo, *Japan* **72 D4** 33 45N 132 45 E
Iyo-Mishima, *Japan* **72 D5** 33 58N 133 30 E
Iyo-Nada, *Japan* **72 D4** 33 40N 132 20 E
Izabal, L. de, *Guatemala* **164 C2** 15 30N 89 10W
Izamal, *Mexico* **163 C7** 20 56N 89 1W
Izberbash, *Russia* **61 J8** 42 35N 47 52 E
Izbica, *Poland* **55 H10** 50 53N 23 10 E
Izbica Kujawska, *Poland* **55 F5** 52 25N 18 40 E
Izbiceni, *Romania* **53 G9** 43 45N 24 40 E
Izena-Shima, *Japan* **71 L3** 26 56N 127 56 E
Izgrev, *Bulgaria* **51 C10** 43 36N 26 58 E
Izh →, *Russia* **64 C4** 56 9N 53 0 E
Izhevsk, *Russia* **64 C4** 56 51N 53 14 E
Izhma = Sosnogorsk, *Russia* **56 B9** 63 37N 53 51 E
Izhma →, *Russia* **56 A9** 65 19N 52 54 E
Izileg, *Algeria* **111 D6** 20 20N 6 4 E
Izkī, *Oman* **99 B7** 22 56N 57 46 E
Izmayil, *Ukraine* **53 E13** 45 22N 28 46 E
İzmir, *Turkey* **49 C9** 38 25N 27 8 E
İzmir □, *Turkey* **49 C9** 38 15N 27 40 E
İzmir Adnan Menderes ✈ (ADB), *Turkey* **49 C9** 38 23N 27 6 E
İzmir Körfezi, *Turkey* **49 C8** 38 30N 26 50 E
İzmit = Kocaeli, *Turkey* **51 F13** 40 45N 29 50 E
Iznájar, *Spain* **43 H6** 37 15N 4 19W
Iznalloz, *Spain* **43 H7** 37 24N 3 30W
İznik, *Turkey* **100 B3** 40 23N 29 46 E
İznik Gölü, *Turkey* **51 F13** 40 27N 29 30 E
Izobilno-Tishchenskoye = Izobil'nyy, *Russia* **61 H5** 45 25N 41 44 E
Izobil'nyy, *Russia* **61 H5** 45 25N 41 44 E
Izola, *Slovenia* **45 C10** 45 32N 13 39 E
Izozog, Bañados de, *Bolivia* **173 D5** 18 48 S 62 10W
Izra, *Syria* **103 C5** 32 51N 36 15 E
Iztochni Rodopi, *Bulgaria* **51 E9** 41 45N 25 30 E
Izu-Hantō, *Japan* **73 C11** 34 45N 139 0 E
Izu-Shotō, *Japan* **71 G10** 34 30N 140 0 E
Izúcar de Matamoros, *Mexico* **163 D5** 18 36N 98 28W
Izuhara, *Japan* **72 C1** 34 12N 129 17 E
Izumi, *Kagoshima, Japan* **72 E2** 32 5N 130 22 E
Izumi, *Ōsaka, Japan* **73 C7** 34 28N 135 24 E
Izumi-Sano, *Japan* **73 C7** 34 23N 135 18 E
Izumo, *Japan* **72 B4** 35 20N 132 46 E
Izyaslav, *Ukraine* **59 G4** 50 5N 26 50 E
Izyum, *Ukraine* **59 H9** 49 12N 37 19 E

J

J.F. Rodrigues, *Brazil* **170 B1** 2 55 S 50 20W
J.P. Koch Fjord, *Greenland* **10 A6** 82 45N 44 0W
J. Strom Thurmond L., *U.S.A.* **152 B7** 33 40N 82 12W
Ja-ela, *Sri Lanka* **95 L4** 7 5N 79 53 E
Jaba, *Ethiopia* **107 F4** 6 20N 35 7 E
Jabal at Tā'ir, *Red Sea* **107 D5** 15 35N 41 52 E
Jabalón →, *Spain* **43 G6** 38 53N 4 5W
Jabalpur, *India* **93 H8** 23 9N 79 58 E
Jabbūl, *Syria* **96 B3** 36 4N 37 30 E
Jabiru, *Australia* **124 B5** 12 40 S 132 53 E
Jablah, *Syria* **100 E6** 35 20N 36 0 E
Jablanac, *Croatia* **45 D11** 44 42N 14 56 E
Jablanica, *Bos.-H.* **52 G2** 43 40N 17 45 E
Jablonec nad Nisou, *Czech Rep.* **34 A8** 50 43N 15 10 E
Jablonica, *Slovak Rep.* **35 C10** 48 37N 17 26 E
Jabłonowo Pomorskie, *Poland* **54 E6** 53 23N 19 10 E
Jablunkov, *Czech Rep.* **35 B11** 49 35N 18 46 E
Jaboatão, *Brazil* **170 C4** 8 7 S 35 1W
Jabonga, *Phil.* **81 G5** 9 20N 125 32 E
Jaboticabal, *Brazil* **175 A6** 21 15 S 48 17W
Jabukovac, *Serbia & M.* **50 B6** 44 22N 22 21 E
Jaburu, *Brazil* **173 B5** 5 30 S 64 0W
Jaca, *Spain* **40 C4** 42 35N 0 33W
Jacaré →, *Brazil* **170 D3** 10 3 S 42 13W
Jacareí, *Brazil* **175 A6** 23 20 S 46 0W
Jacarèzinho, *Brazil* **175 A6** 23 5 S 49 58W
Jaciara, *Brazil* **173 D7** 15 59 S 54 57W
Jacinto, *Brazil* **171 E3** 16 10 S 40 17W
Jaciparaná, *Brazil* **173 B5** 9 15 S 64 23W
Jackman, *U.S.A.* **149 C10** 45 35N 70 17W
Jacksboro, *U.S.A.* **155 J5** 33 14N 98 15W
Jackson, *Barbados* **165 g** 13 7N 59 36W
Jackson, *Ala., U.S.A.* **149 K2** 31 31N 87 53W
Jackson, *Calif., U.S.A.* **160 G6** 38 21N 120 46W
Jackson, *Ga., U.S.A.* **152 B6** 33 20N 83 57W
Jackson, *Ky., U.S.A.* **148 G4** 37 33N 83 23W
Jackson, *Mich., U.S.A.* **157 B12** 42 15N 84 24W
Jackson, *Minn., U.S.A.* **154 D7** 43 37N 95 1W
Jackson, *Miss., U.S.A.* **155 J9** 32 18N 90 12W
Jackson, *Mo., U.S.A.* **155 G10** 37 23N 89 40W
Jackson, *N.H., U.S.A.* **151 B13** 44 10N 71 11W
Jackson, *Ohio, U.S.A.* **148 F4** 39 3N 82 39W
Jackson, *S.C., U.S.A.* **152 B8** 33 20N 81 47W
Jackson, *Tenn., U.S.A.* **149 H1** 35 37N 88 49W
Jackson, *Wyo., U.S.A.* **158 E8** 43 29N 110 46W
Jackson, C., *N.Z.* **131 A9** 40 59 S 174 20 E
Jackson B., *N.Z.* **131 D3** 43 58 S 168 42 E
Jackson Center, *U.S.A.* **157 D12** 40 27N 84 4W
Jackson Hd., *N.Z.* **131 D3** 43 58 S 168 37 E
Jackson L., *Fla., U.S.A.* **152 E5** 30 30N 84 17W
Jackson L., *Ga., U.S.A.* **152 B6** 33 19N 83 50W
Jackson L., *Wyo., U.S.A.* **158 E8** 43 52N 110 36W
Jacksons, *N.Z.* **131 C6** 42 46 S 171 32 E
Jackson's Arm, *Canada* **141 C8** 49 52N 56 47W
Jacksonville, *Ala., U.S.A.* **152 B4** 33 49N 85 46W
Jacksonville, *Ark., U.S.A.* **155 H8** 34 52N 92 7W
Jacksonville, *Calif., U.S.A.* **160 H6** 37 52N 120 24W
Jacksonville, *Fla., U.S.A.* **152 E8** 30 20N 81 39W
Jacksonville, *Ga., U.S.A.* **152 D7** 31 49N 82 59W
Jacksonville, *Ill., U.S.A.* **156 E6** 39 44N 90 14W
Jacksonville, *N.C., U.S.A.* **149 H7** 34 45N 77 26W
Jacksonville, *Tex., U.S.A.* **155 K7** 31 58N 95 17W
Jacksonville Beach, *U.S.A.* **152 E8** 30 17N 81 24W
Jacksonville International ✈ (JAX), *U.S.A.* **152 E8** 30 30N 81 41W
Jacmel, *Haiti* **165 C5** 18 14N 72 32W
Jacob Lake, *U.S.A.* **159 H7** 36 43N 112 13W
Jacobabad, *Pakistan* **91 C3** 28 20N 68 29 E
Jacobina, *Brazil* **170 D3** 11 11 S 40 30W
Jacobshagen = Dobrzany, *Poland* **54 E2** 53 22N 15 25 E
Jacques-Cartier ⌂, *Canada* **141 C5** 47 15N 71 33W
Jacques-Cartier, Dét. de, *Canada* **141 C7** 50 0N 63 30W
Jacques-Cartier, Mt., *Canada* **141 C6** 48 57N 66 0W
Jacqueville, *Ivory C.* **112 D4** 5 12N 4 25W
Jacuí →, *Brazil* **175 C5** 30 2 S 51 15W
Jacumba, *U.S.A.* **161 N10** 32 37N 116 11W
Jacundá →, *Brazil* **170 B1** 1 57 S 50 26W
Jadcherla, *India* **94 F4** 16 46N 78 9 E
Jade, *Germany* **30 B4** 53 20N 8 14 E
Jadebusen, *Germany* **30 B4** 53 29N 8 12 E
Jadotville = Likasi, *Dem. Rep. of the Congo* **119 E2** 10 55 S 26 48 E
Jadovnik, *Serbia & M.* **50 C3** 43 20N 19 45 E
Jadraque, *Spain* **40 E2** 40 55N 2 55W
Jādū, *Libya* **108 B2** 32 0N 12 0 E
Jaén, *Peru* **172 B2** 5 25 S 78 40W
Jaén, *Spain* **43 H7** 37 44N 3 43W
Jaén □, *Spain* **43 H7** 37 50N 3 30W
Jæren, *Norway* **18 F2** 58 42N 5 47 E
Jærens rev, *Norway* **18 F2** 58 45N 5 45 E
Jafarabad, *India* **92 J4** 20 52N 71 22 E
Jafène, *Africa* **110 D3** 20 35N 5 30W
Jaffa = Tel Aviv-Yafo, *Israel* **103 C3** 32 4N 34 48 E
Jaffa, C., *Australia* **128 D3** 36 58 S 139 40 E
Jaffna, *Sri Lanka* **95 K5** 9 45N 80 2 E
Jaffray, *Canada* **143 D10** 49 47N 94 26W
Jaffrey, *U.S.A.* **151 D12** 42 49N 72 2W
Jagadhri, *India* **92 D7** 30 10N 77 20 E
Jagadishpur, *India* **93 G11** 25 30N 84 21 E
Jagdalpur, *India* **94 E6** 19 3N 82 0 E
Jagersfontein, *S. Africa* **116 D4** 29 44 S 25 27 E
Jaghīn →, *Iran* **97 E8** 27 17N 57 13 E
Jagna, *Phil.* **81 G5** 9 39N 124 22 E
Jagodina, *Serbia & M.* **50 B5** 44 5N 21 15 E
Jagst →, *Germany* **31 F5** 49 14N 9 10 E
Jagtial, *India* **94 E4** 18 50N 79 0 E
Jaguaquara, *Brazil* **171 D4** 13 32 S 39 58W
Jaguariaíva, *Brazil* **175 A6** 24 10 S 49 50W
Jaguaribe, *Brazil* **170 C4** 5 53 S 38 37W
Jaguaribe →, *Brazil* **170 B4** 4 25 S 37 45W
Jaguaruana, *Brazil* **170 B4** 4 50 S 37 47W
Jagüey Grande, *Cuba* **164 B3** 22 35N 81 7W
Jagungal, Mt., *Australia* **129 D8** 36 8 S 148 22 E
Jahanabad, *India* **93 G11** 25 13N 84 59 E
Jahazpur, *India* **92 G6** 25 37N 75 17 E
Jahrom, *Iran* **97 D7** 28 30N 53 31 E
Jaicós, *Brazil* **170 C3** 7 21 S 41 8W
Jaigarh, *India* **94 F1** 17 17N 73 13 E
Jaijon, *India* **92 D7** 31 21N 76 9 E
Jailolo, *Indonesia* **82 A3** 1 5N 127 30 E
Jailolo, Selat, *Indonesia* **83 A3** 0 5N 129 5 E
Jaintiapur, *Bangla.* **90 C4** 25 8N 92 7 E
Jaipur, *Assam, India* **90 B5** 27 16N 95 24 E
Jaipur, *Raj., India* **92 F6** 27 0N 75 50 E
Jais, *India* **93 F9** 26 15N 81 32 E
Jaisalmer, *India* **92 F4** 26 55N 70 54 E
Jaisinghnagar, *India* **93 H8** 23 38N 78 34 E
Jaitaran, *India* **92 F5** 26 12N 73 56 E
Jaithari, *India* **93 H8** 23 14N 78 37 E
Jājarm, *Iran* **97 B8** 36 58N 56 27 E
Jajce, *Bos.-H.* **52 F2** 44 19N 17 17 E
Jajpur, *India* **94 D8** 20 53N 86 22 E
Jakam →, *India* **92 H6** 23 54N 74 13 E
Jakarta, *Indonesia* **84 D3** 6 9 S 106 49 E
Jakhal, *India* **92 E6** 29 48N 75 50 E
Jakhau, *India* **92 H3** 23 13N 68 43 E
Jakobshavn = Illulissat, *Greenland* **10 D5** 69 12N 51 10W
Jakobstad = Pietarsaari, *Finland* **14 E20** 63 40N 22 43 E
Jakupica, *Macedonia* **50 E5** 41 45N 21 22 E
Jal, *U.S.A.* **155 J3** 32 7N 103 12W
Jalal-Abad, *Kyrgyzstan* **65 C6** 40 56N 73 0 E
Jalālābād, *Afghan.* **91 B3** 34 30N 70 29 E
Jalalabad, *India* **93 F8** 27 41N 79 42 E
Jalalpur Jattan, *Pakistan* **92 C6** 32 38N 74 11 E
Jalama, *U.S.A.* **161 L6** 34 29N 120 29W
Jalapa, *Guatemala* **164 D2** 14 39N 89 59W
Jalapa Enríquez = Xalapa, *Mexico* **163 D5** 19 32N 96 55W
Jalasjärvi, *Finland* **15 E20** 62 29N 22 47 E
Jalaun, *India* **93 F8** 26 8N 79 25 E
Jalāzin, *Afghan.* **65 E2** 37 2N 64 49 E
Jaldak, *Afghan.* **91 C2** 31 58N 66 43 E
Jaldhaka →, *Bangla.* **90 B2** 26 16N 89 16 E
Jales, *Brazil* **171 F1** 20 10 S 50 33W
Jalesar, *India* **92 F8** 27 29N 78 19 E
Jaleswar, *Nepal* **93 F11** 26 38N 85 48 E
Jalgaon, *India* **94 D2** 21 0N 75 42 E
Jalībah, *Iraq* **96 D5** 30 35N 46 32 E
Jalingo, *Nigeria* **113 D7** 8 55N 11 25 E
Jalisco □, *Mexico* **162 D4** 20 0N 104 0W
Jalkot, *Pakistan* **93 B5** 35 14N 73 24 E
Jallas →, *Spain* **42 C1** 42 54N 9 8W
Jalna, *India* **94 E2** 19 48N 75 38 E
Jalón →, *Spain* **40 D3** 41 47N 1 4W
Jalor, *India* **92 G5** 25 21N 72 37 E
Jalpa, *Mexico* **162 C4** 21 38N 102 58W
Jalpaiguri, *India* **90 B2** 26 32N 88 46 E
Jālq, *Iran* **91 D1** 27 35N 62 46 E
Jaluit I., *Marshall Is.* **134 G8** 6 0N 169 30 E
Jalūlā, *Iraq* **101 E11** 34 16N 45 10 E
Jamaane = Giamama, *Somali Rep.* **120 D2** 0 4N 42 44 E
Jamaari, *Nigeria* **113 C6** 11 44N 9 53 E
Jamaica ■, *W. Indies* **164 a** 18 10N 77 30W
Jamalpur, *Bangla.* **90 C2** 24 52N 89 56 E
Jamalpur, *India* **93 G12** 25 18N 86 28 E
Jamalpurganj, *India* **93 H13** 23 2N 87 59 E
Jamanxim →, *Brazil* **173 A6** 4 43 S 56 18W
Jamari, *Brazil* **173 B5** 8 45 S 63 27W
Jamari →, *Brazil* **173 B5** 8 27 S 63 30W
Jamba, *Angola* **115 E3** 14 40 S 16 2 E
Jambewangi, *Indonesia* **79 J17** 8 17 S 114 7 E
Jambi, *Indonesia* **84 C2** 1 38 S 103 30 E
Jambi □, *Indonesia* **84 C2** 1 30 S 102 30 E
Jambongan, Pulau, *Malaysia* **78 C5** 6 45N 117 20 E
Jambusar, *India* **92 H5** 22 3N 72 51 E
James, *U.S.A.* **152 C6** 32 58N 83 29W
James →, *S. Dak., U.S.A.* **154 D6** 42 52N 97 18W
James →, *Va., U.S.A.* **148 G7** 36 56N 76 27W
James, I. = San Salvador, I., *Ecuador* **172 a** 0 16 S 90 42W
James B., *Canada* **140 B3** 54 0N 80 0W
James Island, *U.S.A.* **152 C10** 32 45N 79 55W
James Ranges, *Australia* **124 D5** 24 10 S 132 30 E
James Ross I., *Antarctica* **7 C18** 63 58 S 57 50W
Jamesabad, *Pakistan* **92 G3** 25 17N 69 15 E
Jameson Land, *Greenland* **10 C8** 71 0N 23 30W
Jamesport, *U.S.A.* **156 E3** 39 58N 93 48W
Jamestown = Wawa, *Canada* **140 C3** 47 59N 84 47W
Jamestown, *Australia* **128 B3** 33 10 S 138 32 E
Jamestown, *St. Helena* **9 h** 15 55 S 5 43W
Jamestown, *S. Africa* **116 E4** 31 6 S 26 45 E
Jamestown, *Ind., U.S.A.* **157 E10** 39 56N 86 38W
Jamestown, *Mo., U.S.A.* **156 F4** 38 48N 92 30W
Jamestown, *N. Dak., U.S.A.* **154 B5** 46 54N 98 42W
Jamestown, *N.Y., U.S.A.* **150 D5** 42 6N 79 14W
Jamestown, *Ohio, U.S.A.* **157 E13** 39 39N 83 33W
Jamestown, *Pa., U.S.A.* **150 E4** 41 29N 80 27W
Jamestown, *S.C., U.S.A.* **152 B10** 33 17N 79 42W
Jamīlābād, *Iran* **97 C6** 34 24N 48 28 E
Jamiltepec, *Mexico* **163 D5** 16 17N 97 49W
Jamira →, *India* **93 J13** 21 35N 88 28 E
Jämjö, *Sweden* **17 H9** 56 12N 15 49 E
Jamkhandi, *India* **94 F2** 16 30N 75 15 E
Jamkhed, *India* **94 E2** 18 43N 75 19 E
Jammalamadugu, *India* **95 G4** 14 51N 78 25 E
Jammerbugt, *Denmark* **17 G3** 57 15N 9 20 E
Jammu, *India* **92 C6** 32 43N 74 54 E
Jammu & Kashmir □, *India* **93 B7** 34 25N 77 0 E
Jamnagar, *India* **92 H4** 22 30N 70 6 E
Jamner, *India* **94 D2** 20 45N 75 52 E
Jamni →, *India* **93 G8** 25 13N 78 35 E
Jampur, *Pakistan* **91 C3** 29 39N 70 40 E
Jamrud, *Pakistan* **92 C4** 33 59N 71 24 E
Jämsä, *Finland* **15 F21** 61 53N 25 10 E
Jamshedpur, *India* **93 H12** 22 44N 86 12 E
Jamtara, *India* **93 H12** 23 59N 86 49 E
Jämtland, *Sweden* **14 E15** 63 31N 14 0 E
Jämtlands län □, *Sweden* **16 B7** 63 0N 14 40 E
Jamuna →, *Bangla.* **90 D2** 23 51N 89 45 E
Jamunamukh, *India* **90 B4** 26 6N 92 44 E
Jamurki, *Bangla.* **90 C3** 24 9N 90 2 E
Jan L., *Canada* **143 C8** 54 56N 102 55W
Jan Mayen, *Arctic* **6 B7** 71 0N 9 0W
Janakkala, *Finland* **15 F21** 60 54N 24 36 E
Janaúba, *Brazil* **171 E3** 15 48 S 43 19W
Janaucu, I., *Brazil* **170 A1** 0 30N 50 10W
Jand, *Pakistan* **92 C5** 33 30N 72 6 E
Jandaia, *Brazil* **171 E1** 17 6 S 50 7W
Jandaq, *Iran* **97 C7** 34 3N 54 22 E
Jandía, *Canary Is.* **9 e2** 28 6N 14 21W
Jandía △, *Canary Is.* **9 e2** 28 4N 14 19W
Jandía, Pta. de, *Canary Is.* **9 e2** 28 3N 14 31W
Jandiatuba →, *Brazil* **168 D4** 3 28 S 68 42W
Jandola, *Pakistan* **92 C4** 32 20N 70 9 E
Jandowae, *Australia* **127 D5** 26 45 S 151 7 E
Jándula →, *Spain* **43 G6** 38 3N 4 6W
Jane Pk., *N.Z.* **131 F3** 45 15 S 168 20 E
Janesville, *U.S.A.* **156 B7** 42 41N 89 1W
Janga, *Ghana* **113 C4** 10 5N 1 0W
Jangamo, *Mozam.* **117 C6** 24 6 S 35 21 E
Janghai, *India* **93 G10** 25 33N 82 19 E
Jango, *Brazil* **173 E6** 20 27 S 55 29W
Jangoon, *India* **94 F4** 17 44N 79 5 E
Jangy-Bazar, *Kyrgyzstan* **65 C5** 41 40N 70 53 E
Jangy-Jol, *Kyrgyzstan* **65 C6** 41 36N 72 9 E
Janhtang Ga, *Burma* **90 B6** 26 32N 96 38 E
Jani Khel, *Afghan.* **91 B3** 32 46N 68 24 E
Janikowo, *Poland* **55 F5** 52 45N 18 7 E
Janinà = Ioánnina □, *Greece* **48 B2** 39 39N 20 57 E
Janiuay, *Phil.* **81 F4** 10 58N 122 30 E
Janja, *Bos.-H.* **52 F4** 44 40N 19 14 E
Janjanbureh, *Gambia* **112 C2** 13 30N 14 47W
Janjevo, *Serbia & M.* **50 D5** 42 35N 21 19 E
Janjgir, *India* **93 J10** 22 1N 82 34 E
Janjina, *Croatia* **45 F14** 42 58N 17 25 E
Janjina, *Madag.* **117 C8** 20 30 S 45 50 E
Jankau = Janikowo, *Poland* **55 F5** 52 45N 18 7 E
Janos, *Mexico* **162 A3** 30 45N 108 10W
Jánoshalma, *Hungary* **52 D4** 46 18N 19 21 E
Jánosháza, *Hungary* **52 C2** 47 8N 17 12 E
Jánossomorja, *Hungary* **52 C2** 47 47N 17 11 E
Janów, *Poland* **55 H6** 50 44N 19 27 E
Janów Lubelski, *Poland* **55 H9** 50 48N 22 23 E
Janów Podlaski, *Poland* **55 F10** 52 11N 23 11 E
Janowiec Wielkopolski, *Poland* **55 F4** 52 45N 17 30 E
Januária, *Brazil* **171 E3** 15 25 S 44 25W
Janub △, *Sudan* **107 F2** 6 50N 28 45 E
Janub Dârfûr □, *Sudan* **107 E2** 11 0N 25 0 E
Janub Kordofân □, *Sudan* **107 E3** 12 0N 30 0 E
Janûb Sînî □, *Egypt* **103 F2** 29 30N 33 50 E
Janubio, *Canary Is.* **9 e2** 28 56N 13 50W
Janville, *France* **27 D8** 48 10N 1 50 E
Janwada, *India* **94 E3** 18 0N 77 29 E
Janzé, *France* **26 E5** 47 55N 1 28W
Jaora, *India* **92 H6** 23 40N 75 10 E
Japan ■, *Asia* **71 G8** 36 0N 136 0 E
Japan, Sea of, *Asia* **70 E7** 40 0N 135 0 E
Japan Trench, *Pac. Oc.* **62 F18** 32 0N 142 0 E
Japen = Yapen, *Indonesia* **83 B5** 1 50 S 136 0 E
Japiim, *Brazil* **172 B3** 7 37 S 72 54W
Japla, *India* **93 G11** 24 33N 84 1 E
Japurá, *Brazil* **168 D4** 1 48 S 66 34W
Japurá →, *Brazil* **168 D4** 3 8 S 65 46W
Jaquarão, *Brazil* **175 C5** 32 34 S 53 23W
Jaqué, *Panama* **164 E4** 7 27N 78 8W
Jarābulus, *Syria* **101 D8** 36 49N 38 1 E
Jaraguá, *Brazil* **171 E2** 15 45 S 49 20W
Jaraguari, *Brazil* **173 E7** 20 9 S 54 35W
Jaraicejo, *Spain* **43 F5** 39 40N 5 49W
Jaraíz de la Vera, *Spain* **42 E5** 40 4N 5 45W
Jarama →, *Spain* **42 E7** 40 24N 3 32W
Jaramānah, *Syria* **100 F7** 33 29N 36 21 E
Jaramillo, *Argentina* **176 C3** 47 10 S 67 7W
Jarandilla, *Spain* **42 E5** 40 8N 5 39W
Jaranwala, *Pakistan* **91 C4** 31 15N 73 26 E
Jarash, *Jordan* **103 C4** 32 17N 35 54 E
Jarash □, *Jordan* **103 C4** 32 17N 35 54 E
Jarauçu →, *Brazil* **169 D7** 1 48 S 52 22W
Järbo, *Sweden* **16 D10** 60 43N 16 36 E
Jarboesville = Lexington Park, *U.S.A.* **148 F7** 38 16N 76 27W
Jardas al 'Abīd, *Libya* **108 B4** 32 18N 20 59 E
Jardim, *Brazil* **174 A4** 21 28 S 56 2W
Jardín →, *Spain* **41 G2** 38 50N 2 10W
Jardine River △, *Australia* **126 A3** 11 9 S 142 21 E
Jardines de la Reina, Arch. de los, *Cuba* **164 B4** 20 50N 78 50W
Jargalang, *China* **75 C12** 43 5N 122 55 E
Jargalant = Hovd, *Mongolia* **68 B4** 48 2N 91 37 E
Jari →, *Brazil* **169 D7** 1 9 S 51 54W
Jaria Janjail, *Bangla.* **90 C3** 25 0N 90 40 E
Jarīr, W. al →, *Si. Arabia* **96 E4** 25 38N 42 30 E
Järlåsa, *Sweden* **16 E11** 59 53N 17 12 E
Jarlsberg og Larvik = Vestfold □, *Norway* **18 E7** 59 15N 10 0 E
Jarmen, *Germany* **30 B9** 53 54N 13 20 E
Järna, *Dalarna, Sweden* **16 D8** 60 33N 14 26 E
Järna, *Stockholm, Sweden* **16 E11** 59 6N 17 34 E
Jarnac, *France* **28 C3** 45 40N 0 11W
Jarny, *France* **27 C12** 49 9N 5 53 E
Jaro, *Phil.* **81 F5** 11 11N 124 47 E
Jarocin, *Poland* **55 G4** 51 59N 17 29 E
Jaroměř, *Czech Rep.* **34 A8** 50 22N 15 52 E
Jarosław, *Poland* **55 H9** 50 2N 22 42 E
Järpås, *Sweden* **17 F6** 58 23N 12 57 E
Järpen, *Sweden* **16 A7** 63 21N 13 26 E
Jarqŭrghon, *Uzbekistan* **65 E3** 37 31N 67 25 E
Jarrahdale, *Australia* **125 F2** 32 24 S 116 5 E
Jarrahi →, *Iran* **97 D6** 30 49N 48 48 E
Jarres, Plaine des, *Laos* **86 C4** 19 27N 103 10 E
Jarso, *Ethiopia* **107 F4** 5 15N 37 30 E
Jartai, *China* **74 E3** 39 45N 105 48 E
Jaru, *Brazil* **173 C5** 10 26 S 62 27W
Jaru →, *Brazil* **173 C5** 10 5 S 61 59W
Jarud Qi, *China* **75 B11** 44 28N 120 50 E
Järvenpää, *Finland* **15 F21** 60 29N 25 5 E
Jarvis, *Canada* **150 D4** 42 53N 80 6W
Jarvis I., *Pac. Oc.* **135 H12** 0 15 S 160 5W
Jarvorník, *Czech Rep.* **35 A10** 50 23N 17 2 E
Järvsö, *Sweden* **16 C10** 61 43N 16 10 E
Jarwa, *India* **93 F10** 27 38N 82 30 E
Jaša Tomić, *Serbia & M.* **52 E5** 45 26N 20 50 E
Jasaan, *Phil.* **81 G5** 8 39N 124 45 E
Jasdan, *India* **92 H4** 22 2N 71 12 E
Jashpurnagar, *India* **93 H11** 22 54N 84 9 E
Jasidih, *India* **93 G12** 24 31N 86 39 E
Jasień, *Poland* **55 G2** 51 46N 15 0 E
Jāsimīyah, *Iraq* **101 F11** 33 45N 44 41 E
Jasin, *Malaysia* **87 L4** 2 20N 102 26 E
Jāsk, *Iran* **97 E8** 25 38N 57 45 E
Jasło, *Poland* **55 J8** 49 45N 21 30 E
Jasmund, *Germany* **30 A9** 54 32N 13 35 E
Jasmund △, *Germany* **30 A9** 54 31N 13 38 E
Jaso, *India* **93 G9** 24 30N 80 29 E
Jason Is., *Falk. Is.* **9 f** 51 0 S 61 0W
Jasonville, *U.S.A.* **157 E9** 39 10N 87 12W
Jasper, *Alta., Canada* **142 C5** 52 55N 118 5W
Jasper, *Ont., Canada* **151 B9** 44 52N 75 57W
Jasper, *Ala., U.S.A.* **149 J2** 33 50N 87 17W

Jasper, *Fla., U.S.A.* **152 E7** 30 31N 82 57W
Jasper, *Ind., U.S.A.* **157 F10** 38 24N 86 56W
Jasper, *Tex., U.S.A.* **155 K8** 30 56N 94 1W
Jasper △, *Canada* **142 C5** 52 50N 118 8W
Jasrasar, *India* **92 F5** 27 43N 73 49 E
Jassey = Iaşi, *Romania* **53 C12** 47 10N 27 40 E
Jastarnia, *Poland* **54 D5** 54 42N 18 40 E
Jastrebarsko, *Croatia* **45 C12** 45 41N 15 39 E
Jastrow = Jastrowie, *Poland* **54 E3** 53 26N 16 49 E
Jastrowie, *Poland* **54 E3** 53 26N 16 49 E
Jastrzębie Zdrój, *Poland* **55 J5** 49 57N 18 35 E
Jász-Nagykun-Szolnok □, *Hungary* **52 C5** 47 15N 20 30 E
Jászapáti, *Hungary* **52 C5** 47 32N 20 10 E
Jászárokszállás, *Hungary* **52 C4** 47 39N 19 58 E
Jászberény, *Hungary* **52 C4** 47 30N 19 55 E
Jászkisér, *Hungary* **52 C5** 47 27N 20 20 E
Jászladány, *Hungary* **52 C5** 47 23N 20 10 E
Jataí, *Brazil* **171 E1** 17 58 S 51 48W
Jatapu →, *Brazil* **169 D6** 2 13 S 58 17W
Jath, *India* **94 F2** 17 3N 75 13 E
Jati, *Pakistan* **92 G3** 24 20N 68 19 E
Jatibarang, *Indonesia* **85 D3** 6 28 S 108 18 E
Jatiluwih, *Indonesia* **79 J18** 8 23 S 115 8 E
Jatinegara, *Indonesia* **84 D3** 6 13 S 106 52 E
Játiva = Xátiva, *Spain* **41 G4** 38 59N 0 32W
Jatobá = Petrolândia, *Brazil* **170 C4** 9 5 S 38 20W
Jättendal, *Sweden* **16 C11** 61 58N 17 15 E
Jaú, *Angola* **115 F2** 15 12 S 13 31 E
Jaú, *Brazil* **175 A6** 22 10 S 48 30W
Jaú →, *Brazil* **169 D5** 1 54 S 61 26W
Jauaperí →, *Brazil* **169 D5** 1 26 S 61 35W
Jauer = Jawor, *Poland* **55 G3** 51 4N 16 11 E
Jauja, *Peru* **172 C2** 11 45 S 75 15W
Jaunpur, *India* **93 G10** 25 46N 82 44 E
Jauru →, *Brazil* **173 D6** 16 22 S 57 46W
Java = Jawa, *Indonesia* **85 D4** 7 0 S 110 0 E
Java Sea, *Indonesia* **85 C3** 4 35 S 107 15 E
Java Trench, *Ind. Oc.* **84 D2** 9 0 S 105 0 E
Javadi Hills, *India* **95 H4** 12 40N 78 40 E
Javalambre, Sa. de, *Spain* **40 E4** 40 6N 1 0W
Jávea, *Spain* **41 G5** 38 48N 0 10 E
Javhlant = Uliastay, *Mongolia* **68 B4** 47 56N 97 28 E
Javier, I., *Chile* **176 C2** 47 5 S 74 25W
Javla, *India* **94 F2** 17 18N 75 9 E
Jawa, *Indonesia* **85 D4** 7 0 S 110 0 E
Jawa Barat □, *Indonesia* **79 G12** 7 0 S 107 0 E
Jawa Tengah □, *Indonesia* **79 G14** 7 0 S 110 0 E
Jawa Timur □, *Indonesia* **79 G15** 8 0 S 113 0 E
Jawad, *India* **92 G6** 24 36N 74 51 E
Jawf, W. al →, *Yemen* **98 D4** 15 50N 45 30 E
Jawhar, *India* **94 E1** 19 55N 73 14 E
Jawor, *Poland* **55 G3** 51 4N 16 11 E
Jaworzno, *Poland* **55 H6** 50 13N 19 11 E
Jaworzyna Śląska, *Poland* **55 H3** 50 55N 16 28 E
Jay, *U.S.A.* **153 E2** 30 57N 87 9W
Jay Peak, *U.S.A.* **151 B12** 44 55N 72 32W
Jaya, Puncak, *Indonesia* **83 B5** 3 57 S 137 17 E
Jayanca, *Peru* **172 B2** 6 24 S 79 50W
Jayanti, *India* **90 B2** 26 45N 89 40 E
Jayapura, *Indonesia* **83 B6** 2 28 S 140 38 E
Jayawijaya, Pegunungan, *Indonesia* **83 B5** 5 0 S 139 0 E
Jayrūd, *Syria* **100 F7** 33 49N 36 44 E
Jayton, *U.S.A.* **155 J4** 33 15N 100 34W
Jāz Mūrīān, Hāmūn-e, *Iran* **97 E8** 27 20N 58 55 E
Jazīreh-ye Shīf, *Iran* **97 D6** 29 4N 50 54 E
Jazminal, *Mexico* **162 C4** 24 56N 101 25W
Jazzīn, *Lebanon* **103 B4** 33 31N 35 35 E
Jean, *U.S.A.* **161 K11** 35 47N 115 20W
Jean Marie River, *Canada* **142 A4** 61 32N 120 38W
Jean-Rabel, *Haiti* **165 C5** 19 50N 73 5W
Jeanerette, *U.S.A.* **155 L9** 29 55N 91 40W
Jeanette, Ostrov = Zhannetty, Ostrov, *Russia* **67 B16** 76 43N 158 0 E
Jeannette, *U.S.A.* **150 F5** 40 20N 79 36W
Jebāl Bārez, Kūh-e, *Iran* **97 D8** 28 30N 58 20 E
Jebba, *Nigeria* **113 D5** 9 9N 4 48 E
Jebel, Bahr el →, *Sudan* **107 F3** 9 30N 30 25 E
Jebel Dud, *Sudan* **107 E3** 13 25N 33 9 E
Jebel Qerri, *Sudan* **107 D3** 16 16N 32 50 E
Jeberos, *Peru* **172 B2** 5 15 S 76 10W
Jedburgh, *U.K.* **22 F6** 55 29N 2 33W
Jedda = Jiddah, *Si. Arabia* **98 B2** 21 29N 39 10 E
Jeddore L., *Canada* **141 C8** 48 3N 55 55W
Jedlicze, *Poland* **55 J8** 49 43N 21 40 E
Jędrzejów, *Poland* **55 H7** 50 35N 20 15 E
Jedwabne, *Poland* **55 E9** 53 17N 22 18 E
Jeetzel →, *Germany* **30 B7** 53 9N 11 3 E
Jefferson, *Ga., U.S.A.* **152 A6** 34 7N 83 35W
Jefferson, *Iowa, U.S.A.* **156 B2** 42 1N 94 23W
Jefferson, *Ohio, U.S.A.* **150 E4** 41 44N 80 46W
Jefferson, *Tex., U.S.A.* **155 J7** 32 46N 94 21W
Jefferson, *Wis., U.S.A.* **157 B8** 43 0N 88 48W
Jefferson, Mt., *Nev., U.S.A.* **158 G5** 38 51N 117 0W
Jefferson, Mt., *Oreg., U.S.A.* **158 D3** 44 41N 121 48W
Jefferson City, *Mo., U.S.A.* **156 F4** 38 34N 92 10W
Jefferson City, *Tenn., U.S.A.* **149 G4** 36 7N 83 30W
Jeffersontown, *U.S.A.* **157 F11** 38 12N 85 35W
Jeffersonville, *Ga., U.S.A.* **152 C6** 32 41N 83 20W
Jeffersonville, *Ind., U.S.A.* **157 F11** 38 17N 85 44W
Jeffersonville, *Ohio, U.S.A.* **157 E13** 39 39N 83 34W
Jeffrey City, *U.S.A.* **158 E10** 42 30N 107 49W
Jega, *Nigeria* **113 C5** 12 15N 4 23 E
Jejevo, *Solomon Is.* **133 M10** 8 6 S 159 8 E
Jeju = Cheju do, *S. Korea* **75 H14** 33 29N 126 34 E
Jēkabpils, *Latvia* **15 H21** 56 29N 25 57 E
Jekyll I., *U.S.A.* **152 D8** 31 4N 81 25W
Jelcz-Laskowice, *Poland* **55 G4** 51 2N 17 19 E
Jelenia Góra, *Poland* **55 H2** 50 50N 15 45 E
Jelgava, *Latvia* **15 H20** 56 41N 23 49 E
Jelgava □, *Latvia* **54 B10** 56 35N 23 45 E
Jelica, *Serbia & M.* **50 C4** 43 50N 20 17 E
Jelli, *Sudan* **107 F3** 5 25N 31 45 E
Jelšava, *Slovak Rep.* **35 C13** 48 37N 20 15 E
Jema'a Mallam = Kafanchan, *Nigeria* **113 D6** 9 40N 8 20 E
Jemaja, *Indonesia* **87 L5** 3 5N 105 45 E
Jemaluang, *Malaysia* **87 L4** 2 16N 103 52 E
Jember, *Indonesia* **85 D4** 8 11 S 113 41 E
Jena, *Germany* **30 E7** 50 54N 11 35 E
Jena, *U.S.A.* **155 K8** 31 41N 92 8W
Jenbach, *Austria* **34 D4** 47 24N 11 47 E
Jendouba, *Tunisia* **108 A1** 36 29N 8 47 E
Jenīn, *West Bank* **103 C4** 32 28N 35 18 E
Jenison, *U.S.A.* **157 B11** 42 54N 85 47W
Jenkins, *U.S.A.* **148 G4** 37 10N 82 38W
Jenner, *U.S.A.* **160 G3** 38 27N 123 7W
Jennings, *Fla., U.S.A.* **152 E6** 30 36N 83 6W
Jennings, *La., U.S.A.* **155 K8** 30 13N 92 40W
Jennings, *Mo., U.S.A.* **156 F6** 38 43N 90 16W
Jensen Beach, *U.S.A.* **153 H9** 27 15N 80 14W
Jepara, *Indonesia* **85 D3** 7 40 S 109 14 E
Jeparit, *Australia* **128 D5** 36 8 S 142 1 E
Jequié, *Brazil* **171 D3** 13 51 S 40 5W
Jequitaí →, *Brazil* **171 E3** 17 4 S 44 50W
Jequitinhonha, *Brazil* **171 E3** 16 30 S 41 0W
Jequitinhonha →, *Brazil* **171 E4** 15 51 S 38 53W
Jerada, *Morocco* **111 B4** 34 17N 2 10W
Jerantut, *Malaysia* **87 L4** 3 56N 102 22 E
Jerejak, Pulau, *Malaysia* **87 c** 5 19N 100 19 E
Jérémie, *Haiti* **165 C5** 18 40N 74 10W
Jeremoabo, *Brazil* **170 D4** 10 4 S 38 21W
Jerez, Punta, *Mexico* **163 C5** 22 58N 97 40W
Jerez de García Salinas, *Mexico* **162 C4** 22 39N 103 0W
Jerez de la Frontera, *Spain* **43 J4** 36 41N 6 7W
Jerez de los Caballeros, *Spain* **43 G4** 38 20N 6 45W
Jericho = El Arīḩā, *West Bank* **103 D4** 31 52N 35 27 E
Jericho, *Australia* **126 C4** 23 38 S 146 6 E
Jerichow, *Germany* **30 C8** 52 30N 12 1 E
Jerico Springs, *U.S.A.* **156 G2** 37 37N 94 1W
Jerid, Chott el = Djerid, Chott, *Tunisia* **108 B1** 33 42N 8 30 E
Jerilderie, *Australia* **129 C6** 35 20 S 145 41 E
Jermyn, *U.S.A.* **151 E9** 41 31N 75 31W
Jerome, *U.S.A.* **158 E6** 42 44N 114 31W
Jerramungup, *Australia* **125 F2** 33 55 S 118 55 E
Jersey, *U.K.* **21 H5** 49 11N 2 7W
Jersey City, *U.S.A.* **151 F10** 40 44N 74 4W
Jersey Shore, *U.S.A.* **150 E7** 41 12N 77 15W
Jerseyville, *U.S.A.* **156 E6** 39 7N 90 20W
Jerumenha, *Brazil* **170 C3** 7 5 S 43 30W
Jerusalem, *Israel* **103 D4** 31 47N 35 10 E
Jervis B., *Australia* **129 C9** 35 8 S 150 46 E
Jervis Inlet, *Canada* **142 C4** 50 0N 123 57W
Jerzu, *Italy* **46 C2** 39 47N 9 31 E
Jesenice, *Slovenia* **45 B11** 46 28N 14 3 E
Jeseník, *Czech Rep.* **35 A10** 50 14N 17 8 E
Jesenké, *Slovak Rep.* **35 C13** 48 20N 20 10 E
Jesi = Iesi, *Italy* **45 E10** 43 31N 13 14 E
Jessel = Jasło, *Poland* **55 J8** 49 45N 21 30 E
Jesselton = Kota Kinabalu, *Malaysia* **85 A5** 6 0N 116 4 E
Jessheim, *Norway* **18 D8** 60 9N 11 10 E
Jessnitz, *Germany* **30 D8** 51 40N 12 18 E
Jessore, *Bangla.* **90 D2** 23 10N 89 10 E
Jessup L., *U.S.A.* **153 G8** 28 43N 81 14W
Jesup, *Ga., U.S.A.* **152 D8** 31 36N 81 53W
Jesup, *Iowa, U.S.A.* **156 B4** 42 29N 92 4W
Jesús, *Peru* **172 B2** 7 15 S 78 25W
Jesús Carranza, *Mexico* **163 D5** 17 28N 95 1W
Jesús María, *Argentina* **174 C3** 30 59 S 64 5W
Jetmore, *U.S.A.* **155 F5** 38 4N 99 54W
Jetpur, *India* **92 J4** 21 45N 70 10 E
Jeumont, *France* **27 B11** 50 18N 4 6 E
Jevnaker, *Norway* **18 D7** 60 15N 10 26 E
Jewell, *U.S.A.* **156 B3** 42 20N 93 39W
Jewett, *U.S.A.* **150 F3** 40 22N 81 2W
Jewett City, *U.S.A.* **151 E13** 41 36N 71 59W
Jeyḩūnābād, *Iran* **97 C6** 34 58N 48 59 E
Jeypore, *India* **94 E6** 18 50N 82 38 E
Jeziorak, Jezioro, *Poland* **54 E6** 53 40N 19 35 E
Jeziorany, *Poland* **54 E7** 53 58N 20 46 E
Jeziorka →, *Poland* **55 F8** 52 8N 21 9 E
Jha Jha, *India* **93 G12** 24 46N 86 22 E
Jhaarkand = Jharkhand □, *India* **93 H11** 24 0N 85 50 E
Jhabua, *India* **92 H6** 22 46N 74 36 E
Jhajjar, *India* **92 E7** 28 37N 76 42 E
Jhal, *Pakistan* **92 E2** 28 17N 67 27 E
Jhal Jhao, *Pakistan* **91 D2** 26 20N 65 35 E
Jhalakati, *Bangla.* **90 D3** 22 39N 90 12 E
Jhalawar, *India* **92 G7** 24 40N 76 10 E
Jhalida, *India* **93 H11** 23 22N 85 58 E
Jhalrapatan, *India* **92 G7** 24 33N 76 10 E
Jhang Maghiana, *Pakistan* **91 C4** 31 15N 72 22 E
Jhansi, *India* **93 G8** 25 30N 78 36 E
Jhargram, *India* **93 H12** 22 27N 86 59 E
Jharia, *India* **93 H12** 23 45N 86 26 E
Jharkhand □, *India* **93 H11** 24 0N 85 50 E
Jharsuguda, *India* **94 D7** 21 56N 84 5 E
Jhelum, *Pakistan* **91 B4** 33 0N 73 45 E
Jhelum →, *Pakistan* **92 D5** 31 20N 72 10 E
Jhilmilli, *India* **93 H10** 23 24N 82 51 E
Jhudo, *Pakistan* **92 G3** 24 58N 69 18 E
Jhunjhunu, *India* **92 E6** 28 10N 75 30 E
Ji-Paraná, *Brazil* **173 C5** 10 50 S 61 58W
Ji Xian, *Hebei, China* **74 F8** 37 35N 115 30 E
Ji Xian, *Henan, China* **74 G8** 35 22N 114 5 E
Ji Xian, *Shanxi, China* **74 F6** 36 7N 110 40 E
Jia Xian, *Henan, China* **74 H7** 33 59N 113 12 E
Jia Xian, *Shaanxi, China* **74 E6** 38 12N 110 28 E
Jiading, *China* **77 B13** 31 22N 121 15 E
Jiahe, *China* **77 E9** 25 38N 112 19 E
Jiaji = Qionghai, *China* **86 C8** 19 15N 110 26 E
Jialing Jiang →, *China* **76 C6** 29 30N 106 20 E
Jiamusi, *China* **69 B8** 46 40N 130 26 E
Ji'an, *Jiangxi, China* **77 D10** 27 6N 114 59 E
Ji'an, *Jilin, China* **75 D14** 41 5N 126 10 E
Jianchang, *China* **75 D11** 40 55N 120 35 E
Jianchangying, *China* **75 D10** 40 10N 118 50 E
Jianchuan, *China* **76 D2** 26 38N 99 55 E
Jiande, *China* **77 C12** 29 23N 119 15 E
Jiang'an, *China* **76 C5** 28 40N 105 3 E
Jiangbei, *China* **76 C6** 29 40N 106 34 E
Jiangcheng, *China* **76 F3** 22 36N 101 52 E
Jiangchuan, *China* **76 E4** 24 8N 102 39 E
Jiangdi, *China* **76 D4** 26 57N 103 37 E
Jiangdu, *China* **77 A12** 32 27N 119 36 E
Jiange, *China* **76 A5** 32 4N 105 32 E
Jianghua, *China* **77 E8** 25 0N 111 47 E
Jiangjin, *China* **76 C6** 29 14N 106 14 E
Jiangkou, *China* **76 D7** 27 40N 108 49 E
Jiangle, *China* **77 D11** 26 42N 117 23 E
Jiangling, *China* **77 B9** 30 25N 112 12 E
Jiangmen, *China* **77 F9** 22 32N 113 0 E
Jiangning, *China* **77 B12** 31 55N 118 50 E
Jiangshan, *China* **77 C12** 28 40N 118 37 E
Jiangsu □, *China* **75 H11** 33 0N 120 0 E
Jiangxi □, *China* **77 D11** 27 30N 116 0 E
Jiangyan, *China* **77 A13** 32 30N 120 7 E
Jiangyin, *China* **77 B13** 31 54N 120 17 E
Jiangyong, *China* **77 E8** 25 20N 111 22 E
Jiangyou, *China* **76 B5** 31 44N 104 43 E
Jianhe, *China* **76 D7** 26 37N 108 31 E
Jianli, *China* **77 C9** 29 46N 112 56 E
Jianning, *China* **77 D11** 26 50N 116 50 E
Jian'ou, *China* **77 D12** 27 3N 118 17 E
Jianshi, *China* **76 B7** 30 37N 109 38 E
Jianshui, *China* **76 F4** 23 36N 102 43 E
Jianyang, *Fujian, China* **77 D12** 27 20N 118 5 E
Jianyang, *Sichuan, China* **76 B5** 30 24N 104 33 E
Jiao Xian = Jiaozhou, *China* **75 F11** 36 18N 120 1 E
Jiaohe, *Hebei, China* **74 E9** 38 2N 116 20 E
Jiaohe, *Jilin, China* **75 C14** 43 40N 127 22 E
Jiaojiang, *China* **77 C13** 28 40N 121 24 E
Jiaoling, *China* **77 E11** 24 41N 116 12 E
Jiaozhou, *China* **75 F11** 36 18N 120 1 E
Jiaozhou Wan, *China* **75 F11** 36 5N 120 10 E
Jiaozuo, *China* **74 G7** 35 16N 113 12 E
Jiashan, *China* **77 B13** 30 55N 120 55 E
Jiashi, *China* **65 D8** 39 29N 76 39 E
Jiawang, *China* **75 G9** 34 28N 117 26 E
Jiaxiang, *China* **74 G9** 35 25N 116 20 E
Jiaxing, *China* **77 B13** 30 49N 120 45 E
Jiayi = Chiai, *Taiwan* **77 F13** 23 29N 120 25 E
Jiayu, *China* **77 C9** 29 55N 113 55 E
Jibão, Serra do, *Brazil* **171 D3** 14 48 S 45 0W
Jibiya, *Nigeria* **113 C6** 13 5N 7 12 E
Jibou, *Romania* **53 C8** 47 15N 23 17 E
Jibuti = Djibouti ■, *Africa* **107 E5** 12 0N 43 0 E
Jicarón, I., *Panama* **164 E3** 7 10N 81 50W
Jičín, *Czech Rep.* **34 A8** 50 25N 15 28 E
Jiddah, *Si. Arabia* **98 B2** 21 29N 39 10 E
Jido, *India* **90 A5** 29 2N 94 58 E
Jieshou, *China* **74 H8** 33 18N 115 22 E
Jiexiu, *China* **74 F6** 37 2N 111 55 E
Jieyang, *China* **77 F11** 23 35N 116 21 E
Jigawa □, *Nigeria* **113 C6** 12 0N 9 45 E
Jiggalong, *Australia* **124 D3** 23 21 S 120 47 E
Jigni, *India* **93 G8** 25 45N 79 25 E
Jihlava, *Czech Rep.* **34 B8** 49 28N 15 35 E
Jihlava →, *Czech Rep.* **35 C9** 48 55N 16 36 E
Jihlavský □, *Czech Rep.* **34 B8** 49 30N 15 30 E
Jihočeský □, *Czech Rep.* **34 B7** 49 8N 14 35 E
Jihomoravský □, *Czech Rep.* **35 B9** 49 5N 16 30 E
Jijel, *Algeria* **111 A6** 36 52N 5 50 E
Jijiga, *Ethiopia* **120 C2** 9 20N 42 50 E
Jikamshi, *Nigeria* **113 C6** 12 12N 7 45 E
Jikau, *Sudan* **107 F3** 8 28N 33 47 E
Jilib = Gelib, *Somali Rep.* **120 D2** 0 29N 42 46 E
Jilin, *China* **75 C14** 43 44N 126 30 E
Jilin □, *China* **75 C14** 44 0N 127 0 E
Jiloca →, *Spain* **40 D3** 41 21N 1 39W
Jilong = Chilung, *Taiwan* **77 E13** 25 3N 121 45 E
Jim Thorpe, *U.S.A.* **151 F9** 40 52N 75 44W
Jima, *Ethiopia* **107 F4** 7 40N 36 47 E
Jimbaran, Teluk, *Indonesia* **79 K18** 8 46 S 115 9 E
Jimbolia, *Romania* **52 E5** 45 47N 20 43 E
Jimena de la Frontera, *Spain* **43 J5** 36 27N 5 24W
Jiménez, *Mexico* **162 B4** 27 10N 104 54W
Jimenez, *Phil.* **81 G4** 8 20N 123 50 E
Jimo, *China* **75 F11** 36 23N 120 30 E
Jin, Kepulauan, *Indonesia* **83 C4** 6 50 S 134 40 E
Jin Jiang →, *China* **77 C10** 28 24N 115 48 E
Jin Xian = Jinzhou, *China* **74 E8** 38 2N 115 2 E
Jin Xian, *China* **75 E11** 38 55N 121 42 E
Jinan, *China* **74 F9** 36 38N 117 1 E
Jinchang, *China* **68 C5** 38 30N 102 10 E
Jincheng, *China* **74 G7** 35 29N 112 50 E
Jinchuan, *China* **76 B4** 31 30N 102 3 E
Jind, *India* **92 E7** 29 19N 76 22 E
Jindabyne, *Australia* **129 D8** 36 25 S 148 35 E
Jinding, *China* **69 G10** 22 22N 113 33 E
Jindřichův Hradec, *Czech Rep.* **34 B8** 49 10N 15 2 E
Jing He →, *China* **74 G5** 34 27N 109 4 E
Jing Shan, *China* **77 B8** 31 20N 111 35 E
Jing Xian, *China* **77 B12** 30 38N 118 25 E
Jing'an, *China* **77 C10** 28 50N 115 17 E
Jingbian, *China* **74 F5** 37 20N 108 30 E
Jingchuan, *China* **74 G4** 35 20N 107 20 E
Jingde, *China* **77 B12** 30 15N 118 27 E
Jingdezhen, *China* **77 C11** 29 20N 117 11 E
Jingdong, *China* **76 E3** 24 23N 100 47 E
Jinggangshan, *China* **77 D10** 26 58N 114 15 E
Jinggu, *China* **76 F3** 23 35N 100 41 E
Jinghai, *China* **74 E9** 38 55N 116 55 E
Jinghong, *China* **76 G3** 22 0N 100 45 E
Jingjiang, *China* **77 A13** 32 2N 120 16 E
Jingle, *China* **74 E6** 38 20N 111 55 E
Jingmen, *China* **77 B9** 31 0N 112 10 E
Jingning, *China* **74 G3** 35 30N 105 43 E
Jingpo Hu, *China* **75 C15** 43 55N 128 55 E
Jingshan, *China* **77 B9** 31 1N 113 7 E
Jingtai, *China* **74 F3** 37 10N 104 6 E
Jingxi, *China* **76 F6** 23 8N 106 27 E
Jingxing, *China* **74 E8** 38 2N 114 8 E
Jingyang, *China* **74 G5** 34 30N 108 50 E
Jingyu, *China* **75 C14** 42 25N 126 45 E
Jingyuan, *China* **74 F3** 36 30N 104 40 E
Jingzhou, *China* **76 D7** 26 33N 109 40 E
Jingziguan, *China* **74 H6** 33 15N 111 0 E
Jinhua, *China* **77 C12** 29 8N 119 38 E
Jining, *Nei Monggol Zizhiqu, China* **74 D7** 41 5N 113 0 E
Jining, *Shandong, China* **74 G9** 35 22N 116 34 E
Jinja, *Uganda* **118 B3** 0 25N 33 12 E
Jinjang, *Malaysia* **87 L3** 3 13N 101 39 E
Jinji, *China* **74 F4** 37 58N 106 8 E
Jinjiang, *Fujian, China* **77 E12** 24 43N 118 33 E
Jinjiang, *Yunnan, China* **76 D3** 26 14N 100 34 E
Jinjini, *Ghana* **112 D4** 7 26N 2 42W
Jinkou, *China* **77 B10** 30 20N 114 8 E
Jinkouhe, *China* **76 C4** 29 18N 103 4 E
Jinmen Dao, *China* **77 E12** 24 25N 118 25 E
Jinning, *China* **76 E4** 24 38N 102 38 E
Jinotega, *Nic.* **164 D2** 13 6N 85 59W
Jinotepe, *Nic.* **164 D2** 11 50N 86 10W
Jinping, *Guizhou, China* **76 D7** 26 41N 109 10 E
Jinping, *Yunnan, China* **76 F4** 22 45N 103 18 E
Jinsha, *China* **76 D6** 27 29N 106 12 E
Jinsha Jiang →, *China* **76 C5** 28 50N 104 36 E
Jinshan, *China* **77 B13** 30 54N 121 10 E
Jinshi, *China* **77 C8** 29 40N 111 50 E
Jintan, *China* **77 B12** 31 42N 119 36 E
Jintotolo Channel, *Phil.* **81 F4** 11 48N 123 5 E
Jintur, *India* **94 E3** 19 37N 76 42 E
Jinxi, *Jiangxi, China* **77 D11** 27 56N 116 45 E
Jinxi, *Liaoning, China* **75 D11** 40 52N 120 50 E
Jinxian, *China* **77 C11** 28 26N 116 17 E
Jinxiang, *China* **74 G9** 35 5N 116 22 E
Jinyang, *China* **76 D4** 27 28N 103 5 E
Jinyun, *China* **77 C13** 28 35N 120 5 E
Jinzhai, *China* **77 B10** 31 40N 115 53 E
Jinzhou, *Hebei, China* **74 E8** 38 2N 115 2 E
Jinzhou, *Liaoning, China* **75 D11** 41 5N 121 3 E
Jiparaná →, *Brazil* **173 B5** 8 3 S 62 52W
Jipijapa, *Ecuador* **168 D1** 1 0 S 80 40W
Jiquilpan, *Mexico* **162 D4** 19 57N 102 42W
Jishan, *China* **74 G6** 35 34N 110 58 E
Jishou, *China* **76 C7** 28 21N 109 43 E
Jishui, *China* **77 D10** 27 12N 115 8 E
Jisr ash Shughūr, *Syria* **100 E7** 35 49N 36 18 E
Jitarning, *Australia* **125 F2** 32 48 S 117 57 E
Jitra, *Malaysia* **87 J3** 6 16N 100 25 E
Jiu →, *Romania* **53 G8** 43 47N 23 48 E
Jiudengkou, *China* **74 E4** 39 56N 106 40 E
Jiujiang, *Guangdong, China* **77 F9** 22 50N 113 0 E
Jiujiang, *Jiangxi, China* **77 C10** 29 42N 115 58 E
Jiuling Shan, *China* **77 C10** 28 40N 114 40 E
Jiulong = Kowloon, *China* **77 F10** 22 19N 114 11 E
Jiulong, *China* **76 C3** 28 57N 101 31 E
Jiutai, *China* **75 B13** 44 10N 125 50 E
Jiuxincheng, *China* **74 E8** 39 17N 115 59 E
Jiuyuhang, *China* **77 B12** 30 18N 119 56 E
Jiwa, *U.A.E.* **99 B6** 23 0N 54 10 E
Jiwani, Ras, *Pakistan* **91 D1** 25 1N 61 44 E
Jixi, *Anhui, China* **77 B12** 30 5N 118 34 E
Jixi, *Heilongjiang, China* **75 B16** 45 20N 130 50 E
Jiyang, *China* **75 F9** 37 0N 117 12 E
Jiyuan, *China* **74 G7** 35 7N 112 57 E
Jiz', W. →, *Yemen* **99 C6** 16 12N 52 14 E
Jīzān, *Si. Arabia* **98 C3** 17 0N 42 20 E
Jize, *China* **74 F8** 36 54N 114 56 E
Jizera →, *Czech Rep.* **34 A7** 50 10N 14 43 E
Jizl, Wādī al →, *Si. Arabia* **96 E3** 25 39N 38 25 E
Jizō-Zaki, *Japan* **72 B5** 35 34N 133 20 E
Jizzakh, *Uzbekistan* **65 C3** 40 6N 67 50 E
Joaçaba, *Brazil* **175 B5** 27 5 S 51 31W
Joaíma, *Brazil* **171 E3** 16 39 S 41 2W
Joal Fadiout, *Senegal* **112 C1** 14 9N 16 50W
João Amaro, *Brazil* **171 D3** 12 46 S 40 22W
João Belo = Xai-Xai, *Mozam.* **117 D5** 25 6 S 33 31 E
João Câmara, *Brazil* **170 C4** 5 32 S 35 48W
João Pessoa = Eirunepé, *Brazil* **172 B4** 6 35 S 69 53W
João Pessoa = Pôrto, *Brazil* **170 B3** 3 54 S 42 42W
João Pessoa, *Brazil* **170 C5** 7 10 S 34 52W
João Pinheiro, *Brazil* **171 E2** 17 45 S 46 10W
Joaquim Távora, *Brazil* **171 F2** 23 30 S 49 58W
Joaquín V. González, *Argentina* **174 B3** 25 10 S 64 0W
Jobat, *India* **92 H6** 22 25N 74 34 E
Jobourg, Nez de, *France* **26 C5** 49 41N 1 57W
Jódar, *Spain* **43 H7** 37 50N 3 21W
Jodhpur, *India* **92 F5** 26 23N 73 8 E
Jodiya, *India* **92 H4** 22 42N 70 18 E
Joensuu, *Finland* **56 B4** 62 37N 29 49 E
Jōetsu, *Japan* **71 F9** 37 12N 138 10 E
Jœuf, *France* **27 C12** 49 12N 6 0 E
Jofane, *Mozam.* **117 C5** 21 15 S 34 18 E
Jogbani, *India* **93 F12** 26 25N 87 15 E
Jõgeva, *Estonia* **15 G22** 58 45N 26 24 E
Jogjakarta = Yogyakarta, *Indonesia* **85 D4** 7 49 S 110 22 E
Jōhana, *Japan* **73 A8** 36 30N 136 57 E
Johannesburg, *S. Africa* **117 D4** 26 10 S 28 2 E
Johannesburg, *U.S.A.* **161 K9** 35 22N 117 38W
Johannisburg = Pisz, *Poland* **54 E8** 53 38N 21 49 E
Johansfors, *Sweden* **17 H9** 56 42N 15 32 E
Johilla →, *India* **93 H9** 23 37N 81 14 E
John Crow Mts., *Jamaica* **164 a** 18 5N 76 25W
John Day, *U.S.A.* **158 D4** 44 25N 118 57W
John Day →, *U.S.A.* **158 D3** 45 44N 120 39W
John Day Fossil Beds ⌓, *U.S.A.* **158 D4** 44 33N 119 38W
John D'Or Prairie, *Canada* **142 B5** 58 30N 115 8W
John F. Kennedy International, New York ✈ (JFK), *U.S.A.* **151 F11** 40 38N 73 47W
John F. Kennedy Space Center, *U.S.A.* **153 G9** 28 40N 80 42W
John H. Kerr Reservoir, *U.S.A.* **149 G6** 36 36N 78 18W
John o' Groats, *U.K.* **22 C5** 58 38N 3 4W
Johnnie, *U.S.A.* **161 J10** 36 25N 116 5W
Johns I., *U.S.A.* **152 C9** 32 40N 80 10W
John's Ra., *Australia* **126 C1** 21 55 S 133 23 E
Johnson, *U.S.A.* **151 B12** 44 38N 72 41W
Johnson City, *Kans., U.S.A.* **155 G4** 37 34N 101 45W
Johnson City, *N.Y., U.S.A.* **151 D9** 42 7N 75 58W
Johnson City, *Tenn., U.S.A.* **149 G4** 36 19N 82 21W
Johnson City, *Tex., U.S.A.* **155 K5** 30 17N 98 25W
Johnsonburg, *U.S.A.* **150 E6** 41 29N 78 41W
Johnsondale, *U.S.A.* **161 K8** 35 58N 118 32W
Johnsons Crossing, *Canada* **142 A2** 60 29N 133 18W
Johnsonville, *N.Z.* **130 H3** 41 13 S 174 48 E
Johnston, *U.S.A.* **152 B8** 33 50N 81 48W
Johnston, L., *Australia* **125 F3** 32 25 S 120 30 E
Johnston City, *U.S.A.* **156 G8** 37 49N 88 56W
Johnston Falls = Mambilima Falls, *Zambia* **119 E2** 10 31 S 28 45 E
Johnston I., *Pac. Oc.* **135 F11** 17 10N 169 8W
Johnstone Str., *Canada* **142 C3** 50 28N 126 0W
Johnstown, *N.Y., U.S.A.* **151 C10** 43 0N 74 22W
Johnstown, *Ohio, U.S.A.* **150 F2** 40 9N 82 41W
Johnstown, *Pa., U.S.A.* **150 F6** 40 20N 78 55W
Johor □, *Malaysia* **84 B2** 2 5N 103 20 E
Johor, Selat, *Asia* **87 d** 1 28N 103 47 E
Johor Bahru, *Malaysia* **87 d** 1 28N 103 46 E
Jõhvi, *Estonia* **15 G22** 59 22N 27 27 E
Joigny, *France* **27 E10** 47 58N 3 20 E
Joinville, *Brazil* **175 B6** 26 15 S 48 55W
Joinville, *France* **27 D12** 48 27N 5 10 E
Joinville I., *Antarctica* **7 C18** 65 0 S 55 30W
Jojutla, *Mexico* **163 D5** 18 37N 99 11W
Jokkmokk, *Sweden* **14 C18** 66 35N 19 50 E
Jökulsá á Bru →, *Iceland* **11 B12** 65 40N 14 16W
Jökulsá á Fjöllum →, *Iceland* **11 A10** 66 10N 16 30W
Jökulsárgljúfur △, *Iceland* **11 B10** 65 56N 16 31W
Jolfā, *Āzarbājān-e Sharqī, Iran* **101 C11** 38 57N 45 38 E
Jolfā, *Eşfahan, Iran* **97 C6** 32 58N 51 37 E
Joliet, *U.S.A.* **157 C8** 41 32N 88 5W
Joliette, *Canada* **140 C5** 46 3N 73 24W
Jolo, *Phil.* **81 H3** 6 0N 121 0 E
Jolo Group, *Phil.* **81 J3** 6 0N 121 9 E
Jolon, *U.S.A.* **160 K5** 35 58N 121 9W
Jølstravatnet, *Norway* **18 C3** 61 32N 6 23 E
Jomalig I., *Phil.* **80 D4** 14 42N 122 22 E
Jombang, *Indonesia* **85 D4** 7 33 S 112 14 E
Jomda, *China* **76 B2** 31 28N 98 12 E
Jona, *Switz.* **33 B7** 47 14N 8 51 E
Jonava, *Lithuania* **15 J21** 55 8N 24 12 E
Jondal, *Norway* **18 D3** 60 16N 6 15 E
Jones, *Phil.* **80 C3** 16 33N 121 42 E
Jones Sound, *Canada* **6 B3** 76 0N 85 0W
Jonesboro, *Ark., U.S.A.* **155 H9** 35 50N 90 42W
Jonesboro, *Ga., U.S.A.* **152 B5** 33 31N 84 22W
Jonesboro, *La., U.S.A.* **155 J8** 32 15N 92 43W
Jonesburg, *U.S.A.* **156 F5** 38 51N 91 18W
Jonesville, *Ind., U.S.A.* **157 E11** 39 5N 85 54W
Jonesville, *Mich., U.S.A.* **157 C12** 41 59N 84 40W
Jong →, *S. Leone* **112 D2** 7 32N 12 23W
Jonglei, *Sudan* **107 F3** 6 25N 30 50 E
Jonglei □, *Sudan* **107 F3** 7 30N 32 30 E
Joniškis, *Lithuania* **15 H20** 56 13N 23 35 E
Jönköping, *Sweden* **17 G8** 57 45N 14 8 E
Jönköpings län □, *Sweden* **17 G8** 57 30N 14 30 E
Jonquière, *Canada* **141 C5** 48 27N 71 14W
Jonsered, *Sweden* **17 G6** 57 45N 12 10 E
Jonzac, *France* **28 C3** 45 27N 0 28W
Joplin, *U.S.A.* **155 G7** 37 6N 94 31W
Jora, *India* **92 F6** 26 20N 77 49 E
Jordan, *Phil.* **81 F4** 10 40N 122 35 E
Jordan, *Mont., U.S.A.* **158 C10** 47 19N 106 55W
Jordan, *N.Y., U.S.A.* **151 C8** 43 4N 76 29W
Jordan ■, *Asia* **103 E5** 31 0N 36 0 E
Jordan →, *Asia* **103 D4** 31 48N 35 32 E
Jordan Valley, *U.S.A.* **158 E5** 42 59N 117 3W
Jordânia, *Brazil* **171 E3** 15 55 S 40 11W
Jordanów, *Poland* **55 J6** 49 41N 19 49 E
Jordet, *Norway* **18 C9** 61 25N 12 8 E
Jorge, C., *Chile* **176 D1** 51 40 S 75 35W
Jorgen Brønlund Fjord, *Greenland* **10 A8** 82 30N 29 0W
Jorhat, *India* **90 B5** 26 45N 94 12 E
Jorm, *Afghan.* **65 E5** 36 50N 70 52 E
Jörn, *Sweden* **14 D19** 65 4N 20 1 E
Jorong, *Indonesia* **85 C4** 3 58 S 114 56 E
Jørpeland, *Norway* **18 E3** 59 3N 6 1 E
Jorquera →, *Chile* **174 B2** 28 3 S 69 58W
Jos, *Nigeria* **113 D6** 9 53N 8 51 E
Jos Plateau, *Nigeria* **113 D6** 9 55N 9 0 E
Jošanička Banja, *Serbia & M.* **50 C4** 43 24N 20 47 E
Jose Abad Santos, *Phil.* **81 J5** 5 55N 125 39 E
José Batlle y Ordóñez, *Uruguay* **175 C4** 33 20 S 55 10W
José Bonifácio = Erechim, *Brazil* **175 B5** 27 35 S 52 15W
José de San Martín, *Argentina* **176 B2** 44 4 S 70 26W
Jose Panganiban, *Phil.* **80 D4** 14 17N 122 41 E
Joseni, *Romania* **53 D10** 46 42N 25 29 E
Joseph, L., *Nfld. & L., Canada* **141 B6** 52 45N 65 18W
Joseph, L., *Ont., Canada* **150 A5** 45 10N 79 44W
Joseph Bonaparte G., *Australia* **124 B4** 14 35 S 128 50 E
Joshinath, *India* **93 D8** 30 34N 79 34 E
Joshinetsu-Kōgen △, *Japan* **73 A10** 36 42N 138 32 E
Joshua Tree, *U.S.A.* **161 L10** 34 8N 116 19W
Joshua Tree △, *U.S.A.* **161 M10** 33 55N 116 0W
Josselin, *France* **26 E4** 47 57N 2 33W
Jost Van Dyke, *Br. Virgin Is.* **165 e** 18 29N 64 47W
Jostedal, *Norway* **18 C4** 61 35N 7 15 E
Jostedalsbreen, *Norway* **18 C3** 61 40N 6 59 E
Jotunheimen, *Norway* **18 C5** 61 35N 8 25 E
Jotunheimen △, *Norway* **18 C5** 61 32N 8 25 E
Joubertberge, *Namibia* **116 B1** 18 30 S 14 0 E
Joué-lès-Tours, *France* **26 E7** 47 21N 0 40 E
Jourdanton, *U.S.A.* **155 L5** 28 55N 98 33W
Joutseno, *Finland* **58 B5** 61 7N 28 31 E
Jovellanos, *Cuba* **164 B3** 22 40N 81 10W
Jovellar, *Phil.* **80 E4** 13 4N 123 36 E
Jowai, *India* **90 C4** 25 26N 92 12 E
Jowhar = Giohar, *Somali Rep.* **120 D3** 2 48N 45 30 E
Jowzjān □, *Afghan.* **65 E3** 36 10N 66 0 E
Joyeuse, *France* **29 D8** 44 29N 4 16 E
Jōyō, *Japan* **73 C7** 34 50N 135 47 E
Józefów, *Lubelskie, Poland* **55 H10** 50 28N 23 2 E
Józefów, *Mazowieckie, Poland* **55 F8** 52 10N 21 11 E
Ju Xian, *China* **75 F10** 36 35N 118 20 E
Juan Aldama, *Mexico* **162 C4** 24 20N 103 23W
Juan Bautista Alberdi, *Argentina* **174 C3** 34 26 S 61 48W
Juan de Fuca Str., *Canada* **160 B3** 48 15N 124 0W
Juan de Nova, *Ind. Oc.* **117 B7** 17 3 S 43 45 E
Juan Fernández, Arch. de, *Pac. Oc.* **135 L20** 33 50 S 80 0W
Juan José Castelli, *Argentina* **174 B3** 25 27 S 60 57W
Juan L. Lacaze, *Uruguay* **174 C4** 34 26 S 57 25W
Juanjuí, *Peru* **172 B2** 7 10 S 76 45W
Juankoski, *Finland* **14 E23** 63 3N 28 19 E
Juara, *Brazil* **173 C6** 11 20 S 57 25W
Juárez, *Argentina* **174 D4** 37 40 S 59 43W
Juárez, *Mexico* **161 N11** 32 20N 115 57W
Juárez, Sierra de, *Mexico* **162 A1** 32 0N 116 0W
Juatinga, Ponta de, *Brazil* **171 F3** 23 17 S 44 30W
Juàzeiro, *Brazil* **170 C3** 9 30 S 40 30W
Juàzeiro do Norte, *Brazil* **170 C4** 7 10 S 39 18W
Juba = Giuba →, *Somali Rep.* **120 D2** 1 30N 42 35 E
Juba, *Sudan* **107 G3** 4 50N 31 35 E
Jubany, *Antarctica* **7 C18** 62 30 S 58 0W
Jubayl, *Lebanon* **103 A4** 34 5N 35 39 E
Jubbah, *Si. Arabia* **96 D4** 28 2N 40 56 E
Jubbal, *India* **92 D7** 31 5N 77 40 E
Jubbulpore = Jabalpur, *India* **93 H8** 23 9N 79 58 E
Jübek, *Germany* **30 A5** 54 33N 9 22 E
Jubga, *Russia* **61 H4** 44 19N 38 48 E
Jubilee L., *Australia* **125 E4** 29 0 S 126 50 E
Juby, C., *Morocco* **110 C2** 28 0N 12 59W
Júcar = Xúquer →, *Spain* **41 F4** 39 5N 0 10W
Júcaro, *Cuba* **164 B4** 21 37N 78 51W
Juchitán, *Mexico* **163 D5** 16 27N 95 5W
Judaberg, *Norway* **18 E2** 59 10N 5 51 E
Judaea = Har Yehuda, *Israel* **103 D3** 31 35N 34 57 E

Judenburg, Austria 34 D7 47 12N 14 38 E
Judith →, U.S.A. 158 C9 47 44N 109 39W
Judith, Pt., U.S.A. 151 E13 41 22N 71 29W
Judith Gap, U.S.A. 158 C9 46 41N 109 45W
Juelsminde, Denmark 17 J4 55 43N 10 1 E
Jufari →, Brazil 169 D5 1 13 S 62 0W
Jugoslavia = Serbia & Montenegro ■, Europe 50 C4 43 20N 20 0 E
Juigalpa, Nic. 164 D2 12 6N 85 26W
Juillac, France 28 C5 45 20N 1 19 E
Juist, Germany 30 B2 53 40N 6 59 E
Juiz de Fora, Brazil 171 F3 21 43 S 43 19W
Jujuy □, Argentina 174 A2 23 20 S 65 40W
Jukao = Rugao, China 77 A13 32 23N 120 31 E
Julesburg, U.S.A. 154 E3 40 59N 102 16W
Juli, Peru 172 D4 16 10 S 69 25W
Julia Cr. →, Australia 126 C3 20 0 S 141 11 E
Julia Creek, Australia 126 C3 20 39 S 141 44 E
Juliaca, Peru 172 D3 15 25 S 70 10W
Julian, U.S.A. 161 M10 33 4N 116 38W
Julian, L., Canada 140 B4 54 25N 77 57W
Julian Alps = Julijske Alpe, Slovenia 45 B11 46 15N 14 1 E
Juliana Top = Mandala, Puncak, Indonesia 83 B6 4 44 S 140 20 E
Julianatop, Suriname 169 C6 3 40N 56 30W
Julianehåb = Qaqortoq, Greenland 10 E6 60 43N 46 0W
Jülich, Germany 30 E2 50 55N 6 22 E
Julierpass, Switz. 33 D9 46 28N 9 32 E
Juliette, L., U.S.A. 152 B6 33 2N 83 50W
Julijske Alpe, Slovenia 45 B11 46 15N 14 1 E
Julimes, Mexico 162 B3 28 25N 105 27W
Jullundur, India 92 D6 31 20N 75 40 E
Julu, China 74 F8 37 15N 115 2 E
Jumbo, Zimbabwe 119 F3 17 30 S 30 58 E
Jumbo Pk., U.S.A. 161 J12 36 12N 114 11W
Jumentos Cays, Bahamas 164 B4 23 0N 75 40W
Jumilla, Spain 41 G3 38 28N 1 19W
Jumla, Nepal 93 E10 29 15N 82 13 E
Jumna = Yamuna →, India 93 G9 25 30N 81 53 E
Junagadh, India 92 J4 21 30N 70 30 E
Junction, Tex., U.S.A. 155 K5 30 29N 99 46W
Junction, Utah, U.S.A. 159 G7 38 14N 112 13W
Junction B., Australia 126 A1 11 52 S 133 55 E
Junction City, Ga., U.S.A. 152 C5 32 36N 84 28W
Junction City, Kans., U.S.A. 154 F6 39 2N 96 50W
Junction City, Oreg., U.S.A. 158 D2 44 13N 123 12W
Junction Pt., Australia 126 A1 11 45 S 133 50 E
Jundah, Australia 126 C3 24 46 S 143 2 E
Jundiaí, Brazil 175 A6 24 30 S 47 0W
Juneau, U.S.A. 142 B2 58 18N 134 25W
Junee, Australia 129 C7 34 53 S 147 35 E
Jungbunzlau = Mladá Boleslav, Czech Rep. 34 A7 50 27N 14 53 E
Jungfrau, Switz. 32 C5 46 32N 7 58 E
Junggar Pendi, China 68 B3 44 30N 86 0 E
Jungsdalshytta, Norway 18 D4 60 49N 7 55 E
Jungshahi, Pakistan 92 G2 24 52N 67 44 E
Juniata →, U.S.A. 150 F7 40 30N 77 40W
Junín, Argentina 174 C3 34 33 S 60 57W
Junín, Peru 172 C2 11 12 S 76 0W
Junín □, Peru 172 C3 11 30 S 75 0W
Junín de los Andes, Argentina 176 A2 39 45 S 71 0W
Jūniyah, Lebanon 103 B4 33 59N 35 38 E
Junlian, China 76 C5 28 8N 104 29 E
Junnar, India 94 E1 19 12N 73 58 E
Juno Beach, U.S.A. 153 J9 26 52N 80 3W
Juntas, Chile 174 B2 28 24 S 69 58W
Juntura, U.S.A. 158 E4 43 45N 118 5W
Juparanã, L., Brazil 171 E3 19 16 S 40 6W
Jupiter, U.S.A. 153 J9 26 57N 80 6W
Juquiá, Brazil 171 F2 24 19 S 47 38W
Jur, Nahr el →, Sudan 107 F2 8 45N 29 15 E
Jura = Jura, Mts. du, Europe 27 F13 46 40N 6 5 E
Jura = Schwäbische Alb, Germany 31 G5 48 20N 9 30 E
Jura, U.K. 22 F3 56 0N 5 50W
Jura □, France 27 F12 46 47N 5 45 E
Jura □, Switz. 31 H3 47 20N 7 20 E
Jūra →, Lithuania 54 C9 55 3N 22 9 E
Jura, Mts. du, Europe 27 F13 46 40N 6 5 E
Jura, Sd. of, U.K. 22 F3 55 57N 5 45W
Jura Suisse, Switz. 32 B4 47 10N 7 0 E
Jurado, Colombia 168 B2 7 7N 77 46W
Jurbarkas, Lithuania 15 J20 55 4N 22 46 E
Jurien, Australia 125 F2 30 18 S 115 2 E
Jurilovca, Romania 53 F13 44 46N 28 52 E
Jūrmala, Latvia 15 H20 56 58N 23 34 E
Jurong, China 77 B12 31 57N 119 9 E
Jurong, Singapore 87 d 1 19N 103 42 E
Juruá, Brazil 168 D4 3 27 S 66 3W
Juruá →, Brazil 168 D4 2 37 S 65 44W
Juruena, Brazil 173 C6 13 0 S 58 10W
Juruena →, Brazil 173 B6 7 20 S 58 3W
Juruti, Brazil 169 D6 2 9 S 56 4W
Jussey, France 27 E12 47 50N 5 55 E
Justo Daract, Argentina 174 C2 33 52 S 65 12W
Jutaí, Amazonas, Brazil 168 D4 2 44 S 66 57W
Jutaí, Amazonas, Brazil 172 B4 5 11 S 68 54W
Jutaí →, Brazil 168 D4 2 43 S 66 57W
Jüterbog, Germany 30 D9 51 59N 13 5 E
Juticalpa, Honduras 164 D2 14 40N 86 12W
Jutland = Jylland, Denmark 17 H3 56 25N 9 30 E
Juventud, I. de la, Cuba 164 B3 21 40N 82 40W
Juvigny-sous-Andaine, France 26 D6 48 32N 0 30W
Jūy Zar, Iran 101 F12 33 50N 46 18 E
Juye, China 74 G9 35 22N 116 5 E
Juzennecourt, France 27 D11 48 10N 4 58 E
Južni Brod = Brod, Macedonia 50 E5 41 32N 21 17 E
Jvari, Georgia 61 J6 42 42N 42 4 E
Jyderup, Denmark 17 J5 55 40N 11 26 E
Jylland, Denmark 17 H3 56 25N 9 30 E
Jyväskylä, Finland 15 E21 62 14N 25 50 E

K

K2, Pakistan 93 B7 35 58N 76 32 E
Ka →, Nigeria 113 C5 11 40N 4 10 E
Ka Lae, U.S.A. 145 E6 18 55N 155 41W
Kaa-Iya △, Bolivia 173 D5 18 35 S 61 40W
Kaaawa, U.S.A. 145 J14 21 33N 157 51W
Kaala, U.S.A. 145 J13 21 31N 158 9W
Kaala-Gomén, N. Cal. 133 T18 20 40 S 164 25 E
Kaalualu B., U.S.A. 145 E6 18 58N 155 37W
Kaap Plateau, S. Africa 116 D3 28 30 S 24 0 E
Kaapkruis, Namibia 116 C1 21 55 S 13 57 E
Kaapstad = Cape Town, S. Africa 116 E2 33 55 S 18 22 E
Kaataon, Mt., Phil. 81 G5 8 10N 124 52 E
Kaba, Guinea 112 C2 10 9N 11 40W
Kabacan, Phil. 81 H5 7 8N 124 49 E
Kabachishche = Zelenodolsk, Russia 60 C9 55 55N 48 30 E
Kabaena, Indonesia 82 C2 5 15 S 122 0 E
Kabala, S. Leone 112 D2 9 38N 11 37W
Kabale, Uganda 118 C3 1 15 S 30 0 E
Kabalebostuwmeer, Suriname 169 C6 4 45N 57 30W
Kabalo, Dem. Rep. of the Congo 118 D2 6 0 S 27 0 E
Kabambare, Dem. Rep. of the Congo 118 C2 4 41 S 27 39 E
Kabango, Dem. Rep. of the Congo 119 D2 8 35 S 28 30 E
Kabanjahe, Indonesia 84 B1 3 6N 98 30 E
Kabankalan, Phil. 81 G4 9 59N 122 49 E
Kabara, Fiji 133 B3 18 59 S 178 56W
Kabara, Mali 112 B4 16 40N 2 50W
Kabarai, Indonesia 83 B4 0 4 S 130 58 E
Kabardinka, Russia 59 K10 44 40N 37 57 E
Kabardino-Balkar Republic = Kabardino-Balkaria □, Russia 61 J6 43 30N 43 30 E
Kabardino-Balkaria □, Russia 61 J6 43 30N 43 30 E
Kabarega Falls = Murchison Falls, Uganda 118 B3 2 15N 31 30 E
Kabasalan, Phil. 81 H4 7 47N 122 44 E
Kabat, Indonesia 79 J17 8 16 S 114 19 E
Kabba, Nigeria 113 D6 7 50N 6 3 E
Kabbani →, India 95 H3 12 13N 76 54 E
Kabetogama, U.S.A. 154 A8 48 28N 92 59W
Kabi, Niger 113 C7 13 30N 12 35 E
Kabin Buri, Thailand 86 F3 13 57N 101 43 E
Kabinakagami L., Canada 140 C3 48 54N 84 25W
Kabinda, Dem. Rep. of the Congo 115 D4 6 10 S 24 29 E
Kabkabīyah, Sudan 109 F4 13 50N 24 0 E
Kablungu, C., Papua N. G. 132 D6 6 20 S 150 1 E
Kabna, Sudan 106 D3 19 6N 32 40 E
Kabo, C.A.R. 114 A3 7 35N 18 38 E
Kabompo, Zambia 119 E1 13 36 S 24 14 E
Kabompo →, Zambia 115 E4 14 11 S 23 11 E
Kabondo, Dem. Rep. of the Congo 119 D2 8 58 S 25 40 E
Kabongo, Dem. Rep. of the Congo 118 D2 7 22 S 25 33 E
Kabot, Guinea 112 C2 10 48N 14 57W
Kabou, Togo 113 D5 9 28N 0 55 E
Kaboudia, Rass, Tunisia 108 A2 35 13N 11 10 E
Kabr, Sudan 107 E2 10 54N 26 50 E
Kabrousse, Senegal 112 C1 12 25N 16 45W
Kabubu, Dem. Rep. of the Congo 115 D4 9 42 S 24 40 E
Kabūd Gonbad, Iran 97 B8 37 5N 59 45 E
Kabugao, Phil. 80 B3 18 2N 121 11 E
Kābul, Afghan. 91 B3 34 28N 69 11 E
Kābul □, Afghan. 91 B3 34 30N 69 0 E
Kābul →, Pakistan 91 B4 33 55N 72 14 E
Kabuli, Papua N. G. 132 B4 2 7 S 146 40 E
Kabunga, Dem. Rep. of the Congo 118 C2 1 38 S 28 3 E
Kaburuang, Indonesia 82 A3 3 50N 126 30 E
Kabushiya, Sudan 107 D3 16 54N 33 41 E
Kabwanga, Dem. Rep. of the Congo 115 D4 7 2 S 22 36 E
Kabwe, Zambia 119 E2 14 30 S 28 29 E
Kabwum, Papua N. G. 132 D4 6 11 S 147 15 E
Kačanik, Serbia & M. 50 D5 42 13N 21 12 E
Kačerginė, Lithuania 54 D10 54 56N 23 42 E
Kachchh, Gulf of, India 92 H3 22 50N 69 15 E
Kachchh, Rann of, India 92 H4 24 0N 70 0 E
Kachchhidhana, India 93 J8 21 44N 78 46 E
Kachebera, Zambia 119 E3 13 50 S 32 50 E
Kachia, Nigeria 113 D6 9 50N 7 55 E
Kachikau, Botswana 116 B3 18 8 S 24 26 E
Kachin □, Burma 76 D1 26 0N 97 30 E
Kachira, L., Uganda 118 C3 0 40 S 31 7 E
Kachiry, Kazakhstan 66 D8 53 10N 75 50 E
Kachisi, Ethiopia 107 F4 9 40N 37 50 E
Kachkanar, Russia 64 B7 58 42N 59 33 E
Kachnara, India 92 H6 23 50N 75 6 E
Kachot, Cambodia 87 G4 11 30N 103 3 E
Kaçkar, Turkey 101 B9 40 45N 41 10 E
Kada, Chad 109 E3 19 20N 19 39 E
Kadaingti, Burma 90 G6 17 37N 97 32 E
Kadaiyanallur, India 95 K3 9 3N 77 22 E
Kadan, Czech Rep. 34 A6 50 23N 13 16 E
Kadan Kyun, Burma 86 F2 12 30N 98 20 E
Kadanai →, Afghan. 92 D1 31 22N 65 45 E
Kadarkút, Hungary 52 D2 46 13N 17 39 E
Kadavu, Fiji 133 B2 19 0 S 178 15 E
Kadavu Passage, Fiji 133 B2 18 45 S 178 0 E
Kade, Ghana 113 D4 6 7N 0 56W
Kadei →, C.A.R. 114 B3 3 31N 16 3 E
Kademlija = Triglav, Slovenia 45 B10 46 21N 13 50 E
Kadhimain = Al Kāzimīyah, Iraq 101 F11 33 22N 44 18 E
Kadi, India 92 H5 23 18N 72 23 E
Kadiak I. = Kodiak I., U.S.A. 144 H9 57 30N 152 45W
Kadina, Australia 128 B2 33 55 S 137 43 E
Kadınhanı, Turkey 100 C5 38 14N 32 13 E
Kadiolo, Mali 112 C3 10 35N 7 41W
Kadipur, India 93 F10 26 10N 82 23 E
Kadirabad, India 94 E2 19 51N 75 54 E
Kadiri, India 95 G4 14 12N 78 13 E
Kadirli, Turkey 100 D7 37 23N 36 5 E
Kadiyevka = Stakhanov, Ukraine 59 H10 48 35N 38 40 E
Kadja, O. →, Chad 109 F4 12 2N 22 28 E
Kadmat I., India 95 J1 11 14N 72 47 E
Kadodo, Sudan 107 E2 11 4N 29 31 E
Kadoka, U.S.A. 154 D4 43 50N 101 31W
Kadom, Russia 60 C6 54 37N 42 30 E
Kadoma, Zimbabwe 119 F2 18 20 S 29 52 E
Kâdugli, Sudan 107 E2 11 0N 29 45 E
Kaduna, Nigeria 113 C6 10 30N 7 21 E
Kaduna □, Nigeria 113 C6 11 0N 7 30 E
Kadur, India 95 H3 13 34N 76 1 E
Kaduy, Russia 58 C9 59 12N 37 9 E
Kaédi, Mauritania 112 B2 16 9N 13 28W
Kaélé, Cameroon 113 C7 10 7N 14 27 E
Kaena Pt., U.S.A. 145 J13 21 35N 158 17W
Kaeng Khoï, Thailand 86 E3 14 35N 101 0 E
Kaeng Kra Chan △, Thailand 86 F2 12 57N 99 23 E
Kaeng Tana △, Thailand 86 E5 15 25N 105 32 E
Kaeo, N.Z. 130 B5 35 6 S 173 49 E
Kaesŏng, N. Korea 75 F14 37 58N 126 35 E
Kāf, Si. Arabia 96 D3 31 25N 37 29 E
Kafakumba, Dem. Rep. of the Congo 115 D4 9 38 S 23 46 E
Kafan = Kapan, Armenia 101 C12 39 18N 46 27 E
Kafanchan, Nigeria 113 D6 9 40N 8 20 E
Kafareti, Nigeria 113 C7 10 25N 11 12 E
Kaffrine, Senegal 112 C1 14 8N 15 36W
Kafia Kingi, Sudan 114 A4 9 20N 24 25 E
Kafin, Nigeria 113 D6 9 30N 7 4 E
Kafin Madaki, Nigeria 113 C6 10 41N 9 46 E
Kafinda, Zambia 119 E3 12 32 S 30 20 E
Kafirévs, Ákra, Greece 48 C6 38 9N 24 38 E
Kafr el Battikh, Egypt 106 H7 31 25N 31 44 E
Kafr el Dauwâr, Egypt 106 H7 31 8N 30 8 E
Kafr el Sheikh, Egypt 106 H7 31 15N 30 50 E
Kafue, Zambia 119 F2 15 46 S 28 9 E
Kafue △, Zambia 119 F2 15 12 S 25 38 E
Kafue Flats, Zambia 119 F2 15 40 S 27 25 E
Kafulwe, Zambia 119 D2 9 0 S 29 1 E
Kafumba, Dem. Rep. of the Congo 115 D3 5 23 S 18 55 E
Kaga, Afghan. 92 B4 34 14N 70 10 E
Kaga, Japan 73 A8 36 16N 136 15 E
Kaga Bandoro, C.A.R. 114 A3 7 0N 19 10 E
Kagamil I., U.S.A. 144 K5 53 0N 169 43W
Kagan, Uzbekistan 65 D2 39 43N 64 33 E
Kaganovich = Sokuluk, Kyrgyzstan 65 B7 42 52N 74 18 E
Kaganovich = Tovarkovskiy, Russia 58 F10 53 40N 38 14 E
Kaganovichabad = Kolkhozobod, Tajikistan 65 E4 37 35N 68 40 E
Kaganovichevsk = Komsomolsk, Turkmenistan 65 D1 39 2N 63 36 E
Kagarko, Nigeria 113 D6 9 28N 7 36 E
Kagawa □, Japan 72 C6 34 15N 134 0 E
Kagera □, Tanzania 118 C3 2 0 S 31 30 E
Kagera →, Uganda 118 C3 0 57 S 31 47 E
Kağızman, Turkey 101 B10 40 5N 43 10 E
Kagmar, Sudan 107 E3 14 24N 30 25 E
Kagopal, Chad 109 G3 8 16N 16 23 E
Kagoshima, Japan 72 F2 31 35N 130 33 E
Kagoshima □, Japan 72 F2 31 30N 130 30 E
Kagoshima-Wan, Japan 72 F2 31 25N 130 40 E
Kagua, Papua N. G. 132 D2 6 26 S 143 48 E
Kagul = Cahul, Moldova 53 E13 45 50N 28 15 E
Kahak, Iran 97 B6 36 6N 49 46 E
Kahaluu, U.S.A. 145 K14 21 28N 157 50W
Kahama, Tanzania 118 C3 4 8 S 32 30 E
Kahan, Pakistan 92 E3 29 18N 68 54 E
Kahana, U.S.A. 145 J14 21 34N 157 53W
Kahana B., U.S.A. 145 J14 21 35N 157 50W
Kahang, Malaysia 87 L4 2 12N 103 32 E
Kahayan →, Indonesia 85 C4 3 40 S 114 0 E
Kahe, Tanzania 118 C4 3 30 S 37 25 E
Kahemba, Dem. Rep. of the Congo 115 D3 7 18 S 18 55 E
Kaherekoau Mts., N.Z. 131 F2 45 45 S 167 15 E
Kahil, Djebel bou, Algeria 111 B5 34 26N 4 0 E
Kahnūj, Iran 97 E8 27 55N 57 40 E
Kahoka, U.S.A. 156 D5 40 25N 91 44W
Kahoolawe, U.S.A. 145 C5 20 33N 156 37W
Kahramanmaraş, Turkey 100 D7 37 37N 36 53 E
Kâhta, Turkey 101 D8 37 46N 38 36 E
Kahuku, U.S.A. 145 J14 21 41N 157 57W
Kahuku Pt., U.S.A. 145 J14 21 43N 157 59W
Kahul, Ozero, Ukraine 53 E13 45 24N 28 24 E
Kahului, U.S.A. 145 C5 20 54N 156 28W
Kahurangi △, N.Z. 131 B7 41 10 S 172 32 E
Kahurangi Pt., N.Z. 131 A7 40 50 S 172 10 E
Kahuta, Pakistan 92 C5 33 35N 73 24 E
Kahuzi-Biega △, Dem. Rep. of the Congo 118 C2 1 50 S 27 55 E
Kai, Kepulauan, Indonesia 83 C4 5 55 S 132 45 E
Kai Besar, Indonesia 83 C4 5 35 S 133 0 E
Kai Is. = Kai, Kepulauan, Indonesia 83 C4 5 55 S 132 45 E
Kai Kecil, Indonesia 83 C4 5 45 S 132 40 E
Kai Xian, China 76 B7 31 11N 108 21 E
Kaiama, Nigeria 113 D5 9 36N 4 1 E
Kaiapit, Papua N. G. 132 D4 6 18 S 146 18 E
Kaiapoi, N.Z. 131 D7 43 24 S 172 40 E
Kaieteur Falls, Guyana 169 B6 5 1N 59 10W
Kaifeng, China 74 G8 34 48N 114 21 E
Kaihua, China 77 C12 29 12N 118 20 E
Kaijiang, China 76 B6 31 7N 107 55 E
Kaikohe, N.Z. 130 B2 35 25 S 173 49 E
Kaikoura, N.Z. 131 C8 42 25 S 173 43 E
Kaikoura Pen., N.Z. 131 C8 42 25 S 173 43 E
Kailahun, S. Leone 112 D2 8 18N 10 39W
Kailash = Kangrinboqe Feng, China 93 D9 31 0N 81 25 E
Kailashahar, India 90 C4 24 19N 92 0 E
Kaileuna I., Papua N. G. 132 E6 8 32 S 150 57 E
Kaili, China 76 D6 26 33N 107 59 E
Kailu, China 75 C11 43 38N 121 18 E
Kailua, U.S.A. 145 K14 21 24N 157 44W
Kailua B., U.S.A. 145 K14 21 25N 157 40W
Kailua Kona, U.S.A. 145 D6 19 39N 155 59W
Kaim →, Papua N. G. 132 D1 6 55 S 141 33 E
Kaima, Indonesia 83 C5 5 32 S 138 48 E
Kaimana, Indonesia 83 B4 3 39 S 133 45 E
Kaimanawa Mts., N.Z. 130 F4 39 15 S 175 56 E
Kaimata, N.Z. 131 C6 42 34 S 171 28 E
Kaimganj, India 93 F8 27 33N 79 24 E
Kaimon-Dake, Japan 72 F2 31 11N 130 32 E
Kaimuki, U.S.A. 145 K14 21 17N 157 48W
Kaimur Hills, India 93 G10 24 30N 82 0 E
Kainab →, Namibia 116 D2 28 32 S 19 34 E
Kainan, Japan 73 C7 34 9N 135 12 E
Kainantu, Papua N. G. 132 D3 6 18 S 145 52 E
Kainji Dam, Nigeria 113 D5 9 55N 4 35 E
Kainji Lake △, Nigeria 113 C5 10 5N 4 6 E
Kainji Res., Nigeria 113 C5 10 1N 4 40 E
Kainsk = Samara, Russia 60 D10 53 8N 50 6 E
Kainuu, Finland 14 D23 64 30N 29 7 E
Kaipara Harbour, N.Z. 130 C3 36 25 S 174 14 E
Kaiping, China 77 F9 22 23N 112 42 E
Kaipokok B., Canada 141 B8 54 54N 59 47W
Kaira, India 92 H5 22 45N 72 50 E
Kairana, India 92 E7 29 24N 77 15 E
Kairiru I., Papua N. G. 132 B2 3 21 S 143 34 E
Kaironi, Indonesia 83 B4 0 47 S 133 40 E
Kairouan, Tunisia 108 A2 35 45N 10 5 E
Kairuku, Papua N. G. 132 E4 8 51 S 146 35 E
Kaiser Wilhelm Kanal = Nord-Ostsee-Kanal, Germany 30 A5 54 12N 9 32 E
Kaiser-Wilhelmsland = Papua □, Indonesia 83 B5 4 0 S 137 0 E
Kaiserslautern, Germany 31 F3 49 26N 7 45 E
Kaiserstuhl, Germany 31 G3 48 4N 7 40 E
Kaita, Japan 72 C4 34 22N 132 32 E
Kaitaia, N.Z. 130 B2 35 8 S 173 17 E
Kaitangata, N.Z. 131 G4 46 17 S 169 51 E
Kaithal, India 92 E7 29 48N 76 26 E
Kaitu →, Pakistan 92 C4 33 10N 70 30 E
Kaiwi Channel, U.S.A. 145 K14 21 15N 157 30W
Kaiyang, China 76 D6 27 4N 106 59 E
Kaiyuan, Liaoning, China 75 C13 42 28N 124 1 E
Kaiyuan, Yunnan, China 76 F4 23 40N 103 12 E
Kaiyuh Mts., U.S.A. 144 D8 64 30N 158 0W
Kajaani, Finland 14 D22 64 17N 27 46 E
Kajabbi, Australia 126 C3 20 0 S 140 1 E
Kajana = Kajaani, Finland 14 D22 64 17N 27 46 E
Kajang, Malaysia 87 L3 2 59N 101 48 E
Kajaran, Armenia 101 C12 39 10N 46 7 E
Kajiado, Kenya 118 C4 1 53 S 36 48 E
Kajo Kaji, Sudan 107 G3 3 58N 31 40 E
Kajuru, Nigeria 113 C6 10 15N 7 34 E
Kajy-Say, Kyrgyzstan 65 B8 42 8N 77 10 E
Kaka, Sudan 107 E3 10 38N 32 10 E
Kaka Pt., U.S.A. 145 C5 20 31N 156 33W
Kakabeka Falls, Canada 140 C2 48 24N 89 37W
Kakadu △, Australia 124 B5 12 0 S 132 3 E
Kakamas, S. Africa 116 D3 28 45 S 20 33 E
Kakamega, Kenya 118 B3 0 20N 34 46 E
Kakamigahara, Japan 73 B8 35 28N 136 48 E
Kakana, India 95 K11 9 7N 92 48 E
Kakanj, Bos.-H. 52 F3 44 4N 18 4 E
Kakanui Mts., N.Z. 131 F5 45 10 S 170 30 E
Kakata, Liberia 112 D2 6 35N 10 20W
Kakdwip, India 93 J13 21 53N 88 11 E
Kake, Japan 72 C4 34 36N 132 19 E
Kake, U.S.A. 142 B2 56 59N 133 57W
Kakegawa, Japan 73 C10 34 45N 138 1 E
Kakeroma-Jima, Japan 71 K4 28 8N 129 14 E
Kakhib, Russia 61 J8 42 28N 46 34 E
Kakhonak, U.S.A. 144 G9 59 26N 154 51W
Kakhovka, Ukraine 59 J7 46 45N 33 30 E
Kakhovske Vdskh., Ukraine 59 J7 47 5N 34 0 E
Kakinada, India 94 F6 16 57N 82 11 E
Kakisa →, Canada 142 A5 61 3N 118 10W
Kakisa L., Canada 142 A5 60 56N 117 43W
Käkisalmi = Priozersk, Russia 58 B6 61 2N 30 7 E
Kakogawa, Japan 72 C6 34 46N 134 51 E
Kaktovik, U.S.A. 144 A12 70 8N 143 38W
Kakum △, Ghana 113 D4 5 24N 1 20W
Kakwa →, Canada 142 C5 54 37N 118 28W
Kāl Gūsheh, Iran 97 D8 30 59N 58 12 E
Kal Safīd, Iran 101 E12 34 52N 47 23 E
Kala, Nigeria 113 C7 12 2N 14 40 E
Kala Oya →, Sri Lanka 95 K4 8 20N 79 45 E
Kalaa-Kebira, Tunisia 108 A2 35 59N 10 32 E
Kalaallit Nunaat = Greenland ☒, N. Amer. 10 D6 66 0N 45 0W
Kalabagh, Pakistan 92 C4 33 0N 71 28 E
Kalabahi, Indonesia 82 C2 8 13 S 124 31 E
Kalabak = Radomir, Bulgaria 50 D6 42 37N 22 59 E
Kalabáka, Greece 48 B3 39 42N 21 39 E
Kalabakan, Malaysia 85 B5 4 25N 117 29 E
Kalabana, Mali 112 C3 14 10N 8 35W
Kalabo, Zambia 115 E4 14 58 S 22 40 E
Kalach, Russia 61 E5 50 22N 41 0 E
Kalach na Donu, Russia 61 F6 48 43N 43 32 E
Kaladan →, Burma 90 E4 20 20N 93 5 E
Kaladar, Canada 140 D4 44 37N 77 5W
Kalahari, Africa 116 C3 24 0 S 21 30 E
Kalahari Gemsbok △, S. Africa 116 D3 25 30 S 20 30 E
Kalaheo, U.S.A. 145 B2 21 56N 159 32W
Kalaikhum, Tajikistan 65 D5 38 28N 70 46 E
Kalajoki, Finland 14 D20 64 12N 24 10 E
Kalakamati, Botswana 117 C4 20 40 S 27 25 E
Kalakan, Russia 67 D12 55 15N 116 45 E
K'alak'unlun Shank'ou = Karakoram Pass, Asia 93 B7 35 33N 77 50 E
Kalam, Pakistan 93 B5 35 34N 72 30 E
Kalama, Dem. Rep. of the Congo 118 C2 2 52 S 28 35 E
Kalama, U.S.A. 160 E4 46 1N 122 51W
Kalámai, Greece 48 D4 37 3N 22 10 E
Kalamaloué △, Cameroon 109 F2 12 9N 14 58 E
Kalamansig, Phil. 81 H5 6 33N 124 3 E
Kalamariá, Greece 50 F6 40 33N 22 55 E
Kalamata = Kalámai, Greece 48 D4 37 3N 22 10 E
Kalamazoo, U.S.A. 157 B11 42 17N 85 35W
Kalamazoo →, U.S.A. 157 B10 42 40N 86 10W
Kalamb, India 94 E2 18 3N 74 48 E
Kalambo Falls, Tanzania 119 D3 8 37 S 31 35 E
Kalamítsi, Greece 48 B2 38 45N 20 36 E
Kalamnuri, India 94 E3 19 40N 77 20 E
Kálamos, Attikí, Greece 48 C5 38 17N 23 52 E
Kálamos, Levkás, Greece 39 B2 38 37N 20 56 E
Kálamos Nisís, Greece 39 B2 38 37N 20 55 E
Kalan, Turkey 39 B3 39 7N 39 32 E
Kalangadoo, Australia 128 D4 37 34 S 140 41 E
Kalankalan, Guinea 112 C3 10 7N 8 54W
Kalannie, Australia 125 F2 30 22 S 117 5 E
Kalāntarī, Iran 97 C7 32 10N 54 8 E
Kalao, Indonesia 82 C2 7 21 S 121 0 E
Kalaotoa, Indonesia 82 C2 7 20 S 121 50 E
Kalapana, U.S.A. 145 D7 19 21N 154 59W
Kälarne, Sweden 16 B10 62 59N 16 5 E
Kalasin, Thailand 86 D4 16 26N 103 30 E
Kalāt, Iran 97 B8 25 29N 59 22 E
Kalat, Pakistan 91 C2 29 8N 66 31 E
Kalāteh, Iran 97 B7 36 33N 55 41 E
Kalāteh-ye Ganj, Iran 97 E8 27 31N 57 55 E
Kálathos, Greece 38 E12 36 9N 28 8 E
Kalatungan Mt., Phil. 81 H5 7 54N 124 50 E
Kalaupapa, U.S.A. 145 B5 21 12N 156 59W
Kalaupapa △, U.S.A. 145 B5 21 10N 156 59W
Kalaus →, Russia 61 H7 45 40N 44 7 E
Kalávrita, Greece 48 C4 38 3N 22 8 E
Kalaw, Burma 90 E6 20 38N 96 34 E
Kalbān, Oman 99 B7 20 18N 58 38 E
Kalbarri, Australia 125 E1 27 40 S 114 10 E
Kalbarri △, Australia 125 E1 27 51 S 114 30 E
Kalce, Slovenia 36 F8 45 54N 14 13 E
Kaldrananes, Iceland 11 B5 65 45N 21 25W
Kale, Antalya, Turkey 49 E12 36 14N 30 0 E
Kale, Denizli, Turkey 49 D10 37 27N 28 49 E
Kalecik, Turkey 100 B5 40 4N 33 26 E
Kalehe, Dem. Rep. of the Congo 118 C2 2 6 S 28 50 E
Kalema, Tanzania 118 C3 1 12 S 31 55 E
Kalemie, Dem. Rep. of the Congo 118 D2 5 55 S 29 9 E
Kalemyo, Burma 90 D5 23 11N 94 4 E
Kalety, Poland 55 H5 50 35N 18 52 E
Kalewa, Burma 90 D5 23 10N 94 15 E
Kaleybar, Iran 96 B5 38 47N 47 2 E
Kálfafell, Iceland 11 D9 63 57N 17 41W
Kalgan = Zhangjiakou, China 74 D8 40 48N 114 55 E
Kalghatgi, India 95 G2 15 11N 74 58 E
Kalgoorlie-Boulder, Australia 125 F3 30 40 S 121 22 E
Kalhovd, Norway 18 D5 60 4N 8 21 E
Kali →, India 93 F8 27 6N 79 55 E
Kali Sindh →, India 92 G6 25 32N 76 17 E
Kaliakra, Nos, Bulgaria 51 C12 43 21N 28 30 E
Kalianda, Indonesia 84 D3 5 50 S 105 45 E
Kalibo, Phil. 81 F4 11 43N 122 22 E
Kaliganj, Bangla. 90 D2 22 25N 89 8 E
Kalihi, U.S.A. 145 K14 21 20N 157 53W
Kalima, Dem. Rep. of the Congo 118 C2 2 33 S 26 32 E
Kalimantan, Indonesia 85 C4 0 0 114 0 E
Kalimantan Barat □, Indonesia 85 C4 0 0 110 30 E
Kalimantan Selatan □, Indonesia 85 C5 2 30 S 115 30 E
Kalimantan Tengah □, Indonesia 85 C4 2 0 S 113 30 E
Kalimantan Timur □, Indonesia 85 B5 1 30N 116 30 E
Kálimnos, Greece 49 D8 37 0N 27 0 E
Kalimpong, India 90 B2 27 4N 88 35 E
Kalinadi →, India 95 G2 14 50N 74 7 E
Kalinga □, Phil. 80 C3 17 30N 121 20 E
Kalinin = Tver, Russia 58 D8 56 55N 35 55 E
Kaliningrad, Russia 15 J19 54 42N 20 32 E
Kaliningrad ✕ (KGD), Russia 54 D7 54 45N 20 33 E
Kalininsk = Petrozavodsk, Russia 58 B8 61 41N 34 20 E
Kalininsk, Russia 60 E7 51 30N 44 40 E
Kalinkavichy, Belarus 59 F5 52 12N 29 20 E
Kalinkovichi = Kalinkavichy, Belarus 59 F5 52 12N 29 20 E
Kalinovik, Bos.-H. 50 C2 43 31N 18 25 E
Kalipetrovo, Bulgaria 51 B11 44 5N 27 14 E
Kaliro, Uganda 118 B3 0 56N 33 30 E
Kalirrákhi, Greece 51 F8 40 40N 24 35 E
Kalispell, U.S.A. 158 B6 48 12N 114 19W
Kalisz, Poland 55 G5 51 45N 18 8 E
Kalisz Pomorski, Poland 55 E2 53 17N 15 55 E
Kaliua, Tanzania 118 D3 5 5 S 31 48 E
Kaliveli Tank, India 95 H4 12 5N 79 50 E
Kalívia Thorikoú, Greece 48 D5 37 50N 23 55 E
Kalix = Kalixälven →, Sweden 14 D20 65 50N 23 11 E
Kalix, Sweden 14 D20 65 53N 23 12 E
Kalixälven →, Sweden 14 D20 65 50N 23 11 E
Kalka, India 92 D7 30 46N 76 57 E
Kalkali Ghat, India 90 C4 24 36N 92 20 E
Kalkan, Turkey 49 E11 36 15N 29 23 E
Kalkarindji, Australia 124 C5 17 30 S 130 47 E
Kalkaska, U.S.A. 148 C3 44 44N 85 11W
Kalkfeld, Namibia 116 C2 20 57 S 16 14 E
Kalkfontein, Botswana 116 C3 22 4 S 20 57 E
Kalkım, Turkey 49 B9 39 48N 27 13 E
Kalkrand, Namibia 116 C2 24 1 S 17 35 E
Kallakkurichchi, India 95 J4 11 44N 79 1 E
Kallam, India 94 E3 18 36N 76 2 E
Kållandsö, Sweden 17 F7 58 40N 13 5 E
Kallavesi, Finland 14 E22 62 58N 27 30 E
Källby, Sweden 17 F7 58 30N 13 8 E
Kållered, Sweden 17 G6 57 32N 12 4 E
Kallidaikurichi, India 95 K3 8 38N 77 31 E
Kallies = Kalisz Pomorski, Poland 55 E2 53 17N 15 55 E
Kallimasiá, Greece 49 C8 38 18N 26 6 E
Kallinge, Sweden 17 H9 56 15N 15 18 E
Kallithéa, Greece 48 D5 37 55N 23 41 E
Kallmet, Albania 50 E3 41 51N 19 41 E
Kalloní, Greece 49 B8 39 14N 26 12 E
Kallonís, Kólpos, Greece 49 B8 39 10N 26 10 E
Kallsjön, Sweden 14 E15 63 38N 13 0 E
Kalmalo, Nigeria 113 C6 13 40N 5 20 E
Kalmanstunga, Iceland 11 C6 64 44N 20 48W
Kalmar, Sweden 17 H10 56 40N 16 20 E
Kalmar län □, Sweden 17 G10 57 25N 16 0 E
Kalmar sund, Sweden 17 H10 56 40N 16 25 E
Kalmunai, Sri Lanka 95 L5 7 25N 81 49 E
Kalmyk Republic = Kalmykia □, Russia 61 G8 46 5N 46 1 E
Kalmykia □, Russia 61 G8 46 5N 46 1 E
Kalmykovo, Kazakhstan 57 E9 49 0N 51 47 E
Kalna, India 93 H13 23 13N 88 25 E
Kalnai, India 93 H10 22 46N 83 30 E
Kalni →, Bangla. 90 C3 24 21N 91 13 E
Kalo, Papua N. G. 132 F4 10 1 S 147 48 E
Kalocsa, Hungary 52 D4 46 32N 19 0 E
Kalofer, Bulgaria 51 D8 42 37N 24 59 E
Kalohi Channel, U.S.A. 145 C5 21 0N 157 0W
Kalokhorio, Cyprus 39 F9 34 51N 33 2 E
Kaloko, Dem. Rep. of the Congo 118 D2 6 47 S 25 48 E
Kaloko-Honokohau △, U.S.A. 145 D5 19 40N 156 1W
Kalol, Gujarat, India 92 H5 22 37N 73 31 E
Kalol, Gujarat, India 92 H5 23 15N 72 33 E
Kalolímnos, Greece 49 D9 37 4N 27 5 E
Kalomo, Zambia 119 F2 17 0 S 26 30 E
Kalona, U.S.A. 156 C5 41 29N 91 43W
Kalonerón, Greece 48 D3 37 20N 21 38 E
Kalpeni I., India 95 J1 10 5N 73 38 E
Kalpi, India 93 F8 26 8N 79 47 E
Kalpitiya, Sri Lanka 95 K4 8 14N 79 46 E
Kalputhi I., India 95 J1 10 49N 72 10 E
Kalrayan Hills, India 95 J4 11 45N 78 40 E
Kalsubai, India 94 E1 19 35N 73 45 E
Kaltag, U.S.A. 144 D8 64 20N 158 43W
Kaltbrunn, Switz. 33 B8 47 13N 9 2 E
Kaltern = Caldaro, Italy 45 B8 46 25N 11 14 E
Kaltungo, Nigeria 113 D7 9 48N 11 19 E
Kalu, Pakistan 92 G2 25 5N 67 39 E
Kaluga, Russia 58 E9 54 35N 36 10 E
Kalulong, Bukit, Malaysia 85 B4 3 14N 114 39 E
Kalulushi, Zambia 119 E2 12 50 S 28 3 E
Kalundborg, Denmark 17 J5 55 41N 11 5 E
Kalush, Ukraine 59 H3 49 3N 24 23 E
Kałuszyn, Poland 55 F8 52 13N 21 52 E
Kalutara, Sri Lanka 95 L5 6 35N 80 0 E
Kalvåg, Norway 18 C1 61 46N 4 51 E
Kalvarija, Lithuania 54 D10 54 24N 23 14 E
Kalwakurti, India 94 F4 16 41N 78 30 E
Kalya, Russia 64 A7 60 15N 59 59 E
Kalyan, Maharashtra, India 94 D2 20 30N 74 3 E
Kalyan, Maharashtra, India 94 E1 19 15N 73 9 E
Kalyandurg, India 95 G3 14 33N 77 6 E
Kalyani, India 94 F3 17 52N 76 57 E
Kalyansingapuram, India 94 E6 19 30N 83 19 E
Kalyazin, Russia 58 D9 57 15N 37 55 E
Kam, Albania 50 D4 42 17N 20 18 E
Kam →, Nigeria 113 D7 8 15N 1 10 E
Kama, Burma 90 F5 19 1N 95 4 E
Kama, Dem. Rep. of the Congo 118 C2 3 30 S 27 5 E
Kama →, Russia 64 C5 55 45N 52 0 E
Kamachumu, Tanzania 118 C3 1 37 S 31 37 E
Kamae, Japan 72 E3 32 48N 131 56 E

Kamaing, *Burma* 90 C6 25 26N 96 35 E
Kamaishi, *Japan* 70 E10 39 16N 141 53 E
Kamakou, *U.S.A.* 145 B5 21 7N 156 52W
Kamakura, *Japan* 73 B11 35 19N 139 33 E
Kamalapurum, *India* 95 G4 14 35N 78 39 E
Kamalété, *Gabon* 114 C2 0 43 S 11 49 E
Kamalia, *Pakistan* 92 D5 30 44N 72 42 E
Kaman, *India* 92 F6 27 39N 77 16 E
Kaman, *Turkey* 100 C5 39 22N 33 44 E
Kamana, *Dem. Rep. of the Congo* 115 D4 5 59 S 24 58 E
Kamananui →, *U.S.A.* 145 J13 21 38N 158 4W
Kamanjab, *Namibia* 116 B2 19 35 S 14 51 E
Kamapanda, *Zambia* 119 E1 12 5 S 24 0 E
Kamarān, *Yemen* 98 D3 15 21N 42 35 E
Kamareddi, *India* 94 E4 18 19N 78 21 E
Kamashi, *Uzbekistan* 65 D5 38 51N 65 23 E
Kamativi, *Zimbabwe* 116 B4 18 20 S 27 6 E
Kamba, *Dem. Rep. of the Congo* 115 C4 4 0 S 22 22 E
Kamba, *Nigeria* 113 C5 11 50N 3 45 E
Kambalda, *Australia* 125 F3 31 10 S 121 37 E
Kambam, *India* 95 K3 9 45N 77 16 E
Kambar, *Pakistan* 92 F3 27 37N 68 1 E
Kambarka, *Russia* 64 C5 56 15N 54 11 E
Kambia, *S. Leone* 112 D2 9 3N 12 53W
Kambolé, *Togo* 113 D5 8 43N 1 39 E
Kambolé, *Zambia* 119 D3 8 47 S 30 48 E
Kambos, *Cyprus* 39 E8 35 2N 32 44 E
Kambove, *Dem. Rep. of the Congo* 119 E2 10 51 S 26 33 E
Kambuie, *Dem. Rep. of the Congo* 115 D4 6 59 S 22 19 E
Kambwata, *Zambia* 115 E4 14 3 S 23 43 E
Kamchatka, Poluostrov, *Russia* 67 D16 57 0N 160 0 E
Kamchatka Pen. = Kamchatka, Poluostrov, *Russia* 67 D16 57 0N 160 0 E
Kamchiya →, *Bulgaria* 51 C11 43 4N 27 44 E
Kame Ruins, *Zimbabwe* 119 G2 20 7 S 28 25 E
Kamehameha Heights, *U.S.A.* 145 K14 21 21N 157 52W
Kamen, *Russia* 66 D9 53 50N 81 30 E
Kamen-Rybolov, *Russia* 70 B6 44 46N 132 2 E
Kamende, *Dem. Rep. of the Congo* 115 D4 6 26 S 24 35 E
Kamenica, *Serbia & M.* 50 C6 43 27N 22 27 E
Kamenica, *Serbia & M.* 50 B3 44 25N 19 45 E
Kamenice nad Lipou, *Czech Rep.* 34 B8 49 18N 15 2 E
Kamenjak, Rt, *Croatia* 45 D10 44 47N 13 55 E
Kamenka = Kaminka, *Ukraine* 59 H7 49 3N 32 6 E
Kamenka, *Kazakhstan* 60 E10 51 7N 50 19 E
Kamenka, *Arkhangelsk, Russia* 56 A7 65 58N 44 0 E
Kamenka, *Penza, Russia* 60 D6 53 10N 44 5 E
Kamenka, *Voronezh, Russia* 59 G10 50 47N 39 20 E
Kamenka Bugskaya = Kamyanka-Buzka, *Ukraine* 59 G3 50 8N 24 16 E
Kamenka Dneprovskaya = Kamyanka-Dniprovska, *Ukraine* 59 J8 47 29N 34 28 E
Kamenka-Shevchenkovskaya = Kamyanka-Buzka, *Ukraine* 59 G3 50 8N 24 16 E
Kamennomostskiy, *Russia* 61 H5 44 18N 40 13 E
Kameno, *Bulgaria* 51 D11 42 34N 27 18 E
Kamenolomini, *Russia* 61 G5 47 40N 40 14 E
Kamensk-Shakhtinskiy, *Russia* 61 F5 48 23N 40 20 E
Kamensk Uralskiy, *Russia* 64 C9 56 25N 62 2 E
Kamenskaya = Kamensk-Shakhtinskiy, *Russia* 61 F5 48 23N 40 20 E
Kamenskiy, *Russia* 60 E7 50 48N 45 25 E
Kamenskoye = Dniprodzerzhynsk, *Ukraine* 59 H8 48 32N 34 37 E
Kamenskoye, *Russia* 67 C17 62 45N 165 30 E
Kamenyak, *Bulgaria* 51 C10 43 24N 26 57 E
Kamenz, *Germany* 30 D10 51 15N 14 5 E
Kameoka, *Japan* 73 C7 35 0N 135 35 E
Kameyama, *Japan* 73 C8 34 51N 136 27 E
Kami-Jima, *Japan* 72 E2 32 27N 130 20 E
Kami-Koshiki-Jima, *Japan* 72 F1 31 50N 129 52 E
Kamiagata, *Japan* 72 C1 34 47N 129 24 E
Kamiah, *U.S.A.* 158 C5 46 14N 116 2W
Kamień Krajeński, *Poland* 54 E4 53 32N 17 32 E
Kamień Pomorski, *Poland* 54 E1 53 57N 14 43 E
Kamienna →, *Poland* 55 G8 51 6N 21 47 E
Kamienna Góra, *Poland* 55 H3 50 47N 16 2 E
Kamieńsk, *Poland* 55 G6 51 12N 19 29 E
Kamieskroon, *S. Africa* 116 E2 30 9 S 17 56 E
Kamilukuak L., *Canada* 143 A8 62 22N 101 40W
Kamin-Kashyrskyy, *Ukraine* 59 G3 51 39N 24 56 E
Kamina, *Dem. Rep. of the Congo* 119 D2 8 45 S 25 0 E
Kaminak L., *Canada* 143 A10 62 10N 95 0W
Kaministiquia, *Canada* 140 C1 48 32N 89 35W
Kaminka, *Ukraine* 59 H7 49 3N 32 6 E
Kaminoyama, *Japan* 70 E10 38 9N 140 17 E
Kamioka, *Japan* 73 A9 36 25N 137 15 E
Kamiros, *Greece* 38 E11 36 20N 27 56 E
Kamishak Bay, *U.S.A.* 144 G9 59 15N 153 45W
Kamitsushima, *Japan* 72 C1 34 50N 129 28 E
Kamituga, *Dem. Rep. of the Congo* 118 C2 3 2 S 28 10 E
Kamla →, *India* 93 G12 25 35N 86 36 E
Kamloops, *Canada* 142 C4 50 40N 120 20W
Kamnik, *Slovenia* 45 B11 46 14N 14 37 E
Kamo, *Armenia* 61 K7 40 21N 45 7 E
Kamo, *Japan* 70 F9 37 39N 139 3 E
Kamo, *N.Z.* 130 B3 35 42 S 174 20 E
Kamoa Mts., *Guyana* 169 C6 1 30N 59 0W
Kamogawa, *Japan* 73 B12 35 5N 140 5 E
Kamojima, *Japan* 72 C6 34 4N 134 21 E
Kamoke, *Pakistan* 92 C6 32 4N 74 4 E
Kamooloa, *U.S.A.* 145 J13 21 34N 158 7W
Kamp →, *Austria* 34 C8 48 23N 15 42 E
Kampala, *Uganda* 118 B3 0 20N 32 30 E
Kampar, *Malaysia* 87 K3 4 18N 101 9 E
Kampar →, *Indonesia* 84 B2 0 30N 103 8 E
Kampen, *Neths.* 24 B5 52 33N 5 53 E
Kamphaeng Phet, *Thailand* 86 D2 16 28N 99 30 E
Kampinoski △, *Poland* 55 F7 52 21N 20 40 E
Kampolombo, L., *Zambia* 119 E2 11 37 S 29 42 E
Kampong Chhnang, *Cambodia* 87 F5 12 20N 104 35 E
Kampong Pengerang, *Malaysia* 87 d 1 22N 104 7 E
Kampong Punggai, *Malaysia* 87 d 1 27N 104 18 E
Kampong Saom, *Cambodia* 87 G4 10 38N 103 30 E
Kampong Saom, Chaak, *Cambodia* 87 G4 10 50N 103 32 E
Kampong Tanjong Langsat, *Malaysia* 87 d 1 28N 104 1 E
Kampong Telok Ramunia, *Malaysia* 87 d 1 22N 104 15 E
Kampong To, *Thailand* 87 J3 6 3N 101 13 E
Kampot, *Cambodia* 87 G5 10 36N 104 10 E
Kampsville, *U.S.A.* 156 E6 39 18N 90 37W
Kampti, *Burkina Faso* 112 C4 10 7N 3 25W
Kampuchea = Cambodia ■, *Asia* 86 F5 12 15N 105 0 E
Kampung Air Putih, *Malaysia* 87 K4 4 15N 103 10 E
Kampung Jerangau, *Malaysia* 87 K4 4 50N 103 10 E
Kampung Raja, *Malaysia* 87 K4 5 45N 102 35 E
Kampungbaru = Tolitoli, *Indonesia* 82 A2 1 5N 120 50 E
Kamrau, Teluk, *Indonesia* 83 B4 3 30 S 133 36 E
Kamsack, *Canada* 143 C8 51 34N 101 54W
Kamsai, *Guinea* 112 C2 10 40N 14 36W
Kamskoye Ustye, *Russia* 60 C9 55 10N 49 20 E
Kamskoye Vdkhr., *Russia* 64 B6 58 41N 56 7 E
Kamthi, *India* 94 D4 21 9N 79 19 E
Kamuchawie L., *Canada* 143 B8 56 18N 101 59W
Kamuela, *U.S.A.* 145 C6 20 1N 155 41W
Kamui-Misaki, *Japan* 70 C10 43 20N 140 21 E
Kamundan →, *Indonesia* 83 B4 2 17 S 132 39 E
Kamyanets-Podilskyy, *Ukraine* 53 B11 48 45N 26 40 E
Kamyanka-Buzka, *Ukraine* 59 G3 50 8N 24 16 E
Kamyanka-Dniprovska, *Ukraine* 59 J8 47 29N 34 28 E
Kamyanyets, *Belarus* 55 F10 52 23N 23 49 E
Kamyanyuki, *Belarus* 55 F10 52 32N 23 49 E
Kāmyārān, *Iran* 101 E12 34 47N 46 56 E
Kamyshin, *Russia* 60 E7 50 10N 45 24 E
Kamyshlov, *Russia* 64 C9 56 50N 62 43 E
Kamyzyak, *Russia* 61 G9 46 4N 48 10 E
Kan = Gan Jiang →, *China* 77 C11 29 15N 116 0 E
Kan, *Burma* 90 D5 22 25N 94 5 E
Kan, *Sudan* 107 F3 9 1N 31 47 E
Kanaaupscow, *Canada* 139 C12 53 39N 77 9W
Kanaaupscow →, *Canada* 140 B4 54 2N 76 30W
Kanab, *U.S.A.* 159 H7 37 3N 112 32W
Kanab Cr. →, *U.S.A.* 159 H7 36 24N 112 38W
Kanacea, *Lau Group, Fiji* 133 A3 17 15 S 179 6W
Kanacea, *Taveuni, Fiji* 133 A2 16 59 S 179 56 E
Kanaga I., *U.S.A.* 144 L3 51 45N 177 22W
Kanagawa □, *Japan* 73 B11 35 20N 139 20 E
Kanagi, *Japan* 70 D10 40 54N 140 27 E
Kanairiktok →, *Canada* 141 A7 55 2N 60 18W
Kanakanak, *U.S.A.* 144 G8 59 0N 158 32W
Kanakapura, *India* 95 H3 12 33N 77 28 E
Kanália, *Greece* 48 B4 39 30N 22 53 E
Kananga, *Dem. Rep. of the Congo* 115 D4 5 55 S 22 18 E
Kanangra-Boyd △, *Australia* 129 B9 33 57 S 150 15 E
Kanash, *Russia* 60 C8 55 30N 47 32 E
Kanaskat, *U.S.A.* 160 C5 47 19N 121 54W
Kanastraíon, Ákra = Palioúrion, Ákra, *Greece* 50 G7 39 57N 23 45 E
Kanawha →, *U.S.A.* 148 F4 38 50N 82 9W
Kanazawa, *Japan* 73 A8 36 30N 136 38 E
Kanbalu, *Burma* 90 D5 23 12N 95 31 E
Kanchanaburi, *Thailand* 86 E2 14 2N 99 31 E
Kanchenjunga, *Nepal* 93 F13 27 50N 88 10 E
Kanchipuram, *India* 95 H4 12 52N 79 45 E
Kanchow = Ganzhou, *China* 77 E10 25 51N 114 56 E
Kańczuga, *Poland* 55 J9 49 59N 22 25 E
Kanda Kanda, *Dem. Rep. of the Congo* 115 D4 6 52 S 23 48 E
Kandagach = Oktyabrsk, *Kazakhstan* 57 E10 49 28N 57 25 E
Kandaghat, *India* 92 D7 30 59N 77 7 E
Kandahar = Qandahār, *Afghan.* 91 C2 31 32N 65 43 E
Kandahar, *India* 94 E3 18 52N 77 12 E
Kandala, *Dem. Rep. of the Congo* 115 D3 6 20 S 19 40 E
Kandalaksha, *Russia* 56 A5 67 9N 32 30 E
Kandalakshskiy Zaliv, *Russia* 56 A6 66 0N 35 0 E
Kandangan, *Indonesia* 85 C5 2 50 S 115 20 E
Kandanghaur, *Indonesia* 79 G13 6 21 S 108 6 E
Kandanos, *Greece* 39 E4 35 19N 23 44 E
Kandava, *Latvia* 54 A9 57 2N 22 46 E
Kandavu = Kadavu, *Fiji* 133 B2 19 0 S 178 15 E
Kandavu Passage = Kadavu Passage, *Fiji* 133 B2 18 45 S 178 0 E
Kandep, *Papua N. G.* 132 C2 5 54 S 143 32 E
Kander →, *Switz.* 32 C5 46 33N 7 38 E
Kandersteg, *Switz.* 32 D5 46 28N 7 40 E
Kandhíla, *Aitolía kai Akarnanía, Greece* 39 B2 38 42N 20 56 E
Kandhíla, *Arkadhía, Greece* 48 D4 37 46N 22 22 E
Kandhkot, *Pakistan* 92 E3 28 16N 69 8 E
Kandhla, *India* 92 E7 29 18N 77 19 E
Kandi, *Benin* 113 C5 11 7N 2 55 E
Kandi, *India* 93 H13 23 58N 88 5 E
Kandiaro, *Pakistan* 92 F3 27 4N 68 13 E
Kandıra, *Turkey* 100 B4 41 4N 30 9 E
Kandla, *India* 92 H4 23 0N 70 10 E
Kandor, O. →, *Chad* 109 E4 17 13N 20 52 E
Kandos, *Australia* 129 B8 32 45 S 149 58 E
Kandreho, *Madag.* 117 B8 17 29 S 46 6 E
Kandrian, *Papua N. G.* 132 D5 6 14 S 149 37 E
Kandy, *Sri Lanka* 95 L5 7 18N 80 43 E
Kane, *U.S.A.* 150 E6 41 40N 78 49W
Kane Basin, *Greenland* 10 B4 79 1N 70 0W
Kaneilio Pt., *U.S.A.* 145 K13 21 27N 158 12W
Kanel, *Senegal* 112 B2 15 30N 13 18W
Kaneohe, *U.S.A.* 145 K14 21 25N 157 48W
Kaneohe B., *U.S.A.* 145 K14 21 30N 157 50W
Kanevskaya, *Russia* 61 G4 46 3N 38 57 E
Kanfanar, *Croatia* 45 C10 45 7N 13 50 E
Kang, *Botswana* 116 C3 23 41 S 22 50 E
Kang Krung △, *Thailand* 87 H2 9 30N 98 50 E
Kangaamiut, *Greenland* 10 D5 65 50N 53 20W
Kangaba, *Mali* 112 C3 11 56N 8 25W
Kangal, *Turkey* 100 C7 39 14N 37 23 E
Kangān, *Fārs, Iran* 97 E7 27 50N 52 3 E
Kangān, *Hormozgān, Iran* 97 E8 25 48N 57 28 E
Kangar, *Malaysia* 87 J3 6 27N 100 12 E
Kangaré, *Mali* 112 C3 11 36N 8 4W
Kangaroo I., *Australia* 128 C2 35 45 S 137 0 E
Kangaroo Mts., *Australia* 126 C3 23 29 S 141 51 E
Kangasala, *Finland* 15 F21 61 28N 24 4 E
Kangāvar, *Iran* 97 C6 34 40N 48 0 E
Kangding, *China* 76 B3 30 2N 101 57 E
Kangdong, *N. Korea* 75 E14 39 9N 126 5 E
Kangean, Kepulauan, *Indonesia* 85 D5 6 55 S 115 23 E
Kangean Is. = Kangean, Kepulauan, *Indonesia* 85 D5 6 55 S 115 23 E
Kangen →, *Sudan* 107 F3 6 47N 33 9 E
Kangerdlugssuak, *Greenland* 10 D7 68 10N 32 20W
Kangerluarsoruseq, *Greenland* 10 E5 63 45N 51 27W
Kangerluarsoruset = Kangerluarsoruseq, *Greenland* 10 E5 63 45N 51 27W
Kangerlussuaq, *Greenland* 10 D5 66 59N 50 40W
Kanggye, *N. Korea* 75 D14 41 0N 126 35 E
Kanggyŏng, *S. Korea* 75 F14 36 10N 127 0 E
Kanghwa, *S. Korea* 75 F14 37 45N 126 30 E
Kangikajik, *Greenland* 10 C8 70 7N 22 0W
Kangilinnguit, *Greenland* 10 E6 61 20N 47 57W
Kangiqliniq = Rankin Inlet, *Canada* 138 B10 62 30N 93 0W
Kangiqsualujjuaq, *Canada* 139 C13 58 30N 65 59W
Kangiqsujuaq, *Canada* 139 B12 61 30N 72 0W
Kangiqtugaapik = Clyde River, *Canada* 139 A13 70 30N 68 30W
Kangirsuk, *Canada* 139 B13 60 0N 70 0W
Kangkar Chemaran, *Malaysia* 87 d 1 34N 104 12 E
Kangkar Sungai Tiram, *Malaysia* 87 d 1 35N 103 55 E
Kangkar Teberau, *Malaysia* 87 d 1 32N 103 51 E
Kangnŭng, *S. Korea* 75 F15 37 45N 128 54 E
Kango, *Gabon* 114 B2 0 11N 10 5 E
Kangoya, *Dem. Rep. of the Congo* 115 D4 9 55 S 22 48 E
Kangping, *China* 75 C12 42 43N 123 18 E
Kangpokpi, *India* 90 C4 25 8N 93 58 E
Kangra, *India* 92 C7 32 6N 76 16 E
Kangrinboqe Feng, *China* 93 D9 31 0N 81 25 E
Kangyidaung, *Burma* 90 G5 16 56N 94 54 E
Kanha △, *India* 93 H9 22 15N 80 40 E
Kanhan →, *India* 94 D4 21 4N 79 34 E
Kanhangad, *India* 95 H2 12 21N 74 58 E
Kanhar →, *India* 93 G10 24 28N 83 8 E
Kanheri, *India* 94 E1 19 13N 72 50 E
Kani, *Sagaing, Burma* 90 D5 23 52N 95 22 E
Kani, *Sagaing, Burma* 90 D5 22 26N 94 51 E
Kani, *Ivory C.* 112 D3 8 29N 6 36W
Kaniama, *Dem. Rep. of the Congo* 118 D1 7 30 S 24 12 E
Kaniapiskau = Caniapiscau →, *Canada* 141 A6 56 40N 69 30W
Kaniapiskau, L. = Caniapiscau, L. de, *Canada* 141 B6 54 10N 69 55W
Kanibadam, *Tajikistan* 65 C5 40 17N 70 25 E
Kaniere, L., *N.Z.* 131 C6 42 50 S 171 10 E
Kanigiri, *India* 95 G4 15 24N 79 31 E
Kanimekh, *Uzbekistan* 65 C2 40 16N 65 7 E
Kanin, Poluostrov, *Russia* 56 A8 68 0N 45 0 E
Kanin Nos, Mys, *Russia* 56 A7 68 39N 43 32 E
Kanin Pen. = Kanin, Poluostrov, *Russia* 56 A8 68 0N 45 0 E
Kaninë, *Albania* 50 F3 40 23N 19 30 E
Kaniva, *Australia* 128 D4 36 22 S 141 18 E
Kanjiža, *Serbia & M.* 52 D5 46 3N 20 4 E
Kanjut Sar, *Pakistan* 93 A6 36 7N 75 25 E
Kankaanpää, *Finland* 15 F20 61 44N 22 50 E
Kankakee, *U.S.A.* 157 C9 41 7N 87 52W
Kankakee →, *U.S.A.* 157 C8 41 23N 88 15W
Kankan, *Guinea* 112 C3 10 23N 9 15W
Kankendy = Xankändi, *Azerbaijan* 101 C12 39 52N 46 49 E
Kanker, *India* 94 D5 20 10N 81 40 E
Kankesanturai, *Sri Lanka* 95 K5 9 49N 80 2 E
Kankossa, *Mauritania* 112 B2 15 54N 11 31W
Kankroli, *India* 92 G5 25 4N 73 53 E
Kanmuri-Yama, *Japan* 72 C4 34 30N 132 4 E
Kannabe, *Japan* 72 C5 34 32N 133 23 E
Kannapolis, *U.S.A.* 149 H5 35 30N 80 37W
Kannauj, *India* 93 F8 27 3N 79 56 E
Kanniyakumari, *India* 95 K3 8 5N 77 34 E
Kano, *Nigeria* 113 C6 12 2N 8 30 E
Kano □, *Nigeria* 113 C6 11 30N 8 30 E
Kan'onji, *Japan* 72 C5 34 7N 133 39 E
Kanoroba, *Ivory C.* 112 D3 9 7N 6 8W
Kanowha, *U.S.A.* 156 B3 42 57N 93 47W
Kanowit, *Malaysia* 85 B4 2 14N 112 20 E
Kanoya, *Japan* 72 F2 31 25N 130 50 E
Kanpetlet, *Burma* 90 E4 21 10N 93 59 E
Kanpur, *India* 93 F9 26 28N 80 20 E
Kansai International ✈ (KIX), *Japan* 73 C7 34 27N 135 12 E
Kansas, *U.S.A.* 157 E9 39 33N 87 56W
Kansas □, *U.S.A.* 154 F6 38 30N 99 0W
Kansas →, *U.S.A.* 154 F7 39 7N 94 37W
Kansas City, *Kans., U.S.A.* 156 E2 39 7N 94 38W
Kansas City, *Mo., U.S.A.* 156 E2 39 6N 94 35W
Kansas City International ✈ (MCI), *U.S.A.* 156 E2 39 18N 94 43W
Kansenia, *Dem. Rep. of the Congo* 119 E2 10 20 S 26 0 E
Kansk, *Russia* 67 D10 56 20N 95 37 E
Kansŏng, *S. Korea* 75 E15 38 24N 128 30 E
Kansu = Gansu □, *China* 74 G3 36 0N 104 0 E
Kansu, *China* 65 D7 39 46N 75 2 E
Kant, *Kyrgyzstan* 65 B7 42 53N 74 51 E
Kantaphor, *India* 92 H7 22 35N 76 34 E
Kantchari, *Burkina Faso* 113 C5 12 37N 1 37 E
Kantché, *Niger* 113 C6 13 31N 8 30 E
Kanté, *Togo* 113 D5 9 57N 1 3 E
Kantemirovka, *Russia* 59 H10 49 43N 39 55 E
Kanth = Kąty Wrocławskie, *Poland* 55 G3 51 2N 16 45 E
Kantharalak, *Thailand* 86 E5 14 39N 104 39 E
Kantishna, *U.S.A.* 144 E10 63 31N 150 57W
Kantishna →, *U.S.A.* 144 D10 64 45N 149 58W
Kantli →, *India* 92 E6 28 20N 75 30 E
Kantō □, *Japan* 73 A11 36 15N 139 30 E
Kantō-Sanchi, *Japan* 73 B10 35 59N 138 50 E
Kantu-long, *Burma* 90 F6 19 57N 97 36 E
Kanturk, *Ireland* 23 D3 52 11N 8 54W
Kanuma, *Japan* 73 A11 36 34N 139 42 E
Kanus, *Namibia* 116 D2 27 50 S 18 39 E
Kanye, *Botswana* 116 C4 24 55 S 25 28 E
Kanzenze, *Dem. Rep. of the Congo* 119 E2 10 30 S 25 12 E
Kanzi, Ras, *Tanzania* 118 D4 7 1 S 39 33 E
Kao, *Tonga* 133 P13 19 40 S 175 1W
Kao Phara, *Thailand* 87 a 8 3N 98 22 E
Kaoe, *Indonesia* 82 A3 1 11N 127 54 E
Kaohsiung, *Taiwan* 77 F13 22 35N 120 16 E
Kaoka, *Solomon Is.* 133 M11 9 42 S 160 43 E
Kaokaona, *Solomon Is.* 133 N11 10 27 S 161 56 E
Kaokoveld, *Namibia* 116 B1 19 15 S 14 30 E
Kaolack, *Senegal* 112 C1 14 5N 16 8W
Kaolan = Lanzhou, *China* 74 F2 36 1N 103 52 E
Kaolo, *Solomon Is.* 133 M10 8 24 S 159 38 E
Kaoma, *Zambia* 115 E4 14 47 S 24 48 E
Kaoshan, *China* 75 B13 44 38N 124 50 E
Kaouar, *Niger* 109 E2 19 5N 12 52 E
Kaoyao = Zhaoqing, *China* 77 F9 23 0N 112 20 E
Kapaa, *U.S.A.* 145 A2 22 5N 159 19W
Kapadvanj, *India* 92 H5 23 5N 73 0 E
Kapagere, *Papua N. G.* 132 E4 9 46 S 147 42 E
Kapahulu, *U.S.A.* 145 K14 21 16N 157 49W
Kapaklı, *Turkey* 51 E11 41 19N 27 59 E
Kapan, *Armenia* 101 C12 39 18N 46 27 E
Kapanga, *Bandundu, Dem. Rep. of the Congo* 115 D3 5 4 S 16 58 E
Kapanga, *Katanga, Dem. Rep. of the Congo* 115 D4 8 30 S 22 40 E
Kapapa I., *U.S.A.* 145 K14 21 29N 157 48W
Kapatagan, *Phil.* 81 H4 7 52N 123 44 E
Kapchagai = Qapshaghay, *Kazakhstan* 65 B8 43 51N 77 14 E
Kapchagaiskoye Vdkhr. = Qapshaghay Bögeni, *Kazakhstan* 65 B8 43 45N 77 50 E
Kapela = Velika Kapela, *Croatia* 45 C12 45 10N 15 5 E
Kapéllo, Ákra, *Greece* 48 E5 36 9N 23 3 E
Kapema, *Dem. Rep. of the Congo* 119 E2 10 45 S 28 22 E
Kapfenberg, *Austria* 34 D8 47 26N 15 18 E
Kapı Dağı, *Turkey* 51 F11 40 28N 27 50 E
Kapia, *Dem. Rep. of the Congo* 115 C3 4 17 S 19 46 E
Kapiri Mposhi, *Zambia* 119 E2 13 59 S 28 43 E
Kāpīsā □, *Afghan.* 91 B3 35 0N 69 20 E
Kapiskau →, *Canada* 140 B3 52 47N 81 55W
Kapit, *Malaysia* 85 B4 2 0N 112 55 E
Kapiti I., *N.Z.* 130 G3 40 50 S 174 56 E
Kapka, Massif du, *Chad* 109 E4 15 7N 21 45 E
Kaplan, *U.S.A.* 155 K8 30 0N 92 17W
Kaplice, *Czech Rep.* 34 C7 48 42N 14 30 E
Kapoe, *Thailand* 87 H2 9 34N 98 32 E
Kapoeta, *Sudan* 107 G3 4 50N 33 35 E
Kápolnásnyék, *Hungary* 52 C3 47 16N 18 41 E
Kapombo, *Dem. Rep. of the Congo* 115 E4 10 40 S 23 30 E
Kaponga, *N.Z.* 130 F3 39 29 S 174 9 E
Kapos →, *Hungary* 52 D3 46 44N 18 30 E
Kaposvár, *Hungary* 52 D2 46 25N 17 47 E
Kapowsin, *U.S.A.* 160 D4 46 59N 122 13W
Kapp, *Norway* 18 D7 60 43N 10 52 E
Kappeln, *Germany* 30 A5 54 40N 9 55 E
Kappelshamn, *Sweden* 17 G12 57 52N 18 47 E
Kaprije, *Croatia* 45 E12 43 42N 15 43 E
Kapsan, *N. Korea* 75 D15 41 4N 128 19 E
Kapsukas = Marijampolė, *Lithuania* 15 J20 54 33N 23 19 E
Kaptai, *Bangla.* 90 D4 22 21N 92 17 E
Kaptai L., *Bangla.* 90 D4 22 40N 92 20 E
Kapuas, *Indonesia* 85 C4 3 10 S 114 5 E
Kapuas →, *Indonesia* 85 C3 0 25 S 109 20 E
Kapuas Hulu, Pegunungan, *Malaysia* 85 B4 1 30N 113 30 E
Kapuas Hulu Ra. = Kapuas Hulu, Pegunungan, *Malaysia* 85 B4 1 30N 113 30 E
Kapulo, *Dem. Rep. of the Congo* 119 D2 8 18 S 29 15 E
Kapunda, *Australia* 128 C3 34 20 S 138 56 E
Kapuni, *N.Z.* 130 F3 39 29 S 174 8 E
Kapurthala, *India* 92 D6 31 23N 75 25 E
Kapuskasing, *Canada* 140 C3 49 25N 82 30W
Kapuskasing →, *Canada* 140 C3 49 49N 82 0W
Kapustin Yar, *Russia* 61 F7 48 37N 45 40 E
Kaputar, *Australia* 127 E5 30 15 S 150 10 E
Kaputir, *Kenya* 118 B4 2 5N 35 28 E
Kapuvár, *Hungary* 52 C2 47 36N 17 1 E
Kaqung, *China* 65 E8 38 0N 76 50 E
Kara, *Russia* 66 C7 69 10N 65 0 E
Karā, W. →, *Si. Arabia* 106 C5 20 45N 41 42 E
Kara Ada, *Turkey* 49 E9 36 58N 27 28 E
Kara-Balta, *Kyrgyzstan* 65 B6 42 50N 73 49 E
Kara Bogaz Gol, Zaliv = Garabogazköl Aylagy, *Turkmenistan* 57 F9 41 0N 53 30 E
Kara Burun, *Turkey* 49 E9 36 32N 27 58 E
Kara-Darya = Payshanba, *Uzbekistan* 65 C3 40 0N 66 14 E
Kara Kalpak Republic = Qoraqalpoghistan □, *Uzbekistan* 66 E6 43 0N 58 0 E
Kara-Köl, *Kyrgyzstan* 65 C6 41 40N 72 43 E
Kara-Kulja, *Kyrgyzstan* 65 C6 40 39N 73 26 E
Kara Kum, *Turkmenistan* 66 F6 39 30N 60 0 E
Kara-Saki, *Japan* 72 C1 34 41N 129 30 E
Kara-Say, *Kyrgyzstan* 65 C8 41 33N 77 54 E
Kara Sea, *Russia* 66 B7 75 0N 70 0 E
Kara-Suu, *Kyrgyzstan* 65 C6 40 44N 72 53 E
Karaadilli, *Turkey* 49 C12 38 18N 30 37 E
Karabash, *Russia* 64 D8 55 29N 60 14 E
Karabekaul = Garabekewül, *Turkmenistan* 65 D2 38 30N 64 8 E
Karabiğa, *Turkey* 51 F11 40 23N 27 17 E
Karabük, *Turkey* 100 B5 41 12N 32 37 E
Karabulak = Qarabulaq, *Kazakhstan* 65 A9 44 54N 78 30 E
Karabulak, *China* 65 C8 40 48N 77 32 E
Karaburun, *Albania* 50 F3 40 25N 19 20 E
Karaburun, *Turkey* 49 C8 38 41N 26 28 E
Karabutak = Qarabutaq, *Kazakhstan* 64 G8 49 59N 60 14 E
Karacabey, *Turkey* 51 F12 40 12N 28 21 E
Karacakılavuz, *Turkey* 51 E11 41 8N 27 21 E
Karacaköy, *Turkey* 51 E12 41 24N 28 22 E
Karacasu, *Turkey* 49 D10 37 43N 28 35 E
Karachala = Qaraçala, *Azerbaijan* 61 L9 39 45N 48 53 E
Karachayevsk, *Russia* 61 J5 43 50N 41 55 E
Karachev, *Russia* 59 F8 53 10N 35 5 E
Karachey-Cherkessia □, *Russia* 61 J5 43 40N 41 30 E
Karachi, *Pakistan* 91 D2 24 53N 67 0 E
Karad, *India* 94 F2 17 15N 74 10 E
Karadirek, *Turkey* 49 C12 38 34N 30 11 E
Karaga, *Ghana* 113 D4 9 58N 0 28W
Karaganda = Qaraghandy, *Kazakhstan* 66 E8 49 50N 73 10 E
Karagayly = Qaraghayly, *Kazakhstan* 66 E8 49 26N 76 0 E
Karaginskiy, Ostrov, *Russia* 67 D17 58 45N 164 0 E
Karagiye, Vpadina, *Kazakhstan* 57 F9 43 27N 51 45 E
Karagiye Depression = Karagiye, Vpadina, *Kazakhstan* 57 F9 43 27N 51 45 E
Karagola Road, *India* 93 G12 25 29N 87 23 E
Karagüney Dağları, *Turkey* 100 B6 40 30N 34 40 E
Karahallı, *Turkey* 49 C11 38 21N 29 33 E
Karaikal, *India* 95 J4 10 59N 79 50 E
Karaikkudi, *India* 95 J4 10 5N 78 45 E
Karaisali, *Turkey* 100 D6 37 16N 35 2 E
Karaiskákis, *Greece* 39 B3 38 35N 21 4 E
Karaitivu I., *Sri Lanka* 95 K4 9 45N 79 52 E
Karaj, *Iran* 97 C6 35 48N 51 0 E
Karak, *Malaysia* 87 L4 3 25N 102 2 E
Karakalpakstan = Qoraqalpoghistan □, *Uzbekistan* 66 E6 43 0N 58 0 E
Karakelong, *Indonesia* 82 A3 4 35N 126 50 E
Karakitang, *Indonesia* 82 A3 3 14N 125 28 E
Karaklis = Vanadzor, *Armenia* 61 K7 40 48N 44 30 E
Karakoçan, *Turkey* 101 C9 38 57N 40 2 E
Karakol, *Kyrgyzstan* 65 B9 42 30N 78 20 E
Karakoram Pass, *Asia* 93 B7 35 33N 77 50 E
Karakoram Ra., *Pakistan* 93 B7 35 30N 77 0 E
Karakul, *Tajikistan* 65 D6 39 2N 73 33 E
Karakul, *Uzbekistan* 65 D1 39 22N 63 50 E
Karakul, Ozero, *Tajikistan* 65 D6 39 5N 73 25 E
Karakurt, *Turkey* 101 B10 40 10N 42 37 E
Karakuwisa, *Namibia* 116 B2 18 56 S 19 40 E
Karal, *Chad* 109 F2 12 50N 14 46 E
Karalon, *Russia* 67 D12 57 5N 115 50 E
Karama, *Jordan* 103 D4 31 57N 35 35 E
Karaman, *Balıkesir, Turkey* 49 B9 39 39N 28 0 E
Karaman, *Konya, Turkey* 100 D5 37 14N 33 13 E
Karamanlı, *Turkey* 49 D11 37 23N 29 47 E
Karamay, *China* 68 B3 45 30N 84 58 E
Karambu, *Indonesia* 85 C5 3 53 S 116 6 E
Karamea, *N.Z.* 131 B7 41 14 S 172 6 E
Karamea →, *N.Z.* 131 B7 41 13 S 172 26 E
Karamea Bight, *N.Z.* 131 B6 41 22 S 171 40 E
Karamet Niyaz = Garamätnyýaz, *Turkmenistan* 65 E2 37 45N 64 34 E
Karamnasa →, *India* 93 G10 25 31N 83 52 E
Karamürsel, *Turkey* 51 F13 40 41N 29 36 E
Karand, *Iran* 101 E12 34 16N 46 15 E
Karangana, *Mali* 112 C3 12 15N 5 4W
Karanganyar, *Indonesia* 85 D3 7 38 S 109 37 E
Karangasem, *Indonesia* 79 J18 8 27 S 115 37 E
Karanja, *Maharashtra, India* 94 D4 21 11N 78 24 E
Karanja, *Maharashtra, India* 94 D3 20 29N 77 31 E
Karanjia, *India* 93 J11 21 47N 85 58 E
Karankasso, *Burkina Faso* 112 C4 10 50N 3 53W
Karaova, *Turkey* 49 D9 37 5N 27 40 E
Karapınar, *Turkey* 100 D5 37 41N 33 30 E
Karapiro, *N.Z.* 130 D4 37 53 S 175 32 E
Karas, *Indonesia* 83 B4 3 27 S 132 40 E
Karasburg, *Namibia* 116 D2 28 0 S 18 44 E
Karasino, *Russia* 66 C9 66 50N 86 50 E
Karasjok, *Norway* 14 B21 69 27N 25 30 E
Karasu, *Turkey* 100 B4 41 4N 30 46 E
Karasu →, *Turkey* 49 E12 36 18N 30 10 E
Karasubazar = Bilohirsk, *Ukraine* 59 K8 45 3N 34 35 E
Karasuk, *Russia* 66 D8 53 44N 78 2 E
Karasuyama, *Japan* 73 A12 36 39N 140 9 E
Karataş, *Adana, Turkey* 100 D6 36 36N 35 21 E
Karataş, *Manisa, Turkey* 49 C10 38 35N 28 16 E
Karataş Burnu, *Turkey* 100 D6 36 31N 35 24 E
Karatau, Khrebet = Qarataū, *Kazakhstan* 65 B4 43 30N 69 30 E
Karateki Shan, *China* 65 C8 40 40N 77 50 E
Karativu, *Sri Lanka* 95 K4 8 22N 79 47 E
Karatobe, *Kazakhstan* 64 G4 49 44N 53 30 E
Karatoprak, *Turkey* 49 D9 37 2N 27 15 E
Karatoya →, *India* 90 C2 24 7N 89 36 E
Karatsu, *Japan* 72 D1 33 26N 129 58 E
Karaturuk = Qaraturyq, *Kazakhstan* 65 B8 43 35N 77 50 E
Karaul, *Russia* 66 B9 70 6N 82 15 E
Karaulbazar, *Uzbekistan* 65 D2 39 30N 64 48 E
Karauli, *India* 92 F7 26 30N 77 4 E
Karavastasë, L. e, *Albania* 50 F3 40 55N 19 30 E
Karávi, *Greece* 48 E5 36 49N 23 37 E
Karavostasi, *Cyprus* 39 E8 35 8N 32 50 E
Karawa, *Dem. Rep. of the Congo* 114 B4 3 18N 20 17 E
Karawang, *Indonesia* 85 D3 6 30 S 107 15 E
Karawanken, *Europe* 34 E7 46 30N 14 40 E
Karayazı, *Turkey* 101 C10 39 41N 42 9 E
Karazhal, *Kazakhstan* 66 E8 48 2N 70 49 E
Karbalā', *Iraq* 101 F11 32 36N 44 3 E
Kärböle, *Sweden* 16 C9 61 59N 15 22 E
Karcag, *Hungary* 52 C5 47 19N 20 57 E
Karcha →, *Pakistan* 93 B7 34 45N 76 10 E
Karchana, *India* 93 G9 25 17N 81 56 E
Karczew, *Poland* 55 F8 52 5N 21 15 E
Kardam, *Bulgaria* 51 C12 43 45N 28 6 E
Kardeljovo = Ploče, *Croatia* 45 E14 43 4N 17 26 E
Kardhakata, *Greece* 39 C1 38 17N 20 28 E
Kardhámila, *Greece* 49 C8 38 35N 26 5 E
Kardhamíli, *Greece* 48 E4 36 53N 22 13 E

Kardhítsa, *Greece* **48 B3** 39 23N 21 54 E
Kardhítsa □, *Greece* **48 B3** 39 15N 21 50 E
Karditsa = Kardhítsa, *Greece* **48 B3** 39 23N 21 54 E
Kärdla, *Estonia* **15 G20** 59 0N 22 45 E
Kareeberge, *S. Africa* **116 E3** 30 59 S 21 50 E
Kareha →, *India* **93 G12** 25 44N 86 21 E
Kareima, *Sudan* **106 D3** 18 30N 31 49 E
Karelia □, *Russia* **56 A5** 65 30N 32 30 E
Karelian Republic = Karelia □, *Russia* **56 A5** 65 30N 32 30 E
Karelo-Finnish SSR = Karelia □, *Russia* **56 A5** 65 30N 32 30 E
Karema, *Papua N. G.* **132 E4** 9 12 S 147 18 E
Karen = Kayin □, *Burma* **90 G6** 18 0N 97 30 E
Karenni = Kayah □, *Burma* **90 F6** 19 15N 97 15 E
Karera, *India* **92 G8** 25 32N 78 9 E
Kārevāndar, *Iran* **97 E9** 27 53N 60 44 E
Kargasok, *Russia* **66 D9** 59 3N 80 53 E
Kargat, *Russia* **66 D9** 55 10N 80 15 E
Kargı, *Turkey* **100 B6** 41 11N 34 30 E
Kargil, *India* **93 B7** 34 32N 76 12 E
Kargopol, *Russia* **58 B10** 61 30N 38 58 E
Kargowa, *Poland* **55 F2** 52 5N 15 51 E
Karguéri, *Niger* **113 C7** 13 27N 10 30 E
Karhal, *India* **93 F8** 27 1N 78 57 E
Kariá, *Greece* **39 B2** 38 45N 20 39 E
Karia ba Mohammed, *Morocco* **110 B3** 34 22N 5 12W
Kariaí, *Greece* **51 F8** 40 14N 24 19 E
Karīān, *Iran* **97 E8** 26 57N 57 14 E
Karianga, *Madag.* **117 C8** 22 25 S 47 22 E
Kariba, *Zimbabwe* **119 F2** 16 28 S 28 50 E
Kariba, L., *Zimbabwe* **119 F2** 16 40 S 28 25 E
Kariba Dam, *Zimbabwe* **119 F2** 16 30 S 28 35 E
Kariba Gorge, *Zambia* **119 F2** 16 30 S 28 50 E
Karibib, *Namibia* **116 C2** 22 0 S 15 56 E
Karijini △, *Australia* **124 D2** 23 8 S 118 15 E
Karikari, C., *N.Z.* **130 A2** 34 46 S 173 24 E
Karimata, Kepulauan, *Indonesia* **85 C3** 1 25 S 109 0 E
Karimata, Selat, *Indonesia* **85 C3** 2 0 S 108 40 E
Karimata Is. = Karimata, Kepulauan, *Indonesia* **85 C3** 1 25 S 109 0 E
Karimganj, *India* **90 C4** 24 52N 92 20 E
Karimnagar, *India* **94 E4** 18 26N 79 10 E
Karimun Kecil, Pulau, *Indonesia* **87 d** 1 8N 103 22 E
Karimunjawa, Kepulauan, *Indonesia* **85 D4** 5 50 S 110 30 E
Karin, *Somali Rep.* **120 B3** 10 50N 45 52 E
Káristos, *Greece* **48 C6** 38 1N 24 29 E
Karīt, *Iran* **97 C8** 33 29N 56 55 E
Kariya, *Japan* **73 C9** 34 58N 137 1 E
Kariyangwe, *Zimbabwe* **117 B4** 18 0 S 27 38 E
Karjala, *Finland* **58 A5** 62 0N 30 25 E
Karjat, *Maharashtra, India* **94 E2** 18 33N 75 0 E
Karjat, *Maharashtra, India* **94 E1** 18 55N 73 20 E
Karkal, *India* **95 H2** 13 15N 74 56 E
Karkar, *Papua N. G.* **132 C3** 4 32 S 145 57 E
Karkar I., *Papua N. G.* **132 C4** 4 40 S 146 0 E
Karkaralinsk = Qarqaraly, *Kazakhstan* **66 E8** 49 26N 75 30 E
Karkheh →, *Iran* **96 D5** 31 2N 47 29 E
Karkinitska Zatoka, *Ukraine* **59 K7** 45 56N 33 0 E
Karkinitskiy Zaliv = Karkinitska Zatoka, *Ukraine* **59 K7** 45 56N 33 0 E
Karkuk = Kirkūk, *Iraq* **101 E11** 35 30N 44 21 E
Karkur Tohl, *Egypt* **106 C2** 22 5N 25 5 E
Karl Liebknecht, *Russia* **59 G8** 51 40N 35 35 E
Karl-Marx-Stadt = Chemnitz, *Germany* **30 E8** 50 51N 12 54 E
Karleby = Kokkola, *Finland* **14 E20** 63 50N 23 8 E
Karlholmsbruk, *Sweden* **16 D11** 60 31N 17 37 E
Karlino, *Poland* **54 D2** 54 3N 15 53 E
Karlivka, *Ukraine* **59 H8** 49 29N 35 8 E
Karlobag, *Croatia* **45 D12** 44 32N 15 5 E
Karlovac, *Croatia* **45 C12** 45 31N 15 36 E
Karlovarský □, *Czech Rep.* **34 A5** 50 10N 12 50 E
Karlovka = Karlivka, *Ukraine* **59 H8** 49 29N 35 8 E
Karlovo, *Bulgaria* **51 D8** 42 38N 24 47 E
Karlovy Vary, *Czech Rep.* **34 A5** 50 13N 12 51 E
Karlowitz = Sremski Karlovci, *Serbia & M.* **52 E4** 45 12N 19 56 E
Karlowitz = Velké Karlovice, *Czech Rep.* **35 B11** 49 20N 18 17 E
Karlsbad = Karlovy Vary, *Czech Rep.* **34 A5** 50 13N 12 51 E
Karlsborg, *Sweden* **17 F8** 58 33N 14 33 E
Karlsburg = Alba-Iulia, *Romania* **53 D8** 46 8N 23 39 E
Karlshamn, *Sweden* **17 H8** 56 10N 14 51 E
Karlshus, *Norway* **18 E7** 59 21N 10 52 E
Karlskoga, *Sweden* **16 E8** 59 28N 14 33 E
Karlskrona, *Sweden* **17 H9** 56 10N 15 35 E
Karlsruhe, *Germany* **31 F4** 49 0N 8 23 E
Karlstad = Karlovac, *Croatia* **45 C12** 45 31N 15 36 E
Karlstad, *Sweden* **16 E7** 59 23N 13 30 E
Karlstad, *U.S.A.* **154 A6** 48 35N 96 31W
Karlstadt, *Germany* **31 F5** 49 57N 9 47 E
Karluk, *U.S.A.* **144 H9** 57 34N 154 28W
Karma, *Niger* **113 C5** 13 38N 1 52 E
Karmala, *India* **94 E2** 18 25N 75 12 E
Karmana, *Uzbekistan* **65 C2** 40 8N 65 21 E
Karmėlava, *Lithuania* **54 D11** 54 58N 24 4 E
Karmi'el, *Israel* **103 C4** 32 55N 35 18 E
Karmøy, *Norway* **18 E2** 59 15N 5 15 E
Karnak, *Egypt* **106 B3** 25 43N 32 39 E
Karnal, *India* **92 E7** 29 42N 77 2 E
Karnali →, *Nepal* **93 E9** 28 45N 81 16 E
Karnaphuli Res. = Kaptai L., *Bangla.* **90 D4** 22 40N 92 20 E
Karnaprayag, *India* **93 D8** 30 16N 79 15 E
Karnataka □, *India* **95 H3** 13 15N 77 0 E
Karnes City, *U.S.A.* **155 L6** 28 53N 97 54W
Karnische Alpen, *Europe* **34 E6** 46 36N 13 0 E
Karnobat, *Bulgaria* **51 D10** 42 39N 26 59 E
Kärnten □, *Austria* **34 E6** 46 52N 13 30 E
Karo, *Mali* **112 C4** 12 16N 3 18W
Karoi, *Zimbabwe* **119 F2** 16 48 S 29 45 E
Karomatan, *Phil.* **81 H4** 7 55N 123 44 E
Karon, Ao, *Thailand* **87 a** 7 51N 98 17 E
Karonga, *Malawi* **119 D3** 9 57 S 33 55 E
Karoo △, *S. Africa* **116 E3** 32 18 S 22 27 E
Karoonda, *Australia* **128 C3** 35 1 S 139 59 E
Karor, *Pakistan* **92 D4** 31 15N 70 59 E
Karora, *Sudan* **106 D4** 17 44N 38 15 E
Káros, *Greece* **49 E7** 36 54N 25 40 E
Karosa, *Indonesia* **82 B1** 1 48 S 119 20 E
Karounga, *Mali* **112 B3** 15 20N 7 35W
Karousádhes, *Greece* **38 B9** 39 47N 19 45 E
Karpacz, *Poland* **55 H2** 50 46N 15 46 E
Karpasia, *Cyprus* **39 E10** 35 32N 34 15 E
Kárpathos, *Greece* **49 F9** 35 37N 27 10 E
Kárpathos, Stenón, *Greece* **49 F9** 36 0N 27 30 E
Karpatsky △, *Ukraine* **53 B9** 48 20N 24 35 E
Karpenísion, *Greece* **48 C3** 38 55N 21 40 E
Karpilovka = Aktsyabrski, *Belarus* **59 F5** 52 38N 28 53 E
Karpinsk, *Russia* **64 B8** 59 45N 60 1 E
Karpogory, *Russia* **56 B7** 64 0N 44 27 E
Karpuz Burnu = Apostolos Andreas, C., *Cyprus* **39 E10** 35 42N 34 35 E
Karpuzlu, *Turkey* **49 D9** 37 33N 27 51 E
Karratha, *Australia* **124 D2** 20 53 S 116 40 E
Kars, *Turkey* **101 B10** 40 40N 43 5 E
Karsakpay, *Kazakhstan* **66 E7** 47 55N 66 40 E
Karsha, *Kazakhstan* **60 F10** 49 45N 51 35 E
Karshi = Qarshi, *Uzbekistan* **65 D2** 38 53N 65 48 E
Karsiyang, *India* **90 B2** 26 56N 88 18 E
Karsog, *India* **92 D7** 31 23N 77 12 E
Karst = Kras, *Croatia* **45 C10** 45 35N 14 0 E
Kartal, *Turkey* **51 F13** 40 53N 29 11 E
Kartál Óros, *Greece* **51 E9** 41 15N 25 13 E
Kartaly, *Russia* **64 E8** 53 3N 60 40 E
Kartapur, *India* **92 D6** 31 27N 75 32 E
Karthaus, *U.S.A.* **150 E6** 41 8N 78 9W
Kartuzy, *Poland* **54 D5** 54 22N 18 10 E
Karuah, *Australia* **129 B9** 32 37 S 151 56 E
Karufa, *Indonesia* **83 B4** 3 50 S 133 20 E
Karuma ⌂, *Uganda* **118 B3** 2 5N 32 15 E
Karumba, *Australia* **126 B3** 17 31 S 140 50 E
Karumo, *Tanzania* **118 C3** 2 25 S 32 50 E
Karumwa, *Tanzania* **118 C3** 3 12 S 32 38 E
Kārūn →, *Iran* **97 D6** 30 26N 48 10 E
Karungu, *Kenya* **118 C3** 0 50 S 34 10 E
Karup, *Denmark* **17 H3** 56 19N 9 10 E
Karur, *India* **95 J4** 10 59N 78 2 E
Karviná, *Czech Rep.* **35 B11** 49 53N 18 31 E
Karwan →, *India* **92 F8** 27 26N 78 4 E
Karwendel ⌂, *Austria* **34 D4** 47 25N 11 30 E
Karwi, *India* **93 G9** 25 12N 80 57 E
Kaş, *Turkey* **49 E11** 36 11N 29 37 E
Kasaan, *U.S.A.* **144 J14** 55 32N 132 24W
Kasaba, *Turkey* **49 E11** 36 18N 29 44 E
Kasabi, *Zambia* **115 E4** 14 52 S 23 45 E
Kasache, *Malawi* **119 E3** 13 25 S 34 20 E
Kasai, *Japan* **72 C6** 34 55N 134 52 E
Kasai →, *Dem. Rep. of the Congo* **115 C3** 3 30 S 16 10 E
Kasai-Occidental □, *Dem. Rep. of the Congo* **115 D4** 6 0 S 22 0 E
Kasai-Oriental □, *Dem. Rep. of the Congo* **118 D1** 5 0 S 24 30 E
Kasaji, *Dem. Rep. of the Congo* **119 E1** 10 25 S 23 27 E
Kasama, *Japan* **73 A12** 36 23N 140 16 E
Kasama, *Zambia* **119 E3** 10 16 S 31 9 E
Kasan, *Uzbekistan* **65 D2** 39 2N 65 35 E
Kasan-dong, *N. Korea* **75 D14** 41 18N 126 55 E
Kasane, *Namibia* **116 B3** 17 34 S 24 50 E
Kasanga, *Tanzania* **119 D3** 8 30 S 31 10 E
Kasangaie, *Dem. Rep. of the Congo* **115 D4** 6 20 S 22 42 E
Kasangulu, *Dem. Rep. of the Congo* **115 C3** 4 33 S 15 15 E
Kasanka △, *Zambia* **119 E3** 11 34 S 30 15 E
Kasansay, *Uzbekistan* **65 C5** 41 15N 71 31 E
Kasaoka, *Japan* **72 C5** 34 30N 133 30 E
Kasar, Ras, *Sudan* **106 D4** 18 2N 38 36 E
Kasaragod, *India* **95 H2** 12 30N 74 58 E
Kasat, *Burma* **90 G7** 15 56N 98 13 E
Kasba, *Bangla.* **90 D3** 23 45N 91 2 E
Kasba L., *Canada* **143 A8** 60 20N 102 10W
Kasba Tadla, *Morocco* **110 B3** 32 36N 6 17W
Kaschau = Košice, *Slovak Rep.* **35 C14** 48 42N 21 15 E
Kaseda, *Japan* **72 F2** 31 25N 130 19 E
Kāseh Garān, *Iran* **96 C5** 34 5N 46 2 E
Kasempa, *Zambia* **119 E2** 13 30 S 25 44 E
Kasenga, *Dem. Rep. of the Congo* **119 E2** 10 20 S 28 45 E
Kasese, *Uganda* **118 B3** 0 13N 30 3 E
Kasevo = Neftekamsk, *Russia* **64 C5** 56 6N 54 17 E
Kasewa, *Zambia* **119 E2** 14 28 S 28 53 E
Kasganj, *India* **93 F8** 27 48N 78 42 E
Kashabowie, *Canada* **140 C1** 48 40N 90 26W
Kashaf, *Iran* **97 C9** 35 58N 61 7 E
Kāshān, *Iran* **97 C6** 34 5N 51 30 E
Kashechewan, *Canada* **140 B3** 52 18N 81 37W
Kashgar = Kashi, *China* **65 D8** 39 30N 76 2 E
Kashi, *China* **65 D8** 39 30N 76 2 E
Kashihara, *Japan* **73 C7** 34 27N 135 46 E
Kashiji Plain, *Zambia* **115 E4** 13 12 S 22 20 E
Kashima, *Ibaraki, Japan* **73 B12** 35 58N 140 38 E
Kashima, *Saga, Japan* **72 D2** 33 7N 130 6 E
Kashima-Nada, *Japan* **73 B12** 36 0N 140 45 E
Kashimbo, *Dem. Rep. of the Congo* **119 E2** 11 12 S 26 19 E
Kashin, *Russia* **58 D9** 57 20N 37 36 E
Kashing = Jiaxing, *China* **77 B13** 30 49N 120 45 E
Kashipur, *Orissa, India* **94 E6** 19 16N 83 3 E
Kashipur, *Uttaranchal, India* **93 E8** 29 15N 79 0 E
Kashira, *Russia* **58 E10** 54 45N 38 10 E
Kashiwa, *Japan* **73 B11** 35 52N 139 59 E
Kashiwabara = Severo-Kurilsk, *Russia* **67 D16** 50 40N 156 8 E
Kashiwazaki, *Japan* **71 F9** 37 22N 138 33 E
Kashk-e Kohneh, *Afghan.* **91 B1** 34 55N 62 30 E
Kashkū'īyeh, *Iran* **97 D7** 30 31N 55 40 E
Kāshmar, *Iran* **97 C8** 35 16N 58 26 E
Kashmir, *Asia* **93 C7** 34 0N 76 0 E
Kashmor, *Pakistan* **91 C3** 28 28N 69 32 E
Kashpirovka, *Russia* **60 D9** 53 0N 48 30 E
Kashun Noerh = Gaxun Nur, *China* **68 B5** 42 22N 100 30 E
Kasiari, *India* **93 H12** 22 8N 87 14 E
Kasilof, *U.S.A.* **144 F10** 60 23N 151 18W
Kasimov, *Russia* **60 C5** 54 55N 41 20 E
Kasinge, *Dem. Rep. of the Congo* **118 D2** 6 15 S 26 58 E
Kasiruta, *Indonesia* **82 B3** 0 25 S 127 12 E
Kaskaskia →, *U.S.A.* **156 G7** 37 58N 89 57W
Kaskattama →, *Canada* **143 B10** 57 3N 90 4W
Kaskelen = Qaskeleng, *Kazakhstan* **65 B8** 43 20N 76 35 E
Kaskinen, *Finland* **15 E19** 62 22N 21 15 E
Kaskö = Kaskinen, *Finland* **15 E19** 62 22N 21 15 E
Kasli, *Russia* **64 D8** 55 53N 60 46 E
Kaslo, *Canada* **142 D5** 49 55N 116 55W
Kasmere L., *Canada* **143 B8** 59 34N 101 10W
Kasongan, *Indonesia* **85 C4** 2 0 S 113 23 E
Kasongo, *Dem. Rep. of the Congo* **118 C2** 4 30 S 26 33 E
Kasongo Lunda, *Dem. Rep. of the Congo* **115 D3** 6 35 S 16 49 E
Kásos, *Greece* **49 F8** 35 20N 26 55 E
Kásos, Stenón, *Greece* **49 F8** 35 30N 26 30 E
Kaspi, *Georgia* **61 K7** 41 59N 44 26 E
Kaspichan, *Bulgaria* **51 C11** 43 18N 27 11 E
Kaspiysk, *Russia* **61 J8** 42 52N 47 40 E
Kaspiyskiy, *Russia* **61 H8** 45 22N 47 23 E
Kassab ed Doleib, *Sudan* **107 E3** 13 30N 33 35 E
Kassaba, *Egypt* **106 C2** 22 40N 29 55 E
Kassalâ, *Sudan* **107 D4** 15 30N 36 0 E
Kassalâ □, *Sudan* **107 D4** 15 20N 36 26 E
Kassándra, *Greece* **50 F7** 40 0N 23 30 E
Kassándrinon, *Greece* **50 F7** 40 1N 23 27 E
Kassel, *Germany* **30 D5** 51 18N 9 26 E
Kassinger, *Sudan* **106 D3** 18 46N 31 51 E
Kassiópi, *Greece* **38 B9** 39 48N 19 53 E
Kasson, *U.S.A.* **154 C8** 44 2N 92 45W
Kassue, *Indonesia* **83 C5** 6 58 S 139 21 E
Kastamonu, *Turkey* **100 B5** 41 25N 33 43 E
Kastav, *Croatia* **45 C11** 45 22N 14 20 E
Kastélli, *Greece* **39 E4** 35 29N 23 38 E
Kastéllion, *Greece* **39 E6** 35 12N 25 20 E
Kastellórizon = Megiste, *Greece* **49 E11** 36 8N 29 34 E
Kástellos, *Greece* **49 E9** 36 16N 27 49 E
Kastellou, Ákra, *Greece* **49 F9** 35 30N 27 15 E
Kasterlee, *Belgium* **24 C4** 51 15N 4 59 E
Kastlösa, *Sweden* **17 H10** 56 26N 16 25 E
Kastóri, *Greece* **48 D4** 37 10N 22 17 E
Kastoría, *Greece* **50 F5** 40 30N 21 19 E
Kastoría □, *Greece* **50 F5** 40 30N 21 15 E
Kastorías, Límni, *Greece* **50 F5** 40 30N 21 20 E
Kastornoye, *Russia* **59 G10** 51 55N 38 2 E
Kastós, *Greece* **39 B2** 38 34N 20 55 E
Kastós Nisís, *Greece* **39 B2** 38 35N 20 55 E
Kastrosikiá, *Greece* **39 A2** 39 6N 20 38 E
Kastrup, København ✈ (CPH), *Denmark* **17 J6** 55 37N 12 39 E
Kastsyukovichy, *Belarus* **58 F7** 53 20N 32 4 E
Kasuga, *Japan* **72 D2** 33 32N 130 26 E
Kasugai, *Japan* **73 B8** 35 12N 136 59 E
Kasukabe, *Japan* **73 B11** 35 58N 139 49 E
Kasulu, *Tanzania* **118 C3** 4 37 S 30 5 E
Kasumi, *Japan* **72 B6** 35 38N 134 38 E
Kasumiga-Ura, *Japan* **73 B12** 36 0N 140 25 E
Kasumkent, *Russia* **61 K9** 41 47N 48 15 E
Kasungu, *Malawi* **119 E3** 13 0 S 33 29 E
Kasungu △, *Malawi* **119 E3** 12 53 S 33 9 E
Kasur, *Pakistan* **91 C4** 31 5N 74 25 E
Kata Tjuta = Olga, Mt., *Australia* **125 E5** 25 20 S 130 50 E
Kataba, *Zambia* **119 F2** 16 5 S 25 10 E
Katagum, *Nigeria* **113 C7** 12 18N 10 21 E
Katahdin, Mt., *U.S.A.* **149 C11** 45 54N 68 56W
Katako Kombe, *Dem. Rep. of the Congo* **118 C1** 3 25 S 24 20 E
Katákolon, *Greece* **48 D3** 37 38N 21 19 E
Katale, *Tanzania* **118 C3** 4 52 S 31 7 E
Katalla, *U.S.A.* **144 F11** 60 12N 144 31W
Katamatite, *Australia* **129 D6** 36 6 S 145 41 E
Katanda, *Katanga, Dem. Rep. of the Congo* **118 D1** 7 52 S 24 13 E
Katanda, *Nord-Kivu, Dem. Rep. of the Congo* **118 C2** 0 55 S 29 21 E
Katanga □, *Dem. Rep. of the Congo* **118 D2** 8 0 S 25 0 E
Katangi, *India* **94 D4** 21 56N 79 50 E
Katanning, *Australia* **125 F2** 33 40 S 117 33 E
Katapakishi, *Dem. Rep. of the Congo* **115 D4** 8 15 S 22 49 E
Katastári, *Greece* **39 D2** 37 50N 20 45 E
Katav Ivanovsk, *Russia* **64 D7** 54 45N 58 12 E
Katavi △, *Tanzania* **118 D3** 6 51 S 31 3 E
Katavi Swamp, *Tanzania* **118 D3** 6 50 S 31 10 E
Kataysk, *Russia* **64 C9** 56 20N 62 30 E
Katchall, *India* **95 L11** 7 57N 93 22 E
Katchiungo, *Angola* **115 E3** 12 35 S 16 13 E
Kateríni, *Greece* **50 F6** 40 18N 22 37 E
Katghora, *India* **93 H10** 22 30N 82 33 E
Katha, *Burma* **90 C6** 24 10N 96 30 E
Katherîna, Gebel, *Egypt* **96 D2** 28 30N 33 57 E
Katherine, *Australia* **124 B5** 14 27 S 132 20 E
Katherine →, *Australia* **122 C5** 14 40 S 131 42 E
Katherine Gorge, *Australia* **124 B5** 14 18 S 132 28 E
Kathi, *India* **92 J6** 21 47N 74 3 E
Kathiawar, *India* **92 H4** 22 20N 71 0 E
Kathikas, *Cyprus* **39 F8** 34 55N 32 25 E
Kathleen, *U.S.A.* **153 G7** 28 7N 82 2W
Kathmandu = Katmandu, *Nepal* **93 F11** 27 45N 85 20 E
Kathua, *India* **92 C6** 32 23N 75 34 E
Kati, *Mali* **112 C3** 12 41N 8 4W
Katihar, *India* **93 G12** 25 34N 87 36 E
Katikati, *N.Z.* **130 D4** 37 32 S 175 57 E
Katima Mulilo, *Zambia* **116 B3** 17 28 S 24 13 E
Katimbira, *Malawi* **119 E3** 12 40 S 34 0 E
Katingan = Mendawai →, *Indonesia* **85 C4** 3 30 S 113 0 E
Katiola, *Ivory C.* **112 D3** 8 10N 5 10W
Katipunan, *Phil.* **81 G4** 8 31N 123 17 E
Katla, *Iceland* **11 D7** 63 36N 19 7W
Katlabukh, Ozero, *Ukraine* **53 E14** 45 28N 29 0 E
Katlanovo, *Macedonia* **50 E5** 41 52N 21 40 E
Katmai △, *U.S.A.* **144 G9** 58 20N 155 0W
Katmandu, *Nepal* **93 F11** 27 45N 85 20 E
Katni, *India* **93 H9** 23 51N 80 24 E
Káto Akhaïa, *Greece* **48 C3** 38 8N 21 33 E
Káto Arkhánai, *Greece* **39 E6** 35 15N 25 10 E
Káto Khorió, *Greece* **39 E6** 35 3N 25 47 E
Káto Pyrgos, *Cyprus* **39 E8** 35 11N 32 41 E
Káto Stavros, *Greece* **50 F7** 40 39N 23 43 E
Katokhí, *Greece* **48 C3** 38 26N 21 15 E
Katol, *India* **94 D4** 21 17N 78 38 E
Katompe, *Dem. Rep. of the Congo* **118 D2** 6 2 S 26 23 E
Katong, *Singapore* **87 d** 1 18N 103 53 E
Katonga →, *Uganda* **118 B3** 0 34N 31 50 E
Katoomba, *Australia* **129 B9** 33 41 S 150 19 E
Katoúna, *Greece* **48 C3** 38 47N 21 7 E
Katowice, *Poland* **55 H6** 50 17N 19 5 E
Katrancı Dağı, *Turkey* **49 D12** 37 27N 30 25 E
Katrine, L., *U.K.* **22 E4** 56 15N 4 30W
Katrineholm, *Sweden* **16 E10** 59 9N 16 12 E
Katsepe, *Madag.* **117 B8** 15 45 S 46 15 E
Katsina, *Nigeria* **113 C6** 13 0N 7 32 E
Katsina □, *Nigeria* **113 C6** 12 30N 7 30 E
Katsina Ala, *Nigeria* **113 D6** 7 10N 9 30 E
Katsina Ala →, *Nigeria* **113 D6** 7 10N 9 20 E
Katsumoto, *Japan* **72 D1** 33 51N 129 42 E
Katsuta, *Japan* **73 A12** 36 25N 140 31 E
Katsuura, *Japan* **73 B12** 35 10N 140 20 E
Katsuyama, *Fukui, Japan* **73 A8** 36 3N 136 30 E
Katsuyama, *Okayama, Japan* **72 B5** 35 5N 133 41 E
Kattakŭrgan, *Uzbekistan* **65 D3** 39 55N 66 15 E
Kattaviá, *Greece* **38 F11** 35 57N 27 46 E
Kattegat, *Denmark* **17 H5** 56 40N 11 20 E
Katthammarsvik, *Sweden* **17 G12** 57 26N 18 51 E
Kattowitz = Katowice, *Poland* **55 H6** 50 17N 19 5 E
Katul, J., *Sudan* **107 E2** 14 12N 29 25 E
Katumba, *Dem. Rep. of the Congo* **118 D2** 7 40 S 25 17 E
Katwa, *India* **93 H13** 23 30N 88 5 E
Katwijk, *Neths.* **24 B4** 52 12N 4 24 E
Kąty Wrocławskie, *Poland* **55 G3** 51 2N 16 45 E
Kauai, *U.S.A.* **145 A2** 22 3N 159 30W
Kauai Channel, *U.S.A.* **145 B3** 21 45N 158 50W
Kaub, *Germany* **31 E3** 50 5N 7 46 E
Kaudom ⌂, *Namibia* **116 B3** 18 45 S 20 51 E
Kaufbeuren, *Germany* **31 H6** 47 53N 10 37 E
Kaufman, *U.S.A.* **155 J6** 32 35N 96 19W
Kaufman Peak = Lenina, Pik, *Kyrgyzstan* **65 D6** 39 20N 72 55 E
Kauhajoki, *Finland* **15 E20** 62 25N 22 10 E
Kauhola Pt., *U.S.A.* **145 C6** 20 15N 155 47W
Kaukauna, *U.S.A.* **148 C1** 44 17N 88 17W
Kaukauveld, *Namibia* **116 C3** 20 0 S 20 15 E
Kaukonahua →, *U.S.A.* **145 J13** 21 35N 158 7W
Kaula I., *U.S.A.* **145 B1** 21 40N 160 33W
Kaulakahi Channel, *U.S.A.* **145 B2** 22 0N 159 55W
Kaumalapau, *U.S.A.* **145 C5** 20 47N 156 59W
Kauna Pt., *U.S.A.* **145 D6** 19 2N 155 53W
Kaunakakai, *U.S.A.* **145 B4** 21 6N 157 1W
Kaunas, *Lithuania* **15 J20** 54 54N 23 54 E
Kaunas ✈ (KUN), *Lithuania* **54 D11** 54 57N 24 3 E
Kaunchi = Yangiyul, *Uzbekistan* **65 C4** 41 0N 69 3 E
Kaunghein, *Burma* **90 C5** 25 41N 95 26 E
Kaunia, *Bangla.* **90 C2** 25 46N 89 26 E
Kaunos, *Turkey* **49 E10** 36 49N 28 39 E
Kaupalatmada, *Indonesia* **82 B3** 3 30 S 126 10 E
Kaupangur, *Iceland* **11 B8** 65 38N 18 2W
Kaupo, *U.S.A.* **145 C5** 20 38N 156 8W
Kaura Namoda, *Nigeria* **113 C6** 12 37N 6 33 E
Kauru, *Nigeria* **113 C6** 10 33N 8 12 E
Kautokeino, *Norway* **14 B20** 69 0N 23 4 E
Kauwapur, *India* **93 F10** 27 31N 82 18 E
Kavacha, *Russia* **67 C17** 60 16N 169 51 E
Kavadarci, *Macedonia* **50 E6** 41 26N 22 3 E
Kavajë, *Albania* **50 E3** 41 11N 19 33 E
Kavak, *Turkey* **100 B7** 41 4N 36 3 E
Kavak Dağı, *Turkey* **49 D10** 37 10N 28 2 E
Kavaklı, *Turkey* **51 E11** 41 39N 27 10 E
Kavaklıdere, *Turkey* **49 D10** 37 27N 28 21 E
Kavaklii = Topolovgrad, *Bulgaria* **51 D10** 42 5N 26 20 E
Kavala = Kaválla, *Greece* **51 F8** 40 57N 24 28 E
Kavalerovo, *Russia* **70 B7** 44 15N 135 4 E
Kavali, *India* **95 G5** 14 55N 80 1 E
Kavála, *Greece* **51 F8** 40 57N 24 28 E
Kavála □, *Greece* **51 E8** 41 5N 24 30 E
Kavála Kólpos, *Greece* **51 F8** 40 50N 24 25 E
Kavār, *Iran* **97 D7** 29 11N 52 44 E
Kavaratti, *India* **95 J1** 10 34N 72 37 E
Kavaratti I., *India* **95 J1** 10 33N 72 38 E
Kavarna, *Bulgaria* **51 C12** 43 26N 28 22 E
Kavava, *Dem. Rep. of the Congo* **115 D4** 8 52 S 22 19 E
Kavi, *India* **92 H5** 22 12N 72 38 E
Kavieng, *Papua N. G.* **132 B6** 2 36 S 150 51 E
Kavimba, *Botswana* **116 B3** 18 2 S 24 38 E
Kavīr, Dasht-e, *Iran* **97 C7** 34 30N 55 0 E
Kavirondo G. = Winam G., *Kenya* **118 C3** 0 20 S 34 15 E
Kavkaz, *Russia* **59 K9** 45 20N 36 40 E
Kävlinge, *Sweden* **17 J7** 55 47N 13 9 E
Kavos, *Greece* **38 C10** 39 23N 20 3 E
Kavoúsi, *Greece* **39 E6** 35 7N 25 51 E
Kavungo, *Angola* **115 E4** 11 31 S 23 3 E
Kaw, *Fr. Guiana* **169 C7** 4 30N 52 15W
Kawa, *Sudan* **107 E3** 13 42N 32 34 E
Kawachi-Nagano, *Japan* **73 C7** 34 28N 135 31 E
Kawagama L., *Canada* **150 A6** 45 18N 78 45W
Kawagoe, *Japan* **73 B11** 35 55N 139 29 E
Kawaguchi, *Japan* **73 B11** 35 52N 139 45 E
Kawaihae B., *U.S.A.* **145 D6** 20 0N 155 50W
Kawaihoa Pt., *U.S.A.* **145 B1** 21 47N 160 12W
Kawaikimi, *U.S.A.* **145 A2** 22 5N 159 29W
Kawailoa Beach, *U.S.A.* **145 J13** 21 37N 158 5W
Kawakawa, *N.Z.* **130 B3** 35 23 S 174 6 E
Kawambwa, *Zambia* **119 D2** 9 48 S 29 3 E
Kawanabe, *Japan* **72 F2** 31 23N 130 24 E
Kawanoe, *Japan* **72 C5** 34 1N 133 34 E
Kawardha, *India* **93 J9** 22 0N 81 17 E
Kawasaki, *Japan* **73 B11** 35 31N 139 43 E
Kawasi, *Indonesia* **82 B3** 1 38 S 127 28 E
Kawau I., *N.Z.* **130 C3** 36 25 S 174 52 E
Kaweka Ra., *N.Z.* **130 F5** 39 17 S 176 19 E
Kawela, *U.S.A.* **145 J13** 21 42N 158 1W
Kawerau, *N.Z.* **130 E5** 38 7 S 176 42 E
Kawhia, *N.Z.* **130 E3** 38 4 S 174 49 E
Kawhia Harbour, *N.Z.* **130 E3** 38 5 S 174 51 E
Kawio, Kepulauan, *Indonesia* **79 D7** 4 30N 125 30 E
Kawkareik, *Burma* **90 G7** 16 33N 98 14 E
Kawlin, *Burma* **90 D5** 23 47N 95 41 E
Kawthaung, *Burma* **87 H2** 10 5N 98 36 E
Kawthoolei = Kayin □, *Burma* **90 G6** 18 0N 97 30 E
Kawthule = Kayin □, *Burma* **90 G6** 18 0N 97 30 E
Kawya, *Burma* **90 C5** 24 50N 94 58 E
Kaxholmen, *Sweden* **17 G8** 57 51N 14 19 E
Kay, *Russia* **64 B4** 59 57N 52 59 E
Kaya, *Burkina Faso* **113 C4** 13 4N 1 10W
Kayah □, *Burma* **90 F6** 19 15N 97 15 E
Kayak I., *U.S.A.* **144 G11** 59 56N 144 23W
Kayalıköy Barajı, *Turkey* **51 E11** 41 50N 27 5 E
Kayan, *Burma* **90 G6** 16 54N 96 34 E
Kayan →, *Indonesia* **85 B5** 2 55N 117 35 E
Kayankulam, *India* **95 K3** 9 10N 76 33 E
Kayasa, *Indonesia* **82 A3** 0 47N 127 38 E
Kaycee, *U.S.A.* **158 E10** 43 43N 106 38W
Kayeli, *Indonesia* **82 B3** 3 20 S 127 10 E
Kayenda, *Dem. Rep. of the Congo* **115 E4** 10 48 S 23 6 E
Kayenta, *U.S.A.* **159 H8** 36 44N 110 15W
Kayes, *Congo* **115 C2** 4 25 S 11 41 E
Kayes, *Mali* **112 C2** 14 25N 11 30W
Kayı, *Turkey* **49 B12** 39 12N 30 46 E
Kayima, *S. Leone* **112 D2** 8 54N 11 15W
Kayin □, *Burma* **90 G6** 18 0N 97 30 E
Kaymakçı, *Turkey* **49 C10** 38 10N 28 8 E
Kayoa, *Indonesia* **82 A3** 0 1N 127 28 E
Kayomba, *Zambia* **119 E1** 13 11 S 24 2 E
Kayombo, *Zambia* **115 E4** 13 3 S 23 51 E
Kayrakkumskoye Vdkhr., *Tajikistan* **65 C4** 40 20N 70 0 E
Kaysatskoye, *Russia* **60 F8** 49 47N 46 49 E
Kayseri, *Turkey* **100 C6** 38 45N 35 30 E
Kaysville, *U.S.A.* **158 F8** 41 2N 111 56W
Kayts, *Sri Lanka* **95 K4** 9 42N 79 51 E
Kayuagung, *Indonesia* **84 C2** 3 24 S 104 50 E
Kayyngdy, *Kyrgyzstan* **65 B6** 42 49N 73 41 E
Kaz Dağı, *Turkey* **49 B8** 39 42N 26 50 E
Kazachye, *Russia* **67 B14** 70 52N 135 58 E
Kazakhstan ■, *Asia* **66 E7** 50 0N 70 0 E
Kazan, *Russia* **60 C9** 55 50N 49 10 E
Kazan →, *Canada* **143 A9** 64 2N 95 29W
Kazan-Kuygan, *Kyrgyzstan* **65 C7** 41 34N 75 42 E
Kazan-Rettō, *Pac. Oc.* **134 E6** 25 0N 141 0 E
Kazanlŭk, *Bulgaria* **51 D9** 42 38N 25 20 E
Kazanskaya, *Russia* **60 F5** 49 50N 41 10 E
Kazarman, *Kyrgyzstan* **65 C6** 41 24N 73 59 E
Kazatin = Kozyatyn, *Ukraine* **59 H5** 49 45N 28 50 E
Kazaure, *Nigeria* **113 C6** 12 42N 8 28 E
Kazbek, *Russia* **61 J7** 42 42N 44 30 E
Kāzerūn, *Iran* **97 D6** 29 38N 51 40 E
Kazhim, *Russia* **64 A3** 60 21N 51 33 E
Kazi Magomed = Qazimämmäd, *Azerbaijan* **61 K9** 40 3N 49 0 E
Kazimierz Dolny, *Poland* **55 G8** 51 19N 21 57 E
Kazimierza Wielka, *Poland* **55 H7** 50 15N 20 30 E
Kazincbarcika, *Hungary* **52 B5** 48 17N 20 36 E
Kazipet, *India* **94 F4** 17 58N 79 30 E
Kaziza, *Dem. Rep. of the Congo* **115 E4** 10 42 S 23 52 E
Kazlų Rūda, *Lithuania* **54 D10** 54 46N 23 30 E
Kazo, *Japan* **73 A11** 36 7N 139 36 E
Kaztalovka, *Kazakhstan* **60 F9** 49 47N 48 43 E
Kazu, *Burma* **90 C6** 25 27N 97 46 E
Kazuma Pan △, *Zimbabwe* **119 F2** 18 20 S 25 48 E
Kazumba, *Dem. Rep. of the Congo* **115 D4** 6 25 S 22 5 E
Kazungula, *Zambia* **115 F5** 17 35 S 25 15 E
Kazuno, *Japan* **70 D10** 40 10N 140 45 E
Kazym →, *Russia* **66 C7** 63 54N 65 50 E
Kcynia, *Poland* **55 F4** 53 0N 17 30 E
Ke-hsi Mansam, *Burma* **90 E6** 21 56N 97 50 E
Ké-Macina, *Mali* **112 C3** 13 58N 5 22W
Kéa, *Greece* **48 D6** 37 35N 24 22 E
Keaau, *U.S.A.* **145 D6** 19 37N 155 2W
Keady, *U.K.* **23 B5** 54 15N 6 42W
Keahi Pt., *U.S.A.* **145 K14** 21 19N 157 59W
Keahole Pt., *U.S.A.* **145 D5** 19 44N 156 4W
Kealaikahiki Channel, *U.S.A.* **145 C5** 20 35N 156 50W
Kealaikahiki Pt., *U.S.A.* **145 C5** 20 32N 156 42W
Kealakekua, *U.S.A.* **145 D6** 19 31N 155 55W
Kealia, *U.S.A.* **145 D6** 19 24N 155 53W
Kearney, *Mo., U.S.A.* **156 E2** 39 22N 94 22W
Kearney, *Nebr., U.S.A.* **154 E5** 40 42N 99 5W
Kearny, *U.S.A.* **159 K8** 33 3N 110 55W
Kearsarge, Mt., *U.S.A.* **151 C13** 43 22N 71 50W
Keawakapu, *U.S.A.* **145 C5** 20 43N 156 27W
Keban, *Turkey* **101 C8** 38 50N 38 50 E
Keban Barajı, *Turkey* **101 C8** 38 41N 38 33 E
Kebara, *Congo* **114 C2** 2 27 S 14 25 E
Kebbi □, *Nigeria* **113 C5** 11 35N 4 0 E
Kébi, *Ivory C.* **112 D3** 9 18N 6 37W
Kebi, Mayo →, *Cameroon* **114 A2** 9 18N 13 33 E
Kebili, *Tunisia* **108 B1** 33 47N 9 0 E
Kebnekaise, *Sweden* **14 C18** 67 53N 18 33 E
Kebri Dehar, *Ethiopia* **120 C2** 6 45N 44 17 E
Kebumen, *Indonesia* **85 D3** 7 42 S 109 40 E
Kecel, *Hungary* **52 D4** 46 31N 19 16 E
Kechika →, *Canada* **142 B3** 59 41N 127 12W
Keçiborlu, *Turkey* **49 D12** 37 57N 30 18 E
Kecskemét, *Hungary* **52 D4** 46 57N 19 42 E
Kedada, *Ethiopia* **107 F4** 5 25N 35 58 E
Kedah □, *Malaysia* **84 A2** 5 50N 100 40 E
Kėdainiai, *Lithuania* **15 J21** 55 15N 24 2 E
Kedarnath, *India* **93 D8** 30 44N 79 4 E
Kedgwick, *Canada* **141 C6** 47 40N 67 20W
Kédhros Óros, *Greece* **39 E5** 35 11N 24 37 E
Kediet Ijill, *Mauritania* **110 D2** 22 38N 12 33W
Kediri, *Indonesia* **85 D4** 7 51 S 112 1 E
Kedja, *Dem. Rep. of the Congo* **114 B3** 4 50N 19 16 E
Kedjebi, *Ghana* **113 D5** 8 12N 0 25 E
Kédougou, *Senegal* **112 C2** 12 35N 12 10W
Kędzierzyn-Koźle, *Poland* **55 H5** 50 20N 18 12 E
Keehi Lagoon, *U.S.A.* **145 K14** 21 20N 157 54W
Keeler, *U.S.A.* **160 J9** 36 29N 117 52W
Keeley L., *Canada* **143 C7** 54 54N 108 8W
Keeling Is. = Cocos Is., *Ind. Oc.* **121 F8** 12 10 S 96 55 E
Keelung = Chilung, *Taiwan* **77 E13** 25 3N 121 45 E
Keene, *Canada* **150 B6** 44 15N 78 10W
Keene, *Calif., U.S.A.* **161 K8** 35 13N 118 33W
Keene, *N.H., U.S.A.* **151 D12** 42 56N 72 17W
Keene, *N.Y., U.S.A.* **151 B11** 44 16N 73 46W
Keep River △, *Australia* **124 C4** 15 49 S 129 8 E
Keeper Hill, *Ireland* **23 D3** 52 45N 8 16W
Keepit, L., *Australia* **129 A9** 30 50 S 150 30 E
Keer-Weer, C., *Australia* **126 A3** 14 0 S 141 32 E
Keeseville, *U.S.A.* **151 B11** 44 29N 73 30W
Keetmanshoop, *Namibia* **116 D2** 26 35 S 18 8 E
Keewatin, *Canada* **143 D10** 49 46N 94 34W
Keewatin →, *Canada* **143 B8** 56 29N 100 46W
Kefa, *Ethiopia* **107 F4** 6 55N 36 30 E
Kefallinía, *Greece* **39 C2** 38 15N 20 30 E
Kefallinía □, *Greece* **39 C2** 38 15N 20 30 E
Kefallinía ✈ (EFL), *Greece* **39 C1** 38 10N 20 30 E
Kefalonia = Kefallinía, *Greece* **39 C2** 38 15N 20 30 E
Kéfalos, *Greece* **49 E8** 36 45N 26 59 E
Kefamenanu, *Indonesia* **82 C2** 9 28 S 124 29 E
Kefar Sava, *Israel* **103 C3** 32 11N 34 54 E
Keffi, *Nigeria* **113 D6** 8 55N 7 43 E
Keffin Hausa, *Nigeria* **113 C6** 12 13N 9 59 E
Keflavík, *Iceland* **11 C4** 64 2N 22 35W
Keflavík ✈ (KEF), *Iceland* **11 C4** 64 0N 22 45W
Keftya, *Ethiopia* **107 E4** 13 54N 37 7 E
Keg River, *Canada* **142 B5** 57 54N 117 55W
Kegalla, *Sri Lanka* **95 L5** 7 15N 80 21 E

Kegaska, Canada 141 B7 50 9N 61 18W
Keheili, Sudan 106 D3 19 25N 32 50 E
Kehl, Germany 31 G3 48 34N 7 50 E
Keighley, U.K. 20 D6 53 52N 1 54W
Keijo = Sŏul, S. Korea 75 F14 37 31N 126 58 E
Keikiwaha Pt., U.S.A. 145 D6 19 31N 155 58W
Keila, Estonia 15 G21 59 18N 24 25 E
Keimoes, S. Africa 116 D3 28 41 S 20 59 E
Keita, Niger 113 C6 14 46N 5 56 E
Keïta, B. →, Chad 109 G3 9 14N 18 21 E
Keitele, Finland 14 E22 63 10N 26 20 E
Keith, Australia 128 D4 36 6 S 140 20 E
Keith, U.K. 22 D6 57 32N 2 57W
Keithsburg, U.S.A. 156 C6 41 6N 90 56W
Keiyasi, Fiji 133 A1 17 53 S 177 46 E
Keizer, U.S.A. 158 D2 44 57N 123 1W
Kejimkujik △, Canada 141 D6 44 25N 65 25W
Kejserr Franz Joseph Fd., Greenland 10 C8 73 30N 24 30W
Kekaha, U.S.A. 145 B2 21 58N 159 43W
Kekri, India 92 G6 26 0N 75 10 E
Keksgolm = Priozersk, Russia 58 B6 61 2N 30 7 E
Kelam, Ethiopia 107 G4 4 48N 35 58 E
Kelamet, Eritrea 107 D4 16 0N 38 30 E
Kelan, China 74 E6 38 43N 111 31 E
Kelang = Klang, Malaysia 87 L3 3 2N 101 26 E
Kelang, Indonesia 82 B3 3 12 S 127 44 E
Kelani Ganga →, Sri Lanka 95 L4 6 58N 79 50 E
Kelantan □, Malaysia 84 A2 5 10N 102 0 E
Kelantan →, Malaysia 87 J4 6 13N 102 14 E
Këlcyrë, Albania 50 F4 40 20N 20 12 E
Kelekçi, Turkey 49 D11 37 15N 29 20 E
Keles, Turkey 51 G13 39 54N 29 14 E
Keles, Uzbekistan 65 C4 41 24N 69 12 E
Keles →, Kazakhstan 65 C4 41 1N 68 37 E
Keleti-főcsatorna, Hungary 52 C6 47 45N 21 20 E
Kelheim, Germany 31 G7 48 54N 11 52 E
Kelibia, Tunisia 108 A2 36 50N 11 3 E
Kelkit, Turkey 101 B8 40 7N 39 16 E
Kelkit →, Turkey 100 B7 40 45N 36 32 E
Kellé, Congo 114 C2 0 8 S 14 38 E
Keller, U.S.A. 152 D8 31 50N 81 15W
Kellerberrin, Australia 125 F2 31 36 S 117 38 E
Kellett, C., Canada 6 B1 72 0N 126 0W
Kelleys I., U.S.A. 150 E2 41 36N 82 42W
Kellogg, U.S.A. 158 C5 47 32N 116 7W
Kells = Ceanannus Mor, Ireland 23 C5 53 44N 6 53W
Kelmė, Lithuania 54 C9 55 38N 22 56 E
Kelmentsi, Ukraine 53 B11 48 28N 26 50 E
Kélo, Chad 109 G3 9 10N 15 45 E
Kelokedhara, Cyprus 39 F8 34 48N 32 39 E
Kelowna, Canada 142 D5 49 50N 119 25W
Kelsey Creek, Australia 126 J6 20 26 S 148 31 E
Kelseyville, U.S.A. 160 G4 38 59N 122 50W
Kelso, N.Z. 131 F4 45 54 S 169 15 E
Kelso, U.K. 22 F6 55 36N 2 26W
Kelso, U.S.A. 160 D4 46 9N 122 54W
Keluang = Kluang, Malaysia 87 L4 2 3N 103 18 E
Kelvington, Canada 143 C8 52 10N 103 30W
Kem, Russia 56 B5 65 0N 34 38 E
Kem →, Russia 56 B5 64 57N 34 41 E
Kem-Kem, Morocco 110 B4 30 40N 4 30W
Kema, Indonesia 79 D7 1 22N 125 8 E
Kemah, Turkey 101 C8 39 32N 39 5 E
Kemaliye, Erzincan, Turkey 101 C8 39 16N 38 29 E
Kemaliye, Manisa, Turkey 49 C10 38 27N 28 25 E
Kemalpaşa, Turkey 49 C9 38 25N 27 27 E
Kemaman, Malaysia 78 D2 4 12N 103 18 E
Kemano, Canada 142 C3 53 35N 128 0W
Kemapyu, Burma 90 F6 18 49N 97 19 E
Kemasik, Malaysia 87 K4 4 25N 103 27 E
Kembani, Indonesia 82 B2 1 34 S 122 54 E
Kembé, C.A.R. 114 B4 4 36N 21 54 E
Kembolcha, Ethiopia 107 E4 11 2N 39 42 E
Kemer, Antalya, Turkey 49 E12 36 36N 30 34 E
Kemer, Burdur, Turkey 49 D12 37 21N 30 4 E
Kemer, Muğla, Turkey 49 E11 36 40N 29 22 E
Kemer Barajı, Turkey 49 D10 37 30N 28 37 E
Kemerovo, Russia 66 D9 55 20N 86 5 E
Ķemeru △, Latvia 54 B10 56 58N 23 25 E
Kemi, Finland 14 D21 65 44N 24 34 E
Kemi älv = Kemijoki →, Finland 14 D21 65 47N 24 32 E
Kemi träsk = Kemijärvi, Finland 14 C22 66 43N 27 22 E
Kemijärvi, Finland 14 C22 66 43N 27 22 E
Kemijoki →, Finland 14 D21 65 47N 24 32 E
Kemin, Kyrgyzstan 65 B7 42 47N 75 42 E
Kemmerer, U.S.A. 158 F8 41 48N 110 32W
Kemmuna = Comino, Malta 38 E7 36 1N 14 20 E
Kemp, L., U.S.A. 155 J5 33 46N 99 9W
Kemp Land, Antarctica 7 C5 69 0 S 55 0 E
Kempas, Malaysia 87 d 1 33N 103 42 E
Kempen = Kępno, Poland 55 G4 51 18N 17 58 E
Kempsey, Australia 129 A10 31 1 S 152 50 E
Kempt, L., Canada 140 C5 47 25N 74 22W
Kempten, Germany 31 H6 47 45N 10 17 E
Kempton, Australia 127 G4 42 31 S 147 12 E
Kempton, U.S.A. 157 D10 40 17N 86 14W
Kemptville, Canada 140 D4 45 0N 75 38W
Ken →, India 93 G9 25 13N 80 27 E
Kenadsa, Algeria 111 B4 31 48N 2 26W
Kenai, U.S.A. 144 F10 60 33N 151 16W
Kenai Fjords △, U.S.A. 144 E10 59 40N 149 50W
Kenai Mts., U.S.A. 144 G10 60 0N 150 0W
Kenansville, U.S.A. 153 H9 27 53N 80 59W
Kendai, India 93 H10 22 45N 82 37 E
Kendal, Indonesia 85 D4 6 56 S 110 14 E
Kendal, U.K. 20 C5 54 20N 2 44W
Kendall, Australia 129 A10 31 35 S 152 44 E
Kendall, U.S.A. 153 K9 25 41N 80 19W
Kendall →, Australia 126 A3 14 4 S 141 35 E
Kendallville, U.S.A. 157 C11 41 27N 85 16W
Kendari, Indonesia 82 B2 3 50 S 122 30 E
Kendawangan, Indonesia 85 C4 2 32 S 110 17 E
Kende, Nigeria 113 C5 11 30N 4 12 E
Kendi, Pulau, Malaysia 87 c 5 13N 100 11 E
Kendigué, Chad 109 F3 10 0N 18 36 E
Kendrapara, India 94 D8 20 35N 86 30 E
Këndrevicës, Maja e, Albania 50 F3 40 15N 19 52 E
Kendrew, S. Africa 116 E3 32 32 S 24 30 E
Kendrick, U.S.A. 153 F7 29 15N 82 10W
Kene Thao, Laos 86 D3 17 44N 101 10 E
Kenedy, U.S.A. 155 L6 28 49N 97 51W
Kenema, S. Leone 112 D2 7 50N 11 14W
Keng Kok, Laos 86 D5 16 26N 105 12 E
Keng Tawng, Burma 90 E7 20 45N 98 18 E
Keng Tung, Burma 76 G2 21 0N 99 30 E
Kengani, Dem. Rep. of the Congo 114 C3 2 59 S 17 36 E
Kenge, Dem. Rep. of the Congo 115 C3 4 50 S 17 4 E
Kengeja, Tanzania 118 D4 5 26 S 39 45 E
Kenhardt, S. Africa 116 D3 29 19 S 21 12 E
Kéniéba, Mali 112 C2 12 54N 11 17W
Kenitra, Morocco 110 B3 34 15N 6 40W
Kenli, China 75 F10 37 30N 118 20 E
Kenmare, Ireland 23 E2 51 53N 9 36W
Kenmare, U.S.A. 154 A3 48 41N 102 5W
Kenmare River, Ireland 23 E2 51 48N 9 51W
Kennebago Lake, U.S.A. 151 A14 45 4N 70 40W
Kennebec, U.S.A. 154 D5 43 54N 99 52W
Kennebec →, U.S.A. 149 D11 43 45N 69 46W
Kennebunk, U.S.A. 151 C14 43 23N 70 33W
Kennedy, Zimbabwe 116 B4 18 52 S 27 10 E
Kennedy, C. = Canaveral, C., U.S.A. 153 G9 28 27N 80 32W
Kennedy Kanal, Arctic 10 A4 80 50N 66 0W
Kennedy Ra., Australia 125 D2 24 45 S 115 10 E
Kennedy Range △, Australia 125 D2 24 34 S 115 2 E
Kennedy Space Center, U.S.A. 153 G9 28 40N 80 42W
Kenner, U.S.A. 155 L9 29 59N 90 15W
Kennesaw, U.S.A. 152 A5 34 1N 84 37W
Kennet →, U.K. 21 F7 51 27N 0 57W
Kenneth Ra., Australia 125 D2 23 50 S 117 8 E
Kennett, U.S.A. 155 G9 36 14N 90 3W
Kennewick, U.S.A. 158 C4 46 12N 119 7W
Kenogami →, Canada 140 B3 51 6N 84 28W
Kenora, Canada 143 D10 49 47N 94 29W
Kenosha, U.S.A. 157 B9 42 35N 87 49W
Kensington, Canada 141 C7 46 28N 63 34W
Kent, Ohio, U.S.A. 150 E3 41 9N 81 22W
Kent, Tex., U.S.A. 155 K2 31 4N 104 13W
Kent, Wash., U.S.A. 160 C4 47 23N 122 14W
Kent □, U.K. 21 F8 51 12N 0 40 E
Kent Group, Australia 127 F4 39 30 S 147 20 E
Kent Pen., Canada 138 B9 68 30N 107 0W
Kentaū, Kazakhstan 65 B4 43 32N 68 36 E
Kentland, U.S.A. 157 D9 40 46N 87 27W
Kenton, U.S.A. 157 D13 40 39N 83 37W
Kentucky □, U.S.A. 148 G3 37 0N 84 0W
Kentucky →, U.S.A. 157 F11 38 41N 85 11W
Kentucky L., U.S.A. 149 G2 37 1N 88 16W
Kentville, Canada 141 C7 45 6N 64 29W
Kentwood, La., U.S.A. 155 K9 30 56N 90 31W
Kentwood, Mich., U.S.A. 157 B11 42 52N 85 37W
Kenya ■, Africa 118 B4 1 0N 38 0 E
Kenya, Mt., Kenya 118 C4 0 10 S 37 18 E
Kenzou, Cameroon 114 B3 4 10N 15 2 E
Keo Neua, Deo, Vietnam 86 C5 18 23N 105 10 E
Keokea, U.S.A. 145 C5 20 43N 156 22W
Keokuk, U.S.A. 156 D5 40 24N 91 24W
Keoladeo △, India 92 F7 27 0N 77 20 E
Keonjhargarh, India 93 J11 21 28N 85 35 E
Keosauqua, U.S.A. 156 D5 40 44N 91 58W
Keota, U.S.A. 156 C5 41 22N 91 57W
Kep, Cambodia 87 G5 10 29N 104 19 E
Kep, Vietnam 86 B6 21 24N 106 16 E
Kepala Batas, Malaysia 87 c 5 31N 100 26 E
Kepez, Turkey 51 F10 40 5N 26 24 E
Kepi, Indonesia 83 C5 6 32 S 139 19 E
Kępice, Poland 54 D3 54 16N 16 51 E
Kepler Mts., N.Z. 131 F2 45 25 S 167 20 E
Kępno, Poland 55 G4 51 18N 17 58 E
Keppel Pt., Papua N. G. 132 F4 10 10 S 147 58 E
Kepsut, Turkey 49 B10 39 40N 28 9 E
Kepuhi Pt., U.S.A. 145 K13 21 29N 158 14W
Kerala □, India 95 J3 11 0N 76 15 E
Keram →, Papua N. G. 132 C3 4 7 S 144 5 E
Kerama-Rettō, Japan 71 L3 26 5N 127 15 E
Keran, Pakistan 93 B5 34 35N 73 59 E
Keran △, Togo 113 C5 10 9N 0 41 E
Kerang, Australia 128 C5 35 40 S 143 55 E
Keranyo, Ethiopia 107 F4 5 3N 38 18 E
Kerao →, Sudan 107 E3 11 0N 32 41 E
Keratéa, Greece 48 D5 37 48N 23 58 E
Keraudren, C., Australia 124 C2 19 58 S 119 45 E
Kerava, Finland 15 F21 60 25N 25 5 E
Keravat, Papua N. G. 132 C7 4 17 S 152 2 E
Kerben, Kyrgyzstan 65 C5 41 30N 71 45 E
Kerch, Ukraine 59 K9 45 20N 36 20 E
Kerchenskiy Proliv, Black Sea 59 K9 45 10N 36 30 E
Kerchoual, Mali 113 B5 17 12N 0 20 E
Kerema, Papua N. G. 132 D3 7 58 S 145 50 E
Kerempe Burnu, Turkey 100 A5 42 2N 33 20 E
Keren, Eritrea 107 D4 15 45N 38 28 E
Kerewan, Gambia 112 C1 13 29N 16 10W
Kerguelen, Ind. Oc. 121 J5 49 15 S 69 10 E
Keri, Greece 39 D2 37 40N 20 49 E
Keri Kera, Sudan 107 E3 12 21N 32 42 E
Kericho, Kenya 118 C4 0 22 S 35 15 E
Kerikeri, N.Z. 130 B2 35 12 S 173 59 E
Kerinci, Indonesia 84 C2 1 40 S 101 15 E
Kerintji = Kerinci, Indonesia 84 C2 1 40 S 101 15 E
Kerkenna, Îs., Tunisia 108 B2 34 48N 11 11 E
Kerki, Turkmenistan 65 E2 37 50N 65 12 E
Kerkinítis, Límni, Greece 50 E7 41 12N 23 10 E
Kérkira, Greece 38 B9 39 38N 19 50 E
Kérkira □, Greece 38 B9 39 37N 19 50 E
Kérkira ✕ (CFU), Greece 48 B1 39 35N 19 54 E
Kerkouane, Tunisia 46 F4 36 58N 11 2 E
Kerkrade, Neths. 24 D6 50 53N 6 4 E
Kerma, Sudan 106 D3 19 33N 30 32 E
Kermadec Is., Pac. Oc. 134 L10 30 0 S 178 15W
Kermadec Trench, Pac. Oc. 134 L10 30 30 S 176 0W
Kermān, Iran 97 D8 30 15N 57 1 E
Kerman, U.S.A. 160 J6 36 43N 120 4W
Kermān □, Iran 97 D8 30 0N 57 0 E
Kermān, Bīābān-e, Iran 97 D8 28 45N 59 45 E
Kermānshāh = Bākhtarān, Iran 101 E12 34 23N 47 0 E
Kermen, Bulgaria 51 D10 42 30N 26 16 E
Kermine = Nawoiy, Uzbekistan 65 C2 40 9N 65 22 E
Kermit, U.S.A. 155 K3 31 52N 103 6W
Kern →, U.S.A. 161 K7 35 16N 119 18W
Kernhof, Austria 34 D8 47 49N 15 32 E
Kernow = Cornwall □, U.K. 21 G3 50 26N 4 40W
Kerns, Switz. 33 C6 46 54N 8 17 E
Kernville, U.S.A. 161 K8 35 45N 118 26W
Keroh, Malaysia 87 K3 5 43N 101 1 E
Kérou, Benin 113 C5 10 50N 2 5 E
Kérouane, Guinea 112 D3 9 15N 9 0W
Kerowagi, Papua N. G. 132 C3 5 51 S 144 51 E
Kerpen, Germany 30 E2 50 51N 6 41 E
Kerrera, U.K. 22 E3 56 24N 5 33W
Kerrobert, Canada 143 C7 51 56N 109 8W
Kerrville, U.S.A. 155 K5 30 3N 99 8W
Kerry □, Ireland 23 D2 52 7N 9 35W
Kerry Hd., Ireland 23 D2 52 25N 9 56W
Kersa, Ethiopia 107 F5 9 28N 41 48 E
Kertosono, Indonesia 85 D4 7 38 S 112 9 E
Kerulen →, Asia 69 B6 48 48N 117 0 E
Kervo = Kerava, Finland 15 F21 60 25N 25 5 E
Kerzaz, Algeria 111 C4 29 29N 1 37W
Kerzers, Switz. 32 C4 46 59N 7 12 E
Kesagami →, Canada 140 B4 51 40N 79 45W
Kesagami L., Canada 140 B3 50 23N 80 15W
Keşan, Turkey 51 F10 40 49N 26 38 E
Kesch, Piz, Switz. 33 C9 46 38N 9 53 E
Kesennuma, Japan 70 E10 38 54N 141 35 E
Keshit, Iran 97 D8 29 43N 58 17 E
Kesigi = Kosgi, India 95 G3 15 51N 77 16 E
Keşiş Dağ, Turkey 101 C8 39 47N 39 46 E
Keskal, India 94 D5 20 5N 81 35 E
Keskin, Turkey 100 C5 39 40N 33 36 E
Kestell, S. Africa 117 D4 28 17 S 28 42 E
Kestenga, Russia 56 A5 65 50N 31 45 E
Keswick, U.K. 20 C4 54 36N 3 8W
Keszthely, Hungary 52 D2 46 50N 17 15 E
Ket →, Russia 66 D9 58 55N 81 32 E
Keta, Ghana 113 D5 5 49N 1 0 E
Keta Lagoon, Ghana 113 D5 5 55N 1 0 E
Ketapang, Bali, Indonesia 79 J17 8 9 S 114 23 E
Ketapang, Kalimantan, Indonesia 85 C4 1 55 S 110 0 E
Ketchenery, Russia 61 G7 47 18N 44 32 E
Ketchikan, U.S.A. 142 B2 55 21N 131 39W
Ketchum, U.S.A. 158 E6 43 41N 114 22W
Kete Krachi, Ghana 113 D4 7 46N 0 1W
Ketef, Khalîg Umm el, Egypt 96 F2 23 40N 35 35 E
Keti Bandar, Pakistan 92 G2 24 8N 67 27 E
Kétou, Benin 113 D5 7 25N 2 45 E
Ketri, India 92 E6 28 1N 75 50 E
Kętrzyn, Poland 54 D8 54 7N 21 22 E
Kettering, U.K. 21 E7 52 24N 0 43W
Kettering, U.S.A. 157 E12 39 41N 84 10W
Kettle →, Canada 143 B11 56 40N 89 34W
Kettle Falls, U.S.A. 158 B4 48 37N 118 3W
Kettle Pt., Canada 150 C2 43 13N 82 1W
Kettleman City, U.S.A. 160 J7 36 1N 119 58W
Kęty, Poland 55 J6 49 51N 19 16 E
Keuka L., U.S.A. 150 D7 42 30N 77 9W
Keuruu, Finland 15 E21 62 16N 24 41 E
Kevelaer, Germany 30 D2 51 36N 6 15 E
Kewanee, U.S.A. 156 C7 41 14N 89 56W
Kewanna, U.S.A. 157 C10 41 1N 86 25W
Kewaunee, U.S.A. 148 C2 44 27N 87 31W
Keweenaw B., U.S.A. 148 B1 47 0N 88 15W
Keweenaw Pen., U.S.A. 148 B2 47 30N 88 0W
Keweenaw Pt., U.S.A. 148 B2 47 25N 87 43W
Kexholm = Priozersk, Russia 58 B6 61 2N 30 7 E
Key Colony Beach, U.S.A. 153 L9 24 45N 80 57W
Key Largo, U.S.A. 153 K9 25 5N 80 27W
Key West, U.S.A. 153 L8 24 33N 81 48W
Keyala, Sudan 107 G3 4 27N 32 52 E
Keynsham, U.K. 21 F5 51 24N 2 29W
Keyser, U.S.A. 148 F6 39 26N 78 59W
Keystone Heights, U.S.A. 152 F7 29 47N 82 1W
Keytesville, U.S.A. 156 E4 39 26N 92 56W
Kez, Russia 64 C4 57 55N 53 46 E
Kezhma, Russia 67 D11 58 59N 101 9 E
Kezi, Zimbabwe 117 C4 20 58 S 28 32 E
Kežmarok, Slovak Rep. 35 B13 49 10N 20 28 E
Kgalagadi Transfrontier ⌓, Africa 116 D3 25 10 S 21 0 E
Khabarovsk, Russia 67 E14 48 30N 135 5 E
Khabr, Iran 97 D8 28 51N 56 22 E
Khābūr →, Syria 101 E9 35 17N 40 35 E
Khachmas = Xaçmaz, Azerbaijan 61 K9 41 31N 48 42 E
Khachrod, India 92 H6 23 25N 75 20 E
Khadari, W. el →, Sudan 107 E2 10 29N 27 15 E
Khadro, Pakistan 92 F3 26 11N 68 50 E
Khadyzhensk, Russia 61 H4 44 26N 39 32 E
Khadzhilyangar, China 93 B8 35 45N 79 20 E
Khaga, India 93 G9 25 47N 81 7 E
Khagaria, India 93 G12 25 30N 86 32 E
Khaipur, Pakistan 92 E5 29 34N 72 17 E
Khair, India 92 F7 27 57N 77 46 E
Khairabad, India 93 F9 27 33N 80 47 E
Khairagarh, India 93 J9 21 27N 81 2 E
Khairpur, Pakistan 91 D3 27 32N 68 49 E
Khairpur Nathan Shah, Pakistan 92 F2 27 6N 67 44 E
Khairwara, India 92 H5 23 58N 73 38 E
Khaisor →, Pakistan 92 D3 31 17N 68 59 E
Khajuri Kach, Pakistan 92 C3 32 4N 69 51 E
Khāk Dow, Afghan. 91 B2 34 57N 67 16 E
Khakassia □, Russia 66 D9 53 0N 90 0 E
Khakhea, Botswana 116 C3 24 48 S 23 22 E
Khalafābād, Iran 97 D6 30 54N 49 24 E
Khalfallah, Algeria 111 B5 34 20N 0 16 E
Khalfūt, Yemen 99 D6 15 52N 52 10 E
Khalilabad, India 93 F10 26 48N 83 5 E
Khalīlī, Iran 97 E7 27 38N 53 17 E
Khalkhāl, Iran 97 B6 37 37N 48 32 E
Khálki, Dhodhekánisos, Greece 49 E9 36 17N 27 35 E
Khálki, Thessalía, Greece 48 B4 39 36N 22 30 E
Khalkidhikí □, Greece 50 F7 40 25N 23 20 E
Khalkís, Greece 48 C5 38 27N 23 42 E
Khalmer-Sede = Tazovskiy, Russia 66 C8 67 30N 78 44 E
Khalmer Yu, Russia 66 C7 67 58N 65 1 E
Khalturin, Russia 64 B2 58 40N 48 50 E
Khalūf, Oman 102 C6 20 30N 58 13 E
Kham Keut, Laos 86 C5 18 15N 104 43 E
Khamaria, India 93 H9 23 5N 80 48 E
Khambhaliya, India 92 H3 22 14N 69 41 E
Khambhat, India 92 H5 22 23N 72 33 E
Khambhat, G. of, India 89 C6 20 45N 72 30 E
Khamgaon, India 94 D3 20 42N 76 37 E
Khamilonísion, Greece 49 F8 35 50N 26 15 E
Khamīr, Iran 97 E7 26 57N 55 36 E
Khamir, Yemen 98 C3 16 2N 44 0 E
Khamīs Mushayţ, Si. Arabia 98 C3 18 18N 42 44 E
Khammam, India 94 F5 17 11N 80 6 E
Khamsa, Egypt 103 E1 30 27N 32 23 E
Khamza, Uzbekistan 65 C5 40 25N 71 29 E
Khan →, Namibia 116 C2 22 37 S 14 56 E
Khān Abū Shāmat, Syria 103 B5 33 39N 36 53 E
Khān Azād, Iraq 96 C5 33 7N 44 22 E
Khān Mujiddah, Iraq 96 C4 32 21N 43 48 E
Khān Shaykhūn, Syria 100 E7 35 26N 36 38 E
Khān Yūnis, Gaza Strip 103 D3 31 21N 34 18 E
Khānābād, Afghan. 65 E4 36 45N 69 5 E
Khanabad, Uzbekistan 65 C6 40 47N 73 0 E
Khanai, Pakistan 92 D2 30 30N 67 8 E
Khānaqīn, Iraq 101 E11 34 23N 45 25 E
Khānbāghī, Iran 97 B7 36 10N 55 25 E
Khandrá, Greece 49 F8 35 3N 26 8 E
Khandūd, Afghan. 65 E6 36 57N 72 19 E
Khandwa, India 94 D3 21 49N 76 22 E
Khandyga, Russia 67 C14 62 42N 135 35 E
Khāneh, Iran 96 B5 36 41N 45 8 E
Khanewal, Pakistan 91 C3 30 20N 71 55 E
Khangah Dogran, Pakistan 92 D5 31 50N 73 37 E
Khanh Duong, Vietnam 86 F7 12 44N 108 44 E
Khaniá, Greece 39 E5 35 30N 24 4 E
Khaniá □, Greece 39 E5 35 30N 24 0 E
Khanía ✕ (CHQ), Greece 39 E5 35 30N 24 6 E
Khaniadhana, India 92 G8 25 1N 78 8 E
Khaníon, Kólpos, Greece 39 E4 35 33N 23 55 E
Khanka, L., Asia 67 E14 45 0N 132 24 E
Khankendy = Xankändi, Azerbaijan 101 C12 39 52N 46 49 E
Khanna, India 92 D7 30 42N 76 16 E
Khanozai, Pakistan 92 D2 30 37N 67 19 E
Khanpur, Pakistan 91 C3 28 42N 70 35 E
Khantaū, Kazakhstan 65 A6 44 13N 73 48 E
Khanty-Mansiysk, Russia 66 C7 61 0N 69 0 E
Khao Laem △, Thailand 86 E2 14 56N 98 31 E
Khao Laem Res., Thailand 86 E2 14 50N 98 30 E
Khao Luang △, Thailand 87 H2 8 34N 99 42 E
Khao Phlu, Thailand 87 b 9 29N 99 59 E
Khao Pu-Khao Ya △, Thailand 87 J2 7 26N 99 57 E
Khao Sam Roi Yot △, Thailand 87 F2 12 13N 99 57 E
Khao Sok △, Thailand 87 H2 8 55N 98 38 E
Khao Yai △, Thailand 86 E3 14 21N 101 29 E
Khaoen Si Nakarin △, Thailand 86 E2 14 47N 99 0 E
Khapalu, Pakistan 93 B7 35 10N 76 20 E
Khapcheranga, Russia 67 E12 49 42N 112 24 E
Khaptao △, Nepal 93 E9 29 20N 81 10 E
Kharabali, Russia 61 G8 47 25N 47 15 E
Kharaghoda, India 92 H4 23 11N 71 46 E
Kharagpur, India 93 H12 22 20N 87 25 E
Khárakas, Greece 39 E6 35 1N 25 7 E
Kharan Kalat, Pakistan 91 C2 28 34N 65 21 E
Kharānaq, Iran 97 C7 32 20N 54 45 E
Kharda, India 94 E2 18 40N 75 34 E
Khardung La, India 93 B7 34 20N 77 43 E
Kharg = Khārk, Jazīreh-ye, Iran 97 D6 29 15N 50 28 E
Khârga, El Wâhât-el, Egypt 106 B3 25 10N 30 35 E
Khargon, India 94 D2 21 45N 75 40 E
Khari →, India 92 G6 25 54N 74 31 E
Kharian, Pakistan 92 C5 32 49N 73 52 E
Khariar, India 94 D6 20 17N 82 46 E
Kharit, Wadi el →, Egypt 106 C3 24 26N 33 3 E
Khārk, Jazīreh-ye, Iran 97 D6 29 15N 50 28 E
Kharkiv, Ukraine 59 H9 49 58N 36 20 E
Kharkov = Kharkiv, Ukraine 59 H9 49 58N 36 20 E
Kharmanli, Bulgaria 51 E9 41 55N 25 55 E
Kharovsk, Russia 58 C11 59 56N 40 13 E
Kharsawangarh, India 93 H11 22 48N 85 50 E
Kharta, Turkey 100 B3 40 55N 29 7 E
Khartoum = El Khartûm, Sudan 107 D3 15 31N 32 35 E
Khasan, Russia 70 C5 42 25N 130 40 E
Khasavyurt, Russia 61 J8 43 16N 46 40 E
Khāsh, Iran 91 C1 28 15N 61 15 E
Khāsh, Dasht-e, Afghan. 91 C1 31 50N 62 30 E
Khashm el Girba, Sudan 107 E4 14 59N 35 58 E
Khashum, Sudan 107 E2 12 27N 28 2 E
Khashuri, Georgia 61 J6 42 3N 43 35 E
Khasi Hills, India 90 C3 25 30N 91 30 E
Khaskovo, Bulgaria 51 E9 41 56N 25 30 E
Khaskovo □, Bulgaria 51 E9 42 0N 25 40 E
Khatanga, Russia 67 B11 72 0N 102 20 E
Khatanga →, Russia 67 B11 72 55N 106 0 E
Khatauli, India 92 E7 29 17N 77 43 E
Khatra, India 93 H12 22 59N 86 51 E
Khātūnābād, Iran 97 D7 30 1N 55 25 E
Khatyrka, Russia 67 C18 62 3N 175 15 E
Khavast, Uzbekistan 65 C4 40 10N 68 49 E
Khavda, India 92 H3 23 51N 69 43 E
Khavdháta, Greece 39 D1 38 12N 20 23 E
Khawlaf, Ra's, Yemen 99 D6 12 40N 54 7 E
Khay', Si. Arabia 98 C3 18 45N 41 24 E
Khaybar, Ḥarrat, Si. Arabia 96 E4 25 45N 40 0 E
Khaydarken, Kyrgyzstan 65 D5 39 57N 71 20 E
Khāzimiyah, Iraq 96 C4 34 46N 43 37 E
Khazzān Jabal al Awliyā, Sudan 107 D3 15 24N 32 20 E
Khe Bo, Vietnam 86 C5 19 8N 104 41 E
Khe Long, Vietnam 86 B5 21 29N 104 46 E
Khe Sanh, Vietnam 86 D6 16 37N 106 45 E
Khed, Maharashtra, India 94 F1 17 43N 73 27 E
Khed, Maharashtra, India 94 E1 18 51N 73 56 E
Khekra, India 92 E7 28 52N 77 20 E
Khem-Beldyr = Kyzyl, Russia 67 D10 51 50N 94 30 E
Khemarak Phouminville, Cambodia 87 G4 11 37N 102 59 E
Khemis Miliana, Algeria 111 A5 36 11N 2 14 E
Khemisset, Morocco 110 B3 33 50N 6 1W
Khemmarat, Thailand 86 D5 16 10N 105 15 E
Khenāmān, Iran 97 D8 30 27N 56 29 E
Khenchela, Algeria 111 A6 35 28N 7 11 E
Khenifra, Morocco 110 B3 32 58N 5 46W
Kherrata, Algeria 111 A6 36 27N 5 13 E
Khersān →, Iran 97 D6 31 33N 50 22 E
Khérson, Greece 50 E6 41 5N 22 47 E
Kherson, Ukraine 59 J7 46 35N 32 35 E
Khersónisos Akrotíri, Greece 39 E5 35 30N 24 10 E
Kheta →, Russia 67 B11 71 54N 102 6 E
Khewari, Pakistan 92 F3 26 36N 68 52 E
Khibinogorsk = Kirovsk, Russia 56 A5 67 32N 33 41 E
Khilchipur, India 92 G7 24 2N 76 34 E
Khiliomódhion, Greece 48 D4 37 48N 22 51 E
Khilok, Russia 67 D12 51 30N 110 45 E
Khimki, Russia 58 E9 55 50N 37 20 E
Khíos, Greece 49 C8 38 27N 26 9 E
Khíos □, Greece 49 C8 38 27N 26 9 E
Khirsadoh, India 93 H8 22 11N 78 47 E
Khiuma = Hiiumaa, Estonia 15 G20 58 50N 22 45 E
Khiva, Uzbekistan 66 E7 41 30N 60 18 E
Khīyāv, Iran 96 B5 38 30N 47 45 E
Khlebarovo, Bulgaria 51 C10 43 37N 26 15 E
Khlong Khlung, Thailand 86 D2 16 12N 99 43 E
Khmelnik, Ukraine 59 H4 49 33N 27 58 E
Khmelnitskiy = Khmelnytskyy, Ukraine 59 H4 49 23N 27 0 E
Khmelnytskyy, Ukraine 59 H4 49 23N 27 0 E
Khmer Rep. = Cambodia ■, Asia 86 F5 12 15N 105 0 E
Khoai, Hon, Vietnam 87 H5 8 26N 104 50 E
Khodoriv, Ukraine 59 H3 49 24N 24 19 E
Khodzent = Khŭjand, Tajikistan 65 C4 40 17N 69 37 E
Khojak Pass, Afghan. 91 C2 30 51N 66 34 E
Khok Kloi, Thailand 87 a 8 17N 98 19 E
Khok Pho, Thailand 87 J3 6 43N 101 6 E
Khokhropār, Pakistan 91 D3 25 42N 70 12 E
Kholm, Afghan. 65 E3 36 45N 67 40 E
Kholm, Russia 58 D6 57 10N 31 15 E
Kholmsk, Russia 67 E15 47 40N 142 5 E
Khomas Hochland, Namibia 116 C2 22 40 S 16 0 E
Khombole, Senegal 112 C1 14 43N 16 42W
Khomeyn, Iran 97 C6 33 40N 50 7 E
Khomeynī Shahr, Iran 97 C6 32 41N 51 31 E
Khomodino, Botswana 116 C3 22 46 S 23 52 E
Khon Kaen, Thailand 86 D4 16 30N 102 47 E
Khong →, Cambodia 86 F5 13 32N 105 58 E
Khong Sedone, Laos 86 E5 15 34N 105 49 E
Khonuu, Russia 67 C15 66 30N 143 12 E
Khoper →, Russia 60 F6 49 30N 42 20 E
Khor el 'Atash, Sudan 107 E3 13 20N 34 15 E
Khóra, Greece 48 D3 37 3N 21 42 E
Khóra Sfakíon, Greece 39 E5 35 15N 24 9 E
Khorāsān □, Iran 97 C8 34 0N 58 0 E
Khorat = Nakhon Ratchasima, Thailand 86 E4 14 59N 102 12 E
Khorat, Cao Nguyen, Thailand 86 E4 15 30N 102 50 E
Khorb el Ethel, Algeria 110 C3 28 30N 6 17W
Khorixas, Namibia 116 C1 20 16 S 14 59 E
Khorol, Ukraine 59 H7 49 48N 33 15 E
Khorramābād, Khorāsān, Iran 97 C8 35 6N 57 57 E
Khorramābād, Lorestān, Iran 97 C6 33 30N 48 25 E
Khorrāmshahr, Iran 97 D6 30 29N 48 15 E
Khorugh, Tajikistan 65 E5 37 30N 71 36 E
Khosravī, Iran 97 D6 30 48N 51 28 E
Khosrowābād, Khuzestān, Iran 97 D6 30 10N 48 25 E
Khosrowābād, Kordestān, Iran 101 E12 35 31N 47 38 E
Khost, Pakistan 92 D2 30 13N 67 35 E
Khosūyeh, Iran 97 D7 28 32N 54 26 E
Khotan = Hotan, China 68 C2 37 25N 79 55 E
Khotyn, Ukraine 53 B11 48 31N 26 27 E
Khouribga, Morocco 110 B3 32 58N 6 57W
Khowai, Bangla. 90 C3 24 5N 91 40 E
Khowst, Afghan. 91 B3 33 22N 69 58 E
Khoyniki, Belarus 59 G5 51 54N 29 55 E
Khrami →, Georgia 61 K7 41 25N 45 0 E
Khrenovoye, Russia 60 E5 51 4N 40 16 E
Khrisoúpolis, Greece 51 F8 40 58N 24 42 E
Khristianá, Greece 49 E7 36 14N 25 13 E
Khromtau, Kazakhstan 64 F7 50 17N 58 27 E
Khrysokhou B., Cyprus 39 E8 35 6N 32 25 E
Khtapodhiá, Greece 49 D7 37 24N 25 34 E
Khu Khan, Thailand 86 E5 14 42N 104 12 E
Khuan Wa, Thailand 87 a 7 53N 98 17 E
Khudrah, W. →, Yemen 99 C5 18 10N 50 20 E
Khudzhand = Khŭjand, Tajikistan 65 C4 40 17N 69 37 E
Khuff, Si. Arabia 96 E5 24 55N 44 53 E
Khūgīānī, Afghan. 91 C2 31 34N 66 32 E
Khuis, Botswana 116 D3 26 40 S 21 49 E
Khuiyala, India 92 F4 27 9N 70 25 E
Khŭjand, Tajikistan 65 C4 40 17N 69 37 E
Khujner, India 92 H7 23 47N 76 36 E
Khulayş, Si. Arabia 98 B2 22 9N 39 19 E
Khulna, Bangla. 90 D2 22 45N 89 34 E
Khulna □, Bangla. 90 D2 22 25N 89 35 E
Khulo, Georgia 61 K6 41 33N 42 19 E
Khumago, Botswana 116 C3 20 26 S 24 32 E
Khumrah, Si. Arabia 98 B2 21 22N 39 13 E
Khunjerab △, Pakistan 93 A6 36 40N 75 30 E
Khunjerab Pass = Kinjirap Daban, Asia 91 A4 36 40N 75 25 E
Khūnsorkh, Iran 97 E8 27 9N 56 7 E
Khunti, India 93 H11 23 5N 85 17 E
Khūr, Iran 97 C8 32 55N 58 18 E
Khurai, India 92 G8 24 3N 78 23 E
Khuraydah, Yemen 99 D5 15 33N 48 18 E
Khurayş, Si. Arabia 97 E6 25 6N 48 2 E
Khurda, India 94 D7 20 11N 85 37 E
Khureit, Sudan 107 E2 13 59N 26 3 E
Khurīyā Murīyā, Ghubbat, Oman 99 C6 17 40N 55 45 E
Khurīyā Murīyā, Jazā'ir, Oman 99 C6 17 30N 55 58 E
Khurja, India 92 E7 28 15N 77 58 E
Khūrmāl, Iraq 96 C5 35 18N 46 2 E
Khurr, Wādī al, Iraq 96 C4 32 3N 43 52 E
Khūsf, Iran 97 C8 32 46N 58 53 E
Khushab, Pakistan 91 B4 32 20N 72 20 E
Khust, Ukraine 53 B8 48 10N 23 18 E
Khutse ⌓, Botswana 116 C3 23 31 S 24 12 E
Khuzdar, Pakistan 91 D2 27 52N 66 30 E
Khūzestān □, Iran 97 D6 31 0N 49 0 E
Khvāf, Iran 97 C9 34 33N 60 8 E
Khvājeh, Iran 96 B5 38 9N 46 35 E
Khvājeh Moḩammad, Kūh-e, Afghan. 65 E5 36 22N 70 17 E
Khvalynsk, Russia 60 D9 52 30N 48 2 E
Khvānsār, Iran 97 D7 29 56N 54 8 E
Khvatovka, Russia 60 D8 52 24N 46 32 E
Khvor, Iran 97 C7 33 45N 55 0 E
Khvorgū, Iran 97 E8 27 34N 56 27 E
Khvormūj, Iran 97 D6 28 40N 51 30 E
Khvoy, Iran 101 C11 38 35N 45 0 E
Khvoynaya, Russia 58 C8 58 58N 34 28 E
Khyber Pass, Afghan. 91 B3 34 10N 71 8 E
Khyriv, Ukraine 55 J9 49 32N 22 50 E
Kia, Fiji 133 A2 16 16 S 179 8 E
Kia, Solomon Is. 133 L10 7 32 S 158 26 E
Kiabukwa, Dem. Rep. of the Congo 119 D1 8 40 S 24 48 E
Kiadho →, India 94 E3 19 37N 77 40 E
Kiama, Australia 129 C9 34 40 S 150 50 E
Kiama, Dem. Rep. of the Congo 115 D3 7 19 S 17 49 E
Kiamba, Phil. 81 H5 6 2N 124 46 E
Kiambi, Dem. Rep. of the Congo 118 D2 7 15 S 28 0 E
Kiambu, Kenya 118 C4 1 8 S 36 50 E
Kiamusze = Jiamusi, China 69 B8 46 40N 130 26 E
Kian = Ji'an, China 75 D14 41 5N 126 10 E
Kiana, U.S.A. 144 C7 66 58N 160 26W
Kiang West △, Gambia 112 C1 13 25N 15 50W
Kiangara, Madag. 117 B8 17 58 S 47 2 E
Kiangsi = Jiangxi □, China 77 D11 27 30N 116 0 E
Kiangsu = Jiangsu □, China 75 H11 33 0N 120 0 E
Kiáton, Greece 48 C4 38 1N 22 45 E
Kibæk, Denmark 17 H2 56 2N 8 51 E
Kibale △, Uganda 118 B3 0 16N 30 18 E
Kibanga Port, Uganda 118 B3 0 10N 32 58 E

Kibangou, Congo 114 C2 3 26 S 12 22 E
Kibara, Tanzania 118 C3 2 8 S 33 30 E
Kibare, Mts., Dem. Rep. of the Congo 118 D2 8 25 S 27 10 E
Kibawe, Phil. 81 H5 7 34N 125 0 E
Kibenga, Dem. Rep. of the Congo 115 D3 7 56 S 17 30 E
Kibira △, Burundi 118 C3 3 6 S 30 24 E
Kibombo, Dem. Rep. of the Congo 118 C2 3 57 S 25 53 E
Kibondo, Tanzania 118 C3 3 35 S 30 45 E
Kibray, Uzbekistan 65 C4 41 23N 69 27 E
Kibre Mengist, Ethiopia 107 F4 5 54N 38 59 E
Kıbrıs = Cyprus ■, Asia 39 F9 35 0N 33 0 E
Kibumbu, Burundi 118 C2 3 32 S 29 45 E
Kibungo, Rwanda 118 C3 2 10 S 30 32 E
Kibuye, Burundi 118 C2 3 39 S 29 59 E
Kibuye, Rwanda 118 C2 2 3 S 29 21 E
Kibwesa, Tanzania 118 D2 6 30 S 29 58 E
Kibwezi, Kenya 118 C4 2 27 S 37 57 E
Kicasalih, Turkey 51 E10 41 23N 26 48 E
Kičevo, Macedonia 50 E4 41 34N 20 59 E
Kichha, India 93 E8 28 53N 79 30 E
Kichha →, India 93 E8 28 41N 79 18 E
Kichmengskiy Gorodok, Russia 56 B8 59 59N 45 48 E
Kicking Horse Pass, Canada 142 C5 51 28N 116 16W
Kidal, Mali 113 B5 18 26N 1 22 E
Kidapawan, Phil. 81 H5 7 1N 125 3 E
Kidderminster, U.K. 21 E5 52 24N 2 15W
Kidepo Valley △, Uganda 118 B3 3 52N 33 50 E
Kidete, Tanzania 118 D4 6 25 S 37 17 E
Kidira, Senegal 112 C2 14 28N 12 13W
Kidnappers, C., N.Z. 130 F6 39 38 S 177 5 E
Kidsgrove, U.K. 20 D5 53 5N 2 14W
Kidston, Australia 126 B3 18 52 S 144 8 E
Kidugallo, Tanzania 118 D4 6 49 S 38 15 E
Kidurong, Tanjong, Malaysia 85 B4 3 16N 113 3 E
Kiel, Germany 30 A6 54 19N 10 8 E
Kiel Canal = Nord-Ostsee-Kanal, Germany 30 A5 54 12N 9 32 E
Kiel-Kanal = Nord-Ostsee-Kanal, Germany 30 A5 54 12N 9 32 E
Kielce, Poland 55 H7 50 52N 20 42 E
Kielder Water, U.K. 20 B5 55 11N 2 31W
Kieler Bucht, Germany 30 A6 54 35N 10 25 E
Kiembara, Burkina Faso 112 C4 13 15N 2 44W
Kien Binh, Vietnam 87 H5 9 55N 105 19 E
Kien Tan, Vietnam 87 G5 10 7N 105 17 E
Kienge, Dem. Rep. of the Congo 119 E2 10 30 S 27 30 E
Kiessé, Niger 113 C5 13 29N 4 1 E
Kieta, Papua N. G. 132 D8 6 12 S 155 36 E
Kiev = Kyyiv, Ukraine 59 G6 50 30N 30 28 E
Kifaya, Guinea 112 C2 12 10N 13 4W
Kiffa, Mauritania 112 B2 16 37N 11 24W
Kifisiá, Greece 48 C5 38 4N 23 49 E
Kifissós →, Greece 48 C5 38 35N 23 20 E
Kifrī, Iraq 101 E11 34 45N 45 0 E
Kigali, Rwanda 118 C3 1 59 S 30 4 E
Kigarama, Tanzania 118 C3 1 1 S 31 50 E
Kigelle, Sudan 107 F3 8 40N 34 2 E
Kigezi ⊂, Uganda 118 C2 0 34 S 29 55 E
Kigoma □, Tanzania 118 D3 5 0 S 30 0 E
Kigoma-Ujiji, Tanzania 118 C2 4 55 S 29 36 E
Kigomasha, Ras, Tanzania 118 C4 4 58 S 38 58 E
Kığzı, Turkey 96 B4 38 18N 43 25 E
Kihei, U.S.A. 145 C5 20 47N 156 28W
Kihikihi, N.Z. 130 E4 38 2 S 175 22 E
Kihnu, Estonia 15 G21 58 9N 24 1 E
Kiholo B., U.S.A. 145 D6 19 50N 155 55W
Kii-Hantō, Japan 73 D7 34 0N 135 45 E
Kii-Nagashima, Japan 73 C8 34 12N 136 20 E
Kii-Sanchi, Japan 73 C8 34 20N 136 0 E
Kii-Suidō, Japan 72 D6 33 40N 134 45 E
Kiire, Japan 72 F2 31 22N 130 33 E
Kijik, U.S.A. 144 F9 60 20N 154 20W
Kikaiga-Shima, Japan 71 K4 28 19N 129 59 E
Kikinda, Serbia & M. 52 E5 45 50N 20 30 E
Kikládhes, Greece 48 E6 37 0N 24 30 E
Kikládhes □, Greece 48 D6 37 0N 25 0 E
Kikoira, Australia 129 B7 33 39 S 146 40 E
Kikombo, Bandundu, Dem. Rep. of the Congo 115 D3 5 37 S 18 50 E
Kikombo, Bandundu, Dem. Rep. of the Congo 115 D3 5 49 S 17 45 E
Kikongo, Dem. Rep. of the Congo 115 C3 4 16 S 17 17 E
Kikori, Papua N. G. 132 D3 7 25 S 144 15 E
Kikori →, Papua N. G. 132 D3 7 38 S 144 20 E
Kikuchi, Japan 72 E2 32 59N 130 47 E
Kikwit, Dem. Rep. of the Congo 115 D3 5 0 S 18 45 E
Kil, Sweden 16 E7 59 30N 13 20 E
Kilafors, Sweden 16 C10 61 14N 16 36 E
Kilakkarai, India 95 K4 9 12N 78 47 E
Kilar, India 92 C7 33 6N 76 25 E
Kilauea, U.S.A. 145 A2 22 13N 159 25W
Kilauea Crater, U.S.A. 145 D6 19 25N 155 17W
Kilbrannan Sd., U.K. 22 F3 55 37N 5 26W
Kilchberg, Switz. 33 B7 47 18N 8 33 E
Kilchu, N. Korea 75 D15 40 57N 129 25 E
Kilcoy, Australia 127 D5 26 59 S 152 30 E
Kildare, Ireland 23 C5 53 9N 6 55W
Kildare □, Ireland 23 C5 53 10N 6 50W
Kileikli, Sudan 107 E2 11 25N 25 31 E
Kilembe, Dem. Rep. of the Congo 115 D3 5 42 S 19 55 E
Kilen, Norway 18 E5 59 20N 8 49 E
Kilfinnane, Ireland 23 D3 52 21N 8 28W
Kilgore, U.S.A. 155 J7 32 23N 94 53W
Kilibo, Benin 113 D5 8 32N 2 38 E
Kilifi, Kenya 118 C4 3 40 S 39 48 E
Kilimanjaro, Tanzania 118 C4 3 7 S 37 20 E
Kilimanjaro □, Tanzania 118 C4 4 0 S 38 0 E
Kilimli, Turkey 100 B4 41 28N 31 50 E
Kilinailau Is., Papua N. G. 132 C8 4 45 S 155 20 E
Kilindini, Kenya 118 C4 4 4 S 39 40 E
Kilis, Turkey 100 D7 36 42N 37 6 E
Kiliya, Ukraine 53 E14 45 28N 29 16 E
Kilkee, Ireland 23 D2 52 41N 9 39W
Kilkeel, U.K. 23 B5 54 4N 6 0W
Kilkenny, Ireland 23 D4 52 39N 7 15W
Kilkenny □, Ireland 23 D4 52 35N 7 15W
Kilkieran B., Ireland 23 C2 53 20N 9 41W
Kilkís, Greece 50 F6 40 58N 22 57 E
Kilkís □, Greece 50 E6 41 5N 22 50 E
Killala, Ireland 23 B2 54 13N 9 12W
Killala B., Ireland 23 B2 54 16N 9 8W
Killaloe, Canada 150 A7 45 33N 77 25W
Killaloe, Ireland 23 D3 52 48N 8 28W
Killarney, Australia 127 D5 28 20 S 152 18 E
Killarney, Canada 143 D9 49 10N 99 40W
Killarney, Ireland 23 D2 52 4N 9 30W
Killarney △, Ireland 23 D2 52 0N 9 33W
Killarney, L., Bahamas 9 b 25 3N 77 27W
Killary Harbour, Ireland 23 C2 53 38N 9 52W
Killdeer, U.S.A. 154 B3 47 26N 102 48W
Killeberg, Sweden 17 H8 56 29N 14 5 E
Killeen, U.S.A. 155 K6 31 7N 97 44W
Killin, U.K. 22 E4 56 28N 4 19W
Killíni, Ilía, Greece 39 D3 37 55N 21 8 E
Killíni, Korinthía, Greece 48 D4 37 54N 22 25 E
Killíni, Ákra, Greece 39 D3 37 57N 21 8 E
Killorglin, Ireland 23 D2 52 6N 9 47W
Killybegs, Ireland 23 B3 54 38N 8 26W
Kilmarnock, U.K. 22 F4 55 37N 4 29W
Kilmez, Russia 60 B10 56 58N 50 55 E
Kilmez →, Russia 60 B10 56 58N 50 28 E
Kilmore, Australia 129 D6 37 25 S 144 53 E
Kilómetro 1082 = Joaquín V. González, Argentina 174 B3 25 10 S 64 0W
Kilondo, Tanzania 119 D3 9 45 S 34 20 E
Kilosa, Tanzania 118 D4 6 48 S 37 0 E
Kilrush, Ireland 23 D2 52 38N 9 29W
Kiltan I., India 95 J1 11 29N 73 0 E
Kilwa Kisiwani, Tanzania 119 D4 8 58 S 39 32 E
Kilwa Kivinje, Tanzania 119 D4 8 45 S 39 25 E
Kilwa Masoko, Tanzania 119 D4 8 55 S 39 30 E
Kilwinning, U.K. 22 F4 55 39N 4 43W
Kim, U.S.A. 155 G3 37 15N 103 21W
Kim →, Cameroon 113 D7 5 28N 11 7 E
Kimaam, Indonesia 83 C5 7 58 S 138 53 E
Kimamba, Tanzania 118 D4 6 45 S 37 10 E
Kimba, Australia 128 B2 33 8 S 136 23 E
Kimball, Nebr., U.S.A. 154 E3 41 14N 103 40W
Kimball, S. Dak., U.S.A. 154 D5 43 45N 98 57W
Kimbanda, Dem. Rep. of the Congo 115 C3 4 16 S 18 30 E
Kimbe, Papua N. G. 132 C6 5 33 S 150 11 E
Kimbe B., Papua N. G. 132 C6 5 15 S 150 30 E
Kimberley, Australia 124 C4 16 20 S 127 0 E
Kimberley, Canada 142 D5 49 40N 115 59W
Kimberley, S. Africa 116 D3 28 43 S 24 46 E
Kimberly, U.S.A. 158 E6 42 32N 114 22W
Kimbongo, Dem. Rep. of the Congo 115 D3 6 8 S 18 1 E
Kimch'aek, N. Korea 75 D15 40 40N 129 10 E
Kimch'ŏn, S. Korea 75 F15 36 11N 128 4 E
Kími, Greece 48 C6 38 38N 24 6 E
Kimitsu, Japan 73 B10 35 19N 139 54 E
Kimje, S. Korea 75 G14 35 48N 126 45 E
Kimmirut, Canada 139 B13 62 50N 69 50W
Kímolos, Greece 48 E6 36 48N 24 37 E
Kimongo, Congo 115 C2 4 27 S 12 53 E
Kimovsk, Moskva, Russia 58 E9 55 21N 37 28 E
Kimovsk, Tula, Russia 58 E10 54 0N 38 29 E
Kimpangu, Dem. Rep. of the Congo 115 D3 5 52 S 15 3 E
Kimparana, Mali 112 C4 12 48N 5 0W
Kimry, Russia 58 D9 56 55N 37 15 E
Kimstad, Sweden 17 F9 58 35N 15 58 E
Kimvula, Dem. Rep. of the Congo 115 D3 5 44 S 15 58 E
Kin, Burma 90 D5 22 46N 94 42 E
Kin-u, Burma 90 D5 22 46N 95 37 E
Kinabalu, Gunung, Malaysia 85 A5 6 3N 116 14 E
Kinard, U.S.A. 152 E4 30 16N 85 15W
Kínaros, Greece 49 E8 36 59N 26 15 E
Kinaskan L., Canada 142 B2 57 38N 130 8W
Kinbasket L., Canada 142 C5 52 0N 118 10W
Kincaid, U.S.A. 156 E7 39 35N 89 25W
Kincardine, Canada 140 D3 44 10N 81 40W
Kinchafoonee Cr. →, U.S.A. 152 D5 31 38N 84 10W
Kinchega △, Australia 128 B5 32 27 S 142 15 E
Kincolith, Canada 142 C3 55 0N 129 57W
Kinda, Kasai-Or., Dem. Rep. of the Congo 119 D2 9 18 S 25 4 E
Kinda, Katanga, Dem. Rep. of the Congo 115 C4 4 47 S 21 48 E
Kindambi, Dem. Rep. of the Congo 115 D4 5 6 S 18 14 E
Kindberg, Austria 34 D8 47 30N 15 27 E
Kinde, U.S.A. 150 C2 43 56N 83 0W
Kindele, Dem. Rep. of the Congo 115 D4 8 39 S 24 10 E
Kinder Scout, U.K. 20 D6 53 24N 1 52W
Kinderhook, U.S.A. 156 E5 39 42N 91 10W
Kindersley, Canada 143 C7 51 30N 109 10W
Kindia, Guinea 112 D2 10 0N 12 52W
Kindley U.S.A.F. Base, Bermuda 9 a 32 22N 64 42W
Kindongo, Dem. Rep. of the Congo 114 C3 3 58 S 17 30 E
Kindu, Dem. Rep. of the Congo 118 C2 2 55 S 25 50 E
Kinel, Russia 60 D10 53 15N 50 40 E
Kineshma, Russia 60 B6 57 30N 42 5 E
Kinesi, Tanzania 118 C3 1 25 S 33 50 E
King, L., Australia 125 F2 33 10 S 119 35 E
King, Mt., Australia 126 D4 25 10 S 147 30 E
King City, Calif., U.S.A. 160 J5 36 13N 121 8W
King City, Mo., U.S.A. 156 D2 40 3N 94 31W
King Cove, U.S.A. 144 J7 55 3N 162 19W
King Cr. →, Australia 126 C2 24 35 S 139 30 E
King Edward →, Australia 124 B4 14 14 S 126 35 E
King Frederick VI Land = Kong Frederik VI Kyst, Greenland 10 E6 63 0N 43 0W
King George B., Falk. Is. 9 f 51 30 S 60 30W
King George I., Antarctica 7 C18 60 0 S 60 0W
King George Is., Canada 139 C11 57 20N 80 30W
King I. = Kadan Kyun, Burma 86 F2 12 30N 98 20 E
King I., Australia 127 F3 39 50 S 144 0 E
King I., Canada 142 C3 52 10N 127 40W
King Leopold Ranges, Australia 124 C4 17 30 S 125 45 E
King of Prussia, U.S.A. 151 F9 40 5N 75 23W
King Salmon, U.S.A. 144 G8 58 42N 156 40W
King Sd., Australia 124 C3 16 50 S 123 20 E
King Sejong, Antarctica 7 C18 62 30 S 58 0W
King William I., Canada 138 B10 69 10N 97 25W
King William's Town, S. Africa 116 E4 32 51 S 27 22 E
Kingait = Cape Dorset, Canada 139 B12 64 14N 76 32W
Kingaok = Bathurst Inlet, Canada 138 B9 66 50N 108 1W
Kingaroy, Australia 127 D5 26 32 S 151 51 E
Kingdom City, U.S.A. 156 F5 38 56N 91 56W
Kingfisher, U.S.A. 155 H6 35 52N 97 56W
Kingirbān, Iraq 96 C5 34 40N 44 54 E
Kingisepp = Kuressaare, Estonia 15 G20 58 15N 22 30 E
Kingisepp, Russia 58 C5 59 25N 28 40 E
Kingking = Pantukan, Phil. 81 H5 7 9N 125 54 E
Kinglake △, Australia 129 D6 37 30 S 145 22 E
Kingman, Ariz., U.S.A. 161 K12 35 12N 114 4W
Kingman, Ind., U.S.A. 157 E9 39 58N 87 18W
Kingman, Kans., U.S.A. 155 G5 37 39N 98 7W
Kingoonya, Australia 127 E2 30 55 S 135 19 E
Kingri, Pakistan 92 D3 30 27N 69 49 E
Kings →, U.S.A. 160 J7 36 3N 119 50W
Kings Canyon △, U.S.A. 160 J8 36 50N 118 40W
Kings County = Offaly □, Ireland 23 C4 53 15N 7 30W
King's Lynn, U.K. 20 E8 52 45N 0 24 E
Kings Park, U.S.A. 151 F11 40 53N 73 16W
King's Peak, U.S.A. 158 F8 40 46N 110 27W
Kingsbridge, U.K. 21 G4 50 17N 3 47W
Kingsburg, U.S.A. 160 J7 36 31N 119 33W
Kingscote, Australia 128 C2 35 40 S 137 38 E
Kingscourt, Ireland 23 C5 53 55N 6 48W
Kingsford, U.S.A. 148 C1 45 48N 88 4W
Kingsland, U.S.A. 152 E8 30 48N 81 41W
Kingsport, U.S.A. 153 G4 36 33N 82 33W
Kingston, Canada 140 D4 44 14N 76 30W
Kingston, Jamaica 164 a 18 0N 76 50W
Kingston, N.Z. 131 F3 45 20 S 168 43 E
Kingston, N.H., U.S.A. 151 D13 42 56N 71 3W
Kingston, N.Y., U.S.A. 151 E11 41 56N 73 59W
Kingston, Pa., U.S.A. 151 E9 41 16N 75 54W
Kingston, R.I., U.S.A. 151 E13 41 29N 71 30W
Kingston Pk., U.S.A. 161 K11 35 45N 115 54W
Kingston South East, Australia 128 D3 36 51 S 139 55 E
Kingston upon Hull, U.K. 20 D7 53 45N 0 21W
Kingston upon Hull □, U.K. 20 D7 53 45N 0 21W
Kingston-upon-Thames □, U.K. 21 F7 51 24N 0 17W
Kingstown = Dún Laoghaire, Ireland 23 C5 53 17N 6 8W
Kingstown, Australia 129 A9 30 29 S 151 6 E
Kingstown, St. Vincent 165 D7 13 10N 61 10W
Kingstree, U.S.A. 152 B10 33 40N 79 50W
Kingsville, Canada 140 D3 42 2N 82 45W
Kingsville, U.S.A. 155 M6 27 31N 97 52W
Kingtechen = Jingdezhen, China 77 C11 29 20N 117 11 E
Kingunda, Dem. Rep. of the Congo 115 D3 6 36 S 16 58 E
Kingussie, U.K. 22 D4 57 6N 4 2W
Kingwood, U.S.A. 155 K7 29 54N 95 18W
Kinhwa = Jinhua, China 77 C12 29 8N 119 38 E
Kınık, Antalya, Turkey 49 E11 36 20N 29 20 E
Kınık, İzmir, Turkey 49 B9 39 6N 27 24 E
Kinistino, Canada 143 C7 52 57N 105 2W
Kinjirap Daban, Asia 91 A4 36 40N 75 25 E
Kinkala, Congo 115 C2 4 18 S 14 49 E
Kinki □, Japan 73 D8 33 45N 136 0 E
Kinleith, N.Z. 130 E4 38 20 S 175 56 E
Kinlochleven, U.K. 22 E4 56 43N 5 0W
Kinmount, Canada 150 B6 44 48N 78 45W
Kinmundy, U.S.A. 157 F8 38 46N 88 51W
Kinn, Norway 18 C1 61 34N 4 45 E
Kinna, Sweden 17 G6 57 32N 12 42 E
Kinnairds Hd., U.K. 22 D6 57 43N 2 1W
Kinnared, Sweden 17 G7 57 2N 13 7 E
Kinnarp, Sweden 17 F7 58 5N 13 32 E
Kinneviken, Sweden 17 F7 58 35N 13 15 E
Kino, Mexico 162 B2 28 45N 111 59W
Kinogitan, Phil. 81 G5 9 0N 124 48 E
Kinoje →, Canada 140 B3 52 8N 81 25W
Kinomoto, Japan 73 B8 35 30N 136 13 E
Kinoni, Uganda 118 C3 0 41 S 30 28 E
Kinoosao, Canada 143 B8 57 5N 102 1W
Kinross, U.K. 22 E5 56 13N 3 25W
Kinsale, Ireland 23 E3 51 42N 8 31W
Kinsale, Old Hd. of, Ireland 23 E3 51 37N 8 33W
Kinsarvik, Norway 18 D3 60 22N 6 43 E
Kinsha = Chang Jiang →, China 77 B13 31 48N 121 10 E
Kinshasa, Dem. Rep. of the Congo 115 C3 4 20 S 15 15 E
Kinsley, U.S.A. 155 G5 37 55N 99 25W
Kinsman, U.S.A. 150 E4 41 26N 80 35W
Kinston, Ala., U.S.A. 152 D3 31 13N 86 10W
Kinston, N.C., U.S.A. 149 H7 35 16N 77 35W
Kintamani, Indonesia 79 J18 8 14 S 115 19 E
Kintampo, Ghana 113 D4 8 5N 1 41W
Kintap, Indonesia 85 C5 3 51 S 115 13 E
Kintore, U.K. 22 D6 57 14N 2 20W
Kintore Ra., Australia 124 D4 23 15 S 128 47 E
Kintshua, Dem. Rep. of the Congo 115 C3 4 27 S 19 38 E
Kintyre, U.K. 22 F3 55 30N 5 35W
Kintyre, Mull of, U.K. 22 F3 55 17N 5 47W
Kinu-Gawa →, Japan 73 B11 35 36N 139 57 E
Kinushseo →, Canada 140 A3 55 15N 83 45W
Kinuso, Canada 142 B5 55 20N 115 25W
Kinwat, India 94 E4 19 38N 78 12 E
Kinyangiri, Tanzania 118 C3 4 25 S 34 37 E
Kinyeti, Sudan 107 G3 3 57N 32 54 E
Kinzia, Dem. Rep. of the Congo 114 C3 3 36 S 18 26 E
Kinzig →, Germany 31 G3 48 36N 7 49 E
Kinzua, U.S.A. 150 E6 41 52N 78 58W
Kinzua Dam, U.S.A. 150 E6 41 53N 79 0W
Kióni, Greece 39 C2 38 27N 20 41 E
Kiosk, Canada 140 C4 46 6N 78 53W
Kiowa, Kans., U.S.A. 155 G5 37 1N 98 29W
Kiowa, Okla., U.S.A. 155 H7 34 43N 95 54W
Kipahigan L., Canada 143 B8 55 20N 101 55W
Kipanga, Tanzania 118 D4 6 15 S 35 20 E
Kipapa →, U.S.A. 145 K13 21 24N 158 1W
Kiparissía, Greece 48 D3 37 15N 21 40 E
Kiparissiakós Kólpos, Greece 48 D3 37 25N 21 25 E
Kipawa, L., Canada 140 C4 46 50N 79 0W
Kipembawe, Tanzania 118 D3 7 38 S 33 27 E
Kipengere Ra., Tanzania 119 D3 9 12 S 34 15 E
Kipili, Tanzania 118 D3 7 28 S 30 32 E
Kipini, Kenya 118 C5 2 30 S 40 32 E
Kipling, Canada 143 C8 50 6N 102 38W
Kipnuk, U.S.A. 144 G6 59 56N 164 3W
Kippure, Ireland 23 C5 53 11N 6 21W
Kipushi, Dem. Rep. of the Congo 119 E2 11 48 S 27 12 E
Kirandul, India 94 E5 18 33N 81 10 E
Kirane, Mali 112 B2 15 20N 10 20W
Kiranomena, Madag. 117 B8 18 17 S 46 2 E
Kiraz, Turkey 49 C10 38 14N 28 13 E
Kirazlı, Turkey 51 F10 40 2N 26 41 E
Kirchberg, Bern, Switz. 32 B5 47 5N 7 35 E
Kirchberg, St. Gallen, Switz. 33 B8 47 25N 9 2 E
Kirchhain, Germany 30 E4 50 47N 8 56 E
Kirchheim, Germany 31 G5 48 39N 9 27 E
Kirchheimbolanden, Germany 31 F3 49 40N 8 0 E
Kirchschlag, Austria 35 D9 47 30N 16 19 E
Kirdimi, Chad 109 E3 18 11N 18 31 E
Kireç, Turkey 49 B10 39 33N 28 22 E
Kirensk, Russia 67 D11 57 50N 107 55 E
Kirghiz Range, Asia 65 B6 42 40N 73 40 E
Kirghizia = Kyrgyzstan ■, Asia 65 C6 42 0N 75 0 E
Kirghizstan = Kyrgyzstan ■, Asia 65 C6 42 0N 75 0 E
Kirgiz-Kulak = Chirchiq, Uzbekistan 65 C4 41 29N 69 35 E
Kirgiziya Steppe, Eurasia 57 E10 50 0N 55 0 E
Kiri, Dem. Rep. of the Congo 114 C3 1 29 S 19 0 E
Kiri Buru, India 94 D7 22 0N 85 0 E
Kiribati ■, Pac. Oc. 134 H10 5 0 S 180 0 E
Kırıkhan, Turkey 100 D7 36 31N 36 21 E
Kırıkkale, Turkey 100 C5 39 51N 33 32 E
Kirikopuni, N.Z. 130 B3 35 50 S 174 1 E
Kirillov, Russia 58 C10 59 49N 38 24 E
Kirin = Jilin, China 75 C14 43 44N 126 30 E
Kirindi Oya →, Sri Lanka 95 L5 6 15N 81 20 E
Kirinyaga = Kenya, Mt., Kenya 118 C4 0 10 S 37 18 E
Kirishi, Russia 58 C7 59 28N 31 59 E
Kirishima Yaku △, Japan 71 J5 31 24N 130 50 E
Kirishima-Yama, Japan 72 F2 31 58N 130 55 E
Kiritimati, Kiribati 135 G12 1 58N 157 27W
Kiriwina I., Papua N. G. 132 E6 8 40 S 151 6 E
Kırka, Turkey 49 B12 39 17N 30 33 E
Kırkağaç, Turkey 49 B9 39 8N 27 40 E
Kirkby, U.K. 20 D5 53 30N 2 54W
Kirkby-in-Ashfield, U.K. 20 D6 53 6N 1 14W
Kirkby Lonsdale, U.K. 20 C5 54 12N 2 36W
Kirkby Stephen, U.K. 20 C5 54 29N 2 21W
Kirkcaldy, U.K. 22 E5 56 7N 3 9W
Kirkcudbright, U.K. 22 G4 54 50N 4 2W
Kirkee, India 94 E1 18 34N 73 56 E
Kirkehamn, Norway 18 F3 58 14N 6 31 E
Kirkenær, Norway 18 D9 60 27N 12 3 E
Kirkenes, Norway 14 B23 69 40N 30 5 E
Kirkfield, Canada 150 B6 44 34N 78 59W
Kirkintilloch, U.K. 22 F4 55 56N 4 8W
Kirkjubæjarklaustur, Iceland 11 D8 63 47N 18 4W
Kirkkonummi, Finland 15 F21 60 8N 24 26 E
Kirkland, U.S.A. 157 B8 42 6N 88 51W
Kirkland Lake, Canada 140 C3 48 9N 80 2W
Kırklareli, Turkey 51 E11 41 44N 27 15 E
Kırklareli □, Turkey 51 E11 41 45N 27 15 E
Kirklin, U.S.A. 157 D10 40 12N 86 22W
Kirkliston Ra., N.Z. 131 E5 44 25 S 170 34 E
Kirknitz = Cerknica, Slovenia 45 C11 45 48N 14 21 E
Kirksville, U.S.A. 156 D4 40 12N 92 35W
Kirkūk, Iraq 101 E11 35 30N 44 21 E
Kirkwall, U.K. 22 C6 58 59N 2 58W
Kirkwood, S. Africa 116 E4 33 22 S 25 15 E
Kirkwood, U.S.A. 156 F6 38 35N 90 24W
Kirlampudi, India 94 F6 17 12N 82 12 E
Kirmasti = Mustafakemalpaşa, Turkey 51 F12 40 2N 28 24 E
Kirn, Germany 31 F3 49 47N 7 26 E
Kirov, Kaluga, Russia 58 E8 54 3N 34 20 E
Kirov, Kirov, Russia 64 B2 58 35N 49 40 E
Kirovabad = Gäncä, Azerbaijan 61 K8 40 45N 46 20 E
Kirovabad = Pyandzh, Tajikistan 65 E4 37 14N 69 6 E
Kirovakan = Vanadzor, Armenia 61 K7 40 48N 44 30 E
Kirovo = Kirovohrad, Ukraine 59 H7 48 35N 32 20 E
Kirovo-Chepetsk, Russia 64 B3 58 28N 50 0 E
Kirovograd = Kirovohrad, Ukraine 59 H7 48 35N 32 20 E
Kirovohrad, Ukraine 59 H7 48 35N 32 20 E
Kirovsk, Russia 56 A5 67 32N 33 41 E
Kirovskiy = Balpyq Bī, Kazakhstan 65 A9 44 52N 78 12 E
Kirovskiy, Astrakhan, Russia 61 H9 45 51N 48 11 E
Kirovskiy, Kamchatka, Russia 67 D16 54 27N 155 42 E
Kirovskiy, Primorsk, Russia 70 B6 45 7N 133 30 E
Kirriemuir, U.K. 22 E5 56 41N 3 1W
Kirs, Russia 64 B4 59 21N 52 14 E
Kirsanov, Russia 60 D6 52 35N 42 40 E
Kırşehir, Turkey 100 C6 39 14N 34 5 E
Kirtachi, Niger 113 C5 12 52N 2 30 E
Kīrteh, Afghan. 91 B1 32 15N 63 0 E
Kirthar △, Pakistan 92 F2 25 45N 67 30 E
Kirthar Range, Pakistan 91 D2 27 0N 67 0 E
Kirtland, U.S.A. 159 H9 36 44N 108 21W
Kiruna, Sweden 14 C19 67 52N 20 15 E
Kirundu, Dem. Rep. of the Congo 118 C2 0 50 S 25 35 E
Kirya, Russia 60 C8 55 8N 46 55 E
Kiryū, Japan 73 A11 36 24N 139 20 E
Kisa, Sweden 17 G9 58 0N 15 39 E
Kisaga, Tanzania 118 C3 4 30 S 34 23 E
Kisalaya, Nic. 164 D3 14 40N 84 3W
Kisalföld, Hungary 52 C2 47 30N 17 0 E
Kisambo, Dem. Rep. of the Congo 115 D3 6 25 S 18 14 E
Kisámou, Kólpos, Greece 39 E4 35 30N 23 38 E
Kisandji, Dem. Rep. of the Congo 115 D3 6 18 S 19 16 E
Kisanga, Dem. Rep. of the Congo 118 B2 2 30N 26 35 E
Kisangani, Dem. Rep. of the Congo 118 B2 0 35N 25 15 E
Kisantu, Dem. Rep. of the Congo 115 D3 5 7 S 15 5 E
Kisar, Indonesia 82 C3 8 5 S 127 10 E
Kisaran, Indonesia 84 B1 3 0N 99 37 E
Kisarawe, Tanzania 118 D4 6 53 S 39 0 E
Kisarazu, Japan 73 B11 35 23N 139 55 E
Kisbér, Hungary 52 C3 47 30N 18 2 E
Kishanganga →, Pakistan 93 B5 34 18N 73 28 E
Kishanganj, India 90 B2 26 3N 88 14 E
Kishangarh, Raj., India 92 F6 26 34N 74 52 E
Kishangarh, Raj., India 92 F4 27 50N 70 30 E
Kishb, Ḩarrat al, Si. Arabia 98 B3 22 30N 40 15 E
Kishi, Nigeria 113 D5 9 1N 3 52 E
Kishinev = Chişinău, Moldova 53 C13 47 2N 28 50 E
Kishiwada, Japan 73 C7 34 28N 135 22 E
Kishkareny = Lazo, Moldova 53 C13 47 33N 28 2 E
Kishorganj, Bangla. 90 C3 24 26N 90 40 E
Kishtwar, India 92 C6 33 20N 75 50 E
Kishtwar, Jammu & Kashmir, India 93 C6 33 20N 75 48 E
Kishwaukee →, U.S.A. 156 B7 42 12N 89 8W
Kisielice, Poland 54 E6 53 36N 19 16 E
Kisigo ⊂, Tanzania 118 D3 6 27 S 34 17 E
Kisii, Kenya 118 C3 0 40 S 34 45 E
Kisiju, Tanzania 118 D4 7 23 S 39 19 E
Kisir, Turkey 101 B10 41 0N 43 5 E
Kisizi, Uganda 118 C2 1 0 S 29 58 E
Kiska I., U.S.A. 144 L2 51 59N 177 30 E
Kiskomárom = Zalakomár, Hungary 52 D2 46 33N 17 10 E
Kiskörei-víztároló, Hungary 52 C5 47 31N 20 36 E
Kiskőrös, Hungary 52 D4 46 37N 19 20 E
Kiskundorozsma, Hungary 52 D5 46 16N 20 5 E
Kiskunfélegyháza, Hungary 52 D4 46 42N 19 53 E
Kiskunhalas, Hungary 52 D4 46 28N 19 37 E
Kiskunmajsa, Hungary 52 D4 46 30N 19 48 E
Kiskunsági △, Hungary 52 D4 46 39N 19 30 E
Kislovodsk, Russia 61 J6 43 50N 42 45 E
Kismayu = Chisimaio, Somali Rep. 120 E2 0 22 S 42 32 E
Kismayu △, Somali Rep. 120 D2 1 25N 41 30 E
Kiso-Gawa →, Japan 73 B8 35 20N 136 45 E
Kiso-Sammyaku, Japan 73 B9 35 45N 137 45 E
Kisofukushima, Japan 73 B9 35 52N 137 43 E
Kisoro, Uganda 118 C2 1 17 S 29 48 E
Kissidougou, Guinea 112 D2 9 5N 10 5W
Kissimmee, U.S.A. 153 G8 28 18N 81 24W
Kissimmee →, U.S.A. 153 H8 27 9N 80 52W
Kissimmee, L., U.S.A. 153 H8 27 55N 81 17W
Kississing L., Canada 143 B8 55 10N 101 20W
Kissónerga, Cyprus 39 F8 34 49N 32 24 E
Kissu, J., Sudan 106 C2 21 37N 25 10 E
Kistanje, Croatia 45 E12 43 58N 15 55 E
Kistna = Krishna →, India 95 G5 15 57N 80 59 E
Kisújszállás, Hungary 52 C5 47 12N 20 50 E
Kisuki, Japan 72 B4 35 17N 132 54 E
Kisumu, Kenya 118 C3 0 3 S 34 45 E
Kisvárda, Hungary 52 B7 48 14N 22 4 E
Kiswani, Tanzania 118 C4 4 5 S 37 57 E
Kiswere, Tanzania 119 D4 9 27 S 39 30 E
Kit Carson, U.S.A. 154 F3 38 46N 102 48W
Kita, Mali 112 C3 13 5N 9 25W
Kita-Ura, Japan 73 B12 36 0N 140 34 E
Kitaa □, Greenland 10 C6 70 0N 47 0W
Kitab, Uzbekistan 65 D3 39 7N 66 52 E
Kitaibaraki, Japan 71 F10 36 50N 140 45 E
Kitakami, Japan 70 E10 39 20N 141 10 E
Kitakami-Gawa →, Japan 70 E10 38 25N 141 19 E
Kitakami-Sammyaku, Japan 70 E10 39 30N 141 30 E
Kitakata, Japan 70 F9 37 39N 139 52 E
Kitakyūshū, Japan 72 D2 33 50N 130 50 E
Kitale, Kenya 118 B4 1 0N 35 0 E
Kitami, Japan 70 C11 43 48N 143 54 E
Kitami-Sammyaku, Japan 70 B11 44 22N 142 43 E
Kitangiri, L., Tanzania 118 C3 4 5 S 34 20 E
Kitano-Kaikyō, Japan 72 C6 34 17N 134 58 E
Kitaotao, Phil. 81 H5 7 40N 125 1 E
Kitava I., Papua N. G. 132 E6 8 40 S 151 20 E
Kitaya, Tanzania 119 E5 10 38 S 40 8 E
Kitcharao, Phil. 81 G5 9 27N 125 36 E
Kitchener, Canada 140 D3 43 27N 80 29W
Kitee, Finland 58 A6 62 5N 30 8 E
Kitega = Gitega, Burundi 118 C2 3 26 S 29 56 E
Kitengo, Dem. Rep. of the Congo 118 D1 7 26 S 24 8 E
Kitgum, Uganda 118 B3 3 17N 32 52 E
Kíthira, Greece 48 E5 36 8N 23 0 E
Kíthnos, Greece 48 D6 37 26N 24 27 E
Kiti, Cyprus 39 F9 34 50N 33 34 E
Kiti, C., Cyprus 39 F9 34 48N 33 36 E
Kitimat, Canada 142 C3 54 3N 128 38W
Kitinen →, Finland 14 C22 67 14N 27 27 E
Kitiyab, Sudan 107 D3 17 13N 33 35 E
Kitombe, Dem. Rep. of the Congo 115 D3 5 22 S 18 59 E
Kítros, Greece 50 F6 40 22N 22 34 E
Kitsman, Ukraine 53 B10 48 26N 25 46 E
Kitsuki, Japan 72 D3 33 25N 131 37 E
Kittakittaooloo, L., Australia 127 D2 28 3 S 138 14 E
Kittanning, U.S.A. 150 F5 40 49N 79 31W
Kittatinny Mts., U.S.A. 151 F10 41 0N 75 0W
Kittery, U.S.A. 149 D10 43 5N 70 45W
Kittilä, Finland 14 C21 67 40N 24 51 E
Kitui, Kenya 118 C4 1 17 S 38 0 E
Kitwanga, Canada 142 B3 55 6N 128 4W
Kitwe, Zambia 119 E2 12 54 S 28 13 E
Kityang = Jieyang, China 77 F11 23 35N 116 21 E
Kitzbühel, Austria 34 D5 47 27N 12 24 E
Kitzbühler Alpen, Austria 34 D5 47 20N 12 20 E
Kitzingen, Germany 31 F6 49 44N 10 9 E
Kiukiang = Jiujiang, China 77 C10 29 42N 115 58 E
Kiunga, Papua N. G. 132 D1 6 7 S 141 18 E
Kivalina, U.S.A. 144 C6 67 44N 164 33W
Kivarli, India 92 G5 24 33N 72 46 E
Kivertsi, Ukraine 59 G3 50 50N 25 28 E
Kividhes, Cyprus 39 F8 34 46N 32 51 E
Kivik, Sweden 17 J8 55 41N 14 13 E
Kivotós, Greece 50 F5 40 13N 21 25 E
Kivu, L., Dem. Rep. of the Congo 118 C2 1 48 S 29 0 E
Kiwai I., Papua N. G. 132 E2 8 35 S 143 30 E
Kiyev = Kyyiv, Ukraine 59 G6 50 30N 30 28 E
Kiyevskoye Vdkhr. = Kyyivske Vdskh., Ukraine 59 G6 51 0N 30 25 E
Kıyıköy, Turkey 51 E12 41 38N 28 5 E
Kizel, Russia 64 B6 59 3N 57 40 E
Kiziguru, Rwanda 118 C3 1 46 S 30 23 E
Kızıl Adalar, Turkey 51 F13 40 52N 29 5 E
Kızıl Irmak →, Turkey 100 B6 41 44N 35 58 E
Kizil Jilga, China 93 B8 35 26N 78 50 E
Kizil Yurt, Russia 61 J8 43 13N 46 54 E
Kızılcabölük, Turkey 49 D11 37 37N 29 1 E
Kızılcadağ, Turkey 49 D11 37 1N 29 58 E
Kızılcahamam, Turkey 100 B5 40 30N 32 30 E
Kızılhisar, Turkey 100 D3 37 32N 29 17 E
Kızılırmak, Turkey 100 B5 40 21N 33 59 E
Kızılkaya, Turkey 49 D12 37 18N 30 27 E
Kızılören, Turkey 49 C12 38 15N 30 10 E
Kizilskoye, Russia 64 E7 52 44N 58 54 E
Kızıltepe, Turkey 101 D9 37 12N 40 35 E
Kizimkazi, Tanzania 118 D4 6 28 S 39 30 E
Kizlyar, Russia 61 J8 43 51N 46 40 E
Kizyl-Arvat = Gyzylarbat, Turkmenistan 66 F6 39 4N 56 23 E

Kjellerup, *Denmark* **17 H3** 56 17N 9 25 E
Kjellmyra, *Norway* **18 D9** 60 39N 12 1 E
Kjølen, *Norway* **18 C5** 62 3N 8 45 E
Kjölur, *Iceland* **11 C7** 64 50N 19 25W
Kjósarsýsla □, *Iceland* **11 C5** 64 15N 21 30W
Kladanj, *Bos.-H.* **52 F3** 44 14N 18 42 E
Kladnica, *Serbia & M.* **50 C4** 43 23N 20 2 E
Kladno, *Czech Rep.* **34 A7** 50 10N 14 7 E
Kladovo, *Serbia & M.* **50 B6** 44 36N 22 33 E
Klæbu, *Norway* **18 A7** 63 18N 10 29 E
Klaeng, *Thailand* **86 F3** 12 47N 101 39 E
Klagan, *Malaysia* **85 A5** 5 58N 117 27 E
Klagenfurt, *Austria* **34 E7** 46 38N 14 20 E
Klaipėda, *Lithuania* **15 J19** 55 43N 21 10 E
Klaipėda □, *Lithuania* **54 C8** 55 43N 21 7 E
Klaksvík, *Færoe Is.* **14 E9** 62 14N 6 35W
Klamath →, *U.S.A.* **158 F1** 41 33N 124 5W
Klamath Falls, *U.S.A.* **158 E3** 42 13N 121 46W
Klamath Mts., *U.S.A.* **158 F2** 41 20N 123 0W
Klamono, *Indonesia* **83 B4** 1 8 S 131 30 E
Klang, *Malaysia* **87 L3** 3 2N 101 26 E
Klangklang, *Burma* **90 D4** 22 41N 93 26 E
Klanjec, *Croatia* **45 B12** 46 3N 15 45 E
Klappan →, *Canada* **142 B3** 58 0N 129 43W
Klara = Trysilelva →,
Norway **18 C9** 61 2N 12 35 E
Klarälven →, *Sweden* **16 E7** 59 23N 13 32 E
Klässbol, *Sweden* **16 E6** 59 33N 12 45 E
Klaten, *Indonesia* **85 D4** 7 43 S 110 36 E
Klatovy, *Czech Rep.* **34 B6** 49 23N 13 18 E
Klausenburg = Cluj-
Napoca, *Romania* **53 D8** 46 47N 23 38 E
Klawer, *S. Africa* **116 E2** 31 44 S 18 36 E
Klawock, *U.S.A.* **144 J14** 55 33N 133 6W
Klazienaveen, *Neths.* **24 B6** 52 44N 7 0 E
Klé, *Mali* **112 C3** 12 0N 6 28W
Klecko, *Poland* **55 F4** 52 38N 17 25 E
Kleczew, *Poland* **55 F5** 52 22N 18 9 E
Kleena Kleene, *Canada* **142 C4** 52 0N 124 59W
Klein-Karas, *Namibia* **116 D2** 27 33 S 18 7 E
Klein-Schlatten =
Zlatna, *Romania* **53 D8** 46 8N 23 11 E
Klekovača, *Bos.-H.* **45 D13** 44 25N 16 32 E
Klembivka, *Ukraine* **53 B13** 48 23N 28 25 E
Klenoec, *Macedonia* **50 E4** 41 32N 20 49 E
Klenovec, *Slovak Rep.* **35 C12** 48 36N 19 54 E
Klerksdorp, *S. Africa* **116 D4** 26 53 S 26 38 E
Kleszczele, *Poland* **55 F10** 52 35N 23 19 E
Kletnya, *Russia* **58 F7** 53 23N 33 12 E
Kletsk = Klyetsk,
Belarus **59 F4** 53 5N 26 45 E
Kletskiy, *Russia* **61 F6** 49 16N 43 11 E
Kleve, *Germany* **30 D2** 51 47N 6 7 E
Klickitat, *U.S.A.* **158 D3** 45 49N 121 9W
Klickitat →, *U.S.A.* **160 E5** 45 42N 121 17W
Klidhes, *Cyprus* **39 E10** 35 42N 34 36 E
Klimovichi, *Belarus* **58 F6** 53 36N 32 0 E
Klin, *Russia* **58 D9** 56 20N 36 48 E
Klina, *Serbia & M.* **50 D4** 42 37N 20 35 E
Klinaklini →, *Canada* **142 C3** 51 21N 125 40W
Klintehamn, *Sweden* **17 G12** 57 24N 18 12 E
Klintsy, *Russia* **59 F7** 52 50N 32 10 E
Klip →, *S. Africa* **117 D4** 27 3 S 29 3 E
Klipdale, *S. Africa* **116 E2** 34 19 S 19 57 E
Klippan, *Sweden* **17 H7** 56 8N 13 10 E
Klipplaat, *S. Africa* **116 E3** 33 1 S 24 22 E
Klishkivtsi, *Ukraine* **53 B11** 48 26N 26 16 E
Klisura, *Bulgaria* **51 D8** 42 40N 24 28 E
Kljajićevo, *Serbia & M.* **52 E4** 45 45N 19 17 E
Ključ, *Bos.-H.* **45 D13** 44 32N 16 48 E
Kłobuck, *Poland* **55 H5** 50 55N 18 55 E
Klockestrand, *Sweden* **16 B11** 62 53N 17 55 E
Kłodawa, *Poland* **55 F5** 52 15N 18 55 E
Kłodzko, *Poland* **55 H3** 50 28N 16 38 E
Kløfta, *Norway* **18 D8** 60 4N 11 10 E
Klondike Goldrush △,
U.S.A. **144 E14** 59 27N 135 19W
Klong Wang Chao △,
Thailand **86 D2** 16 20N 99 9 E
Klos, *Albania* **50 E4** 41 28N 20 10 E
Klosterneuburg, *Austria* **35 C9** 48 18N 16 19 E
Klosters, *Switz.* **33 C9** 46 52N 9 52 E
Kloten, *Switz.* **33 B7** 47 27N 8 35 E
Klötze, *Germany* **30 C7** 52 37N 11 10 E
Klouto, *Togo* **113 D5** 6 57N 0 44 E
Kluane △, *Canada* **142 A1** 60 45N 139 30W
Kluane L., *Canada* **138 B6** 61 15N 138 40W
Kluang, *Malaysia* **87 L4** 2 3N 103 18 E
Kluczbork, *Poland* **55 H5** 50 58N 18 12 E
Klukhori =
Karachayevsk, *Russia* **61 J5** 43 50N 41 55 E
Klukwan, *U.S.A.* **142 B1** 59 24N 135 54W
Klungkung, *Indonesia* **79 K18** 8 32 S 115 24 E
Klyetsk, *Belarus* **59 F4** 53 5N 26 45 E
Klyuchevskaya, Gora,
Russia **67 D17** 55 50N 160 30 E
Knaben, *Norway* **18 F4** 58 40N 7 4 E
Knappavellir, *Iceland* **11 D10** 63 54N 16 36W
Knäred, *Sweden* **17 H7** 56 31N 13 19 E
Knaresborough, *U.K.* **20 C6** 54 1N 1 28W
Knarvik, *Norway* **18 D2** 60 32N 5 19 E
Knee L., *Man., Canada* **140 A1** 55 3N 94 45W
Knee L., *Sask., Canada* **143 B7** 55 51N 107 0W
Kneïss, Is., *Tunisia* **108 B2** 34 22N 10 18 E
Knezha, *Bulgaria* **51 C8** 43 30N 24 5 E
Knight I., *U.S.A.* **144 F11** 60 21N 147 45W
Knight Inlet, *Canada* **142 C3** 50 45N 125 40W
Knighton, *U.K.* **21 E4** 52 21N 3 3W
Knights Ferry, *U.S.A.* **160 H6** 37 50N 120 40W
Knights Landing,
U.S.A. **160 G5** 38 48N 121 43W
Knightstown, *U.S.A.* **157 E11** 39 48N 85 32W
Knin, *Croatia* **45 D13** 44 3N 16 17 E
Knislinge, *Sweden* **17 H8** 56 12N 14 5 E
Knittelfeld, *Austria* **34 D7** 47 13N 14 51 E
Knivsta, *Sweden* **16 E11** 59 43N 17 48 E
Knjaževac, *Serbia & M.* **50 C6** 43 35N 22 18 E
Knob, C., *Australia* **125 F2** 34 32 S 119 16 E
Knob Lake =
Schefferville, *Canada* **141 B6** 54 48N 66 50W
Knob Noster, *U.S.A.* **156 F3** 38 46N 93 33W
Knock, *Ireland* **23 C3** 53 48N 8 55W
Knockmealdown Mts.,
Ireland **23 D4** 52 14N 7 56W
Knokke-Heist, *Belgium* **24 C3** 51 21N 3 17 E
Knossós, *Greece* **39 D6** 35 16N 25 10 E
Knowlton, *Canada* **151 A12** 45 13N 72 31W
Knox, *U.S.A.* **157 C10** 41 18N 86 37W
Knox Coast, *Antarctica* **7 C8** 66 30 S 108 0 E
Knoxville, *Ga., U.S.A.* **152 C4** 32 47N 83 59W
Knoxville, *Ill., U.S.A.* **156 D6** 40 55N 90 17W
Knoxville, *Iowa, U.S.A.* **156 C4** 41 19N 93 6W
Knoxville, *Pa., U.S.A.* **150 E7** 41 57N 77 27W
Knoxville, *Tenn.,*
U.S.A. **149 H4** 35 58N 83 55W
Knud Rasmussen Land,
Greenland **10 B4** 79 0N 60 0W
Knysna, *S. Africa* **116 E3** 34 2 S 23 2 E
Knyszyn, *Poland* **54 E9** 53 20N 22 56 E
Ko Kha, *Thailand* **86 C2** 18 11N 99 24 E
Kō-Saki, *Japan* **72 C1** 34 5N 129 13 E
Ko Tarutao △,
Thailand **87 J2** 6 31N 99 26 E
Ko Yao, *Thailand* **87 a** 8 7N 98 35 E
Koartac = Quaqtaq,
Canada **139 B13** 60 55N 69 40W
Koba, *Aru, Indonesia* **83 C4** 6 37 S 134 37 E
Koba, *Bangka,*
Indonesia **84 C3** 2 26 S 106 14 E
Kobarid, *Slovenia* **45 B10** 46 15N 13 30 E
Kobayashi, *Japan* **72 F2** 31 56N 130 59 E
Kobdo = Hovd,
Mongolia **68 B4** 48 2N 91 37 E
Kobe, *Indonesia* **82 A3** 0 26N 127 54 E
Kōbe, *Japan* **73 C7** 34 45N 135 10 E
Kobelyaky, *Ukraine* **59 H8** 49 11N 34 9 E
København, *Denmark* **17 J6** 55 41N 12 34 E
København ✕ (CPH),
Denmark **17 J6** 55 37N 12 39 E
Københavns
Amtskommune □,
Denmark **17 J6** 55 42N 12 21 E
Kobenni, *Mauritania* **112 B3** 15 58N 9 24W
Kōbi-Sho, *Japan* **71 M1** 25 56N 123 41 E
Koblenz, *Germany* **31 E3** 50 21N 7 36 E
Koblenz, *Switz.* **32 A6** 47 37N 8 14 E
Kobo, *Dem. Rep. of*
the Congo **115 C3** 4 54 S 17 9 E
Kobo, *Ethiopia* **107 E4** 12 2N 39 56 E
Kobroor, *Indonesia* **83 C4** 6 10 S 134 30 E
Kobryn, *Belarus* **59 F3** 52 15N 24 22 E
Kobuchizawa, *Japan* **73 B10** 35 52N 138 19 E
Kobuk, *U.S.A.* **144 C8** 66 55N 156 52W
Kobuk →, *U.S.A.* **144 C7** 66 54N 160 38W
Kobuk Valley △,
U.S.A. **144 C8** 67 0N 160 0W
Kobuleti, *Georgia* **61 K5** 41 55N 41 45 E
Kobyletska Polyana,
Ukraine **53 B9** 48 3N 24 4 E
Kobylin, *Poland* **55 G4** 51 43N 17 12 E
Kobyłka, *Poland* **55 F8** 52 21N 21 10 E
Kobylkino, *Russia* **60 C6** 54 8N 43 56 E
Koca →, *Turkey* **51 F11** 40 8N 27 57 E
Kocabaş, *Turkey* **49 D11** 37 49N 29 20 E
Kocaeli, *Turkey* **51 F13** 40 45N 29 50 E
Kocaeli □, *Turkey* **51 F13** 40 45N 29 55 E
Kočane, *Serbia & M.* **50 C5** 43 12N 21 52 E
Kočani, *Macedonia* **50 E6** 41 55N 22 25 E
Koçarlı, *Turkey* **49 D9** 37 45N 27 43 E
Koceljevo, *Serbia & M.* **50 B3** 44 28N 19 50 E
Kočevje, *Slovenia* **45 C11** 45 39N 14 50 E
Kocgiri = Zara, *Turkey* **100 C7** 39 58N 37 43 E
Koch Bihar, *India* **90 B2** 26 22N 89 29 E
Kochang, *S. Korea* **75 G14** 35 41N 127 55 E
Kochas, *India* **93 G10** 25 15N 83 56 E
Kocher →, *Germany* **31 F5** 49 13N 9 12 E
Kochi = Cochin, *India* **95 K3** 9 58N 76 20 E
Kōchi, *Japan* **72 D5** 33 30N 133 35 E
Kōchi □, *Japan* **72 D5** 33 40N 133 30 E
Kochiu = Gejiu, *China* **76 F4** 23 20N 103 10 E
Kochkor, *Kyrgyzstan* **65 E8** 42 13N 75 46 E
Kochkor-Ata,
Kyrgyzstan **65 C6** 41 1N 72 29 E
Kock, *Poland* **55 G9** 51 38N 22 27 E
Kodaira, *Japan* **73 B11** 35 44N 139 29 E
Kodala, *India* **94 E7** 19 38N 84 57 E
Kodarma, *India* **93 G11** 24 28N 85 36 E
Koddiyar B., *Sri Lanka* **95 K5** 8 33N 81 15 E
Kode, *Sweden* **17 G5** 57 57N 11 51 E
Kodi, *Dem. Rep. of*
the Congo **114 C4** 3 34 S 22 12 E
Kodi, *Indonesia* **82 C1** 9 33 S 119 0 E
Kodiak, *U.S.A.* **144 H9** 57 47N 152 24W
Kodiak I., *U.S.A.* **144 H9** 57 30N 152 45W
Kodinar, *India* **92 J4** 20 46N 70 46 E
Kodlipet, *India* **95 H2** 12 48N 75 53 E
Kodok = Fashoda,
Sudan **107 F3** 9 50N 32 2 E
Kodok, *Sudan* **107 F3** 9 53N 32 7 E
Kodori →, *Georgia* **61 J5** 42 47N 41 10 E
Kodoro, *Dem. Rep. of*
the Congo **114 B4** 1 16N 20 6 E
Kodyma, *Ukraine* **53 B14** 48 6N 29 7 E
Koedoesberge,
S. Africa **116 E3** 32 40 S 20 11 E
Koes, *Namibia* **116 D2** 26 0 S 19 15 E
Kofarnikhon, *Tajikistan* **65 D4** 38 34N 69 1 E
Kofçaz, *Turkey* **51 E11** 41 58N 27 12 E
Koffiefontein, *S. Africa* **116 D4** 29 30 S 25 0 E
Kofiau, *Indonesia* **83 B3** 1 11 S 129 50 E
Köflach, *Austria* **34 D8** 47 4N 15 5 E
Koforidua, *Ghana* **113 D4** 6 3N 0 17W
Kōfu, *Japan* **73 B10** 35 40N 138 30 E
Koga, *Japan* **73 A11** 36 11N 139 43 E
Kogaluc →, *Canada* **141 A7** 56 12N 61 44W
Kögart, *Kyrgyzstan* **65 C7** 40 15N 74 25 E
Køge, *Denmark* **17 J6** 55 27N 12 11 E
Køge Bugt, *Denmark* **17 J6** 55 30N 12 20 E
Kogi □, *Nigeria* **113 D6** 7 45N 6 45 E
Kogin Baba, *Nigeria* **113 D7** 7 55N 11 35 E
Kogo, *Eq. Guin.* **114 B1** 1 5N 9 42 E
Koh-i-Khurd, *Afghan.* **91 B2** 33 30N 65 59 E
Koh-i-Maran, *Pakistan* **92 E2** 29 18N 66 50 E
Kohala Mts., *U.S.A.* **145 C6** 20 5N 155 45W
Kohat, *Pakistan* **91 B3** 33 40N 71 29 E
Kohima, *India* **90 C5** 25 35N 94 10 E
Kohkīlūyeh va Būyer
Aḥmadi □, *Iran* **97 D6** 31 30N 50 30 E
Kohler Ra., *Antarctica* **7 D15** 77 0 S 110 0W
Kohlfurt = Węgliniec,
Poland **55 G2** 51 18N 15 10 E
Kohlu, *Pakistan* **92 E3** 29 54N 69 15 E
Kohtla-Järve, *Estonia* **15 G22** 59 20N 27 20 E
Kohukohu, *N.Z.* **130 B2** 35 22 S 173 38 E
Kohylnyk →, *Ukraine* **53 E14** 45 49N 29 40 E
Koi Sanjaq, *Iraq* **101 D11** 36 5N 44 38 E
Koihoa, *India* **95 K11** 8 12N 93 29 E
Koilkuntla, *India* **95 G4** 15 14N 78 19 E
Koillismaa, *Finland* **14 D23** 65 44N 28 36 E
Koin-dong, *N. Korea* **75 D14** 40 28N 126 18 E
Koinare, *Bulgaria* **51 C8** 43 21N 24 8 E
Koindu, *S. Leone* **112 D2** 8 26N 10 19W
Koivisto = Primorsk,
Russia **58 B5** 60 22N 28 37 E
Kojetín, *Czech Rep.* **35 B10** 49 21N 17 20 E
Kojō, *N. Korea* **75 E14** 38 58N 127 58 E
Kojonup, *Australia* **125 F2** 33 48 S 117 10 E
Kojūr, *Iran* **97 B6** 36 23N 51 43 E
Kök-Aygyr, *Kyrgyzstan* **65 C7** 40 42N 75 32 E
Kök-Janggak,
Kyrgyzstan **65 C6** 41 2N 73 12 E
Koka, *Sudan* **106 C3** 20 5N 30 35 E
Kokand = Qŭqon,
Uzbekistan **65 C5** 40 30N 70 57 E
Kokankishlak =
Pakhtaabad,
Uzbekistan **65 C6** 40 55N 72 29 E
Kokas, *Indonesia* **83 B4** 2 42 S 132 26 E
Kokava, *Slovak Rep.* **35 C12** 48 35N 19 50 E
Kokcha →, *Afghan.* **91 A3** 37 9N 69 24 E
Kokchetav =
Kökshetaū,
Kazakhstan **66 D7** 53 20N 69 25 E
Kokemäenjoki →,
Finland **15 F19** 61 32N 21 44 E
Kokerite, *Guyana* **169 B6** 7 12N 59 35W
Kokhma, *Russia* **60 B5** 56 57N 41 8 E
Koki, *Senegal* **112 B1** 15 30N 15 59W
Kokiu = Gejiu, *China* **76 F4** 23 20N 103 10 E
Kokkilai, *Sri Lanka* **95 K5** 9 0N 80 57 E
Kokkina, *Cyprus* **39 E8** 35 11N 32 36 E
Kokkola, *Finland* **14 E20** 63 50N 23 8 E
Koko, *Nigeria* **113 C5** 11 28N 4 29 E
Koko Head, *U.S.A.* **145 K14** 21 16N 157 43W
Kokoda, *Papua N. G.* **132 E4** 8 54 S 147 47 E
Kokolopozo, *Ivory C.* **112 D3** 5 8N 6 5W
Kokomo, *U.S.A.* **157 D10** 40 29N 86 8W
Kokonau, *Indonesia* **83 B5** 4 43 S 136 26 E
Kokopo, *Papua N. G.* **132 C7** 4 22 S 152 19 E
Kokoro, *Niger* **113 C5** 14 12N 0 55 E
Koksan, *N. Korea* **75 E14** 38 46N 126 40 E
Köksaray, *Kazakhstan* **65 B4** 42 38N 68 9 E
Kökshetaū, *Kazakhstan* **66 D7** 53 20N 69 25 E
Koksoak →, *Canada* **139 C13** 58 30N 68 10W
Kokstad, *S. Africa* **117 E4** 30 32 S 29 29 E
Köksū, *Kazakhstan* **65 C4** 41 28N 68 1 E
Köktal, *Kazakhstan* **65 B5** 43 16N 70 18 E
Koktash = Leninskiy,
Tajikistan **65 D4** 38 26N 68 46 E
Kokubu, *Japan* **72 F2** 31 44N 130 46 E
Kokyar, *China* **65 E8** 37 23N 77 10 E
Kola, *Indonesia* **83 C4** 5 35 S 134 30 E
Kola, *Russia* **56 A5** 68 45N 33 8 E
Kola Pen. = Kolskiy
Poluostrov, *Russia* **56 A6** 67 30N 38 0 E
Kolachel, *India* **95 K3** 8 10N 77 15 E
Kolachi →, *Pakistan* **92 F2** 27 8N 67 2 E
Kolahoi, *India* **93 B6** 34 12N 75 22 E
Kolahun, *Liberia* **112 D2** 8 15N 10 4W
Kolaka, *Indonesia* **82 B2** 4 3 S 121 46 E
Kolar, *India* **95 H4** 13 12N 78 15 E
Kolar Gold Fields,
India **95 H4** 12 58N 78 16 E
Kolaras, *India* **92 G6** 25 14N 77 36 E
Kolari, *Finland* **14 C20** 67 20N 23 48 E
Kolarovgrad = Shumen,
Bulgaria **51 C10** 43 18N 26 55 E
Kolárovo, *Slovak Rep.* **35 D10** 47 54N 18 0 E
Kolašin, *Serbia & M.* **50 D3** 42 50N 19 31 E
Kolbäck, *Sweden* **16 E10** 59 34N 16 15 E
Kolbäcksån →, *Sweden* **16 E10** 59 36N 16 16 E
Kolbeinsstaðir, *Iceland* **11 C4** 64 59N 22 16W
Kolberg = Kołobrzeg,
Poland **54 D2** 54 10N 15 35 E
Kolbermoor, *Germany* **31 H8** 47 51N 12 4 E
Kolbu, *Norway* **18 D7** 60 39N 10 45 E
Kolbuszowa, *Poland* **55 H8** 50 15N 21 46 E
Kolchugino = Leninsk-
Kuznetskiy, *Russia* **66 D9** 54 44N 86 10 E
Kolchugino, *Russia* **58 D10** 56 17N 39 22 E
Kolda, *Senegal* **112 C2** 12 55N 14 57W
Koldegi, *Sudan* **107 E3** 12 3N 30 16 E
Kolding, *Denmark* **17 J3** 55 30N 9 29 E
Kole, *Dem. Rep. of*
the Congo **114 C4** 3 16 S 22 42 E
Koléa, *Algeria* **111 A5** 36 38N 2 46 E
Kolepom = Dolak,
Pulau, *Indonesia* **83 C5** 8 0 S 138 30 E
Kolguyev, Ostrov,
Russia **56 A8** 69 20N 48 30 E
Kolhapur, *India* **94 F2** 16 43N 74 15 E
Koli, *Ivory C.* **112 D3** 9 46N 6 28W
Koliganek, *U.S.A.* **144 G8** 59 48N 157 25W
Kolín, *Czech Rep.* **34 A8** 50 2N 15 9 E
Kolind, *Denmark* **17 H4** 56 21N 10 34 E
Kolkas rags, *Latvia* **15 H20** 57 46N 22 37 E
Kolkata, *India* **93 H13** 22 36N 88 24 E
Kolkhozobod,
Tajikistan **65 E4** 37 35N 68 40 E
Kollam = Quilon, *India* **95 K4** 8 50N 76 38 E
Kölleda, *Germany* **30 D7** 51 11N 11 15 E
Kollegal, *India* **95 H3** 12 9N 77 9 E
Kolleru L., *India* **94 F5** 16 40N 81 10 E
Kollum, *Neths.* **24 A6** 53 17N 6 10 E
Kolmanskop, *Namibia* **116 D2** 26 45 S 15 14 E
Köln, *Germany* **30 E2** 50 56N 6 57 E
Kolno, *Poland* **54 E8** 53 25N 21 56 E
Koło, *Poland* **55 F5** 52 14N 18 40 E
Koloa, *U.S.A.* **145 B2** 21 55N 159 28W
Kołobrzeg, *Poland* **54 D2** 54 10N 15 35 E
Kolochava, *Ukraine* **53 B8** 48 26N 23 41 E
Kolokani, *Mali* **112 C3** 13 35N 7 45W
Koloko, *Burkina Faso* **112 C3** 11 5N 5 19W
Kololo, *Ethiopia* **107 F5** 7 29N 41 58 E
Kolombangara,
Solomon Is. **133 M9** 8 0 S 157 5 E
Kolomna, *Russia* **58 E10** 55 8N 38 45 E
Kolomyya, *Ukraine* **53 B10** 48 31N 25 2 E
Kolondiéba, *Mali* **112 C3** 11 5N 6 54W
Kolonodale, *Indonesia* **82 B2** 2 0 S 121 19 E
Kolonowskie, *Poland* **55 H5** 50 39N 18 22 E
Kolosib, *India* **90 C4** 24 15N 92 45 E
Kolpashevo, *Russia* **66 D9** 58 20N 83 5 E
Kolpino, *Russia* **58 C6** 59 44N 30 39 E
Kolpny, *Russia* **59 F9** 52 17N 37 1 E
Kolskiy Poluostrov,
Russia **56 A6** 67 30N 38 0 E
Kolskiy Zaliv, *Russia* **56 A5** 69 23N 34 0 E
Kolsva, *Sweden* **16 E9** 59 36N 15 51 E
Kolubara →,
Serbia & M. **50 B4** 44 35N 20 15 E
Koluszki, *Poland* **55 G6** 51 45N 19 46 E
Kolwezi, *Dem. Rep. of*
the Congo **119 E2** 10 40 S 25 25 E
Kolyma →, *Russia* **67 C17** 69 30N 161 0 E
Kolymskoye Nagorye,
Russia **67 C16** 63 0N 157 0 E
Kôm Hamâda, *Egypt* **106 H7** 30 46N 30 41 E
Kôm Ombo, *Egypt* **106 C3** 24 25N 32 52 E
Komadugu Gana →,
Nigeria **113 C7** 13 5N 12 24 E
Komagane, *Japan* **73 B9** 35 44N 137 58 E
Komaki, *Japan* **73 B8** 35 17N 136 55 E
Komandorskiye Is. =
Komandorskiye
Ostrova, *Russia* **67 D17** 55 0N 167 0 E
Komandorskiye
Ostrova, *Russia* **67 D17** 55 0N 167 0 E
Komárno, *Slovak Rep.* **35 D11** 47 49N 18 5 E
Komarnyky, *Ukraine* **52 B8** 48 59N 23 3 E
Komárom, *Hungary* **52 C3** 47 43N 18 7 E
Komárom-
Esztergom □,
Hungary **52 C3** 47 35N 18 20 E
Komáromújváros =
Komárom, *Hungary* **52 C3** 47 43N 18 7 E
Komatipoort, *S. Africa* **117 D5** 25 25 S 31 55 E
Komatou Yialou,
Cyprus **39 E10** 35 25N 34 8 E
Komatsu, *Japan* **73 A8** 36 25N 136 30 E
Komatsushima, *Japan* **72 D6** 34 0N 134 35 E
Komavangard =
Sobinka, *Russia* **58 E11** 56 0N 40 0 E
Komba, *Dem. Rep. of*
the Congo **114 B4** 2 52N 24 3 E
Kombissiri,
Burkina Faso **113 C4** 12 4N 1 20W
Kombo, *Gabon* **114 C2** 0 20 S 12 22 E
Kombong, *India* **90 A5** 28 7N 94 51 E
Kombori, *Burkina Faso* **112 C4** 13 26N 3 56W
Kombóti, *Greece* **48 B3** 39 6N 21 5 E
Komen, *Slovenia* **45 C10** 45 49N 13 45 E
Komenda, *Ghana* **113 D4** 5 4N 1 28W
Komi □, *Russia* **56 B10** 64 0N 55 0 E
Kominter =
Novoshakhtinsk,
Russia **59 J10** 47 46N 39 58 E
Komintern =
Marhanets, *Ukraine* **59 J8** 47 40N 34 40 E
Komiža, *Croatia* **45 E13** 43 3N 16 11 E
Komló, *Hungary* **52 D3** 46 15N 18 16 E
Kommamur Canal,
India **95 G5** 16 0N 80 25 E
Kommunarsk =
Alchevsk, *Ukraine* **59 H10** 48 30N 38 45 E
Kommunizma, Pik,
Tajikistan **65 D6** 39 0N 72 2 E
Komodo, *Indonesia* **82 C1** 8 37 S 119 20 E
Komoé →, *Ivory C.* **112 D4** 5 12N 3 44W
Komono, *Congo* **114 C2** 3 10 S 13 20 E
Komoran, Pulau,
Indonesia **83 C5** 8 18 S 138 45 E
Komoro, *Japan* **73 A10** 36 19N 138 26 E
Komotau = Chomutov,
Czech Rep. **34 A6** 50 28N 13 23 E
Komotini, *Greece* **51 E9** 41 9N 25 26 E
Komovi, *Serbia & M.* **50 D3** 42 41N 19 39 E
Kompasberg, *S. Africa* **116 E3** 31 45 S 24 32 E
Kompong Bang,
Cambodia **87 F5** 12 24N 104 40 E
Kompong Cham,
Cambodia **87 F5** 12 0N 105 30 E
Kompong Chhnang =
Kampong Chhnang,
Cambodia **87 F5** 12 20N 104 35 E
Kompong Chikreng,
Cambodia **86 F5** 13 5N 104 18 E
Kompong Kleang,
Cambodia **86 F5** 13 6N 104 8 E
Kompong Luong,
Cambodia **87 G5** 11 49N 104 48 E
Kompong Pranak,
Cambodia **86 F5** 13 35N 104 55 E
Kompong Som =
Kampong Saom,
Cambodia **87 G4** 10 38N 103 30 E
Kompong Som,
Chhung = Kampong
Saom, Chaak,
Cambodia **87 G4** 10 50N 103 32 E
Kompong Speu,
Cambodia **87 G5** 11 26N 104 32 E
Kompong Sralau,
Cambodia **86 E5** 14 5N 105 46 E
Kompong Thom,
Cambodia **86 F5** 12 35N 104 51 E
Kompong Trabeck,
Cambodia **86 F5** 13 6N 105 14 E
Kompong Trabeck,
Cambodia **87 G5** 11 9N 105 28 E
Kompong Trach,
Cambodia **87 G5** 11 25N 105 48 E
Kompong Tralach,
Cambodia **87 G5** 11 54N 104 47 E
Komrat = Comrat,
Moldova **53 D13** 46 18N 28 40 E
Komsberg, *S. Africa* **116 E3** 32 40 S 20 45 E
Komsomolabad,
Tajikistan **65 D4** 38 50N 69 55 E
Komsomolets,
Kazakhstan **64 E9** 53 45N 62 2 E
Komsomolets, Ostrov,
Russia **67 A10** 80 30N 95 0 E
Komsomolsk, *Amur,*
Russia **67 D14** 50 30N 137 0 E
Komsomolsk, *Ivanovo,*
Russia **58 D11** 57 2N 40 20 E
Komsomolsk,
Turkmenistan **65 D1** 39 2N 63 36 E
Komsomolsk, *Russia* **60 C7** 54 27N 45 33 E
Komsomolsky =
Chirchiq, *Uzbekistan* **65 C4** 41 29N 69 35 E
Kömür Burnu, *Turkey* **49 C8** 38 39N 26 12 E
Kon Tum, *Vietnam* **86 E7** 14 24N 108 0 E
Kon Tum, Plateau du,
Vietnam **86 E7** 14 30N 108 30 E
Kona, *Mali* **112 C4** 14 57N 3 53W
Konakovo, *Russia* **58 D9** 56 40N 36 51 E
Konarak, *India* **94 E8** 19 54N 86 7 E
Konarhā □, *Afghan.* **91 B3** 34 30N 71 3 E
Konārī, *Iran* **97 D6** 28 13N 51 36 E
Konch, *India* **93 G8** 26 0N 79 10 E
Konda, *Indonesia* **83 B4** 1 34 S 131 57 E
Kondagaon, *India* **94 E5** 19 35N 81 35 E
Konde, *Tanzania* **118 C4** 4 57 S 39 45 E
Kondiá, *Greece* **49 B7** 39 49N 25 10 E
Kondinin, *Australia* **125 F2** 32 34 S 118 8 E
Kondo, *Dem. Rep. of*
the Congo **115 D2** 5 35 S 13 0 E
Kondoa, *Tanzania* **118 C4** 4 55 S 35 50 E
Kondókali, *Greece* **38 B9** 39 38N 19 51 E
Kondopaga, *Russia* **58 A8** 62 12N 34 17 E
Kondratyevo, *Russia* **67 D10** 57 22N 98 15 E
Kondrovo, *Russia* **58 E8** 54 48N 35 56 E
Konduga, *Nigeria* **113 C7** 11 35N 13 26 E
Kondukur, *India* **95 G4** 15 12N 79 57 E
Koné, *Cameroon* **114 A2** 8 50N 13 17 E
Koné, *N. Cal.* **133 U18** 21 4 S 164 52 E
Köneürgench,
Turkmenistan **66 E6** 42 19N 59 10 E
Konevo, *Russia* **58 A10** 62 8N 39 20 E
Kong = Khong →,
Cambodia **86 F5** 13 32N 105 58 E
Kong, *Ivory C.* **112 D4** 8 54N 4 36W
Kong, Koh, *Cambodia* **87 G4** 11 20N 103 0 E
Kong Christian IX
Land, *Greenland* **10 D7** 68 0N 36 0W
Kong Christian X Land,
Greenland **10 C8** 74 0N 29 0W
Kong Frederik IX
Land, *Greenland* **10 D5** 67 0N 52 0W
Kong Frederik VI Kyst,
Greenland **10 E6** 63 0N 43 0W
Kong Frederik VIII
Land, *Greenland* **10 B8** 78 30N 26 0W
Kong Karls Land,
Svalbard **10 B13** 79 0N 28 0 E
Kong Oscar Fjord,
Greenland **10 C8** 72 20N 24 0W
Kongbo, *C.A.R.* **114 B4** 4 44N 21 23 E
Kongeå →, *Denmark* **17 J2** 55 23N 8 39 E
Kongerslev, *Denmark* **17 H4** 56 54N 10 6 E
Kongju, *S. Korea* **75 F14** 36 30N 127 0 E
Kongkemul, *Indonesia* **85 B4** 1 52N 112 11 E
Konglu, *Burma* **90 B6** 27 13N 97 57 E
Kongmoon = Jiangmen,
China **77 F9** 22 32N 113 0 E
Kongola, *Namibia* **116 B3** 17 45 S 23 20 E
Kongolo, *Kasai-Or.,*
Dem. Rep. of
the Congo **118 D1** 5 26 S 24 49 E
Kongolo, *Katanga,*
Dem. Rep. of
the Congo **118 D2** 5 22 S 27 0 E
Kongor, *Sudan* **107 F3** 7 1N 31 27 E
Kongoulou, *Cameroon* **114 B2** 2 59N 11 7 E
Kongoussi,
Burkina Faso **113 C4** 13 19N 1 32W
Kongsberg, *Norway* **18 E6** 59 39N 9 39 E
Kongsvinger, *Norway* **18 D9** 60 12N 12 2 E
Kongwa, *Tanzania* **118 D4** 6 11 S 36 26 E
Koni, *Dem. Rep. of*
the Congo **119 E2** 10 40 S 27 11 E
Koni, Mts., *Dem. Rep.*
of the Congo **119 E2** 10 36 S 27 10 E
Koniakari, *Mali* **112 C2** 14 35N 10 50W
Koniecpol, *Poland* **55 H6** 50 46N 19 40 E
Königgrätz = Hradec
Králové, *Czech Rep.* **34 A8** 50 15N 15 50 E
Königs Wusterhausen,
Germany **30 C9** 52 19N 13 38 E
Königsberg = Chojna,
Poland **55 F1** 52 58N 14 25 E
Königsberg =
Kaliningrad, *Russia* **15 J19** 54 42N 20 32 E
Königsbrunn, *Germany* **31 G6** 48 16N 10 54 E
Königshütte =
Chorzów, *Poland* **55 H5** 50 18N 18 57 E
Königslutter, *Germany* **30 C6** 52 15N 10 49 E
Konin, *Poland* **55 F5** 52 12N 18 15 E
Königinhof an der
Elbe = Dvůr Králové
nad Labem,
Czech Rep. **34 A8** 50 27N 15 50 E
Konispol, *Albania* **38 B10** 39 42N 20 10 E
Konitsa, *Greece* **48 A2** 40 5N 20 48 E
Köniz, *Switz.* **32 C4** 46 56N 7 25 E
Konjic, *Bos.-H.* **52 G2** 43 42N 17 58 E
Konkiep, *Namibia* **116 D2** 26 49 S 17 15 E
Konkō, *Japan* **72 C4** 34 33N 133 36 E
Konkouré →, *Guinea* **112 D2** 9 50N 13 42W
Könnern, *Germany* **30 D7** 51 41N 11 47 E
Konnur, *India* **95 F2** 16 14N 74 49 E
Kono, *S. Leone* **112 D2** 8 30N 11 5W
Konogogo, *Papua N. G.* **132 B7** 3 29 S 152 10 E
Konolfingen, *Switz.* **32 C5** 46 54N 7 38 E
Konongo, *Ghana* **113 D4** 6 40N 1 15W
Konos, *Papua N. G.* **132 B6** 3 10 S 151 44 E
Konosha, *Russia* **58 B11** 61 0N 40 5 E
Kōnosu, *Japan* **73 A11** 36 3N 139 31 E
Konotop, *Ukraine* **59 G7** 51 12N 33 7 E
Konradshof = Skawina,
Poland **55 J6** 49 59N 19 50 E
Konsankoro, *Guinea* **112 D3** 9 2N 9 0W
Końskie, *Poland* **55 G7** 51 15N 20 23 E
Konsmo, *Norway* **18 F4** 58 16N 7 23 E
Konstadt = Wołczyn,
Poland **55 G5** 51 1N 18 3 E
Konstancin-Jeziorna,
Poland **55 F8** 52 5N 21 7 E
Konstantinograd =
Krasnohrad, *Ukraine* **59 H8** 49 27N 35 27 E
Konstantinovka =
Kostyantynivka,
Ukraine **59 H9** 48 32N 37 39 E
Konstantinovsk, *Russia* **61 G5** 47 33N 41 10 E
Konstantynów Łódzki,
Poland **55 G6** 51 45N 19 20 E
Konstanz, *Germany* **31 H5** 47 40N 9 10 E
Kont, *Iran* **97 E9** 26 55N 61 50 E
Konta, *India* **94 F5** 17 48N 81 23 E
Kontagora, *Nigeria* **113 C6** 10 23N 5 27 E
Kontcha, *Cameroon* **113 D7** 7 59N 12 15 E
Konya, *Turkey* **100 D5** 37 52N 32 35 E
Konya Ovası, *Turkey* **100 C5** 38 9N 33 5 E
Konyin, *Burma* **90 D5** 22 58N 94 42 E
Konz, *Germany* **31 F2** 49 42N 6 34 E
Konza, *Kenya* **118 C4** 1 45 S 37 7 E
Konzhakovskiy Kamen,
Gora, *Russia* **64 B7** 59 38N 59 8 E
Koo-wee-rup, *Australia* **129 E6** 38 13 S 145 28 E
Koocanusa, L., *Canada* **158 B6** 49 20N 115 15W
Kookynie, *Australia* **125 E3** 29 17 S 121 22 E
Koolau Range, *U.S.A.* **145 J14** 21 35N 157 50W
Koolyanobbing,
Australia **125 F2** 30 48 S 119 36 E
Koondrook, *Australia* **128 C6** 35 33 S 144 8 E
Koonibba, *Australia* **127 E1** 31 54 S 133 25 E
Koorawatha, *Australia* **129 C8** 34 2 S 148 33 E
Koorda, *Australia* **125 F2** 30 48 S 117 35 E
Kooskia, *U.S.A.* **158 C6** 46 9N 115 59W
Kootenay △, *Canada* **142 C5** 51 0N 116 0W
Kootenay →, *U.S.A.* **142 D5** 49 19N 117 39W
Kootenay L., *Canada* **158 B5** 49 45N 116 50W
Kootingal, *Australia* **129 A9** 31 3 S 151 4 E
Kootjieskolk, *S. Africa* **116 E3** 31 15 S 20 21 E
Kopa = Qopa,
Kazakhstan **65 B7** 43 31N 75 50 E
Kopanovka, *Russia* **61 G8** 47 28N 46 50 E
Kopaonik, *Serbia & M.* **50 C4** 43 10N 20 50 E
Kopaonik △,
Serbia & M. **50 C4** 43 20N 20 50 E
Koppargaon, *India* **94 E2** 19 51N 74 28 E
Kópasker, *Iceland* **11 A10** 66 18N 16 27W
Kópavogur, *Iceland* **11 C5** 64 6N 21 55W
Kopayhorod, *Ukraine* **53 B12** 48 52N 27 47 E
Koper, *Slovenia* **45 C10** 45 31N 13 44 E
Kopervik, *Norway* **18 E2** 59 17N 5 17 E
Kopet Dagh, *Asia* **97 B8** 38 0N 58 0 E
Kopeysk, *Russia* **64 D8** 55 7N 61 37 E
Kopi, *Australia* **127 E2** 33 24 S 135 40 E
Köping, *Sweden* **16 E10** 59 31N 16 3 E
Köpingsvik, *Sweden* **17 H10** 56 53N 16 43 E
Kopište, *Croatia* **45 F13** 42 48N 16 42 E
Koplik, *Albania* **50 D3** 42 15N 19 25 E
Köpmanholmen,
Sweden **16 A12** 63 10N 18 35 E
Koppa, *India* **95 H2** 13 33N 75 21 E
Koppal, *India* **95 G3** 15 23N 76 5 E
Koppang, *Norway* **18 C8** 61 34N 11 3 E
Kopparberg, *Sweden* **16 E9** 59 52N 15 0 E
Koppeh Dāgh = Kopet
Dagh, *Asia* **97 B8** 38 0N 58 0 E
Kopperå, *Norway* **18 A8** 63 24N 11 50 E
Koppies, *S. Africa* **117 D4** 27 20 S 27 30 E
Koppom, *Sweden* **16 E6** 59 43N 12 10 E
Koprivlen, *Bulgaria* **51 E7** 41 31N 23 53 E
Koprivnica, *Croatia* **45 B13** 46 12N 16 45 E
Kopřivnice, *Czech Rep.* **35 B11** 49 36N 18 9 E
Koprivshtitsa, *Bulgaria* **51 D8** 42 40N 24 19 E
Köprübaşı, *Turkey* **49 C10** 38 43N 28 23 E
Kopychyntsi, *Ukraine* **59 H3** 49 7N 25 58 E
Kora △, *Kenya* **118 C4** 0 14 S 38 44 E
Korab, *Macedonia* **50 E4** 41 44N 20 40 E
Korakiána, *Greece* **38 B9** 39 42N 19 45 E
Koral, *India* **92 J5** 21 50N 73 12 E
Korangal, *India* **94 E3** 17 6N 77 38 E
Koraput, *India* **94 E6** 18 50N 82 40 E
Korarou, L., *Mali* **112 B4** 15 15N 3 15W
Korba, *India* **93 H10** 22 20N 82 45 E
Korbach, *Germany* **30 D4** 51 16N 8 52 E
Korbu, G., *Malaysia* **87 K3** 4 41N 101 18 E
Korçë, *Albania* **50 F4** 40 37N 20 50 E
Korčula, *Croatia* **45 F13** 42 56N 16 57 E
Korčulanski Kanal,
Croatia **45 E13** 43 3N 16 40 E
Kord Kūy, *Iran* **97 B7** 36 48N 54 7 E
Kord Sheykh, *Iran* **97 D7** 28 31N 52 53 E
Korday, *Kazakhstan* **65 B7** 43 3N 74 43 E
Kordestan = Kurdistan,
Asia **101 D10** 37 20N 43 30 E

Kordestān □, *Iran* **96 C5** 36 0N 47 0 E
Koré Mayroua, *Niger* **113 C5** 13 18N 3 55 E
Korea, North ■, *Asia* **75 E14** 40 0N 127 0 E
Korea, South ■, *Asia* **75 G15** 36 0N 128 0 E
Korea Bay, *Korea* **75 E13** 39 0N 124 0 E
Korea Strait, *Asia* **75 H15** 34 0N 129 30 E
Koregaon, *India* **94 F2** 17 40N 74 10 E
Korem, *Ethiopia* **107 E4** 12 30N 39 32 E
Korenevo, *Russia* **59 G8** 51 27N 34 55 E
Korenica = Titova Korenica, *Croatia* **45 D12** 44 45N 15 41 E
Korenovsk, *Russia* **61 H4** 45 30N 39 22 E
Korets, *Ukraine* **59 G4** 50 40N 27 5 E
Korfantów, *Poland* **55 H4** 50 29N 17 36 E
Korgan, *Turkey* **100 B7** 40 44N 37 13 E
Korgus, *Sudan* **106 D3** 19 16N 33 29 E
Korhogo, *Ivory C.* **112 D3** 9 29N 5 28W
Koribundu, *S. Leone* **112 D2** 7 41N 11 46W
Korienzé, *Mali* **112 B4** 15 22N 3 50W
Korim, *Indonesia* **83 B5** 0 58 S 136 10 E
Korinthía □, *Greece* **48 D4** 37 50N 22 35 E
Korinthiakós Kólpos, *Greece* **48 C4** 38 16N 22 30 E
Kórinthos, *Greece* **48 D4** 37 56N 22 55 E
Korioumé, *Mali* **112 B4** 16 35N 3 0W
Koríssa, Límni, *Greece* **38 C9** 39 27N 19 53 E
Korithi, *Greece* **39 D2** 37 55N 20 42 E
Kōriyama, *Japan* **70 F10** 37 24N 140 23 E
Korkino, *Russia* **64 D8** 54 54N 61 23 E
Korkuteli, *Turkey* **49 D12** 37 4N 30 13 E
Korla, *China* **68 B3** 41 45N 86 4 E
Kormakiti, C., *Cyprus* **39 E8** 35 23N 32 56 E
Körmend, *Hungary* **52 C1** 47 5N 16 35 E
Kornat, *Croatia* **45 E12** 43 50N 15 20 E
Kornat △, *Croatia* **45 E12** 43 50N 15 12 E
Korneshty = Corneşti, *Moldova* **53 C13** 47 21N 28 1 E
Korneuburg, *Austria* **35 C9** 48 20N 16 20 E
Kórnik, *Poland* **55 F4** 52 15N 17 6 E
Kornsjø, *Norway* **18 F8** 58 57N 11 39 E
Koro, *Fiji* **133 A2** 17 19 S 179 23 E
Koro, *Ivory C.* **112 D3** 8 32N 7 30W
Koro, *Mali* **112 C4** 14 1N 2 58W
Koro Sea, *Fiji* **133 A3** 17 30 S 179 45W
Koro Toro, *Chad* **109 E3** 16 5N 18 30 E
Koroba, *Papua N. G.* **132 C2** 5 44 S 142 47 E
Korobkovo = Gubkin, *Russia* **59 G9** 51 17N 37 32 E
Korocha, *Russia* **59 G9** 50 54N 37 19 E
Köroğlu Dağları, *Turkey* **100 B5** 40 38N 33 0 E
Korogwe, *Tanzania* **118 D4** 5 5 S 38 25 E
Koroit, *Australia* **128 E5** 38 18 S 142 24 E
Koroleve, *Ukraine* **53 B8** 48 9N 23 8 E
Korolevu, *Fiji* **133 B1** 18 12 S 177 46 E
Korona, *U.S.A.* **153 F8** 29 25N 81 12W
Koronadal, *Phil.* **81 H5** 6 12N 125 1 E
Korong Vale, *Australia* **128 D5** 36 22 S 143 45 E
Koróni, *Greece* **48 E3** 36 48N 21 57 E
Korónia, Límni, *Greece* **50 F7** 40 47N 23 10 E
Koronís, *Greece* **49 D7** 37 12N 25 35 E
Koronowo, *Poland* **55 E4** 53 19N 17 55 E
Koropelé, *C.A.R.* **114 B3** 4 44N 17 11 E
Koropets, *Ukraine* **53 B10** 48 56N 25 10 E
Koror, *Palau* **134 G5** 7 20N 134 28 E
Körös →, *Hungary* **52 D5** 46 43N 20 12 E
Körös Maros △, *Hungary* **52 C5** 47 8N 20 52 E
Köröstarcsa, *Hungary* **52 D6** 46 53N 21 3 E
Korosten, *Ukraine* **59 G5** 50 54N 28 36 E
Korostyshev, *Ukraine* **59 G5** 50 19N 29 4 E
Korotoyak, *Russia* **59 G10** 51 1N 39 2 E
Korovou, *Fiji* **133 A2** 17 47 S 178 32 E
Koroyanitu △, *Fiji* **133 A1** 17 40 S 177 35 E
Korraraika, Helodranon' i, *Madag.* **117 B7** 17 45 S 43 57 E
Korsakov, *Russia* **67 E15** 46 36N 142 42 E
Korsberga, *Sweden* **17 G9** 57 19N 15 7 E
Korshiv, *Ukraine* **53 B10** 48 39N 25 1 E
Korshunovo, *Russia* **67 D12** 58 37N 110 10 E
Korsør, *Denmark* **17 J5** 55 20N 11 9 E
Korsun Shevchenkovskiy, *Ukraine* **59 H6** 49 26N 31 16 E
Korsze, *Poland* **54 D8** 54 11N 21 9 E
Korti, *Sudan* **106 D3** 18 6N 31 33 E
Kortrijk, *Belgium* **24 D3** 50 50N 3 17 E
Korucu, *Turkey* **49 B9** 39 28N 27 22 E
Korumburra, *Australia* **129 E6** 38 26 S 145 50 E
Korup △, *Cameroon* **114 A1** 5 15N 9 2 E
Korwai, *India* **92 G8** 24 7N 78 5 E
Koryakskoye Nagorye, *Russia* **67 C18** 61 0N 171 0 E
Koryŏng, *S. Korea* **75 G15** 35 44N 128 15 E
Koryukovka, *Ukraine* **59 G7** 51 46N 32 16 E
Kos, *Greece* **49 E9** 36 50N 27 15 E
Kos-Istek = Leninskoye, *Kazakhstan* **64 F6** 50 44N 57 53 E
Kosa, *Ethiopia* **107 F4** 7 50N 36 50 E
Kosa, *Russia* **64 B5** 59 56N 55 0 E
Kosa →, *Russia* **64 A5** 60 11N 55 10 E
Kosai, *Japan* **73 C9** 34 42N 137 32 E
Kosaya Gora, *Russia* **58 E9** 54 10N 37 30 E
Koschagyl, *Kazakhstan* **57 E9** 46 40N 54 0 E
Kościan, *Poland* **55 F3** 52 5N 16 40 E
Kościerzyna, *Poland* **54 D4** 54 8N 17 59 E
Kosciusko, *U.S.A.* **155 J10** 33 4N 89 35W
Kosciusko △, *Australia* **129 D8** 36 30 S 148 20 E
Kosciuszko, Mt., *Australia* **129 D8** 36 27 S 148 16 E
Kösély →, *Hungary* **52 C6** 47 25N 21 5 E
Kosgi, *Andhra Pradesh, India* **94 F3** 16 58N 77 43 E
Kosgi, *Andhra Pradesh, India* **95 G3** 15 51N 77 16 E
Kosh-Döbö, *Kyrgyzstan* **65 C7** 41 5N 74 15 E
Kosha, *Sudan* **106 C3** 20 50N 30 30 E
Koshava, *Bulgaria* **50 B7** 44 4N 23 2 E
Koshigaya, *Japan* **73 B11** 35 54N 139 48 E
K'oshih = Kashi, *China* **65 D8** 39 30N 76 2 E
Koshiki-Rettō, *Japan* **72 F1** 31 45N 129 49 E
Koshkonong L., *U.S.A.* **157 B8** 42 52N 88 58W
Kōshoku, *Japan* **73 A10** 36 38N 138 6 E
Koshrabad, *Uzbekistan* **65 C3** 40 18N 66 32 E
Koshu-Kavak = Krumovgrad, *Bulgaria* **51 E9** 41 29N 25 38 E
Kosi, *India* **92 F7** 27 48N 77 29 E
Kosi →, *India* **93 E8** 28 41N 78 57 E
Košice, *Slovak Rep.* **35 C14** 48 42N 21 15 E
Košický □, *Slovak Rep.* **35 C14** 48 45N 21 0 E
Kosiv, *Ukraine* **53 B10** 48 19N 25 6 E
Kosjerić, *Serbia & M.* **50 B3** 44 0N 19 55 E
Köşk, *Turkey* **49 D10** 37 50N 28 3 E
Koskinoú, *Greece* **38 E12** 36 23N 28 13 E
Koslan, *Russia* **56 B8** 63 34N 49 14 E
Köslin = Koszalin, *Poland* **54 D3** 54 11N 16 8 E
Kosmach, *Ukraine* **53 B9** 48 20N 24 50 E
Kosŏng, *N. Korea* **75 E15** 38 40N 128 22 E
Kosovo □, *Serbia & M.* **50 D4** 42 30N 21 0 E
Kosovo Polje, *Serbia & M.* **50 D5** 42 40N 21 5 E
Kosovska Kamenica, *Serbia & M.* **50 D5** 42 35N 21 35 E
Kosovska Mitrovica, *Serbia & M.* **50 D4** 42 54N 20 52 E
Kosrap, *China* **65 E8** 38 0N 76 12 E
Kossou, L. de, *Ivory C.* **112 D3** 6 59N 5 31W
Kosta, *Sweden* **17 H9** 56 50N 15 24 E
Kostajnica, *Croatia* **45 C13** 45 17N 16 30 E
Kostanjevica, *Slovenia* **45 C12** 45 51N 15 27 E
Kostenets = Pernik, *Bulgaria* **50 D7** 42 35N 23 2 E
Kostenets, *Bulgaria* **50 D7** 42 15N 23 52 E
Koster, *S. Africa* **116 D4** 25 52 S 26 54 E
Kôstî, *Sudan* **107 E3** 13 8N 32 43 E
Kostinbrod, *Bulgaria* **50 D7** 42 49N 23 13 E
Kostolac, *Serbia & M.* **50 B5** 44 37N 21 15 E
Kostopil, *Ukraine* **59 G4** 50 51N 26 22 E
Kostroma, *Russia* **58 D11** 57 50N 40 58 E
Kostromskoye Vdkhr., *Russia* **58 D11** 57 52N 40 49 E
Kostryzhivka, *Ukraine* **53 B10** 48 39N 25 43 E
Kostrzyn, *Lubuskie, Poland* **55 F1** 52 35N 14 39 E
Kostrzyn, *Wielkopolskie, Poland* **55 F4** 52 24N 17 14 E
Kostyantynivka, *Ukraine* **59 H9** 48 32N 37 39 E
Kostyukovichi = Kastsyukovichy, *Belarus* **58 F7** 53 20N 32 4 E
Koszalin, *Poland* **54 D3** 54 11N 16 8 E
Kőszeg, *Hungary* **52 C1** 47 23N 16 33 E
Kot Addu, *Pakistan* **91 C3** 30 30N 71 0 E
Kot Kapura, *India* **92 D6** 30 35N 74 50 E
Kot Moman, *Pakistan* **92 C5** 32 13N 73 0 E
Kot Sultan, *Pakistan* **92 D4** 30 46N 70 56 E
Kota, *India* **92 G6** 25 14N 75 49 E
Kota Barrage, *India* **92 G6** 25 6N 75 51 E
Kota Belud, *Malaysia* **85 A5** 6 21N 116 26 E
Kota Bharu, *Malaysia* **87 J4** 6 7N 102 14 E
Kota Kinabalu, *Malaysia* **85 A5** 6 0N 116 4 E
Kota Kubu Bharu, *Malaysia* **87 L3** 3 34N 101 39 E
Kota Tinggi, *Malaysia* **87 M4** 1 44N 103 53 E
Kotaagung, *Indonesia* **84 D2** 5 38 S 104 29 E
Kotabaru, *Indonesia* **85 C5** 3 20 S 116 20 E
Kotabumi, *Indonesia* **84 C2** 4 49 S 104 54 E
Kotagede, *Indonesia* **85 D4** 7 54 S 110 26 E
Kotamobagu, *Indonesia* **82 A2** 0 57N 124 31 E
Kotapad, *India* **94 E6** 19 9N 82 21 E
Kotawaringin, *Indonesia* **85 C4** 2 28 S 111 27 E
Kotchandpur, *Bangla.* **90 D2** 23 24N 89 1 E
Kotcho L., *Canada* **142 B4** 59 7N 121 12W
Kotdwara, *India* **93 E8** 29 45N 78 32 E
Kotel, *Bulgaria* **51 D10** 42 52N 26 26 E
Kotelnich, *Russia* **60 A9** 58 22N 48 24 E
Kotelnikovo, *Russia* **61 G6** 47 38N 43 8 E
Kotelnyy, Ostrov, *Russia* **67 B14** 75 10N 139 0 E
Kothagudam, *India* **94 F5** 17 30N 80 40 E
Kothapet, *India* **94 E4** 19 21N 79 28 E
Kothari →, *India* **92 G6** 25 20N 75 4 E
Köthen, *Germany* **30 D7** 51 45N 11 59 E
Kothi, *Chhattisgarh, India* **93 H10** 23 21N 82 3 E
Kothi, *Mad. P., India* **93 G9** 24 45N 80 40 E
Kotiro, *Pakistan* **92 F2** 26 17N 67 13 E
Kotka, *Finland* **15 F22** 60 28N 26 58 E
Kotlas, *Russia* **56 B8** 61 17N 46 43 E
Kotlenska Planina, *Bulgaria* **51 D10** 42 56N 26 30 E
Kotli, *Pakistan* **92 C5** 33 30N 73 55 E
Kotlik, *U.S.A.* **144 E7** 63 2N 163 33W
Kotma, *India* **93 H9** 23 12N 81 58 E
Kotmul, *Pakistan* **93 B6** 35 32N 75 10 E
Kotohira, *Japan* **72 C5** 34 11N 133 49 E
Koton-Karifi, *Nigeria* **113 D6** 8 0N 6 48 E
Kotonkoro, *Nigeria* **113 C6** 11 3N 5 58 E
Kotor, *Serbia & M.* **50 D2** 42 25N 18 47 E
Kotor Varoš, *Bos.-H.* **52 F2** 44 38N 17 22 E
Kotoriba, *Croatia* **45 B13** 46 23N 16 48 E
Kotovo, *Russia* **60 E7** 50 22N 44 45 E
Kotovsk, *Russia* **60 D5** 52 36N 41 32 E
Kotovsk, *Ukraine* **59 J5** 47 45N 29 35 E
Kotputli, *India* **92 F7** 27 43N 76 12 E
Kotri, *Pakistan* **91 D3** 25 22N 68 22 E
Kotri →, *India* **94 E5** 19 15N 80 35 E
Kótronas, *Greece* **48 E4** 36 38N 22 29 E
Kötschach-Mauthen, *Austria* **34 E6** 46 41N 13 1 E
Kottayam, *India* **95 K3** 9 35N 76 33 E
Kotto →, *C.A.R.* **114 B4** 4 14N 22 2 E
Kottur, *India* **95 J3** 10 34N 76 56 E
Kotu Group, *Tonga* **133 Q14** 20 0 S 173 35 E
Kotuy →, *Russia* **67 B11** 71 54N 102 6 E
Kotyuzhany, *Ukraine* **53 B12** 48 48N 27 42 E
Kotzebue, *U.S.A.* **144 C7** 66 53N 162 39W
Kotzebue Sound, *U.S.A.* **144 C7** 66 20N 163 0W
Kotzenau = Chocianów, *Poland* **55 G2** 51 27N 15 55 E
Kouango, *C.A.R.* **114 B4** 5 0N 20 10 E
Kouchibouguac △, *Canada* **141 C6** 46 50N 65 0W
Koudougou, *Burkina Faso* **112 C4** 12 10N 2 20W
Koufonísi, *Greece* **39 F7** 34 56N 26 8 E
Koufonísia, *Greece* **49 E7** 36 57N 25 35 E
Kougaberge, *S. Africa* **116 E3** 33 48 S 23 50 E
Kouibli, *Ivory C.* **112 D3** 7 15N 7 14W
Kouilou →, *Congo* **115 C2** 4 10 S 12 5 E
Kouki, *C.A.R.* **114 A3** 7 22N 17 3 E
Koula Moutou, *Gabon* **114 C2** 1 15 S 12 25 E
Koulen = Kulen, *Cambodia* **86 F5** 13 50N 104 40 E
Koulikoro, *Mali* **112 C3** 12 40N 7 50W
Kouloúra, *Greece* **38 B9** 39 42N 19 54 E
Koúm-bournoú, Ákra, *Greece* **38 E12** 36 15N 28 11 E
Koumac, *N. Cal.* **133 T18** 20 33 S 164 17 E
Koumala, *Australia* **126 C4** 21 38 S 149 15 E
Koumameyong, *Gabon* **114 B2** 0 11N 11 51 E
Koumankou, *Mali* **112 C3** 11 58N 6 6W
Koumbia, *Burkina Faso* **112 C4** 11 10N 3 50W
Koumbia, *Guinea* **112 C2** 11 48N 13 29W
Koumboum, *Guinea* **112 C2** 10 25N 13 0W
Koumpenntoum, *Senegal* **112 C2** 13 59N 14 34W
Koumra, *Chad* **109 G3** 8 50N 17 35 E
Koun-Fao, *Ivory C.* **112 D4** 7 30N 3 15W
Koundara, *Guinea* **112 C2** 12 29N 13 18W
Koundé, *C.A.R.* **114 A2** 6 7N 14 38 E
Koundian, *Guinea* **112 C3** 13 10N 10 35W
Koungheul, *Senegal* **112 C2** 14 0N 14 50W
Koungoulou, *Congo* **114 C2** 3 31 S 13 20 E
Kounradskiy, *Kazakhstan* **66 E8** 46 59N 75 0 E
Kountze, *U.S.A.* **155 K7** 30 22N 94 19W
Koupéla, *Burkina Faso* **113 C4** 12 11N 0 21W
Kourémalé, *Mali* **112 C3** 11 59N 8 42W
Kouris →, *Cyprus* **39 F8** 34 38N 32 54 E
Kourizo, P. de, *Chad* **108 D3** 22 28N 15 27 E
Kourou, *Fr. Guiana* **169 B7** 5 9N 52 39W
Kourouba, *Mali* **112 C2** 13 22N 10 57W
Kouroukoto, *Mali* **112 C2** 12 35N 10 5W
Kourouma, *Burkina Faso* **112 C4** 11 35N 4 50W
Kourouninkoto, *Mali* **112 C3** 13 52N 9 35W
Kouroussa, *Guinea* **112 C3** 10 45N 9 45W
Koussanar, *Senegal* **112 C2** 13 52N 14 5W
Koussané, *Mali* **112 C2** 14 53N 11 14W
Koussane, *Senegal* **112 C2** 14 10N 12 22W
Kousseri, *Cameroon* **109 F2** 12 0N 14 55 E
Koutiala, *Mali* **112 C3** 12 25N 5 23W
Kouto, *Ivory C.* **112 D3** 9 53N 6 25W
Kouts, *U.S.A.* **157 C9** 41 19N 87 2W
Kouvé, *Togo* **113 D5** 6 25N 1 25 E
Kouvola, *Finland* **15 F22** 60 52N 26 43 E
Kouyi, *Congo* **114 C2** 2 29 S 12 25 E
Kouyou →, *Congo* **114 C3** 0 44 S 16 38 E
Kovačica, *Serbia & M.* **52 E5** 45 5N 20 38 E
Kovdor, *Russia* **56 A5** 67 34N 30 24 E
Kovel, *Ukraine* **59 G3** 51 11N 24 38 E
Kovilpatti, *India* **95 K3** 9 10N 77 50 E
Kovin, *Serbia & M.* **52 F5** 44 44N 20 59 E
Kovno = Kaunas, *Lithuania* **15 J20** 54 54N 23 54 E
Kovrov, *Russia* **60 B5** 56 25N 41 25 E
Kovur, *Andhra Pradesh, India* **94 F5** 17 3N 81 39 E
Kovur, *Andhra Pradesh, India* **95 G5** 14 30N 80 1 E
Kowal, *Poland* **55 F6** 52 32N 19 7 E
Kowalewo Pomorskie, *Poland* **55 E5** 53 10N 18 52 E
Kowanyama, *Australia* **126 B3** 15 29 S 141 44 E
Kowlīnī, *Afghan.* **65 E2** 37 39N 65 58 E
Kowloon, *China* **77 F10** 22 19N 114 11 E
Kowŏn, *N. Korea* **75 E14** 39 26N 127 14 E
Kōyama, *Japan* **72 F2** 31 20N 130 56 E
Koyampattur = Coimbatore, *India* **95 J3** 11 2N 76 59 E
Köyceğiz, *Turkey* **49 E10** 36 57N 28 40 E
Köyceğiz Gölü, *Turkey* **49 E10** 36 56N 28 42 E
Koytash, *Uzbekistan* **65 C3** 40 11N 67 19 E
Koyuk, *U.S.A.* **144 D7** 64 56N 161 9W
Koyukuk, *U.S.A.* **144 D8** 64 53N 157 42W
Koyukuk →, *U.S.A.* **144 D8** 64 55N 157 32W
Koyulhisar, *Turkey* **100 B7** 40 20N 37 52 E
Koyunyeri, *Turkey* **51 F10** 40 50N 26 26 E
Koza, *Japan* **71 L3** 26 19N 127 46 E
Kozak, *Turkey* **49 B9** 39 15N 27 6 E
Kozan, *Turkey* **100 D6** 37 26N 35 50 E
Kozáni, *Greece* **50 F5** 40 19N 21 47 E
Kozáni □, *Greece* **50 F5** 40 18N 21 45 E
Kozara, *Bos.-H.* **45 D14** 45 0N 17 0 E
Kozara △, *Bos.-H.* **52 F2** 45 0N 17 0 E
Kozarac, *Bos.-H.* **45 D13** 44 58N 16 48 E
Kozelets, *Ukraine* **59 G6** 50 55N 31 7 E
Kozelsk, *Russia* **58 E8** 54 2N 35 48 E
Kozhemyaki = Pervomayskiy, *Russia* **64 F5** 51 32N 55 2 E
Kozhikode = Calicut, *India* **95 J2** 11 15N 75 43 E
Kozhva, *Russia* **56 A10** 65 10N 57 0 E
Koziegłowy, *Poland* **55 H6** 50 37N 19 8 E
Kozienice, *Poland* **55 G8** 51 35N 21 34 E
Kozje, *Slovenia* **45 B12** 46 5N 15 35 E
Kozloduy, *Bulgaria* **50 C7** 43 45N 23 42 E
Kozlov = Michurinsk, *Russia* **60 D5** 52 58N 40 27 E
Kozlovets, *Bulgaria* **51 C9** 43 30N 25 20 E
Kozlovka, *Russia* **60 C9** 55 52N 48 14 E
Kozlu, *Turkey* **100 B4** 41 26N 31 45 E
Kozluk, *Turkey* **101 C9** 38 11N 41 31 E
Koźmin, *Poland* **55 G4** 51 48N 17 27 E
Kozmodemyansk, *Russia* **60 B8** 56 20N 46 36 E
Kōzu-Shima, *Japan* **73 C11** 34 13N 139 10 E
Kożuchów, *Poland* **55 G2** 51 45N 15 31 E
Kozyatyn, *Ukraine* **59 H5** 49 45N 28 50 E
Kpabia, *Ghana* **113 D4** 9 10N 0 20W
Kpalimé, *Togo* **113 D5** 6 57N 0 44 E
Kpandae, *Ghana* **113 D4** 8 30N 0 2W
Kpessi, *Togo* **113 D5** 8 4N 1 16 E
Kra, Isthmus of = Kra, Kho Khot, *Thailand* **87 G2** 10 15N 99 30 E
Kra, Kho Khot, *Thailand* **87 G2** 10 15N 99 30 E
Kra Buri, *Thailand* **87 G2** 10 22N 98 46 E
Kraai →, *S. Africa* **116 E4** 30 40 S 26 45 E
Krabi, *Thailand* **87 H2** 8 4N 98 55 E
Kracheh, *Cambodia* **86 F6** 12 32N 106 10 E
Kragan, *Indonesia* **85 D4** 6 43 S 111 38 E
Kragerø, *Norway* **18 F8** 58 52N 9 25 E
Kragujevac, *Serbia & M.* **50 B4** 44 2N 20 56 E
Krainburg = Kranj, *Slovenia* **45 B11** 46 16N 14 22 E
Krajenka, *Poland* **55 E3** 53 18N 16 59 E
Krakatau = Rakata, Pulau, *Indonesia* **84 D3** 6 10 S 105 20 E
Krakatoa = Rakata, Pulau, *Indonesia* **84 D3** 6 10 S 105 20 E
Krakau = Kraków, *Poland* **55 H6** 50 4N 19 57 E
Krakor, *Cambodia* **86 F5** 12 32N 104 12 E
Kraków, *Poland* **55 H6** 50 4N 19 57 E
Kraków ✕ (KRK), *Poland* **55 H6** 50 5N 19 52 E
Kraksaan, *Indonesia* **85 D4** 7 43 S 113 23 E
Kralanh, *Cambodia* **86 F4** 13 35N 103 25 E
Králíky, *Czech Rep.* **35 A9** 50 6N 16 45 E
Kraljevo, *Serbia & M.* **50 C4** 43 44N 20 41 E
Kralovéhradecký □, *Czech Rep.* **34 A8** 50 25N 15 50 E
Královský Chlmec, *Slovak Rep.* **35 C14** 48 27N 22 0 E
Kralupy nad Vltavou, *Czech Rep.* **34 A7** 50 13N 14 20 E
Kramatorsk, *Ukraine* **59 H9** 48 50N 37 30 E
Kramfors, *Sweden* **16 B11** 62 55N 17 48 E
Kramis, C., *Algeria* **111 A5** 36 26N 0 45 E
Kraniá, *Greece* **50 G5** 39 53N 21 18 E
Kraniá Elassónas, *Greece* **48 B4** 39 57N 22 2 E
Kranídhion, *Greece* **48 D5** 37 20N 23 10 E
Kranj, *Slovenia* **45 B11** 46 16N 14 22 E
Kranjska Gora, *Slovenia* **45 B10** 46 29N 13 48 E
Krankskop, *S. Africa* **117 D5** 28 0 S 30 47 E
Kranz = Zelenogradsk, *Russia* **15 J19** 54 53N 20 29 E
Krapina, *Croatia* **45 B12** 46 10N 15 52 E
Krapina →, *Croatia* **45 C12** 45 50N 15 50 E
Krapkowice, *Poland* **55 H4** 50 29N 17 56 E
Krappitz = Krapkowice, *Poland* **55 H4** 50 29N 17 56 E
Kras, *Croatia* **45 C10** 45 35N 14 0 E
Krasavino, *Russia* **56 B8** 60 58N 46 29 E
Krashyy Klyuch, *Russia* **64 D6** 55 23N 56 39 E
Kraskino, *Russia* **67 E14** 42 44N 130 48 E
Krāslava, *Latvia* **58 E4** 55 54N 27 10 E
Kraslice, *Czech Rep.* **34 A5** 50 19N 12 31 E
Krasnaya Gorbatka, *Russia* **60 C5** 55 52N 41 45 E
Krasnaya Polyana, *Russia* **61 J5** 43 40N 40 13 E
Krasnaya Sloboda = Krasnoslobodsk, *Russia* **61 F7** 48 42N 44 33 E
Krasne, *Ukraine* **53 D14** 46 7N 29 15 E
Krasni Okny, *Ukraine* **53 C14** 47 32N 29 27 E
Kraśnik, *Poland* **55 H9** 50 55N 22 15 E
Krasnoarmeisk, *Ukraine* **59 H9** 48 18N 37 11 E
Krasnoarmeysk, *Russia* **60 E7** 51 0N 45 42 E
Krasnoarmeyskiy, *Russia* **61 G6** 47 0N 42 12 E
Krasnoarmeyskoye = Volnansk, *Ukraine* **59 H8** 48 2N 35 29 E
Krasnoarmeysky Rudnik = Dobropole, *Ukraine* **59 H9** 48 25N 37 2 E
Krasnobrod, *Poland* **55 H10** 50 33N 23 12 E
Krasnodar, *Russia* **61 H4** 45 5N 39 0 E
Krasnodon, *Ukraine* **59 H10** 48 17N 39 44 E
Krasnogorskiy, *Russia* **60 B9** 56 10N 48 28 E
Krasnograd = Krasnohrad, *Ukraine* **59 H8** 49 27N 35 27 E
Krasnogvardeysk = Bulungur, *Uzbekistan* **65 D3** 39 46N 67 16 E
Krasnogvardeysk = Gatchina, *Russia* **58 C6** 59 35N 30 9 E
Krasnogvardeyskiy, *Ukraine* **59 K8** 45 32N 34 16 E
Krasnogvardeyskoye, *Russia* **61 H5** 45 52N 41 33 E
Krasnohrad, *Ukraine* **59 H8** 49 27N 35 27 E
Krasnokamsk, *Russia* **64 B5** 58 4N 55 48 E
Krasnokokshaysk = Yoshkar Ola, *Russia* **60 B8** 56 38N 47 55 E
Krasnokutsk, *Ukraine* **59 G8** 50 10N 34 50 E
Krasnolesnyy, *Russia* **59 G10** 51 53N 39 35 E
Krasnoperekopsk, *Ukraine* **59 J7** 46 0N 33 54 E
Krasnorechenskiy, *Russia* **70 B7** 44 41N 135 14 E
Krasnoselkup, *Russia* **66 C9** 65 20N 82 10 E
Krasnoslobodsk, *Mordvinia, Russia* **60 C6** 54 25N 43 45 E
Krasnoslobodsk, *Volgograd, Russia* **61 F7** 48 42N 44 33 E
Krasnoturinsk, *Russia* **64 B8** 59 46N 60 12 E
Krasnoufimsk, *Russia* **64 C6** 56 36N 57 38 E
Krasnouralsk, *Russia* **64 B8** 58 21N 60 3 E
Krasnousolskiy, *Russia* **64 E6** 53 54N 56 27 E
Krasnovishersk, *Russia* **64 A6** 60 23N 57 3 E
Krasnovodsk = Türkmenbashi, *Turkmenistan* **57 G9** 40 5N 53 5 E
Krasnoyarsk, *Russia* **67 D10** 56 8N 93 0 E
Krasnoyarskiy, *Russia* **64 F7** 51 58N 59 55 E
Krasnoyarskoye, *Russia* **54 D8** 54 31N 21 56 E
Krasnoye = Krasnyy, *Russia* **58 E6** 54 25N 31 30 E
Krasnoye = Ulan Erge, *Russia* **61 G7** 46 19N 44 53 E
Krasnoye, *Russia* **64 B1** 59 15N 47 40 E
Krasnoyilsk **53 C10** 47 59N 25 38 E
Krasnozavodsk, *Russia* **58 D10** 56 27N 38 25 E
Krasnoznamensk, *Russia* **54 D9** 54 57N 22 30 E
Krasny = Kyzyl, *Russia* **67 D10** 51 50N 94 30 E
Krasny = Mozhga, *Russia* **60 B11** 56 26N 52 15 E
Krasny Boyevik = Kotovsk, *Russia* **60 D5** 52 36N 41 32 E
Krasny Sulin, *Russia* **59 J11** 47 52N 40 8 E
Krasnystaw, *Poland* **55 H10** 50 57N 23 5 E
Krasnyy, *Russia* **58 E6** 54 25N 31 30 E
Krasnyy Kholm, *Orenburg, Russia* **64 F5** 51 35N 54 9 E
Krasnyy Kholm, *Tver, Russia* **58 C9** 58 10N 37 10 E
Krasnyy Kut, *Russia* **60 E8** 50 50N 47 0 E
Krasnyy Liman, *Ukraine* **59 H9** 48 58N 37 50 E
Krasnyy Luch, *Ukraine* **59 H10** 48 13N 39 0 E
Krasnyy Profintern, *Russia* **58 D11** 57 45N 40 27 E
Krasnyy Yar, *Astrakhan, Russia* **61 G9** 46 43N 48 23 E
Krasnyy Yar, *Samara, Russia* **60 D10** 53 30N 50 22 E
Krasnyy Yar, *Volgograd, Russia* **60 E7** 50 42N 44 45 E
Krasnyye Baki, *Russia* **60 B7** 57 8N 45 10 E
Krasnyyoskolske Vdskh., *Ukraine* **59 H9** 49 27N 37 40 E
Kraszna →, *Hungary* **52 B7** 48 4N 22 20 E
Kratie = Kracheh, *Cambodia* **86 F6** 12 32N 106 10 E
Kratke Ra., *Papua N. G.* **132 D3** 6 45 S 146 0 E
Kratovo, *Macedonia* **50 D6** 42 6N 22 10 E
Krau, *Indonesia* **83 B6** 3 19 S 140 5 E
Kraulshavn = Nuussuaq, *Greenland* **10 C5** 74 8N 57 3W
Kravanh, Chuor Phnum, *Cambodia* **87 G4** 12 0N 103 32 E
Kreb es Sefia, *Algeria* **110 C3** 27 12N 7 11W
Kreb n-Naga, *Algeria* **110 C3** 27 3N 7 9W
Kreb n-Neggar, *Algeria* **110 C3** 27 20N 7 15W
Krefeld, *Germany* **30 D2** 51 20N 6 33 E
Krémaston, Límni, *Greece* **48 C3** 38 52N 21 30 E
Kremen, *Croatia* **45 D12** 44 28N 15 53 E
Kremenchuk, *Ukraine* **59 H7** 49 5N 33 25 E
Kremenchuksk Vdskh., *Ukraine* **59 H7** 49 20N 32 30 E
Kremenets, *Ukraine* **59 G3** 50 8N 25 43 E
Kremennaya, *Ukraine* **59 H10** 49 1N 38 10 E
Kremges = Svitlovodsk, *Ukraine* **59 H7** 49 2N 33 13 E
Kremmen, *Germany* **30 C9** 52 45N 13 1 E
Kremmling, *U.S.A.* **158 F10** 40 4N 106 24W
Kremnica, *Slovak Rep.* **35 C11** 48 45N 18 50 E
Krems, *Austria* **34 C8** 48 25N 15 36 E
Kremsmünster, *Austria* **34 C7** 48 3N 14 8 E
Krenau = Chrzanów, *Poland* **55 H6** 50 10N 19 21 E
Kretinga, *Lithuania* **15 J19** 55 53N 21 15 E
Krettamia, *Algeria* **110 C4** 28 47N 3 27W
Krettsy, *Russia* **58 C7** 58 15N 32 30 E
Kreuzberg, *Germany* **31 E5** 50 22N 9 58 E
Kreuzburg = Kluczbork, *Poland* **55 H5** 50 58N 18 12 E
Kreuzlingen, *Switz.* **33 A8** 47 38N 9 10 E
Kreuztal, *Germany* **30 E4** 50 57N 8 0 E
Kría Vrísi, *Greece* **50 F6** 40 41N 22 18 E
Kribi, *Cameroon* **113 E6** 2 57N 9 56 E
Krichem, *Bulgaria* **51 D8** 42 8N 24 28 E
Krichev = Krychaw, *Belarus* **58 F6** 53 40N 31 41 E
Kriens, *Switz.* **33 B6** 47 2N 8 17 E
Krim, *Slovenia* **45 C11** 45 53N 14 30 E
Krim-Krim, *Chad* **109 G3** 9 0N 15 24 E
Krindachyovka = Krasnyy Luch, *Ukraine* **59 H10** 48 13N 39 0 E
Kriós, Ákra, *Greece* **39 E4** 35 13N 23 34 E
Krishna →, *India* **95 G5** 15 57N 80 59 E
Krishnagiri, *India* **95 H4** 12 32N 78 16 E
Krishnanagar, *India* **93 H13** 23 24N 88 33 E
Krishnaraja Sagara, *India* **95 H3** 12 20N 76 30 E
Kristdala, *Sweden* **17 G10** 57 24N 16 13 E
Kristians = Oppland □, *Norway* **18 C6** 61 15N 9 40 E
Kristiansand, *Norway* **18 F5** 58 8N 8 1 E
Kristianstad, *Sweden* **17 H8** 56 2N 14 9 E
Kristiansund, *Norway* **18 A4** 63 7N 7 45 E
Kristiinankaupunki, *Finland* **15 E19** 62 16N 21 21 E
Kristinehamn, *Sweden* **16 E8** 59 18N 14 7 E
Kristinestad = Kristiinankaupunki, *Finland* **15 E19** 62 16N 21 21 E
Kristinopol = Chervonohrad, *Ukraine* **59 G3** 50 25N 24 10 E
Krithotí, Ákra, *Greece* **39 B3** 38 30N 21 2 E
Kríti, *Greece* **39 E6** 35 15N 25 0 E
Kritsá, *Greece* **39 E6** 35 10N 25 41 E
Kriva →, *Macedonia* **50 D5** 42 5N 21 47 E
Kriva Palanka, *Macedonia* **50 D6** 42 11N 22 19 E
Krivaja →, *Bos.-H.* **52 F3** 44 27N 18 9 E
Krivelj, *Serbia & M.* **50 B6** 44 10N 22 5 E
Křivoklátsko △, *Czech Rep.* **34 A6** 50 1N 13 51 E
Krivoy Rog = Kryvyy Rih, *Ukraine* **59 J7** 47 51N 33 20 E
Križevci, *Croatia* **45 B13** 46 3N 16 32 E
Krk, *Croatia* **45 C11** 45 8N 14 40 E
Krka △, *Croatia* **45 E12** 43 53N 15 56 E
Krka →, *Slovenia* **45 C12** 45 50N 15 30 E
Krkonoše, *Czech Rep.* **34 A8** 50 50N 15 35 E
Krkonoše △, *Czech Rep.* **34 A8** 50 43N 15 39 E
Krnjaja = Kljajićevo, *Serbia & M.* **52 E4** 45 45N 19 17 E
Krnov, *Czech Rep.* **35 A10** 50 5N 17 40 E
Krobia, *Poland* **55 G3** 51 47N 16 59 E
Krøderen, *Norway* **18 D6** 60 9N 9 49 E
Krokeaí, *Greece* **48 E4** 36 53N 22 32 E
Krokek, *Sweden* **17 F10** 58 40N 16 24 E
Krokodil →, *Mozam.* **117 D5** 25 14 S 32 18 E
Krokom, *Sweden* **16 A8** 63 20N 14 30 E
Krokowa, *Poland* **54 D5** 54 47N 18 9 E
Króksfjarðarnes, *Iceland* **11 B5** 65 27N 21 56W
Krokstadelva, *Norway* **18 E7** 59 56N 10 1 E
Krolevets, *Ukraine* **59 G7** 51 35N 33 20 E
Królewska Huta = Chorzów, *Poland* **55 H5** 50 18N 18 57 E
Kroměříž, *Czech Rep.* **35 B10** 49 18N 17 21 E
Krompachy, *Slovak Rep.* **35 C13** 48 54N 20 52 E
Kromy, *Russia* **59 F8** 52 48N 35 48 E
Kronach, *Germany* **31 E7** 50 14N 11 19 E
Kronau = Kranjska Gora, *Slovenia* **45 B10** 46 29N 13 48 E
Krong Kaoh Kong, *Cambodia* **78 B2** 11 35N 103 0 E
Kronobergs län □, *Sweden* **17 H8** 56 45N 14 30 E
Kronprins Christian Land, *Greenland* **10 A8** 80 30N 22 0W
Kronprins Frederik Land, *Greenland* **10 B5** 79 0N 55 0W
Kronprins Olav Kyst, *Antarctica* **7 C5** 69 0 S 42 0 E
Kronprinsesse Märtha Kyst, *Antarctica* **7 D2** 73 30 S 10 0W
Kronshtadt, *Russia* **58 C5** 59 57N 29 51 E
Kronstadt = Braşov, *Romania* **53 E10** 45 38N 25 35 E
Kroonstad, *S. Africa* **116 D4** 27 43 S 27 19 E
Kröpelin, *Germany* **30 A7** 54 4N 11 47 E
Kropotkin, *Russia* **61 H5** 45 28N 40 28 E
Kropp, *Germany* **30 A5** 54 24N 9 31 E
Krosna, *Lithuania* **54 D10** 54 23N 23 33 E
Krośniewice, *Poland* **55 F6** 52 15N 19 11 E
Krosno, *Poland* **55 J8** 49 42N 21 46 E
Krosno Odrzańskie, *Poland* **55 F2** 52 3N 15 7 E
Krotoszyn, *Poland* **55 G4** 51 42N 17 23 E
Krotovka, *Russia* **60 D10** 53 18N 51 10 E
Kroussón, *Greece* **39 E5** 35 13N 24 59 E
Krrabë, *Albania* **50 E3** 41 13N 20 0 E
Krško, *Slovenia* **45 C12** 45 57N 15 30 E
Krstača, *Serbia & M.* **50 D4** 42 57N 20 8 E
Kruger △, *S. Africa* **117 C5** 24 50 S 26 10 E
Krugersdorp, *S. Africa* **117 D4** 26 5 S 27 46 E
Kruisfontein, *S. Africa* **116 E3** 33 59 S 24 43 E
Krujë, *Albania* **50 E3** 41 32N 19 46 E
Krulevshchina = Krulyewshchyna, *Belarus* **58 E4** 55 5N 27 45 E
Krulyewshchyna, *Belarus* **58 E4** 55 5N 27 45 E
Krumbach, *Germany* **31 G6** 48 13N 10 22 E
Krumë, *Albania* **50 D4** 42 14N 20 28 E
Krummau = Český Krumlov, *Czech Rep.* **34 C7** 48 43N 14 21 E
Krummhübel = Karpacz, *Poland* **55 H2** 50 46N 15 46 E
Krumovgrad, *Bulgaria* **51 E9** 41 29N 25 38 E
Krung Thep = Bangkok, *Thailand* **86 F3** 13 45N 100 35 E
Krupanj, *Serbia & M.* **50 B3** 44 25N 19 22 E
Krupina, *Slovak Rep.* **35 C12** 48 22N 19 5 E
Krupinica →, *Slovak Rep.* **35 C11** 48 4N 18 55 E
Krupki, *Belarus* **58 E5** 54 19N 29 8 E
Krusenstern, C., *U.S.A.* **144 C7** 67 8N 163 45W
Kruševac, *Serbia & M.* **50 C5** 43 35N 21 28 E
Kruševo, *Macedonia* **50 E5** 41 23N 21 19 E
Krushchyov = Svitlovodsk, *Ukraine* **59 H7** 49 2N 33 13 E
Krushelnyksya, *Ukraine* **55 J10** 49 7N 23 29 E
Kruszwica, *Poland* **55 F5** 52 40N 18 20 E
Krychaw, *Belarus* **58 F6** 53 40N 31 41 E
Krymsk, *Russia* **59 K10** 44 50N 38 0 E
Krymskyy Poluostrov = Krymskyy Pivostriv, *Ukraine* **59 K8** 45 0N 34 0 E
Krymskyy Pivostriv, *Ukraine* **59 K8** 45 0N 34 0 E
Krynica, *Poland* **55 J7** 49 25N 20 57 E
Krynica Morska, *Poland* **54 D6** 54 23N 19 28 E
Krynki, *Poland* **55 E10** 53 17N 23 43 E
Krynychne, *Ukraine* **53 E13** 45 32N 28 40 E
Kryvyy Rih, *Ukraine* **59 J7** 47 51N 33 20 E
Kryzhopil, *Ukraine* **53 B13** 48 23N 28 53 E
Krzemieniec = Kremenets, *Ukraine* **59 G3** 50 8N 25 43 E
Krzepice, *Poland* **55 H5** 50 58N 18 50 E

Krzeszów, *Poland* **55 H9** 50 24N 22 21 E
Krzna →, *Poland* **55 F10** 52 8N 23 32 E
Krzywiń, *Poland* **55 G3** 51 58N 16 50 E
Krzyż Wielkopolski, *Poland* **55 F2** 52 52N 16 0 E
Ksabi, *Morocco* **110 B4** 32 51N 4 13W
Ksar Chellala, *Algeria* **111 A5** 35 13N 2 19 E
Ksar el Boukhari, *Algeria* **111 A5** 35 51N 2 52 E
Ksar el Kebir, *Morocco* **110 B3** 35 0N 6 0W
Ksar es Souk = Er Rachidia, *Morocco* **110 B4** 31 58N 4 20W
Ksar Rhilane, *Tunisia* **108 B1** 33 0N 9 39 E
Ksiąz Wielkopolski, *Poland* **55 F4** 52 4N 17 14 E
Ksour, Mts. des, *Algeria* **111 B4** 32 45N 0 30W
Kstovo, *Russia* **60 B7** 56 12N 44 13 E
Ku, W. el →, *Sudan* **107 E2** 13 37N 25 15 E
Ku-Ring-Gai Chase △, *Australia* **129 B9** 33 39 S 151 14 E
Ku Tree Reservoir, *U.S.A.* **145 K14** 21 30N 157 59W
Kuah, *Malaysia* **87 J2** 6 19N 99 51 E
Kuala, *Indonesia* **84 B3** 2 55N 105 47 E
Kuala Belait, *Malaysia* **85 B4** 4 35N 114 11 E
Kuala Berang, *Malaysia* **87 K4** 5 5N 103 1 E
Kuala Dungun = Dungun, *Malaysia* **87 K4** 4 45N 103 25 E
Kuala Kangsar, *Malaysia* **87 K3** 4 46N 100 56 E
Kuala Kelawang, *Malaysia* **87 L4** 2 56N 102 5 E
Kuala Kerai, *Malaysia* **87 K4** 5 30N 102 12 E
Kuala Kerian, *Malaysia* **87 c** 5 10N 100 25 E
Kuala Lipis, *Malaysia* **87 K4** 4 10N 102 3 E
Kuala Lumpur, *Malaysia* **87 L3** 3 9N 101 41 E
Kuala Nerang, *Malaysia* **87 J3** 6 16N 100 37 E
Kuala Pilah, *Malaysia* **87 L4** 2 45N 102 15 E
Kuala Rompin, *Malaysia* **87 L4** 2 49N 103 29 E
Kuala Selangor, *Malaysia* **87 L3** 3 20N 101 15 E
Kuala Sepetang, *Malaysia* **87 K3** 4 49N 100 28 E
Kuala Terengganu, *Malaysia* **87 K4** 5 20N 103 8 E
Kualajelai, *Indonesia* **85 C4** 2 58 S 110 46 E
Kualakapuas, *Indonesia* **85 C4** 2 55 S 114 20 E
Kualakurun, *Indonesia* **85 C4** 1 10 S 113 50 E
Kualapembuang, *Indonesia* **85 C4** 3 14 S 112 38 E
Kualapuu, *U.S.A.* **145 B4** 21 10N 157 2W
Kualasimpang, *Indonesia* **84 B1** 4 17N 98 3 E
Kualoa Pt., *U.S.A.* **145 J14** 21 31N 157 50W
Kuamat, *Malaysia* **85 A5** 5 13N 117 30 E
Kuancheng, *China* **75 D10** 40 37N 118 30 E
Kuandang, *Indonesia* **82 A2** 0 56N 123 1 E
Kuandian, *China* **75 D13** 40 45N 124 45 E
Kuangchou = Guangzhou, *China* **77 F9** 23 5N 113 10 E
Kuanshan, *Taiwan* **77 F13** 23 3N 121 9 E
Kuantan, *Malaysia* **87 L4** 3 49N 103 20 E
Kuapa Pond, *U.S.A.* **145 K14** 21 17N 157 43W
Kuba = Quba, *Azerbaijan* **61 K9** 41 21N 48 32 E
Kuban →, *Russia* **59 K9** 45 20N 37 30 E
Kuban Depression = Prikubanskaya Nizmennost, *Russia* **61 H4** 45 39N 38 33 E
Kubenskoye, Ozero, *Russia* **58 C10** 59 40N 39 25 E
Kuberle = Krasnoarmeyskiy, *Russia* **61 G6** 47 0N 42 12 E
Küblis, *Switz.* **33 C9** 46 54N 9 45 E
Kubokawa, *Japan* **72 D5** 33 12N 133 8 E
Kubor, Mt., *Papua N. G.* **132 D3** 6 10 S 144 44 E
Kubrat, *Bulgaria* **51 C10** 43 49N 26 31 E
Kubu, *Indonesia* **79 J18** 8 16 S 115 35 E
Kubutambahan, *Indonesia* **79 J18** 8 5 S 115 10 E
Kucar, Tanjung, *Indonesia* **79 K18** 8 39 S 114 34 E
Kučevo, *Serbia & M.* **50 B5** 44 30N 21 40 E
Kucha Gompa, *India* **93 B7** 34 25N 76 56 E
Kuchaman, *India* **92 F6** 27 13N 74 47 E
Kuchchaveli, *Sri Lanka* **95 K5** 8 49N 81 6 E
Kuchenspitze, *Austria* **34 D3** 47 7N 10 12 E
Kuchinda, *India* **93 J11** 21 44N 84 21 E
Kuching, *Malaysia* **85 B4** 1 33N 110 25 E
Kuchino-eruba-Jima, *Japan* **71 J5** 30 28N 130 12 E
Kuchino-Shima, *Japan* **71 K4** 29 57N 129 55 E
Kuchinotsu, *Japan* **72 E2** 32 36N 130 11 E
Kuchl, *Austria* **34 D6** 47 37N 13 9 E
Kūchnay Darvīshān, *Afghan.* **91 C2** 30 59N 64 10 E
Kuchurhan →, *Ukraine* **53 D14** 46 33N 29 57 E
Kucing = Kuching, *Malaysia* **85 B4** 1 33N 110 25 E
Kuçovë, *Albania* **50 F3** 40 47N 19 57 E
Küçükbahçe, *Turkey* **49 C8** 38 33N 26 24 E
Küçükköy, *Turkey* **49 B8** 39 16N 26 42 E
Küçükkuyu, *Turkey* **49 B8** 39 32N 26 36 E
Küçükmenderes →, *Turkey* **49 D9** 37 57N 27 16 E
Kud →, *Pakistan* **92 F2** 26 5N 66 20 E
Kudal, *India* **95 F1** 16 2N 73 41 E
Kudalier →, *India* **94 E4** 18 35N 79 48 E
Kudamatsu, *Japan* **72 D3** 34 0N 131 52 E
Kudara, *Tajikistan* **65 D6** 38 25N 72 39 E
Kudat, *Malaysia* **85 A5** 6 55N 116 55 E
Kudelka = Asbest, *Russia* **64 C8** 57 0N 61 30 E
Kudirkos Naumiestis, *Lithuania* **54 D9** 54 46N 22 53 E
Kudowa-Zdrój, *Poland* **55 H3** 50 27N 16 15 E
Kudremukh, *India* **95 H2** 13 15N 75 20 E
Kudus, *Indonesia* **85 D4** 6 48 S 110 51 E
Kudymkar, *Russia* **64 B5** 59 1N 54 39 E
Kueiyang = Guiyang, *China* **76 D6** 26 32N 106 40 E
Kufra Oasis = Al Kufrah, *Libya* **108 D4** 24 17N 23 15 E
Kufstein, *Austria* **34 D5** 47 35N 12 11 E
Kugaaruk = Pelly Bay, *Canada* **139 B11** 68 38N 89 50W
Kugluktuk, *Canada* **138 B8** 67 50N 115 5W
Kugong I., *Canada* **140 A4** 56 18N 79 50W
Kūhak, *Iran* **91 D1** 27 12N 63 10 E
Kuhan, *Pakistan* **92 E2** 28 19N 67 14 E
Kūhbonān, *Iran* **97 D8** 31 23N 56 19 E
Kūhestak, *Iran* **97 E8** 26 47N 57 2 E
Kūhestān, *Afghan.* **91 B1** 34 39N 61 12 E
Kuhin, *Iran* **97 B6** 36 22N 49 40 E
Kūhīrī, *Iran* **97 E9** 26 55N 61 2 E
Kuhnsdorf, *Austria* **34 E7** 46 37N 14 38 E
Kūhpāyeh, *Eşfahan, Iran* **97 C7** 32 44N 52 20 E
Kūhpāyeh, *Kermān, Iran* **97 D8** 30 35N 57 15 E
Kūhrān, Kūh-e, *Iran* **97 E8** 26 46N 58 12 E
Kui Buri, *Thailand* **87 F2** 12 3N 99 52 E
Kuichong, *China* **69 F11** 22 38N 114 25 E
Kuiseb →, *Namibia* **116 C1** 22 59 S 14 31 E
Kuito, *Angola* **115 E3** 12 22 S 16 55 E
Kuiu I., *U.S.A.* **142 B2** 57 45N 134 10W
Kujang, *N. Korea* **75 E14** 39 57N 126 1 E
Kujawsko-Pomorskie □, *Poland* **54 E5** 53 20N 18 30 E
Kuji, *Japan* **70 D10** 40 11N 141 46 E
Kujū-San, *Japan* **72 D3** 33 5N 131 15 E
Kukarka = Sovetsk, *Russia* **60 B9** 57 38N 48 53 E
Kukava, *Ukraine* **53 B12** 48 37N 27 43 E
Kukavica, *Serbia & M.* **50 D5** 42 48N 21 57 E
Kukawa, *Nigeria* **113 C7** 12 58N 13 27 E
Kukës, *Albania* **50 D4** 42 5N 20 27 E
Kuki, *Japan* **73 A11** 36 4N 139 40 E
Kukipi, *Papua N. G.* **132 E4** 8 10 S 146 6 E
Kukmor, *Russia* **60 B10** 56 11N 50 54 E
Kükong = Shaoguan, *China* **77 E9** 24 48N 113 35 E
Kukuihaele, *U.S.A.* **145 C6** 20 5N 155 35W
Kukup, *Malaysia* **87 d** 1 20N 103 27 E
Kukup, Pulau, *Malaysia* **87 d** 1 18N 103 25 E
Kukvidze, *Russia* **60 E6** 50 40N 43 0 E
Kula, *Bulgaria* **50 C6** 43 52N 22 36 E
Kula, *Serbia & M.* **52 E4** 45 37N 19 32 E
Kula, *Turkey* **49 C10** 38 32N 28 40 E
Kula Gulf, *Solomon Is.* **133 M9** 8 5 S 157 18 E
Kulachi, *Pakistan* **92 D4** 31 56N 70 27 E
Kulai, *Malaysia* **87 M4** 1 44N 103 35 E
Kulaly, Ostrov, *Kazakhstan* **61 H10** 45 0N 50 0 E
Kulanak, *Kyrgyzstan* **65 C7** 41 22N 75 30 E
Kulasekarappattinam, *India* **95 K4** 8 20N 78 5 E
Kulassein I., *Phil.* **81 H3** 6 25N 120 41 E
Kulaura, *Bangla.* **90 C4** 24 32N 92 3 E
Kulautuva, *Lithuania* **54 D10** 54 56N 23 36 E
Kuldīga, *Latvia* **15 H19** 56 58N 21 59 E
Kuldīga □, *Latvia* **54 B8** 56 55N 22 0 E
Kuldja = Yining, *China* **66 E9** 43 58N 81 10 E
Kuldu, *Sudan* **107 E2** 12 50N 28 30 E
Kulebaki, *Russia* **60 C6** 55 22N 42 25 E
Kulen, *Cambodia* **86 F5** 13 50N 104 40 E
Kulen Vakuf, *Bos.-H.* **45 D13** 44 35N 16 2 E
Kulgam, *India* **93 C6** 33 36N 75 2 E
Kulgera, *Australia* **126 D1** 25 50 S 133 18 E
Kulim, *Malaysia* **87 K3** 5 22N 100 34 E
Kulin, *Australia* **125 F2** 32 40 S 118 2 E
Kulittalai, *India* **95 J4** 10 55N 78 25 E
Kulkayu = Hartley Bay, *Canada* **142 C3** 53 25N 129 15W
Kullen, *Sweden* **17 H6** 56 18N 12 26 E
Kulma Pass, *Asia* **65 D7** 38 5N 74 50 E
Kulmbach, *Germany* **31 E7** 50 6N 11 26 E
Kŭlob, *Tajikistan* **65 E4** 37 55N 69 50 E
Kulp, *Turkey* **101 C9** 38 29N 41 2 E
Kulpawn →, *Ghana* **113 D4** 10 20N 1 5W
Kulsary, *Kazakhstan* **57 E9** 46 59N 54 1 E
Kulti, *India* **93 H12** 23 43N 86 50 E
Kulu, *India* **92 D7** 31 58N 77 6 E
Kulu, *Turkey* **100 C5** 39 5N 33 4 E
Kulumadau, *Papua N. G.* **132 E7** 9 3 S 152 43 E
Kulumbura, *Australia* **124 B4** 13 55 S 126 35 E
Kulunda, *Russia* **66 D8** 52 35N 78 57 E
Kulungar, *Afghan.* **92 C3** 34 0N 69 2 E
Kūlvand, *Iran* **97 D7** 31 21N 54 35 E
Kulwin, *Australia* **128 C5** 35 0 S 142 42 E
Kulyab = Kŭlob, *Tajikistan* **65 E4** 37 55N 69 50 E
Kuma, *Japan* **72 D4** 33 39N 132 54 E
Kuma →, *Russia* **61 H8** 44 55N 47 0 E
Kumafşarı, *Turkey* **49 D11** 37 19N 29 32 E
Kumaganum, *Nigeria* **113 C7** 13 8N 10 38 E
Kumagaya, *Japan* **73 A11** 36 9N 139 22 E
Kumai, *Indonesia* **85 C4** 2 44 S 111 43 E
Kumak, *Russia* **64 F8** 51 10N 60 8 E
Kumalar Dağı, *Turkey* **49 C12** 38 15N 30 20 E
Kumamba, Kepulauan, *Indonesia* **83 B5** 1 36 S 138 45 E
Kumamoto, *Japan* **72 E2** 32 45N 130 45 E
Kumamoto □, *Japan* **72 E2** 32 55N 130 55 E
Kumano, *Japan* **73 D8** 33 54N 136 5 E
Kumano-Nada, *Japan* **73 D8** 33 47N 136 20 E
Kumanovo, *Macedonia* **50 D5** 42 9N 21 42 E
Kumar →, *Afghan.* **91 B3** 34 30N 70 28 E
Kumara, *N.Z.* **131 C6** 42 37 S 171 12 E
Kumarina, *Australia* **125 D2** 24 41 S 119 32 E
Kumarkhali, *Bangla.* **90 D2** 23 51N 89 15 E
Kumasi, *Ghana* **112 D4** 6 41N 1 38W
Kumba, *Cameroon* **113 E6** 4 36N 9 24 E
Kumbağ, *Turkey* **51 F11** 40 51N 27 27 E
Kumbakonam, *India* **95 J4** 10 58N 79 25 E
Kumbarilla, *Australia* **127 D5** 27 15 S 150 55 E
Kumbe, *Indonesia* **83 C6** 8 21 S 140 13 E
Kumbhraj, *India* **92 G7** 24 22N 77 3 E
Kumbia, *Australia* **127 D5** 26 41 S 151 39 E
Kumbo, *Cameroon* **113 D7** 6 15N 10 36 E
Kumbukkan Oya →, *Sri Lanka* **95 L5** 6 35N 81 40 E
Kŭmch'ŏn, *N. Korea* **75 E14** 38 10N 126 29 E
Kumdah, *Si. Arabia* **98 B4** 20 23N 45 5 E
Kumdok, *India* **93 C8** 33 32N 78 10 E
Kume-Shima, *Japan* **71 L3** 26 20N 126 47 E
Kumeny, *Russia* **60 A9** 58 10N 49 47 E
Kumertau, *Russia* **64 E5** 52 45N 55 57 E
Kumharsain, *India* **92 D7** 31 19N 77 27 E
Kŭmhwa, *S. Korea* **75 E14** 38 17N 127 28 E
Kumi, *Uganda* **118 B3** 1 30N 33 58 E
Kumkale, *Turkey* **51 G10** 39 59N 26 11 E
Kumkurgan = Qumqŭrghan, *Uzbekistan* **65 E3** 37 49N 67 35 E
Kumla, *Sweden* **16 E9** 59 8N 15 10 E
Kumluca, *Turkey* **49 E12** 36 22N 30 20 E
Kummerower See, *Germany* **30 B8** 53 49N 12 51 E
Kumo, *Nigeria* **113 C7** 10 1N 11 12 E
Kumo älv = Kokemäenjoki →, *Finland* **15 F19** 61 32N 21 44 E
Kumon Bum, *Burma* **90 B6** 26 30N 97 15 E
Kumotori-Yama, *Japan* **73 B10** 35 51N 138 57 E
Kumta, *India* **95 G2** 14 29N 74 25 E
Kumukahi, C., *U.S.A.* **145 D7** 19 31N 154 49W
Kumusi →, *Papua N. G.* **132 E5** 8 16 S 148 13 E
Kumylzhenskaya, *Russia* **60 F6** 49 51N 42 38 E
Kunágota, *Hungary* **52 D6** 46 26N 21 3 E
Kunak, *Malaysia* **85 B5** 4 41N 118 15 E
Kunashir, Ostrov, *Russia* **67 E15** 44 0N 146 0 E
Kunchaung, *Burma* **90 D6** 23 50N 96 35 E
Kunda, *Estonia* **15 G22** 59 30N 26 34 E
Kunda, *India* **93 G9** 25 43N 81 31 E
Kundar →, *Pakistan* **92 D3** 31 56N 69 19 E
Kundelungu △, *Dem. Rep. of the Congo* **119 E2** 10 30 S 27 40 E
Kundelungu Ouest △, *Dem. Rep. of the Congo* **119 D2** 9 55 S 27 17 E
Kundian, *Pakistan* **92 C4** 32 27N 71 28 E
Kundiawa, *Papua N. G.* **132 D3** 6 2 S 145 1 E
Kundla, *India* **92 J4** 21 21N 71 25 E
Kundur, *Indonesia* **84 C3** 3 8 S 107 48 E
Kung, Ao, *Thailand* **87 a** 8 5N 98 24 E
Kunga →, *Bangla.* **90 E2** 21 46N 89 30 E
Kungälv, *Sweden* **17 G5** 57 53N 11 59 E
Kunghit I., *Canada* **142 C2** 52 6N 131 3W
Kungrad = Qŭnghirot, *Uzbekistan* **66 E6** 43 6N 58 54 E
Kungsängen, *Sweden* **16 E11** 59 29N 17 45 E
Kungsbacka, *Sweden* **17 G6** 57 30N 12 5 E
Kungsgården, *Sweden* **16 D10** 60 37N 16 35 E
Kungshamn, *Sweden* **17 F5** 58 22N 11 15 E
Kungsör, *Sweden* **16 E10** 59 25N 16 5 E
Kungu, *Dem. Rep. of the Congo* **114 B3** 2 47N 19 12 E
Kungur, *Russia* **64 C6** 57 25N 56 57 E
Kungurri, *Australia* **126 K6** 21 4 S 148 45 E
Kungyangon, *Burma* **90 G6** 16 27N 96 20 E
Kunhar →, *Pakistan* **93 B5** 34 20N 73 30 E
Kunhegyes, *Hungary* **52 C5** 47 22N 20 36 E
Kunia, *U.S.A.* **145 K13** 21 28N 158 4W
Kunimi-Dake, *Japan* **72 E3** 32 33N 131 1 E
Kuningan, *Indonesia* **85 D3** 6 59 S 108 29 E
Kunisaki, *Japan* **72 D3** 33 33N 131 45 E
Kunjirap Daban, *Pakistan* **65 E7** 36 52N 75 27 E
Kunlara, *Australia* **128 C3** 34 54 S 139 55 E
Kunlong, *Burma* **76 F2** 23 20N 98 50 E
Kunlun Shan, *Asia* **68 C3** 36 0N 86 30 E
Kunmadaras, *Hungary* **52 C5** 47 28N 20 45 E
Kunming, *China* **76 E4** 25 1N 102 41 E
Kunnamkulam, *India* **95 J3** 10 38N 76 7 E
Kunów, *Poland* **55 H8** 50 57N 21 17 E
Kunsan, *S. Korea* **75 G14** 35 59N 126 45 E
Kunshan, *China* **77 B13** 31 22N 120 58 E
Kunszentmárton, *Hungary* **52 D5** 46 50N 20 20 E
Kunszentmiklós, *Hungary* **52 C4** 47 2N 19 8 E
Kuntaur, *Senegal* **112 C2** 13 40N 14 48W
Kunua, *Papua N. G.* **132 C8** 5 46 S 154 43 E
Kununurra, *Australia* **124 C4** 15 40 S 128 50 E
Kunwari →, *India* **93 F8** 26 26N 79 11 E
Kunya-Urgench = Köneürgench, *Turkmenistan* **66 E6** 42 19N 59 10 E
Künzelsau, *Germany* **31 F5** 49 17N 9 42 E
Kunzulu, *Dem. Rep. of the Congo* **114 C3** 3 28 S 16 12 E
Kuopio, *Finland* **14 E22** 62 53N 27 35 E
Kupa →, *Croatia* **45 C13** 45 28N 16 24 E
Kupang, *Indonesia* **82 D2** 10 19 S 123 39 E
Kupiano, *Papua N. G.* **132 F5** 10 4 S 148 14 E
Kupreanof I., *U.S.A.* **142 B2** 56 50N 133 30W
Kupres, *Bos.-H.* **52 G2** 43 56N 17 15 E
Kupyansk, *Ukraine* **59 H9** 49 52N 37 35 E
Kupyansk-Uzlovoi, *Ukraine* **59 H9** 49 40N 37 43 E
Kuqa, *China* **68 B3** 41 35N 82 30 E
Kur, *Indonesia* **83 C4** 5 20 S 132 0 E
Kür →, *Azerbaijan* **101 C13** 39 29N 49 15 E
Kur →, *Bhutan* **90 B3** 26 50N 91 0 E
Kür Dili, *Azerbaijan* **97 B6** 39 3N 49 13 E
Kura = Kür →, *Azerbaijan* **101 C13** 39 29N 49 15 E
Kurahashi-Jima, *Japan* **72 C4** 34 8N 132 31 E
Kuranda, *Australia* **126 B4** 16 48 S 145 35 E
Kuranga, *India* **92 H3** 22 4N 69 10 E
Kurashiki, *Japan* **72 C5** 34 40N 133 50 E
Kurayoshi, *Japan* **72 B5** 35 26N 133 50 E
Kürdämir, *Azerbaijan* **61 K9** 40 25N 48 3 E
Kurday = Qorday, *Kazakhstan* **65 B7** 43 21N 74 59 E
Kurdistan, *Asia* **101 D10** 37 20N 43 30 E
Kurduvadi, *India* **94 E2** 18 8N 75 29 E
Kŭrdzhali, *Bulgaria* **51 E9** 41 38N 25 21 E
Kure, *Japan* **72 C4** 34 14N 132 32 E
Küre, *Turkey* **100 B5** 41 48N 33 43 E
Küre Dağları, *Turkey* **100 B6** 41 50N 34 10 E
Kure I., *U.S.A.* **145 F8** 28 25N 178 25W
Kuressaare, *Estonia* **15 G20** 58 15N 22 30 E
Kurgan, *Russia* **66 D7** 55 26N 65 18 E
Kurgan-Tyube = Qŭrghonteppa, *Tajikistan* **65 E4** 37 50N 68 47 E
Kurganinsk, *Russia* **61 H5** 44 54N 40 34 E
Kurgannaya = Kurganinsk, *Russia* **61 H5** 44 54N 40 34 E
Kuri, *India* **92 F4** 26 37N 70 43 E
Kuria Maria Is. = Khurīyā Murīyā, Jazā'ir, *Oman* **99 C6** 17 30N 55 58 E
Kurichchi, *India* **95 J3** 11 36N 77 35 E
Kuridala, *Australia* **126 C3** 21 16 S 140 29 E
Kurigram, *Bangla.* **90 C2** 25 49N 89 39 E
Kurik, *Indonesia* **83 C5** 8 9 S 139 59 E
Kurikka, *Finland* **15 E20** 62 36N 22 24 E
Kuril Is. = Kurilskiye Ostrova, *Russia* **67 E15** 45 0N 150 0 E
Kuril Trench, *Pac. Oc.* **62 E19** 44 0N 153 0 E
Kurilsk, *Russia* **67 E15** 45 14N 147 53 E
Kurilskiye Ostrova, *Russia* **67 E15** 45 0N 150 0 E
Kurino, *Japan* **72 F2** 31 57N 130 43 E
Kurinskaya Kosa = Kür Dili, *Azerbaijan* **97 B6** 39 3N 49 13 E
Kurisches Haff = Kurshskiy Zaliv, *Russia* **15 J19** 55 9N 21 6 E
Kurkheda, *India* **94 D5** 20 37N 80 12 E
Kurkur, *Egypt* **106 C3** 23 50N 32 0 E
Kurla, *India* **94 E1** 19 5N 72 52 E
Kurlovskiy, *Russia* **60 C5** 55 25N 40 40 E
Kurmuk, *Sudan* **107 E3** 10 33N 34 21 E
Kurnool, *India* **95 G4** 15 45N 78 0 E
Kuro-Shima, *Kagoshima, Japan* **71 J4** 30 50N 129 57 E
Kuro-Shima, *Okinawa, Japan* **71 M2** 24 14N 124 1 E
Kurobe-Gawe →, *Japan* **73 A9** 36 55N 137 25 E
Kurogi, *Japan* **72 D2** 33 12N 130 40 E
Kuror, J., *Sudan* **106 C3** 20 27N 31 30 E
Kurow, *N.Z.* **131 E5** 44 44 S 170 29 E
Kurów, *Poland* **55 G9** 51 23N 22 12 E
Kurrajong, *Australia* **129 B9** 33 33 S 150 42 E
Kurram →, *Pakistan* **91 B3** 32 36N 71 20 E
Kurri Kurri, *Australia* **129 B9** 32 50 S 151 28 E
Kurrimine, *Australia* **126 B4** 17 47 S 146 6 E
Kursavka, *Russia* **61 H6** 44 29N 42 32 E
Kurse Korhi, *India* **94 D5** 20 14N 80 46 E
Kurshskaya Kosa ⌓, *Russia* **54 C7** 55 7N 20 45 E
Kurshskiy Zaliv, *Russia* **15 J19** 55 9N 21 6 E
Kuršių Nerijos △, *Lithuania* **54 C8** 55 30N 21 6 E
Kursk, *Russia* **59 G9** 51 42N 36 11 E
Kursu = Salla, *Finland* **14 C23** 66 50N 28 49 E
Kuršumlija, *Serbia & M.* **50 C5** 43 9N 21 19 E
Kuršumlijska Banja, *Serbia & M.* **50 C5** 43 3N 21 11 E
Kurşunlu, *Bursa, Turkey* **51 F13** 40 3N 29 40 E
Kurşunlu, *Çankırı, Turkey* **100 B5** 40 51N 33 15 E
Kurtalan, *Turkey* **101 D9** 37 56N 41 44 E
Kurtbey, *Turkey* **51 E10** 41 9N 26 35 E
Kürti →, *Kazakhstan* **65 A8** 44 16N 76 42 E
Kurtistown, *U.S.A.* **145 D6** 19 36N 155 4W
Kuru, *Sudan* **107 F2** 7 43N 26 31 E
Kuru, Bahr el →, *Sudan* **107 F2** 8 10N 26 50 E
Kurucaşile, *Turkey* **100 B5** 41 49N 32 42 E
Kuruçay, *Turkey* **96 B3** 39 39N 38 29 E
Kuruktag, *China* **68 B3** 41 0N 89 0 E
Kuruman, *S. Africa* **116 D3** 27 28 S 23 28 E
Kuruman →, *S. Africa* **116 D3** 26 56 S 20 39 E
Kurume, *Japan* **72 D2** 33 15N 130 30 E
Kurun →, *Sudan* **107 F3** 5 30N 34 17 E
Kurunegala, *Sri Lanka* **95 L5** 7 30N 80 23 E
Kurupukari, *Guyana* **169 C6** 4 43N 58 37W
Kurya, *Russia* **56 B10** 61 42N 57 9 E
Kus Gölü, *Turkey* **51 F11** 40 10N 27 55 E
Kusa, *Russia* **64 D7** 55 20N 59 29 E
Kuşadası, *Turkey* **100 D2** 37 52N 27 15 E
Kuşadası Körfezı, *Turkey* **49 D8** 37 56N 27 0 E
Kusamba, *Indonesia* **79 K18** 8 34 S 115 27 E
Kusatsu, *Gumma, Japan* **73 A10** 36 37N 138 36 E
Kusatsu, *Shiga, Japan* **73 C7** 34 58N 135 57 E
Kusawa L., *Canada* **142 A1** 60 20N 136 13W
Kusel, *Germany* **31 F3** 49 32N 7 24 E
Kushaka, *Nigeria* **113 C6** 10 32N 6 48 E
Kushalgarh, *India* **92 H6** 23 10N 74 27 E
Kushalnagar, *India* **95 H2** 12 14N 75 57 E
Kushchevskaya, *Russia* **61 G4** 46 33N 39 35 E
Kusheriki, *Nigeria* **113 C6** 10 33N 6 28 E
Kushikino, *Japan* **72 F2** 31 44N 130 16 E
Kushima, *Japan* **72 F3** 31 29N 131 14 E
Kushimoto, *Japan* **73 D7** 33 28N 135 47 E
Kushiro, *Japan* **70 C12** 43 0N 144 25 E
Kushiro-Gawa →, *Japan* **70 C12** 42 59N 144 23 E
Kushiro Shitsugen △, *Japan* **70 C12** 43 9N 144 26 E
Kūshk, *Iran* **97 D8** 28 46N 56 51 E
Kushka = Gushgy, *Turkmenistan* **66 F7** 35 20N 62 18 E
Kūshkī, *Iran* **96 C5** 33 31N 47 13 E
Kushnarenkovo, *Russia* **64 D5** 55 6N 55 22 E
Kushnytsya, *Ukraine* **53 B8** 48 27N 23 15 E
Kushol, *India* **93 C7** 33 40N 76 36 E
Kushrabat = Koshrabad, *Uzbekistan* **65 C3** 40 18N 66 32 E
Kushtia, *Bangla.* **90 D2** 23 55N 89 5 E
Kushum →, *Kazakhstan* **60 F10** 49 20N 50 30 E
Kushva, *Russia* **64 B7** 58 18N 59 45 E
Kuskokwim →, *U.S.A.* **144 F7** 60 5N 162 25W
Kuskokwim B., *U.S.A.* **144 G7** 59 45N 162 25W
Kuskokwim Mts., *U.S.A.* **144 E9** 62 30N 156 0W
Kusmi, *India* **93 H10** 23 17N 83 55 E
Küsnacht, *Switz.* **33 B7** 47 19N 8 35 E
Kussharo-Ko, *Japan* **70 C12** 43 38N 144 21 E
Küssnacht, *Switz.* **33 B6** 47 5N 8 26 E
Kustanay = Qostanay, *Kazakhstan* **66 D7** 53 10N 63 35 E
Küstenje = Constanţa, *Romania* **53 F13** 44 14N 28 38 E
Küstrin = Kostrzyn, *Poland* **55 F1** 52 35N 14 39 E
Kusu, *Indonesia* **82 A3** 0 53N 127 43 E
Kusu, *Japan* **72 D3** 33 16N 131 9 E
Kut, Ko, *Thailand* **87 G4** 11 40N 102 35 E
Kuta, *Indonesia* **79 K18** 8 43 S 115 11 E
Kutacane, *Indonesia* **84 B1** 3 50N 97 50 E
Kütahya, *Turkey* **49 B12** 39 30N 30 2 E
Kütahya □, *Turkey* **49 B11** 39 10N 29 30 E
Kutaisi, *Georgia* **61 J6** 42 19N 42 40 E
Kutaraja = Banda Aceh, *Indonesia* **84 A1** 5 35N 95 20 E
Kutch, Gulf of = Kachchh, Gulf of, *India* **92 H3** 22 50N 69 15 E
Kutch, Rann of = Kachchh, Rann of, *India* **92 H4** 24 0N 70 0 E
Kutina, *Croatia* **45 C13** 45 29N 16 48 E
Kutiyana, *India* **92 J4** 21 36N 70 2 E
Kutjevo, *Croatia* **52 E2** 45 23N 17 55 E
Kutkai, *Burma* **90 D6** 23 27N 97 56 E
Kutkashen, *Azerbaijan* **61 K8** 40 58N 47 47 E
Kutná Hora, *Czech Rep.* **34 B8** 49 57N 15 16 E
Kutno, *Poland* **55 F6** 52 15N 19 23 E
Kutru, *India* **94 E5** 19 5N 80 46 E
Kutse, *Botswana* **116 C3** 21 7 S 22 16 E
Kuttabul, *Australia* **126 K6** 21 1 S 148 54 E
Kutu, *Dem. Rep. of the Congo* **114 C3** 2 40 S 18 11 E
Kutu Moke, *Dem. Rep. of the Congo* **114 C3** 3 12 S 17 21 E
Kutum, *Sudan* **107 E1** 14 10N 24 40 E
Kúty, *Slovak Rep.* **35 C10** 48 40N 17 3 E
Kuty, *Ukraine* **53 B10** 48 16N 25 11 E
Kuujjuaq, *Canada* **139 C13** 58 6N 68 15W
Kuujjuarapik, *Canada* **140 A4** 55 20N 77 35W
Kuŭp-tong, *N. Korea* **75 D14** 40 45N 126 1 E
Kuusamo, *Finland* **14 D23** 65 57N 29 8 E
Kuusankoski, *Finland* **15 F22** 60 55N 26 38 E
Kuvandyk, *Russia* **64 F6** 51 28N 57 21 E
Kuvango, *Angola* **115 E3** 14 28 S 16 20 E
Kuvasay, *Uzbekistan* **65 C5** 40 18N 71 59 E
Kuvshinovo, *Russia* **58 D8** 57 2N 34 11 E
Kuwait = Al Kuwayt, *Kuwait* **96 D5** 29 30N 48 0 E
Kuwait ■, *Asia* **96 D5** 29 30N 47 30 E
Kuwana, *Japan* **73 B8** 35 5N 136 43 E
Kuwana →, *India* **93 F10** 26 25N 83 15 E
Kuybyshev = Samara, *Russia* **60 D10** 53 8N 50 6 E
Kuybyshev, *Russia* **66 D8** 55 27N 78 19 E
Kuybyshevabad = Kuybyshevskiy, *Tajikistan* **65 E4** 37 52N 68 44 E
Kuybyshevka-Vostochnaya = Belogorsk, *Russia* **67 D13** 51 0N 128 20 E
Kuybyshevo, *Ukraine* **59 J9** 47 25N 36 40 E
Kuybyshevskiy, *Tajikistan* **65 E4** 37 52N 68 44 E
Kuybyshevskoye Vdkhr., *Russia* **60 C9** 55 2N 49 30 E
Kuye He →, *China* **74 E6** 38 23N 110 46 E
Kūyeh, *Iran* **96 B5** 38 45N 47 57 E
Kuylyuk, *Uzbekistan* **65 C4** 41 14N 69 17 E
Kuyto, Ozero, *Russia* **56 B5** 65 6N 31 20 E
Kuyucak, *Turkey* **49 D10** 37 55N 28 28 E
Kuyumba, *Russia* **67 C10** 60 58N 96 59 E
Kuzey Anadolu Dağları, *Turkey* **100 B7** 41 30N 35 0 E
Kuzhitturai, *India* **95 K3** 8 18N 77 11 E
Kuzino, *Russia* **64 C7** 57 1N 59 27 E
Kuzitrin →, *U.S.A.* **144 D6** 65 10N 165 25W
Kuzmin, *Serbia & M.* **52 E4** 45 2N 19 25 E
Kuznetsk, *Russia* **60 D8** 53 12N 46 40 E
Kuznetsovo = Konakovo, *Russia* **58 D9** 56 40N 36 51 E
Kuzomen, *Russia* **56 A6** 66 22N 36 50 E
Kvænangen, *Norway* **14 A19** 70 5N 21 15 E
Kværndrup, *Denmark* **17 J4** 55 10N 10 31 E
Kvaløy, *Norway* **14 B18** 69 40N 18 30 E
Kvam, *Norway* **18 C6** 61 40N 9 42 E
Kvänum, *Sweden* **17 F7** 58 18N 13 11 E
Kvareli = Qvareli, *Georgia* **61 K7** 41 57N 45 47 E
Kvarner, *Croatia* **45 D11** 44 50N 14 10 E
Kvarnerič, *Croatia* **45 D11** 44 43N 14 37 E
Kvås, *Norway* **18 F4** 58 16N 7 14 E
Kvernaland, *Norway* **18 F2** 58 47N 5 45 E
Kvichak B., *U.S.A.* **144 G8** 58 48N 157 30W
Kvicksund, *Sweden* **16 E10** 59 27N 16 19 E
Kvikne, *Norway* **18 B7** 62 35N 10 16 E
Kvillsfors, *Sweden* **17 G9** 57 24N 15 29 E
Kvina →, *Norway* **18 F3** 58 19N 6 55 E
Kvinlog, *Norway* **18 F3** 58 31N 6 55 E
Kvirily = Zestaponi, *Georgia* **61 J6** 42 6N 43 0 E
Kvismare kanal, *Sweden* **16 E9** 59 11N 15 35 E
Kvissleby, *Sweden* **16 B11** 62 18N 17 22 E
Kviteseid, *Norway* **18 E5** 59 24N 8 29 E
Kvitøya, *Svalbard* **10 A14** 80 8N 32 35 E
Kwabhaca, *S. Africa* **117 E4** 30 51 S 29 0 E
Kwajalein, *Marshall Is.* **134 G8** 9 5N 167 20 E
Kwakhanai, *Botswana* **116 C3** 21 39 S 21 16 E
Kwakoegron, *Suriname* **169 B6** 5 12N 55 25W
Kwale, *Kenya* **118 C4** 4 15 S 39 31 E
Kwale, *Nigeria* **113 D6** 5 46N 6 26 E
Kwamalasamutu, *Suriname* **169 C6** 2 20N 56 47W
KwaMashu, *S. Africa* **117 D5** 29 45 S 30 58 E
Kwamouth, *Dem. Rep. of the Congo* **114 C3** 3 9 S 16 12 E
Kwando →, *Africa* **116 B3** 18 27 S 23 32 E
Kwangchow = Guangzhou, *China* **77 F9** 23 5N 113 10 E
Kwangdaeri, *N. Korea* **75 D14** 40 31N 127 32 E
Kwangju, *S. Korea* **75 G14** 35 9N 126 54 E
Kwango →, *Dem. Rep. of the Congo* **114 C3** 3 14 S 17 22 E
Kwangsi-Chuang = Guangxi Zhuangzu Zizhiqu □, *China* **76 F7** 24 0N 109 0 E
Kwangtung = Guangdong □, *China* **77 F9** 23 0N 113 0 E
Kwara □, *Nigeria* **113 D6** 8 45N 4 30 E
Kwataboahegan →, *Canada* **140 B3** 51 9N 80 50W
Kwatisore, *Indonesia* **83 B4** 3 18 S 134 50 E
KwaZulu Natal □, *S. Africa* **117 D5** 29 0 S 30 0 E
Kweichow = Guizhou □, *China* **76 D6** 27 0N 107 0 E
Kweilin = Guilin, *China* **77 E8** 25 18N 110 15 E
Kweisui = Hohhot, *China* **74 D6** 40 52N 111 40 E
Kweiyang = Guiyang, *China* **76 D6** 26 32N 106 40 E
Kwekwe, *Zimbabwe* **119 F2** 18 58 S 29 48 E
Kwenge →, *Dem. Rep. of the Congo* **115 C3** 4 50 S 18 44 E
Kwethluk, *U.S.A.* **144 F7** 60 49N 161 26W
Kwidzyn, *Poland* **54 E5** 53 44N 18 55 E
Kwigillingok, *U.S.A.* **144 G7** 59 51N 163 8W
Kwiguk, *U.S.A.* **144 E6** 62 46N 164 30W
Kwiha, *Ethiopia* **107 E4** 13 29N 39 32 E
Kwikila, *Papua N. G.* **132 E4** 9 49 S 147 38 E
Kwilu →, *Dem. Rep. of the Congo* **115 C3** 3 22 S 17 22 E
Kwinana New Town, *Australia* **125 F2** 32 15 S 115 47 E
Kwinbet, *Burma* **90 G5** 16 20N 94 14 E
Kwisa →, *Poland* **55 G2** 51 34N 15 24 E
Kwoka, *Indonesia* **83 B4** 0 31 S 132 27 E
Kwolla, *Nigeria* **113 D6** 9 0N 9 15 E
Kwun Tong, *China* **69 G11** 22 19N 114 13 E
Kya-in-Seikkyi, *Burma* **90 G7** 16 2N 98 8 E
Kyabé, *Chad* **109 G3** 9 30N 19 0 E
Kyabra Cr. →, *Australia* **127 D3** 25 36 S 142 55 E
Kyabram, *Australia* **129 D6** 36 19 S 145 4 E
Kyaikkami, *Burma* **90 G6** 16 4N 97 34 E
Kyaiklat, *Burma* **90 G5** 16 25N 95 40 E
Kyaikmaraw, *Burma* **90 G6** 16 23N 97 44 E
Kyaikthin, *Burma* **90 D5** 23 32N 95 40 E
Kyaikto, *Burma* **86 D1** 17 20N 97 3 E
Kyakhta, *Russia* **67 D11** 50 30N 106 25 E
Kyambura ⌓, *Uganda* **118 C3** 0 7 S 30 9 E
Kyancutta, *Australia* **127 E2** 33 8 S 135 33 E
Kyangin, *Burma* **90 F5** 18 20N 95 20 E
Kyaukhnyat, *Burma* **90 F6** 18 15N 97 31 E
Kyaukki, *Burma* **90 F6** 18 27N 96 56 E
Kyaukkyi, *Burma* **90 F5** 18 15N 94 29 E
Kyaukme, *Burma* **90 D6** 22 32N 97 2 E
Kyaukpadaung, *Burma* **90 E5** 20 52N 95 8 E
Kyaukpyu, *Burma* **90 F4** 19 28N 93 30 E
Kyaukse, *Burma* **90 E6** 21 36N 96 10 E
Kyauktaga, *Burma* **90 F6** 18 10N 96 37 E
Kyauktan, *Burma* **90 G6** 16 38N 96 19 E
Kyauktaw, *Burma* **90 E4** 20 51N 92 59 E
Kyaunggon, *Burma* **90 G5** 17 6N 95 11 E
Kyawkku, *Burma* **90 E6** 21 48N 96 56 E
Kybartai, *Lithuania* **54 D9** 54 39N 22 45 E
Kyburz, *U.S.A.* **160 G6** 38 47N 120 18W
Kyeintali, *Burma* **90 G5** 18 0N 94 29 E
Kyelang, *India* **92 C7** 32 35N 77 2 E
Kyenjojo, *Uganda* **118 B3** 0 40N 30 37 E
Kyidaunggan, *Burma* **90 F6** 19 53N 96 12 E
Kyjov, *Czech Rep.* **35 B10** 49 1N 17 7 E
Kyle, *Canada* **143 C7** 50 50N 108 2W
Kyle Dam, *Zimbabwe* **119 G3** 20 15 S 31 0 E
Kyle of Lochalsh, *U.K.* **22 D3** 57 17N 5 44W
Kyll →, *Germany* **31 F2** 49 48N 6 41 E
Kyllburg, *Germany* **31 E2** 50 2N 6 34 E
Kymijoki →, *Finland* **15 F22** 60 30N 26 55 E
Kymmene älv = Kymijoki →, *Finland* **15 F22** 60 30N 26 55 E
Kyneton, *Australia* **128 D6** 37 10 S 144 29 E
Kynuna, *Australia* **126 C3** 21 37 S 141 55 E
Kyō-ga-Saki, *Japan* **73 B7** 35 45N 135 15 E
Kyoga, L., *Uganda* **118 B3** 1 35N 33 0 E
Kyogle, *Australia* **127 D5** 28 40 S 153 0 E
Kyom →, *Sudan* **107 F2** 8 58N 28 13 E
Kyongju, *S. Korea* **75 G15** 35 51N 129 14 E
Kyŏngsŏng, *N. Korea* **75 D15** 41 35N 129 36 E
Kyōto, *Japan* **73 C7** 35 0N 135 45 E
Kyōto □, *Japan* **73 B7** 35 15N 135 45 E
Kyparissovouno, *Cyprus* **39 E9** 35 19N 33 10 E
Kyperounda, *Cyprus* **39 F8** 34 56N 32 58 E
Kypros = Cyprus ■, *Asia* **39 F9** 35 0N 33 0 E
Kyrenia, *Cyprus* **39 E9** 35 20N 33 20 E
Kyrgyzstan ■, *Asia* **65 C6** 42 0N 75 0 E
Kyritz, *Germany* **30 C8** 52 56N 12 24 E

Kyrkhult, *Sweden* **17 H8** 56 22N 14 34 E
Kyrksæterøra, *Norway* **18 A6** 63 18N 9 5 E
Kyrnasivka, *Ukraine* **53 B13** 48 35N 28 58 E
Kyrnychky, *Ukraine* **53 E14** 45 42N 29 4 E
Kyro älv = Kyrönjoki →, *Finland* **14 E19** 63 14N 21 45 E
Kyrönjoki →, *Finland* **14 E19** 63 14N 21 45 E
Kyshtym, *Russia* **64 D8** 55 42N 60 34 E
Kystatyam, *Russia* **67 C13** 67 20N 123 10 E
Kysucké Nové Mesto, *Slovak Rep.* **35 B11** 49 18N 18 47 E
Kytay, Ozero, *Ukraine* **53 E14** 45 40N 29 13 E
Kythira = Kíthira, *Greece* **48 E5** 36 8N 23 0 E
Kythréa, *Cyprus* **39 E9** 35 15N 33 29 E
Kytlym, *Russia* **64 B7** 59 30N 59 12 E
Kyu-hkok, *Burma* **90 C7** 24 4N 98 4 E
Kyunhla, *Burma* **90 D5** 23 25N 95 15 E
Kyuquot Sound, *Canada* **142 D3** 50 2N 127 22W
Kyurdamir = Kürdämir, *Azerbaijan* **61 K9** 40 25N 48 3 E
Kyūshū, *Japan* **72 E3** 33 0N 131 0 E
Kyūshū □, *Japan* **72 E3** 33 0N 131 0 E
Kyūshū-Sanchi, *Japan* **72 E3** 32 35N 131 17 E
Kyustendil, *Bulgaria* **50 D6** 42 16N 22 41 E
Kyusyur, *Russia* **67 B13** 70 19N 127 30 E
Kywong, *Australia* **129 C7** 34 58 S 146 44 E
Kyyiv, *Ukraine* **59 G6** 50 30N 30 28 E
Kyyivske Vdskh., *Ukraine* **59 G6** 51 0N 30 25 E
Kyzyl, *Russia* **67 D10** 51 50N 94 30 E
Kyzyl-Adyr, *Kyrgyzstan* **65 B5** 42 39N 71 35 E
Kyzyl-Burun = Siyäzän, *Azerbaijan* **61 K9** 41 3N 49 10 E
Kyzyl-Khoto = Kyzyl, *Russia* **67 D10** 51 50N 94 30 E
Kyzyl Kum, *Uzbekistan* **65 B2** 42 30N 65 0 E
Kyzyl-Kyya, *Kyrgyzstan* **65 C6** 40 16N 72 8 E
Kyzyl-Orda = Qyzylorda, *Kazakhstan* **65 A2** 44 48N 65 28 E
Kyzyl-Suu, *Kyrgyzstan* **65 B9** 42 20N 78 0 E
Kyzyl-Suu →, *Kyrgyzstan* **65 D6** 38 50N 70 0 E
Kyzyltepa, *Uzbekistan* **65 C2** 40 1N 64 51 E

L

La Albuera, *Spain* **43 G4** 38 45N 6 49W
La Alcarria, *Spain* **40 E2** 40 31N 2 45W
La Almarcha, *Spain* **40 F2** 39 41N 2 24W
La Almunia de Doña Godina, *Spain* **40 D3** 41 29N 1 23W
La Amistad △, *Cent. Amer.* **164 E3** 9 28N 83 18W
La Asunción, *Venezuela* **169 A5** 11 2N 63 53W
La Baie, *Canada* **141 C5** 48 19N 70 53W
La Banda, *Argentina* **174 B3** 27 45 S 64 10W
La Bañeza, *Spain* **42 C5** 42 17N 5 54W
La Barca, *Mexico* **162 C4** 20 20N 102 40W
La Barge, *U.S.A.* **158 E8** 42 16N 110 12W
La Bastide-Puylaurent, *France* **28 D7** 44 35N 3 55 E
La Baule, *France* **26 E4** 47 17N 2 24W
La Belle, *Fla., U.S.A.* **153 J8** 26 46N 81 26W
La Belle, *Mo., U.S.A.* **156 D5** 40 7N 91 55W
La Biche →, *Canada* **142 B4** 59 57N 123 50W
La Biche, L., *Canada* **142 C6** 54 50N 112 5W
La Bisbal d'Empordà, *Spain* **40 D8** 41 58N 3 2 E
La Blanquilla, *Venezuela* **169 A5** 11 51N 64 37W
La Bomba, *Mexico* **162 A1** 31 53N 115 2W
La Brea, *Trin. & Tob.* **169 F9** 10 15N 61 37W
La Brède, *France* **28 D3** 44 41N 0 32W
La Bresse, *France* **27 D13** 48 2N 6 53 E
La Bureba, *Spain* **42 C7** 42 36N 3 24W
La Cal →, *Bolivia* **173 D6** 17 27 S 58 15W
La Calera, *Chile* **174 C1** 32 50 S 71 10W
La Calle = El Kala, *Algeria* **111 A6** 36 50N 8 30 E
La Campana △, *Chile* **174 C1** 32 58 S 71 14W
La Campiña, *Spain* **43 H6** 37 45N 4 45W
La Canal = Sa Canal, *Spain* **38 D1** 38 51N 1 23 E
La Cañiza = A Cañiza, *Spain* **42 C2** 42 13N 8 16W
La Canourgue, *France* **28 D7** 44 26N 3 13 E
La Capelle, *France* **27 C10** 49 59N 3 50 E
La Carlota, *Argentina* **174 C3** 33 30 S 63 20W
La Carlota, *Phil.* **81 F4** 10 25N 122 55 E
La Carlota, *Spain* **43 H6** 37 40N 4 56W
La Carolina, *Spain* **43 G7** 38 17N 3 38W
La Castellana, *Phil.* **81 F4** 10 20N 123 3 E
La Cavalerie, *France* **28 D7** 44 1N 3 10 E
La Ceiba, *Honduras* **164 C2** 15 40N 86 50W
La Ceiba, *Venezuela* **168 C3** 9 28N 71 4W
La Chaise-Dieu, *France* **28 C7** 45 18N 3 42 E
La Chapelle d'Angillon, *France* **27 E9** 47 21N 2 25 E
La Chapelle-St-Luc, *France* **27 D11** 48 20N 4 3 E
La Chapelle-sur-Erdre, *France* **26 E5** 47 18N 1 34W
La Charité-sur-Loire, *France* **27 E10** 47 10N 3 1 E
La Chartre-sur-le-Loir, *France* **26 E7** 47 44N 0 34 E
La Châtaigneraie, *France* **28 B3** 46 39N 0 44W
La Châtre, *France* **27 F9** 46 35N 2 0 E
La Chaux-de-Fonds, *Switz.* **32 B3** 47 7N 6 50 E
La Chorrera, *Colombia* **168 D3** 0 44 S 73 1W
La Chorrera, *Panama* **164 E4** 8 53N 79 47W
La Ciotat, *France* **29 E9** 43 10N 5 37 E
La Clayette, *France* **27 F11** 46 17N 4 19 E
La Cocha, *Argentina* **174 B2** 27 50 S 65 40W
La Concepción = Ri-Aba, *Eq. Guin.* **113 E6** 3 28N 8 40 E
La Concepción, *Panama* **164 E3** 8 31N 82 37W
La Concepción, *Venezuela* **168 A3** 10 30N 71 50W
La Concordia, *Mexico* **163 D6** 16 8N 92 38W
La Coruña = A Coruña, *Spain* **42 B2** 43 20N 8 25W
La Coruña □, *Spain* **42 B2** 43 10N 8 30W
La Côte, *Switz.* **32 D2** 46 25N 6 15 E
La Côte-St-André, *France* **29 C9** 45 24N 5 15 E
La Courtine, *France* **28 C6** 45 41N 2 15 E
La Crau, *Bouches-du-Rhône, France* **29 E8** 43 32N 4 40 E
La Crau, *Var, France* **29 E10** 43 9N 6 4 E
La Crescent, *U.S.A.* **154 D9** 43 50N 91 18W
La Crete, *Canada* **142 B5** 58 11N 116 24W
La Crosse, *Fla., U.S.A.* **152 F7** 29 51N 82 24W
La Crosse, *Kans., U.S.A.* **154 F5** 38 32N 99 18W
La Crosse, *Wis., U.S.A.* **154 D9** 43 48N 91 15W
La Cruz, *Costa Rica* **164 D2** 11 4N 85 39W
La Cruz, *Mexico* **162 C3** 23 55N 106 54W
La Cumbre, Volcán, *Ecuador* **172 a** 0 21 S 91 32W
La Désirade, *Guadeloupe* **164 b** 16 18N 61 3W
La Digue, *Seychelles* **121 b** 4 20 S 55 51 E
La Dorada, *Colombia* **168 B3** 5 30N 74 40W
La Ensenada, *Chile* **176 B2** 41 12 S 72 33W
La Escondida, *Mexico* **162 C5** 24 6N 99 55W
La Esmeralda, *Paraguay* **174 A3** 22 16 S 62 33W
La Esperanza, *Argentina* **176 B3** 40 26 S 68 32W
La Esperanza, *Cuba* **164 B3** 22 46N 83 44W
La Esperanza, *Honduras* **164 D2** 14 15N 88 10W
La Estrada = A Estrada, *Spain* **42 C2** 42 43N 8 27W
La Faouët, *France* **26 D3** 48 2N 3 30W
La Fayette, *U.S.A.* **149 H3** 34 42N 85 17W
La Fé, *Cuba* **164 B3** 22 2N 84 15W
La Fère, *France* **27 C10** 49 39N 3 21 E
La Ferté-Bernard, *France* **26 D7** 48 10N 0 40 E
La Ferté-Gaucher, *France* **27 D10** 48 47N 3 19 E
La Ferté-Macé, *France* **26 D6** 48 35N 0 22W
La Ferté-St-Aubin, *France* **27 E8** 47 42N 1 57 E
La Ferté-sous-Jouarre, *France* **27 D10** 48 56N 3 8 E
La Ferté-Vidame, *France* **26 D7** 48 37N 0 53 E
La Flèche, *France* **26 E6** 47 42N 0 4W
La Foa, *N. Cal.* **133 U19** 21 43 S 165 50 E
La Follette, *U.S.A.* **149 G3** 36 23N 84 7W
La Fontaine, *U.S.A.* **157 D11** 40 40N 85 43W
La Fregeneda, *Spain* **42 E4** 40 58N 6 54W
La Fría, *Venezuela* **168 B3** 8 13N 72 15W
La Fuente de San Esteban, *Spain* **42 E4** 40 49N 6 15W
La Gacilly, *France* **26 E4** 47 45N 2 8W
La Gineta, *Spain* **41 F2** 39 8N 2 1W
La Gloria, *Colombia* **168 B3** 8 37N 73 48W
La Goulette = Halq el Oued, *Tunisia* **108 A2** 36 53N 10 18 E
La Gran Sabana, *Venezuela* **169 B5** 5 30N 61 30W
La Grand'Combe, *France* **29 D8** 44 13N 4 2 E
La Grande, *U.S.A.* **158 D4** 45 20N 118 5W
La Grande →, *Canada* **140 B5** 53 50N 79 0W
La Grande Deux, Rés., *Canada* **140 B4** 53 40N 76 55W
La Grande-Motte, *France* **29 E8** 43 23N 4 5 E
La Grande Quatre, Rés., *Canada* **140 B5** 54 0N 73 15W
La Grande Trois, Rés., *Canada* **140 B4** 53 40N 75 10W
La Grange, *Calif., U.S.A.* **160 H6** 37 42N 120 27W
La Grange, *Ga., U.S.A.* **152 B4** 33 2N 85 2W
La Grange, *Ky., U.S.A.* **148 F3** 38 25N 85 23W
La Grange, *Ky., U.S.A.* **157 F11** 38 24N 85 22W
La Grange, *Mo., U.S.A.* **156 D5** 40 3N 91 35W
La Grange, *Tex., U.S.A.* **155 L6** 29 54N 96 52W
La Grave, *France* **29 C10** 45 3N 6 18 E
La Grita, *Venezuela* **168 B3** 8 8N 71 59W
La Guaira, *Venezuela* **168 A4** 10 36N 66 56W
La Guardia = A Guarda, *Spain* **42 D2** 41 56N 8 52W
La Gudiña = A Gudiña, *Spain* **42 C3** 42 4N 7 8W
La Güera, *Mauritania* **110 D1** 20 51N 17 0W
La Guerche-de-Bretagne, *France* **26 E5** 47 57N 1 16W
La Guerche-sur-l'Aubois, *France* **27 F9** 46 58N 2 56 E
La Habana, *Cuba* **164 B3** 23 8N 82 22W
La Harpe, *U.S.A.* **156 D6** 40 35N 90 58W
La Haute Vallée de Chevreuse ⌓, *France* **27 D8** 48 35N 1 58 E
La Haye-du-Puits, *France* **26 C5** 49 17N 1 33W
La Horqueta, *Venezuela* **169 B5** 7 55N 60 20W
La Horra, *Spain* **42 D7** 41 44N 3 53W
La Independencia, *Mexico* **163 D6** 16 31N 91 47W
La Isabela, *Dom. Rep.* **165 C5** 19 58N 71 2W
La Jonquera, *Spain* **40 C7** 42 25N 2 53 E
La Joya, *Peru* **172 D3** 16 43 S 71 52W
La Junta, *U.S.A.* **155 F3** 37 59N 103 33W
La Laguna, *Canary Is.* **9 e1** 28 28N 16 18W
La Libertad, *Guatemala* **164 C1** 16 47N 90 7W
La Libertad, *Mexico* **162 B2** 29 55N 112 41W
La Libertad □, *Peru* **172 B2** 8 0 S 78 30W
La Ligua, *Chile* **174 C1** 32 30 S 71 16W
La Línea de la Concepción, *Spain* **43 J5** 36 15N 5 23W
La Loche, *Canada* **143 B7** 56 29N 109 26W
La Londe-les-Maures, *France* **29 E10** 43 8N 6 14 E
La Lora, *Spain* **42 C7** 42 45N 4 0W
La Loupe, *France* **26 D8** 48 29N 1 0 E
La Louvière, *Belgium* **24 D4** 50 27N 4 10 E
La Lune, *Trin. & Tob.* **169 F9** 10 3N 61 22W
La Machine, *France* **27 F10** 46 54N 3 27 E
La Maddalena, *Italy* **46 A2** 41 13N 9 24 E
La Malbaie, *Canada* **141 C5** 47 40N 70 10W
La Malinche △, *Mexico* **163 D5** 19 15N 98 3W
La Mancha, *Spain* **41 F2** 39 10N 2 54W
La Mariña, *Spain* **42 B3** 43 30N 7 40W
La Martre, L., *Canada* **142 A5** 63 15N 117 55W
La Mesa, *U.S.A.* **161 N9** 32 46N 117 3W
La Misión, *Mexico* **162 A1** 32 5N 116 50W
La Moille, *U.S.A.* **156 C7** 41 32N 89 17W
La Moine →, *U.S.A.* **156 E6** 39 59N 90 31W
La Monte, *U.S.A.* **156 F3** 38 46N 93 26W
La Mothe-Achard, *France* **26 F5** 46 37N 1 40W
La Motte-Chalançon, *France* **29 D9** 44 30N 5 21 E
La Motte-du-Caire, *France* **29 D10** 44 20N 6 3 E
La Motte-Servolex, *France* **29 C9** 45 35N 5 53 E
La Moure, *U.S.A.* **154 B5** 46 21N 98 18W
La Muela, *Spain* **40 D3** 41 36N 1 7W
La Mure, *France* **29 D9** 44 55N 5 48 E
La Negra, *Chile* **174 A1** 23 46 S 70 18W
La Neuveville, *Switz.* **32 B4** 47 4N 7 6 E
La Oliva, *Canary Is.* **9 e2** 28 36N 13 57W
La Oraya, *Peru* **172 C2** 11 32 S 75 54W
La Orotava, *Canary Is.* **9 e1** 28 22N 16 31W
La Oroya, *Peru* **172 C2** 11 32 S 75 54W
La Pacaudière, *France* **27 F10** 46 11N 3 52 E
La Palma, *Canary Is.* **9 e1** 28 40N 17 50W
La Palma, *Panama* **164 E4** 8 15N 78 0W
La Palma del Condado, *Spain* **43 H4** 37 21N 6 38W
La Paloma, *Chile* **174 C1** 30 35 S 71 0W
La Pampa □, *Argentina* **174 D2** 36 50 S 66 0W
La Paragua, *Venezuela* **169 B5** 6 50N 63 20W
La Paya △, *Colombia* **168 C2** 0 0 75 5W
La Paz, *Entre Ríos, Argentina* **174 C4** 30 50 S 59 45W
La Paz, *San Luis, Argentina* **174 C2** 33 30 S 67 20W
La Paz, *Bolivia* **172 D4** 16 20 S 68 10W
La Paz, *Honduras* **164 D2** 14 20N 87 47W
La Paz, *Mexico* **162 C2** 24 10N 110 20W
La Paz, *Abra, Phil.* **80 C3** 17 40N 120 41 E
La Paz, *Tarlac, Phil.* **80 D3** 15 26N 120 45 E
La Paz □, *Bolivia* **172 D4** 15 30 S 68 0W
La Paz Centro, *Nic.* **164 D2** 12 20N 86 41W
La Pedrera, *Colombia* **168 D4** 1 18 S 69 43W
La Pérade, *Canada* **141 C5** 46 35N 72 12W
La Perouse, Bahía, *Chile* **172 b** 27 5 S 109 18W
La Perouse Str., *Asia* **70 B11** 45 40N 142 0 E
La Pesca, *Mexico* **163 C5** 23 46N 97 47W
La Piedad, *Mexico* **162 C4** 20 20N 102 1W
La Pine, *U.S.A.* **158 E3** 43 40N 121 30W
La Plata, *Argentina* **174 D4** 35 0 S 57 55W
La Plata, *Colombia* **168 C2** 2 23N 75 53W
La Plata, *U.S.A.* **156 D4** 40 2N 92 29W
La Plata, L., *Argentina* **176 B2** 44 55 S 71 50W
La Pobla de Lillet, *Spain* **40 C6** 42 16N 1 59 E
La Pocatière, *Canada* **141 C5** 47 22N 70 2W
La Pola de Gordón, *Spain* **42 C5** 42 51N 5 41W
La Porta, *France* **29 F13** 42 25N 9 21 E
La Porte, *Ind., U.S.A.* **157 C10** 41 36N 86 43W
La Porte, *Tex., U.S.A.* **155 L7** 29 39N 95 1W
La Porte City, *U.S.A.* **156 B4** 42 19N 92 12W
La Presanella, *Italy* **44 B7** 46 13N 10 40 E
La Puebla = Sa Pobla, *Spain* **38 B4** 39 46N 3 1 E
La Puebla de Cazalla, *Spain* **43 H5** 37 10N 5 20W
La Puebla de los Infantes, *Spain* **43 H5** 37 47N 5 24W
La Puebla de Montalbán, *Spain* **42 F6** 39 52N 4 22W
La Puebla del Río, *Spain* **43 H4** 37 16N 6 3W
La Puerta de Segura, *Spain* **43 G8** 38 22N 2 45W
La Punt, *Switz.* **33 C9** 46 35N 9 56 E
La Purísima, *Mexico* **162 B2** 26 10N 112 4W
La Push, *U.S.A.* **160 C2** 47 55N 124 38W
La Quiaca, *Argentina* **174 A2** 22 5 S 65 35W
La Réole, *France* **28 D3** 44 35N 0 1W
La Restinga, *Canary Is.* **9 e1** 27 38N 17 59W
La Rioja, *Argentina* **174 B2** 29 20 S 67 0W
La Rioja □, *Argentina* **174 B2** 29 30 S 67 0W
La Rioja □, *Spain* **40 C2** 42 20N 2 20W
La Robla, *Spain* **42 C5** 42 50N 5 41W
La Roche, *N. Cal.* **133 U22** 21 26 S 168 2 E
La Roche, *Switz.* **32 C4** 46 42N 7 7 E
La Roche-Bernard, *France* **26 E4** 47 31N 2 19W
La Roche-Canillac, *France* **28 C5** 45 12N 1 57 E
La Roche-en-Ardenne, *Belgium* **24 D5** 50 11N 5 35 E
La Roche-sur-Foron, *France* **27 F13** 46 4N 6 19 E
La Roche-sur-Yon, *France* **26 F5** 46 40N 1 25W
La Rochefoucauld, *France* **28 C4** 45 44N 0 24 E
La Rochelle, *France* **28 B2** 46 10N 1 9W
La Roda, *Spain* **41 F2** 39 13N 2 15W
La Roda de Andalucía, *Spain* **43 H6** 37 12N 4 46W
La Romana, *Dom. Rep.* **165 C6** 18 27N 68 57W
La Ronge, *Canada* **143 B7** 55 5N 105 20W
La Rue, *U.S.A.* **157 D13** 40 35N 83 23W
La Rumorosa, *Mexico* **161 N10** 32 33N 116 4W
La Sabina = Sa Savina, *Spain* **38 D1** 38 44N 1 25 E
La Sagra, *Spain* **41 H2** 37 57N 2 35W
La Salle, *U.S.A.* **156 C7** 41 20N 89 6W
La Sanabria, *Spain* **42 C4** 42 0N 6 30W
La Santa, *Canary Is.* **9 e2** 29 5N 13 40W
La Sarraz, *Switz.* **32 C3** 46 38N 6 32 E
La Sarre, *Canada* **140 C4** 48 45N 79 15W
La Scie, *Canada* **141 C8** 49 57N 55 36W
La Selva, *Spain* **40 C7** 42 0N 2 45 E
La Selva Beach, *U.S.A.* **160 J5** 36 56N 121 51W
La Selva del Camp, *Spain* **40 D6** 41 13N 1 8 E
La Serena, *Chile* **174 B1** 29 55 S 71 10W
La Serena, *Spain* **43 G5** 38 45N 5 40W
La Seu d'Urgell, *Spain* **40 C6** 42 22N 1 23 E
La Seyne-sur-Mer, *France* **29 E9** 43 7N 5 52 E
La Sila, *Italy* **47 C9** 39 15N 16 35 E
La Solana, *Spain* **43 G7** 38 59N 3 14W
La Soufrière, *St. Vincent* **165 D7** 13 20N 61 11W
La Souterraine, *France* **27 F8** 46 15N 1 30 E
La Spézia, *Italy* **44 D6** 44 7N 9 50 E
La Suze-sur-Sarthe, *France* **26 E7** 47 53N 0 2 E
La Tagua, *Colombia* **168 C3** 0 3N 74 40W
La Teste-de-Buch, *France* **28 D2** 44 37N 1 8W
La Tortuga, *Venezuela* **169 A4** 11 0N 65 22W
La Tour de Peilz, *Switz.* **32 D3** 46 27N 6 52 E
La Tour-du-Pin, *France* **29 C9** 45 33N 5 27 E
La Tournette, *France* **32 E2** 45 46N 6 15 E
La Tranche-sur-Mer, *France* **26 F5** 46 20N 1 27W
La Tremblade, *France* **28 C2** 45 46N 1 8W
La Trinidad, *Phil.* **80 C3** 16 28N 120 35 E
La Trinité, *Martinique* **164 c** 14 43N 60 58W
La Tuque, *Canada* **140 C5** 47 30N 72 50W
La Unión, *Chile* **176 B2** 40 10 S 73 0W
La Unión, *Colombia* **168 C2** 1 35N 77 5W
La Unión, *El Salv.* **164 D2** 13 20N 87 50W
La Unión, *Mexico* **162 D4** 17 58N 101 49W
La Unión, *Peru* **172 B2** 9 43 S 76 45W
La Unión, *Spain* **41 H4** 37 38N 0 53W
La Union □, *Phil.* **80 C3** 16 30N 120 25 E
La Urbana, *Venezuela* **168 B4** 7 8N 66 56W
La Vache Pt., *Trin. & Tob.* **169 F9** 10 47N 61 28W
La Vall d'Uixó, *Spain* **40 F4** 39 49N 0 15W
La Vecilla de Curveño, *Spain* **42 C5** 42 51N 5 27W
La Vega, *Dom. Rep.* **165 C5** 19 20N 70 30W
La Vega, *Peru* **172 C2** 10 41 S 77 44W
La Vela de Coro, *Venezuela* **168 A4** 11 27N 69 34W
La Veleta, *Spain* **43 H7** 37 1N 3 22W
La Venta, *Mexico* **163 D6** 18 8N 94 3W
La Ventura, *Mexico* **162 C4** 24 38N 100 54W
La Venturosa, *Colombia* **168 B4** 6 8N 68 48W
La Vergne, *U.S.A.* **149 G2** 36 1N 86 35W
La Victoria, *Venezuela* **168 A4** 10 14N 67 20W
La Voulte-sur-Rhône, *France* **29 D8** 44 48N 4 46 E
Laa an der Thaya, *Austria* **35 C9** 48 43N 16 23 E
Laaber, Grosse →, *Germany* **31 G8** 48 55N 12 30 E
Laage, *Germany* **30 B8** 53 55N 12 21 E
Laas Caanood = Las Anod, *Somali Rep.* **120 C3** 8 26N 47 19 E
Laatzen, *Germany* **30 C5** 52 19N 9 48 E
Laau Pt., *U.S.A.* **145 B4** 21 6N 157 19W
Laba →, *Russia* **61 H4** 45 11N 39 42 E
Laban, *Burma* **90 C6** 25 52N 96 40 E
Labasa, *Fiji* **133 A2** 16 30 S 179 27 E
Labason, *Phil.* **81 G4** 8 4N 122 31 E
Labastide-Murat, *France* **28 D5** 44 39N 1 33 E
Labastide-Rouairoux, *France* **28 E6** 43 28N 2 39 E
Labbézenga, *Mali* **113 B5** 15 2N 0 48 E
Labdah = Leptis Magna, *Libya* **108 B2** 32 40N 14 12 E
Labe = Elbe →, *Europe* **30 B4** 53 50N 9 0 E
Labé, *Guinea* **112 C2** 11 24N 12 16W
Laberge, L., *Canada* **142 A1** 61 11N 135 12W
Labes = Łobez, *Poland* **54 E2** 53 38N 15 39 E
Labian, Tanjong, *Malaysia* **85 A5** 5 9N 119 13 E
Labiau = Polessk, *Russia* **15 J19** 54 50N 21 8 E
Labig Pt. = Iligan Pt., *Phil.* **80 B4** 18 25N 122 25 E
Labin, *Croatia* **45 C11** 45 5N 14 8 E
Labinsk, *Russia* **61 H5** 44 40N 40 48 E
Labis, *Malaysia* **87 L4** 2 22N 103 2 E
Łabiszyn, *Poland* **55 F4** 52 57N 17 54 E
Labo, *Phil.* **80 D4** 14 9N 122 51 E
Laboe, *Germany* **30 A6** 54 24N 10 13 E
Laboka, *Gabon* **114 B2** 0 19N 11 32 E
Laborec →, *Slovak Rep.* **35 C14** 48 37N 21 58 E
Laborie, *St. Lucia* **165 f** 13 45N 61 2W
Labouheyre, *France* **28 D3** 44 13N 0 55W
Laboulaye, *Argentina* **174 C3** 34 10 S 63 30W
Labrador, *Canada* **141 B7** 53 20N 61 0W
Labrador City, *Canada* **141 B6** 52 57N 66 55W
Labrador Sea, *Atl. Oc.* **139 C14** 57 0N 54 0W
Lábrea, *Brazil* **173 B5** 7 15 S 64 51W
Labruguière, *France* **28 E6** 43 31N 2 16 E
Labuan, *Malaysia* **85 A5** 5 20N 115 14 E
Labuan, Pulau, *Malaysia* **85 A5** 5 21N 115 13 E
Labuha, *Indonesia* **82 B3** 0 30 S 127 30 E
Labuhan, *Indonesia* **84 D3** 6 22 S 105 50 E
Labuhanbajo, *Indonesia* **82 D2** 8 28 S 119 54 E
Labuk, Telok, *Malaysia* **85 A5** 6 10N 117 50 E
Labutta, *Burma* **90 G5** 16 9N 94 46 E
Labyrinth, L., *Australia* **127 E2** 30 40 S 135 11 E
Labytnangi, *Russia* **66 C7** 66 39N 66 21 E
Laç, *Albania* **50 E3** 41 38N 19 43 E
Lac-Bouchette, *Canada* **141 C5** 48 16N 72 11W
Lac Édouard, *Canada* **140 C5** 47 40N 72 16W
Lac La Biche, *Canada* **142 C6** 54 45N 111 58W
Lac la Martre = Wha Ti, *Canada* **138 B8** 63 8N 117 16W
Lac La Ronge ⌓, *Canada* **143 B7** 55 9N 104 41W
Lac-Mégantic, *Canada* **141 C5** 45 35N 70 53W
Lac Thien, *Vietnam* **86 F7** 12 25N 108 11 E
Lacanau, *France* **28 D2** 44 58N 1 5W
Lacanau, Étang de, *France* **28 D2** 44 58N 1 7W
Lacantúm →, *Mexico* **163 D6** 16 36N 90 40W
Lacara →, *Spain* **43 G4** 38 55N 6 25W
Lacaune, *France* **28 E6** 43 43N 2 40 E
Lacaune, Mts. de, *France* **28 E6** 43 43N 2 50 E
Laccadive Is. = Lakshadweep Is., *India* **95 J1** 10 0N 72 30 E
Lacepede B., *Australia* **128 D3** 36 40 S 139 40 E
Lacepede Is., *Australia* **124 C3** 16 55 S 122 0 E
Lacerdónia, *Mozam.* **119 F4** 18 3 S 35 35 E
Lacey, *U.S.A.* **160 C4** 47 7N 122 49W
Lachay, Pta., *Peru* **172 C2** 11 17 S 77 44W
Lachen, *India* **90 B2** 27 46N 88 36 E
Lachen, *Switz.* **33 B7** 47 12N 8 51 E
Lachhmangarh, *India* **92 F6** 27 50N 75 4 E
Lachi, *Pakistan* **92 C4** 33 25N 71 20 E
Lachine, *Canada* **140 C5** 45 30N 73 40W
Lachlan →, *Australia* **128 C5** 34 22 S 143 55 E
Lachoc, *Peru* **172 C2** 12 50 S 75 6W
Lachute, *Canada* **140 C5** 45 39N 74 21W
Lackawanna, *U.S.A.* **150 D6** 42 50N 78 50W
Lackawaxen, *U.S.A.* **151 E10** 41 29N 74 59W
Lacolle, *Canada* **151 A11** 45 5N 73 22W
Lacombe, *Canada* **142 C6** 52 30N 113 44W
Lacon, *U.S.A.* **156 C7** 41 2N 89 24W
Lacona, *Iowa, U.S.A.* **156 C3** 41 12N 93 23W
Lacona, *N.Y., U.S.A.* **151 C8** 43 39N 76 10W
Láconi, *Italy* **46 C2** 39 54N 9 4 E
Laconia, *U.S.A.* **151 C13** 43 32N 71 28W
Lacoochee, *U.S.A.* **153 G7** 28 28N 82 11W
Lacq, *France* **28 E3** 43 25N 0 35W
Ladakh Ra., *India* **93 C8** 34 0N 78 0 E
Ladário, *Brazil* **173 D6** 19 1 S 57 35W
Ladd, *U.S.A.* **156 C7** 41 23N 89 13W
Laddonia, *U.S.A.* **156 E5** 39 15N 91 39W
Lądek-Zdrój, *Poland* **55 H3** 50 21N 16 53 E
Ládhon →, *Greece* **48 D3** 37 40N 21 50 E
Ladik, *Turkey* **100 B6** 40 57N 35 58 E
Ladismith, *S. Africa* **116 E3** 33 28 S 21 15 E
Ladíspoli, *Italy* **45 G9** 41 56N 12 5 E
Lādīz, *Iran* **97 D9** 28 55N 61 15 E
Ladnun, *India* **92 F6** 27 38N 74 25 E
Ladoga, L. = Ladozhskoye Ozero, *Russia* **58 B6** 61 15N 30 30 E
Ladozhskoye Ozero, *Russia* **58 B6** 61 15N 30 30 E
Ladrillero, G., *Chile* **176 C1** 49 20 S 75 35W
Ladson, *U.S.A.* **152 C9** 32 59N 80 6W
Ladushkin, *Russia* **54 D7** 54 34N 20 10 E
Lady Elliott I., *Australia* **126 C5** 24 7 S 152 42 E
Lady Grey, *S. Africa* **116 E4** 30 43 S 27 13 E
Lady Lake, *U.S.A.* **153 G8** 28 55N 81 55W
Ladybrand, *S. Africa* **116 D4** 29 9 S 27 29 E
Ladysmith, *Canada* **142 D4** 49 0N 123 49W
Ladysmith, *S. Africa* **117 D4** 28 32 S 29 46 E
Ladysmith, *U.S.A.* **154 C9** 45 28N 91 12W
Ladyznyn, *Ukraine* **53 B14** 48 40N 29 15 E
Lae, *Papua N. G.* **132 D4** 6 40 S 147 2 E
Laem Hin Khom, *Thailand* **87 b** 9 25N 99 56 E
Laem Khat, *Thailand* **87 a** 8 6N 98 26 E
Laem Nga, *Thailand* **87 a** 7 55N 98 27 E
Laem Ngop, *Thailand* **87 F4** 12 10N 102 26 E
Laem Phan Wa, *Thailand* **87 a** 7 47N 98 25 E
Laem Pho, *Thailand* **87 J3** 6 55N 101 19 E
Laem Phrom Thep, *Thailand* **87 a** 7 45N 98 19 E
Laem Riang, *Thailand* **87 a** 8 7N 98 27 E
Laem Sam Rong, *Thailand* **87 b** 9 35N 100 4 E
Laem Son, *Thailand* **87 a** 7 59N 98 16 E
Laem Yamu, *Thailand* **87 a** 7 59N 98 26 E
Lærdalsøyri, *Norway* **18 C4** 61 6N 7 28 E
Læsø, *Denmark* **17 G5** 57 15N 11 5 E
Læsø Rende, *Denmark* **17 G4** 57 20N 10 45 E
Lafayette, *Ala., U.S.A.* **152 C4** 32 54N 85 24W
Lafayette, *Ind., U.S.A.* **157 D10** 40 25N 86 54W
Lafayette, *La., U.S.A.* **155 K9** 30 14N 92 1W
Lafayette, *Tenn., U.S.A.* **149 G2** 36 31N 86 2W
Laferte →, *Canada* **142 A5** 61 53N 117 44W
Lafia, *Nigeria* **113 D6** 8 30N 8 34 E
Lafiagi, *Nigeria* **113 D6** 8 52N 5 20 E
Lafleche, *Canada* **143 D7** 49 45N 106 40W
Lafon, *Sudan* **107 F3** 5 5N 32 29 E
Laful, *India* **95 L11** 7 10N 93 52 E
Lagaip →, *Papua N. G.* **132 C2** 5 4 S 142 52 E
Lagan = Kaspiyskiy, *Russia* **61 H8** 45 22N 47 23 E
Lagan, *Sweden* **17 H7** 56 56N 13 58 E
Lagan →, *Sweden* **17 H6** 56 30N 12 58 E
Lagan →, *U.K.* **23 B6** 54 36N 5 55W
Laganás, *Greece* **39 D2** 37 44N 20 53 E
Lagangilang, *Phil.* **80 C3** 17 37N 120 44 E
Lagarfljót →, *Iceland* **11 B12** 65 40N 14 18W
Lagarto, *Brazil* **170 D4** 10 54 S 37 41W
Lagawe, *Phil.* **80 C3** 16 49N 121 6 E
Lagdo, Rés. de, *Cameroon* **114 A2** 8 40N 14 0 E
Lage, *Germany* **30 D4** 51 59N 8 48 E
Lågen →, *Oppland, Norway* **18 C7** 61 8N 10 25 E
Lågen →, *Vestfold, Norway* **18 E7** 59 3N 10 3 E
Lägerdorf, *Germany* **30 B5** 53 53N 9 34 E
Laggan = Lake Louise, *Canada* **142 C5** 51 30N 116 10W
Laghmān □, *Afghan.* **91 B3** 34 20N 70 0 E
Laghouat, *Algeria* **111 B5** 33 50N 2 59 E
Lagnieu, *France* **29 C9** 45 55N 5 20 E
Lagny-sur-Marne, *France* **27 D9** 48 52N 2 44 E
Lago = Niassa □, *Mozam.* **119 E4** 13 30 S 36 0 E
Lago, *Italy* **47 C9** 39 10N 16 9 E
Lago de Sanabria y Entorno ⌓, *Spain* **42 C4** 42 9N 6 45W
Lago Posadas, *Argentina* **176 C2** 47 30 S 71 40W
Lago Puelo △, *Argentina* **176 B2** 42 30 S 71 55W
Lago Ranco, *Chile* **176 B2** 40 19 S 72 30W
Lagoa, *Azores* **9 d3** 37 45N 25 20W
Lagôa, *Portugal* **43 H2** 37 8N 8 27W
Lagoa do Peixe △, *Brazil* **175 C5** 31 12 S 50 55W
Lagoa Vermelha, *Brazil* **175 B5** 28 13 S 51 32W
Lagoaça, *Portugal* **42 D4** 41 11N 6 44W
Lagodekhi, *Georgia* **61 K8** 41 50N 46 22 E
Lagona = Laguna Beach, *U.S.A.* **161 M9** 33 33N 117 47W
Lagónegro, *Italy* **47 B8** 40 8N 15 45 E
Lagonoy G., *Phil.* **80 E4** 13 35N 123 50 E
Lagos, *Angola* **115 F3** 16 3 S 16 35 E
Lagos, *Nigeria* **113 D5** 6 25N 3 27 E
Lagos, *Portugal* **43 H2** 37 5N 8 41W
Lagos □, *Nigeria* **113 D5** 6 28N 3 25 E
Lagos de Moreno, *Mexico* **162 C4** 21 21N 101 55W
Lagrange, *Australia* **124 C3** 18 45 S 121 43 E
Lagrange, *U.S.A.* **157 C11** 41 39N 85 25W
Lagrange B., *Australia* **124 C3** 18 38 S 121 42 E
Laguardia, *Spain* **40 C2** 42 33N 2 35W
Laguépie, *France* **28 D5** 44 8N 1 57 E
Laguna = Padilla, *Bolivia* **173 D5** 19 19 S 64 20W
Laguna, *Brazil* **175 B6** 28 30 S 48 50W
Laguna, *U.S.A.* **159 J10** 35 2N 107 25W
Laguna □, *Phil.* **80 D3** 14 10N 121 20 E
Laguna Beach, *U.S.A.* **161 M9** 33 33N 117 47W
Laguna Blanca △, *Argentina* **176 A2** 39 0 S 70 5W
Laguna de Duera, *Spain* **42 D6** 41 35N 4 43W
Laguna de la Restinga △, *Venezuela* **165 D6** 10 58N 64 0W
Laguna de Tacarigua △, *Venezuela* **168 A4** 10 59N 64 7W
Laguna del Laja △, *Chile* **174 D1** 37 27 S 71 20W
Laguna del Tigre △, *Guatemala* **164 C1** 17 32N 90 56W
Laguna Limpia, *Argentina* **174 B4** 26 32 S 59 45W
Laguna San Rafael △, *Chile* **176 C2** 46 54 S 73 31W
Lagunas, *Chile* **174 A2** 21 0 S 69 45W
Lagunas, *Peru* **172 B2** 5 10 S 75 35W
Lagunas de Chacahua △, *Mexico* **163 D5** 16 0N 97 43W
Lagunas de Montebello △, *Mexico* **163 D6** 16 6N 91 41W
Lagunas de Ruidera ⌓, *Spain* **41 G2** 38 57N 2 52W
Lagunillas, *Bolivia* **173 D5** 19 38 S 63 43W
Lahad Datu, *Malaysia* **85 A5** 5 0N 118 20 E
Lahad Datu, Telok, *Malaysia* **85 B5** 4 50N 118 20 E
Lahaina, *U.S.A.* **145 C5** 20 53N 156 41W
Lahan Sai, *Thailand* **86 E4** 14 25N 102 52 E
Lahanam, *Laos* **86 D5** 16 16N 105 16 E
Lahar, *India* **93 F8** 26 12N 78 57 E
Laharpur, *India* **93 F9** 27 43N 80 56 E
Lahat, *Indonesia* **84 C2** 3 45 S 103 30 E
Lahe, *Burma* **90 B5** 26 20N 95 26 E
Lahewa, *Indonesia* **84 B1** 1 22N 97 12 E
Laḥij, *Yemen* **98 D4** 13 4N 44 53 E
Lāhījān, *Iran* **97 B6** 37 10N 50 6 E
Lahilahi Pt., *U.S.A.* **145 K13** 21 28N 158 13W
Lahn = Wleń, *Poland* **55 G2** 51 2N 15 39 E
Lahn →, *Germany* **31 E3** 50 19N 7 37 E
Lahnstein, *Germany* **31 E3** 50 19N 7 37 E
Laholm, *Sweden* **17 H7** 56 30N 13 2 E
Laholmsbukten, *Sweden* **17 H6** 56 30N 12 45 E
Lahore, *Pakistan* **91 C4** 31 32N 74 22 E
Lahpongsel, *Burma* **90 B7** 27 7N 98 25 E
Lahr, *Germany* **31 G3** 48 20N 7 53 E
Lahri, *Pakistan* **92 E3** 29 11N 68 13 E
Lahti, *Finland* **15 F21** 60 58N 25 40 E
Lahtis = Lahti, *Finland* **15 F21** 60 58N 25 40 E
Lahugala Kitulana △, *Sri Lanka* **95 L5** 6 50N 81 40 E
Laï, *Chad* **109 G3** 9 25N 16 18 E
Lai Chau, *Vietnam* **76 F4** 22 5N 103 3 E
Lai-hka, *Burma* **90 E6** 21 16N 97 40 E
Laiagam, *Papua N. G.* **132 C2** 5 33 S 143 30 E

Lai'an, China 77 A12 32 28N 118 30 E
Laibach = Ljubljana, Slovenia 45 B11 46 4N 14 33 E
Laibin, China 76 F7 23 42N 109 14 E
Laie, U.S.A. 145 J14 21 39N 157 56W
Laifeng, China 76 C7 29 27N 109 20 E
L'Aigle, France 26 D7 48 46N 0 38 E
Laignes, France 27 E11 47 50N 4 20 E
L'Aiguillon-sur-Mer, France 28 B2 46 20N 1 18W
Laila = Layla, Si. Arabia 98 B4 22 10N 46 40 E
Laingsburg, S. Africa 116 E3 33 9S 20 52 E
Lainioälven →, Sweden 14 C20 67 35N 22 40 E
Lairg, U.K. 22 C4 58 2N 4 24W
Laïri, B. de, Chad 109 F3 12 28N 16 45 E
Lais, Phil. 81 H5 6 20N 125 39 E
Laishui, China 78 E8 39 23N 115 45 E
Laissac, France 28 D6 44 23N 2 50 E
Láives, Italy 45 B8 46 26N 11 20 E
Laiwu, China 75 F9 36 15N 117 40 E
Laixi, China 75 F11 36 50N 120 31 E
Laiyang, China 75 F11 36 59N 120 45 E
Laiyuan, China 74 E8 39 20N 114 40 E
Laizhou, China 75 F10 37 8N 119 57 E
Laizhou Wan, China 75 F10 37 30N 119 30 E
Laja →, Mexico 162 C4 20 55N 100 46W
Lajeado = Guiratinga, Brazil 173 D7 16 21 S 53 45W
Lajedo, Azores 9 d2 39 23N 31 15W
Lajere, Nigeria 113 C7 12 10N 11 25 E
Lajes, Azores 9 d1 38 46N 27 6W
Lajes, Rio Grande do N., Brazil 170 C4 5 41 S 36 14W
Lajes, Sta. Catarina, Brazil 175 B5 27 48 S 50 20W
Lajes das Flores, Azores 9 d2 39 23N 31 10W
Lajes do Pico, Azores 9 d1 38 23N 28 16W
Lajinha, Brazil 171 F3 20 9 S 41 37W
Lajkovac, Serbia & M. 50 B4 44 27N 20 14 E
Lajosmizse, Hungary 52 C4 47 3N 19 32 E
Lak Sao, Laos 86 C5 18 11N 104 59 E
Láka, Greece 38 C10 39 17N 20 9 E
Lakaband, Pakistan 92 D3 31 2N 69 15 E
Lakamané, Mali 112 C3 14 35N 9 44W
Lakatoro, Vanuatu 133 F5 16 6 S 167 25 E
Lake Alfred, U.S.A. 153 G8 28 6N 81 44W
Lake Alpine, U.S.A. 160 G7 38 29N 120 0W
Lake Andes, U.S.A. 154 D5 43 9N 98 32W
Lake Arthur, U.S.A. 155 K8 30 5N 92 41W
Lake Bindegolly △, Australia 127 D3 28 0 S 144 12 E
Lake Boga, Australia 128 C5 35 26 S 143 38 E
Lake Butler, U.S.A. 152 E7 30 1N 82 21W
Lake Cargelligo, Australia 129 B7 33 15 S 146 22 E
Lake Charles, U.S.A. 155 K8 30 14N 93 13W
Lake City, Colo., U.S.A. 159 G10 38 2N 107 19W
Lake City, Fla., U.S.A. 152 E7 30 11N 82 38W
Lake City, Iowa, U.S.A. 156 B2 42 16N 94 44W
Lake City, Mich., U.S.A. 148 C3 44 20N 85 13W
Lake City, Minn., U.S.A. 154 C8 44 27N 92 16W
Lake City, Pa., U.S.A. 150 D4 42 1N 80 21W
Lake City, S.C., U.S.A. 152 B10 33 52N 79 45W
Lake Clark △, U.S.A. 144 D9 61 0N 154 0W
Lake Clarke Shores, U.S.A. 153 J9 26 39N 80 5W
Lake Coleridge, N.Z. 131 D6 43 17 S 171 30 E
Lake Cowichan, Canada 142 D4 48 49N 124 3W
Lake District △, U.K. 20 C4 54 30N 3 21W
Lake Elsinore, U.S.A. 161 M9 33 38N 117 20W
Lake Eyre △, Australia 127 D2 28 40 S 137 31 E
Lake Forest, U.S.A. 157 B9 42 15N 87 50W
Lake Gairdner △, Australia 127 E2 31 41 S 135 51 E
Lake Geneva, U.S.A. 157 B8 42 36N 88 26W
Lake George, U.S.A. 151 C11 43 26N 73 43W
Lake Grace, Australia 125 F2 33 7 S 118 28 E
Lake Harbor, U.S.A. 153 J9 26 42N 80 48W
Lake Harbour = Kimmirut, Canada 139 B13 62 50N 69 50W
Lake Havasu City, U.S.A. 161 L12 34 27N 114 22W
Lake Helen, U.S.A. 153 G8 28 59N 81 14W
Lake Hughes, U.S.A. 161 L8 34 41N 118 26W
Lake Isabella, U.S.A. 161 K8 35 38N 118 28W
Lake Jackson, U.S.A. 155 L7 29 3N 95 27W
Lake Junction, U.S.A. 158 D8 44 35N 110 28W
Lake King, Australia 125 F2 33 5 S 119 45 E
Lake Kopiago, Papua N. G. 132 C2 5 23 S 142 31 E
Lake Kutubu, Papua N. G. 132 D2 6 20 S 143 18 E
Lake Lenore, Canada 143 C8 52 24N 104 59W
Lake Louise, Canada 142 C5 51 30N 116 10W
Lake Malawi △, Malawi 119 E3 14 2 S 34 53 E
Lake Mburo △, Uganda 118 C3 0 33 S 30 56 E
Lake Mead ⌂, U.S.A. 161 K12 36 15N 114 30W
Lake Meredith ⌂, U.S.A. 155 H4 35 50N 101 50W
Lake Mills, Iowa, U.S.A. 154 D8 43 25N 93 32W
Lake Mills, Wis., U.S.A. 157 A8 43 5N 88 55W
Lake Murray, Papua N. G. 132 D1 6 48 S 141 29 E
Lake Nakura △, Kenya 118 C4 0 21 S 36 8 E
Lake Naujan △, Phil. 80 E3 13 9N 121 20 E
Lake Odessa, U.S.A. 157 B11 42 47N 85 8W
Lake Orion, U.S.A. 157 B13 42 47N 83 14W
Lake Park, Fla., U.S.A. 153 J9 26 48N 80 3W
Lake Park, Ga., U.S.A. 152 E6 30 41N 83 11W
Lake Placid, Fla., U.S.A. 153 H8 27 18N 81 22W
Lake Placid, N.Y., U.S.A. 151 B11 44 17N 73 59W
Lake Pleasant, U.S.A. 151 C10 43 28N 74 25W
Lake Providence, U.S.A. 155 J9 32 48N 91 10W
Lake Pukaki, N.Z. 131 E5 44 11 S 170 8 E
Lake Roosevelt ⌂, U.S.A. 158 C4 47 57N 118 59W
Lake St. Peter, Canada 150 A6 45 18N 78 2W
Lake Superior ⌂, Canada 140 C3 47 45N 84 45W
Lake Tekapo, N.Z. 131 D5 44 0 S 170 30 E
Lake Torrens △, Australia 127 E2 30 55 S 137 40 E
Lake View, U.S.A. 156 B1 42 18N 95 3W
Lake Villa, U.S.A. 157 B8 42 25N 88 5W
Lake Village, U.S.A. 155 J9 33 20N 91 17W
Lake Wales, U.S.A. 153 H8 27 54N 81 35W
Lake Worth, U.S.A. 153 J9 26 37N 80 3W
Lake Zurich, U.S.A. 157 B8 42 12N 88 5W
Lakeba, Fiji 133 B3 18 13 S 178 47W
Lakeba Passage, Fiji 133 B3 18 0 S 178 45W
Lakefield, Canada 140 D4 44 25N 78 16W
Lakefield △, Australia 126 B3 15 24 S 144 26 E
Lakehurst, U.S.A. 151 F10 40 1N 74 19W
Lakeland, Australia 126 B3 15 49 S 144 57 E
Lakeland, Fla., U.S.A. 153 G8 28 3N 81 57W
Lakeland, Ga., U.S.A. 152 D6 31 2N 83 4W
Lakemba = Lakeba, Fiji 133 B3 18 13 S 178 47W
Lakeport, Calif., U.S.A. 160 F4 39 3N 122 55W
Lakeport, Mich., U.S.A. 150 C2 43 7N 82 30W
Lakes Entrance, Australia 129 D8 37 50 S 148 0 E
Lakeside, Calif., U.S.A. 161 N10 32 52N 116 55W
Lakeside, Nebr., U.S.A. 154 D3 42 3N 102 26W
Lakeside, Ohio, U.S.A. 150 E2 41 32N 82 46W
Lakeview, U.S.A. 158 E3 42 11N 120 21W
Lakeville, U.S.A. 154 C8 44 39N 93 14W
Lakewood, Colo., U.S.A. 154 F2 39 44N 105 5W
Lakewood, N.J., U.S.A. 151 F10 40 6N 74 13W
Lakewood, N.Y., U.S.A. 150 D5 42 6N 79 19W
Lakewood, Ohio, U.S.A. 150 E3 41 29N 81 48W
Lakewood, Wash., U.S.A. 160 C4 47 11N 122 32W
Lakewood Park, U.S.A. 153 H9 27 30N 80 23W
Lakha, India 92 F4 26 9N 70 54 E
Lakhaniá, Greece 38 F11 35 58N 27 54 E
Lakhimpur, India 93 F9 27 57N 80 46 E
Lakhipur, Assam, India 90 C4 24 48N 93 0 E
Lakhipur, Assam, India 90 B3 26 2N 90 18 E
Lakhnadon, India 93 H8 22 36N 79 36 E
Lakhnau = Lucknow, India 93 F9 26 50N 81 0 E
Lakhonpheng, Laos 86 E5 15 54N 105 34 E
Lakhpat, India 92 H3 23 48N 68 47 E
Läki, Azerbaijan 61 K8 40 34N 47 22 E
Laki, Iceland 11 C8 64 4N 18 14W
Lakin, U.S.A. 155 G4 37 57N 101 15W
Lakitusaki →, Canada 140 B3 54 21N 82 25W
Lakki, Pakistan 92 C4 32 36N 70 55 E
Lákkoi, Greece 39 E4 35 24N 23 57 E
Lakonía □, Greece 48 E4 36 55N 22 30 E
Lakonikós Kólpos, Greece 48 E4 36 40N 22 40 E
Lakor, Indonesia 82 C3 8 15 S 128 17 E
Lakota, Ivory C. 112 D3 5 50N 5 30W
Lakota, U.S.A. 154 A5 48 2N 98 21W
Laksar, India 92 E8 29 46N 78 3 E
Laksefjorden, Norway 14 A22 70 45N 26 50 E
Lakselv, Norway 14 A21 70 2N 25 0 E
Laksettipet, India 94 E4 18 52N 79 13 E
Lakshadweep □, India 95 J1 10 0N 72 30 E
Lakshadweep Is., India 95 J1 10 0N 72 30 E
Laksham, Bangla. 90 D3 23 14N 91 8 E
Lakshimpur, Bangla. 90 D3 22 58N 90 50 E
Lakshmanpur, India 93 H10 22 58N 83 3 E
Lakshmeshwar, India 95 G2 15 9N 75 28 E
Lakshmikantapur, India 93 H13 22 5N 88 20 E
Lakuramau, Papua N. G. 132 B6 2 54 S 151 15 E
Lal-lo, Phil. 80 B3 18 12N 121 40 E
Lala, Dem. Rep. of the Congo 115 C4 4 10 S 20 30 E
Lala, Phil. 81 H4 7 59N 123 46 E
Lala Musa, Pakistan 92 C5 32 40N 73 57 E
Lalaghat, India 90 C4 24 30N 92 40 E
Lalago, Tanzania 118 C3 3 28 S 33 58 E
Lalapanzi, Zimbabwe 119 F3 19 20 S 30 15 E
Lalapaşa, Turkey 51 E10 41 49N 26 44 E
Lalbenque, France 28 D5 44 19N 1 34 E
Lalbert, Australia 128 C5 35 38 S 143 20 E
L'Albufera, Spain 41 F4 39 20N 0 27W
Lalganj, India 93 G11 25 52N 85 13 E
Lalgola, India 93 G13 24 25N 88 15 E
Lālī, Iran 97 C6 32 21N 49 6 E
Lalibela, Ethiopia 107 E4 12 3N 39 0 E
Lalin, China 75 B14 45 12N 127 0 E
Lalín, Spain 42 C2 42 40N 8 5W
Lalin He →, China 75 B13 45 32N 125 40 E
Lalinde, France 28 D4 44 50N 0 44 E
Lalitapur, Nepal 93 F11 27 40N 85 20 E
Lalitpur, India 93 G8 24 42N 78 28 E
Lalkua, India 93 E8 29 5N 79 31 E
Lalm, Norway 18 C6 61 50N 9 17 E
Lalsot, India 92 F7 26 34N 76 20 E
Lam, Vietnam 86 B6 21 21N 106 31 E
Lam Pao Res., Thailand 86 D4 16 50N 103 15 E
Lama Kara, Togo 113 D5 9 30N 1 15 E
Lamag, Malaysia 85 A5 5 29N 117 49 E
Lamaipum, Burma 90 C6 25 40N 97 57 E
Lamap, Vanuatu 133 F5 16 26 S 167 43 E
Lamar, Colo., U.S.A. 154 F3 38 5N 102 37W
Lamar, Mo., U.S.A. 155 G7 37 30N 94 16W
Lamarque, Argentina 176 A3 39 24 S 65 40W
Lamas, Peru 172 B2 6 28 S 76 31W
Lamastre, France 29 D8 44 59N 4 35 E
Lambach, Austria 34 C6 48 6N 13 51 E
Lamballe, France 26 D4 48 29N 2 31W
Lambaréné, Gabon 114 C2 0 41 S 10 12 E
Lambasa = Labasa, Fiji 133 A2 16 30 S 179 27 E
Lambay I., Ireland 23 C5 53 29N 6 1W
Lambayeque □, Peru 172 B2 6 45 S 80 0W
Lambert, C., Papua N. G. 132 C6 4 11 S 151 31 E
Lambert Glacier, Antarctica 7 D6 71 0 S 70 0 E
Lambert-St. Louis International ✕ (STL), U.S.A. 156 F6 38 45N 90 22W
Lambert's Bay, S. Africa 116 E2 32 5 S 18 17 E
Lambertville, U.S.A. 157 C13 41 46N 83 35W
Lambesc, France 29 E9 43 39N 5 16 E
Lambèse = Tazoult, Algeria 111 A6 35 29N 6 11 E
Lambeth, Canada 150 D3 42 54N 81 18W
Lambi, Solomon Is. 133 M10 9 22 S 159 39 E
Lámbia, Greece 48 D3 37 52N 21 53 E
Lambomakondro, Madag. 117 C7 22 41 S 44 44 E
Lambon, Papua N. G. 132 C7 4 45 S 152 48 E
Lambro →, Italy 44 C6 45 8N 9 32 E
Lambton Shores, Canada 150 C3 43 10N 81 56W
Lambu, Papua N. G. 132 B6 3 18 S 151 43 E
Lambunao, Phil. 81 F4 11 3N 122 29 E
Lamé, Chad 109 G2 9 15N 14 32 E
Lame, Nigeria 113 C6 10 30N 9 20 E
Lame Deer, U.S.A. 158 D10 45 37N 106 40W
Lamego, Portugal 42 D3 41 5N 7 52W
Lamèque, Canada 141 C7 47 45N 64 38W
Lameroo, Australia 128 C4 35 19 S 140 33 E
Lamesa, U.S.A. 155 J4 32 44N 101 58W
Lamía, Greece 48 C4 38 55N 22 26 E
Lamigan Pt., Phil. 81 H6 6 48N 126 21 E
Lamine →, U.S.A. 156 F4 38 59N 92 51W
Lamington △, Australia 127 D5 28 13 S 153 12 E
Lamitan, Phil. 81 H4 6 39N 122 8 E
Lamlan, Mt., Guam 133 R15 13 22N 144 41 E
Lamma I., China 69 G11 22 12N 114 8 E
Lammermuir Hills, U.K. 22 F6 55 50N 2 40W
Lammhult, Sweden 17 G8 57 10N 14 35 E
Lamoille →, U.S.A. 151 B11 44 38N 73 13W
Lamon B., Phil. 80 D4 14 30N 122 20 E
Lamongan, Indonesia 85 D4 7 7 S 112 25 E
Lamoni, U.S.A. 156 D3 40 37N 93 56W
Lamont, Canada 142 C6 53 46N 112 50W
Lamont, Calif., U.S.A. 161 K8 35 15N 118 55W
Lamont, Fla., U.S.A. 152 E6 30 23N 83 49W
Lamont, Iowa, U.S.A. 156 A5 42 35N 91 40W
Lamont, Wyo., U.S.A. 158 E10 42 13N 107 29W
Lamotte-Beuvron, France 27 E9 47 36N 2 2 E
Lampa, Peru 172 D3 15 22 S 70 22W
Lampang, Thailand 86 C2 18 16N 99 32 E
Lampasas, U.S.A. 155 K5 31 4N 98 11W
Lampazos de Naranjo, Mexico 162 B4 27 2N 100 32W
Lampedusa, Medit. S. 111 A7 35 36N 12 40 E
Lampertheim, Germany 31 F4 49 35N 8 27 E
Lampeter, U.K. 21 E3 52 7N 4 4W
Lampione, Medit. S. 108 A2 35 33N 12 20 E
Lampman, Canada 143 D8 49 25N 102 50W
Lamprechtshausen, Austria 34 D5 48 0N 12 58 E
Lampung □, Indonesia 84 D2 5 30 S 104 30 E
Lamta, India 93 H9 22 8N 80 7 E
Lamu, Burma 90 F5 19 14N 94 10 E
Lamu, Kenya 118 C5 2 16 S 40 55 E
Lamud, Peru 172 B2 6 10 S 77 57W
Lamy, U.S.A. 159 J11 35 29N 105 53W
Lan Xian, China 74 E6 38 15N 111 35 E
Lan Yu = Hungt'ou Hsü, Taiwan 77 G13 22 0N 121 30 E
Lanai, U.S.A. 145 C5 20 50N 156 55W
Lanai City, U.S.A. 145 C5 20 50N 156 55W
Lanaihale, U.S.A. 145 C5 20 49N 156 53W
Lanak La, China 93 B8 34 27N 79 32 E
Lanak'o Shank'ou = Lanak La, China 93 B8 34 27N 79 32 E
Lanao, L., Phil. 81 H5 7 52N 124 15 E
Lanao del Norte □, Phil. 81 H5 8 0N 124 10 E
Lanao del Sur □, Phil. 81 H5 7 40N 124 15 E
Lanark, Canada 151 A8 45 1N 76 22W
Lanark, U.K. 22 F5 55 40N 3 47W
Lanark, U.S.A. 156 B7 42 6N 89 50W
Lanbi Kyun, Burma 87 G2 10 50N 98 20 E
Lancang, China 76 F2 22 36N 99 58 E
Lancang Jiang →, China 76 G3 21 40N 101 10 E
Lancashire □, U.K. 20 D5 53 50N 2 48W
Lancaster, Canada 151 A10 45 10N 74 30W
Lancaster, U.K. 20 C5 54 3N 2 48W
Lancaster, Calif., U.S.A. 161 L8 34 42N 118 8W
Lancaster, Ky., U.S.A. 148 G3 37 37N 84 35W
Lancaster, Mo., U.S.A. 156 D4 40 31N 92 32W
Lancaster, N.H., U.S.A. 151 B13 44 29N 71 34W
Lancaster, N.Y., U.S.A. 150 D6 42 54N 78 40W
Lancaster, Ohio, U.S.A. 148 F4 39 43N 82 36W
Lancaster, Pa., U.S.A. 151 F8 40 2N 76 19W
Lancaster, S.C., U.S.A. 149 H5 34 43N 80 46W
Lancaster, Wis., U.S.A. 156 B6 42 51N 90 43W
Lancaster Sd., Canada 139 A11 74 13N 84 0W
Lancelin, Australia 125 F2 31 0 S 115 18 E
Lanchow = Lanzhou, China 74 F2 36 1N 103 52 E
Lanchyn, Ukraine 53 B9 48 33N 24 45 E
Lanciano, Italy 45 F11 42 14N 14 23 E
Lanco, Chile 176 A2 39 24 S 72 46W
Lancones, Peru 172 A1 4 30 S 80 30W
Lancun, China 75 F11 36 25N 120 10 E
Łańcut, Poland 55 H9 50 10N 22 13 E
Lancy, Switz. 32 D2 46 12N 6 8 E
Land Between the Lakes ⌂, U.S.A. 149 G1 36 55N 88 7W
Landau, Bayern, Germany 31 G8 48 40N 12 41 E
Landau, Rhld-Pfz., Germany 31 F4 49 12N 8 6 E
Landay, Afghan. 91 C1 30 31N 63 47 E
Landeck, Austria 34 D3 47 9N 10 34 E
Lander, U.S.A. 158 E9 42 50N 108 44W
Lander →, Australia 124 D5 22 0 S 132 0 E
Landerneau, France 26 D2 48 28N 4 17W
Landeryd, Sweden 17 G7 57 7N 13 15 E
Landes, France 28 D2 44 0N 1 0W
Landes □, France 28 E3 43 57N 0 48W
Landes de Gascogne ⌂, France 28 D3 44 23N 0 50W
Landeshut = Kamienna Góra, Poland 55 H3 50 47N 16 2 E
Landete, Spain 40 F3 39 56N 1 25W
Landfall I., India 95 H11 13 40N 93 2 E
Landi Kotal, Pakistan 92 B4 34 7N 71 6 E
Landisburg, U.S.A. 150 F7 40 21N 77 19W
Landivisiau, France 26 D2 48 31N 4 6W
Landquart, Switz. 33 C9 46 58N 9 32 E
Landquart →, Switz. 33 C9 46 50N 9 47 E
Landrecies, France 27 B10 50 7N 3 40 E
Land's End, U.K. 21 G2 50 4N 5 44W
Landsberg = Górowo Iławeckie, Poland 54 D7 54 17N 20 30 E
Landsberg, Germany 31 G6 48 2N 10 53 E
Landsberg an der Warthe = Gorzów Wielkopolski, Poland 55 F2 52 43N 15 15 E
Landsberg in Oberschlesien = Gorzów Śląski, Poland 55 G5 51 3N 18 22 E
Landsborough Cr. →, Australia 126 C3 22 28 S 144 35 E
Landsbro, Sweden 17 G8 57 24N 14 56 E
Landshut, Germany 31 G8 48 34N 12 8 E
Landskrona, Sweden 17 J6 55 53N 12 50 E
Landstuhl, Germany 31 F3 49 24N 7 33 E
Landvetter, Sweden 17 G6 57 41N 12 17 E
Lane, U.S.A. 152 B10 33 32N 79 53W
Lanesboro, U.S.A. 151 E9 41 57N 75 34W
Lanester, France 26 E3 47 46N 3 22W
Lanett, U.S.A. 152 C4 32 52N 85 12W
Lang Qua, Vietnam 86 A5 22 16N 104 27 E
Lang Shan, China 74 D4 41 0N 106 30 E
Lang Son, Vietnam 76 G6 21 52N 106 42 E
Lang Suan, Thailand 87 H2 9 57N 99 4 E
Langå, Denmark 17 H3 56 23N 9 54 E
Langa-Langa, Dem Rep. of the Congo 114 C3 3 50 S 15 59 E
Langádhás, Greece 50 F7 40 46N 23 6 E
Langádhia, Greece 48 D4 37 43N 22 1 E
Långan →, Sweden 16 A8 63 19N 14 44 E
Langanes, Iceland 11 A12 66 20N 14 53W
Langano, L., Ethiopia 107 F4 7 36N 38 43 E
Langar, Afghan. 65 E6 37 2N 73 47 E
Langar, Iran 97 C9 35 23N 60 25 E
Langara I., Canada 142 C2 54 14N 133 1W
Långås, Sweden 17 H6 56 58N 12 26 E
Langatabbetje, Suriname 169 C7 4 59N 54 28W
Langdai, China 76 D5 26 6N 105 21 E
Langdon, U.S.A. 154 A5 48 45N 98 22W
Långe Jan = Ölands södra udde, Sweden 17 H10 56 12N 16 23 E
Langeac, France 28 C7 45 7N 3 29 E
Langeais, France 26 E7 47 20N 0 24 E
Langeb Baraka →, Sudan 106 D4 17 28N 36 50 E
Langeberg, S. Africa 116 E3 33 55 S 21 0 E
Langeberge, S. Africa 116 D3 28 15 S 22 33 E
Langeland, Denmark 17 K4 54 56N 10 48 E
Langelands Bælt, Denmark 17 K4 54 50N 10 55 E
Langen, Austria 33 B10 47 8N 10 7 E
Langen, Hessen, Germany 31 F4 49 59N 8 40 E
Langen, Niedersachsen, Germany 30 B4 53 36N 8 36 E
Langenargen, Germany 33 A9 47 36N 9 33 E
Langenbielau = Bielawa, Poland 55 H3 50 43N 16 37 E
Langenburg, Canada 143 C8 50 51N 101 43W
Langeneß, Germany 30 A4 54 38N 8 36 E
Langenlois, Austria 34 C8 48 29N 15 40 E
Langenthal, Switz. 32 B5 47 13N 7 47 E
Langeoog, Germany 30 B3 53 45N 7 32 E
Langeskov, Denmark 17 J4 55 22N 10 35 E
Langesund, Norway 18 F6 59 0N 9 45 E
Langevåg, Norway 18 B3 62 26N 6 13 E
Långhem, Sweden 17 G7 57 36N 13 14 E
Langhirano, Italy 44 D7 44 37N 10 16 E
Langholm, U.K. 22 F5 55 9N 3 0W
Langisjór, Iceland 11 C8 64 11N 18 15W
Langjökull, Iceland 11 C6 64 39N 20 12W
Langkawi, Pulau, Malaysia 87 J2 6 25N 99 45 E
Langklip, S. Africa 116 D3 28 12 S 20 20 E
Langkon, Malaysia 85 A5 6 30N 116 40 E
Langlade, St-P. & M. 141 C8 46 50N 56 20W
Langley, Canada 160 A4 49 7N 122 39W
Langnau, Switz. 32 C5 46 56N 7 47 E
Langogne, France 28 D7 44 43N 3 50 E
Langon, France 28 D3 44 33N 0 16W
Langøya, Norway 14 B16 68 45N 14 50 E
Langreo, Spain 42 B5 43 18N 5 40W
Langres, France 27 E12 47 52N 5 20 E
Langres, Plateau de, France 27 E12 47 45N 5 3 E
Langsa, Indonesia 84 B1 4 30N 97 57 E
Långsele, Sweden 16 A11 63 12N 17 4 E
Långshyttan, Sweden 16 D10 60 27N 16 2 E
Langtang △, Nepal 93 E11 28 10N 85 30 E
Langtao, Burma 90 B6 27 15N 97 34 E
Langting, India 90 C4 25 31N 93 7 E
Langtry, U.S.A. 155 L4 29 49N 101 34W
Langu, Thailand 87 J2 6 53N 99 47 E
Langue de Barbarie △, Senegal 112 C1 14 54N 16 30W
Languedoc, France 28 E7 43 58N 3 55 E
Languedoc-Roussillon □, France 28 E6 43 25N 3 0 E
Langwang, China 69 F9 22 38N 113 27 E
Langwies, Switz. 33 C9 46 50N 9 44 E
Langxi, China 77 B12 31 10N 119 12 E
Langxiangzhen, China 74 E9 39 43N 116 8 E
Langzhong, China 76 B5 31 38N 105 58 E
Lanigan, Canada 143 C7 51 51N 105 2W
Lanín △, Argentina 176 A2 40 0 S 71 58W
Lanjigarh, India 94 E6 19 43N 83 23 E
Lankao, China 74 G8 34 48N 114 50 E
Länkäran, Azerbaijan 97 B6 38 48N 48 52 E
Lanmeur, France 26 D3 48 39N 3 43W
Lannemezan, France 28 E4 43 8N 0 23 E
Lannilis, France 26 D2 48 35N 4 32W
Lannion, France 26 D3 48 46N 3 29W
L'Annonciation, Canada 140 C5 46 25N 74 55W
Lanouaille, France 28 C5 45 24N 1 9 E
Lanping, China 76 D2 26 28N 99 15 E
Lansdale, U.S.A. 151 F9 40 14N 75 17W
Lansdowne, Australia 129 A10 31 48 S 152 30 E
Lansdowne, Canada 151 B8 44 24N 76 1W
Lansdowne, India 93 E8 29 50N 78 41 E
Lansdowne House, Canada 140 B2 52 14N 87 53W
L'Anse, U.S.A. 148 B1 46 45N 88 27W
L'Anse au Loup, Canada 141 B8 51 32N 56 50W
L'Anse aux Meadows, Canada 141 B8 51 36N 55 32W
Lansford, U.S.A. 151 F9 40 50N 75 53W
Lanshan, China 77 E9 25 24N 112 10 E
Lansing, U.S.A. 157 B12 42 44N 84 33W
Lanslebourg-Mont-Cenis, France 29 C10 45 17N 6 52 E
Lanta Yai, Ko, Thailand 87 J2 7 35N 99 3 E
Lantana, U.S.A. 153 J9 26 35N 80 3W
Lantau I., China 69 G10 22 15N 113 56 E
Lantewa, Nigeria 113 C7 12 16N 11 44 E
Lantian, China 74 G5 34 11N 109 20 E
Lanus, Argentina 174 C4 34 44 S 58 27W
Lanusei, Italy 46 C2 39 52N 9 34 E
Lanuza, Phil. 81 G6 9 14N 126 4 E
Lanxi, China 77 C12 29 13N 119 28 E
Lanzarote, Canary Is. 9 e2 29 0N 13 40W
Lanzarote ✕ (ACE), Canary Is. 9 e2 28 57N 13 40W
Lanzhou, China 74 F2 36 1N 103 52 E
Lanzo Torinese, Italy 44 C4 45 16N 7 28 E
Lao →, Italy 47 C8 39 47N 15 48 E
Lao Bao, Laos 86 D6 16 35N 106 30 E
Lao Cai, Vietnam 76 F4 22 30N 103 57 E
Laoag, Phil. 80 B3 18 7N 120 34 E
Laoang, Phil. 80 E5 12 32N 125 8 E
Laoha He →, China 75 C11 43 25N 120 35 E
Laohekou, China 77 A8 32 22N 111 38 E
Laois □, Ireland 23 D4 52 57N 7 36W
Laon, France 27 C10 49 33N 3 35 E
Laona, U.S.A. 148 C1 45 34N 88 40W
Laos ■, Asia 86 D5 17 45N 105 0 E
Lapa, Brazil 175 B6 25 46 S 49 44W
Lapac I., Phil. 81 J3 5 32N 120 47 E
Lapai, Nigeria 113 D6 9 5N 6 32 E
Lapalisse, France 27 F10 46 15N 3 38 E
Lapara I., Phil. 81 J2 5 57N 120 0 E
Lapeer, U.S.A. 157 A13 43 3N 83 19W
Lapeyrade, France 28 D3 44 4N 0 3W
Lapithos, Cyprus 39 E9 35 21N 33 11 E
Lapland = Lappland, Europe 14 B21 68 7N 24 0 E
Laporte, U.S.A. 151 E8 41 25N 76 30W
Lapovo, Serbia & M. 50 B5 44 10N 21 7 E
Lappeenranta, Finland 15 F23 61 3N 28 12 E
Lappland, Europe 14 B21 68 7N 24 0 E
Lappo = Lapua, Finland 14 E20 62 58N 23 0 E
Laprida, Argentina 174 D3 37 34 S 60 45W
Lapseki, Turkey 51 F10 40 20N 26 41 E
Laptev Sea, Russia 67 B13 76 0N 125 0 E
Lapu-Lapu, Phil. 81 F4 10 20N 123 55 E
Lapua, Finland 14 E20 62 58N 23 0 E
Lăpuş →, Romania 53 C8 47 25N 23 40 E
Lapuş, Munţii, Romania 53 C8 47 20N 23 50 E
Lăpuşna, Moldova 53 D13 46 53N 28 25 E
Łapy, Poland 55 F9 52 59N 22 52 E
Laqiya Arba'in, Sudan 106 C2 20 1N 28 1 E
Laqiya Umran, Sudan 106 D2 19 55N 28 18 E
L'Àquila, Italy 45 F10 42 22N 13 22 E
Lār, Āzarbājān-e Sharqī, Iran 96 B5 38 30N 47 52 E
Lār, Fārs, Iran 97 E7 27 40N 54 14 E
Lara, Australia 128 E6 38 2 S 144 26 E
Lara □, Venezuela 168 A4 10 10N 69 50W
Larabanga, Ghana 112 D4 9 16N 1 56W
Laracha, Spain 42 B2 43 15N 8 35W
Larache, Morocco 110 A3 35 10N 6 5W
Laragaran = Plaridel, Phil. 81 G4 8 37N 123 43 E
Laragne-Montéglin, France 29 D9 44 18N 5 49 E
Laramie, U.S.A. 154 E2 41 19N 105 35W
Laramie Mts., U.S.A. 154 E2 42 0N 105 30W
Laranjeiras, Brazil 170 D4 10 48 S 37 10W
Laranjeiras do Sul, Brazil 175 B5 25 23 S 52 23W
Larantuka, Indonesia 82 C2 8 21 S 122 55 E
Larat, Indonesia 83 C4 7 0 S 132 0 E
L'Arbresle, France 29 C8 45 50N 4 36 E
Lärbro, Sweden 17 G12 57 47N 18 50 E
Lårdal, Norway 18 E5 59 25N 8 10 E
Larde, Mozam. 119 F4 16 28 S 39 43 E
Larder Lake, Canada 140 C4 48 5N 79 40W
Lardhos, Ákra = Líndhos, Ákra, Greece 38 E12 36 4N 28 10 E
Lardhos, Órmos, Greece 38 E12 36 4N 28 2 E
Laredo, Spain 42 B7 43 26N 3 28W
Laredo, U.S.A. 155 M5 27 30N 99 30W
Laredo Sd., Canada 142 C3 52 30N 128 53W
Larena, Phil. 81 G4 9 15N 123 35 E
Largentière, France 29 D8 44 34N 4 18 E
L'Argentière-la-Bessée, France 29 D10 44 47N 6 33 E
Largo, U.S.A. 153 H7 27 55N 82 47W
Largo, Key, U.S.A. 153 K9 25 15N 80 15W
Largs, U.K. 22 F4 55 47N 4 52W
Lari, Italy 44 E7 43 34N 10 35 E
Lariang, Indonesia 82 B1 1 26 S 119 17 E
Larimore, U.S.A. 154 B6 47 54N 97 38W
Larino, Italy 45 G11 41 48N 14 54 E
Lárisa, Greece 48 B4 39 36N 22 27 E
Lárisa □, Greece 48 B4 39 39N 22 24 E
Larissa = Lárisa, Greece 48 B4 39 36N 22 27 E
Larkana, Pakistan 91 D3 27 32N 68 18 E
Larkins = South Miami, U.S.A. 153 K9 25 42N 80 18W
Larnaca, Cyprus 39 F9 34 55N 33 38 E
Larnaca ✕ (LCA), Cyprus 39 F9 34 50N 33 34 E
Larnaca Bay, Cyprus 39 F9 34 53N 33 45 E
Larne, U.K. 23 B6 54 51N 5 51W
Larned, U.S.A. 154 F5 38 11N 99 6W
Laroquebrou, France 28 D6 44 58N 2 12 E
Larose, U.S.A. 155 L9 29 34N 90 23W
Larrimah, Australia 124 C5 15 35 S 133 12 E
Larsen Bay, U.S.A. 144 H9 57 32N 153 59W
Larsen Ice Shelf, Antarctica 7 C17 67 0 S 62 0W
Laruns, France 28 F3 43 0N 0 26W
Larvik, Norway 18 E7 59 4N 10 2 E
Larzac, Causse du, France 28 E7 43 50N 3 17 E
Las Alpujarras, Spain 41 J1 36 55N 3 20W
Las Animas, U.S.A. 154 F3 38 4N 103 13W
Las Anod, Somali Rep. 120 C3 8 26N 47 19 E
Las Arenas, Spain 42 B6 43 17N 4 50W
Las Batuecas ⌂, Spain 42 E4 40 32N 6 5W
Las Bonitas, Venezuela 168 B4 7 52N 65 40W
Las Breñas, Argentina 174 B3 27 5 S 61 7W
Las Cabezas de San Juan, Spain 43 J5 36 57N 5 58W
Las Cañadas del Teide △, Canary Is. 9 e1 28 15N 16 37W
Las Chimeneas, Mexico 161 N10 32 8N 116 5W
Las Coloradas, Argentina 176 A2 39 34 S 70 36W
Las Cruces, U.S.A. 159 K10 32 19N 106 47W
Las Flores, Argentina 174 D4 36 10 S 59 7W
Las Heras, Argentina 174 C2 32 51 S 68 49W
Las Hermosas △, Colombia 168 C2 3 48N 75 51W
Las Horquetas, Argentina 176 C2 48 14 S 71 11W
Las Khoreh, Somali Rep. 120 B3 11 10N 48 20 E
Las Lajas, Argentina 176 A2 38 30 S 70 25W
Las Lomas, Peru 172 A1 4 40 S 80 10W
Las Lomitas, Argentina 174 A3 24 43 S 60 35W
Las Marismas, Spain 43 H4 37 5N 6 20W
Las Mercedes, Venezuela 168 B4 9 7N 66 24W
Las Minas, Spain 41 G3 38 20N 1 41W
Las Navas de la Concepción, Spain 43 H5 37 56N 5 30W
Las Navas del Marqués, Spain 42 E6 40 36N 4 20W
Las Nieves, Phil. 81 G5 8 46N 125 34 E
Las Orquideas △, Colombia 168 B2 6 36N 76 16W
Las Palmas, Argentina 174 B4 27 8 S 58 45W
Las Palmas, Canary Is. 9 e1 28 7N 15 26W
Las Palmas →, Mexico 161 N10 32 26N 116 54W
Las Palmas ✕ (LPA), Canary Is. 9 e1 27 55N 15 25W
Las Palmas de Cocalán △, Chile 174 C1 34 18 S 71 4W
Las Pedroñas, Spain 41 F2 39 26N 2 40W
Las Piedras, Uruguay 175 C4 34 44 S 56 14W
Las Pipinas, Argentina 174 D4 35 30 S 57 19W
Las Plumas, Argentina 176 B3 43 40 S 67 15W
Las Rosas, Argentina 174 C3 32 30 S 61 35W
Las Rozas, Spain 42 E7 40 29N 3 52W
Las Tablas, Panama 164 E3 7 49N 80 14W
Las Termas, Argentina 174 B3 27 29 S 64 52W
Las Toscas, Argentina 174 B4 28 21 S 59 18W
Las Truchas, Mexico 162 D4 17 57N 102 13W
Las Varillas, Argentina 174 C3 31 50 S 62 50W
Las Vegas, N. Mex., U.S.A. 159 J11 35 36N 105 13W
Las Vegas, Nev., U.S.A. 161 J11 36 10N 115 9W
Las Vegas McCarran International ✕ (LAS), U.S.A. 161 J11 36 5N 115 9W
Lasa = Lhasa, China 68 D4 29 25N 90 58 E
Lasanga I., Papua N. G. 132 D4 7 25 S 147 15 E
Lasarte, Spain 40 B2 43 16N 2 1W
Lascano, Uruguay 175 C5 33 35 S 54 12W
Lascelles, Australia 128 C5 35 34 S 142 34 E
Lash-e Joveyn, Afghan. 91 C1 31 45N 61 30 E
Lashburn, Canada 143 C7 53 10N 109 40W
Lashio, Burma 90 D6 22 56N 97 45 E
Lashkar, India 92 F8 26 10N 78 10 E
Lashkar Gāh, Afghan. 91 C2 31 35N 64 21 E
Łasin, Poland 54 E6 53 30N 19 2 E
Lasíthi, Greece 39 E6 35 11N 25 31 E
Lasíthi □, Greece 39 E6 35 5N 25 50 E
Lāsjerd, Iran 97 C7 35 24N 53 4 E
Lask, Poland 55 G6 51 34N 19 8 E
Łaskarzew, Poland 55 G8 51 48N 21 36 E
Laško, Slovenia 45 B12 46 10N 15 16 E
Lassance, Brazil 171 E3 17 54 S 44 34W
Lassay-les-Châteaux, France 26 D6 48 27N 0 30W
Lassen Pk., U.S.A. 158 F3 40 29N 121 31W

Lassen Volcanic △, U.S.A. 158 F3 40 30N 121 20W
Lassongo, Angola 115 E4 12 5S 22 46 E
Last Mountain L., Canada 143 C7 51 5N 105 14W
Lastchance Cr. →, U.S.A. 160 E5 40 2N 121 15W
Lastoursville, Gabon 114 C2 0 55 S 12 38 E
Lastovo, Croatia 45 F13 42 46N 16 55 E
Lastovski Kanal, Croatia 45 F14 42 50N 17 0 E
Lat Yao, Thailand 86 E2 15 45N 99 48 E
Latacunga, Ecuador 168 D2 0 50 S 78 35W
Latakia = Al Lādhiqīyah, Syria 100 E6 35 30N 35 45 E
Latchford, Canada 140 C4 47 20N 79 50W
Late, Tonga 133 P13 18 48 S 174 39W
Latehar, India 93 H11 23 45N 84 30 E
Laterza, Italy 47 B9 40 37N 16 48 E
Latham, Australia 125 E2 29 44 S 116 20 E
Lathen, Germany 30 C3 52 52N 7 19 E
Lathi, India 92 F4 27 43N 71 23 E
Lathi, Vanuatu 133 D5 14 57 S 167 8 E
Lathrop, U.S.A. 156 E2 39 33N 94 20W
Lathrop Wells, U.S.A. 161 J10 36 39N 116 24W
Latiano, Italy 47 B10 40 33N 17 43 E
Latina, Italy 46 A5 41 28N 12 52 E
Latisana, Italy 45 C10 45 47N 13 0 E
Latium = Lazio □, Italy 45 F9 42 10N 12 30 E
Laton, U.S.A. 160 J7 36 26N 119 41W
Latorytsya →, Slovak Rep. 35 C14 48 28N 21 50 E
Latouche Treville, C., Australia 124 C3 18 27 S 121 49 E
Latouma, Niger 109 D2 22 10N 14 50 E
Látrar, Iceland 11 A3 66 24N 23 2W
Latrobe, Australia 127 G4 41 14 S 146 30 E
Latrobe, U.S.A. 150 F5 40 19N 79 23W
Latrónico, Italy 47 B9 40 5N 16 1 E
Latur, India 94 E3 18 25N 76 40 E
Latvia ■, Europe 15 H20 56 50N 24 0 E
Lau, Nigeria 113 D7 9 11N 11 19 E
Lau Fau Shan, China 69 G10 22 28N 113 59 E
Lau Group, Fiji 133 A3 17 0 S 178 30W
Lauban = Lubań, Poland 55 G2 51 5N 15 15 E
Lauca →, Bolivia 172 D4 19 9 S 68 10W
Lauchhammer, Germany 30 D9 51 29N 13 47 E
Lauda-Königshofen, Germany 31 F5 49 33N 9 42 E
Laudal, Norway 18 F4 58 15N 7 30 E
Lauenburg = Lębork, Poland 54 D4 54 33N 17 46 E
Lauenburg, Germany 30 B6 53 22N 10 32 E
Lauenburgische Seen △, Germany 30 B6 53 38N 10 45 E
Lauf, Germany 31 F7 49 30N 11 16 E
Laufás, Iceland 11 B8 65 53N 18 4W
Läufelfingen, Switz. 32 B5 47 24N 7 52 E
Laufen, Switz. 32 B5 47 25N 7 30 E
Laugar, Iceland 11 B5 65 15N 21 48W
Laugarás, Iceland 11 C6 64 7N 20 30W
Laugarbakki, Iceland 11 B6 65 20N 20 55W
Laugarvatn, Iceland 11 C6 64 13N 20 44W
Laughlin, U.S.A. 159 J6 35 8N 114 35W
Laujar de Andarax, Spain 41 H2 37 0N 2 54W
Laukaa, Finland 15 E21 62 24N 25 56 E
Launceston, Australia 127 G4 41 24 S 147 8 E
Launceston, U.K. 21 G3 50 38N 4 22W
Laune →, Ireland 23 D2 52 7N 9 47W
Launglon Bok, Burma 86 F1 13 50N 97 54 E
Laupheim, Germany 31 G5 48 14N 9 52 E
Laura, Queens., Australia 126 B3 15 32 S 144 32 E
Laura, S. Austral., Australia 128 B3 33 10 S 138 18 E
Laureana di Borrello, Italy 47 D9 38 30N 16 5 E
Laurel, Fla., U.S.A. 153 H7 27 8N 82 27W
Laurel, Ind., U.S.A. 157 E11 39 31N 85 11W
Laurel, Miss., U.S.A. 155 K10 31 41N 89 8W
Laurel, Mont., U.S.A. 158 D9 45 40N 108 46W
Laurel Bay, U.S.A. 152 C9 32 27N 80 47W
Laurencekirk, U.K. 22 E6 56 50N 2 28W
Laurens, Iowa, U.S.A. 156 B2 42 51N 94 52W
Laurens, S.C., U.S.A. 149 H4 34 30N 82 1W
Laurentian Plateau, Canada 141 B6 52 0N 70 0W
Lauria, Italy 47 B8 40 2N 15 50 E
Laurie L., Canada 143 B8 56 35N 101 57W
Laurinburg, U.S.A. 149 H6 34 47N 79 28W
Laurium, U.S.A. 148 B1 47 14N 88 27W
Lausanne, Switz. 32 C3 46 32N 6 38 E
Laut, Indonesia 85 B3 4 45N 108 0 E
Laut, Pulau, Indonesia 85 C5 3 40 S 116 10 E
Laut Kecil, Kepulauan, Indonesia 85 C5 4 45 S 115 40 E
Lautaro, Chile 176 A2 38 31 S 72 27W
Lautem, E. Timor 82 C3 8 22 S 126 54 E
Lauterbach, Germany 30 E5 50 37N 9 24 E
Lauterbrunnen, Switz. 32 C5 46 36N 7 55 E
Lauterecken, Germany 31 F3 49 38N 7 35 E
Lautoka, Fiji 133 A1 17 37 S 177 27 E
Lauzès, France 28 D5 44 34N 1 35 E
Lava →, Russia 54 D8 54 37N 21 14 E
Lava Beds △, U.S.A. 158 F3 41 40N 121 30W
Lavagh More, Ireland 23 B3 54 46N 8 6W
Lavagna, Italy 44 D6 44 18N 9 20 E
Laval, France 26 D6 48 4N 0 48W
Lavalle, Argentina 174 B2 28 15 S 65 15W
Lavanggu, Solomon Is. 133 N11 11 36 S 160 16 E
Lavant Station, Canada 151 A8 45 3N 76 42W
Lāvar Meydān, Iran 97 D7 30 20N 54 30 E
Lávara, Greece 51 E10 41 19N 26 22 E
Lavardac, France 28 D4 44 12N 0 20 E
Lavaur, France 28 E5 43 40N 1 49 E
Lavaux, Switz. 32 D3 46 30N 6 45 E
Lavelanet, France 28 F5 42 57N 1 51 E
Lavello, Italy 47 A8 41 3N 15 48 E
L'Averdy, C., Papua N. G. 132 C8 5 33 S 155 4 E
Lavers Hill, Australia 128 E5 38 40 S 143 25 E
Laverton, Australia 125 E3 28 44 S 122 29 E
Lavik, Norway 18 C2 61 6N 5 25 E
Lavis, Italy 44 B8 46 8N 11 7 E
Lávkos, Greece 48 B5 39 9N 23 14 E
Lavos, Portugal 42 E2 40 6N 8 49W
Lavradio, Portugal 43 G1 38 40N 9 3W
Lavras, Brazil 171 F3 21 20 S 45 0W
Lavre, Portugal 43 G2 38 46N 8 22W
Lavrio = Lávrion, Greece 48 D6 37 40N 24 4 E
Lávrion, Greece 48 D6 37 40N 24 4 E
Lávris, Greece 39 E5 35 25N 24 40 E
Lavumisa, Swaziland 117 D5 27 20 S 31 55 E
Lavushi Manda △, Zambia 119 E3 12 46 S 31 0 E
Lawa, Phil. 81 H5 6 12N 125 41 E
Lawa-an, Phil. 81 F5 11 51N 125 5 E
Lawaki, Fiji 133 A2 17 40 S 178 35 E
Lawas, Malaysia 85 B5 4 55N 115 25 E
Lawdar, Yemen 98 D4 13 53N 45 52 E
Lawele, Indonesia 82 C2 5 13 S 122 57 E
Lawksawk, Burma 90 E6 21 15N 96 52 E
Lawn Hill △, Australia 126 B2 18 15 S 138 6 E
Lawowa, Indonesia 82 B2 4 26 S 122 56 E
Lawqah, Si. Arabia 96 D4 29 49N 42 45 E
Lawra, Ghana 112 C4 10 39N 2 51W
Lawrence, N.Z. 131 F4 45 55 S 169 41 E
Lawrence, Ind., U.S.A. 157 E10 39 50N 86 2W
Lawrence, Kans., U.S.A. 154 F7 38 58N 95 14W
Lawrence, Mass., U.S.A. 151 D13 42 43N 71 10W
Lawrence, Ohio, U.S.A. 148 F2 39 50N 86 2W
Lawrenceburg, Ind., U.S.A. 157 E12 39 6N 84 52W
Lawrenceburg, Ky., U.S.A. 157 F12 38 2N 84 54W
Lawrenceburg, Tenn., U.S.A. 149 H2 35 14N 87 20W
Lawrenceville, Ga., U.S.A. 152 B6 33 57N 83 59W
Lawrenceville, Ill., U.S.A. 157 F9 38 44N 87 41W
Lawrenceville, Pa., U.S.A. 150 E7 41 59N 77 8W
Laws, U.S.A. 160 H8 37 24N 118 20W
Lawson, U.S.A. 156 E2 39 26N 94 12W
Lawtey, U.S.A. 152 E7 30 3N 82 5W
Lawton, Mich., U.S.A. 157 B11 42 10N 85 50W
Lawton, Okla., U.S.A. 155 H5 34 37N 98 25W
Lawu, Indonesia 85 D4 7 40 S 111 13 E
Lawz, J. al, Si. Arabia 106 B4 28 39N 35 18 E
Laxå, Sweden 17 F8 58 59N 14 37 E
Laxamýri, Iceland 11 B9 65 58N 17 24W
Laxford, L., U.K. 22 C3 58 24N 5 6W
Laxou, France 27 D13 48 41N 6 8 E
Lay →, France 28 B2 46 18N 1 17W
Layla, Si. Arabia 98 B4 22 10N 46 40 E
Laylān, Iraq 96 C5 35 18N 44 31 E
Layon →, France 26 E6 47 20N 0 45W
Laysan I., U.S.A. 145 F9 25 50N 171 50W
Layton, Fla., U.S.A. 153 L9 24 50N 80 47W
Layton, Utah, U.S.A. 158 F7 41 4N 111 58W
Laytonville, U.S.A. 158 G2 39 41N 123 29W
Laza, Burma 90 B6 26 30N 97 38 E
Lazaráta, Greece 39 B2 38 47N 20 40 E
Lazarevac, Serbia & M. 50 B4 44 23N 20 17 E
Lazarevskoye, Russia 61 J4 43 55N 39 21 E
Lazarivo, Madag. 117 C8 23 54 S 44 59 E
Lazdijai, Lithuania 54 D10 54 14N 23 31 E
Lazi, Phil. 81 G4 9 8N 123 38 E
Lazio □, Italy 45 F9 42 10N 12 30 E
Lazo, Moldova 53 C13 47 33N 28 2 E
Lazo, Russia 70 C6 43 25N 133 55 E
Lbishchensk = Chapayev, Kazakhstan 60 E10 50 25N 51 10 E
Le Beausset, France 29 E9 43 12N 5 48 E
Le Bic, Canada 141 C6 48 20N 68 41W
Le Blanc, France 28 B5 46 37N 1 3 E
Le Bleymard, France 28 D7 44 30N 3 42 E
Le Bourgneuf-la-Fôret, France 26 D6 48 10N 0 59W
Le Brassus, Switz. 32 C2 46 35N 6 13 E
Le Bugue, France 28 D4 44 55N 0 56 E
Le Cateau Cambrésis, France 27 B10 50 7N 3 32 E
Le Caylar, France 28 E7 43 51N 3 19 E
Le Châble, Switz. 32 D4 46 5N 7 12 E
Le Chambon-Feugerolles, France 29 C8 45 24N 4 19 E
Le Châtelard, Switz. 32 D3 46 4N 6 57 E
Le Châtelet, France 27 F9 46 38N 2 16 E
Le Chesne, France 27 C11 49 30N 4 45 E
Le Cheylard, France 29 D8 44 55N 4 25 E
Le Claire, U.S.A. 156 C6 41 36N 90 21W
Le Conquet, France 26 D2 48 21N 4 46W
Le Creusot, France 27 F11 46 48N 4 24 E
Le Croisic, France 26 E4 47 18N 2 30W
Le Donjon, France 27 F10 46 22N 3 48 E
Le Dorat, France 28 B5 46 14N 1 5 E
Le François, Martinique 164 c 14 38N 60 57W
Le Gosier, Guadeloupe 164 b 16 14N 61 29W
Le Grand-Lucé, France 26 E7 47 52N 0 28 E
Le Grand-Pressigny, France 26 F7 46 55N 0 48 E
Le Grand-Quevilly, France 26 C8 49 24N 1 3 E
Le Gris Gris, Mauritius 121 d 20 31 S 57 32 E
Le Havre, France 26 C7 49 30N 0 5 E
Le Lamentin, Martinique 164 c 14 35N 61 2W
Le Lavandou, France 29 E10 43 8N 6 22 E
Le Lion-d'Angers, France 26 E6 47 37N 0 43W
Le Locle, Switz. 32 B3 47 3N 6 44 E
Le Louroux-Béconnais, France 26 E6 47 30N 0 55W
Le Luc, France 29 E10 43 23N 6 21 E
Le Lude, France 26 E7 47 39N 0 9 E
Le Maire, Estr. de, Argentina 176 D4 54 50 S 65 0W
Le Mans, France 26 E7 48 0N 0 10 E
Le Marin, Martinique 164 c 14 27N 60 55W
Le Mars, U.S.A. 154 D6 42 47N 96 10W
Le Mayet-de-Montagne, France 27 F10 46 4N 3 40 E
Le Mêle-sur-Sarthe, France 26 D7 48 31N 0 22 E
Le Moléson, Switz. 32 C4 46 33N 7 1 E
Le Monastier-sur-Gazeille, France 28 D7 44 57N 3 59 E
Le Monêtier-les-Bains, France 29 D10 44 58N 6 30 E
Le Mont-Dore, France 28 C6 45 35N 2 49 E
Le Mont-St-Michel, France 26 D5 48 40N 1 30W
Le Moule, Guadeloupe 164 b 16 20N 61 22W
Le Muy, France 29 E10 43 28N 6 34 E
Le Palais, France 26 E3 47 20N 3 10W
Le Perthus, France 28 F6 42 30N 2 53 E
Le Pont, Switz. 32 C2 46 41N 6 20 E
Le Port, Réunion 121 c 20 56 S 55 18 E
Le Prêcheur, Martinique 164 c 14 50N 61 12W
Le Puy-en-Velay, France 28 C7 45 3N 3 52 E
Le Robert, Martinique 164 c 14 40N 60 56W
Le Roy, U.S.A. 157 D8 40 21N 88 46W
Le St-Esprit, Martinique 164 c 14 34N 60 56W
Le Sentier, Switz. 32 C2 46 37N 6 15 E
Le Sueur, U.S.A. 154 C8 44 28N 93 55W
Le Tampon, Réunion 121 c 21 16 S 55 32 E
Le Teil, France 29 D8 44 33N 4 40 E
Le Teilleul, France 26 D6 48 32N 0 53W
Le Theil, France 26 D7 48 16N 0 42 E
Le Thillot, France 27 E13 47 53N 6 46 E
Le Thuy, Vietnam 86 D6 17 14N 106 49 E
Le Touquet-Paris-Plage, France 27 B8 50 30N 1 36 E
Le Tréport, France 26 B8 50 3N 1 20 E
Le Val-d'Ajol, France 27 E13 47 55N 6 30 E
Le Verdon-sur-Mer, France 28 C2 45 33N 1 4W
Le Vigan, France 28 E7 43 59N 3 36 E
Lea →, U.K. 21 F8 51 31N 0 1 E
Lea Lea, Papua N. G. 132 E4 9 17 S 146 59 E
Leach, Cambodia 87 F4 12 21N 103 46 E
Lead, U.S.A. 154 C3 44 21N 103 46W
Leader, Canada 143 C7 50 50N 109 30W
Leadville, U.S.A. 159 G10 39 15N 106 18W
Leaf →, U.S.A. 155 K10 30 59N 88 44W
Leaf Rapids, Canada 143 B9 56 30N 99 59W
Leaghur, L., Australia 128 B5 33 35 S 143 3 E
Leaksville = Eden, U.S.A. 149 G6 36 29N 79 53W
Lealui, Zambia 115 F4 15 10 S 23 2 E
Leamington, Canada 140 D3 42 3N 82 36W
Leamington, N.Z. 130 D4 37 55 S 175 30 E
Leamington, U.S.A. 158 G7 39 32N 112 17W
Leamington Spa = Royal Leamington Spa, U.K. 21 E6 52 18N 1 31W
Le'an, China 77 D10 27 22N 115 48 E
Leandro Norte Alem, Argentina 175 B4 27 34 S 55 15W
Leane, L., Ireland 23 D2 52 2N 9 32W
Learmonth, Australia 124 D1 22 13 S 114 10 E
Leary, U.S.A. 152 D5 31 29N 84 31W
Leask, Canada 143 C7 53 5N 106 45W
Leatherhead, U.K. 21 F7 51 18N 0 20W
Leavenworth, Ind., U.S.A. 157 F10 38 12N 86 21W
Leavenworth, Kans., U.S.A. 154 F7 39 19N 94 55W
Leavenworth, Wash., U.S.A. 158 C3 47 36N 120 40W
Leawood, U.S.A. 156 F2 38 57N 94 37W
Łeba, Poland 54 D4 54 45N 17 32 E
Łeba →, Poland 54 D4 54 46N 17 33 E
Lebach, Germany 31 F2 49 25N 6 54 E
Lebak, Phil. 81 H5 6 32N 124 5 E
Lebam, U.S.A. 160 D3 46 34N 123 33W
Lebane, Serbia & M. 50 D5 42 56N 21 44 E
Lebango, Congo 114 B2 0 39N 14 21 E
Lebango →, Congo 114 B2 0 2N 14 52 E
Lebanon, Ill., U.S.A. 156 F7 38 36N 89 49W
Lebanon, Ind., U.S.A. 157 D10 40 3N 86 28W
Lebanon, Kans., U.S.A. 154 F5 39 49N 98 33W
Lebanon, Ky., U.S.A. 148 G3 37 34N 85 15W
Lebanon, Mo., U.S.A. 155 G8 37 41N 92 40W
Lebanon, N.H., U.S.A. 151 C12 43 39N 72 15W
Lebanon, Ohio, U.S.A. 157 E12 39 26N 84 13W
Lebanon, Oreg., U.S.A. 158 D2 44 32N 122 55W
Lebanon, Pa., U.S.A. 151 F8 40 20N 76 26W
Lebanon, Tenn., U.S.A. 149 G2 36 12N 86 18W
Lebanon ■, Asia 103 B5 34 0N 36 0 E
Lebanon Junction, U.S.A. 157 G11 37 50N 85 44W
Lebanon Station, U.S.A. 153 F7 29 10N 82 37W
Lebec, U.S.A. 161 L8 34 50N 118 52W
Lebedyan, Russia 59 F10 53 0N 39 10 E
Lebedyn, Ukraine 59 G8 50 35N 34 30 E
Lebel-sur-Quévillon, Canada 140 C4 49 3N 76 59W
Lebo, Dem. Rep. of the Congo 114 B4 4 30N 23 58 E
Lebomboberge, S. Africa 117 C5 24 30 S 32 0 E
Lębork, Poland 54 D4 54 33N 17 46 E
Lebrija, Spain 43 J4 36 53N 6 5W
Łebsko, Jezioro, Poland 54 D4 54 40N 17 25 E
Lebu, Chile 174 D1 37 40 S 73 47W
Leca da Palmeira, Portugal 42 D2 41 12N 8 42W
Lecce, Italy 47 B11 40 23N 18 11 E
Lecco, Italy 44 C6 45 51N 9 23 E
Lecco, L. di, Italy 44 C6 45 55N 9 19 E
Lécera, Spain 40 D4 41 13N 0 43W
Lech, Austria 34 D3 47 13N 10 9 E
Lech →, Germany 31 G6 48 43N 10 56 E
Lechang, China 77 E9 25 10N 113 20 E
Lechtaler Alpen, Austria 34 D3 47 15N 10 30 E
Léconi, Gabon 114 C2 1 35 S 14 14 E
Léconi →, Gabon 114 C2 1 11 S 13 16 E
Lecontes Mills, U.S.A. 150 E6 41 5N 78 17W
Lectoure, France 28 E4 43 56N 0 38 E
Łęczna, Poland 55 G9 51 18N 22 53 E
Łęczyca, Poland 55 F6 52 5N 19 15 E
Ledang, Gunung, Malaysia 84 B2 2 22N 102 37 E
Ledesma, Spain 42 D5 41 6N 5 59W
Lediba, Dem. Rep. of the Congo 114 C3 3 1 S 16 34 E
Lédo, Cabo, Angola 115 D2 9 43 S 13 12 E
Ledong, China 86 C7 18 41N 109 5 E
Leduc, Canada 142 C6 53 15N 113 30W
Lee, Fla., U.S.A. 152 E6 30 25N 83 18W
Lee, Mass., U.S.A. 151 D11 42 19N 73 15W
Lee →, Ireland 23 E3 51 53N 8 56W
Lee Vining, U.S.A. 160 H7 37 58N 119 7W
Leech L., U.S.A. 154 B7 47 10N 94 24W
Leechburg, U.S.A. 150 F5 40 37N 79 36W
Leeds, U.K. 20 D6 53 48N 1 33W
Leeds, U.S.A. 149 J2 33 33N 86 33W
Leek, Neths. 24 A6 53 10N 6 24 E
Leek, U.K. 20 D5 53 7N 2 1W
Leeman, Australia 125 E1 29 57 S 114 58 E
Leeper, U.S.A. 150 E5 41 22N 79 18W
Leer, Germany 30 B3 53 13N 7 26 E
Lee's Summit, U.S.A. 156 F2 38 55N 94 23W
Leesburg, Fla., U.S.A. 153 G8 28 49N 81 53W
Leesburg, Ga., U.S.A. 152 D5 31 44N 84 10W
Leesburg, Ohio, U.S.A. 157 E13 39 21N 83 33W
Leeston, N.Z. 131 D7 43 45 S 172 19 E
Leesville, U.S.A. 155 K8 31 9N 93 16W
Leeton, Australia 129 C7 34 33 S 146 23 E
Leetonia, U.S.A. 150 F4 40 53N 80 45W
Leeu Gamka, S. Africa 116 E3 32 47 S 21 59 E
Leeuwarden, Neths. 24 A5 53 15N 5 48 E
Leeuwin, C., Australia 125 F2 34 20 S 115 9 E
Leeuwin Naturaliste △, Australia 125 F2 34 6 S 115 3 E
Leeward Is., Atl. Oc. 165 C7 16 30N 63 30W
Léfini, Congo 114 C3 2 55 S 15 39 E
Léfini △, Congo 114 C3 2 55 S 15 20 E
Léfini →, Congo 114 C3 2 55 S 16 9 E
Lefka, Cyprus 39 E8 35 6N 32 51 E
Lefkada = Levkás, Greece 39 B2 38 40N 20 43 E
Lefkoniko, Cyprus 39 E9 35 18N 33 44 E
Lefroy, Canada 150 B5 44 16N 79 34W
Lefroy, L., Australia 125 F3 31 21 S 121 40 E
Łeg →, Poland 55 H8 50 42N 21 50 E
Leganés, Spain 42 E7 40 19N 3 45W
Legazpi, Phil. 80 E4 13 10N 123 45 E
Lège-Cap-Ferret, France 28 D2 44 48N 1 9W
Lege Hida, Ethiopia 107 F5 7 56N 41 4 E
Legendre I., Australia 124 D2 20 22 S 116 55 E
Leghorn = Livorno, Italy 44 E7 43 33N 10 19 E
Legionowo, Poland 55 F7 52 25N 20 50 E
Legnago, Italy 45 C8 45 11N 11 18 E
Legnano, Italy 44 C5 45 36N 8 54 E
Legnica, Poland 55 G3 51 12N 16 10 E
Legrad, Croatia 45 B13 46 17N 16 51 E
Leh, India 93 B7 34 9N 77 35 E
Lehigh Acres, U.S.A. 153 J8 26 36N 81 39W
Lehighton, U.S.A. 151 F9 40 50N 75 43W
Lehliu, Romania 53 F11 44 29N 26 50 E
Leho, Sudan 107 F3 7 7N 33 52 E
Lehrte, Germany 30 C5 52 22N 9 58 E
Lehua I., U.S.A. 145 A1 22 1N 160 6W
Lehututu, Botswana 116 C3 23 54 S 21 55 E
Lei Shui →, China 77 D9 26 55N 112 35 E
Leiah, Pakistan 91 C3 30 58N 70 58 E
Leibnitz, Austria 34 E8 46 47N 15 34 E
Leibo, China 76 C4 28 11N 103 34 E
Leicester, U.K. 21 E6 52 38N 1 8W
Leicester City □, U.K. 21 E6 52 38N 1 8W
Leicestershire □, U.K. 21 E6 52 41N 1 17W
Leichhardt →, Australia 126 B2 17 35 S 139 48 E
Leichhardt Ra., Australia 126 C4 20 46 S 147 40 E
Leiden, Neths. 24 B4 52 9N 4 30 E
Leie →, Belgium 24 C3 51 2N 3 45 E
Leifers = Láives, Italy 45 B8 46 26N 11 20 E
Leigh →, Australia 128 E6 38 18 S 144 30 E
Leigh Creek, Australia 128 A3 30 38 S 138 26 E
Leikanger, Sogn og Fjordane, Norway 18 B2 62 8N 5 18 E
Leikanger, Sogn og Fjordane, Norway 18 C3 61 10N 6 51 E
Leikong, Norway 18 B2 62 15N 5 47 E
Leiktho, Burma 90 F6 19 13N 96 35 E
Leimen, Germany 31 F4 49 21N 8 41 E
Leine →, Germany 30 C5 52 43N 9 36 E
Leinefelde, Germany 30 D6 51 23N 10 19 E
Leinster, Australia 125 E3 27 51 S 120 36 E
Leinster □, Ireland 23 C4 53 3N 7 8W
Leinster, Mt., Ireland 23 D5 52 37N 6 46W
Leipalingis, Lithuania 54 D10 54 5N 23 51 E
Leipe = Lipno, Poland 55 F6 52 49N 19 15 E
Leipzig, Germany 30 D8 51 18N 12 22 E
Leira, Norway 18 D6 60 58N 9 17 E
Leiria, Portugal 42 F2 39 46N 8 53W
Leiria □, Portugal 42 F2 39 46N 8 53W
Leirvassbu, Norway 18 C5 61 33N 8 13 E
Leirvik, Norway 18 E2 59 47N 5 28 E
Leishan, China 76 D7 26 15N 108 20 E
Leisler, Mt., Australia 124 D4 23 23 S 129 20 E
Leisure City, U.S.A. 153 K9 25 31N 80 26W
Leith, U.K. 22 F5 55 59N 3 11W
Leith Hill, U.K. 21 F7 51 11N 0 22W
Leitha →, Europe 35 D10 47 50N 17 15 E
Leitrim, Ireland 23 B3 54 0N 8 5W
Leitrim □, Ireland 23 B4 54 8N 8 0W
Leitza, Spain 40 B3 43 5N 1 55W
Leiyang, China 77 D9 26 27N 112 45 E
Leizhou, China 77 G8 20 52N 110 8 E
Leizhou Bandao, China 76 G7 21 0N 110 0 E
Leizhou Wan, China 77 G8 20 50N 110 20 E
Lek →, Neths. 24 C4 51 54N 4 35 E
Leka, Norway 14 D14 65 5N 11 35 E
Lekáni, Greece 51 E8 41 10N 24 35 E
Lekbibaj, Albania 50 D3 42 17N 19 56 E
Lekeitio, Spain 40 B2 43 20N 2 32W
Lekhainá, Greece 48 D3 37 57N 21 16 E
Lekitobi, Indonesia 82 B2 1 58 S 124 33 E
Lékoli-Pandaka △, Congo 114 B2 0 41N 14 50 E
Lekoui, Burkina Faso 112 C4 12 37N 3 40W
Leksand, Sweden 16 D9 60 44N 15 1 E
Leksula, Indonesia 82 B3 3 46 S 126 31 E
Leksura = Lentekhi, Georgia 61 J6 42 47N 42 45 E
Lékva Óros, Greece 39 E5 35 18N 24 3 E
Leland, Mich., U.S.A. 148 C3 45 1N 85 45W
Leland, Miss., U.S.A. 155 J9 33 24N 90 54W
Lelång, Sweden 16 E6 59 10N 12 5 E
Leleiwi Pt., U.S.A. 145 D7 19 44N 155 0W
Lelepa, Vanuatu 133 G6 17 35 S 168 11 E
Leleque, Argentina 176 B2 42 28 S 71 0W
Lelewau, Indonesia 82 B2 3 2 S 121 5 E
Leli, Solomon Is. 133 M11 8 42 S 161 4 E
Lelu, Burma 90 F5 19 4N 95 30 E
Lelydorp, Suriname 169 B6 5 42N 55 14W
Lelystad, Neths. 24 B5 52 30N 5 25 E
Lem, Denmark 17 H2 56 1N 8 24 E
Lema, Nigeria 113 C5 12 58N 4 13 E
Lema Shilindi, Ethiopia 107 G5 4 50N 42 6 E
Léman, L., Europe 27 F13 46 26N 6 30 E
Lemanoka, Papua N. G. 132 C8 5 3 S 154 34 E
Lembar, Indonesia 79 K19 8 45 S 116 4 E
Lemberg = Lviv, Ukraine 59 H3 49 50N 24 0 E
Lembuak, Indonesia 79 K19 8 36 S 116 11 E
Lemera, Dem. Rep. of the Congo 118 C2 3 0 S 28 55 E
Lemery, Phil. 80 E3 13 51N 120 56 E
Lemeta, U.S.A. 144 D11 64 52N 147 44W
Lemfu, Dem. Rep. of the Congo 115 D3 5 18 S 15 13 E
Lemhi Ra., U.S.A. 158 D7 44 30N 113 30W
Lemmer, Neths. 24 B5 52 51N 5 43 E
Lemmon, U.S.A. 154 C3 45 57N 102 10W
Lemon Grove, U.S.A. 161 N9 32 45N 117 2W
Lemoore, U.S.A. 160 J7 36 18N 119 46W
Lempdes, France 28 C7 45 22N 3 17 E
Lemsid, W. Sahara 110 C2 26 33N 13 51W
Lemvig, Denmark 17 H2 56 33N 8 20 E
Lemyethna, Burma 90 G5 17 36N 95 9 E
Lena, U.S.A. 156 B7 42 23N 89 49W
Lena →, Russia 67 B13 72 52N 126 40 E
Lenakel, Vanuatu 133 J7 19 38 S 169 16 E
Lenart, Slovenia 45 B12 46 36N 15 48 E
Lenartovce, Slovak Rep. 35 C13 48 18N 20 19 E
Lencloître, France 26 F7 46 50N 0 20 E
Lençóis, Brazil 171 D3 12 35 S 41 24W
Lençóis Maranhenses △, Brazil 170 B3 2 30 S 43 0W
Léndas, Greece 39 F5 34 56N 24 56 E
Lendava, Slovenia 45 B13 46 35N 16 25 E
Lendeh, Iran 97 D6 30 58N 50 25 E
Lendinara, Italy 45 C8 45 5N 11 36 E
Lenger, Kazakhstan 65 B4 42 12N 69 54 E
Lengerich, Germany 30 C3 52 11N 7 52 E
Lenggong, Malaysia 87 K3 5 6N 100 58 E
Lenggries, Germany 31 H7 47 41N 11 35 E
Lengoué, Congo 114 B3 1 15N 15 38 E
Lengshuijiang, China 77 D8 27 40N 111 26 E
Lengshuitan, China 77 D8 26 27N 111 35 E
Lengua de Vaca, Pta., Chile 174 C1 30 14 S 71 38W
Lengwe △, Malawi 119 F3 16 14 S 34 45 E
Lengwethen = Lunino, Russia 60 D7 53 38N 45 18 E
Lengyeltóti, Hungary 52 D2 46 40N 17 40 E
Lengyeltóthiács = Lengyeltóti, Hungary 52 D2 46 40N 17 40 E
Lenhovda, Sweden 17 G9 57 0N 15 16 E
Lenina, Kanal →, Russia 61 J7 43 44N 45 17 E
Lenina, Pik, Kyrgyzstan 65 D6 39 20N 72 55 E
Leninabad = Khŭjand, Tajikistan 65 C4 40 17N 69 37 E
Leninakan = Gyumri, Armenia 61 K6 40 47N 43 50 E
Leningrad = Sankt-Peterburg, Russia 58 C6 59 55N 30 20 E
Leningradskiy, Tajikistan 65 D5 38 6N 70 1 E
Lenino = Leninsk-Kuznetskiy, Russia 66 D9 54 44N 86 10 E
Lenino, Ukraine 59 K8 45 17N 35 46 E
Leninogorsk, Kazakhstan 66 D9 50 20N 83 30 E
Leninogorsk, Russia 64 D4 54 36N 52 30 E
Leninpol, Kyrgyzstan 65 B5 42 29N 71 55 E
Leninsk = Petrodvorets, Russia 58 C5 59 52N 29 54 E
Leninsk, Russia 61 F7 48 40N 45 15 E
Leninsk-Kuznetskiy, Russia 66 D9 54 44N 86 10 E
Leninsk-Turkmensky = Chärjew, Turkmenistan 65 D1 39 6N 63 34 E
Leninskiy, Tajikistan 65 D4 38 26N 68 46 E
Leninskoe, Kyrgyzstan 65 C6 40 40N 73 9 E
Leninskoye, Kazakhstan 64 F6 50 44N 57 53 E
Leninskoye, Russia 60 A8 58 23N 47 3 E
Lenk, Switz. 32 D4 46 27N 7 28 E
Lenkoran = Länkäran, Azerbaijan 97 B6 38 48N 48 52 E
Lenmalu, Indonesia 83 B4 1 45 S 130 15 E
Lenne →, Germany 30 D3 51 25N 7 29 E
Lennestadt, Germany 30 D4 51 8N 8 2 E
Lennox, U.S.A. 154 D6 43 21N 96 53W
Lennox, I., Chile 176 E3 55 18 S 66 50W
Lennoxville, Canada 151 A13 45 22N 71 51W
Leno, Italy 44 C7 45 22N 10 13 E
Lenoir, U.S.A. 149 H5 35 55N 81 32W
Lenoir City, U.S.A. 149 H3 35 48N 84 16W
Lenore L., Canada 143 C8 52 30N 104 59W
Lenox, Ga., U.S.A. 152 D6 31 16N 83 28W
Lenox, Iowa, U.S.A. 156 D2 40 53N 94 34W
Lenox, Mass., U.S.A. 151 D11 42 22N 73 17W
Lens, France 27 B9 50 26N 2 50 E
Lensahn, Germany 30 A6 54 13N 10 53 E
Lensk, Russia 67 C12 60 48N 114 55 E
Lensvik, Norway 18 A6 63 31N 9 48 E
Lentekhi, Georgia 61 J6 42 47N 42 45 E
Lenti, Hungary 52 D1 46 37N 16 33 E
Lentini, Italy 47 E8 37 17N 15 0 E
Lentschütz = Łęczyca, Poland 55 F6 52 5N 19 15 E
Lenwood, U.S.A. 161 L9 34 53N 117 7W
Lenya, Burma 78 B1 11 33N 98 57 E
Lenzburg, Switz. 32 B6 47 23N 8 11 E
Lenzen, Germany 30 B7 53 5N 11 29 E
Lenzerheide, Switz. 33 C9 46 44N 9 34 E
Léo, Burkina Faso 112 C4 11 3N 2 2W
Leoben, Austria 34 D8 47 22N 15 5 E
Leobschütz = Głubczyce, Poland 55 H4 50 13N 17 52 E
Leodhas = Lewis, U.K. 22 C2 58 9N 6 40W
Leola, U.S.A. 154 C5 45 43N 98 56W
Leominster, U.K. 21 E5 52 14N 2 43W
Leominster, U.S.A. 151 D13 42 32N 71 46W
León = Cotopaxi □, Ecuador 168 D2 0 5 S 78 55W
Léon, France 28 E2 43 53N 1 18W
León, Mexico 162 C4 21 7N 101 40W
León, Nic. 164 D2 12 20N 86 51W
León, Spain 42 C5 42 38N 5 34W
Leon, U.S.A. 156 D3 40 44N 93 45W
León □, Spain 42 C5 42 40N 5 55W
Leon →, U.S.A. 155 K6 31 14N 97 28W
León, Montes de, Spain 42 C4 42 30N 6 18W
Leonardo da Vinci, Roma ✈ (FCO), Italy 45 G9 41 48N 12 15 E
Leonardtown, U.S.A. 148 F7 38 17N 76 38W
Leonardville, Namibia 116 C2 23 29 S 18 49 E
Leonberg, Germany 31 G5 48 48N 9 1 E
Leonding, Austria 34 C7 48 16N 14 15 E
Leone, Amer. Samoa 133 X24 14 23 S 170 48W
Leone, Mte., Switz. 32 D6 46 15N 8 5 E
Leonessa, Italy 45 F9 42 34N 12 58 E
Leonforte, Italy 47 E7 37 38N 14 23 E
Leongatha, Australia 129 E6 38 30 S 145 58 E
Leonia, U.S.A. 152 E3 30 55N 86 1W
Leonídhion, Greece 48 D4 37 9N 22 52 E
Leonora, Australia 125 E3 28 49 S 121 19 E
Leopold II, L. = Mai-Ndombe, L., Dem. Rep. of the Congo 114 C3 2 0 S 18 20 E
Leopoldina = Aruanã, Brazil 171 D1 14 54 S 51 10W
Leopoldina = Parnamirim, Brazil 170 C4 8 5 S 39 34W
Leopoldina, Brazil 171 F3 21 28 S 42 40W
Leopoldo Bulhões, Brazil 171 E2 16 37 S 48 46W
Leopoldsburg, Belgium 24 C5 51 7N 5 13 E
Leopoldville = Kinshasa, Dem. Rep. of the Congo 115 C3 4 20 S 15 15 E
Leoti, U.S.A. 154 F4 38 29N 101 21W
Leova, Moldova 53 D13 46 28N 28 15 E
Leoville, Canada 143 C7 53 39N 107 33W
Lepe, Spain 43 H3 37 15N 7 12W
Lepel = Lyepyel, Belarus 58 E5 54 50N 28 40 E
Lepenoú, Greece 48 C3 38 42N 21 17 E
Leping, China 77 C11 28 47N 117 7 E
Lépo, L. do, Angola 116 B2 17 0 S 19 0 E
Lepontine, Alpi, Italy 33 D6 46 22N 8 27 E
Leppävirta, Finland 15 E22 62 29N 27 46 E
Lepsény, Hungary 52 D3 47 0N 18 15 E
Leptis Magna, Libya 108 B2 32 40N 14 12 E
Lequeitio = Lekeitio, Spain 40 B2 43 20N 2 32W
Lercara Friddi, Italy 46 E6 37 45N 13 36 E
Lerdo, Mexico 162 B4 25 32N 103 32W
Léré, C.A.R. 114 A3 6 46N 17 25 E
Léré, Chad 113 D7 9 39N 14 13 E
Léré, Mali 112 B4 15 45N 4 55W
Lere, Bauchi, Nigeria 113 D6 9 43N 9 18 E
Lere, Kaduna, Nigeria 113 C6 10 23N 8 35 E
Leribe, Lesotho 117 D4 28 51 S 28 3 E
Lérici, Italy 44 D6 44 4N 9 55 E
Lérida = Lleida, Spain 40 D5 41 37N 0 39 E
Lérins, Îs. de, France 29 E11 43 31N 7 3 E
Lerma, Spain 42 C7 42 0N 3 47W
Léros, Greece 49 D8 37 10N 26 50 E
Lérouville, France 27 D12 48 44N 5 30 E
Lerum, Sweden 17 G6 57 46N 12 16 E
Lerwick, U.K. 22 A7 60 9N 1 9W
Leş, Romania 52 D6 46 58N 21 50 E
Les Abrets, France 29 C9 45 32N 5 35 E
Les Andelys, France 26 C8 49 15N 1 25 E
Les Bois, Switz. 32 B3 47 11N 6 50 E

Les Borges Blanques, Spain 40 D5 41 31N 0 52 E
Les Cayes, Haiti 165 C5 18 15N 73 46W
Les Coteaux, Canada 151 A10 45 15N 74 13W
Les Diablerets, Switz. 32 D4 46 22N 7 10 E
Les Essarts, France 26 F5 46 47N 1 12W
Les Herbiers, France 26 F5 46 52N 1 1W
Les Minquiers, Plateau des, Chan. Is. 26 D4 48 58N 2 8W
Les Moroubas, C.A.R. 114 A4 6 11N 20 13 E
Les Pieux, France 26 C5 49 30N 1 48W
Les Ponts-de-Cé, France 26 E6 47 25N 0 30W
Les Riceys, France 27 E11 47 59N 4 22 E
Les Sables-d'Olonne, France 28 B2 46 30N 1 45W
Les Vans, France 29 D8 44 25N 4 7 E
Les Verrières, Switz. 32 C2 46 55N 6 28 E
Lesbos = Lésvos, Greece 49 B8 39 10N 26 20 E
L'Escala, Spain 40 C8 42 7N 3 8 E
Leschnitz = Leśnica, Poland 55 H5 50 26N 18 11 E
Leshan, China 76 C4 29 33N 103 41 E
Leshukonskoye, Russia 56 B8 64 54N 45 46 E
Leshwe ⌓, Dem. Rep. of the Congo 119 E2 12 45 S 29 30 E
Lésina, Italy 45 G12 41 52N 15 21 E
Lésina, L. di, Italy 45 G12 41 53N 15 26 E
Lesjaskog, Norway 18 B5 62 14N 8 22 E
Lesjaverk, Norway 18 B5 62 12N 8 34 E
Lesjöfors, Sweden 16 E8 59 58N 14 11 E
Leskhimstroy = Syeverodonetsk, Ukraine 59 H10 48 58N 38 35 E
Lesko, Poland 55 J9 49 30N 22 23 E
Leskov I., Antarctica 7 B1 56 0S 28 0W
Leskovac, Serbia & M. 50 C5 43 0N 21 58 E
Leskovik, Albania 50 F4 40 10N 20 34 E
Leslau = Włocławek, Poland 55 F6 52 40N 19 3 E
Leslie, Ga., U.S.A. 152 D5 31 57N 84 5W
Leslie, Mich., U.S.A. 157 B12 42 27N 84 26W
Leśna, Poland 55 G2 51 1N 15 15 E
Lesneven, France 26 D2 48 35N 4 20W
Leśnica, Poland 55 H5 50 26N 18 11 E
Lešnica, Serbia & M. 50 B3 44 39N 19 20 E
Lesnoi = Umba, Russia 56 A5 66 42N 34 11 E
Lesnoy, Russia 64 B4 59 47N 52 9 E
Lesnoye, Russia 58 C8 58 15N 35 18 E
Lesopilnoye, Russia 70 A7 46 44N 134 20 E
Lesotho ■, Africa 117 D4 29 40 S 28 0 E
Lesozavodsk, Russia 67 E14 45 30N 133 29 E
Lesozavodsky = Novovyatsk, Russia 64 B2 58 24N 49 45 E
Lesparre-Médoc, France 28 C3 45 18N 0 57W
Lessay, France 26 C5 49 14N 1 30W
Lesse →, Belgium 24 D4 50 15N 4 54 E
Lesse et Lomme ⌓, Belgium 24 D5 50 8N 5 9 E
Lessebo, Sweden 17 H9 56 45N 15 16 E
Lesser Antilles, W. Indies 165 D7 15 0N 61 0W
Lesser Slave L., Canada 142 B5 55 30N 115 25W
Lesser Sunda Is., Indonesia 82 C1 8 0 S 120 0 E
Lessines, Belgium 24 D3 50 42N 3 50 E
Lester, U.S.A. 160 C5 47 12N 121 29W
Lester B. Pearson International, Toronto ✕ (YYZ), Canada 150 C5 43 40N 79 34W
Lestershire = Johnson City, U.S.A. 151 D9 42 7N 75 58W
Lestock, Canada 143 C8 51 19N 103 59W
Lesuer I., Australia 124 B4 13 50 S 127 17 E
Lesueur △, Australia 125 F2 30 11 S 115 10 E
Lésvos, Greece 49 B8 39 10N 26 20 E
Leszno, Poland 55 G3 51 50N 16 30 E
Letaba, S. Africa 117 C5 23 59 S 31 50 E
Letälven, Sweden 16 E8 59 5N 14 20 E
Létavértes, Hungary 52 C6 47 23N 21 55 E
Letchworth, U.K. 21 F7 51 59N 0 13W
Letea, Ostrov, Romania 53 E14 45 18N 29 20 E
Lethbridge, Canada 142 D6 49 45N 112 45W
Lethem, Guyana 169 C6 3 20N 59 50W
Leti, Kepulauan, Indonesia 82 C3 8 10 S 128 0 E
Leti Is. = Leti, Kepulauan, Indonesia 82 C3 8 10 S 128 0 E
Letiahau →, Botswana 116 C3 21 16 S 24 0 E
Leticia, Colombia 168 D4 4 9 S 70 0W
Leting, China 75 E10 39 23N 118 55 E
Letjiesbos, S. Africa 116 E3 32 34 S 22 16 E
Letlhakane, Botswana 116 C4 21 27 S 25 30 E
Letlhakeng, Botswana 116 C3 24 0 S 24 59 E
Letong, Indonesia 78 D3 2 58N 105 42 E
Letpadan, Burma 90 G5 17 45N 95 45 E
Letpan, Burma 90 F5 19 28N 94 10 E
Letsôk-aw Kyun, Burma 87 G2 11 30N 98 25 E
Letterkenny, Ireland 23 B4 54 57N 7 45W
Leu, Romania 53 F9 44 10N 24 0 E
Léua, Angola 115 E4 11 34 S 20 32 E
Leucadia, U.S.A. 161 M9 33 4N 117 18W
Leucate, France 28 F7 42 56N 3 3 E
Leucate, Étang de, France 28 F7 42 50N 3 0 E
Leuchars, U.K. 22 E6 56 24N 2 53W
Leuk, Switz. 32 D5 46 19N 7 37 E
Leukerbad, Switz. 32 D5 46 24N 7 36 E
Leuşeni, Moldova 53 D13 46 49N 28 12 E
Leuser, G., Indonesia 84 B1 3 46N 97 12 E
Leutkirch, Germany 31 H6 47 49N 10 1 E
Leutschau = Levoča, Slovak Rep. 35 B13 49 2N 20 35 E
Leuven, Belgium 24 D4 50 52N 4 42 E
Leuze-en-Hainaut, Belgium 24 D3 50 36N 3 37 E
Lev Tolstoy, Russia 58 F10 53 13N 39 29 E
Levádhia, Greece 48 C4 38 27N 22 54 E
Levan, Albania 50 F3 40 40N 19 28 E
Levanger, Norway 14 E14 63 45N 11 19 E
Levant, Î. du, France 29 E10 43 3N 6 28 E
Lévanto, Italy 44 D6 44 10N 9 38 E
Lévanzo, Italy 46 D5 38 0N 12 20 E
Leveld, Norway 18 D5 60 44N 8 33 E
Levelland, U.S.A. 155 J3 33 35N 102 23W
Levelock, U.S.A. 144 G8 59 7N 156 51W
Leven, U.K. 22 E6 56 12N 3 0W
Leven, L., U.K. 22 E5 56 12N 3 22W
Leven, Toraka, Madag. 117 A8 12 30 S 47 45 E
Leveque C., Australia 124 C3 16 20 S 123 0 E
Leverano, Italy 47 B10 40 17N 18 0 E
Leverger = Santo Antônio do Leverger, Brazil 173 D6 15 52 S 56 5W
Leverkusen, Germany 30 D3 51 1N 7 1 E
Levice, Slovak Rep. 35 C11 48 13N 18 35 E
Lévico Terme, Italy 45 C8 46 0N 11 18 E
Levie, France 29 G13 41 40N 9 7 E
Levier, France 27 F13 46 58N 6 8 E
Levin, N.Z. 130 G4 40 37 S 175 18 E
Lévis, Canada 141 C5 46 48N 71 9W
Levis, L., Canada 142 A5 62 37N 117 58W
Levítha, Greece 49 D8 37 0N 26 28 E
Levittown = Willingboro, U.S.A. 148 E8 40 3N 74 54W
Levittown, N.Y., U.S.A. 151 F11 40 44N 73 31W
Levittown, Pa., U.S.A. 151 F10 40 9N 74 51W
Levka, Bulgaria 51 E10 41 52N 26 15 E
Levkás, Greece 39 B2 38 40N 20 43 E
Levkás □, Greece 39 B2 38 45N 20 40 E
Levkímmi, Greece 38 C10 39 25N 20 3 E
Levkímmi, Ákra, Greece 38 C10 39 29N 20 4 E
Levkôsia = Nicosia, Cyprus 39 E9 35 10N 33 25 E
Levoča, Slovak Rep. 35 B13 49 2N 20 35 E
Levroux, France 27 F8 46 59N 1 38 E
Levski, Bulgaria 51 C9 43 21N 25 10 E
Levskigrad = Karlovo, Bulgaria 51 D8 42 38N 24 47 E
Levuka, Fiji 133 A2 17 34 S 179 0 E
Lewe, Burma 90 F6 19 38N 96 7 E
Lewes, U.K. 21 G8 50 52N 0 1 E
Lewes, U.S.A. 148 F8 38 46N 75 9W
Lewin Brzeski, Poland 55 H4 50 45N 17 37 E
Lewis, U.K. 22 C2 58 9N 6 40W
Lewis →, U.S.A. 160 E4 45 51N 122 48W
Lewis, Butt of, U.K. 22 C2 58 31N 6 16W
Lewis Pass, N.Z. 131 C7 42 31 S 172 11 E
Lewis Ra., Australia 124 D4 20 3 S 128 50 E
Lewis Range, U.S.A. 158 C7 48 5N 113 5W
Lewis Run, U.S.A. 150 E6 41 52N 78 40W
Lewisburg, Ohio, U.S.A. 157 E12 39 51N 84 33W
Lewisburg, Pa., U.S.A. 150 F8 40 58N 76 54W
Lewisburg, Tenn., U.S.A. 149 H2 35 27N 86 48W
Lewisburg, W. Va., U.S.A. 148 G5 37 48N 80 27W
Lewisport, U.S.A. 157 G10 37 56N 86 54W
Lewisporte, Canada 141 C8 49 15N 55 3W
Lewiston, Idaho, U.S.A. 158 C5 46 25N 117 1W
Lewiston, Maine, U.S.A. 149 C11 44 6N 70 13W
Lewiston, N.Y., U.S.A. 150 C5 43 11N 79 3W
Lewistown, Ill., U.S.A. 156 D6 40 24N 90 9W
Lewistown, Mo., U.S.A. 156 D5 40 5N 91 49W
Lewistown, Mont., U.S.A. 158 C9 47 4N 109 26W
Lewistown, Pa., U.S.A. 150 F7 40 36N 77 34W
Lexington, Ga., U.S.A. 152 B6 33 52N 83 7W
Lexington, Ill., U.S.A. 154 E10 40 39N 88 47W
Lexington, Ky., U.S.A. 157 F12 38 3N 84 30W
Lexington, Mich., U.S.A. 150 C2 43 16N 82 32W
Lexington, Mo., U.S.A. 156 E3 39 11N 93 52W
Lexington, N.C., U.S.A. 149 H5 35 49N 80 15W
Lexington, N.Y., U.S.A. 151 D10 42 15N 74 22W
Lexington, Nebr., U.S.A. 154 E5 40 47N 99 45W
Lexington, Ohio, U.S.A. 150 F2 40 41N 82 35W
Lexington, S.C., U.S.A. 152 B8 33 59N 81 11W
Lexington, Tenn., U.S.A. 149 H1 35 39N 88 24W
Lexington, Va., U.S.A. 148 G6 37 47N 79 27W
Lexington Park, U.S.A. 148 F7 38 16N 76 27W
Leyburn, U.K. 20 C6 54 19N 1 48W
Leye, China 76 E6 24 48N 106 29 E
Leyland, U.K. 20 D5 53 42N 2 43W
Leyre →, France 28 D2 44 39N 1 1W
Leysin, Switz. 32 D4 46 21N 7 1 E
Leyte, Phil. 81 F5 10 30N 125 0 E
Leyte □, Phil. 81 F5 11 0N 125 0 E
Leyte Gulf, Phil. 81 F5 10 50N 125 25 E
Leżajsk, Poland 55 H9 50 16N 22 25 E
Lezay, France 28 B3 46 15N 0 1W
Lezhë, Albania 50 E3 41 47N 19 39 E
Lezhi, China 76 B5 30 19N 104 58 E
Lézignan-Corbières, France 28 E6 43 13N 2 43 E
Lezoux, France 28 C7 45 49N 3 21 E
Lgov, Russia 59 G8 51 42N 35 16 E
Lhasa, China 68 D4 29 25N 90 58 E
Lhazê, China 68 D3 29 5N 87 38 E
Lhokkruet, Indonesia 84 B1 4 55N 95 24 E
Lhokseumawe, Indonesia 84 A1 5 10N 97 10 E
L'Hospitalet de Llobregat, Spain 40 D7 41 21N 2 6 E
Lhuntsi Dzong, Bhutan 90 B3 27 39N 91 10 E
Li, Thailand 86 D2 17 48N 98 57 E
Li Shui →, China 77 C9 29 24N 112 1 E
Li Xian, Gansu, China 74 G3 34 10N 105 5 E
Li Xian, Hebei, China 74 E8 38 30N 115 35 E
Li Xian, Hunan, China 77 C8 29 36N 111 42 E
Lia-Moya, C.A.R. 114 A3 6 54N 16 17 E
Liádhoi, Greece 49 E8 36 50N 26 11 E
Lian, Phil. 80 D3 14 3N 120 39 E
Liancheng, China 77 E11 25 42N 116 40 E
Liancourt Rocks = Tok-do, Asia 71 F5 37 15N 131 52 E
Lianga, Phil. 81 G6 8 38N 126 6 E
Lianga Bay, Phil. 81 G6 8 37N 126 12 E
Liangcheng, Nei Monggol Zizhiqu, China 74 D7 40 28N 112 25 E
Liangcheng, Shandong, China 75 G10 35 32N 119 37 E
Liangdang, China 74 H4 33 56N 106 18 E
Lianghe, China 76 E2 24 50N 98 20 E
Lianghekou, China 76 C7 29 11N 108 44 E
Liangping, China 76 B6 30 38N 107 47 E
Liangpran, Indonesia 78 D4 1 4N 114 23 E
Lianhua, China 77 D9 27 3N 113 54 E
Lianjiang, Fujian, China 77 D12 26 12N 119 27 E
Lianjiang, Guangdong, China 77 G8 21 40N 110 20 E
Lianping, China 77 E10 24 26N 114 30 E
Lianshan, China 77 E9 24 38N 112 8 E
Lianshanguan, China 75 D12 40 53N 123 43 E
Lianshui, China 75 H10 33 42N 119 20 E
Lianyuan, China 77 D8 27 40N 111 38 E
Lianyungang, China 75 G10 34 40N 119 11 E
Lianzhou, China 77 E9 24 51N 112 22 E
Liao He →, China 75 D11 41 0N 121 50 E
Liaocheng, China 74 F8 36 28N 115 58 E
Liaodong Bandao, China 75 E12 40 0N 122 30 E
Liaodong Wan, China 75 D11 40 20N 121 10 E
Liaoning □, China 75 D12 41 40N 122 30 E
Liaotung, G. of = Liaodong Wan, China 75 D11 40 20N 121 10 E
Liaoyang, China 75 D12 41 15N 122 58 E
Liaoyuan, China 75 C13 42 58N 125 2 E
Liaozhong, China 75 D12 41 23N 122 50 E
Liapádhes, Greece 38 B9 39 42N 19 40 E
Liard →, Canada 142 A4 61 51N 121 18W
Liard River, Canada 142 B3 59 25N 126 5W
Liari, Pakistan 92 G2 25 37N 66 30 E
Libano, Colombia 168 C2 4 55N 75 4W
Libau = Liepāja, Latvia 15 H19 56 30N 21 0 E
Libby, U.S.A. 158 B6 48 23N 115 33W
Libenge, Dem. Rep. of the Congo 114 B3 3 40N 18 55 E
Liberal, U.S.A. 155 G4 37 3N 100 55W
Liberdade, Brazil 172 C3 10 5 S 70 20W
Liberdade →, Brazil 173 B7 9 40 S 52 17W
Liberec, Czech Rep. 34 A8 50 47N 15 7 E
Liberecký □, Czech Rep. 34 A8 50 45N 15 0 E
Liberia, Costa Rica 164 D2 10 40N 85 30W
Liberia ■, W. Afr. 112 D3 6 30N 9 30W
Libertad, Phil. 81 F3 11 46N 121 55 E
Libertad, Venezuela 168 B4 8 20N 69 37W
Liberty, Ind., U.S.A. 157 E12 39 38N 84 56W
Liberty, Mo., U.S.A. 156 E2 39 15N 94 25W
Liberty, N.Y., U.S.A. 151 E10 41 48N 74 45W
Liberty, Pa., U.S.A. 150 E7 41 34N 77 6W
Liberty, Tex., U.S.A. 155 K7 30 3N 94 48W
Liberty Center, U.S.A. 157 C12 41 27N 84 1W
Libertyville, U.S.A. 157 B9 42 18N 87 57W
Libiąż, Poland 55 H6 50 7N 19 21 E
Libibi, Angola 115 E3 14 42 S 17 44 E
Lîbîya, Sahrâ', Africa 108 C4 25 0N 25 0 E
Libjo, Phil. 81 F5 10 12N 125 32 E
Libmanan, Phil. 80 E4 13 42N 123 4 E
Libo, China 76 E6 25 22N 107 53 E
Libobo, Tanjung, Indonesia 83 B3 0 54 S 128 28 E
Libode, S. Africa 117 E4 31 33 S 29 2 E
Libohovë, Albania 50 F4 40 3N 20 10 E
Libona, Phil. 81 G5 8 20N 124 44 E
Libonda, Zambia 115 E4 14 28 S 23 12 E
Libourne, France 28 D3 44 55N 0 14W
Libramont, Belgium 24 E5 49 55N 5 23 E
Librazhd, Albania 50 E4 41 12N 20 22 E
Libreville, Gabon 114 B1 0 25N 9 26 E
Libya ■, N. Afr. 108 C3 27 0N 17 0 E
Libyan Desert = Lîbîya, Sahrâ', Africa 108 C4 25 0N 25 0 E
Libyan Plateau = Ed-Déffa, Egypt 106 A2 30 40N 26 30 E
Licantén, Chile 174 D1 35 55 S 72 0W
Licata, Italy 46 E6 37 6N 13 56 E
Lice, Turkey 101 C9 38 27N 40 39 E
Licheng, China 74 F7 36 28N 113 20 E
Lichfield, U.K. 21 E6 52 41N 1 49W
Lichinga, Mozam. 119 E4 13 13 S 35 11 E
Lichtenburg, S. Africa 116 D4 26 8 S 26 8 E
Lichtenfels, Germany 31 E7 50 8N 11 4 E
Lichuan, Hubei, China 76 B7 30 18N 108 57 E
Lichuan, Jiangxi, China 77 D11 27 18N 116 55 E
Licking →, U.S.A. 157 F12 39 6N 84 30W
Licosa, Punta, Italy 47 B7 40 15N 14 54 E
Licungo →, Mozam. 119 F4 17 40 S 37 15 E
Lida, Belarus 15 K21 53 53N 25 15 E
Liden, Sweden 16 B10 62 42N 16 48 E
Lidhoríkion, Greece 48 C4 38 32N 22 12 E
Lidhult, Sweden 17 H7 56 50N 13 27 E
Lidköping, Sweden 17 F7 58 31N 13 7 E
Lido, Italy 45 C9 45 25N 12 22 E
Lido, Niger 113 C5 12 54N 3 44 E
Lido di Roma = Ostia, Lido di, Italy 45 G9 41 43N 12 17 E
Lidzbark, Poland 55 E6 53 15N 19 49 E
Lidzbark Warmiński, Poland 54 D7 54 7N 20 34 E
Liebenthal = Lubomierz, Poland 55 G2 51 1N 15 31 E
Liebenwalde, Germany 30 C9 52 52N 13 24 E
Lieberose, Germany 30 D10 51 59N 14 17 E
Liebig, Mt., Australia 124 D5 23 18 S 131 22 E
Liebling, Romania 52 E6 45 36N 21 20 E
Liechtenstein ■, Europe 33 B9 47 8N 9 35 E
Liège, Belgium 24 D5 50 38N 5 35 E
Liège □, Belgium 24 D5 50 32N 5 35 E
Liegnitz = Legnica, Poland 55 G3 51 12N 16 10 E
Lienart, Dem. Rep. of the Congo 118 B2 3 3N 25 31 E
Lienyünchiangshih = Lianyungang, China 75 G10 34 40N 119 11 E
Lienz, Austria 34 E5 46 50N 12 46 E
Liepāja, Latvia 15 H19 56 30N 21 0 E
Liepāja □, Latvia 54 B8 56 30N 21 30 E
Liepājas ezers, Latvia 54 B8 56 27N 21 3 E
Lier, Belgium 24 C4 51 7N 4 34 E
Liernais, France 27 E11 47 13N 4 16 E
Liestal, Switz. 32 B5 47 29N 7 44 E
Liești, Romania 53 E12 45 38N 27 34 E
Lietuva = Lithuania ■, Europe 15 J20 55 30N 24 0 E
Liévin, France 27 B9 50 24N 2 47 E
Lièvre →, Canada 140 C4 45 31N 75 26W
Liezen, Austria 34 D7 47 34N 14 15 E
Liffey →, Ireland 23 C5 53 21N 6 13W
Lifford, Ireland 23 B4 54 51N 7 29W
Liffré, France 26 D5 48 12N 1 30W
Lifjell, Norway 18 E5 59 27N 8 45 E
Lifou, I., N. Cal. 133 K5 20 53 S 167 13 E
Lifudzin, Russia 70 B7 44 21N 134 58 E
Lifuka, Tonga 133 P13 19 48 S 174 21W
Ligao, Phil. 80 E4 13 14N 123 32 E
Ligasa, Dem. Rep. of the Congo 114 B4 0 44N 23 49 E
Lighthouse Point, U.S.A. 153 J9 26 15N 80 7W
Lighthouse Pt., U.S.A. 152 F5 29 54N 84 21W
Lightning Ridge, Australia 127 D4 29 22 S 148 0 E
Lignano Sabbiadoro, Italy 45 C10 45 42N 13 9 E
Ligny-en-Barrois, France 27 D12 48 36N 5 20 E
Ligonha →, Mozam. 119 F4 16 54 S 39 9 E
Ligonier, Ind., U.S.A. 157 C11 41 28N 85 35W
Ligonier, Pa., U.S.A. 150 F5 40 15N 79 14W
Ligourion, Greece 48 D5 37 37N 23 4 E
Ligueil, France 26 E7 47 2N 0 49 E
Liguria □, Italy 44 D5 44 30N 8 50 E
Ligurian Sea, Medit. S. 12 G7 43 20N 9 0 E
Lihir Group, Papua N. G. 132 B7 3 0 S 152 35 E
Lihir I., Papua N. G. 132 B7 3 5 S 152 35 E
Lihou Reefs and Cays, Australia 126 B5 17 25 S 151 40 E
Lihue, U.S.A. 145 B2 21 59N 159 23W
Lihué Calel △, Argentina 174 D2 38 0 S 65 10W
Lijiang, China 76 D3 26 55N 100 20 E
Likasi, Dem. Rep. of the Congo 119 E2 10 55 S 26 48 E
Likati, Dem. Rep. of the Congo 114 B4 3 20N 24 0 E
Likati →, Dem. Rep. of the Congo 114 B4 2 53N 24 3 E
Likenäs, Sweden 16 D7 60 37N 13 3 E
Likete, Dem. Rep. of the Congo 114 C4 0 48 S 21 31 E
Likhaya = Likhovskoy, Russia 59 H11 48 10N 40 10 E
Likhoslavl, Russia 58 D8 57 12N 35 30 E
Likhovskoy, Russia 59 H11 48 10N 40 10 E
Likhvin = Chekalin, Russia 58 E9 54 10N 36 10 E
Likimi, Dem. Rep. of the Congo 114 B4 2 44N 20 47 E
Likisia = Liquica, E. Timor 82 C3 8 36 S 125 19 E
Likita, Dem. Rep. of the Congo 114 B4 4 15N 23 36 E
Liknes, Norway 18 F3 58 19N 6 59 E
Likokou, Gabon 114 C2 0 12 S 12 48 E
Likoma I., Malawi 119 E3 12 3 S 34 45 E
Likouala →, Congo 114 C3 0 2N 14 53 E
Likouala aux Herbes →, Congo 114 C3 0 52 S 17 8 E
Likumburu, Tanzania 119 D4 9 43 S 35 8 E
Lilanga, Dem. Rep. of the Congo 114 C4 0 34 S 23 56 E
L'Île-Bouchard, France 26 E7 47 7N 0 26 E
L'Île-Rousse, France 29 F12 42 38N 8 57 E
Lilenga, Dem. Rep. of the Congo 114 B4 1 4N 22 2 E
Liling, China 77 D9 27 42N 113 29 E
Lilla Edet, Sweden 17 F6 58 9N 12 8 E
Lille, France 27 B10 50 38N 3 3 E
Lille Bælt, Denmark 17 J3 55 20N 9 45 E
Lillebonne, France 26 C7 49 30N 0 32 E
Lillehammer, Norway 18 C7 61 8N 10 30 E
Lillesand, Norway 18 F5 58 15N 8 23 E
Lillestrøm, Norway 18 E8 59 58N 11 5 E
Lillhärdal, Sweden 16 C8 61 51N 14 5 E
Lillian Pt., Australia 125 E4 27 40 S 126 6 E
Lillo, Spain 42 F7 39 45N 3 20W
Lillooet, Canada 142 C4 50 44N 121 57W
Lillooet →, Canada 142 D4 49 15N 121 57W
Lilongwe, Malawi 119 E3 14 0 S 33 48 E
Liloy, Phil. 81 G4 8 4N 122 39 E
Lim →, Bos.-H. 50 C3 43 45N 19 15 E
Lim Chu Kang, Singapore 87 d 1 26N 103 43 E
Lima, Brazil 169 D5 4 36 S 63 40W
Lima, Indonesia 82 B3 3 39 S 127 58 E
Lima, Peru 172 C2 12 0 S 77 0W
Lima, Ill., U.S.A. 156 D5 40 11N 91 23W
Lima, Mont., U.S.A. 158 D7 44 38N 112 36W
Lima, Ohio, U.S.A. 157 D12 40 44N 84 6W
Lima □, Peru 172 C2 12 3 S 77 3W
Lima →, Portugal 42 D2 41 41N 8 50W
Liman = Krasnyy Liman, Ukraine 59 H9 48 58N 37 50 E
Liman, Indonesia 79 G14 7 48 S 111 45 E
Liman, Russia 61 H8 45 45N 47 12 E
Limanowa, Poland 55 J7 49 42N 20 22 E
Limassol, Cyprus 39 F9 34 42N 33 1 E
Limavady, U.K. 23 A5 55 3N 6 56W
Limay →, Argentina 176 A3 39 0 S 68 0W
Limay Mahuida, Argentina 174 D2 37 10 S 66 45W
Limbach-Oberfrohna, Germany 30 E8 50 52N 12 43 E
Limbang, Brunei 85 B5 4 42N 115 6 E
Limbara, Mte., Italy 46 B2 40 51N 9 10 E
Limbaži, Latvia 15 H21 57 31N 24 42 E
Limbdi, India 92 H4 22 34N 71 51 E
Limbe, Cameroon 113 E6 4 1N 9 10 E
Limboto, Indonesia 82 A2 0 37N 122 57 E
Limbueta, Angola 115 E3 12 30 S 18 42 E
Limbuhan = Pio V. Corpuz, Phil. 81 F5 11 55N 124 2 E
Limburg, Germany 31 E4 50 22N 8 4 E
Limburg □, Belgium 24 C5 51 2N 5 25 E
Limburg □, Neths. 24 C5 51 20N 5 55 E
Lime Village, U.S.A. 144 F9 61 21N 155 28W
Limedsforsen, Sweden 16 D7 60 52N 13 25 E
Limeira = Joaçaba, Brazil 175 B5 27 5 S 51 31W
Limeira, Brazil 175 A6 22 35 S 47 28W
Limenária, Greece 51 F8 40 38N 24 32 E
Limerick, Ireland 23 D3 52 40N 8 37W
Limerick, U.S.A. 151 C14 43 41N 70 48W
Limerick □, Ireland 23 D3 52 30N 8 50W
Limestone, U.S.A. 150 D6 42 2N 78 38W
Limestone →, Canada 143 B10 56 31N 94 7W
Limestone Hill = Lackawanna, U.S.A. 150 D6 42 50N 78 50W
Limfjorden, Denmark 17 H3 56 55N 9 0 E
Limia = Lima →, Portugal 42 D2 41 41N 8 50W
Limín Khersonísou, Greece 39 E6 35 18N 25 21 E
Limingen, Norway 14 D15 64 48N 13 35 E
Limmared, Sweden 17 G7 57 34N 13 20 E
Limmat →, Switz. 33 B6 47 26N 8 20 E
Limmen Bight, Australia 126 A2 14 40 S 135 35 E
Limmen Bight →, Australia 126 B2 15 7 S 135 44 E
Límni, Greece 48 C5 38 43N 23 18 E
Límni Voulkariá, Greece 39 B2 38 52N 20 50 E
Límnos, Greece 49 B7 39 50N 25 5 E
Limoeiro, Brazil 170 C4 7 52 S 35 27W
Limoeiro do Norte, Brazil 170 C4 5 5 S 38 0W
Limoges, Canada 151 A9 45 20N 75 16W
Limoges, France 28 C5 45 50N 1 15 E
Limón, Costa Rica 164 E3 10 0N 83 2W
Limon, U.S.A. 154 F3 39 16N 103 41W
Limone Piemonte, Italy 44 D4 44 12N 7 34 E
Limousin □, France 28 C5 45 30N 1 30 E
Limousin, Plateaux du, France 28 C5 45 45N 1 15 E
Limoux, France 28 E6 43 4N 2 12 E
Limpopo □, S. Africa 117 C4 24 5 S 29 0 E
Limpopo →, Africa 117 D5 25 5 S 33 30 E
Limuru, Kenya 118 C4 1 2 S 36 35 E
Lin Xian, China 74 F6 37 57N 110 58 E
Lin'an, China 77 B12 30 15N 119 42 E
Linao Pt., Phil. 81 H4 6 46N 123 58 E
Linapacan, Phil. 81 F2 11 30N 119 52 E
Linapacan I., Phil. 81 F2 11 27N 119 49 E
Linapacan Str., Phil. 81 F2 11 37N 119 56 E
Linares, Chile 174 D1 35 50 S 71 40W
Linares, Colombia 168 C2 1 23N 77 31W
Linares, Mexico 163 C5 24 50N 99 40W
Linares, Spain 43 G7 38 10N 3 40W
Linaro, Capo, Italy 45 F8 42 2N 11 50 E
Línas Mte., Italy 46 C1 39 25N 8 38 E
Linate, Milano ✕ (LIN), Italy 44 C6 45 27N 9 16 E
Lincang, China 76 F3 23 58N 100 1 E
Lincheng, China 74 F8 37 25N 114 30 E
Linchuan, China 77 D11 27 57N 116 15 E
Lincoln = Beamsville, Canada 150 C5 43 12N 79 28W
Lincoln, Argentina 174 C3 34 55 S 61 30W
Lincoln, N.Z. 131 D7 43 38 S 172 30 E
Lincoln, U.K. 20 D7 53 14N 0 32W
Lincoln, Calif., U.S.A. 160 G5 38 54N 121 17W
Lincoln, Ill., U.S.A. 156 D7 40 9N 89 22W
Lincoln, Kans., U.S.A. 154 F5 39 3N 98 9W
Lincoln, Maine, U.S.A. 149 C11 45 22N 68 30W
Lincoln, N.H., U.S.A. 151 B13 44 3N 71 40W
Lincoln, N. Mex., U.S.A. 159 K11 33 30N 105 23W
Lincoln, Nebr., U.S.A. 154 E6 40 49N 96 41W
Lincoln Boyhood ⌓, U.S.A. 157 F10 38 7N 86 58W
Lincoln City, U.S.A. 158 D1 44 57N 124 1W
Lincoln Hav = Lincoln Sea, Arctic 10 A5 84 0N 55 0W
Lincoln Park, Ga., U.S.A. 152 C5 32 52N 84 20W
Lincoln Park, Mich., U.S.A. 157 B13 42 15N 83 11W
Lincoln Sea, Arctic 10 A5 84 0N 55 0W
Lincolnshire □, U.K. 20 D7 53 14N 0 32W
Lincolnshire Wolds, U.K. 20 D7 53 26N 0 13W
Lincolnton, Ga., U.S.A. 152 B7 33 48N 82 29W
Lincolnton, N.C., U.S.A. 149 H5 35 29N 81 16W
Lind, U.S.A. 158 C4 46 58N 118 37W
Linda, U.S.A. 160 F5 39 8N 121 34W
Lindale, U.S.A. 152 A4 34 11N 85 11W
Lindås, Norway 18 D2 60 44N 5 9 E
Lindau, Germany 31 H5 47 33N 9 42 E
Lindeman I., Australia 126 J7 20 27 S 149 3 E
Linden = Gladstone, U.S.A. 156 E2 39 13N 94 35W
Linden, Guyana 169 B6 6 0N 58 10W
Linden, Ala., U.S.A. 149 J2 32 18N 87 48W
Linden, Calif., U.S.A. 160 G5 38 1N 121 5W
Linden, Ind., U.S.A. 157 D10 40 11N 86 54W
Linden, Mich., U.S.A. 157 B13 42 49N 83 47W
Linden, Tex., U.S.A. 155 J7 33 1N 94 22W
Lindenhurst, U.S.A. 151 F11 40 41N 73 23W
Lindenow Fjord, Greenland 10 E6 60 30N 43 25W
Lindesberg, Sweden 16 E9 59 36N 15 15 E
Lindesnes, Norway 18 G4 57 58N 7 3 E
Líndhos, Greece 38 E12 36 6N 28 4 E
Líndhos, Ákra, Greece 38 E12 36 4N 28 10 E
Lindi, Tanzania 119 D4 9 58 S 39 38 E
Lindi □, Tanzania 119 D4 9 40 S 38 30 E
Lindi →, Dem. Rep. of the Congo 118 B2 0 33N 25 5 E
Lindö, Sweden 17 F10 58 37N 16 15 E
Lindome, Sweden 17 G6 57 35N 12 5 E
Lindos = Líndhos, Greece 38 E12 36 6N 28 4 E
Lindoso, Portugal 42 D2 41 52N 8 11W
Lindow, Germany 30 C8 52 58N 12 59 E
Lindsay, Canada 140 D4 44 22N 78 43W
Lindsay, Calif., U.S.A. 160 J7 36 12N 119 5W
Lindsay, Okla., U.S.A. 155 H6 34 50N 97 38W
Lindsborg, U.S.A. 154 F6 38 35N 97 40W
Lindsdal, Sweden 17 H10 56 44N 16 18 E
Line Islands, Pac. Oc. 135 H12 7 0N 160 0W
Linesville, U.S.A. 150 E4 41 39N 80 26W
Lineville, Ala., U.S.A. 152 B4 33 19N 85 45W
Lineville, Iowa, U.S.A. 156 D3 40 35N 93 32W
Linfen, China 74 F6 36 3N 111 30 E
Ling Xian, Hunan, China 77 D9 26 29N 113 48 E
Ling Xian, Shandong, China 74 F9 37 22N 116 30 E
Lingal, India 95 F4 16 17N 78 31 E
Lingao, China 86 C7 19 56N 109 42 E
Lingayen, Phil. 80 C3 16 1N 120 14 E
Lingayen G., Phil. 80 C3 16 10N 120 15 E
Lingbi, China 75 H9 33 33N 117 33 E
Lingbo, Sweden 16 C10 61 3N 16 41 E
Lingchuan, Guangxi Zhuangzu, China 77 E8 25 26N 110 21 E
Lingchuan, Shanxi, China 74 G7 35 45N 113 12 E
Lingding Yang, China 69 G10 22 25N 113 44 E
Lingen, Germany 30 C3 52 31N 7 19 E
Lingga, Indonesia 84 C2 0 12 S 104 37 E
Lingga, Kepulauan, Indonesia 84 C2 0 10 S 104 30 E
Lingga Arch. = Lingga, Kepulauan, Indonesia 84 C2 0 10 S 104 30 E
Linghem, Sweden 17 F9 58 26N 15 47 E
Lingig, Phil. 81 G6 8 2N 126 24 E
Lingle, U.S.A. 154 D2 42 8N 104 21W
Lingomo, Dem. Rep. of the Congo 114 B4 0 38N 22 3 E
Lingqiu, China 74 E8 39 28N 114 22 E
Lingshan, China 76 F7 22 25N 109 18 E
Lingshi, China 74 F6 36 48N 111 48 E
Lingshou, China 74 E8 38 20N 114 20 E
Lingshui, China 86 C8 18 27N 110 0 E
Lingsugur, India 95 F3 16 10N 76 31 E
Lingtai, China 74 G4 35 0N 107 40 E
Linguère, Senegal 112 B1 15 25N 15 5W
Lingui, China 77 E8 25 12N 110 2 E
Lingunda, Dem. Rep. of the Congo 114 C3 0 49N 21 8 E
Lingwu, China 74 E4 38 6N 106 20 E
Lingyuan, China 75 D10 41 10N 119 15 E
Lingyun, China 76 E6 25 2N 106 35 E
Linhai, China 77 C13 28 50N 121 8 E
Linhares, Brazil 171 E3 19 25 S 40 4W
Linhe, China 74 D4 40 48N 107 20 E
Linjiang, China 75 D14 41 50N 127 0 E
Linköping, Sweden 17 F9 58 28N 15 36 E
Linkou, China 75 B16 45 15N 130 18 E
Linli, China 77 C8 29 27N 111 30 E
Linlithgow = West Lothian □, U.K. 22 F5 55 54N 3 36W
Linn, U.S.A. 156 F5 38 29N 91 51W
Linneus, U.S.A. 156 E3 39 53N 93 11W
Linnhe, L., U.K. 22 E3 56 36N 5 25W
Linosa, Medit. S. 108 A2 35 51N 12 50 E
Linqi, China 74 G7 35 45N 113 52 E
Linqing, China 74 F8 36 50N 115 42 E
Linqu, China 75 F10 36 25N 118 30 E
Linru, China 74 G7 34 11N 112 52 E
Lins, Brazil 175 A6 21 40 S 49 44W
Linshui, China 76 B6 30 21N 106 57 E
Linsia = Linxia, China 68 C5 35 36N 103 10 E
Linstead, Jamaica 164 a 18 8N 77 2W
Linta →, Madag. 117 D7 25 2 S 44 5 E
Linth →, Switz. 31 H5 47 7N 9 7 E
Linthal, Switz. 33 C8 46 54N 9 0 E
Linton, Ind., U.S.A. 157 F9 39 2N 87 10W
Linton, N. Dak., U.S.A. 154 B4 46 16N 100 14W
Lintong, China 74 G5 34 20N 109 10 E
Linwood, Canada 150 C4 43 35N 80 43W
Linwu, China 77 E9 25 19N 112 31 E
Linxi, China 75 C10 43 36N 118 2 E
Linxia, China 68 C5 35 36N 103 10 E
Linxiang, China 77 C9 29 28N 113 23 E
Linyanti →, Africa 116 B4 17 50 S 25 5 E
Linyi, China 75 G10 35 5N 118 21 E
Linz, Austria 34 C7 48 18N 14 18 E
Linz, Germany 30 E3 50 34N 7 17 E
Linzhenzhen, China 74 F5 36 30N 109 59 E
Linzi, China 75 F10 36 50N 118 20 E
Lioko, Équateur, Dem. Rep. of the Congo 114 B4 0 2N 22 4 E
Lioko, Orientale, Dem. Rep. of the Congo 114 B4 1 25N 23 7 E
Liomseter, Norway 18 C6 61 15N 9 35 E
Lion, G. du, France 28 E7 43 10N 4 0 E

Lionárisso, *Cyprus* **39 E10** 35 28N 34 8 E
Lioni, *Italy* **47 B8** 40 52N 15 11 E
Lions, G. of = Lion, G. du, *France* **28 E7** 43 10N 4 0 E
Lion's Den, *Zimbabwe* **119 F3** 17 15 S 30 5 E
Lion's Head, *Canada* **150 B3** 44 58N 81 15W
Liouesso, *Congo* **114 B3** 1 2N 15 43 E
Liozno = Lyozna, *Belarus* **58 E6** 55 0N 30 50 E
Lipa, *Phil.* **80 E3** 13 57N 121 10 E
Lipali, *Mozam.* **119 F4** 15 50 S 35 50 E
Lipany, *Slovak Rep.* **35 B13** 49 9N 20 58 E
Lípari, *Italy* **47 D7** 38 26N 14 58 E
Lípari, I., *Italy* **47 D7** 38 29N 14 56 E
Lípari, Is. = Eólie, Ís., *Italy* **47 D7** 38 30N 14 57 E
Lipcani, *Moldova* **53 B11** 48 14N 26 48 E
Lipetsk, *Russia* **59 F10** 52 37N 39 35 E
Lipiany, *Poland* **55 E1** 53 2N 14 58 E
Liping, *China* **76 D7** 26 15N 109 7 E
Lipkany = Lipcani, *Moldova* **53 B11** 48 14N 26 48 E
Lipljan, *Serbia & M.* **50 D5** 42 31N 21 7 E
Lipník nad Bečvou, *Czech Rep.* **35 B10** 49 32N 17 36 E
Lipno, *Poland* **55 F6** 52 49N 19 15 E
Lipova, *Romania* **52 D6** 46 8N 21 42 E
Lipovcy Manzovka, *Russia* **70 B5** 44 12N 132 26 E
Lipovets, *Ukraine* **59 H5** 49 12N 29 1 E
Lippe →, *Germany* **30 D2** 51 39N 6 36 E
Lippehne = Lipiany, *Poland* **55 E1** 53 2N 14 58 E
Lippstadt, *Germany* **30 D4** 51 41N 8 22 E
Lipscomb, *U.S.A.* **155 G4** 36 14N 100 16W
Lipsk, *Poland* **54 E10** 53 44N 23 24 E
Lipsko, *Poland* **55 G8** 51 9N 21 40 E
Lipsói, *Greece* **49 D8** 37 19N 26 50 E
Liptovský Hrádok, *Slovak Rep.* **35 B12** 49 2N 19 44 E
Liptovský Milkuláš, *Slovak Rep.* **35 B12** 49 6N 19 35 E
Liptrap, C., *Australia* **129 E6** 38 50 S 145 55 E
Lipu, *China* **77 E8** 24 30N 110 22 E
Liquica, *E. Timor* **82 C3** 8 36 S 125 19 E
Liquillo, Sierra de, *Puerto Rico* **165 d** 18 20N 65 47W
Lira, *Uganda* **118 B3** 2 17N 32 57 E
Liranga, *Congo* **114 C3** 0 43 S 17 32 E
Liri →, *Italy* **46 A6** 41 25N 13 52 E
Liria = Llíria, *Spain* **41 F4** 39 37N 0 35W
Lisakovsk, *Kazakhstan* **64 E9** 52 33N 62 37 E
Lisala, *Dem. Rep. of the Congo* **114 B4** 2 12N 21 38 E
Lisboa, *Portugal* **43 G1** 38 42N 9 10W
Lisboa □, *Portugal* **43 F1** 39 0N 9 12W
Lisboa ✕ (LIS), *Portugal* **43 G1** 38 46N 9 8W
Lisbon = Lisboa, *Portugal* **43 G1** 38 42N 9 10W
Lisbon, *N. Dak., U.S.A.* **154 B6** 46 27N 97 41W
Lisbon, *N.H., U.S.A.* **151 B13** 44 13N 71 55W
Lisbon, *Ohio, U.S.A.* **150 F4** 40 46N 80 46W
Lisbon Falls, *U.S.A.* **149 D10** 44 0N 70 4W
Lisburn, *U.K.* **23 B5** 54 31N 6 3W
Lisburn, C., *Vanuatu* **133 E4** 15 39 S 166 46 E
Lisburne, C., *U.S.A.* **6 C17** 68 53N 166 13W
Liscannor B., *Ireland* **23 D2** 52 55N 9 24W
Liscia →, *Italy* **46 A2** 41 11N 9 9 E
Lishe Jiang →, *China* **76 E3** 24 15N 101 35 E
Lishi, *China* **74 F6** 37 31N 111 8 E
Lishu, *China* **75 C13** 43 20N 124 18 E
Lishui, *Jiangsu, China* **77 B12** 31 38N 119 2 E
Lishui, *Zhejiang, China* **77 C12** 28 28N 119 54 E
Lisianski I., *Pac. Oc.* **145 F9** 26 2N 174 0W
Lisichansk = Lysychansk, *Ukraine* **59 H10** 48 55N 38 30 E
Lisieux, *France* **26 C7** 49 10N 0 12 E
Liski, *Russia* **59 G10** 51 3N 39 30 E
L'Isle-Jourdain, *Gers, France* **28 E5** 43 36N 1 5 E
L'Isle-Jourdain, *Vienne, France* **28 B4** 46 13N 0 31 E
L'Isle-Mont-la-Ville, *Switz.* **32 C2** 46 37N 6 25 E
L'Isle-sur-la-Sorgue, *France* **29 E9** 43 54N 5 2 E
Lisle-sur-Tarn, *France* **28 E5** 43 52N 1 49 E
Lismore, *Australia* **127 D5** 28 44 S 153 21 E
Lismore, *Ireland* **23 D4** 52 8N 7 55W
Lissa = Leszno, *Poland* **55 G3** 51 50N 16 30 E
Lista, *Norway* **18 F3** 58 7N 6 39 E
Lister, Mt., *Antarctica* **7 D11** 78 0 S 162 0 E
Lister og Mandals = Vest-Agder □, *Norway* **18 F4** 58 30N 7 15 E
Liston, *Australia* **127 D5** 28 39 S 152 6 E
Listowel, *Canada* **140 D3** 43 44N 80 58W
Listowel, *Ireland* **23 D2** 52 27N 9 29W
Lit, *Sweden* **16 A8** 63 19N 14 51 E
Lit-et-Mixe, *France* **28 D2** 44 2N 1 15W
Litang, *Guangxi Zhuangzu, China* **76 F7** 23 12N 109 8 E
Litang, *Sichuan, China* **76 B3** 30 1N 100 17 E
Litang, *Malaysia* **85 A5** 5 27N 118 31 E
Litang Qu →, *China* **76 C3** 28 4N 101 32 E
Litani →, *Lebanon* **103 B4** 33 20N 35 15 E
Litchfield, *Australia* **128 D5** 36 18 S 142 52 E
Litchfield, *Calif., U.S.A.* **160 E6** 40 24N 120 23W
Litchfield, *Conn., U.S.A.* **151 E11** 41 45N 73 11W
Litchfield, *Ill., U.S.A.* **156 E7** 39 11N 89 39W
Litchfield, *Minn., U.S.A.* **154 C7** 45 8N 94 32W
Litchfield △, *Australia* **124 B5** 13 14 S 131 1 E
Liteni, *Romania* **53 C11** 47 32N 26 32 E
Lithakiá, *Greece* **39 D2** 37 43N 20 50 E
Lithgow, *Australia* **129 B9** 33 25 S 150 8 E
Líthinon, Ákra, *Greece* **39 F5** 34 55N 24 44 E
Lithuania ■, *Europe* **15 J20** 55 30N 24 0 E
Litija, *Slovenia* **45 B11** 46 3N 14 50 E
Lititz, *U.S.A.* **151 F8** 40 9N 76 18W
Litókhoron, *Greece* **50 F6** 40 8N 22 34 E
Litoko, *Dem. Rep. of the Congo* **114 C4** 1 13 S 24 47 E
Litoměřice, *Czech Rep.* **34 A7** 50 33N 14 10 E
Litomyšl, *Czech Rep.* **35 B9** 49 52N 16 20 E
Litschau, *Austria* **34 C8** 48 58N 15 4 E
Little Abaco, *Bahamas* **164 A4** 26 50N 77 30W
Little Andaman I., *India* **95 J11** 10 45N 92 30 E
Little Barrier I., *N.Z.* **130 C4** 36 12 S 175 8 E
Little Basses, *Sri Lanka* **95 L5** 6 24N 81 43 E
Little Belt Mts., *U.S.A.* **158 C8** 46 40N 110 45W
Little Bighorn Battlefield ⌂, *U.S.A.* **158 D10** 45 34N 107 26W
Little Blue →, *U.S.A.* **154 F6** 39 42N 96 41W
Little Buffalo →, *Canada* **142 A6** 61 0N 113 46W
Little Cayman, *Cayman Is.* **164 C3** 19 41N 80 3W
Little Churchill →, *Canada* **143 B9** 57 30N 95 22W
Little Coco I., *Burma* **95 H11** 14 0N 93 13 E
Little Colorado →, *U.S.A.* **159 H8** 36 12N 111 48W
Little Current, *Canada* **140 C3** 45 55N 82 0W
Little Current →, *Canada* **140 B3** 50 57N 84 36W
Little Desert △, *Australia* **128 D4** 37 25 S 141 30 E
Little Diomede I., *U.S.A.* **144 D5** 65 45N 168 56W
Little Falls, *Minn., U.S.A.* **154 C7** 45 59N 94 22W
Little Falls, *N.Y., U.S.A.* **151 C10** 43 3N 74 51W
Little Fork →, *U.S.A.* **154 A8** 48 31N 93 35W
Little Grand Rapids, *Canada* **143 C9** 52 0N 95 29W
Little Humboldt →, *U.S.A.* **158 F5** 41 1N 117 43W
Little Inagua I., *Bahamas* **165 B5** 21 40N 73 50W
Little Karoo, *S. Africa* **116 E3** 33 45 S 21 0 E
Little Khingan Mts. = Xiao Hinggan Ling, *China* **69 B7** 49 0N 127 0 E
Little Lake, *U.S.A.* **161 K9** 35 56N 117 55W
Little Laut Is. = Laut Kecil, Kepulauan, *Indonesia* **85 C5** 4 45 S 115 40 E
Little Mecatina = Petit-Mécatina →, *Canada* **141 B8** 50 40N 59 30W
Little Minch, *U.K.* **22 D2** 57 35N 6 45W
Little Missouri →, *U.S.A.* **154 B3** 47 36N 102 25W
Little Nicobar, *India* **95 L11** 7 20N 93 40 E
Little Ouse →, *U.K.* **21 E9** 52 22N 1 12 E
Little Rann, *India* **92 H4** 23 25N 71 25 E
Little Red →, *U.S.A.* **155 H9** 35 11N 91 27W
Little River, *N.Z.* **131 D7** 43 45 S 172 49 E
Little Rock, *U.S.A.* **155 H8** 34 45N 92 17W
Little Ruaha →, *Tanzania* **118 D4** 7 57 S 37 53 E
Little Sable Pt., *U.S.A.* **148 D2** 43 38N 86 33W
Little Scarcies →, *S. Leone* **112 D2** 8 50N 13 10W
Little Sioux →, *U.S.A.* **154 E6** 41 48N 96 4W
Little Sitkin I., *U.S.A.* **144 L2** 51 57N 178 31 E
Little Smoky →, *Canada* **142 C5** 54 44N 117 11W
Little Snake →, *U.S.A.* **158 F9** 40 27N 108 26W
Little Sound, *Bermuda* **9 a** 32 15N 64 50W
Little Tobago, *Trin. & Tob.* **169 E10** 11 18N 60 30W
Little Valley, *U.S.A.* **150 D6** 42 15N 78 48W
Little Wabash →, *U.S.A.* **157 G8** 37 55N 88 5W
Little White →, *U.S.A.* **154 D4** 43 40N 100 40W
Little York, *U.S.A.* **156 C6** 41 1N 90 45W
Little Zab = Zāb aş Şaghīr →, *Iraq* **101 E10** 35 17N 43 29 E
Littlefield, *U.S.A.* **155 J3** 33 55N 102 20W
Littlehampton, *U.K.* **21 G7** 50 49N 0 32W
Littleton, *U.S.A.* **151 B13** 44 18N 71 46W
Littoria = Latina, *Italy* **46 A5** 41 28N 12 52 E
Litunga, *Angola* **115 E3** 13 19 S 16 48 E
Litvínov, *Czech Rep.* **34 A6** 50 36N 13 37 E
Liu He →, *China* **75 D11** 40 55N 121 35 E
Liu Jiang →, *China* **76 F7** 23 55N 109 30 E
Liuba, *China* **74 H4** 33 38N 106 55 E
Liucheng, *China* **76 E7** 24 38N 109 14 E
Liugou, *China* **75 D10** 40 57N 118 15 E
Liuhe, *China* **75 C13** 42 17N 125 43 E
Liuheng Dao, *China* **77 C14** 29 40N 122 5 E
Liujiang, *China* **76 E7** 24 26N 109 11 E
Liukang Tenggaja = Sabalana, Kepulauan, *Indonesia* **82 C1** 6 45 S 118 50 E
Liuli, *Tanzania* **119 E3** 11 3 S 34 38 E
Liuwa Plain, *Zambia* **115 E4** 14 20 S 22 30 E
Liuwa Plain △, *Zambia* **115 E4** 14 45 S 22 35 E
Liuyang, *China* **77 C9** 28 10N 113 37 E
Liuzhou, *China* **76 E7** 24 22N 109 22 E
Liuzhuang, *China* **75 H11** 33 12N 120 18 E
Livada, *Romania* **52 C8** 47 52N 23 5 E
Livadherón, *Greece* **50 F5** 40 2N 21 57 E
Livadhia, *Cyprus* **39 F9** 34 57N 33 38 E
Livádhion, *Greece* **48 A4** 40 8N 22 9 E
Livadhje, *Albania* **38 B10** 39 47N 20 7 E
Livadia = Levádhia, *Greece* **48 C4** 38 27N 22 54 E
Livarot, *France* **26 D7** 48 58N 0 9 E
Live Oak, *Calif., U.S.A.* **160 F5** 39 17N 121 40W
Live Oak, *Fla., U.S.A.* **152 E7** 30 18N 82 59W
Lively, *Canada* **148 B5** 46 26N 81 9W
Livengood, *U.S.A.* **144 D10** 65 32N 148 33W
Liveras, *Cyprus* **39 E8** 35 23N 32 57 E
Livermore, *U.S.A.* **160 H5** 37 41N 121 47W
Livermore, Mt., *U.S.A.* **155 K2** 30 38N 104 11W
Livermore Falls, *U.S.A.* **149 C11** 44 29N 70 11W
Liverpool, *Australia* **129 B9** 33 54 S 150 58 E
Liverpool, *Canada* **141 D7** 44 5N 64 41W
Liverpool, *U.K.* **20 D4** 53 25N 3 0W
Liverpool, *U.S.A.* **151 C8** 43 6N 76 13W
Liverpool Bay, *U.K.* **20 D4** 53 30N 3 20W
Liverpool Plains, *Australia* **129 A9** 31 15 S 150 15 E
Liverpool Ra., *Australia* **129 A9** 31 50 S 150 30 E
Livigno, *Italy* **44 B7** 46 35N 10 10 E
Livingston, *Guatemala* **164 C2** 15 50N 88 50W
Livingston, *U.K.* **22 F5** 55 54N 3 30W
Livingston, *Ala., U.S.A.* **149 J1** 32 35N 88 11W
Livingston, *Calif., U.S.A.* **160 H6** 37 23N 120 43W
Livingston, *Mont., U.S.A.* **158 D8** 45 40N 110 34W
Livingston, *S.C., U.S.A.* **149 J5** 33 32N 80 53W
Livingston, *Tenn., U.S.A.* **149 G3** 36 23N 85 19W
Livingston, *Tex., U.S.A.* **155 K7** 30 43N 94 56W
Livingston, *Wis., U.S.A.* **156 B6** 42 54N 90 26W
Livingston, L., *U.S.A.* **155 K7** 30 50N 95 10W
Livingston Manor, *U.S.A.* **151 E10** 41 54N 74 50W
Livingstone, *Zambia* **119 F2** 17 46 S 25 52 E
Livingstone Mts., *N.Z.* **131 F3** 45 15 S 168 9 E
Livingstone Mts., *Tanzania* **119 D3** 9 40 S 34 20 E
Livingstonia, *Malawi* **119 E3** 10 38 S 34 5 E
Livno, *Bos.-H.* **52 G2** 43 50N 17 1 E
Livny, *Russia* **59 F9** 52 30N 37 30 E
Livonia, *Mich., U.S.A.* **157 B13** 42 23N 83 23W
Livonia, *N.Y., U.S.A.* **150 D7** 42 49N 77 40W
Livorno, *Italy* **44 E7** 43 33N 10 19 E
Livradois-Forez ⌂, *France* **28 E7** 44 0N 3 0 E
Livramento = Nossa Senhora do Livramento, *Brazil* **173 D6** 15 48 S 56 22W
Livramento, *Brazil* **175 C4** 30 55 S 55 30W
Livramento do Brumado, *Brazil* **171 D3** 13 39 S 41 50W
Livron-sur-Drôme, *France* **29 D8** 44 46N 4 51 E
Livyntsi, *Ukraine* **53 B11** 48 25N 26 37 E
Liwale, *Tanzania* **119 D4** 9 48 S 37 58 E
Liwiec →, *Poland* **55 F8** 52 36N 21 34 E
Liwonde △, *Malawi* **119 E4** 14 48 S 35 20 E
Lixi, *China* **76 D3** 26 23N 101 59 E
Lixian, *China* **76 B4** 31 23N 103 13 E
Lixoúrion, *Greece* **39 C2** 38 12N 20 26 E
Liyang, *China* **77 B12** 31 26N 119 28 E
Lizard I., *Australia* **126 A4** 14 42 S 145 30 E
Lizard Pt., *U.K.* **21 H2** 49 57N 5 13W
Lizarda, *Brazil* **170 C2** 9 36 S 46 41W
Lizella, *U.S.A.* **152 C6** 32 48N 83 49W
Lizzano, *Italy* **47 B10** 40 23N 17 27 E
Ljig, *Serbia & M.* **50 B4** 44 13N 20 18 E
Ljøra →, *Norway* **18 C9** 61 24N 12 35 E
Ljørdal, *Norway* **18 C9** 61 23N 12 41 E
Ljosland, *Norway* **18 F4** 58 47N 7 22 E
Ljubija, *Bos.-H.* **45 D13** 44 55N 16 35 E
Ljubinje, *Bos.-H.* **50 D2** 42 58N 18 5 E
Ljubljana, *Slovenia* **45 B11** 46 4N 14 33 E
Ljubljana ✕ (LJU), *Slovenia* **45 B11** 46 14N 14 33 E
Ljubno, *Slovenia* **45 B11** 46 25N 14 46 E
Ljubovija, *Serbia & M.* **50 B3** 44 11N 19 22 E
Ljugarn, *Sweden* **17 G12** 57 20N 18 43 E
Ljung, *Sweden* **17 G7** 57 59N 13 3 E
Ljungan →, *Sweden* **16 B11** 62 18N 17 23 E
Ljungaverk, *Sweden* **16 B10** 62 30N 16 5 E
Ljungby, *Sweden* **17 H7** 56 49N 13 55 E
Ljungbyholm, *Sweden* **17 H10** 56 39N 16 5 E
Ljungdalen, *Sweden* **16 B6** 62 51N 12 47 E
Ljungsbro, *Sweden* **17 F9** 58 31N 15 30 E
Ljungskile, *Sweden* **17 F5** 58 14N 11 55 E
Ljusdal, *Sweden* **16 C10** 61 46N 16 3 E
Ljusfallshammar, *Sweden* **17 F9** 58 48N 15 30 E
Ljusnan →, *Sweden* **16 C11** 61 12N 17 8 E
Ljusne, *Sweden* **16 C11** 61 13N 17 7 E
Ljutomer, *Slovenia* **45 B13** 46 31N 16 11 E
Llagostera, *Spain* **40 D7** 41 50N 2 54 E
Llamellín, *Peru* **172 B2** 9 0 S 76 54W
Llancanelo, Salina, *Argentina* **174 D2** 35 40 S 69 8W
Llandeilo, *U.K.* **21 F4** 51 53N 3 59W
Llandovery, *U.K.* **21 F4** 51 59N 3 48W
Llandrindod Wells, *U.K.* **21 E4** 52 14N 3 22W
Llandudno, *U.K.* **20 D4** 53 19N 3 50W
Llanelli, *U.K.* **21 F3** 51 41N 4 10W
Llanes, *Spain* **42 B6** 43 25N 4 50W
Llanganates △, *Ecuador* **168 D3** 0 51 S 72 20W
Llangollen, *U.K.* **20 E4** 52 58N 3 11W
Llanidloes, *U.K.* **21 E4** 52 27N 3 31W
Llano, *U.S.A.* **155 K5** 30 45N 98 41W
Llano →, *U.S.A.* **155 K5** 30 39N 98 26W
Llano Estacado, *U.S.A.* **155 J3** 33 30N 103 0W
Llanos, *S. Amer.* **166 C3** 5 0N 71 35W
Llanos de Challe △, *Chile* **174 B1** 28 8 S 71 1W
Llanquihue, L., *Chile* **176 B1** 41 10 S 72 50W
Llanwrtyd Wells, *U.K.* **21 E4** 52 7N 3 38W
Llata, *Peru* **172 B2** 9 25 S 76 47W
Llebeig, C. des, *Spain* **38 B3** 39 33N 2 18 E
Lleida, *Spain* **40 D5** 41 37N 0 39 E
Lleida □, *Spain* **40 C6** 42 6N 1 0 E
Llentrisca, C., *Spain* **38 D1** 38 52N 1 15 E
Llera, *Mexico* **163 C5** 23 19N 99 1W
Llerena, *Spain* **43 G5** 38 17N 6 0W
Lleyn Peninsula, *U.K.* **20 E3** 52 51N 4 36W
Llica, *Bolivia* **172 D4** 19 52 S 68 16W
Llico, *Chile* **174 C1** 34 46 S 72 5W
Llíria, *Spain* **41 F4** 39 37N 0 35W
Llobregat →, *Spain* **40 D7** 41 19N 2 9 E
Llodio, *Spain* **40 B2** 43 9N 2 58W
Llorente, *Phil.* **81 F5** 11 25N 125 33 E
Lloret de Mar, *Spain* **40 D7** 41 41N 2 53 E
Lloyd B., *Australia* **126 A3** 12 45 S 143 27 E
Lloyd L., *Canada* **143 B7** 57 22N 108 57W
Lloydminster, *Canada* **143 C7** 53 17N 110 0W
Llucena del Cid, *Spain* **40 E4** 40 9N 0 17W
Llucmajor, *Spain* **38 B3** 39 29N 2 53 E
Llullaillaco △, *Chile* **174 A2** 24 50 S 68 51W
Llullaillaco, Volcán, *S. Amer.* **174 A2** 24 43 S 68 30W
Lo →, *Vietnam* **86 B5** 21 18N 105 25 E
Loa, *U.S.A.* **159 G8** 38 24N 111 39W
Loa →, *Chile* **174 A1** 21 26 S 70 41W
Loaita I., *S. China Sea* **78 B4** 10 41N 114 25 E
Loange →, *Dem. Rep. of the Congo* **115 C4** 4 17 S 20 2 E
Loango, *Congo* **115 C2** 4 38 S 11 50 E
Loano, *Italy* **44 D5** 44 8N 8 15 E
Loay, *Phil.* **81 G5** 9 36N 124 1 E
Lobatse, *Botswana* **116 D4** 25 12 S 25 40 E
Löbau, *Germany* **30 D10** 51 5N 14 40 E
Lobaye →, *C.A.R.* **114 B3** 3 41N 18 35 E
Loben = Lubliniec, *Poland* **55 H5** 50 43N 18 45 E
Lobenstein, *Germany* **30 E7** 50 25N 11 39 E
Lobería, *Argentina* **174 D4** 38 10 S 58 40W
Loberöd, *Sweden* **17 J7** 55 47N 13 31 E
Łobez, *Poland* **54 E2** 53 38N 15 39 E
Lobito, *Angola* **115 E2** 12 18 S 13 35 E
Lobo, *Indonesia* **83 B4** 3 45 S 134 5 E
Lobo, *Phil.* **80 E3** 13 39N 121 13 E
Lobo →, *Ivory C.* **112 D3** 6 2N 6 45W
Lobos, *Argentina* **174 D4** 35 10 S 59 0W
Lobos, I., *Mexico* **162 B2** 27 15N 110 30W
Lobos, I. de, *Canary Is.* **9 e2** 28 45N 13 50W
Lobos de Afuera, Islas, *Peru* **172 B1** 6 57 S 80 42W
Lobos de Tierra, I., *Peru* **172 B1** 6 27 S 80 52W
Lobva, *Russia* **64 B8** 59 10N 60 30 E
Lobva →, *Russia* **64 B8** 59 8N 60 48 E
Łobżenica, *Poland* **55 E4** 53 18N 17 15 E
Loc Binh, *Vietnam* **86 B6** 21 46N 106 54 E
Loc Ninh, *Vietnam* **87 G6** 11 50N 106 34 E
Locarno, *Switz.* **33 D7** 46 10N 8 47 E
Loch Baghasdail = Lochboisdale, *U.K.* **22 D1** 57 9N 7 20W
Loch Garman = Wexford, *Ireland* **23 D5** 52 20N 6 28W
Loch Lomond and the Trossachs △, *U.K.* **22 E4** 56 10N 4 40W
Loch Nam Madadh = Lochmaddy, *U.K.* **22 D1** 57 36N 7 10W
Lochaber, *U.K.* **22 E3** 56 59N 5 1W
Locharbriggs, *U.K.* **22 F5** 55 7N 3 35W
Lochboisdale, *U.K.* **22 D1** 57 9N 7 20W
Loche, L. La, *Canada* **143 B7** 56 30N 109 30W
Lochem, *Neths.* **24 B6** 52 9N 6 26 E
Loches, *France* **26 E7** 47 7N 1 0 E
Lochgilphead, *U.K.* **22 E3** 56 2N 5 26W
Lochinvar △, *Zambia* **119 F2** 15 55 S 27 15 E
Lochinver, *U.K.* **22 C3** 58 9N 5 14W
Lochloosa L., *U.S.A.* **153 F7** 29 30N 82 7W
Lochmaddy, *U.K.* **22 D1** 57 36N 7 10W
Lochnagar, *Australia* **126 C4** 23 33 S 145 38 E
Lochnagar, *U.K.* **22 E5** 56 57N 3 15W
Łochów, *Poland* **55 F8** 52 33N 21 42 E
Lochy, L., *U.K.* **22 E4** 57 0N 4 53W
Lock, *Australia* **127 E2** 33 34 S 135 46 E
Lock Haven, *U.S.A.* **150 E7** 41 8N 77 28W
Lockeford, *U.S.A.* **160 G5** 38 10N 121 9W
Lockeport, *Canada* **141 D6** 43 47N 65 4W
Lockerbie, *U.K.* **22 F5** 55 7N 3 21W
Lockhart, *Australia* **129 C7** 35 14 S 146 40 E
Lockhart, *U.S.A.* **155 L6** 29 53N 97 40W
Lockhart, L., *Australia* **125 F2** 33 15 S 119 3 E
Lockhart River, *Australia* **126 A3** 12 58 S 143 30 E
Lockney, *U.S.A.* **155 H4** 34 7N 101 27W
Lockport, *Ill., U.S.A.* **157 C8** 41 35N 88 3W
Lockport, *N.Y., U.S.A.* **150 C6** 43 10N 78 42W
Locminé, *France* **26 E4** 47 54N 2 51W
Locri, *Italy* **47 D9** 38 14N 16 16 E
Locronan, *France* **26 D2** 48 7N 4 15W
Locust Cr. →, *U.S.A.* **156 E3** 39 40N 93 17W
Locust Grove, *U.S.A.* **152 B5** 33 21N 84 7W
Lod, *Israel* **103 D3** 31 57N 34 54 E
Lodalskåpa, *Norway* **18 C4** 61 47N 7 13 E
Lodeinoye Pole, *Russia* **58 B7** 60 44N 33 33 E
Lodève, *France* **28 E7** 43 44N 3 19 E
Lodge Bay, *Canada* **141 B8** 52 14N 55 51W
Lodge Grass, *U.S.A.* **158 D10** 45 19N 107 22W
Lodgepole Cr. →, *U.S.A.* **154 E2** 41 20N 104 30W
Lodhran, *Pakistan* **92 E4** 29 32N 71 30 E
Lodi, *Italy* **44 C6** 45 19N 9 30 E
Lodi, *Calif., U.S.A.* **160 G5** 38 8N 121 16W
Lodi, *Ohio, U.S.A.* **150 E3** 41 2N 82 0W
Lodja, *Dem. Rep. of the Congo* **118 C1** 3 30 S 23 23 E
Lodosa, *Spain* **40 C2** 42 25N 2 4W
Lödöse, *Sweden* **17 F6** 58 2N 12 9 E
Lodwar, *Kenya* **118 B4** 3 10N 35 40 E
Łódź, *Poland* **55 G6** 51 45N 19 27 E
Łódzkie □, *Poland* **55 G6** 51 30N 19 30 E
Loei, *Thailand* **86 D3** 17 29N 101 35 E
Loengo, *Dem. Rep. of the Congo* **118 C2** 4 48 S 26 30 E
Loeriesfontein, *S. Africa* **116 E2** 31 0 S 19 26 E
Lofa →, *Liberia* **113 D2** 6 35N 11 8W
Lofa Mano △, *Liberia* **112 D2** 7 55N 10 25W
Lofer, *Austria* **34 D5** 47 35N 12 41 E
Lofoten, *Norway* **14 B15** 68 30N 14 0 E
Lofsdalen, *Sweden* **16 B7** 62 10N 13 20 E
Lofsen →, *Sweden* **16 B7** 62 7N 13 57 E
Loftahammar, *Sweden* **17 G10** 57 54N 16 41 E
Loga, *Niger* **113 C5** 13 40N 3 15 E
Logan, *Iowa, U.S.A.* **154 E7** 41 39N 95 47W
Logan, *Ohio, U.S.A.* **148 F4** 39 32N 82 25W
Logan, *Utah, U.S.A.* **158 F8** 41 44N 111 50W
Logan, *W. Va., U.S.A.* **148 G5** 37 51N 81 59W
Logan, Mt., *Canada* **138 B5** 60 34N 140 23W
Logan Martin L., *U.S.A.* **152 B3** 33 26N 86 20W
Logandale, *U.S.A.* **161 J12** 36 36N 114 29W
Logansport, *Ind., U.S.A.* **157 D10** 40 45N 86 22W
Logansport, *La., U.S.A.* **155 K8** 31 58N 94 0W
Logirim, *Sudan* **107 G3** 4 43N 33 14 E
Logo, *Sudan* **107 F3** 5 20N 30 18 E
Logone →, *Chad* **109 F3** 12 6N 15 2 E
Logone Gana, *Chad* **109 F3** 11 36N 15 4 E
Logone Occidental →, *Chad* **109 G3** 8 50N 16 0 E
Logone Orientale →, *Chad* **109 G3** 9 7N 16 26 E
Logroño, *Spain* **40 C2** 42 28N 2 27W
Logrosán, *Spain* **43 F5** 39 20N 5 32W
Løgstør, *Denmark* **17 H3** 56 58N 9 14 E
Logtak Lake, *India* **90 C4** 24 33N 93 50 E
Løgumkloster, *Denmark* **17 J2** 55 4N 8 57 E
Loh, *Vanuatu* **133 C4** 13 21 S 166 38 E
Lohals, *Denmark* **17 J4** 55 8N 10 55 E
Lohardaga, *India* **93 H11** 23 27N 84 45 E
Loharia, *India* **92 H6** 23 45N 74 14 E
Loharu, *India* **92 E6** 28 27N 75 49 E
Lohja, *Finland* **15 F21** 60 12N 24 5 E
Löhne, *Germany* **30 C4** 52 11N 8 40 E
Loho = Luohe, *China* **74 H8** 33 32N 114 2 E
Lohr, *Germany* **31 F5** 49 59N 9 35 E
Lohri Wah →, *Pakistan* **92 F2** 27 27N 67 37 E
Loi-kaw, *Burma* **90 F6** 19 40N 97 17 E
Loi-lem, *Burma* **90 E6** 20 52N 97 28 E
Loimaa, *Finland* **15 F20** 60 50N 23 5 E
Loir →, *France* **26 E6** 47 33N 0 32W
Loir-et-Cher □, *France* **26 E8** 47 40N 1 20 E
Loire □, *France* **29 C8** 45 40N 4 5 E
Loire →, *France* **26 E4** 47 16N 2 10W
Loire Anjou Touraine ⌂, *France* **26 E6** 47 14N 0 5W
Loire-Atlantique □, *France* **26 E5** 47 25N 1 40W
Loire Inférieure = Loire-Atlantique □, *France* **26 E5** 47 25N 1 40W
Loiret □, *France* **27 E9** 47 55N 2 30 E
Loitz, *Germany* **30 B9** 53 58N 13 8 E
Loja, *Ecuador* **172 A2** 3 59 S 79 16W
Loja, *Spain* **43 H6** 37 10N 4 10W
Loja □, *Ecuador* **168 D2** 4 0 S 79 13W
Loje →, *Angola* **115 D2** 7 49 S 13 6 E
Loji = Kawasi, *Indonesia* **82 B3** 1 38 S 127 28 E
Lojo = Lohja, *Finland* **15 F21** 60 12N 24 5 E
Løjt Kirkeby, *Denmark* **17 J3** 55 7N 9 26 E
Lojung, *China* **76 E7** 24 27N 109 36 E
Loka, *Dem. Rep. of the Congo* **114 B3** 0 22N 18 2 E
Loka, *Sudan* **107 G3** 4 13N 31 0 E
Lokako, *Dem. Rep. of the Congo* **114 C4** 0 57 S 18 55 E
Lokandu, *Dem. Rep. of the Congo* **118 C2** 2 30 S 25 45 E
Lokaw, *Dem. Rep. of the Congo* **114 C4** 2 40 S 20 12 E
Løken, *Norway* **18 E8** 59 48N 11 29 E
Lokeren, *Belgium* **24 C3** 51 6N 3 59 E
Lokgwabe, *Botswana* **116 C3** 24 10 S 21 50 E
Lokhvitsa, *Ukraine* **59 G7** 50 25N 33 18 E
Lokichokio, *Kenya* **118 B3** 4 19N 34 13 E
Lokitaung, *Kenya* **118 B4** 4 12N 35 48 E
Lokkan tekojärvi, *Finland* **14 C22** 67 55N 27 35 E
Løkken, *Denmark* **17 G3** 57 22N 9 41 E
Løkken, *Norway* **18 A6** 63 9N 9 41 E
Loknya, *Russia* **58 D6** 56 49N 30 4 E
Loko, *C.A.R.* **114 B3** 3 38N 18 2 E
Loko, *Nigeria* **113 D6** 8 1N 7 53 E
Lokoja, *Nigeria* **113 D6** 7 47N 6 45 E
Lokolama, *Dem. Rep. of the Congo* **114 C3** 2 35 S 19 50 E
Lokolenge, *Dem. Rep. of the Congo* **114 B4** 1 12N 22 38 E
Lokolo →, *Dem. Rep. of the Congo* **114 C3** 0 43 S 19 40 E
Lokoro →, *Dem. Rep. of the Congo* **114 C3** 1 43 S 18 23 E
Lokot, *Russia* **59 F8** 52 34N 34 36 E
Lokuru, *Solomon Is.* **133 M9** 8 20 S 157 0 E
Lol →, *Sudan* **107 F2** 9 13N 26 30 E
Lola, *Angola* **115 E2** 14 19 S 13 37 E
Lola, *Guinea* **112 D3** 7 52N 8 29W
Lola, Mt., *U.S.A.* **160 F6** 39 26N 120 22W
Lolibai, Gebel, *Sudan* **107 G3** 3 50N 33 0 E
Lolimi, *Sudan* **107 G3** 4 35N 34 0 E
Loliondo, *Tanzania* **118 C4** 2 2 S 35 39 E
Lolland, *Denmark* **17 K5** 54 45N 11 30 E
Lollar, *Germany* **30 E4** 50 37N 8 43 E
Lolo, *U.S.A.* **158 C6** 46 45N 114 5W
Lolo →, *Eq. Guin.* **114 B1** 1 36N 9 37 E
Lolo →, *Gabon* **114 C2** 0 18 S 12 18 E
Lolobau I., *Papua N. G.* **132 C6** 4 55 S 151 10 E
Lolodorf, *Cameroon* **113 E7** 3 16N 10 49 E
Loloma, *Zambia* **115 E4** 13 24 S 24 21 E
Loltong, *Vanuatu* **133 E6** 15 32 S 168 10 E
Lom, *Bulgaria* **50 C7** 43 48N 23 12 E
Lom, *Norway* **18 C5** 61 50N 8 34 E
Lom →, *Bulgaria* **50 C7** 43 45N 23 15 E
Lom →, *Cameroon* **114 A2** 5 20N 13 24 E
Lom Kao, *Thailand* **86 D3** 16 53N 101 14 E
Lom Sak, *Thailand* **86 D3** 16 47N 101 15 E
Loma, *U.S.A.* **158 C8** 47 56N 110 30W
Loma Linda, *U.S.A.* **161 L9** 34 3N 117 16W
Lomako →, *Dem. Rep. of the Congo* **114 B4** 0 50N 20 50 E
Lomaloma, *Fiji* **133 A3** 17 17 S 178 59W
Lomami →, *Dem. Rep. of the Congo* **118 B1** 0 46N 24 16 E
Lomas de Zamóra, *Argentina* **174 C4** 34 45 S 58 25W
Lombadina, *Australia* **124 C3** 16 31 S 122 54 E
Lombard, *U.S.A.* **157 C8** 41 53N 88 1W
Lombárdia □, *Italy* **44 C6** 45 40N 9 30 E
Lombardy = Lombárdia □, *Italy* **44 C6** 45 40N 9 30 E
Lombe, *Angola* **115 D3** 9 27 S 16 13 E
Lombez, *France* **28 E4** 43 29N 0 55 E
Lomblen, *Indonesia* **82 C2** 8 30 S 123 32 E
Lombok, *Indonesia* **85 D5** 8 45 S 116 30 E
Lombok, Selat, *Indonesia* **79 K18** 8 30 S 115 50 E
Lomé, *Togo* **113 D5** 6 9N 1 20 E
Lomela, *Dem. Rep. of the Congo* **114 C4** 2 19 S 23 15 E
Lomela →, *Dem. Rep. of the Congo* **114 C4** 0 15 S 20 40 E
Lomianki, *Poland* **55 F7** 52 21N 20 54 E
Lomié, *Cameroon* **114 B2** 3 13N 13 38 E
Lomma, *Sweden* **17 J7** 55 43N 13 6 E
Lommel, *Belgium* **24 C5** 51 14N 5 19 E
Lomond, *Canada* **142 C6** 50 24N 112 36W
Lomond, L., *U.K.* **22 E4** 56 8N 4 38W
Lomonosov Ridge, *Arctic* **6 A** 88 0N 140 0 E
Lomphat, *Cambodia* **86 F6** 13 30N 106 59 E
Lompobatang, *Indonesia* **82 C1** 5 24 S 119 56 E
Lompoc, *U.S.A.* **161 L6** 34 38N 120 28W
Lomseggi, *Norway* **18 C5** 61 49N 8 21 E
Łomża, *Poland* **55 E9** 53 10N 22 2 E
Lon, Ko, *Thailand* **87 a** 7 47N 98 23 E
Lonavale, *India* **94 E1** 18 46N 73 29 E
Loncoche, *Chile* **176 A2** 39 20 S 72 50W
Loncopuè, *Argentina* **176 A2** 38 4 S 70 37W
Londa, *India* **95 G2** 15 30N 74 30 E
Londiani, *Kenya* **118 C4** 0 10 S 35 33 E
Londinières, *France* **26 C8** 49 50N 1 25 E
London, *Canada* **140 D3** 42 59N 81 15W
London, *U.K.* **21 F7** 51 30N 0 3W
London, *Ky., U.S.A.* **148 G3** 37 8N 84 5W
London, *Ohio, U.S.A.* **157 E13** 39 53N 83 27W
London, Greater □, *U.K.* **21 F7** 51 36N 0 5W
London Gatwick ✕ (LGW), *U.K.* **21 F7** 51 10N 0 11W
London Heathrow ✕ (LHR), *U.K.* **21 F7** 51 28N 0 27W
London Mills, *U.S.A.* **156 D6** 40 43N 90 11W
London Stansted ✕ (STN), *U.K.* **21 F8** 51 54N 0 14 E
Londonderry, *U.K.* **23 B4** 55 0N 7 20W
Londonderry □, *U.K.* **23 B4** 55 0N 7 20W
Londonderry, C., *Australia* **124 B4** 13 45 S 126 55 E
Londonderry, I., *Chile* **176 E2** 55 0 S 71 0W
Londrina, *Brazil* **175 A5** 23 18 S 51 10W
Londuimbale, *Angola* **115 E3** 12 15 S 15 19 E
Lone Pine, *U.S.A.* **160 J8** 36 36N 118 4W
Lonely Mine, *Zimbabwe* **117 B4** 19 30 S 28 49 E
Long Akah, *Malaysia* **85 B4** 3 19N 114 47 E
Long B., *U.S.A.* **149 J6** 33 35N 78 45W
Long Beach, *Calif., U.S.A.* **161 M8** 33 47N 118 11W
Long Beach, *N.Y., U.S.A.* **151 F11** 40 35N 73 39W
Long Beach, *Wash., U.S.A.* **160 D2** 46 21N 124 3W
Long Branch, *U.S.A.* **151 F11** 40 18N 74 0W
Long Cay, *Bahamas* **9 b** 25 6N 77 22W
Long Creek, *U.S.A.* **158 D4** 44 43N 119 6W
Long Eaton, *U.K.* **20 E6** 52 53N 1 15W
Long I., *Australia* **126 J6** 20 22 S 148 51 E
Long I., *Bahamas* **165 B4** 23 20N 75 10W
Long I., *Canada* **140 B4** 54 50N 79 20W
Long I., *Ireland* **23 E2** 51 30N 9 34W
Long I., *Papua N. G.* **132 C4** 5 20 S 147 5 E
Long I., *U.S.A.* **151 F11** 40 45N 73 30W
Long Island Sd., *U.S.A.* **151 E12** 41 10N 73 0W
Long L., *Canada* **140 C2** 49 30N 86 50W
Long Lake, *U.S.A.* **151 C10** 43 58N 74 25W
Long Point B., *Canada* **150 D4** 42 40N 80 10W
Long Prairie, *U.S.A.* **154 C7** 45 59N 94 52W
Long Prairie →, *U.S.A.* **154 C7** 46 20N 94 36W
Long Pt., *Bahamas* **9 b** 25 1N 77 20W
Long Pt., *Canada* **150 D4** 42 35N 80 2W
Long Pt., *N.Z.* **131 G4** 46 34 S 169 36 E
Long Range Mts., *Canada* **141 C8** 49 30N 57 30W
Long Reef, *Australia* **124 B4** 14 1 S 125 48 E
Long Spruce, *Canada* **143 B10** 56 24N 94 21W
Long Str. = Longa, Proliv, *Russia* **6 C16** 70 0N 175 0 E
Long Thanh, *Vietnam* **87 G6** 10 47N 106 57 E
Long Xian, *China* **74 G4** 34 55N 106 55 E
Long Xuyen, *Vietnam* **87 G5** 10 19N 105 28 E
Longa, *Angola* **115 E3** 14 42 S 18 32 E
Longá, *Greece* **48 E3** 36 53N 21 55 E
Longa →, *Angola* **115 E2** 10 14 S 13 29 E
Longa, Proliv, *Russia* **6 C16** 70 0N 175 0 E
Longa Mavinga ⌂, *Angola* **115 F4** 16 20 S 20 15 E
Long'an, *China* **76 F6** 23 10N 107 40 E
Longana, *Vanuatu* **133 E5** 15 18 S 168 0 E
Longarone, *Italy* **45 B9** 46 16N 12 18 E
Longbenton, *U.K.* **20 B6** 55 1N 1 31W
Longboat Key, *U.S.A.* **153 H7** 27 23N 82 39W
Longburn, *N.Z.* **130 G4** 40 23 S 175 35 E
Longchang, *China* **76 C5** 29 18N 105 15 E
Longchi, *China* **76 C4** 29 25N 103 24 E
Longchuan, *Guangdong, China* **77 E10** 24 5N 115 17 E
Longchuan, *Yunnan, China* **76 E1** 24 23N 97 58 E

Longde, *China* 74 G4 35 30N 106 20 E
Longeau, *France* 27 E12 47 47N 5 20 E
Longford, *Australia* 127 G4 41 32 S 147 3 E
Longford, *Ireland* 23 C4 53 43N 7 49W
Longford □, *Ireland* 23 C4 53 42N 7 45W
Longhai, *China* 77 E11 24 25N 117 46 E
Longhua, *Guangdong, China* 69 F11 22 39N 114 0 E
Longhua, *Hebei, China* 75 D9 41 18N 117 45 E
Longhui, *China* 77 D8 27 7N 111 2 E
Longido, *Tanzania* 118 C4 2 43 S 36 42 E
Longiram, *Indonesia* 85 C5 0 5 S 115 45 E
Longkou, *Jiangxi, China* 77 D10 26 8N 115 10 E
Longkou, *Shandong, China* 75 F11 37 40N 120 18 E
Longlac, *Canada* 140 C2 49 45N 86 25W
Longli, *China* 76 D6 26 25N 106 58 E
Longlin, *China* 76 E5 24 47N 105 20 E
Longling, *China* 76 E2 24 37N 98 39 E
Longmeadow, *U.S.A.* 151 D12 42 3N 72 34W
Longmen, *China* 77 F10 23 40N 114 18 E
Longming, *China* 76 F6 22 59N 107 7 E
Longmont, *U.S.A.* 154 E2 40 10N 105 6W
Longnan, *China* 77 E10 24 55N 114 47 E
Longnawan, *Indonesia* 85 B4 1 51N 114 55 E
Longobucco, *Italy* 47 C9 39 27N 16 37 E
Longonot △, *Kenya* 120 E1 0 55 S 36 28 E
Longos, *Greece* 38 C10 39 16N 20 7 E
Longquan, *China* 77 C12 28 7N 119 10 E
Longreach, *Australia* 126 C3 23 28 S 144 14 E
Longshan, *China* 76 C7 29 29N 109 25 E
Longsheng, *China* 77 E8 25 48N 110 0 E
Longué-Jumelles, *France* 26 E6 47 22N 0 8W
Longueau, *France* 27 C9 49 52N 2 21 E
Longueuil, *Canada* 151 A11 45 32N 73 28W
Longuy, *Cameroon* 114 B1 3 5N 9 58 E
Longuyon, *France* 27 C12 49 27N 5 35 E
Longvic, *France* 27 E12 47 17N 5 4 E
Longview, *Tex., U.S.A.* 155 J7 32 30N 94 44W
Longview, *Wash., U.S.A.* 160 D4 46 8N 122 57W
Longwood, *St. Helena* 9 h 15 57 S 5 41W
Longwood, *U.S.A.* 153 G8 28 42N 81 21W
Longwy, *France* 27 C12 49 30N 5 46 E
Longxi, *China* 74 G3 34 53N 104 40 E
Longxue Dao, *China* 69 F10 22 41N 113 38 E
Longyan, *China* 77 E11 25 10N 117 0 E
Longyearbyen, *Svalbard* 6 B8 78 13N 15 40 E
Longyou, *China* 77 C12 29 1N 119 8 E
Longzhou, *China* 76 F6 22 22N 106 50 E
Lonigo, *Italy* 45 C8 45 23N 11 23 E
Löningen, *Germany* 30 C3 52 44N 7 46 E
Lonja →, *Croatia* 45 C13 45 22N 16 40 E
Lonkala, *Dem. Rep. of the Congo* 115 C4 4 37 S 23 14 E
Lonkin, *Burma* 90 C6 25 39N 96 22 E
Lonoke, *U.S.A.* 155 H9 34 47N 91 54W
Lonquimay, *Chile* 176 A2 38 26 S 71 14W
Lons-le-Saunier, *France* 27 F12 46 40N 5 31 E
Lönsboda, *Sweden* 17 H8 56 24N 14 20 E
Lønset, *Norway* 18 B4 62 46N 7 24 E
Lonton, *Burma* 90 C6 25 6N 96 17 E
Looe, *U.K.* 21 G3 50 22N 4 28W
Loogootee, *U.S.A.* 157 F10 38 41N 86 55W
Lookout, C., *Canada* 140 A3 55 18N 83 56W
Lookout, C., *U.S.A.* 149 H7 34 35N 76 32W
Loolmalasin, *Tanzania* 118 C4 3 0 S 35 53 E
Loon →, *Alta., Canada* 142 B5 57 8N 115 3W
Loon →, *Man., Canada* 143 B8 55 53N 101 59W
Loon Lake, *Canada* 143 C7 54 2N 109 10W
Loongana, *Australia* 125 F4 30 52 S 127 5 E
Loop Hd., *Ireland* 23 D2 52 34N 9 56W
Lop Buri, *Thailand* 86 E3 14 48N 100 37 E
Lop Nor = Lop Nur, *China* 68 B4 40 20N 90 10 E
Lop Nur, *China* 68 B4 40 20N 90 10 E
Lopare, *Bos.-H.* 52 F3 44 39N 18 46 E
Lopatin, *Russia* 61 J8 43 50N 47 35 E
Lopatina, Gora, *Russia* 67 D15 50 47N 143 10 E
Lopatino = Volzhsk, *Russia* 60 C9 55 57N 48 23 E
Lopaye, *Sudan* 107 F3 6 37N 33 40 E
Lopé-Okanda △, *Gabon* 114 C2 0 45 S 11 34 E
Lopevi, *Vanuatu* 133 F6 16 30 S 168 21 E
Lopez, *Phil.* 80 E4 13 53N 122 15 E
Lopez, *U.S.A.* 151 E8 41 27N 76 20W
Lopez, C., *Gabon* 114 C1 0 47 S 8 40 E
López de Filippis = Mariscal Estigarribia, *Paraguay* 174 A3 22 3 S 60 40W
Lopori →, *Dem. Rep. of the Congo* 114 B3 1 14N 19 49 E
Lopphavet, *Norway* 14 A19 70 27N 21 15 E
Lora, *Norway* 18 B5 62 8N 8 45 E
Lora →, *Afghan.* 91 C2 31 35N 66 32 E
Lora →, *Norway* 18 B5 62 8N 8 42 E
Lora, Hāmūn-i-, *Pakistan* 91 C2 29 38N 64 58 E
Lora Cr. →, *Australia* 127 D2 28 10 S 135 22 E
Lora del Río, *Spain* 43 H5 37 39N 5 33W
Lorain, *U.S.A.* 150 E2 41 28N 82 11W
Loraine, *U.S.A.* 156 D5 40 9N 91 13W
Loralai, *Pakistan* 91 C3 30 20N 68 41 E
Lorca, *Spain* 41 H3 37 41N 1 42W
Lord Howe I., *Pac. Oc.* 134 L7 31 33 S 159 6 E
Lord Howe Ridge, *Pac. Oc.* 134 L8 30 0 S 162 30 E
Lordsburg, *U.S.A.* 159 K9 32 21N 108 43W
Lorengau, *Papua N. G.* 132 B4 2 1 S 147 15 E
Lorestan □, *Iran* 97 C6 33 30N 48 40 E
Loreto, *Bolivia* 173 D5 15 13 S 64 40W
Loreto, *Brazil* 170 C2 7 5 S 45 10W
Loreto, *Italy* 45 E10 43 26N 13 36 E
Loreto, *Mexico* 162 B2 26 1N 111 21W
Loreto, *Phil.* 81 F5 10 21N 125 34 E
Loreto □, *Peru* 168 D3 5 0 S 75 0W
Lorgues, *France* 29 E10 43 28N 6 22 E
Lorhosso, *Burkina Faso* 112 C4 10 17N 3 38W
Lorica, *Colombia* 168 B2 9 14N 75 49W
Lorient, *France* 26 E3 47 45N 3 23W
Lorimor, *U.S.A.* 156 C2 41 8N 94 3W
Lőrinci, *Hungary* 52 C4 47 44N 19 41 E
Lormi, *India* 93 H9 22 17N 81 41 E
Lorn, *U.K.* 22 E3 56 26N 5 10W
Lorn, Firth of, *U.K.* 22 E3 56 20N 5 40W
Lorne, *Australia* 128 E5 38 33 S 143 59 E
Loronyo, *Sudan* 107 G3 4 38N 32 38 E
Lorovouno, *Cyprus* 39 E8 35 8N 32 36 E
Lörrach, *Germany* 31 H3 47 36N 7 40 E
Lorraine = Baker, *U.S.A.* 154 B2 46 22N 104 17W
Lorraine △, *France* 27 D12 48 55N 5 50 E
Lorraine □, *France* 27 D13 48 53N 6 0 E
Los, *Sweden* 16 C9 61 45N 15 10 E
Los, Îles de, *Guinea* 112 D2 9 30N 13 50W
Los Alamos, *Calif., U.S.A.* 161 L6 34 44N 120 17W
Los Alamos, *N. Mex., U.S.A.* 159 J10 35 53N 106 19W
Los Alcornocales △, *Spain* 43 J5 36 21N 5 32W
Los Alerces △, *Argentina* 176 B2 42 55 S 71 55W
Los Altos, *U.S.A.* 160 H4 37 23N 122 7W
Los Andes, *Chile* 174 C1 32 50 S 70 40W
Los Angeles, *Chile* 174 D1 37 28 S 72 23W
Los Angeles, *U.S.A.* 161 M8 34 4N 118 15W
Los Angeles, Bahia de, *Mexico* 162 B2 28 56N 113 34W
Los Angeles Aqueduct, *U.S.A.* 161 K9 35 22N 118 5W
Los Angeles International ✕ (LAX), *U.S.A.* 161 M8 33 57N 118 25W
Los Antiguos, *Argentina* 176 C2 46 35 S 71 40W
Los Banos, *U.S.A.* 160 H6 37 4N 120 51W
Los Barrios, *Spain* 43 J5 36 11N 5 30W
Los Blancos, *Argentina* 174 A3 23 40 S 62 30W
Los Cardones △, *Argentina* 174 B2 25 8 S 65 55W
Los Chiles, *Costa Rica* 164 D3 11 2N 84 43W
Los Corrales de Buelna, *Spain* 42 B6 43 16N 4 4W
Los Cristianos, *Canary Is.* 9 e1 28 3N 16 42W
Los Gallardos, *Spain* 41 H3 37 10N 1 57W
Los Gatos, *U.S.A.* 160 H5 37 14N 121 59W
Los Glaciares △, *Argentina* 176 C2 50 0 S 73 55W
Los Haïtises △, *Dom. Rep.* 165 C6 19 4N 69 36W
Los Hermanos Is., *Venezuela* 169 A5 11 45N 64 25W
Los Islotes, *Canary Is.* 9 e2 29 4N 13 44W
Los Katios △, *Colombia* 168 B2 7 50N 77 10W
Los Lagos, *Chile* 176 A2 39 51 S 72 50W
Los Llanos de Aridane, *Canary Is.* 9 e1 28 38N 17 54W
Los Lomas, *Peru* 172 A1 4 40 S 80 10W
Los Loros, *Chile* 174 B1 27 50 S 70 6W
Los Lunas, *U.S.A.* 159 J10 34 48N 106 44W
Los Menucos, *Argentina* 176 B3 40 50 S 68 10W
Los Mochis, *Mexico* 162 B3 25 45N 108 57W
Los Monegros, *Spain* 40 D4 41 29N 0 13W
Los Monos, *Argentina* 176 C3 46 1 S 69 36W
Los Muermos, *Chile* 176 B2 41 24 S 73 29W
Los Nevados △, *Colombia* 168 C2 4 41N 75 21W
Los Nietos, *Spain* 41 H4 37 39N 0 47W
Los Olivos, *U.S.A.* 161 L6 34 40N 120 7W
Los Palacios, *Cuba* 164 B3 22 35N 83 15W
Los Palacios y Villafranca, *Spain* 43 H5 37 10N 5 55W
Los Reyes, *Mexico* 162 D4 19 34N 102 30W
Los Ríos □, *Ecuador* 168 D2 1 30 S 79 25W
Los Roques Is., *Venezuela* 165 D6 11 50N 66 45W
Los Santos de Maimona, *Spain* 43 G4 38 27N 6 22W
Los Teques, *Venezuela* 168 A4 10 21N 67 2W
Los Testigos, Is., *Venezuela* 169 A5 11 23N 63 6W
Los Vilos, *Chile* 174 C1 32 10 S 71 30W
Los Yébenes, *Spain* 43 F7 39 36N 3 55W
Loshan = Leshan, *China* 76 C4 29 33N 103 41 E
Łosice, *Poland* 55 F9 52 13N 22 43 E
Lošinj, *Croatia* 36 F8 44 30N 14 30 E
Loskop Dam, *S. Africa* 117 D4 25 23 S 29 20 E
Løsning, *Denmark* 17 J3 55 48N 9 42 E
Losombo, *Dem. Rep. of the Congo* 114 B3 1 2N 19 4 E
Losone, *Switz.* 33 D7 46 10N 8 45 E
Lossiemouth, *U.K.* 22 D5 57 42N 3 17W
Lossnen △, *Sweden* 16 B6 62 26N 12 45 E
Lostwithiel, *U.K.* 21 G3 50 24N 4 41W
Losuia, *Papua N. G.* 132 E6 8 30 S 151 4 E
Lot □, *France* 28 D5 44 39N 1 40 E
Lot →, *France* 28 D4 44 18N 0 20 E
Lot-et-Garonne □, *France* 28 D4 44 22N 0 30 E
Lota, *Chile* 174 D1 37 5 S 73 10W
Lotagipi Swamp, *Sudan* 107 G3 4 36N 34 55 E
Løten, *Norway* 18 D8 60 51N 11 21 E
Lotfābād, *Iran* 97 B8 37 32N 59 20 E
Lothair, *S. Africa* 117 D5 26 22 S 30 27 E
Loto, *Dem. Rep. of the Congo* 114 C4 2 48 S 22 3 E
Lotoi →, *Dem. Rep. of the Congo* 114 C3 1 35 S 18 30 E
Lotorp, *Sweden* 17 F9 58 44N 15 50 E
Lötschbergtunnel, *Switz.* 32 D5 46 26N 7 43 E
Löttorp, *Sweden* 17 G11 57 10N 17 0 E
Lotung, *Taiwan* 77 E13 24 41N 121 46 E
Lötzen = Giżycko, *Poland* 54 D8 54 2N 21 48 E
Lotzwil, *Switz.* 32 B5 47 12N 7 48 E
Lou I., *Papua N. G.* 132 B4 2 25 S 147 22 E
Loubomo, *Congo* 114 C2 4 9 S 12 47 E
Loudéac, *France* 26 D4 48 11N 2 47W
Loudi, *China* 77 D8 27 42N 111 59 E
Loudima, *Congo* 114 C2 4 6 S 13 5 E
Loudonville, *U.S.A.* 150 F2 40 38N 82 14W
Loudun, *France* 26 E7 47 3N 0 5 E
Loue →, *France* 27 E12 47 1N 5 28 E
Louga, *Senegal* 112 B1 15 45N 16 5W
Loughborough, *U.K.* 20 E6 52 47N 1 11W
Loughman, *U.S.A.* 153 G8 28 14N 81 34W
Loughrea, *Ireland* 23 C3 53 12N 8 33W
Loughros More B., *Ireland* 23 B3 54 48N 8 32W
Louhans, *France* 27 F12 46 38N 5 12 E
Louis-Gentil = Youssoufia, *Morocco* 110 B3 32 16N 8 31W
Louis Trichardt, *S. Africa* 117 C4 23 1 S 29 43 E
Louis XIV, Pte., *Canada* 140 B4 54 37N 79 45W
Louisa, *U.S.A.* 148 F4 38 7N 82 36W
Louisbourg, *Canada* 141 C8 45 55N 60 0W
Louisburg, *U.S.A.* 156 F2 38 37N 94 41W
Louise I., *Canada* 142 C2 52 55N 131 50W
Louiseville, *Canada* 140 C5 46 20N 72 56W
Louisiade Arch., *Papua N. G.* 132 F7 11 10 S 153 0 E
Louisiana, *U.S.A.* 156 E6 39 27N 91 3W
Louisiana □, *U.S.A.* 155 K9 30 50N 92 0W
Louisville, *Ala., U.S.A.* 152 D4 31 47N 85 33W
Louisville, *Ga., U.S.A.* 152 B7 33 0N 82 25W
Louisville, *Ill., U.S.A.* 157 F8 38 46N 88 30W
Louisville, *Ky., U.S.A.* 157 F11 38 15N 85 46W
Louisville, *Miss., U.S.A.* 155 J10 33 7N 89 3W
Louisville, *Ohio, U.S.A.* 150 F3 40 50N 81 16W
Loukoléla, *Congo* 114 C3 1 4 S 17 10 E
Loukouo, *Congo* 114 C2 3 38 S 14 39 E
Loulay, *France* 28 B3 46 3N 0 30W
Loulé, *Portugal* 43 H3 37 9N 8 0W
Louny, *Czech Rep.* 34 A6 50 20N 13 48 E
Loup City, *U.S.A.* 154 E5 41 17N 98 58W
Loups Marins, Lacs des, *Canada* 140 A5 56 30N 73 45W
Lourdes, *France* 28 E3 43 6N 0 3W
Lourenço, *Brazil* 169 C7 2 30N 51 40W
Lourenço Marques = Maputo, *Mozam.* 117 D5 25 58 S 32 32 E
Lourinhã, *Portugal* 43 F1 39 14N 9 17W
Loúros, *Greece* 39 A2 39 3N 20 47 E
Lousã, *Portugal* 42 E2 40 7N 8 14W
Louta, *Burkina Faso* 112 C4 13 30N 3 10W
Louth, *Australia* 129 A6 30 30 S 145 8 E
Louth, *Ireland* 23 C5 53 58N 6 32W
Louth, *U.K.* 20 D7 53 22N 0 1W
Louth □, *Ireland* 23 C5 53 56N 6 34W
Louth Bay, *Australia* 128 C1 34 33 S 135 56 E
Loutrá Aidhipsoú, *Greece* 48 C5 38 54N 23 2 E
Loutrá Killínis, *Greece* 39 D3 37 52N 21 7 E
Loutráki, *Greece* 48 D4 37 58N 22 57 E
Louvain = Leuven, *Belgium* 24 D4 50 52N 4 42 E
Louvale, *U.S.A.* 152 C5 32 10N 84 50W
Louviers, *France* 26 C8 49 12N 1 10 E
Louwsburg, *S. Africa* 117 D5 27 37 S 31 7 E
Lovat →, *Russia* 58 C6 58 14N 31 28 E
Lovćen, *Serbia & M.* 50 D2 42 23N 18 51 E
Lovćen △, *Serbia & M.* 50 D2 42 20N 18 50 E
Lovech, *Bulgaria* 51 C8 43 8N 24 42 E
Lovech □, *Bulgaria* 51 C8 43 15N 24 45 E
Loveland, *Colo., U.S.A.* 154 E2 40 24N 105 5W
Loveland, *Ohio, U.S.A.* 157 E12 39 16N 84 16W
Lovell, *U.S.A.* 158 D9 44 50N 108 24W
Lovelock, *U.S.A.* 158 F4 40 11N 118 28W
Lóvere, *Italy* 44 C7 45 49N 10 4 E
Loves Park, *U.S.A.* 156 B7 42 19N 89 3W
Lövestad, *Sweden* 17 J7 55 40N 13 54 E
Loviisa, *Finland* 15 F22 60 28N 26 12 E
Lovilia, *U.S.A.* 156 C4 41 8N 92 55W
Loving, *U.S.A.* 155 J2 32 17N 104 6W
Lovington, *Ill., U.S.A.* 157 E8 39 43N 88 38W
Lovington, *N. Mex., U.S.A.* 155 J3 32 57N 103 21W
Lovisa = Loviisa, *Finland* 15 F22 60 28N 26 12 E
Lovosice, *Czech Rep.* 34 A7 50 30N 14 2 E
Lovran, *Croatia* 45 C11 45 18N 14 15 E
Lovrin, *Romania* 52 E5 45 58N 20 48 E
Lövstabruk, *Sweden* 16 D11 60 25N 17 53 E
Lövstabukten, *Sweden* 16 D11 60 35N 17 45 E
Lóvua, *Lunda Norte, Angola* 115 D4 7 19 S 20 12 E
Lóvua, *Moxico, Angola* 115 E4 11 33 S 23 33 E
Lóvua →, *Dem. Rep. of the Congo* 115 D4 6 6 S 20 37 E
Low, L., *Canada* 140 B4 52 29N 76 17W
Low Pt., *Australia* 125 F4 32 25 S 127 25 E
Low Tatra = Nízké Tatry, *Slovak Rep.* 35 C12 48 55N 19 30 E
Lowa, *Dem. Rep. of the Congo* 118 C2 1 25 S 25 47 E
Lowa →, *Dem. Rep. of the Congo* 118 C2 1 24 S 25 51 E
Lowden, *U.S.A.* 156 C6 41 52N 90 56W
Lowell, *Ind., U.S.A.* 157 C9 41 18N 87 25W
Lowell, *Mass., U.S.A.* 151 D13 42 38N 71 19W
Lowell, *Mich., U.S.A.* 157 B11 42 56N 85 20W
Lowellville, *U.S.A.* 150 E4 41 2N 80 32W
Löwen = Lewin Brzeski, *Poland* 55 H4 50 45N 17 37 E
Löwen →, *Namibia* 116 D2 26 51 S 18 17 E
Löwenberg = Lwówek Śląski, *Poland* 55 G2 51 7N 15 38 E
Löwenstadt = Brzeziny, *Poland* 55 G6 51 49N 19 42 E
Lower Alkali L., *U.S.A.* 158 F3 41 16N 120 2W
Lower Arrow L., *Canada* 142 D5 49 40N 118 5W
Lower Austria = Niederösterreich □, *Austria* 34 C8 48 25N 15 40 E
Lower California = Baja California, *Mexico* 162 A1 31 10N 115 12W
Lower Glenelg △, *Australia* 128 E4 38 4 S 141 41 E
Lower Hutt, *N.Z.* 130 H3 41 10 S 174 55 E
Lower Kalskag, *U.S.A.* 144 F7 61 31N 160 22W
Lower Lake, *U.S.A.* 160 G4 38 55N 122 37W
Lower Manitou L., *Canada* 143 D10 49 15N 93 0W
Lower Paia, *U.S.A.* 145 C5 20 55N 156 23W
Lower Post, *Canada* 142 B3 59 58N 128 30W
Lower Red L., *U.S.A.* 154 B7 47 58N 95 0W
Lower Saxony = Niedersachsen □, *Germany* 30 C4 52 50N 9 0 E
Lower Tunguska = Tunguska, Nizhnyaya →, *Russia* 67 C9 65 48N 88 4 E
Lower Zambezi △, *Zambia* 119 F2 15 25 S 29 40 E
Lowestoft, *U.K.* 21 E9 52 29N 1 45 E
Lowgar □, *Afghan.* 91 B3 34 0N 69 0 E
Łowicz, *Poland* 55 F6 52 6N 19 55 E
Lowly, Pt., *Australia* 128 B2 33 0 S 137 46 E
Lowry City, *U.S.A.* 156 F3 38 8N 93 44W
Lowville, *U.S.A.* 151 C9 43 47N 75 29W
Loxton, *Australia* 128 C4 34 28 S 140 31 E
Loxton, *S. Africa* 116 E3 31 30 S 22 22 E
Loyalton, *U.S.A.* 160 F6 39 41N 120 14W
Loyalty Is. = Loyauté, Îs., *N. Cal.* 133 K4 20 50 S 166 30 E
Loyang = Luoyang, *China* 74 G7 34 40N 112 26 E
Loyauté, Îs., *N. Cal.* 133 K4 20 50 S 166 30 E
Loyev = Loyew, *Belarus* 59 G6 51 56N 30 46 E
Loyew, *Belarus* 59 G6 51 56N 30 46 E
Loyoro, *Uganda* 118 B3 3 22N 34 14 E
Lož, *Slovenia* 45 C11 45 43N 14 30 E
Lozère □, *France* 28 D7 44 35N 3 30 E
Loznica, *Serbia & M.* 50 B3 44 32N 19 12 E
Lozova, *Ukraine* 59 H9 49 0N 36 20 E
Lozva →, *Russia* 64 B9 59 36N 62 20 E
Lu, *India* 90 B5 26 58N 95 14 E
Lü Shan, *China* 77 C11 29 30N 115 55 E
Lü-Tao, *Taiwan* 77 F13 22 40N 121 30 E
Lu Verne, *U.S.A.* 156 B2 42 55N 94 5W
Lu Wo, *China* 69 F11 22 33N 114 6 E
Lua →, *Dem. Rep. of the Congo* 114 B3 2 46N 18 26 E
Lua Makika, *U.S.A.* 145 C5 20 33N 156 37W
Luachimo, *Angola* 115 D4 7 23 S 20 48 E
Luacono, *Angola* 115 E4 11 15 S 21 37 E
Luajan →, *India* 93 G11 24 44N 85 1 E
Lualaba →, *Dem. Rep. of the Congo* 118 B2 0 26N 25 20 E
Luale, *Dem. Rep. of the Congo* 114 B4 1 9N 23 5 E
Luampa, *Zambia* 119 F1 15 4 S 24 20 E
Lu'an, *China* 77 B11 31 45N 116 29 E
Luan Chau, *Vietnam* 76 G4 21 38N 103 24 E
Luan He →, *China* 75 E10 39 20N 119 5 E
Luan Xian, *China* 75 E10 39 40N 118 40 E
Luancheng, *Guangxi Zhuangzu, China* 76 F7 22 48N 108 55 E
Luancheng, *Hebei, China* 74 F8 37 53N 114 40 E
Luanco, *Spain* 42 B5 43 37N 5 48W
Luanda, *Angola* 115 D2 8 50 S 13 15 E
Luando △, *Angola* 115 E3 11 0 S 17 32 E
Luang, Thale, *Thailand* 87 J3 7 30N 100 15 E
Luang Prabang, *Laos* 76 H4 19 52N 102 10 E
Luanginga →, *Zambia* 115 F4 15 11 S 22 55 E
Luangwa, *Zambia* 119 F3 15 35 S 30 16 E
Luangwa →, *Zambia* 119 E3 14 25 S 30 25 E
Luangwa Valley, *Zambia* 119 E3 13 30 S 31 30 E
Luania-Bubi, *Dem. Rep. of the Congo* 115 D4 7 28 S 24 49 E
Luanne, *China* 75 D9 40 55N 117 40 E
Luanping, *China* 75 D9 40 53N 117 23 E
Luanshya, *Zambia* 119 E2 13 3 S 28 28 E
Luapula □, *Zambia* 119 E2 11 0 S 29 0 E
Luapula →, *Africa* 119 D2 9 26 S 28 33 E
Luarca, *Spain* 42 B4 43 32N 6 32W
Luashi, *Dem. Rep. of the Congo* 119 E1 10 50 S 23 36 E
Luatamba, *Angola* 115 E4 12 6 S 20 19 E
Luatira, *Angola* 115 E3 12 52 S 17 14 E
Luau, *Angola* 115 E4 10 40 S 22 10 E
Luba, *Phil.* 80 C3 17 19N 120 42 E
Lubaczów, *Poland* 55 H10 50 10N 23 8 E
Lubalo, *Angola* 115 D3 9 10 S 19 15 E
Lubamiti, *Dem. Rep. of the Congo* 114 C3 2 28 S 17 47 E
Lubań, *Poland* 55 G2 51 5N 15 15 E
Lubana, Ozero = Lubānas Ezers, *Latvia* 15 H22 56 45N 27 0 E
Lubānas Ezers, *Latvia* 15 H22 56 45N 27 0 E
Lubang, *Phil.* 80 E3 13 52N 120 7 E
Lubang Is., *Phil.* 80 E3 13 50N 120 12 E
Lubango, *Angola* 115 E2 14 55 S 13 30 E
Lubao, *Dem. Rep. of the Congo* 118 D2 5 17 S 25 42 E
Lubartów, *Poland* 55 G9 51 28N 22 42 E
Lubawa, *Poland* 54 E6 53 30N 19 48 E
Lübbecke, *Germany* 30 C4 52 18N 8 37 E
Lübben, *Germany* 30 D9 51 56N 13 54 E
Lübbenau, *Germany* 30 D9 51 52N 13 57 E
Lubbock, *U.S.A.* 155 J4 33 35N 101 51W
Lübeck, *Germany* 30 B6 53 52N 10 40 E
Lübecker Bucht, *Germany* 30 A6 54 3N 10 54 E
Lubefu, *Dem. Rep. of the Congo* 118 C1 4 47 S 24 27 E
Lubefu →, *Dem. Rep. of the Congo* 118 C1 4 10 S 23 0 E
Lubelskie □, *Poland* 55 G9 51 20N 22 50 E
Lüben = Lubin, *Poland* 55 G3 51 24N 16 11 E
Lubero = Luofu, *Dem. Rep. of the Congo* 118 C2 0 10 S 29 15 E
Luberon △, *France* 29 E9 43 52N 5 25 E
Lubersac, *France* 28 C5 45 26N 1 23 E
Lubicon L., *Canada* 142 B5 56 23N 115 56W
Lubień Kujawski, *Poland* 55 F6 52 23N 19 9 E
Lubilash →, *Dem. Rep. of the Congo* 115 D4 6 2 S 23 45 E
Lubin, *Poland* 55 G3 51 24N 16 11 E
Lublin, *Poland* 55 G9 51 12N 22 38 E
Lubliniec, *Poland* 55 H5 50 43N 18 45 E
Lubnān = Lebanon ■, *Asia* 103 B5 34 0N 36 0 E
Lubnān, Jabal, *Lebanon* 103 B4 33 45N 35 40 E
Lubniewice, *Poland* 55 F2 52 31N 15 15 E
Lubny, *Ukraine* 59 G7 50 3N 32 58 E
Lubomierz, *Poland* 55 G2 51 1N 15 31 E
Luboń, *Poland* 55 F3 52 21N 16 51 E
Lubondaie, *Dem. Rep. of the Congo* 115 D4 8 1 S 26 32 E
Lubongola, *Dem. Rep. of the Congo* 118 C2 2 35 S 27 50 E
L'ubotín, *Slovak Rep.* 35 B13 49 17N 20 53 E
Lubraniec, *Poland* 55 F5 52 33N 18 50 E
Lubsko, *Poland* 55 G1 51 45N 14 57 E
Lübtheen, *Germany* 30 B7 53 18N 11 5 E
Lubuagan, *Phil.* 80 C3 17 21N 121 10 E
Lubudi, *Dem. Rep. of the Congo* 115 D4 6 51 S 21 18 E
Lubudi →, *Kasai-Occ., Dem. Rep. of the Congo* 115 C4 4 19 S 20 23 E
Lubudi →, *Katanga, Dem. Rep. of the Congo* 119 D2 9 0 S 25 35 E
Lubuklinggau, *Indonesia* 84 C2 3 15 S 102 55 E
Lubuksikaping, *Indonesia* 84 B2 0 10N 100 15 E
Lubumbashi, *Dem. Rep. of the Congo* 119 E2 11 40 S 27 28 E
Lubunda, *Dem. Rep. of the Congo* 118 D2 5 12 S 26 41 E
Lubungu, *Zambia* 119 E2 14 35 S 26 24 E
Lubuskie □, *Poland* 55 F2 52 10N 15 20 E
Lubutu, *Dem. Rep. of the Congo* 118 C2 0 45 S 26 30 E
Luc An Chau, *Vietnam* 86 A5 22 6N 104 43 E
Luc-en-Diois, *France* 29 D9 44 36N 5 28 E
Lucala, *Angola* 115 D3 9 7 S 15 58 E
Lucala →, *Angola* 115 D3 9 38 S 14 12 E
Lucan, *Canada* 150 C3 43 11N 81 24W
Lucania, Mt., *Canada* 138 B5 61 1N 140 27W
Lucapa, *Angola* 115 D4 8 25 S 20 45 E
Lucas, *U.S.A.* 156 C3 41 2N 93 29W
Lucas Channel, *Canada* 150 A3 45 21N 81 45W
Lucban, *Phil.* 80 D3 14 6N 121 33 E
Lucca, *Italy* 44 E7 43 50N 10 29 E
Lucé, *France* 26 D8 48 26N 1 27 E
Luce Bay, *U.K.* 22 G4 54 45N 4 48W
Lucea, *Jamaica* 164 a 18 27N 78 10W
Lucedale, *U.S.A.* 149 K1 30 56N 88 35W
Lucena, *Phil.* 80 E3 13 56N 121 37 E
Lucena, *Spain* 43 H6 37 27N 4 31W
Lučenec, *Slovak Rep.* 35 C12 48 18N 19 42 E
Lucens, *Switz.* 32 C3 46 43N 6 51 E
Lucera, *Italy* 47 A8 41 30N 15 20 E
Lucerne = Lake Worth, *U.S.A.* 153 J9 26 37N 80 3W
Lucerne = Luzern, *Switz.* 33 B6 47 3N 8 18 E
Lucerne, *U.S.A.* 160 F4 39 6N 122 48W
Lucerne Valley, *U.S.A.* 161 L10 34 27N 116 57W
Lucero, *Mexico* 162 A3 30 49N 106 30W
Luchena →, *Spain* 41 H3 37 44N 1 50W
Lucheng, *China* 74 F7 36 20N 113 11 E
Lucheringo →, *Mozam.* 119 E4 11 43 S 36 17 E
Luchow = Luzhou, *China* 76 C5 28 52N 105 20 E
Lüchow, *Germany* 30 C7 52 58N 11 8 E
Luchuan, *China* 77 F8 22 21N 110 12 E
Lucia, *U.S.A.* 160 J5 36 2N 121 33W
Lucie →, *Suriname* 169 C6 3 35N 57 38W
Lucinda, *Australia* 126 B4 18 32 S 146 20 E
Lucindale, *Australia* 128 D4 36 58 S 140 26 E
Luciras, *Angola* 115 E2 14 0 S 12 35 E
Luciras, B. das, *Angola* 115 E2 13 52 S 12 31 E
Luckau, *Germany* 30 D9 51 50N 13 42 E
Luckenwalde, *Germany* 30 C9 52 5N 13 10 E
Luckey, *U.S.A.* 157 C13 41 27N 83 29W
Luckhoff, *S. Africa* 116 D3 29 44 S 24 43 E
Lucknow, *Canada* 150 C3 43 57N 81 31W
Lucknow, *India* 93 F9 26 50N 81 0 E
Luçon, *France* 28 B2 46 28N 1 10W
Lucusse, *Angola* 115 E4 12 32 S 20 48 E
Lüda = Dalian, *China* 75 E11 38 50N 121 40 E
Luda Kamchiya →, *Bulgaria* 51 C11 43 3N 27 29 E
Ludbreg, *Croatia* 45 B13 46 15N 16 38 E
Lüdenscheid, *Germany* 30 D3 51 13N 7 37 E
Lüderitz, *Namibia* 116 D2 26 41 S 15 8 E
Lüderitzbaai, *Namibia* 116 D2 26 36 S 15 8 E
Ludhiana, *India* 92 D6 30 57N 75 56 E
Ludian, *China* 76 D4 27 10N 103 33 E
Luding Qiao, *China* 76 C4 29 53N 102 12 E
Lüdinghausen, *Germany* 30 D3 51 46N 7 27 E
Ludington, *U.S.A.* 148 D2 43 57N 86 27W
Ludlow, *U.K.* 21 E5 52 22N 2 42W
Ludlow, *Calif., U.S.A.* 161 L10 34 43N 116 10W
Ludlow, *Pa., U.S.A.* 150 E6 41 43N 78 56W
Ludlow, *Vt., U.S.A.* 151 C12 43 24N 72 42W
Ludowici, *U.S.A.* 152 D8 31 43N 81 45W
Ludus, *Romania* 53 D9 46 29N 24 5 E
Ludvika, *Sweden* 16 D9 60 8N 15 14 E
Ludwigsburg, *Germany* 31 G5 48 53N 9 11 E
Ludwigsfelde, *Germany* 30 C9 52 17N 13 17 E
Ludwigshafen, *Germany* 31 F4 49 29N 8 26 E
Ludwigslust, *Germany* 30 B7 53 19N 11 30 E
Ludza, *Latvia* 58 D4 56 32N 27 43 E
Lue, *Australia* 129 B8 32 38 S 149 50 E
Luebo, *Dem. Rep. of the Congo* 115 D4 5 21 S 21 23 E
Lueki, *Dem. Rep. of the Congo* 118 C2 3 20 S 25 48 E
Luena, *Angola* 115 E3 12 13 S 19 51 E
Luena, *Dem. Rep. of the Congo* 119 D2 9 28 S 25 43 E
Luena, *Zambia* 119 E3 10 40 S 30 25 E
Luena →, *Angola* 115 E4 12 30 S 22 34 E
Luena →, *Zambia* 115 E4 14 46 S 23 30 E
Luena Flats, *Zambia* 115 E4 14 47 S 23 17 E
Luengué △, *Angola* 115 F3 16 55 S 19 55 E
Luenha = Ruenya →, *Africa* 119 F3 16 24 S 33 48 E
Luepa, *Venezuela* 169 B5 5 43N 61 31W
Lueta →, *Dem. Rep. of the Congo* 115 D4 7 4 S 21 40 E
Luete →, *Zambia* 115 F4 15 46 S 23 10 E
Lüeyang, *China* 74 H4 33 22N 106 10 E
Lufeng, *Guangdong, China* 77 F10 22 57N 115 38 E
Lufeng, *Yunnan, China* 76 E4 25 0N 102 5 E
Lufico, *Angola* 115 D2 6 24 S 13 23 E
Lufira →, *Dem. Rep. of the Congo* 119 D2 9 30 S 27 0 E
Lufkin, *U.S.A.* 155 K7 31 21N 94 44W
Lufupa, *Dem. Rep. of the Congo* 119 E1 10 37 S 24 56 E
Luga, *Russia* 58 C5 58 40N 29 55 E
Luga →, *Russia* 58 C5 59 40N 28 18 E
Lugano, *Switz.* 33 E7 46 1N 8 57 E
Lugano, L. di, *Switz.* 33 E8 46 0N 9 0 E
Lugansk = Luhansk, *Ukraine* 59 H10 48 38N 39 15 E
Luganville, *Vanuatu* 133 E5 15 27 S 167 10 E
Lugard's Falls, *Kenya* 118 C4 3 6 S 38 41 E
Lugela, *Mozam.* 119 F4 16 25 S 36 43 E
Lugenda →, *Mozam.* 119 E4 11 25 S 38 33 E
Lugh Ganana, *Somali Rep.* 120 D2 3 48N 42 34 E
Lugnaquillia, *Ireland* 23 D5 52 58N 6 28W
Lugo, *Italy* 45 D8 44 25N 11 54 E
Lugo, *Spain* 42 B3 43 2N 7 35W
Lugo □, *Spain* 42 C3 43 0N 7 30W
Lugoj, *Romania* 52 E6 45 42N 21 57 E
Lugovoy = Qulan, *Kazakhstan* 65 B6 42 55N 72 43 E
Lugus I., *Phil.* 81 J3 5 41N 120 50 E
Luhansk, *Ukraine* 59 H10 48 38N 39 15 E
Luhe, *China* 77 A12 32 19N 118 50 E
Luhe →, *Germany* 30 B6 53 18N 10 11 E
Luhit →, *India* 90 B5 27 48N 95 28 E
Luhuo, *China* 76 B3 31 21N 100 48 E
Lui →, *Angola* 115 D3 8 21 S 17 33 E
Lui →, *Zambia* 115 F4 16 18 S 23 17 E
Luia, *Angola* 115 D4 8 10 S 21 32 E
Luia →, *Angola* 115 D4 8 32 S 21 47 E
Luiana, *Angola* 116 B3 17 25 S 22 59 E
Luiana △, *Angola* 115 F4 16 55 S 22 20 E
Luiana →, *Angola* 115 F4 17 24 S 23 3 E
Luichow = Liuzhou, *China* 76 E7 24 22N 109 22 E
Luichow Pen. = Leizhou Bandao, *China* 76 G7 21 0N 110 0 E
Luilaka →, *Dem. Rep. of the Congo* 114 C4 0 52 S 20 12 E
Luimneach = Limerick, *Ireland* 23 D3 52 40N 8 37W
Luing, *U.K.* 22 E3 56 14N 5 39W
Luino, *Italy* 44 C5 45 59N 8 44 E
Luio →, *Angola* 115 E4 13 17 S 21 37 E
Luís Correia, *Brazil* 170 B3 3 0 S 41 35W
Luís Gonçalves, *Brazil* 170 C1 5 37 S 50 25W
Luitpold Coast, *Antarctica* 7 D1 78 30 S 32 0W
Luiza, *Dem. Rep. of the Congo* 115 D4 7 40 S 22 30 E
Luizi, *Dem. Rep. of the Congo* 118 D2 6 0 S 27 25 E
Luján, *Argentina* 174 C4 34 45 S 59 5W
Lujiang, *China* 77 B11 31 20N 117 15 E
Lukala, *Dem. Rep. of the Congo* 115 D2 5 31 S 14 32 E
Lukang, *Taiwan* 77 E13 24 1N 120 22 E
Lukanga, *Bandundu, Dem. Rep. of the Congo* 114 C3 1 41 S 18 9 E
Lukanga, *Équateur, Dem. Rep. of the Congo* 114 C3 1 0 S 18 8 E
Lukanga Swamp, *Zambia* 119 E2 14 30 S 27 40 E
Lukavac, *Bos.-H.* 52 F3 44 33N 18 32 E
Lukenie →, *Dem. Rep. of the Congo* 114 C3 3 0 S 18 50 E
Lukhisaral, *India* 93 G12 25 11N 86 5 E
Lŭki, *Bulgaria* 51 E8 41 50N 24 43 E
Lukk, *Libya* 108 B4 32 1N 24 46 E
Lukolela, *Équateur, Dem. Rep. of the Congo* 114 C3 1 10 S 17 12 E

Lukolela, *Kasai-Or., Dem. Rep. of the Congo* **118 D1** 5 23 S 24 32 E
Lukosi, *Zimbabwe* **119 F2** 18 30 S 26 30 E
Lukovë, *Albania* **50 G3** 39 59N 19 54 E
Lukovit, *Bulgaria* **51 C8** 43 13N 24 11 E
Łuków, *Poland* **55 G9** 51 55N 22 23 E
Lukoyanov, *Russia* **60 C7** 55 2N 44 29 E
Luksefjell, *Norway* **18 E6** 59 23N 9 34 E
Lukuni, *Dem. Rep. of the Congo* **115 D3** 5 50 S 17 16 E
Lukusuzi △, *Zambia* **119 E3** 12 43 S 32 36 E
Lula, *Dem. Rep. of the Congo* **115 D3** 5 22 S 16 2 E
Luleå, *Sweden* **14 D20** 65 35N 22 10 E
Luleälven →, *Sweden* **14 D19** 65 35N 22 10 E
Lüleburgaz, *Turkey* **51 E11** 41 23N 27 22 E
Luliang, *China* **76 E4** 25 0N 103 40 E
Luling, *U.S.A.* **155 L6** 29 41N 97 39W
Lulong, *China* **75 E10** 39 53N 118 51 E
Lulonga →, *Dem. Rep. of the Congo* **114 B3** 1 0N 18 10 E
Lulu, *U.S.A.* **152 E7** 30 7N 82 29W
Lulu →, *Dem. Rep. of the Congo* **114 B4** 1 18N 23 42 E
Lulua →, *Dem. Rep. of the Congo* **115 C4** 4 30 S 20 30 E
Luluaburg = Kananga, *Dem. Rep. of the Congo* **115 D4** 5 55 S 22 18 E
Luma, *Amer. Samoa* **133 X25** 14 16 S 169 33W
Lumai, *Angola* **115 E4** 13 13 S 21 25 E
Lumajang, *Indonesia* **85 D4** 8 8 S 113 13 E
Lumaku, Gunong, *Malaysia* **85 B5** 4 52N 115 38 E
Lumbala →, *Angola* **115 E4** 12 39 S 22 35 E
Lumbala Kaquengue, *Angola* **115 E4** 12 39 S 22 34 E
Lumbala N'guimbo, *Angola* **115 E4** 14 18 S 21 18 E
Lumbe →, *Zambia* **115 F4** 16 44 S 23 41 E
Lumber City, *U.S.A.* **152 D7** 31 56N 82 41W
Lumberton, *U.S.A.* **149 H6** 34 37N 79 0W
Lumding, *India* **90 C4** 25 46N 93 10 E
Lumi, *Papua N. G.* **132 B2** 3 30 S 142 2 E
Lumpkin, *U.S.A.* **152 C5** 32 3N 84 48W
Lumsden, *Canada* **143 C8** 50 39N 104 52W
Lumsden, *N.Z.* **131 F3** 45 44 S 168 27 E
Lumut, *Malaysia* **87 K3** 4 13N 100 37 E
Lumut, Tanjung, *Indonesia* **84 C3** 3 50 S 105 58 E
Luna, *India* **92 H3** 23 43N 69 16 E
Luna, *Phil.* **80 B3** 18 18N 121 21 E
Lunan, *China* **76 E4** 24 40N 103 18 E
Lunavada, *India* **92 H5** 23 8N 73 37 E
Lunca, *Romania* **53 C10** 47 22N 25 1 E
Lunca Corbului, *Romania* **53 F9** 44 42N 24 45 E
Lund, *Sweden* **17 J7** 55 44N 13 12 E
Lunda Norte □, *Angola* **115 D3** 8 0 S 20 0 E
Lunda Sul □, *Angola* **115 D4** 10 0 S 20 0 E
Lundamo, *Norway* **18 A7** 63 9N 10 19 E
Lundazi, *Zambia* **119 E3** 12 20 S 33 7 E
Lundenburg = Břeclav, *Czech Rep.* **35 C9** 48 46N 16 53 E
Lunderskov, *Denmark* **17 J3** 55 29N 9 19 E
Lundi →, *Zimbabwe* **119 G3** 21 43 S 32 34 E
Lundu, *Malaysia* **85 B3** 1 40N 109 50 E
Lundy, *U.K.* **21 F3** 51 10N 4 41W
Lune →, *U.K.* **20 C5** 54 0N 2 51W
Lüneburg, *Germany* **30 B6** 53 15N 10 24 E
Lüneburg Heath = Lüneburger Heide, *Germany* **30 B6** 53 10N 10 12 E
Lüneburger Heide, *Germany* **30 B6** 53 10N 10 12 E
Lunel, *France* **29 E8** 43 39N 4 9 E
Lünen, *Germany* **30 D3** 51 37N 7 32 E
Lunenburg, *Canada* **141 D7** 44 22N 64 18W
Lunéville, *France* **27 D13** 48 36N 6 30 E
Lunga, *Dem. Rep. of the Congo* **115 C4** 5 46 S 12 14 E
Lunga →, *Zambia* **119 E2** 14 34 S 26 25 E
Lunge, *Angola* **115 E3** 12 13 S 16 7 E
Lungern, *Switz.* **32 C6** 46 48N 8 10 E
Lungga, *Solomon Is.* **133 M11** 9 25 S 160 3 E
Lungi Airport, *S. Leone* **112 D2** 8 40N 13 17W
Lunglei, *India* **90 D4** 22 55N 92 45 E
Lungngo, *Burma* **90 E4** 21 57N 93 36 E
Lungwebungu →, *Zambia* **115 E4** 14 19 S 23 14 E
Luni, *India* **92 G5** 26 0N 73 6 E
Luni →, *India* **92 G4** 24 41N 71 14 E
Luninets = Luninyets, *Belarus* **59 F4** 52 15N 26 50 E
Luning, *U.S.A.* **158 G4** 38 30N 118 11W
Lunino, *Russia* **60 D7** 53 38N 45 18 E
Luninyets, *Belarus* **59 F4** 52 15N 26 50 E
Lunkaransar, *India* **92 E5** 28 29N 73 44 E
Lunner, *Norway* **18 D7** 60 19N 10 35 E
Lunsemfwa →, *Zambia* **119 E3** 14 54 S 30 12 E
Lunsemfwa Falls, *Zambia* **119 E2** 14 30 S 29 6 E
Luo He →, *China* **74 G6** 34 35N 110 20 E
Luocheng, *China* **76 E7** 24 48N 108 53 E
Luochuan, *China* **74 G5** 35 45N 109 26 E
Luoci, *China* **76 E4** 25 19N 102 18 E
Luodian, *China* **76 E6** 25 24N 106 43 E
Luoding, *China* **77 F8** 22 45N 111 40 E
Luofu, *Dem. Rep. of the Congo* **118 C2** 0 10 S 29 15 E
Luohe, *China* **74 H8** 33 32N 114 2 E
Luojiang, *China* **76 B5** 31 18N 104 33 E
Luonan, *China* **74 G6** 34 5N 110 10 E
Luoning, *China* **74 G6** 34 35N 111 40 E
Luoshan, *China* **77 A10** 32 13N 114 30 E
Luotian, *China* **77 B10** 30 46N 115 22 E
Luoxiao Shan, *China* **77 D10** 26 30N 114 1 E
Luoyang, *China* **74 G7** 34 40N 112 26 E
Luoyuan, *China* **77 D12** 26 28N 119 30 E
Luozi, *Dem. Rep. of the Congo* **115 C2** 4 54 S 14 0 E
Luozigou, *China* **75 C16** 43 42N 130 18 E
Lupanshui, *China* **76 D5** 26 38N 104 48 E
Lupeni, *Romania* **53 E8** 45 21N 23 13 E
Lupilichi, *Mozam.* **119 E4** 11 47 S 35 13 E
Lupire, *Angola* **115 E3** 14 36 S 19 29 E
Łupków, *Poland* **55 J9** 49 15N 22 4 E
Lupoing, *China* **76 E5** 24 53N 104 21 E
Lupon, *Phil.* **81 H6** 6 54N 126 0 E
Luputa, *Dem. Rep. of the Congo* **115 D4** 7 7 S 23 43 E
Luqa, *Malta* **38 F7** 35 52N 14 29 E
Luquan, *China* **76 E4** 25 35N 102 25 E
Luque, *Paraguay* **174 B4** 25 19 S 57 25W
Luquembo, *Angola* **115 E3** 10 44 S 17 43 E
Lūras, *Italy* **46 B2** 40 56N 9 10 E
Luray, *U.S.A.* **148 F6** 38 40N 78 28W
Lure, *France* **27 E13** 47 40N 6 30 E
Luremo, *Angola* **115 D3** 8 30 S 17 50 E
Lurgan, *U.K.* **23 B5** 54 28N 6 19W
Luribay, *Bolivia* **172 D4** 17 6 S 67 39W
Lurin, *Peru* **172 C2** 12 17 S 76 52W
Lusaka, *Zambia* **119 F2** 15 28 S 28 16 E
Lusaka □, *Zambia* **119 F2** 15 30 S 29 0 E
Lusambo, *Dem. Rep. of the Congo* **118 C1** 4 58 S 23 28 E
Lusancay Is. and Reefs, *Papua N. G.* **132 E6** 8 30 S 150 30 E
Lusangaye, *Dem. Rep. of the Congo* **118 C2** 4 54 S 26 0 E
Luseland, *Canada* **143 C7** 52 5N 109 24W
Lusenga Plain △, *Zambia* **119 D2** 9 22 S 29 14 E
Lusengo, *Dem. Rep. of the Congo* **114 B3** 1 47N 19 31 E
Lushan, *Henan, China* **74 H7** 33 45N 112 55 E
Lushan, *Sichuan, China* **76 B4** 30 12N 102 52 E
Lushi, *China* **74 G6** 34 3N 111 3 E
Lushnjë, *Albania* **50 F3** 40 55N 19 41 E
Lushoto, *Tanzania* **118 C4** 4 47 S 38 20 E
Lushui, *China* **76 E2** 25 58N 98 44 E
Lüshun, *China* **75 E11** 38 45N 121 15 E
Lusignan, *France* **28 B4** 46 26N 0 8 E
Lusigny-sur-Barse, *France* **27 D11** 48 16N 4 15 E
Lusiye, *Zambia* **115 F4** 15 30 S 23 57 E
Lusk, *U.S.A.* **154 D2** 42 46N 104 27W
Lussac-les-Châteaux, *France* **28 B4** 46 24N 0 43 E
Lustenau, *Austria* **34 D2** 47 26N 9 39 E
Lustrafjorden, *Norway* **18 C4** 61 23N 7 25 E
Lūt, Dasht-e, *Iran* **97 D8** 31 30N 58 0 E
Luta = Dalian, *China* **75 E11** 38 50N 121 40 E
Lutembo, *Angola* **115 E4** 13 26 S 21 16 E
Lutherstadt Wittenberg, *Germany* **30 D8** 51 53N 12 39 E
Luthersville, *U.S.A.* **152 B5** 33 13N 84 45W
Luti, *Solomon Is.* **133 L9** 7 14 S 157 0 E
Luton, *U.K.* **21 F7** 51 53N 0 24W
Luton □, *U.K.* **21 F7** 51 53N 0 24W
Lutong, *Malaysia* **85 B4** 4 28N 114 0 E
Lutry, *Switz.* **32 C3** 46 31N 6 42 E
Łutselk'e, *Canada* **143 A6** 62 24N 110 44W
Lutshima →, *Dem. Rep. of the Congo* **115 D3** 5 22 S 18 59 E
Lutsk, *Ukraine* **59 G3** 50 50N 25 15 E
Luttenberg = Ljutomer, *Slovenia* **45 B13** 46 31N 16 11 E
Lutuai, *Angola* **115 E4** 12 41 S 20 7 E
Lutz, *U.S.A.* **153 G7** 28 9N 82 28W
Lützow Holmbukta, *Antarctica* **7 C4** 69 10 S 37 30 E
Lutzputs, *S. Africa* **116 D3** 28 3 S 20 40 E
Luuk, *Phil.* **81 J3** 5 58N 121 18 E
Luuq = Lugh Ganana, *Somali Rep.* **120 D2** 3 48N 42 34 E
Luverne, *Ala., U.S.A.* **152 D3** 31 43N 86 16W
Luverne, *Minn., U.S.A.* **154 D6** 43 39N 96 13W
Luvo, *Angola* **115 D2** 5 51 S 14 5 E
Luvua, *Angola* **115 E4** 8 49 S 25 19 E
Luvua, *Dem. Rep. of the Congo* **119 D2** 8 48 S 25 17 E
Luvua →, *Dem. Rep. of the Congo* **118 D2** 6 50 S 27 30 E
Luvuvhu →, *S. Africa* **117 C5** 22 25 S 31 18 E
Luwegu →, *Tanzania* **119 D4** 8 31 S 37 23 E
Luwuk, *Indonesia* **82 B2** 0 56 S 122 47 E
Luxembourg, *Lux.* **24 E6** 49 37N 6 9 E
Luxembourg □, *Belgium* **24 E5** 49 58N 5 30 E
Luxembourg ■, *Europe* **25 B7** 49 45N 6 0 E
Luxembourg ✕ (LUX), *Lux.* **24 E6** 49 37N 6 10 E
Luxemburg, *U.S.A.* **156 B5** 44 32N 91 5W
Luxeuil-les-Bains, *France* **27 E13** 47 49N 6 24 E
Luxi, *Hunan, China* **77 C8** 28 20N 110 7 E
Luxi, *Yunnan, China* **76 E4** 24 40N 103 55 E
Luxi, *Yunnan, China* **76 E2** 24 27N 98 36 E
Luxor = El Uqsur, *Egypt* **106 B3** 25 41N 32 38 E
Luy-de-Béarn →, *France* **28 E3** 43 39N 0 48W
Luy-de-France →, *France* **28 E3** 43 39N 0 48W
Luyi, *China* **74 H8** 33 50N 115 35 E
Luz, *Azores* **9 d1** 39 1N 28 0W
Luz-St-Sauveur, *France* **28 F4** 42 53N 0 0W
Luza, *Russia* **56 B8** 60 39N 47 10 E
Luzern, *Switz.* **33 B6** 47 3N 8 18 E
Luzern □, *Switz.* **32 B5** 47 2N 7 55 E
Luzhai, *China* **76 E7** 24 29N 109 42 E
Luzhany, *Ukraine* **53 B10** 48 22N 25 47 E
Luzhi, *China* **76 D5** 26 21N 105 16 E
Luzhou, *China* **76 C5** 28 52N 105 20 E
Luziânia, *Brazil* **171 E2** 16 20 S 48 0W
Luzilândia, *Brazil* **170 B3** 3 28 S 42 22W
Lužnice →, *Czech Rep.* **34 B7** 49 14N 14 23 E
Luzon, *Phil.* **80 C3** 16 0N 121 0 E
Luzon Strait, *Asia* **77 G13** 21 0N 120 40 E
Luzy, *France* **27 F10** 46 47N 3 58 E
Luzzi, *Italy* **47 C9** 39 27N 16 17 E
Lviv, *Ukraine* **59 H3** 49 50N 24 0 E
Lvov = Lviv, *Ukraine* **59 H3** 49 50N 24 0 E
Lwówek, *Poland* **55 F3** 52 28N 16 10 E
Lwówek Śląski, *Poland* **55 G2** 51 7N 15 38 E
Lyakhavichy, *Belarus* **59 F4** 53 2N 26 32 E
Lyakhovskiye, Ostrova, *Russia* **67 B15** 73 40N 141 0 E
Lyaki = Läki, *Azerbaijan* **61 K8** 40 34N 47 22 E
Lyal I., *Canada* **150 B3** 44 57N 81 24W
Lyall Mt., *N.Z.* **131 F2** 45 16 S 167 32 E
Lyallpur = Faisalabad, *Pakistan* **91 C4** 31 30N 73 5 E
Lyalya →, *Russia* **64 B8** 59 9N 61 29 E
Lyangar, *Tajikistan* **65 E6** 37 3N 72 40 E
Lyaskovets, *Bulgaria* **51 C9** 43 6N 25 44 E
Lyasnaya, *Belarus* **55 F10** 52 9N 23 31 E
Lybster, *U.K.* **22 C5** 58 18N 3 15W
Lycaonia, *Turkey* **100 D5** 38 0N 33 0 E
Lychen, *Germany* **30 B9** 53 12N 13 18 E
Lychkova, *Russia* **58 D7** 57 55N 32 24 E
Lycia, *Turkey* **49 E11** 36 30N 29 30 E
Lyck = Ełk, *Poland* **54 E9** 53 50N 22 21 E
Lyckebyån →, *Sweden* **17 H9** 56 12N 15 39 E
Lycksele, *Sweden* **14 D18** 64 38N 18 40 E
Lycosura, *Greece* **48 D4** 37 20N 22 3 E
Lydda = Lod, *Israel* **103 D3** 31 57N 34 54 E
Lydenburg, *S. Africa* **117 D5** 25 10 S 30 29 E
Lydia, *Turkey* **49 C10** 38 48N 28 19 E
Łydynia →, *Poland* **55 F7** 52 43N 20 26 E
Lyell, *N.Z.* **131 B7** 41 48 S 172 4 E
Lyell I., *Canada* **142 C2** 52 40N 131 35W
Lyepyel, *Belarus* **58 E5** 54 50N 28 40 E
Lyford Cay, *Bahamas* **9 b** 25 2N 77 33W
Lygnern, *Sweden* **17 G6** 57 30N 12 15 E
Lykens, *U.S.A.* **151 F8** 40 34N 76 42W
Lyman, *Ukraine* **53 E14** 45 41N 29 45 E
Lyman, *Iowa, U.S.A.* **156 C2** 30 29N 94 59W
Lyman, *Wyo., U.S.A.* **158 F8** 41 20N 110 18W
Lymanske, *Ukraine* **53 D14** 46 40N 29 58 E
Lyme B., *U.K.* **21 G4** 50 42N 2 53W
Lyme Regis, *U.K.* **21 G5** 50 43N 2 57W
Lymington, *U.K.* **21 G6** 50 45N 1 32W
Łyna →, *Poland* **15 J19** 54 37N 21 14 E
Lynchburg, *Ohio, U.S.A.* **157 E13** 39 15N 83 48W
Lynchburg, *S.C., U.S.A.* **152 A9** 34 3N 80 4W
Lynchburg, *Va., U.S.A.* **148 G6** 37 25N 79 9W
Lynd →, *Australia* **126 B3** 16 28 S 143 18 E
Lynd Ra., *Australia* **127 D4** 25 30 S 149 20 E
Lynden, *Canada* **150 C4** 43 14N 80 9W
Lynden, *U.S.A.* **160 B4** 48 57N 122 27W
Lyndhurst, *Australia* **127 E2** 30 15 S 138 18 E
Lyndon →, *Australia* **125 D1** 23 29 S 114 6 E
Lyndonville, *N.Y., U.S.A.* **150 C6** 43 20N 78 23W
Lyndonville, *Vt., U.S.A.* **151 B12** 44 31N 72 1W
Lyngdal, *Buskerud, Norway* **18 E6** 59 54N 9 32 E
Lyngdal, *Vest-Agder, Norway* **18 F4** 58 8N 7 7 E
Lyngen, *Norway* **14 B19** 69 45N 20 30 E
Lyngør, *Norway* **18 F6** 58 38N 9 8 E
Lynher Reef, *Australia* **124 C3** 15 27 S 121 55 E
Lynn, *Ind., U.S.A.* **157 D12** 40 3N 84 56W
Lynn, *Mass., U.S.A.* **151 D14** 42 28N 70 57W
Lynn Canal, *U.S.A.* **144 G14** 58 50N 135 15W
Lynn Haven, *U.S.A.* **152 E4** 30 15N 85 39W
Lynn Lake, *Canada* **143 B8** 56 51N 101 3W
Lynne, *U.S.A.* **153 F8** 29 12N 81 55W
Lynnville, *U.S.A.* **157 F9** 38 12N 87 19W
Lynnwood, *U.S.A.* **160 C4** 47 49N 122 19W
Lynton, *U.K.* **21 F4** 51 13N 3 50W
Lyntupy, *Belarus* **15 J22** 55 4N 26 23 E
Lynx L., *Canada* **143 A7** 62 25N 106 15W
Lyon, *France* **29 C8** 45 46N 4 50 E
Lyon St-Exupery ✕ (LYS), *France* **29 C9** 45 44N 5 2 E
Lyonnais, *France* **29 C8** 45 45N 4 15 E
Lyons = Lyon, *France* **29 C8** 45 46N 4 50 E
Lyons, *Ga., U.S.A.* **152 C7** 32 12N 82 19W
Lyons, *Kans., U.S.A.* **154 F5** 38 21N 98 12W
Lyons, *N.Y., U.S.A.* **150 C8** 43 5N 77 0W
Lyons →, *Australia* **125 E2** 25 2 S 115 9 E
Lyons Falls, *U.S.A.* **151 C9** 43 37N 75 22W
Lyozna, *Belarus* **58 E6** 55 0N 30 50 E
Lyra Reef, *Papua N. G.* **132 A7** 1 50 S 153 35 E
Lys = Leie →, *Belgium* **24 C3** 51 2N 3 45 E
Lysá nad Labem, *Czech Rep.* **34 A7** 50 11N 14 51 E
Lysebotn, *Norway* **18 E3** 59 3N 6 37 E
Lysefjorden, *Norway* **18 E3** 59 0N 6 23 E
Lysekil, *Sweden* **17 F5** 58 17N 11 26 E
Lyskovo, *Russia* **60 B7** 56 0N 45 3 E
Lyss, *Switz.* **32 B4** 47 4N 7 19 E
Lystrup, *Denmark* **17 H4** 56 14N 10 14 E
Lysva, *Russia* **64 B6** 58 7N 57 49 E
Lysvik, *Sweden* **16 D7** 60 1N 13 9 E
Lysychansk, *Ukraine* **59 H10** 48 55N 38 30 E
Lytham St. Anne's, *U.K.* **20 D4** 53 45N 3 0W
Lyttelton, *N.Z.* **131 D7** 43 35 S 172 44 E
Lytton, *Canada* **142 C4** 50 13N 121 31W
Lyuban, *Russia* **58 C6** 59 16N 31 18 E
Lyubertsy, *Russia* **58 E9** 55 39N 37 50 E
Lyubim, *Russia* **58 C11** 58 20N 40 39 E
Lyubimets, *Bulgaria* **51 E10** 41 50N 26 5 E
Lyuboml, *Ukraine* **55 G11** 51 11N 24 4 E
Lyubotyn, *Ukraine* **59 H8** 50 0N 36 0 E
Lyubytino, *Russia* **58 C7** 58 50N 33 16 E
Lyudinovo, *Russia* **58 F8** 53 52N 34 28 E

M

M.R. Gomez, Presa, *Mexico* **163 B5** 26 10N 99 0W
M.R. Stefanik, Bratislava ✕ (BTS), *Slovak Rep.* **35 C10** 48 11N 17 9 E
Ma →, *Vietnam* **76 H5** 19 47N 105 56 E
Ma, O. el →, *Algeria* **110 C3** 27 45N 7 52W
Ma'adaba, *Jordan* **103 E4** 30 43N 35 47 E
Maamba, *Zambia* **116 B4** 17 17 S 26 28 E
Ma'ān, *Jordan* **103 E4** 30 12N 35 44 E
Ma'ān □, *Jordan* **103 F5** 30 0N 36 0 E
Maana'oba, *Solomon Is.* **133 M11** 8 17 S 160 50 E
Maanselkä, *Finland* **14 C23** 63 52N 28 32 E
Ma'anshan, *China* **77 B12** 31 44N 118 29 E
Maarianhamina, *Finland* **15 F18** 60 5N 19 55 E
Maarmorilik, *Greenland* **10 C5** 71 3N 51 0W
Ma'arrat an Nu'mān, *Syria* **100 E7** 35 43N 36 43 E
Maas →, *Neths.* **24 C4** 51 45N 4 32 E
Maaseik, *Belgium* **24 C5** 51 6N 5 45 E
Maasim, *Phil.* **81 J5** 5 52N 125 0 E
Maasin, *Phil.* **79 B6** 10 8N 124 50 E
Maastricht, *Neths.* **24 D5** 50 50N 5 40 E
Maasupa, *Solomon Is.* **133 M11** 9 16 S 161 17 E
Maave, *Mozam.* **117 C5** 21 4 S 34 47 E
Mababe Depression, *Botswana* **116 B3** 18 50 S 24 15 E
Mabaia, *Angola* **115 D2** 7 12 S 14 2 E
Mabalane, *Mozam.* **117 C5** 23 37 S 32 31 E
Mabanga, *Dem. Rep. of the Congo* **114 B3** 1 30N 19 6 E
Ma'bar, *Yemen* **98 D4** 14 48N 44 17 E
Mabaruma, *Guyana* **169 B6** 8 10N 59 50W
Mabein, *Burma* **90 D6** 23 29N 96 37 E
Mabel L., *Canada* **142 C5** 50 35N 118 43W
Mabenga, *Dem. Rep. of the Congo* **114 C3** 3 39 S 18 40 E
Mabenge, *Dem. Rep. of the Congo* **118 B1** 4 15N 24 12 E
Maberly, *Canada* **151 B8** 44 50N 76 32W
Mabian, *China* **76 C4** 28 47N 103 37 E
Mabil, *Ethiopia* **107 E4** 10 26N 36 52 E
Mabinay, *Phil.* **81 G4** 9 48N 122 54 E
Mabirou, *Congo* **114 C3** 1 3 S 15 42 E
Mablethorpe, *U.K.* **20 D8** 53 20N 0 15 E
Mableton, *U.S.A.* **152 B5** 33 49N 84 35W
Mably, *France* **27 F11** 46 5N 4 4 E
Maboma, *Dem. Rep. of the Congo* **118 B2** 2 30N 28 10 E
Mabonto, *S. Leone* **112 D2** 8 53N 11 50W
Maboukou, *Congo* **114 C2** 3 39 S 12 31 E
Mabrouk, *Mali* **113 B4** 19 29N 1 15W
Mabrous, *Niger* **109 B2** 21 14N 13 35 E
Mabuasehube ⌂, *Botswana* **116 D3** 25 5 S 21 10 E
Mabungo, *Somali Rep.* **120 D2** 0 49N 42 35 E
Mac Bac, *Vietnam* **87 H6** 9 46N 106 7 E
Macachín, *Argentina* **174 D3** 37 10 S 63 43W
Macaé, *Brazil* **171 F3** 22 20 S 41 43W
Macael, *Spain* **41 H2** 37 20N 2 18W
Macaíba, *Brazil* **170 C4** 5 51 S 35 21W
Macajuba, *Brazil* **171 D3** 12 9 S 40 22W
McAlester, *U.S.A.* **155 H7** 34 56N 95 46W
McAllen, *U.S.A.* **155 M5** 26 12N 98 14W
McAlpin, *U.S.A.* **152 E7** 30 8N 82 57W
MacAlpine L., *Canada* **138 B9** 66 32N 102 45W
Macamic, *Canada* **140 C4** 48 45N 79 0W
Macao = Macau, *China* **77 F9** 22 12N 113 33 E
Macão, *Portugal* **43 F3** 39 35N 7 59W
Macapá, *Brazil* **169 C7** 0 5N 51 4W
Macará, *Ecuador* **168 D2** 4 23 S 79 57W
Macarani, *Brazil* **171 E3** 15 33 S 40 24W
Macarao △, *Venezuela* **165 D6** 10 22N 67 7W
Macarena, Serranía de la, *Colombia* **168 C3** 2 45N 73 55W
Macareo, Caño →, *Venezuela* **169 B5** 9 47N 61 36W
Macarthur, *Australia* **128 E5** 38 5 S 142 0 E
McArthur →, *Australia* **126 B2** 15 54 S 136 40 E
McArthur, Port, *Australia* **126 B2** 16 4 S 136 23 E
Macas, *Ecuador* **168 D2** 2 19 S 78 7W
Macate, *Peru* **172 B2** 8 48 S 78 7W
Macau, *Brazil* **170 C4** 5 15 S 36 40W
Macau, *China* **77 F9** 22 12N 113 33 E
Macaúbas, *Brazil* **171 D3** 13 2 S 42 42W
Macaya →, *Colombia* **168 C3** 0 59N 72 20W
McBride, *Canada* **142 C4** 53 20N 120 19W
McCall, *U.S.A.* **158 D5** 44 55N 116 6W
McCamey, *U.S.A.* **155 K3** 31 8N 102 14W
McCammon, *U.S.A.* **158 E7** 42 39N 112 12W
McCarthy, *U.S.A.* **144 F12** 61 26N 142 56W
McCauley I., *Canada* **142 C2** 53 40N 130 15W
McCleary, *U.S.A.* **160 C3** 47 3N 123 16W
Macclenny, *U.S.A.* **152 E7** 30 17N 82 7W
Macclesfield, *U.K.* **20 D5** 53 15N 2 8W
M'Clintock Chan., *Canada* **138 A9** 72 0N 102 0W
McClintock Ra., *Australia* **124 C4** 18 44 S 127 38 E
McCloud, *U.S.A.* **158 F2** 41 15N 122 8W
McCluer I., *Australia* **124 B5** 11 5 S 133 0 E
McClure, *U.S.A.* **150 F7** 40 42N 77 19W
McClure, L., *U.S.A.* **160 H6** 37 35N 120 16W
M'Clure Str., *Canada* **6 B2** 75 0N 119 0W
McClusky, *U.S.A.* **154 B4** 47 29N 100 27W
McComb, *U.S.A.* **155 K9** 31 15N 90 27W
McCook, *U.S.A.* **154 E4** 40 12N 100 38W
McCormick, *U.S.A.* **152 B7** 33 55N 82 17W
McCreary, *Canada* **143 C9** 50 47N 99 29W
McCullough Mt., *U.S.A.* **161 K11** 35 35N 115 13W
McCusker →, *Canada* **143 B7** 55 32N 108 39W
McDame, *Canada* **142 B3** 59 44N 128 59W
McDavid, *U.S.A.* **153 E2** 30 52N 87 19W
McDermitt, *U.S.A.* **158 F5** 41 59N 117 43W
McDonald, *U.S.A.* **150 F4** 40 22N 80 14W
Macdonald, L., *Australia* **124 D4** 23 30 S 129 0 E
Macdonald, Mt., *Vanuatu* **133 G6** 17 36 S 168 23 E
McDonald Is., *Ind. Oc.* **121 K6** 53 0 S 73 0 E
MacDonnell Ranges, *Australia* **124 D5** 23 40 S 133 0 E
McDonough, *U.S.A.* **152 B5** 33 27N 84 9W
McDougalls Well, *Australia* **128 A4** 31 8 S 141 15 E
MacDowell L., *Canada* **140 B1** 52 15N 92 45W
Macduff, *U.K.* **22 D6** 57 40N 2 31W
Maceda, *Spain* **42 C3** 42 16N 7 39W
Macedonia, *U.S.A.* **150 E3** 41 19N 81 31W
Macedonia ■, *Europe* **50 E5** 41 53N 21 40 E
Maceió, *Brazil* **170 C4** 9 40 S 35 41W
Maceira, *Portugal* **42 F2** 39 41N 8 55W
Macenta, *Guinea* **112 D3** 8 35N 9 32W
Macerata, *Italy* **45 E10** 43 18N 13 27 E
McFarland, *U.S.A.* **161 K7** 35 41N 119 14W
McFarlane →, *Canada* **143 B7** 59 12N 107 58W
Macfarlane, L., *Australia* **128 B2** 32 0 S 136 40 E
McGehee, *U.S.A.* **155 J9** 33 38N 91 24W
McGill, *U.S.A.* **158 G6** 39 23N 114 47W
Macgillycuddy's Reeks, *Ireland* **23 E2** 51 58N 9 45W
McGrath, *U.S.A.* **144 E9** 62 58N 155 36W
McGraw, *U.S.A.* **151 D8** 42 36N 76 8W
McGregor, *U.S.A.* **156 A5** 43 1N 91 11W
McGregor Ra., *Australia* **127 D3** 27 0 S 142 45 E
McGuire, Mt., *Australia* **126 J6** 20 18 S 148 23 E
Māch Kowr, *Iran* **97 E9** 25 48N 61 28 E
Machacalis, *Brazil* **171 E3** 17 5 S 40 45W
Machado = Jiparaná →, *Brazil* **173 B5** 8 3 S 62 52W
Machagai, *Argentina* **174 B3** 26 56 S 60 2W
Machakos, *Kenya* **118 C4** 1 30 S 37 15 E
Machala, *Ecuador* **168 D2** 3 20 S 79 57W
Machalilla △, *Ecuador* **168 D1** 1 24 S 80 42W
Machanga, *Mozam.* **117 C6** 20 59 S 35 0 E
Machattie, L., *Australia* **126 C2** 24 50 S 139 48 E
Machault, *France* **27 C11** 49 21N 4 29 E
Machava, *Mozam.* **117 D5** 25 54 S 32 28 E
Machece, *Mozam.* **119 F4** 19 15 S 35 32 E
Machecoul, *France* **26 F5** 47 0N 1 49W
Macheke, *Zimbabwe* **117 B5** 18 5 S 31 51 E
Macheng, *China* **77 B10** 31 12N 115 2 E
McHenry, *U.S.A.* **157 B8** 42 21N 88 16W
Macherla, *India* **94 F4** 16 29N 79 26 E
Machero, *Spain* **43 F6** 39 21N 4 20W
Machgaon, *India* **94 D8** 20 5N 86 17 E
Machhu →, *India* **92 H4** 23 6N 70 46 E
Machiara △, *Pakistan* **93 B5** 34 40N 73 30 E
Machias, *Maine, U.S.A.* **149 C12** 44 43N 67 28W
Machias, *N.Y., U.S.A.* **150 D6** 42 25N 78 30W
Machichi →, *Canada* **143 B10** 57 3N 92 6W
Machico, *Madeira* **9 c** 32 43N 16 44W
Machida, *Japan* **73 B11** 35 28N 139 23 E
Machilipatnam, *India* **95 F5** 16 12N 81 8 E
Machiques, *Venezuela* **168 A3** 10 4N 72 34W
Machupicchu, *Peru* **172 C3** 13 8 S 72 30W
Machynlleth, *U.K.* **21 E4** 52 35N 3 50W
Macia, *Mozam.* **117 D5** 25 2 S 33 8 E
Macias Nguema Biyoga = Bioko, *Eq. Guin.* **113 E6** 3 30N 8 40 E
Maciejowice, *Poland* **55 G8** 51 36N 21 26 E
McIlwraith Ra., *Australia* **126 A3** 13 50 S 143 20 E
Măcin, *Romania* **53 E13** 45 16N 28 8 E
Macina, *Mali* **112 C4** 14 50N 5 0W
McInnes L., *Canada* **143 C10** 52 13N 93 45W
McIntosh, *U.S.A.* **154 C4** 45 55N 101 21W
McIntosh L., *Canada* **143 B8** 55 45N 105 0W
Macintosh Ra., *Australia* **125 E4** 27 39 S 125 32 E
Macintyre →, *Australia* **127 D5** 28 37 S 150 47 E
Macizo Galaico, *Spain* **42 C3** 42 30N 7 30W
Mackay, *Australia* **126 K7** 21 8 S 149 11 E
Mackay, *U.S.A.* **158 E7** 43 55N 113 37W
MacKay →, *Canada* **142 B6** 57 10N 111 38W
Mackay, L., *Australia* **124 D4** 22 30 S 129 0 E
McKay Ra., *Australia* **124 D3** 23 0 S 122 30 E
McKeesport, *U.S.A.* **150 F5** 40 21N 79 52W
McKellar, *Canada* **150 A5** 45 30N 79 55W
McKenna, *U.S.A.* **160 D4** 46 56N 122 33W
Mackenzie, *Canada* **142 B4** 55 20N 123 5W
McKenzie, *U.S.A.* **149 G1** 36 8N 88 31W
Mackenzie →, *Australia* **126 C4** 23 38 S 149 46 E
Mackenzie →, *Canada* **138 B6** 69 10N 134 20W
McKenzie →, *U.S.A.* **158 D2** 44 7N 123 6W
Mackenzie Bay, *Canada* **6 B1** 69 0N 137 30W
Mackenzie City = Linden, *Guyana* **169 B6** 6 0N 58 10W
Mackenzie Mts., *Canada* **138 B6** 64 0N 130 0W
Mackenzie Plains, *N.Z.* **131 E5** 44 10 S 170 25 E
McKerrow, L., *N.Z.* **131 E3** 44 25 S 168 5 E
Mackheim = Maków Mazowiecki, *Poland* **55 F8** 52 52N 21 6 E
Mackinaw, *U.S.A.* **156 D7** 40 32N 89 21W
Mackinaw →, *U.S.A.* **156 D7** 40 33N 89 44W
Mackinaw City, *U.S.A.* **148 C3** 45 47N 84 44W
McKinlay, *Australia* **126 C3** 21 16 S 141 18 E
McKinlay →, *Australia* **126 C3** 20 50 S 141 28 E
McKinley, Mt., *U.S.A.* **144 E10** 63 4N 151 0W
McKinley Park, *U.S.A.* **144 E10** 63 44N 148 55W
McKinley Sea, *Arctic* **10 A11** 82 0N 0 0W
McKinleyville, *U.S.A.* **158 F1** 40 57N 124 6W
McKinney, *U.S.A.* **155 J6** 33 12N 96 37W
Mackinnon Road, *Kenya* **118 C4** 3 40 S 39 1 E
McKittrick, *Calif., U.S.A.* **161 K7** 35 18N 119 37W
McKittrick, *Mo., U.S.A.* **156 F5** 38 44N 91 27W
Macklin, *Canada* **143 C7** 52 20N 109 56W
Macksville, *Australia* **129 A10** 30 40 S 152 56 E
McLaren Vale, *Australia* **128 C3** 35 13 S 138 31 E
McLaughlin, *U.S.A.* **154 C4** 45 49N 100 49W
Maclean, *Australia* **127 D5** 29 26 S 153 16 E
McLean, *Ill., U.S.A.* **156 D7** 40 19N 89 10W
McLean, *Tex., U.S.A.* **155 H4** 35 14N 100 36W
McLeansboro, *U.S.A.* **154 F10** 38 6N 88 32W
Maclear, *S. Africa* **117 E4** 31 2 S 28 23 E
Maclear, C., *Malawi* **119 E3** 13 58 S 34 49 E
Macleay →, *Australia* **129 A10** 30 56 S 153 0 E
McLennan, *Canada* **142 B5** 55 42N 116 50W
MacLeod = Fort Macleod, *Canada* **142 D6** 49 45N 113 30W
McLeod →, *Canada* **142 C5** 54 9N 115 44W
MacLeod, B., *Canada* **143 A7** 62 53N 110 0W
McLeod, L., *Australia* **125 D1** 24 9 S 113 47 E
MacLeod Lake, *Canada* **142 C4** 54 58N 123 0W
McLoughlin, Mt., *U.S.A.* **158 E2** 42 27N 122 19W
McMahon = Aïn Touta, *Algeria* **111 A6** 35 26N 5 54 E
McMechen, *U.S.A.* **150 G4** 39 57N 80 44W
McMinnville, *Oreg., U.S.A.* **158 D2** 45 13N 123 12W
McMinnville, *Tenn., U.S.A.* **149 H3** 35 41N 85 46W
McMurdo Sd., *Antarctica* **7 D11** 77 0 S 170 0 E
McMurray = Fort McMurray, *Canada* **142 B6** 56 44N 111 7W
McMurray, *U.S.A.* **160 B4** 48 19N 122 14W
Maco, *Phil.* **81 H5** 7 20N 125 50 E
Macocolo, *Angola* **115 D3** 6 47 S 16 8 E
Macodoene, *Mozam.* **117 C6** 23 32 S 35 5 E
Macolo, *Angola* **115 D3** 7 5 S 16 42 E
Macomb, *U.S.A.* **156 D6** 40 27N 90 40W
Macomer, *Italy* **46 B1** 40 16N 8 47 E
Mâcon, *France* **27 F11** 46 19N 4 50 E
Macon, *Ga., U.S.A.* **152 C6** 32 51N 83 38W
Macon, *Ill., U.S.A.* **156 E8** 39 43N 89 0W
Macon, *Miss., U.S.A.* **149 J1** 33 7N 88 34W
Macon, *Mo., U.S.A.* **156 E4** 39 44N 92 28W
Macondo, *Angola* **115 E4** 12 37 S 23 46 E
Macossa, *Mozam.* **119 F3** 17 55 S 33 56 E
Macoun L., *Canada* **143 B8** 56 32N 103 40W
Macoupin Cr. →, *U.S.A.* **156 E6** 39 11N 90 38W
Macovane, *Mozam.* **117 C6** 21 30 S 35 2 E
MacPherson = Kapuskasing, *Canada* **140 C3** 49 25N 82 30W
McPherson, *U.S.A.* **154 F6** 38 22N 97 40W
McPherson Pk., *U.S.A.* **161 L7** 34 53N 119 53W
McPherson Ra., *Australia* **127 D5** 28 15 S 153 15 E
Macquarie →, *Australia* **129 A7** 30 7 S 147 24 E
Macquarie Harbour, *Australia* **127 G4** 42 15 S 145 23 E
Macquarie Is., *Pac. Oc.* **134 N7** 54 36 S 158 55 E
McRae, *U.S.A.* **152 C7** 32 4N 82 54W
MacRobertson Land, *Antarctica* **7 D6** 71 0 S 64 0 E
Macroom, *Ireland* **23 E3** 51 54N 8 57W
MacTier, *Canada* **150 A5** 45 9N 79 46W
Macubela, *Mozam.* **119 F4** 16 53 S 37 49 E
Macugnaga, *Italy* **44 C4** 45 58N 7 58 E
Macuira △, *Colombia* **165 D5** 12 9N 71 21W
Macuiza, *Mozam.* **119 F3** 18 7 S 34 29 E
Macujer, *Colombia* **168 C3** 0 24N 73 10W
Macumba, The →, *Australia* **127 D2** 27 52 S 137 12 E
Macuro, *Venezuela* **169 F9** 10 42N 61 55W
Macusani, *Peru* **172 C3** 14 4 S 70 29W
Macuse, *Mozam.* **119 F4** 17 45 S 37 10 E
Macuspana, *Mexico* **163 D6** 17 46N 92 36W
Macusse, *Angola* **116 B3** 17 48 S 20 23 E
Mada →, *Nigeria* **113 D6** 7 59N 7 55 E
Ma'dabā □, *Jordan* **103 D4** 31 43N 35 47 E
Madadeni, *S. Africa* **117 D5** 27 43 S 30 3 E
Madadi, *Chad* **109 E4** 18 28N 20 45 E
Madagali, *Nigeria* **113 C7** 10 56N 13 33 E
Madagascar ■, *Africa* **117 C8** 20 0 S 47 0 E
Madagascar Basin, *Ind. Oc.* **121 G4** 27 0 S 55 0 E
Madagascar Plateau, *Ind. Oc.* **121 G3** 30 0 S 45 0 E
Madā'in Sālih, *Si. Arabia* **96 E3** 26 46N 37 57 E
Madakasira, *India* **95 H3** 13 56N 77 16 E
Madalena, *Azores* **9 d1** 38 32N 28 32W
Madama, *Niger* **109 D2** 22 0N 13 40 E
Madame, I., *Canada* **141 C7** 45 30N 60 58W
Madan, *Bulgaria* **51 E8** 41 30N 24 57 E
Madanapalle, *India* **95 H4** 13 33N 78 28 E
Madang, *Papua N. G.* **132 C3** 5 12 S 145 49 E
Madang □, *Papua N. G.* **132 C3** 5 0 S 145 30 E
Madaoua, *Niger* **113 C6** 14 5N 6 27 E
Madara, *Nigeria* **113 C7** 11 45N 10 35 E
Madaripur, *Bangla.* **90 D3** 23 19N 90 15 E
Madau I., *Papua N. G.* **132 E7** 8 58 S 152 28 E
Madauk, *Burma* **90 G6** 17 56N 96 52 E
Madawaska, *Canada* **150 A7** 45 30N 78 0W
Madawaska →, *Canada* **140 C4** 45 27N 76 21W
Madaya, *Burma* **90 D6** 22 12N 96 10 E
Madbar, *Sudan* **107 F3** 6 17N 30 45 E
Maddalena, *Italy* **46 A2** 41 16N 9 23 E
Maddaloni, *Italy* **47 A7** 41 2N 14 23 E
Maddela, *Phil.* **80 C3** 16 21N 121 41 E
Maddur, *India* **95 H3** 12 36N 77 4 E
Madeira, *Atl. Oc.* **9 c** 32 50N 17 0W
Madeira, *U.S.A.* **157 E12** 39 11N 84 22W
Madeira →, *Brazil* **169 D6** 3 22 S 58 45W
Mädelegabel, *Germany* **33 B10** 47 18N 10 18 E
Madeleine, Îs. de la, *Canada* **141 C7** 47 30N 61 40W
Maden, *Turkey* **101 C8** 38 23N 39 40 E

Madera, Mexico 162 B3 29 12N 108 7W
Madera, Calif., U.S.A. 160 J6 36 57N 120 3W
Madera, Pa., U.S.A. 150 F6 40 49N 78 26W
Madgaon, India 95 G1 15 12N 73 58 E
Madha, India 94 F2 18 0N 75 30 E
Madhavpur, India 92 J3 21 15N 69 58 E
Madhepura, India 93 F12 26 11N 86 23 E
Madhira, India 94 F5 16 55N 80 22 E
Madhubani, India 93 F12 26 21N 86 7 E
Madhugiri, India 95 H3 13 40N 77 12 E
Madhumati →, Bangla. 90 D2 22 53N 89 52 E
Madhupur, Bangla. 90 C3 24 37N 90 2 E
Madhupur, India 93 G12 24 16N 86 39 E
Madhya Pradesh □, India 92 J8 22 50N 78 0 E
Madidi →, Bolivia 172 C4 12 32 S 66 52W
Madikeri, India 95 H2 12 30N 75 45 E
Madikwe ⌂, S. Africa 117 D5 27 38 S 32 15 E
Madill, U.S.A. 155 H6 34 6N 96 46W
Madimba, Angola 115 D2 6 36 S 14 23 E
Madimba, Dem. Rep. of the Congo 115 C3 4 58 S 15 5 E
Ma'din, Syria 101 E8 35 45N 39 36 E
Madina, Mali 112 C3 13 25N 8 50W
Madinani, Ivory C. 112 D3 9 37N 6 57W
Madīnat ash Sha'b, Yemen 98 D4 12 50N 45 0 E
Madingo, Congo 114 C2 4 5 S 11 24 E
Madingou, Congo 114 C2 4 10 S 13 33 E
Madirovalo, Madag. 117 B8 16 26 S 46 32 E
Madison, Calif., U.S.A. 160 G5 38 41N 121 59W
Madison, Fla., U.S.A. 152 E6 30 28N 83 25W
Madison, Ga., U.S.A. 152 B6 33 36N 83 28W
Madison, Ind., U.S.A. 157 F11 38 44N 85 23W
Madison, Mo., U.S.A. 156 E4 39 28N 92 13W
Madison, Nebr., U.S.A. 154 E6 41 50N 97 27W
Madison, Ohio, U.S.A. 150 E3 41 46N 81 3W
Madison, S. Dak., U.S.A. 154 D6 44 0N 97 7W
Madison, Wis., U.S.A. 156 A7 43 4N 89 24W
Madison →, U.S.A. 158 D8 45 56N 111 31W
Madison Heights, U.S.A. 148 G6 37 25N 79 8W
Madisonville, Ky., U.S.A. 148 G2 37 20N 87 30W
Madisonville, Tex., U.S.A. 155 K7 30 57N 95 55W
Madista, Botswana 116 C4 21 15 S 25 6 E
Madiun, Indonesia 85 D4 7 38 S 111 32 E
Madjingo, Gabon 114 B2 1 20N 14 4 E
Madoc, Canada 150 B7 44 30N 77 28W
Madol, Sudan 107 F2 9 3N 27 45 E
Madon →, France 27 D13 48 36N 6 6 E
Madona, Latvia 15 H22 56 53N 26 5 E
Madonie, Italy 46 E6 37 50N 13 50 E
Madonna di Campíglio, Italy 33 D11 46 14N 10 49 E
Madra Dağı, Turkey 49 B9 39 23N 27 12 E
Madrakah, Ra's al, Oman 99 C7 19 0N 57 50 E
Madras = Chennai, India 95 H5 13 8N 80 19 E
Madras = Tamil Nadu □, India 95 J3 11 0N 77 0 E
Madras, U.S.A. 158 D3 44 38N 121 8W
Madre, Laguna, U.S.A. 155 M6 27 0N 97 30W
Madre, Sierra, Phil. 80 C4 17 0N 122 0 E
Madre de Dios □, Peru 172 C3 12 0 S 70 15W
Madre de Dios →, Bolivia 172 C4 10 59 S 66 8W
Madre de Dios, I., Chile 176 D1 50 20 S 75 10W
Madre del Sur, Sierra, Mexico 163 D5 17 30N 100 0W
Madre Occidental, Sierra, Mexico 162 B3 27 0N 107 0W
Madre Oriental, Sierra, Mexico 162 C5 25 0N 100 0W
Madri, India 92 G5 24 16N 73 32 E
Madrid, Spain 42 E7 40 25N 3 45W
Madrid, Ala., U.S.A. 152 D4 31 2N 85 24W
Madrid, Iowa, U.S.A. 156 C3 41 53N 93 49W
Madrid, N.Y., U.S.A. 151 B9 44 45N 75 8W
Madrid □, Spain 42 E7 40 30N 3 45W
Madrid Barajas ✈ (MAD), Spain 42 E7 40 26N 3 34W
Madridejos, Spain 43 F7 39 28N 3 33W
Madrigal de las Altas Torres, Spain 42 D6 41 5N 5 0W
Madrona, Sierra, Spain 43 G6 38 27N 4 16W
Madroñera, Spain 43 F5 39 26N 5 42W
Madrusah, Libya 108 D2 24 48N 14 32 E
Madu, Sudan 107 E2 14 37N 26 4 E
Maduo, Dem. Rep. of the Congo 114 C4 1 24 S 20 44 E
Madura, Australia 125 F4 31 55 S 127 0 E
Madura, Indonesia 79 G15 7 30 S 114 0 E
Madura, Selat, Indonesia 85 D4 7 30 S 113 20 E
Madura Oya △, Sri Lanka 95 L5 7 20N 81 10 E
Madurai, India 95 K4 9 55N 78 10 E
Madurantakam, India 95 H4 12 30N 79 50 E
Madzhalis, Russia 61 J8 42 9N 47 47 E
Mae Chan, Thailand 86 B2 20 9N 99 52 E
Mae Hong Son, Thailand 86 C2 19 16N 97 56 E
Mae Khlong →, Thailand 86 F3 13 24N 100 0 E
Mae Phrik, Thailand 86 D2 17 27N 99 7 E
Mae Ping △, Thailand 86 D2 17 37N 98 51 E
Mae Ramat, Thailand 86 D2 16 58N 98 31 E
Mae Rim, Thailand 86 C2 18 54N 98 57 E
Mae Sot, Thailand 86 D2 16 43N 98 34 E
Mae Suai, Thailand 86 C2 19 39N 99 33 E
Mae Tha, Thailand 86 C2 18 28N 99 8 E
Mae Wong △, Thailand 86 E2 15 54N 99 12 E
Mae Yom △, Thailand 86 C3 18 43N 100 15 E
Maebaru, Japan 72 D2 33 33N 130 12 E
Maebashi, Japan 73 A11 36 24N 139 4 E
Maella, Spain 40 D5 41 8N 0 7 E
Maesteg, U.K. 21 F4 51 36N 3 40W
Maestra, Sierra, Cuba 164 B4 20 15N 77 0W
Maestre de Campo I., Phil. 80 E3 12 56N 121 42 E
Maetambe, Mt., Solomon Is. 133 L9 7 3 S 157 1 E
Maevatanana, Madag. 117 B8 16 56 S 46 49 E
Maéwo, Vanuatu 133 E6 15 10 S 168 10 E
Mafa, Indonesia 82 A3 0 3N 127 53 E
Ma'fan, Libya 108 C2 25 56N 14 29 E
Mafeking = Mafikeng, S. Africa 116 D4 25 50 S 25 38 E
Mafeking, Canada 143 C8 52 40N 101 10W
Maféré, Ivory C. 112 D4 5 30N 3 2W
Mafeteng, Lesotho 116 D4 29 51 S 27 15 E
Maffra, Australia 129 D7 37 53 S 146 58 E
Mafia I., Tanzania 118 D4 7 45 S 39 50 E
Mafikeng, S. Africa 116 D4 25 50 S 25 38 E
Mafra, Brazil 175 B6 26 10 S 49 55W
Mafra, Portugal 43 G1 38 55N 9 20W
Mafungabusi Plateau, Zimbabwe 119 F2 18 30 S 29 8 E
Magadan, Russia 67 D16 59 38N 150 50 E
Magadi, India 95 H3 12 58N 77 14 E
Magadi, Kenya 118 C4 1 54 S 36 19 E
Magadi, L., Kenya 118 C4 1 54 S 36 19 E
Magaliesburg, S. Africa 117 D4 26 0 S 27 32 E
Magallanes = Punta Arenas, Chile 176 D2 53 10 S 71 0W
Magallanes, Phil. 80 E4 12 50N 123 50 E
Magallanes □, Chile 176 D2 52 0 S 72 0W
Magallanes, Estrecho de, Chile 176 D2 52 30 S 75 0W
Magaluf, Spain 38 B3 39 29N 2 32 E
Magangué, Colombia 168 B3 9 14N 74 45W
Maganoy, Phil. 81 H5 6 51N 124 31 E
Magaria, Niger 113 C6 13 4N 9 5 E
Magarida, Papua N. G. 132 F5 10 18 S 149 20 E
Magburaka, S. Leone 112 D2 8 47N 12 0W
Magdalen Is. = Madeleine, Îs. de la, Canada 141 C7 47 30N 61 40W
Magdalena, Argentina 174 D4 35 5 S 57 30W
Magdalena, Bolivia 173 C5 13 13 S 63 57W
Magdalena, Malaysia 83 B5 4 25N 117 55 E
Magdalena, Mexico 162 A2 30 50N 112 0W
Magdalena, U.S.A. 159 J10 34 7N 107 15W
Magdalena □, Colombia 168 A3 10 0N 74 0W
Magdalena →, Colombia 168 A3 11 6N 74 51W
Magdalena →, Mexico 162 A2 30 40N 112 25W
Magdalena, B., Mexico 162 C2 24 30N 112 10W
Magdalena, I., Chile 176 B2 44 40 S 73 0W
Magdalena, Llano de la, Mexico 162 C2 25 0N 111 30W
Magdeburg, Germany 30 C7 52 7N 11 38 E
Magdelaine Cays, Australia 126 B5 16 33 S 150 18 E
Magdub, Sudan 107 E2 13 42N 25 5 E
Magee, U.S.A. 155 K10 31 52N 89 44W
Magelang, Indonesia 85 D4 7 29 S 110 13 E
Magellan's Str. = Magallanes, Estrecho de, Chile 176 D2 52 30 S 75 0W
Magenta, Italy 44 C5 45 28N 8 53 E
Magenta, L., Australia 125 F2 33 30 S 119 2 E
Magerøya, Norway 14 A21 71 3N 25 40 E
Maggea, Australia 128 C4 34 28 S 140 2 E
Maggia, Switz. 33 D7 46 15N 8 42 E
Maggia →, Switz. 33 D7 46 18N 8 36 E
Maggiorasca, Mte., Italy 44 D6 44 33N 9 29 E
Maggiore, Lago, Italy 44 B5 45 57N 8 39 E
Maggotty, Jamaica 164 a 18 9N 77 46W
Maghâgha, Egypt 106 B3 28 38N 30 50 E
Maghama, Mauritania 112 B2 15 32N 12 57W
Magherafelt, U.K. 23 B5 54 45N 6 37W
Maghnia, Algeria 111 B4 34 50N 1 43W
Maghreb, N. Afr. 104 C3 32 0N 4 0W
Magione, Italy 45 E9 43 8N 12 12 E
Magistralnyy, Russia 67 D11 56 16N 107 36 E
Maglaj, Bos.-H. 52 F3 44 33N 18 7 E
Magliano in Toscana, Italy 45 F8 42 36N 11 17 E
Máglie, Italy 47 B11 40 7N 18 18 E
Magnac-Laval, France 28 B5 46 13N 1 11 E
Magnetic Pole (North), Canada 6 A2 88 30N 107 0W
Magnetic Pole (South), Antarctica 7 C9 64 8 S 138 8 E
Magnisía □, Greece 48 B5 39 15N 23 0 E
Magnitogorsk, Russia 64 E7 53 27N 59 4 E
Magnolia, Ark., U.S.A. 155 J8 33 16N 93 14W
Magnolia, Miss., U.S.A. 155 K9 31 9N 90 28W
Magnor, Norway 18 E9 59 56N 12 15 E
Magny-en-Vexin, France 27 C8 49 9N 1 47 E
Mago, Fiji 133 A3 17 26 S 179 8W
Mago △, Ethiopia 107 F4 5 40N 36 18 E
Magog, Canada 141 C5 45 18N 72 9W
Magoro, Uganda 118 B3 1 45N 34 12 E
Magoša = Famagusta, Cyprus 39 E9 35 8N 33 55 E
Magouládhes, Greece 38 B9 39 45N 19 42 E
Magoye, Zambia 119 F2 16 1 S 27 30 E
Magozal, Mexico 163 C5 21 34N 97 59W
Magpie, L., Canada 141 B7 51 0N 64 41W
Magrath, Canada 142 D6 49 25N 112 50W
Magre →, Spain 41 F4 39 11N 0 25W
Magrur, Sudan 107 E3 14 1N 30 27 E
Magrur, Wadi →, Sudan 107 D2 16 5N 26 30 E
Magsingal, Phil. 80 C3 17 41N 120 25 E
Magta Lahjar, Mauritania 112 B2 17 28N 13 17W
Maguan, China 76 F5 23 0N 104 21 E
Maguarinho, C., Brazil 170 B2 0 15 S 48 30W
Magude, Mozam. 117 D5 25 2 S 32 40 E
Maguindanao □, Phil. 81 H5 7 5N 124 0 E
Magurski △, Poland 55 J8 49 30N 21 30 E
Maġusa = Famagusta, Cyprus 39 E9 35 8N 33 55 E
Maguse L., Canada 143 A9 61 37N 95 10W
Maguse Pt., Canada 143 A10 61 20N 93 50W
Magvana, India 92 H3 23 13N 69 22 E
Magwe, Burma 90 E5 20 10N 95 0 E
Magwe, Sudan 107 G3 4 8N 32 17 E
Magwe □, Burma 90 F5 20 0N 95 0 E
Magyarorszag = Hungary ■, Europe 35 D12 47 20N 19 20 E
Maha Oya, Sri Lanka 95 L5 7 31N 81 22 E
Maha Sarakham, Thailand 86 D4 16 12N 103 16 E
Mahābād, Iran 101 D11 36 50N 45 45 E
Mahabaleshwar, India 94 F1 17 58N 73 43 E
Mahabharat Lekh, Nepal 93 E10 28 30N 82 0 E
Mahabo, Madag. 117 C7 20 23 S 44 40 E
Mahad, India 94 E1 18 6N 73 29 E
Mahaddei Uen, Somali Rep. 120 D3 2 58N 45 32 E
Mahadeo Hills, India 93 H8 22 20N 78 30 E
Mahadeopur, India 94 E5 18 48N 80 0 E
Mahaffey, U.S.A. 150 F6 40 53N 78 44W
Mahagi, Dem. Rep. of the Congo 118 B3 2 20N 31 0 E
Mahaicony, Guyana 169 B6 6 36N 57 48W
Mahajamba →, Madag. 117 B8 15 33 S 47 8 E
Mahajamba, Helodranon' i, Madag. 117 B8 15 24 S 47 5 E
Mahajan, India 92 E5 28 48N 73 56 E
Mahajanga, Madag. 117 B8 15 40 S 46 25 E
Mahajanga □, Madag. 117 B8 17 0 S 47 0 E
Mahajilo →, Madag. 117 B8 19 42 S 45 22 E
Mahakam →, Indonesia 85 C5 0 35 S 117 17 E
Mahalapye, Botswana 116 C4 23 1 S 26 51 E
Mahalchhar, Bangla. 90 D4 22 55N 92 2 E
Mahale Mts., Tanzania 118 D3 6 20 S 30 0 E
Mahale Mts. △, Tanzania 118 D2 6 10 S 29 50 E
Maḥallāt, Iran 97 C6 33 55N 50 30 E
Māhān, Iran 97 D8 30 5N 57 18 E
Mahan →, India 93 H10 23 30N 82 50 E
Mahanadi →, India 94 D8 20 20N 86 25 E
Mahananda →, India 93 G12 25 12N 87 52 E
Mahanoro, Madag. 117 B8 19 54 S 48 48 E
Mahanoy City, U.S.A. 151 F8 40 49N 76 9W
Mahaplag, Phil. 81 F5 10 35N 124 57 E
Maharashtra □, India 94 D2 20 30N 75 30 E
Maharès, Tunisia 108 B2 34 32N 10 29 E
Mahasamund, India 94 D6 21 6N 82 6 E
Mahasham, W. →, Egypt 103 E3 30 15N 34 10 E
Mahasoa, Madag. 117 C8 22 12 S 46 6 E
Mahasolo, Madag. 117 B8 19 7 S 46 22 E
Mahattat ash Shīdīyah, Jordan 103 F4 29 55N 35 55 E
Mahattat 'Unayzah, Jordan 103 E4 30 30N 35 47 E
Mahavavy →, Madag. 117 B8 15 57 S 45 54 E
Mahaweli Ganga →, Sri Lanka 95 K5 8 27N 81 13 E
Mahaxay, Laos 86 D5 17 22N 105 12 E
Mahbubabad, India 94 F5 17 42N 80 2 E
Mahbubnagar, India 94 F3 16 45N 77 59 E
Mahd adh Dhahab, Si. Arabia 98 B3 23 30N 40 52 E
Mahdah, Oman 97 E7 24 24N 55 59 E
Mahdia, Guyana 169 B6 5 13N 59 8W
Mahdia, Tunisia 108 A2 35 28N 11 0 E
Mahe, Jammu & Kashmir, India 93 C8 33 10N 78 32 E
Mahé, Pondicherry, India 95 J2 11 42N 75 34 E
Mahé, Seychelles 121 b 5 0 S 55 30 E
Mahé ✈ (SEZ), Seychelles 121 b 4 40 S 55 31 E
Mahebourg, Mauritius 121 d 20 24 S 57 42 E
Mahendra Giri, India 95 K3 8 20N 77 30 E
Mahendraganj, India 90 C2 25 20N 89 45 E
Mahendragarh, India 92 E7 28 17N 76 14 E
Mahenge, Tanzania 119 D4 8 45 S 36 41 E
Maheno, N.Z. 131 F5 45 10 S 170 50 E
Mahesana, India 92 H5 23 39N 72 26 E
Maheshwar, India 92 H6 22 11N 75 35 E
Mahgawan, India 93 F8 26 29N 78 37 E
Mahi →, India 92 H5 22 15N 72 55 E
Mahia Pen., N.Z. 130 F6 39 9 S 177 55 E
Mahighe, Solomon Is. 133 M10 8 30 S 159 58 E
Mahilyow, Belarus 58 F6 53 55N 30 18 E
Mahim, India 94 E1 19 39N 72 44 E
Mahina, Tahiti 133 S16 17 30 S 149 27W
Mahirija, Morocco 111 B4 34 0N 3 16W
Mahlaing, Burma 90 E5 21 6N 95 39 E
Mahmiya, Sudan 107 D3 17 12N 33 43 E
Mahmud Kot, Pakistan 92 D4 30 16N 71 0 E
Mahmudia, Romania 53 E14 45 5N 29 5 E
Mahmudiye, Turkey 49 B12 39 30N 30 15 E
Mahmutbey, Turkey 51 E12 41 3N 28 49 E
Mahnomen, U.S.A. 154 B7 47 19N 95 58W
Maho, Sri Lanka 95 L5 7 49N 80 16 E
Mahoba, India 93 G8 25 15N 79 55 E
Mahomet, U.S.A. 157 D8 40 12N 88 24W
Mahón = Maó, Spain 38 B5 39 53N 4 16 E
Mahon, Menorca ✈ (MAH), Spain 40 F9 39 50N 4 16 E
Mahone Bay, Canada 141 D7 44 30N 64 20W
Mahopac, U.S.A. 151 E11 41 22N 73 45W
Mahoua, Chad 109 F3 11 49N 18 26 E
Mährisch-Budwitz = Moravské Budějovice, Czech Rep. 34 B8 49 4N 15 49 E
Mährisch-Schönberg = Šumperk, Czech Rep. 35 B9 49 59N 16 59 E
Mährisch-Trubau = Moravská Třebová, Czech Rep. 35 B9 49 45N 16 40 E
Mahuta, Nigeria 113 C5 11 32N 4 58 E
Mahuva, India 92 J4 21 5N 71 48 E
Mahya Dağı, Turkey 51 E11 41 47N 27 36 E
Mai-Ndombe, L., Dem. Rep. of the Congo 114 C3 2 0 S 18 20 E
Mai-Sai, Thailand 76 G2 20 20N 99 55 E
Mai Thon, Ko, Thailand 87 a 7 40N 98 28 E
Maia, Azores 9 d4 36 56N 25 1W
Maia, Portugal 42 D2 41 14N 8 37W
Maia, Spain 40 B3 43 12N 1 29W
Maials, Spain 40 D5 41 22N 0 30 E
Maibong, India 90 C4 25 18N 93 10 E
Maicao, Colombia 168 A3 11 23N 72 13W
Maîche, France 27 E13 47 16N 6 48 E
Maici →, Brazil 173 B5 6 30 S 61 43W
Maicuru →, Brazil 169 D7 2 14 S 54 17W
Máida, Italy 47 D9 38 51N 16 22 E
Maidan Khula, Afghan. 91 B3 33 36N 69 50 E
Maidenhead, U.K. 21 F7 51 31N 0 42W
Maidstone, Canada 143 C7 53 5N 109 20W
Maidstone, U.K. 21 F8 51 16N 0 32 E
Maiduguri, Nigeria 113 C7 12 0N 13 20 E
Maiella △, Italy 45 F11 42 5N 14 5 E
Măieruş, Romania 53 E10 45 53N 25 31 E
Maigatari, Nigeria 113 C6 12 46N 9 27 E
Maignelay Montigny, France 27 C9 49 32N 2 30 E
Maigo, Phil. 81 G4 8 10N 123 57 E
Maigualida, Sierra, Venezuela 169 B4 5 30N 65 10W
Maigudo, Ethiopia 107 F4 7 30N 37 8 E
Maihar, India 93 G9 24 16N 80 45 E
Maihara, Japan 73 B8 35 19N 136 17 E
Maijdi, Bangla. 90 D3 22 48N 91 10 E
Maikala Ra., India 94 D5 22 0N 81 0 E
Maiko △, Dem. Rep. of the Congo 118 C2 0 30 S 27 50 E
Maikoor, Indonesia 83 C4 6 8 S 134 6 E
Mailani, India 93 E9 28 17N 80 21 E
Maili, U.S.A. 145 K13 21 25N 158 11W
Maili Pt, U.S.A. 145 K13 21 24N 158 11W
Maillezais, France 28 B3 46 22N 0 45W
Mailsi, Pakistan 92 E5 29 48N 72 15 E
Maimbung, Phil. 81 J3 5 56N 121 2 E
Main →, Germany 31 F4 50 0N 8 18 E
Main →, U.K. 23 B5 54 48N 6 18W
Main Range △, Australia 127 D5 28 11 S 152 27 E
Main Ridge, Trin. & Tob. 169 E10 11 16N 60 40W
Mainburg, Germany 31 G7 48 38N 11 47 E
Maindargi, India 94 F3 17 28N 76 18 E
Maine, France 26 D6 48 20N 0 15W
Maine □, U.S.A. 149 C11 45 20N 69 0W
Maine →, Ireland 23 D2 52 9N 9 45W
Maine-et-Loire □, France 26 E6 47 31N 0 30W
Maïne-Soroa, Niger 113 C7 13 13N 12 2 E
Maingkaing, Burma 90 C5 24 48N 95 16 E
Maingkwan, Burma 90 B6 26 15N 96 37 E
Mainit, Phil. 81 G5 9 32N 125 32 E
Mainit, L., Phil. 81 G5 9 31N 125 30 E
Mainland, Orkney, U.K. 22 C5 58 59N 3 8W
Mainland, Shet., U.K. 22 A7 60 15N 1 22W
Mainoru, Australia 126 A1 14 0 S 134 6 E
Mainpuri, India 93 F8 27 18N 79 4 E
Maintal, Germany 31 E4 50 7N 8 52 E
Maintenon, France 27 D8 48 35N 1 35 E
Maintirano, Madag. 117 B7 18 3 S 44 1 E
Mainz, Germany 31 E4 50 1N 8 14 E
Maio, C. Verde Is. 9 j 15 10N 23 10W
Maipú, Argentina 174 D4 36 52 S 57 50W
Maiquetía, Venezuela 168 A4 10 36N 66 57W
Máira →, Italy 44 D4 44 49N 7 38 E
Mairabari, India 90 B4 26 30N 92 22 E
Mairipotaba, Brazil 171 E2 17 18 S 49 28W
Maisí, Cuba 165 B5 20 17N 74 9W
Maisí, Pta. de, Cuba 165 B5 20 10N 74 10W
Maitland, N.S.W., Australia 129 B9 32 33 S 151 36 E
Maitland, S. Austral., Australia 128 C2 34 23 S 137 40 E
Maitland →, Canada 150 C3 43 45N 81 43W
Maitland, Banjaran, Malaysia 85 B5 4 55N 116 37 E
Maitri, Antarctica 7 D3 70 0 S 3 0W
Maitum, Phil. 81 H5 6 2N 124 30 E
Maiyema, Nigeria 113 C5 12 5N 4 25 E
Maiyuan, China 77 E11 25 34N 117 28 E
Maiz, Is. del, Nic. 164 D3 12 15N 83 4W
Maizuru, Japan 73 B7 35 25N 135 22 E
Majagual, Colombia 168 B3 8 33N 74 38W
Majalengka, Indonesia 85 D3 6 50 S 108 13 E
Majari →, Brazil 169 C5 3 29N 60 58W
Majdūl, Libya 108 C3 25 51N 15 7 E
Majene, Indonesia 82 B1 3 38 S 118 57 E
Majes →, Peru 172 D3 16 40 S 72 44W
Majete ⌂, Malawi 119 F3 15 54 S 34 34 E
Majevica, Bos.-H. 52 F3 44 45N 18 50 E
Maji, Ethiopia 107 F4 6 12N 35 30 E
Majiang, China 76 D6 26 28N 107 32 E
Majorca = Mallorca, Spain 38 B4 39 30N 3 0 E
Majors Creek, Australia 129 C8 35 33 S 149 45 E
Majuriã, Brazil 173 B5 7 30 S 64 55W
Majuro, Marshall Is. 134 G9 7 9N 171 12 E
Maka, Senegal 112 C2 13 40N 14 10W
Makaha, U.S.A. 145 K13 21 29N 158 13W
Makaha, Zimbabwe 117 B5 17 20 S 32 39 E
Makahoa Pt., U.S.A. 145 J14 21 41N 157 56W
Makahuena Pt., U.S.A. 145 B2 21 52N 159 27W
Makak, Cameroon 113 E7 3 36N 11 0 E
Makakilo City, U.S.A. 145 K13 21 22N 158 5W
Makakou, Gabon 114 C2 0 11 S 12 12 E
Makalamabedi, Botswana 116 C3 20 19 S 23 51 E
Makale, Indonesia 82 B1 3 6 S 119 51 E
Makalu-Barun △, Nepal 93 F12 27 45N 87 10 E
Makamba, Burundi 118 C2 4 8 S 29 49 E
Makapu Pt., U.S.A. 145 K14 21 19N 157 39W
Makarewa, N.Z. 131 G3 46 20 S 168 21 E
Makari, Cameroon 109 F2 12 35N 10 27 E
Makari, Cameroon 113 C7 12 35N 10 27 E
Makarikari = Makgadikgadi Salt Pans, Botswana 116 C4 20 40 S 25 45 E
Makarov Basin, Arctic 6 A 87 0N 150 0W
Makarovo, Russia 67 D11 57 40N 107 45 E
Makarska, Croatia 45 E14 43 20N 17 2 E
Makaryev, Russia 60 B6 57 52N 43 50 E
Makasar = Ujung Pandang, Indonesia 82 C1 5 10 S 119 20 E
Makasar, Selat, Indonesia 85 C5 1 0 S 118 20 E
Makasar, Str. of = Makasar, Selat, Indonesia 85 C5 1 0 S 118 20 E
Makat, Kazakhstan 57 E9 47 39N 53 19 E
Makaw, Dem. Rep. of the Congo 114 C3 3 29 S 18 20 E
Makawao, U.S.A. 145 C5 20 52N 156 17W
Makaya, Dem. Rep. of the Congo 114 C3 3 21 S 18 1 E
Makbon, Indonesia 83 B4 0 45 S 131 32 E
Makedonija = Macedonia ■, Europe 50 E5 41 53N 21 40 E
Makeni, S. Leone 112 D2 8 55N 12 5W
Makeyevka = Makiyivka, Ukraine 59 H9 48 0N 38 0 E
Makgadikgadi △, Botswana 116 C3 20 27 S 24 47 E
Makgadikgadi Salt Pans, Botswana 116 C4 20 40 S 25 45 E
Makhachkala, Russia 61 J8 43 0N 47 30 E
Makhado = Louis Trichardt, S. Africa 117 C4 23 1 S 29 43 E
Makhairádhon, Greece 39 D2 37 46N 20 49 E
Makharadze = Ozurgeti, Georgia 61 K5 41 55N 42 2 E
Makhfar al Buşayyah, Iraq 96 D5 30 0N 46 10 E
Makhmūr, Iraq 101 E10 35 46N 43 35 E
Makhtal, India 95 E3 16 30N 77 31 E
Makhyah, W. →, Yemen 99 C5 17 40N 49 1 E
Makian, Indonesia 82 A3 0 20N 127 20 E
Makina, Solomon Is. 133 M11 9 50 S 160 50 E
Makindu, Kenya 118 C4 2 18 S 37 50 E
Makinka = Makinsk, Kazakhstan 66 D8 52 37N 70 26 E
Makinsk, Kazakhstan 66 D8 52 37N 70 26 E
Makiv, Ukraine 53 B11 48 48N 26 43 E
Makiyivka, Ukraine 59 H9 48 0N 38 0 E
Makkah, Si. Arabia 98 B2 21 30N 39 54 E
Makkovik, Canada 141 A8 55 10N 59 10W
Makó, Hungary 52 D5 46 14N 20 33 E
Mako, Senegal 112 C2 12 52N 12 20W
Makogai, Fiji 133 A2 17 28 S 179 0 E
Makok, Gabon 114 C1 0 1 S 9 35 E
Makokou, Gabon 114 B2 0 40N 12 50 E
Makongo, Dem. Rep. of the Congo 118 B2 3 25N 26 17 E
Makoro, Dem. Rep. of the Congo 118 B2 3 10N 29 59 E
Makoua, Congo 114 C3 0 5 S 15 50 E
Maków Mazowiecki, Poland 55 F8 52 52N 21 6 E
Maków Podhalański, Poland 55 J6 49 43N 19 45 E
Makrá, Greece 49 E7 36 15N 25 54 E
Makran, Asia 91 D1 26 13N 61 30 E
Makran Coast Range, Pakistan 91 D2 25 40N 64 0 E
Makrana, India 92 F6 27 2N 74 46 E
Makrany, Belarus 55 G11 51 48N 24 17 E
Mákri, Greece 51 F9 40 52N 25 40 E
Makri, India 94 E5 19 46N 81 55 E
Makriyialos, Greece 39 E6 35 2N 25 59 E
Mākū, Iran 101 C11 39 15N 44 31 E
Makum, India 90 B5 27 30N 95 23 E
Makumbi, Dem. Rep. of the Congo 115 D4 5 50 S 20 43 E
Makunda, Botswana 116 C3 22 30 S 20 7 E
Makung, Taiwan 77 F12 23 34N 119 34 E
Makunza, Dem. Rep. of the Congo 115 D4 8 52 S 24 19 E
Makurazaki, Japan 72 F2 31 15N 130 20 E
Makurdi, Nigeria 113 D6 7 43N 8 35 E
Makushin Volcano, U.S.A. 144 K6 53 53N 166 55W
Mākūyeh, Iran 97 D7 28 7N 53 9 E
Makwassie, S. Africa 116 D4 27 17 S 26 0 E
Makwiro, Zimbabwe 117 B5 17 58 S 30 25 E
Mal, India 90 B2 26 51N 88 45 E
Mâl, Mauritania 112 B2 16 58N 13 23W
Mal B., Ireland 23 D2 52 50N 9 30W
Mala, Peru 172 C2 12 40 S 76 38W
Mala, Pta., Panama 164 E3 7 28N 80 2W
Mala Belozërka, Ukraine 59 J8 47 12N 34 56 E
Malá Fatra △, Slovak Rep. 35 B12 49 10N 19 0 E
Mala Kapela, Croatia 45 D12 44 45N 15 30 E
Mała Panew →, Poland 55 H4 50 43N 17 54 E
Mala Vyska, Ukraine 59 H6 48 39N 31 36 E
Malabang, Phil. 81 H5 7 36N 124 3 E
Malabar, U.S.A. 153 H9 28 0N 80 34W
Malabar Coast, India 95 J2 11 0N 75 0 E
Malabo = Rey Malabo, Eq. Guin. 113 E6 3 45N 8 50 E
Malabon, Phil. 80 D3 14 21N 121 0 E
Malabrigo = Puerto Chicama, Peru 172 B2 7 45 S 79 20W
Malabrigo Pt., Phil. 80 E3 13 36N 121 15 E
Malabu, Nigeria 113 D7 9 32N 12 48 E
Malabuñgan, Phil. 81 G1 9 3N 117 38 E
Malacca, Straits of, Indonesia 87 L3 3 0N 101 0 E
Malacky, Slovak Rep. 35 C10 48 27N 17 0 E
Malad City, U.S.A. 158 E7 42 12N 112 15W
Maladeta, Spain 40 C5 42 39N 0 39 E
Maladzyechna, Belarus 58 E4 54 20N 26 50 E
Malae Pt., U.S.A. 145 C6 20 7N 155 53W
Málaga, Colombia 168 B3 6 42N 72 44W
Málaga, Spain 43 J6 36 43N 4 23W
Málaga □, Spain 43 J6 36 38N 4 58W
Malagarasi, Tanzania 118 D3 5 5 S 30 50 E
Malagarasi →, Tanzania 118 D2 5 12 S 29 47 E
Malagasy Rep. = Madagascar ■, Africa 117 C8 20 0 S 47 0 E
Malagón, Spain 43 F7 39 11N 3 52W
Malagón →, Spain 43 H3 37 35N 7 29W
Malahide, Ireland 23 C5 53 26N 6 9W
Malaimbandy, Madag. 117 C8 20 20 S 45 36 E
Malaita, Solomon Is. 133 M11 9 0 S 161 0 E
Malakâl, Sudan 107 F3 9 33N 31 40 E
Malakanagiri, India 94 E5 18 21N 81 54 E
Malakand, Pakistan 91 B3 34 40N 71 55 E
Malakula, Vanuatu 133 F5 16 15 S 167 30 E
Malakwal, Pakistan 92 C5 32 34N 73 13 E
Malalag, Phil. 81 H5 6 36N 125 24 E
Malalaua, Papua N. G. 132 E4 8 4 S 146 10 E
Malam, Chad 109 F4 11 27N 20 59 E
Malamala, Indonesia 82 B2 3 21 S 120 55 E
Malanda, Australia 126 B4 17 22 S 145 35 E
Malang, Indonesia 85 D4 7 59 S 112 45 E
Malangas, Phil. 81 H4 7 37N 123 1 E
Malange □, Angola 115 D3 9 30 S 16 0 E
Malangen, Norway 14 B18 69 24N 18 37 E
Malanje, Angola 115 D3 9 36 S 16 17 E
Malapatan, Phil. 81 J5 5 59N 125 18 E
Mälaren, Sweden 16 E11 59 30N 17 10 E
Malargüe, Argentina 174 D2 35 32 S 69 30W
Malartic, Canada 140 C4 48 9N 78 9W
Malaryta, Belarus 55 G11 51 50N 24 3 E
Malaspina Glacier, U.S.A. 144 G12 59 50N 140 30W
Malatya, Turkey 101 C8 38 25N 38 20 E
Malawali, Malaysia 85 A5 7 3N 117 18 E
Malawi ■, Africa 119 E3 11 55 S 34 0 E
Malawi, L. = Nyasa, L., Africa 119 E3 12 30 S 34 30 E
Malay, Phil. 81 F3 11 54N 121 55 E
Malay Pen., Asia 87 J3 7 25N 100 0 E
Malaya Belozërka = Mala Belozërka, Ukraine 59 J8 47 12N 34 56 E
Malaya Vishera, Russia 58 C7 58 55N 32 25 E
Malaya Viska = Mala Vyska, Ukraine 59 H6 48 39N 31 36 E
Malaybalay, Phil. 81 G5 8 5N 125 7 E
Malāyer, Iran 97 C6 34 19N 48 51 E
Malaysia ■, Asia 85 B4 5 0N 110 0 E
Malazgirt, Turkey 101 C10 39 10N 42 33 E
Malbaza, Niger 113 C6 13 59N 5 38 E
Malbon, Australia 126 C3 21 5 S 140 17 E
Malbooma, Australia 127 E1 30 41 S 134 11 E
Malbork, Poland 54 D6 54 3N 19 1 E
Malca Dube, Ethiopia 120 C2 6 47N 42 4 E
Malcésine, Italy 44 C7 45 46N 10 48 E
Malchin, Germany 30 B8 53 44N 12 44 E
Malchow, Germany 30 B8 53 28N 12 25 E
Malcolm, Australia 125 E3 28 51 S 121 25 E
Malcolm, Pt., Australia 125 F3 33 48 S 123 45 E
Malczyce, Poland 55 G3 51 14N 16 29 E
Maldah, India 93 G13 25 2N 88 9 E
Maldegem, Belgium 24 C3 51 14N 3 26 E
Malden, Mass., U.S.A. 151 D13 42 26N 71 4W
Malden, Mo., U.S.A. 155 G10 36 34N 89 57W
Malden I., Kiribati 135 H12 4 3 S 155 1W
Maldives ■, Ind. Oc. 89 E6 5 0N 73 0 E
Maldon, Australia 128 D6 37 0 S 144 6 E
Maldon, U.K. 21 F8 51 44N 0 42 E
Maldonado, Uruguay 175 C5 34 59 S 55 0W
Maldonado, Punta, Mexico 163 D5 16 19N 98 35W
Malè, Italy 44 B7 46 21N 10 55 E
Male, Maldives 121 D6 4 0N 73 28 E
Malé Karpaty, Slovak Rep. 35 C10 48 30N 17 20 E
Maléa, Ákra, Greece 48 E5 36 28N 23 7 E
Maleas, Ákra = Maléa, Ákra, Greece 48 E5 36 28N 23 7 E
Malebo, Pool, Africa 115 C3 4 17 S 15 20 E
Malegaon, India 94 D2 20 30N 74 38 E
Malei, Mozam. 119 F4 17 12 S 36 58 E
Malek, Sudan 107 F3 6 4N 31 36 E
Malek Kandī, Iran 101 D12 37 9N 46 6 E
Malela, Bas-Congo, Dem. Rep. of the Congo 115 D2 5 59 S 12 37 E
Malela, Maniema, Dem. Rep. of the Congo 118 C2 4 22 S 26 8 E
Malema, Mozam. 119 E4 14 57 S 37 20 E
Malème, Greece 39 E4 35 31N 23 49 E
Malendok I., Papua N. G. 132 B7 3 28 S 153 13 E
Malerås, Sweden 17 H9 56 54N 15 34 E
Malerkotla, India 92 D6 30 32N 75 58 E
Máles, Greece 39 E6 35 6N 25 35 E
Malesherbes, France 27 D9 48 15N 2 24 E
Maleshevska Planina, Europe 50 E7 41 38N 23 7 E
Malesína, Greece 48 C5 38 37N 23 14 E
Malestroit, France 26 E4 47 49N 2 25W
Malfa, Italy 47 D7 38 35N 14 50 E
Malgobek, Russia 61 J7 43 30N 44 34 E
Malgomaj, Sweden 14 D17 64 40N 16 30 E
Malgrat de Mar, Spain 40 D7 41 39N 2 46 E
Malha, Sudan 107 D2 15 8N 25 10 E
Malhada, Brazil 171 D3 14 21 S 43 47W

Malhargarh, *India* **92 G6** 24 17N 74 59 E
Malheur →, *U.S.A.* **158 D5** 44 4N 116 59W
Malheur L., *U.S.A.* **158 E4** 43 20N 118 48W
Mali, *Guinea* **112 C2** 12 10N 12 20W
Mali ■, *Africa* **112 B4** 17 0N 3 0W
Mali →, *Burma* **90 C6** 25 42N 97 30 E
Mali Kanal, *Serbia & M.* **52 E4** 45 36N 19 24 E
Mali Kyun, *Burma* **86 F2** 13 0N 98 20 E
Malibu, *U.S.A.* **161 L8** 34 2N 118 41W
Maligaya = Gloria, *Phil.* **80 E3** 12 59N 121 30 E
Maliku, *Indonesia* **82 B2** 0 39 S 123 16 E
Malili, *Indonesia* **82 B2** 2 42 S 121 6 E
Målilla, *Sweden* **17 G9** 57 23N 15 48 E
Malimba, Mts., *Dem. Rep. of the Congo* **118 D2** 7 30 S 29 30 E
Malin Hd., *Ireland* **23 A4** 55 23N 7 23W
Malin Pen., *Ireland* **23 A4** 55 20N 7 17W
Malindang, Mt., *Phil.* **81 G4** 8 13N 123 38 E
Malindi, *Kenya* **118 C5** 3 12 S 40 5 E
Malines = Mechelen, *Belgium* **24 C4** 51 2N 4 29 E
Malino, *Indonesia* **82 A2** 1 0N 121 0 E
Malinyi, *Tanzania* **119 D4** 8 56 S 36 0 E
Malipo, *China* **76 F5** 23 7N 104 42 E
Maliq, *Albania* **50 F4** 40 45N 20 48 E
Malita, *Phil.* **81 H5** 6 19N 125 39 E
Maliwun, *Burma* **78 B1** 10 17N 98 40 E
Maliya, *India* **92 H4** 23 5N 70 46 E
Maljenik, *Serbia & M.* **50 C5** 43 54N 21 43 E
Malka Mari △, *Kenya* **118 B5** 4 11N 40 46 E
Malkapur, *India* **94 D1** 20 53N 73 58 E
Malkara, *Turkey* **51 F10** 40 53N 26 53 E
Malkhangiri = Malakanagiri, *India* **94 E5** 18 21N 81 54 E
Małkinia Górna, *Poland* **55 F9** 52 42N 22 5 E
Malko Tŭrnovo, *Bulgaria* **51 E11** 41 59N 27 31 E
Mallacoota, *Australia* **129 D8** 37 40 S 149 40 E
Mallacoota Inlet, *Australia* **129 D8** 37 34 S 149 40 E
Mallaig, *U.K.* **22 D3** 57 0N 5 50W
Mallala, *Australia* **128 C3** 34 26 S 138 30 E
Mallaoua, *Niger* **113 C6** 13 2N 9 36 E
Mallard, *U.S.A.* **156 B2** 42 56N 94 41W
Mallawan, *India* **93 F9** 27 4N 80 12 E
Mallawi, *Egypt* **106 B3** 27 44N 30 44 E
Mallee Cliffs △, *Australia* **128 C5** 34 16 S 142 32 E
Mallembe, *Gabon* **114 C2** 3 34 S 10 53 E
Mallemort, *France* **29 E9** 43 43N 5 11 E
Málles Venosta, *Italy* **44 B7** 46 41N 10 32 E
Mállia, *Greece* **39 E6** 35 17N 25 32 E
Mallicolo = Malakula, *Vanuatu* **133 F5** 16 15 S 167 30 E
Mallión, Kólpos, *Greece* **39 E6** 35 19N 25 27 E
Mallorca, *Spain* **38 B4** 39 30N 3 0 E
Mallorytown, *Canada* **151 B9** 44 29N 75 53W
Mallow, *Ireland* **23 D3** 52 8N 8 39W
Malmbäck, *Sweden* **17 G8** 57 34N 14 28 E
Malmberget, *Sweden* **14 C19** 67 11N 20 40 E
Malmédy, *Belgium* **24 D6** 50 25N 6 2 E
Malmesbury, *S. Africa* **116 E2** 33 28 S 18 41 E
Malmivaara = Malmberget, *Sweden* **14 C19** 67 11N 20 40 E
Malmköping, *Sweden* **16 E10** 59 8N 16 44 E
Malmö, *Sweden* **17 J7** 55 36N 12 59 E
Malmslätt, *Sweden* **17 F9** 58 27N 15 33 E
Malmyzh, *Russia* **60 B10** 56 31N 50 41 E
Malnaş, *Romania* **53 D10** 46 2N 25 49 E
Malo, *Vanuatu* **133 E5** 15 40 S 167 11 E
Malo Konare, *Bulgaria* **51 D8** 42 12N 24 24 E
Maloarkhangelsk, *Russia* **59 F9** 52 28N 36 30 E
Maloca, *Brazil* **169 C6** 0 43N 55 57W
Maloja, *Switz.* **33 D9** 46 25N 9 35 E
Malojapass, *Switz.* **33 D9** 46 23N 9 42 E
Malolo, *Fiji* **133 A1** 17 45 S 177 11 E
Malolos, *Phil.* **80 D3** 14 50N 120 49 E
Malolotja ⊂, *Swaziland* **117 D5** 26 4 S 31 6 E
Malombe L., *Malawi* **119 E4** 14 40 S 35 15 E
Małomice, *Poland* **55 G2** 51 34N 15 29 E
Malomir, *Bulgaria* **51 D10** 42 16N 26 32 E
Malone, *Fla., U.S.A.* **152 E4** 30 57N 85 10W
Malone, *N.Y., U.S.A.* **151 B10** 44 51N 74 18W
Malong, *China* **76 E4** 25 24N 103 34 E
Malonga, *Dem. Rep. of the Congo* **115 E4** 10 24 S 23 10 E
Malonno, *Italy* **33 D10** 46 7N 10 18 E
Małopolskie □, *Poland* **55 J7** 49 50N 20 20 E
Malorad, *Bulgaria* **50 C7** 43 28N 23 41 E
Måløy, *Norway* **18 C2** 61 57N 5 6 E
Maloyaroslovets, *Russia* **58 E9** 55 2N 36 20 E
Malpartida, *Spain* **43 F4** 39 26N 6 30W
Malpaso, *Canary Is.* **9 e1** 27 43N 18 3W
Malpelo, I. de, *Colombia* **135 G19** 4 3N 81 35W
Malpica de Bergantiños, *Spain* **42 B2** 43 19N 8 50W
Malprabha →, *India* **95 F3** 16 20N 76 5 E
Malpur, *India* **92 H5** 23 21N 73 27 E
Malpura, *India* **92 F6** 26 17N 75 23 E
Mals = Málles Venosta, *Italy* **44 B7** 46 41N 10 32 E
Malsiras, *India* **94 F2** 17 52N 74 55 E
Malta, *Brazil* **170 C4** 6 54 S 37 31W
Malta, *Idaho, U.S.A.* **158 E7** 42 18N 113 22W
Malta, *Mont., U.S.A.* **158 B10** 48 21N 107 52W
Malta ■, *Europe* **38 F7** 35 55N 14 26 E
Malta ✕ (MLA), *Malta* **38 F7** 35 52N 14 29 E
Maltahöhe, *Namibia* **116 C2** 24 55 S 17 0 E
Maltepe, *Turkey* **51 F13** 40 55N 29 8 E
Malters, *Switz.* **32 B6** 47 3N 8 11 E
Malton, *Canada* **150 C5** 43 42N 79 38W
Malton, *U.K.* **20 C7** 54 8N 0 49W
Malu'a, *Solomon Is.* **133 M11** 8 20 S 160 38 E
Maluko = Manolo Fortich, *Phil.* **81 G5** 8 28N 124 50 E
Maluku, *Dem. Rep. of the Congo* **114 C3** 4 3 S 15 34 E
Maluku, *Indonesia* **79 E7** 1 0 S 127 0 E
Maluku □, *Indonesia* **82 B3** 3 0 S 128 0 E
Maluku Sea = Molucca Sea, *Indonesia* **82 A3** 0 0 125 0 E
Maluku Utara □, *Indonesia* **79 D7** 1 0N 129 0 E
Malumfashi, *Nigeria* **113 C6** 11 48N 7 39 E
Malunda, *Indonesia* **82 B1** 3 0 S 118 50 E
Malundo, *Angola* **115 E4** 14 51 S 22 0 E
Malung, *Sweden* **16 D7** 60 42N 13 44 E
Malungon, *Phil.* **81 H5** 6 16N 125 14 E
Malungsfors, *Sweden* **16 D7** 60 44N 13 33 E
Malur, *India* **95 H3** 13 0N 77 55 E
Maluso, *Phil.* **81 H3** 6 33N 121 53 E
Maluwe, *Ghana* **112 D4** 8 40N 2 17W
Malvaglia, *Switz.* **33 D7** 46 24N 8 59 E
Malvalli, *India* **95 H3** 12 28N 77 8 E
Malvan, *India* **95 F1** 16 2N 73 30 E
Malvern, *U.S.A.* **155 H8** 34 22N 92 49W
Malvern Hills, *U.K.* **21 E5** 52 0N 2 19W
Malvik, *Norway* **18 A7** 63 25N 10 40 E
Malvinas, Is. = Falkland Is. ☑, *Atl. Oc.* **9 f** 51 30 S 59 0W
Malý Dunaj →, *Slovak Rep.* **35 D11** 47 45N 18 9 E
Malya, *Tanzania* **118 C3** 3 5 S 33 38 E
Malybay, *Kazakhstan* **65 B9** 43 30N 78 25 E
Malye Derbety, *Russia* **61 G7** 47 57N 44 42 E
Malyn, *Ukraine* **59 G5** 50 46N 29 3 E
Malyy Lyakhovskiy, Ostrov, *Russia* **67 B15** 74 7N 140 36 E
Mama, *Russia* **67 D12** 58 18N 112 54 E
Mamadysh, *Russia* **60 C10** 55 44N 51 23 E
Mamaku, *N.Z.* **130 E5** 38 5 S 176 8 E
Mamala B., *U.S.A.* **145 K14** 21 15N 157 55W
Mamanguape, *Brazil* **170 C4** 6 50 S 35 4W
Mamanuca Group, *Fiji* **133 A1** 17 35 S 177 5 E
Mamarr Mitlā, *Egypt* **103 E1** 30 2N 32 54 E
Mamasa, *Indonesia* **82 B1** 2 55 S 119 20 E
Mambajao, *Phil.* **81 G5** 9 15N 124 43 E
Mambasa, *Dem. Rep. of the Congo* **118 B2** 1 22N 29 3 E
Mamberamo →, *Indonesia* **83 B5** 2 0 S 137 50 E
Mambéré →, *C.A.R.* **114 B3** 3 31N 16 3 E
Mambili →, *Congo* **114 B3** 0 6N 16 5 E
Mambilima Falls, *Zambia* **119 E2** 10 31 S 28 45 E
Mambirima, *Dem. Rep. of the Congo* **119 E2** 11 25 S 27 33 E
Mambo, *Tanzania* **118 C4** 4 52 S 38 22 E
Mambrui, *Kenya* **118 C5** 3 5 S 40 5 E
Mamburao, *Phil.* **80 E3** 13 13N 120 39 E
Mameigwess L., *Canada* **140 B2** 52 35N 87 50W
Mamers, *France* **26 D7** 48 21N 0 22 E
Mamfé, *Cameroon* **113 D6** 5 50N 9 15 E
Māmī, Ra's, *Yemen* **99 D6** 12 32N 54 30 E
Mamiña, *Chile* **172 E4** 20 5 S 69 14W
Mammoth, *U.S.A.* **159 K8** 32 43N 110 39W
Mammoth Cave △, *U.S.A.* **148 G3** 37 8N 86 13W
Mamonovo, *Russia* **54 D6** 54 28N 19 55 E
Mamoré →, *Bolivia* **173 C4** 10 23 S 65 53W
Mamou, *Guinea* **112 C2** 10 15N 12 0W
Mamoudzou, *Mayotte* **121 a** 12 48 S 45 14 E
Mampatá, *Guinea-Biss.* **112 C2** 11 54N 14 53W
Mampikony, *Madag.* **117 B8** 16 6 S 47 38 E
Mampoko, *Dem. Rep. of the Congo* **114 B3** 0 51N 18 42 E
Mampong, *Ghana* **113 D4** 7 6N 1 26W
Mamry, Jezioro, *Poland* **54 D8** 54 5N 21 50 E
Mamuil Malal, Paso, *S. Amer.* **176 A2** 39 35 S 71 28W
Mamuju, *Indonesia* **82 B1** 2 41 S 118 50 E
Ma'mūl, *Oman* **99 C6** 18 8N 55 16 E
Mamuno, *Botswana* **116 C3** 22 16 S 20 1 E
Mamuras, *Albania* **50 E3** 41 34N 19 41 E
Man, *Ivory C.* **112 D3** 7 30N 7 40W
Man →, *India* **94 F2** 17 31N 75 32 E
Man, I. of, *India* **95 K11** 8 28N 93 36 E
Man, I. of, *U.K.* **20 C3** 54 15N 4 30W
Man-Bazar, *India* **93 H12** 23 4N 86 39 E
Man Kat, *Burma* **90 D7** 22 5N 98 1 E
Man Na, *Burma* **90 D6** 23 27N 97 19 E
Man Tun, *Burma* **90 D7** 23 52N 98 38 E
Mana, *Fr. Guiana* **169 B7** 5 45N 53 55W
Mana, *U.S.A.* **145 A2** 22 2N 159 47W
Mana →, *Fr. Guiana* **169 B7** 5 45N 53 55W
Mana Pools △, *Zimbabwe* **119 F2** 15 56 S 29 25 E
Manaar, G. of = Mannar, G. of, *Asia* **95 K4** 8 30N 79 0 E
Manabí □, *Ecuador* **168 D1** 0 40 S 80 5W
Manacacías →, *Colombia* **168 C3** 4 23N 72 4W
Manacapuru, *Brazil* **169 D5** 3 16 S 60 37W
Manacapuru →, *Brazil* **169 D5** 3 18 S 60 37W
Manacor, *Spain* **38 B4** 39 34N 3 13 E
Manadas, *Azores* **9 d1** 38 38N 28 6W
Manado, *Indonesia* **82 A2** 1 29N 124 51 E
Managua, *Nic.* **164 D2** 12 6N 86 20W
Managua, L. de, *Nic.* **164 D2** 12 20N 86 30W
Manaia, *N.Z.* **130 F3** 39 33 S 174 8 E
Manakara, *Madag.* **117 C8** 22 8 S 48 1 E
Manakau, *N.Z.* **131 C8** 42 15 S 173 42 E
Manākhah, *Yemen* **98 D3** 15 5N 43 44 E
Manali, *India* **92 C7** 32 16N 77 10 E
Manam I., *Papua N. G.* **132 C3** 4 5 S 145 0 E
Manama = Al Manāmah, *Bahrain* **97 E6** 26 10N 50 30 E
Manambao →, *Madag.* **117 B7** 17 35 S 44 0 E
Manambato, *Madag.* **117 A8** 13 43 S 49 7 E
Manambolo →, *Madag.* **117 B7** 19 18 S 44 22 E
Manambolosy, *Madag.* **117 B8** 16 2 S 49 40 E
Mánamo, Caño →, *Venezuela* **169 B5** 9 55N 62 16W
Manana I., *U.S.A.* **145 K14** 21 20N 157 40W
Mananara, *Madag.* **117 B8** 16 10 S 49 46 E
Mananara ⊂, *Madag.* **117 B8** 16 14 S 49 45 E
Mananara →, *Madag.* **117 C8** 23 21 S 47 42 E
Manangatang, *Australia* **128 C5** 35 5 S 142 54 E
Mananjary, *Madag.* **117 C8** 21 13 S 48 20 E
Manankoro, *Mali* **112 C3** 10 28N 7 25W
Manantavadi, *India* **95 J3** 11 49N 76 1 E
Manantenina, *Madag.* **117 C8** 24 17 S 47 19 E
Manaos = Manaus, *Brazil* **169 D6** 3 0 S 60 0W
Manapala, *Phil.* **81 F4** 10 58N 123 5 E
Manapire →, *Venezuela* **168 B4** 7 42N 66 7W
Manapouri, *N.Z.* **131 F2** 45 34 S 167 39 E
Manapouri, L., *N.Z.* **131 F2** 45 32 S 167 32 E
Manapparai, *India* **95 J4** 10 36N 78 25 E
Manaqil, *Sudan* **107 E3** 14 15N 32 59 E
Manar →, *India* **94 E3** 18 50N 77 20 E
Manār, Jabal, *Yemen* **98 D4** 14 2N 44 17 E
Manaravolo, *Madag.* **117 C8** 23 59 S 45 39 E
Manas, *China* **68 B3** 44 17N 85 56 E
Manas, *Somali Rep.* **120 D2** 2 57N 43 28 E
Manas →, *India* **90 B3** 26 12N 90 40 E
Manas, Gora, *Kyrgyzstan* **65 B5** 42 22N 71 2 E
Manaslu, *Nepal* **93 E11** 28 33N 84 33 E
Manasquan, *U.S.A.* **151 F10** 40 8N 74 3W
Manassa, *U.S.A.* **159 H11** 37 11N 105 56W
Manatí, *Puerto Rico* **165 d** 18 26N 66 29W
Manati B., *St. Helena* **9 h** 16 0 S 5 46W
Manatuto, *E. Timor* **82 C3** 8 30 S 126 1 E
Manau, *Papua N. G.* **132 E2** 8 4 S 148 0 E
Manaung, *Burma* **90 F4** 18 45N 93 40 E
Manaus, *Brazil* **169 D6** 3 0 S 60 0W
Manavgat, *Turkey* **100 D4** 36 47N 31 26 E
Manawan = Rizal, *Phil.* **80 C3** 17 51N 121 21 E
Manawan L., *Canada* **143 B8** 55 24N 103 14W
Manawatu →, *N.Z.* **130 G4** 40 28 S 175 12 E
Manawatu-Wanganui □, *N.Z.* **130 F4** 39 50 S 175 30 E
Manay, *Phil.* **81 H6** 7 17N 126 33 E
Manbij, *Syria* **100 D7** 36 31N 37 57 E
Mancha Real, *Spain* **43 H7** 37 48N 3 39W
Manche □, *France* **26 C5** 49 10N 1 20W
Manchegorsk, *Russia* **66 C4** 67 54N 32 58 E
Manchester, *U.K.* **20 D5** 53 29N 2 12W
Manchester, *Calif., U.S.A.* **160 G3** 38 58N 123 41W
Manchester, *Conn., U.S.A.* **151 E12** 41 47N 72 31W
Manchester, *Ga., U.S.A.* **152 C5** 32 51N 84 37W
Manchester, *Iowa, U.S.A.* **156 B5** 42 29N 91 27W
Manchester, *Ky., U.S.A.* **148 G4** 37 9N 83 46W
Manchester, *Mich., U.S.A.* **157 B12** 42 9N 84 2W
Manchester, *N.H., U.S.A.* **151 D13** 42 59N 71 28W
Manchester, *N.Y., U.S.A.* **150 D7** 42 56N 77 16W
Manchester, *Ohio, U.S.A.* **157 F13** 38 41N 83 36W
Manchester, *Pa., U.S.A.* **151 F8** 40 4N 76 43W
Manchester, *Tenn., U.S.A.* **149 H2** 35 29N 86 5W
Manchester, *Vt., U.S.A.* **151 C11** 43 10N 73 5W
Manchester International ✕ (MAN), *U.K.* **20 D5** 53 21N 2 17W
Manchester L., *Canada* **143 A7** 61 28N 107 29W
Manchhar L., *Pakistan* **92 F2** 26 25N 67 39 E
Manchuria = Dongbei, *China* **67 E13** 45 0N 125 0 E
Manchurian Plain, *China* **62 E16** 47 0N 124 0 E
Manciano, *Italy* **45 F8** 42 35N 11 31 E
Mancifa, *Ethiopia* **107 F5** 6 53N 41 50 E
Mancora, *Peru* **172 A1** 4 9 S 81 1W
Mand →, *India* **93 J10** 21 42N 83 15 E
Mand →, *Iran* **97 D7** 28 20N 52 30 E
Manda, *Ludewe, Tanzania* **119 E3** 10 30 S 34 40 E
Manda, *Mbeya, Tanzania* **118 D3** 7 58 S 32 29 E
Manda, *Mbeya, Tanzania* **119 D3** 8 30 S 32 49 E
Manda △, *Chad* **109 G3** 9 45N 17 52 E
Mandabé, *Madag.* **117 C7** 21 0 S 44 55 E
Mandaguari, *Brazil* **175 A5** 23 32 S 51 42W
Mandah = Töhöm, *Mongolia* **74 B5** 44 27N 108 2 E
Mandal, *Norway* **18 F4** 58 2N 7 25 E
Mandala, Puncak, *Indonesia* **83 B6** 4 44 S 140 20 E
Mandalay, *Burma* **90 D6** 22 0N 96 4 E
Mandalay □, *Burma* **90 E5** 22 0N 96 5 E
Mandale = Mandalay, *Burma* **90 D6** 22 0N 96 4 E
Mandalgarh, *India* **92 G6** 25 12N 75 6 E
Mandalgovi, *Mongolia* **74 B4** 45 45N 106 10 E
Mandalī, *Iraq* **101 F11** 33 43N 45 28 E
Mandan, *U.S.A.* **154 B4** 46 50N 100 54W
Mandaon, *Phil.* **80 E4** 12 13N 123 17 E
Mandar, Teluk, *Indonesia* **82 B1** 3 35 S 119 15 E
Mandara Mts., *Nigeria* **109 F2** 10 40N 13 40 E
Mándas, *Italy* **46 C2** 39 40N 9 8 E
Mandasor = Mandsaur, *India* **92 G6** 24 3N 75 8 E
Mandaue, *Phil.* **81 F4** 10 20N 123 56 E
Mandelieu-la-Napoule, *France* **29 E10** 43 34N 6 57 E
Mandera, *Kenya* **118 B5** 3 55N 41 53 E
Mandeville, *Jamaica* **164 a** 18 2N 77 31W
Mandi, *India* **92 D7** 31 39N 76 58 E
Mandi Dabwali, *India* **92 E6** 29 58N 74 42 E
Mandiana, *Guinea* **112 C3** 10 37N 8 39W
Mandigos = Manica, *Mozam.* **117 B5** 18 58 S 32 59 E
Mandimba, *Mozam.* **119 E4** 14 20 S 35 40 E
Mandioli, *Indonesia* **82 B3** 0 40 S 127 20 E
Mandioré, L., *S. Amer.* **173 D6** 18 8 S 57 33W
Mandla, *India* **93 H9** 22 39N 80 30 E
Mandø, *Denmark* **17 J2** 55 18N 8 33 E
Mandorah, *Australia* **124 B5** 12 32 S 130 42 E
Mandoto, *Madag.* **117 B8** 19 34 S 46 17 E
Mandoúdhion, *Greece* **48 C5** 38 48N 23 29 E
Mándra, *Greece* **48 C5** 38 4N 23 30 E
Mandra, *Pakistan* **92 C5** 33 23N 73 12 E
Mandrákhi, *Greece* **49 E9** 36 36N 27 11 E
Mandrare →, *Madag.* **117 D8** 25 10 S 46 30 E
Mandritsara, *Madag.* **117 B8** 15 50 S 48 49 E
Mandronarivo, *Madag.* **117 C8** 21 7 S 45 38 E
Mandsaur, *India* **92 G6** 24 3N 75 8 E
Mandurah, *Australia* **125 F2** 32 36 S 115 48 E
Mandúria, *Italy* **47 B10** 40 24N 17 38 E
Mandvi, *India* **92 H3** 22 51N 69 22 E
Mandya, *India* **95 H3** 12 30N 77 0 E
Mandzai, *Pakistan* **92 D2** 30 55N 67 6 E
Mané, *Burkina Faso* **113 C4** 12 59N 1 21W
Maneh, *Iran* **97 B8** 37 39N 57 7 E
Manengouba, Mts., *Cameroon* **113 E6** 5 0N 9 50 E
Maner →, *India* **94 E4** 18 30N 79 40 E
Manera, *Madag.* **117 C7** 22 55 S 44 20 E
Manérbio, *Italy* **44 C7** 45 21N 10 8 E
Maneroo Cr. →, *Australia* **126 C3** 23 21 S 143 53 E
Manfalût, *Egypt* **106 B3** 27 20N 30 52 E
Manfred, *Australia* **128 B5** 33 19 S 143 45 E
Manfredónia, *Italy* **45 G12** 41 38N 15 55 E
Manfredónia, G. di, *Italy* **45 G13** 41 35N 16 5 E
Manga, *Brazil* **171 D3** 14 46 S 43 56W
Manga, *Burkina Faso* **113 C4** 11 40N 1 4W
Manga, *Congo* **114 C3** 0 13 S 16 5 E
Manga, *Niger* **113 C7** 15 0N 14 0 E
Mangabeiras, Chapada das, *Brazil* **170 D2** 10 0 S 46 30W
Mangai, *Dem. Rep. of the Congo* **115 C3** 4 2 S 19 33 E
Mangaia, *Cook Is.* **135 K12** 21 55 S 157 55W
Mangakino, *N.Z.* **130 E4** 38 22 S 175 47 E
Mangal, *Phil.* **81 H3** 6 25N 121 58 E
Mangalagiri, *India* **95 F5** 16 26N 80 36 E
Mangaldai, *India* **90 B4** 26 26N 92 2 E
Mangaldan, *Phil.* **80 C3** 16 4N 120 24 E
Mangalia, *Romania* **53 G13** 43 50N 28 35 E
Mangalmé, *Chad* **109 F3** 12 26N 19 37 E
Mangalore, *India* **95 H2** 12 55N 74 47 E
Mangalvedha, *India* **94 F2** 17 31N 75 28 E
Mangan, *India* **90 B2** 27 31N 88 32 E
Mangaon, *India* **94 E1** 18 15N 73 20 E
Mangawan, *India* **93 G9** 24 41N 81 33 E
Mangaweka, *N.Z.* **130 F4** 39 48 S 175 47 E
Mangaweka, Mt., *N.Z.* **130 F5** 39 49 S 176 5 E
Mange, *Dem. Rep. of the Congo* **114 B4** 0 54N 20 30 E
Manger, *Norway* **18 D2** 60 38N 5 3 E
Manggar, *Indonesia* **85 C3** 2 50 S 108 10 E
Manggawitu, *Indonesia* **83 B4** 4 8 S 133 32 E
Manggis, *Indonesia* **79 J18** 8 29 S 115 31 E
Mangin Taungdan, *Burma* **90 C5** 24 15N 95 45 E
Mangindrano, *Madag.* **117 A8** 14 17 S 48 58 E
Mangkalihat, Tanjung, *Indonesia* **85 B5** 1 2N 118 59 E
Mangla, *Pakistan* **92 C5** 33 7N 73 39 E
Mangla Dam, *Pakistan* **93 C5** 33 9N 73 44 E
Manglares, C., *Colombia* **168 C2** 1 36N 79 2W
Manglaur, *India* **92 E7** 29 44N 77 49 E
Mangnai, *China* **68 C4** 37 52N 91 43 E
Mango, *Togo* **113 C5** 10 20N 0 30 E
Mango, *Tonga* **133 Q14** 20 17 S 173 25W
Mangoche, *Malawi* **119 E4** 14 25 S 35 16 E
Mangoky →, *Madag.* **117 C7** 21 29 S 43 41 E
Mangole, *Indonesia* **82 B3** 1 50 S 125 55 E
Mangombe, *Dem. Rep. of the Congo* **118 C2** 1 20 S 26 48 E
Mangonui, *N.Z.* **130 B2** 35 1 S 173 32 E
Mangoro →, *Madag.* **117 B8** 20 0 S 48 45 E
Mangrol, *Mad. P., India* **92 J4** 21 7N 70 7 E
Mangrol, *Raj., India* **92 G6** 25 20N 76 31 E
Mangrul Pir, *India* **94 D3** 20 19N 77 21 E
Manguaba = Pilar, *Brazil* **170 C4** 9 36 S 35 56W
Mangualde, *Portugal* **42 E3** 40 38N 7 48W
Mangueigne, *Chad* **109 F4** 10 30N 21 15 E
Mangueira, L. da, *Brazil* **175 C5** 33 0 S 52 50W
Manguéni, Hamada, *Niger* **108 D2** 22 35N 12 40 E
Mangum, *U.S.A.* **155 H5** 34 53N 99 30W
Mangungu, *Dem. Rep. of the Congo* **115 D3** 5 16 S 19 36 E
Mangyshlak, Poluostrov, *Kazakhstan* **66 E6** 44 30N 52 30 E
Manhattan, *U.S.A.* **154 F6** 39 11N 96 35W
Manhatten, *U.S.A.* **157 C9** 41 26N 87 59W
Manhiça, *Mozam.* **117 D5** 25 23 S 32 49 E
Manhuaçu, *Brazil* **171 F3** 20 15 S 42 2W
Manhumirim, *Brazil* **171 F3** 20 22 S 41 57W
Maní, *Colombia* **168 C3** 4 49N 72 17W
Mania →, *Madag.* **117 B8** 19 42 S 45 22 E
Maniago, *Italy* **45 B9** 46 10N 12 43 E
Manica, *Mozam.* **117 B5** 18 58 S 32 59 E
Manica □, *Mozam.* **117 B5** 19 10 S 33 45 E
Manicaland □, *Zimbabwe* **119 F3** 19 0 S 32 30 E
Manicoré, *Brazil* **173 B5** 5 48 S 61 16W
Manicoré →, *Brazil* **173 B5** 5 51 S 61 19W
Manicouagan →, *Canada* **141 C6** 49 30N 68 30W
Manicouagan, Rés., *Canada* **141 B6** 51 5N 68 40W
Maniema □, *Dem. Rep. of the Congo* **118 C2** 3 0 S 26 0 E
Manīfah, *Si. Arabia* **97 E6** 27 44N 49 0 E
Manifold, C., *Australia* **126 C5** 22 41 S 150 50 E
Maniganggo, *China* **76 B2** 31 56N 99 10 E
Manigotagan, *Canada* **143 C9** 51 6N 96 18W
Manigotagan →, *Canada* **143 C9** 51 7N 96 20W
Manihari, *India* **93 G12** 25 21N 87 38 E
Manihiki, *Cook Is.* **135 J11** 10 24 S 161 1W
Manihiki Plateau, *Pac. Oc.* **135 J11** 11 0 S 164 0W
Maniitsoq, *Greenland* **10 D5** 65 26N 52 55W
Manika, Plateau de la, *Dem. Rep. of the Congo* **119 E2** 10 0 S 25 5 E
Manikchhari, *Bangla.* **90 D3** 22 51N 91 50 E
Manikganj, *Bangla.* **90 D3** 23 52N 90 0 E
Manikpur, *India* **93 G9** 25 4N 81 7 E
Manila, *Phil.* **80 D3** 14 40N 121 3 E
Manila, *U.S.A.* **158 F9** 40 59N 109 43W
Manila B., *Phil.* **80 D3** 14 40N 120 35 E
Manildra, *Australia* **129 B8** 33 11 S 148 41 E
Manilla, *Australia* **129 A9** 30 45 S 150 43 E
Manimpé, *Mali* **112 C3** 14 11N 5 28W
Maningrida, *Australia* **126 A1** 12 3 S 134 13 E
Maninian, *Ivory C.* **112 C3** 10 3N 7 52W
Manipa, *Indonesia* **82 B3** 3 17 S 127 35 E
Manipur □, *India* **90 C4** 25 0N 94 0 E
Manipur →, *Burma* **90 D5** 23 45N 94 20 E
Manisa, *Turkey* **49 C9** 38 38N 27 30 E
Manisa □, *Turkey* **49 C9** 38 40N 28 0 E
Manistee, *U.S.A.* **148 C2** 44 15N 86 19W
Manistee →, *U.S.A.* **148 C2** 44 15N 86 21W
Manistique, *U.S.A.* **148 C2** 45 57N 86 15W
Manito, *U.S.A.* **156 D7** 40 26N 89 47W
Manitoba □, *Canada* **143 B9** 53 30N 97 0W
Manitoba, L., *Canada* **143 C9** 51 0N 98 45W
Manitou, *Canada* **143 D9** 49 15N 98 32W
Manitou, L., *Canada* **141 B6** 50 55N 65 17W
Manitou Beach, *U.S.A.* **157 C12** 41 58N 84 19W
Manitou Is., *U.S.A.* **148 C3** 45 8N 86 0W
Manitou L., *Canada* **143 C7** 52 43N 109 43W
Manitou Springs, *U.S.A.* **154 F2** 38 52N 104 55W
Manitoulin I., *Canada* **140 C3** 45 40N 82 30W
Manitouwadge, *Canada* **140 C2** 49 8N 85 48W
Manitowoc, *U.S.A.* **148 C2** 44 5N 87 40W
Manitsauá-Missu →, *Brazil* **173 C7** 10 58 S 53 20W
Maniyachi, *India* **95 K3** 8 51N 77 55 E
Manizales, *Colombia* **168 B2** 5 5N 75 32W
Manja, *Madag.* **117 C7** 21 26 S 44 20 E
Manjacaze, *Mozam.* **117 C5** 24 45 S 34 0 E
Manjakandriana, *Madag.* **117 B8** 18 55 S 47 47 E
Manjeri, *India* **95 J3** 11 7N 76 11 E
Manjhand, *Pakistan* **91 D3** 25 50N 68 10 E
Manjil, *Iran* **97 B6** 36 46N 49 30 E
Manjimup, *Australia* **125 F2** 34 15 S 116 6 E
Manjlegaon, *India* **94 E3** 19 9N 76 14 E
Manjra →, *India* **94 E3** 18 49N 77 52 E
Mankato, *Kans., U.S.A.* **154 F5** 39 47N 98 13W
Mankato, *Minn., U.S.A.* **154 C8** 44 10N 94 0W
Mankayan, *Phil.* **80 C3** 16 52N 120 47 E
Mankayane, *Swaziland* **117 D5** 26 40 S 31 4 E
Mankera, *Pakistan* **92 D4** 31 23N 71 26 E
Mankim, *Cameroon* **113 D7** 5 6N 12 3 E
Mankono, *Ivory C.* **112 D3** 8 1N 6 10W
Mankota, *Canada* **143 D7** 49 25N 107 5W
Mankulam, *Sri Lanka* **95 K5** 9 8N 80 26 E
Manlay = Üydzin, *Mongolia* **74 B4** 44 9N 107 0 E
Manley Hot Springs, *U.S.A.* **144 D10** 65 0N 150 38W
Manlleu, *Spain* **40 C7** 42 2N 2 17 E
Manly, *Australia* **129 B9** 33 48 S 151 17 E
Manmad, *India* **94 D2** 20 18N 74 28 E
Mann Ranges, *Australia* **125 E5** 26 6 S 130 5 E
Manna, *Indonesia* **84 C2** 4 25 S 102 55 E
Mannahill, *Australia* **128 B4** 32 25 S 140 0 E
Mannar, *Sri Lanka* **95 K4** 9 1N 79 54 E
Mannar, G. of, *Asia* **95 K4** 8 30N 79 0 E
Mannar I., *Sri Lanka* **95 K4** 9 5N 79 45 E
Mannargudi, *India* **95 J4** 10 45N 79 51 E
Männedorf, *Switz.* **33 B7** 47 15N 8 43 E
Mannheim, *Germany* **31 F4** 49 29N 8 29 E
Manning, *Canada* **142 B5** 56 53N 117 39W
Manning, *Oreg., U.S.A.* **160 E3** 45 45N 123 13W
Manning, *S.C., U.S.A.* **152 B9** 33 42N 80 13W
Manning →, *Australia* **129 A10** 31 52 S 152 43 E
Manning Str., *Solomon Is.* **133 L10** 7 30 S 158 0 E
Mannu →, *Italy* **46 C2** 39 16N 9 0 E
Mannu, C., *Italy* **46 B1** 40 3N 8 21 E
Mannum, *Australia* **128 C3** 34 50 S 139 20 E
Mano, *S. Leone* **112 D2** 8 3N 12 2W
Mano →, *Liberia* **112 D2** 6 56N 11 30W
Mano River, *Liberia* **112 D2** 7 20N 11 6W
Manoa, *Bolivia* **173 B4** 9 40 S 65 27W
Manoharpur, *India* **93 H11** 22 23N 85 12 E
Manokotak, *U.S.A.* **144 G8** 58 58N 159 3W
Manokwari, *Indonesia* **83 B4** 0 54 S 134 0 E
Manolás, *Greece* **48 C3** 38 4N 21 21 E
Manolo Fortich, *Phil.* **81 G5** 8 28N 124 50 E
Manombo, *Madag.* **117 C7** 22 57 S 43 28 E
Manono, *Dem. Rep. of the Congo* **118 D2** 7 15 S 27 25 E
Manono, *Samoa* **133 W23** 13 50 S 172 5W
Manoppello, *Italy* **45 F11** 42 15N 14 3 E
Manosque, *France* **29 E9** 43 49N 5 47 E
Manotick, *Canada* **151 A9** 45 13N 75 41W
Manouane →, *Canada* **141 C5** 49 30N 71 10W
Manouane, L., *Canada* **141 B5** 50 45N 70 45W
Manovo-Gounda Saint Floris △, *C.A.R.* **114 A4** 9 30N 21 25 E
Manp'o, *N. Korea* **75 D14** 41 6N 126 24 E
Manpojin = Manp'o, *N. Korea* **75 D14** 41 6N 126 24 E
Manpur, *Chhattisgarh, India* **93 H10** 23 17N 83 35 E
Manpur, *Chhattisgarh, India* **94 D5** 20 22N 80 43 E
Manpur, *Mad. P., India* **92 H6** 22 26N 75 37 E
Manresa, *Spain* **40 D6** 41 48N 1 50 E
Mansa, *Gujarat, India* **92 H5** 23 27N 72 45 E
Mansa, *Punjab, India* **92 E6** 30 0N 75 27 E
Mansa, *Zambia* **119 E2** 11 13 S 28 55 E
Mansalay, *Phil.* **80 E3** 12 31N 121 26 E
Månsåsen, *Sweden* **16 A8** 63 5N 14 18 E
Mansehra, *Pakistan* **92 B5** 34 20N 73 15 E
Mansel I., *Canada* **139 B11** 62 0N 80 0W
Mansfield, *Australia* **129 D7** 37 4 S 146 6 E
Mansfield, *U.K.* **20 D6** 53 9N 1 11W
Mansfield, *Ga., U.S.A.* **152 B6** 33 31N 83 44W
Mansfield, *La., U.S.A.* **155 J8** 32 2N 93 43W
Mansfield, *Mass., U.S.A.* **151 D13** 42 2N 71 13W
Mansfield, *Ohio, U.S.A.* **150 F2** 40 45N 82 31W
Mansfield, *Pa., U.S.A.* **150 E7** 41 48N 77 5W
Mansfield, *Tex., U.S.A.* **155 J6** 32 34N 97 9W
Mansfield, Mt., *U.S.A.* **151 B12** 44 33N 72 49W
Mansi, *Burma* **90 C5** 24 48N 95 52 E
Mansidão, *Brazil* **170 D3** 10 43 S 44 2W
Mansilla de las Mulas, *Spain* **42 C5** 42 30N 5 25W
Mansle, *France* **28 C4** 45 52N 0 12 E
Manso →, *Brazil* **171 D2** 13 50 S 47 0W
Mansoa, *Guinea-Biss.* **112 C1** 12 0N 15 20W
Manson, *U.S.A.* **156 B2** 42 32N 94 32W
Manson Creek, *Canada* **142 B4** 55 37N 124 32W
Mansoura, *Algeria* **111 A5** 36 1N 4 31 E
Manta, *Ecuador* **168 D1** 1 0 S 80 40W
Manta, B. de, *Ecuador* **168 D1** 0 54 S 80 44W
Mantadia △, *Madag.* **117 B8** 18 54 S 48 21 E
Mantalingajan, Mt., *Phil.* **81 G1** 8 55N 117 45 E
Mantantale, *Dem. Rep. of the Congo* **114 C4** 2 10 S 20 11 E
Mantare, *Tanzania* **118 C3** 2 42 S 33 13 E
Mantaro →, *Peru* **172 C3** 12 16 S 73 57W
Manteca, *U.S.A.* **160 H5** 37 48N 121 13W
Mantecal, *Venezuela* **168 B4** 7 34N 69 17W
Mantena, *Brazil* **171 E3** 18 47 S 40 59W
Manteno, *U.S.A.* **157 C9** 41 15N 87 50W
Manteo, *U.S.A.* **149 H8** 35 55N 75 40W
Mantes-la-Jolie, *France* **27 D8** 48 58N 1 41 E
Mantha, *India* **94 E3** 19 40N 76 23 E
Manthani, *India* **94 E4** 18 40N 79 35 E
Manti, *U.S.A.* **158 G8** 39 16N 111 38W
Mantiqueira, Serra da, *Brazil* **171 F3** 22 0 S 44 0W
Manton, *U.S.A.* **148 C3** 44 25N 85 24W
Mantorp, *Sweden* **17 F9** 58 21N 15 20 E
Mántova, *Italy* **44 C7** 45 9N 10 48 E
Mänttä, *Finland* **15 E21** 62 3N 24 40 E
Mantua = Mántova, *Italy* **44 C7** 45 9N 10 48 E
Mantung, *Australia* **128 C4** 34 35 S 140 3 E
Manturovo, *Russia* **60 A7** 58 23N 44 45 E
Manu, *Peru* **172 C3** 12 10 S 70 51W
Manu →, *Peru* **172 C3** 12 16 S 70 55W
Manu'a Is., *Amer. Samoa* **133 X25** 14 13 S 169 35W
Manuel Alves →, *Brazil* **171 D2** 11 19 S 48 28W
Manuel Alves Grande →, *Brazil* **170 C2** 7 27 S 47 35W
Manuel Urbano, *Brazil* **172 B4** 8 53 S 69 18W
Manui, *Indonesia* **82 B2** 3 35 S 123 5 E
Manukan, *Phil.* **81 G4** 8 32N 123 12 E
Manukau, *N.Z.* **130 D3** 37 0 S 174 52 E
Manukau Harbour, *N.Z.* **130 D3** 37 3 S 174 45 E
Manunui, *N.Z.* **130 E4** 38 54 S 175 21 E
Manuohou, *N.Z.* **130 E6** 38 39 S 177 7 E
Manuripi →, *Bolivia* **172 C4** 11 6 S 67 36W
Manus □, *Papua N. G.* **132 B4** 2 0 S 147 0 E
Manus I., *Papua N. G.* **132 B4** 2 0 S 147 0 E
Manvi, *India* **95 G3** 15 57N 76 59 E
Manwath, *India* **94 E3** 19 19N 76 32 E
Many, *U.S.A.* **155 K8** 31 34N 93 29W
Manyara, L., *Tanzania* **118 C4** 3 40 S 35 50 E
Manyas, *Turkey* **51 F11** 40 2N 27 59 E
Manyas Gölü = Kus Gölü, *Turkey* **51 F11** 40 10N 27 55 E
Manyava, *Ukraine* **53 B9** 48 39N 24 21 E
Manych →, *Russia* **61 G5** 47 13N 40 40 E
Manych-Gudilo, Ozero, *Russia* **61 G6** 46 24N 42 38 E
Manyonga →, *Tanzania* **118 C3** 4 10 S 34 15 E
Manyoni, *Tanzania* **118 D3** 5 45 S 34 55 E
Manzai, *Pakistan* **92 C4** 32 12N 70 15 E
Manzala, Bahra el, *Egypt* **106 H7** 31 10N 31 56 E
Manzanar ⊂, *U.S.A.* **160 J7** 36 44N 119 5W
Manzanares, *Spain* **43 F7** 39 2N 3 22W
Manzaneda, *Spain* **42 C3** 42 12N 7 15W
Manzanillo, *Cuba* **164 B4** 20 20N 77 31W
Manzanillo, *Mexico* **162 D4** 19 0N 104 20W
Manzanillo, Pta., *Panama* **164 E4** 9 30N 79 40W
Manzano Mts., *U.S.A.* **159 J10** 34 40N 106 20W
Manzariyeh, *Iran* **97 C6** 34 53N 50 50 E
Manzhouli, *China* **69 B6** 49 35N 117 25 E
Manzini, *Swaziland* **117 D5** 26 30 S 31 25 E
Mao, *Chad* **109 F3** 14 4N 15 19 E
Maó, *Spain* **38 B5** 39 53N 4 16 E
Maoka = Kholmsk, *Russia* **67 E15** 47 40N 142 5 E
Maoke, Pegunungan, *Indonesia* **83 B5** 3 40 S 137 30 E
Maolin, *China* **75 C12** 43 58N 123 30 E
Maoming, *China* **77 G8** 21 50N 110 54 E
Maopi T'ou, *China* **77 G13** 21 56N 120 43 E
Maouri, Dallol →, *Niger* **113 C5** 12 5N 3 30 E
Maoxian, *China* **76 B4** 31 41N 103 49 E
Maoxing, *China* **75 B13** 45 28N 124 40 E

Mapalma, Dem. Rep. of the Congo 114 B4 2 3N 24 30 E
Mapam Yumco, China 68 C3 30 45N 81 28 E
Mapastepec, Mexico 163 D6 15 26N 92 54W
Mapfongui, Gabon 114 C2 1 15 S 12 59 E
Maphrao, Ko, Thailand 88 E4 7 56N 98 26 E
Mapi →, Indonesia 83 C5 6 55 S 139 14 E
Mapia, Kepulauan, Indonesia 83 A4 0 50N 134 20 E
Mapimí, Mexico 162 B4 25 50N 103 50W
Mapimí, Bolsón de, Mexico 162 B4 27 30N 104 15W
Maping, China 77 B9 31 34N 113 32 E
Mapinga, Tanzania 118 D4 6 40 S 39 12 E
Mapinhane, Mozam. 117 C6 22 20 S 35 0 E
Mapire, Venezuela 169 B5 7 45N 64 42W
Maple →, U.S.A. 157 B12 42 59N 84 57W
Maple Creek, Canada 143 D7 49 55N 109 29W
Maple Valley, U.S.A. 160 C4 47 25N 122 3W
Mapleton, U.S.A. 158 D2 44 2N 123 52W
Mapourika, L., N.Z. 131 D5 43 16 S 170 12 E
Maprik, Papua N. G. 132 B2 3 44 S 143 3 E
Mapuca, India 95 G1 15 36N 73 46 E
Mapuera →, Brazil 169 D6 1 5 S 57 2W
Mapulanguene, Mozam. 117 C5 24 29 S 32 6 E
Maputo, Mozam. 117 D5 25 58 S 32 32 E
Maputo ⌓, Mozam. 117 D5 26 23 S 32 48 E
Maputo □, Mozam. 117 D5 26 0 S 32 25 E
Maputo, B. de, Mozam. 117 D5 25 50 S 32 45 E
Maqiaohe, China 75 B16 44 40N 130 30 E
Maqnā, Si. Arabia 96 D2 28 25N 34 50 E
Maqran, W. →, Si. Arabia 98 B4 20 55N 47 12 E
Maqteïr, Mauritania 110 D2 21 50N 11 40W
Maquan He = Brahmaputra →, Asia 68 D3 23 40N 90 35 E
Maqueda, Spain 42 E6 40 4N 4 22W
Maqueda Channel, Phil. 80 E5 13 42N 124 1 E
Maquela do Zombo, Angola 115 D3 6 0 S 15 15 E
Maquinchao, Argentina 176 B3 41 15 S 68 50W
Maquoketa, U.S.A. 156 B6 42 4N 90 40W
Mar, Serra do, Brazil 175 B6 25 30 S 49 0W
Mar Chiquita, L., Argentina 174 C3 30 40 S 62 50W
Mar del Plata, Argentina 174 D4 38 0 S 57 30W
Mar Menor, Spain 41 H4 37 40N 0 45W
Mara, Guyana 169 B6 6 0N 57 36W
Mara, India 90 A5 28 11N 94 14 E
Mara, Tanzania 118 C3 1 30 S 34 32 E
Mara □, Tanzania 118 C3 1 45 S 34 20 E
Maraã, Brazil 168 D4 1 52 S 65 25W
Marabá, Brazil 170 C2 5 20 S 49 5W
Maracá, I. de, Brazil 169 C7 2 10N 50 30W
Maracaibo, Venezuela 168 A3 10 40N 71 37W
Maracaibo, L. de, Venezuela 168 B3 9 40N 71 30W
Maracaju, Brazil 175 A4 21 38 S 55 9W
Maracajú, Serra de, Brazil 173 E6 20 57 S 55 1W
Maracanã, Brazil 170 B2 0 46 S 47 27W
Maracás, Brazil 171 D3 13 26 S 40 18W
Maracas Bay Village, Trin. & Tob. 169 F9 10 46N 61 28W
Maracay, Venezuela 168 A4 10 15N 67 28W
Maracena, Spain 43 H7 37 12N 3 38W
Marādah, Libya 108 C3 29 15N 19 15 E
Maradi, Niger 113 C6 13 29N 7 20 E
Maraetiria, Pte., Tahiti 133 S16 17 51 S 149 10W
Marāgheh, Iran 101 D12 37 30N 46 12 E
Maragogipe, Brazil 171 D4 12 46 S 38 55W
Marāh, Si. Arabia 96 E5 25 0N 45 35 E
Marahoue △, Ivory C. 112 D3 8 0N 7 8W
Marais du Cotentin et du Bessin △, France 26 C5 49 10N 1 30W
Marais Poitevin, Val de Sèvre et Vendée △, France 28 B3 46 18N 0 35W
Maraisburg = Hofmeyr, S. Africa 116 E4 31 39 S 25 50 E
Marajó, B. de, Brazil 170 B2 1 0 S 48 30W
Marajó, I. de, Brazil 170 B2 1 0 S 49 30W
Marākand, Iran 96 B5 38 51N 45 16 E
Marakele △, S. Africa 117 E4 32 14 S 25 27 E
Maralal, Kenya 118 B4 1 0N 36 38 E
Maralinga, Australia 125 F5 30 13 S 131 32 E
Maram, India 90 C5 25 25N 94 6 E
Marama, Australia 128 C4 35 10 S 140 10 E
Maramag, Phil. 81 H5 7 46N 125 0 E
Maramaraereğlisi, Turkey 51 F11 40 57N 27 57 E
Maramasike, Solomon Is. 133 M11 9 30 S 161 25 E
Marambio, Antarctica 7 C18 64 0 S 56 0W
Marampa, S. Leone 112 D2 8 45N 12 28W
Maramureş □, Romania 53 C9 47 45N 24 0 E
Maran, Malaysia 87 L4 3 35N 102 45 E
Marana, U.S.A. 159 K8 32 27N 111 13W
Maranboy, Australia 124 B5 14 40 S 132 39 E
Maranchón, Spain 40 D2 41 6N 2 15W
Marand, Iran 101 C11 38 30N 45 45 E
Marandokhóri, Greece 39 B2 38 38N 20 39 E
Marang, Malaysia 87 K4 5 12N 103 13 E
Maranguape, Brazil 170 B4 3 55 S 38 50W
Maranhão = São Luís, Brazil 170 B3 2 39 S 44 15W
Maranhão □, Brazil 170 C3 5 0 S 46 0W
Marano, L. di, Italy 45 C10 45 44N 13 10 E
Maranoa →, Australia 127 D4 27 50 S 148 37 E
Marañón →, Peru 172 A3 4 30 S 73 35W
Marão, Mozam. 117 C5 24 18 S 34 2 E
Marapi →, Brazil 169 C6 0 37N 55 58W
Marari, Brazil 172 B4 5 43 S 67 47W
Maraş = Kahramanmaraş, Turkey 100 D7 37 37N 36 53 E
Mărăşeşti, Romania 53 E12 45 52N 27 14 E
Maratea, Italy 47 C8 39 59N 15 43 E
Marateca, Portugal 43 G2 38 34N 8 40W
Marathasa, Cyprus 39 F8 34 59N 32 51 E
Marathiás, Ákra, Greece 39 D2 37 39N 20 50 E
Marathókambos, Greece 49 D8 37 43N 26 42 E
Marathon, Australia 126 C3 20 51 S 143 32 E
Marathon, Canada 140 C2 48 44N 86 23W
Marathón, Greece 48 C5 38 11N 23 58 E
Marathon, Fla., U.S.A. 153 L8 24 43N 81 5W
Marathon, N.Y., U.S.A. 151 D8 42 27N 76 2W
Marathon, Tex., U.S.A. 155 K3 30 12N 103 15W
Marathóvouno, Cyprus 39 E9 35 13N 33 37 E
Maratua, Indonesia 85 B5 2 10N 118 35 E
Maraú, Brazil 171 D4 14 6 S 39 0W
Marau, Solomon Is. 133 N11 10 31 S 161 31 E
Maraval, Trin. & Tob. 169 F9 10 42N 61 31W
Maravari, Solomon Is. 133 L9 7 50 S 156 42 E
Maravatío, Mexico 162 D4 19 51N 100 25W
Marawi City, Phil. 81 G5 8 0N 124 21 E
Marāwih, U.A.E. 97 E7 24 18N 53 18 E
Marazliyivka 53 D15 46 8N 30 3 E
Marbach, Switz. 32 C5 46 51N 7 53 E
Marbella, Spain 43 J6 36 30N 4 57W
Marble Bar, Australia 124 D2 21 9 S 119 44 E
Marble Falls, U.S.A. 155 K5 30 35N 98 16W
Marblehead, U.S.A. 151 D14 42 30N 70 51W
Mårbu, Norway 18 D5 60 11N 8 9 E
Marburg = Maribor, Slovenia 45 B12 46 36N 15 40 E
Marburg, Germany 30 E4 50 47N 8 46 E
Marcal →, Hungary 52 C2 47 41N 17 40 E
Marcali, Hungary 52 D2 46 35N 17 25 E
Marcapata, Peru 172 C3 13 31 S 70 52W
Marcaria, Italy 44 C7 45 7N 10 32 E
Mărcăuţi, Moldova 53 B12 48 20N 27 14 E
Marceline, U.S.A. 156 E4 39 43N 92 57W
March, U.K. 21 E8 52 33N 0 5 E
Marchal, Dem. Rep. of the Congo 115 D2 5 16 S 14 58 E
Marchand = Rommani, Morocco 110 B3 33 31N 6 40W
Marche, France 28 B5 46 5N 1 20 E
Marche □, Italy 45 E10 43 30N 13 15 E
Marche-en-Famenne, Belgium 24 D5 50 14N 5 19 E
Marchena, Spain 43 H5 37 18N 5 23W
Marchena, Canal de, Ecuador 172 a 0 19N 90 12W
Marchena, I., Ecuador 172 a 0 19N 90 29W
Marches = Marche □, Italy 45 E10 43 30N 13 15 E
Marchesale ⌓, Italy 47 D9 38 32N 16 13 E
Marciana Marina, Italy 44 F7 42 48N 10 12 E
Marcianise, Italy 47 A7 41 2N 14 17 E
Marcigny, France 27 F11 46 17N 4 2 E
Marcillat-en-Combraille, France 27 F9 46 12N 2 38 E
Marck, France 27 B8 50 57N 1 57 E
Marckolsheim, France 27 D14 48 10N 7 30 E
Marco Island, U.S.A. 153 K8 25 58N 81 44W
Marco Rondon, Brazil 173 C5 12 0 S 60 56W
Marcona, Peru 172 D2 15 10 S 75 0W
Marcos Juárez, Argentina 174 C3 32 42 S 62 5W
Mărculeşti, Moldova 53 C13 47 52N 28 14 E
Marcus Baker, Mt., U.S.A. 144 F11 61 26N 147 45W
Marcus I. = Minami-Tori-Shima, Pac. Oc. 134 E7 24 20N 153 58 E
Marcus Necker Ridge, Pac. Oc. 134 F9 20 0N 175 0 E
Marcy, Mt., U.S.A. 151 B11 44 7N 73 56W
Mardan, Pakistan 91 B4 34 20N 72 0 E
Mardarivka, Ukraine 53 C14 47 32N 29 44 E
Mardin, Turkey 101 D9 37 20N 40 43 E
Mårdsjö, Sweden 16 A9 63 18N 15 35 E
Maré, Î., N. Cal. 133 U22 21 30 S 168 0 E
Marécchia →, Italy 45 D9 44 4N 12 34 E
Marechal Deodoro, Brazil 170 C4 9 43 S 35 54W
Marechal Floriano = Piranhas, Brazil 170 C4 9 27 S 37 46W
Maree, L., U.K. 22 D3 57 40N 5 26W
Mareeba, Australia 126 B4 16 59 S 145 28 E
Mareetsane, S. Africa 116 D4 26 9 S 25 25 E
Marek, Indonesia 82 B2 4 41 S 120 24 E
Maremma, Italy 45 F8 42 30N 11 30 E
Maremma ⌓, Italy 44 F8 42 35N 11 8 E
Maréna, Kayes, Mali 112 C2 14 36N 10 45W
Maréna, Koulikouro, Mali 112 C3 13 55N 7 20W
Marengo, Ind., U.S.A. 157 F10 38 22N 86 21W
Marengo, Iowa, U.S.A. 156 C4 41 48N 92 4W
Marennes, France 28 C2 45 49N 1 7W
Marerano, Madag. 117 C7 21 23 S 44 52 E
Maréttimo, Italy 46 E5 37 58N 12 4 E
Mareuil, France 28 C4 45 26N 0 29 E
Marfa, U.S.A. 155 K2 30 19N 104 1W
Marganets = Marhanets, Ukraine 59 J8 47 40N 34 40 E
Margaret →, Australia 124 C4 18 9 S 125 41 E
Margaret Bay, Canada 142 C3 51 20N 127 35W
Margaret L., Canada 142 B5 58 56N 115 25W
Margaret River, Australia 125 F2 33 57 S 115 4 E
Margarita, I. de, Venezuela 169 A5 11 0N 64 0W
Margarítion, Greece 48 B2 39 22N 20 26 E
Margaritovo, Russia 52 C7 43 25N 134 45 E
Margate, S. Africa 117 E5 30 50 S 30 20 E
Margate, U.K. 21 F9 51 23N 1 23 E
Margate, U.S.A. 153 J9 26 15N 80 12W
Margeride, Mts. de la, France 28 D7 44 43N 3 38 E
Marggrabowa = Olecko, Poland 54 D9 54 2N 22 31 E
Margherita, India 90 B5 27 16N 95 40 E
Margherita di Savóia, Italy 47 A9 41 22N 16 9 E
Margherita Pk., Uganda 118 B3 0 22N 29 51 E
Marghilon = Margilan, Uzbekistan 65 C5 40 27N 71 42 E
Marghita, Romania 52 C7 47 22N 22 22 E
Margilan, Uzbekistan 65 C5 40 27N 71 42 E
Margonin, Poland 55 F4 52 58N 17 5 E
Margosatubig, Phil. 81 H4 7 34N 123 10 E
Marguerite, Canada 142 C4 52 30N 122 25W
Marhanets, Ukraine 59 J8 47 40N 34 40 E
Marhoum, Algeria 111 B4 34 27N 0 11W
Mari, Papua N. G. 132 E1 9 11 S 141 42 E
Mari El □, Russia 60 B8 56 30N 48 0 E
Mari Indus, Pakistan 92 C4 32 57N 71 34 E
Mari Republic = Mari El □, Russia 60 B8 56 30N 48 0 E
María, Sa. de, Spain 41 H2 37 39N 2 14W
Maria Aurora, Phil. 80 D3 15 48N 121 28 E
Maria Elena, Chile 174 A2 22 18 S 69 40W
María Grande, Argentina 174 C4 31 45 S 59 55W
Maria I., N. Terr., Australia 126 A2 14 52 S 135 45 E
Maria I., Tas., Australia 127 G4 42 35 S 148 0 E
Maria Island △, Australia 127 G4 42 38 S 148 5 E
Maria Pereira = Mombaça, Brazil 170 C4 5 43 S 39 45W
Maria Theresiopel = Subotica, Serbia & M. 52 D4 46 6N 19 39 E
Maria van Diemen, C., N.Z. 130 A1 34 29 S 172 40 E
Mariager, Denmark 17 H3 56 40N 9 59 E
Mariager Fjord, Denmark 17 H4 56 42N 10 19 E
Mariakani, Kenya 118 C4 3 50 S 39 27 E
Mariala △, Australia 127 D4 25 57 S 145 2 E
Marian, Australia 126 K6 21 9 S 148 57 E
Marian L., Canada 142 A5 63 0N 116 15W
Mariana Trench, Pac. Oc. 62 H18 13 0N 145 0 E
Marianao, Cuba 164 B3 23 8N 82 24W
Mariani, India 90 B5 26 39N 94 19 E
Marianica, Cord. = Morena, Sierra, Spain 43 G7 38 20N 4 0W
Marianna, Ark., U.S.A. 155 H9 34 46N 90 46W
Marianna, Fla., U.S.A. 152 E4 30 46N 85 14W
Mariannelund, Sweden 17 G9 57 37N 15 35 E
Mariánské Lázně, Czech Rep. 34 B5 49 58N 12 41 E
Marias →, U.S.A. 158 C8 47 56N 110 30W
Mariato, Punta, Panama 164 E3 7 12N 80 52W
Mariazell, Austria 34 D8 47 47N 15 19 E
Ma'rib, Yemen 98 D4 15 25N 45 21 E
Maribo, Denmark 17 K5 54 48N 11 30 E
Maribor, Slovenia 45 B12 46 36N 15 40 E
Maricaban I., Phil. 80 E3 13 39N 120 53 E
Marico →, Africa 116 C4 23 35 S 26 57 E
Maricopa, Ariz., U.S.A. 159 K7 33 4N 112 3W
Maricopa, Calif., U.S.A. 161 K7 35 4N 119 24W
Marīdī, Sudan 107 G2 4 55N 29 25 E
Marīdī, Wadi →, Sudan 107 F2 6 15N 29 21 E
Marié →, Brazil 168 D4 0 27 S 66 26W
Marie Byrd Land, Antarctica 7 D14 79 30 S 125 0W
Marie-Galante, Guadeloupe 164 b 15 56N 61 16W
Mariecourt = Kangiqsujuaq, Canada 139 B12 61 30N 72 0W
Mariefred, Sweden 16 E11 59 15N 17 12 E
Mariehamn = Maarianhamina, Finland 15 F18 60 5N 19 55 E
Marieholm, Sweden 17 J7 55 53N 13 10 E
Mariembourg, Belgium 24 D4 50 6N 4 31 E
Marienbad = Mariánské Lázně, Czech Rep. 34 B5 49 58N 12 41 E
Marienberg, Germany 30 E9 50 39N 13 9 E
Marienburg = Malbork, Poland 54 D6 54 3N 19 1 E
Mariental, Namibia 116 C2 24 36 S 18 0 E
Marienville, U.S.A. 150 E5 41 28N 79 8W
Mariestad, Sweden 17 F7 58 43N 13 50 E
Marietta, Ga., U.S.A. 152 B5 33 57N 84 33W
Marietta, Ohio, U.S.A. 148 F5 39 25N 81 27W
Marieville, Canada 151 A11 45 26N 73 10W
Mariga →, Nigeria 113 C6 9 40N 5 55 E
Marignane, France 29 E9 43 25N 5 13 E
Marignier, France 32 D3 46 6N 6 31 E
Marihatag, Phil. 81 G6 8 48N 126 18 E
Mariinsk, Russia 66 D9 56 10N 87 20 E
Mariinsk Water = Volgo-Baltiyskiy Kanal, Russia 58 B9 60 0N 38 0 E
Mariinskiy Posad, Russia 60 B8 56 10N 47 45 E
Marijampolė, Lithuania 15 J20 54 33N 23 19 E
Marijampolės □, Lithuania 54 D10 54 34N 23 21 E
Marília, Brazil 175 A6 22 13 S 50 0W
Marimba, Angola 115 D3 8 28 S 17 8 E
Marín, Spain 42 C2 42 23N 8 42W
Marina, U.S.A. 160 J5 36 41N 121 48W
Marinduque, Phil. 79 B6 13 25N 122 0 E
Marinduque □, Phil. 80 E4 13 18N 122 0 E
Marine City, U.S.A. 150 D2 42 43N 82 30W
Marineland, U.S.A. 152 F8 29 40N 81 13W
Marineo, Italy 46 E6 37 57N 13 25 E
Marinette, U.S.A. 148 C2 45 6N 87 38W
Maringá, Brazil 175 A5 23 26 S 52 2W
Maringa →, Dem. Rep. of the Congo 114 B3 1 14N 19 48 E
Marinha Grande, Portugal 42 F2 39 45N 8 56W
Marinho dos Abrolhos △, Brazil 171 E4 17 50 S 39 0W
Marino, Italy 45 G9 41 46N 12 39 E
Marion, Ala., U.S.A. 149 J2 32 38N 87 19W
Marion, Ill., U.S.A. 155 G10 37 44N 88 56W
Marion, Ind., U.S.A. 157 D11 40 32N 85 40W
Marion, Iowa, U.S.A. 156 B5 42 2N 91 36W
Marion, Kans., U.S.A. 154 F6 38 21N 97 1W
Marion, N.C., U.S.A. 149 H5 35 41N 82 1W
Marion, Ohio, U.S.A. 157 D13 40 35N 83 8W
Marion, S.C., U.S.A. 149 H6 34 11N 79 24W
Marion, Va., U.S.A. 149 G5 36 50N 81 31W
Marion, L., U.S.A. 152 B9 33 28N 80 10W
Marion Bay, Australia 128 C2 35 12 S 136 59 E
Marion I., Ind. Oc. 121 J2 47 0 S 38 0 E
Maripa, Venezuela 169 B5 7 26N 65 9W
Maripasoula, Fr. Guiana 169 C7 3 40N 54 4W
Mariposa, U.S.A. 160 H7 37 29N 119 58W
Mariscal Estigarribia, Paraguay 174 A3 22 3 S 60 40W
Maritime Alps = Maritimes, Alpes, Europe 29 D11 44 10N 7 10 E
Maritimes, Alpes, Europe 29 D11 44 10N 7 10 E
Maritsa = Évros →, Greece 100 B2 41 40N 26 34 E
Maritsá, Greece 38 E12 36 22N 28 8 E
Marium, Mt., Vanuatu 133 F6 16 15 S 168 7 E
Mariupol, Ukraine 59 J9 47 5N 37 31 E
Mariusa △, Venezuela 165 E7 9 24N 61 27W
Marīvān, Iran 101 E12 35 30N 46 25 E
Mariveles, Phil. 80 D3 14 26N 120 29 E
Marj 'Uyūn, Lebanon 103 B4 33 20N 35 35 E
Marjan = Wazikhwah, Afghan. 91 B3 32 11N 68 21 E
Mark Twain L., U.S.A. 156 E5 39 28N 91 55W
Marka = Merca, Somali Rep. 120 D2 1 48N 44 50 E
Marka, Si. Arabia 106 D5 18 14N 41 19 E
Markam, China 76 C2 29 42N 98 38 E
Markapur, India 95 G4 15 44N 79 19 E
Markaryd, Sweden 17 H7 56 28N 13 35 E
Markat, Albania 38 B10 39 44N 20 12 E
Markdale, Canada 150 B4 44 19N 80 39W
Marked Tree, U.S.A. 155 H9 35 32N 90 25W
Markelsdorfer Huk, Germany 30 A7 54 33N 11 4 E
Market Drayton, U.K. 20 E5 52 54N 2 29W
Market Harborough, U.K. 21 E7 52 29N 0 55W
Market Rasen, U.K. 20 D7 53 24N 0 20W
Markham, Canada 150 C5 43 52N 79 16W
Markham →, Papua N. G. 132 D4 6 41 S 147 2 E
Markham, Mt., Antarctica 7 E11 83 0 S 164 0 E
Marki, Poland 55 F8 52 20N 21 2 E
Märkisch Friedland = Mirosławiec, Poland 54 E3 53 20N 16 5 E
Märkische Schweiz ⌓, Germany 30 C10 52 34N 14 2 E
Markit, China 65 D8 38 53N 77 23 E
Markkleeberg, Germany 30 D8 51 16N 12 23 E
Markleeville, U.S.A. 160 G7 38 42N 119 47W
Markounda, C.A.R. 114 A3 7 39N 16 55 E
Markoupoulon, Greece 48 D5 37 53N 23 57 E
Markovac, Serbia & M. 50 B5 44 14N 21 7 E
Markovo, Russia 67 C17 64 40N 170 24 E
Markoye, Burkina Faso 113 C5 14 39N 0 2 E
Marks, Russia 60 E8 51 45N 46 50 E
Marksshtadt = Marks, Russia 60 E8 51 45N 46 50 E
Marksville, U.S.A. 155 K8 31 8N 92 4W
Markt Schwaben, Germany 31 G7 48 11N 11 52 E
Marktoberdorf, Germany 31 H6 47 45N 10 37 E
Marktredwitz, Germany 31 E8 50 1N 12 6 E
Marl, Germany 30 D3 51 39N 7 4 E
Marla, Australia 127 D1 27 19 S 133 33 E
Marlbank, Canada 150 B7 44 26N 77 6W
Marlboro, Mass., U.S.A. 151 D13 42 19N 71 33W
Marlboro, N.Y., U.S.A. 151 E11 41 36N 73 59W
Marlborough, Australia 126 C4 22 46 S 149 52 E
Marlborough, U.K. 21 F6 51 25N 1 43W
Marlborough □, N.Z. 131 B8 41 40 S 173 50 E
Marlborough Downs, U.K. 21 F6 51 27N 1 53W
Marle, France 27 C10 49 43N 3 47 E
Marlin, U.S.A. 155 K6 31 18N 96 54W
Marlow, Germany 30 A8 54 9N 12 33 E
Marlow, U.K. 21 F7 51 34N 0 46W
Marlow, U.S.A. 155 H6 34 39N 97 58W
Marly, Switz. 32 C4 46 47N 7 10 E
Marmagao, India 95 G1 15 25N 73 56 E
Marmande, France 28 D4 44 30N 0 10 E
Marmara, Turkey 51 F11 40 35N 27 34 E
Marmara, Sea of = Marmara Denizi, Turkey 51 F12 40 45N 28 15 E
Marmara Denizi, Turkey 51 F12 40 45N 28 15 E
Marmara Gölü, Turkey 49 C10 38 37N 28 2 E
Marmaris, Turkey 49 E10 36 50N 28 14 E
Marmaris Limanı, Turkey 49 E10 36 50N 28 19 E
Marmelos →, Brazil 173 B5 6 6 S 61 46W
Marmion, Mt., Australia 125 E2 29 16 S 119 50 E
Marmion L., Canada 140 C1 48 55N 91 20W
Marmolada, Mte., Italy 45 B8 46 26N 11 51 E
Marmolejo, Spain 43 G6 38 3N 4 13W
Marmora, Canada 140 D4 44 28N 77 41W
Mármora, La, Italy 46 C2 39 59N 9 20 E
Marnay, France 27 E12 47 16N 5 48 E
Marne, Germany 30 B5 53 56N 9 2 E
Marne □, France 27 D11 48 50N 4 10 E
Marne →, France 27 D9 48 48N 2 24 E
Marneuli, Georgia 61 K7 41 30N 44 48 E
Marnia = Maghnia, Algeria 111 B4 34 50N 1 43W
Marnoo, Australia 128 D5 36 40 S 142 52 E
Maro, Chad 109 G3 8 30N 19 0 E
Maro Reef, U.S.A. 145 F9 25 25N 170 35W
Maroa, U.S.A. 156 D8 40 2N 88 57W
Maroa, Venezuela 168 C4 2 43N 67 33W
Maroala, Madag. 117 B8 15 23 S 47 59 E
Maroantsetra, Madag. 117 B8 15 26 S 49 44 E
Maroelaboom, Namibia 116 B2 19 15 S 18 53 E
Marofandilia, Madag. 117 C7 20 7 S 44 34 E
Marojejy ⌓, Madag. 117 A8 14 26 S 49 21 E
Marolambo, Madag. 117 C8 20 2 S 48 7 E
Maromandia, Madag. 117 A8 14 13 S 48 5 E
Maromokotro, Madag. 117 A8 14 0 S 49 0 E
Marondera, Zimbabwe 119 F3 18 5 S 31 42 E
Maroni →, Fr. Guiana 169 B7 5 30N 54 0W
Marónia, Greece 51 F9 40 53N 25 30 E
Maronne →, France 28 C5 45 5N 1 56 E
Maroochydore, Australia 127 D5 26 29 S 153 5 E
Maroona, Australia 128 D5 37 27 S 142 54 E
Maros, Indonesia 82 C1 5 0 S 119 34 E
Maros →, Hungary 52 D5 46 15N 20 13 E
Marosakoa, Madag. 117 B8 15 26 S 46 38 E
Maroseranana, Madag. 117 B8 18 32 S 48 51 E
Maróstica, Italy 45 C8 45 44N 11 40 E
Marotandrano, Madag. 117 B8 16 10 S 48 50 E
Marotaolano, Madag. 117 A8 12 47 S 49 15 E
Maroua, Cameroon 113 C7 10 40N 14 20 E
Marovato, Madag. 117 B8 15 48 S 48 5 E
Marovoay, Madag. 117 B8 16 6 S 46 39 E
Marowijne □, Suriname 169 C7 4 0N 55 0W
Marowijne →, Suriname 169 B7 5 45N 53 58W
Marquard, S. Africa 116 D4 28 40 S 27 28 E
Marquesas Fracture Zone, Pac. Oc. 135 H15 9 0 S 125 0W
Marquesas Is. = Marquises, Îs., French Polynesia 135 H14 9 30 S 140 0W
Marquesas Keys, U.S.A. 153 L7 24 35N 82 10W
Marquette, U.S.A. 148 B2 46 33N 87 24W
Marquis, St. Lucia 165 f 14 2N 60 54W
Marquise, France 27 B8 50 50N 1 40 E
Marquises, Îs., French Polynesia 135 H14 9 30 S 140 0W
Marra, Gebel, Sudan 107 F2 7 20N 27 35 E
Marra, Pta. da, Angola 115 F2 16 31 S 11 43 E
Marra Cr. →, Australia 129 A7 30 8 S 147 15 E
Marra Marra △, Australia 129 B9 33 30 S 151 4 E
Marracuene, Mozam. 117 D5 25 45 S 32 35 E
Marradi, Italy 45 D8 44 4N 11 37 E
Marrakech, Morocco 110 B3 31 9N 8 0W
Marratxi, Spain 38 B3 39 39N 2 48 E
Marrawah, Australia 127 G3 40 55 S 144 42 E
Marrecas, Serra das, Brazil 170 C3 9 0 S 41 0W
Marree, Australia 127 D2 29 39 S 138 1 E
Marrero, U.S.A. 155 L9 29 54N 90 6W
Marrimane, Mozam. 117 C5 22 58 S 33 34 E
Marromeu, Mozam. 117 B6 18 15 S 36 25 E
Marromeu ⌓, Mozam. 117 B6 19 0 S 36 0 E
Marroquí, Punta, Spain 43 K5 36 0N 5 37W
Marrowie Cr. →, Australia 129 B6 33 23 S 145 40 E
Marruás = Pôrto, Brazil 170 B3 3 54 S 42 42W
Marrubane, Mozam. 119 F4 18 0 S 37 0 E
Marrúbiu, Italy 46 C1 39 40N 8 35 E
Marrupa, Mozam. 119 E4 13 8 S 37 30 E
Mars Bl., Ascension I. 9 g 7 59 S 14 24W
Mars Hill, U.S.A. 149 B12 46 31N 67 52W
Marsá 'Alam, Egypt 106 B3 25 5N 34 54 E
Marsá el Brega, Libya 108 B3 30 24N 19 37 E
Marsá Matrūh, Egypt 106 A2 31 19N 27 9 E
Marsá Sha'b, Sudan 106 C4 22 52N 35 47 E
Marsá Susah, Libya 108 B4 32 52N 21 59 E
Marsabit, Kenya 118 B4 2 18N 38 0 E
Marsabit △, Kenya 118 B4 2 23N 37 56 E
Marsala, Italy 46 E5 37 48N 12 26 E
Marsalforn, Malta 38 E7 36 4N 14 16 E
Mârşani, Romania 53 F9 44 1N 24 1 E
Marsaskala, Malta 38 F8 35 52N 14 34 E
Marsaxlokk, Malta 38 F8 35 51N 14 33 E
Marsaxlokk Bay, Malta 38 F8 35 49N 14 33 E
Marsberg, Germany 30 D4 51 28N 8 52 E
Marsciano, Italy 45 F9 42 54N 12 20 E
Marsden, Australia 129 B7 33 47 S 147 32 E
Marseillan, France 28 E7 43 23N 3 31 E
Marseille, France 29 E9 43 18N 5 23 E
Marseille ✕ (MRS), France 29 E9 43 26N 5 14 E
Marseilles = Marseille, France 29 E9 43 18N 5 23 E
Marseilles, U.S.A. 157 C8 41 20N 88 43W
Marsh I., U.S.A. 155 L9 29 34N 91 53W
Marshall = Fortuna Ledge, U.S.A. 144 F7 61 53N 162 5W
Marshall, Liberia 112 D2 6 8N 10 22W
Marshall, Ark., U.S.A. 155 H8 35 55N 92 38W
Marshall, Ill., U.S.A. 157 E9 39 23N 87 42W
Marshall, Mich., U.S.A. 157 B12 42 16N 84 58W
Marshall, Minn., U.S.A. 154 C7 44 25N 95 45W
Marshall, Mo., U.S.A. 156 E3 39 7N 93 12W
Marshall, Tex., U.S.A. 155 J7 32 33N 94 23W
Marshall →, Australia 126 C2 22 59 S 136 59 E
Marshall, C., Ecuador 172 a 0 1 S 91 12W
Marshall Bennett Is., Papua N. G. 132 E6 8 50 S 151 55 E
Marshall Is. ■, Pac. Oc. 134 G9 9 0N 171 0 E
Marshalltown, U.S.A. 156 B4 42 3N 92 55W
Marshallville = Lewisporte, Canada 141 C8 49 15N 55 3W
Marshallville, U.S.A. 152 C6 32 27N 83 56W
Marshbrook, Zimbabwe 117 B5 18 33 S 31 9 E
Marshfield = Coos Bay, U.S.A. 158 E1 43 22N 124 13W
Marshfield, Mo., U.S.A. 155 G8 37 15N 92 54W
Marshfield, Vt., U.S.A. 151 B12 44 20N 72 20W
Marshfield, Wis., U.S.A. 154 C9 44 40N 90 10W
Marshūn, Iran 97 B6 36 19N 49 23 E
Màrsico Nuovo, Italy 47 B8 40 25N 15 44 E
Märsta, Sweden 16 E11 59 37N 17 52 E
Marstal, Denmark 17 K4 54 51N 10 30 E
Marstrand, Sweden 17 G5 57 53N 11 35 E
Mart, U.S.A. 155 K6 31 33N 96 50W
Marta →, Italy 45 F8 42 14N 11 42 E
Martaban, Burma 90 G6 16 30N 97 35 E
Martaban, G. of, Burma 90 G6 16 5N 96 30 E
Martano, Italy 47 B11 40 12N 18 18 E
Martapura, Kalimantan, Indonesia 85 C4 3 22 S 114 47 E
Martapura, Sumatera, Indonesia 84 C2 4 19 S 104 22 E
Marte, Nigeria 113 C7 12 23N 13 46 E
Martel, France 28 D5 44 57N 1 37 E
Martelange, Belgium 24 E5 49 49N 5 43 E
Martellago, Italy 45 C9 45 33N 12 9 E
Martés, Sierra, Spain 41 F4 39 20N 1 0W
Martfű, Hungary 52 C5 47 1N 20 17 E
Marthaguy Cr. →, Australia 129 A7 30 16 S 147 35 E
Marthapal, India 94 E5 19 24N 81 37 E
Martha's Vineyard, U.S.A. 151 E14 41 25N 70 38W
Martigné-Ferchaud, France 26 E5 47 50N 1 20W
Martigny, Switz. 32 D4 46 6N 7 3 E
Martigues, France 29 E9 43 24N 5 4 E
Martil, Morocco 110 A3 35 36N 5 15W
Martin, Slovak Rep. 35 B11 49 6N 18 58 E
Martin, S. Dak., U.S.A. 154 D4 43 11N 101 44W
Martin, Tenn., U.S.A. 155 G10 36 21N 88 51W
Martín →, Spain 40 D4 41 18N 0 19W
Martin, L., U.S.A. 152 C4 32 41N 85 55W
Martin Pt., U.S.A. 144 A12 70 8N 143 16W
Martin Vaz, Atl. Oc. 8 J9 20 30 S 28 51W
Martina, Switz. 33 C10 46 53N 10 28 E
Martina Franca, Italy 47 B10 40 42N 17 20 E
Martinborough, N.Z. 130 H4 41 14 S 175 29 E
Martinez, Calif., U.S.A. 160 G4 38 1N 122 8W
Martinez, Ga., U.S.A. 149 J4 33 31N 82 4W
Martinho Campos, Brazil 171 E2 19 20 S 45 13W
Martinique ☒, W. Indies 164 c 14 40N 61 0W
Martinique Passage, W. Indies 165 C7 15 15N 61 0W
Martínon, Greece 48 C5 38 35N 23 12 E
Martinópolis, Brazil 175 A5 22 11 S 51 12W
Martin's Bay, Barbados 165 g 13 12N 59 29W
Martins Ferry, U.S.A. 150 F4 40 6N 80 44W
Martinsberg, Austria 34 C8 48 22N 15 9 E
Martinsburg, Pa., U.S.A. 150 F6 40 19N 78 20W
Martinsburg, W. Va., U.S.A. 148 F7 39 27N 77 58W
Martinsicuro, Italy 45 F10 42 54N 13 54 E
Martinsville, Ill., U.S.A. 157 E9 39 20N 87 53W
Martinsville, Ind., U.S.A. 157 E10 39 26N 86 25W
Martinsville, Va., U.S.A. 149 G6 36 41N 79 52W
Marton, N.Z. 130 G4 40 4 S 175 23 E
Martorell, Spain 40 D6 41 28N 1 56 E
Martos, Spain 43 H7 37 44N 3 58W
Martūbah, Libya 108 B4 32 35N 22 46 E
Martuk, Kazakhstan 64 F6 50 46N 56 31 E
Martuni, Armenia 61 K7 40 8N 45 20 E
Maru, Nigeria 113 C6 12 22N 6 22 E
Marudi, Malaysia 85 B4 4 11N 114 19 E
Maruf, Afghan. 91 C2 31 30N 67 6 E
Marugame, Japan 72 C5 34 15N 133 40 E
Marui = Pagwi, Papua N. G. 132 C2 4 4 S 143 2 E
Maruia →, N.Z. 131 B7 41 47 S 172 13 E
Maruim, Brazil 170 D4 10 45 S 37 5W
Marulan, Australia 129 C9 34 43 S 150 3 E
Marunga, Angola 116 B3 17 28 S 20 2 E
Marungu, Mts., Dem. Rep. of the Congo 118 D3 7 30 S 30 0 E
Maruoka, Japan 73 A8 36 9N 136 16 E
Marv Dasht, Iran 97 D7 29 50N 52 40 E
Marvão = Castelo do Piauí, Brazil 170 C3 5 20 S 41 33W
Marvast, Iran 97 D7 30 30N 54 15 E
Marvejols, France 28 D7 44 33N 3 19 E
Marvel Loch, Australia 125 F2 31 28 S 119 29 E
Marwar, India 92 G5 25 43N 73 45 E
Mary, Turkmenistan 66 F7 37 40N 61 50 E
Mary Esther, U.S.A. 153 E3 30 27N 86 38W
Maryborough = Port Laoise, Ireland 23 C4 53 2N 7 18W
Maryborough, Queens., Australia 127 D5 25 31 S 152 37 E
Maryborough, Vic., Australia 128 D5 37 0 S 143 44 E
Maryfield, Canada 143 D8 49 50N 101 35W
Maryino = Pristen, Russia 59 G9 51 15N 36 44 E
Maryland □, U.S.A. 148 F7 39 0N 76 30W
Maryland Junction, Zimbabwe 119 F3 17 45 S 30 31 E
Maryport, U.K. 20 C4 54 44N 3 28W
Mary's Harbour, Canada 141 B8 52 18N 55 51W
Marystown, Canada 141 C8 47 10N 55 10W
Marysville, Canada 142 D5 49 35N 116 0W
Marysville, Calif., U.S.A. 160 F5 39 9N 121 35W
Marysville, Kans., U.S.A. 154 F6 39 51N 96 39W
Marysville, Mich., U.S.A. 150 D2 42 54N 82 29W

Marysville, *Ohio, U.S.A.* **157 D13** 40 14N 83 22W
Marysville, *Wash., U.S.A.* **160 B4** 48 3N 122 11W
Maryville, *Mo., U.S.A.* **156 D2** 40 21N 94 52W
Maryville, *Tenn., U.S.A.* **149 H4** 35 46N 83 58W
Marzo, Punta, *Colombia* **168 B2** 6 50N 77 42W
Marzūq, *Libya* **108 C2** 25 53N 13 57 E
Marzūq □, *Libya* **108 D3** 25 0N 16 0 E
Marzūq, Idehan, *Libya* **108 D2** 24 50N 13 51 E
Masada, *Israel* **103 D4** 31 15N 35 20 E
Masahunga, *Tanzania* **118 C3** 2 6 S 33 18 E
Masai, *Malaysia* **87 d** 1 29N 103 53 E
Masai Mara △, *Kenya* **118 C4** 1 25 S 35 5 E
Masai Steppe, *Tanzania* **118 C4** 4 30 S 36 30 E
Masaka, *Uganda* **118 C3** 0 21 S 31 45 E
Masalembo, Kepulauan, *Indonesia* **85 D4** 5 35 S 114 30 E
Masalima, Kepulauan, *Indonesia* **85 D5** 5 4 S 117 5 E
Masallı, *Azerbaijan* **101 C13** 39 3N 48 40 E
Masamba, *Indonesia* **82 B2** 2 30 S 120 15 E
Masan, *S. Korea* **75 G15** 35 11N 128 32 E
Masandam, Ra's, *Oman* **97 E8** 26 30N 56 30 E
Masasi, *Tanzania* **119 E4** 10 45 S 38 52 E
Masaya, *Nic.* **164 D2** 12 0N 86 7W
Masba, *Nigeria* **113 C7** 11 35N 13 1 E
Masbate, *Phil.* **80 E4** 12 21N 123 36 E
Masbate □, *Phil.* **80 E4** 12 20N 123 30 E
Masbate Pass, *Phil.* **80 E4** 12 30N 123 35 E
Máscali, *Italy* **47 E8** 37 45N 15 12 E
Mascara, *Algeria* **111 A5** 35 26N 0 6 E
Mascarene Is., *Ind. Oc.* **121 G4** 22 0 S 55 0 E
Mascarene Plain, *Ind. Oc.* **121 F4** 13 0 S 53 0 E
Mascarene Ridge, *Ind. Oc.* **121 F5** 11 0 S 61 0 E
Mascota, *Mexico* **162 C4** 20 30N 104 50W
Mascoutah, *U.S.A.* **156 F7** 38 29N 89 48W
Masein, *Burma* **90 D5** 23 22N 94 21 E
Masela, *Indonesia* **83 C3** 8 9 S 129 51 E
Maseru, *Lesotho* **116 D4** 29 18 S 27 30 E
Masfjorden, *Norway* **18 D2** 60 48N 5 18 E
Mashaba, *Zimbabwe* **119 G3** 20 2 S 30 29 E
Mashābih, *Si. Arabia* **96 E3** 25 35N 36 30 E
Mashan, *China* **76 F7** 23 40N 108 11 E
Mashar, *Sudan* **107 F2** 9 16N 26 51 E
Mashatu △, *Botswana* **117 C4** 22 5 S 29 5 E
Mashegu, *Nigeria* **113 D6** 10 0N 5 35 E
Masherbrum, *Pakistan* **93 B7** 35 38N 76 18 E
Mashhad, *Iran* **97 B8** 36 20N 59 35 E
Mashi, *Nigeria* **113 C6** 13 0N 7 54 E
Mashiki, *Japan* **72 E2** 32 51N 130 53 E
Mashīz, *Iran* **97 D8** 29 56N 56 37 E
Mashkel →, *Pakistan* **91 D2** 26 2N 65 19 E
Māshkel, Hāmūn-i-, *Pakistan* **91 C1** 28 20N 62 56 E
Mashki Chāh, *Pakistan* **91 C1** 29 5N 62 30 E
Mashonaland Central □, *Zimbabwe* **117 B5** 17 30 S 31 0 E
Mashonaland East □, *Zimbabwe* **117 B5** 18 0 S 32 0 E
Mashonaland West □, *Zimbabwe* **117 B4** 17 30 S 29 30 E
Mashrakh, *India* **93 F11** 26 7N 84 48 E
Mashtaga = Maştağa, *Azerbaijan* **61 K10** 40 35N 49 57 E
Masi Manimba, *Dem. Rep. of the Congo* **115 C3** 4 40 S 17 54 E
Masibi, *Angola* **115 E4** 11 6 S 22 41 E
Masindi, *Uganda* **118 B3** 1 40N 31 43 E
Masindi Port, *Uganda* **118 B3** 1 43N 32 2 E
Masinloc, *Phil.* **80 D2** 15 32N 119 57 E
Maşīrah, *Oman* **99 B7** 21 0N 58 50 E
Maşīrah, Khalīj, *Oman* **99 B7** 20 10N 58 10 E
Maşīrah, Tur'at, *Oman* **99 B7** 20 30N 58 40 E
Masisea, *Peru* **172 B3** 8 35 S 74 22W
Masisi, *Dem. Rep. of the Congo* **118 C2** 1 23 S 28 49 E
Masjed Soleyman, *Iran* **97 D6** 31 55N 49 18 E
Mask, L., *Ireland* **23 C2** 53 36N 9 22W
Maskelyne Is., *Vanuatu* **133 F5** 16 32 S 167 49 E
Maski, *India* **95 G3** 15 56N 76 46 E
Maskin, *Oman* **97 F8** 23 30N 56 50 E
Maslen Nos, *Bulgaria* **51 D11** 42 18N 27 48 E
Maslinica, *Croatia* **45 E13** 43 24N 16 13 E
Maşna'ah, *Yemen* **99 D5** 14 27N 48 17 E
Masnou = El Masnou, *Spain* **40 D7** 41 28N 2 20 E
Masoala △, *Madag.* **117 B9** 15 30 S 50 12 E
Masoala, Tanjon' i, *Madag.* **117 B9** 15 59 S 50 13 E
Masoarivo, *Madag.* **117 B7** 19 3 S 44 19 E
Masohi = Amahai, *Indonesia* **83 C3** 3 20 S 128 55 E
Masomeloka, *Madag.* **117 C8** 20 17 S 48 37 E
Mason, *Mich., U.S.A.* **157 B12** 42 35N 84 27W
Mason, *Nev., U.S.A.* **160 G7** 38 56N 119 8W
Mason, *Ohio, U.S.A.* **157 E12** 39 22N 84 19W
Mason, *Tex., U.S.A.* **155 K5** 30 45N 99 14W
Mason B., *N.Z.* **131 G2** 46 55 S 167 45 E
Mason City, *Ill., U.S.A.* **156 D7** 40 12N 89 42W
Mason City, *Iowa, U.S.A.* **156 A3** 43 9N 93 12W
Maspalomas, *Canary Is.* **9 e1** 27 46N 15 35W
Maspalomas, Pta., *Canary Is.* **9 e1** 27 43N 15 36W
Masqat, *Oman* **99 B7** 23 37N 58 36 E
Massa, *Congo* **114 C3** 3 45 S 15 29 E
Massa, *Italy* **44 D7** 44 1N 10 9 E
Massa, O. →, *Morocco* **110 B3** 30 2N 9 40W
Massa Maríttima, *Italy* **44 E7** 43 3N 10 52 E
Massachusetts □, *U.S.A.* **151 D13** 42 30N 72 0W
Massachusetts B., *U.S.A.* **151 D14** 42 20N 70 50W
Massafra, *Italy* **47 B10** 40 35N 17 7 E
Massaguet, *Chad* **109 F3** 12 28N 15 26 E
Massakory, *Chad* **109 F3** 13 0N 15 49 E
Massanella, *Spain* **38 B3** 39 48N 2 51 E
Massangano, *Angola* **115 D2** 9 40 S 14 13 E
Massangena, *Mozam.* **117 C5** 21 34 S 33 0 E
Massango, *Angola* **115 D3** 8 1 S 16 10 E
Massapê, *Brazil* **170 B3** 3 31 S 40 19W
Massat, *France* **28 F5** 42 53N 1 21 E
Massawa = Mitsiwa, *Eritrea* **107 D4** 15 35N 39 25 E
Massena, *U.S.A.* **151 B10** 44 56N 74 54W
Massénya, *Chad* **109 F3** 11 21N 16 9 E
Masset, *Canada* **142 C2** 54 2N 132 10W
Masseube, *France* **28 E4** 43 25N 0 34 E
Massiac, *France* **28 C7** 45 15N 3 11 E
Massiah Street, *Barbados* **165 g** 13 9N 59 29W
Massif Central, *France* **28 D7** 44 55N 3 0 E
Massif des Bauges △, *France* **27 G13** 45 40N 6 10 E
Massigui, *Mali* **112 C3** 11 48N 6 50W
Massillon, *U.S.A.* **150 F3** 40 48N 81 32W
Massima, *Gabon* **114 C2** 1 27 S 11 33 E
Massine, O. →, *Algeria* **111 C5** 36 13N 2 12 E
Massinga, *Mozam.* **117 C6** 23 15 S 35 22 E
Massingir, *Mozam.* **117 C5** 23 51 S 32 4 E
Masson-Angers, *Canada* **151 A9** 45 32N 75 25W
Masson I., *Antarctica* **7 C7** 66 10 S 93 20 E
Massouka, *Gabon* **114 C1** 1 37 S 9 56 E
Massow = Maszewo, *Poland* **54 E2** 53 29N 15 3 E
Mastābah, *Si. Arabia* **98 B2** 20 49N 39 26 E
Maştağa, *Azerbaijan* **61 K10** 40 35N 49 57 E
Mastanli = Momchilgrad, *Bulgaria* **51 E9** 41 33N 25 23 E
Masterton, *N.Z.* **130 G4** 40 56 S 175 39 E
Mastic, *U.S.A.* **151 F12** 40 47N 72 54W
Mástikho, Ákra, *Greece* **49 C8** 38 10N 26 2 E
Mastuj, *Pakistan* **93 A5** 36 20N 72 36 E
Mastung, *Pakistan* **91 C2** 29 50N 66 56 E
Mastūrah, *Si. Arabia* **98 B2** 23 7N 38 52 E
Masty, *Belarus* **58 F3** 53 27N 24 38 E
Masuda, *Japan* **72 C3** 34 40N 131 51 E
Masuika, *Dem. Rep. of the Congo* **115 D4** 7 37 S 22 32 E
Masvingo, *Zimbabwe* **119 G3** 20 8 S 30 49 E
Masvingo □, *Zimbabwe* **119 G3** 21 0 S 31 30 E
Maswa △, *Tanzania* **118 C3** 2 58 S 34 19 E
Maşyāf, *Syria* **100 E7** 35 4N 36 20 E
Maszewo, *Poland* **54 E2** 53 29N 15 3 E
Mat →, *Albania* **50 E3** 41 40N 19 35 E
Mata de São João, *Brazil* **171 D4** 12 31 S 38 17W
Mata Utu, *Wall. & F. Is.* **123 C15** 13 17 S 176 8W
Matabele Plain, *Zambia* **115 F4** 16 20 S 23 10 E
Matabeleland North □, *Zimbabwe* **119 F2** 19 0 S 28 0 E
Matabeleland South □, *Zimbabwe* **119 G2** 21 0 S 29 0 E
Mataboor, *Indonesia* **83 B5** 1 41 S 138 3 E
Matachel →, *Spain* **43 G4** 38 50N 6 17W
Matachewan, *Canada* **140 C3** 47 56N 80 39W
Matacuni →, *Venezuela* **169 C4** 3 2N 65 16W
Matadi, *Dem. Rep. of the Congo* **115 D2** 5 52 S 13 31 E
Matagalpa, *Nic.* **164 D2** 13 0N 85 58W
Matagami, *Canada* **140 C4** 49 45N 77 34W
Matagami, L., *Canada* **140 C4** 49 50N 77 40W
Matagorda B., *U.S.A.* **155 L6** 28 40N 96 0W
Matagorda I., *U.S.A.* **155 L6** 28 15N 96 30W
Mataguinao, *Phil.* **80 E5** 12 5N 124 55 E
Matak, *Indonesia* **84 B3** 3 18N 106 16 E
Matakana, *Australia* **129 B6** 32 59 S 145 54 E
Matakana, *N.Z.* **130 C3** 36 21 S 174 43 E
Matala, *Angola* **115 E3** 14 46 S 15 4 E
Mátala, *Greece* **39 F5** 34 59N 24 45 E
Matalaque, *Peru* **172 D3** 16 26 S 70 49W
Matale, *Sri Lanka* **95 L5** 7 30N 80 37 E
Matam, *Senegal* **112 B2** 15 34N 13 17W
Matamata, *N.Z.* **130 D4** 37 48 S 175 47 E
Matameye, *Niger* **113 C6** 13 26N 8 28 E
Matamoros, *Campeche, Mexico* **163 D6** 18 50N 90 50W
Matamoros, *Coahuila, Mexico* **162 B4** 25 33N 103 15W
Matamoros, *Tamaulipas, Mexico* **163 B5** 25 50N 97 30W
Ma'ţan as Sarra, *Libya* **109 D4** 21 45N 22 0 E
Ma'ţan Bishārah, *Libya* **108 D4** 23 0N 22 32 E
Matana, Danau, *Indonesia* **82 B2** 2 28 S 121 20 E
Matandu →, *Tanzania* **119 D3** 8 45 S 34 19 E
Matane, *Canada* **141 C6** 48 50N 67 33W
Matang, *China* **76 F5** 23 30N 104 7 E
Matankari, *Niger* **113 C5** 13 46N 4 1 E
Matanomadh, *India* **92 H3** 23 33N 68 57 E
Matanzas, *Cuba* **164 B3** 23 0N 81 40W
Matapa, *Botswana* **116 C3** 23 11 S 24 39 E
Matapan, C. = Taínaron, Ákra, *Greece* **48 E4** 36 22N 22 27 E
Matapédia, *Canada* **141 C6** 48 0N 66 59W
Matapo △, *Zimbabwe* **119 G2** 20 30 S 29 40 E
Matara, *Sri Lanka* **95 M5** 5 58N 80 30 E
Mataram, *Indonesia* **85 D5** 8 35 S 116 7 E
Matarani, *Peru* **172 D3** 17 0 S 72 10W
Mataranka, *Australia* **124 B5** 14 55 S 133 4 E
Matarma, Râs, *Egypt* **103 E1** 30 27N 32 44 E
Mataró, *Spain* **40 D7** 41 32N 2 29 E
Matarraña →, *Spain* **40 D5** 41 14N 0 22 E
Mataruška Banja, *Serbia & M.* **50 C4** 43 40N 20 40 E
Matasao, *Vanuatu* **133 G6** 17 14 S 168 26 E
Matata, *N.Z.* **130 D5** 37 54 S 176 48 E
Matatiele, *S. Africa* **117 E4** 30 20 S 28 49 E
Mataura, *N.Z.* **131 G3** 46 11 S 168 51 E
Mataura →, *N.Z.* **131 G3** 46 34 S 168 44 E
Mataveri, *Chile* **172 b** 27 9 S 109 27W
Mategua, *Bolivia* **173 C5** 13 1 S 62 48W
Matehuala, *Mexico* **162 C4** 23 40N 100 40W
Mateira, *Brazil* **171 E1** 18 54 S 50 30W
Mateke, *Dem. Rep. of the Congo* **114 C3** 4 52 S 24 25 E
Mateke Hills, *Zimbabwe* **119 G3** 21 48 S 31 0 E
Matelot, *Trin. & Tob.* **169 F9** 10 50N 61 7W
Matera, *Italy* **47 B9** 40 40N 16 36 E
Matese △, *Italy* **47 A7** 41 24N 14 23 E
Matese, Monti del, *Italy* **47 A7** 41 27N 14 22 E
Mátészalka, *Hungary* **52 C7** 47 58N 22 20 E
Matetsi, *Zimbabwe* **119 F2** 18 12 S 26 0 E
Mateur, *Tunisia* **108 A1** 37 0N 9 40 E
Matfors, *Sweden* **16 B11** 62 21N 17 2 E
Matha, *France* **28 C3** 45 52N 0 20W
Matheniko △, *Uganda* **118 B3** 2 49N 34 27 E
Mathis, *U.S.A.* **155 L6** 28 6N 97 50W
Mathoura, *Australia* **129 C6** 35 50 S 144 55 E
Mathráki, *Greece* **38 B9** 39 48N 19 31 E
Mathura, *India* **92 F7** 27 30N 77 40 E
Mati, *Phil.* **81 H6** 6 55N 126 15 E
Matiakoali, *Burkina Faso* **113 C5** 12 28N 1 2 E
Matiali, *India* **93 F13** 26 56N 88 49 E
Matías Romero, *Mexico* **163 D5** 16 53N 95 2W
Matibane, *Mozam.* **119 E5** 14 49 S 40 45 E
Matinhos, *Brazil* **171 G2** 25 49 S 48 32W
Matiri Ra., *N.Z.* **131 B7** 41 38 S 172 20 E
Matjiesfontein, *S. Africa* **116 E3** 33 14 S 20 35 E
Matla →, *India* **93 J13** 21 40N 88 40 E
Matlamanyane, *Botswana* **116 B4** 19 33 S 25 57 E
Matli, *Pakistan* **92 G3** 25 2N 68 39 E
Matlock, *U.K.* **20 D6** 53 9N 1 33W
Matmata, *Tunisia* **108 B1** 33 37N 9 59 E
Matna, *Sudan* **107 E4** 13 49N 35 10 E
Matnog, *Phil.* **80 E5** 12 35N 124 5 E
Mato, *Dem. Rep. of the Congo* **115 D4** 8 1 S 24 24 E
Mato →, *Venezuela* **169 B4** 7 9N 65 7W
Mato, Serrania de, *Venezuela* **168 B4** 6 25N 65 25W
Mato Grosso □, *Brazil* **173 C6** 14 0 S 55 0W
Mato Grosso, Planalto do, *Brazil* **173 C7** 15 0 S 55 0W
Mato Grosso do Sul □, *Brazil* **173 D7** 18 0 S 55 0W
Mato Verde, *Brazil* **171 D1** 11 13 S 50 40W
Matobo = Matapo △, *Zimbabwe* **119 G2** 20 30 S 29 40 E
Matochkin Shar, *Russia* **66 B6** 73 10N 56 40 E
Matong, *Papua N. G.* **132 C6** 5 36 S 151 50 E
Matopo Hills, *Zimbabwe* **119 G2** 20 36 S 28 20 E
Matopos, *Zimbabwe* **119 G2** 20 20 S 28 29 E
Matosinhos, *Portugal* **42 D2** 41 11N 8 42W
Matour, *France* **27 F11** 46 19N 4 29 E
Matroosberg, *S. Africa* **116 E2** 33 23 S 19 40 E
Maţruḩ, *Oman* **99 B7** 23 37N 58 30 E
Matsena, *Nigeria* **113 C7** 13 5N 10 5 E
Matsesta, *Russia* **61 J4** 43 34N 39 51 E
Matsu Tao, *Taiwan* **77 E13** 26 9N 119 56 E
Matsubara = Takahagi, *Japan* **71 F10** 36 43N 140 45 E
Matsudo, *Japan* **73 B11** 35 47N 139 54 E
Matsue, *Japan* **72 B5** 35 25N 133 10 E
Matsum, Ko, *Thailand* **87 b** 9 22N 99 59 E
Matsumae, *Japan* **70 D10** 41 26N 140 7 E
Matsumoto, *Japan* **73 A10** 36 15N 138 0 E
Matsusaka, *Japan* **73 C8** 34 34N 136 32 E
Matsushima, *Japan* **72 E2** 32 30N 130 25 E
Matsuura, *Japan* **72 D1** 33 20N 129 49 E
Matsuyama, *Japan* **72 D4** 33 45N 132 45 E
Matsuzaki, *Japan* **73 C10** 34 43N 138 50 E
Mattagami →, *Canada* **140 B3** 50 43N 81 29W
Mattancheri, *India* **95 K3** 9 50N 76 15 E
Mattawa, *Canada* **140 C4** 46 20N 78 45W
Matterhorn, *Switz.* **32 E5** 45 58N 7 39 E
Mattersburg, *Austria* **35 D9** 47 44N 16 24 E
Matteson, *U.S.A.* **157 C9** 41 30N 87 42W
Matthew, I., *N. Cal.* **123 E13** 22 29 S 171 15 E
Matthew Town, *Bahamas* **165 B5** 20 57N 73 40W
Matthews, *U.S.A.* **157 D11** 40 23N 85 30W
Matthews Ridge, *Guyana* **169 B5** 7 37N 60 10W
Mattice, *Canada* **140 C3** 49 40N 83 20W
Mattili, *India* **94 E6** 18 33N 82 12 E
Mattituck, *U.S.A.* **151 F12** 40 59N 72 32W
Mattō, *Japan* **73 A8** 36 31N 136 34 E
Mattoon, *U.S.A.* **154 F10** 39 29N 88 23W
Matuba, *Mozam.* **117 C5** 24 28 S 32 49 E
Matucana, *Peru* **172 C2** 11 55 S 76 25W
Matugama, *Sri Lanka* **95 L5** 6 31N 80 7 E
Matuka, *Papua N. G.* **132 C3** 4 54 S 145 47 E
Matuku, *Fiji* **133 B2** 19 10 S 179 44 E
Matūn = Khowst, *Afghan.* **91 B3** 33 22N 69 58 E
Matura B., *Trin. & Tob.* **169 F10** 10 39N 61 1W
Maturín, *Venezuela* **169 B5** 9 45N 63 11W
Matusadona △, *Zimbabwe* **119 F2** 16 58 S 28 42 E
Matutum, Mt., *Phil.* **81 H5** 6 22N 125 5 E
Matveyev Kurgan, *Russia* **59 J10** 47 35N 38 57 E
Matxitxako, C., *Spain* **40 B2** 43 28N 2 47W
Mau, *Mad. P., India* **93 F8** 26 17N 78 41 E
Mau, *Ut. P., India* **93 G10** 25 56N 83 33 E
Mau, *Ut. P., India* **93 G9** 25 17N 81 23 E
Mau Escarpment, *Kenya* **118 C4** 0 40 S 36 0 E
Mau Ranipur, *India* **93 G8** 25 16N 79 8 E
Mauban, *Phil.* **80 D3** 14 12N 121 44 E
Maubeuge, *France* **27 B10** 50 17N 3 57 E
Maubin, *Burma* **90 G5** 16 44N 95 39 E
Maubourguet, *France* **28 E4** 43 29N 0 1 E
Maud, Pt., *Australia* **124 D1** 23 6 S 113 45 E
Maude, *Australia* **128 C6** 34 29 S 144 18 E
Maudin Sun, *Burma* **90 G5** 16 0N 94 30 E
Maués, *Brazil* **169 D6** 3 20 S 57 45W
Maués-Acu →, *Brazil* **169 D6** 3 22 S 57 44W
Maughold Hd., *I. of Man* **20 C3** 54 18N 4 18W
Mauguio, *France* **28 E7** 43 37N 4 1 E
Maui, *U.S.A.* **145 C5** 20 48N 156 20W
Maulamyaing = Moulmein, *Burma* **90 G6** 16 30N 97 40 E
Maule □, *Chile* **174 D1** 36 5 S 72 30W
Mauléon-Licharre, *France* **28 E3** 43 14N 0 54W
Maullín, *Chile* **176 B2** 41 38 S 73 37W
Maulvibazar, *Bangla.* **90 C3** 24 29N 91 42 E
Maumee, *U.S.A.* **157 C13** 41 34N 83 39W
Maumee →, *U.S.A.* **157 C13** 41 42N 83 28W
Maumere, *Indonesia* **82 C2** 8 38 S 122 13 E
Maumusson, Pertuis de, *France* **28 C2** 45 48N 1 14W
Maun, *Botswana* **116 C3** 20 0 S 23 26 E
Mauna Kea, *U.S.A.* **145 D6** 19 50N 155 28W
Mauna Loa, *U.S.A.* **145 D6** 19 30N 155 35W
Maunaloa, *U.S.A.* **145 B4** 21 8N 157 13W
Maunalua B., *U.S.A.* **145 K14** 21 15N 157 45W
Maunawili, *U.S.A.* **145 K14** 21 23N 157 46W
Maunga Orito, *Chile* **172 b** 27 10 S 109 25W
Maunga Puakatiki, *Chile* **172 b** 27 6 S 109 15W
Maunga Terevaka, *Chile* **172 b** 27 5 S 109 23W
Maungaturoto, *N.Z.* **130 C3** 36 6 S 174 23 E
Maungdow, *Burma* **90 E4** 20 50N 92 21 E
Maungmagan Kyunzu, *Burma* **86 E1** 14 0N 97 48 E
Maupin, *U.S.A.* **158 D3** 45 11N 121 5W
Maure-de-Bretagne, *France* **26 E5** 47 59N 1 58W
Maurepas, L., *U.S.A.* **155 K9** 30 15N 90 30W
Maures, *France* **29 E10** 43 15N 6 15 E
Mauriac, *France* **28 C6** 45 13N 2 19 E
Maurice, L., *Australia* **125 E5** 29 30 S 131 0 E
Mauriceville, *N.Z.* **130 G4** 40 45 S 175 42 E
Mauricie △, *Canada* **140 C5** 46 45N 73 0W
Maurienne, *France* **29 C10** 45 13N 6 30 E
Mauritania ■, *Africa* **110 D3** 20 50N 10 0W
Mauritius ■, *Ind. Oc.* **121 d** 20 0 S 57 0 E
Mauritius ✕ (MRU), *Mauritania* **121 d** 20 25 S 57 40 E
Mauron, *France* **26 D4** 48 9N 2 18W
Maurs, *France* **28 D6** 44 43N 2 12 E
Mauston, *U.S.A.* **154 D9** 43 48N 90 5W
Mauterndorf, *Austria* **34 D6** 47 9N 13 40 E
Mauthen, *Austria* **34 E6** 46 40N 13 0 E
Mauvezin, *France* **28 E4** 43 44N 0 53 E
Mauvoisin, Barr. de, *Switz.* **32 E4** 45 58N 7 20 E
Mauzé-sur-le-Mignon, *France* **28 B3** 46 12N 0 41W
Mavaca →, *Venezuela* **169 C4** 2 31N 65 11W
Mavinga, *Angola* **115 F4** 15 50 S 20 21 E
Mavli, *India* **92 G5** 24 45N 73 55 E
Mavráta, *Greece* **39 C2** 38 4N 20 44 E
Mavrovë, *Albania* **50 F3** 40 26N 19 32 E
Mavrovo △, *Macedonia* **50 E4** 41 36N 20 45 E
Mavuradonha Mts., *Zimbabwe* **119 F3** 16 30 S 31 30 E
Mawa, *Dem. Rep. of the Congo* **118 B2** 2 45N 26 40 E
Mawai, *India* **93 H9** 22 30N 81 4 E
Mawana, *India* **92 E7** 29 6N 77 58 E
Mawand, *Pakistan* **92 E3** 29 33N 68 38 E
Mawasangka, *Indonesia* **82 C2** 5 17 S 122 18 E
Mawk Mai, *Burma* **90 E6** 20 14N 97 37 E
Mawlaik, *Burma* **90 D5** 23 40N 94 26 E
Mawlamyine = Moulmein, *Burma* **90 G6** 16 30N 97 40 E
Mawlawkho, *Burma* **90 G6** 17 50N 97 38 E
Mawqaq, *Si. Arabia* **96 E4** 27 25N 41 8 E
Mawshij, *Yemen* **98 D3** 13 43N 43 17 E
Mawson Base, *Antarctica* **7 C6** 67 30 S 62 53 E
Mawson Coast, *Antarctica* **7 C6** 68 30 S 63 0 E
Mawsynram, *India* **90 C3** 25 15N 91 30 E
Max, *U.S.A.* **154 B4** 47 49N 101 18W
Maxambamba = Nova Iguaçu, *Brazil* **171 F3** 22 45 S 43 28W
Maxcanú, *Mexico* **163 C6** 20 40N 92 0W
Maxesibeni, *S. Africa* **117 E4** 30 49 S 29 23 E
Maxeys, *U.S.A.* **152 B6** 33 45N 83 11W
Maxhamish L., *Canada* **142 B4** 59 50N 123 17W
Maxixe, *Mozam.* **117 C6** 23 54 S 35 17 E
Maxville, *Canada* **151 A10** 45 17N 74 51W
Maxwell, *N.Z.* **130 F3** 39 51 S 174 49 E
Maxwell, *U.S.A.* **160 F4** 39 17N 122 11W
Maxwelton, *Australia* **126 C3** 20 43 S 142 41 E
May, C., *U.S.A.* **148 F8** 38 56N 74 58W
May Jirgui, *Niger* **109 F1** 13 44N 8 8 E
May Pen, *Jamaica* **164 a** 17 58N 77 15W
May River, *Papua N. G.* **132 C1** 4 19 S 141 58 E
Maya, *Indonesia* **85 C3** 1 10 S 109 35 E
Maya →, *Russia* **67 D14** 60 28N 134 28 E
Maya Mts., *Belize* **163 D7** 16 30N 89 0W
Mayabandar, *India* **95 H11** 12 56N 92 56 E
Mayaguana, *Bahamas* **165 B5** 22 30N 72 44W
Mayagüez, *Puerto Rico* **165 d** 18 12N 67 9W
Mayahi, *Niger* **113 C6** 13 58N 7 40 E
Mayaky, *Ukraine* **53 C14** 47 26N 29 33 E
Mayals = Maials, *Spain* **40 D5** 41 22N 0 30 E
Mayama, *Congo* **114 C2** 3 51 S 14 54 E
Mayāmey, *Iran* **97 B7** 36 24N 55 42 E
Mayang, *China* **76 D7** 27 53N 109 49 E
Mayanup, *Australia* **125 F2** 33 57 S 116 27 E
Mayapán, *Mexico* **163 C7** 20 28N 89 11W
Mayapan, *Yucatán, Mexico* **163 C7** 20 30N 89 25W
Mayaqum, *Kazakhstan* **65 B4** 42 51N 68 3 E
Mayarí, *Cuba* **165 B4** 20 40N 75 41W
Mayaro B., *Trin. & Tob.* **169 F10** 10 14N 60 59W
Mayavaram = Mayuram, *India* **95 J4** 11 3N 79 42 E
Maybell, *U.S.A.* **158 F9** 40 31N 108 5W
Maybole, *U.K.* **22 F4** 55 21N 4 42W
Maychew, *Ethiopia* **107 E4** 12 50N 39 31 E
Maydān, *Iraq* **101 E11** 34 55N 45 37 E
Maydan, *Ukraine* **53 B8** 48 36N 23 29 E
Maydena, *Australia* **127 G4** 42 45 S 146 30 E
Maydī, *Yemen* **98 C3** 16 19N 42 48 E
Mayen, *Germany* **31 E3** 50 19N 7 13 E
Mayenne, *France* **26 D6** 48 20N 0 38W
Mayenne □, *France* **26 D6** 48 10N 0 40W
Mayenne →, *France* **26 E6** 47 30N 0 32W
Mayer, *U.S.A.* **159 J7** 34 24N 112 14W
Mayerthorpe, *Canada* **142 C5** 53 57N 115 8W
Mayesville, *U.S.A.* **152 A9** 34 0N 80 12W
Mayfield, *Ky., U.S.A.* **149 G1** 36 44N 88 38W
Mayfield, *N.Y., U.S.A.* **151 C10** 43 6N 74 16W
Mayhill, *U.S.A.* **159 K11** 32 53N 105 29W
Maykop, *Russia* **61 H5** 44 35N 40 10 E
Mayli-Say = Mayluu-Suu, *Kyrgyzstan* **65 C6** 41 17N 72 24 E
Mayluu-Suu, *Kyrgyzstan* **65 C6** 41 17N 72 24 E
Maymak, *Kyrgyzstan* **65 B5** 42 42N 71 13 E
Maymyo, *Burma* **86 A1** 22 2N 96 28 E
Maynard, *Mass., U.S.A.* **151 D13** 42 26N 71 27W
Maynard, *Wash., U.S.A.* **160 C4** 47 59N 122 55W
Maynard Hills, *Australia* **125 E2** 28 28 S 119 49 E
Mayne →, *Australia* **126 C3** 23 40 S 141 55 E
Maynooth, *Ireland* **23 C5** 53 23N 6 34W
Mayo, *Canada* **138 B6** 63 38N 135 57W
Mayo, *U.S.A.* **152 E6** 30 3N 83 10W
Mayo □, *Ireland* **23 C2** 53 53N 9 3W
Mayo →, *Argentina* **176 C3** 45 45 S 69 45W
Mayo →, *Peru* **172 B2** 6 38 S 76 15W
Mayo Bay, *Phil.* **81 H6** 6 56N 126 22 E
Mayo Daga, *Nigeria* **113 D7** 6 59N 11 25 E
Mayo Faran, *Nigeria* **113 D7** 8 57N 12 4 E
Mayoko, *Congo* **114 C2** 2 18 S 12 49 E
Mayoko, *Dem. Rep. of the Congo* **114 C4** 1 6 S 23 50 E
Mayon Volcano, *Phil.* **80 E4** 13 15N 123 41 E
Mayor Buratovich, *Argentina* **176 A4** 39 15 S 62 37W
Mayor I., *N.Z.* **130 D5** 37 16 S 176 17 E
Mayorga, *Spain* **42 C5** 42 10N 5 16W
Mayotte ⧄, *Ind. Oc.* **121 a** 12 50 S 45 10 E
Mayoyao, *Phil.* **80 C3** 16 59N 121 14 E
Mayraira Pt., *Phil.* **80 B3** 18 39N 120 51 E
Maysān □, *Iraq* **96 D5** 31 55N 47 15 E
Mayskiy, *Russia* **61 J7** 43 47N 44 2 E
Maysville, *Ky., U.S.A.* **157 F13** 38 39N 83 46W
Maysville, *Mo., U.S.A.* **156 E2** 39 53N 94 22W
Mayu, *Indonesia* **82 A3** 1 30N 126 30 E
Mayumba, *Gabon* **114 C2** 3 25 S 10 39 E
Mayuram, *India* **95 J4** 11 3N 79 42 E
Mayville, *N. Dak., U.S.A.* **154 B6** 47 30N 97 20W
Mayville, *N.Y., U.S.A.* **150 D5** 42 15N 79 30W
Mayya, *Russia* **67 C14** 61 44N 130 18 E
Mazabuka, *Zambia* **119 F2** 15 52 S 27 44 E
Mazagán = El Jadida, *Morocco* **110 B3** 33 11N 8 17W
Mazagão, *Brazil* **169 D7** 0 7 S 51 16W
Mazamet, *France* **28 E6** 43 30N 2 20 E
Mazán, *Peru* **168 D3** 3 30 S 73 0W
Māzandarān □, *Iran* **97 B7** 36 30N 52 0 E
Mazapil, *Mexico* **162 C4** 24 38N 101 34W
Mazar, *China* **65 E8** 36 32N 77 1 E
Mazar, O. →, *Algeria* **111 B5** 31 50N 1 36 E
Mazār-e Sharīf, *Afghan.* **65 E3** 36 41N 67 0 E
Mazara del Vallo, *Italy* **46 E5** 37 39N 12 35 E
Mazarredo, *Argentina* **176 C3** 47 10 S 66 50W
Mazarrón, *Spain* **41 H3** 37 38N 1 19W
Mazarrón, G. de, *Spain* **41 H3** 37 27N 1 19W
Mazaruni →, *Guyana* **169 B6** 6 25N 58 35W
Mazatán, *Mexico* **162 B2** 29 0N 110 8W
Mazatenango, *Guatemala* **164 D1** 14 35N 91 30W
Mazatlán, *Mexico* **162 C3** 23 13N 106 25W
Mažeikiai, *Lithuania* **15 H20** 56 20N 22 20 E
Māzhān, *Iran* **97 C8** 32 30N 59 0 E
Mazīnān, *Iran* **97 B8** 36 19N 56 56 E
Mazo Cruz, *Peru* **172 D4** 16 45 S 69 44W
Mazoe, *Mozam.* **119 F3** 16 42 S 33 7 E
Mazoe →, *Mozam.* **119 F3** 16 20 S 33 30 E
Mazomanie, *U.S.A.* **156 A7** 43 11N 89 48W
Mazon, *U.S.A.* **157 C8** 41 14N 88 25W
Mazowe, *Zimbabwe* **119 F3** 17 28 S 30 58 E
Mazowieckie □, *Poland* **55 F8** 52 40N 21 0 E
Mazrûb, *Sudan* **107 E2** 14 0N 29 20 E
Mazu Dao, *China* **77 D12** 26 10N 119 55 E
Mazurian Lakes = Mazurski, Pojezierze, *Poland* **54 E7** 53 50N 21 0 E
Mazurski, Pojezierze, *Poland* **54 E7** 53 50N 21 0 E
Mazyr, *Belarus* **59 F5** 51 59N 29 15 E
Mba, *Fiji* **133 A1** 17 33 S 177 41 E
Mbaba, *Senegal* **112 C1** 14 59N 16 44W
Mbabane, *Swaziland* **117 D5** 26 18 S 31 6 E
Mbaéré →, *C.A.R.* **114 B3** 3 47N 17 31 E
Mbagne, *Mauritania* **112 B2** 16 6N 14 47W
M'bahiakro, *Ivory C.* **112 D4** 7 33N 4 19W
Mbaïki, *C.A.R.* **114 B3** 3 53N 18 1 E
Mbakana, Mt. de, *Cameroon* **114 A3** 7 57N 15 6 E
Mbala, *Zambia* **119 D3** 8 46 S 31 24 E
Mbalabala, *Zimbabwe* **117 C4** 20 27 S 29 3 E
Mbale, *Uganda* **118 B3** 1 8N 34 12 E
Mbali →, *C.A.R.* **114 B3** 4 27N 18 20 E
Mbalmayo, *Cameroon* **113 E7** 3 33N 11 33 E
Mbam →, *Cameroon* **113 E7** 4 24N 11 17 E
Mbamba Bay, *Tanzania* **119 E3** 11 13 S 34 49 E
Mbandaka, *Dem. Rep. of the Congo* **114 B3** 0 1N 18 18 E
Mbanga, *Cameroon* **113 E6** 4 30N 9 33 E
Mbanika, *Solomon Is.* **133 M10** 9 3 S 159 13 E
M'Banio, Lagune, *Gabon* **114 C2** 3 35 S 11 0 E
Mbanza Congo, *Angola* **115 D2** 6 18 S 14 16 E
Mbanza Ngungu, *Dem. Rep. of the Congo* **115 D2** 5 12 S 14 53 E
Mbarangandu, *Tanzania* **119 D4** 10 11 S 36 48 E
Mbarara, *Uganda* **118 C3** 0 35 S 30 40 E
Mbari →, *C.A.R.* **114 B4** 4 34N 22 43 E
Mbashe →, *S. Africa* **117 E4** 32 15 S 28 54 E
Mbatto, *Ivory C.* **112 D4** 6 28N 4 22W
Mbava, *Solomon Is.* **133 L9** 7 47 S 156 33 E
Mbé, *Congo* **114 C3** 3 14 S 15 50 E
Mbe, *Eq. Guin.* **114 B1** 1 47N 9 56 E
Mbengga = Beqa, *Fiji* **133 B2** 18 23 S 178 8 E
Mbengué, *Gabon* **114 C2** 2 2 S 11 7 E
Mbengui, *Gabon* **114 C2** 2 3 S 10 4 E
Mbenkuru →, *Tanzania* **119 D4** 9 25 S 39 50 E
Mbéré →, *Cameroon* **114 A3** 7 45N 15 36 E
Mberengwa, *Zimbabwe* **119 G2** 20 29 S 29 57 E
Mberengwa, Mt., *Zimbabwe* **119 G2** 20 37 S 29 55 E
Mberubu, *Nigeria* **113 D6** 6 10N 7 38 E
Mbesuma, *Zambia* **119 E3** 10 0 S 32 2 E
Mbeya, *Tanzania* **119 D3** 8 54 S 33 29 E
Mbeya □, *Tanzania* **118 D3** 8 15 S 33 30 E
Mbigou, *Gabon* **114 C2** 1 53 S 11 56 E
M'bili, *Sudan* **107 F2** 7 35N 28 15 E
Mbinga, *Tanzania* **119 E4** 10 50 S 35 0 E
Mbini = Río Muni □, *Eq. Guin.* **114 B2** 1 30N 10 0 E
Mbini, *Eq. Guin.* **114 B1** 1 35N 9 37 E
Mboi, *Dem. Rep. of the Congo* **115 D4** 6 57 S 21 54 E
Mboki, *C.A.R.* **107 F2** 5 19N 25 58 E
Mbokonimbeti, *Solomon Is.* **133 M11** 8 57 S 160 7 E
Mboli, *Dem. Rep. of the Congo* **114 B4** 4 8N 23 9 E
M'bonge, *Cameroon* **113 E6** 4 33N 9 5 E
Mboro, *Senegal* **112 B1** 15 9N 16 54W
Mboua, *Cameroon* **114 A2** 4 25N 14 16 E
M'boukou, Rés. de, *Cameroon* **113 D7** 6 23N 12 50 E
Mboune, *Senegal* **112 C2** 14 42N 13 34W
Mbouoma, *Congo* **114 C3** 0 52 S 15 4 E
Mbour, *Senegal* **112 C1** 14 22N 16 54W
Mbout, *Mauritania* **112 B2** 16 1N 12 38W
Mbrés, *C.A.R.* **114 A3** 6 40N 19 48 E
M'Bridge →, *Angola* **115 D2** 7 12 S 12 51 E
Mbuji-Mayi, *Dem. Rep. of the Congo* **118 D1** 6 9 S 23 40 E
Mbulu, *Tanzania* **118 C4** 3 45 S 35 30 E
Mbuma, *Dem. Rep. of the Congo* **114 B4** 3 32N 24 50 E
Mbuma, *Solomon Is.* **133 M11** 8 59 S 160 46 E
Mburucuyá, *Argentina* **174 B4** 28 1 S 58 14W
M'bwat, *Cameroon* **114 A2** 6 29N 10 45 E
McCarran International, Las Vegas ✕ (LAS), *U.S.A.* **161 J11** 36 5N 115 9W
Mcherrah, *Algeria* **110 C4** 27 0N 4 30W
Mchinja, *Tanzania* **119 D4** 9 44 S 39 45 E
Mchinji, *Malawi* **119 E3** 13 47 S 32 58 E
McMurdo, *Antarctica* **7 D11** 77 0 S 140 0 E
Mdennah, *Mauritania* **110 D3** 24 37N 6 0W
Mé Maoya, *N. Cal.* **133 U19** 21 22 S 165 22 E
Mead, L., *U.S.A.* **161 J12** 36 1N 114 44W
Meade, *U.S.A.* **155 G4** 37 17N 100 20W
Meade →, *U.S.A.* **144 A9** 70 52N 155 55W
Meade River, *U.S.A.* **144 A8** 70 28N 157 24W
Meadow Lake, *Canada* **143 C7** 54 10N 108 26W
Meadow Lake △, *Canada* **143 C7** 54 27N 109 0W
Meadow Valley Wash →, *U.S.A.* **161 J12** 36 40N 114 34W
Meadville, *Mo., U.S.A.* **156 E3** 39 47N 93 18W
Meadville, *Pa., U.S.A.* **150 E4** 41 39N 80 9W
Meaford, *Canada* **140 D3** 44 36N 80 35W
Mealhada, *Portugal* **42 E2** 40 22N 8 27W
Mealy Mts., *Canada* **141 B8** 53 10N 58 0W
Meander River, *Canada* **142 B5** 59 2N 117 42W
Meares, C., *U.S.A.* **158 D2** 45 37N 124 0W
Mearim →, *Brazil* **170 B3** 3 4 S 44 35W
Meath □, *Ireland* **23 C5** 53 40N 6 57W
Meath Park, *Canada* **143 C7** 53 27N 105 22W
Meaulne, *France* **27 F9** 46 36N 2 36 E
Meaux, *France* **27 D9** 48 58N 2 50 E
Mebechi-Gawa →, *Japan* **70 D10** 40 31N 141 31 E
Mebonden, *Norway* **18 A8** 63 13N 11 2 E
Mebulu, Tanjung, *Indonesia* **79 K18** 8 50 S 115 5 E
Mecanhelas, *Mozam.* **119 F4** 15 12 S 35 54 E
Mecaya →, *Colombia* **168 C2** 0 29N 75 11W
Mecca = Makkah, *Si. Arabia* **98 B2** 21 30N 39 54 E
Mecca, *U.S.A.* **161 M10** 33 34N 116 5W
Mechanicsburg, *Ohio, U.S.A.* **157 D13** 40 4N 83 33W
Mechanicsburg, *Pa., U.S.A.* **150 F8** 40 13N 77 1W
Mechanicsville, *U.S.A.* **156 C5** 41 54N 91 16W
Mechanicville, *U.S.A.* **151 D11** 42 54N 73 41W
Mechara, *Ethiopia* **107 F5** 8 36N 40 20 E
Mechelen, *Belgium* **24 C4** 51 2N 4 29 E
Mecheria, *Algeria* **111 B4** 33 35N 0 18W
Mechernich, *Germany* **30 E2** 50 35N 6 39 E
Mechetinskaya, *Russia* **61 G5** 46 45N 40 32 E
Mechra Bel Ksiri, *Morocco* **110 B3** 34 34N 5 57W
Mechra Benâbbou, *Morocco* **110 B3** 32 39N 7 48W
Mecidiye, *Turkey* **51 F10** 40 38N 26 32 E
Mecitözü, *Turkey* **100 B6** 40 32N 35 17 E

Mecklenburg, Germany 36 B6 53 33N 11 40 E
Mecklenburg-Vorpommern □, Germany 30 B8 53 45N 12 15 E
Mecklenburger Bucht, Germany 30 A7 54 20N 11 40 E
Meconta, Mozam. 119 E4 14 59 S 39 50 E
Mecsek, Hungary 52 D3 46 10N 18 18 E
Meda, Portugal 42 E3 40 57N 7 18W
Medak, India 94 E4 18 1N 78 15 E
Medan, Indonesia 84 B1 3 40N 98 38 E
Médanos, Argentina 176 A4 38 50 S 62 42W
Médanos de Coro △, Venezuela 165 D6 11 35N 69 44W
Medanosa, Pta., Argentina 176 C3 48 8 S 66 0W
Medart, U.S.A. 152 E5 30 5N 84 23W
Medaryville, U.S.A. 157 C10 41 5N 86 55W
Medawachchiya, Sri Lanka 95 K5 8 30N 80 30 E
Medchal, India 94 F4 17 37N 78 29 E
Mede, Italy 44 C5 45 6N 8 44 E
Médéa, Algeria 111 A5 36 12N 2 50 E
Mededa, Bos.-H. 52 G4 43 44N 19 10 E
Médégué, Gabon 114 B2 0 37N 10 8 E
Medeiros Neto, Brazil 171 E3 17 20 S 40 14W
Medel, Pic, Switz. 33 C7 46 34N 8 55 E
Medellín, Colombia 168 B2 6 15N 75 35W
Medelpad, Sweden 16 B10 62 33N 16 30 E
Medemblik, Neths. 24 B5 52 46N 5 8 E
Médenine, Tunisia 108 B2 33 21N 10 30 E
Mederdra, Mauritania 112 B1 17 0N 15 38W
Medford, Mass., U.S.A. 151 D13 42 25N 71 7W
Medford, Oreg., U.S.A. 158 E2 42 19N 122 52W
Medford, Wis., U.S.A. 154 C9 45 9N 90 20W
Medgidia, Romania 53 F13 44 15N 28 19 E
Medi, Sudan 107 F3 5 4N 30 42 E
Media Agua, Argentina 174 C2 31 58 S 68 25W
Media Luna, Argentina 174 C2 34 45 S 66 44W
Medianeira, Brazil 175 B5 25 17 S 54 5W
Mediapolis, U.S.A. 156 D5 41 0N 91 10W
Mediaş, Romania 53 D9 46 9N 24 22 E
Medicilândia, Brazil 169 D7 3 33 S 53 8W
Medicina, Italy 45 D8 44 28N 11 38 E
Medicine Bow, U.S.A. 158 F10 41 54N 106 12W
Medicine Bow Mts., U.S.A. 158 F10 41 10N 106 25W
Medicine Bow Pk., U.S.A. 158 F10 41 21N 106 19W
Medicine Hat, Canada 143 D6 50 0N 110 45W
Medicine Lake, U.S.A. 154 A2 48 30N 104 30W
Medicine Lodge, U.S.A. 155 G5 37 17N 98 35W
Medina = Al Madīnah, Si. Arabia 96 E3 24 35N 39 52 E
Medina, Brazil 171 E3 16 15 S 41 29W
Medina, Colombia 168 C3 4 30N 73 21W
Medina, Phil. 81 G5 8 55N 125 0 E
Medina, N. Dak., U.S.A. 154 B5 46 54N 99 18W
Medina, N.Y., U.S.A. 150 C6 43 13N 78 23W
Medina, Ohio, U.S.A. 150 E3 41 8N 81 52W
Medina →, U.S.A. 155 L5 29 16N 98 29W
Medina de Pomar, Spain 42 C7 42 56N 3 29W
Medina de Ríoseco, Spain 42 D5 41 53N 5 3W
Medina del Campo, Spain 42 D6 41 18N 4 55W
Medina L., U.S.A. 155 L5 29 32N 98 56W
Medina Sidonia, Spain 43 J5 36 28N 5 57W
Medinaceli, Spain 40 D2 41 12N 2 30W
Medinipur, India 93 H12 22 25N 87 21 E
Mediterranean Sea, Europe 12 H7 35 0N 15 0 E
Medjerda, O. →, Tunisia 108 A2 37 7N 10 13 E
Mednogorsk, Russia 64 F6 51 24N 57 37 E
Medny = Mednogorsk, Russia 64 F6 51 24N 57 37 E
Médoc, France 28 C3 45 10N 0 50W
Medora, U.S.A. 157 F10 38 49N 86 10W
Médouneu, Gabon 114 B2 0 57N 10 47 E
Medulin, Croatia 45 D10 44 49N 13 55 E
Medveđa, Serbia & M. 50 D5 42 50N 21 32 E
Medvedevo, Russia 60 B8 56 37N 47 47 E
Medveditsa →, Tver, Russia 58 D9 57 5N 37 30 E
Medveditsa →, Volgograd, Russia 60 F6 49 35N 42 41 E
Medvedok, Russia 60 B10 57 20N 50 1 E
Medvezhi, Ostrava, Russia 67 B17 71 0N 161 0 E
Medvezhye = Krasnogvardeyskoye, Russia 61 H5 45 52N 41 33 E
Medvezhyegorsk, Russia 56 B5 63 0N 34 25 E
Medway □, U.K. 21 F8 51 25N 0 32 E
Medway →, U.K. 21 F8 51 27N 0 46 E
Medzev, Slovak Rep. 35 C13 48 43N 20 55 E
Medzilaborce, Slovak Rep. 35 B14 49 17N 21 52 E
Medžitlija, Macedonia 50 F5 40 56N 21 26 E
Meekatharra, Australia 125 E2 26 32 S 118 29 E
Meeker, U.S.A. 158 F10 40 2N 107 55W
Meelpaeg Res., Canada 141 C8 48 15N 56 33W
Meeniyan, Australia 129 E7 38 35 S 146 0 E
Meersburg, Germany 31 H5 47 41N 9 16 E
Meerut, India 92 E7 29 1N 77 42 E
Meeteetse, U.S.A. 158 D9 44 9N 108 52W
Mega, Ethiopia 107 G4 3 57N 38 19 E
Megálo Khorío, Greece 49 E9 36 27N 27 24 E
Megálo Petalí, Greece 48 D6 38 0N 24 15 E
Megalópolis, Greece 48 D4 37 25N 22 7 E
Meganísi Nisís, Greece 39 B2 38 38N 20 46 E
Mégara, Greece 48 D5 37 58N 23 22 E
Megasini, India 93 J12 21 38N 86 21 E
Megdhova →, Greece 48 B3 39 10N 21 45 E
Megève, France 29 C10 45 51N 6 37 E
Meghalaya □, India 90 C3 25 50N 91 0 E
Meghezez, Ethiopia 107 F4 9 18N 39 26 E
Meghna →, Bangla. 90 D3 22 50N 90 50 E
Mégiscane, L., Canada 140 C4 48 35N 75 55W
Megiste, Greece 49 E11 36 8N 29 34 E
Megra, Russia 58 B9 60 11N 37 14 E
Mehadia, Romania 52 F7 44 56N 22 23 E
Mehaïguene, O. →, Algeria 111 B5 32 15N 2 59 E
Meharry, Mt., Australia 124 D2 22 59 S 118 35 E
Mehedeby, Sweden 16 D11 60 27N 17 25 E
Mehedinţi □, Romania 52 F7 44 40N 22 45 E
Meheisa, Sudan 106 D3 19 38N 32 57 E
Mehekar, India 94 D3 20 9N 76 34 E
Mehlville, U.S.A. 154 F9 38 30N 90 19W
Mehndawal, India 93 F10 26 58N 83 5 E
Mehr Jān, Iran 97 C7 33 50N 55 6 E
Mehrābād, Iran 101 D12 36 53N 47 55 E
Mehrān, Iran 101 F12 33 7N 46 10 E
Mehrīz, Iran 97 D7 31 35N 54 28 E
Mehun-sur-Yèvre, France 27 E9 47 10N 2 13 E
Mei Jiang →, China 77 E11 24 25N 116 35 E
Mei Xian, China 74 G4 34 18N 107 55 E
Meia Ponte →, Brazil 171 E2 18 32 S 49 36W
Meicheng, China 77 C12 29 29N 119 16 E
Meichengzhen, China 77 C8 28 9N 111 40 E
Meichuan, China 77 B10 30 8N 115 31 E
Meiganga, Cameroon 114 A2 6 30N 14 25 E
Meigs, U.S.A. 152 D5 31 4N 84 6W
Meigu, China 76 C4 28 16N 103 20 E
Meiktila, Burma 90 E5 20 53N 95 54 E
Meilen, Switz. 33 B7 47 16N 8 39 E
Meinerzhagen, Germany 30 D3 51 6N 7 38 E
Meiningen, Germany 30 E6 50 34N 10 25 E
Meio →, Brazil 171 D3 13 36 S 44 7W
Meira, Serra de, Spain 42 B3 43 15N 7 15W
Meiringen, Switz. 32 C6 46 43N 8 12 E
Meishan, China 76 B4 30 3N 103 23 E
Meissen, Germany 30 D9 51 9N 13 29 E
Meissner, Germany 30 D5 51 14N 9 50 E
Meissner-Kaufunger Wald ⌓, Germany 30 D5 51 16N 9 45 E
Meitan, China 76 D6 27 45N 107 29 E
Meizhou, China 77 E11 24 16N 116 6 E
Meja, India 93 G10 25 9N 82 7 E
Mejillones, Chile 174 A1 23 10 S 70 30W
Mékambo, Gabon 114 B2 1 2N 13 50 E
Mekdela, Ethiopia 107 E4 11 24N 39 10 E
Mekele, Ethiopia 107 E4 13 33N 39 30 E
Mekerghene, Sebkra, Algeria 111 C5 26 21N 1 30 E
Mekhomiya = Razlog, Bulgaria 50 E7 41 53N 23 28 E
Mekhtar, Pakistan 91 C3 30 30N 69 15 E
Meknès, Morocco 110 B3 33 57N 5 33W
Meko, Nigeria 113 D5 7 27N 2 52 E
Mekong →, Asia 87 H6 9 30N 106 15 E
Mekongga, Indonesia 82 B2 3 39 S 121 15 E
Mekoryuk, U.S.A. 144 F6 60 23N 166 11W
Mekrou →, Benin 113 C5 12 25N 2 50 E
Mekvari = Kür →, Azerbaijan 101 C13 39 29N 49 15 E
Mel, Italy 45 B9 46 4N 12 5 E
Melagiri Hills, India 95 H3 12 20N 77 30 E
Melah, Oued el →, Algeria 111 C6 32 20N 2 28 E
Melah, Sebkhet el, Algeria 111 C4 29 20N 1 30W
Melaka, Malaysia 87 L4 2 15N 102 15 E
Melaka □, Malaysia 84 B2 2 15N 102 15 E
Melalap, Malaysia 78 C5 5 10N 116 5 E
Mélambes, Greece 39 E5 35 8N 24 40 E
Melanesia, Pac. Oc. 134 H7 4 0 S 155 0 E
Melapalaiyam, India 95 K3 8 39N 77 44 E
Melawi →, Indonesia 85 B4 0 5N 111 29 E
Melaya, Indonesia 79 J17 8 17 S 114 30 E
Melbourne, Australia 129 D6 37 50 S 145 0 E
Melbourne, Fla., U.S.A. 153 G9 28 5N 80 37W
Melbourne, Iowa, U.S.A. 156 C3 41 57N 93 6W
Melcher-Dallas, U.S.A. 156 C3 41 14N 93 15W
Melchor Múzquiz, Mexico 162 B4 27 50N 101 30W
Melchor Ocampo, Mexico 162 C4 24 52N 101 40W
Meldal, Norway 18 A6 63 3N 9 44 E
Méldola, Italy 45 D9 44 7N 12 5 E
Meldorf, Germany 30 A5 54 5N 9 5 E
Mélé, C.A.R. 114 A4 9 46N 21 33 E
Mele B., Vanuatu 133 G6 17 44 S 168 14 E
Meleden, Somali Rep. 120 B3 10 25N 49 51 E
Melegnano, Italy 44 C6 45 21N 9 19 E
Meleizem, Mauritania 110 D2 22 19N 11 24W
Melekess = Dimitrovgrad, Russia 60 C9 54 14N 49 39 E
Melenci, Serbia & M. 52 E5 45 32N 20 20 E
Melenki, Russia 60 C5 55 20N 41 37 E
Meleuz, Russia 64 E6 52 58N 55 55 E
Mélèzes →, Canada 140 A5 57 40N 69 29W
Melfi, Chad 109 F3 11 0N 17 59 E
Melfi, Italy 47 B8 41 0N 15 39 E
Melfort, Canada 143 C8 52 50N 104 37W
Melfort, Zimbabwe 119 F3 18 0 S 31 25 E
Melgaço, Portugal 42 C2 42 7N 8 15W
Melgar de Fernamental, Spain 42 C6 42 27N 4 17W
Melgraseyri, Iceland 11 A4 66 1N 22 27W
Melhus, Norway 18 A7 63 17N 10 18 E
Melide, Spain 42 C2 42 55N 8 1W
Melide, Switz. 33 E7 45 57N 8 57 E
Meligalá, Greece 48 D3 37 15N 21 59 E
Melilla, N. Afr. 111 A4 35 21N 2 57W
Melilli, Italy 47 E8 37 11N 15 7 E
Melipilla, Chile 174 C1 33 42 S 71 15W
Mélissa, Ákra, Greece 39 E5 35 6N 24 33 E
Mélissa Óros, Greece 49 D8 37 32N 26 4 E
Melissani Cave, Greece 39 C2 38 15N 20 38 E
Melita, Canada 143 D8 49 15N 101 0W
Mélito di Porto Salvo, Italy 47 E8 37 55N 15 47 E
Melitopol, Ukraine 59 J8 46 50N 35 22 E
Melk, Austria 34 C8 48 13N 15 20 E
Mellan Fryken, Sweden 16 E7 59 45N 13 10 E
Mellansel, Sweden 14 E18 63 26N 18 19 E
Mellbystrand, Sweden 17 H6 56 30N 12 56 E
Melle, France 28 B3 46 14N 0 10W
Melle, Germany 30 C4 52 12N 8 20 E
Mellègue, O. →, Tunisia 108 A1 36 36N 9 14 E
Mellen, U.S.A. 154 B9 46 20N 90 40W
Mellerud, Sweden 17 F6 58 41N 12 28 E
Mellette, U.S.A. 154 C5 45 9N 98 30W
Mellid = Melide, Spain 42 C2 42 55N 8 1W
Mellieha, Malta 38 F7 35 57N 14 22 E
Mellieha Bay, Malta 38 F7 35 59N 14 22 E
Mellit, Sudan 107 E2 14 7N 25 34 E
Mellizo Sur, Cerro, Chile 176 C2 48 33 S 73 10W
Mellrichstadt, Germany 30 E6 50 25N 10 17 E
Melnik, Bulgaria 50 E7 41 30N 23 25 E
Mělník, Czech Rep. 34 A7 50 22N 14 23 E
Melnytsya Podilska, Ukraine 53 B11 48 37N 26 10 E
Melo, Uruguay 175 C5 32 20 S 54 10W
Melolo, Indonesia 82 C2 9 53 S 120 40 E
Melouprey, Cambodia 86 F5 13 48N 105 16 E
Melrhir, Chott, Algeria 111 B6 34 13N 6 30 E
Melrose, Australia 129 B7 32 42 S 146 57 E
Melrose, U.K. 22 F6 55 36N 2 43W
Melrose, Minn., U.S.A. 154 C7 45 40N 94 49W
Melrose, N. Mex., U.S.A. 155 H3 34 26N 103 38W
Mels, Switz. 33 B8 47 3N 9 25 E
Melsisi, Vanuatu 133 E6 15 46 S 168 10 E
Melstone, U.S.A. 158 C10 46 36N 107 52W
Melsungen, Germany 30 D5 51 7N 9 32 E
Melton, Australia 128 D6 37 41 S 144 35 E
Melton Mowbray, U.K. 20 E7 52 47N 0 54W
Melun, France 27 D9 48 32N 2 39 E
Melur, India 95 J4 10 2N 78 23 E
Melut, Sudan 107 E3 10 30N 32 13 E
Melville, Canada 143 C8 50 55N 102 50W
Melville, C., Australia 126 A3 14 11 S 144 30 E
Melville, C., Phil. 81 H1 7 49N 117 0 E
Melville, L., Canada 141 B8 53 30N 60 0W
Melville B., Australia 126 A2 12 0 S 136 45 E
Melville B., Greenland 10 B4 75 30N 63 0W
Melville I., Australia 124 B5 11 30 S 131 0 E
Melville I., Canada 6 B2 75 30N 112 0W
Melville Pen., Canada 139 B11 68 0N 84 0W
Mélykút, Hungary 52 D4 46 11N 19 25 E
Memaliaj, Albania 50 F3 40 25N 19 56 E
Memba, Mozam. 119 E5 14 11 S 40 30 E
Memboro, Indonesia 82 C1 9 30 S 119 30 E
Membrilla, Spain 43 G7 38 59N 3 21W
Memel = Klaipėda, Lithuania 15 J19 55 43N 21 10 E
Memel, S. Africa 117 D4 27 38 S 29 36 E
Memmingen, Germany 31 H6 47 58N 10 10 E
Mempawah, Indonesia 85 B3 0 30N 109 5 E
Memphis, Egypt 106 J7 29 52N 31 12 E
Memphis, Mich., U.S.A. 150 D2 42 54N 82 46W
Memphis, Mo., U.S.A. 156 D4 40 28N 92 10W
Memphis, Tenn., U.S.A. 155 H10 35 8N 90 3W
Memphis, Tex., U.S.A. 155 H4 34 44N 100 33W
Memphremagog, L., U.S.A. 151 B12 45 0N 72 12W
Mena, Ukraine 59 G7 51 31N 32 13 E
Mena, U.S.A. 155 H7 34 35N 94 15W
Mena →, Ethiopia 107 F5 5 40N 40 50 E
Menai Strait, U.K. 20 D3 53 11N 4 13W
Ménaka, Mali 113 B5 15 59N 2 18 E
Menan = Chao Phraya →, Thailand 86 F3 13 32N 100 36 E
Menarandra →, Madag. 117 D7 25 17 S 44 30 E
Menard, U.S.A. 155 K5 30 55N 99 47W
Menard Fracture Zone, Pac. Oc. 135 M18 43 0 S 97 0W
Menate, Indonesia 85 C4 0 12 S 113 3 E
Menawashei, Sudan 107 E1 12 41N 24 59 E
Mendawai →, Indonesia 85 C4 3 30 S 113 0 E
Mende, France 28 D7 44 31N 3 30 E
Mendebo Mts., Ethiopia 107 F4 7 0N 39 22 E
Mendeleyev Ridge, Arctic 6 B17 80 0N 178 0W
Menden, Germany 30 D3 51 26N 7 47 E
Mendenhall, C., U.S.A. 144 G6 59 45N 166 10W
Menderes, Turkey 49 C9 38 14N 27 8 E
Mendez, Mexico 163 B5 25 7N 98 34W
Mendhar, India 93 C6 33 35N 74 10 E
Mendi, Ethiopia 107 F4 9 47N 35 4 E
Mendi, Papua N. G. 132 D2 6 11 S 143 39 E
Mendip Hills, U.K. 21 F5 51 17N 2 40W
Mendocino, U.S.A. 158 G2 39 19N 123 48W
Mendocino, C., U.S.A. 158 F1 40 26N 124 25W
Mendocino Fracture Zone, Pac. Oc. 135 D13 40 0N 142 0W
Mendon, U.S.A. 157 B11 42 0N 85 27W
Mendooran, Australia 129 A8 31 50 S 149 6 E
Mendota, Calif., U.S.A. 160 J6 36 45N 120 23W
Mendota, Ill., U.S.A. 156 C7 41 33N 89 7W
Mendoyo, Indonesia 79 J17 8 23 S 114 42 E
Mendoza, Argentina 174 C2 32 50 S 68 52W
Mendoza □, Argentina 174 C2 33 0 S 69 0W
Mendrisio, Switz. 33 E7 45 52N 8 59 E
Mene Grande, Venezuela 168 B3 9 49N 70 56W
Menemen, Turkey 49 C9 38 34N 27 3 E
Menen, Belgium 24 D3 50 47N 3 7 E
Menéndez, L., Argentina 176 B2 42 40 S 71 51W
Ménerville = Thenia, Algeria 111 A5 36 44N 3 33 E
Menfi, Italy 46 E5 37 36N 12 58 E
Mengdingjie, China 76 F2 23 31N 98 58 E
Mengeš, Slovenia 45 B11 46 10N 14 35 E
Menggala, Indonesia 84 C3 4 30 S 105 15 E
Menghai, China 76 G3 21 49N 100 55 E
Mengíbar, Spain 43 H7 37 58N 3 48W
Mengjin, China 74 G7 34 55N 112 45 E
Mengla, China 76 G3 21 20N 101 25 E
Menglian, China 76 F2 22 21N 99 27 E
Mengoub, Algeria 110 C3 29 49N 5 26W
Mengshan, China 77 E8 24 14N 110 55 E
Mengyin, China 75 G9 35 40N 117 58 E
Mengzhe, China 76 F3 22 2N 100 15 E
Mengzi, China 76 F4 23 20N 103 22 E
Menihek, Canada 141 B6 54 28N 56 36W
Menihek L., Canada 141 B6 54 0N 67 0W
Menin = Menen, Belgium 24 D3 50 47N 3 7 E
Menindee, Australia 128 B5 32 20 S 142 25 E
Menindee L., Australia 128 B5 32 20 S 142 25 E
Meningie, Australia 128 C3 35 50 S 139 18 E
Menjangan, Pulau, Indonesia 79 J17 8 7 S 114 31 E
Menkrour, Algeria 111 C6 26 27N 8 9 E
Menlo Park, U.S.A. 160 H4 37 27N 122 12W
Menominee, U.S.A. 148 C2 45 6N 87 37W
Menominee →, U.S.A. 148 C2 45 6N 87 36W
Menomonee Falls, U.S.A. 157 A8 43 11N 88 7W
Menomonie, U.S.A. 154 C9 44 53N 91 55W
Menongue, Angola 115 E3 14 48 S 17 52 E
Menorca, Spain 38 B5 40 0N 4 0 E
Menorca ✈ (MAH), Spain 40 F9 39 50N 4 16 E
Mentakab, Malaysia 87 L4 3 29N 102 21 E
Mentasta Lake, U.S.A. 144 E12 62 55N 143 45W
Mentawai, Kepulauan, Indonesia 84 C1 2 0 S 99 0 E
Menton, France 29 E11 43 50N 7 29 E
Mentone, U.S.A. 157 C10 41 10N 86 2W
Mentor, U.S.A. 150 E3 41 40N 81 21W
Menyamya, Papua N. G. 132 D3 7 10 S 145 59 E
Menzel-Bourguiba, Tunisia 108 A1 37 9N 9 49 E
Menzel-Chaker, Tunisia 108 B2 35 0N 10 26 E
Menzel-Temime, Tunisia 108 A2 36 46N 11 0 E
Menzelinsk, Russia 64 D4 55 47N 53 11 E
Menzies, Australia 125 E3 29 40 S 121 2 E
Meob B., Namibia 116 C1 24 25 S 14 34 E
Me'ona, Israel 103 B4 33 1N 35 15 E
Meoqui, Mexico 162 B3 28 17N 105 29W
Mepaco, Mozam. 119 F3 15 57 S 30 48 E
Meppel, Neths. 24 B6 52 42N 6 12 E
Meppen, Germany 30 C3 52 42N 7 17 E
Mequinenza, Spain 40 D5 41 22N 0 17 E
Mequinenza, Embalse de, Spain 40 D5 41 25N 0 15 E
Mequon, U.S.A. 157 A9 43 14N 87 59W
Mer, France 26 E8 47 42N 1 30 E
Merabéllou, Kólpos, Greece 39 E6 35 10N 25 50 E
Merai, Papua N. G. 132 C7 4 52 S 152 19 E
Merak, Indonesia 79 F12 6 10N 106 26 E
Meråker, Norway 18 A8 63 25N 11 46 E
Meramangye, L., Australia 125 E5 28 25 S 132 13 E
Meramec →, U.S.A. 156 F6 38 24N 90 21W
Meran = Merano, Italy 45 B8 46 40N 11 9 E
Merano, Italy 45 B8 46 40N 11 9 E
Merate, Italy 44 C6 45 42N 9 25 E
Merauke, Indonesia 83 C6 8 29 S 140 24 E
Merauke →, Indonesia 83 C6 8 30 S 140 24 E
Merbabu, Indonesia 85 D4 7 30 S 110 40 E
Merbein, Australia 128 C5 34 10 S 142 2 E
Merbuk, Gunung, Indonesia 79 J17 8 13 S 114 39 E
Merca, Somali Rep. 120 D2 1 48N 44 50 E
Mercantour △, France 29 D10 44 16N 6 43 E
Mercato Saraceno, Italy 45 E9 43 57N 12 12 E
Merced, U.S.A. 160 H6 37 18N 120 29W
Merced →, U.S.A. 160 H6 37 21N 120 59W
Merced Pk., U.S.A. 160 H7 37 36N 119 24W
Mercedes, Buenos Aires, Argentina 174 C4 34 40 S 59 30W
Mercedes, Corrientes, Argentina 174 B4 29 10 S 58 5W
Mercedes, San Luis, Argentina 174 C2 33 40 S 65 21W
Mercedes, Phil. 80 D4 14 7N 123 1 E
Mercedes, Uruguay 174 C4 33 12 S 58 0W
Merceditas, Chile 174 B1 28 20 S 70 35W
Mercer, N.Z. 130 D4 37 16 S 175 5 E
Mercer, Mo., U.S.A. 156 D3 40 31N 93 32W
Mercer, Pa., U.S.A. 150 E4 41 14N 80 15W
Mercer Island, U.S.A. 160 C4 47 35N 122 15W
Mercier, Bolivia 172 C4 10 42 S 68 5W
Mercury, U.S.A. 161 J11 36 40N 115 58W
Mercury B., N.Z. 130 C4 36 48 S 175 45 E
Mercury Is., N.Z. 130 C4 36 37 S 175 52 E
Mercy, C., Canada 139 B13 65 0N 63 30W
Merdrignac, France 26 D4 48 11N 2 27W
Mere, U.K. 21 F5 51 6N 2 16W
Mere Lava, Vanuatu 133 D6 14 25 S 168 3 E
Meredith, Australia 128 D6 37 49 S 144 5 E
Meredith, C., Falk. Is. 9 f 52 15 S 60 40W
Meredith, L., U.S.A. 155 H4 35 43N 101 33W
Meredosia, U.S.A. 156 E6 39 50N 90 34W
Merefa, Ukraine 59 H9 49 48N 36 3 E
Meregh, Somali Rep. 120 D3 3 46N 47 18 E
Merei, Romania 53 E11 45 7N 26 43 E
Merga = Nukheila, Sudan 106 D2 19 1N 26 21 E
Mergui, Burma 86 F2 12 26N 98 34 E
Mergui Arch. = Myeik Kyunzu, Burma 87 G1 11 30N 97 30 E
Meribah, Australia 128 C4 34 43 S 140 51 E
Méribel-les-Allues, France 29 C10 45 25N 6 34 E
Meriç, Turkey 51 E10 41 11N 26 25 E
Meriç →, Turkey 51 F10 40 52N 26 12 E
Mérida, Mexico 163 C7 20 58N 89 37W
Merida, Phil. 81 F5 10 55N 124 32 E
Mérida, Spain 43 G4 38 55N 6 25W
Mérida, Venezuela 168 B3 8 24N 71 8W
Mérida □, Venezuela 168 B3 8 30N 71 10W
Mérida, Cord. de, Venezuela 168 B3 9 0N 71 0W
Meriden, U.K. 21 E6 52 26N 1 38W
Meriden, U.S.A. 151 E12 41 32N 72 48W
Meridian, Calif., U.S.A. 160 F5 39 9N 121 55W
Meridian, Ga., U.S.A. 152 D8 31 27N 81 23W
Meridian, Idaho, U.S.A. 158 E5 43 37N 116 24W
Meridian, Miss., U.S.A. 149 J1 32 22N 88 42W
Mérignac, France 28 D3 44 51N 0 39W
Merimbula, Australia 129 D8 36 53 S 149 54 E
Mérinaghène, Senegal 112 B1 15 57N 15 55W
Merinda, Australia 126 C4 20 2 S 148 11 E
Mering, Germany 31 G6 48 16N 10 59 E
Meringa, Nigeria 113 C7 10 44N 12 9 E
Meringur, Australia 128 C4 34 20 S 141 19 E
Merir, Pac. Oc. 79 D8 4 10N 132 30 E
Merirumã, Brazil 169 C7 1 15N 54 50W
Merke, Kazakhstan 65 B6 42 52N 73 11 E
Merkel, U.S.A. 155 J5 32 28N 100 1W
Mermaid Reef, Australia 124 C2 17 6 S 119 36 E
Meroe, India 95 L11 7 33N 93 33 E
Merowe, Sudan 106 D3 18 29N 31 46 E
Merredin, Australia 125 F2 31 28 S 118 18 E
Merrick, U.K. 22 F4 55 8N 4 28W
Merrickville, Canada 151 B9 44 55N 75 50W
Merrill, Oreg., U.S.A. 158 E3 42 1N 121 36W
Merrill, Wis., U.S.A. 154 C10 45 11N 89 41W
Merrillville, U.S.A. 157 C9 41 29N 87 20W
Merrimack →, U.S.A. 151 D14 42 49N 70 49W
Merriman, U.S.A. 154 D4 42 55N 101 42W
Merritt, Canada 142 C4 50 10N 120 45W
Merritt Island, U.S.A. 153 G9 28 21N 80 42W
Merriwa, Australia 129 B9 32 6 S 150 22 E
Merriwagga, Australia 129 B6 33 47 S 145 43 E
Merry I., Canada 140 A4 55 29N 77 31W
Merrygoen, Australia 129 A8 31 51 S 149 12 E
Merryville, U.S.A. 155 K8 30 45N 93 33W
Mersa Fatma, Eritrea 107 E5 14 57N 40 17 E
Mersch, Lux. 24 E6 49 44N 6 7 E
Merse →, Italy 45 E8 43 5N 11 22 E
Mersea I., U.K. 21 F8 51 47N 0 58 E
Merseburg, Germany 30 D7 51 22N 11 59 E
Mersey →, U.K. 20 D4 53 25N 3 1W
Merseyside □, U.K. 20 D4 53 31N 3 2W
Mersin, Turkey 100 D6 36 51N 34 36 E
Mersing, Malaysia 87 L4 2 25N 103 50 E
Merta, India 92 F6 26 39N 74 4 E
Merta Road, India 92 F5 26 43N 73 55 E
Merthyr Tydfil, U.K. 21 F4 51 45N 3 22W
Merthyr Tydfil □, U.K. 21 F4 51 46N 3 21W
Mértola, Portugal 43 H3 37 40N 7 40W
Mertzon, U.S.A. 155 K4 31 16N 100 49W
Méru, France 27 C9 49 13N 2 8 E
Meru, Kenya 118 B4 0 3N 37 40 E
Meru, Tanzania 118 C4 3 15 S 36 46 E
Meru △, Kenya 118 B4 0 5N 38 10 E
Merv = Mary, Turkmenistan 66 F7 37 40N 61 50 E
Merville, France 27 B9 50 38N 2 38 E
Méry-sur-Seine, France 27 D10 48 31N 3 54 E
Merzifon, Turkey 100 B6 40 53N 35 32 E
Merzig, Germany 31 F2 49 26N 6 38 E
Merzouga, Erg Tin, Algeria 111 D7 24 0N 11 4 E
Mesa, U.S.A. 159 K8 33 25N 111 50W
Mesa Verde △, U.S.A. 159 H9 37 11N 108 29W
Mesach Mellet, Libya 108 D2 24 30N 11 30 E
Mesagne, Italy 47 B10 40 34N 17 48 E
Mesanagrós, Greece 38 E11 36 1N 27 49 E
Mesaoría, Cyprus 39 E9 35 12N 33 14 E
Mesarás, Kólpos, Greece 39 E5 35 6N 24 47 E
Meschede, Germany 30 D4 51 20N 8 18 E
Mescit, Turkey 101 B9 40 21N 41 11 E
Mesemvriya = Nesebŭr, Bulgaria 51 D11 42 41N 27 46 E
Mesfinto, Ethiopia 107 E4 13 20N 37 22 E
Mesgouez, L., Canada 140 B5 51 20N 75 0W
Meshchovsk, Russia 58 E8 54 22N 35 17 E
Meshed = Mashhad, Iran 97 B8 36 20N 59 35 E
Meshkede-Ser = Bābol Sar, Iran 97 B7 36 45N 52 45 E
Meshoppen, U.S.A. 151 E8 41 36N 76 3W
Meshra er Req, Sudan 107 F2 8 25N 29 18 E
Mesilinka →, Canada 142 B4 56 6N 124 30W
Mesilla, U.S.A. 159 K10 32 16N 106 48W
Meslay-du-Maine, France 26 E6 47 58N 0 33W
Mesocco, Switz. 33 D8 46 23N 9 12 E
Mesologi = Mesolóngion, Greece 48 C3 38 21N 21 28 E
Mesolóngion, Greece 48 C3 38 21N 21 28 E
Mesopotamia = Al Jazirah, Iraq 101 E10 33 30N 44 0 E
Mesopotamia, U.S.A. 150 E4 41 27N 80 57W
Mesopótamon, Greece 48 B2 39 14N 20 32 E
Mesoraca, Italy 47 C9 39 5N 16 48 E
Mésou Volímais = Volímai, Greece 39 D2 37 52N 20 39 E
Mesquite, U.S.A. 159 H6 36 47N 114 6W
Messaad, Algeria 111 B5 34 8N 3 30 E
Messac, France 26 E5 47 49N 1 50W
Messalo →, Mozam. 119 E4 12 25 S 39 15 E
Méssaména, Cameroon 113 E7 3 48N 12 49 E
Messeue, Greece 48 D3 37 12N 21 58 E
Messier, Canal, Chile 176 C2 48 20 S 74 33W
Messina = Musina, S. Africa 117 C5 22 20 S 30 5 E
Messina, Italy 47 D8 38 11N 15 34 E
Messina, Str. di, Italy 47 D8 38 15N 15 35 E
Messíni, Greece 48 D4 37 4N 22 1 E
Messínia □, Greece 48 D3 37 10N 22 0 E
Messiniakós Kólpos, Greece 48 E4 36 45N 22 5 E
Messkirch, Germany 31 H5 47 59N 9 7 E
Messlingen, Sweden 16 B6 62 40N 12 50 E
Messonghi, Greece 38 C9 39 29N 19 56 E
Mesta →, Bulgaria 50 E7 40 54N 24 49 E
Mestá, Ákra, Greece 49 C7 38 16N 25 53 E
Mestanza, Spain 43 G6 38 35N 4 4W
Mestersvig, Greenland 10 C8 72 10N 23 40W
Mestre, Italy 45 C9 45 29N 12 15 E
Mestre, Espigão, Brazil 171 D2 12 30 S 46 10W
Mesudiye, Turkey 100 B7 40 28N 37 46 E
Meta, U.S.A. 156 F4 38 19N 92 10W
Meta □, Colombia 168 C3 3 30N 73 0W
Meta →, S. Amer. 168 B4 6 12N 67 28W
Meta Incognita Pen., Canada 139 B13 62 45N 68 30W
Metabetchouan, Canada 141 C5 48 26N 71 52W
Metairie, U.S.A. 155 L9 29 58N 90 10W
Metalici, Munţii, Romania 52 D7 46 15N 22 50 E
Metaline Falls, U.S.A. 158 B5 48 52N 117 22W
Metallifere, Colline, Italy 44 E8 43 10N 11 0 E
Metamora, U.S.A. 156 D7 40 47N 89 22W
Metán, Argentina 174 B3 25 30 S 65 0W
Metangula, Mozam. 119 E3 12 40 S 34 50 E
Metauro →, Italy 45 E10 43 50N 13 3 E
Metcalf, U.S.A. 152 E6 30 43N 83 59W
Metema, Ethiopia 107 E4 12 56N 36 13 E
Metengobalame, Mozam. 119 E3 14 49 S 34 30 E
Méthana, Greece 48 D5 37 35N 23 23 E
Methóni, Greece 48 E3 36 49N 21 42 E
Methven, N.Z. 131 D6 43 38 S 171 40 E
Metil, Mozam. 119 F4 16 24 S 39 0 E
Metkovets, Bulgaria 50 C7 43 37N 23 10 E
Metković, Croatia 45 E14 43 6N 17 39 E
Metlakatla, U.S.A. 144 J15 55 8N 131 35W
Metlaoui, Tunisia 108 B1 34 24N 8 24 E
Metlik, Papua N. G. 132 C7 4 46 S 152 55 E
Metlika, Slovenia 45 C12 45 40N 15 20 E
Metro, Indonesia 84 D3 5 5 S 105 20 E
Metropolis, U.S.A. 155 G10 37 9N 88 44W
Métsovon, Greece 48 B3 39 48N 21 12 E
Metter, U.S.A. 152 C7 32 24N 82 3W
Mettuppalaiyam, India 95 J3 11 18N 76 59 E
Mettur, India 95 J3 11 48N 77 47 E
Metu, Ethiopia 107 F4 8 18N 35 35 E
Metz, France 27 C13 49 8N 6 10 E
Metzingen, Germany 31 G5 48 31N 9 17 E
Meulaboh, Indonesia 84 B1 4 11N 96 3 E
Meung-sur-Loire, France 27 E8 47 50N 1 40 E
Meurcourt, France 32 A2 47 46N 6 14 E
Meureudu, Indonesia 84 A1 5 19N 96 10 E
Meurthe →, France 27 D13 48 47N 6 9 E
Meurthe-et-Moselle □, France 27 D13 48 52N 6 0 E
Meuse □, France 27 C12 49 8N 5 25 E
Meuse →, Europe 24 D5 50 45N 5 41 E
Meuselwitz, Germany 30 D8 51 2N 12 17 E
Meutapok, Mt., Malaysia 85 A5 5 40N 117 0 E
Mexia, U.S.A. 155 K6 31 41N 96 29W
Mexiana, I., Brazil 170 A2 0 0 49 30W
Mexicali, Mexico 161 N11 32 40N 115 30W
Mexican Plateau, Mexico 136 G9 25 0N 104 0W
Mexican Water, U.S.A. 159 H9 36 57N 109 32W
México, Mexico 163 D5 19 20N 99 10W
Mexico, Maine, U.S.A. 151 B14 44 34N 70 33W
Mexico, Mo., U.S.A. 156 E5 39 10N 91 53W
Mexico, N.Y., U.S.A. 151 C8 43 28N 76 18W
México □, Mexico 163 D5 19 20N 99 10W
Mexico ■, Cent. Amer. 162 C4 25 0N 105 0W
Mexico, G. of, Cent. Amer. 163 C7 25 0N 90 0W
Mexico B., U.S.A. 151 C8 43 35N 76 20W
Mexico Beach, U.S.A. 152 F4 29 57N 85 25W
Meydān-e Naftūn, Iran 97 D6 31 56N 49 18 E
Meydani, Ra's-e, Iran 97 E8 25 24N 59 6 E
Meyenburg, Germany 30 B8 53 18N 12 14 E
Meyers Chuck, U.S.A. 144 J14 55 45N 132 15W
Meymac, France 28 C6 45 32N 2 10 E
Meymaneh, Afghan. 91 B2 35 53N 64 38 E
Meyo, Cameroon 114 B2 2 50N 11 1 E
Meyrueis, France 28 D7 44 12N 3 27 E
Meyssac, France 28 C5 45 3N 1 40 E
Meyzieu, France 29 C8 45 46N 4 59 E
Mezdra, Bulgaria 50 C7 43 12N 23 42 E
Mèze, France 28 E7 43 27N 3 36 E
Mezen, Russia 56 A7 65 50N 44 20 E
Mezen →, Russia 56 A7 65 44N 44 22 E
Mézenc, Mt., France 29 D8 44 54N 4 11 E
Mezeş, Munţii, Romania 52 C8 47 5N 23 5 E
Mezha →, Russia 58 E6 55 44N 31 33 E
Mezhdurechenskiy, Russia 66 D7 59 36N 65 56 E
Mezhdurechye = Shali, Russia 61 J7 43 9N 45 55 E
Mezhevaya Utka = Sinegorskiy, Russia 61 G5 47 55N 40 52 E
Mézidon-Canon, France 26 C6 49 5N 0 1W
Mézières-en-Brenne, France 28 B5 46 49N 1 13 E
Mézilhac, France 29 D8 44 49N 4 21 E
Mézin, France 28 D4 44 4N 0 16 E
Mezőberény, Hungary 52 D6 46 49N 21 3 E
Mezőfalva, Hungary 52 D3 46 55N 18 49 E
Mezőhegyes, Hungary 52 D5 46 19N 20 49 E
Mezőkövácsháza, Hungary 52 D5 46 25N 20 57 E
Mezőkövesd, Hungary 52 C5 47 49N 20 35 E
Mézos, France 28 D2 44 5N 1 10W
Mezőtúr, Hungary 52 C5 47 1N 20 41 E
Mezquital, Mexico 162 C4 23 29N 104 23W
Mezzolombardo, Italy 44 B8 46 13N 11 5 E
Mfolozi →, S. Africa 117 D5 28 25 S 32 26 E

Mgarr, Malta 38 F7 35 55N 14 22 E
Mgarr, Gozo, Malta 38 E7 36 2N 14 18 E
Mgeta, Tanzania 119 D4 8 22 S 36 6 E
Mglin, Russia 59 F7 53 2N 32 50 E
Mhlaba Hills, Zimbabwe 119 F3 18 30 S 30 30 E
Mhow, India 92 H6 22 33N 75 50 E
Mi-Shima, Japan 72 C3 34 46N 131 9 E
Miagao, Phil. 81 F4 10 39N 122 14 E
Miahuatlán, Mexico 163 D5 16 21N 96 36W
Miajadas, Spain 43 F5 39 9N 5 54W
Miami, Fla., U.S.A. 153 K9 25 47N 80 11W
Miami, Okla., U.S.A. 155 G7 36 53N 94 53W
Miami, Tex., U.S.A. 155 H4 35 42N 100 38W
Miami Beach, U.S.A. 153 K9 25 47N 80 8W
Miami Canal, U.S.A. 153 J9 26 30N 80 45W
Miami International ✈ (MIA), U.S.A. 153 K9 25 48N 80 17W
Miami Shores, U.S.A. 153 K9 25 52N 80 12W
Miami Springs, U.S.A. 153 K9 25 49N 80 17W
Miamisburg, U.S.A. 157 E12 39 38N 84 17W
Mian Xian, China 74 H4 33 10N 106 32 E
Mianchi, China 74 G6 34 48N 111 48 E
Mīāndarreh, Iran 97 C7 35 37N 53 39 E
Mīāndowāb, Iran 101 D12 37 0N 46 5 E
Miandrivazo, Madag. 117 B8 19 31 S 45 29 E
Mīāneh, Iran 101 D12 37 30N 47 40 E
Mianning, China 76 C4 28 32N 102 9 E
Mianwali, Pakistan 91 B3 32 38N 71 28 E
Mianyang, China 76 B5 31 22N 104 47 E
Mianzhu, China 76 B5 31 22N 104 7 E
Miaoli, Taiwan 77 E13 24 37N 120 49 E
Miarinarivo, Antananarivo, Madag. 117 B8 18 57 S 46 55 E
Miarinarivo, Toamasina, Madag. 117 B8 16 38 S 48 15 E
Miarinavaratra, Madag. 117 C8 20 13 S 47 31 E
Miass, Russia 64 D8 54 59N 60 6 E
Miasteczko Krajeńskie, Poland 55 E4 53 7N 17 1 E
Miastko, Poland 54 E3 54 0N 16 58 E
Mica, S. Africa 117 C5 24 10 S 30 48 E
Micanopy, U.S.A. 153 F7 29 30N 82 17W
Micăsasa, Romania 53 D9 46 7N 24 7 E
Micco, U.S.A. 153 H9 27 53N 80 30W
Miccosukee, U.S.A. 152 E5 30 36N 84 3W
Miccosukee, L., U.S.A. 152 E6 30 33N 83 53W
Michael, Mt., Papua N. G. 132 D3 6 27 S 145 22 E
Michalovce, Slovak Rep. 35 C14 48 47N 21 58 E
Michigan □, U.S.A. 148 C3 44 0N 85 0W
Michigan, L., U.S.A. 148 D2 44 0N 87 0W
Michigan Center, U.S.A. 157 B12 42 14N 84 20W
Michigan City, U.S.A. 157 C10 41 43N 86 54W
Michika, Nigeria 113 C7 10 36N 13 23 E
Michipicoten I., Canada 140 C2 47 40N 85 40W
Michoacan □, Mexico 162 D4 19 0N 102 0W
Michurin, Bulgaria 51 D11 42 9N 27 51 E
Michurinsk, Russia 60 D5 52 58N 40 27 E
Mico, Pta., Nic. 164 D3 12 0N 83 30W
Miconje, Angola 115 C2 4 26 S 12 48 E
Micoud, St. Lucia 165 f 13 49N 60 54W
Micronesia, Pac. Oc. 134 G7 11 0N 160 0 E
Micronesia, Federated States of ■, Pac. Oc. 134 G7 9 0N 150 0 E
Mid-Indian Ridge, Ind. Oc. 121 H6 30 0 S 75 0 E
Mid-Oceanic Ridge, Ind. Oc. 134 M1 42 0 S 90 0 E
Mid-Pacific Mts., Pac. Oc. 134 F10 18 0N 177 0W
Midai, Indonesia 85 B3 3 0N 107 47 E
Midale, Canada 143 D8 49 25N 103 20W
Middelburg, Neths. 24 C3 51 30N 3 36 E
Middelburg, Eastern Cape, S. Africa 116 E4 31 30 S 25 0 E
Middelburg, Mpumalanga, S. Africa 117 D4 25 49 S 29 28 E
Middelfart, Denmark 17 J3 55 30N 9 43 E
Middelpos, S. Africa 116 E3 31 55 S 20 13 E
Middelwit, S. Africa 116 C4 24 51 S 27 3 E
Middle →, U.S.A. 156 C3 41 26N 93 30W
Middle Alkali L., U.S.A. 158 F3 41 27N 120 5W
Middle America Trench, Pac. Oc. 135 F18 14 0N 95 0W
Middle Andaman I., India 95 H11 12 30N 92 50 E
Middle Bass I., U.S.A. 150 E2 41 41N 82 49W
Middle East, Asia 88 B2 38 0N 40 0 E
Middle Fork Feather →, U.S.A. 160 F5 38 33N 121 30W
Middle I., Australia 125 F3 34 6 S 123 11 E
Middle Loup →, U.S.A. 154 E5 41 17N 98 24W
Middle Raccoon →, U.S.A. 156 C3 41 35N 93 35W
Middle Sackville, Canada 141 D7 44 47N 63 42W
Middleboro, U.S.A. 151 E14 41 54N 70 55W
Middleburg, Fla., U.S.A. 152 E8 30 4N 81 52W
Middleburg, Pa., U.S.A. 150 F7 40 47N 77 3W
Middleburgh, U.S.A. 151 D10 42 36N 74 20W
Middlebury, Ind., U.S.A. 157 C11 41 41N 85 42W
Middlebury, Vt., U.S.A. 151 B11 44 1N 73 10W
Middlemarch, N.Z. 131 F5 45 30 S 170 9 E
Middlemount, Australia 126 C4 22 50 S 148 40 E
Middleport, N.Y., U.S.A. 150 C6 43 13N 78 29W
Middleport, Ohio, U.S.A. 148 F4 39 0N 82 3W
Middlesboro, U.S.A. 149 G4 36 36N 83 43W
Middlesbrough, U.K. 20 C6 54 35N 1 13W
Middlesbrough □, U.K. 20 C6 54 28N 1 13W
Middlesex, Belize 164 C2 17 2N 88 31W
Middlesex, N.J., U.S.A. 151 F10 40 36N 74 30W
Middlesex, N.Y., U.S.A. 150 D7 42 42N 77 16W
Middleton, Australia 126 C3 22 22 S 141 32 E
Middleton, Canada 141 D6 44 57N 65 4W
Middleton, U.S.A. 156 A7 43 6N 89 30W
Middleton Basin, Pac. Oc. 134 K7 25 0 S 156 0 E
Middleton Cr. →, Australia 126 C3 22 35 S 141 51 E
Middleton I., U.S.A. 144 G11 59 26N 146 20W
Middletown, U.K. 23 B5 54 17N 6 51W
Middletown, Calif., U.S.A. 160 G4 38 45N 122 37W
Middletown, Conn., U.S.A. 151 E12 41 34N 72 39W
Middletown, Ky., U.S.A. 157 F11 38 14N 85 32W
Middletown, N.Y., U.S.A. 151 E10 41 27N 74 25W
Middletown, Ohio, U.S.A. 157 E12 39 31N 84 24W
Middletown, Pa., U.S.A. 151 F8 40 12N 76 44W
Middleville, U.S.A. 157 B11 42 43N 85 28W
Midelt, Morocco 110 B4 32 46N 4 44W
Midge Point, Australia 126 J6 20 39 S 148 43 E
Midhirst, N.Z. 130 F3 39 17 S 174 18 E
Miðsandur, Iceland 11 C5 64 24N 21 28W
Midhurst, U.K. 21 G7 50 59N 0 44W
Mīdī, Yemen 107 D5 16 20N 42 45 E
Midi, Canal du →, France 28 E5 43 45N 1 21 E
Midi d'Ossau, Pic du, France 28 F3 42 50N 0 26W
Midi-Pyrénées □, France 28 E5 43 55N 1 45 E
Midland, Australia 125 F2 31 54 S 116 1 E
Midland, Canada 140 D4 44 45N 79 50W
Midland, Calif., U.S.A. 161 M12 33 52N 114 48W
Midland, Mich., U.S.A. 148 D3 43 37N 84 14W
Midland, Pa., U.S.A. 150 F4 40 39N 80 27W
Midland, Tex., U.S.A. 155 K3 32 0N 102 3W
Midlands □, Zimbabwe 119 F2 19 40 S 29 0 E
Midleton, Ireland 23 E3 51 55N 8 10W
Midlothian □, U.K. 22 F5 55 51N 3 5W
Midongy, Tangorombohitr' i, Madag. 117 C8 23 30 S 47 0 E
Midongy Atsimo, Madag. 117 C8 23 35 S 47 1 E
Midou →, France 28 E3 43 54N 0 30W
Midouze →, France 28 E3 43 48N 0 51W
Midsayap, Phil. 81 H5 7 12N 124 32 E
Midsund, Norway 18 B3 62 41N 6 40 E
Midtgulen, Norway 18 C2 61 44N 5 11 E
Midu, China 76 E3 25 18N 100 30 E
Midville, U.S.A. 152 C7 32 49N 82 14W
Midway, Ala., U.S.A. 152 C4 32 5N 85 31W
Midway, Fla., U.S.A. 152 E5 30 30N 84 27W
Midway Is., Pac. Oc. 134 E10 28 13N 177 22W
Midway Wells, U.S.A. 161 N11 32 41N 115 7W
Midwest, U.S.A. 147 B9 42 0N 90 0W
Midwest, Wyo., U.S.A. 158 E10 43 25N 106 16W
Midwest City, U.S.A. 155 H6 35 27N 97 24W
Midyat, Turkey 101 D9 37 25N 41 23 E
Midžor, Bulgaria 50 C6 43 24N 22 40 E
Mie, Japan 72 E3 32 58N 131 35 E
Mie □, Japan 73 C8 34 30N 136 10 E
Miechów, Poland 55 H7 50 21N 20 5 E
Miedwie, Jezioro, Poland 55 E1 53 17N 14 54 E
Międzybórz, Poland 55 G4 51 25N 17 34 E
Międzychód, Poland 55 F2 52 35N 15 53 E
Międzylesie, Poland 55 H3 50 8N 16 40 E
Międzyrzec Podlaski, Poland 55 G9 51 58N 22 45 E
Międzyrzecz, Poland 55 F2 52 26N 15 35 E
Międzyzdroje, Poland 54 E1 53 56N 14 26 E
Miejska Górka, Poland 55 G3 51 39N 16 58 E
Miélan, France 28 E4 43 27N 0 19 E
Mielau = Mława, Poland 55 E7 53 9N 20 25 E
Mielec, Poland 55 H8 50 15N 21 25 E
Mienga, Angola 116 B2 17 12 S 19 48 E
Miercurea-Ciuc, Romania 53 D10 46 21N 25 48 E
Miercurea Sibiului, Romania 53 E8 45 53N 23 48 E
Mieres, Spain 42 B5 43 18N 5 48W
Mieroszów, Poland 55 H3 50 40N 16 11 E
Mies = Stříbro, Czech Rep. 34 A6 49 44N 13 0 E
Mieso, Ethiopia 107 F5 9 15N 40 43 E
Mieszkowice, Poland 55 F1 52 47N 14 30 E
Mifflintown, U.S.A. 150 F7 40 34N 77 24W
Mifraz Hefa, Israel 103 C4 32 52N 35 0 E
Migennes, France 27 E10 47 58N 3 31 E
Migliarino, Italy 45 D8 44 46N 11 56 E
Migliarino-San Rossore-Massaciuccoli △, Italy 44 E7 43 44N 10 20 E
Miguel Alemán, Presa, Mexico 163 D5 18 15N 96 40W
Miguel Alves, Brazil 170 B3 4 11 S 42 55W
Miguel Calmon, Brazil 170 D3 11 26 S 40 36W
Miguelturra, Spain 43 G7 38 58N 3 53W
Mihăileni, Romania 53 C11 47 58N 26 9 E
Mihăilești, Romania 53 F10 44 20N 25 54 E
Mihailovca, Moldova 53 D13 46 33N 28 56 E
Mihalgazi, Turkey 49 A12 40 2N 30 34 E
Mihaliççik, Turkey 100 C4 39 53N 31 30 E
Mihara, Japan 72 C5 34 24N 133 5 E
Mihara-Yama, Japan 73 C11 34 43N 139 23 E
Miheşu de Cîmpie, Romania 53 D9 46 41N 24 9 E
Mijas, Spain 43 J6 36 36N 4 40W
Mikese, Tanzania 118 D4 6 48 S 37 55 E
Mikha-Tskhakaya = Senaki, Georgia 61 J6 42 15N 42 7 E
Mikhailovka = Mykhaylivka, Ukraine 59 J8 47 12N 35 15 E
Mikhaylov, Russia 58 E10 54 14N 39 0 E
Mikhaylovgrad = Montana, Bulgaria 50 C7 43 27N 23 16 E
Mikhaylovka = Kimovsk, Russia 58 E10 54 0N 38 29 E
Mikhaylovka, Kyrgyzstan 65 B9 42 37N 78 20 E
Mikhaylovka, Russia 60 E6 50 3N 43 5 E
Mikhaylovski, Russia 64 C7 56 27N 59 7 E
Mikhnevo, Russia 58 E9 55 4N 37 59 E
Miki, Hyōgo, Japan 72 C6 34 48N 134 59 E
Miki, Kagawa, Japan 72 C6 34 12N 134 7 E
Mikínai, Greece 48 D4 37 43N 22 46 E
Mikir Hills, India 90 B4 26 10N 93 30 E
Mikkeli, Finland 15 F22 61 43N 27 15 E
Mikkwa →, Canada 142 B6 58 25N 114 46W
Mikniya, Sudan 107 D3 17 0N 33 45 E
Mikołajki, Poland 54 E8 53 49N 21 37 E
Míkonos, Greece 49 D7 37 30N 25 25 E
Mikope, Dem. Rep. of the Congo 115 C4 4 58 S 20 43 E
Mikoyan-Shakhar = Karachayevsk, Russia 61 J5 43 50N 41 55 E
Mikrí Préspa, Límni, Greece 50 F5 40 47N 21 3 E
Mikrón Dhérion, Greece 51 E10 41 19N 26 6 E
Mikstat, Poland 55 G4 51 32N 17 59 E
Mikulov, Czech Rep. 35 C9 48 48N 16 39 E
Mikumi, Tanzania 118 D4 7 26 S 37 0 E
Mikumi △, Tanzania 118 D4 7 35 S 37 15 E
Mikun, Russia 56 B9 62 20N 50 0 E
Mikuni, Japan 73 A8 36 13N 136 9 E
Mikuni-Tōge, Japan 73 A10 36 50N 138 50 E
Mikura-Jima, Japan 73 D11 33 52N 139 36 E
Milaca, U.S.A. 154 C8 45 45N 93 39W
Milagro, Ecuador 168 D2 2 11 S 79 36W
Milagros, Phil. 80 E4 12 13N 123 30 E
Milan = Milano, Italy 44 C6 45 28N 9 12 E
Milan, Ga., U.S.A. 152 C6 32 1N 83 4W
Milan, Ill., U.S.A. 156 C6 41 27N 90 34W
Milan, Mich., U.S.A. 157 B13 42 5N 83 41W
Milan, Mo., U.S.A. 156 D3 40 12N 93 7W
Milan, Tenn., U.S.A. 149 H1 35 55N 88 46W
Miland, Norway 18 E5 59 54N 8 45 E
Milando, Angola 115 D3 8 45 S 17 36 E
Milando △, Angola 115 D3 8 45 S 17 10 E
Milang, Australia 128 C3 35 24 S 138 58 E
Milange, Mozam. 119 F4 16 3 S 35 45 E
Milano, Italy 44 C6 45 28N 9 12 E
Milano Linate ✈ (LIN), Italy 44 C6 45 27N 9 16 E
Milanoa, Madag. 117 A8 13 35 S 49 47 E
Milâs, Turkey 49 D9 37 20N 27 50 E
Milatos, Greece 39 E6 35 18N 25 34 E
Milazzo, Italy 47 D8 38 13N 15 15 E
Milbank, U.S.A. 154 C6 45 13N 96 38W
Milbanke Sd., Canada 142 C3 52 15N 128 35W
Milden, Canada 143 C7 51 29N 107 32W
Mildenhall, U.K. 21 E8 52 21N 0 32 E
Mildmay, Canada 150 B3 44 3N 81 7W
Mildura, Australia 128 C5 34 13 S 142 9 E
Mile, China 76 E4 24 28N 103 20 E
Miléai, Greece 48 B5 39 20N 23 9 E
Miles, Australia 127 D5 26 40 S 150 9 E
Miles City, U.S.A. 154 B2 46 25N 105 51W
Milești, Moldova 53 C13 47 13N 28 3 E
Milestone, Canada 143 D8 49 59N 104 31W
Mileto, Italy 47 D9 38 36N 16 4 E
Miletto, Mte., Italy 47 A7 41 27N 14 22 E
Miletus, Turkey 49 D9 37 30N 27 18 E
Milevsko, Czech Rep. 34 B7 49 27N 14 21 E
Milford, Calif., U.S.A. 160 E6 40 10N 120 22W
Milford, Conn., U.S.A. 151 E11 41 14N 73 3W
Milford, Del., U.S.A. 148 F8 38 55N 75 26W
Milford, Ill., U.S.A. 157 D9 40 38N 87 42W
Milford, Mass., U.S.A. 151 D13 42 8N 71 31W
Milford, Mich., U.S.A. 157 B13 42 35N 83 36W
Milford, N.H., U.S.A. 151 D13 42 50N 71 39W
Milford, Pa., U.S.A. 151 E10 41 19N 74 48W
Milford, Utah, U.S.A. 159 G7 38 24N 113 1W
Milford Haven, U.K. 21 F2 51 42N 5 7W
Milford Sd., N.Z. 131 E2 44 41 S 167 47 E
Milḥ, Baḥr al = Razāzah, Buḥayrat ar, Iraq 101 F10 32 40N 43 35 E
Miliana, Aïn Salah, Algeria 111 C5 27 20N 2 32 E
Miliana, Médéa, Algeria 111 A5 36 20N 2 15 E
Milicz, Poland 55 G4 51 31N 17 19 E
Milikapiti, Australia 124 B5 11 26 S 130 40 E
Mililani Town, U.S.A. 145 K13 21 28N 158 1W
Miling, Australia 125 F2 30 30 S 116 17 E
Militello in Val di Catània, Italy 47 E7 37 16N 14 48 E
Militsch = Milicz, Poland 55 G4 51 31N 17 19 E
Milk →, U.S.A. 158 B10 48 4N 106 19W
Milk, Wadi el →, Sudan 106 D3 17 55N 30 20 E
Milk River, Canada 142 D6 49 10N 112 5W
Mill I., Antarctica 7 C8 66 0 S 101 30 E
Mill Shoals, U.S.A. 157 F8 38 15N 88 21W
Mill Valley, U.S.A. 160 H4 37 54N 122 32W
Millárs →, Spain 40 F4 39 55N 0 1W
Millau, France 28 D7 44 8N 3 4 E
Millbridge, Canada 150 B7 44 41N 77 36W
Millbrook, Canada 150 B6 44 10N 78 29W
Millbrook, Ala., U.S.A. 149 J2 32 29N 86 22W
Millbrook, N.Y., U.S.A. 151 E11 41 47N 73 42W
Mille Lacs, L. des, Canada 140 C1 48 45N 90 35W
Mille Lacs L., U.S.A. 154 B8 46 15N 93 39W
Milledgeville, Ga., U.S.A. 152 B6 33 5N 83 14W
Milledgeville, Ill., U.S.A. 156 C7 41 58N 89 46W
Millen, U.S.A. 152 C8 32 48N 81 57W
Millennium I. = Caroline I., Kiribati 135 H12 9 58 S 150 13W
Miller, U.S.A. 154 C5 44 31N 98 59W
Millerovo, Russia 61 F5 48 57N 40 28 E
Miller's Flat, N.Z. 131 F4 45 39 S 169 23 E
Millersburg, Ind., U.S.A. 157 C11 41 32N 85 42W
Millersburg, Ohio, U.S.A. 150 F3 40 33N 81 55W
Millersburg, Pa., U.S.A. 150 F8 40 32N 76 58W
Millerton, N.Z. 131 B6 41 39 S 171 54 E
Millerton, U.S.A. 151 E11 41 57N 73 31W
Millerton L., U.S.A. 160 J7 37 1N 119 41W
Millet, St. Lucia 165 f 13 55N 60 59W
Millevaches, Plateau de, France 28 C6 45 45N 2 0 E
Millheim, U.S.A. 150 F7 40 54N 77 29W
Millicent, Australia 128 D4 37 34 S 140 21 E
Milligan, U.S.A. 153 E3 30 45N 86 38W
Millington, U.S.A. 155 H10 35 20N 89 53W
Millinocket, U.S.A. 149 C11 45 39N 68 43W
Millmerran, Australia 127 D5 27 53 S 151 16 E
Millom, U.K. 20 C4 54 13N 3 16W
Mills L., Canada 142 A5 61 30N 118 20W
Millsboro, U.S.A. 150 G5 40 0N 80 0W
Millstream-Chichester △, Australia 124 D2 21 35 S 117 6 E
Millthorpe, Australia 129 B8 33 26 S 149 12 E
Milltown Malbay, Ireland 23 D2 52 52N 9 24W
Millville, N.J., U.S.A. 148 F8 39 24N 75 2W
Millville, Pa., U.S.A. 151 E8 41 7N 76 32W
Millwood L., U.S.A. 155 J8 33 42N 93 58W
Milna, Croatia 45 E13 43 20N 16 28 E
Milne →, Australia 126 C2 21 10 S 137 33 E
Milne Bay □, Papua N. G. 132 E7 10 0 S 152 30 E
Milne Land, Greenland 10 C8 70 40N 26 30W
Milo, U.S.A. 149 C11 45 15N 68 59W
Milolii, U.S.A. 145 D6 19 11N 155 55W
Milos, Greece 49 E6 36 44N 24 25 E
Miłosław, Poland 55 F4 52 12N 17 32 E
Milot, Albania 50 E3 41 41N 19 43 E
Milparinka, Australia 127 D3 29 46 S 141 57 E
Milroy, U.S.A. 157 E11 39 30N 85 28W
Miltenberg, Germany 31 F5 49 41N 9 16 E
Milton, Australia 129 C9 35 20 S 150 27 E
Milton, N.S., Canada 141 D7 44 4N 64 45W
Milton, Ont., Canada 150 C5 43 31N 79 53W
Milton, N.Z. 131 G4 46 7 S 169 59 E
Milton, Calif., U.S.A. 160 G6 38 3N 120 51W
Milton, Fla., U.S.A. 153 E2 30 38N 87 3W
Milton, Iowa, U.S.A. 156 D4 40 41N 92 10W
Milton, Pa., U.S.A. 150 F8 41 1N 76 51W
Milton, Vt., U.S.A. 151 B11 44 38N 73 7W
Milton, Wis., U.S.A. 157 B8 42 47N 88 56W
Milton-Freewater, U.S.A. 158 D4 45 56N 118 23W
Milton Keynes, U.K. 21 E7 52 1N 0 44W
Milton Keynes □, U.K. 21 E7 52 1N 0 44W
Miltou, Chad 109 F3 10 14N 17 26 E
Miluo, China 77 C9 29 0N 112 59 E
Milverton, Canada 150 C4 43 34N 80 55W
Milwaukee, U.S.A. 157 A9 43 2N 87 55W
Milwaukee Deep, Atl. Oc. 165 C6 19 50N 68 0W
Milwaukie, U.S.A. 160 E4 45 27N 122 38W
Mim, Ghana 112 D4 6 57N 2 33W
Mimizan, France 28 D2 44 12N 1 13W
Mimoň, Czech Rep. 34 A7 50 38N 14 43 E
Mimongo, Gabon 114 C2 1 11 S 11 36 E
Mimoso, Brazil 171 E2 15 10 S 48 5W
Mims, U.S.A. 153 G9 28 40N 80 51W
Min Jiang →, Fujian, China 77 E12 26 0N 119 35 E
Min Jiang →, Sichuan, China 76 C5 28 45N 104 40 E
Min Xian, China 74 G3 34 25N 104 5 E
Mina Pirquitas, Argentina 174 A2 22 40 S 66 30W
Mīnā Su'ud, Si. Arabia 97 D6 28 45N 48 28 E
Mīnā'al Aḥmadī, Kuwait 97 D6 29 5N 48 10 E
Minago →, Canada 143 C9 54 33N 98 59W
Minakami, Japan 73 A10 36 49N 138 59 E
Minaki, Canada 143 D10 49 59N 94 40W
Minakuchi, Japan 73 C8 34 58N 136 10 E
Minamata, Japan 72 E2 32 10N 130 30 E
Minami-Arapusa △, Japan 73 B10 35 30N 138 9 E
Minami-Tori-Shima, Pac. Oc. 134 E7 24 20N 153 58 E
Minas, Uruguay 175 C4 34 20 S 55 10W
Minas, Sierra de las, Guatemala 164 C2 15 9N 89 31W
Minas Basin, Canada 141 C7 45 20N 64 12W
Minas de Riotinto, Spain 43 H4 37 42N 6 35W
Minas Gerais □, Brazil 171 E2 18 50 S 46 0W
Minas Novas, Brazil 171 E3 17 15 S 42 36W
Minatitlán, Mexico 163 D6 17 59N 94 31W
Minbu, Burma 90 E5 20 10N 94 52 E
Minbya, Burma 90 E4 20 22N 93 16 E
Minchinabad, Pakistan 92 D5 30 10N 73 34 E
Mincio →, Italy 44 C7 45 4N 10 59 E
Minčol, Slovak Rep. 35 B13 49 15N 20 58 E
Mindanao, Phil. 81 H5 8 0N 125 0 E
Mindanao Sea = Bohol Sea, Phil. 81 G5 9 0N 124 0 E
Mindanao Trench, Pac. Oc. 80 E5 12 0N 126 6 E
Mindel →, Germany 31 G6 48 31N 10 23 E
Mindelheim, Germany 31 G6 48 2N 10 29 E
Mindelo, C. Verde Is. 9 j 16 24N 25 0W
Minden, Canada 150 B6 44 55N 78 43W
Minden, Germany 30 C4 52 17N 8 55 E
Minden, La., U.S.A. 155 J8 32 37N 93 17W
Minden, Nev., U.S.A. 160 G7 38 57N 119 46W
Mindiptana, Indonesia 83 C6 5 55 S 140 22 E
Mindon, Burma 90 F5 19 21N 94 44 E
Mindona L., Australia 128 B5 33 6 S 142 6 E
Mindoro, Phil. 80 E3 13 0N 121 0 E
Mindoro Occidental □, Phil. 80 E3 13 0N 120 55 E
Mindoro Oriental □, Phil. 80 E3 13 0N 121 5 E
Mindoro Str., Phil. 80 E3 12 30N 120 30 E
Mindouli, Congo 115 C2 4 12 S 14 28 E
Mindourou, Cameroon 114 B2 3 29N 13 26 E
Mine, Japan 72 C3 34 12N 131 7 E
Minehead, U.K. 21 F4 51 12N 3 29W
Mineiros, Brazil 173 D7 17 34 S 52 34W
Mineola, N.Y., U.S.A. 151 F11 40 45N 73 39W
Mineola, Tex., U.S.A. 155 J7 32 40N 95 29W
Mineral King, U.S.A. 160 J8 36 27N 118 36W
Mineral Point, U.S.A. 156 B6 42 52N 90 11W
Mineral Wells, U.S.A. 155 J5 32 48N 98 7W
Mineralnyye Vody, Russia 61 H6 44 15N 43 8 E
Minersville, U.S.A. 151 F8 40 41N 76 16W
Minerva, U.S.A. 150 F3 40 44N 81 6W
Minervino Murge, Italy 47 A9 41 5N 16 5 E
Minetto, U.S.A. 151 C8 43 24N 76 28W
Ming-Kush, Kyrgyzstan 65 C7 41 40N 74 28 E
Mingäçevir, Azerbaijan 61 K8 40 45N 47 0 E
Mingäçevir Su Anbarı, Azerbaijan 61 K8 40 57N 46 50 E
Mingala, C.A.R. 114 A4 5 6N 21 49 E
Mingan, Canada 141 B7 50 20N 64 0W
Mingary, Australia 128 B4 32 8 S 140 45 E
Mingechaur = Mingäçevir, Azerbaijan 61 K8 40 45N 47 0 E
Mingechaurskoye Vdkhr. = Mingäçevir Su Anbarı, Azerbaijan 61 K8 40 57N 46 50 E
Mingela, Australia 126 B4 19 52 S 146 38 E
Mingenew, Australia 125 E2 29 12 S 115 21 E
Mingera Cr. →, Australia 126 C2 20 38 S 137 45 E
Minggang, China 77 A10 32 24N 114 3 E
Mingguang, China 77 A11 32 46N 117 59 E
Mingin, Burma 90 D5 22 50N 94 30 E
Mingir, Moldova 53 D13 46 38N 28 20 E
Minglanilla, Spain 41 F3 39 34N 1 38W
Minglun, China 76 E7 25 10N 108 21 E
Mingo, Congo 114 C3 1 55 S 15 1 E
Mingo Junction, U.S.A. 150 F4 40 19N 80 37W
Mingorria, Spain 42 E6 40 45N 4 40W
Mingshan, China 76 B4 30 6N 103 10 E
Mingteke, China 65 E7 37 7N 75 4 E
Mingteke Daban = Mintaka Pass, Pakistan 65 E7 37 0N 74 58 E
Mingxi, China 77 D11 26 18N 117 12 E
Mingyuegue, China 75 C15 43 2N 128 50 E
Minhla, Magwe, Burma 90 F5 19 58N 95 3 E
Minhla, Pegu, Burma 90 G5 17 59N 95 43 E
Minho = Miño →, Spain 42 D2 41 52N 8 40W
Minhou, China 77 E12 26 0N 119 15 E
Miničevo, Serbia & M. 52 G7 43 42N 22 18 E
Minicoy I., India 95 K1 8 17N 73 2 E
Minidoka, U.S.A. 158 E7 42 45N 113 29W
Minier, U.S.A. 156 D7 40 26N 89 19W
Minigwal, L., Australia 125 E3 29 31 S 123 14 E
Minilya →, Australia 125 D1 23 45 S 114 0 E
Minilya Roadhouse, Australia 125 D1 23 55 S 114 0 E
Mininera, Australia 128 D5 37 37 S 142 58 E
Minipi L., Canada 141 B7 52 25N 60 45W
Minj, Papua N. G. 132 C3 5 54 S 144 37 E
Mink L., Canada 142 A5 61 54N 117 40W
Minkammen, Sudan 107 F3 6 3N 31 32 E
Minkebé, Gabon 114 B2 1 45N 12 45 E
Minlaton, Australia 128 C2 34 45 S 137 35 E
Minna, Nigeria 113 D6 9 37N 6 30 E
Minneapolis, Kans., U.S.A. 154 F6 39 8N 97 42W
Minneapolis, Minn., U.S.A. 154 C8 44 59N 93 16W
Minnedosa, Canada 143 C9 50 14N 99 50W
Minnesota □, U.S.A. 154 B8 46 0N 94 15W
Minnesota →, U.S.A. 154 C8 44 54N 93 9W
Minnesund, Norway 18 D8 60 23N 11 14 E
Minnewaukan, U.S.A. 154 A5 48 4N 99 15W
Minnipa, Australia 127 E2 32 51 S 135 9 E
Minnitaki L., Canada 140 C1 49 57N 92 10W
Mino, Japan 73 B8 35 32N 136 55 E
Miño, Spain 42 B2 43 21N 8 12W
Miño →, Spain 42 D2 41 52N 8 40W
Mino-Kamo, Japan 73 B9 35 23N 137 2 E
Mino-Mikawa-Kōgen, Japan 73 B9 35 10N 137 23 E
Minoa, Greece 49 F7 35 6N 25 45 E
Minobu, Japan 73 B10 35 22N 138 26 E
Minobu-Sanchi, Japan 73 B10 35 14N 138 20 E
Minonk, U.S.A. 156 D7 40 54N 89 2W
Minooka, U.S.A. 157 C8 41 27N 88 16W
Minorca = Menorca, Spain 38 B5 40 0N 4 0 E
Minore, Australia 129 B8 32 14 S 148 27 E
Minot, U.S.A. 154 A4 48 14N 101 18W
Minqin, China 74 E2 38 38N 103 20 E
Minqing, China 77 D12 26 15N 118 50 E
Minsen, Germany 30 B3 53 41N 7 58 E
Minsk, Belarus 58 F4 53 52N 27 30 E
Mińsk Mazowiecki, Poland 55 F8 52 10N 21 33 E
Minster, U.S.A. 157 D12 40 24N 84 23W
Mintabie, Australia 127 D1 27 15 S 133 7 E
Mintaka Pass, Pakistan 65 E7 37 0N 74 58 E
Minthami, Burma 90 D5 23 55N 94 16 E
Minto, Canada 141 C6 46 5N 66 5W
Minto, U.S.A. 144 D10 64 53N 149 11W
Minto, L., Canada 140 A5 57 13N 75 0W
Minton, Canada 143 D8 49 10N 104 35W
Mintoum, Gabon 114 B2 0 27N 12 16 E
Minturn, U.S.A. 158 G10 39 35N 106 26W
Minturno, Italy 46 A6 41 15N 13 45 E
Minûf, Egypt 106 H7 30 26N 30 52 E
Minusinsk, Russia 67 D10 53 43N 91 20 E
Minusio, Switz. 33 D7 46 11N 8 49 E
Minutang, India 90 A6 28 15N 96 30 E
Minvoul, Gabon 114 B2 2 9N 12 8 E
Minwakh, Yemen 99 C5 16 48N 48 6 E
Minya el Qamh, Egypt 106 H7 30 31N 31 21 E
Minya Konka = Gongga Shan, China 76 C3 29 40N 101 55 E
Minyar, Russia 64 D6 55 4N 57 33 E
Minyarskiy Zavod = Minyar, Russia 64 D6 55 4N 57 33 E
Minyip, Australia 128 D5 36 29 S 142 36 E
Minzhong, China 69 F10 22 37N 113 30 E
Mionica, Bos.-H. 52 F3 44 51N 18 29 E
Mionica, Serbia & M. 50 B4 44 14N 20 6 E
Miquelon, Canada 140 C4 49 25N 76 27W
Miquelon, St-P. & M. 141 C8 47 8N 56 22W
Mir, Niger 113 C7 14 5N 11 59 E
Mīr Kūh, Iran 97 E8 26 22N 58 55 E
Mīr Shahdād, Iran 97 E8 26 15N 58 29 E
Mira, Italy 45 C9 45 26N 12 8 E
Mira, Portugal 42 E2 40 26N 8 44W
Mira →, Colombia 168 C2 1 36N 79 1W
Mira →, Portugal 43 H2 37 43N 8 47W
Mira por vos Cay, Bahamas 165 B5 22 9N 74 30W
Mīrābād, Afghan. 91 C1 30 25N 61 50 E
Mirabella Eclano, Italy 47 A7 41 2N 14 59 E
Miracema do Norte, Brazil 170 C2 9 33 S 48 24W
Mirador, Brazil 170 C3 6 22 S 44 22W
Mirador-Río Azul △, Guatemala 164 C2 17 45N 89 50W
Miraflores = Rovira, Colombia 168 C2 4 15N 75 20W
Miraflores, Colombia 168 C3 1 25N 72 13W
Miraj, India 94 F2 16 50N 74 45 E
Miram Shah, Pakistan 91 B3 33 0N 70 2 E
Miramar, Argentina 174 D4 38 15 S 57 50W
Miramar, Mozam. 117 C6 23 50 S 35 35 E
Miramas, France 29 E8 43 33N 4 59 E
Mirambeau, France 28 C3 45 23N 0 35W
Miramichi, Canada 141 C6 47 2N 65 28W
Miramichi B., Canada 141 C7 47 15N 65 0W
Miramont-de-Guyenne, France 28 D4 44 37N 0 21 E
Miranda, Brazil 173 E6 20 10 S 56 15W
Miranda □, Venezuela 168 A4 10 15N 66 25W
Miranda →, Brazil 173 D6 19 25 S 57 20W
Miranda de Ebro, Spain 40 C2 42 41N 2 57W
Miranda do Corvo, Portugal 42 E2 40 6N 8 20W
Miranda do Douro, Portugal 42 D4 41 30N 6 16W
Mirande, France 28 E4 43 31N 0 25 E
Mirandela, Portugal 42 D3 41 32N 7 10W
Mirándola, Italy 44 D8 44 53N 11 4 E
Mirandópolis, Brazil 175 A5 21 9 S 51 6W
Mirango, Malawi 119 E3 13 32 S 34 58 E
Mirani, Australia 126 K6 21 8 S 148 53 E
Mirano, Italy 45 C9 45 30N 12 7 E
Miras, Albania 50 F4 40 30N 20 56 E
Mirassol, Brazil 175 A6 20 46 S 49 28W
Mirbāṭ, Oman 99 C6 17 0N 54 45 E
Mirboo North, Australia 129 E7 38 24 S 146 10 E
Mirear, Egypt 106 C4 23 15N 35 41 E
Mirebeau, France 26 F7 46 49N 0 10 E
Mirebeau-sur-Bèze, France 27 E12 47 25N 5 20 E
Mirecourt, France 27 D13 48 20N 6 10 E
Mirgorod = Myrhorod, Ukraine 59 H7 49 58N 33 37 E
Miri, Malaysia 85 B4 4 23N 113 59 E
Mirialguda, India 94 F4 16 52N 79 35 E
Miriam Vale, Australia 126 C5 24 20 S 151 33 E
Miribel, France 27 G11 45 50N 4 57 E
Mirim, L., S. Amer. 175 C5 32 45 S 52 50W
Mirimire, Venezuela 168 A4 11 10N 68 43W
Miriti, Brazil 173 B6 6 15 S 59 0W
Mīrjāveh, Iran 88 C5 29 1N 61 30 E
Mirnyy, Russia 67 C12 62 33N 113 53 E
Miroč, Serbia & M. 50 B6 44 32N 22 16 E
Mirokhan, Pakistan 92 F3 27 46N 68 6 E
Mirond L., Canada 143 B8 55 6N 102 47W
Mirosławiec, Poland 54 E3 53 20N 16 5 E
Mirpur, Pakistan 93 C5 33 32N 73 56 E
Mirpur Batoro, Pakistan 92 G3 24 44N 68 16 E
Mirpur Bibiwari, Pakistan 92 E2 28 33N 67 44 E
Mirpur Khas, Pakistan 91 D3 25 30N 69 0 E
Mirpur Sakro, Pakistan 92 G2 24 33N 67 41 E
Mirria, Niger 113 C6 13 43N 9 7 E
Mirrool, Australia 129 C7 34 19 S 147 10 E
Mirs Bay = Tai Pang Wan, China 69 F11 22 33N 114 24 E
Mirsk, Poland 55 H2 50 58N 15 23 E
Mirtağ, Turkey 96 B4 38 23N 41 56 E
Mírtou, Kólpos, Greece 39 C1 38 20N 20 27 E
Miryang, S. Korea 75 G15 35 31N 128 44 E
Mirzaani, Georgia 61 K8 41 24N 46 5 E
Mirzachul = Guliston, Uzbekistan 65 C4 40 29N 68 46 E
Mirzapur, India 93 G10 25 10N 82 34 E
Mirzapur-cum-Vindhyachal = Mirzapur, India 93 G10 25 10N 82 34 E
Mirzoyan = Taraz, Kazakhstan 65 B5 42 54N 71 22 E
Misaki, Japan 73 C7 34 18N 135 9 E
Misamis = Ozamiz, Phil. 81 G4 8 15N 123 50 E

Misamis Occidental □, Phil. 81 G4 8 20N 123 42 E
Misamis Oriental □, Phil. 81 G5 8 45N 125 0 E
Misantla, Mexico 163 D5 19 56N 96 50W
Misawa, Japan 70 D10 40 41N 141 24 E
Miscou I., Canada 141 C7 47 57N 64 31W
Misdroy = Międzyzdroje, Poland 54 E1 53 56N 14 26 E
Misericordia = Itaporanga, Brazil 170 C4 7 18 S 38 0W
Misha, India 95 L10 7 59N 93 20 E
Mish'āb, Ra's al, Si. Arabia 97 D6 28 15N 48 43 E
Mishagua →, Peru 172 C3 11 12 S 72 58W
Mishan, China 69 B8 45 37N 131 48 E
Mishawaka, U.S.A. 157 C10 41 40N 86 11W
Mishbih, Gebel, Egypt 106 C3 22 38N 34 44 E
Mishima, Japan 73 B10 35 10N 138 52 E
Mishmi Hills, India 90 A5 29 0N 96 0 E
Mishō, Japan 72 E4 32 57N 132 35 E
Misima I., Papua N. G. 132 F7 10 40 S 152 45 E
Misión, Mexico 161 N10 32 6N 116 53W
Misión Fagnano, Argentina 176 D3 54 32 S 67 17W
Misiones □, Argentina 175 B5 27 0 S 55 0W
Misiones □, Paraguay 174 B4 27 0 S 56 0W
Miskah, Si. Arabia 96 E4 24 49N 42 56 E
Miski, E. →, Chad 109 E3 20 0N 17 55 E
Miskitos, Cayos, Nic. 164 D3 14 26N 82 50W
Miskolc, Hungary 52 B5 48 7N 20 50 E
Misoke, Dem. Rep. of the Congo 118 C2 0 42 S 28 2 E
Misool, Indonesia 83 B4 1 52 S 130 10 E
Miṣr = Egypt ■, Africa 106 B3 28 0N 31 0 E
Miṣrātah, Libya 108 B3 32 24N 15 3 E
Miṣrātah □, Libya 108 C3 33 30N 15 0 E
Missanabie, Canada 140 C3 48 20N 84 6W
Missão Catrimani, Brazil 169 C5 2 48N 62 18W
Missão Velha, Brazil 170 C4 7 15 S 39 10W
Missinaibi →, Canada 140 B3 50 43N 81 29W
Missinaibi L., Canada 140 C3 48 23N 83 40W
Mission, Canada 142 D4 49 10N 122 15W
Mission, S. Dak., U.S.A. 154 D4 43 18N 100 39W
Mission, Tex., U.S.A. 155 M5 26 13N 98 20W
Mission Beach, Australia 126 B4 17 53 S 146 6 E
Mission Viejo, U.S.A. 161 M9 33 36N 117 40W
Missirah, Senegal 112 C1 13 40N 16 30W
Missisa L., Canada 140 B2 52 20N 85 7W
Missisicabi →, Canada 140 B4 51 14N 79 31W
Mississagi →, Canada 140 C3 46 15N 83 9W
Mississauga, Canada 150 C5 43 32N 79 35W
Mississinewa L., U.S.A. 157 D10 40 46N 86 3W
Mississippi □, U.S.A. 155 J10 33 0N 90 0W
Mississippi →, U.S.A. 155 L10 29 9N 89 15W
Mississippi L., Canada 151 A8 45 5N 76 10W
Mississippi River Delta, U.S.A. 155 L9 29 10N 89 15W
Mississippi Sd., U.S.A. 155 K10 30 20N 89 0W
Missoula, U.S.A. 158 C7 46 52N 114 1W
Missour, Morocco 110 B4 33 3N 4 0W
Missouri □, U.S.A. 156 E3 38 25N 92 30W
Missouri →, U.S.A. 156 F6 38 49N 90 7W
Missouri City, U.S.A. 155 L7 29 37N 95 32W
Missouri Valley, U.S.A. 154 E7 41 34N 95 53W
Mist, U.S.A. 160 E3 45 59N 123 15W
Mistassibi →, Canada 141 B5 48 53N 72 13W
Mistassini →, Canada 141 C5 48 42N 72 20W
Mistassini, L., Canada 140 B5 51 0N 73 30W
Mistastin L., Canada 141 A7 55 57N 63 20W
Mistelbach, Austria 35 C9 48 34N 16 34 E
Misterbianco, Italy 47 E8 37 31N 15 1 E
Misti, Volcán, Peru 172 D3 16 18 S 71 24W
Mistinibi, L., Canada 141 A7 55 56N 64 17W
Mistissini, Canada 141 C5 48 53N 72 12W
Mistretta, Italy 47 E7 37 56N 14 22 E
Misty L., Canada 143 B8 58 53N 101 40W
Misugi, Japan 73 C8 34 31N 136 16 E
Misumi, Japan 72 E2 32 37N 130 27 E
Misurata = Miṣrātah, Libya 108 B3 32 24N 15 3 E
Mît Ghamr, Egypt 106 H7 30 42N 31 12 E
Mitaka, Japan 73 B11 35 40N 139 33 E
Mitatib, Sudan 107 D4 15 59N 36 12 E
Mitau = Jelgava, Latvia 15 H20 56 41N 23 49 E
Mitava = Jelgava, Latvia 15 H20 56 41N 23 49 E
Mitchell, Australia 127 D4 26 29 S 147 58 E
Mitchell, Canada 150 C3 43 28N 81 12W
Mitchell, Ga., U.S.A. 152 B7 33 13N 82 42W
Mitchell, Ind., U.S.A. 157 F10 38 44N 86 28W
Mitchell, Nebr., U.S.A. 154 E3 41 57N 103 49W
Mitchell, Oreg., U.S.A. 158 D3 44 34N 120 9W
Mitchell, S. Dak., U.S.A. 154 D6 43 43N 98 2W
Mitchell →, Australia 126 B3 15 12 S 141 35 E
Mitchell, Mt., U.S.A. 149 H4 35 46N 82 16W
Mitchell and Alice Rivers △, Australia 126 B3 15 28 S 142 5 E
Mitchell Ranges, Australia 126 A2 12 49 S 135 36 E
Mitchell River △, Australia 129 D7 37 37 S 147 22 E
Mitchelstown, Ireland 23 D3 52 15N 8 16W
Mitha Tiwana, Pakistan 92 C5 32 13N 72 6 E
Mithi, Pakistan 92 G3 24 44N 69 48 E
Míthimna, Greece 49 B8 39 20N 26 12 E
Mithrao, Pakistan 92 F3 27 28N 69 40 E
Mitiamo, Australia 128 D6 36 12 S 144 15 E
Mítikas, Aitolía kai Akarnanía, Greece 39 B2 38 40N 20 56 E
Mítikas, Prévéza, Greece 39 B2 39 0N 20 42 E
Mitilíni, Greece 49 B8 39 6N 26 35 E
Mitilinoí, Greece 49 D8 37 42N 26 56 E
Mito, Japan 73 A12 36 20N 140 30 E
Mitra, Mt., Eq. Guin. 114 B1 1 23N 9 19 E
Mitre, Mt., N.Z. 130 G4 40 50 S 175 30 E
Mitrofanovka, Russia 59 H10 49 58N 39 42 E
Mitrovica = Kosovska Mitrovica, Serbia & M. 50 D4 42 54N 20 52 E
Mitrowitz = Sremska Mitrovica, Serbia & M. 52 F4 44 59N 19 38 E
Mitsamiouli, Comoros Is. 121 a 11 20 S 43 16 E
Mitsang, Gabon 114 B2 0 42N 12 33 E
Mitsinjo, Madag. 117 B8 16 1 S 45 52 E
Mitsiwa, Eritrea 107 D4 15 35N 39 25 E
Mitsiwa Channel, Eritrea 107 D5 15 30N 40 0 E
Mitsukaidō, Japan 73 A11 36 1N 139 59 E
Mitsushima, Japan 72 C1 34 15N 129 20 E
Mittagong, Australia 129 C9 34 28 S 150 29 E
Mittel Schreiberhau = Szklarska Poreba, Poland 55 H2 50 50N 15 33 E
Mittelberg, Tirol, Austria 33 C11 46 57N 10 53 E
Mittelberg, Vorarlberg, Austria 33 B10 47 20N 10 10 E
Mittelberg, Germany 33 A10 47 38N 10 26 E
Mittelfranken □, Germany 31 F6 49 25N 10 40 E
Mittelland, Switz. 32 C4 46 50N 7 23 E
Mittellandkanal →, Germany 30 C4 52 20N 8 28 E
Mittelwalde = Międzylesie, Poland 55 H3 50 8N 16 40 E
Mittenwalde, Germany 30 C9 52 15N 13 31 E
Mittersill, Austria 34 D5 47 16N 12 29 E
Mitterteich, Germany 31 F8 49 57N 12 14 E
Mittimatalik = Pond Inlet, Canada 139 A12 72 40N 77 0W
Mittweida, Germany 30 E8 50 59N 12 59 E
Mitú, Colombia 168 C3 1 15N 70 13W
Mituas, Colombia 168 C4 3 52N 68 49W
Mitumba, Tanzania 118 D3 7 8 S 31 2 E
Mitumba, Mts., Dem. Rep. of the Congo 118 D2 7 0 S 27 30 E
Mitwaba, Dem. Rep. of the Congo 119 D2 8 2 S 27 17 E
Mityana, Uganda 118 B3 0 23N 32 2 E
Mitzic, Gabon 114 B2 0 45N 11 40 E
Miura, Japan 73 B11 35 12N 139 40 E
Mixteco →, Mexico 163 D5 18 11N 98 30W
Miyagi □, Japan 70 E10 38 15N 140 45 E
Miyāh, W. el →, Egypt 106 C3 25 0N 33 23 E
Miyāh, W. el →, Syria 96 C3 34 44N 39 57 E
Miyake-Jima, Japan 73 C11 34 5N 139 30 E
Miyako, Japan 70 E10 39 40N 141 59 E
Miyako-Jima, Japan 71 M2 24 45N 125 20 E
Miyako-Rettō, Japan 71 M2 24 24N 125 0 E
Miyakonojō, Japan 72 F3 31 40N 131 5 E
Miyani, India 92 J3 21 50N 69 26 E
Miyanojō, Japan 72 F3 31 54N 130 27 E
Miyanoura-Dake, Japan 71 J5 30 20N 130 31 E
Miyata, Japan 72 D2 33 49N 130 42 E
Miyazaki, Japan 72 F3 31 56N 131 30 E
Miyazaki □, Japan 72 E3 32 30N 131 30 E
Miyazu, Japan 73 B7 35 35N 135 10 E
Miyet, Bahr el = Dead Sea, Asia 100 D4 31 30N 35 30 E
Miyi, China 76 D4 26 47N 102 9 E
Miyoshi, Japan 72 C4 34 48N 132 51 E
Miyun, China 74 D9 40 28N 116 50 E
Miyun Shuiku, China 75 D9 40 30N 117 0 E
Mizan Teferi, Ethiopia 107 F4 6 57N 35 3 E
Mizdah, Libya 108 B2 31 30N 13 0 E
Mizen Hd., Cork, Ireland 23 E2 51 27N 9 50W
Mizen Hd., Wicklow, Ireland 23 D5 52 51N 6 4W
Mizhhirya, Ukraine 53 B8 48 32N 23 30 E
Mizhi, China 74 F6 37 47N 110 12 E
Mizil, Romania 53 F11 44 59N 26 29 E
Mizo Hills = Mizoram □, India 90 D4 23 30N 92 40 E
Mizoram □, India 90 D4 23 30N 92 40 E
Mizpe Ramon, Israel 103 E3 30 34N 34 49 E
Mizuho, Antarctica 7 D5 70 30 S 41 0 E
Mizuho, Japan 73 B7 35 6N 135 17 E
Mizunami, Japan 73 B9 35 22N 137 15 E
Mizusawa, Japan 70 E10 39 8N 141 8 E
Mjällby, Sweden 17 H8 56 3N 14 40 E
Mjöbäck, Sweden 17 G6 57 28N 12 53 E
Mjölby, Sweden 17 F9 58 20N 15 10 E
Mjølfjell, Norway 18 D3 60 41N 6 55 E
Mjømna, Norway 18 D1 60 55N 4 55 E
Mjörn, Sweden 17 G6 57 55N 12 25 E
Mjøsa, Norway 18 D8 60 40N 11 0 E
Mkata, Tanzania 118 D4 5 45 S 38 20 E
Mkhaya ⌓, Swaziland 117 D5 26 34 S 31 45 E
Mkokotoni, Tanzania 118 D4 5 55 S 39 15 E
Mkomazi, Tanzania 118 C4 4 40 S 38 7 E
Mkomazi ⌓, Tanzania 118 C3 4 4 S 30 2 E
Mkomazi →, S. Africa 117 E5 30 12 S 30 50 E
Mkulwe, Tanzania 119 D3 8 37 S 32 20 E
Mkumbi, Ras, Tanzania 118 D4 7 38 S 39 55 E
Mkushi, Zambia 119 E2 14 25 S 29 15 E
Mkushi River, Zambia 119 E2 13 32 S 29 45 E
Mkuze, S. Africa 117 D5 27 10 S 32 0 E
Mkuze ⌓, S. Africa 117 D4 29 27 S 29 30 E
Mladá Boleslav, Czech Rep. 34 A7 50 27N 14 53 E
Mladenovac, Serbia & M. 50 B4 44 28N 20 44 E
Mlala Hills, Tanzania 118 D3 6 50 S 31 40 E
Mlange = Mulanje, Malawi 119 F4 16 2 S 35 33 E
Mlava →, Serbia & M. 50 B5 44 45N 21 13 E
Mława, Poland 55 E7 53 9N 20 25 E
Mlawula ⌓, Swaziland 117 D5 26 12 S 32 2 E
Mlinište, Bos.-H. 45 D13 44 15N 16 50 E
Mljet, Croatia 45 F14 42 43N 17 30 E
Mljet △, Croatia 45 F14 42 45N 17 25 E
Mljetski Kanal, Croatia 45 F14 42 48N 17 35 E
Młynary, Poland 54 D6 54 12N 19 46 E
Mmabatho, S. Africa 116 D4 25 49 S 25 30 E
Mme, Cameroon 113 D7 6 18N 10 14 E
Mnichovo Hradiště, Czech Rep. 34 A7 50 32N 14 59 E
Mo, Hordaland, Norway 18 D2 60 49N 5 48 E
Mo, Møre og Romsdal, Norway 18 A5 63 0N 8 59 E
Mo, Telemark, Norway 18 E4 59 28N 7 50 E
Mo i Rana, Norway 14 C16 66 20N 14 7 E
Moa, Cuba 165 B4 20 40N 74 56W
Moa, Indonesia 82 C3 8 0 S 128 0 E
Moa →, S. Leone 112 D2 6 59N 11 36W
Moa, I., Papua N. G. 132 F2 10 10 S 142 15 E
Moab, U.S.A. 159 G9 38 35N 109 33W
Moabi, Gabon 114 C2 2 24 S 10 59 E
Moaco →, Brazil 172 B4 7 41 S 68 18W
Moala, Fiji 133 B2 18 36 S 179 53 E
Moama, Australia 127 F3 36 7 S 144 46 E
Moamba, Mozam. 117 D5 25 36 S 32 15 E
Moapa, U.S.A. 161 J12 36 40N 114 37W
Moate, Ireland 23 C4 53 24N 7 44W
Moba, Dem. Rep. of the Congo 118 D2 7 0 S 29 48 E
Mobara, Japan 73 B12 35 25N 140 18 E
Mobārakābād, Iran 97 D7 28 24N 53 20 E
Mobaye, C.A.R. 114 B4 4 25N 21 5 E
Mobayi, Dem. Rep. of the Congo 114 B4 4 15N 21 8 E
Mobeka, Dem. Rep. of the Congo 114 B3 1 52N 19 49 E
Mobenzélé, Congo 114 B3 0 56N 17 50 E
Moberley Lake, Canada 142 B4 55 50N 121 44W
Moberly, U.S.A. 156 E4 39 25N 92 26W
Mobile, U.S.A. 149 K1 30 41N 88 3W
Mobile B., U.S.A. 149 K2 30 30N 88 0W
Mobridge, U.S.A. 154 C4 45 32N 100 26W
Mobutu Sese Seko, L. = Albert, L., Africa 118 B3 1 30N 31 0 E
Moc Chau, Vietnam 86 B5 20 50N 104 38 E
Moc Hoa, Vietnam 87 G5 10 46N 105 56 E
Mocaba, Sa. de, Angola 115 D3 7 12 S 15 0 E
Mocabe Kasari, Dem. Rep. of the Congo 119 D2 9 58 S 26 12 E
Mocajuba, Brazil 170 B2 2 35 S 49 30W
Moçambique = Mozambique ■, Africa 119 F4 19 0 S 35 0 E
Moçambique, Mozam. 119 F5 15 3 S 40 42 E
Moçâmedes = Namibe, Angola 115 F2 15 7 S 12 11 E
Mocanaqua, U.S.A. 151 E8 41 9N 76 8W
Mocapra →, Venezuela 168 B4 7 56N 66 46W
Moce, Fiji 133 B3 18 40 S 178 29W
Mocha = Al Mukhā, Yemen 98 D3 13 18N 43 15 E
Mocha, I., Chile 176 A2 38 22 S 73 56W
Mochima △, Venezuela 165 D7 10 30N 64 5W
Mochudi, Botswana 116 C4 24 27 S 26 7 E
Mocimboa da Praia, Mozam. 119 E5 11 25 S 40 20 E
Mociu, Romania 53 D9 46 46N 24 3 E
Möckeln, Sweden 17 H8 56 40N 14 15 E
Mockfjärd, Sweden 16 D8 60 30N 14 57 E
Mocklips, U.S.A. 160 C2 47 14N 124 13W
Mocoa, Colombia 168 C2 1 7N 76 35W
Mococa, Brazil 175 A6 21 28 S 47 0W
Mocorito, Mexico 162 B3 25 30N 107 53W
Moctezuma, Mexico 162 B3 29 50N 109 0W
Moctezuma →, Mexico 163 C5 21 59N 98 34W
Mocuba, Mozam. 119 F4 16 54 S 36 57 E
Mocúzari, Presa, Mexico 162 B3 27 10N 109 10W
Moda, Burma 90 C6 24 22N 96 29 E
Modane, France 29 C10 45 12N 6 40 E
Modasa, India 92 H5 23 30N 73 21 E
Modder →, S. Africa 116 D3 29 2 S 24 37 E
Modderfontein = Niekerkshoop, S. Africa 116 D3 29 19 S 22 51 E
Modderrivier, S. Africa 116 D3 29 2 S 24 38 E
Módena, Italy 44 D7 44 40N 10 55 E
Modena, U.S.A. 159 H7 37 48N 113 56W
Modesto, U.S.A. 160 H6 37 39N 121 0W
Möðrudalur, Iceland 11 B11 65 22N 15 53W
Möðruvellir, Iceland 11 B8 65 46N 18 15W
Módica, Italy 47 F7 36 52N 14 46 E
Modimolle, S. Africa 117 C4 24 42 S 28 22 E
Modjamboli, Dem. Rep. of the Congo 114 B4 2 28N 22 6 E
Mödling, Austria 35 C9 48 5N 16 17 E
Modo, Sudan 107 F3 5 31N 30 33 E
Modoc, U.S.A. 152 B7 33 44N 82 13W
Modowi, Indonesia 83 B4 4 5 S 134 39 E
Modra, Slovak Rep. 35 C10 48 19N 17 20 E
Modriča, Bos.-H. 52 F3 44 57N 18 17 E
Moe, Australia 129 E7 38 12 S 146 19 E
Moebase, Mozam. 119 F4 17 3 S 38 41 E
Moëlan-sur-Mer, France 26 E3 47 49N 3 38W
Moelv, Norway 18 D7 60 56N 10 43 E
Moengo, Suriname 169 B7 5 45N 54 20W
Moerewa, N.Z. 130 B3 35 8 S 174 1 E
Moësa →, Switz. 33 D8 46 12N 9 10 E
Moffat, U.K. 22 F5 55 21N 3 27W
Moga, India 92 D6 30 48N 75 8 E
Mogadishu = Muqdisho, Somali Rep. 120 D3 2 2N 45 25 E
Mogador = Essaouira, Morocco 110 B3 31 32N 9 42W
Mogadouro, Portugal 42 D4 41 22N 6 47W
Mogalakwena →, S. Africa 117 C4 22 38 S 28 40 E
Mogami-Gawa →, Japan 70 E10 38 45N 140 0 E
Mogán, Canary Is. 9 e1 27 53N 15 43W
Mogandjo, Dem. Rep. of the Congo 114 B4 1 23N 24 15 E
Mogaung, Burma 90 C6 25 20N 97 0 E
Mogen, Norway 18 D4 60 2N 7 52 E
Mogente = Moixent, Spain 41 G4 38 52N 0 45W
Mogho, Ethiopia 107 G5 4 54N 40 16 E
Mogi das Cruzes, Brazil 175 A6 23 31 S 46 11W
Mogi-Guaçu →, Brazil 175 A6 20 53 S 48 10W
Mogi-Mirim, Brazil 175 A6 22 29 S 47 0W
Mogielnica, Poland 55 G7 51 42N 20 41 E
Mogige, Ethiopia 107 F4 5 24N 36 14 E
Mogilev = Mahilyow, Belarus 58 F6 53 55N 30 18 E
Mogilev-Podolskiy = Mohyliv-Podilskyy, Ukraine 53 B12 48 26N 27 48 E
Mogilno, Poland 55 F4 52 39N 17 55 E
Mogincual, Mozam. 119 F5 15 35 S 40 25 E
Mogliano Véneto, Italy 45 C9 45 33N 12 14 E
Mogocha, Russia 67 D12 53 40N 119 50 E
Mogoi, Indonesia 83 B4 1 55 S 133 10 E
Mogok, Burma 90 D6 23 0N 96 40 E
Mogollon Rim, U.S.A. 159 J8 34 10N 110 50W
Mogoro, Italy 46 C1 39 41N 8 47 E
Mograt, Sudan 106 D3 19 28N 33 16 E
Mogroum, Chad 109 F3 11 6N 15 25 E
Moguer, Spain 43 H4 37 15N 6 52W
Mogumber, Australia 125 F2 31 2 S 116 3 E
Mohács, Hungary 52 E3 45 58N 18 41 E
Mohaka →, N.Z. 130 F6 39 7 S 177 12 E
Mohala, India 94 D5 20 35N 80 44 E
Mohales Hoek, Lesotho 116 E4 30 7 S 27 26 E
Mohali, Congo 114 B3 0 15N 15 29 E
Mohall, U.S.A. 154 A4 48 46N 101 31W
Moḩammadābād, Iran 97 B8 37 52N 59 5 E
Mohammadia, Algeria 111 A5 35 33N 0 3 E
Mohammedia, Morocco 110 B3 33 44N 7 21W
Mohammerah = Khorramshahr, Iran 97 D6 30 29N 48 15 E
Mohana, India 94 E7 19 27N 84 16 E
Mohana →, India 93 G11 24 43N 85 0 E
Mohanganj, Bangla. 90 C3 24 54N 90 59 E
Mohanlalganj, India 93 F9 26 41N 80 58 E
Mohave, L., U.S.A. 161 K12 35 12N 114 34W
Mohawk →, U.S.A. 151 D11 42 47N 73 41W
Moheda, Sweden 17 G8 57 1N 14 35 E
Mohéli, Comoros Is. 121 a 12 20 S 43 40 E
Mohenjodaro, Pakistan 91 D3 27 19N 68 7 E
Moher, Cliffs of, Ireland 23 D2 52 58N 9 27W
Mohican, C., U.S.A. 144 F6 60 12N 167 25W
Mohicanville Reservoir, U.S.A. 150 F3 40 45N 82 0W
Möhlin, Switz. 32 A5 47 33N 7 51 E
Möhne →, Germany 30 D3 51 29N 7 57 E
Mohnyin, Burma 90 C6 24 47N 96 22 E
Mohoro, Tanzania 118 D4 8 6 S 39 8 E
Mohrin = Moryń, Poland 55 F1 52 51N 14 22 E
Mohyliv-Podilskyy, Ukraine 53 B12 48 26N 27 48 E
Moi, Norway 18 F3 58 27N 6 32 E
Moia, Sudan 107 F2 5 3N 28 2 E
Moidart L., U.K. 22 E3 56 47N 5 52W
Moinabad, India 94 F3 17 44N 77 16 E
Moindou, N. Cal. 133 U19 21 42 S 165 41 E
Moineşti, Romania 53 D11 46 28N 26 31 E
Moira →, Canada 150 B7 44 21N 77 24W
Moirang, India 90 C4 24 30N 93 46 E
Moirans, France 29 C9 45 20N 5 33 E
Moirans-en-Montagne, France 27 F12 46 26N 5 43 E
Moíres, Greece 39 E5 35 4N 24 56 E
Moisaküla, Estonia 15 G21 58 3N 25 12 E
Moisie, Canada 141 B6 50 12N 66 1W
Moisie →, Canada 141 B6 50 14N 66 5W
Moissac, France 28 D5 44 7N 1 5 E
Moïssala, Chad 109 G3 8 21N 17 46 E
Moita, Portugal 43 G2 38 38N 8 58W
Moixent, Spain 41 G4 38 52N 0 45W
Möja, Sweden 16 E12 59 26N 18 55 E
Mojácar, Spain 41 H3 37 6N 1 55W
Mojados, Spain 42 D6 41 26N 4 40W
Mojave, U.S.A. 161 K8 35 3N 118 10W
Mojave ⌓, U.S.A. 161 K11 35 7N 115 30W
Mojave Desert, U.S.A. 161 L10 35 0N 116 30W
Moji, China 65 D7 39 0N 74 27 E
Mojiang, China 76 F3 23 37N 101 35 E
Mojjo →, Ethiopia 107 F5 7 55N 42 0 E
Mojkovac, Serbia & M. 50 D3 42 58N 19 35 E
Mojo, Bolivia 174 A2 21 48 S 65 33W
Mojo, Ethiopia 107 F4 8 35N 39 5 E
Mojokerto, Indonesia 85 D4 7 28 S 112 26 E
Mojos, Llanos de, Bolivia 173 D5 15 10 S 65 0W
Moju, Brazil 170 B2 1 53 S 48 46W
Moju →, Brazil 170 B2 1 40 S 48 25W
Mokai, N.Z. 130 E4 38 32 S 175 56 E
Mokambo, Dem. Rep. of the Congo 119 E2 12 25 S 28 20 E
Mokameh, India 93 G11 25 24N 85 55 E
Mokane, U.S.A. 156 F5 38 41N 91 53W
Mokapu Peninsula, U.S.A. 145 K14 21 25N 157 45W
Mokau, N.Z. 130 E3 38 42 S 174 39 E
Mokau →, N.Z. 130 E3 38 35 S 174 35 E
Mokelumne →, U.S.A. 160 G5 38 13N 121 28W
Mokelumne Hill, U.S.A. 160 G6 38 18N 120 43W
Mokhós, Greece 39 E6 35 16N 25 27 E
Mokhotlong, Lesotho 117 D4 29 22 S 29 2 E
Mokihinui →, N.Z. 131 B6 41 33 S 171 58 E
Möklinta, Sweden 16 D10 60 4N 16 33 E
Moknine, Tunisia 108 A2 35 35N 10 58 E
Mokoan, L., Australia 129 D7 36 27 S 146 5 E
Mokokchung, India 90 B5 26 15N 94 30 E
Mokolea Rock, U.S.A. 145 K14 21 27N 157 44W
Mokolo, Cameroon 109 F2 10 49N 13 54 E
Mokolo, Cameroon 113 C7 10 50N 13 55 E
Mokolo, Dem. Rep. of the Congo 114 B3 1 55N 18 6 E
Mokolo →, S. Africa 117 C4 23 14 S 27 43 E
Mokombe, Dem. Rep. of the Congo 114 C4 0 14 S 23 48 E
Mokopane, S. Africa 117 C4 24 10 S 28 55 E
Mokpalin, Burma 90 G6 17 26N 96 53 E
Mokp'o, S. Korea 75 G14 34 50N 126 25 E
Mokra Gora, Serbia & M. 50 D4 42 50N 20 30 E
Mokronog, Slovenia 45 C12 45 57N 15 9 E
Moksha →, Russia 60 C6 54 45N 41 53 E
Mokshan, Russia 60 D7 53 25N 44 35 E
Mokuaeae I., U.S.A. 145 A2 22 14N 159 25W
Mokuauia I., U.S.A. 145 J14 21 40N 157 56W
Mokulua Is., U.S.A. 145 K14 21 24N 157 42W
Mokwa, Nigeria 113 D6 9 19N 5 0 E
Mol, Belgium 24 C5 51 11N 5 5 E
Mola di Bari, Italy 47 A10 41 4N 17 5 E
Molakalmuru, India 95 G3 14 55N 76 50 E
Molale, Ethiopia 107 E4 10 10N 39 41 E
Molanda, Dem. Rep. of the Congo 114 B4 2 28N 20 48 E
Moláoi, Greece 48 E4 36 49N 22 56 E
Molara, Italy 46 B2 40 52N 9 43 E
Molat, Croatia 45 D11 44 15N 14 50 E
Molave, Phil. 81 G4 8 5N 123 30 E
Molchanovo, Russia 66 D9 57 40N 83 50 E
Mold, U.K. 20 D4 53 9N 3 8W
Moldava nad Bodvou, Slovak Rep. 35 C14 48 38N 21 0 E
Moldavia = Moldova ■, Europe 53 C13 47 0N 28 0 E
Moldavia, Romania 53 D12 46 30N 27 0 E
Molde, Norway 18 B4 62 45N 7 9 E
Moldo Too, Kyrgyzstan 65 C7 41 35N 75 0 E
Moldotau = Moldo Too, Kyrgyzstan 65 C7 41 35N 75 0 E
Moldova ■, Europe 53 C13 47 0N 28 0 E
Moldova Nouă, Romania 52 F6 44 45N 21 41 E
Moldoveanu, Vf., Romania 53 E9 45 36N 24 45 E
Moldoviţa, Romania 53 C10 47 41N 25 32 E
Mole △, Ghana 113 D4 9 43N 1 44W
Mole →, U.K. 21 F7 51 24N 0 21W
Mole Creek, Australia 127 G4 41 34 S 146 24 E
Molegbwe, Dem. Rep. of the Congo 114 B4 4 12N 20 53 E
Molepolole, Botswana 116 C4 24 28 S 25 28 E
Molesworth, N.Z. 131 C8 42 5 S 173 16 E
Molfetta, Italy 47 A9 41 12N 16 36 E
Molii Pond, U.S.A. 145 J14 21 31N 157 51W
Molina de Aragón, Spain 40 E3 40 46N 1 52W
Molina de Segura, Spain 41 G3 38 3N 1 12W
Moline, U.S.A. 156 C6 41 30N 90 31W
Molinella, Italy 45 D8 44 37N 11 40 E
Molino, U.S.A. 153 E2 30 43N 87 20W
Molinos, Argentina 174 B2 25 28 S 66 15W
Moliro, Dem. Rep. of the Congo 118 D3 8 12 S 30 30 E
Moliterno, Italy 47 B8 40 14N 15 52 E
Molkom, Sweden 16 E7 59 37N 13 44 E
Mölle, Sweden 17 H6 56 17N 12 31 E
Molledo, Spain 42 B6 43 8N 4 6W
Mollendo, Peru 172 D3 17 0 S 72 0W
Mollerin, L., Australia 125 F2 30 30 S 117 35 E
Mollerussa, Spain 40 D5 41 37N 0 54 E
Mollina, Spain 43 H6 37 8N 4 38W
Mölln, Germany 30 B6 53 39N 10 32 E
Mölltorp, Sweden 17 F8 58 30N 14 26 E
Mölnlycke, Sweden 17 G6 57 40N 12 8 E
Molo, Burma 90 D6 23 22N 96 53 E
Molochansk, Ukraine 59 J8 47 15N 35 35 E
Molochnoye, Ozero, Ukraine 59 J8 46 30N 35 20 E
Molodechno = Maladzyechna, Belarus 58 E4 54 20N 26 50 E
Molodove, Ukraine 53 D14 46 13N 29 39 E
Molokai, U.S.A. 145 B5 21 8N 157 0W
Molokai Fracture Zone, Pac. Oc. 135 E15 28 0N 125 0W
Molokini I., U.S.A. 145 C5 20 38N 156 30W
Moloma →, Russia 64 B2 58 29N 48 33 E
Molong, Australia 129 B8 33 5 S 148 54 E
Molopo →, Africa 116 D3 28 30 S 20 12 E
Mólos, Greece 48 C4 38 47N 22 37 E
Molotov = Perm, Russia 64 C6 58 0N 56 10 E
Molotov, Mys = Arkticheskiy, Mys, Russia 67 A10 81 10N 95 0 E
Molotovsk = Nolinsk, Russia 60 B9 57 28N 49 57 E
Molotovsk = Severodvinsk, Russia 56 B6 64 27N 39 58 E
Molotovskoye = Krasnogvardeyskoye, Russia 61 H5 45 52N 41 33 E
Moloundou, Cameroon 114 B3 2 8N 15 15 E
Molowaie, Dem. Rep. of the Congo 115 D4 5 47 S 23 18 E
Molsheim, France 27 D14 48 33N 7 29 E
Molson L., Canada 143 C9 54 22N 96 40W
Molteno, S. Africa 116 E4 31 22 S 26 22 E
Moltràsio, Italy 44 C6 45 52N 9 6 E
Molu, Indonesia 83 C4 6 45 S 131 40 E
Molucca Sea, Indonesia 82 A3 0 0 125 0 E
Moluccas = Maluku, Indonesia 79 E7 1 0 S 127 0 E
Molundo, Phil. 81 H5 7 57N 124 23 E
Moma, Dem. Rep. of the Congo 118 C1 1 35 S 23 52 E
Moma, Mozam. 119 F4 16 47 S 39 4 E
Momba, Australia 128 A5 30 58 S 143 30 E
Mombaça, Brazil 170 C4 5 43 S 39 45W
Mombango, Dem. Rep. of the Congo 114 B4 1 45N 24 26 E
Mombasa, Kenya 118 C4 4 2 S 39 43 E
Mombetsu, Japan 70 B11 44 21N 143 22 E
Mombil, Burma 90 B7 27 46N 98 6 E
Momboyo →, Dem. Rep. of the Congo 114 C3 0 16 S 19 0 E
Mombuey, Spain 42 C4 42 3N 6 20W
Momchilgrad, Bulgaria 51 E9 41 33N 25 23 E
Momence, U.S.A. 157 C9 41 10N 87 40W
Momi, Dem. Rep. of the Congo 118 C2 1 42 S 27 0 E
Momote, Papua N. G. 132 B4 2 4 S 147 27 E
Mompog Pass, Phil. 80 E4 13 34N 122 13 E
Mompós, Colombia 168 B3 9 14N 74 26W
Møn, Denmark 17 K6 54 57N 12 20 E
Mon □, Burma 90 G6 16 0N 97 30 E
Mona, Canal de la = Mona Passage, W. Indies 165 C6 18 30N 67 45W
Mona, Isla, Puerto Rico 165 C6 18 5N 67 54W
Mona, Pta., Costa Rica 164 E3 9 37N 82 36W
Mona Passage, W. Indies 165 C6 18 30N 67 45W
Mona Quimbundo, Angola 115 D3 9 55 S 19 58 E
Monaca, U.S.A. 150 F4 40 41N 80 17W
Monaco ■, Europe 29 E11 43 46N 7 23 E
Monadhliath Mts., U.K. 22 D4 57 10N 4 4W
Monadnock, Mt., U.S.A. 151 D12 42 52N 72 7W
Monagas □, Venezuela 169 B5 9 20N 63 0W
Monaghan, Ireland 23 B5 54 15N 6 57W
Monaghan □, Ireland 23 B5 54 11N 6 56W
Monahans, U.S.A. 155 K3 31 36N 102 54W
Monapo, Mozam. 119 E5 14 56 S 40 19 E
Monar, L., U.K. 22 D3 57 26N 5 8W
Monaragala, Sri Lanka 95 L5 6 52N 81 22 E
Monarch Mt., Canada 142 C3 51 55N 125 57W
Monashee Mts., Canada 142 C5 51 0N 118 43W
Monasterevin, Ireland 23 C4 53 8N 7 4W
Monastir = Bitola, Macedonia 50 E5 41 1N 21 20 E
Monastir, Tunisia 108 A2 35 50N 10 49 E
Moncada, Phil. 80 D3 15 44N 120 34 E
Moncalieri, Italy 44 D4 45 0N 7 41 E
Moncalvo, Italy 44 C5 45 3N 8 16 E
Monção, Portugal 42 C2 42 4N 8 27W
Moncarapacho, Portugal 43 H3 37 5N 7 46W
Moncayo, Sierra del, Spain 40 D3 41 48N 1 50W
Moncha-Guba = Monchegorsk, Russia 56 A5 67 54N 32 58 E
Monchegorsk, Russia 56 A5 67 54N 32 58 E
Mönchengladbach, Germany 30 D2 51 11N 6 27 E
Monchique, Portugal 43 H2 37 19N 8 38W
Moncks Corner, U.S.A. 152 B9 33 12N 80 1W
Monclova, Mexico 162 B4 26 50N 101 30W
Moncontour, France 26 D4 48 22N 2 38W
Moncton, Canada 141 C7 46 7N 64 51W
Mondariz, Spain 42 C2 42 14N 8 27W
Mondego →, Portugal 42 E2 40 9N 8 52W
Mondego, C., Portugal 42 E2 40 11N 8 54W
Mondeodo, Indonesia 82 B2 3 34 S 122 9 E
Mondeville, France 26 C6 49 10N 0 18W
Mondimbi, Dem. Rep. of the Congo 114 B4 1 48N 22 46 E
Mondjuku, Dem. Rep. of the Congo 114 C4 1 41 S 21 12 E
Mondo, Chad 109 F3 13 47N 15 32 E
Mondolfo, Italy 45 E10 43 45N 13 6 E
Mondoñedo, Spain 42 B3 43 25N 7 23W
Mondovì, Italy 44 D4 44 23N 7 49 E
Mondragon, Phil. 80 E5 12 31N 124 45 E
Mondragone, Italy 46 A6 41 7N 13 53 E
Mondrain I., Australia 125 F3 34 9 S 122 14 E
Moneague, Jamaica 164 a 18 16N 77 7W
Monemvasía, Greece 48 E5 36 41N 23 3 E
Monessen, U.S.A. 150 F5 40 9N 79 54W
Monesterio, Spain 43 G4 38 6N 6 15W
Monestier-de-Clermont, France 29 D9 44 55N 5 38 E
Monett, U.S.A. 155 G8 36 55N 93 55W
Moneymore, U.K. 23 B5 54 41N 6 40W
Monfalcone, Italy 45 C10 45 49N 13 32 E
Monflanquin, France 28 D4 44 32N 0 47 E
Monforte, Portugal 43 F3 39 6N 7 25W
Monforte de Lemos, Spain 42 C3 42 31N 7 33W
Mong Cai, Vietnam 86 B6 21 27N 107 54 E
Mong Hsu, Burma 76 G2 21 54N 98 30 E
Mong Hta, Burma 90 F7 19 50N 98 35 E
Mong Ket, Burma 90 D7 23 8N 98 22 E
Mong Kung, Burma 90 E6 21 35N 97 35 E
Mong Kyawt, Burma 90 F7 19 56N 98 45 E
Möng Long, Burma 90 D6 22 47N 96 37 E
Möng Mit, Burma 90 D6 23 7N 96 41 E
Möng Nai, Burma 90 E6 20 32N 97 46 E
Mong Pan, Burma 90 E7 20 19N 98 22 E
Mong Ping, Burma 76 G2 21 22N 99 2 E
Mong Pu, Burma 90 E7 20 55N 98 44 E
Mong Ton, Burma 90 E7 20 17N 98 45 E
Mong Tung, Burma 90 D6 22 2N 97 41 E
Mong Yai, Burma 90 D7 22 21N 98 3 E
Möng Yu, Burma 90 D6 23 30N 97 47 E
Monga, Dem. Rep. of the Congo 114 B4 4 12N 22 49 E
Mongala →, Dem. Rep. of the Congo 114 B3 1 53N 19 46 E
Mongalla, Sudan 107 F3 5 8N 31 42 E
Mongandia, Congo 114 B3 0 45N 17 11 E
Mongers, L., Australia 125 E2 29 25 S 117 5 E
Mongga, Solomon Is. 133 L9 7 52 S 157 0 E

Monghyr = Munger, *India* **93 G12** 25 23N 86 30 E
Mongibello = Etna, *Italy* **47 E7** 37 50N 14 55 E
Mongla, *Bangla.* **90 D2** 22 8N 89 35 E
Mongnngaw, *Burma* **90 D6** 22 47N 96 59 E
Mongo, *Chad* **109 F3** 12 14N 18 43 E
Mongó, *Eq. Guin.* **114 B2** 1 52N 10 10 E
Mongo →, *S. Leone* **112 D2** 9 35N 12 10W
Mongolia ■, *Asia* **67 E10** 47 0N 103 0 E
Mongolia, Plateau of, *Asia* **62 E14** 45 0N 105 0 E
Mongomo, *Eq. Guin.* **114 B2** 1 38N 11 19 E
Mongonu, *Nigeria* **113 C7** 12 40N 13 32 E
Mongororo, *Chad* **109 F4** 12 3N 22 26 E
Mongstad, *Norway* **18 D2** 60 49N 5 2 E
Mongu, *Zambia* **115 F4** 15 16 S 23 12 E
Môngua, *Angola* **116 B2** 16 43 S 15 20 E
Moniac, *U.S.A.* **152 E7** 30 31N 82 14W
Monifieth, *U.K.* **22 E6** 56 30N 2 48W
Monistrol-sur-Loire, *France* **29 C8** 45 17N 4 11 E
Monkayo, *Phil.* **81 H6** 7 50N 126 5 E
Monkey Bay, *Malawi* **119 E4** 14 7 S 35 1 E
Monkey Mia, *Australia* **125 E1** 25 48 S 113 43 E
Monkey River Town, *Belize* **163 D7** 16 22N 88 29W
Mońki, *Poland* **54 E9** 53 23N 22 48 E
Monkoto, *Dem. Rep. of the Congo* **114 C4** 1 38 S 20 35 E
Monkton, *Canada* **150 C3** 43 35N 81 5W
Monmouth, *U.K.* **21 F5** 51 48N 2 42W
Monmouth, *Ill., U.S.A.* **156 D6** 40 55N 90 39W
Monmouth, *Oreg., U.S.A.* **158 D2** 44 51N 123 14W
Monmouthshire □, *U.K.* **21 F5** 51 48N 2 54W
Mono, *Solomon Is.* **133 L8** 7 20 S 155 35 E
Mono L., *U.S.A.* **160 H7** 38 1N 119 1W
Monolith, *U.S.A.* **161 K8** 35 7N 118 22W
Monólithos, *Greece* **38 E11** 36 7N 27 45 E
Monon, *U.S.A.* **157 D10** 40 52N 86 53W
Monona, *Iowa, U.S.A.* **156 A5** 43 3N 91 23W
Monona, *Wis., U.S.A.* **156 A7** 43 4N 89 20W
Monongahela, *U.S.A.* **150 F5** 40 12N 79 56W
Monópoli, *Italy* **47 B10** 40 57N 17 18 E
Monor, *Hungary* **52 C4** 47 21N 19 27 E
Monos I., *Trin. & Tob.* **169 F9** 10 42N 61 44W
Monóvar, *Spain* **41 G4** 38 28N 0 53W
Monowai, *N.Z.* **131 F2** 45 53 S 167 31 E
Monowai, L., *N.Z.* **131 F2** 45 53 S 167 25 E
Monqoumba, *C.A.R.* **114 B3** 3 33N 18 40 E
Monreal del Campo, *Spain* **40 E3** 40 47N 1 20W
Monreale, *Italy* **46 D6** 38 5N 13 17 E
Monroe, *Ga., U.S.A.* **152 B6** 33 47N 83 43W
Monroe, *Iowa, U.S.A.* **156 C3** 41 31N 93 6W
Monroe, *La., U.S.A.* **155 J8** 32 30N 92 7W
Monroe, *Mich., U.S.A.* **157 C13** 41 55N 83 24W
Monroe, *N.C., U.S.A.* **149 H5** 34 59N 80 33W
Monroe, *N.Y., U.S.A.* **151 E10** 41 20N 74 11W
Monroe, *Ohio, U.S.A.* **157 E12** 39 27N 84 22W
Monroe, *Utah, U.S.A.* **159 G7** 38 38N 112 7W
Monroe, *Wash., U.S.A.* **160 C5** 47 51N 121 58W
Monroe, *Wis., U.S.A.* **156 B7** 42 36N 89 38W
Monroe, L., *U.S.A.* **153 G8** 28 50N 81 19W
Monroe City, *Ind., U.S.A.* **157 F9** 38 37N 87 20W
Monroe City, *Mo., U.S.A.* **156 E5** 39 39N 91 44W
Monroe L., *U.S.A.* **157 E10** 39 1N 86 31W
Monroeton, *U.S.A.* **151 E8** 41 43N 76 29W
Monroeville, *Ala., U.S.A.* **149 K2** 31 31N 87 20W
Monroeville, *Ind., U.S.A.* **157 D12** 40 59N 84 52W
Monroeville, *Pa., U.S.A.* **150 F5** 40 26N 79 45W
Monrovia, *Liberia* **112 D2** 6 18N 10 47W
Mons, *Belgium* **24 D3** 50 27N 3 58 E
Møns Klint, *Denmark* **17 K6** 54 57N 12 33 E
Monsaraz, *Portugal* **43 G3** 38 28N 7 22W
Monse, *Indonesia* **82 B2** 4 7 S 123 15 E
Monsefú, *Peru* **172 B2** 6 52 S 79 52W
Monségur, *France* **28 D4** 44 38N 0 4 E
Monsélice, *Italy* **45 C8** 45 14N 11 45 E
Mønshaug, *Norway* **18 D3** 60 37N 6 31 E
Mönsterås, *Sweden* **17 G10** 57 3N 16 26 E
Mont Cenis, Col du, *France* **29 C10** 45 15N 6 55 E
Mont-de-Marsan, *France* **28 E3** 43 54N 0 31W
Mont-Dore, *N. Cal.* **133 V20** 22 16 S 166 34 E
Mont Fouari ⌂, *Congo* **114 C2** 2 52 S 11 32 E
Mont-Joli, *Canada* **141 C6** 48 37N 68 10W
Mont-Laurier, *Canada* **140 C4** 46 35N 75 30W
Mont-Louis, *Canada* **141 C6** 49 15N 65 44W
Mont Peko ⌂, *Ivory C.* **112 D3** 9 5N 7 15W
Mont-roig del Camp, *Spain* **40 D5** 41 5N 0 58 E
Mont-St-Michel, Le, *France* **26 D5** 48 40N 1 30W
Mont Sangbe △, *Ivory C.* **112 D3** 8 0N 7 10W
Mont-Tremblant ⌂, *Canada* **140 C5** 46 30N 74 30W
Montabaur, *Germany* **30 E3** 50 25N 7 50 E
Montagnac = Remchi, *Algeria* **111 A4** 35 2N 1 26W
Montagnac, *France* **28 E7** 43 29N 3 28 E
Montagnana, *Italy* **45 C8** 45 14N 11 28 E
Montagne d'Ambre △, *Madag.* **117 A8** 12 37 S 49 8 E
Montagne de Reims ⌂, *France* **27 C11** 49 8N 4 0 E
Montagu, *S. Africa* **116 E3** 33 45 S 20 8 E
Montagu I., *Antarctica* **7 B1** 58 25 S 26 20W
Montague, *Canada* **141 C7** 46 10N 62 39W
Montague, I., *Mexico* **162 A2** 31 40N 114 56W
Montague I., *Australia* **129 D9** 36 16 S 150 13 E
Montague I., *U.S.A.* **144 G11** 60 0N 147 30W
Montague Ra., *Australia* **127 E2** 27 15 S 119 30 E
Montague Sd., *Australia* **124 B4** 14 28 S 125 20 E
Montaigu, *France* **26 F5** 46 59N 1 18W
Montalbán, *Spain* **40 E4** 40 50N 0 45W
Montalbano Iónico, *Italy* **47 B9** 40 17N 16 34 E
Montalbo, *Spain* **40 F2** 39 53N 2 42W
Montalcino, *Italy* **45 E8** 43 3N 11 29 E
Montalegre, *Angola* **115 D3** 8 45 S 17 4 E
Montalegre, *Portugal* **42 D3** 41 49N 7 47W
Montalto, *Italy* **47 D8** 38 10N 15 55 E
Montalto di Castro, *Italy* **45 F8** 42 21N 11 37 E
Montalto Uffugo, *Italy* **47 C9** 39 24N 16 9 E
Montalvo, *U.S.A.* **161 L7** 34 15N 119 12W
Montamarta, *Spain* **42 D5** 41 39N 5 49W
Montana, *Bulgaria* **50 C7** 43 27N 23 16 E
Montaña, *Peru* **172 B3** 6 0 S 73 0W
Montana, *Switz.* **32 D4** 46 19N 7 29 E
Montana □, *Bulgaria* **50 C7** 43 30N 23 20 E
Montana □, *U.S.A.* **158 C9** 47 0N 110 0W
Montaña Clara, I., *Canary Is.* **9 e2** 29 17N 13 33W
Montañas de Malaga ⌂, *Spain* **43 J6** 36 48N 4 32W
Montánchez, *Spain* **43 F4** 39 15N 6 8W
Montañita, *Colombia* **168 C2** 1 22N 75 28W
Montargil, *Portugal* **43 F2** 39 5N 8 10W
Montargis, *France* **27 E9** 47 59N 2 43 E
Montauban, *France* **28 D5** 44 2N 1 21 E
Montauk, *U.S.A.* **151 E13** 41 3N 71 57W
Montauk Pt., *U.S.A.* **151 E13** 41 4N 71 52W
Montaytas, *Kazakhstan* **65 B4** 42 5N 68 59 E
Montbard, *France* **27 E11** 47 38N 4 20 E
Montbarrey, *France* **27 E12** 47 1N 5 39 E
Montbéliard, *France* **27 E13** 47 31N 6 48 E
Montblanc, *Spain* **40 D6** 41 23N 1 4 E
Montbrison, *France* **29 C8** 45 36N 4 3 E
Montcalm, Pic de, *France* **28 F5** 42 40N 1 25 E
Montceau-les-Mines, *France* **27 F11** 46 40N 4 23 E
Montcenis, *France* **29 B8** 46 47N 4 23 E
Montclair, *U.S.A.* **151 F10** 40 49N 74 13W
Montcornet, *France* **27 C11** 49 40N 4 1 E
Montcuq, *France* **28 D5** 44 21N 1 13 E
Montdidier, *France* **27 C9** 49 38N 2 35 E
Monte Albán, *Mexico* **163 D5** 17 2N 96 45W
Monte Alegre, *Brazil* **169 D7** 2 0 S 54 0W
Monte Alegre de Goiás, *Brazil* **171 D2** 13 14 S 47 10W
Monte Alegre de Minas, *Brazil* **171 E2** 18 52 S 48 52W
Monte Alegre do Piauí, *Brazil* **170 C2** 9 46 S 45 18W
Monte Azul, *Brazil* **171 E3** 15 9 S 42 53W
Monte-Carlo, *Monaco* **29 E11** 43 44N 7 25 E
Monte Carmelo, *Brazil* **171 E2** 18 43 S 47 29W
Monte Caseros, *Argentina* **174 C4** 30 10 S 57 50W
Monte Comán, *Argentina* **174 C2** 34 40 S 67 53W
Monte Cristi, *Dom. Rep.* **165 C5** 19 52N 71 39W
Monte Cucco ⌂, *Italy* **45 E9** 43 22N 12 43 E
Monte Dinero, *Argentina* **176 D3** 52 18 S 68 33W
Monte Dourado, *Brazil* **169 D7** 0 52 S 52 31W
Monte Lindo →, *Paraguay* **174 A4** 23 56 S 57 12W
Monte Pascoal △, *Brazil* **171 E4** 16 51 S 39 21W
Monte Patria, *Chile* **174 C1** 30 42 S 70 58W
Monte Quemado, *Argentina* **174 B3** 25 53 S 62 41W
Monte Redondo, *Portugal* **42 F2** 39 53N 8 50W
Monte Rio, *U.S.A.* **160 G4** 38 28N 123 0W
Monte San Giovanni Campano, *Italy* **46 A6** 41 38N 13 31 E
Monte San Giuliano = Érice, *Italy* **46 D5** 38 2N 12 35 E
Monte San Savino, *Italy* **45 E8** 43 20N 11 43 E
Monte Sant' Ángelo, *Italy* **45 G12** 41 42N 15 59 E
Monte Santu, C. di, *Italy* **46 B2** 40 5N 9 44 E
Monte Sibillini △, *Italy* **45 F10** 42 55N 13 15 E
Monte Subasio ⌂, *Italy* **45 E9** 43 5N 12 40 E
Monte Vista, *U.S.A.* **159 H10** 37 35N 106 9W
Monteagudo, *Argentina* **175 B5** 27 14 S 54 8W
Monteagudo, *Bolivia* **173 D5** 19 49 S 63 59W
Montealegre del Castillo, *Spain* **41 G3** 38 48N 1 17W
Montebello, *Canada* **140 C5** 45 40N 74 55W
Montebello Iónico, *Italy* **47 E8** 37 59N 15 45 E
Montebello Is., *Australia* **124 D2** 20 30 S 115 45 E
Montebelluna, *Italy* **45 C9** 45 47N 12 3 E
Montebourg, *France* **26 C5** 49 30N 1 20W
Montecastrilli, *Italy* **45 F9** 42 39N 12 29 E
Montecatini Terme, *Italy* **44 E7** 43 53N 10 46 E
Montecito, *U.S.A.* **161 L7** 34 26N 119 40W
Montecristi, *Ecuador* **168 D1** 1 0 S 80 40W
Montecristo, *Italy* **44 F7** 42 20N 10 19 E
Montefalco, *Italy* **45 F9** 42 54N 12 39 E
Montefiascone, *Italy* **45 F9** 42 32N 12 2 E
Montefrío, *Spain* **43 H7** 37 20N 4 0W
Montegiórgio, *Italy* **45 E10** 43 6N 13 33 E
Montego Bay, *Jamaica* **164 a** 18 28N 77 55W
Montehermoso, *Spain* **42 E4** 40 5N 6 21W
Monteiro, *Brazil* **170 C4** 7 48 S 37 2W
Montejicar, *Spain* **43 H7** 37 33N 3 30W
Monteleone di Calabria = Vibo Valéntia, *Italy* **47 D9** 38 40N 16 6 E
Montelíbano, *Colombia* **168 B2** 8 5N 75 29W
Montélimar, *France* **29 D8** 44 33N 4 45 E
Montella, *Italy* **47 B8** 40 51N 15 1 E
Montellano, *Spain* **43 J5** 36 59N 5 29W
Montello, *U.S.A.* **154 D10** 43 48N 89 20W
Montemayor, Meseta de, *Argentina* **176 B3** 44 20 S 66 10W
Montemor-o-Novo, *Portugal* **43 G2** 38 40N 8 12W
Montemor-o-Velho, *Portugal* **42 E2** 40 11N 8 40W
Montemorelos, *Mexico* **163 B5** 25 11N 99 42W
Montendre, *France* **28 C3** 45 16N 0 26W
Montenegro, *Brazil* **175 B5** 29 39 S 51 29W
Montenegro □, *Serbia & M.* **50 D3** 42 40N 19 20 E
Montenero di Bisáccia, *Italy* **45 G11** 41 57N 14 47 E
Montepuez, *Mozam.* **119 E4** 13 8 S 38 59 E
Montepuez →, *Mozam.* **119 E5** 12 32 S 40 27 E
Montepulciano, *Italy* **45 E8** 43 5N 11 47 E
Montereale, *Italy* **45 F10** 42 31N 13 15 E
Montereau-Faut-Yonne, *France* **27 D9** 48 22N 2 57 E
Monterey, *Calif., U.S.A.* **160 J5** 36 37N 121 55W
Monterey, *Ind., U.S.A.* **157 C10** 41 11N 86 30W
Monterey B., *U.S.A.* **160 J5** 36 45N 122 0W
Montería, *Colombia* **168 B2** 8 46N 75 53W
Montero, *Bolivia* **173 D5** 17 20 S 63 15W
Monteros, *Argentina* **174 B2** 27 11 S 65 30W
Monterotondo, *Italy* **45 F9** 42 3N 12 37 E
Monterrey, *Mexico* **162 B4** 25 40N 100 30W
Montes Altos, *Brazil* **170 C2** 5 50 S 47 4W
Montes Azules ⌂, *Mexico* **163 D6** 16 21N 91 3W
Montes Claros, *Brazil* **171 E3** 16 30 S 43 50W
Montesano, *U.S.A.* **160 D3** 46 59N 123 36W
Montesano sulla Marcellana, *Italy* **47 B8** 40 16N 15 42 E
Montesárchio, *Italy* **47 A7** 41 4N 14 38 E
Montescaglioso, *Italy* **47 B9** 40 33N 16 40 E
Montesilvano, *Italy* **45 F11** 42 29N 14 8 E
Montesinho ⌂, *Portugal* **42 D4** 41 54N 6 52W
Montevarchi, *Italy* **45 E8** 43 31N 11 34 E
Montevideo, *Uruguay* **175 C4** 34 50 S 56 11W
Montevideo, *U.S.A.* **154 C7** 44 57N 95 43W
Montezuma, *Ga., U.S.A.* **152 C5** 32 18N 84 2W
Montezuma, *Ind., U.S.A.* **157 E9** 39 48N 87 22W
Montezuma, *Iowa, U.S.A.* **156 C4** 41 35N 92 32W
Montezuma Castle ⌂, *U.S.A.* **159 J8** 34 34N 111 45W
Montfaucon, *France* **26 E5** 47 6N 1 7W
Montfaucon-d'Argonne, *France* **27 C12** 49 16N 5 8 E
Montfaucon-en-Velay, *France* **29 C8** 45 11N 4 20 E
Montfort-le-Gesnois, *France* **26 D7** 48 3N 0 25 E
Montfort-sur-Meu, *France* **26 D5** 48 9N 1 58W
Montfragüe ⌂, *Spain* **42 F5** 39 48N 5 52W
Montgenèvre, *France* **29 D10** 44 56N 6 43 E
Montgomery = Sahiwal, *Pakistan* **91 C4** 30 45N 73 8 E
Montgomery, *U.K.* **21 E4** 52 34N 3 8W
Montgomery, *Ala., U.S.A.* **152 C3** 32 23N 86 19W
Montgomery, *Ill., U.S.A.* **157 C8** 41 44N 88 21W
Montgomery, *Pa., U.S.A.* **150 E8** 41 10N 76 53W
Montgomery, *W. Va., U.S.A.* **148 F5** 38 11N 81 19W
Montgomery City, *U.S.A.* **156 F5** 38 59N 91 30W
Montguyon, *France* **28 C3** 45 12N 0 12W
Monthermé, *France* **27 C11** 49 52N 4 42 E
Monthey, *Switz.* **32 D3** 46 15N 6 56 E
Monthois, *France* **27 C11** 49 19N 4 43 E
Monti, *Italy* **46 B2** 40 49N 9 19 E
Monti Lucrétili ⌂, *Italy* **45 F9** 42 5N 12 50 E
Monti Picentini ⌂, *Italy* **47 B8** 40 45N 15 2 E
Monti Simbruini ⌂, *Italy* **45 G10** 41 55N 13 13 E
Monticelli d'Ongina, *Italy* **44 C6** 45 5N 9 56 E
Monticello, *Ark., U.S.A.* **155 J9** 33 38N 91 47W
Monticello, *Fla., U.S.A.* **152 E6** 30 33N 83 52W
Monticello, *Ga., U.S.A.* **152 B6** 33 18N 83 40W
Monticello, *Ill., U.S.A.* **157 D8** 40 1N 88 34W
Monticello, *Ind., U.S.A.* **157 D10** 40 45N 86 46W
Monticello, *Iowa, U.S.A.* **156 B5** 42 15N 91 12W
Monticello, *Ky., U.S.A.* **149 G3** 36 50N 84 51W
Monticello, *Minn., U.S.A.* **154 C8** 45 18N 93 48W
Monticello, *Miss., U.S.A.* **155 K9** 31 33N 90 7W
Monticello, *Mo., U.S.A.* **156 D5** 40 7N 91 43W
Monticello, *N.Y., U.S.A.* **151 E10** 41 39N 74 42W
Monticello, *Utah, U.S.A.* **159 H9** 37 52N 109 21W
Montichiari, *Italy* **44 C7** 45 25N 10 23 E
Montier-en-Der, *France* **27 D11** 48 30N 4 45 E
Montignac, *France* **28 C5** 45 4N 1 10 E
Montigny-les-Metz, *France* **27 C13** 49 7N 6 10 E
Montigny-sur-Aube, *France* **27 E11** 47 57N 4 45 E
Montijo, *Portugal* **43 G2** 38 41N 8 54W
Montijo, *Spain* **43 G4** 38 52N 6 39W
Montilla, *Spain* **43 H6** 37 36N 4 40W
Montivilliers, *France* **26 C7** 49 33N 0 12 E
Montluçon, *France* **27 F9** 46 22N 2 36 E
Montmagny, *Canada* **141 C5** 46 58N 70 34W
Montmarault, *France* **27 F9** 46 19N 2 57 E
Montmartre, *Canada* **143 C8** 50 14N 103 27W
Montmédy, *France* **27 C12** 49 30N 5 20 E
Montmélian, *France* **29 C10** 45 30N 6 4 E
Montmirail, *France* **27 D10** 48 51N 3 30 E
Montmoreau-St-Cybard, *France* **28 C4** 45 23N 0 8 E
Montmorillon, *France* **28 B4** 46 26N 0 50 E
Montmort-Lucy, *France* **27 D10** 48 55N 3 49 E
Monto, *Australia* **126 C5** 24 52 S 151 6 E
Montohora, *N.Z.* **130 E6** 38 17 S 177 32 E
Montoire-sur-le-Loir, *France* **26 E7** 47 45N 0 52 E
Montongbuwoh, *Indonesia* **79 K19** 8 33 S 116 4 E
Montório al Vomano, *Italy* **45 F10** 42 35N 13 38 E
Montoro, *Spain* **43 G6** 38 1N 4 27W
Montour Falls, *U.S.A.* **150 D8** 42 21N 76 51W
Montoursville, *U.S.A.* **150 E8** 41 15N 76 55W
Montpelier, *Idaho, U.S.A.* **158 E8** 42 19N 111 18W
Montpelier, *Ind., U.S.A.* **157 D11** 40 33N 85 17W
Montpelier, *Ohio, U.S.A.* **157 C12** 41 35N 84 37W
Montpelier, *Vt., U.S.A.* **151 B12** 44 16N 72 35W
Montpellier, *France* **28 E7** 43 37N 3 52 E
Montpezat-de-Quercy, *France* **28 D5** 44 15N 1 30 E
Montpon-Ménestérol, *France* **28 D4** 45 0N 0 11 E
Montréal, *Canada* **140 C5** 45 31N 73 34W
Montréal, *Aude, France* **28 E6** 43 13N 2 8 E
Montréal, *Gers, France* **28 E4** 43 56N 0 11 E
Montreal →, *Canada* **140 C3** 47 14N 84 39W
Montreal L., *Canada* **143 C7** 54 20N 105 45W
Montreal Lake, *Canada* **143 C7** 54 3N 105 46W
Montredon-Labessonnié, *France* **28 E6** 43 45N 2 18 E
Montrésor, *France* **26 E8** 47 10N 1 10 E
Montret, *France* **27 F12** 46 40N 5 7 E
Montreuil, *Pas-de-Calais, France* **27 B8** 50 27N 1 45 E
Montreuil, *Seine-St-Denis, France* **27 D9** 48 51N 2 27 E
Montreuil-Bellay, *France* **26 E6** 47 8N 0 9W
Montreux, *Switz.* **32 D3** 46 26N 6 55 E
Montrevel-en-Bresse, *France* **27 F12** 46 21N 5 8 E
Montrichard, *France* **26 E8** 47 20N 1 10 E
Montrose, *U.K.* **22 E6** 56 44N 2 27W
Montrose, *Colo., U.S.A.* **159 G10** 38 29N 107 53W
Montrose, *Pa., U.S.A.* **151 E9** 41 50N 75 53W
Montrose, L., *U.S.A.* **156 F3** 38 18N 93 50W
Monts, Pte. des, *Canada* **141 C6** 49 20N 67 12W
Montsalvy, *France* **28 D6** 44 41N 2 30 E
Montsant, Serra de, *Spain* **40 D6** 41 17N 1 0 E
Montsauche-les-Settons, *France* **27 E11** 47 13N 4 2 E
Montsec, Serra del, *Spain* **40 C5** 42 5N 0 45 E
Montseny ⌂, *Spain* **40 D7** 41 43N 2 22W
Montserrat, *Spain* **40 D6** 41 36N 1 49 E
Montserrat ☒, *W. Indies* **165 C7** 16 40N 62 10W
Montuenga, *Spain* **42 D6** 41 3N 4 38W
Montuiri, *Spain* **38 B3** 39 34N 2 59 E
Monveda, *Dem. Rep. of the Congo* **114 B4** 2 52N 21 30 E
Monyo, *Burma* **90 G5** 17 59N 95 30 E
Monywa, *Burma* **90 D5** 22 7N 95 11 E
Monza, *Italy* **44 C6** 45 35N 9 16 E
Monze, *Zambia* **119 F2** 16 17 S 27 29 E
Monze, C., *Pakistan* **91 D2** 24 47N 66 37 E
Monzón, *Spain* **40 D5** 41 52N 0 10 E
Moodyville = North Vancouver, *Canada* **142 D4** 49 19N 123 4W
Mooers, *U.S.A.* **151 B11** 44 58N 73 35W
Mooi →, *S. Africa* **117 D5** 28 45 S 30 34 E
Mooi River, *S. Africa* **117 D4** 29 13 S 29 50 E
Mo'oka, *Japan* **73 A12** 36 26N 140 1 E
Moonah →, *Australia* **126 C2** 22 3 S 138 33 E
Moonda, L., *Australia* **126 D3** 25 52 S 140 25 E
Moonie, *Australia* **127 D5** 27 46 S 150 20 E
Moonie →, *Australia* **127 D4** 29 19 S 148 43 E
Moonta, *Australia* **128 C2** 34 6 S 137 32 E
Moor, Kepulauan, *Indonesia* **83 B5** 2 57 S 135 45 E
Moora, *Australia* **125 F2** 30 37 S 115 58 E
Moorcroft, *U.S.A.* **154 C2** 44 16N 104 57W
Moore →, *Australia* **125 F2** 31 22 S 115 30 E
Moore, L., *Australia* **125 F2** 29 50 S 117 35 E
Moore Haven, *U.S.A.* **153 J8** 26 50N 81 6W
Moore Park, *Australia* **126 C5** 24 43 S 152 17 E
Moore River △, *Australia* **125 F2** 31 7 S 115 39 E
Mooréa, *French Polynesia* **133 S16** 17 30 S 149 50W
Moorefield, *U.S.A.* **148 F6** 39 5N 78 59W
Moores Res., *U.S.A.* **151 B13** 44 45N 71 50W
Mooresville, *U.S.A.* **157 E10** 39 37N 86 22W
Moorfoot Hills, *U.K.* **22 F5** 55 44N 3 8W
Moorhead, *U.S.A.* **154 B6** 46 53N 96 45W
Moorland, *U.S.A.* **156 B2** 42 26N 94 18W
Moormerland, *Germany* **30 B3** 53 20N 7 20 E
Moornanyah L., *Australia* **128 B5** 33 15 S 143 42 E
Mooroopna, *Australia* **129 D6** 36 25 S 145 22 E
Moorpark, *U.S.A.* **161 L8** 34 17N 118 53W
Moorreesburg, *S. Africa* **116 E2** 33 6 S 18 38 E
Moorrinya △, *Australia* **126 C3** 21 42 S 144 58 E
Moosburg, *Germany* **31 G7** 48 27N 11 56 E
Moose →, *Canada* **140 B3** 51 20N 80 25W
Moose →, *U.S.A.* **151 C9** 43 38N 75 24W
Moose Creek, *Canada* **151 A10** 45 15N 74 58W
Moose Factory, *Canada* **140 B3** 51 16N 80 32W
Moose Jaw, *Canada* **143 C7** 50 24N 105 30W
Moose Jaw →, *Canada* **143 C7** 50 34N 105 18W
Moose Lake, *U.S.A.* **154 B8** 46 27N 92 46W
Moose Mountain ⌂, *Canada* **143 D8** 49 48N 102 25W
Moose Pass, *U.S.A.* **144 F10** 60 29N 149 22W
Moosehead L., *U.S.A.* **149 C11** 45 38N 69 40W
Mooselookmeguntic L., *U.S.A.* **149 C10** 44 55N 70 49W
Moosilauke, Mt., *U.S.A.* **151 B13** 44 3N 71 40W
Moosomin, *Canada* **143 C8** 50 9N 101 40W
Moosonee, *Canada* **140 B3** 51 17N 80 39W
Moosup, *U.S.A.* **151 E13** 41 43N 71 53W
Mootwingee △, *Australia* **128 A5** 31 10 S 142 30 E
Mopane, *S. Africa* **117 C4** 22 37 S 29 52 E
Mopeia Velha, *Mozam.* **119 F4** 17 30 S 35 40 E
Mopipi, *Botswana* **116 C3** 21 6 S 24 55 E
Mopoi, *C.A.R.* **118 A2** 5 6N 26 54 E
Mopti, *Mali* **112 C4** 14 30N 4 0W
Moqatta, *Sudan* **107 E4** 14 38N 35 50 E
Moqor, *Afghan.* **91 B2** 32 50N 67 42 E
Moquegua, *Peru* **172 D3** 17 15 S 70 46W
Moquegua □, *Peru* **172 D3** 16 50 S 70 55W
Mór, *Hungary* **52 C3** 47 25N 18 12 E
Mora, *Cameroon* **109 F2** 11 3N 14 9 E
Mora, *Cameroon* **113 C7** 11 2N 14 7 E
Móra, *Portugal* **43 G2** 38 55N 8 10W
Mora, *Spain* **43 F7** 39 41N 3 46W
Mora, *Sweden* **16 C8** 61 2N 14 38 E
Mora, *Minn., U.S.A.* **154 C8** 45 53N 93 18W
Mora, *N. Mex., U.S.A.* **159 J11** 35 58N 105 20W
Mora de Rubielos, *Spain* **40 E4** 40 15N 0 45W
Mòra d'Ebre, *Spain* **40 D5** 41 6N 0 38 E
Mòra la Nova, *Spain* **40 D5** 41 7N 0 39 E
Morača →, *Serbia & M.* **50 D3** 42 20N 19 9 E
Morada Nova, *Brazil* **170 C4** 5 7 S 38 23W
Morada Nova de Minas, *Brazil* **171 E2** 18 37 S 45 22W
Moradabad, *India* **93 E8** 28 50N 78 50 E
Morafenobe, *Madag.* **117 B7** 17 50 S 44 53 E
Morąg, *Poland* **54 E6** 53 55N 19 56 E
Moral de Calatrava, *Spain* **43 G7** 38 51N 3 33W
Moraleda, Canal, *Chile* **176 B2** 44 30 S 73 30W
Moraleja, *Spain* **42 E4** 40 6N 6 43W
Morales, *Bolívar, Colombia* **168 B3** 8 16N 73 51W
Morales, *Cauca, Colombia* **168 C2** 2 45N 76 38W
Moramanga, *Madag.* **117 B8** 18 56 S 48 12 E
Moran, *Kans., U.S.A.* **155 G7** 37 55N 95 10W
Moran, *Wyo., U.S.A.* **158 E8** 43 53N 110 37W
Moranbah, *Australia* **126 C4** 22 1 S 148 6 E
Moranhat, *India* **90 B5** 27 10N 94 50 E
Morano Cálabro, *Italy* **47 C9** 39 50N 16 8 E
Morant Bay, *Jamaica* **164 a** 17 53N 76 25W
Morant Cays, *Jamaica* **164 C4** 17 22N 76 0W
Morant Pt., *Jamaica* **164 a** 17 55N 76 12W
Morar, *India* **92 F8** 26 14N 78 14 E
Morar, L., *U.K.* **22 E3** 56 57N 5 40W
Moratalla, *Spain* **41 G3** 38 14N 1 49W
Moratuwa, *Sri Lanka* **95 L4** 6 45N 79 55 E
Morava →, *Slovak Rep.* **35 C9** 48 10N 16 59 E
Moravia, *Iowa, U.S.A.* **156 D4** 40 53N 92 49W
Moravia, *N.Y., U.S.A.* **151 D8** 42 43N 76 25W
Moravian Hts. = Českomoravská Vrchovina, *Czech Rep.* **34 B8** 49 30N 15 40 E
Moravica →, *Serbia & M.* **50 C4** 43 52N 20 8 E
Moravița, *Romania* **52 E6** 45 17N 21 14 E
Moravská Třebová, *Czech Rep.* **35 B9** 49 45N 16 40 E
Moravské Budějovice, *Czech Rep.* **34 B8** 49 4N 15 49 E
Morawa, *Australia* **125 E2** 29 13 S 116 0 E
Morawhanna, *Guyana* **169 B6** 8 30N 59 40W
Moray □, *U.K.* **22 D5** 57 31N 3 18W
Moray Firth, *U.K.* **22 D5** 57 40N 3 52W
Morbach, *Germany* **31 F3** 49 48N 7 6 E
Morbegno, *Italy* **44 B6** 46 8N 9 34 E
Morbi, *India* **92 H4** 22 50N 70 42 E
Morbihan □, *France* **26 E4** 47 55N 2 50W
Mörbylånga, *Sweden* **17 H10** 56 32N 16 22 E
Morcenx, *France* **28 D3** 44 3N 0 55W
Morcone, *Italy* **47 A7** 41 20N 14 40 E
Mordelles, *France* **26 D5** 48 5N 1 52W
Morden, *Canada* **143 D9** 49 15N 98 10W
Mordoğan, *Turkey* **49 C8** 38 30N 26 37 E
Mordovian Republic = Mordvinia □, *Russia* **60 C7** 54 20N 44 30 E
Mordovo, *Russia* **60 D5** 52 6N 40 50 E
Mordvinia □, *Russia* **60 C7** 54 20N 44 30 E
Mordy, *Poland* **55 F9** 52 13N 22 31 E
Møre og Romsdal □, *Norway* **18 B4** 62 30N 8 0 E
Morea, *Greece* **12 H10** 37 45N 22 10 E
Moreau →, *U.S.A.* **154 C4** 45 18N 100 43W
Morecambe, *U.K.* **20 C5** 54 5N 2 52W
Morecambe B., *U.K.* **20 C5** 54 7N 3 0W
Moree, *Australia* **127 D4** 29 28 S 149 54 E
Morehead, *Papua N. G.* **132 E1** 8 41 S 141 41 E
Morehead, *U.S.A.* **157 F13** 38 11N 83 26W
Morehead City, *U.S.A.* **149 H7** 34 43N 76 43W
Mörel, *Switz.* **32 D6** 46 22N 8 2 E
Morel →, *India* **92 F7** 26 13N 76 36 E
Moreland, *U.S.A.* **152 B5** 33 17N 84 46W
Morelia, *Mexico* **162 D4** 19 42N 101 7W
Morella, *Australia* **126 C3** 23 0 S 143 52 E
Morella, *Spain* **40 E4** 40 35N 0 5W
Morelos, *Mexico* **162 B3** 26 42N 107 40W
Morelos □, *Mexico* **163 D5** 18 40N 99 10W
Moremi ⌂, *Botswana* **116 B3** 19 18 S 23 10 E
Morena, *India* **92 F8** 26 30N 78 4 E
Morena, Sierra, *Spain* **43 G7** 38 20N 4 0W
Morenci, *U.S.A.* **157 C12** 41 43N 84 13W
Moreni, *Romania* **53 F10** 44 59N 25 36 E
Moreno Valley, *U.S.A.* **161 M10** 33 56N 117 15W
Morero, *Bolivia* **173 C4** 11 9 S 66 15W
Moreru →, *Brazil* **173 C6** 10 10 S 59 15W
Moresby I., *Canada* **142 C2** 52 30N 131 40W
Morestel, *France* **29 C9** 45 40N 5 28 E
Moreton I., *Australia* **127 D5** 27 10 S 153 25 E
Moreton Island △, *Australia* **127 D5** 27 2 S 153 24 E
Moreuil, *France* **27 C9** 49 46N 2 30 E
Morey, *Spain* **38 B4** 39 44N 3 20 E
Morez, *France* **27 F13** 46 31N 6 2 E
Morgan, *Australia* **128 C3** 34 2 S 139 35 E
Morgan, *Ga., U.S.A.* **152 D5** 31 32N 84 36W
Morgan, *Utah, U.S.A.* **158 F8** 41 2N 111 41W
Morgan City, *U.S.A.* **155 L9** 29 42N 91 12W
Morgan Hill, *U.S.A.* **160 H5** 37 8N 121 39W
Morganfield, *U.S.A.* **148 G2** 37 41N 87 55W
Morganton, *U.S.A.* **149 H5** 35 45N 81 41W
Morgantown, *Ind., U.S.A.* **157 E10** 39 22N 86 16W
Morgantown, *W. Va., U.S.A.* **148 F6** 39 38N 79 57W
Morgenzon, *S. Africa* **117 D4** 26 45 S 29 36 E
Morges, *Switz.* **32 C2** 46 31N 6 29 E
Morghak, *Iran* **97 D8** 29 7N 57 54 E
Morgongåva, *Sweden* **16 E10** 59 57N 16 58 E
Morhange, *France* **27 D13** 48 55N 6 38 E
Morhar →, *India* **93 G11** 25 29N 85 11 E
Mori, *Italy* **44 C7** 45 51N 10 59 E
Mori, *Japan* **70 C10** 42 6N 140 35 E
Moriarty, *U.S.A.* **159 J10** 34 59N 106 3W
Moribaya, *Guinea* **112 D3** 9 53N 9 32W
Morice L., *Canada* **142 C3** 53 50N 127 40W
Morichal, *Colombia* **168 C3** 2 10N 70 34W
Morichal Largo →, *Venezuela* **169 B5** 9 27N 62 25W
Moriguchi, *Japan* **73 C7** 34 44N 135 34 E
Moriki, *Nigeria* **113 C6** 12 52N 6 30 E
Morinville, *Canada* **142 C6** 53 49N 113 41W
Morioka, *Japan* **70 E10** 39 45N 141 8 E
Moris, *Mexico* **162 B3** 28 8N 108 52W
Morisset, *Australia* **129 B9** 33 6 S 151 30 E
Moriyama, *Japan* **73 B7** 35 4N 135 59 E
Morlaàs, *France* **28 E3** 43 21N 0 18W
Morlaix, *France* **26 D3** 48 36N 3 52W
Mörlunda, *Sweden* **17 G9** 57 19N 15 52 E
Mormanno, *Italy* **47 C8** 39 53N 15 59 E
Mormant, *France* **27 D9** 48 37N 2 52 E
Mornington, *Australia* **129 E6** 38 15 S 145 5 E
Mornington, I., *Chile* **176 C1** 49 50 S 75 30W
Mornington I., *Australia* **126 B2** 16 30 S 139 30 E
Mórnos →, *Greece* **48 C3** 38 25N 21 50 E
Moro, *Pakistan* **92 F2** 26 40N 68 0 E
Moro, *Sudan* **107 E3** 10 50N 30 9 E
Moro →, *Pakistan* **92 E2** 29 42N 67 22 E
Moro G., *Phil.* **81 H4** 6 30N 123 0 E
Morobe, *Papua N. G.* **132 D4** 7 49 S 147 38 E
Morobe □, *Papua N. G.* **132 D4** 7 0 S 147 0 E
Morocco, *U.S.A.* **157 D9** 40 57N 87 27W
Morocco ■, *N. Afr.* **110 B3** 32 0N 5 50W
Morococha, *Peru* **172 C2** 11 40 S 76 5W
Morogoro, *Tanzania* **118 D4** 6 50 S 37 40 E
Morogoro □, *Tanzania* **118 D4** 8 0 S 37 0 E
Moroleón, *Mexico* **162 C4** 20 8N 101 32W
Morombe, *Madag.* **117 C7** 21 45 S 43 22 E
Moron = Morong, *Phil.* **80 D3** 14 41N 120 16 E
Morón, *Argentina* **174 C4** 34 39 S 58 37W
Morón, *Cuba* **164 B4** 22 8N 78 39W
Morón de Almazán, *Spain* **40 D2** 41 29N 2 27W
Morón de la Frontera, *Spain* **43 H5** 37 6N 5 28W
Morona →, *Peru* **168 D2** 4 40 S 77 10W
Morona-Santiago □, *Ecuador* **168 D2** 2 30 S 78 0W
Morondava, *Madag.* **117 C7** 20 17 S 44 17 E
Morondo, *Ivory C.* **112 D3** 8 57N 6 47W
Morong, *Phil.* **80 D3** 14 41N 120 16 E
Morongo Valley, *U.S.A.* **161 L10** 34 3N 116 37W
Moroni, *Comoros Is.* **121 a** 11 40 S 43 16 E
Moroni, *U.S.A.* **158 G8** 39 32N 111 35W
Moronou, *Ivory C.* **112 D4** 6 16N 4 59W
Morotai, *Indonesia* **82 A3** 2 10N 128 30 E
Moroto, *Uganda* **118 B3** 2 28N 34 42 E
Moroto, Mt., *Uganda* **118 B3** 2 30N 34 43 E
Morowali, *Indonesia* **82 B2** 1 52 S 121 30 E
Morozov, *Bulgaria* **51 D9** 42 30N 25 10 E
Morozovsk, *Russia* **61 F5** 48 25N 41 50 E
Morpeth, *U.K.* **20 B6** 55 10N 1 41W
Morphou, *Cyprus* **39 E8** 35 12N 32 59 E
Morphou Bay, *Cyprus* **39 E8** 35 15N 32 50 E
Morrelganj, *Bangla.* **90 D2** 22 28N 89 51 E
Morrilton, *U.S.A.* **155 H8** 35 9N 92 44W
Morrinhos, *Ceará, Brazil* **170 B3** 3 14 S 40 7W
Morrinhos, *Minas Gerais, Brazil* **171 E2** 17 45 S 49 10W
Morrinsville, *N.Z.* **130 D4** 37 40 S 175 32 E
Morris, *Canada* **143 D9** 49 25N 97 22W
Morris, *Ill., U.S.A.* **154 E10** 41 22N 88 26W
Morris, *Minn., U.S.A.* **154 C7** 45 35N 95 55W
Morris, *N.Y., U.S.A.* **151 D9** 42 33N 75 15W
Morris, *Pa., U.S.A.* **150 E7** 41 35N 77 17W
Morris, Mt., *Australia* **125 E5** 26 9 S 131 4 E
Morris Jesup, Kap, *Greenland* **10 A7** 83 40N 34 0W
Morrisburg, *Canada* **151 B9** 44 55N 75 7W
Morrison, *U.S.A.* **156 C7** 41 49N 89 58W
Morrisonville, *U.S.A.* **156 E7** 39 25N 89 27W
Morristown, *Ariz., U.S.A.* **159 K7** 33 51N 112 37W
Morristown, *Ind., U.S.A.* **157 E11** 39 40N 85 42W
Morristown, *N.J., U.S.A.* **151 F10** 40 48N 74 29W

Morristown, *N.Y., U.S.A.* **151 B9** 44 35N 75 39W
Morristown, *Tenn., U.S.A.* **149 G4** 36 13N 83 18W
Morrisville, *N.Y., U.S.A.* **151 D9** 42 53N 75 35W
Morrisville, *Pa., U.S.A.* **151 F10** 40 13N 74 47W
Morrisville, *Vt., U.S.A.* **151 B12** 44 34N 72 36W
Morro, Pta., *Chile* **174 B1** 27 6 S 71 0W
Morro Bay, *U.S.A.* **160 K6** 35 22N 120 51W
Morro Chico, *Chile* **176 D2** 52 2 S 71 26W
Morro del Jable, *Canary Is.* **9 e2** 28 3N 14 23W
Morro do Chapéu, *Brazil* **171 D3** 11 33 S 41 9W
Morro Grande = Barão de Cocais, *Brazil* **171 E3** 19 56 S 43 28W
Morro Jable, Pta. de, *Canary Is.* **9 e2** 28 2N 14 20W
Morrocoy △, *Venezuela* **165 D6** 10 48N 68 13W
Morros, *Brazil* **170 B3** 2 52 S 44 3W
Morrosquillo, G. de, *Colombia* **164 E4** 9 35N 75 40W
Morrow, *U.S.A.* **157 E12** 39 21N 84 8W
Mörrum, *Sweden* **17 H8** 56 12N 14 45 E
Morrumbene, *Mozam.* **117 C6** 23 31 S 35 16 E
Mörrumsån →, *Sweden* **17 H8** 56 10N 14 45 E
Mors, *Denmark* **17 H2** 56 50N 8 45 E
Morshansk, *Russia* **60 D5** 53 28N 41 50 E
Morsi, *India* **94 D4** 21 21N 78 0 E
Mörsil, *Sweden* **16 A7** 63 19N 13 40 E
Mortagne →, *France* **27 D13** 48 33N 6 27 E
Mortagne-au-Perche, *France* **26 D7** 48 31N 0 33 E
Mortagne-sur-Gironde, *France* **28 C3** 45 28N 0 47W
Mortagne-sur-Sèvre, *France* **26 F6** 47 0N 0 59W
Mortain, *France* **26 D6** 48 40N 0 57W
Mortara, *Italy* **44 C5** 45 15N 8 44 E
Morteau, *France* **27 E13** 47 3N 6 35 E
Morteros, *Argentina* **174 C3** 30 50 S 62 0W
Mortes, R. das →, *Brazil* **171 D1** 11 45 S 50 44W
Mortlach, *Canada* **143 C7** 50 27N 106 4W
Mortlake, *Australia* **128 E5** 38 5 S 142 50 E
Morton, *Ill., U.S.A.* **156 D7** 40 37N 89 28W
Morton, *Tex., U.S.A.* **155 J3** 33 44N 102 46W
Morton, *Wash., U.S.A.* **160 D4** 46 34N 122 17W
Morton △, *Australia* **129 C9** 35 0 S 150 12 E
Moruga, *Trin. & Tob.* **169 F9** 10 4N 61 16W
Morundah, *Australia* **129 C7** 34 57 S 146 19 E
Moruya, *Australia* **129 C9** 35 58 S 150 3 E
Morvan, *France* **27 E11** 47 5N 4 3 E
Morvan ⌂, *France* **27 E11** 47 12N 4 3 E
Morven, *Australia* **127 D4** 26 22 S 147 5 E
Morven, *N.Z.* **131 E6** 44 50 S 171 6 E
Morven, *U.S.A.* **152 E6** 30 57N 83 30W
Morvern, *U.K.* **22 E3** 56 38N 5 44W
Morwell, *Australia* **129 E7** 38 10 S 146 22 E
Moryń, *Poland* **55 F1** 52 51N 14 22 E
Morzhovets, Ostrov, *Russia* **56 A7** 66 44N 42 35 E
Morzine, *France* **27 F13** 46 11N 6 42 E
Mosalsk, *Russia* **58 E8** 54 30N 34 55 E
Mosbach, *Germany* **25 F5** 49 21N 9 9 E
Mosby, *Norway* **18 F4** 58 12N 7 55 E
Moščenice, *Croatia* **45 C11** 45 17N 14 16 E
Mosciano Sant' Ángelo, *Italy* **45 F10** 42 42N 13 52 E
Moscos Is., *Burma* **86 E1** 14 0N 97 30 E
Moscow = Moskva, *Russia* **58 E9** 55 45N 37 35 E
Moscow, *Idaho, U.S.A.* **158 C5** 46 44N 117 0W
Moscow, *Mich., U.S.A.* **157 B12** 42 3N 84 30W
Moscow, *Pa., U.S.A.* **151 E9** 41 20N 75 31W
Moscow Mills, *U.S.A.* **156 F6** 38 57N 90 55W
Mosel →, *Europe* **27 B14** 50 22N 7 36 E
Moselle = Mosel →, *Europe* **27 B14** 50 22N 7 36 E
Moselle □, *France* **27 D13** 48 59N 6 33 E
Moses Lake, *U.S.A.* **158 C4** 47 8N 119 17W
Mosgiel, *N.Z.* **131 F5** 45 53 S 170 21 E
Moshaweng →, *S. Africa* **116 D3** 26 35 S 22 50 E
Moshi, *Tanzania* **118 C4** 3 22 S 37 18 E
Moshupa, *Botswana* **116 C4** 24 46 S 25 29 E
Mosina, *Poland* **55 F3** 52 15N 16 50 E
Mosite, *Dem. Rep. of the Congo* **114 B4** 0 53N 23 40 E
Mosjøen, *Norway* **14 D15** 65 51N 13 12 E
Moskenesøya, *Norway* **14 C15** 67 58N 13 0 E
Moskenstraumen, *Norway* **14 C15** 67 47N 12 45 E
Moskog, *Norway* **18 C2** 61 26N 6 0 E
Moskovskiy, *Tajikistan* **65 E4** 37 37N 69 42 E
Moskovsky = Shakhrikhan, *Uzbekistan* **65 C6** 40 42N 72 3 E
Moskva, *Russia* **58 E9** 55 45N 37 35 E
Moskva →, *Russia* **58 E10** 55 5N 38 51 E
Moslavačka Gora, *Croatia* **45 C13** 45 40N 16 37 E
Moso, *Vanuatu* **133 G6** 17 30 S 168 15 E
Mosomane, *Botswana* **116 C4** 24 2 S 26 19 E
Mosonmagyaróvár, *Hungary* **52 C2** 47 52N 17 18 E
Mošorin, *Serbia & M.* **52 E5** 45 19N 20 4 E
Mospino, *Ukraine* **59 J9** 47 52N 38 0 E
Mosqueiro, *Brazil* **170 B2** 1 10 S 48 28W
Mosquera, *Colombia* **168 C2** 2 35N 78 24W
Mosquero, *U.S.A.* **155 H3** 35 47N 103 58W
Mosqueruela, *Spain* **40 E4** 40 21N 0 27W
Mosquitia, *Honduras* **164 C3** 15 20N 84 10W
Mosquito Coast = Mosquitia, *Honduras* **164 C3** 15 20N 84 10W
Mosquito Creek L., *U.S.A.* **150 E4** 41 18N 80 46W
Mosquito L., *Canada* **143 A8** 62 35N 103 20W
Mosquitos, G. de los, *Panama* **164 E3** 9 15N 81 10W
Moss, *Norway* **18 E7** 59 27N 10 40 E
Moss Vale, *Australia* **129 C9** 34 32 S 150 25 E
Mossaka, *Congo* **114 C3** 1 15 S 16 45 E
Mossâmedes, *Brazil* **171 E1** 16 7 S 50 11W
Mossbank, *Canada* **143 D7** 49 56N 105 56W
Mossburn, *N.Z.* **131 F3** 45 41 S 168 15 E
Mosselbaai, *S. Africa* **116 E3** 34 11 S 22 8 E
Mossendjo, *Congo* **114 C2** 2 55 S 12 42 E
Mosses, Col des, *Switz.* **32 D4** 46 25N 7 7 E
Mossfellsbær, *Iceland* **11 C5** 64 11N 21 45W
Mossgiel, *Australia* **128 B6** 33 15 S 144 5 E
Mössingen, *Germany* **31 G5** 48 24N 9 4 E
Mossman, *Australia* **126 B4** 16 21 S 145 15 E
Mossoró, *Brazil* **170 C4** 5 10 S 37 15W
Mossuril, *Mozam.* **119 E5** 14 58 S 40 42 E
Mossy Head, *U.S.A.* **153 E3** 30 45N 86 19W
Mossy Point, *Australia* **129 C9** 35 50 S 150 11 E
Most, *Czech Rep.* **34 A6** 50 31N 13 38 E
Mosta, *Malta* **38 F7** 35 55N 14 26 E
Mostaganem, *Algeria* **111 A5** 35 54N 0 5 E
Mostar, *Bos.-H.* **52 G2** 43 22N 17 50 E
Mostardas, *Brazil* **175 C5** 31 2 S 50 51W
Mostefa, Rass, *Tunisia* **108 A2** 36 55N 11 3 E
Mosteiros, *Azores* **9 d3** 37 53N 25 49W
Mosterhamn, *Norway* **18 E2** 59 42N 5 21 E
Mostiska = Mostyska, *Ukraine* **55 J10** 49 48N 23 4 E
Móstoles, *Spain* **42 E7** 40 19N 3 53W
Mosty = Masty, *Belarus* **58 F3** 53 27N 24 38 E
Mostyska, *Ukraine* **55 J10** 49 48N 23 4 E
Mosul = Al Mawşil, *Iraq* **101 D10** 36 15N 43 5 E
Mosŭlpo, *S. Korea* **75 H14** 33 20N 126 17 E
Møsvatnet, *Norway* **18 E5** 59 52N 8 5 E
Mota, *Ethiopia* **107 E4** 11 5N 37 52 E
Mota, *Vanuatu* **133 C5** 13 49 S 167 42 E
Mota del Cuervo, *Spain* **41 F2** 39 30N 2 52W
Mota del Marqués, *Spain* **42 D5** 41 38N 5 11W
Mota Lava, *Vanuatu* **133 C5** 13 40 S 167 40 E
Motaba, *Congo* **114 B3** 2 6N 18 2 E
Motagua →, *Guatemala* **164 C2** 15 44N 88 14W
Motala, *Sweden* **17 F9** 58 32N 15 1 E
Motaze, *Mozam.* **117 C5** 24 48 S 32 52 E
Moţca, *Romania* **53 C11** 47 15N 26 37 E
Motegi, *Japan* **73 A12** 36 32N 140 11 E
Moth, *India* **93 G8** 25 43N 78 57 E
Motherwell, *U.K.* **22 F5** 55 47N 3 58W
Motihari, *India* **93 F11** 26 30N 84 55 E
Motilla del Palancar, *Spain* **41 F3** 39 34N 1 55W
Motiti I., *N.Z.* **130 D5** 37 38 S 176 25 E
Motnik, *Slovenia* **45 B11** 46 14N 14 54 E
Motocurunya, *Venezuela* **169 C5** 4 24N 64 5W
Motovun, *Croatia* **45 C10** 45 20N 13 50 E
Motozintla de Mendoza, *Mexico* **163 D6** 15 21N 92 14W
Motril, *Spain* **43 J7** 36 31N 3 37W
Motru, *Romania* **52 F7** 44 48N 22 59 E
Motru →, *Romania* **53 F8** 44 32N 23 31 E
Mott, *U.S.A.* **154 B3** 46 23N 102 20W
Möttling = Metlika, *Slovenia* **45 C12** 45 40N 15 20 E
Móttola, *Italy* **47 B10** 40 38N 17 2 E
Motu →, *N.Z.* **130 D6** 37 51 S 177 35 E
Motu Nui, *Chile* **172 b** 27 12 S 109 28W
Motuba, *Dem. Rep. of the Congo* **114 B3** 2 20N 18 34 E
Motueka, *N.Z.* **131 B8** 41 7 S 173 1 E
Motueka →, *N.Z.* **131 B8** 41 5 S 173 1 E
Motul, *Mexico* **163 C7** 21 0N 89 20W
Motupena Pt., *Papua N. G.* **132 D8** 6 30 S 155 10 E
Mou, *N. Cal.* **133 U19** 21 5 S 165 26 E
Mouanda, *Gabon* **114 C2** 1 28 S 13 7 E
Mouchalagane →, *Canada* **141 B6** 50 56N 68 41W
Moúdhros, *Greece* **49 B7** 39 50N 25 18 E
Mouding, *China* **76 E3** 25 20N 101 28 E
Moudjeria, *Mauritania* **112 B2** 17 50N 12 28W
Moudon, *Switz.* **32 C3** 46 40N 6 49 E
Moudros = Moúdhros, *Greece* **49 B7** 39 50N 25 18 E
Mougoundou, *Congo* **114 C2** 2 40 S 12 41 E
Mouila, *Gabon* **114 C2** 1 50 S 11 0 E
Mouka, *C.A.R.* **114 A4** 7 16N 21 52 E
Moukabala ⌂, *Gabon* **114 C2** 2 50 S 10 35 E
Moukambo, *Gabon* **114 C2** 3 5 S 11 38 E
Moul, *Niger* **109 F2** 15 5N 13 11 E
Moulamein, *Australia* **128 C6** 35 3 S 144 1 E
Moule à Chique, C., *St. Lucia* **165 f** 13 43N 60 57W
Mouliana, *Greece* **39 E6** 35 10N 25 59 E
Moulins, *France* **27 F10** 46 35N 3 19 E
Moulmein, *Burma* **90 G6** 16 30N 97 40 E
Moulmeingyun, *Burma* **90 G5** 16 23N 95 16 E
Moulouya, O. →, *Morocco* **111 A4** 35 5N 2 25W
Moulton, *U.S.A.* **156 D4** 40 41N 92 41W
Moultrie, *U.S.A.* **152 D6** 31 11N 83 47W
Moultrie, L., *U.S.A.* **152 B9** 33 20N 80 5W
Mouly, *N. Cal.* **133 K4** 20 47 S 166 26 E
Mounana, *Gabon* **114 C2** 1 18 S 13 13 E
Mound City, *Mo., U.S.A.* **154 E7** 40 7N 95 14W
Mound City, *S. Dak., U.S.A.* **154 C4** 45 44N 100 4W
Moúnda, Ákra, *Greece* **39 C2** 38 3N 20 47 E
Moundou, *Chad* **109 G3** 8 40N 16 10 E
Moundsville, *U.S.A.* **150 G4** 39 55N 80 44W
Mounembé, *Congo* **114 C2** 3 20 S 12 32 E
Moung, *Cambodia* **86 F4** 12 46N 103 27 E
Moungoudi, *Congo* **114 C2** 2 45 S 11 46 E
Mount Airy, *U.S.A.* **149 G5** 36 31N 80 37W
Mount Albert, *Canada* **150 B5** 44 8N 79 19W
Mount Apo △, *Phil.* **81 H5** 7 0N 125 10 E
Mount Aspiring △, *N.Z.* **131 E3** 44 19 S 168 47 E
Mount Ayliff = Maxesibeni, *S. Africa* **117 E4** 30 49 S 29 23 E
Mount Ayr, *U.S.A.* **156 D2** 40 43N 94 14W
Mount Barker, *S. Austral., Australia* **128 C3** 35 5 S 138 52 E
Mount Barker, *W. Austral., Australia* **125 F2** 34 38 S 117 40 E
Mount Beauty, *Australia* **129 D7** 36 47 S 147 10 E
Mount Brydges, *Canada* **150 D3** 42 54N 81 29W
Mount Buffalo △, *Australia* **129 D7** 36 43 S 146 46 E
Mount Burr, *Australia* **127 F3** 37 34 S 140 26 E
Mount Carmel = Ha Karmel △, *Israel* **103 C4** 32 45N 35 5 E
Mount Carmel, *Ill., U.S.A.* **157 F9** 38 25N 87 46W
Mount Carmel, *Pa., U.S.A.* **151 F8** 40 47N 76 24W
Mount Carroll, *U.S.A.* **156 B7** 42 6N 89 59W
Mount Charleston, *U.S.A.* **161 J11** 36 16N 115 37W
Mount Clemens, *U.S.A.* **150 D2** 42 35N 82 53W
Mount Cook, *N.Z.* **131 D5** 43 44 S 170 5 E
Mount Cook △, *N.Z.* **131 D5** 43 35 S 170 15 E
Mount Coolon, *Australia* **126 C4** 21 25 S 147 25 E
Mount Darwin, *Zimbabwe* **119 F3** 16 47 S 31 38 E
Mount Desert I., *U.S.A.* **149 C11** 44 21N 68 20W
Mount Dora, *U.S.A.* **153 G8** 28 48N 81 38W
Mount Eccles △, *Australia* **128 E4** 38 5 S 141 54 E
Mount Eden, *U.S.A.* **157 F11** 38 3N 85 9W
Mount Edgecumbe, *U.S.A.* **144 H14** 57 3N 135 21W
Mount Edziza ⌂, *Canada* **142 B2** 57 30N 130 45W
Mount Elgon △, *E. Afr.* **118 B3** 1 4N 34 42 E
Mount Field △, *Australia* **127 G4** 42 39 S 146 35 E
Mount Fletcher, *S. Africa* **117 E4** 30 40 S 28 30 E
Mount Forest, *Canada* **140 D3** 43 59N 80 43W
Mount Frere = Kwabhaca, *S. Africa* **117 E4** 30 51 S 29 0 E
Mount Gambier, *Australia* **128 D4** 37 50 S 140 46 E
Mount Garnet, *Australia* **126 B4** 17 37 S 145 6 E
Mount Hagen, *Papua N. G.* **132 C3** 5 52 S 144 16 E
Mount Holly, *U.S.A.* **151 G10** 39 59N 74 47W
Mount Holly Springs, *U.S.A.* **150 F7** 40 7N 77 12W
Mount Hope, *N.S.W., Australia* **129 B6** 32 51 S 145 51 E
Mount Hope, *S. Austral., Australia* **127 E2** 34 7 S 135 23 E
Mount Horeb, *U.S.A.* **156 B7** 43 1N 89 44W
Mount Isa, *Australia* **126 C2** 20 42 S 139 26 E
Mount Isarog △, *Phil.* **80 E4** 13 38N 123 24 E
Mount Jewett, *U.S.A.* **150 E6** 41 44N 78 39W
Mount Kaputar △, *Australia* **127 E5** 30 16 S 150 10 E
Mount Kenya △, *Kenya* **118 C4** 0 7 S 37 21 E
Mount Kilimanjaro △, *Tanzania* **118 C4** 3 2 S 37 19 E
Mount Kisco, *U.S.A.* **151 E11** 41 12N 73 44W
Mount Laguna, *U.S.A.* **161 N10** 32 52N 116 25W
Mount Larcom, *Australia* **126 C5** 23 48 S 150 59 E
Mount Lofty Ra., *Australia* **128 C3** 34 35 S 139 5 E
Mount McKinley = Denali △, *U.S.A.* **144 E10** 63 30N 152 0W
Mount Magnet, *Australia* **125 E2** 28 2 S 117 47 E
Mount Malindang △, *Phil.* **81 G4** 8 17N 123 32 E
Mount Manara, *Australia* **128 B5** 32 29 S 143 58 E
Mount Maunganui, *N.Z.* **130 D5** 37 40 S 176 14 E
Mount Molloy, *Australia* **126 B4** 16 42 S 145 20 E
Mount Morgan, *Australia* **126 C5** 23 40 S 150 25 E
Mount Morris, *Mich., U.S.A.* **157 A13** 43 7N 83 42W
Mount Morris, *N.Y., U.S.A.* **150 D7** 42 44N 77 52W
Mount Olive, *U.S.A.* **156 E7** 39 4N 89 44W
Mount Olivet, *U.S.A.* **157 F12** 38 32N 84 2W
Mount Orab, *U.S.A.* **157 E13** 39 2N 83 55W
Mount Pearl, *Canada* **141 C9** 47 31N 52 47W
Mount Penn, *U.S.A.* **151 F9** 40 20N 75 54W
Mount Perry, *Australia* **127 D5** 25 13 S 151 42 E
Mount Pleasant, *Iowa, U.S.A.* **156 D5** 40 58N 91 33W
Mount Pleasant, *Mich., U.S.A.* **148 D3** 43 36N 84 46W
Mount Pleasant, *Pa., U.S.A.* **150 F5** 40 9N 79 33W
Mount Pleasant, *S.C., U.S.A.* **152 C10** 32 47N 79 52W
Mount Pleasant, *Tenn., U.S.A.* **149 H2** 35 32N 87 12W
Mount Pleasant, *Tex., U.S.A.* **155 J7** 33 9N 94 58W
Mount Pleasant, *Utah, U.S.A.* **158 G8** 39 33N 111 27W
Mount Pocono, *U.S.A.* **151 E9** 41 7N 75 22W
Mount Pulaski, *U.S.A.* **156 D7** 40 1N 89 17W
Mount Pulog △, *Phil.* **80 C3** 16 35N 120 57 E
Mount Rainier △, *U.S.A.* **160 D5** 46 55N 121 50W
Mount Remarkable △, *Australia* **128 B3** 32 47 S 138 3 E
Mount Revelstoke △, *Canada* **142 C5** 51 5N 118 30W
Mount Robson ⌂, *Canada* **142 C5** 53 0N 119 0W
Mount St. Helens ⌂, *U.S.A.* **160 D4** 46 14N 122 11W
Mount Selinda, *Zimbabwe* **117 C5** 20 24 S 32 43 E
Mount Shasta, *U.S.A.* **158 F2** 41 19N 122 19W
Mount Signal, *U.S.A.* **161 N11** 32 39N 115 37W
Mount Somers, *N.Z.* **131 D6** 43 45 S 171 27 E
Mount Sterling, *Ill., U.S.A.* **156 E6** 39 59N 90 45W
Mount Sterling, *Ky., U.S.A.* **157 F13** 38 4N 83 56W
Mount Sterling, *Ohio, U.S.A.* **157 E13** 39 43N 83 16W
Mount Surprise, *Australia* **126 B3** 18 10 S 144 17 E
Mount Union, *U.S.A.* **150 F7** 40 23N 77 53W
Mount Upton, *U.S.A.* **151 D9** 42 26N 75 23W
Mount Vernon, *Ga., U.S.A.* **152 C7** 32 11N 82 36W
Mount Vernon, *Ill., U.S.A.* **148 F1** 38 19N 88 55W
Mount Vernon, *Ind., U.S.A.* **154 F10** 38 17N 88 57W
Mount Vernon, *Ind., U.S.A.* **157 G9** 37 56N 87 54W
Mount Vernon, *Iowa, U.S.A.* **156 C5** 41 55N 91 23W
Mount Vernon, *N.Y., U.S.A.* **151 F11** 40 55N 73 50W
Mount Vernon, *Ohio, U.S.A.* **150 F2** 40 23N 82 29W
Mount Vernon, *Wash., U.S.A.* **160 B4** 48 25N 122 20W
Mount Victor, *Australia* **128 B3** 32 11 S 139 44 E
Mount Washington, *U.S.A.* **157 F11** 38 3N 85 33W
Mount Wellington, *N.Z.* **130 C3** 36 55 S 174 52 E
Mount William △, *Australia* **127 G4** 40 56 S 148 14 E
Mount Zion, *U.S.A.* **157 E8** 39 46N 88 53W
Mountain □, *Phil.* **80 C3** 17 20N 121 10 E
Mountain Ash, *U.K.* **21 F4** 51 40N 3 23W
Mountain Center, *U.S.A.* **161 M10** 33 42N 116 44W
Mountain City, *Nev., U.S.A.* **158 F6** 41 50N 115 58W
Mountain City, *Tenn., U.S.A.* **149 G5** 36 29N 81 48W
Mountain Dale, *U.S.A.* **151 E10** 41 41N 74 32W
Mountain Grove, *U.S.A.* **155 G8** 37 8N 92 16W
Mountain Home, *Ark., U.S.A.* **155 G8** 36 20N 92 23W
Mountain Home, *Idaho, U.S.A.* **158 E6** 43 8N 115 41W
Mountain Iron, *U.S.A.* **154 B8** 47 32N 92 37W
Mountain Pass, *U.S.A.* **161 K11** 35 29N 115 35W
Mountain View, *Ark., U.S.A.* **155 H8** 35 52N 92 7W
Mountain View, *Calif., U.S.A.* **160 H4** 37 23N 122 5W
Mountain View, *Hawaii, U.S.A.* **145 D6** 19 33N 155 7W
Mountain Village, *U.S.A.* **144 E7** 62 5N 163 43W
Mountain Zebra △, *S. Africa* **116 E4** 32 14 S 25 27 E
Mountainair, *U.S.A.* **159 J10** 34 31N 106 15W
Mountlake Terrace, *U.S.A.* **160 C4** 47 47N 122 19W
Mountmellick, *Ireland* **23 C4** 53 7N 7 20W
Mountrath, *Ireland* **23 D4** 53 0N 7 28W
Moura, *Australia* **126 C4** 24 35 S 149 58 E
Moura, *Brazil* **169 D5** 1 32 S 61 38W
Moura, *Portugal* **43 G3** 38 7N 7 30W
Mourão, *Portugal* **43 G3** 38 22N 7 22W
Mourdi, Dépression du, *Chad* **109 E4** 18 10N 23 0 E
Mourdiah, *Mali* **112 C3** 14 35N 7 25W
Mourenx, *France* **28 E3** 43 22N 0 38W
Mouri, *Ghana* **113 D4** 5 6N 1 14W
Mourilyan, *Australia* **126 B4** 17 35 S 146 3 E
Mourmelon-le-Grand, *France* **27 C11** 49 8N 4 22 E
Mourne →, *U.K.* **23 B4** 54 52N 7 26W
Mourne Mts., *U.K.* **23 B5** 54 10N 6 0W
Mourniaí, *Greece* **39 E5** 35 29N 24 1 E
Mournies = Mourniaí, *Greece* **39 E5** 35 29N 24 1 E
Mouscron, *Belgium* **24 D3** 50 45N 3 12 E
Mousgougou, *Chad* **109 F3** 10 47N 16 9 E
Moussoro, *Chad* **109 F3** 13 41N 16 35 E
Mouthe, *France* **27 F13** 46 44N 6 12 E
Moutier, *Switz.* **32 B4** 47 16N 7 21 E
Moûtiers, *France* **29 C10** 45 29N 6 32 E
Moutohara, *N.Z.* **130 E6** 38 27 S 177 32 E
Moutong, *Indonesia* **82 A2** 0 28N 121 13 E
Mouy, *France* **27 C9** 49 18N 2 20 E
Mouyondzi, *Congo* **114 C2** 4 1 S 13 59 E
Mouzáki, *Greece* **48 B3** 39 25N 21 37 E
Mouzon, *France* **27 C12** 49 36N 5 3 E
Movas, *Mexico* **162 B3** 28 10N 109 25W
Moville, *Ireland* **23 A4** 55 11N 7 3W
Mowandjum, *Australia* **124 C3** 17 22 S 123 40 E
Moweaqua, *U.S.A.* **156 E7** 39 38N 89 1W
Moxico □, *Angola* **115 E4** 12 0 S 20 30 E
Moxotó →, *Brazil* **170 C4** 9 19 S 38 14W
Moy →, *Ireland* **23 B2** 54 8N 9 8W
Moya, *Comoros Is.* **121 a** 12 18 S 44 18 E
Moyale, *Kenya* **107 G4** 3 30N 39 0 E
Moyamba, *S. Leone* **112 D2** 8 4N 12 30W
Moyen Atlas, *Morocco* **110 B4** 33 0N 5 0W
Moyne, L. le, *Canada* **141 A6** 56 45N 68 47W
Moyo, *Indonesia* **85 D5** 8 10 S 117 40 E
Moyobamba, *Peru* **172 B2** 6 0 S 77 0W
Moyto, *Chad* **109 F3** 12 35N 16 33 E
Moyyero →, *Russia* **67 C11** 68 44N 103 42 E
Moyynqum, *Kazakhstan* **65 A6** 44 17N 72 57 E
Moyynty, *Kazakhstan* **66 E8** 47 10N 73 18 E
Mozambique = Moçambique, *Mozam.* **119 F5** 15 3 S 40 42 E
Mozambique ■, *Africa* **119 F4** 19 0 S 35 0 E
Mozambique Chan., *Africa* **117 B7** 17 30 S 42 30 E
Mozambique Ridge, *Ind. Oc.* **121 H2** 32 0 S 36 0 E
Mozdok, *Russia* **61 J7** 43 45N 44 48 E
Mozdūrān, *Iran* **97 B9** 36 9N 60 35 E
Mozhaysk, *Russia* **58 E9** 55 30N 36 2 E
Mozhga, *Russia* **60 B11** 56 26N 52 15 E
Mozhnābād, *Iran* **97 C9** 34 7N 60 6 E
Mozirje, *Slovenia* **45 B11** 46 22N 14 58 E
Mozyr = Mazyr, *Belarus* **59 F5** 51 59N 29 15 E
Mpanda, *Tanzania* **118 D3** 6 23 S 31 1 E
Mpé, *Congo* **114 C2** 2 58 S 14 38 E
Mpese, *Dem. Rep. of the Congo* **115 D3** 5 16 S 15 30 E
Mpésoba, *Mali* **112 C3** 12 31N 5 39W
Mphoengs, *Zimbabwe* **117 C4** 21 10 S 27 51 E
Mpika, *Zambia* **119 E3** 11 51 S 31 25 E
Mpoko →, *C.A.R.* **114 B3** 4 19N 18 33 E
Mpouya, *Congo* **114 C3** 2 38 S 16 13 E
Mpulungu, *Zambia* **119 D3** 8 51 S 31 5 E
Mpumalanga, *S. Africa* **117 D5** 29 50 S 30 33 E
Mpumalanga □, *S. Africa* **117 D5** 26 0 S 30 0 E
Mpwapwa, *Tanzania* **118 D4** 6 23 S 36 30 E
Mqabba, *Malta* **38 F7** 35 51N 14 28 E
Mqanduli, *S. Africa* **117 E4** 31 49 S 28 45 E
Mqinvartsveri = Kazbek, *Russia* **61 J7** 42 42N 44 30 E
Mrągowo, *Poland* **54 E8** 53 52N 21 18 E
Mramor, *Serbia & M.* **50 C5** 43 20N 21 45 E
Mrimina, *Morocco* **110 C3** 29 50N 7 9W
Mrkonjić Grad, *Bos.-H.* **52 F2** 44 26N 17 4 E
Mrkopalj, *Croatia* **45 C11** 45 21N 14 52 E
Mrocza, *Poland* **55 E4** 53 16N 17 35 E
Msaken, *Tunisia* **108 A2** 35 49N 10 33 E
Msambansovu, *Zimbabwe* **119 F3** 15 50 S 30 3 E
Msida, *Malta* **38 F7** 35 54N 14 29 E
M'sila, *Algeria* **111 A5** 35 46N 4 30 E
Msoro, *Zambia* **119 E3** 13 35 S 31 50 E
Msta →, *Russia* **58 C6** 58 25N 31 20 E
Mstislavl = Mstsislaw, *Belarus* **58 E6** 54 0N 31 50 E
Mstsislaw, *Belarus* **58 E6** 54 0N 31 50 E
Mszana Dolna, *Poland* **55 J7** 49 41N 20 5 E
Mszczonów, *Poland* **55 G7** 51 58N 20 33 E
Mtama, *Tanzania* **119 E4** 10 17 S 39 21 E
Mtamvuna →, *S. Africa* **117 E5** 31 6 S 30 12 E
Mtilikwe →, *Zimbabwe* **119 G3** 21 9 S 31 30 E
Mtima, *Congo* **114 C2** 3 49 S 12 7 E
Mtsensk, *Russia* **58 F9** 53 17N 36 36 E
Mtskheta, *Georgia* **61 K7** 41 52N 44 45 E
Mtubatuba, *S. Africa* **117 D5** 28 30 S 32 8 E
Mtwalume, *S. Africa* **117 E5** 30 30 S 30 38 E
Mtwara-Mikindani, *Tanzania* **119 E5** 10 20 S 40 20 E
Mu →, *Burma* **90 E5** 21 56N 95 38 E
Mu Gia, Deo, *Vietnam* **86 D5** 17 40N 105 47 E
Mu Ko Chang △, *Thailand* **87 G4** 11 59N 102 22 E
Mu Us Shamo, *China* **74 E5** 39 0N 109 0 E
Muacandala, *Angola* **115 E3** 10 2 S 19 40 E
Muaná, *Brazil* **170 B2** 1 25 S 49 15W
Muanda, *Dem. Rep. of the Congo* **115 D2** 6 0 S 12 20 E
Muang Chiang Rai = Chiang Rai, *Thailand* **76 H2** 19 52N 99 50 E
Muang Khong, *Laos* **86 E5** 14 7N 105 51 E
Muang Lamphun, *Thailand* **86 C2** 18 40N 99 2 E
Muang Mai, *Thailand* **87 a** 8 5N 98 21 E
Muang Pak Beng, *Laos* **76 H3** 19 54N 101 8 E
Muangai, *Angola* **115 E3** 12 32 S 19 55 E
Muar, *Malaysia* **87 L4** 2 3N 102 34 E
Muarabungo, *Indonesia* **84 C2** 1 28 S 102 52 E
Muaraenim, *Indonesia* **84 C2** 3 40 S 103 50 E
Muarajuloi, *Indonesia* **85 C4** 0 12 S 114 3 E
Muarakaman, *Indonesia* **85 C5** 0 2 S 116 45 E
Muaratebo, *Indonesia* **84 C2** 1 30 S 102 26 E
Muaratembesi, *Indonesia* **84 C2** 1 42 S 103 8 E
Muaratewe, *Indonesia* **85 C4** 0 58 S 114 52 E
Mubarakpur, *India* **93 F10** 26 6N 83 18 E
Mubarek, *Uzbekistan* **65 D2** 39 15N 65 9 E
Mubarraz = Al Mubarraz, *Si. Arabia* **97 E6** 25 30N 49 40 E
Mubende, *Uganda* **118 B3** 0 33N 31 22 E
Mubi, *Nigeria* **113 C7** 10 18N 13 16 E
Mucajá, *Brazil* **169 D6** 3 57 S 57 32W
Mucajaí →, *Brazil* **169 C5** 2 25N 60 52W
Mucajaí, Serra do, *Brazil* **169 C5** 2 23N 61 10W
Mucari, *Angola* **115 D3** 9 30 S 16 54 E
Muchachos, Roque de los, *Canary Is.* **9 e1** 28 44N 17 52W
Mücheln, *Germany* **30 D7** 51 17N 11 47 E
Muchinga Mts., *Zambia* **119 E3** 11 30 S 31 30 E
Muchkapskiy, *Russia* **60 E6** 51 52N 42 28 E
Muchuan, *China* **76 C5** 28 57N 103 55 E
Muck, *U.K.* **22 E2** 56 50N 6 15W
Muckadilla, *Australia* **127 D4** 26 35 S 148 23 E
Muckalee Cr. →, *U.S.A.* **152 D5** 31 38N 84 9W
Muckle Flugga, *U.K.* **22 A8** 60 51N 0 54W
Muco →, *Colombia* **168 C3** 4 15N 70 21W
Mucoma, *Angola* **115 F2** 15 18 S 13 39 E
Muconda, *Angola* **115 E4** 10 31 S 21 15 E
Mucope, *Angola* **115 F2** 16 24 S 14 52 E
Mucugê, *Brazil* **171 D3** 13 0 S 41 23W
Mucuim →, *Brazil* **173 B5** 6 33 S 64 18W
Mucur, *Turkey* **100 C6** 39 3N 34 22 E
Mucura, *Brazil* **169 D5** 2 31 S 62 43W
Mucuri, *Brazil* **171 E4** 18 0 S 39 36W
Mucurici, *Brazil* **171 E3** 18 6 S 40 31W
Mucusso, *Angola* **116 B3** 18 1 S 21 25 E
Mucusso ⌂, *Angola* **115 F4** 17 27 S 21 0 E
Muda, *Canary Is.* **9 e2** 28 34N 13 57W
Mudanjiang, *China* **75 B15** 44 38N 129 30 E
Mudanya, *Turkey* **51 F12** 40 25N 28 50 E
Muddebihal, *India* **95 F3** 16 20N 76 8 E
Muddy Cr. →, *U.S.A.* **159 H8** 38 24N 110 42W
Mudgee, *Australia* **129 B8** 32 32 S 149 31 E
Mudhol, *Andhra Pradesh, India* **94 E3** 18 58N 77 55 E
Mudhol, *Karnataka, India* **95 F2** 16 21N 75 17 E
Mudiata, *Dem. Rep. of the Congo* **115 D4** 7 15 S 22 1 E
Mudigere, *India* **95 H2** 13 8N 75 38 E
Mudjatik →, *Canada* **143 B7** 56 1N 107 36W
Mudon, *Burma* **90 G6** 16 15N 97 44 E
Mudugh, *Somali Rep.* **120 C3** 7 0N 47 30 E
Mudukulattur, *India* **95 K4** 9 21N 78 31 E
Mudurnu, *Turkey* **100 B4** 40 27N 31 12 E
Muecate, *Mozam.* **119 E4** 14 55 S 39 40 E
Mueda, *Mozam.* **119 E4** 11 36 S 39 28 E
Mueller Ra., *Australia* **124 C4** 18 18 S 126 46 E
Muende, *Mozam.* **119 E3** 14 28 S 33 0 E
Muerto, Mar, *Mexico* **163 D6** 16 10N 94 10W
Mufu Shan, *China* **77 C10** 29 20N 114 30 E
Mufulira, *Zambia* **119 E2** 12 32 S 28 15 E
Mufumbwe, *Zambia* **115 E4** 13 34 S 24 54 E
Mufumbiro Range, *Africa* **118 C2** 1 25 S 29 30 E
Mugardos, *Spain* **42 B2** 43 27N 8 15W
Muge →, *Portugal* **43 F2** 39 8N 8 44W
Múggia, *Italy* **45 C10** 45 36N 13 46 E
Mughal Sarai, *India* **93 G10** 25 18N 83 7 E
Mughayrā', *Si. Arabia* **96 D3** 29 17N 37 41 E
Mugi, *Japan* **72 D6** 33 40N 134 25 E
Mugia = Muxía, *Spain* **42 B1** 43 3N 9 10W
Mugila, Mts., *Dem. Rep. of the Congo* **118 D2** 7 0 S 28 50 E
Muginga, *Angola* **115 D3** 8 21 S 17 36 E
Muğla, *Turkey* **49 D10** 37 15N 28 22 E
Muğla □, *Turkey* **49 D10** 37 15N 28 0 E
Muglad, *Sudan* **107 E2** 11 1N 27 50 E
Mŭglizh, *Bulgaria* **51 D9** 42 37N 25 32 E
Mugodzhary, *Kazakhstan* **64 G7** 49 0N 58 40 E
Mugu, *Nepal* **93 E10** 29 45N 82 30 E
Muhammad, Râs, *Egypt* **96 E2** 27 44N 34 16 E
Muhammad Qol, *Sudan* **106 C4** 20 53N 37 9 E
Muhammadabad, *India* **93 F10** 26 4N 83 25 E
Muḩayriqah, *Si. Arabia* **98 B4** 23 59N 45 4 E
Muhesi →, *Tanzania* **118 D4** 7 0 S 35 20 E
Mühlacker, *Germany* **31 G4** 48 57N 8 51 E
Mühldorf, *Germany* **31 G8** 48 14N 12 32 E
Mühlhausen = Milevsko, *Czech Rep.* **34 B7** 49 27N 14 21 E
Mühlhausen, *Germany* **30 D6** 51 12N 10 27 E
Mühlig Hofmann fjell, *Antarctica* **7 D3** 72 30 S 5 0 E
Mühlviertel, *Austria* **34 C7** 48 30N 14 10 E
Muhos, *Finland* **14 D22** 64 47N 25 59 E
Muhu, *Estonia* **15 G20** 58 36N 23 11 E
Muhutwe, *Tanzania* **118 C3** 1 35 S 31 45 E
Mui Wo, *China* **69 G10** 22 16N 113 59 E
Muie, *Angola* **115 E4** 14 23 S 20 48 E
Muine Bheag, *Ireland* **23 D5** 52 42N 6 58W
Muir, L., *Australia* **125 F2** 34 30 S 116 40 E
Muir of Ord, *U.K.* **22 D4** 57 32N 4 28W
Muisné, *Ecuador* **168 C1** 0 36N 80 2W
Mujnak = Muynak, *Uzbekistan* **66 E6** 43 44N 59 10 E
Mujuí dos Campos, *Brazil* **169 D7** 2 35 S 54 41W
Muka, Tanjung, *Malaysia* **87 c** 5 28N 100 11 E
Mukacheve, *Ukraine* **52 B7** 48 27N 22 45 E
Mukachevo = Mukacheve, *Ukraine* **52 B7** 48 27N 22 45 E
Mukah, *Malaysia* **85 B4** 2 55N 112 5 E
Mukandwara, *India* **92 G6** 24 49N 75 59 E
Mukawa, *Papua N. G.* **132 E5** 9 38 S 149 59 E
Mukawwa, Geziret, *Egypt* **106 C4** 23 55N 35 53 E
Mukawwar, *Sudan* **106 C4** 20 50N 37 17 E
Mukdahan, *Thailand* **86 D5** 16 32N 104 43 E
Mukden = Shenyang, *China* **75 D12** 41 48N 123 27 E
Mukerian, *India* **92 D6** 31 57N 75 37 E
Mukhavyets, *Belarus* **55 F10** 52 5N 23 39 E
Mukher, *India* **94 E3** 18 42N 77 22 E
Mukhtolovo, *Russia* **60 C6** 55 29N 43 15 E
Mukhtuya = Lensk, *Russia* **67 C12** 60 48N 114 55 E
Mukinbudin, *Australia* **125 F2** 30 55 S 118 5 E
Mukishi, *Kasai-Occ., Dem. Rep. of the Congo* **115 D4** 5 39 S 21 3 E
Mukishi, *Katanga, Dem. Rep. of the Congo* **119 D1** 8 30 S 24 44 E
Mukomuko, *Indonesia* **84 C2** 2 30 S 101 10 E
Mukomwenze, *Dem. Rep. of the Congo* **118 D2** 6 49 S 27 15 E
Mukry, *Turkmenistan* **65 E2** 37 54N 65 12 E
Muktsar, *India* **92 D6** 30 30N 74 30 E
Mukur = Moqor, *Afghan.* **91 B2** 32 50N 67 42 E
Mukutawa →, *Canada* **143 C9** 53 10N 97 24W
Mukwela, *Zambia* **119 F2** 17 0 S 26 40 E
Mukwonago, *U.S.A.* **157 B8** 42 52N 88 20W

Mul, *India* **94 D4** 20 4N 79 40 E
Mula, *Spain* **41 G3** 38 3N 1 33W
Mula →, *India* **94 E2** 18 34N 74 21 E
Mula →, *Pakistan* **92 F2** 27 57N 67 36 E
Mulamba, *Dem. Rep. of the Congo* **115 D4** 6 0 S 21 13 E
Mulanay, *Phil.* **80 E4** 13 31N 122 24 E
Mulange, *Dem. Rep. of the Congo* **118 C2** 3 40 S 27 10 E
Mulanje, *Malawi* **119 F4** 16 2 S 35 33 E
Mulanje, Mt., *Malawi* **119 F4** 16 0 S 35 30 E
Mulatupo, *Panama* **168 B2** 8 57N 77 45W
Mulbagal, *India* **95 H4** 13 10N 78 24 E
Mulberry, *U.S.A.* **153 H8** 27 54N 81 59W
Mulberry Grove, *U.S.A.* **156 F7** 38 56N 89 16W
Mulchatna →, *U.S.A.* **144 G8** 59 40N 157 7W
Mulchén, *Chile* **174 D1** 37 45 S 72 20W
Mulde →, *Germany* **30 D8** 51 53N 12 15 E
Muldraugh, *U.S.A.* **157 G11** 37 56N 85 59W
Mule Creek Junction, *U.S.A.* **154 D2** 43 19N 104 8W
Muleba, *Tanzania* **118 C3** 1 50 S 31 37 E
Mulegns, *Switz.* **33 C9** 46 32N 9 38 E
Mulejé, *Mexico* **162 B2** 26 53N 112 1W
Muleshoe, *U.S.A.* **155 H3** 34 13N 102 43W
Muletta, Gara, *Ethiopia* **107 F5** 9 15N 41 44 E
Mulgrave, *Canada* **141 C7** 45 38N 61 31W
Mulgrave I. = Badu I., *Papua N. G.* **132 F2** 10 5 S 142 10 E
Mulhacén, *Spain* **43 H7** 37 4N 3 20W
Mülheim, *Germany* **30 D2** 51 25N 6 54 E
Mulhouse, *France* **27 E14** 47 40N 7 20 E
Muli, *China* **76 D3** 27 52N 101 8 E
Muli →, *Indonesia* **83 C5** 7 16 S 138 45 E
Mulifanua, *Samoa* **133 W24** 13 50 S 171 59W
Muling, *China* **75 B16** 44 35N 130 10 E
Mulki, *India* **95 H2** 13 6N 74 48 E
Mull, *U.K.* **22 E3** 56 25N 5 56W
Mull, Sound of, *U.K.* **22 E3** 56 30N 5 50W
Mullaittivu, *Sri Lanka* **95 K5** 9 15N 80 49 E
Mullen, *U.S.A.* **154 D4** 42 3N 101 1W
Mullens, *U.S.A.* **148 G5** 37 35N 81 23W
Muller, Pegunungan, *Indonesia* **85 B4** 0 30N 113 30 E
Muller Ra., *Papua N. G.* **132 C2** 5 35 S 142 20 E
Mullet Pen., *Ireland* **23 B1** 54 13N 10 2W
Mullewa, *Australia* **125 E2** 28 29 S 115 30 E
Müllheim, *Germany* **31 H3** 47 47N 7 36 E
Mulligan →, *Australia* **126 D2** 25 0 S 139 0 E
Mullingar, *Ireland* **23 C4** 53 31N 7 21W
Mullins, *U.S.A.* **149 H6** 34 12N 79 15W
Mullsjö, *Sweden* **17 G7** 57 56N 13 55 E
Mullumbimby, *Australia* **127 D5** 28 30 S 153 30 E
Mulobezi, *Zambia* **119 F2** 16 45 S 25 7 E
Mulondo, *Angola* **115 F3** 15 41 S 15 12 E
Mulonga Plain, *Zambia* **115 F4** 16 20 S 22 40 E
Mulroy B., *Ireland* **23 A4** 55 15N 7 46W
Mulshi L., *India* **94 E1** 18 30N 73 48 E
Multai, *India* **94 D4** 21 50N 78 21 E
Multan, *Pakistan* **91 C3** 30 15N 71 36 E
Mulu, Gunung, *Malaysia* **85 B4** 4 3N 114 56 E
Mulug, *India* **94 E4** 18 11N 79 57 E
Mulumbe, Mts., *Dem. Rep. of the Congo* **119 D2** 8 40 S 27 30 E
Mulundu, *Dem. Rep. of the Congo* **115 D4** 6 40 S 20 33 E
Mulungushi Dam, *Zambia* **119 E2** 14 48 S 28 48 E
Mulurulu L., *Australia* **128 B5** 33 15 S 143 20 E
Mulvane, *U.S.A.* **155 G6** 37 29N 97 15W
Mulwad, *Sudan* **106 D3** 18 45N 30 39 E
Mulwala, *Australia* **129 C7** 35 59 S 146 0 E
Muma, *Dem. Rep. of the Congo* **114 B4** 3 25N 23 21 E
Mumbai, *India* **94 E1** 18 55N 72 50 E
Mumbeji, *Zambia* **115 E4** 13 51 S 23 39 E
Mumbondo, *Angola* **115 E2** 10 9 S 14 15 E
Mumbwa, *Zambia* **119 F2** 15 0 S 27 0 E
Mumeng, *Papua N. G.* **132 D4** 7 1 S 146 37 E
Muminabad = Leningradskiy, *Tajikistan* **65 D5** 38 6N 70 1 E
Mumra, *Russia* **61 H8** 45 45N 47 41 E
Mun →, *Thailand* **86 E5** 15 19N 105 30 E
Muna, *Indonesia* **82 B2** 5 0 S 122 30 E
Munabao, *India* **92 G4** 25 45N 70 17 E
Munakata, *Japan* **72 D2** 33 48N 130 38 E
Munamagi, *Estonia* **15 H22** 57 43N 27 4 E
Muncan, *Indonesia* **79 K18** 8 34 S 115 11 E
Muncar, *Indonesia* **79 J17** 8 26 S 114 20 E
Münchberg, *Germany* **31 E7** 50 11N 11 47 E
Müncheberg, *Germany* **30 C10** 52 30N 14 9 E
München, *Germany* **31 G7** 48 8N 11 34 E
Munchen-Gladbach = Mönchengladbach, *Germany* **30 D2** 51 11N 6 27 E
München International ✕ (MUC), *Germany* **31 G7** 48 20N 11 50 E
Münchenbuchsee, *Switz.* **32 B4** 47 1N 7 27 E
Munchique △, *Colombia* **168 C2** 2 44N 77 1W
Muncho Lake, *Canada* **142 B3** 59 0N 125 50W
Munch'ŏn, *N. Korea* **75 E14** 39 14N 127 19 E
Münchwilen, *Switz.* **33 B7** 47 28N 8 59 E
Muncie, *U.S.A.* **157 D11** 40 12N 85 23W
Muncoonie, L., *Australia* **126 D2** 25 12 S 138 40 E
Munda, *Solomon Is.* **133 M9** 8 20 S 157 16 E
Mundabbera, *Australia* **127 D5** 25 36 S 151 18 E
Mundakayam, *India* **95 K3** 9 30N 76 50 E
Mundal, *Sri Lanka* **95 L4** 7 48N 79 48 E
Munday, *U.S.A.* **155 J5** 33 27N 99 38W
Mundelein, *U.S.A.* **157 B8** 42 16N 88 0W
Münden, *Germany* **30 D5** 51 25N 9 38 E
Münden ⌂, *Germany* **30 D5** 51 28N 9 42 E
Mundiwindi, *Australia* **124 D3** 23 47 S 120 9 E
Mundo →, *Spain* **41 G2** 38 30N 2 15W
Mundo Novo, *Brazil* **171 D3** 11 50 S 40 29W
Mundra, *India* **92 H3** 22 54N 69 48 E
Mundrabilla, *Australia* **125 F4** 31 52 S 127 51 E
Munducurus, *Brazil* **169 D6** 4 47 S 58 16W
Munenga, *Angola* **115 E2** 10 2 S 14 41 E
Munera, *Spain* **41 F2** 39 2N 2 29W
Muneru →, *India* **94 F5** 16 45N 80 3 E
Mungallala, *Australia* **127 D4** 26 28 S 147 34 E
Mungallala Cr. →, *Australia* **127 D4** 28 53 S 147 5 E
Mungana, *Australia* **126 B3** 17 8 S 144 27 E
Mungaoli, *India* **92 G8** 24 24N 78 7 E
Mungari, *Mozam.* **119 F3** 17 12 S 33 30 E
Mungbere, *Dem. Rep. of the Congo* **118 B2** 2 36N 28 28 E
Mungeli, *India* **93 H9** 22 4N 81 41 E
Munger, *India* **93 G12** 25 23N 86 30 E
Mungkan Kandju △, *Australia* **126 A3** 13 35 S 142 52 E
Mungo, *Angola* **115 E3** 11 49 S 16 16 E
Mungo △, *Australia* **128 B5** 33 44 S 143 6 E
Mungo, L., *Australia* **128 B5** 33 45 S 143 0 E
Munhango, *Angola* **115 E3** 12 10 S 18 38 E
Munhango →, *Angola* **115 E4** 11 17 S 19 44 E
Munich = München, *Germany* **31 G7** 48 8N 11 34 E
Munirabad, *India* **95 F3** 15 20N 76 20 E
Munising, *U.S.A.* **148 B2** 46 25N 86 40W
Munka-Ljungby, *Sweden* **17 H6** 56 16N 12 58 E
Munkebo, *Denmark* **17 J4** 55 27N 10 34 E
Munkedal, *Sweden* **17 F5** 58 28N 11 40 E
Munkfors, *Sweden* **16 E7** 59 47N 13 30 E
Munku-Sardyk, *Russia* **67 D11** 51 45N 100 20 E
Münnerstadt, *Germany* **31 E6** 50 14N 10 12 E
Munoz, *Phil.* **80 D3** 15 43N 120 54 E
Muñoz Gamero, Pen., *Chile* **176 D2** 52 30 S 73 5W
Munroe L., *Canada* **143 B9** 59 13N 98 35W
Munsan, *S. Korea* **75 F14** 37 51N 126 48 E
Munshiganj, *Bangla.* **90 D3** 23 33N 90 32 E
Münsingen, *Switz.* **32 C5** 46 52N 7 32 E
Munson, *U.S.A.* **153 E3** 30 52N 86 52W
Munster, *France* **27 D14** 48 2N 7 8 E
Münster, *Niedersachsen, Germany* **30 C6** 52 58N 10 5 E
Münster, *Nordrhein-Westfalen, Germany* **30 D3** 51 58N 7 37 E
Münster, *Switz.* **33 D6** 46 29N 8 17 E
Munster □, *Ireland* **23 D3** 52 18N 8 44W
Münsterberg = Ziębice, *Poland* **55 H4** 50 37N 17 2 E
Muntadgin, *Australia* **125 F2** 31 45 S 118 33 E
Muntele Mare, Vf., *Romania* **53 D8** 46 30N 23 12 E
Muntok, *Indonesia* **84 C3** 2 5 S 105 10 E
Munyama, *Zambia* **119 F2** 16 5 S 28 31 E
Munzur Dağları, *Turkey* **101 C8** 39 30N 39 10 E
Muong Beng, *Laos* **76 G3** 20 23N 101 46 E
Muong Boum, *Vietnam* **76 F4** 22 24N 102 49 E
Muong Et, *Laos* **86 B5** 20 49N 104 1 E
Muong Hai, *Laos* **76 G3** 21 3N 101 49 E
Muong Hiem, *Laos* **86 B4** 20 5N 103 22 E
Muong Houn, *Laos* **76 G3** 20 8N 101 23 E
Muong Hung, *Vietnam* **76 G4** 20 56N 103 53 E
Muong Kau, *Laos* **86 E5** 15 6N 105 47 E
Muong Khao, *Laos* **86 C4** 19 38N 103 32 E
Muong Khoua, *Laos* **76 G4** 21 5N 102 31 E
Muong Liep, *Laos* **86 C3** 18 29N 101 40 E
Muong May, *Laos* **86 E6** 14 49N 106 56 E
Muong Ngeun, *Laos* **76 G3** 20 36N 101 3 E
Muong Ngoi, *Laos* **76 G4** 20 43N 102 41 E
Muong Nhie, *Vietnam* **76 F4** 22 12N 102 28 E
Muong Nong, *Laos* **86 D6** 16 22N 106 30 E
Muong Ou Tay, *Laos* **76 F3** 22 7N 101 48 E
Muong Oua, *Laos* **86 C3** 18 18N 101 20 E
Muong Peun, *Laos* **76 G4** 20 13N 103 52 E
Muong Phalane, *Laos* **86 D5** 16 39N 105 34 E
Muong Phieng, *Laos* **86 C3** 19 6N 101 32 E
Muong Phine, *Laos* **86 D6** 16 32N 106 2 E
Muong Sai, *Laos* **76 G3** 20 42N 101 59 E
Muong Saiapoun, *Laos* **86 C3** 18 24N 101 31 E
Muong Sen, *Vietnam* **86 C5** 19 24N 104 8 E
Muong Sing, *Laos* **76 G3** 21 11N 101 9 E
Muong Son, *Laos* **76 G4** 20 27N 103 19 E
Muong Soui, *Laos* **86 C4** 19 33N 102 52 E
Muong Va, *Laos* **76 G4** 21 53N 102 19 E
Muong Xia, *Vietnam* **86 B5** 20 19N 104 50 E
Muonio, *Finland* **14 C20** 67 57N 23 40 E
Muonio älv = Muonionjoki →, *Finland* **14 C20** 67 11N 23 34 E
Muonioälven = Muonionjoki →, *Finland* **14 C20** 67 11N 23 34 E
Muonionjoki →, *Finland* **14 C20** 67 11N 23 34 E
Muotathal, *Switz.* **33 C7** 46 58N 8 46 E
Mupa, *Angola* **115 F3** 16 5 S 15 50 E
Mupa △, *Angola* **115 F3** 15 55 S 15 35 E
Muping, *China* **75 F11** 37 22N 121 36 E
Mupoi, *Sudan* **107 F2** 5 28N 27 40 E
Muqaddam, Wadi →, *Sudan* **106 D3** 18 4N 31 30 E
Muqdisho, *Somali Rep.* **120 D3** 2 2N 45 25 E
Muqshin, W. →, *Oman* **99 C6** 19 44N 55 14 E
Muquequete, *Angola* **115 E2** 14 50 S 14 16 E
Mur →, *Austria* **35 E9** 46 18N 16 52 E
Mûr-de-Bretagne, *France* **26 D4** 48 12N 3 0W
Muradiye, *Manisa, Turkey* **49 C9** 38 39N 27 21 E
Muradiye, *Van, Turkey* **101 C10** 39 0N 43 44 E
Murakami, *Japan* **70 E9** 38 14N 139 29 E
Murallón, Cerro, *Chile* **176 C2** 49 48 S 73 30W
Muranda, *Rwanda* **118 C2** 1 52 S 29 20 E
Murang'a, *Kenya* **118 C4** 0 45 S 37 9 E
Murashi, *Russia* **64 B2** 59 30N 49 0 E
Murat, *France* **28 C6** 45 7N 2 53 E
Murat →, *Turkey* **101 C9** 38 46N 40 0 E
Murat Bay = Ceduna, *Australia* **127 E1** 32 7 S 133 46 E
Murat Dağı, *Turkey* **49 C11** 38 55N 29 43 E
Muratlı, *Turkey* **51 E11** 41 10N 27 29 E
Murato, *France* **29 F13** 42 35N 9 20 E
Murau, *Austria* **34 D7** 47 6N 14 10 E
Murava, *Belarus* **55 F11** 52 39N 24 15 E
Muravera, *Italy* **46 C2** 39 25N 9 34 E
Muravyevo = Mažeikiai, *Lithuania* **15 H20** 56 20N 22 20 E
Muravyovsky = Korsakov, *Russia* **67 E15** 46 36N 142 42 E
Murayama, *Japan* **70 E10** 38 30N 140 25 E
Murça, *Portugal* **42 D3** 41 24N 7 28W
Murchison, *N.Z.* **131 B7** 41 49 S 172 21 E
Murchison →, *Australia* **125 E1** 27 45 S 114 0 E
Murchison, Mt., *Antarctica* **7 D11** 73 0 S 168 0 E
Murchison, Mt., *N.Z.* **131 D6** 43 0 S 171 22 E
Murchison Falls, *Uganda* **118 B3** 2 15N 31 30 E
Murchison Falls △, *Uganda* **118 B3** 2 17N 31 48 E
Murchison Mts., *N.Z.* **131 F2** 45 13 S 167 23 E
Murchison Ra., *Australia* **126 C1** 20 0 S 134 10 E
Murchison Rapids, *Malawi* **119 F3** 15 55 S 34 35 E
Murcia, *Spain* **41 G3** 38 5N 1 10W
Murcia □, *Spain* **41 H3** 37 50N 1 30W
Murdo, *U.S.A.* **154 D4** 43 53N 100 43W
Murdoch Pt., *Australia* **126 A3** 14 37 S 144 55 E
Mürefte, *Turkey* **51 F11** 40 40N 27 14 E
Mureş □, *Romania* **53 D9** 46 45N 24 40 E
Mureş →, *Romania* **52 D5** 46 15N 20 13 E
Mureşul = Mureş →, *Romania* **52 D5** 46 15N 20 13 E
Muret, *France* **28 E5** 43 30N 1 20 E
Murewa, *Zimbabwe* **117 B5** 17 39 S 31 47 E
Murfreesboro, *N.C., U.S.A.* **149 G7** 36 27N 77 6W
Murfreesboro, *Tenn., U.S.A.* **149 H2** 35 51N 86 24W
Murg, *Switz.* **33 B8** 47 6N 9 13 E
Murgab = Murghob, *Tajikistan* **65 D7** 38 10N 74 2 E
Murgab →, *Turkmenistan* **97 B9** 38 18N 61 12 E
Murgenella, *Australia* **124 B5** 11 34 S 132 56 E
Murgeni, *Romania* **53 D13** 46 12N 28 1 E
Murgenthal, *Switz.* **32 B5** 47 16N 7 50 E
Murgha Kibzai, *Pakistan* **92 D3** 30 44N 69 25 E
Murghob, *Tajikistan* **65 D7** 38 10N 74 2 E
Murgon, *Australia* **127 D5** 26 15 S 151 54 E
Muri, *India* **93 H11** 23 22N 85 52 E
Muri, *Switz.* **33 B6** 47 17N 8 21 E
Muria, *Indonesia* **85 D4** 6 36 S 110 53 E
Muriaé, *Brazil* **171 F3** 21 8 S 42 23W
Murias de Paredes, *Spain* **42 C4** 42 52N 6 11W
Murici, *Brazil* **170 C4** 9 19 S 35 56W
Muriége, *Angola* **115 D4** 9 58 S 21 11 E
Muriel Mine, *Zimbabwe* **119 F3** 17 14 S 30 40 E
Murila, *Angola* **115 E4** 10 44 S 20 20 E
Müritz, *Germany* **30 B8** 53 25N 12 42 E
Müritz △, *Germany* **30 B8** 53 22N 12 55 E
Muriwai Beach, *N.Z.* **130 C3** 36 50 S 174 26 E
Murkong Selek, *India* **90 B5** 27 44N 95 18 E
Murliganj, *India* **93 G12** 25 54N 86 59 E
Murmansk, *Russia* **56 A5** 68 57N 33 10 E
Murnau, *Germany* **31 H7** 47 40N 11 12 E
Muro, *France* **29 F12** 42 34N 8 54 E
Muro, *Spain* **38 B4** 39 44N 3 3 E
Muro, C. de, *France* **29 G12** 41 44N 8 37 E
Muro de Alcoy, *Spain* **41 G4** 38 46N 0 26W
Muro Lucano, *Italy* **47 B8** 40 45N 15 29 E
Murom, *Russia* **60 C6** 55 35N 42 3 E
Muroran, *Japan* **70 C10** 42 25N 141 0 E
Muros, *Spain* **42 C1** 42 45N 9 5W
Muros y de Noya, Ría de, *Spain* **42 C1** 42 45N 9 0W
Muroto, *Japan* **72 D6** 33 18N 134 9 E
Muroto-Misaki, *Japan* **72 D6** 33 15N 134 10 E
Murovani Kurylivtsi, *Ukraine* **53 B12** 48 44N 27 31 E
Murowana Goślina, *Poland* **55 F3** 52 35N 17 0 E
Murphy, *U.S.A.* **158 E5** 43 13N 116 33W
Murphys, *U.S.A.* **160 G6** 38 8N 120 28W
Murphy's Station = Sunnyvale, *U.S.A.* **160 H4** 37 23N 122 2W
Murphysboro, *U.S.A.* **156 G7** 37 46N 89 20W
Murrat, *Sudan* **106 D2** 18 51N 29 33 E
Murrat Wells, *Sudan* **106 C3** 21 3N 32 55 E
Murray, *Iowa, U.S.A.* **156 C3** 41 3N 93 57W
Murray, *Ky., U.S.A.* **149 G1** 36 37N 88 19W
Murray, *Utah, U.S.A.* **158 F8** 40 40N 111 53W
Murray →, *Australia* **128 C3** 35 20 S 139 22 E
Murray, L., *Papua N. G.* **132 D1** 7 0 S 141 35 E
Murray, L., *U.S.A.* **152 A8** 34 3N 81 13W
Murray Bridge, *Australia* **128 C3** 35 6 S 139 14 E
Murray Fracture Zone, *Pac. Oc.* **135 D14** 35 0N 130 0W
Murray Harbour, *Canada* **141 C7** 46 0N 62 28W
Murray River △, *Australia* **127 E3** 34 23 S 140 32 E
Murray-Sunset △, *Australia* **128 C4** 34 45 S 141 30 E
Murraysburg, *S. Africa* **116 E3** 31 58 S 23 47 E
Murrayville, *U.S.A.* **156 E6** 39 35N 90 15W
Murree, *Pakistan* **92 C5** 33 56N 73 28 E
Murren, *Switz.* **32 C5** 46 34N 7 53 E
Murrieta, *U.S.A.* **161 M9** 33 33N 117 13W
Murro di Porco, Capo, *Italy* **47 F8** 37 0N 15 20 E
Murrumbateman, *Australia* **129 C8** 34 58 S 149 0 E
Murrumbidgee →, *Australia* **128 C5** 34 43 S 143 12 E
Murrumburrah, *Australia* **129 C8** 34 32 S 148 22 E
Murrurundi, *Australia* **129 A9** 31 42 S 150 51 E
Murshid, *Sudan* **106 C3** 21 40N 31 10 E
Murshidabad, *India* **93 G13** 24 11N 88 19 E
Murska Sobota, *Slovenia* **45 B13** 46 39N 16 12 E
Murtazapur, *India* **94 D3** 20 40N 77 25 E
Murten, *Switz.* **32 C4** 46 56N 7 4 E
Murtensee, *Switz.* **32 C4** 46 56N 7 7 E
Murtle L., *Canada* **142 C5** 52 8N 119 38W
Murtoa, *Australia* **128 D5** 36 35 S 142 28 E
Murtosa, *Portugal* **42 E2** 40 44N 8 40W
Muru →, *Brazil* **172 B3** 8 9 S 70 45W
Murud, *India* **94 E1** 18 19N 72 58 E
Murungu, *Tanzania* **118 C3** 4 12 S 31 10 E
Muruntau, *Uzbekistan* **65 C2** 41 30N 64 37 E
Murupara, *N.Z.* **130 E5** 38 28 S 176 42 E
Mururoa, *French Polynesia* **135 K14** 21 52 S 138 55W
Murwara, *India* **93 H9** 23 46N 80 28 E
Murwillumbah, *Australia* **127 D5** 28 18 S 153 27 E
Mürz →, *Austria* **34 D8** 47 30N 15 25 E
Mürzzuschlag, *Austria* **34 D8** 47 36N 15 41 E
Mus, *India* **95 K11** 9 14N 92 47 E
Muş, *Turkey* **101 C9** 38 45N 41 30 E
Musa, *Dem. Rep. of the Congo* **114 B3** 2 40N 19 18 E
Musa →, *Papua N. G.* **132 E5** 9 3 S 148 55 E
Mûsa, Gebel, *Egypt* **96 D2** 28 33N 33 59 E
Musa Khel, *Pakistan* **92 D3** 30 59N 69 52 E
Mûsa Qal'eh, *Afghan.* **91 B2** 32 20N 64 50 E
Musadi, *Dem. Rep. of the Congo* **114 C4** 2 31 S 22 50 E
Musafirkhana, *India* **93 F9** 26 22N 81 48 E
Musala, *Bulgaria* **50 D7** 42 13N 23 37 E
Musala, *Indonesia* **84 B1** 1 41N 98 28 E
Musan, *N. Korea* **75 C15** 42 12N 129 12 E
Musandam, Ra's, *Oman* **99 A7** 26 20N 56 20 E
Musangu, *Dem. Rep. of the Congo* **119 E1** 10 28 S 23 55 E
Musasa, *Tanzania* **118 C3** 3 25 S 31 30 E
Musashino, *Japan* **73 B11** 35 42N 139 34 E
Musay'īd, *Qatar* **97 E6** 25 0N 51 33 E
Musaymīr, *Yemen* **98 D4** 13 27N 44 37 E
Muscat = Masqat, *Oman* **99 B7** 23 37N 58 36 E
Muscat & Oman = Oman ■, *Asia* **99 B7** 23 0N 58 0 E
Muscatatuc →, *U.S.A.* **157 F10** 38 47N 86 9W
Muscatine, *U.S.A.* **156 C5** 41 25N 91 3W
Muschu I., *Papua N. G.* **132 B2** 3 25 S 143 35 E
Muscle Shoals, *U.S.A.* **149 H2** 34 45N 87 40W
Muscoda, *U.S.A.* **156 A6** 43 11N 90 27W
Musengezi = Unsengedsi →, *Zimbabwe* **119 F3** 15 43 S 31 14 E
Musgrave Harbour, *Canada* **141 C9** 49 27N 53 58W
Musgrave Ranges, *Australia* **125 E5** 26 0 S 132 0 E
Mushie, *Dem. Rep. of the Congo* **114 C3** 2 56 S 16 55 E
Mushima, *Zambia* **115 E4** 14 10 S 24 56 E
Mushin, *Nigeria* **113 D5** 6 32N 3 21 E
Musi →, *India* **94 F4** 16 41N 79 40 E
Musi →, *Indonesia* **84 C2** 2 20 S 104 56 E
Musina, *S. Africa* **117 C5** 22 20 S 30 5 E
Musiri, *India* **95 J4** 10 56N 78 27 E
Muskeg →, *Canada* **142 A4** 60 20N 123 20W
Muskego, *U.S.A.* **157 B8** 42 55N 88 8W
Muskegon, *U.S.A.* **157 A10** 43 14N 86 16W
Muskegon →, *U.S.A.* **148 D2** 43 14N 86 21W
Muskegon Heights, *U.S.A.* **157 A10** 43 12N 86 16W
Muskogee, *U.S.A.* **155 H7** 35 45N 95 22W
Muskoka, L., *Canada* **150 B5** 45 0N 79 25W
Muskwa →, *Canada* **142 B4** 58 47N 122 48W
Muslīmiyah, *Syria* **96 B3** 36 19N 37 12 E
Musmar, *Sudan* **106 D4** 18 13N 35 40 E
Musofu, *Zambia* **119 E2** 13 30 S 29 0 E
Musoma, *Tanzania* **118 C3** 1 30 S 33 48 E
Musquaro, L., *Canada* **141 B7** 50 38N 61 5W
Musquodoboit Harbour, *Canada* **141 D7** 44 50N 63 9W
Mussau I., *Papua N. G.* **132 A5** 1 30 S 149 40 E
Musselburgh, *U.K.* **22 F5** 55 57N 3 2W
Musselshell →, *U.S.A.* **158 C10** 47 21N 107 57W
Mussende, *Angola* **115 E3** 10 32 S 16 5 E
Mussidan, *France* **28 C4** 45 2N 0 22 E
Mussolinea di Sardegna = Arboréa, *Italy* **46 C1** 39 46N 8 35 E
Mussolo, *Angola* **115 D3** 9 59 S 17 19 E
Mussomeli, *Italy* **46 E6** 37 35N 13 45 E
Mussoorie, *India* **92 D8** 30 27N 78 6 E
Mussuco, *Angola* **116 B2** 17 2 S 19 3 E
Mustafakemalpaşa, *Turkey* **51 F12** 40 2N 28 24 E
Mustahil, *Ethiopia* **120 C2** 5 16N 44 45 E
Mustang, *Nepal* **93 E10** 29 10N 83 55 E
Musters, L., *Argentina* **176 C3** 45 20 S 69 25W
Musudan, *N. Korea* **75 D15** 40 50N 129 43 E
Muswellbrook, *Australia* **129 B9** 32 16 S 150 56 E
Muszyna, *Poland* **55 J7** 49 22N 20 55 E
Mût, *Egypt* **106 B2** 25 28N 28 58 E
Mut, *Turkey* **100 D5** 36 40N 33 28 E
Mutanda, *Dem. Rep. of the Congo* **115 D3** 5 17 S 16 34 E
Mutanda, *Mozam.* **117 C5** 21 0 S 33 34 E
Mutanda, *Zambia* **119 E2** 12 24 S 26 13 E
Mutankiang = Mudanjiang, *China* **75 B15** 44 38N 129 30 E
Mutare, *Zimbabwe* **119 F3** 18 58 S 32 38 E
Muting, *Indonesia* **83 C6** 7 23 S 140 20 E
Mutis, *Indonesia* **82 C2** 9 30 S 124 14 E
Mutki = Mirtağ, *Turkey* **96 B4** 38 23N 41 56 E
Mutoko, *Zimbabwe* **117 B5** 17 24 S 32 13 E
Mutoray, *Russia* **67 C11** 60 56N 101 0 E
Mutoto, *Dem. Rep. of the Congo* **115 D4** 5 42 S 22 42 E
Mutoxo, *Angola* **115 E4** 12 17 S 21 40 E
Mutshatsha, *Dem. Rep. of the Congo* **119 E1** 10 35 S 24 20 E
Mutsu, *Japan* **70 D10** 41 5N 140 55 E
Mutsu-Wan, *Japan* **70 D10** 41 5N 140 55 E
Muttaburra, *Australia* **126 C3** 22 38 S 144 29 E
Muttalip, *Turkey* **49 B12** 39 50N 30 32 E
Mutton I., *Ireland* **23 D2** 52 49N 9 32W
Muttra = Mathura, *India* **92 F7** 27 30N 77 40 E
Muttukuru, *India* **95 G5** 14 16N 80 6 E
Mutuáli, *Mozam.* **119 E4** 14 55 S 37 0 E
Mutum Biyu, *Nigeria* **113 D7** 8 40N 10 50 E
Mutunópolis, *Brazil* **171 D2** 13 40 S 49 15W
Mutur, *Sri Lanka* **95 K5** 8 27N 81 16 E
Muweilih, *Egypt* **103 E3** 30 42N 34 19 E
Muxaluando, *Angola* **115 D2** 8 8 S 14 18 E
Muxía, *Spain* **42 B1** 43 3N 9 10W
Muxima, *Angola* **115 D2** 9 33 S 13 58 E
Muy Muy, *Nic.* **164 D2** 12 39N 85 36W
Muyinga, *Burundi* **118 C3** 3 14 S 30 33 E
Muynak, *Uzbekistan* **66 E6** 43 44N 59 10 E
Muyunkum, Peski, *Kazakhstan* **65 A4** 44 12N 71 0 E
Muzaffarabad, *Pakistan* **93 B5** 34 25N 73 30 E
Muzaffargarh, *Pakistan* **92 D4** 30 5N 71 14 E
Muzaffarnagar, *India* **92 E7** 29 26N 77 40 E
Muzaffarpur, *India* **93 F11** 26 7N 85 23 E
Muzafirpur, *Pakistan* **92 D3** 30 58N 69 9 E
Muzeze, *Angola* **115 F3** 15 3 S 17 43 E
Muzhi, *Russia* **56 A11** 65 25N 64 40 E
Muzillac, *France* **26 E4** 47 35N 2 30W
Muzon, C., *U.S.A.* **144 J14** 54 40N 132 42W
Muztagh-Ata, *China* **65 D7** 38 17N 75 7 E
Muztor = Toktogul, *Kyrgyzstan* **65 C6** 41 50N 72 50 E
Muzūra, *Egypt* **106 J7** 28 53N 30 48 E
Mvadhi-Ousyé, *Gabon* **114 B2** 1 13N 13 12 E
Mvam, *Gabon* **114 C1** 0 13 S 9 39 E
Mvangan, *Cameroon* **114 B2** 2 17N 11 43 E
Mvôlô, *Sudan* **107 F2** 6 2N 29 53 E
Mvuma, *Zimbabwe* **119 F3** 19 16 S 30 30 E
Mvurwi, *Zimbabwe* **119 F3** 17 0 S 30 57 E
Mwabvi ⌂, *Malawi* **119 F3** 16 42 S 35 0 E
Mwadi-Kalumbu, *Dem. Rep. of the Congo* **115 D3** 7 53 S 18 43 E
Mwadui, *Tanzania* **118 C3** 3 26 S 33 32 E
Mwali = Mohéli, *Comoros Is.* **121 a** 12 20 S 43 40 E
Mwambo, *Tanzania* **119 E5** 10 30 S 40 22 E
Mwandi, *Zambia* **119 F1** 17 30 S 24 51 E
Mwanza, *Dem. Rep. of the Congo* **118 D2** 7 55 S 26 43 E
Mwanza, *Tanzania* **118 C3** 2 30 S 32 58 E
Mwanza, *Zambia* **119 F1** 16 58 S 24 28 E
Mwanza □, *Tanzania* **118 C3** 2 0 S 33 0 E
Mwaya, *Tanzania* **119 D3** 9 32 S 33 55 E
Mweelrea, *Ireland* **23 C2** 53 39N 9 49W
Mweka, *Dem. Rep. of the Congo* **115 C4** 4 50 S 21 34 E
Mwendjila, *Dem. Rep. of the Congo* **115 D3** 7 12 S 18 51 E
Mwene-Ditu, *Dem. Rep. of the Congo* **115 D4** 6 35 S 22 27 E
Mwenezi, *Zimbabwe* **119 G3** 21 15 S 30 48 E
Mwenezi →, *Mozam.* **119 G3** 22 40 S 31 50 E
Mwenga, *Dem. Rep. of the Congo* **118 C2** 3 1 S 28 28 E
Mweru, L., *Zambia* **119 D2** 9 0 S 28 40 E
Mweru Wantipa △, *Zambia* **119 D2** 8 39 S 29 25 E
Mwetshi, *Dem. Rep. of the Congo* **115 C4** 4 50 S 21 34 E
Mweza Range, *Zimbabwe* **119 G3** 21 0 S 30 0 E
Mwilambwe, *Dem. Rep. of the Congo* **118 D2** 8 7 S 25 5 E
Mwimbi, *Tanzania* **119 D3** 8 38 S 31 39 E
Mwinilunga, *Zambia* **119 E1** 11 43 S 24 25 E
My Tho, *Vietnam* **87 G6** 10 29N 106 23 E
Mya, O. →, *Algeria* **111 B5** 30 46N 4 54 E
Myajlar, *India* **92 F4** 26 15N 70 20 E
Myakka →, *U.S.A.* **153 J7** 26 56N 82 11W
Myall Lakes △, *Australia* **129 B10** 32 25 S 152 30 E
Myanaung, *Burma* **90 F5** 18 18N 95 22 E
Myanmar = Burma ■, *Asia* **90 E6** 21 0N 96 30 E
Myaung, *Burma* **90 E5** 21 50N 95 25 E
Myaungmya, *Burma* **90 G5** 16 30N 94 40 E
Myebon, *Burma* **90 E4** 20 3N 93 22 E
Myedna, *Belarus* **55 G10** 51 52N 23 42 E
Myeik Kyunzu, *Burma* **87 G1** 11 30N 97 30 E
Myers Chuck, *U.S.A.* **142 B2** 55 44N 132 11W
Myerstown, *U.S.A.* **151 F8** 40 22N 76 19W
Myingyan, *Burma* **90 E5** 21 30N 95 20 E
Myitkyina, *Burma* **90 C6** 25 24N 97 26 E
Myitson, *Burma* **90 D6** 23 16N 96 34 E
Myittha, *Burma* **90 E6** 21 25N 96 8 E
Myittha →, *Burma* **90 D5** 23 12N 94 17 E
Myjava, *Slovak Rep.* **35 C10** 48 41N 17 37 E
Mykhaylivka, *Ukraine* **59 J8** 47 12N 35 15 E
Mykines, *Færoe Is.* **14 E9** 62 7N 7 35W
Myking, *Norway* **18 D2** 60 41N 5 19 E
Mykolayiv, *Ukraine* **59 J7** 46 58N 32 0 E
Mylius Erichsen Land, *Greenland* **10 A8** 81 30N 27 0W
Mymensingh, *Bangla.* **90 C3** 24 45N 90 24 E
Mynydd Du, *U.K.* **21 F4** 51 52N 3 50W
Myo-gyi, *Burma* **90 E6** 21 27N 96 22 E
Myohaung, *Burma* **90 E4** 20 35N 93 11 E
Myohla, *Burma* **90 F5** 19 16N 95 25 E
Myotha, *Burma* **90 E5** 21 41N 95 43 E
Myothit, *Kachin, Burma* **90 C6** 24 24N 97 24 E
Myothit, *Magwe, Burma* **90 E5** 20 12N 95 27 E
Myrasýsla □, *Iceland* **11 C5** 64 45N 21 30W
Mýrdalsjökull, *Iceland* **11 D7** 63 40N 19 6W
Myrhorod, *Ukraine* **59 H7** 49 58N 33 37 E
Mýri, *Iceland* **11 B9** 65 23N 17 23W
Myrtle Beach, *U.S.A.* **149 J6** 33 42N 78 53W
Myrtle Creek, *U.S.A.* **158 E2** 43 1N 123 17W
Myrtle Grove, *U.S.A.* **153 E2** 30 23N 87 17W
Myrtle Point, *U.S.A.* **158 E1** 43 4N 124 8W
Myrtleford, *Australia* **129 D7** 36 34 S 146 44 E
Myrtou, *Cyprus* **39 E9** 35 18N 33 4 E
Myrzakent, *Kazakhstan* **65 C4** 40 40N 68 32 E
Mysen, *Norway* **18 E8** 59 33N 11 20 E
Mysia, *Turkey* **51 G11** 39 50N 27 0 E
Myślenice, *Poland* **55 J6** 49 51N 19 57 E
Myślibórz, *Poland* **55 F1** 52 55N 14 50 E
Mysłowice, *Poland* **55 H6** 50 15N 19 12 E
Myslowitz = Mysłowice, *Poland* **55 H6** 50 15N 19 12 E
Mysore = Karnataka □, *India* **95 H3** 13 15N 77 0 E
Mysore, *India* **95 H3** 12 17N 76 41 E
Mystic, *Conn., U.S.A.* **151 E13** 41 21N 71 58W
Mystic, *Iowa, U.S.A.* **156 D4** 40 47N 92 57W
Myszków, *Poland* **55 H6** 50 45N 19 22 E
Myszyniec, *Poland* **54 E8** 53 23N 21 21 E
Mythen, *Switz.* **33 B7** 47 2N 8 42 E
Mytishchi, *Russia* **58 E9** 55 50N 37 50 E
Mývatn, *Iceland* **11 B10** 65 36N 17 0W
Mzab, Oued en →, *Algeria* **111 B6** 32 15N 5 0 E
Mže →, *Czech Rep.* **34 B6** 49 46N 13 24 E
Mzimba, *Malawi* **119 E3** 11 55 S 33 39 E
Mzimkulu →, *S. Africa* **117 E5** 30 44 S 30 28 E
Mzimvubu →, *S. Africa* **117 E4** 31 38 S 29 33 E
Mzuzu, *Malawi* **119 E3** 11 30 S 33 55 E

N

Na Hearadh = Harris, *U.K.* **22 D2** 57 50N 6 55W
Na-lang, *Burma* **90 D6** 22 42N 97 33 E
Na Noi, *Thailand* **86 C3** 18 19N 100 43 E
Na Phao, *Laos* **86 D5** 17 35N 105 44 E
Na Sam, *Vietnam* **76 F6** 22 3N 106 37 E
Na San, *Vietnam* **86 B5** 21 12N 104 2 E
Na Thon, *Thailand* **87 b** 9 32N 99 56 E
Naab →, *Germany* **31 F8** 49 1N 12 2 E
Naalehu, *U.S.A.* **145 D6** 19 4N 155 35W
Na'am, *Sudan* **107 F2** 9 42N 28 27 E
Na'am →, *Sudan* **107 F2** 6 48N 29 57 E
Naantali, *Finland* **15 F19** 60 29N 22 2 E
Naas, *Ireland* **23 C5** 53 12N 6 40W
Nababeep, *S. Africa* **116 D2** 29 36 S 17 46 E
Nabadwip = Navadwip, *India* **93 H13** 23 34N 88 20 E
Nabari, *Japan* **73 C8** 34 37N 136 5 E
Nabawa, *Australia* **125 E1** 28 30 S 114 48 E
Nabberu, L., *Australia* **125 E3** 25 50 S 120 30 E
Nabburg, *Germany* **31 F8** 49 27N 12 11 E
Naberezhnyye Chelny, *Russia* **60 C11** 55 42N 52 19 E
Nabesna, *U.S.A.* **144 E12** 62 22N 143 0W
Nabeul, *Tunisia* **108 A2** 36 30N 10 44 E
Nabha, *India* **92 D7** 30 26N 76 14 E
Nabīd, *Iran* **97 D8** 29 40N 57 38 E
Nabire, *Indonesia* **83 B5** 3 15 S 135 26 E
Nabisar, *Pakistan* **92 G3** 25 8N 69 40 E
Nabisipi →, *Canada* **141 B7** 50 14N 62 13W
Nabiswera, *Uganda* **118 B3** 1 27N 32 15 E
Nāblus = Nābulus, *West Bank* **103 C4** 32 14N 35 15 E
Naboomspruit, *S. Africa* **117 C4** 24 32 S 28 40 E
Nabou, *Burkina Faso* **112 C4** 11 25N 2 50W
Nabouwalu, *Fiji* **133 A2** 17 0 S 178 45 E
Nabua, *Phil.* **80 E4** 13 24N 123 22 E
Nābulus, *West Bank* **103 C4** 32 14N 35 15 E
Nabunturan, *Phil.* **81 H5** 7 35N 125 58 E
Nacala, *Mozam.* **119 E5** 14 31 S 40 34 E
Nacala-Velha, *Mozam.* **119 E5** 14 32 S 40 34 E
Nacaome, *Honduras* **164 D2** 13 31N 87 30W
Nacaroa, *Mozam.* **119 E4** 14 22 S 39 56 E
Naches, *U.S.A.* **158 C3** 46 44N 120 42W
Naches →, *U.S.A.* **160 D6** 46 38N 120 31W
Nachicapau, L., *Canada* **141 A6** 56 40N 68 5W
Nachikatsuura, *Japan* **73 D7** 33 33N 135 58 E
Nachingwea, *Tanzania* **119 E4** 10 23 S 38 49 E
Nachna, *India* **92 F4** 27 34N 71 41 E
Náchod, *Czech Rep.* **34 A9** 50 25N 16 8 E
Nachuge, *India* **95 J11** 10 47N 92 21 E
Nacimiento L., *U.S.A.* **160 K6** 35 46N 120 53W
Nackara, *Australia* **128 B3** 32 48 S 139 12 E
Naco, *Mexico* **162 A3** 31 20N 109 56W
Nacogdoches, *U.S.A.* **155 K7** 31 36N 94 39W
Nácori Chico, *Mexico* **162 B3** 29 39N 109 1W
Nacozari, *Mexico* **162 A3** 30 24N 109 39W
Nacula, *Fiji* **133 A1** 16 54 S 177 27 E
Nådendal = Naantali, *Finland* **15 F19** 60 29N 22 2 E
Nadezhdinsky = Serov, *Russia* **64 B8** 59 29N 60 35 E
Nadi, *Fiji* **133 A1** 17 42 S 177 20 E

Nadi, Sudan 106 D3 18 40N 33 41 E
Nadiad, India 92 H5 22 41N 72 56 E
Nădlac, Romania 52 D5 46 10N 20 50 E
Nador, Morocco 111 A4 35 14N 2 58W
Nadur, Malta 38 F7 35 54N 14 22 E
Nadur, Gozo, Malta 38 E7 36 2N 14 18 E
Nadūshan, Iran 97 C7 32 2N 53 35 E
Nadvirna, Ukraine 53 B9 48 37N 24 30 E
Nadvoitsy, Russia 56 B5 63 52N 34 14 E
Nadvornaya = Nadvirna, Ukraine 53 B9 48 37N 24 30 E
Nadym, Russia 66 C8 65 35N 72 42 E
Nadym →, Russia 66 C8 66 12N 72 0 E
Nærbø, Norway 18 F2 58 40N 5 39 E
Næstved, Denmark 17 J5 55 13N 11 44 E
Nafada, Nigeria 113 C7 11 8N 11 20 E
Näfels, Switz. 33 B8 47 6N 9 4 E
Nafpaktos = Návpaktos, Greece 48 C3 38 24N 21 50 E
Nafplio = Návplion, Greece 48 D4 37 33N 22 50 E
Naft-e Safīd, Iran 97 D6 31 40N 49 17 E
Naftshahr, Iran 101 E11 34 0N 45 30 E
Nafud Desert = An Nafūd, Si. Arabia 96 D4 28 15N 41 0 E
Nafūsah, Jabal, Libya 108 B2 32 12N 12 30 E
Nag Hammâdi, Egypt 106 B3 26 2N 32 18 E
Naga, Camarines S., Phil. 80 E4 13 38N 123 15 E
Naga, Cebu, Phil. 81 F4 10 13N 123 45 E
Naga, Zamboanga del S., Phil. 81 H4 7 46N 122 45 E
Naga, Kreb en, Africa 110 D3 24 12N 6 0W
Naga Hills = Nagaland □, India 90 B5 26 0N 94 30 E
Naga-Shima, Kagoshima, Japan 72 E2 32 10N 130 9 E
Naga-Shima, Yamaguchi, Japan 72 D4 33 49N 132 5 E
Nagahama, Ehime, Japan 72 D4 33 36N 132 29 E
Nagahama, Shiga, Japan 73 B8 35 23N 136 16 E
Nagai, Japan 70 E10 38 6N 140 2 E
Nagai I., U.S.A. 144 J8 55 5N 160 0W
Nagaland □, India 90 B5 26 0N 94 30 E
Nagambie, Australia 129 D6 36 47 S 145 10 E
Nagano, Japan 73 A10 36 40N 138 10 E
Nagano □, Japan 73 A10 36 15N 138 0 E
Nagaoka, Japan 71 F9 37 27N 138 51 E
Nagappattinam, India 95 J4 10 46N 79 51 E
Nagar →, Bangla. 90 C2 24 27N 89 12 E
Nagar Karnul, India 95 F4 16 29N 78 20 E
Nagar Parkar, Pakistan 92 G4 24 28N 70 46 E
Nagara-Gawa →, Japan 73 B8 35 40N 136 43 E
Nagaram, India 94 E5 18 21N 80 26 E
Nagarhole △, India 95 J3 12 0N 76 10 E
Nagari Hills, India 95 H4 13 3N 79 45 E
Nagasaki, Japan 72 E1 32 47N 129 50 E
Nagasaki □, Japan 72 E1 32 50N 129 40 E
Nagato, Japan 72 C3 34 19N 131 5 E
Nagaur, India 92 F5 27 15N 73 45 E
Nagbhir, India 94 D4 20 34N 79 55 E
Nagda, India 92 H6 23 27N 75 25 E
Nagercoil, India 95 K3 8 12N 77 26 E
Nagina, India 93 E8 29 30N 78 30 E
Nagīneh, Iran 97 C8 34 20N 57 15 E
Naginimara, India 90 B5 26 49N 94 50 E
Nagir, Pakistan 93 A6 36 12N 74 42 E
Naglarby, Sweden 16 D9 60 25N 15 34 E
Nagod, India 93 G9 24 34N 80 36 E
Nagold, Germany 31 G4 48 32N 8 43 E
Nagold →, Germany 31 G4 48 52N 8 42 E
Nagoorin, Australia 126 C5 24 17 S 151 15 E
Nagorno-Karabakh □, Azerbaijan 101 C12 39 55N 46 45 E
Nagornyy, Russia 67 D13 55 58N 124 57 E
Nagorsk, Russia 64 B3 59 18N 50 48 E
Nagoya, Japan 73 B8 35 10N 136 50 E
Nagoya ✕ (NGO), Japan 73 B8 35 14N 136 57 E
Nagpartian = Burgos, Phil. 80 B3 18 31N 120 39 E
Nagpur, India 94 D4 21 8N 79 10 E
Nagua, Dom. Rep. 165 C6 19 23N 69 50W
Naguabo, Puerto Rico 165 d 18 13N 65 44W
Nagyatád, Hungary 52 D2 46 14N 17 22 E
Nagyecsed, Hungary 52 C7 47 53N 22 24 E
Nagykálló, Hungary 52 C6 47 53N 21 51 E
Nagykanizsa, Hungary 52 D2 46 28N 17 0 E
Nagykáta, Hungary 52 C4 47 25N 19 45 E
Nagykőrös, Hungary 52 C4 47 5N 19 48 E
Nagyszombat = Trnava, Slovak Rep. 35 C10 48 23N 17 35 E
Nagyvárad = Oradea, Romania 52 C6 47 2N 21 58 E
Naha, Japan 71 L3 26 13N 127 42 E
Nahan, India 92 D7 30 33N 77 18 E
Nahanni △, Canada 142 A4 61 36N 125 41W
Nahanni Butte, Canada 142 A4 61 2N 123 31W
Nahargarh, Mad. P., India 92 G6 24 10N 75 14 E
Nahargarh, Raj., India 92 G7 24 55N 76 50 E
Nahariyya, Israel 100 F6 33 1N 35 5 E
Nahāvand, Iran 97 C6 34 10N 48 22 E
Nahe →, Germany 31 F3 49 58N 7 54 E
Nahirne, Ukraine 53 E13 45 26N 28 17 E
Nahîya, W. →, Egypt 106 B3 28 55N 31 0 E
Nahuel Huapi △, Argentina 176 B2 41 3 S 71 59W
Nahuel Huapi, L., Argentina 176 B2 41 0 S 71 32W
Nahuelbuta △, Chile 174 D1 37 44 S 72 57W
Nahunta, U.S.A. 152 D8 31 12N 81 59W
Nai Yong, Thailand 87 a 8 14N 98 22 E
Naic, Phil. 80 D3 14 19N 120 46 E
Naicá, Mexico 162 B3 27 53N 105 31W
Naicam, Canada 143 C8 52 30N 104 30W
Naikliu, Indonesia 82 C2 9 30 S 123 50 E
Naikoon △, Canada 142 C2 53 55N 131 55W
Naikul, India 94 D7 21 20N 84 58 E
Naila, Germany 31 E7 50 19N 11 42 E
Naimisharanya, India 93 F9 27 21N 80 30 E
Nain, Canada 141 A7 56 34N 61 40W
Nā'īn, Iran 97 C7 32 54N 53 0 E
Naini Tal, India 93 E8 29 30N 79 30 E
Naintré, France 26 F7 46 46N 0 29 E
Nainwa, India 92 G6 25 46N 75 51 E
Naipu, Romania 53 F10 44 12N 25 47 E
Nairai, Fiji 133 A2 17 49 S 179 15 E
Nairn, U.K. 22 D5 57 35N 3 53W
Nairobi, Kenya 118 C4 1 17 S 36 48 E
Nairobi △, Kenya 118 C4 1 22 S 36 50 E
Naissaar, Estonia 15 G21 59 34N 24 29 E
Naita, Mt., Ethiopia 107 F4 5 30N 35 18 E
Naitaba, Fiji 133 A3 17 0 S 179 16W
Naivasha, Kenya 118 C4 0 40 S 36 30 E
Naivasha, L., Kenya 118 C4 0 48 S 36 20 E
Najac, France 28 D5 44 14N 1 58 E
Najaf = An Najaf, Iraq 101 G11 32 3N 44 15 E
Najafābād, Iran 97 C6 32 40N 51 15 E
Najd, Si. Arabia 88 C3 26 30N 42 0 E
Nájera, Spain 40 C2 42 26N 2 48W
Najerilla →, Spain 40 C2 42 32N 2 48W
Najibabad, India 92 E8 29 40N 78 20 E
Najin, N. Korea 75 C16 42 12N 130 15 E
Najmah, Si. Arabia 97 E6 26 42N 50 6 E
Najrān, Si. Arabia 98 C4 17 34N 44 18 E
Naju, S. Korea 75 G14 35 3N 126 43 E
Naka-Gawa →, Japan 73 A12 36 20N 140 36 E
Nakadōri-Shima, Japan 71 H4 32 57N 129 4 E
Nakał = Nakło nad Notecią, Poland 55 E4 53 9N 17 38 E
Nakalagba, Dem. Rep. of the Congo 118 B2 2 50N 27 58 E
Nakalele Pt., U.S.A. 145 B5 21 2N 156 35W
Nakama, Japan 72 D2 33 56N 130 43 E
Nakaminato, Japan 73 A12 36 21N 140 36 E
Nakamura, Japan 72 E4 32 59N 132 56 E
Nakanai Mts., Papua N. G. 132 C6 5 40 S 151 0 E
Nakano, Japan 73 A10 36 45N 138 22 E
Nakano-Shima, Japan 71 K4 29 51N 129 52 E
Nakanojō, Japan 73 A10 36 35N 138 51 E
Nakashibetsu, Japan 70 C12 43 33N 144 59 E
Nakatsu, Japan 72 D3 33 34N 131 15 E
Nakatsugawa, Japan 73 B9 35 29N 137 30 E
Nakfa, Eritrea 107 D4 16 40N 38 32 E
Nakfa △, Eritrea 107 D4 17 28N 38 55 E
Nakha Yai, Ko, Thailand 87 a 8 3N 98 28 E
Nakhichevan = Naxçıvan, Azerbaijan 101 C11 39 12N 45 15 E
Nakhichevan Rep. = Naxçıvan □, Azerbaijan 101 C11 39 25N 45 26 E
Nakhl, Egypt 103 F2 29 55N 33 43 E
Nakhl-e Taqī, Iran 97 E7 27 28N 52 36 E
Nakhodka, Russia 67 E14 42 53N 132 54 E
Nakhon Nayok, Thailand 86 E3 14 12N 101 13 E
Nakhon Pathom, Thailand 86 F3 13 49N 100 3 E
Nakhon Phanom, Thailand 86 D5 17 23N 104 43 E
Nakhon Ratchasima, Thailand 86 E4 14 59N 102 12 E
Nakhon Sawan, Thailand 86 E3 15 35N 100 10 E
Nakhon Si Thammarat, Thailand 87 H3 8 29N 100 0 E
Nakhon Thai, Thailand 86 D3 17 5N 100 44 E
Nakhtarana, India 92 H3 23 20N 69 15 E
Nakina, Canada 140 B2 50 10N 86 40W
Nakło nad Notecią, Poland 55 E4 53 9N 17 38 E
Naknek, U.S.A. 144 G8 58 44N 157 1W
Nako, Burkina Faso 112 C4 10 40N 3 4W
Nakodar, India 92 D6 31 8N 75 31 E
Nakskov, Denmark 17 K5 54 50N 11 8 E
Naktong →, S. Korea 75 G15 35 7N 128 57 E
Nakuru, Kenya 118 C4 0 15 S 36 4 E
Nakuru, L., Kenya 118 C4 0 23 S 36 5 E
Nakusp, Canada 142 C5 50 20N 117 45W
Nal, Pakistan 92 F2 27 40N 66 12 E
Nal →, Pakistan 91 D2 25 20N 65 30 E
Nalázi, Mozam. 117 C5 24 3 S 33 20 E
Nalchik, Russia 61 J6 43 30N 43 33 E
Nałęczów, Poland 55 G9 51 17N 22 9 E
Nalerigu, Ghana 113 C4 10 35N 0 25W
Nalgonda, India 94 F4 17 6N 79 15 E
Nalhati, India 93 G12 24 17N 87 52 E
Naliya, India 92 H3 23 16N 68 50 E
Nallamalai Hills, India 95 G4 15 30N 78 50 E
Nallıhan, Turkey 100 B4 40 11N 31 20 E
Nalolo, Zambia 115 F4 15 33 S 23 7 E
Nalón →, Spain 42 B4 43 32N 6 4W
Nalong, Burma 90 C6 24 44N 97 28 E
Nālūt, Libya 108 B2 31 54N 11 0 E
Nam Can, Vietnam 87 H5 8 46N 104 59 E
Nam-ch'on, N. Korea 75 E14 38 15N 126 26 E
Nam Co, China 68 C4 30 30N 90 45 E
Nam Dinh, Vietnam 76 G6 20 25N 106 5 E
Nam Du, Hon, Vietnam 87 H5 9 41N 104 21 E
Nam Nao △, Thailand 86 D3 16 44N 101 32 E
Nam Ngum Dam, Laos 86 C4 18 35N 102 34 E
Nam-Phan, Vietnam 87 G6 10 30N 106 0 E
Nam Phong, Thailand 86 D4 16 42N 102 52 E
Nam Tha, Laos 76 G3 20 58N 101 30 E
Nam Tok, Thailand 86 E2 14 21N 99 4 E
Namachire, Angola 115 E4 11 26 S 22 43 E
Namacunde, Angola 116 B2 17 18 S 15 50 E
Namacurra, Mozam. 117 B6 17 30 S 36 50 E
Namadgi △, Australia 129 C8 35 42 S 149 0 E
Namak, Daryācheh-ye, Iran 97 C7 34 30N 52 0 E
Namak, Kavir-e, Iran 97 C8 34 30N 57 30 E
Namakkal, India 95 J4 11 13N 78 13 E
Namakzār, Daryācheh-ye, Iran 91 B1 34 0N 60 30 E
Namaland, Namibia 116 C2 26 0 S 17 0 E
Namangan, Uzbekistan 65 C5 41 0N 71 40 E
Namapa, Mozam. 119 E4 13 43 S 39 50 E
Namaqualand, S. Africa 116 E2 30 0 S 17 25 E
Namasagali, Uganda 118 B3 1 2N 33 0 E
Namatanai, Papua N. G. 132 B7 3 40 S 152 29 E
Namber, Indonesia 83 B4 1 2 S 134 49 E
Nambour, Australia 127 D5 26 32 S 152 58 E
Nambouwalu = Nabouwalu, Fiji 133 A2 17 0 S 178 45 E
Nambuangongo, Angola 115 D2 8 1 S 14 12 E
Nambucca Heads, Australia 129 A10 30 37 S 153 0 E
Nambung △, Australia 125 F2 30 30 S 115 5 E
Namcha Barwa, China 68 D4 29 40N 95 10 E
Namche Bazar, Nepal 93 F12 27 51N 86 47 E
Namchonjŏm = Nam-ch'on, N. Korea 75 E14 38 15N 126 26 E
Namecunda, Mozam. 119 E4 14 54 S 37 37 E
Nameh, Indonesia 85 B5 2 34N 116 21 E
Namen = Namur, Belgium 24 D4 50 27N 4 52 E
Namenalala, Fiji 133 A2 17 8 S 179 9 E
Nameponda, Mozam. 119 F4 15 50 S 39 50 E
Namerikawa, Japan 73 A9 36 46N 137 20 E
Náměšť nad Oslavou, Czech Rep. 35 B9 49 12N 16 10 E
Námestovo, Slovak Rep. 35 B12 49 24N 19 25 E
Nametil, Mozam. 119 F4 15 40 S 39 21 E
Namew L., Canada 143 C8 54 14N 101 56W
Namgia, India 93 D8 31 48N 78 40 E
Namhkam, Burma 76 E1 23 50N 97 41 E
Namho, Burma 90 D7 22 4N 99 1 E
Namhsan, Burma 90 D6 22 48N 97 2 E
Namib Desert, Namibia 116 C2 22 30 S 15 0 E
Namib-Naukluft △, Namibia 116 C2 24 40 S 15 16 E
Namibe, Angola 115 F2 15 7 S 12 11 E
Namibe △, Angola 115 F2 16 35 S 12 20 E
Namibe □, Angola 116 B1 16 35 S 12 30 E
Namibia ■, Africa 116 C2 22 0 S 18 9 E
Namibwoestyn = Namib Desert, Namibia 116 C2 22 30 S 15 0 E
Namīn, Iran 101 C13 38 25N 48 30 E
Namlan, Burma 90 D6 22 15N 97 24 E
Namlea, Indonesia 82 B3 3 18 S 127 5 E
Namoi →, Australia 129 A9 30 12 S 149 30 E
Namous, O. en →, Algeria 111 B4 31 0N 0 15W
Nampa, U.S.A. 158 E5 43 34N 116 34W
Nampala, Mali 112 B3 15 20N 5 30W
Namp'o, N. Korea 75 E13 38 52N 125 10 E
Nampō-Shotō, Japan 71 J10 32 0N 140 0 E
Nampula, Mozam. 119 F4 15 6 S 39 15 E
Namrole, Indonesia 82 B3 3 46 S 126 46 E
Namsang, Burma 90 E6 20 53N 97 43 E
Namsen →, Norway 14 D14 64 28N 11 37 E
Namslau = Namysłów, Poland 55 G4 51 6N 17 42 E
Namsos, Norway 14 D14 64 29N 11 30 E
Namtok Chat Trakan △, Thailand 86 D3 17 17N 100 40 E
Namtok Mae Surin △, Thailand 86 C2 18 55N 98 2 E
Namtsy, Russia 67 C13 62 43N 129 37 E
Namtu, Burma 90 D6 23 5N 97 28 E
Namtumbo, Tanzania 119 E4 10 30 S 36 4 E
Namu, Canada 142 C3 51 52N 127 50W
Namuka-i-Lau, Fiji 133 B3 18 53 S 178 37W
Namumea, Tuvalu 123 B14 5 41 S 176 9 E
Namur, Belgium 24 D4 50 27N 4 52 E
Namur □, Belgium 24 D4 50 17N 5 0 E
Namutoni, Namibia 116 B2 18 49 S 16 55 E
Namwala, Zambia 119 F2 15 44 S 26 30 E
Namwŏn, S. Korea 75 G14 35 23N 127 23 E
Namysłów, Poland 55 G4 51 6N 17 42 E
Nan, Thailand 86 C3 18 48N 100 46 E
Nan →, Thailand 86 E3 15 42N 100 9 E
Nan-ch'ang = Nanchang, China 77 C10 28 42N 115 55 E
Nan Ling, China 77 E8 25 0N 112 30 E
Nan Xian, China 77 C9 29 20N 112 22 E
Nana, C.A.R. 114 A3 5 0N 15 50 E
Nana, Romania 53 F11 44 17N 26 34 E
Nana-Barya △, C.A.R. 114 A3 7 40N 17 29 E
Nana Kru, Liberia 112 E3 4 55N 8 45W
Nanaimo, Canada 142 D4 49 10N 124 0W
Nanakuli, U.S.A. 145 K13 21 24N 158 9W
Nanam, N. Korea 75 D15 41 44N 129 40 E
Nanan, China 77 E12 24 59N 118 21 E
Nanango, Australia 127 D5 26 40 S 152 0 E
Nan'ao, China 77 F11 23 28N 117 5 E
Nanao, Japan 71 F8 37 0N 137 0 E
Nanbu, China 76 B6 31 18N 106 3 E
Nanchang, Jiangxi, China 77 C10 28 42N 115 55 E
Nanchang, Kiangsi, China 77 C10 28 34N 115 48 E
Nancheng, China 77 D11 27 33N 116 35 E
Nanching = Nanjing, China 77 A12 32 2N 118 47 E
Nanchong, China 76 B6 30 43N 106 2 E
Nanchuan, China 76 C6 29 9N 107 6 E
Nanchung = Nanchong, China 76 B6 30 43N 106 2 E
Nancowry, India 95 L11 7 59N 93 32 E
Nancy, France 27 D13 48 42N 6 12 E
Nanda Devi, India 93 D8 30 23N 79 59 E
Nanda Devi △, India 93 D8 30 30N 79 50 E
Nanda Kot, India 93 D9 30 17N 80 5 E
Nandan, China 76 E6 24 58N 107 29 E
Nandan, Japan 72 C6 34 10N 134 42 E
Nanded, India 94 E3 19 10N 77 20 E
Nandewar Ra., Australia 127 E5 30 15 S 150 35 E
Nandgaon, India 94 D2 20 19N 74 39 E
Nandi = Nadi, Fiji 133 A1 17 42 S 177 20 E
Nandiarane, Pte., N. Cal. 133 T18 20 14 S 164 19 E
Nandigama, India 94 F5 16 47N 80 18 E
Nandigram, India 93 H12 22 1N 87 58 E
Nandikotkur, India 95 G4 15 52N 78 18 E
Nandura, India 94 D3 20 52N 76 25 E
Nandurbar, India 94 D2 21 20N 74 15 E
Nandyal, India 95 G4 15 30N 78 30 E
Nanfeng, Guangdong, China 77 F8 23 45N 111 47 E
Nanfeng, Jiangxi, China 77 D11 27 12N 116 28 E
Nanga-Eboko, Cameroon 113 E7 4 41N 12 22 E
Nanga Parbat, Pakistan 93 B6 35 10N 74 35 E
Nangade, Mozam. 119 E4 11 5 S 39 36 E
Nangapinoh, Indonesia 85 C4 0 20 S 111 44 E
Nangarhār □, Afghan. 91 B3 34 20N 70 0 E
Nangatayap, Indonesia 85 C4 1 32 S 110 34 E
Nangeya Mts., Uganda 118 B3 3 30N 33 30 E
Nangis, France 27 D10 48 33N 3 1 E
Nangong, China 74 F8 37 23N 115 22 E
Nangtud, Mt., Phil. 81 F4 11 17N 122 11 E
Nanguneri, India 95 K3 8 29N 77 40 E
Nangwarry, Australia 128 D4 37 33 S 140 48 E
Nanhua, China 76 E3 25 13N 101 21 E
Nanhuang, China 75 F11 36 58N 121 48 E
Nanhui, China 77 B13 31 5N 121 44 E
Nanjangud, India 95 H3 12 6N 76 43 E
Nanjeko, Zambia 119 F1 15 31 S 23 30 E
Nanji Shan, China 77 D13 27 27N 121 4 E
Nanjian, China 76 E3 25 2N 100 25 E
Nanjiang, China 76 A6 32 28N 106 51 E
Nanjing, Fujian, China 77 E11 24 25N 117 20 E
Nanjing, Jiangsu, China 77 A12 32 2N 118 47 E
Nanjirinji, Tanzania 119 D4 9 41 S 39 5 E
Nankana Sahib, Pakistan 92 D5 31 27N 73 38 E
Nankang, China 77 E10 25 40N 114 45 E
Nanking = Nanjing, China 77 A12 32 2N 118 47 E
Nankoku, Japan 72 D5 33 39N 133 44 E
Nanlang, China 69 G10 22 30N 113 32 E
Nanling, China 77 B12 30 55N 118 20 E
Nannial, India 94 E4 19 4N 79 40 E
Nanning, China 76 F7 22 48N 108 20 E
Nannup, Australia 125 F2 33 59 S 115 48 E
Nanortalik, Greenland 10 E6 60 10N 45 17W
Nanpan Jiang →, China 76 E6 25 10N 106 5 E
Nanpara, India 93 F9 27 52N 81 33 E
Nanpi, China 74 E9 38 2N 116 45 E
Nanping, Fujian, China 77 D12 26 38N 118 10 E
Nanping, Henan, China 77 C9 29 55N 112 3 E
Nanri Dao, China 77 E12 25 15N 119 25 E
Nanripe, Mozam. 119 E4 13 52 S 38 52 E
Nansei-Shotō = Ryūkyū-rettō, Japan 71 M3 26 0N 126 0 E
Nansen Basin, Arctic 6 A10 84 0N 50 0 E
Nansen Cordillera, Arctic 6 A 87 0N 90 0 E
Nansen Land, Greenland 10 A6 83 0N 43 0W
Nansen Sd., Canada 6 A3 81 0N 91 0W
Nanshan, China 69 F10 22 45N 113 34 E
Nanshan I., S. China Sea 78 B5 10 45N 115 49 E
Nansio, Tanzania 118 C3 2 3 S 33 4 E
Nant, France 28 D7 44 1N 3 18 E
Nanterre, France 27 D9 48 53N 2 13 E
Nantes, France 26 E5 47 12N 1 33W
Nantiat, France 28 B5 46 1N 1 11 E
Nanticoke, U.S.A. 151 E8 41 12N 76 0W
Nanton, Canada 142 C6 50 21N 113 46W
Nantong, China 77 A13 32 1N 120 52 E
Nantou, China 69 F10 22 32N 113 55 E
Nantou, Taiwan 77 F13 23 57N 120 35 E
Nantua, France 27 F12 46 10N 5 35 E
Nantucket I., U.S.A. 148 E10 41 16N 70 5W
Nantung = Nantong, China 77 A13 32 1N 120 52 E
Nantwich, U.K. 20 D5 53 4N 2 31W
Nanty Glo, U.S.A. 150 F6 40 28N 78 50W
Nanuku Passage, Fiji 133 A3 16 45 S 179 15W
Nanuque, Brazil 171 E3 17 50 S 40 21W
Nanusa, Kepulauan, Indonesia 79 D7 4 45N 127 1 E
Nanutarra Roadhouse, Australia 124 D2 22 32 S 115 30 E
Nanxi, China 76 C5 28 54N 104 59 E
Nanxiong, China 77 E10 25 6N 114 15 E
Nanyang, China 74 H7 33 11N 112 30 E
Nanyi Hu, China 77 B12 31 5N 119 0 E
Nanyuki, Kenya 118 B4 0 2N 37 4 E
Nanzhang, China 77 B8 31 45N 111 50 E
Nao, C. de la, Spain 41 G5 38 44N 0 14 E
Naococane, L., Canada 141 B5 52 50N 70 45W
Naogaon, Bangla. 90 C2 24 52N 88 52 E
Naoné, Vanuatu 133 E6 15 0 S 168 8 E
Náousa, Imathía, Greece 50 F6 40 42N 22 9 E
Náousa, Kikládhes, Greece 49 D7 37 7N 25 14 E
Naozhou Dao, China 77 G8 20 55N 110 20 E
Napa, U.S.A. 160 G4 38 18N 122 17W
Napa →, U.S.A. 160 G4 38 10N 122 19W
Napakiak, U.S.A. 144 F7 60 42N 161 57W
Napamute, U.S.A. 144 F8 61 33N 158 42W
Napanee, Canada 140 D4 44 15N 77 0W
Napanoch, U.S.A. 151 E10 41 44N 74 22W
Napanwainami, Indonesia 83 B5 3 3 S 135 45 E
Napaskiak, U.S.A. 144 F7 60 43N 161 55W
Nape, Laos 86 C5 18 18N 105 6 E
Nape Pass = Keo Neua, Deo, Vietnam 86 C5 18 23N 105 10 E
Naperville, U.S.A. 157 C8 41 46N 88 9W
Napf, Switz. 32 B5 47 1N 7 56 E
Napier, N.Z. 130 F5 39 30 S 176 56 E
Napier Broome B., Australia 124 B4 14 2 S 126 37 E
Napier Pen., Australia 126 A2 12 4 S 135 43 E
Napierville, Canada 151 A11 45 11N 73 25W
Naples = Nápoli, Italy 47 B7 40 50N 14 15 E
Naples, U.S.A. 153 J8 26 8N 81 48W
Naples Park, U.S.A. 153 J8 26 17N 81 46W
Napo, China 76 F5 23 22N 105 50 E
Napo □, Ecuador 168 D2 0 30 S 77 0W
Napo →, Peru 168 D3 3 20 S 72 40W
Napoleon, N. Dak., U.S.A. 154 B5 46 30N 99 46W
Napoleon, Ohio, U.S.A. 157 C12 41 23N 84 8W
Napoleon's Tomb, St. Helena 9 h 15 56 S 5 42W
Nápoli, Italy 47 B7 40 50N 14 15 E
Nápoli, G. di, Italy 47 B7 40 43N 14 10 E
Nápoli Capodichino ✕ (NAP), Italy 47 B7 40 53N 14 16 E
Napopo, Dem. Rep. of the Congo 118 B2 4 15N 28 0 E
Nappanee, U.S.A. 157 C11 41 27N 86 0W
Napperby, Australia 128 B3 33 9 S 138 7 E
Naqâda, Egypt 106 B3 25 53N 32 42 E
Naqadeh, Iran 101 D11 36 57N 45 23 E
Naqb, Ra's an, Jordan 103 F4 30 0N 35 29 E
Naqqāsh, Iran 97 C6 35 40N 49 6 E
Nara, Japan 73 C7 34 40N 135 49 E
Nara, Mali 112 B3 15 10N 7 20W
Nara □, Japan 73 C8 34 30N 136 0 E
Nara Canal, Pakistan 92 G3 24 30N 69 20 E
Nara Visa, U.S.A. 155 H3 35 37N 103 6W
Naracoorte, Australia 128 D4 36 58 S 140 45 E
Naradhan, Australia 129 B7 33 34 S 146 17 E
Naraini, India 93 G9 25 11N 80 29 E
Narasannapeta, India 94 E7 18 25N 84 3 E
Narasapur, India 95 F5 16 26N 81 40 E
Narasaropet, India 95 F5 16 14N 80 4 E
Narathiwat, Thailand 87 J3 6 30N 101 48 E
Narayanapatnam, India 94 E6 18 53N 83 10 E
Narayanganj, Bangla. 90 D3 23 40N 90 33 E
Narayanpet, India 94 F3 16 45N 77 30 E
Narbada = Narmada →, India 92 J5 21 38N 72 36 E
Narberth, U.K. 21 F3 51 47N 4 44W
Narbonne, France 28 E7 43 11N 3 0 E
Narborough, I. = Fernandina, I., Ecuador 172 a 0 25 S 91 30W
Narbuvollen, Norway 18 B8 62 21N 11 27 E
Narcea →, Spain 42 B4 43 33N 6 44W
Narcondam I., India 95 H12 13 20N 94 16 E
Nardīn, Iran 97 B7 37 3N 55 59 E
Nardò, Italy 47 B11 40 11N 18 2 E
Narembeen, Australia 125 F2 32 7 S 118 24 E
Narendranagar, India 92 D8 30 10N 78 18 E
Nares Deep, Atl. Oc. 8 D6 26 0N 57 0W
Nares Plain, Atl. Oc. 8 D6 22 0N 67 0W
Nares Str., Arctic 10 B3 80 0N 70 0W
Naretha, Australia 125 F3 31 0 S 124 45 E
Narew →, Poland 55 F7 52 26N 20 41 E
Nari →, Pakistan 92 F2 28 0N 67 40 E
Narin, Afghan. 91 A3 36 5N 69 0 E
Narinda, Helodranon' i, Madag. 117 A8 14 55 S 47 30 E
Narino □, Colombia 168 C2 1 30N 78 0W
Narita, Japan 73 B12 35 47N 140 19 E
Narita, Tokyo ✕ (NRT), Japan 73 B12 35 45N 140 25 E
Nariva Swamp, Trin. & Tob. 169 F9 10 26N 61 4W
Närke, Sweden 16 E8 59 10N 15 0 E
Narmada →, India 92 J5 21 38N 72 36 E
Narman, Turkey 101 B9 40 26N 41 57 E
Narmland, Sweden 15 F15 60 0N 13 30 E
Narnaul, India 92 E7 28 5N 76 11 E
Narni, Italy 45 F9 42 30N 12 30 E
Naro, Ghana 112 C4 10 22N 2 27W
Naro Fominsk, Russia 58 E9 55 23N 36 43 E
Narodnaya, Russia 56 A10 65 5N 59 58 E
Narok, Kenya 118 C4 1 55 S 35 52 E
Narón, Spain 42 B2 43 32N 8 9W
Narooma, Australia 129 D9 36 14 S 150 4 E
Narowal, Pakistan 91 B4 32 6N 74 52 E
Narra, Phil. 81 G2 9 18N 118 28 E
Narrabri, Australia 127 E4 30 19 S 149 46 E
Narran →, Australia 127 D4 28 37 S 148 12 E
Narrandera, Australia 129 C7 34 42 S 146 31 E
Narrogin, Australia 125 F2 32 58 S 117 14 E
Narromine, Australia 129 B8 32 12 S 148 12 E
Narrow Hills △, Canada 143 C8 54 0N 104 37W
Narsampet, India 94 F4 17 57N 79 58 E
Narsaq, Greenland 10 E6 60 57N 46 4W
Narsimhapur, India 93 H8 22 54N 79 14 E
Narsinghgarh, India 92 H7 23 45N 76 40 E
Narsinghpur, India 94 D7 20 28N 85 5 E
Narsipatnam, India 94 F6 17 40N 82 37 E
Nartes, L. e, Albania 50 F3 40 32N 19 25 E
Nartkala, Russia 61 J6 43 33N 43 51 E
Naruto, Kantō, Japan 72 C6 34 11N 134 37 E
Narutō, Shikoku, Japan 73 B12 35 36N 140 25 E
Naruto-Kaikyō, Japan 72 C6 34 14N 134 39 E
Narva, Estonia 58 C5 59 23N 28 12 E
Narva →, Russia 15 G22 59 27N 28 2 E
Narva Bay = Narva Laht, Estonia 15 G19 59 35N 27 35 E
Narva Laht, Estonia 15 G19 59 35N 27 35 E
Narvacan, Phil. 80 C3 17 25N 120 28 E
Narvik, Norway 14 B17 68 28N 17 26 E
Narvskoye Vdkhr., Russia 58 C5 59 18N 28 14 E
Narwana, India 92 E7 29 39N 76 6 E
Narwiański △, Poland 55 F9 52 5N 22 53 E
Naryan-Mar, Russia 56 A9 67 42N 53 12 E
Narym, Russia 66 D9 59 0N 81 30 E
Naryn, Kyrgyzstan 65 C7 41 26N 75 58 E
Naryn →, Uzbekistan 65 C5 40 52N 71 36 E
Nasa, Norway 14 C16 66 29N 15 23 E
Nasau, Fiji 133 A2 17 19 S 179 27 E
Năsăud, Romania 53 C9 47 19N 24 29 E
Nasawa, Vanuatu 133 E6 15 0 S 168 9 E
Naseby, N.Z. 131 F5 45 1 S 170 10 E
Naselle, U.S.A. 160 D3 46 22N 123 49W
Naser, Buheirat en, Egypt 106 C3 23 0N 32 30 E
Nashua, Iowa, U.S.A. 156 B4 42 57N 92 32W
Nashua, Mont., U.S.A. 158 B10 48 8N 106 22W
Nashua, N.H., U.S.A. 151 D13 42 45N 71 28W
Nashville, Ark., U.S.A. 155 J8 33 57N 93 51W
Nashville, Ga., U.S.A. 152 D6 31 12N 83 15W
Nashville, Ill., U.S.A. 156 F7 38 21N 89 23W
Nashville, Ind., U.S.A. 157 E10 39 12N 86 15W
Nashville, Mich., U.S.A. 157 B11 42 36N 85 5W
Nashville, Tenn., U.S.A. 149 G2 36 10N 86 47W
Našice, Croatia 52 E3 45 32N 18 4 E
Nasielsk, Poland 55 F7 52 35N 20 50 E
Nasik, India 94 E1 19 58N 73 50 E
Nasipit, Phil. 81 G5 8 57N 125 19 E
Nasir, Sudan 107 F3 8 36N 33 4 E
Nasirabad = Mymensingh, Bangla. 90 C3 24 45N 90 24 E
Nasirabad, India 92 F6 26 15N 74 45 E
Nasirabad, Pakistan 92 E3 28 23N 68 24 E
Nasiriyah = An Nāşirīyah, Iraq 96 D5 31 0N 46 15 E
Naskaupi →, Canada 141 B7 53 47N 60 51W
Naso, Italy 47 D7 38 7N 14 47 E
Naso Pt., Phil. 81 F3 10 25N 121 57 E
Naşrābād, Iran 97 C6 34 8N 51 26 E
Naşriān-e Pā'īn, Iran 96 C5 32 52N 46 52 E
Nass →, Canada 142 C3 55 0N 129 40W
Nassarawa, Nigeria 113 D6 8 32N 7 41 E
Nassarawa □, Nigeria 113 D6 8 30N 8 20 E
Nassau, Bahamas 9 b 25 5N 77 20W
Nassau, U.S.A. 151 D11 42 31N 73 37W
Nassau, B., Chile 176 E3 55 20 S 68 0W
Nassau International ✕ (NAS), Bahamas 9 b 25 3N 77 28W
Nasser, L. = Naser, Buheirat en, Egypt 106 C3 23 0N 32 30 E
Nasser City = Kôm Ombo, Egypt 106 C3 24 25N 32 52 E
Nassereith, Austria 33 B11 47 19N 10 50 E
Nassian, Ivory C. 112 D4 8 28N 3 28W
Nässjö, Sweden 17 G8 57 39N 14 42 E
Nastapoka →, Canada 140 A4 56 55N 76 33W
Nastapoka, Is., Canada 140 A4 56 55N 76 50W
Nasugbu, Phil. 80 D3 14 5N 120 38 E
Näsum, Sweden 17 H8 56 10N 14 29 E
Näsviken, Sweden 16 C10 61 46N 16 52 E
Nata, Botswana 116 C4 20 12 S 26 12 E
Nata →, Botswana 116 C4 20 14 S 26 10 E
Natagaima, Colombia 168 C2 3 37N 75 6W
Natal, Brazil 170 C4 5 47 S 35 13W
Natal, Indonesia 84 B1 0 35N 99 7 E
Natal Basin, Ind. Oc. 121 H2 35 0 S 40 0 E
Natal Drakensberg △, S. Africa 117 D4 29 27 S 29 30 E
Natalinci, Serbia & M. 52 F5 44 15N 20 49 E
Naţanz, Iran 97 C6 33 30N 51 55 E
Natashquan, Canada 141 B7 50 14N 61 46W
Natashquan →, Canada 141 B7 50 7N 61 50W
Natchez, U.S.A. 155 K9 31 34N 91 24W
Natchitoches, U.S.A. 155 K8 31 46N 93 5W
Naters, Switz. 32 D5 46 19N 7 58 E
Natewa B., Fiji 133 A2 16 35 S 179 40 E
Nathalia, Australia 129 D6 36 1 S 145 13 E
Nathdwara, India 92 G5 24 55N 73 50 E
Nati, Pta., Spain 38 A4 40 3N 3 50 E
Natimuk, Australia 128 D5 36 42 S 142 0 E
Nation →, Canada 142 B4 55 30N 123 32W
National Capital District □, Papua N. G. 132 E4 9 25 S 147 10 E
National City, U.S.A. 161 N9 32 41N 117 6W
Natitingou, Benin 113 C5 10 20N 1 26 E
Natividad, I., Mexico 162 B1 27 50N 115 10W
Natividade, Brazil 171 D2 11 43 S 47 47W
Natkyizin, Burma 86 E1 14 57N 97 59 E
Natmauk, Burma 90 E5 20 20N 95 24 E
Natogyi, Burma 90 E5 21 25N 95 39 E
Natonin, Phil. 80 C3 17 6N 121 18 E
Natron, L., Tanzania 118 C4 2 20 S 36 0 E
Natrona Heights, U.S.A. 150 F5 40 37N 79 44W
Natrûn, W. el →, Egypt 106 H7 30 25N 30 13 E
Nattai △, Australia 129 C9 34 12 S 150 22 E
Nättraby, Sweden 17 H9 56 13N 15 31 E
Natukanaoka Pan, Namibia 116 B2 18 40 S 15 45 E
Natuna Besar, Kepulauan, Indonesia 84 B3 4 0N 108 15 E
Natuna Is. = Natuna Besar, Kepulauan, Indonesia 84 B3 4 0N 108 15 E
Natuna Selatan, Kepulauan, Indonesia 85 B3 2 45N 109 0 E
Natural Bridge, U.S.A. 151 B9 44 5N 75 30W
Natural Bridges △, U.S.A. 159 H8 37 36N 110 1W
Naturaliste, C., Australia 127 G4 40 50 S 148 15 E
Naturaliste Plateau, Ind. Oc. 121 H10 34 0 S 112 0 E
Nau, Tajikistan 65 C4 40 9N 69 22 E
Nau Qala, Afghan. 92 B3 34 5N 68 5 E
Naucelle, France 28 D6 44 13N 2 20 E
Nauders, Austria 34 E3 46 54N 10 30 E
Nauen, Germany 30 C8 52 36N 12 52 E
Naugard = Nowogard, Poland 54 E2 53 41N 15 10 E
Naugatuck, U.S.A. 151 E11 41 30N 73 3W
Naujaat = Repulse Bay, Canada 139 B11 66 30N 86 30W
Naujan, Phil. 80 E3 13 20N 121 18 E

Naujoji Akmenė, Lithuania 54 B9 56 19N 22 54 E
Naulila, Angola 115 F2 17 13 S 14 39 E
Naumburg, Germany 30 D7 51 9N 11 47 E
Naumburg am Queis = Nowogrodziec, Poland 55 G2 51 12N 15 24 E
Naupada, India 94 E7 18 34N 84 18 E
Nā'ūr at Tunayb, Jordan 103 D4 31 48N 35 57 E
Nauru ■, Pac. Oc. 134 H8 1 0 S 166 0 E
Naushahra = Nowshera, Pakistan 91 B3 34 0N 72 0 E
Naushahro, Pakistan 92 F3 26 50N 68 7 E
Naushon I., U.S.A. 151 E14 41 29N 70 45W
Nausori, Fiji 133 B2 18 2 S 178 32 E
Naustdal, Norway 18 C2 61 31N 5 43 E
Nauta, Peru 168 D3 4 31 S 73 35W
Naute ⌂, Namibia 116 D2 26 55 S 17 57 E
Nautla, Mexico 163 C5 20 20N 96 50W
Nauvoo, U.S.A. 156 D5 40 33N 91 23W
Nava, Mexico 162 B4 28 25N 100 46W
Nava, Spain 42 B5 43 21N 5 31W
Nava del Rey, Spain 42 D5 41 22N 5 6W
Navadwip, India 93 H13 23 34N 88 20 E
Navahermosa, Spain 43 F6 39 41N 4 28W
Navahrudak, Belarus 58 F3 53 40N 25 50 E
Navai, Fiji 133 A1 17 36 S 177 57 E
Navajo Reservoir, U.S.A. 159 H10 36 48N 107 36W
Naval, Phil. 81 F5 11 34N 124 23 E
Navalcarnero, Spain 42 E6 40 17N 4 5W
Navalgund, India 95 G2 15 34N 75 22 E
Navalmoral de la Mata, Spain 42 F5 39 52N 5 33W
Navalvillar de Pela, Spain 43 F5 39 9N 5 24W
Navan = An Uaimh, Ireland 23 C5 53 39N 6 41W
Navanagar = Jamnagar, India 92 H4 22 30N 70 6 E
Navapolatsk, Belarus 58 E5 55 32N 28 37 E
Navarin, Mys, Russia 6 C16 62 15N 179 5 E
Navarino, I., Chile 176 E3 55 0 S 67 40W
Navarra □, Spain 40 C3 42 40N 1 40W
Navarre, Fla., U.S.A. 153 E3 30 24N 86 52W
Navarre, Ohio, U.S.A. 150 F3 40 43N 81 31W
Navarro →, U.S.A. 160 F3 39 11N 123 45W
Navas de San Juan, Spain 43 G7 38 30N 3 19W
Navasota, U.S.A. 155 K6 30 23N 96 5W
Navassa I., W. Indies 165 C5 18 30N 75 0W
Nävekvarn, Sweden 17 F10 58 38N 16 49 E
Naver →, U.K. 22 C4 58 32N 4 14W
Navia, Spain 42 B4 43 35N 6 42W
Navia →, Spain 42 B4 43 15N 6 50W
Navia de Suarna, Spain 42 C3 42 58N 7 3W
Navibandar, India 92 J3 21 26N 69 48 E
Navidad, Chile 174 C1 33 57 S 71 50W
Naviraí, Brazil 175 A5 23 8 S 54 13W
Naviti, Fiji 133 A1 17 7 S 177 15 E
Navlakhi, India 92 H4 22 58N 70 28 E
Navlya, Russia 59 F8 52 53N 34 30 E
Năvodari, Romania 53 F13 44 19N 28 36 E
Navoi = Nawoiy, Uzbekistan 65 C2 40 9N 65 22 E
Navojoa, Mexico 162 B3 27 0N 109 30W
Navolato, Mexico 162 C3 24 47N 107 42W
Návpaktos, Greece 48 C3 38 24N 21 50 E
Návplion, Greece 48 D4 37 33N 22 50 E
Navrongo, Ghana 113 C4 10 51N 1 3W
Navsari, India 94 D1 20 57N 72 59 E
Navua, Fiji 133 B2 18 12 S 178 11 E
Nawa Kot, Pakistan 92 E4 28 21N 71 24 E
Nawab Khan, Pakistan 92 D3 30 17N 69 12 E
Nawabganj, Bangla. 90 C2 24 35N 88 14 E
Nawabganj, Ut. P., India 93 F9 26 56N 81 14 E
Nawabganj, Ut. P., India 93 E8 28 32N 79 40 E
Nawabshah, Pakistan 91 D3 26 15N 68 25 E
Nawada, India 93 G11 24 50N 85 33 E
Nāwah, Afghan. 91 B2 32 19N 67 53 E
Nawakot, Nepal 93 F11 27 55N 85 10 E
Nawalgarh, India 92 F6 27 50N 75 15 E
Nawanshahr, India 93 C6 32 33N 74 48 E
Nawapara, India 94 D6 20 46N 82 33 E
Nawar, Dasht-i-, Afghan. 91 B2 33 52N 68 0 E
Nawāsīf, Ḥarrat, Si. Arabia 98 B3 21 20N 42 10 E
Nawi, Sudan 106 D3 18 32N 30 50 E
Nawng Hpa, Burma 90 D7 22 30N 98 30 E
Nawoiy, Uzbekistan 65 C2 40 9N 65 22 E
Nawş, Ra's, Oman 99 C6 17 15N 55 16 E
Naxçıvan, Azerbaijan 101 C11 39 12N 45 15 E
Naxçıvan □, Azerbaijan 101 C11 39 25N 45 26 E
Náxos, Greece 49 D7 37 8N 25 25 E
Naxxar, Malta 38 F7 35 55N 14 27 E
Nay, France 28 E3 43 10N 0 18W
Nay, Mui, Vietnam 78 B3 12 55N 109 23 E
Nāy Band, Būshehr, Iran 97 E7 27 20N 52 40 E
Nāy Band, Khorāsān, Iran 97 C8 32 20N 57 34 E
Naya →, Colombia 168 C2 3 13N 77 22W
Nayagarh, India 94 D7 20 8N 85 6 E
Nayakhan, Russia 67 C16 61 56N 159 0 E
Nayarit □, Mexico 162 C4 22 0N 105 0W
Nayau, Fiji 133 B2 18 6 S 178 10 E
Nayé, Senegal 112 C2 14 28N 12 12W
Nayong, China 76 D5 26 50N 105 20 E
Nayoro, Japan 70 B11 44 21N 142 28 E
Nayudupeta, India 95 H4 13 54N 79 54 E
Nayyāl, W. →, Si. Arabia 96 D3 28 35N 39 4 E
Nazaré, Bahia, Brazil 171 D4 13 2 S 39 0W
Nazaré, Pará, Brazil 173 B7 6 25 S 52 29W
Nazaré, Tocantins, Brazil 170 C2 6 23 S 47 40W
Nazaré, Portugal 43 F1 39 36N 9 4W
Nazareth = Nazerat, Israel 103 C4 32 42N 35 17 E
Nazareth, U.S.A. 151 F9 40 44N 75 19W
Nazas, Mexico 162 B4 25 10N 104 6W
Nazas →, Mexico 162 B4 25 35N 103 25W
Nazca, Peru 172 C3 14 50 S 74 57W
Nazca Ridge, Pac. Oc. 135 K19 20 0 S 80 0W
Naze, The, U.K. 21 F9 51 53N 1 18 E
Nazerat, Israel 103 C4 32 42N 35 17 E
Nāzīk, Iran 101 C11 39 1N 45 4 E
Nazilli, Turkey 49 D10 37 55N 28 15 E
Nazir Hat, Bangla. 90 D3 22 35N 91 49 E
Nazko, Canada 142 C4 53 1N 123 37W
Nazko →, Canada 142 C4 53 7N 123 34W
Nazret, Ethiopia 107 F4 8 32N 39 22 E
Nazwa, Oman 99 B7 22 56N 57 32 E
Ncama, Eq. Guin. 114 B2 1 55N 10 56 E
Nchanga, Zambia 119 E2 12 30 S 27 49 E
Ncheu, Malawi 119 E3 14 50 S 34 47 E
Ndala, Tanzania 118 C3 4 45 S 33 15 E
Ndalatando, Angola 115 D2 9 12 S 14 48 E
Ndali, Benin 113 D5 9 50N 2 46 E
Ndareda, Tanzania 118 C4 4 12 S 35 30 E
Ndélé, C.A.R. 114 A4 8 25N 20 36 E
Ndendé, Gabon 114 C2 2 22 S 11 23 E
Ndiael ⌂, Senegal 112 B1 16 15N 16 0W
Ndikinimeki, Cameroon 113 E7 4 46N 10 50 E
Ndindi, Gabon 114 C2 3 46 S 11 9 E
N'Dioum, Senegal 112 B2 16 31N 14 39W
Ndjamena, Chad 109 F2 12 10N 14 59 E
Ndjolé, Gabon 114 C2 0 10 S 10 45 E
Ndogo, Lagune, Gabon 114 C2 2 35 S 10 0 E
Ndoki-Nouabalé ⌂, Congo 114 B3 2 32N 16 32 E
Ndola, Zambia 119 E2 13 0 S 28 34 E
Ndoto Mts., Kenya 118 B4 2 0N 37 0 E
Ndoua, C., N. Cal. 133 V20 22 24 S 166 56 E
Ndouba, Congo 114 C2 0 9 S 14 4 E
Nduguti, Tanzania 118 C3 4 18 S 34 41 E
Ndumu ⌂, S. Africa 117 D5 26 52 S 32 15 E
Nea →, Norway 18 A8 63 15N 11 0 E
Néa Alikarnassós, Greece 49 F7 35 18N 25 13 E
Néa Ankhíalos, Greece 48 B4 39 16N 22 49 E
Néa Epídhavros, Greece 48 D5 37 40N 23 7 E
Néa Flippiás, Greece 48 B2 39 12N 20 53 E
Néa Ionia, Greece 48 B4 39 21N 22 56 E
Néa Kallikrátia, Greece 50 F7 40 21N 23 3 E
Néa Mákri, Greece 48 C5 38 5N 23 59 E
Néa Moudhaniá, Greece 50 F7 40 15N 23 17 E
Néa Péramos, Attikí, Greece 48 C5 38 0N 23 26 E
Néa Péramos, Kavála, Greece 51 F8 40 50N 24 18 E
Néa Víssi, Greece 51 E10 41 34N 26 33 E
Néa Zíkhna, Greece 50 E7 41 2N 23 49 E
Neagari, Japan 73 A8 36 26N 136 25 E
Neagh, Lough, U.K. 23 B5 54 37N 6 25W
Neah Bay, U.S.A. 160 B2 48 22N 124 37W
Neale, L., Australia 124 D5 24 15 S 130 0 E
Neales, The →, Australia 127 D2 28 8 S 136 47 E
Neamati, India 90 B5 26 50N 94 20 E
Neamţ □, Romania 53 C11 47 0N 26 20 E
Neápolis, Kozáni, Greece 50 F5 40 20N 21 24 E
Neápolis, Kríti, Greece 39 E6 35 15N 25 37 E
Neápolis, Lakonía, Greece 48 E5 36 27N 23 8 E
Near Is., U.S.A. 144 K1 52 30N 174 0 E
Neath, U.K. 21 F4 51 39N 3 48W
Neath Port Talbot □, U.K. 21 F4 51 42N 3 45W
Neba, Î., N. Cal. 133 T17 20 10 S 163 57 E
Nebbou, Burkina Faso 113 C4 11 9N 1 51W
Nebelat el Hagana, Sudan 107 E2 13 13N 29 2 E
Nebine Cr. →, Australia 127 D4 29 27 S 146 56 E
Nebitdag, Turkmenistan 57 G9 39 30N 54 22 E
Nebka, Algeria 110 C4 27 28N 3 12W
Nebo, Australia 126 C4 21 42 S 148 42 E
Nebolchy, Russia 58 C7 59 8N 33 18 E
Nebraska □, U.S.A. 154 E5 41 30N 99 30W
Nebraska City, U.S.A. 154 E7 40 41N 95 52W
Nébrodi, Monti, Italy 47 E7 37 54N 14 35 E
Necedah, U.S.A. 154 C9 44 2N 90 4W
Nechako →, Canada 142 C4 53 55N 122 42W
Neches →, U.S.A. 155 L8 29 58N 93 51W
Nechisar ⌂, Ethiopia 107 F4 5 58N 37 55 E
Neckar →, Germany 31 F4 49 27N 8 29 E
Neckartal-Odenwald ⌂, Germany 31 F5 49 30N 9 5 E
Necker I., U.S.A. 145 G11 23 35N 164 42W
Necochea, Argentina 174 D4 38 30 S 58 50W
Nectar Brook, Australia 128 B2 32 43 S 137 57 E
Neda, Spain 42 B2 43 30N 8 9W
Nedalshytta, Norway 18 B9 62 59N 12 3 E
Nedelino, Bulgaria 51 E9 41 27N 25 3 E
Nedelišće, Croatia 45 B13 46 23N 16 22 E
Nederland = Netherlands ■, Europe 24 C5 52 0N 5 30 E
Nédha →, Greece 48 D3 37 25N 21 45 E
Nedoboyivtsi, Ukraine 53 B11 48 26N 26 21 E
Nedreberg, Norway 18 D8 60 59N 11 41 E
Nedroma, Algeria 111 A4 35 1N 1 45W
Nedstrand, Norway 18 E2 59 21N 5 49 E
Needles, Canada 142 D5 49 53N 118 7W
Needles, U.S.A. 161 L12 34 51N 114 37W
Needles, The, U.K. 21 G6 50 39N 1 35W
Needles Pt., N.Z. 130 C4 36 3 S 175 25 E
Neely Henry L., U.S.A. 152 B3 33 55N 86 2W
Ñeembucú □, Paraguay 174 B4 27 0 S 58 0W
Neemuch = Nimach, India 92 G6 24 30N 74 56 E
Neenah, U.S.A. 148 C1 44 11N 88 28W
Neepawa, Canada 143 C9 50 15N 99 30W
Neeses, U.S.A. 152 B8 33 33N 81 7W
Nefta, Tunisia 108 B1 33 53N 7 50 E
Neftah Sidi Boubekeur, Algeria 111 A5 35 1N 0 4 E
Neftçala, Azerbaijan 97 B6 39 19N 49 12 E
Neftechala = Neftçala, Azerbaijan 97 B6 39 19N 49 12 E
Neftegorsk, Russia 61 H4 44 25N 39 45 E
Neftekamsk, Russia 64 C5 56 5N 54 17 E
Neftekumsk, Russia 61 H7 44 46N 44 50 E
Neftenbach, Switz. 33 A7 47 32N 8 41 E
Nefyn, U.K. 20 E3 52 56N 4 31W
Négala, Mali 112 C3 12 52N 8 30W
Negapatam = Nagappattinam, India 95 J4 10 46N 79 51 E
Negara, Indonesia 79 J17 8 22 S 114 37 E
Negaunee, U.S.A. 148 B2 46 30N 87 36W
Negele, Ethiopia 107 F4 5 20N 39 36 E
Negeri Sembilan □, Malaysia 84 B2 2 45N 102 10 E
Negev Desert = Hanegev, Israel 103 E4 30 50N 35 0 E
Negoiul, Vf., Romania 53 E9 45 38N 24 35 E
Negombo, Sri Lanka 95 L4 7 12N 79 50 E
Negotin, Serbia & M. 50 B6 44 16N 22 37 E
Negotino, Macedonia 50 E6 41 29N 22 7 E
Negra, Peña, Spain 42 C4 42 11N 6 30W
Negra, Pta., Mauritania 110 D1 22 54N 16 18W
Negra, Pta., Peru 172 B1 6 6 S 81 10W
Negra Pt., Phil. 80 B3 18 40N 120 50 E
Negrais, C. = Maudin Sun, Burma 90 G5 16 0N 94 30 E
Negreşti, Romania 53 D12 46 50N 27 30 E
Negreşti-Oaş, Romania 53 C8 47 52N 23 26 E
Negril, Jamaica 164 a 18 22N 78 20W
Négrine, Algeria 111 B6 34 30N 7 30 E
Negro →, Argentina 176 B4 41 2 S 62 47W
Negro →, Bolivia 173 C5 14 11 S 63 7W
Negro →, Brazil 169 D6 3 0 S 60 0W
Negro →, Uruguay 174 C4 33 24 S 58 22W
Negros, Phil. 81 G4 9 30N 122 40 E
Negros Occidental □, Phil. 81 F4 10 0N 122 55 E
Negros Oriental □, Phil. 81 G4 9 45N 123 0 E
Negru Vodă, Romania 53 G13 43 47N 28 21 E
Neguac, Canada 141 C6 47 15N 65 5W
Nehalem →, U.S.A. 160 E3 45 40N 123 56W
Nehāvand, Iran 97 C6 35 56N 49 31 E
Nehbandān, Iran 97 D9 31 35N 60 5 E
Nehoiu, Romania 53 E11 45 24N 26 20 E
Nei Monggol Zizhiqu □, China 74 D7 42 0N 112 0 E
Neiafu, Tonga 133 P14 18 39 S 173 59W
Neidenburg = Nidzica, Poland 55 E7 53 25N 20 28 E
Neiges, Piton des, Réunion 121 c 21 5 S 55 29 E
Neijiang, China 76 C5 29 35N 104 55 E
Neikiang = Neijiang, China 76 C5 29 35N 104 55 E
Neilingding Dao, China 69 G10 22 25N 113 48 E
Neill I., India 95 J11 11 50N 93 3 E
Neillsville, U.S.A. 154 C9 44 34N 90 36W
Neilton, U.S.A. 158 C2 47 25N 123 53W
Neiqiu, China 74 F8 37 15N 114 30 E
Neisse = Nysa →, Europe 30 C10 52 4N 14 46 E
Neiva, Colombia 168 C2 2 56N 75 18W
Neixiang, China 74 H6 33 10N 111 52 E
Nejanilini L., Canada 143 B9 59 33N 97 48W
Nejd = Najd, Si. Arabia 88 C3 26 30N 42 0 E
Nejo, Ethiopia 107 F4 9 30N 35 28 E
Nekā, Iran 97 B7 36 39N 53 19 E
Nekemte, Ethiopia 107 F4 9 4N 36 30 E
Nêkheb, Egypt 106 B3 25 10N 32 48 E
Neksø, Denmark 17 J9 55 4N 15 8 E
Nelamangala, India 95 H3 13 6N 77 24 E
Nelas, Portugal 42 E3 40 32N 7 52W
Nelaug, Norway 18 F5 58 39N 8 40 E
Nelia, Australia 126 C3 20 39 S 142 12 E
Nelidovo, Russia 58 D7 56 13N 32 49 E
Neligh, U.S.A. 154 D5 42 8N 98 2W
Nelkan, Russia 67 D14 57 40N 136 4 E
Nellikuppam, India 95 J4 11 46N 79 43 E
Nellore, India 95 G4 14 27N 79 59 E
Nelson, Canada 142 D5 49 30N 117 20W
Nelson, N.Z. 131 B8 41 18 S 173 16 E
Nelson, U.K. 20 D5 53 50N 2 13W
Nelson, Ariz., U.S.A. 159 J7 35 31N 113 19W
Nelson, Nev., U.S.A. 161 K12 35 42N 114 50W
Nelson □, N.Z. 131 B8 41 20 S 173 20 E
Nelson →, Canada 143 C9 54 33N 98 2W
Nelson, C., Australia 128 E4 38 26 S 141 32 E
Nelson, C., Papua N. G. 132 E5 9 0 S 149 20 E
Nelson, Estrecho, Chile 176 D2 51 30 S 75 0W
Nelson Bay, Australia 129 B10 32 43 S 152 9 E
Nelson Forks, Canada 142 B4 59 30N 124 0W
Nelson House, Canada 143 B9 55 47N 98 51W
Nelson L., Canada 143 B8 55 48N 100 7W
Nelson Lakes ⌂, N.Z. 131 B7 41 55 S 172 44 E
Nelspoort, S. Africa 116 E3 32 7 S 23 0 E
Nelspruit, S. Africa 117 D5 25 29 S 30 59 E
Néma, Mauritania 112 B3 16 40N 7 15W
Neman = Nemunas →, Lithuania 15 J19 55 25N 21 10 E
Neman, Russia 15 J20 55 2N 22 2 E
Nembrala, Indonesia 82 D2 10 53 S 122 50 E
Neméa, Greece 48 D4 37 49N 22 40 E
Nemecký Brod = Havlíčkův Brod, Czech Rep. 34 B8 49 36N 15 33 E
Nemeiben L., Canada 143 B7 55 20N 105 20W
Nemërçkë, Mal, Albania 50 F4 40 15N 20 15 E
Nemira, Vf., Romania 53 D11 46 17N 26 19 E
Nemiscau, Canada 140 B4 51 18N 76 54W
Nemiscau, L., Canada 140 B4 51 25N 76 40W
Nemours = Ghazaouet, Algeria 111 A4 35 8N 1 50W
Nemours, France 27 D9 48 16N 2 40 E
Nemšová, Slovak Rep. 35 C11 48 58N 18 7 E
Nemunas →, Lithuania 15 J19 55 25N 21 10 E
Nemuro, Japan 70 C12 43 20N 145 35 E
Nemuro-Kaikyō, Japan 70 C12 43 30N 145 30 E
Nemyriv, Ukraine 55 H10 50 7N 23 27 E
Nen Jiang →, China 75 B13 45 28N 124 30 E
Nenagh, Ireland 23 D3 52 52N 8 11W
Nenana, U.S.A. 144 D10 64 34N 149 5W
Nenasi, Malaysia 87 L4 3 9N 103 23 E
Nene →, U.K. 21 E8 52 49N 0 11 E
Nénita, Greece 49 C8 38 14N 26 6 E
Nenjiang, China 69 B7 49 10N 125 10 E
Neno, Malawi 119 F3 15 25 S 34 40 E
Nenzing, Austria 33 B9 47 11N 9 42 E
Neodesha, U.S.A. 155 G7 37 25N 95 41W
Neoga, U.S.A. 157 E8 39 19N 88 27W
Neokhórion, Aitolía kai Akarnanía, Greece 48 C3 38 25N 21 17 E
Neokhórion, Árta, Greece 48 B2 39 4N 21 0 E
Néon Karlovásion, Greece 49 D8 37 45N 26 42 E
Néon Petrítsi, Greece 50 E7 41 16N 23 15 E
Neópolis, Brazil 170 D4 10 18 S 36 35W
Neora Valley, India 93 F13 27 0N 88 45 E
Neosho, U.S.A. 155 G7 36 52N 94 22W
Neosho →, U.S.A. 155 H7 36 48N 95 18W
Nepal ■, Asia 93 F11 28 0N 84 30 E
Nepalganj, Nepal 93 E9 28 5N 81 40 E
Nepalganj Road, India 93 E9 28 1N 81 41 E
Nepean B., Australia 128 C2 35 42 S 137 37 E
Nephi, U.S.A. 158 G8 39 43N 111 50W
Nephin, Ireland 23 B2 54 1N 9 22W
Nepi, Italy 45 F9 42 14N 12 21 E
Nepomuk, Czech Rep. 34 B6 49 29N 13 35 E
Neppel = Moses Lake, U.S.A. 158 C4 47 8N 119 17W
Neptune, U.S.A. 151 F10 40 13N 74 2W
Neptune Is., Australia 128 C2 35 17 S 136 10 E
Nera →, Italy 45 F9 42 26N 12 24 E
Nera →, Romania 52 F6 44 48N 21 25 E
Nérac, France 28 D4 44 8N 0 21 E
Nerang, Australia 127 D5 27 58 S 153 20 E
Nerastro, Sarîr, Libya 108 D4 24 20N 20 37 E
Neratovice, Czech Rep. 34 A7 50 16N 14 31 E
Nerchinsk, Russia 67 D12 52 0N 116 39 E
Nereju, Romania 53 E11 45 43N 26 43 E
Nerekhta, Russia 58 D11 57 26N 40 38 E
Neresnytsya, Ukraine 53 B8 48 7N 23 46 E
Néret, L., Canada 141 B5 54 45N 70 44W
Neretvanski Kanal, Croatia 45 E14 43 7N 17 10 E
Neringa, Lithuania 15 J19 55 20N 21 5 E
Neris →, Lithuania 15 J21 55 8N 24 16 E
Nerja, Spain 43 J7 36 43N 3 55W
Nerl →, Russia 58 D11 56 11N 40 34 E
Nerpio, Spain 41 G2 38 11N 2 16W
Nerva, Spain 43 H4 37 42N 6 30W
Nervi, Italy 44 D6 44 23N 9 2 E
Neryungri, Russia 67 D13 57 38N 124 28 E
Nes, Iceland 11 B9 65 53N 17 24W
Nes, Norway 18 D6 60 34N 9 59 E
Nesbyen, Norway 18 D6 60 34N 9 8 E
Nescopeck, U.S.A. 151 E8 41 3N 76 12W
Nesebūr, Bulgaria 51 D11 42 41N 27 46 E
Neset, Norway 18 C7 61 53N 10 7 E
Nesflaten, Norway 18 E3 59 38N 6 48 E
Neskaupstaður, Iceland 11 B13 65 9N 13 42W
Nesland, Norway 18 E4 59 31N 7 59 E
Neslandsvatn, Norway 18 F6 58 57N 9 10 E
Nesoddtangen, Norway 18 E7 59 48N 10 40 E
Ness, L., U.K. 22 D4 57 15N 4 32W
Ness City, U.S.A. 154 F5 38 27N 99 54W
Nesslau, Switz. 33 B8 47 14N 9 13 E
Nesterov, Russia 54 D9 54 38N 22 41 E
Nesterov, Ukraine 59 G2 50 4N 23 58 E
Nestórion, Greece 50 F5 40 24N 21 5 E
Néstos →, Greece 51 E8 41 20N 24 35 E
Nesttun, Norway 18 D2 60 19N 5 20 E
Nesvady, Slovak Rep. 35 D11 47 56N 18 7 E
Nesvizh = Nyasvizh, Belarus 59 F4 53 14N 26 38 E
Netanya, Israel 103 C3 32 20N 34 51 E
Netarhat, India 93 H11 23 29N 84 16 E
Nete →, Belgium 24 C4 51 7N 4 14 E
Netherdale, Australia 126 K6 21 10 S 148 33 E
Netherlands ■, Europe 24 C5 52 0N 5 30 E
Netherlands Antilles ☒, W. Indies 168 A4 12 15N 69 0W
Netherlands East Indies = Indonesia ■, Asia 85 C4 5 0 S 115 0 E
Netherlands Guiana = Suriname ■, S. Amer. 169 C6 4 0N 56 0W
Neto →, Italy 47 C10 39 12N 17 9 E
Netrakona, Bangla. 90 C3 24 53N 90 47 E
Netrang, India 92 J5 21 39N 73 21 E
Netstal, Switz. 33 B8 47 3N 9 3 E
Nettancourt, France 27 D11 48 51N 4 57 E
Nettetal, Germany 30 D2 51 19N 6 12 E
Nettilling L., Canada 139 B12 66 30N 71 0W
Nettuno, Italy 46 A5 41 27N 12 39 E
Netzahualcoyotl, Presa, Mexico 163 D6 17 10N 93 30W
Neu-Bentschen = Zbąszynek, Poland 55 F2 52 16N 15 51 E
Neu-Isenburg, Germany 31 E4 50 3N 8 42 E
Neu-Langenburg = Tukuyu, Tanzania 119 D3 9 17 S 33 35 E
Neu-Mecklenberg = New Ireland, Papua N. G. 132 B6 3 20 S 151 50 E
Neu Pommern = New Britain, Papua N. G. 132 C6 5 50 S 150 20 E
Neu-Sandec = Nowy Sącz, Poland 55 J7 49 40N 20 41 E
Neu Sandez = Nowy Sącz, Poland 55 J7 49 40N 20 41 E
Neu-Ulm, Germany 31 G6 48 22N 10 0 E
Neubrandenburg, Germany 30 B9 53 33N 13 15 E
Neubukow, Germany 30 A7 54 2N 11 39 E
Neuburg, Germany 31 G7 48 44N 11 11 E
Neuchâtel, Switz. 32 C3 47 0N 6 55 E
Neuchâtel □, Switz. 32 C3 47 0N 6 55 E
Neuchâtel, Lac de, Switz. 32 C3 46 53N 6 50 E
Neudau, Austria 34 D9 47 11N 16 6 E
Neuenberg an der Elbe = Nymburk, Czech Rep. 34 A8 50 10N 15 1 E
Neuenegg, Switz. 32 C4 46 54N 7 18 E
Neuenhagen, Germany 30 C9 52 30N 13 38 E
Neuenhaus, Germany 30 C2 52 30N 6 58 E
Neuenhof, Switz. 33 B6 47 27N 8 19 E
Neuf-Brisach, France 27 D14 48 1N 7 30 E
Neufahrn, Bayern, Germany 31 G8 48 41N 12 11 E
Neufahrn, Bayern, Germany 31 G7 48 18N 11 40 E
Neufchâteau, Belgium 24 E5 49 50N 5 25 E
Neufchâteau, France 27 D12 48 21N 5 40 E
Neufchâtel-en-Bray, France 26 C8 49 44N 1 26 E
Neufchâtel-sur-Aisne, France 27 C11 49 26N 4 1 E
Neuhaus = Jindřichův Hradec, Czech Rep. 34 B8 49 10N 15 2 E
Neuhaus, Germany 30 B6 53 17N 10 56 E
Neuhäusel = Nové Zámky, Slovak Rep. 35 C11 48 2N 18 8 E
Neuhausen, Switz. 33 A7 47 41N 8 37 E
Neuillé-Pont-Pierre, France 26 E7 47 33N 0 33 E
Neuilly-St-Front, France 27 C10 49 10N 3 15 E
Neukalen, Germany 30 B8 53 49N 12 46 E
Neumarkt = Nowy Targ, Poland 55 J7 49 29N 20 2 E
Neumarkt = Środa Śląska, Poland 55 G3 51 10N 16 36 E
Neumarkt, Germany 31 F7 49 16N 11 27 E
Neumarktl = Tržič, Slovenia 45 B11 46 22N 14 18 E
Neumittelwalde = Międzybórz, Poland 55 G4 51 25N 17 34 E
Neumünster, Germany 30 A5 54 4N 9 58 E
Neung-sur-Beuvron, France 27 E8 47 30N 1 50 E
Neunkirch, Switz. 33 A7 47 42N 8 30 E
Neunkirchen, Austria 34 D9 47 43N 16 4 E
Neunkirchen, Germany 31 F3 49 20N 7 9 E
Neuquén, Argentina 176 A3 38 55 S 68 0W
Neuquén □, Argentina 174 D2 38 0 S 69 50W
Neuquén →, Argentina 176 A3 38 59 S 68 0W
Neuruppin, Germany 30 C8 52 55N 12 48 E
Neusalz an der Oder = Nowa Sól, Poland 55 G2 51 48N 15 44 E
Neusäss, Germany 31 G6 48 24N 10 50 E
Neusatz = Novi Sad, Serbia & M. 52 E4 45 18N 19 52 E
Neuse →, U.S.A. 149 H7 35 6N 76 29W
Neusiedl, Austria 35 D9 47 57N 16 50 E
Neusiedler See, Austria 35 D9 47 50N 16 47 E
Neusiedler See-Seewinkel ⌂, Austria 35 D9 47 50N 16 45 E
Neusohl = Banská Bystrica, Slovak Rep. 35 C12 48 46N 19 14 E
Neuss, Germany 30 D2 51 11N 6 42 E
Neussargues-Moissac, France 28 C7 45 9N 3 0 E
Neustadt = Lwówek, Poland 55 F3 52 28N 16 10 E
Neustadt = Prudnik, Poland 55 H4 50 20N 17 38 E
Neustadt = Wejherowo, Poland 54 D5 54 35N 18 12 E
Neustadt, Bayern, Germany 31 F8 49 44N 12 10 E
Neustadt, Bayern, Germany 31 G7 48 48N 11 46 E
Neustadt, Bayern, Germany 31 F6 49 34N 10 37 E
Neustadt, Bayern, Germany 31 E7 50 19N 11 7 E
Neustadt, Brandenburg, Germany 30 C8 52 50N 12 27 E
Neustadt, Hessen, Germany 30 E5 50 51N 9 9 E
Neustadt, Niedersachsen, Germany 30 C5 52 30N 9 30 E
Neustadt, Rhld-Pfz., Germany 31 F4 49 21N 8 10 E
Neustadt, Sachsen, Germany 30 D10 51 2N 14 12 E
Neustadt, Schleswig-Holstein, Germany 30 A6 54 6N 10 49 E
Neustadt, Thüringen, Germany 30 E7 50 45N 11 43 E
Neustädtel = Nowe Miasteczko, Poland 55 G2 51 42N 15 42 E
Neustädtl = Novo Mesto, Slovenia 45 C12 45 47N 15 12 E
Neustettin = Szczecinek, Poland 54 E3 53 43N 16 41 E
Neustrelitz, Germany 30 B9 53 21N 13 4 E
Neutitschein = Nový Jičín, Czech Rep. 35 B11 49 30N 18 2 E
Neuvic, France 28 C6 45 23N 2 16 E
Neuville-sur-Saône, France 29 C8 45 52N 4 51 E
Neuvy-le-Roi, France 26 E7 47 36N 0 36 E
Neuvy-St-Sépulchre, France 27 F8 46 35N 1 48 E
Neuvy-sur-Barangeon, France 27 E9 47 20N 2 15 E
Neuwedell = Drawno, Poland 55 E2 53 13N 15 46 E
Neuwerk, Germany 30 B4 53 55N 8 30 E
Neuwied, Germany 30 E3 50 26N 7 29 E
Neva →, Russia 58 C6 59 50N 30 30 E
Nevada, Iowa, U.S.A. 156 B3 42 1N 93 27W
Nevada, Mo., U.S.A. 155 G7 37 51N 94 22W
Nevada □, U.S.A. 158 G5 39 0N 117 0W
Nevada City, U.S.A. 160 F6 39 16N 121 1W
Nevado, Cerro, Argentina 174 D2 35 30 S 68 32W
Nevado de Colima = Volcán de Colima ⌂, Mexico 162 D4 19 30N 103 40W
Nevado de Tres Cruces ⌂, Chile 174 B2 27 13 S 69 5W
Nevado del Huila ⌂, Colombia 168 C2 3 5N 75 58W
Nevasa, India 94 E2 19 34N 75 0 E
Neve, Sa. da, Angola 115 E2 13 43 S 13 10 E
Nevel, Russia 58 D5 56 0N 29 55 E
Nevers, France 27 F10 47 0N 3 9 E
Nevertire, Australia 129 A7 31 50 S 147 44 E
Nevesinje, Bos.-H. 50 C2 43 14N 18 6 E
Neville, Canada 143 D7 49 58N 107 39W
Nevinnomyssk, Russia 61 H6 44 40N 42 0 E
Nevis, St. Kitts & Nevis 165 C7 17 0N 62 30W
Nevlunghavn, Norway 18 F6 58 58N 9 53 E
Nevoso, Mte. = Snežnik, Slovenia 45 C11 45 36N 14 35 E
Nevrokop = Gotse Delchev, Bulgaria 50 E7 41 36N 23 46 E
Nevşehir, Turkey 100 C6 38 33N 34 40 E
Nevskoye, Russia 54 D9 54 32N 22 39 E
Nevyansk, Russia 64 C8 57 30N 60 13 E
New →, Guyana 169 C6 3 20N 57 37W
New →, U.S.A. 148 F5 38 10N 81 12W
New Aiyansh, Canada 142 B3 55 12N 129 4W
New Albany, Ind., U.S.A. 157 F11 38 18N 85 49W
New Albany, Miss., U.S.A. 155 H10 34 29N 89 0W
New Albany, Pa., U.S.A. 151 E8 41 36N 76 27W
New Amsterdam, Guyana 169 B6 6 15N 57 36W
New Angledool, Australia 127 D4 29 5 S 147 55 E
New Athens, U.S.A. 156 F7 38 19N 89 53W
New Baltimore, U.S.A. 150 D2 42 41N 82 44W
New Barbadoes = Hackensack, U.S.A. 151 F10 40 53N 74 3W
New Bedford, U.S.A. 151 E14 41 38N 70 56W
New Berlin = North Canton, U.S.A. 150 F3 40 53N 81 24W
New Berlin, Ill., U.S.A. 156 E7 39 44N 89 55W
New Berlin, N.Y., U.S.A. 151 D9 42 37N 75 20W
New Berlin, Pa., U.S.A. 150 F8 40 50N 76 57W
New Berlin, Wis., U.S.A. 157 B8 42 59N 88 6W
New Bern, U.S.A. 149 H7 35 7N 77 3W
New Bethlehem, U.S.A. 150 F5 41 0N 79 20W
New Bloomfield, U.S.A. 150 F7 40 25N 77 11W
New Boston, U.S.A. 155 J7 33 28N 94 25W
New Braunfels, U.S.A. 155 L5 29 42N 98 8W
New Brighton, N.Z. 131 D7 43 29 S 172 43 E
New Brighton, U.S.A. 150 F4 40 42N 80 19W
New Britain, Papua N. G. 132 C6 5 50 S 150 20 E
New Britain, U.S.A. 151 E12 41 40N 72 47W
New Brockton, U.S.A. 152 D4 31 23N 85 56W
New Brookland = West Columbia, U.S.A. 152 B8 33 59N 81 4W
New Brunswick, U.S.A. 151 F10 40 30N 74 27W
New Brunswick □, Canada 141 C6 46 50N 66 30W
New Buffalo, U.S.A. 157 C10 41 47N 86 45W
New Bussa, Nigeria 113 D5 9 53N 4 31 E
New Caledonia ☒, Pac. Oc. 133 U19 21 0 S 165 0 E
New Carlisle, Ind., U.S.A. 157 C10 41 45N 86 32W
New Carlisle, Ohio, U.S.A. 157 E12 39 56N 84 2W
New Castile = Castilla-La Mancha □, Spain 12 H5 39 30N 3 30W
New Castle, Ind., U.S.A. 157 E11 39 55N 85 22W
New Castle, Ky., U.S.A. 157 F11 38 26N 85 10W
New Castle, Pa., U.S.A. 150 F4 41 0N 80 21W
New City, U.S.A. 151 E11 41 9N 73 59W
New Concord, U.S.A. 150 G3 39 59N 81 54W
New Cumberland, U.S.A. 150 F4 40 30N 80 36W
New Cuyama, U.S.A. 161 L7 34 57N 119 38W
New Delhi, India 92 E7 28 37N 77 13 E
New Denver, Canada 142 D5 50 0N 117 25W
New Don Pedro Reservoir, U.S.A. 160 H6 37 43N 120 24W
New Ellenton, U.S.A. 152 B8 33 28N 81 41W
New England, U.S.A. 147 B12 43 0N 71 0W
New England, N. Dak., U.S.A. 154 B3 46 32N 102 52W
New England ⌂, Australia 129 A10 30 25 S 152 30 E
New England Ra., Australia 127 E5 30 20 S 151 45 E
New England Seamounts, Atl. Oc. 6 C5 38 0N 63 0W
New Forest, U.K. 21 G6 50 53N 1 34W
New Franklin, U.S.A. 156 E4 39 1N 92 44W
New Galloway, U.K. 22 F4 55 5N 4 9W
New Georgia Is., Solomon Is. 133 M9 8 15 S 157 30 E
New Georgia Sound, Solomon Is. 133 L9 8 0 S 158 20 E
New Glarus, U.S.A. 156 B7 42 49N 89 38W

New Glasgow, *Canada* **141 C7** 45 35N 62 36W
New Guinea, *Oceania* **132 C1** 4 0S 136 0E
New Hamburg, *Canada* **150 C4** 43 23N 80 42W
New Hampshire □, *U.S.A.* **151 C13** 44 0N 71 30W
New Hampton, *U.S.A.* **156 A4** 43 3N 92 19W
New Hanover, *Papua N. G.* **132 B6** 2 30S 150 10E
New Hanover, *S. Africa* **117 D5** 29 22S 30 31E
New Harmony, *U.S.A.* **157 F9** 38 8N 87 56W
New Hartford, *U.S.A.* **151 C9** 43 4N 75 18W
New Haven, *Conn., U.S.A.* **151 E12** 41 18N 72 55W
New Haven, *Ill., U.S.A.* **157 G8** 37 55N 88 8W
New Haven, *Ind., U.S.A.* **157 C11** 41 4N 85 1W
New Haven, *Mich., U.S.A.* **150 D2** 42 44N 82 48W
New Haven, *Mo., U.S.A.* **156 F5** 38 37N 91 13W
New Hazelton, *Canada* **142 B3** 55 20N 127 30W
New Hebrides = Vanuatu ■, *Pac. Oc.* **133 E6** 15 0S 168 0E
New Holland, *U.S.A.* **151 F8** 40 6N 76 5W
New Iberia, *U.S.A.* **155 K9** 30 1N 91 49W
New Ireland, *Papua N. G.* **132 B6** 3 20S 151 50E
New Ireland □, *Papua N. G.* **132 B6** 3 0S 151 30E
New Jersey □, *U.S.A.* **148 E8** 40 0N 74 30W
New Kensington, *U.S.A.* **150 F5** 40 34N 79 46W
New Lexington, *U.S.A.* **148 F4** 39 43N 82 13W
New Liskeard, *Canada* **140 C4** 47 31N 79 41W
New London, *Conn., U.S.A.* **151 E12** 41 22N 72 6W
New London, *Iowa, U.S.A.* **156 D5** 40 55N 91 24W
New London, *Mo., U.S.A.* **156 E5** 39 35N 91 24W
New London, *Ohio, U.S.A.* **150 E2** 41 5N 82 24W
New London, *Wis., U.S.A.* **154 C10** 44 23N 88 45W
New Madrid, *U.S.A.* **155 G10** 36 36N 89 32W
New Martinsville, *U.S.A.* **148 F5** 39 39N 80 52W
New Meadows, *U.S.A.* **158 D5** 44 58N 116 18W
New Melones L., *U.S.A.* **160 H6** 37 57N 120 31W
New Mexico □, *U.S.A.* **159 J10** 34 30N 106 0W
New Miami, *U.S.A.* **157 E12** 39 26N 84 32W
New Milford, *Conn., U.S.A.* **151 E11** 41 35N 73 25W
New Milford, *Pa., U.S.A.* **151 E9** 41 52N 75 44W
New Norcia, *Australia* **125 F2** 30 57S 116 13E
New Norfolk, *Australia* **127 G4** 42 46S 147 2E
New Orleans, *U.S.A.* **155 L9** 29 58N 90 4W
New Palestine, *U.S.A.* **157 E11** 39 45N 85 52W
New Panamao, *Phil.* **81 J3** 5 59N 121 13E
New Paris, *U.S.A.* **157 E12** 39 51N 84 48W
New Pekin, *U.S.A.* **157 F10** 38 31N 86 2W
New Philadelphia, *U.S.A.* **150 F3** 40 30N 81 27W
New Plymouth, *N.Z.* **130 F3** 39 4S 174 5E
New Plymouth, *U.S.A.* **158 E5** 43 58N 116 49W
New Pomerania = New Britain, *Papua N. G.* **132 C6** 5 50S 150 20E
New Port Richey, *U.S.A.* **153 G7** 28 16N 82 43W
New Providence, *Bahamas* **9 b** 25 25N 78 35W
New Quay, *U.K.* **21 E3** 52 13N 4 21W
New Radnor, *U.K.* **21 E4** 52 15N 3 9W
New Richmond, *Canada* **141 C6** 48 15N 65 45W
New Richmond, *Ohio, U.S.A.* **157 F12** 38 57N 84 17W
New Richmond, *Wis., U.S.A.* **154 C8** 45 7N 92 32W
New River Gorge △, *U.S.A.* **148 G5** 37 53N 81 5W
New Roads, *U.S.A.* **155 K9** 30 42N 91 26W
New Rochelle, *U.S.A.* **151 F11** 40 55N 73 47W
New Rockford, *U.S.A.* **154 B5** 47 41N 99 8W
New Romney, *U.K.* **21 G8** 50 59N 0 57E
New Ross, *Ireland* **23 D5** 52 23N 6 57W
New Salem, *U.S.A.* **154 B4** 46 51N 101 25W
New Scone = Scone, *U.K.* **22 E5** 56 25N 3 24W
New Sharon, *U.S.A.* **156 C4** 41 28N 92 39W
New Siberian I. = Novaya Sibir, Ostrov, *Russia* **67 B16** 75 10N 150 0E
New Siberian Is. = Novosibirskiye Ostrova, *Russia* **67 B15** 75 0N 142 0E
New Smyrna Beach, *U.S.A.* **153 F9** 29 1N 80 56W
New South Wales □, *Australia* **129 B7** 33 0S 146 0E
New Stuyahok, *U.S.A.* **144 G8** 59 29N 157 20W
New Tecumseth, *Canada* **140 D4** 44 9N 79 52W
New Town, *U.S.A.* **154 B3** 47 59N 102 30W
New Tredegar, *U.K.* **21 F4** 51 44N 3 16W
New Ulm, *U.S.A.* **154 C7** 44 19N 94 28W
New Vienna, *U.S.A.* **157 E13** 39 19N 83 42W
New Washington, *Phil.* **81 F4** 11 39N 122 26E
New Waterford, *Canada* **141 C7** 46 13N 60 4W
New-Wes-Valley, *Canada* **141 C9** 49 8N 53 36W
New Westminster, *Canada* **160 A4** 49 13N 122 55W
New York, *U.S.A.* **151 F11** 40 45N 74 0W
New York □, *U.S.A.* **151 D9** 43 0N 75 0W
New York J.F. Kennedy International ✈ (JFK), *U.S.A.* **151 F11** 40 38N 73 47W
New York Mts., *U.S.A.* **159 J6** 35 0N 115 20W
New Zealand ■, *Oceania* **130 G5** 40 0S 176 0E
Newaj →, *India* **92 G7** 24 24N 76 49E
Newala, *Tanzania* **119 E4** 10 58S 39 18E
Newark, *Del., U.S.A.* **148 F8** 39 41N 75 46W
Newark, *N.J., U.S.A.* **151 F10** 40 44N 74 10W
Newark, *N.Y., U.S.A.* **150 C7** 43 3N 77 6W
Newark, *Ohio, U.S.A.* **150 F2** 40 3N 82 24W
Newark International ✈ (EWR), *U.S.A.* **151 F10** 40 42N 74 10W
Newark-on-Trent, *U.K.* **20 D7** 53 5N 0 48W
Newark Valley, *U.S.A.* **151 D8** 42 14N 76 11W
Newberg, *Mo., U.S.A.* **156 G5** 37 55N 91 54W
Newberg, *Oreg., U.S.A.* **158 D2** 45 18N 122 58W
Newberry, *Fla., U.S.A.* **153 F7** 29 39N 82 37W
Newberry, *Mich., U.S.A.* **148 B3** 46 21N 85 30W
Newberry, *S.C., U.S.A.* **149 H5** 34 17N 81 37W
Newberry ⌂, *U.S.A.* **158 E2** 43 42N 121 15W
Newberry Springs, *U.S.A.* **161 L10** 34 50N 116 41W
Newboro L., *Canada* **151 B8** 44 38N 76 20W
Newbridge = Droichead Nua, *Ireland* **23 C5** 53 11N 6 48W
Newburgh, *Canada* **150 B8** 44 19N 76 52W
Newburgh, *Ind., U.S.A.* **157 G9** 37 57N 87 24W
Newburgh, *N.Y., U.S.A.* **151 E10** 41 30N 74 1W
Newbury, *U.K.* **21 F6** 51 24N 1 20W
Newbury, *N.H., U.S.A.* **151 B12** 43 19N 72 3W
Newbury, *Vt., U.S.A.* **151 B12** 44 5N 72 4W
Newburyport, *U.S.A.* **149 D10** 42 49N 70 53W
Newcastle, *Australia* **129 B9** 33 0S 151 46E
Newcastle, *N.B., Canada* **141 C6** 47 1N 65 38W
Newcastle, *Ont., Canada* **140 D4** 43 55N 78 35W
Newcastle, *S. Africa* **117 D4** 27 45S 29 58E
Newcastle, *U.K.* **23 B6** 54 13N 5 54W
Newcastle, *Calif., U.S.A.* **160 G5** 38 53N 121 8W
Newcastle, *Wyo., U.S.A.* **154 D2** 43 50N 104 11W
Newcastle Emlyn, *U.K.* **21 E3** 52 2N 4 28W
Newcastle Ra., *Australia* **124 C5** 15 45S 130 15E
Newcastle-under-Lyme, *U.K.* **20 D5** 53 1N 2 14W
Newcastle-upon-Tyne, *U.K.* **20 C6** 54 58N 1 36W
Newcastle Waters, *Australia* **126 B1** 17 30S 133 28E
Newcastle West, *Ireland* **23 D2** 52 27N 9 3W
Newcomb, *U.S.A.* **151 C10** 43 58N 74 10W
Newcomerstown, *U.S.A.* **150 F3** 40 16N 81 36W
Newdegate, *Australia* **125 F2** 33 6S 119 0E
Newell, *Australia* **126 B4** 16 20S 145 16E
Newell, *Iowa, U.S.A.* **156 B1** 42 36N 95 0W
Newell, *S. Dak., U.S.A.* **154 C3** 44 43N 103 25W
Newenham, C., *U.S.A.* **144 G7** 58 39N 162 11W
Newfane, *U.S.A.* **150 C6** 43 17N 78 43W
Newfield, *U.S.A.* **151 D8** 42 18N 76 33W
Newfound L., *U.S.A.* **151 C13** 43 40N 71 47W
Newfoundland, *Canada* **141 C8** 49 0N 55 0W
Newfoundland, *U.S.A.* **151 E9** 41 18N 75 19W
Newfoundland & Labrador □, *Canada* **141 B8** 53 0N 58 0W
Newhalen, *U.S.A.* **144 G9** 59 43N 154 54W
Newhall, *U.S.A.* **161 L8** 34 23N 118 32W
Newhaven, *U.K.* **21 G8** 50 47N 0 3E
Newington, *U.S.A.* **152 C8** 32 35N 81 30W
Newkirk, *U.S.A.* **155 G6** 36 53N 97 3W
Newlyn, *U.K.* **21 G2** 50 6N 5 34W
Newman, *Australia* **124 D2** 23 18S 119 45E
Newman, *Calif., U.S.A.* **160 H5** 37 19N 121 1W
Newman, *Ill., U.S.A.* **157 E9** 39 48N 87 59W
Newmarket, *Canada* **150 B5** 44 3N 79 28W
Newmarket, *Ireland* **23 D2** 52 13N 9 0W
Newmarket, *U.K.* **21 E8** 52 15N 0 25E
Newmarket, *U.S.A.* **151 C14** 43 4N 70 56W
Newnan, *U.S.A.* **152 B5** 33 23N 84 48W
Newport, *Ireland* **23 C2** 53 53N 9 33W
Newport, *I. of W., U.K.* **21 G6** 50 42N 1 17W
Newport, *Newp., U.K.* **21 F5** 51 35N 3 0W
Newport, *Ark., U.S.A.* **155 H9** 35 37N 91 16W
Newport, *Fla., U.S.A.* **152 E5** 30 11N 84 10W
Newport, *Ind., U.S.A.* **157 E9** 39 53N 87 25W
Newport, *Ky., U.S.A.* **157 E12** 39 5N 84 30W
Newport, *N.H., U.S.A.* **151 C12** 43 22N 72 10W
Newport, *N.Y., U.S.A.* **151 C9** 43 11N 75 1W
Newport, *Oreg., U.S.A.* **158 D1** 44 39N 124 3W
Newport, *Pa., U.S.A.* **150 F7** 40 29N 77 8W
Newport, *R.I., U.S.A.* **151 E13** 41 29N 71 19W
Newport, *Tenn., U.S.A.* **149 H4** 35 58N 83 11W
Newport, *Vt., U.S.A.* **151 B12** 44 56N 72 13W
Newport, *Wash., U.S.A.* **158 B5** 48 11N 117 3W
Newport □, *U.K.* **21 F4** 51 33N 3 1W
Newport Beach, *U.S.A.* **161 M9** 33 37N 117 56W
Newport News, *U.S.A.* **148 G7** 36 59N 76 25W
Newport Pagnell, *U.K.* **21 E7** 52 5N 0 43W
Newquay, *U.K.* **21 G2** 50 25N 5 6W
Newry, *U.K.* **23 B5** 54 11N 6 21W
Newtok, *U.S.A.* **144 F6** 60 56N 164 38W
Newton, *Ga., U.S.A.* **152 D5** 31 19N 84 20W
Newton, *Ill., U.S.A.* **154 F10** 38 59N 88 10W
Newton, *Iowa, U.S.A.* **156 C3** 41 42N 93 3W
Newton, *Kans., U.S.A.* **155 F6** 38 3N 97 21W
Newton, *Mass., U.S.A.* **151 D13** 42 21N 71 12W
Newton, *Miss., U.S.A.* **155 J10** 32 19N 89 10W
Newton, *N.C., U.S.A.* **149 H5** 35 40N 81 13W
Newton, *N.J., U.S.A.* **151 E10** 41 3N 74 45W
Newton, *Tex., U.S.A.* **155 K8** 30 51N 93 46W
Newton Abbot, *U.K.* **21 G4** 50 32N 3 37W
Newton Aycliffe, *U.K.* **20 C6** 54 37N 1 34W
Newton Falls, *U.S.A.* **150 E4** 41 11N 80 59W
Newton L., *U.S.A.* **157 F8** 38 55N 88 15W
Newton Stewart, *U.K.* **22 G4** 54 57N 4 30W
Newtonmore, *U.K.* **22 D4** 57 4N 4 8W
Newtontoppen, *Svalbard* **10 B12** 79 0N 17 30E
Newtown, *U.K.* **21 E4** 52 31N 3 19W
Newtown, *Ind., U.S.A.* **157 D9** 40 13N 87 9W
Newtown, *Mo., U.S.A.* **156 D3** 40 22N 93 20W
Newtownabbey, *U.K.* **23 B6** 54 40N 5 56W
Newtownards, *U.K.* **23 B6** 54 36N 5 42W
Newtownbarry = Bunclody, *Ireland* **23 D5** 52 39N 6 40W
Newtownstewart, *U.K.* **23 B4** 54 43N 7 23W
Newville, *U.S.A.* **150 F7** 40 10N 77 24W
Nexon, *France* **28 C5** 45 41N 1 11E
Neya, *Russia* **60 A6** 58 21N 43 49E
Neyrīz, *Iran* **97 D7** 29 15N 54 19E
Néyruz, *Switz.* **32 C4** 46 47N 7 4E
Neyshābūr, *Iran* **97 B8** 36 10N 58 50E
Neyyattinkara, *India* **95 K3** 8 26N 77 5E
Nezametny = Aldan, *Russia* **67 D13** 58 40N 125 30E
Nezhin = Nizhyn, *Ukraine* **59 G6** 51 5N 31 55E
Nezperce, *U.S.A.* **158 C5** 46 14N 116 14W
Nezvysko, *Ukraine* **53 B10** 48 46N 25 15E
Ngabang, *Indonesia* **85 B3** 0 23N 109 55E
Ngabe, *Congo* **114 C3** 3 12S 16 12E
Ngabordamlu, Tanjung, *Indonesia* **83 C4** 6 56S 134 11E
N'Gage, *Angola* **115 D3** 7 46S 15 15E
Ngaiphaipi, *Burma* **90 D4** 22 14N 93 15E
Ngala, *Nigeria* **113 C7** 12 20N 14 11E
Ngama, *Chad* **109 F3** 11 45N 17 6E
Ngambé, *Centre, Cameroon* **113 D7** 5 48N 11 29E
Ngambé, *Littoral, Cameroon* **113 E7** 4 21N 10 40E
Ngami Depression, *Botswana* **116 C3** 20 30S 22 46E
Ngamo, *Zimbabwe* **119 F2** 19 3S 27 32E
Ngangala, *Sudan* **107 G3** 4 42N 31 55E
Nganglong Kangri, *China* **93 C9** 33 0N 81 0E
Nganjuk, *Indonesia* **85 D4** 7 32S 111 55E
Ngao, *Thailand* **86 C2** 18 46N 99 59E
Ngaoundéré, *Cameroon* **114 A2** 7 15N 13 35E
Ngapara, *N.Z.* **131 E5** 44 57S 170 46E
Ngape, *Burma* **90 E5** 20 2N 94 28E
Ngara, *Tanzania* **118 C3** 2 29S 30 40E
Ngaruawahia, *N.Z.* **130 D4** 37 42S 175 11E
Ngaruroro →, *N.Z.* **130 F5** 39 34S 176 55E
Ngatapa, *N.Z.* **130 E6** 38 32S 177 45E
Ngathainggyaung, *Burma* **90 G5** 17 24N 95 5E
Ngauruhoe, Mt., *N.Z.* **130 F4** 39 13S 175 45E
Ngawi, *Indonesia* **85 D4** 7 24S 111 26E
Ngele, *Dem. Rep. of the Congo* **114 C4** 0 30S 20 22E
Ngelebok, *Cameroon* **114 B2** 4 16N 14 3E
Ngatokae, *Solomon Is.* **133 M10** 8 45S 158 15E
Nggela, *Solomon Is.* **133 M11** 9 5S 160 15E
Nggela Pile, *Solomon Is.* **133 M11** 9 5S 160 20E
Nggela Sule, *Solomon Is.* **133 M11** 9 2S 160 12E
Nghia Lo, *Vietnam* **76 G5** 21 33N 104 28E
Ngidinga, *Dem. Rep. of the Congo* **115 D3** 5 37S 15 17E
Ngo, *Congo* **114 C3** 2 29S 15 45E
Ngoap, *Cameroon* **114 B2** 4 9N 12 51E
Ngoboli, *Sudan* **107 G3** 4 57N 32 37E
N'Gola, *Angola* **115 E2** 14 10S 14 30E
Ngoma, *Malawi* **119 E3** 13 8S 33 45E
Ngomahura, *Zimbabwe* **119 G3** 20 26S 30 43E
Ngomba, *Tanzania* **119 D3** 8 20S 32 53E
Ngongotaha, *N.Z.* **130 E5** 38 5S 176 12E
Ngonye Falls, *Zambia* **115 F4** 16 40S 23 25E
Ngop, *Sudan* **107 F3** 6 17N 30 9E
Ngoring Hu, *China* **68 C4** 34 55N 97 5E
Ngorkou, *Mali* **112 B4** 15 40N 3 41W
Ngorongoro, *Tanzania* **118 C4** 3 11S 35 32E
Ngorongoro ⌂, *Tanzania* **118 C4** 2 40S 35 30E
Ngoto, *C.A.R.* **114 B3** 3 59N 17 19E
Ngouo, Dj., *C.A.R.* **114 A4** 7 55N 24 38E
Ngoura, *Chad* **109 F3** 12 44N 16 21E
Ngouri, *Chad* **109 F3** 13 38N 15 22E
Ngourti, *Niger* **109 E2** 15 19N 13 12E
Ngoussou, *Gabon* **114 C2** 3 0S 11 7E
Ngozi, *Burundi* **118 C2** 2 54S 29 50E
Ngudu, *Tanzania* **118 C3** 2 58S 33 25E
Nguigmi, *Niger* **109 F2** 14 20N 13 20E
Nguila, *Cameroon* **113 E7** 4 41N 11 43E
Nguiu, *Australia* **124 B5** 11 46S 130 38E
Ngukurr, *Australia* **126 A1** 14 44S 134 44E
Nguna, *Vanuatu* **133 G6** 17 26S 168 22E
Ngunga, *Tanzania* **118 C3** 3 37S 33 37E
Nguru, *Nigeria* **113 C7** 12 56N 10 29E
Nguru Mts., *Tanzania* **118 D4** 6 0S 37 30E
Ngusi, *Malawi* **119 E3** 14 0S 34 50E
Nguyen Binh, *Vietnam* **76 F5** 22 39N 105 56E
Ngwedaung, *Burma* **90 F6** 19 31N 97 9E
Nha Trang, *Vietnam* **87 F7** 12 16N 109 10E
Nhacoongo, *Mozam.* **117 C6** 24 18S 35 14E
Nhamaabué, *Mozam.* **119 F4** 17 25S 35 5E
Nhambiquara, *Brazil* **173 C6** 12 50S 59 49W
Nhamundá, *Brazil* **169 D6** 2 14S 56 43W
Nhamundá →, *Brazil* **169 D6** 2 12S 56 41W
Nhangulaze, L., *Mozam.* **117 C5** 24 0S 34 30E
Nharêa, *Angola* **115 E3** 11 38S 16 58E
Nhecolândia, *Brazil* **173 D6** 19 17S 56 58W
Nhill, *Australia* **128 D4** 36 18S 141 40E
Nho Quan, *Vietnam* **76 G5** 20 18N 105 45E
Nhulunbuy, *Australia* **126 A2** 12 10S 137 20E
Nhundo, *Angola* **115 E4** 14 25S 21 23E
Nia-nia, *Dem. Rep. of the Congo* **118 B2** 1 30N 27 40E
Niafounké, *Mali* **112 B4** 16 0N 4 5W
Niagara Falls, *Canada* **140 D4** 43 7N 79 5W
Niagara Falls, *U.S.A.* **150 C6** 43 5N 79 4W
Niagara-on-the-Lake, *Canada* **150 C5** 43 15N 79 4W
Niah, *Malaysia* **85 B4** 3 58N 113 46E
Nialaha'u Pt., *Solomon Is.* **133 M11** 9 47S 161 34E
Niamey, *Niger* **113 C5** 13 27N 2 6E
Niandan-Koro, *Guinea* **112 C3** 11 5N 9 15W
Nianforando, *Guinea* **112 D2** 9 37N 10 36W
Niangara, *Dem. Rep. of the Congo* **118 B2** 3 42N 27 50E
Niangbo, *Ivory C.* **112 D3** 8 49N 5 10W
Niangoloko, *Burkina Faso* **112 C4** 10 15N 4 55W
Niangua →, *U.S.A.* **156 G4** 38 0N 92 48W
Niantic, *U.S.A.* **151 E12** 41 20N 72 11W
Niari, *Congo* **114 C2** 4 9S 14 9E
Niaro, *Sudan* **107 E3** 10 38N 31 31E
Nias, *Indonesia* **84 B1** 1 0N 97 30E
Niassa ⌂, *Mozam.* **119 E4** 12 4S 36 57E
Niassa □, *Mozam.* **119 E4** 13 30S 36 0E
Nībāk, *Si. Arabia* **97 E7** 24 25N 50 50E
Nibe, *Denmark* **17 H3** 56 59N 9 38E
Nicaragua ■, *Cent. Amer.* **164 D2** 11 40N 85 30W
Nicaragua, L. de, *Nic.* **164 D2** 12 0N 85 30W
Nicastro, *Italy* **47 D9** 38 59N 16 19E
Nice, *France* **29 E11** 43 42N 7 14E
Nice ✈ (NCE), *France* **29 E11** 43 41N 7 12E
Niceville, *U.S.A.* **153 E3** 30 31N 86 30W
Nichicun, L., *Canada* **141 B5** 53 5N 71 0W
Nichinan, *Japan* **72 F3** 31 38N 131 23E
Nicholas Channel, *W. Indies* **164 B3** 23 30N 80 5W
Nicholasville, *U.S.A.* **157 G12** 37 53N 84 34W
Nicholls, *U.S.A.* **152 D7** 31 31N 82 38W
Nichols, *U.S.A.* **151 D8** 42 1N 76 22W
Nicholson, *Australia* **124 C4** 18 2S 128 54E
Nicholson, *U.S.A.* **151 E9** 41 37N 75 47W
Nicholson →, *Australia* **126 B2** 17 31S 139 36E
Nicholson L., *Canada* **143 A8** 62 40N 102 40W
Nicholson Ra., *Australia* **125 E2** 27 15S 116 45E
Nicholville, *U.S.A.* **151 B10** 44 41N 74 39W
Nickerie →, *Suriname* **169 B6** 5 58N 57 0W
Nico Pérez = José Batlle y Ordóñez, *Uruguay* **175 C4** 33 20S 55 10W
Nicobar Is., *Ind. Oc.* **95 L11** 8 0N 93 30E
Nicola, *Canada* **142 C4** 50 12N 120 40W
Nicolls Town, *Bahamas* **164 A4** 25 8N 78 0W
Nicopolis, *Greece* **39 A2** 39 5N 20 43E
Nicosia, *Cyprus* **39 E9** 35 10N 33 25E
Nicosia, *Italy* **47 E7** 37 45N 14 24E
Nicótera, *Italy* **47 D8** 38 33N 15 56E
Nicoya, *Costa Rica* **164 D2** 10 9N 85 27W
Nicoya, G. de, *Costa Rica* **164 E3** 10 0N 85 0W
Nicoya, Pen. de, *Costa Rica* **164 E2** 9 45N 85 40W
Nictheroy = Niterói, *Brazil* **171 F3** 22 52S 43 0W
Nida, *Lithuania* **54 C8** 55 20N 21 4E
Nidaros = Trondheim, *Norway* **18 A7** 63 36N 10 25E
Nidau, *Switz.* **32 B4** 47 7N 7 15E
Nidd →, *U.K.* **20 D6** 53 59N 1 23W
Nidda, *Germany* **31 E5** 50 23N 9 1E
Nidda →, *Germany* **31 E4** 50 17N 8 48E
Nidri, *Greece* **39 B2** 38 43N 20 42E
Nidwalden □, *Switz.* **33 C6** 46 50N 8 25E
Nidzica, *Poland* **55 E7** 53 25N 20 28E
Niē, Ī., *N. Cal.* **133 U21** 21 8S 167 35E
Niebüll, *Germany* **30 A4** 54 46N 8 48E
Nied →, *Germany* **27 C13** 49 23N 6 40E
Niederaula, *Germany* **30 E5** 50 47N 9 36E
Niederbayern □, *Germany* **31 G8** 48 40N 12 50E
Niederbipp, *Switz.* **32 B5** 47 16N 7 42E
Niederbronn-les-Bains, *France* **27 D14** 48 57N 7 39E
Niedere Tauern, *Austria* **34 D7** 47 20N 14 0E
Niederlausitz, *Germany* **30 D9** 51 42N 13 59E
Niederösterreich □, *Austria* **34 C8** 48 25N 15 40E
Niedersachsen □, *Germany* **30 C4** 52 50N 9 0E
Niedersächsisches Wattenmeer △, *Germany* **30 B3** 53 45N 7 30E
Niefang, *Eq. Guin.* **114 B2** 1 50N 10 14E
Niekerkshoop, *S. Africa* **116 D3** 29 19S 22 51E
Niellé, *Ivory C.* **112 C3** 10 5N 5 38W
Niellim, *Chad* **109 G3** 9 42N 17 49E
Niem, *C.A.R.* **114 A3** 6 12N 15 14E
Niemba, *Dem. Rep. of the Congo* **118 D2** 5 58S 28 24E
Niemen = Nemunas →, *Lithuania* **15 J19** 55 25N 21 10E
Niemodlin, *Poland* **55 H4** 50 38N 17 38E
Niemur, *Australia* **128 C6** 35 17S 144 9E
Nienburg, *Germany* **30 C5** 52 39N 9 13E
Niepołomice, *Poland* **55 H7** 50 3N 20 13E
Niers →, *Germany* **30 D1** 51 43N 5 57E
Niesen, *Switz.* **32 C5** 46 38N 7 39E
Niesky, *Germany* **30 D10** 51 17N 14 49E
Nieszawa, *Poland* **55 F5** 52 52N 18 50E
Nieu Bethesda, *S. Africa* **116 E3** 31 51S 24 34E
Nieuw Amsterdam, *Suriname* **169 B6** 5 53N 55 5W
Nieuw Nickerie, *Suriname* **169 B6** 6 0N 56 59W
Nieuwoudtville, *S. Africa* **116 E2** 31 23S 19 7E
Nieuwpoort, *Belgium* **24 C2** 51 8N 2 45E
Nieves, Pico de las, *Canary Is.* **9 e1** 27 57N 15 35W
Nièvre □, *France* **27 E10** 47 10N 3 40E
Niga, *Mali* **112 C3** 13 38N 5 27W
Niğde, *Turkey* **100 D6** 37 58N 34 40E
Nigel, *S. Africa* **117 D4** 26 27S 28 25E
Niger □, *Nigeria* **113 D6** 10 0N 5 30E
Niger ■, *W. Afr.* **113 B7** 17 30N 10 0E
Niger →, *W. Afr.* **113 D6** 5 33N 6 33E
Niger Delta, *Africa* **113 E6** 5 0N 6 0E
Nigeria ■, *W. Afr.* **113 D6** 8 30N 8 0E
Nighasin, *India* **93 E9** 28 14N 80 52E
Nightcaps, *N.Z.* **131 F3** 45 57S 168 2E
Nightmute, *U.S.A.* **144 F6** 60 29N 164 44W
Nigríta, *Greece* **50 F7** 40 56N 23 29E
Nihoa, *U.S.A.* **145 G11** 23 6N 161 58W
Nihon = Japan ■, *Asia* **71 G8** 36 0N 136 0E
Nii-Jima, *Japan* **73 C11** 34 20N 139 15E
Niigata, *Japan* **70 F9** 37 58N 139 0E
Niigata □, *Japan* **71 F9** 37 15N 138 45E
Niihama, *Japan* **72 D5** 33 55N 133 16E
Niihau, *U.S.A.* **145 B1** 21 54N 160 9W
Niimi, *Japan* **72 C5** 34 59N 133 28E
Niisle Khureheh = Ulaanbaatar, *Mongolia* **67 E11** 47 55N 106 53E
Niitsu, *Japan* **70 F9** 37 48N 139 7E
Nij Laluk, *India* **90 B4** 27 7N 93 56E
Níjar, *Spain* **41 J2** 36 53N 2 15W
Nijil, *Jordan* **103 E4** 30 32N 35 33E
Nijkerk, *Neths.* **24 B5** 52 13N 5 30E
Nijmegen, *Neths.* **24 C5** 51 50N 5 52E
Nijverdal, *Neths.* **24 B6** 52 22N 6 28E
Nīk Pey, *Iran* **97 B6** 36 50N 48 10E
Nikaweratiya, *Sri Lanka* **95 L5** 7 45N 80 7E
Nike, *Nigeria* **113 D6** 6 26N 7 29E
Nikiniki, *Indonesia* **82 C2** 9 49S 124 30E
Nikísiani, *Greece* **51 F8** 40 57N 24 9E
Nikítas, *Greece* **50 F7** 40 13N 23 43E
Nikitinskiye promysly = Kirovskiy, *Russia* **61 H9** 45 51N 48 11E
Nikki, *Benin* **113 D5** 9 58N 3 12E
Nikkō, *Japan* **73 A11** 36 45N 139 35E
Nikkō △, *Japan* **71 F9** 36 56N 139 37E
Nikolai, *U.S.A.* **144 E9** 62 58N 154 10W
Nikolaikaupunki = Vaasa, *Finland* **14 E19** 63 6N 21 38E
Nikolaistad = Vaasa, *Finland* **14 E19** 63 6N 21 38E
Nikolayev = Mykolayiv, *Ukraine* **59 J7** 46 58N 32 0E
Nikolayevsk, *Russia* **60 E7** 50 0N 45 35E
Nikolayevsk-na-Amur, *Russia* **67 D15** 53 8N 140 44E
Nikolsburg = Mikulov, *Czech Rep.* **35 C9** 48 48N 16 39E
Nikolsk, *Russia* **60 D8** 53 49N 46 4E
Nikolsk-Ussuriysky = Ussuriysk, *Russia* **67 E14** 43 48N 131 59E
Nikolskaya Pestravka = Nikolsk, *Russia* **60 D8** 53 49N 46 4E
Nikolski, *U.S.A.* **144 K5** 52 56N 168 52W
Nikolskoye = Ussuriysk, *Russia* **67 E14** 43 48N 131 59E
Nikolskoye, *Russia* **67 D17** 55 12N 166 0E
Nikolsky Khutor = Sursk, *Russia* **60 D7** 53 3N 45 40E
Nikopol, *Bulgaria* **51 C8** 43 43N 24 54E
Nikopol, *Ukraine* **59 J8** 47 35N 34 25E
Niksar, *Turkey* **100 B7** 40 31N 37 2E
Nīkshahr, *Iran* **97 E9** 26 15N 60 10E
Nikšić, *Serbia & M.* **50 D2** 42 50N 18 57E
Nîl, Nahr en →, *Africa* **106 H7** 30 10N 31 6E
Nîl el Abyad →, *Sudan* **107 D3** 15 38N 32 31E
Nîl el Azraq →, *Sudan* **107 D3** 15 38N 32 31E
Nila, *Indonesia* **83 C3** 6 44S 129 31E
Nilakkottai, *India* **95 J3** 10 10N 77 52E
Niland, *U.S.A.* **161 M11** 33 14N 115 31W
Nilanga, *India* **94 E3** 18 6N 76 46E
Nile = Nîl, Nahr en →, *Africa* **106 H7** 30 10N 31 6E
Nile Delta, *Egypt* **106 H7** 31 40N 31 0E
Niles, *Mich., U.S.A.* **157 C10** 41 50N 86 15W
Niles, *Ohio, U.S.A.* **150 E4** 41 11N 80 46W
Niles Center = Skokie, *U.S.A.* **157 B9** 42 3N 87 45W
Nileshwar, *India* **95 H2** 12 15N 75 6E
Nilgiri Hills, *India* **95 J3** 11 30N 76 30E
Nilo Peçanha, *Brazil* **171 D4** 13 37S 39 6W
Nilsebu, *Norway* **18 E3** 59 11N 6 39E
Nilüfer →, *Turkey* **51 F12** 40 18N 28 27E
Nim Ka Thana, *India* **92 F6** 27 44N 75 48E
Nimach, *India* **92 G6** 24 30N 74 56E
Nimbahera, *India* **92 G6** 24 37N 74 45E
Nîmes, *France* **29 E8** 43 50N 4 23E
Nimfaíon, Ákra = Pínnes, Ákra, *Greece* **51 F8** 40 5N 24 20E
Nimmitabel, *Australia* **129 D8** 36 29S 149 15E
Nīmrūz □, *Afghan.* **91 C1** 30 0N 62 0E
Nimule, *Sudan* **107 G3** 3 32N 32 3E
Nimule △, *Sudan* **107 G3** 3 38N 32 2E
Nin, *Croatia* **45 D12** 44 16N 15 12E
Nīnawá, *Iraq* **101 D10** 36 25N 43 10E
Nīnawá □, *Iraq* **96 B4** 36 15N 43 0E
Ninda, *Angola* **115 E4** 14 47S 21 24E
Nindigully, *Australia* **127 D4** 28 21S 148 50E
Nine Degree Channel, *India* **95 K1** 9 0N 73 0E
Ninepin Group, *China* **69 G11** 22 16N 114 21E
Ninety East Ridge, *Ind. Oc.* **121 E7** 1 0S 90 0E
Ninety Mile Beach, *N.Z.* **130 A1** 34 48S 173 0E
Ninety Mile Beach, The, *Australia* **129 E7** 38 15S 147 24E
Ninety Six, *U.S.A.* **152 A7** 34 11N 82 1W
Nineveh = Nīnawá, *Iraq* **101 D10** 36 25N 43 10E
Ning Xian, *China* **74 G4** 35 30N 107 58E
Ningaloo ⌂, *Australia* **124 D1** 22 23S 113 32E
Ning'an, *China* **75 B15** 44 22N 129 20E
Ningbo, *China* **77 C13** 29 51N 121 28E
Ningcheng, *China* **75 D10** 41 32N 119 53E
Ningde, *China* **77 D12** 26 38N 119 23E
Ningdu, *China* **77 D10** 26 25N 115 59E
Ningerum, *Papua N. G.* **132 C1** 5 41S 141 8E
Ninggang, *China* **77 D9** 26 42N 113 55E
Ningguo, *China* **77 B12** 30 35N 119 0E
Ninghai, *China* **77 C13** 29 15N 121 27E
Ninghua, *China* **77 D11** 26 14N 116 45E
Ningi, *Nigeria* **113 C6** 10 55N 9 30E
Ningjin, *China* **74 F8** 37 35N 114 57E
Ningjing Shan, *China* **76 C2** 30 0N 98 20E
Ninglang, *China* **76 D3** 27 20N 100 55E
Ningling, *China* **74 G8** 34 25N 115 22E
Ningming, *China* **76 F6** 22 8N 107 4E
Ningnan, *China* **76 D4** 27 5N 102 36E
Ningpo = Ningbo, *China* **77 C13** 29 51N 121 28E
Ningqiang, *China* **74 H4** 32 47N 106 15E
Ningshan, *China* **74 H5** 33 21N 108 21E
Ningsia Hui A.R. = Ningxia Huizu Zizhiqu □, *China* **74 F4** 38 0N 106 0E
Ningwu, *China* **74 E7** 39 0N 112 18E
Ningxia Huizu Zizhiqu □, *China* **74 F4** 38 0N 106 0E
Ningxiang, *China* **77 C9** 28 15N 112 30E
Ningyang, *China* **74 G9** 35 47N 116 45E
Ningyuan, *China* **77 E8** 25 37N 111 57E
Ninh Binh, *Vietnam* **76 G5** 20 15N 105 55E
Ninh Giang, *Vietnam* **86 B6** 20 44N 106 24E
Ninh Hoa, *Vietnam* **86 F7** 12 30N 109 7E
Ninh Ma, *Vietnam* **86 F7** 12 48N 109 21E
Nini-Suhien △, *Ghana* **112 D4** 5 20N 2 34W
Ninigo Group, *Papua N. G.* **132 A3** 1 22S 144 17E
Ninini Pt., *U.S.A.* **145 B2** 21 58N 159 20W
Ninove, *Belgium* **24 D4** 50 51N 4 2E
Nioaque, *Brazil* **175 A4** 21 5S 55 50W
Niobrara, *U.S.A.* **154 D6** 42 45N 98 2W
Niobrara →, *U.S.A.* **154 D6** 42 46N 98 3W
Nioki, *Dem. Rep. of the Congo* **114 C3** 2 47S 17 40E
Niokolo-Koba △, *Senegal* **112 C2** 13 3N 13 2W
Niono, *Mali* **112 C3** 14 15N 6 0W
Nionsamoridougou, *Guinea* **112 D3** 8 45N 8 50W
Nioro du Rip, *Senegal* **112 C1** 13 40N 15 50W
Nioro du Sahel, *Mali* **112 B3** 15 15N 9 30W
Niort, *France* **28 B3** 46 19N 0 29W
Nipa, *Papua N. G.* **132 D2** 6 9S 143 29E
Nipani, *India* **95 F2** 16 20N 74 25E
Nipawin, *Canada* **143 C8** 53 20N 104 0W
Nipfjället, *Sweden* **16 C6** 61 59N 12 50E
Nipigon, *Canada* **140 C2** 49 0N 88 17W
Nipigon, L., *Canada* **140 C2** 49 50N 88 30W
Nipishish L., *Canada* **141 B7** 54 12N 60 45W
Nipissing, L., *Canada* **140 C4** 46 20N 80 0W
Nipomo, *U.S.A.* **161 K6** 35 3N 120 29W
Nippon = Japan ■, *Asia* **71 G8** 36 0N 136 0E
Nipton, *U.S.A.* **161 K11** 35 28N 115 16W
Niquelândia, *Brazil* **171 D2** 14 33S 48 23W
Nīr, *Iran* **101 C12** 38 2N 47 59E
Nira →, *India* **94 F2** 17 58N 75 8E
Nirasaki, *Japan* **73 B10** 35 42N 138 27E
Nirmal, *India* **94 E4** 19 3N 78 20E
Nirmali, *India* **93 F12** 26 20N 86 35E
Niš, *Serbia & M.* **50 C5** 43 19N 21 58E
Nisa = Nysa →, *Europe* **30 C10** 52 4N 14 46E
Nisa, *Portugal* **43 F3** 39 30N 7 41W
Nişāb, *Si. Arabia* **96 D5** 29 11N 44 43E
Nişāb, *Yemen* **98 D4** 14 25N 46 29E
Nišava →, *Serbia & M.* **50 C5** 43 20N 21 46E
Niscemi, *Italy* **47 E7** 37 9N 14 23E
Nishi-Sonogi-Hantō, *Japan* **72 E1** 32 55N 129 45E
Nishi-Tosa, *Japan* **72 D4** 33 13N 132 46E
Nishinomiya, *Japan* **73 C7** 34 45N 135 20E
Nishino'omote, *Japan* **71 J5** 30 43N 130 59E
Nishio, *Japan* **73 C9** 34 52N 137 3E
Nishiwaki, *Japan* **72 C6** 34 59N 134 58E
Nisibin = Nusaybin, *Turkey* **101 D9** 37 3N 41 10E
Nisíros, *Greece* **49 E9** 36 35N 27 12E
Niška Banja, *Serbia & M.* **50 C6** 43 18N 22 1E
Niskibi →, *Canada* **140 A2** 56 29N 88 9W
Nisko, *Poland* **55 H9** 50 35N 22 7E
Nisporeni, *Moldova* **53 C13** 47 4N 28 10E
Nisqually →, *U.S.A.* **160 C4** 47 6N 122 42W
Nissáki, *Greece* **38 B9** 39 43N 19 52E
Nissan →, *Sweden* **17 H6** 56 40N 12 51E
Nissedal, *Norway* **18 E5** 59 10N 8 30E
Nisser, *Norway* **18 E5** 59 7N 8 28E
Nissum Bredning, *Denmark* **17 H2** 56 40N 8 20E
Nissum Fjord, *Denmark* **17 H2** 56 20N 8 11E
Nistru = Dnister →, *Europe* **59 J6** 46 18N 30 17E
Nisutlin →, *Canada* **142 A2** 60 14N 132 34W
Nitchequon, *Canada* **141 B5** 53 10N 70 58W
Niterói, *Brazil* **171 F3** 22 52S 43 0W
Nith →, *Canada* **150 C4** 43 12N 80 23W
Nith →, *U.K.* **22 F5** 55 14N 3 33W
Nitmiluk △, *Australia* **124 B5** 14 6S 132 15E
Nitra, *Slovak Rep.* **35 C11** 48 19N 18 4E
Nitra →, *Slovak Rep.* **35 D11** 47 46N 18 10E
Nitriansky □, *Slovak Rep.* **35 C11** 48 10N 18 30E
Nittenau, *Germany* **31 F8** 49 12N 12 16E
Niu, *U.S.A.* **145 K14** 21 19N 157 44W
Niuafo'ou, *Tonga* **123 D15** 15 30S 175 58W
Niue, *Cook Is.* **135 J11** 19 2S 169 54W
Niulan Jiang →, *China* **76 D4** 27 30N 103 5E
Niut, *Indonesia* **85 B4** 0 55N 110 6E
Niutou Shan, *China* **77 C13** 29 5N 121 59E
Niuzhuang, *China* **75 D12** 40 58N 122 28E
Nivala, *Finland* **14 E21** 63 56N 24 57E
Nivelles, *Belgium* **24 D4** 50 35N 4 20E
Nivernais, *France* **27 E10** 47 15N 3 30E
Niwas, *India* **93 H9** 23 3N 80 26E
Nixa, *U.S.A.* **155 G8** 37 3N 93 18W

Nixon, *U.S.A.* **155 L6** 29 16N 97 46W
Nizam Sagar, *India* **94 E3** 18 10N 77 58 E
Nizamabad, *India* **94 E4** 18 45N 78 7 E
Nizamghat, *India* **90 A5** 28 20N 95 45 E
Nizhne Kolymsk, *Russia* **67 C17** 68 34N 160 55 E
Nizhneangarsk, *Russia* **67 D11** 55 47N 109 30 E
Nizhnegorskiy = Nyzhnohirskyy, *Ukraine* **59 K8** 45 27N 34 38 E
Nizhnekamsk, *Russia* **60 C10** 55 38N 51 49 E
Nizhnekamskoye Vdkhr., *Russia* **64 D4** 55 56N 52 56 E
Nizhnesaldinsky Zavod = Nizhnyaya Salda, *Russia* **64 B8** 58 8N 60 42 E
Nizhneserginsky Zavod = Nizhniye Sergi, *Russia* **64 C7** 56 40N 59 18 E
Nizhneudinsk, *Russia* **67 D10** 54 54N 99 3 E
Nizhnevartovsk, *Russia* **66 C8** 60 56N 76 38 E
Nizhniy Chir, *Russia* **61 F6** 48 22N 43 5 E
Nizhniy Lomov, *Russia* **60 D6** 53 34N 43 38 E
Nizhniy Novgorod, *Russia* **60 B7** 56 20N 44 0 E
Nizhniy Tagil, *Russia* **64 C7** 57 55N 59 57 E
Nizhniye Kresty = Cherskiy, *Russia* **67 C17** 68 45N 161 18 E
Nizhniye Sergi, *Russia* **64 C7** 56 40N 59 18 E
Nizhnyaya Salda, *Russia* **64 B8** 58 8N 60 42 E
Nizhyn, *Ukraine* **59 G6** 51 5N 31 55 E
Nizina Mazowiecka, *Poland* **55 F8** 52 30N 21 0 E
Nizip, *Turkey* **100 D7** 37 5N 37 50 E
Nízké Tatry, *Slovak Rep.* **35 C12** 48 55N 19 30 E
Nízké Tatry △, *Slovak Rep.* **35 C12** 48 55N 19 37 E
Nízký Jeseník, *Czech Rep.* **35 B10** 49 50N 17 30 E
Nizza Monferrato, *Italy* **44 D5** 44 46N 8 21 E
Njakwa, *Malawi* **119 E3** 11 1 S 33 56 E
Njanji, *Zambia* **119 E3** 14 25 S 31 46 E
Njarðvík, *Iceland* **11 D4** 63 59N 22 32W
Njazidja = Grande Comore, *Comoros Is.* **121 a** 11 35 S 43 20 E
Njegoš, *Serbia & M.* **50 D2** 42 53N 18 45 E
Njinjo, *Tanzania* **119 D4** 8 48 S 38 54 E
Njoko →, *Zambia* **115 F4** 17 8 S 24 4 E
Njombe, *Tanzania* **119 D3** 9 20 S 34 50 E
Njombe →, *Tanzania* **118 D4** 6 56 S 35 6 E
Njurundabommen, *Sweden* **16 B11** 62 15N 17 25 E
Nkambe, *Cameroon* **113 D7** 6 35N 10 40 E
Nkana, *Zambia* **119 E2** 12 50 S 28 8 E
Nkandla, *S. Africa* **117 D5** 28 37 S 31 5 E
Nkawkaw, *Ghana* **113 D4** 6 36N 0 49W
Nkayi, *Zimbabwe* **119 F2** 19 41 S 29 20 E
Nkhotakota, *Malawi* **119 E3** 12 56 S 34 15 E
Nkhotakota ⌂, *Malawi* **119 E3** 12 50 S 34 0 E
Nkolabona, *Gabon* **114 B2** 1 14N 11 43 E
Nkomi, Lagune, *Gabon* **114 C1** 1 35 S 9 17 E
Nkone, *Dem. Rep. of the Congo* **114 C4** 1 2 S 22 20 E
Nkongsamba, *Cameroon* **113 E6** 4 55N 9 55 E
Nkunga, *Dem. Rep. of the Congo* **115 C3** 4 41 S 18 34 E
Nkurenkuru, *Namibia* **116 B2** 17 42 S 18 32 E
Nkwanta, *Ghana* **112 D4** 6 10N 2 10W
Nmai →, *Burma* **76 F2** 25 30N 97 25 E
Noakhali = Maijdi, *Bangla.* **90 D3** 22 48N 91 10 E
Noatak, *U.S.A.* **144 C7** 67 34N 162 58W
Noatak ⌂, *U.S.A.* **144 B8** 68 10N 160 0W
Nobel, *Canada* **150 A4** 45 25N 80 6W
Nobeoka, *Japan* **72 E3** 32 36N 131 41 E
Noble, *U.S.A.* **157 F8** 38 42N 88 14W
Noblejas, *Spain* **42 F7** 39 58N 3 26W
Noblesville, *U.S.A.* **157 D11** 40 3N 86 1W
Noboribetsu, *Japan* **70 C10** 42 24N 141 6 E
Nocatee, *U.S.A.* **153 H8** 27 10N 81 53W
Noce →, *Italy* **44 B8** 46 9N 11 4 E
Nocera Inferiore, *Italy* **47 B7** 40 44N 14 38 E
Nocera Umbra, *Italy* **45 E9** 43 5N 12 47 E
Noci, *Italy* **47 B10** 40 48N 17 7 E
Nocona, *U.S.A.* **155 J6** 33 47N 97 44W
Nocrich, *Romania* **53 E9** 45 55N 24 26 E
Noda, *Japan* **73 B11** 35 56N 139 52 E
Nodeland, *Norway* **18 F4** 58 8N 7 51 E
Noel Kempff Mercado △, *Bolivia* **173 C5** 14 9 S 60 49W
Nogal Valley = Nugaaleed, Dooxo, *Somali Rep.* **120 C3** 8 35N 48 35 E
Nogales, *Mexico* **162 A2** 31 20N 110 56W
Nogales, *U.S.A.* **159 L8** 31 20N 110 56W
Nogaro, *France* **28 E3** 43 45N 0 2W
Nogat →, *Poland* **54 D6** 54 17N 19 17 E
Nōgata, *Japan* **72 D2** 33 48N 130 44 E
Nogaysk = Primorskoye, *Ukraine* **59 J9** 46 48N 36 20 E
Nogent, *France* **27 D12** 48 1N 5 20 E
Nogent-le-Rotrou, *France* **26 D7** 48 20N 0 50 E
Nogent-sur-Seine, *France* **27 D10** 48 30N 3 30 E
Noggerup, *Australia* **125 F2** 33 32 S 116 5 E
Noginsk, *Moskva, Russia* **58 E10** 55 50N 38 25 E
Noginsk, *Tunguska, Russia* **67 C10** 64 30N 90 50 E
Nogoa →, *Australia* **126 C4** 23 40 S 147 55 E
Nogoyá, *Argentina* **174 C4** 32 24 S 59 48W
Nógrád □, *Hungary* **52 C4** 48 0N 19 30 E
Noguera Pallaresa →, *Spain* **40 D5** 41 55N 0 55 E
Noguera Ribagorzana →, *Spain* **40 D5** 41 40N 0 43 E
Nohar, *India* **92 E6** 29 11N 74 49 E
Nohfelden, *Germany* **31 F3** 49 35N 7 7 E
Nohili Pt., *U.S.A.* **145 A2** 22 4N 159 47W
Nohta, *India* **93 H8** 23 40N 79 34 E
Noia, *Spain* **42 C2** 42 48N 8 53W
Noichi, *Japan* **72 D5** 33 33N 133 42 E
Noing, *Phil.* **81 J5** 5 40N 125 28 E
Noipuos, *Papua N. G.* **132 B6** 2 25 S 150 7 E
Noire, Montagne, *France* **28 E6** 43 28N 2 18 E
Noires, Mts., *France* **26 D3** 48 11N 3 40W
Noirétable, *France* **28 C7** 45 48N 3 46 E
Noirmoutier, Î. de, *France* **26 F4** 46 58N 2 10W
Noirmoutier-en-l'Île, *France* **26 F4** 47 0N 2 14W
Nojane, *Botswana* **116 C3** 23 15 S 20 14 E
Nojima-Zaki, *Japan* **73 C11** 34 54N 139 53 E
Nok Kundi, *Pakistan* **91 C1** 28 50N 62 45 E
Nok Ta Phao, Ko, *Thailand* **87 b** 9 23N 99 40 E
Nokaneng, *Botswana* **116 B3** 19 40 S 22 17 E
Nokia, *Finland* **15 F20** 61 30N 23 30 E
Nokkeushi = Kitami, *Japan* **70 C11** 43 48N 143 54 E
Nokomis, *Canada* **143 C8** 51 35N 105 0W
Nokomis, *Fla., U.S.A.* **153 H7** 27 7N 82 27W
Nokomis, *Ill., U.S.A.* **156 E7** 39 18N 89 18W
Nokomis L., *Canada* **143 B8** 57 0N 103 0W
Nokou, *Chad* **109 F2** 14 35N 14 47 E
Nokuku, *Vanuatu* **133 D4** 14 54 S 166 35 E
Nola, *C.A.R.* **114 B3** 3 35N 16 4 E
Nola, *Italy* **47 B7** 40 55N 14 33 E
Nolay, *France* **27 F11** 46 58N 4 35 E
Noli, C. di, *Italy* **44 D5** 44 12N 8 25 E
Nolinsk, *Russia* **60 B9** 57 28N 49 57 E
Noma, *U.S.A.* **152 E4** 30 59N 85 37W
Noma Omuramba →, *Namibia* **116 B3** 18 52 S 20 53 E
Noma-Saki, *Japan* **72 F2** 31 25N 130 7 E
Nomad, *Papua N. G.* **132 D2** 6 19 S 142 13 E
Nombre de Dios, *Panama* **164 E4** 9 34N 79 28W
Nome, *U.S.A.* **144 D6** 64 30N 165 25W
Nomo-Zaki, *Japan* **72 E1** 32 35N 129 44 E
Nomuka, *Tonga* **133 Q13** 20 17 S 174 48W
Nomuka Group, *Tonga* **133 Q13** 20 20 S 174 48W
Nonacho L., *Canada* **143 A7** 61 42N 109 40W
Nonancourt, *France* **26 D8** 48 47N 1 11 E
Nonda, *Australia* **126 C3** 20 40 S 142 28 E
Nondalton, *U.S.A.* **144 G9** 60 0N 154 51W
None, *Italy* **44 D4** 44 56N 7 32 E
Nong Chang, *Thailand* **86 E2** 15 23N 99 51 E
Nong Het, *Laos* **86 C4** 19 29N 103 59 E
Nong Khai, *Thailand* **86 D4** 17 50N 102 46 E
Nong'an, *China* **75 B13** 44 25N 125 5 E
Nongjrong, *India* **90 C4** 25 29N 92 6 E
Nongoma, *S. Africa* **117 D5** 27 58 S 31 35 E
Nongsa, *Indonesia* **87 d** 1 11N 104 8 E
Nongstoin, *India* **90 C3** 25 31N 91 16 E
Nonoava, *Mexico* **162 B3** 27 28N 106 44W
Nonoava →, *Mexico* **162 B3** 27 29N 106 45W
Nonoc I., *Phil.* **81 G5** 9 51N 125 37 E
Nonthaburi, *Thailand* **86 F3** 13 51N 100 34 E
Nontron, *France* **28 C4** 45 31N 0 40 E
Nonza, *France* **29 F13** 42 47N 9 21 E
Noonamah, *Australia* **124 B5** 12 40 S 131 4 E
Noondie, L., *Australia* **125 E2** 28 30 S 119 30 E
Noord Brabant □, *Neths.* **24 C5** 51 40N 5 0 E
Noord Holland □, *Neths.* **24 B4** 52 30N 4 45 E
Noordbeveland, *Neths.* **24 C3** 51 35N 3 50 E
Noordoostpolder, *Neths.* **24 B5** 52 45N 5 45 E
Noordwijk, *Neths.* **24 B4** 52 14N 4 26 E
Noorvik, *U.S.A.* **144 C7** 66 50N 161 3W
Noosa Heads, *Australia* **127 D5** 26 25 S 153 6 E
Nootka I., *Canada* **142 D3** 49 32N 126 42W
Nopiming ⌂, *Canada* **143 C9** 50 30N 95 37W
Nóqui, *Angola* **115 D2** 5 55 S 13 30 E
Nor-Bayazet = Kamo, *Armenia* **61 K7** 40 21N 45 7 E
Nora, *Eritrea* **107 D5** 16 6N 40 4 E
Nora, *Sweden* **16 E9** 59 32N 15 2 E
Nora Springs, *U.S.A.* **156 A4** 43 9N 93 0W
Norak = Nurek, *Tajikistan* **65 D4** 38 23N 69 19 E
Norala, *Phil.* **81 H5** 6 32N 124 40 E
Noralee, *Canada* **142 C3** 53 59N 126 26W
Noranda = Rouyn-Noranda, *Canada* **140 C4** 48 20N 79 0W
Norberg, *Sweden* **16 D9** 60 4N 15 56 E
Norborne, *U.S.A.* **156 E3** 39 18N 93 40W
Nórcia, *Italy* **45 F10** 42 48N 13 5 E
Norco, *U.S.A.* **161 M9** 33 56N 117 33W
Norcross, *U.S.A.* **152 B5** 33 56N 84 13W
Nord □, *France* **27 B10** 50 15N 3 30 E
Nord-Kivu □, *Dem. Rep. of the Congo* **118 C2** 1 0 S 29 0 E
Nord-og-Østgrønland △, *Greenland* **10 C7** 75 0N 35 0W
Nord-Ostsee-Kanal, *Germany* **30 A5** 54 12N 9 32 E
Nord-Pas-de-Calais □, *France* **27 B9** 50 30N 2 50 E
Nordagutu, *Norway* **18 E6** 59 25N 9 20 E
Nordaustlandet, *Svalbard* **6 B9** 79 14N 23 0 E
Nordberg, *Norway* **18 C5** 61 54N 8 10 E
Nordborg, *Denmark* **17 J3** 55 5N 9 50 E
Nordby, *Denmark* **17 J2** 55 27N 8 24 E
Norddeich, *Germany* **30 B3** 53 36N 7 9 E
Nordegg, *Canada* **142 C5** 52 29N 116 5W
Norden, *Germany* **30 B3** 53 35N 7 12 E
Nordenham, *Germany* **30 B4** 53 30N 8 30 E
Nordenskjöld Sea = Laptev Sea, *Russia* **67 B13** 76 0N 125 0 E
Norderhov, *Norway* **18 D7** 60 7N 10 17 E
Norderney, *Germany* **30 B3** 53 42N 7 9 E
Norderstedt, *Germany* **30 B6** 53 42N 10 1 E
Nordeste, *Azores* **9 d3** 37 50N 25 10W
Nordfjord, *Norway* **18 C2** 61 55N 5 30 E
Nordfjordeid, *Norway* **18 C2** 61 54N 6 0 E
Nordfriesische Inseln, *Germany* **30 A4** 54 40N 8 20 E
Nordgrønland = Avannaarsua □, *Greenland* **10 B5** 80 0N 55 0W
Nordhausen, *Germany* **30 D6** 51 30N 10 47 E
Nordhorn, *Germany* **30 C3** 52 26N 7 4 E
Norðoyar, *Færoe Is.* **14 E9** 62 17N 6 35W
Norðtunga, *Iceland* **11 C5** 64 44N 21 24W
Norður-múlasýsla □, *Iceland* **11 B11** 65 30N 15 0W
Norðurbotn, *Iceland* **11 B3** 65 36N 23 46W
Nördinge-Nol, *Sweden* **17 G6** 57 56N 12 5 E
Nordingrå, *Sweden* **16 B12** 62 56N 18 17 E
Nordjyllands Amtskommune □, *Denmark* **17 G4** 57 20N 10 0 E
Nordkapp, *Norway* **14 A21** 71 10N 25 50 E
Nordkapp, *Svalbard* **6 A9** 80 31N 20 0 E
Nordkinnhalvøya, *Norway* **14 A22** 70 55N 27 40 E
Nördlicher Teutoburger Wald-Wiehengebirge ⌂, *Germany* **30 C4** 52 18N 8 10 E
Nördlingen, *Germany* **31 G6** 48 48N 10 30 E
Nordmøre, *Norway* **18 B4** 63 6N 8 15 E
Nordostrundingen, *Greenland* **10 A9** 81 22N 11 40W
Nordøyane, *Norway* **18 B3** 62 40N 6 0 E
Nordre Bergenhus = Sogn og Fjordane □, *Norway* **18 C3** 61 40N 6 45 E
Nordre Osen, *Norway* **18 C8** 61 18N 11 45 E
Nordre Strømfjord, *Greenland* **10 D5** 67 10N 53 35W
Nordrhein-Westfalen □, *Germany* **30 D3** 51 45N 7 30 E
Nordsinni, *Norway* **18 D6** 60 50N 9 57 E
Nørdstedalsseter, *Norway* **18 C4** 61 40N 7 48 E
Nordstrand, *Germany* **30 A4** 54 30N 8 52 E
Nordvik, *Russia* **67 B12** 74 2N 111 32 E
Nore →, *Ireland* **23 D4** 52 25N 6 58W
Norefjell, *Norway* **18 D6** 60 16N 9 29 E
Noresund, *Norway* **18 D6** 60 11N 9 37 E
Norfolk, *Canada* **150 D4** 42 50N 80 23W
Norfolk, *Nebr., U.S.A.* **154 D6** 42 2N 97 25W
Norfolk, *Va., U.S.A.* **148 G7** 36 51N 76 17W
Norfolk □, *U.K.* **21 E8** 52 39N 0 54 E
Norfolk I., *Pac. Oc.* **134 K8** 28 58 S 168 3 E
Norfork L., *U.S.A.* **155 G8** 36 15N 92 14W
Norge = Norway ■, *Europe* **14 E14** 63 0N 11 0 E
Norheimsund, *Norway* **18 D3** 60 23N 6 6 E
Norilsk, *Russia* **67 C9** 69 20N 88 6 E
Norma, Mt., *Australia* **126 C3** 20 55 S 140 42 E
Normal, *U.S.A.* **156 D8** 40 31N 88 59W
Norman, *U.S.A.* **155 H6** 35 13N 97 26W
Norman →, *Australia* **126 B3** 19 18 S 141 51 E
Norman Park, *U.S.A.* **152 D6** 31 16N 83 41W
Norman Wells, *Canada* **138 B7** 65 17N 126 51W
Normanby, *N.Z.* **130 F3** 39 32 S 174 18 E
Normanby →, *Australia* **126 A3** 14 23 S 144 10 E
Normanby I., *Papua N. G.* **132 F6** 10 5 S 151 5 E
Normandie, *France* **25 B4** 48 45N 0 10 E
Normandie-Maine ⌂, *France* **26 D6** 48 30N 0 20W
Normandin, *Canada* **140 C5** 48 49N 72 31W
Normandy = Normandie, *France* **25 B4** 48 45N 0 10 E
Normanhurst, Mt., *Australia* **125 E3** 25 4 S 122 30 E
Normanton, *Australia* **126 B3** 17 40 S 141 10 E
Normanville, *Australia* **128 C3** 35 27 S 138 18 E
Normétal, *Canada* **140 C4** 49 0N 79 22W
Norquay, *Canada* **143 C8** 51 53N 102 5W
Norquinco, *Argentina* **176 B2** 41 51 S 70 55W
Norra Dellen, *Sweden* **16 C10** 61 53N 16 43 E
Norra Kvill △, *Sweden* **17 G9** 57 46N 15 35 E
Norra Ulvön, *Sweden* **16 A12** 63 3N 18 40 E
Norrahammar, *Sweden* **17 G8** 57 43N 14 7 E
Norrbottens län □, *Sweden* **14 C19** 66 50N 20 0 E
Nørre Åby, *Denmark* **17 J3** 55 27N 9 52 E
Nørre Alslev, *Denmark* **17 K5** 54 54N 11 52 E
Nørresundby, *Denmark* **17 G3** 57 5N 9 52 E
Norrhult-Klavreström, *Sweden* **17 G9** 57 7N 15 10 E
Norris City, *U.S.A.* **157 G8** 37 59N 88 20W
Norris Point, *Canada* **141 C8** 49 31N 57 53W
Norristown, *Ga., U.S.A.* **152 C7** 32 30N 82 30W
Norristown, *Pa., U.S.A.* **151 F9** 40 7N 75 21W
Norrköping, *Sweden* **17 F10** 58 37N 16 11 E
Norrland, *Sweden* **16 E16** 62 15N 15 45 E
Norrsundet, *Sweden* **16 D11** 60 56N 17 8 E
Norrtälje, *Sweden* **16 E12** 59 46N 18 42 E
Norseman, *Australia* **125 F3** 32 8 S 121 43 E
Norsewood, *N.Z.* **130 G5** 40 3 S 176 13 E
Norsjø, *Norway* **18 E6** 59 18N 9 20 E
Norsk, *Russia* **67 D14** 52 30N 130 5 E
Norsup, *Vanuatu* **133 F5** 16 3 S 167 24 E
Norte, C., *Chile* **172 b** 27 3 S 109 24W
Norte, Canal do →, *Brazil* **169 C7** 0 40N 50 20W
Norte, Pta., *Argentina* **176 B4** 42 5 S 63 46W
Norte, Pta. del, *Canary Is.* **9 e1** 27 51N 17 57W
Norte, Pta. do, *Azores* **9 d4** 37 1N 25 4W
Norte, Serra do, *Brazil* **173 C6** 11 20 S 59 0W
Norte de Santander □, *Colombia* **168 B3** 8 0N 73 0W
Norte Grande, *Azores* **9 d1** 38 40N 28 4W
Nortelândia, *Brazil* **173 C6** 14 25 S 56 48W
North, *U.S.A.* **152 B8** 33 37N 81 6W
North, C., *Canada* **141 C7** 47 2N 60 20W
North Adams, *U.S.A.* **151 D11** 42 42N 73 7W
North America **136 F10** 40 0N 100 0W
North Andaman I., *India* **95 H11** 13 15N 92 55 E
North Arm, *Canada* **142 A5** 62 0N 114 30W
North Atlantic Ocean, *Atl. Oc.* **8 C7** 30 0N 50 0W
North Augusta, *U.S.A.* **152 B8** 33 30N 81 59W
North Ayrshire □, *U.K.* **22 F4** 55 45N 4 44W
North Baltimore, *U.S.A.* **157 C13** 41 11N 83 41W
North Bass I., *U.S.A.* **150 E2** 41 44N 82 53W
North Battleford, *Canada* **143 C7** 52 50N 108 17W
North Bay, *Canada* **140 C4** 46 20N 79 30W
North Belcher Is., *Canada* **140 A4** 56 50N 79 50W
North Bend, *Oreg., U.S.A.* **158 E1** 43 24N 124 14W
North Bend, *Pa., U.S.A.* **150 E7** 41 20N 77 42W
North Bend, *Wash., U.S.A.* **160 C5** 47 30N 121 47W
North Bennington, *U.S.A.* **151 D11** 42 56N 73 15W
North Berwick, *U.K.* **22 E6** 56 4N 2 42W
North Berwick, *U.S.A.* **151 C14** 43 18N 70 44W
North Borneo = Sabah □, *Malaysia* **85 A5** 6 0N 117 0 E
North Brother I., *India* **95 J11** 10 59N 92 40 E
North C., *Canada* **141 C7** 47 5N 64 0W
North C., *N.Z.* **130 A2** 34 23 S 173 4 E
North C., *Papua N. G.* **132 B6** 2 32 S 150 50 E
North Canadian →, *U.S.A.* **155 H7** 35 16N 95 31W
North Canton, *U.S.A.* **150 F3** 40 53N 81 24W
North Cape = Nordkapp, *Norway* **14 A21** 71 10N 25 50 E
North Cape = Nordkapp, *Svalbard* **6 A9** 80 31N 20 0 E
North Caribou L., *Canada* **140 B1** 52 50N 90 40W
North Carolina □, *U.S.A.* **149 H6** 35 30N 80 0W
North Cascades △, *U.S.A.* **158 B3** 48 45N 121 10W
North Cay, *Bahamas* **9 b** 25 6N 77 26W
North Channel, *Canada* **140 C3** 46 0N 83 0W
North Channel, *U.K.* **22 F3** 55 13N 5 52W
North Charleston, *U.S.A.* **152 C10** 32 53N 79 58W
North Chicago, *U.S.A.* **157 B9** 42 19N 87 51W
North College Hill, *U.S.A.* **157 E12** 39 13N 84 33W
North Comino Channel, *Malta* **38 E7** 36 1N 14 20 E
North Creek, *U.S.A.* **151 C11** 43 41N 73 59W
North Dakota □, *U.S.A.* **154 B5** 47 30N 100 15W
North Downs, *U.K.* **21 F8** 51 19N 0 21 E
North East, *U.S.A.* **150 D5** 42 13N 79 50W
North East B., *Ascension I.* **9 g** 7 55 S 14 21W
North East Frontier Agency = Arunachal Pradesh □, *India* **90 A5** 28 0N 95 0 E
North East Lincolnshire □, *U.K.* **20 D7** 53 34N 0 2W
North Eastern □, *Kenya* **118 B5** 1 30N 40 0 E
North Esk →, *U.K.* **22 E6** 56 46N 2 24W
North European Plain, *Europe* **12 E10** 55 0N 25 0 E
North Fabius →, *U.S.A.* **156 E5** 39 54N 91 30W
North Foreland, *U.K.* **21 F9** 51 22N 1 28 E
North Fork, *U.S.A.* **160 H7** 37 14N 119 21W
North Fork, Salt →, *U.S.A.* **156 E5** 39 26N 91 53W
North Fork American →, *U.S.A.* **160 G5** 38 57N 120 59W
North Fork Edisto →, *U.S.A.* **152 B9** 33 16N 80 54W
North Fork Feather →, *U.S.A.* **160 F5** 38 33N 121 30W
North Fork Grand →, *U.S.A.* **154 C3** 45 47N 102 16W
North Fork Red →, *U.S.A.* **155 H5** 34 24N 99 14W
North Fort Myers, *U.S.A.* **153 J8** 26 41N 81 53W
North Frisian Is. = Nordfriesische Inseln, *Germany* **30 A4** 54 40N 8 20 E
North Gower, *Canada* **151 A9** 45 8N 75 43W
North Greenfield = West Allis, *U.S.A.* **157 B8** 43 1N 88 0W
North Hd., *Australia* **125 F1** 30 14 S 114 59 E
North Henik L., *Canada* **143 A9** 61 45N 97 40W
North Highlands, *U.S.A.* **160 G5** 38 40N 121 23W
North Horr, *Kenya* **118 B4** 3 20N 37 8 E
North I., *India* **95 J1** 10 8N 72 20 E
North I., *Kenya* **118 B4** 4 5N 36 5 E
North I., *N.Z.* **130 E4** 38 0 S 175 0 E
North I., *Seychelles* **121 b** 4 25 S 55 13 E
North Judson, *U.S.A.* **157 C10** 41 13N 86 46W
North Kingsville, *U.S.A.* **150 E4** 41 54N 80 42W
North Kitui ⌂, *Kenya* **118 C4** 0 15 S 38 29 E
North Knife →, *Canada* **143 B10** 58 53N 94 45W
North Koel →, *India* **93 G10** 24 45N 83 50 E
North Korea ■, *Asia* **75 E14** 40 0N 127 0 E
North L., *Australia* **128 B5** 32 30 S 143 5 E
North Lakhimpur, *India* **90 B5** 27 14N 94 7 E
North Lanarkshire □, *U.K.* **22 F5** 55 52N 3 56W
North Las Vegas, *U.S.A.* **161 J11** 36 12N 115 7W
North Liberty, *U.S.A.* **157 C10** 41 32N 86 26W
North Lincolnshire □, *U.K.* **20 D7** 53 36N 0 30W
North Little Rock, *U.S.A.* **155 H8** 34 45N 92 16W
North Loup →, *U.S.A.* **154 E5** 41 17N 98 24W
North Luangwa △, *Zambia* **119 E3** 11 49 S 32 9 E
North Magnetic Pole, *Canada* **6 A2** 88 30N 107 0W
North Manchester, *U.S.A.* **157 D11** 41 0N 85 46W
North Mankato, *U.S.A.* **154 C8** 44 10N 94 0W
North Miami Beach, *U.S.A.* **153 K9** 25 56N 80 10W
North Minch, *U.K.* **22 C3** 58 5N 5 55W
North Moose L., *Canada* **143 C8** 54 11N 100 6W
North Moose L., *Man., Canada* **143 C8** 54 4N 100 12W
North Myrtle Beach, *U.S.A.* **149 J6** 33 48N 78 42W
North Nahanni →, *Canada* **142 A4** 62 15N 123 20W
North Naples, *U.S.A.* **153 J8** 26 12N 81 48W
North New River Canal, *U.S.A.* **153 J9** 26 30N 80 30W
North Olmsted, *U.S.A.* **150 E3** 41 25N 81 56W
North Ossetia □, *Russia* **61 J7** 43 30N 44 30 E
North Pagai, I. = Pagai Utara, Pulau, *Indonesia* **84 C2** 2 35 S 100 0 E
North Palisade, *U.S.A.* **160 H8** 37 6N 118 31W
North Platte, *U.S.A.* **154 E4** 41 8N 100 46W
North Platte →, *U.S.A.* **154 E4** 41 7N 100 42W
North Pole, *Arctic* **6 A** 90 0N 0 0W
North Pole, *U.S.A.* **144 D11** 64 45N 147 21W
North Portal, *Canada* **143 D8** 49 0N 102 33W
North Powder, *U.S.A.* **158 D5** 45 2N 117 55W
North Pt., *Ascension I.* **9 g** 7 53 S 14 23W
North Pt., *Barbados* **165 g** 13 20N 59 37W
North Pt., *Trin. & Tob.* **169 E10** 11 21N 60 31W
North Pt., *U.S.A.* **150 A1** 45 2N 83 16W
North Pt., *Vanuatu* **133 D6** 14 56 S 168 6 E
North Reef I., *India* **95 H11** 13 5N 92 43 E
North Rhine Westphalia = Nordrhein-Westfalen □, *Germany* **30 D3** 51 45N 7 30 E
North River, *Canada* **141 B8** 53 49N 57 6W
North Ronaldsay, *U.K.* **22 B6** 59 22N 2 26W
North Salem, *U.S.A.* **157 E10** 39 52N 86 39W
North Saskatchewan →, *Canada* **143 C7** 53 15N 105 5W
North Sea, *Europe* **19 C7** 56 0N 4 0 E
North Seal →, *Canada* **143 B9** 58 50N 98 7W
North Sentinel I., *India* **95 J11** 11 33N 92 15 E
North Shields, *Australia* **128 C1** 34 38 S 135 52 E
North Solomons □, *Papua N. G.* **132 B8** 4 0 S 155 0 E
North Somerset □, *U.K.* **21 F5** 51 24N 2 45W
North Sporades = Vóriai Sporádhes, *Greece* **48 B5** 39 15N 23 30 E
North Sydney, *Canada* **141 C7** 46 12N 60 15W
North Syracuse, *U.S.A.* **151 C8** 43 8N 76 7W
North Taranaki Bight, *N.Z.* **130 E3** 38 50 S 174 15 E
North Thompson →, *Canada* **142 C4** 50 40N 120 20W
North Tonawanda, *U.S.A.* **150 C6** 43 2N 78 53W
North Troy, *U.S.A.* **151 B12** 45 0N 72 24W
North Twin I., *Canada* **140 B4** 53 20N 80 0W
North Tyne →, *U.K.* **20 B5** 55 0N 2 8W
North Ubian I., *Phil.* **81 H3** 6 9N 120 27 E
North Uist, *U.K.* **22 D1** 57 40N 7 15W
North Union = Shaker Heights, *U.S.A.* **150 E3** 41 29N 81 32W
North Vancouver, *Canada* **142 D4** 49 19N 123 4W
North Vernon, *U.S.A.* **157 F11** 39 0N 85 38W
North Wabasca L., *Canada* **142 B6** 56 0N 113 55W
North Walsham, *U.K.* **20 E9** 52 50N 1 22 E
North Webster, *U.S.A.* **157 C11** 41 25N 85 48W
North West = Severo-Zapadnyy □, *Russia* **66 C4** 65 0N 40 0 E
North-West □, *S. Africa* **116 D4** 27 0 S 25 0 E
North West C., *Australia* **124 D1** 21 45 S 114 9 E
North West Christmas I. Ridge, *Pac. Oc.* **135 G11** 6 30N 165 0W
North West Frontier □, *Pakistan* **91 B3** 34 0N 72 0 E
North West Highlands, *U.K.* **22 D4** 57 33N 4 58W
North West River, *Canada* **141 B7** 53 30N 60 10W
North Western □, *Zambia* **119 E2** 13 30 S 25 30 E
North-Western Provinces and Oudh = Uttar Pradesh □, *India* **93 F9** 27 0N 80 0 E
North Wildwood, *U.S.A.* **148 F8** 39 0N 74 48W
North Yakima = Yakima, *U.S.A.* **158 C3** 46 36N 120 31W
North York Moors, *U.K.* **20 C7** 54 23N 0 53W
North York Moors △, *U.K.* **20 C7** 54 27N 0 51W
North Yorkshire □, *U.K.* **20 C6** 54 15N 1 25W
Northallerton, *U.K.* **20 C6** 54 20N 1 26W
Northam, *Australia* **125 F2** 31 35 S 116 42 E
Northam, *S. Africa* **116 C4** 24 56 S 27 18 E
Northampton, *Australia* **125 E1** 28 27 S 114 33 E
Northampton, *U.K.* **21 E7** 52 15N 0 53W
Northampton, *Mass., U.S.A.* **151 D12** 42 19N 72 38W
Northampton, *Pa., U.S.A.* **151 F9** 40 41N 75 30W
Northamptonshire □, *U.K.* **21 E7** 52 16N 0 55W
Northbridge, *U.S.A.* **151 D13** 42 9N 71 39W
Northcliffe, *Australia* **125 F2** 34 39 S 116 7 E
Northeast C., *U.S.A.* **144 E5** 63 18N 168 42W
Northeast Pacific Basin, *Pac. Oc.* **135 D13** 32 0N 145 0W
Northeast Providence Chan., *W. Indies* **164 A4** 26 0N 76 0W
Northeim, *Germany* **30 D6** 51 42N 10 0 E
Northern = Limpopo □, *S. Africa* **117 C4** 24 5 S 29 0 E
Northern □, *Ghana* **113 D4** 9 30N 1 0W
Northern □, *Malawi* **119 E3** 11 0 S 34 0 E
Northern □, *Papua N. G.* **132 E5** 9 0 S 148 30 E
Northern □, *S. Leone* **112 D2** 9 15N 11 30W
Northern □, *Zambia* **119 E3** 10 30 S 31 0 E
Northern Areas □, *Pakistan* **65 E6** 36 30N 73 0 E
Northern Cape □, *S. Africa* **116 D3** 30 0 S 20 0 E
Northern Circars, *India* **94 F6** 17 30N 82 30 E
Northern Indian L., *Canada* **143 B9** 57 20N 97 20W
Northern Ireland □, *U.K.* **23 B5** 54 45N 7 0W
Northern Lau Group, *Fiji* **133 A3** 17 30 S 178 59W
Northern Light L., *Canada* **140 C1** 48 15N 90 39W
Northern Marianas ☑, *Pac. Oc.* **134 F6** 17 0N 145 0 E
Northern Mid-Atlantic Ridge, *Atl. Oc.* **8 C8** 35 0N 35 0W
Northern Province □, *S. Africa* **117 C4** 24 0 S 29 0 E
Northern Range, *Trin. & Tob.* **169 F9** 10 46N 61 15W
Northern Rhodesia = Zambia ■, *Africa* **119 F2** 15 0 S 28 0 E
Northern Samar □, *Phil.* **80 E5** 12 30N 124 40 E
Northern Territory □, *Australia* **124 D5** 20 0 S 133 0 E
Northfield, *Minn., U.S.A.* **154 C8** 44 27N 93 9W
Northfield, *Vt., U.S.A.* **151 B12** 44 9N 72 40W
Northland □, *N.Z.* **130 B2** 35 30 S 173 30 E
Northome, *U.S.A.* **154 B7** 47 52N 94 17W
Northport, *Ala., U.S.A.* **149 J2** 33 14N 87 35W
Northport, *Wash., U.S.A.* **158 B5** 48 55N 117 48W
Northumberland □, *U.K.* **20 B6** 55 12N 2 0W
Northumberland, C., *Australia* **128 E4** 38 5 S 140 40 E
Northumberland Is., *Australia* **126 C4** 21 30 S 149 50 E
Northumberland Str., *Canada* **141 C7** 46 20N 64 0W
Northville, *U.S.A.* **151 C10** 43 13N 74 11W
Northway, *U.S.A.* **144 E12** 62 58N 141 56W
Northwest Pacific Basin, *Pac. Oc.* **134 D8** 33 0N 165 0 E
Northwest Providence Channel, *W. Indies* **164 A4** 26 0N 78 0W
Northwest Pt., *Bahamas* **9 b** 25 4N 77 31W
Northwest Territories □, *Canada* **138 B9** 63 0N 118 0W
Northwich, *U.K.* **20 D5** 53 15N 2 31W
Northwood, *Iowa, U.S.A.* **154 D8** 43 27N 93 13W
Northwood, *N. Dak., U.S.A.* **154 B6** 47 44N 97 34W
Norton, *U.S.A.* **154 F5** 39 50N 99 53W
Norton, *Zimbabwe* **119 F3** 17 52 S 30 40 E
Norton B., *U.S.A.* **144 D7** 64 45N 161 15W
Norton Sd., *U.S.A.* **144 E7** 63 50N 164 0W
Norton Shores, *U.S.A.* **157 A10** 43 8N 86 15W
Nortorf, *Germany* **30 A5** 54 10N 9 50 E
Norwalk, *Calif., U.S.A.* **161 M8** 33 54N 118 5W
Norwalk, *Conn., U.S.A.* **151 E11** 41 7N 73 22W
Norwalk, *Iowa, U.S.A.* **156 C3** 41 29N 93 41W
Norwalk, *Ohio, U.S.A.* **150 E2** 41 15N 82 37W
Norway, *Maine, U.S.A.* **149 C10** 44 13N 70 32W
Norway, *Mich., U.S.A.* **148 C2** 45 47N 87 55W
Norway ■, *Europe* **14 E14** 63 0N 11 0 E
Norway House, *Canada* **143 C9** 53 59N 97 50W
Norwegian Sea, *Atl. Oc.* **6 C8** 66 0N 1 0 E
Norwich, *Canada* **150 D4** 42 59N 80 36W
Norwich, *U.K.* **21 E9** 52 38N 1 18 E
Norwich, *Conn., U.S.A.* **151 E12** 41 31N 72 5W
Norwich, *N.Y., U.S.A.* **151 D9** 42 32N 75 32W
Norwood, *Canada* **150 B7** 44 23N 77 59W
Norwood, *Mass., U.S.A.* **151 B10** 44 45N 75 0W
Norwood, *Ohio, U.S.A.* **157 E12** 39 10N 84 27W
Noshiro, *Japan* **70 D10** 40 12N 140 0 E
Nosivka, *Ukraine* **59 G6** 50 50N 31 37 E
Nosovka = Nosivka, *Ukraine* **59 G6** 50 50N 31 37 E
Noşratābād, *Iran* **97 D8** 29 55N 60 0 E

O

Oasis, Nev., U.S.A. 160 H9 37 29N 117 55W
Oates Land, Antarctica 7 C11 69 0S 160 0E
Oatlands, Australia 127 G4 42 17S 147 21E
Oatman, U.S.A. 161 K12 35 1N 114 19W
Oaxaca, Mexico 163 D5 17 2N 96 40W
Oaxaca □, Mexico 163 D5 17 0N 97 0W
Ob →, Russia 66 C7 66 45N 69 30E
Oba, Canada 140 C3 49 4N 84 7W
Obala, Cameroon 113 E7 4 9N 11 32E
Obama, Fukui, Japan 73 B7 35 30N 135 45E
Obama, Nagasaki, Japan 72 E2 32 43N 130 13E
Oban, Nigeria 113 D6 5 17N 8 33E
Oban, U.K. 22 E3 56 25N 5 29W
Obbia, Somali Rep. 120 C3 5 25N 48 30E
Obdorsk = Salekhard, Russia 66 C7 66 30N 66 35E
Ober-Aargau, Switz. 32 B5 47 10N 7 45E
Ober-engadin, Switz. 33 C9 46 35N 9 55E
Obera, Argentina 175 B4 27 21S 55 2W
Oberalppass, Switz. 33 C7 46 39N 8 35E
Oberalpstock, Switz. 33 C7 46 45N 8 47E
Oberammergau, Germany 31 H7 47 36N 11 4E
Oberasbach, Germany 31 F6 49 25N 10 57E
Oberbayern □, Germany 31 G7 48 5N 11 50E
Oberburg = Gornji Grad, Slovenia 45 B11 46 20N 14 52E
Oberdiessbach, Switz. 32 C5 46 51N 7 40E
Oberdonau = Oberösterreich □, Austria 34 C7 48 10N 14 0E
Oberdrauburg, Austria 34 E5 46 44N 12 58E
Obere Donau ⌓, Germany 31 G5 48 5N 9 0E
Oberentfelden, Switz. 32 B6 47 21N 8 2E
Oberer Bayerischer Wald ⌓, Germany 31 F8 49 15N 12 40E
Oberfranken □, Germany 31 E7 50 10N 11 20E
Oberglogau = Głogówek, Poland 55 H4 50 21N 17 53E
Oberhausen, Germany 30 D2 51 28N 6 51E
Oberkirch, Germany 31 G4 48 31N 8 4E
Oberlaibach = Vrhnika, Slovenia 45 C11 45 58N 14 15E
Oberland, Switz. 32 C5 46 35N 7 38E
Oberlausitz, Germany 30 D10 51 16N 14 18E
Oberlin, Kans., U.S.A. 154 F4 39 49N 100 32W
Oberlin, La., U.S.A. 155 K8 30 37N 92 46W
Oberlin, Ohio, U.S.A. 150 E2 41 18N 82 13W
Obernai, France 27 D14 48 28N 7 30E
Oberndorf, Germany 31 G4 48 17N 8 34E
Obernigk = Oborniki Śląskie, Poland 55 G3 51 17N 16 53E
Oberon, Australia 129 B8 33 45S 149 52E
Oberösterreich □, Austria 34 C7 48 10N 14 0E
Oberpfalz □, Germany 31 F8 49 20N 12 10E
Oberpfälzer Wald, Germany 31 F8 49 30N 12 30E
Oberpfälzer Wald ⌓, Germany 31 F8 49 40N 12 20E
Oberriet, Switz. 33 B9 47 19N 9 34E
Obersiggenthal, Switz. 33 B6 47 29N 8 18E
Oberstdorf, Germany 31 H6 47 24N 10 15E
Oberting, Gabon 114 C1 0 22S 9 46E
Obertyn, Ukraine 53 B10 48 42N 25 10E
Oberursel, Germany 31 E4 50 11N 8 35E
Oberwart, Austria 35 D9 47 17N 16 12E
Oberwil, Switz. 32 A5 47 32N 7 33E
Obi, Indonesia 82 B3 1 23S 127 45E
Obiaruku, Nigeria 113 D6 5 51N 6 9E
Óbidos, Brazil 169 D6 1 50S 55 30W
Óbidos, Portugal 43 F1 39 19N 9 10W
Obigarm, Tajikistan 65 D4 38 43N 69 42E
Obihiro, Japan 70 C11 42 56N 143 12E
Obīkiik, Tajikistan 65 D4 38 9N 68 39E
Obilatu, Indonesia 82 B3 1 25S 127 20E
Obilnoye, Russia 61 G7 47 32N 44 30E
Obing, Germany 31 G8 48 0N 12 24E
Objat, France 28 C5 45 16N 1 24E
Oblong, U.S.A. 157 F9 39 0N 87 55W
Obluchye, Russia 67 E14 49 1N 131 4E
Obninsk, Russia 58 E9 55 8N 36 37E
Obo, C.A.R. 118 A2 5 20N 26 32E
Oboa, Mt., Uganda 118 B3 1 45N 34 45E
Obock, Djibouti 107 E5 12 0N 43 20E
Obodivka, Ukraine 53 B14 48 24N 29 15E
Oborniki, Poland 55 F3 52 39N 16 50E
Oborniki Śląskie, Poland 55 G3 51 17N 16 53E
Obouya, Congo 114 C3 0 56S 15 43E
Oboyan, Russia 59 G9 51 15N 36 21E
Obozerskaya = Obozerskiy, Russia 56 B7 63 34N 40 21E
Obozerskiy, Russia 56 B7 63 34N 40 21E
Obrenovac, Serbia & M. 50 B4 44 40N 20 11E
O'Brien, U.S.A. 152 E7 30 2N 82 57W
Obrovac, Croatia 45 D12 44 11N 15 41E
Obruk, Turkey 100 C5 38 7N 33 12E
Obrzycko, Poland 55 F3 52 42N 16 32E
Observatory Inlet, Canada 142 B3 55 10N 129 54W
Obshchi Syrt, Russia 64 E4 52 0N 53 0E
Obskaya Guba, Russia 66 C8 69 0N 73 0E
Obuasi, Ghana 113 D4 6 17N 1 40W
Obubra, Nigeria 113 D6 6 8N 8 20E
Obudu, Nigeria 113 D6 6 38N 9 5E
Obura, Papua N. G. 132 D3 6 33S 145 58E
Obwalden □, Switz. 32 C6 46 55N 8 15E
Obzor, Bulgaria 51 D11 42 50N 27 52E
Ocala, U.S.A. 153 F7 29 11N 82 8W
Ocamo →, Venezuela 169 C4 2 48N 65 14W
Ocampo, Chihuahua, Mexico 162 B3 28 9N 108 24W
Ocampo, Tamaulipas, Mexico 163 C5 22 50N 99 20W
Ocaña, Colombia 168 B3 8 15N 73 20W
Ocaña, Spain 42 F7 39 55N 3 30W
Ocanomowoc, U.S.A. 154 D10 43 7N 88 30W
Occidental, Cordillera, Colombia 168 C3 5 0N 76 0W
Occidental, Cordillera, Peru 172 C3 14 0S 74 0W
Occidental, Grand Erg, Algeria 111 B5 30 20N 1 0E
Ocean City, Md., U.S.A. 148 F8 38 20N 75 5W
Ocean City, N.J., U.S.A. 148 F8 39 17N 74 35W
Ocean City, Wash., U.S.A. 160 C2 47 4N 124 10W
Ocean Falls, Canada 142 C3 52 18N 127 48W
Ocean I. = Banaba, Kiribati 134 H8 0 45S 169 50E
Ocean Park, U.S.A. 160 D2 46 30N 124 3W
Oceano, U.S.A. 161 K6 35 6N 120 37W
Oceanport, U.S.A. 151 F10 40 19N 74 3W
Oceanside, U.S.A. 161 M9 33 12N 117 23W
Ochagavía, Spain 40 C3 42 55N 1 5W
Ochakiv, Ukraine 59 J6 46 37N 31 33E
Ochamchira, Georgia 61 J5 42 46N 41 32E
Ocher, Russia 64 C5 57 53N 54 42E
Ochiai, Japan 72 B5 35 1N 133 45E
Ochil Hills, U.K. 22 E5 56 14N 3 40W
Ochlocknee, U.S.A. 152 E5 30 58N 84 3W
Ochlockonee →, U.S.A. 152 F5 29 59N 84 26W
Ocho Rios, Jamaica 164 a 18 24N 77 6W
Ochopee, U.S.A. 153 K8 25 54N 81 18W
Ochsenfurt, Germany 31 F6 49 40N 10 4E
Ochsenhausen, Germany 31 G5 48 4N 9 57E
Ocilla, U.S.A. 152 D6 31 36N 83 15W
Ockelbo, Sweden 16 D10 60 54N 16 45E
Ocmulgee ⌓, U.S.A. 152 C6 32 49N 83 37W
Ocmulgee →, U.S.A. 152 D7 31 58N 82 33W
Ocna Mureş, Romania 53 D8 46 23N 23 55E
Ocna Sibiului, Romania 53 E9 45 52N 24 2E
Ocnele Mari, Romania 53 E9 45 8N 24 18E
Ocniţa, Moldova 53 B12 48 25N 27 30E
Ocoee, U.S.A. 153 G8 28 34N 81 33W
Ocoña, Peru 172 D3 16 26S 73 8W
Ocoña →, Peru 172 D3 16 28S 73 8W
Oconee →, U.S.A. 152 D7 31 58N 82 33W
Oconee, L., U.S.A. 152 B6 33 28N 83 15W
Oconomowoc, U.S.A. 157 A8 43 7N 88 30W
Oconto, U.S.A. 148 C2 44 53N 87 52W
Oconto Falls, U.S.A. 148 C1 44 52N 88 9W
Ocosingo, Mexico 163 D6 17 10N 92 15W
Ocotal, Nic. 164 D2 13 41N 86 31W
Ocotlán, Mexico 162 C4 20 21N 102 42W
Ocotlán de Morelos, Mexico 163 D5 16 48N 96 40W
Ocreza →, Portugal 43 F3 39 32N 7 50W
Ócsa, Hungary 52 C4 47 17N 19 15E
Octeville, France 26 C5 49 38N 1 40W
Ocumare del Tuy, Venezuela 168 A4 10 7N 66 46W
Ocuri, Bolivia 173 D4 18 45S 65 50W
Oda, Ghana 113 D4 5 50N 0 51W
Ōda, Japan 72 B4 35 11N 132 30E
Oda, J., Sudan 106 C4 20 21N 36 39E
Ódáðahraun, Iceland 11 B9 65 5N 17 0W
Ödåkra, Sweden 17 H6 56 7N 12 45E
Odammun →, Indonesia 83 C5 6 50S 138 45E
Odate, Japan 70 D10 40 16N 140 34E
Odawara, Japan 73 B11 35 20N 139 6E
Odda, Norway 18 D3 60 3N 6 35E
Odder, Denmark 17 J4 55 58N 10 10E
Oddur, Somali Rep. 120 D2 4 11N 43 52E
Odei →, Canada 143 B9 56 6N 96 54W
Odell, U.S.A. 157 C8 41 0N 88 31W
Odemira, Portugal 43 H2 37 35N 8 40W
Ödemiş, Turkey 49 C9 38 15N 28 0E
Ödenburg = Sopron, Hungary 52 C1 47 45N 16 32E
Odendaalsrus, S. Africa 116 D4 27 48S 26 45E
Odensbacken, Sweden 16 E9 59 10N 15 32E
Odense, Denmark 17 J4 55 22N 10 23E
Odenwald = Neckartal-Odenwald ⌓, Germany 31 F5 49 30N 9 5E
Odenwald, Germany 31 F5 49 35N 9 0E
Oder →, Europe 30 B10 53 33N 14 38E
Oder-Havel Kanal, Germany 30 C10 52 52N 14 2E
Oderzo, Italy 45 C9 45 47N 12 29E
Odesa, Ukraine 59 J6 46 30N 30 45E
Ödeshög, Sweden 17 F8 58 14N 14 39E
Odessa = Odesa, Ukraine 59 J6 46 30N 30 45E
Odessa, Canada 151 B8 44 17N 76 43W
Odessa, Mo., U.S.A. 156 F3 39 0N 93 57W
Odessa, Tex., U.S.A. 155 K3 31 52N 102 23W
Odessa, Wash., U.S.A. 158 C4 47 20N 118 41W
Odiakwe, Botswana 116 C4 20 12S 25 17E
Odiel →, Spain 43 H4 37 10N 6 55W
Odienné, Ivory C. 112 D3 9 30N 7 34W
Odimba, Gabon 114 C2 2 2S 9 33E
Odintsovo, Russia 58 E9 55 39N 37 15E
Odiongan, Phil. 80 E3 12 24N 121 59E
Odobeşti, Romania 53 E12 45 43N 27 4E
Odolanów, Poland 55 G4 51 34N 17 40E
O'Donnell, U.S.A. 155 J4 32 58N 101 50W
Odorheiu Secuiesc, Romania 53 D10 46 21N 25 21E
Odoyevo, Russia 58 F9 53 56N 36 42E
Odra = Oder →, Europe 30 B10 53 33N 14 38E
Odra →, Spain 42 C6 42 14N 4 17W
Odum, U.S.A. 152 D7 31 40N 82 2W
Odweina, Somali Rep. 120 C3 9 25N 45 4E
Odžaci, Serbia & M. 52 E4 45 30N 19 17E
Odžak, Bos.-H. 52 E3 45 3N 18 18E
Odzala, Congo 114 B2 0 37N 14 37E
Odzala △, Congo 114 B2 0 55N 14 55E
Odzi, Zimbabwe 117 B5 19 0S 32 20E
Odzi →, Zimbabwe 117 B5 19 45S 32 23E
Oebisfelde, Germany 30 C6 52 27N 10 57E
Oeiras = Araticu, Brazil 170 B2 1 58S 49 51W
Oeiras, Brazil 170 C3 7 0S 42 8W
Oeiras, Portugal 43 G1 38 41N 9 18W
Oeiras do Para, Brazil 169 D8 1 58S 49 51W
Oelrichs, U.S.A. 154 D3 43 11N 103 14W
Oels in Schlesien = Oleśnica, Poland 55 G4 51 13N 17 22E
Oelsnitz, Germany 31 E8 50 24N 12 10E
Oelwein, U.S.A. 156 B5 42 41N 91 55W
Oeno I., Pac. Oc. 135 K14 24 0S 131 0W
Oenpelli, Australia 124 B5 12 20S 133 4E
Oetz, Austria 34 D3 47 13N 10 53E
Of, Turkey 101 B9 40 59N 40 23E
O'Fallon, U.S.A. 156 F6 38 49N 90 42W
Ofanto →, Italy 47 A9 41 22N 16 13E
Offa, Nigeria 113 D5 8 13N 4 42E
Offaly □, Ireland 23 C4 53 15N 7 30W
Offenbach, Germany 31 E4 50 6N 8 44E
Offenburg, Germany 31 G3 48 28N 7 56E
Officer, The →, Australia 125 E5 27 46S 132 30E
Offida, Italy 45 F10 42 56N 13 41E
Offoué →, Gabon 114 C2 0 4S 11 44E
Ofidhousa, Greece 49 E8 36 33N 26 8E
Öflingen, Germany 32 A5 47 36N 7 55E
Ofolanga, Tonga 133 P14 19 38S 173 35W
Ofotfjorden, Norway 14 B17 68 27N 17 0E
Ofte, Norway 18 E5 59 30N 8 12E
Ofu, Amer. Samoa 133 X25 14 11S 169 41W
Ōfunato, Japan 70 E10 39 4N 141 43E
Oga, Japan 70 E9 39 55N 139 50E
Oga-Hantō, Japan 70 E9 39 58N 139 47E
Ogaden, Ethiopia 120 C3 7 30N 45 30E
Ōgaki, Japan 73 B8 35 21N 136 37E
Ogallala, U.S.A. 154 E4 41 8N 101 43W
Ogan →, Indonesia 84 C2 3 1S 104 44E
Ogasawara Gunto, Pac. Oc. 62 G18 27 0N 142 0E
Ogbomosho, Nigeria 113 D5 8 1N 4 11E
Ogden, Iowa, U.S.A. 156 B2 42 2N 94 2W
Ogden, Utah, U.S.A. 158 F7 41 13N 111 58W
Ogdensburg, U.S.A. 151 B9 44 42N 75 30W
Ogea Driki, Fiji 133 B3 19 12S 178 27W
Ogea Levu, Fiji 133 B3 19 8S 178 24W
Ogeechee →, U.S.A. 152 D8 31 50N 81 3W
Ogilby, U.S.A. 161 N12 32 49N 114 50W
Oglat Beraber, Algeria 110 B4 30 15N 3 34W
Oglats de Khenachiche, Mali 110 D4 21 51N 3 58W
Oglesby, U.S.A. 156 C7 41 18N 89 4W
Oglethorpe, U.S.A. 152 C5 32 18N 84 4W
Oglio →, Italy 44 C7 45 2N 10 39E
Óglio Nord ⌓, Italy 44 C6 45 22N 9 54E
Óglio Sud ⌓, Italy 44 C7 45 7N 10 24E
Ogmore, Australia 126 C4 22 37S 149 35E
Ognon →, France 27 E12 47 16N 5 28E
Ogoamas, Indonesia 82 A2 0 50N 120 5E
Ogoja, Nigeria 113 D6 6 38N 8 39E
Ogoki, Canada 140 B2 51 38N 85 58W
Ogoki →, Canada 140 B2 51 38N 85 57W
Ogoki L., Canada 140 B2 50 50N 87 10W
Ogoki Res., Canada 140 B2 50 45N 88 15W
Ogooué →, Gabon 114 C1 1 0S 9 0E
Ogōri, Japan 72 C3 34 6N 131 24E
Ogosta →, Bulgaria 50 C7 43 48N 23 55E
Ogowe = Ogooué →, Gabon 114 C1 1 0S 9 0E
Ogr = Sharafa, Sudan 107 E2 11 59N 27 7E
Ograźden, Macedonia 50 E6 41 30N 22 50E
Ogre, Latvia 15 H21 56 49N 24 36E
Ogrein, Sudan 106 D3 17 55N 34 50E
Ogulin, Croatia 45 C12 45 16N 15 16E
Ogun □, Nigeria 113 D5 7 0N 3 0E
Oguni, Japan 72 D3 33 11N 131 8E
Ögur, Iceland 11 A4 66 2N 22 44W
Ogurchinskiy, Ostrov, Turkmenistan 97 B7 38 55N 53 2E
Oguta, Nigeria 113 D6 5 44N 6 44E
Ogwashi-Uku, Nigeria 113 D6 6 15N 6 30E
Ogwe, Nigeria 113 E6 5 0N 7 14E
Ohai, N.Z. 131 F3 45 55S 168 0E
Ohakune, N.Z. 130 F4 39 24S 175 24E
Ohanet, Algeria 111 C6 28 44N 8 46E
Ōhara, Japan 73 B12 35 15N 140 23E
O'Hare International, Chicago ✕ (ORD), U.S.A. 157 C9 41 59N 87 54W
Ohata, Japan 70 D10 41 24N 141 10E
Ohatchee, U.S.A. 152 B4 33 47N 86 0W
Ohau, L., N.Z. 131 E4 44 15S 169 53E
Ohaupo, N.Z. 130 D4 37 56S 175 20E
O'Higgins, C., Chile 172 b 27 5S 109 15W
Ohio □, U.S.A. 150 F2 40 15N 82 45W
Ohio →, U.S.A. 157 G8 36 59N 89 8W
Ohio City, U.S.A. 157 D12 40 46N 84 37W
Ohiwa Harbour, N.Z. 130 D6 37 59S 177 10E
Ohlau = Oława, Poland 55 H4 50 57N 17 20E
Ohře →, Czech Rep. 34 A7 50 30N 14 10E
Ohre →, Germany 30 C7 52 18N 11 46E
Ohrid, Macedonia 50 E4 41 8N 20 52E
Ohridsko Jezero, Macedonia 50 E4 41 8N 20 52E
Ohrigstad, S. Africa 117 C5 24 39S 30 36E
Öhringen, Germany 31 F5 49 12N 9 31E
Ohura, N.Z. 130 E3 38 51S 174 59E
Oi Qu, China 76 C2 28 37N 98 16E
Oiapoque, Brazil 169 C7 3 50N 51 50W
Oiapoque →, S. Amer. 169 C7 4 8N 51 40W
Oikou, China 75 E9 38 35N 117 42E
Oil City, U.S.A. 150 E5 41 26N 79 42W
Oil Springs, Canada 150 D2 42 47N 82 7W
Oildale, U.S.A. 161 K7 35 25N 119 1W
Oinousa, Greece 49 C8 38 33N 26 14E
Oise □, France 27 C9 49 28N 2 30E
Oise →, France 27 C9 49 0N 2 4E
Oiseaux du Djoudj △, Senegal 112 B1 16 24N 16 14W
Oistins, Barbados 165 g 13 4N 59 33W
Oistins B., Barbados 165 g 13 4N 59 33W
Ōita, Japan 72 D3 33 14N 131 36E
Ōita □, Japan 72 D3 33 15N 131 30E
Oiticica, Brazil 170 C3 5 3S 41 5W
Ojacaliente, Mexico 162 C4 22 34N 102 15W
Ojai, U.S.A. 161 L7 34 27N 119 15W
Ojcowski △, Poland 55 H6 50 15N 19 50E
Ojhar, India 94 D1 20 6N 73 56E
Ojinaga, Mexico 162 B4 29 34N 104 25W
Ojiya, Japan 71 F9 37 18N 138 48E
Ojo de Liebre ⌓, Mexico 162 B2 27 50N 114 0W
Ojos del Salado, Cerro, Argentina 174 B2 27 0S 68 40W
Oka →, Russia 60 B7 56 20N 43 59E
Okaba, Indonesia 83 C5 8 6S 139 42E
Okahandja, Namibia 116 C2 22 0S 16 59E
Okahukura, N.Z. 130 E4 38 48S 175 14E
Okaihau, N.Z. 130 B2 35 19S 173 47E
Okalataka, Congo 114 C2 0 18S 14 54E
Okanagan L., Canada 142 D5 50 0N 119 30W
Okandja, Gabon 114 C2 0 35S 13 45E
Okano →, Gabon 114 C2 0 5S 10 57E
Okanogan, U.S.A. 158 B4 48 22N 119 35W
Okanogan →, U.S.A. 158 B4 48 6N 119 44W
Okány, Hungary 52 D6 46 52N 21 21E
Okapa, Papua N. G. 132 D3 6 38S 145 39E
Okapi △, Dem. Rep. of the Congo 118 B2 2 30N 27 20E
Okaputa, Namibia 116 C2 20 5S 17 0E
Okara, Pakistan 91 C4 30 50N 73 31E
Okarito, N.Z. 131 D5 43 15S 170 9E
Okato, N.Z. 130 F2 39 12S 173 53E
Okaukuejo, Namibia 116 B2 19 10S 16 0E
Okavango Delta, Botswana 116 B3 18 45S 22 45E
Okavango Swamp = Okavango Delta, Botswana 116 B3 18 45S 22 45E
Ōkawa, Japan 72 D2 33 9N 130 21E
Okawville, U.S.A. 156 F7 38 26N 89 33W
Okaya, Japan 73 A10 36 5N 138 10E
Okayama, Japan 72 C5 34 40N 133 54E
Okayama □, Japan 72 C5 35 0N 133 50E
Okazaki, Japan 73 C9 34 57N 137 10E
Oke-Iho, Nigeria 113 D5 8 1N 3 18E
Okęcie, Warszawa ✕ (WAW), Poland 55 F7 52 9N 20 59E
Okeechobee, U.S.A. 153 H9 27 15N 80 50W
Okeechobee, L., U.S.A. 153 J9 27 0N 80 50W
Okefenokee ⌓, U.S.A. 152 E7 30 44N 82 7W
Okefenokee Swamp, U.S.A. 152 E7 30 40N 82 20W
Okehampton, U.K. 21 G4 50 44N 4 0W
Okemos, U.S.A. 157 B12 42 43N 84 26W
Okene, Nigeria 113 D6 7 32N 6 11E
Oker →, Germany 30 C6 52 32N 10 22E
Okha, India 92 H3 22 27N 69 4E
Okha, Russia 67 D15 53 40N 143 0E
Ókhi Óros, Greece 48 C6 38 5N 24 25E
Okhotsk, Russia 67 D15 59 20N 143 10E
Okhotsk, Sea of, Asia 67 D15 55 0N 145 0E
Okhotskiy Perevoz, Russia 67 C14 61 52N 135 35E
Okhtyrka, Ukraine 59 G8 50 25N 35 0E
Oki-no-Shima, Japan 72 E4 32 44N 132 33E
Oki-Shotō, Japan 72 A5 36 5N 133 15E
Okiep, S. Africa 116 D2 29 39S 17 53E
Okigwi, Nigeria 113 D6 5 52N 7 20E
Okija, Nigeria 113 D6 5 54N 6 55E
Okinawa □, Japan 71 L4 26 40N 128 0E
Okinawa-Guntō, Japan 71 L4 26 40N 128 0E
Okinawa-Jima, Japan 71 L4 26 32N 128 0E
Okino-erabu-Shima, Japan 71 L4 27 21N 128 33E
Okitipupa, Nigeria 113 D5 6 31N 4 50E
Oklahoma □, U.S.A. 155 H6 35 20N 97 30W
Oklahoma City, U.S.A. 155 H6 35 30N 97 30W
Oklawaha →, U.S.A. 153 F8 29 28N 81 41W
Okmulgee, U.S.A. 155 H7 35 37N 95 58W
Oknitsa = Ocniţa, Moldova 53 B12 48 25N 27 30E
Oko, W. →, Sudan 106 C4 21 15N 35 56E
Okolo, Uganda 118 B3 2 37N 31 8E
Okolona, Ky., U.S.A. 157 F11 38 8N 85 41W
Okolona, Miss., U.S.A. 155 J10 34 0N 88 45W
Okombahe, Namibia 116 C2 21 23S 15 22E
Okonek, Poland 54 E3 53 32N 16 51E
Okotoks, Canada 142 C6 50 43N 113 58W
Okoyo, Congo 114 C3 1 28S 15 0E
Okrika, Nigeria 113 E6 4 40N 7 10E
Oksapmin, Papua N. G. 132 C2 5 17S 142 15E
Øksendal, Norway 18 B5 62 42N 8 27E
Oksibil, Indonesia 83 B6 4 59S 140 35E
Øksna, Norway 18 D8 60 58N 11 27E
Oksovskiy, Russia 56 B6 62 33N 39 57E
Oktabrsk = Oktyabrsk, Kazakhstan 57 E10 49 28N 57 25E
Oktwin, Burma 90 F6 18 49N 96 26E
Oktyabr, Kazakhstan 65 B8 43 41N 77 12E
Oktyabrsk, Kazakhstan 57 E10 49 28N 57 25E
Oktyabrsk, Russia 60 D9 53 11N 48 40E
Oktyabrskiy = Aktsyabrski, Belarus 59 F5 52 38N 28 53E
Oktyabrskiy, Bashkortostan, Russia 64 D4 54 28N 53 28E
Oktyabrskiy, Perm, Russia 64 C6 56 31N 57 12E
Oktyabrskiy, Rostov, Russia 61 G5 47 30N 40 4E
Oktyabrskoy Revolyutsii, Ostrov, Russia 67 B10 79 30N 97 0E
Oktyabrskoye = Zhovtneve, Ukraine 59 J7 46 54N 32 3E
Oktyabrskoye, Russia 64 D9 54 26N 62 44E
Ōkuchi, Japan 72 E2 32 4N 130 37E
Okulovka, Russia 58 C7 58 25N 33 19E
Okuru, N.Z. 131 D3 43 55S 168 55E
Okushiri-Tō, Japan 70 C9 42 15N 139 30E
Okuta, Nigeria 113 D5 9 14N 3 12E
Okwa →, Botswana 116 C3 22 30S 23 0E
Ola, U.S.A. 155 H8 35 2N 93 13W
Ólafsfjörður, Iceland 11 A8 66 4N 18 39W
Ólafsvík, Iceland 11 C3 64 53N 23 43W
Olaine, Latvia 54 B10 56 48N 23 59E
Olancha, U.S.A. 161 J8 36 17N 118 1W
Olancha Pk., U.S.A. 161 J8 36 15N 118 7W
Olanchito, Honduras 164 C2 15 30N 86 30W
Öland, Sweden 17 H10 56 45N 16 38E
Ölands norra udde, Sweden 17 G11 57 22N 17 5E
Ölands södra udde, Sweden 17 H10 56 12N 16 23E
Olanta, U.S.A. 152 B10 33 56N 79 56W
Olar, U.S.A. 152 B8 33 11N 81 11W
Olargues, France 28 E6 43 34N 2 53E
Olary, Australia 128 B4 32 18S 140 19E
Olascoaga, Argentina 174 D3 35 15S 60 39W
Olathe, U.S.A. 154 F7 38 53N 94 49W
Olavarría, Argentina 174 D3 36 55S 60 20W
Oława, Poland 55 H4 50 57N 17 20E
Olbernhau, Germany 30 E9 50 40N 13 19E
Ólbia, Italy 46 B2 40 55N 9 31E
Ólbia, G. di, Italy 46 B2 40 55N 9 39E
Olching, Germany 31 G7 48 12N 11 21E
Olcott, U.S.A. 150 C6 43 20N 78 42W
Old Bahama Chan. = Bahama, Canal Viejo de, W. Indies 164 B4 22 10N 77 30W
Old Baldy Pk. = San Antonio, Mt., U.S.A. 161 L9 34 17N 117 38W
Old Bar, Australia 129 A10 31 58S 152 35E
Old Castile = Castilla y Leon □, Spain 42 D6 42 0N 5 0W
Old Crow, Canada 138 B6 67 30N 139 55W
Old Dale, U.S.A. 161 L11 34 8N 115 47W
Old Forge, N.Y., U.S.A. 151 C10 43 43N 74 58W
Old Forge, Pa., U.S.A. 151 E9 41 22N 75 45W
Old Fort B., Bahamas 9 b 25 3N 77 32W
Old Harbor, U.S.A. 144 H9 57 12N 153 18W
Old Perlican, Canada 141 C9 48 5N 53 1W
Old Shinyanga, Tanzania 118 C3 3 33S 33 27E
Old Speck Mt., U.S.A. 151 B14 44 34N 70 57W
Old Town, Fla., U.S.A. 153 F7 29 36N 82 59W
Old Town, Maine, U.S.A. 149 C11 44 56N 68 39W
Old Washington, U.S.A. 150 F3 40 2N 81 27W
Old Wives L., Canada 143 C7 50 5N 106 0W
Oldbury, U.K. 21 F5 51 38N 2 33W
Oldcastle, Ireland 23 C4 53 46N 7 10W
Oldeani, Tanzania 118 C4 3 22S 35 35E
Olden, Norway 18 C3 61 49N 6 49E
Oldenburg, Niedersachsen, Germany 30 B4 53 9N 8 13E
Oldenburg, Schleswig-Holstein, Germany 30 A6 54 17N 10 52E
Oldenzaal, Neths. 24 B6 52 19N 6 53E
Oldham, U.K. 20 D5 53 33N 2 7W
Oldman →, Canada 142 D6 49 57N 111 42W
Oldmeldrum, U.K. 22 D6 57 20N 2 19W
Olds, Canada 142 C6 51 50N 114 10W
Oldsmar, U.S.A. 153 G7 28 2N 82 40W
Olduvai Gorge, Tanzania 118 C4 2 57S 35 23E
Oldziyt, Mongolia 74 B5 44 40N 109 1E
Ole Rømer Land, Greenland 10 C8 74 10N 24 30W
Olean, U.S.A. 150 D6 42 5N 78 26W
Olecko, Poland 54 D9 54 2N 22 31E
Oléggio, Italy 44 C5 45 36N 8 38E
Oleiros, Portugal 42 F3 39 56N 7 56W
Oleiros, Spain 42 B2 43 20N 8 19W
Olekma →, Russia 67 C13 60 22N 120 42E
Olekminsk, Russia 67 C13 60 25N 120 30E
Oleksandriya, Kirovohrad, Ukraine 59 H7 48 42N 33 3E
Oleksandriya, Rivne, Ukraine 59 G4 50 37N 26 19E
Oleksandrovka, Ukraine 59 H7 48 55N 32 20E
Olema, U.S.A. 160 G4 38 3N 122 47W
Ølen, Norway 18 E2 59 36N 5 48E
Olenegorsk, Russia 56 A5 68 9N 33 18E
Olenek, Russia 67 C12 68 28N 112 18E
Olenek →, Russia 67 B13 73 0N 120 10E
Olenino, Russia 58 D7 56 15N 33 30E
Olenya = Olenegorsk, Russia 56 A5 68 9N 33 18E
Oléron, Î. d', France 28 C2 45 55N 1 15W
Olesk, Ukraine 55 G11 51 6N 24 11E
Oleśnica, Poland 55 G4 51 13N 17 22E
Olesno, Poland 55 H5 50 51N 18 26E
Olevsk, Ukraine 59 G4 51 12N 27 39E
Olga, Russia 67 E14 43 50N 135 14E
Olga, L., Canada 140 C4 49 47N 77 15W
Olga, Mt., Australia 125 E5 25 20S 130 50E
Ölgiy, Mongolia 68 B3 48 56N 89 57E
Ølgod, Denmark 17 J2 55 49N 8 36E
Olhão, Portugal 43 H3 37 3N 7 48W
Olhopil, Ukraine 53 B14 48 12N 29 30E
Olhovatka, Russia 54 D9 54 30N 22 18E
Olib, Croatia 45 D11 44 23N 14 44E
Oliena, Italy 46 B2 40 16N 9 24E
Oliete, Spain 40 D4 41 1N 0 41W
Olifants = Elefantes →, Africa 117 C5 24 10S 32 40E
Olifants →, Namibia 116 C2 25 30S 19 30E
Olifantshoek, S. Africa 116 D3 27 57S 22 42E
Ólimbos, Greece 49 F9 35 44N 27 11E
Ólimbos, Óros, Greece 50 F6 40 6N 22 23E
Olímpia, Brazil 175 A6 20 44S 48 54W
Olimpos-Beydaglari △, Turkey 49 E12 36 36N 30 30E
Olin, U.S.A. 156 C5 42 0N 91 9W
Olinda, Brazil 170 C5 8 1S 34 51W
Olindiná, Brazil 170 D4 11 22S 38 21W
Olite, Spain 40 C3 42 29N 1 40W
Oliva, Argentina 174 C3 32 0S 63 38W
Oliva, Spain 41 G4 38 58N 0 9W
Oliva, Punta del, Spain 42 B5 43 37N 5 28W
Oliva de la Frontera, Spain 43 G4 38 17N 6 54W
Olivares, Spain 40 F2 39 46N 2 20W
Olive Branch, U.S.A. 155 H10 34 58N 89 50W
Olive Hill, U.S.A. 157 F13 38 18N 83 13W
Olivehurst, U.S.A. 160 F5 39 6N 121 34W
Oliveira, Brazil 171 F3 20 39S 44 50W
Oliveira de Azeméis, Portugal 42 E2 40 49N 8 29W
Oliveira do Douro, Portugal 42 D2 41 5N 8 2W
Oliveira dos Brejinhos, Brazil 171 D3 12 19S 42 54W
Olivenza, Spain 43 G3 38 41N 7 9W
Oliver, Canada 142 D5 49 13N 119 37W
Oliver L., Canada 143 B8 56 56N 103 22W
Olivet, France 27 E8 47 51N 1 55E
Olivet, U.S.A. 157 B12 42 27N 84 56W
Olivine Ra., N.Z. 131 E3 44 15S 168 30E
Olivone, Switz. 33 C7 46 32N 8 57E
Olkhovka, Russia 60 F7 49 48N 44 32E
Olkusz, Poland 55 H6 50 18N 19 33E
Ollachea, Peru 172 C3 13 49S 70 29W
Ollagüe, Chile 174 A2 21 15S 68 10W
Ollon, Switz. 32 D3 46 18N 7 0E
Olloua, Congo 114 C2 0 54S 14 34E
Olmaliq, Uzbekistan 65 C4 40 50N 69 35E
Olmedo, Spain 42 D6 41 20N 4 43W
Olmeto, France 29 G12 41 43N 8 55E
Olmos, Peru 172 B2 5 59S 79 45W
Olmütz = Olomouc, Czech Rep. 35 B10 49 38N 17 12E
Olney, Ill., U.S.A. 157 F8 38 44N 88 5W
Olney, Tex., U.S.A. 155 J5 33 22N 98 45W
Olofström, Sweden 17 H8 56 17N 14 32E
Ololi, Congo 114 C2 0 15S 14 36E
Oloma, Cameroon 113 E7 3 29N 11 19E
Olomane →, Canada 141 B7 50 14N 60 37W
Olombo, Congo 114 C3 1 18S 15 53E
Olomouc, Czech Rep. 35 B10 49 38N 17 12E
Olomoucký □, Czech Rep. 35 B10 49 45N 17 5E
Olonets, Russia 58 B7 61 0N 32 54E
Olongapo, Phil. 80 D3 14 50N 120 18E
Olonne-sur-Mer, France 28 B2 46 32N 1 47W
Oloron, Gave d' →, France 28 E2 43 33N 1 5W
Oloron-Ste-Marie, France 28 E3 43 11N 0 38W
Olosega, Amer. Samoa 133 X25 14 12S 169 40W
Olosenga = Swains I., Amer. Samoa 135 J11 11 11S 171 4W
Olot, Spain 40 C7 42 11N 2 30E
Olovo, Bos.-H. 52 F3 44 8N 18 35E
Olovyannaya, Russia 67 D12 50 58N 115 35E
Olowalu, U.S.A. 145 C5 20 49N 156 38W
Oloy →, Russia 67 C16 66 29N 159 29E
Olsberg, Germany 30 D4 51 21N 8 31E
Olshammar, Sweden 17 F8 58 45N 14 48E
Olshanka, Ukraine 59 H6 48 16N 30 58E
Olshany, Ukraine 59 G8 50 3N 35 53E
Olsztyn, Poland 54 E7 53 48N 20 29E
Olsztynek, Poland 54 E7 53 34N 20 19E
Olt □, Romania 53 F9 44 20N 24 30E
Olt →, Romania 53 G9 43 43N 24 51E
Oltedal, Norway 18 F3 58 49N 6 2E
Olten, Switz. 32 B5 47 21N 7 53E
Olteniţa, Romania 53 F11 44 7N 26 42E
Olton, U.S.A. 155 H3 34 11N 102 8W
Oltu, Turkey 101 B9 40 35N 41 58E
Oluanpi, Taiwan 77 G13 21 54N 120 51E
Olula del Rio, Spain 41 H2 37 21N 2 18W
Olur, Turkey 101 B10 40 49N 42 8E
Olustee, U.S.A. 152 E7 30 12N 82 26W
Olutanga, Phil. 81 H4 7 26N 122 54E
Olutanga I., Phil. 81 H4 7 22N 122 52E
Olvega, Spain 40 D2 41 47N 2 0W
Olvera, Spain 43 J5 36 55N 5 18W
Olymbos, Cyprus 39 E9 35 21N 33 45E
Olympia, Greece 48 D3 37 39N 21 39E
Olympia, U.S.A. 160 D4 47 3N 122 53W
Olympic △, U.S.A. 160 C3 47 48N 123 30W
Olympic Dam, Australia 128 A2 30 30S 136 55E
Olympic Mts., U.S.A. 160 C3 47 55N 123 45W
Olympus, Cyprus 39 F8 34 56N 32 52E
Olympus, Mt. = Ólimbos, Óros, Greece 50 F6 40 6N 22 23E
Olympus, Mt. = Uludağ, Turkey 51 F13 40 4N 29 13E
Olympus, Mt., U.S.A. 160 C3 47 48N 123 43W
Olyphant, U.S.A. 151 E9 41 27N 75 36W
Om →, Russia 66 D8 54 59N 73 22E
Om Hajer, Eritrea 107 E4 14 20N 36 41E
Om Koi, Thailand 86 D2 17 48N 98 22E
Ōma, Japan 70 D10 41 45N 141 5E
Ōmachi, Japan 73 A9 36 30N 137 50E
Omae-Zaki, Japan 73 C10 34 36N 138 14E
Ōmagari, Japan 70 E10 39 27N 140 29E
Omagh, U.K. 23 B4 54 36N 7 19W
Omagh □, U.K. 23 B4 54 35N 7 15W
Omaha, U.S.A. 154 E7 41 17N 95 58W
Omak, U.S.A. 158 B4 48 25N 119 31W
Omalos, Greece 39 E4 35 19N 23 55E
Omalur, India 95 J4 11 44N 78 4E
Oman ■, Asia 99 B7 23 0N 58 0E
Oman, G. of, Asia 97 E8 24 30N 58 30E
Omapere, N.Z. 130 B2 35 37S 173 25E
Omar Combon, Somali Rep. 120 D3 3 10N 45 47E
Omaruru, Namibia 116 C2 21 26S 16 0E
Omaruru →, Namibia 116 C1 22 7S 14 15E

Omate, *Peru* **172 D3** 16 45 S 71 0W
Ombai, Selat, *Indonesia* **82 C2** 8 30 S 124 50 E
Omboué, *Gabon* **114 C1** 1 35 S 9 15 E
Ombrone →, *Italy* **44 F8** 42 42N 11 5 E
Omchi, *Chad* **109 D3** 21 22N 17 53 E
Omdurmân, *Sudan* **111 D3** 15 40N 32 28 E
Ōme, *Japan* **73 B11** 35 47N 139 15 E
Omega, *U.S.A.* **152 D6** 31 21N 83 36W
Omegna, *Italy* **44 C5** 45 53N 8 24 E
Omemee, *Canada* **150 B6** 44 18N 78 33W
Omeo, *Australia* **129 D7** 37 6 S 147 36 E
Omeonga, *Dem. Rep. of the Congo* **118 C1** 3 40 S 24 22 E
Ometepe, I. de, *Nic.* **164 D2** 11 32N 85 35W
Ometepec, *Mexico* **163 D5** 16 39N 98 23W
Ōmi-Shima, *Ehime, Japan* **72 C5** 34 15N 133 0 E
Ōmi-Shima, *Yamaguchi, Japan* **72 C3** 34 25N 131 9 E
Omihachiman, *Japan* **73 B8** 35 7N 136 3 E
Ominato, *Japan* **70 D10** 41 17N 141 10 E
Omineca →, *Canada* **142 B4** 56 3N 124 16W
Omiš, *Croatia* **45 E13** 43 28N 16 40 E
Omišalj, *Croatia* **45 C11** 45 13N 14 32 E
Omitara, *Namibia* **116 C2** 22 16 S 18 2 E
Ōmiya, *Japan* **73 B11** 35 54N 139 38 E
Ommaney, C., *U.S.A.* **144 H14** 56 10N 134 40W
Omme Å →, *Denmark* **17 J2** 55 56N 8 32 E
Ommen, *Neths.* **24 B6** 52 31N 6 26 E
Ömnögovĭ □, *Mongolia* **74 C3** 43 15N 104 0 E
Omo △, *Ethiopia* **107 F4** 5 54N 35 55 E
Omo →, *Ethiopia* **107 F4** 6 25N 36 10 E
Omo Valley, *Ethiopia* **107 F4** 5 7N 36 0 E
Omodeo, L., *Italy* **46 B1** 40 8N 8 56 E
Omodhos, *Cyprus* **39 F8** 34 51N 32 48 E
Omoi, *Congo* **114 C2** 2 56 S 13 13 E
Omoko, *Nigeria* **113 D6** 5 19N 6 40 E
Omolon →, *Russia* **67 C16** 68 42N 158 36 E
Omona, *Solomon Is.* **133 L10** 7 30 S 158 43 E
Omono-Gawa →, *Japan* **70 E10** 39 46N 140 3 E
Omsk, *Russia* **66 D8** 55 0N 73 12 E
Omsukchan, *Russia* **67 C16** 62 32N 155 48 E
Ōmu, *Japan* **70 B11** 44 34N 142 58 E
Omul, Vf., *Romania* **53 E10** 45 27N 25 29 E
Omulew →, *Poland* **55 E8** 53 5N 21 33 E
Ōmura, *Japan* **72 E1** 32 56N 129 57 E
Ōmura-Wan, *Japan* **72 E1** 32 57N 129 52 E
Omuramba Omatako →, *Namibia* **116 B2** 17 45 S 20 25 E
Omuramba Ovambo →, *Namibia* **116 B2** 18 45 S 16 59 E
Omurtag, *Bulgaria* **51 C10** 43 8N 26 26 E
Ōmuta, *Japan* **72 D2** 33 5N 130 26 E
Omutninsk, *Russia* **64 B4** 58 45N 52 4 E
On-ma-thi, *Burma* **90 D6** 22 17N 96 41 E
On-Take, *Japan* **72 F2** 31 35N 130 39 E
Oña, *Spain* **42 C7** 42 43N 3 25W
Ona, *U.S.A.* **153 H8** 27 29N 81 55W
Ona Dikonde, *Dem. Rep. of the Congo* **114 C4** 3 51 S 24 11 E
Onaga, *U.S.A.* **154 F6** 39 29N 96 10W
Onalaska, *U.S.A.* **154 D9** 43 53N 91 14W
Onancock, *U.S.A.* **148 G8** 37 43N 75 45W
Onang, *Indonesia* **82 B1** 3 2 S 118 49 E
Onangue, L., *Gabon* **114 C1** 0 57 S 10 4 E
Onaping L., *Canada* **140 C3** 47 3N 81 30W
Onarga, *U.S.A.* **157 D8** 40 43N 88 1W
Ōnati, *Spain* **40 B2** 43 3N 2 25W
Onavas, *Mexico* **162 B3** 28 28N 109 30W
Onawa, *U.S.A.* **154 D6** 42 2N 96 6W
Oncócua, *Angola* **116 B1** 16 30 S 13 25 E
Onda, *Spain* **40 F4** 39 55N 0 17W
Ondaejin, *N. Korea* **75 D15** 41 34N 129 40 E
Ondangwa, *Namibia* **116 B2** 17 57 S 16 4 E
Ondarroa, *Spain* **40 B2** 43 19N 2 25W
Ondas →, *Brazil* **171 D3** 12 8 S 44 55W
Ondava →, *Slovak Rep.* **35 C14** 48 27N 21 48 E
Ondjiva, *Angola* **116 B2** 16 48 S 15 50 E
Ondo, *Japan* **72 C4** 34 11N 132 32 E
Ondo, *Nigeria* **113 D5** 7 4N 4 47 E
Ondo □, *Nigeria* **113 D6** 6 45N 5 0 E
Öndörshil, *Mongolia* **74 B5** 45 13N 108 5 E
Öndverðarnes, *Iceland* **11 C2** 64 52N 24 0W
One Tree, *Australia* **127 E3** 34 11 S 144 43 E
Oneata, *Fiji* **133 B3** 18 26 S 178 25W
Oneco, *U.S.A.* **153 H7** 27 25N 82 31W
Onega, *Russia* **56 B6** 64 0N 38 10 E
Onega →, *Russia* **56 B6** 63 58N 38 2 E
Onega, G. of = Onezhskaya Guba, *Russia* **56 B6** 64 24N 36 38 E
Onega, L. = Onezhskoye Ozero, *Russia* **58 B8** 61 44N 35 22 E
Onehunga, *N.Z.* **130 C3** 36 55 S 174 48 E
Oneida, *Ill., U.S.A.* **156 C6** 41 4N 90 13W
Oneida, *N.Y., U.S.A.* **151 C9** 43 6N 75 39W
Oneida L., *U.S.A.* **151 C9** 43 12N 75 54W
O'Neill, *U.S.A.* **154 D5** 42 27N 98 39W
Onekotan, Ostrov, *Russia* **67 E16** 49 25N 154 45 E
Onema, *Dem. Rep. of the Congo* **118 C1** 4 35 S 24 30 E
Oneonta, *U.S.A.* **151 D9** 42 27N 75 4W
Onerahi, *N.Z.* **130 B3** 35 45 S 174 22 E
Onești, *Romania* **53 D11** 46 17N 26 47 E
Onezhskaya Guba, *Russia* **56 B6** 64 24N 36 38 E
Onezhskoye Ozero, *Russia* **58 B8** 61 44N 35 22 E
Ongarue, *N.Z.* **130 E4** 38 42 S 175 19 E
Ongea Levu = Ogea Levu, *Fiji* **133 B3** 19 8 S 178 24W
Ongers →, *S. Africa* **116 E3** 31 4 S 23 13 E
Ongerup, *Australia* **125 F2** 33 58 S 118 28 E
Ongjin, *N. Korea* **75 F13** 37 56N 125 21 E
Ongkharak, *Thailand* **86 E3** 14 8N 101 1 E
Ongniud Qi, *China* **75 C10** 43 0N 118 38 E
Ongoka, *Dem. Rep. of the Congo* **118 C2** 1 20 S 26 0 E
Ongole, *India* **95 G5** 15 33N 80 2 E
Ongon = Havirga, *Mongolia* **74 B7** 45 41N 113 5 E
Ongouendjo, *Gabon* **114 C1** 1 23 S 9 5 E
Oni, *Georgia* **61 J6** 42 33N 43 26 E
Onida, *U.S.A.* **154 C4** 44 42N 100 4W
Onilahy →, *Madag.* **117 C7** 23 34 S 43 45 E
Onitsha, *Nigeria* **113 D6** 6 6N 6 42 E
Ono, *Fiji* **133 B2** 18 55 S 178 29 E
Ono, *Fukui, Japan* **73 B8** 35 59N 136 29 E
Ono, *Hyōgo, Japan* **72 C6** 34 51N 134 56 E
Onoda, *Japan* **72 C3** 33 59N 131 11 E
Onohara, *Japan* **72 C5** 34 5N 133 40 E
Onoke, L., *N.Z.* **130 H4** 41 22 S 175 8 E
Onomichi, *Japan* **72 C5** 34 25N 133 12 E
Onpyŏng-ni, *S. Korea* **75 H14** 33 25N 126 55 E
Ons, I. de, *Spain* **42 C2** 42 23N 8 55W
Onsala, *Sweden* **17 G6** 57 26N 12 0 E
Onslow, *Australia* **124 D2** 21 40 S 115 12 E
Onslow B., *U.S.A.* **149 H7** 34 20N 77 15W
Ontake-San, *Japan* **73 B9** 35 53N 137 29 E
Ontar, *Vanuatu* **133 D5** 14 17 S 167 27 E
Ontario, *Calif., U.S.A.* **161 L9** 34 4N 117 39W
Ontario, *Oreg., U.S.A.* **158 D5** 44 2N 116 58W
Ontario □, *Canada* **140 B2** 48 0N 83 0W
Ontario, L., *N. Amer.* **150 C7** 43 20N 78 0W
Ontinyent, *Spain* **41 G4** 38 50N 0 35W
Ontonagon, *U.S.A.* **154 B10** 46 52N 89 19W
Ontur, *Spain* **41 G3** 38 38N 1 29W
Onverwacht, *Suriname* **169 B6** 5 35N 55 11W
Onyx, *U.S.A.* **161 K8** 35 41N 118 14W
Oodnadatta, *Australia* **127 D2** 27 33 S 135 30 E
Ookala, *U.S.A.* **145 C6** 20 1N 155 17W
Ooku = Ōma, *Japan* **70 D10** 41 45N 141 5 E
Ooldea, *Australia* **125 F5** 30 27 S 131 50 E
Oombulgurri, *Australia* **124 C4** 15 15 S 127 45 E
Oorindi, *Australia* **126 C3** 20 40 S 141 1 E
Oost-Vlaanderen □, *Belgium* **24 C3** 51 5N 3 50 E
Oostende, *Belgium* **24 C2** 51 15N 2 54 E
Oosterhout, *Neths.* **24 C4** 51 39N 4 47 E
Oosterschelde →, *Neths.* **24 C4** 51 33N 4 0 E
Oosterwolde, *Neths.* **24 B6** 53 0N 6 17 E
Ootacamund = Udagamandalam, *India* **95 J3** 11 30N 76 44 E
Ootha, *Australia* **129 B7** 33 6 S 147 29 E
Ootsa L., *Canada* **142 C3** 53 50N 126 2W
Op Luang △, *Thailand* **86 C2** 18 12N 98 32 E
Opaka, *Bulgaria* **51 C10** 43 28N 26 10 E
Opala, *Dem. Rep. of the Congo* **118 C1** 0 40 S 24 20 E
Opalenica, *Poland* **55 F3** 52 18N 16 24 E
Opan, *Bulgaria* **51 D9** 42 13N 25 41 E
Opanake, *Sri Lanka* **95 L5** 6 35N 80 40 E
Opapa, *N.Z.* **130 F5** 39 47 S 176 42 E
Opasatika, *Canada* **140 C3** 49 30N 82 50W
Opasquia ⌓, *Canada* **140 B1** 53 33N 93 5W
Opatija, *Croatia* **45 C11** 45 21N 14 17 E
Opatów, *Poland* **55 H8** 50 50N 21 27 E
Opava, *Czech Rep.* **35 B10** 49 57N 17 58 E
Opelika, *U.S.A.* **152 C4** 32 39N 85 23W
Opelousas, *U.S.A.* **155 K8** 30 32N 92 5W
Opémisca, L., *Canada* **140 C5** 49 56N 74 52W
Opheim, *U.S.A.* **158 B10** 48 51N 106 24W
Ophir, *U.S.A.* **144 E8** 63 10N 156 31W
Ophthalmia Ra., *Australia* **124 D2** 23 15 S 119 30 E
Opi, *Nigeria* **113 D6** 6 36N 7 28 E
Opihikao, *U.S.A.* **145 D7** 19 26N 154 53W
Opinaca →, *Canada* **140 B4** 52 15N 78 2W
Opinaca, Rés., *Canada* **140 B4** 52 39N 76 20W
Opinnagau →, *Canada* **140 B3** 54 12N 82 25W
Opiscotéo, L., *Canada* **141 B6** 53 10N 68 10W
Opobo, *Nigeria* **113 E6** 4 35N 7 34 E
Opochka, *Russia* **58 D5** 56 42N 28 45 E
Opoczno, *Poland* **55 G7** 51 22N 20 18 E
Opol, *Phil.* **81 G5** 8 31N 124 34 E
Opole, *Poland* **55 H4** 50 42N 17 58 E
Opole Lubelskie, *Poland* **55 G8** 51 9N 21 58 E
Opolskie □, *Poland* **55 H5** 50 30N 18 0 E
Opon = Lapu-Lapu, *Phil.* **81 F4** 10 20N 123 55 E
Opononono L., *Namibia* **116 B2** 18 8 S 15 45 E
Oporto = Porto, *Portugal* **42 D2** 41 8N 8 40W
Opotiki, *N.Z.* **130 E6** 38 1 S 177 19 E
Opp, *U.S.A.* **152 D3** 31 17N 86 16W
Oppdal, *Norway* **18 B6** 62 35N 9 41 E
Oppeln = Opole, *Poland* **55 H4** 50 42N 17 58 E
Óppido Mamertina, *Italy* **47 D8** 38 16N 15 59 E
Oppland □, *Norway* **16 C6** 61 15N 9 40 E
Opportunity, *U.S.A.* **158 C5** 47 39N 117 15W
Oprișor, *Romania* **52 F8** 44 17N 23 5 E
Oprtalj, *Croatia* **45 C10** 45 23N 13 50 E
Opua, *N.Z.* **130 B3** 35 19 S 174 9 E
Opunake, *N.Z.* **130 F2** 39 26 S 173 52 E
Opuwo, *Namibia* **116 B1** 18 3 S 13 45 E
Opuzen, *Croatia* **45 E14** 43 1N 17 34 E
Oquawka, *U.S.A.* **156 D6** 40 56N 90 57W
Ora, *Cyprus* **39 F9** 34 51N 33 12 E
Oracle, *U.S.A.* **159 K8** 32 37N 110 46W
Oracuzar, *Peru* **168 D2** 4 42 S 78 6W
Oradea, *Romania* **52 C6** 47 2N 21 58 E
Öræfajökull, *Iceland* **11 C10** 64 2N 16 39W
Orahovac, *Serbia & M.* **50 D4** 42 24N 20 40 E
Orahovica, *Croatia* **52 E2** 45 35N 17 52 E
Orai, *India* **93 G8** 25 58N 79 30 E
Oraison, *France* **29 E9** 43 55N 5 55 E
Oral = Zhayyq →, *Kazakhstan* **57 E9** 47 0N 51 48 E
Oral, *Kazakhstan* **60 E10** 51 20N 51 20 E
Oran, *Algeria* **111 A4** 35 45N 0 39W
Orange, *Australia* **129 B8** 33 15 S 149 7 E
Orange, *France* **29 D8** 44 8N 4 47 E
Orange, *Calif., U.S.A.* **161 M9** 33 47N 117 51W
Orange, *Mass., U.S.A.* **151 D12** 42 35N 72 19W
Orange, *Tex., U.S.A.* **155 K8** 30 6N 93 44W
Orange, *Va., U.S.A.* **148 F6** 38 15N 78 7W
Orange →, *S. Africa* **116 D2** 28 41 S 16 28 E
Orange, C., *Brazil* **169 C7** 4 20N 51 30W
Orange City, *U.S.A.* **153 G8** 28 57N 81 18W
Orange Cove, *U.S.A.* **160 J7** 36 38N 119 19W
Orange Free State = Free State □, *S. Africa* **116 D4** 28 30 S 27 0 E
Orange Grove, *U.S.A.* **155 M6** 27 58N 97 56W
Orange L., *U.S.A.* **153 F7** 29 25N 82 13W
Orange Park, *U.S.A.* **152 E8** 30 10N 81 42W
Orange River Colony = Free State □, *S. Africa* **116 D4** 28 30 S 27 0 E
Orange Walk, *Belize* **163 D7** 18 6N 88 33W
Orangeburg, *U.S.A.* **152 B9** 33 30N 80 52W
Orangeville, *Canada* **140 D3** 43 55N 80 5W
Orangeville, *U.S.A.* **156 B7** 42 28N 89 39W
Orango, *Guinea-Biss.* **112 C1** 11 5N 16 0W
Orani, *Phil.* **80 D3** 14 49N 120 32 E
Oranienburg, *Germany* **30 C9** 52 45N 13 14 E
Oranje = Orange →, *S. Africa* **116 D2** 28 41 S 16 28 E
Oranjemund, *Namibia* **116 D2** 28 38 S 16 29 E
Oranjerivier, *S. Africa* **116 D3** 29 40 S 24 12 E
Oranjestad, *Aruba* **165 D5** 12 32N 70 2W
Orap, *Vanuatu* **133 E5** 15 58 S 167 20 E
Orarak, *Sudan* **107 F3** 6 15N 32 23 E
Oras, *Phil.* **80 E5** 12 9N 125 28 E
Orašje, *Bos.-H.* **52 E3** 45 1N 18 42 E
Orăștie, *Romania* **53 E8** 45 50N 23 10 E
Orava →, *Slovak Rep.* **35 B12** 49 9N 19 8 E
Orava, Vodna nádrž, *Slovak Rep.* **35 B12** 49 25N 19 35 E
Oravița, *Romania* **52 E6** 45 2N 21 43 E
Orawia, *N.Z.* **131 G2** 46 1 S 167 50 E
Orb →, *France* **28 E7** 43 15N 3 18 E
Orba →, *Italy* **44 D5** 44 53N 8 37 E
Ørbæk, *Denmark* **17 J4** 55 17N 10 39 E
Orbe, *Switz.* **32 C3** 46 43N 6 32 E
Orbec, *France* **26 C7** 49 1N 0 23 E
Orbetello, *Italy* **45 F8** 42 27N 11 13 E
Órbigo →, *Spain* **42 C5** 42 5N 5 42W
Orbisonia, *U.S.A.* **150 F7** 40 15N 77 54W
Orbost, *Australia* **129 D8** 37 40 S 148 29 E
Örbyhus, *Sweden* **16 D11** 60 15N 17 43 E
Orcadas, *Antarctica* **7 C18** 60 44 S 44 37W
Orcas I., *U.S.A.* **160 B4** 48 42N 122 56W
Orce, *Spain* **41 H2** 37 44N 2 28W
Orce →, *Spain* **41 H2** 37 44N 2 28W
Orchard City, *U.S.A.* **159 G10** 38 50N 107 58W
Orchard Homes, *U.S.A.* **158 C6** 46 55N 114 4W
Orchies, *France* **27 B10** 50 28N 3 14 E
Orchila, I., *Venezuela* **165 D6** 11 48N 66 10W
Orchilla, Pta., *Canary Is.* **9 e1** 27 42N 18 10W
Órcia →, *Italy* **45 F8** 42 58N 11 21 E
Orco →, *Italy* **44 C4** 45 10N 7 52 E
Orcopampa, *Peru* **172 D3** 15 20 S 72 23W
Orcutt, *U.S.A.* **161 L6** 34 52N 120 27W
Ord, *U.S.A.* **154 E5** 41 36N 98 56W
Ord →, *Australia* **124 C4** 15 33 S 128 15 E
Ord, Mt., *Australia* **124 C4** 17 20 S 125 34 E
Ordenes = Ordes, *Spain* **42 B2** 43 5N 8 29W
Orderville, *U.S.A.* **159 H7** 37 17N 112 38W
Ordes, *Spain* **42 B2** 43 5N 8 29W
Ordesa y Monte Perido △, *Spain* **40 C4** 42 40N 0 10W
Ording = St-Peter-Ording, *Germany* **30 A4** 54 20N 8 36 E
Ordos = Mu Us Shamo, *China* **74 E5** 39 0N 109 0 E
Ordu, *Turkey* **100 B7** 40 55N 37 53 E
Ordubad, *Azerbaijan* **101 C12** 38 54N 46 1 E
Orduña, *Álava, Spain* **40 C2** 42 58N 2 58W
Orduña, *Granada, Spain* **43 H7** 37 20N 3 30W
Ordway, *U.S.A.* **154 F3** 38 13N 103 46W
Ordzhonikidze = Vladikavkaz, *Russia* **61 J7** 43 0N 44 35 E
Ordzhonikidze = Yenakiyeve, *Ukraine* **59 H10** 48 15N 38 15 E
Ordzhonikidze, *Kazakhstan* **64 E8** 52 27N 61 39 E
Ordzhonikidze, *Ukraine* **59 J8** 47 39N 34 3 E
Ordzhonikidzeabad = Kofarnikhon, *Tajikistan* **65 D4** 38 34N 69 1 E
Ore, *Dem. Rep. of the Congo* **118 B2** 3 17N 29 30 E
Ore Mts. = Erzgebirge, *Germany* **30 E8** 50 27N 12 55 E
Orealla, *Guyana* **169 B6** 5 15N 57 23W
Orebić, *Croatia* **45 F14** 43 0N 17 11 E
Örebro, *Sweden* **16 E9** 59 20N 15 18 E
Örebro län □, *Sweden* **16 E8** 59 27N 15 0 E
Orecchiella ⌓, *Italy* **44 D7** 44 16N 10 22 E
Oregon, *Ill., U.S.A.* **156 B7** 42 1N 89 20W
Oregon, *Ohio, U.S.A.* **157 C13** 41 38N 83 25W
Oregon, *Wis., U.S.A.* **156 B7** 42 56N 89 23W
Oregon □, *U.S.A.* **158 E3** 44 0N 121 0W
Oregon City, *U.S.A.* **160 E4** 45 21N 122 36W
Oregon Dunes ⌓, *U.S.A.* **158 E1** 42 3N 124 5W
Öregrund, *Sweden* **16 D12** 60 21N 18 30 E
Öregrundsgrepen, *Sweden* **16 D12** 60 25N 18 15 E
Orekhov = Orikhiv, *Ukraine* **59 J8** 47 30N 35 48 E
Orekhovo-Zuyevo, *Russia* **58 E10** 55 50N 38 55 E
Orel, *Russia* **59 F9** 52 57N 36 3 E
Orel →, *Ukraine* **59 H8** 48 40N 34 39 E
Orellana, *Spain* **43 F5** 39 1N 5 32W
Orellana, Canal de, *Spain* **43 F5** 39 2N 6 0W
Orellana, Embalse de, *Spain* **43 F5** 39 5N 5 10W
Orem, *U.S.A.* **158 F8** 40 19N 111 42W
Ören, *Turkey* **49 D9** 37 3N 27 57 E
Orenburg, *Russia* **64 F5** 51 45N 55 6 E
Örencik, *Turkey* **49 B11** 39 16N 29 33 E
Orense = Ourense, *Spain* **42 C3** 42 19N 7 55W
Orense □, *Spain* **42 C3** 42 15N 7 51W
Orepuki, *N.Z.* **131 G2** 46 19 S 167 46 E
Orestiada = Orestiás, *Greece* **51 E10** 41 30N 26 33 E
Orestiás *Greece* **51 E10** 41 30N 26 33 E
Orestos Pereyra, *Mexico* **162 B3** 26 31N 105 40W
Øresund, *Europe* **17 J6** 55 45N 12 45 E
Oretana, Cordillera = Toledo, Montes de, *Spain* **43 F6** 39 33N 4 20W
Oreti →, *N.Z.* **131 G3** 46 28 S 168 14 E
Orford Ness, *U.K.* **21 E9** 52 5N 1 35 E
Organ Pipe Cactus ⌓, *U.S.A.* **159 K7** 32 0N 113 10W
Organos Pta. de los, *Canary Is.* **9 e1** 28 12N 17 17W
Organyà, *Spain* **40 C6** 42 13N 1 20 E
Orgaz, *Spain* **43 F7** 39 39N 3 53W
Ørgenvika, *Norway* **18 D6** 60 17N 9 42 E
Orgeyev = Orhei, *Moldova* **53 C13** 47 24N 28 50 E
Orgūn, *Afghan.* **91 B3** 32 55N 69 12 E
Orhaneli, *Turkey* **51 G12** 39 54N 28 59 E
Orhaneli →, *Turkey* **51 G12** 39 50N 28 55 E
Orhangazi, *Turkey* **51 F13** 40 29N 29 18 E
Orhei, *Moldova* **53 C13** 47 24N 28 50 E
Orhon Gol →, *Mongolia* **68 A5** 50 21N 106 0 E
Oria, *Italy* **47 B10** 40 30N 17 38 E
Orida, *Niger* **111 D7** 21 20N 12 15 E
Oriental, Cordillera, *Bolivia* **173 D4** 17 0 S 66 0W
Oriental, Cordillera, *Colombia* **168 B3** 6 0N 73 0W
Oriental, Grand Erg, *Algeria* **111 C6** 30 0N 6 30 E
Orientale □, *Dem. Rep. of the Congo* **118 B2** 2 20N 26 0 E
Oriente, *Argentina* **174 D3** 38 44 S 60 37W
Orihuela, *Spain* **41 G4** 38 7N 0 55W
Orihuela del Tremedal, *Spain* **40 E3** 40 33N 1 39W
Orikhiv, *Ukraine* **59 J8** 47 30N 35 48 E
Orikum, *Albania* **50 F3** 40 20N 19 26 E
Orillia, *Canada* **140 D4** 44 40N 79 24W
Orinduik, *Guyana* **169 C5** 4 40N 60 3W
Orinoco →, *Venezuela* **169 B5** 9 15N 61 30W
Orion, *Canada* **143 D6** 49 27N 110 49W
Orion, *Ala., U.S.A.* **152 D4** 31 58N 86 0W
Orion, *Ill., U.S.A.* **156 C6** 41 21N 90 23W
Oriskany, *U.S.A.* **151 C9** 43 10N 75 20W
Orissa □, *India* **94 E7** 20 0N 84 0 E
Orissaare, *Estonia* **15 G20** 58 34N 23 5 E
Oristano, *Italy* **46 C1** 39 54N 8 36 E
Oristano, G. di, *Italy* **46 C1** 39 50N 8 29 E
Orituco →, *Venezuela* **168 B4** 8 45N 67 27W
Oriximiná, *Brazil* **169 D6** 1 45 S 55 52W
Orizaba, *Mexico* **163 D5** 18 51N 97 6W
Orizaba, Pico de, *Mexico* **163 D5** 19 0N 97 20W
Orizare, *Bulgaria* **51 D11** 42 44N 27 39 E
Orizona, *Brazil* **171 E2** 17 3 S 48 18W
Ørje, *Norway* **18 E8** 59 29N 11 39 E
Orjen, *Bos.-H.* **50 D2** 42 35N 18 34 E
Orjiva, *Spain* **43 J7** 36 53N 3 24W
Orkanger, *Norway* **18 A6** 63 18N 9 52 E
Örkelljunga, *Sweden* **17 H7** 56 17N 13 17 E
Örken, *Sweden* **17 G9** 57 6N 15 1 E
Örkény, *Hungary* **52 C4** 47 9N 19 26 E
Orkhaniye = Botevgrad, *Bulgaria* **50 D7** 42 55N 23 47 E
Orkla →, *Norway* **18 A6** 63 18N 9 51 E
Orkney, *S. Africa* **116 D4** 26 58 S 26 40 E
Orkney □, *U.K.* **22 B5** 59 2N 3 13W
Orkney Is., *U.K.* **22 B6** 59 0N 3 0W
Orland, *Calif., U.S.A.* **160 F4** 39 45N 122 12W
Orland, *Ind., U.S.A.* **157 C11** 41 47N 85 12W
Orlando, *U.S.A.* **153 G8** 28 33N 81 23W
Orlando, C. d', *Italy* **47 D7** 38 10N 14 43 E
Orlando International ✈ (MCO), *U.S.A.* **153 G8** 28 26N 81 19W
Orléanais, *France* **27 E9** 48 0N 2 0 E
Orléans, *France* **27 E8** 47 54N 1 52 E
Orleans, *Ind., U.S.A.* **157 F10** 38 40N 86 27W
Orleans, *Vt., U.S.A.* **151 B12** 44 49N 72 12W
Orléans, Î. d', *Canada* **141 C5** 46 54N 70 58W
Orléansville = Ech Chéliff, *Algeria* **111 A5** 36 10N 1 20 E
Orlice →, *Czech Rep.* **34 A8** 50 13N 15 50 E
Orlivka, *Ukraine* **53 E13** 45 19N 28 27 E
Orlov = Khalturin, *Russia* **64 B2** 58 40N 48 50 E
Orlov, *Slovak Rep.* **35 B13** 49 17N 20 51 E
Orlov Gay, *Russia* **60 E9** 50 56N 48 19 E
Orlová, *Czech Rep.* **35 B11** 49 51N 18 26 E
Orlovat, *Serbia & M.* **52 E5** 45 14N 20 33 E
Orlovka, *Kyrgyzstan* **65 B7** 42 45N 75 36 E
Orly, Paris ✈ (ORY), *France* **27 D9** 48 44N 2 23 E
Ormara, *Pakistan* **91 D2** 25 16N 64 33 E
Ormea, *Italy* **44 D4** 44 9N 7 54 E
Ormília, *Greece* **50 F7** 40 16N 23 39 E
Ormoc, *Phil.* **81 F5** 11 0N 124 37 E
Ormond, *N.Z.* **130 E6** 38 33 S 177 56 E
Ormond Beach, *U.S.A.* **153 F8** 29 17N 81 3W
Ormond by the Sea, *U.S.A.* **153 F8** 29 21N 81 4W
Ormondville, *N.Z.* **130 G5** 40 5 S 176 19 E
Örmos Keríou, *Greece* **39 D2** 37 42N 20 53 E
Ormož, *Slovenia* **45 B13** 46 25N 16 10 E
Ormskirk, *U.K.* **20 D5** 53 35N 2 54W
Ormstown, *Canada* **151 A11** 45 8N 74 0W
Ormtjernkampen △, *Norway* **18 C6** 61 12N 9 48 E
Ornans, *France* **27 E13** 47 7N 6 10 E
Ornavasso, *Italy* **33 E6** 45 58N 8 24 E
Orne □, *France* **26 D7** 48 40N 0 5 E
Orne →, *France* **26 C6** 49 18N 0 15W
Orneta, *Poland* **54 D7** 54 8N 20 9 E
Ornö, *Sweden* **16 E12** 59 4N 18 24 E
Örnsköldsvik, *Sweden* **16 A12** 63 17N 18 40 E
Oro, *N. Korea* **75 D14** 40 1N 127 27 E
Oro →, *Mexico* **162 B3** 25 35N 105 2W
Oro Grande, *U.S.A.* **161 L9** 34 36N 117 20W
Oro Valley, *U.S.A.* **159 K8** 32 26N 110 58W
Orobie, Alpi, *Italy* **44 B6** 46 7N 10 0 E
Orobie Bergamasche ⌓, *Italy* **44 C6** 46 0N 9 45 E
Orobie Valtellinesi ⌓, *Italy* **44 B6** 46 5N 9 45 E
Orocué, *Colombia* **168 C3** 4 48N 71 20W
Orodara, *Burkina Faso* **112 C4** 11 0N 4 55W
Orodo, *Nigeria* **113 D6** 5 34N 7 4 E
Orofino, *U.S.A.* **158 C5** 46 29N 116 15W
Orohena, Mt., *Tahiti* **133 S16** 17 37 S 149 28W
Orol Dengizi = Aral Sea, *Asia* **66 E7** 44 30N 60 0 E
Oromiya □, *Ethiopia* **107 F5** 7 0N 40 0 E
Oromocto, *Canada* **141 C6** 45 54N 66 29W
Oron, *Nigeria* **113 E6** 4 48N 8 14 E
Oron, *Switz.* **32 C3** 46 34N 6 50 E
Orongo, *Chile* **172 b** 27 11 S 109 27W
Orono, *Canada* **150 C6** 43 59N 78 37W
Orono, *U.S.A.* **149 C11** 44 53N 68 40W
Oronsay, *U.K.* **22 E2** 56 1N 6 15W
Oropesa, *Spain* **42 F5** 39 57N 5 10W
Oroqen Zizhiqi, *China* **69 A7** 50 34N 123 43 E
Oroquieta, *Phil.* **81 G4** 8 32N 123 44 E
Orós, *Brazil* **170 C4** 6 15 S 38 55W
Orosei, *Italy* **46 B2** 40 23N 9 42 E
Orosei, G. di, *Italy* **46 B2** 40 15N 9 44 E
Orosháza, *Hungary* **52 D5** 46 32N 20 42 E
Oroszlány, *Hungary* **52 C3** 47 29N 18 19 E
Orote Pen., *Guam* **133 R15** 13 26N 144 38 E
Orotukan, *Russia* **67 C16** 62 16N 151 42 E
Oroville, *Calif., U.S.A.* **160 F5** 39 31N 121 33W
Oroville, *Wash., U.S.A.* **158 B4** 48 56N 119 26W
Oroville, L., *U.S.A.* **160 F5** 39 33N 121 29W
Orrefors, *Sweden* **17 H9** 56 50N 15 45 E
Orrick, *U.S.A.* **156 E2** 39 13N 94 7W
Orroroo, *Australia* **128 B3** 32 43 S 138 38 E
Orrviken, *Sweden* **16 A8** 63 6N 14 26 E
Orrville, *U.S.A.* **150 F3** 40 50N 81 46W
Orsa, *Sweden* **16 C8** 61 7N 14 37 E
Orsara di Púglia, *Italy* **47 A8** 41 17N 15 16 E
Orsasjön, *Sweden* **16 C8** 61 7N 14 37 E
Orsha, *Belarus* **58 E6** 54 30N 30 25 E
Orsières, *Switz.* **32 D4** 46 2N 7 9 E
Örsjö, *Sweden* **17 H9** 56 42N 15 45 E
Orsk, *Russia* **64 F7** 51 12N 58 34 E
Orșova, *Romania* **52 F7** 44 41N 22 25 E
Ørsta, *Norway* **18 B3** 62 13N 6 8 E
Ørsted, *Denmark* **17 H4** 56 30N 10 20 E
Örsundsbro, *Sweden* **16 E11** 59 44N 17 18 E
Orta, L. d', *Italy* **44 C5** 45 49N 8 24 E
Orta Nova, *Italy* **47 A8** 41 19N 15 42 E
Ortaca, *Turkey* **49 E10** 36 49N 28 45 E
Ortakent, *Turkey* **49 D9** 37 5N 27 21 E
Ortaklar, *Turkey* **49 D9** 37 53N 27 30 E
Ortaköy, *Çorum, Turkey* **100 B6** 40 16N 35 15 E
Ortaköy, *Niğde, Turkey* **100 C6** 38 44N 34 3 E
Orte, *Italy* **45 F9** 42 27N 12 23 E
Ortegal, C., *Spain* **42 B3** 43 43N 7 52W
Orteguaza →, *Colombia* **168 C2** 0 43N 75 16W
Ortelsburg = Szczytno, *Poland* **54 E7** 53 33N 21 0 E
Orthez, *France* **28 E3** 43 29N 0 48W
Ortigueira, *Spain* **42 B3** 43 40N 7 50W
Orting, *U.S.A.* **160 C4** 47 6N 122 12W
Ortisei, *Italy* **45 B8** 46 34N 11 40 E
Ortles, *Italy* **44 B7** 46 31N 10 33 E
Ortnevik, *Norway* **18 C3** 61 6N 6 7 E
Orto-Tokoy, *Kyrgyzstan* **65 B8** 42 20N 76 1 E
Ortón →, *Bolivia* **172 C4** 10 50 S 67 0W
Ortona, *Italy* **45 F11** 42 21N 14 24 E
Ortonville, *U.S.A.* **154 C6** 45 19N 96 27W
Orūmīyeh, *Iran* **101 D11** 37 40N 45 0 E
Orūmīyeh, Daryācheh-ye, *Iran* **101 D11** 37 50N 45 30 E
Orune, *Italy* **46 B2** 40 24N 9 22 E
Oruro, *Bolivia* **172 D4** 18 0 S 67 9W
Oruro □, *Bolivia* **172 D4** 18 40 S 67 30W
Orust, *Sweden* **17 F5** 58 10N 11 40 E
Oruzgān □, *Afghan.* **91 B2** 33 30N 66 0 E
Orvault, *France* **26 E5** 47 17N 1 38W
Orvieto, *Italy* **45 F9** 42 43N 12 7 E
Orwell, *N.Y., U.S.A.* **151 C9** 43 35N 75 50W
Orwell, *Ohio, U.S.A.* **150 E4** 41 32N 80 52W
Orwell →, *U.K.* **21 F9** 51 59N 1 18 E
Orwigsburg, *U.S.A.* **151 F8** 40 38N 76 6W
Oryakhovo, *Bulgaria* **50 C7** 43 40N 23 57 E
Orynyn, *Ukraine* **53 B11** 48 46N 26 24 E
Orzinuovi, *Italy* **44 C6** 45 24N 9 55 E
Orzyc →, *Poland* **55 F8** 52 46N 21 14 E
Orzysz, *Poland* **54 E8** 53 50N 21 58 E
Os, *Norway* **18 B8** 62 30N 11 14 E
Osa, *Russia* **64 C5** 57 17N 55 26 E
Osa →, *Norway* **18 C8** 61 18N 11 46 E
Osa →, *Poland* **54 E5** 53 33N 18 46 E
Osa, Pen. de, *Costa Rica* **164 E3** 8 0N 84 0W
Osage, *U.S.A.* **154 D8** 43 17N 92 49W
Osage →, *U.S.A.* **156 F5** 38 35N 91 57W
Osage City, *U.S.A.* **154 F7** 38 38N 95 50W
Ōsaka, *Japan* **73 C7** 34 40N 135 30 E
Ōsaka □, *Japan* **73 C7** 34 30N 135 30 E
Osaka Kansai International ✈ (KIX), *Japan* **73 C7** 34 27N 135 12 E
Ōsaka-Wan, *Japan* **73 C7** 34 30N 135 18 E
Ōsaki, *Japan* **72 F3** 31 25N 131 2 E
Osan, *S. Korea* **75 F14** 37 11N 127 4 E
Osawatomie, *U.S.A.* **154 F7** 38 31N 94 57W
Osborne, *U.S.A.* **154 F5** 39 26N 98 42W
Osby, *Sweden* **17 H7** 56 23N 13 59 E
Osceola, *Ark., U.S.A.* **155 H10** 35 42N 89 58W
Osceola, *Iowa, U.S.A.* **156 C3** 41 2N 93 46W
Osceola, *Mo., U.S.A.* **156 F3** 38 3N 93 42W
Oschatz, *Germany* **30 D9** 51 17N 13 6 E
Oschersleben, *Germany* **30 C7** 52 2N 11 14 E
Óschiri, *Italy* **46 B2** 40 43N 9 6 E
Oscoda, *U.S.A.* **150 B1** 44 26N 83 20W
Osečina, *Serbia & M.* **50 B3** 44 23N 19 34 E
Ösel = Saaremaa, *Estonia* **15 G20** 58 30N 22 30 E
Osensjøen, *Norway* **18 C8** 61 13N 11 50 E
Osery, *Russia* **58 E10** 54 52N 38 28 E
Osgood, *U.S.A.* **157 E11** 39 8N 85 18W
Osgoode, *Canada* **151 A9** 45 8N 75 36W
Osh, *Kyrgyzstan* **65 C6** 40 37N 72 49 E
Oshawa, *Canada* **140 D4** 43 50N 78 50W
Oshigambo, *Namibia* **116 B2** 17 45 S 16 5 E
Oshkosh, *Nebr., U.S.A.* **154 E3** 41 24N 102 21W
Oshkosh, *Wis., U.S.A.* **154 C10** 44 1N 88 33W
Oshmyany = Ashmyany, *Belarus* **15 J21** 54 26N 25 52 E
Oshnovīyeh, *Iran* **96 B5** 37 2N 45 6 E
Oshogbo, *Nigeria* **113 D5** 7 48N 4 37 E
Oshtorīnān, *Iran* **97 C6** 34 1N 48 38 E
Oshwe, *Dem. Rep. of the Congo* **114 C3** 3 25 S 19 28 E
Osi, *Nigeria* **113 D6** 8 8N 5 14 E
Osieczna, *Poland* **55 G3** 51 55N 16 40 E
Osijek, *Croatia* **52 E3** 45 34N 18 41 E
Ósilo, *Italy* **46 B1** 40 45N 8 40 E
Ósimo, *Italy* **45 E10** 43 28N 13 30 E
Osintorf, *Belarus* **58 E6** 54 40N 30 39 E
Osipenko = Berdyansk, *Ukraine* **59 J9** 46 45N 36 50 E
Osipovichi = Asipovichy, *Belarus* **58 F5** 53 19N 28 33 E
Osiyan, *India* **92 F5** 26 43N 72 55 E
Osizweni, *S. Africa* **117 D5** 27 49 S 30 7 E
Oskaloosa, *U.S.A.* **156 C4** 41 18N 92 39W
Oskarshamn, *Sweden* **17 G10** 57 15N 16 27 E
Oskarström, *Sweden* **17 H6** 56 48N 12 58 E
Oskélanéo, *Canada* **140 C4** 48 5N 75 15W
Öskemen, *Kazakhstan* **66 E9** 50 0N 82 36 E
Oskol →, *Ukraine* **59 H9** 49 6N 37 25 E
Oslo, *Norway* **18 E7** 59 55N 10 45 E
Oslo □, *Norway* **18 D7** 59 54N 10 43 E
Oslo ✈ (OSL), *Norway* **18 D8** 60 10N 11 8 E
Oslob, *Phil.* **81 G4** 9 31N 123 26 E
Oslofjorden, *Norway* **18 E7** 59 20N 10 35 E
Osmanabad, *India* **94 E3** 18 5N 76 10 E
Osmancık, *Turkey* **100 B6** 40 58N 34 47 E
Osmaniye, *Turkey* **100 D7** 37 5N 36 10 E
Osmanlı, *Turkey* **51 E10** 41 35N 26 51 E
Osmannagar, *India* **94 E4** 18 32N 79 20 E
Ösmo, *Sweden* **16 F11** 58 58N 17 55 E
Osnabrück, *Germany* **30 C4** 52 17N 8 3 E
Ośno Lubuskie, *Poland* **55 F1** 52 28N 14 51 E
Osoblaha, *Czech Rep.* **35 A10** 50 17N 17 44 E
Osogovska Planina, *Macedonia* **50 D6** 42 10N 22 30 E
Osor, *Italy* **45 D11** 44 42N 14 24 E
Osorio, *Brazil* **175 B5** 29 53 S 50 17W
Osório da Fonseca, *Brazil* **169 D6** 3 52 S 58 14W
Osorno, *Chile* **176 B2** 40 25 S 73 0W
Osorno, *Spain* **42 C6** 42 24N 4 22W
Osorno □, *Chile* **176 B2** 40 34 S 73 9W
Osorno, Vol., *Chile* **176 B2** 41 0 S 72 30W
Osoyoos, *Canada* **142 D5** 49 0N 119 30W
Osøyro, *Norway* **18 D2** 60 9N 5 30 E
Ospakseyri, *Iceland* **11 B5** 65 27N 21 26W
Ospika →, *Canada* **142 B4** 56 20N 124 0W
Osprey, *U.S.A.* **153 H7** 27 12N 82 29W
Osprey Reef, *Australia* **126 A4** 13 52 S 146 36 E
Oss, *Neths.* **24 C5** 51 46N 5 32 E
Ossa, Mt., *Australia* **127 G4** 41 52 S 146 3 E
Óssa, Óros, *Greece* **48 B4** 39 47N 22 42 E
Ossa de Montiel, *Spain* **41 G2** 38 58N 2 45W
Ossabaw I., *U.S.A.* **152 D8** 31 50N 81 5W
Ossabaw Sd., *U.S.A.* **152 D8** 31 50N 81 6W
Osse →, *France* **28 D4** 44 7N 0 17 E
Osse →, *Nigeria* **113 D6** 6 10N 5 20 E
Ossersee = Zarasai, *Lithuania* **15 J22** 55 40N 26 20 E
Ossi, *Italy* **46 B1** 40 40N 8 35 E
Ossining, *U.S.A.* **151 E11** 41 10N 73 55W
Ossipee, *U.S.A.* **151 C13** 43 41N 71 7W
Ossokmanuan L., *Canada* **141 B7** 53 25N 65 0W
Ossora, *Russia* **67 D17** 59 20N 163 13 E
Ostashkov, *Russia* **58 D7** 57 4N 33 2 E
Östavall, *Sweden* **16 B9** 62 26N 15 29 E
Østby, *Norway* **18 C9** 61 15N 12 33 E
Oste →, *Germany* **30 B5** 53 49N 9 2 E
Ostenburg = Pułtusk, *Poland* **55 F8** 52 43N 21 6 E
Ostend = Oostende, *Belgium* **24 C2** 51 15N 2 54 E
Ostend, *N.Z.* **130 C4** 36 48 S 175 2 E
Oster, *Ukraine* **59 G6** 50 57N 30 53 E
Österbotten = Pohjanmaa, *Finland* **14 E20** 62 58N 22 50 E
Osterburg, *Germany* **30 C7** 52 47N 11 45 E
Osterburg, *U.S.A.* **150 F6** 40 16N 78 31W
Osterburken, *Germany* **31 F5** 49 25N 9 26 E
Österbybruk, *Sweden* **16 D11** 60 13N 17 55 E
Österbymo, *Sweden* **17 G9** 57 49N 15 15 E
Österdalälven, *Sweden* **16 C7** 61 30N 13 45 E
Østerdalen, *Norway* **15 F14** 61 40N 10 50 E
Österfärnebo, *Sweden* **16 D10** 60 19N 16 48 E

Österforse, *Sweden* **16 A11** 63 9N 17 3 E
Östergötlands län □, *Sweden* **17 F9** 58 35N 15 45 E
Osterholz-Scharmbeck, *Germany* **30 B4** 53 13N 8 47 E
Østerild, *Denmark* **17 G2** 57 2N 8 51 E
Ostermundigen, *Switz.* **32 C4** 46 58N 7 27 E
Östermyra = Seinäjoki, *Finland* **15 E20** 62 40N 22 51 E
Osterode, *Germany* **30 D6** 51 43N 10 15 E
Osterode in Ostpreussen = Ostróda, *Poland* **54 E6** 53 42N 19 58 E
Österreich = Austria ■, *Europe* **34 E7** 47 0N 14 0 E
Österreich ober der Ems = Oberösterreich □, *Austria* **34 C7** 48 10N 14 0 E
Östersund, *Sweden* **16 A8** 63 10N 14 38 E
Östervåla, *Sweden* **16 D11** 60 11N 17 11 E
Østfold □, *Norway* **18 E8** 59 25N 11 25 E
Ostfriesische Inseln, *Germany* **30 B3** 53 42N 7 0 E
Ostfriesland, *Germany* **30 B3** 53 20N 7 30 E
Östhammar, *Sweden* **16 D12** 60 16N 18 22 E
Óstia, Lido di, *Italy* **45 G9** 41 43N 12 17 E
Ostíglia, *Italy* **45 C8** 45 4N 11 8 E
Östmark, *Sweden* **16 D6** 60 17N 12 45 E
Östra Husby, *Sweden* **17 F10** 58 35N 16 33 E
Ostrava, *Czech Rep.* **35 B11** 49 51N 18 18 E
Ostravský □, *Czech Rep.* **35 B10** 49 55N 17 58 E
Ostróda, *Poland* **54 E6** 53 42N 19 58 E
Ostrogozhsk, *Russia* **59 G10** 50 55N 39 7 E
Ostroh, *Ukraine* **59 G4** 50 20N 26 30 E
Ostrołęka, *Poland* **55 E8** 53 4N 21 32 E
Ostrov, *Bulgaria* **51 C8** 43 40N 24 9 E
Ostrov, *Czech Rep.* **34 A5** 50 18N 12 57 E
Ostrov, *Romania* **53 F12** 44 6N 27 24 E
Ostrov, *Russia* **58 D5** 57 25N 28 20 E
Ostrów Lubelski, *Poland* **55 G9** 51 29N 22 51 E
Ostrów Mazowiecka, *Poland* **55 F8** 52 50N 21 51 E
Ostrów Wielkopolski, *Poland* **55 G4** 51 36N 17 44 E
Ostrowiec-Świętokrzyski, *Poland* **55 H8** 50 55N 21 22 E
Ostrowo = Ostrów Wielkopolski, *Poland* **55 G4** 51 36N 17 44 E
Ostrožac, *Bos.-H.* **52 G2** 43 43N 17 49 E
Ostrzeszów, *Poland* **55 G4** 51 25N 17 52 E
Ostseebad Kühlungsborn, *Germany* **30 A7** 54 8N 11 44 E
Osttirol □, *Austria* **34 E5** 46 50N 12 30 E
Ostuni, *Italy* **47 B10** 40 44N 17 35 E
Ostyako-Vogulsk = Khanty-Mansiysk, *Russia* **66 C7** 61 0N 69 0 E
Osum →, *Albania* **50 F4** 40 40N 20 10 E
Osŭm →, *Bulgaria* **51 C8** 43 40N 24 50 E
Ōsumi-Hantō, *Japan* **72 F2** 31 20N 130 55 E
Ōsumi-Kaikyō, *Japan* **71 J5** 30 55N 131 0 E
Ōsumi-Shotō, *Japan* **71 J5** 30 30N 130 0 E
Osun □, *Nigeria* **113 D5** 7 30N 4 30 E
Osuna, *Spain* **43 H5** 37 14N 5 8W
Oswegatchie →, *U.S.A.* **151 B9** 44 42N 75 30W
Oswego, *U.S.A.* **151 C8** 43 27N 76 31W
Oswego →, *U.S.A.* **151 C8** 43 27N 76 30W
Oswestry, *U.K.* **20 E4** 52 52N 3 3W
Oświęcim, *Poland* **55 H6** 50 2N 19 11 E
Ōta, *Fukui, Japan* **73 B8** 35 57N 136 3 E
Ōta, *Gumma, Japan* **73 A11** 36 18N 139 22 E
Ōta-Gawa →, *Japan* **72 C4** 34 21N 132 18 E
Otaci, *Moldova* **53 B12** 48 27N 27 47 E
Otago □, *N.Z.* **131 E4** 45 15 S 170 0 E
Otago Harbour, *N.Z.* **131 F5** 45 47 S 170 42 E
Otago Pen., *N.Z.* **131 F5** 45 48 S 170 39 E
Otaheite B., *Trin. & Tob.* **169 F9** 10 15N 61 30W
Otahuhu, *N.Z.* **130 C3** 36 56 S 174 51 E
Ōtake, *Japan* **72 C4** 34 12N 132 13 E
Ōtaki, *Japan* **73 B12** 35 17N 140 15 E
Otaki, *N.Z.* **130 G4** 40 45 S 175 10 E
Otane, *N.Z.* **130 F5** 39 54 S 176 39 E
Otar, *Kazakhstan* **65 B7** 43 32N 75 12 E
Otaru, *Japan* **70 C10** 43 10N 141 0 E
Otaru-Wan = Ishikari-Wan, *Japan* **70 C10** 43 25N 141 1 E
Otautau, *N.Z.* **131 G3** 46 9 S 168 1 E
Otava →, *Czech Rep.* **34 B7** 49 26N 14 12 E
Otavalo, *Ecuador* **168 C2** 0 13N 78 20W
Otavi, *Namibia* **116 B2** 19 40 S 17 24 E
Otchinjau, *Angola* **116 B1** 16 30 S 13 56 E
Oteiza = Marihatag, *Phil.* **81 G6** 8 48N 126 18 E
Otelec, *Romania* **52 E5** 45 36N 20 50 E
Otelnuk, L., *Canada* **141 A6** 56 9N 68 12W
Oţelu Roşu, *Romania* **52 E7** 45 32N 22 22 E
Otero de Rey = Outeiro de Rei, *Spain* **42 B3** 43 6N 7 36W
Othello, *U.S.A.* **158 C4** 46 50N 119 10W
Othonoí, *Greece* **38 B9** 39 52N 19 22 E
Óthris, Óros, *Greece* **48 B4** 39 2N 22 37 E
Oti ⌓, *Togo* **113 C5** 10 40N 0 35 E
Otira, *N.Z.* **131 C6** 42 49 S 171 35 E
Otira Gorge, *N.Z.* **131 C6** 42 53 S 171 33 E
Otjiwarongo, *Namibia* **116 C2** 20 30 S 16 33 E
Ötmök, *Kyrgyzstan* **65 B6** 42 20N 73 10 E
Otmuchów, *Poland* **55 H4** 50 28N 17 10 E
Oto Tolu Group, *Tonga* **133 Q13** 20 21 S 174 32W
Otočac, *Croatia* **45 D12** 44 53N 15 12 E
Otoineppu, *Japan* **70 B11** 44 44N 142 16 E
Otok, *Croatia* **45 E13** 43 42N 16 44 E
Otomavi = Korsakov, *Russia* **67 E15** 46 36N 142 42 E
Oton, *Phil.* **81 F4** 10 42N 122 29 E
Otopeni, Bucureşti ✈ (OTP), *Romania* **53 F11** 44 30N 26 11 E
Otorohanga, *N.Z.* **130 E4** 38 12 S 175 14 E
Otoskwin →, *Canada* **140 B2** 52 13N 88 6W
Ōtoyo, *Japan* **72 D5** 33 43N 133 45 E
Otpor = Zabaykalsk, *Russia* **67 E12** 49 40N 117 25 E
Otra →, *Norway* **18 F5** 58 9N 8 1 E
Otradnyy, *Russia* **60 D10** 53 22N 51 21 E
Otranto, *Italy* **47 B11** 40 9N 18 28 E
Otranto, C. d', *Italy* **47 B11** 40 7N 18 30 E
Otranto, Str. of, *Italy* **47 B11** 40 15N 18 40 E
Otrogovo = Stepnoye, *Russia* **64 D8** 54 4N 60 26 E
Otrokovice, *Czech Rep.* **35 B10** 49 12N 17 32 E
Otse, *S. Africa* **116 D4** 25 2 S 25 45 E
Otsego, *U.S.A.* **157 B11** 42 27N 85 42W
Ōtsu, *Japan* **73 C7** 35 0N 135 50 E
Ōtsuki, *Japan* **73 B10** 35 36N 138 57 E
Otta, *Norway* **18 C6** 61 46N 9 32 E
Otta →, *Norway* **18 C6** 61 46N 9 31 E
Ottapalam, *India* **95 J3** 10 46N 76 23 E
Ottawa = Outaouais →, *Canada* **140 C5** 45 27N 74 8W
Ottawa, *Canada* **140 C4** 45 27N 75 42W
Ottawa, *Ill., U.S.A.* **154 E10** 41 21N 88 51W
Ottawa, *Kans., U.S.A.* **154 F7** 38 37N 95 16W
Ottawa, *Ohio, U.S.A.* **157 C12** 41 1N 84 3W
Ottawa Is., *Canada* **139 C11** 59 35N 80 10W
Ottélé, *Cameroon* **113 E7** 3 38N 11 19 E
Ottensheim, *Austria* **34 C7** 48 21N 14 12 E
Otter Cr. →, *U.S.A.* **151 B11** 44 13N 73 17W
Otter Creek, *U.S.A.* **153 F7** 29 19N 82 46W
Otter L., *Canada* **143 B8** 55 35N 104 39W
Otterbein, *U.S.A.* **157 D9** 40 29N 87 6W
Otterndorf, *Germany* **30 B4** 53 48N 8 53 E
Otterøya, *Norway* **18 B3** 62 45N 6 50 E
Otterup, *Denmark* **17 J4** 55 30N 10 22 E
Otterville, *Canada* **150 D4** 42 55N 80 36W
Otterville, *U.S.A.* **156 F4** 38 42N 93 0W
Ottery St. Mary, *U.K.* **21 G4** 50 44N 3 17W
Ottilien Reef, *Papua N. G.* **132 C5** 4 33 S 148 49 E
Ottmachau = Otmuchów, *Poland* **55 H4** 50 28N 17 10 E
Otto Beit Bridge, *Zimbabwe* **119 F2** 15 59 S 28 56 E
Ottosdal, *S. Africa* **116 D4** 26 46 S 25 59 E
Ottoville, *U.S.A.* **157 D12** 40 57N 84 22W
Ottumwa, *U.S.A.* **156 D4** 41 1N 92 25W
Otu, *Nigeria* **113 D5** 8 14N 3 22 E
Otukpa, *Nigeria* **113 D6** 7 9N 7 41 E
Oturkpo, *Nigeria* **113 D6** 7 16N 8 8 E
Otvazhnoye = Zhigulevsk, *Russia* **60 D9** 53 28N 49 30 E
Otvazhny = Zhigulevsk, *Russia* **60 D9** 53 28N 49 30 E
Otway △, *Australia* **128 E5** 38 47 S 143 34 E
Otway, B., *Chile* **176 D2** 53 30 S 74 0W
Otway, C., *Australia* **128 E5** 38 52 S 143 30 E
Otway, Seno de, *Chile* **176 D2** 53 0 S 71 30W
Otwock, *Poland* **55 F8** 52 5N 21 20 E
Otyniya, *Ukraine* **53 B9** 48 44N 24 51 E
Ötztaler Ache →, *Austria* **34 D3** 47 14N 10 50 E
Ötztaler Alpen, *Austria* **34 E3** 46 56N 11 0 E
Ou →, *Laos* **86 B4** 20 4N 102 13 E
Ou Neua, *Laos* **76 F3** 22 18N 101 48 E
Ou-Sammyaku, *Japan* **70 E10** 39 20N 140 35 E
Ouachita →, *U.S.A.* **155 K9** 31 38N 91 49W
Ouachita, L., *U.S.A.* **155 H8** 34 34N 93 12W
Ouachita Mts., *U.S.A.* **155 H7** 34 40N 94 25W
Ouaco, *N. Cal.* **133 T18** 20 50 S 164 29 E
Ouadâne, *Mauritania* **110 D2** 20 50N 11 40W
Ouadda, *C.A.R.* **114 A4** 8 15N 22 20 E
Ouagadougou, *Burkina Faso* **113 C4** 12 25N 1 30W
Ouagam, *Chad* **109 F2** 14 22N 14 42 E
Ouaham →, *C.A.R.* **114 A3** 6 35N 15 12 E
Ouahigouya, *Burkina Faso* **112 C4** 13 31N 2 25W
Ouahila, *Algeria* **110 C4** 27 50N 5 0W
Ouahran = Oran, *Algeria* **111 A4** 35 45N 0 39W
Oualâta, *Mauritania* **112 B3** 17 20N 6 55W
Ouallam, *Niger* **113 C5** 14 23N 2 10 E
Ouallene, *Algeria* **111 D5** 24 41N 1 11 E
Ouanary, *Fr. Guiana* **169 C7** 4 13N 51 40W
Ouanda Djallé, *C.A.R.* **114 A4** 8 55N 22 53 E
Ouandago, *C.A.R.* **114 A3** 7 13N 18 50 E
Ouandjia, Bahr →, *C.A.R.* **114 A4** 9 35N 21 43 E
Ouandjia-Vakaga ⌓, *C.A.R.* **114 A4** 9 2N 22 18 E
Ouango, *C.A.R.* **114 B4** 4 19N 22 30 E
Ouani, *Comoros Is.* **121 a** 12 9 S 44 18 E
Ouantonou, *C.A.R.* **114 A3** 7 19N 15 18 E
Ouarâne, *Mauritania* **110 D2** 21 0N 10 30W
Ouargaye, *Burkina Faso* **113 C5** 11 40N 0 5 E
Ouargla, *Algeria* **111 B6** 31 59N 5 16 E
Ouarkoye, *Burkina Faso* **112 C4** 12 5N 3 40W
Ouarkziz, Jebel, *Algeria* **110 C3** 28 50N 8 0W
Ouarra →, *C.A.R.* **114 A4** 5 5N 24 26 E
Ouarzazate, *Morocco* **110 B3** 30 55N 6 50W
Ouassouas, *Mali* **113 B5** 16 10N 1 23 E
Ouatagouna, *Mali* **113 B5** 15 11N 0 43 E
Ouatere, *C.A.R.* **114 A3** 5 30N 19 8 E
Oubangi →, *Dem. Rep. of the Congo* **114 C3** 0 30 S 17 50 E
Oubarakai, O. →, *Algeria* **111 C6** 27 20N 9 0 E
Ouche →, *France* **27 E12** 47 6N 5 16 E
Ouddorp, *Neths.* **24 C3** 51 50N 3 57 E
Oude Rijn →, *Neths.* **24 B4** 52 12N 4 24 E
Oudeïka, *Mali* **113 B4** 17 30N 1 40W
Oudenaarde, *Belgium* **24 D3** 50 50N 3 37 E
Oudon →, *France* **26 E6** 47 41N 0 53W
Oudtshoorn, *S. Africa* **116 E3** 33 35 S 22 14 E
Oued Zem, *Morocco* **110 B3** 32 52N 6 34W
Ouégoa, *N. Cal.* **133 T18** 20 20 S 164 26 E
Oueita, *Chad* **109 E4** 17 47N 20 39 E
Ouellé, *Ivory C.* **112 D4** 7 26N 4 1W
Ouéme →, *Benin* **113 D5** 6 30N 2 30 E
Ouen, Î., *N. Cal.* **133 V20** 22 26 S 166 49 E
Ouenza, *Algeria* **111 A6** 35 57N 8 4 E
Ouessa, *Burkina Faso* **112 C4** 11 4N 2 47W
Ouessant, Î. d', *France* **26 D1** 48 28N 5 6W
Ouesso, *Congo* **114 B3** 1 37N 16 5 E
Ouest, Pte. de l', *Canada* **141 C7** 49 52N 64 40W
Ouezzane, *Morocco* **110 B3** 34 51N 5 35W
Ougarou, *Burkina Faso* **113 C5** 12 10N 0 58 E
Oughterard, *Ireland* **23 C2** 53 26N 9 18W
Ouhan →, *Chad* **109 G3** 9 18N 18 14 E
Ouidah, *Benin* **113 D5** 6 25N 2 0 E
Ouidi, *Niger* **113 C7** 14 10N 13 0 E
Ouissongo, *Angola* **115 E3** 7 40 S 15 41 E
Ouistreham, *France* **26 C6** 49 17N 0 18W
Oujda, *Morocco* **111 B4** 34 41N 1 55W
Oujeft, *Mauritania* **112 A2** 20 2N 13 0W
Oulainen, *Finland* **14 D21** 64 17N 24 47 E
Ould Yenjé, *Mauritania* **112 B2** 15 38N 12 16W
Ouled Djellal, *Algeria* **111 B6** 34 28N 5 2 E
Ouled Naïl, Mts. des, *Algeria* **111 B5** 34 30N 3 30 E
Ouli, *Cameroon* **114 A2** 5 12N 14 33 E
Oullins, *France* **29 C8** 45 43N 4 49 E
Oulmès, *Morocco* **110 B3** 33 17N 6 0W
Oulou, Bahr →, *C.A.R.* **114 A4** 9 48N 21 32 E
Oulu, *Finland* **14 D21** 65 1N 25 29 E
Oulujärvi, *Finland* **14 D22** 64 25N 27 15 E
Oulujoki →, *Finland* **14 D21** 65 1N 25 30 E
Oulx, *Italy* **44 C3** 45 2N 6 50 E
Oum Chalouba, *Chad* **109 E4** 15 48N 20 46 E
Oum-el-Bouaghi, *Algeria* **111 A6** 35 55N 7 6 E
Oum-el-Ksi, *Algeria* **110 C3** 29 4N 6 59W
Oum-er-Rbia, O. →, *Morocco* **110 B3** 33 19N 8 21W
Oum Hadjer, *Chad* **109 F3** 13 18N 19 41 E
Oum Hadjer, O. →, *Chad* **109 E4** 16 38N 20 14 E
Oumé, *Ivory C.* **112 D3** 6 21N 5 27W
Oumm ed Droûs Guebli, Sebkhet, *Mauritania* **110 D2** 24 3N 11 45W
Oumm ed Droûs Telli, Sebkhet, *Mauritania* **110 D2** 24 20N 11 30W
Ounane, Dj., *Algeria* **111 C6** 25 4N 7 19 E
Ounasjoki →, *Finland* **14 C21** 66 31N 25 40 E
Ounguati, *Namibia* **116 C2** 22 0 S 15 46 E
Ounianga Kébir, *Chad* **109 E4** 19 4N 20 29 E
Ounianga Sérir, *Chad* **109 E4** 18 54N 20 51 E
Ounissoui, *Niger* **109 E2** 17 34N 12 13 E
Our →, *Lux.* **24 E6** 49 55N 6 5 E
Ouranópolis, *Greece* **50 F7** 40 20N 23 59 E
Ourârene, *Niger* **113 B6** 19 30N 7 10 E
Ourari, Tarso, *Chad* **109 D3** 21 27N 17 27 E
Ouray, *U.S.A.* **159 G10** 38 1N 107 40W
Ourcq →, *France* **27 C10** 49 1N 3 1 E
Ourém, *Brazil* **170 B2** 1 33 S 47 6W
Ourense, *Spain* **42 C3** 42 19N 7 55W
Ouricuri, *Brazil* **170 C3** 7 53 S 40 5W
Ourinhos, *Brazil* **175 A6** 23 0 S 49 54W
Ourique, *Portugal* **43 H2** 37 38N 8 16W
Ouro Fino, *Brazil* **175 A6** 22 16 S 46 25W
Ouro-Ndia, *Mali* **112 B4** 15 8N 4 35W
Ouro Prêto, *Brazil* **171 F3** 20 20 S 43 30W
Ouro Prêto do Oeste, *Brazil* **173 C5** 10 40 S 62 18W
Ouro Sogui, *Senegal* **112 B2** 15 36N 13 19W
Oursi, *Burkina Faso* **113 C4** 14 41N 0 27W
Ourthe →, *Belgium* **24 D5** 50 29N 5 35 E
Ouse →, *E. Susx., U.K.* **21 G8** 50 47N 0 4 E
Ouse →, *N. Yorks., U.K.* **20 D7** 53 44N 0 55W
Oust, *France* **28 F5** 42 52N 1 13 E
Oust →, *France* **26 E4** 47 35N 2 6W
Outamba-Kilimi △, *S. Leone* **112 D2** 9 50N 12 40W
Outaouais →, *Canada* **140 C5** 45 27N 74 8W
Outardes →, *Canada* **141 C6** 49 24N 69 30W
Outat Oulad el Haj, *Morocco* **111 B4** 33 22N 3 42W
Outeiro de Rei, *Spain* **42 B3** 43 6N 7 36W
Outer Hebrides, *U.K.* **22 D1** 57 30N 7 40W
Outes = Serra de Outes, *Spain* **42 C2** 42 52N 8 55W
Outjo, *Namibia* **116 C2** 20 5 S 16 7 E
Outlook, *Canada* **143 C7** 51 30N 107 0W
Outokumpu, *Finland* **14 E23** 62 43N 29 1 E
Outreau, *France* **27 B8** 50 40N 1 36 E
Ouvéa, Î., *N. Cal.* **133 K4** 20 35 S 166 35 E
Ouvèze →, *France* **29 E8** 43 59N 4 51 E
Ouyen, *Australia* **128 C5** 35 1 S 142 22 E
Ouzinkie, *U.S.A.* **144 H9** 57 56N 152 30W
Ouzouer-le-Marché, *France* **27 E8** 47 54N 1 32 E
Ovada, *Italy* **44 D5** 44 38N 8 38 E
Ovahe, *Chile* **172 b** 27 5 S 109 19W
Ovalau, *Fiji* **133 A2** 17 40 S 178 48 E
Ovalle, *Chile* **174 C1** 30 33 S 71 18W
Ovamboland, *Namibia* **116 B2** 18 30 S 16 0 E
Ovar, *Portugal* **42 E2** 40 51N 8 40W
Ovau, *Solomon Is.* **133 L9** 6 40 S 156 8 E
Overath, *Germany* **30 E3** 50 56N 7 17 E
Overflakkee, *Neths.* **24 C4** 51 44N 4 10 E
Overijssel □, *Neths.* **24 B6** 52 25N 6 35 E
Overland, *U.S.A.* **156 F6** 38 41N 90 22W
Overland Park, *U.S.A.* **154 F7** 38 55N 94 50W
Overton, *U.S.A.* **161 J12** 36 33N 114 27W
Övertorneå, *Sweden* **14 C20** 66 23N 23 38 E
Överum, *Sweden* **17 F10** 58 0N 16 20 E
Ovid, *Mich., U.S.A.* **157 A12** 43 1N 84 22W
Ovid, *N.Y., U.S.A.* **151 D8** 42 41N 76 49W
Ovidiopol, *Ukraine* **59 J6** 46 15N 30 30 E
Ovidiu, *Romania* **53 F13** 44 16N 28 34 E
Oviedo, *Spain* **42 B5** 43 25N 5 50W
Oviedo, *U.S.A.* **153 G8** 28 40N 81 13W
Oviksfjällen, *Sweden* **16 A7** 63 0N 13 49 E
Oviši, *Latvia* **15 H19** 57 33N 21 44 E
Ovoot, *Mongolia* **74 B7** 45 21N 113 45 E
Övör Hangay □, *Mongolia* **74 B2** 45 0N 102 30 E
Ovoro, *Nigeria* **113 D6** 5 26N 7 16 E
Øvre Årdal, *Norway* **18 C4** 61 19N 7 48 E
Övre Fryken, *Sweden* **16 E7** 60 0N 13 7 E
Øvre Rendal, *Norway* **18 C8** 61 54N 11 4 E
Øvre Rindal, *Norway* **18 A6** 63 6N 9 10 E
Øvre Sirdal, *Norway* **18 F3** 58 48N 6 43 E
Ovruch, *Ukraine* **59 G5** 51 25N 28 45 E
Owaka, *N.Z.* **131 G4** 46 27 S 169 40 E
Owambo = Ovamboland, *Namibia* **116 B2** 18 30 S 16 0 E
Owando, *Congo* **114 C3** 0 29 S 15 55 E
Owasco L., *U.S.A.* **151 D8** 42 50N 76 31W
Owase, *Japan* **73 C8** 34 7N 136 12 E
Owatonna, *U.S.A.* **154 C8** 44 5N 93 14W
Owbeh, *Afghan.* **91 B1** 34 28N 63 10 E
Owego, *U.S.A.* **151 D8** 42 6N 76 16W
Owen, *Australia* **128 C3** 34 15 S 138 32 E
Owen, Mt., *N.Z.* **131 B7** 41 35 S 172 33 E
Owen Falls Dam, *Uganda* **118 B3** 0 30N 33 5 E
Owen Sound, *Canada* **140 D3** 44 35N 80 55W
Owen Stanley Ra., *Papua N. G.* **132 E4** 8 30 S 147 0 E
Owendo, *Gabon* **114 B1** 0 17N 9 30 E
Owens →, *U.S.A.* **160 J9** 36 32N 117 59W
Owens L., *U.S.A.* **161 J9** 36 26N 117 57W
Owensboro, *U.S.A.* **157 G9** 37 46N 87 7W
Owensville, *Ind., U.S.A.* **157 F9** 38 16N 87 41W
Owensville, *Mo., U.S.A.* **156 F5** 38 21N 91 30W
Owenteik, *Guyana* **169 C6** 4 27N 59 35W
Owenton, *U.S.A.* **157 F12** 38 32N 84 50W
Owerri, *Nigeria* **113 D6** 5 29N 7 0 E
Owhango, *N.Z.* **130 F4** 39 0 S 175 23 E
Owingsville, *U.S.A.* **157 F13** 38 9N 83 46W
Owl →, *Canada* **143 B10** 57 51N 92 44W
Owo, *Nigeria* **113 D6** 7 10N 5 39 E
Owosso, *U.S.A.* **157 B12** 43 0N 84 10W
Owyhee, *U.S.A.* **158 F5** 41 57N 116 6W
Owyhee →, *U.S.A.* **158 E5** 43 49N 117 2W
Owyhee, L., *U.S.A.* **158 E5** 43 38N 117 14W
Ox Mts. = Slieve Gamph, *Ireland* **23 B3** 54 6N 9 0W
Oxapampa, *Peru* **172 C2** 10 33 S 75 26W
Öxarfjörður, *Iceland* **11 A10** 66 15N 16 45W
Oxbow, *Canada* **143 D8** 49 14N 102 10W
Oxelösund, *Sweden* **17 F11** 58 43N 17 5 E
Oxford, *N.Z.* **131 D7** 43 18 S 172 11 E
Oxford, *U.K.* **21 F6** 51 46N 1 15W
Oxford, *Ala., U.S.A.* **152 B4** 33 36N 85 51W
Oxford, *Iowa, U.S.A.* **156 C5** 41 43N 91 47W
Oxford, *Mass., U.S.A.* **151 D13** 42 7N 71 52W
Oxford, *Mich., U.S.A.* **157 B13** 42 49N 83 16W
Oxford, *Miss., U.S.A.* **155 H10** 34 22N 89 31W
Oxford, *N.C., U.S.A.* **149 G6** 36 19N 78 35W
Oxford, *N.Y., U.S.A.* **151 D9** 42 27N 75 36W
Oxford, *Ohio, U.S.A.* **157 E12** 39 31N 84 45W
Oxford L., *Canada* **143 C9** 54 51N 95 37W
Oxfordshire □, *U.K.* **21 F6** 51 48N 1 16W
Oxía Nisís, *Greece* **39 C3** 38 18N 21 6 E
Oxie, *Sweden* **17 J7** 55 33N 13 6 E
Oxílithos, *Greece* **48 C6** 38 35N 24 7 E
Oxley, *Australia* **128 C6** 34 11 S 144 6 E
Oxley Wild Rivers △, *Australia* **129 A10** 30 57 S 152 12 E
Oxnard, *U.S.A.* **161 L7** 34 12N 119 11W
Oxsjövålen, *Sweden* **16 B7** 62 34N 13 57 E
Oxus = Amudarya →, *Uzbekistan* **66 E6** 43 58N 59 34 E
Oy-Tal, *Kyrgyzstan* **65 C7** 40 24N 74 6 E
Oya, *Malaysia* **85 B4** 2 55N 111 55 E
Oyabe, *Japan* **73 A8** 36 47N 136 56 E
Oyama, *Japan* **73 A11** 36 18N 139 48 E
Oyambre ⌓, *Spain* **42 B6** 43 22N 4 21W
Oyapock →, *Fr. Guiana* **169 C7** 4 8N 51 40W
Øye, *Norway* **18 F3** 58 16N 6 49 E
Oyem, *Gabon* **114 B2** 1 34N 11 31 E
Oyen, *Canada* **143 C6** 51 22N 110 28W
Øyer, *Norway* **18 C7** 61 16N 10 25 E
Øyeren, *Norway* **18 E8** 59 50N 11 15 E
Oykel →, *U.K.* **22 D4** 57 56N 4 26W
Oymyakon, *Russia* **67 C15** 63 25N 142 44 E
Oyo, *Nigeria* **113 D5** 7 46N 3 56 E
Oyo □, *Nigeria* **113 D5** 8 15N 3 30 E
Oyón, *Peru* **172 C2** 10 37 S 76 47W
Oyonnax, *France* **27 F12** 46 16N 5 40 E
Oyrot = Gorno-Altay □, *Russia* **66 D9** 51 0N 86 0 E
Oyrot-Tura = Gorno-Altaysk, *Russia* **66 D9** 51 50N 86 5 E
Øyslebø, *Norway* **18 F4** 58 9N 7 34 E
Oyster Bay, *U.S.A.* **151 F11** 40 52N 73 32W
Oyster Harbour = Ladysmith, *Canada* **142 D4** 49 0N 123 49W
Øystese, *Norway* **18 D3** 60 22N 6 9 E
Oytal, *Kazakhstan* **65 B6** 42 54N 73 17 E
Ōyūbari, *Japan* **70 C11** 43 1N 142 5 E
Oyyq, *Kazakhstan* **65 B5** 43 36N 71 16 E
Özalp, *Turkey* **101 C10** 38 39N 43 59 E
Ozamiz, *Phil.* **81 G4** 8 15N 123 50 E
Ozark, *Ala., U.S.A.* **152 D4** 31 28N 85 39W
Ozark, *Ark., U.S.A.* **155 H8** 35 29N 93 50W
Ozark, *Mo., U.S.A.* **155 G8** 37 1N 93 12W
Ozark Plateau, *U.S.A.* **155 G9** 37 20N 91 40W
Ozarks, L. of the, *U.S.A.* **156 F4** 38 12N 92 38W
Ożarów, *Poland* **55 H8** 50 53N 21 40 E
Ózd, *Hungary* **52 B5** 48 14N 20 15 E
Ozernoye, *Russia* **60 E10** 51 46N 51 28 E
Ozërnyy, *Russia* **64 F8** 51 8N 60 50 E
Ozero Svityaz, *Ukraine* **55 G10** 51 30N 23 50 E
Ozersk, *Russia* **54 D8** 54 25N 22 0 E
Ozette L., *U.S.A.* **160 B2** 48 6N 124 38W
Özgön, *Kyrgyzstan* **65 C6** 40 46N 73 18 E
Ozieri, *Italy* **46 B2** 40 35N 9 0 E
Ozimek, *Poland* **55 H5** 50 41N 18 11 E
Ozinki, *Russia* **60 E9** 51 12N 49 44 E
Ozona, *U.S.A.* **155 K4** 30 43N 101 12W
Ozorków, *Poland* **55 G6** 51 57N 19 16 E
Ozren, *Bos.-H.* **52 G3** 43 55N 18 29 E
Ōzu, *Ehime, Japan* **72 D4** 33 30N 132 33 E
Ōzu, *Kumamoto, Japan* **72 E2** 32 52N 130 52 E
Ozuluama, *Mexico* **163 C5** 21 40N 97 50W
Ozun, *Romania* **53 E10** 45 47N 25 50 E
Ozurgeti, *Georgia* **61 K5** 41 55N 42 2 E

P

Pa, *Burkina Faso* **112 C4** 11 33N 3 19W
Pa-an, *Burma* **90 G6** 16 51N 97 40 E
Pa Mong Dam, *Thailand* **86 D4** 18 0N 102 22 E
Pa Sak →, *Thailand* **78 B2** 15 30N 101 0 E
Paagoumène, *N. Cal.* **133 T18** 20 29 S 164 11 E
Paama, *Vanuatu* **133 F6** 16 28 S 168 14 E
Paamiut, *Greenland* **10 E6** 62 0N 49 43W
Paar →, *Germany* **31 G7** 48 46N 11 36 E
Paarl, *S. Africa* **116 E2** 33 45 S 18 56 E
Paauilo, *U.S.A.* **145 C6** 20 2N 155 22W
Pab Hills, *Pakistan* **91 D2** 26 30N 66 45 E
Pabbay, *U.K.* **22 D1** 57 46N 7 14W
Pabianice, *Poland* **55 G6** 51 40N 19 20 E
Pabna, *Bangla.* **90 C2** 24 1N 89 18 E
Pabo, *Uganda* **118 B3** 3 1N 32 10 E
Pacaás Novos △, *Brazil* **173 C5** 11 0 S 63 0W
Pacaás Novos, Serra dos, *Brazil* **173 C5** 10 45 S 64 15W
Pacaipampa, *Peru* **172 B2** 5 35 S 79 39W
Pacaja →, *Brazil* **170 B1** 1 56 S 50 50W
Pacajus, *Brazil* **170 B4** 4 10 S 38 31W
Pacaraima, Sa., *S. Amer.* **169 C5** 4 0N 62 30W
Pacarán, *Peru* **172 C2** 12 50 S 76 3W
Pacaraos, *Peru* **172 C2** 11 12 S 76 42W
Pacasmayo, *Peru* **172 B2** 7 20 S 79 35W
Pace, *U.S.A.* **153 E2** 30 36N 87 10W
Paceco, *Italy* **46 E5** 37 59N 12 33 E
Pachacamac, *Peru* **172 C2** 12 14 S 77 53W
Pachhar, *India* **92 G7** 24 40N 77 42 E
Pachino, *Italy* **47 F8** 36 43N 15 5 E
Pachitea →, *Peru* **172 B3** 8 46 S 74 33W
Pachiza, *Peru* **172 B2** 7 16 S 76 46W
Pachmarhi, *India* **93 H8** 22 28N 78 26 E
Pachnai, *India* **90 B4** 26 57N 92 19 E
Pacho, *Colombia* **168 B3** 5 8N 74 10W
Pachora, *India* **94 D2** 20 38N 75 29 E
Pachuca, *Mexico* **163 C5** 20 10N 98 40W
Pacific, *Canada* **142 C3** 54 48N 128 28W
Pacific, *U.S.A.* **156 F6** 38 29N 90 45W
Pacific-Antarctic Ridge, *Pac. Oc.* **7 B13** 43 0 S 115 0W
Pacific City = Huntington Beach, *U.S.A.* **161 M9** 33 40N 118 5W
Pacific Grove, *U.S.A.* **160 J5** 36 38N 121 56W
Pacific Ocean **135 G14** 10 0N 140 0W
Pacific Palisades, *U.S.A.* **145 K14** 21 25N 157 58W
Pacific Rim △, *Canada* **142 D4** 48 40N 124 45W
Pacifica, *U.S.A.* **160 H4** 37 36N 122 30W
Pacitan, *Indonesia* **85 D4** 8 12 S 111 7 E
Packsaddle, *Australia* **128 A4** 30 36 S 141 58 E
Packwood, *U.S.A.* **160 D5** 46 36N 121 40W
Pacov, *Czech Rep.* **34 B8** 49 27N 15 0 E
Pacoval, *Brazil* **169 D7** 2 40 S 54 11W
Pacuí →, *Brazil* **171 E2** 16 46 S 45 1W
Pacy-sur-Eure, *France* **26 C8** 49 1N 1 23 E
Padaido, Kepulauan, *Indonesia* **83 B5** 1 15 S 136 30 E
Padali = Amursk, *Russia* **67 D14** 50 14N 136 54 E
Padampur, *India* **94 D6** 20 59N 83 4 E
Padang, *Indonesia* **84 C2** 1 0 S 100 20 E
Padang Endau, *Malaysia* **87 L4** 2 40N 103 38 E
Padangpanjang, *Indonesia* **84 C2** 0 40 S 100 20 E
Padangsidempuan, *Indonesia* **84 B1** 1 30N 99 15 E
Padangtikar, *Indonesia* **85 C3** 0 44 S 109 15 E
Padatchaung, *Burma* **90 F5** 19 46N 94 48 E
Padauari →, *Brazil* **169 D5** 0 15 S 64 5W
Padaung, *Burma* **90 F5** 18 43N 95 9 E
Padborg, *Denmark* **17 K3** 54 49N 9 21 E
Padcaya, *Bolivia* **173 E5** 21 52 S 64 48W
Paddle Prairie, *Canada* **142 B5** 57 57N 117 29W
Paddockwood, *Canada* **143 C7** 53 30N 105 30W
Paderborn, *Germany* **30 D4** 51 42N 8 45 E
Paderoo, *India* **94 E6** 18 5N 82 40 E
Padeş, Vf., *Romania* **52 E7** 45 40N 22 22 E
Padilla, *Bolivia* **173 D5** 19 19 S 64 20W
Padina, *Romania* **53 F12** 44 50N 27 8 E
Padma, *India* **93 G11** 24 12N 85 22 E
Padma →, *Bangla.* **90 D3** 23 22N 90 32 E
Pádova, *Italy* **45 C8** 45 25N 11 53 E
Padra, *India* **92 H5** 22 15N 73 7 E
Padrauna, *India* **93 F10** 26 54N 83 59 E
Padre Burgos, *Phil.* **81 F5** 10 1N 125 0 E
Padre I., *U.S.A.* **155 M6** 27 10N 97 25W
Padre Island ⌓, *U.S.A.* **155 M6** 26 36N 97 17W
Padrón, *Spain* **42 C2** 42 41N 8 39W
Padstow, *U.K.* **21 G3** 50 33N 4 58W
Padthaway, *Australia* **128 D4** 36 36 S 140 31 E
Padua = Pádova, *Italy* **45 C8** 45 25N 11 53 E
Paducah, *Ky., U.S.A.* **148 G1** 37 5N 88 37W
Paducah, *Tex., U.S.A.* **155 H4** 34 1N 100 18W
Padukka, *Sri Lanka* **95 L5** 6 50N 80 5 E
Padul, *Spain* **43 H7** 37 1N 3 38W
Padwa, *India* **94 E6** 18 27N 82 47 E
Paekakariki, *N.Z.* **130 G3** 40 59 S 174 58 E
Paengaroa, *N.Z.* **130 D5** 37 49 S 176 29 E
Paengnyŏng-do, *S. Korea* **75 F13** 37 57N 124 40 E
Paeroa, *N.Z.* **130 D4** 37 23 S 175 41 E
Paesana, *Italy* **44 D4** 44 41N 7 16 E
Paete, *Phil.* **80 D3** 14 23N 121 29 E
Pafúri, *Mozam.* **117 C5** 22 28 S 31 17 E
Pag, *Croatia* **45 D12** 44 25N 15 3 E
Paga, *Gabon* **114 C2** 0 45 S 10 21 E
Paga, *Ghana* **113 C4** 11 1N 1 8W
Pagadian, *Phil.* **81 H4** 7 55N 123 30 E
Pagai Selatan, Pulau, *Indonesia* **84 C2** 3 0 S 100 15 E
Pagai Utara, Pulau, *Indonesia* **84 C2** 2 35 S 100 0 E
Pagalu = Annobón, *Atl. Oc.* **105 G4** 1 25 S 5 36 E
Pagalungan, *Phil.* **81 H5** 7 4N 124 41 E
Pagan, *Burma* **90 E5** 21 10N 94 52 E
Pagara, *India* **93 G9** 24 22N 80 1 E
Pagastikós Kólpos, *Greece* **48 B5** 39 15N 23 0 E
Pagatan, *Indonesia* **85 C5** 3 33 S 115 59 E
Page, *U.S.A.* **159 H8** 36 57N 111 27W
Pagėgiai, *Lithuania* **54 C8** 55 9N 21 54 E
Pagei, *Papua N. G.* **132 B1** 3 2 S 141 10 E
Paget I., *India* **95 H11** 13 26N 92 50 E
Pago Pago, *Amer. Samoa* **133 X24** 14 16 S 170 43W
Pagosa Springs, *U.S.A.* **159 H10** 37 16N 107 1W
Pagudpud, *Phil.* **80 B3** 18 34N 120 47 E
Pagwa River, *Canada* **140 B2** 50 2N 85 14W
Pagwi, *Papua N. G.* **132 C2** 4 4 S 143 2 E
Pahala, *U.S.A.* **145 D6** 19 12N 155 29W
Pahang □, *Malaysia* **84 B2** 3 30N 102 45 E
Pahang →, *Malaysia* **87 L4** 3 30N 103 9 E
Pahia Pt., *N.Z.* **131 G2** 46 20 S 167 41 E
Pahiatua, *N.Z.* **130 G4** 40 27 S 175 50 E
Pahoa, *U.S.A.* **145 D7** 19 30N 154 57W
Pahokee, *U.S.A.* **153 J9** 26 50N 80 40W
Pahrump, *U.S.A.* **161 J11** 36 12N 115 59W
Pahute Mesa, *U.S.A.* **160 H10** 37 20N 116 45W
Pai, *Thailand* **86 C2** 19 19N 98 27 E
Paia, *U.S.A.* **145 C5** 20 54N 156 22W
Paicines, *U.S.A.* **160 J5** 36 44N 121 17W
Paide, *Estonia* **15 G21** 58 53N 25 33 E
Paignton, *U.K.* **21 G4** 50 26N 3 35W
Paihia, *N.Z.* **130 B3** 35 17 S 174 6 E
Paiho, *Taiwan* **77 F13** 23 21N 120 25 E
Paiján, *Peru* **172 B2** 7 42 S 79 20W
Päijänne, *Finland* **15 F21** 61 30N 25 30 E
Pailani, *India* **93 G9** 25 45N 80 26 E
Pailin, *Cambodia* **86 F4** 12 46N 102 36 E
Pailolo Channel, *U.S.A.* **145 C5** 21 0N 156 40W
Paimpol, *France* **26 D3** 48 48N 3 4W
Painan, *Indonesia* **84 C2** 1 21 S 100 34 E
Paine, Cerro, *Chile* **176 D2** 50 59 S 73 4W
Painesville, *U.S.A.* **150 E3** 41 43N 81 15W
Paint Hills = Wemindji, *Canada* **140 B4** 53 0N 78 49W
Paint L., *Canada* **143 B9** 55 28N 97 57W
Painted Desert, *U.S.A.* **159 J8** 36 0N 111 0W
Paintsville, *U.S.A.* **148 G4** 37 49N 82 48W
País Vasco □, *Spain* **40 C2** 42 50N 2 45W
Paishambe = Payshanba, *Uzbekistan* **65 C3** 40 0N 66 14 E
Paisley, *Canada* **150 B3** 44 18N 81 16W
Paisley, *U.K.* **22 F4** 55 50N 4 25W
Paisley, *U.S.A.* **158 E3** 42 42N 120 32W
Païta, *N. Cal.* **133 V20** 22 8 S 166 22 E
Paita, *Peru* **172 B1** 5 11 S 81 9W
Paithan, *India* **94 E2** 19 29N 75 23 E
Paiva →, *Portugal* **42 D2** 41 4N 8 16W
Paizhou, *China* **77 B9** 30 12N 113 55 E
Paja, Cerro, *Ecuador* **172 a** 1 17 S 90 26W
Pajares, *Spain* **42 B5** 43 1N 5 46W
Pajares, Puerto de, *Spain* **42 C5** 42 58N 5 46W
Pajarito, *Colombia* **168 B3** 5 17N 72 43W
Pajęczno, *Poland* **55 G5** 51 10N 19 0 E
Pak Lay, *Laos* **86 C3** 18 15N 101 27 E
Pak Phanang, *Thailand* **87 H3** 8 21N 100 12 E
Pak Sane, *Laos* **86 C4** 18 22N 103 39 E
Pak Song, *Laos* **86 E6** 15 11N 106 14 E
Pak Suong, *Laos* **76 H4** 19 58N 102 15 E
Pak Tam Chung, *China* **69 G11** 22 24N 114 19 E
Pakala, *India* **95 H4** 13 29N 79 8 E
Pakaraima Mts., *Guyana* **169 B5** 6 0N 60 0W
Pakaur, *India* **93 G12** 24 38N 87 51 E
Pakenham, *Australia* **129 E6** 38 6 S 145 30 E
Pakenham, *Canada* **151 A8** 45 18N 76 18W
Pákhnes, *Greece* **39 E5** 35 16N 24 4 E
Pakhoi = Beihai, *China* **76 G7** 21 28N 109 6 E
Pakhtaabad, *Uzbekistan* **65 C6** 40 55N 72 29 E
Pakhuis, *S. Africa* **116 E2** 32 9 S 19 5 E
Pakistan ■, *Asia* **91 C3** 30 0N 70 0 E
Pakkading, *Laos* **86 C4** 18 19N 103 59 E
Paklay = Sayaboury, *Laos* **86 C3** 19 15N 101 45 E
Paklenica △, *Croatia* **45 D12** 44 20N 15 39 E
Pakokku, *Burma* **90 E5** 21 20N 95 0 E
Pakość, *Poland* **55 F5** 52 48N 18 6 E
Pakowki L., *Canada* **143 D6** 49 20N 111 0W
Pakpattan, *Pakistan* **91 C4** 30 25N 73 27 E
Pakrac, *Croatia* **52 E2** 45 27N 17 12 E
Pakruojis, *Lithuania* **54 C10** 55 58N 23 52 E
Paks, *Hungary* **52 D3** 46 38N 18 55 E
Paktīā □, *Afghan.* **91 B3** 33 30N 69 15 E
Paktīkā □, *Afghan.* **91 B3** 32 30N 69 0 E
Pakwach, *Uganda* **118 B3** 2 28N 31 27 E
Pakxe, *Laos* **86 E5** 15 5N 105 52 E
Pal Lahara, *India* **93 J11** 21 27N 85 11 E
Pala, *Chad* **109 G3** 9 25N 15 5 E
Pala, *Dem. Rep. of the Congo* **118 D2** 6 45 S 29 30 E
Pala, *U.S.A.* **161 M9** 33 22N 117 5W
Palabek, *Uganda* **118 B3** 3 22N 32 33 E
Palacios, *U.S.A.* **155 L6** 28 42N 96 13W

Palafrugell, *Spain* **40 D8** 41 55N 3 10 E
Palagiano, *Italy* **47 B10** 40 35N 17 2 E
Palagonía, *Italy* **47 E7** 37 19N 14 45 E
Palagruža, *Croatia* **45 F13** 42 24N 16 15 E
Palaiókastron, *Greece* **39 E7** 35 12N 26 15 E
Palaiokhóra, *Greece* **39 E4** 35 16N 23 39 E
Pálairos, *Greece* **39 B2** 38 47N 20 53 E
Palaiseau, *France* **27 D9** 48 43N 2 15 E
Palakol, *India* **95 F5** 16 31N 81 46 E
Palalankwe, *India* **95 J11** 10 52N 92 29 E
Palam, *India* **94 E3** 19 0N 77 0 E
Palamás, *Greece* **48 B4** 39 26N 22 4 E
Palamós, *Spain* **40 D8** 41 50N 3 10 E
Palampur, *India* **92 C7** 32 10N 76 30 E
Palamut, *Turkey* **49 C9** 38 59N 27 41 E
Palana, *Australia* **127 F4** 39 45 S 147 55 E
Palana, *Russia* **67 D16** 59 10N 159 59 E
Palanan, *Phil.* **80 C4** 17 8N 122 29 E
Palanan Bay, *Phil.* **80 C4** 17 9N 122 27 E
Palanan Pt., *Phil.* **80 C4** 17 17N 122 30 E
Palandri, *Pakistan* **93 C5** 33 42N 73 40 E
Palanga, *Lithuania* **15 J19** 55 58N 21 3 E
Palanganene, *Dem. Rep. of the Congo* **115 D3** 6 32 S 18 52 E
Palangkaraya, *Indonesia* **85 C4** 2 16 S 113 56 E
Palani, *India* **95 J3** 10 30N 77 30 E
Palani Hills, *India* **95 J3** 10 14N 77 33 E
Palanpur, *India* **92 G5** 24 10N 72 25 E
Palanro, *Indonesia* **82 B1** 3 21 S 119 23 E
Palaoa Pt., *U.S.A.* **145 C5** 20 44N 156 58W
Palapag, *Phil.* **80 E5** 12 33N 125 7 E
Palapye, *Botswana* **116 C4** 22 30 S 27 7 E
Palar →, *India* **95 H5** 12 27N 80 13 E
Palas, *Pakistan* **93 B5** 35 4N 73 14 E
Palas de Rei, *Spain* **42 C3** 42 52N 7 52W
Palashi, *India* **93 H13** 23 47N 88 15 E
Palasponga, *India* **93 J11** 21 47N 85 34 E
Palatine, *U.S.A.* **157 B8** 42 7N 88 3W
Palatka, *Russia* **67 C16** 60 6N 150 54 E
Palatka, *U.S.A.* **152 F8** 29 39N 81 38W
Palau, *Italy* **46 A2** 41 11N 9 23 E
Palau ■, *Pac. Oc.* **62 J17** 7 30N 134 30 E
Palauk, *Burma* **86 F2** 13 10N 98 40 E
Palawan, *Phil.* **81 G2** 9 30N 118 30 E
Palawan □, *Phil.* **81 G2** 10 0N 119 0 E
Palawan Passage, *Phil.* **81 G2** 10 0N 118 0 E
Palayan, *Phil.* **80 D3** 15 36N 121 8 E
Palayankottai, *India* **95 K3** 8 45N 77 45 E
Palazzo, Pte., *France* **29 F12** 42 28N 8 30 E
Palazzo San Gervásio, *Italy* **47 B8** 40 56N 15 59 E
Palazzolo Acréide, *Italy* **47 E7** 37 4N 14 54 E
Palca, *Chile* **172 D4** 19 7 S 69 9W
Paldiski, *Estonia* **15 G21** 59 23N 24 9 E
Pale, *Bos.-H.* **52 G3** 43 50N 18 38 E
Palel, *India* **90 C5** 24 27N 94 2 E
Paleleh, *Indonesia* **82 A2** 1 10N 121 50 E
Palembang, *Indonesia* **84 C2** 3 0 S 104 50 E
Palena →, *Chile* **176 B2** 43 50 S 73 50W
Palena, L., *Chile* **176 B2** 43 55 S 71 40W
Palencia, *Spain* **42 C6** 42 1N 4 34W
Palencia □, *Spain* **42 C6** 42 31N 4 33W
Palenque, *Mexico* **163 D6** 17 31N 91 58W
Paleokastrítsa, *Greece* **38 B9** 39 40N 19 41 E
Paleometokho, *Cyprus* **39 E9** 35 7N 33 11 E
Palermo, *Colombia* **168 C2** 2 54N 75 26W
Palermo, *Italy* **46 D6** 38 7N 13 22 E
Palermo, *U.S.A.* **158 G3** 39 26N 121 33W
Palermo ✗ (PMO), *Italy* **46 D6** 38 11N 13 5 E
Palestina = Jordânia, *Brazil* **171 E3** 15 55 S 40 11W
Palestine, *Asia* **103 D4** 32 0N 35 0 E
Palestine, *Ill., U.S.A.* **157 F9** 39 0N 87 37W
Palestine, *Tex., U.S.A.* **155 K7** 31 46N 95 38W
Palestrina, *Italy* **45 G9** 41 50N 12 53 E
Paletwa, *Burma* **90 E4** 21 10N 92 50 E
Palghat, *India* **95 J3** 10 46N 76 42 E
Palgrave, Mt., *Australia* **124 D2** 23 22 S 115 58 E
Pali, *India* **92 G5** 25 50N 73 20 E
Pali-Aike △, *Chile* **176 D3** 52 6 S 69 44W
Palikea Pk., *U.S.A.* **145 K13** 21 26N 158 6W
Palikir, *Micronesia* **134 G7** 6 55N 158 9 E
Palimbang, *Phil.* **81 H5** 6 12N 124 12 E
Palin, Mt., *Malaysia* **85 A5** 6 10N 117 10 E
Palinuro, *Italy* **47 B8** 40 2N 15 17 E
Palinuro, C., *Italy* **47 B8** 40 2N 15 16 E
Palioúri, Ákra = Paliouríon, Ákra, *Greece* **50 G7** 39 57N 23 45 E
Paliouríon, Ákra, *Greece* **50 G7** 39 57N 23 45 E
Palisades Reservoir, *U.S.A.* **158 E8** 43 20N 111 12W
Paliseul, *Belgium* **24 E5** 49 54N 5 8 E
Palitana, *India* **92 J4** 21 32N 71 49 E
Palizada, *Mexico* **163 D6** 18 18N 92 8W
Palk Bay, *Asia* **95 K4** 9 30N 79 15 E
Palk Strait, *Asia* **95 K4** 10 0N 79 45 E
Palkānah, *Iraq* **96 C5** 35 49N 44 26 E
Palkonda, *India* **94 E6** 18 36N 83 48 E
Palkonda Ra., *India* **95 H4** 13 50N 79 20 E
Palkot, *India* **93 H11** 22 53N 84 39 E
Palla Road = Dinokwe, *Botswana* **116 C4** 23 29 S 26 37 E
Pallanza = Verbània, *Italy* **44 C5** 45 56N 8 33 E
Pallarenda, *Australia* **126 B4** 19 12 S 146 46 E
Pallasovka, *Russia* **60 E8** 50 4N 47 0 E
Palleru →, *India* **94 F5** 16 45N 80 2 E
Pallës, Bishti i, *Albania* **50 E3** 41 24N 19 24 E
Pallinup →, *Australia* **125 F2** 34 27 S 118 50 E
Pallisa, *Uganda* **118 B3** 1 12N 33 43 E
Palliser, C., *N.Z.* **130 H4** 41 37 S 175 14 E
Palliser B., *N.Z.* **130 H4** 41 26 S 175 5 E
Pallu, *India* **92 E6** 28 59N 74 14 E
Palm Bay, *U.S.A.* **153 G9** 28 2N 80 35W
Palm Beach, *U.S.A.* **153 J9** 26 43N 80 2W
Palm Coast, *U.S.A.* **153 F8** 29 32N 81 10W
Palm Desert, *U.S.A.* **161 M10** 33 43N 116 22W
Palm Harbor, *U.S.A.* **153 G7** 28 5N 82 47W
Palm Is., *Australia* **126 B4** 18 40 S 146 35 E
Palm Springs, *U.S.A.* **161 M10** 33 50N 116 33W
Palma = Paraná, *Brazil* **171 D2** 12 30 S 47 48W
Palma, *Mozam.* **119 E5** 10 46 S 40 29 E
Palma →, *Brazil* **171 D2** 12 33 S 47 52W
Palma, B. de, *Spain* **38 B3** 39 30N 2 39 E
Palma de Mallorca, *Spain* **38 B3** 39 35N 2 39 E
Palma de Mallorca ✗ (PMI), *Spain* **41 F7** 39 34N 2 43 E
Palma del Río, *Spain* **43 H5** 37 43N 5 17W
Palma di Montechiaro, *Italy* **46 E6** 37 11N 13 46 E
Palma Nova, *Spain* **38 B3** 39 32N 2 34 E
Palma Soriano, *Cuba* **164 B4** 20 15N 76 0W
Palmaner, *India* **95 H4** 13 12N 78 45 E
Palmares, *Brazil* **170 C4** 8 41 S 35 28W
Palmarito, *Venezuela* **168 B3** 7 37N 70 10W
Palmarola, *Italy* **46 B5** 40 56N 12 51 E
Palmas, *Brazil* **175 B5** 26 29 S 52 0W
Palmas, C., *Liberia* **112 E3** 4 27N 7 46W
Pálmas, G. di, *Italy* **46 D1** 39 0N 8 30 E
Palmas de Monte Alto, *Brazil* **171 D3** 14 16 S 43 10W
Palmdale, *Calif., U.S.A.* **161 L8** 34 35N 118 7W
Palmdale, *Fla., U.S.A.* **153 J8** 26 57N 81 19W
Palmeira, *Brazil* **171 G2** 25 25 S 50 0W
Palmeira das Missões, *Brazil* **175 B5** 27 55 S 53 17W
Palmeira dos Índios, *Brazil* **170 C4** 9 25 S 36 37W
Palmeirais, *Brazil* **170 C3** 6 0 S 43 0W
Palmeiras, *Brazil* **171 D3** 12 31 S 41 34W
Palmeiras →, *Brazil* **171 D2** 12 22 S 47 8W
Palmeirinhas, Pta. das, *Angola* **115 D2** 9 2 S 12 57 E
Palmela, *Portugal* **43 G2** 38 32N 8 57W
Palmelo, *Brazil* **171 E2** 17 20 S 48 27W
Palmer, *Antarctica* **7 C17** 64 35 S 60 0W
Palmer, *U.S.A.* **144 F10** 61 36N 149 7W
Palmer →, *Australia* **126 B3** 16 0 S 142 26 E
Palmer Arch., *Antarctica* **7 C17** 64 15 S 65 0W
Palmer Lake, *U.S.A.* **154 F2** 39 7N 104 55W
Palmer Land, *Antarctica* **7 D18** 73 0 S 63 0W
Palmerston = Darwin, *Australia* **124 B5** 12 25 S 130 51 E
Palmerston, *Australia* **124 B5** 12 31 S 130 59 E
Palmerston, *Canada* **150 C4** 43 50N 80 51W
Palmerston, *N.Z.* **131 F5** 45 29 S 170 43 E
Palmerston North, *N.Z.* **130 G4** 40 21 S 175 39 E
Palmerton, *U.S.A.* **151 F9** 40 48N 75 37W
Palmetto, *Fla., U.S.A.* **153 H7** 27 31N 82 34W
Palmetto, *Ga., U.S.A.* **152 B5** 33 31N 84 40W
Palmi, *Italy* **47 D8** 38 21N 15 51 E
Palmira, *Argentina* **174 C2** 32 59 S 68 34W
Palmira, *Colombia* **168 C2** 3 32N 76 16W
Palmyra = Tudmur, *Syria* **101 E8** 34 36N 38 15 E
Palmyra, *Ill., U.S.A.* **156 E7** 39 26N 90 0W
Palmyra, *Mo., U.S.A.* **156 E5** 39 48N 91 32W
Palmyra, *N.J., U.S.A.* **151 F9** 40 1N 75 1W
Palmyra, *N.Y., U.S.A.* **150 C7** 43 5N 77 18W
Palmyra, *Pa., U.S.A.* **151 F8** 40 18N 76 36W
Palmyra, *Wis., U.S.A.* **157 B8** 42 52N 88 36W
Palmyra Is., *Pac. Oc.* **135 G11** 5 52N 162 5W
Palmyras Pt., *India* **94 D8** 20 46N 87 1 E
Palo, *Phil.* **81 F5** 11 10N 124 59 E
Palo Alto, *U.S.A.* **160 H4** 37 27N 122 10W
Palo Seco, *Trin. & Tob.* **169 F9** 10 4N 61 36W
Palo Verde, *U.S.A.* **161 M12** 33 26N 114 44W
Palo Verde △, *Costa Rica* **164 D2** 10 21N 85 21W
Paloich, *Sudan* **107 E3** 10 28N 32 32 E
Palomar Mt., *U.S.A.* **161 M10** 33 22N 116 50W
Palompon, *Phil.* **81 F5** 11 3N 124 23 E
Palopo, *Indonesia* **82 B2** 3 0 S 120 16 E
Palos, C. de, *Spain* **41 H4** 37 38N 0 40W
Palos de la Frontera, *Spain* **43 H4** 37 14N 6 53W
Palos Verdes, *U.S.A.* **161 M8** 33 48N 118 23W
Palos Verdes, Pt., *U.S.A.* **161 M8** 33 43N 118 26W
Palpa, *Peru* **172 C2** 14 30 S 75 15W
Pålsboda, *Sweden* **16 E9** 59 3N 15 22 E
Palu, *Indonesia* **82 B1** 1 0 S 119 52 E
Palu, *Turkey* **101 C9** 38 45N 40 0 E
Paluan, *Phil.* **80 E3** 13 26N 120 29 E
Paluke, *Liberia* **112 D3** 5 2N 8 5W
Paluzza, *Italy* **45 B10** 46 32N 13 1 E
Palwal, *India* **92 E7** 28 8N 77 19 E
Pama, *Burkina Faso* **113 C5** 11 19N 0 44 E
Pama △, *Burkina Faso* **113 C5** 11 27N 0 40 E
Pama →, *C.A.R.* **114 B3** 4 23N 18 43 E
Pamanukan, *Indonesia* **85 D3** 6 16 S 107 49 E
Pamban I., *India* **95 K4** 9 15N 79 20 E
Pamekasan, *Indonesia* **85 D4** 7 10 S 113 28 E
Pamenang, *Indonesia* **79 J19** 8 24 S 116 6 E
Pamiers, *France* **28 E5** 43 7N 1 39 E
Pamir, *Tajikistan* **65 E6** 37 40N 73 0 E
Pamir →, *Tajikistan* **65 E6** 37 1N 72 41 E
Pamirsky Post = Murghob, *Tajikistan* **65 D7** 38 10N 74 2 E
Pamlico →, *U.S.A.* **149 H7** 35 20N 76 28W
Pamlico Sd., *U.S.A.* **149 H8** 35 20N 76 0W
Pampa, *U.S.A.* **155 H4** 35 32N 100 58W
Pampa de Agma, *Argentina* **176 B3** 43 45 S 69 40W
Pampa de las Salinas, *Argentina* **174 C2** 32 1 S 66 58W
Pampa Grande, *Bolivia* **173 D5** 18 5 S 64 6W
Pampa Hermosa, *Peru* **172 B2** 7 7 S 75 4W
Pampanga □, *Phil.* **80 D3** 15 4N 120 40 E
Pampanua, *Indonesia* **82 B2** 4 16 S 120 8 E
Pampas, *Argentina* **174 D3** 35 0 S 63 0W
Pampas, *Peru* **172 C3** 12 20 S 74 50W
Pampas →, *Peru* **172 C3** 13 24 S 73 12W
Pamphylia, *Turkey* **100 D4** 37 0N 31 20 E
Pamplona, *Colombia* **168 B3** 7 23N 72 39W
Pamplona, *Phil.* **80 B3** 18 31N 121 20 E
Pamplona, *Spain* **40 C3** 42 48N 1 38W
Pampoenpoort, *S. Africa* **116 E3** 31 3 S 22 40 E
Pamukçu, *Turkey* **49 B9** 39 30N 27 54 E
Pamukkale, *Turkey* **49 D11** 37 55N 29 8 E
Pan de Azúcar △, *Chile* **174 B1** 26 0 S 70 40W
Pan Xian, *China* **76 E5** 25 46N 104 38 E
Pana, *U.S.A.* **156 E7** 39 23N 89 5W
Panabo, *Phil.* **81 H5** 7 19N 125 42 E
Panaca, *U.S.A.* **159 H6** 37 47N 114 23W
Panacea, *U.S.A.* **152 E5** 30 2N 84 23W
Panagyurishte, *Bulgaria* **51 D8** 42 30N 24 15 E
Panaitan, *Indonesia* **84 D3** 6 36 S 105 12 E
Panaji, *India* **95 G1** 15 25N 73 50 E
Panamá, *Panama* **164 E4** 9 0N 79 25W
Panama, *Sri Lanka* **95 L5** 6 45N 81 48 E
Panama ■, *Cent. Amer.* **164 E4** 8 48N 79 55W
Panamá, G. de, *Panama* **164 E4** 8 4N 79 20W
Panama Canal, *Panama* **164 E4** 9 10N 79 37W
Panama City, *U.S.A.* **152 E4** 30 10N 85 40W
Panama City Beach, *U.S.A.* **152 E4** 30 11N 85 48W
Panamint Range, *U.S.A.* **161 J9** 36 20N 117 20W
Panamint Springs, *U.S.A.* **161 J9** 36 20N 117 28W
Panão, *Peru* **172 B2** 9 55 S 75 55W
Panaon I., *Phil.* **81 F5** 10 3N 125 13 E
Panare, *Thailand* **87 J3** 6 51N 101 30 E
Panarea, *Italy* **47 D8** 38 38N 15 4 E
Panaro →, *Italy* **45 D8** 44 55N 11 25 E
Panarukan, *Indonesia* **85 D4** 7 42 S 113 56 E
Panay, *Phil.* **81 F4** 11 10N 122 30 E
Panay, G., *Phil.* **79 B6** 11 0N 122 30 E
Pančevo, *Serbia & M.* **52 F5** 44 52N 20 41 E
Panch'iao, *Taiwan* **77 E13** 25 1N 121 27 E
Panciu, *Romania* **53 E12** 45 54N 27 8 E
Pancol, *Phil.* **81 F2** 10 52N 119 25 E
Pancorbo, Desfiladero, *Spain* **42 C7** 42 32N 3 5W
Pâncota, *Romania* **52 D6** 46 20N 21 45 E
Panda, *Mozam.* **117 C5** 24 2 S 34 45 E
Pandan, *Malaysia* **87 d** 1 32N 103 46 E
Pandan, *Antique, Phil.* **81 F4** 11 45N 122 10 E
Pandan, *Catanduanes, Phil.* **80 D5** 14 3N 124 10 E
Pandan, Selat, *Singapore* **87 d** 1 15N 103 44 E
Pandan Bay, *Phil.* **81 F4** 11 43N 122 0 E
Pandan Tampoi = Tampoi, *Malaysia* **87 d** 1 30N 103 39 E
Pandegelang, *Indonesia* **84 D3** 6 25 S 106 5 E
Pandhana, *India* **92 J7** 21 42N 76 13 E
Pandharkawada, *India* **94 D4** 20 1N 78 32 E
Pandharpur, *India* **94 F2** 17 41N 75 20 E
Pandhurna, *India* **94 D4** 21 36N 78 35 E
Pando, *Uruguay* **175 C4** 34 44 S 56 0W
Pando □, *Bolivia* **172 C4** 11 20 S 67 40W
Pando, L. = Hope, L., *Australia* **127 D2** 28 24 S 139 18 E
Pandokrátor, *Greece* **38 B9** 39 45N 19 50 E
Pandora, *Costa Rica* **164 E3** 9 43N 83 3W
Pandrup, *Denmark* **17 G3** 57 14N 9 40 E
Pandu, *Dem. Rep. of the Congo* **114 B3** 4 59N 19 16 E
Panevéggio-Pale di San Martino △, *Italy* **45 B8** 46 14N 11 46 E
Panevėžys, *Lithuania* **15 J21** 55 42N 24 25 E
Panfilov, *Kazakhstan* **66 E8** 44 10N 80 0 E
Panfilov Atyndaghy, *Kazakhstan* **65 B8** 43 23N 77 7 E
Panfilovo, *Russia* **60 E6** 50 25N 42 46 E
Pang Sida △, *Thailand* **86 E4** 14 5N 102 17 E
Panga, *Dem. Rep. of the Congo* **118 B2** 1 52N 26 18 E
Pangaion Óros, *Greece* **51 F8** 40 50N 24 0 E
Pangala, *Congo* **114 C2** 3 16 S 14 34 E
Pangalanes, Canal des = Ampangalana, Lakandranon', *Madag.* **117 C8** 22 48 S 47 50 E
Pangani, *Tanzania* **118 D4** 5 25 S 38 58 E
Pangani →, *Tanzania* **118 D4** 5 26 S 38 58 E
Pangantocan, *Phil.* **81 H5** 7 50N 124 49 E
Pangar Djérem △, *Cameroon* **114 A2** 5 50N 13 10 E
Pangasinan □, *Phil.* **80 D3** 15 55N 120 20 E
Pangfou = Bengbu, *China* **75 H9** 32 58N 117 20 E
Pangil, *Dem. Rep. of the Congo* **118 C2** 3 10 S 26 35 E
Pangkah, Tanjung, *Indonesia* **85 D4** 6 51 S 112 33 E
Pangkai, *Burma* **90 D7** 22 40N 98 40 E
Pangkajene, *Indonesia* **82 B1** 4 46 S 119 34 E
Pangkalanbrandan, *Indonesia* **84 B1** 4 1N 98 20 E
Pangkalanbuun, *Indonesia* **85 C4** 2 41 S 111 37 E
Pangkalansusu, *Indonesia* **84 B1** 4 2N 98 13 E
Pangkalpinang, *Indonesia* **84 C3** 2 0 S 106 0 E
Pangkoh, *Indonesia* **85 C4** 3 5 S 114 8 E
Panglao, *Phil.* **81 G4** 9 35N 123 45 E
Panglao I., *Phil.* **81 G4** 9 35N 123 48 E
Pangnirtung, *Canada* **139 B13** 66 8N 65 43W
Pango Aluquem, *Angola* **115 D2** 8 43 S 14 33 E
Pangong Tso, *India* **93 B8** 34 40N 78 40 E
Pangrango, *Indonesia* **84 D3** 6 46 S 107 1 E
Pangsau Pass, *Burma* **90 B6** 27 15N 96 10 E
Pangtara, *Burma* **90 E6** 20 57N 96 40 E
Panguipulli, *Chile* **176 A2** 39 38 S 72 20W
Panguitch, *U.S.A.* **159 H7** 37 50N 112 26W
Panguna, *Papua N. G.* **132 D8** 6 21 S 155 25 E
Pangutaran, *Phil.* **81 H3** 6 18N 120 35 E
Pangutaran Group, *Phil.* **81 H3** 6 18N 120 34 E
Panhala, *India* **94 F2** 16 49N 74 7 E
Panhandle, *U.S.A.* **155 H4** 35 21N 101 23W
Pani Mines, *India* **92 H5** 22 29N 73 50 E
Pania-Mutombo, *Dem. Rep. of the Congo* **118 D1** 5 11 S 23 51 E
Paniau, *U.S.A.* **145 B1** 21 56N 160 5W
Panié, Mt., *N. Cal.* **133 T18** 20 36 S 164 46 E
Panikota I., *India* **92 J4** 20 46N 71 21 E
Panipat, *India* **92 E7** 29 25N 77 2 E
Panitan, *Phil.* **81 F4** 11 28N 122 46 E
Panj = Pyandzh, *Tajikistan* **65 E4** 37 14N 69 6 E
Panj = Pyandzh →, *Asia* **65 E4** 37 6N 68 20 E
Panjab, *Afghan.* **91 B2** 34 23N 67 1 E
Panjakent = Pendzhikent, *Tajikistan* **65 D3** 39 29N 67 37 E
Panjal Range = Pir Panjal Range, *India* **92 C7** 32 30N 76 50 E
Panjang, Hon, *Vietnam* **87 H4** 9 20N 103 28 E
Panjgur, *Pakistan* **91 D2** 27 0N 64 5 E
Panjhra →, *India* **94 D2** 21 13N 74 57 E
Panji Poyon, *Tajikistan* **65 E4** 37 12N 68 35 E
Panjim = Panaji, *India* **95 G1** 15 25N 73 50 E
Panjin, *China* **75 D12** 41 3N 122 2 E
Panjnad →, *Pakistan* **92 E4** 28 57N 70 30 E
Panjwai, *Afghan.* **92 D1** 31 26N 65 27 E
Pankshin, *Nigeria* **113 D6** 9 16N 9 25 E
Panmunjŏm, *N. Korea* **75 F14** 37 59N 126 38 E
Panna, *India* **93 G9** 24 40N 80 15 E
Panna △, *India* **93 G8** 24 40N 80 0 E
Panna Hills, *India* **93 G9** 24 40N 81 15 E
Pannawonica, *Australia* **124 D2** 21 39 S 116 19 E
Pannga, Tanjung, *Indonesia* **79 K19** 8 54 S 116 2 E
Panngi, *Vanuatu* **133 E6** 15 58 S 168 12 E
Pannirtuuq = Pangnirtung, *Canada* **139 B13** 66 8N 65 43W
Pano Akil, *Pakistan* **92 F3** 27 51N 69 7 E
Pano Lefkara, *Cyprus* **39 F9** 34 53N 33 20 E
Pano Panayia, *Cyprus* **39 F8** 34 55N 32 38 E
Panora, *U.S.A.* **156 C2** 41 42N 94 22W
Panorama, *Brazil* **175 A5** 21 21 S 51 51W
Pánormon, *Greece* **39 E5** 35 25N 24 41 E
Panruti, *India* **95 J4** 11 46N 79 35 E
Pansemal, *India* **92 J6** 21 39N 74 42 E
Panshan = Panjin, *China* **75 D12** 41 3N 122 2 E
Panshi, *China* **75 C14** 42 58N 126 5 E
Pantanal Matogrossense △, *Brazil* **173 D6** 17 35 S 57 27W
Pantanaw, *Burma* **90 G5** 16 59N 95 28 E
Pantanos de Centla △, *Mexico* **163 D6** 18 25N 92 25W
Pantar, *Indonesia* **82 C2** 8 28 S 124 10 E
Pante Macassar, *E. Timor* **82 C2** 9 30 S 123 58 E
Pante Makasar = Pante Macassar, *E. Timor* **82 C2** 9 30 S 123 58 E
Pantelleria, *Italy* **46 F4** 36 50N 11 57 E
Pantin Sakan, *Burma* **90 F6** 18 38N 97 33 E
Pantoja, *Peru* **168 D2** 0 58 S 75 10W
Pantón, *Spain* **42 C3** 42 31N 7 37W
Pantukan, *Phil.* **81 H5** 7 9N 125 54 E
Panu, *Dem. Rep. of the Congo* **114 C3** 3 50 S 19 10 E
Pánuco, *Mexico* **163 C5** 22 0N 98 15W
Panukulan, *Phil.* **80 D3** 14 56N 121 49 E
Panvel, *India* **94 E1** 18 59N 73 4 E
Panyam, *Nigeria* **113 D6** 9 27N 9 8 E
Panyu = Guangzhou, *China* **77 F9** 23 5N 113 10 E
Panyu, *China* **77 F9** 22 51N 113 20 E
Panzhihua, *China* **76 D3** 26 33N 101 44 E
Panzi, *Dem. Rep. of the Congo* **115 D3** 7 17 S 18 1 E
Pao →, *Anzoátegui, Venezuela* **169 B5** 8 6N 64 17W
Pao →, *Apure, Venezuela* **168 B4** 8 33N 68 1W
Paochi = Baoji, *China* **74 G4** 34 20N 107 5 E
Paoki = Baoji, *China* **74 G4** 34 20N 107 5 E
Páola, *Italy* **47 C9** 39 21N 16 2 E
Paola, *Malta* **38 F8** 35 52N 14 30 E
Paola, *U.S.A.* **154 F7** 38 35N 94 53W
Paoli, *U.S.A.* **157 F10** 38 33N 86 28W
Paonia, *U.S.A.* **159 G10** 38 52N 107 36W
Paoting = Baoding, *China* **74 E8** 38 50N 115 28 E
Paot'ou = Baotou, *China* **74 D6** 40 32N 110 2 E
Paoua, *C.A.R.* **114 A3** 7 9N 16 20 E
Pap, *Uzbekistan* **65 C5** 40 52N 71 6 E
Pápa, *Hungary* **52 C2** 47 22N 17 30 E
Papa, *U.S.A.* **145 D6** 19 13N 155 52W
Papa Stour, *U.K.* **22 A7** 60 20N 1 42W
Papa Westray, *U.K.* **22 B6** 59 20N 2 55W
Papaaloa, *U.S.A.* **145 D6** 19 59N 155 13W
Papagayo →, *Mexico* **163 D5** 16 36N 99 43W
Papagayo, G. de, *Costa Rica* **164 D2** 10 30N 85 50W
Papagni →, *India* **95 G3** 15 35N 77 45 E
Papaïchton, *Fr. Guiana* **169 C7** 3 48N 54 10W
Papaikou, *U.S.A.* **145 D6** 19 47N 155 6W
Papakura, *N.Z.* **130 D3** 37 4 S 174 59 E
Papantla, *Mexico* **163 C5** 20 30N 97 30W
Papar, *Malaysia* **78 C5** 5 45N 116 0 E
Papara, *Tahiti* **133 S16** 17 43 S 149 22W
Paparoa, *N.Z.* **130 C3** 36 6 S 174 16 E
Paparoa △, *N.Z.* **131 C6** 42 7 S 171 26 E
Paparoa Ra., *N.Z.* **131 C6** 42 5 S 171 35 E
Pápas, Ákra, *Greece* **48 C3** 38 13N 21 20 E
Papatoetoe, *N.Z.* **130 C3** 36 59 S 174 51 E
Papatura, *Solomon Is.* **133 L10** 7 32 S 158 47 E
Papawai Pt., *U.S.A.* **145 C5** 20 47N 156 32W
Papeete, *Tahiti* **133 S16** 17 32 S 149 34W
Papenburg, *Germany* **30 B3** 53 5N 7 23 E
Papetoai, *Tahiti* **133 S16** 17 29 S 149 52W
Paphlagonia, *Turkey* **100 B5** 41 30N 33 0 E
Paphos, *Cyprus* **39 F8** 34 46N 32 25 E
Paphos ✗ (PFO), *Cyprus* **39 F8** 34 43N 32 30 E
Papien Chiang = Da →, *Vietnam* **76 G5** 21 15N 105 20 E
Papigochic →, *Mexico* **162 B3** 29 9N 109 40W
Paposo, *Chile* **174 B1** 25 0 S 70 30W
Papoutsa, *Cyprus* **39 F9** 34 54N 33 4 E
Papua □, *Indonesia* **83 B5** 4 0 S 137 0 E
Papua, G. of, *Papua N. G.* **132 E3** 9 0 S 144 50 E
Papua New Guinea ■, *Oceania* **132 D3** 8 0 S 145 0 E
Papudo, *Chile* **174 C1** 32 29 S 71 27W
Papuk, *Croatia* **52 E2** 45 30N 17 30 E
Papun, *Burma* **90 F6** 18 2N 97 30 E
Papunya, *Australia* **124 D5** 23 15 S 131 54 E
Pará = Belém, *Brazil* **170 B2** 1 20 S 48 30W
Pará □, *Brazil* **173 A7** 3 20 S 52 0W
Paraburdoo, *Australia* **124 D2** 23 14 S 117 32 E
Paracale, *Phil.* **80 D4** 14 17N 122 48 E
Paracas, Pen., *Peru* **172 C2** 13 53 S 76 20W
Paracatu, *Brazil* **171 E2** 17 10 S 46 50W
Paracatu →, *Brazil* **171 E2** 16 30 S 45 4W
Paracel Is., *S. China Sea* **78 A4** 15 50N 112 0 E
Parachilna, *Australia* **128 A3** 31 10 S 138 21 E
Parachinar, *Pakistan* **91 B3** 33 55N 70 5 E
Paraćin, *Serbia & M.* **50 C5** 43 54N 21 27 E
Paracuru, *Brazil* **170 B4** 3 24 S 39 4W
Parada, Punta, *Peru* **172 D2** 15 22 S 75 11W
Paradas, *Spain* **43 H5** 37 18N 5 29W
Paradela, *Spain* **42 C3** 42 44N 7 37W
Paradhísi, *Greece* **38 E12** 36 18N 28 7 E
Paradip, *India* **94 D8** 20 15N 86 35 E
Paradise, *Calif., U.S.A.* **160 F5** 39 46N 121 37W
Paradise, *Nev., U.S.A.* **161 J11** 36 9N 115 10W
Paradise →, *Canada* **141 B8** 53 27N 57 19W
Paradise Hill, *Canada* **143 C7** 53 32N 109 28W
Paradise I., *Bahamas* **9 b** 25 6N 77 19W
Paradise River, *Canada* **141 B8** 53 27N 57 17W
Paradise Valley, *U.S.A.* **158 F5** 41 30N 117 32W
Parado, *Indonesia* **85 D5** 8 42 S 118 30 E
Paragould, *U.S.A.* **155 G9** 36 3N 90 29W
Paragua = Palawan, *Phil.* **81 G2** 9 30N 118 30 E
Paraguá →, *Bolivia* **173 C5** 13 34 S 61 53W
Paragua →, *Venezuela* **169 B5** 6 55N 62 55W
Paraguaçu = Paraguaçu Paulista, *Brazil* **175 A5** 22 22 S 50 35W
Paraguaçu →, *Brazil* **171 D4** 12 45 S 38 54W
Paraguaçu Paulista, *Brazil* **175 A5** 22 22 S 50 35W
Paraguaipoa, *Venezuela* **168 A3** 11 21N 71 57W
Paraguaná, Pen. de, *Venezuela* **168 A3** 12 0N 70 0W
Paraguarí, *Paraguay* **174 B4** 25 36 S 57 0W
Paraguarí □, *Paraguay* **174 B4** 26 0 S 57 10W
Paraguay ■, *S. Amer.* **174 A4** 23 0 S 57 0W
Paraguay →, *Paraguay* **174 B4** 27 18 S 58 38W
Paraíba = João Pessoa, *Brazil* **170 C5** 7 10 S 34 52W
Paraíba □, *Brazil* **170 C4** 7 0 S 36 0W
Paraíba do Sul →, *Brazil* **171 F3** 21 37 S 41 3W
Parainen, *Finland* **15 F20** 60 18N 22 18 E
Paraiso, *Brazil* **173** 19 3 S 52 59W
Paraiso, *Mexico* **163 D6** 18 24N 93 14W
Parak, *Iran* **97 E7** 27 38N 52 25 E
Parakhino Paddubye, *Russia* **58 C7** 58 26N 33 10 E
Parakou, *Benin* **113 D5** 9 25N 2 40 E
Parakylia, *Australia* **128 A2** 30 24 S 136 25 E
Paralimni, *Cyprus* **39 E9** 35 2N 33 58 E
Parálion-Astrous, *Greece* **48 D4** 37 25N 22 45 E
Paralkote, *India* **94 E5** 19 47N 80 41 E
Parama I., *Papua N. G.* **132 E2** 9 0 S 143 25 E
Paramaribo, *Suriname* **169 B6** 5 50N 55 10W
Parambu, *Brazil* **170 C3** 6 13 S 40 43W
Paramillo △, *Colombia* **168 B2** 7 37N 76 13W
Paramillo, Nudo del, *Colombia* **168 B2** 7 4N 75 55W
Paramirim, *Brazil* **171 D3** 13 26 S 42 15W
Paramirim →, *Brazil* **171 D3** 11 34 S 43 18W
Paramithiá, *Greece* **48 B2** 39 30N 20 35 E
Páramos del Batallón y La Negra △, *Venezuela* **165 E5** 8 2N 71 55W
Paramushir, Ostrov, *Russia* **67 D16** 50 24N 156 0 E
Paran →, *Israel* **103 E4** 30 20N 35 10 E
Paraná, *Argentina* **174 C3** 31 45 S 60 30W
Paranã, *Brazil* **171 D2** 12 30 S 47 48W
Paraná □, *Brazil* **175 A5** 24 30 S 51 0W
Paraná →, *Argentina* **174 C4** 33 43 S 59 15W
Paranã →, *Brazil* **171 D2** 12 30 S 48 14W
Paranaguá, *Brazil* **175 B6** 25 30 S 48 30W
Paranaíba, *Brazil* **173 D7** 19 40 S 51 11W
Paranaíba →, *Brazil* **171 F1** 20 6 S 51 4W
Paranapanema →, *Brazil* **175 A5** 22 40 S 53 9W
Paranapiacaba, Serra do, *Brazil* **175 A6** 24 31 S 48 35W
Paranas, *Phil.* **81 F5** 11 42N 125 2 E
Paranavaí, *Brazil* **175 A5** 23 4 S 52 56W
Parang, *Maguindanao, Phil.* **81 H5** 7 23N 124 16 E
Parang, *Sulu, Phil.* **81 J3** 5 55N 120 54 E
Parangaba, *Brazil* **170 B4** 3 45 S 38 33W
Parangippettai, *India* **95 J4** 11 30N 79 38 E
Parângul Mare, Vf., *Romania* **53 E8** 45 20N 23 37 E
Paranthan, *Sri Lanka* **95 K5** 9 26N 80 24 E
Paraparaumu, *N.Z.* **130 G4** 40 57 S 175 3 E
Parapetí →, *Bolivia* **173 D5** 18 58 S 62 21W
Parapóla, *Greece* **48 E5** 36 55N 23 27 E
Paraspóri, Ákra, *Greece* **49 F9** 35 55N 27 15 E
Paratinga, *Brazil* **171 D3** 12 40 S 43 10W
Paratoo, *Australia* **128 B3** 32 42 S 139 20 E
Paraúna, *Brazil* **171 E1** 16 55 S 50 26W
Paray-le-Monial, *France* **27 F11** 46 27N 4 7 E
Parbati →, *Mad. P., India* **92 G7** 25 50N 76 30 E
Parbati →, *Raj., India* **92 F7** 26 54N 77 53 E
Parbatipur, *Bangla.* **90 C2** 25 39N 88 55 E
Parbhani, *India* **94 E3** 19 8N 76 52 E
Parchim, *Germany* **30 B7** 53 26N 11 52 E
Parchwitz = Prochowice, *Poland* **55 G3** 51 17N 16 20 E
Parco = Sinclair, *U.S.A.* **158 F10** 41 47N 107 7W
Parczew, *Poland* **55 G9** 51 40N 22 52 E
Pardes Hanna-Karkur, *Israel* **103 C3** 32 28N 34 57 E
Pardilla, *Spain* **42 D7** 41 33N 3 43W
Pardo →, *Bahia, Brazil* **171 E4** 15 40 S 39 0W
Pardo →, *Mato Grosso, Brazil* **175 A5** 21 46 S 52 9W
Pardo →, *Minas Gerais, Brazil* **171 E3** 15 48 S 44 48W
Pardo →, *São Paulo, Brazil* **171 F2** 20 10 S 48 38W
Pardubice, *Czech Rep.* **34 A8** 50 3N 15 45 E
Pardubický □, *Czech Rep.* **34 B8** 49 50N 16 0 E
Pardubitz = Pardubice, *Czech Rep.* **34 A8** 50 3N 15 45 E
Pare, *Indonesia* **85 D4** 7 43 S 112 12 E
Pare Mts., *Tanzania* **118 C4** 4 0 S 37 45 E
Parecis, Serra dos, *Brazil* **173 C6** 13 0 S 60 0W
Paredes de Nava, *Spain* **42 C6** 42 9N 4 42W
Parelhas, *Brazil* **170 C4** 6 41 S 36 39W
Paren, *Russia* **67 C17** 62 30N 163 15 E
Parenda, *India* **94 E2** 18 16N 75 28 E
Parengarenga Harbour, *N.Z.* **130 A1** 34 31 S 173 0 E
Parent, *Canada* **140 C5** 47 55N 74 35W
Parent, L., *Canada* **140 C4** 48 31N 77 1W
Parentis-en-Born, *France* **28 D2** 44 21N 1 4W
Parepare, *Indonesia* **82 B1** 4 0 S 119 40 E
Parfino, *Russia* **58 D6** 57 59N 31 34 E
Párga, *Greece* **48 B2** 39 15N 20 29 E
Pargas = Parainen, *Finland* **15 F20** 60 18N 22 18 E
Pargi, *India* **94 E3** 17 11N 77 53 E
Pargo, Pta. do, *Madeira* **9 c** 32 49N 17 17W
Paria →, *U.S.A.* **159 H8** 36 52N 111 36W
Paria, G. de, *Venezuela* **169 A5** 10 20N 62 0W
Paria, Pen. de, *Venezuela* **169 A5** 10 50N 62 30W
Pariaguán, *Venezuela* **169 B5** 8 51N 64 34W
Pariaman, *Indonesia* **84 C2** 0 47 S 100 11 E
Paricatuba, *Brazil* **169 D5** 4 26 S 61 53W
Paricutín, Cerro, *Mexico* **162 D4** 19 28N 102 15W
Parigi, *Java, Indonesia* **85 D3** 7 42 S 108 29 E
Parigi, *Sulawesi, Indonesia* **82 B2** 0 50 S 120 5 E
Parika, *Guyana* **169 B6** 6 50N 58 20W
Parikkala, *Finland* **58 B5** 61 33N 29 31 E
Parima, Serra, *Brazil* **169 C5** 2 30N 64 0W
Parinari, *Peru* **172 A3** 4 35 S 74 25W
Pariñas, Pta., *S. Amer.* **166 D2** 4 30 S 82 0W
Parincea, *Romania* **53 D12** 46 27N 27 9 E
Paringa, *Australia* **128 C4** 34 10 S 140 46 E
Parintins, *Brazil* **169 D6** 2 40 S 56 50W
Paris, *Canada* **150 C4** 43 12N 80 25W
Paris, *France* **27 D9** 48 50N 2 20 E
Paris, *Idaho, U.S.A.* **158 E8** 42 14N 111 24W
Paris, *Ill., U.S.A.* **157 E9** 39 36N 87 42W
Paris, *Ky., U.S.A.* **157 F12** 38 13N 84 15W
Paris, *Mo., U.S.A.* **156 E5** 39 29N 92 0W
Paris, *Tenn., U.S.A.* **153 C2** 36 18N 88 19W
Paris, *Tex., U.S.A.* **155 J7** 33 40N 95 33W
Paris, Ville de □, *France* **27 D9** 48 50N 2 20 E
Paris Charles de Gaulle ✗ (CDG), *France* **27 D9** 49 0N 2 32 E
Paris Orly ✗ (ORY), *France* **27 D9** 48 44N 2 24 E
Parish, *U.S.A.* **151 C8** 43 25N 76 8W
Parishville, *U.S.A.* **151 B10** 44 38N 74 49W
Pariti, *Indonesia* **82 D2** 10 1 S 123 45 E
Park, *U.S.A.* **160 B4** 48 45N 122 18W
Park City, *U.S.A.* **155 G6** 37 48N 97 20W
Park Falls, *U.S.A.* **154 C9** 45 56N 90 27W
Park Forest, *U.S.A.* **157 C9** 41 29N 87 40W
Park Head, *Canada* **150 B3** 44 36N 81 9W
Park Hills, *Mo., U.S.A.* **155 G9** 37 53N 90 28W
Park Hills, *Mo., U.S.A.* **156 G6** 37 51N 90 31W
Park Range, *U.S.A.* **158 G10** 40 0N 106 30W
Park Rapids, *U.S.A.* **154 B7** 46 55N 95 4W
Park Ridge, *U.S.A.* **157 B9** 42 2N 87 51W
Park River, *U.S.A.* **154 A6** 48 24N 97 45W
Park Rynie, *S. Africa* **117 E5** 30 25 S 30 45 E
Parkā Bandar, *Iran* **97 E8** 25 55N 59 35 E
Parkal, *India* **94 E4** 18 12N 79 43 E
Parkán = Štúrovo, *Slovak Rep.* **35 D11** 47 48N 18 41 E
Parkano, *Finland* **15 E20** 62 1N 23 0 E
Parkent, *Uzbekistan* **65 C4** 41 18N 69 40 E
Parker, *Ariz., U.S.A.* **161 L12** 34 9N 114 17W
Parker, *Pa., U.S.A.* **150 E5** 41 5N 79 41W
Parker Dam, *U.S.A.* **161 L12** 34 18N 114 8W
Parkersburg, *Iowa, U.S.A.* **156 B4** 42 35N 92 47W
Parkersburg, *W. Va., U.S.A.* **148 F5** 39 16N 81 34W
Parkes, *Australia* **129 B8** 33 9 S 148 11 E
Parkfield, *U.S.A.* **160 K6** 35 54N 120 26W

Parkhar, Tajikistan . . . 65 E4 37 30N 69 34 E
Parkhill, Canada 150 C3 43 15N 81 38W
Parkland, U.S.A. 160 C4 47 9N 122 26W
Parkston, U.S.A. 154 D6 43 24N 97 59W
Parksville, Canada . . . 142 D4 49 20N 124 21W
Parla, Spain 42 E7 40 14N 3 46W
Parlakimidi, India . . . . 94 E7 18 45N 84 5 E
Parli, India . . . . 94 E3 18 50N 76 35 E
Pârliţa, Moldova . . . . . 53 C12 47 19N 27 52 E
Parma, Italy . . . . 44 D7 44 48N 10 20 E
Parma, Idaho, U.S.A. . . 158 E5 43 47N 116 57W
Parma, Ohio, U.S.A. . . 150 E3 41 23N 81 43W
Parma →, Italy . . . . . . 44 D7 44 56N 10 26 E
Parnaguá, Brazil . . . . . 170 D3 10 10 S 44 38W
Parnaíba, Brazil . . . . . 170 B3 2 54 S 41 47W
Parnaíba →, Brazil . . . 170 B3 3 0 S 41 50W
Parnamirim, Brazil . . . 170 C4 8 5 S 39 34W
Parnarama, Brazil . . . . 170 C3 5 31 S 43 6W
Parnassós, Greece . . . . 48 C4 38 35N 22 30 E
Parnassus, N.Z. . . . . . . 131 C8 42 42 S 173 23 E
Parndana, Australia . . 128 C2 35 48 S 137 12 E
Parner, India . . . . 94 E2 19 0N 74 26 E
Párnis, Greece . . . . 48 C5 38 14N 23 45 E
Párnitha △, Greece . . . 48 C5 38 12N 23 44 E
Párnon Óros, Greece . . 48 D4 37 15N 22 45 E
Pärnu, Estonia . . . . . . 15 G21 58 28N 24 33 E
Parola, India . . . . 94 D2 20 47N 75 7 E
Paroo →, Australia . . . 128 A5 31 28 S 143 32 E
Páros, Greece . . . . 49 D7 37 5N 25 12 E
Parowan, U.S.A. 159 H7 37 51N 112 50W
Parpaillon, France . . . . 29 D10 44 30N 6 40 E
Parral, Chile . . . . 174 D1 36 10 S 71 52W
Parramatta, Australia . 129 B9 33 48 S 151 1 E
Parras, Mexico 162 B4 25 30N 102 20W
Parrett →, U.K. 21 F4 51 12N 3 1W
Parris I., U.S.A. 152 C9 32 20N 80 41W
Parrish, U.S.A. 153 H7 27 35N 82 26W
Parrott, U.S.A. 152 D5 31 54N 84 31W
Parrsboro, Canada 141 C7 45 30N 64 25W
Parry I., Canada 150 A4 45 18N 80 10W
Parry Is., Canada 6 B2 77 0N 110 0W
Parry Sound, Canada . . 140 C4 45 20N 80 0W
Parsberg, Germany . . . 31 F7 49 10N 11 43 E
Parseier Spitze, Austria 33 B10 47 10N 10 28 E
Parsęta →, Poland . . . . 54 D2 54 11N 15 34 E
Parsnip →, Canada . . . 142 B4 55 10N 123 2W
Parsons, U.S.A. 155 G7 37 20N 95 16W
Parsons Ra., Australia 126 A2 13 30 S 135 15 E
Partabpur, India . . . . . 94 E5 20 0N 80 42 E
Partanna, Italy . . . . 46 E5 37 43N 12 53 E
Partenio △, Italy . . . . . 47 B7 40 56N 14 38 E
Parthenay, France 26 F6 46 38N 0 16W
Partinico, Italy . . . . 46 D6 38 3N 13 7 E
Partizánske,
Slovak Rep. . . . . 35 C11 48 38N 18 23 E
Partridge I., Canada . . 140 A2 55 59N 87 37W
Partur, India . . . . 94 E3 19 40N 76 14 E
Paru →, Brazil . . . . . . 169 D7 1 33 S 52 38W
Parú →, Venezuela . . . 168 C4 4 20N 66 27W
Paru de Oeste →,
Brazil 169 C6 1 30N 56 0W
Parucito →, Venezuela 168 B4 5 18N 65 59W
Parur, India . . . . 95 J3 10 13N 76 14 E
Paruro, Peru . . . . 172 C3 13 45 S 71 50W
Parvān □, Afghan. . . . 91 B3 35 0N 69 0 E
Parvatipuram, India . . 94 E6 18 50N 83 25 E
Parvatsar, India . . . . . . 92 F6 26 52N 74 49 E
Påryd, Sweden . . . . 17 H9 56 34N 15 55 E
Parys, S. Africa . . . . . . 116 D4 26 52 S 27 29 E
Pas, Pta. des, Spain . . . 38 D1 38 46N 1 26 E
Pas-de-Calais □, France 27 B9 50 30N 2 10 E
Pasada, Spain 42 B5 43 23N 5 40W
Pasadena, Canada 141 C8 49 1N 57 36W
Pasadena, Calif., U.S.A. 161 L8 34 9N 118 9W
Pasadena, Tex., U.S.A. 155 L7 29 43N 95 13W
Pasaje, Ecuador . . . . . . 168 D2 3 23 S 79 50W
Pasaje →, Argentina . . 174 B3 25 39 S 63 56W
Paşalimanı, Turkey . . . 51 F11 40 29N 27 36 E
Pasar, Indonesia . . . . . 79 J17 8 27 S 114 54 E
Pasay, Phil. . . . . 80 D3 14 33N 121 0 E
Pascagoula, U.S.A. . . . 155 K10 30 21N 88 33W
Pascagoula →, U.S.A. 155 K10 30 23N 88 37W
Paşcani, Romania . . . . 53 C11 47 14N 26 45 E
Pasco, U.S.A. 158 C4 46 14N 119 6W
Pasco □, Peru . . . . 172 C2 10 40 S 75 0W
Pasco, Cerro de, Peru . 172 C2 10 45 S 76 10W
Pasco I., Australia . . . 124 D2 20 57 S 115 20 E
Pascoag, U.S.A. 151 E13 41 57N 71 42W
Pascua, I. de, Chile . . . 172 b 27 7 S 109 23W
Pasewalk, Germany . . 30 B9 53 30N 13 58 E
Pasfield L., Canada . . . 143 B7 58 24N 105 20W
Pasha →, Russia . . . . . 58 B7 60 29N 32 55 E
Pashiya, Russia . . . . . . 64 B7 58 33N 58 26 E
Pashmakli = Smolyan,
Bulgaria . . . . 51 E8 41 36N 24 38 E
Pasig, Phil. . . . . 80 D3 14 35N 121 5 E
Pasighat, India . . . . . . 90 A5 28 4N 95 21 E
Pasinler, Turkey . . . . . 101 C9 39 59N 41 41 E
Pasir Mas, Malaysia . . 87 J4 6 2N 102 8 E
Pasir Panjang,
Singapore . . . . 87 d 1 18N 103 46 E
Pasir Putih, Malaysia . 87 K4 5 50N 102 24 E
Pasirian, Indonesia . . . 85 D4 8 13 S 113 8 E
Pasirkuning, Indonesia 84 C2 0 30 S 104 33 E
Påskallavik, Sweden . . 17 G10 57 10N 16 26 E
Paskūh, Iran . . . . 97 E9 27 34N 61 39 E
Pasłęk, Poland . . . . . . 54 D6 54 3N 19 41 E
Pasłęka →, Poland . . . 54 D6 54 26N 19 46 E
Pasley, C., Australia . . 125 F3 33 52 S 123 35 E
Pašman, Croatia . . . . . 45 E12 43 58N 15 20 E
Pasmore →, Australia 128 A3 31 5 S 139 49 E
Pasni, Pakistan . . . . . . 91 D1 25 15N 63 27 E
Paso Cantinela, Mexico 161 N11 32 33N 115 47W
Paso de Indios,
Argentina . . . . 176 B3 43 55 S 69 0W
Paso de los Indios,
Argentina . . . . 176 A3 38 32 S 69 25W
Paso de los Libres,
Argentina . . . . 174 B4 29 44 S 57 10W
Paso de los Toros,
Uruguay . . . . 174 C4 32 45 S 56 30W
Paso Flores, Argentina 176 B2 40 35 S 70 38W
Paso Robles, U.S.A. . . 159 J3 35 38N 120 41W
Pasorapa, Bolivia . . . . 173 D5 18 16 S 64 37W
Paspébiac, Canada . . . 141 C6 48 3N 65 17W
Pasrur, Pakistan . . . . . 92 C6 32 16N 74 43 E
Passage West, Ireland . 23 E3 51 52N 8 21W
Passaic, U.S.A. 151 F10 40 51N 74 7W
Passam, Papua N. G. . 132 B2 3 41 S 143 38 E
Passau, Germany . . . . . 31 G9 48 34N 13 28 E
Passenheim = Pasym,
Poland . . . . 54 E7 53 48N 20 49 E
Passero, C., Italy . . . . . 47 F8 36 41N 15 10 E
Passi, Phil. . . . . 81 F4 11 6N 122 38 E
Passo Fundo, Brazil . . 175 B5 28 10 S 52 20W
Passos, Brazil . . . . 171 F2 20 45 S 46 37W
Passow, Germany . . . . 30 B10 53 8N 14 6 E
Passwang, Switz. . . . . . 32 B5 47 22N 7 41 E
Passy, France . . . . 29 C10 45 55N 6 41 E
Pastavy, Belarus . . . . . 15 J22 55 4N 26 50 E
Pastaza □, Ecuador . . 168 D2 2 0 S 77 0W
Pastaza →, Peru . . . . . 168 D2 4 50 S 76 52W
Pasto, Colombia 168 C2 1 13N 77 17W
Pastol B., U.S.A. 144 E7 63 7N 163 15W
Pastos Bons, Brazil . . . 170 C3 6 36 S 44 5W
Pastrana, Spain 40 E2 40 27N 2 53W
Pasuquin, Phil. . . . . . . 80 B3 18 20N 120 37 E
Pasuruan, Indonesia . . 85 D4 7 40 S 112 44 E
Pasym, Poland . . . . 54 E7 53 48N 20 49 E
Pásztó, Hungary . . . . . 52 C4 47 52N 19 43 E
Pata, Phil. . . . . 81 J3 5 51N 121 10 E
Pata I., Phil. . . . . 81 J3 5 49N 121 10 E
Patagonia, Argentina . 176 C2 45 0 S 69 0W
Patagonia, U.S.A. 159 L8 31 33N 110 45W
Patalasang, Indonesia . 82 C1 5 26 S 119 26 E
Patambar, Iran . . . . . . 97 D9 29 45N 60 17 E
Patan = Lalitapur,
Nepal . . . . 93 F11 27 40N 85 20 E
Patan, Gujarat, India . 94 F1 17 22N 73 57 E
Patan, Maharashtra,
India . . . . 92 H5 23 54N 72 14 E
Patani, Indonesia . . . . 82 A3 0 20N 128 50 E
Pătârlagele, Romania . 53 E11 45 19N 26 21 E
Pataudi, India . . . . 92 E7 28 18N 76 48 E
Patchewollock,
Australia . . . . 128 C5 35 22 S 142 12 E
Patchogue, U.S.A. . . . 151 F11 40 46N 73 1W
Pate, Kenya . . . . 118 C5 2 10 S 41 0 E
Patea, N.Z. . . . . 130 F3 39 45 S 174 30 E
Pategi, Nigeria . . . . . . 113 D6 8 50N 5 45 E
Patensie, S. Africa . . . 116 E3 33 46 S 24 49 E
Paterna, Spain 41 F4 39 30N 0 26W
Paternion, Austria . . . 34 E6 46 43N 13 38 E
Paternò, Italy . . . . 47 E7 37 34N 14 54 E
Pateros, U.S.A. 158 B4 48 3N 119 54W
Paterson, Australia . . . 129 B9 32 35 S 151 36 E
Paterson, U.S.A. 151 F10 40 55N 74 11W
Paterson Inlet, N.Z. . . 131 G3 46 56 S 168 12 E
Paterson Ra., Australia 124 D3 21 45 S 122 10 E
Pathankot, India . . . . . 92 C6 32 18N 75 45 E
Pathardi, India . . . . . . 94 E2 19 10N 75 11 E
Patharghata, Bangla. . . 90 D2 22 2N 89 58 E
Pathein = Bassein,
Burma . . . . 90 G5 16 45N 94 30 E
Pathfinder Reservoir,
U.S.A. 158 E10 42 28N 106 51W
Pathiu, Thailand . . . . . 87 G2 10 42N 99 19 E
Pathri, India . . . . 94 E3 19 15N 76 27 E
Pathum Thani,
Thailand . . . . 86 E3 14 1N 100 32 E
Pati, Indonesia . . . . . . 85 D4 6 45 S 111 1 E
Pati Pt., Guam . . . . . . 133 R15 13 40N 144 50 E
Patía, Colombia 168 C2 2 4N 77 4W
Patía →, Colombia . . . 168 C2 2 13N 78 40W
Patiala, Punjab, India . 92 D7 30 23N 76 26 E
Patiala, Ut. P., India . . 93 F8 27 43N 79 1 E
Patine Kouka, Senegal 112 C2 12 45N 13 45W
Patitírion, Greece . . . . 48 B5 39 8N 23 50 E
Pativilca, Peru . . . . . . 172 C2 10 42 S 77 48W
Patkai Bum, India . . . . 90 B5 27 0N 95 30 E
Pátmos, Greece . . . . . . 49 D8 37 21N 26 36 E
Patna, India . . . . 93 G11 25 35N 85 12 E
Patnagarh, India . . . . . 94 D6 20 43N 83 9 E
Patnanongan I., Phil. . 80 D4 14 48N 122 11 E
Patnongon, Phil. . . . . 81 F4 10 55N 122 0 E
Patnos, Turkey . . . . . . 101 C10 39 13N 42 51 E
Pato Branco, Brazil . . 175 B5 26 13 S 52 40W
Patoka L., U.S.A. 157 F10 38 20N 86 40W
Patong, Ao, Thailand . 87 a 7 54N 98 17 E
Patonga, Uganda . . . . . 118 B3 2 45N 33 15 E
Patos, Albania . . . . 50 F3 40 42N 19 38 E
Patos, Brazil . . . . 170 C4 6 55 S 37 16W
Patos, L. dos, Brazil . . 175 C5 31 20 S 51 0W
Patos, Río de los →,
Argentina . . . . 174 C2 31 18 S 69 25W
Patos de Minas, Brazil 171 E2 18 35 S 46 32W
Patquía, Argentina . . . 174 C2 30 2 S 66 55W
Pátra = Pátrai, Greece 48 C3 38 14N 21 47 E
Pátrai, Greece . . . . 48 C3 38 14N 21 47 E
Pátraikós Kólpos,
Greece . . . . 48 C3 38 17N 21 30 E
Patras = Pátrai, Greece 48 C3 38 14N 21 47 E
Patreksfjörður, Iceland 11 B2 65 34N 24 0W
Patriarsheye =
Donskoy, Russia . . . . 58 F10 53 55N 38 15 E
Patricio Lynch, I., Chile 176 C1 48 35 S 75 30W
Patrocínio, Brazil . . . . 171 E2 18 57 S 47 0W
Pattada, Italy . . . . 46 B2 40 35N 9 6 E
Pattani, Thailand . . . . 87 J3 6 48N 101 15 E
Pattaya, Thailand . . . . 78 B2 12 52N 100 55 E
Patten, U.S.A. 149 C11 46 0N 68 38W
Patterson, Calif., U.S.A. 160 H5 37 28N 121 8W
Patterson, Ga., U.S.A. 152 D7 31 23N 82 8W
Patterson, La., U.S.A. . 155 L9 29 42N 91 18W
Patterson, Mt., U.S.A. 160 G7 38 29N 119 20W
Patteson, Passage,
Vanuatu . . . . 133 E6 15 26 S 168 12 E
Patti, Punjab, India . . 92 D6 31 17N 74 54 E
Patti, Ut. P., India . . . . 93 G10 25 55N 82 12 E
Patti, Italy . . . . 47 D7 38 8N 14 58 E
Pattoki, Pakistan . . . . 92 D5 31 5N 73 52 E
Patton = Monroeville,
U.S.A. 150 F5 40 26N 79 45W
Patton, U.S.A. 150 F6 40 38N 78 39W
Pattonsburg, U.S.A. . . 156 D2 40 3N 94 8W
Pattukkattai, India . . . 95 J4 10 25N 79 20 E
Patu, Brazil . . . . 170 C4 6 6 S 37 38W
Patuakhali, Bangla. . . . 90 D3 22 20N 90 25 E
Patuanak, Canada 143 B7 55 55N 107 43W
Patuca △, Honduras . . 164 D2 14 30N 85 30W
Patuca →, Honduras . 164 C3 15 50N 84 18W
Patuca, Punta,
Honduras 164 C3 15 49N 84 14W
Pătulele, Romania . . . . 52 F7 44 21N 22 47 E
Patur, India . . . . 94 D3 20 27N 76 56 E
Pátzcuaro, Mexico . . . 162 D4 19 30N 101 40W
Pau, France 28 E3 43 19N 0 25W
Pau, Gave de →,
France 28 E2 43 33N 1 12W
Pau d' Arco, Brazil . . . 170 C2 7 30 S 49 22W
Pau dos Ferros, Brazil 170 C4 6 7 S 38 10W
Pauanui, N.Z. . . . . 130 D4 37 1 S 175 52 E
Paucartambo, Peru . . . 172 C3 13 19 S 71 35W
Pauillac, France 28 C3 45 11N 0 46W
Pauini, Brazil . . . . 172 B4 7 40 S 66 58W
Pauini →, Brazil . . . . 169 D5 1 42 S 62 50W
Pauk, Burma . . . . 90 E5 21 27N 94 30 E
Paukkaung, Burma . . . 90 F5 18 54N 95 33 E
Pauktaw, Burma . . . . . 90 E4 20 11N 93 4 E
Paul I., Canada 141 A7 56 30N 61 20W
Paul Isnard, Fr. Guiana 169 C7 4 47N 54 1W
Paul Smiths, U.S.A. . . 151 B10 44 26N 74 15W
Paulatuk, Canada 138 B7 69 25N 124 0W
Paulding, U.S.A. 157 C12 41 8N 84 35W
Paulhan, France . . . . . 28 E7 43 33N 3 28 E
Paulis = Isiro,
Dem. Rep. of
the Congo . . . . 118 B2 2 53N 27 40 E
Paulista = Paulistana,
Brazil . . . . 170 C3 8 9 S 41 9W
Paulista, Brazil . . . . . . 170 C5 7 57 S 34 53W
Paulistana, Brazil . . . . 170 C3 8 9 S 41 9W
Paulo Afonso, Brazil . . 170 C4 9 21 S 38 15W
Paulo de Faria, Brazil . 171 F2 20 2 S 49 24W
Paulpietersburg,
S. Africa . . . . 117 D5 27 23 S 30 50 E
Pauls Valley, U.S.A. . . 155 H6 34 44N 97 13W
Pauma Valley, U.S.A. . 161 M10 33 16N 116 58W
Paung, Burma . . . . 90 G5 16 37N 94 28 E
Paungde, Burma . . . . . 90 F5 18 29N 95 30 E
Pauni, India . . . . 94 D4 20 48N 79 40 E
Pauri, India . . . . 93 D8 30 9N 78 47 E
Pausa, Peru . . . . 172 D3 15 16 S 73 22W
Pauto →, Colombia . . 168 B3 5 9N 70 55W
Pauwela, U.S.A. 145 C5 20 56N 156 19W
Pavagada, India . . . . . 95 G3 14 6N 77 16 E
Pāveh, Iran . . . . 101 E12 35 3N 46 22 E
Pavelets, Russia . . . . . 58 F10 53 49N 39 14 E
Pavia, Italy . . . . 44 C6 45 7N 9 8 E
Pavilion, U.S.A. 150 D6 42 52N 78 1W
Pavilly, France . . . . . . 26 C7 49 34N 0 57 E
Pāvilosta, Latvia . . . . 15 H19 56 53N 21 14 E
Pavlikeni, Bulgaria . . . 51 C9 43 14N 25 20 E
Pavlodar, Kazakhstan . 66 D8 52 33N 77 0 E
Pavlograd = Pavlohrad,
Ukraine . . . . 59 H8 48 30N 35 52 E
Pavlohrad, Ukraine . . . 59 H8 48 30N 35 52 E
Pavlovo, Russia . . . . . . 60 C6 55 58N 43 5 E
Pavlovsk, Russia . . . . . 60 E5 50 26N 40 5 E
Pavlovskaya, Russia . . 61 G4 46 17N 39 47 E
Pavlovskiy-Posad,
Russia . . . . 58 E10 55 47N 38 42 E
Pavo, U.S.A. 152 E6 30 58N 83 45W
Pavullo nel Frignano,
Italy . . . . 44 D7 44 20N 10 50 E
Pavuvu, Solomon Is. . . 133 M10 9 4 S 159 8 E
Paw Paw, U.S.A. 157 B11 42 13N 85 53W
Pawahku, Burma . . . . . 90 B7 26 11N 98 40 E
Pawai, Pulau, Singapore 87 d 1 11N 103 44 E
Pawan →, Indonesia . . 85 C4 1 55 S 110 0 E
Pawayan, India . . . . . . 93 E9 28 4N 80 6 E
Pawhuska, U.S.A. 155 G6 36 40N 96 20W
Pawling, U.S.A. 151 E11 41 34N 73 36W
Pawnee, Ill., U.S.A. . . 156 E7 39 36N 89 35W
Pawnee, Okla., U.S.A. . 155 G6 36 20N 96 48W
Pawnee City, U.S.A. . . 154 E6 40 7N 96 9W
Pawpaw, U.S.A. 156 C8 41 41N 88 59W
Pawtucket, U.S.A. . . . 151 E13 41 53N 71 23W
Paxi = Paxoí, Greece . . 38 C10 39 14N 20 12 E
Paximádhia, Greece . . . 39 F5 35 0N 24 35 E
Paxoí, Greece . . . . 38 C10 39 14N 20 12 E
Paxson, U.S.A. 144 E11 63 2N 145 30W
Paxton, U.S.A. 157 D8 40 27N 88 6W
Payagyi, Burma . . . . . 90 G6 17 29N 96 32 E
Payakumbuh, Indonesia 84 C2 0 20 S 100 35 E
Payapa = General
Tinio, Phil. . . . . 80 D3 15 39N 121 10 E
Payerne, Switz. . . . . . . 32 C3 46 49N 6 56 E
Payette, U.S.A. 158 D5 44 5N 116 56W
Paymogo, Spain 43 H3 37 44N 7 21W
Payne, U.S.A. 157 C12 41 5N 84 44W
Payne Bay = Kangirsuk,
Canada 139 B13 60 0N 70 0W
Payne L., Canada 139 C12 59 30N 74 30W
Payne Pt., Ascension I. 9 g 7 57 S 14 25W
Paynes Find, Australia 125 E2 29 15 S 117 42 E
Paynesville, Liberia . . 112 D2 6 20N 10 45W
Paynesville, U.S.A. . . . 154 C7 45 23N 94 43W
Payo Obispo =
Chetumal, Mexico . . 163 D7 18 30N 88 20W
Pays de la Loire □,
France 26 E6 47 45N 0 25W
Paysandú, Uruguay . . . 174 C4 32 19 S 58 8W
Payshanba, Uzbekistan 65 C3 40 0N 66 14 E
Payson, Ariz., U.S.A. . 159 J8 34 14N 111 20W
Payson, Utah, U.S.A. . 158 F8 40 3N 111 44W
Paz →, Guatemala . . . 164 D1 13 44N 90 10W
Paz, B. de la, Mexico . 162 C2 24 15N 110 25W
Pāzanān, Iran . . . . 97 D6 30 35N 49 59 E
Pazar, Turkey . . . . 101 B9 41 10N 40 50 E
Pazarcık, Turkey . . . . 100 D7 37 30N 37 17 E
Pazardzhik, Bulgaria . . 51 D8 42 12N 24 20 E
Pazarköy, Turkey . . . . 49 B9 39 51N 27 24 E
Pazarlar, Turkey . . . . . 49 C11 39 0N 29 7 E
Pazaryeri, Turkey . . . . 49 B11 40 0N 29 56 E
Pazaryolu, Turkey . . . . 101 B9 40 21N 40 47 E
Pazin, Croatia . . . . 45 C10 45 14N 13 56 E
Pazña, Bolivia . . . . 172 D4 18 36 S 66 55W
Pčinja →, Macedonia . 50 E5 41 50N 21 45 E
Pe Ell, U.S.A. 160 D3 46 34N 123 18W
Pea →, U.S.A. 152 D4 31 1N 85 51W
Peabody, U.S.A. 151 D14 42 31N 70 56W
Peace →, Canada 142 B6 59 0N 111 25W
Peace →, U.S.A. 153 J7 26 56N 82 6W
Peace Point, Canada . . 142 B6 59 7N 112 27W
Peace River, Canada . . 142 B5 56 15N 117 18W
Peach Springs, U.S.A. . 159 J7 35 32N 113 25W
Peachland, Canada . . . 142 D5 49 47N 119 45W
Peachtree City, U.S.A. 152 B5 33 25N 84 35W
Peak, The = Kinder
Scout, U.K. 20 D6 53 24N 1 52W
Peak, The, Ascension I. 9 g 7 57 S 14 20W
Peak Charles △,
Australia . . . . 125 F3 32 42 S 121 10 E
Peak District △, U.K. . 20 D6 53 24N 1 46W
Peak Hill, N.S.W.,
Australia . . . . 129 B8 32 47 S 148 11 E
Peak Hill, W. Austral.,
Australia . . . . 125 E2 25 35 S 118 43 E
Peak Ra., Australia . . . 126 C4 22 50 S 148 20 E
Peake, Australia . . . . . 128 C3 35 25 S 139 55 E
Peake Cr. →, Australia 127 D2 28 2 S 136 7 E
Peal de Becerro, Spain 43 H7 37 55N 3 7W
Peale, Mt., U.S.A. 159 G9 38 26N 109 14W
Pearblossom, U.S.A. . . 161 L9 34 30N 117 55W
Pearl, U.S.A. 156 E6 39 28N 90 38W
Pearl →, U.S.A. 155 K10 30 11N 89 32W
Pearl and Hermes Reef,
U.S.A. 145 F8 27 55N 175 45W
Pearl Banks, Sri Lanka 95 K4 8 45N 79 45 E
Pearl City, U.S.A. . . . 145 K14 21 24N 157 59W
Pearl Harbor, U.S.A. . 145 K14 21 21N 157 57W
Pearl River = Zhu
Jiang →, China . . . . 77 F9 22 45N 113 37 E
Pearl River, U.S.A. . . . 151 E10 41 4N 74 2W
Pearsall, U.S.A. 155 L5 28 54N 99 6W
Pearson, U.S.A. 152 D7 31 18N 82 51W
Peary Land, Greenland 10 A7 82 40N 33 0W
Pease →, U.S.A. 155 H5 34 12N 99 2W
Peawanuck, Canada . . 139 C11 55 15N 85 12W
Pebane, Mozam. . . . . . 119 F4 17 10 S 38 8 E
Pebas, Peru . . . . 168 D3 3 10 S 71 46W
Pebble, I., Falk. Is. . . . 9 f 51 20 S 59 40W
Pebble Beach, U.S.A. . 160 J5 36 34N 121 57W
Peć, Serbia & M. . . . . 50 D4 42 40N 20 17 E
Peçanha, Brazil . . . . . 171 E3 18 33 S 42 34W
Pecatonica, U.S.A. . . . 156 B7 42 19N 89 22W
Pecatonica →, U.S.A. 156 B7 42 26N 89 12W
Péccioli, Italy . . . . 44 E7 43 33N 10 43 E
Pechea, Romania . . . . 53 E12 45 36N 27 49 E
Pechenga, Russia . . . . 56 A5 69 29N 31 4 E
Pechenizhyn, Ukraine . 53 B9 48 30N 24 48 E
Pechiguera, Pta.,
Canary Is. 9 e2 28 51N 13 53W
Pechnezhskoye Vdkhr.,
Ukraine . . . . 59 G9 50 5N 36 54 E
Pechora, Russia . . . . . 56 A10 65 10N 57 11 E
Pechora →, Russia . . . 56 A9 68 13N 54 15 E
Pechorskaya Guba,
Russia . . . . 56 A9 68 40N 54 0 E
Pechory, Russia . . . . . 15 H22 57 48N 27 40 E
Pecica, Romania . . . . . 52 D6 46 10N 21 3 E
Pecka, Serbia & M. . . . 50 B3 44 18N 19 33 E
Pécora, C., Italy . . . . . 46 C1 39 27N 8 23 E
Pecos, N. Mex., U.S.A. 159 J11 35 35N 105 41W
Pecos, Tex., U.S.A. . . . 155 K3 31 26N 103 30W
Pecos →, U.S.A. 155 L3 29 42N 101 22W
Pécs, Hungary . . . . 52 D3 46 5N 18 15 E
Pedda Bellala, India . . 94 E4 19 4N 78 49 E
Peddapalli, India . . . . . 94 E4 18 40N 79 24 E
Peddapuram, India . . . 94 F6 17 6N 82 8 E
Pedder, L., Australia . . 127 G4 42 55 S 146 10 E
Peddie, S. Africa . . . . . 117 E4 33 14 S 27 7 E
Pedernales, Dom. Rep. 165 C5 18 2N 71 44W
Pedernales, Ecuador . . 168 C1 0 5N 80 3W
Pedieos →, Cyprus . . . 39 E9 35 10N 33 54 E
Pedirka, Australia . . . . 127 D2 26 40 S 135 14 E
Pedra Azul, Brazil . . . . 171 E3 16 2 S 41 17W
Pedra Branca, Brazil . . 169 C7 0 51N 51 58W
Pedra Grande, Recifes
de, Brazil . . . . 171 E4 17 45 S 38 58W
Pedra Lume,
C. Verde Is. . . . . 9 j 16 40N 22 52W
Pedras Negras, Brazil . 173 C5 12 51 S 62 54W
Pedras Tinhosas, I.,
São Tomé & Príncipe 115 G6 1 22N 7 17 E
Pedreguer, Spain . . . . . 41 G5 38 48N 0 3 E
Pedreiras, Brazil . . . . . 170 B3 4 32 S 44 40W
Pedro Afonso, Brazil . . 170 C2 9 0 S 48 10W
Pedro Bay, U.S.A. 144 G9 59 47N 154 7W
Pedro Cays, Jamaica . . 164 C4 17 5N 77 48W
Pedro Chico, Colombia 168 C3 1 4N 70 25W
Pedro de Valdivia,
Chile . . . . 174 A2 22 55 S 69 38W
Pedro Dorado,
Colombia 168 C3 1 0N 70 14W
Pedro Juan Caballero,
Paraguay . . . . 175 A4 22 30 S 55 40W
Pedro Muñoz, Spain . . 43 F8 39 25N 2 56W
Pedrógão Grande,
Portugal 42 F2 39 55N 8 9W
Pee Dee →, U.S.A. . . . 149 J6 33 22N 79 16W
Peebinga, Australia . . . 128 C4 34 52 S 140 57 E
Peebles, U.K. 22 F5 55 40N 3 11W
Peebles, U.S.A. 157 F13 38 57N 83 24W
Peekskill, U.S.A. 151 E11 41 17N 73 55W
Peel, I. of Man 20 C3 54 13N 4 40W
Peel →, Australia . . . . 129 A9 30 50 S 150 29 E
Peel →, Canada 138 B6 67 0N 135 0W
Peel Sd., Canada 138 A10 73 0N 96 0W
Peene →, Germany . . . 30 A9 54 9N 13 46 E
Peera Peera Poolanna
L., Australia . . . . 127 D2 26 30 S 138 0 E
Peerless Lake, Canada 142 B6 56 37N 114 40W
Peers, Canada 142 C5 53 40N 116 0W
Peery L., Australia . . . 128 A5 30 45 S 143 35 E
Pegasus Bay, N.Z. . . . 131 D8 43 20 S 173 10 E
Peggau, Austria . . . . . . 34 D8 47 12N 15 21 E
Pegnitz, Germany . . . . 31 F7 49 44N 11 31 E
Pegnitz →, Germany . . 31 F6 49 30N 10 59 E
Pego, Spain 41 G4 38 51N 0 8W
Pegu, Burma . . . . 90 G6 17 20N 96 29 E
Pegu □, Burma . . . . . . 90 G6 17 30N 96 30 E
Pegu Yoma, Burma . . . 90 F5 19 0N 96 0 E
Pehčevo, Macedonia . . 50 E6 41 41N 22 55 E
Pehlivanköy, Turkey . . 51 E10 41 20N 26 55 E
Pehuajó, Argentina . . . 174 D3 35 45 S 62 0W
Pei Xian = Pizhou,
China . . . . 74 G9 34 44N 116 55 E
Peian = Bei'an, China . 69 B7 48 10N 126 20 E
Peihai = Beihai, China 76 G7 21 28N 109 6 E
Peine, Chile . . . . 174 A2 23 45 S 68 8W
Peine, Germany . . . . . . 30 C6 52 19N 10 14 E
Peip'ing = Beijing,
China . . . . 74 E9 39 55N 116 20 E
Peipus, L. =
Chudskoye, Ozero,
Russia . . . . 15 G22 58 13N 27 30 E
Peissenberg, Germany 31 H7 47 48N 11 4 E
Peitz, Germany . . . . . . 30 D10 51 51N 14 24 E
Peixe, Brazil . . . . 171 D2 12 0 S 48 40W
Peixe →, Brazil . . . . . 171 F1 21 31 S 51 58W
Peixoto de Azeredo →,
Brazil . . . . 173 C6 10 6 S 55 31W
Pek →, Serbia & M. . . 50 B5 44 45N 21 29 E
Pekalongan, Indonesia 85 D3 6 53 S 109 40 E
Pekan, Malaysia . . . . . 87 L4 3 30N 103 25 E
Pekan Nenas, Malaysia 87 d 1 31N 103 31 E
Pekanbaru, Indonesia . 84 B2 0 30N 101 15 E
Pekang, Taiwan . . . . . 77 F13 23 34N 120 18 E
Pekin, U.S.A. 156 D7 40 35N 89 40W
Peking = Beijing, China 74 E9 39 55N 116 20 E
Peklevskaya =
Troitskiy, Russia . . . 64 C9 57 5N 63 43 E
Pekutatan, Indonesia . 79 J17 8 25 S 114 49 E
Péla, Guinea 112 D3 7 37N 9 7W
Pelabuhan Klang,
Malaysia . . . . 87 L3 3 0N 101 23 E
Pelabuhan Ratu, Teluk,
Indonesia . . . . 84 D3 7 5 S 106 30 E
Pelabuhanratu,
Indonesia . . . . 84 D3 7 0 S 106 32 E
Pélagos, Greece . . . . . . 48 B6 39 17N 24 4 E
Pelaihari, Indonesia . . 85 C4 3 55 S 114 45 E
Pelat, Mt., France . . . . 29 D10 44 16N 6 42 E
Pełczyce, Poland . . . . . 55 E2 53 3N 15 16 E
Peleaga, Vf., Romania . 52 E7 45 22N 22 55 E
Pelechuco, Bolivia . . . 172 C4 14 48 S 69 4W
Pelée, Mt., Martinique 164 c 14 48N 61 10W
Pelee, Pt., Canada 140 D3 41 54N 82 31W
Pelee I., Canada 140 D3 41 47N 82 40W
Pelejo, Peru . . . . 172 B2 6 10 S 75 49W
Pelekech, Kenya . . . . . 118 B4 3 52N 35 8 E
Peleng, Indonesia . . . . 82 B2 1 20 S 123 30 E
Pelenge, Dem. Rep. of
the Congo . . . . 114 C4 2 44 S 22 39 E
Pelentong, Malaysia . . 87 d 1 32N 103 49 E
Pélézi, Ivory C. 112 D3 7 17N 6 54W
Pelham, U.S.A. 152 D5 31 8N 84 9W
Pelhřimov, Czech Rep. 34 B8 49 24N 15 12 E
Pelican, U.S.A. 142 B1 57 58N 136 14W
Pelican L., Canada . . . 143 C8 52 28N 100 20W
Pelican Narrows,
Canada 143 B8 55 10N 102 56W
Pelion, U.S.A. 152 B8 33 46N 81 15W
Pelister △, Macedonia 50 F5 41 0N 21 10 E
Pelješac, Croatia . . . . . 45 F14 42 55N 17 25 E
Pelkosenniemi, Finland 14 C22 67 6N 27 28 E
Pell City, U.S.A. 152 B3 33 35N 86 17W
Pella, Greece . . . . 50 F6 40 46N 22 23 E
Pella, S. Africa . . . . . . 116 D2 29 1 S 19 6 E
Pella, U.S.A. 156 C4 41 25N 92 55W
Pélla □, Greece . . . . . . 50 F6 40 52N 22 0 E
Pello, Finland . . . . 14 C21 66 47N 23 59 E
Pellworm, Germany . . . 30 A4 54 31N 8 39 E
Pelly →, Canada 138 B6 62 47N 137 19W
Pelly Bay, Canada 139 B11 68 38N 89 50W
Peloponnese =
Pelopónnisos □,
Greece . . . . 48 D4 37 10N 22 0 E
Pelopónnisos □, Greece 48 D4 37 10N 22 0 E
Peloritani, Monti, Italy 47 D8 38 3N 15 20 E
Pelorus →, N.Z. . . . . . 131 B8 41 16 S 173 45 E
Pelorus Sd., N.Z. . . . . 131 A8 40 59 S 173 59 E
Pelotas, Brazil . . . . . . 175 C5 31 42 S 52 23W
Pelotas →, Brazil . . . . 175 B5 27 28 S 51 55W
Pelovo, Bulgaria . . . . . 51 C8 43 26N 24 17 E
Pelplin, Poland . . . . . . 54 E5 53 55N 18 42 E
Pelvoux, Massif du,
France . . . . 29 D10 44 52N 6 20 E
Pelym, Russia . . . . 64 B9 59 34N 63 27 E
Pelym →, Russia . . . . 64 B9 59 39N 63 26 E
Pemalang, Indonesia . . 85 D3 6 53 S 109 23 E
Pemanggil, Pulau,
Malaysia . . . . 87 L5 2 37N 104 21 E
Pematangsiantar,
Indonesia . . . . 84 B1 2 57N 99 5 E
Pemba, Mozam. . . . . . . 119 E5 12 58 S 40 30 E
Pemba, Zambia . . . . . . 119 F2 16 30 S 27 28 E
Pemba Channel,
Tanzania . . . . 118 D4 5 0 S 39 37 E
Pemba I., Tanzania . . . 118 D4 5 0 S 39 45 E
Pemberton, Australia . 125 F2 34 30 S 116 0 E
Pemberton, Canada . . . 142 C4 50 25N 122 50W
Pembina, U.S.A. 154 A6 48 58N 97 15W
Pembroke, Canada 140 C4 45 50N 77 7W
Pembroke, U.K. 21 F3 51 41N 4 55W
Pembroke, U.S.A. 152 C8 32 8N 81 37W
Pembroke Pines, U.S.A. 153 J9 26 5N 80 14W
Pembrokeshire □, U.K. 21 F3 51 52N 4 56W
Pembrokeshire
Coast △, U.K. 21 F2 51 50N 5 2W
Pembuang →,
Indonesia . . . . 85 C4 3 24 S 112 33 E
Pen, India . . . . 94 E1 18 45N 73 5 E
Pen-y-Ghent, U.K. . . . 20 C5 54 10N 2 14W
Peña, Sierra de la,
Spain 40 C4 42 32N 0 45W
Peña de Francia, Sierra
de la, Spain 42 E4 40 32N 6 10W
Penafiel, Portugal 42 D2 41 12N 8 17W
Peñafiel, Spain 42 D6 41 35N 4 7W
Peñaflor, Spain 43 H5 37 43N 5 21W
Penal, Trin. & Tob. . . . 169 F9 10 9N 61 29W
Peñalara, Spain 42 E7 40 51N 3 57W
Penalva, Brazil . . . . . . 170 B2 3 18 S 45 10W
Penamacôr, Portugal . . 42 E3 40 10N 7 10W
Penambulai, Indonesia 83 C4 6 24 S 134 48 E
Penang = Pinang,
Malaysia . . . . 87 c 5 25N 100 15 E
Penápolis, Brazil . . . . 175 A6 21 30 S 50 0W
Peñaranda de
Bracamonte, Spain . . 42 E5 40 53N 5 13W
Peñarroya, Spain 40 E4 40 25N 0 40W
Peñarroya-
Pueblonuevo, Spain . 43 G5 38 19N 5 16W
Penarth, U.K. 21 F4 51 26N 3 11W
Peñas, C. de, Spain . . . 42 B5 43 42N 5 52W
Penas, G. de, Chile . . . 176 C2 47 0 S 75 0W
Peñas, Pta., Venezuela 169 A5 11 17N 62 0W
Peñas de San Pedro,
Spain 41 G3 38 44N 2 0W
Peñas del Chache,
Canary Is. 9 e2 29 6N 13 33W
Peñausende, Spain . . . 42 D5 41 17N 5 52W
Pench △, India . . . . . . 93 J8 21 45N 79 20 E
Pench →, India . . . . . 94 D4 21 17N 79 10 E
Pench'i = Benxi, China 75 D12 41 20N 123 48 E
Pend Oreille →, U.S.A. 158 B5 49 4N 117 37W
Pend Oreille, L., U.S.A. 158 C5 48 10N 116 21W
Pendálofon, Greece . . . 50 F5 40 14N 21 12 E
Pendé →, C.A.R. . . . . 114 A3 7 55N 16 36 E
Pendembu, Eastern,
S. Leone 112 D2 8 10N 10 42W
Pendembu, Northern,
S. Leone 112 D2 9 7N 11 14W
Pendências, Brazil . . . 170 C4 5 15 S 36 43W
Pender B., Australia . . 124 C3 16 45 S 122 42 E
Pendik, Turkey . . . . . . 51 F13 40 53N 29 13 E
Pendjari △, Benin . . . 113 C5 11 15N 1 32 E
Pendjari →, Benin . . . 113 C5 10 55N 0 50 E
Pendleton, Ind., U.S.A. 157 E11 40 0N 85 45W
Pendleton, Oreg.,
U.S.A. 158 D4 45 40N 118 47W
Pendra, India . . . . 93 H9 22 46N 81 57 E
Pendzhikent, Tajikistan 65 D3 39 29N 67 37 E
Peneda-Gerês △,
Portugal 42 D2 41 57N 8 15W
Penedo, Brazil . . . . . . 170 D4 10 15 S 36 36W
Penelokan, Indonesia . 79 J18 8 17 S 115 22 E
Penetanguishene,
Canada 140 D4 44 50N 79 55W
Penfield, U.S.A. 150 E6 41 13N 78 35W
Peng Chau, China . . . . 69 G11 22 17N 114 2 E
Pengalengan, Indonesia 85 D3 7 9 S 107 30 E
Penganga →, India . . . 94 E4 19 53N 79 9 E
Penge, Kasai-Or.,
Dem. Rep. of
the Congo . . . . 118 D1 5 30 S 24 33 E
Penge, Sud-Kivu,
Dem. Rep. of
the Congo . . . . 118 C2 4 27 S 28 25 E
P'enghu Ch'üntou,
Taiwan . . . . 77 F12 23 34N 119 30 E
Penglai, China . . . . . . 75 F11 37 48N 120 42 E
Pengshan, China . . . . . 76 B4 30 14N 103 58 E
Pengshui, China . . . . . 76 C7 29 17N 108 12 E
Penguin, Australia . . . 127 G4 41 8 S 146 6 E
Pengxi, China . . . . 76 B5 30 44N 105 45 E
Pengze, China . . . . 77 C11 29 52N 116 32 E
Penhalonga, Zimbabwe 119 F3 18 52 S 32 40 E
Peniche, Portugal 43 F1 39 19N 9 22W
Penicuik, U.K. 22 F5 55 50N 3 13W
Penida, Nusa, Indonesia 85 D5 8 45 S 115 30 E
Peninnes, Alpes =
Pennine, Alpi, Alps . 31 J3 46 4N 7 30 E
Peninsular Malaysia □,
Malaysia . . . . 87 L4 4 0N 102 0 E
Peñíscola, Spain . . . . . 40 E5 40 22N 0 24 E
Penitente, Serra do,
Brazil . . . . 170 C2 8 45 S 46 20W
Penki = Benxi, China . 75 D12 41 20N 123 48 E
Penkridge, U.K. 20 E5 52 44N 2 6W
Penmarch, France 26 E2 47 49N 4 21W
Penmarch, Pte. de,
France 26 E2 47 48N 4 22W
Penn = Penn Hills,
U.S.A. 150 F5 40 28N 79 52W
Penn Hills, U.S.A. . . . 150 F5 40 28N 79 52W
Penn Yan, U.S.A. 150 D7 42 40N 77 3W
Penna, Punta della,
Italy . . . . 45 F11 42 10N 14 43 E
Pennant, Canada 143 C7 50 32N 108 14W
Penne, Italy . . . . 45 F10 42 27N 13 55 E
Penner →, India . . . . . 95 G5 14 35N 80 10 E
Penneshaw, Australia . 128 C2 35 44 S 137 56 E
Pennine, Alpi, Alps . . 31 J3 46 4N 7 30 E
Pennines, U.K. 20 C5 54 45N 2 27W
Pennington, U.S.A. . . . 160 F5 39 15N 121 47W
Pennington →, Nigeria 113 E6 4 45N 5 35 E
Pennino, Mte., Italy . . 45 E9 43 6N 12 53 E
Pennsburg, U.S.A. . . . 151 F9 40 23N 75 29W
Pennsylvania □, U.S.A. 148 E7 40 45N 77 30W
Pennville, U.S.A. 157 D11 40 30N 85 9W
Penny, Canada 142 C4 53 51N 121 20W
Peno, Russia . . . . 58 D7 57 2N 32 49 E
Penobscot →, U.S.A. . 149 C11 44 30N 68 48W
Penobscot B., U.S.A. . 149 C11 44 35N 68 50W
Penola, Australia . . . . 128 D4 37 25 S 140 48 E
Penong, Australia . . . . 125 F5 31 56 S 133 1 E

Penonomé, *Panama* **164 E3** 8 31N 80 21W
Penot, Mt., *Vanuatu* **133 F5** 16 20 S 167 31 E
Penrith, *Australia* **129 B9** 33 43 S 150 38 E
Penrith, *U.K.* **20 C5** 54 40N 2 45W
Penryn, *U.K.* **21 G2** 50 9N 5 7W
Pensacola, *U.S.A.* **153 E2** 30 25N 87 13W
Pensacola Bay, *U.S.A.* **153 E2** 30 25N 87 5W
Pensacola Mts., *Antarctica* **7 E1** 84 0 S 40 0W
Pense, *Canada* **143 C8** 50 25N 104 59W
Penshurst, *Australia* **128 D5** 37 49 S 142 20 E
Pensiangan, *Malaysia* **85 B5** 4 33N 116 19 E
Pentecost = Pentecôte, *Vanuatu* **133 E6** 15 42 S 168 10 E
Pentecoste, *Brazil* **170 B4** 3 48 S 39 17W
Pentecôte, *Vanuatu* **133 E6** 15 42 S 168 10 E
Penticton, *Canada* **142 D5** 49 30N 119 38W
Pentland, *Australia* **126 C4** 20 32 S 145 25 E
Pentland Firth, *U.K.* **22 C5** 58 43N 3 10W
Pentland Hills, *U.K.* **22 F5** 55 48N 3 25W
Pentland Hills ⌂, *U.K.* **22 F5** 55 50N 3 20W
Penukonda, *India* **95 G3** 14 5N 77 38 E
Penza, *Russia* **60 D7** 53 15N 45 5 E
Penzance, *U.K.* **21 G2** 50 7N 5 33W
Penzberg, *Germany* **31 H7** 47 45N 11 22 E
Penzhino, *Russia* **67 C17** 63 30N 167 55 E
Penzhinskaya Guba, *Russia* **67 C17** 61 30N 163 0 E
Penzhou, *China* **76 B4** 31 4N 103 32 E
Penzlin, *Germany* **30 B9** 53 30N 13 5 E
Peoria, *Ariz., U.S.A.* **159 K7** 33 35N 112 14W
Peoria, *Ill., U.S.A.* **156 D7** 40 42N 89 36W
Peoria Heights, *U.S.A.* **156 D7** 40 45N 89 35W
Peotone, *U.S.A.* **157 C9** 41 20N 87 48W
Pepacton Reservoir, *U.S.A.* **151 D10** 42 5N 74 58W
Pepani →, *S. Africa* **116 D3** 25 49 S 22 47 E
Pepeekeo, *U.S.A.* **145 D6** 19 51N 155 6W
Pepel, *S. Leone* **112 D2** 8 40N 13 5W
Peqin, *Albania* **50 E3** 41 3N 19 44 E
Pera Hd., *Australia* **126 A3** 12 55 S 141 37 E
Perabumulih, *Indonesia* **84 C2** 3 27 S 104 15 E
Perak □, *Malaysia* **84 A2** 5 0N 101 0 E
Perak →, *Malaysia* **87 K3** 4 0N 100 50 E
Perakhóra, *Greece* **48 C4** 38 2N 22 56 E
Perakhórion, *Greece* **39 C2** 38 21N 20 43 E
Perales de Alfambra, *Spain* **40 E4** 40 38N 1 0W
Perales del Puerto, *Spain* **42 E4** 40 10N 6 40W
Pérama, *Kérkira, Greece* **38 B9** 39 34N 19 54 E
Pérama, *Kriti, Greece* **39 E5** 35 20N 24 40 E
Perancak, *Indonesia* **79 J17** 8 24 S 114 37 E
Peräpohjola, *Finland* **14 C22** 66 16N 26 10 E
Perast, *Serbia & M.* **50 D2** 42 31N 18 47 E
Peratiá, *Greece* **39 B2** 38 49N 20 45 E
Percé, *Canada* **141 C7** 48 31N 64 13W
Perche, *France* **26 D8** 48 31N 1 1 E
Perche ⌂, *France* **26 D7** 48 24N 0 46 E
Perche, Collines du, *France* **25 B4** 48 30N 0 40 E
Perchtoldsdorf, *Austria* **35 C9** 48 7N 16 16 E
Percival Lakes, *Australia* **124 D4** 21 25 S 125 0 E
Percy, *France* **26 D5** 48 55N 1 11W
Percy, *U.S.A.* **156 F7** 38 5N 89 41W
Percy Is., *Australia* **126 C5** 21 39 S 150 16 E
Perdido →, *Argentina* **176 B3** 42 55 S 67 0W
Perdido, Mte., *Spain* **40 C5** 42 40N 0 5 E
Perdu, Mt. = Perdido, Mte., *Spain* **40 C5** 42 40N 0 5 E
Perechyn, *Ukraine* **52 B7** 48 44N 22 28 E
Perehinske, *Ukraine* **53 B9** 48 49N 24 11 E
Pereira, *Colombia* **168 C2** 4 49N 75 43W
Perelazovskiy, *Russia* **61 F6** 49 8N 42 35 E
Peremul Par, *India* **95 J1** 11 10N 72 4 E
Peremyshl = Przemyśl, *Poland* **55 J9** 49 50N 22 45 E
Perené →, *Peru* **172 C3** 11 9 S 74 14W
Perenjori, *Australia* **125 E2** 29 26 S 116 16 E
Peresecina, *Moldova* **53 C13** 47 16N 28 46 E
Pereslavl-Zalesskiy, *Russia* **58 D10** 56 45N 38 50 E
Peretu, *Romania* **53 F10** 44 3N 25 5 E
Perevolotskiy, *Russia* **64 F5** 51 51N 54 12 E
Pereyaslav-Khmelnytskyy, *Ukraine* **59 G6** 50 3N 31 28 E
Pereyma, *Ukraine* **53 B14** 48 4N 29 30 E
Pérez, I., *Mexico* **163 C7** 22 24N 89 42W
Perg, *Austria* **34 C7** 48 15N 14 38 E
Pergamino, *Argentina* **174 C3** 33 52 S 60 30W
Pergau →, *Malaysia* **87 K3** 5 23N 102 2 E
Pergine Valsugana, *Italy* **45 B8** 46 4N 11 14 E
Pérgola, *Italy* **45 E9** 43 34N 12 50 E
Perham, *U.S.A.* **154 B7** 46 36N 95 34W
Perhentian, Kepulauan, *Malaysia* **87 K4** 5 54N 102 42 E
Periam, *Romania* **52 D5** 46 2N 20 52 E
Péribonka →, *Canada* **141 C5** 48 45N 72 5W
Péribonka, L., *Canada* **141 B5** 50 1N 71 10W
Perico, *Argentina* **174 A2** 24 20 S 65 5W
Pericos, *Mexico* **162 B3** 25 3N 107 42W
Périers, *France* **26 C5** 49 11N 1 25W
Périgord, *France* **28 D4** 45 0N 0 40 E
Périgord-Limousin ⌂, *France* **28 C4** 45 40N 0 50 E
Périgueux, *France* **28 C4** 45 10N 0 42 E
Perijá △, *Venezuela* **165 E5** 9 30N 72 55W
Perijá, Sierra de, *Colombia* **168 B3** 9 30N 73 3W
Perisher Valley, *Australia* **129 D8** 36 27 S 148 25 E
Peristéra, *Greece* **48 B5** 39 15N 23 58 E
Peristerona →, *Cyprus* **39 E9** 35 8N 33 5 E
Perito Moreno, *Argentina* **176 C2** 46 36 S 70 56W
Perito Moreno △, *Argentina* **176 C2** 47 49 S 72 17W
Peritoró, *Brazil* **170 B3** 4 20 S 44 18W
Perivol = Dragovishtitsa, *Bulgaria* **50 D6** 42 22N 22 39 E
Periyakulam, *India* **95 J3** 10 5N 77 30 E
Periyar △, *India* **95 K3** 9 25N 77 10 E
Periyar →, *India* **95 J3** 10 15N 76 10 E
Periyar, L., *India* **95 K3** 9 25N 77 10 E
Perkasie, *U.S.A.* **151 F9** 40 22N 75 18W
Perković, *Croatia* **45 E13** 43 41N 16 10 E
Perlas, Arch. de las, *Panama* **164 E4** 8 41N 79 7W
Perlas, Punta de, *Nic.* **164 D3** 12 30N 83 30W
Perleberg, *Germany* **30 B7** 53 5N 11 52 E
Perlez, *Serbia & M.* **52 E5** 45 11N 20 22 E
Perlis □, *Malaysia* **84 A2** 6 30N 100 15 E
Perm, *Russia* **64 C6** 58 0N 56 10 E
Përmet, *Albania* **50 F4** 40 15N 20 21 E
Permskoye = Komsomolsk, *Russia* **67 D14** 50 30N 137 0 E
Pernambuco = Recife, *Brazil* **170 C5** 8 0 S 35 0W
Pernambuco □, *Brazil* **170 C4** 8 0 S 37 0W
Pernambuco Plain, *Atl. Oc.* **8 G9** 5 0 S 24 0W
Pernatty Lagoon, *Australia* **128 A2** 31 30 S 137 12 E
Pernik, *Bulgaria* **50 D7** 42 35N 23 2 E
Pernov = Pärnu, *Estonia* **15 G21** 58 28N 24 33 E
Peron Is., *Australia* **124 B5** 13 9 S 130 4 E
Peron Pen., *Australia* **125 E1** 26 0 S 113 10 E
Péronne, *France* **27 C9** 49 55N 2 57 E
Perosa Argentina, *Italy* **44 D4** 44 58N 7 10 E
Perovsk = Qyzylorda, *Kazakhstan* **65 A2** 44 48N 65 28 E
Perow, *Canada* **142 C3** 54 35N 126 10W
Perparim = Pogradec, *Albania* **50 F4** 40 54N 20 37 E
Perpignan, *France* **28 F6** 42 42N 2 53 E
Perrégaux = Mohammadia, *Algeria* **111 A5** 35 33N 0 3 E
Perrine, *U.S.A.* **153 K9** 25 36N 80 21W
Perris, *U.S.A.* **161 M9** 33 47N 117 14W
Perros-Guirec, *France* **26 D3** 48 49N 3 28W
Perry, *Fla., U.S.A.* **152 E6** 30 7N 83 35W
Perry, *Ga., U.S.A.* **152 C6** 32 28N 83 44W
Perry, *Iowa, U.S.A.* **156 C2** 41 51N 94 6W
Perry, *Mich., U.S.A.* **157 B12** 42 50N 84 13W
Perry, *Mo., U.S.A.* **156 E5** 39 26N 91 40W
Perry, *Okla., U.S.A.* **155 G6** 36 17N 97 14W
Perrysburg, *U.S.A.* **157 C13** 41 34N 83 38W
Perryton, *U.S.A.* **155 G4** 36 24N 100 48W
Perryville, *Alaska, U.S.A.* **144 J8** 55 55N 159 9W
Perryville, *Mo., U.S.A.* **155 G10** 37 43N 89 52W
Persan, *France* **27 C9** 49 9N 2 16 E
Persberg, *Sweden* **16 E8** 59 47N 14 15 E
Perşembe, *Turkey* **100 B7** 41 5N 37 46 E
Persepolis, *Iran* **97 D7** 29 55N 52 50 E
Perseverancia, *Bolivia* **173 C5** 14 44 S 62 48W
Pershotravensk, *Ukraine* **59 G4** 50 13N 27 40 E
Pershotravnevoye = Pershotravensk, *Ukraine* **59 G4** 50 13N 27 40 E
Persia = Iran ■, *Asia* **97 C7** 33 0N 53 0 E
Persian Gulf, *Asia* **97 E6** 27 0N 50 0 E
Perstorp, *Sweden* **17 H7** 56 10N 13 25 E
Pertek, *Turkey* **101 C8** 38 51N 39 19 E
Perth, *Australia* **125 F2** 31 57 S 115 52 E
Perth, *Canada* **140 D4** 44 55N 76 15W
Perth, *U.K.* **22 E5** 56 24N 3 26W
Perth & Kinross □, *U.K.* **22 E5** 56 45N 3 55W
Perth Amboy, *U.S.A.* **151 F10** 40 31N 74 16W
Perth-Andover, *Canada* **141 C6** 46 44N 67 42W
Perth Basin, *Ind. Oc.* **121 H9** 30 0 S 108 0 E
Pertuis, *France* **29 E9** 43 42N 5 30 E
Pertusato, C., *France* **29 G13** 41 21N 9 11 E
Peru, *Ill., U.S.A.* **156 C7** 41 20N 89 8W
Peru, *Ind., U.S.A.* **157 D10** 40 45N 86 4W
Peru, *N.Y., U.S.A.* **151 B11** 44 35N 73 32W
Peru ■, *S. Amer.* **168 D2** 4 0 S 75 0W
Peru Basin, *Pac. Oc.* **135 J18** 20 0 S 95 0W
Peru-Chile Trench, *Pac. Oc.* **135 K20** 20 0 S 72 0W
Perúgia, *Italy* **45 E9** 43 7N 12 23 E
Perušić, *Croatia* **45 D12** 44 40N 15 22 E
Pervomaysk, *Russia* **60 C6** 54 56N 43 58 E
Pervomaysk, *Ukraine* **59 H6** 48 10N 30 46 E
Pervomayskiy, *Russia* **64 F5** 51 32N 55 2 E
Pervouralsk, *Russia* **64 C7** 56 59N 59 59 E
Pervouralsky = Pervouralsk, *Russia* **64 C7** 56 59N 59 59 E
Pésaro, *Italy* **45 E9** 43 54N 12 55 E
Pescadores = P'enghu Ch'üntou, *Taiwan* **77 F12** 23 34N 119 30 E
Pescara, *Italy* **45 F11** 42 28N 14 13 E
Pescara →, *Italy* **45 F11** 42 28N 14 13 E
Peschanokopskoye, *Russia* **61 G5** 46 14N 41 4 E
Peschanoye = Yashkul, *Russia* **61 G7** 46 11N 45 21 E
Péscia, *Italy* **44 E7** 43 54N 10 41 E
Pescina, *Italy* **45 F10** 42 2N 13 39 E
Peseux, *Switz.* **32 C3** 46 59N 6 53 E
Peshawar, *Pakistan* **91 B3** 34 2N 71 37 E
Peshkopi, *Albania* **50 E4** 41 41N 20 25 E
Peshtera, *Bulgaria* **51 D8** 42 2N 24 18 E
Peshtigo, *U.S.A.* **148 C2** 45 4N 87 46W
Peski, *Russia* **60 E6** 51 14N 42 29 E
Peskova, *Russia* **64 B4** 59 4N 52 22 E
Pêso da Régua, *Portugal* **42 D3** 41 10N 7 47W
Pesochnya = Kirov, *Russia* **58 E8** 54 3N 34 20 E
Pesqueira, *Brazil* **170 C4** 8 20 S 36 42W
Pessac, *France* **28 D3** 44 48N 0 37W
Pessádhes, *Greece* **39 C2** 38 7N 20 35 E
Pest □, *Hungary* **52 C4** 47 29N 19 5 E
Pestovo = Zavolzhye, *Russia* **60 B6** 56 37N 43 26 E
Pestovo, *Russia* **58 C8** 58 33N 35 42 E
Pestravka, *Russia* **60 D9** 52 28N 49 57 E
Péta, *Greece* **48 B3** 39 10N 21 2 E
Petah Tiqwa, *Israel* **103 C3** 32 6N 34 53 E
Petalás, Nisís, *Greece* **39 C3** 38 25N 21 5 E
Petalídhion, *Greece* **48 E3** 36 57N 21 55 E
Petaling Jaya, *Malaysia* **87 L3** 3 4N 101 42 E
Petaloudhes, *Greece* **38 E12** 36 18N 28 5 E
Petaluma, *U.S.A.* **160 G4** 38 14N 122 39W
Pétange, *Lux.* **24 E5** 49 33N 5 55 E
Petaro, *Pakistan* **92 G3** 25 31N 68 18 E
Petatlán, *Mexico* **162 D4** 17 31N 101 16W
Petauke, *Zambia* **119 E3** 14 14 S 31 20 E
Petawawa, *Canada* **140 C4** 45 54N 77 17W
Petén Itzá, L., *Guatemala* **164 C2** 16 58N 89 50W
Peter I., *Br. Virgin Is.* **165 e** 18 22N 64 35W
Peter I.s Øy, *Antarctica* **7 C16** 69 0 S 91 0W
Peter Pond L., *Canada* **143 B7** 55 55N 108 44W
Peterbell, *Canada* **140 C3** 48 36N 83 21W
Peterborough, *Australia* **128 B3** 32 58 S 138 51 E
Peterborough, *Canada* **140 D4** 44 20N 78 20W
Peterborough, *U.K.* **21 E7** 52 35N 0 15W
Peterborough, *U.S.A.* **151 D13** 42 53N 71 57W
Peterborough □, *U.K.* **21 E7** 52 35N 0 15W
Peterculter, *U.K.* **22 D6** 57 6N 2 16W
Peterhead, *U.K.* **22 D7** 57 31N 1 48W
Peterhof = Petrodvorets, *Russia* **58 C5** 59 52N 29 54 E
Peterlee, *U.K.* **20 C6** 54 47N 1 20W
Petermann Bjerg, *Greenland* **10 C8** 73 7N 28 25W
Petermann Gletscher, *Greenland* **10 A4** 80 30N 60 0W
Petermann Ranges, *Australia* **125 E5** 26 0 S 130 30 E
Peter's Mine, *Guyana* **169 B6** 6 14N 59 20W
Petersburg = Peterborough, *Australia* **128 B3** 32 58 S 138 51 E
Petersburg, *Alaska, U.S.A.* **144 H14** 56 48N 132 58W
Petersburg, *Ill., U.S.A.* **156 D7** 40 1N 89 51W
Petersburg, *Ind., U.S.A.* **157 F9** 38 30N 87 17W
Petersburg, *Mich., U.S.A.* **157 C13** 41 54N 83 43W
Petersburg, *Pa., U.S.A.* **150 F6** 40 34N 78 3W
Petersburg, *Va., U.S.A.* **148 G7** 37 14N 77 24W
Petersburg, *W. Va., U.S.A.* **148 F6** 39 1N 79 5W
Petersfield, *U.K.* **21 F7** 51 1N 0 56W
Petershagen, *Germany* **30 C4** 52 23N 8 58 E
Petília Policastro, *Italy* **47 C9** 39 7N 16 48 E
Petit Batanga, *Cameroon* **114 B1** 3 15N 9 54 E
Petit-Canal, *Guadeloupe* **164 b** 16 25N 61 31W
Petit Goâve, *Haiti* **165 C5** 18 27N 72 51W
Petit Jardin, *Canada* **141 C8** 48 28N 59 14W
Petit Lac Manicouagan, *Canada* **141 B6** 51 25N 67 40W
Petit-Mécatina →, *Canada* **141 B8** 50 40N 59 30W
Petit-Mécatina, Î. du, *Canada* **141 B8** 50 30N 59 25W
Petit Piton, *St. Lucia* **165 f** 13 51N 61 5W
Petit-Saguenay, *Canada* **141 C5** 48 15N 70 4W
Petit Saint Bernard, Col du, *Italy* **29 C10** 45 40N 6 52 E
Petitcodiac, *Canada* **141 C6** 45 57N 65 11W
Petite Terre, Îles de la, *Guadeloupe* **164 b** 16 13N 61 9W
Petitjean = Sidi Kacem, *Morocco* **110 B3** 34 11N 5 49W
Petitot →, *Canada* **142 A4** 60 14N 123 29W
Petitsikapau L., *Canada* **141 B6** 54 37N 66 25W
Petlad, *India* **92 H5** 22 30N 72 45 E
Peto, *Mexico* **163 C7** 20 10N 88 53W
Petone, *N.Z.* **130 H3** 41 13 S 174 53 E
Petorca, *Chile* **174 C1** 32 15 S 70 56W
Petoskey, *U.S.A.* **148 C3** 45 22N 84 57W
Petra, *Jordan* **103 E4** 30 20N 35 22 E
Petra, *Spain* **38 B4** 39 37N 3 6 E
Petra, Ostrova, *Russia* **6 B13** 76 15N 118 30 E
Petra Velikogo, Zaliv, *Russia* **70 C6** 42 40N 132 0 E
Petrel = Petrer, *Spain* **41 G4** 38 30N 0 46W
Petrella, Monte, *Italy* **46 A6** 41 18N 13 40 E
Petrer, *Spain* **41 G4** 38 30N 0 46W
Petreto-Bicchisano, *France* **29 G12** 41 47N 8 58 E
Petrich, *Bulgaria* **50 E7** 41 24N 23 13 E
Petrified Forest △, *U.S.A.* **159 J9** 35 0N 109 30W
Petrijanec, *Croatia* **45 B13** 46 23N 16 17 E
Petrikov = Pyetrikaw, *Belarus* **59 F5** 52 11N 28 29 E
Petrila, *Romania* **53 E8** 45 29N 23 29 E
Petrinja, *Croatia* **45 C13** 45 28N 16 18 E
Petrodvorets, *Russia* **58 C5** 59 52N 29 54 E
Petrograd = Sankt-Peterburg, *Russia* **58 C6** 59 55N 30 20 E
Petrolândia, *Brazil* **170 C4** 9 5 S 38 20W
Petrolia, *Canada* **140 D3** 42 54N 82 9W
Petrolina, *Brazil* **170 C3** 9 24 S 40 30W
Petromaryevka = Pervomaysk, *Ukraine* **59 H6** 48 10N 30 46 E
Petropavl, *Kazakhstan* **66 D7** 54 53N 69 13 E
Petropavlovsk = Petropavl, *Kazakhstan* **66 D7** 54 53N 69 13 E
Petropavlovsk-Kamchatskiy, *Russia* **67 D16** 53 3N 158 43 E
Petropavlovskiy = Akhtubinsk, *Russia* **61 F8** 48 13N 46 7 E
Petropavlovsky = Severouralsk, *Russia* **64 A7** 60 9N 59 57 E
Petrópolis, *Brazil* **171 F3** 22 33 S 43 9W
Petroşani, *Romania* **53 E8** 45 28N 23 20 E
Petrova Gora, *Croatia* **45 C12** 45 15N 15 45 E
Petrovac, *Serbia & M.* **50 D2** 42 13N 18 57 E
Petrovac, *Serbia & M.* **50 B5** 44 22N 21 26 E
Petrovaradin, *Serbia & M.* **52 E4** 45 16N 19 55 E
Petrovgrad = Zrenjanin, *Serbia & M.* **52 E5** 45 22N 20 23 E
Petrovsk, *Russia* **60 D7** 52 22N 45 19 E
Petrovsk-Port = Makhachkala, *Russia* **61 J8** 43 0N 47 30 E
Petrovsk-Zabaykalskiy, *Russia* **67 D11** 51 20N 108 55 E
Petrovskaya, *Russia* **59 K9** 45 25N 37 58 E
Petrovskoye = Svetlograd, *Russia* **61 H6** 45 25N 42 58 E
Petrovskoye, *Russia* **64 E6** 53 37N 56 23 E
Petrovsky Zavod = Petrovsk-Zabaykalskiy, *Russia* **67 D11** 51 20N 108 55 E
Petrozavodsk, *Russia* **58 B8** 61 41N 34 20 E
Petrus Steyn, *S. Africa* **117 D4** 27 38 S 28 8 E
Petrusburg, *S. Africa* **116 D4** 29 4 S 25 26 E
Petsamo = Pechenga, *Russia* **56 A5** 69 29N 31 4 E
Petuna = Fuyu, *China* **75 B13** 45 12N 124 43 E
Petzeck, *Austria* **34 E5** 46 57N 12 48 E
Peumo, *Chile* **174 C1** 34 21 S 71 12W
Peureulak, *Indonesia* **84 B1** 4 48N 97 45 E
Peusangan →, *Indonesia* **84 A1** 5 16N 96 51 E
Pevek, *Russia* **67 C18** 69 41N 171 19 E
Pevely, *U.S.A.* **156 F6** 38 17N 90 24W
Peveragno, *Italy* **44 D4** 44 20N 7 37 E
Peyrehorade, *France* **28 E2** 43 34N 1 7W
Peyruis, *France* **29 D9** 44 1N 5 56 E
Pézenas, *France* **28 E7** 43 28N 3 24 E
Pezinok, *Slovak Rep.* **35 C10** 48 17N 17 17 E
Pfaffenhofen, *Germany* **31 G7** 48 31N 11 31 E
Pfäffikon, *Schwyz, Switz.* **33 B7** 47 13N 8 46 E
Pfäffikon, *Zürich, Switz.* **33 B7** 47 22N 8 47 E
Pfälzerwald ⌂, *Germany* **31 F5** 49 18N 9 55 E
Pfarrkirchen, *Germany* **31 G8** 48 25N 12 56 E
Pfeffenhausen, *Germany* **31 G7** 48 39N 11 58 E
Pforzheim, *Germany* **31 G4** 48 52N 8 41 E
Pfullendorf, *Germany* **31 H5** 47 55N 9 15 E
Pfungstadt, *Germany* **31 F4** 49 48N 8 35 E
Pha Taem △, *Thailand* **86 E5** 15 32N 105 30 E
Phaistós, *Greece* **39 E5** 35 2N 24 50 E
Phala, *Botswana* **116 C4** 23 45 S 26 50 E
Phalera = Phulera, *India* **92 F6** 26 52N 75 16 E
Phalodi, *India* **92 F5** 27 12N 72 24 E
Phalsbourg, *France* **27 D14** 48 46N 7 15 E
Phaltan, *India* **94 F2** 17 59N 74 26 E
Phaluai, Ko, *Thailand* **87 b** 9 32N 99 41 E
Phan, *Thailand* **86 C2** 19 28N 99 43 E
Phan Rang, *Vietnam* **87 G7** 11 34N 109 0 E
Phan Ri = Hoa Da, *Vietnam* **87 G7** 11 16N 108 40 E
Phan Thiet, *Vietnam* **87 G7** 11 1N 108 9 E
Phanae, *Greece* **49 C7** 38 8N 25 57 E
Phanat Nikhom, *Thailand* **86 F3** 13 27N 101 11 E
Phangan, Ko, *Thailand* **87 H3** 9 45N 100 0 E
Phangnga, *Thailand* **87 H2** 8 28N 98 30 E
Phangnga, Ao, *Thailand* **87 a** 8 16N 98 33 E
Phanom Sarakham, *Thailand* **86 F3** 13 45N 101 21 E
Phaphund, *India* **93 F8** 26 36N 79 28 E
Pharenda, *India* **93 F10** 27 5N 83 17 E
Pharr, *U.S.A.* **155 M5** 26 12N 98 11W
Phatthalung, *Thailand* **87 J3** 7 39N 100 6 E
Phayao, *Thailand* **86 C2** 19 11N 99 55 E
Phelps, *U.S.A.* **150 D7** 42 58N 77 3W
Phelps L., *Canada* **143 B8** 59 15N 103 15W
Phenix City, *U.S.A.* **149 J3** 32 28N 85 0W
Phet Buri, *Thailand* **86 F2** 13 1N 99 55 E
Phetchabun, *Thailand* **86 D3** 16 25N 101 8 E
Phetchabun, Thiu Khao, *Thailand* **86 E3** 16 0N 101 20 E
Phetchaburi = Phet Buri, *Thailand* **86 F2** 13 1N 99 55 E
Phi Phi, Ko, *Thailand* **87 J2** 7 45N 98 46 E
Phiafay, *Laos* **86 E6** 14 48N 106 0 E
Phibun Mangsahan, *Thailand* **86 E5** 15 14N 105 14 E
Phichai, *Thailand* **86 D3** 17 22N 100 10 E
Phichit, *Thailand* **86 D3** 16 26N 100 22 E
Philadelphia, *Miss., U.S.A.* **155 J10** 32 46N 89 7W
Philadelphia, *N.Y., U.S.A.* **151 B9** 44 9N 75 43W
Philadelphia, *Pa., U.S.A.* **151 G9** 39 57N 75 10W
Philip, *U.S.A.* **154 C4** 44 2N 101 40W
Philip Smith Mts., *U.S.A.* **144 C11** 68 0N 148 0W
Philippeville = Skikda, *Algeria* **111 A6** 36 50N 6 58 E
Philippeville, *Belgium* **24 D4** 50 12N 4 33 E
Philippi, *Greece* **51 E8** 41 1N 24 16 E
Philippi, *U.S.A.* **148 F5** 39 9N 80 3W
Philippi L., *Australia* **126 C2** 24 20 S 138 55 E
Philippine Sea, *Pac. Oc.* **62 H16** 18 0N 125 0 E
Philippines ■, *Asia* **80 E4** 12 0N 123 0 E
Philippolis, *S. Africa* **116 E4** 30 15 S 25 16 E
Philippopolis = Plovdiv, *Bulgaria* **51 D8** 42 8N 24 44 E
Philipsburg, *Canada* **151 A11** 45 2N 73 5W
Philipsburg, *Mont., U.S.A.* **158 C7** 46 20N 113 18W
Philipsburg, *Pa., U.S.A.* **150 F6** 40 54N 78 13W
Philipstown = Daingean, *Ireland* **23 C4** 53 18N 7 17W
Philipstown, *S. Africa* **116 E3** 30 28 S 24 30 E
Phillip I., *Australia* **129 E6** 38 30 S 145 12 E
Phillips, *U.S.A.* **154 C9** 45 42N 90 24W
Phillipsburg, *Ga., U.S.A.* **152 D6** 31 25N 83 30W
Phillipsburg, *Kans., U.S.A.* **154 F5** 39 45N 99 19W
Phillipsburg, *N.J., U.S.A.* **151 F9** 40 42N 75 12W
Philmont, *U.S.A.* **151 D11** 42 15N 73 39W
Philomath, *Ga., U.S.A.* **152 B7** 33 44N 82 59W
Philomath, *Oreg., U.S.A.* **158 D2** 44 32N 123 22W
Phimai, *Thailand* **86 E4** 15 13N 102 30 E
Phitsanulok, *Thailand* **86 D3** 16 50N 100 12 E
Phnom Dangrek, *Thailand* **78 B2** 14 20N 104 0 E
Phnom Penh, *Cambodia* **87 G5** 11 33N 104 55 E
Phnum Penh = Phnom Penh, *Cambodia* **87 G5** 11 33N 104 55 E
Phoenicia, *U.S.A.* **151 D10** 42 5N 74 14W
Phoenix, *Mauritius* **121 d** 20 17 S 57 30 E
Phoenix, *Ariz., U.S.A.* **159 K7** 33 27N 112 4W
Phoenix, *N.Y., U.S.A.* **151 C8** 43 14N 76 18W
Phoenix Is., *Kiribati* **134 H10** 3 30 S 172 0W
Phoenixville, *U.S.A.* **151 F9** 40 8N 75 31W
Phon, *Thailand* **86 E4** 15 49N 102 36 E
Phon Tiou, *Laos* **86 D5** 17 53N 104 37 E
Phong →, *Thailand* **86 D4** 16 23N 102 56 E
Phong Saly, *Laos* **76 G4** 21 42N 102 9 E
Phong Tho, *Vietnam* **86 A4** 22 32N 103 21 E
Phonhong, *Laos* **86 C4** 18 30N 102 25 E
Phonum, *Thailand* **87 H2** 8 49N 98 48 E
Phosphate Hill, *Australia* **126 C2** 21 53 S 139 58 E
Photharam, *Thailand* **86 F2** 13 41N 99 51 E
Phra Nakhon Si Ayutthaya, *Thailand* **86 E3** 14 25N 100 30 E
Phra Thong, Ko, *Thailand* **87 H2** 9 5N 98 17 E
Phrae, *Thailand* **86 C3** 18 7N 100 9 E
Phrom Phiram, *Thailand* **86 D3** 17 2N 100 12 E
Phrygia, *Turkey* **100 C4** 38 40N 30 0 E
Phu Bia, *Laos* **86 C4** 19 10N 103 0 E
Phu Chong-Na Yoi △, *Thailand* **86 E5** 14 25N 105 30 E
Phu Dien, *Vietnam* **86 C5** 18 58N 105 31 E
Phu Hin Rang Kla △, *Thailand* **86 D3** 17 0N 100 59 E
Phu Kradung △, *Thailand* **86 D3** 17 2N 101 44 E
Phu Loi, *Laos* **86 B4** 20 14N 103 14 E
Phu Luang △, *Thailand* **86 D3** 17 15N 101 29 E
Phu Ly, *Vietnam* **76 G5** 20 35N 105 50 E
Phu Phan △, *Thailand* **86 D4** 17 0N 103 56 E
Phu Quoc, Dao, *Vietnam* **87 G4** 10 20N 104 0 E
Phu Tho, *Vietnam* **76 G5** 21 24N 105 13 E
Phuc Yen, *Vietnam* **76 G5** 21 16N 105 45 E
Phuket, *Thailand* **87 a** 7 53N 98 24 E
Phuket, Ko, *Thailand* **87 a** 8 0N 98 22 E
Phul, *India* **92 D6** 30 19N 75 14 E
Phulad, *India* **92 G5** 25 38N 73 49 E
Phulbani, *India* **94 D7** 20 28N 84 14 E
Phulbari, *India* **93 G13** 25 55N 90 2 E
Phulchari, *Bangla.* **90 C2** 25 11N 89 37 E
Phulera, *India* **92 F6** 26 52N 75 16 E
Phulpur, *India* **93 G10** 25 31N 82 49 E
Phun Phin, *Thailand* **87 H2** 9 7N 99 12 E
Piacá, *Brazil* **170 C2** 7 42 S 47 18W
Piacenza, *Italy* **44 C6** 45 1N 9 40 E
Piaçubaçu, *Brazil* **170 D4** 10 24 S 36 25W
Piai, Tanjung, *Malaysia* **87 d** 1 17N 103 30 E
Piako →, *N.Z.* **130 D4** 37 12 S 175 30 E
Pian Cr. →, *Australia* **127 E4** 30 2 S 148 12 E
Pian-Upe ⌂, *Uganda* **118 B3** 1 44N 34 20 E
Piana, *France* **29 F12** 42 15N 8 34 E
Pianella, *Italy* **45 F11** 42 24N 14 2 E
Piangil, *Australia* **128 C5** 35 5 S 143 20 E
Pianosa, *Puglia, Italy* **45 F12** 42 12N 15 44 E
Pianosa, *Toscana, Italy* **44 F7** 42 35N 10 5 E
Piapot, *Canada* **143 D7** 49 59N 109 8W
Pias, *Portugal* **43 G3** 38 1N 7 29W
Piaseczno, *Poland* **55 F8** 52 5N 21 2 E
Piaski, *Poland* **55 G9** 51 8N 22 52 E
Piastów, *Poland* **55 F7** 52 12N 20 48 E
Piatã, *Brazil* **171 D3** 13 9 S 41 48W
Piatra, *Romania* **53 G10** 43 51N 25 9 E
Piatra Craiului ⌂, *Romania* **53 E10** 45 30N 25 12 E
Piatra Neamţ, *Romania* **53 D11** 46 56N 26 21 E
Piatra Olt, *Romania* **53 F9** 44 22N 24 16 E
Piauí □, *Brazil* **170 C3** 7 0 S 43 0W
Piauí →, *Brazil* **170 C3** 6 38 S 42 42W
Piave →, *Italy* **45 C9** 45 32N 12 44 E
Piazza Ármerina, *Italy* **47 E7** 37 21N 14 20 E
Pibor →, *Sudan* **107 F3** 7 35N 33 0 E
Pibor Post, *Sudan* **107 F3** 6 47N 33 3 E
Pica, *Chile* **172 E4** 20 35 S 69 25W
Picardie □, *France* **27 C10** 49 50N 3 0 E
Picardie, Plaine de, *France* **27 C9** 50 0N 2 0 E
Picardy = Picardie □, *France* **27 C10** 49 50N 3 0 E
Picayune, *U.S.A.* **155 K10** 30 32N 89 41W
Picerno, *Italy* **47 B8** 40 38N 15 38 E
Pichhor, *India* **93 G8** 25 58N 78 20 E
Pichilemu, *Chile* **174 C1** 34 22 S 72 0W
Pichincha, □, *Ecuador* **168 D2** 0 10 S 78 40W
Pichor, *India* **92 G8** 25 11N 78 11 E
Pickerel L., *Canada* **140 C1** 48 40N 91 25W
Pickering, *U.K.* **20 C7** 54 15N 0 46W
Pickering, Vale of, *U.K.* **20 C7** 54 14N 0 45W
Pickle Lake, *Canada* **140 B1** 51 30N 90 12W
Pickwick L., *U.S.A.* **149 H1** 35 4N 88 15W
Pico, *Azores* **9 d1** 38 28N 28 20W
Pico, Ponta do, *Azores* **9 d1** 38 28N 28 25W
Pico Bonito △, *Honduras* **164 C2** 15 34N 86 48W
Pico da Neblina △, *Brazil* **168 C4** 0 19N 66 28W
Pico Truncado, *Argentina* **176 C3** 46 40 S 68 0W
Picos = Colinas, *Brazil* **170 C3** 6 0 S 44 10W
Picos, *Brazil* **170 C3** 7 5 S 41 28W
Picos de Europa △, *Spain* **42 B6** 43 14N 4 59W
Picota, *Peru* **172 B2** 6 54 S 76 24W
Picton, *Australia* **129 C9** 34 12 S 150 34 E
Picton, *Canada* **140 D4** 44 1N 77 9W
Picton, *N.Z.* **131 B9** 41 18 S 174 3 E
Picton, I., *Chile* **176 E3** 55 2 S 66 57W
Pictou, *Canada* **141 C7** 45 41N 62 42W
Picture Butte, *Canada* **142 D6** 49 55N 112 45W
Pictured Rocks ⌂, *U.S.A.* **148 B2** 46 30N 86 30W
Picuí, *Brazil* **170 C4** 6 31 S 36 21W
Picún Leufú, *Argentina* **176 A3** 39 30 S 69 5W
Pidbuzh, *Ukraine* **55 J10** 49 19N 23 14 E
Pidurutalagala, *Sri Lanka* **95 L5** 7 10N 80 50 E
Piechowice, *Poland* **55 H2** 50 51N 15 36 E
Piedecuesta, *Colombia* **168 B3** 6 59N 73 3W
Piedimonte Matese, *Italy* **47 A7** 41 22N 14 22 E
Piedmont = Piemonte □, *Italy* **44 D5** 45 0N 8 0 E
Piedmont, *Ala., U.S.A.* **152 B4** 33 55N 85 37W
Piedmont, *S.C., U.S.A.* **147 D10** 34 0N 81 30W
Piedra →, *Spain* **40 D3** 41 18N 1 47W
Piedra del Anguila, *Argentina* **176 B2** 40 2 S 70 4W
Piedra Lais, *Venezuela* **168 C4** 3 10N 65 50W
Piedrabuena, *Spain* **43 G6** 39 0N 4 10W
Piedrahita, *Spain* **42 E5** 40 28N 5 23W
Piedralaves, *Spain* **42 E6** 40 19N 4 42W
Piedras, R. de las →, *Peru* **172 C4** 12 30 S 69 15W
Piedras Blancas, *Spain* **42 B5** 43 33N 5 58W
Piedras Negras, *Mexico* **162 B4** 28 42N 100 31W
Piedras Pt., *Phil.* **81 F2** 10 11N 118 48 E
Piekar = Piekary Śląskie, *Poland* **55 H5** 50 24N 18 57 E
Piekary Śląskie, *Poland* **55 H5** 50 24N 18 57 E
Pieksämäki, *Finland* **15 E22** 62 18N 27 10 E
Piemonte □, *Italy* **44 D5** 45 0N 8 0 E
Pienaarsrivier, *S. Africa* **117 D4** 25 15 S 28 18 E
Pieniężno, *Poland* **54 D7** 54 14N 20 8 E
Pieninský △, *Europe* **35 B13** 49 25N 20 28 E
Pieńsk, *Poland* **55 G2** 51 16N 15 2 E
Piercefield, *U.S.A.* **151 B10** 44 13N 74 35W
Pierceland, *Canada* **143 C7** 54 20N 109 46W
Piería □, *Greece* **50 F6** 40 13N 22 25 E
Pierpont, *U.S.A.* **150 E4** 41 45N 80 34W
Pierre, *U.S.A.* **154 C4** 44 22N 100 21W
Pierre-Buffière, *France* **28 C5** 45 41N 1 22 E
Pierre-de-Bresse, *France* **27 F12** 46 54N 5 13 E
Pierrefontaine-les-Varans, *France* **27 E13** 47 14N 6 32 E
Pierrefort, *France* **28 D6** 44 55N 2 50 E
Pierrelatte, *France* **29 D8** 44 23N 4 43 E
Pierreville, *Trin. & Tob.* **169 D9** 10 16N 61 0W
Pierson, *U.S.A.* **153 F8** 29 14N 81 28W
Piešťany, *Slovak Rep.* **35 C10** 48 38N 17 55 E
Piesting →, *Austria* **35 C9** 48 6N 16 40 E
Pieszyce, *Poland* **55 H3** 50 43N 16 33 E
Piet Retief, *S. Africa* **117 D5** 27 1 S 30 50 E
Pietarsaari, *Finland* **14 E20** 63 40N 22 43 E
Pietermaritzburg, *S. Africa* **117 D5** 29 35 S 30 25 E
Pietersburg = Polokwane, *S. Africa* **117 C4** 23 54 S 29 25 E
Pietragalla, *Italy* **47 B8** 40 45N 15 53 E
Pietrasanta, *Italy* **44 E7** 43 57N 10 14 E
Pietroşiţa, *Romania* **53 E10** 45 11N 25 26 E
Pietrosul, Vf., *Maramureş, Romania* **53 C9** 47 35N 24 43 E
Pietrosul, Vf., *Suceava, Romania* **53 C10** 47 12N 25 18 E
Pieve di Cadore, *Italy* **45 B9** 46 26N 12 22 E
Pieve di Teco, *Italy* **44 D4** 44 3N 7 56 E
Pievepélago, *Italy* **44 D7** 44 12N 10 37 E
Pigadhítsa, *Greece* **50 G5** 39 59N 21 23 E
Pigeon I., *India* **95 G2** 14 2N 74 20 E
Pigeon L., *Canada* **150 B6** 44 27N 78 30W
Piggott, *U.S.A.* **155 G9** 36 23N 90 11W
Pigna, *Italy* **44 E4** 43 56N 7 40 E
Pigüe, *Argentina* **174 D3** 37 36 S 62 25W
Piha, *N.Z.* **130 C3** 36 57 S 174 28 E
Pihani, *India* **93 F9** 27 36N 80 15 E
Pihlajavesi, *Finland* **15 F23** 61 45N 28 45 E
Pijijiapan, *Mexico* **163 D6** 15 42N 93 14W
Pikalevo, *Russia* **58 C8** 59 37N 34 9 E
Pikangikum Berens, *Canada* **143 C10** 51 49N 94 0W
Pikes Peak, *U.S.A.* **154 F2** 38 50N 105 3W
Piketberg, *S. Africa* **116 E2** 32 55 S 18 40 E
Pikeville, *U.S.A.* **148 G4** 37 29N 82 31W
Pikit, *Phil.* **81 H5** 7 4N 124 41 E
Pikou, *China* **75 E12** 39 18N 122 22 E
Pikounda, *Congo* **114 B3** 0 30N 16 44 E
Pikwitonei, *Canada* **143 B9** 55 35N 97 9W
Piła, *Poland* **55 E3** 53 10N 16 48 E
Pila, *Spain* **41 G3** 38 16N 1 11W
Piláia, *Greece* **50 F6** 40 32N 22 59 E
Pilanesberg △, *S. Africa* **116 D4** 25 15 S 27 4 E
Pilani, *India* **92 E6** 28 22N 75 33 E
Pilar, *Brazil* **170 C4** 9 36 S 35 56W
Pilar, *Paraguay* **174 B4** 26 50 S 58 20W
Pilar, *Capiz, Phil.* **81 F4** 11 29N 123 0 E
Pilar, *Sorsogon, Phil.* **80 E4** 12 56N 123 40 E
Pilar de la Horadada, *Spain* **41 H4** 37 52N 0 47W
Pilas Group, *Phil.* **81 H3** 6 45N 121 35 E

Pilat ⌓, France 29 C8 45 20N 4 30 E
Pilawa, Poland 55 G8 51 57N 21 32 E
Pilaya →, Bolivia 173 E5 20 55 S 64 4W
Pilbara, Australia 124 D2 23 35 S 117 25 E
Pilcomayo →,
Paraguay 174 B4 25 21 S 57 42W
Pilgrim's Rest, S. Africa 117 C5 24 55 S 30 44 E
Pilgrimstad, Sweden 16 B9 62 57N 15 2 E
Píli, Greece 49 E9 36 50N 27 15 E
Pili, Phil. 80 E4 13 33N 123 19 E
Pilibhit, India 93 E8 28 40N 79 50 E
Pilica →, Poland 55 G8 51 52N 21 17 E
Pílion, Greece 48 B5 39 27N 23 3 E
Pilipinas =
Philippines ■, Asia 80 E4 12 0N 123 0 E
Pilis, Hungary 52 C4 47 17N 19 35 E
Pilisvörösvár, Hungary 52 C3 47 38N 18 56 E
Pilkhawa, India 92 E7 28 43N 77 42 E
Pillar B., Ascension I. 9 g 7 59 S 14 21W
Pillaro, Ecuador 168 D2 1 10 S 78 32W
Pillau = Baltiysk, Russia 15 J18 54 41N 19 58 E
Pilliga, Australia 127 E4 30 21 S 148 54 E
Pílos, Greece 48 E3 36 55N 21 42 E
Pilot Grove, U.S.A. 156 F4 38 53N 92 55W
Pilot Mound, Canada 143 D9 49 15N 98 54W
Pilot Point, Alaska,
U.S.A. 144 H8 57 34N 157 35W
Pilot Point, Tex., U.S.A. 155 J6 33 24N 96 58W
Pilot Rock, U.S.A. 158 D4 45 29N 118 50W
Pilot Station, U.S.A. 144 F7 61 56N 162 53W
Pilsen = Plzno, Poland 55 J8 49 58N 21 16 E
Pilsen = Plzeň,
Czech Rep. 34 B6 49 45N 13 22 E
Pilštanj, Slovenia 45 B12 46 8N 15 39 E
Piltene, Latvia 54 A8 57 13N 21 40 E
Pilzno, Poland 55 J8 49 58N 21 16 E
Pima, U.S.A. 159 K9 32 54N 109 50W
Pimba, Australia 128 A2 31 18 S 136 46 E
Pimenta Bueno, Brazil 173 C5 11 35 S 61 10W
Pimenteiras, Brazil 173 C5 13 40 S 60 58W
Pimentel, Peru 172 B2 6 45 S 79 55W
Pimu, Dem. Rep. of
the Congo 114 B4 1 42N 20 58 E
Pin Valley △, India 92 D7 31 50N 77 50 E
Pina de Ebro, Spain 40 D4 41 29N 0 33W
Pinamalayan, Phil. 80 E3 13 2N 121 29 E
Pinang, Malaysia 87 c 5 25N 100 15 E
Pinang □, Malaysia 84 A2 5 20N 100 20 E
Pinar, C. des, Spain 38 B4 39 53N 3 12 E
Pinar del Río, Cuba 164 B3 22 26N 83 40W
Pınarbaşı, Çanakkale,
Turkey 49 B8 39 53N 26 15 E
Pınarbaşı, Kayseri,
Turkey 100 C7 38 43N 36 23 E
Pınarhisar, Turkey 51 E11 41 37N 27 30 E
Pinatubo, Mt., Phil. 80 D3 15 8N 120 21 E
Pincehely, Hungary 52 D3 46 41N 18 27 E
Pinchang, China 76 B6 31 36N 107 3 E
Pincher Creek, Canada 142 D6 49 30N 113 57W
Pinchi L., Canada 142 C4 54 38N 124 30W
Pinckard, U.S.A. 152 D4 31 19N 85 33W
Pinckneyville, U.S.A. 156 F7 38 5N 89 23W
Pińczów, Poland 55 H7 50 32N 20 32 E
Pindaí, Presqu'île de,
N. Cal. 133 U18 21 20 S 164 56 E
Pindar, Australia 125 E2 28 30 S 115 47 E
Pindaré →, Brazil 170 B3 3 17 S 44 47W
Pindaré Mirim, Brazil 170 B2 3 37 S 45 21W
Pindi Gheb, Pakistan 92 C5 33 14N 72 21 E
Pindiga, Nigeria 113 D7 9 58N 10 53 E
Pindobal, Brazil 170 B2 3 16 S 48 25W
Pindos △, Greece 48 B3 39 52N 21 11 E
Pindos Óros, Greece 48 B3 40 0N 21 0 E
Pindus Mts. = Pindos
Óros, Greece 48 B3 40 0N 21 0 E
Pine →, B.C., Canada 142 B4 56 8N 120 43W
Pine →, Sask., Canada 143 B7 58 50N 105 38W
Pine, C., Canada 141 C9 46 37N 53 32W
Pine Bluff, U.S.A. 155 H9 34 13N 92 1W
Pine Bluffs, U.S.A. 154 E2 41 11N 104 4W
Pine City, U.S.A. 154 C8 45 50N 92 59W
Pine Cr. →, U.S.A. 150 E7 41 10N 77 16W
Pine Creek, Australia 124 B5 13 50 S 131 50 E
Pine Falls, Canada 143 C9 50 34N 96 11W
Pine Flat Res., U.S.A. 160 J7 36 50N 119 20W
Pine Grove, U.S.A. 151 F8 40 33N 76 23W
Pine Is., U.S.A. 153 J7 26 36N 82 7W
Pine Level, U.S.A. 152 C3 32 4N 86 4W
Pine Mountain, U.S.A. 152 C5 32 52N 84 51W
Pine Pass, Canada 142 B4 55 25N 122 42W
Pine Point, Canada 142 A6 60 50N 114 28W
Pine Ridge, Australia 129 A9 31 30 S 150 28 E
Pine Ridge, U.S.A. 154 D3 43 2N 102 33W
Pine River, Canada 143 C8 51 45N 100 30W
Pine River, U.S.A. 154 B7 46 43N 94 24W
Pine Valley, U.S.A. 161 N10 32 50N 116 32W
Pinecrest, U.S.A. 160 G6 38 12N 120 1W
Pineda de Mar, Spain 40 D7 41 37N 2 42 E
Pinedale, Calif., U.S.A. 160 J7 36 50N 119 48W
Pinedale, Wyo., U.S.A. 158 E9 42 52N 109 52W
Pinega →, Russia 56 B8 64 30N 44 19 E
Pinehill, Australia 126 C4 23 38 S 146 57 E
Pinehouse L., Canada 143 B7 55 32N 106 35W
Pineimuta →, Canada 140 B1 52 8N 88 33W
Pinellas Park, U.S.A. 153 H7 27 50N 82 43W
Pinerolo, Italy 44 D4 44 53N 7 21 E
Pines, Ákra = Pínnes,
Ákra, Greece 51 F8 40 5N 24 20 E
Pineto, Italy 45 F11 42 36N 14 4 E
Pinetop-Lakeside,
U.S.A. 159 J9 34 9N 109 58W
Pinetown, S. Africa 117 D5 29 48 S 30 54 E
Pinetta, U.S.A. 152 E6 30 36N 83 21W
Pineview, U.S.A. 152 C6 32 7N 83 30W
Pineville, La., U.S.A. 155 K8 31 19N 92 26W
Pineville, S.C., U.S.A. 152 B9 33 26N 80 1W
Pinewood, U.S.A. 152 B9 33 44N 80 27W
Piney, France 27 D11 48 22N 4 21 E
Ping →, Thailand 86 E3 15 42N 100 9 E
Pingaring, Australia 125 F2 32 40 S 118 32 E
Pingba, China 76 D6 26 23N 106 12 E
Pingbian, China 76 F4 23 0N 103 45 E
Pingchuan, China 76 D3 27 35N 101 55 E
Pingding, China 74 F7 37 47N 113 38 E
Pingdingshan, China 74 H7 33 43N 113 27 E
Pingdong, Taiwan 77 F13 22 39N 120 30 E
Pingdu, China 75 F10 36 42N 119 59 E
Pingelly, Australia 125 F2 32 32 S 117 5 E
Pingguo, China 76 F6 23 19N 107 36 E
Pinghe, China 77 E11 24 17N 117 21 E
Pinghu, China 77 B13 30 40N 121 2 E
Pingjiang, China 77 C9 28 45N 113 36 E
Pingle, China 77 E8 24 40N 110 40 E
Pingli, China 76 A7 32 27N 109 22 E
Pingliang, China 74 G4 35 35N 106 31 E
Pinglu, China 74 E7 39 31N 112 30 E
Pingluo, China 74 E4 38 52N 106 30 E
Pingnan, Fujian, China 77 D12 26 55N 119 0 E
Pingnan,
Guangxi Zhuangzu,
China 77 F8 23 33N 110 22 E
Pingo, Gabon 114 C2 1 19 S 10 55 E
Pingquan, China 75 D10 41 1N 118 37 E
Pingrup, Australia 125 F2 33 32 S 118 29 E
Pingshan, China 76 C5 28 39N 104 3 E
Pingtan, China 77 E12 25 31N 119 47 E
Pingtang, China 76 E6 25 49N 107 17 E
P'ingtung, Taiwan 77 F13 22 38N 120 30 E
Pingwu, China 74 H3 32 25N 104 30 E
Pingxiang,
Guangxi Zhuangzu,
China 76 F6 22 6N 106 46 E
Pingxiang, Jiangxi,
China 77 D9 27 43N 113 48 E
Pingyao, China 74 F7 37 12N 112 10 E
Pingyi, China 75 G9 35 30N 117 35 E
Pingyin, China 74 F9 36 20N 116 25 E
Pingyuan, Guangdong,
China 77 E10 24 37N 115 57 E
Pingyuan, Shandong,
China 74 F9 37 10N 116 22 E
Pingyuanjie, China 76 F4 23 45N 103 48 E
Pinhal, Brazil 175 A6 22 10 S 46 46W
Pinhal Novo, Portugal 43 G2 38 38N 8 55W
Pinheiro = Icoraci,
Brazil 170 B2 1 18 S 48 28W
Pinheiro, Brazil 170 B2 2 31 S 45 5W
Pinheiro Machado,
Brazil 175 C5 31 34 S 53 23W
Pinhel, Portugal 42 E3 40 50N 7 1W
Pinhuá →, Brazil 173 B4 6 21 S 65 0W
Pini, Indonesia 84 B1 0 10N 98 40 E
Piniós →, Ilía, Greece 48 D3 37 48N 21 20 E
Piniós →, Trikkala,
Greece 48 B4 39 55N 22 41 E
Pinjarra, Australia 125 F2 32 37 S 115 52 E
Pink Mountain, Canada 142 B4 57 3N 122 52W
Pinkafeld, Austria 35 D9 47 22N 16 9 E
Pinlaung, Burma 90 E6 20 8N 96 47 E
Pinlebu, Burma 90 C5 24 5N 95 22 E
Pinnacles, U.S.A. 160 J5 36 33N 121 19W
Pinnacles ⌓, U.S.A. 160 J5 36 25N 121 12W
Pinnaroo, Australia 128 C4 35 17 S 140 53 E
Pinneberg, Germany 30 B5 53 40N 9 48 E
Pínnes, Ákra, Greece 51 F8 40 5N 24 20 E
Pino Hachado, Paso,
S. Amer. 176 A2 38 39 S 70 54W
Pinon Hills, U.S.A. 161 L9 34 26N 117 39W
Pinos, Mexico 162 C4 22 20N 101 40W
Pinos, Mt., U.S.A. 161 L7 34 49N 119 8W
Pinos Pt., U.S.A. 159 H3 36 38N 121 57W
Pinos Puente, Spain 43 H7 37 15N 3 45W
Pinotepa Nacional,
Mexico 163 D5 16 19N 98 3W
Pinrang, Indonesia 82 B1 3 46 S 119 41 E
Pins, Î. des, N. Cal. 133 V21 22 37 S 167 30 E
Pins, Pte. aux, Canada 150 D3 42 15N 81 51W
Pinsk, Belarus 59 F4 52 10N 26 1 E
Pinta, Canal de,
Ecuador 172 a 0 27N 90 38W
Pinta, I., Ecuador 172 a 0 35N 90 44W
Pintados, Chile 172 E4 20 35 S 69 40W
Pintuyan, Phil. 81 G5 9 57N 125 15 E
Pinukpuk, Phil. 80 C3 17 35N 121 22 E
Pinyang, China 77 D13 27 42N 120 31 E
Pinyug, Russia 64 A1 60 5N 48 0 E
Pio Duran, Phil. 80 E4 13 2N 123 25 E
Pio V. Corpuz, Phil. 81 F5 11 55N 124 2 E
Pio XII, Brazil 170 B2 3 53 S 45 17W
Pioche, U.S.A. 159 H6 37 56N 114 27W
Piombino, Italy 44 F7 42 55N 10 32 E
Piombino, Canale di,
Italy 44 F7 42 53N 10 30 E
Pioner, Ostrov, Russia 67 B10 79 50N 92 0 E
Pionerskiy, Russia 54 D7 54 56N 20 14 E
Pionki, Poland 55 G8 51 29N 21 28 E
Piorini →, Brazil 169 D5 3 23 S 63 30W
Piorini, L., Brazil 169 D5 3 15 S 62 35W
Piotrków Trybunalski,
Poland 55 G6 51 23N 19 43 E
Piove di Sacco, Italy 45 C9 45 18N 12 2 E
Pip, Iran 97 E9 26 45N 60 10 E
Pipar, India 92 F5 26 25N 73 31 E
Pipar Road, India 92 F5 26 27N 73 27 E
Piparia, Mad. P., India 92 H8 22 45N 78 23 E
Piparia, Mad. P., India 92 J7 21 49N 77 37 E
Pipas, Angola 115 E2 14 57 S 12 11 E
Pipéri, Greece 48 B6 39 20N 24 19 E
Piperno = Priverno,
Italy 46 A6 41 28N 13 11 E
Pipestone, U.S.A. 154 D6 44 0N 96 19W
Pipestone →, Canada 140 B2 52 53N 89 23W
Pipestone Cr. →,
Canada 143 D8 49 38N 100 15W
Pipiriki, N.Z. 130 F4 39 28 S 175 5 E
Piplan, Pakistan 92 C4 32 17N 71 21 E
Piploda, India 92 H6 23 37N 74 56 E
Pipmuacan, Rés.,
Canada 141 C5 49 45N 70 30W
Pippingarra, Australia 124 D2 20 27 S 118 42 E
Pipriac, France 26 E5 47 59N 1 58W
Piqua, U.S.A. 157 D12 40 9N 84 15W
Piquet Carneiro, Brazil 170 C4 5 48 S 39 25W
Piquiri →, Brazil 175 A5 24 3 S 54 14W
Pir Panjal Range, India 92 C7 32 30N 76 50 E
Pīr Sohrāb, Iran 97 E9 25 44N 60 54 E
Pira, Benin 113 D5 8 28N 1 48 E
Piracanjuba, Brazil 171 E2 17 18 S 49 1W
Piracicaba, Brazil 175 A6 22 45 S 47 40W
Piracuruca, Brazil 170 B3 3 50 S 41 50W
Piræus = Piraiévs,
Greece 48 D5 37 57N 23 42 E
Piraiévs, Greece 48 D5 37 57N 23 42 E
Pirajuí, Brazil 175 A6 21 59 S 49 29W
Piram I., India 92 J5 21 36N 72 21 E
Piran, Slovenia 45 C10 45 31N 13 33 E
Pirané, Argentina 174 B4 25 42 S 59 6W
Piranhas, Brazil 170 C4 9 27 S 37 46W
Pirano = Piran, Slovenia 45 C10 45 31N 13 33 E
Pirapemas, Brazil 170 B3 3 43 S 44 14W
Pirapora, Brazil 171 E3 17 20 S 44 56W
Pirara, Guyana 169 C6 3 37N 59 40W
Pirawa, India 92 G7 24 10N 76 2 E
Piray →, Bolivia 173 D5 16 32 S 63 45W
Pirdop, Bulgaria 51 D8 42 40N 24 10 E
Pireas = Piraiévs,
Greece 48 D5 37 57N 23 42 E
Pires do Rio, Brazil 171 E2 17 18 S 48 17W
Pirganj, Bangla. 90 C2 25 51N 88 24 E
Pírgos, Ilía, Greece 48 D3 37 40N 21 27 E
Pírgos, Kríti, Greece 39 E6 35 0N 25 9 E
Pirgovo, Bulgaria 51 C9 43 44N 25 43 E
Piribebuy, Paraguay 174 B4 25 26 S 57 2W
Pirimapun, Indonesia 83 C5 6 20 S 138 24 E
Pirin △, Bulgaria 50 E7 41 48N 23 22 E
Pirin Planina, Bulgaria 50 E7 41 40N 23 30 E
Pírineos = Pyrénées,
Europe 28 F4 42 45N 0 18 E
Piripiri, Brazil 170 B3 4 15 S 41 46W
Piritu, Venezuela 168 B4 9 23N 69 12W
Pirmasens, Germany 31 F3 49 12N 7 36 E
Pirna, Germany 30 E9 50 57N 13 56 E
Pirojpur, Bangla. 90 D3 22 35N 90 1 E
Pirot, Serbia & M. 50 C6 43 9N 22 33 E
Piru, Indonesia 82 B3 3 4 S 128 12 E
Piru, U.S.A. 161 L8 34 25N 118 48W
Piryatin = Pyryatyn,
Ukraine 59 G7 50 15N 32 25 E
Piryí, Greece 49 C7 38 13N 25 59 E
Pisa, Italy 44 E7 43 43N 10 23 E
Pisa →, Poland 55 E8 53 14N 21 52 E
Pisa, Firenze ✕ (PSA),
Italy 44 E7 43 40N 10 22 E
Pisa Ra., N.Z. 131 E4 44 52 S 169 12 E
Pisac, Peru 172 C3 13 25 S 71 50W
Pisagne, Italy 44 C7 45 45N 10 10 E
Pisagua, Chile 172 D3 19 40 S 70 15W
Pisarovina, Croatia 45 C12 45 35N 15 50 E
Pisau, Tanjong,
Malaysia 85 A5 6 4N 117 59 E
Pisba △, Colombia 168 A3 10 39N 74 30W
Pisco, Peru 172 C2 13 50 S 76 12W
Piscu, Romania 53 E12 45 30N 27 43 E
Písek, Czech Rep. 34 B7 49 19N 14 10 E
Pishan, China 68 C2 37 30N 78 33 E
Pishcha, Ukraine 55 G10 51 35N 23 50 E
Pishchanka, Ukraine 53 B13 48 12N 28 54 E
Pīshīn, Iran 97 E9 26 6N 61 47 E
Pishin, Pakistan 92 D2 30 35N 67 0 E
Pishin Lora →,
Pakistan 92 E1 29 9N 64 5 E
Pishpek = Bishkek,
Kyrgyzstan 65 B7 42 54N 74 46 E
Pisidia, Turkey 100 D4 37 30N 31 40 E
Pising, Indonesia 82 C2 5 8 S 121 53 E
Pismo Beach, U.S.A. 161 K6 35 9N 120 38W
Piso, L., Liberia 112 D2 6 50N 11 15W
Pissila, Burkina Faso 113 C4 13 7N 0 50W
Pissis, Cerro, Argentina 174 B2 27 45 S 68 48W
Pissos, France 28 D3 44 19N 0 49W
Pissouri, Cyprus 39 F8 34 40N 32 42 E
Pisticci, Italy 47 B9 40 23N 16 33 E
Pistóia, Italy 44 E7 43 55N 10 54 E
Pistol B., Canada 143 A10 62 25N 92 37W
Pisuerga →, Spain 42 D6 41 33N 4 52W
Pisz, Poland 54 E8 53 38N 21 49 E
Pit →, U.S.A. 158 F2 40 47N 122 6W
Pita, Guinea 112 C2 11 5N 12 15W
Pitalito, Colombia 168 C2 1 51N 76 2W
Pitanga, Brazil 171 F1 24 46 S 51 44W
Pitangui, Brazil 171 E3 19 40 S 44 54W
Pitarpunga, L.,
Australia 128 C5 34 24 S 143 30 E
Pitcairn I., Pac. Oc. 135 K14 25 5 S 130 5W
Pitch L., Trin. & Tob. 169 F9 10 12N 61 39W
Piteå, Sweden 14 D19 65 20N 21 25 E
Piteälven →, Sweden 14 D19 65 20N 21 25 E
Piterka, Russia 60 E8 50 41N 47 29 E
Piteşti, Romania 53 F9 44 52N 24 54 E
Pithapuram, India 94 F6 17 10N 82 15 E
Pithara, Australia 125 F2 30 20 S 116 35 E
Píthion, Greece 51 E10 41 24N 26 40 E
Pithiviers, France 27 D9 48 10N 2 13 E
Pithora, India 94 D6 21 16N 82 31 E
Pithoragarh, India 93 E9 29 35N 80 13 E
Pithoro, Pakistan 92 G3 25 31N 69 23 E
Pitigliano, Italy 45 F8 42 38N 11 40 E
Pitkyaranta, Russia 58 B6 61 34N 31 37 E
Pitlochry, U.K. 22 E5 56 42N 3 44W
Pitogo, Phil. 80 E4 13 47N 122 5 E
Pitrufquén, Chile 176 A2 38 59 S 72 39W
Pitschen = Byczyna,
Poland 55 G5 51 7N 18 12 E
Pitsilia, Cyprus 39 F9 34 55N 33 0 E
Pitt, Pta., Ecuador 172 a 0 43 S 89 14W
Pitt I., Canada 142 C3 53 30N 129 50W
Pitt I., N.Z. 131 a 44 15 S 176 15W
Pitti I., India 95 J1 10 50N 72 38 E
Pittsburg, Calif., U.S.A. 160 G5 38 2N 121 53W
Pittsburg, Kans., U.S.A. 155 G7 37 25N 94 42W
Pittsburg, Tex., U.S.A. 155 J7 33 0N 94 59W
Pittsburgh, U.S.A. 150 F5 40 26N 80 1W
Pittsfield, Ill., U.S.A. 156 E6 39 36N 90 49W
Pittsfield, Maine, U.S.A. 149 C11 44 47N 69 23W
Pittsfield, Mass., U.S.A. 151 D11 42 27N 73 15W
Pittsfield, N.H., U.S.A. 151 C13 43 18N 71 20W
Pittston, U.S.A. 151 E9 41 19N 75 47W
Pittsview, U.S.A. 152 C4 32 11N 85 10W
Pittsworth, Australia 127 D5 27 41 S 151 37 E
Pituri →, Australia 126 C2 22 35 S 138 30 E
Piuí, Brazil 171 F2 20 28 S 45 58W
Pium, Brazil 170 D2 10 27 S 49 11W
Piura, Peru 172 B1 5 15 S 80 38W
Piura □, Peru 172 A2 5 10 S 80 0W
Piva →, Serbia & M. 50 C2 43 20N 18 50 E
Pivijay, Colombia 168 A3 10 28N 74 37W
Piwniczna, Poland 55 J7 49 27N 20 42 E
Pixley, U.S.A. 160 K7 35 58N 119 18W
Piyai, Greece 48 B3 39 17N 21 25 E
Pizarra, Spain 43 J6 36 36N 4 42W
Pizarro, Colombia 168 C2 4 58N 77 22W
Pizhou, China 74 G9 34 44N 116 55 E
Pizol, Switz. 33 C8 46 57N 9 23 E
Pizzo, Italy 47 D9 38 44N 16 10 E
Placentia, Canada 141 C9 47 20N 54 0W
Placentia B., Canada 141 C9 47 0N 54 40W
Placer, Masbate, Phil. 81 F4 11 52N 123 55 E
Placer, Surigao N., Phil. 81 G5 9 36N 125 38 E
Placerville, U.S.A. 160 G6 38 44N 120 48W
Placetas, Cuba 164 B4 22 15N 79 44W
Plácido de Castro,
Brazil 172 C4 10 20 S 67 11W
Plačkovica, Macedonia 50 E6 41 45N 22 30 E
Plaffeien, Switz. 32 C4 46 45N 7 17 E
Plainfield, Ill., U.S.A. 157 C8 41 37N 88 12W
Plainfield, Ind., U.S.A. 157 E10 39 42N 86 24W
Plainfield, N.J., U.S.A. 151 F10 40 37N 74 25W
Plainfield, Ohio, U.S.A. 150 F3 40 13N 81 43W
Plainfield, Vt., U.S.A. 151 B12 44 17N 72 26W
Plains, Ga., U.S.A. 152 C5 32 2N 84 24W
Plains, Mont., U.S.A. 158 C6 47 28N 114 53W
Plains, Tex., U.S.A. 155 J3 33 11N 102 50W
Plainview, Nebr., U.S.A. 154 D6 42 21N 97 47W
Plainview, Tex., U.S.A. 155 H4 34 11N 101 43W
Plainwell, U.S.A. 157 B11 42 27N 85 38W
Plaisance, France 28 E4 43 36N 0 3 E
Plaistow, U.S.A. 151 D13 42 50N 71 6W
Pláka, Greece 49 B7 40 0N 25 24 E
Pláka, Ákra, Greece 39 E7 35 11N 26 19 E
Plakenska Planina,
Macedonia 50 E5 41 14N 21 2 E
Planá, Czech Rep. 34 B5 49 50N 12 44 E
Plana Cays, Bahamas 165 B5 22 38N 73 30W
Planada, U.S.A. 160 H6 37 16N 120 19W
Plancoët, France 26 D4 48 32N 2 13W
Plandište, Serbia & M. 52 E6 45 16N 21 10 E
Planeta Rica, Colombia 168 B2 8 25N 75 36W
Plano, U.S.A. 155 J6 33 1N 96 42W
Plant City, U.S.A. 153 G7 28 1N 82 7W
Plantation, U.S.A. 153 J9 26 8N 80 15W
Plaquemine, U.S.A. 155 K9 30 17N 91 14W
Plaridel, Phil. 81 G4 8 37N 123 43 E
Plasencia, Spain 42 E4 40 3N 6 8W
Plaški, Croatia 45 C12 45 4N 15 22 E
Plassen, Norway 18 C9 61 9N 12 30 E
Plast, Russia 64 D8 54 22N 60 50 E
Plaster City, U.S.A. 161 N11 32 47N 115 51W
Plaster Rock, Canada 141 C6 46 53N 67 22W
Plastun, Russia 70 B8 44 45N 136 19 E
Plasy, Czech Rep. 34 B6 49 56N 13 24 E
Plata, Río de la,
S. Amer. 174 C4 34 45 S 57 30W
Plátani →, Italy 46 E6 37 23N 13 16 E
Plátanos, Greece 39 E4 35 28N 23 33 E
Plataria, Greece 38 C10 39 27N 20 16 E
Plateau □, Nigeria 113 D6 8 30N 9 0 E
Plateau d'Ipassa ⌓,
Gabon 114 B2 0 26N 12 40 E
Plathe = Płoty, Poland 54 E2 53 48N 15 18 E
Platí, Ákra, Greece 51 F8 40 27N 24 0 E
Platinum, U.S.A. 144 G7 59 1N 161 49W
Plato, Colombia 168 B3 9 47N 74 47W
Platta, Piz, Switz. 33 D9 46 28N 9 35 E
Platte, U.S.A. 154 D5 43 23N 98 51W
Platte →, Mo., U.S.A. 156 E2 39 16N 94 50W
Platte →, Nebr., U.S.A. 154 E7 41 4N 95 53W
Platte City, U.S.A. 156 E2 39 22N 94 47W
Platteville, U.S.A. 156 B6 42 44N 90 29W
Plattling, Germany 31 G8 48 46N 12 53 E
Plattsburg, U.S.A. 156 E2 39 34N 94 27W
Plattsburgh, U.S.A. 151 B11 44 42N 73 28W
Plattsmouth, U.S.A. 154 E7 41 1N 95 53W
Plau, Germany 30 B8 53 27N 12 15 E
Plauen, Germany 30 E8 50 30N 12 8 E
Plauer See, Germany 30 B8 53 28N 12 17 E
Plav, Serbia & M. 50 D3 42 38N 19 57 E
Plavinas, Latvia 15 H21 56 35N 25 46 E
Plavnica, Serbia & M. 50 D3 42 20N 19 13 E
Plavno, Croatia 45 D13 44 9N 16 10 E
Plavsk, Russia 58 F9 53 40N 37 18 E
Playa Blanca,
Canary Is. 9 e2 28 55N 13 37W
Playa Blanca Sur,
Canary Is. 9 e2 28 51N 13 50W
Playa de las Americas,
Canary Is. 9 e1 28 5N 16 43W
Playa de Mogán,
Canary Is. 9 e1 27 48N 15 47W
Playa del Inglés,
Canary Is. 9 e1 27 45N 15 33W
Playa Esmerelda,
Canary Is. 9 e2 28 8N 14 16W
Playgreen L., Canada 143 C9 54 0N 98 15W
Playiá, Greece 39 C2 38 24N 20 35 E
Pleasant Bay, Canada 141 C7 46 51N 60 48W
Pleasant Hill, Calif.,
U.S.A. 160 H4 37 57N 122 4W
Pleasant Hill, Ill.,
U.S.A. 156 E6 39 27N 90 52W
Pleasant Hill, Mo.,
U.S.A. 156 F2 38 47N 94 16W
Pleasant Mount, U.S.A. 151 E9 41 44N 75 26W
Pleasant Point, N.Z. 131 E6 44 16 S 171 9 E
Pleasanton, Calif.,
U.S.A. 160 H5 37 39N 121 52W
Pleasanton, Tex., U.S.A. 155 L5 28 58N 98 29W
Pleasantville, Iowa,
U.S.A. 156 C3 41 23N 93 18W
Pleasantville, N.J.,
U.S.A. 148 F8 39 24N 74 32W
Pleasantville, Pa.,
U.S.A. 150 E5 41 35N 79 34W
Pleasure Ridge Park,
U.S.A. 157 F11 38 9N 85 50W
Pléaux, France 28 C6 45 8N 2 13 E
Plei Ku, Vietnam 86 F7 13 57N 108 0 E
Plélan-le-Grand, France 26 D4 48 0N 2 7W
Pléneuf-Val-André,
France 26 D4 48 35N 2 32W
Pleniţa, Romania 53 F8 44 14N 23 10 E
Plenty →, Australia 126 C2 23 25 S 136 31 E
Plenty, B. of, N.Z. 130 D6 37 45 S 177 0 E
Plentywood, U.S.A. 154 A2 48 47N 104 34W
Plérin, France 26 D4 48 32N 2 46W
Plesetsk, Russia 56 B7 62 43N 40 20 E
Pleskau = Pskov, Russia 58 D5 57 50N 28 25 E
Plessisville, Canada 141 C5 46 14N 71 47W
Plestin-les-Grèves,
France 26 D3 48 40N 3 39W
Pleszew, Poland 55 G4 51 53N 17 47 E
Pleternica, Croatia 52 E2 45 17N 17 48 E
Plétipi, L., Canada 141 B5 51 44N 70 6W
Pleven, Bulgaria 51 C8 43 26N 24 37 E
Plevlja, Serbia & M. 50 C3 43 21N 19 21 E
Plevna, Canada 150 B8 44 58N 76 59W
Plitvička Jezera △,
Croatia 45 D12 44 54N 15 35 E
Plješevica, Croatia 45 D12 44 45N 15 45 E
Ploaghe, Italy 46 B1 40 40N 8 45 E
Ploče, Croatia 45 E14 43 4N 17 26 E
Płock, Poland 55 F6 52 32N 19 40 E
Plöckenpass, Italy 45 B9 46 37N 12 57 E
Plöckenstein, Germany 31 G9 48 46N 13 51 E
Ploemeur, France 26 E3 47 44N 3 26W
Ploërmel, France 26 E4 47 55N 2 26W
Plöhnen = Płońsk,
Poland 55 F7 52 37N 20 21 E
Ploieşti, Romania 53 F11 44 57N 26 5 E
Plomárion, Greece 49 C8 38 59N 26 22 E
Plombières-les-Bains,
France 27 E13 47 58N 6 27 E
Plomin, Croatia 45 C11 45 8N 14 10 E
Plön, Germany 30 A6 54 9N 10 24 E
Plonge, Lac la, Canada 143 B7 55 8N 107 20W
Płońsk, Poland 55 F7 52 37N 20 21 E
Plopeni, Romania 53 E10 45 4N 25 59 E
Plopişului, Munţii,
Romania 52 C7 47 5N 22 30 E
Plotsk = Płock, Poland 55 F6 52 32N 19 40 E
Płoty, Poland 54 E2 53 48N 15 18 E
Plouaret, France 26 D3 48 37N 3 28W
Plouay, France 26 E3 47 55N 3 21W
Ploučnice →,
Czech Rep. 34 A7 50 46N 14 13 E
Ploudalmézeau, France 26 D2 48 34N 4 41W
Plouescat, France 26 D2 48 39N 4 10W
Plougasnou, France 26 D3 48 42N 3 49W
Plougastel-Daoulas,
France 26 D2 48 22N 4 17W
Plouguerneau, France 26 D2 48 36N 4 30W
Plouha, France 26 D4 48 41N 2 57W
Plouhinec, France 26 E2 48 0N 4 29W
Plovdiv, Bulgaria 51 D8 42 8N 24 44 E
Plovdiv □, Bulgaria 51 D8 42 15N 24 30 E
Plover Cove Res.,
China 69 G11 22 28N 114 15 E
Plum, U.S.A. 150 F5 40 29N 79 47W
Plum I., U.S.A. 151 E12 41 11N 72 12W
Plumas, U.S.A. 160 F7 39 45N 120 4W
Plummer, U.S.A. 158 C5 47 20N 116 53W
Plumtree, Zimbabwe 119 G2 20 27 S 27 55 E
Plungė, Lithuania 15 J19 55 53N 21 59 E
Pluvigner, France 26 E3 47 46N 3 1W
Plymouth, Trin. & Tob. 169 E10 11 14N 60 48W
Plymouth, U.K. 21 G3 50 22N 4 10W
Plymouth, Calif., U.S.A. 160 G6 38 29N 120 51W
Plymouth, Ill., U.S.A. 156 D6 40 18N 90 58W
Plymouth, Ind., U.S.A. 157 C10 41 21N 86 19W
Plymouth, Mass.,
U.S.A. 151 E14 41 57N 70 40W
Plymouth, N.C., U.S.A. 149 H7 35 52N 76 43W
Plymouth, N.H., U.S.A. 151 C13 43 46N 71 41W
Plymouth, Pa., U.S.A. 151 E9 41 14N 75 57W
Plymouth, Wis., U.S.A. 148 D2 43 45N 87 59W
Plympton-Wyoming,
Canada 150 D2 42 57N 82 7W
Plynlimon = Pumlumon
Fawr, U.K. 21 E4 52 28N 3 46W
Plyusa, Russia 58 C5 58 28N 29 27 E
Plyusa →, Russia 58 C5 59 4N 28 6 E
Plzeň, Czech Rep. 34 B6 49 45N 13 22 E
Plzeňský □, Czech Rep. 34 B6 49 35N 13 0 E
Pniewy, Poland 55 F3 52 31N 16 16 E
Pô, Burkina Faso 113 C4 11 14N 1 5W
Pô △, Burkina Faso 113 C4 11 25N 1 5W
Po →, Italy 45 D9 44 57N 12 4 E
Po, Foci del, Italy 45 D9 44 55N 12 30 E
Po Hai = Bo Hai, China 75 E10 39 0N 119 0 E
Po Toi, China 69 G11 22 10N 114 16 E
Pobé, Benin 113 D5 7 0N 2 56 E
Pobé, Burkina Faso 113 C4 13 53N 1 42W
Pobeda, Russia 67 C15 65 12N 146 12 E
Pobedy, Pik,
Kyrgyzstan 66 E8 42 0N 79 58 E
Pobiedziska, Poland 55 F4 52 29N 17 11 E
Pobla de Segur, Spain 40 C5 42 15N 0 58 E
Pobladura del Valle,
Spain 42 C5 42 6N 5 44W
Pobra de Trives, Spain 42 C3 42 20N 7 10W
Pocahontas, Ark.,
U.S.A. 155 G9 36 16N 90 58W
Pocahontas, Ill., U.S.A. 156 F7 38 50N 89 33W
Pocahontas, Iowa,
U.S.A. 156 B2 42 44N 94 40W
Pocatello, U.S.A. 158 E7 42 52N 112 27W
Počátky, Czech Rep. 34 B8 49 15N 15 14 E
Pochep, Russia 59 F7 52 58N 33 29 E
Pochinki, Russia 60 C7 54 41N 44 59 E
Pochinok, Russia 58 E7 54 28N 32 29 E
Pöchlarn, Austria 34 C8 48 12N 15 12 E
Pochutla, Mexico 163 D5 15 50N 96 31W
Poci, Venezuela 169 B5 5 57N 61 29W
Pocinhos, Brazil 170 C4 7 4 S 36 3W
Pocito Casas, Mexico 162 B2 28 32N 111 6W
Pocking, Germany 31 G9 48 23N 13 19 E
Pocklington Reef,
Papua N. G. 132 F8 10 51 S 155 44 E
Poções, Brazil 171 D3 14 31 S 40 21W
Pocomoke City, U.S.A. 148 F8 38 5N 75 34W
Poconé, Brazil 173 D6 16 15 S 56 37W
Poços de Caldas, Brazil 175 A6 21 50 S 46 33W
Podbořany, Czech Rep. 34 A6 50 14N 13 25 E
Poddębice, Poland 55 G5 51 54N 18 58 E
Poděbrady, Czech Rep. 34 A8 50 9N 15 8 E
Podensac, France 28 D3 44 40N 0 22W
Podenzano, Italy 44 D6 44 57N 9 41 E
Podgorač, Croatia 52 E3 45 27N 18 13 E
Podgorica, Serbia & M. 50 D3 42 30N 19 19 E
Podgorie, Albania 50 F4 40 49N 20 48 E
Podile, India 95 G4 15 37N 79 37 E
Podilska Vysochyna,
Ukraine 53 B13 49 0N 28 0 E
Podkarpackie □,
Poland 55 H9 50 0N 22 10 E
Podkova, Bulgaria 51 E9 41 24N 25 24 E
Podlapača, Croatia 45 D12 44 37N 15 47 E
Podlaskie □, Poland 55 E10 53 10N 23 0 E
Podocarpus △, Ecuador 168 D2 4 13 S 79 2W
Podoleni, Romania 53 D11 46 46N 26 39 E
Podolínec, Slovak Rep. 35 B13 49 16N 20 31 E
Podolsk, Russia 58 E9 55 25N 37 30 E
Podor, Senegal 112 B1 16 40N 15 2W
Podporozhye, Russia 58 B8 60 55N 34 2 E
Podu Iloaiei, Romania 53 C12 47 13N 27 16 E
Podu Turcului,
Romania 53 D12 46 11N 27 25 E
Podujevo, Serbia & M. 50 D5 42 54N 21 10 E
Podyji △, Czech Rep. 34 C8 48 51N 15 57 E
Poechos, Peru 168 D1 4 41 S 80 34W
Poel, Germany 30 B6 54 0N 11 25 E
Pofadder, S. Africa 116 D2 29 10 S 19 22 E
Poggiardo, Italy 47 B11 40 3N 18 23 E
Poggibonsi, Italy 44 E8 43 28N 11 9 E
Póggio Mirteto, Italy 45 F9 42 16N 12 41 E
Pogoanele, Romania 53 F12 44 55N 27 0 E
Pogorzela, Poland 55 G4 51 50N 17 12 E
Pogoso, Dem. Rep. of
the Congo 115 D3 6 46 S 17 12 E
Pogradec, Albania 50 F4 40 54N 20 37 E
Pogranichnyy, Russia 70 B5 44 25N 131 24 E
Poh, Indonesia 82 B2 0 46 S 122 51 E
P'ohang, S. Korea 75 F15 36 1N 129 23 E
Pohjanmaa, Finland 14 E20 62 58N 22 50 E
Pohjois-Pirkkala =
Nokia, Finland 15 F20 61 30N 23 30 E
Pohnpei, Micronesia 134 G7 6 55N 158 10 E
Pohorelá, Slovak Rep. 35 C13 48 50N 20 2 E
Pohořelice, Czech Rep. 35 C9 48 59N 16 31 E
Pohorje, Slovenia 45 B12 46 30N 15 20 E
Pohri, India 92 G6 25 32N 77 22 E
Pohue B., U.S.A. 145 E6 19 0N 155 48W
Poi, Solomon Is. 133 N11 10 9 S 161 42 E
Poiana Mare, Romania 52 G8 43 57N 23 5 E
Poiana Ruscăi, Munţii,
Romania 52 E7 45 45N 22 25 E
Poiana Stampei,
Romania 53 C10 47 19N 25 8 E
Poike, Península, Chile 172 b 27 6 S 109 15W
Poindimié, N. Cal. 133 T19 20 56 S 165 20 E
Poinsett, C., Antarctica 7 C8 65 42 S 113 18 E
Point Arena, U.S.A. 160 G3 38 55N 123 41W
Point Baker, U.S.A. 142 B2 56 21N 133 37W
Point Calimere, India 95 J4 10 17N 79 49 E
Point Edward, Canada 140 D3 43 0N 82 30W
Point Fortin,
Trin. & Tob. 169 F9 10 10N 61 42W
Point Hope, U.S.A. 144 B6 68 21N 166 47W
Point L., Canada 138 B8 65 15N 113 4W
Point Lay, U.S.A. 144 B7 69 46N 163 3W
Point Lisas,
Trin. & Tob. 169 F9 10 32N 61 30W
Point Pedro, Sri Lanka 95 K5 9 50N 80 15 E
Point Pelee △, Canada 140 D3 41 57N 82 31W
Point Pleasant, N.J.,
U.S.A. 151 F10 40 5N 74 4W
Point Pleasant, W. Va.,
U.S.A. 148 F4 38 51N 82 8W
Point Reyes ⌓, U.S.A. 160 G2 38 10N 122 55W
Pointe-à-Pitre,
Guadeloupe 164 b 16 10N 61 32W
Pointe-au-Pic = La
Malbaie, Canada 141 C5 47 40N 70 10W
Pointe-Claire, Canada 151 A11 45 26N 73 50W
Pointe-Gatineau,
Canada 151 A9 45 28N 75 42W
Pointe-Noire, Congo 115 C2 4 48 S 11 53 E
Pointe Noire,
Guadeloupe 164 b 16 14N 61 47W
Poio, Spain 42 C2 42 28N 8 41W
Poirino, Italy 44 D4 44 56N 7 48 E
Poisonbush Ra.,
Australia 124 D3 22 30 S 121 30 E
Poissonnier Pt.,
Australia 124 C2 19 57 S 119 10 E
Poitiers, France 26 F7 46 35N 0 20 E
Poitou, France 28 B3 46 40N 0 10W
Poitou-Charentes □,
France 28 B4 46 10N 0 15 E
Poix-de-Picardie,
France 27 C8 49 47N 1 58 E

Poix-Terron, France 27 C11 49 38N 4 38 E
Pojoaque, U.S.A. 159 J11 35 54N 106 1W
Pokai B., U.S.A. 145 K13 21 27N 158 12W
Pokataroo, Australia 127 D4 29 30 S 148 36 E
Pokhara, Nepal 93 E10 28 14N 83 58 E
Pokhvistnevo, Russia 60 D11 53 36N 52 0 E
Pokigron, Suriname 169 C6 4 30N 55 22W
Poko, Dem. Rep. of the Congo 118 B2 3 7N 26 52 E
Poko, Sudan 107 F3 5 41N 31 55 E
Pokrov, Russia 58 E10 55 55N 39 7 E
Pokrovka = Kyzyl-Suu, Kyrgyzstan 65 B9 42 20N 78 0 E
Pokrovka, Kyrgyzstan 65 B5 42 45N 71 36 E
Pokrovsk = Engels, Russia 60 E8 51 28N 46 6 E
Pokrovsk, Russia 67 C13 61 29N 129 0 E
Pokrovsk-Uralskiy, Russia 64 A7 60 10N 59 49 E
Pokrovskoye = Priazovskoye, Ukraine 59 J8 46 44N 35 40 E
Pokrovskoye, Russia 59 J10 47 25N 38 54 E
Pol-e Khomri, Afghan. 91 B3 35 56N 68 42 E
Pola = Istra, Croatia 45 C10 45 10N 14 0 E
Pola = Pula, Croatia 45 D10 44 54N 13 57 E
Pola, Russia 58 D7 57 55N 32 0 E
Pola de Allande, Spain 42 B4 43 16N 6 37W
Pola de Lena, Spain 42 B5 43 10N 5 49W
Pola de Siero, Spain 42 B5 43 24N 5 39W
Pola de Somiedo, Spain 42 B4 43 5N 6 15W
Polacca, U.S.A. 159 J8 35 50N 110 23W
Polan, Iran 97 E9 25 30N 61 10 E
Pol'ana, Slovak Rep. 35 C12 48 38N 19 29 E
Poland ■, Europe 55 G3 52 0N 20 0 E
Polanica-Zdrój, Poland 55 H3 50 24N 16 32 E
Połaniec, Poland 55 H8 50 26N 21 17 E
Polanów, Poland 54 D3 54 7N 16 41 E
Polar Bear △, Canada 140 A2 55 0N 83 45W
Polatlı, Turkey 100 C5 39 36N 32 9 E
Polatsk, Belarus 58 E5 55 30N 28 50 E
Polavaram, India 94 F5 17 15N 81 38 E
Polcura, Chile 174 D1 37 17 S 71 43W
Połczyn-Zdrój, Poland 54 E3 53 47N 16 5 E
Poleski △, Poland 55 G10 51 29N 23 5 E
Polessk, Russia 15 J19 54 50N 21 8 E
Polesye = Pripet Marshes, Europe 59 F5 52 10N 28 10 E
Polevskoy, Russia 64 C8 56 26N 60 11 E
Polewali, Indonesia 82 B1 3 25 S 119 20 E
Polgar, Hungary 52 C6 47 54N 21 6 E
Pŏlgyo-ri, S. Korea 75 G14 34 51N 127 21 E
Poli, Cameroon 113 C7 8 34N 13 15 E
Políaigos, Greece 46 E6 36 45N 24 38 E
Policastro, G. di, Italy 47 C8 40 0N 15 35 E
Police, Poland 54 E1 53 33N 14 33 E
Police, Pte., Seychelles 121 b 4 51 S 55 32 E
Polička, Czech Rep. 35 B9 49 43N 16 15 E
Policoro, Italy 47 B9 40 13N 16 41 E
Poligiros = Políyiros, Greece 50 F7 40 23N 23 25 E
Polignano a Mare, Italy 47 A9 41 0N 17 13 E
Poligny, France 27 F12 46 50N 5 42 E
Polikhnitas, Greece 49 B8 39 6N 26 10 E
Polillo, Phil. 80 D3 14 43N 121 56 E
Polillo Is., Phil. 80 D4 14 56N 122 0 E
Polillo Strait, Phil. 80 D3 14 44N 121 51 E
Polis, Cyprus 39 E8 35 2N 32 26 E
Polístena, Italy 47 D9 38 24N 16 4 E
Pölitz = Police, Poland 54 E1 53 33N 14 33 E
Políyiros, Greece 50 F7 40 23N 23 25 E
Polk, U.S.A. 150 E5 41 22N 79 56W
Polkowice, Poland 55 G3 51 29N 16 3 E
Polkwitz = Polkowice, Poland 55 G3 51 29N 16 3 E
Polla, Italy 47 B8 40 31N 15 29 E
Pollachi, India 95 J3 10 35N 77 0 E
Pollença, Spain 38 B4 39 54N 3 1 E
Pollença, B. de, Spain 38 B4 39 53N 3 8 E
Pollfoss, Norway 18 C4 61 58N 7 54 E
Póllica, Italy 47 B8 40 11N 15 3 E
Pollino △, Italy 47 C9 40 0N 16 12 E
Pollino, Mte., Italy 47 C9 39 55N 16 11 E
Polna, Russia 58 C5 58 31N 28 5 E
Polnovat, Russia 66 C7 63 50N 65 54 E
Polo, Ill., U.S.A. 156 C7 41 59N 89 35W
Polo, Mo., U.S.A. 156 E2 39 33N 94 3W
Pology, Ukraine 59 J9 47 29N 36 15 E
Polokwane, S. Africa 117 C4 23 54 S 29 25 E
Polonnaruwa, Sri Lanka 95 L5 7 56N 81 0 E
Polonne, Ukraine 59 G4 50 6N 27 30 E
Polonnoye = Polonne, Ukraine 59 G4 50 6N 27 30 E
Polovinka = Ugleuralskiy, Russia 64 B6 59 8N 57 35 E
Polski Trŭmbesh, Bulgaria 51 C9 43 20N 25 38 E
Polsko Kosovo, Bulgaria 51 C9 43 23N 25 38 E
Polson, U.S.A. 158 C6 47 41N 114 9W
Poltár, Slovak Rep. 35 C12 48 26N 19 48 E
Poltava, Ukraine 59 H8 49 35N 34 35 E
Poltoratsk = Ashgabat, Turkmenistan 66 F6 38 0N 57 50 E
Põltsamaa, Estonia 15 G21 58 39N 25 58 E
Polunochnoye, Russia 66 C7 60 52N 60 25 E
Polur, India 95 H4 12 32N 79 11 E
Põlva, Estonia 15 G22 58 3N 27 3 E
Polyana, Ukraine 52 B7 48 38N 22 58 E
Polyarny, Russia 56 A5 69 8N 33 20 E
Polynesia, Pac. Oc. 135 F11 10 0 S 162 0W
Polynésie française = French Polynesia ☑, Pac. Oc. 135 K13 20 0 S 145 0W
Pomabamba = Azurduy, Bolivia 173 D5 19 59 S 64 29W
Pomabamba, Peru 172 B2 8 50 S 77 28W
Pomarance, Italy 44 E7 43 18N 10 52 E
Pomaro, Mexico 162 D4 18 20N 103 18W
Pombachi = Komsomolabad, Tajikistan 65 D4 38 50N 69 55 E
Pombal, Brazil 170 C4 6 45 S 37 50W
Pombal, Portugal 42 F2 39 55N 8 40W
Pómbia, Greece 39 F5 35 0N 24 51 E
Pombos, B. dos, Angola 115 E2 11 40 S 13 47 E
Pomene, Mozam. 117 C6 22 53 S 35 33 E
Pomeroy, Ohio, U.S.A. 148 F4 39 2N 82 2W
Pomeroy, Wash., U.S.A. 158 C5 46 28N 117 36W
Pomézia, Italy 46 A5 41 40N 12 30 E
Pomichna, Ukraine 59 H6 48 13N 31 36 E
Pomio, Papua N. G. 132 C6 5 32 S 151 33 E
Pomme de Terre L., U.S.A. 156 G3 37 54N 93 19W
Pomona, Australia 127 D5 26 22 S 152 52 E
Pomona, U.S.A. 161 L9 34 4N 117 45W
Pomona Park, U.S.A. 153 F8 29 30N 81 36W
Pomorie, Bulgaria 51 D11 42 32N 27 41 E
Pomorskie □, Poland 54 D5 54 30N 18 0 E
Pomorskie, Pojezierze, Poland 54 E3 53 40N 16 37 E
Pomos, Cyprus 39 E8 35 9N 32 33 E
Pomos, C., Cyprus 39 E8 35 10N 32 33 E
Pompano Beach, U.S.A. 153 J9 26 14N 80 8W
Pompei, Italy 47 B7 40 45N 14 30 E
Pompey, France 27 D13 48 46N 6 6 E
Pompeys Pillar, U.S.A. 158 D10 45 59N 107 57W
Pompeys Pillar △, U.S.A. 158 D10 46 0N 108 0W
Pompton Lakes, U.S.A. 151 F10 41 0N 74 17W
Ponape = Pohnpei, Micronesia 134 G7 6 55N 158 10 E
Ponask L., Canada 140 B1 54 0N 92 41W
Ponca, U.S.A. 154 D6 42 34N 96 43W
Ponca City, U.S.A. 155 G6 36 42N 97 5W
Ponce, Puerto Rico 165 d 18 1N 66 37W
Ponce de Leon, U.S.A. 152 E4 30 44N 85 56W
Ponce de Leon B., U.S.A. 153 K8 25 15N 81 10W
Ponchatoula, U.S.A. 155 K9 30 26N 90 26W
Poncheville, L., Canada 140 B4 50 10N 76 55W
Pond, U.S.A. 161 K7 35 43N 119 20W
Pond Inlet, Canada 139 A12 72 40N 77 0W
Pondicherry, India 95 J4 11 59N 79 50 E
Pondo, Papua N. G. 132 C6 4 33 S 151 38 E
Ponds, I. of, Canada 141 B8 53 27N 55 52W
Ponérihouen, N. Cal. 133 U19 21 5 S 165 24 E
Ponferrada, Spain 42 C4 42 32N 6 35W
Pongo, Wadi →, Sudan 107 F2 8 42N 27 40 E
Poniatowa, Poland 55 G9 51 11N 22 3 E
Poniec, Poland 55 G3 51 48N 16 50 E
Ponikva, Slovenia 45 B12 46 16N 15 26 E
Ponizovkino = Krasnyy Profintern, Russia 58 D11 57 45N 40 27 E
Ponnaiyar →, India 95 J4 11 50N 79 45 E
Ponnani, India 95 J3 10 45N 75 59 E
Ponneri, India 95 H5 13 20N 80 15 E
Ponnuru, India 95 F5 16 5N 80 34 E
Ponoka, Canada 142 C6 52 42N 113 40W
Ponomarevka, Russia 64 E5 53 19N 54 8 E
Ponorogo, Indonesia 85 D4 7 52 S 111 27 E
Ponot, Phil. 81 G4 8 25N 123 0 E
Ponoy, Russia 56 A7 67 0N 41 13 E
Ponoy →, Russia 56 A7 66 59N 41 17 E
Pons = Ponts, Spain 40 D6 41 55N 1 12 E
Pons, France 28 C3 45 35N 0 34W
Ponsul →, Portugal 42 F3 39 40N 7 31W
Pont-à-Mousson, France 27 D13 48 54N 6 1 E
Pont-Audemer, France 26 C7 49 21N 0 30 E
Pont-Aven, France 26 E3 47 51N 3 47W
Pont Canavese, Italy 44 C4 45 25N 7 36 E
Pont-d'Ain, France 27 F12 46 3N 5 21 E
Pont-de-Roide, France 27 E13 47 23N 6 45 E
Pont-de-Salars, France 28 D6 44 18N 2 44 E
Pont-de-Vaux, France 27 F11 46 26N 4 56 E
Pont-de-Veyle, France 27 F11 46 17N 4 53 E
Pont-du-Château, France 27 G10 45 47N 3 15 E
Pont-l'Abbé, France 26 E2 47 52N 4 15W
Pont-l'Évêque, France 26 C7 49 18N 0 11 E
Pont-St-Esprit, France 29 D8 44 16N 4 40 E
Pont-St-Martin, Italy 44 C4 45 36N 7 48 E
Pont-Ste-Maxence, France 27 C9 49 18N 2 35 E
Pont-sur-Yonne, France 27 D10 48 18N 3 10 E
Ponta de Pedras, Brazil 170 B2 1 23 S 48 52W
Ponta Delgada, Flores, Azores 9 d2 39 31N 31 13W
Ponta Delgada, São Miguel, Azores 9 d3 37 44N 25 40W
Ponta Delgada ✕ (PDL), Azores 9 d3 37 44N 25 41W
Ponta do Sol, Madeira 9 c 32 42N 17 7W
Ponta Grossa, Brazil 175 B5 25 7 S 50 10W
Ponta Pora, Brazil 175 A4 22 20 S 55 35W
Pontacq, France 28 E3 43 11N 0 8W
Pontailler-sur-Saône, France 27 E12 47 13N 5 25 E
Pontal →, Brazil 170 C3 9 8 S 40 12W
Pontalina, Brazil 171 E2 17 31 S 49 27W
Pontarlier, France 27 F13 46 54N 6 20 E
Pontassieve, Italy 45 E8 43 46N 11 26 E
Pontaumur, France 28 C6 45 52N 2 40 E
Pontcharra, France 29 C10 45 26N 6 1 E
Pontchartrain, L., U.S.A. 155 K10 30 5N 90 5W
Pontchâteau, France 26 E4 47 25N 2 5W
Ponte Alta, Serra do, Brazil 171 E2 19 42 S 47 40W
Ponte Alta do Norte, Brazil 170 D2 10 45 S 47 34W
Ponte Branca, Brazil 173 D7 16 27 S 52 40W
Ponte da Barca, Portugal 42 D2 41 48N 8 25W
Ponte de Sor, Portugal 43 F2 39 17N 8 1W
Ponte dell'Ólio, Italy 44 D6 44 52N 9 39 E
Ponte di Legno, Italy 44 B7 46 16N 10 31 E
Ponte do Lima, Portugal 42 D2 41 46N 8 35W
Ponte do Pungué, Mozam. 119 F3 19 30 S 34 33 E
Ponte-Leccia, France 29 F13 42 28N 9 13 E
Ponte nelle Alpi, Italy 45 B9 46 11N 12 16 E
Ponte Nova, Brazil 171 F3 20 25 S 42 54W
Ponte Tresa, Italy 33 E7 45 58N 8 51 E
Ponte Vedra Beach, U.S.A. 152 E8 30 15N 81 23W
Ponteareas, Spain 42 C2 42 10N 8 28W
Pontebba, Italy 45 B10 46 30N 13 18 E
Ponteceso, Spain 42 B2 43 15N 8 54W
Pontecorvo, Italy 46 A6 41 27N 13 40 E
Pontedeume, Spain 42 B2 43 24N 8 10W
Ponteix, Canada 143 D7 49 46N 107 29W
Pontes e Lacerda, Brazil 173 D6 15 12 S 59 22W
Pontevedra, Capiz, Phil. 81 F4 11 29N 122 50 E
Pontevedra, Neg. Occ., Phil. 81 F4 10 22N 122 52 E
Pontevedra, Spain 42 C2 42 26N 8 40W
Pontevedra □, Spain 42 C2 42 25N 8 39W
Pontevedra, R. de →, Spain 42 C2 42 22N 8 45W
Pontevico, Italy 44 C7 45 16N 10 5 E
Pontiac, Ill., U.S.A. 154 E10 40 53N 88 38W
Pontiac, Mich., U.S.A. 157 B13 42 38N 83 18W
Pontian Kechil, Malaysia 87 d 1 29N 103 23 E
Pontianak, Indonesia 85 C3 0 3 S 109 15 E
Pontine Is. = Ponziane, Ísole, Italy 46 B5 40 55N 12 57 E
Pontine Mts. = Kuzey Anadolu Dağları, Turkey 100 B7 41 30N 35 0 E
Pontínia, Italy 46 A6 41 25N 13 2 E
Pontivy, France 26 D4 48 5N 2 58W
Pontoise, France 27 C9 49 3N 2 5 E
Ponton →, Canada 142 B5 58 27N 116 11W
Pontorson, France 26 D5 48 34N 1 30W
Pontrémoli, Italy 44 D6 44 22N 9 53 E
Pontresina, Switz. 33 D9 46 29N 9 48 E
Pontrieux, France 26 D3 48 42N 3 10W
Ponts, Spain 40 D6 41 55N 1 12 E
Pontypool, Canada 150 B6 44 6N 78 38W
Pontypool, U.K. 21 F4 51 42N 3 2W
Ponza, Italy 46 B5 40 54N 12 58 E
Ponziane, Ísole, Italy 46 B5 40 55N 12 57 E
Poochera, Australia 127 E1 32 43 S 134 51 E
Poole, U.K. 21 G6 50 43N 1 59W
Poole □, U.K. 21 G6 50 43N 1 59W
Pooler, U.S.A. 152 C8 32 7N 81 15W
Poona = Pune, India 94 E1 18 29N 73 57 E
Poonamallee, India 95 H5 13 3N 80 10 E
Pooncarie, Australia 128 B5 33 22 S 142 31 E
Poopelloe L., Australia 128 A6 31 40 S 144 0 E
Poopó, Bolivia 172 D4 18 23 S 66 59W
Poopó, L. de, Bolivia 172 D4 18 30 S 67 35W
Poor Knights Is., N.Z. 130 B3 35 29 S 174 43 E
Poorman, U.S.A. 144 D9 64 5N 155 33W
Popa, Gabon 114 C2 1 35 S 12 32 E
Popayán, Colombia 168 C2 2 27N 76 36W
Poperinge, Belgium 24 D2 50 51N 2 42 E
Popilta L., Australia 128 B4 33 10 S 141 42 E
Popina, Bulgaria 51 B10 44 7N 26 57 E
Popio L., Australia 128 B4 33 10 S 141 52 E
Poplar, U.S.A. 154 A2 48 7N 105 12W
Poplar →, Canada 143 C9 53 0N 97 19W
Poplar Bluff, U.S.A. 155 G9 36 46N 90 24W
Poplar Head = Dothan, U.S.A. 152 D4 31 13N 85 24W
Poplarville, U.S.A. 155 K10 30 51N 89 32W
Popocatépetl, Volcán, Mexico 163 D5 19 2N 98 38W
Popokabaka, Dem. Rep. of the Congo 115 D3 5 41 S 16 40 E
Pópoli, Italy 45 F10 42 10N 13 50 E
Popolo, Dem. Rep. of the Congo 114 B4 2 22N 21 8 E
Popomanaseu, Mt., Solomon Is. 133 M11 9 40 S 160 1 E
Popondetta, Papua N. G. 132 E5 8 48 S 148 17 E
Popovača, Croatia 45 C13 45 30N 16 41 E
Popovo, Bulgaria 51 C10 43 21N 26 18 E
Poppberg, Germany 31 F7 49 26N 11 37 E
Poppi, Italy 45 E8 43 43N 11 46 E
Poprad, Slovak Rep. 35 B13 49 3N 20 18 E
Poprad →, Slovak Rep. 35 B13 49 38N 20 42 E
Poradaha, Bangla. 90 D2 23 51N 89 1 E
Porali →, Pakistan 91 D2 25 58N 66 26 E
Porangaba, Brazil 172 B3 8 48 S 70 36W
Porangahau, N.Z. 130 G5 40 17 S 176 37 E
Porangatu, Brazil 171 D2 13 26 S 49 10W
Porbandar, India 92 J3 21 44N 69 43 E
Porce →, Colombia 168 B3 7 28N 74 53W
Porcher I., Canada 142 C2 53 50N 130 30W
Porco, Bolivia 173 D4 19 50 S 65 59W
Porcos →, Brazil 171 D2 12 42 S 45 7W
Porcuna, Spain 43 H6 37 52N 4 11W
Porcupine →, Canada 143 B8 59 11N 104 46W
Porcupine →, U.S.A. 144 C11 66 34N 145 19W
Porcupine Gorge △, Australia 126 C3 20 22 S 144 26 E
Porcupine Plain, Atl. Oc. 8 B10 48 0N 8 0W
Pordenone, Italy 45 C9 45 57N 12 39 E
Pordim, Bulgaria 51 C8 43 23N 24 51 E
Pore, Colombia 168 B3 5 43N 72 0W
Poreč, Croatia 45 C10 45 14N 13 36 E
Porecatu, Brazil 171 F1 22 43 S 51 24W
Porechye = Demidov, Russia 58 E6 55 16N 31 30 E
Poretskoye, Russia 60 C8 55 9N 46 21 E
Porgera, Papua N. G. 132 C2 5 28 S 143 12 E
Pori, Finland 15 F19 61 29N 21 48 E
Pori, Greece 48 F5 35 58N 23 13 E
Porkhov, Russia 58 D5 57 45N 29 38 E
Porlamar, Venezuela 169 A5 10 57N 63 51W
Porlezza, Italy 44 B6 46 2N 9 7 E
Porma →, Spain 42 C5 42 49N 5 28W
Pornic, France 26 E4 47 7N 2 5W
Poronaysk, Russia 67 E15 49 13N 143 0 E
Póros, Attikí, Greece 48 D5 37 30N 23 30 E
Póros, Kefallinía, Greece 39 C2 38 9N 20 47 E
Póros, Levkás, Greece 39 B2 38 38N 20 43 E
Poroshiri-Dake, Japan 70 C11 42 41N 142 52 E
Poroszló, Hungary 52 C5 47 39N 20 40 E
Poroto Mts., Tanzania 119 D3 9 0 S 33 30 E
Porpoise B., Antarctica 7 C9 66 0 S 127 0 E
Porpoise Pt., Ascension I. 9 g 7 54 S 14 21W
Porquerolles, Î. de, France 29 F10 43 0N 6 13 E
Porrentruy, Switz. 32 B4 47 25N 7 6 E
Porreres, Spain 38 B4 39 31N 3 2 E
Porsangen, Norway 14 A21 70 40N 25 40 E
Porsgrunn, Norway 18 E6 59 10N 9 40 E
Port Adelaide, Australia 128 C3 34 46 S 138 30 E
Port Alberni, Canada 142 D4 49 14N 124 50W
Port Albert, Australia 129 E7 38 42 S 146 42 E
Port Alexander, U.S.A. 144 H14 56 15N 134 38W
Port Alfred, S. Africa 116 E4 33 36 S 26 55 E
Port Alice, Canada 142 C3 50 20N 127 25W
Port Allegany, U.S.A. 150 E6 41 48N 78 17W
Port Allen, U.S.A. 155 K9 30 27N 91 12W
Port Alma, Australia 126 C5 23 38 S 150 53 E
Port Angeles, U.S.A. 160 B3 48 7N 123 27W
Port Antonio, Jamaica 164 a 18 10N 76 26W
Port Aransas, U.S.A. 155 M6 27 50N 97 4W
Port Arthur, Australia 127 G4 43 7 S 147 50 E
Port Arthur, U.S.A. 155 L8 29 54N 93 56W
Port au Choix, Canada 141 B8 50 43N 57 22W
Port au Port B., Canada 141 C8 48 40N 58 50W
Port-au-Prince, Haiti 165 C5 18 40N 72 20W
Port Augusta, Australia 128 B2 32 30 S 137 50 E
Port Austin, U.S.A. 150 B2 44 3N 83 1W
Port Bell, Uganda 118 B3 0 18N 32 35 E
Port Bergé Vaovao, Madag. 117 B8 15 33 S 47 40 E
Port Blair, India 95 J11 11 40N 92 45 E
Port Blandford, Canada 141 C9 48 20N 54 10W
Port-Bouët, Ivory C. 112 D4 5 16N 3 57W
Port Bradshaw, Australia 126 A2 12 30 S 137 20 E
Port Broughton, Australia 128 B2 33 37 S 137 56 E
Port Burwell, Canada 150 D4 42 40N 80 48W
Port Byron, U.S.A. 156 C6 41 37N 90 19W
Port Campbell, Australia 128 E5 38 37 S 143 1 E
Port Campbell, India 95 J11 11 56N 92 37 E
Port Campbell △, Australia 128 E5 38 8 S 143 6 E
Port Canning, India 93 H13 22 23N 88 40 E
Port-Cartier, Canada 141 B6 50 2N 66 50W
Port Chalmers, N.Z. 131 F5 45 49 S 170 30 E
Port Charles, N.Z. 130 C4 36 33 S 175 30 E
Port Charlotte, U.S.A. 153 J7 26 59N 82 6W
Port Chester, U.S.A. 151 F11 41 0N 73 40W
Port Clements, Canada 142 C2 53 40N 132 10W
Port Clinton, U.S.A. 157 C14 41 31N 82 56W
Port Colborne, Canada 150 D4 42 50N 79 10W
Port Coquitlam, Canada 142 D4 49 15N 122 45W
Port Cornwallis, India 95 H11 13 17N 93 5 E
Port Credit, Canada 150 C5 43 33N 79 35W
Port-Cros △, France 29 F10 43 0N 6 24 E
Port Curtis, Australia 126 C5 23 57 S 151 20 E
Port d'Alcúdia, Spain 38 B4 39 50N 3 7 E
Port Dalhousie, Canada 150 C5 43 13N 79 16W
Port d'Andratx, Spain 38 B3 39 32N 2 23 E
Port Darwin, Australia 124 B5 12 24 S 130 45 E
Port Darwin, Falk. Is. 9 f 51 50 S 59 0W
Port Davey, Australia 127 G4 43 16 S 145 55 E
Port-de-Bouc, France 29 E8 43 24N 4 59 E
Port-de-Paix, Haiti 165 C5 19 50N 72 50W
Port de Pollença, Spain 38 B4 39 54N 3 4 E
Port de Sóller, Spain 38 B3 39 48N 2 42 E
Port Dickson, Malaysia 87 L3 2 30N 101 49 E
Port Douglas, Australia 126 B4 16 30 S 145 30 E
Port Dover, Canada 150 D4 42 47N 80 12W
Port Edward, Canada 142 C2 54 12N 130 10W
Port Elgin, Canada 140 D3 44 25N 81 25W
Port Elizabeth, S. Africa 116 E4 33 58 S 25 40 E
Port Ellen, U.K. 22 F2 55 38N 6 11W
Port Elliot, Australia 128 C3 35 32 S 138 41 E
Port-en-Bessin-Huppain, France 26 C6 49 21N 0 45W
Port Erin, I. of Man 20 C3 54 5N 4 45W
Port Essington, Australia 124 B5 11 15 S 132 10 E
Port Etienne = Nouâdhibou, Mauritania 110 D1 20 54N 17 0W
Port Ewen, U.S.A. 151 E11 41 54N 73 59W
Port Fairy, Australia 128 E5 38 22 S 142 12 E
Port Fitzroy, N.Z. 130 C4 36 8 S 175 20 E
Port Florence = Kisumu, Kenya 118 C3 0 3 S 34 45 E
Port Fouâd = Bûr Fuad, Egypt 106 H8 31 15N 32 20 E
Port Francqui = Ilebo, Dem. Rep. of the Congo 115 C4 4 17 S 20 55 E
Port Gamble, U.S.A. 160 C4 47 51N 122 35W
Port-Gentil, Gabon 114 C1 0 40 S 8 50 E
Port Germein, Australia 127 E2 33 1 S 138 1 E
Port Gibson, U.S.A. 155 K9 31 58N 90 59W
Port Glasgow, U.K. 22 F4 55 56N 4 41W
Port-Gueydon = Azeffoun, Algeria 111 A5 36 51N 4 26 E
Port Harcourt, Nigeria 113 E6 4 40N 7 10 E
Port Hardy, Canada 142 C3 50 41N 127 30W
Port Harrison = Inukjuak, Canada 139 C12 58 25N 78 15W
Port Hawkesbury, Canada 141 C7 45 36N 61 22W
Port Hedland, Australia 124 D2 20 25 S 118 35 E
Port Heiden, U.S.A. 144 H8 56 55N 158 41W
Port Henry, U.S.A. 151 B11 44 3N 73 28W
Port Herald = Nsanje, Malawi 119 F4 16 55 S 35 12 E
Port Hood, Canada 141 C7 46 0N 61 32W
Port Hope, Canada 140 D4 43 56N 78 20W
Port Hope, U.S.A. 150 C2 43 57N 82 43W
Port Hope Simpson, Canada 141 B8 52 33N 56 18W
Port Hueneme, U.S.A. 161 L7 34 7N 119 12W
Port Huron, U.S.A. 150 D2 42 58N 82 26W
Port Iliç, Azerbaijan 101 C13 38 53N 48 47 E
Port Jefferson, U.S.A. 151 F11 40 57N 73 3W
Port Jervis, U.S.A. 151 E10 41 22N 74 41W
Port-Joinville, France 26 F4 46 45N 2 23W
Port Katon, Russia 59 J10 46 52N 38 46 E
Port Kelang = Pelabuhan Klang, Malaysia 87 L3 3 0N 101 23 E
Port Kembla, Australia 129 C9 34 52 S 150 49 E
Port Kenny, Australia 127 E1 33 10 S 134 41 E
Port-la-Nouvelle, France 28 E7 43 1N 3 3 E
Port Lairge = Waterford, Ireland 23 D4 52 15N 7 8W
Port Laoise, Ireland 23 C4 53 2N 7 18W
Port Lavaca, U.S.A. 155 L6 28 37N 96 38W
Port Leyden, U.S.A. 151 C9 43 35N 75 21W
Port Lincoln, Australia 128 C1 34 42 S 135 52 E
Port Lions, U.S.A. 144 H9 57 52N 152 53W
Port Loko, S. Leone 112 D2 8 48N 12 46W
Port Louis, France 26 E3 47 42N 3 22W
Port-Louis, Guadeloupe 164 b 16 28N 61 32W
Port Louis, Mauritius 121 d 20 10 S 57 30 E
Port Lyautey = Kenitra, Morocco 110 B3 34 15N 6 40W
Port MacDonnell, Australia 128 E4 38 5 S 140 48 E
Port McNeill, Canada 142 C3 50 35N 127 6W
Port Macquarie, Australia 129 A10 31 25 S 152 25 E
Port Maria, Jamaica 164 a 18 22N 76 54W
Port Matilda, U.S.A. 150 F6 40 48N 78 3W
Port Mayaca, U.S.A. 153 J9 26 59N 80 36W
Port Mellon, Canada 142 D4 49 32N 123 31W
Port-Menier, Canada 141 C7 49 51N 64 15W
Port Moller, U.S.A. 144 J7 55 59N 160 34W
Port Moody, Canada 160 A4 49 17N 122 51W
Port Morant, Jamaica 164 a 17 54N 76 19W
Port Moresby, Papua N. G. 132 E4 9 24 S 147 8 E
Port Mourant, Guyana 169 B6 6 15N 57 20W
Port Musgrave, Australia 126 A3 11 55 S 141 50 E
Port Narevin, Vanuatu 133 H7 18 45 S 169 10 E
Port-Navalo, France 26 E4 47 34N 2 54W
Port Neches, U.S.A. 155 L8 30 0N 93 59W
Port Nicholson, N.Z. 130 H3 41 20 S 174 52 E
Port Nolloth, S. Africa 116 D2 29 17 S 16 52 E
Port Nouveau-Québec = Kangiqsualujjuaq, Canada 139 C13 58 30N 65 59W
Port of Spain, Trin. & Tob. 169 F9 10 40N 61 31W
Port Olry, Vanuatu 133 E5 15 1 S 167 4 E
Port Orange, U.S.A. 153 F9 29 9N 80 59W
Port Orchard, U.S.A. 160 C4 47 32N 122 38W
Port Orford, U.S.A. 158 E1 42 45N 124 30W
Port Pegasus, N.Z. 131 H2 47 12 S 167 41 E
Port Perry, Canada 140 D4 44 6N 78 56W
Port Phillip B., Australia 129 E6 38 10 S 144 50 E
Port Pirie, Australia 128 B3 33 10 S 138 1 E
Port Renfrew, Canada 142 D4 48 30N 124 20W
Port Roper, Australia 126 A2 14 45 S 135 25 E
Port Rowan, Canada 150 D4 42 40N 80 30W
Port Royal Sd., U.S.A. 152 C9 32 15N 80 40W
Port Safaga = Bûr Safâga, Egypt 96 E2 26 43N 33 57 E
Port Said = Bûr Sa'îd, Egypt 106 H8 31 16N 32 18 E
Port St. Joe, U.S.A. 152 F4 29 49N 85 18W
Port St. Johns = Umzimvubu, S. Africa 117 E4 31 38 S 29 33 E
Port-St-Louis-du-Rhône, France 29 E8 43 23N 4 49 E
Port St. Lucie, U.S.A. 153 H9 27 20N 80 20W
Port-Ste-Marie, France 28 D4 44 15N 0 25 E
Port Salerno, U.S.A. 153 H9 27 9N 80 12W
Port Sanilac, U.S.A. 150 C2 43 26N 82 33W
Port Severn, Canada 150 B5 44 48N 79 43W
Port Shepstone, S. Africa 117 E5 30 44 S 30 28 E
Port Simpson, Canada 142 C2 54 30N 130 20W
Port Stanley = Stanley, Falk. Is. 9 f 51 40 S 59 51W
Port Stanley, Canada 140 D3 42 40N 81 10W
Port Sudan = Bûr Sûdân, Sudan 106 D4 19 32N 37 9 E
Port Sulphur, U.S.A. 155 L10 29 29N 89 42W
Port-sur-Saône, France 27 E13 47 42N 6 2 E
Port Swettenham = Pelabuhan Klang, Malaysia 87 L3 3 0N 101 23 E
Port Talbot, U.K. 21 F4 51 35N 3 47W
Port Taufiq = Bûr Taufiq, Egypt 106 J8 29 54N 32 32 E
Port Townsend, U.S.A. 160 B4 48 7N 122 45W
Port-Vato, Vanuatu 133 F6 16 20 S 168 1 E
Port-Vendres, France 28 F7 42 32N 3 8 E
Port Victoria, Australia 128 C2 34 30 S 137 29 E
Port Vila, Vanuatu 133 G6 17 45 S 168 18 E
Port Vladimir, Russia 56 A5 69 25N 33 6 E
Port Wakefield, Australia 128 C3 34 12 S 138 10 E
Port Washington, U.S.A. 148 D2 43 23N 87 53W
Port Weld = Kuala Sepetang, Malaysia 87 K3 4 49N 100 28 E
Port Wentworth, U.S.A. 152 C8 32 9N 81 10W
Porta Orientalis, Romania 37 F12 45 6N 22 18 E
Portachuelo, Bolivia 173 D5 17 10 S 63 20W
Portadown, U.K. 23 B5 54 25N 6 27W
Portaferry, U.K. 23 B6 54 23N 5 33W
Portage, Mich., U.S.A. 157 B11 42 12N 85 35W
Portage, Pa., U.S.A. 150 F6 40 23N 78 41W
Portage, Wis., U.S.A. 154 D10 43 33N 89 28W
Portage →, U.S.A. 157 C14 41 31N 83 5W
Portage la Prairie, Canada 143 D9 49 58N 98 18W
Portageville, U.S.A. 155 G10 36 26N 89 42W
Portal, U.S.A. 152 C8 32 33N 81 56W
Portalegre, Portugal 43 F3 39 19N 7 25W
Portalegre □, Portugal 43 F3 39 20N 7 40W
Portales, U.S.A. 155 H3 34 11N 103 20W
Portarlington, Ireland 23 C4 53 9N 7 14W
Portbou, Spain 40 C8 42 25N 3 9 E
Porteira, Brazil 169 D6 1 5 S 57 4W
Porteirinha, Brazil 171 E3 15 44 S 43 2W
Portel, Brazil 170 B1 1 57 S 50 49W
Portel, Portugal 43 G3 38 19N 7 41W
Portela, Lisboa ✕ (LIS), Portugal 43 G1 38 46N 9 8W
Porter, U.S.A. 157 C9 41 36N 87 4W
Porter L., N.W.T., Canada 143 A7 61 41N 108 5W
Porter L., Sask., Canada 143 B7 56 20N 107 20W
Porterville, S. Africa 116 E2 33 0 S 19 0 E
Porterville, U.S.A. 160 J8 36 4N 119 1W
Portes-lès-Valence, France 29 D8 44 52N 4 54 E
Porthcawl, U.K. 21 F4 51 29N 3 42W
Porthill, U.S.A. 158 B5 48 59N 116 30W
Porthmadog, U.K. 20 E3 52 55N 4 8W
Portile de Fier, Europe 52 F7 44 44N 22 30 E
Portimão, Portugal 43 H2 37 8N 8 32W
Portishead, U.K. 21 F5 51 29N 2 46W
Portiţei, Gura, Romania 53 F14 44 41N 29 0 E
Portknockie, U.K. 22 D6 57 42N 2 51W
Portland, N.S.W., Australia 129 B9 33 20 S 150 0 E
Portland, Vic., Australia 128 E4 38 20 S 141 35 E
Portland, Canada 151 B8 44 42N 76 12W
Portland, Conn., U.S.A. 151 E12 41 34N 72 38W
Portland, Fla., U.S.A. 152 E3 30 31N 86 12W
Portland, Ind., U.S.A. 157 D12 40 26N 84 59W
Portland, Maine, U.S.A. 139 D12 43 39N 70 16W
Portland, Mich., U.S.A. 157 B12 42 52N 84 54W
Portland, Oreg., U.S.A. 160 E4 45 32N 122 37W
Portland, Pa., U.S.A. 151 F9 40 55N 75 6W
Portland, Tex., U.S.A. 155 M6 27 53N 97 20W
Portland ✕ (PDX), U.S.A. 160 E4 45 35N 122 36W
Portland, I. of, U.K. 21 G5 50 33N 2 26W
Portland B., Australia 128 E4 38 15 S 141 45 E
Portland Bight, Jamaica 164 a 17 52N 77 5W
Portland Bill, U.K. 21 G5 50 31N 2 28W
Portland Canal, U.S.A. 142 B2 55 56N 130 0W
Portland I., N.Z. 130 F6 39 20 S 177 51 E
Portland Pt., Ascension I. 9 g 7 59 S 14 25W
Portland Pt., Jamaica 164 a 17 42N 77 11W
Portmadoc = Porthmadog, U.K. 20 E3 52 55N 4 8W
Portmore, Jamaica 164 a 17 53N 77 53W
Pôrto, Brazil 170 B3 3 54 S 42 42W
Porto, France 29 F12 42 16N 8 42 E
Porto, Portugal 42 D2 41 8N 8 40W
Porto □, Portugal 42 D2 41 8N 8 20W
Porto, G. de, France 29 F12 42 17N 8 34 E
Pôrto Acre, Brazil 172 B4 9 34 S 67 31W
Pôrto Alegre = Luzilândia, Brazil 170 B3 3 28 S 42 22W
Pôrto Alegre, Pará, Brazil 169 D7 4 22 S 52 44W
Pôrto Alegre, Rio Grande do S., Brazil 175 C5 30 5 S 51 10W
Porto Alegre, São Tomé & Principe 115 G6 0 2N 6 32 E
Porto Amboim = Gunza, Angola 115 E2 10 50 S 13 50 E
Porto Amélia = Pemba, Mozam. 119 E5 12 58 S 40 30 E
Porto Azzurro, Italy 44 F7 42 46N 10 24 E
Pôrto Cajueiro, Brazil 173 C6 11 3 S 55 53W
Porto Cristo, Spain 38 B4 39 33N 3 20 E
Pôrto da Fôlha, Brazil 170 C4 9 55 S 37 17W
Pôrto de Móz, Brazil 169 D7 1 41 S 52 13W
Pôrto de Pedras, Brazil 170 C4 9 10 S 35 17W
Pôrto des Meinacos, Brazil 173 C7 12 33 S 53 7W
Pôrto dos Gaúchos, Brazil 173 C6 11 32 S 57 16W
Porto Empédocle, Italy 46 E6 37 17N 13 32 E
Pôrto Esperança, Brazil 173 D6 19 37 S 57 29W
Pôrto Esperidão, Brazil 173 D6 15 51 S 58 28W
Porto Formoso, Azores 9 d3 37 49N 25 25W
Pôrto Franco, Brazil 170 C2 6 20 S 47 24W
Pôrto Grande, Brazil 169 C7 0 42N 51 24W
Porto Inglês, C. Verde Is. 9 j 15 21N 23 10W
Pôrto Jofre, Brazil 173 D6 17 20 S 56 48W
Pôrto Lágos, Greece 51 E9 41 1N 25 6 E
Porto Lengone = Porto Azzurro, Italy 44 F7 42 46N 10 24 E
Porto Maurizio = Impéria, Italy 44 E5 43 53N 8 3 E
Pôrto Mendes, Brazil 175 A5 24 30 S 54 15W
Porto Moniz, Madeira 9 c 32 52N 17 11W
Pôrto Murtinho, Brazil 173 E6 21 45 S 57 55W
Pôrto Nacional, Brazil 170 D2 10 40 S 48 30W

Porto-Novo, *Benin* **113 D5** 6 23N 2 42 E
Porto Petro, *Spain* **38 B4** 39 22N 3 13 E
Porto San Giórgio, *Italy* **45 E10** 43 11N 13 48 E
Porto Sant' Elpídio, *Italy* **45 E10** 43 15N 13 43 E
Pôrto Santana, *Brazil* **169 D7** 0 3 S 51 11W
Porto Santo, I. de, *Madeira* **110 B1** 33 45N 16 25W
Porto Santo Stéfano, *Italy* **44 F8** 42 26N 11 7 E
Pôrto São José, *Brazil* **175 A5** 22 43 S 53 10W
Porto Seguro = Guadalupe, *Brazil* **170 C3** 6 44 S 43 47W
Pôrto Seguro, *Brazil* **171 E4** 16 26 S 39 5W
Porto Tolle, *Italy* **45 D9** 44 56N 12 22 E
Porto Tórres, *Italy* **46 B1** 40 50N 8 24 E
Pôrto União, *Brazil* **175 B5** 26 10 S 51 10W
Pôrto Válter, *Brazil* **172 B3** 8 15 S 72 40W
Porto-Vecchio, *France* **29 G13** 41 35N 9 16 E
Pôrto Velho, *Brazil* **173 B5** 8 46 S 63 54W
Portobelo, *Panama* **164 E4** 9 35N 79 42W
Portoferráio, *Italy* **44 F7** 42 48N 10 20 E
Portogruaro, *Italy* **45 C9** 45 47N 12 50 E
Portola, *U.S.A.* **160 F6** 39 49N 120 28W
Portomaggiore, *Italy* **45 D8** 44 42N 11 48 E
Portør, *Norway* **18 F6** 58 48N 9 28 E
Portoscuso, *Italy* **46 C1** 39 12N 8 24 E
Portovénere, *Italy* **44 D6** 44 3N 9 51 E
Portoviejo, *Ecuador* **168 D1** 1 7 S 80 28W
Portpatrick, *U.K.* **22 G3** 54 51N 5 7W
Portree, *U.K.* **22 D2** 57 25N 6 12W
Portrush, *U.K.* **23 A5** 55 12N 6 40W
Portsmouth, *Dominica* **165 C7** 15 34N 61 27W
Portsmouth, *U.K.* **21 G6** 50 48N 1 6W
Portsmouth, *N.H., U.S.A.* **149 D10** 43 5N 70 45W
Portsmouth, *Ohio, U.S.A.* **148 F4** 38 44N 82 57W
Portsmouth, *R.I., U.S.A.* **151 E13** 41 36N 71 15W
Portsmouth, *Va., U.S.A.* **148 G7** 36 50N 76 18W
Portsmouth □, *U.K.* **21 G6** 50 48N 1 6W
Portsoy, *U.K.* **22 D6** 57 41N 2 41W
Portstewart, *U.K.* **23 A5** 55 11N 6 43W
Porttipahdan tekojärvi, *Finland* **14 B22** 68 5N 26 40 E
Portugal ■, *Europe* **42 F3** 40 0N 8 0W
Portugalete, *Spain* **40 B1** 43 19N 3 4W
Portuguesa □, *Venezuela* **168 B4** 9 10N 69 15W
Portuguese East Africa = Mozambique ■, *Africa* **119 F4** 19 0 S 35 0 E
Portuguese Guinea = Guinea-Bissau ■, *Africa* **112 C2** 12 0N 15 0W
Portuguese Timor = East Timor ■, *Asia* **82 C3** 8 50 S 126 0 E
Portuguese West Africa = Angola ■, *Africa* **115 E3** 12 0 S 18 0 E
Portumna, *Ireland* **23 C3** 53 6N 8 14W
Portville, *U.S.A.* **150 D6** 42 3N 78 20W
Porvenir, *Bolivia* **172 C4** 11 10 S 68 50W
Porvenir, *Chile* **176 D2** 53 10 S 70 16W
Porvoo, *Finland* **15 F21** 60 24N 25 40 E
Porzuna, *Spain* **43 F6** 39 9N 4 9W
Posada, *Italy* **46 B2** 40 38N 9 43 E
Posada →, *Italy* **46 B2** 40 39N 9 45 E
Posadas, *Argentina* **175 B4** 27 30 S 55 50W
Posadas, *Spain* **43 H5** 37 47N 5 11W
Poschiavo, *Switz.* **33 D10** 46 19N 10 4 E
Posen = Poznań, *Poland* **55 F3** 52 25N 16 55 E
Posets, *Spain* **40 C5** 42 39N 0 25 E
Poseyville, *U.S.A.* **157 F9** 38 10N 87 47W
Poshan = Boshan, *China* **75 F9** 36 28N 117 49 E
Posht-e Badam, *Iran* **97 C7** 33 2N 55 23 E
Posídhion, Ákra, *Greece* **50 G7** 39 57N 23 30 E
Posidium, *Greece* **49 F9** 35 30N 27 10 E
Poso, *Indonesia* **82 B2** 1 20 S 120 55 E
Poso, Danau, *Indonesia* **82 B2** 1 52 S 120 35 E
Posoegroenoe, *Suriname* **169 C6** 4 23N 55 43W
Posong, *S. Korea* **75 G14** 34 46N 127 5 E
Posse, *Brazil* **171 D2** 14 4 S 46 18W
Possedimenti Italiani dell'Egeo = Dhodhekánisos, *Greece* **49 E8** 36 35N 27 0 E
Possel, *C.A.R.* **114 A3** 5 5N 19 10 E
Possession I., *Antarctica* **7 D11** 72 4 S 172 0 E
Pössneck, *Germany* **30 E7** 50 42N 11 35 E
Possum Kingdom L., *U.S.A.* **155 J5** 32 52N 98 26W
Post, *U.S.A.* **155 J4** 33 12N 101 23W
Post Falls, *U.S.A.* **158 C5** 47 43N 116 57W
Postavy = Pastavy, *Belarus* **15 J22** 55 4N 26 50 E
Poste-de-la-Baleine = Kuujjuarapik, *Canada* **140 A4** 55 20N 77 35W
Poste Maurice Cortier, *Algeria* **111 D5** 22 14N 1 2 E
Postmasburg, *S. Africa* **116 D3** 28 18 S 23 5 E
Postojna, *Slovenia* **45 C11** 45 46N 14 12 E
Poston, *U.S.A.* **161 M12** 34 0N 114 24W
Postumia = Postojna, *Slovenia* **45 C11** 45 46N 14 12 E
Postville, *Canada* **141 B8** 54 54N 59 47W
Postville, *U.S.A.* **156 A5** 43 5N 91 34W
Potamós, *Andikíthira, Greece* **48 F5** 35 52N 23 15 E
Potamós, *Kíthira, Greece* **48 E4** 36 15N 22 58 E
Potchefstroom, *S. Africa* **116 D4** 26 41 S 27 7 E
Potcoava, *Romania* **53 F9** 44 30N 24 39 E
Poté, *Brazil* **171 E3** 17 49 S 41 49W
Poteau, *U.S.A.* **155 H7** 35 3N 94 37W
Poteet, *U.S.A.* **155 L5** 29 2N 98 35W
Potenza, *Italy* **47 B8** 40 38N 15 48 E
Potenza →, *Italy* **45 E10** 43 25N 13 40 E
Potenza Picena, *Italy* **45 E10** 43 22N 13 37 E
Poteriteri, L., *N.Z.* **131 G2** 46 5 S 167 10 E
Potgietersrus = Mokopane, *S. Africa* **117 C4** 24 10 S 28 55 E
Poti, *Georgia* **61 J5** 42 10N 41 38 E
Potiraguá, *Brazil* **171 E4** 15 36 S 39 53W
Potiskum, *Nigeria* **113 C7** 11 39N 11 2 E
Potlogi, *Romania* **53 F10** 44 34N 25 34 E
Potomac →, *U.S.A.* **148 G7** 38 0N 76 23W
Potosí, *Bolivia* **173 D4** 19 38 S 65 50W
Potosi, *U.S.A.* **156 G6** 37 56N 90 47W
Potosí □, *Bolivia* **172 E4** 20 31 S 67 0W
Potosi Mt., *U.S.A.* **161 K11** 35 57N 115 29W
Pototan, *Phil.* **81 F4** 10 54N 122 38 E
Potrerillos, *Chile* **174 B2** 26 30 S 69 30W
Potsdam, *Germany* **30 C9** 52 25N 13 4 E
Potsdam, *U.S.A.* **151 B10** 44 40N 74 59W
Pottangi, *India* **94 E6** 18 34N 82 58 E
Pottenstein, *Germany* **31 F7** 49 46N 11 24 E
Pottersville, *U.S.A.* **151 C11** 43 43N 73 50W
Pottery Hill = Abu Ballas, *Egypt* **106 C2** 24 26N 27 36 E
Pottstown, *U.S.A.* **151 F9** 40 15N 75 39W
Pottsville, *U.S.A.* **151 F8** 40 41N 76 12W
Pottuvil, *Sri Lanka* **95 L5** 6 55N 81 50 E
P'otzu, *Taiwan* **77 F13** 23 30N 120 25 E
Pouancé, *France* **26 E5** 47 44N 1 10W
Pouce Coupé, *Canada* **142 B4** 55 40N 120 10W
Pouébo, *N. Cal.* **133 T18** 20 24 S 164 36 E
Pouembout, *N. Cal.* **133 U18** 21 8 S 164 53 E
Poughkeepsie, *U.S.A.* **151 E11** 41 42N 73 56W
Pouilly-sur-Loire, *France* **27 E9** 47 17N 2 57 E
Poulan, *U.S.A.* **152 D6** 31 31N 83 47W
Poulaphouca Res., *Ireland* **23 C5** 53 8N 6 30W
Pouláta, *Greece* **39 C2** 38 14N 20 36 E
Poulsbo, *U.S.A.* **160 C4** 47 44N 122 39W
Poultney, *U.S.A.* **151 C11** 43 31N 73 14W
Poulton-le-Fylde, *U.K.* **20 D5** 53 51N 2 58W
Poum, *N. Cal.* **133 T18** 20 14 S 164 2 E
Pounga-Nganda, *Gabon* **114 C2** 2 58 S 10 51 E
Pouso Alegre, *Mato Grosso, Brazil* **173 C6** 11 46 S 57 16W
Pouso Alegre, *Minas Gerais, Brazil* **175 A6** 22 14 S 45 57W
Pouso Alto = Piracanjuba, *Brazil* **171 E2** 17 18 S 49 1W
Pout, *Senegal* **112 C1** 14 45N 17 0W
Pouthisat, *Cambodia* **86 F4** 12 34N 103 50 E
Pouzauges, *France* **26 F6** 46 47N 0 50W
Pova de Santa Iria, *Portugal* **43 G1** 38 51N 9 4W
Považská Bystrica, *Slovak Rep.* **35 B11** 49 8N 18 27 E
Povenets, *Russia* **56 B5** 62 50N 34 50 E
Poverty B., *N.Z.* **130 E7** 38 43 S 178 2 E
Povlen, *Serbia & M.* **50 B3** 44 9N 19 44 E
Póvoa de Lanhosa, *Portugal* **42 D2** 41 33N 8 15W
Póvoa de Varzim, *Portugal* **42 D2** 41 25N 8 46W
Povoação, *Azores* **9 d3** 37 45N 25 15W
Povorino, *Russia* **60 E6** 51 12N 42 5 E
Povungnituk = Puvirnituq, *Canada* **139 B12** 60 2N 77 10W
Powassan, *Canada* **140 C4** 46 5N 79 25W
Poway, *U.S.A.* **161 N9** 32 58N 117 2W
Powder →, *U.S.A.* **154 B2** 46 45N 105 26W
Powder River, *U.S.A.* **158 E10** 43 2N 106 59W
Powder Springs, *U.S.A.* **152 B5** 33 52N 84 41W
Powell, *U.S.A.* **158 D9** 44 45N 108 46W
Powell, L., *U.S.A.* **159 H8** 36 57N 111 29W
Powell River, *Canada* **142 D4** 49 50N 124 35W
Powelton, *U.S.A.* **152 B7** 33 26N 82 52W
Power House = Drayton Valley, *Canada* **142 C6** 53 12N 114 58W
Powers, *U.S.A.* **148 C2** 45 41N 87 32W
Powys □, *U.K.* **21 E4** 52 20N 3 20W
Poxoreu, *Brazil* **173 D7** 15 50 S 54 23W
Poya, *N. Cal.* **133 U19** 21 19 S 165 7 E
Poyang Hu, *China* **77 C11** 29 5N 116 20 E
Poyarkovo, *Russia* **67 E13** 49 36N 128 41 E
Poysdorf, *Austria* **35 C9** 48 40N 16 37 E
Poza de la Sal, *Spain* **42 C7** 42 35N 3 31W
Poza Rica, *Mexico* **163 C5** 20 33N 97 27W
Pozanti, *Turkey* **100 D6** 37 25N 34 50 E
Požarevac, *Serbia & M.* **50 B5** 44 35N 21 18 E
Pozazal, Puerto, *Spain* **42 C6** 42 56N 4 10W
Požega, *Croatia* **52 E2** 45 20N 17 40 E
Požega, *Serbia & M.* **50 C4** 43 53N 20 2 E
Pozhva, *Russia* **64 B6** 59 5N 56 5 E
Poznań, *Poland* **55 F3** 52 25N 16 55 E
Poznań ✕ (POZ), *Poland* **55 F3** 52 26N 16 45 E
Pozo, *U.S.A.* **161 K6** 35 20N 120 24W
Pozo Alcón, *Spain* **43 H8** 37 42N 2 56W
Pozo Almonte, *Chile* **172 E4** 20 10 S 69 50W
Pozo Colorado, *Paraguay* **174 A4** 23 30 S 58 45W
Pozoblanco, *Spain* **43 G6** 38 23N 4 51W
Pozorrubio, *Phil.* **80 C3** 16 7N 120 33 E
Pozuzo, *Peru* **172 C2** 10 5 S 75 35W
Pozzallo, *Italy* **47 F7** 36 43N 14 51 E
Pozzomaggiore, *Italy* **46 B1** 40 24N 8 39 E
Pozzuoli, *Italy* **47 B7** 40 49N 14 7 E
Pra →, *Ghana* **113 D4** 5 1N 1 37W
Prabuty, *Poland* **54 E6** 53 47N 19 15 E
Prača, *Bos.-H.* **52 G3** 43 47N 18 43 E
Prachatice, *Czech Rep.* **34 B6** 49 1N 14 0 E
Prachin Buri, *Thailand* **86 E3** 14 0N 101 25 E
Prachuap Khiri Khan, *Thailand* **87 G2** 11 49N 99 48 E
Pradelles, *France* **28 D7** 44 46N 3 52 E
Pradera, *Colombia* **168 C2** 3 25N 76 15W
Prades, *France* **28 F6** 42 38N 2 23 E
Prado, *Brazil* **171 E4** 17 20 S 39 13W
Prado del Rey, *Spain* **43 J5** 36 48N 5 33W
Præstø, *Denmark* **17 J6** 55 8N 12 2 E
Pragersko, *Slovenia* **45 B12** 46 27N 15 42 E
Prague = Praha, *Czech Rep.* **34 A7** 50 5N 14 22 E
Praha, *Czech Rep.* **34 A7** 50 5N 14 22 E
Praha ✕ (PRG), *Czech Rep.* **34 A7** 50 7N 14 15 E
Prahecq, *France* **28 B3** 46 19N 0 26W
Prahita →, *India* **94 E4** 19 0N 79 55 E
Prahova □, *Romania* **53 E10** 45 10N 26 0 E
Prahova →, *Romania* **53 F10** 44 50N 25 50 E
Prahovo, *Serbia & M.* **50 B6** 44 18N 22 39 E
Praia, *Azores* **9 d1** 39 3N 27 58W
Praia, *C. Verde Is.* **9 j** 15 2N 23 34W
Praia a Mare, *Italy* **47 C8** 39 50N 15 45 E
Praia da Vitória, *Azores* **9 d1** 38 44N 27 4W
Praia do Norte, *Azores* **9 d1** 38 36N 28 46W
Praid, *Romania* **53 D10** 46 32N 25 10 E
Prainha, *Azores* **9 d1** 38 27N 28 12W
Prainha, *Amazonas, Brazil* **173 B5** 7 10 S 60 30W
Prainha, *Pará, Brazil* **169 D7** 1 45 S 53 30W
Prairie, *Australia* **126 C3** 20 50 S 144 35 E
Prairie City, *U.S.A.* **158 D4** 44 28N 118 43W
Prairie Dog Town Fork →, *U.S.A.* **155 H5** 34 30N 99 23W
Prairie du Chien, *U.S.A.* **156 A5** 43 3N 91 9W
Prairie du Rocher, *U.S.A.* **156 F6** 38 5N 90 6W
Prairie Village, *U.S.A.* **156 F2** 38 58N 94 38W
Prairies, L. of the, *Canada* **143 C8** 51 16N 101 32W
Pramánda, *Greece* **48 B3** 39 32N 21 8 E
Prampram, *Ghana* **113 D5** 5 43N 0 8 E
Pran Buri, *Thailand* **86 F2** 12 23N 99 55 E
Prándarjökull, *Iceland* **11 C12** 64 40N 14 55W
Prang, *Ghana* **113 D4** 8 1N 0 56W
Prapat, *Indonesia* **78 D1** 2 41N 98 58 E
Praslin, *Seychelles* **121 b** 4 18 S 55 45 E
Prasonísi, Ákra, *Greece* **38 F11** 35 42N 27 46 E
Prassberg = Mozirje, *Slovenia* **45 B11** 46 22N 14 58 E
Prästmon, *Sweden* **16 A11** 63 5N 17 45 E
Praszka, *Poland* **55 G5** 51 5N 18 31 E
Prata, *Brazil* **171 E2** 19 25 S 48 54W
Pratabpur, *India* **93 H10** 23 28N 83 15 E
Pratapgarh, *Raj., India* **92 G6** 24 2N 74 40 E
Pratapgarh, *Ut. P., India* **93 G9** 25 56N 81 59 E
Pratas Is. = Dongsha Dao, *China* **77 G11** 20 45N 116 43 E
Prätigau, *Switz.* **33 C9** 46 56N 9 44 E
Prato, *Italy* **44 E8** 43 53N 11 6 E
Prato allo Stelvio, *Italy* **33 C11** 46 37N 10 35 E
Prátola Peligna, *Italy* **45 F10** 42 6N 13 52 E
Prats-de-Mollo-la-Preste, *France* **28 F6** 42 25N 2 27 E
Pratt, *U.S.A.* **155 G5** 37 39N 98 44W
Pratteln, *Switz.* **32 A5** 47 31N 7 41 E
Prattville, *U.S.A.* **149 J2** 32 28N 86 29W
Praust = Pruszcz Gdański, *Poland* **54 D5** 54 17N 18 40 E
Pravara →, *India* **94 E2** 19 35N 74 45 E
Pravdinsk, *Russia* **54 D8** 54 27N 21 1 E
Pravdinsk, *Russia* **60 B6** 56 29N 43 28 E
Pravets, *Bulgaria* **50 D7** 42 53N 23 55 E
Pravia, *Spain* **42 B4** 43 30N 6 12W
Praya, *Indonesia* **85 D5** 8 39 S 116 17 E
Pré-en-Pail, *France* **26 D6** 48 28N 0 12W
Precipice △, *Australia* **127 D5** 25 18 S 150 5 E
Precordillera, *Argentina* **174 C2** 30 0 S 69 1W
Predáppio, *Italy* **45 D8** 44 6N 11 59 E
Predazzo, *Italy* **45 B8** 46 19N 11 36 E
Predeal, *Romania* **53 E10** 45 30N 25 34 E
Predejane, *Serbia & M.* **50 D6** 42 51N 22 9 E
Preeceville, *Canada* **143 C8** 51 57N 102 40W
Preetz, *Germany* **30 A6** 54 14N 10 18 E
Pregolya →, *Russia* **54 D7** 54 41N 20 22 E
Pregrada, *Croatia* **45 B12** 46 11N 15 45 E
Preiļi, *Latvia* **15 H22** 56 18N 26 43 E
Preko, *Croatia* **45 D12** 44 7N 15 10 E
Prelog, *Croatia* **45 B13** 46 18N 16 32 E
Premer, *Australia* **129 A8** 31 29 S 149 56 E
Prémery, *France* **27 E10** 47 10N 3 18 E
Prémia, *Italy* **33 D6** 46 17N 8 20 E
Premià de Mar, *Spain* **40 D7** 41 29N 2 22 E
Premont, *U.S.A.* **155 M5** 27 22N 98 7W
Premuda, *Croatia* **45 D11** 44 20N 14 36 E
Prentice, *U.S.A.* **154 C9** 45 33N 90 17W
Prenzlau, *Germany* **30 B9** 53 19N 13 50 E
Preobrazheniye, *Russia* **70 C6** 42 54N 133 54 E
Preparis I., *Burma* **95 G11** 14 52N 93 41 E
Preparis North Channel, *Burma* **95 G11** 15 27N 94 5 E
Preparis South Channel, *Burma* **95 G11** 14 33N 93 30 E
Přerov, *Czech Rep.* **35 B10** 49 28N 17 27 E
Prescott, *Canada* **140 D4** 44 45N 75 30W
Prescott, *Ariz., U.S.A.* **159 J7** 34 33N 112 28W
Prescott, *Ark., U.S.A.* **155 J8** 33 48N 93 23W
Prescott Valley, *U.S.A.* **159 J7** 34 40N 112 18W
Preservation Inlet, *N.Z.* **131 G1** 46 8 S 166 35 E
Preševo, *Serbia & M.* **50 D5** 42 19N 21 39 E
Presho, *U.S.A.* **154 D4** 43 54N 100 3W
Presicce, *Italy* **47 C11** 39 54N 18 16 E
Presidencia de la Plaza, *Argentina* **174 B4** 27 0 S 59 50W
Presidencia Roque Saenz Peña, *Argentina* **174 B3** 26 45 S 60 30W
Presidente Dutra, *Brazil* **170 C3** 5 15 S 44 30W
Presidente Epitácio, *Brazil* **171 F1** 21 56 S 52 6W
Presidente Figueiredo, *Brazil* **169 D5** 1 57 S 60 2W
Presidente Hayes □, *Paraguay* **174 A4** 24 0 S 59 0W
Presidente Hermes, *Brazil* **173 C5** 11 17 S 61 55W
Presidente Juán Perón = Chaco □, *Argentina* **174 B3** 26 30 S 61 0W
Presidente Prudente, *Brazil* **175 A5** 22 5 S 51 25W
Presidente Vargas = Nova Era, *Brazil* **171 E3** 19 45 S 43 3W
Presidio, *Mexico* **162 B4** 29 29N 104 23W
Presidio, *U.S.A.* **155 L2** 29 34N 104 22W
Preslav, *Bulgaria* **51 C10** 43 10N 26 52 E
Preslavska Planina, *Bulgaria* **51 C10** 43 10N 26 45 E
Prešov, *Slovak Rep.* **35 B14** 49 0N 21 15 E
Prešovský □, *Slovak Rep.* **35 B13** 49 10N 21 0 E
Prespa, *Bulgaria* **51 E8** 41 44N 24 55 E
Préspa △, *Greece* **50 F5** 40 48N 21 4 E
Prespa, L. = Prespansko Jezero, *Macedonia* **50 F5** 40 55N 21 0 E
Prespansko Jezero, *Macedonia* **50 F5** 40 55N 21 0 E
Presque I., *U.S.A.* **150 D4** 42 9N 80 6W
Presque Isle, *U.S.A.* **149 B12** 46 41N 68 1W
Pressburg = Bratislava, *Slovak Rep.* **35 C10** 48 10N 17 7 E
Prestatyn, *U.K.* **20 D4** 53 20N 3 24W
Prestea, *Ghana* **112 D4** 5 22N 2 7W
Presteigne, *U.K.* **21 E5** 52 17N 3 0W
Přeštice, *Czech Rep.* **34 B6** 49 34N 13 20 E
Presto, *Bolivia* **173 D5** 18 55 S 64 56W
Preston, *Canada* **150 C4** 43 23N 80 21W
Preston, *U.K.* **20 D5** 53 46N 2 42W
Preston, *Ga., U.S.A.* **152 C5** 32 4N 84 32W
Preston, *Idaho, U.S.A.* **158 E8** 42 6N 111 53W
Preston, *Iowa, U.S.A.* **156 B6** 42 3N 90 24W
Preston, *Minn., U.S.A.* **154 D8** 43 40N 92 5W
Preston, *Mo., U.S.A.* **156 G3** 37 56N 93 13W
Preston, C., *Australia* **124 D2** 20 51 S 116 12 E
Prestonsburg, *U.S.A.* **148 G4** 37 39N 82 46W
Prestrand, *Norway* **18 E6** 59 6N 9 4 E
Prestwick, *U.K.* **22 F4** 55 29N 4 37W
Prêto →, *Amazonas, Brazil* **169 D5** 0 8 S 64 6W
Prêto →, *Bahia, Brazil* **170 D3** 11 21 S 43 52W
Prêto do Igapó-Açu →, *Brazil* **169 D6** 4 26 S 59 48W
Pretoria, *S. Africa* **117 D4** 25 44 S 28 12 E
Preuilly-sur-Claise, *France* **26 F7** 46 51N 0 56 E
Preussisch-Eylau = Bagrationovsk, *Russia* **15 J19** 54 23N 20 39 E
Preussisch Friedland = Debrzno, *Poland* **54 E4** 53 31N 17 14 E
Preussisch Holland = Pasłęk, *Poland* **54 D6** 54 5N 19 41 E
Preussisch-Stargard = Starogard Gdański, *Poland* **54 E5** 53 59N 18 30 E
Préveza, *Greece* **39 B2** 38 57N 20 45 E
Préveza □, *Greece* **48 B2** 39 10N 20 40 E
Préveza-Levkás ✕ (PVK), *Greece* **39 B2** 38 57N 20 45 E
Prey Veng, *Cambodia* **87 G5** 11 35N 105 29 E
Priazovskoye, *Ukraine* **59 J8** 46 44N 35 40 E
Pribalkhash = Balqash, *Kazakhstan* **66 E8** 46 50N 74 50 E
Pribilof Is., *U.S.A.* **144 H5** 57 0N 170 0W
Priboj, *Serbia & M.* **50 C3** 43 35N 19 32 E
Příbram, *Czech Rep.* **34 B7** 49 41N 14 2 E
Price, *U.S.A.* **158 G8** 39 36N 110 49W
Price, C., *India* **95 H11** 13 34N 93 3 E
Price I., *Canada* **142 C3** 52 23N 128 41W
Prichard, *U.S.A.* **149 K1** 30 44N 88 5W
Priego, *Spain* **40 E2** 40 26N 2 21W
Priego de Córdoba, *Spain* **43 H6** 37 27N 4 12W
Priekule, *Latvia* **15 H19** 56 26N 21 35 E
Priekulė, *Lithuania* **54 C8** 55 33N 21 19 E
Prien, *Germany* **31 H8** 47 51N 12 20 E
Prienai, *Lithuania* **15 J20** 54 38N 23 57 E
Prieska, *S. Africa* **116 D3** 29 40 S 22 42 E
Priest L., *U.S.A.* **158 B5** 48 35N 116 52W
Priest River, *U.S.A.* **158 B5** 48 10N 116 54W
Priest Valley, *U.S.A.* **160 J6** 36 10N 120 39W
Prieto Diaz, *Phil.* **80 E5** 13 2N 124 12 E
Prievidza, *Slovak Rep.* **35 C11** 48 46N 18 36 E
Prignitz, *Germany* **30 B7** 53 6N 11 45 E
Prijedor, *Bos.-H.* **45 D13** 44 58N 16 41 E
Prijepolje, *Serbia & M.* **50 C3** 43 27N 19 40 E
Prikaspiyskaya Nizmennost = Caspian Depression, *Eurasia* **61 G9** 47 0N 48 0 E
Prikro, *Ivory C.* **112 D4** 7 40N 3 59W
Prikubanskaya Nizmennost, *Russia* **61 H4** 45 39N 38 33 E
Prilep, *Macedonia* **50 E5** 41 21N 21 32 E
Priluki = Pryluky, *Ukraine* **59 G7** 50 30N 32 24 E
Prime Seal I., *Australia* **127 G4** 40 3 S 147 43 E
Primeira Cruz, *Brazil* **170 B3** 2 30 S 43 26W
Primkenau = Przemków, *Poland* **55 G2** 51 31N 15 48 E
Primorsk, *Russia* **54 D6** 54 44N 20 0 E
Primorsk, *Russia* **58 B5** 60 22N 28 37 E
Primorsko, *Bulgaria* **51 D11** 42 15N 27 44 E
Primorsko-Akhtarsk, *Russia* **59 J10** 46 2N 38 10 E
Primorskoye, *Ukraine* **59 J9** 46 48N 36 20 E
Primrose L., *Canada* **143 C7** 54 55N 109 45W
Prince Albert, *Canada* **143 C7** 53 15N 105 50W
Prince Albert, *S. Africa* **116 E3** 33 12 S 22 2 E
Prince Albert △, *Canada* **143 C7** 54 0N 106 25W
Prince Albert Mts., *Antarctica* **7 D11** 76 0 S 161 30 E
Prince Albert Pen., *Canada* **138 A8** 72 30N 116 0W
Prince Albert Sd., *Canada* **138 A8** 70 25N 115 0W
Prince Alfred, C., *Canada* **6 B1** 74 20N 124 40W
Prince Charles I., *Canada* **139 B12** 67 47N 76 12W
Prince Charles Mts., *Antarctica* **7 D6** 72 0 S 67 0 E
Prince Edward I. □, *Canada* **141 C7** 46 20N 63 20W
Prince Edward Is., *Ind. Oc.* **121 J2** 46 35 S 38 0 E
Prince Edward Pt., *Canada* **150 C8** 43 56N 76 52W
Prince George, *Canada* **142 C4** 53 55N 122 50W
Prince of Wales, C., *U.S.A.* **144 D5** 65 36N 168 5W
Prince of Wales I., *Australia* **126 A3** 10 40 S 142 10 E
Prince of Wales I., *Canada* **138 A10** 73 0N 99 0W
Prince of Wales I., *U.S.A.* **144 J14** 55 47N 132 50W
Prince Patrick I., *Canada* **6 B2** 77 0N 120 0W
Prince Regent Inlet, *Canada* **6 B3** 73 0N 90 0W
Prince Rupert, *Canada* **142 C2** 54 20N 130 20W
Prince William Sd., *U.S.A.* **144 F11** 60 40N 147 0W
Princes Town, *Trin. & Tob.* **169 F9** 10 16N 61 23W
Princesa Isabel, *Brazil* **170 C4** 7 44 S 38 0W
Princess Charlotte B., *Australia* **126 A3** 14 25 S 144 0 E
Princess May Ranges, *Australia* **124 C4** 15 30 S 125 30 E
Princess Royal I., *Canada* **142 C3** 53 0N 128 40W
Princeton, *Canada* **142 D4** 49 27N 120 30W
Princeton, *Calif., U.S.A.* **160 F4** 39 24N 122 1W
Princeton, *Ill., U.S.A.* **156 C7** 41 23N 89 28W
Princeton, *Ind., U.S.A.* **157 F9** 38 21N 87 34W
Princeton, *Ky., U.S.A.* **148 G2** 37 7N 87 53W
Princeton, *Mo., U.S.A.* **156 D3** 40 24N 93 35W
Princeton, *N.J., U.S.A.* **151 F10** 40 21N 74 39W
Princeton, *W. Va., U.S.A.* **148 G5** 37 22N 81 6W
Princeville, *U.S.A.* **156 D7** 40 56N 89 46W
Príncipe, *São Tomé & Príncipe* **115 G6** 1 37N 7 25 E
Príncipe, I. de, *Atl. Oc.* **104 F4** 1 37N 7 27 E
Príncipe da Beira, *Brazil* **173 C5** 12 20 S 64 30W
Prineville, *U.S.A.* **158 D3** 44 18N 120 51W
Prins Christian Sund, *Greenland* **10 E6** 60 4N 43 10W
Prins Harald Kyst, *Antarctica* **7 D4** 70 0 S 35 1 E
Prins Karls Forland, *Svalbard* **10 B12** 78 30N 11 0 E
Prinsesse Astrid Kyst, *Antarctica* **7 D3** 70 45 S 12 30 E
Prinsesse Ragnhild Kyst, *Antarctica* **7 D4** 70 15 S 27 30 E
Prinzapolca, *Nic.* **164 D3** 13 20N 83 35W
Prior, C., *Spain* **42 B2** 43 34N 8 17W
Priozersk, *Russia* **58 B6** 61 2N 30 7 E
Pripet = Prypyat →, *Europe* **59 G6** 51 20N 30 15 E
Pripet Marshes, *Europe* **59 F5** 52 10N 28 10 E
Pripyat Marshes = Pripet Marshes, *Europe* **59 F5** 52 10N 28 10 E
Pripyats = Prypyat →, *Europe* **59 G6** 51 20N 30 15 E
Prishib = Leninsk, *Russia* **61 F7** 48 40N 45 15 E
Prislop, Pasul, *Romania* **53 C9** 47 37N 24 48 E
Pristen, *Russia* **59 G9** 51 15N 36 44 E
Priština, *Serbia & M.* **50 D5** 42 40N 21 13 E
Pritzwalk, *Germany* **30 B8** 53 9N 12 10 E
Privas, *France* **29 D8** 44 45N 4 37 E
Priverno, *Italy* **46 A6** 41 28N 13 11 E
Privolzhsk, *Russia* **60 B5** 57 23N 41 16 E
Privolzhskaya Vozvyshennost, *Russia* **60 E7** 51 0N 46 0 E
Privolzhskiy, *Russia* **60 E8** 51 25N 46 3 E
Privolzhskiy □, *Russia* **60 B10** 56 0N 50 0 E
Privolzhye, *Russia* **60 D9** 52 52N 48 33 E
Priyutnoye, *Russia* **61 G6** 46 12N 43 40 E
Priyutovo, *Russia* **64 E4** 53 55N 53 59 E
Prizren, *Serbia & M.* **50 D4** 42 13N 20 45 E
Prizzi, *Italy* **46 E6** 37 43N 13 26 E
Prnjavor, *Bos.-H.* **52 F2** 44 52N 17 43 E
Probolinggo, *Indonesia* **85 D4** 7 46 S 113 13 E
Prochowice, *Poland* **55 G3** 51 17N 16 20 E
Proctor, *U.S.A.* **151 C11** 43 40N 73 2W
Proddatur, *India* **95 G4** 14 45N 78 30 E
Prodhromos, *Cyprus* **39 F8** 34 57N 32 50 E
Proença-a-Nova, *Portugal* **42 F3** 39 45N 7 54W
Profítis Ilías, *Greece* **38 E11** 36 17N 27 56 E
Profondeville, *Belgium* **24 D4** 50 23N 4 52 E
Progreso, *Coahuila, Mexico* **162 B4** 27 28N 101 4W
Progreso, *Yucatán, Mexico* **163 C7** 21 20N 89 40W
Prokhladnyy, *Russia* **61 J7** 43 50N 44 2 E
Prokletije, *Albania* **50 D3** 42 30N 19 45 E
Prokopyevsk, *Russia* **66 D9** 54 0N 86 45 E
Prokuplje, *Serbia & M.* **50 C5** 43 16N 21 36 E
Proletarsk, *Russia* **61 G5** 46 42N 41 50 E
Proletarskaya = Proletarsk, *Russia* **61 G5** 46 42N 41 50 E
Prome, *Burma* **90 F5** 18 49N 95 13 E
Promise City, *U.S.A.* **156 D3** 40 45N 93 9W
Promzino = Surskoye, *Russia* **60 C8** 54 30N 46 44 E
Prophet →, *Canada* **142 B4** 58 48N 122 40W
Prophet River, *Canada* **142 B4** 58 6N 122 43W
Prophetstown, *U.S.A.* **156 C7** 41 40N 89 56W
Propriá, *Brazil* **170 D4** 10 13 S 36 51W
Propriano, *France* **29 G12** 41 41N 8 52 E
Proserpine, *Australia* **126 J6** 20 21 S 148 36 E
Proskurov = Khmelnytskyy, *Ukraine* **59 H4** 49 23N 27 0 E
Prosna →, *Poland* **55 F4** 52 6N 17 44 E
Prospect, *N.Y., U.S.A.* **151 C9** 43 18N 75 9W
Prospect, *Ohio, U.S.A.* **157 D13** 40 27N 83 11W
Prosperidad, *Phil.* **81 G5** 8 34N 125 52 E
Prosperity, *U.S.A.* **152 E4** 30 51N 85 56W
Prosperous B., *St. Helena* **9 h** 15 56 S 5 39W
Prosser, *U.S.A.* **158 C4** 46 12N 119 46W
Prossnitz = Prostějov, *Czech Rep.* **35 B10** 49 30N 17 9 E
Prostějov, *Czech Rep.* **35 B10** 49 30N 17 9 E
Prostki, *Poland* **54 E9** 53 42N 22 25 E
Proston, *Australia* **127 D5** 26 8 S 151 32 E
Proszowice, *Poland* **55 H7** 50 13N 20 16 E
Próti, *Greece* **48 D3** 37 5N 21 32 E
Provadiya, *Bulgaria* **51 C11** 43 12N 27 30 E
Provence, *France* **29 E9** 43 40N 5 46 E
Provence-Alpes-Côte d'Azur □, *France* **29 D10** 44 0N 6 15 E
Providence, *Seychelles* **121 E4** 9 14 S 51 2 E
Providence, *Ky., U.S.A.* **148 G2** 37 24N 87 46W
Providence, *R.I., U.S.A.* **151 E13** 41 49N 71 24W
Providence, C., *N.Z.* **131 F1** 45 59 S 166 29 E
Providence Bay, *Canada* **140 C3** 45 41N 82 15W
Providence Mts., *U.S.A.* **161 K11** 35 10N 115 15W
Providencia, I. de, *Colombia* **164 D3** 13 25N 81 26W
Provideniya, *Russia* **67 C19** 64 23N 173 18W
Provins, *France* **27 D10** 48 33N 3 15 E
Provo, *U.S.A.* **158 F8** 40 14N 111 39W
Provost, *Canada* **143 C6** 52 25N 110 20W
Prozor, *Bos.-H.* **52 G2** 43 50N 17 34 E
Prrenjas, *Albania* **50 E4** 41 4N 20 32 E
Prudentópolis, *Brazil* **171 G1** 25 12 S 50 57W
Prudhoe Bay, *U.S.A.* **144 A10** 70 18N 148 22W
Prudhoe I., *Australia* **126 C4** 21 19 S 149 41 E
Prud'homme, *Canada* **143 C7** 52 20N 105 54W
Prudnik, *Poland* **55 H4** 50 20N 17 38 E
Prüm, *Germany* **31 E2** 50 12N 6 25 E
Prundu, *Romania* **53 F11** 44 6N 26 14 E
Pruszcz Gdański, *Poland* **54 D5** 54 17N 18 40 E
Pruszków, *Poland* **55 F7** 52 9N 20 49 E
Prut →, *Romania* **53 E13** 45 28N 28 10 E
Prutz, *Austria* **33 B11** 47 5N 10 40 E
Pruzhany, *Belarus* **59 F3** 52 33N 24 28 E
Prvič, *Croatia* **45 D11** 44 55N 14 47 E
Prydz B., *Antarctica* **7 C6** 69 0 S 74 0 E
Pryluky, *Ukraine* **59 G7** 50 30N 32 24 E
Pryor, *U.S.A.* **155 G7** 36 19N 95 19W
Prypyat →, *Europe* **59 G6** 51 20N 30 15 E
Przasnysz, *Poland* **55 E7** 53 2N 20 54 E
Przedbórz, *Poland* **55 G6** 51 6N 19 53 E
Przedecz, *Poland* **55 F5** 52 20N 18 53 E
Przemków, *Poland* **55 G2** 51 31N 15 48 E
Przemyśl, *Poland* **55 J9** 49 50N 22 45 E
Przeworsk, *Poland* **55 H9** 50 6N 22 32 E
Przewóz, *Poland* **55 G1** 51 28N 14 57 E
Przhevalsk = Karakol, *Kyrgyzstan* **65 B9** 42 30N 78 20 E
Przysucha, *Poland* **55 G7** 51 22N 20 38 E
Psakhná, *Greece* **48 C5** 38 34N 23 35 E
Psará, *Greece* **49 C7** 38 37N 25 38 E
Psathoúra, *Greece* **48 B6** 39 30N 24 12 E
Psel →, *Ukraine* **59 H7** 49 10N 33 37 E
Pserimos, *Greece* **49 E9** 36 56N 27 8 E
Psíra, *Greece* **39 E6** 35 12N 25 52 E
Pskem →, *Uzbekistan* **65 C5** 41 38N 70 1 E
Pskem Tizmasi, *Uzbekistan* **65 C5** 42 0N 70 45 E
Pskent, *Uzbekistan* **65 C4** 40 54N 69 20 E
Pskov, *Russia* **58 D5** 57 50N 28 25 E
Pskovskoye, Ozero, *Russia* **58 D5** 58 0N 27 58 E
Psunj, *Croatia* **52 E2** 45 25N 17 19 E
Pteleón, *Greece* **48 B4** 39 3N 22 57 E
Ptich = Ptsich →, *Belarus* **59 F5** 52 9N 28 52 E
Ptolemaïda = Ptolemaïs, *Greece* **50 F5** 40 30N 21 43 E
Ptolemaïs, *Greece* **50 F5** 40 30N 21 43 E
Ptsich →, *Belarus* **59 F5** 52 9N 28 52 E
Ptuj, *Slovenia* **45 B12** 46 28N 15 50 E
Ptujska Gora, *Slovenia* **45 B12** 46 23N 15 47 E
Pu Xian, *China* **74 F6** 36 24N 111 6 E
Pua, *Thailand* **86 C3** 19 11N 100 55 E
Puaena Pt., *U.S.A.* **145 J13** 21 36N 158 6W
Puán, *Argentina* **174 D3** 37 30 S 62 45W
Pu'an, *China* **76 E5** 25 46N 104 57 E
Puan, *S. Korea* **75 G14** 35 44N 126 44 E
Pu'apu'a, *Samoa* **133 W23** 13 34 S 172 9W
Pubei, *China* **76 F7** 22 16N 109 31 E
Pucacuro →, *Peru* **168 D3** 3 20 S 74 58W
Pucallpa, *Peru* **172 B3** 8 25 S 74 30W
Pucará, *Bolivia* **173 D5** 18 43 S 64 11W
Pucará, *Cajamarca, Peru* **172 B2** 6 0 S 79 7W
Pucará, *Puno, Peru* **172 D3** 15 5 S 70 24W
Pucarani, *Bolivia* **172 D4** 16 23 S 68 30W
Pucheng, *China* **77 D12** 27 59N 118 31 E
Pucheni, *Romania* **53 E10** 45 12N 25 17 E
Puchheim, *Germany* **31 G7** 48 9N 11 21 E
Puch'ŏn, *S. Korea* **57 F14** 37 30N 126 50 E
Púchov, *Slovak Rep.* **35 B11** 49 8N 18 20 E

Pucio Pt., *Phil.* **81 F3** 11 46N 121 51 E
Pucioasa, *Romania* **53 E10** 45 5N 25 25 E
Pučišća, *Croatia* **45 E13** 43 22N 16 43 E
Puck, *Poland* **54 D5** 54 45N 18 23 E
Pucka, Zatoka, *Poland* **54 D5** 54 30N 18 40 E
Puçol, *Spain* **41 F4** 39 37N 0 18W
Pudasjärvi, *Finland* **14 D22** 65 23N 26 53 E
Puding, *China* **76 D5** 26 18N 105 44 E
Pudozh, *Russia* **58 B9** 61 48N 36 32 E
Puduchcheri = Pondicherry, *India* **95 J4** 11 59N 79 50 E
Pudukkottai, *India* **95 J4** 10 28N 78 47 E
Puebla, *Mexico* **163 D5** 19 3N 98 12W
Puebla □, *Mexico* **163 D5** 18 30N 98 0W
Puebla de Alcocer, *Spain* **43 G5** 38 59N 5 14W
Puebla de Don Fadrique, *Spain* **41 H2** 37 58N 2 25W
Puebla de Don Rodrigo, *Spain* **43 F6** 39 5N 4 37W
Puebla de Guzmán, *Spain* **43 H3** 37 37N 7 15W
Puebla de la Calzada, *Spain* **43 G4** 38 54N 6 37W
Puebla de Sanabria, *Spain* **42 C4** 42 4N 6 38W
Puebla de Trives = Pobra de Trives, *Spain* **42 C3** 42 20N 7 10W
Pueblo, *U.S.A.* **154 F2** 38 16N 104 37W
Pueblo Hundido, *Chile* **174 B1** 26 20 S 70 5W
Puelches, *Argentina* **174 D2** 38 5 S 65 51W
Puelén, *Argentina* **174 D2** 37 32 S 67 38W
Puente Alto, *Chile* **174 C1** 33 32 S 70 35W
Puente-Genil, *Spain* **43 H6** 37 22N 4 47W
Puente la Reina, *Spain* **40 C3** 42 40N 1 49W
Puenteareas = Ponteareas, *Spain* **42 C2** 42 10N 8 28W
Puentedeume = Pontedeume, *Spain* **42 B2** 43 24N 8 10W
Puentes de Garcia Rodriguez = As Pontes de García Rodríguez, *Spain* **42 B3** 43 27N 7 50W
Pueo Pt., *U.S.A.* **145 B1** 21 54N 160 4W
Pu'er, *China* **76 F3** 23 0N 101 15 E
Puerca, Pta., *Puerto Rico* **165 d** 18 13N 65 36W
Puerco →, *U.S.A.* **159 J10** 34 22N 107 50W
Puerto Acosta, *Bolivia* **172 D4** 15 32 S 69 15W
Puerto Aisén, *Chile* **176 C2** 45 27 S 73 0W
Puerto Ángel, *Mexico* **163 D5** 15 40N 96 29W
Puerto Arista, *Mexico* **163 D6** 15 56N 93 48W
Puerto Armuelles, *Panama* **164 E3** 8 20N 82 51W
Puerto Asis, *Colombia* **168 C2** 0 30N 76 30W
Puerto Ayacucho, *Venezuela* **168 B4** 5 40N 67 35W
Puerto Ayora, *Ecuador* **172 a** 0 45 S 90 19W
Puerto Baquerizo Moreno, *Ecuador* **172 a** 0 54 S 89 36W
Puerto Barrios, *Guatemala* **164 C2** 15 40N 88 32W
Puerto Bermejo, *Argentina* **174 B4** 26 55 S 58 34W
Puerto Bermúdez, *Peru* **172 C3** 10 20 S 74 58W
Puerto Bolívar, *Ecuador* **168 D2** 3 19 S 79 55W
Puerto Cabello, *Venezuela* **168 A4** 10 28N 68 1W
Puerto Cabezas, *Nic.* **164 D3** 14 0N 83 30W
Puerto Cabo Gracias á Dios, *Nic.* **164 D3** 15 0N 83 10W
Puerto Capaz = El Jebha, *Morocco* **110 A4** 35 11N 4 43W
Puerto Carreño, *Colombia* **168 B4** 6 12N 67 22W
Puerto Castilla, *Honduras* **164 C2** 16 0N 86 0W
Puerto Chicama, *Peru* **172 B2** 7 45 S 79 20W
Puerto Cisnes, *Chile* **176 B2** 44 45 S 72 42W
Puerto Coig, *Argentina* **176 D3** 50 54 S 69 15W
Puerto Cortés, *Costa Rica* **164 E3** 8 55N 84 0W
Puerto Cortés, *Honduras* **164 C2** 15 51N 88 0W
Puerto Cumarebo, *Venezuela* **168 A4** 11 29N 69 30W
Puerto de Alcudia = Port d'Alcúdia, *Spain* **38 B4** 39 50N 3 7 E
Puerto de Cabras = Puerto del Rosario, *Canary Is.* **9 e2** 28 30N 13 52W
Puerto de Cabrera, *Spain* **38 B3** 39 8N 2 56 E
Puerto de Gran Tarajal, *Canary Is.* **9 e2** 28 13N 14 1W
Puerto de la Cruz, *Canary Is.* **9 e1** 28 24N 16 32W
Puerto de los Angeles ⌂, *Mexico* **162 C3** 23 39N 105 45W
Puerto de Mazarrón, *Spain* **41 H3** 37 34N 1 15W
Puerto de Pozo Negro, *Canary Is.* **9 e2** 28 19N 13 55W
Puerto de Sóller = Port de Sóller, *Spain* **38 B3** 39 48N 2 42 E
Puerto de Somosierra, *Spain* **42 D7** 41 9N 3 35W
Puerto del Carmen, *Canary Is.* **9 e2** 28 55N 13 38W
Puerto del Rosario, *Canary Is.* **9 e2** 28 30N 13 52W
Puerto Deseado, *Argentina* **176 C3** 47 55 S 66 0W
Puerto Escondido, *Mexico* **163 D5** 15 50N 97 3W
Puerto Gaitán, *Colombia* **168 C3** 4 19N 72 4W
Puerto Galera, *Phil.* **80 E3** 13 30N 120 57 E
Puerto Guaraní, *Paraguay* **173 E6** 21 18 S 57 55W
Puerto Heath, *Bolivia* **172 C4** 12 34 S 68 39W
Puerto Huitoto, *Colombia* **168 C3** 0 18N 74 3W
Puerto Inca, *Peru* **172 B3** 9 22 S 74 54W
Puerto Inírida, *Colombia* **168 C4** 3 53N 67 52W
Puerto Juárez, *Mexico* **163 C7** 21 11N 86 49W
Puerto La Cruz, *Venezuela* **169 A5** 10 13N 64 38W
Puerto Leguízamo, *Colombia* **168 D3** 0 12 S 74 46W
Puerto Limón, *Colombia* **168 C3** 3 23N 73 30W
Puerto Lobos, *Argentina* **176 B3** 42 0 S 65 3W
Puerto López, *Colombia* **168 C3** 4 5N 72 58W
Puerto Lumbreras, *Spain* **41 H3** 37 34N 1 48W
Puerto Madryn, *Argentina* **176 B3** 42 48 S 65 4W
Puerto Maldonado, *Peru* **172 C4** 12 30 S 69 10W
Puerto Manatí, *Cuba* **164 B4** 21 22N 76 50W
Puerto Mariti, *Colombia* **168 D4** 1 10 S 69 59W
Puerto Mercedes, *Colombia* **168 C3** 1 11N 72 53W
Puerto Mexico = Coatzacoalcos, *Mexico* **163 D6** 18 7N 94 25W
Puerto Miraña, *Colombia* **168 D3** 1 20 S 70 19W
Puerto Montt, *Chile* **176 B2** 41 28 S 73 0W
Puerto Morazán, *Nic.* **164 D2** 12 51N 87 11W
Puerto Morelos, *Mexico* **163 C7** 20 49N 86 52W
Puerto Mutis, *Colombia* **168 B2** 6 14N 77 25W
Puerto Nariño, *Colombia* **168 C4** 4 56N 67 48W
Puerto Natales, *Chile* **176 D2** 51 45 S 72 15W
Puerto Nuevo, *Colombia* **168 B4** 5 53N 69 56W
Puerto Nutrias, *Venezuela* **168 B4** 8 5N 69 18W
Puerto Ordaz, *Venezuela* **169 B5** 8 16N 62 44W
Puerto Padre, *Cuba* **164 B4** 21 13N 76 35W
Puerto Páez, *Venezuela* **168 B4** 6 13N 67 28W
Puerto Peñasco, *Mexico* **162 A2** 31 20N 113 33W
Puerto Pinasco, *Paraguay* **174 A4** 22 36 S 57 50W
Puerto Pirámides, *Argentina* **176 B4** 42 35 S 64 20W
Puerto Piritu, *Venezuela* **169 A4** 10 4N 65 3W
Puerto Plata, *Dom. Rep.* **165 C5** 19 48N 70 45W
Puerto Pollensa = Port de Pollença, *Spain* **38 B4** 39 54N 3 4 E
Puerto Portillo, *Peru* **172 B3** 9 45 S 72 42W
Puerto Princesa, *Phil.* **81 G2** 9 46N 118 45 E
Puerto Quellón, *Chile* **176 B2** 43 7 S 73 37W
Puerto Quepos, *Costa Rica* **164 E3** 9 29N 84 6W
Puerto Real, *Spain* **43 J4** 36 33N 6 12W
Puerto Rico, *Bolivia* **172 C4** 11 5 S 67 38W
Puerto Rico, *Canary Is.* **9 e1** 27 47N 15 42W
Puerto Rico ⊠, *W. Indies* **165 d** 18 15N 66 45W
Puerto Rico Trench, *Atl. Oc.* **165 C6** 19 50N 66 0W
Puerto Rondón, *Colombia* **168 B3** 6 17N 71 6W
Puerto Saavedra, *Chile* **176 A2** 38 47 S 73 24W
Puerto Sastre, *Paraguay* **174 A4** 22 2 S 57 55W
Puerto Serrano, *Spain* **43 J5** 36 56N 5 33W
Puerto Siles, *Bolivia* **173 C4** 12 48 S 65 5W
Puerto Suárez, *Bolivia* **173 D6** 18 58 S 57 52W
Puerto Tejada, *Colombia* **168 C2** 3 14N 76 24W
Puerto Umbría, *Colombia* **168 C2** 0 52N 76 33W
Puerto Vallarta, *Mexico* **162 C3** 20 36N 105 15W
Puerto Varas, *Chile* **176 B2** 41 19 S 72 59W
Puerto Velasco Ibarra, *Ecuador* **172 a** 1 17 S 90 29W
Puerto Villamil, *Ecuador* **172 a** 0 56 S 91 1W
Puerto Villazón, *Bolivia* **173 C5** 13 32 S 61 57W
Puerto Wilches, *Colombia* **168 B3** 7 21N 73 54W
Puertollano, *Spain* **43 G6** 38 43N 4 7W
Puesto Cunambo, *Peru* **168 D2** 2 10 S 76 0W
Pueyrredón, L., *Argentina* **176 C2** 47 20 S 72 0W
Púez Odle ⌂, *Italy* **45 B8** 46 37N 11 48 E
Puffin I., *Ireland* **23 E1** 51 50N 10 24W
Pugachev, *Russia* **60 D9** 52 0N 48 49 E
Pugal, *India* **92 E5** 28 30N 72 48 E
Puge, *China* **76 D4** 27 20N 102 31 E
Puge, *Tanzania* **118 C3** 4 45 S 33 11 E
Puget Sound, *U.S.A.* **158 C2** 47 50N 122 30W
Puget-Théniers, *France* **29 E10** 43 58N 6 53 E
Púglia □, *Italy* **47 A9** 41 15N 16 15 E
Pugŏdong, *N. Korea* **75 C16** 42 5N 130 0 E
Pugu, *Tanzania* **118 D4** 6 55 S 39 4 E
Pūgūnzī, *Iran* **97 E8** 25 49N 59 10 E
Puha, *N.Z.* **130 E6** 38 30 S 177 50 E
Pui, *Romania* **52 E8** 45 30N 23 4 E
Puica, *Peru* **172 C3** 15 0 S 72 33W
Puieşti, *Romania* **53 D12** 46 25N 27 33 E
Puig Major, *Spain* **38 B3** 39 48N 2 47 E
Puigcerdà, *Spain* **40 C6** 42 24N 1 50 E
Puigmal, *Spain* **40 C7** 42 23N 2 7 E
Puigpunyent, *Spain* **38 B3** 39 38N 2 32 E
Puijiang, *China* **76 B4** 30 14N 103 30 E
Puisaye, Collines de la, *France* **27 E10** 47 37N 3 20 E
Puiseaux, *France* **27 D9** 48 11N 2 30 E
Pujehun, *S. Leone* **112 D2** 7 23N 11 45W
Pujiang, *China* **77 C12** 29 29N 119 54 E
Pujilí, *Ecuador* **168 D2** 0 57 S 78 41W
Pujols, *France* **28 D3** 44 48N 0 2W
Pujon-chŏsuji, *N. Korea* **75 D14** 40 35N 127 35 E
Pukaki, L., *N.Z.* **131 E5** 44 4 S 170 1 E
Pukalani, *U.S.A.* **145 C5** 20 51N 156 20W
Pukapuka, *Cook Is.* **135 J11** 10 53 S 165 49W
Pukaskwa △, *Canada* **140 C2** 48 20N 86 0W
Pukatawagan, *Canada* **143 B8** 55 45N 101 20W
Pukchin, *N. Korea* **75 D13** 40 12N 125 45 E
Pukch'ŏng, *N. Korea* **75 D15** 40 14N 128 10 E
Pukë, *Albania* **50 D3** 42 2N 19 53 E
Pukearuhe, *N.Z.* **130 E3** 38 55 S 174 31 E
Pukekohe, *N.Z.* **130 D3** 37 12 S 174 55 E
Puketeraki Ra., *N.Z.* **131 C7** 42 58 S 172 13 E
Puketoi Ra., *N.Z.* **130 G5** 40 30 S 176 5 E
Pukeuri, *N.Z.* **131 F6** 45 4 S 171 2 E
Pukhrayan, *India* **93 F8** 26 14N 79 51 E
Pukoo, *U.S.A.* **145 B5** 21 4N 156 48W
Pukou, *China* **77 A12** 32 7N 118 38 E
Pula, *Croatia* **45 D10** 44 54N 13 57 E
Pula, *Italy* **46 C1** 39 1N 9 0 E
Pulacayo, *Bolivia* **172 E4** 20 25 S 66 41W
Pulai, *Malaysia* **87 d** 1 20N 103 31 E
Pulandian, *China* **75 E11** 39 25N 121 58 E
Pularumpi, *Australia* **124 B5** 11 24 S 130 26 E
Pulaski, *N.Y., U.S.A.* **151 C8** 43 34N 76 8W
Pulaski, *Tenn., U.S.A.* **149 H2** 35 12N 87 2W
Pulaski, *Va., U.S.A.* **148 G5** 37 3N 80 47W
Pulau →, *Indonesia* **83 C5** 5 50 S 138 15 E
Pulau Miangas, *Indonesia* **81 J6** 5 35N 126 34 E
Puławy, *Poland* **55 G8** 51 23N 21 59 E
Pulga, *U.S.A.* **160 F5** 39 48N 121 29W
Pulgaon, *India* **94 D4** 20 44N 78 21 E
Pulicat, *India* **95 H5** 13 25N 80 19 E
Pulicat L., *India* **95 H5** 13 40N 80 15 E
Pulivendla, *India* **95 G4** 14 25N 78 14 E
Puliyangudi, *India* **95 K3** 9 11N 77 24 E
Pullman, *U.S.A.* **158 C5** 46 44N 117 10W
Pulog, Mt., *Phil.* **80 C3** 16 40N 120 50 E
Púlpito do Sul, *Angola* **115 F2** 15 46 S 12 0 E
Pułtusk, *Poland* **55 F8** 52 43N 21 6 E
Pülümür, *Turkey* **101 C8** 39 30N 39 51 E
Pumlumon Fawr, *U.K.* **21 E4** 52 28N 3 46W
Puna, *Bolivia* **173 D4** 19 45 S 65 28W
Puná, I., *Ecuador* **168 D1** 2 55 S 80 5W
Punaauia, *Tahiti* **133 S16** 17 37 S 149 34W
Punakha, *Bhutan* **90 B2** 27 42N 89 52 E
Punalur, *India* **95 K3** 9 0N 76 56 E
Punaluu, *U.S.A.* **145 J14** 21 35N 157 53W
Punasar, *India* **92 F5** 27 6N 73 6 E
Punata, *Bolivia* **173 D4** 17 32 S 65 50W
Punch, *India* **93 C6** 33 48N 74 4 E
Punch →, *Pakistan* **92 C5** 33 12N 73 40 E
Punda Maria, *S. Africa* **117 C5** 22 40 S 31 5 E
Pune, *India* **94 E1** 18 29N 73 57 E
Pungo Andongo, *Angola* **115 D3** 9 44 S 15 35 E
P'ungsan, *N. Korea* **75 D15** 40 50N 128 9 E
Pungue, Ponte de, *Mozam.* **119 F3** 19 0 S 34 0 E
Puning, *China* **77 F11** 23 20N 116 12 E
Punjab □, *India* **92 D7** 31 0N 76 0 E
Punjab □, *Pakistan* **91 C4** 32 0N 72 30 E
Puno, *Peru* **172 D3** 15 55 S 70 3W
Punpun →, *India* **93 G11** 25 31N 85 18 E
Punta, Cerro de, *Puerto Rico* **165 d** 18 10N 66 37W
Punta Alta, *Argentina* **176 A4** 38 53 S 62 4W
Punta Arenas, *Chile* **176 D2** 53 10 S 71 0W
Punta Cardón, *Venezuela* **168 A3** 11 38N 70 14W
Punta Coles, *Peru* **172 D3** 17 43 S 71 23W
Punta de Bombón, *Peru* **172 D3** 17 10 S 71 48W
Punta de Díaz, *Chile* **174 B1** 28 0 S 70 45W
Punta del Hidalgo, *Canary Is.* **9 e1** 28 33N 16 19W
Punta Delgado, *Argentina* **176 B4** 42 43 S 63 38W
Punta Gorda, *Belize* **163 D7** 16 10N 88 45W
Punta Gorda, *U.S.A.* **153 J7** 26 56N 82 3W
Punta Prieta, *Mexico* **162 B2** 28 58N 114 17W
Punta Prima, *Spain* **38 B5** 39 48N 4 16 E
Punta Umbria, *Spain* **43 H4** 37 10N 6 56W
Puntarenas, *Costa Rica* **164 E3** 10 0N 84 50W
Punto Fijo, *Venezuela* **168 A3** 11 50N 70 13W
Punxsatawney, *U.S.A.* **150 F6** 40 57N 78 59W
Punyu = Guangzhou, *China* **77 F9** 23 5N 113 10 E
Puolo Pt., *U.S.A.* **145 B2** 21 54N 159 36W
Pupuan, *Indonesia* **79 J18** 8 19 S 115 0 E
Puqi, *China* **77 C9** 29 40N 113 50 E
Puquio, *Peru* **172 C3** 14 45 S 74 10W
Pur →, *Russia* **66 C8** 67 31N 77 55 E
Puracé △, *Colombia* **168 C2** 2 10N 76 21W
Puracé, Vol., *Colombia* **168 C2** 2 21N 76 23W
Puračić, *Bos.-H.* **52 F3** 44 33N 18 28 E
Puralia = Puruliya, *India* **93 H12** 23 17N 86 24 E
Puranpur, *India* **93 E9** 28 31N 80 9 E
Purari →, *Papua N. G.* **132 D3** 7 49 S 145 0 E
Purbeck, Isle of, *U.K.* **21 G5** 50 39N 1 59W
Purcell, *U.S.A.* **155 H6** 35 1N 97 22W
Purcell Mts., *Canada* **142 D5** 49 55N 116 15W
Puri, *India* **94 E7** 19 50N 85 58 E
Purificación, *Colombia* **168 C3** 3 51N 74 55W
Purmerend, *Neths.* **24 B4** 52 32N 4 58 E
Purna →, *India* **94 E3** 19 6N 77 2 E
Purnia, *India* **93 G12** 25 45N 87 31 E
Purnululu Nat. Park △, *Australia* **124 C4** 17 20 S 128 20 E
Pursat = Pouthisat, *Cambodia* **86 F4** 12 34N 103 50 E
Purukcahu, *Indonesia* **85 C4** 0 35 S 114 35 E
Puruliya, *India* **93 H12** 23 17N 86 24 E
Purus →, *Brazil* **169 D5** 3 42 S 61 28W
Purutu I., *Papua N. G.* **132 E2** 8 24 S 143 27 E
Puruvesi, *Finland* **58 B5** 61 50N 29 30 E
Purvis, *U.S.A.* **155 K10** 31 9N 89 25W
Pŭrvomay, *Bulgaria* **51 D9** 42 8N 25 17 E
Purwa, *India* **93 F9** 26 28N 80 47 E
Purwakarta, *Indonesia* **85 D3** 6 35 S 107 29 E
Purwo, Tanjung, *Indonesia* **79 K18** 8 44 S 114 21 E
Purwodadi, *Jawa, Indonesia* **85 D4** 7 7 S 110 55 E
Purwodadi, *Jawa, Indonesia* **85 D3** 7 51 S 110 0 E
Purwokerto, *Indonesia* **85 D3** 7 25 S 109 14 E
Purworejo, *Indonesia* **85 D4** 7 43 S 110 2 E
Puryŏng, *N. Korea* **75 C15** 42 5N 129 43 E
Pus →, *India* **94 E3** 19 55N 77 55 E
Pusa, *India* **93 G11** 25 59N 85 41 E
Pusad, *India* **94 E3** 19 56N 77 36 E
Pusan, *S. Korea* **75 G15** 35 5N 129 0 E
Pushkin, *Russia* **58 C6** 59 45N 30 25 E
Pushkino, *Moskva, Russia* **58 D9** 56 2N 37 49 E
Pushkino, *Saratov, Russia* **60 E8** 51 16N 47 0 E
Püspökladány, *Hungary* **52 C6** 47 19N 21 6 E
Pustoshka, *Russia* **58 D5** 56 20N 29 30 E
Puszczykowo, *Poland* **55 F3** 52 18N 16 49 E
Putahow L., *Canada* **143 B8** 59 54N 100 40W
Putao, *Burma* **90 B6** 27 28N 97 30 E
Putaruru, *N.Z.* **130 E4** 38 2 S 175 50 E
Putbus, *Germany* **30 A9** 54 22N 13 28 E
Putian, *China* **77 E12** 25 23N 119 0 E
Putignano, *Italy* **47 B10** 40 51N 17 7 E
Putina, *Peru* **172 C4** 14 55 S 69 55W
Puting, Tanjung, *Indonesia* **85 C4** 3 31 S 111 46 E
Putlitz, *Germany* **30 B8** 53 15N 12 2 E
Putna, *Romania* **53 C10** 47 50N 25 33 E
Putna →, *Romania* **53 E12** 45 42N 27 26 E
Putnam, *U.S.A.* **151 E13** 41 55N 71 55W
Putney, *U.S.A.* **152 D5** 31 29N 84 8W
Putnok, *Hungary* **52 B5** 48 18N 20 26 E
Putorana, Gory, *Russia* **67 C10** 69 0N 95 0 E
Putorino, *N.Z.* **130 F5** 39 4 S 176 58 E
Putrajaya, *Malaysia* **87 L3** 2 55N 101 40 E
Putre, *Chile* **172 D4** 18 12 S 69 35W
Puttalam, *Sri Lanka* **95 K5** 8 1N 79 55 E
Puttalam Lagoon, *Sri Lanka* **95 K4** 8 15N 79 45 E
Puttgarden, *Germany* **30 A7** 54 30N 11 10 E
Püttlingen, *Germany* **31 F2** 49 17N 6 53 E
Puttur, *Andhra Pradesh, India* **95 H4** 13 27N 79 33 E
Puttur, *Karnataka, India* **95 H2** 12 46N 75 12 E
Putty, *Australia* **129 B9** 32 57 S 150 42 E
Putumayo →, *S. Amer.* **168 D4** 3 7 S 67 58W
Putuo, *China* **77 C14** 29 56N 122 20 E
Putussibau, *Indonesia* **85 B4** 0 50N 112 56 E
Pututahi, *N.Z.* **130 E6** 38 39 S 177 53 E
Putyla, *Ukraine* **53 B10** 48 0N 25 5 E
Puu Kaaumakua, *U.S.A.* **145 K14** 21 30N 157 54W
Puu Keahiakahoe, *U.S.A.* **145 K14** 21 23N 157 49W
Puu o Keokeo, *U.S.A.* **145 D6** 19 13N 155 44W
Puuanahulu, *U.S.A.* **145 D6** 19 49N 155 51W
Pu'uhonua o Hōnaunau △, *U.S.A.* **145 D6** 19 25N 155 55W
Pu'ukoholā Heiau ⌂, *U.S.A.* **145 C6** 20 1N 155 51W
Puukolii, *U.S.A.* **145 C5** 20 56N 156 41W
Puunene, *U.S.A.* **145 C5** 20 53N 156 23W
Puuwai, *U.S.A.* **145 B1** 21 54N 160 12W
Puvirnituq, *Canada* **139 B12** 60 2N 77 10W
Puy-de-Dôme, *France* **28 C6** 45 46N 2 57 E
Puy-de-Dôme □, *France* **28 C7** 45 40N 3 5 E
Puy-l'Évêque, *France* **28 D5** 44 31N 1 9 E
Puyallup, *U.S.A.* **160 C4** 47 12N 122 18W
Puyang, *China* **74 G8** 35 40N 115 1 E
Puyehue, *Chile* **176 B2** 40 40 S 72 37W
Puyehue △, *Chile* **176 B2** 40 27 S 72 6W
Puylaurens, *France* **28 E6** 43 35N 2 0 E
Puyo, *Ecuador* **168 D2** 1 28 S 77 59W
Puysegur Pt., *N.Z.* **131 G1** 46 9 S 166 37 E
Pūzeh Rīg, *Iran* **97 E8** 27 20N 58 40 E
Puzhaykove, *Ukraine* **53 B14** 48 7N 29 50 E
Pwani □, *Tanzania* **118 D4** 7 0 S 39 0 E
Pweto, *Dem. Rep. of the Congo* **119 D2** 8 25 S 28 51 E
Pwinbyu, *Burma* **90 E5** 20 23N 94 40 E
Pwllheli, *U.K.* **20 E3** 52 53N 4 25W
Pya-ozero, *Russia* **56 A5** 66 5N 30 58 E
Pyana →, *Russia* **60 C8** 55 43N 46 1 E
Pyandzh = Dusti, *Tajikistan* **65 E4** 37 20N 68 40 E
Pyandzh, *Tajikistan* **65 E4** 37 14N 69 6 E
Pyandzh →, *Asia* **65 E4** 37 6N 68 20 E
Pyapon, *Burma* **90 G5** 16 20N 95 40 E
Pyasina →, *Russia* **67 B9** 73 30N 87 0 E
Pyatigorsk, *Russia* **61 H6** 44 2N 43 6 E
Pyatykhatky, *Ukraine* **59 H7** 48 28N 33 38 E
Pyawbwe, *Burma* **90 E6** 20 35N 96 4 E
Pyaye, *Burma* **90 F5** 19 12N 95 10 E
Pydna, *Greece* **50 F6** 40 20N 22 34 E
Pyè = Prome, *Burma* **90 F5** 18 49N 95 13 E
Pyetrikaw, *Belarus* **59 F5** 52 11N 28 29 E
Pyhäjoki, *Finland* **14 D21** 64 28N 24 14 E
Pyinbauk, *Burma* **90 F5** 19 10N 95 12 E
Pyingaing, *Burma* **90 D5** 23 9N 94 50 E
Pyinkayaing, *Burma* **90 H5** 15 58N 94 24 E
Pyinmana, *Burma* **90 F6** 19 45N 96 12 E
Pyinyaung, *Burma* **90 E6** 20 49N 96 25 E
Pyla, C., *Cyprus* **39 F9** 34 56N 33 51 E
Pymatuning Reservoir, *U.S.A.* **150 E4** 41 30N 80 28W
Pyŏktong, *N. Korea* **75 D13** 40 50N 125 50 E
Pyŏnggang, *N. Korea* **75 E14** 38 24N 127 17 E
P'yŏngt'aek, *S. Korea* **75 F14** 37 1N 127 4 E
P'yŏngyang, *N. Korea* **75 E13** 39 0N 125 30 E
Pyote, *U.S.A.* **155 K3** 31 32N 103 8W
Pyramid L., *U.S.A.* **158 G4** 40 1N 119 35W
Pyramid Pk., *U.S.A.* **161 J10** 36 25N 116 37W
Pyramid Pt., *Ascension I.* **9 g** 7 55 S 14 24W
Pyramids, *Egypt* **106 J7** 29 58N 31 9 E
Pyrénées, *Europe* **28 F4** 42 45N 0 18 E
Pyrénées △, *France* **28 F3** 42 52N 0 10W
Pyrénées-Atlantiques □, *France* **28 E3** 43 10N 0 50W
Pyrénées-Orientales □, *France* **28 F6** 42 35N 2 26 E
Pyryatyn, *Ukraine* **59 G7** 50 15N 32 25 E
Pyrzyce, *Poland* **55 E1** 53 10N 14 55 E
Pyskowice, *Poland* **55 H5** 50 24N 18 38 E
Pytalovo, *Russia* **58 D4** 57 5N 27 55 E
Pyttegga, *Norway* **18 B4** 62 13N 7 42 E
Pyu, *Burma* **90 F6** 18 30N 96 28 E
Pyzdry, *Poland* **55 F4** 52 11N 17 42 E

Q

Qaanaaq, *Greenland* **10 B4** 77 40N 69 0W
Qabirri →, *Azerbaijan* **61 K8** 41 3N 46 17 E
Qabr Hūd, *Yemen* **99 C5** 16 9N 49 34 E
Qachasnek, *S. Africa* **117 E4** 30 6 S 28 42 E
Qādib, *Yemen* **99 D6** 12 37N 53 57 E
Qa'el Jafr, *Jordan* **103 E5** 30 20N 36 25 E
Qa'emābād, *Iran* **97 D9** 31 44N 60 2 E
Qā'emshahr, *Iran* **97 B7** 36 30N 52 53 E
Qagan Nur, *China* **74 C8** 43 30N 114 55 E
Qahar Youyi Zhongqi, *China* **74 D7** 41 12N 112 40 E
Qahremānshahr = Bākhtarān, *Iran* **101 E12** 34 23N 47 0 E
Qaidam Pendi, *China* **68 C4** 37 0N 95 0 E
Qajarīyeh, *Iran* **97 D6** 31 1N 48 22 E
Qala, *Malta* **38 E7** 36 2N 14 19 E
Qala, Ras il, *Malta* **38 E7** 36 2N 14 20 E
Qala-i-Jadid = Spīn Būldak, *Afghan.* **91 C2** 31 1N 66 25 E
Qala Point = Qala, Ras il, *Malta* **38 E7** 36 2N 14 20 E
Qala Viala, *Pakistan* **92 D2** 30 49N 67 17 E
Qala Yangi, *Afghan.* **92 B2** 34 20N 66 30 E
Qalācheh, *Afghan.* **91 B2** 35 30N 67 43 E
Qalaikhum = Kalaikhum, *Tajikistan* **65 D5** 38 28N 70 46 E
Qalansīyah, *Yemen* **99 D6** 12 41N 53 29 E
Qal'at al Akhḑar, *Si. Arabia* **96 E3** 28 0N 37 10 E
Qal'at Bīshah, *Si. Arabia* **98 C3** 20 0N 42 36 E
Qal'at Dīzah, *Iraq* **101 D11** 36 11N 45 7 E
Qalāt-i-Ghilzai, *Afghan.* **91 B2** 32 15N 66 58 E
Qal'at Şāliḩ, *Iraq* **96 D5** 31 31N 47 16 E
Qal'at Sukkar, *Iraq* **101 G12** 31 51N 46 5 E
Qal'eh-ye Bost, *Afghan.* **91 C2** 31 30N 64 21 E
Qal'eh-ye Now, *Afghan.* **91 B1** 35 0N 63 5 E
Qal'eh-ye Panjeh, *Afghan.* **65 E6** 37 0N 72 35 E
Qal'eh-ye Sarkari, *Afghan.* **91 B2** 35 54N 67 17 E
Qal'eh-ye Valī, *Afghan.* **91 B1** 35 46N 63 45 E
Qalyûb, *Egypt* **106 H7** 30 12N 31 11 E
Qamani'tuaq = Baker Lake, *Canada* **138 B10** 64 20N 96 3W
Qamar, Ghubbat al, *Yemen* **99 C6** 16 20N 52 30 E
Qamar, Jabal al, *Oman* **99 C6** 16 48N 53 15 E
Qamashi, *Uzbekistan* **65 D3** 38 49N 66 28 E
Qamdo, *China* **76 B1** 31 15N 97 6 E
Qamea, *Fiji* **133 A3** 16 45 S 179 45W
Qammieh Point, *Malta* **38 F7** 35 58N 14 19 E
Qamruddin Karez, *Pakistan* **91 C3** 31 45N 68 20 E
Qandahār, *Afghan.* **91 C2** 31 32N 65 43 E
Qandahār □, *Afghan.* **91 C2** 31 0N 65 0 E
Qanshenggel, *Kazakhstan* **65 A7** 44 19N 75 33 E
Qapān, *Iran* **97 B7** 37 40N 55 47 E
Qapshaghay, *Kazakhstan* **65 B8** 43 51N 77 14 E
Qapshaghay Bögeni, *Kazakhstan* **65 B8** 43 45N 77 50 E
Qaqortoq, *Greenland* **10 E6** 60 43N 46 0W
Qâra, *Egypt* **106 B2** 29 38N 26 30 E
Qarā', Jabal al, *Oman* **99 C6** 17 15N 54 15 E
Qara Qash →, *China* **93 B8** 35 0N 78 30 E
Qarabulaq, *Kazakhstan* **65 A9** 44 54N 78 30 E
Qarabulaq, *Kazakhstan* **65 B4** 42 31N 69 46 E
Qarabutaq, *Kazakhstan* **64 G8** 49 59N 60 14 E
Qaraçala, *Azerbaijan* **61 L9** 39 45N 48 53 E
Qaradarya = Zeravshan →, *Asia* **65 D1** 39 22N 63 45 E
Qaradarya →, *Uzbekistan* **65 C2** 39 0N 63 35 E
Qaraghandy, *Kazakhstan* **66 E8** 49 50N 73 10 E
Qaraghayly, *Kazakhstan* **66 E8** 49 26N 76 0 E
Qārah, *Si. Arabia* **96 D4** 29 55N 40 3 E
Qarak, *China* **65 D8** 38 25N 77 0 E
Qarataū, *Kazakhstan* **65 B5** 43 10N 70 28 E
Qarataū, *Kazakhstan* **65 B4** 43 30N 69 30 E
Qaraturyq, *Kazakhstan* **65 B8** 43 35N 77 50 E
Qarāvol, *Afghan.* **65 E4** 37 14N 68 46 E
Qardho = Gardo, *Somali Rep.* **120 C3** 9 30N 49 6 E
Qardud, *Sudan* **107 E2** 10 20N 29 56 E
Qareh →, *Iran* **101 C12** 39 25N 47 22 E
Qareh Tekān, *Iran* **97 B6** 36 38N 49 29 E
Qarqan He →, *China* **68 C3** 39 30N 88 30 E
Qarqaraly, *Kazakhstan* **66 E8** 49 26N 75 30 E
Qarqin, *Afghan.* **65 E3** 37 24N 66 4 E
Qarrasa, *Sudan* **107 E3** 14 38N 32 5 E
Qarshi, *Uzbekistan* **65 D2** 38 53N 65 48 E
Qartabā, *Lebanon* **103 A4** 34 4N 35 50 E
Qaryat al Gharab, *Iraq* **96 D5** 31 27N 44 48 E
Qaryat al 'Ulyā, *Si. Arabia* **96 E5** 27 33N 47 42 E
Qasigiannguit, *Greenland* **10 D5** 68 50N 51 18W
Qaskeleng, *Kazakhstan* **65 B8** 43 20N 76 35 E
Qasr 'Amra, *Jordan* **96 D3** 31 48N 36 35 E
Qaşr Bū Hadi, *Libya* **108 B3** 31 1N 16 45 E
Qaşr-e Qand, *Iran* **97 E9** 26 15N 60 45 E
Qasr Farâfra, *Egypt* **106 B2** 27 0N 28 1 E
Qa'ţabah, *Yemen* **98 D4** 13 51N 44 42 E
Qatanā, *Syria* **103 B5** 33 26N 36 4 E
Qaţānan, Ra's, *Yemen* **99 D6** 12 21N 53 33 E
Qatar ■, *Asia* **97 E6** 25 30N 51 15 E
Qatlīsh, *Iran* **97 B8** 37 50N 57 19 E
Qattâra, *Egypt* **106 A2** 30 12N 27 3 E
Qattâra, Munkhafed el, *Egypt* **106 B2** 29 30N 27 30 E
Qattâra Depression = Qattâra, Munkhafed el, *Egypt* **106 B2** 29 30N 27 30 E
Qawām al Ḩamzah = Al Ḩamzah, *Iraq* **96 D5** 31 43N 44 58 E
Qawra Point, *Malta* **38 F7** 35 58N 14 26 E
Qāyen, *Iran* **97 C8** 33 40N 59 10 E
Qazaqstan = Kazakhstan ■, *Asia* **66 E7** 50 0N 70 0 E
Qazimämmäd, *Azerbaijan* **61 K9** 40 3N 49 0 E
Qazvin, *Iran* **97 B6** 36 15N 50 0 E
Qazvin □, *Iran* **97 B6** 36 20N 50 0 E
Qazyghurt, *Kazakhstan* **65 C4** 41 45N 69 23 E
Qeisari = Caesarea, *Israel* **103 C3** 32 30N 34 53 E
Qeissan, *Sudan* **107 E3** 11 4N 34 40 E
Qena, *Egypt* **106 B3** 26 10N 32 43 E
Qena, W. →, *Egypt* **106 B3** 26 12N 32 44 E
Qeqertarsuaq, *Greenland* **10 D5** 69 45N 53 30W
Qeqertarsuaq, *Greenland* **10 D5** 69 15N 53 38W
Qeqertarsuatsiaat, *Greenland* **10 E5** 63 5N 50 45W
Qeshlāq, *Iran* **101 E12** 34 55N 46 28 E
Qeshm, *Iran* **97 E8** 26 55N 56 10 E
Qeys, *Iran* **97 E7** 26 32N 53 58 E
Qezel Owzen →, *Iran* **97 B6** 36 45N 49 22 E
Qezi'ot, *Israel* **103 E3** 30 52N 34 26 E
Qi Xian, *China* **74 G8** 34 40N 114 48 E
Qian Gorlos, *China* **75 B13** 45 5N 124 42 E
Qian Hai, *China* **69 F10** 22 32N 113 54 E
Qian Xian, *China* **74 G5** 34 31N 108 15 E
Qiancheng, *China* **76 D7** 27 12N 109 50 E
Qianjiang, *Guangxi Zhuangzu, China* **76 F7** 23 38N 108 58 E
Qianjiang, *Hubei, China* **77 B9** 30 24N 112 55 E
Qianjiang, *Sichuan, China* **76 C7** 29 33N 108 47 E
Qianshan, *Anhui, China* **77 B11** 30 37N 116 35 E
Qianshan, *Guangdong, China* **69 G10** 22 15N 113 31 E
Qianwei, *China* **76 C4** 29 13N 103 56 E
Qianxi, *China* **76 D6** 27 3N 106 3 E
Qianyang, *Hunan, China* **77 D8** 27 18N 110 10 E
Qianyang, *Shaanxi, China* **74 G4** 34 40N 107 8 E
Qianyang, *Zhejiang, China* **77 B12** 30 11N 119 25 E
Qi'ao, *China* **69 G10** 22 25N 113 39 E
Qi'ao Dao, *China* **69 G10** 22 25N 113 38 E
Qiaojia, *China* **76 D4** 26 56N 102 58 E
Qichun, *China* **77 B10** 30 18N 115 25 E
Qidong, *Hunan, China* **77 D9** 26 49N 112 7 E
Qidong, *Jiangsu, China* **77 B13** 31 48N 121 38 E
Qijiang, *China* **76 C6** 28 57N 106 35 E
Qikiqtarjuaq, *Canada* **139 B13** 67 33N 63 0W
Qila Safed, *Pakistan* **91 C1** 29 0N 61 30 E
Qila Saifullāh, *Pakistan* **91 C3** 30 45N 68 17 E
Qilian Shan, *China* **68 C4** 38 30N 96 0 E
Qimen, *China* **77 C11** 29 50N 117 42 E
Qin He →, *China* **74 G7** 35 1N 113 22 E
Qin Jiang →, *Guangxi Zhuangzu, China* **76 F7** 21 53N 108 35 E
Qin Jiang →, *Jiangxi, China* **77 D10** 26 15N 115 55 E
Qin Ling = Qinling Shandi, *China* **74 H5** 33 50N 108 10 E
Qināb, W. →, *Yemen* **99 C5** 17 55N 49 59 E
Qin'an, *China* **74 G3** 34 48N 105 40 E
Qing Xian, *China* **74 E9** 38 35N 116 45 E
Qingcheng, *China* **75 F9** 37 15N 117 40 E
Qingdao, *China* **75 F11** 36 5N 120 20 E
Qingfeng, *China* **74 G8** 35 52N 115 8 E
Qinghai □, *China* **68 C4** 36 0N 98 0 E
Qinghai Hu, *China* **68 C5** 36 40N 100 10 E
Qinghecheng, *China* **75 D13** 41 28N 124 15 E
Qinghemen, *China* **75 D11** 41 48N 121 25 E
Qingjian, *China* **74 F6** 37 8N 110 8 E
Qingjiang = Huaiyin, *China* **75 H10** 33 30N 119 2 E
Qingliu, *China* **77 D11** 26 11N 116 48 E
Qinglong, *China* **76 E5** 25 49N 105 12 E
Qingping, *China* **76 D6** 26 39N 107 47 E
Qingpu, *China* **77 B13** 31 10N 121 6 E
Qingshui, *China* **74 G4** 34 48N 106 8 E
Qingshuihe, *China* **74 E6** 39 55N 111 35 E
Qingtian, *China* **77 C13** 28 12N 120 15 E

Qingtongxia Shuiku, China 74 F3 37 50N 105 58 E
Qingxi, China 76 D7 27 8N 108 43 E
Qingxu, China 74 F7 37 34N 112 22 E
Qingyang, Anhui, China 77 B11 30 38N 117 50 E
Qingyang, Gansu, China 74 F4 36 2N 107 55 E
Qingyi Jiang →, China 76 C4 29 32N 103 44 E
Qingyuan, Guangdong, China 77 F9 23 40N 112 59 E
Qingyuan, Liaoning, China 75 C13 42 10N 124 55 E
Qingyuan, Zhejiang, China 77 D12 27 36N 119 3 E
Qingyun, China 75 F9 37 45N 117 20 E
Qingzhen, China 76 D6 26 31N 106 25 E
Qinhuangdao, China 75 E10 39 56N 119 30 E
Qinling Shandi, China 74 H5 33 50N 108 10 E
Qinshui, China 74 G7 35 40N 112 8 E
Qinyang = Jiyuan, China 74 G7 35 7N 112 57 E
Qinyuan, China 74 F7 36 29N 112 20 E
Qinzhou, China 76 G7 21 58N 108 38 E
Qionghai, China 86 C8 19 15N 110 26 E
Qionglai, China 76 B4 30 25N 103 31 E
Qionglai Shan, China 76 B4 31 0N 102 30 E
Qiongzhou Haixia, China 86 B8 20 10N 110 15 E
Qiqihar, China 67 E13 47 26N 124 0 E
Qiraîya, W. →, Egypt 103 E3 30 27N 34 0 E
Qiryat Ata, Israel 103 C4 32 47N 35 6 E
Qiryat Gat, Israel 103 D3 31 32N 34 46 E
Qiryat Mal'akhi, Israel 103 D3 31 44N 34 44 E
Qiryat Shemona, Israel 103 B4 33 13N 35 35 E
Qiryat Yam, Israel 103 C4 32 51N 35 4 E
Qirzah, W. →, Libya 108 B2 30 56N 14 31 E
Qishan, China 74 G4 34 25N 107 38 E
Qishn, Yemen 99 D5 15 26N 51 40 E
Qitai, China 68 B3 44 2N 89 35 E
Qitbīt, W. →, Oman 99 C6 19 15N 54 23 E
Qiubei, China 76 E5 24 2N 104 12 E
Qixia, China 75 F11 37 17N 120 52 E
Qiyang, China 77 D8 26 35N 111 50 E
Qızılağac Körfäzi, Azerbaijan 97 B6 39 9N 49 0 E
Qoghaly, Kazakhstan 65 A9 44 29N 78 39 E
Qojūr, Iran 96 B5 36 12N 47 55 E
Qom, Iran 97 C6 34 40N 51 0 E
Qom □, Iran 97 C6 34 40N 51 0 E
Qomolangma Feng = Everest, Mt., Nepal 93 E12 28 5N 86 58 E
Qomsheh, Iran 97 D6 32 0N 51 55 E
Qondūz, Afghan. 65 E4 36 50N 68 50 E
Qondūz □, Afghan. 65 E4 36 50N 68 50 E
Qondūz →, Afghan. 91 A3 37 0N 68 16 E
Qopa, Kazakhstan 65 B7 43 31N 75 50 E
Qoraqalpoghistan □, Uzbekistan 66 E6 43 0N 58 0 E
Qorday, Kazakhstan 65 B7 43 21N 74 59 E
Qormi, Malta 38 F7 35 53N 14 28 E
Qorveh, Iran 101 E12 35 10N 47 48 E
Qosqudyq, Kazakhstan 65 A8 44 10N 77 18 E
Qostanay, Kazakhstan 66 D7 53 10N 63 35 E
Qotūr, Iran 101 C11 38 28N 44 25 E
Qoz Salsilgo, C.A.R. 114 A4 10 45N 22 54 E
Qrejten Point, Malta 38 F7 35 57N 14 27 E
Qu Jiang →, China 76 B6 30 1N 106 24 E
Qu Xian, China 76 B6 30 48N 106 58 E
Quabbin Reservoir, U.S.A. 151 D12 42 20N 72 20W
Quairading, Australia 125 F2 32 0 S 117 21 E
Quakenbrück, Germany 30 C3 52 41N 7 57 E
Quakertown, U.S.A. 151 F9 40 26N 75 21W
Qualicum Beach, Canada 142 D4 49 22N 124 26W
Quambatook, Australia 128 C5 35 49 S 143 34 E
Quambone, Australia 129 A7 30 57 S 147 53 E
Quamby, Australia 126 C3 20 22 S 140 17 E
Quan Long = Ca Mau, Vietnam 87 H5 9 7N 105 8 E
Quanah, U.S.A. 155 H5 34 18N 99 44W
Quandialla, Australia 129 C7 34 1 S 147 47 E
Quang Ngai, Vietnam 86 E7 15 13N 108 58 E
Quang Tri, Vietnam 86 D6 16 45N 107 13 E
Quang Yen, Vietnam 76 G6 20 56N 106 52 E
Quannan, China 77 E10 24 45N 114 33 E
Quantock Hills, U.K. 21 F4 51 8N 3 10W
Quanzhou, Fujian, China 77 E12 24 55N 118 34 E
Quanzhou, Guangxi Zhuangzu, China 77 E8 25 57N 111 5 E
Qu'Appelle, Canada 143 C8 50 33N 103 53W
Quaqtaq, Canada 139 B13 60 55N 69 40W
Quaraí, Brazil 174 C4 30 15 S 56 20W
Quarré-les-Tombes, France 27 E11 47 21N 4 0 E
Quarteira, Portugal 43 H2 37 4N 8 6W
Quartu Sant'Élena, Italy 46 C2 39 15N 9 10 E
Quartzsite, U.S.A. 161 M12 33 40N 114 13W
Quatre Bornes, Mauritius 121 d 20 15 S 57 28 E
Quatsino Sd., Canada 142 C3 50 25N 127 58W
Quba, Azerbaijan 61 K9 41 21N 48 32 E
Qūchān, Iran 97 B8 37 10N 58 27 E
Queanbeyan, Australia 129 C8 35 17 S 149 14 E
Québec, Canada 141 C5 46 52N 71 13W
Québec □, Canada 141 C6 48 0N 74 0W
Quebrada del Condorito △, Argentina 174 C3 31 49 S 64 40W
Quedlinburg, Germany 30 D7 51 47N 11 8 E
Queen Alexandra Ra., Antarctica 7 E11 85 0 S 170 0 E
Queen Charlotte B., Falk. Is. 9 f 51 50 S 60 40W
Queen Charlotte City, Canada 142 C2 53 15N 132 2W
Queen Charlotte Is., Canada 142 C2 53 20N 132 10W
Queen Charlotte Sd., Canada 142 C3 51 0N 128 0W
Queen Charlotte Sd., N.Z. 131 B9 41 10 S 174 15 E
Queen Charlotte Strait, Canada 142 C3 50 45N 127 10W
Queen City, U.S.A. 156 D4 40 25N 92 34W
Queen Elizabeth △, U.K. 22 E4 56 7N 4 30W
Queen Elizabeth △, Uganda 118 C3 0 0 30 0 E
Queen Elizabeth Is., Canada 136 B10 76 0N 95 0W
Queen Elizabeth Nat. Park = Ruwenzori △, Uganda 118 B2 0 20 S 30 0 E
Queen Mary Land, Antarctica 7 D7 70 0 S 95 0 E
Queen Maud G., Canada 138 B9 68 15N 102 30W
Queen Maud Land = Dronning Maud Land, Antarctica 7 D3 72 30 S 12 0 E
Queen Maud Mts., Antarctica 7 E13 86 0 S 160 0W
Queens Chan., Australia 124 C4 15 0 S 129 30 E
Queenscliff, Australia 128 E6 38 16 S 144 39 E
Queensland, U.S.A. 152 D6 31 46N 83 14W
Queensland □, Australia 126 C3 22 0 S 142 0 E
Queenstown = Cóbh, Ireland 23 E3 51 51N 8 17W
Queenstown, Australia 127 G4 42 4 S 145 35 E
Queenstown, N.Z. 131 F3 45 1 S 168 40 E
Queenstown, Singapore 87 d 1 18N 103 48 E
Queenstown, S. Africa 116 E4 31 52 S 26 52 E
Queets, U.S.A. 160 C2 47 32N 124 20W
Queguay Grande →, Uruguay 174 C4 32 9 S 58 9W
Queimada, Pta. da, Azores 9 d1 38 23N 28 14W
Queimadas, Brazil 170 D4 11 0 S 39 38W
Queiros, C., Vanuatu 133 D5 14 55 S 167 1 E
Quela, Angola 115 D3 9 10 S 16 56 E
Quelimane, Mozam. 119 F4 17 53 S 36 58 E
Quelo, Angola 115 D2 6 29 S 12 36 E
Quelpart = Cheju do, S. Korea 75 H14 33 29N 126 34 E
Queluz, Portugal 43 G1 38 45N 9 15W
Quemado, N. Mex., U.S.A. 159 J9 34 20N 108 30W
Quemado, Tex., U.S.A. 155 L4 28 58N 100 35W
Quemoy = Chinmen, Taiwan 77 E13 24 26N 118 19 E
Quemú-Quemú, Argentina 174 D3 36 3 S 63 36W
Quepem, India 95 G2 15 13N 74 3 E
Quequén, Argentina 174 D4 38 30 S 58 30W
Querco, Peru 172 C3 13 50 S 74 52W
Querétaro, Mexico 162 C4 20 36N 100 23W
Querétaro □, Mexico 162 C5 20 30N 100 0W
Querfurt, Germany 30 D7 51 23N 11 35 E
Quérigut, France 28 F6 42 42N 2 6 E
Querqueville, France 26 C5 49 40N 1 42W
Quesada, Spain 43 H7 37 51N 3 4W
Queshan, China 74 H8 32 55N 114 2 E
Quesnel, Canada 142 C4 53 0N 122 30W
Quesnel →, Canada 142 C4 52 58N 122 29W
Quesnel L., Canada 142 C4 52 30N 121 20W
Questa, U.S.A. 159 H11 36 42N 105 36W
Questembert, France 26 E4 47 40N 2 28W
Quetena, Bolivia 172 E4 22 10 S 67 25W
Quetico △, Canada 140 C1 48 30N 91 45W
Quetrequile, Argentina 176 B3 41 33 S 69 22W
Quetta, Pakistan 91 C2 30 15N 66 55 E
Queulat △, Chile 176 B2 44 29 S 72 24W
Quevedo, Ecuador 168 D2 1 2 S 79 29W
Queyras △, France 29 D10 44 45N 6 50 E
Quezaltenango, Guatemala 164 D1 14 50N 91 30W
Quezon, Phil. 81 G1 9 15N 117 59 E
Quezon □, Phil. 80 D3 14 40N 121 30 E
Quezon △, Phil. 80 D3 14 0N 121 55 E
Quezon City, Phil. 80 D3 14 38N 121 0 E
Qufār, Si. Arabia 96 E4 27 26N 41 37 E
Qui Nhon, Vietnam 86 F7 13 40N 109 13 E
Quibala, Angola 115 E2 10 46 S 14 59 E
Quibaxe, Angola 115 D2 8 24 S 14 27 E
Quibdo, Colombia 168 B2 5 42N 76 40W
Quiberon, France 26 E3 47 29N 3 9W
Quiberon, Presqu'île de, France 26 E3 47 30N 3 8W
Quiçama △, Angola 115 D2 9 41 S 13 35 E
Quickborn, Germany 30 B5 53 42N 9 52 E
Quiet L., Canada 142 A2 61 5N 133 5W
Quiindy, Paraguay 174 B4 25 58 S 57 14W
Quila, Mexico 162 C3 24 23N 107 13W
Quilán, C., Chile 176 B2 43 15 S 74 30W
Quilcene, U.S.A. 160 C4 47 49N 122 53W
Quilenda, Angola 115 E2 10 39 S 14 23 E
Quilengues, Angola 115 E2 14 12 S 14 12 E
Quilimarí, Chile 174 C1 32 5 S 71 30W
Quilino, Argentina 174 C3 30 14 S 64 29W
Quill Lakes, Canada 143 C8 51 55N 104 13W
Quillabamba, Peru 172 C3 12 50 S 72 50W
Quillacollo, Bolivia 172 D4 17 26 S 66 17W
Quillagua, Chile 174 A2 21 40 S 69 40W
Quillaicillo, Chile 174 C1 31 17 S 71 40W
Quillan, France 28 F6 42 53N 2 10 E
Quillota, Chile 174 C1 32 54 S 71 16W
Quilmes, Argentina 174 C4 34 43 S 58 15W
Quilon, India 95 K3 8 50N 76 38 E
Quilpie, Australia 127 D3 26 35 S 144 11 E
Quilpué, Chile 174 C1 33 5 S 71 33W
Quilua, Mozam. 119 F4 16 17 S 39 54 E
Quimbele, Angola 115 D3 6 17 S 16 41 E
Quimbo, Angola 115 E3 14 4 S 16 11 E
Quimbonge, Angola 115 D3 8 36 S 18 30 E
Quime, Bolivia 172 D4 17 2 S 67 15W
Quimilí, Argentina 174 B3 27 40 S 62 30W
Quimper, France 26 E2 48 0N 4 9W
Quimperlé, France 26 E3 47 53N 3 33W
Quinault →, U.S.A. 160 C2 47 21N 124 18W
Quincemil, Peru 172 C3 13 15 S 70 40W
Quincy, Calif., U.S.A. 160 F6 39 56N 120 57W
Quincy, Fla., U.S.A. 152 E5 30 35N 84 34W
Quincy, Ill., U.S.A. 156 E5 39 56N 91 23W
Quincy, Mass., U.S.A. 151 D14 42 15N 71 0W
Quincy, Mich., U.S.A. 157 C12 41 57N 84 53W
Quincy, Wash., U.S.A. 158 C4 47 22N 119 56W
Quines, Argentina 174 C2 32 13 S 65 48W
Quinga, Mozam. 119 F5 15 49 S 40 15 E
Quingey, France 27 E12 47 7N 5 52 E
Quingombe, Angola 115 D2 6 38 S 13 1 E
Quinhagak, U.S.A. 144 G7 59 45N 161 54W
Quiniluban Group, Phil. 81 F3 11 27N 120 48 E
Quintana de la Serena, Spain 43 G5 38 45N 5 40W
Quintana Roo □, Mexico 163 D7 19 0N 88 0W
Quintanar de la Orden, Spain 43 F7 39 36N 3 5W
Quintanar de la Sierra, Spain 40 D2 41 57N 2 55W
Quintanar del Rey, Spain 41 F3 39 21N 1 56W
Quinte West, Canada 140 D4 44 10N 77 34W
Quintero, Chile 174 C1 32 45 S 71 30W
Quintin, France 26 D4 48 26N 2 56W
Quinto, Spain 40 D4 41 25N 0 32W
Quinzáu, Angola 115 D2 6 51 S 12 44 E
Quípar →, Spain 41 G3 38 15N 1 40W
Quipeio, Angola 115 E3 12 27 S 15 30 E
Quirihue, Chile 174 D1 36 15 S 72 35W
Quirima, Angola 115 E3 10 47 S 18 6 E
Quirimbo, Angola 115 E2 10 36 S 14 12 E
Quirindi, Australia 129 A9 31 28 S 150 40 E
Quirino □, Phil. 80 C3 16 15N 121 40 E
Quirinópolis, Brazil 171 E1 18 32 S 50 30W
Quiroga, Spain 42 C3 42 28N 7 18W
Quiruvilca, Peru 172 B2 8 1 S 78 19W
Quissac, France 29 E8 43 55N 4 0 E
Quissanga, Mozam. 119 E5 12 24 S 40 28 E
Quissico, Mozam. 117 C5 24 42 S 34 44 E
Quitapa, Angola 115 E3 10 20 S 18 19 E
Quitilipi, Argentina 174 B3 26 50 S 60 13W
Quitman, U.S.A. 152 E6 30 47N 83 34W
Quito, Ecuador 168 D2 0 15 S 78 35W
Quixadá, Brazil 170 B4 4 55 S 39 0W
Quixaxe, Mozam. 119 F5 15 17 S 40 4 E
Quixeramobim, Brazil 170 C4 5 12 S 39 17W
Quixico, Angola 115 D2 7 59 S 14 25 E
Quixinge, Angola 115 D2 9 52 S 14 23 E
Quizenga, Angola 115 D3 9 21 S 15 28 E
Qujing, China 76 E4 25 32N 103 41 E
Qulan, Kazakhstan 65 B6 42 55N 72 43 E
Qul'ân, Jazâ'ir, Egypt 96 E2 24 22N 35 31 E
Qumbu, S. Africa 117 E4 31 10 S 28 48 E
Qumqūrghan, Uzbekistan 65 E3 37 49N 67 35 E
Quneitra, Syria 103 B4 33 7N 35 48 E
Qūnghirot, Uzbekistan 66 E6 43 6N 58 54 E
Qu'nyido, China 76 B2 31 15N 98 6 E
Quoin I., Australia 124 B4 14 54 S 129 32 E
Quoin Pt., S. Africa 116 E2 34 46 S 19 37 E
Quorn, Australia 128 B3 32 25 S 138 5 E
Qūqon, Uzbekistan 65 C5 40 30N 70 57 E
Qurein, Sudan 107 E3 13 30N 34 50 E
Qŭrghonteppa, Tajikistan 65 E4 37 50N 68 47 E
Qurnat as Sawdā', Lebanon 103 A5 34 18N 36 6 E
Qûs, Egypt 106 B3 25 55N 32 50 E
Qusar, Azerbaijan 61 K9 41 25N 48 26 E
Quşaybā', Si. Arabia 96 E4 26 53N 43 35 E
Qusaybah, Iraq 101 E9 34 24N 40 59 E
Quşay'ir, Yemen 99 D5 14 55N 50 20 E
Quseir, Egypt 96 E2 26 7N 34 16 E
Qūshchī, Iran 101 D11 37 59N 45 3 E
Quthing, Lesotho 117 E4 30 25 S 27 36 E
Qūţīābād, Iran 97 C6 35 47N 48 30 E
Quwo, China 74 G6 35 38N 111 25 E
Quyang, China 74 E8 38 35N 114 40 E
Quynh Nhai, Vietnam 86 B4 21 49N 103 33 E
Quyon, Canada 151 A8 45 31N 76 14W
Quzhou, China 77 C12 28 57N 118 54 E
Quzi, China 74 F4 36 20N 107 20 E
Qvareli, Georgia 61 K7 41 57N 45 47 E
Qytet Stalin = Kuçovë, Albania 50 F3 40 47N 19 57 E
Qyzylorda, Kazakhstan 65 A2 44 48N 65 28 E

R

Ra, Ko, Thailand 87 H2 9 13N 98 16 E
Raab, Austria 34 C6 48 21N 13 39 E
Raahe, Finland 14 D21 64 40N 24 28 E
Raalte, Neths. 24 B6 52 23N 6 16 E
Raasay, U.K. 22 D2 57 25N 6 4W
Raasay, Sd. of, U.K. 22 D2 57 30N 6 8W
Rab, Croatia 45 D11 44 45N 14 45 E
Raba, Indonesia 85 D5 8 36 S 118 55 E
Rába →, Hungary 52 C2 47 38N 17 38 E
Raba →, Poland 55 H7 50 8N 20 30 E
Rabaçal →, Portugal 42 D3 41 30N 7 12W
Rabah, Nigeria 113 C6 13 5N 5 30 E
Rabai, Kenya 118 C4 3 50 S 39 31 E
Rabak, Sudan 107 E3 13 9N 32 44 E
Rabaraba, Papua N. G. 132 E5 9 58 S 149 49 E
Rabastens, France 28 E5 43 50N 1 43 E
Rabastens-de-Bigorre, France 28 E4 43 23N 0 9 E
Rabat = Victoria, Malta 38 E6 36 3N 14 14 E
Rabat, Kazakhstan 65 B4 42 2N 69 31 E
Rabat, Malta 38 F7 35 53N 14 24 E
Rabat, Morocco 110 B3 34 2N 6 48W
Rabaul, Papua N. G. 132 C7 4 24 S 152 18 E
Rabi, Fiji 133 A3 16 30 S 179 59W
Rābigh, Si. Arabia 98 B2 22 50N 39 5 E
Rabka, Poland 55 J6 49 37N 19 59 E
Râbniţa, Moldova 53 C14 47 45N 29 0 E
Rābor, Iran 97 D8 29 17N 56 55 E
Rabyānah, Libya 108 D4 24 15N 22 0 E
Rača, Serbia & M. 50 B4 44 14N 21 0 E
Răcăciuni, Romania 53 D11 46 20N 26 59 E
Răcăşdia, Romania 52 F6 44 59N 21 36 E
Racconigi, Italy 44 D4 44 46N 7 46 E
Raccoon →, U.S.A. 156 C3 41 35N 93 37W
Raccoon Cr. →, U.S.A. 157 E9 39 47N 87 23W
Race, C., Canada 141 C9 46 40N 53 5W
Rach Gia, Vietnam 87 G5 10 5N 105 5 E
Rachid, Mauritania 112 B2 18 45N 11 35W
Raciąż, Poland 55 F7 52 46N 20 10 E
Racibórz, Poland 55 H5 50 7N 18 18 E
Racichy, Belarus 54 E10 53 44N 23 42 E
Racine, U.S.A. 157 B9 42 41N 87 51W
Račisdorf = Rača, Serbia & M. 50 B4 44 14N 21 0 E
Rackerby, U.S.A. 160 F5 39 26N 121 22W
Radama, Nosy, Madag. 117 A8 14 0 S 47 47 E
Radama, Saikanosy, Madag. 117 A8 14 16 S 47 53 E
Radan, Serbia & M. 50 D5 42 59N 21 29 E
Rădăuţi, Romania 53 C10 47 50N 25 59 E
Rădăuţi-Prut, Romania 53 B11 48 14N 26 48 E
Radbuza →, Czech Rep. 34 B6 49 45N 13 22 E
Radcliff, U.S.A. 157 G11 37 51N 85 57W
Radeberg, Germany 30 D9 51 7N 13 53 E
Radebeul, Germany 30 D9 51 6N 13 39 E
Radeče, Slovenia 45 B12 46 5N 15 14 E
Radekhiv, Ukraine 59 G3 50 25N 24 32 E
Radekhov = Radekhiv, Ukraine 59 G3 50 25N 24 32 E
Radenthein, Austria 34 E6 46 48N 13 43 E
Radew →, Poland 54 D2 54 2N 15 52 E
Radford, U.S.A. 148 G5 37 8N 80 34W
Radhanpur, India 92 H4 23 50N 71 38 E
Radhwa, Jabal, Si. Arabia 96 E3 24 34N 38 18 E
Radika →, Macedonia 50 E4 41 38N 20 37 E
Radisson, Qué., Canada 140 B4 53 47N 77 37W
Radisson, Sask., Canada 143 C7 52 30N 107 20W
Radium Hot Springs, Canada 142 C5 50 35N 116 2W
Radlje ob Dravi, Slovenia 45 B12 46 38N 15 13 E
Radmannsdorf = Radovljica, Slovenia 45 B11 46 22N 14 12 E
Radnevo, Bulgaria 51 D9 42 17N 25 58 E
Radnice, Czech Rep. 34 B6 49 51N 13 35 E
Radnor Forest, U.K. 21 E4 52 17N 3 10W
Radolfzell, Germany 31 H4 47 39N 8 59 E
Radom, Poland 55 G8 51 23N 21 12 E
Radom △, Sudan 114 A4 9 20N 23 50 E
Radomir, Bulgaria 50 D6 42 37N 22 59 E
Radomka →, Poland 55 G8 51 43N 21 28 E
Radomsko, Poland 55 G6 51 5N 19 28 E
Radomyshl, Ukraine 59 G5 50 30N 29 12 E
Radomyśl Wielki, Poland 55 H8 50 14N 21 15 E
Radoszyce, Poland 55 G7 51 4N 20 15 E
Radoviš, Macedonia 50 E6 41 38N 22 28 E
Radovljica, Slovenia 45 B11 46 22N 14 12 E
Radstadt, Austria 34 D6 47 24N 13 28 E
Radstock, C., Australia 127 E1 33 12 S 134 20 E
Răducăneni, Romania 53 D12 46 58N 27 54 E
Raduša, Macedonia 50 D5 42 7N 21 15 E
Radvanichy, Belarus 55 F11 52 1N 24 0 E
Radviliškis, Lithuania 15 J20 55 49N 23 33 E
Radville, Canada 143 D8 49 30N 104 15W
Raḍwā, J., Si. Arabia 106 C4 24 34N 38 18 E
Radymno, Poland 55 J9 49 59N 22 52 E
Radzanów, Poland 55 F7 52 56N 20 8 E
Radziejów, Poland 55 F5 52 40N 18 30 E
Radzyń Chełmiński, Poland 54 E5 53 23N 18 55 E
Radzyń Podlaski, Poland 55 G9 51 47N 22 37 E
Rae, Canada 142 A5 62 50N 116 3W
Rae Bareli, India 93 F9 26 18N 81 20 E
Rae Isthmus, Canada 139 B11 66 40N 87 30W
Raeren, Belgium 24 D6 50 41N 6 7 E
Raeside, L., Australia 125 E3 29 20 S 122 0 E
Raetihi, N.Z. 130 F4 39 25 S 175 17 E
Rafaela, Argentina 174 C3 31 10 S 61 30W
Rafah, Gaza Strip 103 D3 31 18N 34 14 E
Rafai, C.A.R. 118 B1 4 59N 23 58 E
Raffadali, Italy 46 E6 37 24N 13 32 E
Raffili, Sudan 107 F2 6 50N 28 0 E
Rafḥā, Si. Arabia 96 D4 29 35N 43 35 E
Rafsanjān, Iran 97 D8 30 30N 56 5 E
Raft Pt., Australia 124 C3 16 4 S 124 26 E
Râgâ, Sudan 107 F2 8 28N 25 41 E
Raga →, Sudan 107 F2 8 41N 25 52 E
Ragachow, Belarus 59 F6 53 8N 30 5 E
Ragag, Sudan 107 E1 10 59N 24 40 E
Ragang, Mt., Phil. 81 H5 7 43N 124 32 E
Ragay, Phil. 80 E4 13 49N 122 47 E
Ragay G., Phil. 80 E4 13 30N 122 45 E
Ragged, Mt., Australia 125 F3 33 27 S 123 25 E
Ragged Pt., Barbados 165 g 13 10N 59 26W
Rāgh, Afghan. 65 E5 37 32N 70 27 E
Raghunathpalli, India 93 H11 22 14N 84 48 E
Raghunathpur, India 93 H12 23 33N 86 40 E
Raglan, N.Z. 130 D3 37 55 S 174 55 E
Raglan Harbour, N.Z. 130 D3 37 47 S 174 50 E
Ragland, U.S.A. 152 B3 33 45N 86 9W
Ragnit = Neman, Russia 15 J20 55 2N 22 2 E
Ragusa = Dubrovnik, Croatia 50 D2 42 39N 18 6 E
Ragusa, Italy 47 F7 36 55N 14 44 E
Raha, Indonesia 82 B2 4 55 S 123 0 E
Rahad, Nahr ed →, Sudan 107 E3 14 28N 33 31 E
Rahad al Bardī, Sudan 109 F4 11 20N 23 40 E
Rahaeng = Tak, Thailand 86 D2 16 52N 99 8 E
Rahatgarh, India 93 H8 23 47N 78 22 E
Rahden, Germany 30 C4 52 26N 8 36 E
Raheb, Ras ir-, Malta 38 F7 35 54N 14 20 E
Raheita, Eritrea 107 E5 12 46N 43 4 E
Raheng = Tak, Thailand 86 D2 16 52N 99 8 E
Rahimyar Khan, Pakistan 91 C3 28 30N 70 25 E
Rāhjerd, Iran 97 C6 34 22N 50 22 E
Rahole △, Kenya 118 B4 0 5N 38 57 E
Råholt, Norway 16 D5 60 16N 11 11 E
Rahon, India 92 D7 31 3N 76 7 E
Rahotu, N.Z. 130 F2 39 20 S 173 49 E
Rahuri, India 94 E2 19 23N 74 39 E
Raiatéa, I., French Polynesia 135 J12 16 50 S 151 25W
Raichur, India 95 F3 16 10N 77 20 E
Raiford, U.S.A. 152 E7 30 4N 82 14W
Raiganj, India 93 G13 25 37N 88 10 E
Raigarh, India 94 D6 21 56N 83 25 E
Raighar, India 94 E6 19 51N 82 6 E
Raijua, Indonesia 82 D2 10 37 S 121 36 E
Raikot, India 92 D6 30 41N 75 42 E
Railton, Australia 127 G4 41 25 S 146 28 E
Rainbow Bridge △, U.S.A. 159 H8 37 5N 110 58W
Rainbow City, U.S.A. 152 B3 33 57N 86 5W
Rainbow Lake, Canada 142 B5 58 30N 119 23W
Rainier, U.S.A. 160 D4 46 53N 122 41W
Rainier, Mt., U.S.A. 160 D5 46 52N 121 46W
Rainy L., Canada 143 D10 48 42N 93 10W
Rainy River, Canada 143 D10 48 43N 94 29W
Raippaluoto, Finland 14 E19 63 13N 21 14 E
Raipur, India 94 D5 21 17N 81 45 E
Rairakhol, India 94 D7 21 4N 84 21 E
Ra'is, Si. Arabia 106 C4 23 33N 38 43 E
Raisen, India 92 H8 23 20N 77 48 E
Raisio, Finland 15 F20 60 28N 22 11 E
Raj Nandgaon, India 94 D5 21 5N 81 5 E
Raj Nilgiri, India 93 J12 21 28N 86 46 E
Raja, Ujung, Indonesia 84 B1 3 40N 96 25 E
Raja Ampat, Kepulauan, Indonesia 83 B4 0 30 S 130 0 E
Rajah Sikatuna △, Phil. 81 G5 9 40N 124 20 E
Rajahmundry, India 94 F5 17 1N 81 48 E
Rajaji △, India 92 D8 30 10N 78 20 E
Rajampet, India 95 G4 14 11N 79 10 E
Rajang →, Malaysia 85 B4 2 30N 112 0 E
Rajanpur, Pakistan 92 E4 29 6N 70 19 E
Rajapalaiyam, India 95 K3 9 25N 77 35 E
Rajapur, India 94 F1 16 40N 73 31 E
Rajasthan □, India 92 F5 26 45N 73 30 E
Rajasthan Canal = Indira Gandhi Canal, India 92 F5 28 0N 72 0 E
Rajauri, India 93 C6 33 25N 74 21 E
Rajbari, Bangla. 90 D2 23 47N 89 41 E
Rajgarh, Mad. P., India 92 G7 24 2N 76 45 E
Rajgarh, Raj., India 92 F7 27 14N 76 38 E
Rajgarh, Raj., India 92 E6 28 40N 75 25 E
Rajgir, India 93 G11 25 2N 85 25 E
Rajgród, Poland 54 E9 53 42N 22 42 E
Rajkot, India 92 H4 22 15N 70 56 E
Rajmahal Hills, India 93 G12 24 30N 87 30 E
Rajpipla, India 94 D1 21 50N 73 30 E
Rajpur, India 92 H6 22 18N 74 21 E
Rajpura, India 92 D7 30 25N 76 32 E
Rajputana = Rajasthan □, India 92 F5 26 45N 73 30 E
Rajshahi, Bangla. 90 C2 24 22N 88 39 E
Rajshahi □, Bangla. 90 C2 25 0N 89 0 E
Rajula, India 92 J4 21 3N 71 26 E
Rajur, India 94 D4 20 7N 78 55 E
Rajura, India 94 E4 19 47N 79 22 E
Rakaia, N.Z. 131 D7 43 45 S 172 1 E
Rakaia →, N.Z. 131 D7 43 36 S 172 15 E
Rakan, Ra's, Qatar 97 E6 26 10N 51 20 E
Rakaposhi, Pakistan 93 A6 36 10N 74 25 E
Rakata, Pulau, Indonesia 84 D3 6 10 S 105 20 E
Rakhiv, Ukraine 53 B9 48 3N 24 12 E
Rakhni, Pakistan 92 D3 30 4N 69 56 E
Rakhni →, Pakistan 92 E3 29 31N 69 36 E
Rakhny-Lisovi, Ukraine 53 B13 48 47N 28 29 E
Rakhyūt, Oman 99 C6 16 44N 53 20 E
Rakiraki, Fiji 133 A2 17 22 S 178 11 E
Rakitnoye, Russia 70 B7 45 36N 134 17 E
Rakitovo, Bulgaria 51 E8 41 59N 24 5 E
Rakkestad, Norway 18 E8 59 25N 11 21 E
Rakoniewice, Poland 55 F3 52 10N 16 16 E
Rakops, Botswana 116 C3 21 1 S 24 28 E
Rakovica, Croatia 45 D12 44 59N 15 38 E
Rakovník, Czech Rep. 34 A6 50 6N 13 42 E
Rakovski, Bulgaria 51 D8 42 21N 24 57 E
Rakshan →, Pakistan 91 D1 27 10N 63 25 E
Rakvere, Estonia 15 G22 59 20N 26 25 E
Raleigh, Fla., U.S.A. 153 F7 29 25N 82 32W
Raleigh, N.C., U.S.A. 149 H6 35 47N 78 39W
Rali Salem, Algeria 111 D5 21 3N 1 9 E
Ralik Chain, Pac. Oc. 134 G8 8 0N 168 0 E
Ralja, Serbia & M. 50 B4 44 33N 20 34 E
Ralls, U.S.A. 155 J4 33 41N 101 24W
Ralston, U.S.A. 150 E8 41 30N 76 57W
Ram →, Canada 142 A4 62 1N 123 41W
Rām Allāh, West Bank 103 D4 31 55N 35 10 E
Rama, Nic. 164 D3 12 9N 84 15W
Ramacca, Italy 47 E7 37 23N 14 42 E
Ramachandrapuram, India 94 F6 16 50N 82 4 E
Ramagiri Udayagiri, India 94 E7 19 5N 84 18 E
Ramakona, India 93 J8 21 43N 78 50 E
Ramales de la Victoria, Spain 42 B7 43 15N 3 28W
Ramalho, Serra do, Brazil 171 D3 13 45 S 44 0W
Rāmallāh = Rām Allāh, West Bank 103 D4 31 55N 35 10 E
Raman, Thailand 87 J3 6 29N 101 18 E
Ramanathapuram, India 95 K4 9 25N 78 55 E
Ramanetaka, B. de, Madag. 117 A8 14 13 S 47 52 E
Ramanujganj, India 93 H10 23 48N 83 42 E
Ramas C., India 95 G1 15 5N 73 55 E
Ramat Gan, Israel 103 C3 32 4N 34 48 E
Ramatlhabama, S. Africa 116 D4 25 37 S 25 33 E
Ramban, India 93 C6 33 14N 75 12 E
Rambervillers, France 27 D13 48 20N 6 38 E
Rambi = Rabi, Fiji 133 A3 16 30 S 179 59W
Rambipuji, Indonesia 85 D4 8 12 S 113 37 E
Rambouillet, France 27 D8 48 39N 1 50 E
Rambrai, India 90 C3 25 40N 91 19 E
Rambutyo I., Papua N. G. 132 B4 2 18 S 147 49 E
Ramdurg, India 95 G2 15 58N 75 22 E
Rame Hd., Australia 129 D8 37 47 S 149 30 E
Ramechhap, Nepal 93 F12 27 25N 86 10 E
Ramenskoye, Russia 58 E10 55 32N 38 15 E
Ramer, U.S.A. 152 C3 32 3N 86 13W
Rameswaram, India 95 K4 9 17N 79 18 E
Ramganga →, India 93 F8 27 5N 79 58 E
Ramgarh, Bangla. 90 D3 22 59N 91 44 E
Ramgarh, Jharkhand, India 93 H11 23 40N 85 35 E
Ramgarh, Raj., India 92 F6 27 16N 75 14 E
Ramgarh, Raj., India 92 F4 27 30N 70 36 E
Rāmhormoz, Iran 97 D6 31 15N 49 35 E
Ramīān, Iran 97 B7 37 3N 55 16 E
Ramingining, Australia 126 A2 12 19 S 135 3 E
Ramla, Israel 103 D3 31 55N 34 52 E
Ramlat Zaltan, Libya 108 C3 28 30N 19 30 E
Ramlu, Eritrea 107 E5 13 32N 41 40 E
Ramm = Rum, Jordan 103 F4 29 39N 35 26 E
Ramm, Jabal, Jordan 103 F4 29 35N 35 24 E
Râmna →, Romania 53 E12 45 36N 27 3 E
Ramnad = Ramanathapuram, India 95 K4 9 25N 78 55 E
Ramnagar, Jammu & Kashmir, India 93 C6 32 47N 75 18 E
Ramnagar, Uttaranchal, India 93 E8 29 24N 79 7 E
Ramnäs, Sweden 16 E10 59 46N 16 12 E
Râmnicu Sărat, Romania 53 E12 45 26N 27 3 E
Râmnicu Vâlcea, Romania 53 E9 45 9N 24 21 E
Ramon, Phil. 80 C3 16 50N 121 31 E
Ramon, Russia 59 G10 51 55N 39 21 E
Ramona, U.S.A. 161 M10 33 2N 116 52W
Ramonville-St-Agne, France 28 E5 43 33N 1 28 E
Ramore, Canada 140 C3 48 30N 80 25W
Ramos →, Nigeria 113 D6 5 8N 5 22 E
Ramotswa, Botswana 116 C4 24 50 S 25 52 E
Rampart, U.S.A. 144 D10 65 30N 150 10W
Rampur, H.P., India 92 D7 31 26N 77 43 E
Rampur, Mad. P., India 92 H5 23 25N 73 53 E
Rampur, Orissa, India 94 D6 21 48N 83 58 E
Rampur, Ut. P., India 93 E8 28 50N 79 5 E
Rampur Hat, India 93 G12 24 10N 87 50 E
Rampura, India 92 G6 24 30N 75 27 E
Ramrama Tola, India 93 J8 21 52N 79 55 E
Ramree I., Burma 90 F5 19 0N 93 40 E
Rāmsar, Iran 97 B6 36 53N 50 41 E
Ramsey, I. of Man 20 C3 54 20N 4 22W
Ramsey, Ill., U.S.A. 156 E7 39 8N 89 7W
Ramsey, N.J., U.S.A. 151 E10 41 4N 74 9W
Ramsey L., Canada 140 C3 47 13N 82 15W
Ramsgate, U.K. 21 F9 51 20N 1 25 E
Ramshai, India 90 B2 26 44N 88 51 E
Ramsjö, Sweden 16 B9 62 11N 15 37 E
Ramstein, Germany 31 F3 49 27N 7 32 E
Ramtek, India 94 D4 21 20N 79 15 E
Ramu →, Papua N. G. 132 C3 4 0 S 144 41 E
Ramvik, Sweden 16 B11 62 49N 17 51 E
Rana Pratap Sagar Dam, India 92 G6 24 58N 75 38 E
Ranaghat, India 93 H13 23 15N 88 35 E
Ranahu, Pakistan 92 G3 25 55N 69 45 E
Ranau, Malaysia 78 C5 6 2N 116 40 E
Rancagua, Chile 174 C1 34 10 S 70 50W
Rance →, France 26 D5 48 34N 1 59W
Rancharia, Brazil 171 F1 22 15 S 50 55W
Rancheria →, Canada 142 A3 60 13N 129 7W
Ranchester, U.S.A. 158 D10 44 54N 107 10W
Ranchi, India 93 H11 23 19N 85 27 E
Rancho Cucamonga, U.S.A. 161 L9 34 10N 117 30W
Ranco, L., Chile 176 B2 40 15 S 72 25W
Rand, Australia 129 C7 35 33 S 146 32 E
Randaberg, Norway 18 E2 59 1N 5 36 E
Randabygd, Norway 18 C3 61 51N 6 20 E
Randalstown, U.K. 23 B5 54 45N 6 19W
Randan, France 27 F10 46 2N 3 21 E
Randazzo, Italy 47 E7 37 53N 14 57 E
Rander, India 94 D1 21 14N 72 47 E
Randers, Denmark 17 H4 56 29N 10 1 E
Randers Fjord, Denmark 17 H4 56 37N 10 20 E
Randfontein, S. Africa 117 D4 26 8 S 27 45 E
Randle, U.S.A. 160 D5 46 32N 121 57W
Randolph, Mass., U.S.A. 151 D13 42 10N 71 2W
Randolph, N.Y., U.S.A. 150 D6 42 10N 78 59W
Randolph, Utah, U.S.A. 158 F8 41 40N 111 11W

Randolph, Vt., U.S.A. 151 C12 43 55N 72 40W
Randsburg, U.S.A. 161 K9 35 22N 117 39W
Randsfjorden, Norway 18 D7 60 25N 10 24 E
Randsverk, Norway 18 C6 61 44N 9 3 E
Råneälven →, Sweden 14 D20 65 50N 22 20 E
Ranenburg = Chaplygin, Russia 58 F11 53 15N 40 0 E
Ranfurly, N.Z. 131 F5 45 7 S 170 6 E
Rangae, Thailand 87 J3 6 19N 101 44 E
Rangamati, Bangla. 90 D4 22 38N 92 12 E
Rangapara, India 90 B4 26 49N 92 39 E
Rangárvallasýsla □, Iceland 11 D7 63 55N 20 0W
Rangataua, N.Z. 130 F4 39 26 S 175 28 E
Rangaunu B., N.Z. 130 A2 34 51 S 173 15 E
Rangeley, U.S.A. 149 C10 44 58N 70 39W
Rangeley L., U.S.A. 151 B14 44 55N 70 43W
Rangely, U.S.A. 158 F9 40 5N 108 48W
Ranger, U.S.A. 155 J5 32 28N 98 41W
Rangia, India 90 B3 26 28N 91 38 E
Rangiora, N.Z. 131 D7 43 19 S 172 36 E
Rangitaiki, N.Z. 130 E5 38 52 S 176 24 E
Rangitaiki →, N.Z. 130 D5 37 54 S 176 49 E
Rangitata →, N.Z. 131 D6 43 45 S 171 15 E
Rangitikei →, N.Z. 130 G4 40 17 S 175 15 E
Rangitoto ke te tonga = D'Urville I., N.Z. 131 A8 40 50 S 173 55 E
Rangitoto Ra., N.Z. 130 E4 38 25 S 175 35 E
Rangkasbitung, Indonesia 84 D3 6 21 S 106 15 E
Rangoon, Burma 90 G6 16 45N 96 20 E
Rangoon □, Burma 90 G6 17 0N 96 10 E
Rangpur, Bangla. 90 C2 25 42N 89 22 E
Rangsang, Indonesia 84 B2 1 20N 103 30 E
Rangsit, Thailand 86 F3 13 59N 100 37 E
Ranheim, Norway 18 A7 63 26N 10 32 E
Rānibennur, India 95 G2 14 35N 75 30 E
Raniganj, India 93 F9 27 3N 82 13 E
Ranikhet, India 93 E8 29 39N 79 25 E
Ranippettai, India 95 H4 12 56N 79 23 E
Rāniyah, Iraq 96 B5 36 15N 44 53 E
Ranka, India 93 H10 23 59N 83 47 E
Ranken →, Australia 126 C2 20 31 S 137 36 E
Rankin, Ill., U.S.A. 157 D9 40 28N 87 54W
Rankin, Tex., U.S.A. 155 K4 31 13N 101 56W
Rankin Inlet, Canada 138 B10 62 30N 93 0W
Rankins Springs, Australia 129 B7 33 49 S 146 14 E
Rankovicevo = Kraljevo, Serbia & M. 50 C4 43 44N 20 41 E
Rankweil, Austria 34 D2 47 17N 9 39 E
Rannoch, L., U.K. 22 E4 56 41N 4 20W
Rannoch Moor, U.K. 22 E4 56 38N 4 48W
Rano Kau, Chile 172 b 27 11 S 109 26W
Rano Raraku, Volcán, Chile 172 b 27 7 S 109 17W
Ranobe, Helodranon' i, Madag. 117 C7 23 3 S 43 33 E
Ranohira, Madag. 117 C8 22 29 S 45 24 E
Ranomafana, Toamasina, Madag. 117 B8 18 57 S 48 50 E
Ranomafana, Toliara, Madag. 117 C8 24 34 S 47 0 E
Ranomafana △, Madag. 117 C8 21 16 S 47 25 E
Ranomena, Madag. 117 C8 23 25 S 47 17 E
Ranon, Vanuatu 133 F6 16 8 S 168 7 E
Ranong, Thailand 87 H2 9 56N 98 40 E
Ranongga, Solomon Is. 133 M9 8 5 S 156 35 E
Ranotsara Nord, Madag. 117 C8 22 48 S 46 36 E
Ranpur, India 94 D7 20 5N 85 20 E
Rānsa, Iran 97 C6 33 39N 48 18 E
Ransiki, Indonesia 83 B4 1 30 S 134 10 E
Ransom, U.S.A. 157 C8 41 9N 88 39W
Rantabe, Madag. 117 B8 15 42 S 49 39 E
Rantau, Indonesia 85 C5 2 56 S 115 9 E
Rantauprapat, Indonesia 84 B1 2 15N 99 50 E
Rantemario, Indonesia 82 B1 3 15 S 119 57 E
Ranthambore △, India 92 F7 26 10N 76 30 E
Rantoul, U.S.A. 157 D8 40 19N 88 9W
Ranum, Denmark 17 H3 56 54N 9 14 E
Ranyah, W. →, Si. Arabia 98 B3 21 18N 43 20 E
Raon l'Étape, France 27 D13 48 24N 6 50 E
Raoping, China 77 F11 23 42N 117 1 E
Raoui, Erg er, Algeria 111 C4 29 0N 2 0W
Raoyang, China 78 E8 38 15N 115 45 E
Rap, Ko, Thailand 87 b 9 19N 99 58 E
Rapa, French Polynesia 135 K13 27 35 S 144 20W
Rapa Nui = Pascua, I. de, Chile 172 b 27 7 S 109 23W
Rapallo, Italy 44 D6 44 21N 9 14 E
Rapang, Indonesia 82 B1 3 50 S 119 48 E
Rapar, India 92 H4 23 34N 70 38 E
Rāpch, Iran 97 E8 25 40N 59 15 E
Raper, C., Canada 139 B13 69 44N 67 6W
Rapid City, U.S.A. 154 D3 44 5N 103 14W
Rapid River, U.S.A. 148 C2 45 55N 86 58W
Rapla, Estonia 15 G21 59 1N 24 52 E
Rapperswil, Switz. 33 B7 47 14N 8 45 E
Rapti →, India 93 F10 26 18N 83 41 E
Rapu Rapu I., Phil. 80 E5 13 12N 124 9 E
Raqaba ez Zarqa →, Sudan 107 F2 9 14N 29 44 E
Raqūbah, Libya 108 C3 28 58N 19 2 E
Raquette →, U.S.A. 151 B10 45 0N 74 42W
Raquette Lake, U.S.A. 151 C10 43 49N 74 40W
Rara △, Nepal 93 E10 29 30N 82 10 E
Rarotonga, Cook Is. 135 K12 21 30 S 160 0W
Ra's al 'Ayn, Syria 101 D9 36 45N 40 12 E
Ra's al Khaymah, U.A.E. 97 E7 25 50N 55 59 E
Ras el Ma, Algeria 111 B4 34 26N 0 50W
Râs el Mâ, Mali 112 B4 16 35N 4 30W
Râs Ghârib, Egypt 106 B3 28 6N 33 18 E
Ras Kōh, Pakistan 91 C2 28 43N 64 55 E
Ra's Lānūf, Libya 108 B3 30 46N 18 11 E
Râs Mallap, Egypt 106 B3 29 18N 32 50 E
Râs Muhammad △, Egypt 106 B3 27 45N 34 16 E
Rasa, Punta, Argentina 176 B4 40 50 S 62 15W
Rasca, Pta. de la, Canary Is. 9 e1 27 59N 16 41W
Râşcani, Moldova 53 C12 47 58N 27 33 E
Raseiniai, Lithuania 15 J20 55 25N 23 5 E
Rashad, Sudan 107 E3 11 55N 31 0 E
Rashîd, Egypt 106 H7 31 21N 30 22 E
Rashîd, Masabb, Egypt 106 H7 31 22N 30 17 E
Rashin = Najin, N. Korea 75 C16 42 12N 130 15 E
Rashmi, India 92 G6 25 4N 74 22 E
Rasht, Iran 97 B6 37 20N 49 40 E
Rasi Salai, Thailand 86 E5 15 20N 104 9 E
Rasipuram, India 95 J4 11 30N 78 15 E
Raška, Serbia & M. 50 C4 43 19N 20 39 E
Râşnov, Romania 53 E10 45 35N 25 27 E
Rason L., Australia 125 E3 28 45 S 124 25 E
Raşova, Romania 53 F12 44 15N 27 55 E
Rasovo, Bulgaria 50 C7 43 42N 23 17 E
Rasra, India 93 G10 25 50N 83 50 E
Rass el Oued, Algeria 111 A6 35 57N 5 2 E
Rasskazovo, Russia 60 D5 52 35N 41 50 E
Rast, Romania 53 G8 43 53N 23 16 E
Rastatt, Germany 31 G4 48 50N 8 11 E
Rastede, Germany 30 B4 53 15N 8 12 E
Rastenburg = Kętrzyn, Poland 54 D8 54 7N 21 22 E
Răstoliţa, Romania 53 D9 46 59N 24 58 E
Rastyapino = Dzerzhinsk, Russia 60 B6 56 14N 43 30 E
Rasul, Pakistan 92 C5 32 42N 73 34 E
Raszków, Poland 55 G4 51 43N 17 40 E
Rat Buri, Thailand 86 F2 13 30N 99 54 E
Rat Islands, U.S.A. 144 L2 52 0N 178 0 E
Rat L., Canada 143 B9 56 10N 99 40W
Ratak Chain, Pac. Oc. 134 G8 1 0N 170 0 E
Rätan, Sweden 16 B8 62 29N 14 33 E
Ratangarh, India 92 E6 28 5N 74 35 E
Raţāwī, Iraq 96 D5 30 38N 47 13 E
Ratcatchers L., Australia 128 B5 32 30 S 143 12 E
Rath, India 93 G8 25 36N 79 37 E
Rath Luirc, Ireland 23 D3 52 21N 8 40W
Rathbun L., U.S.A. 156 D4 40 49N 92 53W
Rathdrum, Ireland 23 D5 52 56N 6 14W
Rathedaung, Burma 90 E4 20 29N 92 45 E
Rathenow, Germany 30 C8 52 37N 12 19 E
Rathkeale, Ireland 23 D3 52 32N 8 56W
Rathlin I., U.K. 23 A5 55 18N 6 14W
Rathmelton, Ireland 23 A4 55 2N 7 38W
Ratibor = Racibórz, Poland 55 H5 50 7N 18 18 E
Rätikon, Austria 33 B9 47 0N 9 55 E
Ratingen, Germany 30 D2 51 18N 6 52 E
Ratlam, India 92 H6 23 20N 75 0 E
Ratnagiri, India 94 F1 16 57N 73 18 E
Ratnapura, Sri Lanka 95 L5 6 40N 80 20 E
Ratodero, Pakistan 92 F3 27 48N 68 18 E
Raton, U.S.A. 155 G2 36 54N 104 24W
Ratschach = Radeče, Slovenia 45 B12 46 5N 15 14 E
Rattaphum, Thailand 87 J3 7 8N 100 16 E
Ratten, Austria 34 D8 47 28N 15 44 E
Rattray Hd., U.K. 22 D7 57 38N 1 50W
Rättvik, Sweden 16 D9 60 52N 15 7 E
Ratz, Mt., Canada 142 B2 57 23N 132 12W
Ratzebuhr = Okonek, Poland 54 E3 53 32N 16 51 E
Ratzeburg, Germany 30 B6 53 40N 10 46 E
Rau, Indonesia 82 A3 2 20N 128 10 E
Raub, Malaysia 87 L3 3 47N 101 52 E
Rauch, Argentina 174 D4 36 45 S 59 5W
Raudales de Malpaso, Mexico 163 D6 17 30N 93 30W
Raudeberg, Norway 18 C2 61 59N 5 7 E
Raufarhöfn, Iceland 11 A11 66 27N 15 57W
Raufoss, Norway 18 D7 60 44N 10 37 E
Rauhellern, Norway 18 D4 60 15N 7 50 E
Raukumara Ra., N.Z. 130 E6 38 5 S 177 55 E
Raul Soares, Brazil 171 F3 20 5 S 42 22W
Rauma, Finland 15 F19 61 10N 21 30 E
Rauma →, Norway 18 B4 62 34N 7 43 E
Raumo = Rauma, Finland 15 F19 61 10N 21 30 E
Raung, Gunung, Indonesia 79 J17 8 8 S 114 3 E
Raurkela, India 93 H11 22 14N 84 50 E
Rausu-Dake, Japan 70 B12 44 4N 145 7 E
Răut →, Moldova 53 C14 47 15N 29 9 E
Rava-Ruska, Ukraine 55 H10 50 15N 23 42 E
Rava Russkaya = Rava-Ruska, Ukraine 55 H10 50 15N 23 42 E
Ravalli, U.S.A. 158 C6 47 17N 114 11W
Ravānsar, Iran 101 E12 34 43N 46 40 E
Ravanusa, Italy 46 E6 37 16N 13 58 E
Rāvar, Iran 97 D8 31 20N 56 51 E
Ravena, U.S.A. 151 D11 42 28N 73 49W
Ravenel, U.S.A. 152 C9 32 46N 80 15W
Ravenna, Italy 45 D9 44 25N 12 12 E
Ravenna, Ky., U.S.A. 157 G13 37 42N 83 55W
Ravenna, Nebr., U.S.A. 154 E5 41 1N 98 55W
Ravenna, Ohio, U.S.A. 150 E3 41 9N 81 15W
Ravensburg, Germany 31 H5 47 46N 9 36 E
Ravenshoe, Australia 126 B4 17 37 S 145 29 E
Ravensthorpe, Australia 125 F3 33 35 S 120 2 E
Ravenswood, Australia 126 C4 20 6 S 146 54 E
Ravenswood, U.S.A. 148 F5 38 57N 81 46W
Ravensworth, Australia 129 B9 32 26 S 151 4 E
Ravenwood, U.S.A. 156 D2 40 22N 94 41W
Raver, India 94 D3 21 15N 76 2 E
Ravi →, Pakistan 92 D4 30 35N 71 49 E
Ravna Gora, Croatia 45 C11 45 24N 14 50 E
Ravna Reka, Serbia & M. 50 B5 44 1N 21 35 E
Ravne na Koroškem, Slovenia 45 B11 46 36N 14 59 E
Rawa Mazowiecka, Poland 55 G7 51 46N 20 12 E
Rawalpindi, Pakistan 91 B4 33 38N 73 8 E
Rawāndūz, Iraq 101 D11 36 40N 44 30 E
Rawang, Malaysia 87 L3 3 20N 101 35 E
Rawene, N.Z. 130 B2 35 25 S 173 32 E
Rawicz, Poland 55 G3 51 36N 16 52 E
Rawitsch = Rawicz, Poland 55 G3 51 36N 16 52 E
Rawka →, Poland 55 F7 52 9N 20 8 E
Rawlinna, Australia 125 F4 30 58 S 125 28 E
Rawlins, U.S.A. 158 F10 41 47N 107 14W
Rawlinson Ra., Australia 125 D4 24 40 S 128 30 E
Rawson, Argentina 176 B3 43 15 S 65 5W
Raxaul, India 93 F11 26 59N 84 51 E
Ray, U.S.A. 154 A3 48 21N 103 10W
Ray, C., Canada 141 C8 47 33N 59 15W
Ray City, U.S.A. 152 D6 31 5N 83 11W
Ray Mts., U.S.A. 144 D10 66 0N 152 0W
Raya Ring, Ko, Thailand 87 a 8 18N 98 29 E
Rayachoti, India 95 G4 14 4N 78 50 E
Rayadurg, India 95 G3 14 40N 76 50 E
Rayagada, India 94 E6 19 15N 83 20 E
Raychikhinsk, Russia 67 E13 49 46N 129 25 E
Rāyen, Iran 97 D8 29 34N 57 26 E
Rayevskiy, Russia 64 D5 54 4N 54 56 E
Rayle, U.S.A. 152 B7 33 48N 82 54W
Rayleigh, U.K. 21 F8 51 36N 0 37 E
Raymond, Canada 142 D6 49 30N 112 35W
Raymond, Calif., U.S.A. 160 H7 37 13N 119 54W
Raymond, Ill., U.S.A. 156 E7 39 19N 89 34W
Raymond, N.H., U.S.A. 151 C13 43 2N 71 11W
Raymond, Wash., U.S.A. 160 D3 46 41N 123 44W
Raymond Terrace, Australia 129 B9 32 45 S 151 44 E
Raymondville, U.S.A. 155 M6 26 29N 97 47W
Raymore, Canada 143 C8 51 25N 104 31W
Rayón, Mexico 162 B2 29 43N 110 35W
Rayong, Thailand 86 F3 12 40N 101 20 E
Raytown, U.S.A. 156 E2 39 1N 94 28W
Rayville, U.S.A. 155 J9 32 29N 91 46W
Raz, Pte. du, France 26 D2 48 2N 4 47W
Razan, Iran 97 C6 35 23N 49 2 E
Ražana, Serbia & M. 50 B3 44 6N 19 55 E
Ražanj, Serbia & M. 50 C5 43 40N 21 31 E
Razāzah, Buḩayrat ar, Iraq 101 F10 32 40N 43 35 E
Razazah, L. = Razāzah, Buḩayrat ar, Iraq 101 F10 32 40N 43 35 E
Razdelna, Bulgaria 51 C11 43 13N 27 41 E
Razdel'naya = Rozdilna, Ukraine 53 D15 46 50N 30 2 E
Razdolnoye, Russia 70 C5 43 30N 131 52 E
Razdolnoye, Ukraine 59 K7 45 46N 33 29 E
Razeh, Iran 97 C6 32 47N 48 9 E
Razgrad, Bulgaria 51 C10 43 33N 26 34 E
Razim, Lacul, Romania 53 F14 44 50N 29 0 E
Razlog, Bulgaria 50 E7 41 53N 23 28 E
Razmak, Pakistan 91 B3 32 45N 69 50 E
Ré, Î. de, France 28 B2 46 12N 1 30W
Reading, U.K. 21 F7 51 27N 0 58W
Reading, Mich., U.S.A. 157 C12 41 50N 84 45W
Reading, Ohio, U.S.A. 157 E12 39 13N 84 26W
Reading, Pa., U.S.A. 151 F9 40 20N 75 56W
Reading □, U.K. 21 F7 51 27N 0 58W
Real, Cordillera, Bolivia 172 D4 17 0 S 67 10W
Realicó, Argentina 174 D3 35 0 S 64 15W
Réalmont, France 28 E6 43 48N 2 10 E
Realp, Switz. 33 C6 46 36N 8 30 E
Ream, Cambodia 87 G4 10 34N 103 39 E
Reata, Mexico 162 B4 26 8N 101 5W
Reay Forest, U.K. 22 C4 58 22N 4 55W
Rebais, France 27 D10 48 50N 3 10 E
Rebi, Indonesia 83 C4 6 23 S 134 7 E
Rebiana, Libya 108 D4 24 12N 22 10 E
Rebiana, Sahrâ', Libya 108 D3 24 30N 21 0 E
Rebun-Tō, Japan 70 B10 45 23N 141 2 E
Recanati, Italy 45 E10 43 24N 13 32 E
Recaş, Romania 52 E6 45 46N 21 30 E
Recco, Italy 44 D6 44 22N 9 9 E
Recherche, Arch. of the, Australia 125 F3 34 15 S 122 50 E
Rechna Doab, Pakistan 92 D5 31 35N 73 30 E
Rechytsa, Belarus 59 F6 52 21N 30 24 E
Recife, Brazil 170 C5 8 0 S 35 0W
Recife, Seychelles 121 b 4 36 S 55 42 E
Recklinghausen, Germany 24 C7 51 37N 7 12 E
Reconquista, Argentina 174 B4 29 10 S 59 45W
Recreio, Brazil 173 B6 8 0 S 58 25W
Recreo, Argentina 174 B2 29 25 S 65 10W
Recuay, Peru 172 B2 9 43 S 77 28W
Recz, Poland 55 E2 53 16N 15 31 E
Red →, La., U.S.A. 155 K9 31 1N 91 45W
Red →, N. Dak., U.S.A. 138 C10 49 0N 97 15W
Red Bank, U.S.A. 151 F10 40 21N 74 5W
Red Bay, Canada 141 B8 51 44N 56 25W
Red Bluff, U.S.A. 158 F2 40 11N 122 15W
Red Bluff Res., U.S.A. 155 K3 31 54N 103 55W
Red Bud, U.S.A. 156 F7 38 13N 89 59W
Red Cliffs, Australia 128 C5 34 19 S 142 11 E
Red Cloud, U.S.A. 154 E5 40 5N 98 32W
Red Creek, U.S.A. 151 C8 43 14N 76 45W
Red Deer, Canada 142 C6 52 20N 113 50W
Red Deer →, Alta., Canada 143 C7 50 58N 110 0W
Red Deer →, Man., Canada 143 C8 52 53N 101 1W
Red Deer L., Canada 143 C8 52 55N 101 20W
Red Devil, U.S.A. 144 F8 61 46N 157 19W
Red Hook, U.S.A. 151 E11 41 55N 73 53W
Red Indian L., Canada 141 C8 48 35N 57 0W
Red L., Canada 143 C10 51 3N 93 49W
Red Lake, Canada 143 C10 51 3N 93 49W
Red Lake Falls, U.S.A. 154 B6 47 53N 96 16W
Red Lake Road, Canada 143 C10 49 59N 93 25W
Red Lodge, U.S.A. 158 D9 45 11N 109 15W
Red Mountain, U.S.A. 161 K9 35 37N 117 38W
Red Oak, U.S.A. 154 E7 41 1N 95 14W
Red Rock, Canada 140 C2 48 55N 88 15W
Red Rock, L., U.S.A. 156 C3 41 22N 92 59W
Red Rocks Pt., Australia 125 F4 32 13 S 127 32 E
Red Sea, Asia 88 C2 25 0N 36 0 E
Red Slate Mt., U.S.A. 160 H8 37 31N 118 52W
Red Sucker L., Canada 140 B1 54 9N 93 40W
Red Tower Pass = Turnu Roşu, P., Romania 53 E9 45 33N 24 17 E
Red Wing, U.S.A. 154 C8 44 34N 92 31W
Reda, Poland 54 D5 54 40N 18 19 E
Redang, Malaysia 87 K4 5 49N 103 2 E
Redange, Lux. 24 E5 49 46N 5 52 E
Redcar, U.K. 20 C6 54 37N 1 4W
Redcar & Cleveland □, U.K. 20 C7 54 29N 1 0W
Redcliff, Canada 158 A8 50 10N 110 50W
Redcliffe, Australia 127 D5 27 12 S 153 0 E
Redcliffe, Mt., Australia 125 E3 28 30 S 121 30 E
Reddersburg, S. Africa 116 D4 29 41 S 26 10 E
Reddick, Fla., U.S.A. 153 F7 29 22N 82 12W
Reddick, Ill., U.S.A. 157 C8 41 6N 88 15W
Redding, Calif., U.S.A. 158 F2 40 35N 122 24W
Redding, Iowa, U.S.A. 156 D2 40 36N 94 23W
Redditch, U.K. 21 E6 52 18N 1 55W
Redenção, Brazil 170 B4 4 13 S 38 43W
Redfield, U.S.A. 154 C5 44 53N 98 31W
Redford, U.S.A. 151 B11 44 38N 73 48W
Redhead, Trin. & Tob. 169 F10 10 44N 60 58W
Redkey, U.S.A. 157 D11 40 21N 85 9W
Redkino, Russia 58 D9 56 39N 36 16 E
Redlands, U.S.A. 161 M9 34 4N 117 11W
Redmond, Oreg., U.S.A. 158 D3 44 17N 121 11W
Redmond, Wash., U.S.A. 160 C4 47 41N 122 7W
Redon, France 26 E4 47 40N 2 6W
Redonda, Antigua & B. 165 C7 16 58N 62 19W
Redondela, Pta., Chile 172 b 27 10 S 109 22W
Redondela, Spain 42 C2 42 15N 8 38W
Redondo, Portugal 43 G3 38 39N 7 37W
Redondo Beach, U.S.A. 161 M8 33 50N 118 23W
Redoubt Volcano, U.S.A. 144 F9 60 29N 152 45W
Redruth, U.K. 21 G2 50 14N 5 14W
Redvers, Canada 143 D8 49 35N 101 40W
Redwater, Canada 142 C6 53 55N 113 6W
Redwood, U.S.A. 151 B9 44 18N 75 48W
Redwood △, U.S.A. 158 F1 41 40N 124 5W
Redwood City, U.S.A. 160 H4 37 30N 122 15W
Redwood Falls, U.S.A. 154 C7 44 32N 95 7W
Ree, L., Ireland 23 C3 53 35N 8 0W
Reed, L., Canada 143 C8 54 38N 100 30W
Reed City, U.S.A. 148 D3 43 53N 85 31W
Reedley, U.S.A. 160 J7 36 36N 119 27W
Reedsburg, U.S.A. 154 D9 43 32N 90 0W
Reedsport, U.S.A. 158 E1 43 42N 124 6W
Reedsville, U.S.A. 150 F7 40 39N 77 35W
Reedy Creek, Australia 128 D4 36 58 S 140 2 E
Reefton, N.Z. 131 C6 42 6 S 171 51 E
Rees, Germany 30 D2 51 46N 6 24 E
Reese →, U.S.A. 158 F5 40 48N 117 4W
Refahiye, Turkey 101 C8 39 54N 38 47 E
Reftele, Sweden 17 G7 57 11N 13 35 E
Refugio, U.S.A. 155 L6 28 18N 97 17W
Rega →, Poland 54 D2 54 10N 15 18 E
Regalbuto, Italy 47 E7 37 39N 14 38 E
Regar = Tursunzade, Tajikistan 65 D4 38 30N 68 14 E
Regen, Germany 31 G9 48 58N 13 8 E
Regen →, Germany 31 F8 49 1N 12 6 E
Regeneração, Brazil 170 C3 6 15 S 42 41W
Regensburg, Germany 31 F8 49 1N 12 6 E
Regensdorf, Switz. 33 B6 47 26N 8 28 E
Regenstauf, Germany 31 F8 49 7N 12 8 E
Regenwalde = Resko, Poland 54 E2 53 47N 15 25 E
Reggâne = Zaouiet Reggâne, Algeria 111 C5 26 32N 0 3 E
Reggello, Italy 45 E8 43 41N 11 32 E
Réggio di Calábria, Italy 47 D8 38 6N 15 39 E
Réggio nell'Emília, Italy 44 D7 44 43N 10 36 E
Reghin, Romania 53 D9 46 46N 24 42 E
Regina, Canada 143 C8 50 27N 104 35W
Régina, Fr. Guiana 169 C7 4 19N 52 8W
Regina Beach, Canada 143 C8 50 47N 105 0W
Register, U.S.A. 152 C8 32 22N 81 53W
Registro, Brazil 175 A6 24 29 S 47 49W
Reguengos de Monsaraz, Portugal 43 G3 38 25N 7 32W
Reh, Erg er, Algeria 111 C5 27 48N 4 30 E
Rehar →, India 93 H10 23 55N 82 40 E
Rehli, India 93 H8 23 38N 79 5 E
Rehoboth, Namibia 116 C2 23 15 S 17 4 E
Rehovot, Israel 103 D3 31 54N 34 48 E
Reïbell = Ksar Chellala, Algeria 111 A5 35 13N 2 19 E
Reichenau = Rychnov nad Kněžnou, Czech Rep. 35 A9 50 10N 16 17 E
Reichenbach = Dzierżoniów, Poland 55 H3 50 45N 16 39 E
Reichenbach, Germany 30 E8 50 37N 12 17 E
Reichenbach, Switz. 32 C5 46 38N 7 42 E
Reichenberg = Liberec, Czech Rep. 34 A8 50 47N 15 7 E
Reichshof = Rzeszów, Poland 55 H8 50 5N 21 58 E
Reid, Australia 125 F4 30 49 S 128 26 E
Reiden, Switz. 32 B5 47 14N 7 59 E
Reidsville, Ga., U.S.A. 152 C7 32 6N 82 7W
Reidsville, N.C., U.S.A. 149 G6 36 21N 79 40W
Reifnig = Ribnica, Slovenia 45 C11 45 45N 14 45 E
Reigate, U.K. 21 F7 51 14N 0 12W
Reillo, Spain 40 F3 39 54N 1 53W
Reims, France 27 C11 49 15N 4 1 E
Reina Adelaida, Arch., Chile 176 D2 52 20 S 74 0W
Reina Sofia, Tenerife ✕ (TFS), Canary Is. 9 e1 28 3N 16 33W
Reinach, Aargau, Switz. 32 B6 47 14N 8 11 E
Reinach, Basel, Switz. 32 B5 47 29N 7 35 E
Reinbeck, U.S.A. 156 B4 42 19N 92 36W
Reinbek, Germany 30 B6 53 30N 10 15 E
Reindeer →, Canada 143 B8 55 36N 103 11W
Reindeer I., Canada 143 C9 52 30N 98 0W
Reindeer L., Canada 143 B8 57 15N 102 15W
Reinga, C., N.Z. 130 A1 34 25 S 172 43 E
Reinosa, Spain 42 B6 43 2N 4 15W
Reinsvoll, Norway 18 D7 60 40N 10 38 E
Reitan, Norway 18 B8 62 49N 11 22 E
Reitz, S. Africa 117 D4 27 48 S 28 29 E
Reivilo, S. Africa 116 D3 27 36 S 24 8 E
Rejaf, Sudan 107 G3 4 45N 31 35 E
Rejmyre, Sweden 17 F9 58 50N 15 55 E
Rejowiec Fabryczny, Poland 55 G10 51 5N 23 17 E
Reka →, Slovenia 45 C11 45 40N 14 0 E
Rekohua = Chatham I., N.Z. 131 a 43 50 S 176 20W
Rekovac, Serbia & M. 50 C5 43 51N 21 3 E
Reliance, Canada 143 A7 63 0N 109 20W
Relizane, Algeria 111 A5 35 44N 0 31 E
Remad, Oued →, Algeria 111 B4 33 28N 1 20W
Rémalard, France 26 D7 48 26N 0 47 E
Remarkable, Mt., Australia 128 B3 32 48 S 138 10 E
Remarkables, The, N.Z. 131 F3 45 10 S 168 50 E
Rembang, Indonesia 85 D4 6 42 S 111 21 E
Rembau, Malaysia 84 B2 2 35N 102 6 E
Rembert, U.S.A. 152 A9 34 6N 80 32W
Remchi, Algeria 111 A4 35 2N 1 26W
Remedios, Colombia 168 B3 7 2N 74 41W
Remedios, Panama 164 E3 8 15N 81 50W
Remeshk, Iran 97 E8 26 55N 58 50 E
Remetea, Romania 53 D10 46 45N 25 29 E
Remich, Lux. 24 E6 49 32N 6 22 E
Remington, U.S.A. 157 D9 40 46N 87 9W
Rémire, Fr. Guiana 169 C7 4 53N 52 17W
Remiremont, France 27 D13 48 2N 6 36 E
Remo, Ethiopia 107 F5 6 48N 41 20 E
Remontnoye, Russia 61 G6 46 34N 43 37 E
Remoulins, France 29 E8 43 55N 4 35 E
Remscheid, Germany 24 C7 51 11N 7 12 E
Ren Xian, China 74 F8 37 8N 114 40 E
Rena, Norway 18 C8 61 8N 11 20 E
Rena →, Norway 18 C8 61 8N 11 23 E
Renascença, Brazil 168 D4 3 50 S 66 21W
Rend Lake, U.S.A. 156 F8 38 2N 88 58W
Rendang, Indonesia 79 J18 8 26 S 115 25 E
Rende, Italy 47 C9 39 20N 16 11 E
Rendína, Greece 48 B3 39 4N 21 58 E
Rendova, Solomon Is. 133 M9 8 33 S 157 17 E
Rendsburg, Germany 30 A5 54 17N 9 39 E
Renens, Switz. 32 C3 46 32N 6 35 E
Renfrew, Canada 140 C4 45 30N 76 40W
Renfrewshire □, U.K. 22 F4 55 49N 4 38W
Renfroe, U.S.A. 152 C5 32 14N 84 43W
Rengat, Indonesia 84 C2 0 30 S 102 45 E
Rengo, Chile 174 C1 34 24 S 70 50W
Renhua, China 77 E9 25 5N 113 40 E
Renhuai, China 76 D6 27 48N 106 24 E
Reni, Ukraine 53 E13 45 28N 28 15 E
Renigunta, India 95 H4 13 38N 79 30 E
Renk, Sudan 107 E3 11 50N 32 50 E
Renland, Greenland 10 C8 71 10N 26 30W
Renmark, Australia 128 C4 34 11 S 140 43 E
Rennebu, Norway 18 B6 62 52N 9 49 E
Rennell, Solomon Is. 133 N11 11 40 S 160 10 E
Rennell Sd., Canada 142 C2 53 23N 132 35W
Renner Springs, Australia 126 B1 18 20 S 133 47 E
Rennes, France 26 D5 48 7N 1 41W
Rennie L., Canada 143 A7 61 32N 105 35W
Reno, U.S.A. 160 F7 39 31N 119 48W
Reno →, Italy 45 D9 44 38N 12 16 E
Renovo, U.S.A. 150 E7 41 20N 77 45W
Renqiu, China 74 E9 38 43N 116 5 E
Rens, Denmark 17 K3 54 54N 9 5 E
Renshou, China 76 C5 30 3N 104 9 E
Rensselaer, Ind., U.S.A. 157 D9 40 57N 87 9W
Rensselaer, N.Y., U.S.A. 151 D11 42 38N 73 45W
Rentería, Spain 40 B3 43 19N 1 54W
Renton, U.S.A. 160 C4 47 29N 122 12W
Renwick, N.Z. 131 B8 41 30 S 173 51 E
Réo, Burkina Faso 112 C4 12 28N 2 35W
Reo, Indonesia 82 C2 8 19 S 120 30 E
Reocín, Spain 42 B6 43 21N 4 5W
Reotipur, India 93 G10 25 33N 83 45 E
Repalle, India 95 F5 16 2N 80 45 E
Répcelak, Hungary 52 C2 47 24N 17 1 E
Reppen = Rzepin, Poland 55 F1 52 20N 14 49 E
Republic, Mo., U.S.A. 155 G8 37 7N 93 29W
Republic, Wash., U.S.A. 158 B4 48 39N 118 44W
Republican →, U.S.A. 154 F6 39 4N 96 48W
Republiek, Suriname 169 B6 5 30N 55 13W
Repulse B., Australia 126 J6 20 35 S 148 46 E
Repulse Bay, Canada 139 B11 66 30N 86 30W
Requena, Peru 172 B3 5 5 S 73 52W
Requena, Spain 41 F3 39 30N 1 4W
Réquista, France 28 D6 44 1N 2 31 E
Reşadiye = Datça, Turkey 49 E9 36 46N 27 40 E
Reşadiye, Turkey 100 B7 40 23N 37 20 E
Reşadiye Yarımadası, Turkey 49 E9 36 40N 27 45 E
Resavica, Serbia & M. 50 B5 44 4N 21 31 E
Resen, Macedonia 50 E5 41 5N 21 0 E
Reserve, U.S.A. 159 K9 33 43N 108 45W
Resht = Rasht, Iran 97 B6 37 20N 49 40 E
Résia, Italy 33 C11 46 50N 10 31 E
Resistencia, Argentina 174 B4 27 30 S 59 0W
Reşiţa, Romania 52 E6 45 18N 21 53 E
Resko, Poland 54 E2 53 47N 15 25 E
Reso = Raisio, Finland 15 F20 60 28N 22 11 E
Resolution I., Canada 139 B13 61 30N 65 0W
Resolution I., N.Z. 131 F1 45 40 S 166 40 E
Resplandes, Brazil 170 C2 6 17 S 45 13W
Resplendor, Brazil 171 E3 19 20 S 41 15W
Ressano Garcia, Mozam. 117 D5 25 25 S 32 0 E
Restinga de Jurubatiba △, Brazil 171 F3 22 5 S 41 20W
Reston, Canada 143 D8 49 33N 101 6W
Resulayn = Ceylânpınar, Turkey 101 D9 36 50N 40 2 E
Reszel, Poland 54 D8 54 4N 21 10 E
Retalhuleu, Guatemala 164 D1 14 33N 91 46W
Retenue, L. de, Dem. Rep. of the Congo 119 E2 11 0 S 27 0 E
Retezat △, Romania 52 E7 45 23N 22 56 E
Retezat, Munţii, Romania 52 E8 45 25N 23 0 E
Retford, U.K. 20 D7 53 19N 0 56W
Rethel, France 27 C11 49 30N 4 20 E
Rethem, Germany 30 C5 52 47N 9 22 E
Rethimno = Réthímnon, Greece 39 E5 35 18N 24 30 E
Réthímnon, Greece 39 E5 35 18N 24 30 E
Réthímnon □, Greece 39 E5 35 23N 24 28 E
Reti, Pakistan 92 E3 28 5N 69 48 E
Retiche, Alpi, Switz. 33 D10 46 30N 10 0 E
Retiers, France 26 E5 47 55N 1 23W
Retortillo, Spain 42 E4 40 48N 6 21W
Retournac, France 29 C8 45 12N 4 2 E
Rétság, Hungary 52 C4 47 58N 19 10 E
Rettenberg, Germany 33 A10 47 35N 10 18 E
Réunion ☑, Ind. Oc. 121 c 21 0 S 56 0 E
Reus, Spain 40 D6 41 10N 1 5 E
Reuss →, Switz. 33 B6 47 16N 8 24 E
Reuterstadt Stavenhagen, Germany 30 B8 53 42N 12 54 E
Reutlingen, Germany 31 G5 48 29N 9 12 E
Reutte, Austria 34 D3 47 29N 10 42 E
Reval = Tallinn, Estonia 15 G21 59 22N 24 48 E
Revda, Russia 64 C7 56 48N 59 57 E
Revel = Tallinn, Estonia 15 G21 59 22N 24 48 E
Revel, France 28 E6 43 28N 2 1 E
Revelganj, India 93 G11 25 50N 84 40 E
Revelstoke, Canada 142 C5 51 0N 118 10W
Reventazón, Peru 172 B1 6 10 S 80 58W
Revigny-sur-Ornain, France 27 D11 48 49N 4 59 E
Revillagigedo, Is. de, Pac. Oc. 162 D2 18 40N 112 0W
Revin, France 27 C11 49 55N 4 39 E
Revolyutsii, Pik, Tajikistan 65 D6 38 31N 72 21 E
Revolyutsiya, Qullai = Revolyutsii, Pik, Tajikistan 65 D6 38 31N 72 21 E
Revúca, Slovak Rep. 35 C13 48 41N 20 7 E
Revuè →, Mozam. 119 F3 19 50 S 34 0 E
Rewa, India 93 G9 24 33N 81 25 E
Rewa →, Guyana 169 C6 3 19N 58 42W
Rewari, India 92 E7 28 15N 76 40 E
Rex, U.S.A. 144 D10 64 13N 149 16W
Rexburg, U.S.A. 158 E8 43 49N 111 47W
Rey, Iran 97 C6 35 35N 51 25 E
Rey, I. del, Panama 164 E4 8 20N 78 30W
Rey, Mayo →, Cameroon 114 A2 8 47N 14 1 E
Rey, Rio-del-→, Cameroon 114 B1 4 31N 8 45 E
Rey Bouba, Cameroon 114 A2 8 40N 14 15 E
Rey Malabo, Eq. Guin. 113 E6 3 45N 8 50 E
Reyðarfjörður, Iceland 11 B12 65 2N 14 13W
Reyes, Bolivia 172 C4 14 19 S 67 23W
Reyes, Pt., U.S.A. 160 H3 38 0N 123 0W
Reyhanlı, Turkey 100 D7 36 16N 36 35 E
Reykholt, Árnessýsla, Iceland 11 C5 64 40N 21 18W
Reykholt, Borgarfjarðarsýsla, Iceland 11 C6 64 10N 20 25W
Reykjahlið, Iceland 11 B10 65 40N 16 55W
Reykjanes, Iceland 11 D4 63 48N 22 40W
Reykjanes Ridge, Atl. Oc. 8 A8 59 0N 31 0W
Reykjavík, Iceland 11 C5 64 10N 21 57W
Reykjavík Keflavík ✕ (KEF), Iceland 11 C4 64 0N 22 45W
Reynolds, Ga., U.S.A. 152 C5 32 33N 84 6W
Reynolds, Ill., U.S.A. 156 C6 41 20N 90 40W
Reynolds Ra., Australia 124 D5 22 30 S 133 0 E
Reynoldsville, Ga., U.S.A. 152 E5 30 51N 84 47W
Reynoldsville, Pa., U.S.A. 150 E6 41 5N 78 58W
Reynosa, Mexico 163 B5 26 5N 98 18W
Reza'iyeh = Orūmīyeh, Iran 101 D11 37 40N 45 0 E
Rezāiyeh, L. = Orūmīyeh, Daryācheh-ye, Iran 101 D11 37 50N 45 30 E
Rēzekne, Latvia 15 H22 56 30N 27 17 E
Rezh, Russia 64 C8 57 23N 61 24 E
Rezhitsa = Rēzekne, Latvia 15 H22 56 30N 27 17 E
Rezina, Moldova 53 C13 47 45N 28 58 E
Rezovo, Bulgaria 51 D12 42 0N 28 0 E
Rezvān, Iran 97 E8 27 34N 56 6 E
Rgotina, Serbia & M. 50 B6 44 1N 22 17 E

Rhamnus, *Greece* **48 C6** 38 12N 24 3 E
Rharbi, Zahrez, *Algeria* **111 B5** 34 50N 2 55 E
Rharis, O. →, *Algeria* **111 C6** 26 0N 5 4 E
Rhayader, *U.K.* **21 E4** 52 18N 3 29W
Rheda-Wiedenbrück, *Germany* **30 D4** 51 50N 8 20 E
Rhede, *Germany* **30 D2** 51 50N 6 42 E
Rhein →, *Europe* **24 C6** 51 52N 6 2 E
Rhein-Main-Donau-Kanal, *Germany* **31 F7** 49 1N 11 27 E
Rhein-Ruhr, Düsseldorf ✈ (DUS), *Germany* **30 D2** 51 17N 6 46 E
Rhein-Taunus ⌓, *Germany* **31 E4** 50 10N 8 10 E
Rhein-Westerwald ⌓, *Germany* **30 E3** 50 32N 7 20 E
Rheinbach, *Germany* **30 E2** 50 38N 6 57 E
Rheine, *Germany* **30 C3** 52 17N 7 26 E
Rheineck, *Switz.* **33 B9** 47 28N 9 31 E
Rheinfall, *Switz.* **33 A7** 47 40N 8 37 E
Rheinfelden, *Germany* **31 H3** 47 33N 7 47 E
Rheinfelden, *Switz.* **32 A5** 47 32N 7 47 E
Rheinhessen-Pfalz □, *Germany* **31 F3** 49 20N 8 0 E
Rheinland-Pfalz □, *Germany* **31 E2** 50 0N 7 0 E
Rheinsberg, *Germany* **30 B8** 53 6N 12 54 E
Rheinwaldhorn, *Switz.* **33 D8** 46 30N 9 3 E
Rheris, Oued →, *Morocco* **110 B4** 30 50N 4 34W
Rhin = Rhein →, *Europe* **24 C6** 51 52N 6 2 E
Rhine = Rhein →, *Europe* **24 C6** 51 52N 6 2 E
Rhine, *U.S.A.* **152 D6** 31 59N 83 12W
Rhinebeck, *U.S.A.* **151 E11** 41 56N 73 55W
Rhineland-Palatinate = Rheinland-Pfalz □, *Germany* **31 E2** 50 0N 7 0 E
Rhinelander, *U.S.A.* **154 C10** 45 38N 89 25W
Rhinns Pt., *U.K.* **22 F2** 55 40N 6 29W
Rhino Camp, *Uganda* **118 B3** 3 0N 31 22 E
Rhir, Cap, *Morocco* **110 B3** 30 38N 9 54W
Rho, *Italy* **44 C6** 45 32N 9 2 E
Rhode Island □, *U.S.A.* **151 E13** 41 40N 71 30W
Rhodes = Ródhos, *Greece* **38 E12** 36 15N 28 10 E
Rhodesia = Zimbabwe ■, *Africa* **119 F3** 19 0 S 30 0 E
Rhodope Mts. = Rhodopi Planina, *Bulgaria* **51 E8** 41 40N 24 20 E
Rhodopi Planina, *Bulgaria* **51 E8** 41 40N 24 20 E
Rhön, *Germany* **30 E5** 50 24N 9 58 E
Rhondda, *U.K.* **21 F4** 51 39N 3 31W
Rhondda Cynon Taff □, *U.K.* **21 F4** 51 42N 3 27W
Rhône □, *France* **29 C8** 45 54N 4 35 E
Rhône →, *France* **29 E8** 43 28N 4 42 E
Rhône-Alpes □, *France* **29 C9** 45 40N 6 0 E
Rhum, *U.K.* **22 E2** 57 0N 6 20W
Rhyl, *U.K.* **20 D4** 53 20N 3 29W
Ri-Aba, *Eq. Guin.* **113 E6** 3 28N 8 40 E
Ria Formosa ⌓, *Portugal* **43 H3** 37 1N 7 48W
Riachão, *Brazil* **170 C2** 7 20 S 46 37W
Riacho de Santana, *Brazil* **171 D3** 13 37 S 42 57W
Rialma, *Brazil* **171 E2** 15 18 S 49 34W
Riang, *India* **90 B4** 27 31N 92 56 E
Riangnom, *Sudan* **107 F3** 9 55N 30 1 E
Riaño, *Spain* **42 C6** 42 59N 4 59W
Rians, *France* **29 E9** 43 37N 5 44 E
Riansáres →, *Spain* **43 F7** 39 32N 3 18W
Riasi, *India* **93 C6** 33 10N 74 50 E
Riau □, *Indonesia* **84 B2** 0 0 102 35 E
Riau, Kepulauan, *Indonesia* **84 B2** 0 30N 104 20 E
Riau Arch. = Riau, Kepulauan, *Indonesia* **84 B2** 0 30N 104 20 E
Riaza, *Spain* **42 D7** 41 18N 3 30W
Riaza →, *Spain* **42 D7** 41 42N 3 55W
Riba de Saelices, *Spain* **40 E2** 40 55N 2 17W
Riba-Roja de Turia, *Spain* **41 F4** 39 33N 0 34W
Ribadavia, *Spain* **42 C2** 42 17N 8 8W
Ribadeo, *Spain* **42 B3** 43 35N 7 5W
Ribadesella, *Spain* **42 B5** 43 30N 5 7W
Ribado, *Nigeria* **113 D7** 9 16N 12 47 E
Ribamar, *Brazil* **170 B3** 2 33 S 44 3W
Ribao, *Cameroon* **113 D7** 6 32N 11 30 E
Ribas = Ribes de Freser, *Spain* **40 C7** 42 19N 2 15 E
Ribas do Rio Pardo, *Brazil* **173 E7** 20 27 S 53 46W
Ribauè, *Mozam.* **119 E4** 14 57 S 38 17 E
Ribble →, *U.K.* **20 D5** 53 52N 2 25W
Ribe, *Denmark* **17 J2** 55 19N 8 44 E
Ribe Amtskommune □, *Denmark* **17 J2** 55 35N 8 45 E
Ribeauvillé, *France* **27 D14** 48 10N 7 20 E
Ribécourt-Dreslincourt, *France* **27 C9** 49 30N 2 55 E
Ribeira = Santa Uxía, *Spain* **42 C2** 42 36N 8 58W
Ribeira Brava, *Madeira* **9 c** 32 41N 17 4W
Ribeira do Pombal, *Brazil* **170 D4** 10 50 S 38 32W
Ribeira Grande, *Azores* **9 d3** 37 49N 25 31W
Ribeira Grande, *C. Verde Is.* **9 j** 17 0N 25 4W
Ribeirão, *Brazil* **170 C4** 8 31 S 35 23W
Ribeirão Prêto, *Brazil* **175 A6** 21 10 S 47 50W
Ribeiro Gonçalves, *Brazil* **170 C2** 7 32 S 45 14W
Ribemont, *France* **27 C10** 49 47N 3 27 E
Ribera, *Italy* **46 E6** 37 30N 13 16 E
Ribérac, *France* **28 C4** 45 15N 0 20 E
Riberalta, *Bolivia* **173 C4** 11 0 S 66 0W
Ribes de Freser, *Spain* **40 C7** 42 19N 2 15 E
Ribnica, *Slovenia* **45 C11** 45 45N 14 45 E
Ribnitz-Damgarten, *Germany* **30 A8** 54 15N 12 27 E
Ričany, *Czech Rep.* **34 B7** 50 0N 14 40 E
Riccarton, *N.Z.* **131 D7** 43 32 S 172 37 E
Ríccia, *Italy* **47 A7** 41 30N 14 50 E
Riccione, *Italy* **45 E9** 43 59N 12 39 E
Rice, *U.S.A.* **161 L12** 34 5N 114 51W
Rice L., *Canada* **150 B6** 44 12N 78 10W
Rice Lake, *U.S.A.* **154 C9** 45 30N 91 44W
Riceboro, *U.S.A.* **152 D8** 31 44N 81 26W
Rich, *Morocco* **110 B4** 32 16N 4 30W
Rich, C., *Canada* **150 B4** 44 43N 80 38W
Richard Toll, *Senegal* **112 B1** 16 25N 15 42W
Richards Bay, *S. Africa* **117 D5** 28 48 S 32 6 E
Richardson →, *Canada* **143 B6** 58 25N 111 14W
Richardson Lakes, *U.S.A.* **148 C10** 44 46N 70 58W
Richardson Mts., *N.Z.* **131 E3** 44 49 S 168 34 E
Richardson Springs, *U.S.A.* **160 F5** 39 51N 121 46W
Riche, C., *Australia* **125 F2** 34 36 S 118 47 E
Richelieu, *France* **26 E7** 47 1N 0 20 E
Richey, *U.S.A.* **154 B2** 47 39N 105 4W
Richfield, *U.S.A.* **159 G8** 38 46N 112 5W
Richfield Springs, *U.S.A.* **151 D10** 42 51N 74 59W
Richford, *U.S.A.* **151 B12** 45 0N 72 40W
Richibucto, *Canada* **141 C7** 46 42N 64 54W
Richland, *Ga., U.S.A.* **152 C5** 32 5N 84 40W
Richland, *Iowa, U.S.A.* **156 C5** 41 13N 92 0W
Richland, *Mo., U.S.A.* **156 G4** 37 51N 92 26W
Richland, *Wash., U.S.A.* **158 C4** 46 17N 119 18W
Richland Center, *U.S.A.* **154 D9** 43 21N 90 23W
Richlands, *U.S.A.* **148 G5** 37 6N 81 48W
Richmond, *N.S.W., Australia* **129 B9** 33 35 S 150 42 E
Richmond, *Queens., Australia* **126 C3** 20 43 S 143 8 E
Richmond, *N.Z.* **131 B8** 41 20 S 173 12 E
Richmond, *U.K.* **20 C6** 54 25N 1 43W
Richmond, *Calif., U.S.A.* **160 H4** 37 56N 122 21W
Richmond, *Ind., U.S.A.* **157 E12** 39 50N 84 53W
Richmond, *Ky., U.S.A.* **157 G12** 37 45N 84 18W
Richmond, *Mich., U.S.A.* **150 D2** 42 49N 82 45W
Richmond, *Mo., U.S.A.* **156 E3** 39 17N 93 58W
Richmond, *Tex., U.S.A.* **155 L7** 29 35N 95 46W
Richmond, *Utah, U.S.A.* **158 F8** 41 56N 111 48W
Richmond, *Va., U.S.A.* **148 G7** 37 33N 77 27W
Richmond, *Vt., U.S.A.* **151 B12** 44 24N 72 59W
Richmond, Mt., *N.Z.* **131 B8** 41 32 S 173 22 E
Richmond Hill, *Canada* **150 C5** 43 52N 79 27W
Richmond Hill, *U.S.A.* **152 D8** 31 56N 81 18W
Richmond Ra., *Australia* **127 D5** 29 0 S 152 45 E
Richmond Ra., *N.Z.* **131 B8** 41 32 S 173 22 E
Richtersveld △, *S. Africa* **116 D2** 28 15 S 17 10 E
Richterswil, *Switz.* **33 B7** 47 13N 8 43 E
Richwood, *Ohio, U.S.A.* **157 D13** 40 26N 83 18W
Richwood, *W. Va., U.S.A.* **148 F5** 38 14N 80 32W
Ricla, *Spain* **40 D3** 41 31N 1 24W
Ricupe, *Angola* **115 E4** 14 37 S 21 25 E
Ridā', *Yemen* **98 D4** 14 25N 44 50 E
Ridder = Leninogorsk, *Kazakhstan* **66 D9** 50 20N 83 30 E
Riddes, *Switz.* **32 D4** 46 11N 7 14 E
Riddlesburg, *U.S.A.* **150 F6** 40 9N 78 15W
Ridge Farm, *U.S.A.* **157 E9** 39 54N 87 39W
Ridge Spring, *U.S.A.* **152 B8** 33 51N 81 40W
Ridgecrest, *U.S.A.* **161 K9** 35 38N 117 40W
Ridgefield, *Conn., U.S.A.* **151 E11** 41 17N 73 30W
Ridgefield, *Wash., U.S.A.* **160 E4** 45 49N 122 45W
Ridgeland, *Miss., U.S.A.* **155 J9** 32 26N 90 8W
Ridgeland, *S.C., U.S.A.* **152 C9** 32 29N 80 59W
Ridgetown, *Canada* **140 D3** 42 26N 81 52W
Ridgeville, *Ind., U.S.A.* **157 D11** 40 18N 85 2W
Ridgeville, *S.C., U.S.A.* **152 B9** 33 6N 80 19W
Ridgewood, *U.S.A.* **151 F10** 40 59N 74 7W
Ridgway, *Ill., U.S.A.* **157 G8** 37 48N 88 16W
Ridgway, *Pa., U.S.A.* **150 E6** 41 25N 78 44W
Riding Mountain △, *Canada* **143 C9** 50 50N 100 0W
Ridley, Mt., *Australia* **125 F3** 33 12 S 122 7 E
Riebeek-Oos, *S. Africa* **116 E4** 33 10 S 26 10 E
Ried, *Austria* **34 C6** 48 14N 13 30 E
Riedlingen, *Germany* **31 G5** 48 9N 9 28 E
Riedstadt, *Germany* **31 F4** 49 45N 8 30 E
Riehen, *Switz.* **32 A5** 47 37N 7 38 E
Rienza →, *Italy* **45 B8** 46 49N 11 47 E
Riesa, *Germany* **30 D9** 51 17N 13 17 E
Riesco, I., *Chile* **176 D2** 52 55 S 72 40W
Riesenburg = Prabuty, *Poland* **54 E6** 53 47N 19 15 E
Riesi, *Italy* **47 E7** 37 17N 14 5 E
Riet →, *S. Africa* **116 D3** 29 0 S 23 54 E
Rietavas, *Lithuania* **54 C8** 55 44N 21 56 E
Rietbron, *S. Africa* **116 E3** 32 54 S 23 10 E
Rietfontein, *Namibia* **116 C3** 21 58 S 20 58 E
Rieti, *Italy* **45 F9** 42 24N 12 51 E
Rieupeyroux, *France* **28 D6** 44 19N 2 12 E
Riez, *France* **29 E10** 43 49N 6 6 E
Rif = Er Rif, *Morocco* **111 A4** 35 1N 4 1W
Riffe L., *U.S.A.* **160 D4** 46 32N 122 26W
Rifle, *U.S.A.* **158 G10** 39 32N 107 47W
Rift Valley, *Africa* **104 G7** 7 0N 30 0 E
Rift Valley □, *Kenya* **118 B4** 0 20N 36 0 E
Rig Rig, *Chad* **109 F2** 14 13N 14 25 E
Riga, *India* **90 A5** 28 26N 95 2 E
Rīga, *Latvia* **15 H21** 56 53N 24 8 E
Rīga ✈ (RIX), *Latvia* **54 B10** 56 54N 23 59 E
Riga, G. of, *Latvia* **15 H20** 57 40N 23 45 E
Rigacikun, *Nigeria* **113 C6** 10 40N 7 28 E
Rīgān, *Iran* **97 D8** 28 37N 58 58 E
Rīgas Jūras Līcis = Riga, G. of, *Latvia* **15 H20** 57 40N 23 45 E
Rigaud, *Canada* **151 A10** 45 29N 74 18W
Rigby, *U.S.A.* **158 E8** 43 40N 111 55W
Rīgestān, *Afghan.* **91 C2** 30 15N 65 0 E
Riggins, *U.S.A.* **158 D5** 45 25N 116 19W
Rignac, *France* **28 D6** 44 25N 2 16 E
Rigolet, *Canada* **141 B8** 54 10N 58 23W
Rihand Dam, *India* **93 G10** 24 9N 83 2 E
Riihimäki, *Finland* **15 F21** 60 45N 24 48 E
Riiser-Larsen-halvøya, *Antarctica* **7 C4** 68 0 S 35 0 E
Rijau, *Nigeria* **113 C6** 11 8N 5 17 E
Rijeka, *Croatia* **45 C11** 45 20N 14 21 E
Rijeka Crnojevića, *Serbia & M.* **50 D3** 42 24N 19 1 E
Rijssen, *Neths.* **24 B6** 52 19N 6 31 E
Rika →, *Ukraine* **53 B8** 48 11N 23 16 E
Rikā', W. ar →, *Si. Arabia* **98 B4** 22 25N 44 50 E
Rike, *Ethiopia* **107 E4** 10 50N 39 53 E
Rikuchū-Kaigan △, *Japan* **70 E11** 39 20N 142 0 E
Rikuzentakada, *Japan* **70 E10** 39 0N 141 40 E
Rila, *Bulgaria* **50 D7** 42 7N 23 7 E
Rila Planina, *Bulgaria* **50 D7** 42 10N 23 20 E
Riley, *U.S.A.* **158 E4** 43 32N 119 28W
Rima →, *Nigeria* **113 C6** 13 4N 5 10 E
Rimah, Wadi ar →, *Si. Arabia* **96 E4** 26 5N 41 30 E
Rimau, Pulau, *Malaysia* **87 c** 5 15N 100 16 E
Rimavská Sobota, *Slovak Rep.* **35 C13** 48 22N 20 2 E
Rimbey, *Canada* **142 C6** 52 35N 114 15W
Rimbo, *Sweden* **16 E12** 59 44N 18 21 E
Rimersburg, *U.S.A.* **150 E5** 41 3N 79 30W
Rimforsa, *Sweden* **17 F9** 58 6N 15 43 E
Rimi, *Nigeria* **113 C6** 12 58N 7 43 E
Rímini, *Italy* **45 D9** 44 3N 12 33 E
Rimouski, *Canada* **141 C6** 48 27N 68 30W
Rimrock, *U.S.A.* **160 D5** 46 38N 121 10W
Rinca, *Indonesia* **82 C1** 8 45 S 119 35 E
Rincon, *U.S.A.* **152 C8** 32 18N 81 14W
Rincón de la Victoria, *Spain* **43 J6** 36 43N 4 18W
Rincón de Romos, *Mexico* **162 C4** 22 14N 102 18W
Rinconada, *Argentina* **174 A2** 22 26 S 66 10W
Rind →, *India* **93 G9** 25 53N 80 33 E
Rindal, *Norway* **18 A6** 63 3N 9 13 E
Ringarum, *Sweden* **17 F10** 58 21N 16 26 E
Ringas, *India* **92 F6** 27 21N 75 34 E
Ringdove, *Vanuatu* **133 F6** 16 40 S 168 10 E
Ringe, *Denmark* **17 J4** 55 13N 10 28 E
Ringebu, *Norway* **18 C7** 61 32N 10 7 E
Ringgi, *Solomon Is.* **133 M9** 8 5 S 157 10 E
Ringgold Is., *Fiji* **133 A3** 16 15 S 179 25W
Ringim, *Nigeria* **113 C6** 12 13N 9 10 E
Ringkøbing, *Denmark* **17 H2** 56 5N 8 15 E
Ringkøbing Amtskommune □, *Denmark* **17 H2** 56 10N 8 45 E
Ringkøbing Fjord, *Denmark* **17 H2** 56 0N 8 15 E
Ringoma, *Angola* **115 E3** 12 25 S 17 32 E
Ringsaker, *Norway* **18 D7** 60 54N 10 45 E
Ringsjön, *Sweden* **17 J7** 55 55N 13 30 E
Ringsted, *Denmark* **17 J5** 55 25N 11 46 E
Ringvassøy, *Norway* **14 B18** 69 56N 19 15 E
Ringwood, *U.S.A.* **151 E10** 41 7N 74 15W
Rinía, *Greece* **49 D7** 37 23N 25 13 E
Rinjani, *Indonesia* **85 D5** 8 24 S 116 28 E
Rinteln, *Germany* **30 C5** 52 10N 9 8 E
Río, Punta del, *Spain* **41 J2** 36 49N 2 24W
Rio Bonito = Caiapônia, *Brazil* **173 D7** 16 57 S 51 49W
Rio Branco = Arcoverde, *Brazil* **170 C4** 8 25 S 37 4W
Rio Branco = Paratinga, *Brazil* **171 D3** 12 40 S 43 10W
Rio Branco = Roraima □, *Brazil* **169 C5** 2 0N 61 30W
Rio Branco, *Brazil* **172 B4** 9 58 S 67 49W
Río Branco, *Uruguay* **175 C5** 32 40 S 53 40W
Río Bravo ⌓, *N. Amer.* **162 B4** 29 2N 102 45W
Río Bravo del Norte →, *Mexico* **163 B5** 25 57N 97 9W
Rio Brilhante, *Brazil* **175 A5** 21 48 S 54 33W
Río Bueno, *Chile* **176 B2** 40 19 S 72 58W
Río Caribe, *Venezuela* **169 A5** 10 42N 63 7W
Río Chico, *Venezuela* **168 A4** 10 19N 65 59W
Rio Claro, *Brazil* **175 A6** 22 19 S 47 35W
Rio Claro, *Trin. & Tob.* **169 F9** 10 20N 61 25W
Río Colorado, *Argentina* **176 A4** 39 0 S 64 0W
Río Cuarto, *Argentina* **174 C3** 33 10 S 64 25W
Rio das Pedras, *Mozam.* **117 C6** 23 8 S 35 28 E
Rio de Contas, *Brazil* **171 D3** 13 36 S 41 48W
Rio de Janeiro, *Brazil* **171 F3** 23 0 S 43 12W
Rio de Janeiro □, *Brazil* **171 F3** 22 50 S 43 0W
Río de Oro, B. de, *W. Sahara* **110 D1** 23 45N 15 50W
Rio do Prado, *Brazil* **171 E3** 16 35 S 40 34W
Rio do Sul, *Brazil* **175 B6** 27 13 S 49 37W
Río Dulce △, *Guatemala* **164 C2** 15 43N 88 50W
Río Gallegos, *Argentina* **176 D3** 51 35 S 69 15W
Río Grande, *Argentina* **176 D3** 53 50 S 67 45W
Río Grande, *Bolivia* **172 E4** 20 51 S 67 17W
Rio Grande, *Brazil* **175 C5** 32 0 S 52 20W
Río Grande, *Mexico* **162 C4** 23 50N 103 2W
Río Grande, *Nic.* **164 D3** 12 54N 83 33W
Rio Grande, *Puerto Rico* **165 d** 18 23N 65 50W
Rio Grande, *U.S.A.* **155 N6** 25 58N 97 9W
Rio Grande City, *U.S.A.* **155 M5** 26 23N 98 49W
Río Grande de Santiago →, *Mexico* **162 C3** 21 36N 105 26W
Rio Grande do Norte □, *Brazil* **170 C4** 5 40 S 36 0W
Rio Grande do Sul □, *Brazil* **175 C5** 30 0 S 53 0W
Rio Grande Rise, *Atl. Oc.* **8 K8** 31 0 S 35 0W
Río Hato, *Panama* **164 E3** 8 22N 80 10W
Río Lagartos, *Mexico* **163 C7** 21 36N 88 10W
Rio Largo, *Brazil* **170 C4** 9 28 S 35 50W
Rio Maior, *Portugal* **43 F2** 39 19N 8 57W
Rio Marina, *Italy* **44 F7** 42 49N 10 25 E
Río Mayo, *Argentina* **176 C2** 45 40 S 70 15W
Río Mulatos, *Bolivia* **172 D4** 19 40 S 66 50W
Río Muni □, *Eq. Guin.* **114 B2** 1 30N 10 0 E
Rio Negro, *Brazil* **175 B6** 26 0 S 49 55W
Río Negro, *Chile* **176 B2** 40 47 S 73 14W
Rio Negro, Pantanal do, *Brazil* **173 D6** 19 0 S 56 0W
Rio Novo = Ipiaú, *Brazil* **171 D4** 14 8 S 39 44W
Rio Pardo = Ribas do Rio Pardo, *Brazil* **173 E7** 20 27 S 53 46W
Rio Pardo, *Brazil* **175 C5** 30 0 S 52 30W
Río Pico, *Argentina* **176 B2** 44 0 S 70 22W
Río Pilcomayo △, *Argentina* **174 B4** 25 5 S 58 5W
Río Platano ⌓, *Honduras* **164 C3** 15 45N 85 0W
Rio Prêto = Ibipetuba, *Brazil* **170 D3** 11 0 S 44 32W
Rio Preto da Eva, *Brazil* **169 D6** 2 46 S 59 41W
Rio Rancho, *U.S.A.* **159 J10** 35 14N 106 38W
Rio Real, *Brazil* **171 D4** 11 28 S 37 56W
Río Seco = Villa de María, *Argentina* **174 B3** 29 55 S 63 43W
Río Segundo, *Argentina* **174 C3** 31 40 S 63 59W
Río Simpson △, *Chile* **176 C2** 45 27 S 73 30W
Río Tercero, *Argentina* **174 C3** 32 15 S 64 8W
Rio Tinto, *Brazil* **170 C4** 6 48 S 35 5W
Rio Tinto, *Portugal* **42 D2** 41 11N 8 34W
Río Turbio, *Argentina* **176 D2** 51 32 S 72 18W
Rio Verde, *Brazil* **171 E1** 17 50 S 51 0W
Río Verde, *Mexico* **163 C5** 21 56N 99 59W
Rio Verde de Mato Grosso, *Brazil* **173 D7** 18 56 S 54 52W
Río Viejo △, *Venezuela* **168 B3** 7 15N 71 20W
Rio Vista, *U.S.A.* **160 G5** 38 10N 121 42W
Ríobamba, *Ecuador* **168 D2** 1 50 S 78 45W
Ríohacha, *Colombia* **168 A3** 11 33N 72 55W
Rioja, *Peru* **172 B2** 6 11 S 77 5W
Riom, *France* **28 C7** 45 54N 3 7 E
Riom-ès-Montagnes, *France* **28 C6** 45 17N 2 39 E
Rion-des-Landes, *France* **28 E3** 43 55N 0 56W
Rionegro, *Antioquía, Colombia* **168 B2** 6 9N 75 22W
Rionegro, *Santander, Colombia* **168 B3** 7 15N 73 9W
Rionero in Vúlture, *Italy* **47 B8** 40 55N 15 40 E
Rioni →, *Georgia* **61 J5** 42 14N 41 44 E
Riós, *Spain* **42 D3** 41 58N 7 16W
Riosinho →, *Brazil* **173 B7** 7 7 S 51 39W
Ríosucio, *Caldas, Colombia* **168 B2** 5 30N 75 40W
Ríosucio, *Choco, Colombia* **168 B2** 7 27N 77 7W
Riou L., *Canada* **143 B7** 59 7N 106 25W
Rioz, *France* **27 E13** 47 26N 6 5 E
Riozinho →, *Brazil* **168 D4** 2 55 S 67 7W
Ripatransone, *Italy* **45 F10** 42 59N 13 46 E
Ripley, *Canada* **150 B3** 44 4N 81 35W
Ripley, *Calif., U.S.A.* **161 M12** 33 32N 114 39W
Ripley, *N.Y., U.S.A.* **150 D5** 42 16N 79 43W
Ripley, *Ohio, U.S.A.* **157 F13** 38 45N 83 51W
Ripley, *Tenn., U.S.A.* **155 H10** 35 45N 89 32W
Ripley, *W. Va., U.S.A.* **148 F5** 38 49N 81 43W
Ripoll, *Spain* **40 C7** 42 15N 2 13 E
Ripon, *U.K.* **20 C6** 54 9N 1 31W
Ripon, *Calif., U.S.A.* **160 H5** 37 44N 121 7W
Ripon, *Wis., U.S.A.* **148 D1** 43 51N 88 50W
Riposto, *Italy* **47 E8** 37 44N 15 12 E
Rippin = Rypin, *Poland* **55 E6** 53 3N 19 25 E
Risan, *Serbia & M.* **50 D2** 42 32N 18 42 E
Risaralda □, *Colombia* **168 B2** 5 0N 76 10W
Riscle, *France* **28 E3** 43 39N 0 5W
Rishā', W. ar →, *Si. Arabia* **96 E5** 25 33N 44 5 E
Rishiri-Rebun-Sarobetsu △, *Japan* **70 B10** 45 26N 141 30 E
Rishiri-Tō, *Japan* **70 B10** 45 11N 141 15 E
Rishon le Ẕiyyon, *Israel* **103 D3** 31 58N 34 48 E
Rishtan, *Uzbekistan* **65 C5** 40 20N 71 15 E
Rising Sun, *U.S.A.* **157 F12** 38 57N 84 51W
Risle →, *France* **26 C7** 49 26N 0 23 E
Risnjak △, *Croatia* **45 C11** 45 25N 14 36 E
Rison, *U.S.A.* **155 J8** 33 58N 92 11W
Risør, *Norway* **18 F6** 58 43N 9 13 E
Rissani, *Morocco* **110 B4** 31 18N 4 12W
Rita Blanca Cr. →, *U.S.A.* **155 H3** 35 40N 102 29W
Ritchie's Arch., *India* **95 H11** 12 14N 93 10 E
Riti, *Nigeria* **113 D6** 7 57N 9 41 E
Ritidian Pt., *Guam* **133 R15** 13 39N 144 51 E
Ritter, Mt., *U.S.A.* **160 H7** 37 41N 119 12W
Rittman, *U.S.A.* **150 F3** 40 58N 81 47W
Ritzville, *U.S.A.* **158 C4** 47 8N 118 23W
Riu, *India* **90 A5** 28 19N 95 3 E
Riva del Garda, *Italy* **44 C7** 45 53N 10 50 E
Riva Lígure, *Italy* **44 E4** 43 50N 7 50 E
Rivadavia, *Buenos Aires, Argentina* **174 D3** 35 29 S 62 59W
Rivadavia, *Mendoza, Argentina* **174 C2** 33 13 S 68 30W
Rivadavia, *Salta, Argentina* **174 A3** 24 5 S 62 54W
Rivadavia, *Chile* **174 B1** 29 57 S 70 35W
Rivarolo Canavese, *Italy* **44 C4** 45 19N 7 43 E
Rivas, *Nic.* **164 D2** 11 30N 85 50W
Rive-de-Gier, *France* **29 C8** 45 32N 4 37 E
River Cess, *Liberia* **112 D3** 5 30N 9 32W
River Jordan, *Canada* **160 B2** 48 26N 124 3W
Rivera, *Argentina* **174 D3** 37 12 S 63 14W
Rivera, *Uruguay* **175 C4** 31 0 S 55 50W
Riverbank, *U.S.A.* **160 H6** 37 44N 120 56W
Riverdale, *Calif., U.S.A.* **160 J7** 36 26N 119 52W
Riverdale, *Ga., U.S.A.* **152 B5** 33 34N 84 25W
Riverhead, *U.S.A.* **151 F12** 40 55N 72 40W
Riverhurst, *Canada* **143 C7** 50 55N 106 50W
Rivers, *Canada* **143 C8** 50 2N 100 14W
Rivers □, *Nigeria* **113 E6** 4 30N 7 10 E
Rivers Inlet, *Canada* **142 C3** 51 42N 127 15W
Riversdale, *N.Z.* **131 F3** 45 54 S 168 44 E
Riversdale, *S. Africa* **116 E3** 34 7 S 21 15 E
Riverside, *U.S.A.* **161 M9** 33 59N 117 22W
Riverton, *Australia* **128 C3** 34 10 S 138 46 E
Riverton, *Canada* **143 C9** 51 1N 97 0W
Riverton, *N.Z.* **131 G2** 46 21 S 168 0 E
Riverton, *Ill., U.S.A.* **156 E7** 39 51N 89 33W
Riverton, *Wyo., U.S.A.* **158 E9** 43 2N 108 23W
Riverton Heights, *U.S.A.* **160 C4** 47 28N 122 17W
Riverview, *Fla., U.S.A.* **153 H7** 27 52N 82 20W
Riverview, *Fla., U.S.A.* **153 E2** 30 32N 87 12W
Rives, *France* **29 C9** 45 21N 5 31 E
Rivesaltes, *France* **28 F6** 42 47N 2 50 E
Riviera, *U.S.A.* **161 K12** 35 4N 114 35W
Riviera Beach, *U.S.A.* **153 J9** 26 47N 80 3W
Riviera di Levante, *Italy* **44 D6** 44 15N 9 30 E
Riviera di Ponente, *Italy* **44 D5** 44 10N 8 20 E
Rivière-au-Renard, *Canada* **141 C7** 48 59N 64 23W
Rivière Bleue ⌓, *N. Cal.* **133 V20** 22 6 S 166 38 E
Rivière-du-Loup, *Canada* **141 C6** 47 50N 69 30W
Rivière-Pentecôte, *Canada* **141 C6** 49 57N 67 1W
Rivière-Pilote, *Martinique* **164 c** 14 26N 60 53W
Rivière St-Paul, *Canada* **141 B8** 51 28N 57 45W
Rivière-Salée, *Martinique* **164 c** 14 31N 61 0W
Rivne, *Ukraine* **53 D14** 46 1N 29 10 E
Rivne, *Ukraine* **59 G4** 50 40N 26 10 E
Rívoli, *Italy* **44 C4** 45 3N 7 31 E
Rivoli B., *Australia* **128 D4** 37 32 S 140 3 E
Riwaka, *N.Z.* **131 B7** 41 5 S 172 59 E
Rixheim, *France* **27 E14** 47 40N 7 24 E
Riyadh = Ar Riyāḍ, *Si. Arabia* **96 E5** 24 41N 46 42 E
Rizal, *Cagayan, Phil.* **80 C3** 17 51N 121 21 E
Rizal, *Nueva Ecija, Phil.* **80 D3** 15 43N 121 6 E
Rizal, *Zamboanga del N., Phil.* **81 G4** 8 35N 123 26 E
Rize, *Turkey* **101 B9** 41 0N 40 30 E
Rizhao, *China* **75 G10** 35 25N 119 30 E
Rizokarpaso, *Cyprus* **39 E10** 35 36N 34 23 E
Rizzuto, C., *Italy* **47 D10** 38 53N 17 5 E
Rjukan, *Norway* **18 E5** 59 54N 8 33 E
Rjuven, *Norway* **18 E4** 59 9N 7 8 E
Ro, *Greece* **49 E11** 36 9N 29 33 E
Rô, *N. Cal.* **133 U21** 21 22 S 167 50 E
Roa, *Dem. Rep. of the Congo* **114 B4** 3 49N 24 56 E
Roa, *Norway* **18 D7** 60 17N 10 37 E
Roa, *Spain* **42 D7** 41 41N 3 56W
Roachdale, *U.S.A.* **157 E10** 39 51N 86 48W
Road Town, *Br. Virgin Is.* **165 e** 18 27N 64 37W
Roan Plateau, *U.S.A.* **158 G9** 39 20N 109 20W
Roanne, *France* **27 F11** 46 3N 4 4 E
Roanoke, *Ala., U.S.A.* **152 B4** 33 9N 85 22W
Roanoke, *Ind., U.S.A.* **157 D11** 40 58N 85 22W
Roanoke, *Va., U.S.A.* **148 G6** 37 16N 79 56W
Roanoke →, *U.S.A.* **149 H7** 35 57N 76 42W
Roanoke I., *U.S.A.* **149 H8** 35 55N 75 40W
Roanoke Rapids, *U.S.A.* **149 G7** 36 28N 77 40W
Roatán, *Honduras* **164 C2** 16 18N 86 35W
Rob Roy, *Solomon Is.* **133 L9** 7 23 S 157 36 E
Robāt Sang, *Iran* **97 C8** 35 35N 59 10 E
Robāṭkarīm, *Iran* **97 C6** 35 25N 50 59 E
Robāṭkarīm □, *Iran* **97 B6** 35 26N 50 59 E
Robbins I., *Australia* **127 G4** 40 42 S 145 0 E
Róbbio, *Italy* **44 C5** 45 17N 8 35 E
Robe, *Australia* **128 D3** 37 11 S 139 45 E
Robe →, *Australia* **124 D2** 21 42 S 116 15 E
Röbel, *Germany* **30 B8** 53 22N 12 35 E
Robert Lee, *U.S.A.* **155 K4** 31 54N 100 29W
Roberta, *U.S.A.* **152 C5** 32 43N 84 1W
Roberts, *U.S.A.* **157 D8** 40 37N 88 11W
Robertsdale, *U.S.A.* **150 F6** 40 11N 78 6W
Robertsganj, *India* **93 G10** 24 44N 83 4 E
Robertson, *S. Africa* **116 E2** 33 46 S 19 50 E
Robertson I., *Antarctica* **7 C18** 65 15 S 59 30W
Robertson Ra., *Australia* **124 D3** 23 15 S 121 0 E
Robertsport, *Liberia* **112 D2** 6 45N 11 26W
Robertstown, *Australia* **128 B3** 33 58 S 139 5 E
Roberval, *Canada* **141 C5** 48 32N 72 15W
Robeson Chan., *N. Amer.* **10 A4** 82 0N 61 30W
Robesonia, *U.S.A.* **151 F8** 40 21N 76 8W
Robi, *Ethiopia* **107 F4** 7 52N 39 38 E
Robinson, *U.S.A.* **157 F9** 39 0N 87 44W
Robinson →, *Australia* **126 B2** 16 3 S 137 16 E
Robinson Ra., *Australia* **125 E2** 25 40 S 119 0 E
Robinvale, *Australia* **128 C5** 34 40 S 142 45 E
Robledo, *Spain* **41 G2** 38 46N 2 26W
Roblin, *Canada* **143 C8** 51 14N 101 21W
Roboré, *Bolivia* **173 D6** 18 10 S 59 45W
Robson, *Canada* **142 D5** 49 20N 117 41W
Robson, Mt., *Canada* **142 C5** 53 10N 119 10W
Robstown, *U.S.A.* **155 M6** 27 47N 97 40W
Roca, C. da, *Portugal* **43 G1** 38 40N 9 31W
Roca Partida, I., *Mexico* **162 D2** 19 1N 112 2W
Rocamadour, *France* **28 D5** 44 48N 1 37 E
Rocca San Casciano, *Italy* **45 D8** 44 3N 11 50 E
Roccadáspide, *Italy* **47 B8** 40 27N 15 10 E
Roccastrada, *Italy* **45 F8** 43 0N 11 10 E
Roccella Iónica, *Italy* **47 D9** 38 19N 16 24 E
Rocha, *Uruguay* **175 C5** 34 30 S 54 25W
Rochdale, *U.K.* **20 D5** 53 38N 2 9W
Rochechouart, *France* **28 C4** 45 50N 0 49 E
Rochedo, *Brazil* **173 D7** 19 57 S 54 52W
Rochefort, *Belgium* **24 D5** 50 9N 5 12 E
Rochefort, *France* **28 C3** 45 56N 0 57W
Rochefort-en-Terre, *France* **26 E4** 47 42N 2 22W
Rochelle, *Ga., U.S.A.* **152 D6** 31 57N 83 27W
Rochelle, *Ill., U.S.A.* **156 C7** 41 56N 89 4W
Rocher River, *Canada* **142 A6** 61 23N 112 44W
Rocheservière, *France* **26 F5** 46 57N 1 30W
Rochester, *Australia* **128 D6** 36 22 S 144 41 E
Rochester, *U.K.* **21 F8** 51 23N 0 31 E
Rochester, *Ind., U.S.A.* **157 C10** 41 4N 86 13W
Rochester, *Minn., U.S.A.* **154 C8** 44 1N 92 28W
Rochester, *N.H., U.S.A.* **151 C14** 43 18N 70 59W
Rochester, *N.Y., U.S.A.* **150 C7** 43 10N 77 37W
Rochester Hills, *U.S.A.* **157 B13** 42 41N 83 8W
Rociu, *Romania* **53 F10** 44 43N 25 2 E
Rock →, *Canada* **142 A3** 60 7N 127 7W
Rock →, *U.S.A.* **156 C6** 41 29N 90 37W
Rock Creek, *U.S.A.* **150 E4** 41 40N 80 52W
Rock Falls, *U.S.A.* **156 C7** 41 47N 89 41W
Rock Flat, *Australia* **129 D8** 36 21 S 149 13 E
Rock Hill, *U.S.A.* **149 H5** 34 56N 81 1W
Rock Island, *U.S.A.* **156 C6** 41 30N 90 34W
Rock Port, *U.S.A.* **154 E7** 40 25N 95 31W
Rock Rapids, *U.S.A.* **154 D6** 43 26N 96 10W
Rock Sound, *Bahamas* **164 B4** 24 54N 76 12W
Rock Springs, *Mont., U.S.A.* **158 C10** 46 49N 106 15W
Rock Springs, *Wyo., U.S.A.* **158 F9** 41 35N 109 14W
Rock Valley, *U.S.A.* **154 D6** 43 12N 96 18W
Rockall, *Atl. Oc.* **8 A10** 57 37N 13 42W
Rockdale, *Tex., U.S.A.* **155 K6** 30 39N 97 0W
Rockdale, *Wash., U.S.A.* **160 C5** 47 22N 121 28W
Rockeby = Mungkan Kandju △, *Australia* **126 A3** 13 35 S 142 52 E
Rockefeller Plateau, *Antarctica* **7 E14** 80 0 S 140 0W
Rockford, *Ala., U.S.A.* **152 C3** 32 53N 86 13W
Rockford, *Ill., U.S.A.* **156 B7** 42 16N 89 6W
Rockford, *Iowa, U.S.A.* **156 A4** 43 3N 92 57W
Rockford, *Mich., U.S.A.* **157 A11** 43 7N 85 34W
Rockford, *Ohio, U.S.A.* **157 D12** 40 41N 84 39W
Rockglen, *Canada* **143 D7** 49 11N 105 57W
Rockhampton, *Australia* **126 C5** 23 22 S 150 32 E
Rockingham, *Australia* **125 F2** 32 15 S 115 38 E
Rockingham, *U.S.A.* **149 H6** 34 57N 79 46W
Rockingham B., *Australia* **126 B4** 18 5 S 146 10 E
Rocklake, *U.S.A.* **154 A5** 48 47N 99 15W
Rockland, *Canada* **151 A9** 45 33N 75 17W
Rockland, *Idaho, U.S.A.* **158 E7** 42 34N 112 53W
Rockland, *Maine, U.S.A.* **149 C11** 44 6N 69 7W
Rockland, *Mich., U.S.A.* **154 B10** 46 44N 89 11W
Rocklands Reservoir, *Australia* **128 D5** 37 15 S 142 5 E
Rockledge, *U.S.A.* **153 G9** 28 20N 80 43W
Rocklin, *U.S.A.* **160 G5** 38 48N 121 14W
Rockly B., *Trin. & Tob.* **169 E10** 11 9N 60 46W
Rockmart, *U.S.A.* **149 H3** 34 0N 85 3W
Rockport, *Ind., U.S.A.* **157 G9** 37 53N 87 3W
Rockport, *Mass., U.S.A.* **151 D14** 42 39N 70 37W
Rockport, *Tex., U.S.A.* **155 L6** 28 2N 97 3W
Rocksprings, *U.S.A.* **155 K4** 30 1N 100 13W
Rockstone, *Guyana* **169 B6** 5 59N 58 33W
Rockville, *Conn., U.S.A.* **151 E12** 41 52N 72 28W
Rockville, *Ind., U.S.A.* **157 E9** 39 46N 87 14W
Rockville, *Md., U.S.A.* **148 F7** 39 5N 77 9W
Rockwall, *U.S.A.* **155 J6** 32 56N 96 28W
Rockwell City, *U.S.A.* **156 B2** 42 24N 94 38W
Rockwood, *Canada* **150 C4** 43 37N 80 8W
Rockwood, *Maine, U.S.A.* **149 C11** 45 41N 69 45W
Rockwood, *Tenn., U.S.A.* **149 H3** 35 52N 84 41W
Rocky Ford, *U.S.A.* **154 F3** 38 3N 103 43W
Rocky Fork Lake, *U.S.A.* **157 E13** 39 12N 83 23W
Rocky Gully, *Australia* **125 F2** 34 30 S 116 57 E
Rocky Harbour, *Canada* **141 C8** 49 36N 57 55W
Rocky Island L., *Canada* **140 C3** 46 55N 83 0W
Rocky Lane, *Canada* **142 B5** 58 31N 116 22W
Rocky Mount, *U.S.A.* **149 H7** 35 57N 77 48W
Rocky Mountain △, *U.S.A.* **158 F11** 40 25N 105 45W
Rocky Mountain House, *Canada* **142 C6** 52 22N 114 55W
Rocky Mts., *N. Amer.* **158 G10** 49 0N 115 0W
Rocky Point, *Namibia* **116 B2** 19 3 S 12 30 E

Rocroi, *France* **27 C11** 49 55N 4 30 E
Rod, *Pakistan* **91 C1** 28 10N 63 5 E
Roda = Stadtroda, *Germany* **30 E7** 50 52N 11 44 E
Rødberg, *Norway* **18 D5** 60 17N 8 56 E
Rødby, *Denmark* **17 K5** 54 41N 11 23 E
Rødbyhavn, *Denmark* **17 K5** 54 39N 11 22 E
Roddickton, *Canada* **141 B8** 50 51N 56 8W
Rødding, *Denmark* **17 J3** 55 23N 9 3 E
Rödeby, *Sweden* **17 H9** 56 15N 15 37 E
Rødekro, *Denmark* **17 J3** 55 4N 9 20 E
Rodenkirchen, *Germany* **30 B4** 53 23N 8 26 E
Rodez, *France* **28 D6** 44 21N 2 33 E
Rodholívas, *Greece* **50 F7** 40 55N 24 0 E
Rodhópi □, *Greece* **51 E9** 41 5N 25 30 E
Rodhopoú, *Greece* **39 E4** 35 34N 23 45 E
Ródhos, *Greece* **38 E12** 36 15N 28 10 E
Ródhos ✕ (RHO), *Greece* **49 E10** 36 23N 28 12 E
Rodi Gargánico, *Italy* **45 G12** 41 55N 15 53 E
Rodna, *Romania* **53 C9** 47 25N 24 50 E
Rodnei, Munţii, *Romania* **53 C9** 47 35N 24 35 E
Rodney, *Canada* **150 D3** 42 34N 81 41W
Rodney, C., *N.Z.* **130 C3** 36 17 S 174 50 E
Rodniki, *Russia* **60 B5** 57 7N 41 47 E
Rodonit, Kepi i, *Albania* **50 E3** 41 35N 19 27 E
Rodriguez, *Ind. Oc.* **121 F5** 19 45 S 63 20 E
Roe ➛, *U.K.* **23 A5** 55 6N 6 59W
Roebling, *U.S.A.* **151 F10** 40 7N 74 47W
Roebourne, *Australia* **124 D2** 20 44 S 117 9 E
Roebuck B., *Australia* **124 C3** 18 5 S 122 20 E
Roermond, *Neths.* **24 C6** 51 12N 6 0 E
Roes Welcome Sd., *Canada* **139 B11** 65 0N 87 0W
Roeselare, *Belgium* **24 D3** 50 57N 3 7 E
Rogachev = Ragachow, *Belarus* **59 F6** 53 8N 30 5 E
Rogačica, *Serbia & M.* **50 B3** 44 4N 19 40 E
Rogagua, L., *Bolivia* **172 C4** 13 43 S 66 50W
Rogaland □, *Norway* **18 E3** 59 12N 6 20 E
Rogaška Slatina, *Slovenia* **45 B12** 46 15N 15 42 E
Rogatec, *Slovenia* **45 B12** 46 15N 15 46 E
Rogatica, *Bos.-H.* **52 G4** 43 47N 19 0 E
Rogatyn, *Ukraine* **59 H3** 49 24N 24 36 E
Rogdhia, *Greece* **39 E6** 35 22N 25 1 E
Rogers, *U.S.A.* **155 G7** 36 20N 94 7W
Rogers City, *U.S.A.* **148 C4** 45 25N 83 49W
Rogersville, *Canada* **141 C6** 46 44N 65 26W
Roggan ➛, *Canada* **140 B4** 54 24N 79 25W
Roggan L., *Canada* **140 B4** 54 8N 77 50W
Roggeveldberge, *S. Africa* **116 E3** 32 10 S 20 10 E
Roggiano Gravina, *Italy* **47 C9** 39 37N 16 9 E
Rogliano, *France* **29 F13** 42 57N 9 30 E
Rogliano, *Italy* **47 C9** 39 10N 16 19 E
Rogoaguado, L., *Bolivia* **173 C4** 13 0 S 65 30W
Rogojampi, *Indonesia* **79 J17** 8 19 S 114 17 E
Rogoźno, *Poland* **55 F3** 52 45N 16 59 E
Rogue ➛, *U.S.A.* **158 E1** 42 26N 124 26W
Roha, *India* **94 E1** 18 26N 73 7 E
Rohan, *France* **26 D4** 48 4N 2 45W
Róhda, *Greece* **38 B9** 39 48N 19 46 E
Rohnert Park, *U.S.A.* **160 G4** 38 16N 122 40W
Rohri, *Pakistan* **91 D3** 27 45N 68 51 E
Rohri Canal, *Pakistan* **92 F3** 26 15N 68 27 E
Rohtak, *India* **92 E7** 28 55N 76 43 E
Rohtisch-Sauerbrunn = Rogaška Slatina, *Slovenia* **45 B12** 46 15N 15 42 E
Roi Et, *Thailand* **86 D4** 16 4N 103 40 E
Roja, *Latvia* **15 H20** 57 29N 22 43 E
Rojas, *Argentina* **174 C3** 34 10 S 60 45W
Rojište, *Romania* **53 F8** 44 4N 23 56 E
Rojo, C., *Mexico* **163 C5** 21 33N 97 20W
Rokan ➛, *Indonesia* **84 B2** 2 0N 100 50 E
Rokel ➛, *S. Leone* **112 D2** 8 30N 12 48W
Rokiškis, *Lithuania* **15 J21** 55 55N 25 35 E
Rokitno, *Russia* **59 G8** 50 57N 35 56 E
Rokycany, *Czech Rep.* **34 B6** 49 43N 13 35 E
Rolândia, *Brazil* **175 A5** 23 18 S 51 23W
Røldal, *Norway* **18 E3** 59 47N 6 50 E
Rolfe, *U.S.A.* **156 B2** 42 49N 94 31W
Rolla, *Mo., U.S.A.* **155 G9** 37 57N 91 46W
Rolla, *N. Dak., U.S.A.* **154 A5** 48 52N 99 37W
Rolle, *Switz.* **32 D2** 46 28N 6 20 E
Rolleston, *Australia* **126 C4** 24 28 S 148 35 E
Rolleston, *N.Z.* **131 D7** 43 35 S 172 24 E
Rolling Fork ➛, *U.S.A.* **157 G11** 37 55N 85 50W
Rollingstone, *Australia* **126 B4** 19 2 S 146 24 E
Rom, *Norway* **18 F4** 58 8N 7 5 E
Rom, *Sudan* **107 F3** 9 54N 32 16 E
Roma, *Australia* **127 D4** 26 32 S 148 49 E
Roma, *Italy* **45 G9** 41 54N 12 29 E
Roma, *Sweden* **17 G12** 57 32N 18 26 E
Roma, *U.S.A.* **155 M5** 26 25N 99 1W
Roma Fiumicino ✕ (FCO), *Italy* **45 G9** 41 48N 12 15 E
Romain C., *U.S.A.* **149 J6** 33 0N 79 22W
Romaine, *Canada* **141 B7** 50 13N 60 40W
Romaine ➛, *Canada* **141 B7** 50 18N 63 47W
Roman, *Bulgaria* **50 C7** 43 8N 23 57 E
Roman, *Romania* **53 D11** 46 57N 26 55 E
Roman-Kosh, Gora, *Ukraine* **59 K8** 44 37N 34 15 E
Romanche ➛, *France* **29 C9** 45 5N 5 43 E
Romang, *Indonesia* **82 C3** 7 30 S 127 20 E
Români, *Egypt* **103 E1** 30 59N 32 38 E
Romania ■, *Europe* **53 D10** 46 0N 25 0 E
Romanija, *Bos.-H.* **52 G3** 43 50N 18 45 E
Romano, C., *U.S.A.* **153 K8** 25 51N 81 41W
Romano, Cayo, *Cuba* **164 B4** 22 0N 77 30W
Romanov-Borisoglebsk = Tutayev, *Russia* **58 D10** 57 53N 39 32 E
Romanovka = Basarabeasca, *Moldova* **53 D13** 46 21N 28 58 E
Romanovna-Murmane = Murmansk, *Russia* **56 A5** 68 57N 33 10 E
Romanovsk = Kropotkin, *Russia* **61 H5** 45 28N 40 28 E
Romanovskiy Khutor = Kropotkin, *Russia* **61 H5** 45 28N 40 28 E
Romans-sur-Isère, *France* **29 C9** 45 3N 5 3 E
Romanshorn, *Switz.* **33 A8** 47 33N 9 22 E
Romanzof C., *U.S.A.* **144 F6** 61 49N 166 6W
Rombari, *Sudan* **107 G3** 4 33N 31 2 E
Rombebai, Danau, *Indonesia* **83 B5** 1 50 S 137 53 E
Romblon, *Phil.* **80 E4** 12 33N 122 17 E
Romblon □, *Phil.* **80 E4** 12 30N 122 15 E
Romblon Pass, *Phil.* **80 E4** 12 27N 122 12 E
Rome = Roma, *Italy* **45 G9** 41 54N 12 29 E
Rome, *Ga., U.S.A.* **149 H3** 34 15N 85 10W
Rome, *N.Y., U.S.A.* **151 C9** 43 13N 75 27W
Rome, *Pa., U.S.A.* **151 E8** 41 51N 76 21W
Romeoville, *U.S.A.* **157 C8** 41 39N 88 3W
Rometta, *Italy* **47 D8** 38 10N 15 25 E
Romilly-sur-Seine, *France* **27 D10** 48 31N 3 44 E
Romitan, *Uzbekistan* **65 D2** 39 56N 64 23 E
Rommani, *Morocco* **110 B3** 33 31N 6 40W
Romney, *U.S.A.* **148 F6** 39 21N 78 45W
Romney Marsh, *U.K.* **21 F8** 51 2N 0 54 E
Romny, *Ukraine* **59 G7** 50 48N 33 28 E
Rømø, *Denmark* **17 J2** 55 10N 8 30 E
Romodan, *Ukraine* **59 G7** 49 55N 33 15 E
Romodanovo, *Russia* **60 C7** 54 26N 45 23 E
Romont, *Switz.* **32 C3** 46 42N 6 54 E
Romorantin-Lanthenay, *France* **27 E8** 47 21N 1 45 E
Rompin ➛, *Malaysia* **84 B2** 2 49N 103 29 E
Romsdalen, *Norway* **18 B4** 62 25N 7 52 E
Romsdalsfjorden, *Norway* **18 B4** 62 38N 7 20 E
Romsey, *U.K.* **21 G6** 51 0N 1 29W
Ron, *India* **95 G2** 15 40N 75 44 E
Ron, *Vietnam* **86 D6** 17 53N 106 27 E
Rona, *U.K.* **22 D3** 57 34N 5 59W
Ronan, *U.S.A.* **158 C6** 47 32N 114 6W
Roncador, Cayos, *Colombia* **164 D3** 13 32N 80 4W
Roncador, Serra do, *Brazil* **171 D1** 12 30 S 52 30W
Ronciglione, *Italy* **45 F9** 42 17N 12 13 E
Ronco ➛, *Italy* **45 D9** 44 24N 12 12 E
Ronda, *Spain* **43 J5** 36 46N 5 12W
Ronda, Serranía de, *Spain* **43 J5** 36 44N 5 3W
Rondane, *Norway* **18 C6** 61 57N 9 50 E
Rondane △, *Norway* **18 C6** 61 55N 9 44 E
Rondón, *Colombia* **168 B3** 6 17N 71 6W
Rondônia, *Brazil* **173 C5** 10 52 S 61 57W
Rondônia □, *Brazil* **173 C5** 11 0 S 63 0W
Rondonópolis, *Brazil* **173 D7** 16 28 S 54 38W
Rondslottet, *Norway* **18 C6** 61 55N 9 45 E
Rong, Koh, *Cambodia* **87 G4** 10 45N 103 15 E
Rong Jiang ➛, *China* **76 E7** 24 35N 109 20 E
Rong Xian, *Guangxi Zhuangzu, China* **77 F8** 22 50N 110 31 E
Rong Xian, *Sichuan, China* **76 C5** 29 23N 104 22 E
Rong'an, *China* **76 E7** 25 14N 109 22 E
Rongchang, *China* **76 C5** 29 20N 105 32 E
Ronge, L. la, *Canada* **143 B7** 55 6N 105 17W
Rongjiang, *China* **76 E7** 25 57N 108 28 E
Rongotea, *N.Z.* **130 G4** 40 19 S 175 25 E
Rongshui, *China* **76 E7** 25 5N 109 12 E
Rønne, *Denmark* **17 J8** 55 6N 14 43 E
Ronne Ice Shelf, *Antarctica* **7 D18** 78 0 S 60 0W
Ronneby, *Sweden* **17 H9** 56 12N 15 17 E
Ronnebyån ➛, *Sweden* **17 H9** 56 11N 15 18 E
Rönneshytta, *Sweden* **17 F9** 58 56N 15 2 E
Ronsard, C., *Australia* **125 D1** 24 46 S 113 10 E
Ronse, *Belgium* **24 D3** 50 45N 3 35 E
Ronuro ➛, *Brazil* **173 C7** 11 56 S 53 33W
Roodepoort, *S. Africa* **117 D4** 26 11 S 27 54 E
Roodhouse, *U.S.A.* **156 E6** 39 29N 90 24W
Roof Butte, *U.S.A.* **159 H9** 36 28N 109 5W
Rooiboklaagte ➛, *Namibia* **116 C3** 20 50 S 21 0 E
Roon, *Indonesia* **83 B4** 2 23 S 134 33 E
Rooniu, Mt., *Tahiti* **133 S16** 17 49 S 149 12W
Roopville, *U.S.A.* **152 B4** 33 27N 85 8W
Roorkee, *India* **92 E7** 29 52N 77 59 E
Roosendaal, *Neths.* **24 C4** 51 32N 4 29 E
Roosevelt, *U.S.A.* **158 F8** 40 18N 109 59W
Roosevelt ➛, *Brazil* **173 B5** 7 35 S 60 20W
Roosevelt, Mt., *Canada* **142 B3** 58 26N 125 20W
Roosevelt I., *Antarctica* **7 D12** 79 30 S 162 0W
Root, *Switz.* **33 B6** 47 5N 8 23 E
Ropczyce, *Poland* **55 H8** 50 4N 21 38 E
Roper ➛, *Australia* **126 A2** 14 43 S 135 27 E
Roper Bar, *Australia* **126 A1** 14 44 S 134 44 E
Roque Pérez, *Argentina* **174 D4** 35 25 S 59 24W
Roquefort, *France* **28 D3** 44 2N 0 20W
Roquemaure, *France* **29 D8** 44 3N 4 48 E
Roquetas de Mar, *Spain* **41 J2** 36 46N 2 36W
Roquetes, *Spain* **40 E5** 40 50N 0 30 E
Roquevaire, *France* **29 E9** 43 20N 5 36 E
Roraima □, *Brazil* **169 C5** 2 0N 61 30W
Roraima, Mt., *Venezuela* **169 B5** 5 10N 60 40W
Røros, *Norway* **18 B8** 62 35N 11 23 E
Rorschach, *Switz.* **33 B8** 47 28N 9 28 E
Rosa, *Zambia* **119 D3** 9 33 S 31 15 E
Rosa, C., *Algeria* **111 A6** 37 0N 8 16 E
Rosa, C., *Ecuador* **172 a** 1 4 S 91 10W
Rosa, L., *Bahamas* **165 B5** 21 0N 73 30W
Rosa, Monte, *Europe* **32 E5** 45 57N 7 53 E
Rosais, Pta. dos, *Azores* **9 d1** 38 45N 28 19W
Rosal de la Frontera, *Spain* **43 H3** 37 59N 7 13W
Rosales, *Phil.* **80 D3** 15 54N 120 38 E
Rosalia, *U.S.A.* **158 C5** 47 14N 117 22W
Rosamond, *U.S.A.* **161 L8** 34 52N 118 10W
Rosans, *France* **29 D9** 44 24N 5 29 E
Rosario, *Argentina* **174 C3** 33 0 S 60 40W
Rosário, *Brazil* **170 B3** 3 0 S 44 15W
Rosario, *Baja Calif., Mexico* **162 B1** 30 0N 115 50W
Rosario, *Sinaloa, Mexico* **162 C3** 23 0N 105 52W
Rosario, *Paraguay* **174 A4** 24 30 S 57 35W
Rosario, *Phil.* **81 G5** 8 24N 125 59 E
Rosario, Villa del, *Venezuela* **168 A3** 10 19N 72 19W
Rosario de la Frontera, *Argentina* **174 B3** 25 50 S 65 0W
Rosario de Lerma, *Argentina* **174 A2** 24 59 S 65 35W
Rosario del Tala, *Argentina* **174 C4** 32 20 S 59 10W
Rosário do Sul, *Brazil* **175 C5** 30 15 S 54 55W
Rosário Oeste, *Brazil* **173 C6** 14 50 S 56 25W
Rosarito, *Mexico* **161 N9** 32 18N 117 4W
Rosarno, *Italy* **47 D8** 38 29N 15 58 E
Rosas = Roses, *Spain* **40 C8** 42 19N 3 10 E
Roscoe, *Miss., U.S.A.* **156 G3** 37 58N 93 48W
Roscoe, *N.Y., U.S.A.* **151 E10** 41 56N 74 55W
Roscoff, *France* **26 D3** 48 44N 3 58W
Roscommon, *Ireland* **23 C3** 53 38N 8 11W
Roscommon □, *Ireland* **23 C3** 53 49N 8 23W
Roscrea, *Ireland* **23 D4** 52 57N 7 49W
Rose ➛, *Australia* **126 A2** 14 16 S 135 45 E
Rose Belle, *Mauritius* **121 d** 20 24 S 57 36 E
Rose Blanche-Harbour Le Cou, *Canada* **141 C8** 47 38N 58 45W
Rose Hill, *Mauritius* **121 d** 20 14 S 57 27 E
Rose Pt., *Canada* **142 C2** 54 11N 131 39W
Rose Valley, *Canada* **143 C8** 52 19N 103 49W
Roseau, *Dominica* **165 C7** 15 17N 61 24W
Roseau, *U.S.A.* **154 A7** 48 51N 95 46W
Rosebery, *Australia* **127 G4** 41 46 S 145 33 E
Rosebud, *Australia* **128 E6** 38 21 S 144 54 E
Rosebud, *S. Dak., U.S.A.* **154 D4** 43 14N 100 51W
Rosebud, *Tex., U.S.A.* **155 K6** 31 4N 96 59W
Roseburg, *U.S.A.* **158 E2** 43 13N 123 20W
Rosedale, *U.S.A.* **155 J9** 33 51N 91 2W
Rosehearty, *U.K.* **22 D6** 57 42N 2 7W
Roseland, *U.S.A.* **160 G4** 38 25N 122 43W
Rosemary, *Canada* **142 C6** 50 46N 112 5W
Rosenberg = Olesno, *Poland* **55 H5** 50 51N 18 26 E
Rosenberg = Susz, *Poland* **54 E6** 53 44N 19 20 E
Rosenberg, *U.S.A.* **155 L7** 29 34N 95 49W
Rosendaël, *France* **27 A9** 51 3N 2 24 E
Rosendal, *Norway* **18 E3** 59 59N 6 0 E
Rosendale, *U.S.A.* **156 D2** 40 4N 94 51W
Rosenheim, *Germany* **31 H8** 47 51N 12 7 E
Roses, *Spain* **40 C8** 42 19N 3 10 E
Roses, G. de, *Spain* **40 C8** 42 10N 3 15 E
Roseto degli Abruzzi, *Italy* **45 F11** 42 41N 14 1 E
Rosetown, *Canada* **143 C7** 51 35N 107 59W
Rosetta = Rashîd, *Egypt* **106 H7** 31 21N 30 22 E
Roseville, *Calif., U.S.A.* **160 G5** 38 45N 121 17W
Roseville, *Ill., U.S.A.* **156 D6** 40 44N 90 40W
Roseville, *Mich., U.S.A.* **150 D2** 42 30N 82 56W
Rosewood, *Australia* **127 D5** 27 38 S 152 36 E
Roshkhvār, *Iran* **97 C8** 34 58N 59 37 E
Roshtqala, *Tajikistan* **65 E5** 37 16N 71 49 E
Rosières-en-Santerre, *France* **27 C9** 49 49N 2 42 E
Rosignano Maríttimo, *Italy* **44 E7** 43 24N 10 28 E
Rosignol, *Guyana* **169 B6** 6 15N 57 30W
Roşiori de Vede, *Romania* **53 F10** 44 9N 25 0 E
Rositsa, *Bulgaria* **51 C11** 43 57N 27 57 E
Rositsa ➛, *Bulgaria* **51 C9** 43 10N 25 30 E
Roskilde, *Denmark* **17 J6** 55 38N 12 3 E
Roskilde Amtskommune □, *Denmark* **17 J6** 55 35N 12 5 E
Roskovec, *Albania* **50 F3** 40 44N 19 43 E
Roslavl, *Russia* **58 F7** 53 57N 32 55 E
Rosmaninhal, *Portugal* **42 F3** 39 44N 7 5W
Rosmead, *S. Africa* **116 E4** 31 29 S 25 8 E
Røsnæs, *Denmark* **17 J4** 55 44N 10 55 E
Rosolini, *Italy* **47 F7** 36 49N 14 57 E
Rosporden, *France* **26 E3** 47 57N 3 50W
Ross, *Australia* **127 G4** 42 2 S 147 30 E
Ross, *N.Z.* **131 C5** 42 53 S 170 49 E
Ross Béthio, *Mauritania* **112 B1** 16 15N 16 8W
Ross Dependency, *Antarctica* **7 D12** 76 0 S 170 0W
Ross I., *Antarctica* **7 D11** 77 30 S 168 0 E
Ross Ice Shelf, *Antarctica* **7 E12** 80 0 S 180 0 E
Ross L., *U.S.A.* **158 B3** 48 44N 121 4W
Ross-on-Wye, *U.K.* **21 F5** 51 54N 2 34W
Ross River, *Australia* **126 C1** 23 44 S 134 30 E
Ross River, *Canada* **142 A2** 62 30N 131 30W
Ross Sea, *Antarctica* **7 D11** 74 0 S 178 0 E
Rossa, *Switz.* **33 D8** 46 23N 9 8 E
Rossall Pt., *U.K.* **20 D4** 53 55N 3 3W
Rossan Pt., *Ireland* **23 B3** 54 42N 8 47W
Rossano, *Italy* **47 C9** 39 36N 16 39 E
Rossburn, *Canada* **143 C8** 50 40N 100 49W
Rosseau, *Canada* **150 A5** 45 16N 79 39W
Rosseau, L., *Canada* **150 A5** 45 10N 79 35W
Rössel = Reszel, *Poland* **54 D8** 54 4N 21 10 E
Rossel, C., *Vanuatu* **133 K4** 20 23 S 166 36 E
Rossel I., *Papua N. G.* **132 F8** 11 21 S 154 9 E
Rossens, *Switz.* **32 C4** 46 43N 7 7 E
Rosses, The, *Ireland* **23 A3** 55 2N 8 20W
Rossford, *U.S.A.* **157 C13** 41 36N 83 34W
Rossignol, L., *Canada* **140 B5** 52 43N 73 40W
Rossignol L., *Canada* **141 D6** 44 12N 65 10W
Rossiya = Russia ■, *Eurasia* **67 C11** 62 0N 105 0 E
Rosskreppfjorden, *Norway* **18 E4** 59 4N 7 10 E
Rossland, *Canada* **142 D5** 49 6N 117 50W
Rosslare, *Ireland* **23 D5** 52 17N 6 24W
Rosslare Harbour, *Ireland* **23 D5** 52 15N 6 20W
Rosslau, *Germany* **30 D8** 51 52N 12 15 E
Rosso, *Mauritania* **112 B1** 16 40N 15 45W
Rosso, C., *France* **29 F12** 42 13N 8 32 E
Rossosh, *Russia* **59 G10** 50 15N 39 28 E
Røssvatnet, *Norway* **14 D16** 65 45N 14 5 E
Rossville, *Ill., U.S.A.* **157 D9** 40 23N 87 40W
Rossville, *Ind., U.S.A.* **157 D10** 40 25N 86 36W
Røst, *Norway* **14 C15** 67 32N 12 0 E
Rostāq, *Afghan.* **65 E4** 37 7N 69 49 E
Rosthern, *Canada* **143 C7** 52 40N 106 20W
Rostock, *Germany* **30 A8** 54 5N 12 8 E
Rostov, *Don, Russia* **59 J10** 47 15N 39 45 E
Rostov, *Yaroslavl, Russia* **58 D10** 57 14N 39 25 E
Rostovsevo = Bulungur, *Uzbekistan* **65 D3** 39 46N 67 16 E
Rostrenen, *France* **26 D3** 48 14N 3 21W
Roswell, *Ga., U.S.A.* **152 A5** 34 2N 84 22W
Roswell, *N. Mex., U.S.A.* **155 J2** 33 24N 104 32W
Rot-Front = Dobropole, *Ukraine* **59 H9** 48 25N 37 2 E
Rota, *Spain* **43 J4** 36 37N 6 20W
Rotan, *U.S.A.* **155 J4** 32 51N 100 28W
Rote Wand, *Austria* **33 B9** 47 11N 9 59 E
Rotenburg, *Hessen, Germany* **30 E5** 50 59N 9 44 E
Rotenburg, *Niedersachsen, Germany* **30 B5** 53 6N 9 25 E
Roth, *Germany* **31 F7** 49 15N 11 5 E
Rothaargebirge, *Germany* **30 D4** 51 2N 8 13 E
Rothaargebirge △, *Germany* **30 E4** 51 0N 8 15 E
Rothenburg, *Switz.* **33 B6** 47 6N 8 16 E
Rothenburg ob der Tauber, *Germany* **31 F6** 49 23N 10 11 E
Rother ➛, *U.K.* **21 G8** 50 59N 0 45 E
Rothera, *Antarctica* **7 C17** 67 20 S 63 0W
Rotherham, *U.K.* **20 D6** 53 26N 1 20W
Rothes, *U.K.* **22 D5** 57 32N 3 13W
Rothesay, *Canada* **141 C6** 45 23N 66 0W
Rothesay, *U.K.* **22 F3** 55 50N 5 3W
Rothrist, *Switz.* **32 B5** 47 18N 7 54 E
Roti, *Indonesia* **82 D2** 10 50 S 123 0 E
Rotja, Pta., *Spain* **38 D2** 38 38N 1 35 E
Rotnes, *Norway* **18 D7** 60 3N 10 51 E
Roto, *Australia* **129 B6** 33 0 S 145 30 E
Rotoaira, L., *N.Z.* **130 F4** 39 3 S 175 45 E
Rotoehu, L., *N.Z.* **130 E5** 38 1 S 176 32 E
Rotoiti, L., *Bay of Plenty, N.Z.* **130 E5** 38 2 S 176 26 E
Rotoiti, L., *W. Coast, N.Z.* **131 B7** 41 51 S 172 49 E
Rotoma, L., *N.Z.* **130 E5** 38 2 S 176 35 E
Rotondo, Mte., *France* **29 F13** 42 14N 9 8 E
Rotoroa, L., *N.Z.* **131 B7** 41 55 S 172 39 E
Rotorua, *N.Z.* **130 E5** 38 9 S 176 16 E
Rotorua, L., *N.Z.* **130 E5** 38 5 S 176 18 E
Rott ➛, *Germany* **31 G9** 48 27N 13 25 E
Rotten ➛, *Switz.* **32 D5** 46 18N 7 36 E
Rottenburg, *Germany* **31 G4** 48 28N 8 55 E
Rottenmann, *Austria* **34 D7** 47 31N 14 22 E
Rotterdam, *Neths.* **24 C4** 51 55N 4 30 E
Rotterdam, *U.S.A.* **151 D10** 42 48N 74 1W
Rottne, *Sweden* **17 G8** 57 1N 14 54 E
Rottnest I., *Australia* **125 F2** 32 0 S 115 27 E
Rottumeroog, *Neths.* **24 A6** 53 33N 6 34 E
Rottweil, *Germany* **31 G4** 48 9N 8 37 E
Rotuma, *Fiji* **134 J9** 12 25 S 177 5 E
Roubaix, *France* **27 B10** 50 40N 3 10 E
Roudnice nad Labem, *Czech Rep.* **34 A7** 50 25N 14 15 E
Rouen, *France* **26 C8** 49 27N 1 4 E
Rouergue, *France* **28 D5** 44 15N 2 0 E
Rough Ridge, *N.Z.* **131 F4** 45 10 S 169 55 E
Rouillac, *France* **28 C3** 45 47N 0 4W
Rouleau, *Canada* **143 C8** 50 10N 104 56W
Roulers = Roeselare, *Belgium* **24 D3** 50 57N 3 7 E
Round I., *Mauritius* **121 d** 19 51 S 57 45 E
Round Mountain, *U.S.A.* **158 G5** 38 43N 117 4W
Round Mt., *Australia* **129 A10** 30 26 S 152 16 E
Round Rock, *U.S.A.* **155 K6** 30 31N 97 41W
Roundup, *U.S.A.* **158 C9** 46 27N 108 33W
Roura, *Fr. Guiana* **169 C7** 4 44N 52 20W
Rousay, *U.K.* **22 B5** 59 10N 3 2W
Rouses Point, *U.S.A.* **151 B11** 44 59N 73 22W
Rouseville, *U.S.A.* **150 E5** 41 28N 79 42W
Rousse = Ruse, *Bulgaria* **51 C9** 43 48N 25 59 E
Roussenski Lom △, *Bulgaria* **51 C10** 43 40N 26 10 E
Roussillon, *Isère, France* **29 C8** 45 24N 4 49 E
Roussillon, *Pyrénées-Or., France* **28 F6** 42 30N 2 35 E
Roussin, C., *N. Cal.* **133 U21** 21 20 S 167 59 E
Rouxville, *S. Africa* **116 E4** 30 25 S 26 50 E
Rouyn-Noranda, *Canada* **140 C4** 48 20N 79 0W
Rovaniemi, *Finland* **14 C21** 66 29N 25 41 E
Rovato, *Italy* **44 C7** 45 34N 10 0 E
Rovenki, *Ukraine* **59 H10** 48 5N 39 21 E
Rovereto, *Italy* **44 C8** 45 53N 11 3 E
Roverud, *Norway* **18 D9** 60 15N 12 3 E
Rovigno = Rovinj, *Croatia* **45 C10** 45 5N 13 40 E
Rovigo, *Italy* **45 C8** 45 4N 11 47 E
Rovinj, *Croatia* **45 C10** 45 5N 13 40 E
Rovira, *Colombia* **168 C2** 4 15N 75 20W
Rovno = Rivne, *Ukraine* **59 G4** 50 40N 26 10 E
Rovnoye, *Russia* **60 E8** 50 52N 46 3 E
Rovuma = Ruvuma ➛, *Tanzania* **119 E5** 10 29 S 40 28 E
Row'ān, *Iran* **97 C6** 35 8N 48 51 E
Rowena, *Australia* **127 D4** 29 48 S 148 55 E
Rowley Shoals, *Australia* **124 C2** 17 30 S 119 0 E
Roxa, *Guinea-Biss.* **112 C1** 11 15N 15 45W
Roxas, *Capiz, Phil.* **81 F4** 11 36N 122 49 E
Roxas, *Isabela, Phil.* **80 C3** 17 8N 121 36 E
Roxas, *Mind. Or., Phil.* **80 E3** 12 35N 121 31 E
Roxas, *Palawan, Phil.* **81 F2** 10 20N 119 21 E
Roxboro, *U.S.A.* **149 G6** 36 24N 78 59W
Roxborough, *Trin. & Tob.* **169 E10** 11 15N 60 35W
Roxburgh, *N.Z.* **131 F4** 45 33 S 169 19 E
Roxbury, *U.S.A.* **150 F7** 40 6N 77 39W
Roxen, *Sweden* **17 F9** 58 30N 15 40 E
Roy, *Mont., U.S.A.* **158 C9** 47 20N 108 58W
Roy, *N. Mex., U.S.A.* **155 H2** 35 57N 104 12W
Roy, *Utah, U.S.A.* **158 F7** 41 10N 112 2W
Royal △, *Australia* **129 C9** 34 5 S 151 5 E
Royal Bardia △, *Nepal* **93 E9** 28 20N 81 20 E
Royal Canal, *Ireland* **23 C4** 53 30N 7 13W
Royal Center, *U.S.A.* **157 D10** 40 52N 86 30W
Royal Chitawan △, *Nepal* **93 F11** 26 30N 84 30 E
Royal Leamington Spa, *U.K.* **21 E6** 52 18N 1 31W
Royal Natal △, *S. Africa* **117 D4** 28 43 S 28 51 E
Royal Oak, *U.S.A.* **157 B13** 42 30N 83 9W
Royal Palm Beach, *U.S.A.* **153 J9** 26 41N 80 14W
Royal Tunbridge Wells, *U.K.* **21 F8** 51 7N 0 16 E
Royale, Isle, *U.S.A.* **154 B10** 48 0N 88 54W
Royalla, *Australia* **129 C8** 35 30 S 149 9 E
Royan, *France* **28 C2** 45 37N 1 2W
Roye, *France* **27 C9** 49 42N 2 48 E
Royston, *U.K.* **21 E7** 52 3N 0 0W
Rožaj, *Serbia & M.* **50 D4** 42 50N 20 11 E
Różan, *Poland* **55 F8** 52 52N 21 25 E
Rozay-en-Brie, *France* **27 D9** 48 41N 2 58 E
Rozdilna, *Ukraine* **53 D15** 46 50N 30 2 E
Rozhnyativ, *Ukraine* **53 B9** 48 56N 24 9 E
Rozhyshche, *Ukraine* **59 G3** 50 54N 25 15 E
Rožmitál pod Třemšínem, *Czech Rep.* **34 B6** 49 36N 13 53 E
Rožňava, *Slovak Rep.* **35 C13** 48 37N 20 35 E
Rozogi, *Poland* **54 E8** 53 28N 21 19 E
Rozoy-sur-Serre, *France* **27 C11** 49 40N 4 8 E
Roztoczański △, *Poland* **55 H10** 50 37N 23 0 E
Rozzano, *Italy* **44 C6** 45 22N 9 10 E
Rrëshen, *Albania* **50 E3** 41 47N 19 49 E
Rrogozhine, *Albania* **50 E3** 41 4N 19 50 E
Rtanj, *Serbia & M.* **50 C5** 43 45N 21 50 E
Rtem, O. el ➛, *Algeria* **111 B6** 33 29N 5 38 E
Rtishchevo, *Russia* **60 D6** 52 18N 43 46 E
Rúa = A Rúa, *Spain* **42 C3** 42 24N 7 6W
Ruacaná, *Namibia* **116 B1** 17 27 S 14 21 E
Ruaha △, *Tanzania* **118 D3** 7 41 S 34 30 E
Ruahine Ra., *N.Z.* **130 F5** 39 55 S 176 2 E
Ruamahanga ➛, *N.Z.* **130 H4** 41 24 S 175 8 E
Ruapehu, *N.Z.* **130 F4** 39 17 S 175 35 E
Ruapuke I., *N.Z.* **131 G3** 46 46 S 168 31 E
Ruâq, W. ➛, *Egypt* **103 F2** 30 0N 33 49 E
Ruatoria, *N.Z.* **130 D7** 37 55 S 178 20 E
Ruavatu, *Solomon Is.* **133 M11** 9 26 S 160 26 E
Ruawai, *N.Z.* **130 C2** 36 8 S 173 59 E
Rub' al Khālī, *Si. Arabia* **99 C5** 19 0N 48 0 E
Rubeho Mts., *Tanzania* **118 D4** 6 50 S 36 25 E
Rubezhnaya = Rubizhne, *Ukraine* **59 H10** 49 6N 38 25 E
Rubezhnoye = Rubizhne, *Ukraine* **59 H10** 49 6N 38 25 E
Rubh a' Mhail, *U.K.* **22 F2** 55 56N 6 8W
Rubha Hunish, *U.K.* **22 D2** 57 42N 6 20W
Rubha Robhanais = Lewis, Butt of, *U.K.* **22 C2** 58 31N 6 16W
Rubí, *Spain* **40 D7** 41 29N 2 2 E
Rubiataba, *Brazil* **171 E2** 15 8 S 49 48W
Rubicon ➛, *U.S.A.* **160 G5** 38 53N 121 4W
Rubicone ➛, *Italy* **45 D9** 44 8N 12 28 E
Rubik, *Albania* **50 E3** 41 46N 19 48 E
Rubinéia, *Brazil* **171 F1** 20 13 S 51 2W
Rubino, *Ivory C.* **112 D4** 6 4N 4 18W
Rubio, *Venezuela* **168 B3** 7 43N 72 22W
Rubizhne, *Ukraine* **59 H10** 49 6N 38 25 E
Rubondo △, *Tanzania* **118 C3** 2 18 S 31 58 E
Rubtsovsk, *Russia* **66 D9** 51 30N 81 10 E
Ruby, *U.S.A.* **144 D9** 64 45N 155 30W
Ruby Beach = Jacksonville Beach, *U.S.A.* **152 E8** 30 17N 81 24W
Ruby L., *U.S.A.* **158 F6** 40 10N 115 28W
Ruby Mts., *U.S.A.* **158 F6** 40 30N 115 20W
Rubyvale, *Australia* **126 C4** 23 25 S 147 42 E
Rucheng, *China* **77 E9** 25 33N 113 38 E
Ruciane-Nida, *Poland* **54 E8** 53 40N 21 32 E
Rūd Sar, *Iran* **97 B6** 37 8N 50 18 E
Ruda, *Sweden* **17 G10** 57 6N 16 7 E
Ruda Śląska, *Poland* **55 H5** 50 16N 18 50 E
Rudall, *Australia* **128 B2** 33 43 S 136 17 E
Rudall ➛, *Australia* **124 D3** 22 34 S 122 13 E
Rudall River △, *Australia* **124 D3** 22 38 S 122 30 E
Rūdbār, *Afghan.* **91 C1** 30 9N 62 36 E
Rüdersdorf, *Germany* **30 C9** 52 27N 13 47 E
Rudewa, *Tanzania* **119 E3** 10 7 S 34 40 E
Rudkøbing, *Denmark* **17 K4** 54 56N 10 41 E
Rudky, *Ukraine* **55 J10** 49 38N 23 29 E
Rudna, *Poland* **55 G3** 51 30N 16 17 E
Rudnichnyy, *Kazakhstan* **65 A9** 44 40N 78 54 E
Rudnik, *Bulgaria* **51 D11** 42 36N 27 30 E
Rudnik, *Poland* **55 H9** 50 26N 22 15 E
Rudnik, *Serbia & M.* **50 B4** 44 7N 20 35 E
Rudnik Ingichka = Ingichka, *Uzbekistan* **65 D2** 39 47N 65 58 E
Rudnya, *Russia* **58 E6** 54 55N 31 7 E
Rudnytsa, *Ukraine* **53 B13** 48 16N 28 54 E
Rudnyy, *Kazakhstan* **64 E9** 52 57N 63 7 E
Rudo, *Bos.-H.* **52 G4** 43 41N 19 23 E
Rudolfa, Ostrov, *Russia* **66 A6** 81 45N 58 30 E
Rudolstadt, *Germany* **30 E7** 50 44N 11 19 E
Rudong, *China* **77 A13** 32 20N 121 12 E
Rudozem, *Bulgaria* **51 E8** 41 29N 24 51 E
Rudyard, *U.S.A.* **148 B3** 46 14N 84 36W
Rue, *France* **27 B8** 50 15N 1 40 E
Ruenya ➛, *Africa* **119 F3** 16 24 S 33 48 E
Rufa'a, *Sudan* **107 E3** 14 44N 33 22 E
Ruffec, *France* **28 B4** 46 2N 0 12 E
Rufflin, *U.S.A.* **152 B9** 33 0N 80 49W
Rufiji ➛, *Tanzania* **118 D4** 7 50 S 39 15 E
Rufino, *Argentina* **174 C3** 34 20 S 62 50W
Rufisque, *Senegal* **112 C1** 14 40N 17 15W
Rufling Pt., *Br. Virgin Is.* **165 e** 18 44N 64 27W
Rufunsa, *Zambia* **119 F2** 15 4 S 29 34 E
Rugao, *China* **77 A13** 32 23N 120 31 E
Rugby, *U.K.* **21 E6** 52 23N 1 16W
Rugby, *U.S.A.* **154 A5** 48 22N 100 0W
Rügen, *Germany* **30 A9** 54 22N 13 24 E
Rügen △, *Germany* **30 A9** 54 25N 13 25 E
Rugles, *France* **26 D7** 48 50N 0 40 E
Ruhea, *Bangla.* **90 B2** 26 10N 88 25 E
Ruhengeri, *Rwanda* **118 C2** 1 30 S 29 36 E
Ruhla, *Germany* **30 E6** 50 54N 10 23 E
Ruhland, *Germany* **30 D9** 51 27N 13 51 E
Ruhnu, *Estonia* **15 H20** 57 48N 23 15 E
Ruhr ➛, *Germany* **30 D2** 51 27N 6 43 E
Ruhuhu ➛, *Tanzania* **119 E3** 10 31 S 34 34 E
Rui Barbosa, *Brazil* **171 D3** 12 18 S 40 27W
Rui'an, *China* **77 D13** 27 47N 120 40 E
Ruichang, *China* **77 C10** 29 40N 115 39 E
Ruidoso, *U.S.A.* **159 K11** 33 20N 105 41W
Ruijin, *China* **77 E10** 25 48N 116 0 E
Ruili, *China* **76 E1** 24 1N 97 43 E
Ruivo, Pico, *Madeira* **9 c** 32 45N 16 56W
Ruj, *Bulgaria* **50 D6** 42 52N 22 34 E
Rujen, *Macedonia* **50 D6** 42 9N 22 30 E
Rujm Tal'at al Jamā'ah, *Jordan* **103 E4** 30 24N 35 30 E
Ruk, *Pakistan* **92 F3** 27 50N 68 42 E
Rukhla, *Pakistan* **92 C4** 32 27N 71 57 E
Rukwa □, *Tanzania* **118 D3** 7 0 S 31 30 E
Rukwa, L., *Tanzania* **118 D3** 8 0 S 32 20 E
Rulhieres, C., *Australia* **124 B4** 13 56 S 127 22 E
Rum = Rhum, *U.K.* **22 E2** 57 0N 6 20W
Rum, *Jordan* **103 F4** 29 39N 35 26 E
Rum Cay, *Bahamas* **165 B5** 23 40N 74 58W
Rum Jungle, *Australia* **124 B5** 13 0 S 130 59 E
Ruma, *Serbia & M.* **52 E4** 45 0N 19 50 E
Ruma △, *Kenya* **118 C3** 0 39 S 34 18 E
Rumāh, *Si. Arabia* **96 E5** 25 29N 47 10 E
Rumania = Romania ■, *Europe* **53 D10** 46 0N 25 0 E
Rumaylah, *Iraq* **96 D5** 30 47N 47 37 E
Rumbêk, *Sudan* **107 F2** 6 54N 29 37 E
Rumberpon, *Indonesia* **83 B4** 1 50 S 134 15 E
Rumburk, *Czech Rep.* **34 A7** 50 57N 14 32 E
Rumford, *U.S.A.* **149 C10** 44 33N 70 33W
Rumia, *Poland* **54 D5** 54 37N 18 25 E
Rumilly, *France* **29 C9** 45 53N 5 56 E
Rummelsburg = Miastko, *Poland* **54 E3** 54 0N 16 58 E
Rumoi, *Japan* **70 C10** 43 56N 141 39 E
Rumonge, *Burundi* **118 C2** 3 59 S 29 26 E
Rumson, *U.S.A.* **151 F11** 40 23N 74 0W
Rumuruti, *Kenya* **118 B4** 0 17N 36 32 E
Runan, *China* **74 H8** 33 0N 114 30 E
Runanga, *N.Z.* **131 C6** 42 25 S 171 15 E
Runaway, C., *N.Z.* **130 D6** 37 32 S 177 59 E
Runaway Bay, *Jamaica* **164 a** 18 27N 77 20W
Runcorn, *U.K.* **20 D5** 53 21N 2 44W
Rundu, *Namibia* **116 B2** 17 52 S 19 43 E
Rungwa, *Tanzania* **118 D3** 6 55 S 33 32 E
Rungwa △, *Tanzania* **118 D3** 6 53 S 34 2 E
Rungwa ➛, *Tanzania* **118 D3** 7 36 S 31 50 E
Rungwe, *Tanzania* **119 D3** 9 11 S 33 32 E
Runka, *Nigeria* **113 C6** 12 28N 7 20 E
Runn, *Sweden* **16 D9** 60 30N 15 40 E
Runton Ra., *Australia* **124 D3** 23 31 S 123 6 E
Ruokolahti, *Finland* **58 B5** 61 17N 28 50 E
Ruoqiang, *China* **68 C3** 38 55N 88 10 E
Rupa, *India* **90 B4** 27 15N 92 21 E
Rupar, *India* **92 D7** 31 2N 76 38 E
Rupat, *Indonesia* **84 B2** 1 45N 101 40 E
Rupea, *Romania* **53 D10** 46 2N 25 13 E
Rupen ➛, *India* **92 H4** 23 28N 71 31 E
Rupert, *U.S.A.* **158 E7** 42 37N 113 41W
Rupert ➛, *Canada* **140 B4** 51 29N 78 45W
Rupert B., *Canada* **140 B4** 51 35N 79 0W
Rupert House = Waskaganish, *Canada* **140 B4** 51 30N 78 40W
Rupsa, *India* **93 J12** 21 37N 87 1 E
Rupununi ➛, *Guyana* **169 C6** 4 3N 58 35W
Rur ➛, *Germany* **30 D1** 51 11N 5 59 E
Rurópolis, *Brazil* **169 D7** 4 3 S 54 59W
Rurrenabaque, *Bolivia* **172 C4** 14 30 S 67 32W
Rus ➛, *Spain* **41 F2** 39 30N 2 30W
Rusambo, *Zimbabwe* **119 F3** 16 30 S 32 4 E
Rusape, *Zimbabwe* **119 F3** 18 35 S 32 8 E
Ruschuk = Ruse, *Bulgaria* **51 C9** 43 48N 25 59 E
Ruse, *Bulgaria* **51 C9** 43 48N 25 59 E
Ruse □, *Bulgaria* **51 C10** 43 35N 26 20 E
Ruşeţu, *Romania* **53 F12** 44 57N 27 14 E
Rush, *Ireland* **23 C5** 53 31N 6 6W

Rushan, *China* 75 F11 36 56N 121 30 E
Rushden, *U.K.* 21 E7 52 18N 0 35W
Rushikulya →, *India* 94 E7 19 23N 85 5 E
Rushmore, Mt., *U.S.A.* 154 D3 43 53N 103 28W
Rushon, *Tajikistan* 65 E5 37 57N 71 33 E
Rushville, *Ill., U.S.A.* 156 D6 40 7N 90 34W
Rushville, *Ind., U.S.A.* 157 E11 39 37N 85 27W
Rushville, *Nebr., U.S.A.* 154 D3 42 43N 102 28W
Rushworth, *Australia* 129 D6 36 32 S 145 1 E
Ruskin, *U.S.A.* 153 H7 27 43N 82 26W
Russas, *Brazil* 170 B4 4 55 S 37 50W
Russell, *Canada* 143 C8 50 50N 101 20W
Russell, *N.Z.* 130 B3 35 16 S 174 10 E
Russell, *Fla., U.S.A.* 152 E8 30 3N 81 45W
Russell, *Kans., U.S.A.* 154 F5 38 54N 98 52W
Russell, *N.Y., U.S.A.* 151 B9 44 27N 75 9W
Russell, *Pa., U.S.A.* 150 E5 41 56N 79 8W
Russell Cave ⌂, *U.S.A.* 149 H3 34 59N 85 49W
Russell Is., *Solomon Is.* 133 M10 9 4 S 159 12 E
Russell L., *Man., Canada* 143 B8 56 15N 101 30W
Russell L., *N.W.T., Canada* 142 A5 63 5N 115 44W
Russellkonda, *India* 94 E7 19 57N 84 42 E
Russells Point, *U.S.A.* 157 D13 40 28N 83 54W
Russellville, *Ala., U.S.A.* 149 H2 34 30N 87 44W
Russellville, *Ark., U.S.A.* 155 H8 35 17N 93 8W
Russellville, *Ky., U.S.A.* 149 G2 36 51N 86 53W
Rüsselsheim, *Germany* 31 F4 49 59N 8 23 E
Russi, *Italy* 45 D9 44 22N 12 2 E
Russia ■, *Eurasia* 67 C11 62 0N 105 0 E
Russian →, *U.S.A.* 160 G3 38 27N 123 8W
Russian Mission, *U.S.A.* 144 F7 61 47N 161 19W
Russiaville, *U.S.A.* 157 D10 40 25N 86 16W
Russkoye Ustie, *Russia* 6 B15 71 0N 149 0 E
Rust, *Austria* 35 D9 47 49N 16 42 E
Rustam, *Pakistan* 92 B5 34 25N 72 13 E
Rustam Shahr, *Pakistan* 92 F2 26 58N 66 6 E
Rustavi, *Georgia* 61 K7 41 30N 45 0 E
Rustenburg, *S. Africa* 116 D4 25 41 S 27 14 E
Ruston, *U.S.A.* 155 J8 32 32N 92 38W
Ruswil, *Switz.* 32 B6 47 5N 8 8 E
Rutana, *Burundi* 118 C3 3 55 S 30 0 E
Rute, *Spain* 43 H6 37 19N 4 23W
Ruteng, *Indonesia* 82 C2 8 35 S 120 30 E
Ruth, *U.S.A.* 150 C2 43 42N 82 45W
Rutherford, *U.S.A.* 160 G4 38 26N 122 24W
Rutherglen, *Australia* 129 D7 36 5 S 146 29 E
Rüti, *Switz.* 33 B7 47 16N 8 51 E
Rutland, *U.S.A.* 151 C12 43 37N 72 58W
Rutland □, *U.K.* 21 E7 52 38N 0 40W
Rutland I., *India* 95 J11 11 25N 92 10 E
Rutland Water, *U.K.* 21 E7 52 39N 0 38W
Rutledal, *Norway* 18 C2 61 4N 5 10 E
Rutledge, *U.S.A.* 152 B6 33 38N 83 37W
Rutledge →, *Canada* 143 A6 61 4N 112 0W
Rutledge L., *Canada* 143 A6 61 33N 110 47W
Rutqa, W. →, *Syria* 101 E9 34 30N 41 3 E
Rutshuru, *Dem. Rep. of the Congo* 118 C2 1 13 S 29 25 E
Ruvo di Púglia, *Italy* 47 A9 41 7N 16 29 E
Ruvu, *Tanzania* 118 D4 6 49 S 38 43 E
Ruvu →, *Tanzania* 118 D4 6 23 S 38 52 E
Ruvuba △, *Burundi* 118 C2 3 3 S 29 33 E
Ruvuma □, *Tanzania* 119 E4 10 20 S 36 0 E
Ruvuma →, *Tanzania* 119 E5 10 29 S 40 28 E
Ruwais, *U.A.E.* 97 E7 24 5N 52 50 E
Ruwenzori, *Africa* 118 B2 0 30N 29 55 E
Ruwenzori △, *Uganda* 118 B2 0 20 S 30 0 E
Ruya →, *Zimbabwe* 117 B5 16 27 S 32 5 E
Ruyigi, *Burundi* 118 C3 3 29 S 30 15 E
Ruyuan, *China* 77 E9 24 46N 113 16 E
Ruzayevka, *Russia* 60 C7 54 4N 45 0 E
Růzhevo Konare, *Bulgaria* 51 D8 42 23N 24 46 E
Ružomberok, *Slovak Rep.* 35 B12 49 3N 19 17 E
Ruzyne, Praha ✈ (PRG), *Czech Rep.* 34 A7 50 7N 14 15 E
Rwanda ■, *Africa* 118 C3 2 0 S 30 0 E
Ryakhovo, *Bulgaria* 51 C10 43 58N 26 18 E
Ryan, L., *U.K.* 22 G3 55 0N 5 2W
Ryazan, *Russia* 58 E10 54 40N 39 40 E
Ryazhsk, *Russia* 58 F11 53 45N 40 3 E
Rybache = Rybachye, *Kazakhstan* 66 E9 46 40N 81 20 E
Rybachiy, *Russia* 54 C7 55 10N 20 50 E
Rybachiy Poluostrov, *Russia* 56 A5 69 43N 32 0 E
Rybachye = Balykchy, *Kyrgyzstan* 65 B8 42 26N 76 12 E
Rybachye, *Kazakhstan* 66 E9 46 40N 81 20 E
Rybinsk, *Russia* 58 C10 58 5N 38 50 E
Rybinskoye Vdkhr., *Russia* 58 C10 58 30N 38 25 E
Rybnik, *Poland* 55 H5 50 6N 18 32 E
Rybnitsa = Râbniţa, *Moldova* 53 C14 47 45N 29 0 E
Rybnoye, *Russia* 58 E10 54 45N 39 30 E
Rychnov nad Kněžnou, *Czech Rep.* 35 A9 50 10N 16 17 E
Rychwał, *Poland* 55 F5 52 4N 18 10 E
Rycroft, *Canada* 142 B5 55 45N 118 40W
Ryd, *Sweden* 17 H8 56 27N 14 42 E
Rydaholm, *Sweden* 17 H8 56 59N 14 18 E
Ryde, *U.K.* 21 G6 50 43N 1 9W
Ryderwood, *U.S.A.* 160 D3 46 23N 123 3W
Rydzyna, *Poland* 55 G3 51 47N 16 39 E
Rye, *U.K.* 21 G8 50 57N 0 45 E
Rye →, *U.K.* 20 C7 54 11N 0 44W
Rye Bay, *U.K.* 21 G8 50 52N 0 49 E
Rye Patch Reservoir, *U.S.A.* 158 F4 40 28N 118 19W
Ryegate, *U.S.A.* 158 C9 46 18N 109 15W
Ryfylke, *Norway* 18 E3 59 25N 6 25 E
Rykene, *Norway* 18 F5 58 24N 8 37 E
Ryki, *Poland* 55 G8 51 38N 21 56 E
Rykovo = Yenakiyeve, *Ukraine* 59 H10 48 15N 38 15 E
Ryley, *Canada* 142 C6 53 17N 112 26W
Rylsk, *Russia* 59 G8 51 36N 34 43 E
Rylstone, *Australia* 129 B8 32 46 S 149 58 E
Rymanów, *Poland* 55 J8 49 35N 21 51 E
Ryn, *Poland* 54 E8 53 57N 21 34 E
Ryn Peski, *Kazakhstan* 61 G9 47 30N 49 0 E
Ryōhaku-Sanchi, *Japan* 73 A8 36 9N 136 49 E
Ryojun = Lüshun, *China* 75 E11 38 45N 121 15 E
Ryōtsu, *Japan* 70 E9 38 5N 138 26 E
Rypin, *Poland* 55 E6 53 3N 19 25 E
Ryssby, *Sweden* 17 H8 56 52N 14 10 E
Rysy, *Europe* 35 B13 49 10N 20 4 E
Ryūgasaki, *Japan* 73 B12 35 54N 140 11 E
Ryūkyū Is. = Ryūkyū-rettō, *Japan* 71 M3 26 0N 126 0 E
Ryūkyū-rettō, *Japan* 71 M3 26 0N 126 0 E
Rzepin, *Poland* 55 F1 52 20N 14 49 E
Rzeszów, *Poland* 55 H8 50 5N 21 58 E
Rzhev, *Russia* 58 D8 56 20N 34 20 E

S

Sa, *Thailand* 86 C3 18 34N 100 45 E
Sa Canal, *Spain* 38 D1 38 51N 1 23 E
Sa Conillera, *Spain* 38 D1 38 59N 1 13 E
Sa Dec, *Vietnam* 87 G5 10 20N 105 46 E
Sa Dragonera, *Spain* 38 B3 39 35N 2 19 E
Sa-koi, *Burma* 90 F6 19 54N 97 3 E
Sa Mesquida, *Spain* 38 B5 39 55N 4 16 E
Sa Pobla, *Spain* 38 B4 39 46N 3 1 E
Sa Savina, *Spain* 38 D1 38 44N 1 25 E
Sa'a, *Solomon Is.* 133 M11 9 43 S 161 35 E
Sa'ādatābād, *Fārs, Iran* 97 D7 30 10N 53 5 E
Sa'ādatābād, *Hormozgān, Iran* 97 D7 28 3N 55 53 E
Sa'ādatābād, *Kermān, Iran* 97 D7 29 40N 55 51 E
Saale →, *Germany* 30 D7 51 56N 11 54 E
Saaler Bodden, *Germany* 30 A8 54 20N 12 27 E
Saalfeld, *Germany* 30 E7 50 38N 11 21 E
Saalfelden, *Austria* 34 D5 47 25N 12 51 E
Saane →, *Switz.* 32 B4 47 8N 7 10 E
Saanen, *Switz.* 32 D4 46 29N 7 15 E
Saanich, *Canada* 160 B3 48 29N 123 26W
Saar →, *Europe* 24 E6 49 41N 6 32 E
Saar-Hunsrück ⌂, *Germany* 31 F2 49 30N 6 50 E
Saar in Mähren = Ždár nad Sázavov, *Czech Rep.* 34 B8 49 34N 15 57 E
Saarbrücken, *Germany* 31 F2 49 14N 6 59 E
Saarburg, *Germany* 31 F2 49 36N 6 32 E
Saaremaa, *Estonia* 15 G20 58 30N 22 30 E
Saarijärvi, *Finland* 15 E21 62 43N 25 16 E
Saariselkä, *Finland* 14 B23 68 16N 28 15 E
Saarland □, *Germany* 31 F2 49 20N 7 0 E
Saarlautern = Saarlouis, *Germany* 31 F2 49 18N 6 45 E
Saarlouis, *Germany* 31 F2 49 18N 6 45 E
Saas Fee, *Switz.* 32 D5 46 7N 7 56 E
Saaz = Žatec, *Czech Rep.* 34 A6 50 20N 13 32 E
Sab 'Ābar, *Syria* 100 F7 33 46N 37 41 E
Saba, *W. Indies* 165 C7 17 38N 63 14W
Šabac, *Serbia & M.* 50 B3 44 48N 19 42 E
Sabadell, *Spain* 40 D7 41 28N 2 7 E
Sabae, *Japan* 73 B8 35 57N 136 11 E
Sabah □, *Malaysia* 85 A5 6 0N 117 0 E
Sabak Bernam, *Malaysia* 87 L3 3 46N 100 58 E
Sabalān, Kūhhā-ye, *Iran* 101 C12 38 15N 47 45 E
Sabalana, Kepulauan, *Indonesia* 82 C1 6 45 S 118 50 E
Sábana de la Mar, *Dom. Rep.* 165 C6 19 7N 69 24W
Sábanalarga, *Colombia* 168 A3 10 38N 74 55W
Sabang, *Indonesia* 84 A1 5 50N 95 15 E
Săbăoani, *Romania* 53 C11 47 1N 26 51 E
Sabará, *Brazil* 171 E3 19 55 S 43 46W
Sabari →, *India* 94 F5 17 35N 81 16 E
Sabarmati →, *India* 92 H5 22 18N 72 22 E
Sab'atayn, Ramlat as, *Yemen* 98 D4 15 30N 46 10 E
Sabattis, *U.S.A.* 151 B10 44 6N 74 40W
Sabáudia, *Italy* 46 A6 41 18N 13 1 E
Sabaya, *Bolivia* 172 D4 19 1 S 68 23W
Şābāyā, Jaza'ir, *Si. Arabia* 98 C3 18 35N 41 3 E
Sabbio Chiese, *Italy* 33 E10 45 39N 10 25 E
Saberania, *Indonesia* 83 B5 2 5 S 138 18 E
Sabhah, *Libya* 108 C2 27 9N 14 29 E
Sabhah □, *Libya* 108 C2 26 0N 14 0 E
Sabi →, *India* 92 E7 28 29N 76 44 E
Sabi Game Reserve = Kruger △, *S. Africa* 117 C5 24 50 S 26 10 E
Sabidana, J., *Sudan* 106 D4 18 4N 36 50 E
Sabie, *S. Africa* 117 D5 25 10 S 30 48 E
Sabina, *U.S.A.* 157 E13 39 29N 83 38W
Sabinal, *Mexico* 162 A3 30 58N 107 25W
Sabinal, *U.S.A.* 155 L5 29 19N 99 28W
Sabiñánigo, *Spain* 40 C4 42 31N 0 22W
Sabinar, Punta del, *Spain* 41 J2 36 43N 2 44W
Sabinas, *Mexico* 162 B4 27 50N 101 10W
Sabinas →, *Mexico* 162 B4 27 37N 100 42W
Sabinas Hidalgo, *Mexico* 162 B4 26 33N 100 10W
Sabine →, *U.S.A.* 155 L8 29 59N 93 47W
Sabine L., *U.S.A.* 155 L8 29 53N 93 51W
Sabine Pass, *U.S.A.* 155 L8 29 44N 93 54W
Sabinópolis, *Brazil* 171 E3 18 40 S 43 6W
Sabinov, *Slovak Rep.* 35 B14 49 6N 21 5 E
Sabinsville, *U.S.A.* 150 E7 41 52N 77 31W
Sabirabad, *Azerbaijan* 61 K9 40 5N 48 30 E
Sabka, *Chad* 109 E3 19 15N 16 35 E
Sablayan, *Phil.* 80 E3 12 50N 120 50 E
Sable, *Canada* 141 A6 55 30N 68 21W
Sable, C., *Canada* 141 D6 43 29N 65 38W
Sable, C., *U.S.A.* 153 K8 25 9N 81 8W
Sable I., *Canada* 141 D8 44 0N 60 0W
Sable I., *Papua N. G.* 132 B8 3 38 S 154 42 E
Sablé-sur-Sarthe, *France* 26 E6 47 50N 0 20W
Saboeiro, *Brazil* 170 C4 6 32 S 39 54W
Sabonkafi, *Niger* 113 C6 14 40N 8 45 E
Sabor →, *Portugal* 42 D3 41 10N 7 7W
Sabou, *Burkina Faso* 112 C4 12 1N 2 15W
Şabrātah, *Libya* 108 B2 32 47N 12 29 E
Sabres, *France* 28 D3 44 9N 0 43W
Sabria, *Tunisia* 108 B1 33 22N 8 45 E
Sabrina Coast, *Antarctica* 7 C9 68 0 S 120 0 E
Sabtang I., *Phil.* 80 A3 20 19N 121 52 E
Sabugal, *Portugal* 42 E3 40 20N 7 5W
Sabula, *U.S.A.* 156 B6 42 4N 90 10W
Sabulubbek, *Indonesia* 84 C1 1 36 S 98 40 E
Sabuncu, *Turkey* 49 B12 39 33N 30 12 E
Şabyā, *Si. Arabia* 98 C3 17 9N 42 37 E
Sabzevār, *Iran* 97 B8 36 15N 57 40 E
Sabzvārān, *Iran* 97 D8 28 45N 57 50 E
Sac City, *U.S.A.* 156 B2 42 25N 95 0W
Sacaolo, *Angola* 115 E4 12 58 S 22 28 E
Sacatengo, *Angola* 115 E4 13 16 S 21 20 E
Sacedón, *Spain* 40 E2 40 29N 2 41W
Săcele, *Romania* 53 E10 45 37N 25 41 E
Sachigo →, *Canada* 140 A2 55 6N 88 58W
Sachigo, L., *Canada* 140 B1 53 50N 92 12W
Sachimbo, *Angola* 115 D4 9 14 S 20 16 E
Sachin, *India* 94 D1 21 5N 72 53 E
Sachkhere, *Georgia* 61 J6 42 25N 43 28 E
Sachseln, *Switz.* 33 C6 46 52N 8 15 E
Sachsen □, *Germany* 30 E9 50 55N 13 10 E
Sachsen-Anhalt □, *Germany* 30 D7 52 0N 12 0 E
Sächsische Schweiz △, *Germany* 30 E10 50 55N 14 10 E
Sacile, *Italy* 45 C9 45 57N 12 30 E
Sackets Harbor, *U.S.A.* 151 C8 43 57N 76 7W
Sackville, *Canada* 141 C7 45 54N 64 22W
Saco, *Maine, U.S.A.* 149 D10 43 30N 70 27W
Saco, *Mont., U.S.A.* 158 B10 48 28N 107 21W
Sacramento = Itatupa, *Brazil* 169 D7 0 37 S 51 12W
Sacramento, *Brazil* 171 E2 19 53 S 47 27W
Sacramento, *U.S.A.* 160 G5 38 35N 121 29W
Sacramento →, *U.S.A.* 160 G5 38 3N 121 56W
Sacramento Mts., *U.S.A.* 159 K11 32 30N 105 30W
Sacramento Valley, *U.S.A.* 160 G5 39 30N 122 0W
Sacratif, C., *Spain* 43 J7 36 42N 3 28W
Săcueni, *Romania* 52 C7 47 20N 22 5 E
Sada, *Spain* 42 B2 43 22N 8 15W
Sada-Misaki, *Japan* 71 H6 33 20N 132 1 E
Sada-Misaki-Hantō, *Japan* 72 D4 33 22N 132 1 E
Sádaba, *Spain* 40 C3 42 19N 1 12W
Sadabad, *India* 92 F8 27 27N 78 3 E
Şa'dah, *Yemen* 98 C3 16 15N 43 37 E
Sadani, *Tanzania* 118 D4 5 58 S 38 35 E
Sadao, *Thailand* 87 J3 6 38N 100 26 E
Sadaseopet, *India* 94 F3 17 38N 77 59 E
Sadd el Aali, *Egypt* 106 C3 23 54N 32 54 E
Saddle Mt., *U.S.A.* 160 E3 45 58N 123 41W
Saddle Pk., *India* 95 H11 13 9N 93 1 E
Saddle Pt., *St. Helena* 9 h 15 57 S 5 38W
Sade, *Nigeria* 113 C7 11 22N 10 45 E
Şadh, *Oman* 99 C6 17 3N 55 4 E
Sadimi, *Dem. Rep. of the Congo* 119 D1 9 25 S 23 32 E
Sadiola, *Mali* 112 C2 13 50N 11 40W
Sadiya, *India* 90 B5 27 50N 95 40 E
Sa'dīyah, Hawr as, *Iraq* 101 F12 32 15N 46 30 E
Sado, *Japan* 70 F9 38 0N 138 25 E
Sado →, *Portugal* 43 G2 38 29N 8 55W
Sadon, *Russia* 61 J6 42 52N 43 58 E
Sadovoye, *Russia* 61 G7 47 47N 44 31 E
Sadowara, *Japan* 72 E3 32 2N 131 26 E
Sadra, *India* 92 H5 23 21N 72 43 E
Sadri, *India* 92 G5 25 11N 73 26 E
Sæbøvik, *Norway* 18 E2 59 47N 5 40 E
Sæby, *Denmark* 17 G4 57 21N 10 30 E
Saegertown, *U.S.A.* 150 E4 41 43N 80 9W
Saelices, *Spain* 40 F2 39 55N 2 49W
Sætre, *Norway* 18 E7 59 41N 10 33 E
Sævareid, *Norway* 18 D2 60 11N 5 46 E
Safaalan, *Turkey* 51 E12 41 26N 28 6 E
Safaga, *Egypt* 106 B3 26 42N 34 0 E
Şafājah, *Si. Arabia* 96 E3 26 25N 39 0 E
Šafárikovo = Tornal'a, *Slovak Rep.* 35 C13 48 25N 20 20 E
Safata B., *Samoa* 133 X24 14 0 S 171 50W
Safed Koh, *Afghan.* 91 B3 34 0N 70 0 E
Säffle, *Sweden* 16 E6 59 8N 12 55 E
Safford, *U.S.A.* 159 K9 32 50N 109 43W
Saffron Walden, *U.K.* 21 E8 52 1N 0 16 E
Safi, *Morocco* 110 B3 32 18N 9 20W
Safia, *Papua N. G.* 132 E5 9 35 S 148 38 E
Safia, Hamada, *Mali* 110 D4 23 10N 4 15W
Şafīābād, *Iran* 97 B8 36 45N 57 58 E
Safīd Dasht, *Iran* 97 C6 33 27N 48 11 E
Safīd Kūh, *Afghan.* 91 B1 34 45N 63 0 E
Safīd Rūd →, *Iran* 97 B6 37 23N 50 11 E
Safipur, *India* 93 F9 26 44N 80 21 E
Safonovo, *Russia* 58 E7 55 4N 33 16 E
Safranbolu, *Turkey* 100 B5 41 15N 32 41 E
Saft Rashîn, *Egypt* 106 J7 28 58N 30 55 E
Safune, *Samoa* 133 W23 13 25 S 172 21W
Şafwān, *Iraq* 96 D5 30 7N 47 43 E
Sag Harbor, *U.S.A.* 151 F12 41 0N 72 18W
Sag Sag, *Papua N. G.* 132 C5 5 32 S 148 23 E
Saga, *Indonesia* 83 B4 2 40 S 132 55 E
Saga, *Kōchi, Japan* 72 D5 33 5N 133 6 E
Saga, *Saga, Japan* 72 D2 33 15N 130 16 E
Saga □, *Japan* 72 D2 33 15N 130 20 E
Sagae, *Japan* 70 E10 38 22N 140 17 E
Sagaing, *Burma* 90 E5 21 52N 95 59 E
Sagaing □, *Burma* 90 D5 23 55N 95 56 E
Sagala, *Mali* 112 C3 14 9N 6 38W
Sagami-Nada, *Japan* 73 C11 34 58N 139 30 E
Sagami-Wan, *Japan* 73 B11 35 15N 139 25 E
Sagamihara, *Japan* 73 B11 35 33N 139 25 E
Sagamore, *U.S.A.* 150 F5 40 46N 79 14W
Sagan = Żagań, *Poland* 55 G2 51 39N 15 22 E
Saganaga L., *Canada* 154 A9 48 14N 90 52W
Saganoseki, *Japan* 72 D3 33 15N 131 53 E
Sagar, *Karnataka, India* 94 F3 16 38N 76 48 E
Sagar, *Karnataka, India* 95 G2 14 14N 75 6 E
Sagar, *Mad. P., India* 93 H8 23 50N 78 44 E
Sagara, *Japan* 73 C10 34 41N 138 12 E
Sagara, L., *Tanzania* 118 D3 5 20 S 31 0 E
Sagarmatha = Everest, Mt., *Nepal* 93 E12 28 5N 86 58 E
Sagarmatha △, *Nepal* 93 F12 27 55N 86 45 E
Sagavanirktok →, *U.S.A.* 144 A11 70 19N 147 53W
Sagay, *Phil.* 81 F4 10 57N 123 25 E
Saginaw, *U.S.A.* 148 D4 43 26N 83 56W
Saginaw B., *U.S.A.* 148 D4 43 50N 83 40W
Sagleipie, *Liberia* 112 D3 7 0N 8 52W
Saglouc = Salluit, *Canada* 139 B12 62 14N 75 38W
Sagŏ-ri, *S. Korea* 75 G14 35 25N 126 49 E
Sagone, *France* 29 F12 42 7N 8 42 E
Sagone, G. de, *France* 29 F12 42 4N 8 40 E
Sagres, *Portugal* 43 J2 37 0N 8 58W
Sagu, *Burma* 90 E5 20 13N 94 46 E
Sagua la Grande, *Cuba* 164 B3 22 50N 80 10W
Saguache, *U.S.A.* 159 G10 38 5N 106 8W
Saguaro △, *U.S.A.* 159 K8 32 12N 110 38W
Saguenay →, *Canada* 141 C5 48 22N 71 0W
Saguia el Hamra →, *W. Sahara* 110 C2 27 24N 13 43W
Sagunt, *Spain* 40 F4 39 42N 0 18W
Sagunto = Sagunt, *Spain* 40 F4 39 42N 0 18W
Sagvåg, *Norway* 18 E2 59 46N 5 25 E
Sagwara, *India* 92 H6 23 41N 74 1 E
Sahaba, *Sudan* 106 D3 18 57N 30 25 E
Sahagún, *Colombia* 168 B2 8 57N 75 27W
Sahagún, *Spain* 42 C5 42 18N 5 2W
Saḩam al Jawlān, *Syria* 103 C4 32 45N 35 55 E
Sahamandrevo, *Madag.* 117 C8 23 15 S 45 35 E
Sahand, Kūh-e, *Iran* 101 D12 37 44N 46 27 E
Sahara, *Africa* 104 D4 23 0N 5 0 E
Saharan Atlas = Saharien, Atlas, *Algeria* 111 B5 33 30N 1 0 E
Saharanpur, *India* 92 E7 29 58N 77 33 E
Saharien, Atlas, *Algeria* 111 B5 33 30N 1 0 E
Saharsa, *India* 93 G12 25 53N 86 36 E
Sahasinaka, *Madag.* 117 C8 21 49 S 47 49 E
Sahaswan, *India* 93 E8 28 5N 78 45 E
Sahel, *Africa* 104 E3 12 0N 8 0W
Sahel, Canal du, *Mali* 112 C3 14 20N 6 0W
Sahibganj, *India* 93 G12 25 12N 87 40 E
Sāḩilīyah, *Iraq* 101 F10 33 43N 42 42 E
Sahiwal, *Pakistan* 91 C4 30 45N 73 8 E
Şaḩneh, *Iran* 101 E12 34 29N 47 41 E
Sahrawi = Western Sahara ■, *Africa* 110 D2 25 0N 13 0W
Sahrawi = Western Sahara ■, *Africa* 110 D2 25 0N 13 0W
Sahuaripa, *Mexico* 162 B3 29 0N 109 13W
Sahuarita, *U.S.A.* 159 L8 31 57N 110 58W
Sahuayo, *Mexico* 162 C4 20 4N 102 43W
Šahy, *Slovak Rep.* 35 C11 48 4N 18 55 E
Sai →, *India* 93 G10 25 39N 82 47 E
Sai Buri, *Thailand* 87 J3 6 43N 101 45 E
Sai-Cinza, *Brazil* 173 B6 6 17 S 57 42W
Sai Kung, *China* 69 G11 22 23N 114 16 E
Saibai I., *Australia* 132 E2 9 25 S 142 40 E
Sa'id Bundas, *Sudan* 109 G4 8 24N 24 48 E
Saïda, *Algeria* 111 B5 34 50N 0 11 E
Sa'īdābād = Sīrjān, *Iran* 97 D7 29 30N 55 45 E
Sa'īdābād, *Iran* 97 B7 36 8N 54 11 E
Saidaiji, *Japan* 72 C6 34 39N 134 2 E
Saïdia, *Morocco* 111 A4 35 5N 2 14W
Sa'īdīyeh, *Iran* 97 B6 36 20N 48 55 E
Saidor, *Papua N. G.* 132 C4 5 40 S 146 29 E
Saidpur, *Bangla.* 90 C2 25 48N 89 0 E
Saidpur, *India* 93 G10 25 33N 83 11 E
Saidu, *Pakistan* 93 B5 34 43N 72 24 E
Saignelégier, *Switz.* 32 B4 47 15N 7 0 E
Saignes, *France* 28 C6 45 20N 2 31 E
Saigō, *Japan* 72 A5 36 12N 133 20 E
Saigon = Thanh Pho Ho Chi Minh, *Vietnam* 87 G6 10 58N 106 40 E
Saijō, *Japan* 72 D5 33 55N 133 11 E
Saikai △, *Japan* 72 D1 33 12N 129 36 E
Saikanosy Masoala, *Madag.* 117 B9 15 45 S 50 10 E
Saikhoa Ghat, *India* 90 B5 27 50N 95 40 E
Saiki, *Japan* 72 E3 32 58N 131 51 E
Sailana, *India* 92 H6 23 28N 74 55 E
Saillans, *France* 29 D9 44 42N 5 12 E
Sailolof, *Indonesia* 83 B4 1 15 S 130 46 E
Sailu, *India* 94 E3 19 28N 76 28 E
Saimaa, *Finland* 15 F23 61 15N 28 15 E
Saimbeyli, *Turkey* 100 D7 37 59N 36 6 E
Saimen = Saimaa, *Finland* 15 F23 61 15N 28 15 E
Şa'in Dezh, *Iran* 101 D12 36 40N 46 25 E
St. Abb's Head, *U.K.* 22 F6 55 55N 2 8W
St-Affrique, *France* 28 E6 43 57N 2 53 E
St-Agrève, *France* 29 C8 45 0N 4 23 E
St-Aignan, *France* 26 E8 47 16N 1 22 E
St. Alban's, *Canada* 141 C8 47 51N 55 50W
St. Albans, *U.K.* 21 F7 51 45N 0 19W
St. Albans, *Vt., U.S.A.* 151 B11 44 49N 73 5W
St. Albans, *W. Va., U.S.A.* 148 F5 38 23N 81 50W
St. Alban's Head, *U.K.* 21 G5 50 34N 2 4W
St. Albert, *Canada* 142 C6 53 37N 113 32W
St-Amand-en-Puisaye, *France* 27 E10 47 32N 3 5 E
St-Amand-les-Eaux, *France* 27 B10 50 27N 3 25 E
St-Amand-Montrond, *France* 27 F9 46 43N 2 30 E
St-Amarin, *France* 27 E14 47 54N 7 2 E
St-Amour, *France* 27 F12 46 26N 5 21 E
St-André, *Réunion* 121 c 20 57 S 55 39 E
St-André-de-Cubzac, *France* 28 D3 44 59N 0 26W
St-André-les-Alpes, *France* 29 E10 43 58N 6 30 E
St. Andrew Sd., *U.S.A.* 152 E8 31 0N 81 25W
St. Andrew's, *Canada* 141 C8 47 45N 59 15W
St. Andrews, *N.Z.* 131 E6 44 33 S 171 10 E
St. Andrews, *U.K.* 22 E6 56 20N 2 47W
St. Andrews, *U.S.A.* 152 C9 32 47N 80 0W
St-Anicet, *Canada* 151 A10 45 8N 74 22W
St. Anne, *U.S.A.* 157 C9 41 1N 87 43W
St. Anns B., *Canada* 141 C7 46 22N 60 25W
St. Ann's Bay, *Jamaica* 164 a 18 26N 77 12W
St. Anthony, *Canada* 141 B8 51 22N 55 35W
St. Anthony, *U.S.A.* 158 E8 43 58N 111 41W
St-Antoine, *Canada* 141 C7 46 22N 64 45W
St. Anton am Arlberg, *Austria* 33 B10 47 8N 10 16 E
St-Antonin-Noble-Val, *France* 28 D5 44 10N 1 45 E
St. Arnaud = El Eulma, *Algeria* 111 A6 36 9N 5 42 E
St. Arnaud, *Australia* 128 D5 36 40 S 143 16 E
St. Arnaud Ra., *N.Z.* 131 C7 42 1 S 172 53 E
St-Astier, *France* 28 C4 45 8N 0 31 E
St-Aubin, *Switz.* 32 C3 46 54N 6 47 E
St-Aubin-du-Cormier, *France* 26 D5 48 15N 1 26W
St-Augustin, *Canada* 141 B8 51 13N 58 38W
St-Augustin →, *Canada* 141 B8 51 16N 58 40W
St. Augustine, *U.S.A.* 152 F8 29 54N 81 19W
St. Augustine Beach, *U.S.A.* 152 F8 29 51N 81 16W
St-Aulaye, *France* 28 C4 45 12N 0 9 E
St. Austell, *U.K.* 21 G3 50 20N 4 47W
St-Avold, *France* 27 C13 49 6N 6 43 E
St. Barbe, *Canada* 141 B8 51 12N 56 46W
St-Barthélemy, *W. Indies* 165 C7 17 50N 62 50W
St. Bathans, *N.Z.* 131 E4 44 53 S 169 50 E
St. Bathan's, Mt., *N.Z.* 131 E4 44 45 S 169 45 E
St-Béat, *France* 28 F4 42 55N 0 41 E
St. Bees Hd., *U.K.* 20 C4 54 31N 3 38W
St. Bees I., *Australia* 126 J7 20 56 S 149 26 E
St-Benoît, *Réunion* 121 c 21 2 S 55 43 E
St-Benoît-du-Sault, *France* 28 B5 46 26N 1 24 E
St-Bernard, Col du Grand, *Europe* 32 E4 45 53N 7 11 E
St-Blaise, *Switz.* 32 B3 47 1N 6 59 E
St-Bonnet-en-Champsaur, *France* 29 D10 44 40N 6 5 E
St-Brevin-les-Pins, *France* 26 E4 47 14N 2 10W
St-Brice-en-Coglès, *France* 26 D5 48 25N 1 22W
St. Bride's, *Canada* 141 C9 46 56N 54 10W
St. Brides B., *U.K.* 21 F2 51 49N 5 9W
St-Brieuc, *France* 26 D4 48 30N 2 46W
St-Calais, *France* 26 E7 47 55N 0 45 E
St-Cast-le-Guildo, *France* 26 D4 48 37N 2 18W
St. Catharines, *Canada* 140 D4 43 10N 79 15W
St. Catherine Pt., *Bermuda* 9 a 32 23N 64 40W
St. Catherines I., *U.S.A.* 152 D8 31 40N 81 10W
St. Catherine's Pt., *U.K.* 21 G6 50 34N 1 18W
St-Céré, *France* 28 D5 44 51N 1 54 E
St-Cergue, *Switz.* 32 D2 46 27N 6 10 E
St-Cernin, *France* 28 C6 45 5N 2 25 E
St-Chamond, *France* 29 C8 45 28N 4 31 E
St. Charles, *Ill., U.S.A.* 157 C8 41 54N 88 19W
St. Charles, *Md., U.S.A.* 148 F7 38 36N 76 56W
St. Charles, *Mo., U.S.A.* 156 F6 38 47N 90 29W
St-Chély-d'Apcher, *France* 28 D7 44 48N 3 17 E
St-Chinian, *France* 28 E6 43 25N 2 56 E
St. Christopher-Nevis = St. Kitts & Nevis ■, *W. Indies* 165 C7 17 20N 62 40W
St-Ciers-sur-Gironde, *France* 28 C3 45 17N 0 37W
St. Clair, *Ga., U.S.A.* 152 B7 33 9N 82 13W
St. Clair, *Mich., U.S.A.* 150 D2 42 50N 82 30W
St. Clair, *Mo., U.S.A.* 156 F6 38 21N 90 59W
St. Clair, *Pa., U.S.A.* 151 F8 40 43N 76 12W
St. Clair →, *U.S.A.* 150 D2 42 38N 82 31W
St. Clair, L., *Australia* 128 D3 37 20 S 139 55 E
St. Clair, L., *Canada* 140 D3 42 30N 82 45W
St. Clair, L., *U.S.A.* 150 D2 42 27N 82 39W
St. Clair Shores, *U.S.A.* 157 B14 42 30N 82 53W
St. Clairsville, *U.S.A.* 150 F4 40 5N 80 54W
St-Claud, *France* 28 C4 45 54N 0 28 E
St. Claude, *Canada* 143 D9 49 40N 98 20W
St-Claude, *France* 27 F12 46 22N 5 52 E
St. Clears, *U.K.* 21 F3 51 49N 4 31W
St-Clet, *Canada* 151 A10 45 21N 74 13W
St. Cloud, *Fla., U.S.A.* 153 G8 28 15N 81 17W
St. Cloud, *Minn., U.S.A.* 154 C7 45 34N 94 10W
St. Cricq, C., *Australia* 125 E1 25 17 S 113 6 E
St. Croix, *U.S. Virgin Is.* 165 C7 17 45N 64 45W
St. Croix →, *U.S.A.* 154 C8 44 45N 92 48W
St. Croix Falls, *U.S.A.* 154 C8 45 24N 92 38W
St-Cyprien, *France* 28 F7 42 37N 3 2 E
St-Cyr-sur-Mer, *France* 29 E9 43 11N 5 43 E
St. David, *U.S.A.* 156 D6 40 30N 90 3W
St. David's, *Canada* 141 C8 48 12N 58 52W
St. David's, *U.K.* 21 F2 51 53N 5 16W
St. David's Head, *U.K.* 21 F2 51 54N 5 19W
St. David's I., *Bermuda* 9 a 32 21N 64 39W
St-Denis = Sig, *Algeria* 111 A4 35 32N 0 12W
St-Denis, *France* 27 D9 48 56N 2 22 E
St-Denis, *Réunion* 121 c 20 52 S 55 27 E
St-Denis ✈ (RUN), *Réunion* 121 c 20 53 S 55 32 E
St-Dié, *France* 27 D13 48 17N 6 56 E
St-Dizier, *France* 27 D11 48 38N 4 56 E
St-Égrève, *France* 29 C9 45 14N 5 41 E
St. Elias, Mt., *U.S.A.* 144 F12 60 18N 140 56W
St. Elias Mts., *N. Amer.* 142 A1 60 33N 139 28W
St-Élie, *Fr. Guiana* 169 C7 4 49N 53 17W
St. Elmo, *U.S.A.* 157 E8 39 2N 88 51W
St-Eloy-les-Mines, *France* 27 F9 46 10N 2 51 E
St-Émilion, *France* 28 D3 44 53N 0 9W
St-Étienne, *France* 29 C8 45 27N 4 22 E
St-Étienne-de-Tinée, *France* 29 D10 44 16N 6 56 E
St-Étienne-du-Rouvray, *France* 26 C8 49 23N 1 6 E
St. Eugène, *Canada* 151 A10 45 30N 74 28W
St. Eustatius, *W. Indies* 165 C7 17 20N 63 0W
St-Exupery, Lyon ✈ (LYS), *France* 29 C9 45 44N 5 2 E
St-Fargeau, *France* 27 E10 47 39N 3 4 E
St-Félicien, *Canada* 140 C5 48 40N 72 25W
St. Ferdinand = Florissant, *U.S.A.* 156 F6 38 48N 90 20W
St-Florent, *France* 29 F13 42 41N 9 18 E
St-Florent, G. de, *France* 29 F13 42 47N 9 12 E
St-Florent-sur-Cher, *France* 27 F9 46 59N 2 15 E
St-Florentin, *France* 27 E10 48 0N 3 45 E
St-Flour, *France* 28 C7 45 2N 3 6 E
St. Francis, *U.S.A.* 154 F4 39 47N 101 48W
St. Francis →, *U.S.A.* 155 H9 34 38N 90 36W
St. Francis, C., *S. Africa* 116 E3 34 14 S 24 49 E
St. Francisville, *Ill., U.S.A.* 157 F9 38 36N 87 39W
St. Francisville, *La., U.S.A.* 155 K9 30 47N 91 23W
St-François, L., *Canada* 151 A10 45 10N 74 22W
St-Fulgent, *France* 26 F5 46 50N 1 10W
St-Gabriel, *Canada* 140 C5 46 17N 73 24W
St. Gallen = Sankt Gallen, *Switz.* 33 B8 47 26N 9 22 E
St. Gallenkirch, *Austria* 33 B9 47 1N 9 58 E
St-Galmier, *France* 27 G11 45 35N 4 19 E
St-Gaudens, *France* 28 E4 43 6N 0 44 E
St-Gaultier, *France* 26 F8 46 39N 1 26 E
St-Gengoux-le-National, *France* 27 F11 46 37N 4 40 E
St-Geniez-d'Olt, *France* 28 D6 44 27N 2 58 E
St. George, *Australia* 127 D4 28 1 S 148 30 E
St. George, *Bermuda* 9 a 32 22N 64 40W
St. George, *Canada* 141 C6 45 11N 66 50W
St. George, *Ga., U.S.A.* 152 E7 30 31N 82 2W
St. George, *S.C., U.S.A.* 152 B9 33 11N 80 35W
St. George, *Utah, U.S.A.* 159 H7 37 6N 113 35W
St. George, C., *Canada* 141 C8 48 30N 59 16W
St. George, C., *Papua N. G.* 132 C7 4 49 S 152 53 E
St. George, C., *U.S.A.* 152 F4 29 40N 85 5W
St. George I., *Alaska, U.S.A.* 144 H5 56 35N 169 35W
St. George I., *Fla., U.S.A.* 152 F5 29 35N 84 55W
St. George Ra., *Australia* 124 C4 18 40 S 125 0 E
St. George's, *Canada* 141 C8 48 26N 58 31W
St-Georges, *Canada* 141 C5 46 8N 70 40W
St-Georges, *Fr. Guiana* 169 C7 3 53N 51 50W
St. George's, *Grenada* 165 D7 12 5N 61 43W
St. George's B., *Canada* 141 C8 48 24N 58 53W
St. Georges Basin, *N.S.W., Australia* 129 C9 35 7 S 150 36 E
St. Georges Basin, *W. Austral., Australia* 124 C4 15 23 S 125 2 E
St. George's Channel, *Europe* 23 E6 52 0N 6 0W
St. George's Channel, *India* 95 L11 7 15N 93 43 E
St. George's Channel, *Papua N. G.* 132 C7 4 10 S 152 20 E
St. Georges Hd., *Australia* 129 C9 35 12 S 150 42 E
St. Georges I., *Bermuda* 9 a 32 23N 64 40W
St-Georges-lès-Baillargeaux, *France* 28 B4 46 41N 0 22 E
St-Germain-de-Calberte, *France* 28 D7 44 13N 3 48 E
St-Germain-en-Laye, *France* 27 D9 48 54N 2 6 E
St-Germain-Lembron, *France* 28 C7 45 27N 3 14 E
St-Gervais-d'Auvergne, *France* 27 F9 46 4N 2 50 E
St-Gervais-les-Bains, *France* 29 C10 45 53N 6 42 E
St-Gildas, Pte. de, *France* 26 E4 47 8N 2 14W
St-Gilles, *France* 29 E8 43 40N 4 26 E
St-Gingolph, *Switz.* 32 D3 46 24N 6 48 E
St-Girons, *Ariège, France* 28 F5 42 59N 1 8 E
St-Girons, *Landes, France* 28 E2 43 56N 1 18W
St. Gotthard P. = San Gottardo, P. del, *Switz.* 33 C7 46 33N 8 33 E
St. Helena, *Atl. Oc.* 9 h 15 58 S 5 42W
St. Helena, *U.S.A.* 158 G2 38 30N 122 28W
St. Helena, Mt., *U.S.A.* 160 G4 38 40N 122 36W
St. Helena B., *S. Africa* 116 E2 32 40 S 18 10 E
St. Helena Sd., *U.S.A.* 152 C9 32 15N 80 25W
St. Helens, *Australia* 127 G4 41 20 S 148 15 E

St. Helens, *U.K.* **20 D5** 53 27N 2 44W
St. Helens, *U.S.A.* **160 E4** 45 52N 122 48W
St. Helens, Mt., *U.S.A.* **160 D4** 46 12N 122 12W
St. Helier, *U.K.* **21 H5** 49 10N 2 7W
St-Herblain, *France* **26 E5** 47 13N 1 40W
St-Hilaire-du-Harcouët, *France* **26 D5** 48 35N 1 5W
St-Hippolyte, *France* **27 E13** 47 19N 6 50 E
St-Hippolyte-du-Fort, *France* **28 E7** 43 58N 3 52 E
St-Honoré-les-Bains, *France* **27 F10** 46 54N 3 50 E
St-Hubert, *Belgium* **24 D5** 50 2N 5 23 E
St-Hyacinthe, *Canada* **140 C5** 45 40N 72 58W
St. Ignace, *U.S.A.* **148 C3** 45 52N 84 44W
St. Ignace I., *Canada* **140 C2** 48 45N 88 0W
St. Ignatius, *U.S.A.* **158 C6** 47 19N 114 6W
St-Imier, *Switz.* **32 B3** 47 9N 6 58 E
St. Ives, *Cambs., U.K.* **21 E7** 52 20N 0 4W
St. Ives, *Corn., U.K.* **21 G2** 50 12N 5 30W
St-James, *France* **26 D5** 48 31N 1 20W
St. James, *Minn., U.S.A.* **154 D7** 43 59N 94 38W
St. James, *Mo., U.S.A.* **156 G5** 38 0N 91 37W
St-Jean →, *Canada* **141 B7** 50 17N 64 20W
St-Jean, L., *Canada* **141 C5** 48 40N 72 0W
St-Jean-d'Angély, *France* **28 C3** 45 57N 0 31W
St-Jean-de-Braye, *France* **27 E8** 47 53N 1 58 E
St-Jean-de-Luz, *France* **28 E2** 43 23N 1 39W
St-Jean-de-Maurienne, *France* **29 C10** 45 16N 6 21 E
St-Jean-de-Monts, *France* **26 F4** 46 47N 2 4W
St-Jean-du-Gard, *France* **28 D7** 44 7N 3 52 E
St-Jean-en-Royans, *France* **29 C9** 45 1N 5 18 E
St-Jean-Pied-de-Port, *France* **28 E2** 43 10N 1 14W
St-Jean-Port-Joli, *Canada* **141 C5** 47 15N 70 13W
St-Jean-sur-Richelieu, *Canada* **140 C5** 45 20N 73 20W
St-Jérôme, *Canada* **140 C5** 45 47N 74 0W
St. Joe, *U.S.A.* **157 C12** 41 19N 84 54W
St. John, *Canada* **141 C6** 45 20N 66 8W
St. John, *U.S.A.* **155 G5** 38 0N 98 46W
St. John →, *Liberia* **112 D2** 6 40N 9 10W
St. John →, *U.S.A.* **149 C12** 45 12N 66 5W
St. John, C., *Canada* **141 C8** 50 0N 55 32W
St. John I., *U.S. Virgin Is.* **165 e** 18 20N 64 42W
St. John's, *Antigua & B.* **165 C7** 17 6N 61 51W
St. John's, *Canada* **141 C9** 47 35N 52 40W
St. Johns, *Ariz., U.S.A.* **159 J9** 34 30N 109 22W
St. Johns, *Mich., U.S.A.* **157 B12** 43 0N 84 33W
St. Johns →, *U.S.A.* **152 E8** 30 24N 81 24W
St. John's Pt., *Ireland* **23 B3** 54 34N 8 27W
St. Johnsbury, *U.S.A.* **151 B12** 44 25N 72 1W
St. Johnsville, *U.S.A.* **151 D10** 43 0N 74 43W
St-Joseph, *Martinique* **164 c** 14 39N 61 4W
St-Joseph, *N. Cal.* **133 K4** 20 27 S 166 36 E
St-Joseph, *Réunion* **121 c** 21 22 S 55 37 E
St. Joseph, *Ill., U.S.A.* **157 D8** 40 7N 88 2W
St. Joseph, *La., U.S.A.* **155 K9** 31 55N 91 14W
St. Joseph, *Mich., U.S.A.* **157 B10** 42 6N 86 29W
St. Joseph, *Mo., U.S.A.* **156 E2** 39 46N 94 50W
St. Joseph →, *U.S.A.* **157 B10** 42 7N 86 29W
St. Joseph, I., *Canada* **140 C3** 46 12N 83 58W
St. Joseph, L., *Canada* **140 B1** 51 10N 90 35W
St. Joseph Pt., *U.S.A.* **152 F4** 29 52N 85 24W
St-Jovite, *Canada* **140 C5** 46 8N 74 38W
St-Juéry, *France* **28 E6** 43 57N 2 12 E
St. Julian's, *Malta* **38 F7** 35 55N 14 29 E
St-Julien-Chapteuil, *France* **29 C8** 45 2N 4 4 E
St-Julien-de-Vouvantes, *France* **26 E5** 47 38N 1 13W
St-Julien-en-Genevois, *France* **27 F13** 46 9N 6 5 E
St-Junien, *France* **28 C4** 45 53N 0 55 E
St-Just-en-Chaussée, *France* **27 C9** 49 30N 2 25 E
St-Just-en-Chevalet, *France* **28 C7** 45 55N 3 50 E
St. Kilda, *N.Z.* **131 F5** 45 53 S 170 31 E
St. Kilda, *U.K.* **19 C2** 57 49N 8 34W
St. Kitts & Nevis ■, *W. Indies* **165 C7** 17 20N 62 40W
St. Laurent, *Canada* **143 C9** 50 25N 97 58W
St-Laurent, *Fr. Guiana* **169 B7** 5 29N 54 3W
St-Laurent-de-la-Salanque, *France* **28 F6** 42 46N 2 59 E
St-Laurent-du-Pont, *France* **29 C9** 45 23N 5 45 E
St-Laurent-en-Grandvaux, *France* **27 F12** 46 35N 5 58 E
St-Laurent-Médoc, *France* **28 C3** 45 8N 0 49W
St. Lawrence, *Australia* **126 C4** 22 16 S 149 31 E
St. Lawrence, *Canada* **141 C8** 46 54N 55 23W
St. Lawrence →, *Canada* **141 C6** 49 30N 66 0W
St. Lawrence, Gulf of, *Canada* **141 C7** 48 25N 62 0W
St. Lawrence I., *U.S.A.* **144 E5** 63 30N 170 30W
St. Lawrence Islands △, *Canada* **151 B9** 44 27N 75 52W
St. Leonard, *Canada* **141 C6** 47 12N 67 58W
St-Léonard-de-Noblat, *France* **28 C5** 45 49N 1 29 E
St. Leonhard im Pitztal, *Austria* **33 B11** 47 4N 10 51 E
St-Leu, *Réunion* **121 c** 21 9 S 55 18 E
St. Lewis →, *Canada* **141 B8** 52 26N 56 11W
St-Lô, *France* **26 C5** 49 7N 1 5W
St-Louis, *France* **27 E14** 47 30N 7 34 E
St-Louis, *Guadeloupe* **164 b** 15 56N 61 19W
St-Louis, *Réunion* **121 c** 21 16 S 55 25 E
St. Louis, *Senegal* **112 B1** 16 8N 16 27W
St. Louis, *U.S.A.* **156 F6** 38 37N 90 12W
St. Louis →, *U.S.A.* **154 B8** 47 15N 92 45W
St. Louis Lambert International ✈ (STL), *U.S.A.* **156 F6** 38 45N 90 22W
St-Loup-sur-Semouse, *France* **27 E13** 47 53N 6 16 E
St. Lucia ■, *W. Indies* **165 f** 14 0N 60 57W
St. Lucia, L., *S. Africa* **117 D5** 28 5 S 32 30 E
St. Lucia Channel, *W. Indies* **165 D7** 14 15N 61 0W
St. Lucie, *U.S.A.* **153 H9** 27 29N 80 20W
St. Lucie Canal, *U.S.A.* **153 H9** 27 10N 80 18W
St. Maarten ⊘, *W. Indies* **165 C7** 18 0N 63 5W
St. Magnus B., *U.K.* **22 A7** 60 25N 1 35W
St-Maixent-l'École, *France* **28 B3** 46 24N 0 12W
St-Malo, *France* **26 D4** 48 39N 2 1W
St-Malo, G. de, *France* **26 D4** 48 50N 2 30W
St-Mandrier-sur-Mer, *France* **29 E9** 43 4N 5 57 E
St-Marc, *Haiti* **165 C5** 19 10N 72 41W
St-Marcellin, *France* **29 C9** 45 9N 5 20 E
St-Marcouf, Îs., *France* **26 C5** 49 30N 1 10W
St. Maries, *U.S.A.* **158 C5** 47 19N 116 35W
St. Marks, *U.S.A.* **152 E5** 30 9N 84 12W
St-Martin ⊘, *W. Indies* **165 C7** 18 0N 63 0W
St-Martin, C., *Martinique* **164 c** 14 52N 61 14W
St. Martin, L., *Canada* **143 C9** 51 40N 98 30W
St-Martin-de-Crau, *France* **29 E8** 43 38N 4 48 E
St-Martin-de-Ré, *France* **28 B2** 46 12N 1 21W
St-Martin-d'Hères, *France* **29 C9** 45 9N 5 45 E
St-Martin-Vésubie, *France* **29 D11** 44 4N 7 15 E
St. Martins, *Barbados* **165 g** 13 5N 59 28W
St-Martory, *France* **28 E4** 43 9N 0 56 E
St. Mary, *U.S.A.* **156 G7** 37 53N 89 57W
St. Mary, Mt., *Papua N. G.* **132 E4** 8 8 S 147 2 E
St. Mary Is., *India* **95 H2** 13 20N 74 35 E
St. Mary Pk., *Australia* **128 A3** 31 32 S 138 34 E
St. Marys, *Australia* **127 G4** 41 35 S 148 11 E
St. Marys, *Canada* **150 C3** 43 20N 81 10W
St. Mary's, *Corn., U.K.* **21 H1** 49 55N 6 18W
St. Mary's, *Orkney, U.K.* **22 C6** 58 54N 2 54W
St. Mary's, *Alaska, U.S.A.* **144 E7** 62 4N 163 10W
St. Marys, *Ga., U.S.A.* **152 E8** 30 44N 81 33W
St. Marys, *Ohio, U.S.A.* **157 D12** 40 33N 84 24W
St. Marys, *Pa., U.S.A.* **150 E6** 41 26N 78 34W
St. Marys →, *U.S.A.* **152 E8** 30 43N 81 27W
St. Mary's, C., *Canada* **141 C9** 46 50N 54 12W
St. Mary's B., *Canada* **141 C9** 46 50N 53 50W
St. Marys Bay, *Canada* **141 D6** 44 25N 66 10W
St-Mathieu, Pte., *France* **26 D2** 48 20N 4 45W
St. Matthew I., *U.S.A.* **144 F4** 60 24N 172 42W
St. Matthews, *Ky., U.S.A.* **157 F11** 38 15N 85 39W
St. Matthews, *S.C., U.S.A.* **152 B9** 33 40N 80 46W
St. Matthews, I. = Zadetkyi Kyun, *Burma* **87 G2** 10 0N 98 25 E
St. Matthias Group, *Papua N. G.* **132 A5** 1 30 S 150 0 E
St-Maurice, *Switz.* **32 D4** 46 13N 7 0 E
St-Maurice →, *Canada* **140 C5** 46 21N 72 31W
St. Mawes, *U.K.* **21 G2** 50 10N 5 2W
St-Maximin-la-Ste-Baume, *France* **29 E9** 43 27N 5 52 E
St-Médard-en-Jalles, *France* **28 D3** 44 53N 0 43W
St-Méen-le-Grand, *France* **26 D4** 48 11N 2 12W
St. Meinrad, *U.S.A.* **157 F10** 38 10N 86 49W
St. Michael, *U.S.A.* **144 E7** 63 29N 162 2W
St-Mihiel, *France* **27 D12** 48 54N 5 32 E
St. Moritz, *Switz.* **31 J5** 46 30N 9 51 E
St-Nazaire, *France* **26 E4** 47 17N 2 12W
St. Neots, *U.K.* **21 E7** 52 14N 0 15W
St-Nicolas-de-Port, *France* **27 D13** 48 38N 6 18 E
St-Niklaas, *Belgium* **24 C4** 51 10N 4 8 E
St. Niklaus, *Switz.* **32 D5** 46 10N 7 49 E
St-Omer, *France* **27 B9** 50 45N 2 15 E
St-Palais-sur-Mer, *France* **28 C2** 45 38N 1 5W
St-Pamphile, *Canada* **141 C6** 46 58N 69 48W
St-Pardoux-la-Rivière, *France* **28 C4** 45 29N 0 45 E
St. Paris, *U.S.A.* **157 D13** 40 8N 83 58W
St-Pascal, *Canada* **141 C6** 47 32N 69 48W
St. Paul, *Canada* **142 C6** 54 0N 111 17W
St-Paul, *France* **29 D10** 44 31N 6 45 E
St-Paul, *Réunion* **121 c** 20 59 S 55 17 E
St. Paul, *Alaska, U.S.A.* **144 H5** 57 7N 170 17W
St. Paul, *Ind., U.S.A.* **157 E11** 39 26N 85 38W
St. Paul, *Minn., U.S.A.* **154 C8** 44 57N 93 6W
St. Paul, *Nebr., U.S.A.* **154 E5** 41 13N 98 27W
St-Paul →, *Canada* **141 B8** 51 27N 57 42W
St. Paul →, *Liberia* **112 D2** 6 25N 10 48W
St. Paul, I., *Ind. Oc.* **121 H6** 38 55 S 77 34 E
St-Paul-de-Fenouillet, *France* **28 F6** 42 48N 2 30 E
St. Paul I., *Canada* **141 C7** 47 12N 60 9W
St. Paul I., *U.S.A.* **144 H5** 57 10N 170 15W
St-Paul-lès-Dax, *France* **28 E2** 43 44N 1 3W
St. Paul Subterranean River △, *Phil.* **81 F2** 10 10N 118 55 E
St. Paul's Bay, *Malta* **38 F7** 35 57N 14 24 E
St-Péray, *France* **29 D8** 44 57N 4 50 E
St. Peter, *U.S.A.* **154 C8** 44 20N 93 57W
St-Peter-Ording, *Germany* **30 A4** 54 20N 8 36 E
St. Peter Port, *U.K.* **21 H5** 49 26N 2 33W
St. Peters, *N.S., Canada* **141 C7** 45 40N 60 53W
St. Peters, *P.E.I., Canada* **141 C7** 46 25N 62 35W
St. Petersburg = Sankt-Peterburg, *Russia* **58 C6** 59 55N 30 20 E
St. Petersburg, *U.S.A.* **153 H7** 27 46N 82 39W
St. Petersburg Beach, *U.S.A.* **153 H7** 27 45N 82 45W
St-Philbert-de-Grand-Lieu, *France* **26 E5** 47 2N 1 39W
St-Philippe, *Réunion* **121 c** 21 21 S 55 44 E
St-Pie, *Canada* **151 A12** 45 30N 72 54W
St-Pierre, *Martinique* **164 c** 14 45N 61 10W
St-Pierre, *Réunion* **121 c** 21 19 S 55 28 E
St-Pierre, *St-P. & M.* **141 C8** 46 46N 56 12W
St. Pierre, *Seychelles* **121 E3** 9 20 S 46 0 E
St-Pierre, L., *Canada* **140 C5** 46 12N 72 52W
St-Pierre-de-la-Pointe-aux-Esquimaux = Havre-St.-Pierre, *Canada* **141 B7** 50 18N 63 33W
St-Pierre-d'Oléron, *France* **28 C2** 45 57N 1 19W
St-Pierre-en-Port, *France* **26 C7** 49 48N 0 30 E
St-Pierre-et-Miquelon ⊘, *N. Amer.* **141 C8** 46 55N 56 10W
St-Pierre-le-Moûtier, *France* **27 F10** 46 47N 3 7 E
St-Pierre-sur-Dives, *France* **26 C6** 49 2N 0 1W
St-Pol-de-Léon, *France* **26 D3** 48 41N 4 0W
St-Pol-sur-Mer, *France* **27 A9** 51 1N 2 20 E
St-Pol-sur-Ternoise, *France* **27 B9** 50 23N 2 20 E
St-Pons, *France* **28 E6** 43 30N 2 45 E
St-Pourçain-sur-Sioule, *France* **27 F10** 46 18N 3 18 E
St-Priest, *France* **29 C8** 45 42N 4 57 E
St-Quay-Portrieux, *France* **26 D4** 48 39N 2 51W
St-Quentin, *Canada* **141 C6** 47 30N 67 23W
St-Quentin, *France* **27 C10** 49 50N 3 16 E
St-Rambert-d'Albon, *France* **29 C8** 45 17N 4 49 E
St-Raphaël, *France* **29 E10** 43 25N 6 46 E
St. Regis, *U.S.A.* **158 C6** 47 18N 115 6W
St-Renan, *France* **26 D2** 48 26N 4 37W
St. Robert, *U.S.A.* **156 G4** 37 48N 92 9W
St-Saëns, *France* **26 C8** 49 41N 1 16 E
St-Savin, *France* **28 B4** 46 34N 0 53 E
St-Savinien, *France* **28 C3** 45 53N 0 42W
St. Sebastien, Tanjon' i, *Madag.* **117 A8** 12 26 S 48 44 E
St-Seine-l'Abbaye, *France* **27 E11** 47 26N 4 47 E
St-Sernin-sur-Rance, *France* **28 E6** 43 54N 2 35 E
St-Sever, *France* **28 E3** 43 45N 0 35W
St-Siméon, *Canada* **141 C6** 47 51N 69 54W
St. Simons I., *U.S.A.* **152 D8** 31 12N 81 15W
St. Simons Island, *U.S.A.* **149 K5** 31 9N 81 22W
St. Stephen, *Canada* **141 C6** 45 16N 67 17W
St. Stephen, *U.S.A.* **152 B10** 33 24N 79 55W
St-Sulpice, *France* **28 E5** 43 46N 1 41 E
St-Sulpice-Laurière, *France* **28 B5** 46 3N 1 29 E
St-Sulpice-les-Feuilles, *France* **28 B5** 46 19N 1 21 E
St-Syprien = St-Cyprien, *France* **28 F7** 42 37N 3 2 E
St. Teresa, *U.S.A.* **152 F5** 29 55N 84 27W
St-Thégonnec, *France* **26 D3** 48 31N 3 57W
St. Thomas = Charlotte Amalie, *U.S. Virgin Is.* **165 e** 18 21N 64 56W
St. Thomas, *Canada* **140 D3** 42 45N 81 10W
St. Thomas Bay, *Malta* **38 F8** 35 51N 14 34 E
St. Thomas I., *U.S. Virgin Is.* **165 e** 18 20N 64 55W
St-Tite, *Canada* **140 C5** 46 45N 72 34W
St-Tropez, *France* **29 E10** 43 17N 6 38 E
St-Troud = St. Truiden, *Belgium* **24 D5** 50 48N 5 10 E
St. Truiden, *Belgium* **24 D5** 50 48N 5 10 E
St-Vaast-la-Hougue, *France* **26 C5** 49 35N 1 17W
St-Valery-en-Caux, *France* **26 C7** 49 52N 0 43 E
St-Valéry-sur-Somme, *France* **27 B8** 50 11N 1 38 E
St-Vallier, *France* **27 F11** 46 38N 4 22 E
St-Vallier-de-Thiey, *France* **29 E10** 43 42N 6 51 E
St-Varent, *France* **26 F6** 46 53N 0 13W
St-Vaury, *France* **28 B5** 46 12N 1 46 E
St. Vincent = São Vicente, *C. Verde Is.* **9 j** 17 0N 25 0W
St. Vincent, *Italy* **44 C4** 45 45N 7 39 E
St. Vincent, G., *Australia* **128 C3** 35 0 S 138 0 E
St. Vincent & the Grenadines ■, *W. Indies* **165 D7** 13 0N 61 10W
St-Vincent-de-Tyrosse, *France* **28 E2** 43 39N 1 19W
St. Vincent I., *U.S.A.* **153 F4** 29 42N 85 3W
St. Vincent Passage, *W. Indies* **165 D7** 13 30N 61 0W
St-Vith, *Belgium* **24 D6** 50 17N 6 9 E
St-Vivien-de-Médoc, *France* **28 C2** 45 25N 1 2W
St. Walburg, *Canada* **143 C7** 53 39N 109 12W
St-Yrieix-la-Perche, *France* **28 C5** 45 31N 1 12 E
Saintala, *India* **94 D6** 20 26N 83 20 E
Ste-Adresse, *France* **26 C7** 49 31N 0 5 E
Ste-Agathe-des-Monts, *Canada* **140 C5** 46 3N 74 17W
Ste-Anne, *Guadeloupe* **164 b** 16 13N 61 24W
Ste-Anne, *Seychelles* **121 b** 4 36 S 55 1 E
Ste-Anne, L., *Canada* **141 B6** 50 0N 67 42W
Ste-Anne-des-Monts-Tourelle, *Canada* **141 C6** 49 8N 66 30W
Ste-Croix, *Switz.* **32 C3** 46 49N 6 34 E
Ste-Enimie, *France* **28 D7** 44 22N 3 26 E
Ste-Foy-la-Grande, *France* **28 D4** 44 50N 0 13 E
Ste. Genevieve, *U.S.A.* **156 G6** 37 59N 90 2W
Ste-Hermine, *France* **28 B2** 46 32N 1 4W
Ste-Livrade-sur-Lot, *France* **28 D4** 44 24N 0 36 E
Ste-Marguerite →, *Canada* **141 B6** 50 9N 66 36W
Ste-Marie, *Canada* **141 C5** 46 26N 71 0W
Ste. Marie, *Gabon* **114 C2** 3 48 S 11 1 E
Ste-Marie, *Martinique* **164 c** 14 48N 61 1W
Ste-Marie, *Réunion* **121 c** 20 53 S 55 33 E
Ste-Marie-aux-Mines, *France* **27 D14** 48 15N 7 12 E
Ste-Maure-de-Touraine, *France* **26 E7** 47 7N 0 37 E
Ste-Maxime, *France* **29 E10** 43 19N 6 39 E
Ste-Menehould, *France* **27 C11** 49 5N 4 54 E
Ste-Mère-Église, *France* **26 C5** 49 24N 1 19W
Ste-Rose, *Guadeloupe* **164 b** 16 20N 61 45W
Ste-Rose, *Réunion* **121 c** 21 8 S 55 45 E
Ste. Rose du Lac, *Canada* **143 C9** 51 4N 99 30W
Ste-Savine, *France* **27 D11** 48 18N 4 3 E
Ste-Sigolène, *France* **29 C8** 45 15N 4 14 E
Saintes, *France* **28 C3** 45 45N 0 37W
Saintes, Îs. des, *Guadeloupe* **164 b** 15 50N 61 35W
Stes-Maries-de-la-Mer, *France* **29 E8** 43 26N 4 26 E
Saintfield, *U.K.* **23 B6** 54 28N 5 49W
Saintonge, *France* **28 C3** 45 40N 0 50W
Saipan, *Pac. Oc.* **134 F6** 15 12N 145 45 E
Sairang, *India* **90 D4** 23 50N 92 45 E
Sairecábur, Cerro, *Bolivia* **174 A2** 22 43 S 67 54W
Saitama □, *Japan* **73 A11** 36 25N 139 30 E
Saiteli = Kadınhanı, *Turkey* **100 C5** 38 14N 32 13 E
Saiţi, *Moldova* **53 D14** 46 30N 29 24 E
Saito, *Japan* **72 E3** 32 3N 131 24 E
Saiyid, *Pakistan* **92 C5** 33 7N 73 2 E
Saja-Besaya ⌂, *Spain* **42 B6** 43 10N 4 9W
Sajama, *Bolivia* **172 D4** 18 7 S 69 0W
Sajama, Nevado, *Bolivia* **172 D4** 18 6 S 68 54W
Sajan, *Serbia & M.* **52 E5** 45 50N 20 20 E
Sajó →, *Hungary* **52 C6** 47 56N 21 7 E
Sajókazinc = Kazincbarcika, *Hungary* **52 B5** 48 17N 20 36 E
Sajószentpéter, *Hungary* **52 B5** 48 12N 20 44 E
Sajum, *India* **93 C8** 33 20N 79 0 E
Sak →, *S. Africa* **116 E3** 30 52 S 20 25 E
Saka Kalat, *Pakistan* **91 D2** 27 3N 65 3 E
Sakaba, *Nigeria* **113 C6** 11 4N 5 35 E
Sakai, *Japan* **73 C7** 34 30N 135 30 E
Sakaide, *Japan* **72 C5** 34 19N 133 50 E
Sakaiminato, *Japan* **72 B5** 35 38N 133 11 E
Sakākah, *Si. Arabia* **96 D4** 30 0N 40 8 E
Sakakawea, L., *U.S.A.* **154 B4** 47 30N 101 25W
Sakami →, *Canada* **140 B4** 53 40N 76 40W
Sakami, L., *Canada* **140 B4** 53 15N 77 0W
Sâkâne, 'Erg i-n, *Mali* **113 A4** 20 30N 1 30W
Sakania, *Dem. Rep. of the Congo* **119 E2** 12 43 S 28 30 E
Sakar I., *Papua N. G.* **132 C5** 5 25 S 148 6 E
Sakaraha, *Madag.* **117 C7** 22 55 S 44 32 E
Sakartvelo = Georgia ■, *Asia* **61 J6** 42 0N 43 0 E
Sakarya, *Turkey* **100 B4** 40 48N 30 25 E
Sakarya →, *Turkey* **100 B4** 41 7N 30 39 E
Sakashima-Guntō, *Japan* **71 M2** 24 46N 124 0 E
Sakassou, *Ivory C.* **112 D3** 7 29N 5 19W
Sakata, *Japan* **70 E9** 38 55N 139 50 E
Sakawa, *Japan* **72 D5** 33 28N 133 11 E
Sakchu, *N. Korea* **75 D13** 40 23N 125 2 E
Sakeny →, *Madag.* **117 C8** 20 0 S 45 25 E
Sakété, *Benin* **113 D5** 6 40N 2 45 E
Sakha □, *Russia* **67 C13** 66 0N 130 0 E
Sakhalin, *Russia* **67 D15** 51 0N 143 0 E
Sakhalinskiy Zaliv, *Russia* **67 D15** 54 0N 141 0 E
Sakhi Gopal, *India* **94 E7** 19 58N 85 50 E
Şaki, *Azerbaijan* **61 K8** 41 10N 47 5 E
Šakiai, *Lithuania* **15 J20** 54 59N 23 2 E
Sakiz-Adasi = Khíos, *Greece* **49 C8** 38 27N 26 9 E
Sakmara →, *Russia* **64 F5** 51 46N 55 1 E
Sakoli, *India* **94 D4** 21 5N 79 59 E
Sakon Nakhon, *Thailand* **86 D5** 17 10N 104 9 E
Sakrand, *Pakistan* **92 F3** 26 10N 68 15 E
Sakri, *Maharashtra, India* **93 F12** 26 13N 86 5 E
Sakri, *Maharashtra, India* **94 D2** 21 2N 74 20 E
Sakrivier, *S. Africa* **116 E3** 30 54 S 20 28 E
Sakskøbing, *Denmark* **17 K5** 54 49N 11 39 E
Sakti, *India* **93 H10** 22 2N 82 58 E
Saku, *Japan* **73 A10** 36 17N 138 31 E
Sakuma, *Japan* **73 B9** 35 3N 137 49 E
Sakura, *Japan* **73 B12** 35 43N 140 14 E
Sakurai, *Japan* **73 C7** 34 30N 135 51 E
Saky, *Ukraine* **59 K7** 45 9N 33 34 E
Sal →, *Russia* **61 G5** 47 31N 40 45 E
Sal Rei, *C. Verde Is.* **9 j** 16 11N 22 53W
Sala, *Eritrea* **107 D4** 16 53N 37 36 E
Šal'a, *Slovak Rep.* **35 C10** 48 10N 17 50 E
Sala, *Sweden* **16 E10** 59 58N 16 35 E
Sala →, *Eritrea* **107 D4** 16 53N 37 36 E
Sala, O. →, *Chad* **109 E4** 17 0N 20 53 E
Sala Consilina, *Italy* **45 B8** 40 23N 15 36 E
Sala-y-Gómez, *Pac. Oc.* **135 K17** 26 28 S 105 28W
Salaberry-de-Valleyfield, *Canada* **140 C5** 45 15N 74 8W
Salacgrīva, *Latvia* **54 A11** 57 45N 24 21 E
Salada, L., *Mexico* **159 K6** 32 20N 115 40W
Saladas, *Argentina* **174 B4** 28 15 S 58 40W
Saladillo, *Argentina* **174 D4** 35 40 S 59 55W
Salado →, *Buenos Aires, Argentina* **174 D4** 35 44 S 57 22W
Salado →, *La Pampa, Argentina* **176 A3** 37 30 S 67 0W
Salado →, *Río Negro, Argentina* **176 B3** 41 34 S 65 3W
Salado →, *Santa Fe, Argentina* **174 C3** 31 40 S 60 41W
Salado →, *Mexico* **155 M5** 26 52N 99 19W
Salaga, *Ghana* **113 D4** 8 31N 0 31W
Şālah, *Syria* **103 C5** 32 40N 36 45 E
Şalāḩ ad Dīn □, *Iraq* **96 C4** 34 35N 43 35 E
Sălaj □, *Romania* **52 C8** 47 15N 23 0 E
Sálakhos, *Greece* **38 E11** 36 17N 27 57 E
Salal, *Chad* **109 F3** 14 48N 17 12 E
Salala, *Liberia* **112 D2** 6 42N 10 7W
Salala, *Sudan* **106 C4** 21 17N 36 16 E
Şalālah, *Oman* **99 C6** 16 56N 53 59 E
Salamanca, *Chile* **174 C1** 31 46 S 70 59W
Salamanca, *Spain* **42 E5** 40 58N 5 39W
Salamanca, *U.S.A.* **150 D6** 42 10N 78 43W
Salamanca □, *Spain* **42 E5** 40 57N 5 40W
Salamat, Bahr →, *Chad* **109 G3** 9 20N 18 0 E
Salāmatābād, *Iran* **96 C5** 35 39N 47 50 E
Salamina = Salamís, *Greece* **48 D5** 37 56N 23 30 E
Salamina, *Colombia* **168 B2** 5 25N 75 29W
Salamis, *Cyprus* **39 E9** 35 11N 33 54 E
Salamís, *Greece* **48 D5** 37 56N 23 30 E
Salamonie L., *U.S.A.* **157 D11** 40 46N 85 37W
Salaóra, *Greece* **39 A2** 39 2N 20 52 E
Salar de Atacama, *Chile* **174 A2** 23 30 S 68 25W
Salar de Uyuni, *Bolivia* **172 E4** 20 30 S 67 45W
Sălard, *Romania* **52 C7** 47 12N 22 3 E
Salas, *Spain* **42 B4** 43 25N 6 15W
Salas de los Infantes, *Spain* **42 C7** 42 2N 3 17W
Salatiga, *Indonesia* **85 D4** 7 19 S 110 30 E
Salavat, *Russia* **64 E5** 53 21N 55 55 E
Salaverry, *Peru* **172 B2** 8 15 S 79 0W
Salawati, *Indonesia* **83 B4** 1 7 S 130 52 E
Salay, *Phil.* **81 G5** 8 52N 124 47 E
Salaya, *India* **92 H3** 22 19N 69 35 E
Salayar, *Indonesia* **82 C2** 6 7 S 120 30 E
Salazar →, *Spain* **40 C3** 42 40N 1 20W
Salbris, *France* **27 E9** 47 25N 2 3 E
Salcedo, *Phil.* **81 F5** 11 9N 125 40 E
Salcia, *Romania* **53 G9** 43 56N 24 55 E
Sălciua, *Romania* **53 D8** 46 24N 23 26 E
Salcombe, *U.K.* **21 G4** 50 14N 3 47W
Saldaña, *Spain* **42 C6** 42 32N 4 48W
Saldanha, *S. Africa* **116 E2** 33 0 S 17 58 E
Saldanha B., *S. Africa* **116 E2** 33 6 S 18 0 E
Saldus, *Latvia* **15 H20** 56 38N 22 30 E
Saldus □, *Latvia* **54 B9** 56 35N 22 30 E
Sale, *Australia* **129 E7** 38 6 S 147 6 E
Sale, *Burma* **90 E5** 20 50N 94 45 E
Sale, *Italy* **44 D5** 44 59N 8 48 E
Salé, *Morocco* **110 B3** 34 3N 6 48W
Sale, *U.K.* **20 D5** 53 26N 2 19W
Sale City, *U.S.A.* **152 D5** 31 16N 84 1W
Salegard = Salekhard, *Russia* **66 C7** 66 30N 66 35 E
Salekhard, *Russia* **66 C7** 66 30N 66 35 E
Salelologa, *Samoa* **133 W23** 13 41 S 172 11W
Salem, *India* **95 J4** 11 40N 78 11 E
Salem, *Fla., U.S.A.* **152 F6** 29 53N 83 25W
Salem, *Ill., U.S.A.* **156 F8** 38 38N 88 57W
Salem, *Ind., U.S.A.* **157 F10** 38 36N 86 6W
Salem, *Mass., U.S.A.* **151 D14** 42 31N 70 53W
Salem, *Mo., U.S.A.* **155 G9** 37 39N 91 32W
Salem, *N.H., U.S.A.* **151 D13** 42 45N 71 12W
Salem, *N.J., U.S.A.* **148 F8** 39 34N 75 28W
Salem, *N.Y., U.S.A.* **151 C11** 43 10N 73 20W
Salem, *Ohio, U.S.A.* **150 F4** 40 54N 80 52W
Salem, *Oreg., U.S.A.* **158 D2** 44 56N 123 2W
Salem, *S. Dak., U.S.A.* **154 D6** 43 44N 97 23W
Salem, *Va., U.S.A.* **148 G5** 37 18N 80 3W
Salemi, *Italy* **46 E5** 37 49N 12 48 E
Sälen, *Sweden* **16 C7** 61 15N 13 22 E
Salernes, *France* **29 E10** 43 34N 6 15 E
Salerno, *Italy* **47 B7** 40 41N 14 47 E
Salerno, G. di, *Italy* **47 B7** 40 32N 14 42 E
Sales, *Brazil* **169 D5** 4 2 S 63 40W
Salford, *U.K.* **20 D5** 53 30N 2 18W
Salgir →, *Ukraine* **59 K8** 45 38N 35 1 E
Salgótarján, *Hungary* **52 B4** 48 5N 19 47 E
Salgueiro, *Brazil* **170 C4** 8 4 S 39 6W
Salher, *India* **94 D1** 20 40N 73 55 E
Salhus, *Norway* **18 D2** 60 30N 5 15 E
Salibabu, *Indonesia* **79 D7** 3 51N 126 40 E
Salibea = Salybia, *Trin. & Tob.* **169 F9** 10 43N 61 2W
Salida, *U.S.A.* **146 C5** 38 32N 106 0W
Salies-de-Béarn, *France* **28 E3** 43 28N 0 56W
Şalif, *Yemen* **98 D3** 15 18N 42 41 E
Salihli, *Turkey* **100 C3** 38 28N 28 8 E
Salihorsk, *Belarus* **59 F4** 52 51N 27 27 E
Salin, *Burma* **90 E5** 20 35N 94 40 E
Salina, *Italy* **47 D7** 38 34N 14 50 E
Salina, *Kans., U.S.A.* **154 F6** 38 50N 97 37W
Salina, *Utah, U.S.A.* **159 G8** 38 58N 111 51W
Salina Cruz, *Mexico* **163 D5** 16 10N 95 10W
Salina di Margherita di Savoia ⌂, *Italy* **47 A9** 41 23N 16 4 E
Salinas = Salinópolis, *Brazil* **170 B2** 0 40 S 47 20W
Salinas, *Brazil* **171 E3** 16 10 S 42 10W
Salinas, *Chile* **174 A2** 23 31 S 69 29W
Salinas, *Ecuador* **168 D1** 2 10 S 80 58W
Salinas, *U.S.A.* **160 J5** 36 40N 121 39W
Salinas →, *Guatemala* **163 D6** 16 28N 90 31W
Salinas →, *U.S.A.* **160 J5** 36 45N 121 48W
Salinas, B. das, *Angola* **115 E2** 14 11 S 12 21 E
Salinas, B. de, *Nic.* **164 D2** 11 4N 85 45W
Salinas, Pampa de las, *Argentina* **174 C2** 31 58 S 66 42W
Salinas Ambargasta, *Argentina* **174 B3** 29 0 S 65 0W
Salinas de Hidalgo, *Mexico* **162 C4** 22 30N 101 40W
Salinas Grandes, *Argentina* **174 C3** 30 0 S 65 0W
Salinas Pueblo Missions ⌂, *U.S.A.* **159 J10** 34 16N 106 5W
Saline, *U.S.A.* **157 B13** 42 10N 83 47W
Saline →, *Ark., U.S.A.* **155 J8** 33 10N 92 8W
Saline →, *Kans., U.S.A.* **154 F6** 38 52N 97 30W
Saline di Trapani e Paceco ⌂, *Italy* **46 E5** 37 59N 12 28 E
Salines, C. de ses, *Spain* **38 B4** 39 16N 3 4 E
Salinópolis, *Brazil* **170 B2** 0 40 S 47 20W
Salins-les-Bains, *France* **27 F12** 46 58N 5 52 E
Salir, *Portugal* **43 H2** 37 14N 8 2W
Salisbury = Harare, *Zimbabwe* **119 F3** 17 43 S 31 2 E
Salisbury, *U.K.* **21 F6** 51 4N 1 47W
Salisbury, *Md., U.S.A.* **148 F8** 38 22N 75 36W
Salisbury, *Mo., U.S.A.* **156 E4** 39 25N 92 48W
Salisbury, *N.C., U.S.A.* **149 H5** 35 40N 80 29W
Salisbury I., *Canada* **139 B12** 63 30N 77 0W
Salisbury Plain, *U.K.* **21 F6** 51 14N 1 55W
Săliște, *Romania* **53 E8** 45 45N 23 56 E
Salitre →, *Brazil* **170 C3** 9 29 S 40 39W
Salka, *Nigeria* **113 C5** 10 20N 4 58 E
Salkehatchie →, *U.S.A.* **152 C9** 32 37N 80 53W
Şalkhad, *Syria* **103 C5** 32 29N 36 43 E
Salkove, *Ukraine* **53 B14** 48 15N 29 59 E
Salla, *Finland* **14 C23** 66 50N 28 49 E
Sallanches, *France* **29 C10** 45 55N 6 38 E
Sallent, *Spain* **40 D6** 41 49N 1 54 E
Salles, *France* **28 D3** 44 33N 0 52W
Salles-Curan, *France* **28 D6** 44 11N 2 48 E
Salling, *Denmark* **17 H2** 56 40N 8 55 E
Salliq = Coral Harbour, *Canada* **139 B11** 64 8N 83 10W
Sallisaw, *U.S.A.* **155 H7** 35 28N 94 47W
Sallom Junction, *Sudan* **106 D4** 19 17N 37 6 E
Salluit, *Canada* **139 B12** 62 14N 75 38W
Salmās, *Iran* **101 C11** 38 11N 44 47 E
Salmerón, *Spain* **40 E2** 40 33N 2 29W
Salmo, *Canada* **142 D5** 49 10N 117 20W
Salmon, *U.S.A.* **158 D7** 45 11N 113 54W
Salmon →, *Canada* **142 C4** 54 3N 122 40W
Salmon →, *U.S.A.* **158 D5** 45 51N 116 47W
Salmon Arm, *Canada* **142 C5** 50 40N 119 15W
Salmon Gums, *Australia* **125 F3** 32 59 S 121 38 E
Salmon River Mts., *U.S.A.* **158 D6** 45 0N 114 30W
Salo, *C.A.R.* **114 B3** 3 10N 16 8 E
Salo, *Finland* **15 F20** 60 22N 23 10 E
Salò, *Italy* **44 C7** 45 36N 10 31 E
Salobreña, *Spain* **43 J7** 36 44N 3 35W
Salome, *U.S.A.* **161 M13** 33 47N 113 37W
Salon, *India* **93 F9** 26 2N 81 27 E
Salon-de-Provence, *France* **29 E9** 43 39N 5 6 E
Salonga →, *Dem. Rep. of the Congo* **114 C4** 0 10 S 19 50 E
Salonga-Nord △, *Dem. Rep. of the Congo* **114 C4** 1 55 S 21 45 E
Salonga-Sud △, *Dem. Rep. of the Congo* **114 C4** 2 25 S 21 0 E
Salonica = Thessaloníki, *Greece* **50 F6** 40 38N 22 58 E
Salonta, *Romania* **52 D6** 46 49N 21 42 E
Salop = Shropshire □, *U.K.* **21 E5** 52 36N 2 45W
Salor →, *Spain* **43 F3** 39 39N 7 3W
Salou, *Spain* **40 D6** 41 4N 1 8 E
Salou, C. de, *Spain* **40 D6** 41 3N 1 10 E
Saloum →, *Senegal* **112 C1** 13 50N 16 45W
Salpausselkä, *Finland* **15 F22** 61 3N 26 15 E
Salsacate, *Argentina* **174 C2** 31 20 S 65 5W
Salses, *France* **28 F6** 42 50N 2 55 E
Salsette I., *India* **94 E1** 19 5N 72 50 E
Salsk, *Russia* **61 G5** 46 28N 41 30 E
Salso →, *Italy* **46 E6** 37 6N 13 57 E
Salsomaggiore Terme, *Italy* **44 D6** 44 49N 9 59 E
Salt, *Spain* **40 D7** 41 59N 2 47 E
Salt →, *Canada* **142 B6** 60 0N 112 25W
Salt →, *Ariz., U.S.A.* **159 K7** 33 23N 112 19W
Salt →, *Mo., U.S.A.* **156 E5** 39 28N 91 4W
Salt Cay, *Bahamas* **9 b** 25 6N 77 18W
Salt Fork Red →, *U.S.A.* **155 H5** 34 27N 99 21W
Salt L., *U.S.A.* **145 K14** 21 21N 157 55W
Salt L., The, *Australia* **127 E3** 30 6 S 142 8 E
Salt Lake City, *U.S.A.* **158 F8** 40 45N 111 53W
Salt Range, *Pakistan* **92 C5** 32 30N 72 25 E
Salt Springs, *U.S.A.* **153 F8** 29 21N 81 44W
Salta, *Argentina* **174 A2** 24 57 S 65 25W
Salta □, *Argentina* **174 A2** 24 48 S 65 30W
Saltara, *Italy* **45 E9** 43 45N 12 50 E
Saltash, *U.K.* **21 G3** 50 24N 4 14W
Saltburn by the Sea, *U.K.* **20 C7** 54 35N 0 58W
Saltcoats, *U.K.* **22 F4** 55 38N 4 47W
Saltee Is., *Ireland* **23 D5** 52 7N 6 37W
Salters, *U.S.A.* **152 B10** 33 36N 79 51W
Saltfjellet, *Norway* **14 C16** 66 40N 15 15 E

Saltfjorden, *Norway* **14 C16** 67 15N 14 10 E
Saltholm, *Denmark* **17 J6** 55 38N 12 43 E
Salthólmavík, *Iceland* **11 B5** 65 24N 21 57W
Saltillo, *Mexico* **162 B4** 25 25N 101 0W
Salto, *Argentina* **174 C3** 34 20 S 60 15W
Salto, *Uruguay* **174 C4** 31 27 S 57 50W
Salto da Divisa, *Brazil* **171 E4** 16 0 S 39 57W
Salto del Guaíra, *Paraguay* **175 A5** 24 3 S 54 17W
Salton City, *U.S.A.* **161 M11** 33 29N 115 51W
Salton Sea, *U.S.A.* **161 M11** 33 15N 115 45W
Saltpond, *Ghana* **113 D4** 5 15N 1 3W
Saltrød, *Norway* **18 F5** 58 30N 8 49 E
Saltsburg, *U.S.A.* **150 F5** 40 29N 79 27W
Saltsjöbaden, *Sweden* **16 E12** 59 15N 18 20 E
Saluda, *U.S.A.* **152 A8** 34 0N 81 46W
Saluda →, *U.S.A.* **149 J5** 34 1N 81 4W
Salug, *Phil.* **81 G4** 8 7N 122 47 E
Salûm, *Egypt* **106 A2** 31 31N 25 7 E
Salûm, Khâlig el, *Egypt* **106 A2** 31 35N 25 24 E
Salur, *India* **94 E6** 18 27N 83 18 E
Salut, Is. du, *Fr. Guiana* **169 B7** 5 15N 52 35W
Saluzzo, *Italy* **44 D4** 44 39N 7 29 E
Salvación, B., *Chile* **176 D1** 50 50 S 75 10W
Salvador, *Brazil* **171 D4** 13 0 S 38 30W
Salvador, *Canada* **143 C7** 52 10N 109 32W
Salvador, El ■, *Cent. Amer.* **164 D2** 13 50N 89 0W
Salvador, L., *U.S.A.* **155 L9** 29 43N 90 15W
Salvaterra, *Brazil* **170 B2** 0 46 S 48 31W
Salvaterra de Magos, *Portugal* **43 F2** 39 1N 8 47W
Salvisa, *U.S.A.* **157 G12** 37 54N 84 51W
Sálvora, I. de, *Spain* **42 C2** 42 30N 8 58W
Salween →, *Burma* **90 G6** 16 31N 97 37 E
Salyan, *Azerbaijan* **101 C13** 39 33N 48 59 E
Salybia, *Trin. & Tob.* **169 F9** 10 43N 61 2W
Salza →, *Austria* **34 D7** 47 40N 14 43 E
Salzach →, *Austria* **34 C5** 48 12N 12 56 E
Salzburg, *Austria* **34 D6** 47 48N 13 2 E
Salzburg □, *Austria* **34 D6** 47 15N 13 0 E
Salzburgen = Château-Salins, *France* **27 D13** 48 50N 6 30 E
Salzgitter, *Germany* **30 C6** 52 9N 10 19 E
Salzkotten, *Germany* **30 D4** 51 40N 8 37 E
Salzwedel, *Germany* **30 C7** 52 52N 11 10 E
Sam, *Gabon* **114 B2** 0 58N 11 16 E
Sam, *India* **92 F4** 26 50N 70 31 E
Sam Neua, *Laos* **76 G5** 20 29N 104 5 E
Sam Ngao, *Thailand* **86 D2** 17 18N 99 0 E
Sam Rayburn Reservoir, *U.S.A.* **155 K7** 31 4N 94 5W
Sam Son, *Vietnam* **86 C5** 19 44N 105 54 E
Sam Teu, *Laos* **86 C5** 19 59N 104 38 E
Sama de Langreo = Langreo, *Spain* **42 B5** 43 18N 5 40W
Samacimbo, *Angola* **115 E3** 13 33 S 16 59 E
Samagaltay, *Russia* **67 D10** 50 36N 95 3 E
Samā'il, *Oman* **99 B7** 23 40N 57 50 E
Samaipata, *Bolivia* **173 D5** 18 9 S 63 52W
Samal, *Phil.* **81 H5** 7 5N 125 42 E
Samal I., *Phil.* **81 H5** 7 3N 125 44 E
Samales Group, *Phil.* **81 J3** 6 0N 122 0 E
Samalkot, *India* **94 F6** 17 3N 82 13 E
Samâlût, *Egypt* **106 B3** 28 20N 30 42 E
Samana, *India* **92 D7** 30 10N 76 13 E
Samana Cay, *Bahamas* **165 B5** 23 3N 73 45W
Samandağı, *Turkey* **100 D6** 36 5N 35 59 E
Samandıra, *Turkey* **51 F13** 40 59N 29 13 E
Samanga, *Tanzania* **119 D4** 8 20 S 39 13 E
Samangān □, *Afghan.* **91 A3** 36 15N 68 3 E
Samangwa, *Dem. Rep. of the Congo* **118 C1** 4 23 S 24 10 E
Samani, *Japan* **70 C11** 42 7N 142 56 E
Samanli Dağları, *Turkey* **51 F13** 40 32N 29 10 E
Samar, *Phil.* **81 E5** 12 0N 125 0 E
Samar □, *Phil.* **81 F5** 11 50N 125 0 E
Samar Sea, *Phil.* **80 E5** 12 0N 124 15 E
Samara, *Russia* **60 D10** 53 8N 50 6 E
Samara →, *Russia* **60 D10** 53 10N 50 4 E
Samara →, *Ukraine* **59 H8** 48 28N 35 7 E
Samarai, *Papua N. G.* **132 F6** 10 39 S 150 41 E
Samaria = Shōmrōn, *West Bank* **103 C4** 32 15N 35 13 E
Samariá, *Greece* **39 E4** 35 17N 23 58 E
Samaria △, *Greece* **48 F5** 35 18N 23 57 E
Samariapo, *Venezuela* **168 B4** 5 15N 67 48W
Samarinda, *Indonesia* **85 C5** 0 30 S 117 9 E
Samarkand = Samarqand, *Uzbekistan* **65 D3** 39 40N 66 55 E
Samarkandsky = Temirtau, *Kazakhstan* **66 D8** 50 5N 72 56 E
Samarqand, *Uzbekistan* **65 D3** 39 40N 66 55 E
Sāmarrā', *Iraq* **101 E10** 34 12N 43 52 E
Samastipur, *India* **93 G11** 25 50N 85 50 E
Samate, *Indonesia* **83 B4** 0 58 S 131 4 E
Samaúma, *Brazil* **173 B5** 7 50 S 60 2W
Şamaxi, *Azerbaijan* **61 K9** 40 38N 48 37 E
Samba, *Équateur, Dem. Rep. of the Congo* **114 B4** 0 13N 21 25 E
Samba, *Maniema, Dem. Rep. of the Congo* **118 C2** 4 38 S 26 22 E
Samba, *India* **93 C6** 32 32N 75 10 E
Samba Caju, *Angola* **115 D3** 8 46 S 15 24 E
Sambaíba, *Brazil* **170 C2** 7 8 S 45 21W
Sambalpur, *India* **94 D7** 21 28N 84 4 E
Sambar, Tanjung, *Indonesia* **85 C4** 2 59 S 110 19 E
Sambas, *Indonesia* **85 B3** 1 20N 109 20 E
Sambava, *Madag.* **117 A9** 14 16 S 50 10 E
Sambawizi, *Zimbabwe* **119 F2** 18 24 S 26 13 E
Sambhal, *India* **93 E8** 28 35N 78 37 E
Sambhar, *India* **92 F6** 26 52N 75 6 E
Sambhar L., *India* **92 F6** 26 55N 75 12 E
Sambiase, *Italy* **47 D9** 38 58N 16 17 E
Sambir, *Ukraine* **55 J10** 49 30N 23 10 E
Sambo, *Angola* **115 E3** 13 3 S 16 8 E
Sambor, *Cambodia* **86 F6** 12 46N 106 0 E
Samborombón, B., *Argentina* **174 D4** 36 5 S 57 20W
Sambuca di Sicília, *Italy* **46 E6** 37 39N 13 7 E
Samburu ⌓, *Kenya* **118 B4** 0 37N 37 31 E
Samch'ŏk, *S. Korea* **75 F15** 37 30N 129 10 E
Samch'onp'o, *S. Korea* **75 G15** 35 0N 128 6 E
Same, *Tanzania* **118 C4** 4 2 S 37 38 E
Samedan, *Switz.* **33 C9** 46 32N 9 52 E
Samer, *France* **27 B8** 50 38N 1 44 E
Samfya, *Zambia* **119 E2** 11 22 S 29 31 E
Samḩān, Jabal, *Oman* **99 C6** 17 12N 54 55 E
Sámi, *Greece* **39 C2** 38 15N 20 39 E
Samka, *Burma* **90 E6** 20 9N 96 57 E
Şämkir, *Azerbaijan* **61 K8** 40 50N 46 0 E
Şamlı, *Turkey* **49 B9** 39 48N 27 51 E
Sammanturai, *Sri Lanka* **95 L5** 7 36N 81 39 E
Samnah, *Si. Arabia* **96 E3** 25 10N 37 15 E
Samnaun, *Switz.* **33 C10** 46 57N 10 22 E
Samnū, *Libya* **108 C2** 27 15N 14 55 E
Samo Alto, *Chile* **174 C1** 30 22 S 71 0W
Samoa ■, *Pac. Oc.* **133 X24** 14 0 S 172 0W
Samoan Is., *Pac. Oc.* **133 X24** 14 0 S 171 0W
Samobor, *Croatia* **45 C12** 45 47N 15 44 E
Samoëns, *France* **27 F13** 46 5N 6 45 E
Samokov, *Bulgaria* **50 D7** 42 18N 23 35 E
Šamorín, *Slovak Rep.* **35 C10** 48 2N 17 19 E
Samorogouan, *Burkina Faso* **112 C4** 11 21N 4 57W
Sámos, *Greece* **49 D8** 37 45N 26 50 E
Samoš, *Serbia & M.* **52 E5** 45 13N 20 46 E
Samos, *Spain* **42 C3** 42 44N 7 20W
Sámos □, *Greece* **49 D8** 37 45N 26 50 E
Samoset, *U.S.A.* **153 H7** 27 28N 82 33W
Samosir, *Indonesia* **84 B1** 2 55N 98 50 E
Samothráki = Mathráki, *Greece* **38 B9** 39 48N 19 31 E
Samothráki, *Greece* **51 F9** 40 28N 25 28 E
Samoylovka, *Russia* **60 E6** 51 12N 43 43 E
Sampa, *Angola* **115 E3** 10 38 S 18 56 E
Sampa, *Ghana* **112 D4** 8 0N 2 36W
Sampacho, *Argentina* **174 C3** 33 20 S 64 50W
Sampalan, *Indonesia* **79 K18** 8 41 S 115 34 E
Sampang, *Indonesia* **85 D4** 7 11 S 113 13 E
Samper de Calanda, *Spain* **40 D4** 41 11N 0 28W
Sampéyre, *Italy* **44 D4** 44 34N 7 11 E
Sampit, *Indonesia* **85 C4** 2 34 S 113 0 E
Sampit →, *Indonesia* **85 C4** 2 44 S 112 54 E
Sampit, Teluk, *Indonesia* **85 C4** 3 5 S 113 3 E
Sampsoús, *Greece* **39 A2** 39 5N 20 45 E
Sampun, *Papua N. G.* **132 C7** 5 21 S 152 8 E
Samrong, *Cambodia* **86 E4** 14 15N 103 30 E
Samrong, *Thailand* **86 E3** 15 10N 100 40 E
Samsø, *Denmark* **17 J4** 55 50N 10 35 E
Samsø Bælt, *Denmark* **17 J4** 55 45N 10 45 E
Samson, *U.S.A.* **152 D3** 31 7N 86 3W
Samsun, *Turkey* **100 B7** 41 15N 36 22 E
Samtredia, *Georgia* **61 J6** 42 7N 42 24 E
Samui, Ko, *Thailand* **87 b** 9 30N 100 0 E
Samur →, *Russia* **61 K9** 41 53N 48 32 E
Samurskiy Khrebet, *Russia* **61 K8** 41 55N 47 11 E
Samusole, *Dem. Rep. of the Congo* **119 E1** 10 2 S 24 0 E
Samut Prakan, *Thailand* **86 F3** 13 32N 100 40 E
Samut Songkhram →, *Thailand* **78 B1** 13 24N 100 1 E
Samwari, *Pakistan* **92 E2** 28 30N 66 46 E
San, *Mali* **112 C4** 13 15N 4 57W
San →, *Cambodia* **86 F5** 13 32N 105 57 E
San →, *Poland* **55 H8** 50 45N 21 51 E
San Adrián, *Spain* **40 C3** 42 20N 1 56W
San Adrián, C. de, *Spain* **42 B2** 43 21N 8 50W
San Agustín, *Colombia* **168 C2** 1 53N 76 16W
San Agustin, *Phil.* **80 E4** 12 34N 122 6 E
San Agustin, C., *Phil.* **81 H6** 6 20N 126 13 E
San Agustín de Valle Fértil, *Argentina* **174 C2** 30 35 S 67 30W
San Ambrosio, *Pac. Oc.* **135 K20** 26 28 S 79 53W
San Andreas, *U.S.A.* **160 G6** 38 12N 120 41W
San Andres, *Catanduanes, Phil.* **80 E5** 13 36N 124 6 E
San Andres, *Romblon, Phil.* **80 E4** 13 19N 122 41 E
San Andres, *Romblon, Phil.* **80 E4** 12 31N 122 2 E
San Andrés, I. de, *Caribbean* **164 D3** 12 42N 81 46W
San Andrés del Rabanedo, *Spain* **42 C5** 42 37N 5 36W
San Andres Mts., *U.S.A.* **159 K10** 33 0N 106 30W
San Andrés Tuxtla, *Mexico* **163 D5** 18 30N 95 20W
San Angelo, *U.S.A.* **155 K4** 31 28N 100 26W
San Anselmo, *U.S.A.* **160 H4** 37 59N 122 34W
San Antonio, *Belize* **163 D7** 16 15N 89 2W
San Antonio, *Chile* **174 C1** 33 40 S 71 40W
San Antonio, *Phil.* **80 D3** 14 57N 120 5 E
San Antonio, *N. Mex., U.S.A.* **159 K10** 33 55N 106 52W
San Antonio, *Tex., U.S.A.* **155 L5** 29 25N 98 30W
San Antonio, *Venezuela* **168 C4** 3 30N 66 44W
San Antonio →, *U.S.A.* **155 L6** 28 30N 96 54W
San Antonio, C., *Argentina* **174 D4** 36 15 S 56 40W
San Antonio, C. de, *Cuba* **164 B3** 21 50N 84 57W
San Antonio, C. de, *Spain* **41 G5** 38 48N 0 12 E
San Antonio, Mt., *U.S.A.* **161 L9** 34 17N 117 38W
San Antonio Bay, *Phil.* **81 G1** 8 38N 117 35 E
San Antonio de los Baños, *Cuba* **164 B3** 22 54N 82 31W
San Antonio de los Cobres, *Argentina* **174 A2** 24 10 S 66 17W
San Antonio Oeste, *Argentina* **176 B4** 40 40 S 65 0W
San Arcángelo, *Italy* **47 B9** 40 14N 16 14 E
San Ardo, *U.S.A.* **160 J6** 36 1N 120 54W
San Augustín, *Canary Is.* **9 e1** 27 47N 15 32W
San Augustine, *U.S.A.* **155 K7** 31 30N 94 7W
San Bartolomé, *Canary Is.* **9 e2** 28 59N 13 37W
San Bartolomé de Tirajana, *Canary Is.* **9 e1** 27 54N 15 34W
San Bartolomeo in Galdo, *Italy* **47 A8** 41 24N 15 1 E
San Benedetto del Tronto, *Italy* **45 F10** 42 57N 13 53 E
San Benedetto Po, *Italy* **44 C7** 45 2N 10 55 E
San Benedicto, I., *Mexico* **162 D2** 19 18N 110 49W
San Benito, *U.S.A.* **155 M6** 26 8N 97 38W
San Benito →, *U.S.A.* **160 J5** 36 53N 121 34W
San Benito Mt., *U.S.A.* **160 J6** 36 22N 120 37W
San Bernardino, *Switz.* **33 D8** 46 27N 9 12 E
San Bernardino, *U.S.A.* **161 L9** 34 7N 117 19W
San Bernardino, Paso del, *Switz.* **33 D8** 46 28N 9 11 E
San Bernardino Mts., *U.S.A.* **161 L10** 34 10N 116 45W
San Bernardino Str., *Phil.* **80 E5** 13 0N 125 0 E
San Bernardo, *Chile* **174 C1** 33 40 S 70 50W
San Bernardo, I. de, *Colombia* **168 B2** 9 45N 75 50W
San-Beyse = Choybalsan, *Mongolia* **69 B6** 48 4N 114 30 E
San Blas, *Mexico* **162 B3** 26 4N 108 46W
San Blas, Arch. de, *Panama* **164 E4** 9 50N 78 31W
San Blas, C., *U.S.A.* **152 F4** 29 40N 85 21W
San Bonifacio, *Italy* **45 C8** 45 24N 11 16 E
San Borja, *Bolivia* **172 C4** 14 50 S 66 52W
San Buenaventura = Ventura, *U.S.A.* **161 L7** 34 17N 119 18W
San Buenaventura, *Bolivia* **172 C4** 14 28 S 67 35W
San Buenaventura, *Mexico* **162 B4** 27 5N 101 32W
San Carlo Park, *U.S.A.* **153 J8** 26 28N 81 49W
San Carlos = Butuku-Luba, *Eq. Guin.* **113 E6** 3 29N 8 33 E
San Carlos = Sant Carles, *Spain* **38 C2** 39 3N 1 34 E
San Carlos, *Argentina* **174 C2** 33 50 S 69 0W
San Carlos, *Bolivia* **173 D5** 17 24 S 63 45W
San Carlos, *Chile* **174 D1** 36 10 S 72 0W
San Carlos, *Baja Calif. S., Mexico* **162 C2** 24 47N 112 6W
San Carlos, *Coahuila, Mexico* **162 B4** 29 0N 100 54W
San Carlos, *Nic.* **164 D3** 11 12N 84 50W
San Carlos, *Neg. Occ., Phil.* **81 F4** 10 29N 123 25 E
San Carlos, *Pangasinan, Phil.* **80 D3** 15 55N 120 20 E
San Carlos, *Uruguay* **175 C5** 34 46 S 54 58W
San Carlos, *U.S.A.* **159 K8** 33 21N 110 27W
San Carlos, *Amazonas, Venezuela* **168 C4** 1 55N 67 4W
San Carlos, *Cojedes, Venezuela* **168 B4** 9 40N 68 36W
San Carlos de Bariloche, *Argentina* **176 B2** 41 10 S 71 25W
San Carlos de la Rápita = Sant Carles de la Ràpita, *Spain* **40 E5** 40 37N 0 35 E
San Carlos de Río Negro, *Venezuela* **168 C4** 1 55N 67 4W
San Carlos del Zulia, *Venezuela* **168 B3** 9 1N 71 55W
San Carlos L., *U.S.A.* **159 K8** 33 11N 110 32W
San Cataldo, *Italy* **46 E6** 37 29N 13 59 E
San Celoni = Sant Celoni, *Spain* **40 D7** 41 42N 2 30 E
San Clemente, *Chile* **174 D1** 35 30 S 71 29W
San Clemente, *Spain* **41 F2** 39 24N 2 25W
San Clemente, *U.S.A.* **161 M9** 33 26N 117 37W
San Clemente I., *U.S.A.* **161 N8** 32 53N 118 29W
San Cristóbal = Es Migjorn Gran, *Spain* **38 B5** 39 57N 4 3 E
San Cristóbal, *Argentina* **174 C3** 30 20 S 61 10W
San Cristóbal, *Colombia* **168 D3** 2 18 S 73 2W
San Cristóbal, *Dom. Rep.* **165 C5** 18 25N 70 6W
San Cristóbal, *Solomon Is.* **133 N11** 10 30 S 161 0 E
San Cristóbal, *Venezuela* **168 B3** 7 46N 72 14W
San Cristóbal, I., *Ecuador* **172 a** 0 50 S 89 26W
San Cristóbal de la Casas, *Mexico* **163 D6** 16 50N 92 33W
San Damiano d'Asti, *Italy* **44 D5** 44 50N 8 4 E
San Daniele del Friuli, *Italy* **45 B10** 46 9N 13 1 E
San Diego, *Calif., U.S.A.* **161 N9** 32 43N 117 9W
San Diego, *Tex., U.S.A.* **155 M5** 27 46N 98 14W
San Diego, C., *Argentina* **176 D3** 54 40 S 65 10W
San Diego de la Unión, *Mexico* **162 C4** 21 28N 100 52W
San Diego International ✕ (SAN), *U.S.A.* **161 N9** 32 44N 117 11W
San Dimitri, Ras, *Malta* **38 E6** 36 4N 14 11 E
San Dimitri Point = San Dimitri, Ras, *Malta* **38 E6** 36 4N 14 11 E
San Donà di Piave, *Italy* **45 C9** 45 38N 12 34 E
San Estanislao, *Paraguay* **174 A4** 24 39 S 56 26W
San Esteban △, *Venezuela* **168 A4** 10 24N 67 58W
San Esteban de Gormaz, *Spain* **40 D1** 41 34N 3 13W
San Eugenio = Artigas, *Uruguay* **174 C4** 30 20 S 56 30W
San Felice Circeo, *Italy* **46 A6** 41 14N 13 5 E
San Felice sul Panaro, *Italy* **45 D8** 44 50N 11 8 E
San Felipe, *Chile* **174 C1** 32 43 S 70 42W
San Felipe, *Colombia* **168 C4** 1 55N 67 6W
San Felipe, *Mexico* **162 A2** 31 0N 114 52W
San Felipe, *Phil.* **80 D3** 15 4N 120 4 E
San Felipe, *Venezuela* **168 A4** 10 20N 68 44W
San Felipe →, *U.S.A.* **161 M11** 33 12N 115 49W
San Félix, *Chile* **174 B1** 28 56 S 70 28W
San Félix, *Pac. Oc.* **135 K20** 26 23 S 80 0W
San Fernando = Sant Ferran, *Spain* **38 D1** 38 42N 1 28 E
San Fernando, *Chile* **174 C1** 34 30 S 71 0W
San Fernando, *Baja Calif., Mexico* **162 B1** 29 55N 115 10W
San Fernando, *Tamaulipas, Mexico* **163 C5** 24 51N 98 10W
San Fernando, *Cebu, Phil.* **81 F4** 10 10N 123 42 E
San Fernando, *La Union, Phil.* **80 C3** 16 40N 120 23 E
San Fernando, *Pampanga, Phil.* **80 D3** 15 5N 120 37 E
San Fernando, *Romblon, Phil.* **80 E4** 12 18N 122 36 E
San Fernando, *Spain* **43 J4** 36 28N 6 17W
San Fernando, *Trin. & Tob.* **169 F9** 10 16N 61 28W
San Fernando, *U.S.A.* **161 L8** 34 17N 118 26W
San Fernando de Apure, *Venezuela* **168 B4** 7 54N 67 15W
San Fernando de Atabapo, *Venezuela* **168 C4** 4 3N 67 42W
San Fernando di Púglia, *Italy* **47 A9** 41 18N 16 5 E
San Francisco, *Argentina* **174 C3** 31 30 S 62 5W
San Francisco, *Bolivia* **173 D4** 15 16 S 65 31W
San Francisco, *Peru* **172 C3** 12 36 S 73 49W
San Francisco, *Agusan del S., Phil.* **81 G5** 8 30N 125 56 E
San Francisco, *Cebu, Phil.* **81 F5** 10 39N 124 23 E
San Francisco, *Quezon, Phil.* **80 E4** 13 21N 122 31 E
San Francisco, *S. Leyte, Phil.* **81 F5** 10 4N 125 9 E
San Francisco, *U.S.A.* **160 H4** 37 47N 122 25W
San Francisco →, *U.S.A.* **159 K9** 32 59N 109 22W
San Francisco, C. de, *Colombia* **168 B2** 6 18N 77 29W
San Francisco, Paso de, *S. Amer.* **174 B2** 27 0 S 68 0W
San Francisco de Macorís, *Dom. Rep.* **165 C5** 19 19N 70 15W
San Francisco del Monte de Oro, *Argentina* **174 C2** 32 36 S 66 8W
San Francisco del Oro, *Mexico* **162 B3** 26 52N 105 50W
San Francisco International ✕ (SFO), *U.S.A.* **160 H4** 37 37N 122 22W
San Francisco Javier = Sant Francesc de Formentera, *Spain* **38 D1** 38 42N 1 26 E
San Fratello, *Italy* **47 D7** 38 1N 14 36 E
San Gabriel, *Chile* **174 C1** 33 47 S 70 15W
San Gabriel, *Ecuador* **168 C2** 0 36N 77 49W
San Gabriel Mts., *U.S.A.* **161 L9** 34 20N 118 0W
San Gavino Monreale, *Italy* **46 C1** 39 33N 8 47 E
San German, *Puerto Rico* **165 d** 18 4N 67 4W
San Gil, *Colombia* **168 B3** 6 33N 73 8W
San Giljan = St. Julian's, *Malta* **38 F7** 35 55N 14 29 E
San Gimignano, *Italy* **44 E8** 43 28N 11 2 E
San Giórgio di Nogaro, *Italy* **45 C10** 45 50N 13 13 E
San Giórgio Iónico, *Italy* **47 B10** 40 27N 17 23 E
San Giovanni Bianco, *Italy* **44 C6** 45 52N 9 39 E
San Giovanni in Fiore, *Italy* **47 C9** 39 15N 16 42 E
San Giovanni in Persiceto, *Italy* **45 D8** 44 38N 11 11 E
San Giovanni Rotondo, *Italy* **45 G12** 41 42N 15 44 E
San Giovanni Valdarno, *Italy* **45 E8** 43 34N 11 32 E
San Giuliano Terme, *Italy* **44 E7** 43 46N 10 26 E
San Gorgonio Mt., *U.S.A.* **161 L10** 34 7N 116 51W
San Gottardo, P. del, *Switz.* **33 C7** 46 33N 8 33 E
San Gregorio, *Uruguay* **175 C4** 32 37 S 55 40W
San Gregorio, *U.S.A.* **160 H4** 37 20N 122 23W
San Guiseppe Jato, *Italy* **46 E6** 37 57N 13 11 E
San Ignacio, *Belize* **163 D7** 17 10N 89 5W
San Ignacio, *Beni, Bolivia* **173 C4** 14 53 S 65 36W
San Ignacio, *Santa Cruz, Bolivia* **173 D5** 16 20 S 60 55W
San Ignacio, *Mexico* **162 B2** 27 27N 113 0W
San Ignacio, *Paraguay* **174 B4** 26 52 S 57 3W
San Ignacio, *Peru* **172 B2** 5 8 S 78 59W
San Ignacio ⌓, *Mexico* **162 B2** 27 0N 113 10W
San Ignacio, L., *Mexico* **162 B2** 26 50N 113 11W
San Ildefonso, C., *Phil.* **80 C4** 16 0N 122 1 E
San Isidro, *Argentina* **174 C4** 34 29 S 58 31W
San Isidro, *Phil.* **81 H6** 6 50N 126 5 E
San Isidro de Potot = Burgos, *Phil.* **80 C2** 16 4N 119 52 E
San Jacinto, *Colombia* **168 B2** 9 50N 75 8W
San Jacinto, *Phil.* **80 E4** 12 34N 123 44 E
San Jacinto, *U.S.A.* **161 M10** 33 47N 116 57W
San Jaime = Sant Jaume, *Spain* **38 B5** 39 54N 4 4 E
San Javier, *Misiones, Argentina* **175 B4** 27 55 S 55 5W
San Javier, *Santa Fe, Argentina* **174 C4** 30 40 S 59 55W
San Javier, *Beni, Bolivia* **173 C5** 14 34 S 64 42W
San Javier, *Santa Cruz, Bolivia* **173 D5** 16 18 S 62 30W
San Javier, *Chile* **174 D1** 35 40 S 71 45W
San Javier, *Spain* **41 H4** 37 49N 0 50W
San Jeronimo Taviche, *Mexico* **163 D5** 16 38N 96 32W
San Joaquín, *Bolivia* **173 C5** 13 4 S 64 49W
San Joaquin, *Phil.* **81 F4** 10 35N 122 8 E
San Joaquin, *U.S.A.* **160 J6** 36 36N 120 11W
San Joaquín →, *Bolivia* **173 C5** 13 8 S 63 41W
San Joaquin →, *U.S.A.* **160 G5** 38 4N 121 51W
San Joaquín, Cerro, *Ecuador* **172 a** 0 53 S 89 30W
San Joaquin Valley, *U.S.A.* **160 J6** 37 20N 121 0W
San Jon, *U.S.A.* **155 H3** 35 6N 103 20W
San Jordi = Sant Jordi, *Spain* **38 B3** 39 33N 2 46 E
San Jorge, *Argentina* **174 C3** 31 54 S 61 50W
San Jorge, *Solomon Is.* **133 M10** 8 28 S 159 38 E
San Jorge, B. de, *Mexico* **162 A2** 31 20N 113 20W
San Jorge, G., *Argentina* **176 C3** 46 0 S 66 0W
San José = San Josep, *Spain* **38 D1** 38 55N 1 18 E
San José, *Costa Rica* **164 E3** 9 55N 84 2W
San José, *Guatemala* **164 D1** 14 0N 90 50W
San José, *Mexico* **162 C2** 25 0N 110 50W
San Jose, *Mind. Occ., Phil.* **80 E3** 12 27N 121 4 E
San Jose, *Nueva Ecija, Phil.* **80 D3** 15 45N 120 55 E
San Jose, *Calif., U.S.A.* **160 H5** 37 20N 121 53W
San Jose, *Ill., U.S.A.* **156 D7** 40 18N 89 36W
San Jose →, *U.S.A.* **159 J10** 34 25N 106 45W
San José, Golfo, *Argentina* **176 B4** 42 20 S 64 18W
San Jose de Buenavista, *Phil.* **79 B6** 10 45N 121 56 E
San José de Chiquitos, *Bolivia* **173 D5** 17 53 S 60 50W
San José de Feliciano, *Argentina* **174 C4** 30 26 S 58 46W
San José de Jáchal, *Argentina* **174 C2** 30 15 S 68 46W
San José de Mayo, *Uruguay* **174 C4** 34 27 S 56 40W
San José de Ocune, *Colombia* **168 C3** 4 15N 70 20W
San José de Uchapiamonas, *Bolivia* **172 C4** 14 13 S 68 5W
San José del Cabo, *Mexico* **162 C3** 23 0N 109 40W
San José del Guaviare, *Colombia* **168 C3** 2 35N 72 38W
San Jose del Monte, *Phil.* **80 D3** 14 49N 121 3 E
San José do Anauá, *Brazil* **169 C5** 0 58N 61 22W
San Josep, *Spain* **38 D1** 38 55N 1 18 E
San Juan, *Argentina* **174 C2** 31 30 S 68 30W
San Juan, *Colombia* **168 B2** 8 46N 76 32W
San Juan, *Mexico* **162 C4** 21 20N 102 50W
San Juan, *Ica, Peru* **172 D2** 15 22 S 75 7W
San Juan, *Puno, Peru* **172 C4** 14 2 S 69 19W
San Juan, *Batangas, Phil.* **80 E3** 13 50N 121 24 E
San Juan, *S. Leyte, Phil.* **81 F5** 10 16N 125 10 E
San Juan, *Puerto Rico* **165 d** 18 28N 66 7W
San Juan, *Trin. & Tob.* **169 F9** 10 39N 61 29W
San Juan □, *Argentina* **174 C2** 31 9 S 69 0W
San Juan →, *Argentina* **174 C2** 32 20 S 67 25W
San Juan →, *Bolivia* **173 E4** 21 2 S 65 19W
San Juan →, *Colombia* **168 C2** 4 3N 77 27W
San Juan →, *Nic.* **164 D3** 10 56N 83 42W
San Juan →, *U.S.A.* **159 H8** 37 16N 110 26W
San Juan →, *Venezuela* **169 A5** 10 14N 62 38W
San Juan, C., *Eq. Guin.* **114 B1** 1 5N 9 20 E
San Juan Bautista = Sant Joan Baptista, *Spain* **38 C2** 39 5N 1 31 E
San Juan Bautista = Villahermosa, *Mexico* **163 D6** 17 59N 92 55W
San Juan Bautista, *Paraguay* **174 B4** 26 37 S 57 6W
San Juan Bautista, *U.S.A.* **160 J5** 36 51N 121 32W
San Juan Bautista Valle Nacional, *Mexico* **163 D5** 17 47N 96 19W
San Juan Capistrano, *U.S.A.* **161 M9** 33 30N 117 40W
San Juan Cr. →, *U.S.A.* **160 J5** 35 40N 120 22W
San Juan de Alicante, *Spain* **41 G4** 38 24N 0 26W
San Juan de Guadalupe, *Mexico* **162 C4** 24 38N 102 44W
San Juan de Guía, Cabo de, *Colombia* **168 A3** 11 21N 73 59W
San Juan de la Costa, *Mexico* **162 C2** 24 23N 110 45W
San Juan de los Morros, *Venezuela* **168 B4** 9 55N 67 21W
San Juan de Manapiare, *Venezuela* **168 B4** 5 15N 66 5W
San Juan de Villa Hermosa = Villahermosa, *Mexico* **163 D6** 17 59N 92 55W
San Juan del César, *Colombia* **168 A3** 10 46N 73 1W
San Juan del Norte, *Nic.* **164 D3** 10 58N 83 40W
San Juan del Norte, B. de, *Nic.* **164 D3** 11 0N 83 40W
San Juan del Río, *Mexico* **163 C5** 20 25N 100 0W
San Juan del Sur, *Nic.* **164 D2** 11 20N 85 51W
San Juan I., *U.S.A.* **160 B3** 48 32N 123 5W
San Juan Island △, *U.S.A.* **160 B4** 48 27N 123 0W
San Juan Mts., *U.S.A.* **159 H10** 37 30N 107 0W
San Julián, *Argentina* **176 C3** 49 15 S 67 45W
San Julian, *Phil.* **81 F5** 11 45N 125 27 E
San Just, Sierra de, *Spain* **40 E4** 40 45N 0 49W
San Justo, *Argentina* **174 C3** 30 47 S 60 30W
San Kamphaeng, *Thailand* **86 C2** 18 45N 99 8 E
San Lázaro, C., *Mexico* **162 C2** 24 50N 112 18W
San Lázaro, Sa., *Mexico* **162 C3** 23 25N 110 0W
San Leandro, *U.S.A.* **160 H4** 37 44N 122 9W
San Leonardo de Yagüe, *Spain* **40 D1** 41 51N 3 5W
San Lorenzo = Sant Llorenç des Cardassar, *Spain* **38 B4** 39 37N 3 17 E
San Lorenzo, *Argentina* **174 C3** 32 45 S 60 45W
San Lorenzo, *Beni, Bolivia* **173 D4** 15 22 S 65 48W
San Lorenzo, *Tarija, Bolivia* **173 E5** 21 26 S 64 47W
San Lorenzo, *Ecuador* **168 C2** 1 15N 78 50W
San Lorenzo, *Paraguay* **174 B4** 25 20 S 57 32W
San Lorenzo →, *Mexico* **162 C3** 24 15N 107 24W
San Lorenzo, I., *Mexico* **162 B2** 28 35N 112 50W
San Lorenzo, I., *Peru* **172 C2** 12 7 S 77 15W
San Lorenzo, Mte., *Argentina* **176 C2** 47 40 S 72 20W
San Lorenzo de la Parrilla, *Spain* **40 F2** 39 51N 2 22W
San Lorenzo de Morunys = Sant Llorenç de Morunys, *Spain* **40 C6** 42 8N 1 35 E
San Lucas, *Bolivia* **173 E4** 20 5 S 65 7W
San Lucas, *Baja Calif. S., Mexico* **162 C3** 22 53N 109 54W
San Lucas, *Baja Calif. S., Mexico* **162 B2** 27 10N 112 14W
San Lucas, *U.S.A.* **160 J5** 36 8N 121 1W
San Lucas, C., *Mexico* **162 C3** 22 50N 110 0W
San Lúcido, *Italy* **47 C9** 39 18N 16 3 E
San Luis = Entre Ríos, *Bolivia* **174 A3** 21 30 S 64 25W
San Luis = Sevilla, *Colombia* **168 C2** 4 16N 75 57W
San Luis, *Argentina* **174 C2** 33 20 S 66 20W
San Luis, *Cuba* **164 B3** 22 17N 83 46W
San Luis, *Guatemala* **164 C2** 16 14N 89 27W
San Luis, *Ariz., U.S.A.* **159 K6** 32 29N 114 47W
San Luis, *Colo., U.S.A.* **159 H11** 37 12N 105 25W
San Luis □, *Argentina* **174 C2** 34 0 S 66 0W
San Luis, I., *Mexico* **162 B2** 29 58N 114 26W
San Luis, L. de, *Bolivia* **173 C5** 13 45 S 64 0W
San Luis, Sierra de, *Argentina* **174 C2** 32 30 S 66 10W
San Luis de la Paz, *Mexico* **162 C4** 21 19N 100 32W
San Luis Obispo, *U.S.A.* **161 K6** 35 17N 120 40W
San Luis Potosí, *Mexico* **162 C4** 22 9N 100 59W
San Luis Potosí □, *Mexico* **162 C4** 22 10N 101 0W
San Luis Reservoir, *U.S.A.* **160 H5** 37 4N 121 5W
San Luis Río Colorado, *Mexico* **162 A2** 32 29N 114 58W
San Manuel, *Phil.* **80 C3** 16 4N 120 40 E
San Manuel, *U.S.A.* **159 K8** 32 36N 110 38W
San Marco, C., *Italy* **46 C1** 39 51N 8 26 E
San Marco Argentano, *Italy* **47 C9** 39 33N 16 7 E
San Marco in Lámis, *Italy* **45 G12** 41 43N 15 38 E
San Marcos, *Colombia* **168 B2** 8 39N 75 8W
San Marcos, *Guatemala* **164 D1** 14 59N 91 52W
San Marcos, *Mexico* **162 B2** 27 13N 112 6W
San Marcos, *Calif., U.S.A.* **161 M9** 33 9N 117 10W
San Marcos, *Tex., U.S.A.* **155 L6** 29 53N 97 56W
San Mariano, *Phil.* **80 C4** 17 0N 122 2 E
San Marino, *San Marino* **45 E9** 43 55N 12 30 E
San Marino ■, *Europe* **45 E9** 43 56N 12 25 E
San Martín = Tarapoto, *Peru* **172 B2** 6 30 S 76 20W
San Martin, *Antarctica* **7 C17** 68 11 S 67 0W
San Martín, *Argentina* **174 C2** 33 5 S 68 28W
San Martín, *Colombia* **168 E3** 3 42N 73 42W
San Martín □, *Peru* **172 B2** 7 0 S 76 50W
San Martín →, *Bolivia* **173 C5** 13 8 S 63 43W

San Martín, L., *Argentina* **176 C2** 48 50 S 72 50W
San Martín de la Vega, *Spain* **42 E7** 40 13N 3 34W
San Martín de los Andes, *Argentina* **176 B2** 40 10 S 71 20W
San Martín de Valdeiglesias, *Spain* **42 E6** 40 21N 4 24W
San Mateo = Sant Mateu, *Baleares, Spain* **38 C1** 39 3N 1 23 E
San Mateo = Sant Mateu, *Valencia, Spain* **40 E5** 40 28N 0 10 E
San Mateo, *Phil.* **80 C3** 16 54N 121 33 E
San Mateo, *U.S.A.* **160 H4** 37 34N 122 19W
San Matías, *Bolivia* **173 D6** 16 25 S 58 20W
San Matías, G., *Argentina* **176 B4** 41 30 S 64 0W
San Miguel = Linapacan, *Phil.* **81 F2** 11 30N 119 52 E
San Miguel = Sant Miguel, *Spain* **38 C1** 39 3N 1 26 E
San Miguel = Sarrat, *Phil.* **80 B3** 18 9N 120 39 E
San Miguel, *Bolivia* **173 C5** 16 42 S 61 1W
San Miguel, *El Salv.* **164 D2** 13 30N 88 12W
San Miguel, *Panama* **164 E4** 8 27N 78 55W
San Miguel, *Bulacan, Phil.* **80 D3** 15 9N 120 59 E
San Miguel, *Palawan, Phil.* **81 F2** 11 30N 119 51 E
San Miguel, *Surigao S., Phil.* **81 G5** 9 3N 125 59 E
San Miguel, *U.S.A.* **160 K6** 35 45N 120 42W
San Miguel →, *Bolivia* **173 C5** 13 52 S 63 56W
San Miguel →, *S. Amer.* **168 C2** 0 25N 76 30W
San Miguel, Golfo de, *Panama* **168 B2** 8 22N 78 17W
San Miguel de Huachi, *Bolivia* **172 D4** 15 40 S 67 15W
San Miguel de Tucumán, *Argentina* **174 B2** 26 50 S 65 20W
San Miguel del Monte, *Argentina* **174 D4** 35 23 S 58 50W
San Miguel I., *U.S.A.* **161 L6** 34 2N 120 23W
San Miguel Is., *Phil.* **81 H2** 7 45N 118 28 E
San Miniato, *Italy* **44 E7** 43 41N 10 51 E
San Narciso, *Phil.* **80 E4** 13 34N 122 34 E
San Nicolás, *Canary Is.* **9 e1** 27 58N 15 47W
San Nicolas, *Phil.* **80 B3** 18 10N 120 36 E
San Nicolás de los Arroyas, *Argentina* **174 C3** 33 25 S 60 10W
San Nicolas I., *U.S.A.* **161 M7** 33 15N 119 30W
San Onofre, *Colombia* **168 B2** 9 44N 75 32W
San Onofre, *U.S.A.* **161 M9** 33 22N 117 34W
San Pablo, *Bolivia* **174 A2** 21 43 S 66 38W
San Pablo, *Isabela, Phil.* **80 C3** 17 27N 121 48 E
San Pablo, *Laguna, Phil.* **80 D3** 14 11N 121 31 E
San Pablo, *U.S.A.* **160 H4** 37 58N 122 21W
San Pablo de Manta = Manta, *Ecuador* **168 D1** 1 0 S 80 40W
San Páolo di Civitate, *Italy* **45 G12** 41 44N 15 15 E
San Pascual, *Phil.* **80 E4** 13 8N 122 59 E
San Pedro, *Buenos Aires, Argentina* **174 C4** 33 40 S 59 40W
San Pedro, *Misiones, Argentina* **175 B5** 26 30 S 54 10W
San Pedro, *Chile* **174 C1** 33 54 S 71 28W
San Pedro, *Colombia* **168 C3** 4 56N 71 53W
San Pédro, *Ivory C.* **112 E3** 4 50N 6 33W
San Pedro, *Mexico* **162 C2** 23 55N 110 17W
San Pedro, *Peru* **172 C3** 14 49 S 74 5W
San Pedro □, *Paraguay* **174 A4** 24 0 S 57 0W
San Pedro →, *Chihuahua, Mexico* **162 B3** 28 20N 106 10W
San Pedro →, *Nayarit, Mexico* **162 C3** 21 45N 105 30W
San Pedro →, *U.S.A.* **159 K8** 32 59N 110 47W
San Pedro, Pta., *Chile* **174 B1** 25 30 S 70 38W
San Pedro, Sierra de, *Spain* **43 F4** 39 18N 6 40W
San Pedro Channel, *U.S.A.* **161 M8** 33 30N 118 25W
San Pedro de Arimena, *Colombia* **168 C3** 4 37N 71 42W
San Pedro de Atacama, *Chile* **174 A2** 22 55 S 68 15W
San Pedro de Jujuy, *Argentina* **174 A3** 24 12 S 64 55W
San Pedro de las Colonias, *Mexico* **162 B4** 25 50N 102 59W
San Pedro de Lloc, *Peru* **172 B2** 7 15 S 79 28W
San Pedro de Macorís, *Dom. Rep.* **165 C6** 18 30N 69 18W
San Pedro del Norte, *Nic.* **164 D3** 13 4N 84 33W
San Pedro del Paraná, *Paraguay* **174 B4** 26 43 S 56 13W
San Pedro del Pinatar, *Spain* **41 H4** 37 50N 0 50W
San Pedro Mártir △, *Mexico* **162 A1** 31 0N 115 21W
San Pedro Mártir, Sierra, *Mexico* **162 A1** 31 0N 115 30W
San Pedro Mixtepec, *Mexico* **163 D5** 16 2N 97 7W
San Pedro Ocampo = Melchor Ocampo, *Mexico* **162 C4** 24 52N 101 40W
San Pedro Sula, *Honduras* **164 C2** 15 30N 88 0W
San Pietro, *Italy* **46 C1** 39 8N 8 17 E
San Pietro Vernótico, *Italy* **47 B11** 40 29N 18 0 E
San Quintín, *Mexico* **162 A1** 30 29N 115 57W
San Rafael, *Argentina* **174 C2** 34 40 S 68 21W
San Rafael, *Bolivia* **173 D5** 16 45 S 60 34W
San Rafael, *Calif., U.S.A.* **160 H4** 37 58N 122 32W
San Rafael, *N. Mex., U.S.A.* **159 J10** 35 7N 107 53W
San Rafael, *Venezuela* **168 A3** 10 58N 71 46W
San Rafael Mt., *U.S.A.* **161 L7** 34 41N 119 52W
San Rafael Mts., *U.S.A.* **161 L7** 34 40N 119 50W
San Ramón, *Bolivia* **173 C5** 13 17 S 64 43W
San Ramón, *Peru* **172 C2** 11 8 S 75 20W
San Ramón de la Nueva Orán, *Argentina* **174 A3** 23 10 S 64 20W
San Remo, *Australia* **129 E6** 38 33 S 145 22 E
San Remo, *Italy* **44 E4** 43 49N 7 46 E
San Román, C., *Venezuela* **168 A3** 12 12N 70 0W
San Roque, *Argentina* **174 B4** 28 25 S 58 45W
San Roque, *Phil.* **80 E5** 12 37N 124 52 E
San Roque, *Spain* **43 J5** 36 17N 5 21W
San Rosendo, *Chile* **174 D1** 37 16 S 72 43W
San Saba, *U.S.A.* **155 K5** 31 12N 98 43W
San Salvador, *El Salv.* **164 D2** 13 40N 89 10W
San Salvador, *Spain* **38 B4** 39 27N 3 11 E
San Salvador, Canal de, *Ecuador* **172 a** 0 25 S 90 30W
San Salvador, I., *Ecuador* **172 a** 0 16 S 90 42W
San Salvador de Jujuy, *Argentina* **174 A3** 24 10 S 64 48W
San Salvador I., *Bahamas* **165 B5** 24 0N 74 40W
San Salvo, *Italy* **45 F11** 42 3N 14 44 E
San Sebastián = Donostia-San Sebastián, *Spain* **40 B3** 43 17N 1 58W
San Sebastián, *Argentina* **176 D3** 53 10 S 68 30W
San Sebastian, *Puerto Rico* **165 d** 18 20N 66 59W
San Sebastián de la Gomera, *Canary Is.* **9 e1** 28 5N 17 7W
San Serra = Son Serra, *Spain* **38 B4** 39 43N 3 13 E
San Serverino Marche, *Italy* **45 E10** 43 13N 13 10 E
San Severo, *Italy* **45 G12** 41 41N 15 23 E
San Simeon, *U.S.A.* **160 K5** 35 39N 121 11W
San Simon, *U.S.A.* **159 K9** 32 16N 109 14W
San Stéfano di Cadore, *Italy* **45 B9** 46 34N 12 33 E
San Stino di Livenza, *Italy* **45 C9** 45 44N 12 41 E
San Telmo = Sant Telm, *Spain* **38 B3** 39 35N 2 21 E
San Telmo, *Mexico* **162 A1** 30 58N 116 6W
San Teodoro, *Phil.* **80 E3** 13 26N 121 1 E
San Tiburcio, *Mexico* **162 C4** 24 8N 101 32W
San Valentin, Mte., *Chile* **176 C2** 46 30 S 73 30W
San Vicente de Alcántara, *Spain* **43 F3** 39 22N 7 8W
San Vicente de la Barquera, *Spain* **42 B6** 43 23N 4 29W
San Vicente del Caguán, *Colombia* **168 C3** 2 7N 74 46W
San Vincente del Raspeig, *Spain* **41 G4** 38 24N 0 31W
San Vincenzo, *Italy* **44 E7** 43 6N 10 32 E
San Vito, *Costa Rica* **164 E3** 8 50N 82 58W
San Vito, *Italy* **46 C2** 39 26N 9 32 E
San Vito, C., *Italy* **46 D5** 38 11N 12 41 E
San Vito al Tagliamento, *Italy* **45 C9** 45 54N 12 52 E
San Vito Chietino, *Italy* **45 F11** 42 18N 14 27 E
San Vito dei Normanni, *Italy* **47 B10** 40 39N 17 42 E
San Yanaro, *Colombia* **168 C4** 2 47N 69 42W
Saña, *Peru* **172 B2** 6 54 S 79 36W
Sana', *Yemen* **98 D4** 15 27N 44 12 E
Sana →, *Bos.-H.* **45 C13** 45 3N 16 23 E
Sanaba, *Burkina Faso* **112 C4** 12 25N 3 47W
Şanāfīr, *Si. Arabia* **106 B3** 27 56N 34 42 E
Sanaga →, *Cameroon* **113 E6** 3 35N 9 38 E
Sanak I., *U.S.A.* **144 J7** 54 25N 162 40W
Sanaloa, Presa, *Mexico* **162 C3** 24 50N 107 20W
Sanām, *Si. Arabia* **98 B4** 23 40N 44 45 E
Sanana, *Indonesia* **82 B3** 2 4 S 125 58 E
Sanand, *India* **92 H5** 22 59N 72 25 E
Sanandaj, *Iran* **101 E12** 35 18N 47 1 E
Sanandita, *Bolivia* **174 A3** 21 40 S 63 45W
Sanaroa I., *Papua N. G.* **132 E6** 9 37 S 151 0 E
Sanary-sur-Mer, *France* **29 E9** 43 7N 5 49 E
Sanāw, *Yemen* **99 C5** 17 50N 51 5 E
Sanawad, *India* **92 H7** 22 11N 76 5 E
Sanbe-San, *Japan* **72 B4** 35 6N 132 38 E
Sancellas = Sencelles, *Spain* **38 B3** 39 39N 2 54 E
Sancergues, *France* **27 E9** 47 10N 2 54 E
Sancerre, *France* **27 E9** 47 20N 2 50 E
Sancerrois, Collines du, *France* **27 E9** 47 20N 2 40 E
Sancha He →, *China* **76 D6** 26 48N 106 7 E
Sanchahe, *China* **75 B14** 44 50N 126 2 E
Sanchakou, *China* **65 D9** 39 47N 78 20 E
Sánchez, *Dom. Rep.* **165 C6** 19 15N 69 36W
Sanchez-Mira, *Phil.* **80 B3** 18 34N 121 14 E
Sanchor, *India* **92 G4** 24 45N 71 55 E
Sanco Pt., *Phil.* **81 G6** 8 15N 126 27 E
Sancoins, *France* **27 F9** 46 47N 2 55 E
Sancti Spíritus, *Cuba* **164 B4** 21 52N 79 33W
Sancy, Puy de, *France* **28 C6** 45 32N 2 50 E
Sand, *Norway* **18 E3** 59 29N 6 16 E
Sand →, *S. Africa* **117 C5** 22 25 S 30 5 E
Sand Cr. →, *U.S.A.* **157 E11** 39 3N 85 51W
Sand Hills, *Guyana* **169 B6** 6 27N 58 19W
Sand Hills, *U.S.A.* **154 D4** 42 10N 101 30W
Sand I., *U.S.A.* **145 K14** 21 19N 157 53W
Sand Lakes ⌓, *Canada* **143 B9** 57 51N 98 32W
Sand Point, *U.S.A.* **144 J7** 55 20N 160 30W
Sand Springs, *U.S.A.* **155 G6** 36 9N 96 7W
Sanda, *Japan* **73 C7** 34 53N 135 14 E
Sandakan, *Malaysia* **85 A5** 5 53N 118 4 E
Sandalwood, *Australia* **128 C4** 34 55 S 140 9 E
Sandan = Sambor, *Cambodia* **86 F6** 12 46N 106 0 E
Sandane, *Norway* **18 C3** 61 46N 6 13 E
Sandanski, *Bulgaria* **50 E7** 41 35N 23 16 E
Sandaré, *Mali* **112 C2** 14 40N 10 15W
Sandared, *Sweden* **17 G6** 57 43N 12 47 E
Sandarne, *Sweden* **16 C11** 61 16N 17 9 E
Sanday, *U.K.* **22 B6** 59 16N 2 31W
Sande, *Møre og Romsdal, Norway* **18 B2** 62 15N 5 27 E
Sande, *Sogn og Fjordane, Norway* **18 C2** 61 20N 5 47 E
Sande, *Vestfold, Norway* **18 E7** 59 36N 10 12 E
Sandefjord, *Norway* **18 E7** 59 10N 10 15 E
Sandeid, *Norway* **18 E2** 59 33N 5 52 E
Sanders, *Ariz., U.S.A.* **159 J9** 35 13N 109 20W
Sanders, *Ky., U.S.A.* **157 F12** 38 40N 84 56W
Sanderson, *Fla., U.S.A.* **152 E7** 30 15N 82 16W
Sanderson, *Tex., U.S.A.* **155 K3** 30 9N 102 24W
Sandersville, *U.S.A.* **152 C7** 32 59N 82 48W
Sandfire Roadhouse, *Australia* **124 C3** 19 45 S 121 15 E
Sandfloegga, *Norway* **18 E4** 59 58N 7 10 E
Sandfly L., *Canada* **143 B7** 55 43N 106 6W
Sandfontein, *Namibia* **116 C2** 23 48 S 19 1 E
Sandhammaren, C., *Sweden* **17 J8** 55 23N 14 14 E
Sandheads, The, *India* **90 E2** 21 10N 88 20 E
Sandía, *Peru* **172 C4** 14 10 S 69 30W
Sandıklı, *Turkey* **49 C12** 38 28N 30 17 E
Sandila, *India* **93 F9** 27 5N 80 31 E
Sandilands, *Bahamas* **9 b** 25 3N 77 19W
Sandnes, *Aust-Agder, Norway* **18 F4** 58 53N 7 45 E
Sandnes, *Rogaland, Norway* **18 F2** 58 50N 5 45 E
Sandnessjøen, *Norway* **14 C15** 66 2N 12 38 E
Sandoa, *Dem. Rep. of the Congo* **115 D4** 9 41 S 23 0 E
Sandomierz, *Poland* **55 H8** 50 40N 21 43 E
Sândominic, *Romania* **53 D10** 46 35N 25 47 E
Sandona, *Colombia* **168 C2** 1 17N 77 28W
Sandongo, *Angola* **115 F4** 15 30 S 21 28 E
Sandoval, *U.S.A.* **156 F7** 38 37N 89 7W
Sandover →, *Australia* **126 C2** 21 43 S 136 32 E
Sandoway, *Burma* **90 F5** 18 20N 94 30 E
Sandoy, *Færoe Is.* **14 F9** 61 52N 6 46W
Sandpoint, *U.S.A.* **158 B5** 48 17N 116 33W
Sandray, *U.K.* **22 E1** 56 53N 7 31W
Sandringham, *U.K.* **20 E8** 52 51N 0 31 E
Sandstone, *Australia* **125 E2** 27 59 S 119 16 E
Sandu, *China* **76 E6** 26 0N 107 52 E
Sandumba, *Angola* **115 E3** 13 45 S 17 34 E
Sandur, *India* **95 F3** 15 6N 76 33 E
Sandusky, *Mich., U.S.A.* **150 C2** 43 25N 82 50W
Sandusky, *Ohio, U.S.A.* **150 E2** 41 27N 82 42W
Sandusky →, *U.S.A.* **157 C14** 41 27N 83 0W
Sandvig, *Sweden* **17 J8** 55 18N 14 47 E
Sandvika, *Norway* **18 E7** 59 54N 10 31 E
Sandviken, *Sweden* **16 D10** 60 38N 16 46 E
Sandwich, *U.S.A.* **157 C8** 41 39N 88 37W
Sandwich, C., *Australia* **126 B4** 18 14 S 146 18 E
Sandwich B., *Canada* **141 B8** 53 40N 57 15W
Sandwich B., *Namibia* **116 C1** 23 25 S 14 20 E
Sandwip I., *Bangla.* **90 D3** 22 30N 91 25 E
Sandy, *Oreg., U.S.A.* **160 E4** 45 24N 122 16W
Sandy, *Pa., U.S.A.* **150 E6** 41 6N 78 46W
Sandy, *Utah, U.S.A.* **158 F8** 40 35N 111 50W
Sandy B., *St. Helena* **9 h** 16 0 S 5 43W
Sandy Bay, *Canada* **143 B8** 55 31N 102 19W
Sandy Bight, *Australia* **125 F3** 33 50 S 123 20 E
Sandy C., *Queens., Australia* **126 C5** 24 42 S 153 15 E
Sandy C., *Tas., Australia* **127 G3** 41 25 S 144 45 E
Sandy Cay, *Bahamas* **165 B4** 23 13N 75 18W
Sandy Cr. →, *U.S.A.* **158 F9** 41 51N 109 47W
Sandy L., *Canada* **140 B1** 53 2N 93 0W
Sandy Lake, *Canada* **140 B1** 53 0N 93 15W
Sandy Point, *India* **95 J11** 10 32N 92 22 E
Sandy Springs, *U.S.A.* **152 B5** 33 56N 84 23W
Sandy Valley, *U.S.A.* **161 K11** 35 49N 115 36W
Sånfjällets △, *Sweden* **16 B7** 62 17N 13 35 E
Sanford, *Fla., U.S.A.* **153 G8** 28 48N 81 16W
Sanford, *Maine, U.S.A.* **149 D10** 43 27N 70 47W
Sanford, *N.C., U.S.A.* **149 H6** 35 29N 79 10W
Sanford →, *Australia* **125 E2** 27 22 S 115 53 E
Sanford, Mt., *U.S.A.* **144 E11** 62 13N 144 8W
Sang-i-Masha, *Afghan.* **92 C2** 33 8N 67 27 E
Sanga, *Angola* **115 E3** 11 9 S 15 21 E
Sanga, *Mozam.* **119 E4** 12 22 S 35 21 E
Sanga →, *Congo* **114 C3** 1 5 S 17 0 E
Sangaie, *Dem. Rep. of the Congo* **115 D4** 6 48 S 22 46 E
Sangamner, *India* **94 E2** 19 37N 74 15 E
Sangamon →, *U.S.A.* **156 D6** 40 7N 90 20W
Sanganeb Atoll △, *Sudan* **106 D4** 19 33N 37 11 E
Sangar, *Afghan.* **92 C1** 32 56N 65 30 E
Sangar, *Russia* **67 C13** 64 2N 127 31 E
Sangar Sarai, *Afghan.* **92 B4** 34 27N 70 35 E
Sangareddi, *India* **94 F4** 17 38N 78 7 E
Sangaredi, *Guinea* **112 C2** 11 7N 13 52W
Sangarh →, *Pakistan* **92 D4** 30 43N 70 44 E
Sangasangadalam, *Indonesia* **85 C5** 0 36 S 117 13 E
Sangasso, *Mali* **112 C3** 12 5N 5 35W
Sangatte, *France* **27 B8** 50 56N 1 44 E
Sangay, *Ecuador* **168 D2** 2 0 S 78 20W
Sangay △, *Ecuador* **168 D2** 2 15 S 78 26W
Sangchris L., *U.S.A.* **156 E7** 39 35N 89 30W
Sange, *Dem. Rep. of the Congo* **118 D2** 6 58 S 28 21 E
Sangeang, *Indonesia* **85 D5** 8 12 S 119 6 E
Sângeorz-Băi, *Romania* **53 C9** 47 22N 24 41 E
Sanger, *U.S.A.* **160 J7** 36 42N 119 33W
Sângera, *Moldova* **53 D13** 46 55N 28 58 E
Sangerhausen, *Germany* **30 D7** 51 28N 11 18 E
Sanggan He →, *China* **74 E9** 38 12N 117 15 E
Sanggau, *Indonesia* **85 B4** 0 5N 110 30 E
Sanghar, *Pakistan* **92 F3** 26 2N 68 57 E
Sangihe, Kepulauan, *Indonesia* **82 A3** 3 0N 125 30 E
Sangihe, Pulau, *Indonesia* **82 A3** 3 35N 125 30 E
Sangju, *S. Korea* **75 F15** 36 25N 128 10 E
Sangkapura, *Indonesia* **85 D4** 5 52 S 112 40 E
Sangkhla, *Thailand* **86 E2** 14 57N 98 28 E
Sangkulirang, *Indonesia* **83 B5** 0 59N 117 58 E
Sangla, *Pakistan* **92 D5** 31 43N 73 23 E
Sangli, *India* **94 F2** 16 55N 74 33 E
Sangmélima, *Cameroon* **113 E7** 2 57N 12 1 E
Sango, *Angola* **115 D2** 9 51 S 15 44 E
Sangod, *India* **92 G7** 24 55N 76 17 E
Sangole, *India* **94 F2** 17 26N 75 12 E
Sangorodok = Ust-Vorkuta, *Russia* **56 A11** 67 24N 64 0 E
Sangpang Bum, *Burma* **90 B5** 26 30N 95 50 E
Sangre de Cristo Mts., *U.S.A.* **155 G2** 37 30N 105 20W
Sangre Grande, *Trin. & Tob.* **169 F9** 10 35N 61 8W
Sangro →, *Italy* **45 F11** 42 14N 14 32 E
Sangrur, *India* **92 D6** 30 14N 75 50 E
Sangudo, *Canada* **142 C6** 53 50N 114 54W
Sangue →, *Brazil* **173 C6** 11 1 S 58 39W
Sangüesa, *Spain* **40 C3** 42 37N 1 17W
Sanguinaires, Îs., *France* **29 G12** 41 51N 8 36 E
Sangzhi, *China* **77 C8** 29 25N 110 12 E
Sanhala, *Ivory C.* **112 C3** 10 3N 6 51W
Sanibel, *U.S.A.* **153 J7** 26 26N 82 1W
Sanibel I., *U.S.A.* **153 J7** 26 26N 82 6W
Sanikiluaq, *Canada* **139 C12** 56 32N 79 14W
Sanin-Kaigan △, *Japan* **72 B6** 35 39N 134 37 E
Sanirajak, *Canada* **139 B11** 68 46N 81 12W
Sanjawi, *Pakistan* **92 D3** 30 17N 68 21 E
Sanje, *Uganda* **118 C3** 0 49 S 31 30 E
Sanjiang, *China* **76 E7** 25 48N 109 37 E
Sanjo, *Japan* **70 F9** 37 37N 138 57 E
Sankarankovil, *India* **95 K3** 9 10N 77 35 E
Sankeshwar, *India* **95 F2** 16 23N 74 32 E
Sankh →, *India* **93 H11** 22 15N 84 48 E
Sankosh →, *India* **90 B2** 26 24N 89 47 E
Sankt Andrä, *Austria* **34 E7** 46 46N 14 50 E
Sankt Antönien, *Switz.* **33 C9** 46 58N 9 48 E
Sankt Augustin, *Germany* **30 E3** 50 45N 7 10 E
Sankt Blasien, *Germany* **31 H4** 47 47N 8 7 E
Sankt Gallen, *Switz.* **33 B8** 47 26N 9 22 E
Sankt Gallen □, *Switz.* **33 B8** 47 25N 9 22 E
Sankt Goar, *Germany* **31 E3** 50 12N 7 43 E
Sankt Ingbert, *Germany* **31 F3** 49 16N 7 6 E
Sankt Johann im Pongau, *Austria* **34 D6** 47 22N 13 12 E
Sankt Johann in Tirol, *Austria* **34 D5** 47 30N 12 25 E
Sankt Marein = Smarje, *Slovenia* **45 B12** 46 15N 15 34 E
Sankt Margrethen, *Switz.* **33 B9** 47 28N 9 37 E
Sankt Michel = Mikkeli, *Finland* **15 F22** 61 43N 27 15 E
Sankt Moritz, *Switz.* **33 D9** 46 30N 9 50 E
Sankt-Peterburg, *Russia* **58 C6** 59 55N 30 20 E
Sankt Pölten, *Austria* **34 C8** 48 12N 15 38 E
Sankt Ulrich = Ortisei, *Italy* **45 B8** 46 34N 11 40 E
Sankt Valentin, *Austria* **34 C7** 48 11N 14 33 E
Sankt Veit an der Glan, *Austria* **34 E7** 46 47N 14 22 E
Sankt Wendel, *Germany* **31 F3** 49 27N 7 9 E
Sankt Wolfgang, *Austria* **34 D6** 47 43N 13 27 E
Sankuru →, *Dem. Rep. of the Congo* **115 C4** 4 17 S 20 25 E
Sanliurfa, *Turkey* **101 D8** 37 12N 38 50 E
Sanlúcar de Barrameda, *Spain* **43 J4** 36 46N 6 21W
Sanluri, *Italy* **46 C1** 39 34N 8 54 E
Sânmartin, *Romania* **53 D10** 46 19N 25 58 E
Sanmen, *China* **77 C13** 29 5N 121 35 E
Sanmenxia, *China* **74 G6** 34 47N 111 12 E
Sanming, *China* **77 D11** 26 15N 117 40 E
Sannan, *Japan* **73 B7** 35 2N 135 1 E
Sannaspos, *S. Africa* **116 D4** 29 6 S 26 34 E
Sannat, *Malta* **38 E6** 36 1N 14 15 E
Sannicandro Gargánico, *Italy* **45 G12** 41 50N 15 34 E
Sânnicolau Mare, *Romania* **52 D5** 46 5N 20 39 E
Sannieshof, *S. Africa* **116 D4** 26 30 S 25 47 E
Sannīn, J., *Lebanon* **103 B4** 33 57N 35 52 E
Sanniquellie, *Liberia* **112 D3** 7 19N 8 38W
Sannûr, W. →, *Egypt* **106 B3** 28 59N 31 3 E
Sano, *Japan* **73 A11** 36 19N 139 35 E
Sanoe, *Antarctica* **7 D2** 70 20 S 9 0W
Sanok, *Poland* **55 J9** 49 35N 22 10 E
Sanquhar, *U.K.* **22 F5** 55 22N 3 54W
Sanquianga △, *Colombia* **168 C2** 2 33N 78 14W
Sans Souci, *Trin. & Tob.* **169 F9** 10 50N 61 0W
Sansanding, *Mali* **112 C3** 13 48N 6 0W
Sansepolcro, *Italy* **45 E9** 43 34N 12 8 E
Sansha, *China* **77 D13** 26 58N 120 12 E
Sanshui, *China* **77 F9** 23 10N 112 56 E
Sanski Most, *Bos.-H.* **45 D13** 44 46N 16 40 E
Sansui, *China* **76 D7** 26 58N 108 39 E
Sant Antoni Abat, *Spain* **38 D1** 38 59N 1 19 E
Sant Boi de Llobregat, *Spain* **40 D7** 41 21N 2 2 E
Sant Carles, *Spain* **38 C2** 39 3N 1 34 E
Sant Carles de la Ràpita, *Spain* **40 E5** 40 37N 0 35 E
Sant Celoni, *Spain* **40 D7** 41 42N 2 30 E
Sant Feliu de Guíxols, *Spain* **40 D8** 41 45N 3 1 E
Sant Feliu de Llobregat, *Spain* **40 D7** 41 23N 2 2 E
Sant Ferran, *Spain* **38 D1** 38 42N 1 28 E
Sant Francesc de Formentera, *Spain* **38 D1** 38 42N 1 26 E
Sant Jaume, *Spain* **38 B5** 39 54N 4 4 E
Sant Joan Baptista, *Spain* **38 C2** 39 5N 1 31 E
Sant Jordi, *Ibiza, Spain* **38 D1** 38 53N 1 24 E
Sant Jordi, *Mallorca, Spain* **38 B3** 39 33N 2 46 E
Sant Jordi, G. de, *Spain* **40 E6** 40 53N 1 2 E
Sant Llorenç de Morunys, *Spain* **40 C6** 42 8N 1 35 E
Sant Llorenç del Munt y l'Obac ⌓, *Spain* **40 D3** 41 39N 1 55W
Sant Llorenç des Cardassar, *Spain* **38 B4** 39 37N 3 17 E
Sant Mateu, *Baleares, Spain* **38 C1** 39 3N 1 23 E
Sant Mateu, *Valencia, Spain* **40 E5** 40 28N 0 10 E
Sant Miguel, *Spain* **38 C1** 39 3N 1 26 E
Sant Telm, *Spain* **38 B3** 39 35N 2 21 E
Santa, *Peru* **172 B2** 8 59 S 78 40W
Sant' Ágata Militello, *Italy* **47 D7** 38 2N 14 8 E
Santa Agnés, *Spain* **38 C1** 39 3N 1 21 E
Santa Ana, *Beni, Bolivia* **173 C4** 13 50 S 65 40W
Santa Ana, *La Paz, Bolivia* **172 D4** 15 31 S 67 30W
Santa Ana, *Santa Cruz, Bolivia* **173 D6** 18 43 S 58 44W
Santa Ana, *Santa Cruz, Bolivia* **173 D5** 16 37 S 60 43W
Santa Ana, *Ecuador* **168 D1** 1 16 S 80 20W
Santa Ana, *El Salv.* **164 D2** 14 0N 89 31W
Santa Ana, *Mexico* **162 A2** 30 31N 111 8W
Santa Ana, *Phil.* **80 B4** 18 28N 122 20 E
Santa Ana, *Solomon Is.* **133 N12** 10 50 S 162 30 E
Santa Ana, *U.S.A.* **161 M9** 33 46N 117 52W
Santa Ana →, *Venezuela* **168 B3** 9 30N 71 57W
Sant' Ángelo Lodigiano, *Italy* **44 C6** 45 14N 9 25 E
Sant' Antíoco, *Italy* **46 C1** 39 4N 8 27 E
Santa Bárbara, *Santa Maria, Azores* **9 d4** 36 59N 25 4W
Santa Bárbara, *Terciera, Azores* **9 d1** 38 41N 27 20W
Santa Bárbara, *Chile* **174 D1** 37 40 S 72 1W
Santa Bárbara, *Colombia* **168 B2** 5 53N 75 35W
Santa Barbara, *Honduras* **164 D2** 14 53N 88 14W
Santa Bárbara, *Mexico* **162 B3** 26 48N 105 50W
Santa Barbara, *Phil.* **81 F4** 10 50N 122 32 E
Santa Bárbara, *Spain* **40 E5** 40 42N 0 29 E
Santa Barbara, *U.S.A.* **161 L7** 34 25N 119 42W
Santa Bárbara, *Amazonas, Venezuela* **168 C4** 3 57N 67 6W
Santa Bárbara, *Barinas, Venezuela* **168 B3** 7 47N 71 10W
Santa Bárbara, Mt., *Spain* **41 H2** 37 23N 2 50W
Santa Bárbara, Serra de, *Azores* **9 d1** 38 44N 27 19W
Santa Barbara Channel, *U.S.A.* **161 L7** 34 15N 120 0W
Santa Barbara I., *U.S.A.* **161 M7** 33 29N 119 2W
Santa Catalina, *Colombia* **168 A2** 10 36N 75 17W
Santa Catalina, *Phil.* **81 G4** 9 20N 122 52 E
Santa Catalina, *Solomon Is.* **133 N12** 10 53 S 162 29 E
Santa Catalina, Gulf of, *U.S.A.* **161 N9** 33 10N 117 50W
Santa Catalina, I., *Mexico* **162 B2** 25 40N 110 50W
Santa Catalina I., *U.S.A.* **161 M8** 33 23N 118 25W
Santa Catarina □, *Brazil* **175 B6** 27 25 S 48 30W
Santa Catarina, I. de, *Brazil* **175 B6** 27 30 S 48 40W
Santa Caterina di Pittinuri, *Italy* **46 B1** 40 6N 8 27 E
Santa Caterina Villarmosa, *Italy* **47 E7** 37 35N 14 2 E
Santa Cecília, *Brazil* **175 B5** 26 56 S 50 18W
Santa Clara, *Cuba* **164 B4** 22 20N 80 0W
Santa Clara, *Calif., U.S.A.* **160 H5** 37 21N 121 57W
Santa Clara, *Utah, U.S.A.* **159 H7** 37 8N 113 39W
Santa Clara, El Golfo de, *Mexico* **162 A2** 31 42N 114 30W
Santa Clara de Olimar, *Uruguay* **175 C5** 32 50 S 54 54W
Santa Clarita, *U.S.A.* **161 L8** 34 24N 118 30W
Santa Clotilde, *Peru* **168 D3** 2 33 S 73 45W
Santa Coloma de Farners, *Spain* **40 D7** 41 50N 2 39 E
Santa Coloma de Gramenet, *Spain* **40 D7** 41 27N 2 13 E
Santa Comba, *Spain* **42 B2** 43 2N 8 49W
Santa Croce Camerina, *Italy* **47 F7** 36 50N 14 31 E
Santa Croce di Magliano, *Italy* **45 G11** 41 42N 14 59 E
Santa Cruz, *Argentina* **176 D3** 50 0 S 68 32W
Santa Cruz, *Bolivia* **173 D5** 17 43 S 63 10W
Santa Cruz, *Brazil* **170 C4** 6 13 S 36 1W
Santa Cruz, *Chile* **174 C1** 34 38 S 71 27W
Santa Cruz, *Costa Rica* **164 D2** 10 15N 85 35W
Santa Cruz, *Madeira* **9 c** 32 42N 16 46W
Santa Cruz, *Peru* **172 B2** 5 40 S 75 56W
Santa Cruz, *Davao del S., Phil.* **81 H5** 6 50N 125 25 E
Santa Cruz, *Laguna, Phil.* **80 D3** 14 20N 121 24 E
Santa Cruz, *Marinduque, Phil.* **80 E4** 13 28N 122 2 E
Santa Cruz, *Mind. Occ., Phil.* **80 E3** 13 4N 120 43 E
Santa Cruz, *Zambales, Phil.* **80 D2** 15 46N 119 55 E
Santa Cruz, *U.S.A.* **160 J4** 36 58N 122 1W
Santa Cruz, *Venezuela* **169 B5** 8 3N 64 27W
Santa Cruz □, *Argentina* **176 C3** 49 0 S 70 0W
Santa Cruz □, *Bolivia* **173 D5** 17 43 S 63 10W
Santa Cruz →, *Argentina* **176 D3** 50 10 S 68 20W
Santa Cruz, I., *Ecuador* **172 a** 0 38 S 90 23W
Santa Cruz Cabrália, *Brazil* **171 E4** 16 17 S 39 2W
Santa Cruz da Graciosa, *Azores* **9 d1** 39 5N 28 1W
Santa Cruz das Flores, *Azores* **9 d2** 39 27N 31 7W
Santa Cruz de Bravo = Felipe Carrillo Puerto, *Mexico* **163 D7** 19 38N 88 3W
Santa Cruz de la Palma, *Canary Is.* **9 e1** 28 41N 17 46W
Santa Cruz de la Palma ✈ (SPC), *Canary Is.* **9 e1** 28 40N 17 45W
Santa Cruz de Mudela, *Spain* **43 G7** 38 39N 3 28W
Santa Cruz de Tenerife, *Canary Is.* **9 e1** 28 28N 16 15W
Santa Cruz del Norte, *Cuba* **164 B3** 23 9N 81 55W
Santa Cruz del Retamar, *Spain* **42 E6** 40 8N 4 14W
Santa Cruz del Sur, *Cuba* **164 B4** 20 44N 78 0W
Santa Cruz do Rio Pardo, *Brazil* **175 A6** 22 54 S 49 37W
Santa Cruz do Sul, *Brazil* **175 B5** 29 42 S 52 25W
Santa Cruz I., *U.S.A.* **161 M7** 34 1N 119 43W
Santa Cruz Is., *Solomon Is.* **134 J8** 10 30 S 166 0 E
Santa Cruz la Vieja △, *Bolivia* **173 D5** 17 55 S 60 50W
Santa Cruz Mts., *Jamaica* **164 a** 17 58N 77 43W
Santa Domingo, Cay, *Bahamas* **164 B4** 21 25N 75 15W
Sant' Egídio alla Vibrata, *Italy* **45 F10** 42 49N 13 42 E
Santa Elena, *Argentina* **174 C4** 30 58 S 59 47W
Santa Elena, *Ecuador* **168 D1** 2 16 S 80 52W
Santa Elena, *Phil.* **80 D4** 14 12N 122 24 E
Santa Elena, C., *Costa Rica* **164 D2** 10 54N 85 56W
Sant' Eufémia, G. di, *Italy* **47 D9** 38 51N 16 4 E
Santa Eulàlia des Riu, *Spain* **38 D2** 38 59N 1 32 E
Santa Fe, *Argentina* **174 C3** 31 35 S 60 41W
Santa Fe, *Nueva Viscaya, Phil.* **80 C3** 16 10N 120 57 E
Santa Fe, *Romblon, Phil.* **80 E4** 12 10N 122 0 E
Santa Fe, *Spain* **43 H7** 37 11N 3 43W
Santa Fe, *U.S.A.* **159 J11** 35 41N 105 57W
Santa Fé □, *Argentina* **174 C3** 31 50 S 60 55W
Santa Fé, Canal de, *Ecuador* **172 a** 0 48 S 89 55W
Santa Fé, I., *Ecuador* **172 a** 0 49 S 90 5W
Santa Fé do Sul, *Brazil* **171 F1** 20 13 S 50 56W
Santa Filomena, *Brazil* **170 C2** 9 6 S 45 50W
Santa Fiora, *Italy* **45 F8** 42 50N 11 35 E
Santa Gertrudis, *Spain* **38 C1** 39 0N 1 26 E
Santa Giustina, *Italy* **45 B9** 46 10N 12 5 E
Santa Helena, *Brazil* **170 B2** 2 14 S 45 18W
Santa Helena de Goiás, *Brazil* **171 E1** 17 53 S 50 35W
Santa Inês, *Bahia, Brazil* **171 D4** 13 17 S 39 48W
Santa Inês, *Maranhão, Brazil* **170 B2** 3 39 S 45 20W
Santa Inés, *Spain* **43 G5** 38 32N 5 37W
Santa Inés, I., *Chile* **176 D2** 54 0 S 73 0W
Santa Isabel = Rey Malabo, *Eq. Guin.* **113 E6** 3 45N 8 50 E
Santa Isabel, *Argentina* **174 D2** 36 10 S 66 54W
Santa Isabel, *Solomon Is.* **133 M10** 8 0 S 159 0 E
Santa Isabel, Pico, *Eq. Guin.* **113 E6** 3 36N 8 49 E
Santa Isabel do Araguaia, *Brazil* **170 C2** 6 7 S 48 19W
Santa Isabel do Morro, *Brazil* **171 D1** 11 34 S 50 40W
Santa Isabel do Río Negro, *Brazil* **169 D4** 0 24 S 65 2W
Santa Lucía, *Corrientes, Argentina* **174 B4** 28 58 S 59 5W
Santa Lucía, *San Juan, Argentina* **174 C2** 31 30 S 68 30W
Santa Lucia, *Phil.* **80 C3** 17 7N 120 27 E
Santa Lucía, *Spain* **41 H4** 37 35N 0 58W

Santa Lucia, Uruguay 174 C4 34 27 S 56 24W
Santa Lucia Range, U.S.A. 160 K5 36 0N 121 20W
Santa Luzia = Luziânia, Brazil 171 E2 16 20 S 48 0W
Santa Luzia, C. Verde Is. 9 j 16 50N 24 35W
Santa Magdalena, I., Mexico 162 C2 24 40N 112 15W
Santa Margarita, Argentina 174 D3 38 28 S 61 35W
Santa Margarita, Spain 38 B4 39 42N 3 6 E
Santa Margarita, U.S.A. 160 K6 35 23N 120 37W
Santa Margarita →, U.S.A. 161 M9 33 13N 117 23W
Santa Margarita, I., Mexico 162 C2 24 30N 111 50W
Santa Margherita, Italy 46 D1 38 58N 8 58 E
Santa Margherita Ligure, Italy 44 D6 44 20N 9 11 E
Santa María, Argentina 174 B2 26 40 S 66 0W
Santa Maria, Azores 9 d4 36 58N 25 6W
Santa Maria, Brazil 175 B5 29 40 S 53 48W
Santa Maria, C. Verde Is. 9 j 16 31N 22 53W
Santa Maria, Ilocos S., Phil. 80 C3 17 22N 120 29 E
Santa Maria, Isabela, Phil. 80 C3 17 28N 121 45 E
Santa Maria, Switz. 33 C10 46 36N 10 25 E
Santa Maria, U.S.A. 161 L6 34 57N 120 26W
Santa María →, Mexico 162 A3 31 0N 107 14W
Santa María, B. de, Mexico 162 B3 25 10N 108 40W
Santa Maria, C. de, Portugal 43 J3 36 58N 7 53W
Santa María, I., Ecuador 172 a 1 17 S 90 26W
Santa Maria Cápua Vétere, Italy 47 A7 41 5N 14 15 E
Santa Maria da Feira, Portugal 42 E2 40 55N 8 35W
Santa Maria da Vitória, Brazil 171 D3 13 24 S 44 12W
Santa María de Ipire, Venezuela 169 B4 8 49N 65 19W
Santa Maria del Camí, Spain 38 B3 39 38N 2 47 E
Santa Maria di Léuca, C., Italy 47 C11 39 47N 18 22 E
Santa Maria do Boiaçu, Brazil 169 D5 0 25 S 61 48W
Santa Maria do Suaçuí, Brazil 171 E3 18 12 S 42 25W
Santa Maria dos Marmelos, Brazil 173 B5 6 7 S 61 51W
Santa María la Real de Nieva, Spain 42 D6 41 4N 4 24W
Santa Marinella, Italy 45 F8 42 2N 11 52 E
Santa Marta, Colombia 168 A3 11 15N 74 13W
Santa Marta, Sierra Nevada de, Colombia 168 A3 10 55N 73 50W
Santa Marta de Tormes, Spain 42 E5 40 57N 5 38W
Santa Marta Grande, C., Brazil 175 B6 28 43 S 48 50W
Santa Marta Ortigueira, Ría de, Spain 42 B3 43 44N 7 45W
Santa Maura = Levkás, Greece 39 B2 38 40N 20 43 E
Santa Monica, U.S.A. 161 M8 34 1N 118 29W
Santa Monica Mts. △, U.S.A. 161 L8 34 4N 118 44W
Santa Olalla, Huelva, Spain 43 H4 37 54N 6 14W
Santa Olalla, Toledo, Spain 42 E6 40 2N 4 25W
Santa Paula, U.S.A. 161 L7 34 21N 119 4W
Santa Pola, Spain 41 G4 38 13N 0 35W
Santa Ponça, Spain 38 B3 39 30N 2 28 E
Santa Quitéria, Brazil 170 B3 4 20 S 40 10W
Santa Rita = Itumbiara, Brazil 171 E2 18 20 S 49 10W
Santa Rita, Brazil 168 D4 3 29 S 69 19W
Santa Rita, Colombia 168 C4 4 53N 68 24W
Santa Rita, Phil. 81 F5 11 27N 124 56 E
Santa Rita, U.S.A. 159 K10 32 48N 108 4W
Santa Rita, Venezuela 168 A3 10 32N 71 32W
Santa Rita do Araguaia = Guiratinga, Brazil 173 D7 16 21 S 53 45W
Santa Rita do Araquaia, Brazil 173 D7 17 20 S 53 12W
Santa Rosa = Bella Unión, Uruguay 174 C4 30 15 S 57 40W
Santa Rosa, La Pampa, Argentina 174 D3 36 40 S 64 17W
Santa Rosa, San Luis, Argentina 174 C2 32 21 S 65 10W
Santa Rosa, Beni, Bolivia 172 C4 14 10 S 66 53W
Santa Rosa, Pando, Bolivia 172 C4 10 36 S 67 20W
Santa Rosa, Santa Cruz, Bolivia 173 D5 17 7 S 63 35W
Santa Rosa, Brazil 175 B5 27 52 S 54 29W
Santa Rosa, Colombia 168 C4 3 32N 69 48W
Santa Rosa, El Oro, Ecuador 168 D2 3 27 S 79 58W
Santa Rosa, Galápagos Is., Ecuador 172 a 0 40 S 90 25W
Santa Rosa, Puno, Peru 172 C3 14 30 S 70 50W
Santa Rosa, San Martin, Peru 172 B2 6 41 S 76 37W
Santa Rosa, Phil. 80 D3 15 25N 120 57 E
Santa Rosa, Calif., U.S.A. 160 G4 38 26N 122 43W
Santa Rosa, N. Mex., U.S.A. 155 H2 34 57N 104 41W
Santa Rosa, Venezuela 168 C4 1 29N 66 55W
Santa Rosa and San Jacinto Mts. △, U.S.A. 161 M10 33 28N 116 20W
Santa Rosa Beach, U.S.A. 152 E3 30 22N 86 14W
Santa Rosa de Amanadona, Venezuela 168 C4 1 29N 66 55W
Santa Rosa de Cabal, Colombia 168 C2 4 52N 75 38W
Santa Rosa de Copán, Honduras 164 D2 14 47N 88 46W
Santa Rosa de la Roca, Bolivia 173 D5 16 3 S 61 34W
Santa Rosa de Osos, Colombia 168 B2 6 39N 75 28W
Santa Rosa de Río Primero, Argentina 174 C3 31 8 S 63 20W
Santa Rosa de Viterbo, Colombia 168 B3 5 53N 72 59W
Santa Rosa del Palmar, Bolivia 173 D5 16 54 S 62 24W
Santa Rosa I., Calif., U.S.A. 161 M6 33 58N 120 6W
Santa Rosa I., Fla., U.S.A. 153 E3 30 20N 86 50W
Santa Rosa Range, U.S.A. 158 F5 41 45N 117 40W
Santa Rosalía, Mexico 162 B2 27 20N 112 20W
Santa Sylvina, Argentina 174 B3 27 50 S 61 10W
Santa Tecla = Nueva San Salvador, El Salv. 164 D2 13 40N 89 18W
Santa Teresa, Argentina 174 C3 33 25 S 60 47W
Santa Teresa, Australia 126 C1 24 8 S 134 22 E
Santa Teresa, Brazil 171 E3 19 55 S 40 36W
Santa Teresa, Mexico 163 B5 25 17N 97 51W
Santa Teresa, Venezuela 169 C5 4 43N 61 4W
Santa Teresa △, Uruguay 175 C5 33 57 S 53 31W
Santa Teresa di Riva, Italy 47 E8 37 57N 15 22 E
Santa Teresa Gallura, Italy 46 A2 41 14N 9 11 E
Santa Teresinha, Brazil 170 D1 10 28 S 50 31W
Santa Uxía, Spain 42 C2 42 36N 8 58W
Santa Vitória, Brazil 171 E1 18 50 S 50 8W
Santa Vitória do Palmar, Brazil 175 C5 33 32 S 53 25W
Santa Ynez →, U.S.A. 161 L6 35 41N 120 36W
Santa Ynez Mts., U.S.A. 161 L6 34 30N 120 0W
Santa Ysabel, U.S.A. 161 M10 33 7N 116 40W
Santadi, Italy 46 C1 39 5N 8 43 E
Santaella, Spain 43 H6 37 34N 4 51W
Santahar, Bangla. 90 C2 24 48N 88 59 E
Santai, China 76 B5 31 5N 104 58 E
Santaluz, Brazil 170 D4 11 15 S 39 22W
Santana = Uruaçu, Brazil 171 D2 14 30 S 49 10W
Santana, Brazil 171 D3 13 2 S 44 5W
Santana, Madeira 9 c 32 48N 16 52W
Sântana, Romania 52 D6 46 20N 21 30 E
Santana, Coxilha de, Brazil 175 C4 30 50 S 55 35W
Santana do Ipanema, Brazil 170 C4 9 22 S 37 14W
Santana do Livramento, Brazil 175 C4 30 55 S 55 30W
Santana do Paranaíba = Paranaíba, Brazil 173 D7 19 40 S 51 11W
Santander, Colombia 168 C2 3 1N 76 28W
Santander, Phil. 81 G4 9 25N 123 20 E
Santander, Spain 42 B7 43 27N 3 51W
Santander □, Colombia 168 B3 7 0N 73 15W
Santander Jiménez, Mexico 163 C5 24 11N 98 29W
Santanilla, Is., Honduras 164 C3 17 22N 83 57W
Santanyí, Spain 38 B4 39 20N 3 5 E
Santaquin, U.S.A. 158 G8 39 59N 111 47W
Santarcángelo di Romagna, Italy 45 D9 44 4N 12 26 E
Santarém, Brazil 169 D7 2 25 S 54 42W
Santarém, Portugal 43 F2 39 12N 8 42W
Santarém □, Portugal 43 F2 39 10N 8 40W
Santaren Channel, W. Indies 164 B4 24 0N 79 30W
Santee, U.S.A. 161 N10 32 50N 116 58W
Santee →, U.S.A. 149 J6 33 7N 79 17W
Santéramo in Colle, Italy 47 B9 40 49N 16 45 E
Santerno →, Italy 45 D8 44 34N 11 58 E
Santhià, Italy 44 C5 45 22N 8 10 E
Santi-Quaranta = Sarandë, Albania 38 B9 39 52N 19 55 E
Santiago = São Tiago, C. Verde Is. 9 j 15 0N 23 40W
Santiago, Bolivia 173 D6 18 19 S 59 34W
Santiago, Brazil 175 B5 29 11 S 54 52W
Santiago, Canary Is. 9 e1 28 2N 17 12W
Santiago, Chile 174 C1 33 24 S 70 40W
Santiago, Panama 164 E3 8 0N 81 0W
Santiago, Peru 172 C2 14 11 S 75 43W
Santiago, Ilocos S., Phil. 80 C3 17 18N 120 27 E
Santiago, Isabela, Phil. 80 C3 16 41N 121 33 E
Santiago □, Chile 174 C1 33 30 S 70 50W
Santiago →, Mexico 136 G9 25 11N 105 26W
Santiago →, Peru 168 D2 4 27 S 77 38W
Santiago, C., Chile 176 D1 50 46 S 75 27W
Santiago, I. = San Salvador, I., Ecuador 172 a 0 16 S 90 42W
Santiago, Punta de, Eq. Guin. 113 E6 3 12N 8 40 E
Santiago, Serranía de, Bolivia 173 D6 18 25 S 59 25W
Santiago de Chuco, Peru 172 B2 8 9 S 78 11W
Santiago de Compostela, Spain 42 C2 42 52N 8 37W
Santiago de Cuba, Cuba 164 C4 20 0N 75 49W
Santiago de los Cabelleros, Dom. Rep. 165 C5 19 30N 70 40W
Santiago del Estero, Argentina 174 B3 27 50 S 64 15W
Santiago del Estero □, Argentina 174 B3 27 40 S 63 15W
Santiago del Teide, Canary Is. 9 e1 28 17N 16 48W
Santiago do Boqueirão = Santiago, Brazil 175 B5 29 11 S 54 52W
Santiago do Cacém, Portugal 43 G2 38 1N 8 42W
Santiago Ixcuintla, Mexico 162 C3 21 50N 105 11W
Santiago Papasquiaro, Mexico 162 C3 25 0N 105 20W
Santiaguillo, L. de, Mexico 162 C4 24 50N 104 50W
Santiguila, Mali 112 C3 12 42N 7 25W
Santillana, Spain 42 B6 43 24N 4 6W
Säntis, Switz. 33 B8 47 15N 9 22 E
Santisteban del Puerto, Spain 43 G7 38 17N 3 15W
Santo →, Peru 172 B2 8 56 S 78 37W
Santo Amaro, Brazil 171 D4 12 30 S 38 43W
Santo Anastácio, Brazil 175 A5 21 58 S 51 39W
Santo André, Brazil 175 A6 23 39 S 46 29W
Santo Ângelo, Brazil 175 B5 28 15 S 54 15W
Santo Antão, C. Verde Is. 9 j 16 52N 25 10W
Santo Antônio, São Tomé & Príncipe 115 G6 1 37N 7 27 E
Santo Antonio, Brazil 169 D5 2 24 S 60 58W
Santo Antônio da Cachoeira = Itaguatins, Brazil 170 C2 5 47 S 47 29W
Santo Antônio de Jesus, Brazil 171 D4 12 58 S 39 16W
Santo Antônio do Abaixo = Santo Antônio do Leverger, Brazil 173 D6 15 52 S 56 5W
Santo Antônio do Içá, Brazil 168 D4 3 5 S 67 57W
Santo Antônio do Leverger, Brazil 173 D6 15 52 S 56 5W
Santo Corazón, Bolivia 173 D6 18 0 S 58 45W
Santo Domingo, Dom. Rep. 165 C6 18 30N 69 59W
Santo Domingo, Baja Calif., Mexico 162 A1 30 43N 116 2W
Santo Domingo, Baja Calif. S., Mexico 162 B2 25 32N 112 2W
Santo Domingo, Nic. 164 D3 12 14N 84 59W
Santo Domingo de la Calzada, Spain 40 C2 42 26N 2 57W
Santo Domingo de los Colorados, Ecuador 168 D2 0 15 S 79 9W
Santo Domingo Pueblo, U.S.A. 159 J10 35 31N 106 22W
Santo Stéfano di Camastro, Italy 47 D7 38 1N 14 22 E
Santo Tirso, Portugal 42 D2 41 21N 8 28W
Santo Tomás, Ecuador 172 a 0 51 S 91 2W
Santo Tomás, Mexico 162 A1 31 33N 116 24W
Santo Tomás, Peru 172 C3 14 26 S 72 8W
Santo Tomás, Volcán, Ecuador 172 a 0 48 S 91 7W
Santo Tomé, Argentina 175 B4 28 40 S 56 5W
Santo Tomé de Guayana = Ciudad Guayana, Venezuela 169 B5 8 0N 62 30W
Santomera, Spain 41 G3 38 4N 1 3W
Santoña, Spain 42 B7 43 29N 3 27W
Santoríni = Thíra, Greece 49 E7 36 23N 25 27 E
Santos, Brazil 175 A6 24 0 S 46 20W
Santos, Sierra de los, Spain 43 G5 38 7N 5 12W
Santos Dumont, Brazil 171 F3 22 55 S 43 10W
Santos Plateau, India 8 J7 26 0 S 42 0W
Sanur, Indonesia 79 K18 8 41 S 115 15 E
Sanwer, India 92 H6 22 59N 75 50 E
Sanxenxo, Spain 42 C2 42 24N 8 49W
Sanxiang, China 69 G9 22 21N 113 25 E
Sanya, China 86 C7 18 14N 109 29 E
San'yō, Japan 72 C3 34 2N 131 5 E
Sanyuan, China 74 G5 34 35N 108 58 E
Sanyuki-Sammyaku, Japan 72 C6 34 5N 134 0 E
Sanza Pombo, Angola 115 D3 7 18 S 15 56 E
São Bartolomeu de Messines, Portugal 43 H2 37 15N 8 17W
São Benedito = Beneditinos, Brazil 170 C3 5 27 S 42 22W
São Benedito, Brazil 170 B3 4 3 S 40 53W
São Benedito →, Brazil 173 B6 9 11 S 57 2W
São Bento, Brazil 170 B3 2 42 S 44 50W
São Bento do Norte, Brazil 170 C4 5 4 S 36 2W
São Bernardo do Campo, Brazil 171 F2 23 45 S 46 34W
São Borja, Brazil 175 B4 28 39 S 56 0W
São Brás de Alportel, Portugal 43 H3 37 8N 7 37W
São Braz, C. de, Angola 115 D2 9 58 S 13 19 E
São Caitano, Brazil 170 C4 8 21 S 36 6W
São Carlos, Brazil 175 A6 22 0 S 47 50W
São Cristóvão, Brazil 170 D4 11 1 S 37 15W
São Domingos, Brazil 171 D2 13 25 S 46 19W
São Domingos, Guinea-Biss. 112 C1 12 19N 16 13W
São Domingos da Boa Vista = Capim, Brazil 170 B2 1 41 S 47 47W
São Domingos do Capim = Capim, Brazil 170 B2 1 41 S 47 47W
São Domingos do Maranhão, Brazil 170 C3 5 42 S 44 22W
São Felipe = Içana, Brazil 168 C4 0 21N 67 19W
São Felippe = Eirunepé, Brazil 172 B4 6 35 S 69 53W
São Félix, Brazil 171 D1 11 36 S 50 39W
São Felix do Xingu, Brazil 173 B7 6 38 S 51 59W
São Filipe, C. Verde Is. 9 j 15 2N 24 30W
São Francisco = Itapagé, Brazil 170 B4 3 41 S 39 34W
São Francisco, Brazil 171 E3 16 0 S 44 50W
São Francisco →, Brazil 170 D4 10 30 S 36 24W
São Francisco do Maranhão, Brazil 170 C3 6 15 S 42 52W
São Francisco do Sul, Brazil 175 B6 26 15 S 48 36W
São Gabriel, Brazil 175 C5 30 20 S 54 20W
São Gabriel da Cachoeira, Brazil 168 D4 0 8 S 67 5W
São Gabriel da Palha, Brazil 171 E3 18 47 S 40 39W
São Gonçalo = Araripina, Brazil 170 C3 7 33 S 40 34W
São Gonçalo, Brazil 171 F3 22 48 S 43 5W
São Gotardo, Brazil 171 E2 19 19 S 46 3W
Sao Hill, Tanzania 119 D4 8 20 S 35 12 E
São João, Guinea-Biss. 112 C1 11 32N 15 25W
São João da Baliza, Brazil 169 C6 0 52N 59 52W
São João da Boa Vista, Brazil 175 A6 22 0 S 46 52W
São João da Madeira, Portugal 42 E2 40 54N 8 30W
São João da Pesqueira, Portugal 42 D3 41 8N 7 24W
São João da Ponte, Brazil 171 E3 15 56 S 44 1W
São João do Montenegro = Montenegro, Brazil 175 B5 29 39 S 51 29W
São João del Rei, Brazil 171 F3 21 8 S 44 15W
São João do Araguaia, Brazil 170 C2 5 23 S 48 46W
São João do Paraíso, Brazil 171 E3 15 19 S 42 1W
São João do Piauí, Brazil 170 C3 8 21 S 42 15W
São João dos Patos, Brazil 170 C3 6 30 S 43 42W
São Joaquim, Amazonas, Brazil 168 D4 0 1 S 67 16W
São Joaquim, Sta. Catarina, Brazil 175 B6 28 18 S 49 56W
São Joaquim △, Brazil 175 B6 28 12 S 49 37W
São Joaquim da Barra, Brazil 171 F2 20 35 S 47 53W
São Jorge, Azores 9 d1 38 38N 28 3W
São Jorge, Canal de, Azores 9 d1 38 30N 28 0W
São Jorge, Pta. de, Azores 9 d1 38 42N 27 3W
São Jorge, Pta. de, Madeira 9 c 32 50N 16 53W
São José, Brazil 175 B5 27 38 S 48 39W
São José, B. de, Brazil 170 B3 2 38 S 44 4W
São José da Lagoa = Nova Era, Brazil 171 E3 19 45 S 43 3W
São José da Laje, Brazil 170 C4 9 1 S 36 3W
São José de Mipibu, Brazil 170 C4 6 5 S 35 15W
São José de Tocantins = Niquelândia, Brazil 171 D2 14 33 S 48 23W
São José do Norte, Brazil 175 C5 32 1 S 52 3W
São José do Peixe, Brazil 170 C3 7 24 S 42 34W
São José do Rio Prêto, Brazil 175 A6 20 50 S 49 20W
São José dos Campos, Brazil 175 A6 23 7 S 45 52W
São José dos Cocais = Nossa Senhora do Livramento, Brazil 173 D6 15 48 S 56 22W
São José dos Matões = Parnarama, Brazil 170 C3 5 31 S 43 6W
São Leopoldo, Brazil 175 B5 29 50 S 51 10W
São Lourenço, Brazil 171 F2 22 7 S 45 3W
São Lourenço →, Brazil 173 D6 17 53 S 57 27W
São Lourenço, Pantanal do, Brazil 173 D6 17 30 S 56 20W
São Lourenço, Pta. de, Madeira 9 c 32 44N 16 39W
São Lourenço do Sul, Brazil 175 C5 31 22 S 51 58W
São Luís, Brazil 170 B3 2 39 S 44 15W
São Luís do Curu, Brazil 170 B4 3 40 S 39 14W
São Luís do Tapajós, Brazil 169 D6 4 25 S 56 12W
São Luís Gonzaga = Ipixuna, Brazil 172 B3 7 0 S 71 40W
São Luís Gonzaga, Brazil 175 B5 28 25 S 55 0W
São Marcos →, Brazil 171 E2 18 15 S 47 37W
São Marcos, B. de, Brazil 170 B3 2 0 S 44 0W
São Martinho da Cortiça, Portugal 42 E2 40 18N 8 8W
São Mateus, Azores 9 d1 38 26N 28 27W
São Mateus, Brazil 171 E4 18 44 S 39 50W
São Mateus →, Brazil 171 E4 18 35 S 39 44W
São Mateus do Sul, Brazil 175 B5 25 52 S 50 23W
São Miguel, Azores 9 d3 37 47N 25 30W
São Miguel do Araguaia, Brazil 171 D1 13 19 S 50 13W
São Miguel do Guamá = Guamá, Brazil 170 B2 1 37 S 47 29W
São Miguel do Oeste, Brazil 175 B5 26 45 S 53 34W
São Miguel dos Campos, Brazil 170 C4 9 47 S 36 5W
São Nicolau, C. Verde Is. 9 j 16 20N 24 20W
São Nicolau →, Angola 115 E2 14 16 S 12 22 E
São Nicolau →, Brazil 170 C3 5 45 S 42 2W
São Paulo, Brazil 175 A6 23 32 S 46 37W
São Paulo □, Brazil 175 A6 22 0 S 49 0W
São Paulo, I., Atl. Oc. 8 F9 0 56N 29 22W
São Paulo de Olivença, Brazil 168 D4 3 27 S 68 48W
São Pedro, Atl. Oc. 8 F9 0 56N 29 22W
São Pedro do Sul, Portugal 42 E2 40 46N 8 4W
São Rafael, Brazil 170 C4 5 47 S 36 55W
São Raimundo das Mangabeiras, Brazil 170 C2 7 1 S 45 29W
São Raimundo Nonato, Brazil 170 C3 9 1 S 42 42W
São Romão, Brazil 171 E2 16 22 S 45 4W
São Roque, Madeira 9 c 32 46N 16 48W
São Roque, C. de, Brazil 170 C4 5 30 S 35 16W
São Roque do Pico, Azores 9 d1 38 31N 28 19W
São Salvador do Congo = Mbanza Congo, Angola 115 D2 6 18 S 14 16 E
São Sebastião, Azores 9 d1 38 39N 27 6W
São Sebastião, I. de, Brazil 175 A6 23 50 S 45 18W
São Sebastião do Paraíso, Brazil 175 A6 20 54 S 46 59W
São Simão, Brazil 171 E1 18 56 S 50 30W
São Teotónio, Portugal 43 H2 37 30N 8 42W
São Tiago, C. Verde Is. 9 j 15 0N 23 40W
São Tomé, Brazil 170 C4 5 58 S 36 4W
São Tomé, São Tomé & Príncipe 115 G6 0 10N 6 39 E
São Tomé, C. de, Brazil 171 F3 22 0 S 40 59W
São Tomé, Pico de, São Tomé & Príncipe 115 G6 0 16N 6 33 E
São Tomé & Príncipe ■, Africa 115 G6 0 12N 6 39 E
São Vicente = Araguatins, Brazil 170 C2 5 38 S 48 7W
São Vicente, Brazil 175 A6 23 57 S 46 23W
São Vicente, C. Verde Is. 9 j 17 0N 25 0W
São Vicente, Madeira 9 c 32 48N 17 3W
São Vicente, C. de, Portugal 43 H1 37 0N 9 0W
Saona, I., Dom. Rep. 165 C6 18 10N 68 40W
Saône →, France 27 G11 45 44N 4 50 E
Saône-et-Loire □, France 27 F11 46 30N 4 50 E
Saonek, Indonesia 83 B4 0 22 S 130 55 E
Saoura, O. →, Algeria 111 C4 29 0N 0 55W
Sápai, Greece 51 E9 41 2N 25 43 E
Sapam, Ao, Thailand 87 a 8 0N 98 26 E
Sapanca, Turkey 100 B4 40 41N 30 16 E
Sapão →, Brazil 170 D2 11 1 S 45 32W
Saparua, Indonesia 82 B3 3 33 S 128 40 E
Sapé, Brazil 170 C4 7 6 S 35 13W
Sape, Indonesia 85 D5 8 34 S 118 59 E
Sapele, Nigeria 113 D6 5 50N 5 40 E
Sapelo I., U.S.A. 152 D8 31 25N 81 12W
Sapelo Sound, U.S.A. 152 D8 31 30N 81 10W
Şaphane, Turkey 49 B11 39 1N 29 13 E
Sapi △, Zimbabwe 119 F2 15 48 S 29 42 E
Sapiéntza, Greece 48 E3 36 45N 21 43 E
Sapindji, Dem. Rep. of the Congo 115 D4 9 39 S 23 12 E
Sapo △, Liberia 112 D3 5 15N 8 30W
Sapone, Burkina Faso 113 C4 12 3N 1 35W
Saposoa, Peru 172 B2 6 55 S 76 45W
Sapotskina, Belarus 54 E10 53 49N 23 40 E
Sapouy, Burkina Faso 113 C4 11 34N 1 44W
Sapozhok, Russia 60 D5 53 59N 40 41 E
Sapphire, Australia 126 C4 23 28 S 147 43 E
Sappho, U.S.A. 160 B2 48 4N 124 16W
Sapporo, Japan 70 C10 43 0N 141 21 E
Sapri, Italy 47 B8 40 4N 15 38 E
Sapu, Angola 115 E3 12 28 S 19 26 E
Sapudi, Indonesia 85 D4 7 6 S 114 20 E
Sapulpa, U.S.A. 155 H6 35 59N 96 5W
Saqqez, Iran 101 D12 36 15N 46 20 E
Sar Dasht, Āzarbāyjān-e Gharbī, Iran 101 D11 36 9N 45 28 E
Sar Dasht, Khuzestān, Iran 97 C6 32 32N 48 52 E
Sar-e Pol, Afghan. 91 A2 36 10N 66 0 E
Sar-e Pol □, Afghan. 91 A2 36 20N 65 50 E
Sar Gachīneh = Yāsūj, Iran 97 D6 30 31N 51 31 E
Sar Planina, Macedonia 50 E4 42 0N 21 0 E
Sara, Burkina Faso 112 C4 11 40N 3 53W
Sara, Niger 109 D2 20 46N 12 35 E
Sara, Phil. 81 F4 11 16N 123 1 E
Šara △, Serbia & M. 50 D5 42 12N 21 0 E
Sara Buri = Saraburi, Thailand 86 E3 14 30N 100 55 E
Sarāb, Iran 101 D12 37 55N 47 40 E
Sarabadi, Iraq 96 C5 33 1N 44 48 E
Saraburi, Thailand 86 E3 14 30N 100 55 E
Saradiya, India 92 J4 21 34N 70 2 E
Saraféré, Mali 112 B4 15 50N 3 40W
Saragossa = Zaragoza, Spain 40 D4 41 39N 0 53W
Saraguro, Ecuador 168 D2 3 35 S 79 16W
Sarai Naurang, Pakistan 92 C4 32 50N 70 47 E
Saraikela, India 93 H11 22 42N 85 56 E
Saraipali, India 94 D6 21 20N 82 59 E
Saraiu, Romania 53 F13 44 43N 28 10 E
Sarajevo, Bos.-H. 52 G3 43 52N 18 26 E
Sarakhs, Turkmenistan 97 B9 36 32N 61 13 E
Saraktash, Russia 64 F6 51 47N 56 22 E
Saramacca →, Suriname 169 B6 5 50N 55 55W
Saramati, Burma 90 C5 25 44N 95 2 E
Saran, Gunung, Indonesia 85 C4 0 30 S 111 25 E
Saranac, U.S.A. 157 B11 42 56N 85 13W
Saranac L., U.S.A. 151 B10 44 20N 74 10W
Saranac Lake, U.S.A. 151 B10 44 20N 74 8W
Saranda, Tanzania 118 D3 5 45 S 34 59 E
Sarandë, Albania 38 B9 39 52N 19 55 E
Sarandí del Yi, Uruguay 175 C4 33 18 S 55 38W
Sarandí Grande, Uruguay 174 C4 33 44 S 56 20W
Sarangani □, Phil. 81 J5 5 45N 125 20 E
Sarangani B., Phil. 81 J5 6 0N 125 13 E
Sarangani Is., Phil. 81 J5 5 25N 125 25 E
Sarangarh, India 94 D6 21 30N 83 5 E
Saranovo = Septemvri, Bulgaria 51 D8 42 13N 24 6 E
Saransk, Russia 60 C7 54 10N 45 10 E
Sarapul, Russia 64 C4 56 28N 53 48 E
Sarar Plain = Bannaanka Saraar, Somali Rep. 120 C3 9 25N 46 17 E
Sarasota, U.S.A. 153 H7 27 20N 82 32W
Sarata, Ukraine 53 D14 46 1N 29 40 E
Sarata →, Ukraine 53 E14 45 51N 29 42 E
Saratoga, Calif., U.S.A. 160 H4 37 16N 122 2W
Saratoga, Wyo., U.S.A. 158 F10 41 27N 106 49W
Saratoga △, U.S.A. 151 D11 43 0N 73 37W
Saratoga Springs, U.S.A. 151 C11 43 5N 73 47W
Saratok, Malaysia 78 D4 1 55N 111 17 E
Saratov, Russia 60 E7 51 30N 46 2 E
Sarāvān, Iran 97 E9 27 25N 62 15 E
Saravane, Laos 86 E6 15 43N 106 25 E
Sarawak □, Malaysia 85 B4 2 0N 113 0 E
Saray, Tekirdağ, Turkey 51 E11 41 26N 27 55 E
Saray, Van, Turkey 101 C11 38 38N 44 9 E
Saray Komar = Pyandzh, Tajikistan 65 E4 37 14N 69 6 E
Saraya, Guinea 112 C2 12 50N 11 45W
Saraya, Senegal 112 C2 12 50N 11 45W
Saraycık, Turkey 49 B11 39 1N 29 49 E
Sarayköy, Turkey 49 D10 37 55N 28 54 E
Saraylar, Turkey 51 F11 40 39N 27 40 E
Sarayönü, Turkey 100 C5 38 16N 32 24 E
Sarbāz, Iran 97 E9 26 38N 61 19 E
Sarbīsheh, Iran 97 C8 32 30N 59 40 E
Sárbogárd, Hungary 52 D3 46 50N 18 40 E
Sarca →, Italy 44 C7 45 52N 10 52 E
Sarcelles, France 27 D9 49 1N 2 23 E
Sardalas, Libya 108 C2 25 50N 10 34 E
Sardarova Karakhana = Leninskiy, Tajikistan 65 D4 38 26N 68 46 E
Sardarshahr, India 92 E6 28 30N 74 29 E
Sardegna □, Italy 46 B1 40 0N 9 0 E
Sardhana, India 92 E7 29 9N 77 39 E
Sardina, Pta., Canary Is. 9 e1 28 9N 15 44W
Sardinata, Colombia 168 B3 8 5N 72 48W
Sardinia = Sardegna □, Italy 46 B1 40 0N 9 0 E
Sardinia, U.S.A. 157 F13 39 0N 83 49W
Sardis, Turkey 49 C10 38 28N 28 2 E
Sardis, U.S.A. 152 C8 32 58N 81 46W
Sārdūīyeh = Dar Mazār, Iran 97 D8 29 14N 57 20 E
Saren, Indonesia 79 J18 8 26 S 115 34 E
S'Arenal, Spain 38 B3 39 30N 2 45 E
Sarentino, Italy 45 B8 46 38N 11 21 E
Saréyamou, Mali 112 B4 16 7N 3 10W
Sargans, Switz. 33 B8 47 3N 9 15 E
Sargasso Sea, Atl. Oc. 8 D4 27 0N 72 0W
Sargent, U.S.A. 152 B5 33 26N 84 52W
Sargodha, Pakistan 91 B4 32 10N 72 40 E
Sarh, Chad 109 G3 9 5N 18 23 E
Sarhala, Ivory C. 112 D3 8 22N 6 8W
Sarhro, Jebel, Morocco 110 B4 31 6N 5 0W
Sārī, Iran 97 B7 36 30N 53 4 E
Sari d'Orcino, France 29 F12 42 3N 8 49 E
Sária, Greece 49 F9 35 54N 27 17 E
Saria, India 93 J10 21 38N 83 22 E
Sariab, Pakistan 92 D2 30 6N 66 59 E
Sarıbeyler, Turkey 49 B9 39 24N 27 35 E
Saricumbe, Angola 115 E3 12 12 S 19 46 E
Sarıgöl, Turkey 100 C3 38 14N 28 41 E
Sarıkamış, Turkey 101 B10 40 22N 42 35 E
Sarıkaya, Turkey 100 C6 39 29N 35 22 E
Sarikei, Malaysia 85 B4 2 8N 111 30 E
Sarıköy, Turkey 51 F11 40 12N 27 37 E
Sarila, India 93 G8 25 46N 79 41 E
Sarina, Australia 126 C4 21 22 S 149 13 E
Sariñena, Spain 40 D4 41 47N 0 10W
Sariri, Papua N. G. 132 E5 9 11 S 148 35 E
Sarita, U.S.A. 155 M6 27 13N 97 47W
Sariwŏn, N. Korea 75 E13 38 31N 125 46 E
Sariyar Barajı, Turkey 100 B4 40 2N 31 33 E
Sarıyer, Turkey 51 E13 41 10N 29 3 E
Sarju →, India 93 F9 27 21N 81 23 E
Sark, U.K. 21 H5 49 25N 2 22W
Sarkad, Hungary 52 D6 46 47N 21 23 E
Sarkari Tala, India 92 F4 27 39N 70 52 E
Şarkışla, Turkey 100 C7 39 21N 36 25 E
Şarköy, Turkey 51 F11 40 36N 27 6 E
Sarlat-la-Canéda, France 28 D5 44 54N 1 13 E
Sărmaşag, Romania 52 C7 47 21N 22 50 E
Sărmaşu, Romania 53 D9 46 45N 24 13 E
Sarmi, Indonesia 83 B5 1 49 S 138 44 E
Sarmiento, Argentina 176 C3 45 35 S 69 5W
Sarmizegetusa, Romania 52 E7 45 31N 22 47 E
Särna, Sweden 16 C7 61 41N 13 8 E

Sarnano, *Italy* **45 E10** 43 2N 13 18 E
Sarnen, *Switz.* **32 C6** 46 53N 8 13 E
Sarnia, *Canada* **140 D3** 42 58N 82 23W
Sarno, *Italy* **47 B7** 40 49N 14 37 E
Sarnthein = Sarentino, *Italy* **45 B8** 46 38N 11 21 E
Särö, *Sweden* **17 G5** 57 31N 11 57 E
Saroako, *Indonesia* **82 B2** 2 31 S 121 22 E
Sarolangun, *Indonesia* **84 C2** 2 19 S 102 42 E
Saronikós Kólpos, *Greece* **48 D5** 37 45N 23 45 E
Saronno, *Italy* **44 C6** 45 38N 9 2 E
Saros Körfezi, *Turkey* **51 F10** 40 30N 26 15 E
Sárospatak, *Hungary* **52 B6** 48 18N 21 33 E
Sarowbī, *Afghan.* **91 B3** 34 36N 69 44 E
Sarpsborg, *Norway* **18 E8** 59 16N 11 7 E
Sarracín, *Spain* **42 C7** 42 15N 3 45W
Sarralbe, *France* **27 D14** 49 0N 7 1 E
Sarrat, *Phil.* **80 B3** 18 9N 120 39 E
Sarre = Saar →, *Europe* **24 E6** 49 41N 6 32 E
Sarre, *Italy* **44 C4** 45 40N 7 15 E
Sarre-Union, *France* **27 D14** 48 57N 7 4 E
Sarrebourg, *France* **27 D14** 48 43N 7 3 E
Sarreguemines, *France* **27 C14** 49 5N 7 4 E
Sarria, *Spain* **42 C3** 42 49N 7 29W
Sarrión, *Spain* **40 E4** 40 9N 0 49W
Sarro, *Mali* **112 C3** 13 40N 5 15W
Sarstedt, *Germany* **30 C5** 52 14N 9 52 E
Sartène, *France* **29 G12** 41 38N 8 58 E
Sarthe □, *France* **26 D7** 48 10N 0 10 E
Sarthe →, *France* **26 E6** 47 33N 0 31W
Sartilly, *France* **26 D5** 48 45N 1 28W
Saruhanlı, *Turkey* **49 C9** 38 44N 27 36 E
Sărulești, *Romania* **53 F11** 44 25N 26 39 E
Saruna →, *Pakistan* **92 F2** 26 31N 67 7 E
Sarupeta, *India* **90 B3** 26 30N 91 5 E
Saruwaged Ra., *Papua N. G.* **132 D4** 6 13 S 146 45 E
Sárvár, *Hungary* **52 C1** 47 15N 16 56 E
Sarvar, *India* **92 F6** 26 4N 75 0 E
Sarvestān, *Iran* **97 D7** 29 20N 53 10 E
Särvfjället, *Sweden* **16 B7** 62 42N 13 30 E
Sárviz →, *Hungary* **52 D3** 46 24N 18 41 E
Sary-Tash, *Kyrgyzstan* **65 D6** 39 44N 73 15 E
Saryaghash, *Kazakhstan* **65 C4** 41 27N 69 9 E
Sarybulaq, *Kazakhstan* **65 B5** 43 23N 71 29 E
Sarych, Mys, *Ukraine* **59 K7** 44 25N 33 45 E
Sarykemer, *Kazakhstan* **65 B5** 43 0N 71 30 E
Sarykolskiy Khrebet, *Tajikistan* **65 D7** 38 30N 74 30 E
Saryözek, *Kazakhstan* **65 A8** 44 22N 77 59 E
Saryshagan, *Kazakhstan* **66 E8** 46 12N 73 38 E
Sarzana, *Italy* **44 D6** 44 7N 9 58 E
Sarzeau, *France* **26 E4** 47 31N 2 48W
Sasabeneh, *Ethiopia* **120 C2** 7 59N 44 43 E
Sasamungga, *Solomon Is.* **133 L9** 7 0 S 156 50 E
Sasan Gir, *India* **92 J4** 21 10N 70 36 E
Sasaram, *India* **93 G11** 24 57N 84 5 E
Sasari, Mt., *Solomon Is.* **133 M10** 8 10 S 159 30 E
Sasayama, *Japan* **73 B7** 35 4N 135 13 E
Sasebo, *Japan* **72 D1** 33 10N 129 43 E
Saser, *India* **93 B7** 34 50N 77 50 E
Saskatchewan □, *Canada* **143 C7** 54 40N 106 0W
Saskatchewan →, *Canada* **143 C8** 53 37N 100 40W
Saskatoon, *Canada* **143 C7** 52 10N 106 38W
Saskylakh, *Russia* **67 B12** 71 55N 114 1 E
Saslaya △, *Nic.* **164 D2** 13 45N 85 4W
Sasolburg, *S. Africa* **117 D4** 26 46 S 27 49 E
Sasovo, *Russia* **60 C5** 54 25N 41 55 E
Sassandra, *Ivory C.* **112 E3** 4 55N 6 8W
Sassandra →, *Ivory C.* **112 E3** 4 58N 6 5W
Sássari, *Italy* **46 B1** 40 43N 8 34 E
Sassnitz, *Germany* **30 A9** 54 29N 13 39 E
Sasso Marconi, *Italy* **45 D8** 44 24N 11 15 E
Sassocorvaro, *Italy* **45 E9** 43 47N 12 30 E
Sassoferrato, *Italy* **45 E9** 43 26N 12 51 E
Sasstown, *Liberia* **112 E3** 4 45N 8 27W
Sassuolo, *Italy* **44 D7** 44 33N 10 47 E
Sástago, *Spain* **40 D4** 41 19N 0 21W
Sastöbe, *Kazakhstan* **65 B4** 42 33N 70 0 E
Sasvad, *India* **94 E2** 18 20N 74 2 E
Sasyk, Ozero, *Ukraine* **53 E14** 45 45N 29 20 E
Sata-Misaki, *Japan* **72 F2** 31 0N 130 40 E
Satadougou, *Mali* **112 C2** 12 25N 11 25W
Satakunda = Satakunta, *Finland* **15 F20** 61 45N 23 0 E
Satakunta, *Finland* **15 F20** 61 45N 23 0 E
Satama-Soukoura, *Ivory C.* **112 D4** 7 55N 4 27W
Satara, *India* **94 F1** 17 44N 73 58 E
Satara, *S. Africa* **117 C5** 24 29 S 31 47 E
Satbarwa, *India* **93 H11** 23 55N 84 16 E
Satellite Beach, *U.S.A.* **153 G9** 28 10N 80 36W
Såtenäs, *Sweden* **17 F6** 58 27N 12 41 E
Säter, *Sweden* **16 D9** 60 21N 15 45 E
Satevó, *Mexico* **162 B3** 27 57N 106 7W
Satilla →, *U.S.A.* **152 E8** 30 59N 81 29W
Satipo, *Peru* **172 C3** 11 15 S 74 25W
Satka, *Russia* **64 D7** 55 3N 59 1 E
Satkania, *Bangla.* **90 D4** 22 4N 92 3 E
Satkhira, *Bangla.* **90 D2** 22 43N 89 8 E
Satmala Hills, *Andhra Pradesh, India* **94 E4** 19 45N 78 45 E
Satmala Hills, *Maharashtra, India* **94 D2** 20 15N 74 40 E
Satna, *India* **93 G9** 24 35N 80 50 E
Šator, *Bos.-H.* **45 D13** 44 11N 16 37 E
Sátoraljaújhely, *Hungary* **52 B6** 48 25N 21 41 E
Satpura △, *India* **92 H8** 22 40N 78 15 E
Satpura Ra., *India* **94 D3** 21 25N 76 10 E
Satrup, *Germany* **30 A5** 54 41N 9 36 E
Satsuma-Hantō, *Japan* **72 F2** 31 25N 130 25 E
Satsuna-Shotō, *Japan* **71 K5** 30 0N 130 0 E
Sattahip, *Thailand* **86 F3** 12 41N 100 54 E
Sattenapalle, *India* **95 F5** 16 25N 80 6 E
Satu Mare, *Romania* **52 C7** 47 46N 22 55 E
Satu Mare □, *Romania* **52 C8** 47 45N 23 0 E
Satui, *Indonesia* **85 C5** 3 50 S 115 27 E
Satun, *Thailand* **87 J3** 6 43N 100 2 E
Satupa'itea, *Samoa* **133 W23** 13 45 S 172 18W
Saturnina →, *Brazil* **173 C6** 12 15 S 58 10W
Sauce = Juan L. Lacaze, *Uruguay* **174 C4** 34 26 S 57 25W
Sauce, *Argentina* **174 C4** 30 5 S 58 46W
Sauceda, *Mexico* **162 B4** 25 55N 101 18W
Saucillo, *Mexico* **162 B3** 28 1N 105 17W
Sauda, *Norway* **18 E3** 59 40N 6 20 E
Saūdakent, *Kazakhstan* **65 B4** 43 48N 69 58 E
Saudasjøen, *Norway* **18 E3** 59 38N 6 17 E
Saúde, *Brazil* **170 D3** 10 56 S 40 24W
Sauðarkrókur, *Iceland* **11 B7** 65 45N 19 40W
Saudi Arabia ■, *Asia* **96 B3** 26 0N 44 0 E
Sauerland, *Germany* **36 C4** 51 12N 7 59 E
Saugatuck, *U.S.A.* **157 B10** 42 40N 86 12W
Saugeen →, *Canada* **150 B3** 44 30N 81 22W
Saugerties, *U.S.A.* **151 D11** 42 5N 73 57W
Saugues, *France* **28 D7** 44 58N 3 32 E
Saugus, *U.S.A.* **161 L8** 34 25N 118 32W
Saujbulagh = Mahābād, *Iran* **101 D11** 36 50N 45 45 E
Saujon, *France* **28 C3** 45 41N 0 55W
Sauk Centre, *U.S.A.* **154 C7** 45 44N 94 57W
Sauk City, *U.S.A.* **156 A7** 43 17N 89 43W
Sauk Rapids, *U.S.A.* **154 C7** 45 35N 94 10W
Saül, *Fr. Guiana* **169 C7** 3 37N 53 12W
Sauland, *Norway* **18 E5** 59 37N 8 56 E
Saulgau, *Germany* **31 G5** 48 1N 9 29 E
Saulieu, *France* **27 E11** 47 17N 4 14 E
Sault, *France* **29 D9** 44 6N 5 24 E
Sault Ste. Marie, *Canada* **140 C3** 46 30N 84 20W
Sault Ste. Marie, *U.S.A.* **139 D11** 46 30N 84 21W
Saumlaki, *Indonesia* **83 C4** 7 55 S 131 20 E
Saumur, *France* **26 E6** 47 15N 0 5W
Saundatti, *India* **95 G2** 15 47N 75 7 E
Saunders, C., *N.Z.* **131 F5** 45 53 S 170 45 E
Saunders I., *Antarctica* **7 B1** 57 48 S 26 28W
Saunders Point, *Australia* **125 E4** 27 52 S 125 38 E
Saunemin, *U.S.A.* **157 D8** 40 54N 88 24W
Saupite, *Angola* **115 E3** 13 54 S 17 43 E
Saurbær, *Borgarfjarðarsýsla, Iceland* **11 C5** 64 24N 21 35W
Saurbær, *Eyjafjarðarsýsla, Iceland* **11 B8** 65 27N 18 13W
Sauri, *Nigeria* **113 C6** 11 42N 6 44 E
Saurimo, *Angola* **115 D4** 9 40 S 20 12 E
Sausalito, *U.S.A.* **160 H4** 37 51N 122 29W
Sausapor, *Indonesia* **83 B4** 0 31 S 132 4 E
Sautatá, *Colombia* **168 B2** 7 50N 77 4W
Sauveterre-de-Béarn, *France* **28 E3** 43 24N 0 57W
Sauzé-Vaussais, *France* **28 B4** 46 8N 0 8 E
Savá, *Honduras* **164 C2** 15 32N 86 15W
Sava, *Italy* **47 B10** 40 24N 17 33 E
Sava →, *Serbia & M.* **52 F5** 44 50N 20 26 E
Savage, *U.S.A.* **154 B2** 47 27N 104 21W
Savage I. = Niue, *Cook Is.* **135 J11** 19 2 S 169 54W
Savage River, *Australia* **127 G4** 41 31 S 145 14 E
Savai'i, *Samoa* **133 W23** 13 28 S 172 24W
Savalou, *Benin* **113 D5** 7 57N 1 58 E
Savane, *Mozam.* **119 F4** 19 37 S 35 8 E
Savanna, *U.S.A.* **156 B6** 42 5N 90 8W
Savanna-la-Mar, *Jamaica* **164 a** 18 10N 78 10W
Savannah, *Ga., U.S.A.* **152 C8** 32 5N 81 6W
Savannah, *Mo., U.S.A.* **156 E2** 39 56N 94 50W
Savannah, *Tenn., U.S.A.* **149 H1** 35 14N 88 15W
Savannah →, *U.S.A.* **152 C9** 32 2N 80 53W
Savannah Beach = Tybee Island , *U.S.A.* **152 C9** 32 1N 80 51W
Savannakhet, *Laos* **86 D5** 16 30N 104 49 E
Savant L., *Canada* **140 B1** 50 16N 90 44W
Savant Lake, *Canada* **140 B1** 50 14N 90 40W
Savantvadi, *India* **95 G1** 15 55N 73 54 E
Savanur, *India* **95 G2** 14 59N 75 21 E
Săvârşin, *Romania* **52 D7** 46 1N 22 14 E
Savaştepe, *Turkey* **49 B9** 39 22N 27 42 E
Savda, *India* **94 D2** 21 9N 75 56 E
Savé, *Benin* **113 D5** 8 2N 2 29 E
Save →, *France* **28 E5** 43 47N 1 17 E
Save →, *Mozam.* **117 C5** 21 16 S 34 0 E
Sāveh, *Iran* **97 C6** 35 2N 50 20 E
Savelugu, *Ghana* **113 D4** 9 38N 0 54W
Savenay, *France* **26 E5** 47 20N 1 55W
Săveni, *Romania* **53 C11** 47 57N 26 52 E
Saverdun, *France* **28 E5** 43 14N 1 34 E
Saverne, *France* **27 D14** 48 43N 7 20 E
Savièse, *Switz.* **32 D4** 46 17N 7 22 E
Savigliano, *Italy* **44 D4** 44 38N 7 40 E
Savigny-sur-Braye, *France* **26 E7** 47 53N 0 49 E
Sávio →, *Italy* **45 D9** 44 19N 12 20 E
Šavnik, *Serbia & M.* **50 D3** 42 59N 19 10 E
Savo, *Finland* **14 E22** 62 45N 27 30 E
Savo, *Solomon Is.* **133 M10** 9 8 S 159 48 E
Savognin, *Switz.* **33 C9** 46 36N 9 37 E
Savoie □, *France* **29 C10** 45 26N 6 25 E
Savolax = Savo, *Finland* **14 E22** 62 45N 27 30 E
Savona, *Italy* **44 D5** 44 17N 8 30 E
Savona, *U.S.A.* **150 D7** 42 17N 77 13W
Savonlinna, *Finland* **58 B5** 61 52N 28 53 E
Savoonga, *U.S.A.* **144 E5** 63 42N 170 29W
Savoy = Savoie □, *France* **29 C10** 45 26N 6 25 E
Şavşat, *Turkey* **101 B10** 41 15N 42 20 E
Sävsjö, *Sweden* **17 G8** 57 20N 14 40 E
Savur, *Turkey* **96 B4** 37 34N 40 53 E
Savusavu, *Fiji* **133 A2** 16 34 S 179 15 E
Savusavu B., *Fiji* **133 A2** 16 45 S 179 15 E
Sawahlunto, *Indonesia* **84 C2** 0 40 S 100 52 E
Sawai, *Indonesia* **83 B3** 3 0 S 129 5 E
Sawai Madhopur, *India* **92 G7** 26 0N 76 25 E
Sawaleke, *Fiji* **133 A2** 17 59 S 179 18 E
Sawang Daen Din, *Thailand* **86 D4** 17 28N 103 28 E
Sawankhalok, *Thailand* **86 D2** 17 19N 99 50 E
Sawara, *Japan* **73 B12** 35 55N 140 30 E
Sawatch Range, *U.S.A.* **159 G10** 38 30N 106 30W
Sawdā', Jabal as, *Libya* **108 C3** 28 51N 15 12 E
Sawel Mt., *U.K.* **23 B4** 54 50N 7 2W
Sawfajjin □, *Libya* **108 B3** 31 0N 15 0 E
Sawfajjin, W. →, *Libya* **108 B2** 31 41N 14 44 E
Sawi, *Thailand* **87 G2** 10 14N 99 5 E
Sawla, *Ghana* **112 D4** 9 17N 2 25W
Sawmills, *Zimbabwe* **119 F2** 19 30 S 28 2 E
Şawqirah, *Oman* **99 C7** 18 7N 56 32 E
Şawqirah, Ghubbat, *Oman* **99 C7** 18 35N 57 0 E
Sawtell, *Australia* **129 A10** 30 19 S 153 6 E
Sawtooth ⌓, *U.S.A.* **158 D6** 44 0N 114 50W
Sawtooth Range, *U.S.A.* **158 E6** 44 3N 114 58W
Sawu, *Indonesia* **82 C2** 10 35 S 121 50 E
Sawu Sea, *Indonesia* **82 C2** 9 30 S 121 50 E
Saxby →, *Australia* **126 B3** 18 25 S 140 53 E
Saxmundham, *U.K.* **21 E9** 52 13N 1 30 E
Saxon, *Switz.* **32 D4** 46 9N 7 11 E
Saxony = Sachsen □, *Germany* **30 E9** 50 55N 13 10 E
Saxony, Lower = Niedersachsen □, *Germany* **30 C4** 52 50N 9 0 E
Saxton, *U.S.A.* **150 F6** 40 13N 78 15W
Say, *Mali* **112 C4** 13 50N 4 57W
Say, *Niger* **113 C5** 13 8N 2 22 E
Saya, *Nigeria* **113 D5** 9 30N 3 18 E
Sayabec, *Canada* **141 C6** 48 35N 67 41W
Sayaboury, *Laos* **86 C3** 19 15N 101 45 E
Sayán, *Peru* **172 C2** 11 8 S 77 12W
Sayan, Vostochnyy, *Russia* **67 D10** 54 0N 96 0 E
Sayan, Zapadnyy, *Russia* **67 D10** 52 30N 94 0 E
Saydā, *Lebanon* **103 B4** 33 35N 35 25 E
Sayghān, *Afghan.* **91 B2** 35 10N 67 55 E
Sayhandulaan = Oldziyt, *Mongolia* **74 B5** 44 40N 109 1 E
Sayḩūt, *Yemen* **99 D5** 15 12N 51 10 E
Sayiádha, *Greece* **38 B10** 39 38N 20 12 E
Saykhin, *Kazakhstan* **61 F8** 48 50N 46 47 E
Saylac = Zeila, *Somali Rep.* **120 B2** 11 21N 43 30 E
Saylorville L., *U.S.A.* **156 C3** 41 48N 93 46W
Saynshand, *Mongolia* **69 B6** 44 55N 110 11 E
Sayō, *Japan* **72 C6** 34 59N 134 22 E
Sayre, *Okla., U.S.A.* **155 H5** 35 18N 99 38W
Sayre, *Pa., U.S.A.* **151 E8** 41 59N 76 32W
Sayreville, *U.S.A.* **151 F10** 40 28N 74 22W
Sayula, *Mexico* **162 D4** 19 50N 103 40W
Sayward, *Canada* **142 C3** 50 21N 125 55W
Saywūn, *Yemen* **99 D5** 15 56N 48 47 E
Saza, *Japan* **72 D1** 33 14N 129 39 E
Sazanit, *Albania* **50 F3** 40 30N 19 20 E
Sázava →, *Czech Rep.* **34 B7** 49 53N 14 24 E
Sazin, *Pakistan* **93 B5** 35 35N 73 30 E
Sazlika →, *Bulgaria* **51 E9** 41 59N 25 50 E
Sbeïtla, *Tunisia* **108 A1** 35 12N 9 7 E
Scaër, *France* **26 D3** 48 2N 3 42W
Scafell Pike, *U.K.* **20 C4** 54 27N 3 14W
Scalea, *Italy* **47 C8** 39 49N 15 47 E
Scalloway, *U.K.* **22 A7** 60 9N 1 17W
Scalpay, *U.K.* **22 D3** 57 18N 6 0W
Scammon Bay, *U.S.A.* **144 F6** 61 51N 165 35W
Scandia, *Canada* **142 C6** 50 20N 112 2W
Scandiano, *Italy* **44 D7** 44 36N 10 43 E
Scandicci, *Italy* **45 E8** 43 45N 11 11 E
Scandinavia, *Europe* **14 E16** 64 0N 12 0 E
Scansano, *Italy* **45 F8** 42 41N 11 20 E
Scapa Flow, *U.K.* **22 C5** 58 53N 3 3W
Scappoose, *U.S.A.* **160 E4** 45 45N 122 53W
Scarámia, Capo, *Italy* **47 F7** 36 47N 14 29 E
Scarba, *U.K.* **22 E3** 56 11N 5 43W
Scarborough, *Trin. & Tob.* **169 E10** 11 11N 60 42W
Scarborough, *U.K.* **20 C7** 54 17N 0 24W
Scarborough Shoal, *S. China Sea* **80 D1** 15 0N 117 50 E
Scargill, *N.Z.* **131 C7** 42 56 S 172 58 E
Scariff I., *Ireland* **23 E1** 51 44N 10 15W
Scarp, *U.K.* **22 C1** 58 1N 7 8W
Scarpanto = Kárpathos, *Greece* **49 F9** 35 37N 27 10 E
Scarpe-Escaut ⌓, *France* **27 B10** 50 26N 3 23 E
Scarsdale, *Australia* **128 D5** 37 41 S 143 39 E
Scebeli, Wabi →, *Somali Rep.* **120 D2** 2 0N 44 0 E
Šćedro, *Croatia* **45 E13** 43 6N 16 43 E
Schaal See, *Germany* **30 B6** 53 36N 10 55 E
Schaalsee ⌓, *Germany* **30 B6** 53 40N 10 59 E
Schaan, *Liech.* **33 B9** 47 10N 9 31 E
Schaffhausen, *Switz.* **33 A7** 47 42N 8 39 E
Schaffhausen □, *Switz.* **33 A7** 47 42N 8 36 E
Schagen, *Neths.* **24 B4** 52 49N 4 48 E
Schaghticoke, *U.S.A.* **151 D11** 42 54N 73 35W
Schangnau, *Switz.* **32 C5** 46 50N 7 47 E
Schänis, *Switz.* **33 B8** 47 10N 9 3 E
Schärding, *Austria* **34 C6** 48 27N 13 27 E
Scharfenwiese = Ostrołęka, *Poland* **55 E8** 53 4N 21 32 E
Scharhörn, *Germany* **30 B4** 53 57N 8 24 E
Schässburg = Sighişoara, *Romania* **53 D9** 46 12N 24 50 E
Scheessel, *Germany* **30 B5** 53 10N 9 29 E
Schefferville, *Canada* **141 B6** 54 48N 66 50W
Scheibbs, *Austria* **34 C8** 48 1N 15 9 E
Scheidt = Schelde →, *Belgium* **24 C4** 51 15N 4 16 E
Schelde →, *Belgium* **24 C4** 51 15N 4 16 E
Schell City, *U.S.A.* **156 F2** 38 1N 94 7W
Schell Creek Ra., *U.S.A.* **158 G6** 39 15N 114 30W
Schellsburg, *U.S.A.* **150 F6** 40 3N 78 39W
Schemnitz = Banská Štiavnica, *Slovak Rep.* **35 C11** 48 25N 18 55 E
Schenectady, *U.S.A.* **151 D11** 42 49N 73 57W
Schenevus, *U.S.A.* **151 D10** 42 33N 74 50W
Scherfede, *Germany* **30 D5** 51 32N 9 2 E
Schesaplana, *Switz.* **33 B9** 47 5N 9 43 E
Schesslitz, *Germany* **31 F7** 49 58N 11 1 E
Schiedam, *Neths.* **24 C4** 51 55N 4 25 E
Schieratz = Sieradz, *Poland* **55 G5** 51 37N 18 41 E
Schiermonnikoog, *Neths.* **24 A6** 53 30N 6 15 E
Schiers, *Switz.* **33 C9** 46 58N 9 41 E
Schiltigheim, *France* **27 D14** 48 35N 7 45 E
Schio, *Italy* **45 C8** 45 43N 11 21 E
Schiphol, Amsterdam ✈ (AMS), *Neths.* **24 B4** 52 18N 4 45 E
Schippenbeil = Sępopol, *Poland* **54 D8** 54 16N 21 2 E
Schivelbein = Świdwin, *Poland* **54 E2** 53 47N 15 49 E
Schladming, *Austria* **34 D6** 47 23N 13 41 E
Schlanders = Silandro, *Italy* **44 B7** 46 38N 10 46 E
Schlawa = Sława, *Poland* **55 G3** 51 52N 16 2 E
Schlei →, *Germany* **30 A5** 54 40N 10 0 E
Schleiden, *Germany* **30 E2** 50 31N 6 28 E
Schleinitz Ra., *Papua N. G.* **132 B6** 3 0 S 151 30 E
Schleiz, *Germany* **30 E7** 50 35N 11 49 E
Schlesiersee = Sława, *Poland* **55 G3** 51 52N 16 2 E
Schleswig, *Germany* **30 A5** 54 31N 9 34 E
Schleswig-Holstein □, *Germany* **30 A5** 54 30N 9 30 E
Schlettstadt = Sélestat, *France* **27 D14** 48 16N 7 26 E
Schlichtingsheim = Szlichtyngowa, *Poland* **55 G3** 51 42N 16 15 E
Schlieren, *Switz.* **33 B6** 47 26N 8 27 E
Schlochau = Człuchów, *Poland* **54 E4** 53 41N 17 22 E
Schloppe = Człopa, *Poland* **55 E3** 53 6N 16 6 E
Schlüchtern, *Germany* **31 E5** 50 20N 9 32 E
Schmalkalden, *Germany* **30 E6** 50 44N 10 26 E
Schmölln, *Germany* **30 E8** 50 54N 12 19 E
Schneeberg, *Austria* **34 D8** 47 47N 15 48 E
Schneeberg, *Germany* **30 E8** 50 35N 12 38 E
Schneidemühl = Piła, *Poland* **55 E3** 53 10N 16 48 E
Schneider, *U.S.A.* **157 C9** 41 13N 87 28W
Schneverdingen, *Germany* **30 B5** 53 7N 9 48 E
Schœlcher, *Martinique* **164 c** 14 36N 61 7W
Schoharie, *U.S.A.* **151 D10** 42 40N 74 19W
Schoharie Cr. →, *U.S.A.* **151 D10** 42 57N 74 18W
Scholls, *U.S.A.* **160 E4** 45 24N 122 56W
Schönau = Swierzawa, *Poland* **55 G2** 51 1N 15 54 E
Schönberg, *Mecklenburg-Vorpommern, Germany* **30 B6** 53 52N 10 56 E
Schönberg, *Schleswig-Holstein, Germany* **30 A6** 54 23N 10 21 E
Schönbuch ⌓, *Germany* **31 G5** 48 35N 9 2 E
Schönebeck, *Germany* **30 C7** 52 2N 11 44 E
Schönenwerd, *Switz.* **32 B6** 47 23N 8 0 E
Schongau, *Germany* **31 H6** 47 47N 10 53 E
Schöningen, *Germany* **30 C6** 52 8N 10 56 E
Schönlanke = Trzcianka, *Poland* **55 E3** 53 3N 16 25 E
Schönstein = Šoštanj, *Slovenia* **45 B12** 46 23N 15 4 E
Schoolcraft, *U.S.A.* **157 B11** 42 7N 85 38W
Schopfheim, *Germany* **31 H3** 47 38N 7 50 E
Schorndorf, *Germany* **31 G5** 48 47N 9 32 E
Schortens, *Germany* **30 B3** 53 31N 7 56 E
Schouten I., *Australia* **127 G4** 42 20 S 148 20 E
Schouten Is. = Supiori, *Indonesia* **83 B5** 1 0 S 136 0 E
Schouten Is., *Papua N. G.* **132 B3** 3 30 S 144 30 E
Schouwen, *Neths.* **24 C3** 51 43N 3 45 E
Schramberg, *Germany* **31 G4** 48 13N 8 22 E
Schrankogel, *Austria* **34 D4** 47 3N 11 7 E
Schreckhorn, *Switz.* **32 C6** 46 36N 8 7 E
Schreiber, *Canada* **140 C2** 48 45N 87 20W
Schrems, *Austria* **34 C8** 48 47N 15 4 E
Schrobenhausen, *Germany* **31 G7** 48 34N 11 16 E
Schröcken, *Austria* **33 B10** 47 17N 10 5 E
Schroffenstein, *Namibia* **116 D2** 27 11 S 18 42 E
Schroon Lake, *U.S.A.* **151 C11** 43 50N 73 46W
Schröttersberg = Płock, *Poland* **55 F6** 52 32N 19 40 E
Schruns, *Austria* **34 D2** 47 5N 9 56 E
Schuchye = Shchuchinsk, *Kazakhstan* **66 D8** 52 56N 70 12 E
Schuler, *Canada* **143 C6** 50 20N 110 6W
Schuls, *Switz.* **33 C10** 46 48N 10 18 E
Schumacher, *Canada* **140 C3** 48 30N 81 16W
Schüpfen, *Switz.* **32 B4** 47 2N 7 24 E
Schüpfheim, *Switz.* **32 C6** 46 57N 8 2 E
Schurz, *U.S.A.* **158 G4** 38 57N 118 49W
Schuyler, *U.S.A.* **154 E6** 41 27N 97 4W
Schuylerville, *U.S.A.* **151 C11** 43 6N 73 35W
Schuylkill →, *U.S.A.* **151 G9** 39 53N 75 12W
Schuylkill Haven, *U.S.A.* **151 F8** 40 37N 76 11W
Schwabach, *Germany* **31 F7** 49 19N 11 2 E
Schwaben □, *Germany* **31 G6** 48 15N 10 30 E
Schwäbisch-Fränkischer Wald ⌓, *Germany* **31 G5** 49 0N 9 30 E
Schwäbisch Gmünd, *Germany* **31 G5** 48 48N 9 47 E
Schwäbisch Hall, *Germany* **31 F5** 49 6N 9 44 E
Schwäbische Alb, *Germany* **31 G5** 48 20N 9 30 E
Schwabmünchen, *Germany* **31 G6** 48 10N 10 46 E
Schwalmstadt, *Germany* **30 E5** 50 55N 9 10 E
Schwanden, *Switz.* **33 C8** 46 58N 9 5 E
Schwandorf, *Germany* **31 F8** 49 20N 12 7 E
Schwaner, Pegunungan, *Indonesia* **85 C4** 1 0 S 112 30 E
Schwanewede, *Germany* **30 B4** 53 14N 8 35 E
Schwarmstedt, *Germany* **30 C5** 52 39N 9 38 E
Schwarze Elster →, *Germany* **30 D8** 51 48N 12 50 E
Schwarzenberg, *Germany* **30 E8** 50 32N 12 47 E
Schwarzenburg, *Switz.* **32 C4** 46 49N 7 20 E
Schwarzrand, *Namibia* **116 D2** 25 37 S 16 50 E
Schwarzwald, *Germany* **31 G4** 48 30N 8 20 E
Schwatka Mts., *U.S.A.* **144 C8** 67 20N 156 30W
Schwaz, *Austria* **34 D4** 47 20N 11 44 E
Schwechat, *Austria* **35 C9** 48 8N 16 28 E
Schwechat, Wien ✈ (VIA), *Austria* **35 C9** 48 7N 16 35 E
Schwedt, *Germany* **30 B10** 53 3N 14 16 E
Schweidnitz = Świdnica, *Poland* **55 H3** 50 50N 16 30 E
Schweinfurt, *Germany* **31 E6** 50 3N 10 14 E
Schweiz = Svizzer △, *Switz.* **33 C10** 46 40N 10 10 E
Schweiz = Switzerland ■, *Europe* **32 D6** 46 30N 8 0 E
Schweizer Mittelland, *Switz.* **32 C4** 47 0N 7 15 E
Schweizer-Reneke, *S. Africa* **116 D4** 27 11 S 25 18 E
Schwenningen = Villingen-Schwenningen, *Germany* **31 G4** 48 3N 8 26 E
Schwerin = Skwierzyna, *Poland* **55 F2** 52 33N 15 30 E
Schwerin, *Germany* **30 B7** 53 36N 11 22 E
Schweriner See, *Germany* **30 B7** 53 43N 11 28 E
Schwetzingen, *Germany* **31 F4** 49 23N 8 35 E
Schwiebus = Świebodzin, *Poland* **55 F2** 52 15N 15 31 E
Schwyz, *Switz.* **33 B7** 47 2N 8 39 E
Schwyz □, *Switz.* **33 B7** 47 2N 8 39 E
Sciacca, *Italy* **46 E6** 37 31N 13 3 E
Sciao, *Somali Rep.* **120 D3** 3 26N 45 21 E
Scicli, *Italy* **47 F7** 36 47N 14 42 E
Sciliar ⌓, *Italy* **45 B8** 46 28N 11 35 E
Scilla, *Italy* **47 D8** 38 15N 15 43 E
Scilly, Isles of, *U.K.* **21 H1** 49 56N 6 22W
Ścinawa, *Poland* **55 G3** 51 25N 16 26 E
Scione, *Greece* **50 G7** 39 57N 23 36 E
Scioto →, *U.S.A.* **157 D13** 38 44N 83 1W
Scituate, *U.S.A.* **151 D14** 42 12N 70 44W
Scobey, *U.S.A.* **154 A2** 48 47N 105 25W
Scone, *Australia* **129 B9** 32 5 S 150 52 E
Scone, *U.K.* **22 E5** 56 25N 3 24W
Scordia, *Italy* **47 E7** 37 18N 14 51 E
Scoresby Sund, *Greenland* **10 C8** 70 28N 21 46W
Scoresbysund = Ittoqqortoormiit, *Greenland* **10 C8** 70 20N 23 0W
Scorniceşti, *Romania* **53 F9** 44 34N 24 33 E
Scotia, *Calif., U.S.A.* **158 F1** 40 29N 124 6W
Scotia, *N.Y., U.S.A.* **151 D11** 42 50N 73 58W
Scotia Sea, *Antarctica* **7 B18** 56 5 S 56 0W
Scotland, *Canada* **150 C4** 43 1N 80 22W
Scotland □, *U.K.* **22 E5** 57 0N 4 0W
Scott, *Antarctica* **7 D11** 77 0 S 165 0 E
Scott, C., *Australia* **124 B4** 13 30 S 129 49 E
Scott City, *U.S.A.* **154 F4** 38 29N 100 54W
Scott Glacier, *Antarctica* **7 C8** 66 15 S 100 5 E
Scott I., *Antarctica* **7 C11** 67 0 S 179 0 E
Scott Is., *Canada* **142 C3** 50 48N 128 40W
Scott L., *Canada* **143 B7** 59 55N 106 18W
Scott Reef, *Australia* **124 B3** 14 0 S 121 50 E
Scottburgh, *S. Africa* **117 E5** 30 15 S 30 47 E
Scottdale, *U.S.A.* **150 F5** 40 6N 79 35W
Scottish Borders □, *U.K.* **22 F6** 55 35N 2 50W
Scotts Head, *Australia* **129 A10** 30 45 S 153 0 E
Scottsbluff, *U.S.A.* **154 E3** 41 52N 103 40W
Scottsboro, *U.S.A.* **149 H3** 34 40N 86 2W
Scottsburg, *U.S.A.* **157 F11** 38 41N 85 47W
Scottsdale, *Australia* **127 G4** 41 9 S 147 31 E
Scottsdale, *U.S.A.* **159 K7** 33 29N 111 56W
Scottsville, *Ky., U.S.A.* **149 G2** 36 45N 86 11W
Scottsville, *N.Y., U.S.A.* **150 C7** 43 2N 77 47W
Scottville, *U.S.A.* **148 D2** 43 58N 86 17W
Scranton, *U.S.A.* **151 E9** 41 25N 75 40W
Screven, *U.S.A.* **152 D7** 31 29N 82 1W
Scugog, L., *Canada* **150 B6** 44 10N 78 55W
Sculeni, *Moldova* **53 C12** 47 20N 27 37 E
Scunthorpe, *U.K.* **20 D7** 53 36N 0 39W
Scuol Schuls, *Switz.* **33 C10** 46 48N 10 17 E
Scusciuban, *Somali Rep.* **120 B4** 10 18N 50 12 E
Scutari = Shkodër, *Albania* **50 D3** 42 4N 19 32 E
Scutari = Üsküdar, *Turkey* **51 F13** 41 0N 29 5 E
Sea Lake, *Australia* **128 C5** 35 28 S 142 55 E
Seabra = Tarauacá, *Brazil* **172 B3** 8 6 S 70 48W
Seabra, *Brazil* **171 D3** 12 25 S 41 46W
Seabrook, L., *Australia* **125 F2** 30 55 S 119 40 E
Seaford, *U.K.* **21 G8** 50 47N 0 7 E
Seaford, *U.S.A.* **148 F8** 38 39N 75 37W
Seaforth, *Australia* **126 J6** 20 55 S 148 57 E
Seaforth, *Canada* **150 C3** 43 35N 81 25W
Seaforth, L., *U.K.* **22 D2** 57 52N 6 36W
Seagraves, *U.S.A.* **155 J3** 32 57N 102 34W
Seaham, *U.K.* **20 C6** 54 50N 1 20W
Seal →, *Canada* **143 B10** 59 4N 94 48W
Seal L., *Canada* **141 B7** 54 20N 61 30W
Seale, *U.S.A.* **152 C4** 32 18N 85 10W
Sealy, *U.S.A.* **155 L6** 29 47N 96 9W
Seaman, *U.S.A.* **157 F13** 38 57N 83 34W
Searchlight, *U.S.A.* **161 K12** 35 28N 114 55W
Searcy, *U.S.A.* **155 H9** 35 15N 91 44W
Searles L., *U.S.A.* **161 K9** 35 44N 117 21W
Seascale, *U.K.* **20 C4** 54 24N 3 29W
Seaside, *Calif., U.S.A.* **160 J5** 36 37N 121 50W
Seaside, *Oreg., U.S.A.* **160 E3** 46 0N 123 56W
Seaspray, *Australia* **129 E7** 38 25 S 147 15 E
Seattle, *U.S.A.* **160 C4** 47 36N 122 20W
Seattle-Tacoma International ✈ (SEA), *U.S.A.* **160 C4** 47 27N 122 18W
Seaview Ra., *Australia* **126 B4** 18 40 S 145 45 E
Seaward Kaikoura Ra., *N.Z.* **131 C8** 42 10 S 173 44 E
Seba, *Indonesia* **82 D2** 10 29 S 121 50 E
Sebago L., *U.S.A.* **151 C14** 43 52N 70 34W
Sebago Lake, *U.S.A.* **151 C14** 43 51N 70 34W
Sebangka, *Indonesia* **84 B2** 0 7N 104 36 E
Sebastian, *U.S.A.* **153 H9** 27 49N 80 28W
Sebastián Vizcaíno, B., *Mexico* **162 B2** 28 0N 114 30W
Sebastopol = Sevastopol, *Ukraine* **59 K7** 44 35N 33 30 E
Sebastopol, *U.S.A.* **160 G4** 38 24N 122 49W
Sebba, *Burkina Faso* **113 C5** 13 35N 0 32 E
Sebderat, *Eritrea* **107 D4** 15 26N 36 42 E
Sebdou, *Algeria* **111 B4** 34 38N 1 19W
Sébé →, *Gabon* **114 C2** 1 2 S 13 6 E
Sébékoro, *Mali* **112 C3** 12 58N 9 0W
Seben, *Turkey* **100 B4** 40 24N 31 34 E
Sebeş, *Romania* **53 E8** 45 58N 23 34 E
Sebeşului, Munţii, *Romania* **53 E8** 45 36N 23 40 E
Sebewaing, *U.S.A.* **148 D4** 43 44N 83 27W
Sebezh, *Russia* **58 D5** 56 14N 28 22 E
Sebha = Sabhah, *Libya* **108 C2** 27 9N 14 29 E
Sébi, *Mali* **112 B4** 15 50N 4 12W
Şebinkarahisar, *Turkey* **101 B8** 40 22N 38 28 E
Sebiş, *Romania* **52 D7** 46 23N 22 13 E
Seblat, *Indonesia* **84 C2** 3 14 S 101 38 E
Sebnitz, *Germany* **30 E10** 50 58N 14 15 E
Sebou, Oued →, *Morocco* **110 B3** 34 16N 6 40W
Sebring, *Fla., U.S.A.* **153 H8** 27 30N 81 27W
Sebring, *Ohio, U.S.A.* **150 F3** 40 55N 81 2W
Sebringville, *Canada* **150 C3** 43 24N 81 4W
Sebta = Ceuta, *N. Afr.* **110 A3** 35 52N 5 18W
Sebuku, *Indonesia* **85 C5** 3 30 S 116 25 E
Sebuku, Teluk, *Malaysia* **85 B5** 4 0N 118 10 E
Sečanj, *Serbia & M.* **52 E5** 45 25N 20 47 E
Secchia →, *Italy* **44 C8** 45 4N 11 0 E
Sechelt, *Canada* **142 D4** 49 25N 123 42W
Sechura, *Peru* **172 B1** 5 39 S 80 50W
Sechura, Desierto de, *Peru* **172 B1** 6 0 S 80 30W
Seclin, *France* **27 B10** 50 33N 3 2 E
Secondigny, *France* **26 F6** 46 37N 0 26W
Sečovce, *Slovak Rep.* **35 C14** 48 42N 21 40 E
Secretary I., *N.Z.* **131 F1** 45 15 S 166 56 E
Secunderabad, *India* **94 F4** 17 28N 78 30 E
Sécure →, *Bolivia* **173 D5** 15 10 S 64 52W
Security, *U.S.A.* **154 F2** 38 45N 104 45W
Sedalia, *U.S.A.* **156 F3** 38 42N 93 14W
Sedam, *India* **94 E3** 17 11N 77 17 E
Sedan, *Australia* **128 C3** 34 34 S 139 19 E
Sedan, *France* **27 C11** 49 43N 4 57 E
Sedan, *U.S.A.* **155 G6** 37 8N 96 11W
Sedano, *Spain* **42 C7** 42 43N 3 49W
Sedaw, *Burma* **90 D6** 22 19N 96 19 E
Sedbergh, *U.K.* **20 C5** 54 20N 2 31W
Seddon, *N.Z.* **131 B9** 41 40 S 174 7 E
Seddonville, *N.Z.* **131 B7** 41 33 S 172 1 E
Sedé Boqér, *Israel* **103 E3** 30 52N 34 47 E
Sedeh, *Fārs, Iran* **97 D7** 30 45N 52 11 E
Sedeh, *Khorāsān, Iran* **97 C8** 33 20N 59 14 E
Séderon, *France* **29 D9** 44 12N 5 32 E
Sederot, *Israel* **103 D3** 31 32N 34 37 E
Sédhiou, *Senegal* **112 C1** 12 44N 15 30W
Sedico, *Italy* **45 B9** 46 8N 12 6 E
Sedlčany, *Czech Rep.* **34 B7** 49 40N 14 25 E
Sedley, *Canada* **143 C8** 50 10N 104 0W
Sedona, *U.S.A.* **159 J8** 34 52N 111 46W
Sedova, Pik, *Russia* **66 B6** 73 29N 54 58 E
Sedrata, *Algeria* **111 A6** 36 7N 7 31 E
Sedro Woolley, *U.S.A.* **160 B4** 48 30N 122 14W
Sedrun, *Switz.* **33 C7** 46 36N 8 47 E
Šeduva, *Lithuania* **54 C10** 55 45N 23 45 E
Sędziszów, *Poland* **55 H7** 50 35N 20 4 E
Sędziszów Małapolski, *Poland* **55 H8** 50 5N 21 45 E
Seebad Ahlbeck, *Germany* **30 B10** 53 56N 14 10 E
Seeburg = Jeziorany, *Poland* **54 E7** 53 58N 20 46 E
Seefeld in Tirol, *Austria* **34 D4** 47 19N 11 13 E
Seehausen, *Germany* **30 C7** 52 54N 11 45 E
Seeheim, *Namibia* **116 D2** 26 50 S 17 45 E

Seeheim-Jugenheim, Germany 31 F4 49 49N 8 40 E
Seeis, Namibia 116 C2 22 29 S 17 39 E
Seekoei →, S. Africa 116 E4 30 18 S 25 1 E
Seeley's Bay, Canada 151 B8 44 29N 76 14W
Seelow, Germany 30 C10 52 32N 14 23 E
Sées, France 26 D7 48 38N 0 10 E
Seesen, Germany 30 D6 51 54N 10 10 E
Seevetal, Germany 30 B6 53 26N 10 1 E
Seewinkel = Neusiedler See-Seewinkel △, Austria 35 D9 47 50N 16 45 E
Sefadu, S. Leone 112 D2 8 35N 10 58W
Seferihisar, Turkey 49 C8 38 10N 26 50 E
Séféto, Mali 112 C3 14 8N 9 49W
Sefrou, Morocco 110 B4 33 52N 4 52W
Sefton, N.Z. 131 D7 43 15 S 172 41 E
Sefuri-San, Japan 72 D2 33 28N 130 18 E
Sefwi Bekwai, Ghana 112 D4 6 10N 2 25W
Seg-ozero, Russia 56 B5 63 20N 33 46 E
Segaf, Kepulauan, Indonesia 83 B4 2 10 S 130 28 E
Segag, Ethiopia 120 C2 7 39N 42 50 E
Segamat, Malaysia 87 L4 2 30N 102 50 E
Şegarcea, Romania 53 F8 44 6N 23 43 E
Ségbana, Benin 113 C5 10 55N 3 42 E
Segbwema, S. Leone 112 D2 8 0N 11 0W
Seget, Indonesia 83 B4 1 24 S 130 58 E
Segewold = Sigulda, Latvia 15 H21 57 10N 24 55 E
Segezha, Russia 56 B5 63 44N 34 19 E
Seggueur, O. →, Algeria 111 B5 32 14N 1 48 E
Seghe, Solomon Is. 133 M9 8 32 S 157 54 E
Segonzac, France 28 C3 45 36N 0 14W
Segorbe, Spain 40 F4 39 50N 0 30W
Ségou, Mali 112 C3 13 30N 6 16W
Segovia = Coco →, Cent. Amer. 164 D3 15 0N 83 8W
Segovia, Colombia 168 B3 7 7N 74 42W
Segovia, Spain 42 E6 40 57N 4 10W
Segovia □, Spain 42 E6 40 55N 4 10W
Segré, France 26 E6 47 40N 0 52W
Segre →, Spain 40 D5 41 40N 0 43 E
Seguam I., U.S.A. 144 K4 52 19N 172 30W
Seguam Pass, U.S.A. 144 L4 52 0N 172 30W
Séguédine, Niger 109 D2 20 12N 12 59 E
Séguéla, Ivory C. 112 D3 7 55N 6 40W
Séguénéga, Burkina Faso 113 C4 13 25N 1 58W
Seguin, U.S.A. 155 L6 29 34N 97 58W
Segundo →, Argentina 174 C3 30 53 S 62 44W
Segura →, Spain 41 G4 38 3N 0 44W
Segura, Sierra de, Spain 41 G2 38 5N 2 45W
Seh Konj, Kūh-e, Iran 97 D8 30 6N 57 30 E
Seh Qal'eh, Iran 97 C8 33 40N 58 24 E
Sehitwa, Botswana 116 C3 20 30 S 22 30 E
Sehlabathebe △, Lesotho 117 D4 29 53 S 29 7 E
Sehore, India 92 H7 23 10N 77 5 E
Sehulea, Papua N. G. 132 E6 9 58 S 151 10 E
Sehwan, Pakistan 91 D2 26 28N 67 53 E
Şeica Mare, Romania 53 D9 46 1N 24 7 E
Seikpyu, Burma 90 E5 20 54N 94 48 E
Seil, U.K. 22 E3 56 18N 5 38W
Seiland, Norway 14 A20 70 25N 23 15 E
Seilhac, France 28 C5 45 22N 1 43 E
Seiling, U.S.A. 155 G5 36 9N 98 56W
Seille →, Moselle, France 27 C13 49 7N 6 11 E
Seille →, Saône-et-Loire, France 27 F11 46 31N 4 57 E
Sein, Î. de, France 26 D2 48 2N 4 52W
Seinäjoki, Finland 15 E20 62 40N 22 51 E
Seine →, France 26 C7 49 26N 0 26 E
Seine, B. de la, France 26 C6 49 40N 0 40W
Seine-et-Marne □, France 27 D10 48 45N 3 0 E
Seine-Inférieure = Seine-Maritime □, France 26 C7 49 40N 1 0 E
Seine-Maritime □, France 26 C7 49 40N 1 0 E
Seine-St-Denis □, France 27 D9 48 58N 2 24 E
Seini, Romania 53 C8 47 44N 23 21 E
Seirijai, Lithuania 54 D10 54 14N 23 49 E
Seis de Septiembre = Moron, Argentina 174 C4 34 39 S 58 37W
Seistan = Sīstān, Asia 97 D9 30 50N 61 0 E
Seistan, Daryācheh-ye = Sīstān, Daryācheh-ye, Iran 97 D9 31 0N 61 0 E
Seitler = Nyzhnohirskyy, Ukraine 59 K8 45 27N 34 38 E
Sejerø, Denmark 17 J5 55 54N 11 9 E
Sejerø Bugt, Denmark 17 J5 55 53N 11 15 E
Sejny, Poland 54 D10 54 6N 23 21 E
Seka, Ethiopia 107 F4 8 10N 36 52 E
Sekayu, Indonesia 84 C2 2 51 S 103 51 E
Seke, Tanzania 118 C3 3 20 S 33 31 E
Seke-Banza, Dem. Rep. of the Congo 115 D2 5 20 S 13 16 E
Sekenke, Tanzania 118 C3 4 18 S 34 11 E
Sekhira, Tunisia 108 B2 34 20N 10 5 E
Seki, Japan 73 B8 35 29N 136 55 E
Seki, Turkey 49 E11 36 48N 29 33 E
Sekigahara, Japan 73 B8 35 22N 136 28 E
Sekondi-Takoradi, Ghana 112 E4 4 58N 1 45W
Sekota, Ethiopia 107 E4 12 40N 39 2 E
Seksna, Russia 58 C10 59 13N 38 30 E
Sekudai, Malaysia 87 d 1 32N 103 39 E
Sekuma, Botswana 116 C3 24 36 S 23 50 E
Selah, U.S.A. 158 C3 46 39N 120 32W
Selama, Malaysia 87 K3 5 12N 100 42 E
Selangor □, Malaysia 84 B2 3 10N 101 30 E
Selárgius, Italy 46 C2 39 16N 9 10 E
Selaru, Indonesia 83 C4 8 9 S 131 0 E
Selatan, Selat, Malaysia 87 c 5 15N 100 20 E
Selawik, U.S.A. 144 C8 66 36N 160 0W
Selawik L., U.S.A. 144 C7 66 30N 160 45W
Selb, Germany 31 E8 50 10N 12 7 E
Selbusjøen, Norway 18 A7 63 15N 10 50 E
Selby, U.K. 20 D6 53 47N 1 5W
Selby, U.S.A. 154 C4 45 31N 100 2W
Selca, Croatia 45 E13 43 20N 16 50 E
Selçuk, Turkey 49 D9 37 56N 27 22 E
Selden, U.S.A. 154 F4 39 33N 100 34W
Seldovia, U.S.A. 144 G10 59 26N 151 43W
Sele →, Italy 47 B7 40 29N 14 56 E
Selebi-Pikwe, Botswana 117 C4 21 58 S 27 48 E
Selemdzha →, Russia 67 D13 51 42N 128 53 E
Selendi, Manisa, Turkey 49 C10 38 43N 28 50 E
Selendi, Manisa, Turkey 49 C9 38 46N 27 56 E
Selenga = Selenge Mörön →, Asia 68 A5 52 16N 106 16 E
Selenge, Dem. Rep. of the Congo 114 C3 1 58 S 18 11 E
Selenge Mörön →, Asia 68 A5 52 16N 106 16 E
Selenicë, Albania 50 F3 40 33N 19 39 E
Selenter See, Germany 30 A6 54 18N 10 26 E
Sélestat, France 27 D14 48 16N 7 26 E
Seletan, Tanjung, Indonesia 85 C4 4 10 S 114 40 E
Selevac, Serbia & M. 50 B4 44 28N 20 52 E
Selfoss, Iceland 11 D6 63 56N 21 0W
Sélibabi, Mauritania 112 B2 15 10N 12 15W
Seliger, Ozero, Russia 58 D7 57 15N 33 0 E
Seligman, U.S.A. 159 J7 35 20N 112 53W
Şelim, Turkey 101 B10 40 30N 42 46 E
Selîma, El Wâhât el, Sudan 106 C2 21 22N 29 19 E
Selimiye, Turkey 49 D9 37 24N 27 40 E
Selinda Spillway →, Botswana 116 B3 18 35 S 23 10 E
Selinoús, Greece 48 D3 37 35N 21 37 E
Selinsgrove, U.S.A. 150 F8 40 48N 76 52W
Selizharovo, Russia 58 D7 56 51N 33 27 E
Selje, Norway 18 B2 62 3N 5 22 E
Seljord, Norway 18 E5 59 30N 8 40 E
Selkirk, Canada 143 C9 50 10N 96 55W
Selkirk, U.K. 22 F6 55 33N 2 50W
Selkirk I. = Horse I., Canada 143 C9 53 20N 99 6W
Selkirk Mts., Canada 138 C8 51 15N 117 40W
Sellafield, U.K. 20 C4 54 25N 3 29W
Sellama, Sudan 107 E2 12 51N 29 46 E
Selliá, Greece 39 E5 35 12N 24 23 E
Sellières, France 27 F12 46 50N 5 32 E
Sells, U.S.A. 159 L8 31 55N 111 53W
Sellye, Hungary 52 E2 45 52N 17 51 E
Selma, Ala., U.S.A. 149 J2 32 25N 87 1W
Selma, Calif., U.S.A. 160 J7 36 34N 119 37W
Selma, N.C., U.S.A. 149 H6 35 32N 78 17W
Selmer, U.S.A. 149 H1 35 10N 88 36W
Selong, Indonesia 85 D5 8 39 S 116 32 E
Selongey, France 27 E12 47 36N 5 11 E
Selouane, Morocco 111 A4 35 7N 2 57W
Selous ⌓, Tanzania 119 D4 8 37 S 37 42 E
Selowandoma Falls, Zimbabwe 119 G3 21 15 S 31 50 E
Selpele, Indonesia 83 B4 0 1 S 130 5 E
Selsey Bill, U.K. 21 G7 50 43N 0 47W
Seltso, Russia 58 F8 53 22N 34 4 E
Seltz, France 27 D15 48 54N 8 4 E
Selu, Indonesia 83 C4 7 32 S 130 55 E
Sélune →, France 26 D5 48 38N 1 22W
Selva = La Selva del Camp, Spain 40 D6 41 13N 1 8 E
Selva, Argentina 174 B3 29 50 S 62 0W
Selva Lancandona = Montes Azules ⌓, Mexico 163 D6 16 21N 91 3W
Selvagens, Ilhas, Madeira 110 B1 30 5N 15 55W
Selvas, Brazil 172 B4 6 30 S 67 0W
Selwyn L., Canada 143 B8 60 0N 104 30W
Selwyn Mts., Canada 138 B6 63 0N 130 0W
Selwyn Passage, Vanuatu 133 F6 16 3 S 168 12 E
Selwyn Ra., Australia 126 C3 21 10 S 140 0 E
Selyatyn, Ukraine 53 C10 47 50N 25 12 E
Sem, Norway 18 E7 59 14N 10 17 E
Sem Kolodezey = Lenino, Ukraine 59 K8 45 17N 35 46 E
Semadrek = Samothráki, Greece 51 F9 40 28N 25 28 E
Seman →, Albania 50 F3 40 47N 19 30 E
Semara, W. Sahara 110 C2 26 48N 11 41W
Semarang, Indonesia 85 D4 7 0 S 110 26 E
Sematan, Malaysia 85 B3 1 48N 109 46 E
Semau, Indonesia 82 D2 10 13 S 123 22 E
Sembabule, Uganda 118 C3 0 4 S 31 25 E
Sembawang, Singapore 87 d 1 27N 103 50 E
Sembé, Congo 114 B2 1 39N 14 36 E
Sembung, Indonesia 79 J18 8 28 S 115 11 E
Şemdinli, Turkey 101 D11 37 18N 44 35 E
Sémé, Senegal 112 B2 15 4N 13 41W
Semeih, Sudan 107 E3 12 43N 30 53 E
Semenanjung Blambangan, Indonesia 79 K17 8 42 S 114 29 E
Semendua, Dem. Rep. of the Congo 114 C3 3 10 S 18 6 E
Semenov, Russia 60 B7 56 43N 44 30 E
Semenovka, Chernihiv, Ukraine 59 F7 52 8N 32 36 E
Semenovka, Kremenchuk, Ukraine 59 H7 49 37N 33 10 E
Semeru, Indonesia 85 D4 8 4 S 112 55 E
Semey, Kazakhstan 66 D9 50 30N 80 10 E
Semichi Is., U.S.A. 144 K1 52 42N 174 0 E
Semikarakorskiy, Russia 61 G5 47 31N 40 48 E
Semiluki, Russia 59 G10 51 41N 39 2 E
Seminoe Reservoir, U.S.A. 158 F10 42 9N 106 55W
Seminole, Fla., U.S.A. 153 H7 27 50N 82 47W
Seminole, Okla., U.S.A. 155 H6 35 14N 96 41W
Seminole, Tex., U.S.A. 155 J3 32 43N 102 39W
Seminole, L., U.S.A. 152 E5 30 43N 84 52W
Seminole Draw →, U.S.A. 155 J3 32 27N 102 20W
Semipalatinsk = Semey, Kazakhstan 66 D9 50 30N 80 10 E
Semirara I., Phil. 80 E3 12 4N 121 23 E
Semirara Is., Phil. 81 F3 12 0N 121 20 E
Semisopochnoi I., U.S.A. 144 L2 51 55N 179 36 E
Semitau, Indonesia 85 B4 0 29N 111 57 E
Semiyarka, Kazakhstan 66 D8 50 55N 78 23 E
Semiyarskoye = Semiyarka, Kazakhstan 66 D8 50 55N 78 23 E
Semlin = Zemun, Serbia & M. 50 B4 44 51N 20 25 E
Semmering P., Austria 34 D8 47 41N 15 45 E
Semnān, Iran 97 C7 35 40N 53 23 E
Semnān □, Iran 97 C7 36 0N 54 0 E
Sempang Mengayou, Tanjong, Malaysia 85 A5 7 0N 116 40 E
Semporna, Malaysia 85 B5 4 30N 118 33 E
Semuda, Indonesia 85 C4 2 51 S 112 58 E
Semur-en-Auxois, France 27 E11 47 30N 4 20 E
Semyonovka = Arsenev, Russia 70 B6 44 10N 133 15 E
Semyonovskoye = Bereznik, Russia 56 B7 62 51N 42 40 E
Sen →, Cambodia 78 B3 13 45N 105 12 E
Senā, Bolivia 172 C4 11 32 S 67 11W
Senā, Iran 97 D6 28 27N 51 36 E
Sena, Mozam. 119 F4 17 25 S 35 0 E
Sena →, Bolivia 172 C4 11 31 S 67 11W
Sena Madureira, Brazil 172 B4 9 5 S 68 45W
Senachwine L., U.S.A. 156 C7 41 10N 89 18W
Senador José Porfírio, Brazil 169 D7 2 35 S 51 55W
Senador Pompeu, Brazil 170 C4 5 40 S 39 20W
Senaja, Malaysia 85 A5 6 45N 117 3 E
Senaki, Georgia 61 J6 42 15N 42 7 E
Senang, Pulau, Singapore 87 d 1 10N 103 44 E
Senanga, Zambia 115 F4 16 7 S 23 16 E
Senatobia, U.S.A. 155 H10 34 37N 89 58W
Sencelles, Spain 38 B3 39 39N 2 54 E
Sendafa, Ethiopia 107 F4 9 11N 39 3 E
Sendai, Kagoshima, Japan 72 F2 31 50N 130 20 E
Sendai, Miyagi, Japan 70 E10 38 15N 140 53 E
Sendai-Wan, Japan 70 E10 38 15N 141 0 E
Senden, Bayern, Germany 31 G6 48 19N 10 4 E
Senden, Nordrhein-Westfalen, Germany 30 D3 51 52N 7 22 E
Sendhwa, India 92 J6 21 41N 75 6 E
Sendurjana, India 94 D4 21 32N 78 17 E
Sene →, Ghana 113 D4 7 30N 0 33W
Senec, Slovak Rep. 35 C10 48 12N 17 23 E
Seneca, Ill., U.S.A. 157 C8 41 19N 88 37W
Seneca, S.C., U.S.A. 149 H4 34 41N 82 57W
Seneca Falls, U.S.A. 151 D8 42 55N 76 48W
Seneca L., U.S.A. 150 D8 42 40N 76 54W
Senecaville L., U.S.A. 150 G3 39 55N 81 25W
Senegal ■, W. Afr. 112 C2 14 30N 14 30W
Sénégal →, W. Afr. 112 B1 15 48N 16 32W
Senegambia, Africa 104 E2 12 45N 12 0W
Senegambia & Niger = Mali ■, Africa 112 B4 17 0N 3 0W
Senekal, S. Africa 117 D4 28 20 S 27 36 E
Senftenberg, Germany 30 D10 51 32N 14 0 E
Senga Hill, Zambia 119 D3 9 19 S 31 11 E
Senge Khambab = Indus →, Pakistan 91 D2 24 20N 67 47 E
Sengiley, Russia 60 D9 53 58N 48 46 E
Sengua →, Zimbabwe 119 F2 17 7 S 28 5 E
Senguerr →, Argentina 176 C3 45 35 S 68 50W
Senhor-do-Bonfim, Brazil 170 D3 10 30 S 40 10W
Senica, Slovak Rep. 35 C10 48 41N 17 25 E
Senigállia, Italy 45 E10 43 43N 13 13 E
Seniku, Burma 90 C6 25 32N 97 48 E
Senio →, Italy 45 D9 44 35N 12 15 E
Senirkent, Turkey 49 C12 38 6N 30 33 E
Senise, Italy 47 B9 40 9N 16 17 E
Senj, Croatia 45 D11 45 0N 14 58 E
Senja, Norway 14 B17 69 25N 17 30 E
Senkaku-Shotō, Japan 71 L1 25 45N 124 0 E
Senkuang, Indonesia 87 d 1 11N 104 2 E
Senlis, France 27 C9 49 13N 2 35 E
Senmonorom, Cambodia 86 F6 12 27N 107 12 E
Sennār, Sudan 107 E3 13 30N 33 35 E
Sennar □, Sudan 107 E3 13 0N 34 0 E
Senneterre, Canada 140 C4 48 25N 77 15W
Senno, Belarus 58 E5 54 45N 29 43 E
Sènnori, Italy 46 B1 40 47N 8 35 E
Seno, Laos 86 D5 16 35N 104 50 E
Senoia, U.S.A. 152 B5 33 18N 84 33W
Senonches, France 26 D8 48 34N 1 2 E
Senorbì, Italy 46 C2 39 32N 9 8 E
Senožeče, Slovenia 45 C11 45 43N 14 3 E
Sens, France 27 D10 48 11N 3 15 E
Senta, Serbia & M. 52 E5 45 55N 20 3 E
Sentani, Indonesia 83 B6 2 36 S 140 37 E
Sentani, Danau, Indonesia 83 B6 2 36 S 140 34 E
Sentery = Lubao, Dem. Rep. of the Congo 118 D2 5 17 S 25 42 E
Sentinel, U.S.A. 159 K7 32 52N 113 13W
Šentjur, Slovenia 45 B12 46 14N 15 24 E
Sentolo, Indonesia 85 D4 7 55 S 110 13 E
Sentosa, Singapore 87 d 1 15N 103 50 E
Senya Beraku, Ghana 113 D4 5 28N 0 31W
Seo de Urgel = La Seu d'Urgell, Spain 40 C6 42 22N 1 23 E
Seohara, India 93 E8 29 15N 78 33 E
Seonath →, India 93 J10 21 44N 82 28 E
Seondha, India 93 F8 26 9N 78 48 E
Seoni, India 93 H8 22 5N 79 30 E
Seoni Malwa, India 92 H8 22 27N 77 28 E
Seoriuarayan, India 94 D6 21 45N 82 34 E
Seoul = Sŏul, S. Korea 75 F14 37 31N 126 58 E
Separation Pt., N.Z. 131 A7 40 47 S 172 59 E
Sepatini →, Brazil 172 B4 7 36 S 65 24W
Sepi, Solomon Is. 133 M10 8 31 S 159 52 E
Sepīdān, Iran 97 D7 30 20N 52 5 E
Sepik →, Papua N. G. 132 B3 3 49 S 144 30 E
Sepo-ri, N. Korea 75 E14 38 57N 127 25 E
Sępólno Krajeńskie, Poland 54 E4 53 26N 17 30 E
Sepone, Laos 86 D6 16 45N 106 13 E
Sępopol, Poland 54 D8 54 16N 21 2 E
Sept-Îles, Canada 141 B6 50 13N 66 22W
Septemvri, Bulgaria 51 D8 42 13N 24 6 E
Sepúlveda, Spain 42 D7 41 18N 3 45W
Sequeros, Spain 42 E4 40 31N 6 2W
Sequim, U.S.A. 160 B3 48 5N 123 6W
Sequoia ⌓, U.S.A. 160 J8 36 30N 118 30W
Sera, Indonesia 83 C4 7 40 S 131 5 E
Serafimovich, Russia 60 F6 49 36N 42 43 E
Seraing, Belgium 24 D5 50 35N 5 32 E
Serakhis →, Cyprus 39 E8 35 13N 32 55 E
Seram, Indonesia 83 B3 3 10 S 129 0 E
Seram Sea, Indonesia 82 B3 2 30 S 128 30 E
Seranantsara, Madag. 117 B8 18 30 S 49 5 E
Serang, Indonesia 84 D3 6 8 S 106 10 E
Serangoon, Singapore 87 d 1 23N 103 54 E
Serasan, Indonesia 85 B3 2 29N 109 4 E
Seravezza, Italy 44 E7 43 59N 10 13 E
Şerbettar, Turkey 51 E10 41 27N 26 46 E
Serbia □, Serbia & M. 50 C5 43 30N 21 0 E
Serbia & Montenegro ■, Europe 50 C4 43 20N 20 0 E
Şercaia, Romania 53 E10 45 49N 25 9 E
Serdo, Ethiopia 107 E5 11 56N 41 14 E
Serdobol = Sortavala, Russia 58 B6 61 42N 30 41 E
Serdobsk, Russia 60 D7 52 28N 44 10 E
Sered', Slovak Rep. 35 C10 48 17N 17 44 E
Sereda = Furmanov, Russia 60 B5 57 10N 41 9 E
Seredka, Russia 58 C5 58 12N 28 10 E
Serednye, Ukraine 52 B7 48 32N 22 30 E
Şereflikoçhisar, Turkey 100 C5 38 56N 33 32 E
Seregno, Italy 44 C6 45 39N 9 12 E
Seremban, Malaysia 87 L3 2 43N 101 53 E
Serengeti △, Tanzania 118 C3 2 11 S 35 0 E
Serengeti Plain, Tanzania 118 C4 2 40 S 35 0 E
Serenje, Zambia 119 E3 13 14 S 30 15 E
Sereth = Siret →, Romania 53 E12 45 24N 28 1 E
Sergach, Russia 60 C7 55 30N 45 30 E
Sergen, Turkey 51 E11 41 41N 27 42 E
Sergino, Russia 66 C7 62 25N 65 12 E
Sergiopol = Ayaguz, Kazakhstan 66 E9 48 10N 80 10 E
Sergipe □, Brazil 170 D4 10 30 S 37 30W
Sergiyev Posad, Russia 58 D10 56 20N 38 10 E
Sergo = Stakhanov, Ukraine 59 H10 48 35N 38 40 E
Seria, Brunei 85 B4 4 37N 114 23 E
Serian, Malaysia 85 B4 1 10N 110 31 E
Seriate, Italy 44 C6 45 41N 9 43 E
Seribu, Kepulauan, Indonesia 84 D3 5 36 S 106 33 E
Sérifontaine, France 27 C8 49 20N 1 45 E
Sérifos, Greece 48 D6 37 9N 24 30 E
Sérignan, France 28 E7 43 17N 3 17 E
Sérigny →, Canada 141 A6 56 47N 66 0W
Serik, Turkey 100 D4 36 55N 31 7 E
Serikbuya, China 65 D8 39 21N 77 50 E
Seringapatam Reef, Australia 124 B3 13 38 S 122 5 E
Serinhisar, Turkey 49 D11 37 36N 29 18 E
Seririt, Indonesia 79 J17 8 12 S 114 56 E
Sermaize-les-Bains, France 27 D11 48 47N 4 54 E
Sermata, Indonesia 83 C3 8 15 S 128 50 E
Sermersuaq, Greenland 10 B4 79 30N 62 0W
Sérmide, Italy 45 D8 45 0N 11 18 E
Sernovodsk, Russia 60 D10 53 54N 51 16 E
Sernur, Russia 60 B9 56 52N 49 2 E
Serock, Poland 55 F8 52 31N 21 4 E
Serón, Spain 41 H2 37 20N 2 29W
Serós, Spain 40 D5 41 27N 0 24 E
Serouenout, Algeria 111 D6 24 18N 7 25 E
Serov, Russia 64 B8 59 29N 60 35 E
Serowe, Botswana 116 C4 22 25 S 26 43 E
Serpa, Portugal 43 H3 37 57N 7 38W
Serpeddí, Punta, Italy 46 C2 39 22N 9 18 E
Serpentara, Italy 46 C2 39 8N 9 36 E
Serpentine Lakes, Australia 125 E4 28 30 S 129 10 E
Serpent's Mouth = Sierpe, Bocas de la, Venezuela 169 G9 10 0N 61 30W
Serpis →, Spain 41 G4 38 59N 0 9W
Serpneve, Ukraine 53 D14 46 18N 29 1 E
Serpukhov, Russia 58 E9 54 55N 37 28 E
Serra da Bocaina △, Brazil 171 F3 23 0 S 44 40W
Serra da Canastra △, Brazil 171 F2 20 3 S 46 50W
Serra da Capivara △, Brazil 170 C3 8 42 S 42 15W
Serra da Estrela ⌓, Portugal 42 E3 40 27N 7 33W
Serra das Confusões △, Brazil 170 C3 8 50 S 43 50W
Serra de Outes, Spain 42 C2 42 52N 8 55W
Serra do Cipó △, Brazil 171 E3 19 14 S 43 23W
Serra do Navio, Brazil 169 C7 0 59N 52 3W
Serra do Salitre, Brazil 171 E2 19 6 S 46 41W
Serra dos Orgãos △, Brazil 171 F3 22 25 S 43 8W
Serra San Bruno, Italy 47 D9 38 35N 16 20 E
Serra Talhada, Brazil 170 C4 7 59 S 38 18W
Serradilla, Spain 42 F4 39 50N 6 9W
Sérrai, Greece 50 E7 41 5N 23 31 E
Sérrai □, Greece 50 E7 41 5N 23 37 E
Serramanna, Italy 46 C1 39 25N 8 55 E
Serranía de la Neblina △, Venezuela 168 C4 1 5N 65 51W
Serranía San Luís △, Paraguay 174 A4 22 35 S 57 22W
Serranópolis, Brazil 173 18 16 S 52 0W
Serras d'Aire e Candeeiros ⌓, Portugal 43 F2 39 31N 8 48W
Serrat, C., Tunisia 108 A1 37 14N 9 10 E
Serravalle, Italy 33 E6 45 41N 8 18 E
Serravalle Scrívia, Italy 44 D5 44 43N 8 51 E
Serre-Ponçon, L. de, France 29 D10 44 22N 6 20 E
Serres = Sérrai, Greece 50 E7 41 5N 23 31 E
Serres, France 29 D9 44 26N 5 43 E
Serrezuela, Argentina 174 C2 30 40 S 65 20W
Serrinha, Brazil 171 D4 11 39 S 39 0W
Serrita, Brazil 170 C4 7 56 S 39 19W
Sersale, Italy 47 C9 39 1N 16 43 E
Sertã, Portugal 42 F2 39 48N 8 6W
Sertânia, Brazil 170 C4 8 5 S 37 20W
Sertanópolis, Brazil 175 A5 23 4 S 51 2W
Sêrtar, China 76 A3 32 20N 100 41 E
Sertig, Switz. 33 C9 46 44N 9 52 E
Serua, Indonesia 83 C4 6 18 S 130 1 E
Serui, Indonesia 83 B5 1 53 S 136 10 E
Serule, Botswana 116 C4 21 57 S 27 20 E
Sérvia, Greece 50 F6 40 11N 22 0 E
Serzedelo, Portugal 42 D2 41 24N 8 14W
Ses Salines, Spain 38 B4 39 21N 3 3 E
Sesayap →, Indonesia 85 B5 3 36N 117 15 E
Sese Is., Uganda 118 C3 0 20 S 32 20 E
Sesepe, Indonesia 83 B3 1 30 S 127 59 E
Sesfontein, Namibia 116 B1 19 7 S 13 39 E
Sesheke, Zambia 116 B3 17 29 S 24 13 E
Sésia →, Italy 44 C5 45 5N 8 37 E
Sesimbra, Portugal 43 G1 38 28N 9 6W
S'Espalmador, Spain 38 D1 38 47N 1 26 E
S'Espardell, Spain 38 D1 38 48N 1 29 E
Sessa, Angola 115 E4 13 56 S 20 38 E
Sessa Aurunca, Italy 46 A6 41 14N 13 56 E
Sesser, U.S.A. 156 F7 38 5N 89 1W
S'Estanyol, Spain 38 B3 39 22N 2 54 E
Sestao, Spain 40 B2 43 18N 3 0W
Sesto Calende, Italy 44 C5 45 44N 8 37 E
Sesto San Giovanni, Italy 44 C6 45 32N 9 14 E
Sestri Levante, Italy 44 D6 44 16N 9 24 E
Sestriere, Italy 44 D3 44 57N 6 53 E
Sestroretsk, Russia 58 B6 60 5N 29 58 E
Sestrunj, Croatia 45 D11 44 10N 15 0 E
Sestu, Italy 46 C2 39 18N 9 5 E
Sesvenna, Switz. 33 C10 46 42N 10 25 E
Setaka, Japan 72 D2 33 9N 130 28 E
Setana, Japan 70 C9 42 26N 139 51 E
Sète, France 28 E7 43 25N 3 42 E
Sete Cidades △, Brazil 170 B3 4 0 S 41 37W
Sete Lagôas, Brazil 171 E3 19 27 S 44 16W
Setesdalsheiene, Norway 18 E3 59 28N 7 10 E
Sétif, Algeria 111 A6 36 9N 5 26 E
Seto, Japan 73 B9 35 14N 137 6 E
Setonaikai, Japan 72 C5 34 20N 133 30 E
Setonaikai △, Japan 72 C5 34 15N 133 15 E
Setsan, Burma 90 G5 16 3N 95 23 E
Settat, Morocco 110 B3 33 0N 7 40W
Setté-Cama, Gabon 114 C1 2 32 S 9 45 E
Séttimo Torinese, Italy 44 C4 45 9N 7 46 E
Setting L., Canada 143 C9 55 0N 98 38W
Settle, U.K. 20 C5 54 5N 2 16W
Settlement Pt., Bahamas 149 M6 26 40N 79 0W
Settlers, S. Africa 117 C4 25 2 S 28 30 E
Setúbal, Portugal 43 G2 38 30N 8 58W
Setúbal □, Portugal 43 G2 38 25N 8 35W
Setúbal, B. de, Portugal 43 G2 38 40N 8 56W
Seugne →, France 28 C3 45 42N 0 32W
Seul, Lac, Canada 140 B1 50 20N 92 30W
Seulimeum, Indonesia 84 A1 5 27N 95 15 E
Seurre, France 27 F12 47 0N 5 8 E
Seuzach, Switz. 33 A7 47 32N 8 49 E
Sevan, Armenia 61 K7 40 33N 44 56 E
Sevan, Ozero = Sevana Lich, Armenia 61 K7 40 30N 45 20 E
Sevana Lich, Armenia 61 K7 40 30N 45 20 E
Sevastopol, Ukraine 59 K7 44 35N 33 30 E
Sevelen, Switz. 33 B8 47 7N 9 28 E
Seven Islands = Sept-Îles, Canada 141 B6 50 13N 66 22W
Seven Sisters, Canada 142 C3 54 56N 128 10W
Sever →, Spain 43 F3 39 40N 7 32W
Sévérac-le-Château, France 28 D7 44 20N 3 5 E
Severn →, Canada 140 A2 56 2N 87 36W
Severn →, U.K. 21 F5 51 35N 2 40W
Severn L., Canada 140 B1 53 54N 90 48W
Severnaya Zemlya, Russia 67 B10 79 0N 100 0 E
Severnyye Uvaly, Russia 64 B2 60 0N 50 0 E
Severo-Kurilsk, Russia 67 D16 50 40N 156 8 E
Severo-Yeniseyskiy, Russia 67 C10 60 22N 93 1 E
Severo-Zapadnyy □, Russia 66 C4 65 0N 40 0 E
Severočeský □, Czech Rep. 34 A7 50 30N 14 0 E
Severodonetsk = Syeverodonetsk, Ukraine 59 H10 48 58N 38 35 E
Severodvinsk, Russia 56 B6 64 27N 39 58 E
Severomoravský □, Czech Rep. 35 B10 49 38N 17 40 E
Severomorsk, Russia 56 A5 69 5N 33 27 E
Severouralsk, Russia 64 A7 60 9N 59 57 E
Sevier, U.S.A. 159 G7 38 39N 112 11W
Sevier →, U.S.A. 159 G7 39 4N 113 6W
Sevier Desert, U.S.A. 158 G7 39 40N 112 45W
Sevier L., U.S.A. 158 G7 38 54N 113 9W
Sevilla, Colombia 168 C2 4 16N 75 57W
Sevilla, Spain 43 H5 37 23N 5 58W
Sevilla □, Spain 43 H5 37 25N 5 30W
Seville = Sevilla, Spain 43 H5 37 23N 5 58W
Seville, Fla., U.S.A. 153 F8 29 19N 81 30W
Seville, Ga., U.S.A. 152 D6 31 58N 83 36W
Sevlievo, Bulgaria 51 C9 43 2N 25 6 E
Sevnica, Slovenia 45 B12 46 2N 15 19 E
Sèvre-Nantaise →, France 26 E5 47 12N 1 33W
Sèvre-Niortaise →, France 28 B3 46 28N 0 50W
Sevsk, Russia 59 F8 52 10N 34 30 E
Sewa →, S. Leone 112 D2 7 20N 12 10W
Sewani, India 92 E6 28 58N 75 39 E
Seward, Alaska, U.S.A. 144 F10 60 7N 149 27W
Seward, Nebr., U.S.A. 154 E6 40 55N 97 6W
Seward, Pa., U.S.A. 150 F5 40 25N 79 1W
Seward Peninsula, U.S.A. 144 D6 65 30N 166 0W
Sewell, Chile 174 C1 34 10 S 70 23W
Sewer, Indonesia 83 C4 5 53 S 134 40 E
Sewickley, U.S.A. 150 F4 40 32N 80 12W
Sexsmith, Canada 142 B5 55 21N 118 47W
Seychelles ■, Ind. Oc. 121 b 5 0 S 56 0 E
Seyðisfjörður, Iceland 11 B13 65 16N 13 57W
Seydişehir, Turkey 100 D4 37 25N 31 51 E
Seydvān, Iran 101 C11 38 34N 45 2 E
Seyhan →, Turkey 100 D6 36 43N 34 53 E
Seyhan Barajı, Turkey 100 D6 37 2N 35 18 E
Seyitgazi, Turkey 49 B12 39 27N 30 43 E
Seyitömer, Turkey 49 B11 39 34N 29 52 E
Seym →, Ukraine 59 G7 51 27N 32 34 E
Seymen, Turkey 51 E11 41 6N 27 57 E
Seymour, Australia 129 D6 37 0 S 145 10 E
Seymour, S. Africa 117 E4 32 33 S 26 46 E
Seymour, Conn., U.S.A. 151 E11 41 24N 73 4W
Seymour, Ind., U.S.A. 157 F11 38 58N 85 53W
Seymour, Tex., U.S.A. 155 J5 33 35N 99 16W
Seyne, France 29 D10 44 21N 6 22 E
Seyssel, France 29 C9 45 57N 5 50 E
Sežana, Slovenia 45 C10 45 43N 13 41 E
Sézanne, France 27 D10 48 40N 3 40 E
Sezze, Italy 46 A6 41 30N 13 3 E
Sfântu Gheorghe, Covasna, Romania 53 E10 45 52N 25 48 E
Sfântu Gheorghe, Tulcea, Romania 53 F14 44 53N 29 36 E
Sfântu Gheorghe, Braţul →, Romania 53 F14 44 51N 29 36 E
Sfax, Tunisia 108 B2 34 49N 10 48 E
Sha Tau Kok, China 69 F11 22 33N 114 13 E
Sha Tin, China 69 G11 22 23N 114 12 E
Sha Xi →, China 77 D12 26 35N 118 0 E
Sha Xian, China 77 D11 26 23N 117 45 E
Shaanxi □, China 74 G5 35 0N 109 0 E
Shaarikhan = Shakhrikhan, Uzbekistan 65 C6 40 42N 72 3 E
Shaartuz, Tajikistan 65 E4 37 16N 68 8 E
Shaba = Katanga □, Dem. Rep. of the Congo 118 D2 8 0 S 25 0 E
Shaba ⌓, Kenya 118 B4 0 38N 37 48 E
Shaballe = Scebeli, Wabi →, Somali Rep. 120 D2 2 0N 44 0 E
Shabla, Bulgaria 51 C12 43 31N 28 32 E
Shabogamo L., Canada 141 B6 53 15N 66 30W
Shabunda, Dem. Rep. of the Congo 118 C2 2 40 S 27 16 E
Shabwah, Yemen 98 D4 15 22N 47 1 E
Shache, China 65 D8 38 20N 77 10 E
Shackleton Ice Shelf, Antarctica 7 C8 66 0 S 100 0 E
Shackleton Inlet, Antarctica 7 E11 83 0 S 160 0 E
Shādegān, Iran 97 D6 30 40N 48 38 E
Shadi, China 77 D10 26 7N 114 47 E
Shadi, India 93 C7 33 24N 77 14 E
Shadrinsk, Russia 64 C9 56 5N 63 32 E
Shady Dale, U.S.A. 152 B6 33 24N 83 36W
Shady Grove, U.S.A. 152 E6 30 17N 83 38W
Shadyside, U.S.A. 150 G4 39 58N 80 45W
Shafer, L., U.S.A. 157 D10 40 46N 86 46W
Shaffa, Nigeria 113 C7 10 30N 12 6 E
Shafter, U.S.A. 161 K7 35 30N 119 16W
Shaftesbury, U.K. 21 F5 51 0N 2 11W
Shag Pt., N.Z. 131 F5 45 29 S 170 52 E
Shag Rocks, Atl. Oc. 8 M7 53 0 S 41 0W
Shagamu, Nigeria 113 D5 6 51N 3 39 E
Shageluk, U.S.A. 144 E8 62 41N 159 34W
Shaghan, Kazakhstan 65 A2 44 53N 64 57 E
Shagram, Pakistan 93 A5 36 24N 72 20 E
Shah Alam, Malaysia 84 B2 3 5N 101 30 E
Shah Alizai, Pakistan 92 E2 29 25N 66 33 E
Shah Bunder, Pakistan 92 G2 24 13N 67 56 E
Shāh Jūy, Afghan. 91 B2 32 31N 67 25 E
Shahabad, Andhra Pradesh, India 94 F4 17 10N 78 7 E
Shahabad, Karnataka, India 94 F3 17 10N 76 54 E
Shahabad, Punjab, India 92 D7 30 10N 76 55 E
Shahabad, Raj., India 92 G7 25 15N 77 11 E
Shahabad, Ut. P., India 93 F8 27 36N 79 56 E

Shahada, *India* **94 D2** 21 33N 74 30 E
Shahadpur, *Pakistan* **92 G3** 25 55N 68 35 E
Shahapur, *India* **95 G2** 15 50N 74 34 E
Shahba, *Syria* **103 C5** 32 52N 36 38 E
Shahbazpur I., *Bangla.* **90 D3** 22 30N 90 45 E
Shahdād, *Iran* **97 D8** 30 30N 57 40 E
Shahdād, Namakzār-e, *Iran* **97 D8** 30 20N 58 20 E
Shahdadkot, *Pakistan* **91 D2** 27 50N 67 55 E
Shahdol, *India* **93 H9** 23 19N 81 26 E
Shahe, *China* **74 F8** 37 0N 114 32 E
Shahganj, *India* **93 F10** 26 3N 82 44 E
Shaḥḥāt, *Libya* **108 B4** 32 48N 21 54 E
Shahīdān, *Afghan.* **91 A2** 36 42N 67 49 E
Shahjahanpur, *India* **93 F8** 27 54N 79 57 E
Shahpur, *Karnataka, India* **94 F3** 16 40N 76 48 E
Shahpur, *Mad. P., India* **92 H7** 22 12N 77 58 E
Shahpur, *Baluchistan, Pakistan* **92 E3** 28 46N 68 27 E
Shahpur, *Punjab, Pakistan* **92 C5** 32 17N 72 26 E
Shahpur Chakar, *Pakistan* **92 F3** 26 9N 68 39 E
Shahpura, *Mad. P., India* **93 H9** 23 10N 80 45 E
Shahpura, *Raj., India* **92 G6** 25 38N 74 56 E
Shahr-e Bābak, *Iran* **97 D7** 30 7N 55 9 E
Shahr-e Kord, *Iran* **97 C6** 32 15N 50 55 E
Shāhrakht, *Iran* **97 C9** 33 38N 60 16 E
Shahrig, *Pakistan* **91 C2** 30 15N 67 40 E
Shahukou, *China* **74 D7** 40 20N 112 18 E
Shaikhabad, *Afghan.* **91 B3** 34 2N 68 45 E
Shajapur, *India* **92 H7** 23 27N 76 21 E
Shajing, *China* **69 F10** 22 44N 113 48 E
Shakargarh, *Pakistan* **92 C6** 32 17N 75 10 E
Shakawe, *Botswana* **116 B3** 18 28 S 21 49 E
Shakenge, *Dem. Rep. of the Congo* **115 D3** 6 14 S 18 41 E
Shaker Heights, *U.S.A.* **150 E3** 41 29N 81 32W
Shakhimardan = Khamza, *Uzbekistan* **65 C5** 40 25N 71 29 E
Shakhrikhan, *Uzbekistan* **65 C6** 40 42N 72 3 E
Shakhrisabz, *Uzbekistan* **65 D3** 39 3N 66 50 E
Shakhristan, *Tajikistan* **65 D4** 39 47N 68 49 E
Shakhty, *Russia* **61 G5** 47 40N 40 16 E
Shakhtyorskoye = Pershotravensk, *Ukraine* **59 G4** 50 13N 27 40 E
Shakhunya, *Russia* **60 B8** 57 40N 46 46 E
Shaki, *Nigeria* **113 D5** 8 41N 3 21 E
Shākir, *Egypt* **106 B3** 27 30N 33 59 E
Shakpak, *Kazakhstan* **65 B4** 43 15N 69 20 E
Shaksam Valley, *Asia* **93 A7** 36 0N 76 20 E
Shaktoolik, *U.S.A.* **144 D7** 64 20N 161 9W
Shala, L., *Ethiopia* **107 F4** 7 30N 38 30 E
Shali, *Russia* **61 J7** 43 9N 45 55 E
Shalkar, *Kazakhstan* **64 F3** 50 40N 51 53 E
Shalkar, Ozero, *Kazakhstan* **64 F3** 50 35N 51 47 E
Shallow Lake, *Canada* **150 B3** 44 36N 81 5W
Shalqar, *Kazakhstan* **66 E6** 47 48N 59 39 E
Shalskiy, *Russia* **58 B8** 61 48N 35 58 E
Shaluli Shan, *China* **76 B2** 30 40N 99 55 E
Shām, *Iran* **97 E8** 26 39N 57 21 E
Shām, Bādiyat ash, *Asia* **96 C3** 32 0N 40 0 E
Shām, J. ash, *Oman* **99 B7** 23 10N 57 5 E
Shamâl Bahr el Ghazal □, *Sudan* **107 F2** 8 0N 27 30 E
Shamâl Dârfûr □, *Sudan* **107 E2** 15 0N 25 0 E
Shamâl Kordofân □, *Sudan* **107 E3** 15 0N 30 0 E
Shamâl Sînî □, *Egypt* **103 E2** 30 30N 33 30 E
Shamaldy-Say, *Kyrgyzstan* **65 C6** 41 12N 72 11 E
Shamattawa, *Canada* **140 A1** 55 51N 92 5W
Shamattawa →, *Canada* **140 A2** 55 1N 85 23W
Shambe, *Sudan* **107 F3** 7 8N 30 46 E
Shambe ⌓, *Sudan* **107 F3** 6 57N 30 50 E
Shambu, *Ethiopia* **107 F4** 9 32N 37 3 E
Shamgong Dzong, *Bhutan* **90 B3** 27 13N 90 35 E
Shamīl, *Iran* **97 E8** 27 30N 56 55 E
Shamkhor = Şämkir, *Azerbaijan* **61 K8** 40 50N 46 0 E
Shāmkūh, *Iran* **97 C8** 35 47N 57 50 E
Shamli, *India* **92 E7** 29 32N 77 18 E
Shammar, Jabal, *Si. Arabia* **96 E4** 27 40N 41 0 E
Shamo = Gobi, *Asia* **74 C6** 44 0N 110 0 E
Shamo, L., *Ethiopia* **107 F4** 5 45N 37 30 E
Shamokin, *U.S.A.* **151 F8** 40 47N 76 34W
Shamrock, *U.S.A.* **155 H4** 35 13N 100 15W
Shamshabad, *India* **94 F4** 17 15N 78 25 E
Shamva, *Zimbabwe* **119 F3** 17 20 S 31 32 E
Shan □, *Burma* **90 E7** 21 30N 98 30 E
Shan Xian, *China* **74 G9** 34 50N 116 5 E
Shana = Kurilsk, *Russia* **67 E15** 45 14N 147 53 E
Shanan →, *Ethiopia* **107 F5** 8 0N 40 20 E
Shanchengzhen, *China* **75 C13** 42 20N 125 20 E
Shāndak, *Iran* **97 D9** 28 28N 60 27 E
Shandon, *U.S.A.* **160 K6** 35 39N 120 23W
Shandong □, *China* **75 G10** 36 0N 118 0 E
Shandong Bandao, *China* **75 F11** 37 0N 121 0 E
Shang Xian = Shangzhou, *China* **74 H5** 33 50N 109 58 E
Shangalowe, *Dem. Rep. of the Congo* **119 E2** 10 50 S 26 30 E
Shangani, *Zimbabwe* **117 B4** 19 41 S 29 20 E
Shangani →, *Zimbabwe* **119 F2** 18 41 S 27 10 E
Shangbancheng, *China* **75 D10** 40 50N 118 1 E
Shangcheng, *China* **77 B10** 31 47N 115 26 E
Shangchuan Dao, *China* **77 G9** 21 40N 112 50 E
Shangdu, *China* **74 D7** 41 30N 113 30 E
Shanggao, *China* **77 C10** 28 17N 114 55 E
Shanghai, *China* **77 B13** 31 15N 121 26 E
Shanghai Shi □, *China* **77 B13** 31 0N 121 30 E
Shanghang, *China* **77 E11** 25 2N 116 23 E
Shanghe, *China* **75 F9** 37 20N 117 10 E
Shangjao = Shangrao, *China* **77 C11** 28 25N 117 59 E
Shanglin, *China* **76 F7** 23 27N 108 33 E
Shangnan, *China* **74 H6** 33 32N 110 50 E
Shangqiu, *China* **74 G8** 34 26N 115 36 E
Shangrao, *China* **77 C11** 28 25N 117 59 E
Shangshui, *China* **69 C6** 33 42N 114 35 E
Shangsi, *China* **76 F6** 22 8N 107 58 E
Shangyou, *China* **77 E10** 25 48N 114 32 E
Shangyu, *China* **77 B13** 30 3N 120 52 E
Shangzhi, *China* **75 B14** 45 22N 127 56 E
Shangzhou, *China* **74 H5** 33 50N 109 58 E
Shanhetun, *China* **75 B14** 44 33N 127 15 E
Shani, *Nigeria* **113 C7** 10 14N 12 2 E
Shanklin, *U.K.* **21 G6** 50 38N 1 11W
Shannon, *Greenland* **10 B9** 75 10N 18 30W
Shannon, *N.Z.* **130 G4** 40 33 S 175 25 E
Shannon ⌓, *Australia* **125 F2** 31 55 S 117 51 E
Shannon →, *Ireland* **23 D2** 52 35N 9 30W
Shannon, Mouth of the, *Ireland* **23 D2** 52 30N 9 55W
Shannon Airport, *Ireland* **23 D3** 52 42N 8 57W
Shannontown, *U.S.A.* **152 B9** 33 53N 80 21W
Shansi = Shanxi □, *China* **74 F7** 37 0N 112 0 E
Shantar, Ostrov Bolshoy, *Russia* **67 D14** 55 9N 137 40 E
Shantipur, *India* **93 H13** 23 17N 88 25 E
Shantou, *China* **77 F11** 23 18N 116 40 E
Shantung = Shandong □, *China* **75 G10** 36 0N 118 0 E
Shanwei, *China* **77 F10** 22 48N 115 22 E
Shanxi □, *China* **74 F7** 37 0N 112 0 E
Shanyang, *China* **74 H5** 33 31N 109 55 E
Shanyin, *China* **74 E7** 39 25N 112 56 E
Shaodong, *China* **77 D8** 27 15N 111 43 E
Shaoguan, *China* **77 E9** 24 48N 113 35 E
Shaohing = Shaoxing, *China* **77 C13** 30 0N 120 35 E
Shaoshan, *China* **77 D9** 27 55N 112 33 E
Shaowu, *China* **77 D11** 27 22N 117 28 E
Shaoxing, *China* **77 C13** 30 0N 120 35 E
Shaoyang, *Hunan, China* **77 D8** 26 59N 111 20 E
Shaoyang, *Hunan, China* **77 D8** 27 14N 111 25 E
Shap, *U.K.* **20 C5** 54 32N 2 40W
Shapinsay, *U.K.* **22 B6** 59 3N 2 51W
Shaqq el Gi'eifer →, *Sudan* **107 D2** 15 16N 26 0 E
Shaqra', *Si. Arabia* **96 E5** 25 15N 45 16 E
Shaqrā', *Yemen* **98 D4** 13 22N 45 44 E
Sharafa, *Sudan* **107 E2** 11 59N 27 7 E
Sharafkhāneh, *Iran* **101 C11** 38 11N 45 29 E
Sharashova, *Belarus* **55 F11** 52 34N 24 12 E
Sharavati →, *India* **95 G2** 14 20N 74 25 E
Sharbatāt, Ra's ash, *Oman* **99 C7** 17 56N 56 21 E
Sharbot Lake, *Canada* **151 B8** 44 46N 76 41W
Shardara, *Kazakhstan* **65 C3** 41 15N 67 0 E
Shardara, Step, *Kazakhstan* **65 C3** 42 20N 68 0 E
Shardara Bögeni, *Kazakhstan* **65 C4** 41 10N 68 15 E
Shargun, *Uzbekistan* **65 D3** 38 35N 67 58 E
Sharhorod, *Ukraine* **53 B13** 48 45N 28 5 E
Shari, *Japan* **70 C12** 43 55N 144 40 E
Sharjah = Ash Shāriqah, *U.A.E.* **97 E7** 25 23N 55 26 E
Shark B., *Australia* **125 E1** 25 30 S 113 32 E
Shark Bay ⌓, *Australia* **125 F2** 32 49 S 118 49 E
Sharm el Sheikh, *Egypt* **106 B3** 27 53N 34 18 E
Sharon, *Mass., U.S.A.* **151 D13** 42 7N 71 11W
Sharon, *Pa., U.S.A.* **150 E4** 41 14N 80 31W
Sharon, *Wis., U.S.A.* **157 B8** 42 30N 88 44W
Sharon Springs, *Kans., U.S.A.* **154 F4** 38 54N 101 45W
Sharon Springs, *N.Y., U.S.A.* **151 D10** 42 48N 74 37W
Sharonville, *U.S.A.* **157 E12** 39 16N 84 25W
Sharp Pk., *Phil.* **81 J5** 5 58N 125 31 E
Sharp Pt., *Australia* **126 A3** 10 58 S 142 43 E
Sharpe L., *Canada* **140 B1** 54 24N 93 40W
Sharpes, *U.S.A.* **153 G9** 28 26N 80 46W
Sharpsville, *U.S.A.* **150 E4** 41 15N 80 29W
Sharq el Istiwa'iya □, *Sudan* **107 G3** 5 0N 33 0 E
Sharya, *Russia* **60 A7** 58 22N 45 20 E
Shasha, *Ethiopia* **107 F4** 6 29N 35 59 E
Shashemene, *Ethiopia* **107 F4** 7 13N 38 33 E
Shashi, *Botswana* **117 C4** 21 15 S 27 27 E
Shashi, *China* **77 B9** 30 25N 112 14 E
Shashi →, *Africa* **119 G2** 21 14 S 29 20 E
Shasta, Mt., *U.S.A.* **158 F2** 41 25N 122 12W
Shasta L., *U.S.A.* **158 F2** 40 43N 122 25W
Shatawi, *Sudan* **107 E3** 14 39N 32 6 E
Shāṭi', Wādī ash →, *Libya* **108 C3** 27 30N 15 0 E
Shatilki = Svyetlahorsk, *Belarus* **59 F5** 52 38N 29 46 E
Shatsk, *Russia* **60 C5** 54 5N 41 45 E
Shatsk, *Ukraine* **55 G10** 51 29N 23 55 E
Shatskiy Rise, *Pac. Oc.* **134 D7** 34 0N 157 0 E
Shatskyi ⌓, *Ukraine* **55 G10** 51 30N 23 52 E
Shatt al Arab, *Asia* **97 D6** 30 0N 48 31 E
Shatt al'Arab →, *Iraq* **88 C3** 29 57N 48 34 E
Shatura, *Russia* **58 E10** 55 33N 39 21 E
Shaturtorf = Shatura, *Russia* **58 E10** 55 33N 39 21 E
Shaŭildir, *Kazakhstan* **65 B4** 42 47N 68 3 E
Shaumyani = Shulaveri, *Georgia* **61 K7** 41 22N 44 45 E
Shaunavon, *Canada* **143 D7** 49 35N 108 25W
Shaver L., *U.S.A.* **160 H7** 37 9N 119 18W
Shavli = Šiauliai, *Lithuania* **15 J20** 55 56N 23 15 E
Shaw →, *Australia* **124 D2** 20 21 S 119 17 E
Shaw I., *Australia* **126 J7** 20 30 S 149 2 E
Shawanaga, *Canada* **150 A4** 45 31N 80 17W
Shawangunk Mts., *U.S.A.* **151 E10** 41 35N 74 30W
Shawano, *U.S.A.* **156 C1** 44 47N 88 36W
Shawinigan, *Canada* **140 C5** 46 35N 72 50W
Shawnee, *Ga., U.S.A.* **152 C8** 32 29N 81 25W
Shawnee, *Kans., U.S.A.* **156 E2** 39 1N 94 43W
Shawnee, *Okla., U.S.A.* **155 H6** 35 20N 96 55W
Shay Gap, *Australia* **124 D3** 20 30 S 120 10 E
Shayan, *Kazakhstan* **65 B4** 43 5N 69 25 E
Shayang, *China* **77 B9** 30 42N 112 29 E
Shaybārā, *Si. Arabia* **96 E3** 25 26N 36 47 E
Shayib el Banat, Gebel, *Egypt* **106 B3** 26 59N 33 29 E
Shaykh, J. ash, *Lebanon* **103 B4** 33 25N 35 50 E
Shaykh Miskīn, *Syria* **103 C5** 32 49N 36 9 E
Shaykh Sa'īd, *Iraq* **101 F12** 32 34N 46 17 E
Shaykh 'Uthmān, *Yemen* **98 D4** 12 52N 44 59 E
Shaymak, *Tajikistan* **65 E7** 37 33N 74 50 E
Shaytansky Zavod = Pervouralsk, *Russia* **64 C7** 56 59N 59 59 E
Shazud, *Tajikistan* **65 E6** 37 45N 72 25 E
Shcheglovo = Kemerovo, *Russia* **66 D9** 55 20N 86 5 E
Shchekino, *Russia* **58 E9** 54 1N 37 34 E
Shcherbakov = Rybinsk, *Russia* **58 C10** 58 5N 38 50 E
Shchigry, *Russia* **59 G9** 51 55N 36 58 E
Shchors, *Ukraine* **59 G6** 51 48N 31 56 E
Shchuchinsk, *Kazakhstan* **66 D8** 52 56N 70 12 E
Shchuchye, *Russia* **64 D9** 55 12N 62 46 E
She Xian, *Anhui, China* **77 C12** 29 50N 118 25 E
She Xian, *Hebei, China* **74 F7** 36 30N 113 40 E
Shea, *Guyana* **169 C6** 2 48N 59 4W
Shebekino, *Russia* **59 G9** 50 28N 36 54 E
Shebele = Scebeli, Wabi →, *Somali Rep.* **120 D2** 2 0N 44 0 E
Sheberghān, *Afghan.* **65 E2** 36 40N 65 45 E
Sheboygan, *U.S.A.* **148 D2** 43 46N 87 45W
Shebshi Mts., *Nigeria* **113 D7** 8 30N 12 0 E
Shediac, *Canada* **141 C7** 46 14N 64 32W
Sheelin, L., *Ireland* **23 C4** 53 48N 7 20W
Sheenjek →, *U.S.A.* **144 C11** 66 45N 144 33W
Sheep Haven, *Ireland* **23 A4** 55 11N 7 52W
Sheerness, *U.K.* **21 F8** 51 26N 0 47 E
Sheet Harbour, *Canada* **141 D7** 44 56N 62 31W
Sheffield, *N.Z.* **131 D7** 43 23 S 172 1 E
Sheffield, *U.K.* **20 D6** 53 23N 1 28W
Sheffield, *Ala., U.S.A.* **149 H2** 34 46N 87 41W
Sheffield, *Ill., U.S.A.* **156 C7** 41 21N 89 44W
Sheffield, *Iowa, U.S.A.* **156 B3** 42 54N 93 13W
Sheffield, *Mass., U.S.A.* **151 D11** 42 5N 73 21W
Sheffield, *Pa., U.S.A.* **150 E5** 41 42N 79 3W
Shegaon, *India* **94 D3** 20 48N 76 47 E
Sheghnān, *Afghan.* **65 E5** 37 37N 71 36 E
Shehojele, *Ethiopia* **107 E4** 10 40N 35 9 E
Shehong, *China* **76 B5** 30 54N 105 18 E
Shehuen →, *Argentina* **176 C3** 49 35 S 69 34W
Sheikh Idris, *Sudan* **107 E3** 11 43N 33 30 E
Sheikhpura, *India* **93 G11** 25 9N 85 53 E
Shek Hasan, *Ethiopia* **107 E4** 12 5N 35 58 E
Shekhupura, *Pakistan* **91 C4** 31 42N 73 58 E
Sheki = Şaki, *Azerbaijan* **61 K8** 41 10N 47 5 E
Shekki = Zhongshan, *China* **77 F9** 22 26N 113 20 E
Shekou, *China* **69 G10** 22 30N 113 55 E
Shelbina, *U.S.A.* **156 E4** 39 47N 92 2W
Shelburn, *U.S.A.* **157 E9** 39 11N 87 24W
Shelburne, *N.S., Canada* **141 D6** 43 47N 65 20W
Shelburne, *Ont., Canada* **140 D3** 44 4N 80 15W
Shelburne, *U.S.A.* **151 B11** 44 23N 73 14W
Shelburne B., *Australia* **126 A3** 11 50 S 142 50 E
Shelburne Falls, *U.S.A.* **151 D12** 42 36N 72 45W
Shelby, *Mich., U.S.A.* **148 D2** 43 37N 86 22W
Shelby, *Miss., U.S.A.* **155 J9** 33 57N 90 46W
Shelby, *Mont., U.S.A.* **158 B8** 48 30N 111 51W
Shelby, *N.C., U.S.A.* **149 H5** 35 17N 81 32W
Shelby, *Ohio, U.S.A.* **150 F2** 40 53N 82 40W
Shelbyville, *Ill., U.S.A.* **154 F10** 39 24N 88 48W
Shelbyville, *Ind., U.S.A.* **157 E11** 39 31N 85 47W
Shelbyville, *Ky., U.S.A.* **157 F11** 38 13N 85 14W
Shelbyville, *Mo., U.S.A.* **156 E4** 39 48N 92 2W
Shelbyville, *Tenn., U.S.A.* **149 H2** 35 29N 86 28W
Shelbyville, L., *U.S.A.* **157 E8** 39 26N 88 46W
Sheldon, *Ill., U.S.A.* **157 D9** 40 46N 87 34W
Sheldon, *Iowa, U.S.A.* **154 D7** 43 11N 95 51W
Sheldon, *Mo., U.S.A.* **156 G2** 37 40N 94 18W
Sheldon, *S.C., U.S.A.* **152 C9** 32 36N 80 48W
Sheldon Point, *U.S.A.* **144 E6** 62 32N 164 52W
Sheldrake, *Canada* **141 B7** 50 20N 64 51W
Shelek, *Kazakhstan* **65 B9** 43 33N 78 17 E
Shelengo, Khawr →, *Sudan* **107 E2** 10 33N 28 40 E
Shelikhova, Zaliv, *Russia* **67 D16** 59 30N 157 0 E
Shelikof Strait, *U.S.A.* **144 H9** 57 30N 155 0W
Shell Beach = Huntington Beach, *U.S.A.* **161 M9** 33 40N 118 5W
Shell Lakes, *Australia* **125 E4** 29 20 S 127 30 E
Shellbrook, *Canada* **143 C7** 53 13N 106 24W
Shellharbour, *Australia* **129 C9** 34 31 S 150 51 E
Shellman, *U.S.A.* **152 D5** 31 46N 84 37W
Shellsburg, *U.S.A.* **156 B5** 42 6N 91 52W
Shelon →, *Russia* **58 C6** 58 13N 30 47 E
Shelter Bay = Port-Cartier, *Canada* **141 B6** 50 2N 66 50W
Shelter I, *U.S.A.* **151 E12** 41 5N 72 21W
Shelton, *Conn., U.S.A.* **151 E11** 41 19N 73 5W
Shelton, *Wash., U.S.A.* **160 C3** 47 13N 123 6W
Shemakha = Şamaxi, *Azerbaijan* **61 K9** 40 38N 48 37 E
Shëmri, *Albania* **50 D4** 42 7N 20 13 E
Shemsi, *Sudan* **106 D2** 19 2N 29 57 E
Shen Xian, *China* **74 F8** 36 15N 115 40 E
Shenandoah, *Iowa, U.S.A.* **154 E7** 40 46N 95 22W
Shenandoah, *Pa., U.S.A.* **151 F8** 40 49N 76 12W
Shenandoah, *Va., U.S.A.* **148 F6** 38 29N 78 37W
Shenandoah ⌓, *U.S.A.* **148 F6** 38 35N 78 22W
Shenandoah →, *U.S.A.* **148 F7** 39 19N 77 44W
Shenchi, *China* **74 E7** 39 8N 112 10 E
Shencottah, *India* **95 K3** 8 59N 77 18 E
Shendam, *Nigeria* **113 D6** 8 49N 9 30 E
Shendî, *Sudan* **107 D3** 16 46N 33 22 E
Shendurni, *India* **94 D2** 20 39N 75 36 E
Shenge, *S. Leone* **112 D2** 7 54N 12 55W
Shengfang, *China* **74 E9** 39 3N 116 42 E
Shenggeldi, *Kazakhstan* **65 B8** 43 59N 77 27 E
Shëngjergj, *Albania* **50 E4** 41 17N 20 10 E
Shëngjin, *Albania* **50 E3** 41 50N 19 35 E
Shengzhou, *China* **77 C13** 29 35N 120 50 E
Shenjingzi, *China* **75 B13** 44 40N 124 30 E
Shenmu, *China* **74 E6** 38 50N 110 29 E
Shennongjia, *China* **77 B8** 31 43N 110 44 E
Shenqiu, *China* **74 H8** 33 25N 115 5 E
Shensi = Shaanxi □, *China* **74 G5** 35 0N 109 0 E
Shenyang, *China* **75 D12** 41 48N 123 27 E
Shenzhen, *China* **77 F10** 22 32N 114 5 E
Shenzhen ✕ (SZX), *China* **69 F10** 22 41N 113 49 E
Shenzhen Shuiku, *China* **69 F11** 22 34N 114 8 E
Shenzhen Wan, *China* **69 G10** 22 27N 113 55 E
Sheo, *India* **92 F4** 26 11N 71 15 E
Sheopur Kalan, *India* **92 G7** 25 40N 76 40 E
Shepetivka, *Ukraine* **59 G4** 50 10N 27 10 E
Shepetovka = Shepetivka, *Ukraine* **59 G4** 50 10N 27 10 E
Shepherd Is., *Vanuatu* **133 F6** 16 55 S 168 36 E
Shepherdsville, *U.S.A.* **157 G11** 37 59N 85 43W
Shepparton, *Australia* **129 D6** 36 23 S 145 26 E
Sheppey, I. of, *U.K.* **21 F8** 51 25N 0 48 E
Shepton Mallet, *U.K.* **21 F5** 51 11N 2 33W
Sheqi, *China* **74 H7** 33 12N 112 57 E
Sher Khan Qala, *Afghan.* **91 C2** 29 53N 66 13 E
Sher Qila, *Pakistan* **93 A6** 36 7N 74 2 E
Sherab, *Sudan* **107 E1** 10 44N 24 41 E
Sherabad, *Uzbekistan* **65 E3** 37 40N 67 1 E
Sherborne, *U.K.* **21 G5** 50 57N 2 31W
Sherbro →, *S. Leone* **112 D2** 7 45N 12 55W
Sherbro I., *S. Leone* **112 D2** 7 30N 12 40W
Sherbrooke, *N.S., Canada* **141 C7** 45 8N 61 59W
Sherbrooke, *Qué., Canada* **141 C5** 45 28N 71 57W
Sherburne, *U.S.A.* **151 D9** 42 41N 75 30W
Sherburne Reef, *Papua N. G.* **132 B5** 3 20 S 148 0 E
Sherda, *Chad* **109 D3** 20 7N 16 46 E
Shereik, *Sudan* **106 D3** 18 44N 33 47 E
Shergaon, *India* **90 B4** 27 7N 92 16 E
Shergarh, *India* **92 F5** 26 20N 72 18 E
Sherghati, *India* **93 G11** 24 34N 84 47 E
Sheridan, *Ark., U.S.A.* **155 H8** 34 19N 92 24W
Sheridan, *Ill., U.S.A.* **157 C8** 41 32N 88 41W
Sheridan, *Ind., U.S.A.* **157 D10** 40 8N 86 13W
Sheridan, *Wyo., U.S.A.* **158 D10** 44 48N 106 58W
Sheringham, *U.K.* **20 E9** 52 56N 1 13 E
Sherkin I., *Ireland* **23 E2** 51 28N 9 26W
Sherkot, *India* **93 E8** 29 22N 78 35 E
Sherman, *U.S.A.* **155 J6** 33 40N 96 35W
Sherpur, *Bangla.* **90 C3** 25 0N 90 0 E
Sherpur, *India* **93 G10** 25 34N 83 47 E
Sherridon, *Canada* **143 B8** 55 8N 101 5W
Sherwood, *U.S.A.* **157 C12** 41 17N 84 33W
Sherwood Forest, *U.K.* **20 D6** 53 6N 1 7W
Sherwood Park, *Canada* **142 C6** 53 31N 113 19W
Sheslay →, *Canada* **142 B2** 58 48N 132 5W
Shethanei L., *Canada* **143 B9** 58 48N 97 50W
Shetland □, *U.K.* **22 A7** 60 30N 1 30W
Shetland Is., *U.K.* **22 A7** 60 30N 1 30W
Shetrunji →, *India* **92 J5** 21 19N 72 7 E
Sheung Shui, *China* **69 F11** 22 31N 114 7 E
Shevaroy Hills, *India* **95 J4** 11 58N 78 12 E
Shevchenkovo = Dolynska, *Ukraine* **59 H7** 48 6N 32 46 E
Shevchenkovo, *Ukraine* **53 E14** 45 33N 29 20 E
Shevgaon, *India* **94 E2** 19 21N 75 14 E
Shewa, *Ethiopia* **107 F4** 9 33N 38 10 E
Shewa Gimira, *Ethiopia* **107 F4** 7 4N 35 51 E
Shey-Phoksundo ⌓, *Nepal* **93 E10** 29 30N 82 45 E
Sheyenne →, *U.S.A.* **154 B6** 47 2N 96 50W
Shibām, *Yemen* **99 D5** 15 59N 48 36 E
Shibata, *Japan* **70 F9** 37 57N 139 20 E
Shibecha, *Japan* **70 C12** 43 17N 144 36 E
Shibetsu, *Japan* **70 B11** 44 10N 142 23 E
Shibîn el Kôm, *Egypt* **106 H7** 30 31N 30 55 E
Shibîn el Qanâtir, *Egypt* **106 H7** 30 19N 31 19 E
Shibing, *China* **76 D7** 27 2N 108 7 E
Shibogama L., *Canada* **140 B2** 53 35N 88 15W
Shibukawa, *Japan* **73 A11** 36 29N 139 0 E
Shibushi, *Japan* **72 F3** 31 25N 131 8 E
Shibushi-Wan, *Japan* **72 F3** 31 24N 131 8 E
Shicheng, *China* **77 D11** 26 22N 116 20 E
Shickshinny, *U.S.A.* **151 E8** 41 9N 76 9W
Shickshock Mts. = Chic-Chocs, Mts., *Canada* **141 C6** 48 55N 66 0W
Shidād, *Si. Arabia* **98 B3** 21 19N 40 3 E
Shidao, *China* **75 F12** 36 50N 122 25 E
Shidian, *China* **76 E2** 24 40N 99 5 E
Shido, *Japan* **72 C6** 34 19N 134 10 E
Shiel, L., *U.K.* **22 E3** 56 48N 5 34W
Shield, C., *Australia* **126 A2** 13 20 S 136 20 E
Shīeli, *Kazakhstan* **65 A3** 44 20N 66 15 E
Shifang, *China* **76 B5** 31 8N 104 10 E
Shiga □, *Japan* **73 B8** 35 20N 136 0 E
Shigaib, *Sudan* **109 E4** 15 5N 23 35 E
Shigu, *China* **76 D2** 26 51N 99 56 E
Shiguaigou, *China* **74 D6** 40 52N 110 15 E
Shihan, W. →, *Yemen* **99 C5** 17 24N 51 26 E
Shihchiachuangi = Shijiazhuang, *China* **74 E8** 38 2N 114 28 E
Shihezi, *China* **68 B3** 44 15N 86 2 E
Shiiba, *Japan* **72 E3** 32 29N 131 4 E
Shijak, *Albania* **50 E3** 41 21N 19 33 E
Shijiazhuang, *China* **74 E8** 38 2N 114 28 E
Shijiu Hu, *China* **77 B12** 31 25N 118 50 E
Shikarpur, *India* **92 E8** 28 17N 78 7 E
Shikarpur, *Pakistan* **91 D3** 27 57N 68 39 E
Shikhrany = Kanash, *Russia* **60 C8** 55 30N 47 32 E
Shikine-Jima, *Japan* **73 C11** 34 19N 139 13 E
Shikohabad, *India* **93 F8** 27 6N 78 36 E
Shikoku, *Japan* **72 D5** 33 30N 133 30 E
Shikoku □, *Japan* **72 D5** 33 30N 133 30 E
Shikoku-Sanchi, *Japan* **72 D5** 33 30N 133 30 E
Shikotsu-Ko, *Japan* **70 C10** 42 45N 141 25 E
Shikotsu-Tōya ⌓, *Japan* **70 C10** 44 4N 145 8 E
Shikuka = Poronaysk, *Russia* **67 E15** 49 13N 143 0 E
Shiliguri, *India* **90 B2** 26 45N 88 25 E
Shiliu = Changjiang, *China* **86 C7** 19 20N 108 55 E
Shilka, *Russia* **67 D12** 52 0N 115 55 E
Shilka →, *Russia* **67 D13** 53 20N 121 26 E
Shillelagh, *Ireland* **23 D5** 52 45N 6 32W
Shillington, *U.S.A.* **151 F9** 40 18N 75 58W
Shillong, *India* **90 C3** 25 35N 91 53 E
Shilo, *West Bank* **103 C4** 32 4N 35 18 E
Shilong, *China* **77 F9** 23 5N 113 52 E
Shilou, *China* **74 F6** 37 0N 110 48 E
Shilovo, *Russia* **60 C5** 54 25N 40 57 E
Shima-Hantō, *Japan* **73 C8** 34 22N 136 45 E
Shimabara, *Japan* **72 E2** 32 48N 130 20 E
Shimada, *Japan* **73 C10** 34 49N 138 10 E
Shimane □, *Japan* **72 C4** 35 0N 132 30 E
Shimane-Hantō, *Japan* **72 B5** 35 30N 133 0 E
Shimanovsk, *Russia* **67 D13** 52 15N 127 30 E
Shimba Hills ⌓, *Kenya* **118 C4** 4 14 S 39 25 E
Shimen, *China* **77 C8** 29 35N 111 20 E
Shimenjie, *China* **77 C11** 29 29N 116 48 E
Shimian, *China* **76 C4** 29 17N 102 23 E
Shimizu, *Japan* **73 C10** 35 0N 138 30 E
Shimo-Jima, *Japan* **72 E2** 32 15N 130 7 E
Shimo-Koshiki-Jima, *Japan* **72 F1** 31 40N 129 43 E
Shimoda, *Japan* **73 C10** 34 40N 138 57 E
Shimodate, *Japan* **73 A11** 36 20N 139 55 E
Shimoga, *India* **95 H2** 13 57N 75 32 E
Shimoni, *Kenya* **118 C4** 4 38 S 39 20 E
Shimonita, *Japan* **73 A10** 36 13N 138 47 E
Shimonoseki, *Japan* **72 D2** 33 58N 130 55 E
Shimotsuma, *Japan* **73 A11** 36 11N 139 58 E
Shimpuru Rapids, *Namibia* **116 B2** 17 45 S 19 55 E
Shimsha →, *India* **95 H3** 13 15N 77 10 E
Shimsk, *Russia* **58 C6** 58 15N 30 50 E
Shin, L., *U.K.* **22 C4** 58 5N 4 30W
Shin-Nan'yō, *Japan* **72 C3** 34 3N 131 49 E
Shin-Tone-Gawa →, *Japan* **73 B12** 35 44N 140 51 E
Shinan, *China* **76 F7** 22 44N 109 53 E
Shinano-Gawa →, *Japan* **71 F9** 36 50N 138 30 E
Shināş, *Oman* **97 E8** 24 46N 56 28 E
Shīndand, *Afghan.* **91 B1** 33 12N 62 8 E
Shingbwiyang, *Burma* **90 B6** 26 41N 96 13 E
Shinglehouse, *U.S.A.* **150 E6** 41 58N 78 12W
Shingū, *Japan* **73 D7** 33 40N 135 55 E
Shingwidzi, *S. Africa* **117 C5** 23 5 S 31 25 E
Shinji, *Japan* **72 B4** 35 24N 132 54 E
Shinji-Ko, *Japan* **72 B4** 35 26N 132 57 E
Shinjō, *Japan* **70 E10** 38 46N 140 18 E
Shinkafe, *Nigeria* **113 C6** 13 8N 6 29 E
Shinminato, *Japan* **73 A9** 36 47N 137 4 E
Shinshār, *Syria* **103 A5** 34 36N 36 43 E
Shinshiro, *Japan* **73 C9** 34 54N 137 30 E
Shintuya, *Peru* **172 C3** 12 41 S 71 15W
Shinyanga, *Tanzania* **118 C3** 3 45 S 33 27 E
Shinyanga □, *Tanzania* **118 C3** 3 50 S 34 0 E
Shio-no-Misaki, *Japan* **73 D7** 33 25N 135 45 E
Shiogama, *Japan* **70 E10** 38 19N 141 1 E
Shiojiri, *Japan* **73 A9** 36 6N 137 58 E
Shipchenski Prokhod, *Bulgaria* **51 D9** 42 45N 25 15 E
Shiping, *China* **76 F4** 23 45N 102 23 E
Shippagan, *Canada* **141 C7** 47 45N 64 45W
Shippensburg, *U.S.A.* **150 F7** 40 3N 77 31W
Shippenville, *U.S.A.* **150 E5** 41 15N 79 28W
Shiprock, *U.S.A.* **159 H9** 36 47N 108 41W
Shiqian, *China* **76 D7** 27 32N 108 13 E
Shiqma, N. →, *Israel* **103 D3** 31 37N 34 30 E
Shiquan, *China* **74 H5** 33 5N 108 15 E
Shiquan He = Indus →, *Pakistan* **91 D2** 24 20N 67 47 E
Shīr Khān, *Afghan.* **65 E4** 37 11N 68 36 E
Shīr Kūh, *Iran* **97 D7** 31 39N 54 3 E
Shirabad = Sherabad, *Uzbekistan* **65 E3** 37 40N 67 1 E
Shiragami-Misaki, *Japan* **70 D10** 41 24N 140 12 E
Shirahama, *Japan* **73 D7** 33 41N 135 20 E
Shirakawa, *Fukushima, Japan* **71 F10** 37 7N 140 13 E
Shirakawa, *Gifu, Japan* **73 A8** 36 17N 136 56 E
Shirane-San, *Gumma, Japan* **73 A11** 36 48N 139 22 E
Shirane-San, *Yamanashi, Japan* **73 B10** 35 42N 138 9 E
Shiraoi, *Japan* **70 C10** 42 33N 141 21 E
Shīrāz, *Iran* **97 D7** 29 42N 52 30 E
Shirbîn, *Egypt* **106 H7** 31 11N 31 32 E
Shire →, *Africa* **119 F4** 17 42 S 35 19 E
Shiretoko-Misaki, *Japan* **70 B12** 44 21N 145 20 E
Shirin, *Uzbekistan* **65 C4** 40 14N 69 7 E
Shirinab →, *Pakistan* **92 D2** 30 15N 66 28 E
Shiriya-Zaki, *Japan* **70 D10** 41 25N 141 30 E
Shirley, *U.S.A.* **157 E11** 39 53N 85 35W
Shiroishi, *Japan* **70 F10** 38 0N 140 37 E
Shirol, *India* **94 F2** 16 47N 74 41 E
Shirpur, *India* **94 D2** 21 21N 74 57 E
Shirshow Ridge, *Pac. Oc.* **134 B8** 58 0N 170 0 E
Shīrvān, *Iran* **97 B8** 37 30N 57 50 E
Shirwa, L. = Chilwa, L., *Malawi* **119 F4** 15 15 S 35 40 E
Shishaldin Volcano, *U.S.A.* **144 J7** 54 45N 163 58W
Shishi, *China* **77 E12** 24 44N 118 37 E
Shishmaref, *U.S.A.* **144 C6** 66 15N 166 4W
Shishou, *China* **77 C9** 29 38N 112 22 E
Shitai, *China* **77 B11** 30 12N 117 25 E
Shively, *U.S.A.* **157 F11** 38 12N 85 49W
Shivpuri, *India* **92 G7** 25 26N 77 42 E
Shixian, *China* **75 C15** 43 5N 129 50 E
Shixing, *China* **77 E10** 24 46N 114 5 E
Shiyan, *Guangdong, China* **69 F10** 22 42N 113 56 E
Shiyan, *Hubei, China* **77 A8** 32 35N 110 45 E
Shiyan Shuiku, *China* **69 F10** 22 42N 113 54 E
Shiyata, *Egypt* **106 B2** 29 25N 25 7 E
Shizhu, *China* **76 C7** 29 58N 108 7 E
Shizong, *China* **76 E5** 24 50N 104 0 E
Shizuishan, *China* **74 E4** 39 15N 106 50 E
Shizuoka, *Japan* **73 C10** 34 57N 138 24 E
Shizuoka □, *Japan* **73 B10** 35 15N 138 40 E
Shklov = Shklow, *Belarus* **58 E6** 54 16N 30 15 E
Shklow, *Belarus* **58 E6** 54 16N 30 15 E
Shkodër, *Albania* **50 D3** 42 4N 19 32 E
Shkodra = Shkodër, *Albania* **50 D3** 42 4N 19 32 E
Shkumbini →, *Albania* **50 E3** 41 2N 19 31 E
Shmidta, Ostrov, *Russia* **67 A10** 81 0N 91 0 E
Shō-Gawa →, *Japan* **73 A9** 36 47N 137 4 E
Shoal Cr. →, *U.S.A.* **156 E3** 39 44N 93 32W
Shoal L., *Canada* **143 D9** 49 33N 95 1W
Shoal Lake, *Canada* **143 C8** 50 30N 100 35W
Shoalhaven →, *Australia* **129 C9** 34 54 S 150 42 E
Shoals, *U.S.A.* **157 F10** 38 40N 86 47W
Shōbara, *Japan* **72 C5** 34 51N 133 1 E
Shōdo-Shima, *Japan* **72 C6** 34 30N 134 15 E
Shokpar = Shoqpar, *Kazakhstan* **65 B7** 43 49N 74 21 E
Sholapur = Solapur, *India* **94 F2** 17 43N 75 56 E
Sholaqqūrghan, *Kazakhstan* **65 B4** 43 46N 69 9 E
Shōmrōn, *West Bank* **103 C4** 32 15N 35 13 E
Shoqpar, *Kazakhstan* **65 B7** 43 49N 74 21 E
Shoranur, *India* **95 J3** 10 46N 76 19 E
Shorapur, *India* **95 F3** 16 31N 76 48 E
Shoreham by Sea, *U.K.* **21 G7** 50 50N 0 16W
Shorewood, *U.S.A.* **157 A9** 43 5N 87 54W
Shori →, *Pakistan* **92 E3** 28 29N 69 44 E
Shorkot Road, *Pakistan* **92 D5** 30 47N 72 15 E
Shornak, *Kazakhstan* **65 B4** 43 24N 68 2 E
Shorter, *U.S.A.* **152 C4** 32 24N 85 57W
Shorterville, *U.S.A.* **152 D4** 31 34N 85 6W
Shortland I., *Solomon Is.* **133 L8** 7 0 S 155 45 E
Shortland Is., *Solomon Is.* **133 L8** 7 0 S 156 0 E
Shortt's I., *India* **94 D8** 20 47N 87 4 E
Shoshone, *Calif., U.S.A.* **161 K10** 35 58N 116 16W
Shoshone, *Idaho, U.S.A.* **158 E6** 42 56N 114 25W
Shoshone L., *U.S.A.* **158 D8** 44 22N 110 43W
Shoshone Mts., *U.S.A.* **158 G5** 39 20N 117 25W
Shoshong, *Botswana* **116 C4** 22 56 S 26 31 E
Shoshoni, *U.S.A.* **158 E9** 43 14N 108 7W
Shostka, *Ukraine* **59 G7** 51 57N 33 32 E
Shotor Khūn, *Afghan.* **91 B2** 34 19N 64 56 E
Shotover →, *N.Z.* **131 E3** 44 59 S 168 41 E
Shou Xian, *China* **77 A11** 32 37N 116 42 E
Shouchang, *China* **77 C12** 29 18N 119 12 E
Shouguang, *China* **75 F10** 37 52N 118 45 E
Shouning, *China* **77 D12** 27 27N 119 31 E
Shouyang, *China* **74 F7** 37 54N 113 8 E
Show Low, *U.S.A.* **159 J9** 34 15N 110 2W
Showa, *Japan* **73 B10** 35 36N 138 29 E
Shpola, *Ukraine* **59 H6** 49 1N 31 30 E
Shpykiv, *Ukraine* **53 B13** 48 47N 28 34 E
Shqipëria = Albania ■, *Europe* **50 E4** 41 0N 20 0 E
Shreveport, *U.S.A.* **155 J8** 32 31N 93 45W
Shrewsbury, *U.K.* **21 E5** 52 43N 2 45W
Shri Mohangarh, *India* **92 F4** 27 17N 71 18 E
Shrigonda, *India* **94 E2** 18 37N 74 41 E
Shrirampur, *India* **93 H13** 22 44N 88 21 E
Shropshire □, *U.K.* **21 E5** 52 36N 2 45W
Shū, *Kazakhstan* **65 B6** 43 36N 73 42 E
Shū →, *Kazakhstan* **65 A3** 45 0N 67 44 E
Shuangbai, *China* **76 E3** 24 42N 101 38 E
Shuangcheng, *China* **75 B14** 45 20N 126 15 E
Shuangfeng, *China* **77 D9** 27 29N 112 11 E
Shuanggou, *China* **75 G9** 34 2N 117 30 E
Shuangjiang, *China* **76 F2** 23 26N 99 58 E
Shuangliao, *China* **75 C12** 43 29N 123 30 E
Shuangshanzi, *China* **75 D10** 40 20N 119 8 E
Shuangyang, *China* **75 C13** 43 28N 125 40 E
Shuangyashan, *China* **69 B8** 46 28N 131 5 E
Shu'b, Ra's, *Yemen* **99 D6** 12 30N 53 25 E
Shubra el Kheima, *Egypt* **106 H7** 30 6N 31 15 E
Shubra Khit, *Egypt* **106 H7** 31 2N 30 42 E
Shucheng, *China* **77 B11** 31 28N 116 57 E
Shufu, *China* **65 D7** 39 27N 75 52 E
Shugozero, *Russia* **58 C8** 59 54N 34 10 E
Shuguri Falls, *Tanzania* **119 D4** 8 33 S 37 22 E
Shuḥayr, *Yemen* **99 D5** 14 41N 49 23 E

Shuiji, China 77 D12 27 13N 118 20 E
Shuiye, China 74 F8 36 7N 114 8 E
Shujalpur, India 92 H7 23 18N 76 46 E
Shukpa Kunzang, India 93 B8 34 22N 78 22 E
Shulan, China 75 B14 44 28N 127 0 E
Shulaveri, Georgia 61 K7 41 22N 44 45 E
Shule, China 65 D8 39 25N 76 3 E
Shullsburg, U.S.A. 156 B6 42 35N 90 13W
Shumagin Is., U.S.A. 144 J8 55 7N 160 30W
Shumen, Bulgaria 51 C10 43 18N 26 55 E
Shumerlya, Russia 60 C8 55 30N 46 25 E
Shumikha, Russia 64 D9 55 10N 63 15 E
Shunchang, China 77 D11 26 54N 117 48 E
Shunde, China 77 F9 22 42N 113 14 E
Shungay, Kazakhstan 61 F8 48 30N 46 45 E
Shungnak, U.S.A. 144 C8 66 52N 157 9W
Shuo Xian = Shuozhou, China 74 E7 39 20N 112 33 E
Shuozhou, China 74 E7 39 20N 112 33 E
Shūr →, Fārs, Iran 97 D7 28 30N 55 0 E
Shūr →, Kermān, Iran 97 D8 30 52N 57 37 E
Shūr →, Yazd, Iran 97 D7 31 45N 55 15 E
Shūr Āb, Iran 97 C6 34 23N 51 11 E
Shūr Gaz, Iran 97 D8 29 10N 59 20 E
Shūrāb, Iran 97 C8 33 43N 56 29 E
Shurab, Tajikistan 65 C5 40 3N 70 33 E
Shurchi, Uzbekistan 65 E3 37 59N 67 47 E
Shūrjestān, Iran 97 D7 31 24N 52 25 E
Shurkhua, Burma 90 D4 22 15N 93 38 E
Shurugwi, Zimbabwe 119 F3 19 40 S 30 0 E
Shūsf, Iran 97 D9 31 50N 60 5 E
Shūsh, Iran 101 F13 32 11N 48 15 E
Shūshtar, Iran 97 D6 32 0N 48 50 E
Shuswap L., Canada 142 C5 50 55N 119 3W
Shuya, Russia 60 B5 56 50N 41 28 E
Shuyak I., U.S.A. 144 G9 58 31N 152 30W
Shuyang, China 75 G10 34 10N 118 42 E
Shuzenji, Japan 73 C10 34 58N 138 56 E
Shūzū, Iran 97 D7 29 52N 54 30 E
Shwangliao = Liaoyuan, China 75 C13 42 58N 125 2 E
Shwebo, Burma 90 D5 22 30N 95 45 E
Shwegu, Burma 90 C6 24 15N 96 26 E
Shwegun, Burma 90 G6 17 9N 97 39 E
Shwegyin, Burma 90 G6 17 55N 96 53 E
Shweli →, Burma 90 D6 23 45N 96 45 E
Shwenyaung, Burma 90 E6 20 46N 96 57 E
Shyamnagar, India 95 H11 13 21N 92 57 E
Shyghanaq, Kazakhstan 65 A6 45 6N 73 59 E
Shyghanaq, Kazakhstan 65 A5 44 49N 70 0 E
Shymkent, Kazakhstan 65 B4 42 18N 69 36 E
Shyok, India 93 B8 34 13N 78 12 E
Shyok →, Pakistan 93 B6 35 13N 75 53 E
Shyroke, Ukraine 52 B8 48 13N 23 6 E
Shyroke, Ukraine 53 E15 45 59N 30 5 E
Si Chon, Thailand 87 H2 9 0N 99 54 E
Si Kiang = Xi Jiang →, China 77 F9 22 5N 113 20 E
Si Lanna △, Thailand 86 C2 19 17N 99 12 E
Si-ngan = Xi'an, China 74 G5 34 15N 109 0 E
Si Prachan, Thailand 86 E3 14 37N 100 9 E
Si Racha, Thailand 86 F3 13 10N 100 48 E
Si Xian, China 75 H9 33 30N 117 50 E
Siachen Glacier, Asia 93 B7 35 20N 77 30 E
Siahaf →, Pakistan 92 E3 29 3N 68 57 E
Siahan Range, Pakistan 91 D2 27 30N 64 40 E
Siak →, Indonesia 84 B2 1 13N 102 9 E
Siaksriindrapura, Indonesia 84 B2 0 51N 102 0 E
Sialkot, Pakistan 91 B4 32 32N 74 30 E
Sialsuk, India 90 D4 23 24N 92 45 E
Sialum, Papua N. G. 132 D4 6 5 S 147 36 E
Siam = Thailand ■, Asia 86 E4 16 0N 102 0 E
Sian = Xi'an, China 74 G5 34 15N 109 0 E
Sian Ka'an ⌓, Mexico 163 D7 19 35N 87 40W
Siangtan = Xiangtan, China 77 D9 27 51N 112 54 E
Sianów, Poland 54 D3 54 13N 16 18 E
Siantan, Indonesia 84 B3 3 10N 106 15 E
Siàpo →, Venezuela 168 C4 2 7N 66 28W
Sīāreh, Iran 97 D9 28 5N 60 14 E
Siargao I., Phil. 81 G6 9 52N 126 3 E
Siari, Pakistan 93 B7 34 55N 76 40 E
Siasi, Phil. 79 C6 5 34N 120 50 E
Siasi I., Phil. 81 J3 5 33N 120 51 E
Siassi, Papua N. G. 132 C4 5 40 S 147 51 E
Siátista, Greece 50 F5 40 15N 21 33 E
Siaton, Phil. 81 G4 9 4N 123 2 E
Siau, Indonesia 82 A3 2 50N 125 25 E
Šiauliai, Lithuania 15 J20 55 56N 23 15 E
Šiauliai □, Lithuania 54 C10 55 56N 23 19 E
Siazan = Siyäzän, Azerbaijan 61 K9 41 3N 49 10 E
Sibâi, Gebel el, Egypt 96 E2 25 45N 34 10 E
Sibang, Gabon 114 B1 0 25N 9 31 E
Sibang, Indonesia 79 K18 8 34 S 115 13 E
Sibay, Russia 64 E7 52 42N 58 39 E
Sibay I., Phil. 81 F3 11 51N 121 29 E
Sibayi, L., S. Africa 117 D5 27 20 S 32 45 E
Sibdu, Sudan 107 E2 10 57N 26 17 E
Šibenik, Croatia 45 E12 43 48N 15 54 E
Siberia = Sibirskiy □, Russia 67 D10 58 0N 90 0 E
Siberia, Russia 6 D13 60 0N 100 0 E
Siberut, Indonesia 84 C1 1 30 S 99 0 E
Sibi, Pakistan 91 C2 29 30N 67 54 E
Sibil = Oksibil, Indonesia 83 B6 4 59 S 140 35 E
Sibiloi △, Kenya 118 B4 4 0N 36 20 E
Sibirskiy □, Russia 67 D10 58 0N 90 0 E
Sibiti, Congo 114 C2 3 38 S 13 19 E
Sibiu, Romania 53 E9 45 45N 24 9 E
Sibiu □, Romania 53 E9 45 50N 24 15 E
Sibium Mts., Papua N. G. 132 E5 9 19 S 148 25 E
Sibley, Ill., U.S.A. 157 D8 40 35N 88 23W
Sibley, Iowa, U.S.A. 154 D7 43 24N 95 45W
Sibolga, Indonesia 84 B1 1 42N 98 45 E
Sibsagar, India 90 B5 27 0N 94 36 E
Sibu, Malaysia 85 B4 2 18N 111 49 E
Sibuco, Phil. 81 H4 7 20N 122 10 E
Sibuguey B., Phil. 81 H4 7 50N 122 45 E
Sibut, C.A.R. 114 A3 5 46N 19 10 E
Sibutu, Phil. 85 B5 4 45N 119 30 E
Sibutu Group, Phil. 81 J2 4 45N 119 20 E
Sibutu Passage, E. Indies 81 J3 4 50N 120 0 E
Sibuyan I., Phil. 80 E4 12 25N 122 40 E
Sibuyan Sea, Phil. 80 E4 12 30N 122 20 E
Sic, Romania 53 D8 46 56N 23 53 E
Sicamous, Canada 142 C5 50 49N 119 0W
Sicapoo, Mt., Phil. 80 B3 18 1N 120 56 E
Sicasica, Bolivia 172 D4 17 22 S 67 45W
Siccus →, Australia 128 A3 31 55 S 139 17 E
Sichelberg = Sierpc, Poland 55 F6 52 55N 19 43 E
Sichuan □, China 76 B5 30 30N 103 0 E
Sichuan Pendi, China 76 B5 31 0N 105 0 E
Sicilia, Italy 47 E7 37 30N 14 30 E
Sicily = Sicilia, Italy 47 E7 37 30N 14 30 E
Sicily, Str. of 46 E4 37 35N 11 56 E
Sicuani, Peru 172 C3 14 21 S 71 10W
Šid, Serbia & M. 52 E4 45 8N 19 14 E
Sidamo, Ethiopia 107 G4 5 0N 37 50 E
Sidaouet, Niger 113 B6 18 34N 8 3 E
Sidári, Greece 38 B9 39 47N 19 41 E
Siddapur, India 95 G2 14 20N 74 53 E
Siddhapur, India 92 H5 23 56N 72 25 E
Siddipet, India 94 E4 18 5N 78 51 E
Sidensjö, Sweden 16 A12 63 18N 18 17 E
Sidéradougou, Burkina Faso 112 C4 10 42N 4 12W
Siderno, Italy 47 D9 38 16N 16 18 E
Sidhauli, India 93 F9 27 17N 80 50 E
Sídheros, Ákra, Greece 39 E7 35 19N 26 19 E
Sidhi, India 93 G9 24 25N 81 53 E
Sidhirókastron, Greece 50 E7 41 13N 23 24 E
Sîdi Abd el Rahmân, Egypt 106 A2 30 55N 29 44 E
Sidi Ahmed Rgueibi, W. Sahara 110 C2 27 32N 11 16W
Sîdi Barrâni, Egypt 106 A2 31 38N 25 58 E
Sidi-bel-Abbès, Algeria 111 A4 35 13N 0 39W
Sidi Bennour, Morocco 110 B3 32 40N 8 25W
Sîdi Haneish, Egypt 106 A2 31 10N 27 35 E
Sidi Ifni, Morocco 110 C2 29 29N 10 12W
Sidi Kacem, Morocco 110 B3 34 11N 5 49W
Sîdi Omar, Egypt 106 A1 31 24N 24 57 E
Sidi Slimane, Morocco 110 B3 34 16N 5 56W
Sidi Smaïl, Morocco 110 B3 32 50N 8 31W
Sīdī 'Uzayz, Libya 108 B4 31 41N 24 55 E
Siding No 14 = Ponoka, Canada 142 C6 52 42N 113 40W
Sidlaw Hills, U.K. 22 E5 56 32N 3 2W
Sidley, Mt., Antarctica 7 D14 77 2 S 126 2W
Sidmouth, U.K. 21 G4 50 40N 3 15W
Sidmouth, C., Australia 126 A3 13 25 S 143 36 E
Sidney, Canada 142 D4 48 39N 123 24W
Sidney, Mont., U.S.A. 154 B2 47 43N 104 9W
Sidney, N.Y., U.S.A. 151 D9 42 19N 75 24W
Sidney, Nebr., U.S.A. 154 E3 41 8N 102 59W
Sidney, Ohio, U.S.A. 157 D12 40 17N 84 9W
Sidney Lanier, L., U.S.A. 152 A5 34 10N 84 4W
Sido, Mali 112 C3 11 37N 7 29W
Sidoarjo, Indonesia 85 D4 7 27 S 112 43 E
Sidoktaya, Burma 90 E5 20 27N 94 15 E
Sidon = Saydā, Lebanon 103 B4 33 35N 35 25 E
Sidra, G. of = Surt, Khalīj, Libya 108 B3 31 40N 18 30 E
Sidrolândia, Brazil 173 20 55 S 54 58W
Siedlce, Poland 55 F9 52 10N 22 20 E
Sieg →, Germany 30 E3 50 46N 7 6 E
Siegburg, Germany 30 E3 50 47N 7 12 E
Siegen, Germany 30 E4 50 51N 8 0 E
Siem Pang, Cambodia 86 E6 14 7N 106 23 E
Siem Reap = Siemreab, Cambodia 86 F4 13 20N 103 52 E
Siemiatycze, Poland 55 F9 52 27N 22 53 E
Siemreab, Cambodia 86 F4 13 20N 103 52 E
Siena, Italy 45 E8 43 19N 11 21 E
Sieniawa, Poland 55 H9 50 11N 22 38 E
Sienyang = Xianyang, China 74 G5 34 20N 108 40 E
Sieradz, Poland 55 G5 51 37N 18 41 E
Sieraków, Poland 55 F3 52 39N 16 2 E
Sierck-les-Bains, France 27 C13 49 26N 6 20 E
Sierning, Austria 34 C7 48 2N 14 18 E
Sierpc, Poland 55 F6 52 55N 19 43 E
Sierpe, Bocas de la, Venezuela 169 G9 10 0N 61 30W
Sierra Blanca, U.S.A. 159 L11 31 11N 105 22W
Sierra Blanca Peak, U.S.A. 159 K11 33 23N 105 49W
Sierra City, U.S.A. 160 F6 39 34N 120 38W
Sierra Colorada, Argentina 176 B3 40 35 S 67 50W
Sierra de Aracena y Picas de Aroche ⌓, Spain 43 H4 37 53N 6 41W
Sierra de Bahoruco △, Dom. Rep. 165 C5 18 10N 71 25W
Sierra de Baza ⌓, Spain 41 H2 37 20N 2 48W
Sierra de Castril ⌓, Spain 41 H2 37 54N 2 50W
Sierra de Espuña ⌓, Spain 41 H3 37 50N 1 31W
Sierra de Grazalema ⌓, Spain 43 J5 36 31N 5 28W
Sierra de Gredos ⌓, Spain 42 E5 40 17N 5 17W
Sierra de Hornachuelos ⌓, Spain 43 H5 37 56N 5 14W
Sierra de Huétor ⌓, Spain 43 H7 37 14N 3 30W
Sierra de La Culata △, Venezuela 165 E5 8 45N 71 10W
Sierra de la Culata △, Venezuela 168 B3 8 48N 70 56W
Sierra de la Macarena △, Colombia 168 A3 11 19N 74 1W
Sierra de Lancandón △, Guatemala 164 C1 16 59N 90 23W
Sierra de las Nieves ⌓, Spain 43 J6 36 42N 5 0W
Sierra de las Quijadas △, Argentina 174 C2 32 29 S 67 5W
Sierra de María-Los Vélez ⌓, Spain 41 H2 37 41N 2 10W
Sierra de San Luis △, Venezuela 165 D6 11 20N 69 43W
Sierra de San Luis △, Venezuela 168 A4 11 11N 69 33W
Sierra de Yeguas, Spain 43 H6 37 7N 4 52W
Sierra del São Mamede ⌓, Portugal 43 F3 39 17N 7 18W
Sierra Gorda, Chile 174 A2 22 50 S 69 15W
Sierra Grande, Argentina 176 B3 41 36 S 65 22W
Sierra Leone ■, W. Afr. 112 D2 9 0N 12 0W
Sierra Leone Rise, Atl. Oc. 8 F9 7 0N 22 0W
Sierra Madre, Mexico 163 D6 16 0N 93 0W
Sierra Mágina ⌓, Spain 43 H7 37 44N 3 28W
Sierra Mojada, Mexico 162 B4 27 19N 103 42W
Sierra Nevada, Spain 43 H7 37 3N 3 15W
Sierra Nevada, U.S.A. 160 H8 39 0N 120 30W
Sierra Nevada ⌓, Spain 43 H7 37 4N 3 7W
Sierra Nevada △, Venezuela 165 E5 8 35N 70 45W
Sierra Nevada de Santa Marta △, Colombia 165 D5 10 56N 73 36W
Sierra Norte de Seville ⌓, Spain 43 H5 37 55N 5 46W
Sierra Subbéticas ⌓, Spain 43 H6 37 26N 4 18W
Sierra Vista, U.S.A. 159 L8 31 33N 110 18W
Sierras de Cardeña y Montoro ⌓, Spain 43 G6 38 13N 4 15W
Sierras de Cazorla, Segura y las Villas ⌓, Spain 41 J2 37 0N 2 45W
Sierraville, U.S.A. 160 F6 39 36N 120 22W
Sierre, Switz. 32 D5 46 17N 7 31 E
Sifani, Ethiopia 107 E5 12 18N 40 19 E
Sifié, Ivory C. 112 D3 8 0N 7 5W
Sífnos, Greece 48 E6 37 0N 24 45 E
Sifton, Canada 143 C8 51 21N 100 8W
Sifton Pass, Canada 142 B3 57 52N 126 15W
Sig, Algeria 111 A4 35 32N 0 12W
Sigaboy = Governor Generoso, Phil. 81 H6 6 39N 126 5 E
Sigatoka, Fiji 133 B1 18 8 S 177 32 E
Sigdal, Norway 18 D6 60 3N 9 38 E
Sigean, France 28 E6 43 2N 2 58 E
Siggiewi, Malta 38 F7 35 51N 14 26 E
Sighetu-Marmaţiei, Romania 53 C8 47 57N 23 52 E
Sighişoara, Romania 53 D9 46 12N 24 50 E
Sigira, Yemen 99 D6 12 37N 54 20 E
Sigiriya, Sri Lanka 95 L5 7 57N 80 45 E
Sigli, Indonesia 84 A1 5 25N 96 0 E
Siglufjörður, Iceland 11 A8 66 12N 18 55W
Siglunes, Iceland 11 A8 66 12N 18 50W
Sigmaringen, Germany 31 G5 48 5N 9 12 E
Signa, Italy 44 E8 43 45N 11 10 E
Signakhi = Tsnori, Georgia 61 K7 41 40N 45 57 E
Signal, U.S.A. 161 L13 34 30N 113 38W
Signal de Botrang, Belgium 24 D6 50 29N 6 4 E
Signal Pk., U.S.A. 161 M12 33 20N 114 2W
Signau, Switz. 32 C5 46 56N 7 45 E
Signy I., Antarctica 7 C18 60 45 S 45 56W
Signy-l'Abbaye, France 27 C11 49 40N 4 25 E
Sigourney, U.S.A. 156 C4 41 20N 92 12W
Sigsbee, U.S.A. 152 D6 31 16N 83 52W
Sigsig, Ecuador 168 D2 3 0 S 78 50W
Sigüenza, Spain 40 D2 41 3N 2 40W
Siguiri, Guinea 112 C3 11 31N 9 10W
Sigulda, Latvia 15 H21 57 10N 24 55 E
Sihanoukville = Kampong Saom, Cambodia 87 G4 10 38N 103 30 E
Sihaus, Peru 172 B2 8 40 S 77 40W
Sihawa, India 94 D5 20 19N 81 55 E
Sihora, India 93 H9 23 29N 80 6 E
Sihui, China 77 F9 23 20N 112 40 E
Siikajoki →, Finland 14 D21 64 50N 24 43 E
Siilinjärvi, Finland 14 E22 63 4N 27 39 E
Siirt, Turkey 101 D9 37 57N 41 55 E
Sijarira Ra. = Chizarira, Zimbabwe 119 F2 17 36 S 27 45 E
Sijungjung, Indonesia 84 C2 0 42 S 100 58 E
Sika, India 92 H3 22 26N 69 47 E
Sikani Chief →, Canada 142 B4 57 47N 122 15W
Sikao, Thailand 87 J2 7 34N 99 21 E
Sikar, India 92 F6 27 33N 75 10 E
Sikasso, Mali 112 C3 11 18N 5 35W
Sikelenge, Zambia 115 E4 14 53 S 24 14 E
Sikeston, U.S.A. 155 G10 36 53N 89 35W
Sikhote Alin, Khrebet, Russia 67 E14 45 0N 136 0 E
Sikhote Alin Ra. = Sikhote Alin, Khrebet, Russia 67 E14 45 0N 136 0 E
Sikiá, Greece 50 F7 40 2N 23 56 E
Síkinos, Greece 49 E7 36 40N 25 8 E
Sikkim □, India 90 B2 27 50N 88 30 E
Siklós, Hungary 52 E3 45 50N 18 19 E
Sil →, Spain 42 C3 42 27N 7 43W
Silacayoapan, Mexico 163 D5 17 30N 98 9W
Šilalė, Lithuania 54 C9 55 28N 22 12 E
Silam, Malaysia 81 J2 4 59N 118 12 E
Silandro, Italy 44 B7 46 38N 10 46 E
Silang, Phil. 80 D3 14 14N 120 58 E
Silawad, India 92 J6 21 54N 74 54 E
Silay, Phil. 81 F4 10 47N 122 58 E
Silba, Croatia 45 D11 44 24N 14 41 E
Silchar, India 90 C4 24 49N 92 48 E
Sildegapet, Norway 18 B2 62 5N 5 0 E
Şile, Turkey 51 E13 41 10N 29 37 E
Silent Valley △, India 95 J3 11 10N 76 20 E
Siler City, U.S.A. 149 H6 35 44N 79 28W
Sileru →, India 94 F5 17 49N 81 24 E
Silesia = Śląsk, Poland 36 C9 51 0N 16 30 E
Silet, Algeria 111 D5 22 44N 4 37 E
Silgarhi Doti, Nepal 93 E9 29 15N 81 0 E
Silghat, India 90 B4 26 35N 93 0 E
Silhouette, Seychelles 121 b 4 29 S 55 12 E
Sili, Burkina Faso 112 C4 11 37N 2 30W
Silifke, Turkey 100 D5 36 22N 33 58 E
Siliguri = Shiliguri, India 90 B2 26 45N 88 25 E
Siling Co, China 68 C3 31 50N 89 20 E
Silistea Nouă, Romania 53 F10 44 23N 25 1 E
Silistra, Bulgaria 51 B11 44 6N 27 19 E
Silivri, Turkey 51 E12 41 4N 28 14 E
Siljan, Norway 18 E6 59 18N 9 42 E
Siljan, Sweden 16 D8 60 55N 14 45 E
Siljansnäs, Sweden 16 D8 60 47N 14 52 E
Silkeborg, Denmark 17 H3 56 10N 9 32 E
Silkwood, Australia 126 B4 17 45 S 146 2 E
Silla, Spain 41 F4 39 22N 0 25W
Sillajhuay, Cordillera, Chile 172 D4 19 46 S 68 40W
Sillamäe, Estonia 15 G22 59 24N 27 45 E
Sillé-le-Guillaume, France 26 D6 48 10N 0 8W
Silleda, Spain 42 C2 42 42N 8 14W
Sillein = Žilina, Slovak Rep. 35 B11 49 12N 18 42 E
Sillod, India 94 D2 20 18N 75 39 E
Silloth, U.K. 20 C4 54 52N 3 23W
Sillustani, Peru 172 D3 15 50 S 70 7W
Sílo, Greece 51 E9 41 10N 25 53 E
Siloam Springs, U.S.A. 155 G7 36 11N 94 32W
Silopi, Turkey 101 D10 37 15N 42 27 E
Silsbee, U.S.A. 155 K7 30 21N 94 11W
Siltou, Chad 109 E3 16 46N 15 33 E
Siluko, Nigeria 113 D6 6 35N 5 10 E
Šilutė, Lithuania 15 J19 55 21N 21 33 E
Silva Porto = Kuito, Angola 115 E3 12 22 S 16 55 E
Silvan, Turkey 101 C9 38 7N 41 2 E
Silvani, India 93 H8 23 18N 78 25 E
Silvaplana, Switz. 33 D9 46 28N 9 48 E
Silver City, U.S.A. 159 K9 32 46N 108 17W
Silver Cr. →, U.S.A. 158 E4 43 16N 119 13W
Silver Creek, U.S.A. 150 D5 42 33N 79 10W
Silver Grove, U.S.A. 157 E12 39 2N 84 24W
Silver L., U.S.A. 160 G6 38 39N 120 6W
Silver Lake, Calif., U.S.A. 161 K10 35 21N 116 7W
Silver Lake, Ind., U.S.A. 157 C11 41 4N 85 53W
Silver Lake, Oreg., U.S.A. 158 E3 43 8N 121 3W
Silver Lake, Wis., U.S.A. 157 B8 42 33N 88 13W
Silver Springs, U.S.A. 153 F7 29 13N 82 3W
Silverdalen, Sweden 17 G9 57 32N 15 45 E
Silverton, Australia 128 A4 31 52 S 141 10 E
Silverton, Colo., U.S.A. 159 H10 37 49N 107 40W
Silverton, Tex., U.S.A. 155 H4 34 28N 101 19W
Silves, Brazil 169 D6 2 54 S 58 27W
Silves, Portugal 43 H2 37 11N 8 26W
Silvi Marina, Italy 45 F11 42 34N 14 5 E
Silvia, Colombia 168 C2 2 37N 76 21W
Silvies →, U.S.A. 158 E4 43 34N 119 2W
Silvrettahorn, Switz. 33 C10 46 50N 10 6 E
Silwa Bahari, Egypt 106 C3 24 45N 32 55 E
Silz, Austria 34 D3 47 16N 10 56 E
Sim, C., Morocco 110 B3 31 26N 9 51W
Simakumba, Zambia 115 E4 14 12 S 23 16 E
Simaltala, India 93 G12 24 43N 86 33 E
Simaluguri, India 90 B5 26 55N 94 46 E
Simanggang = Sri Aman, Malaysia 85 B4 1 15N 111 32 E
Simao, China 76 F3 22 47N 101 5 E
Simão Dias, Brazil 170 D4 10 44 S 37 49W
Simara I., Phil. 80 E4 12 48N 122 3 E
Simard, L., Canada 140 C4 47 40N 78 40W
Şīmareh →, Iran 101 F12 33 9N 47 41 E
Simav, Turkey 49 B10 39 4N 28 58 E
Simav →, Turkey 51 F12 40 23N 28 31 E
Simav Dağları, Turkey 49 B10 39 10N 28 30 E
Simba, Dem. Rep. of the Congo 114 B4 0 38N 22 59 E
Simba, Tanzania 118 C4 2 10 S 37 36 E
Simbach, Germany 31 G9 48 16N 13 2 E
Simberi I., Papua N. G. 132 B7 2 38 S 152 0 E
Simbirsk, Russia 60 C9 54 20N 48 25 E
Simbo, Solomon Is. 133 M9 8 16 S 156 33 E
Simbo, Tanzania 118 C2 4 51 S 29 41 E
Simcoe, Canada 140 D3 42 50N 80 20W
Simcoe, L., Canada 140 D4 44 25N 79 20W
Simdega, India 93 H11 22 37N 84 31 E
Simeonovgrad, Bulgaria 51 D9 42 1N 25 50 E
Simeria, Romania 52 E8 45 51N 23 1 E
Simeto →, Italy 47 E8 37 24N 15 6 E
Simeulue, Indonesia 84 B1 2 45N 95 45 E
Simferopol, Ukraine 59 K8 44 55N 34 3 E
Sími, Greece 49 E9 36 35N 27 50 E
Simi Valley, U.S.A. 161 L8 34 16N 118 47W
Simien Mts. △, Ethiopia 107 E4 13 19N 38 0 E
Simikot, Nepal 93 E9 30 0N 81 50 E
Simití, Colombia 168 B3 7 58N 73 57W
Simitli, Bulgaria 50 E7 41 52N 23 7 E
Simla, India 92 D7 31 2N 77 9 E
Simlångsdalen, Sweden 17 H7 56 43N 13 6 E
Şimleu-Silvaniei, Romania 52 C7 47 17N 22 50 E
Simlipal △, India 93 J12 21 45N 86 30 E
Simme →, Switz. 32 C4 46 38N 7 25 E
Simmern, Germany 31 F3 49 58N 7 30 E
Simmie, Canada 143 D7 49 56N 108 6W
Simmler, U.S.A. 161 K7 35 21N 119 59W
Simnas, Lithuania 54 D10 54 24N 23 39 E
Simo älv = Simojoki →, Finland 14 D21 65 35N 25 1 E
Simões, Brazil 170 C3 7 36 S 40 49W
Simojoki →, Finland 14 D21 65 35N 25 1 E
Simojovel, Mexico 163 D6 17 12N 92 38W
Simonette →, Canada 142 B5 55 9N 118 15W
Šimonovany = Partizánske, Slovak Rep. 35 C11 48 38N 18 23 E
Simonstown, S. Africa 116 E2 34 14 S 18 26 E
Simontornya, Hungary 52 D3 46 45N 18 33 E
Simpang Empat, Malaysia 87 c 5 27N 100 29 E
Simpangkiri →, Indonesia 84 B1 2 50N 97 40 E
Simplício Mendes, Brazil 170 C3 7 51 S 41 54W
Simplon, Switz. 32 D6 46 12N 8 4 E
Simplonpass, Switz. 32 D6 46 15N 8 3 E
Simplontunnel, Switz. 32 D6 46 15N 8 7 E
Simpson, Mt., Papua N. G. 132 F5 10 2 S 149 34 E
Simpson Desert, Australia 126 D2 25 0 S 137 0 E
Simpson Desert △, Australia 126 C2 24 59 S 138 21 E
Simpson Pen., Canada 139 B11 68 34N 88 45W
Simpungdong, N. Korea 75 D15 40 56N 129 29 E
Simrishamn, Sweden 17 J8 55 33N 14 22 E
Simsbury, U.S.A. 151 E12 41 53N 72 48W
Simunjan, Malaysia 85 B4 1 25N 110 45 E
Simunul, Phil. 81 J2 4 54N 119 51 E
Simushir, Ostrov, Russia 67 E16 46 50N 152 30 E
Sin Cowe I., S. China Sea 78 C4 9 53N 114 19 E
Sina →, India 94 F2 17 30N 75 55 E
Sinabang, Indonesia 84 B1 2 30N 96 24 E
Sinadogo, Somali Rep. 120 C3 5 50N 47 0 E
Sinai = Es Sînâ', Egypt 103 F3 29 0N 34 0 E
Sinai, Mt. = Mûsa, Gebel, Egypt 96 D2 28 33N 33 59 E
Sinai Peninsula, Egypt 62 G7 29 30N 34 0 E
Sinaia, Romania 53 E10 45 21N 25 38 E
Sinait, Phil. 80 C3 17 52N 120 27 E
Sinako, Mt., Phil. 81 H5 7 30N 125 17 E
Sinaloa □, Mexico 162 C3 25 0N 107 30W
Sinaloa de Leyva, Mexico 162 B3 25 50N 108 20W
Sinalunga, Italy 45 E8 43 12N 11 44 E
Sinan, China 76 D7 27 56N 108 13 E
Sînandrei, Romania 52 E6 45 52N 21 13 E
Sinarádhes, Greece 38 B9 39 34N 19 51 E
Sīnāwan, Libya 108 B2 31 0N 10 37 E
Sinbaungwe, Burma 90 F5 19 43N 95 10 E
Sinbo, Burma 90 C6 24 46N 97 3 E
Sincan, Turkey 100 B5 39 58N 32 36 E
Sincanlı, Turkey 49 C12 38 45N 30 15 E
Sincé, Colombia 168 B2 9 15N 75 9W
Sincelejo, Colombia 168 B2 9 18N 75 24W
Sinch'ang, N. Korea 75 D15 40 7N 128 28 E
Sinchang-ni, N. Korea 75 E14 39 24N 126 8 E
Sinclair, U.S.A. 158 F10 41 47N 107 7W
Sinclair, L., U.S.A. 152 B6 33 8N 83 12W
Sinclair Mills, Canada 142 C4 54 5N 121 40W
Sinclair's B., U.K. 22 C5 58 31N 3 5W
Sinclairville, U.S.A. 150 D5 42 16N 79 16W
Sind = Sindh □, Pakistan 91 D3 26 0N 69 0 E
Sind, Pakistan 92 G3 26 0N 68 30 E
Sind →, Jammu & Kashmir, India 93 B6 34 18N 74 45 E
Sind →, Mad. P., India 93 F8 26 26N 79 13 E
Sind Sagar Doab, Pakistan 92 D4 32 0N 71 30 E
Sindal, Denmark 17 G4 57 28N 10 10 E
Sindangan, Phil. 81 G4 8 10N 123 5 E
Sindangan Bay, Phil. 81 G4 8 11N 122 50 E
Sindangbarang, Indonesia 85 D3 7 27 S 107 1 E
Sindara, Gabon 114 C2 1 7 S 10 41 E
Sinde, Zambia 119 F2 17 28 S 25 51 E
Sindelfingen, Germany 31 G4 48 42N 9 0 E
Sindewahi, India 94 D4 20 17N 79 39 E
Sindgi, India 94 F3 16 55N 76 14 E
Sindh □, Pakistan 91 D3 26 0N 69 0 E
Sindhnur, India 95 F3 15 47N 76 46 E
Sindi, India 94 D4 20 48N 78 52 E
Sındırgı, Turkey 49 B10 39 13N 28 10 E
Sindou, Burkina Faso 112 C3 10 35N 5 4W
Sindri, India 93 H12 23 45N 86 42 E
Sine →, Senegal 112 C1 14 10N 16 28W
Sineglazovo = Novosineglazovskiy, Russia 64 D8 55 2N 61 21 E
Sinegorskiy, Russia 61 G5 47 55N 40 52 E
Sinekli, Turkey 51 E12 41 14N 28 12 E
Sinelnikovo = Synelnykove, Ukraine 59 H8 48 25N 35 30 E
Sinendé, Benin 113 C5 10 20N 2 22 E
Sines, Portugal 43 H2 37 56N 8 51W
Sines, C. de, Portugal 43 H2 37 58N 8 53W
Sineu, Spain 38 B4 39 38N 3 1 E
Sinewit, Mt., Papua N. G. 132 C7 4 44 S 152 2 E
Sinfra, Ivory C. 112 D3 6 35N 5 56W
Sing Buri, Thailand 86 E3 14 53N 100 25 E
Sing Sing = Ossining, U.S.A. 151 E11 41 10N 73 55W
Singa, Sudan 107 E3 13 10N 33 57 E
Singako, Chad 109 G3 9 50N 19 24 E
Singalila △, India 93 F13 27 10N 88 5 E
Singanallur, India 95 J3 11 2N 77 1 E
Singapore ■, Asia 87 d 1 17N 103 51 E
Singapore, Straits of, Asia 87 d 1 15N 104 0 E
Singapore Changi ✕ (SIN), Singapore 87 M4 1 23N 103 59 E
Singaraja, Indonesia 85 D5 8 7 S 115 6 E
Singatoka = Sigatoka, Fiji 133 B1 18 8 S 177 32 E
Singen, Germany 31 H4 47 45N 8 50 E
Singida, Tanzania 118 C3 4 49 S 34 48 E
Singida □, Tanzania 118 D3 6 0 S 34 30 E
Singitikós Kólpos, Greece 50 F7 40 6N 24 0 E
Singkaling Hkamti, Burma 90 C5 26 0N 95 39 E
Singkang, Indonesia 82 B2 4 8 S 120 1 E
Singkawang, Indonesia 85 B3 1 0N 108 57 E
Singkep, Indonesia 78 E2 0 30 S 104 25 E
Singleton, Australia 129 B9 32 33 S 151 0 E
Singleton, Mt., N. Terr., Australia 124 D5 22 0 S 130 46 E
Singleton, Mt., W. Austral., Australia 125 E2 29 27 S 117 15 E
Singö, Sweden 16 D12 60 12N 18 45 E
Singoli, India 92 G6 25 0N 75 22 E
Singora = Songkhla, Thailand 87 J3 7 13N 100 37 E
Singosan, N. Korea 75 E14 38 52N 127 25 E
Singri, India 90 B4 26 36N 92 29 E
Singsås, Norway 18 B7 62 56N 10 37 E
Singu, Burma 90 D6 22 33N 96 0 E
Sinhgarh, India 94 E1 18 22N 73 45 E
Sinhung, N. Korea 75 D14 40 11N 127 34 E
Siniátsikon, Óros, Greece 50 F5 40 25N 21 35 E
Siniloan, Phil. 80 D3 14 25N 121 27 E
Sining = Xining, China 68 C5 36 34N 101 40 E
Siniscóla, Italy 46 B2 40 34N 9 41 E
Sinj, Croatia 45 E13 43 42N 16 39 E
Sinjai, Indonesia 82 C2 5 7 S 120 20 E
Sinjajevina, Serbia & M. 50 D3 42 57N 19 22 E
Sinjār, Iraq 101 D9 36 19N 41 52 E
Sinkat, Sudan 106 D4 18 55N 35 49 E
Sinkiang Uighur = Xinjiang Uygur Zizhiqu □, China 68 C3 42 0N 86 0 E
Sinlumkaba, Burma 90 C6 24 16N 97 31 E
Sinmak, N. Korea 75 E14 38 25N 126 14 E
Sínnai, Italy 46 C2 39 18N 9 13 E
Sinnar, India 94 E2 19 48N 74 0 E
Sinni →, Italy 47 B9 40 8N 16 41 E
Sinnuris, Egypt 106 J7 29 26N 30 31 E
Sinoie, Lacul, Romania 53 F13 44 35N 28 50 E
Sinop, Turkey 100 A6 42 1N 35 11 E
Sinor, India 92 J5 21 55N 73 20 E
Sinp'o, N. Korea 75 E15 40 0N 128 13 E
Sins, Switz. 33 B6 47 12N 8 24 E
Sinsheim, Germany 31 F4 49 15N 8 52 E
Sinsiang = Xinxiang, China 74 G7 35 18N 113 50 E
Sinsk, Russia 67 C13 61 8N 126 48 E
Sintang, Indonesia 85 B4 0 5N 111 35 E
Sinton, U.S.A. 155 L6 28 2N 97 31W
Sintra, Portugal 43 G1 38 47N 9 25W
Sintra-Cascais ⌓, Portugal 43 G1 38 50N 9 25W
Sinugif, Somali Rep. 120 C3 8 33N 48 59 E
Sinŭiju, N. Korea 75 D13 40 5N 124 24 E
Sinyukha →, Ukraine 59 H6 48 3N 30 51 E
Sinzig, Germany 30 E3 50 32N 7 14 E
Sio →, Hungary 52 D3 46 20N 18 53 E
Siocon, Phil. 81 H4 7 40N 122 10 E
Siófok, Hungary 52 D3 46 54N 18 3 E
Sioma, Zambia 115 F4 16 40 S 23 32 E
Sioma Ngwezi △, Zambia 115 F4 17 14 S 23 26 E
Sion, Switz. 32 D4 46 14N 7 20 E
Sion Mills, U.K. 23 B4 54 48N 7 29W
Sioux Center, U.S.A. 154 D6 43 5N 96 11W
Sioux City, U.S.A. 154 D6 42 30N 96 24W
Sioux Falls, U.S.A. 154 D6 43 33N 96 44W
Sioux Lookout, Canada 140 B1 50 10N 91 50W
Sioux Narrows, Canada 143 D10 49 25N 94 10W
Sipalay, Phil. 81 G4 9 45N 122 24 E
Šipan, Croatia 50 D1 42 45N 17 52 E
Sipang, Tanjong, Malaysia 85 B4 1 48N 110 20 E
Siparia, Trin. & Tob. 169 F9 10 8N 61 31W
Sipil Daği △, Turkey 49 C9 38 35N 27 30 E
Siping, China 75 C13 43 8N 124 21 E
Sipiwesk L., Canada 143 B9 55 5N 97 35W
Siple, Antarctica 7 D7 75 0 S 74 0 E
Sipocot, Phil. 80 E4 13 46N 122 58 E
Šipovo, Bos.-H. 52 F2 44 16N 17 6 E
Sipra →, India 92 H6 23 55N 75 28 E
Sipur, India 94 D7 21 11N 85 9 E
Sipura, Indonesia 84 C1 2 18 S 99 40 E
Siquia →, Nic. 164 D3 12 10N 84 20W
Siquijor, Phil. 81 G4 9 12N 123 35 E
Siquijor □, Phil. 81 G4 9 11N 123 35 E
Siquirres, Costa Rica 164 D3 10 6N 83 30W
Siquisique, Venezuela 168 A4 10 34N 69 42W
Şīr Abu Nu'ayr, U.A.E. 97 E7 25 20N 54 20 E
Şīr Banī Yās, U.A.E. 97 E7 24 19N 52 37 E
Sir Edward Pellew Group, Australia 126 B2 15 40 S 137 10 E
Sir Graham Moore Is., Australia 124 B4 13 53 S 126 34 E
Sir James MacBrien, Mt., Canada 138 B7 62 7N 127 41W
Sir Joseph Banks Group, Australia 128 C2 34 36 S 136 16 E
Sira, India 95 H3 13 41N 76 49 E
Sira, Norway 18 F3 58 24N 6 40 E
Sira →, Norway 18 F3 58 23N 6 34 E
Siracusa, Italy 47 E8 37 4N 15 17 E
Sirajganj, Bangla. 90 C2 24 25N 89 47 E
Sirakoro, Mali 112 C3 12 41N 9 14W
Şiran, Turkey 101 B8 40 11N 39 7 E

Sirasso, Ivory C. 112 D3 9 16N 6 6W
Sirathu, India 93 G9 25 39N 81 19 E
Sirawai, Phil. 81 H4 7 34N 122 8 E
Sirdalsvatnet, Norway 18 F3 58 34N 6 43 E
Sīrdān, Iran 97 B6 36 39N 49 12 E
Sirdaryo = Syrdarya, Uzbekistan 65 C4 40 50N 68 40 E
Sirdaryo = Syrdarya →, Kazakhstan 66 E7 46 3N 61 0 E
Sire, Ethiopia 107 F4 6 55N 35 36 E
Siren, U.S.A. 154 C8 45 47N 92 24W
Sirente-Velino △, Italy 45 F10 42 10N 13 32 E
Sirer, Spain 38 D1 38 56N 1 22 E
Siret, Romania 53 C11 47 55N 26 5 E
Siret →, Romania 53 E12 45 24N 28 1 E
Sirevåg, Norway 18 G3 58 30N 5 48 E
Sirghāyā, Syria 103 B5 33 51N 36 8 E
Şiria, Romania 52 D6 46 16N 21 38 E
Sirik, Tanjong, Malaysia 85 B4 2 47N 111 15 E
Sirinath △, Thailand 87 a 8 6N 98 17 E
Sirino, Mte., Italy 47 B8 40 7N 15 50 E
Sīrjān, Iran 97 D7 29 30N 55 45 E
Sirkali = Sirkazhi, India 95 J4 11 15N 79 41 E
Sirkazhi, India 95 J4 11 15N 79 41 E
Sirmans, U.S.A. 152 E6 30 21N 83 39W
Sirmaur, India 93 G9 24 51N 81 23 E
Sírna, Greece 49 E8 36 22N 26 42 E
Sirnach, Switz. 33 B7 47 28N 8 59 E
Şirnak, Turkey 101 D10 37 32N 42 28 E
Sirohi, India 92 G5 24 52N 72 53 E
Sironj, India 92 G7 24 5N 77 39 E
Síros, Greece 48 D6 37 28N 24 57 E
Siroz = Sérrai, Greece 50 E7 41 5N 23 31 E
Sirpur, India 94 E4 19 29N 79 36 E
Sirrayn, Si. Arabia 98 C3 19 38N 40 36 E
Sirretta Pk., U.S.A. 161 K8 35 56N 118 19W
Sīrrī, Iran 97 E7 25 55N 54 32 E
Sirsa, India 92 E6 29 33N 75 4 E
Sirsa →, India 93 F8 26 51N 79 4 E
Sirsi, India 95 G2 14 40N 74 49 E
Sirsilla, India 94 E4 18 23N 78 50 E
Siruela, Spain 43 G5 38 58N 5 3W
Siruguppa, India 95 F3 15 38N 76 54 E
Sirur, India 94 E2 18 50N 74 23 E
Sisak, Croatia 45 C13 45 30N 16 21 E
Sisaket, Thailand 86 E5 15 8N 104 23 E
Sisante, Spain 41 F2 39 25N 2 12W
Sisargas, Is., Spain 42 B2 43 21N 8 50W
Sishen, S. Africa 116 D3 27 47 S 22 59 E
Sishui, Henan, China 74 G7 34 48N 113 15 E
Sishui, Shandong, China 75 G9 35 42N 117 18 E
Sisiga, Solomon Is. 133 L10 7 54 S 159 10 E
Sisimiut, Greenland 10 D5 66 40N 53 30W
Sisipuk L., Canada 143 B8 55 45N 101 50W
Sisophon, Cambodia 86 F4 13 38N 102 59 E
Sissach, Switz. 32 B5 47 27N 7 48 E
Sissano, Papua N. G. 132 B2 3 0 S 142 3 E
Sisseton, U.S.A. 154 C6 45 40N 97 3W
Sisson = Mount Shasta, U.S.A. 158 F2 41 19N 122 19W
Sissonne, France 27 C10 49 34N 3 51 E
Sīstān, Asia 97 D9 30 50N 61 0 E
Sīstān, Daryācheh-ye, Iran 97 D9 31 0N 61 0 E
Sīstān va Balūchestān □, Iran 97 E9 27 0N 62 0 E
Sisteron, France 29 D9 44 12N 5 57 E
Sisters, U.S.A. 158 D3 44 18N 121 33W
Sisters, The, Seychelles 121 b 4 16 S 55 52 E
Sisters Pk., Ascension I. 9 g 7 56 S 14 22W
Siswa Bazar, India 93 F10 27 9N 83 46 E
Sitakili, Mali 112 C2 13 7N 11 14W
Sitakunda, Bangla. 90 D3 22 37N 91 39 E
Sitamarhi, India 93 F11 26 37N 85 30 E
Sitampiky, Madag. 117 B8 16 41 S 46 6 E
Sitangkai, Phil. 81 J2 4 40N 119 24 E
Sitapur, India 93 F9 27 38N 80 45 E
Siteki, Swaziland 117 D5 26 32 S 31 58 E
Sitges, Spain 40 D6 41 17N 1 47 E
Sithoniá, Greece 50 F7 40 0N 23 45 E
Sitía, Greece 39 E7 35 13N 26 6 E
Sitía ✕ (JSH), Greece 39 E7 35 15N 26 5 E
Sítio da Abadia, Brazil 171 D2 14 48 S 46 16W
Sitka, U.S.A. 142 B1 57 3N 135 20W
Sitka △, U.S.A. 144 E14 57 3N 135 19W
Sitkinak I., U.S.A. 144 H9 56 33N 154 10W
Sitoti, Botswana 116 C3 23 15 S 23 40 E
Sitra, Egypt 106 B2 28 40N 26 53 E
Sittang Myit →, Burma 90 G6 17 20N 96 45 E
Sittard, Neths. 24 C5 51 0N 5 52 E
Sittaung, Burma 90 C5 24 10N 94 35 E
Sittensen, Germany 30 B5 53 17N 9 32 E
Sittingbourne, U.K. 21 F8 51 21N 0 45 E
Sittona, Eritrea 107 E4 14 25N 37 23 E
Sittoung = Sittang Myit →, Burma 90 G6 17 20N 96 45 E
Sittwe, Burma 90 E4 20 18N 92 45 E
Situbondo, Indonesia 79 G16 7 42 S 114 0 E
Si'umu, Samoa 133 X24 14 1 S 171 48W
Siuna, Nic. 164 D3 13 37N 84 45W
Siuri, India 93 H12 23 50N 87 34 E
Siutghiol, Lacul, Romania 53 F13 44 15N 28 35 E
Sivaganga, India 95 K4 9 50N 78 28 E
Sivagiri, India 95 K3 9 16N 77 26 E
Sivakasi, India 95 K3 9 24N 77 47 E
Sīvand, Iran 97 D7 30 5N 52 55 E
Sivas, Turkey 100 C7 39 43N 36 58 E
Sivasamudram, India 95 H3 12 16N 77 10 E
Sivaslı, Turkey 49 C11 38 31N 29 42 E
Siverek, Turkey 101 D8 37 50N 39 19 E
Sivomaskinskiy, Russia 56 A11 66 40N 62 35 E
Sivota, Greece 38 C10 39 24N 20 13 E
Sivrihisar, Turkey 100 C4 39 30N 31 35 E
Sívros, Greece 39 B2 38 40N 20 39 E
Sîwa, Egypt 106 B2 29 11N 25 31 E
Sîwa, El Wâhât es, Egypt 106 B2 29 10N 25 30 E
Siwa Oasis = Sîwa, El Wâhât es, Egypt 106 B2 29 10N 25 30 E
Siwalik Range, Nepal 93 F10 28 0N 83 0 E
Siwan, India 93 F11 26 13N 84 21 E
Siwana, India 92 G5 25 38N 72 25 E
Six Cross Roads, Barbados 165 g 13 7N 59 28W
Sixmilebridge, Ireland 23 D3 52 44N 8 46W
Sixth Cataract, Sudan 107 D3 16 20N 32 42 E
Siyāh Kuh, Afghan. 91 B2 34 7N 64 10 E
Siyâl, Jazâ'ir, Egypt 106 C4 22 49N 36 12 E
Siyäzän, Azerbaijan 61 K9 41 3N 49 10 E
Siziwang Qi, China 74 D6 41 25N 111 40 E
Sjælland, Denmark 17 J5 55 30N 11 30 E
Sjællands Odde, Denmark 17 J5 55 58N 11 24 E
Sjenica, Serbia & M. 50 C3 43 16N 20 0 E
Sjoa, Norway 18 C6 61 41N 9 33 E
Sjöbo, Sweden 17 J7 55 37N 13 45 E
Sjøholt, Norway 18 B3 62 27N 6 52 E
Sjøli, Norway 18 C8 61 29N 11 18 E
Sjötofta, Sweden 17 G7 57 22N 13 17 E
Sjötorp, Sweden 17 F8 58 50N 14 0 E
Sjumen = Shumen, Bulgaria 51 C10 43 18N 26 55 E
Sjuntorp, Sweden 17 F6 58 12N 12 13 E
Skåbu, Norway 18 C6 61 32N 9 24 E
Skadarsko Jezero, Serbia & M. 50 D3 42 10N 19 20 E
Skadovsk, Ukraine 59 J7 46 17N 32 52 E
Skælskør, Denmark 17 J5 55 15N 11 18 E
Skærbæk, Denmark 17 J2 55 9N 8 45 E
Skaftafell, Iceland 11 C9 64 1N 17 0W
Skaftafell △, Iceland 11 C9 64 9N 16 50W
Skagafjarðarsýsla □, Iceland 11 B7 65 30N 19 0W
Skagafjörður, Iceland 11 B7 65 54N 19 35W
Skagastølstindane, Norway 18 C4 61 28N 7 52 E
Skagaströnd, Iceland 11 B6 65 50N 20 19W
Skagatá, Iceland 11 A6 66 7N 20 6W
Skagen, Denmark 17 G4 57 43N 10 35 E
Skagern, Sweden 16 E8 59 0N 14 20 E
Skagerrak, Denmark 17 G2 57 30N 9 0 E
Skagit →, U.S.A. 160 B4 48 23N 122 22W
Skagway, U.S.A. 144 G14 59 28N 135 19W
Skála 39 C2 38 5N 20 47 E
Skala nad Zbruczem = Skala-Podilska, Ukraine 53 B11 48 50N 26 15 E
Skala-Podilska, Ukraine 53 B11 48 50N 26 15 E
Skala Podolskaya = Skala-Podilska, Ukraine 53 B11 48 50N 26 15 E
Skalat, Ukraine 59 H3 49 23N 25 55 E
Skálavík, Iceland 11 A3 66 11N 23 29W
Skalbmierz, Poland 55 H7 50 20N 20 25 E
Skälderviken, Sweden 17 H6 56 22N 12 30 E
Skålevik, Norway 18 F5 58 5N 8 1 E
Skalica, Slovak Rep. 35 C10 48 50N 17 15 E
Skallingen, Denmark 17 J2 55 32N 8 13 E
Skalni Dol = Kamenyak, Bulgaria 51 C10 43 24N 26 57 E
Skanderborg, Denmark 17 H3 56 2N 9 55 E
Skåne, Sweden 17 J7 55 59N 13 30 E
Skåne län □, Sweden 17 H7 56 15N 14 0 E
Skaneateles, U.S.A. 151 D8 42 57N 76 26W
Skaneateles L., U.S.A. 151 D8 42 51N 76 22W
Skånevik, Norway 18 E2 59 43N 5 53 E
Skänninge, Sweden 17 F9 58 24N 15 5 E
Skanör med Falsterbo, Sweden 17 J6 55 24N 12 50 E
Skantzoúra, Greece 48 B6 39 5N 24 6 E
Skara, Sweden 17 F7 58 25N 13 30 E
Skärblacka, Sweden 17 F9 58 35N 15 54 E
Skarð, Iceland 11 B4 65 17N 22 19W
Skardu, Pakistan 93 B6 35 20N 75 44 E
Skare, Norway 18 E3 59 55N 6 36 E
Skåre, Sweden 16 E7 59 26N 13 26 E
Skärhamn, Sweden 17 G5 57 59N 11 34 E
Skarnes, Norway 18 D8 60 15N 11 41 E
Skarszewy, Poland 54 D5 54 4N 18 25 E
Skaryszew, Poland 55 G8 51 19N 21 15 E
Skarżysko-Kamienna, Poland 55 G7 51 7N 20 52 E
Skattkärr, Sweden 16 E7 59 25N 13 40 E
Skattungbyn, Sweden 16 C8 61 10N 14 56 E
Skawina, Poland 55 J6 49 59N 19 50 E
Skebobruk, Sweden 16 E12 59 58N 18 36 E
Skeena →, Canada 142 C2 54 9N 130 5W
Skeena Mts., Canada 142 B3 56 40N 128 30W
Skegness, U.K. 20 D8 53 9N 0 20 E
Skei, Norway 18 C3 61 34N 6 28 E
Skeiðarársandur, Iceland 11 D9 63 54N 17 14W
Skeiðflötur, Iceland 11 D7 63 26N 19 11W
Skeldon, Guyana 169 B6 5 55N 57 20W
Skeleton Coast ⌂, Namibia 116 C1 20 0 S 13 20 E
Skellefteå, Sweden 14 D19 64 45N 20 50 E
Skellefteälven →, Sweden 14 D19 64 45N 21 10 E
Skelleftehamn, Sweden 14 D19 64 40N 21 9 E
Skender Vakuf, Bos.-H. 52 F2 44 29N 17 22 E
Skerries, The, U.K. 20 D3 53 25N 4 36W
Skhidnytsya, Ukraine 55 J10 49 13N 23 20 E
Skhíza, Greece 48 E3 36 41N 21 40 E
Skhoinoúsa, Greece 49 E7 36 53N 25 31 E
Ski, Norway 18 E7 59 43N 10 52 E
Skíathos, Greece 48 B5 39 12N 23 30 E
Skibbereen, Ireland 23 E2 51 33N 9 16W
Skiddaw, U.K. 20 C4 54 39N 3 9W
Skidegate, Canada 142 C2 53 15N 132 1W
Skídhra, Greece 50 F6 40 46N 22 10 E
Skien, Norway 18 E6 59 12N 9 35 E
Skierniewice, Poland 55 G7 51 58N 20 10 E
Skikda, Algeria 111 A6 36 50N 6 58 E
Skillet →, U.S.A. 157 F8 38 5N 88 5W
Skillingaryd, Sweden 17 G8 57 27N 14 5 E
Skillinge, Sweden 17 J8 55 30N 14 16 E
Skilloura, Cyprus 39 E9 35 14N 33 10 E
Skinári, Ákra, Greece 39 D2 37 56N 20 42 E
Skinnastaður, Iceland 11 A10 66 4N 16 27W
Skinnskatteberg, Sweden 16 E9 59 50N 15 42 E
Skipton, Australia 128 D5 37 39 S 143 40 E
Skipton, U.K. 20 D5 53 58N 2 3W
Skiptvet, Norway 18 E8 59 28N 11 11 E
Skiring, C., Senegal 112 C1 12 26N 16 46W
Skirmish Pt., Australia 126 A1 11 59 S 134 17 E
Skiropoúla, Greece 48 C6 38 50N 24 21 E
Skíros, Greece 48 C6 38 55N 24 34 E
Skivarp, Sweden 17 J7 55 26N 13 34 E
Skive, Denmark 17 H3 56 33N 9 2 E
Skjærhalden, Norway 18 E8 59 2N 11 2 E
Skjálfandafljót →, Iceland 11 B9 65 59N 17 25W
Skjálfandi, Iceland 11 A9 66 5N 17 30W
Skjeberg, Norway 18 E8 59 12N 11 12 E
Skjern, Denmark 17 J2 55 57N 8 30 E
Skjold, Norway 18 E2 59 31N 5 34 E
Skjolden, Norway 18 C4 61 29N 7 36 E
Skjöldólfsstaðir, Iceland 11 B11 65 19N 15 7W
Skjønhaug, Norway 18 E8 59 39N 11 19 E
Skobelev = Farghona, Uzbekistan 65 C5 40 23N 71 19 E
Skobeleva, Pik, Kyrgyzstan 65 D6 39 48N 72 36 E
Skoczów, Poland 55 J5 49 49N 18 45 E
Skodje, Norway 18 B3 62 30N 6 43 E
Škofja Loka, Slovenia 45 B11 46 9N 14 19 E
Skógar, Iceland 11 D7 63 32N 19 28W
Skógarnes, Iceland 11 C4 64 46N 22 34W
Skoghall, Sweden 16 E7 59 20N 13 30 E
Skogstorp, Sweden 16 E10 59 19N 16 29 E
Skoki, Poland 55 F4 52 40N 17 11 E
Skokie, U.S.A. 157 B9 42 3N 87 45W
Skole, Ukraine 59 H2 49 3N 23 30 E
Skollenborg, Norway 18 E6 59 38N 9 43 E
Skópelos, Greece 48 B5 39 9N 23 47 E
Skopí, Greece 39 E7 35 11N 26 2 E
Skopin, Russia 58 F10 53 55N 39 32 E
Skopje, Macedonia 50 D5 42 1N 21 26 E
Skopje ✕ (SKP), Macedonia 50 E5 41 59N 21 29 E
Skoppum, Norway 18 E7 59 23N 10 26 E
Skórcz, Poland 54 E5 53 47N 18 30 E
Skørping, Denmark 17 H3 56 50N 9 53 E
Skotfoss, Norway 18 E6 59 12N 9 30 E
Skotterud, Norway 18 D9 60 0N 12 7 E
Skövde, Sweden 17 F8 58 24N 13 50 E
Skovorodino, Russia 67 D13 54 0N 124 0 E
Skowhegan, U.S.A. 149 C11 44 46N 69 43W
Skradin, Croatia 45 E12 43 52N 15 53 E
Skrea, Sweden 17 H6 56 53N 12 34 E
Skreia, Norway 18 D7 60 40N 10 56 E
Skrim, Norway 18 E6 59 31N 9 38 E
Skrunda, Latvia 54 B9 56 41N 22 1 E
Skrwa →, Poland 55 F6 52 35N 19 32 E
Skudeneshavn, Norway 18 E2 59 10N 5 10 E
Skuleskogen △, Sweden 16 A12 63 6N 18 30 E
Skull, Ireland 23 E2 51 32N 9 34W
Skultorp, Sweden 17 F7 58 24N 13 51 E
Skultuna, Sweden 16 E10 59 43N 16 25 E
Skunk →, U.S.A. 156 D5 40 42N 91 7W
Skuodas, Lithuania 15 H19 56 16N 21 33 E
Skurup, Sweden 17 J7 55 28N 13 30 E
Skutskär, Sweden 16 D11 60 37N 17 25 E
Skútustaðir, Iceland 11 B9 65 34N 17 2W
Skvyra, Ukraine 59 H5 49 44N 29 40 E
Skwierzyna, Poland 55 F2 52 33N 15 30 E
Skye, U.K. 22 D2 57 15N 6 10W
Skykomish, U.S.A. 158 C3 47 42N 121 22W
Skyring, Seno, Chile 176 D3 52 35 S 72 0W
Skyros = Skíros, Greece 48 C6 38 55N 24 34 E
Skyttorp, Sweden 16 D11 60 5N 17 44 E
Slade Pt., Australia 126 K7 21 5 S 149 13 E
Slættaratindur, Færoe Is. 14 E9 62 18N 7 1W
Slagelse, Denmark 17 J5 55 23N 11 19 E
Slamet, Indonesia 85 D3 7 16 S 109 8 E
Slaney →, Ireland 23 D5 52 26N 6 33W
Slangberge, S. Africa 116 E3 31 32 S 20 48 E
Slănic, Romania 53 E10 45 14N 25 58 E
Slano, Croatia 50 D1 42 48N 17 53 E
Slantsy, Russia 58 C5 59 7N 28 5 E
Slaný, Czech Rep. 34 A7 50 13N 14 6 E
Śląsk, Poland 36 C9 51 0N 16 30 E
Śląskie □, Poland 55 H6 50 30N 19 0 E
Slätbaken, Sweden 17 F10 58 25N 16 45 E
Slate Is., Canada 140 C2 48 40N 87 0W
Slater, U.S.A. 156 E3 39 13N 93 4W
Slatina, Croatia 52 E2 45 42N 17 45 E
Slatina, Romania 53 F9 44 28N 24 22 E
Slatina Timiş, Romania 52 E7 45 15N 22 17 E
Slatington, U.S.A. 151 F9 40 45N 75 37W
Slaton, U.S.A. 155 J4 33 26N 101 39W
Slave →, Canada 142 A6 61 18N 113 39W
Slave Coast, W. Afr. 113 D5 6 0N 2 30 E
Slave Lake, Canada 142 B6 55 17N 114 43W
Slave Pt., Canada 142 A5 61 11N 115 56W
Slavgorod, Russia 66 D8 53 1N 78 37 E
Slavinja, Serbia & M. 50 C6 43 9N 22 50 E
Slavkov u Brna, Czech Rep. 35 B9 49 10N 16 52 E
Slavkovský Les ⌂, Czech Rep. 34 A5 50 5N 12 44 E
Slavonija, Europe 52 E2 45 20N 17 40 E
Slavonski Brod, Croatia 52 E3 45 11N 18 1 E
Slavsk, Russia 54 C8 55 3N 21 41 E
Slavska, Ukraine 53 B8 48 51N 23 27 E
Slavskoye, Russia 54 D7 54 30N 20 27 E
Slavuta, Ukraine 59 G4 50 15N 27 2 E
Slavyanka, Russia 70 C5 42 53N 131 21 E
Slavyanovo, Bulgaria 51 C8 43 28N 24 52 E
Slavyansk = Slovyansk, Ukraine 59 H9 48 55N 37 36 E
Slavyansk-na-Kubani, Russia 59 K10 45 15N 38 11 E
Sława, Poland 55 G3 51 52N 16 2 E
Slawharad, Belarus 58 F6 53 27N 31 0 E
Sławno, Poland 54 D3 54 20N 16 41 E
Sławoborze, Poland 54 E2 53 55N 15 42 E
Sleaford, U.K. 20 D7 53 0N 0 24W
Sleaford B., Australia 127 E2 34 55 S 135 45 E
Sleat, Sd. of, U.K. 22 D3 57 5N 5 47W
Sleðbrjótur, Iceland 11 B12 65 34N 14 30W
Sleeper Is., Canada 139 C11 58 30N 81 0W
Sleeping Bear Dunes ⌂, U.S.A. 148 C2 44 50N 86 5W
Sleepy Eye, U.S.A. 154 C7 44 18N 94 43W
Sleetmute, U.S.A. 144 F8 61 42N 157 10W
Sleman, Indonesia 85 D4 7 40 S 110 20 E
Slemon L., Canada 142 A5 63 13N 116 4W
Ślesin, Poland 55 F5 52 22N 18 14 E
Slide Mt., U.S.A. 151 E10 42 0N 74 25W
Slidell, U.S.A. 155 K10 30 17N 89 47W
Sliema, Malta 38 F8 35 55N 14 30 E
Slieve Aughty, Ireland 23 C3 53 4N 8 30W
Slieve Bloom, Ireland 23 C4 53 4N 7 40W
Slieve Donard, U.K. 23 B6 54 11N 5 55W
Slieve Gamph, Ireland 23 B3 54 6N 9 0W
Slieve Gullion, U.K. 23 B5 54 7N 6 26W
Slieve League, Ireland 23 B3 54 40N 8 42W
Slieve Mish, Ireland 23 D2 52 12N 9 50W
Slievenamon, Ireland 23 D4 52 25N 7 34W
Sligeach = Sligo, Ireland 23 B3 54 16N 8 28W
Sligo, Ireland 23 B3 54 16N 8 28W
Sligo, U.S.A. 150 E5 41 6N 79 29W
Sligo □, Ireland 23 B3 54 8N 8 42W
Sligo B., Ireland 23 B3 54 18N 8 40W
Slippery Rock, U.S.A. 150 E4 41 3N 80 3W
Slite, Sweden 17 G12 57 42N 18 48 E
Slīteres ⌂, Latvia 54 A9 57 41N 22 21 E
Sliven, Bulgaria 51 D10 42 42N 26 19 E
Slivnitsa, Bulgaria 50 D7 42 50N 23 2 E
Sljeme, Croatia 45 C12 45 57N 15 58 E
Sloan, U.S.A. 161 K11 35 57N 115 13W
Sloansville, U.S.A. 151 D10 42 45N 74 22W
Slobidka, Ukraine 53 C14 47 54N 29 21 E
Slobodskoy, Russia 64 B3 58 40N 50 6 E
Slobozia, Moldova 53 D14 46 45N 29 42 E
Slobozia, Argeş, Romania 53 F10 44 30N 25 14 E
Slobozia, Ialomiţa, Romania 53 F12 44 34N 27 23 E
Slocan, Canada 142 D5 49 48N 117 28W
Slocomb, U.S.A. 152 D4 31 7N 85 36W
Slomikhino = Furmanovo, Kazakhstan 60 F9 49 42N 49 25 E
Słomniki, Poland 55 H7 50 16N 20 4 E
Slonim, Belarus 59 F3 53 4N 25 19 E
Slot, The = New Georgia Sound, Solomon Is. 133 L9 8 0 S 158 20 E
Slough, U.K. 21 F7 51 30N 0 36W
Slough □, U.K. 21 F7 51 30N 0 36W
Sloughhouse, U.S.A. 160 G5 38 26N 121 12W
Slovak Rep. ■, Europe 35 C13 48 30N 20 0 E
Slovakia = Slovak Rep. ■, Europe 35 C13 48 30N 20 0 E
Slovakian Ore Mts. = Slovenské Rudohorie, Slovak Rep 35 C12 48 45N 20 0 E
Slovenia ■, Europe 45 C11 45 58N 14 30 E
Slovenija = Slovenia ■, Europe 45 C11 45 58N 14 30 E
Slovenj Gradec, Slovenia 45 B12 46 31N 15 5 E
Slovenska = Slovak Rep. ■, Europe 35 C13 48 30N 20 0 E
Slovenska Bistrica, Slovenia 45 B12 46 24N 15 35 E
Slovenské Konjice, Slovenia 45 B12 46 20N 15 28 E
Slovenské Rudohorie, Slovak Rep. 35 C12 48 45N 20 0 E
Slovenský Raj △, Slovak Rep. 35 C13 48 53N 20 25 E
Slovyansk, Ukraine 59 H9 48 55N 37 36 E
Słowiński △, Poland 54 D4 54 43N 17 26 E
Słubice, Poland 55 F1 52 22N 14 35 E
Sluch →, Ukraine 59 G4 51 37N 26 38 E
Sluis, Neths. 24 C3 51 18N 3 23 E
Slŭnchev Bryag, Bulgaria 51 D11 42 40N 27 41 E
Slunj, Croatia 45 C12 45 6N 15 33 E
Słupca, Poland 55 F4 52 15N 17 52 E
Słupia →, Poland 54 D3 54 35N 16 51 E
Słupsk, Poland 54 D4 54 30N 17 3 E
Slurry, S. Africa 116 D4 25 49 S 25 42 E
Slutsk = Pavlovsk, Russia 60 E5 50 26N 40 5 E
Slutsk, Belarus 59 F4 53 2N 27 31 E
Slyne Hd., Ireland 23 C1 53 25N 10 10W
Slyudyanka, Russia 67 D11 51 40N 103 40 E
Smaalenene = Østfold □, Norway 18 E8 59 25N 11 25 E
Småland, Sweden 17 G9 57 15N 15 25 E
Smålandsfarvandet, Denmark 17 J5 55 10N 11 20 E
Smålandsstenar, Sweden 17 G7 57 10N 13 25 E
Smaldeel = Theunissen, S. Africa 116 D4 28 26 S 26 43 E
Smalltree L., Canada 143 A8 61 0N 105 0W
Smallwood Res., Canada 141 B7 54 5N 64 30W
Smarhon, Belarus 58 E4 54 20N 26 24 E
Smarje, Slovenia 45 B12 46 15N 15 34 E
Smartt Syndicate Dam, S. Africa 116 E3 30 45 S 23 10 E
Smartville, U.S.A. 160 F5 39 13N 121 18W
Smeaton, Canada 143 C8 53 30N 104 49W
Smedby, Sweden 17 H10 56 41N 16 13 E
Smederevo, Serbia & M. 50 B4 44 40N 20 57 E
Smederevska Palanka, Serbia & M. 50 B4 44 22N 20 58 E
Smedjebacken, Sweden 16 D9 60 8N 15 25 E
Smela = Smila, Ukraine 59 H6 49 15N 31 58 E
Smerwick Harbour, Ireland 23 D1 52 12N 10 23W
Smethport, U.S.A. 150 E6 41 49N 78 27W
Smidovich, Russia 67 E14 48 36N 133 49 E
Śmigiel, Poland 55 F3 52 1N 16 32 E
Smila, Ukraine 59 H6 49 15N 31 58 E
Smilyan, Bulgaria 51 E8 41 29N 24 46 E
Smith, Canada 142 B6 55 10N 114 0W
Smith B., U.S.A. 144 A9 70 30N 154 20W
Smith Center, U.S.A. 154 F5 39 47N 98 47W
Smith I., India 95 H11 13 20N 93 4 E
Smith River, U.S.A. 158 F2 41 55N 124 0W
Smith Sd., N. Amer. 10 B3 78 25N 74 0W
Smithburne →, Australia 126 B3 17 3 S 140 57 E
Smithers, Canada 142 C3 54 45N 127 10W
Smithfield, S. Africa 117 E4 30 9 S 26 30 E
Smithfield, N.C., U.S.A. 153 H6 35 31N 78 21W
Smithfield, Utah, U.S.A. 158 F8 41 50N 111 50W
Smiths, U.S.A. 152 C4 32 32N 85 6W
Smiths Falls, Canada 140 D4 44 55N 76 0W
Smithton, Australia 127 G4 40 53 S 145 6 E
Smithville, Canada 150 C5 43 6N 79 33W
Smithville, Ga., U.S.A. 152 D5 31 54N 84 15W
Smithville, Mo., U.S.A. 156 E2 39 23N 94 35W
Smithville, Tex., U.S.A. 155 K6 30 1N 97 10W
Smoky →, Canada 142 B5 56 10N 117 21W
Smoky Bay, Australia 127 E1 32 22 S 134 13 E
Smoky Hill →, U.S.A. 154 F6 39 4N 96 48W
Smoky Hills, U.S.A. 154 F5 39 15N 99 30W
Smoky Lake, Canada 142 C6 54 10N 112 30W
Smøla, Norway 18 A5 63 23N 8 3 E
Smolensk, Russia 58 E7 54 45N 32 5 E
Smolikas, Óros, Greece 50 F4 40 9N 20 58 E
Smolník, Slovak Rep. 35 C13 48 43N 20 44 E
Smolyan, Bulgaria 51 E8 41 36N 24 38 E
Smooth Rock Falls, Canada 140 C3 49 17N 81 37W
Smoothstone L., Canada 143 C7 54 40N 106 50W
Smorgon = Smarhon, Belarus 58 E4 54 20N 26 24 E
Smotrych, Ukraine 53 B11 48 57N 26 33 E
Smotrych →, Ukraine 53 B11 48 34N 26 39 E
Smulţi, Romania 53 E12 45 57N 27 44 E
Smyadovo, Bulgaria 51 C11 43 2N 27 1 E
Smygehamn, Sweden 17 J7 55 21N 13 22 E
Smyrna = İzmir, Turkey 49 C9 38 25N 27 8 E
Smyrna, Del., U.S.A. 148 F8 39 18N 75 36W
Smyrna, Ga., U.S.A. 152 B5 33 53N 84 31W
Snæfell, Iceland 11 B11 64 48N 15 34W
Snaefell, I. of Man 20 C3 54 16N 4 27W
Snæfellsjökull, Iceland 11 C3 64 49N 23 46W
Snæfellsnessýsla □, Iceland 11 C3 65 0N 23 0W
Snake →, U.S.A. 158 C4 46 12N 119 2W
Snake I., Australia 129 E7 38 47 S 146 33 E
Snake Range, U.S.A. 158 G6 39 0N 114 20W
Snake River Plain, U.S.A. 158 E7 42 50N 113 0W
Snasahögarna, Sweden 16 A6 63 13N 12 21 E
Snåsavatnet, Norway 14 D14 64 12N 12 0 E
Snedsted, Denmark 17 H2 56 55N 8 32 E
Sneek, Neths. 24 A5 53 2N 5 40 E
Sneeuberge, S. Africa 116 E3 31 46 S 24 20 E
Snegurovka = Tetiyev, Ukraine 59 H5 49 22N 29 38 E
Snejbjerg, Denmark 17 H2 56 8N 8 54 E
Snelling, Calif., U.S.A. 160 H6 37 31N 120 26W
Snelling, S.C., U.S.A. 152 B8 33 15N 81 27W
Snells Beach, N.Z. 130 C3 36 25 S 174 44 E
Snezhnoye, Ukraine 59 J10 48 0N 38 58 E
Sněžka, Europe 36 C8 50 41N 15 50 E
Snežnik, Slovenia 45 C11 45 36N 14 35 E
Śniadowo, Poland 55 E8 53 2N 22 0 E
Sniardwy, Jezioro, Poland 54 E8 53 48N 21 50 E
Śnieżka, Europe 34 A8 50 44N 15 44 E
Snigirevka = Snihurivka, Ukraine 59 J7 47 2N 32 49 E
Snihurivka, Ukraine 59 J7 47 2N 32 49 E
Snillfjord, Norway 18 A6 63 24N 9 30 E
Snina, Slovak Rep. 35 C15 48 58N 22 9 E
Snizort, L., U.K. 22 D2 57 33N 6 28W
Snøhetta, Norway 18 B6 62 19N 9 16 E
Snohomish, U.S.A. 160 C4 47 55N 122 6W
Snønuten, Norway 18 E3 59 31N 6 52 E
Snoul, Cambodia 87 F6 12 4N 106 26 E
Snovsk = Shchors, Ukraine 59 G6 51 48N 31 56 E
Snow Hill, U.S.A. 148 F8 38 11N 75 24W
Snow Lake, Canada 143 C8 54 52N 100 3W
Snow Mt., Calif., U.S.A. 160 F4 39 23N 122 45W
Snow Mt., Maine, U.S.A. 151 A14 45 18N 70 48W
Snow Shoe, U.S.A. 150 E7 41 2N 77 57W
Snowbird L., Canada 143 A8 60 45N 103 0W
Snowdon, U.K. 20 D3 53 4N 4 5W
Snowdonia △, U.K. 20 D4 53 7N 3 59W
Snowdoun, U.S.A. 152 C3 32 15N 86 18W
Snowdrift = Łutselk'e, Canada 143 A6 62 24N 110 44W
Snowdrift →, Canada 143 A6 62 24N 110 44W
Snowflake, U.S.A. 159 J8 34 30N 110 5W
Snowshoe Pk., U.S.A. 158 B6 48 13N 115 41W
Snowtown, Australia 128 B3 33 46 S 138 14 E
Snowville, U.S.A. 158 F7 41 58N 112 43W
Snowy →, Australia 129 D8 37 46 S 148 30 E
Snowy Mt., U.S.A. 151 C10 43 42N 74 23W
Snowy Mts., Australia 129 D8 36 30 S 148 20 E
Snowy River △, Australia 129 D7 37 15 S 147 29 E
Snug Corner, Bahamas 165 B5 22 33N 73 52W
Snyatyn, Ukraine 53 B10 48 27N 25 38 E
Snyder, Okla., U.S.A. 155 H5 34 40N 98 57W
Snyder, Tex., U.S.A. 155 J4 32 44N 100 55W
Soacha, Colombia 168 C3 4 35N 74 13W
Soahanina, Madag. 117 B7 18 42 S 44 13 E
Soalala, Madag. 117 B8 16 6 S 45 20 E
Soaloka, Madag. 117 B8 18 32 S 45 15 E
Soamanonga, Madag. 117 C7 23 52 S 44 47 E
Soan →, Pakistan 92 C4 33 1N 71 44 E
Soanierana-Ivongo, Madag. 117 B8 16 55 S 49 35 E
Soanindrariny, Madag. 117 B8 19 54 S 47 14 E
Şoarş, Romania 53 E9 45 56N 24 55 E
Soasiu, Indonesia 82 A3 0 40N 127 26 E
Soavina, Madag. 117 C8 20 23 S 46 56 E
Soavinandriana, Madag. 117 B8 19 9 S 46 45 E
Sob →, Ukraine 53 B14 48 40N 29 15 E
Soba, Nigeria 113 C6 10 58N 8 4 E
Sobat, Nahr →, Sudan 107 F3 9 22N 31 33 E
Soběslav, Czech Rep. 34 B7 49 16N 14 45 E
Sobger →, Indonesia 83 B6 3 42 S 140 16 E
Sobhapur, India 92 H8 22 47N 78 17 E
Sobinka, Russia 58 E11 56 0N 40 0 E
Sobo-Yama, Japan 72 E3 32 51N 131 22 E
Sobótka, Poland 55 H3 50 54N 16 44 E
Sobra, Croatia 45 F14 42 44N 17 34 E
Sobradinho, Represa de, Brazil 170 C3 9 30 S 42 0W
Sobral, Brazil 170 B3 3 50 S 40 20W
Sobrance, Slovak Rep. 35 C15 48 45N 22 11 E
Sobreira Formosa, Portugal 42 F3 39 46N 7 51W
Soc Giang, Vietnam 76 F6 22 54N 106 1 E
Soc Trang, Vietnam 87 H5 9 37N 105 50 E
Soča →, Europe 34 E6 46 20N 13 40 E
Socastee, U.S.A. 149 J6 33 41N 79 1W
Sochaczew, Poland 55 F7 52 15N 20 13 E
Soch'e = Shache, China 65 D8 38 20N 77 10 E
Sochi, Russia 61 J4 43 35N 39 40 E
Social Circle, U.S.A. 152 B6 33 39N 83 43W
Société, Is. de la, French Polynesia 135 J12 17 0 S 151 0W
Society Hill, U.S.A. 152 C4 32 26N 85 27W
Society Is. = Société, Is. de la, French Polynesia 135 J12 17 0 S 151 0W
Socompa, Portezuelo de, Chile 174 A2 24 27 S 68 18W
Socorro = Fronteiras, Brazil 170 C3 7 5 S 40 37W
Socorro, Colombia 168 B3 6 29N 73 16W
Socorro, Phil. 81 G5 9 37N 125 58 E
Socorro, N. Mex., U.S.A. 159 J10 34 4N 106 54W
Socorro, Tex., U.S.A. 159 L10 31 39N 106 18W
Socorro, I., Mexico 162 D2 18 45N 110 58W
Socotra, Yemen 99 D6 12 30N 54 0 E
Socovos, Spain 41 G3 38 20N 1 58W
Socuéllamos, Spain 41 F2 39 16N 2 47W
Soda L., U.S.A. 159 J5 35 10N 116 4W
Soda Plains, India 93 B8 35 30N 79 0 E
Soda Springs, U.S.A. 158 E8 42 39N 111 36W
Sodankylä, Finland 14 C22 67 29N 26 40 E
Soddy-Daisy, U.S.A. 149 H3 35 17N 85 10W
Söderala, Sweden 16 C10 61 17N 16 55 E
Söderåsen △, Sweden 17 H7 56 2N 13 13 E
Söderbärke, Sweden 16 D9 60 5N 15 33 E
Söderfors, Sweden 16 D11 60 23N 17 25 E
Söderhamn, Sweden 16 C11 61 18N 17 10 E
Söderköping, Sweden 17 F10 58 31N 16 20 E
Södermanland, Sweden 15 G17 58 56N 16 55 E
Södermanlands län □, Sweden 16 E10 59 10N 16 30 E
Södertälje, Sweden 16 E11 59 12N 17 39 E
Sodiri, Sudan 107 E2 14 27N 29 0 E
Sodo, Ethiopia 107 F4 7 0N 37 41 E
Södra Dellen, Sweden 16 C10 61 48N 16 43 E
Södra Finnskoga, Sweden 16 D6 60 42N 12 34 E
Södra Sandby, Sweden 17 J7 55 43N 13 21 E
Södra Ulvön, Sweden 16 B12 62 59N 18 38 E
Södra Vi, Sweden 17 G9 57 45N 15 45 E
Sodražica, Slovenia 45 C11 45 45N 14 39 E
Sodus, U.S.A. 150 C7 43 14N 77 4W
Sodwana Bay △, S. Africa 117 D5 27 35 S 32 43 E
Soe, Indonesia 82 C2 9 52 S 124 17 E
Soekmekaar, S. Africa 117 C4 23 30 S 29 55 E
Soest, Germany 30 D4 51 34N 8 7 E
Soest, Neths. 24 B5 52 9N 5 19 E
Sofádhes, Greece 48 B4 39 20N 22 4 E
Sofala □, Mozam. 117 B5 19 30 S 34 30 E
Sofara, Mali 112 C4 13 59N 4 9W
Sofia = Sofiya, Bulgaria 50 D7 42 45N 23 20 E
Sofia →, Madag. 117 B8 15 27 S 47 23 E
Sofievka, Ukraine 59 H7 48 6N 33 55 E
Sofikón, Greece 48 D5 37 47N 23 3 E
Sofiya, Bulgaria 50 D7 42 45N 23 20 E
Sofiya □, Bulgaria 50 D7 42 45N 23 20 E
Sofiya ✕ (SOF), Bulgaria 50 D7 42 46N 23 28 E
Sofiyevka = Volnansk, Ukraine 59 H8 48 2N 35 29 E
Sōfu-Gan, Japan 71 K10 29 49N 140 21 E
Sogakofe, Ghana 113 D5 6 2N 0 39 E
Sogamoso, Colombia 168 B3 5 43N 72 56W
Soğar, Iran 97 E8 25 53N 58 6 E
Sögel, Germany 30 C3 52 50N 7 31 E
Sogeri, Papua N. G. 132 E4 9 26 S 147 35 E
Sogn og Fjordane □, Norway 18 C3 61 40N 6 45 E
Sogndalsfjøra, Norway 18 C4 61 14N 7 5 E
Søgne, Norway 18 F4 58 5N 7 48 E
Sognefjorden, Norway 18 C2 61 10N 5 50 E
Sogod, Phil. 81 F5 10 28N 124 59 E
Söğüt, Bilecik, Turkey 49 A12 40 2N 30 11 E
Söğüt, Burdur, Turkey 49 D11 37 2N 29 50 E
Söğüt Dağı, Turkey 49 D11 37 50N 29 55 E
Söğütköy, Turkey 49 E10 36 40N 28 8 E
Sögwipo, S. Korea 75 H14 33 13N 126 34 E
Soh, Iran 97 C6 33 26N 51 27 E
Sohâg, Egypt 106 B3 26 33N 31 43 E

Sohagpur, India 92 H8 22 42N 78 12 E
Sohano, Papua N. G. 132 C8 5 22 S 154 37 E
Sohela, India 94 D6 21 18N 83 24 E
Sŏhori, N. Korea 75 D15 40 7N 128 23 E
Soignies, Belgium 24 D4 50 35N 4 5 E
Soin, Burkina Faso 112 C4 12 47N 3 50W
Soira, Eritrea 107 E4 14 45N 39 30 E
Soissons, France 27 C10 49 25N 3 19 E
Sōja, Japan 72 C5 34 40N 133 45 E
Sojat, India 92 G5 25 55N 73 45 E
Sok →, Russia 60 D10 53 24N 50 8 E
Sokal, Ukraine 59 G3 50 31N 24 15 E
Söke, Turkey 49 D9 37 48N 27 28 E
Sokelo, Dem. Rep. of the Congo 119 D1 9 55 S 24 36 E
Sokh, Uzbekistan 65 D5 39 56N 71 9 E
Sokhós, Greece 50 F7 40 48N 23 22 E
Sokhumi, Georgia 61 J5 43 0N 41 0 E
Sokki, Oued In →, Algeria 111 C5 29 30N 3 42 E
Sokna, Norway 18 D6 60 16N 9 58 E
Soknedal, Norway 18 B7 62 57N 10 13 E
Soko Banja, Serbia & M. 50 C5 43 40N 21 51 E
Soko Islands, China 69 G10 22 10N 113 54 E
Sokodé, Togo 113 D5 9 0N 1 11 E
Sokol, Russia 58 C11 59 30N 40 5 E
Sokolac, Bos.-H. 52 G3 43 56N 18 48 E
Sokółka, Poland 54 E10 53 25N 23 30 E
Sokolo, Ségou, Mali 112 C3 14 53N 6 8W
Sokolo, Sikasso, Mali 112 C3 10 52N 6 59W
Sokolov, Czech Rep. 34 A5 50 12N 12 40 E
Sokołów Małpolski, Poland 55 H9 50 12N 22 7 E
Sokołów Podlaski, Poland 55 F9 52 25N 22 15 E
Sokoły, Poland 55 F9 52 59N 22 42 E
Sokoto, Nigeria 113 C6 13 2N 5 16 E
Sokoto □, Nigeria 113 C6 12 30N 6 0 E
Sokoto →, Nigeria 113 C5 11 20N 4 10 E
Sokuluk, Kyrgyzstan 65 B7 42 52N 74 18 E
Sokyrnytsya, Ukraine 53 B8 48 7N 23 23 E
Sokyryany, Ukraine 53 B12 48 27N 27 25 E
Sol Iletsk, Russia 64 F5 51 10N 55 0 E
Sola, Norway 18 F2 58 53N 5 36 E
Sola, Vanuatu 133 C5 13 51 S 167 33 E
Sola →, Poland 55 H6 50 4N 19 15 E
Solai, Kenya 118 B4 0 2N 36 12 E
Solan, India 92 D7 30 55N 77 7 E
Solana, Phil. 80 C3 17 39N 121 41 E
Solander I., N.Z. 131 G1 46 34 S 166 54 E
Solano, Phil. 80 C3 16 31N 121 15 E
Solapur, India 94 F2 17 43N 75 56 E
Solca, Romania 53 C10 47 40N 25 50 E
Solda Gölü, Turkey 49 D11 37 33N 29 42 E
Soldănești, Moldova 53 C13 47 49N 28 48 E
Soldeu, Andorra 40 C6 42 35N 1 40 E
Soldin = Myślibórz, Poland 55 F1 52 55N 14 50 E
Soldotna, U.S.A. 144 F10 60 29N 151 3W
Soléa, Cyprus 39 E9 35 5N 33 4 E
Solec Kujawski, Poland 55 E5 53 5N 18 14 E
Soledad, Colombia 168 A3 10 55N 74 46W
Soledad, U.S.A. 160 J5 36 26N 121 20W
Soledad, Venezuela 169 B5 8 10N 63 34W
Sølen, Norway 18 C8 61 53N 11 31 E
Solent, The, U.K. 21 G6 50 45N 1 25W
Solenzara, France 29 G13 41 53N 9 23 E
Solesmes, France 27 B10 50 10N 3 30 E
Solfonn, Norway 18 D3 60 2N 6 57 E
Solhan, Turkey 101 C9 38 57N 41 3 E
Sølheim, Norway 18 D2 60 53N 5 27 E
Soligalich, Russia 56 C7 59 5N 42 10 E
Soligorsk = Salihorsk, Belarus 59 F4 52 51N 27 27 E
Solihull, U.K. 21 E6 52 26N 1 47W
Solikamsk, Russia 64 B6 59 38N 56 50 E
Solila, Madag. 117 C8 21 25 S 46 37 E
Solimões = Amazonas →, S. Amer. 169 D7 0 5 S 50 0W
Solin, Croatia 45 E13 43 33N 16 30 E
Solingen, Germany 30 D3 51 10N 7 5 E
Sollebrunn, Sweden 17 F6 58 8N 12 32 E
Sollefteå, Sweden 16 A11 63 12N 17 20 E
Sollentuna, Sweden 16 E11 59 26N 17 56 E
Sóller, Spain 38 B3 39 46N 2 43 E
Sollerön, Sweden 16 D8 60 55N 14 37 E
Solling, Germany 30 D5 51 42N 9 38 E
Solling-Vogler ⌓, Germany 30 D5 51 45N 9 32 E
Solnechnogorsk, Russia 58 D9 56 10N 36 57 E
Solo →, Indonesia 79 G15 6 47 S 112 22 E
Solofra, Italy 47 B7 40 50N 14 51 E
Sologne, France 27 E8 47 40N 1 45 E
Solok, Indonesia 84 C2 0 45 S 100 40 E
Sololá, Guatemala 164 D1 14 49N 91 10W
Solomon, N. Fork →, U.S.A. 154 F5 39 29N 98 26W
Solomon, S. Fork →, U.S.A. 154 F5 39 25N 99 12W
Solomon Is., Papua N. G. 132 D8 6 0 S 155 0 E
Solomon Is. ■, Pac. Oc. 133 B8 6 0 S 155 0 E
Solomon Sea, Papua N. G. 132 D6 7 0 S 150 0 E
Solon, China 69 B7 46 32N 121 10 E
Solon Springs, U.S.A. 154 B9 46 22N 91 49W
Solonópole, Brazil 170 C4 5 44 S 39 1W
Solor, Indonesia 82 C2 8 27 S 123 0 E
Solotcha, Russia 58 E10 54 48N 39 53 E
Solothurn, Switz. 32 B5 47 13N 7 32 E
Solothurn □, Switz. 32 B5 47 18N 7 40 E
Solotvyn, Ukraine 53 B9 48 42N 24 25 E
Solsona, Spain 40 C6 42 0N 1 31 E
Solsvik, Norway 18 D1 60 26N 4 58 E
Solt, Hungary 52 D4 46 45N 19 1 E
Šolta, Croatia 45 E13 43 24N 16 15 E
Solṭānābād, Khorāsān, Iran 97 C8 34 13N 59 58 E
Solṭānābād, Khorāsān, Iran 97 B8 36 29N 58 5 E
Soltau, Germany 30 C5 52 59N 9 50 E
Soltsy, Russia 58 C6 58 10N 30 30 E
Solund, Norway 18 C1 61 5N 4 50 E
Solunska Glava, Macedonia 50 E5 41 44N 21 31 E
Solvang, U.S.A. 161 L6 34 36N 120 8W
Solvay, U.S.A. 151 C8 43 3N 76 13W
Sölvesborg, Sweden 17 H8 56 5N 14 35 E
Solvychegodsk, Russia 56 B8 61 21N 46 56 E
Solway Firth, U.K. 20 C4 54 49N 3 35W
Solwezi, Zambia 119 E2 12 11 S 26 21 E
Sōma, Japan 70 F10 37 40N 140 50 E
Soma, Turkey 49 B9 39 10N 27 35 E
Somabhula, Zimbabwe 117 B4 19 42 S 29 40 E
Somali = Sumale □, Ethiopia 120 C2 7 0N 45 0 E
Somali Basin, Ind. Oc. 121 D4 3 0N 53 0 E
Somali Pen., Africa 104 F8 7 0N 46 0 E
Somali Rep. ■, Africa 120 C3 7 0N 47 0 E
Somalia = Somali Rep. ■, Africa 120 C3 7 0N 47 0 E
Sombe Dzong, Bhutan 90 B2 27 13N 89 8 E
Sombernon, France 27 E11 47 20N 4 40 E
Sombo, Angola 115 D4 8 42 S 20 59 E
Sombor, Serbia & M. 52 E4 45 46N 19 9 E
Sombra, Canada 150 D2 42 43N 82 29W
Sombrerete, Mexico 162 C4 23 40N 103 40W
Sombrero, Anguilla 165 C7 18 37N 63 30W
Sombrero Channel, India 95 L11 7 41N 93 35 E
Şomcuta Mare, Romania 53 C8 47 31N 23 28 E
Somdari, India 92 G5 25 47N 72 38 E
Someido ⌓, Spain 42 B4 43 5N 6 11W
Somers, U.S.A. 158 B6 48 5N 114 13W
Somerset, Bermuda 9 a 32 17N 64 52W
Somerset, Ky., U.S.A. 148 G3 37 5N 84 36W
Somerset, Mass., U.S.A. 151 E13 41 47N 71 8W
Somerset, Pa., U.S.A. 150 F5 40 1N 79 5W
Somerset □, U.K. 21 F5 51 9N 3 0W
Somerset East, S. Africa 116 E4 32 42 S 25 35 E
Somerset I., Bermuda 9 a 32 17N 64 52W
Somerset I., Canada 138 A10 73 30N 93 0W
Somerset West, S. Africa 116 E2 34 8 S 18 50 E
Somersworth, U.S.A. 151 C14 43 16N 70 52W
Somerton, U.S.A. 159 K6 32 36N 114 43W
Somerville, U.S.A. 151 F10 40 35N 74 38W
Someş →, Romania 52 C7 47 49N 22 43 E
Someşul Mare →, Romania 53 C8 47 9N 23 55 E
Somme □, France 27 C9 49 57N 2 20 E
Somme →, France 27 B8 50 11N 1 38 E
Somme, B. de la, France 26 B8 50 14N 1 33 E
Sommen, Jönköping, Sweden 17 F8 58 12N 14 58 E
Sommen, Östergötland, Sweden 17 F9 58 0N 15 15 E
Sommepy-Tahure, France 27 C11 49 15N 4 31 E
Sömmerda, Germany 30 D7 51 9N 11 7 E
Sommerfeld = Lubsko, Poland 55 G1 51 45N 14 57 E
Sommesous, France 27 D11 48 44N 4 12 E
Sommières, France 29 E8 43 47N 4 6 E
Somnath, India 92 J4 20 53N 70 22 E
Somogy □, Hungary 52 D2 46 19N 17 30 E
Somogyszob, Hungary 52 D2 46 18N 17 20 E
Somosomo, Fiji 133 A3 16 47 S 179 58W
Somosomo Str., Fiji 133 A3 16 0 S 180 0 E
Somoto, Nic. 164 D2 13 28N 86 37W
Sompolno, Poland 55 F5 52 26N 18 30 E
Somport, Puerto de, Spain 40 C4 42 48N 0 31W
Somuncurá, Meseta de, Argentina 176 B3 41 30 S 67 0W
Somvarpet, India 95 H2 12 36N 75 52 E
Son, Norway 18 E7 59 32N 10 42 E
Son →, India 93 G11 25 42N 84 52 E
Son Ha, Vietnam 86 E7 15 3N 108 34 E
Son Hoa, Vietnam 86 F7 13 2N 108 58 E
Son La, Vietnam 76 G4 21 20N 103 50 E
Son Serra, Spain 38 B4 39 43N 3 13 E
Son Servera, Spain 38 B4 39 37N 3 21 E
Son Tay, Vietnam 76 G5 21 8N 105 30 E
Soná, Panama 164 E3 8 0N 81 20W
Sonamarg, India 93 B6 34 18N 75 21 E
Sonamukhi, India 93 H12 23 18N 87 27 E
Sonamura, India 90 D3 23 29N 91 15 E
Sonar →, India 93 G8 24 24N 79 56 E
Sŏnch'ŏn, N. Korea 75 E13 39 48N 124 55 E
Sondags →, S. Africa 116 E4 33 44 S 25 51 E
Sóndalo, Italy 44 B7 46 20N 10 19 E
Sondar, India 93 C6 33 28N 75 56 E
Søndeled, Norway 18 F6 58 46N 9 3 E
Sønder Felding, Denmark 17 J2 55 57N 8 47 E
Sønder Omme, Denmark 17 J2 55 50N 8 54 E
Sønderborg, Denmark 17 K3 54 55N 9 49 E
Sønderjyllands Amtskommune □, Denmark 17 J3 55 10N 9 10 E
Sondershausen, Germany 30 D6 51 22N 10 51 E
Sondre Bergenhaus = Hordaland □, Norway 18 D3 60 25N 6 15 E
Søndre Strømfjord = Kangerlussuaq, Greenland 10 D5 66 59N 50 40W
Søndre Trøndhjem = Sør-Trøndelag □, Norway 18 A7 63 0N 11 0 E
Sóndrio, Italy 44 B6 46 10N 9 52 E
Sondur →, India 94 D6 20 40N 82 1 E
Sone, Mozam. 119 F3 17 23 S 34 55 E
Sonepur, India 94 D6 20 55N 83 50 E
Sonfim, Brazil 172 B4 6 0 S 67 52W
Song, Nigeria 113 D7 9 49N 12 39 E
Song, Thailand 86 C3 18 28N 100 11 E
Song Cau, Vietnam 86 F7 13 27N 109 18 E
Song-Köl, Kyrgyzstan 65 C7 41 50N 75 12 E
Song Xian, China 74 G7 34 12N 112 8 E
Songadh, India 94 D1 21 9N 73 33 E
Songan, Indonesia 79 J18 8 13 S 115 24 E
Songavatnet, Norway 18 E4 59 52N 7 32 E
Songch'ŏn, N. Korea 75 E14 39 12N 126 15 E
Songea, Tanzania 119 E4 10 40 S 35 40 E
Songeons, France 27 C8 49 32N 1 50 E
Songgang, China 69 F10 22 46N 113 50 E
Songhua Hu, China 75 C14 43 35N 126 50 E
Songhua Jiang →, China 69 B8 47 45N 132 30 E
Songimvelo ⌓, S. Africa 117 D5 25 50 S 31 2 E
Songjiang, China 77 B13 31 1N 121 12 E
Sŏngjin = Kimch'aek, N. Korea 75 D15 40 40N 129 10 E
Songjin, N. Korea 75 D15 40 40N 129 10 E
Songjŏng-ni, S. Korea 75 G14 35 8N 126 47 E
Songkan, China 76 C6 28 35N 106 52 E
Songkhla, Thailand 87 J3 7 13N 100 37 E
Songming, China 76 E4 25 12N 103 2 E
Sŏngnam, S. Korea 57 F14 37 25N 127 10 E
Songnim, N. Korea 75 E13 38 45N 125 39 E
Songo, Angola 115 D2 7 22 S 14 51 E
Songololo = Mbanza Ngungu, Dem. Rep. of the Congo 115 D2 5 12 S 14 53 E
Songololo, Dem. Rep. of the Congo 115 D2 5 42 S 14 2 E
Songpan, China 76 A4 32 40N 103 30 E
Songtao, China 76 C7 28 11N 109 10 E
Songwe, Dem. Rep. of the Congo 118 C2 3 20 S 26 16 E
Songwe →, Africa 119 D3 9 44 S 33 58 E
Songxi, China 77 D12 27 31N 118 44 E
Songzi, China 77 B8 30 12N 111 45 E
Sonhat, India 93 H10 23 29N 82 31 E
Sonid Youqi, China 74 C7 42 45N 112 48 E
Sonipat, India 92 E7 29 0N 77 5 E
Sonkach, India 92 H7 22 59N 76 21 E
Sonkovo, Russia 58 D9 57 50N 37 5 E
Sonmiani, Pakistan 91 D2 25 25N 66 40 E
Sonmiani B., Pakistan 92 G2 25 15N 66 30 E
Sonnino, Italy 46 A6 41 25N 13 14 E
Sono →, Minas Gerais, Brazil 171 E2 17 2 S 45 32W
Sono →, Tocantins, Brazil 170 C2 9 58 S 48 11W
Sonobe, Japan 73 B7 35 6N 135 28 E
Sonogno, Switz. 33 D7 46 22N 8 47 E
Sonoma, U.S.A. 160 G4 38 18N 122 28W
Sonora, Calif., U.S.A. 160 H6 37 59N 120 23W
Sonora, Tex., U.S.A. 155 K4 30 34N 100 39W
Sonora □, Mexico 162 B2 29 0N 111 0W
Sonora →, Mexico 162 B2 28 50N 111 33W
Sonoran Desert, U.S.A. 161 L12 33 40N 114 15W
Sonoyta, Mexico 162 A2 31 51N 112 50W
Sonqor, Iran 101 E12 34 47N 47 36 E
Sŏnsan, S. Korea 75 F15 36 14N 128 17 E
Sonseca, Spain 43 F7 39 42N 3 57W
Sonsón, Colombia 168 B2 5 43N 75 18W
Sonsonate, El Salv. 164 D2 13 43N 89 44W
Sonstorp, Sweden 17 F9 58 44N 15 38 E
Sonthofen, Germany 31 H6 47 30N 10 16 E
Soochow = Suzhou, China 77 B13 31 19N 120 38 E
Sooke, Canada 160 B3 48 13N 123 43W
Soomaaliya = Somali Rep. ■, Africa 120 C3 7 0N 47 0 E
Sop Hao, Laos 76 G5 20 33N 104 27 E
Sop Prap, Thailand 86 D2 17 53N 99 20 E
Sopachuy, Bolivia 173 D5 19 29 S 64 31W
Sopchoppy, U.S.A. 152 E5 30 4N 84 29W
Sopelana, Spain 40 B2 43 23N 2 58W
Soperton, U.S.A. 152 C7 32 23N 82 35W
Sopi, Indonesia 82 A3 2 34N 128 28 E
Sopo, Nahr →, Sudan 107 F2 8 40N 26 30 E
Sopot, Bulgaria 51 D8 42 39N 24 45 E
Sopot, Poland 54 D5 54 27N 18 31 E
Sopot, Serbia & M. 50 B4 44 29N 20 30 E
Sopotnica, Macedonia 50 E5 41 18N 21 13 E
Sopron, Hungary 52 C1 47 45N 16 32 E
Sopur, India 93 B6 34 18N 74 27 E
Sør-Rondane, Antarctica 7 D4 72 0 S 25 0 E
Sør-Trøndelag □, Norway 18 A7 63 0N 11 0 E
Sora, Italy 45 G10 41 43N 13 37 E
Sorab, India 95 G2 14 23N 75 6 E
Sorada, India 94 E7 19 45N 84 26 E
Sorah, Pakistan 92 F3 27 13N 68 56 E
Söråker, Sweden 16 B11 62 30N 17 32 E
Sorano, Italy 45 F8 42 41N 11 43 E
Soraon, India 93 G9 25 37N 81 51 E
Sorata, Bolivia 172 D4 15 50 S 68 40W
Sorbas, Spain 41 H2 37 6N 2 7W
Sörbygden, Sweden 16 B10 62 48N 16 12 E
Sore, France 28 D3 44 18N 0 35W
Sorel-Tracy, Canada 140 C5 46 0N 73 10W
Sörenberg, Switz. 32 C6 46 50N 8 2 E
Soresina, Italy 44 C6 45 17N 9 51 E
Sørfjorden, Norway 18 D3 60 20N 6 37 E
Sörforsa, Sweden 16 C10 61 43N 16 58 E
Sórgono, Italy 46 B2 40 1N 9 6 E
Sorgues, France 29 D8 44 1N 4 53 E
Sorgun, Turkey 100 C6 39 46N 35 11 E
Sori, Papua N. G. 132 A4 1 58 S 146 42 E
Soria, Spain 40 D2 41 43N 2 32W
Soria □, Spain 40 D2 41 46N 2 28W
Soriano, Uruguay 174 C4 33 24 S 58 19W
Soriano nel Cimino, Italy 45 F9 42 25N 12 14 E
Sorkh, Kuh-e, Iran 97 C8 35 40N 58 30 E
Sorø, Denmark 17 J5 55 26N 11 32 E
Soro, Guinea 112 C3 10 9N 9 48W
Soroca, Moldova 53 B13 48 8N 28 12 E
Sorocaba, Brazil 175 A6 23 31 S 47 27W
Sorochinsk, Russia 64 E4 52 26N 53 10 E
Soroka = Belomorsk, Russia 56 B5 64 35N 34 54 E
Soroki = Soroca, Moldova 53 B13 48 8N 28 12 E
Sorokino = Krasnodon, Ukraine 59 H10 48 17N 39 44 E
Sorong, Indonesia 83 B4 0 55 S 131 15 E
Soroni, Greece 38 E12 36 21N 28 1 E
Soroti, Uganda 118 B3 1 43N 33 35 E
Sørøya, Norway 14 A20 70 40N 22 30 E
Sørøyane, Norway 18 B2 62 25N 5 32 E
Sørøysundet, Norway 14 A20 70 25N 23 0 E
Sorraia →, Portugal 43 G2 38 55N 8 53W
Sorrell, Australia 127 G4 42 47 S 147 34 E
Sorrento, Italy 47 B7 40 37N 14 22 E
Sorsele, Sweden 14 D17 65 31N 17 30 E
Sörsjön, Sweden 16 C7 61 24N 13 5 E
Sorso, Italy 46 B1 40 48N 8 34 E
Sorsogon, Phil. 80 E5 13 0N 124 0 E
Sorsogon □, Phil. 80 E4 12 50N 123 55 E
Sortavala, Russia 58 B6 61 42N 30 41 E
Sortino, Italy 47 E8 37 9N 15 2 E
Sortland, Norway 14 B16 68 42N 15 25 E
Sørum, Norway 18 D7 60 30N 10 17 E
Sørvika, Norway 18 B8 62 25N 11 54 E
Sorvizhi, Russia 60 B9 57 52N 48 32 E
Sos del Rey Católico, Spain 40 C3 42 30N 1 13W
Sŏsan, S. Korea 75 F14 36 47N 126 27 E
Sosaq, Kazakhstan 65 A4 44 9N 68 27 E
Soscumica, L., Canada 140 B4 50 15N 77 27W
Sösdala, Sweden 17 H7 56 2N 13 41 E
Sosna →, Russia 59 F10 52 42N 38 55 E
Sosnogorsk, Russia 56 B9 63 37N 53 51 E
Sosnovka, Kyrgyzstan 65 B6 42 40N 73 50 E
Sosnovka, Kirov, Russia 60 B10 56 17N 51 17 E
Sosnovka, Tambov, Russia 60 D5 53 13N 41 24 E
Sosnovyy Bor, Russia 58 C5 59 55N 29 6 E
Sosnowiec, Poland 55 H6 50 20N 19 10 E
Sosnowitz = Sosnowiec, Poland 55 H6 50 20N 19 10 E
Soso, C.A.R. 114 B3 3 55N 15 30 E
Sospel, France 29 E11 43 52N 7 27 E
Sossus Vlei, Namibia 116 C2 24 40 S 15 23 E
Šoštanj, Slovenia 45 B12 46 23N 15 4 E
Sŏsura, N. Korea 75 C16 42 16N 130 36 E
Sosva, Russia 64 B8 59 10N 61 50 E
Sosva →, Russia 64 B9 59 21N 62 23 E
Sosvinsky Zavod = Sosva, Russia 64 B8 59 10N 61 50 E
Sot →, India 93 F8 27 27N 79 37 E
Sotaseter, Norway 18 C4 61 49N 7 43 E
Sotavento, C. Verde Is. 9 j 15 0N 25 0W
Sotkamo, Finland 14 D23 64 8N 28 23 E
Soto del Barco, Spain 42 B4 43 32N 6 4W
Soto la Marina →, Mexico 163 C5 23 40N 97 40W
Soto y Amío, Spain 42 C5 42 46N 5 53W
Sotrondio, Spain 42 B5 43 17N 5 36W
Sotuf, Adrar, W. Sahara 110 D1 21 42N 15 36W
Sotuta, Mexico 163 C7 20 29N 89 43W
Souanké, Congo 114 B2 2 10N 14 3 E
Soubré, Ivory C. 112 D3 5 50N 6 35W
Souderton, U.S.A. 151 F9 40 19N 75 19W
Soúdha, Greece 39 E5 35 29N 24 4 E
Soúdhas, Kólpos, Greece 39 E5 35 25N 24 10 E
Soufflay, Congo 114 B2 2 1N 14 54 E
Souflíon, Greece 51 E10 41 12N 26 18 E
Soufrière, Guadeloupe 164 b 16 5N 61 40W
Soufrière, St. Lucia 165 f 13 51N 61 3W
Soufrière Bay, Dominica 165 f 13 53N 61 6W
Souillac, France 28 D5 44 53N 1 29 E
Souilly, France 27 C12 49 3N 5 17 E
Souk-Ahras, Algeria 111 A6 36 23N 7 57 E
Souk el Arba du Rharb, Morocco 110 B3 34 43N 5 59W
Soukhouma, Laos 86 E5 14 38N 105 48 E
Sŏul, S. Korea 75 F14 37 31N 126 58 E
Soulac-sur-Mer, France 28 C2 45 30N 1 7W
Soulári, Greece 39 C1 38 10N 20 25 E
Soulougou, Burkina Faso 113 C5 13 1N 0 25 E
Soultz-sous-Forêts, France 27 D14 48 57N 7 52 E
Sound, The = Øresund, Europe 17 J6 55 45N 12 45 E
Sound, The, U.K. 21 G3 50 20N 4 10W
Sound I., India 95 H11 12 58N 92 59 E
Soúnion, Ákra, Greece 48 D6 37 37N 24 1 E
Sour el Ghozlane, Algeria 111 A5 36 10N 3 45 E
Sources, Mt. aux, Lesotho 117 D4 28 45 S 28 50 E
Soure, Brazil 170 B2 0 35 S 48 30W
Soure, Portugal 42 E2 40 4N 8 38W
Souris, Man., Canada 143 D8 49 40N 100 20W
Souris, P.E.I., Canada 141 C7 46 21N 62 15W
Souris →, Canada 154 A4 49 40N 99 34W
Sourou →, Africa 112 C4 12 45N 3 25W
Soúrpi, Greece 48 B4 39 6N 22 54 E
Sous, O. →, Morocco 110 B3 30 27N 9 31W
Sousa, Brazil 170 C4 6 45 S 38 10W
Sousel, Brazil 170 B1 2 38 S 52 29W
Sousel, Portugal 43 G3 38 57N 7 40W
Souss-Massa ⌓, Morocco 110 B3 31 26N 9 35W
Sousse, Tunisia 108 A2 35 50N 10 38 E
Soustons, France 28 E2 43 45N 1 19W
Sout →, S. Africa 116 E2 31 35 S 18 24 E
South Africa ■, Africa 116 E3 32 0 S 23 0 E
South America 166 E5 10 0 S 60 0W
South Andaman, India 95 J11 11 45N 92 10 E
South Atlantic Ocean 8 J10 20 0 S 10 0W
South Aulatsivik I., Canada 141 A7 56 45N 61 30W
South Australia □, Australia 128 B3 32 0 S 139 0 E
South Ayrshire □, U.K. 22 F4 55 18N 4 41W
South Baldy, U.S.A. 159 J10 34 6N 107 11W
South Bass I., U.S.A. 150 E2 41 38N 82 53W
South Bay, U.S.A. 153 J9 26 40N 80 43W
South Beach, Bahamas 9 b 25 1N 77 20W
South Beloit, U.S.A. 156 B7 42 29N 89 2W
South Bend, Ind., U.S.A. 157 C10 41 41N 86 15W
South Bend, Wash., U.S.A. 160 D3 46 40N 123 48W
South Boston, U.S.A. 149 G6 36 42N 78 54W
South Branch, Canada 141 C8 47 55N 59 2W
South Brook, Canada 141 C8 49 26N 56 5W
South Brother I., India 95 J11 10 56N 92 37 E
South C. = Ka Lae, U.S.A. 145 E6 18 55N 155 41W
South Carolina □, U.S.A. 149 J5 34 0N 81 0W
South Charleston, U.S.A. 148 F5 38 22N 81 44W
South China Sea, Asia 80 D2 10 0N 113 0 E
South Comino Channel, Malta 38 F7 36 0N 14 20 E
South Congaree, U.S.A. 152 B8 33 53N 81 9W
South Cotabato □, Phil. 81 J5 6 0N 125 0 E
South Cumberland Is. △, Australia 126 J7 20 42 S 149 11 E
South Dakota □, U.S.A. 154 C5 44 15N 100 0W
South Daytona, U.S.A. 153 F8 29 10N 81 0W
South Deerfield, U.S.A. 151 D12 42 29N 72 37W
South Downs, U.K. 21 G7 50 52N 0 25W
South East B., Ascension I. 9 g 7 57 S 14 18W
South East C., Australia 127 G4 43 40 S 146 50 E
South East Forests △, Australia 129 D8 37 0 S 149 30 E
South-East Indian Rise, Ind. Oc. 7 B10 43 0 S 80 0 E
South East Is., Australia 125 F3 34 17 S 123 30 E
South Elgin, U.S.A. 157 C8 42 0N 88 18W
South Esk →, U.K. 22 E6 56 43N 2 31W
South Foreland, U.K. 21 F9 51 8N 1 24 E
South Fork American →, U.S.A. 160 G5 38 45N 121 5W
South Fork Edisto →, U.S.A. 152 B9 33 16N 80 54W
South Fork Feather →, U.S.A. 160 F5 39 17N 121 36W
South Fork Grand →, U.S.A. 154 C3 45 43N 102 17W
South Fork Licking →, U.S.A. 157 F12 38 40N 84 18W
South Fork Republican →, U.S.A. 154 E4 40 3N 101 31W
South Georgia, Antarctica 7 B1 54 30 S 37 0W
South Gloucestershire □, U.K. 21 F5 51 32N 2 28W
South Grand →, U.S.A. 156 F3 38 17N 93 25W
South Hadley, U.S.A. 151 D12 42 16N 72 35W
South Haven, U.S.A. 157 B10 42 24N 86 16W
South Henik L., Canada 143 A9 61 30N 97 20W
South Honshu Ridge, Pac. Oc. 134 E6 23 0N 143 0 E
South Horr, Kenya 118 B4 2 12N 36 56 E
South I., India 95 J1 10 3N 72 17 E
South I., Kenya 118 B4 2 35N 36 35 E
South I., N.Z. 131 E5 44 0 S 170 0 E
South Indian Lake, Canada 143 B9 56 47N 98 56W
South Invercargill, N.Z. 131 G3 46 26 S 168 23 E
South Island △, Kenya 118 B4 2 39N 36 35 E
South Kitui △, Kenya 118 C4 1 48 S 38 46 E
South Knife →, Canada 143 B10 58 55N 94 37W
South Koel →, India 93 H11 22 32N 85 14 E
South Korea ■, Asia 75 G15 36 0N 128 0 E
South Lake Tahoe, U.S.A. 160 G6 38 57N 119 59W
South Lanarkshire □, U.K. 22 F5 55 37N 3 53W
South Loup →, U.S.A. 154 E5 41 4N 98 39W
South Luangwa △, Zambia 119 E3 13 0 S 31 20 E
South Lyon, U.S.A. 157 B13 42 28N 83 39W
South Magnetic Pole, Antarctica 7 C9 64 8 S 138 8 E
South Miami, U.S.A. 153 K9 25 42N 80 18W
South Milwaukee, U.S.A. 157 B9 42 55N 87 52W
South Molton, U.K. 21 F4 51 1N 3 51W
South Monroe, U.S.A. 157 C13 41 54N 83 26W
South Moose L., Canada 143 C8 53 46N 100 8W
South Nahanni →, Canada 142 A4 61 3N 123 21W
South Nation →, Canada 151 A9 45 34N 75 6W
South Natuna Is. = Natuna Selatan, Kepulauan, Indonesia 85 B3 2 45N 109 0 E
South Negril Pt., Jamaica 164 a 18 16N 78 22W
South Newport, U.S.A. 152 D8 31 38N 81 24W
South Orkney Is., Antarctica 7 C18 63 0 S 45 0W
South Ossetia □, Georgia 61 J7 42 21N 44 2 E
South Pagai, I. = Pagai Selatan, Pulau, Indonesia 84 C2 3 0 S 100 15 E
South Paris, U.S.A. 151 B14 44 14N 70 31W
South Pekin, U.S.A. 156 D7 40 30N 89 39W
South Pittsburg, U.S.A. 149 H3 35 1N 85 42W
South Platte →, U.S.A. 154 E4 41 7N 100 42W
South Pole, Antarctica 7 E 90 0 S 0 0W
South Ponte Vedra Beach, U.S.A. 152 E8 30 3N 81 20W
South Porcupine, Canada 140 C3 48 30N 81 12W
South Portland, U.S.A. 149 D10 43 38N 70 15W
South Pt., Ascension I. 9 g 8 0 S 14 24W
South Pt., Barbados 165 g 13 2N 59 32W
South Pt., U.S.A. 150 B1 44 52N 83 19W
South River, Canada 140 C4 45 52N 79 23W
South River, U.S.A. 151 F10 40 27N 74 23W
South Ronaldsay, U.K. 22 C6 58 48N 2 58W
South Sandwich Is., Antarctica 7 B1 57 0 S 27 0W
South Sandwich Trench, Atl. Oc. 8 M9 56 0 S 24 0W
South Saskatchewan →, Canada 143 C7 53 15N 105 5W
South Seal →, Canada 143 B9 58 48N 98 8W
South Sentinel I., India 95 J11 10 59N 92 14 E
South Shetland Is., Antarctica 7 C18 62 0 S 59 0W
South Shields, U.K. 20 C6 55 0N 1 25W
South Sioux City, U.S.A. 154 D6 42 28N 96 24W
South Taranaki Bight, N.Z. 130 F3 39 40 S 174 5 E
South Thompson →, Canada 142 C4 50 40N 120 20W
South Twin I., Canada 140 B4 53 7N 79 52W
South Tyne →, U.K. 20 C5 54 59N 2 8W
South Ubian, Phil. 81 J3 5 11N 120 30 E
South Uist, U.K. 22 D1 57 20N 7 15W
South Valley, U.S.A. 159 J10 35 1N 106 41W
South Venice, U.S.A. 153 H7 27 3N 82 25W
South Wayne, U.S.A. 156 B7 42 34N 89 53W
South West Africa = Namibia ■, Africa 116 C2 22 0 S 18 9 E
South West B., Ascension I. 9 g 7 58 S 14 25W
South West B., Bahamas 9 b 25 0N 77 32W
South West C., Australia 127 G4 43 34 S 146 3 E
South West C., N.Z. 131 H2 47 17 S 167 28 E
South West Pt., Papua N. G. 132 B4 2 14 S 146 34 E
South West Pt., St. Helena 9 h 15 59 S 5 48W
South West Rocks, Australia 129 A10 30 52 S 153 3 E
South Whitley, U.S.A. 157 C11 41 5N 85 38W
South Williamsport, U.S.A. 150 E8 41 13N 77 0W
South Yarmouth, U.S.A. 148 E10 41 40N 70 10W
South Yemen = Yemen ■, Asia 98 D4 15 0N 44 0 E
South Yorkshire □, U.K. 20 D6 53 27N 1 36W
Southampton, Canada 140 D3 44 30N 81 25W
Southampton, U.K. 21 G6 50 54N 1 23W
Southampton, U.S.A. 151 F12 40 53N 72 23W
Southampton □, U.K. 21 G6 50 54N 1 23W
Southampton I., Canada 139 B11 64 30N 84 0W
Southaven, U.S.A. 155 H9 34 59N 90 2W
Southbank, Canada 142 C3 54 2N 125 46W
Southbridge, N.Z. 131 D7 43 48 S 172 16 E
Southbridge, U.S.A. 151 D12 42 5N 72 2W
Southeast C., U.S.A. 144 E5 62 56N 169 39W
Southeast Pacific Basin, Pac. Oc. 7 C15 16 30 S 92 0W
Southend, Canada 143 B8 56 19N 103 22W
Southend-on-Sea, U.K. 21 F8 51 32N 0 44 E
Southend-on-Sea □, U.K. 21 F8 51 32N 0 44 E
Southern = Janub △, Sudan 107 F2 6 50N 28 45 E
Southern = Yedebub Biheroch Bihereseboch na Hizboch □, Ethiopia 107 F4 12 0N 36 0 E
Southern = Yuzhnyy □, Russia 61 H5 44 0N 40 0 E
Southern □, Malawi 119 F4 15 0 S 35 0 E
Southern □, S. Leone 112 D2 8 0N 12 30W
Southern □, Zambia 119 F2 16 20 S 26 20 E
Southern Alps, N.Z. 131 D5 43 41 S 170 11 E
Southern Cross, Australia 125 F2 31 12 S 119 15 E
Southern Highlands □, Papua N. G. 132 D2 6 15 S 143 25 E
Southern Indian L., Canada 143 B9 57 10N 98 30W
Southern Lau Group, Fiji 133 B3 18 40 S 178 40W
Southern Leyte □, Phil. 81 F5 10 30N 125 10 E
Southern Mid-Atlantic Ridge, Atl. Oc. 8 J10 21 0 S 13 0W
Southern Ocean, Antarctica 7 C6 62 0 S 60 0 E
Southern Pines, U.S.A. 149 H6 35 11N 79 24W
Southern Rhodesia = Zimbabwe ■, Africa 119 F3 19 0 S 30 0 E
Southern Uplands, U.K. 22 F5 55 28N 3 52W
Southfield, U.S.A. 157 B13 42 29N 83 17W
Southington, U.S.A. 151 E12 41 36N 72 53W
Southland □, N.Z. 131 F3 45 30 S 168 0 E
Southold, U.S.A. 151 E12 41 4N 72 26W
Southport, Australia 127 D5 27 58 S 153 25 E
Southport, U.K. 20 D4 53 39N 3 0W
Southport, Fla., U.S.A. 152 E4 30 17N 85 38W
Southport, N.Y., U.S.A. 150 D8 42 3N 76 49W
Southwest △, Australia 127 G4 43 8 S 146 5 E

Southwest Indian Ridge, *Ind. Oc.* .... **121 H4** 30 0 S 59 0 E
Southwest Pacific Basin, *Pac. Oc.* .... **135 L13** 40 0 S 140 0W
Southwestern Pacific Basin, *Pac. Oc.* .... **7 A12** 42 0 S 170 0W
Southwold, *U.K.* ..... **21 E9** 52 20N 1 41 E
Southwood △, *Australia* **127 D5** 27 48 S 150 8 E
Soutpansberg, *S. Africa* **117 C4** 23 0 S 29 30 E
Souvigny, *France* ..... **27 F10** 46 33N 3 10 E
Sovata, *Romania* ..... **53 D10** 46 35N 25 3 E
Soverato, *Italy* .... **47 D9** 38 41N 16 33 E
Sovet, *Kyrgyzstan* .... **65 C5** 40 11N 71 20 E
Sovetsk, *Kaliningrad, Russia* .... **15 J19** 55 6N 21 50 E
Sovetsk, *Kirov, Russia* **60 B9** 57 38N 48 53 E
Sovetskaya Gavan = Vanino, *Russia* .... **67 E15** 48 50N 140 5 E
Sovetskoye = Zelenokumsk, *Russia* **61 H6** 44 24N 44 0 E
Sovicille, *Italy* .... **45 E8** 43 17N 11 13 E
Søvik, *Norway* .... **18 B3** 62 33N 6 17 E
Soweto, *S. Africa* ..... **117 D4** 26 14 S 27 54 E
Sōya-Kaikyō = La Perouse Str., *Asia* .. **70 B11** 45 40N 142 0 E
Sōya-Misaki, *Japan* ... **70 B10** 45 30N 141 55 E
Soyaux, *France* ...... **28 C4** 45 39N 0 12 E
Soyo, *Angola* .... **115 D2** 6 13 S 12 20 E
Sozh ➝, *Belarus* ..... **59 F6** 51 57N 30 48 E
Sozopol, *Bulgaria* .... **51 D11** 42 23N 27 42 E
Spa, *Belgium* .... **24 D5** 50 29N 5 53 E
Spaccaforno = Ispica, *Italy* .... **47 F7** 36 47N 14 55 E
Spain ■, *Europe* **13 H5** 39 0N 4 0W
Spalato = Split, *Croatia* **45 E13** 43 31N 16 26 E
Spalding, *Australia* ... **128 B3** 33 30 S 138 37 E
Spalding, *U.K.* **20 E7** 52 48N 0 9W
Spangler, *U.S.A.* **150 F6** 40 39N 78 48W
Spanish, *Canada* **140 C3** 46 12N 82 20W
Spanish Fork, *U.S.A.* . **158 F8** 40 7N 111 39W
Spanish Pt., *Bermuda* . **9 a** 32 18N 64 49W
Spanish Town, *Br. Virgin Is.* ...... **165 e** 17 43N 64 26W
Spanish Town, *Jamaica* **164 a** 18 0N 76 57W
Sparks, *Ga., U.S.A.* ... **152 D6** 31 11N 83 26W
Sparks, *Nev., U.S.A.* .. **160 F7** 39 32N 119 45W
Sparreholm, *Sweden* .. **16 E10** 59 4N 16 49 E
Sparta = Spárti, *Greece* **48 D4** 37 5N 22 25 E
Sparta, *Ga., U.S.A.* ... **152 B7** 33 17N 82 58W
Sparta, *Ill., U.S.A.* **156 F7** 38 8N 89 42W
Sparta, *Mich., U.S.A.* . **157 A11** 43 10N 85 42W
Sparta, *N.J., U.S.A.* ... **151 E10** 41 2N 74 38W
Sparta, *Wis., U.S.A.* .. **154 D9** 43 56N 90 49W
Spartanburg, *U.S.A.* .. **149 H5** 34 56N 81 57W
Spartansburg, *U.S.A.* . **150 E5** 41 49N 79 41W
Spartel, C., *Morocco* .. **110 A3** 35 47N 5 56W
Spárti, *Greece* .... **48 D4** 37 5N 22 25 E
Spartivento, C., *Calabria, Italy* ..... **47 E9** 37 55N 16 4 E
Spartivento, C., *Sard., Italy* .... **46 D1** 38 53N 8 50 E
Spartokhóri, *Greece* .. **39 B2** 38 40N 20 46 E
Sparwood, *Canada* ... **142 D6** 49 44N 114 53W
Spas-Demensk, *Russia* **58 E7** 54 20N 34 0 E
Spas-Klepiki, *Russia* .. **58 E11** 55 10N 40 10 E
Spassk = Bednodemyanovsk, *Russia* .... **60 D6** 53 55N 43 15 E
Spassk Dalniy, *Russia* . **67 E14** 44 40N 132 48 E
Spassk-Ryazanskiy, *Russia* .... **58 E11** 54 24N 40 25 E
Spátha, Ákra, *Greece* . **39 E4** 35 42N 23 43 E
Spatsizi ➝, *Canada* .. **142 B3** 57 42N 128 7W
Spatsizi Plateau Wilderness △, *Canada* **142 B3** 57 40N 128 0W
Spean ➝, *U.K.* **22 E4** 56 55N 4 59W
Spearfish, *U.S.A.* **154 C3** 44 30N 103 52W
Spearman, *U.S.A.* **155 G4** 36 12N 101 12W
Speculator, *U.S.A.* ... **151 C10** 43 30N 74 25W
Speed, *Australia* ..... **128 C5** 35 21 S 142 27 E
Speedway, *U.S.A.* **157 E10** 39 47N 86 15W
Speer, *Switz.* .... **33 B8** 47 12N 9 8 E
Speery I., *St. Helena* .. **9 h** 16 1 S 5 46W
Speia, *Moldova* ...... **53 D14** 46 59N 29 19 E
Speightstown, *Barbados* **165 g** 13 15N 59 39W
Speke Gulf, *Tanzania* . **118 C3** 2 20 S 32 50 E
Spello, *Italy* .... **45 F9** 42 59N 12 40 E
Spenard, *U.S.A.* **144 F10** 61 11N 149 55W
Spence Bay = Taloyoak, *Canada* .. **138 B10** 69 32N 93 32W
Spencer, *Idaho, U.S.A.* **158 D7** 44 22N 112 11W
Spencer, *Ind., U.S.A.* . **157 E10** 39 17N 86 46W
Spencer, *Iowa, U.S.A.* **154 D7** 43 9N 95 9W
Spencer, *N.Y., U.S.A.* . **151 D8** 42 13N 76 30W
Spencer, *Nebr., U.S.A.* **154 D5** 42 53N 98 42W
Spencer, C., *Australia* . **128 C2** 35 20 S 136 53 E
Spencer B., *Namibia* .. **116 D1** 25 30 S 14 47 E
Spencer G., *Australia* . **128 C2** 34 0 S 137 20 E
Spencerville, *Canada* . **151 B9** 44 51N 75 33W
Spencerville, *U.S.A.* .. **157 D12** 40 43N 84 21W
Spences Bridge, *Canada* **142 C4** 50 25N 121 20W
Spennymoor, *U.K.* **20 C6** 54 42N 1 36W
Spenser Mts., *N.Z.* ... **131 C7** 42 15 S 172 45 E
Spentrup, *Denmark* .. **17 H4** 56 33N 10 2 E
Sperillen, *Norway* .... **18 D7** 60 28N 10 3 E
Sperkhiós ➝, *Greece* . **48 C4** 38 57N 22 3 E
Sperrin Mts., *U.K.* **23 B5** 54 50N 7 0W
Spessart, *Germany* .... **31 F5** 49 56N 9 18 E
Spetalen, *Norway* .... **18 E7** 59 18N 10 45 E
Spétsai, *Greece* ...... **48 D5** 37 15N 23 10 E
Spey ➝, *U.K.* **22 D5** 57 40N 3 6W
Speyer, *Germany* .... **31 F4** 49 29N 8 25 E
Spezand, *Pakistan* .... **92 E2** 29 59N 67 0 E
Spezzano Albanese, *Italy* .... **47 C9** 39 40N 16 19 E
Spickard, *U.S.A.* **156 D3** 40 14N 93 36W
Spiekeroog, *Germany* . **30 B3** 53 46N 7 42 E
Spiez, *Switz.* .... **32 C5** 46 40N 7 40 E
Spíli, *Greece* .... **39 E5** 35 13N 24 31 E
Spilimbergo, *Italy* .... **45 B9** 46 7N 12 54 E
Spīn Būldak, *Afghan.* . **91 C2** 31 1N 66 25 E
Spinalónga, *Greece* ... **39 E6** 35 18N 25 44 E
Spinazzola, *Italy* ..... **47 B9** 40 58N 16 5 E
Spineni, *Romania* .... **53 F9** 44 43N 24 37 E
Spirding = Sniardwy, Jezioro, *Poland* .... **54 E8** 53 48N 21 50 E
Spirit Lake, *U.S.A.* ... **160 D4** 46 15N 122 9W
Spirit River, *Canada* .. **142 B5** 55 45N 118 50W
Spiritwood, *Canada* .. **143 C7** 53 24N 107 33W
Spišská Nová Ves, *Slovak Rep.* .... **35 C13** 48 58N 20 34 E
Spišské Podhradie, *Slovak Rep.* .... **35 B13** 49 0N 20 48 E
Spital, *Austria* .... **34 D7** 47 42N 14 18 E
Spithead, *U.K.* **21 G6** 50 45N 1 10W
Spittal an der Drau, *Austria* .... **34 E6** 46 48N 13 31 E
Spitzbergen = Svalbard, *Arctic* .... **6 B8** 78 0N 17 0 E
Spjelkavik, *Norway* ... **18 B3** 62 28N 6 22 E
Split, *Croatia* .... **45 E13** 43 31N 16 26 E
Split ✈ (SPU), *Croatia* **45 E13** 43 33N 16 15 E
Split L., *Canada* **143 B9** 56 8N 96 15W
Split Lake, *Canada* ... **143 B9** 56 8N 96 15W
Splitski Kanal, *Croatia* **45 E13** 43 31N 16 20 E
Splügen, *Switz.* ...... **33 C8** 46 34N 9 21 E
Splügenpass, *Switz.* ... **33 D8** 46 30N 9 20 E
Spofford, *U.S.A.* **155 L4** 29 10N 100 25W
Spokane, *U.S.A.* **158 C5** 47 40N 117 24W
Spoleto, *Italy* .... **45 F9** 42 44N 12 44 E
Sponvika, *Norway* .... **18 E8** 59 7N 11 15 E
Spoon ➝, *U.S.A.* **156 D6** 40 19N 90 4W
Spooner, *U.S.A.* **154 C9** 45 50N 91 53W
Sporyy Navolok, Mys, *Russia* .... **66 B7** 75 50N 68 40 E
Sprague, *U.S.A.* **158 C5** 47 18N 117 59W
Spratly I., *S. China Sea* **78 C4** 8 38N 111 55 E
Spratly Is., *S. China Sea* **78 C4** 8 20N 112 0 E
Spray, *U.S.A.* **158 D4** 44 50N 119 48W
Spreča ➝, *Bos.-H.* .... **52 F3** 44 44N 18 6 E
Spree ➝, *Germany* ... **30 C9** 52 32N 13 13 E
Spreewald, *Germany* . **30 D9** 51 58N 13 51 E
Spremberg, *Germany* . **30 D10** 51 34N 14 22 E
Sprengisandur, *Iceland* **11 C8** 64 52N 18 7W
Spring City, *U.S.A.* ... **151 F9** 40 11N 75 33W
Spring Cr. ➝, *U.S.A.* . **152 E5** 30 54N 84 45W
Spring Creek, *U.S.A.* . **158 F6** 40 45N 115 38W
Spring Garden, *Guyana* **169 B6** 6 59N 58 31W
Spring Garden, *U.S.A.* **160 F6** 39 52N 120 47W
Spring Green, *U.S.A.* . **156 A6** 43 11N 90 4W
Spring Hall, *Barbados* **165 g** 13 18N 59 36W
Spring Hill, *Ala., U.S.A.* **152 D4** 31 42N 85 58W
Spring Hill, *Fla., U.S.A.* **153 G7** 28 27N 82 41W
Spring Mts., *U.S.A.* ... **159 H6** 36 0N 115 45W
Spring Valley, *Calif., U.S.A.* **161 N10** 32 45N 117 5W
Spring Valley, *Ill., U.S.A.* **156 C7** 41 20N 89 12W
Springbok, *S. Africa* .. **116 D2** 29 42 S 17 54 E
Springboro, *U.S.A.* ... **150 E4** 41 48N 80 22W
Springdale, *Canada* ... **141 C8** 49 30N 56 6W
Springdale, *Ark., U.S.A.* **155 G7** 36 11N 94 8W
Springdale, *Ohio, U.S.A.* **157 E12** 39 17N 84 29W
Springe, *Germany* .... **30 C5** 52 13N 9 33 E
Springer, *U.S.A.* **155 G2** 36 22N 104 36W
Springerville, *U.S.A.* .. **159 J9** 34 8N 109 17W
Springfield, *Canada* .. **150 D4** 42 50N 80 56W
Springfield, *N.Z.* ..... **131 D6** 43 19 S 171 56 E
Springfield, *Colo., U.S.A.* **155 G3** 37 24N 102 37W
Springfield, *Fla., U.S.A.* **152 E4** 30 10N 85 37W
Springfield, *Ga., U.S.A.* **152 C8** 32 22N 81 18W
Springfield, *Ill., U.S.A.* **156 E7** 39 48N 89 39W
Springfield, *Ky., U.S.A.* **157 G11** 37 41N 85 13W
Springfield, *Mass., U.S.A.* **151 D12** 42 6N 72 35W
Springfield, *Mo., U.S.A.* **155 G8** 37 13N 93 17W
Springfield, *Ohio, U.S.A.* **157 E13** 39 55N 83 49W
Springfield, *Oreg., U.S.A.* **158 D2** 44 3N 123 1W
Springfield, *S.C., U.S.A.* **152 B8** 33 30N 81 17W
Springfield, *Tenn., U.S.A.* **149 G2** 36 31N 86 53W
Springfield, *Vt., U.S.A.* **151 C12** 43 18N 72 29W
Springfield, L., *U.S.A.* **156 E7** 39 46N 89 36W
Springfontein, *S. Africa* **116 E4** 30 15 S 25 40 E
Springhill, *Canada* **141 C7** 45 40N 64 4W
Springhill, *U.S.A.* **155 J8** 33 0N 93 28W
Springhouse, *Canada* . **142 C4** 51 56N 122 7W
Springs, *S. Africa* .... **117 D4** 26 13 S 28 25 E
Springsure, *Australia* . **126 C4** 24 8 S 148 6 E
Springvale, *Ga., U.S.A.* **152 D5** 31 50N 84 53W
Springvale, *Maine, U.S.A.* **151 C14** 43 28N 70 48W
Springville, *Calif., U.S.A.* **160 J8** 36 8N 118 49W
Springville, *Iowa, U.S.A.* **156 B5** 42 3N 91 27W
Springville, *N.Y., U.S.A.* **150 D6** 42 31N 78 40W
Springville, *Utah, U.S.A.* **158 F8** 40 10N 111 37W
Springwater, *U.S.A.* .. **150 D7** 42 38N 77 35W
Sprottau = Szprotawa, *Poland* .... **55 G2** 51 33N 15 35 E
Spruce-Creek, *U.S.A.* . **150 F6** 40 36N 78 9W
Spruce Knob-Seneca Rocks △, *U.S.A.* **148 F6** 38 50N 79 30W
Spruce Mt., *U.S.A.* ... **151 B12** 44 12N 72 19W
Spur, *U.S.A.* **155 J4** 33 28N 100 52W
Spurn Hd., *U.K.* ..... **20 D8** 53 35N 0 8 E
Spuž, *Serbia & M.* .... **50 D3** 42 32N 19 10 E
Spuzzum, *Canada* **142 D4** 49 37N 121 23W
Spydeberg, *Norway* .. **18 E8** 59 36N 11 5 E
Squam L., *U.S.A.* **151 C13** 43 45N 71 32W
Squamish, *Canada* ... **142 D4** 49 45N 123 10W
Square Islands, *Canada* **141 B8** 52 47N 55 47W
Squillace, G. di, *Italy* . **47 D9** 38 45N 16 50 E
Squinzano, *Italy* ..... **47 B11** 40 26N 18 2 E
Squires, Mt., *Australia* **125 E4** 26 14 S 127 28 E
Sragen, *Indonesia* .... **85 D4** 7 26 S 111 2 E
Srbac, *Bos.-H.* .... **52 E2** 45 7N 17 30 E
Srbica, *Serbia & M.* ... **50 D4** 42 45N 20 47 E
Srbija = Serbia □, *Serbia & M.* .... **50 C5** 43 30N 21 0 E
Srbobran, *Serbia & M.* **52 E4** 45 32N 19 48 E
Sre Ambel, *Cambodia* **87 G4** 11 8N 103 46 E
Sre Khtum, *Cambodia* **87 F6** 12 10N 106 52 E
Sre Umbell = Sre Ambel, *Cambodia* ... **87 G4** 11 8N 103 46 E
Srebrenica, *Bos.-H.* ... **52 F4** 44 6N 19 18 E
Sredinny Ra. = Sredinnyy Khrebet, *Russia* .... **67 D16** 57 0N 160 0 E
Sredinnyy Khrebet, *Russia* .... **67 D16** 57 0N 160 0 E
Središče, *Slovenia* .... **45 B13** 46 24N 16 17 E
Sredna Gora, *Bulgaria* **51 D8** 42 40N 24 20 E
Srednekolymsk, *Russia* **67 C16** 67 27N 153 40 E
Sredni Rodopi, *Bulgaria* .... **51 E8** 41 40N 24 45 E
Srednogorie, *Bulgaria* **51 D8** 42 43N 24 10 E
Śrem, *Poland* .... **55 F4** 52 6N 17 2 E
Sremska Mitrovica, *Serbia & M.* .... **52 F4** 44 59N 19 38 E
Sremski Karlovci, *Serbia & M.* .... **52 E4** 45 12N 19 56 E
Srepok ➝, *Cambodia* **86 F6** 13 33N 106 16 E
Sretensk, *Russia* ..... **67 D12** 52 10N 117 40 E
Sri Aman, *Malaysia* .. **85 B4** 1 15N 111 32 E
Sri Kalahasti, *India* ... **95 H4** 13 45N 79 44 E
Sri Lanka ■, *Asia* .... **95 L5** 7 30N 80 50 E
Sriharikota I., *India* .. **95 H5** 13 40N 80 20 E
Srikakulam, *India* .... **94 E6** 18 14N 83 58 E
Srinagar, *India* ...... **93 B6** 34 5N 74 50 E
Srinagarind Res., *Thailand* .... **86 E2** 14 35N 99 0 E
Sripur, *Bangla.* ...... **90 C3** 24 14N 90 30 E
Srivardhan, *India* .... **94 E1** 18 4N 73 3 E
Srivilliputtur, *India* .. **95 K3** 9 31N 77 40 E
Środa Śląska, *Poland* . **55 G3** 51 10N 16 36 E
Środa Wielkopolski, *Poland* .... **55 F4** 52 15N 17 19 E
Srono, *Indonesia* .... **79 J17** 8 24 S 114 16 E
Srpska Crnja, *Serbia & M.* .... **52 E5** 45 38N 20 44 E
Srpski Itebej, *Serbia & M.* .... **52 E5** 45 35N 20 44 E
Srungavarapukota, *India* .... **94 E6** 18 7N 83 10 E
Staaten ➝, *Australia* . **126 B3** 16 24 S 141 17 E
Staaten River △, *Australia* .... **126 B3** 16 15 S 142 40 E
Staberhuk, *Germany* . **30 A7** 54 23N 11 18 E
Stade, *Germany* ...... **30 B5** 53 35N 9 29 E
Staðarfell, *Iceland* **11 B4** 65 7N 22 12W
Staðarhólskirkja, *Iceland* **11 B5** 65 23N 21 58W
Staðastaður, *Iceland* .. **11 C3** 64 49N 23 1W
Stadhavet, *Norway* ... **18 B2** 62 13N 5 0 E
Staður, *Húnavatnssýsla, Iceland* **11 B5** 65 9N 21 3W
Staður, *Ísafjarðarsýsla, Iceland* **11 A4** 66 15N 22 50W
Stadlandet, *Norway* .. **18 B2** 62 10N 5 10 E
Stadskanaal, *Neths.* ... **24 A6** 53 4N 6 55 E
Stadtallendorf, *Germany* .... **30 E5** 50 48N 9 1 E
Stadthagen, *Germany* . **30 C5** 52 19N 9 13 E
Stadtlohn, *Germany* .. **30 D2** 51 59N 6 55 E
Stadtroda, *Germany* .. **30 E7** 50 52N 11 44 E
Stäfa, *Switz.* .... **33 B7** 47 14N 8 45 E
Stafafell, *Iceland* **11 C12** 64 25N 14 52W
Staffa, *U.K.* **22 E2** 56 27N 6 21W
Staffanstorp, *Sweden* . **17 J7** 55 39N 13 13 E
Stafford, *U.K.* **20 E5** 52 49N 2 7W
Stafford, *U.S.A.* **155 G5** 37 58N 98 36W
Stafford, L., *U.S.A.* ... **153 F7** 29 20N 82 29W
Stafford Springs, *U.S.A.* **151 E12** 41 57N 72 18W
Staffordshire □, *U.K.* . **20 E5** 52 53N 2 10W
Stagnone, *Italy* ...... **46 E5** 37 53N 12 26 E
Stagnone di Marsala △, *Italy* .... **46 E5** 37 52N 12 26 E
Staines, *U.K.* **21 F7** 51 26N 0 29W
Stainz, *Austria* ...... **34 E8** 46 53N 15 17 E
Stakhanov, *Ukraine* .. **59 H10** 48 35N 38 40 E
Stalać, *Serbia & M.* ... **50 C5** 43 43N 21 28 E
Stalden, *Switz.* ...... **32 D5** 46 14N 7 52 E
Stalin = Kuçovë, *Albania* .... **50 F3** 40 47N 19 57 E
Stalin = Varna, *Bulgaria* .... **51 C11** 43 13N 27 56 E
Stalin, Pk. = Musala, *Bulgaria* .... **50 D7** 42 13N 23 37 E
Stalin Pk. = Gerlachovský štit, *Slovak Rep.* .... **35 B13** 49 11N 20 7 E
Stalin Pk. = Kommunizma, Pik, *Tajikistan* .... **65 D6** 39 0N 72 2 E
Stalinabad = Dushanbe, *Tajikistan* .... **65 D4** 38 33N 68 48 E
Stalingrad = Volgograd, *Russia* .... **61 F7** 48 40N 44 25 E
Staliniri = Tskhinvali, *Georgia* .... **61 J7** 42 14N 44 1 E
Stalino = Shakhrikhan, *Uzbekistan* .... **65 C6** 40 42N 72 3 E
Stalinogorsk = Novomoskovsk, *Russia* .... **58 E10** 54 5N 38 15 E
Stalinogrod = Katowice, *Poland* .... **55 H6** 50 17N 19 5 E
Stalinsk = Novokuznetsk, *Russia* .... **66 D9** 53 45N 87 10 E
Stalinstadt = Eisenhüttenstadt, *Germany* .... **30 C10** 52 9N 14 38 E
Stallarholmen, *Sweden* **16 E11** 59 22N 17 12 E
Ställdalen, *Sweden* ... **16 E8** 59 56N 14 56 E
Stalowa Wola, *Poland* **55 H9** 50 34N 22 3 E
Stalybridge, *U.K.* **20 D5** 53 28N 2 3W
Stamford, *Australia* ... **126 C3** 21 15 S 143 46 E
Stamford, *U.K.* **21 E7** 52 39N 0 29W
Stamford, *Conn., U.S.A.* **151 E11** 41 3N 73 32W
Stamford, *N.Y., U.S.A.* **151 D10** 42 25N 74 38W
Stamford, *Tex., U.S.A.* **155 J5** 32 57N 99 48W
Stamnes, *Norway* .... **18 D2** 60 40N 5 45 E
Stamping Ground, *U.S.A.* **157 F12** 38 16N 84 41W
Stampriet, *Namibia* ... **116 C2** 24 20 S 18 28 E
Stamps, *U.S.A.* **155 J8** 33 22N 93 30W
Stanberry, *U.S.A.* **156 D2** 40 13N 94 35W
Stančevo = Kalipetrovo, *Bulgaria* .... **51 B11** 44 5N 27 14 E
Standerton, *S. Africa* . **117 D4** 26 55 S 29 7 E
Standish, *U.S.A.* **148 D4** 43 59N 83 57W
Stanford, *S. Africa* ... **116 E2** 34 26 S 19 29 E
Stanford, *U.S.A.* **158 C8** 47 9N 110 13W
Stånga, *Sweden* ..... **17 G12** 57 17N 18 29 E
Stange, *Norway* ..... **18 D8** 60 43N 11 5 E
Stanger, *S. Africa* .... **117 D5** 29 27 S 31 14 E
Stängselåser = Salpausselkä, *Finland* **15 F22** 61 3N 26 15 E
Stangvik, *Norway* .... **18 B5** 62 55N 8 28 E
Stanhope, *Australia* .. **129 D6** 36 27 S 144 59 E
Stanhope, *U.S.A.* **156 B3** 42 17N 93 48W
Stanimaka = Asenovgrad, *Bulgaria* **51 D8** 42 1N 24 51 E
Stanišić, *Serbia & M.* . **52 E4** 45 56N 19 10 E
Stanislaus ➝, *U.S.A.* . **160 H5** 37 40N 121 14W
Stanislav = Ivano-Frankivsk, *Ukraine* . **53 B9** 48 40N 24 40 E
Stanislavov = Ivano-Frankivsk, *Ukraine* . **53 B9** 48 40N 24 40 E
Stanisławów, *Poland* .. **55 F8** 52 18N 21 33 E
Stanley, *Australia* ... **127 G4** 40 46 S 145 19 E
Stanley, *China* ...... **69 G11** 22 13N 114 12 E
Stanley, *Falk Is.* ...... **9 f** 51 40 S 59 51W
Stanley, *U.K.* **20 C6** 54 53N 1 41W
Stanley, *Idaho, U.S.A.* **158 D6** 44 13N 114 56W
Stanley, *N. Dak., U.S.A.* **154 A3** 48 19N 102 23W
Stanley, *N.Y. U.S.A.* . **150 D7** 42 48N 77 6W
Stanley Falls = Boyoma, Chutes, *Dem. Rep. of the Congo* .... **118 B2** 0 35N 25 23 E
Stanley Mission, *Canada* **143 B8** 55 25N 104 33W
Stanley Pool = Malebo, Pool, *Africa* .... **115 C3** 4 17 S 15 20 E
Stanley Res., *India* ... **95 J3** 11 50N 77 40 E
Stanleyville = Kisangani, *Dem. Rep. of the Congo* ...... **118 B2** 0 35N 25 15 E
Stanovoy Khrebet, *Russia* .... **67 D13** 55 0N 130 0 E
Stanovoy Ra. = Stanovoy Khrebet, *Russia* .... **67 D13** 55 0N 130 0 E
Stans, *Switz.* .... **33 C6** 46 58N 8 21 E
Stansmore Ra., *Australia* .... **124 D4** 21 23 S 128 33 E
Stansted, London ✈ (STN), *U.K* .... **21 F8** 51 54N 0 14 E
Stanthorpe, *Australia* . **127 D5** 28 36 S 151 59 E
Stanton, *Ky., U.S.A.* .. **157 G13** 37 54N 83 52W
Stanton, *Tex., U.S.A.* . **155 J4** 32 8N 101 48W
Stantsiya Regar = Tursunzade, *Tajikistan* .... **65 D4** 38 30N 68 14 E
Stanwood, *U.S.A.* **160 B4** 48 15N 122 23W
Staples, *U.S.A.* **154 B7** 46 21N 94 48W
Stapleton, *U.S.A.* **154 E4** 41 29N 100 31W
Stąporków, *Poland* ... **55 G7** 51 9N 20 31 E
Star City, *Canada* **143 C8** 52 50N 104 20W
Star Harbour, *Solomon Is.* .... **133 N12** 10 47 S 162 19 E
Star Lake, *U.S.A.* **151 B9** 44 10N 75 2W
Stará Ďala = Hurbanovo, *Slovak Rep.* .... **35 D11** 47 51N 18 11 E
Stará L'ubovňa, *Slovak Rep.* .... **35 B13** 49 18N 20 42 E
Stara Moravica, *Serbia & M.* .... **52 E4** 45 50N 19 30 E
Stara Pazova, *Serbia & M.* .... **52 F5** 44 58N 20 10 E
Stara Planina, *Bulgaria* **50 C7** 43 15N 23 0 E
Stara Sil, *Ukraine* .... **55 J9** 49 29N 22 58 E
Stará Turá, *Slovak Rep.* **35 C10** 48 47N 17 42 E
Stara Ushytsya, *Ukraine* .... **53 B12** 48 35N 27 8 E
Stara Zagora, *Bulgaria* **51 D9** 42 26N 25 39 E
Starachowice, *Poland* . **55 G8** 51 3N 21 2 E
Staraya Russa, *Russia* . **58 D6** 57 58N 31 23 E
Starbuck I., *Kiribati* .. **135 H12** 5 37 S 155 55W
Starchiojd, *Romania* .. **53 E11** 45 19N 26 11 E
Starcke △, *Australia* .. **126 A4** 14 56 S 145 2 E
Stargard in Pommern = Stargard Szczeciński, *Poland* .... **54 E2** 53 20N 15 0 E
Stargard Szczeciński, *Poland* .... **54 E2** 53 20N 15 0 E
Ståheim, *Norway* .... **18 C2** 61 56N 5 40 E
Stari Bar, *Serbia & M.* **50 D3** 42 7N 19 10 E
Stari Bečej = Bečej, *Serbia & M.* .... **52 E5** 45 36N 20 3 E
Stari Trg, *Slovenia* ... **45 C12** 45 29N 15 7 E
Staritsa, *Russia* ...... **58 D8** 56 33N 34 55 E
Starke, *U.S.A.* **152 F7** 29 57N 82 7W
Starkville, *U.S.A.* **155 J10** 33 28N 88 49W
Starnberg, *Germany* .. **31 H7** 48 0N 11 21 E
Starnberger See, *Germany* .... **31 H7** 47 54N 11 19 E
Starobilsk, *Ukraine* ... **59 H10** 49 16N 39 0 E
Starodub, *Russia* ..... **59 F7** 52 30N 32 50 E
Starogard Gdański, *Poland* .... **54 E5** 53 59N 18 30 E
Starokonstantinov = Starokonstyantyniv, *Ukraine* .... **59 H4** 49 48N 27 10 E
Starokonstyantyniv, *Ukraine* .... **59 H4** 49 48N 27 10 E
Starokozache, *Ukraine* **53 D14** 46 20N 29 59 E
Starominskaya, *Russia* **59 J10** 46 33N 39 0 E
Staroshcherbinovskaya, *Russia* .... **59 J10** 46 40N 38 53 E
Starrs Mill, *U.S.A.* ... **152 B5** 33 19N 84 31W
Start Pt., *U.K.* **21 G4** 50 13N 3 39W
Stary Chardzhuy = Komsomolsk, *Turkmenistan* ...... **65 D1** 39 2N 63 36 E
Stary Sącz, *Poland* .... **55 J7** 49 33N 20 35 E
Staryy Biryuzyak, *Russia* .... **61 H8** 44 46N 46 50 E
Staryy Chartoriysk, *Ukraine* .... **59 G3** 51 15N 25 54 E
Staryy Krym, *Ukraine* **59 K8** 45 3N 35 8 E
Staryy Margilan = Margilan, *Uzbekistan* **65 C5** 40 27N 71 42 E
Staryy Oskol, *Russia* .. **59 G9** 51 19N 37 55 E
Staryy Sambir, *Ukraine* **55 J9** 49 27N 22 59 E
Stassfurt, *Germany* ... **30 D7** 51 51N 11 35 E
Staszów, *Poland* ..... **55 H8** 50 33N 21 10 E
State Center, *U.S.A.* .. **156 B3** 42 1N 93 10W
State College, *U.S.A.* . **150 F7** 40 48N 77 52W
Stateline, *U.S.A.* **160 G7** 38 57N 119 56W
Staten, I. = Estados, I. de Los, *Argentina* .. **176 D4** 54 40 S 64 30W
Staten I., *U.S.A.* **151 F10** 40 35N 74 9W
Statenville, *U.S.A.* ... **152 E6** 30 42N 83 2W
Statesboro, *U.S.A.* ... **152 C8** 32 27N 81 47W
Statesville, *U.S.A.* ... **149 H5** 35 47N 80 53W
Statham, *U.S.A.* **152 B6** 33 58N 83 35W
Stathelle, *Norway* .... **18 E6** 59 3N 9 41 E
Statia = St. Eustatius, *W. Indies* **165 C7** 17 20N 63 0W
Stauffer, *U.S.A.* **161 L7** 34 45N 119 3W
Staunton, *Ill., U.S.A.* . **156 F7** 39 1N 89 47W
Staunton, *Va., U.S.A.* . **148 F6** 38 9N 79 4W
Stavanger = Rogaland □, *Norway* **18 E3** 59 12N 6 20 E
Stavanger, *Norway* ... **18 F2** 58 57N 5 40 E
Stavelot, *Belgium* .... **24 D5** 50 23N 5 55 E
Stavern, *Norway* ..... **18 F7** 59 0N 10 1 E
Stavoren, *Neths.* ..... **24 B5** 52 53N 5 22 E
Stavropol, *Russia* .... **61 H6** 45 5N 42 0 E
Stavros, *Cyprus* ...... **39 E8** 35 1N 32 38 E
Stavrós, *Ithákí, Greece* **39 C2** 38 27N 20 39 E
Stavrós, *Kríti, Greece* . **39 E5** 35 12N 24 45 E
Stavrós, Ákra, *Greece* . **39 E5** 35 26N 24 58 E
Stavroúpolis, *Greece* .. **51 E8** 41 12N 24 45 E
Stawell, *Australia* .... **128 D5** 37 5 S 142 47 E
Stawell ➝, *Australia* . **126 C3** 20 20 S 142 55 E
Stawiski, *Poland* ..... **54 E9** 53 22N 22 9 E
Stawiszyn, *Poland* .... **55 G5** 51 56N 18 4 E
Stayner, *Canada* **150 B4** 44 25N 80 5W
Stayton, *U.S.A.* **158 D2** 44 48N 122 48W
Steamboat Springs, *U.S.A.* **158 F10** 40 29N 106 50W
Steane, *Norway* ..... **18 E5** 59 16N 8 33 E
Stebbins, *U.S.A.* **144 E7** 63 31N 162 17W
Steblevë, *Albania* .... **50 E4** 41 23N 20 33 E
Steckborn, *Switz.* .... **33 A7** 47 44N 8 59 E
Steele, *Ala., U.S.A.* ... **152 B3** 33 56N 86 12W
Steele, *N. Dak., U.S.A.* **154 B5** 46 51N 99 55W
Steelton, *U.S.A.* **150 F8** 40 14N 76 50W
Steelville, *U.S.A.* **156 G5** 37 58N 91 22W
Steen River, *Canada* .. **142 B5** 59 40N 117 12W
Steenkool = Bintuni, *Indonesia* .... **83 B4** 2 7 S 133 32 E
Steens Mt., *U.S.A.* ... **158 E4** 42 35N 118 40W
Steenstrup Gletscher, *Greenland* **10 B5** 75 15N 57 0W
Steenwijk, *Neths.* .... **24 B6** 52 47N 6 7 E
Steep Pt., *Australia* ... **125 E1** 26 8 S 113 8 E
Steep Rock, *Canada* ... **143 C9** 51 30N 98 48W
Ştefan Vodă, *Moldova* **53 D14** 46 27N 29 42 E
Ştefăneşti, *Romania* .. **53 C12** 47 44N 27 15 E
Stefanie △, *Ethiopia* .. **107 G4** 4 55N 36 55 E
Stefanie L. = Chew Bahir, *Ethiopia* ..... **107 G4** 4 40N 36 50 E
Stefansson Bay, *Antarctica* .... **7 C5** 67 20 S 59 8 E
Steffisburg, *Switz.* .... **32 C5** 46 47N 7 38 E
Stege, *Denmark* ..... **17 K6** 54 59N 12 18 E
Stegi = Siteki, *Swaziland* .... **117 D5** 26 32 S 31 58 E
Stegman = Artesia, *U.S.A.* **155 J2** 32 51N 104 24W
Ştei, *Romania* .... **52 D7** 46 32N 22 27 E
Steiermark □, *Austria* **34 D8** 47 26N 15 0 E
Steigerwald, *Germany* **31 F6** 49 44N 10 26 E
Steigerwald △, *Germany* .... **31 F6** 49 50N 10 30 E
Steilacoom, *U.S.A.* ... **160 C4** 47 10N 122 36W
Steilrandberge, *Namibia* .... **116 B1** 17 45 S 13 20 E
Stein = Kamnik, *Slovenia* .... **45 B11** 46 14N 14 37 E
Stein am Rhein, *Switz.* **33 A7** 47 39N 8 51 E
Steinbach, *Canada* ... **143 D9** 49 32N 96 40W
Steinfurt, *Germany* ... **30 C3** 52 9N 7 20 E
Steinhatchee, *U.S.A.* .. **152 F6** 29 40N 83 23W
Steinhausen, *Namibia* . **116 C2** 21 49 S 18 20 E
Steinheim, *Germany* .. **30 D5** 51 51N 9 5 E
Steinhuder Meer, *Germany* .... **30 C5** 52 29N 9 21 E
Steinhuder Meer △, *Germany* .... **30 C5** 52 30N 9 16 E
Steinkjer, *Norway* .... **14 D14** 64 1N 11 31 E
Steinkopf, *S. Africa* ... **116 D2** 29 18 S 17 43 E
Steinshamn, *Norway* .. **18 B3** 62 47N 6 28 E
Steinwald △, *Germany* **31 F8** 49 55N 12 8 E
Stellarton, *Canada* ... **141 C7** 45 32N 62 30W
Stellenbosch, *S. Africa* **116 E2** 33 58 S 18 50 E
Stelvio, Paso dello, *Italy* **33 C10** 46 32N 10 27 E
Stenay, *France* ...... **27 C12** 49 29N 5 12 E
Stendal, *Germany* .... **30 C7** 52 36N 11 53 E
Stende, *Latvia* ...... **54 A9** 57 11N 22 33 E
Stenhamra, *Sweden* ... **16 E11** 59 20N 17 41 E
Stenón Ithákis, *Greece* **39 C2** 38 22N 20 39 E
Stenón Kerkiras, *Greece* .... **38 B10** 39 36N 20 5 E
Stenshuvud △, *Sweden* **17 J8** 55 39N 14 15 E
Stenstorp, *Sweden* ... **17 F7** 58 17N 13 45 E
Stenungsund, *Sweden* . **17 F5** 58 6N 11 50 E
Steornabhaigh = Stornoway, *U.K.* **22 C2** 58 13N 6 23W
Stepanakert = Xankändi, *Azerbaijan* .... **101 C12** 39 52N 46 49 E
Stepanavan, *Armenia* . **61 K7** 41 1N 44 23 E
Stephens, C., *N.Z.* .... **131 A8** 40 42 S 173 58 E
Stephens Creek, *Australia* .... **128 A4** 31 50 S 141 30 E
Stephens I., *Canada* .. **142 C2** 54 10N 130 45W
Stephens I., *N.Z.* ..... **131 A9** 40 40 S 174 1 E
Stephens L., *Canada* . **143 B9** 56 32N 95 0W
Stephenville, *Canada* . **141 C8** 48 31N 58 35W
Stephenville, *U.S.A.* .. **155 J5** 32 13N 98 12W
Stepnica, *Poland* ..... **54 E1** 53 38N 14 36 E
Stepnoi = Elista, *Russia* **61 G7** 46 16N 44 14 E
Stepnoye, *Russia* .... **61 G8** 54 4N 60 26 E
Steppe, *Asia* .... **62 D9** 50 0N 50 0 E
Stereá Ellas □, *Greece* **48 C4** 38 50N 23 0 E
Sterkstroom, *S. Africa* **116 E4** 31 32 S 26 32 E
Sterling, *Alaska, U.S.A.* **144 F10** 60 32N 150 46W
Sterling, *Colo., U.S.A.* **154 E3** 40 37N 103 13W
Sterling, *Ga., U.S.A.* .. **152 D8** 31 16N 81 34W
Sterling, *Ill., U.S.A.* ... **156 C7** 41 48N 89 42W
Sterling, *Kans., U.S.A.* **154 F5** 38 13N 98 12W
Sterling City, *U.S.A.* .. **155 K4** 31 51N 101 0W
Sterling Heights, *U.S.A.* **157 B13** 42 35N 83 0W
Sterling Run, *U.S.A.* .. **150 E6** 41 25N 78 12W
Sterlitamak, *Russia* ... **64 E6** 53 40N 56 0 E
Sternberg, *Germany* .. **30 B7** 53 42N 11 50 E
Šternberk, *Czech Rep.* **35 B10** 49 45N 17 15 E
Stérnes, *Greece* ..... **39 E5** 35 30N 24 9 E
Sterzing = Vipiteno, *Italy* .... **45 B8** 46 54N 11 26 E
Stettin = Szczecin, *Poland* .... **54 E1** 53 27N 14 27 E
Stettiner Haff, *Germany* .... **30 B10** 53 47N 14 15 E
Stettler, *Canada* **142 C6** 52 19N 112 40W
Steubenville, *U.S.A.* .. **150 F4** 40 22N 80 37W
Stevenage, *U.K.* **21 F7** 51 55N 0 13W
Stevens Point, *U.S.A.* . **154 C10** 44 31N 89 34W
Stevens Pottery, *U.S.A.* **152 C6** 32 57N 83 17W
Stevens Village, *U.S.A.* **144 C10** 66 1N 149 6W
Stevenson, *U.S.A.* ... **160 E5** 45 42N 121 53W
Stevenson, The ➝, *Australia* .... **127 D2** 27 6 S 135 33 E
Stevenson L., *Canada* . **143 C9** 53 55N 96 0W
Stevensville, *U.S.A.* .. **158 C6** 46 30N 114 5W
Stevns Klint, *Denmark* **17 J6** 55 17N 12 28 E
Steward, *U.S.A.* **156 C7** 41 51N 89 1W
Stewardson, *U.S.A.* ... **157 E8** 39 16N 88 38W
Stewart, *Canada* **142 B3** 55 56N 129 57W
Stewart, *Ga., U.S.A.* .. **152 B6** 33 25N 83 52W
Stewart, *Nev., U.S.A.* . **160 F7** 39 5N 119 46W
Stewart ➝, *Canada* .. **138 B6** 63 19N 139 26W
Stewart, C., *Australia* . **126 A1** 11 57 S 134 56 E
Stewart, I., *Chile* ..... **176 D2** 54 50 S 71 15W
Stewart I., *N.Z.* ...... **131 G2** 46 58 S 167 54 E
Stewarts Point, *U.S.A.* **160 G3** 38 39N 123 24W
Stewartsville, *U.S.A.* . **156 E2** 39 45N 94 30W
Stewartville, *U.S.A.* .. **154 D8** 43 51N 92 29W
Stewiacke, *Canada* ... **141 C7** 45 9N 63 22W
Steynsburg, *S. Africa* . **116 E4** 31 15 S 25 49 E
Steyr, *Austria* .... **34 C7** 48 3N 14 25 E
Steyr ➝, *Austria* .... **34 C7** 48 3N 14 25 E
Steytlerville, *S. Africa* . **116 E3** 33 17 S 24 19 E
Stia, *Italy* .... **45 E8** 43 48N 11 42 E
Stigler, *U.S.A.* **155 H7** 35 15N 95 8W
Stigliano, *Italy* ...... **47 B9** 40 24N 16 14 E
Stigtomta, *Sweden* .... **17 F10** 58 47N 16 48 E
Stikine ➝, *Canada* ... **142 B2** 56 40N 132 30W
Stilfontein, *S. Africa* . **116 D4** 26 51 S 26 50 E
Stilís, *Greece* .... **48 C4** 38 55N 22 47 E
Stillmore, *U.S.A.* **152 C7** 32 27N 82 13W
Stillwater, *Minn., U.S.A.* **147 A8** 45 3N 92 49W
Stillwater, *N.Y., U.S.A.* **151 D11** 42 55N 73 41W
Stillwater, *Okla., U.S.A.* **155 G6** 36 7N 97 4W
Stillwater Range, *U.S.A.* **158 G4** 39 50N 118 5W
Stillwater Reservoir, *U.S.A.* **151 C9** 43 54N 75 3W
Stilo, Pta., *Italy* ..... **47 D9** 38 25N 16 35 E
Stilwell, *U.S.A.* **155 H7** 35 49N 94 38W
Stînga Nistrului □, *Moldova* .... **53 C14** 47 20N 29 15 E
Štip, *Macedonia* ..... **50 E6** 41 42N 22 10 E
Stira, *Greece* .... **48 C6** 38 9N 24 14 E
Stirling, *Canada* **150 B7** 44 18N 77 33W
Stirling, *N.Z.* .... **131 G4** 46 14 S 169 49 E
Stirling, *U.K.* **22 E5** 56 8N 3 57W
Stirling □, *U.K.* **22 E4** 56 12N 4 18W
Stirling Ra., *Australia* . **125 F2** 34 23 S 118 0 E
Stirling Range △, *Australia* .... **125 F2** 34 26 S 118 20 E
Stittsville, *Canada* ... **151 A9** 45 15N 75 55W
Stjernøya, *Norway* ... **14 A20** 70 20N 22 40 E
Stjørdalshalsen, *Norway* .... **18 A7** 63 29N 10 51 E
Stock Island, *U.S.A.* .. **153 L8** 24 32N 81 34W
Stockach, *Germany* ... **31 H5** 47 50N 9 1 E
Stockaryd, *Sweden* ... **17 G8** 57 19N 14 36 E
Stockbridge, *Ga., U.S.A.* **152 B5** 33 33N 84 14W

Stockbridge, *Mich., U.S.A.* **157 B12** 42 27N 84 11W
Stockerau, *Austria* **35 C9** 48 24N 16 12 E
Stockholm, *Sweden* **16 E12** 59 20N 18 3 E
Stockholm Arlanda ✈ (ARN), *Sweden* **16 E11** 59 41N 17 56 E
Stockholms län □, *Sweden* **16 E12** 59 30N 18 20 E
Stockhorn, *Switz.* **32 C5** 46 42N 7 33 E
Stockport, *U.K.* **20 D5** 53 25N 2 9W
Stocksbridge, *U.K.* **20 D6** 53 29N 1 35W
Stockton, *Calif., U.S.A.* **160 H5** 37 58N 121 17W
Stockton, *Ill., U.S.A.* **156 B6** 42 21N 90 1W
Stockton, *Kans., U.S.A.* **154 F5** 39 26N 99 16W
Stockton, *Mo., U.S.A.* **155 G8** 37 42N 93 48W
Stockton-on-Tees, *U.K.* **20 C6** 54 35N 1 19W
Stockton-on-Tees □, *U.K.* **20 C6** 54 35N 1 19W
Stockton Plateau, *U.S.A.* **155 K3** 30 30N 102 30W
Stoczek Łukowski, *Poland* **55 G8** 51 58N 21 58 E
Stöde, *Sweden* **16 B10** 62 28N 16 35 E
Stoeng Treng, *Cambodia* **86 F5** 13 31N 105 58 E
Stoer, Pt. of, *U.K.* **22 C3** 58 16N 5 23W
Stogovo, *Macedonia* **50 E4** 41 31N 20 38 E
Stoholm, *Denmark* **17 H3** 56 30N 9 8 E
Stoke, *N.Z.* **131 B8** 41 19 S 173 14 E
Stoke-on-Trent, *U.K.* **20 D5** 53 1N 2 11W
Stoke-on-Trent □, *U.K.* **20 D5** 53 1N 2 11W
Stokes △, *Australia* **125 E2** 29 55 S 115 6 E
Stokes Pt., *Australia* **127 G3** 40 10 S 143 56 E
Stokes Ra., *Australia* **124 C5** 15 50 S 130 50 E
Stokkseyri, *Iceland* **11 D5** 63 50N 21 2W
Stokksnes, *Iceland* **11 C12** 64 14N 14 58W
Stokmarknes, *Norway* **14 B16** 68 34N 14 54 E
Stolac, *Bos.-H.* **50 C1** 43 5N 17 59 E
Stolberg, *Germany* **30 E2** 50 47N 6 13 E
Stolbovoy, Ostrov, *Russia* **67 B14** 74 44N 135 14 E
Stolbtsy = Stowbtsy, *Belarus* **58 F4** 53 30N 26 43 E
Stolin, *Belarus* **59 G4** 51 53N 26 50 E
Stöllet, *Sweden* **16 D7** 60 26N 13 15 E
Stolnici, *Romania* **53 F9** 44 31N 24 48 E
Stolp = Słupsk, *Poland* **54 D4** 54 30N 17 3 E
Stolpmünde = Ustka, *Poland* **54 D3** 54 35N 16 55 E
Stomíon, *Greece* **39 E4** 35 21N 23 32 E
Ston, *Croatia* **45 F14** 42 51N 17 43 E
Stone, *U.K.* **20 E5** 52 55N 2 9W
Stone Mountain, *U.S.A.* **152 B5** 33 49N 84 10W
Stoneboro, *U.S.A.* **150 E4** 41 20N 80 7W
Stonehaven, *U.K.* **22 E6** 56 59N 2 12W
Stonehenge, *Australia* **126 C3** 24 22 S 143 17 E
Stonehenge, *U.K.* **21 F6** 51 9N 1 45W
Stonewall, *Canada* **143 C9** 50 10N 97 19W
Stongfjorden, *Norway* **18 C2** 61 26N 5 10 E
Stonington, *U.S.A.* **156 E7** 39 44N 89 12W
Stony L., *Man., Canada* **143 B9** 58 51N 98 40W
Stony L., *Ont., Canada* **150 B6** 44 30N 78 5W
Stony Point, *U.S.A.* **151 E11** 41 14N 73 59W
Stony Pt., *U.S.A.* **151 C8** 43 50N 76 18W
Stony Rapids, *Canada* **143 B7** 59 16N 105 50W
Stony River, *U.S.A.* **144 F8** 61 47N 156 35W
Stony Tunguska = Tunguska, Podkamennaya ➝, *Russia* **67 C10** 61 50N 90 13 E
Stonyford, *U.S.A.* **160 F4** 39 23N 122 33W
Stopnica, *Poland* **55 H7** 50 27N 20 57 E
Storå, *Sweden* **16 E9** 59 42N 15 6 E
Storå ➝, *Denmark* **17 H2** 56 20N 8 19 E
Stora Gla, *Sweden* **16 E6** 59 30N 12 30 E
Stora Le, *Sweden* **16 E5** 59 5N 11 55 E
Stora Lulevatten, *Sweden* **14 C18** 67 10N 19 30 E
Stóra-Vatnshorn, *Iceland* **11 B5** 65 4N 21 33W
Storavan, *Sweden* **14 D18** 65 45N 18 10 E
Stord, *Norway* **18 E2** 59 52N 5 23 E
Stordal, *Norway* **18 B4** 62 23N 7 0 E
Store Bælt, *Denmark* **17 J4** 55 20N 11 0 E
Store Heddinge, *Denmark* **17 J6** 55 18N 12 23 E
Store Jukleggi, *Norway* **18 C5** 61 3N 8 12 E
Store Koldewey, *Greenland* **10 B9** 76 30N 19 0W
Store Mosse △, *Sweden* **17 G7** 57 18N 13 55 E
Store Sølnkletten, *Norway* **18 C7** 61 59N 10 16 E
Store Sotra, *Norway* **18 D1** 60 18N 5 4 E
Storebro, *Sweden* **17 G9** 57 35N 15 52 E
Støren, *Norway* **18 A7** 63 3N 10 18 E
Storerikvollen, *Norway* **18 A8** 63 7N 11 58 E
Storfjellseter, *Norway* **18 C7** 61 40N 10 30 E
Storfjorden, *Norway* **18 B3** 62 28N 6 35 E
Storfors, *Sweden* **16 E8** 59 32N 14 17 E
Stóridalur, *Iceland* **11 D7** 63 38N 19 57W
Stórinúpur, *Iceland* **11 C6** 64 3N 20 10W
Storli, *Norway* **18 B6** 62 42N 9 5 E
Storlien, *Sweden* **16 A6** 63 19N 12 6 E
Storm B., *Australia* **127 G4** 43 10 S 147 30 E
Storm Lake, *U.S.A.* **154 D7** 42 39N 95 13W
Stormberge, *S. Africa* **116 E4** 31 16 S 26 17 E
Stormsrivier, *S. Africa* **116 E3** 33 59 S 23 52 E
Stornoway, *U.K.* **22 C2** 58 13N 6 23W
Storo, *Italy* **44 C7** 45 51N 10 35 E
Storozhinets = Storozhynets, *Ukraine* **53 B10** 48 14N 25 45 E
Storozhynets, *Ukraine* **53 B10** 48 14N 25 45 E
Storrs, *U.S.A.* **151 E12** 41 49N 72 15W
Storsjøen, *Hedmark, Norway* **18 D8** 60 20N 11 40 E
Storsjøen, *Hedmark, Norway* **18 C8** 61 30N 11 14 E
Storsjön, *Gävleborg, Sweden* **16 D10** 60 35N 16 45 E
Storsjön, *Jämtland, Sweden* **16 B7** 62 48N 13 7 E
Storsjön, *Jämtland, Sweden* **16 A8** 63 9N 14 30 E
Storstrøms Amtskommune □, *Denmark* **17 J5** 54 50N 11 45 E
Storuman, *Sweden* **14 D17** 65 5N 17 10 E
Storuman, *Sweden* **14 D17** 65 13N 16 50 E
Stóruvellir, *Iceland* **11 B9** 65 30N 17 29W
Storvätteshågna, *Sweden* **16 B6** 62 6N 12 30 E
Storvigelen, *Norway* **18 B9** 62 32N 12 2 E
Storvik, *Sweden* **16 D10** 60 35N 16 33 E
Storvreta, *Sweden* **16 E11** 59 58N 17 44 E
Story City, *U.S.A.* **156 B3** 42 11N 93 36W
Stouffville, *Canada* **150 C5** 43 58N 79 15W
Stoughton, *Canada* **143 D8** 49 40N 103 0W
Stoughton, *U.S.A.* **156 B8** 42 55N 89 13W
Stour ➝, *Dorset, U.K.* **21 G6** 50 43N 1 47W
Stour ➝, *Kent, U.K.* **21 F9** 51 18N 1 22 E
Stour ➝, *Suffolk, U.K.* **21 F9** 51 57N 1 4 E
Stourbridge, *U.K.* **21 E5** 52 28N 2 8W
Stout L., *Canada* **143 C10** 52 0N 94 40W
Stove Pipe Wells Village, *U.S.A.* **161 J9** 36 35N 117 11W
Støvring, *Denmark* **17 H3** 56 54N 9 50 E
Stow, *U.S.A.* **150 E3** 41 10N 81 27W
Stowbtsy, *Belarus* **58 F4** 53 30N 26 43 E
Stowmarket, *U.K.* **21 E9** 52 12N 1 0 E
Strabane, *U.K.* **23 B4** 54 50N 7 27W
Stracin, *Macedonia* **50 D6** 42 13N 22 2 E
Stradella, *Italy* **44 C6** 45 5N 9 18 E
Strahan, *Australia* **127 G4** 42 9 S 145 20 E
Strajitsa, *Bulgaria* **51 C9** 43 14N 25 58 E
Strakonice, *Czech Rep.* **34 B6** 49 15N 13 53 E
Straldzha, *Bulgaria* **51 D10** 42 35N 26 40 E
Stralsund, *Germany* **30 A9** 54 18N 13 4 E
Strand, *Norway* **18 C8** 61 17N 11 17 E
Strand, *S. Africa* **116 E2** 34 9 S 18 48 E
Stranda, *Møre og Romsdal, Norway* **18 B3** 62 19N 6 58 E
Stranda, *Nord-Trøndelag, Norway* **14 E14** 63 33N 10 14 E
Strandasýsla □, *Iceland* **11 B5** 65 45N 21 45W
Strandby, *Denmark* **17 G4** 57 30N 10 29 E
Strangford L., *U.K.* **23 B6** 54 30N 5 37W
Strängnäs, *Sweden* **16 E11** 59 23N 17 2 E
Stranraer, *U.K.* **22 G3** 54 54N 5 1W
Strasbourg, *Canada* **143 C8** 51 4N 104 55W
Strasbourg, *France* **27 D14** 48 35N 7 42 E
Strasburg, *Germany* **30 B9** 53 30N 13 43 E
Strășeni, *Moldova* **53 C13** 47 8N 28 36 E
Stråssa, *Sweden* **16 E9** 59 44N 15 12 E
Strassburg = Aiud, *Romania* **53 D8** 46 19N 23 44 E
Stratford, *N.S.W., Australia* **129 B9** 32 7 S 151 55 E
Stratford, *Vic., Australia* **129 D7** 37 59 S 147 7 E
Stratford, *Canada* **140 D3** 43 23N 81 0W
Stratford, *N.Z.* **130 F3** 39 20 S 174 19 E
Stratford, *Calif., U.S.A.* **160 J7** 36 11N 119 49W
Stratford, *Conn., U.S.A.* **151 E11** 41 12N 73 8W
Stratford, *Tex., U.S.A.* **155 G3** 36 20N 102 4W
Stratford-upon-Avon, *U.K.* **21 E6** 52 12N 1 42W
Strath Spey, *U.K.* **22 D5** 57 9N 3 49W
Strathalbyn, *Australia* **128 C3** 35 13 S 138 53 E
Strathaven, *U.K.* **22 F4** 55 40N 4 5W
Strathcona ⌓, *Canada* **142 D3** 49 38N 125 40W
Strathmore, *Canada* **142 C6** 51 5N 113 18W
Strathmore, *U.K.* **22 E5** 56 37N 3 7W
Strathmore, *U.S.A.* **160 J7** 36 9N 119 4W
Strathnaver, *Canada* **142 C4** 53 20N 122 33W
Strathpeffer, *U.K.* **22 D4** 57 35N 4 32W
Strathroy, *Canada* **140 D3** 42 58N 81 38W
Strathy Pt., *U.K.* **22 C4** 58 36N 4 1W
Strattanville, *U.S.A.* **150 E5** 41 12N 79 19W
Stratton, *U.S.A.* **151 A14** 45 8N 70 26W
Stratton Mt., *U.S.A.* **151 C12** 43 4N 72 55W
Straubing, *Germany* **31 G8** 48 52N 12 34 E
Straumnes, *Iceland* **11 A3** 66 26N 23 8W
Strausberg, *Germany* **30 C9** 52 35N 13 54 E
Strawberry ➝, *U.S.A.* **158 F8** 40 10N 110 24W
Strawberry Point, *U.S.A.* **156 B5** 42 41N 91 32W
Strážnice, *Czech Rep.* **35 C10** 48 54N 17 19 E
Streaky B., *Australia* **127 E1** 32 48 S 134 13 E
Streaky Bay, *Australia* **127 E1** 32 51 S 134 18 E
Streator, *U.S.A.* **154 E10** 41 8N 88 50W
Středočeský □, *Czech Rep.* **34 B7** 49 55N 14 30 E
Streetsboro, *U.S.A.* **150 E3** 41 14N 81 21W
Streetsville, *Canada* **150 C5** 43 35N 79 42W
Strehaia, *Romania* **53 F8** 44 37N 23 10 E
Strehlen = Strzelin, *Poland* **55 H4** 50 46N 17 2 E
Strelcha, *Bulgaria* **51 D8** 42 25N 24 19 E
Strelka, *Russia* **67 D10** 58 5N 93 3 E
Streng ➝, *Cambodia* **86 F4** 13 12N 103 37 E
Stresa, *Italy* **44 C5** 45 52N 8 28 E
Streymoy, *Færoe Is.* **14 E9** 62 8N 7 5W
Strezhevoy, *Russia* **66 C8** 60 42N 77 34 E
Stříbro, *Czech Rep.* **34 A6** 49 44N 13 0 E
Strickland ➝, *Papua N. G.* **132 D1** 7 35 S 141 36 E
Striegau = Strzegom, *Poland* **55 H3** 50 58N 16 20 E
Strilky, *Ukraine* **55 J9** 49 20N 22 59 E
Strimón ➝, *Greece* **50 F7** 40 46N 23 51 E
Strimonas = Strimón ➝, *Greece* **50 F7** 40 46N 23 51 E
Strimonikós Kólpos, *Greece* **50 F7** 40 33N 24 0 E
Stroeder, *Argentina* **176 B4** 40 12 S 62 37W
Strofádhes, *Greece* **48 D3** 37 15N 21 0 E
Stroma, *U.K.* **22 C5** 58 41N 3 7W
Stromberg-Heuchelberg ⌓, *Germany* **31 F4** 49 2N 8 50 E
Strómboli, *Italy* **47 D8** 38 47N 15 13 E
Stromeferry, *U.K.* **22 D3** 57 21N 5 33W
Strømmen, *Norway* **18 E7** 59 58N 10 59 E
Stromness, *U.K.* **22 C5** 58 58N 3 17W
Strömsbruk, *Sweden* **16 C11** 61 52N 17 18 E
Stromsburg, *U.S.A.* **154 E6** 41 7N 97 36W
Strömsnäsbruk, *Sweden* **17 H7** 56 35N 13 45 E
Strömstad, *Sweden* **17 F5** 58 56N 11 10 E
Strömsund, *Sweden* **14 E16** 63 51N 15 33 E
Stronghurst, *U.S.A.* **156 D6** 40 45N 90 55W
Strongilí, *Greece* **49 E11** 36 6N 29 42 E
Stróngoli, *Italy* **47 C10** 39 16N 17 3 E
Strongsville, *U.S.A.* **150 E3** 41 19N 81 50W
Stronie Ślaskie, *Poland* **55 H3** 50 18N 16 53 E
Stronsay, *U.K.* **22 B6** 59 7N 2 35W
Stropkov, *Slovak Rep.* **35 B14** 49 13N 21 39 E
Stroud, *U.K.* **21 F5** 51 45N 2 13W
Stroud Road, *Australia* **129 B9** 32 18 S 151 57 E
Stroudsburg, *U.S.A.* **151 F9** 40 59N 75 12W
Stroumbi, *Cyprus* **39 F8** 34 53N 32 29 E
Struer, *Denmark* **17 H2** 56 30N 8 35 E
Struga, *Macedonia* **50 E4** 41 11N 20 44 E
Strugi Krasnyye, *Russia* **58 C5** 58 21N 29 1 E
Strumica, *Macedonia* **50 E6** 41 28N 22 41 E
Strumica ➝, *Europe* **50 E7** 41 20N 23 22 E
Strumok, *Ukraine* **53 E14** 45 43N 29 27 E
Struthers, *Canada* **140 C2** 48 41N 85 51W
Struthers, *U.S.A.* **150 E4** 41 4N 80 39W
Stryama, *Bulgaria* **51 D8** 42 16N 24 54 E
Stryker, *U.S.A.* **158 B6** 48 41N 114 46W
Stryków, *Poland* **55 G6** 51 55N 19 33 E
Stryn, *Norway* **18 C3** 61 54N 6 43 E
Stryy, *Ukraine* **59 H2** 49 16N 23 48 E
Strzegom, *Poland* **55 H3** 50 58N 16 20 E
Strzelce Krajeńskie, *Poland* **55 F2** 52 52N 15 33 E
Strzelce Opolskie, *Poland* **55 H5** 50 31N 18 18 E
Strzelecki Cr. ➝, *Australia* **127 D2** 29 37 S 139 59 E
Strzelin, *Poland* **55 H4** 50 46N 17 2 E
Strzelno, *Poland* **55 F5** 52 35N 18 9 E
Strzybnica, *Poland* **55 H5** 50 28N 18 48 E
Strzyżów, *Poland* **55 J8** 49 52N 21 47 E
Stuart, *Fla., U.S.A.* **153 H9** 27 12N 80 15W
Stuart, *Iowa, U.S.A.* **156 C2** 41 30N 94 19W
Stuart, *Nebr., U.S.A.* **154 D5** 42 36N 99 8W
Stuart ➝, *Canada* **142 C4** 54 0N 123 35W
Stuart Bluff Ra., *Australia* **124 D5** 22 50 S 131 52 E
Stuart I., *U.S.A.* **144 E7** 63 35N 162 30W
Stuart L., *Canada* **142 C4** 54 30N 124 30W
Stuart Mts., *N.Z.* **131 F2** 45 2 S 167 39 E
Stuart Ra., *Australia* **127 D1** 29 10 S 134 56 E
Stubbekøbing, *Denmark* **17 K6** 54 53N 12 9 E
Stuben, *Austria* **34 D3** 47 10N 10 8 E
Štubnianske Teplice = Turčianske Teplice, *Slovak Rep.* **35 C11** 48 52N 18 52 E
Studen Kladenets, Yazovir, *Bulgaria* **51 E9** 41 37N 25 30 E
Studenka, *Czech Rep.* **35 B11** 49 44N 18 5 E
Studholme, *N.Z.* **131 E6** 44 42 S 171 9 E
Stugudal, *Norway* **18 B8** 62 53N 11 53 E
Stugun, *Sweden* **16 A9** 63 10N 15 40 E
Stühlingen, *Germany* **33 A6** 47 44N 8 26 E
Stuhlweissenburg = Székesfehérvár, *Hungary* **52 C3** 47 15N 18 25 E
Stuhm = Sztum, *Poland* **54 E6** 53 55N 19 1 E
Stuhr, *Germany* **30 B4** 53 5N 8 44 E
Stull L., *Canada* **140 B1** 54 24N 92 34W
Stung Treng = Stoeng Treng, *Cambodia* **86 F5** 13 31N 105 58 E
Stupart ➝, *Canada* **140 A1** 56 0N 93 25W
Stupava, *Slovak Rep.* **35 C10** 48 17N 17 2 E
Stupino, *Russia* **58 E10** 54 57N 38 2 E
Sturgeon B., *Canada* **143 C9** 52 0N 97 50W
Sturgeon Bay, *U.S.A.* **148 C2** 44 50N 87 23W
Sturgeon Falls, *Canada* **140 C4** 46 25N 79 57W
Sturgeon L., *Alta., Canada* **142 B5** 55 6N 117 32W
Sturgeon L., *Ont., Canada* **140 C1** 50 0N 90 45W
Sturgeon L., *Ont., Canada* **150 B6** 44 28N 78 43W
Sturgis, *Canada* **143 C8** 51 56N 102 36W
Sturgis, *Mich., U.S.A.* **157 C11** 41 48N 85 25W
Sturgis, *S. Dak., U.S.A.* **154 C3** 44 25N 103 31W
Sturkö, *Sweden* **17 H9** 56 5N 15 42 E
Štúrovo, *Slovak Rep.* **35 D11** 47 48N 18 41 E
Sturt △, *Australia* **127 D3** 27 17 S 141 37 E
Sturt Cr. ➝, *Australia* **124 C4** 19 8 S 127 50 E
Sturt Stony Desert, *Australia* **127 D2** 28 30 S 141 0 E
Sturts Meadows, *Australia* **128 A4** 31 18 S 141 42 E
Stutterheim, *S. Africa* **116 E4** 32 33 S 27 28 E
Stuttgart, *Germany* **31 G5** 48 48N 9 11 E
Stuttgart, *U.S.A.* **155 H9** 34 30N 91 33W
Stuttgart Echterdingen ✈ (STR), *Germany* **31 G5** 48 42N 9 11 E
Stutthof = Sztutowo, *Poland* **54 D6** 54 20N 19 15 E
Stuyvesant, *U.S.A.* **151 D11** 42 23N 73 45W
Stykkishólmur, *Iceland* **11 B4** 65 2N 22 40W
Styria = Steiermark □, *Austria* **34 D8** 47 26N 15 0 E
Styrsö, *Sweden* **17 G5** 57 37N 11 46 E
Su-no-Saki, *Japan* **73 C11** 34 58N 139 45 E
Su Xian = Suzhou, *China* **74 H9** 33 41N 116 59 E
Suakin, *Sudan* **106 D4** 19 8N 37 20 E
Suan, *N. Korea* **75 E14** 38 42N 126 22 E
Süanhwa = Xuanhua, *China* **74 D8** 40 40N 115 2 E
Suapure ➝, *Venezuela* **168 B4** 6 48N 67 1W
Suaqui, *Mexico* **162 B3** 29 12N 109 41W
Suar, *India* **93 E8** 29 2N 79 3 E
Suatá ➝, *Venezuela* **169 B4** 7 52N 65 22W
Suau, *Papua N. G.* **132 F6** 10 37 S 150 2 E
Suavanao, *Solomon Is.* **133 L10** 7 35 S 158 47 E
Suba Talan, *Malaysia* **81 H1** 6 22N 117 38 E
Subang, *Indonesia* **85 D3** 6 34 S 107 45 E
Subankhata, *India* **90 B3** 26 48N 91 25 E
Subansiri ➝, *India* **90 B4** 26 48N 93 50 E
Subarnagiri, *India* **94 E6** 19 50N 83 51 E
Subarnarekha ➝, *India* **93 H12** 22 34N 87 24 E
Subayhah, *Si. Arabia* **96 D3** 30 2N 38 50 E
Subcetate, *Romania* **52 E8** 45 36N 23 0 E
Subi, *Indonesia* **85 B3** 2 58N 108 50 E
Subiaco, *Italy* **45 G10** 41 56N 13 5 E
Subotica, *Serbia & M.* **52 D4** 46 6N 19 39 E
Suca, *Ethiopia* **107 F4** 6 31N 39 14 E
Suceava, *Romania* **53 C11** 47 38N 26 16 E
Suceava □, *Romania* **53 C10** 47 37N 25 40 E
Suceava ➝, *Romania* **53 C11** 47 32N 26 32 E
Sucesso, *Brazil* **170 B3** 4 56 S 40 32W
Sucha-Beskidzka, *Poland* **55 J6** 49 44N 19 35 E
Suchań, *Poland* **55 E2** 53 18N 15 18 E
Suchan, *Russia* **70 C6** 43 8N 133 9 E
Suchedniów, *Poland* **55 G7** 51 3N 20 49 E
Suchitoto, *El Salv.* **164 D2** 13 56N 89 0W
Suchou = Suzhou, *China* **77 B13** 31 19N 120 38 E
Süchow = Xuzhou, *China* **75 G9** 34 18N 117 10 E
Suchowola, *Poland* **54 E10** 53 33N 23 3 E
Sucio ➝, *Colombia* **168 B2** 7 27N 77 7W
Suck ➝, *Ireland* **23 C3** 53 17N 8 3W
Suckling, Mt., *Papua N. G.* **132 E5** 9 49 S 148 53 E
Sucre, *Bolivia* **173 D4** 19 0 S 65 15W
Sucre, *Colombia* **168 B3** 8 49N 74 44W
Sucre □, *Colombia* **168 B2** 8 50N 75 40W
Sucre □, *Venezuela* **169 A5** 10 25N 63 30W
Sucuaro, *Colombia* **168 C4** 4 34N 68 50W
Sućuraj, *Croatia* **45 E14** 43 10N 17 8 E
Sucuriju, *Brazil* **170 A2** 1 39N 49 57W
Sucuriú ➝, *Brazil* **173 E7** 20 47 S 51 38W
Sud, Pte. du, *Canada* **141 C7** 49 3N 62 14W
Sud-Kivu □, *Dem. Rep. of the Congo* **118 C2** 3 0 S 28 30 E
Sud-Ouest, Pte., *Canada* **141 C7** 49 23N 63 36W
Sud-Ouest, Pte., *Mauritius* **121 d** 20 28 S 57 18 E
Suda ➝, *Russia* **58 C9** 59 0N 37 40 E
Sudak, *Ukraine* **59 K8** 44 51N 34 57 E
Sudan, *U.S.A.* **155 H3** 34 4N 102 32W
Sudan ■, *Africa* **107 E3** 15 0N 30 0 E
Sudauen = Suwałki, *Poland* **54 D9** 54 8N 22 59 E
Sudbury, *Canada* **140 C3** 46 30N 81 0W
Sudbury, *U.K.* **21 E8** 52 2N 0 45 E
Sûdd, *Sudan* **107 F3** 8 20N 30 0 E
Suddie, *Guyana* **169 B6** 7 8N 58 29W
Sudeifel = Deutsch-Luxemburgischer ⌓, *Germany* **31 F2** 49 58N 6 12 E
Süderbrarup, *Germany* **30 A5** 54 38N 9 45 E
Süderlügum, *Germany* **30 A4** 54 52N 8 54 E
Süderoogsand, *Germany* **30 A4** 54 27N 8 28 E
Sudeten Mts. = Sudety, *Europe* **35 A9** 50 20N 16 45 E
Sudety, *Europe* **35 A9** 50 20N 16 45 E
Súðavík, *Iceland* **11 A3** 66 2N 23 0W
Südheide ⌓, *Germany* **30 C6** 52 46N 10 10 E
Suður-múlasýsla □, *Iceland* **11 C12** 65 0N 14 30W
Suður-þingeyjarsýsla □, *Iceland* **11 B9** 65 30N 17 0W
Suðureyri, *Iceland* **11 A3** 66 7N 23 32W
Suðuroy, *Færoe Is.* **14 F9** 61 32N 6 50W
Sudi, *Tanzania* **119 E4** 10 11 S 39 57 E
Sudirman, Pegunungan, *Indonesia* **83 B5** 4 30 S 137 0 E
Sudiţi, *Romania* **53 F12** 44 35N 27 38 E
Sudogda, *Russia* **60 C5** 55 55N 40 50 E
Sudong, Pulau, *Singapore* **87 d** 1 12N 103 43 E
Sudostroy = Severodvinsk, *Russia* **56 B6** 64 27N 39 58 E
Sudova Vyshnya, *Ukraine* **55 J10** 49 46N 23 22 E
Sudr, *Egypt* **106 B3** 29 40N 32 42 E
Sudzha, *Russia* **59 G8** 51 14N 35 17 E
Sue ➝, *Sudan* **107 F2** 7 41N 28 3 E
Sueca, *Spain* **41 F4** 39 12N 0 21W
Sŭedinenie, *Bulgaria* **51 D8** 42 16N 24 33 E
Suemez I., *U.S.A.* **142 B2** 55 15N 133 20W
Suez = El Suweis, *Egypt* **106 J8** 29 58N 32 31 E
Suez, G. of = Suweis, Khalîg el, *Egypt* **106 J8** 28 40N 33 0 E
Suez Canal = Suweis, Qanâ es, *Egypt* **106 H8** 31 0N 32 20 E
Suffield, *Canada* **142 C6** 50 12N 111 10W
Suffolk, *U.S.A.* **148 G7** 36 44N 76 35W
Suffolk □, *U.K.* **21 E9** 52 16N 1 0 E
Suga-no-Sen, *Japan* **72 B6** 35 25N 134 25 E
Şugag, *Romania* **53 E8** 45 47N 23 37 E
Sugar ➝, *U.S.A.* **156 B7** 42 26N 89 12W
Sugar Cr. ➝, *Ill., U.S.A.* **156 D7** 40 9N 89 38W
Sugar Cr. ➝, *Ind., U.S.A.* **157 E9** 39 50N 87 23W
Sugar Hill, *U.S.A.* **152 A5** 34 6N 84 2W
Sugar Loaf Pt., *St. Helena* **9 h** 15 54 S 5 42W
Sugargrove, *U.S.A.* **150 E5** 41 59N 79 21W
Sugarive ➝, *India* **93 F12** 26 16N 86 24 E
Sugbai Passage, *Phil.* **81 J3** 5 22N 120 33 E
Suğla Gölü, *Turkey* **100 D5** 37 20N 32 0 E
Sugluk = Salluit, *Canada* **139 B12** 62 14N 75 38W
Sugun, *China* **65 D8** 39 53N 76 47 E
Suhaia, Lacul, *Romania* **53 G10** 43 45N 25 15 E
Şuḥār, *Oman* **97 E8** 24 20N 56 40 E
Sühbaatar □, *Mongolia* **74 B8** 45 30N 114 0 E
Suheli Par, *India* **95 J1** 10 5N 72 17 E
Suhl, *Germany* **30 E6** 50 36N 10 42 E
Suhr, *Switz.* **32 B6** 47 22N 8 5 E
Şuhut, *Turkey* **49 C12** 38 31N 30 32 E
Sui, *Pakistan* **92 E3** 28 37N 69 19 E
Sui Xian, *China* **74 G8** 34 25N 115 2 E
Suiá Missu ➝, *Brazil* **173 C7** 11 13 S 53 15W
Šuica, *Bos.-H.* **52 G2** 43 52N 17 11 E
Suichang, *China* **77 C12** 28 29N 119 15 E
Suichuan, *China* **77 D10** 26 20N 114 32 E
Suide, *China* **74 F6** 37 30N 110 12 E
Suifenhe, *China* **75 B16** 44 25N 131 10 E
Suihua, *China* **69 B7** 46 32N 126 55 E
Suijiang, *China* **76 C4** 28 40N 103 59 E
Suining, *Hunan, China* **77 D8** 26 35N 110 10 E
Suining, *Jiangsu, China* **75 H9** 33 56N 117 58 E
Suining, *Sichuan, China* **76 B5** 30 26N 105 35 E
Suiping, *China* **74 H7** 33 10N 113 59 E
Suippes, *France* **27 C11** 49 8N 4 30 E
Suir ➝, *Ireland* **23 D4** 52 16N 7 9W
Suisse = Switzerland ■, *Europe* **32 D6** 46 30N 8 0 E
Suisun City, *U.S.A.* **160 G4** 38 15N 122 2W
Suita, *Japan* **73 C7** 34 45N 135 32 E
Suixi, *China* **77 G8** 21 19N 110 18 E
Suiyang, *Guizhou, China* **76 D6** 27 58N 107 18 E
Suiyang, *Heilongjiang, China* **75 B16** 44 30N 130 56 E
Suizhong, *China* **75 D11** 40 21N 120 20 E
Suizhou, *China* **77 B9** 31 42N 113 24 E
Sujangarh, *India* **92 F6** 27 42N 74 31 E
Sukabumi, *Indonesia* **84 D3** 6 56 S 106 50 E
Sukadana, *Kalimantan, Indonesia* **85 C4** 1 10 S 110 0 E
Sukadana, *Sumatera, Indonesia* **84 D3** 5 5 S 105 33 E
Sukagawa, *Japan* **71 F10** 37 17N 140 23 E
Sukaraja, *Indonesia* **85 C4** 2 28 S 110 25 E
Sukarnapura = Jayapura, *Indonesia* **83 B6** 2 28 S 140 38 E
Sukarno, Puntjak = Jaya, Puncak, *Indonesia* **83 B5** 3 57 S 137 17 E
Sukawati, *Indonesia* **79 K18** 8 35 S 115 17 E
Sukch'ŏn, *N. Korea* **75 E13** 39 22N 125 35 E
Sukhindol, *Bulgaria* **51 C9** 43 11N 25 10 E
Sukhinichi, *Russia* **58 E8** 54 8N 35 10 E
Sukhona ➝, *Russia* **56 C6** 61 15N 46 39 E
Sukhothai, *Thailand* **86 D2** 17 1N 99 49 E
Sukhoy Log, *Russia* **64 C9** 56 55N 62 1 E
Sukhum = Sokhumi, *Georgia* **61 J5** 43 0N 41 0 E
Sukhumi = Sokhumi, *Georgia* **61 J5** 43 0N 41 0 E
Sukkertoppen = Maniitsoq, *Greenland* **10 D5** 65 26N 52 55W
Sukkur, *Pakistan* **91 D3** 27 42N 68 54 E
Sukkur Barrage, *Pakistan* **92 F3** 27 40N 68 50 E
Sukma, *India* **94 E5** 18 24N 81 45 E
Sukovo, *Serbia & M.* **50 C6** 43 4N 22 37 E
Sukri ➝, *India* **92 G4** 25 4N 71 43 E
Sukumo, *Japan* **72 E4** 32 56N 132 44 E
Sukunka ➝, *Canada* **142 B4** 55 45N 121 15W
Sul, Canal do, *Brazil* **170 B2** 0 10 S 48 30W
Sula, *Norway* **18 C1** 61 7N 4 54 E
Sula ➝, *Ukraine* **59 H7** 49 40N 32 41 E
Sula, Kepulauan, *Indonesia* **82 B3** 1 45 S 125 0 E
Sulaco ➝, *Honduras* **164 C2** 15 2N 87 44W
Sulaiman Range, *Pakistan* **92 D3** 30 30N 69 50 E
Sulak ➝, *Russia* **61 J8** 43 20N 47 34 E
Sūlār, *Iran* **97 D6** 31 53N 51 54 E
Sulawesi □, *Indonesia* **82 B2** 2 0 S 120 0 E
Sulawesi Sea = Celebes Sea, *Indonesia* **82 A2** 3 0N 123 0 E
Sulawesi Selatan □, *Indonesia* **82 B1** 2 30 S 120 0 E
Sulawesi Tengah □, *Indonesia* **82 B2** 1 30 S 121 0 E
Sulawesi Tenggara □, *Indonesia* **82 B2** 3 50 S 122 0 E
Sulawesi Utara □, *Indonesia* **82 A2** 1 0N 124 0 E
Suldalsosen, *Norway* **18 E3** 59 29N 6 29 E
Sulechów, *Poland* **55 F2** 52 5N 15 40 E
Sulęcin, *Poland* **55 F2** 52 26N 15 10 E
Sulei, *Solomon Is.* **133 M10** 8 3 S 159 34 E
Sulejów, *Poland* **55 G6** 51 26N 19 53 E
Sulejówek, *Poland* **55 F8** 52 13N 21 17 E
Süleymanlı, *Turkey* **49 C9** 38 58N 27 47 E
Sulgen, *Switz.* **33 A8** 47 33N 9 7 E
Sulima, *S. Leone* **112 D2** 6 58N 11 32W
Sulina, *Romania* **53 E14** 45 10N 29 40 E
Sulina, Braţul ➝, *Romania* **53 E14** 45 10N 29 40 E
Sulingen, *Germany* **30 C4** 52 41N 8 48 E
Suliţa, *Romania* **53 C11** 47 39N 26 59 E
Sulitjelma, *Norway* **14 C17** 67 9N 16 3 E
Sułkowice, *Poland* **55 J6** 49 50N 19 49 E
Sullana, *Peru* **172 A1** 4 52 S 80 39W
Süller, *Turkey* **49 C11** 38 9N 29 29 E
Sullivan, *Ill., U.S.A.* **154 F10** 39 36N 88 37W
Sullivan, *Ind., U.S.A.* **157 E9** 39 6N 87 24W
Sullivan, *Mo., U.S.A.* **156 F5** 38 13N 91 10W
Sullivan Bay, *Canada* **142 C3** 50 55N 126 50W
Sullivan I. = Lanbi Kyun, *Burma* **87 G2** 10 50N 98 20 E
Sullom Voe, *U.K.* **22 A7** 60 27N 1 20W
Sully, *U.S.A.* **156 C4** 41 34N 92 50W
Sully-sur-Loire, *France* **27 E9** 47 45N 2 20 E
Sulmierzyce, *Poland* **55 G4** 51 37N 17 32 E
Sulmona, *Italy* **45 F10** 42 3N 13 55 E
Süloğlu, *Turkey* **51 E10** 41 44N 26 53 E
Sulphur, *La., U.S.A.* **155 K8** 30 14N 93 23W
Sulphur, *Okla., U.S.A.* **155 H6** 34 31N 96 58W
Sulphur Pt., *Canada* **142 A6** 60 56N 114 48W
Sulphur Springs, *U.S.A.* **155 J7** 33 8N 95 36W
Sulsul, *Ethiopia* **120 C2** 5 5N 44 50 E
Sultan, *Canada* **140 C3** 47 36N 82 47W
Sultan, *U.S.A.* **160 C5** 47 52N 121 49W
Sultan Dağları, *Turkey* **100 C4** 38 20N 31 20 E
Sultan Kudarat, *Phil.* **81 H5** 7 16N 124 18 E
Sultan Kudarat □, *Phil.* **81 H5** 6 30N 124 10 E
Sultan Naga Dimaporo, *Phil.* **81 H4** 7 55N 123 44 E
Sultan sa Barongis, *Phil.* **81 H5** 6 45N 124 35 E
Sultanabad = Arāk, *Iran* **97 C6** 34 0N 49 40 E
Sultanhisar, *Turkey* **49 D10** 37 53N 28 9 E
Sultaniça, *Turkey* **51 F10** 40 37N 26 8 E
Sultaniye, *Turkey* **51 F12** 40 11N 28 12 E
Sultanpur, *Mad. P., India* **92 H8** 23 9N 77 56 E
Sultanpur, *Punjab, India* **92 D6** 31 13N 75 11 E
Sultanpur, *Ut. P., India* **93 F10** 26 18N 82 4 E
Sulu □, *Phil.* **81 J3** 5 30N 120 30 E
Sulu Arch., *Phil.* **81 J3** 6 0N 121 0 E
Sulu Sea, *E. Indies* **81 G3** 8 0N 120 0 E
Sülüklü, *Turkey* **100 C5** 38 53N 32 20 E
Sülüktü, *Kyrgyzstan* **65 D4** 39 56N 69 34 E
Sululta, *Ethiopia* **107 F4** 9 10N 38 43 E
Suluova, *Turkey* **100 B6** 40 46N 35 32 E
Suluq, *Libya* **108 B4** 31 44N 20 14 E
Suluru, *India* **95 H5** 13 42N 80 1 E
Sulütöbe, *Kazakhstan* **65 A3** 44 37N 66 3 E
Sulyukta = Sülüktü, *Kyrgyzstan* **65 D4** 39 56N 69 34 E
Sulzbach, *Germany* **31 F3** 49 18N 7 3 E
Sulzbach-Rosenberg, *Germany* **31 F7** 49 30N 11 44 E
Sulzberg, *Germany* **33 A10** 47 39N 10 39 E
Sulzberger Ice Shelf, *Antarctica* **7 E13** 78 0 S 150 0W
Sumaco -Napo Galeras △, *Ecuador* **168 D2** 0 34 S 77 38W
Sumalata, *Indonesia* **82 A2** 1 0N 122 31 E
Sumale □, *Ethiopia* **120 C2** 7 0N 45 0 E
Sumampa, *Argentina* **174 B3** 29 25 S 63 29W
Sumapaz △, *Colombia* **168 C3** 3 49N 74 13W
Sumatera, *Indonesia* **84 B2** 0 40N 100 20 E
Sumatera Barat □, *Indonesia* **78 E2** 1 0 S 101 0 E
Sumatera Utara □, *Indonesia* **78 D1** 2 30N 98 0 E
Sumatra = Sumatera, *Indonesia* **84 B2** 0 40N 100 20 E
Sumatra, *U.S.A.* **152 E5** 30 1N 84 59W
Sumava △, *Czech Rep.* **34 C6** 49 0N 13 49 E
Sumba, *Angola* **115 D2** 6 15 S 12 38 E
Sumba, *Indonesia* **82 C1** 9 45 S 119 35 E
Sumba, Selat, *Indonesia* **82 C1** 9 0 S 118 40 E
Sumbawa, *Indonesia* **85 D5** 8 26 S 117 30 E
Sumbawa Besar, *Indonesia* **85 D5** 8 30 S 117 26 E
Sumbe, *Angola* **115 E2** 11 10 S 13 48 E
Sumbu △, *Zambia* **119 D3** 8 43 S 30 22 E
Sumburgh Hd., *U.K.* **22 B7** 59 52N 1 17W
Sumdeo, *India* **93 D8** 31 26N 78 44 E
Sumdo, *China* **93 B8** 35 6N 78 41 E
Sumé, *Brazil* **170 C4** 7 39 S 36 55W
Sumedang, *Indonesia* **85 D3** 6 52 S 107 55 E
Sümeg, *Hungary* **52 D2** 46 59N 17 20 E
Sumeih, *Sudan* **107 F2** 9 50N 27 39 E
Šumen = Shumen, *Bulgaria* **51 C10** 43 18N 26 55 E
Sumenep, *Indonesia* **85 D4** 7 1 S 113 52 E
Sumgait = Sumqayıt, *Azerbaijan* **61 K9** 40 34N 49 38 E
Sumisu-Jima, *Japan* **73 F12** 31 27N 140 3 E
Sumiswald, *Switz.* **32 B5** 47 2N 7 44 E
Summer L., *U.S.A.* **158 E3** 42 50N 120 45W
Summerland, *Canada* **142 D5** 49 32N 119 41W
Summerland Key, *U.S.A.* **153 L8** 24 40N 81 27W
Summerside, *Canada* **141 C7** 46 24N 63 47W
Summersville, *U.S.A.* **148 F5** 38 17N 80 51W
Summerton, *U.S.A.* **152 B9** 33 36N 80 20W
Summertown, *U.S.A.* **152 C7** 32 45N 82 16W
Summerville, *Ga., U.S.A.* **149 H3** 34 29N 85 21W
Summerville, *S.C., U.S.A.* **152 B9** 33 1N 80 11W
Summit, *U.S.A.* **144 E10** 63 20N 149 7W
Summit Lake, *Canada* **142 C4** 54 20N 122 40W
Summit Peak, *U.S.A.* **159 H10** 37 21N 106 42W
Sumner, *N.Z.* **131 D7** 43 35 S 172 48 E
Sumner, *Ill., U.S.A.* **157 F9** 38 42N 87 53W
Sumner, *Iowa, U.S.A.* **156 B4** 42 51N 92 6W
Sumner, *Wash., U.S.A.* **160 C4** 47 12N 122 14W
Sumner, L., *N.Z.* **131 C7** 42 42 S 172 15 E
Sumoto, *Japan* **72 C6** 34 21N 134 54 E
Sumpangbinangae, *Indonesia* **82 B1** 4 24 S 119 36 E
Šumperk, *Czech Rep.* **35 B9** 49 59N 16 59 E
Sumprabum, *Burma* **90 B6** 26 33N 97 36 E
Sumqayıt, *Azerbaijan* **61 K9** 40 34N 49 38 E
Sumsar, *Kyrgyzstan* **65 C5** 41 18N 71 19 E
Sumter, *U.S.A.* **152 B9** 33 55N 80 21W
Sumy, *Ukraine* **59 G8** 50 57N 34 50 E
Sun City, *S. Africa* **116 D4** 25 17 S 27 3 E
Sun City, *Ariz., U.S.A.* **159 K7** 33 36N 112 17W
Sun City, *Calif., U.S.A.* **161 M9** 33 42N 117 11W
Sun City Center, *U.S.A.* **153 H7** 27 43N 82 18W
Sun Lakes, *U.S.A.* **159 K8** 33 10N 111 52W
Sun Prairie, *U.S.A.* **156 A7** 43 11N 89 13W
Sun Valley, *U.S.A.* **158 E6** 43 42N 114 21W
Sunagawa, *Japan* **70 C10** 43 29N 141 55 E
Sunan, *N. Korea* **75 E13** 39 15N 125 40 E
Sunart, L., *U.K.* **22 E3** 56 42N 5 43W

Sunburst, *U.S.A.* **158 B8** 48 53N 111 55W
Sunbury, *Australia* ... **129 D6** 37 35 S 144 44 E
Sunbury, *U.S.A.* **151 F8** 40 52N 76 48W
Sunchales, *Argentina* . **174 C3** 30 58 S 61 35W
Suncho Corral,
Argentina .... **174 B3** 27 55 S 63 27W
Sunch'ŏn, *S. Korea* ... **75 G14** 34 52N 127 31 E
Suncook, *U.S.A.* **151 C13** 43 8N 71 27W
Sunda, Selat, *Indonesia* **84 D3** 6 20 S 105 30 E
Sunda Is., *Indonesia* .. **62 K14** 5 0 S 105 0 E
Sunda Str. = Sunda,
Selat, *Indonesia* .... **84 D3** 6 20 S 105 30 E
Sundance, *Canada* ... **143 B10** 56 32N 94 4W
Sundance, *U.S.A.* **154 C2** 44 24N 104 23W
Sundar Nagar, *India* .. **92 D7** 31 32N 76 53 E
Sundarbans, *Asia* .... **90 E2** 22 0N 89 0 E
Sundarbans △, *India* .. **93 J13** 22 0N 88 45 E
Sundargarh, *India* .... **94 C7** 22 4N 84 5 E
Sundays = Sondags ↝,
S. Africa .... **116 E4** 33 44 S 25 51 E
Sunderland, *Canada* .. **150 B5** 44 16N 79 4W
Sunderland, *U.K.* **20 C6** 54 55N 1 23W
Sundi Lutete,
*Dem. Rep. of
the Congo* .... **115 C2** 4 34 S 14 14 E
Sundown △, *Australia* **127 D5** 28 49 S 151 38 E
Sundre, *Canada* **142 C6** 51 49N 114 38W
Sunds, *Denmark* ..... **17 H3** 56 13N 9 1 E
Sundsjö, *Sweden* .... **16 B11** 62 23N 17 17 E
Sundsvallsbukten,
Sweden .... **16 B11** 62 21N 17 25 E
Sung Hei, *Vietnam* ... **87 G6** 10 20N 106 2 E
Sungai Acheh, *Malaysia* **87 c** 5 8N 100 30 E
Sungai Kolok, *Thailand* **87 J3** 6 2N 101 58 E
Sungai Lembing,
Malaysia .... **87 L4** 3 55N 103 3 E
Sungai Petani, *Malaysia* **87 K3** 5 37N 100 30 E
Sungaigerong,
Indonesia .... **84 C2** 2 59 S 104 52 E
Sungailiat, *Indonesia* . **84 C3** 1 51 S 106 8 E
Sungaipenuh, *Indonesia* **84 C2** 2 1 S 101 20 E
Sungaitiram, *Indonesia* **85 C5** 0 45 S 117 8 E
Sungari = Songhua
Jiang ↝, *China* .... **69 B8** 47 45N 132 30 E
Sungguminasa,
Indonesia .... **82 C1** 5 17 S 119 30 E
Sunghua Chiang =
Songhua Jiang ↝,
China .... **69 B8** 47 45N 132 30 E
Sungikai, *Sudan* ..... **107 E2** 12 20N 29 51 E
Sungu, *Dem. Rep. of
the Congo* .... **114 C3** 1 5 S 17 21 E
Sungurlu, *Turkey* .... **100 B6** 40 12N 34 21 E
Sunja, *Croatia* ...... **45 C13** 45 21N 16 35 E
Sunland Park, *U.S.A.* . **159 L10** 31 50N 106 40W
Sunnansjö, *Sweden* ... **16 D8** 60 13N 14 58 E
Sunndalsøra, *Norway* . **18 B5** 62 40N 8 33 E
Sunne, *Sweden* ...... **16 E7** 59 52N 13 5 E
Sunnemo, *Sweden* ... **16 E7** 59 53N 13 44 E
Sunnfjord, *Norway* ... **18 C2** 61 35N 5 45 E
Sunnmøre, *Norway* ... **18 B3** 62 35N 6 30 E
Sunnyside, *U.S.A.* ... **158 C3** 46 20N 120 0W
Sunnyvale, *U.S.A.* ... **160 H4** 37 23N 122 2W
Sunrise Manor, *U.S.A.* . **159 H6** 36 12N 115 3W
Sunset Beach, *U.S.A.* . **145 J13** 21 40N 158 3W
Suntar, *Russia* ...... **67 C12** 62 15N 117 30 E
Suntrana, *U.S.A.* **144 E10** 63 52N 148 51W
Sunyani, *Ghana* **112 D4** 7 21N 2 22W
Suō-Nada, *Japan* .... **72 D3** 33 50N 131 30 E
Suomenselkä, *Finland* **14 E21** 62 52N 24 0 E
Suomi = Finland ■,
Europe .... **14 E22** 63 0N 27 0 E
Suomussalmi, *Finland* **14 D23** 64 54N 29 10 E
Suoyarvi, *Russia* .... **58 A7** 62 3N 32 20 E
Supai, *U.S.A.* **159 H7** 36 15N 112 41W
Supamo ↝, *Venezuela* **169 B5** 6 48N 61 50W
Supaul, *India* .... **93 F12** 26 10N 86 40 E
Supe, *Peru* .... **172 C2** 11 0 S 77 30W
Superagüi △, *Brazil* .. **171 G2** 25 6 S 48 18W
Superior, *Ariz., U.S.A.* **159 K8** 33 18N 111 6W
Superior, *Mont., U.S.A.* **158 C6** 47 12N 114 53W
Superior, *Nebr., U.S.A.* **154 E5** 40 1N 98 4W
Superior, *Wis., U.S.A.* . **154 B8** 46 44N 92 6W
Superior, L., *N. Amer.* **140 C2** 47 0N 87 0W
Supetar, *Croatia* .... **45 E13** 43 25N 16 32 E
Suphan Buri, *Thailand* **86 E3** 14 14N 100 10 E
Suphan Dağı, *Turkey* . **101 C10** 38 54N 42 48 E
Supiori, *Indonesia* ... **83 B5** 1 0 S 136 0 E
Supraśl, *Poland* ..... **55 E10** 53 13N 23 19 E
Supraśl ↝, *Poland* ... **55 E9** 53 11N 22 57 E
Supung Shuiku, *China* **75 D13** 40 35N 124 50 E
Sūq 'Abs, *Yemen* .... **98 D3** 16 0N 43 12 E
Sūq Suwayq, *Si. Arabia* **96 E3** 24 23N 38 27 E
Suqian, *China* ...... **75 H10** 33 54N 118 8 E
Suquṭra = Socotra,
Yemen .... **99 D6** 12 30N 54 0 E
Sūr, *Lebanon* .... **103 B4** 33 19N 35 16 E
Ṣūr, *Oman* .... **99 B7** 22 34N 59 32 E
Sur, C., *Chile* ...... **172 b** 27 12 S 109 26W
Sur, Pt., *U.S.A.* **160 J5** 36 18N 121 54W
Sura ↝, *Russia* ..... **60 C8** 56 6N 46 0 E
Surab, *Pakistan* ..... **91 C2** 28 25N 66 15 E
Surabaja = Surabaya,
Indonesia .... **85 D4** 7 17 S 112 45 E
Surabaya, *Indonesia* .. **85 D4** 7 17 S 112 45 E
Surahammar, *Sweden* . **16 E10** 59 43N 16 13 E
Suraia, *Romania* ..... **53 E12** 45 40N 27 25 E
Surakarta, *Indonesia* . **85 D4** 7 35 S 110 48 E
Surakhany, *Azerbaijan* **61 K10** 40 25N 50 1 E
Šurany, *Slovak Rep.* .. **35 C11** 48 6N 18 10 E
Surat, *Australia* ..... **127 D4** 27 10 S 149 6 E
Surat, *India* .... **94 D1** 21 12N 72 55 E
Surat Thani, *Thailand* **87 H2** 9 6N 99 20 E
Suratgarh, *India* ..... **92 E5** 29 18N 73 55 E
Suraż, *Poland* .... **55 F9** 52 57N 22 57 E
Surazh, *Belarus* ..... **58 E6** 55 25N 30 44 E
Surazh, *Russia* ..... **59 F7** 53 5N 32 27 E
Surduc, *Romania* ..... **53 C8** 47 15N 23 25 E
Surduc Pasul, *Romania* **53 E8** 45 21N 23 23 E
Surdulica, *Serbia & M.* **50 D6** 42 41N 22 11 E
Surendranagar, *India* . **92 H4** 22 45N 71 40 E
Surf, *U.S.A.* **161 L6** 34 41N 120 36W
Surfers Paradise,
Australia .... **127 D5** 28 0 S 153 25 E
Surfside, *U.S.A.* **153 K9** 25 53N 80 8W
Surgana, *India* ...... **94 D1** 20 34N 73 37 E
Surgères, *France* **28 B3** 46 7N 0 47W
Surgut, *Russia* ...... **66 C8** 61 14N 73 20 E
Súria, *Spain* .... **40 D6** 41 50N 1 45 E
Suriapet, *India* ..... **94 F4** 17 10N 79 40 E
Surigao, *Phil.* ...... **81 G5** 9 47N 125 29 E
Surigao del Norte □,
Phil. .... **81 G5** 10 0N 125 40 E
Surigao del Sur □, *Phil.* **81 G6** 8 45N 126 0 E
Surigao Strait, *Phil.* ... **81 F5** 10 15N 125 23 E
Surin, *Thailand* ..... **86 E4** 14 50N 103 34 E
Surin Nua, Ko,
Thailand .... **87 H1** 9 30N 97 55 E
Surinam = Suriname ■,
S. Amer. **169 C6** 4 0N 56 0W
Suriname ■, *S. Amer.* . **169 C6** 4 0N 56 0W
Suriname ↝, *Suriname* **169 B6** 5 50N 55 15W
Surjagarh, *India* ..... **94 E5** 19 36N 80 25 E
Surkhandarya ↝,
Uzbekistan .... **65 E3** 37 12N 67 20 E
Surma ↝, *Bangla.* ... **90 C3** 24 34N 91 14 E
Sürmaq, *Iran* .... **97 D7** 31 3N 52 48 E
Sürmene, *Turkey* .... **101 B9** 41 0N 40 1 E
Surna ↝, *Norway* .... **18 B5** 62 59N 8 40 E
Surnadalsøra, *Norway* **18 B5** 62 58N 8 40 E
Surovikino, *Russia* ... **61 F6** 48 32N 42 55 E
Surrency, *U.S.A.* **152 D7** 31 44N 82 12W
Surrey, *Canada* **160 A4** 49 10N 122 54W
Surrey □, *U.K.* **21 F7** 51 15N 0 31W
Sursand, *India* ...... **93 F11** 26 39N 85 43 E
Sursar ↝, *India* ..... **93 F12** 26 14N 87 3 E
Sursee, *Switz.* ...... **32 B6** 47 11N 8 6 E
Sursk, *Russia* ...... **60 D7** 53 3N 45 40 E
Surskoye, *Russia* .... **60 C8** 54 30N 46 44 E
Surt, *Libya* .... **108 B3** 31 11N 16 39 E
Surt □, *Libya* ...... **108 B3** 30 0N 17 30 E
Surt, Al Hammadah al,
Libya .... **108 C3** 30 0N 17 50 E
Surt, Khalīj, *Libya* ... **108 B3** 31 40N 18 30 E
Surtanahu, *Pakistan* .. **92 F4** 26 22N 70 0 E
Surte, *Sweden* ...... **17 G6** 57 50N 12 1 E
Surtsey, *Iceland* **11 D6** 63 20N 20 30W
Surubim, *Brazil* ..... **170 C4** 7 50 S 35 45W
Sürüç, *Turkey* ...... **101 D8** 36 58N 38 25 E
Surud Ad, *Somali Rep.* **120 B3** 10 42N 47 9 E
Suruga-Wan, *Japan* .. **73 C10** 34 45N 138 30 E
Surumu ↝, *Brazil* ... **169 C5** 3 22N 60 19W
Susa = Sousse, *Tunisia* **108 A2** 35 50N 10 38 E
Susa, *Italy* .... **44 C4** 45 8N 7 3 E
Suså ↝, *Denmark* ... **17 J5** 55 12N 11 42 E
Sušac, *Croatia* ...... **45 F13** 42 46N 16 30 E
Susak, *Croatia* ...... **45 D11** 44 30N 14 18 E
Susaki, *Japan* .... **72 D5** 33 22N 133 17 E
Susam-Adasi = Sámos,
Greece .... **49 D8** 37 45N 26 50 E
Susamyrtau, Khrebet =
Suusamyr Kyrka
Tooloru, *Kyrgyzstan* **65 B6** 42 8N 73 15 E
Süsangerd, *Iran* ..... **97 D6** 31 35N 48 6 E
Susanville, *U.S.A.* ... **158 F3** 40 25N 120 39W
Susch, *Switz.* .... **33 C10** 46 46N 10 5 E
Suşehri, *Turkey* ..... **101 B8** 40 10N 38 6 E
Sušice, *Czech Rep.* .. **34 B6** 49 17N 13 30 E
Susleni, *Moldova* .... **53 C13** 47 25N 28 59 E
Susner, *India* .... **92 H7** 23 57N 76 5 E
Susong, *China* ...... **77 B11** 30 10N 116 5 E
Susquehanna, *U.S.A.* . **151 E9** 41 57N 75 36W
Susquehanna ↝,
U.S.A. **151 G8** 39 33N 76 5W
Susques, *Argentina* ... **174 A2** 23 35 S 66 25W
Sussex, *Canada* **141 C6** 45 45N 65 37W
Sussex, *U.S.A.* **151 E10** 41 13N 74 37W
Sussex, E. □, *U.K.* ... **21 G8** 51 0N 0 20 E
Sussex, W. □, *U.K.* .. **21 G7** 51 0N 0 30W
Sussex Inlet, *Australia* **129 C9** 35 10 S 150 36 E
Sustut ↝, *Canada* ... **142 B3** 56 20N 127 30W
Susuman, *Russia* .... **67 C15** 62 47N 148 10 E
Susunu, *Indonesia* ... **83 B4** 3 7 S 133 39 E
Susurluk, *Turkey* .... **49 B10** 39 54N 28 8 E
Susuz, *Turkey* ...... **101 B10** 40 46N 43 8 E
Susz, *Poland* .... **54 E6** 53 44N 19 20 E
Sütçüler, *Turkey* .... **100 D4** 37 29N 30 57 E
Şuţeşti, *Romania* .... **53 E12** 45 13N 27 27 E
Sutherland, *Australia* . **129 C9** 34 2 S 151 4 E
Sutherland, *S. Africa* . **116 E3** 32 24 S 20 40 E
Sutherland, *U.K.* **22 C4** 58 12N 4 50W
Sutherland, *U.S.A.* ... **154 E4** 41 10N 101 8W
Sutherland Falls, *N.Z.* **131 E2** 44 48 S 167 46 E
Sutherlin, *U.S.A.* **158 E2** 43 23N 123 19W
Suthri, *India* .... **92 H3** 23 3N 68 55 E
Sutjeska △, *Bos.-H.* .. **52 G3** 43 50N 18 32 E
Sutlej ↝, *Pakistan* ... **91 C3** 29 23N 71 3 E
Sutter, *U.S.A.* **160 F5** 39 10N 121 45W
Sutter Creek, *U.S.A.* . **160 G6** 38 24N 120 48W
Sutton, *Canada* **151 A12** 45 6N 72 37W
Sutton, *N.Z.* .... **131 F5** 45 34 S 170 8 E
Sutton, *Nebr., U.S.A.* . **154 E6** 40 36N 97 52W
Sutton, *W. Va., U.S.A.* **148 F5** 38 40N 80 43W
Sutton ↝, *Canada* ... **140 A3** 55 15N 83 45W
Sutton Coldfield, *U.K.* **21 E6** 52 35N 1 49W
Sutton in Ashfield, *U.K.* **20 D6** 53 8N 1 16W
Sutton L., *Canada* ... **140 B3** 54 15N 84 42W
Suttor ↝, *Australia* .. **126 C4** 21 36 S 147 2 E
Suttsu, *Japan* .... **70 C10** 42 48N 140 14 E
Sutwik I., *U.S.A.* **144 H8** 56 34N 157 12W
Susamyr, *Kyrgyzstan* **65 B6** 42 12N 73 58 E
Suusamyr Kyrka
Tooloru, *Kyrgyzstan* **65 B6** 42 8N 73 15 E
Suva, *Fiji* .... **133 B2** 18 6 S 178 30 E
Suva Gora, *Macedonia* **50 E5** 41 45N 21 3 E
Suva Planina,
Serbia & M. .... **50 C6** 43 10N 22 5 E
Suva Reka, *Serbia & M.* **50 D4** 42 21N 20 50 E
Suvorov, *Russia* ..... **58 E9** 54 7N 36 30 E
Suvorov Is. = Suwarrow
Is., *Cook Is.* .... **135 J11** 13 15 S 163 5W
Suvorove, *Ukraine* ... **53 E13** 45 35N 28 59 E
Suvorovo, *Bulgaria* .. **51 C11** 43 20N 27 35 E
Suwa, *Japan* .... **73 A10** 36 2N 138 8 E
Suwa-Ko, *Japan* .... **73 A10** 36 3N 138 5 E
Suwałki, *Poland* ..... **54 D9** 54 8N 22 59 E
Suwana, *Indonesia* ... **79 K18** 8 44 S 115 36 E
Suwanee, *U.S.A.* **152 A5** 34 3N 84 4W
Suwannaphum,
Thailand .... **86 E4** 15 33N 103 47 E
Suwannee, *U.S.A.* ... **153 F6** 29 20N 83 9W
Suwannee ↝, *U.S.A.* . **153 F6** 29 17N 83 10W
Suwannee L., *U.S.A.* . **153 F6** 29 20N 83 15W
Suwanose-Jima, *Japan* **71 K4** 29 38N 129 43 E
Suwarrow Is., *Cook Is.* **135 J11** 13 15 S 163 5W
Suwayq aş Şuqban, *Iraq* **96 D5** 31 32N 46 7 E
Suweis, Khalîg el, *Egypt* **106 J8** 28 40N 33 0 E
Suweis, Qanâ es, *Egypt* **106 H8** 31 0N 32 20 E
Suwŏn, *S. Korea* .... **75 F14** 37 17N 127 1 E
Suzak = Sosaq,
Kazakhstan .... **65 A4** 44 9N 68 27 E
Suzaka, *Japan* ...... **73 A10** 36 39N 138 19 E
Suzdal, *Russia* ...... **58 D11** 56 29N 40 26 E
Suzhou, *Anhui, China* **74 H9** 33 41N 116 59 E
Suzhou, *Jiangsu, China* **77 B13** 31 19N 120 38 E
Suzu, *Japan* .... **71 F8** 37 25N 137 17 E
Suzu-Misaki, *Japan* .. **71 F8** 37 31N 137 21 E
Suzuka, *Japan* ...... **73 C8** 34 55N 136 36 E
Suzuka-Sammyaku,
Japan .... **73 B8** 35 5N 136 30 E
Suzzara, *Italy* ...... **44 D7** 44 59N 10 45 E
Svalbard, *Arctic* ..... **6 B8** 78 0N 17 0 E
Svalbard Radio =
Longyearbyen,
Svalbard .... **6 B8** 78 13N 15 40 E
Svalbarð,
*Norður-þingeyjarsýsla,
Iceland* **11 A11** 66 12N 15 43W
Svalbarð,
*Suður-þingeyjarsýsla,
Iceland* **11 B8** 65 45N 18 5W
Svalöv, *Sweden* ..... **17 J7** 55 57N 13 8 E
Svalyava, *Ukraine* .... **52 B7** 48 33N 22 59 E
Svaneke, *Denmark* ... **17 J9** 55 8N 15 8 E
Svängsta, *Sweden* ... **17 H8** 56 16N 14 47 E
Svanskog, *Sweden* ... **16 E6** 59 11N 12 33 E
Svappavaara, *Sweden* . **14 C19** 67 40N 21 3 E
Svärdsjö, *Sweden* .... **16 D9** 60 45N 15 54 E
Svarstad, *Norway* .... **18 E6** 59 27N 9 56 E
Svartå, *Sweden* ..... **16 E8** 59 8N 14 32 E
Svartárkot, *Iceland* ... **11 B9** 65 20N 17 15W
Svartevatn, *Norway* .. **18 E3** 59 10N 6 56 E
Svartisen, *Norway* ... **14 C15** 66 40N 13 59 E
Svartvik, *Sweden* .... **16 B11** 62 19N 17 24 E
Svatove, *Ukraine* .... **59 H10** 49 22N 38 15 E
Svatovo = Svatove,
Ukraine .... **59 H10** 49 22N 38 15 E
Svatsum, *Norway* .... **18 C6** 61 20N 9 50 E
Svay Chek, *Cambodia* **86 F4** 13 48N 102 58 E
Svay Rieng, *Cambodia* **87 G5** 11 9N 105 45 E
Svealand □, *Sweden* .. **16 D9** 60 20N 15 0 E
Svedala, *Sweden* .... **17 J7** 55 30N 13 15 E
Sveg, *Sweden* .... **16 B8** 62 2N 14 21 E
Sveindal, *Norway* .... **18 F4** 58 29N 7 30 E
Sveinseyri, *Iceland* ... **11 B3** 65 38N 23 51W
Svelgen, *Norway* .... **18 C2** 61 46N 5 17 E
Svelvik, *Norway* ..... **18 E7** 59 37N 10 24 E
Svendborg, *Denmark* . **17 J4** 55 4N 10 35 E
Svene, *Norway* ...... **18 E6** 59 45N 9 31 E
Svenljunga, *Sweden* .. **17 G7** 57 29N 13 5 E
Svenstavik, *Sweden* .. **16 B8** 62 45N 14 26 E
Svenstrup, *Denmark* .. **17 H3** 56 58N 9 50 E
Sverdlovsk =
Yekaterinburg,
Russia .... **64 C8** 56 50N 60 30 E
Sverdlovsk, *Ukraine* .. **59 H10** 48 5N 39 47 E
Sverdrup Is., *Canada* . **6 B3** 79 0N 97 0W
Sverige = Sweden ■,
Europe .... **15 G16** 57 0N 15 0 E
Svetac, *Croatia* ..... **45 E12** 43 3N 15 43 E
Sveti Ivan = Zelina,
Croatia .... **45 C13** 45 57N 16 16 E
Sveti Nikola, Prokhad,
Europe .... **50 C6** 43 27N 22 6 E
Sveti Nikole,
Macedonia .... **50 E5** 41 51N 21 56 E
Sveti Rok, *Croatia* ... **45 D12** 44 22N 15 39 E
Sveti Vrach =
Sandanski, *Bulgaria* **50 E7** 41 35N 23 16 E
Svetlaya, *Russia* .... **70 A9** 46 33N 138 18 E
Svetlogorsk =
Svyetlahorsk, *Belarus* **59 F5** 52 38N 29 46 E
Svetlogorsk, *Russia* .. **54 D7** 54 56N 20 10 E
Svetlograd, *Russia* ... **61 H6** 45 25N 42 58 E
Svetlovodsk =
Svitlovodsk, *Ukraine* **59 H7** 49 2N 33 13 E
Svetlyy, *Russia* ..... **54 D7** 54 41N 20 8 E
Svetlyy, *Russia* ..... **64 F8** 50 48N 60 51 E
Svidník, *Slovak Rep.* .. **35 B14** 49 20N 21 37 E
Svignaskarð, *Iceland* .. **11 C5** 64 40N 21 42W
Svilaja Planina, *Croatia* **45 E13** 43 49N 16 31 E
Svilajnac, *Serbia & M.* **50 B5** 44 15N 21 11 E
Svilengrad, *Bulgaria* .. **51 E10** 41 49N 26 12 E
Svinafell, *Iceland* **11 D10** 63 59N 16 51W
Svir ↝, *Russia* ..... **58 B7** 60 30N 32 48 E
Sviritsa, *Russia* ..... **58 B7** 60 29N 32 51 E
Svishtov, *Bulgaria* ... **51 C9** 43 36N 25 23 E
Svislach, *Belarus* .... **55 E11** 53 3N 24 2 E
Svitava ↝, *Czech Rep.* **35 B9** 49 11N 16 37 E
Svitavy, *Czech Rep.* .. **35 B9** 49 47N 16 28 E
Svitlovodsk, *Ukraine* . **59 H7** 49 2N 33 13 E
Svizzer △, *Switz.* .... **33 C10** 46 40N 10 10 E
Svizzera =
Switzerland ■,
Europe .... **32 D6** 46 30N 8 0 E
Svobodnyy, *Russia* ... **67 D13** 51 20N 128 0 E
Svoge, *Bulgaria* ..... **50 D7** 42 59N 23 23 E
Svolvær, *Norway* .... **14 B16** 68 15N 14 34 E
Svorkmo, *Norway* .... **18 A6** 63 10N 9 46 E
Svoronáta, *Greece* ... **39 C2** 38 7N 20 31 E
Svratka ↝, *Czech Rep.* **35 B9** 49 11N 16 38 E
Svrljig, *Serbia & M.* .. **50 C6** 43 25N 22 6 E
Svullrya, *Norway* .... **18 D9** 60 25N 12 23 E
Svyatogorovsky
Rudnik = Dobropole,
Ukraine .... **59 H9** 48 25N 37 2 E
Svyetlahorsk, *Belarus* . **59 F5** 52 38N 29 46 E
Swa, *Burma* .... **90 F6** 19 15N 96 17 E
Swa Tende, *Dem. Rep.
of the Congo* ...... **115 D3** 7 9 S 17 7 E
Swabian Alps =
Schwäbische Alb,
Germany .... **31 G5** 48 20N 9 30 E
Swaffham, *U.K.* ..... **21 E8** 52 39N 0 42 E
Swains I., *Amer. Samoa* **135 J11** 11 11 S 171 4W
Swainsboro, *U.S.A.* ... **152 C7** 32 36N 82 20W
Swakop ↝, *Namibia* . **116 C2** 22 38 S 14 36 E
Swakopmund, *Namibia* **116 C1** 22 37 S 14 30 E
Swale ↝, *U.K.* **20 C6** 54 5N 1 20W
Swamihalli, *India* .... **95 G3** 14 52N 76 38 E
Swan ↝, *Australia* ... **125 F2** 32 3 S 115 45 E
Swan ↝, *Canada* **143 C8** 52 30N 100 45W
Swan Hill, *Australia* .. **128 C5** 35 20 S 143 33 E
Swan Hills, *Canada* .. **142 C5** 54 43N 115 24W
Swan Is. = Santanilla,
Is., *Honduras* **164 C3** 17 22N 83 57W
Swan L., *Canada* **143 C8** 52 30N 100 40W
Swan Peak, *U.S.A.* ... **158 C7** 47 43N 113 38W
Swan Ra., *U.S.A.* **158 C7** 48 0N 113 45W
Swan Reach, *Australia* **128 C3** 34 35 S 139 37 E
Swan River, *Canada* .. **143 C8** 52 10N 101 16W
Swanage, *U.K.* **21 G6** 50 36N 1 58W
Swansea, *N.S.W.,
Australia* .... **129 B9** 33 3 S 151 35 E
Swansea, *Tas. Australia* **127 G4** 42 8 S 148 4 E
Swansea, *Canada* **150 C5** 43 38N 79 28W
Swansea, *U.K.* **21 F4** 51 37N 3 57W
Swansea, *U.S.A.* **152 B8** 33 44N 81 6W
Swansea □, *U.K.* **21 F3** 51 38N 4 3W
Swanton, *U.S.A.* **157 C13** 41 35N 83 53W
Swar ↝, *Pakistan* .... **93 B5** 34 40N 72 5 E
Swartberge, *S. Africa* . **116 E3** 33 20 S 22 0 E
Swartmodder, *S. Africa* **116 D3** 28 1 S 20 32 E
Swartnossob ↝,
Namibia .... **116 C2** 23 8 S 18 42 E
Swartruggens, *S. Africa* **116 D4** 25 39 S 26 42 E
Swarzędz, *Poland* .... **55 F4** 52 25N 17 4 E
Swastika, *Canada* **140 C3** 48 7N 80 6W
Swatow = Shantou,
China .... **77 F11** 23 18N 116 40 E
Swaziland ■, *Africa* .. **117 D5** 26 30 S 31 30 E
Sweden ■, *Europe* ... **15 G16** 57 0N 15 0 E
Swedru, *Ghana* **113 D4** 5 32N 0 41W
Sweet Home, *U.S.A.* .. **158 D2** 44 24N 122 44W
Sweet Springs, *U.S.A.* . **156 F3** 38 58N 93 25W
Sweetgrass, *U.S.A.* ... **158 B8** 48 59N 111 58W
Sweetwater, *Nev.,
U.S.A.* **160 G7** 38 27N 119 9W
Sweetwater, *Tenn.,
U.S.A.* **149 H3** 35 36N 84 28W
Sweetwater, *Tex.,
U.S.A.* **155 J4** 32 28N 100 25W
Sweetwater ↝, *U.S.A.* **158 E10** 42 31N 107 2W
Swellendam, *S. Africa* **116 E3** 34 1 S 20 26 E
Swider ↝, *Poland* ... **55 F8** 52 6N 21 14 E
Świdnica, *Poland* .... **55 H3** 50 50N 16 30 E
Świdnik, *Poland* ..... **55 G9** 51 13N 22 39 E
Świdwin, *Poland* ..... **54 E2** 53 47N 15 49 E
Świebodzice, *Poland* .. **55 H3** 50 51N 16 20 E
Świebodzin, *Poland* .. **55 F2** 52 15N 15 31 E
Świecie, *Poland* ..... **54 E5** 53 25N 18 30 E
Świerzawa, *Poland* ... **55 G2** 51 1N 15 54 E
Świętokrzyski △,
Poland .... **55 H7** 50 53N 20 59 E
Świętokrzyskie □,
Poland .... **55 H7** 50 45N 20 45 E
Świętokrzyskie, Góry,
Poland .... **55 H7** 51 0N 20 30 E
Swift Current, *Canada* **143 C7** 50 20N 107 45W
Swift Current ↝,
Canada **143 C7** 50 38N 107 44W
Swifts Creek, *Australia* **129 D7** 37 17 S 147 44 E
Swilly, L., *Ireland* **23 A4** 55 12N 7 33W
Swindon, *U.K.* **21 F6** 51 34N 1 46W
Swindon □, *U.K.* **21 F6** 51 34N 1 46W
Swinemünde =
Świnoujście, *Poland* **54 E1** 53 54N 14 16 E
Swinford, *Ireland* **23 C3** 53 57N 8 58W
Świnoujście, *Poland* .. **54 E1** 53 54N 14 16 E
Switzerland ■, *Europe* **32 D6** 46 30N 8 0 E
Swords, *Ireland* **23 C5** 53 28N 6 13W
Swoyerville, *U.S.A.* ... **151 E9** 41 18N 75 53W
Syasstroy, *Russia* .... **58 B7** 60 9N 32 33 E
Sycamore, *Ill., U.S.A.* . **157 C8** 41 59N 88 41W
Sycamore, *Ohio, U.S.A.* **157 D13** 40 57N 83 10W
Sychevka, *Russia* .... **58 E8** 55 59N 34 16 E
Syców, *Poland* ...... **55 G4** 51 19N 17 40 E
Sydenham ↝, *Canada* **150 D2** 42 33N 82 25W
Sydney, *Australia* .... **129 B9** 33 53 S 151 10 E
Sydney, *Canada* **141 C7** 46 7N 60 7W
Sydney L., *Canada* ... **143 C10** 50 41N 94 25W
Sydney Mines, *Canada* **141 C7** 46 18N 60 15W
Sydprøven = Alluitsup
Paa, *Greenland* **10 E6** 60 30N 45 35W
Sydra, G. of = Surt,
Khalīj, *Libya* ...... **108 B3** 31 40N 18 30 E
Syeverodonetsk,
Ukraine .... **59 H10** 48 58N 38 35 E
Syfteland, *Norway* ... **18 D2** 60 14N 5 27 E
Syke, *Germany* ...... **30 C4** 52 55N 8 50 E
Sykesville, *U.S.A.* **150 E6** 41 3N 78 50W
Sykkylven, *Norway* ... **18 B3** 62 23N 6 35 E
Syktyvkar, *Russia* .... **56 B9** 61 45N 50 40 E
Sylacauga, *U.S.A.* **152 B3** 33 10N 86 15W
Sylarna, *Sweden* ..... **18 A9** 63 2N 12 13 E
Sylhet, *Bangla.* ...... **90 C3** 24 54N 91 52 E
Sylt, *Germany* ...... **30 A4** 54 54N 8 22 E
Sylte, *Norway* ...... **18 B4** 62 18N 7 17 E
Sylva ↝, *Russia* ..... **64 B6** 58 0N 56 54 E
Sylvan Beach, *U.S.A.* . **151 C9** 43 12N 75 44W
Sylvan Lake, *Canada* . **142 C6** 52 20N 114 3W
Sylvania, *Ga., U.S.A.* . **152 C8** 32 45N 81 38W
Sylvania, *Ohio, U.S.A.* **157 C13** 41 43N 83 42W
Sylvester, *U.S.A.* **152 D6** 31 32N 83 50W
Sym, *Russia* .... **66 C9** 60 20N 88 18 E
Symón, *Mexico* **162 C4** 24 42N 102 35W
Synelnykove, *Ukraine* **59 H8** 48 25N 35 30 E
Synevyr △, *Ukraine* .. **53 B8** 48 30N 23 40 E
Synevyrska Polyana,
Ukraine .... **53 B8** 48 35N 23 41 E
Synnfjell, *Norway* .... **18 C6** 61 5N 9 46 E
Synnott Ra., *Australia* **124 C4** 16 30 S 125 20 E
Synyak, *Ukraine* ..... **52 B7** 48 35N 22 51 E
Syowa, *Antarctica* ... **7 C5** 68 50 S 12 0 E
Syracuse = Siracusa,
Italy .... **47 E8** 37 4N 15 17 E
Syracuse, *Ind., U.S.A.* . **157 C11** 41 26N 85 45W
Syracuse, *Kans., U.S.A.* **155 G4** 37 59N 101 45W
Syracuse, *N.Y., U.S.A.* **151 C8** 43 3N 76 9W
Syracuse, *Nebr., U.S.A.* **154 E6** 40 39N 96 11W
Syrdarinsky = Syrdarya,
Uzbekistan .... **65 C4** 40 50N 68 40 E
Syrdarya, *Uzbekistan* . **65 C4** 40 50N 68 40 E
Syrdarya ↝,
Kazakhstan .... **66 E7** 46 3N 61 0 E
Syria ■, *Asia* .... **101 E8** 35 0N 38 0 E
Syriam, *Burma* ...... **90 G6** 16 44N 96 19 E
Syrian Desert = Shām,
Bādiyat ash, *Asia* .. **96 C3** 32 0N 40 0 E
Syrnovorossiysk =
Syrdarya, *Uzbekistan* **65 C4** 40 50N 68 40 E
Syros = Síros, *Greece* . **48 D6** 37 28N 24 57 E
Sysert, *Russia* ...... **64 C8** 56 29N 60 49 E
Sysslebäck, *Sweden* .. **16 D6** 60 44N 12 52 E
Syvde, *Norway* ..... **18 B2** 62 5N 5 44 E
Syzran, *Russia* ..... **60 D9** 53 12N 48 30 E
Szabolcs-Szatmár-
Bereg □, *Hungary* . **52 B6** 48 2N 21 45 E
Szadek, *Poland* ..... **55 G5** 51 41N 18 59 E
Szamocin, *Poland* .... **55 E4** 53 2N 17 7 E
Szamos ↝, *Hungary* .. **52 B7** 48 7N 22 20 E
Szamotuły, *Poland* ... **55 F3** 52 37N 16 33 E
Száraz ↝, *Hungary* .. **52 D6** 46 10N 21 15 E
Szarvas, *Hungary* .... **52 D5** 46 50N 20 38 E
Százhalombatta,
Hungary .... **52 C3** 47 20N 18 58 E
Szczawnica, *Poland* .. **55 J7** 49 26N 20 30 E
Szczebrzeszyn, *Poland* **55 H9** 50 42N 22 59 E
Szczecin, *Poland* .... **54 E1** 53 27N 14 27 E
Szczecinek, *Poland* .. **54 E3** 53 43N 16 41 E
Szczeciński, Zalew =
Stettiner Haff,
Germany .... **30 B10** 53 47N 14 15 E
Szczekociny, *Poland* .. **55 H6** 50 38N 19 48 E
Szczuczyn, *Poland* ... **54 E9** 53 36N 22 19 E
Szczyrk, *Poland* ..... **55 J6** 49 43N 19 2 E
Szczytna, *Poland* .... **55 H3** 50 25N 16 28 E
Szczytno, *Poland* .... **54 E7** 53 33N 21 0 E
Szechuan Basin =
Sichuan Pendi, *China* **76 B5** 31 0N 105 0 E
Szechwan = Sichuan □,
China .... **76 B5** 30 30N 103 0 E
Szécsény, *Hungary* ... **52 B4** 48 7N 19 30 E
Szeged, *Hungary* .... **52 D5** 46 16N 20 10 E
Szeghalom, *Hungary* .. **52 C6** 47 1N 21 10 E
Székesfehérvár,
Hungary .... **52 C3** 47 15N 18 25 E
Szekszárd, *Hungary* .. **52 D3** 46 22N 18 42 E
Szendrő, *Hungary* ... **52 B5** 48 24N 20 41 E
Szentendre, *Hungary* . **52 C4** 47 39N 19 4 E
Szentes, *Hungary* .... **52 D5** 46 39N 20 21 E
Szentgotthárd, *Hungary* **52 D1** 46 58N 16 19 E
Szentlőrinc, *Hungary* . **52 D3** 46 3N 18 1 E
Szeping = Siping, *China* **75 C13** 43 8N 124 21 E
Szerencs, *Hungary* ... **52 B6** 48 10N 21 12 E
Szigetszentmiklós,
Hungary .... **52 C4** 47 21N 19 3 E
Szigetvár, *Hungary* ... **52 D2** 46 3N 17 46 E
Szikszó, *Hungary* .... **52 B5** 48 12N 20 56 E
Szklarska Poreba,
Poland .... **55 H2** 50 50N 15 33 E
Szkwa ↝, *Poland* .... **55 E8** 53 11N 21 43 E
Szlichtyngowa, *Poland* **55 G3** 51 42N 16 15 E
Szob, *Hungary* ...... **52 C3** 47 48N 18 53 E
Szolnok, *Hungary* .... **52 C5** 47 10N 20 15 E
Szombathely, *Hungary* **52 C1** 47 14N 16 38 E
Szprotawa, *Poland* ... **55 G2** 51 33N 15 35 E
Sztálinváros =
Dunaújváros,
Hungary .... **52 D3** 46 58N 18 57 E
Sztum, *Poland* ...... **54 E6** 53 55N 19 1 E
Sztutowo, *Poland* .... **54 D6** 54 20N 19 15 E
Szubin, *Poland* ..... **55 E4** 53 1N 17 45 E
Szydłowiec, *Poland* .. **55 G7** 51 15N 20 51 E
Szypliszki, *Poland* ... **54 D10** 54 17N 23 2 E

T

Ta Khli Khok, *Thailand* **86 E3** 15 18N 100 20 E
Ta Lai, *Vietnam* ..... **87 G6** 11 24N 107 23 E
Ta Pieh Shan = Dabie
Shan, *China* ...... **77 B10** 31 20N 115 20 E
Tab, *Hungary* ...... **52 D3** 46 44N 18 2 E
Tabacal, *Argentina* ... **174 A3** 23 15 S 64 15W
Tabaco, *Phil.* .... **80 E4** 13 22N 123 44 E
Tabagné, *Ivory C.* ... **112 D4** 7 59N 3 4W
Ţābah, *Si. Arabia* ... **96 E4** 26 55N 42 38 E
Tabajara, *Brazil* ..... **173 B5** 8 56 S 62 8W
Tabalo, *Papua N. G.* .. **132 A5** 1 24 S 149 40 E
Tabalos, *Peru* ...... **172 B2** 6 26 S 76 37W
Tabanan, *Indonesia* .. **79 K18** 8 32 S 115 8 E
Tabankort, *Niger* .... **113 B5** 17 44N 0 20 E
Tabar I., *Papua N. G.* . **132 B7** 2 56 S 152 0 E
Tabar Is., *Papua N. G.* **132 B7** 2 50 S 152 0 E
Tabarka, *Tunisia* .... **108 A1** 36 56N 8 46 E
Ţabas, *Khorāsān, Iran* **97 C9** 32 48N 60 12 E
Ţabas, *Khorāsān, Iran* **97 C8** 33 35N 56 55 E
Tabasará, Serranía de,
Panama **164 E3** 8 35N 81 40W
Tabasco □, *Mexico* ... **163 D6** 17 45N 93 30W
Tabāsīn, *Iran* .... **97 D8** 31 12N 57 54 E
Tabatinga, *Brazil* .... **172 A4** 4 16 S 69 56W
Tabatinga, Serra da,
Brazil .... **170 D3** 10 30 S 44 0W
Tabayin, *Burma* ..... **90 D5** 22 42N 95 20 E
Tabelbala, Kahal de,
Algeria **111 C4** 28 47N 2 0W
Tabelembila, *Algeria* . **111 D5** 24 43N 4 16 E
Taber, *Canada* **142 D6** 49 47N 112 8W
Taberg, *Sweden* ..... **17 G8** 57 40N 14 6 E
Taberg, *U.S.A.* **151 C9** 43 18N 75 37W
Tabi, *Angola* .... **115 D2** 8 10 S 13 18 E
Tabira, *Brazil* ...... **170 C4** 7 35 S 37 33W
Tabla, *Niger* .... **113 C5** 13 46N 3 1 E
Tablas de Daimiel △,
Spain **43 F7** 39 9N 3 40W
Tablas I., *Phil.* ...... **80 E4** 12 25N 122 2 E
Tablas Strait, *Phil.* ... **80 E3** 12 40N 121 48 E
Table, Pte. de la,
Réunion .... **121 c** 21 14 S 55 48 E
Table B., *Canada* **141 B8** 53 40N 56 25W
Table B., *S. Africa* ... **116 E2** 33 35 S 18 25 E
Table C., *N.Z.* ...... **130 F7** 39 6 S 178 0 E
Table Grove, *U.S.A.* .. **156 D6** 40 20N 90 27W
Table I., *Burma* ..... **95 G11** 14 12N 93 22 E
Table Mt., *S. Africa* .. **116 E2** 34 0 S 18 22 E
Table Rock L., *U.S.A.* . **155 G8** 36 36N 93 19W
Tabletop, Mt., *Australia* **126 C4** 23 24 S 147 11 E
Tabocal, *Brazil* ..... **169 D6** 2 42 S 57 40W
Tábor, *Czech Rep.* ... **34 B7** 49 25N 14 39 E
Tabora, *Tanzania* .... **118 D3** 5 2 S 32 50 E
Tabora □, *Tanzania* .. **118 D3** 5 0 S 33 0 E
Taboshar, *Tajikistan* .. **65 C4** 40 34N 69 38 E
Tabou, *Ivory C.* **112 E3** 4 30N 7 20W
Tabrīz, *Iran* .... **101 C12** 38 7N 46 20 E
Tabuaeran, *Kiribati* .. **135 G12** 3 51N 159 22W
Tabubil, *Papua N. G.* . **132 C1** 5 20 S 141 15 E
Tabuenca, *Spain* **40 D3** 41 42N 1 33W
Tabuk, *Phil.* .... **80 C3** 17 24N 121 25 E
Tabūk, *Si. Arabia* ... **96 D3** 28 23N 36 36 E
Taburno-
Camposauro ⌂, *Italy* **47 A7** 41 8N 14 37 E
Tabwemasana, Mt.,
Vanuatu .... **133 E4** 15 20 S 166 44 E
Täby, *Sweden* ...... **16 E12** 59 28N 18 4 E
Tacámbaro de
Codallos, *Mexico* ... **162 D4** 19 14N 101 28W
Tacarigua, Laguna de,
Venezuela **168 A4** 10 15N 65 50W
Tacheng, *China* ..... **68 B3** 46 40N 82 58 E
Tach'i, *Taiwan* ...... **77 E13** 24 46N 121 0 E
Tachia, *Taiwan* ..... **77 E13** 24 25N 120 28 E
Tachibana-Wan, *Japan* **72 E2** 32 45N 130 7 E
Tachikawa, *Japan* ... **73 B11** 35 42N 139 25 E
Tach'ing Shan = Daqing
Shan, *China* ...... **74 D6** 40 40N 111 0 E
Táchira □, *Venezuela* . **168 B3** 8 7N 72 15W
Tachov, *Czech Rep.* .. **34 B5** 49 47N 12 39 E
Tácina ↝, *Italy* ..... **47 D9** 38 57N 16 55 E
Tacloban, *Phil.* ...... **81 F5** 11 15N 124 58 E
Tacna, *Peru* .... **172 D3** 18 0 S 70 20W
Tacna □, *Peru* ...... **172 D3** 17 40 S 70 20W
Tacoma, *U.S.A.* **160 C4** 47 14N 122 26W
Tacopaya = Zudáñez,
Bolivia .... **173 D5** 19 6 S 64 44W
Tacuarembó, *Uruguay* **175 C4** 31 45 S 56 0W
Tacurong, *Phil.* ..... **81 H5** 6 40N 124 41 E
Tacutu ↝, *Brazil* **169 C5** 3 1N 60 29W
Tada-u, *Burma* ..... **90 E5** 21 49N 95 58 E
Tadahadi, *Solomon Is.* **133 N11** 10 18 S 161 35 E
Tademaït, Plateau du,
Algeria .... **111 C5** 28 30N 2 30 E
Tadent, O. ↝, *Algeria* **111 D6** 22 25N 6 40 E
Tadéra, *Niger* ...... **111 D6** 20 29N 8 18 E
Tadine, *N. Cal.* ..... **133 U21** 21 33 S 167 52 E
Tadio, L., *Ivory C.* ... **112 D3** 5 10N 5 15W
Tadjerdjeri, O. ↝,
Algeria .... **111 C6** 26 0N 8 0 E
Tadjerouna, *Algeria* .. **111 B5** 33 31N 2 3 E
Tadjettaret, O. ↝,
Algeria .... **111 D6** 21 20N 7 22 E
Tadjmout, *Laghouat,
Algeria* .... **111 B5** 33 52N 2 30 E
Tadjmout, *Saoura,
Algeria* .... **111 C5** 25 37N 3 48 E
Tadjoura, *Djibouti* ... **107 E5** 11 50N 42 55 E
Tadjoura, Golfe de,
Djibouti .... **107 E5** 11 50N 43 0 E
Tadmor, *N.Z.* ...... **131 B7** 41 27 S 172 45 E
Tadoba △, *India* .... **94 D4** 20 30N 78 20 E
Tadotsu, *Japan* ..... **72 C5** 34 16N 133 45 E
Tadoule L., *Canada* .. **143 B9** 58 36N 98 20W
Tadoussac, *Canada* .. **141 C6** 48 11N 69 42W
Tadpatri, *India* ..... **95 G4** 14 55N 78 1 E
Tadrés ⌂, *Niger* ..... **113 B6** 16 0N 7 10 E
Tadzhikistan =
Tajikistan ■, *Asia* .. **65 D4** 38 30N 70 0 E
Taechŏn-ni, *S. Korea* . **75 F14** 36 21N 126 36 E
Taegu, *S. Korea* .... **75 G15** 35 50N 128 37 E
Taegwan, *N. Korea* .. **75 D13** 40 13N 125 12 E
Taejŏn, *S. Korea* .... **75 F14** 36 20N 127 28 E
Taen, Ko, *Thailand* ... **87 b** 9 22N 99 57 E
Tafalla, *Spain* **40 C3** 42 30N 1 41W
Tafar, *Sudan* .... **107 F2** 6 52N 28 15 E
Tafassasset, O. ↝,
Algeria .... **111 D6** 22 0N 9 57 E
Tafelbaai = Table B.,
S. Africa .... **116 E2** 33 35 S 18 25 E
Tafelney, C., *Morocco* **110 B3** 31 3N 9 51W
Tafermaar, *Indonesia* . **83 C4** 6 47 S 134 10 E
Taffermit, *Morocco* ... **110 C3** 29 37N 9 15W
Tafí Viejo, *Argentina* . **174 B2** 26 43 S 65 17W
Tafīhān, *Iran* .... **97 D7** 29 25N 52 39 E
Tafilalet, *Morocco* ... **110 B4** 31 20N 4 45W
Tafiré, *Ivory C.* **112 D3** 9 4N 5 4W
Tafjord, *Norway* ..... **18 B4** 62 14N 7 24 E
Tafnidilt, *Morocco* ... **110 C2** 28 47N 10 58W

Tafo, Ghana 113 D4 6 15N 0 20W
Tafraoute, Morocco 110 C3 29 50N 8 58W
Tafresh, Iran 97 C6 34 45N 49 57 E
Taft, Iran 97 D7 31 45N 54 14 E
Taft, Phil. 81 F5 11 57N 125 30 E
Taft, U.S.A. 161 K7 35 8N 119 28W
Taftān, Kūh-e, Iran 97 D9 28 40N 61 0 E
Tafwap, India 95 L11 7 23N 93 43 E
Taga, Samoa 133 W23 13 46 S 172 28W
Taga Dzong, Bhutan 90 B2 27 5N 89 55 E
Tagana-an, Phil. 81 G5 9 42N 125 35 E
Taganrog, Russia 59 J10 47 12N 38 50 E
Taganrogskiy Zaliv, Russia 59 J10 47 0N 38 30 E
Tagânt, Mauritania 112 B2 18 20N 11 0W
Tagap Ga, Burma 90 B6 26 56N 96 13 E
Tagatay, Phil. 80 D3 14 6N 120 56 E
Tagauayan I., Phil. 81 F3 10 58N 121 13 E
Tagaung, Burma 90 D6 23 30N 96 2 E
Tagawa, Japan 72 D2 33 38N 130 51 E
Tagbilaran, Phil. 81 G4 9 39N 123 51 E
Tagdempt = Tiaret, Algeria 111 A5 35 20N 1 21 E
Tage, Papua N. G. 132 D2 6 19 S 143 20 E
Tággia, Italy 44 E4 43 52N 7 51 E
Taghzout, Morocco 110 B4 33 30N 4 49W
Tagish, Canada 142 A2 60 19N 134 16W
Tagish L., Canada 142 A2 60 10N 134 20W
Tagkawayan, Phil. 80 E4 13 58N 122 32 E
Tagliacozzo, Italy 45 F10 42 4N 13 14 E
Tagliamento →, Italy 45 C10 45 38N 13 6 E
Táglio di Po, Italy 45 D9 45 0N 12 12 E
Tagna, Colombia 168 D3 2 24 S 70 37W
Tago, Phil. 81 G6 9 2N 126 13 E
Tago, Mt., Phil. 81 G5 8 23N 125 5 E
Tagomago, Spain 38 C2 39 2N 1 39 E
Tagourāret, Mauritania 112 B3 17 45N 7 45W
Taguatinga, Brazil 171 D3 12 16 S 42 26W
Tagudin, Phil. 80 C3 16 56N 120 27 E
Taguenout Haggueret, Mali 111 D4 21 14N 0 48W
Tagula, Papua N. G. 132 F7 11 22 S 153 15 E
Tagula I., Papua N. G. 132 F7 11 30 S 153 30 E
Tagum, Phil. 81 H5 7 33N 125 53 E
Tagus = Tejo →, Europe 43 F2 38 40N 9 24W
Tahakopa, N.Z. 131 G4 46 30 S 169 23 E
Tahala, Morocco 110 B4 34 0N 4 28W
Tahan, Gunung, Malaysia 87 K4 4 34N 102 17 E
Tahānah-ye sūr Gol, Afghan. 91 C2 31 43N 67 53 E
Tahara, Japan 73 C9 34 40N 137 16 E
Tahat, Algeria 111 D6 23 18N 5 33 E
Tāherī, Iran 97 E7 27 43N 52 20 E
Tahiti, French Polynesia 133 S16 17 37 S 149 27W
Tahlab →, Pakistan 91 C1 28 9N 62 45 E
Tahlequah, U.S.A. 155 H7 35 55N 94 58W
Tahoe, L., U.S.A. 160 G6 39 6N 120 2W
Tahoe City, U.S.A. 160 F6 39 10N 120 9W
Tahoka, U.S.A. 155 J4 33 10N 101 48W
Taholah, U.S.A. 160 C2 47 21N 124 17W
Tahora, N.Z. 130 F3 39 2 S 174 49 E
Tahoua, Niger 113 C6 14 57N 5 16 E
Tahrūd, Iran 97 D8 29 26N 57 49 E
Tahsis, Canada 142 D3 49 55N 126 40W
Tahta, Egypt 106 B3 26 44N 31 32 E
Tahtaköprü, Turkey 51 G13 39 57N 29 39 E
Tahtalı Dağları, Turkey 100 C7 38 20N 36 0 E
Tahuamanu →, Bolivia 172 C4 11 6 S 67 36W
Tahulandang, Indonesia 82 A3 2 27N 125 23 E
Tahuna, Indonesia 82 A3 3 38N 125 30 E
Taï, Ivory C. 112 D3 5 55N 7 30W
Taï △, Ivory C. 112 D3 5 25N 7 5W
Tai Au Mun, China 69 G11 22 18N 114 17 E
Tai Hu, China 77 B12 31 5N 120 10 E
Tai Mo Shan, China 69 G11 22 25N 114 7 E
Tai O, China 69 G10 22 15N 113 52 E
Tai Pang Wan, China 69 F11 22 33N 114 24 E
Tai Po, China 69 G11 22 27N 114 10 E
Tai Rom Yen △, Thailand 87 H2 8 45N 99 30 E
Tai Shan, China 75 F9 36 25N 117 20 E
Tai Yue Shan = Lantau I., China 69 G10 22 15N 113 56 E
Tai'an, China 75 F9 36 12N 117 8 E
Taiarapu, Presq. de, Tahiti 133 S16 17 47 S 149 14W
Taibei = T'aipei, Taiwan 77 E13 25 2N 121 30 E
Taibique, Canary Is. 9 e1 27 42N 17 58W
Taibus Qi, China 74 D8 41 54N 115 22 E
Taicang, China 77 B13 31 30N 121 5 E
Taichow = Taizhou, China 77 A12 32 28N 119 55 E
T'aichung, Taiwan 77 E13 24 9N 120 37 E
Taieri →, N.Z. 131 G5 46 3 S 170 12 E
Taiga Madema, Libya 108 D3 23 46N 15 25 E
Taigu, China 74 F7 37 28N 112 30 E
Taihang Shan, China 74 G7 36 0N 113 30 E
Taihape, N.Z. 130 F4 39 41 S 175 48 E
Taihe, Anhui, China 74 H8 33 20N 115 42 E
Taihe, Jiangxi, China 77 D10 26 47N 114 52 E
Taihoku = T'aipei, Taiwan 77 E13 25 2N 121 30 E
Taihu, China 77 B11 30 22N 116 20 E
Taijiang, China 76 D7 26 39N 108 21 E
Taikang, China 74 G8 34 5N 114 50 E
Taikkyi, Burma 90 G6 17 20N 96 0 E
Tailem Bend, Australia 128 C3 35 12 S 139 29 E
Tailfingen, Germany 31 G5 48 15N 9 1 E
Tailuko, Taiwan 77 E13 24 9N 121 37 E
Taimyr Peninsula = Taymyr, Poluostrov, Russia 67 B11 75 0N 100 0 E
Tain, U.K. 22 D4 57 49N 4 4W
T'ainan, Taiwan 77 F13 23 0N 120 10 E
Taínaron, Ákra, Greece 48 E4 36 22N 22 27 E
Tainggyo, Burma 90 G5 17 49N 94 29 E
Taining, China 77 D11 26 54N 117 9 E
Taiobeiras, Brazil 171 E3 15 49 S 42 14W
Taipa, China 69 G10 22 10N 113 35 E
T'aipei, Taiwan 77 E13 25 2N 121 30 E
Taiping, China 77 B12 30 15N 118 6 E
Taiping, Malaysia 87 K3 4 51N 100 44 E
Taipingzhen, China 74 H6 33 35N 111 42 E
Taipu, Brazil 170 C4 5 37 S 35 36W
Tairbeart = Tarbert, U.K. 22 D2 57 54N 6 49W
Tairenpokpi, India 90 C4 24 39N 93 40 E
Tairua, N.Z. 130 D4 37 0 S 175 51 E
Taisha, Japan 72 B4 35 24N 132 40 E
Taishan, China 77 F9 22 14N 112 41 E
Taishun, China 77 D12 27 30N 119 42 E
Taita Hills, Kenya 118 C4 3 25 S 38 15 E
Taitao, C., Chile 176 C1 45 53 S 75 5W
Taitao, Pen. de, Chile 176 C2 46 30 S 75 0W
T'aitung, Taiwan 77 F13 22 43N 121 4 E
Taivalkoski, Finland 14 D23 65 33N 28 12 E
Taiwan ■, Asia 77 F13 23 30N 121 0 E
Taiwan Strait, Asia 77 E12 24 40N 120 0 E
Taixing, China 77 A13 32 11N 120 0 E
Taiyara, Sudan 107 E3 13 12N 30 47 E
Taïyetos Óros, Greece 48 D4 37 0N 22 23 E
Taiyiba, Israel 103 C4 32 36N 35 27 E
Taiyuan, China 74 F7 37 52N 112 33 E
Taizhong = T'aichung, Taiwan 77 E13 24 9N 120 37 E
Taizhou, China 77 A12 32 28N 119 55 E
Taizhou Liedao, China 77 C13 28 30N 121 55 E
Ta'izz, Yemen 98 D4 13 35N 44 2 E
Tājābād, Iran 97 D7 30 2N 54 24 E
Tajapuru, Furo do, Brazil 170 B1 1 50 S 50 25W
Tajarḥī, Libya 108 D2 24 21N 14 28 E
Tajikistan ■, Asia 65 D4 38 30N 70 0 E
Tajima, Japan 71 F9 37 12N 139 46 E
Tajimi, Japan 73 B9 35 19N 137 8 E
Tajo = Tejo →, Europe 43 F2 38 40N 9 24W
Tajrīsh, Iran 97 C6 35 48N 51 25 E
Tājūrā, Libya 108 B2 32 51N 13 21 E
Tak, Thailand 86 D2 16 52N 99 8 E
Takāb, Iran 101 D12 36 24N 47 7 E
Takachiho, Japan 72 E3 32 42N 131 18 E
Takachu, Botswana 116 C3 22 37 S 21 58 E
Takada, Japan 71 F9 37 7N 138 15 E
Takahagi, Japan 71 F10 36 43N 140 45 E
Takahashi, Japan 72 C5 34 51N 133 39 E
Takaka, N.Z. 131 A7 40 51 S 172 50 E
Takaki = Yamato, Japan 73 B11 35 27N 139 25 E
Takamaka, Seychelles 121 b 4 50 S 55 30 E
Takamatsu, Japan 72 C6 34 20N 134 5 E
Takanabe, Japan 72 E3 32 8N 131 30 E
Takaoka, Japan 73 A9 36 47N 137 0 E
Takapau, N.Z. 130 G5 40 2 S 176 21 E
Takapuna, N.Z. 130 C3 36 47 S 174 47 E
Takasago, Japan 72 C6 34 45N 134 48 E
Takasaki, Japan 73 A11 36 20N 139 0 E
Takatsuki, Japan 73 C7 34 51N 135 37 E
Takaungu, Kenya 118 C4 3 38 S 39 52 E
Takayama, Japan 73 A9 36 18N 137 11 E
Takayama-Bonchi, Japan 73 B9 36 0N 137 18 E
Take-Shima, Japan 71 J5 30 49N 130 26 E
Takefu, Japan 73 B8 35 50N 136 10 E
Takehara, Japan 72 C4 34 21N 132 55 E
Takeli, Tajikistan 65 C4 40 29N 69 26 E
Takengon, Indonesia 84 B1 4 45N 96 50 E
Takeo, Japan 72 D2 33 12N 130 1 E
Tåkern, Sweden 17 F8 58 22N 14 45 E
Takeshima = Tok-do, Asia 71 F5 37 15N 131 52 E
Tākestān, Iran 97 C6 36 0N 49 40 E
Taketa, Japan 72 E3 32 58N 131 24 E
Takev, Cambodia 87 G5 10 59N 104 47 E
Takh, India 93 C7 33 6N 77 32 E
Takhār □, Afghan. 91 A3 36 40N 70 0 E
Takht-Sulaiman, Pakistan 92 D3 31 40N 69 58 E
Taki, Papua N. G. 132 D8 6 29 S 155 52 E
Takikawa, Japan 70 C10 43 33N 141 54 E
Takla L., Canada 142 B3 55 15N 125 45W
Takla Landing, Canada 142 B3 55 30N 125 50W
Takla Makan = Taklamakan Shamo, China 68 C3 38 0N 83 0 E
Taklamakan Shamo, China 68 C3 38 0N 83 0 E
Takotna, U.S.A. 144 E8 62 59N 156 4W
Taku, Japan 72 D2 33 18N 130 3 E
Taku →, Canada 142 B2 58 30N 133 50W
Takua Thung, Thailand 87 a 8 24N 98 27 E
Takum, India 90 B4 27 47N 93 37 E
Takum, Nigeria 113 D6 7 18N 9 36 E
Takundi, Dem. Rep. of the Congo 115 C3 4 45 S 16 34 E
Takutu →, Guyana 169 C5 3 1N 60 29W
Tal Halāl, Iran 97 D7 28 54N 55 1 E
Tala, Uruguay 175 C4 34 21 S 55 46W
Talachyn, Belarus 58 E5 54 25N 29 42 E
Talacogan, Phil. 81 G5 8 32N 125 39 E
Talagang, Pakistan 92 C5 32 55N 72 25 E
Talagante, Chile 174 C1 33 40 S 70 50W
Talahouhait, Algeria 111 D5 24 52N 1 5 E
Talaimannar, Sri Lanka 95 K4 9 6N 79 43 E
Talaïnt, Morocco 110 C3 29 41N 9 40W
Talak, Niger 113 B6 18 0N 5 0 E
Talakag, Phil. 81 G5 8 16N 124 37 E
Talamanca, Cordillera de, Cent. Amer. 164 E3 9 20N 83 20W
Talant, France 27 E11 47 19N 4 58 E
Talara, Peru 172 A1 4 38 S 81 18W
Talas, Kyrgyzstan 65 B6 42 30N 72 13 E
Talas, Turkey 100 C6 38 41N 35 33 E
Talas →, Kazakhstan 65 B5 44 0N 70 20 E
Talas Ala Too, Kyrgyzstan 65 B6 42 15N 72 0 E
Talasea, Papua N. G. 132 C6 5 20 S 150 2 E
Talasskiy Alatau = Talas Ala Too, Kyrgyzstan 65 B6 42 15N 72 0 E
Talâta, Egypt 103 E1 30 36N 32 20 E
Talata Mafara, Nigeria 113 C6 12 38N 6 4 E
Talaud, Kepulauan, Indonesia 82 A3 4 30N 126 50 E
Talaud Is. = Talaud, Kepulauan, Indonesia 82 A3 4 30N 126 50 E
Talavera de la Reina, Spain 42 F6 39 55N 4 46W
Talavera la Real, Spain 43 G4 38 53N 6 46W
Talawgyi, Burma 90 C6 25 4N 97 19 E
Talayan, Phil. 81 H5 6 52N 124 24 E
Talayuela, Spain 42 F5 39 59N 5 36W
Talbandh, India 93 H12 22 3N 86 20 E
Talbert, Sillon de, France 26 D3 48 53N 3 5W
Talbot, Australia 128 D5 37 10 S 143 44 E
Talbot, C., Australia 124 B4 13 48 S 126 43 E
Talbotton, U.S.A. 152 C5 32 41N 84 32W
Talbragar →, Australia 129 B8 32 12 S 148 37 E
Talca, Chile 174 D1 35 28 S 71 40W
Talcahuano, Chile 174 D1 36 40 S 73 10W
Talcher, India 94 D7 21 0N 85 18 E
Talcho, Niger 113 C5 14 44N 3 28 E
Taldy Kurgan = Taldyqorghan, Kazakhstan 66 E8 45 10N 78 45 E
Taldy-Suu, Kyrgyzstan 65 B9 42 48N 78 26 E
Taldyqorghan, Kazakhstan 66 E8 45 10N 78 45 E
Talent, U.S.A. 158 E2 42 15N 122 47W
Tālesh, Iran 97 B6 37 58N 48 58 E
Tālesh, Kūhhā-ye, Iran 97 B6 37 42N 48 55 E
Talgar = Talghar, Kazakhstan 65 B8 43 19N 77 15 E
Talgar, Pik, Kazakhstan 65 B8 43 5N 77 20 E
Talghar, Kazakhstan 65 B8 43 19N 77 15 E
Talguharai, Sudan 106 D4 18 19N 35 56 E
Talguppa, India 95 G2 14 13N 74 56 E
Tali Post, Sudan 107 F3 5 55N 30 44 E
Taliabu, Indonesia 82 B2 1 50 S 125 0 E
Talibon, Phil. 81 F5 10 9N 124 20 E
Talibong, Ko, Thailand 87 J2 7 15N 99 23 E
Talihina, U.S.A. 155 H7 34 45N 95 3W
Talikota, India 95 F3 16 29N 76 17 E
Talimardzhan, Uzbekistan 65 D2 38 17N 65 33 E
Talipao, Phil. 81 J3 5 59N 121 7 E
Talisay, Phil. 81 F4 10 44N 122 58 E
Talisayan, Phil. 81 G5 9 0N 124 55 E
Talitsa, Russia 64 C9 57 0N 63 43 E
Talitsky Zavod = Talitsa, Russia 64 C9 57 0N 63 43 E
Taliwang, Indonesia 85 D5 8 50 S 116 55 E
Talkeetna, U.S.A. 144 E10 62 20N 150 6W
Tall 'Afar, Iraq 101 D10 36 22N 42 27 E
Tall Kalakh, Syria 103 A5 34 41N 36 15 E
Talla, Egypt 106 B3 28 5N 30 43 E
Talladega, U.S.A. 152 B3 33 26N 86 6W
Tallahassee, U.S.A. 152 E5 30 27N 84 17W
Tallangatta, Australia 129 D7 36 15 S 147 19 E
Tallapoosa, U.S.A. 152 B4 33 45N 85 17W
Tallapoosa →, U.S.A. 152 C3 32 30N 86 16W
Tallard, France 29 D10 44 28N 6 3 E
Tallarook, Australia 129 D6 37 5 S 145 6 E
Tallassee, U.S.A. 152 C4 32 32N 85 54W
Tällberg, Sweden 16 D9 60 51N 15 2 E
Tallering Pk., Australia 125 E2 28 6 S 115 37 E
Talli, Pakistan 92 E3 29 32N 68 8 E
Tallinn, Estonia 15 G21 59 22N 24 48 E
Tallmadge, U.S.A. 150 E3 41 6N 81 27W
Tallulah, U.S.A. 155 J9 32 25N 91 11W
Tălmaciu, Romania 53 E9 45 38N 24 19 E
Talmest, Morocco 110 B3 31 48N 9 21W
Talmont-St-Hilaire, France 28 B2 46 27N 1 37W
Talne, Ukraine 59 H6 48 50N 30 44 E
Talnoye = Talne, Ukraine 59 H6 48 50N 30 44 E
Taloda, India 94 D2 21 34N 74 11 E
Talodi, Sudan 107 E3 10 35N 30 22 E
Tālogān, Afghan. 65 E4 36 44N 69 33 E
Talovaya, Russia 60 E5 51 6N 40 45 E
Taloyoak, Canada 138 B10 69 32N 93 32W
Talpa de Allende, Mexico 162 C4 20 23N 104 51W
Talparo, Trin. & Tob. 169 F9 10 30N 61 17W
Talquin, L., U.S.A. 152 E5 30 23N 84 39W
Talsi, Latvia 15 H20 57 10N 22 30 E
Talsi □, Latvia 54 A9 57 20N 22 40 E
Talsinnt, Morocco 111 B4 32 33N 3 27W
Taltal, Chile 174 B1 25 23 S 70 33W
Taltson →, Canada 142 A6 61 24N 112 46W
Talwood, Australia 127 D4 28 29 S 149 29 E
Talyawalka Cr. →, Australia 128 B5 32 28 S 142 22 E
Tam Ky, Vietnam 86 E7 15 34N 108 29 E
Tam Quan, Vietnam 86 E7 14 35N 109 3 E
Tama, U.S.A. 156 C4 41 58N 92 35W
Tama △, Ethiopia 107 F4 5 55N 36 5 E
Tamada, Algeria 111 D5 21 34N 3 20 E
Tamalameque, Colombia 168 B3 8 52N 73 49W
Tamale, Ghana 113 D4 9 22N 0 50W
Taman, Russia 59 K9 45 14N 36 41 E
Taman Negara △, Malaysia 87 K4 4 38N 102 26 E
Tamana, Japan 72 E2 32 58N 130 32 E
Tamana, Kiribati 123 A13 2 30 S 175 59 E
Tamanar, Morocco 110 B3 31 1N 9 46W
Tamani, Mali 112 C3 13 20N 6 50W
Tamano, Japan 72 C5 34 29N 133 59 E
Tamanrasset, Algeria 111 D6 22 50N 5 30 E
Tamanrasset, O. →, Algeria 111 D5 22 0N 2 0 E
Tamanthi, Burma 90 C5 25 19N 95 17 E
Tamaqua, U.S.A. 151 F9 40 48N 75 58W
Tamar →, U.K. 21 G3 50 27N 4 15W
Támara, Colombia 168 B3 5 50N 72 10W
Tamarac, U.S.A. 153 J9 26 12N 80 10W
Tamarin, Mauritius 121 d 20 19 S 57 20 E
Tamarinda, Spain 38 B4 39 55N 3 49 E
Tamarite de Litera, Spain 40 D5 41 52N 0 25 E
Tamaroa, U.S.A. 156 F7 38 8N 89 14W
Tamashima, Japan 72 C5 34 32N 133 40 E
Tamási, Hungary 52 D3 46 40N 18 18 E
Tamaské, Niger 113 C6 14 49N 5 43 E
Tamaulipas □, Mexico 163 C5 24 0N 99 0W
Tamaulipas, Sierra de, Mexico 163 C5 23 30N 98 20W
Tamazula, Mexico 162 C3 24 55N 106 58W
Tamazunchale, Mexico 163 C5 21 16N 98 47W
Tamba-Dabatou, Guinea 112 C2 11 50N 10 40W
Tambacounda, Senegal 112 C2 13 45N 13 40W
Tambaram, India 95 H5 12 55N 80 7 E
Tambea, Solomon Is. 133 M10 9 16 S 159 41 E
Tambelan, Kepulauan, Indonesia 84 B3 1 0N 107 30 E
Tambellup, Australia 125 F2 34 4 S 117 37 E
Tambo, Australia 126 C4 24 54 S 146 14 E
Tambo, Peru 172 C3 12 57 S 74 1W
Tambo →, Peru 172 C3 10 42 S 73 47W
Tambo de Mora, Peru 172 C2 13 30 S 76 8W
Tambobamba, Peru 172 C3 13 54 S 72 8W
Tambohorano, Madag. 117 B7 17 30 S 43 58 E
Tambopata →, Peru 172 C4 13 21 S 69 36W
Tambora, Indonesia 85 D5 8 12 S 118 5 E
Tamboritha, Mt., Australia 129 D7 37 31 S 146 40 E
Tambov, Russia 60 D5 52 45N 41 28 E
Tambre →, Spain 42 C2 42 49N 8 53W
Tambuku, Indonesia 85 D4 7 8 S 113 40 E
Tambul, Papua N. G. 132 C2 5 54 S 143 54 E
Tamburâ, Sudan 107 F2 5 40N 27 25 E
Tambuyukan, Gunong, Malaysia 85 A5 6 13N 116 39 E
Tâmchekket, Mauritania 112 B2 17 25N 10 40W
Tamdybulak, Uzbekistan 65 C2 41 46N 64 36 E
Tame, Colombia 168 B3 6 28N 71 44W
Tâmega →, Portugal 42 D2 41 5N 8 21W
Tamelelt, Morocco 110 B3 31 50N 7 32W
Tamenglong, India 90 C4 25 0N 93 35 E
Tamerza, Tunisia 108 B1 34 23N 7 58 E
Tamgué, Massif du, Guinea 112 C2 12 0N 12 18W
Tami Is., Papua N. G. 132 C4 6 46 S 147 55 E
Tamiahua, L. de, Mexico 163 C5 21 30N 97 30W
Tamiami Canal, U.S.A. 153 K8 25 50N 81 0W
Tamil Nadu □, India 95 J3 11 0N 77 0 E
Tamiš →, Serbia & M. 52 F5 44 51N 20 39 E
Tamluk, India 93 H12 22 18N 87 58 E
Tammerfors = Tampere, Finland 15 F20 61 30N 23 50 E
Tammisaari, Finland 15 F20 60 0N 23 26 E
Tämnaren, Sweden 16 D11 60 10N 17 25 E
Tamo Abu, Banjaran, Malaysia 85 B5 3 10N 115 5 E
Tampa, Angola 115 F2 15 30 S 13 27 E
Tampa, U.S.A. 153 H7 27 57N 82 27W
Tampa, Tanjung, Indonesia 79 K19 8 55 S 116 12 E
Tampa B., U.S.A. 153 H7 27 50N 82 30W
Tampa International ✕ (TPA), U.S.A. 153 H7 27 59N 82 32W
Tamparan, Phil. 81 H5 7 53N 124 20 E
Tampere, Finland 15 F20 61 30N 23 50 E
Tampico, Mexico 163 C5 22 20N 97 50W
Tampico, U.S.A. 156 C7 41 38N 89 47W
Tampin, Malaysia 87 L4 2 28N 102 13 E
Tampoi, Malaysia 87 d 1 30N 103 39 E
Tamrah, Si. Arabia 98 B4 20 24N 45 25 E
Tamrau, Peg., Indonesia 83 B4 0 30 S 132 27 E
Tamri, Morocco 110 B3 30 49N 9 50W
Tamrida = Qādib, Yemen 99 D6 12 37N 53 57 E
Tamsweg, Austria 34 D6 47 7N 13 49 E
Tamu, Burma 90 C5 24 13N 94 12 E
Tamuja →, Spain 43 F4 39 38N 6 29W
Tamworth, Australia 129 A9 31 7 S 150 58 E
Tamworth, Canada 150 B8 44 29N 77 0W
Tamworth, U.K. 21 E6 52 39N 1 41W
Tamyang, S. Korea 75 G14 35 19N 126 59 E
Tan An, Vietnam 87 G6 10 32N 106 25 E
Tan Chau, Vietnam 87 G5 10 48N 105 12 E
Tan Iddah, Algeria 111 C6 26 33N 9 42 E
Tan-Tan, Morocco 110 C2 28 29N 11 1W
Tana →, Kenya 118 C5 2 32 S 40 31 E
Tana →, Norway 14 A23 70 30N 28 14 E
Tana, L., Ethiopia 107 E4 13 5N 37 30 E
Tana River Primate △, Kenya 118 C5 1 55 S 40 7 E
Tanabe, Japan 73 D7 33 44N 135 22 E
Tanabi, Brazil 171 F2 20 37 S 49 37W
Tanacross, U.S.A. 144 E12 63 23N 143 21W
Tanafjorden, Norway 14 A23 70 45N 28 25 E
Tanaga I., U.S.A. 144 L3 51 48N 177 53W
Tanaga Volcano, U.S.A. 144 L3 51 53N 178 8W
Tanah Merah, Malaysia 84 A2 5 48N 102 9 E
Tanahbala, Indonesia 84 C1 0 30 S 98 30 E
Tanahgrogot, Indonesia 85 C5 1 55 S 116 15 E
Tanahjampea, Indonesia 82 C2 7 10 S 120 35 E
Tanahmasa, Indonesia 84 C1 0 12 S 98 39 E
Tanahmerah, Indonesia 83 C6 6 5 S 140 16 E
Tanakpur, India 93 E9 29 5N 80 7 E
Tanakura, Japan 71 F10 37 10N 140 20 E
Tanamalwila, Sri Lanka 95 L5 6 26N 81 8 E
Tanami, Australia 124 C4 19 59 S 129 43 E
Tanami Desert, Australia 124 C5 18 50 S 132 0 E
Tanana, U.S.A. 144 D9 65 10N 152 4W
Tanana →, U.S.A. 144 D10 65 10N 151 58W
Tananarive = Antananarivo, Madag. 117 B8 18 55 S 47 31 E
Tananger, Norway 18 F2 58 57N 5 37 E
Tanannt, Morocco 110 B3 31 54N 6 56W
Tánaro →, Italy 44 D5 44 55N 8 40 E
Tanauan, Phil. 80 D3 14 5N 121 10 E
Tanay, Phil. 80 D3 14 30N 121 17 E
Tanba-Sanchi, Japan 73 B7 35 7N 135 48 E
Tancheng, China 75 G10 34 25N 118 20 E
Tanch'ŏn, N. Korea 75 D15 40 27N 128 54 E
Tanda, Ut. P., India 93 F10 26 33N 82 35 E
Tanda, Ut. P., India 93 E8 28 57N 78 56 E
Tanda, Ivory C. 112 D4 7 48N 3 10W
Tandag, Phil. 81 G6 9 4N 126 9 E
Tandaia, Tanzania 119 D3 9 25 S 34 15 E
Tăndărei, Romania 53 F12 44 39N 27 40 E
Tandaué, Angola 116 B2 16 58 S 18 5 E
Tandil, Argentina 174 D4 37 15 S 59 6W
Tandil, Sa. del, Argentina 174 D4 37 30 S 59 0W
Tandin, Burma 90 F4 19 33N 93 58 E
Tandjilé →, Chad 109 G3 9 45N 15 50 E
Tandlianwala, Pakistan 92 D5 31 3N 73 9 E
Tando Adam, Pakistan 92 G3 25 45N 68 40 E
Tando Allahyar, Pakistan 92 G3 25 28N 68 43 E
Tando Bago, Pakistan 92 G3 24 47N 68 58 E
Tando Mohommed Khan, Pakistan 92 G3 25 8N 68 32 E
Tando-Zinze, Angola 115 D2 5 22 S 12 30 E
Tandou-Bengou, Congo 114 C2 3 50 S 11 44 E
Tandou L., Australia 128 B5 32 40 S 142 5 E
Tandragee, U.K. 23 B5 54 21N 6 24W
Tandsjöborg, Sweden 16 C8 61 42N 14 43 E
Tandubas, Phil. 81 J3 5 8N 120 20 E
Tandula →, India 94 D5 21 6N 81 14 E
Tandula Tank, India 94 D5 20 40N 81 12 E
Tandur, Andhra Pradesh, India 94 E4 19 11N 79 30 E
Tandur, Andhra Pradesh, India 94 F3 17 14N 77 35 E
Tane-ga-Shima, Japan 71 J5 30 30N 131 0 E
Taneatua, N.Z. 130 E6 38 4 S 177 1 E
Tanen Tong Dan = Dawna Ra., Burma 86 D2 16 30N 98 30 E
Tanew →, Poland 55 H9 50 29N 22 16 E
Tanezrouft, Algeria 111 D5 23 9N 0 11 E
Tanezzuft, W. →, Libya 108 C2 25 51N 10 19 E
Tang, Koh, Cambodia 87 G4 10 16N 103 7 E
Tang, Ra's-e, Iran 97 E8 25 21N 59 52 E
Tang Krasang, Cambodia 86 F5 12 34N 105 3 E
Tanga, Tanzania 118 D4 5 5 S 39 2 E
Tanga □, Tanzania 118 D4 5 20 S 38 0 E
Tanga Is., Papua N. G. 132 B7 3 20 S 153 15 E
Tangail, Bangla. 90 C2 24 15N 89 55 E
Tangalla, Sri Lanka 95 L5 6 1N 80 48 E
Tanganyika = Tanzania ■, Africa 118 D3 6 0 S 34 0 E
Tanganyika, L., Africa 118 D3 6 40 S 30 0 E
Tangarare, Solomon Is. 133 M10 9 36 S 159 41 E
Tangariro, Mt., N.Z. 130 F4 39 8 S 175 38 E
Tangasseri, India 95 K3 8 53N 76 35 E
Tangaza, Nigeria 113 C5 13 19N 4 55 E
Tangen, Norway 18 D8 60 37N 11 15 E
Tanger, Morocco 110 A3 35 50N 5 49W
Tangerang, Indonesia 84 D3 6 11 S 106 37 E
Tangerhütte, Germany 30 C7 52 26N 11 48 E
Tangermünde, Germany 30 C7 52 33N 11 58 E
Tanggu, China 75 E9 39 2N 117 40 E
Tanggula Shan, China 68 C4 32 40N 92 10 E
Tanghe, China 74 H7 32 47N 112 50 E
Tanghla Range = Tanggula Shan, China 68 C4 32 40N 92 10 E
Tangi, India 94 E7 19 56N 85 24 E
Tangier = Tanger, Morocco 110 A3 35 50N 5 49W
Tangjia, China 69 G10 22 22N 113 35 E
Tangjia Wan, China 69 G10 22 21N 113 36 E
Tangkeleboke, Indonesia 82 B2 3 10 S 121 30 E
Tangorin, Australia 126 C3 21 47 S 144 12 E
Tangorombohitr'i Makay, Madag. 117 C8 21 0 S 45 15 E
Tangshan, China 75 E10 39 38N 118 10 E
Tangtou, China 75 G10 35 28N 118 30 E
Tangub, Phil. 81 G4 8 3N 123 44 E
Tanguiéta, Benin 113 C5 10 35N 1 21 E
Tangxi, China 77 C12 29 3N 119 25 E
Tangyan He →, China 76 C7 28 54N 108 19 E
Tanimbar, Kepulauan, Indonesia 83 C4 7 30 S 131 30 E
Tanimbar Is. = Tanimbar, Kepulauan, Indonesia 83 C4 7 30 S 131 30 E
Taninthari = Tenasserim, Burma 87 F2 12 6N 99 3 E
Tanjay, Phil. 81 G4 9 30N 123 5 E
Tanjong Malim, Malaysia 87 L3 3 42N 101 31 E
Tanjong Pelepas, Malaysia 87 d 1 21N 103 33 E
Tanjore = Thanjavur, India 95 J4 10 48N 79 12 E
Tanjung, Indonesia 79 J19 8 21 S 116 9 E
Tanjung, Phil. 85 C5 2 10 S 115 25 E
Tanjung Tokong, Malaysia 87 c 5 28N 100 18 E
Tanjungbalai, Indonesia 84 B1 2 55N 99 44 E
Tanjungbatu, Indonesia 85 B5 2 23N 118 3 E
Tanjungkarang Telukbetung, Indonesia 84 D3 5 20 S 105 10 E
Tanjungpandan, Indonesia 85 C3 2 43 S 107 38 E
Tanjungpinang, Indonesia 84 B2 1 5N 104 30 E
Tanjungpriok, Indonesia 84 D3 6 8 S 106 55 E
Tanjungredeb, Indonesia 85 B5 2 9N 117 29 E
Tanjungselor, Indonesia 85 B5 2 55N 117 25 E
Tank, Pakistan 91 B3 32 14N 70 25 E
Tankhala, India 92 J5 21 58N 73 47 E
Tankwa-Karoo △, S. Africa 116 E2 32 14 S 19 50 E
Tanna, Vanuatu 133 J7 19 30 S 169 20 E
Tännäs, Sweden 16 B6 62 26N 12 42 E
Tannersville, U.S.A. 151 E9 41 3N 75 18W
Tannis Bugt, Denmark 17 G4 57 40N 10 15 E
Tannu-Ola, Russia 67 D10 51 0N 94 0 E
Tannum Sands, Australia 126 C5 23 57 S 151 22 E
Tano →, Ghana 112 D4 5 7N 2 56W
Tanombella, Algeria 111 C6 25 30N 5 49 E
Tanon Str., Phil. 81 F4 10 20N 123 30 E
Tanout, Niger 113 C6 14 50N 8 55 E
Tanquinho, Brazil 171 D4 11 58 S 39 6W
Tanshui, Taiwan 77 E13 25 10N 121 28 E
Tansilla, Burkina Faso 112 C4 12 25N 4 23W
Tanta, Egypt 106 H7 30 45N 30 57 E
Tantabin, Burma 90 G5 17 1N 95 59 E
Tantoyuca, Mexico 163 C5 21 21N 98 10W
Tantung = Dandong, China 75 D13 40 10N 124 20 E
Tanuku, India 94 F5 16 45N 81 44 E
Tanumshede, Sweden 17 F5 58 42N 11 20 E
Tanunda, Australia 128 C3 34 30 S 139 0 E
Tanur, India 95 J2 11 1N 75 52 E
Tanus, France 28 D6 44 8N 2 19 E
Tanzania ■, Africa 118 D3 6 0 S 34 0 E
Tanzawa-Sanchi, Japan 73 B11 35 27N 139 0 E
Tanzhou, China 69 G9 22 16N 113 28 E
Tanzilla →, Canada 142 B2 58 8N 130 43W
Tao, Ko, Thailand 87 G2 10 5N 99 52 E
Tao'an = Taonan, China 75 B12 45 22N 122 40 E
Tao'er He →, China 75 B13 45 45N 124 5 E
Taohua Dao, China 77 C14 29 50N 122 20 E
Taolanaro, Madag. 117 D8 25 2 S 47 0 E
Taole, China 74 E4 38 48N 106 40 E
Taonan, China 75 B12 45 22N 122 40 E
Taora, Solomon Is. 133 L9 7 21 S 157 30 E
Taormina, Italy 47 E8 37 51N 15 17 E
Taos, U.S.A. 159 H11 36 24N 105 35W
Taoudenni, Mali 110 D4 22 40N 3 55W
Taoudrart, Adrar, Algeria 111 D5 24 25N 2 24 E
Taounate, Morocco 110 B4 34 25N 4 41W
Taourirt, Dj., Algeria 111 D6 35 52N 1 46 E
Taourirt, Algeria 111 C5 26 37N 0 20 E
Taourirt, Morocco 111 B4 34 25N 2 53W
Taouz, Morocco 110 B4 30 53N 4 0W
Taoyuan, China 77 C8 28 55N 111 16 E
T'aoyüan, Taiwan 77 E13 25 0N 121 4 E
Tapa, Estonia 15 G21 59 15N 25 50 E
Tapa Shan = Daba Shan, China 76 B7 32 0N 109 0 E
Tapachula, Mexico 163 E6 14 54N 92 17W
Tapah, Malaysia 87 K3 4 12N 101 15 E
Tapajós →, Brazil 169 D7 2 24 S 54 41W
Tapaktuan, Indonesia 84 B1 3 15N 97 10 E
Tapanahoni →, Suriname 169 C7 4 20N 54 25W
Tapanui, N.Z. 131 F4 45 56 S 169 18 E
Tapauá, Brazil 173 B5 5 40 S 64 20W
Tapauá →, Brazil 173 B5 5 40 S 64 21W
Tapaz, Phil. 81 F4 11 16N 122 32 E
Tapes, Brazil 175 C5 30 40 S 51 23W
Tapeta, Liberia 112 D3 6 29N 8 52W
Taphan Hin, Thailand 86 D3 16 13N 100 26 E
Tapi →, India 94 D1 21 8N 72 41 E
Tapia de Casariego, Spain 42 B4 43 34N 6 56W
Tapiantana Group, Phil. 81 H4 6 20N 122 0 E
Tapiau = Gvardeysk, Russia 15 J19 54 39N 21 5 E
Tapilon = Daanbantayan, Phil. 81 F5 11 17N 124 2 E
Tapini, Papua N. G. 132 E4 8 19 S 147 0 E
Tapiraí, Brazil 171 E2 19 52 S 46 1W
Tapirapé →, Brazil 170 D1 10 41 S 50 38W
Tapirapecó, Serra, Venezuela 169 C5 1 10N 65 0W
Tapirapuã, Brazil 173 C6 14 51 S 57 45W
Taplan, Australia 128 C4 34 33 S 140 52 E
Tapo-Capara △, Venezuela 165 E5 7 55N 71 15W
Tapoeripa, Suriname 169 B6 5 22N 56 34W
Tapolca, Hungary 52 D2 46 53N 17 29 E
Tapuae-o-Uenuku, N.Z. 131 B8 42 0 S 173 39 E
Tapul, Phil. 81 J3 5 42N 120 55 E
Tapul Group, Phil. 81 J3 5 35N 120 50 E
Tapul I., Phil. 81 J3 5 43N 120 55 E
Tapun, India 90 B6 27 35N 96 22 E
Tapurucuará, Brazil 169 D4 0 24 S 65 2W
Ţaqṭaq, Iraq 101 E11 35 53N 44 35 E
Taquara, Brazil 175 B5 29 36 S 50 46W
Taquari →, Brazil 173 D6 19 15 S 57 17W
Taquaritinga, Brazil 171 F2 21 24 S 48 30W
Tara, Australia 127 D5 27 17 S 150 31 E
Tara, Canada 150 B3 44 28N 81 9W
Tara, Japan 72 D2 33 2N 130 11 E
Tara, Russia 66 D8 56 55N 74 24 E
Tara, Zambia 119 F2 16 58 S 26 45 E
Tara △, Serbia & M. 50 C3 43 55N 19 30 E
Tara →, Serbia & M. 50 C2 43 21N 18 51 E
Tara-Dake, Japan 72 E2 32 58N 130 6 E
Taraba □, Nigeria 113 D7 8 0N 10 30 E
Taraba →, Nigeria 113 D7 8 30N 10 15 E
Tarabuco, Bolivia 173 D5 19 10 S 64 57W

Tarābulus, Lebanon 103 A4 34 31N 35 50 E
Tarābulus, Libya 108 B2 32 49N 13 7 E
Taraclia, Taraclia, Moldova 53 E13 45 54N 28 40 E
Taraclia, Tighina, Moldova 53 D14 46 34N 29 7 E
Taradale, N.Z. 130 F5 39 33 S 176 53 E
Taradehi, India 93 H8 23 18N 79 21 E
Taragi, Japan 72 E2 32 16N 130 56 E
Tarahouahout, Algeria 111 D6 22 41N 5 59 E
Tarajalejo, Canary Is. 9 e2 28 12N 14 7W
Tarakan, Indonesia 85 B5 3 20N 117 35 E
Tarakit, Mt., Kenya 118 B4 2 2N 35 10 E
Taralga, Australia 129 C8 34 26 S 149 52 E
Tarama-Jima, Japan 71 M2 24 39N 124 42 E
Taramakau →, N.Z. 131 C6 42 34 S 171 8 E
Taran, Mys, Russia 15 J18 54 56N 19 59 E
Taranagar, India 92 E6 28 43N 74 50 E
Taranaki □, N.Z. 130 F3 39 25 S 174 30 E
Taranaki, Mt., N.Z. 130 F3 39 17 S 174 5 E
Tarancón, Spain 40 E1 40 1N 3 1W
Tarangire △, Tanzania 118 C4 4 21 S 36 7 E
Taransay, U.K. 22 D1 57 54N 7 0W
Táranto, Italy 47 B10 40 28N 17 14 E
Táranto, G. di, Italy 47 B10 40 8N 17 20 E
Tarapacá, Colombia 168 D4 2 56 S 69 46W
Tarapacá □, Chile 174 A2 20 45 S 69 30W
Tarapoto, Peru 172 B2 6 30 S 76 20W
Taraquá, Brazil 168 C4 0 6N 68 28W
Tarare, France 29 C8 45 54N 4 26 E
Tararua Ra., N.Z. 130 G4 40 45 S 175 25 E
Tarasag, Vanuatu 133 D5 14 12 S 167 36 E
Tarascon, France 29 E8 43 48N 4 39 E
Tarascon-sur-Ariège, France 28 F5 42 50N 1 36 E
Tarashcha, Ukraine 59 H6 49 30N 30 31 E
Tarata, Peru 172 D3 17 27 S 70 2W
Tarauacá, Brazil 172 B3 8 6 S 70 48W
Tarauacá →, Brazil 172 B3 6 42 S 69 48W
Taravo →, France 29 G12 41 42N 8 49 E
Tarawa, Kiribati 134 G9 1 30N 173 0 E
Tarawai I., Papua N. G. 132 B2 3 13 S 143 15 E
Tarawera, N.Z. 130 F5 39 2 S 176 36 E
Tarawera, L., N.Z. 130 E5 38 13 S 176 27 E
Tarawera, Mt., N.Z. 130 E5 38 14 S 176 32 E
Taraz, Kazakhstan 65 B5 42 54N 71 22 E
Tarazona, Spain 40 D3 41 55N 1 43W
Tarazona de la Mancha, Spain 41 F3 39 16N 1 55W
Tarbagatay, Khrebet, Kazakhstan 66 E9 48 0N 83 0 E
Tarbat Ness, U.K. 22 D5 57 52N 3 47W
Tarbela Dam, Pakistan 92 B5 34 8N 72 52 E
Tarbert, Arg. & Bute, U.K. 22 F3 55 52N 5 25W
Tarbert, W. Isles, U.K. 22 D2 57 54N 6 49W
Tarbes, France 28 E4 43 15N 0 3 E
Tarboro, U.S.A. 149 H7 35 54N 77 32W
Tarbū, Libya 108 C3 26 0N 15 5 E
Tărcău, Munţii, Romania 53 D11 46 39N 26 7 E
Tarcento, Italy 45 B10 46 13N 13 13 E
Tarcoola, Australia 127 E1 30 44 S 134 36 E
Tarcoon, Australia 127 E4 30 15 S 146 43 E
Tarcutta, Australia 129 C7 35 16 S 147 44 E
Tardets-Sorholus, France 28 E3 43 8N 0 52W
Tardoire →, France 28 C4 45 52N 0 14 E
Taredjedja, Algeria 111 C5 25 12N 2 32 E
Taree, Australia 129 A10 31 50 S 152 30 E
Tarella, Australia 128 A5 31 2 S 143 2 E
Tarf, Ras, Morocco 110 A3 35 40N 5 11W
Ţarfā, Ra's aţ, Si. Arabia 98 C3 17 2N 42 22 E
Tarfa, W. el →, Egypt 106 B3 28 25N 30 50 E
Tarfaya, Morocco 110 C2 27 55N 12 55W
Târgovişte, Romania 53 F10 44 55N 25 27 E
Târgu Bujor, Romania 53 E12 45 52N 27 54 E
Târgu Cărbuneşti, Romania 53 F8 44 57N 23 31 E
Târgu Frumos, Romania 53 C12 47 12N 27 2 E
Târgu-Jiu, Romania 53 E8 45 5N 23 19 E
Târgu Lăpuş, Romania 53 C8 47 27N 23 52 E
Târgu Mureş, Romania 53 D9 46 31N 24 38 E
Târgu Neamţ, Romania 53 C11 47 12N 26 25 E
Târgu Ocna, Romania 53 D11 46 16N 26 39 E
Târgu Secuiesc, Romania 53 E11 46 0N 26 10 E
Targuist, Morocco 110 B4 34 59N 4 14W
Tărgușor, Romania 53 F13 44 27N 28 25 E
Tărhăus, Vf., Romania 53 D11 46 40N 26 8 E
Tarhbalt, Morocco 110 B3 30 39N 5 20W
Tarhit, Algeria 111 B4 30 58N 2 0W
Tarhūnah, Libya 108 B2 32 27N 13 36 E
Tari, Papua N. G. 132 C2 5 54 S 142 59 E
Táriba, Venezuela 168 B3 7 49N 72 13W
Ţarif, U.A.E. 97 E7 24 3N 53 46 E
Tarifa, Spain 43 J5 36 1N 5 36W
Tarija, Bolivia 174 A3 21 30 S 64 40W
Tarija □, Bolivia 174 A3 21 30 S 63 30W
Tariku →, Indonesia 83 B5 2 55 S 138 26 E
Tarīm, Yemen 99 C5 16 3N 49 0 E
Tarim Basin = Tarim Pendi, China 68 B3 40 0N 84 0 E
Tarim He →, China 68 C3 39 30N 88 30 E
Tarim Pendi, China 68 B3 40 0N 84 0 E
Taritatu →, Indonesia 83 B5 2 54 S 138 27 E
Tarka →, S. Africa 116 E4 32 10 S 26 0 E
Tarkastad, S. Africa 116 E4 32 0 S 26 16 E
Tarkhankut, Mys, Ukraine 59 K7 45 25N 32 30 E
Tarko Sale, Russia 66 C8 64 55N 77 50 E
Tarkwa, Ghana 112 D4 5 20N 2 0W
Tarlac, Phil. 80 D3 15 29N 120 35 E
Tarlac □, Phil. 80 D3 15 30N 120 30 E
Tarm, Denmark 17 J2 55 56N 8 31 E
Tarma, Peru 172 C2 11 25 S 75 45W
Tarn □, France 28 E6 43 49N 2 8 E
Tarn →, France 28 D5 44 5N 1 6 E
Tarn-et-Garonne □, France 28 D5 44 8N 1 20 E
Tarna →, Hungary 52 C4 47 31N 19 59 E
Târnava Mare →, Romania 53 D8 46 10N 23 43 E
Târnava Mică →, Romania 53 D8 46 9N 23 55 E
Târnăveni, Romania 53 D9 46 19N 24 13 E
Tarnica, Poland 55 J9 49 4N 22 44 E
Tarnobrzeg, Poland 55 H8 50 35N 21 41 E
Tarnogród, Poland 55 H9 50 22N 22 45 E
Tarnopol = Ternopil, Ukraine 59 H3 49 30N 25 40 E
Tarnos, France 28 E2 43 32N 1 28W
Târnova, Moldova 53 B12 48 10N 27 40 E
Târnova, Romania 52 E6 45 23N 21 59 E
Tarnów, Poland 55 H8 50 3N 21 0 E
Tarnowitz = Tarnowskie Góry, Poland 55 H5 50 27N 18 54 E
Tarnowskie Góry, Poland 55 H5 50 27N 18 54 E
Tärnsjö, Sweden 16 D10 60 9N 16 56 E
Táro →, Italy 44 C7 45 2N 10 15 E
Ţārom, Iran 97 D7 28 11N 55 46 E
Taroom, Australia 127 D4 25 36 S 149 48 E
Taroudannt, Morocco 110 B3 30 30N 8 52W
Tarp, Germany 30 A5 54 39N 9 24 E
Tarpeena, Australia 128 D4 37 37 S 140 47 E
Tarpon Springs, U.S.A. 153 G7 28 9N 82 45W
Tarquínia, Italy 45 F8 42 15N 11 45 E
Tarrafal, C. Verde Is. 9 j 15 18N 23 39W
Tarragona, Spain 40 D6 41 5N 1 17 E
Tarragona □, Spain 40 D6 41 5N 1 0 E
Tarraleah, Australia 127 G4 42 17 S 146 26 E
Tarrasa = Terrassa, Spain 40 D7 41 34N 2 1 E
Tàrrega, Spain 40 D6 41 39N 1 9 E
Tarrytown, Ga., U.S.A. 152 C7 32 19N 82 34W
Tarrytown, N.Y., U.S.A. 151 E11 41 4N 73 52W
Tårs, Denmark 17 G4 57 23N 10 7 E
Tarshiha = Me'ona, Israel 103 B4 33 1N 35 15 E
Tarsus, Turkey 106 D6 36 58N 34 55 E
Tartagal, Argentina 174 A3 22 30 S 63 50W
Tärtär, Azerbaijan 61 K8 40 20N 46 58 E
Tärtär →, Azerbaijan 61 K8 40 26N 47 20 E
Tartas, France 28 E3 43 50N 0 49W
Tartogay, Kazakhstan 65 A3 44 26N 66 15 E
Tartu, Estonia 15 G22 58 20N 26 44 E
Ţarţūs, Syria 100 E6 34 55N 35 55 E
Tarumirim, Brazil 171 E3 19 16 S 41 59W
Tarumizu, Japan 72 F2 31 29N 130 42 E
Tarussa, Russia 58 E9 54 44N 37 10 E
Tarutao = Ko Tarutao △, Thailand 87 J2 6 31N 99 26 E
Tarutao, Ko, Thailand 87 J2 6 33N 99 40 E
Tarutung, Indonesia 84 B1 2 0N 98 54 E
Tarutyne, Ukraine 53 D14 46 12N 29 9 E
Tarvísio, Italy 45 B10 46 30N 13 35 E
Tarxien, Malta 38 F8 35 52N 14 31 E
Tarz Ulli, Libya 108 C2 25 32N 10 8 E
Tasahku, Burma 90 B6 27 33N 97 52 E
Tasaret, O. →, Algeria 111 C5 26 25N 1 59 E
Tasāwah, Libya 108 C2 26 0N 13 30 E
Tasböget, Kazakhstan 65 A2 44 46N 65 33 E
Täsch, Switz. 32 D5 46 4N 7 46 E
Taseko →, Canada 142 C4 52 8N 123 45W
Tasgaon, India 94 F2 17 2N 74 39 E
Tash-Bashat, Kyrgyzstan 65 C8 41 23N 76 20 E
Tash-Kömür, Kyrgyzstan 65 C6 41 40N 72 10 E
Tash-Kumyr = Tash-Kömür, Kyrgyzstan 65 C6 41 40N 72 10 E
Tashauz = Dashhowuz, Turkmenistan 66 E6 41 49N 59 58 E
Tashi Chho Dzong = Thimphu, Bhutan 90 B2 27 31N 89 45 E
Tashino = Pervomaysk, Russia 60 C6 54 56N 43 58 E
Ţashk, Daryācheh-ye, Iran 97 D7 29 45N 53 35 E
Tashkent = Toshkent, Uzbekistan 65 C4 41 20N 69 10 E
Tashtagol, Russia 66 D9 52 47N 87 53 E
Tasiilaq, Greenland 10 D7 65 40N 37 20W
Tasikmalaya, Indonesia 85 D3 7 18 S 108 12 E
Tåsinge, Denmark 17 J4 55 0N 10 35 E
Tåsjön, Sweden 14 D16 64 15N 15 40 E
Task, Niger 109 F2 14 56N 10 46 E
Taskan, Russia 67 C16 62 59N 150 20 E
Tasker, Niger 113 C7 15 8N 10 40 E
Taşköprü, Turkey 100 B6 41 30N 34 15 E
Taskul, Papua N. G. 132 B6 2 32 S 150 27 E
Taşlâc, Moldova 53 C14 47 4N 29 24 E
Tasman □, N.Z. 131 B7 41 30 S 172 40 E
Tasman →, N.Z. 131 D5 43 48 S 170 8 E
Tasman, Mt., N.Z. 131 D5 43 34 S 170 12 E
Tasman B., N.Z. 131 A8 40 59 S 173 25 E
Tasman Basin, Pac. Oc. 134 M7 46 0 S 158 0 E
Tasman Mts., N.Z. 131 B7 41 3 S 172 25 E
Tasman Pen., Australia 127 G4 43 10 S 148 0 E
Tasman Plateau, S. Ocean 7 A10 48 0 S 146 0 E
Tasman Sea, Pac. Oc. 134 L8 36 0 S 160 0 E
Tasmania □, Australia 127 G4 42 0 S 146 30 E
Tăşnad, Romania 52 C7 47 30N 22 33 E
Tassili n'Ajjer, Algeria 111 C6 25 47N 8 1 E
Tassili-Oua-n-Ahaggar, Algeria 111 D6 20 41N 5 30 E
Tassili Tin-Rerhoh, Algeria 111 D5 20 5N 3 55 E
Tasty, Kazakhstan 65 A4 44 47N 69 7 E
Tata, Hungary 52 C3 47 37N 18 19 E
Tata, Morocco 110 C3 29 46N 7 56W
Tata Mai Lau, E. Timor 82 C3 8 58 S 125 30 E
Tatabánya, Hungary 52 C3 47 32N 18 25 E
Tatamā △, Colombia 168 B2 5 5N 76 9W
Tatamba, Solomon Is. 133 M10 8 21 S 159 51 E
Tataouine, Tunisia 108 B2 32 57N 10 29 E
Tatar-Pazardzhik = Pazardzhik, Bulgaria 51 D8 42 12N 24 20 E
Tatar Republic = Tatarstan □, Russia 60 C10 55 30N 51 30 E
Tatarbunary, Ukraine 53 E14 45 50N 29 39 E
Tatarsk, Russia 66 D8 55 14N 76 0 E
Tatarstan □, Russia 60 C10 55 30N 51 30 E
Tatatóváros = Tata, Hungary 52 C3 47 37N 18 19 E
Tatau, Malaysia 85 B4 2 53N 112 51 E
Tatau I., Papua N. G. 132 B6 2 48 S 151 57 E
Tatebayashi, Japan 73 A11 36 15N 139 32 E
Tateshina-Yama, Japan 73 A10 36 8N 138 11 E
Tateyama, Japan 73 C11 35 0N 139 50 E
Tathlina L., Canada 142 A5 60 33N 117 39W
Tathlīth, Si. Arabia 98 C3 19 32N 43 30 E
Tathlīth, W. →, Si. Arabia 98 B4 20 35N 44 20 E
Tathra, Australia 129 D8 36 44 S 149 59 E
Tatinnai L., Canada 143 A9 60 55N 97 40W
Tatitlek, U.S.A. 144 F11 60 52N 146 41W
Tatkon, Burma 90 E6 20 7N 96 13 E
Tatla L., Canada 142 C4 52 0N 124 20W
Tatlısu, Turkey 51 F11 40 24N 27 55 E
Tatnam, C., Canada 143 B10 57 16N 91 0W
Tatra = Tatry, Slovak Rep. 35 B13 49 20N 20 0 E
Tatranský △, Slovak Rep. 35 B13 49 10N 20 0 E
Tatry, Slovak Rep. 35 B13 49 20N 20 0 E
Tatshenshini →, Canada 142 B1 59 28N 137 45W
Tatsuno, Hyōgo, Japan 72 C6 34 52N 134 33 E
Tatsuno, Nagano, Japan 73 B10 35 58N 138 0 E
Tatta, Pakistan 92 D2 24 42N 67 55 E
Tätti, Kazakhstan 65 B6 43 13N 73 18 E
Tatuí, Brazil 175 A6 23 25 S 47 53W
Tatum, U.S.A. 155 J3 33 16N 103 19W
Tat'ung = Datong, China 74 D7 40 6N 113 18 E
Tatura, Australia 129 D6 36 29 S 145 16 E
Tatvan, Turkey 101 C10 38 31N 42 15 E
Ta'ū, Amer. Samoa 133 X25 14 15 S 169 30W
Tau, Norway 18 E2 59 3N 5 55 E
Tauá, Brazil 170 C3 6 1 S 40 26W
Taubaté, Brazil 175 A6 23 0 S 45 36W
Tauberbischofsheim, Germany 31 F5 49 37N 9 39 E
Taucha, Germany 30 D8 51 23N 12 29 E
Tauern, Austria 36 E7 47 15N 12 40 E
Tauern-tunnel, Austria 34 D6 47 0N 13 12 E
Taufikia, Sudan 107 F3 9 24N 31 37 E
Taulé, France 26 D3 48 37N 3 55W
Taumarunui, N.Z. 130 E4 38 53 S 175 15 E
Taumaturgo, Brazil 172 B3 8 54 S 72 51W
Taung, S. Africa 116 D3 27 33 S 24 47 E
Taungdwingyi, Burma 90 E5 20 1N 95 40 E
Taunggyi, Burma 90 E6 20 50N 97 0 E
Taungtha, Burma 90 E5 21 12N 95 25 E
Taungup, Burma 90 F5 18 51N 94 14 E
Taungup Pass, Burma 90 F5 18 40N 94 45 E
Taunsa, Pakistan 92 D4 30 42N 70 39 E
Taunsa Barrage, Pakistan 92 D4 30 42N 70 50 E
Taunton, U.K. 21 F4 51 1N 3 5W
Taunton, U.S.A. 151 E13 41 54N 71 6W
Taunus, Germany 31 E4 50 13N 8 34 E
Taupo, N.Z. 130 E5 38 41 S 176 7 E
Taupo, L., N.Z. 130 E4 38 46 S 175 55 E
Tauragė, Lithuania 15 J20 55 14N 22 16 E
Tauragė □, Lithuania 54 C9 55 15N 22 17 E
Tauranga, N.Z. 130 D5 37 42 S 176 11 E
Tauranga Harb., N.Z. 130 D5 37 30 S 176 5 E
Taureau, Rés., Canada 140 C5 46 46N 73 50W
Tauri →, Papua N. G. 132 E4 8 8 S 146 8 E
Taurianova, Italy 47 D9 38 21N 16 1 E
Taurus Mts. = Toros Dağlar, Turkey 100 D5 37 0N 32 30 E
Taus = Domažlice, Czech Rep. 34 B5 49 28N 12 58 E
Tauste, Spain 40 D3 41 58N 1 18W
Tautira, Tahiti 133 S16 17 44 S 149 9W
Tauz = Tovuz, Azerbaijan 61 K7 41 0N 45 40 E
Tavaar, Somali Rep. 120 D3 3 6N 46 1 E
Tavannes, Switz. 32 B4 47 13N 7 12 E
Tavares, U.S.A. 153 G8 28 48N 81 44W
Tavas, Turkey 49 D11 37 34N 29 4 E
Tavastehus = Hämeenlinna, Finland 15 F21 61 0N 24 28 E
Tavda, Russia 66 D7 58 7N 65 8 E
Tavda →, Russia 66 D7 57 47N 67 18 E
Tavernes de la Valldigna, Spain 41 F4 39 5N 0 13W
Tavernier, U.S.A. 153 K9 25 1N 80 31W
Taveta, Tanzania 118 C4 3 23 S 37 37 E
Taveuni, Fiji 133 A3 16 51 S 179 58W
Taviano, Italy 47 C11 39 59N 18 5 E
Tavignano →, France 29 F13 42 7N 9 33 E
Tavildara, Tajikistan 65 D5 38 41N 70 29 E
Tavira, Portugal 43 H3 37 8N 7 40W
Tavistock, Canada 150 C4 43 19N 80 50W
Tavistock, U.K. 21 G3 50 33N 4 9W
Tavolara, Italy 46 B2 40 54N 9 42 E
Távora →, Portugal 42 D3 41 8N 7 35W
Tavoy, Burma 86 E2 14 2N 98 12 E
Tavşanlı, Turkey 49 B11 39 32N 29 30 E
Tavua, Fiji 133 A1 17 37 S 177 5 E
Tavuki, Fiji 133 B2 19 7 S 178 8 E
Taw →, U.K. 21 F3 51 4N 4 4W
Tawa →, India 92 H8 22 48N 77 48 E
Tawa Tawa Mal Reef, Papua N. G. 132 F7 11 3 S 152 55 E
Tawai, India 90 B6 27 48N 96 47 E
Tawas City, U.S.A. 148 C4 44 16N 83 31W
Tawau, Malaysia 85 B5 4 20N 117 55 E
Taweisha, Sudan 107 E2 12 19N 26 40 E
Tawi-Tawi □, Phil. 81 J3 5 0N 120 0 E
Tawitawi, Phil. 79 B6 5 10N 120 0 E
Tawitawi Group, Phil. 81 J3 5 10N 120 15 E
Tawngche, Burma 90 B5 26 34N 95 38 E
Tawu, Taiwan 77 F13 22 30N 120 50 E
Tāwurghā', Libya 108 B3 32 1N 15 2 E
Tāwurghā', Sabkhat, Libya 108 B3 31 51N 15 15 E
Taxco de Alarcón, Mexico 163 D5 18 33N 99 36W
Taxila, Pakistan 92 C5 33 42N 72 52 E
Taxkorgan He →, China 65 E8 37 45N 76 10 E
Taxkorgan Tajik Zizhixian, China 65 E7 37 49N 75 14 E
Tay ◠, U.K. 22 E5 56 43N 3 59W
Tay →, U.K. 22 E5 56 37N 3 38W
Tay, Firth of, U.K. 22 E5 56 25N 3 8W
Tay, L., Australia 125 F3 32 55 S 120 48 E
Tay, L., U.K. 22 E4 56 32N 4 8W
Tay Ninh, Vietnam 87 G6 11 20N 106 5 E
Tayabamba, Peru 172 B2 8 15 S 77 16W
Tayabas = Quezon, Phil. 81 G1 9 15N 117 59 E
Tayabas, Phil. 80 D3 14 1N 121 35 E
Tayabas Bay, Phil. 80 E3 13 45N 121 45 E
Tayandu, Kepulauan, Indonesia 83 C4 5 30 S 132 15 E
Taylakova, Russia 66 D8 59 13N 74 0 E
Taylakovy = Taylakova, Russia 66 D8 59 13N 74 0 E
Taylor, Canada 142 B4 56 13N 120 40W
Taylor, Fla., U.S.A. 152 E7 30 26N 82 18W
Taylor, Mich., U.S.A. 157 B13 42 14N 83 16W
Taylor, Nebr., U.S.A. 154 E5 41 46N 99 23W
Taylor, Pa., U.S.A. 151 E9 41 23N 75 43W
Taylor, Tex., U.S.A. 155 K6 30 34N 97 25W
Taylor, Mt., N.Z. 131 D6 43 30 S 171 20 E
Taylor, Mt., U.S.A. 159 J10 35 14N 107 37W
Taylorsville, U.S.A. 157 F11 38 2N 85 21W
Taylorsville L., U.S.A. 157 G11 38 0N 85 15W
Taylorville, U.S.A. 156 E7 39 33N 89 18W
Taymā, Si. Arabia 96 E3 27 35N 38 45 E
Taymyr, Oz., Russia 67 B11 74 20N 102 0 E
Taymyr, Poluostrov, Russia 67 B11 75 0N 100 0 E
Tayport, U.K. 22 E6 56 27N 2 52W
Tayrona △, Colombia 165 D5 11 20N 74 2W
Tayshet, Russia 67 D10 55 58N 98 1 E
Taytay, Phil. 81 F2 10 45N 119 30 E
Taytay Bay, Phil. 81 F2 10 55N 119 35 E
Tayug, Phil. 80 C3 16 2N 120 45 E
Tāyyebād, Iran 97 C9 34 45N 60 45 E
Tayyebād □, Iran 97 C9 34 44N 60 44 E
Taz →, Russia 66 C8 67 32N 78 40 E
Taza, Morocco 110 B4 34 16N 4 6W
Tāza Khurmātū, Iraq 101 E11 35 18N 44 20 E
Tazawa-Ko, Japan 70 E10 39 43N 140 40 E
Taze, Burma 90 D5 22 57N 95 24 E
Tazenakht, Morocco 110 B3 30 35N 7 12W
Tazerbo, Libya 108 C4 25 45N 21 0 E
Tazin, Canada 143 B7 59 48N 109 55W
Tazin L., Canada 143 B7 59 44N 108 42W
Tazlina, U.S.A. 144 E11 62 4N 146 27W
Tazoult, Algeria 111 A6 35 29N 6 11 E
Tazovskiy, Russia 66 C8 67 30N 78 44 E
Tbilisi, Georgia 61 K7 41 43N 44 50 E
Tchad = Chad ■, Africa 109 F3 15 0N 17 15 E
Tchad, L., Chad 109 F2 13 30N 14 30 E
Tchaourou, Benin 113 D5 8 58N 2 40 E
Tch'eng-tou = Chengdu, China 76 B5 30 38N 104 2 E
Tchentlo L., Canada 142 B4 55 15N 125 0W
Tchetti, Benin 113 D5 7 50N 1 40 E
Tchibanga, Gabon 114 C2 2 45 S 11 0 E
Tchien, Liberia 112 D3 5 59N 8 15W
Tchin Tabaraden, Niger 113 B6 15 58N 5 56 E
Tchingou, Massif de, N. Cal. 133 T19 20 54 S 165 0 E
Tcholliré, Cameroon 114 A2 8 24N 14 10 E
Tch'ong-k'ing = Chongqing, China 76 C6 29 35N 106 25 E
Tczew, Poland 54 D5 54 8N 18 50 E
Te Anau, N.Z. 131 F2 45 25 S 167 43 E
Te Anau, L., N.Z. 131 F2 45 15 S 167 45 E
Te Araroa, N.Z. 130 D7 37 39 S 178 25 E
Te Aroha, N.Z. 130 D4 37 32 S 175 44 E
Te Awamutu, N.Z. 130 E4 38 1 S 175 20 E
Te Ika a Maui = North I., N.Z. 130 E4 38 0 S 175 0 E
Te Kaha, N.Z. 130 D6 37 44 S 177 52 E
Te Karaka, N.Z. 130 E6 38 26 S 177 53 E
Te Kauwhata, N.Z. 130 D4 37 25 S 175 9 E
Te Kopuru, N.Z. 130 C2 36 2 S 173 56 E
Te Kuiti, N.Z. 130 E4 38 20 S 175 11 E
Te-n-Dghâmcha, Sebkhet, Mauritania 112 B1 18 30N 15 55W
Te Puke, N.Z. 130 D5 37 46 S 176 22 E
Te Teko, N.Z. 130 E5 38 2 S 176 48 E
Te Waewae B., N.Z. 131 G2 46 13 S 167 33 E
Te Wai Pounamu = South I., N.Z. 131 E5 44 0 S 170 0 E
Tea →, Brazil 168 D4 0 30 S 65 9W
Teaca, Romania 53 D9 46 55N 24 30 E
Teague, U.S.A. 155 K6 31 38N 96 17W
Teano, Italy 47 A7 41 15N 14 4 E
Teapa, Mexico 163 D6 18 35N 92 56W
Teba, Spain 43 J6 36 59N 4 55W
Tebakang, Malaysia 78 D4 1 6N 110 30 E
Teberau, Malaysia 84 B2 1 32N 103 45 E
Teberda, Russia 61 J5 43 30N 41 46 E
Teberu, Malaysia 87 d 1 30N 103 42 E
Tébessa, Algeria 111 A6 35 22N 8 8 E
Tebicuary →, Paraguay 174 B4 26 36 S 58 16W
Tebingtinggi, Riau, Indonesia 84 B2 1 0N 102 45 E
Tebingtinggi, Sumatera Utara, Indonesia 84 B1 3 20N 99 9 E
Tébourba, Tunisia 108 A1 36 49N 9 51 E
Téboursouk, Tunisia 108 A1 36 29N 9 10 E
Tebulos, Georgia 61 J7 42 36N 45 17 E
Tecate, Mexico 161 N10 32 34N 116 38W
Tecer Dağları, Turkey 100 C7 39 27N 37 27 E
Tech →, France 28 F7 42 36N 3 3 E
Techa →, Russia 64 C9 56 13N 62 58 E
Techiman, Ghana 112 D4 7 35N 1 58W
Techirghiol, Romania 53 F13 44 4N 28 32 E
Techou = Dezhou, China 74 F9 37 26N 116 18 E
Tecka, Argentina 176 B2 43 29 S 70 48W
Tecomán, Mexico 162 D4 18 55N 103 53W
Tecopa, U.S.A. 161 K10 35 51N 116 13W
Tecoripa, Mexico 162 B3 28 37N 109 57W
Tecuala, Mexico 162 C3 22 23N 105 27W
Tecuci, Romania 53 E12 45 51N 27 27 E
Tecumseh, Canada 150 D2 42 19N 82 54W
Tecumseh, Mich., U.S.A. 157 B13 42 0N 83 57W
Tecumseh, Okla., U.S.A. 155 H6 35 15N 96 56W
Ted, Somali Rep. 120 D2 4 24N 43 55 E
Tedjert, Algeria 111 D6 21 23N 6 25 E
Tedzhen = Tejen, Turkmenistan 66 F7 37 23N 60 31 E
Tees →, U.K. 20 C6 54 37N 1 10W
Tees B., U.K. 20 C6 54 40N 1 9W
Teeswater, Canada 150 C3 43 59N 81 17W
Tefé, Brazil 169 D5 3 25 S 64 50W
Tefé →, Brazil 169 D5 3 35 S 64 47W
Tefenni, Turkey 49 D11 37 18N 29 45 E
Tegal, Indonesia 85 D3 6 52 S 109 8 E
Tegallalang, Indonesia 79 J18 8 27 S 115 17 E
Tegalsari, Indonesia 79 J17 8 25 S 114 8 E
Tegel, Berlin ✕ (TXL), Germany 30 C9 52 35N 13 14 E
Tegernsee, Germany 31 H7 47 43N 11 46 E
Teggiano, Italy 47 B8 40 23N 15 32 E
Tegid, L. = Bala, L., U.K. 20 E4 52 53N 3 37W
Tegina, Nigeria 113 C6 10 5N 6 11 E
Téglio, Italy 33 D10 46 10N 10 4 E
Tegua, Vanuatu 133 C4 13 15 S 166 37 E
Tegucigalpa, Honduras 164 D2 14 5N 87 14W
Teguidda i-n-Tessoum, Niger 113 B6 17 25N 6 37 E
Tehachapi, U.S.A. 161 K8 35 8N 118 27W
Tehachapi Mts., U.S.A. 161 L8 35 0N 118 30W
Tehamiyam, Sudan 106 D4 18 20N 36 32 E
Teheran = Tehrān, Iran 97 C6 35 44N 51 30 E
Tehilla, Sudan 106 D4 17 42N 36 6 E
Téhini, Ivory C. 112 D4 9 39N 3 40W
Tehoru, Indonesia 83 B3 3 23 S 129 30 E
Tehrān, Iran 97 C6 35 44N 51 30 E
Tehran □, Iran 97 C6 35 30N 51 30 E
Tehri, India 93 D8 30 23N 78 29 E
Tehuacán, Mexico 163 D5 18 30N 97 30W
Tehuantepec, Mexico 163 D5 16 21N 95 13W
Tehuantepec, G. de, Mexico 163 D5 15 50N 95 12W
Tehuantepec, Istmo de, Mexico 163 D6 17 0N 94 30W
Teide, Pico de, Canary Is. 9 e1 28 15N 16 38W
Teifi →, U.K. 21 E3 52 5N 4 41W
Teigebyen, Norway 18 D8 60 12N 11 0 E
Teign →, U.K. 21 G4 50 32N 3 32W
Teignmouth, U.K. 21 G4 50 33N 3 31W
Teiuş, Romania 53 D8 46 12N 23 40 E
Teixeira, Brazil 170 C4 7 13 S 37 15W
Teixeira Pinto, Guinea-Biss. 112 C1 12 3N 16 0W
Tejakula, Indonesia 79 J18 8 8 S 115 20 E
Tejam, India 93 E9 29 57N 80 11 E
Tejen, Turkmenistan 66 F7 37 23N 60 31 E
Tejen →, Turkmenistan 97 B9 37 24N 60 38 E
Tejo →, Europe 43 F2 38 40N 9 24W
Tejon Pass, U.S.A. 161 L8 34 49N 118 53W
Tekamah, U.S.A. 154 E6 41 47N 96 13W
Tekapo →, N.Z. 131 E5 44 13 S 170 21 E
Tekapo, L., N.Z. 131 D5 43 53 S 170 33 E
Tekax, Mexico 163 C7 20 11N 89 18W
Teke, Kazakhstan 65 B4 43 15N 68 10 E
Teke, Turkey 51 E13 41 4N 29 39 E
Tekeli, Kazakhstan 65 A9 44 50N 79 0 E
Tekeze →, Ethiopia 107 E4 14 20N 35 50 E
Tekija, Serbia & M. 50 B6 44 42N 22 26 E
Tekirdağ, Turkey 51 F11 40 58N 27 30 E
Tekirdağ □, Turkey 51 E11 41 0N 27 0 E
Tekirova, Turkey 49 E12 36 30N 30 32 E
Tekkali, India 94 E7 18 37N 84 15 E
Tekke, Turkey 100 B7 40 42N 36 12 E
Tekman, Turkey 101 C9 39 38N 41 30 E
Tekoa, U.S.A. 158 C5 47 14N 117 4W
Tekong Besar, Pulau, Singapore 87 d 1 25N 104 3 E
Tekouiât, O. →, Algeria 111 D5 22 25N 2 35 E
Tekro, Chad 109 E4 19 32N 20 56 E
Teku, Indonesia 82 B2 0 46 S 123 26 E
Tel →, India 94 D6 20 50N 83 54 E
Tel Aviv ✕ (TLV), Israel 103 C3 32 5N 34 49 E
Tel Aviv-Yafo, Israel 103 C3 32 4N 34 48 E
Tel Lakhish, Israel 103 D3 31 34N 34 51 E
Tel Megiddo, Israel 103 C4 32 35N 35 11 E
Tela, Honduras 164 C2 15 40N 87 28W
Télagh, Algeria 111 B4 34 51N 0 32W
Telanaipura = Jambi, Indonesia 84 C2 1 38 S 103 30 E
Telašćica ◠, Croatia 45 E12 43 55N 15 10 E
Telavåg, Norway 18 D1 60 15N 4 58 E
Telavi, Georgia 61 J7 42 0N 45 30 E
Telč, Czech Rep. 34 B8 49 11N 15 28 E
Telciu, Romania 53 C9 47 25N 24 24 E
Telde, Canary Is. 9 e1 27 59N 15 25W
Tele →, Dem. Rep. of the Congo 114 B4 2 48N 23 54 E
Telefomin, Papua N. G. 132 C1 5 10 S 141 31 E
Telegraph Creek, Canada 142 B2 58 0N 131 10W
Telekhany = Tsyelyakhany, Belarus 59 F3 52 30N 25 46 E
Telemark, Norway 15 G12 59 15N 7 40 E
Telemark □, Norway 18 E5 59 25N 8 30 E
Telén, Argentina 174 D2 36 15 S 65 31W
Telen →, Indonesia 85 C5 0 10 S 117 20 E
Teleneşti, Moldova 53 C13 47 30N 28 22 E
Teleng, Iran 97 E9 25 47N 61 3 E
Teleño, Spain 42 C4 42 23N 6 22W
Teleorman □, Romania 53 G10 44 0N 25 0 E
Teleorman →, Romania 53 G10 43 52N 25 26 E
Teles Pires →, Brazil 173 B6 7 21 S 58 3W
Telescope Pk., U.S.A. 161 J9 36 10N 117 5W
Teletaye, Mali 113 B5 16 31N 1 30 E
Telfer Mine, Australia 124 C3 21 40 S 122 12 E
Telford, U.K. 21 E5 52 40N 2 27W
Telford and Wrekin □, U.K. 20 E5 52 45N 2 27W
Telfs, Austria 34 D4 47 19N 11 4 E
Telida, U.S.A. 144 E9 63 23N 153 16W
Télimélé, Guinea 112 C2 10 54N 13 2W
Teljo, J., Sudan 107 E2 14 42N 25 26 E
Telkwa, Canada 142 C3 54 41N 127 5W
Tell City, U.S.A. 157 G10 37 57N 86 46W
Teller, U.S.A. 144 D6 65 16N 166 22W
Tellicherry, India 95 J2 11 45N 75 30 E
Telluride, U.S.A. 159 H10 37 56N 107 49W
Telok Datok, Malaysia 84 B2 2 49N 101 31 E
Teloloapán, Mexico 163 D5 18 21N 99 51W
Telpos Iz, Russia 56 B10 63 16N 59 13 E
Telsen, Argentina 176 B3 42 30 S 66 50W
Telšiai, Lithuania 15 H20 55 59N 22 14 E
Telšiai □, Lithuania 54 C9 55 59N 22 15 E
Teltow, Germany 30 C9 52 23N 13 15 E
Teluk Anson = Teluk Intan, Malaysia 87 K3 4 3N 101 0 E
Teluk Bahang, Malaysia 87 c 5 28N 100 13 E
Teluk Betung = Tanjungkarang Telukbetung, Indonesia 84 D3 5 20 S 105 10 E
Teluk Cenderawasih, Indonesia 83 B5 2 30 S 135 20 E
Teluk Darvel, Malaysia 81 J2 4 45N 118 30 E
Teluk Intan, Malaysia 87 K3 4 3N 101 0 E
Teluk Kumbar, Malaysia 87 c 5 18N 100 14 E
Telukbutun, Indonesia 85 B3 4 13N 108 12 E
Telukdalem, Indonesia 84 B1 0 33N 97 50 E
Tema, Ghana 113 D5 5 41N 0 0W
Temanggung, Indonesia 85 D4 7 18 S 110 10 E
Temasint, Algeria 111 D6 23 18N 7 40 E
Temax, Mexico 163 C7 21 10N 88 50W
Temba, S. Africa 117 D4 25 20 S 28 17 E
Tembagapura, Indonesia 83 B5 4 20 S 137 0 E
Tembe, Dem. Rep. of the Congo 118 C2 0 16 S 28 14 E
Tembe ◠, S. Africa 117 D5 26 51 S 32 24 E
Tembesi, Indonesia 84 C2 1 43 S 103 6 E
Tembilahan, Indonesia 84 C2 0 19 S 103 9 E
Temblador, Venezuela 169 B5 8 59N 62 44W
Tembleque, Spain 42 F7 39 41N 3 30W
Temblor Range, U.S.A. 161 K7 35 20N 119 50W
Teme →, U.K. 21 E5 52 11N 2 13W
Temecula, U.S.A. 161 M9 33 30N 117 9W
Temerloh, Malaysia 84 B2 3 27N 102 25 E
Teminabuan, Indonesia 83 B4 1 26 S 132 1 E
Temir, Kazakhstan 57 E10 49 1N 57 14 E
Temir, Kazakhstan 65 B4 42 49N 68 26 E
Temir-Khan-Shura = Buynaksk, Russia 61 J8 42 48N 47 7 E
Temirlan, Kazakhstan 65 B4 42 36N 69 17 E
Temirtau, Kazakhstan 66 D8 50 5N 72 56 E
Temirtau, Russia 66 D9 53 10N 87 30 E
Témiscamie →, Canada 141 B5 50 59N 73 5W
Témiscaming, Canada 140 C4 46 44N 79 5W
Témiscamingue, L., Canada 140 C4 47 10N 79 25W
Temnikov, Russia 60 C6 54 40N 43 11 E
Temo →, Italy 46 B1 40 17N 8 28 E
Temora, Australia 129 C7 34 30 S 147 30 E
Temosachic, Mexico 162 B3 28 58N 107 50W
Tempe, U.S.A. 159 K8 33 25N 111 56W
Tempelburg = Czaplinek, Poland 54 E3 53 34N 16 14 E
Témpio Pausánia, Italy 46 B2 40 54N 9 6 E
Tempiute, U.S.A. 160 H11 37 39N 115 38W
Templar Bank, S. China Sea 81 F1 9 0N 117 30 E
Temple, U.S.A. 155 K6 31 6N 97 21W
Temple B., Australia 126 A3 12 15 S 143 3 E
Temple Terrace, U.S.A. 153 G7 28 2N 82 23W
Templemore, Ireland 23 D4 52 47N 7 51W
Templeton, U.S.A. 160 K6 35 33N 120 42W
Templeton →, Australia 126 C2 21 0 S 138 40 E
Templin, Germany 30 B9 53 7N 13 28 E
Tempoal, Mexico 163 C5 21 31N 98 23W
Tempué, Angola 115 E3 13 27 S 18 49 E
Temryuk, Russia 59 K9 45 15N 37 24 E
Temska →, Serbia & M. 50 C6 43 17N 22 33 E
Temuco, Chile 176 A2 38 45 S 72 40W
Temuka, N.Z. 131 E6 44 14 S 171 17 E
Ten Degree Channel, India 95 K11 10 0N 92 30 E
Ten Thousand Is., U.S.A. 153 K8 25 55N 81 45W
Tena, Ecuador 168 D2 0 59 S 77 49W
Tenabo, Mexico 163 C6 20 2N 90 12W
Tenaha, U.S.A. 155 K7 31 57N 94 15W
Tenakee Springs, U.S.A. 142 B1 57 47N 135 13W
Tenali, India 95 F5 16 15N 80 35 E
Tenancingo, Mexico 163 D5 19 0N 99 33W

Tenango, *Mexico* **163 D5** 19 7N 99 33W
Tenaro, Ákra = Taínaron, Ákra, *Greece* ..... **48 E4** 36 22N 22 27 E
Tenasserim, *Burma* ... **87 F2** 12 6N 99 3 E
Tenasserim □, *Burma* **86 F2** 14 0N 98 30 E
Tenby, *U.K.* **21 F3** 51 40N 4 42W
Tenda, Colle di, *France* **29 D11** 44 7N 7 36 E
Tendaho, *Ethiopia* ... **107 E5** 11 48N 40 54 E
Tende, *France* ..... **29 D11** 44 5N 7 35 E
Tendelti, *Sudan* ..... **107 E3** 13 1N 31 55 E
Tendjedi, Adrar, *Algeria* ..... **111 D6** 23 41N 7 32 E
Tendrara, *Morocco* ... **111 B4** 33 3N 1 58W
Tendre, Mt., *Switz.* ... **32 C2** 46 35N 6 18 E
Tendrovskaya Kosa, *Ukraine* ..... **59 J6** 46 16N 31 35 E
Tendukhera, *India* ... **93 H8** 23 24N 79 33 E
Tenebroûret, O. →, *Mauritania* **110 D1** 20 35N 16 0W
Teneguía, Volcanes de, *Canary Is.* **9 e1** 28 28N 17 51W
Teneida, *Egypt* ..... **106 B2** 25 30N 29 19 E
Tenenkou, *Mali* **112 C4** 14 28N 4 55W
Tenente Marques →, *Brazil* ..... **173 C6** 11 10 S 59 56W
Ténéré, *Niger* ..... **113 B7** 19 0N 10 30 E
Ténéré, Erg du, *Niger* . **109 E2** 17 35N 10 55 E
Tenerife, *Canary Is.* .. **9 e1** 28 15N 16 35W
Tenerife, Pico, *Canary Is.* **9 e1** 27 43N 18 1W
Tenerife Norte ✈ (TFN), *Canary Is.* .. **9 e1** 28 28N 16 17W
Tenerife Sur ✈ (TFS), *Canary Is.* **9 e1** 28 3N 16 33W
Ténès, *Algeria* ..... **111 A5** 36 31N 1 14 E
Teng Xian, *Guangxi Zhuangzu, China* ..... **77 F8** 23 21N 110 56 E
Teng Xian, *Shandong, China* ..... **75 G9** 35 5N 117 10 E
Tengah, Kepulauan, *Indonesia* ..... **85 D5** 7 5 S 118 15 E
Tengchong, *China* .... **76 E2** 25 0N 98 28 E
Tengchowfu = Penglai, *China* ..... **75 F11** 37 48N 120 42 E
Tenggarong, *Indonesia* **85 C5** 0 24 S 116 58 E
Tenggol, Pulau, *Malaysia* ..... **87 K4** 4 48N 103 41 E
Tengi-Kharam = Dekhkanabad, *Uzbekistan* ..... **65 D3** 38 21N 66 30 E
Tengiz, Ozero, *Kazakhstan* ..... **66 D7** 50 30N 69 0 E
Tenhult, *Sweden* ..... **17 G8** 57 41N 14 20 E
Teniente Enciso △, *Paraguay* ..... **174 A3** 21 5 S 61 8W
Teniente Rodolfo Marsh, *Antarctica* .. **7 C18** 62 30 S 58 0W
Tenigerbad, *Switz.* .... **33 C7** 46 42N 8 57 E
Tenille, *U.S.A.* **152 F6** 29 46N 83 19W
Tenino, *U.S.A.* **160 D4** 46 51N 122 51W
Tenkasi, *India* ..... **95 K3** 8 55N 77 20 E
Tenke, *Katanga, Dem. Rep. of the Congo* ..... **119 E2** 11 22 S 26 40 E
Tenke, *Katanga, Dem. Rep. of the Congo* ..... **119 E2** 10 32 S 26 7 E
Tenkodogo, *Burkina Faso* **113 C4** 11 54N 0 19W
Tenna →, *Italy* ..... **45 E10** 43 14N 13 47 E
Tennant Creek, *Australia* ..... **126 B1** 19 30 S 134 15 E
Tennessee □, *U.S.A.* .. **149 H2** 36 0N 86 30W
Tennessee →, *U.S.A.* . **148 G1** 37 4N 88 34W
Tennille, *U.S.A.* **152 C7** 32 56N 82 48W
Teno, Pta. de, *Canary Is.* **9 e1** 28 21N 16 55W
Tenom, *Malaysia* ..... **85 A5** 5 4N 115 57 E
Tenosique, *Mexico* **163 D6** 17 30N 91 24W
Tenri, *Japan* ..... **73 C7** 34 39N 135 49 E
Tenryū, *Japan* ..... **73 C9** 34 52N 137 49 E
Tenryū-Gawa →, *Japan* ..... **73 B9** 35 39N 137 48 E
Tensift, Oued →, *Morocco* **110 B3** 32 3N 9 28W
Tentelomatinan, *Indonesia* ..... **82 A2** 0 56N 121 48 E
Tentena, *Indonesia* ... **82 B2** 1 47 S 120 39 E
Tenterden, *U.K.* ..... **21 F8** 51 4N 0 42 E
Tenterfield, *Australia* . **127 D5** 29 0 S 152 0 E
Tenuaiur, Uad →, *W. Sahara* **110 D1** 21 36N 16 0W
Teo, *Spain* **42 C2** 42 45N 8 30W
Teófilo Otoni, *Brazil* . **171 E3** 17 50 S 41 30W
Tepa, *Indonesia* ..... **83 C3** 7 52 S 129 31 E
Tepalcatepec →, *Mexico* **162 D4** 18 35N 101 59W
Tepecik, *Bursa, Turkey* **51 F12** 40 7N 28 25 E
Tepecik, *Kütahya, Turkey* ..... **49 B11** 39 32N 29 28 E
Tepehuanes, *Mexico* .. **162 B3** 25 21N 105 44W
Tepelenë, *Albania* .... **50 F4** 40 17N 20 2 E
Tepequem, Serra, *Brazil* **169 C5** 3 45N 61 45W
Tepetongo, *Mexico* ... **162 C4** 22 28N 103 9W
Tepic = Nayarit □, *Mexico* **162 C4** 22 0N 105 0W
Tepic, *Mexico* **162 C4** 21 30N 104 54W
Teplá, *Czech Rep.* .... **34 B5** 49 59N 12 52 E
Teplice, *Czech Rep.* .. **34 A6** 50 40N 13 48 E
Teplitz = Teplice, *Czech Rep.* ..... **34 A6** 50 40N 13 48 E
Teploklyuchenka, *Kyrgyzstan* ..... **65 B9** 42 30N 78 30 E
Teplyk, *Ukraine* ..... **53 B14** 48 40N 29 44 E
Tepoca, C., *Mexico* ... **162 A2** 30 20N 112 25W
Tequila, *Mexico* **162 C4** 20 54N 103 47W
Ter →, *Spain* ..... **40 C8** 42 2N 3 12 E
Ter Apel, *Neths.* ..... **24 B7** 52 53N 7 5 E
Téra, *Niger* ..... **113 C5** 14 0N 0 45 E
Tera →, *Spain* **42 D5** 41 54N 5 44W
Teraina, *Kiribati* **135 G11** 4 43N 160 25W
Terakeka, *Sudan* ..... **107 F3** 5 26N 31 45 E
Téramo, *Italy* ..... **45 F10** 42 39N 13 42 E
Terang, *Australia* .... **128 E5** 38 15 S 142 55 E
Terang, Teluk, *Indonesia* ..... **79 K19** 8 44 S 116 0 E
Terawhiti, C., *N.Z.* ... **130 H3** 41 16 S 174 38 E
Terazit, Massif de, *Niger* ..... **111 D6** 20 2N 8 30 E
Tercan, *Turkey* ..... **101 C9** 39 47N 40 23 E
Terceira, *Azores* **9 d1** 38 43N 27 13W
Tercero →, *Argentina* **174 C3** 32 58 S 61 47W
Terdal, *India* ..... **94 F2** 16 33N 75 3 E
Terebovlya, *Ukraine* .. **59 H3** 49 18N 25 44 E
Teregova, *Romania* ... **52 E7** 45 10N 22 16 E
Tereida, *Sudan* ..... **107 E3** 10 35N 31 17 E
Terek →, *Russia* ..... **61 J8** 44 0N 47 30 E
Terek-Say, *Kyrgyzstan* **65 C5** 41 30N 71 11 E
Terengganu □, *Malaysia* ..... **84 B2** 4 55N 103 0 E
Terengözek, *Kazakhstan* ..... **65 A2** 45 3N 64 59 E
Terenos, *Brazil* ..... **173 E7** 20 26 S 54 50W
Terepaima △, *Venezuela* **165 E6** 9 58N 69 17W
Tereshka →, *Russia* .. **60 E8** 51 48N 46 26 E
Teresina, *Brazil* ..... **170 C3** 5 9 S 42 45W
Teresinha, *Brazil* **169 C7** 0 58N 52 2W
Terespol, *Poland* ..... **55 F10** 52 5N 23 37 E
Teressa, *India* ..... **95 K11** 8 15N 93 10 E
Teresva, *Ukraine* ..... **53 B8** 48 0N 23 42 E
Terewah, L., *Australia* **127 D4** 29 52 S 147 35 E
Terges →, *Portugal* .. **43 H3** 37 49N 7 41W
Tergnier, *France* ..... **27 C10** 49 40N 3 17 E
Terhazza, *Mali* **110 D3** 23 38N 5 22W
Teridgerie Cr. →, *Australia* ..... **129 A8** 30 25 S 148 50 E
Terijoki = Zelenogorsk, *Russia* ..... **58 B5** 60 12N 29 43 E
Terlizzi, *Italy* ..... **47 A9** 41 8N 16 32 E
Terme, *Turkey* ..... **100 B7** 41 11N 37 0 E
Termez = Termiz, *Uzbekistan* ..... **65 E3** 37 15N 67 15 E
Términi Imerese, *Italy* **46 E6** 37 59N 13 42 E
Términos, L. de, *Mexico* **163 D6** 18 35N 91 30W
Termiz, *Uzbekistan* ... **65 E3** 37 15N 67 15 E
Térmoli, *Italy* ..... **45 F12** 42 0N 15 0 E
Ternate, *Indonesia* ... **82 A3** 0 45N 127 25 E
Terneuzen, *Neths.* .... **24 C3** 51 20N 3 50 E
Terney, *Russia* ..... **67 E14** 45 3N 136 37 E
Terni, *Italy* ..... **45 F9** 42 34N 12 37 E
Ternitz, *Austria* ..... **34 D9** 47 43N 16 2 E
Ternivka, *Ukraine* .... **53 B14** 48 32N 29 58 E
Ternopil, *Ukraine* .... **59 H3** 49 30N 25 40 E
Ternopol = Ternopil, *Ukraine* ..... **59 H3** 49 30N 25 40 E
Terowie, *Australia* ... **128 B3** 33 8 S 138 55 E
Terpní, *Greece* ..... **50 F7** 40 55N 23 26 E
Terra Bella, *U.S.A.* ... **161 K7** 35 58N 119 3W
Terra Nova △, *Canada* **141 C9** 48 33N 53 55W
Terrace, *Canada* **142 C3** 54 30N 128 35W
Terrace Bay, *Canada* . **140 C2** 48 47N 87 5W
Terracina, *Italy* ..... **46 A6** 41 17N 13 15 E
Terralba, *Italy* ..... **46 C1** 39 43N 8 39 E
Terranova di Sicilia = Gela, *Italy* ..... **47 E7** 37 4N 14 15 E
Terranova Pausania = Ólbia, *Italy* ..... **46 B2** 40 55N 9 31 E
Terrasini, *Italy* ..... **46 D6** 38 10N 13 4 E
Terrassa, *Spain* ..... **40 D7** 41 34N 2 1 E
Terrasson-la-Villedieu, *France* ..... **28 C5** 45 8N 1 18 E
Terre Haute, *U.S.A.* .. **157 E9** 39 28N 87 25W
Terrebonne B., *U.S.A.* **155 L9** 29 5N 90 35W
Terrecht, *Mali* **111 D4** 20 10N 0 10W
Terrell, *U.S.A.* **155 J6** 32 44N 96 17W
Terrenceville, *Canada* **141 C9** 47 40N 54 44W
Terry, *U.S.A.* **154 B2** 46 47N 105 19W
Terryville, *U.S.A.* **151 E11** 41 41N 73 3W
Terschelling, *Neths.* .. **24 A5** 53 25N 5 20 E
Terskey Ala Too, *Kyrgyzstan* ..... **65 C8** 41 50N 77 0 E
Terskey Alatau = Terskey Ala Too, *Kyrgyzstan* ..... **65 C8** 41 50N 77 0 E
Tersko-Kumskiy Kanal, *Russia* ..... **61 H7** 44 32N 44 38 E
Tertenía, *Italy* ..... **46 C2** 39 42N 9 34 E
Terter = Tärtär →, *Azerbaijan* ..... **61 K8** 40 26N 47 20 E
Teruel, *Spain* **40 E3** 40 22N 1 8W
Teruel □, *Spain* **40 E4** 40 48N 1 0W
Tervel, *Bulgaria* ..... **51 C11** 43 45N 27 28 E
Tervola, *Finland* ..... **14 C21** 66 6N 24 49 E
Teryaweyna L., *Australia* ..... **128 B5** 32 18 S 143 22 E
Tešanj, *Bos.-H.* ..... **52 F3** 44 38N 18 1 E
Teschen = Český Těšín, *Czech Rep.* ..... **35 B11** 49 45N 18 39 E
Teschen = Cieszyn, *Poland* ..... **55 J5** 49 45N 18 35 E
Teseney, *Eritrea* ..... **107 D4** 15 5N 36 42 E
Tesha →, *Russia* ..... **60 C6** 55 38N 42 9 E
Teshekpuk L., *U.S.A.* . **144 A9** 70 35N 153 26W
Teshio, *Japan* ..... **70 B10** 44 53N 141 44 E
Teshio-Gawa →, *Japan* **70 B10** 44 53N 141 45 E
Tešica, *Serbia & M.* .. **50 C5** 43 27N 21 45 E
Tesiyn Gol →, *Mongolia* ..... **68 A4** 50 40N 93 20 E
Teslić, *Bos.-H.* ..... **52 F2** 44 37N 17 54 E
Teslin, *Canada* **142 A2** 60 10N 132 43W
Teslin →, *Canada* **142 A2** 61 34N 134 35W
Teslin L., *Canada* **142 A2** 60 15N 132 57W
Tesouro, *Brazil* ..... **173 D7** 16 4 S 53 34W
Tessalit, *Mali* ..... **111 D5** 20 12N 1 0 E
Tessaoua, *Niger* ..... **113 C6** 13 47N 7 56 E
Tessin, *Germany* ..... **30 A8** 54 2N 12 26 E
Tessit, *Mali* ..... **113 B5** 15 13N 0 18 E
Tessounfat, *Mali* ..... **111 D5** 22 53N 0 32 E
Test →, *U.K.* **21 G6** 50 56N 1 29W
Testa del Gargano, *Italy* **45 G13** 41 50N 16 10 E
Testigos, Is. Las, *Venezuela* **165 D7** 11 23N 63 7W
Tét, *Hungary* ..... **52 C2** 47 30N 17 33 E
Têt →, *France* ..... **28 F7** 42 44N 3 2 E
Tetachuck L., *Canada* . **142 C3** 53 18N 125 55W
Tetas, Pta., *Chile* .... **174 A1** 23 31 S 70 38W
Tete, *Mozam.* ..... **119 F3** 16 13 S 33 33 E
Tete □, *Mozam.* ..... **119 F3** 15 15 S 32 40 E
Tetenga, Caleta, *Chile* **172 b** 27 9 S 109 19W
Tetepare, *Solomon Is.* . **133 M9** 8 45 S 157 35 E
Teterev →, *Ukraine* .. **59 G6** 51 1N 30 5 E
Teterow, *Germany* .... **30 B8** 53 46N 12 34 E
Teteven, *Bulgaria* .... **51 D8** 42 58N 24 17 E
Tethul →, *Canada* **142 A6** 60 35N 112 12W
Tetiyev, *Ukraine* ..... **59 H5** 49 22N 29 38 E
Tetlin, *U.S.A.* **144 E12** 63 8N 142 31W
Tetlin Junction, *U.S.A.* **144 E12** 63 19N 142 36W
Teton →, *U.S.A.* **158 C8** 47 56N 110 31W
Tétouan, *Morocco* **110 A3** 35 35N 5 21W
Tetovo, *Macedonia* ... **50 D4** 42 1N 20 59 E
Tetschen = Děčín, *Czech Rep.* ..... **34 A7** 50 47N 14 12 E
Tetyukhe = Dalnegorsk, *Russia* . **67 E14** 44 32N 135 33 E
Tetyushi, *Russia* ..... **60 C9** 54 55N 48 49 E
Teuco →, *Argentina* . **174 B3** 25 35 S 60 11W
Teufen, *Switz.* ..... **33 B8** 47 24N 9 23 E
Teulada, *Italy* ..... **46 D1** 38 58N 8 46 E
Teulon, *Canada* **143 C9** 50 23N 97 16W
Teun, *Indonesia* ..... **83 C3** 6 59 S 129 8 E
Teutoburger Wald, *Germany* ..... **30 C4** 52 5N 8 22 E
Teutopolis, *U.S.A.* **157 E8** 39 8N 88 29W
Tevere ⌂, *Italy* ..... **45 F9** 42 46N 12 14 E
Tevere →, *Italy* ..... **45 G9** 41 44N 12 14 E
Teverya, *Israel* ..... **103 C4** 32 47N 35 32 E
Teviot →, *U.K.* **22 F6** 55 29N 2 38W
Tewantin, *Australia* .. **127 D5** 26 27 S 153 3 E
Tewkesbury, *U.K.* **21 F5** 51 59N 2 9W
Texada I., *Canada* **142 D4** 49 40N 124 25W
Texarkana, *Ark., U.S.A.* **155 J8** 33 26N 94 2W
Texarkana, *Tex., U.S.A.* **155 J7** 33 26N 94 3W
Texas, *Australia* ..... **127 D5** 28 49 S 151 9 E
Texas □, *U.S.A.* **155 K5** 31 40N 98 30W
Texas City, *U.S.A.* **155 L7** 29 24N 94 54W
Texel, *Neths.* ..... **24 A4** 53 5N 4 50 E
Texline, *U.S.A.* **155 G3** 36 23N 103 2W
Texoma, L., *U.S.A.* ... **155 J6** 33 50N 96 34W
Teykovo, *Russia* ..... **58 D11** 56 55N 40 30 E
Teyvareh, *Afghan.* .... **91 B2** 33 30N 64 24 E
Teza →, *Russia* ..... **60 B5** 56 32N 41 53 E
Tezin, *Afghan.* ..... **91 B3** 34 24N 69 30 E
Teziutlán, *Mexico* **163 D5** 19 50N 97 22W
Tezpur, *India* ..... **90 B4** 26 40N 92 45 E
Tezzeron L., *Canada* .. **142 C4** 54 43N 124 30W
Tha-anne →, *Canada* . **143 A10** 60 31N 94 37W
Tha Deua, *Laos* ..... **86 D4** 17 57N 102 53 E
Tha Deua, *Laos* ..... **86 C3** 19 26N 101 50 E
Tha Pla, *Thailand* .... **86 D3** 17 48N 100 32 E
Tha Rua, *Thailand* .... **86 E3** 14 34N 100 44 E
Tha Sala, *Thailand* ... **87 H2** 8 40N 99 56 E
Tha Song Yang, *Thailand* ..... **86 D1** 17 34N 97 55 E
Thaba Putsoa, *Lesotho* **117 D4** 29 45 S 28 0 E
Thabana Ntlenyana, *Lesotho* ..... **117 D4** 29 30 S 29 16 E
Thabaung, *Burma* .... **90 G5** 17 2N 94 48 E
Thabazimbi, *S. Africa* . **117 C4** 24 40 S 27 21 E
Thabeikkyin, *Burma* .. **90 D5** 22 53N 95 59 E
Thādiq, *Si. Arabia* .... **96 E5** 25 18N 45 52 E
Thai Binh, *Vietnam* ... **76 G6** 20 35N 106 1 E
Thai Muang, *Thailand* . **87 H2** 8 24N 98 16 E
Thai Nguyen, *Vietnam* . **76 G5** 21 35N 105 55 E
Thailand ■, *Asia* ..... **86 E4** 16 0N 102 0 E
Thailand, G. of, *Asia* . **87 G3** 11 30N 101 0 E
Thakhek, *Laos* ..... **86 D5** 17 25N 104 45 E
Thakurgaon, *Bangla.* . **90 B2** 26 2N 88 34 E
Thal, *Pakistan* ..... **91 B3** 33 28N 70 33 E
Thal Desert, *Pakistan* . **92 D4** 31 10N 71 30 E
Thala, *Tunisia* ..... **108 A1** 35 35N 8 40 E
Thalabarivat, *Cambodia* ..... **86 F5** 13 33N 105 57 E
Thalkirch, *Switz.* ..... **33 C8** 46 39N 9 17 E
Thallon, *Australia* .... **127 D4** 28 39 S 148 49 E
Thalu, Ko, *Thailand* .. **87 b** 9 26N 99 54 E
Thalwil, *Switz.* ..... **33 B7** 47 17N 8 35 E
Thamarīt, *Oman* ..... **99 C6** 17 39N 54 2 E
Thames, *N.Z.* ..... **130 D4** 37 7 S 175 34 E
Thames →, *Canada* .. **140 D3** 42 20N 82 25W
Thames →, *U.K.* ..... **21 F8** 51 29N 0 34 E
Thames →, *U.S.A.* ... **151 E12** 41 18N 72 5W
Thames, Firth of, *N.Z.* **130 D4** 37 0 S 175 25 E
Thames Estuary, *U.K.* . **21 F8** 51 29N 0 52 E
Thamesford, *Canada* .. **150 C4** 43 4N 81 0W
Thamesville, *Canada* .. **150 D3** 42 33N 81 59W
Thāmit, W. →, *Libya* . **108 B3** 31 11N 16 8 E
Thamūd, *Yemen* ..... **99 C5** 17 18N 49 55 E
Than, *India* ..... **92 H4** 22 34N 71 11 E
Than Uyen, *Vietnam* .. **86 B4** 22 0N 103 54 E
Thana Gazi, *India* .... **92 F7** 27 25N 76 19 E
Thanbyuzayat, *Burma* . **90 G6** 15 58N 97 44 E
Thandaung, *Burma* ... **90 F6** 19 4N 96 41 E
Thandla, *India* ..... **92 H6** 23 0N 74 34 E
Thane, *India* ..... **94 E1** 19 12N 72 59 E
Thanesar, *India* ..... **92 D7** 30 1N 76 52 E
Thanet, I. of, *U.K.* ... **21 F9** 51 21N 1 20 E
Thangool, *Australia* .. **126 C5** 24 38 S 150 42 E
Thanh Hoa, *Vietnam* .. **86 C5** 19 48N 105 46 E
Thanh Hung, *Vietnam* . **87 H5** 9 55N 105 43 E
Thanh Pho Ho Chi Minh, *Vietnam* ..... **87 G6** 10 58N 106 40 E
Thanh Thuy, *Vietnam* . **86 A5** 22 55N 104 51 E
Thanjavur, *India* ..... **95 J4** 10 48N 79 12 E
Thann, *France* ..... **27 E14** 47 48N 7 5 E
Thano Bula Khan, *Pakistan* ..... **92 G2** 25 22N 67 50 E
Thaolinta L., *Canada* . **143 A9** 61 30N 96 25W
Thaon-les-Vosges, *France* ..... **27 D13** 48 15N 6 24 E
Thap Lan △, *Thailand* . **86 E4** 14 15N 102 16 E
Thap Sakae, *Thailand* . **87 G2** 11 30N 99 37 E
Thap Than, *Thailand* .. **86 E2** 15 27N 99 54 E
Thar Desert, *India* .... **92 F5** 28 0N 72 0 E
Tharad, *India* ..... **92 G4** 24 30N 71 44 E
Thargomindah, *Australia* ..... **127 D3** 27 58 S 143 46 E
Tharrawaddy, *Burma* . **90 G5** 17 38N 95 48 E
Tharrawaw, *Burma* ... **90 G5** 17 41N 95 28 E
Tharthār, Buḥayrat ath, *Iraq* ..... **101 E10** 34 0N 43 15 E
Tharthar, L. = Tharthār, Buḥayrat ath, *Iraq* ..... **101 E10** 34 0N 43 15 E
Tharthār, W. ath →, *Iraq* ..... **101 E10** 33 59N 43 12 E
Thasopoúla, *Greece* .. **51 F8** 40 49N 24 45 E
Thásos, *Greece* ..... **51 F8** 40 40N 24 40 E
That Khe, *Vietnam* ... **76 F6** 22 16N 106 28 E
Thatcher, *Ariz., U.S.A.* **159 K9** 32 51N 109 46W
Thatcher, *Colo., U.S.A.* **155 G2** 37 33N 104 7W
Thaton, *Burma* ..... **90 G6** 16 55N 97 22 E
Thau, Bassin de, *France* **28 E7** 43 23N 3 36 E
Thaungdut, *Burma* .... **90 C5** 24 30N 94 40 E
Thawatti, *Burma* ..... **90 F6** 19 32N 96 16 E
Thayer, *U.S.A.* **155 G9** 36 31N 91 33W
Thayetmyo, *Burma* ... **90 F5** 19 20N 95 10 E
Thayngen, *Switz.* ..... **33 A7** 47 49N 8 43 E
Thazi, *Magwe, Burma* . **90 F5** 19 59N 95 3 E
Thazi, *Mandalay, Burma* ..... **90 E6** 21 0N 96 5 E
The Bight, *Bahamas* .. **165 B4** 24 19N 75 24W
The Briars, *St. Helena* **9 h** 15 56 S 5 43W
The Crane, *Barbados* . **165 g** 13 6N 59 27W
The Dalles, *U.S.A.* **158 D3** 45 36N 121 10W
The Entrance, *Australia* **129 B9** 33 21 S 151 30 E
The Forks = Merritt, *Canada* **142 C4** 50 10N 120 45W
The Great Divide = Great Dividing Ra., *Australia* ..... **126 C4** 23 0 S 146 0 E
The Hague = 's-Gravenhage, *Neths.* . **24 B4** 52 7N 4 17 E
The Oaks, *Australia* .. **129 C9** 34 3 S 150 34 E
The Pas, *Canada* **143 C8** 53 45N 101 15W
The Range, *Zimbabwe* **119 F3** 19 2 S 31 2 E
The Rock, *Australia* .. **129 C7** 35 15 S 147 2 E
The Settlement, *Br. Virgin Is.* ..... **165 e** 18 43N 64 22W
The Woodlands, *U.S.A.* **155 K7** 30 9N 95 27W
Thebes = Thívai, *Greece* ..... **48 C5** 38 19N 23 19 E
Thebes, *Egypt* ..... **106 B3** 25 40N 32 35 E
Thedaw, *Burma* ..... **90 E6** 21 5N 96 4 E
Thedford, *U.S.A.* **154 E4** 41 59N 100 35W
Theebine, *Australia* .. **127 D5** 25 57 S 152 34 E
Thègon, *Burma* ..... **90 F5** 18 39N 95 25 E
Thékli, Ayía, *Greece* .. **39 C1** 38 15N 20 23 E
Thekulthili L., *Canada* **143 A7** 61 3N 110 0W
Thelon →, *Canada* ... **143 A8** 64 16N 96 4W
Thénezay, *France* **26 F6** 46 44N 0 2W
Thenia, *Algeria* ..... **111 A5** 36 44N 3 33 E
Thenon, *France* ..... **28 C5** 45 9N 1 4 E
Theodore, *Australia* .. **126 C5** 24 55 S 150 3 E
Theodore, *Canada* **143 C8** 51 26N 102 55W
Theodore, *U.S.A.* **149 K1** 30 33N 88 10W
Theodore Roosevelt △, *U.S.A.* **154 B3** 47 0N 103 25W
Theodore Roosevelt L., *U.S.A.* **159 K8** 33 40N 111 10W
Thepha, *Thailand* .... **87 J3** 6 52N 100 58 E
Thérain →, *France* ... **27 C9** 49 15N 2 27 E
Theresa, *U.S.A.* **151 B9** 44 13N 75 48W
Theressa, *U.S.A.* **152 F7** 29 50N 82 4W
Therma = Eagle Nest, *U.S.A.* **159 H11** 36 33N 105 16W
Thermaïkós Kólpos, *Greece* ..... **50 F6** 40 15N 22 45 E
Thermí, *Greece* ..... **49 B8** 39 11N 26 29 E
Thermopolis, *U.S.A.* .. **158 E9** 43 39N 108 13W
Thermopylae P., *Greece* **48 C4** 38 48N 22 35 E
Thesprotía □, *Greece* . **48 B2** 39 27N 20 22 E
Thessalía □, *Greece* .. **48 B4** 39 25N 22 0 E
Thessalon, *Canada* ... **140 C3** 46 20N 83 30W
Thessaloníki, *Greece* .. **50 F6** 40 38N 22 58 E
Thessaloníki □, *Greece* **50 F7** 40 45N 23 0 E
Thessaloníki ✈ (SKG), *Greece* ..... **50 F7** 40 30N 23 0 E
Thessaloníki, Gulf of = Thermaïkós Kólpos, *Greece* ..... **50 F6** 40 15N 22 45 E
Thessaly = Thessalía □, *Greece* ..... **48 B4** 39 25N 22 0 E
Thetford, *U.K.* ..... **21 E8** 52 25N 0 45 E
Thetford Mines, *Canada* **141 C5** 46 8N 71 18W
Theun →, *Laos* ..... **86 C5** 18 19N 104 0 E
Theunissen, *S. Africa* . **116 D4** 28 26 S 26 43 E
Thevenard, *Australia* . **127 E1** 32 9 S 133 38 E
Thiámis →, *Greece* ... **48 B2** 39 15N 20 6 E
Thiberville, *France* ... **26 C7** 49 8N 0 27 E
Thibodaux, *U.S.A.* **155 L9** 29 48N 90 49W
Thicket Portage, *Canada* **143 B9** 55 19N 97 42W
Thief River Falls, *U.S.A.* **154 A6** 48 7N 96 10W
Thiel Mts., *Antarctica* . **7 E16** 85 15 S 91 0W
Thiene, *Italy* ..... **45 C8** 45 42N 11 29 E
Thiérache, *France* .... **27 C10** 49 51N 3 45 E
Thiers, *France* ..... **28 C7** 45 52N 3 33 E
Thiès, *Senegal* **112 C1** 14 50N 16 51W
Thiesi, *Italy* ..... **46 B1** 40 31N 8 43 E
Thiet, *Sudan* ..... **107 F2** 7 37N 28 49 E
Thika, *Kenya* ..... **118 C4** 1 1 S 37 5 E
Thille-Boubacar, *Senegal* **112 B1** 16 31N 15 5W
Thimphu, *Bhutan* .... **90 B2** 27 31N 89 45 E
Thingangyun, *Burma* . **90 G6** 16 49N 96 12 E
Þingeyjarsýsla □, *Iceland* **11 B10** 65 40N 16 30W
Þingeyri, *Iceland* **11 B3** 65 52N 23 30W
Þingmúli, *Iceland* **11 B12** 65 2N 14 37W
Þingvallavatn, *Iceland* **11 C5** 64 11N 21 9W
Þingvellir, *Iceland* ... **11 C5** 64 15N 21 7W
Þingvellir △, *Iceland* . **11 C5** 64 16N 21 5W
Thio, *N. Cal.* ..... **133 U20** 21 37 S 166 14 E
Thionville, *France* .... **27 C13** 49 20N 6 10 E
Thíra, *Greece* ..... **49 E7** 36 23N 25 27 E
Thirasía, *Greece* ..... **49 E7** 36 26N 25 21 E
Third Cataract, *Sudan* **106 D3** 19 42N 30 20 E
Thirsk, *U.K.* **20 C6** 54 14N 1 19W
Thiruvananthapuram = Trivandrum, *India* .. **95 K3** 8 41N 77 0 E
Thiruvarur, *India* .... **95 J4** 10 46N 79 38 E
Thisted, *Denmark* .... **17 H2** 56 58N 8 40 E
Þistilfjörður, *Iceland* . **11 A11** 66 18N 15 24W
Thistle I., *Australia* .. **128 C2** 35 0 S 136 8 E
Thityabin, *Burma* .... **90 F6** 18 15N 96 13 E
Thithia = Cicia, *Fiji* .. **133 A3** 17 45 S 179 18W
Thitpokpin, *Burma* ... **90 F5** 19 24N 95 58 E
Thiva = Thívai, *Greece* **48 C5** 38 19N 23 19 E
Thívai, *Greece* ..... **48 C5** 38 19N 23 19 E
Thiviers, *France* ..... **28 C4** 45 25N 0 54 E
Thizy, *France* ..... **27 F11** 46 2N 4 18 E
Þjórsá →, *Iceland* **11 D6** 63 47N 20 48W
Thlewiaza →, *Canada* **143 A10** 60 29N 94 40W
Thmar Puok, *Cambodia* **86 F4** 13 57N 103 4 E
Tho Vinh, *Vietnam* .... **86 C5** 19 16N 105 42 E
Thoa →, *Canada* **143 A7** 60 31N 109 47W
Thoen, *Thailand* ..... **86 D2** 17 43N 99 12 E
Thoeng, *Thailand* .... **86 C3** 19 41N 100 12 E
Tholdi, *Pakistan* ..... **93 B7** 35 5N 76 6 E
Thomas, *U.S.A.* **155 H5** 35 45N 98 45W
Thomas, L., *Australia* . **127 D2** 26 4 S 137 58 E
Thomas Hill Reservoir, *U.S.A.* **156 E4** 39 34N 92 39W
Thomaston, *U.S.A.* ... **152 C5** 32 53N 84 20W
Thomasville, *Ala., U.S.A.* **149 K2** 31 55N 87 44W
Thomasville, *Ga., U.S.A.* **152 E6** 30 50N 83 59W
Thomasville, *N.C., U.S.A.* **149 H5** 35 53N 80 5W
Thompson, *Canada* ... **143 B9** 55 45N 97 52W
Thompson, *U.S.A.* **151 E9** 41 52N 75 31W
Thompson →, *Canada* **142 C4** 50 15N 121 24W
Thompson →, *U.S.A.* . **156 E3** 39 46N 93 37W
Thompson Falls, *U.S.A.* **158 C6** 47 36N 115 21W
Thompson Pk., *U.S.A.* . **158 F2** 41 0N 123 0W
Thompson Sd., *N.Z.* .. **131 F1** 45 8 S 166 46 E
Thompson Springs, *U.S.A.* **159 G9** 38 58N 109 43W
Thompsontown, *U.S.A.* **150 F7** 40 33N 77 14W
Thomson, *Ga., U.S.A.* . **152 B7** 33 28N 82 30W
Thomson, *Ill., U.S.A.* .. **156 C6** 41 58N 90 6W
Thomson →, *Australia* **126 C3** 25 11 S 142 53 E
Thomson's Falls = Nyahururu, *Kenya* .. **118 B4** 0 2N 36 27 E
Thônes, *France* ..... **29 C10** 45 54N 6 18 E
Thong Yang, *Thailand* . **87 b** 9 28N 99 56 E
Thongwa, *Burma* ..... **90 G6** 16 45N 96 33 E
Thonon-les-Bains, *France* ..... **27 F13** 46 22N 6 29 E
Thonze, *Burma* ..... **90 G5** 17 38N 95 47 E
Thorez, *Ukraine* ..... **59 H10** 48 4N 38 34 E
Þórisjökull, *Iceland* .. **11 C6** 64 32N 20 43W
Þórisvatn, *Iceland* **11 C8** 64 20N 18 55W
Þórkötlustaðir, *Iceland* **11 D4** 63 50N 22 24W
Þorlákshöfn, *Iceland* .. **11 D5** 63 51N 21 22W
Thorn = Toruń, *Poland* **55 E5** 53 2N 18 39 E
Thornaby on Tees, *U.K.* **20 C6** 54 33N 1 18W
Thornbury, *Canada* ... **150 B4** 44 34N 80 26W
Thornbury, *N.Z.* ..... **131 G3** 46 17 S 168 9 E
Thorne, *U.K.* **20 D7** 53 37N 0 57W
Thornhill, *Canada* **142 C3** 54 31N 128 32W
Thornton, *Colo., U.S.A.* **154 F2** 39 52N 104 58W
Thornton, *Iowa, U.S.A.* **156 B3** 42 57N 93 23W
Thornton-Beresfield, *Australia* ..... **129 B9** 32 50 S 151 40 E
Thorntown, *U.S.A.* ... **157 D10** 40 8N 86 36W
Thorold, *Canada* **150 C5** 43 7N 79 12W
Þórshöfn, *Iceland* **11 A11** 66 12N 15 20W
Thouarcé, *France* **26 E6** 47 17N 0 30W
Thouars, *France* **26 F6** 46 58N 0 15W
Thouet →, *France* ... **26 E6** 47 17N 0 6W
Thouin, C., *Australia* . **124 D2** 20 20 S 118 10 E
Thousand Oaks, *U.S.A.* **161 L8** 34 10N 118 50W
Thrace, *Turkey* ..... **51 F10** 41 0N 27 0 E
Thrakikón Pélagos, *Greece* ..... **51 F8** 40 30N 25 0 E
Thredbo, *Australia* ... **129 D8** 36 30 S 148 21 E
Three Forks, *U.S.A.* .. **158 D8** 45 54N 111 33W
Three Gorges Dam, *China* ..... **77 B8** 30 45N 111 15 E
Three Hills, *Canada* .. **142 C6** 51 43N 113 15W
Three Hummock I., *Australia* ..... **127 G3** 40 25 S 144 55 E
Three Oaks, *U.S.A.* ... **157 C10** 41 48N 86 36W
Three Pagodas Pass, *Asia* ..... **86 E2** 15 20N 98 30 E
Three Points, C., *Ghana* **112 E4** 4 42N 2 6W
Three Rivers, *Calif., U.S.A.* **160 J8** 36 26N 118 54W
Three Rivers, *Mich., U.S.A.* **157 C11** 41 57N 85 38W
Three Rivers, *Tex., U.S.A.* **155 L5** 28 28N 98 11W
Three Sisters, *U.S.A.* . **158 D3** 44 4N 121 51W
Three Sisters Is., *Solomon Is.* ..... **133 N11** 10 10 S 161 57 E
Three Springs, *Australia* ..... **125 E2** 29 32 S 115 45 E
Throssell, L., *Australia* **125 E3** 27 33 S 124 10 E
Throssell Ra., *Australia* **124 D3** 22 3 S 121 43 E
Thrushton △, *Australia* **127 D4** 27 47 S 147 40 E
Thuamal Rampur, *India* ..... **94 E6** 19 23N 82 56 E
Thuan Hoa, *Vietnam* .. **87 H5** 8 58N 105 30 E
Thubun Lakes, *Canada* **143 A6** 61 30N 112 0W
Thueyts, *France* ..... **29 D8** 44 41N 4 9 E
Thuin, *Belgium* ..... **24 D4** 50 20N 4 17 E
Thuir, *France* ..... **28 F6** 42 38N 2 45 E
Thule = Qaanaaq, *Greenland* **10 B4** 77 40N 69 0W
Thule Air Base = Uummannaq, *Greenland* **6 B5** 70 58N 52 0W
Thun, *Switz.* ..... **32 C5** 46 45N 7 38 E
Thunder B., *U.S.A.* ... **150 B1** 45 0N 83 20W
Thunder Bay, *Canada* . **140 C2** 48 20N 89 15W
Thunderbolt, *U.S.A.* .. **152 C8** 32 3N 81 4W
Thunersee, *Switz.* .... **32 C5** 46 43N 7 39 E
Thung Salaeng Luang △, *Thailand* . **86 D3** 16 43N 100 50 E
Thung Song, *Thailand* . **87 H2** 8 10N 99 40 E
Thunkar, *Bhutan* ..... **90 B3** 27 55N 91 0 E
Thuong Tra, *Vietnam* . **86 D6** 16 2N 107 42 E
Thur →, *Switz.* ..... **33 A8** 47 32N 9 10 E
Thurgau □, *Switz.* .... **33 A8** 47 34N 9 10 E
Thüringen □, *Germany* **30 D6** 51 0N 11 0 E
Thüringer Wald, *Germany* ..... **30 E6** 50 35N 11 0 E
Thurles, *Ireland* **23 D4** 52 41N 7 49W
Thurn P., *Austria* ..... **34 D5** 47 20N 12 25 E
Thurrock □, *U.K.* .... **21 F8** 51 31N 0 23 E
Thursday I., *Australia* . **126 A3** 10 30 S 142 3 E
Thurso, *Canada* **140 C4** 45 36N 75 15W
Thurso, *U.K.* **22 C5** 58 36N 3 32W
Thurso →, *U.K.* **22 C5** 58 36N 3 32W
Thurston I., *Antarctica* **7 D16** 72 0 S 100 0W
Thury-Harcourt, *France* **26 D6** 48 59N 0 30W
Thusis, *Switz.* ..... **33 C8** 46 42N 9 26 E
Thutade L., *Canada* .. **142 B3** 57 0N 126 55W
Thy, *Denmark* ..... **17 H2** 56 52N 8 25 E
Thy ⌂, *N. Cal.* ..... **133 V20** 22 10 S 166 31 E
Thyborøn, *Denmark* .. **17 H2** 56 42N 8 12 E
Þykkvabæjarklaustur, *Iceland* **11 D8** 63 30N 18 22W
Þykkvibær, *Iceland* ... **11 D6** 63 45N 20 37W
Thyolo, *Malawi* ..... **119 F4** 16 7 S 35 5 E
Ti-n-Amzi →, *Niger* .. **113 B5** 18 20N 4 32 E
Ti-n-Barraouene, O. →, *Africa* ..... **113 B5** 18 40N 4 5 E
Ti-n-Barraouene, O. →, *Algeria* ..... **111 E5** 19 2N 4 45 E
Ti-n-Medjerdam, O. →, *Algeria* ..... **111 C5** 25 45N 1 30 E
Ti-n-Rerhoh, *Algeria* . **111 D5** 20 44N 4 2 E
Ti-n-Tanetfirt, *Algeria* **111 D5** 24 49N 3 48 E
Ti-n-Tarabine, O. →, *Algeria* ..... **111 D6** 21 16N 7 25 E
Ti-n-Toumma, *Niger* .. **109 E2** 16 4N 12 40 E
Ti-n-Zaouatene, *Algeria* ..... **111 E5** 19 55N 2 55 E
Ti Tree, *Australia* .... **126 C1** 22 5 S 133 22 E
Tiadiaye, *Senegal* **112 C1** 14 25N 16 40W
Tiahuanacu, *Bolivia* .. **172 D4** 16 33 S 68 42W
Tian Shan, *Asia* ..... **65 C8** 40 30N 76 0 E
Tianchang, *China* .... **77 A12** 32 40N 119 0 E
Tiandeng, *China* ..... **76 F6** 23 6N 107 7 E
Tiandong, *China* ..... **76 F6** 23 36N 107 8 E
Tian'e, *China* ..... **76 E6** 25 1N 107 9 E
Tianguá, *Brazil* ..... **170 B3** 3 44 S 40 59W
Tianhe, *China* ..... **76 E7** 24 48N 108 40 E
Tianjin, *China* ..... **75 E9** 39 8N 117 10 E
Tiankoura, *Burkina Faso* **112 C4** 10 47N 3 17W
Tianlin, *China* ..... **76 E6** 24 21N 106 12 E
Tianmen, *China* ..... **77 B9** 30 39N 113 9 E
Tianquan, *China* ..... **76 B4** 30 7N 102 43 E
Tianshui, *China* ..... **74 G3** 34 32N 105 40 E
Tiantai, *China* ..... **77 C13** 29 10N 121 2 E
Tianyang, *China* ..... **76 F6** 23 42N 106 53 E
Tianyar, *Indonesia* ... **79 J18** 8 12 S 115 30 E
Tianzhen, *China* ..... **74 D8** 40 24N 114 5 E
Tianzhu, *China* ..... **76 D7** 26 54N 109 11 E
Tianzhuangtai, *China* . **75 D12** 40 43N 122 5 E
Tiaret, *Algeria* ..... **111 A5** 35 20N 1 21 E
Tiassalé, *Ivory C.* **112 D4** 5 58N 4 57W
Tibagi, *Brazil* ..... **175 A5** 24 30 S 50 24W
Tibagi →, *Brazil* ..... **175 A5** 22 47 S 51 1W
Tībastī, Sarīr, *Libya* .. **108 D3** 22 50N 18 30 E
Tibati, *Cameroon* .... **113 D7** 6 22N 12 30 E
Tibe, *Ethiopia* ..... **107 F4** 9 2N 37 12 E
Tiber = Tevere →, *Italy* **45 G9** 41 44N 12 14 E
Tiberias = Teverya, *Israel* ..... **103 C4** 32 47N 35 32 E
Tiberias, L. = Yam Kinneret, *Israel* ... **103 C4** 32 45N 35 35 E
Tibesti, *Chad* ..... **109 D3** 21 0N 17 30 E
Tibet = Xizang Zizhiqu □, *China* .. **68 C3** 32 0N 88 0 E
Tibet, Plateau of, *Asia* **62 F12** 32 0N 86 0 E
Tibiao, *Phil.* ..... **81 F4** 11 17N 122 2 E
Tibiri, *Niger* ..... **113 C6** 13 34N 7 4 E
Tibleş, Vf., *Romania* .. **53 C9** 47 32N 24 15 E
Ţibleşului, Munţii, *Romania* ..... **53 C9** 47 38N 24 5 E
Tibnī, *Syria* ..... **101 E8** 35 36N 39 50 E
Tibooburra, *Australia* . **127 D3** 29 26 S 142 1 E
Tibro, *Sweden* ..... **17 F8** 58 28N 14 10 E
Tibugá, G. de, *Colombia* **168 B2** 5 45N 77 20W
Tiburón, I., *Mexico* ... **162 B2** 29 0N 112 30W
Ticao I., *Phil.* ..... **80 E4** 12 31N 123 42 E
Tice, *U.S.A.* **153 J8** 26 40N 81 49W
Tīchīt, *Mauritania* **112 B3** 18 21N 9 29W
Tichla, *Mauritania* **110 D2** 21 36N 14 58W
Ticho, *Ethiopia* ..... **107 F4** 7 50N 39 32 E
Ticino □, *Switz.* ..... **33 D7** 46 20N 8 45 E
Ticino →, *Italy* ..... **31 J4** 45 9N 9 14 E
Ticleni, *Romania* ..... **53 F8** 44 53N 23 24 E
Ticonderoga, *U.S.A.* .. **151 C11** 43 51N 73 26W
Ticul, *Mexico* **163 C7** 20 20N 89 31W

Tidaholm, *Sweden* **17 F7** 58 12N 13 58 E
Tidan, *Sweden* **17 F8** 58 34N 14 1 E
Tiddim, *Burma* **90 D4** 23 28N 93 45 E
Tiden, *India* **95 L11** 7 15N 93 33 E
Tideridjaouine, Adrar, *Algeria* **111 D5** 23 0N 2 15 E
Tidikelt, *Algeria* **111 C5** 26 58N 1 30 E
Tidioute, *U.S.A.* **150 E5** 41 41N 79 24W
Tidjikja, *Mauritania* **112 B2** 18 29N 11 35W
Tidmore = Seminole, *U.S.A.* **155 H6** 35 14N 96 41W
Tidore, *Indonesia* **82 A3** 0 40N 127 25 E
Tiébissou, *Ivory C.* **112 D3** 7 9N 5 10W
Tiéboro, *Chad* **109 D3** 21 20N 17 7 E
Tiefencastel, *Switz.* **33 C9** 46 40N 9 33 E
Tiegang Shuiku, *China* **69 F10** 22 37N 113 53 E
Tiel, *Neths.* **24 C5** 51 53N 5 26 E
Tiel, *Senegal* **112 C1** 14 55N 15 5W
Tieling, *China* **75 C12** 42 20N 123 55 E
Tielt, *Belgium* **24 C3** 51 0N 3 20 E
Tien Shan = Tian Shan, *Asia* **65 C8** 40 30N 76 0 E
Tien-tsin = Tianjin, *China* **75 E9** 39 8N 117 10 E
Tien Yen, *Vietnam* **86 B6** 21 20N 107 24 E
T'ienching = Tianjin, *China* **75 E9** 39 8N 117 10 E
Tienen, *Belgium* **24 D4** 50 48N 4 57 E
Tiénigbé, *Ivory C.* **112 D3** 8 11N 5 43W
Tientsin = Tianjin, *China* **75 E9** 39 8N 117 10 E
Tieri, *Australia* **126 C4** 23 2 S 148 21 E
Tieroko, Tarso, *Chad* **109 D3** 20 45N 17 52 E
Tierp, *Sweden* **16 D11** 60 20N 17 30 E
Tierra Amarilla, *Chile* **174 B1** 27 28 S 70 18W
Tierra Amarilla, *U.S.A.* **159 H10** 36 42N 106 33W
Tierra Colorada, *Mexico* **163 D5** 17 10N 99 35W
Tierra de Barros, *Spain* **43 G4** 38 40N 6 30W
Tierra de Campos, *Spain* **42 C6** 42 10N 4 50W
Tierra del Fuego □, *Argentina* **176 D3** 54 0 S 67 45W
Tierra del Fuego △, *Argentina* **176 D3** 54 50 S 68 23W
Tierra del Fuego, I. Gr. de, *Argentina* **176 D3** 54 0 S 69 0W
Tierralta, *Colombia* **168 B2** 8 11N 76 4W
Tiétar →, *Spain* **42 F4** 39 50N 6 1W
Tieté →, *Brazil* **175 A5** 20 40 S 51 35W
Tifarati, *W. Sahara* **110 C2** 26 9N 10 33W
Tiffin, *U.S.A.* **157 C13** 41 7N 83 11W
Tiffin →, *U.S.A.* **157 C12** 41 20N 84 24W
Tiflèt, *Morocco* **110 B3** 33 54N 6 20W
Tiflis = Tbilisi, *Georgia* **61 K7** 41 43N 44 50 E
Tifton, *U.S.A.* **152 D6** 31 27N 83 31W
Tifu, *Indonesia* **82 B3** 3 39 S 126 24 E
Tiga, Î., *N. Cal.* **133 U21** 21 7 S 167 49 E
Tigalda I., *U.S.A.* **144 J6** 54 6N 165 5W
Tigaon, *Phil.* **80 E4** 13 38N 123 30 E
Tigbauan, *Phil.* **81 F4** 10 41N 122 27 E
Tighina, *Moldova* **53 D14** 46 50N 29 30 E
Tigil, *Russia* **67 D16** 57 49N 158 40 E
Tigiria, *India* **94 D7** 20 29N 85 31 E
Tignall, *U.S.A.* **152 B7** 33 52N 82 44W
Tignish, *Canada* **141 C7** 46 58N 64 2W
Tigray □, *Ethiopia* **107 E4** 13 35N 39 15 E
Tigre →, *Peru* **168 D3** 4 30 S 74 10W
Tigre →, *Venezuela* **169 B5** 9 20N 62 30W
Tigris = Dijlah, Nahr →, *Asia* **96 D5** 31 0N 47 25 E
Tiguentourine, *Algeria* **111 C6** 27 52N 9 8 E
Tigveni, *Romania* **53 E9** 45 10N 24 31 E
Tigyaing, *Burma* **90 D6** 23 45N 96 10 E
Tigzerte, O. →, *Morocco* **110 C3** 28 10N 9 37W
Tîh, Gebel el, *Egypt* **106 B3** 29 32N 33 26 E
Tihodaine, Erg de, *Algeria* **111 C6** 25 15N 7 15 E
Tihwa = Ürümqi, *China* **66 E9** 43 45N 87 45 E
Tijara, *India* **92 F7** 27 56N 76 31 E
Tîjî, *Libya* **108 B2** 32 0N 11 18 E
Tijuana, *Mexico* **161 N9** 32 30N 117 10W
Tijuca △, *Brazil* **171 F3** 22 56 S 43 12W
Tikal, *Guatemala* **164 C2** 17 13N 89 24W
Tikal △, *Guatemala* **164 C2** 17 23N 89 34W
Tikamgarh, *India* **93 G8** 24 44N 78 50 E
Tikaré, *Burkina Faso* **113 C4** 13 15N 1 43W
Tikchik Lakes, *U.S.A.* **144 G8** 60 0N 159 0W
Tikhonkaya = Birobidzhan, *Russia* **67 E14** 48 50N 132 50 E
Tikhoretsk, *Russia* **61 H5** 45 56N 40 5 E
Tikhvin, *Russia* **58 C7** 59 35N 33 30 E
Tikiraqjuaq = Whale Cove, *Canada* **143 A10** 62 10N 92 34W
Tikkadouine, Adrar, *Algeria* **111 D5** 24 28N 1 30 E
Tiko, *Cameroon* **113 E6** 4 4N 9 20 E
Tikrīt, *Iraq* **101 E10** 34 35N 43 37 E
Tiksi, *Russia* **67 B13** 71 40N 128 45 E
Tilamuta, *Indonesia* **82 A2** 0 32N 122 23 E
Tilburg, *Neths.* **24 C5** 51 31N 5 6 E
Tilbury, *Canada* **140 D3** 42 17N 82 23W
Tilbury, *U.K.* **21 F8** 51 27N 0 22 E
Tilcara, *Argentina* **174 A2** 23 36 S 65 23W
Tilden, *U.S.A.* **154 D6** 42 3N 97 50W
Tilemses, *Niger* **113 B5** 15 37N 4 44 E
Tilemsi, Vallée du, *Mali* **113 B5** 17 42N 0 15 E
Tilhar, *India* **93 F8** 28 0N 79 45 E
Tilia, O. →, *Algeria* **111 C5** 27 32N 0 55 E
Tilichiki, *Russia* **67 C17** 60 27N 166 5 E
Tiliane, *Algeria* **111 C4** 27 49N 0 6W
Tilin, *Burma* **90 E5** 21 41N 94 6 E
Tilissos, *Greece* **39 E6** 35 20N 25 1 E
Till →, *U.K.* **20 B5** 55 41N 2 13W
Tillabéri, *Niger* **113 C5** 14 28N 1 28 E
Tillamook, *U.S.A.* **158 D2** 45 27N 123 51W
Tillanchong I., *India* **95 K11** 8 30N 93 37 E
Tillberga, *Sweden* **16 E10** 59 40N 16 39 E
Tillia, *Niger* **113 B5** 16 8N 4 47 E
Tillman, *U.S.A.* **152 C8** 32 28N 81 6W
Tillsonburg, *Canada* **140 D3** 42 53N 80 44W
Tillyeria, *Cyprus* **39 E8** 35 6N 32 40 E
Tilogne, *Senegal* **112 B2** 16 0N 13 40W
Tílos, *Greece* **49 E9** 36 27N 27 27 E
Tilpa, *Australia* **128 A6** 30 57 S 144 24 E
Tilrhemt, *Algeria* **111 B5** 33 9N 3 22 E
Tilsit = Sovetsk, *Russia* **15 J19** 55 6N 21 50 E
Tilt →, *U.K.* **22 E5** 56 46N 3 51W
Tilton, *U.S.A.* **151 C13** 43 27N 71 36W
Tiltonsville, *U.S.A.* **150 F4** 40 10N 80 41W
Tim, *Denmark* **17 H2** 56 12N 8 19 E
Timagami, L., *Canada* **140 C3** 47 0N 80 10W
Timanah, *Asia* **98 C3** 19 0N 41 0 E
Timanfaya △, *Canary Is.* **9 e2** 29 0N 13 46W
Timanskiy Kryazh, *Russia* **56 A9** 65 58N 50 5 E
Timaru, *N.Z.* **131 E6** 44 23 S 171 14 E
Timashevo, *Russia* **60 D10** 53 22N 51 9 E
Timashevsk, *Russia* **61 H4** 45 35N 39 0 E
Timau, *Kenya* **118 B4** 0 4N 37 15 E
Timbákion, *Greece* **39 E6** 35 4N 24 45 E
Timbaúba, *Brazil* **170 C4** 7 31 S 35 19W
Timbedgha, *Mauritania* **112 B3** 16 17N 8 16W
Timber Creek, *Australia* **124 C5** 15 40 S 130 29 E
Timber Lake, *U.S.A.* **154 C4** 45 26N 101 5W
Timber Mt., *U.S.A.* **160 H10** 37 6N 116 28W
Timbío, *Colombia* **168 C2** 2 20N 76 40W
Timbiqui, *Colombia* **168 C2** 2 46N 77 42W
Timbo, *Guinea* **112 C2** 10 35N 11 50W
Timbo, *Liberia* **112 D3** 5 35N 9 45W
Timboon, *Australia* **128 E5** 38 30 S 142 58 E
Timbuktu = Tombouctou, *Mali* **112 B4** 16 50N 3 0W
Timdjaouine, *Algeria* **111 D5** 21 37N 4 30 E
Timeiaouine, *Algeria* **111 D5** 20 27N 1 50 E
Timellouline, *Algeria* **111 C6** 29 22N 8 55 E
Timétrine, Mts., *Mali* **113 B4** 19 25N 1 0W
Timfi Óros, *Greece* **48 B2** 39 59N 20 45 E
Timfristós, Óros, *Greece* **48 C3** 38 57N 21 50 E
Timhadit, *Morocco* **110 B3** 33 15N 5 4W
Timi, *Cyprus* **39 F8** 34 44N 32 31 E
Tîmia, *Niger* **113 B6** 18 4N 8 40 E
Timika, *Indonesia* **83 B5** 4 47 S 136 32 E
Timimoun, *Algeria* **111 C5** 29 14N 0 16 E
Timimoun, Sebkha de, *Algeria* **111 C5** 28 50N 0 46 E
Timirist, Râs, *Mauritania* **112 B1** 19 21N 16 30W
Timiş = Tamis →, *Serbia & M.* **52 F5** 44 51N 20 39 E
Timiş □, *Romania* **52 E6** 45 40N 21 30 E
Timiskaming, L. = Témiscamingue, L., *Canada* **140 C4** 47 10N 79 25W
Timişoara, *Romania* **52 E6** 45 43N 21 15 E
Timmersdala, *Sweden* **17 F7** 58 32N 13 46 E
Timmins, *Canada* **140 C3** 48 28N 81 25W
Timmonsville, *U.S.A.* **152 A10** 34 8N 79 57W
Timok →, *Serbia & M.* **50 B6** 44 10N 22 40 E
Timon, *Brazil* **170 C3** 5 8 S 42 52W
Timor, *Asia* **82 C3** 9 0 S 125 0 E
Timor Leste = East Timor ■, *Asia* **82 C3** 8 50 S 126 0 E
Timor Sea, *Ind. Oc.* **124 B4** 12 0 S 127 0 E
Timrå, *Sweden* **16 B11** 62 29N 17 18 E
Timucuan ⌂, *U.S.A.* **152 E8** 30 28N 81 27W
Tīn, Ra's at, *Libya* **108 B4** 32 37N 23 8 E
Tin Alkoum, *Algeria* **111 D7** 24 42N 10 17 E
Tin Amzi, O. →, *Algeria* **111 D6** 18 20N 4 32 E
Tin Atanai, *Algeria* **111 C5** 25 52N 1 37 E
Tin Can Bay, *Australia* **127 D5** 25 56 S 153 0 E
Tin Ethisane, *Mali* **113 B4** 19 3N 0 52W
Tin Gornai, *Mali* **113 B4** 16 38N 0 38W
Tin Mt., *U.S.A.* **160 J9** 36 50N 117 10W
Tina →, *S. Africa* **117 E4** 31 18 S 29 13 E
Tîna, Khalîg el, *Egypt* **106 A3** 31 20N 32 42 E
Tinaca Pt., *Phil.* **81 J5** 5 30N 125 25 E
Tinaco, *Venezuela* **168 B4** 9 42N 68 26W
Tinafak, O. →, *Algeria* **111 C6** 27 10N 7 0 E
Tinajo, *Canary Is.* **9 e2** 29 4N 13 42W
Tinca, *Romania* **52 D6** 46 46N 21 58 E
Tindal, *Australia* **124 B5** 14 31 S 132 22 E
Tindivanam, *India* **95 H4** 12 15N 79 41 E
Tindouf, *Algeria* **110 C3** 27 42N 8 10W
Tinée →, *France* **29 E11** 43 55N 7 11 E
Tineo, *Spain* **42 B4** 43 21N 6 27W
Tinerhir, *Morocco* **110 B3** 31 29N 5 31W
Tinfouchi, *Algeria* **110 C3** 28 52N 5 49W
Tinfunque △, *Paraguay* **174 A3** 23 55 S 60 17W
Ting Jiang →, *China* **77 E11** 24 45N 116 35 E
Tinggi, Pulau, *Malaysia* **87 L5** 2 18N 104 7 E
Tingkawk Sakan, *Burma* **90 B6** 26 4N 96 44 E
Tinglayan, *Phil.* **80 C3** 17 15N 121 9 E
Tinglev, *Denmark* **17 K3** 54 57N 9 13 E
Tingo Maria, *Peru* **172 B2** 9 10 S 75 54W
Tingrela, *Ivory C.* **112 C3** 10 27N 6 25W
Tingsryd, *Sweden* **17 H9** 56 31N 15 0 E
Tingstäde, *Sweden* **17 G12** 57 44N 18 37 E
Tingvoll, *Norway* **18 B5** 62 55N 8 12 E
Tingwon Group, *Papua N. G.* **132 B5** 2 37 S 149 42 E
Tinh Bien, *Vietnam* **87 G5** 10 36N 104 57 E
Tinharé, I. de, *Brazil* **171 D4** 13 30 S 38 58W
Tinian, *N. Marianas* **134 F6** 15 0N 145 38 E
Tinigua △, *Colombia* **168 C3** 2 30N 74 8W
Tiniguiban, *Phil.* **81 F2** 11 22N 119 30 E
Tinjar →, *Malaysia* **85 B4** 4 4N 114 18 E
Tinn = Atrå, *Norway* **18 E5** 59 59N 8 45 E
Tinnevelly = Tirunelveli, *India* **95 K3** 8 45N 77 45 E
Tinnoset, *Norway* **18 E6** 59 43N 9 3 E
Tinnsjø, *Norway* **18 E5** 59 55N 8 54 E
Tinogasta, *Argentina* **174 B2** 28 5 S 67 32W
Tinos, *Greece* **49 D7** 37 33N 25 8 E
Tiñoso, C., *Spain* **41 H3** 37 32N 1 6W
Tinpahar, *India* **93 G12** 24 59N 87 44 E
Tinputz, *Papua N. G.* **132 C8** 5 33 S 155 0 E
Tinsukia, *India* **90 B5** 27 29N 95 20 E
Tinta, *Peru* **172 C3** 14 3 S 71 20W
Tintina, *Argentina* **174 B3** 27 2 S 62 45W
Tintinara, *Australia* **128 C4** 35 48 S 140 2 E
Tintioulé, *Guinea* **112 C3** 10 13N 9 12W
Tinto →, *Spain* **43 H4** 37 12N 6 55W
Tinui, *N.Z.* **130 G5** 40 52 S 176 5 E
Tinwald, *N.Z.* **131 D6** 43 55 S 171 43 E
Tioga, *N. Dak., U.S.A.* **154 A3** 48 23N 102 56W
Tioga, *Pa., U.S.A.* **150 E7** 41 55N 77 8W
Tioman, Pulau, *Malaysia* **87 L5** 2 50N 104 10 E
Tione di Trento, *Italy* **44 B7** 46 2N 10 43 E
Tionesta, *U.S.A.* **150 E5** 41 30N 79 28W
Tior, *Sudan* **107 F3** 6 26N 31 11 E
Tioulilin, *Algeria* **111 C4** 27 1N 0 2W
Tipp City, *U.S.A.* **157 E12** 39 58N 84 11W
Tippecanoe →, *U.S.A.* **157 D10** 40 30N 86 45W
Tipperary, *Ireland* **23 D3** 52 28N 8 10W
Tipperary □, *Ireland* **23 D4** 52 37N 7 55W
Tipton, *Calif., U.S.A.* **160 J7** 36 4N 119 19W
Tipton, *Ind., U.S.A.* **157 D10** 40 17N 86 2W
Tipton, *Iowa, U.S.A.* **156 C5** 41 46N 91 8W
Tipton, *Mo., U.S.A.* **156 F4** 38 39N 92 47W
Tipton Mt., *U.S.A.* **161 K12** 35 32N 114 12W
Tiptonville, *U.S.A.* **155 G10** 36 23N 89 29W
Tiptur, *India* **95 H3** 13 15N 76 26 E
Tiquié →, *Brazil* **168 C4** 0 5N 68 25W
Tiracambu, Serra do, *Brazil* **170 B2** 3 15 S 46 30W
Tirahart, O. →, *Algeria* **111 D5** 23 45N 3 10 E
Tirān, *Iran* **97 C6** 32 45N 51 8 E
Tirān, *Si. Arabia* **106 B3** 27 57N 34 32 E
Tiranë, *Albania* **50 E3** 41 18N 19 49 E
Tiranë ✈ (TIA), *Albania* **50 E3** 41 57N 19 42 E
Tirano, *Italy* **44 B7** 46 13N 10 10 E
Tiraspol, *Moldova* **53 D14** 46 55N 29 35 E
Tiratimine, *Algeria* **111 C5** 25 56N 3 37 E
Tirau, *N.Z.* **130 D4** 37 58 S 175 46 E
Tirdout, *Mali* **113 B4** 16 7N 1 5W
Tire, *Turkey* **49 C9** 38 5N 27 45 E
Tirebolu, *Turkey* **101 B8** 40 58N 38 45 E
Tiree, *U.K.* **22 E2** 56 31N 6 55W
Tiree, Passage of, *U.K.* **22 E2** 56 30N 6 30W
Tîrgovişte = Târgovişte, *Romania* **53 F10** 44 55N 25 27 E
Tîrgu-Jiu = Târgu-Jiu, *Romania* **53 E8** 45 5N 23 19 E
Tîrgu Mureş = Târgu Mureş, *Romania* **53 D9** 46 31N 24 38 E
Tirgua △, *Venezuela* **168 A4** 10 5N 68 48W
Tirich Mir, *Pakistan* **91 A3** 36 15N 71 55 E
Tiriolo, *Italy* **47 D9** 38 57N 16 30 E
Tiririca, Serra da, *Brazil* **171 E2** 17 6 S 47 6W
Tiriro, *Guinea* **112 C3** 10 27N 8 40W
Tiris, *W. Sahara* **110 D2** 23 10N 13 20W
Tiritiri o te Moana = Southern Alps, *N.Z.* **131 D5** 43 41 S 170 11 E
Tirlyanskiy, *Russia* **64 D7** 54 14N 58 35 E
Tirna →, *India* **94 E3** 18 4N 76 57 E
Tîrnavos, *Greece* **48 B4** 39 45N 22 18 E
Tirodi, *India* **94 D4** 21 40N 79 44 E
Tirol □, *Austria* **34 D3** 47 3N 10 43 E
Tiros, *Brazil* **171 E2** 19 0 S 45 58W
Tirrukkovil, *Sri Lanka* **95 L5** 7 7N 81 51 E
Tirschenreuth, *Germany* **31 F8** 49 53N 12 19 E
Tirschtiegel = Trzciel, *Poland* **55 F2** 52 23N 15 50 E
Tirso →, *Italy* **46 C1** 39 53N 8 32 E
Tirstrup, *Denmark* **17 H4** 56 18N 10 42 E
Tirthahalli, *India* **95 H2** 13 42N 75 14 E
Tirua Pt., *N.Z.* **130 E3** 38 25 S 174 40 E
Tiruchchendur, *India* **95 K4** 8 30N 78 11 E
Tiruchchirappalli, *India* **95 J4** 10 45N 78 45 E
Tirukkoyilur, *India* **95 J4** 11 57N 79 12 E
Tirumangalam, *India* **95 K3** 9 49N 77 58 E
Tirumayam, *India* **95 J4** 10 14N 78 45 E
Tirunelveli, *India* **95 K3** 8 45N 77 45 E
Tirupati, *India* **95 H4** 13 39N 79 25 E
Tiruppattur, *Tamil Nadu, India* **95 J4** 10 8N 78 37 E
Tiruppattur, *Tamil Nadu, India* **95 H4** 12 30N 78 30 E
Tiruppur, *India* **95 J3** 11 5N 77 22 E
Tirur, *India* **95 J2** 10 54N 75 55 E
Tiruttani, *India* **95 H4** 13 11N 79 58 E
Tiruttaraippundi, *India* **95 J4** 10 32N 79 41 E
Tiruvadaimarudur, *India* **95 J4** 11 2N 79 27 E
Tiruvalla, *India* **95 K3** 9 23N 76 34 E
Tiruvallar, *India* **95 H4** 13 9N 79 57 E
Tiruvannamalai, *India* **95 H4** 12 15N 79 5 E
Tiruvettipuram, *India* **95 H4** 12 39N 79 33 E
Tiruvottiyur, *India* **95 H5** 13 10N 80 22 E
Tisa, *India* **92 C7** 32 50N 76 9 E
Tisa →, *Serbia & M.* **52 E5** 45 15N 20 17 E
Tisdale, *Canada* **143 C8** 52 50N 104 0W
Tishomingo, *U.S.A.* **155 H6** 34 14N 96 41W
Tisjön, *Sweden* **16 D7** 60 56N 13 0 E
Tisnaren, *Sweden* **17 F9** 58 58N 15 56 E
Tišnov, *Czech Rep.* **35 B9** 49 21N 16 25 E
Tisovec, *Slovak Rep.* **35 C12** 48 41N 19 56 E
Tissamaharama, *Sri Lanka* **95 L5** 6 17N 81 17 E
Tissemsilt, *Algeria* **111 A5** 35 35N 1 50 E
Tissint, *Morocco* **110 C3** 29 57N 7 16W
Tista →, *India* **90 C2** 25 23N 89 43 E
Tistedal, *Norway* **18 E8** 59 8N 11 27 E
Tisza = Tisa →, *Serbia & M.* **52 E5** 45 15N 20 17 E
Tiszaföldvár, *Hungary* **52 D5** 46 58N 20 14 E
Tiszafüred, *Hungary* **52 C5** 47 38N 20 50 E
Tiszalök, *Hungary* **52 B6** 48 1N 21 20 E
Tiszavasvári, *Hungary* **52 C6** 47 58N 21 18 E
Tit, *Ahaggar, Algeria* **111 D6** 23 0N 5 10 E
Tit, *Tademait, Algeria* **111 C5** 27 0N 1 29 E
Tit-Ary, *Russia* **67 B13** 71 55N 127 2 E
Titabar, *India* **90 B5** 26 36N 94 12 E
Titaguas, *Spain* **40 F3** 39 53N 1 6W
Titao, *Burkina Faso* **113 C4** 13 45N 2 5W
Titel, *Serbia & M.* **52 E5** 45 10N 20 18 E
Tithwal, *Pakistan* **93 B5** 34 21N 73 50 E
Titicaca, L., *S. Amer.* **172 D4** 15 30 S 69 30W
Titisee, *Germany* **31 H4** 47 54N 8 10 E
Tititira Hd., *N.Z.* **131 D4** 43 36 S 169 25 E
Titiwa, *Nigeria* **113 C7** 12 14N 12 53 E
Titlagarh, *India* **94 D6** 20 15N 83 11 E
Titlis, *Switz.* **33 C6** 46 46N 8 27 E
Tito, *Italy* **47 B8** 40 35N 15 40 E
Titograd = Podgorica, *Serbia & M.* **50 D3** 42 30N 19 19 E
Titova Korenica, *Croatia* **45 D12** 44 45N 15 41 E
Titu, *Romania* **53 F10** 44 39N 25 32 E
Titule, *Dem. Rep. of the Congo* **118 B2** 3 15N 25 31 E
Titusville, *Fla., U.S.A.* **153 G9** 28 37N 80 49W
Titusville, *Pa., U.S.A.* **150 E5** 41 38N 79 41W
Tivaouane, *Senegal* **112 C1** 14 56N 16 45W
Tivat, *Serbia & M.* **50 D2** 42 28N 18 43 E
Tivedens △, *Sweden* **17 F8** 58 45N 14 35 E
Tiverton, *U.K.* **21 G4** 50 54N 3 29W
Tívoli, *Italy* **45 G9** 41 58N 12 45 E
Tiwi, *Oman* **99 B7** 22 45N 59 12 E
Tiyo, *Eritrea* **107 E5** 14 41N 40 15 E
Tiyo, Peg., *Indonesia* **83 B5** 4 0 S 135 30 E
Tizga, *Morocco* **110 B3** 32 1N 5 9W
Ti'zi N'Isli, *Morocco* **110 B3** 32 28N 5 47W
Tizi-Ouzou, *Algeria* **111 A5** 36 42N 4 3 E
Tizimín, *Mexico* **163 C7** 21 0N 88 1W
Tiznados →, *Venezuela* **168 B4** 8 16N 67 47W
Tiznap He →, *China* **65 D8** 38 23N 77 24 E
Tiznit, *Morocco* **110 C3** 29 48N 9 45W
Tjæreborg, *Denmark* **17 J2** 55 28N 8 36 E
Tjällmo, *Sweden* **17 F9** 58 43N 15 21 E
Tjeggelvas, *Sweden* **14 C17** 66 37N 17 45 E
Tjieggelvas = Tjeggelvas, *Sweden* **14 C17** 66 37N 17 45 E
Tjirebon = Cirebon, *Indonesia* **85 D3** 6 45 S 108 32 E
Tjluring, *Indonesia* **79 J17** 8 25 S 114 13 E
Tjøme, *Norway* **18 E7** 59 8N 10 26 E
Tjörn, *Sweden* **17 F5** 58 0N 11 35 E
Tkibuli = Tqibuli, *Georgia* **61 J6** 42 26N 43 0 E
Tkvarcheli = Tqvarcheli, *Georgia* **61 J5** 42 47N 41 42 E
Tlacotalpan, *Mexico* **163 D5** 18 37N 95 40W
Tlahualilo, *Mexico* **162 B4** 26 20N 103 30W
Tlaquepaque, *Mexico* **162 C4** 20 39N 103 19W
Tlaxcala, *Mexico* **163 D5** 19 20N 98 14W
Tlaxcala □, *Mexico* **163 D5** 19 25N 98 10W
Tlaxiaco, *Mexico* **163 D5** 17 18N 97 40W
Tlemcen, *Algeria* **111 B4** 34 52N 1 21W
Tleta Sidi Bouguedra, *Morocco* **110 B3** 32 16N 9 59W
Tlumach, *Ukraine* **53 B10** 48 51N 25 0 E
Tłuszcz, *Poland* **55 F8** 52 25N 21 25 E
Tlyarata, *Russia* **61 J8** 42 9N 46 26 E
Tmassah, *Libya* **108 C3** 26 19N 15 51 E
Tnine d'Anglou, *Morocco* **110 C3** 29 50N 9 50W
To Bong, *Vietnam* **86 F7** 12 45N 109 16 E
To-Shima, *Japan* **73 C11** 34 31N 139 17 E
Toa Payoh, *Singapore* **87 d** 1 20N 103 51 E
Toad →, *Canada* **142 B4** 59 25N 124 57W
Toad River, *Canada* **142 B3** 58 51N 125 14W
Toamasina, *Madag.* **117 B8** 18 10 S 49 25 E
Toamasina □, *Madag.* **117 B8** 18 0 S 49 0 E
Toay, *Argentina* **174 D3** 36 43 S 64 38W
Toba, *China* **76 B1** 31 19N 97 42 E
Toba, *Japan* **73 C8** 34 30N 136 51 E
Toba, Danau, *Indonesia* **84 B1** 2 30N 97 30 E
Toba Kakar, *Pakistan* **91 C3** 31 30N 69 0 E
Toba Tek Singh, *Pakistan* **92 D5** 30 55N 72 25 E
Tobago, *Trin. & Tob.* **169 E10** 11 10N 60 30W
Tobarra, *Spain* **41 G3** 38 37N 1 44W
Tobelo, *Indonesia* **82 A3** 1 45N 127 56 E
Tobermory, *Canada* **140 C3** 45 12N 81 40W
Tobermory, *U.K.* **22 E2** 56 38N 6 5W
Tobi, *Pac. Oc.* **83 A4** 2 40N 131 10 E
Tobias Fornier, *Phil.* **81 F3** 10 30N 121 57 E
Tobin, *U.S.A.* **160 F5** 39 55N 121 19W
Tobin, L., *Australia* **124 D4** 21 45 S 125 49 E
Tobin L., *Canada* **143 C8** 53 35N 103 30W
Toblach = Dobbiaco, *Italy* **45 B9** 46 44N 12 14 E
Toboali, *Indonesia* **84 C3** 3 0 S 106 25 E
Tobol, *Kazakhstan* **64 E9** 52 40N 62 39 E
Tobol →, *Russia* **66 D7** 58 10N 68 12 E
Toboli, *Indonesia* **82 B2** 0 38 S 120 5 E
Tobolsk, *Russia* **66 D7** 58 15N 68 10 E
Tobor, *Senegal* **112 C1** 12 40N 16 15W
Toboso, *Phil.* **81 F4** 10 43N 123 31 E
Tobruk = Tubruq, *Libya* **108 B4** 32 7N 23 55 E
Tobyhanna, *U.S.A.* **151 E9** 41 11N 75 25W
Tobyl = Tobol →, *Russia* **66 D7** 58 10N 68 12 E
Tocache Nuevo, *Peru* **172 B2** 8 9 S 76 26W
Tocantínia, *Brazil* **170 C2** 9 33 S 48 22W
Tocantinópolis, *Brazil* **170 C2** 6 20 S 47 25W
Tocantins □, *Brazil* **170 D2** 10 0 S 48 0W
Tocantins →, *Brazil* **170 B2** 1 45 S 49 10W
Toccoa, *U.S.A.* **149 H4** 34 35N 83 19W
Toce →, *Italy* **44 C5** 45 56N 8 29 E
Tochi →, *Pakistan* **92 C4** 32 49N 70 41 E
Tochigi, *Japan* **73 A11** 36 25N 139 45 E
Tochigi □, *Japan* **73 A11** 36 45N 139 45 E
Tocina, *Spain* **43 H5** 37 37N 5 44W
Töcksfors, *Sweden* **16 E5** 59 31N 11 52 E
Toco, *Chile* **172 E4** 22 5 S 69 35W
Toco, *Trin. & Tob.* **169 F10** 10 49N 60 57W
Toconao, *Chile* **174 A2** 23 11 S 68 1W
Tocopilla, *Chile* **174 A1** 22 5 S 70 10W
Tocqueville = Rass el Oued, *Algeria* **111 A6** 35 57N 5 2 E
Tocumwal, *Australia* **129 C6** 35 51 S 145 31 E
Tocuyo →, *Venezuela* **168 A4** 11 3N 68 23W
Tocuyo de la Costa, *Venezuela* **168 A4** 11 2N 68 23W
Todal, *Norway* **18 B5** 62 49N 8 44 E
Todd →, *Australia* **126 C2** 24 52 S 135 48 E
Todeli, *Indonesia* **82 B2** 1 40 S 124 29 E
Todenyang, *Kenya* **118 B4** 4 35N 35 56 E
Todgarh, *India* **92 G5** 25 42N 73 58 E
Todi, *Italy* **45 F9** 42 47N 12 24 E
Tödi, *Switz.* **33 C7** 46 48N 8 55 E
Todos os Santos, B. de, *Brazil* **171 D4** 12 48 S 38 38W
Todos Santos, *Mexico* **162 C2** 23 27N 110 13W
Todtnau, *Germany* **31 H3** 47 49N 7 56 E
Toe Hd., *U.K.* **22 D1** 57 50N 7 8W
Toecé, *Burkina Faso* **113 C4** 11 50N 1 16W
Toetoes B., *N.Z.* **131 G3** 46 42 S 168 41 E
Tofield, *Canada* **142 C6** 53 25N 112 40W
Tofino, *Canada* **142 D3** 49 11N 125 55W
Töfsingdalens △, *Sweden* **16 B6** 62 10N 12 28 E
Tofte, *Norway* **18 E7** 59 33N 10 34 E
Tofua, *Tonga* **133 P13** 19 45 S 175 5W
Toga, *Vanuatu* **133 C4** 13 26 S 166 42 E
Tōgane, *Japan* **73 B12** 35 33N 140 22 E
Togba, *Mauritania* **112 B2** 17 26N 10 12W
Togbo, *C.A.R.* **114 A3** 6 0N 17 27 E
Toggenburg, *Switz.* **33 B8** 47 16N 9 9 E
Togiak, *U.S.A.* **144 G7** 59 4N 160 24W
Togian, Kepulauan, *Indonesia* **82 B2** 0 20 S 121 50 E
Togliatti, *Russia* **60 D9** 53 32N 49 24 E
Togo ■, *W. Afr.* **113 D5** 8 30N 1 35 E
Togtoh, *China* **74 D6** 40 15N 111 10 E
Toguzak →, *Kazakhstan* **64 D9** 54 3N 62 44 E
Tohma →, *Turkey* **100 C7** 38 29N 38 23 E
Tōhoku □, *Japan* **70 E10** 39 50N 141 45 E
Töhöm, *Mongolia* **74 B5** 44 27N 108 2 E
Tohopekaliga, L., *U.S.A.* **153 G8** 28 12N 81 24W
Toi, *Japan* **73 C10** 34 54N 138 47 E
Toibalewe, *India* **95 J11** 10 32N 92 30 E
Toili, *Indonesia* **82 B2** 1 24 S 122 26 E
Toinya, *Sudan* **107 F2** 6 17N 29 46 E
Toiyabe Range, *U.S.A.* **158 G5** 39 30N 117 0W
Tojikiston = Tajikistan ■, *Asia* **65 D4** 38 30N 70 0 E
Tojo, *Indonesia* **82 B2** 1 20 S 121 15 E
Tōjō, *Japan* **72 C5** 34 53N 133 16 E
Tok, *U.S.A.* **144 E12** 63 20N 142 59W
Tok →, *Russia* **64 E4** 52 46N 52 22 E
Tok-do, *Asia* **71 F5** 37 15N 131 52 E
Toka, *Guyana* **169 C6** 3 58N 59 17W
Tokaanu, *N.Z.* **130 E4** 38 58 S 175 46 E
Tokachi-Dake, *Japan* **70 C11** 43 17N 142 5 E
Tokachi-Gawa →, *Japan* **70 C11** 42 44N 143 42 E
Tokai, *Japan* **73 B8** 35 2N 136 55 E
Tokaj, *Hungary* **52 B6** 48 8N 21 27 E
Tokala, *Indonesia* **82 B2** 1 30 S 121 40 E
Tōkamachi, *Japan* **71 F9** 37 8N 138 43 E
Tokanui, *N.Z.* **131 G3** 46 34 S 168 56 E
Tokar, *Sudan* **106 D4** 18 27N 37 56 E
Tokara-Rettō, *Japan* **71 K4** 29 37N 129 43 E
Tokarahi, *N.Z.* **131 E5** 44 56 S 170 39 E
Tokashiki-Shima, *Japan* **71 L3** 26 11N 127 21 E
Tokat, *Turkey* **100 B7** 40 22N 36 35 E
Tŏkch'ŏn, *N. Korea* **75 E14** 39 45N 126 18 E
Tokeland, *U.S.A.* **160 D3** 46 42N 123 59W
Tokelau Is., *Pac. Oc.* **134 H10** 9 0 S 171 45W
Toki, *Japan* **73 B9** 35 18N 137 8 E
Tokmak, *Kyrgyzstan* **65 B7** 42 49N 75 15 E
Tokmak, *Ukraine* **59 J8** 47 16N 35 42 E
Toko Ra., *Australia* **126 C2** 23 5 S 138 20 E
Tokomaru Bay, *N.Z.* **130 E7** 38 8 S 178 22 E
Tokoname, *Japan* **73 C8** 34 53N 136 51 E
Tokoro-Gawa →, *Japan* **70 B12** 44 7N 144 5 E
Tokoroa, *N.Z.* **130 E4** 38 13 S 175 50 E
Tokorozawa, *Japan* **73 B11** 35 47N 139 28 E
Toksook Bay, *U.S.A.* **144 F6** 60 32N 165 0W
Toktogul, *Kyrgyzstan* **65 C6** 41 50N 72 50 E
Toktogul Suu Saktagychy, *Kyrgyzstan* **65 C6** 41 48N 72 51 E
Toku, *Tonga* **133 P13** 18 10 S 174 11W
Tokuji, *Japan* **72 C3** 34 11N 131 42 E
Tokuno-Shima, *Japan* **71 L4** 27 56N 128 55 E
Tokushima, *Japan* **72 C6** 34 4N 134 34 E
Tokushima □, *Japan* **72 D6** 33 55N 134 0 E
Tokuyama, *Japan* **72 C3** 34 3N 131 50 E
Tōkyō, *Japan* **73 B11** 35 45N 139 45 E
Tōkyō □, *Japan* **73 B11** 35 40N 139 30 E
Tokyo Haneda ✈ (HND), *Japan* **73 B11** 35 33N 139 46 E
Tokyo Narita ✈ (NRT), *Japan* **73 B12** 35 45N 140 25 E
Tōkyō-Wan, *Japan* **73 B11** 35 25N 139 47 E
Tokzār, *Afghan.* **91 B2** 35 52N 66 26 E
Tolaga Bay, *N.Z.* **130 E7** 38 21 S 178 20 E
Tolageak, *U.S.A.* **144 A7** 70 3N 162 27W
Tolbukhin = Dobrich, *Bulgaria* **51 C11** 43 37N 27 49 E
Tolé, *C.A.R.* **114 A3** 6 34N 16 1 E
Tōle Bī, *Kazakhstan* **65 B6** 43 42N 73 46 E
Toledo, *Brazil* **175 A5** 24 44 S 53 45W
Toledo, *Phil.* **81 F4** 10 23N 123 38 E
Toledo, *Spain* **42 F6** 39 50N 4 2W
Toledo, *Ill., U.S.A.* **157 E8** 39 16N 88 15W
Toledo, *Iowa, U.S.A.* **156 C4** 42 0N 92 35W
Toledo, *Ohio, U.S.A.* **157 C13** 41 39N 83 33W
Toledo, *Oreg., U.S.A.* **158 D2** 44 37N 123 56W
Toledo, *Wash., U.S.A.* **158 C2** 46 26N 122 51W
Toledo, Montes de, *Spain* **43 F6** 39 33N 4 20W
Toledo Bend Reservoir, *U.S.A.* **155 K8** 31 11N 93 34W
Tolentino, *Italy* **45 E10** 43 12N 13 17 E
Tolfa, *Italy* **45 F8** 42 9N 11 56 E
Tolga, *Algeria* **111 B6** 34 40N 5 22 E
Tolga, *Australia* **126 B4** 17 15 S 145 29 E
Tolga, *Norway* **18 B8** 62 26N 11 1 E
Tolhuaca △, *Chile* **176 A2** 38 15 S 71 50W
Toliara, *Madag.* **117 C7** 23 21 S 43 40 E
Toliara □, *Madag.* **117 C8** 21 0 S 45 0 E
Tolima, *Colombia* **168 C2** 4 40N 75 19W
Tolima □, *Colombia* **168 C2** 3 45N 75 15W
Tolitoli, *Indonesia* **82 A2** 1 5N 120 50 E
Tolkmicko, *Poland* **54 D6** 54 19N 19 31 E
Tollarp, *Sweden* **17 J7** 55 55N 13 58 E
Tollensesee, *Germany* **30 B9** 53 30N 13 13 E
Tollhouse, *U.S.A.* **160 H7** 37 1N 119 24W
Tolmachevo, *Russia* **58 C5** 58 56N 29 51 E
Tolmezzo, *Italy* **45 B10** 46 24N 13 1 E
Tolmin, *Slovenia* **45 B10** 46 11N 13 45 E
Tolna, *Hungary* **52 D3** 46 25N 18 48 E
Tolna □, *Hungary* **52 D3** 46 30N 18 30 E
Tolo, *Dem. Rep. of the Congo* **114 C3** 2 55 S 18 34 E
Tolo, Teluk, *Indonesia* **82 B2** 2 20 S 122 10 E
Tolo Harbour, *China* **69 G11** 22 27N 114 12 E
Tolochin = Talachyn, *Belarus* **58 E5** 54 25N 29 42 E
Tolokiwa I., *Papua N. G.* **132 C4** 5 19 S 147 37 E
Tolong Bay, *Phil.* **81 G4** 9 20N 122 49 E
Tolono, *U.S.A.* **157 E8** 39 59N 88 16W
Tolosa, *Spain* **40 B2** 43 8N 2 5W
Tolox, *Spain* **43 J6** 36 41N 4 54W
Toltén, *Chile* **176 A2** 39 13 S 74 14W
Toluca, *Mexico* **163 D5** 19 20N 99 40W
Toluca, *U.S.A.* **156 C7** 41 0N 89 9W
Tolybay, *Kazakhstan* **64 F9** 50 31N 62 19 E
Tom Burke, *S. Africa* **117 C4** 23 5 S 28 0 E
Tom Price, *Australia* **124 D2** 22 40 S 117 48 E
Toma, *Burkina Faso* **112 C4** 12 45N 2 53W
Tomah, *U.S.A.* **154 D9** 43 59N 90 30W
Tomahawk, *U.S.A.* **154 C10** 45 28N 89 44W
Tomai, *Moldova* **53 D13** 46 34N 28 19 E
Tomakomai, *Japan* **70 C10** 42 38N 141 36 E
Tomales, *U.S.A.* **160 G4** 38 15N 122 53W
Tomales B., *U.S.A.* **160 G3** 38 15N 123 58W
Tomanlivi, *Fiji* **133 A2** 17 37 S 178 1 E
Tomar, *Portugal* **43 F2** 39 36N 8 25W
Tómaros, Óros, *Greece* **48 B2** 39 29N 20 48 E
Tomarza, *Turkey* **100 C6** 38 27N 35 48 E
Tomás Barrón, *Bolivia* **172 D4** 17 35 S 67 31W
Tomashevka, *Belarus* **55 G10** 51 33N 23 36 E
Tomashpil, *Ukraine* **53 B13** 48 32N 28 31 E
Tomaszów Lubelski, *Poland* **55 H10** 50 27N 23 25 E
Tomaszów Mazowiecki, *Poland* **55 G7** 51 30N 20 2 E
Tomatlán, *Mexico* **162 D3** 19 56N 105 15W
Tombadonkéa, *Guinea* **112 C2** 11 0N 14 25W
Tombador, Serra do, *Brazil* **173 C6** 12 0 S 58 0W
Tombe, *Sudan* **107 F3** 5 53N 31 40 E
Tombel, *Cameroon* **114 B1** 4 45N 9 40 E
Tombigbee →, *U.S.A.* **149 K2** 31 8N 87 57W
Tombôco, *Angola* **115 D2** 6 48 S 13 18 E
Tombouctou, *Mali* **112 B4** 16 50N 3 0W
Tombstone, *U.S.A.* **159 L8** 31 43N 110 4W
Tombua, *Angola* **116 B1** 15 55 S 11 55 E
Tomé, *Chile* **174 D1** 36 36 S 72 57W
Tomé-Açu, *Brazil* **170 B2** 2 25 S 48 9W
Tomelilla, *Sweden* **17 J7** 55 33N 13 58 E
Tomelloso, *Spain* **43 F7** 39 10N 3 2W
Tömenaryk, *Kazakhstan* **65 A3** 44 2N 67 1 E
Tomingley, *Australia* **129 B8** 32 26 S 148 16 E
Tomini, *Indonesia* **82 A2** 0 30N 120 30 E
Tomini, Teluk, *Indonesia* **82 B2** 0 10 S 121 0 E
Tominian, *Mali* **112 C4** 13 17N 4 35W
Tomiño, *Spain* **42 D2** 41 59N 8 46W
Tomintoul, *U.K.* **22 D5** 57 15N 3 23W
Tomioka, *Japan* **73 A10** 36 15N 138 54 E
Tomislavgrad, *Bos.-H.* **52 G2** 43 42N 17 13 E
Tomkinson Ranges, *Australia* **125 E4** 26 11 S 129 5 E
Tommot, *Russia* **67 D13** 59 4N 126 20 E
Tomnop Ta Suos, *Cambodia* **87 G5** 11 20N 104 15 E
Tomo, *Colombia* **168 C4** 2 38N 67 32W
Tomo →, *Colombia* **168 B4** 5 20N 67 48W
Tomobe, *Japan* **73 A12** 36 20N 140 20 E
Toms, *Norway* **18 B3** 62 34N 6 56 E
Toms Place, *U.S.A.* **160 H8** 37 34N 118 41W
Toms River, *U.S.A.* **151 G10** 39 58N 74 12W
Tomsk, *Russia* **66 D9** 56 30N 85 5 E
Tomtabacken, *Sweden* **17 G8** 57 30N 14 30 E
Tona, *Spain* **40 D7** 41 51N 2 14 E
Tonalá, *Mexico* **163 D6** 16 8N 93 41W
Tonale, Passo del, *Italy* **44 B7** 46 16N 10 35 E
Tonami, *Japan* **73 A8** 36 40N 136 58 E
Tonantins, *Brazil* **168 D4** 2 45 S 67 45W
Tonasket, *U.S.A.* **158 B4** 48 42N 119 26W
Tonate, *Fr. Guiana* **169 C7** 5 0N 52 28W
Tonawanda, *U.S.A.* **150 D6** 43 1N 78 53W
Tonb, *Iran* **97 E7** 26 15N 55 15 E
Tonbo, *Burma* **90 F5** 18 31N 95 5 E
Tonbridge, *U.K.* **21 F8** 51 11N 0 17 E
Tonda, *Papua N. G.* **132 E1** 8 55 S 141 34 E
Tondabayashi, *Japan* **73 C7** 34 30N 135 36 E
Tondano, *Indonesia* **82 A2** 1 35N 124 54 E
Tondela, *Portugal* **42 E2** 40 31N 8 5W
Tønder, *Denmark* **17 K2** 54 58N 8 50 E
Tondern = Tønder, *Denmark* **17 K2** 54 58N 8 50 E
Tondi, *India* **95 K4** 9 45N 79 4 E
Tondi Kiwindi, *Niger* **113 C5** 14 28N 2 2 E
Tondibi, *Mali* **113 B4** 16 39N 0 14W

Tondoro, *Namibia* **116 B2** 17 45 S 18 50 E
Tone →, *Australia* **125 F2** 34 25 S 116 25 E
Tone-Gawa →, *Japan* **73 B12** 35 44N 140 51 E
Tonekābon, *Iran* **97 B6** 36 45N 51 12 E
Tong I., *Papua N. G.* **132 B4** 2 2 S 147 47 E
Tong Xian, *China* **74 E9** 39 55N 116 35 E
Tōngā, *Sudan* **107 F3** 9 28N 31 3 E
Tonga ■, *Pac. Oc.* **133 P13** 19 50 S 174 30W
Tonga Trench, *Pac. Oc.* **134 J10** 18 0 S 173 0W
Tongaat, *S. Africa* **117 D5** 29 33 S 31 9 E
Tongala, *Australia* **129 D6** 36 14 S 144 56 E
Tong'an, *China* **77 E12** 24 37N 118 8 E
Tongareva, *Cook Is.* **135 H12** 9 0 S 158 0W
Tongariro △, *N.Z.* **130 F4** 39 8 S 175 33 E
Tongatapu, *Tonga* **133 Q14** 21 10 S 174 0W
Tongatapu Group, *Tonga* **133 Q13** 21 0 S 175 0W
Tongbai, *China* **77 A9** 32 20N 113 23 E
Tongcheng, *Anhui, China* **77 B11** 31 4N 116 56 E
Tongcheng, *Hubei, China* **77 C9** 29 15N 113 50 E
Tongchŏn-ni, *N. Korea* **75 E14** 39 50N 127 25 E
Tongchuan, *China* **74 G5** 35 6N 109 3 E
Tongdao, *China* **76 D7** 26 10N 109 42 E
Tongeren, *Belgium* **24 D5** 50 47N 5 28 E
Tonggu, *China* **77 C10** 28 31N 114 20 E
Tonggu Jiao, *China* **69 G10** 22 22N 113 37 E
Tongguan, *China* **74 G6** 34 40N 110 25 E
Tonghae, *S. Korea* **75 F15** 37 29N 129 7 E
Tonghai, *China* **76 E4** 24 10N 102 53 E
Tonghua, *China* **75 D13** 41 42N 125 58 E
Tongjiang, *China* **76 B6** 31 58N 107 11 E
Tongjosŏn Man, *N. Korea* **75 E15** 39 30N 128 0 E
Tongkil, *Phil.* **81 H3** 6 4N 121 48 E
Tongking, G. of = Tonkin, G. of, *Asia* **68 E5** 20 0N 108 0 E
Tongliang, *China* **76 C6** 29 50N 106 3 E
Tongliao, *China* **75 C12** 43 38N 122 18 E
Tongling, *China* **77 B11** 30 55N 117 48 E
Tonglu, *China* **77 C12** 29 45N 119 37 E
Tongnae, *S. Korea* **75 G15** 35 12N 129 5 E
Tongnan = Anyue, *China* **76 B5** 30 9N 105 50 E
Tongoa, *Vanuatu* **133 F6** 16 54 S 168 34 E
Tongobory, *Madag.* **117 C7** 23 32 S 44 20 E
Tongoy, *Chile* **174 C1** 30 16 S 71 31W
Tongquil I., *Phil.* **81 H3** 6 2N 121 51 E
Tongren, *China* **76 D7** 27 43N 109 11 E
Tongres = Tongeren, *Belgium* **24 D5** 50 47N 5 28 E
Tongsa Dzong, *Bhutan* **90 B3** 27 31N 90 31 E
Tongshi, *China* **86 C7** 18 30N 109 20 E
Tongue, *U.K.* **22 C4** 58 29N 4 25W
Tongue →, *U.S.A.* **154 B2** 46 25N 105 52W
Tongwei, *China* **74 G3** 35 0N 105 5 E
Tongxiang, *China* **77 B13** 30 39N 120 34 E
Tongxin, *China* **74 F3** 36 59N 105 58 E
Tongyang, *N. Korea* **75 E14** 39 9N 126 53 E
Tongyu, *China* **75 B12** 44 45N 123 4 E
Tongzi, *China* **76 C6** 28 9N 106 49 E
Tonica, *U.S.A.* **156 C7** 41 13N 89 4W
Tonj, *Sudan* **107 F2** 7 20N 28 44 E
Tonj →, *Sudan* **107 F2** 7 31N 28 55 E
Tonk, *India* **92 F6** 26 6N 75 54 E
Tonkawa, *U.S.A.* **155 G6** 36 41N 97 18W
Tonkin = Bac Phan, *Vietnam* **86 B5** 22 0N 105 0 E
Tonkin, G. of, *Asia* **68 E5** 20 0N 108 0 E
Tonle Sap, *Cambodia* **86 F4** 13 0N 104 0 E
Tonnay-Charente, *France* **28 C3** 45 56N 0 55W
Tonneins, *France* **28 D4** 44 23N 0 19 E
Tonnerre, *France* **27 E10** 47 51N 3 59 E
Tönning, *Germany* **30 A4** 54 19N 8 56 E
Tono, *Japan* **70 E10** 39 19N 141 32 E
Tonopah, *U.S.A.* **159 G5** 38 4N 117 14W
Tonoshō, *Japan* **72 C6** 34 29N 134 11 E
Tonosí, *Panama* **164 E3** 7 20N 80 20W
Tons →, *Haryana, India* **92 D7** 30 30N 77 39 E
Tons →, *Ut. P., India* **93 F10** 26 1N 83 33 E
Tønsberg, *Norway* **18 E7** 59 19N 10 25 E
Tonsina, *U.S.A.* **144 F11** 61 39N 145 11W
Tonstad, *Norway* **18 F3** 58 40N 6 45 E
Tonto ⌓, *U.S.A.* **159 K8** 33 39N 111 7W
Tonumea, *Tonga* **133 Q13** 20 30 S 174 30W
Tonya, *Turkey* **101 B8** 40 53N 39 16 E
Tonzang, *Burma* **90 D4** 23 36N 93 42 E
Tonzi, *Burma* **90 C5** 24 39N 94 57 E
Toobanna, *Australia* **126 B4** 18 42 S 146 9 E
Toodyay, *Australia* **125 F2** 31 34 S 116 28 E
Tooele, *U.S.A.* **158 F7** 40 32N 112 18W
Toompine, *Australia* **127 D3** 27 15 S 144 19 E
Toomsboro, *U.S.A.* **152 C6** 32 50N 83 5W
Toora, *Australia* **129 E7** 38 39 S 146 23 E
Toora-Khem, *Russia* **67 D10** 52 28N 96 17 E
Toowoomba, *Australia* **127 D5** 27 32 S 151 56 E
Top-ozero, *Russia* **56 A5** 65 35N 32 0 E
Top Springs, *Australia* **124 C5** 16 37 S 131 51 E
Topalu, *Romania* **53 F13** 44 31N 28 3 E
Topaz, *U.S.A.* **160 G7** 38 41N 119 30W
Topeka, *U.S.A.* **154 F7** 39 3N 95 40W
Topl'a →, *Slovak Rep.* **35 C14** 48 45N 21 45 E
Topley, *Canada* **142 C3** 54 49N 126 18W
Toplica →, *Serbia & M.* **50 C5** 43 15N 21 49 E
Toplița, *Romania* **53 D10** 46 55N 25 20 E
Topo, *Azores* **9 d1** 38 33N 27 45W
Topo, Pta. do, *Azores* **9 d1** 38 33N 27 46W
Topocalma, Pta., *Chile* **174 C1** 34 10 S 72 2W
Topock, *U.S.A.* **161 L12** 34 46N 114 29W
Topola, *Serbia & M.* **50 B4** 44 17N 20 41 E
Topolčani, *Macedonia* **50 E5** 41 14N 21 25 E
Topol'čany, *Slovak Rep.* **35 C11** 48 35N 18 12 E
Topolnitsa →, *Bulgaria* **51 D8** 42 11N 24 18 E
Topolobampo, *Mexico* **162 B3** 25 40N 109 4W
Topoloveni, *Romania* **53 F10** 44 49N 25 5 E
Topolovgrad, *Bulgaria* **51 D10** 42 5N 26 20 E
Topolvățu Mare, *Romania* **52 E6** 45 46N 21 41 E
Topornino = Kushnarenkovo, *Russia* **64 D5** 55 6N 55 22 E
Toppenish, *U.S.A.* **158 C3** 46 23N 120 19W
Topraisar, *Romania* **53 F13** 44 1N 28 27 E
Topusko, *Croatia* **45 C12** 45 18N 15 59 E
Toquepala, *Peru* **172 D3** 17 24 S 70 25W
Torà, *Spain* **40 D6** 41 49N 1 25 E
Tora Kit, *Sudan* **107 E3** 11 2N 32 36 E
Toraka Vestale, *Madag.* **117 B7** 16 20 S 43 58 E
Torata, *Peru* **172 D3** 17 23 S 70 1W
Torbalı, *Turkey* **49 C9** 38 10N 27 21 E
Torbat-e Heydārīyeh, *Iran* **97 C8** 35 15N 59 12 E
Torbat-e Jām, *Iran* **97 C9** 35 16N 60 35 E
Torbay, *Canada* **141 C9** 47 40N 52 42W
Torbay □, *U.K.* **21 G4** 50 26N 3 31W
Tørberget, *Norway* **18 C9** 61 8N 12 7 E
Torbjörntorp, *Sweden* **17 F7** 58 12N 13 36 E
Tordesillas, *Spain* **42 D6** 41 30N 5 0W
Töreboda, *Sweden* **17 F8** 58 41N 14 7 E
Torekov, *Sweden* **17 H6** 56 26N 12 37 E
Torellò, *Spain* **40 C7** 42 3N 2 16 E
Toreno, *Spain* **42 C4** 42 42N 6 30W
Torfaen □, *U.K.* **21 F4** 51 43N 3 3W
Torfajökull, *Iceland* **11 D7** 63 54N 19 0W
Torgau, *Germany* **30 D8** 51 34N 13 0 E
Torgelow, *Germany* **30 B10** 53 37N 14 1 E
Torgovaya = Salsk, *Russia* **61 G5** 46 28N 41 30 E
Torhamn, *Sweden* **17 H9** 56 6N 15 50 E
Torhout, *Belgium* **24 C3** 51 5N 3 7 E
Torhovytsya, *Ukraine* **53 B10** 48 36N 25 26 E
Tori, *Ethiopia* **107 F3** 7 53N 33 35 E
Tori-Shima, *Japan* **71 J10** 30 29N 140 19 E
Torigni-sur-Vire, *France* **26 C6** 49 3N 0 58W
Torija, *Spain* **40 E1** 40 44N 3 2W
Torin, *Mexico* **162 B2** 27 33N 110 15W
Torino, *Italy* **44 C4** 45 3N 7 40 E
Torit, *Sudan* **107 G3** 4 27N 32 31 E
Torkamān, *Iran* **101 D12** 37 35N 47 23 E
Torkovichi, *Russia* **58 C6** 58 51N 30 21 E
Tormac, *Romania* **52 E6** 45 30N 21 30 E
Tormes →, *Spain* **42 D4** 41 18N 6 29W
Tornado Mt., *Canada* **142 D6** 49 55N 114 40W
Tornal'a, *Slovak Rep.* **35 C13** 48 25N 20 20 E
Torneå = Tornio, *Finland* **14 D21** 65 50N 24 12 E
Torneälven →, *Europe* **14 D21** 65 50N 24 12 E
Torneträsk, *Sweden* **14 B18** 68 24N 19 15 E
Tornio, *Finland* **14 D21** 65 50N 24 12 E
Tornionjoki = Torneälven →, *Europe* **14 D21** 65 50N 24 12 E
Tornquist, *Argentina* **174 D3** 38 8 S 62 15W
Toro, *Baleares, Spain* **38 B5** 39 59N 4 8 E
Toro, *Zamora, Spain* **42 D5** 41 35N 5 24W
Torö, *Sweden* **17 F11** 58 48N 17 50 E
Toro ⌓, *Uganda* **118 C3** 0 5 S 30 22 E
Toro, Cerro del, *Chile* **174 B2** 29 10 S 69 50W
Toro Pk., *U.S.A.* **161 M10** 33 34N 116 24W
Torokina, *Papua N. G.* **132 D8** 6 14 S 155 3 E
Törökszentmiklós, *Hungary* **52 C5** 47 11N 20 27 E
Toronaíos Kólpos, *Greece* **50 F7** 40 5N 23 30 E
Toronto, *Australia* **129 B9** 33 0 S 151 30 E
Toronto, *Canada* **140 D4** 43 39N 79 20W
Toronto, *U.S.A.* **150 F4** 40 28N 80 36W
Toronto Lester B. Pearson International ✈ (YYZ), *Canada* **150 C5** 43 40N 79 34W
Toropets, *Russia* **58 D6** 56 30N 31 40 E
Tororo, *Uganda* **118 B3** 0 45N 34 12 E
Toros Dağları, *Turkey* **100 D5** 37 0N 32 30 E
Torotoro, *Bolivia* **173 D4** 18 7 S 65 46W
Torotoro △, *Bolivia* **173 D4** 18 7 S 65 46W
Torpa, *India* **93 H11** 22 57N 85 6 E
Torpo, *Norway* **18 D5** 60 40N 8 43 E
Torquay, *Australia* **128 E6** 38 20 S 144 19 E
Torquay, *U.K.* **21 G4** 50 27N 3 32W
Torquemada, *Spain* **42 C6** 42 2N 4 19W
Torrais, Pta., *Azores* **9 d2** 39 43N 31 7W
Torrance, *U.S.A.* **161 M8** 33 50N 118 19W
Torrão, *Portugal* **43 G2** 38 16N 8 11W
Torre Annunziata, *Italy* **47 B7** 40 45N 14 27 E
Torre de Moncorvo, *Portugal* **42 D3** 41 12N 7 8W
Torre del Campo, *Spain* **43 H7** 37 46N 3 53W
Torre del Greco, *Italy* **47 B7** 40 47N 14 22 E
Torre del Mar, *Spain* **43 J6** 36 44N 4 6W
Torre-Pacheco, *Spain* **41 H4** 37 44N 0 57W
Torre Péllice, *Italy* **44 D4** 44 49N 7 13 E
Torreblanca, *Spain* **40 E5** 40 14N 0 12 E
Torrecampo, *Spain* **43 G6** 38 29N 4 41W
Torrecilla en Cameros, *Spain* **40 C2** 42 15N 2 38W
Torredembarra, *Spain* **40 D6** 41 9N 1 24 E
Torredonjimeno, *Spain* **43 H7** 37 46N 3 57W
Torrejón de Ardoz, *Spain* **42 E7** 40 27N 3 29W
Torrejoncillo, *Spain* **42 F4** 39 54N 6 28W
Torrelaguna, *Spain* **42 E7** 40 50N 3 38W
Torrelavega, *Spain* **42 B6** 43 20N 4 5W
Torremaggiore, *Italy* **45 G12** 41 41N 15 17 E
Torremolinos, *Spain* **43 J6** 36 38N 4 30W
Torrens, L., *Australia* **128 A2** 31 0 S 137 50 E
Torrens Cr. →, *Australia* **126 C4** 22 23 S 145 9 E
Torrens Creek, *Australia* **126 C4** 20 48 S 145 3 E
Torrent, *Spain* **41 F4** 39 27N 0 28W
Torrenueva, *Spain* **43 G7** 38 38N 3 22W
Torreón, *Mexico* **162 B4** 25 33N 103 26W
Torreperogil, *Spain* **43 G7** 38 2N 3 17W
Torres, *Brazil* **175 B5** 29 21 S 49 44W
Torres, *Mexico* **162 B2** 28 46N 110 47W
Torres, Is., *Vanuatu* **133 C4** 13 15 S 166 37 E
Torres del Paine △, *Chile* **176 D2** 51 3 S 72 58W
Torres Novas, *Portugal* **43 F2** 39 27N 8 33W
Torres Strait, *Australia* **132 E2** 9 50 S 142 20 E
Torres Vedras, *Portugal* **43 F1** 39 5N 9 15W
Torrevieja, *Spain* **41 H4** 37 59N 0 42W
Torrey, *U.S.A.* **159 G8** 38 18N 111 25W
Torricelli Mts., *Papua N. G.* **132 B2** 3 23 S 142 15 E
Torridge →, *U.K.* **21 G3** 51 0N 4 13W
Torridon, L., *U.K.* **22 D3** 57 35N 5 50W
Torrijos, *Phil.* **80 E4** 13 19N 122 5 E
Torrijos, *Spain* **42 F6** 39 59N 4 18W
Tørring, *Denmark* **17 J3** 55 52N 9 29 E
Torrington, *Conn., U.S.A.* **151 E11** 41 48N 73 7W
Torrington, *Wyo., U.S.A.* **154 D2** 42 4N 104 11W
Torroella de Montgrì, *Spain* **40 C8** 42 2N 3 8 E
Torrox, *Spain* **43 J7** 36 46N 3 57W
Torsås, *Sweden* **17 H9** 56 24N 16 0 E
Torsby, *Sweden* **16 D6** 60 7N 13 0 E
Torshälla, *Sweden* **16 E10** 59 25N 16 28 E
Tórshavn, *Færoe Is.* **14 E9** 62 5N 6 56W
Torslanda, *Sweden* **17 G5** 57 44N 11 45 E
Torsö, *Sweden* **17 F7** 58 48N 13 45 E
Tortkŏl, *Kazakhstan* **65 B4** 42 55N 68 57 E
Tortola, *Br. Virgin Is.* **165 e** 18 19N 64 45W
Tórtoles de Esgueva, *Spain* **42 D6** 41 49N 4 2W
Tortolì, *Italy* **46 C2** 39 55N 9 39 E
Tortona, *Italy* **44 D5** 44 54N 8 52 E
Tortorici, *Italy* **47 D7** 38 2N 14 49 E
Tortosa, *Spain* **40 E5** 40 49N 0 31 E
Tortosa, C., *Spain* **40 E5** 40 41N 0 52 E
Tortosendo, *Portugal* **42 E3** 40 15N 7 31W
Tortue, I. de la, *Haiti* **165 B5** 20 5N 72 57W
Tortuguero △, *Costa Rica* **164 D3** 10 31N 83 29W
Tortum, *Turkey* **101 B9** 40 19N 41 35 E
Toru-Aygyr, *Kyrgyzstan* **65 B8** 42 30N 76 26 E
Torūd, *Iran* **97 C7** 35 25N 55 5 E
Torul, *Turkey* **101 B8** 40 34N 39 18 E
Toruń, *Poland* **55 E5** 53 2N 18 39 E
Torun, *Ukraine* **53 B8** 48 40N 23 34 E
Tory I., *Ireland* **23 A3** 55 16N 8 14W
Torysa →, *Slovak Rep.* **35 C14** 48 39N 21 21 E
Torzhok, *Russia* **58 D8** 57 5N 34 55 E
Torzym, *Poland* **55 F2** 52 19N 15 5 E
Tosa, *Japan* **72 D5** 33 24N 133 23 E
Tosa-Shimizu, *Japan* **72 E4** 32 52N 132 58 E
Tosa-Wan, *Japan* **72 D5** 33 15N 133 30 E
Tosa-Yamada, *Japan* **72 D5** 33 36N 133 38 E
Toscana □, *Italy* **44 E8** 43 25N 11 0 E
Toscanella = Tuscánia, *Italy* **45 F8** 42 25N 11 52 E
Toscano, Arcipelago, *Italy* **44 F7** 42 30N 10 30 E
Toshkent, *Uzbekistan* **65 C4** 41 20N 69 10 E
Tosno, *Russia* **58 C6** 59 38N 30 46 E
Tossa de Mar, *Spain* **40 D7** 41 43N 2 56 E
Tösse, *Sweden* **17 F6** 58 58N 12 39 E
Tostado, *Argentina* **174 B3** 29 15 S 61 50W
Tostedt, *Germany* **30 B5** 53 17N 9 42 E
Tostón, Pta. de, *Canary Is.* **9 e2** 28 42N 14 2W
Tosu, *Japan* **72 D2** 33 22N 130 31 E
Tosya, *Turkey* **100 B6** 41 1N 34 2 E
Toszek, *Poland* **55 H5** 50 27N 18 32 E
Totak, *Norway* **18 E5** 59 40N 8 0 E
Totana, *Spain* **41 H3** 37 45N 1 30W
Totebo, *Sweden* **17 G10** 57 38N 16 12 E
Toteng, *Botswana* **116 C3** 20 22 S 22 58 E
Tôtes, *France* **26 C8** 49 41N 1 2 E
Tótkomlós, *Hungary* **52 D5** 46 24N 20 45 E
Totland, *Norway* **18 C2** 61 56N 5 23 E
Totma, *Russia* **56 C7** 60 0N 42 40 E
Totnes, *U.K.* **21 G4** 50 26N 3 42W
Totness, *Suriname* **169 B6** 5 53N 56 19W
Toto, *Nigeria* **113 D6** 8 26N 7 5 E
Totonicapán, *Guatemala* **164 D1** 14 58N 91 12W
Totora, *Bolivia* **173 D4** 17 42 S 65 9W
Totoya, I., *Fiji* **133 B3** 18 57 S 179 50W
Totskoye, *Russia* **64 E4** 52 32N 52 45 E
Totten Glacier, *Antarctica* **7 C8** 66 45 S 116 10 E
Tottenham, *Australia* **129 B7** 32 14 S 147 21 E
Tottenham, *Canada* **150 B5** 44 1N 79 49W
Tottori, *Japan* **72 B6** 35 30N 134 15 E
Tottori □, *Japan* **72 B6** 35 30N 134 12 E
Touaret, *Niger* **111 D6** 20 17N 7 8 E
Touat, *Algeria* **111 C5** 27 27N 0 30 E
Touba, *Ivory C.* **112 D3** 8 22N 7 40W
Touba, *Senegal* **112 C1** 14 50N 15 55W
Toubkal △, *Morocco* **110 B3** 31 0N 8 2W
Toubkal, Djebel, *Morocco* **110 B3** 31 0N 8 0W
Toucy, *France* **27 E10** 47 44N 3 15 E
Tougan, *Burkina Faso* **112 C4** 13 11N 2 58W
Touggourt, *Algeria* **111 B6** 33 6N 6 4 E
Tougouri, *Burkina Faso* **113 C4** 13 20N 0 30W
Tougué, *Guinea* **112 C2** 11 25N 11 50W
Touho, *N. Cal.* **133 T19** 20 47 S 165 14 E
Toukmatine, *Algeria* **111 D6** 24 49N 7 11 E
Toukoto, *Mali* **112 C3** 13 27N 9 52W
Toul, *France* **27 D12** 48 40N 5 53 E
Toulepleu, *Ivory C.* **112 D3** 6 32N 8 24W
Toulon, *France* **29 E9** 43 10N 5 55 E
Toulon, *U.S.A.* **156 C7** 41 6N 89 52W
Toulouse, *France* **28 E5** 43 37N 1 27 E
Toulouse Blagnac ✈ (TLS), *France* **28 E5** 43 37N 1 22 E
Toummo, *Niger* **108 D2** 22 45N 14 8 E
Toummo Dhoba, *Niger* **108 D2** 22 30N 14 31 E
Toumodi, *Ivory C.* **112 D3** 6 32N 5 4W
Tounan, *Taiwan* **77 F13** 23 41N 120 28 E
Tounassine, Hamada, *Algeria* **110 C4** 28 48N 5 0W
Toungo, *Nigeria* **113 D7** 8 20N 12 3 E
Toungoo, *Burma* **90 F6** 19 0N 96 30 E
Touques →, *France* **26 C7** 49 22N 0 8 E
Touraine, *France* **26 E7** 47 20N 0 30 E
Tourane = Da Nang, *Vietnam* **86 D7** 16 4N 108 13 E
Tourcoing, *France* **27 B10** 50 42N 3 10 E
Touriñán, C., *Spain* **42 B1** 43 3N 9 17W
Tourine, *Mauritania* **110 D2** 22 23N 11 50W
Tournai, *Belgium* **24 D3** 50 35N 3 25 E
Tournan-en-Brie, *France* **27 D9** 48 44N 2 46 E
Tournay, *France* **28 E4** 43 13N 0 13 E
Tournon-St-Martin, *France* **26 F7** 46 45N 0 58 E
Tournon-sur-Rhône, *France* **29 C8** 45 4N 4 50 E
Tournus, *France* **27 F11** 46 35N 4 54 E
Touros, *Brazil* **170 C4** 5 12 S 35 28W
Tours, *France* **26 E7** 47 22N 0 40 E
Touside, Pic, *Chad* **109 D3** 21 1N 16 29 E
Touws →, *S. Africa* **116 E3** 33 45 S 21 11 E
Touwsrivier, *S. Africa* **116 E3** 33 20 S 20 2 E
Tovar, *Venezuela* **168 B3** 8 20N 71 46W
Tovarkovskiy, *Russia* **58 F10** 53 40N 38 14 E
Tovdal, *Norway* **18 F5** 58 47N 8 10 E
Tovdalselva →, *Norway* **18 F5** 58 11N 8 7 E
Tovste, *Ukraine* **53 B10** 48 50N 25 44 E
Tovuz, *Azerbaijan* **61 K7** 41 0N 45 40 E
Towada, *Japan* **70 D10** 40 37N 141 13 E
Towada-Hachimantai △, *Japan* **70 D10** 40 20N 140 55 E
Towada-Ko, *Japan* **70 D10** 40 28N 140 55 E
Towanda, *Ill., U.S.A.* **157 D8** 40 36N 88 53W
Towanda, *Pa., U.S.A.* **151 E8** 41 46N 76 27W
Tower, *U.S.A.* **154 B8** 47 48N 92 17W
Tower, I. = Genovesa, I., *Ecuador* **172 a** 0 20N 89 58W
Towerhill Cr. →, *Australia* **126 C3** 22 28 S 144 35 E
Towner, *U.S.A.* **154 A4** 48 21N 100 25W
Townsend, *Ga., U.S.A.* **152 D8** 31 33N 81 31W
Townsend, *Mont., U.S.A.* **158 C8** 46 19N 111 31W
Townshend I., *Australia* **126 C5** 22 10 S 150 31 E
Townsville, *Australia* **126 B4** 19 15 S 146 45 E
Towraghondi, *Afghan.* **91 B1** 35 13N 62 16 E
Towson, *U.S.A.* **148 F7** 39 24N 76 36W
Towuti, Danau, *Indonesia* **82 B2** 2 45 S 121 32 E
Toxkan He →, *China* **65 C9** 41 8N 80 11 E
Toya-Ko, *Japan* **70 C10** 42 35N 140 51 E
Toyama, *Japan* **73 A9** 36 40N 137 15 E
Toyama □, *Japan* **73 A9** 36 45N 137 30 E
Toyama-Wan, *Japan* **73 A9** 37 0N 137 30 E
Toyapakeh, *Indonesia* **79 K18** 8 41 S 115 29 E
Tōyō, *Ehime, Japan* **72 D5** 33 56N 133 5 E
Tōyō, *Kōchi, Japan* **72 D6** 33 26N 134 16 E
Toyohara = Yuzhno-Sakhalinsk, *Russia* **67 E15** 46 58N 142 45 E
Toyohashi, *Japan* **73 C9** 34 45N 137 25 E
Toyokawa, *Japan* **73 C9** 34 48N 137 27 E
Toyonaka, *Japan* **73 C7** 34 50N 135 28 E
Toyooka, *Japan* **72 B6** 35 35N 134 48 E
Toyota, *Japan* **73 B9** 35 3N 137 7 E
Toyoura, *Japan* **72 C2** 34 6N 130 57 E
Toytepa, *Uzbekistan* **65 C4** 41 3N 69 20 E
Tozeur, *Tunisia* **108 B1** 33 56N 8 8 E
Tozkhurmato, *Iraq* **101 E11** 34 56N 44 38 E
Tqibuli, *Georgia* **61 J6** 42 26N 43 0 E
Tqvarcheli, *Georgia* **61 J5** 42 47N 41 42 E
Trá Li = Tralee, *Ireland* **23 D2** 52 16N 9 42W
Tra On, *Vietnam* **87 H5** 9 58N 105 55 E
Trabancos →, *Spain* **42 D5** 41 36N 5 15W
Traben-Trarbach, *Germany* **31 F3** 49 57N 7 7 E
Trabzon, *Turkey* **101 B8** 41 0N 39 45 E
Tracadie-Sheila, *Canada* **141 C7** 47 30N 64 55W
Trachenburg = Żmigród, *Poland* **55 G3** 51 28N 16 53 E
Tracy, *Calif., U.S.A.* **160 H5** 37 44N 121 26W
Tracy, *Minn., U.S.A.* **154 C7** 44 14N 95 37W
Tradate, *Italy* **44 C5** 45 43N 8 54 E
Trade Town, *Liberia* **112 D3** 5 40N 9 50W
Traer, *U.S.A.* **156 B4** 42 12N 92 28W
Trafalgar, *Australia* **129 E7** 38 14 S 146 12 E
Trafalgar, C., *Spain* **43 J4** 36 10N 6 2W
Trāghān, *Libya* **108 C2** 26 0N 14 30 E
Traian, *Brăila, Romania* **53 E12** 45 11N 27 44 E
Traian, *Tulcea, Romania* **53 E13** 45 2N 28 15 E
Traiguén, *Chile* **176 A2** 38 15 S 72 41W
Trail, *Canada* **142 D5** 49 5N 117 40W
Trail Ø, *Greenland* **10 C8** 72 30N 23 0W
Trainor L., *Canada* **142 A4** 60 24N 120 17W
Traíra →, *Brazil* **168 D4** 1 4 S 69 26W
Trákhonas, *Cyprus* **39 E9** 35 12N 33 21 E
Tralee, *Ireland* **23 D2** 52 16N 9 42W
Tralee B., *Ireland* **23 D2** 52 17N 9 55W
Tramelan, *Switz.* **32 B4** 47 13N 7 7 E
Tramore, *Ireland* **23 D4** 52 10N 7 10W
Tramore B., *Ireland* **23 D4** 52 9N 7 10W
Tran Ninh, Cao Nguyen, *Laos* **86 C4** 19 30N 103 10 E
Tranås, *Sweden* **17 F8** 58 3N 14 59 E
Tranbjerg, *Denmark* **17 H4** 56 6N 10 9 E
Tranby, *Norway* **18 E7** 59 49N 10 15 E
Trancas, *Argentina* **174 B2** 26 11 S 65 20W
Trancoso, *Portugal* **42 E3** 40 49N 7 21W
Tranebjerg, *Denmark* **17 J4** 55 51N 10 36 E
Tranemo, *Sweden* **17 G7** 57 30N 13 20 E
Trang, *Thailand* **87 J2** 7 33N 99 38 E
Trangahy, *Madag.* **117 B7** 19 7 S 44 31 E
Trangan, *Indonesia* **83 C4** 6 40 S 134 20 E
Trangie, *Australia* **129 B8** 32 4 S 148 0 E
Trångsviken, *Sweden* **16 A7** 63 19N 13 59 E
Trani, *Italy* **47 A9** 41 17N 16 25 E
Tranoroa, *Madag.* **117 C8** 24 42 S 45 4 E
Tranqueras, *Uruguay* **175 C4** 31 13 S 55 45W
Transantarctic Mts., *Antarctica* **7 E12** 85 0 S 170 0W
Transilvania, *Romania* **53 D9** 46 30N 24 0 E
Transilvanian Alps = Carpaţii Meridionali, *Romania* **53 E9** 45 30N 25 0 E
Transjordan = Jordan ■, *Asia* **103 E5** 31 0N 36 0 E
Transnistria = Stînga Nistrului □, *Moldova* **53 C14** 47 20N 29 15 E
Transtrand, *Sweden* **16 C7** 61 6N 13 20 E
Transtrandsfjällen, *Sweden* **16 C6** 61 8N 13 0 E
Transylvania = Transilvania, *Romania* **53 D9** 46 30N 24 0 E
Trápani, *Italy* **46 D5** 38 1N 12 29 E
Trapper Pk., *U.S.A.* **158 D6** 45 54N 114 18W
Traralgon, *Australia* **129 E7** 38 12 S 146 34 E
Trarza, *Mauritania* **112 B2** 17 30N 15 0W
Trás-os-Montes = Cucumbi, *Angola* **115 E3** 10 17 S 19 5 E
Trasacco, *Italy* **45 G10** 41 57N 13 32 E
Trăscău, Munţii, *Romania* **53 D8** 46 14N 23 14 E
Trasimeno, L., *Italy* **45 E9** 43 8N 12 6 E
Träslövsläge, *Sweden* **17 G6** 57 4N 12 16 E
Trasvase Tajo-Segura, Canal de, *Spain* **40 E2** 40 15N 2 55W
Trat, *Thailand* **87 F4** 12 14N 102 33 E
Tratani →, *Pakistan* **92 E3** 29 19N 68 20 E
Traun, *Austria* **34 C7** 48 14N 14 15 E
Traunreut, *Germany* **31 H8** 47 57N 12 36 E
Traunsee, *Austria* **34 D6** 47 55N 13 50 E
Traunstein, *Germany* **31 H8** 47 52N 12 37 E
Traveller's L., *Australia* **128 B5** 33 20 S 142 0 E
Travemünde, *Germany* **30 B6** 53 57N 10 52 E
Travers, Mt., *N.Z.* **131 C7** 42 1 S 172 45 E
Traverse City, *U.S.A.* **148 C3** 44 46N 85 38W
Travis, L., *U.S.A.* **155 K5** 30 24N 97 55W
Travnik, *Bos.-H.* **52 F2** 44 17N 17 39 E
Trbovlje, *Slovenia* **45 B12** 46 12N 15 5 E
Treasure Island, *U.S.A.* **153 H7** 27 46N 82 46W
Treasury Is., *Solomon Is.* **133 L8** 7 22 S 155 37 E
Trébbia →, *Italy* **44 C6** 45 4N 9 41 E
Trebel →, *Germany* **30 B9** 53 54N 13 2 E
Trébeurden, *France* **26 D3** 48 46N 3 35W
Trebević △, *Bos.-H.* **52 G3** 43 20N 18 45 E
Třebíč, *Czech Rep.* **34 B8** 49 14N 15 55 E
Trebinje, *Bos.-H.* **50 D2** 42 44N 18 22 E
Trebisacce, *Italy* **47 C9** 39 52N 16 32 E
Trebišnjica →, *Bos.-H.* **50 D2** 42 47N 18 8 E
Trebišov, *Slovak Rep.* **35 C14** 48 38N 21 41 E
Trebitsch = Třebíč, *Czech Rep.* **34 B8** 49 14N 15 55 E
Trebižat →, *Bos.-H.* **45 E14** 43 15N 17 30 E
Trebnitz = Trzebnica, *Poland* **55 G4** 51 20N 17 1 E
Trebnje, *Slovenia* **45 C12** 45 54N 15 1 E
Třeboň, *Czech Rep.* **34 B7** 49 1N 14 48 E
Trebonne, *Australia* **126 B4** 18 37 S 146 5 E
Třeboňsko ⌓, *Czech Rep.* **34 B7** 49 1N 14 49 E
Trebujena, *Spain* **43 J4** 36 52N 6 11W
Trecate, *Italy* **44 C5** 45 26N 8 44 E
Tregaron, *U.K.* **21 E4** 52 14N 3 56W
Tregnago, *Italy* **45 C8** 45 31N 11 10 E
Tregrosse Is., *Australia* **126 B5** 17 41 S 150 43 E
Tréguier, *France* **26 D3** 48 47N 3 16W
Trégunc, *France* **26 E3** 47 51N 3 51W
Treherne, *Canada* **143 D9** 49 38N 98 42W
Tréia, *Italy* **45 E10** 43 19N 13 19 E
Treignac, *France* **28 C5** 45 32N 1 48 E
Treinta y Tres, *Uruguay* **175 C5** 33 16 S 54 17W
Treis-karden, *Germany* **31 E3** 50 10N 7 18 E
Treklyano, *Bulgaria* **50 D6** 42 33N 22 36 E
Trelawney, *Zimbabwe* **117 B5** 17 30 S 30 30 E
Trélazé, *France* **26 E6** 47 26N 0 30W
Trelew, *Argentina* **176 B3** 43 10 S 65 20W
Trélissac, *France* **28 C4** 45 11N 0 47 E
Trelleborg, *Sweden* **17 J7** 55 20N 13 10 E
Tremadog Bay, *U.K.* **20 E3** 52 51N 4 18W
Trembowla = Terebovlya, *Ukraine* **59 H3** 49 18N 25 44 E
Tremedal = Monte Azul, *Brazil* **171 E3** 15 9 S 42 53W
Tremezzo, *Italy* **33 E8** 45 59N 9 15 E
Trémiti, *Italy* **45 F12** 42 8N 15 30 E
Tremonton, *U.S.A.* **158 F7** 41 43N 112 10W
Tremp, *Spain* **40 C5** 42 10N 0 52 E
Trenche →, *Canada* **140 C5** 47 46N 72 53W
Trenčiansky □, *Slovak Rep.* **35 C11** 48 45N 18 20 E
Trenčín, *Slovak Rep.* **35 C11** 48 52N 18 4 E
Trengereid, *Norway* **18 D2** 60 26N 5 37 E
Trenggalek, *Indonesia* **85 D4** 8 3 S 111 43 E
Trenque Lauquen, *Argentina* **174 D3** 36 5 S 62 45W
Trent →, *Canada* **150 B7** 44 6N 77 34W
Trent →, *U.K.* **20 D7** 53 41N 0 42W
Trentino-Alto Adige □, *Italy* **45 B8** 46 30N 11 20 E
Trento, *Italy* **44 B8** 46 4N 11 8 E
Trento, *Phil.* **81 G6** 8 3N 126 2 E
Trenton = Quinte West, *Canada* **140 D4** 44 10N 77 34W
Trenton, *Fla., U.S.A.* **153 F7** 29 37N 82 49W
Trenton, *Mich., U.S.A.* **157 B13** 42 8N 83 11W
Trenton, *Mo., U.S.A.* **156 D3** 40 5N 93 37W
Trenton, *N.J., U.S.A.* **151 F10** 40 14N 74 46W
Trenton, *Nebr., U.S.A.* **154 E4** 40 11N 101 1W
Trenton, *Ohio, U.S.A.* **157 E12** 39 29N 84 28W
Trenton, *S.C., U.S.A.* **152 B8** 33 45N 81 51W
Trepassey, *Canada* **141 C9** 46 43N 53 25W
Treptow an der Rega = Trzebiatów, *Poland* **54 D2** 54 3N 15 18 E
Trepuzzi, *Italy* **47 B11** 40 24N 18 4 E
Tres Arroyos, *Argentina* **174 D3** 38 26 S 60 20W
Três Casas, *Brazil* **173 B5** 6 59 S 62 41W
Três Corações, *Brazil* **171 F2** 21 44 S 45 15W
Tres Equinas, *Colombia* **168 C2** 0 43N 75 16W
Três Lagoas, *Brazil* **171 F1** 20 50 S 51 43W
Tres Lagos, *Argentina* **176 C2** 49 35 S 71 25W
Tres Lomas, *Argentina* **174 D3** 36 27 S 62 51W
Tres Marías, Islas, *Mexico* **162 C3** 21 25N 106 28W
Três Marias, Represa, *Brazil* **171 E2** 18 12 S 45 15W
Tres Montes, C., *Chile* **176 C1** 46 50 S 75 30W
Tres Pinos, *U.S.A.* **160 J5** 36 48N 121 19W
Três Pontas, *Brazil* **171 F2** 21 23 S 45 29W
Tres Pontas, C. das, *Angola* **115 E2** 10 28 S 13 32 E
Tres Puentes, *Chile* **174 B1** 27 50 S 70 15W
Tres Puntas, C., *Argentina* **176 C3** 47 0 S 66 0W
Três Rios, *Brazil* **171 F3** 22 6 S 43 15W
Tres Valles, *Mexico* **163 D5** 18 15N 96 8W
Tresco, *U.K.* **21 H1** 49 57N 6 20W
Tresfjord, *Norway* **18 B4** 62 31N 7 7 E
Treska →, *Macedonia* **50 E5** 42 0N 21 20 E
Treskavica, *Bos.-H.* **52 G3** 43 40N 18 20 E
Trespaderne, *Spain* **42 C7** 42 47N 3 24W
Tresticklan △, *Sweden* **17 F5** 59 0N 11 42 E
Trets, *France* **29 E9** 43 27N 5 41 E
Treuburg = Olecko, *Poland* **54 D9** 54 2N 22 31 E
Treuchtlingen, *Germany* **31 G6** 48 58N 10 54 E
Treuenbrietzen, *Germany* **30 C8** 52 5N 12 52 E
Treungen, *Norway* **18 E5** 59 1N 8 31 E
Trèves = Trier, *Germany* **31 F2** 49 45N 6 38 E
Trevi, *Italy* **45 F9** 42 52N 12 45 E
Treviglio, *Italy* **44 C6** 45 31N 9 35 E
Trevinca, Peña, *Spain* **42 C4** 42 15N 6 46W
Treviso, *Italy* **45 C9** 45 40N 12 15 E
Trévoux, *France* **29 C8** 45 57N 4 47 E
Trgovište, *Serbia & M.* **50 D6** 42 20N 22 10 E
Triabunna, *Australia* **127 G4** 42 30 S 147 55 E
Triánda, *Greece* **38 E12** 36 25N 28 10 E
Triangle, *Zimbabwe* **117 C5** 21 2 S 31 28 E
Triaucourt-en-Argonne, *France* **27 D12** 48 59N 5 2 E
Tribal Areas □, *Pakistan* **91 B3** 33 0N 70 0 E
Tribly, *U.S.A.* **153 G7** 28 28N 82 12W
Tribsees, *Germany* **30 A8** 54 5N 12 44 E
Tribulation, C., *Australia* **126 B4** 16 5 S 145 29 E
Tribune, *U.S.A.* **154 F4** 38 28N 101 45W
Tricárico, *Italy* **47 B9** 40 37N 16 9 E
Tricase, *Italy* **47 C11** 39 56N 18 22 E
Trichinopoly = Tiruchchirappalli, *India* **95 J4** 10 45N 78 45 E
Trichur, *India* **95 J3** 10 30N 76 18 E
Trida, *Australia* **129 B6** 33 1 S 145 1 E
Trier, *Germany* **31 F2** 49 45N 6 38 E
Trieste, *Italy* **45 C10** 45 40N 13 46 E
Trieste, G. di, *Italy* **45 C10** 45 40N 13 35 E
Trieux →, *France* **26 D3** 48 43N 3 9W
Triggiano, *Italy* **47 A9** 41 4N 16 55 E
Triglav, *Slovenia* **45 B10** 46 21N 13 50 E
Triglavski △, *Slovenia* **45 B10** 46 20N 13 50 E
Trigno →, *Italy* **45 F11** 42 4N 14 48 E
Trigo de Morais = Guijá, *Mozam.* **117 C5** 24 27 S 33 0 E
Trigueros, *Spain* **43 H4** 37 24N 6 50W
Tríkeri, *Greece* **48 B5** 39 6N 23 5 E
Trikhonis, Límni, *Greece* **48 C3** 38 34N 21 30 E
Tríkkala, *Greece* **48 B3** 39 34N 21 47 E
Tríkkala □, *Greece* **48 B3** 39 41N 21 30 E
Trikomo, *Cyprus* **39 E9** 35 17N 33 52 E
Trikora, Puncak, *Indonesia* **83 B5** 4 15 S 138 45 E
Trilj, *Croatia* **45 E13** 43 38N 16 42 E
Trillo, *Spain* **40 E2** 40 42N 2 35W
Trim, *Ireland* **23 C5** 53 33N 6 48W
Trimbak, *India* **94 E1** 19 56N 73 33 E
Trincomalee, *Sri Lanka* **95 K5** 8 38N 81 15 E
Trindade, *Brazil* **171 E2** 16 40 S 49 30W
Trindade, I., *Atl. Oc.* **8 J9** 20 20 S 29 50W
Třinec, *Czech Rep.* **35 B11** 49 41N 18 39 E
Trinidad = Jose Abad Santos, *Phil.* **81 J5** 5 55N 125 39 E
Trinidad, *Bolivia* **173 C5** 14 46 S 64 50W
Trinidad, *Colombia* **168 B3** 5 25N 71 40W
Trinidad, *Cuba* **164 B4** 21 48N 80 0W
Trinidad, *Trin. & Tob.* **169 F9** 10 30N 61 15W
Trinidad, *Uruguay* **174 C4** 33 30 S 56 50W
Trinidad, *U.S.A.* **155 G2** 37 10N 104 31W
Trinidad →, *Mexico* **163 D5** 17 49N 95 9W
Trinidad, G., *Chile* **176 C1** 49 55 S 75 25W
Trinidad, I., *Argentina* **176 A4** 39 10 S 62 0W
Trinidad & Tobago ■, *W. Indies* **165 D7** 10 30N 61 20W
Trinitápoli, *Italy* **47 A9** 41 21N 16 5 E
Trinity, *Canada* **141 C9** 48 59N 53 55W
Trinity, *U.S.A.* **155 K7** 30 57N 95 22W
Trinity →, *Calif., U.S.A.* **158 F2** 41 11N 123 42W
Trinity →, *Tex., U.S.A.* **155 L7** 29 45N 94 43W
Trinity B., *Canada* **141 C9** 48 20N 53 10W
Trinity Hills, *Trin. & Tob.* **169 F9** 10 7N 61 7W
Trinity Is., *U.S.A.* **144 H9** 56 33N 154 25W
Trinity Range, *U.S.A.* **158 F4** 40 15N 118 45W
Trinkat, *India* **95 K11** 8 5N 93 30 E
Trinkitat, *Sudan* **106 D4** 18 45N 37 51 E

Trino, Italy 44 C5 45 12N 8 18 E
Trinway, U.S.A. 150 F2 40 9N 82 1W
Triolet, Mauritius 121 d 20 4 S 57 32 E
Trionto, C., Italy 47 C9 39 37N 16 43 E
Triora, Italy 44 D4 44 1N 7 46 E
Tripoli = Tarābulus, Lebanon 103 A4 34 31N 35 50 E
Tripoli = Tarābulus, Libya 108 B2 32 49N 13 7 E
Tripoli = Trípolis, Greece 48 D4 37 31N 22 25 E
Tripoli, U.S.A. 156 B4 42 49N 92 16W
Trípolis, Greece 48 D4 37 31N 22 25 E
Tripolitania, N. Afr. 104 C5 31 0N 13 0 E
Tripura □, India 90 D3 24 0N 92 0 E
Tripylos, Cyprus 39 F8 34 59N 32 41 E
Trischen, Germany 30 A4 54 4N 8 40 E
Tristan da Cunha, Atl. Oc. 8 K10 37 6 S 12 20W
Trisul, India 93 D8 30 19N 79 47 E
Trivandrum, India 95 K3 8 41N 77 0 E
Trivento, Italy 45 G11 41 47N 14 33 E
Trnava, Slovak Rep. 35 C10 48 23N 17 35 E
Trnavský □, Slovak Rep. 35 C10 48 30N 17 45 E
Troarn, France 26 C6 49 11N 0 11W
Trobriand Is., Papua N. G. 132 E6 8 30 S 151 0 E
Trochu, Canada 142 C6 51 50N 113 13W
Trodely I., Canada 140 B4 52 15N 79 26W
Troezen, Greece 48 D5 37 25N 23 15 E
Trogen, Switz. 33 B8 47 24N 9 28 E
Trogir, Croatia 45 E13 43 32N 16 15 E
Troglav, Croatia 45 E13 43 56N 16 36 E
Tróia, Italy 47 A8 41 22N 15 18 E
Troilus, L., Canada 140 B5 50 50N 74 35W
Troina, Italy 47 E7 37 47N 14 36 E
Trois Fourches, Cap des, Morocco 111 A4 35 26N 2 58W
Trois-Pistoles, Canada 141 C6 48 5N 69 10W
Trois-Rivières, Canada 140 C5 46 25N 72 34W
Trois-Rivières, Guadeloupe 164 b 15 57N 61 40W
Troisdorf, Germany 30 E3 50 48N 7 11 E
Troitsk, Russia 64 D8 54 10N 61 35 E
Troitskiy, Russia 64 C9 57 5N 63 43 E
Troitsko Pechorsk, Russia 56 B10 62 40N 56 10 E
Troitskosavsk = Kyakhta, Russia 67 D11 50 30N 106 25 E
Troitskoye, Russia 61 G7 46 26N 44 15 E
Troitsky = Troitsk, Russia 64 D8 54 10N 61 35 E
Trölladyngja, Iceland 11 C9 64 54N 17 16W
Trollhättan, Sweden 17 F6 58 17N 12 20 E
Trollheimen, Norway 18 B6 62 46N 9 1 E
Trombetas →, Brazil 169 D6 1 55 S 55 35W
Tromelin I., Ind. Oc. 121 F4 15 52 S 54 25 E
Tromøy, Norway 18 F5 58 27N 8 51 E
Tromsø, Norway 14 B18 69 40N 18 56 E
Trona, U.S.A. 161 K9 35 46N 117 23W
Tronador, Mte., Argentina 176 B2 41 10 S 71 50W
Trøndelag, Norway 14 D14 64 17N 11 50 E
Trondheim, Norway 18 A7 63 36N 10 25 E
Trondheimsfjorden, Norway 14 E14 63 35N 10 30 E
Trondheimsleia, Norway 18 A5 63 25N 8 30 E
Trondhjem = Trondheim, Norway 18 A7 63 36N 10 25 E
Trönninge, Sweden 17 H6 56 37N 12 51 E
Tronto →, Italy 45 F10 42 54N 13 55 E
Troodos, Cyprus 39 F8 34 55N 32 52 E
Troon, U.K. 22 F4 55 33N 4 39W
Tropea, Italy 47 D8 38 41N 15 54 E
Tropic, U.S.A. 159 H7 37 37N 112 5W
Tropojë, Albania 50 D4 42 23N 20 10 E
Troppau = Opava, Czech Rep. 35 B10 49 57N 17 58 E
Trosa, Sweden 17 F11 58 54N 17 33 E
Trostan, U.K. 23 A5 55 3N 6 10W
Trostberg, Germany 31 G8 48 1N 12 33 E
Trostyanets, Ukraine 53 B14 48 31N 29 11 E
Trostyanets, Ukraine 59 G8 50 33N 34 59 E
Trotsk = Chapayevsk, Russia 60 D9 53 0N 49 40 E
Trotsk = Gatchina, Russia 58 C6 59 35N 30 9 E
Trou Gras Pt., St. Lucia 165 f 13 51N 60 53W
Trout →, Canada 142 A5 61 19N 119 51W
Trout L., N.W.T., Canada 142 A4 60 40N 121 14W
Trout L., Ont., Canada 143 C10 51 20N 93 15W
Trout Lake, Canada 142 B6 56 30N 114 32W
Trout Lake, U.S.A. 160 E5 46 0N 121 32W
Trout River, Canada 141 C8 49 29N 58 8W
Trout Run, U.S.A. 150 E7 41 23N 77 3W
Trouville-sur-Mer, France 26 C7 49 21N 0 5 E
Trowbridge, U.K. 21 F5 51 18N 2 12W
Troy, Turkey 49 B8 39 57N 26 12 E
Troy, Ala., U.S.A. 152 D4 31 48N 85 58W
Troy, Ill., U.S.A. 154 F7 38 44N 89 54W
Troy, Ind., U.S.A. 157 G10 37 59N 86 55W
Troy, Kans., U.S.A. 154 F7 39 47N 95 5W
Troy, Mich., U.S.A. 157 B13 42 37N 83 9W
Troy, Mo., U.S.A. 156 F6 38 59N 90 59W
Troy, Mont., U.S.A. 158 B6 48 28N 115 53W
Troy, N.Y., U.S.A. 151 D11 42 44N 73 41W
Troy, Ohio, U.S.A. 157 D12 40 2N 84 12W
Troy, Pa., U.S.A. 151 E8 41 47N 76 47W
Troyan, Bulgaria 51 D8 42 57N 24 43 E
Troyes, France 27 D11 48 19N 4 3 E
Trpanj, Croatia 45 E14 43 1N 17 15 E
Trstenik, Serbia & M. 50 C5 43 36N 21 0 E
Trubchevsk, Russia 59 F7 52 33N 33 47 E
Truchas Peak, U.S.A. 155 H2 35 58N 105 39W
Truchas Pk., U.S.A. 159 J11 36 0N 105 30W
Trucial States = United Arab Emirates ■, Asia 97 F7 23 50N 54 0 E
Truckee, U.S.A. 160 F6 39 20N 120 11W
Trudfront, Russia 61 H8 45 56N 47 40 E
Trudovoye, Russia 70 C6 43 17N 132 5 E
Trujillo, Colombia 168 C2 4 10N 76 19W
Trujillo, Honduras 164 C2 16 0N 86 0W
Trujillo, Peru 172 B2 8 6 S 79 0W
Trujillo, Spain 43 F5 39 28N 5 55W
Trujillo, U.S.A. 155 H2 35 32N 104 42W
Trujillo, Venezuela 168 B3 9 22N 70 38W
Trujillo □, Venezuela 168 B3 9 25N 70 30W
Trujillo, Mte. = Duarte, Pico, Dom. Rep. 165 D5 19 2N 70 59W
Truk, Micronesia 134 G7 7 25N 151 46 E
Trumann, U.S.A. 155 H9 35 41N 90 31W
Trumansburg, U.S.A. 151 D8 42 33N 76 40W
Trumbull, Mt., U.S.A. 159 H7 36 25N 113 8W
Trŭn, Bulgaria 50 D6 42 51N 22 38 E
Trun, France 26 D7 48 50N 0 2 E
Trun, Switz. 33 C7 46 45N 8 59 E
Trundle, Australia 129 B7 32 53 S 147 35 E
Trung-Phan = Annam, Vietnam 86 E7 16 0N 108 0 E
Truro, Australia 128 C3 34 24 S 139 9 E
Truro, Canada 141 C7 45 21N 63 14W
Truro, U.K. 21 G2 50 16N 5 4W
Truskavets, Ukraine 59 H2 49 17N 23 30 E
Trŭstenik, Bulgaria 51 C8 43 31N 24 28 E
Trustrup, Denmark 17 H4 56 20N 10 46 E
Trutch, Canada 142 B4 57 44N 122 57W
Truth or Consequences, U.S.A. 159 K10 33 8N 107 15W
Trutnov, Czech Rep. 34 A8 50 37N 15 54 E
Truxton, U.S.A. 151 D8 42 45N 76 2W
Truyère →, France 28 D6 44 38N 2 34 E
Tryavna, Bulgaria 51 D9 42 54N 25 25 E
Tryonville, U.S.A. 150 E5 41 42N 79 48W
Tryphena, N.Z. 130 C4 36 18 S 175 28 E
Trysilelva →, Norway 18 C9 61 2N 12 35 E
Trzcianka, Poland 55 E3 53 3N 16 25 E
Trzciel, Poland 55 F2 52 23N 15 50 E
Trzcińsko Zdrój, Poland 55 F1 52 58N 14 35 E
Trzebiatów, Poland 54 D2 54 3N 15 18 E
Trzebiez, Poland 54 E1 53 38N 14 31 E
Trzebnica, Poland 55 G4 51 20N 17 1 E
Trzemeszno, Poland 55 F4 52 33N 17 48 E
Tržič, Slovenia 45 B11 46 22N 14 18 E
Tsagan Aman, Russia 61 G8 47 34N 46 43 E
Tsakarisiánon, Greece 39 C2 38 10N 20 40 E
Tsala Apopka L., U.S.A. 153 G7 28 53N 82 19W
Tsamandás, Greece 48 B2 39 46N 20 21 E
Tsamkong = Zhanjiang, China 77 G8 21 15N 110 20 E
Tsandi, Namibia 116 B1 17 42 S 14 50 E
Tsangpo = Brahmaputra →, Asia 68 D3 23 40N 90 35 E
Tsaratanana, Madag. 117 B8 16 47 S 47 39 E
Tsaratanana △, Madag. 117 A8 13 57 S 48 52 E
Tsaratanana, Mt. de = Maromokotro, Madag. 117 A8 14 0 S 49 0 E
Tsarekonstantinovka = Kuybyshevo, Ukraine 59 J9 47 25N 36 40 E
Tsarevo = Michurin, Bulgaria 51 D11 42 9N 27 51 E
Tsarevo, Bulgaria 51 D9 42 28N 25 52 E
Tsaribrod = Dimitrovgrad, Serbia & M. 50 C6 43 2N 22 48 E
Tsaritsáni, Greece 48 B4 39 53N 22 14 E
Tsarskoye Selo = Pushkin, Russia 58 C6 59 45N 30 25 E
Tsaryovokokshaysk = Yoshkar Ola, Russia 60 B8 56 38N 47 55 E
Tsau, Botswana 116 C3 20 8 S 22 22 E
Tsavo East △, Kenya 118 C4 2 44 S 38 47 E
Tsavo West △, Kenya 118 C4 3 19 S 37 57 E
Tsebrykove, Ukraine 59 J6 47 9N 30 10 E
Tselinograd = Astana, Kazakhstan 66 D8 51 10N 71 30 E
Tsementny = Fokino, Russia 58 F8 53 30N 34 22 E
Tsentralnyy □, Russia 60 D4 52 0N 40 0 E
Tses, Namibia 116 D2 25 58 S 18 8 E
Tsetserleg, Mongolia 68 B5 47 36N 101 32 E
Tsévié, Togo 113 D5 6 25N 1 20 E
Tshabong, Botswana 116 D3 26 2 S 22 29 E
Tshabuta, Dem. Rep. of the Congo 115 D4 7 42 S 23 7 E
Tshane, Botswana 116 C3 24 5 S 21 54 E
Tshela, Dem. Rep. of the Congo 115 C2 4 57 S 13 4 E
Tshesebe, Botswana 117 C4 21 51 S 27 32 E
Tshibeke, Dem. Rep. of the Congo 118 C2 2 40 S 28 35 E
Tshibinda, Dem. Rep. of the Congo 118 C2 2 23 S 28 43 E
Tshikapa, Dem. Rep. of the Congo 115 D4 6 28 S 20 48 E
Tshilenge, Dem. Rep. of the Congo 118 D1 6 17 S 23 48 E
Tshindjambo, Dem. Rep. of the Congo 115 E4 10 52 S 22 43 E
Tshinota, Dem. Rep. of the Congo 115 D4 7 2 S 20 58 E
Tshinsenda, Dem. Rep. of the Congo 119 E2 12 20 S 28 0 E
Tshitadi, Dem. Rep. of the Congo 115 D4 6 46 S 21 43 E
Tshofa, Dem. Rep. of the Congo 118 D2 5 13 S 25 16 E
Tshuapa →, Dem. Rep. of the Congo 114 C4 0 14 S 20 42 E
Tshumbiri, Dem. Rep. of the Congo 114 C3 2 38 S 16 18 E
Tshwane, Botswana 116 C3 22 24 S 22 1 E
Tsiaotso = Jiaozuo, China 74 G7 35 16N 113 12 E
Tsigara, Botswana 116 C4 20 22 S 25 54 E
Tsihombe, Madag. 117 D8 25 10 S 45 41 E
Tsiigehtchic, Canada 138 B6 67 15N 134 0W
Tsimlyansk, Russia 61 G6 47 40N 42 6 E
Tsimlyansk Res. = Tsimlyanskoye Vdkhr., Russia 61 F6 48 0N 43 0 E
Tsimlyanskoye Vdkhr., Russia 61 F6 48 0N 43 0 E
Tsinan = Jinan, China 74 F9 36 38N 117 1 E
Tsineng, S. Africa 116 D3 27 5 S 23 5 E
Tsing Yi, China 69 G11 22 21N 114 6 E
Tsínga, Greece 51 E8 41 23N 24 44 E
Tsinghai = Qinghai □, China 68 C4 36 0N 98 0 E
Tsingshih = Jinshi, China 77 C8 29 40N 111 50 E
Tsingtao = Qingdao, China 75 F11 36 5N 120 20 E
Tsingy de Bemaraha △, Madag. 117 B8 18 35 S 45 25 E
Tsingy de Namoraka △, Madag. 117 B8 16 29 S 45 25 E
Tsining = Jining, China 74 G9 35 22N 116 34 E
Tsinjoarivo, Madag. 117 B8 19 37 S 47 40 E
Tsinjomitondraka, Madag. 117 B8 15 40 S 47 8 E
Tsinling Shan = Qinling Shandi, China 74 H5 33 50N 108 10 E
Tsiroanomandidy, Madag. 117 B8 18 46 S 46 2 E
Tsiteli-Tsqaro, Georgia 61 K8 41 33N 46 0 E
Tsitondroina, Madag. 117 C8 21 19 S 46 0 E
Tsitsihar = Qiqihar, China 67 E13 47 26N 124 0 E
Tsitsikamma △, S. Africa 116 E3 34 3 S 23 40 E
Tsivilsk, Russia 60 C8 55 50N 47 25 E
Tsivory, Madag. 117 C8 24 4 S 46 5 E
Tskhinvali, Georgia 61 J7 42 14N 44 1 E
Tsna →, Russia 60 C6 54 55N 41 58 E
Tsnori, Georgia 61 K7 41 40N 45 57 E
Tso Moriri, L., India 93 C8 32 50N 78 20 E
Tsobis, Namibia 116 B2 19 27 S 17 30 E
Tsodilo Hill, Botswana 116 B3 18 49 S 21 43 E
Tsogni, Gabon 114 C2 2 48 S 10 10 E
Tsogttsetsiy = Baruunsuu, Mongolia 74 C3 43 43N 105 35 E
Tsolo, S. Africa 117 E4 31 18 S 28 37 E
Tsomo, S. Africa 117 E4 32 0 S 27 42 E
Tsoukaládes, Greece 39 B2 38 41N 20 47 E
Tsu, Japan 73 C8 34 45N 136 25 E
Tsu L., Canada 142 A6 60 40N 111 52W
Tsubata, Japan 73 A8 36 40N 136 44 E
Tsuchiura, Japan 73 A12 36 5N 140 15 E
Tsuen Wan, China 77 F10 22 22N 114 6 E
Tsugaru-Kaikyō, Japan 70 D10 41 35N 141 0 E
Tsukuba, Japan 73 A12 36 2N 140 4 E
Tsukumi, Japan 72 D3 33 4N 131 52 E
Tsukushi-Sanchi, Japan 72 D2 33 25N 130 30 E
Tsumeb, Namibia 116 B2 19 9 S 17 44 E
Tsumis, Namibia 116 C2 23 39 S 17 29 E
Tsuna, Japan 72 C6 34 28N 134 56 E
Tsuno-Shima, Japan 72 C2 34 21N 130 52 E
Tsuru, Japan 73 B10 35 31N 138 57 E
Tsuruga, Japan 73 B8 35 45N 136 2 E
Tsuruga-Wan, Japan 73 B8 35 50N 136 3 E
Tsurugi, Japan 73 A8 36 29N 136 37 E
Tsurugi-San, Japan 72 D6 33 51N 134 6 E
Tsurumi-Saki, Japan 72 E4 32 56N 132 5 E
Tsuruoka, Japan 70 E9 38 44N 139 50 E
Tsurusaki, Japan 72 D3 33 14N 131 41 E
Tsushima, Ehime, Japan 72 D4 33 7N 132 32 E
Tsushima, Gifu, Japan 73 B8 35 10N 136 43 E
Tsushima, Nagasaki, Japan 72 C1 34 20N 129 20 E
Tsuyama, Japan 72 B6 35 3N 134 0 E
Tsvetkovo, Ukraine 59 H6 49 8N 31 33 E
Tsyelyakhany, Belarus 59 F3 52 30N 25 46 E
Tu →, Burma 90 E6 21 50N 96 15 E
Tua, Dem. Rep. of the Congo 114 C3 3 38 S 16 38 E
Tua →, Papua N. G. 132 D3 6 30 S 144 28 E
Tua →, Portugal 42 D3 41 13N 7 26W
Tuaheni Pt., N.Z. 130 E7 38 43 S 178 4 E
Tuai, N.Z. 130 E6 38 47 S 177 10 E
Tuakau, N.Z. 130 D3 37 16 S 174 59 E
Tual, Indonesia 83 C4 5 38 S 132 44 E
Tuam, Ireland 23 C3 53 31N 8 51W
Tuamarina, N.Z. 131 B8 41 25 S 173 59 E
Tuamotu Arch. = Tuamotu Is., French Polynesia 135 J13 17 0 S 144 0W
Tuamotu Is., French Polynesia 135 J13 17 0 S 144 0W
Tuamotu Ridge, Pac. Oc. 135 K14 20 0 S 138 0W
Tuanfeng, China 77 B10 30 38N 114 52 E
Tuanxi, China 76 D6 27 28N 107 8 E
Tuao, Phil. 80 C3 17 55N 121 22 E
Tuapse, Russia 61 H4 44 5N 39 10 E
Tuas, Singapore 87 d 1 19N 103 39 E
Tuatapere, N.Z. 131 G2 46 8 S 167 41 E
Tuba City, U.S.A. 159 H8 36 8N 111 14W
Tuban, Indonesia 85 D4 6 54 S 112 3 E
Tubani, Botswana 116 C3 24 46 S 24 18 E
Tubarão, Brazil 175 B6 28 30 S 49 0W
Tūbās, West Bank 103 C4 32 20N 35 22 E
Tubas →, Namibia 116 C2 22 54 S 14 35 E
Tubau, Malaysia 85 B4 3 10N 113 40 E
Tubbataha Reefs △, Phil. 81 G2 8 53N 119 53 E
Tubigon, Phil. 81 G4 9 57N 123 58 E
Tübingen, Germany 31 G5 48 31N 9 4 E
Tubod, Phil. 81 G4 8 3N 123 48 E
Tubou, Fiji 133 B3 18 13 S 178 48W
Tubruq, Libya 108 B4 32 7N 23 55 E
Tubruq □, Libya 108 B4 30 30N 24 0 E
Tubuai Is., French Polynesia 135 K13 25 0 S 150 0W
Tuburan, Basilan, Phil. 81 H4 6 39N 122 16 E
Tuburan, Cebu, Phil. 81 F4 10 44N 123 49 E
Tuc Trung, Vietnam 87 G6 11 1N 107 12 E
Tucacas, Venezuela 168 A4 10 48N 68 19W
Tucano, Brazil 170 D4 10 58 S 38 48W
T'uch'ang, Taiwan 77 E13 24 42N 121 25 E
Tuchodi →, Canada 142 B4 58 17N 123 42W
Tuchola, Poland 54 E4 53 33N 17 52 E
Tuchów, Poland 55 J8 49 54N 21 1 E
Tuckanarra, Australia 125 E2 27 7 S 118 5 E
Tucker, U.S.A. 152 B5 33 51N 84 13W
Tuckers Town, Bermuda 9 a 32 20N 64 42W
Tucson, U.S.A. 159 K8 32 13N 110 58W
Tucumán □, Argentina 174 B2 26 48 S 66 2W
Tucumcari, U.S.A. 155 H3 35 10N 103 44W
Tucunaré, Brazil 173 B6 5 18 S 55 51W
Tucupido, Venezuela 168 B4 9 17N 65 47W
Tucupita, Venezuela 169 B5 9 2N 62 3W
Tucuruí, Brazil 170 B2 3 42 S 49 44W
Tucuruí, Reprêsa de, Brazil 170 B2 4 0 S 49 30W
Tuczno, Poland 55 E3 53 13N 16 10 E
Tuddal, Norway 18 E5 59 46N 8 49 E
Tudela, Spain 40 C3 42 4N 1 39W
Tudmur, Syria 101 E8 34 36N 38 15 E
Tudor, L., Canada 141 A6 55 50N 65 25W
Tudora, Romania 53 C11 47 31N 26 45 E
Tuella →, Portugal 42 D3 41 30N 7 12W
Tuen Mun, China 69 G10 22 24N 113 59 E
Tueré →, Brazil 170 B1 2 48 S 50 59W
Tüffer = Laško, Slovenia 45 B12 46 10N 15 16 E
Tufi, Papua N. G. 132 E5 9 8 S 149 19 E
Tufsingdalen, Norway 18 B8 62 18N 11 44 E
Tugalan = Kolkhozobod, Tajikistan 65 E4 37 35N 68 40 E
Tugela →, S. Africa 117 D5 29 14 S 31 30 E
Tugidak I., U.S.A. 144 H9 56 30N 154 40W
Tuguegarao, Phil. 80 C3 17 35N 121 42 E
Tugur, Russia 67 D14 53 44N 136 45 E
Tui, Spain 42 C2 42 3N 8 39W
Tuineje, Canary Is. 9 e2 28 19N 14 3W
Tukangbesi, Kepulauan, Indonesia 82 C2 6 0 S 124 0 E
Tukarak I., Canada 140 A4 56 15N 78 45W
Tukayyid, Iraq 96 D5 29 47N 45 36 E
Tûkh, Egypt 106 H7 30 21N 31 12 E
Tukhlya, Ukraine 53 B8 48 55N 23 28 E
Tukituki →, N.Z. 130 F5 39 36 S 176 56 E
Tukkae, Ao, Thailand 87 a 7 51N 98 25 E
Tukobo, Ghana 112 D4 5 1N 2 47W
Tūkrah, Libya 108 B4 32 30N 20 37 E
Tuktoyaktuk, Canada 138 B6 69 27N 133 2W
Tukums, Latvia 15 H20 56 58N 23 10 E
Tukums □, Latvia 54 B10 56 55N 23 0 E
Tukuran, Phil. 81 H4 7 51N 123 34 E
Tukuyu, Tanzania 119 D3 9 17 S 33 35 E
Tula, Hidalgo, Mexico 163 C5 20 5N 99 20W
Tula, Tamaulipas, Mexico 163 C5 23 0N 99 40W
Tula, Nigeria 113 D7 9 51N 11 27 E
Tula, Russia 58 E9 54 13N 37 38 E
Tulagi, Solomon Is. 133 M11 9 5 S 160 10 E
Tūlak, Afghan. 91 B1 33 55N 63 40 E
Tulancingo, Mexico 163 C5 20 5N 99 22W
Tulangbawang →, Indonesia 84 C3 4 24 S 105 52 E
Tulare, Serbia & M. 50 D5 42 48N 21 28 E
Tulare, U.S.A. 160 J7 36 13N 119 21W
Tulare Lake Bed, U.S.A. 160 K7 36 0N 119 48W
Tularosa, U.S.A. 159 K10 33 5N 106 1W
Tulbagh, S. Africa 116 E2 33 16 S 19 6 E
Tulcán, Ecuador 168 C2 0 48N 77 43W
Tulcea, Romania 53 E13 45 13N 28 46 E
Tulcea □, Romania 53 E13 45 0N 28 30 E
Tulchyn, Ukraine 53 B13 48 41N 28 49 E
Tūleh, Iran 97 C7 34 35N 52 33 E
Tulemalu L., Canada 143 A9 62 58N 99 25W
Tulgheş, Romania 53 D10 46 58N 25 45 E
Tuli, Zimbabwe 119 G2 21 58 S 29 13 E
Tulia, U.S.A. 155 H4 34 32N 101 46W
Tuliszków, Poland 55 F5 52 5N 18 18 E
Tulita, Canada 138 B7 64 57N 125 30W
Ṭulkarm, West Bank 103 C4 32 19N 35 2 E
Tülkibas, Kazakhstan 65 B5 42 29N 70 17 E
Tulla, Ireland 23 D3 52 53N 8 46W
Tullahoma, U.S.A. 149 H2 35 22N 86 13W
Tullamore, Australia 129 B7 32 39 S 147 36 E
Tullamore, Ireland 23 C4 53 16N 7 31W
Tulle, France 28 C5 45 16N 1 46 E
Tulln, Austria 34 C9 48 20N 16 4 E
Tullow, Ireland 23 D5 52 49N 6 45W
Tullus, Sudan 107 E1 11 7N 24 31 E
Tully, Australia 126 B4 17 56 S 145 55 E
Tully, U.S.A. 151 D8 42 48N 76 7W
Ṭulmaythah, Libya 108 B4 32 40N 20 55 E
Tulnici, Romania 53 E11 45 51N 26 38 E
Tulovo, Bulgaria 51 D9 42 33N 25 32 E
Tulsa, U.S.A. 155 G7 36 10N 95 55W
Tulsequah, Canada 142 B2 58 39N 133 35W
Tulu Milki, Ethiopia 107 F4 9 55N 38 20 E
Tulu Welel, Ethiopia 107 F3 8 56N 34 47 E
Tulua, Colombia 168 C2 4 6N 76 11W
Tulucești, Romania 53 E13 45 34N 28 2 E
Tuluksak, U.S.A. 144 F7 61 6N 160 58W
Tulun, Russia 67 D11 54 32N 100 35 E
Tulungagung, Indonesia 85 D4 8 5 S 111 54 E
Tuma, Russia 58 E11 55 10N 40 30 E
Tuma →, Nic. 164 D3 13 6N 84 35W
Tumacacori △, U.S.A. 159 L8 31 34N 111 3W
Tumaco, Colombia 168 C2 1 50N 78 45W
Tumaco, Ensenada, Colombia 168 C2 1 55N 78 45W
Tumatumari, Guyana 169 B6 5 20N 58 55W
Tumauini, Phil. 80 C3 17 17N 121 49 E
Tumba, Dem. Rep. of the Congo 114 C4 3 10 S 23 36 E
Tumba, Sweden 16 E11 59 12N 17 48 E
Tumba, L., Dem. Rep. of the Congo 114 C3 0 50 S 18 0 E
Tumbarumba, Australia 129 C8 35 44 S 148 0 E
Tumbaya, Argentina 174 A2 23 50 S 65 26W
Tumbes, Peru 172 A1 3 37 S 80 27W
Tumbes □, Peru 172 A1 3 50 S 80 30W
Tumbur, Sudan 107 G3 4 20N 31 34 E
Tumbwe, Dem. Rep. of the Congo 119 E2 11 25 S 27 15 E
Tumby Bay, Australia 128 C2 34 21 S 136 8 E
Tumd Youqi, China 74 D6 40 30N 110 30 E
Tumen, China 75 C15 43 0N 129 50 E
Tumen Jiang →, China 75 C16 42 20N 130 35 E
Tumeremo, Venezuela 169 B5 7 18N 61 30W
Tumiritinga, Brazil 171 E3 18 58 S 41 38W
Tumkur, India 95 H3 13 18N 77 6 E
Tump, Pakistan 91 D1 26 7N 62 16 E
Tumpat, Malaysia 87 J4 6 11N 102 10 E
Tumsar, India 94 D4 21 26N 79 45 E
Tumu, Ghana 112 C4 10 56N 1 56W
Tumucumaque, Serra, Brazil 169 C7 2 0N 55 0W
Tumupasa, Bolivia 172 C4 14 9 S 67 55W
Tumut, Australia 129 C8 35 16 S 148 13 E
Tumwater, U.S.A. 160 C4 47 1N 122 54W
Tuna, India 92 H4 22 59N 70 5 E
Tunadal, Sweden 16 B11 62 26N 17 22 E
Tunapuna, Trin. & Tob. 169 F9 10 38N 61 24W
Tunas de Zaza, Cuba 164 B4 21 39N 79 34W
Tunbridge Wells = Royal Tunbridge Wells, U.K. 21 F8 51 7N 0 16 E
Tunçbilek, Turkey 49 B11 39 37N 29 29 E
Tunceli, Turkey 101 C8 39 6N 39 31 E
Tuncurry, Australia 129 B10 32 17 S 152 29 E
Tundla, India 92 F8 27 12N 78 17 E
Tundubai, Sudan 106 D2 18 36N 28 35 E
Tunduru, Tanzania 119 E4 11 8 S 37 25 E
Tundzha →, Bulgaria 51 E10 41 40N 26 35 E
Tung Chung, China 69 G10 22 17N 113 57 E
Tung Lung Chau, China 69 G11 22 15N 114 17 E
Tunga →, India 95 G2 15 0N 75 50 E
Tunga Pass, India 90 A5 29 0N 94 14 E
Tungabhadra →, India 95 G4 15 57N 78 15 E
Tungabhadra Dam, India 95 G2 15 0N 75 50 E
Tungaru, Sudan 107 E3 10 9N 30 52 E
Tungawan, Phil. 81 H4 7 30N 122 20 E
Tungch'uan = Dongchuan, China 76 D4 26 8N 103 1 E
Tunghwa = Tonghua, China 75 D13 41 42N 125 58 E
Tungi, Bangla. 90 D3 23 53N 90 24 E
Tungla, Nic. 164 D3 13 24N 84 21W
Tungnafellsjökull, Iceland 11 C9 64 45N 17 55W
Tungsha Tao = Dongsha Dao, China 77 G11 20 45N 116 43 E
Tungshih, Taiwan 77 E13 24 12N 120 43 E
Tungsten, Canada 142 A3 61 57N 128 16W
Tungufell, Iceland 11 C6 64 17N 20 10W
Tungurahua □, Ecuador 168 D2 1 15 S 78 35W
Tunguska, Nizhnyaya →, Russia 67 C9 65 48N 88 4 E
Tunguska, Podkamennaya →, Russia 67 C10 61 50N 90 13 E
Tuni, India 94 F6 17 22N 82 36 E
Tunia, Colombia 168 C2 2 41N 76 31W
Tunica, U.S.A. 155 H9 34 41N 90 23W
Tunis, Tunisia 108 A2 36 50N 10 11 E
Tunis ✕ (TUN), Tunisia 46 F3 36 52N 10 14 E
Tunis, Golfe de, Tunisia 108 A2 37 0N 10 30 E
Tunisia ■, Africa 108 B1 33 30N 9 10 E
Tunja, Colombia 168 B3 5 33N 73 25W
Tunkhannock, U.S.A. 151 E9 41 32N 75 57W
Tunliu, China 74 F7 36 13N 112 52 E
Tunnel Creek △, Australia 124 C4 17 41 S 125 18 E
Tunnsjøen, Norway 14 D15 64 45N 13 25 E
Tunø, Denmark 17 J4 55 57N 10 27 E
Tuntutuliak, U.S.A. 144 F7 60 22N 162 38W
Tununak, U.S.A. 144 F6 60 37N 165 15W
Tunungayualok I., Canada 141 A7 56 0N 61 0W
Tunuyán, Argentina 174 C2 33 35 S 69 0W
Tunuyán →, Argentina 174 C2 33 33 S 67 30W
Tuo Jiang →, China 76 C5 28 50N 105 35 E
Tuolumne, U.S.A. 160 H6 37 58N 120 15W
Tuolumne →, U.S.A. 160 H5 37 36N 121 13W
Tüp, Kyrgyzstan 65 B9 42 45N 78 20 E
Tūp Āghāj, Iran 101 D12 36 3N 47 50 E
Tupã, Brazil 175 A5 21 57 S 50 28W
Tupaciguara, Brazil 171 E2 18 35 S 48 42W
Tupelo, U.S.A. 149 H1 34 16N 88 43W
Tupik, Russia 58 E7 55 42N 33 22 E
Tupinambaranas, Brazil 169 D6 3 0 S 58 0W
Tupirama, Brazil 170 C2 8 58 S 48 12W
Tupiratins, Brazil 170 C2 8 23 S 48 8W
Tupiza, Bolivia 174 A2 21 30 S 65 40W
Tupižnica, Serbia & M. 50 C6 43 43N 22 10 E
Tupman, U.S.A. 161 K7 35 18N 119 21W
Tupper, Canada 142 B4 55 32N 120 1W
Tupper Lake, U.S.A. 151 B10 44 14N 74 28W
Tupungato, Cerro, S. Amer. 174 C2 33 15 S 69 50W
Tuquan, China 75 B11 45 18N 121 38 E
Túquerres, Colombia 168 C2 1 5N 77 37W
Tura, India 90 C3 25 30N 90 16 E
Tura, Russia 67 C11 64 20N 100 17 E
Turabah, Ḥā'il, Si. Arabia 96 D4 28 20N 43 15 E
Turabah, Makkah, Si. Arabia 98 B3 21 15N 41 34 E
Turagua, Serranía, Venezuela 169 B5 7 20N 64 35W
Turakina, N.Z. 130 G4 40 3 S 175 16 E
Turakina →, N.Z. 130 G4 40 5 S 175 8 E
Turakirae Hd., N.Z. 130 H3 41 26 S 174 56 E
Turakūrghan, Uzbekistan 65 C5 41 0N 71 31 E
Turama →, Papua N. G. 132 D2 7 40 S 143 50 E
Tūrān, Iran 97 C8 35 39N 56 42 E
Turan, Russia 67 D10 51 55N 95 0 E
Turangi, N.Z. 130 E4 38 59 S 175 48 E
Turar Rysqulov, Kazakhstan 65 B5 42 32N 70 20 E
Ṭurayf, Si. Arabia 96 D3 31 41N 38 39 E
Turbaco, Colombia 168 A2 10 21N 75 25W
Turbacz, Poland 55 J7 49 30N 20 8 E
Turbat, Pakistan 91 D1 25 59N 63 4 E
Turbe, Bos.-H. 52 F2 44 15N 17 35 E
Turbenthal, Switz. 33 B7 47 27N 8 51 E
Turbeville, U.S.A. 152 B9 33 54N 80 1W
Turbo, Colombia 168 B2 8 6N 76 43W
Turčianske Teplice, Slovak Rep. 35 C11 48 52N 18 52 E
Turco, Bolivia 172 D4 18 10 S 68 11W
Turcoaia, Romania 53 E13 45 7N 28 11 E
Turda, Romania 53 D8 46 34N 23 47 E
Turek, Poland 55 F5 52 3N 18 30 E
Turfan = Turpan, China 68 B3 43 58N 89 10 E
Turfan Basin = Turpan Pendi, China 62 E12 42 40N 89 25 E
Turfan Depression = Turpan Pendi, China 62 E12 42 40N 89 25 E
Turgayskaya Stolovaya Strana, Asia 64 F8 51 0N 63 0 E
Turgeon →, Canada 140 C4 50 0N 78 56W
Tŭrgovishte, Bulgaria 51 C10 43 17N 26 38 E
Turgut, Turkey 49 D10 37 22N 28 4 E
Turgutlu, Turkey 49 C9 38 30N 27 43 E
Turgwe →, Zimbabwe 117 C5 21 31 S 32 15 E
Turhal, Turkey 100 B7 40 24N 36 5 E
Turia →, Spain 41 F4 39 27N 0 19W
Turiaçu, Brazil 170 B2 1 40 S 45 19W
Turiaçu →, Brazil 170 B2 1 36 S 45 19W
Turiec →, Slovak Rep. 35 B11 49 7N 18 55 E
Turin = Torino, Italy 44 C4 45 3N 7 40 E
Turinsk, Russia 64 B9 58 3N 63 42 E
Turinskaya Kultbaza = Tura, Russia 67 C11 64 20N 100 17 E
Turka, Ukraine 55 J10 49 10N 23 2 E
Turkana, L., Africa 118 B4 3 30N 36 5 E
Türkeli, Turkey 51 F11 40 30N 27 30 E
Turkestan = Türkistan, Kazakhstan 65 B4 43 17N 68 16 E
Turkestan Range, Asia 65 D4 39 35N 69 0 E
Túrkeve, Hungary 52 C5 47 6N 20 44 E
Turkey ■, Eurasia 100 C7 39 0N 36 0 E
Turkey →, U.S.A. 156 B5 42 43N 91 2W
Turkey Creek, Australia 124 C4 17 2 S 128 12 E
Turki, Russia 60 D6 52 0N 43 15 E
Türkistan, Kazakhstan 65 B4 43 17N 68 16 E
Türkmenbashi, Turkmenistan 57 G9 40 5N 53 5 E
Turkmenistan ■, Asia 66 F6 39 0N 59 0 E
Türkmenli, Turkey 49 B8 39 45N 26 30 E
Türkoğlu, Turkey 100 D7 37 23N 36 50 E
Turks & Caicos Is. ☑, W. Indies 165 B5 21 20N 71 20W
Turks Island Passage, W. Indies 165 B5 21 30N 71 30W
Turku, Finland 15 F20 60 30N 22 19 E
Turkwel →, Kenya 118 B4 3 6N 36 6 E
Turlock, U.S.A. 160 H6 37 30N 120 51W
Turnagain →, Canada 142 B3 59 12N 127 35W
Turnagain, C., N.Z. 130 G5 40 28 S 176 38 E
Turneffe Is., Belize 163 D7 17 20N 87 50W
Turner, U.S.A. 158 B9 48 51N 108 24W
Turner Pt., Australia 126 A1 11 47 S 133 32 E
Turner Valley, Canada 142 C6 50 40N 114 17W
Turners Falls, U.S.A. 151 D12 42 36N 72 33W
Turnhout, Belgium 24 C4 51 19N 4 57 E
Türnitz, Austria 34 D8 47 55N 15 29 E
Turnor L., Canada 143 B7 56 35N 108 35W
Tŭrnovo = Veliko Tŭrnovo, Bulgaria 51 C9 43 5N 25 41 E
Turnu Măgurele, Romania 53 G9 43 46N 24 56 E
Turnu Roşu, P., Romania 53 E9 45 33N 24 17 E
Turobin, Poland 55 H9 50 50N 22 44 E
Tuross Head, Australia 129 D9 36 3 S 150 8 E
Turpan, China 68 B3 43 58N 89 10 E
Turpan Pendi, China 62 E12 42 40N 89 25 E
Turrawan, Australia 129 A8 30 28 S 149 53 E
Turrës, Kala e, Albania 50 E3 41 10N 19 28 E
Turriff, U.K. 22 D6 57 32N 2 27W
Tursāq, Iraq 101 F11 33 27N 45 47 E
Tursi, Italy 47 B9 40 15N 16 28 E
Tursunzade, Tajikistan 65 D4 38 30N 68 14 E
Turtle Head I., Australia 126 A3 10 56 S 142 37 E
Turtle Is., Phil. 81 H2 6 7N 118 14 E
Turtle Is., S. Leone 112 D2 7 40N 13 0 E
Turtle L., Canada 143 C7 53 36N 108 38W
Turtle Lake, U.S.A. 154 B4 47 31N 100 53W
Turtleford, Canada 143 C7 53 23N 108 57W
Turtucaia = Tutrakan, Bulgaria 51 B10 44 2N 26 40 E
Turua, N.Z. 130 D4 37 14 S 175 35 E
Turuépano △, Venezuela 165 D7 10 34N 62 43W
Turugart Pass, Kyrgyzstan 65 C7 40 32N 75 24 E
Turukhansk, Russia 67 C9 65 21N 88 5 E

Turyinskiye Rudniki = Krasnoturinsk, Russia **64 B8** 59 46N 60 12 E
Turzovka, Slovak Rep. **35 B11** 49 25N 18 35 E
Tuscaloosa, U.S.A. **149 J2** 33 12N 87 34W
Tuscània, Italy **45 F8** 42 25N 11 52 E
Tuscany = Toscana □, Italy **44 E8** 43 25N 11 0 E
Tuscarawas →, U.S.A. **150 F3** 40 24N 81 25W
Tuscarora Mt., U.S.A. **150 F7** 40 55N 77 55W
Tuscola, Ill., U.S.A. **157 E8** 39 48N 88 17W
Tuscola, Tex., U.S.A. **155 J5** 32 12N 99 48W
Tuscumbia, Ala., U.S.A. **149 H2** 34 44N 87 42W
Tuscumbia, Mo., U.S.A. **156 F4** 38 14N 92 28W
Tuskegee, U.S.A. **152 C4** 32 25N 85 42W
Tusket Wedge = Wedgeport, Canada **141 D6** 43 44N 65 59W
Tustin, U.S.A. **161 M9** 33 44N 117 49W
Tustna, Norway **18 A5** 63 10N 8 5 E
Tuszyn, Poland **55 G6** 51 36N 19 33 E
Tutak, Turkey **101 C10** 39 31N 42 46 E
Tutayev, Russia **58 D10** 57 53N 39 32 E
Tuticorin, India **95 K4** 8 50N 78 12 E
Tutin, Serbia & M. **50 D4** 42 58N 20 20 E
Tutóia, Brazil **170 B3** 2 45 S 42 20W
Tutong, Brunei **85 B4** 4 47N 114 40 E
Tutova →, Romania **53 D12** 46 7N 27 30 E
Tutrakan, Bulgaria **51 B10** 44 2N 26 40 E
Tuttle Creek L., U.S.A. **154 F6** 39 22N 96 40W
Tuttlingen, Germany **31 H4** 47 58N 8 48 E
Tutuala, E. Timor **82 C3** 8 25 S 127 15 E
Tutuba, Vanuatu **133 E5** 15 33 S 167 16 E
Tutubeia, Papua N. G. **132 E6** 9 34 S 150 40 E
Tutuila, Amer. Samoa **133 X24** 14 19 S 170 50W
Tutuko, Mt., N.Z. **131 E3** 44 35 S 168 1 E
Tutun, Egypt **106 J7** 29 9N 30 46 E
Tututepec, Mexico **163 D5** 16 9N 97 38W
Tütz = Tuczno, Poland **55 E3** 53 13N 16 10 E
Tuva □, Russia **67 D10** 51 30N 95 0 E
Tuvalu ■, Pac. Oc. **134 H9** 8 0 S 178 0 E
Tuvuca, Fiji **133 A3** 17 40 S 178 48W
Tūwal, Si. Arabia **98 B2** 22 17N 39 6 E
Tuxer Alpen, Austria **34 D4** 47 10N 11 45 E
Tuxpan, Mexico **163 C5** 20 58N 97 23W
Tuxtla Gutiérrez, Mexico **163 D6** 16 50N 93 10W
Tuy = Tui, Spain **42 C2** 42 3N 8 39W
Tuy An, Vietnam **86 F7** 13 17N 109 16 E
Tuy Duc, Vietnam **87 F6** 12 15N 107 27 E
Tuy Hoa, Vietnam **86 F7** 13 5N 109 10 E
Tuy Phong, Vietnam **87 G7** 11 14N 108 43 E
Tuya L., Canada **142 B2** 59 7N 130 35W
Tuyen Hoa, Vietnam **86 D6** 17 50N 106 10 E
Tuyen Quang, Vietnam **76 G5** 21 50N 105 10 E
Tuymazy, Russia **64 D4** 54 36N 53 42 E
Tūysarkān, Iran **97 C6** 34 33N 48 27 E
Tuyün = Duyun, China **76 D6** 26 18N 107 29 E
Tuz Gölü, Turkey **100 C5** 38 42N 33 18 E
Ṭūz Khurmātū = Tozkhurmato, Iraq **101 E11** 34 56N 44 38 E
Tuzi, Serbia & M. **50 D3** 42 22N 19 20 E
Tuzigoot △, U.S.A. **159 J7** 34 46N 112 2W
Tuzla, Bos.-H. **52 F3** 44 34N 18 41 E
Tuzlov →, Russia **59 J10** 47 17N 39 57 E
Tuzluca, Turkey **101 B10** 40 3N 43 39 E
Tuzly **53 E15** 45 54N 30 6 E
Tvååker, Sweden **17 G6** 57 4N 12 25 E
Tvardiṭa, Moldova **53 D13** 46 9N 28 58 E
Tvedestrand, Norway **18 F5** 58 38N 8 58 E
Tver, Russia **58 D8** 56 55N 35 55 E
Tvrdošín, Slovak Rep. **35 B12** 49 21N 19 35 E
Tvrdošovce, Slovak Rep. **35 C11** 48 6N 18 4 E
Tvŭrditsa, Bulgaria **51 D9** 42 42N 25 53 E
Twain, U.S.A. **160 E5** 40 1N 121 3W
Twain Harte, U.S.A. **160 G6** 38 2N 120 14W
Twann, Switz. **32 B4** 47 6N 7 9 E
Twardogóra, Poland **55 G4** 51 23N 17 28 E
Tweed, Canada **150 B7** 44 29N 77 19W
Tweed →, U.K. **22 F6** 55 45N 2 0W
Tweed Heads, Australia **127 D5** 28 10 S 153 31 E
Tweedsmuir △, Canada **142 C3** 53 0N 126 20W
Twentynine Palms, U.S.A. **161 L10** 34 8N 116 3W
Tweya, Dem. Rep. of the Congo **114 C3** 0 54 S 18 58 E
Twillingate, Canada **141 C9** 49 42N 54 45W
Twin Bridges, U.S.A. **158 D7** 45 33N 112 20W
Twin City, U.S.A. **152 C7** 32 35N 82 10W
Twin Falls, Canada **141 B7** 53 30N 64 32W
Twin Falls, U.S.A. **158 E6** 42 34N 114 28W
Twin Hills, U.S.A. **144 G8** 59 23N 159 58W
Twin Lakes, U.S.A. **152 E6** 30 43N 83 13W
Twin Valley, U.S.A. **154 B6** 47 16N 96 16W
Twinnge, Burma **90 D6** 23 10N 96 2 E
Twinsburg, U.S.A. **150 E3** 41 18N 81 26W
Twistringen, Germany **30 C4** 52 48N 8 37 E
Twitchell Reservoir, U.S.A. **161 L6** 34 59N 120 19W
Two Boats Village, Ascension I. **9 g** 7 56 S 14 22W
Two Harbors, U.S.A. **154 B9** 47 2N 91 40W
Two Hills, Canada **142 C6** 53 43N 111 52W
Two Rivers, U.S.A. **148 C2** 44 9N 87 34W
Two Rocks, Australia **125 F2** 31 30 S 115 35 E
Two Thumbs Ra., N.Z. **131 D5** 43 45 S 170 44 E
Twofold B., Australia **129 D8** 37 8 S 149 59 E
Ty Ty, U.S.A. **152 D6** 31 28N 83 39W
Tyachiv, Ukraine **59 H2** 48 1N 23 35 E
Tybee Island, U.S.A. **152 C9** 32 1N 80 51W
Tychy, Poland **55 H5** 50 9N 18 59 E
Tyczyn, Poland **55 J9** 49 58N 22 2 E
Tydal, Norway **18 A8** 63 4N 11 34 E
Tyin, Norway **18 C5** 61 18N 8 15 E
Tykocin, Poland **55 E9** 53 13N 22 46 E
Tyler, Minn., U.S.A. **154 C6** 44 18N 96 8W
Tyler, Tex., U.S.A. **155 J7** 32 21N 95 18W
Tyligul →, Ukraine **59 J6** 47 4N 30 57 E
Tylldal, Norway **18 B7** 62 8N 10 48 E
Tymanivka, Ukraine **53 B13** 48 34N 28 50 E
Týn nad Vltavou, Czech Rep. **34 B7** 49 13N 14 26 E
Tynda, Russia **67 D13** 55 10N 124 43 E
Tyndall, U.S.A. **154 D6** 43 0N 97 50W
Tyndinsky = Tynda, Russia **67 D13** 55 10N 124 43 E
Tyne →, U.K. **20 C6** 54 59N 1 32W
Tyne & Wear □, U.K. **20 B6** 55 6N 1 17W
Týnec nad Sázavou, Czech Rep. **34 B7** 49 50N 14 36 E
Tynemouth, U.K. **20 B6** 55 1N 1 26W
Tynset, Norway **18 B7** 62 17N 10 47 E
Tyonek, U.S.A. **144 F10** 61 4N 151 8W
Tyre = Sūr, Lebanon **103 B4** 33 19N 35 16 E
Tyresta △, Sweden **16 E12** 59 12N 18 14 E
Tyrifjorden, Norway **18 D7** 60 2N 10 8 E
Tyringe, Sweden **17 H7** 56 9N 13 35 E
Tyristrand, Norway **18 D7** 60 4N 10 6 E
Tyrnyauz, Russia **61 J6** 43 21N 42 45 E
Tyrol = Tirol □, Austria **34 D3** 47 3N 10 43 E
Tyrone, U.S.A. **150 F6** 40 40N 78 14W
Tyrone □, U.K. **23 B4** 54 38N 7 11W
Tyrrell →, Australia **128 C5** 35 26 S 142 51 E
Tyrrell, L., Australia **128 C5** 35 20 S 142 50 E
Tyrrell L., Canada **143 A7** 63 7N 105 27W
Tyrrhenian Sea, Medit. S. **12 G8** 40 0N 12 30 E
Tysfjorden, Norway **14 B17** 68 7N 16 25 E
Tysmenytsya, Ukraine **53 B9** 48 54N 24 51 E
Tysnes, Norway **18 D2** 60 1N 5 30 E
Tysnesøya, Norway **18 D2** 60 0N 5 35 E
Tysse, Norway **18 D2** 60 23N 5 47 E
Tyssedal, Norway **18 D3** 60 7N 6 35 E
Tystberga, Sweden **17 F11** 58 51N 17 15 E
Tytuvėnai, Lithuania **54 C10** 55 36N 23 12 E
Tyub Karagan, Mys, Kazakhstan **61 H10** 44 40N 50 19 E
Tyuleni, Ostrova, Kazakhstan **61 H10** 45 2N 50 16 E
Tyuleniy, Russia **61 H8** 44 28N 47 30 E
Tyuleniy, Mys, Azerbaijan **61 K10** 40 12N 50 22 E
Tyulgan, Russia **64 E6** 52 22N 56 12 E
Tyumen, Russia **66 D7** 57 11N 65 29 E
Tyumen-Aryk = Tömenaryk, Kazakhstan **65 A3** 44 2N 67 1 E
Tyup = Tüp, Kyrgyzstan **65 B9** 42 45N 78 20 E
Tywi →, U.K. **21 F3** 51 48N 4 21W
Tywyn, U.K. **21 E3** 52 35N 4 5W
Tzaneen, S. Africa **117 C5** 23 47 S 30 9 E
Tzermiádhes, Greece **39 E6** 35 12N 25 29 E
Tzia = Kéa, Greece **48 D6** 37 35N 24 22 E
Tzoumérka, Óros, Greece **48 B3** 39 30N 21 26 E
Tzukong = Zigong, China **76 C5** 29 15N 104 48 E
Tzupo = Boshan, China **75 F9** 36 28N 117 49 E

U

U Taphao, Thailand **86 F3** 12 35N 101 0 E
U.S.A. = United States of America ■, N. Amer. **137 F10** 37 0N 96 0W
U.S.S. Arizona △, U.S.A. **145 K14** 21 22N 157 57W
U.S. Virgin Is. ☑, W. Indies **165 e** 18 20N 65 0W
Uacalla Iero, Somali Rep. **120 D2** 1 48N 42 38 E
Uachadi, Sierra = Uasadi-jidi, Venezuela **169 C4** 4 54N 65 18W
Uad Atui →, W. Sahara **110 D2** 20 4N 15 59W
Uad el Jat →, W. Sahara **110 C2** 26 47N 13 3W
Uad Erni, O. →, W. Sahara **110 C3** 26 45N 10 47W
Uainambi, Colombia **168 C4** 1 43N 69 51W
Uamba, Angola **115 D3** 7 21 S 16 10 E
Uanle Uen, Somali Rep. **120 D2** 2 37N 44 54 E
Uarsciek, Somali Rep. **120 D3** 2 28N 45 55 E
Uasadi-jidi, Venezuela **169 C4** 4 54N 65 18W
Uascen, Somali Rep. **120 D2** 4 11N 43 13 E
Uatumã →, Brazil **169 D6** 2 26 S 57 37W
Uauá, Brazil **170 C4** 9 50 S 39 28W
Uaupés, Brazil **168 D4** 0 8 S 67 5W
Uaupés →, Brazil **168 C4** 0 2N 67 16W
Uaxactún, Guatemala **164 C2** 17 25N 89 29W
Ub, Serbia & M. **50 B4** 44 28N 20 6 E
Ubá, Brazil **171 F3** 21 8 S 43 0W
Uba, Nigeria **113 C7** 10 29N 13 13 E
Ubai, Papua N. G. **132 C6** 5 39 S 150 38 E
Ubaitaba, Brazil **171 D4** 14 18 S 39 20W
Ubajara △, Brazil **170 B3** 3 55 S 40 50W
Ubangi = Oubangi →, Dem. Rep. of the Congo **114 C3** 0 30 S 17 50 E
Ubaté, Colombia **168 B3** 5 19N 73 49W
Ubauro, Pakistan **92 E3** 28 15N 69 45 E
Ubay, Phil. **81 F5** 10 3N 124 28 E
Ubaye →, France **29 D10** 44 28N 6 18 E
Ubayyiḍ, W. al →, Iraq **101 F10** 32 34N 43 48 E
Ube, Japan **72 D3** 33 56N 131 15 E
Úbeda, Spain **43 G7** 38 3N 3 23W
Uberaba, Brazil **171 E2** 19 50 S 47 55W
Uberaba, L., Brazil **173 D6** 17 30 S 57 50W
Uberlândia, Minas Gerais, Brazil **171 E2** 19 0 S 48 20W
Uberlândia, Roraima, Brazil **169 C6** 0 48N 59 20W
Überlingen, Germany **31 H5** 47 46N 9 10 E
Überlinger See, Germany **33 A8** 47 45N 9 9 E
Ubiaja, Nigeria **113 D6** 6 41N 6 22 E
Ubin, Pulau, Singapore **87 d** 1 25N 103 56 E
Ubolratna Res., Thailand **86 D4** 16 45N 102 30 E
Ubombo, S. Africa **117 D5** 27 31 S 32 4 E
Ubon Ratchathani, Thailand **86 E5** 15 15N 104 50 E
Ubondo, Dem. Rep. of the Congo **118 C2** 0 55 S 25 42 E
Ubort →, Belarus **59 F5** 52 6N 28 30 E
Ubrique, Spain **43 J5** 36 41N 5 27W
Ubud, Indonesia **79 J18** 8 30 S 115 16 E
Ubuna, Solomon Is. **133 N11** 10 11 S 161 24 E
Ubundu, Dem. Rep. of the Congo **118 C2** 0 22 S 25 30 E
Ucayali →, Peru **172 A3** 4 30 S 73 30W
Uchab, Namibia **116 B2** 19 47 S 17 42 E
Uchaly, Russia **64 D7** 54 19N 59 27 E
Uchiko, Japan **72 D4** 33 33N 132 39 E
Uchiura-Wan, Japan **70 C10** 42 25N 140 40 E
Uchiza, Peru **172 B2** 8 25 S 76 20W
Uchquduq, Uzbekistan **66 E7** 41 50N 62 50 E
Uchqŭrghon, Uzbekistan **65 C6** 41 6N 72 4 E
Uchte, Germany **30 C4** 52 30N 8 54 E
Uchur →, Russia **67 D14** 58 48N 130 35 E
Uckermark, Germany **30 B9** 53 5N 13 30 E
Uckkulach, Uzbekistan **65 C3** 40 33N 67 11 E
Ucluelet, Canada **142 D3** 48 57N 125 32W
Ucua, Angola **115 D2** 8 43 S 14 8 E
Uda →, Russia **67 D14** 54 42N 135 14 E
Uda Walawe △, Sri Lanka **95 L5** 6 20N 81 0 E
Udagamandalam, India **95 J3** 11 30N 76 44 E
Udainagar, India **92 H7** 22 33N 76 13 E
Udaipur, Raj., India **92 G5** 24 36N 73 44 E
Udaipur, Tripura, India **90 D3** 23 32N 91 30 E
Udaipur Garhi, Nepal **93 F12** 27 0N 86 35 E
Udala, India **93 J12** 21 35N 86 34 E
Udalguri, India **90 B4** 26 46N 92 8 E
Udayagiri, Andhra Pradesh, India **95 G4** 14 52N 79 19 E
Udayagiri, Orissa, India **94 D7** 20 8N 84 23 E
Udbina, Croatia **45 D12** 44 31N 15 47 E
Uddeholm, Sweden **16 D7** 60 1N 13 38 E
Uddevalla, Sweden **17 F5** 58 21N 11 55 E
Uddjaure, Sweden **14 D17** 65 56N 17 49 E
Uden, Neths. **24 C5** 51 40N 5 37 E
Udgir, India **94 E3** 18 25N 77 5 E
Udhampur, India **93 C6** 33 0N 75 5 E
Udi, Nigeria **113 D6** 6 17N 7 21 E
Údine, Italy **45 B10** 46 3N 13 14 E
Udmurtia □, Russia **64 C4** 57 30N 52 30 E
Udon Thani, Thailand **86 D4** 17 29N 102 46 E
Udu Pt., Fiji **133 A3** 16 9 S 179 57W
Udumalaippettai, India **95 J3** 10 35N 77 15 E
Udupi, India **95 H2** 13 25N 74 42 E
Udva, India **94 D1** 20 5N 73 0 E
Udvoy Balkan, Bulgaria **51 D10** 42 50N 26 50 E
Udzungwa △, Tanzania **118 D4** 7 52 S 36 35 E
Udzungwa Range, Tanzania **119 D4** 9 30 S 35 10 E
Ueckermünde, Germany **30 B10** 53 44N 14 1 E
Ueda, Japan **73 A10** 36 24N 138 16 E
Uedineniya, Os., Russia **6 B12** 78 0N 85 0 E
Uel Scimbiro, Somali Rep. **120 D2** 2 23N 44 14 E
Uele →, Dem. Rep. of the Congo **114 B4** 3 45N 24 45 E
Uelen, Russia **67 C19** 66 10N 170 0W
Uelzen, Germany **30 C6** 52 57N 10 32 E
Ueno, Japan **73 C8** 34 45N 136 8 E
Uetendorf, Switz. **32 C5** 46 47N 7 34 E
Uetersen, Germany **30 B5** 53 40N 9 40 E
Uetze, Germany **30 C6** 52 28N 10 11 E
Ufa, Russia **64 D6** 54 45N 55 55 E
Ufa →, Russia **64 D6** 54 40N 56 0 E
Uffenheim, Germany **31 F6** 49 33N 10 14 E
Ugab →, Namibia **116 C1** 20 55 S 13 30 E
Ugalla →, Tanzania **118 D3** 5 8 S 30 42 E
Ugalla River △, Tanzania **118 D3** 5 50 S 31 54 E
Ugam Tizmasi, Kazakhstan **65 B5** 42 20N 70 30 E
Uganda ■, Africa **118 B3** 2 0N 32 0 E
Ugento, Italy **47 C11** 39 56N 18 10 E
Ugep, Nigeria **113 D6** 5 53N 8 2 E
Ughelli, Nigeria **113 D6** 5 33N 6 0 E
Ugie, S. Africa **117 E4** 31 10 S 28 13 E
Ugíjar, Spain **43 J7** 36 58N 3 7W
Ugine, France **29 C10** 45 45N 6 25 E
Uglegorsk, Russia **67 E15** 49 5N 142 2 E
Ugleuralskiy, Russia **64 B6** 59 8N 57 35 E
Uglich, Russia **58 D10** 57 33N 38 20 E
Ugljan, Croatia **45 D12** 44 12N 15 10 E
Ugljane, Croatia **45 E13** 43 35N 16 46 E
Ugolny = Beringovskiy, Russia **67 C18** 63 3N 179 19 E
Ugolny = Karpinsk, Russia **64 B8** 59 45N 60 1 E
Ugolnyye Kopi = Kopeysk, Russia **64 D8** 55 7N 61 37 E
Ugra →, Russia **58 E9** 54 30N 36 7 E
Ugŭrchin, Bulgaria **51 C8** 43 6N 24 26 E
Uh →, Slovak Rep. **35 C15** 48 37N 22 0 E
Uherské Hradiště, Czech Rep. **35 B10** 49 4N 17 30 E
Uherský Brod, Czech Rep. **35 B10** 49 1N 17 40 E
Úhlava →, Czech Rep. **34 B6** 49 45N 13 24 E
Uhlenhorst, Namibia **116 C2** 23 45 S 17 55 E
Uhniv, Ukraine **55 H10** 50 22N 23 45 E
Uhrichsville, U.S.A. **150 F3** 40 24N 81 21W
Uibhist a Deas = South Uist, U.K. **22 D1** 57 20N 7 15W
Uibhist a Tuath = North Uist, U.K. **22 D1** 57 40N 7 15W
Uiche, Angola **115 E4** 12 2 S 20 51 E
Uig, U.K. **22 D2** 57 35N 6 21W
Uíge, Angola **115 D2** 7 30 S 14 40 E
Uíge □, Angola **115 D3** 7 0 S 16 0 E
Uiha, Tonga **133 P13** 19 54 S 174 25W
Uijŏngbu, S. Korea **75 F14** 37 48N 127 0 E
Ŭiju, N. Korea **75 D13** 40 15N 124 35 E
Uinta Mts., U.S.A. **158 F8** 40 45N 110 30W
Uis, Namibia **116 C1** 21 8 S 14 49 E
Uitenhage, S. Africa **116 E4** 33 40 S 25 28 E
Uithuizen, Neths. **24 A6** 53 24N 6 41 E
Ujazd, Poland **55 H5** 50 23N 18 21 E
Újfehértó, Hungary **52 C6** 47 49N 21 41 E
Ujh →, India **92 C6** 32 10N 75 18 E
Ujhani, India **93 F8** 28 0N 79 6 E
Uji, Japan **73 C7** 34 53N 135 48 E
Uji-guntō, Japan **71 J4** 31 15N 129 25 E
Ujiyamada = Ise, Japan **73 C8** 34 25N 136 45 E
Ujjain, India **92 H6** 23 9N 75 43 E
Ujście, Poland **55 E3** 53 3N 16 45 E
Újszász, Hungary **52 C5** 47 19N 20 7 E
Ujung Pandang, Indonesia **82 C1** 5 10 S 119 20 E
Uka, Russia **67 D17** 57 50N 162 0 E
Ukara I., Tanzania **118 C3** 1 50 S 33 0 E
Uke-Shima, Japan **71 K4** 28 2N 129 14 E
Ukerewe I., Tanzania **118 C3** 2 0 S 33 0 E
Ukholovo, Russia **60 D5** 53 47N 40 30 E
Ukhrul, India **90 C5** 25 10N 94 25 E
Ukhta, Russia **56 B9** 63 34N 53 41 E
Uki Ni Masi, Solomon Is. **133 N11** 10 15 S 161 47 E
Ukiah, U.S.A. **160 F3** 39 9N 123 13W
Ukmergė, Lithuania **15 J21** 55 15N 24 45 E
Ukraine ■, Europe **59 H7** 49 0N 32 0 E
Uku, Angola **115 E2** 11 24 S 14 22 E
Ukwi, Botswana **116 C3** 23 29 S 20 30 E
Ulaan-Uul, Mongolia **74 B6** 44 13N 111 10 E
Ulaanbaatar, Mongolia **67 E11** 47 55N 106 53 E
Ulaangom, Mongolia **68 A4** 50 5N 92 10 E
Ulaanjirem, Mongolia **74 B3** 45 5N 105 30 E
Ulak I., U.S.A. **144 L3** 51 22N 178 57W
Ulala = Gorno-Altaysk, Russia **66 D9** 51 50N 86 5 E
Ulamambri, Australia **129 A8** 31 19 S 149 23 E
Ulamba, Dem. Rep. of the Congo **119 D1** 9 3 S 23 38 E
Ulamona, Papua N. G. **132 C6** 5 0 S 151 15 E
Ulan Bator = Ulaanbaatar, Mongolia **67 E11** 47 55N 106 53 E
Ulan Erge, Russia **61 G7** 46 19N 44 53 E
Ulan Khol, Russia **61 H8** 45 18N 47 4 E
Ulan Ude, Russia **67 D11** 51 45N 107 40 E
Ulanbel, Kazakhstan **65 A5** 44 50N 71 7 E
Ulanów, Poland **55 H9** 50 30N 22 16 E
Ulaş, Sivas, Turkey **100 C7** 39 26N 37 2 E
Ulaş, Tekirdağ, Turkey **51 E11** 41 14N 27 42 E
Ulawa, Solomon Is. **133 M11** 9 46 S 161 57 E
Ulaya, Morogoro, Tanzania **118 D4** 7 3 S 36 55 E
Ulaya, Tabora, Tanzania **118 C3** 4 25 S 33 30 E
Ulcinj, Serbia & M. **50 E3** 41 58N 19 10 E
Ulco, S. Africa **116 D3** 28 21 S 24 15 E
Ule älv = Oulujoki →, Finland **14 D21** 65 1N 25 30 E
Ule träsk = Oulujärvi, Finland **14 D22** 64 25N 27 15 E
Uleåborg = Oulu, Finland **14 D21** 65 1N 25 29 E
Ulefoss, Norway **18 E6** 59 17N 9 16 E
Ulëz, Albania **50 E3** 41 46N 19 54 E
Ulfborg, Denmark **17 H2** 56 16N 8 20 E
Ulhasnagar, India **94 E1** 19 15N 73 10 E
Uliastay, Mongolia **68 B4** 47 56N 97 28 E
Uljma, Serbia & M. **52 E6** 45 2N 21 10 E
Ulla →, Spain **42 C2** 42 39N 8 44W
Ulladulla, Australia **129 C9** 35 21 S 150 29 E
Ullapool, U.K. **22 D3** 57 54N 5 9W
Ullared, Sweden **17 G6** 57 8N 12 42 E
Ulldecona, Spain **40 E5** 40 36N 0 20 E
Ullswater, U.K. **20 C5** 54 34N 2 52W
Ullŭng-do, S. Korea **71 F5** 37 30N 130 30 E
Ulm, Germany **31 G5** 48 23N 9 58 E
Ulmarra, Australia **127 D5** 29 37 S 153 4 E
Ulmeni, Buzău, Romania **53 E11** 45 4N 26 40 E
Ulmeni, Maramureş, Romania **53 C8** 47 28N 23 18 E
Ulonguè, Mozam. **119 E3** 14 37 S 34 19 E
Ulricehamn, Sweden **17 G7** 57 46N 13 26 E
Ulrichen, Switz. **33 C6** 46 30N 8 18 E
Ulrika, Sweden **17 F9** 58 5N 15 23 E
Ulsan, S. Korea **75 G15** 35 20N 129 15 E
Ulsberg, Norway **18 B6** 62 45N 10 0 E
Ulsta, U.K. **22 A7** 60 30N 1 9W
Ulsteinvik, Norway **18 B2** 62 21N 5 53 E
Ulster □, U.K. **23 B5** 54 35N 6 30W
Ulstrem, Bulgaria **51 D10** 42 1N 26 27 E
Ultima, Australia **128 C5** 35 30 S 143 18 E
Ulubat Gölü, Turkey **51 F12** 40 9N 28 35 E
Ulubey, Turkey **49 C11** 38 25N 29 18 E
Uluborlu, Turkey **49 C12** 38 4N 30 28 E
Uluçinar, Turkey **100 D6** 36 21N 35 57 E
Uludağ, Turkey **51 F13** 40 4N 29 13 E
Uludağ △, Turkey **51 F13** 40 5N 29 12 E
Uludere, Turkey **101 D10** 37 28N 42 42 E
Ulugqat, China **65 D7** 39 48N 74 15 E
Uluguru Mts., Tanzania **118 D4** 7 15 S 37 40 E
Ulukışla, Turkey **100 D6** 37 33N 34 28 E
Ulungur He →, China **68 B3** 47 1N 87 24 E
Ulupalakua, U.S.A. **145 C5** 20 39N 156 24W
Uluru = Ayers Rock, Australia **125 E5** 25 23 S 131 5 E
Uluru-Kata Tjuta △, Australia **125 E5** 25 19 S 131 1 E
Ulutau, Kazakhstan **66 E7** 48 39N 67 1 E
Uluwatu, Indonesia **79 K18** 8 50 S 115 5 E
Ulva, U.K. **22 E2** 56 29N 6 13W
Ulverston, U.K. **20 C4** 54 13N 3 5W
Ulverstone, Australia **127 G4** 41 11 S 146 11 E
Ulvik, Norway **18 D3** 60 35N 6 54 E
Ulya, Russia **67 D15** 59 10N 142 0 E
Ulyanovo, Russia **54 D9** 54 50N 22 6 E
Ulyanovsk = Simbirsk, Russia **60 C9** 54 20N 48 25 E
Ulyasutay = Uliastay, Mongolia **68 B4** 47 56N 97 28 E
Ulysses, U.S.A. **155 G4** 37 35N 101 22W
Umag, Croatia **45 C10** 45 26N 13 31 E
Umala, Bolivia **172 D4** 17 25 S 68 5W
'Umān = Oman ■, Asia **99 B7** 23 0N 58 0 E
Uman, Ukraine **59 H6** 48 40N 30 12 E
Umarkhed, India **94 E3** 19 37N 77 46 E
Umarpada, India **92 J5** 21 27N 73 30 E
Umatac, Guam **133 R15** 13 18N 144 39 E
Umatilla, U.S.A. **158 D4** 45 55N 119 21W
Umba, Russia **56 A5** 66 42N 34 11 E
Umbagog L., U.S.A. **151 B13** 44 46N 71 3W
Umbakumba, Australia **126 A2** 13 47 S 136 50 E
Umbértide, Italy **45 E9** 43 18N 12 20 E
Umboi I., Papua N. G. **132 C4** 5 40 S 148 0 E
Umbrella Mts., N.Z. **131 F4** 45 35 S 169 5 E
Umbria □, Italy **45 F9** 42 53N 12 30 E
Umeå, Sweden **14 E19** 63 45N 20 20 E
Umeälven →, Sweden **14 E19** 63 45N 20 20 E
Umera, Indonesia **83 B3** 0 12 S 129 37 E
Umfolozi △, S. Africa **117 D5** 28 18 S 31 50 E
Umfuli →, Zimbabwe **119 F2** 17 30 S 29 23 E
Umfurudzi △, Zimbabwe **119 F3** 17 6 S 31 40 E
Umgusa, Zimbabwe **119 F2** 19 29 S 27 52 E
Umiat, U.S.A. **144 B9** 69 22N 152 8W
Umim Urūmah, Si. Arabia **106 B4** 25 43N 36 35 E
Umka, Serbia & M. **50 B4** 44 40N 20 19 E
Umkomaas, S. Africa **117 E5** 30 13 S 30 48 E
Umm ad Daraj, J., Jordan **103 C4** 32 18N 35 48 E
Umm al Arānib, Libya **108 C2** 26 10N 14 43 E
Umm al Qaywayn, U.A.E. **97 E7** 25 30N 55 35 E
Umm al Qittayn, Jordan **103 C5** 32 18N 36 40 E
Umm al'Abīd, Libya **108 C3** 27 31N 15 2 E
Umm Arda, Sudan **107 D3** 15 17N 32 31 E
Umm Bāb, Qatar **97 E6** 25 12N 50 48 E
Umm Badr, Sudan **107 E2** 14 13N 27 58 E
Umm Baiyud, Sudan **107 E3** 12 5N 31 40 E
Umm Bel, Sudan **107 E2** 13 35N 28 0 E
Umm Birkah, Si. Arabia **106 B4** 27 44N 36 31 E
Umm Boim, Sudan **107 E2** 11 43N 25 27 E
Umm Dam, Sudan **107 E3** 13 45N 30 59 E
Umm Debi, Sudan **107 E3** 14 37N 30 23 E
Umm Dubban, Sudan **107 D3** 15 23N 32 52 E
Umm Durman = Omdurmân, Sudan **107 D3** 15 40N 32 28 E
Umm el Fahm, Israel **103 C4** 32 31N 35 9 E
Umm Gafala, Sudan **107 E2** 13 22N 27 15 E
Umm Gimala, Sudan **107 E2** 11 27N 28 12 E
Umm Inderaba, Sudan **106 D3** 17 30N 33 13 E
Umm Keddada, Sudan **107 E2** 13 33N 26 35 E
Umm Koweika, Sudan **107 E3** 13 10N 32 16 E
Umm Lajj, Si. Arabia **96 E3** 25 0N 37 23 E
Umm Merwa, Sudan **106 D3** 18 4N 32 30 E
Umm Qantur, Sudan **107 E3** 14 17N 31 22 E
Umm Qurein, Sudan **107 F2** 9 58N 28 55 E
Umm Ruwaba, Sudan **107 E3** 12 50N 31 20 E
Umm Saiyala, Sudan **107 E3** 14 25N 31 10 E
Umm Shanqa, Sudan **107 E2** 13 14N 27 14 E
Umm Shutur, Sudan **107 F3** 7 17N 33 14 E
Umm Sidr, Sudan **107 E2** 14 29N 25 10 E
Umm Zehetir, Egypt **106 J8** 28 48N 32 31 E
Umnak I., U.S.A. **144 K5** 53 15N 168 20W
Umniati →, Zimbabwe **119 F2** 16 49 S 28 45 E
Umpqua →, U.S.A. **158 E1** 43 40N 124 12W
Umpulo, Angola **115 E3** 12 38 S 17 42 E
Umred, India **94 D4** 20 51N 79 18 E
Umreth, India **92 H5** 22 41N 73 4 E
Umri, India **94 E3** 19 2N 77 39 E
Umtata, S. Africa **117 E4** 31 36 S 28 49 E
Umuahia, Nigeria **113 D6** 5 31N 7 26 E
Umuarama, Brazil **175 A5** 23 45 S 53 20W
Umuda I., Papua N. G. **132 E2** 8 29 S 143 46 E
Ümurbey, Turkey **51 F10** 40 13N 26 36 E
Umvukwe Ra., Zimbabwe **119 F3** 16 45 S 30 45 E
Umzimvubu, S. Africa **117 E4** 31 38 S 29 33 E
Umzingwane →, Zimbabwe **119 G2** 22 12 S 29 56 E
Umzinto, S. Africa **117 E5** 30 15 S 30 45 E
Una, India **92 J4** 20 46N 71 8 E
Una →, Bos.-H. **45 D13** 45 0N 16 20 E
Unac →, Bos.-H. **45 D13** 44 30N 16 9 E
Unaðsdalur, Iceland **11 A4** 66 7N 22 36W
Unadilla, Ga., U.S.A. **152 C6** 32 16N 83 44W
Unadilla, N.Y., U.S.A. **151 D9** 42 20N 75 19W
Unaí, Brazil **171 E2** 16 23 S 46 53W
Unalakleet, U.S.A. **144 E7** 63 52N 160 47W
Unalaska, U.S.A. **144 K6** 53 53N 166 32W
Unalaska I., U.S.A. **144 K6** 53 35N 166 50W
'Unayzah, Si. Arabia **96 E4** 26 6N 43 58 E
'Unayzah, J., Asia **101 F8** 32 12N 39 18 E
Uncastillo, Spain **40 C3** 42 21N 1 8W
Uncía, Bolivia **172 D4** 18 25 S 66 40W
Uncompahgre Peak, U.S.A. **159 G10** 38 4N 107 28W
Uncompahgre Plateau, U.S.A. **159 G9** 38 20N 108 15W
Undara Volcanic △, Australia **126 B3** 18 14 S 144 41 E
Unden, Sweden **17 F8** 58 45N 14 25 E
Underbool, Australia **128 C4** 35 10 S 141 51 E
Undersaker, Sweden **16 A7** 63 19N 13 21 E
Undredal, Norway **18 D4** 60 57N 7 6 E
Unea I., Papua N. G. **132 C5** 4 53 S 149 9 E
Unecha, Russia **59 F7** 52 50N 32 37 E
Uneiuxi →, Brazil **168 D4** 0 37 S 65 34W
Unga I., U.S.A. **144 J7** 55 15N 160 40W
Ungarie, Australia **129 B7** 33 38 S 146 56 E
Ungarisch-Hradisch = Uherské Hradiště, Czech Rep. **35 B10** 49 4N 17 30 E
Ungarisch-Ostra = Uherský Brod, Czech Rep. **35 B10** 49 1N 17 40 E
Ungarra, Australia **128 C2** 34 12 S 136 2 E
Ungat, Papua N. G. **132 B6** 2 40 S 150 15 E
Ungava, Pén. d', Canada **139 C12** 60 0N 74 0W
Ungava B., Canada **139 C13** 59 30N 67 30W
Ungeny = Ungheni, Moldova **53 C12** 47 11N 27 51 E
Unggi, N. Korea **75 C16** 42 16N 130 28 E
Ungheni, Moldova **53 C12** 47 11N 27 51 E
Unguala →, Ethiopia **107 F5** 8 6N 41 9 E
Ungvár = Uzhhorod, Ukraine **52 B7** 48 36N 22 18 E
Ungwana B., Kenya **118 C5** 2 40 S 40 20 E
Ungwatiri, Sudan **107 D4** 16 52N 36 10 E
Uni, Russia **60 B10** 57 46N 51 31 E
União, Brazil **170 B3** 4 35 S 42 52W
União da Vitória, Brazil **175 B5** 26 13 S 51 5W
União dos Palmares, Brazil **170 C4** 9 10 S 36 2W
Uničov, Czech Rep. **35 B10** 49 46N 17 8 E
Uniejów, Poland **55 G5** 51 59N 18 46 E
Unije, Croatia **45 D11** 44 40N 14 15 E
Unimak I., U.S.A. **144 J7** 54 45N 164 0W
Unimak Pass, U.S.A. **144 J6** 54 15N 164 30W
Unini →, Brazil **169 D5** 1 41 S 61 31W
Union, Miss., U.S.A. **155 J10** 32 34N 89 7W
Union, Mo., U.S.A. **156 F6** 38 27N 91 0W
Union, Ohio, U.S.A. **157 E12** 39 55N 84 12W
Union, S.C., U.S.A. **149 H5** 34 43N 81 37W
Union City, Calif., U.S.A. **160 H4** 37 36N 122 1W
Union City, Ga., U.S.A. **152 B5** 33 35N 84 33W
Union City, N.J., U.S.A. **151 F10** 40 45N 74 2W
Union City, Ohio, U.S.A. **157 D12** 40 12N 84 48W
Union City, Pa., U.S.A. **150 E5** 41 54N 79 51W
Union City, Tenn., U.S.A. **155 G10** 36 26N 89 3W
Union Gap, U.S.A. **158 C3** 46 33N 120 28W
Union Grove, U.S.A. **157 B8** 42 41N 88 3W
Union Park, U.S.A. **153 G8** 28 34N 81 17W
Union Point, U.S.A. **152 B6** 33 37N 83 4W
Union Springs, U.S.A. **152 C4** 32 9N 85 43W
Union Star, U.S.A. **156 E2** 39 59N 94 36W
Uniondale, S. Africa **116 E3** 33 39 S 23 7 E
Uniontown, Ky., U.S.A. **157 G9** 37 47N 87 56W
Uniontown, Pa., U.S.A. **148 F6** 39 54N 79 44W
Unionville, Ga., U.S.A. **152 D6** 31 26N 83 30W
Unionville, Mo., U.S.A. **156 D3** 40 29N 93 1W
Unirea, Romania **53 F12** 44 15N 27 35 E
United Arab Emirates ■, Asia **97 F7** 23 50N 54 0 E
United Arab Republic = Egypt ■, Africa **106 B3** 28 0N 31 0 E
United Kingdom ■, Europe **19 E6** 53 0N 2 0W
United Provinces = Uttar Pradesh □, India **93 F9** 27 0N 80 0 E
United States of America ■, N. Amer. **137 F10** 37 0N 96 0W
Unity, Canada **143 C7** 52 30N 109 5W
Universales, Mtes., Spain **40 E3** 40 18N 1 33W
University City, U.S.A. **156 F6** 38 40N 90 20W
University Park, U.S.A. **159 K10** 32 17N 106 45W
Unjha, India **92 H5** 23 46N 72 24 E
Unmet, Vanuatu **133 F5** 16 8 S 167 15 E
Unna, Germany **30 D3** 51 32N 7 42 E
Unnao, India **93 F9** 26 35N 80 30 E
Uno, Ilha, Guinea-Biss. **112 C1** 11 15N 16 13W
Unpongkor, Vanuatu **133 H6** 18 50 S 168 59 E
Unruhstadt = Kargowa, Poland **55 F2** 52 5N 15 51 E
Unsengedsi →, Zimbabwe **119 F3** 15 43 S 31 14 E
Unst, U.K. **22 A8** 60 44N 0 53W
Unstrut →, Germany **30 D7** 51 10N 11 48 E
Unter-engadin, Switz. **33 C10** 46 48N 10 20 E
Unterägeri, Switz. **33 B7** 47 8N 8 36 E
Unterdrauburg = Dravograd, Slovenia **45 B12** 46 36N 15 5 E
Unterfranken □, Germany **31 F5** 50 0N 10 0 E
Unterkulm, Switz. **32 B6** 47 18N 8 7 E
Unterschleissheim, Germany **31 G7** 48 17N 11 34 E
Unterseen, Switz. **32 C5** 46 41N 7 50 E
Unterthingau, Germany **33 A11** 47 46N 10 30 E
Unterwaldner Alpen, Switz. **33 C6** 46 55N 8 15 E
Unterwasser, Switz. **33 B8** 47 13N 9 19 E
Unuk →, Canada **142 B2** 56 5N 131 3W
Ünye, Turkey **100 B7** 41 5N 37 15 E
Unzen-Amakusa △, Japan **72 E2** 32 15N 130 10 E
Unzen-Dake, Japan **72 E2** 32 45N 130 17 E
Unzha, Russia **60 A7** 58 0N 44 0 E
Unzha →, Russia **60 B6** 57 49N 43 47 E
Uors, Switz. **33 C8** 46 42N 9 12 E
Uozu, Japan **73 A9** 36 48N 137 24 E
Upata, Venezuela **169 B5** 8 1N 62 24W
Upatoi Cr. →, U.S.A. **152 C5** 32 22N 84 58W
Upemba △, Dem. Rep. of the Congo **119 D2** 9 0 S 26 35 E
Upemba, L., Dem. Rep. of the Congo **119 D2** 8 30 S 26 20 E

Upernavik, *Greenland* **10 C5** 72 49N 56 20W
Upington, *S. Africa* ... **116 D3** 28 25 S 21 15 E
Upleta, *India* .... **92 J4** 21 46N 70 16 E
'Upolu, *Samoa* .... **133 W24** 13 58 S 172 0W
Upolu Pt., *U.S.A.* **145 C6** 20 16N 155 52W
Upper □, *Ghana* **113 C4** 10 30N 1 30W
Upper Alkali L., *U.S.A.* **158 F3** 41 47N 120 8W
Upper Arlington,
U.S.A. **157 E13** 40 0N 83 4W
Upper Arrow L.,
Canada **142 C5** 50 30N 117 50W
Upper Austria =
Oberösterreich □,
Austria .... **34 C7** 48 10N 14 0 E
Upper Darby, *U.S.A.* . **148 F8** 39 58N 75 16W
Upper Foster L.,
Canada **143 B7** 56 47N 105 20W
Upper Hutt, *N.Z.* .... **130 H4** 41 8 S 175 5 E
Upper Juba,
Somali Rep. .... **120 D2** 3 0N 43 0 E
Upper Klamath L.,
U.S.A. **158 E3** 42 25N 121 55W
Upper Lake, *U.S.A.* .. **160 F4** 39 10N 122 54W
Upper Manilla,
Australia .... **129 A9** 30 38 S 150 40 E
Upper Manzanilla,
Trin. & Tob. **169 F9** 10 31N 61 4W
Upper Missouri River
Breaks △, *U.S.A.* ... **158 C9** 47 50N 108 55W
Upper Musquodoboit,
Canada **141 C7** 45 10N 62 58W
Upper Preoria L.,
U.S.A. **156 D7** 40 55N 89 27W
Upper Red L., *U.S.A.* . **154 A7** 48 8N 94 45W
Upper Sandusky,
U.S.A. **157 D13** 40 50N 83 17W
Upper Senegal &
Niger = Mali ■,
Africa **112 B4** 17 0N 3 0W
Upper Sheikh,
Somali Rep. .... **120 C3** 9 56N 45 13 E
Upper Volta = Burkina
Faso ■, *Africa* **112 C4** 12 0N 1 0W
Upphärad, *Sweden* ... **17 F6** 58 9N 12 19 E
Uppland, *Sweden* .... **16 D12** 59 59N 17 48 E
Upplands-Väsby,
Sweden .... **16 E11** 59 31N 17 54 E
Uppsala, *Sweden* ..... **16 E11** 59 53N 17 38 E
Uppsala län □, *Sweden* **16 D11** 60 0N 17 30 E
Upshi, *India* .... **93 C7** 33 48N 77 52 E
Upstart, C., *Australia* . **126 B4** 19 41 S 147 45 E
Upton, *U.S.A.* **154 C2** 44 6N 104 38W
Uqsuqtuuq = Gjoa
Haven, *Canada* **138 B10** 68 38N 95 53W
Ur, *Iraq* .... **96 D5** 30 55N 46 25 E
Ura-Tyube = Uroteppa,
Tajikistan .... **65 D4** 39 55N 69 1 E
Urabá, G. de, *Colombia* **168 B2** 8 25N 76 53W
Urad Qianqi, *China* .. **74 D5** 40 40N 108 30 E
Uraga-Suidō, *Japan* .. **73 B11** 35 13N 139 45 E
Urakawa, *Japan* ..... **70 C11** 42 9N 142 47 E
Ural = Uralskiy □,
Russia .... **66 C7** 64 0N 70 0 E
Ural = Zhayyq ➝,
Kazakhstan .... **57 E9** 47 0N 51 48 E
Ural, *Australia* ...... **129 B7** 33 21 S 146 12 E
Ural Mts. = Uralskie
Gory, *Eurasia* ..... **64 C7** 60 0N 59 0 E
Uralla, *Australia* .... **129 A9** 30 37 S 151 29 E
Uralmedstroy =
Krasnouralsk, *Russia* **64 B8** 58 21N 60 3 E
Uralsk = Oral,
Kazakhstan .... **60 E10** 51 20N 51 20 E
Uralskie Gory, *Eurasia* **64 C7** 60 0N 59 0 E
Uralskiy □, *Russia* ... **66 C7** 64 0N 70 0 E
Urambo, *Tanzania* ... **118 D3** 5 4 S 32 0 E
Urana, *Australia* .... **129 C7** 35 15 S 146 21 E
Urana, L., *Australia* .. **129 C7** 35 16 S 146 10 E
Urandangi, *Australia* . **126 C2** 21 32 S 138 14 E
Uranga, *Australia* ... **129 A10** 30 31 S 153 1 E
Uranium City, *Canada* **143 B7** 59 34N 108 37W
Uraricaá ➝, *Brazil* ... **169 C5** 3 20N 61 56W
Uraricoera, *Brazil* ... **169 C5** 3 27N 60 59W
Uraricoera ➝, *Brazil* . **169 C5** 3 2N 60 30W
Uravakonda, *India* ... **95 G3** 14 57N 77 12 E
Urawa, *Japan* .... **73 B11** 35 50N 139 40 E
Uray, *Russia* .... **66 C7** 60 5N 65 15 E
'Uray'irah, *Si. Arabia* . **97 E6** 25 57N 48 53 E
Urbakh = Pushkino,
Russia .... **60 E8** 51 16N 47 0 E
Urbana, *Ill., U.S.A.* ... **157 D8** 40 7N 88 12W
Urbana, *Ohio, U.S.A.* . **157 D13** 40 7N 83 45W
Urbandale, *U.S.A.* ... **156 C3** 41 38N 93 43W
Urbánia, *Italy* .... **45 E9** 43 40N 12 31 E
Urbano Santos, *Brazil* **170 B3** 3 12 S 43 23W
Urbel ➝, *Spain* **42 C7** 42 21N 3 40W
Urbino, *Italy* .... **45 E9** 43 43N 12 38 E
Urbión, Picos de, *Spain* **40 C2** 42 1N 2 52W
Urcos, *Peru* .... **172 C3** 13 40 S 71 38W
Urdaneta, *Phil.* ...... **80 D3** 15 59N 120 34 E
Urdinarrain, *Argentina* **174 C4** 32 37 S 58 52W
Urdos, *France* **28 F3** 42 51N 0 35W
Urdzhar, *Kazakhstan* . **66 E9** 47 5N 81 38 E
Ure ➝, *U.K.* **20 C6** 54 5N 1 20W
Uren, *Russia* .... **60 B7** 57 35N 45 55 E
Ureparapara, *Vanuatu* **133 C5** 13 32 S 167 20 E
Ures, *Mexico* **162 B2** 29 30N 110 30W
Ureshino, *Japan* ..... **72 D1** 33 6N 129 59 E
Urewera △, *N.Z.* ..... **130 E6** 38 29 S 177 7 E
Urfa = Sanliurfa,
Turkey .... **101 D8** 37 12N 38 50 E
Urga = Ulaanbaatar,
Mongolia .... **67 E11** 47 55N 106 53 E
Urganch, *Uzbekistan* . **66 E7** 41 40N 60 41 E
Urgench = Urganch,
Uzbekistan .... **66 E7** 41 40N 60 41 E
Ürgüp, *Turkey* ...... **96 B2** 38 38N 34 56 E
Urgut, *Uzbekistan* ... **65 D3** 39 23N 67 15 E
Uri, *India* .... **93 B6** 34 8N 74 2 E
Uri □, *Switz.* .... **33 C7** 46 43N 8 35 E
Uribante ➝, *Venezuela* **168 B3** 7 25N 71 50W
Uribe, *Colombia* **168 C3** 3 13N 74 24W
Uribia, *Colombia* **168 A3** 11 43N 72 16W
Uricani, *Romania* .... **52 E8** 45 20N 23 9 E
Urimba, *Angola* ..... **115 E3** 10 56 S 16 32 E
Uriondo, *Bolivia* .... **174 A3** 21 41 S 64 41W
Urique, *Mexico* **162 B3** 27 13N 107 55W
Urique ➝, *Mexico* ... **162 B3** 26 29N 107 58W
Urirotstock, *Switz.* ... **33 C7** 46 52N 8 32 E
Urk, *Neths.* .... **24 B5** 52 39N 5 36 E
Urkiola △, *Spain* **40 B3** 43 6N 1 2W
Urla, *Turkey* .... **49 C8** 38 20N 26 47 E
Urlați, *Romania* ..... **53 F11** 44 59N 26 15 E
Urmia = Orūmīyeh,
Iran .... **100 D11** 37 40N 45 0 E
Urmia, L. = Orūmīyeh,
Daryācheh-ye, *Iran* . **101 D11** 37 50N 45 30 E
Urnäsch, *Switz.* ..... **33 B8** 47 19N 9 17 E
Urner Alpen, *Switz.* .. **33 C7** 46 45N 8 45 E
Uroševac, *Serbia & M.* . **50 D5** 42 23N 21 10 E
Uroteppa, *Tajikistan* .. **65 D4** 39 55N 69 1 E
Uroyan, Montanas de,
Puerto Rico .... **165 d** 18 12N 67 0W
Urrao, *Colombia* **168 B2** 6 20N 76 11W
Ursatyevskaya =
Khavast, *Uzbekistan* **65 C4** 40 10N 68 49 E
Urshult, *Sweden* ..... **17 H8** 56 31N 14 50 E
Uruaçu, *Brazil* ...... **171 D2** 14 30 S 49 10W
Uruana, *Brazil* ...... **171 E2** 15 30 S 49 41W
Uruapan, *Mexico* **162 D4** 19 30N 102 0W
Uruará, *Brazil* ...... **169 D7** 3 42 S 53 51W
Uruará ➝, *Brazil* .... **169 D7** 2 6 S 53 38W
Urubamba, *Peru* ..... **172 C3** 13 20 S 72 10W
Urubamba ➝, *Peru* .. **172 C3** 10 43 S 73 48W
Urubaxi ➝, *Brazil* ... **169 D5** 0 31 S 64 50W
Urubu ➝, *Brazil* ..... **169 D6** 2 55 S 58 25W
Uruçara, *Brazil* ..... **169 D6** 2 32 S 57 45W
Uruçuí, *Brazil* ...... **170 C3** 7 20 S 44 28W
Uruçuí, Serra do, *Brazil* **170 C3** 9 0 S 44 45W
Uruçuí Prêto ➝, *Brazil* **170 C3** 7 20 S 44 38W
Urucuia ➝, *Brazil* ... **171 E2** 16 8 S 45 5W
Urucurituba, *Brazil* .. **169 D6** 2 41 S 57 40W
Uruguai ➝, *Brazil* ... **175 B5** 26 0 S 53 30W
Uruguaiana, *Brazil* ... **174 B4** 29 50 S 57 0W
Uruguay ■, *S. Amer.* . **174 C4** 32 30 S 56 30W
Uruguay ➝, *S. Amer.* . **174 C4** 34 12 S 58 18W
Urumchi = Ürümqi,
China .... **66 E9** 43 45N 87 45 E
Ürümqi, *China* ...... **66 E9** 43 45N 87 45 E
Urundi = Burundi ■,
Africa .... **118 C3** 3 15 S 30 0 E
Urup ➝, *Russia* ..... **61 H5** 45 0N 41 10 E
Urup, Ostrov, *Russia* . **67 E16** 46 0N 151 0 E
Urutaí, *Brazil* ...... **171 E2** 17 28 S 48 12W
Uryupinsk, *Russia* ... **60 E5** 50 45N 41 58 E
Urzhum, *Russia* ..... **60 B9** 57 10N 49 56 E
Urziceni, *Romania* ... **53 F11** 44 40N 26 42 E
Usa, *Japan* .... **72 D3** 33 31N 131 21 E
Usa ➝, *Russia* ...... **56 A10** 66 16N 59 49 E
Uşak, *Turkey* .... **49 C11** 38 43N 29 28 E
Uşak □, *Turkey* ..... **49 C11** 38 30N 29 0 E
Usakos, *Namibia* .... **116 C2** 21 54 S 15 31 E
Usborne, Mt., *Falk. Is.* **9 f** 51 40 S 59 55W
Ušće, *Serbia & M.* .... **50 C4** 43 30N 20 39 E
Usedom, *Germany* ... **30 B10** 53 55N 14 2 E
Usedom △, *Germany* . **30 B10** 53 55N 14 10 E
Useless Loop, *Australia* **125 E1** 26 8 S 113 23 E
'Usfān, *Si. Arabia* ... **98 B2** 21 58N 39 27 E
Ush-Tobe, *Kazakhstan* **66 E8** 45 16N 78 0 E
Ushakova, Ostrov,
Russia .... **6 A12** 82 0N 80 0 E
Ushakovo, *Russia* .... **54 D7** 54 37N 20 16 E
Ushant = Ouessant, Î.
d', *France* **26 D1** 48 28N 5 6W
Usharal, *Kazakhstan* . **65 B5** 43 53N 70 31 E
Ushashi, *Tanzania* ... **118 C3** 1 59 S 33 57 E
Ushat, *Sudan* .... **107 F2** 7 59N 29 28 E
'Ushayrah, *Si. Arabia* . **106 C5** 21 46N 40 42 E
Ushibuka, *Japan* .... **72 E2** 32 11N 130 1 E
Ushuaia, *Argentina* .. **176 D3** 54 50 S 68 23W
Ushumun, *Russia* .... **67 D13** 52 47N 126 32 E
Ushytsya ➝, *Ukraine* . **53 B12** 48 35N 27 8 E
Usino, *Papua N. G.* ... **132 C3** 5 32 S 145 23 E
Usk, *Canada* **142 C3** 54 38N 128 26W
Usk ➝, *U.K.* **21 F5** 51 33N 2 58W
Uska, *India* .... **93 F10** 27 12N 83 7 E
Uskedal, *Norway* ... **18 E2** 59 56N 5 53 E
Üsküb = Skopje,
Macedonia .... **50 D5** 42 1N 21 26 E
Üsküdar, *Turkey* .... **51 F13** 41 0N 29 5 E
Uslar, *Germany* ..... **30 D5** 51 39N 9 38 E
Usman, *Russia* ...... **59 F10** 52 5N 39 48 E
Usmat, *Uzbekistan* ... **65 D3** 39 45N 67 38 E
Usoke, *Tanzania* .... **118 D3** 5 8 S 32 24 E
Usolye, *Russia* ...... **64 B6** 59 28N 56 31 E
Usolye Sibirskoye,
Russia .... **67 D11** 52 48N 103 40 E
Usolye-Solikamskoye =
Bereznik, *Russia* ... **64 B6** 59 24N 56 46 E
Usoro, *Nigeria* ..... **113 D6** 5 33N 6 11 E
Uspallata, P. de,
Argentina .... **174 C2** 32 37 S 69 22W
Uspenka = Kirovskiy,
Russia .... **70 B6** 45 7N 133 30 E
Uspenskiy, *Kazakhstan* **66 E8** 48 41N 72 43 E
Ussel, *France* ...... **28 C6** 45 32N 2 18 E
Usson-du-Poitou,
France .... **28 B4** 46 16N 0 31 E
Ussuriysk, *Russia* ... **67 E14** 43 48N 131 59 E
Ussurka, *Russia* .... **70 B6** 45 12N 133 31 E
Ust-Aldan = Batamay,
Russia .... **67 C13** 63 30N 129 15 E
Ust-Amginskoye =
Khandyga, *Russia* .. **67 C14** 62 42N 135 35 E
Ust-Bolsheretsk, *Russia* **67 D16** 52 50N 156 15 E
Ust-Buzulukskaya,
Russia .... **60 E6** 50 8N 42 11 E
Ust-Chaun, *Russia* ... **67 C18** 68 47N 170 30 E
Ust-Chorna, *Ukraine* . **53 B8** 48 19N 23 56 E
Ust-Donetskiy, *Russia* **61 G5** 47 35N 40 55 E
Ust-Ilimpeya = Yukta,
Russia .... **67 C11** 63 26N 105 42 E
Ust-Ilimsk, *Russia* ... **67 D11** 58 3N 102 39 E
Ust-Ishim, *Russia* ... **66 D8** 57 45N 71 10 E
Ust-Kamchatsk, *Russia* **67 D17** 56 10N 162 28 E
Ust-Kamenogorsk =
Öskemen,
Kazakhstan .... **66 E9** 50 0N 82 36 E
Ust-Khayryuzovo,
Russia .... **67 D16** 57 15N 156 45 E
Ust-Kut, *Russia* ..... **67 D11** 56 50N 105 42 E
Ust-Kuyga, *Russia* ... **67 B14** 70 1N 135 43 E
Ust-Labinsk, *Russia* . **61 H4** 45 15N 39 41 E
Ust-Luga, *Russia* .... **58 C5** 59 35N 28 20 E
Ust-Maya, *Russia* .... **67 C14** 60 30N 134 28 E
Ust-Mil, *Russia* .... **67 D14** 59 40N 133 11 E
Ust-Medveditskaya =
Serafimovich, *Russia* **60 F6** 49 36N 42 43 E
Ust-Nera, *Russia* .... **67 C15** 64 35N 143 15 E
Ust-Nyukzha, *Russia* . **67 D13** 56 34N 121 37 E
Ust-Olenek, *Russia* .. **67 B12** 73 0N 120 5 E
Ust-Omchug, *Russia* . **67 C15** 61 9N 149 38 E
Ust-Port, *Russia* .... **66 C9** 69 40N 84 26 E
Ust-Sysolsk =
Syktyvkar, *Russia* .. **56 B9** 61 45N 50 40 E
Ust-Tsilma, *Russia* .. **56 A9** 65 28N 52 11 E
Ust Urt = Ustyurt
Plateau, *Asia* ...... **66 E6** 44 0N 55 0 E
Ust-Usa, *Russia* ..... **56 A10** 66 2N 56 57 E
Ust-Vorkuta, *Russia* . **56 A11** 67 24N 64 0 E
Ust-Zhuya = Chara,
Russia .... **67 D12** 56 54N 118 20 E
Ustaoset, *Norway* ... **18 D5** 60 30N 8 2 E
Ustaritz, *France* **28 E2** 43 24N 1 27W
Ustecký □, *Czech Rep.* **34 A7** 50 30N 14 0 E
Uster, *Switz.* .... **33 B7** 47 22N 8 43 E
Ústí nad Labem,
Czech Rep. .... **34 A7** 50 41N 14 3 E
Ústí nad Orlicí,
Czech Rep. .... **35 B9** 49 58N 16 24 E
Ustica, *Italy* .... **46 D6** 38 42N 13 11 E
Ustinov = Izhevsk,
Russia .... **64 C4** 56 51N 53 14 E
Ustka, *Poland* ...... **54 D3** 54 35N 16 55 E
Ustroń, *Poland* ..... **55 J5** 49 43N 18 48 E
Ustrzyki Dolne, *Poland* **55 J9** 49 27N 22 40 E
Ustupo, *Panama* **168 B2** 9 27N 78 34W
Ustyluh, *Ukraine* ... **55 H11** 50 51N 24 10 E
Ustyurt Plateau, *Asia* . **66 E6** 44 0N 55 0 E
Ustyuzhna, *Russia* ... **58 C9** 58 50N 36 32 E
Usu, *China* .... **68 B3** 44 27N 84 40 E
Usuki, *Japan* .... **72 D3** 33 8N 131 49 E
Usulután, *El Salv.* **164 D2** 13 25N 88 28W
Usumacinta ➝, *Mexico* **163 D6** 17 0N 91 0W
Usumbura =
Bujumbura, *Burundi* **118 C2** 3 16 S 29 18 E
Usure, *Tanzania* .... **118 C3** 4 40 S 34 22 E
Usutuo ➝, *Mozam.* .. **117 D5** 26 48 S 32 7 E
Usva, *Russia* .... **64 B6** 58 41N 57 37 E
Uta, *Indonesia* ..... **83 B5** 4 33 S 136 0 E
Utah □, *U.S.A.* **158 G8** 39 20N 111 30W
Utah L., *U.S.A.* **158 F8** 40 10N 111 58W
Utansjö, *Sweden* .... **16 B11** 62 46N 17 55 E
Utara, Selat, *Malaysia* **87 c** 5 28N 100 20 E
Utarni, *India* .... **92 F4** 26 5N 71 58 E
Utatlan, *Guatemala* .. **164 C1** 15 2N 91 11W
Ute Creek ➝, *U.S.A.* . **155 H3** 35 21N 103 50W
Utebo, *Spain* **40 D3** 41 43N 1 0W
Utemurat, *Uzbekistan* **65 B2** 42 6N 65 42 E
Utena, *Lithuania* .... **15 J21** 55 27N 25 40 E
Utete, *Tanzania* ..... **118 D4** 8 0 S 38 45 E
Uthai Thani, *Thailand* **86 E3** 15 22N 100 3 E
Uthal, *Pakistan* ..... **92 G2** 25 44N 66 40 E
Utiariti, *Brazil* ..... **173 C6** 13 0 S 58 10W
Utica, *N.Y., U.S.A.* ... **151 C9** 43 6N 75 14W
Utica, *Ohio, U.S.A.* ... **150 F2** 40 14N 82 27W
Utiel, *Spain* **41 F3** 39 37N 1 11W
Utikuma L., *Canada* .. **142 B5** 55 50N 115 30W
Utinga, *Brazil* ...... **171 D3** 12 6 S 41 5W
Utkela, *India* .... **94 D6** 20 6N 83 10 E
Utne, *Norway* ...... **18 D3** 60 25N 6 37 E
Utnur, *India* .... **94 E4** 19 22N 78 46 E
Uto, *Japan* .... **72 E2** 32 41N 130 40 E
Utö, *Sweden* .... **16 F12** 58 56N 18 16 E
Utopia, *Australia* ... **126 C1** 22 14 S 134 33 E
Utraula, *India* ...... **93 F10** 27 19N 82 25 E
Utrecht, *Neths.* ..... **24 B5** 52 5N 5 8 E
Utrecht, *S. Africa* ... **117 D5** 27 38 S 30 20 E
Utrecht □, *Neths.* ... **24 B5** 52 6N 5 7 E
Utrera, *Spain* **43 H5** 37 12N 5 48W
Utría △, *Colombia* ... **168 B2** 5 57N 77 21W
Utsira, *Norway* ..... **18 E1** 59 19N 4 53 E
Utsjoki ➝, *Finland* .. **14 B22** 69 51N 26 59 E
Utsunomiya, *Japan* .. **73 A11** 36 30N 139 50 E
Uttar Pradesh □, *India* **93 F9** 27 0N 80 0 E
Uttaradit, *Thailand* .. **86 D3** 17 36N 100 5 E
Uttaranchal □, *India* . **93 D8** 30 0N 79 30 E
Uttoxeter, *U.K.* **20 E6** 52 54N 1 52W
Utuado, *Puerto Rico* . **165 d** 18 16N 66 42W
Utva ➝, *Kazakhstan* . **64 F4** 51 28N 52 40 E
Uummannaq,
Greenland **10 B4** 77 0N 69 0W
Uummannaq,
Greenland **6 B5** 70 58N 52 0W
Uummannarsuaq =
Nunap Isua,
Greenland **10 F6** 59 48N 43 55W
Uusikaarlepyy, *Finland* **14 E20** 63 32N 22 31 E
Uusikaupunki, *Finland* **15 F19** 60 47N 21 25 E
Uva, *Russia* .... **60 B11** 56 59N 52 13 E
Uvá ➝, *Colombia* **168 C3** 3 41N 70 3W
Uvac ➝, *Serbia & M.* . **50 C3** 43 35N 19 30 E
Uvalda, *U.S.A.* **152 C7** 32 2N 82 31W
Uvalde, *U.S.A.* **155 L5** 29 13N 99 47W
Uvarovo, *Russia* .... **60 E6** 51 59N 42 14 E
Uvat, *Russia* .... **66 D7** 59 5N 68 50 E
Uvdal, *Norway* ..... **18 D5** 60 17N 8 48 E
Uvelskiy, *Russia* .... **64 D8** 54 26N 61 22 E
Uvinza, *Tanzania* ... **118 D3** 5 5 S 30 24 E
Uvira, *Dem. Rep. of
the Congo* .... **118 C2** 3 22 S 29 3 E
Uvs Nuur, *Mongolia* .. **68 A4** 50 20N 92 30 E
Uwa, *Japan* .... **72 D4** 33 22N 132 31 E
'Uwairidh, Ḩarrat al,
Si. Arabia .... **96 E3** 26 50N 38 0 E
Uwajima, *Japan* .... **72 D4** 33 10N 132 35 E
Uwanda △, *Tanzania* . **118 D3** 7 46 S 32 0 E
Uweinat, Jebel, *Sudan* **106 C1** 21 54N 24 58 E
Uwekuli, *Indonesia* .. **82 B2** 1 25 S 121 6 E
Uxbridge, *Canada* ... **150 B5** 44 6N 79 7W
Uxin Qi, *China* ..... **74 E5** 38 50N 109 5 E
Uxmal, *Mexico* **163 C7** 20 22N 89 46W
Uyak, *U.S.A.* **144 H9** 57 38N 154 0W
Üydzin, *Mongolia* ... **74 B4** 44 9N 107 0 E
Uyo, *Nigeria* .... **113 D6** 5 1N 7 53 E
Uyu ➝, *Burma* ..... **90 C5** 24 51N 94 57 E
Uyuk = Oyyq,
Kazakhstan .... **65 B5** 43 36N 71 16 E
Üyüklü Tepe, *Turkey* . **49 D9** 37 5N 27 21 E
Uyûn Mûsa, *Egypt* ... **103 F1** 29 53N 32 40 E
Uyuni, *Bolivia* ..... **172 E4** 20 28 S 66 47W
Uzbekistan ■, *Asia* ... **65 C2** 41 30N 65 0 E
Uzen, *Kazakhstan* ... **57 F9** 43 29N 52 54 E
Uzen, Bolshoi ➝,
Kazakhstan .... **61 F9** 49 6N 49 56 E
Uzen, Mal ➝,
Kazakhstan .... **61 F9** 49 4N 49 44 E
Uzerche, *France* .... **28 C5** 45 25N 1 34 E
Uzès, *France* .... **29 D8** 44 1N 4 26 E
Uzgen = Özgön,
Kyrgyzstan .... **65 C6** 40 46N 73 18 E
Uzh ➝, *Ukraine* ..... **59 G6** 51 15N 30 12 E
Uzhgorod = Uzhhorod,
Ukraine .... **52 B7** 48 36N 22 18 E
Uzhhorod, *Ukraine* .. **52 B7** 48 36N 22 18 E
Uzhok, *Ukraine* ..... **52 B7** 48 59N 22 52 E
Užice, *Serbia & M.* ... **50 C3** 43 55N 19 50 E
Uzlovaya, *Russia* ... **58 F10** 54 0N 38 5 E
Üzümlü, *Turkey* ..... **49 E11** 36 44N 29 14 E
Uzunköprü, *Turkey* .. **51 E10** 41 16N 26 43 E
Uzunkuyu, *Turkey* ... **49 C8** 38 17N 26 33 E
Uzwil, *Switz.* .... **33 B8** 47 26N 9 9 E
Uzynaghash,
Kazakhstan .... **65 B8** 43 35N 76 20 E
Uzynaghash,
Kazakhstan .... **65 B8** 43 13N 76 19 E

V

Vaal ➝, *S. Africa* ... **116 D3** 29 4 S 23 38 E
Vaal Dam, *S. Africa* .. **117 D4** 27 0 S 28 14 E
Vaalbos △, *S. Africa* . **116 D3** 28 22 S 24 20 E
Vaalwater, *S. Africa* . **117 C4** 24 15 S 28 8 E
Vaasa, *Finland* ..... **14 E19** 63 6N 21 38 E
Vabkent, *Uzbekistan* . **65 C2** 40 1N 64 30 E
Vabre, *France* ...... **28 E6** 43 42N 2 24 E
Vác, *Hungary* ...... **52 C4** 47 49N 19 10 E
Vacaria, *Brazil* ..... **175 B5** 28 31 S 50 52W
Vacata, *Fiji* .... **133 A3** 17 15 S 179 31W
Vacaville, *U.S.A.* **160 G5** 38 21N 121 59W
Vaccarès, Étang de,
France .... **29 E8** 43 32N 4 34 E
Vach = Vakh ➝,
Russia .... **66 C8** 60 45N 76 45 E
Vache, Î. à, *Haiti* **165 C5** 18 2N 73 35W
Väckelsång, *Sweden* . **17 H8** 56 37N 14 58 E
Vacoas, *Mauritius* ... **121 d** 20 18 S 57 29 E
Vada, *India* .... **94 E1** 19 39N 73 8 E
Väddö, *Sweden* ..... **16 D12** 60 0N 18 50 E
Väderstad, *Sweden* .. **17 F8** 58 19N 14 55 E
Vadheim, *Norway* ... **18 C2** 61 13N 5 49 E
Vadnagar, *India* .... **92 H5** 23 47N 72 40 E
Vado Lígure, *Italy* ... **44 D5** 44 17N 8 26 E
Vadodara, *India* .... **92 H5** 22 20N 73 10 E
Vadret, Piz, *Switz.* ... **33 C9** 46 51N 9 58 E
Vadsø, *Norway* ..... **14 A23** 70 3N 29 50 E
Vadstena, *Sweden* ... **17 F8** 58 28N 14 54 E
Vaduj, *India* .... **94 F2** 17 36N 74 27 E
Vaduz, *Liech.* ...... **33 B9** 47 8N 9 31 E
Værlandet, *Norway* .. **18 C1** 61 18N 4 44 E
Værøy, *Norway* ..... **14 C15** 67 40N 12 40 E
Vagalat, *Albania* ... **38 B10** 39 44N 20 8 E
Vågåmo, *Norway* ... **18 C6** 61 52N 9 6 E
Vágar, *Færoe Is.* **14 E9** 62 5N 7 15W
Vagarshapat =
Yejmiadzin, *Armenia* **61 K7** 40 12N 44 19 E
Vaggeryd, *Sweden* ... **17 G8** 57 30N 14 10 E
Vaghena, *Solomon Is.* **133 L9** 7 25 S 157 45 E
Vagney, *France* .... **27 D13** 48 1N 6 43 E
Vagnhärad, *Sweden* . **17 F11** 58 57N 17 33 E
Vagos, *Portugal* **42 E2** 40 33N 8 42W
Vågsfjorden, *Norway* . **14 B17** 68 50N 16 50 E
Váh ➝, *Slovak Rep.* .. **35 D11** 47 43N 18 7 E
Vahsel B., *Antarctica* . **7 D1** 75 0 S 35 0W
Våhtjer = Gällivare,
Sweden .... **14 C19** 67 9N 20 40 E
Vaï, *Greece* .... **39 E7** 35 15N 26 18 E
Vaigach, *Russia* .... **66 B6** 70 10N 59 0 E
Vaigai ➝, *India* ..... **95 K4** 9 15N 79 10 E
Vaiges, *France* **26 D6** 48 2N 0 30W
Vaihingen, *Germany* . **31 G4** 48 54N 8 57 E
Vaijapur, *India* ..... **94 E2** 19 58N 74 45 E
Vaikam, *India* ...... **95 K3** 9 45N 76 25 E
Vail, *U.S.A.* **146 C5** 39 40N 106 20W
Vailala ➝, *Papua N. G.* **132 D3** 7 57 S 145 25 E
Vailly-sur-Aisne,
France .... **27 C10** 49 24N 3 31 E
Vaippar ➝, *India* .... **95 K4** 9 0N 78 25 E
Vaisali ➝, *India* .... **93 F8** 26 28N 78 53 E
Vaison-la-Romaine,
France .... **29 D9** 44 14N 5 4 E
Vaitogi, *Amer. Samoa* **133 X24** 14 24 S 170 44W
Vajpur, *India* ...... **94 D1** 21 24N 73 17 E
Vakaga ➝, *C.A.R.* ... **114 A4** 9 48N 21 32 E
Vakarai, *Sri Lanka* ... **95 K5** 8 8N 81 26 E
Vakarel, *Bulgaria* ... **50 D7** 42 35N 23 40 E
Vakfıkebir, *Turkey* ... **101 B8** 41 2N 39 17 E
Vakh ➝, *Russia* ..... **66 C8** 60 45N 76 45 E
Vakhsh, *Tajikistan* .. **65 E4** 37 43N 68 50 E
Vakhsh ➝, *Tajikistan* **65 E4** 37 6N 68 18 E
Vakhshstroy = Vakhsh,
Tajikistan .... **65 E4** 37 43N 68 50 E
Vakhtan, *Russia* .... **60 B8** 57 53N 46 47 E
Vaksdal, *Norway* .... **18 D2** 60 29N 5 45 E
Vakuta I., *Papua N. G.* **132 E6** 8 51 S 151 10 E
Vál, *Hungary* ...... **52 C3** 47 22N 18 40 E
Val-de-Marne □,
France .... **27 D9** 48 45N 2 28 E
Val-d'Isère, *France* .. **29 C10** 45 27N 6 59 E
Val-d'Oise □, *France* . **27 C9** 49 5N 2 10 E
Val-d'Or, *Canada* **140 C4** 48 7N 77 47W
Val Grande △, *Italy* .. **44 B5** 46 3N 8 25 E
Val Marie, *Canada* ... **143 D7** 49 15N 107 45W
Val Thorens, *France* .. **29 C10** 45 20N 6 33 E
Valaam, *Russia* .... **58 B6** 61 22N 30 57 E
Valadares, *Portugal* .. **42 D2** 41 5N 8 38W
Valahia, *Romania* ... **53 F9** 44 35N 25 0 E
Valaichenai, *Sri Lanka* **95 L5** 7 54N 81 32 E
Valais □, *Switz.* ..... **32 D5** 46 12N 7 45 E
Valais, Alpes du, *Switz.* **32 D5** 46 5N 7 35 E
Valandovo, *Macedonia* **50 E6** 41 19N 22 34 E
Valašské Meziříčí,
Czech Rep. .... **35 B10** 49 29N 17 59 E
Valáxa, *Greece* ..... **48 C6** 38 50N 24 29 E
Vålberg, *Sweden* .... **16 E7** 59 23N 13 11 E
Valbo, *Sweden* ..... **16 D10** 60 40N 17 0 E
Valbondione, *Italy* ... **44 B7** 46 2N 10 1 E
Vălcani, *Romania* ... **52 D5** 46 0N 20 26 E
Vâlcea □, *Romania* .. **53 F9** 45 0N 24 10 E
Valcheta, *Argentina* . **176 B3** 40 40 S 66 8W
Valdagno, *Italy* ..... **45 C8** 45 39N 11 18 E
Valdahon, *France* ... **27 E13** 47 8N 6 21 E
Valdai Hills =
Valdayskaya
Vozvyshennost,
Russia .... **58 D7** 57 0N 33 30 E
Valday, *Russia* ..... **58 D7** 57 58N 33 9 E
Valdayskaya
Vozvyshennost,
Russia .... **58 D7** 57 0N 33 30 E
Valdeazogues ➝, *Spain* **43 G6** 38 45N 4 55W
Valdecañas, Embalse
de, *Spain* **42 F5** 39 45N 5 25W
Valdemarsvik, *Sweden* **17 F10** 58 14N 16 40 E
Valdemoro, *Spain* ... **42 E7** 40 12N 3 40W
Valdepeñas, *Spain* ... **43 G7** 38 43N 3 25W
Valderaduey ➝, *Spain* **42 D5** 41 31N 5 42W
Valdérice, *Italy* ..... **46 D5** 38 4N 12 37 E
Valderrobres, *Spain* .. **40 E5** 40 53N 0 9 E
Valdés, Pen., *Argentina* **176 B4** 42 30 S 63 45W
Valdez, *Ecuador* **168 C2** 1 15N 79 0W
Valdez, *U.S.A.* **144 F11** 61 7N 146 16W
Valdgeym =
Dobropole, *Ukraine* **59 H9** 48 25N 37 2 E
Valdivia, *Chile* ..... **176 A2** 39 50 S 73 14W
Valdivia, *Colombia* .. **168 B2** 7 11N 75 27W
Valdobbiádene, *Italy* . **45 C8** 45 54N 12 0 E
Valdosta, *U.S.A.* ... **152 E6** 30 50N 83 17W
Valdoviño, *Spain* **42 B2** 43 36N 8 8W
Valdres, *Norway* .... **18 C6** 61 5N 9 5 E
Vale, *Georgia* ...... **61 K6** 41 30N 42 58 E
Vale, *U.S.A.* **158 E5** 43 59N 117 15W
Vale of Glamorgan □,
U.K. **21 F4** 51 28N 3 25W
Valea lui Mihai,
Romania .... **52 C7** 47 32N 22 11 E
Valea Mărului,
Romania .... **53 E12** 45 49N 27 42 E
Valemount, *Canada* .. **142 C5** 52 50N 119 15W
Valença = Valença do
Piauí, *Brazil* .... **170 C3** 6 20 S 41 45W
Valença, *Brazil* ..... **171 D4** 13 20 S 39 5W
Valença, *Portugal* ... **42 C2** 42 1N 8 34W
Valença do Piauí,
Brazil .... **170 C3** 6 20 S 41 45W
Valençay, *France* ... **27 E8** 47 9N 1 34 E
Valence, *France* .... **29 D8** 44 57N 4 54 E
Valence d'Agen, *France* **28 D4** 44 6N 0 53 E
Valencia, *Phil.* ...... **81 H5** 7 57N 125 3 E
Valencia, *Spain* **41 F4** 39 27N 0 23W
Valencia, *Trin. & Tob.* **169 F9** 10 39N 61 11W
Valencia, *U.S.A.* **159 J10** 34 48N 106 43W
Valencia, *Venezuela* . **168 A4** 10 11N 68 0W
Valencia □, *Spain* ... **41 F4** 39 20N 0 40W
Valencia ✕ (VLC),
Spain **41 F4** 39 20N 0 26W
Valencia, G. de, *Spain* **41 F5** 39 30N 0 20 E
Valencia de Alcántara,
Spain **43 F3** 39 25N 7 14W
Valencia de Don Juan,
Spain **42 C5** 42 17N 5 31W
Valencia I., *Ireland* ... **23 E1** 51 54N 10 22W
Valenciennes, *France* . **27 B10** 50 20N 3 34 E
Văleni, *Romania* .... **53 F9** 44 15N 24 45 E
Vălenii de Munte,
Romania .... **53 E11** 45 11N 26 2 E
Valensole, *France* ... **29 E9** 43 50N 5 59 E
Valentigney, *France* .. **27 E13** 47 27N 6 51 E
Valentim, Sa. do, *Brazil* **170 C3** 6 0 S 43 30W
Valentin, *Russia* .... **70 C7** 43 8N 134 17 E
Valentine, *Nebr.,
U.S.A.* **154 D4** 42 52N 100 33W
Valentine, *Tex., U.S.A.* **155 K2** 30 35N 104 30W
Valenza, *Italy* ...... **44 C5** 45 1N 8 38 E
Våler, *Hedmark,
Norway* .... **18 D8** 60 41N 11 50 E
Våler, *Østfold, Norway* **18 E7** 59 29N 10 51 E
Valera, *Venezuela* ... **168 B3** 9 19N 70 37W
Valesdir, *Vanuatu* ... **133 F6** 16 47 S 168 10 E
Valestrand, *Norway* .. **18 E2** 59 40N 5 26 E
Valga, *Estonia* ...... **15 H22** 57 47N 26 2 E
Valguarnera Caropepe,
Italy .... **47 E7** 37 30N 14 23 E
Valier, *U.S.A.* **158 B7** 48 18N 112 16W
Valinco, G. de, *France* **29 G12** 41 40N 8 52 E
Valjevo, *Serbia & M.* .. **50 B3** 44 18N 19 53 E
Valka, *Latvia* .... **15 H21** 57 46N 26 3 E
Valkeakoski, *Finland* . **15 F20** 61 16N 24 2 E
Valkenswaard, *Neths.* . **24 C5** 51 21N 5 29 E
Vall de Uxó = La Vall
d'Uixó, *Spain* **40 F4** 39 49N 0 15W
Valla, *Sweden* ...... **16 E10** 59 2N 16 20 E
Valladolid, *Mexico* ... **163 C7** 20 40N 88 11W
Valladolid, *Spain* **42 D6** 41 38N 4 43W
Valladolid □, *Spain* .. **42 D6** 41 38N 4 43W
Vallata, *Italy* .... **47 A8** 41 2N 15 15 E
Valldemossa, *Spain* .. **38 B3** 39 43N 2 37 E
Valle, *Norway* ...... **18 E4** 59 13N 7 33 E
Valle d'Aosta □, *Italy* **44 C4** 45 45N 7 15 E
Valle de Arán, *Spain* . **40 C5** 42 50N 0 55 E
Valle de la Pascua,
Venezuela **168 B4** 9 13N 66 0W
Valle de las Palmas,
Mexico **161 N10** 32 20N 116 43W
Valle de Santiago,
Mexico **162 C4** 20 25N 101 15W
Valle de Suchil, *Mexico* **162 C4** 23 38N 103 55W
Valle de Zaragoza,
Mexico **162 B3** 27 28N 105 49W
Valle del Cauca □,
Colombia **168 C2** 3 45N 76 30W
Valle del Ticino △, *Italy* **44 C6** 45 22N 9 0 E
Valle Fértil, Sierra del,
Argentina .... **174 C2** 30 20 S 68 0W
Valle Gran Rey,
Canary Is. **9 e1** 28 5N 17 20W
Valle Hermoso, *Mexico* **163 B5** 25 35N 97 40W
Valledupar, *Colombia* **168 A3** 10 29N 73 15W
Vallehermoso,
Canary Is. **9 e1** 28 10N 17 15W
Vallejo, *U.S.A.* **160 G4** 38 7N 122 14W
Vallenar, *Chile* ..... **174 B1** 28 30 S 70 50W
Vallentuna, *Sweden* .. **16 E12** 59 32N 18 5 E
Valleraugue, *France* . **28 D7** 44 6N 3 39 E
Vallet, *France* **26 E5** 47 10N 1 15W
Valletta, *Malta* ..... **38 F8** 35 54N 14 31 E
Valley Center, *U.S.A.* . **161 M9** 33 13N 117 2W
Valley City, *U.S.A.* ... **154 B6** 46 55N 98 0W
Valley Falls, *Oreg.,
U.S.A.* **158 E3** 42 29N 120 17W
Valley Falls, *R.I.,
U.S.A.* **151 E13** 41 54N 71 24W
Valley Junction = West
Des Moines, *U.S.A.* **156 C3** 41 35N 93 43W
Valley of Flowers △,
India .... **93 D8** 30 50N 79 40 E
Valley of the Kings,
Egypt .... **106 B3** 25 41N 32 34 E
Valley Springs, *U.S.A.* **160 G6** 38 12N 120 50W
Valley Station, *U.S.A.* **157 F11** 38 6N 85 52W
Valley View, *U.S.A.* ... **151 F8** 40 39N 76 33W
Valley Wells, *U.S.A.* .. **161 K11** 35 27N 115 46W
Valleyview, *Canada* .. **142 B5** 55 5N 117 17W
Valli di Comácchio,
Italy .... **45 D9** 44 40N 12 15 E
Vallimanca, Arroyo,
Argentina .... **174 D4** 35 40 S 59 10W
Vallo della Lucánia,
Italy .... **47 B8** 40 14N 15 16 E
Vallon-Pont-d'Arc,
France .... **29 D8** 44 24N 4 24 E
Vallorbe, *Switz.* ..... **32 C2** 46 42N 6 20 E
Valls, *Spain* .... **40 D6** 41 18N 1 15 E
Valmaseda =
Balmaseda, *Spain* .. **40 B1** 43 11N 3 12W
Valmeyer, *U.S.A.* ... **156 F6** 38 18N 90 19W
Valmiera, *Latvia* ..... **15 H21** 57 37N 25 29 E
Valnera, *Spain* **42 B7** 43 9N 3 40W
Valognes, *France* ... **26 C5** 49 30N 1 28W
Valona = Vlorë,
Albania .... **50 F3** 40 32N 19 28 E
Valongo, *Portugal* ... **42 D2** 41 8N 8 30W
Valozhyn, *Belarus* ... **58 E4** 54 3N 26 30 E
Valpaços, *Portugal* .. **42 D3** 41 36N 7 17W
Valparai, *India* ..... **95 J3** 10 22N 76 58 E
Valparaíso, *Chile* .... **174 C1** 33 2 S 71 40W
Valparaíso, *Mexico* ... **162 C4** 22 50N 103 32W
Valparaiso, *Fla., U.S.A.* **153 E3** 30 29N 86 30W
Valparaiso, *Ind., U.S.A.* **157 C9** 41 28N 87 4W
Valparaíso □, *Chile* .. **174 C1** 33 2 S 71 40W
Valpovo, *Croatia* .... **52 E3** 45 39N 18 25 E
Valpoy, *India* .... **95 G2** 15 32N 74 8 E
Valréas, *France* ..... **29 D9** 44 24N 5 0 E
Vals, *Switz.* .... **33 C8** 46 39N 9 11 E
Vals ➝, *S. Africa* .... **116 D4** 27 23 S 26 30 E
Vals, Tanjung,
Indonesia .... **83 C5** 8 26 S 137 25 E
Vals-les-Bains, *France* **29 D8** 44 42N 4 24 E
Valsad, *India* .... **94 D1** 20 40N 72 58 E
Valsamáta, *Greece* ... **39 C2** 38 10N 20 36 E
Valtellina, *Italy* ..... **44 B6** 46 11N 9 55 E
Valþjófsstaður, *Iceland* **11 B12** 65 1N 14 59W
Valtí, *Greece* .... **39 C3** 38 27N 21 7 E
Valuyki, *Russia* ..... **59 G10** 50 10N 38 5 E
Valverde, *Canary Is.* .. **9 e1** 27 48N 17 55W
Valverde del Camino,
Spain **43 H4** 37 35N 6 47W
Valverde del Fresno,
Spain **42 E4** 40 15N 6 51W
Vama, *Romania* ..... **53 C10** 47 34N 25 42 E
Vambori, *India* ..... **94 E2** 19 17N 74 44 E
Vamdrup, *Denmark* .. **17 J3** 55 25N 9 17 E
Våmhus, *Sweden* .... **16 C8** 61 7N 14 29 E
Vammala, *Finland* ... **15 F20** 61 20N 22 54 E
Vámos, *Greece* ..... **39 E5** 35 24N 24 13 E
Vamsadhara ➝, *India* . **94 E7** 18 21N 84 8 E
Van, *Turkey* .... **101 C10** 38 30N 43 20 E
Van, L. = Van Gölü,
Turkey .... **101 C10** 38 30N 43 0 E
Van Alstyne, *U.S.A.* .. **155 J6** 33 25N 96 35W
Van Blommestein
Meer, *Suriname* **169 C6** 4 45N 55 5W
Van Buren = Kettering,
U.S.A. **157 E12** 39 41N 84 10W
Van Buren, *Canada* .. **141 C6** 47 10N 67 55W

Van Buren, *Ark., U.S.A.* **155 H7** 35 26N 94 21W
Van Buren, *Maine, U.S.A.* **149 B11** 47 10N 67 58W
Van Buren, *Mo., U.S.A.* **155 G9** 37 0N 91 1W
Van Canh, *Vietnam* **86 F7** 13 37N 109 0 E
Van Diemen, C., *N. Terr., Australia* **124 B5** 11 9 S 130 24 E
Van Diemen, C., *Queens., Australia* **126 B2** 16 30 S 139 46 E
Van Diemen G., *Australia* **124 B5** 11 45 S 132 0 E
Van Gölü, *Turkey* **101 C10** 38 30N 43 0 E
Van Horn, *U.S.A.* **155 K2** 31 3N 104 50W
Van Horne, *U.S.A.* **156 B4** 42 1N 92 4W
Van Meter, *U.S.A.* **156 C3** 41 32N 93 57W
Van Ninh, *Vietnam* **86 F7** 12 42N 109 14 E
Van Rees, Pegunungan, *Indonesia* **83 B5** 2 35 S 138 15 E
Van Tivu, *India* **95 K4** 8 51N 78 15 E
Van Wert, *U.S.A.* **157 D12** 40 52N 84 35W
Van Yen, *Vietnam* **76 G5** 21 4N 104 42 E
Vanadzor, *Armenia* **61 K7** 40 48N 44 30 E
Vanavara, *Russia* **67 C11** 60 22N 102 16 E
Vanceburg, *U.S.A.* **157 F13** 38 36N 83 19W
Vancouver, *Canada* **142 D4** 49 15N 123 10W
Vancouver, *U.S.A.* **160 E4** 45 38N 122 40W
Vancouver, C., *Australia* **125 G2** 35 2 S 118 11 E
Vancouver, Mt., *U.S.A.* **144 F13** 60 20N 139 41W
Vancouver I., *Canada* **142 D3** 49 50N 126 0W
Vancouver International ✈ (YVR), *U.S.A.* **160 A3** 49 10N 123 10W
Vanda = Vantaa, *Finland* **15 F21** 60 18N 24 58 E
Vandalia, *Ill., U.S.A.* **156 F7** 38 58N 89 6W
Vandalia, *Mo., U.S.A.* **156 E5** 39 19N 91 29W
Vandalia, *Ohio, U.S.A.* **157 E12** 39 54N 84 12W
Vandavasi, *India* **95 H4** 12 30N 79 30 E
Vandeloos B., *Sri Lanka* **95 L5** 8 0N 81 45 E
Vandenburg, *U.S.A.* **161 L6** 34 35N 120 33W
Vanderbijlpark, *S. Africa* **117 D4** 26 42 S 27 54 E
Vandergrift, *U.S.A.* **150 F5** 40 36N 79 34W
Vanderhoof, *Canada* **142 C4** 54 0N 124 0W
Vanderkloof Dam, *S. Africa* **116 E3** 30 4 S 24 40 E
Vanderlin I., *Australia* **126 B2** 15 44 S 137 2 E
Vänern, *Sweden* **17 F7** 58 47N 13 30 E
Vänersborg, *Sweden* **17 F6** 58 26N 12 19 E
Vang, *Norway* **18 C5** 61 7N 8 34 E
Vang Vieng, *Laos* **86 C4** 18 58N 102 32 E
Vanga, *Kenya* **118 C4** 4 35 S 39 12 E
Vangaindrano, *Madag.* **117 C8** 23 21 S 47 36 E
Vangsnes, *Norway* **18 C3** 61 9N 6 39 E
Vanguard, *Canada* **143 D7** 49 55N 107 20W
Vangunu, *Solomon Is.* **133 M10** 8 40 S 158 5 E
Vanimo, *Papua N. G.* **83 B6** 2 42 S 141 21 E
Vanino, *Russia* **67 E15** 48 50N 140 5 E
Vanivilasa Sagara, *India* **95 H3** 13 45N 76 30 E
Vaniyambadi, *India* **95 H4** 12 46N 78 44 E
Vanj, *Tajikistan* **65 D5** 38 22N 71 27 E
Vânju Mare, *Romania* **52 F7** 44 25N 22 52 E
Vanna, *Norway* **14 A18** 70 6N 19 50 E
Vännäs, *Sweden* **14 E18** 63 58N 19 48 E
Vannes, *France* **26 E4** 47 40N 2 47W
Vannovsky = Khamza, *Uzbekistan* **65 C5** 40 25N 71 29 E
Vanoise, Massif de la, *France* **29 C10** 45 25N 6 40 E
Vanrhynsdorp, *S. Africa* **116 E2** 31 36 S 18 44 E
Vansada, *India* **94 D1** 20 47N 73 25 E
Vansbro, *Sweden* **16 D8** 60 32N 14 15 E
Vanse, *Norway* **18 F3** 58 6N 6 41 E
Vansittart B., *Australia* **124 B4** 14 3 S 126 17 E
Vantaa, *Finland* **15 F21** 60 18N 24 58 E
Vanua Balavu, *Fiji* **133 A3** 17 12 S 178 55W
Vanua Lava, *Vanuatu* **133 C5** 13 50 S 167 30 E
Vanua Levu, *Fiji* **133 A2** 16 33 S 179 15 E
Vanua Vatu, *Fiji* **133 B3** 18 22 S 179 15W
Vanuatu ■, *Pac. Oc.* **133 E6** 15 0 S 168 0 E
Vanwyksvlei, *S. Africa* **116 E3** 30 18 S 21 49 E
Vanzylsrus, *S. Africa* **116 D3** 26 52 S 22 4 E
Vapnyarka, *Ukraine* **53 B13** 48 32N 28 45 E
Var □, *France* **29 E10** 43 27N 6 18 E
Var →, *France* **29 E11** 43 39N 7 12 E
Vara, *Sweden* **17 F6** 58 16N 12 55 E
Vara, Pico da, *Azores* **9 d3** 37 48N 25 13W
Varada →, *India* **95 G2** 15 0N 75 40 E
Varades, *France* **26 E5** 47 25N 1 1W
Varáita →, *Italy* **44 D4** 44 9N 7 53 E
Varaldsøy, *Norway* **18 D2** 60 6N 5 59 E
Varallo, *Italy* **44 C5** 45 49N 8 15 E
Varāmīn, *Iran* **97 C6** 35 20N 51 39 E
Varāmīn □, *Iran* **97 B6** 35 18N 51 35 E
Varanasi, *India* **93 G10** 25 22N 83 0 E
Varangerfjorden, *Norway* **14 A23** 70 3N 29 25 E
Varangerhalvøya, *Norway* **14 A23** 70 25N 29 30 E
Varano, Lago di, *Italy* **45 G12** 41 53N 15 45 E
Varaždin, *Croatia* **45 B13** 46 20N 16 20 E
Varazze, *Italy* **44 D5** 44 22N 8 34 E
Varberg, *Sweden* **17 G6** 57 6N 12 20 E
Varcar Vakuf = Mrkonjić Grad, *Bos.-H.* **52 F2** 44 26N 17 4 E
Vardak □, *Afghan.* **91 B3** 34 0N 68 0 E
Vardar = Axiós →, *Greece* **50 F6** 40 57N 22 35 E
Varde, *Denmark* **17 J2** 55 38N 8 29 E
Varde Å →, *Denmark* **17 J2** 55 35N 8 19 E
Vardø, *Norway* **14 A24** 70 23N 31 5 E
Varel, *Germany* **30 B4** 53 23N 8 8 E
Varella, Mui, *Vietnam* **86 F7** 12 54N 109 26 E
Varėna, *Lithuania* **15 J21** 54 12N 24 30 E
Varennes-sur-Allier, *France* **27 F10** 46 19N 3 24 E
Varennes-Vauzelles, *France* **27 E10** 47 3N 3 9 E
Vareš, *Bos.-H.* **52 F3** 44 12N 18 23 E
Varese, *Italy* **44 C5** 45 48N 8 50 E
Vârfurile, *Romania* **52 D7** 46 19N 22 31 E
Vårgårda, *Sweden* **17 F6** 58 2N 12 49 E
Vargem Bonita, *Brazil* **171 F2** 20 20 S 46 22W
Vargem Grande, *Brazil* **170 B3** 3 33 S 43 56W
Varginha, *Brazil* **175 A6** 21 33 S 45 25W
Vargön, *Sweden* **17 F6** 58 22N 12 20 E
Varhaug, *Norway* **18 F2** 58 37N 5 41 E
Varillas, *Chile* **174 A1** 24 0 S 70 10W
Varkaus, *Finland* **15 E22** 62 19N 27 50 E
Värmdölandet, *Sweden* **16 E12** 59 20N 18 33 E
Värmeln, *Sweden* **16 E6** 59 35N 12 54 E
Värmlands län □, *Sweden* **16 E6** 60 0N 13 20 E
Värmlandsbro, *Sweden* **16 E7** 59 11N 13 0 E
Varna, *Bulgaria* **51 C11** 43 13N 27 56 E
Varna, *Russia* **64 E8** 53 24N 60 58 E
Varna □, *Bulgaria* **51 C11** 43 20N 27 30 E
Varna →, *India* **94 F2** 16 48N 74 32 E
Värnamo, *Sweden* **17 G8** 57 10N 14 3 E
Varnsdorf, *Czech Rep.* **34 A7** 50 55N 14 35 E
Varnville, *U.S.A.* **152 C8** 32 51N 81 5W
Várpalota, *Hungary* **52 C3** 47 12N 18 8 E
Vars, *Canada* **151 A9** 45 21N 75 21W
Vars, *France* **29 D10** 44 37N 6 42 E
Vartdal, *Norway* **18 B3** 62 20N 6 8 E
Varto, *Turkey* **101 C9** 39 10N 41 27 E
Varvarin, *Serbia & M.* **50 C5** 43 43N 21 20 E
Varysburg, *U.S.A.* **150 D6** 42 46N 78 19W
Varzaneh, *Iran* **97 C7** 32 25N 52 40 E
Várzea Alegre, *Brazil* **170 C4** 6 47 S 39 17W
Várzea da Palma, *Brazil* **171 E3** 17 36 S 44 44W
Várzea Grande, *Brazil* **173 D6** 15 39 S 56 8W
Varzi, *Italy* **44 D6** 44 49N 9 12 E
Varzo, *Italy* **44 B5** 46 12N 8 15 E
Varzob, *Tajikistan* **65 D4** 38 46N 68 49 E
Varzy, *France* **27 E10** 47 22N 3 20 E
Vas □, *Hungary* **52 C1** 47 10N 16 55 E
Vasa = Vaasa, *Finland* **14 E19** 63 6N 21 38 E
Vasa Barris →, *Brazil* **170 D4** 11 10 S 37 10W
Vásárosnamény, *Hungary* **52 B7** 48 9N 22 19 E
Vascâo →, *Portugal* **43 H3** 37 31N 7 31W
Vaşcău, *Romania* **52 D7** 46 28N 22 30 E
Vascongadas = País Vasco □, *Spain* **40 C2** 42 50N 2 45W
Vāshīr, *Afghan.* **91 B1** 32 16N 63 51 E
Vashkivtsi, *Ukraine* **53 B10** 48 23N 25 31 E
Vasht = Khāsh, *Iran* **91 C1** 28 15N 61 15 E
Vasilevichi, *Belarus* **59 F5** 52 15N 29 50 E
Vasilikí, *Greece* **39 B2** 38 37N 20 36 E
Vasiliko = Michurin, *Bulgaria* **51 D11** 42 9N 27 51 E
Vasilikón, *Greece* **48 C5** 38 25N 23 40 E
Vasilikós, *Greece* **39 D2** 37 43N 20 59 E
Vasilkov = Vasylkiv, *Ukraine* **59 G6** 50 7N 30 15 E
Vasilyova Sloboda = Chkolovsk, *Russia* **60 B6** 56 50N 43 10 E
Vasilyovo = Chkolovsk, *Russia* **60 B6** 56 50N 43 10 E
Vaslui, *Romania* **53 D12** 46 38N 27 42 E
Vaslui □, *Romania* **53 D12** 46 30N 27 45 E
Väsman, *Sweden* **16 D9** 60 9N 15 5 E
Vassar, *Canada* **143 D9** 49 10N 95 55W
Vassar, *U.S.A.* **148 D4** 43 22N 83 35W
Vassfaret, *Norway* **18 D6** 60 38N 9 28 E
Västerås, *Sweden* **16 E10** 59 37N 16 38 E
Västerbotten, *Sweden* **14 D18** 64 36N 20 4 E
Västerdalälven →, *Sweden* **16 D8** 60 30N 14 7 E
Västergötland, *Sweden* **17 F7** 58 0N 13 10 E
Västerhaninge, *Sweden* **16 E12** 59 7N 18 6 E
Västervik, *Sweden* **17 G10** 57 43N 16 33 E
Västmanland, *Sweden* **15 G16** 59 45N 16 20 E
Västmanlands län □, *Sweden* **16 E10** 59 45N 16 20 E
Vasto, *Italy* **45 F11** 42 8N 14 40 E
Västra Götalands Län □, *Sweden* **17 F6** 58 0N 13 0 E
Vasvár, *Hungary* **52 C1** 47 3N 16 47 E
Vasylivka, *Ukraine* **53 E13** 45 38N 28 50 E
Vasylkiv, *Ukraine* **59 G6** 50 7N 30 15 E
Vatan, *France* **27 E8** 47 4N 1 50 E
Vaté = Efate, I., *Vanuatu* **133 G6** 17 40 S 168 25 E
Vatersay, *U.K.* **22 E1** 56 55N 7 32W
Vathí, *Greece* **39 B2** 38 41N 20 47 E
Váthia, *Greece* **48 E4** 36 29N 22 29 E
Vatican City ■, *Europe* **45 G9** 41 54N 12 27 E
Vaticano, C., *Italy* **47 D8** 38 37N 15 50 E
Vatili, *Cyprus* **39 E9** 35 6N 33 40 E
Vatin, *Serbia & M.* **52 E6** 45 12N 21 20 E
Vatiu = Atiu, *Cook Is.* **135 J12** 20 0 S 158 10W
Vatnajökull, *Iceland* **11 C10** 64 30N 16 48W
Vatnås, *Norway* **18 E6** 59 58N 9 37 E
Vatneyri, *Iceland* **11 B2** 65 35N 24 0W
Vatnsfjörður, *Iceland* **11 B4** 65 56N 22 30W
Vatólakkos, *Greece* **39 E4** 35 27N 23 53 E
Vatoloha, *Madag.* **117 B8** 17 52 S 47 48 E
Vatomandry, *Madag.* **117 B8** 19 20 S 48 59 E
Vatra-Dornei, *Romania* **53 C10** 47 22N 25 22 E
Vatrak →, *India* **92 H5** 23 9N 73 2 E
Vättern, *Sweden* **17 F8** 58 25N 14 30 E
Vättis, *Switz.* **33 C8** 46 55N 9 27 E
Vatu Vara, *Fiji* **133 A3** 17 26 S 179 31W
Vatulele, *Fiji* **133 B1** 18 33 S 177 37 E
Vaucluse □, *France* **29 E9** 43 50N 5 20 E
Vaucouleurs, *France* **27 D12** 48 37N 5 40 E
Vaud □, *Switz.* **32 C3** 46 35N 6 30 E
Vaudreuil-Dorion, *Canada* **151 A10** 45 23N 74 3W
Vaughn, *Mont., U.S.A.* **158 C8** 47 33N 111 33W
Vaughn, *N. Mex., U.S.A.* **159 J11** 34 36N 105 13W
Vaujours L., *Canada* **140 A5** 55 27N 74 15W
Vaulruz, *Switz.* **32 C3** 46 38N 6 58 E
Vaupés = Uaupés →, *Brazil* **168 C4** 0 2N 67 16W
Vaupes □, *Colombia* **168 C3** 1 0N 71 0W
Vauvert, *France* **29 E8** 43 42N 4 17 E
Vauxhall, *Canada* **142 C6** 50 5N 112 9W
Vav, *India* **92 G4** 24 22N 71 31 E
Vavatenina, *Madag.* **117 B8** 17 28 S 49 12 E
Vava'u, *Tonga* **133 P14** 18 36 S 174 0W
Vava'u Group, *Tonga* **133 P14** 18 40 S 174 0W
Vavoua, *Ivory C.* **112 D3** 7 23N 6 29W
Vavuniya, *Sri Lanka* **95 K5** 8 45N 80 30 E
Vawkavysk, *Belarus* **59 F3** 53 9N 24 30 E
Vaxholm, *Sweden* **16 E12** 59 25N 18 20 E
Växjö, *Sweden* **17 H8** 56 52N 14 50 E
Våxtorp, *Sweden* **17 H7** 56 25N 13 8 E
Vayalpad, *India* **95 H4** 13 39N 78 38 E
Vayenga = Severomorsk, *Russia* **56 A5** 69 5N 33 27 E
Vaygach, Ostrov, *Russia* **66 C6** 70 0N 60 0 E
Váyia, *Greece* **48 C5** 38 19N 23 11 E
Váyia, Ákra, *Greece* **38 E12** 36 15N 28 11 E
Veadeiros, *Brazil* **171 D2** 14 7 S 47 31W
Veaikevárri = Svappavaara, *Sweden* **14 C19** 67 40N 21 3 E
Vechelde, *Germany* **30 C6** 52 16N 10 22 E
Vechta, *Germany* **30 C4** 52 44N 8 17 E
Vechte →, *Neths.* **24 B6** 52 34N 6 6 E
Vecsés, *Hungary* **52 C4** 47 26N 19 19 E
Vedaranniyam, *India* **95 J4** 10 25N 79 50 E
Vedavågen, *Norway* **18 E2** 59 17N 5 12 E
Veddige, *Sweden* **17 G6** 57 17N 12 20 E
Vedea →, *Romania* **53 G10** 43 42N 25 41 E
Vedia, *Argentina* **174 C3** 34 30 S 61 31W
Vedrette di Ries-Aurina ⌓, *Italy* **45 B9** 46 54N 12 5 E
Vedum, *Sweden* **17 F7** 58 11N 13 0 E
Veedersburg, *U.S.A.* **157 D9** 40 7N 87 16W
Veendam, *Neths.* **24 A6** 53 5N 6 52 E
Veenendaal, *Neths.* **24 B5** 52 2N 5 34 E
Vefsna →, *Norway* **14 D15** 65 48N 13 10 E
Vega, *Norway* **14 D14** 65 40N 11 55 E
Vega, *U.S.A.* **155 H3** 35 15N 102 26W
Vega Baja, *Puerto Rico* **165 d** 18 27N 66 23W
Vega de Ribadeo = Vegadeo, *Spain* **42 B3** 43 27N 7 4W
Vegadeo, *Spain* **42 B3** 43 27N 7 4W
Vegårshei, *Norway* **18 F5** 58 44N 8 51 E
Vegas Verde = North Las Vegas, *U.S.A.* **161 J11** 36 12N 115 7W
Veggli, *Norway* **18 D6** 60 3N 9 9 E
Veglia = Krk, *Croatia* **45 C11** 45 8N 14 40 E
Vegorrítis, Límni, *Greece* **50 F5** 40 45N 21 45 E
Vegreville, *Canada* **142 C6** 53 30N 112 5W
Veidholmen, *Norway* **18 A4** 63 31N 7 58 E
Veinge, *Sweden* **17 H7** 56 33N 13 4 E
Veisiejai, *Lithuania* **54 D10** 54 6N 23 42 E
Vejbystrand, *Sweden* **17 H6** 56 19N 12 45 E
Vejen, *Denmark* **17 J3** 55 30N 9 9 E
Vejer de la Frontera, *Spain* **43 J5** 36 15N 5 59W
Vejle, *Denmark* **17 J3** 55 43N 9 30 E
Vejle Amtskommune □, *Denmark* **17 J3** 55 45N 9 20 E
Vejle Fjord, *Denmark* **17 J3** 55 40N 9 50 E
Vela Luka, *Croatia* **45 F13** 42 59N 16 44 E
Velachha, *India* **94 D1** 21 26N 73 1 E
Velanai I., *Sri Lanka* **95 K4** 9 45N 79 45 E
Velas, *Azores* **9 d1** 38 41N 28 13W
Velas, C., *Costa Rica* **164 D2** 10 21N 85 52W
Velasco, Sierra de, *Argentina* **174 B2** 29 20 S 67 10W
Velay, Mts. du, *France* **28 D7** 45 0N 3 40 E
Velbert, *Germany* **30 D3** 51 20N 7 3 E
Velddrif, *S. Africa* **116 E2** 32 42 S 18 11 E
Velebit ⌓, *Croatia* **45 D12** 44 30N 15 15 E
Velebit Planina, *Croatia* **45 D12** 44 50N 15 20 E
Velebitski Kanal, *Croatia* **45 D11** 44 45N 14 55 E
Veleka →, *Bulgaria* **51 D11** 42 4N 27 58 E
Velencei-tó, *Hungary* **52 C3** 47 13N 18 36 E
Velenje, *Slovenia* **45 B12** 46 23N 15 8 E
Veles, *Macedonia* **50 E5** 41 46N 21 47 E
Velestínon, *Greece* **48 B4** 39 23N 22 43 E
Vélez, *Colombia* **168 B3** 6 1N 73 41W
Vélez-Málaga, *Spain* **43 J6** 36 48N 4 5W
Vélez Rubio, *Spain* **41 H2** 37 41N 2 5W
Velhas →, *Brazil* **171 E3** 17 13 S 44 49W
Velika, *Croatia* **52 E2** 45 27N 17 40 E
Velika Gorica, *Croatia* **45 C13** 45 44N 16 5 E
Velika Kapela, *Croatia* **45 C12** 45 10N 15 5 E
Velika Kikinda = Kikinda, *Serbia & M.* **52 E5** 45 50N 20 30 E
Velika Kladuša, *Bos.-H.* **45 C12** 45 11N 15 48 E
Velika Kruša, *Serbia & M.* **50 D4** 42 19N 20 39 E
Velika Morava →, *Serbia & M.* **50 B5** 44 43N 21 3 E
Velika Plana, *Serbia & M.* **50 B5** 44 20N 21 4 E
Velikaya →, *Russia* **58 D5** 57 48N 28 10 E
Velikaya Kema, *Russia* **70 B8** 45 30N 137 12 E
Velikaya Lepetikha, *Ukraine* **59 J7** 47 2N 33 58 E
Veliké Kapušany, *Slovak Rep.* **35 C15** 48 34N 22 5 E
Velike Lašče, *Slovenia* **45 C11** 45 49N 14 45 E
Veliki Jastrebac, *Serbia & M.* **50 C5** 43 25N 21 30 E
Veliki Kanal, *Serbia & M.* **52 E4** 45 45N 19 15 E
Veliki Popović, *Serbia & M.* **50 B5** 44 8N 21 18 E
Veliki Ustyug, *Russia* **56 B8** 60 47N 46 20 E
Velikiye Luki, *Russia* **58 D6** 56 25N 30 32 E
Veliko Gradište, *Serbia & M.* **50 B5** 44 46N 21 29 E
Veliko Tŭrnovo, *Bulgaria* **51 C9** 43 5N 25 41 E
Velikonda Range, *India* **95 G4** 14 45N 79 10 E
Vélingara, *Kolda, Senegal* **112 C2** 13 12N 14 5W
Vélingara, *Louga, Senegal* **112 B2** 15 0N 14 40W
Velingrad, *Bulgaria* **50 D7** 42 4N 23 58 E
Velino, Mte., *Italy* **45 F10** 42 9N 13 23 E
Velizh, *Russia* **58 E6** 55 36N 31 11 E
Velké Karlovice, *Czech Rep.* **35 B11** 49 20N 18 17 E
Velké Meziříčí, *Czech Rep.* **34 B9** 49 21N 16 1 E
Vel'ký Javorník, *Slovak Rep.* **35 B11** 49 19N 18 22 E
Vel'ký Krtíš, *Slovak Rep.* **35 C12** 48 12N 19 21 E
Vel'ký Meder, *Slovak Rep.* **35 D10** 47 52N 17 46 E
Vel'ký Tribeč, *Slovak Rep.* **35 C11** 48 28N 18 15 E
Vella G., *Solomon Is.* **133 M9** 8 0 S 156 50 E
Vella Lavella, *Solomon Is.* **133 L9** 7 45 S 156 40 E
Vellar →, *India* **95 J4** 11 30N 79 36 E
Velletri, *Italy* **46 A5** 41 41N 12 47 E
Vellinge, *Sweden* **17 J6** 55 29N 13 0 E
Vellmar, *Germany* **30 D5** 51 22N 9 28 E
Vellore, *India* **95 H4** 12 57N 79 10 E
Velsk, *Russia* **58 B11** 61 10N 42 5 E
Velten, *Germany* **30 C9** 52 42N 13 10 E
Veluwezoom △, *Neths.* **24 B6** 52 5N 6 0 E
Velva, *U.S.A.* **154 A4** 48 4N 100 56W
Velvendós, *Greece* **50 F6** 40 15N 22 6 E
Velyka Mykhaylivka, *Ukraine* **53 C14** 47 4N 29 52 E
Velyki Luchky, *Ukraine* **52 B7** 48 25N 22 34 E
Velykyy Bereznyy, *Ukraine* **52 B7** 48 54N 22 28 E
Velykyy Bychkiv, *Ukraine* **53 C9** 47 58N 24 1 E
Vemb, *Denmark* **17 H2** 56 21N 8 21 E
Vembanad L., *India* **95 K3** 9 36N 76 15 E
Vemdalen, *Sweden* **16 B7** 62 27N 13 51 E
Ven, *Sweden* **17 J6** 55 55N 12 45 E
Venaco, *France* **29 F13** 42 14N 9 11 E
Venado Tuerto, *Argentina* **174 C3** 33 50 S 62 0W
Venafro, *Italy* **47 A7** 41 29N 14 2 E
Venarey-les-Laumes, *France* **27 E11** 47 32N 4 26 E
Venaría, *Italy* **44 C4** 45 8N 7 38 E
Venčane, *Serbia & M.* **50 B4** 44 24N 20 28 E
Vence, *France* **29 E11** 43 43N 7 6 E
Vendas Novas, *Portugal* **43 G2** 38 39N 8 27W
Vendée □, *France* **26 F5** 46 50N 1 35W
Vendée →, *France* **26 F5** 46 20N 1 10W
Vendéen, Bocage, *France* **28 B2** 46 40N 1 20W
Vendeuvre-sur-Barse, *France* **27 D11** 48 14N 4 28 E
Vendôme, *France* **26 E8** 47 47N 1 3 E
Vendrell = El Vendrell, *Spain* **40 D6** 41 10N 1 30 E
Vendsyssel, *Denmark* **17 G4** 57 22N 10 0 E
Vendychany, *Ukraine* **53 B12** 48 38N 27 48 E
Venelles, *France* **29 E9** 43 35N 5 28 E
Véneta, L., *Italy* **45 C9** 45 23N 12 25 E
Venetie, *U.S.A.* **144 C11** 67 1N 146 25W
Véneto □, *Italy* **45 C9** 45 30N 12 0 E
Venev, *Russia* **58 E10** 54 22N 38 17 E
Venézia, *Italy* **45 C9** 45 27N 12 21 E
Venézia, G. di, *Italy* **45 C10** 45 15N 13 0 E
Venezia Tridentina = Trentino-Alto Adige □, *Italy* **45 B8** 46 30N 11 20 E
Venezuela ■, *S. Amer.* **168 B4** 8 0N 66 0W
Venezuela, G. de, *Venezuela* **168 A3** 11 30N 71 0W
Vengurla, *India* **95 G1** 15 53N 73 45 E
Vengurla Rocks, *India* **95 G1** 15 55N 73 22 E
Venice = Venézia, *Italy* **45 C9** 45 27N 12 21 E
Venice, *U.S.A.* **153 H7** 27 6N 82 27W
Vénissieux, *France* **29 C8** 45 42N 4 53 E
Venjansjön, *Sweden* **16 D8** 60 54N 14 0 E
Venkatagiri, *India* **95 H4** 14 0N 79 35 E
Venkatapuram, *India* **94 E5** 18 20N 80 30 E
Venlo, *Neths.* **24 C6** 51 22N 6 11 E
Vennesla, *Norway* **18 F4** 58 15N 7 59 E
Venosa, *Italy* **47 B8** 40 58N 15 49 E
Venray, *Neths.* **24 C6** 51 31N 6 0 E
Vent, Îs. du, *French Polynesia* **133 S16** 17 30 S 149 30W
Venta, *Lithuania* **54 B9** 56 12N 22 42 E
Venta →, *Latvia* **54 A8** 57 24N 21 33 E
Venta de Baños, *Spain* **42 D6** 41 55N 4 30W
Venta de Cardeña = Cardeña, *Spain* **43 G6** 38 16N 4 20W
Ventana, Punta de la, *Mexico* **162 C3** 24 4N 109 48W
Ventana, Sa. de la, *Argentina* **174 D3** 38 0 S 62 30W
Ventersburg, *S. Africa* **116 D4** 28 7 S 27 9 E
Ventersburgweg = Hennenman, *S. Africa* **116 D4** 27 59 S 27 1 E
Venterstad, *S. Africa* **116 E4** 30 47 S 25 48 E
Ventimíglia, *Italy* **44 E4** 43 47N 7 36 E
Ventnor, *U.K.* **21 G6** 50 36N 1 12W
Ventoténe, *Italy* **46 B6** 40 47N 13 25 E
Ventoux, Mt., *France* **29 D9** 44 10N 5 17 E
Ventspils, *Latvia* **15 H19** 57 25N 21 32 E
Ventspils □, *Latvia* **54 A8** 57 20N 21 50 E
Ventuarí →, *Venezuela* **168 C4** 3 58N 67 2W
Ventucopa, *U.S.A.* **161 L7** 34 50N 119 29W
Ventura, *U.S.A.* **161 L7** 34 17N 119 18W
Venus, *U.S.A.* **153 H8** 27 4N 81 22W
Venus B., *Australia* **129 E6** 38 40 S 145 42 E
Vera, *Argentina* **174 B3** 29 30 S 60 20W
Vera, *Spain* **41 H3** 37 15N 1 51W
Veracruz, *Mexico* **163 D5** 19 10N 96 10W
Veracruz □, *Mexico* **163 D5** 19 0N 96 15W
Veraval, *India* **92 J4** 20 53N 70 27 E
Verbánia, *Italy* **44 C5** 45 56N 8 33 E
Verbicaro, *Italy* **47 C8** 39 45N 15 55 E
Verbier, *Switz.* **32 D4** 46 6N 7 13 E
Verceia, *Italy* **33 D8** 46 12N 9 27 E
Vercelli, *Italy* **44 C5** 45 19N 8 25 E
Verchovchevo, *Ukraine* **59 H8** 48 32N 34 10 E
Vercors ⌓, *France* **29 D9** 45 0N 5 25 E
Verdalsøra, *Norway* **14 E14** 63 48N 11 30 E
Verde →, *Argentina* **176 B3** 41 56 S 65 5W
Verde →, *Goiás, Brazil* **171 E1** 19 11 S 50 44W
Verde →, *Goiás, Brazil* **171 E1** 18 1 S 50 14W
Verde →, *Mato Grosso, Brazil* **173 C6** 11 54 S 55 48W
Verde →, *Mato Grosso do Sul, Brazil* **173 E7** 21 25 S 52 20W
Verde →, *Chihuahua, Mexico* **162 B3** 26 29N 107 58W
Verde →, *Oaxaca, Mexico* **163 D5** 15 59N 97 50W
Verde →, *Veracruz, Mexico* **162 C4** 21 10N 102 50W
Verde →, *Paraguay* **174 A4** 23 9 S 57 37W
Verde →, *U.S.A.* **146 D4** 33 33N 111 40W
Verde, Cay, *Bahamas* **164 B4** 23 0N 75 5W
Verde Grande →, *Brazil* **171 E3** 16 13 S 43 49W
Verde I., *Phil.* **80 E3** 13 33N 121 5 E
Verde Island Pass, *Phil.* **80 E3** 13 34N 120 51 E
Verde Pequeno →, *Brazil* **171 D3** 14 48 S 43 31W
Verden, *Germany* **30 C5** 52 55N 9 14 E
Verdhikoúsa, *Greece* **48 B3** 39 47N 21 59 E
Verdi, *U.S.A.* **160 F7** 39 31N 119 59W
Verdon ⌓, *France* **29 E10** 43 50N 6 5 E
Verdon →, *France* **29 E9** 43 43N 5 46 E
Verdun, *France* **27 C12** 49 9N 5 24 E
Verdun-sur-le-Doubs, *France* **27 F12** 46 54N 5 2 E
Vereeniging, *S. Africa* **117 D4** 26 38 S 27 57 E
Vereshchagino, *Russia* **64 B5** 58 5N 54 40 E
Verga, C., *Guinea* **112 C2** 10 30N 14 10W
Vergara, *Uruguay* **175 C5** 32 56 S 53 57W
Vergato, *Italy* **44 D8** 44 17N 11 7 E
Vergemont Cr. →, *Australia* **126 C3** 24 16 S 143 16 E
Vergennes, *U.S.A.* **151 B11** 44 10N 73 15W
Vergt, *France* **28 C4** 45 2N 0 43 E
Veria = Véroia, *Greece* **50 F6** 40 34N 22 12 E
Verín, *Spain* **42 D3** 41 57N 7 27W
Verkhne-Saldinsky Zavod = Verkhnyaya Salda, *Russia* **64 C8** 58 2N 60 33 E
Verkhnedvinsk = Vyerkhnyadzvinsk, *Belarus* **58 E4** 55 45N 27 58 E
Verkhneufaleysky Zavod = Verkhniy Ufaley, *Russia* **64 C8** 56 4N 60 14 E
Verkhneuralsk, *Russia* **64 E7** 53 53N 59 13 E
Verkhnevilyuysk, *Russia* **67 C13** 63 27N 120 18 E
Verkhniy Avzyan, *Russia* **64 E6** 53 32N 57 33 E
Verkhniy Baskunchak, *Russia* **61 F8** 48 14N 46 44 E
Verkhniy Tagil, *Russia* **64 C7** 57 22N 59 56 E
Verkhniy Ufaley, *Russia* **64 C8** 56 4N 60 14 E
Verkhniye Kigi, *Russia* **64 D7** 55 25N 58 37 E
Verkhnyaya Salda, *Russia* **64 C8** 58 2N 60 33 E
Verkhnyaya Tura, *Russia* **64 B7** 58 22N 59 50 E
Verkhoturye, *Russia* **64 B8** 58 52N 60 48 E
Verkhovye, *Russia* **59 F9** 52 55N 37 15 E
Verkhovyna, *Ukraine* **53 B9** 48 9N 24 47 E
Verkhoyansk, *Russia* **67 C14** 67 35N 133 25 E
Verkhoyansk Ra. = Verkhoyanskiy Khrebet, *Russia* **67 C13** 66 0N 129 0 E
Verkhoyanskiy Khrebet, *Russia* **67 C13** 66 0N 129 0 E
Verma, *Norway* **18 B5** 62 21N 8 3 E
Vermenton, *France* **27 E10** 47 40N 3 42 E
Vermilion, *Canada* **143 C6** 53 20N 110 50W
Vermilion, *U.S.A.* **150 E2** 41 25N 82 22W
Vermilion →, *Canada* **143 C6** 53 22N 110 51W
Vermilion →, *Ill., U.S.A.* **156 C7** 41 19N 89 4W
Vermilion →, *Ind., U.S.A.* **157 E9** 39 57N 87 27W
Vermilion B., *U.S.A.* **155 L9** 29 45N 91 55W
Vermilion Bay, *Canada* **143 D10** 49 51N 93 34W
Vermilion L., *U.S.A.* **154 B8** 47 53N 92 26W
Vermillion, *U.S.A.* **154 D6** 42 47N 96 56W
Vermillion →, *Canada* **140 C5** 47 38N 72 56W
Vermont, *U.S.A.* **156 D6** 40 18N 90 26W
Vermont □, *U.S.A.* **151 C12** 44 0N 73 0W
Vermosh, *Albania* **50 D3** 42 35N 19 42 E
Verna, *U.S.A.* **153 H7** 27 23N 82 16W
Vernadsky, *Antarctica* **7 C17** 65 0 S 64 0W
Vernal, *U.S.A.* **158 F9** 40 27N 109 32W
Vernalis, *U.S.A.* **160 H5** 37 36N 121 17W
Vernayaz, *Switz.* **32 D4** 46 8N 7 3 E
Vernazza, *Italy* **44 D6** 44 10N 9 45 E
Verner, *Canada* **140 C3** 46 25N 80 8W
Verneuil-sur-Avre, *France* **26 D7** 48 45N 0 55 E
Verneukpan, *S. Africa* **116 E3** 30 0 S 21 0 E
Vernier, *Switz.* **32 D2** 46 11N 6 12 E
Vérnio, *Italy* **44 D8** 44 3N 11 9 E
Vernon, *Canada* **142 C5** 50 20N 119 15W
Vernon, *France* **26 C8** 49 5N 1 30 E
Vernon, *Ill., U.S.A.* **156 F7** 38 48N 89 5W
Vernon, *Ind., U.S.A.* **157 F11** 38 59N 85 36W
Vernon, *Tex., U.S.A.* **155 H5** 34 9N 99 17W
Vernonia, *U.S.A.* **160 E3** 45 52N 123 11W
Verny = Almaty, *Kazakhstan* **65 B8** 43 15N 76 57 E
Vero Beach, *U.S.A.* **153 H9** 27 38N 80 24W
Véroia, *Greece* **50 F6** 40 34N 22 12 E
Véroli, *Italy* **45 G10** 41 41N 13 25 E
Verona, *Canada* **151 B8** 44 29N 76 42W
Verona, *Italy* **44 C7** 45 27N 10 59 E
Verona, *U.S.A.* **156 B7** 42 59N 89 32W
Verrès, *Italy* **44 C4** 45 40N 7 42 E
Verron Ra., *Papua N. G.* **132 C7** 4 21 S 152 46 E
Versailles, *France* **27 D9** 48 48N 2 8 E
Versailles, *Ill., U.S.A.* **156 E6** 39 53N 90 39W
Versailles, *Ind., U.S.A.* **157 E11** 39 4N 85 15W
Versailles, *Ky., U.S.A.* **157 F12** 38 3N 84 44W
Versailles, *Mo., U.S.A.* **156 F4** 38 26N 92 51W
Versailles, *Ohio, U.S.A.* **157 D12** 40 13N 84 29W
Versalles, *Bolivia* **173 C5** 12 44 S 63 18W
Versmold, *Germany* **30 C4** 52 2N 8 9 E
Versoix, *Switz.* **32 D2** 46 17N 6 10 E
Vert, C., *Senegal* **112 C1** 14 45N 17 30W
Vertou, *France* **26 E5** 47 10N 1 28W
Vertus, *France* **27 D11** 48 54N 4 2 E
Verulam, *S. Africa* **117 D5** 29 38 S 31 2 E
Verviers, *Belgium* **24 D5** 50 37N 5 52 E
Vervins, *France* **27 C10** 49 50N 3 53 E
Veržej, *Slovenia* **45 B13** 46 34N 16 13 E
Verzy, *France* **27 C11** 49 9N 4 10 E
Vescovato, *France* **29 F13** 42 30N 9 27 E
Veselí nad Lužnicí, *Czech Rep.* **34 B7** 49 12N 14 43 E
Veselie, *Bulgaria* **51 D11** 42 18N 27 38 E
Veselovskoye Vdkhr., *Russia* **61 G5** 46 58N 41 25 E
Veshenskaya, *Russia* **60 F5** 49 35N 41 44 E
Vesle →, *France* **27 C10** 49 23N 3 28 E
Veslyana →, *Russia* **64 A4** 60 20N 54 0 E
Vesoul, *France* **27 E13** 47 40N 6 11 E
Vessigebro, *Sweden* **17 H6** 56 58N 12 40 E
Vest-Agder □, *Norway* **18 F4** 58 30N 7 15 E
Vestbygd, *Norway* **18 F3** 58 6N 6 34 E
Vesterålen, *Norway* **14 B16** 68 45N 15 0 E
Vestfjorden, *Norway* **14 C15** 67 55N 14 0 E
Vestfold □, *Norway* **18 E7** 59 15N 10 0 E
Vestfossen, *Norway* **18 E6** 59 44N 9 52 E
Vestgrønland = Kitaa □, *Greenland* **10 C6** 70 0N 47 0W
Vestmannaeyjar, *Iceland* **11 D6** 63 27N 20 15W
Vestnes, *Norway* **18 B4** 62 39N 7 5 E
Vestre Gausdal, *Norway* **18 C7** 61 12N 10 8 E
Vestre Slidre, *Norway* **18 C5** 61 5N 8 58 E
Vestsjællands Amtskommune □, *Denmark* **17 J5** 55 30N 11 20 E
Vestspitsbergen, *Svalbard* **6 B8** 78 40N 17 0 E
Vestur-skaftafellssýsla □, *Iceland* **11 D8** 63 50N 18 30W
Vestvågøy, *Norway* **14 B15** 68 18N 13 50 E
Vesul Spitze, *Austria* **33 C10** 47 0N 10 21 E
Vesuvio, *Italy* **47 B7** 40 49N 14 26 E
Vesuvius, Mt. = Vesuvio, *Italy* **47 B7** 40 49N 14 26 E
Vesyegonsk, *Russia* **58 C9** 58 40N 37 16 E
Veszprém, *Hungary* **52 C2** 47 8N 17 57 E
Veszprém □, *Hungary* **52 C2** 47 5N 17 55 E
Vésztő, *Hungary* **52 D6** 46 55N 21 16 E
Vetapalem, *India* **95 G5** 15 47N 80 18 E
Vetlanda, *Sweden* **17 G9** 57 24N 15 3 E
Vetluga, *Russia* **60 B7** 57 53N 45 45 E
Vetlugu →, *Russia* **60 B8** 56 36N 46 4 E
Vetluzhskiy, *Kostroma, Russia* **60 A7** 58 23N 45 26 E
Vetluzhskiy, *Nizhniy Novgorod, Russia* **60 B7** 57 17N 45 12 E
Vetovo, *Bulgaria* **51 C10** 43 42N 26 16 E
Vetralla, *Italy* **45 F9** 42 20N 12 2 E
Vetren, *Bulgaria* **51 D8** 42 15N 24 3 E
Vettore, Mte., *Italy* **45 F10** 42 49N 13 16 E
Veurne, *Belgium* **24 C2** 51 5N 2 40 E
Vevay, *U.S.A.* **157 F11** 38 45N 85 4W
Veveno →, *Sudan* **107 F3** 6 40N 32 58 E
Vevey, *Switz.* **32 D3** 46 28N 6 51 E
Vévi, *Greece* **50 F5** 40 47N 21 38 E
Vex, *Switz.* **32 D4** 46 12N 7 24 E
Veynes, *France* **29 D9** 44 32N 5 49 E
Veys, *Iran* **97 D6** 31 30N 49 0 E
Vézelay, *France* **27 E10** 47 27N 3 45 E
Vézelise, *France* **27 D13** 48 30N 6 5 E
Vézère →, *France* **28 D4** 44 53N 0 53 E
Vezhen, *Bulgaria* **51 D8** 42 50N 24 20 E
Vezirköprü, *Turkey* **100 B6** 41 8N 35 27 E
Vezzani, *France* **29 F13** 42 10N 9 15 E
Vi Thanh, *Vietnam* **87 H5** 9 42N 105 26 E
Viacha, *Bolivia* **172 D4** 16 39 S 68 18W
Viadana, *Italy* **44 D7** 44 56N 10 31 E
Vialar = Tissemsilt, *Algeria* **111 A5** 35 35N 1 50 E
Viamão, *Brazil* **175 C5** 30 5 S 51 0W
Viana, *Brazil* **170 B3** 3 13 S 44 55W
Viana, *Spain* **40 C2** 42 31N 2 22W
Viana do Alentejo, *Portugal* **43 G3** 38 17N 7 59W
Viana do Bolo, *Spain* **42 C3** 42 11N 7 6W
Viana do Castelo, *Portugal* **42 D2** 41 42N 8 50W
Viana do Castelo □, *Portugal* **42 D2** 41 50N 8 30W
Vianden, *Lux.* **24 E6** 49 56N 6 12 E

Viangchan = Vientiane, Laos 86 D4 17 58N 102 36 E
Vianópolis, Brazil 171 E2 16 40 S 48 35W
Viar →, Spain 43 H5 37 36N 5 50W
Viaréggio, Italy 44 E7 43 52N 10 14 E
Viaur →, France 28 D5 44 8N 1 58 E
Vibble, Sweden 17 G12 57 37N 18 16 E
Vibo Valéntia, Italy 47 D9 38 40N 16 6 E
Viborg, Denmark 17 H3 56 27N 9 23 E
Viborg Amtskommune □, Denmark 17 H3 56 30N 9 30 E
Vibraye, France 26 D7 48 3N 0 44 E
Vic, Spain 40 D7 41 58N 2 19 E
Vic, Étang de, France 28 E7 43 29N 3 50 E
Vic-en-Bigorre, France 28 E4 43 24N 0 3 E
Vic-Fezensac, France 28 E4 43 47N 0 19 E
Vic-le-Comte, France 27 G10 45 39N 3 14 E
Vic-sur-Cère, France 28 D6 44 59N 2 38 E
Vícar, Spain 41 J2 36 50N 2 38W
Vicente Pérez Rosales △, Chile 176 B2 41 11 S 72 12W
Vicenza, Italy 45 C8 45 33N 11 33 E
Vich = Vic, Spain 40 D7 41 58N 2 19 E
Vichada □, Colombia 168 C4 5 0N 69 30W
Vichada →, Colombia 168 C4 4 55N 67 50W
Vichuga, Russia 60 B5 57 12N 41 55 E
Vichy, France 27 F10 46 9N 3 26 E
Vicksburg, Ariz., U.S.A. 161 M13 33 45N 113 45W
Vicksburg, Mich., U.S.A. 157 B11 42 7N 85 32W
Vicksburg, Miss., U.S.A. 155 J9 32 21N 90 53W
Vico, France 29 F12 42 10N 8 49 E
Vico, L. di, Italy 45 F9 42 19N 12 10 E
Vico del Gargano, Italy 45 G12 41 54N 15 57 E
Viçosa, Brazil 170 C4 9 28 S 36 14W
Viçosa do Ceará, Brazil 170 B3 3 34 S 41 5W
Vicosoprano, Switz. 33 D9 46 22N 9 38 E
Vicovu de Sus, Romania 53 C10 47 56N 25 41 E
Victor, India 92 J4 21 0N 71 30 E
Victor, U.S.A. 150 D7 42 58N 77 24W
Victor Emanuel Ra., Papua N. G. 132 C2 5 20 S 142 15 E
Victor Harbor, Australia 128 C3 35 30 S 138 37 E
Victor Hugo = Hamadia, Algeria 111 A5 35 28N 1 57 E
Victoria = Labuan, Malaysia 85 A5 5 20N 115 14 E
Victoria, Argentina 174 C3 32 40 S 60 10W
Victoria, Canada 142 D4 48 30N 123 25W
Victoria, Chile 176 A2 38 13 S 72 20W
Victoria, China 69 G1 22 17N 114 9 E
Victoria, Guinea 112 C2 10 50N 14 32W
Victoria, Malta 38 E6 36 3N 14 14 E
Victoria, Mind. Or., Phil. 80 E3 13 12N 121 12 E
Victoria, Tarlac, Phil. 80 D3 15 35N 120 41 E
Victoria, Romania 53 E9 45 44N 24 41 E
Victoria, Seychelles 121 b 4 38 S 55 28 E
Victoria, Kans., U.S.A. 154 F5 38 52N 99 9W
Victoria, Tex., U.S.A. 155 L6 28 48N 97 0W
Victoria □, Australia 128 D6 37 0 S 144 0 E
Victoria →, Australia 124 C4 15 10 S 129 40 E
Victoria, Grand L., Canada 140 C4 47 31N 77 30W
Victoria, L., Africa 118 C3 1 0 S 33 0 E
Victoria, L., Australia 128 B4 33 57 S 141 15 E
Victoria, Mt. = Tomanlivi, Fiji 133 A2 17 37 S 178 1 E
Victoria, Mt., Burma 90 E4 21 14N 93 55 E
Victoria, Mt., Papua N. G. 132 E4 8 55 S 147 32 E
Victoria Beach, Canada 143 C9 50 40N 96 35W
Victoria de Durango = Durango, Mexico 162 C4 24 3N 104 39W
Victoria de las Tunas, Cuba 164 B4 20 58N 76 59W
Victoria Falls, Zimbabwe 119 F2 17 58 S 25 52 E
Victoria Harbour, Canada 150 B5 44 45N 79 45W
Victoria I., Canada 138 A8 71 0N 111 0W
Victoria L., Canada 141 C8 48 20N 57 27W
Victoria Ld., Antarctica 7 D11 75 0 S 160 0 E
Victoria Nile →, Uganda 118 B3 2 14N 31 26 E
Victoria Peaks, Phil. 81 G2 9 22N 118 20 E
Victoria Ra., N.Z. 131 C7 42 12 S 172 7 E
Victoria River, Australia 124 C5 16 25 S 131 0 E
Victoria Str., Canada 138 B9 69 31N 100 30W
Victoria West, S. Africa 116 E3 31 25 S 23 4 E
Victorias, Phil. 81 F4 10 54N 123 5 E
Victoriaville, Canada 141 C5 46 4N 71 56W
Victorica, Argentina 174 D2 36 20 S 65 30W
Victorville, U.S.A. 161 L9 34 32N 117 18W
Vicuña, Chile 174 C1 30 0 S 70 50W
Vicuña Mackenna, Argentina 174 C3 33 53 S 64 25W
Vidal, U.S.A. 161 L12 34 7N 114 31W
Vidal Junction, U.S.A. 161 L12 34 11N 114 34W
Vidalia, U.S.A. 152 C7 32 13N 82 25W
Vidamlya, Belarus 55 F10 52 19N 23 47 E
Vidauban, France 29 E10 43 25N 6 27 E
Videbæk, Denmark 17 H2 56 6N 8 38 E
Videle, Romania 53 F10 44 17N 25 31 E
Videseter, Norway 18 C4 61 57N 7 14 E
Vidette, U.S.A. 152 B7 33 2N 82 15W
Vídho, Greece 38 B9 39 38N 19 55 E
Vidigueira, Portugal 43 G3 38 12N 7 48W
Vidin, Bulgaria 50 C6 43 59N 22 50 E
Vidio, C., Spain 42 B4 43 35N 6 14W
Vidisha, India 92 H7 23 28N 77 53 E
Vidra, Romania 53 E11 45 56N 26 55 E
Viduša, Bos.-H. 50 D2 42 55N 18 21 E
Vidzy, Belarus 15 J22 55 23N 26 37 E
Viechtach, Germany 31 F8 49 4N 12 53 E
Viedma, Argentina 176 B4 40 50 S 63 0W
Viedma, L., Argentina 176 C2 49 30 S 72 30W
Vieira do Minho, Portugal 42 D2 41 38N 8 8W
Vielha, Spain 40 C5 42 43N 0 44 E
Viella = Vielha, Spain 40 C5 42 43N 0 44 E
Vielsalm, Belgium 24 D5 50 17N 5 54 E
Vienenburg, Germany 30 D6 51 57N 10 34 E
Vieng Pou Kha, Laos 76 G3 20 41N 101 4 E
Vienna = Wien, Austria 35 C9 48 12N 16 22 E
Vienna, Ga., U.S.A. 152 C6 32 6N 83 47W
Vienna, Ill., U.S.A. 155 G10 37 25N 88 54W
Vienna, Mo., U.S.A. 156 F5 38 11N 91 57W
Vienne, France 29 C8 45 31N 4 53 E
Vienne □, France 28 B4 46 30N 0 42 E
Vienne →, France 26 E7 47 13N 0 5 E
Vientiane, Laos 86 D4 17 58N 102 36 E
Vientos, Paso de los, Caribbean 165 C5 20 0N 74 0W
Vieques, Isla de, Puerto Rico 165 d 18 8N 65 25W
Vierge Pt., St. Lucia 165 f 13 49N 60 53W
Viernheim, Germany 31 F4 49 31N 8 35 E
Viersen, Germany 30 D2 51 15N 6 23 E
Vierwaldstättersee, Switz. 33 C7 47 0N 8 30 E
Vierzon, France 27 E9 47 13N 2 5 E
Vieste, Italy 45 G13 41 53N 16 10 E
Vietnam ■, Asia 86 C6 19 0N 106 0 E
Vietz = Witnica, Poland 55 F1 52 40N 14 54 E
Vieux-Boucau-les-Bains, France 28 E2 43 48N 1 23W
Vieux Fort, St. Lucia 165 f 13 46N 60 58W
Vif, France 29 C9 45 5N 5 41 E
Viga, Phil. 80 E5 13 52N 124 18 E
Vigan, Phil. 80 C3 17 35N 120 28 E
Vigévano, Italy 44 C5 45 19N 8 51 E
Vigia = Almenara, Brazil 171 E3 16 11 S 40 42W
Vigia, Brazil 170 B2 0 50 S 48 5W
Vigía Chico, Mexico 163 D7 19 46N 87 35W
Vigla, Greece 39 A2 39 7N 20 50 E
Víglas, Ákra, Greece 38 F11 35 54N 27 51 E
Vignemalle, France 28 F3 42 47N 0 10W
Vigneulles-lès-Hattonchâtel, France 27 D12 48 59N 5 43 E
Vignola, Italy 44 D8 44 29N 11 1 E
Vigo, Spain 42 C2 42 12N 8 41W
Vigo, Ría de, Spain 42 C2 42 15N 8 45W
Vigrestad, Norway 18 F2 58 34N 5 42 E
Vigsø Bugt, Denmark 17 G2 57 8N 8 47 E
Vihiers, France 26 E6 47 10N 0 30W
Vihowa, Pakistan 92 D4 31 8N 70 30 E
Vihowa →, Pakistan 92 D4 31 8N 70 41 E
Viipuri = Vyborg, Russia 58 B5 60 43N 28 47 E
Vijayadurg, India 94 F1 16 30N 73 25 E
Vijayawada, India 94 F5 16 31N 80 39 E
Vijosë →, Albania 50 F3 40 37N 19 24 E
Vík, Iceland 11 D7 63 25N 19 1W
Vik, Norway 18 C3 61 21N 6 6 E
Vika, Sweden 16 D8 60 57N 14 28 E
Vikarabad, India 94 E3 17 20N 77 54 E
Vikarbyn, Sweden 16 D9 60 55N 15 1 E
Vike, Norway 18 D2 60 42N 5 35 E
Vikedal, Norway 18 E2 59 30N 5 55 E
Vikeke = Viqueque, E. Timor 82 C3 8 52 S 126 23 E
Vikeland, Norway 18 F4 58 5N 7 18 E
Viken, Skåne, Sweden 17 H6 56 9N 12 34 E
Viken, Västra Götaland, Sweden 17 F8 58 39N 14 20 E
Vikersund, Norway 18 E6 59 58N 9 59 E
Vikeså, Norway 18 F3 58 38N 6 3 E
Vikevåg, Norway 18 E2 59 5N 5 41 E
Viking, Canada 142 C6 53 7N 111 50W
Vikmanshyttan, Sweden 16 D9 60 18N 15 50 E
Vikna, Norway 14 D14 64 55N 10 58 E
Vikos-Aoos △, Greece 48 B2 40 0N 20 45 E
Viksøyri, Norway 18 C3 61 4N 6 34 E
Vila Alferes Chamusca = Guijá, Mozam. 117 C5 24 27 S 33 0 E
Vila António Enes = Angoche, Mozam. 119 F4 16 8 S 39 55 E
Vila Bela da Santissima Trindade, Brazil 173 C6 15 0 S 59 57W
Vila Cabral = Lichinga, Mozam. 119 E4 13 13 S 35 11 E
Vila Cabral = Niassa □, Mozam. 119 E4 13 30 S 36 0 E
Vila da Maganja, Mozam. 119 F4 17 18 S 37 30 E
Vila da Ribeira Brava, C. Verde Is. 9 j 16 32N 24 25W
Vila de Rei, Portugal 42 F2 39 41N 8 9W
Vila do Bispo, Portugal 43 H2 37 5N 8 53W
Vila do Conde, Portugal 42 D2 41 21N 8 45W
Vila do Porto, Azores 9 d4 36 56N 25 9W
Vila Franca de Xira, Portugal 43 G2 38 57N 8 59W
Vila Franca do Campo, Azores 9 d3 37 43N 25 26W
Vila Gamito, Mozam. 119 E3 14 12 S 33 0 E
Vila Gomes da Costa, Mozam. 117 C5 24 20 S 33 37 E
Vila Machado, Mozam. 119 F3 19 15 S 34 14 E
Vila Mouzinho, Mozam. 119 E3 14 48 S 34 25 E
Vila Nova de Famalicão, Portugal 42 D2 41 25N 8 32W
Vila Nova de Fos Côa, Portugal 42 D3 41 5N 7 9W
Vila Nova de Gaia, Portugal 42 D2 41 4N 8 40W
Vila Nova de Gaza = Xai-Xai, Mozam. 117 D5 25 6 S 33 31 E
Vila Nova de Ourém, Portugal 42 F2 39 40N 8 35W
Vila Nova do Corvo, Azores 9 d2 39 40N 31 8W
Vila Pereira de Eça = Ondjiva, Angola 116 B2 16 48 S 15 50 E
Vila Pery = Manica, Mozam. 117 B5 18 58 S 32 59 E
Vila Pouca de Aguiar, Portugal 42 D3 41 30N 7 38W
Vila Real, Portugal 42 D3 41 17N 7 48W
Vila Real □, Portugal 42 D3 41 36N 7 35W
Vila-real de los Infantes, Spain 40 F4 39 55N 0 3W
Vila Real de Santo António, Portugal 43 H3 37 10N 7 28W
Vila Texeira da Silva = Luau, Angola 115 E4 10 40 S 22 10 E
Vila Vasco da Gama, Mozam. 119 E3 14 54 S 32 14 E
Vila Velha, Amapá, Brazil 169 C7 3 13N 51 13W
Vila Velha, Espirito Santo, Brazil 171 F3 20 20 S 40 17W
Vila Viçosa, Portugal 43 G3 38 45N 7 27W
Vilafranca del Maestrat, Spain 40 E4 40 26N 0 16W
Vilafranca del Penedès, Spain 40 D6 41 21N 1 40 E
Vilagarcía de Arousa, Spain 42 C2 42 34N 8 46W
Vilaine →, France 26 E4 47 30N 2 27W
Vilakalaka, Vanuatu 133 E5 15 25 S 167 42 E
Vilanandro, Tanjona, Madag. 117 B7 16 11 S 44 27 E
Vilanculos, Mozam. 117 C6 22 1 S 35 17 E
Vilanova de Castelló, Spain 41 F4 39 5N 0 31W
Vilanova i la Geltrú, Spain 40 D6 41 13N 1 40 E
Vilar Formosa, Portugal 42 E4 40 38N 6 45W
Vilaseca, Spain 40 D6 41 7N 1 9 E
Vilaseca-Salou = Vilaseca, Spain 40 D6 41 7N 1 9 E
Vilbjerg, Denmark 17 H2 56 12N 8 46 E
Vilcabamba, Cordillera, Peru 172 C3 13 0 S 73 0W
Vilcanchos, Peru 172 C3 13 40 S 74 25W
Vilcheka, Zemlya, Russia 6 A11 80 30N 60 30 E
Vilches, Spain 43 G7 38 12N 3 30W
Vileyka, Belarus 58 E4 54 30N 26 53 E
Vilhelmina, Sweden 14 D17 64 35N 16 39 E
Vilhena, Brazil 173 C5 12 40 S 60 5W
Viliya = Neris →, Lithuania 15 J21 55 8N 24 16 E
Viljandi, Estonia 15 G21 58 28N 25 30 E
Viljoensdorp = Newcastle, S. Africa 117 D4 27 45 S 29 58 E
Vilkaviškis, Lithuania 54 D10 54 39N 23 2 E
Vilkija, Lithuania 54 C10 55 3N 23 35 E
Vilkitskogo, Proliv, Russia 67 B11 78 0N 103 0 E
Vilkomir = Ukmergė, Lithuania 15 J21 55 15N 24 45 E
Vilkovo = Vylkove, Ukraine 53 E14 45 28N 29 32 E
Villa Abecia, Bolivia 174 A2 21 0 S 68 18W
Villa Ahumada, Mexico 162 A3 30 38N 106 30W
Villa Ana, Argentina 174 B4 28 28 S 59 40W
Villa Ángela, Argentina 174 B3 27 34 S 60 45W
Villa Bela = Serra Talhada, Brazil 170 C4 7 59 S 38 18W
Villa Bella, Bolivia 173 C4 10 25 S 65 22W
Villa Bruzual, Venezuela 168 C4 9 20N 69 6W
Villa Cañás, Argentina 174 C3 34 0 S 61 35W
Villa Cecilia = Ciudad Madero, Mexico 163 C5 22 19N 97 50W
Villa Cisneros = Dakhla, W. Sahara 110 D1 23 50N 15 53W
Villa Colón, Argentina 174 C2 31 38 S 68 20W
Villa Constitución, Argentina 174 C3 33 15 S 60 20W
Villa de Cura, Venezuela 168 A4 10 2N 67 29W
Villa de María, Argentina 174 B3 29 55 S 63 43W
Villa del Nevoso = Ilirska-Bistrica, Slovenia 45 C11 45 34N 14 14 E
Villa del Rio, Spain 43 H6 37 59N 4 17W
Villa del Rosario, Venezuela 168 A3 10 19N 72 19W
Villa Dolores, Argentina 174 C2 31 58 S 65 15W
Villa Frontera, Mexico 162 B4 26 56N 101 27W
Villa Grove, U.S.A. 157 E8 39 52N 88 10W
Villa Guillermina, Argentina 174 B4 28 15 S 59 29W
Villa Hayes, Paraguay 174 B4 25 5 S 57 20W
Villa Iris, Argentina 174 D3 38 12 S 63 12W
Villa Juárez, Mexico 162 B4 27 37N 100 44W
Villa María, Argentina 174 C3 32 20 S 63 10W
Villa Mazán, Argentina 174 B2 28 40 S 66 30W
Villa Minozzo, Italy 44 D7 44 22N 10 28 E
Villa Montes, Bolivia 174 A3 21 10 S 63 30W
Villa Ocampo, Argentina 174 B4 28 30 S 59 20W
Villa Ocampo, Mexico 162 B3 26 29N 105 30W
Villa Ojo de Agua, Argentina 174 B3 29 30 S 63 44W
Villa Rica, U.S.A. 152 B5 33 44N 84 55W
Villa San Giovanni, Italy 47 D8 38 13N 15 38 E
Villa San José, Argentina 174 C4 32 12 S 58 15W
Villa San Martín, Argentina 174 B3 28 15 S 64 9W
Villa Sanjurjo = Al Hoceïma, Morocco 110 A4 35 8N 3 58W
Villa Santina, Italy 45 B9 46 24N 12 55 E
Villa Unión, Mexico 162 C3 23 12N 106 14W
Villaba, Phil. 81 F5 11 13N 124 24 E
Villablino, Spain 42 C4 42 57N 6 19W
Villacarlos, Spain 38 B5 39 53N 4 17 E
Villacarriedo, Spain 42 B7 43 14N 3 48W
Villacarrillo, Spain 43 G7 38 7N 3 3W
Villacastín, Spain 42 E6 40 46N 4 25W
Villach, Austria 34 E6 46 37N 13 51 E
Villacidro, Italy 46 C1 39 27N 8 44 E
Villada, Spain 42 C6 42 15N 4 59W
Villadiego, Spain 42 C6 42 31N 4 1W
Villadóssola, Italy 44 B5 46 4N 8 16 E
Villafeliche, Spain 40 D3 41 10N 1 30W
Villafranca, Spain 40 C3 42 17N 1 46W
Villafranca de los Barros, Spain 43 G4 38 35N 6 18W
Villafranca de los Caballeros, Spain 43 F7 39 26N 3 21W
Villafranca del Cid = Vilafranca del Maestrat, Spain 40 E4 40 26N 0 16W
Villafranca del Panadés = Vilafranca del Penedès, Spain 40 D6 41 21N 1 40 E
Villafranca di Verona, Italy 44 C7 45 21N 10 50 E
Villafranca Tirrena, Italy 47 D8 38 20N 15 25 E
Villagio Mussolini = Arborea, Italy 46 C1 39 46N 8 35 E
Villagrán, Mexico 163 C5 24 29N 99 29W
Villaguay, Argentina 174 C4 32 0 S 59 0W
Villaharta, Spain 43 G6 38 9N 4 54W
Villahermosa, Mexico 163 D6 17 59N 92 55W
Villahermosa, Spain 41 G2 38 46N 2 52W
Villaines-la-Juhel, France 26 D6 48 21N 0 20W
Villajoyosa, Spain 41 G4 38 30N 0 12W
Villalba, Spain 42 B3 43 26N 7 40W
Villalba de Guardo, Spain 42 C6 42 42N 4 49W
Villalón de Campos, Spain 42 C5 42 5N 5 4W
Villalpando, Spain 42 D5 41 51N 5 25W
Villaluenga, Spain 42 E7 40 2N 3 54W
Villamanán, Spain 42 C5 42 19N 5 35W
Villamartín, Spain 43 J5 36 52N 5 38W
Villamayor de Santiago, Spain 40 F2 39 50N 2 59W
Villamblard, France 28 C4 45 2N 0 32 E
Villanova Monteleone, Italy 46 B1 40 30N 8 28 E
Villanueva, Colombia 168 A3 10 37N 72 59W
Villanueva, U.S.A. 155 H2 35 16N 105 22W
Villanueva de Castellón = Vilanova de Castelló, Spain 41 F4 39 5N 0 31W
Villanueva de Córdoba, Spain 43 G6 38 20N 4 38W
Villanueva de la Fuente, Spain 41 G2 38 42N 2 42W
Villanueva de la Serena, Spain 43 G5 38 59N 5 50W
Villanueva de la Sierra, Spain 42 E4 40 12N 6 24W
Villanueva de los Castillejos, Spain 43 H3 37 30N 7 15W
Villanueva de los Infantes, Spain 43 G7 38 43N 3 1W
Villanueva del Arzobispo, Spain 41 G2 38 10N 3 0W
Villanueva del Fresno, Spain 43 G3 38 23N 7 10W
Villanueva y Geltrú = Vilanova i la Geltrú, Spain 40 D6 41 13N 1 40 E
Villaputzu, Italy 46 C2 39 26N 9 34 E
Villaquilambre, Spain 42 C5 42 39N 5 33W
Villar del Arzobispo, Spain 40 F4 39 44N 0 50W
Villar del Rey, Spain 43 F4 39 7N 6 50W
Villard-de-Lans, France 29 C9 45 3N 5 33 E
Villarramiel, Spain 42 C6 42 2N 4 55W
Villarreal = Vila-real de los Infantes, Spain 40 F4 39 55N 0 3W
Villarrica, Chile 176 A2 39 15 S 72 15W
Villarrica, Paraguay 174 B4 25 40 S 56 30W
Villarrica △, Chile 176 A2 39 24 S 71 46W
Villarrobledo, Spain 41 F2 39 18N 2 36W
Villarroya de la Sierra, Spain 40 D3 41 27N 1 46W
Villarrubia de los Ojos, Spain 43 F7 39 14N 3 36W
Villars-les-Dombes, France 27 F12 46 0N 5 3 E
Villasayas, Spain 40 D2 41 24N 2 39W
Villaseca de los Gamitos = Villaseco de los Gamitos, Spain 42 D4 41 2N 6 7W
Villaseco de los Gamitos, Spain 42 D4 41 2N 6 7W
Villasimíus, Italy 46 C2 39 8N 9 31 E
Villastar, Spain 40 E3 40 17N 1 9W
Villatobas, Spain 42 F7 39 54N 3 20W
Villavicencio, Argentina 174 C2 32 28 S 69 0W
Villavicencio, Colombia 168 C3 4 9N 73 37W
Villaviciosa, Spain 42 B5 43 32N 5 27W
Villazón, Bolivia 174 A2 22 0 S 65 35W
Ville-Marie, Canada 140 C4 47 20N 79 30W
Ville Platte, U.S.A. 155 K8 30 41N 92 17W
Villedieu-les-Poêles, France 26 D5 48 50N 1 13W
Villefort, France 28 D7 44 28N 3 56 E
Villefranche-de-Lauragais, France 28 E5 43 25N 1 44 E
Villefranche-de-Rouergue, France 28 D6 44 21N 2 2 E
Villefranche-du-Périgord, France 28 D5 44 38N 1 5 E
Villefranche-sur-Saône, France 29 C8 45 59N 4 43 E
Villegrande, Bolivia 173 D5 18 30 S 64 10W
Villel, Spain 40 E3 40 14N 1 12W
Villemur-sur-Tarn, France 28 E5 43 51N 1 31 E
Villena, Spain 41 G4 38 39N 0 52W
Villenauxe-la-Grande, France 27 D10 48 35N 3 33 E
Villenave-d'Ornon, France 28 D3 44 46N 0 33W
Villeneuve, Switz. 32 D3 46 24N 6 56 E
Villeneuve-d'Ascq, France 27 B10 50 38N 3 9 E
Villeneuve-l'Archevêque, France 27 D10 48 14N 3 32 E
Villeneuve-lès-Avignon, France 29 E8 43 58N 4 49 E
Villeneuve-sur-Allier, France 27 F10 46 40N 3 13 E
Villeneuve-sur-Lot, France 28 D4 44 24N 0 42 E
Villeneuve-sur-Yonne, France 27 D10 48 5N 3 18 E
Villeréal, France 28 D4 44 38N 0 45 E
Villers-Bocage, France 26 C6 49 3N 0 40W
Villers-Cotterêts, France 27 C10 49 15N 3 4 E
Villers-sur-Mer, France 26 C6 49 21N 0 2W
Villersexel, France 27 E13 47 33N 6 26 E
Villerupt, France 27 C12 49 28N 5 55 E
Villeurbanne, France 29 C8 45 46N 4 55 E
Villiers, S. Africa 117 D4 27 2 S 28 36 E
Villingen-Schwenningen, Germany 31 G4 48 3N 8 26 E
Villisca, U.S.A. 156 D2 40 56N 94 59W
Villmanstrand = Lappeenranta, Finland 15 F23 61 3N 28 12 E
Villupuram, India 95 J4 11 59N 79 31 E
Vilna = Vilnius, Lithuania 15 J21 54 38N 25 19 E
Vilna, Canada 142 C6 54 7N 111 55W
Vilnius, Lithuania 15 J21 54 38N 25 19 E
Vils, Austria 34 D3 47 33N 10 38 E
Vils →, Bayern, Germany 31 G9 48 37N 13 11 E
Vils →, Bayern, Germany 31 F7 49 10N 11 57 E
Vilsbiburg, Germany 31 G8 48 26N 12 22 E
Vilshofen, Germany 31 G9 48 37N 13 11 E
Vilusi, Serbia & M. 50 D2 42 44N 18 34 E
Vilvoorde, Belgium 24 D4 50 56N 4 26 E
Vilyuy →, Russia 67 C13 64 24N 126 26 E
Vilyuysk, Russia 67 C13 63 40N 121 35 E
Vimianzo, Spain 42 B1 43 7N 9 2W
Vimioso, Portugal 42 D4 41 35N 6 31W
Vimmerby, Sweden 17 G9 57 40N 15 55 E
Vimoutiers, France 26 D7 48 57N 0 10 E
Vimperk, Czech Rep. 34 B6 49 3N 13 46 E
Vina →, Cameroon 114 A3 7 45N 15 36 E
Viña del Mar, Chile 174 C1 33 0 S 71 30W
Vinarós, Spain 40 E5 40 30N 0 27 E
Vincennes, U.S.A. 157 F9 38 41N 87 32W
Vincent, U.S.A. 161 L8 34 33N 118 11W
Vinces, Ecuador 168 D2 1 32 S 79 45W
Vinchina, Argentina 174 B2 28 45 S 68 15W
Vindava = Ventspils, Latvia 15 H19 57 25N 21 32 E
Vindelälven →, Sweden 14 E18 63 55N 19 50 E
Vindeln, Sweden 14 D18 64 12N 19 43 E
Vinderup, Denmark 17 H2 56 29N 8 45 E
Vindhya Ra., India 92 H7 22 50N 77 0 E
Vine Grove, U.S.A. 157 G11 37 49N 85 59W
Vineland, U.S.A. 148 F8 39 29N 75 2W
Vineuil, France 26 47 35N 1 22 E
Vinga, Romania 52 D6 46 1N 21 14 E
Vingåker, Sweden 16 E9 59 2N 15 52 E
Vingelen, Norway 18 B7 62 25N 10 52 E
Vingnes, Norway 18 C7 61 7N 10 26 E
Vinh, Vietnam 86 C5 18 45N 105 38 E
Vinh Linh, Vietnam 86 D6 17 4N 107 2 E
Vinh Loi = Bac Lieu, Vietnam 87 H5 9 17N 105 43 E
Vinh Long, Vietnam 87 G5 10 16N 105 57 E
Vinh Yen, Vietnam 76 G5 21 21N 105 35 E
Vinhais, Portugal 42 D3 41 50N 7 5W
Vinica, Croatia 45 B13 46 20N 16 9 E
Vinica, Macedonia 50 E6 41 53N 22 30 E
Vinica, Slovenia 45 C12 45 28N 15 16 E
Vinita, U.S.A. 155 G7 36 39N 95 9W
Vinje, Hordaland, Norway 18 D3 60 48N 6 30 E
Vinje, Sør-Trøndelag, Norway 18 A5 63 12N 9 0 E
Vinje, Telemark, Norway 18 E4 59 37N 7 51 E
Vinkovci, Croatia 52 E3 45 19N 18 48 E
Vinnitsa = Vinnytsya, Ukraine 59 H5 49 15N 28 30 E
Vinnytsya, Ukraine 59 H5 49 15N 28 30 E
Vinodelnoye = Ipatovo, Russia 61 H6 45 45N 42 50 E
Vinslöv, Sweden 17 H7 56 7N 13 55 E
Vinson Massif, Antarctica 7 D16 78 35 S 85 25W
Vinstra, Norway 18 C6 61 37N 9 44 E
Vinstra →, Norway 18 C6 61 37N 9 44 E
Vintar, Phil. 80 B3 18 14N 120 39 E
Vintjärn, Sweden 16 D10 60 50N 16 4 E
Vinton, Calif., U.S.A. 160 F6 39 48N 120 10W
Vinton, Iowa, U.S.A. 156 B4 42 10N 92 1W
Vinton, La., U.S.A. 155 K8 30 11N 93 35W
Vinţu de Jos, Romania 53 D8 46 0N 23 30 E
Vinukonda, India 95 F4 16 4N 79 45 E
Viöl, Germany 30 A5 54 34N 9 11 E
Viola, U.S.A. 156 C6 41 12N 90 35W
Violet Town, Australia 129 D6 36 38 S 145 42 E
Vipacco = Vipava, Slovenia 45 C10 45 51N 13 58 E
Vipava, Slovenia 45 C10 45 51N 13 58 E
Vipiteno, Italy 45 B8 46 54N 11 26 E
Viqueque, E. Timor 82 C3 8 52 S 126 23 E
Vir, Croatia 45 D12 44 17N 15 3 E
Vira, Switz. 33 D7 46 8N 8 50 E
Virac, Phil. 80 E5 13 30N 124 20 E
Virachey, Cambodia 86 F6 13 59N 106 49 E
Virachey △, Cambodia 86 E6 14 14N 106 55 E
Virago Sd., Canada 142 C2 54 0N 132 30W
Virajpet = Virarajendrapet, India 95 H2 12 10N 75 50 E
Viramgam, India 92 H5 23 5N 72 0 E
Viranşehir, Turkey 101 D8 37 13N 39 45 E
Virarajendrapet, India 95 H2 12 10N 75 50 E
Virawah, Pakistan 92 G4 24 31N 70 46 E
Virbalis, Lithuania 54 D9 54 39N 22 49 E
Virden, Canada 143 D8 49 50N 100 56W
Virden, U.S.A. 156 E7 39 30N 89 46W
Vire, France 26 D6 48 50N 0 53W
Vire →, France 26 C5 49 20N 1 7W
Virei, Angola 115 F2 15 43 S 12 52 E
Virgem da Lapa, Brazil 171 E3 16 49 S 42 21W
Vírgenes, C., Argentina 176 D3 52 19 S 68 21W
Virgin →, U.S.A. 159 H6 36 28N 114 21W
Virgin Gorda, Br. Virgin Is. 165 e 18 30N 64 26W
Virgin Is. (British) ☑, W. Indies 165 e 18 30N 64 30W
Virgin Is. (U.S.) ☑, W. Indies 165 e 18 20N 65 0W
Virgin Islands △, U.S. Virgin Is. 165 C7 18 21N 64 43W
Virginia, S. Africa 116 D4 28 8 S 26 55 E
Virginia, Ill., U.S.A. 156 E6 39 57N 90 13W
Virginia, Minn., U.S.A. 154 B8 47 31N 92 32W
Virginia □, U.S.A. 148 G7 37 30N 78 45W
Virginia Beach, U.S.A. 148 G8 36 51N 75 59W
Virginia City, Mont., U.S.A. 158 D8 45 18N 111 56W
Virginia City, Nev., U.S.A. 160 F7 39 19N 119 39W
Virginia Falls, Canada 142 A3 61 38N 125 42W
Virginiatown, Canada 140 C4 48 9N 79 36W
Virje, Croatia 45 B13 46 4N 16 59 E
Viroqua, U.S.A. 154 D9 43 34N 90 53W
Virovitica, Croatia 52 E2 45 51N 17 21 E
Virpazar, Serbia & M. 50 D3 42 14N 19 6 E
Virpur, India 92 J4 21 51N 70 42 E
Virserum, Sweden 17 G9 57 20N 15 35 E
Virton, Belgium 25 E5 49 35N 5 32 E
Virú, Peru 172 B2 8 25 S 78 45W
Virudunagar, India 95 K3 9 30N 77 58 E
Virunga △, Dem. Rep. of the Congo 118 B2 0 5N 29 38 E
Vis, Croatia 45 E13 43 4N 16 10 E
Visalia, U.S.A. 160 J7 36 20N 119 18W
Visayan Sea, Phil. 81 F4 11 30N 123 30 E
Visby, Sweden 17 G12 57 37N 18 18 E
Viscount Melville Sd., Canada 6 B2 74 10N 108 0W
Visé, Belgium 24 D5 50 44N 5 41 E
Višegrad, Bos.-H. 52 G4 43 47N 19 17 E
Viseu, Brazil 170 B2 1 10 S 46 5W
Viseu, Portugal 42 E3 40 40N 7 55W
Viseu □, Portugal 42 E3 40 40N 7 55W
Vişeu de Sus, Romania 53 C9 47 45N 24 25 E
Vishakhapatnam, India 94 F6 17 45N 83 20 E
Vishera →, Russia 64 A6 59 55N 56 25 E
Vişina, Romania 53 G9 43 52N 24 27 E
Vişineşti, Moldova 53 D13 46 20N 28 27 E
Visingsö, Sweden 17 F8 58 2N 14 20 E
Viskafors, Sweden 17 G6 57 37N 12 50 E
Viskan →, Sweden 17 G6 57 14N 12 12 E
Viški Kanal, Croatia 45 E13 43 4N 16 5 E
Vislanda, Sweden 17 H8 56 46N 14 30 E
Visnagar, India 92 H5 23 45N 72 32 E
Višnja Gora, Slovenia 45 C11 45 58N 14 45 E
Viso, Mte., Italy 44 D4 44 38N 7 5 E
Viso del Marqués, Spain 43 G7 38 32N 3 34W
Visoko, Bos.-H. 52 G3 43 58N 18 10 E
Visokoi I., Antarctica 7 B1 56 43 S 27 15W
Visp, Switz. 32 D5 46 17N 7 52 E
Vispa →, Switz. 32 D5 46 9N 7 48 E
Vissefjärda, Sweden 17 H9 56 32N 15 35 E
Visselhövede, Germany 30 C5 52 59N 9 34 E
Vissenbjerg, Denmark 17 J4 55 23N 10 7 E
Vissoie, Switz. 32 D5 46 13N 7 36 E
Vista, U.S.A. 161 M9 33 12N 117 14W
Vistonikos, Ormos = Vistonís, Límni, Greece 51 E9 41 0N 25 7 E
Vistonís, Límni, Greece 51 E9 41 0N 25 7 E
Vistula = Wisła →, Poland 54 D5 54 22N 18 55 E
Vistula Lagoon = Zalew Wiślany, Poland 54 D6 54 20N 19 50 E
Vit →, Bulgaria 51 C8 43 30N 24 30 E
Vita, India 94 F2 17 17N 74 33 E
Vitanje, Slovenia 45 B12 46 25N 15 18 E
Vitebsk = Vitsyebsk, Belarus 58 E6 55 10N 30 15 E
Viterbo, Italy 45 F9 42 25N 12 6 E
Vitez, Bos.-H. 52 F2 44 10N 17 48 E
Viti Levu, Fiji 133 A1 17 30 S 177 30 E
Vitiaz Str., Papua N. G. 132 C4 5 40 S 147 10 E
Vitigudino, Spain 42 D4 41 1N 6 26W
Vitim, Russia 67 D12 59 28N 112 35 E
Vitim →, Russia 67 D12 59 26N 112 34 E
Vitina, Bos.-H. 45 E14 43 17N 17 29 E
Vitina, Greece 48 D4 37 40N 22 10 E
Vítkov, Czech Rep. 35 B10 49 46N 17 45 E
Vitória = Vitória de São Antão, Brazil 170 C4 8 10 S 35 20W
Vitória, Espirito Santo, Brazil 171 F3 20 20 S 40 22W

Vitória, *Pará, Brazil* **169 D7** 2 54 S 52 1W
Vitória da Conquista, *Brazil* **171 D3** 14 51 S 40 51W
Vitória de São Antão, *Brazil* **170 C4** 8 10 S 35 20W
Vitoria-Gasteiz, *Spain* **40 C2** 42 50N 2 41W
Vitória Seamount, *India* **8 J8** 20 0 S 44 0W
Vitorino Friere, *Brazil* **170 B2** 4 4 S 45 10W
Vitosha △, *Bulgaria* **50 D7** 42 36N 23 18 E
Vitré, *France* **26 D5** 48 8N 1 12W
Vitry-le-François, *France* **27 D11** 48 43N 4 33 E
Vitry-sur-Seine, *France* **27 D9** 48 47N 2 24 E
Vitsand, *Sweden* **16 D7** 60 20N 13 0 E
Vitsi, Óros, *Greece* **50 F5** 40 40N 21 25 E
Vitsyebsk, *Belarus* **58 E6** 55 10N 30 15 E
Vittaryd, *Sweden* **17 H7** 56 58N 13 57 E
Vitteaux, *France* **27 E11** 47 24N 4 30 E
Vittel, *France* **27 D12** 48 12N 5 57 E
Vittória, *Italy* **47 F7** 36 57N 14 32 E
Vittório = Vittório Véneto, *Italy* **45 C9** 45 59N 12 18 E
Vittório Véneto, *Italy* **45 C9** 45 59N 12 18 E
Vittoriosa, *Malta* **38 F8** 35 54N 14 31 E
Vittsjö, *Sweden* **17 H7** 56 20N 13 40 E
Vitznau, *Switz.* **33 B6** 47 1N 8 29 E
Viveiro, *Spain* **42 B3** 43 39N 7 38W
Vivian, *U.S.A.* **155 J8** 32 53N 93 59W
Viviers, *France* **29 D8** 44 30N 4 40 E
Vivonne, *Australia* **128 C2** 35 59 S 137 9 E
Vivonne, *France* **28 B4** 46 25N 0 15 E
Vivonne B., *Australia* **128 C2** 35 59 S 137 9 E
Viwa, *Fiji* **133 A1** 17 10 S 177 58 E
Vizagapatam = Vishakhapatnam, *India* **94 F6** 17 45N 83 20 E
Vizcaíno, Desierto de, *Mexico* **162 B2** 27 40N 113 50W
Vizcaíno, Sierra, *Mexico* **162 B2** 27 30N 114 0W
Vizcaya □, *Spain* **40 B2** 43 15N 2 45W
Vize, *Turkey* **51 E11** 41 34N 27 45 E
Vizianagaram, *India* **94 E6** 18 6N 83 30 E
Vizille, *France* **29 C9** 45 5N 5 46 E
Viziňada, *Croatia* **45 C10** 45 20N 13 46 E
Viziru, *Romania* **53 E12** 45 0N 27 43 E
Vizlinsky Zaliv = Zalew Wiślany, *Poland* **54 D6** 54 20N 19 50 E
Vizzini, *Italy* **47 E7** 37 10N 14 45 E
Vlaardingen, *Neths.* **24 C4** 51 55N 4 21 E
Vlădeasa, Vf., *Romania* **52 D7** 46 47N 22 50 E
Vladičin Han, *Serbia & M.* **50 D6** 42 42N 22 1 E
Vladikavkaz, *Russia* **61 J7** 43 0N 44 35 E
Vladimir, *Russia* **58 D11** 56 15N 40 30 E
Vladimir Volynskiy = Volodymyr-Volynskyy, *Ukraine* **59 G3** 50 50N 24 18 E
Vladimirci, *Serbia & M.* **50 B3** 44 36N 19 50 E
Vladimirovac, *Serbia & M.* **52 E5** 45 1N 20 53 E
Vladimirovka = Yuzhno-Sakhalinsk, *Russia* **67 E15** 46 58N 142 45 E
Vladimirovka, *Russia* **61 F8** 48 27N 46 10 E
Vladimirovo, *Bulgaria* **50 C7** 43 32N 23 22 E
Vladimorvka, *Kazakhstan* **60 E10** 50 51N 51 8 E
Vladislavovka, *Ukraine* **59 K8** 45 12N 35 29 E
Vladivostok, *Russia* **67 E14** 43 10N 131 53 E
Vlăhiţa, *Romania* **53 D10** 46 21N 25 31 E
Vlakhiótis, *Greece* **48 E4** 36 52N 22 42 E
Vlasenica, *Bos.-H.* **52 F3** 44 11N 18 59 E
Vlašić, *Bos.-H.* **52 F2** 44 19N 17 37 E
Vlašim, *Czech Rep.* **34 B7** 49 40N 14 53 E
Vlasinsko Jezero, *Serbia & M.* **50 D6** 42 44N 22 22 E
Vlasotince, *Serbia & M.* **50 D6** 42 59N 22 7 E
Vlieland, *Neths.* **24 A4** 53 16N 4 55 E
Vlissingen, *Neths.* **24 C3** 51 26N 3 34 E
Vlorë, *Albania* **50 F3** 40 32N 19 28 E
Vlorës, Gjiri i, *Albania* **50 F3** 40 29N 19 27 E
Vltava →, *Czech Rep.* **34 A7** 50 21N 14 30 E
Vo Dat, *Vietnam* **87 G6** 11 9N 107 31 E
Vobarno, *Italy* **33 E11** 45 39N 10 30 E
Voćin, *Croatia* **52 E2** 45 37N 17 33 E
Vöcklabruck, *Austria* **34 C6** 48 1N 13 39 E
Vodice, *Croatia* **45 E12** 43 47N 15 47 E
Vodňany, *Czech Rep.* **34 B7** 49 9N 14 11 E
Vodnjan, *Croatia* **45 D10** 44 59N 13 52 E
Vodopyanovo = Donskoy, *Russia* **58 F10** 53 55N 38 15 E
Voe, *U.K.* **22 A7** 60 21N 1 16W
Vogar, *Iceland* **11 D4** 63 58N 22 22W
Vogel Pk., *Nigeria* **113 D7** 8 24N 11 47 E
Vogelkop = Doberai, Jazirah, *Indonesia* **83 B4** 1 25 S 133 0 E
Vogelsberg, *Germany* **30 E5** 50 31N 9 12 E
Voghera, *Italy* **44 D6** 44 59N 9 1 E
Vogorno, *Switz.* **33 D7** 46 13N 8 52 E
Voh, *N. Cal.* **133 T18** 20 58 S 164 42 E
Vohibinany, *Madag.* **117 B8** 18 49 S 49 4 E
Vohilava, *Madag.* **117 C8** 21 4 S 48 0 E
Vohimarina = Iharana, *Madag.* **117 A9** 13 25 S 50 0 E
Vohimena, Tanjon' i, *Madag.* **117 D8** 25 36 S 45 8 E
Vohipeno, *Madag.* **117 C8** 22 22 S 47 51 E
Voi, *Kenya* **118 C4** 3 25 S 38 32 E
Void-Vacon, *France* **27 D12** 48 40N 5 36 E
Voineşti, *Iaşi, Romania* **53 C12** 47 5N 27 27 E
Voineşti, *Prahova, Romania* **53 E10** 45 5N 25 14 E
Voíotía □, *Greece* **48 C5** 38 20N 23 0 E
Voiron, *France* **29 C9** 45 22N 5 35 E
Voisey B., *Canada* **141 A7** 56 15N 61 50W
Voitsberg, *Austria* **34 D8** 47 3N 15 9 E
Vojens, *Denmark* **17 J3** 55 16N 9 18 E
Vojmsjön, *Sweden* **14 D17** 65 0N 16 24 E
Vojnić, *Croatia* **45 C12** 45 19N 15 43 E
Vojnik, *Italy* **45 B12** 46 18N 15 19 E
Vojvodina □, *Serbia & M.* **52 E5** 45 20N 20 0 E
Vokeo I., *Papua N. G.* **132 B3** 3 14 S 144 2 E
Vokhtoga, *Russia* **58 C11** 58 46N 41 8 E
Volary, *Czech Rep.* **34 C6** 48 54N 13 52 E
Volborg, *U.S.A.* **154 C2** 45 51N 105 41W
Volcán de Colima △, *Mexico* **162 D4** 19 30N 103 40W
Volcano, *U.S.A.* **145 D6** 19 26N 155 14W
Volcano Is. = Kazan-Rettō, *Pac. Oc.* **134 E6** 25 0N 141 0 E
Volcans △, *Rwanda* **118 C2** 1 30 S 29 26 E
Volcans d'Auvergne ⌓, *France* **28 C6** 45 20N 2 40 E
Volchansk = Vovchansk, *Ukraine* **59 G9** 50 17N 36 58 E
Volchansk, *Russia* **64 B8** 59 56N 60 4 E
Volchya →, *Ukraine* **59 H8** 48 32N 36 0 E
Volda, *Norway* **18 B3** 62 9N 6 5 E
Volga = Privolzhskiy □, *Russia* **60 B10** 56 0N 50 0 E
Volga, *Russia* **58 C10** 57 58N 38 16 E
Volga →, *Russia* **61 G9** 46 0N 48 30 E
Volga Hts. = Privolzhskaya Vozvyshennost, *Russia* **60 E7** 51 0N 46 0 E
Volgo-Baltiyskiy Kanal, *Russia* **58 B9** 60 0N 38 0 E
Volgo-Donskoy Kanal, *Russia* **61 F7** 48 40N 43 37 E
Volgodonsk, *Russia* **61 G6** 47 33N 42 5 E
Volgograd, *Russia* **61 F7** 48 40N 44 25 E
Volgogradskoye Vdkhr., *Russia* **60 E8** 50 0N 45 20 E
Volgorechensk, *Russia* **60 B5** 57 28N 41 14 E
Volímai, *Greece* **39 D2** 37 52N 20 39 E
Volintiri, *Moldova* **53 D14** 46 26N 29 37 E
Volissós, *Greece* **49 C7** 38 29N 25 54 E
Volkach, *Germany* **31 F6** 49 52N 10 14 E
Völkermarkt, *Austria* **34 E7** 46 39N 14 39 E
Volkhov, *Russia* **58 C7** 59 55N 32 15 E
Volkhov →, *Russia* **58 B7** 60 8N 32 20 E
Volkhovstroy = Volkhov, *Russia* **58 C7** 59 55N 32 15 E
Völklingen, *Germany* **31 F2** 49 15N 6 50 E
Volkovysk = Vawkavysk, *Belarus* **59 F3** 53 9N 24 30 E
Volksrust, *S. Africa* **117 D4** 27 24 S 29 53 E
Voll, *Norway* **18 B4** 62 31N 7 27 E
Volnansk, *Ukraine* **59 H8** 48 2N 35 29 E
Volnovakha, *Ukraine* **59 J9** 47 35N 37 30 E
Volochanka, *Russia* **67 B10** 71 0N 94 28 E
Volodarsk, *Russia* **60 B6** 56 12N 43 15 E
Volodymyr-Volynskyy, *Ukraine* **59 G3** 50 50N 24 18 E
Vologda, *Russia* **58 C10** 59 10N 39 45 E
Volokolamsk, *Russia* **58 D8** 56 5N 35 57 E
Volokonovka, *Russia* **59 G9** 50 33N 37 52 E
Vólos, *Greece* **48 B4** 39 24N 22 59 E
Vološinovo = Novi Bečej, *Serbia & M.* **52 E5** 45 36N 20 10 E
Volosovo, *Russia* **58 C5** 59 27N 29 32 E
Volovets, *Ukraine* **53 B8** 48 43N 23 11 E
Volovo, *Russia* **58 F10** 53 35N 38 1 E
Volozhin = Valozhyn, *Belarus* **58 E4** 54 3N 26 30 E
Volsk, *Russia* **60 D8** 52 5N 47 22 E
Volta □, *Ghana* **113 D5** 7 0N 0 30 E
Volta →, *Ghana* **113 D5** 5 46N 0 41 E
Volta, L., *Ghana* **113 D5** 7 30N 0 0W
Volta Blanche = White Volta →, *Ghana* **113 D4** 9 10N 1 15W
Volta Redonda, *Brazil* **171 F3** 22 31 S 44 5W
Voltaire, C., *Australia* **124 B4** 14 16 S 125 35 E
Volterra, *Italy* **44 E7** 43 24N 10 51 E
Voltri, *Italy* **44 D5** 44 26N 8 45 E
Volturno →, *Italy* **46 A6** 41 1N 13 55 E
Volubilis, *Morocco* **110 B3** 34 2N 5 33W
Vólvi, L., *Greece* **50 F7** 40 40N 23 34 E
Volyně, *Czech Rep.* **34 B6** 49 10N 13 53 E
Volzhsk, *Russia* **60 C9** 55 57N 48 23 E
Volzhskiy, *Russia* **61 F7** 48 56N 44 46 E
Vomo, *Fiji* **133 A1** 17 30 S 177 15 E
Vonavona, *Solomon Is.* **133 M9** 8 15 S 157 5 E
Vondrozo, *Madag.* **117 C8** 22 49 S 47 20 E
Vónitsa, *Greece* **39 B2** 38 55N 20 53 E
Vopnafjörður, *Iceland* **11 B12** 65 45N 14 50W
Vorarlberg □, *Austria* **34 D2** 47 20N 10 0 E
Vóras Óros, *Greece* **50 F5** 40 57N 21 45 E
Voray-sur-l'Ognon, *France* **32 B2** 47 20N 6 1 E
Vorbasse, *Denmark* **17 J3** 55 39N 9 6 E
Vorchdorf, *Austria* **34 C6** 48 0N 13 55 E
Vorderrhein →, *Switz.* **33 C8** 46 49N 9 25 E
Vordingborg, *Denmark* **17 J5** 55 0N 11 54 E
Vorë, *Albania* **50 E3** 41 23N 19 40 E
Voreio Aigaio = Vórios Aiyaíon □, *Greece* **49 C7** 38 50N 25 30 E
Voreppe, *France* **29 C9** 45 18N 5 39 E
Vóriai Sporádhes, *Greece* **48 B5** 39 15N 23 30 E
Vórios Aiyaíon □, *Greece* **49 C7** 38 50N 25 30 E
Vórios Evvoïkos Kólpos, *Greece* **48 C5** 38 45N 23 15 E
Vorkuta, *Russia* **56 A11** 67 48N 64 20 E
Vorma →, *Norway* **18 D8** 60 9N 11 29 E
Vormsi, *Estonia* **15 G20** 59 1N 23 13 E
Vóroi, *Greece* **39 E5** 35 4N 24 49 E
Vorona →, *Russia* **60 E6** 51 22N 42 3 E
Voronezh, *Russia* **59 G10** 51 40N 39 10 E
Voronezh, *Ukraine* **59 G7** 51 47N 33 28 E
Voronezh →, *Russia* **59 G10** 51 32N 39 10 E
Vorontsovo-Aleksandrovskoye = Zelenokumsk, *Russia* **61 H6** 44 24N 44 0 E
Voroshilov = Ussuriysk, *Russia* **67 E14** 43 48N 131 59 E
Voroshilovgrad = Luhansk, *Ukraine* **59 H10** 48 38N 39 15 E
Voroshilovsk = Alchevsk, *Ukraine* **59 H10** 48 30N 38 45 E
Voroshilovsk = Stavropol, *Russia* **61 H6** 45 5N 42 0 E
Vorpommersche Boddenlandschaft △, *Germany* **30 A8** 54 25N 12 32 E
Vorskla →, *Ukraine* **59 H8** 48 50N 34 10 E
Võrts Järv, *Estonia* **15 G22** 58 16N 26 3 E
Võru, *Estonia* **15 H22** 57 48N 26 54 E
Vosges, *France* **27 D14** 48 20N 7 10 E
Vosges □, *France* **27 D13** 48 12N 6 20 E
Vosges du Nord ⌓, *France* **27 D14** 49 0N 7 30 E
Voskopojë, *Albania* **50 F4** 40 35N 20 33 E
Voskresensk, *Russia* **58 E10** 55 19N 38 43 E
Voskresenskoye, *Russia* **60 B7** 56 51N 45 30 E
Voss, *Norway* **18 D3** 60 38N 6 26 E
Vostok = Neftegorsk, *Russia* **61 H4** 44 25N 39 45 E
Vostok, *Antarctica* **7 D8** 78 30 S 106 50 E
Vostok I., *Kiribati* **135 J12** 10 5 S 152 23W
Votice, *Czech Rep.* **34 B7** 49 38N 14 39 E
Votkinsk, *Russia* **64 C4** 57 0N 53 55 E
Votkinskoye Vdkhr., *Russia* **64 C5** 57 22N 55 12 E
Votsuri-Shima, *Japan* **71 M1** 25 45N 123 29 E
Votuporanga, *Brazil* **171 F2** 20 24 S 49 59W
Vouga →, *Portugal* **42 E2** 40 41N 8 40W
Vouillé, *France* **26 F7** 46 38N 0 10 E
Voulou, *C.A.R.* **114 A4** 8 33N 22 36 E
Vouma →, *Cameroon* **114 B2** 3 19N 14 9 E
Vouvry, *Switz.* **32 D3** 46 21N 6 51 E
Voúxa, Ákra, *Greece* **39 E4** 35 37N 23 32 E
Vouzela, *Portugal* **42 E2** 40 43N 8 7W
Vouziers, *France* **27 C11** 49 22N 4 40 E
Vovchansk, *Ukraine* **59 G9** 50 17N 36 58 E
Vovodo →, *C.A.R.* **114 A4** 5 40N 24 21 E
Vowchyn, *Belarus* **55 F10** 52 18N 23 18 E
Voyageurs △, *U.S.A.* **154 A8** 48 32N 93 0W
Vozhe, Ozero, *Russia* **58 B10** 60 45N 39 0 E
Vozhega, *Russia* **58 B11** 60 29N 40 12 E
Voznesensk, *Ukraine* **59 J6** 47 35N 31 21 E
Voznesenye, *Russia* **58 B8** 61 0N 35 28 E
Vrå, *Denmark* **17 G3** 57 21N 9 56 E
Vráble, *Slovak Rep.* **35 C11** 48 15N 18 16 E
Vraćevšnica, *Serbia & M.* **50 B4** 44 2N 20 34 E
Vrådal, *Norway* **18 E5** 59 20N 8 25 E
Vrakhnéïka, *Greece* **48 C3** 38 10N 21 40 E
Vrancea □, *Romania* **53 E11** 45 50N 26 45 E
Vrancei, Munţii, *Romania* **53 E11** 46 0N 26 30 E
Vrang, *Tajikistan* **65 E6** 37 0N 72 22 E
Vrangelya, Ostrov, *Russia* **67 B19** 71 0N 180 0 E
Vranica, *Bos.-H.* **52 G2** 43 55N 17 50 E
Vranje, *Serbia & M.* **50 D5** 42 34N 21 54 E
Vranjska Banja, *Serbia & M.* **50 D6** 42 34N 22 1 E
Vranov nad Topl'ou, *Slovak Rep.* **35 C14** 48 53N 21 40 E
Vransko, *Slovenia* **45 B11** 46 17N 14 58 E
Vransko Jezero, *Croatia* **45 E12** 43 53N 15 34 E
Vrapčište, *Macedonia* **50 E4** 41 50N 20 53 E
Vratsa, *Bulgaria* **50 C7** 43 15N 23 30 E
Vråvatn, *Norway* **18 E5** 59 20N 8 8 E
Vrbas, *Serbia & M.* **52 E4** 45 40N 19 40 E
Vrbas →, *Bos.-H.* **52 E2** 45 8N 17 29 E
Vrbnik, *Croatia* **45 C11** 45 4N 14 40 E
Vrbovec, *Croatia* **45 C13** 45 53N 16 28 E
Vrbovsko, *Croatia* **45 C12** 45 24N 15 5 E
Vrchlabí, *Czech Rep.* **34 A8** 50 38N 15 37 E
Vrede, *S. Africa* **117 D4** 27 24 S 29 6 E
Vredefort, *S. Africa* **116 D4** 27 0 S 27 22 E
Vreden, *Germany* **30 C2** 52 2N 6 50 E
Vredenburg, *S. Africa* **116 E2** 32 56 S 18 0 E
Vredendal, *S. Africa* **116 E2** 31 41 S 18 35 E
Vretstorp, *Sweden* **16 E8** 59 1N 14 53 E
Vrgorac, *Croatia* **45 E14** 43 12N 17 20 E
Vrhnika, *Slovenia* **45 C11** 45 58N 14 15 E
Vriddhachalam, *India* **95 J4** 11 30N 79 20 E
Vrïdi, *Ivory C.* **112 D4** 5 15N 4 3W
Vrigstad, *Sweden* **17 G8** 57 22N 14 28 E
Vrin, *Switz.* **33 C8** 46 39N 9 6 E
Vrindavan, *India* **92 F7** 27 37N 77 40 E
Vríses, *Greece* **39 E5** 35 23N 24 13 E
Vrnograč, *Bos.-H.* **45 C12** 45 10N 15 57 E
Vrondádhes, *Greece* **49 C8** 38 25N 26 7 E
Vrpolje, *Croatia* **52 E3** 45 13N 18 24 E
Vršac, *Serbia & M.* **52 E6** 45 8N 21 20 E
Vrsacki Kanal, *Serbia & M.* **52 E5** 45 15N 21 0 E
Vrútky, *Slovak Rep.* **35 B11** 49 7N 18 55 E
Vryburg, *S. Africa* **116 D3** 26 55 S 24 45 E
Vryheid, *S. Africa* **117 D5** 27 45 S 30 47 E
Vsetín, *Czech Rep.* **35 B11** 49 20N 18 0 E
Vu Liet, *Vietnam* **86 C5** 18 43N 105 23 E
Vŭcha →, *Bulgaria* **51 D8** 42 10N 24 26 E
Vučitrn, *Serbia & M.* **50 D4** 42 49N 20 59 E
Vukovar, *Croatia* **52 E3** 45 21N 18 59 E
Vulcan, *Canada* **142 C6** 50 25N 113 15W
Vulcan, *Romania* **53 E8** 45 23N 23 17 E
Vulcaneşti, *Moldova* **53 E13** 45 41N 28 18 E
Vulcano, *Italy* **47 D7** 38 24N 14 58 E
Vŭlchedruma, *Bulgaria* **50 C7** 43 42N 23 27 E
Vulkaneshty = Vulcaneşti, *Moldova* **53 E13** 45 41N 28 18 E
Vunduzi →, *Mozam.* **119 F3** 18 56 S 34 1 E
Vung Tau, *Vietnam* **87 G6** 10 21N 107 4 E
Vunidawa, *Fiji* **133 A2** 17 50 S 178 21 E
Vunisea, *Fiji* **133 B2** 19 3 S 178 10 E
Vuntut △, *Canada* **144 B13** 68 25N 139 41W
Vuranggo, *Solomon Is.* **133 L9** 6 39 S 156 38 E
Vŭrbitsa, *Bulgaria* **51 D10** 42 59N 26 40 E
Vurshets, *Bulgaria* **50 C7** 43 13N 23 23 E
Vutcani, *Romania* **53 D12** 46 26N 27 59 E
Vuya, *Sudan* **107 F2** 5 21N 29 40 E
Vuzlove, *Ukraine* **52 B7** 48 22N 22 24 E
Vwaza ⌓, *Malawi* **119 E3** 10 58 S 33 25 E
Vyara, *India* **94 D1** 21 8N 73 28 E
Vyartsilya, *Russia* **58 A6** 62 8N 30 45 E
Vyatka = Kirov, *Russia* **64 B2** 58 35N 49 40 E
Vyatka →, *Russia* **60 C10** 55 37N 51 28 E
Vyatskiye Polyany, *Russia* **60 B10** 56 14N 51 5 E
Vyazemskiy, *Russia* **67 E14** 47 32N 134 45 E
Vyazma, *Russia* **58 E8** 55 10N 34 15 E
Vyazniki, *Russia* **60 B6** 56 10N 42 10 E
Vyborg, *Russia* **58 B5** 60 43N 28 47 E
Vychegda →, *Russia* **56 B8** 61 18N 46 36 E
Vychodné Beskydy, *Europe* **35 B15** 49 20N 22 0 E
Vyerkhnyadzvinsk, *Belarus* **58 E4** 55 45N 27 58 E
Vyg-ozero, *Russia* **56 B5** 63 47N 34 29 E
Vyhoda, *Ukraine* **53 B8** 48 56N 23 55 E
Vyksa, *Russia* **60 C6** 55 19N 42 11 E
Vylkove, *Ukraine* **53 E14** 45 28N 29 32 E
Vylok, *Ukraine* **52 B7** 48 6N 22 50 E
Vynohradiv, *Ukraine* **52 B8** 48 9N 23 2 E
Vypin, *India* **95 J3** 10 10N 76 15 E
Vyrnwy, L., *U.K.* **20 E4** 52 48N 3 31W
Vyshkiv, *Ukraine* **53 B8** 48 44N 23 39 E
Vyshkove, *Ukraine* **53 B8** 48 3N 23 25 E
Vyshniy Volochek, *Russia* **58 D8** 57 30N 34 30 E
Vyshzha = imeni 26 Bakinskikh Komissarov, *Turkmenistan* **97 B7** 39 22N 54 10 E
Vyškov, *Czech Rep.* **35 B9** 49 17N 17 0 E
Vysokaye, *Belarus* **55 F10** 52 22N 23 22 E
Vysoké Mýto, *Czech Rep.* **35 B9** 49 58N 16 10 E
Vysokovsk, *Russia* **58 D9** 56 22N 36 30 E
Vyšší Brod, *Czech Rep.* **34 C7** 48 37N 14 19 E
Vytegra, *Russia* **58 B9** 61 0N 36 27 E
Vyzhnytsya, *Ukraine* **53 B10** 48 15N 25 11 E
Vyzhnytsya ⌓, *Ukraine* **53 B10** 48 7N 25 15 E

W

W du Benin △, *Benin* **113 C5** 11 57N 2 43 E
W du Burkina Faso △, *Burkina Faso* **113 C4** 11 52N 2 50W
W du Niger △, *Niger* **113 C5** 13 31N 2 28 E
W.A.C. Bennett Dam, *Canada* **142 B4** 56 2N 122 6W
Wa, *Ghana* **112 C4** 10 7N 2 25W
Waal →, *Neths.* **24 C5** 51 37N 5 0 E
Waalwijk, *Neths.* **24 C5** 51 42N 5 4 E
Waar, *Indonesia* **83 B4** 2 5 S 134 23 E
Waat, *Sudan* **107 F3** 8 10N 32 7 E
Wabag, *Papua N. G.* **132 C2** 5 32 S 143 40 E
Wabakimi △, *Canada* **140 B2** 50 43N 89 29W
Wabana, *Canada* **141 C9** 47 40N 53 0W
Wabao, *N. Cal.* **133 U21** 21 36 S 167 57 E
Wabao, C., *N. Cal.* **133 U21** 21 35 S 167 53 E
Wabasca →, *Canada* **142 B5** 58 22N 115 20W
Wabasca-Desmarais, *Canada* **142 B6** 55 57N 113 56W
Wabash, *U.S.A.* **157 D11** 40 48N 85 49W
Wabash →, *U.S.A.* **157 G8** 37 48N 88 2W
Wabasso, *U.S.A.* **153 H9** 27 45N 80 26W
Wabawng, *Burma* **90 B6** 26 20N 97 25 E
Wabi →, *Ethiopia* **107 F5** 7 45N 40 50 E
Wabigoon L., *Canada* **143 D10** 49 44N 92 44W
Wabowden, *Canada* **143 C9** 54 55N 98 38W
Wąbrzeźno, *Poland* **55 E5** 53 16N 18 57 E
Wabu Hu, *China* **77 A11** 32 20N 116 50 E
Wabuda I., *Papua N. G.* **132 E2** 8 23 S 143 37 E
Wabuk Pt., *Canada* **140 A2** 55 20N 85 5W
Wabush, *Canada* **141 B6** 52 55N 66 52W
Waccasassa B., *U.S.A.* **153 F7** 29 10N 82 50W
Wąchock, *Poland* **55 G8** 51 4N 21 1 E
Wächtersbach, *Germany* **31 E5** 50 14N 9 17 E
Wacissa, *U.S.A.* **152 E6** 30 22N 83 59W
Waco, *U.S.A.* **155 K6** 31 33N 97 9W
Waconichi, L., *Canada* **140 B5** 50 8N 74 0W
Wad Ban Naqa, *Sudan* **107 D3** 16 32N 33 9 E
Wad Banda, *Sudan* **107 E2** 13 10N 27 56 E
Wad el Haddad, *Sudan* **107 E3** 13 50N 33 30 E
Wad en Nau, *Sudan* **107 E3** 14 10N 33 34 E
Wad Hamid, *Sudan* **107 D3** 16 30N 32 45 E
Wad Medanî, *Sudan* **107 E3** 14 28N 33 30 E
Wad Thana, *Pakistan* **91 D2** 27 22N 66 23 E
Wadai, *Africa* **104 E5** 12 0N 19 0 E
Wadayama, *Japan* **72 B6** 35 19N 134 52 E
Wadbilliga △, *Australia* **129 D8** 36 25 S 149 35 E
Waddān, *Libya* **108 C3** 29 9N 16 10 E
Waddeneilanden, *Neths.* **24 A5** 53 25N 5 10 E
Waddenzee, *Neths.* **24 A5** 53 6N 5 10 E
Waddi, Chappal, *Nigeria* **113 D7** 7 2N 11 43W
Waddington, *U.S.A.* **151 B9** 44 52N 75 12W
Waddington, Mt., *Canada* **142 C3** 51 23N 125 15W
Waddy Pt., *Australia* **127 C5** 24 58 S 153 21 E
Wadebridge, *U.K.* **21 G3** 50 31N 4 51W
Wadena, *Canada* **143 C8** 51 57N 103 47W
Wadena, *U.S.A.* **154 B7** 46 26N 95 8W
Wädenswil, *Switz.* **33 B7** 47 14N 8 40 E
Wadern, *Germany* **31 F2** 49 32N 6 53 E
Wadeye, *Australia* **124 B4** 14 28 S 129 52 E
Wadgaon, *India* **94 E1** 18 44N 73 39 E
Wadhams, *Canada* **142 C3** 51 30N 127 30W
Wadhwan = Surendranagar, *India* **92 H4** 22 45N 71 40 E
Wadi, *India* **94 F3** 17 4N 76 59 E
Wādī as Sīr, *Jordan* **103 D4** 31 56N 35 49 E
Wādī Banī Walīd, *Libya* **108 B2** 31 49N 14 0 E
Wadi Gemâl, *Egypt* **106 C4** 24 35N 35 10 E
Wadi Halfa, *Sudan* **106 C3** 21 53N 31 19 E
Wadi Rum △, *Jordan* **103 F4** 29 30N 35 20 E
Wadian, *China* **77 A9** 32 42N 112 29 E
Wadlew, *Poland* **55 G6** 51 31N 19 23 E
Wadley, *Ala., U.S.A.* **152 B4** 33 7N 85 34W
Wadley, *Ga., U.S.A.* **152 C7** 32 52N 82 24W
Wadowice, *Poland* **55 J6** 49 52N 19 30 E
Wadsworth, *Nev., U.S.A.* **158 G4** 39 38N 119 17W
Wadsworth, *Ohio, U.S.A.* **150 E3** 41 2N 81 44W
Waegwan, *S. Korea* **75 G15** 35 59N 128 23 E
Waeplau, *Indonesia* **82 B3** 3 8 S 126 55 E
Wafangdian, *China* **75 E11** 39 38N 121 58 E
Wafania, *Dem. Rep. of the Congo* **114 C4** 1 23 S 20 22 E
Wafrah, *Si. Arabia* **96 D5** 28 33N 47 56 E
Wagadugu = Ouagadougou, *Burkina Faso* **113 C4** 12 25N 1 30W
Wagener, *U.S.A.* **152 B8** 33 39N 81 22W
Wageningen, *Neths.* **24 C5** 51 58N 5 40 E
Wageningen, *Suriname* **169 B6** 5 50N 56 50W
Wager B., *Canada* **139 B11** 65 26N 88 40W
Wagga Wagga, *Australia* **129 C7** 35 7 S 147 24 E
Waghai, *India* **94 D1** 20 46N 73 29 E
Waghete, *Indonesia* **83 B5** 4 10 S 135 50 E
Wagin, *Australia* **125 F2** 33 17 S 117 25 E
Wagner, *U.S.A.* **154 D5** 43 5N 98 18W
Wagon Mound, *U.S.A.* **155 G2** 36 1N 104 42W
Wagoner, *U.S.A.* **155 H7** 35 58N 95 22W
Wagrowiec, *Poland* **55 F4** 52 48N 17 11 E
Wah, *Pakistan* **91 B4** 33 45N 72 40 E
Wahai, *Indonesia* **83 B3** 2 48 S 129 35 E
Waharoa, *N.Z.* **130 D4** 37 46 S 175 45 E
Wahiawa, *U.S.A.* **145 K13** 21 30N 158 2W
Wahiawa Reservoir, *U.S.A.* **145 K13** 21 30N 158 3W
Wâḩid, *Egypt* **103 E1** 30 48N 32 21 E
Wahnai, *Afghan.* **92 C1** 32 40N 65 50 E
Wahni, *Ethiopia* **107 E4** 12 40N 36 39 E
Wahoo, *U.S.A.* **154 E6** 41 13N 96 37W
Wahpeton, *U.S.A.* **154 B6** 46 16N 96 36W
Wahx, Ras il-, *Malta* **38 F7** 35 56N 14 20 E
Wai, *India* **94 F1** 17 56N 73 57 E
Waiai →, *N.Z.* **131 G2** 46 12 S 167 38 E
Waialee, *U.S.A.* **145 J13** 21 41N 158 1W
Waialua, *U.S.A.* **145 J13** 21 34N 158 8W
Waialua B., *U.S.A.* **145 J13** 21 35N 158 5W
Waianae, *U.S.A.* **145 K13** 21 27N 158 11W
Waianae Mts., *U.S.A.* **145 K13** 21 30N 158 10W
Waiapu →, *N.Z.* **130 D7** 37 47 S 178 29 E
Waiau, *N.Z.* **131 C8** 42 39 S 173 5 E
Waiau →, *N.Z.* **131 C8** 42 47 S 173 22 E
Waiawa →, *U.S.A.* **145 K14** 21 23N 157 59W
Waiawe Ganga →, *Sri Lanka* **95 L5** 6 15N 81 0 E
Waibeem, *Indonesia* **83 B4** 0 30 S 132 59 E
Waiblingen, *Germany* **31 G5** 48 49N 9 18 E
Waidhofen an der Thaya, *Austria* **34 C8** 48 49N 15 17 E
Waidhofen an der Ybbs, *Austria* **34 D7** 47 57N 14 46 E
Waigeo, *Indonesia* **83 B4** 0 20 S 130 40 E
Waihao →, *N.Z.* **131 E6** 44 52 S 171 11 E
Waihao Downs, *N.Z.* **131 E5** 44 48 S 170 55 E
Waiheke I., *N.Z.* **130 C4** 36 48 S 175 6 E
Waihi, *N.Z.* **130 D4** 37 23 S 175 52 E
Waihi Beach, *N.Z.* **130 D7** 37 25 S 175 57 E
Waihola, *N.Z.* **131 G5** 46 1 S 170 8 E
Waihola L., *N.Z.* **131 F5** 45 59 S 170 8 E
Waihou →, *N.Z.* **130 D4** 37 15 S 175 40 E
Waika, *Dem. Rep. of the Congo* **118 C2** 2 22 S 25 42 E
Waikabubak, *Indonesia* **82 C1** 9 45 S 119 25 E
Waikaia, *N.Z.* **131 F3** 45 44 S 168 51 E
Waikaka, *N.Z.* **131 F4** 45 55 S 169 1 E
Waikare, L., *N.Z.* **130 D4** 37 26 S 175 13 E
Waikareiti, L., *N.Z.* **130 E6** 38 43 S 177 10 E
Waikaremoana, *N.Z.* **130 E6** 38 42 S 177 12 E
Waikaremoana, L., *N.Z.* **130 E6** 38 49 S 177 9 E
Waikari, *N.Z.* **131 C7** 42 58 S 172 41 E
Waikato →, *N.Z.* **130 D3** 37 23 S 174 43 E
Waikelo, *Indonesia* **82 C1** 9 24 S 119 19 E
Waikerie, *Australia* **128 C4** 34 9 S 140 0 E
Waikiekie, *N.Z.* **130 B3** 35 57 S 174 16 E
Waikiki, *U.S.A.* **145 K14** 21 17N 157 50W
Waikokopu, *N.Z.* **130 F6** 39 3 S 177 52 E
Waikouaiti, *N.Z.* **131 F5** 45 36 S 170 41 E
Waikouaiti Downs, *N.Z.* **131 F5** 45 30 S 170 30 E
Wailingding Dao, *China* **69 G11** 22 6N 114 2 E
Wailua, *Hawaii, U.S.A.* **145 A2** 22 3N 159 20W
Wailua, *Hawaii, U.S.A.* **145 C5** 20 51N 156 8W
Wailuku, *U.S.A.* **145 C5** 20 53N 156 30W
Waimakariri →, *N.Z.* **131 D7** 43 24 S 172 42 E
Waimanalo, *U.S.A.* **145 K14** 21 21N 157 43W
Waimanalo B., *U.S.A.* **145 K14** 21 20N 157 40W
Waimanalo Beach, *U.S.A.* **145 K14** 21 21N 157 42W
Waimangaroa, *N.Z.* **131 B6** 41 43 S 171 46 E
Waimano →, *U.S.A.* **145 K14** 21 25N 157 58W
Waimarie, *N.Z.* **131 B6** 41 35 S 171 58 E
Waimate, *N.Z.* **131 E6** 44 45 S 171 3 E
Waimea, *Hawaii, U.S.A.* **145 B2** 21 58N 159 40W
Waimea, *Hawaii, U.S.A.* **145 J13** 21 39N 158 3W
Waimea B., *U.S.A.* **145 J13** 21 40N 158 5W
Waimea Plain, *N.Z.* **131 F3** 45 55 S 168 35 E
Wainganga →, *India* **94 E4** 18 50N 79 55 E
Waingapu, *Indonesia* **82 C2** 9 35 S 120 11 E
Waingmaw, *Burma* **90 C6** 25 21N 97 26 E
Waini →, *Guyana* **169 B6** 8 20N 59 50W
Wainuiomata, *N.Z.* **130 H3** 41 17 S 174 56 E
Wainwright, *Canada* **143 C6** 52 50N 110 50W
Wainwright, *U.S.A.* **144 A7** 70 38N 160 2W
Waiotapu, *N.Z.* **130 E5** 38 21 S 176 25 E
Waiouru, *N.Z.* **130 F4** 39 28 S 175 41 E
Waipa →, *N.Z.* **130 E4** 38 16 S 175 21 E
Waipahi, *N.Z.* **131 G4** 46 6 S 169 15 E
Waipahu, *U.S.A.* **145 K13** 21 23N 158 1W
Waipapa Pt., *N.Z.* **131 G3** 46 40 S 168 51 E
Waipara, *N.Z.* **131 D7** 43 3 S 172 46 E
Waipawa, *N.Z.* **130 F5** 39 56 S 176 38 E
Waipio Acres, *U.S.A.* **145 K13** 21 28N 158 1W
Waipio Peninsula, *U.S.A.* **145 K14** 21 20N 158 0W
Waipiro, *N.Z.* **130 E7** 38 2 S 178 22 E
Waipiro Bay, *N.Z.* **130 E7** 38 1 S 178 21 E
Waipoua Forest, *N.Z.* **130 B2** 35 39 S 173 33 E
Waipu, *N.Z.* **130 B3** 35 59 S 174 29 E
Waipukurau, *N.Z.* **130 G5** 40 1 S 176 33 E
Wairakei, *N.Z.* **130 E5** 38 37 S 176 6 E
Wairarapa, L., *N.Z.* **130 H4** 41 14 S 175 15 E
Wairau →, *N.Z.* **131 B9** 41 32 S 174 7 E
Wairio, *N.Z.* **131 F3** 45 59 S 168 3 E
Wairoa, *N.Z.* **130 F6** 39 3 S 177 25 E
Wairoa →, *Hawke's Bay, N.Z.* **130 F6** 39 4 S 177 25 E
Wairoa →, *Northland, N.Z.* **130 C2** 36 5 S 173 59 E
Waïsisi, *Vanuatu* **133 J7** 19 32 S 169 22 E
Waita Reservoir, *U.S.A.* **145 B2** 21 55N 159 28W
Waitaki →, *N.Z.* **131 E6** 44 56 S 171 7 E
Waitaki Plains, *N.Z.* **131 E5** 44 22 S 170 0 E
Waitangi, *N.Z.* **130 B3** 35 16 S 174 5 E
Waitara, *N.Z.* **130 E3** 38 59 S 174 15 E
Waitara →, *N.Z.* **130 E3** 38 59 S 174 14 E
Waitoa, *N.Z.* **130 D4** 37 37 S 175 35 E
Waitomo Caves, *N.Z.* **130 E4** 38 16 S 175 7 E
Waitotara, *N.Z.* **130 F3** 39 49 S 174 44 E
Waitotara →, *N.Z.* **130 F3** 39 51 S 174 41 E
Waitsburg, *U.S.A.* **158 C5** 46 16N 118 9W
Waitzen = Vác, *Hungary* **52 C4** 47 49N 19 10 E
Waiuku, *N.Z.* **130 D3** 37 15 S 174 45 E
Wajima, *Japan* **71 F8** 37 30N 137 0 E
Wajir, *Kenya* **118 B5** 1 42N 40 5 E
Waka, *Dem. Rep. of the Congo* **114 B4** 1 1N 20 13 E
Waka, *Ethiopia* **107 F4** 7 2N 37 20 E
Wakai, *Suriname* **169 B6** 5 18N 57 14W
Wakarusa, *U.S.A.* **157 C10** 41 32N 86 1W
Wakasa, *Japan* **72 B6** 35 20N 134 24 E
Wakasa-Wan, *Japan* **73 B7** 35 40N 135 30 E
Wakatipu, L., *N.Z.* **131 F3** 45 5 S 168 33 E
Wakaw, *Canada* **143 C7** 52 39N 105 44W
Wakaya, *Fiji* **133 A2** 17 37 S 179 0 E
Wakayama, *Japan* **73 C7** 34 15N 135 15 E
Wakayama □, *Japan* **73 D7** 33 50N 135 30 E
Wake, *Japan* **72 C6** 34 48N 134 8 E
Wake Forest, *U.S.A.* **149 H6** 35 59N 78 30W
Wake I., *Pac. Oc.* **134 F8** 19 18N 166 36 E
WaKeeney, *U.S.A.* **154 F5** 39 1N 99 53W
Wakefield, *Jamaica* **164 a** 18 26N 77 42W
Wakefield, *N.Z.* **131 B8** 41 24 S 173 5 E
Wakefield, *U.K.* **20 D6** 53 41N 1 29W
Wakefield, *Mass., U.S.A.* **151 D13** 42 30N 71 4W
Wakefield, *Mich., U.S.A.* **154 B10** 46 29N 89 56W
Wakema, *Burma* **90 G5** 16 30N 95 11 E
Waki, *Japan* **72 C6** 34 4N 134 9 E
Wakkanai, *Japan* **70 B10** 45 28N 141 35 E
Wakkerstroom, *S. Africa* **117 D5** 27 24 S 30 10 E
Wakool, *Australia* **128 C6** 35 28 S 144 23 E
Wakool →, *Australia* **128 C5** 35 5 S 143 33 E
Wakre, *Indonesia* **83 B4** 0 19 S 131 5 E
Waku, *Papua N. G.* **132 D5** 6 5 S 149 9 E
Wakuach, L., *Canada* **141 A6** 55 34N 67 32W
Wakulla, *U.S.A.* **152 E5** 30 14N 84 14W
Wakunai, *Papua N. G.* **132 C8** 5 52 S 155 13 E
Walamba, *Zambia* **119 E2** 13 30 S 28 42 E
Wałbrzych, *Poland* **55 H3** 50 45N 16 18 E
Walbury Hill, *U.K.* **21 F6** 51 21N 1 28W
Walcha, *Australia* **129 A9** 30 55 S 151 31 E
Walcheren, *Neths.* **24 C3** 51 30N 3 35 E
Walckenaer, Teluk, *Indonesia* **83 B5** 2 20 S 139 50 E
Walcott, *U.S.A.* **158 F10** 41 46N 106 51W
Wałcz, *Poland* **55 E3** 53 17N 16 27 E
Wald, *Switz.* **33 B7** 47 17N 8 56 E
Waldbröl, *Germany* **30 E3** 50 52N 7 37 E
Waldburg Ra., *Australia* **125 D2** 24 40 S 117 35 E
Waldeck, *Germany* **30 D5** 51 12N 9 4 E
Walden, *Colo., U.S.A.* **158 F10** 40 44N 106 17W
Walden, *N.Y., U.S.A.* **151 E10** 41 34N 74 11W
Waldenberg = Wałbrzych, *Poland* **55 H3** 50 45N 16 18 E
Waldenburg, *Switz.* **32 B5** 47 23N 7 45 E
Waldkirch, *Germany* **31 G3** 48 5N 7 58 E
Waldkirchen, *Germany* **31 G9** 48 43N 13 36 E
Waldkraiburg, *Germany* **31 G8** 48 11N 12 24 E
Waldo, *U.S.A.* **152 F7** 29 48N 82 10W
Waldport, *U.S.A.* **158 D1** 44 26N 124 4W
Waldron, *U.S.A.* **155 H7** 34 54N 94 5W
Waldviertel, *Austria* **34 C8** 48 30N 15 30 E
Walebing, *Australia* **125 F2** 30 41 S 116 13 E
Walembele, *Ghana* **112 C4** 10 30N 1 58W
Walensee, *Switz.* **33 B8** 47 7N 9 13 E
Walenstadt, *Switz.* **33 B8** 47 8N 9 19 E
Wales, *U.S.A.* **144 D5** 65 37N 168 5W
Wales □, *U.K.* **21 E3** 52 19N 4 43W
Walewale, *Ghana* **113 C4** 10 21N 0 50W
Walgett, *Australia* **127 E4** 30 0 S 148 5 E
Walgreen Coast, *Antarctica* **7 D15** 75 15 S 105 0W
Walhalla, *Australia* **129 D7** 37 56 S 146 29 E

Walis I., Papua N. G. 132 B2 3 14 S 143 18 E
Walker, Mich., U.S.A. 157 B11 42 58N 85 46W
Walker, Minn., U.S.A. 154 B7 47 6N 94 35W
Walker, L., Canada 141 B6 50 20N 67 11W
Walker L., Canada 143 C9 54 42N 95 57W
Walker L., U.S.A. 158 G4 38 42N 118 43W
Walkerston, Australia 126 K7 21 11 S 149 8 E
Walkerton, Canada 140 D3 44 10N 81 10W
Walkerton, U.S.A. 157 C10 41 28N 86 29W
Wall, U.S.A. 154 D3 44 0N 102 8W
Walla Walla, Australia 129 C7 35 45 S 146 54 E
Walla Walla, U.S.A. 158 C4 46 4N 118 20W
Wallace, Idaho, U.S.A. 158 C6 47 28N 115 56W
Wallace, N.C., U.S.A. 149 H7 34 44N 77 59W
Wallaceburg, Canada 140 D3 42 34N 82 23W
Wallacetown, N.Z. 131 G3 46 21 S 168 19 E
Wallachia = Valahia, Romania 53 F9 44 35N 25 0 E
Wallal, Australia 127 D4 26 32 S 146 7 E
Wallam Cr. →, Australia 127 D4 28 40 S 147 20 E
Wallambin, L., Australia 125 F2 30 57 S 117 35 E
Wallan, Australia 129 D6 37 26 S 144 59 E
Wallangarra, Australia 127 D5 28 56 S 151 58 E
Wallaroo, Australia 128 B2 33 56 S 137 39 E
Walldürn, Germany 31 F5 49 34N 9 22 E
Wallenhorst, Germany 30 C4 52 21N 8 1 E
Wallenpaupack, L., U.S.A. 151 E9 41 25N 75 15W
Wallerawang, Australia 129 B9 33 25 S 150 4 E
Wallingford, U.S.A. 151 E12 41 27N 72 50W
Wallis & Futuna, Is., Pac. Oc. 134 J10 13 18 S 176 10W
Wallisellen, Switz. 33 B7 47 25N 8 36 E
Wallowa, U.S.A. 158 D5 45 34N 117 32W
Wallowa Mts., U.S.A. 158 D5 45 20N 117 30W
Walls, U.K. 22 A7 60 14N 1 33W
Walls of Jerusalem △, Australia 127 G4 41 56 S 146 15 E
Wallsend, Australia 129 B9 32 55 S 151 40 E
Wallula, U.S.A. 158 C4 46 5N 118 54W
Wallumbilla, Australia 127 D4 26 33 S 149 9 E
Walmsley, L., Canada 143 A7 63 25N 108 36W
Walney, I. of, U.K. 20 C4 54 6N 3 15W
Walnut, U.S.A. 156 C7 41 33N 89 36W
Walnut Canyon △, U.S.A. 159 J8 35 15N 111 20W
Walnut Creek, U.S.A. 160 H4 37 54N 122 4W
Walnut Grove, U.S.A. 152 A3 34 4N 86 18W
Walnut Hill, U.S.A. 153 E2 30 53N 87 30W
Walnut Ridge, U.S.A. 155 G9 36 4N 90 57W
Walpeup, Australia 128 C5 35 7 S 142 2 E
Walpole, Australia 125 F2 34 58 S 116 44 E
Walpole, U.S.A. 151 D13 42 9N 71 15W
Wals, Austria 34 D5 47 47N 12 58 E
Walsall, U.K. 21 E6 52 35N 1 58W
Walsenburg, U.S.A. 155 G2 37 38N 104 47W
Walsh, U.S.A. 155 G3 37 23N 102 17W
Walsh →, Australia 126 B3 16 31 S 143 42 E
Walsrode, Germany 30 C5 52 51N 9 35 E
Walt Disney World, U.S.A. 153 G8 28 25N 81 35W
Waltair, India 94 F6 17 44N 83 23 E
Walter F. George Reservoir, U.S.A. 152 D4 31 38N 85 4W
Walterboro, U.S.A. 152 C9 32 55N 80 40W
Walters, U.S.A. 155 H5 34 22N 98 19W
Waltershausen, Germany 30 E6 50 54N 10 33 E
Waltham, U.S.A. 151 D13 42 23N 71 14W
Waltman, U.S.A. 158 E10 43 4N 107 12W
Walton, Ky., U.S.A. 157 F12 38 52N 84 37W
Walton, N.Y., U.S.A. 151 D9 42 10N 75 8W
Walton-on-the-Naze, U.K. 21 F9 51 51N 1 17 E
Waltonville, U.S.A. 156 F7 38 13N 89 2W
Walu, Burma 90 B7 26 28N 98 2 E
Walvis Bay, Namibia 116 C1 23 0 S 14 28 E
Walvis Ridge, Atl. Oc. 8 J12 26 0 S 5 0 E
Walvisbaai = Walvis Bay, Namibia 116 C1 23 0 S 14 28 E
Walwa, Australia 129 C7 35 59 S 147 44 E
Wamba, Équateur, Dem. Rep. of the Congo 114 C4 1 37 S 22 30 E
Wamba, Orientale, Dem. Rep. of the Congo 118 B2 2 10N 27 57 E
Wamba, Kenya 118 B4 0 58N 37 19 E
Wamba, Nigeria 113 D6 8 57N 8 42 E
Wamba →, Dem. Rep. of the Congo 115 C3 3 56 S 17 12 E
Wamego, U.S.A. 154 F6 39 12N 96 18W
Wamena, Indonesia 83 B5 4 4 S 138 57 E
Wamsutter, U.S.A. 158 F9 41 40N 107 58W
Wamulan, Indonesia 82 B3 3 27 S 126 7 E
Wan Hat, Burma 90 E6 20 14N 97 53 E
Wan Kinghao, Burma 90 E7 21 34N 98 17 E
Wan Lai-kam, Burma 90 E7 21 21N 98 22 E
Wan Tup, Burma 90 E7 21 13N 98 42 E
Wan Xian, China 74 E8 38 47N 115 7 E
Wana, Pakistan 91 B3 32 20N 69 32 E
Wanaaring, Australia 127 D3 29 38 S 144 9 E
Wanaka, N.Z. 131 E4 44 42 S 169 9 E
Wanaka, L., N.Z. 131 E4 44 33 S 169 7 E
Wan'an, China 77 D10 26 26N 114 49 E
Wanapiri, Indonesia 83 B5 4 30 S 135 59 E
Wanapitei L., Canada 140 C3 46 45N 80 40W
Wanbi, Australia 128 C4 34 46 S 140 17 E
Wandaik, Guyana 169 C6 4 27N 59 35W
Wandel Sea = McKinley Sea, Arctic 10 A11 82 0N 0 0W
Wandérama, Ivory C. 112 D4 8 37N 4 25W
Wanderer, Zimbabwe 119 F3 19 36 S 30 1 E
Wandhari, Pakistan 92 F2 27 42N 66 48 E
Wanding, China 76 E2 24 5N 98 4 E
Wandoan, Australia 127 D4 26 5 S 149 55 E
Wandur Marine △, India 95 J11 11 30N 92 30 E
Wanfu, China 75 D12 40 8N 122 38 E
Wang →, Thailand 86 D2 17 8N 99 2 E
Wang Kai, Sudan 107 F2 9 3N 29 23 E
Wang Noi, Thailand 86 E3 14 13N 100 44 E
Wang Saphung, Thailand 86 D3 17 18N 101 46 E
Wang Thong, Thailand 86 D3 16 50N 100 26 E
Wanga, Dem. Rep. of the Congo 118 B2 2 58N 29 12 E
Wangal, Indonesia 83 C4 6 8 S 134 9 E
Wanganella, Australia 129 C6 35 6 S 144 49 E
Wanganui, N.Z. 130 F4 39 56 S 175 3 E
Wanganui →, W. Coast, N.Z. 131 D5 43 3 S 170 26 E
Wanganui →, Wanganui-Manawatu, N.Z. 130 F4 39 55 S 175 4 E
Wangaratta, Australia 129 D7 36 21 S 146 19 E
Wangary, Australia 127 E2 34 35 S 135 29 E
Wangcang, China 76 A6 32 18N 106 20 E
Wangcheng, China 77 C9 28 22N 112 49 E
Wangdu, China 74 E8 38 40N 115 7 E
Wangdu Phodrang, Bhutan 90 B2 27 28N 89 54 E
Wangen, Germany 31 H5 47 41N 9 50 E
Wangerin = Węgorzyno, Poland 54 E2 53 32N 15 33 E
Wangerooge, Germany 30 B3 53 47N 7 54 E
Wängi, Switz. 33 B7 47 30N 8 57 E
Wangiwangi, Indonesia 82 C2 5 22 S 123 37 E
Wangjiang, China 77 B11 30 10N 116 42 E
Wangmo, China 76 E6 25 11N 106 5 E
Wangolodougou, Ivory C. 112 D3 9 55N 5 10W
Wangqing, China 75 C15 43 12N 129 42 E
Wani, India 94 D4 20 5N 78 55 E
Wanigela, Papua N. G. 132 E5 9 21 S 149 9 E
Wankaner, India 92 H4 22 35N 71 0 E
Wanlaweyne = Uanle Uen, Somali Rep. 120 D2 2 37N 44 54 E
Wanless, Canada 143 C8 54 11N 101 21W
Wanneroo, Australia 125 F2 31 42 S 115 46 E
Wannian, China 77 C11 28 42N 117 4 E
Wanning, China 86 C8 18 48N 110 22 E
Wanon Niwat, Thailand 86 D4 17 38N 103 46 E
Wanqinsha, China 69 F10 22 43N 113 33 E
Wanquan, China 74 D8 40 50N 114 40 E
Wanrong, China 74 G6 35 25N 110 50 E
Wansen = Wiązów, Poland 55 H4 50 50N 17 10 E
Wanshan, China 76 D7 27 30N 109 12 E
Wanshan Qundao, China 69 G10 21 57N 113 45 E
Wanshengchang, China 76 C6 28 57N 106 53 E
Wanstead, N.Z. 130 G5 40 8 S 176 30 E
Wantage, U.K. 21 F6 51 35N 1 25W
Wanxian, China 76 B7 30 42N 108 20 E
Wanyin, Burma 90 E6 20 23N 97 15 E
Wanyuan, China 76 A7 32 4N 108 3 E
Wanzai, Guangdong, China 69 G10 22 12N 113 31 E
Wanzai, Jiangxi, China 77 C10 28 7N 114 30 E
Wapakoneta, U.S.A. 157 D12 40 34N 84 12W
Wapato, U.S.A. 158 C3 46 27N 120 25W
Wapawekka L., Canada 143 C8 54 55N 104 40W
Wapello, U.S.A. 156 C5 41 11N 91 11W
Wapikopa L., Canada 140 B2 52 56N 87 53W
Wapinda, Dem. Rep. of the Congo 114 B4 3 41N 22 48 E
Wapiti →, Canada 142 B5 55 5N 118 18W
Wappingers Falls, U.S.A. 151 E11 41 36N 73 55W
Wapsipinicon →, U.S.A. 156 C6 41 44N 90 19W
Wapusk △, Canada 143 B10 57 46N 93 22W
Warab □, Sudan 107 F2 7 30N 28 30 E
Warabi, Japan 73 B11 35 49N 139 41 E
Warangal, India 94 F4 17 58N 79 35 E
Waraseoni, India 93 J9 21 45N 80 2 E
Waratah, Australia 127 G4 41 30 S 145 30 E
Waratah B., Australia 129 E7 38 54 S 146 5 E
Warburg, Germany 30 D5 51 28N 9 11 E
Warburton, Vic., Australia 129 D6 37 47 S 145 42 E
Warburton, W. Austral., Australia 125 E4 26 8 S 126 35 E
Warburton, The →, Australia 127 D2 28 4 S 137 28 E
Warburton Ra., Australia 125 E4 25 55 S 126 28 E
Ward, N.Z. 131 B9 41 49 S 174 11 E
Ward →, Australia 127 D4 26 28 S 146 6 E
Ward Hunt, C., Papua N. G. 132 E5 8 2 S 148 10 E
Ward Hunt Str., Papua N. G. 132 E6 9 30 S 150 0 E
Ward Mt., U.S.A. 160 H8 37 12N 118 54W
Wardang I., Australia 128 C2 34 30 S 137 20 E
Warden, S. Africa 117 D4 27 50 S 29 0 E
Wardha, India 94 D4 20 45N 78 39 E
Wardija Point, Malta 38 E6 36 2N 14 11 E
Wardo, Indonesia 83 B5 1 2 S 135 50 E
Ware, Canada 142 B3 57 26N 125 41W
Ware, U.K. 21 F8 51 49N 0 0W
Ware, U.S.A. 151 D12 42 16N 72 14W
Waregem, Belgium 24 D3 50 53N 3 27 E
Wareham, U.S.A. 151 E14 41 46N 70 43W
Waremme, Belgium 24 D5 50 43N 5 15 E
Waren, Germany 30 B8 53 31N 12 40 E
Waren, Indonesia 83 B5 2 16 S 136 20 E
Warendorf, Germany 30 D3 51 57N 8 1 E
Waresboro, U.S.A. 152 D7 31 15N 82 29W
Waria →, Papua N. G. 132 D4 7 49 S 147 41 E
Warialda, Australia 127 D5 29 29 S 150 33 E
Wariap, Indonesia 83 B4 1 30 S 134 5 E
Warin Chamrap, Thailand 86 E5 15 12N 104 53 E
Warka, Poland 55 G8 51 47N 21 12 E
Warkopi, Indonesia 83 B4 1 12 S 134 9 E
Warkworth, N.Z. 130 C3 36 24 S 174 41 E
Warm Baths = Bela Bela, S. Africa 117 C4 24 51 S 28 19 E
Warm Springs, Ga., U.S.A. 152 C5 32 53N 84 41W
Warm Springs, Nev., U.S.A. 159 G5 38 10N 116 20W
Warman, Canada 143 C7 52 19N 106 30W
Warmandi, Indonesia 83 B4 0 22 S 132 39 E
Warmbad = Bela Bela, S. Africa 117 C4 24 51 S 28 19 E
Warmbad, Namibia 116 D2 28 25 S 18 42 E
Warmińsko-Mazurskie □, Poland 54 D8 54 0N 21 0 E
Warminster, U.K. 21 F5 51 12N 2 10W
Warminster, U.S.A. 151 F9 40 12N 75 6W
Warnemünde, Germany 30 A8 54 10N 12 4 E
Warner Mts., U.S.A. 158 F3 41 40N 120 15W
Warner Robins, U.S.A. 152 C6 32 37N 83 36W
Warnes, Bolivia 173 D5 17 30 S 63 10W
Warnow →, Germany 30 A8 54 6N 12 9 E
Waroona, Australia 125 F2 32 50 S 115 58 E
Warora, India 94 D4 20 14N 79 1 E
Warracknabeal, Australia 128 D5 36 9 S 142 26 E
Warragul, Australia 129 E6 38 10 S 145 58 E
Warrego →, Australia 127 E4 30 24 S 145 21 E
Warrego Ra., Australia 126 C4 24 58 S 146 0 E
Warren, Australia 129 A7 31 42 S 147 51 E
Warren, Ark., U.S.A. 155 J8 33 37N 92 4W
Warren, Ill., U.S.A. 156 B7 42 29N 90 0W
Warren, Ind., U.S.A. 157 D11 40 41N 85 26W
Warren, Mich., U.S.A. 157 B13 42 30N 83 0W
Warren, Minn., U.S.A. 154 A6 48 12N 96 46W
Warren, Ohio, U.S.A. 150 E4 41 14N 80 49W
Warren, Pa., U.S.A. 150 E5 41 51N 79 9W
Warrenpoint, U.K. 23 B5 54 6N 6 15W
Warrensburg, Ill., U.S.A. 156 E7 39 56N 89 4W
Warrensburg, Mo., U.S.A. 156 F3 38 46N 93 44W
Warrensburg, N.Y., U.S.A. 151 C11 43 29N 73 46W
Warrenton, S. Africa 116 D3 28 9 S 24 47 E
Warrenton, Ga., U.S.A. 152 B7 33 24N 82 40W
Warrenton, Mo., U.S.A. 156 F5 38 49N 91 9W
Warrenton, Oreg., U.S.A. 160 D3 46 10N 123 56W
Warrenville = Gloverville, U.S.A. 152 B8 33 32N 81 48W
Warri, Nigeria 113 D6 5 30N 5 41 E
Warrina, Australia 127 D2 28 12 S 135 50 E
Warrington, N.Z. 131 F5 45 43 S 170 35 E
Warrington, U.K. 20 D5 53 24N 2 35W
Warrington, U.S.A. 153 E2 30 23N 87 17W
Warrington □, U.K. 20 D5 53 24N 2 35W
Warrnambool, Australia 128 E5 38 25 S 142 30 E
Warroad, U.S.A. 154 A7 48 54N 95 19W
Warrumbungle △, Australia 129 A8 31 18 S 149 1 E
Warruwi, Australia 126 A1 11 36 S 133 20 E
Warsa, Indonesia 83 B5 0 47 S 135 55 E
Warsak Dam, Pakistan 92 B4 34 11N 71 19 E
Warsaw = Warszawa, Poland 55 F8 52 13N 21 0 E
Warsaw, Ill., U.S.A. 156 D5 40 22N 91 26W
Warsaw, Ind., U.S.A. 157 C11 41 14N 85 51W
Warsaw, Ky., U.S.A. 157 F12 38 47N 84 54W
Warsaw, Mo., U.S.A. 156 F3 38 15N 93 23W
Warsaw, N.Y., U.S.A. 150 D6 42 45N 78 8W
Warsaw, Ohio, U.S.A. 150 F3 40 20N 82 0W
Warstein, Germany 30 D4 51 26N 8 22 E
Warszawa, Poland 55 F8 52 13N 21 0 E
Warszawa ✕ (WAW), Poland 55 F7 52 9N 20 59 E
Warta, Poland 55 G5 51 43N 18 38 E
Warta →, Poland 55 F1 52 35N 14 39 E
Wartenburg = Barczewo, Poland 54 E7 53 50N 20 42 E
Warth, Austria 33 B10 47 15N 10 11 E
Warthbrücken = Koło, Poland 55 F5 52 14N 18 40 E
Warthe = Warta →, Poland 55 F1 52 35N 14 39 E
Warthen, U.S.A. 152 B7 33 6N 82 48W
Warthenau = Zawiercie, Poland 55 H6 50 30N 19 24 E
Waru, Indonesia 83 B4 3 30 S 130 36 E
Warud, India 94 D4 21 30N 78 16 E
Warwick, Australia 127 D5 28 10 S 152 1 E
Warwick, U.K. 21 E6 52 18N 1 35W
Warwick, Ga., U.S.A. 152 D6 31 50N 83 57W
Warwick, N.Y., U.S.A. 151 E10 41 16N 74 22W
Warwick, R.I., U.S.A. 151 E13 41 42N 71 28W
Warwickshire □, U.K. 21 E6 52 14N 1 38W
Wasaga Beach, Canada 150 B4 44 31N 80 1W
Wasagaming, Canada 143 C9 50 39N 99 58W
Wasatch Ra., U.S.A. 158 F8 40 30N 111 15W
Wasbank, S. Africa 117 D5 28 15 S 30 9 E
Wasco, Calif., U.S.A. 161 K7 35 36N 119 20W
Wasco, Oreg., U.S.A. 158 D3 45 36N 120 42W
Wase, Nigeria 113 D6 9 4N 9 54 E
Waseca, U.S.A. 154 C8 44 5N 93 30W
Wasekamio L., Canada 143 B7 56 45N 108 45W
Wasgomura △, Sri Lanka 95 L5 7 45N 81 0 E
Wash, The, U.K. 20 E8 52 58N 0 20 E
Washago, Canada 150 B5 44 45N 79 20W
Washburn, Ill., U.S.A. 156 D7 40 55N 89 17W
Washburn, N. Dak., U.S.A. 154 B4 47 17N 101 2W
Washburn, Wis., U.S.A. 154 B9 46 40N 90 54W
Washim, India 94 D3 20 3N 77 0 E
Washington, U.K. 20 C6 54 55N 1 30W
Washington, D.C., U.S.A. 148 F7 38 54N 77 2W
Washington, Ga., U.S.A. 152 B7 33 44N 82 44W
Washington, Ill., U.S.A. 156 D7 40 42N 89 24W
Washington, Ind., U.S.A. 157 F9 38 40N 87 10W
Washington, Iowa, U.S.A. 156 C5 41 18N 91 42W
Washington, Mo., U.S.A. 156 F5 38 33N 91 1W
Washington, N.C., U.S.A. 149 H7 35 33N 77 3W
Washington, N.J., U.S.A. 151 F10 40 46N 74 59W
Washington, Pa., U.S.A. 150 F4 40 10N 80 15W
Washington, Utah, U.S.A. 159 H7 37 8N 113 31W
Washington □, U.S.A. 158 C3 47 30N 120 30W
Washington, Mt., U.S.A. 151 B13 44 16N 71 18W
Washington Court House, U.S.A. 157 E13 39 32N 83 26W
Washington I., U.S.A. 148 C2 45 23N 86 54W
Washington Land, Greenland 10 A4 80 30N 66 0W
Washougal, U.S.A. 160 E4 45 35N 122 21W
Washpool △, Australia 127 D5 29 22 S 152 20 E
Washuk, Pakistan 91 D2 27 42N 64 45 E
Wasian, Indonesia 83 B4 1 47 S 133 19 E
Wasilków, Poland 55 E10 53 12N 23 13 E
Wasilla, U.S.A. 144 F10 61 35N 149 26W
Wasior, Indonesia 83 B4 2 43 S 134 30 E
Wāsiṭ □, Iraq 96 C5 32 30N 46 0 E
Waskaganish, Canada 140 B4 51 30N 78 40W
Waskaiowaka, L., Canada 143 B9 56 33N 96 23W
Waskesiu Lake, Canada 143 C7 53 55N 106 5W
Wassaw I., U.S.A. 152 D9 31 53N 80 58W
Wassaw Sd., U.S.A. 152 D9 31 55N 80 55W
Wassen, Switz. 33 C7 46 42N 8 36 E
Wasserauen, Switz. 33 B8 47 17N 9 26 E
Wasserburg, Germany 31 G8 48 3N 12 14 E
Wasserkuppe, Germany 30 E5 50 29N 9 55 E
Wassy, France 27 D11 48 30N 4 58 E
Wasu, Papua N. G. 132 C4 5 58 S 147 12 E
Wasua, Papua N. G. 132 E2 8 18 S 142 52 E
Waswanipi, Canada 140 C4 49 40N 76 29W
Waswanipi, L., Canada 140 C4 49 35N 76 40W
Watam, Papua N. G. 132 B3 3 55 S 144 33 E
Watampone, Indonesia 82 B2 4 29 S 120 25 E
Watamu, Kenya 118 C5 3 23 S 40 0 E
Watansoppeng, Indonesia 82 B1 4 10 S 119 56 E
Watarrka △, Australia 124 D5 24 20 S 131 30 E
Watee, Solomon Is. 133 N12 10 30 S 162 2 E
Watenstadt-Salzgitter = Salzgitter, Germany 30 C6 52 9N 10 19 E
Water Park Pt., Australia 126 C5 22 56 S 150 47 E
Water Valley, U.S.A. 155 H10 34 10N 89 38W
Waterberg Plateau △, Namibia 116 C2 20 25 S 17 18 E
Waterberge, S. Africa 117 C4 24 10 S 28 0 E
Waterbury, Conn., U.S.A. 151 E11 41 33N 73 3W
Waterbury, Vt., U.S.A. 151 B12 44 20N 72 46W
Waterbury L., Canada 143 B8 58 10N 104 22W
Waterdown, Canada 150 C5 43 20N 79 53W
Wateree →, U.S.A. 152 B9 33 45N 80 37W
Waterford, Canada 150 D4 42 56N 80 17W
Waterford, Ireland 23 D4 52 15N 7 8W
Waterford, Calif., U.S.A. 160 H6 37 38N 120 46W
Waterford, Mich., U.S.A. 157 B13 42 45N 83 32W
Waterford, Pa., U.S.A. 150 E5 41 57N 79 59W
Waterford, Wis., U.S.A. 157 B8 42 46N 88 13W
Waterford □, Ireland 23 D4 52 10N 7 40W
Waterford Harbour, Ireland 23 D5 52 8N 6 58W
Waterhen L., Canada 143 C9 52 10N 99 40W
Waterloo, Belgium 24 D4 50 43N 4 25 E
Waterloo, Ont., Canada 140 D3 43 30N 80 32W
Waterloo, Qué., Canada 151 A12 45 22N 72 32W
Waterloo, S. Leone 112 D2 8 26N 13 8W
Waterloo, Ill., U.S.A. 156 F6 38 20N 90 9W
Waterloo, Ind., U.S.A. 157 C11 41 26N 85 1W
Waterloo, Iowa, U.S.A. 156 B4 42 30N 92 21W
Waterloo, N.Y., U.S.A. 150 D8 42 54N 76 52W
Waterloo, Wis., U.S.A. 156 A8 43 11N 88 59W
Waterman, U.S.A. 157 C8 41 46N 88 47W
Watersmeet, U.S.A. 154 B10 46 16N 89 11W
Waterton Lakes △, Canada 142 D6 48 45N 115 0W
Watertown, Conn., U.S.A. 151 E11 41 36N 73 7W
Watertown, Fla., U.S.A. 152 E7 30 11N 82 36W
Watertown, N.Y., U.S.A. 151 C9 43 59N 75 55W
Watertown, S. Dak., U.S.A. 154 C6 44 54N 97 7W
Watertown, Wis., U.S.A. 154 D10 43 12N 88 43W
Waterval-Boven, S. Africa 117 D5 25 40 S 30 18 E
Waterville, Canada 151 A13 45 16N 71 54W
Waterville, Maine, U.S.A. 149 C11 44 33N 69 38W
Waterville, N.Y., U.S.A. 151 D9 42 56N 75 23W
Waterville, Pa., U.S.A. 150 E7 41 19N 77 21W
Waterville, Wash., U.S.A. 158 C3 47 39N 120 4W
Watervliet, Mich., U.S.A. 157 B10 42 11N 86 18W
Watervliet, N.Y., U.S.A. 151 D11 42 44N 73 42W
Wates, Indonesia 85 D4 7 51 S 110 10 E
Watford, Canada 150 D3 42 57N 81 53W
Watford, U.K. 21 F7 51 40N 0 24W
Watford City, U.S.A. 154 B3 47 48N 103 17W
Wathaman →, Canada 143 B8 57 16N 102 59W
Wathaman L., Canada 143 B8 56 58N 103 44W
Watheroo, Australia 125 F2 30 15 S 116 0 E
Watheroo △, Australia 125 F2 30 19 S 115 48 E
Wating, China 74 G4 35 40N 106 38 E
Watkins Glen, U.S.A. 150 D8 42 23N 76 52W
Watkinsville, U.S.A. 152 B6 33 52N 83 25W
Watling I. = San Salvador I., Bahamas 165 B5 24 0N 74 40W
Watmuri, Indonesia 83 C4 7 25 S 131 42 E
Watom I., Papua N. G. 132 C7 4 7 S 152 4 E
Watonga, U.S.A. 155 H5 35 51N 98 25W
Watrous, Canada 143 C7 51 40N 105 25W
Watrous, U.S.A. 155 H2 35 48N 104 59W
Watsa, Dem. Rep. of the Congo 118 B2 3 4N 29 30 E
Watseka, U.S.A. 157 D9 40 47N 87 44W
Watsi Kenga, Dem. Rep. of the Congo 114 C4 0 49 S 20 34 E
Watson, Australia 125 F5 30 29 S 131 31 E
Watson, Canada 143 C8 52 10N 104 30W
Watson Lake, Canada 142 A3 60 6N 128 49W
Watsontown, U.S.A. 150 E8 41 5N 76 52W
Watsonville, U.S.A. 160 J5 36 55N 121 45W
Wattenwil, Switz. 32 C5 46 46N 7 31 E
Wattiwarriganna Cr. →, Australia 127 D2 28 57 S 136 10 E
Wattwil, Switz. 33 B8 47 18N 9 6 E
Watu, Dem. Rep. of the Congo 114 C4 3 18 S 20 3 E
Watuata = Batuata, Indonesia 82 C2 6 12 S 122 42 E
Watubela, Kepulauan, Indonesia 83 B4 4 28 S 131 35 E
Watubela Is. = Watubela, Kepulauan, Indonesia 83 B4 4 28 S 131 35 E
Wau = Wâw, Sudan 107 F2 7 45N 28 1 E
Wau, Papua N. G. 132 D4 7 21 S 146 47 E
Waubamik, Canada 150 A4 45 27N 80 1W
Waubay, U.S.A. 154 C6 45 20N 97 18W
Waubra, Australia 128 D5 37 21 S 143 39 E
Wauchope, N.S.W., Australia 129 A10 31 28 S 152 45 E
Wauchope, N. Terr., Australia 126 C1 20 36 S 134 15 E
Wauchula, U.S.A. 153 H8 27 33N 81 49W
Waukarlycarly, L., Australia 124 D3 21 18 S 121 56 E
Waukeenah, U.S.A. 152 E6 30 25N 83 57W
Waukegan, U.S.A. 157 B9 42 22N 87 50W
Waukesha, U.S.A. 154 D10 43 1N 88 14W
Waukon, U.S.A. 154 D9 43 16N 91 29W
Waupaca, U.S.A. 154 C10 44 21N 89 5W
Waupun, U.S.A. 154 D10 43 38N 88 44W
Waurika, U.S.A. 155 H6 34 10N 98 0W
Wausau, Fla., U.S.A. 152 E4 30 38N 85 35W
Wausau, Wis., U.S.A. 154 C10 44 58N 89 38W
Wauseon, U.S.A. 157 C12 41 33N 84 8W
Wautoma, U.S.A. 154 C10 44 4N 89 18W
Wauwatosa, U.S.A. 157 A9 43 3N 88 0W
Waveland, U.S.A. 157 E9 39 53N 87 3W
Waveney →, U.K. 21 E9 52 35N 1 39 E
Waverley, N.Z. 130 F3 39 46 S 174 37 E
Waverley Hall, U.S.A. 152 C5 32 41N 84 44W
Waverly, Ala., U.S.A. 152 C4 32 44N 85 35W
Waverly, Fla., U.S.A. 153 H8 27 59N 81 37W
Waverly, Ga., U.S.A. 152 D8 31 6N 81 43W
Waverly, Ill., U.S.A. 156 E7 39 36N 89 57W
Waverly, Iowa, U.S.A. 156 B4 42 44N 92 29W
Waverly, Mo., U.S.A. 156 E3 39 13N 93 31W
Waverly, N.Y., U.S.A. 151 E8 42 1N 76 32W
Wavre, Belgium 24 D4 50 43N 4 38 E
Waw, Burma 90 G6 17 28N 96 41 E
Wâw, Sudan 107 F2 7 45N 28 1 E
Wāw al Kabīr, Libya 108 C3 25 20N 16 43 E
Wāw an Nāmūs, Libya 108 D3 24 55N 17 46 E
Wawa, Canada 140 C3 47 59N 84 47W
Wawa, Nigeria 113 D5 9 54N 4 27 E
Wawa, Sudan 106 C3 20 30N 30 22 E
Wawanesa, Canada 143 D9 49 36N 99 40W
Wawasee, L., U.S.A. 157 C11 41 24N 85 42W
Wawoi →, Papua N. G. 132 D2 7 48 S 143 16 E
Wawona, U.S.A. 160 H7 37 32N 119 39W
Waxahachie, U.S.A. 155 J6 32 24N 96 51W
Way, L., Australia 125 E3 26 45 S 120 16 E
Waya, Fiji 133 A1 17 19 S 177 10 E
Wayabula, Indonesia 82 A3 2 29N 128 17 E
Waycross, U.S.A. 152 D7 31 13N 82 21W
Wayi, Sudan 107 F3 5 8N 30 10 E
Wayland, Mich., U.S.A. 157 B11 42 40N 85 39W
Wayland, N.Y., U.S.A. 150 D7 42 34N 77 35W
Wayne, Nebr., U.S.A. 154 D6 42 14N 97 1W
Wayne, W. Va., U.S.A. 148 F4 38 13N 82 27W
Wayne City, U.S.A. 157 F8 38 21N 88 35W
Wayne County, Detroit ✕ (DTW), U.S.A. 157 B13 42 13N 83 21W
Wayne Lakes, U.S.A. 157 D12 40 1N 84 40W
Waynesboro, Ga., U.S.A. 152 B7 33 6N 82 1W
Waynesboro, Miss., U.S.A. 149 K1 31 40N 88 39W
Waynesboro, Pa., U.S.A. 148 F7 39 45N 77 35W
Waynesboro, Va., U.S.A. 148 F6 38 4N 78 53W
Waynesburg, U.S.A. 148 F5 39 54N 80 11W
Waynesville, Mo., U.S.A. 156 G4 37 50N 92 12W
Waynesville, N.C., U.S.A. 149 H4 35 28N 82 58W
Waynesville, Ohio, U.S.A. 157 E12 39 32N 84 5W
Waynoka, U.S.A. 155 G5 36 35N 98 53W
Wayside, U.S.A. 152 B6 33 4N 83 37W
Waza, Afghan. 91 B3 33 22N 69 26 E
Waza △, Cameroon 109 F2 11 15N 14 38 E
Wazikhwah, Afghan. 91 B3 32 11N 68 21 E
Wāzin, Libya 108 B2 31 58N 10 40 E
Wazirabad, Pakistan 92 C6 32 30N 74 8 E
Wda →, Poland 55 E5 53 25N 18 29 E
We, Indonesia 84 A1 5 51N 95 18 E
Wé, N. Cal. 133 K5 20 55 S 167 16 E
Weald, The, U.K. 21 F8 51 4N 0 20 E
Weam, Papua N. G. 132 E1 8 37 S 141 8 E
Wear →, U.K. 20 C6 54 55N 1 23W
Weatherford, Okla., U.S.A. 155 H5 35 32N 98 43W
Weatherford, Tex., U.S.A. 155 J6 32 46N 97 48W
Weaubleau, U.S.A. 156 G3 37 54N 93 32W
Weaverville, U.S.A. 158 F2 40 44N 122 56W
Webb City, U.S.A. 155 G7 37 9N 94 28W
Webequie, Canada 140 B2 52 59N 87 21W
Weber, N.Z. 130 G5 40 24 S 176 20 E
Webo = Nyaake, Liberia 112 E3 4 52N 7 37W
Webster, Mass., U.S.A. 151 D13 42 3N 71 53W
Webster, N.Y., U.S.A. 150 C7 43 13N 77 26W
Webster, S. Dak., U.S.A. 154 C6 45 20N 97 31W
Webster City, U.S.A. 156 B3 42 28N 93 49W
Webster Springs, U.S.A. 148 F5 38 29N 80 25W
Weda, Indonesia 79 D7 0 21N 127 50 E
Weda, Teluk, Indonesia 82 A3 0 20N 128 0 E
Weddell I., Falk. Is. 9 f 51 50 S 61 0W
Weddell Sea, Antarctica 7 D1 72 30 S 40 0W
Wedderburn, Australia 128 D5 36 26 S 143 33 E
Weddin Mts. △, Australia 129 C8 33 59 S 148 0 E
Wedel, Germany 30 B5 53 34N 9 42 E
Wedemark, Germany 30 C5 52 32N 9 43 E
Wedgeport, Canada 141 D6 43 44N 65 59W
Wednesday I., Australia 132 F2 10 31 S 142 16 E
Wedowee, U.S.A. 152 B4 33 19N 85 29W
Wedza, Zimbabwe 119 F3 18 40 S 31 33 E
Wee Waa, Australia 127 E4 30 11 S 149 26 E
Weed, U.S.A. 158 F2 41 25N 122 23W
Weed Heights, U.S.A. 160 G7 38 59N 119 13W
Weedsport, U.S.A. 151 C8 43 3N 76 35W
Weedville, U.S.A. 150 E6 41 17N 78 30W
Weeki Wachee, U.S.A. 153 G7 28 32N 82 35W
Weenen, S. Africa 117 D5 28 48 S 30 7 E
Weener, Germany 30 B3 53 9N 7 20 E
Weert, Neths. 24 C5 51 15N 5 43 E
Weggis, Switz. 33 B6 47 2N 8 26 E
Węgierska-Górka, Poland 55 J6 49 36N 19 7 E
Węgliniec, Poland 55 G2 51 18N 15 10 E
Węgorzewo, Poland 54 D8 54 13N 21 43 E
Węgorzyno, Poland 54 E2 53 32N 15 33 E
Węgrów, Poland 55 F9 52 24N 22 0 E
Wehda □, Sudan 107 F3 8 30N 30 0 E
Wei He →, Hebei, China 74 F8 36 10N 115 45 E
Wei He →, Shaanxi, China 74 G6 34 38N 110 15 E
Weichang, China 75 D9 41 58N 117 49 E
Weichuan, China 74 G7 34 20N 113 59 E
Weida, Germany 30 E8 50 46N 12 2 E
Weiden, Germany 31 F8 49 41N 12 10 E
Weifang, China 75 F10 36 44N 119 7 E
Weihai, China 75 F12 37 30N 122 6 E
Weil, Germany 31 H3 47 35N 7 37 E
Weilburg, Germany 30 E4 50 28N 8 17 E
Weilheim, Germany 31 H7 47 50N 11 9 E
Weimar, Germany 30 E7 50 58N 11 19 E
Weinan, China 74 G5 34 31N 109 29 E
Weinfelden, Switz. 33 A8 47 34N 9 6 E
Weingarten, Germany 31 F4 49 3N 8 31 E
Weinheim, Germany 31 F4 49 32N 8 39 E
Weining, China 76 D5 26 50N 104 17 E
Weipa, Australia 126 A3 12 40 S 141 50 E
Weir →, Australia 127 D4 28 20 S 149 50 E
Weir →, Canada 143 B10 56 54N 93 21W
Weir, L., U.S.A. 153 F8 29 0N 81 56W
Weir River, Canada 143 B10 56 49N 94 6W
Weirsdale, U.S.A. 153 G8 28 59N 81 55W
Weirton, U.S.A. 150 F4 40 24N 80 35W
Weiser, U.S.A. 158 D5 44 10N 117 0W
Weishan, Shandong, China 75 G9 34 47N 117 5 E
Weishan, Yunnan, China 76 E3 25 12N 100 20 E
Weissenbach, Austria 33 B11 47 26N 10 39 E
Weissenburg, Germany 31 F6 49 2N 10 58 E
Weissenfels, Germany 30 D7 51 11N 12 0 E
Weisshorn, Switz. 32 D5 46 7N 7 43 E
Weisskirchen = Hranice, Czech Rep. 35 B10 49 34N 17 45 E
Weisskugel, Austria 33 C11 46 48N 10 44 E
Weissmies, Switz. 32 D6 46 8N 8 1 E
Weisstannen, Switz. 33 C8 46 59N 9 22 E
Weisswasser, Germany 30 D10 51 30N 14 36 E
Weistritz = Bystrzyca →, Dolnośląskie, Poland 55 G3 51 12N 16 55 E
Weistritz = Bystrzyca →, Lubelskie, Poland 55 G9 51 21N 22 46 E
Weitra, Austria 34 C7 48 41N 14 54 E
Weixi, China 76 D2 27 10N 99 10 E
Weixin, China 76 D5 27 48N 105 3 E
Weiyuan, China 74 G3 35 7N 104 10 E
Weiz, Austria 34 D8 47 13N 15 39 E
Weizhou Dao, China 76 G7 21 0N 109 5 E
Wejherowo, Poland 54 D5 54 35N 18 12 E
Wekusko L., Canada 143 C9 54 40N 99 50W
Welch, U.S.A. 148 G5 37 26N 81 35W
Weldya, Ethiopia 107 E4 11 50N 39 34 E
Welega, Ethiopia 107 F3 9 25N 34 20 E
Welford △, Australia 126 D3 25 5 S 143 16 E
Weligama, Sri Lanka 95 M5 5 58N 80 25 E
Welkite, Ethiopia 107 F4 8 15N 37 42 E
Welkom, S. Africa 116 D4 28 0 S 26 46 E
Welland, Canada 140 D4 43 0N 79 15W
Welland →, U.K. 21 E7 52 51N 0 5W
Wellawaya, Sri Lanka 95 L5 6 44N 81 6 E
Wellesley Is., Australia 126 B2 16 42 S 139 30 E
Wellingborough, U.K. 21 E7 52 19N 0 41W
Wellington, Australia 129 B8 32 35 S 148 59 E
Wellington, Canada 150 C7 43 57N 77 20W

Wellington, N.Z. 130 H3 41 19 S 174 46 E
Wellington, S. Africa 116 E2 33 38 S 19 1 E
Wellington, Somst., U.K. 21 G4 50 58N 3 13W
Wellington, Telford & Wrekin, U.K. 21 E5 52 42N 2 30W
Wellington, Colo., U.S.A. 154 E2 40 42N 105 0W
Wellington, Kans., U.S.A. 155 G6 37 16N 97 24W
Wellington, Mo., U.S.A. 156 E3 39 8N 93 59W
Wellington, Nev., U.S.A. 160 G7 38 45N 119 23W
Wellington, Ohio, U.S.A. 150 E2 41 10N 82 13W
Wellington, Tex., U.S.A. 155 H4 34 51N 100 13W
Wellington □, N.Z. 130 G4 41 0 S 175 30 E
Wellington, I., Chile 176 C2 49 30 S 75 0W
Wellington, L., Australia 129 E7 38 6 S 147 20 E
Wellman, U.S.A. 156 C5 41 28N 91 50W
Wells, U.K. 21 F5 51 13N 2 39W
Wells, Maine, U.S.A. 151 C14 43 20N 70 35W
Wells, N.Y., U.S.A. 151 C10 43 24N 74 17W
Wells, Nev., U.S.A. 158 F6 41 7N 114 58W
Wells, L., Australia 125 E3 26 44 S 123 15 E
Wells, Mt., Australia 124 C4 17 25 S 127 8 E
Wells Gray ⌓, Canada 142 C4 52 30N 120 15W
Wells-next-the-Sea, U.K. 20 E8 52 57N 0 51 E
Wells River, U.S.A. 151 B12 44 9N 72 4W
Wellsboro, U.S.A. 150 E7 41 45N 77 18W
Wellsburg, U.S.A. 150 F4 40 16N 80 37W
Wellsford, N.Z. 130 C3 36 16 S 174 32 E
Wellston = Warner Robins, U.S.A. 152 C6 32 37N 83 36W
Wellsville, Mo., U.S.A. 156 E5 39 4N 91 34W
Wellsville, N.Y., U.S.A. 150 D7 42 7N 77 57W
Wellsville, Ohio, U.S.A. 150 F4 40 36N 80 39W
Wellsville, Utah, U.S.A. 158 F8 41 38N 111 56W
Wellton, U.S.A. 159 K6 32 40N 114 8W
Welmel, Wabi →, Ethiopia 107 F5 5 38N 40 47 E
Welo, Ethiopia 107 E4 11 50N 39 48 E
Welo, Somali Rep. 120 C3 9 25N 48 55 E
Wels, Austria 34 C7 48 9N 14 1 E
Welshpool, Australia 129 E7 38 42 S 146 26 E
Welshpool, U.K. 21 E4 52 39N 3 8W
Welungen = Wieluń, Poland 55 G5 51 15N 18 34 E
Welwitschia = Khorixas, Namibia 116 C1 20 16 S 14 59 E
Welwyn Garden City, U.K. 21 F7 51 48N 0 12W
Wem, U.K. 20 E5 52 52N 2 44W
Wembere →, Tanzania 118 C3 4 10 S 34 15 E
Wemindji, Canada 140 B4 53 0N 78 49W
Wen Xian, China 74 G7 34 55N 113 5 E
Wenatchee, U.S.A. 158 C3 47 25N 120 19W
Wenchang, China 86 C8 19 38N 110 42 E
Wencheng, China 77 D13 27 46N 120 4 E
Wenchi, Ghana 112 D4 7 46N 2 8W
Wenchow = Wenzhou, China 77 D13 28 0N 120 38 E
Wenchuan, China 76 B4 31 22N 103 35 E
Wenden, U.S.A. 161 M13 33 49N 113 33W
Wendeng, China 75 F12 37 15N 122 5 E
Wendesi, Indonesia 83 B4 2 30 S 134 17 E
Wendo, Ethiopia 107 F4 6 40N 38 27 E
Wendover, U.S.A. 158 F6 40 44N 114 2W
Weng'an, China 76 D6 27 5N 107 25 E
Wengcheng, China 77 E9 24 22N 113 50 E
Wengen, Switz. 32 C5 46 37N 7 55 E
Wengyuan, China 77 E10 24 20N 114 9 E
Wenjiang, China 76 B4 30 44N 103 55 E
Wenling, China 77 C13 28 21N 121 20 E
Wenlock →, Australia 126 A3 12 2 S 141 55 E
Wenona, U.S.A. 156 C7 41 3N 89 3W
Wenshan, China 76 F5 23 20N 104 18 E
Wenshang, China 74 G9 35 45N 116 30 E
Wenshui, China 74 F7 37 26N 112 1 E
Wensleydale, U.K. 20 C6 54 17N 2 0W
Wensu, China 68 B3 41 15N 80 10 E
Wensum →, U.K. 20 E8 52 40N 1 15 E
Wentworth, Australia 128 C4 34 2 S 141 54 E
Wentzel L., Canada 142 B6 59 2N 114 28W
Wentzville, U.S.A. 156 F6 38 49N 90 51W
Wenut, Indonesia 83 B4 3 11 S 133 19 E
Wenxi, China 74 G6 35 20N 111 10 E
Wenxian, China 74 H3 32 43N 104 36 E
Wenzhou, China 77 D13 28 0N 120 38 E
Weott, U.S.A. 158 F2 40 20N 123 55W
Wepener, S. Africa 116 D4 29 42 S 27 3 E
Werda, Botswana 116 D3 25 24 S 23 15 E
Werdau, Germany 30 E8 50 44N 12 22 E
Werder, Ethiopia 120 C3 6 58N 45 1 E
Werder, Germany 30 C8 52 23N 12 55 E
Werdohl, Germany 30 D3 51 15N 7 46 E
Wereilu, Ethiopia 107 E4 10 40N 39 28 E
Weri, Indonesia 83 B4 3 10 S 132 38 E
Werneck, Germany 31 F6 49 58N 10 5 E
Wernigerode, Germany 30 D6 51 50N 10 47 E
Werra →, Germany 30 D5 51 24N 9 39 E
Werribee, Australia 128 D6 37 54 S 144 40 E
Werrikimbee △, Australia 129 A10 31 11 S 152 15 E
Werrimull, Australia 128 C4 34 25 S 141 38 E
Werris Creek, Australia 129 A9 31 18 S 150 38 E
Werschetz = Vršac, Serbia & M. 52 E6 45 8N 21 20 E
Wertach →, Germany 31 G6 48 22N 10 54 E
Wertheim, Germany 31 F5 49 45N 9 32 E
Wertingen, Germany 31 G6 48 33N 10 41 E
Wesel, Germany 30 D2 51 39N 6 37 E
Weser →, Germany 30 B4 53 36N 8 28 E
Weser-Ems □, Germany 30 C3 53 0N 7 30 E
Weserbergland, Germany 30 C5 52 12N 9 7 E
Weserbergland Schaumburg Hameln ⌓, Germany 30 C5 52 8N 9 20 E
Wesermünde = Bremerhaven, Germany 30 B4 53 33N 8 36 E
Wesiri, Indonesia 82 C3 7 30 S 126 30 E
Weslaco, U.S.A. 155 M6 26 10N 97 58W
Weslemkoon L., Canada 150 A7 45 2N 77 25W
Wesleyville, U.S.A. 150 D4 42 9N 80 0W
Wessel, C., Australia 126 A2 10 59 S 136 46 E
Wessel Is., Australia 126 A2 11 10 S 136 45 E
Wesselburen, Germany 30 A4 54 13N 8 54 E
Wessington Springs, U.S.A. 154 C5 44 5N 98 34W
West, U.S.A. 155 K6 31 48N 97 6W
West →, U.S.A. 151 D12 42 52N 72 33W
West Allis, U.S.A. 157 B8 43 1N 88 0W
West Antarctica, Antarctica 7 D15 80 0 S 90 0W
West Baines →, Australia 124 C4 15 38 S 129 59 E
West Bank ◪, Asia 103 C4 32 6N 35 13 E
West Bend, U.S.A. 148 D1 43 25N 88 11W
West Bengal □, India 93 H13 23 0N 88 0 E
West Berkshire □, U.K. 21 F6 51 25N 1 17W
West Beskids = Západné Beskydy, Europe 35 B12 49 30N 19 0 E
West Branch, U.S.A. 148 C3 44 17N 84 14W
West Branch Susquehanna →, U.S.A. 151 F8 40 53N 76 48W
West Bromwich, U.K. 21 E6 52 32N 1 59W
West Burra, U.K. 22 A7 60 5N 1 21W
West Canada Cr. →, U.S.A. 151 C10 43 1N 74 58W
West Cape Howe, Australia 125 G2 35 8 S 117 36 E
West Carrollton, U.S.A. 157 E12 39 40N 84 17W
West Chazy, U.S.A. 151 B11 44 49N 73 28W
West Chester, U.S.A. 151 G9 39 58N 75 36W
West Chicago, U.S.A. 157 C8 41 53N 88 12W
West Coast ⌓, Namibia 116 C1 21 53 S 14 14 E
West Coast □, N.Z. 131 D5 43 15 S 170 30 E
West Coast △, S. Africa 116 E2 33 13 S 18 0 E
West Columbia, S.C., U.S.A. 152 B8 33 59N 81 4W
West Columbia, Tex., U.S.A. 155 L7 29 9N 95 39W
West Covina, U.S.A. 161 L9 34 4N 117 54W
West Des Moines, U.S.A. 156 C3 41 35N 93 43W
West Dunbartonshire □, U.K. 22 F4 55 59N 4 30W
West End, Bahamas 164 A4 26 41N 78 58W
West Falkland, Falk. Is. 9 f 51 40 S 60 0W
West Fargo, U.S.A. 154 B6 46 52N 96 54W
West Farmington, U.S.A. 150 E4 41 23N 80 58W
West Fjord = Vestfjorden, Norway 14 C15 67 55N 14 0 E
West Fork Trinity →, U.S.A. 155 J6 32 48N 96 54W
West Frankfort, U.S.A. 156 G8 37 54N 88 55W
West Grand L., U.S.A. 149 C12 45 14N 67 51W
West Green, U.S.A. 152 D7 31 37N 82 44W
West Hartford, U.S.A. 151 E12 41 45N 72 44W
West Haven, U.S.A. 151 E12 41 17N 72 57W
West Hazleton, U.S.A. 151 F9 40 58N 76 0W
West Helena, U.S.A. 155 H9 34 33N 90 38W
West Hurley, U.S.A. 151 E10 41 59N 74 7W
West I., India 95 H11 13 35N 92 54 E
West Ice Shelf, Antarctica 7 C7 67 0 S 85 0 E
West Indies, Cent. Amer. 165 D7 15 0N 65 0W
West Jefferson, U.S.A. 157 E12 39 57N 83 17W
West Jordan, U.S.A. 158 F8 40 36N 111 56W
West Lafayette, U.S.A. 157 D10 40 27N 86 55W
West Lamma Channel, China 69 G11 22 13N 114 4 E
West Liberty, Iowa, U.S.A. 156 C5 41 34N 91 16W
West Liberty, Ky., U.S.A. 157 G13 37 55N 83 16W
West Liberty, Ohio, U.S.A. 157 D13 40 15N 83 45W
West Lorne, Canada 150 D3 42 36N 81 36W
West Lothian □, U.K. 22 F5 55 54N 3 36W
West Lunga △, Zambia 115 E4 12 49 S 24 47 E
West Lunga →, Zambia 119 E1 13 6 S 24 39 E
West MacDonnell △, Australia 124 D5 23 38 S 132 59 E
West Memphis, U.S.A. 155 H9 35 9N 90 11W
West Midlands □, U.K. 21 E6 52 26N 2 0W
West Mifflin, U.S.A. 150 F5 40 22N 79 52W
West Milton, Ohio, U.S.A. 157 E12 39 58N 84 20W
West Milton, Pa., U.S.A. 150 E8 41 1N 76 50W
West Monroe, U.S.A. 155 J8 32 31N 92 9W
West New Britain □, Papua N. G. 132 C5 5 0 S 149 30 E
West Newton, U.S.A. 150 F5 40 14N 79 46W
West Nicholson, Zimbabwe 119 G2 21 2 S 29 20 E
West Odessa, U.S.A. 155 K3 31 50N 102 31W
West Palm Beach, U.S.A. 153 J9 26 43N 80 3W
West Palm Beach Canal, U.S.A. 153 J9 26 40N 80 15W
West Pensacola, U.S.A. 153 E2 30 25N 87 16W
West Plains, U.S.A. 155 G9 36 44N 91 51W
West Point, Ga., U.S.A. 152 C4 32 53N 85 11W
West Point, Iowa, U.S.A. 156 D5 40 43N 91 27W
West Point, Ky., U.S.A. 157 G11 37 59N 85 57W
West Point, Miss., U.S.A. 155 J10 33 36N 88 39W
West Point, N.Y., U.S.A. 151 E11 41 24N 73 58W
West Point, Nebr., U.S.A. 154 E6 41 51N 96 43W
West Point, Va., U.S.A. 148 G7 37 32N 76 48W
West Point L., U.S.A. 152 B4 33 0N 85 5W
West Pt. = Ouest, Pte. de l', Canada 141 C7 49 52N 64 40W
West Pt., Australia 128 C1 35 1 S 135 56 E
West Ra., Papua N. G. 132 C1 4 15 S 141 30 E
West Road →, Canada 142 C4 53 18N 122 53W
West Rutland, U.S.A. 151 C11 43 38N 73 5W
West Salem, U.S.A. 157 F8 38 31N 88 1W
West Schelde = Westerschelde →, Neths. 24 C3 51 25N 3 25 E
West Seneca, U.S.A. 150 D6 42 51N 78 48W
West Sepik □, Papua N. G. 132 B2 3 30 S 142 0 E
West Siberian Plain, Russia 62 C11 62 0N 75 0 E
West Sussex □, U.K. 21 G7 50 55N 0 30W
West Terre Haute, U.S.A. 157 E9 39 28N 87 27W
West-Terschelling, Neths. 24 A5 53 22N 5 13 E
West Union, Iowa, U.S.A. 156 B5 42 57N 91 49W
West Union, Ohio, U.S.A. 157 F13 38 48N 83 33W
West Unity, U.S.A. 157 C12 41 35N 84 26W
West Valley City, U.S.A. 158 F8 40 42N 111 57W
West Virginia □, U.S.A. 148 F5 38 45N 80 30W
West-Vlaanderen □, Belgium 24 D2 51 0N 3 0 E
West Walker →, U.S.A. 160 G7 38 54N 119 9W
West Wyalong, Australia 129 B7 33 56 S 147 10 E
West Yellowstone, U.S.A. 158 D8 44 40N 111 6W
West Yorkshire □, U.K. 20 D6 53 45N 1 40W
Westall, Pt., Australia 127 E1 32 55 S 134 4 E
Westbay, U.S.A. 152 E4 30 18N 85 52W
Westbrook, U.S.A. 149 D10 43 41N 70 22W
Westbury, Australia 127 G4 41 30 S 146 51 E
Westby, U.S.A. 154 A2 48 52N 104 3W
Westend, U.S.A. 161 K9 35 42N 117 24W
Westerland, Germany 15 J13 54 54N 8 17 E
Westerly, U.S.A. 151 E13 41 22N 71 50W
Western □, Ghana 112 D4 5 30N 2 30W
Western □, Kenya 118 B3 0 30N 34 30 E
Western □, Papua N. G. 132 D2 7 30 S 142 0 E
Western □, S. Leone 112 D2 8 30N 13 20W
Western □, Zambia 119 F1 15 0 S 24 4 E
Western Australia □, Australia 125 E2 25 0 S 118 0 E
Western Cape □, S. Africa 116 E3 34 0 S 20 0 E
Western Dvina = Daugava →, Latvia 15 H21 57 4N 24 3 E
Western Ghats, India 95 H2 14 0N 75 0 E
Western Highlands □, Papua N. G. 132 C3 5 45 S 144 30 E
Western Isles □, U.K. 22 D1 57 30N 7 10W
Western Sahara ■, Africa 110 D2 25 0N 13 0W
Western Samoa = Samoa ■, Pac. Oc. 133 X24 14 0 S 172 0W
Westernport, U.S.A. 148 F6 39 29N 79 3W
Westerschelde →, Neths. 24 C3 51 25N 3 25 E
Westerstede, Germany 30 B3 53 15N 7 55 E
Westerwald, Germany 30 E3 50 38N 7 56 E
Westfield, Ill., U.S.A. 157 E8 39 27N 88 0W
Westfield, Ind., U.S.A. 157 D10 40 2N 86 8W
Westfield, Mass., U.S.A. 151 D12 42 7N 72 45W
Westfield, N.Y., U.S.A. 150 D5 42 20N 79 35W
Westfield, Pa., U.S.A. 150 E7 41 55N 77 32W
Westhill, U.K. 22 D6 57 9N 2 19W
Westhope, U.S.A. 154 A4 48 55N 101 1W
Westland, U.S.A. 157 B13 42 15N 83 20W
Westland △, N.Z. 131 D5 43 16 S 170 16 E
Westland Bight, N.Z. 131 C5 42 55 S 170 5 E
Westlock, Canada 142 C6 54 9N 113 55W
Westmar, Australia 127 D4 27 55 S 149 44 E
Westmeath □, Ireland 23 C4 53 33N 7 34W
Westminster, Colo., U.S.A. 154 F2 39 50N 105 2W
Westminster, Md., U.S.A. 148 F7 39 34N 76 59W
Westmont, U.S.A. 150 F6 40 19N 78 58W
Westmoreland, Barbados 165 g 13 13N 59 37W
Westmorland, U.S.A. 161 M11 33 2N 115 37W
Weston, Malaysia 85 A5 5 10N 115 35 E
Weston, Ohio, U.S.A. 157 C13 41 21N 83 47W
Weston, Oreg., U.S.A. 158 D4 45 49N 118 26W
Weston, W. Va., U.S.A. 148 F5 39 2N 80 28W
Weston I., Canada 140 B4 52 33N 79 36W
Weston-super-Mare, U.K. 21 F5 51 21N 2 58W
Westover, U.S.A. 150 F6 40 45N 78 40W
Westphalia, U.S.A. 156 F5 38 26N 92 0W
Westport, Canada 151 B8 44 40N 76 25W
Westport, Ireland 23 C2 53 48N 9 31W
Westport, N.Z. 131 B6 41 46 S 171 37 E
Westport, Ind., U.S.A. 157 E11 39 11N 85 34W
Westport, N.Y., U.S.A. 151 B11 44 11N 73 26W
Westport, Oreg., U.S.A. 160 D3 46 8N 123 23W
Westport, Wash., U.S.A. 160 D2 46 53N 124 6W
Westray, Canada 143 C8 53 36N 101 24W
Westray, U.K. 22 B5 59 18N 3 0W
Westree, Canada 140 C3 47 26N 81 34W
Westville, Calif., U.S.A. 160 F6 39 8N 120 42W
Westville, Fla., U.S.A. 152 E4 30 46N 85 51W
Westville, Ill., U.S.A. 157 D9 40 2N 87 38W
Westville, Ind., U.S.A. 157 C10 41 35N 86 55W
Westwood, U.S.A. 158 F3 40 18N 121 0W
Wetar, Indonesia 82 C3 7 48 S 126 30 E
Wetar, Selat, Indonesia 82 C3 8 20 S 126 30 E
Wetaskiwin, Canada 142 C6 52 55N 113 24W
Wetherby, U.K. 20 D6 53 56N 1 23W
Wethersfield, U.S.A. 151 E12 41 42N 72 40W
Wetlet, Burma 90 D5 22 20N 95 53 E
Wetteren, Belgium 24 D3 51 0N 3 53 E
Wettingen, Switz. 33 B6 47 28N 8 20 E
Wetumpka, U.S.A. 152 C3 32 32N 86 13W
Wetzikon, Switz. 33 B7 47 19N 8 48 E
Wetzlar, Germany 30 E4 50 32N 8 31 E
Wevok, U.S.A. 144 B6 68 53N 166 13W
Wewahitchka, U.S.A. 152 E4 30 7N 85 12W
Wewak, Papua N. G. 132 B2 3 38 S 143 41 E
Wewoka, U.S.A. 155 H6 35 9N 96 30W
Wexford, Ireland 23 D5 52 20N 6 28W
Wexford □, Ireland 23 D5 52 20N 6 25W
Wexford Harbour, Ireland 23 D5 52 20N 6 25W
Weyburn, Canada 143 D8 49 40N 103 50W
Weyer Markt, Austria 34 D7 47 51N 14 40 E
Weyhe, Germany 30 C4 52 58N 8 49 E
Weyib →, Ethiopia 107 F5 7 15N 40 15 E
Weymouth, Canada 141 D6 44 30N 66 1W
Weymouth, U.K. 21 G5 50 37N 2 28W
Weymouth, U.S.A. 151 D14 42 13N 70 58W
Weymouth, C., Australia 126 A3 12 37 S 143 27 E
Wha Ti, Canada 138 B8 63 8N 117 16W
Whakaari = White I., N.Z. 130 D6 37 30 S 177 13 E
Whakamaru, N.Z. 130 E4 38 23 S 175 50 E
Whakatane, N.Z. 130 D6 37 57 S 177 1 E
Whakatane →, N.Z. 130 D6 37 57 S 177 1 E
Whale →, Canada 141 A6 58 15N 67 40W
Whale Cove, Canada 143 A10 62 10N 92 34W
Whale Pt., Ascension I. 9 g 7 57 S 14 18W
Whales, B. of, Antarctica 7 D12 78 0 S 165 0W
Whalsay, U.K. 22 A8 60 22N 0 59W
Whangaehu →, N.Z. 130 G4 40 3 S 175 6 E
Whangamata, N.Z. 130 D4 37 12 S 175 53 E
Whangamomona, N.Z. 130 F3 39 8 S 174 44 E
Whanganui △, N.Z. 130 F3 39 17 S 174 53 E
Whangaparaoa Pen., N.Z. 130 C4 36 40 S 174 45 E
Whangarei, N.Z. 130 B3 35 43 S 174 21 E
Whangarei Harb., N.Z. 130 B3 35 45 S 174 28 E
Whangaroa Harb., N.Z. 130 B2 35 4 S 173 46 E
Whangaruru Harb., N.Z. 130 B3 35 24 S 174 23 E
Wharanui, N.Z. 131 B9 41 55 S 174 6 E
Wharekauri = Chatham Is., Pac. Oc. 130 a 44 0 S 176 40W
Wharfe →, U.K. 20 D6 53 51N 1 9W
Wharfedale, U.K. 20 C5 54 6N 2 1W
Wharton, N.J., U.S.A. 151 F10 40 54N 74 35W
Wharton, Pa., U.S.A. 150 E6 41 31N 78 1W
Wharton, Tex., U.S.A. 155 L6 29 19N 96 6W
Wharton Basin, Ind. Oc. 134 J3 22 0 S 92 0 E
Whataroa, N.Z. 131 D5 43 18 S 170 24 E
Whataroa →, N.Z. 131 D5 43 7 S 170 16 E
Whatcom = Bellingham, U.S.A. 160 B4 48 46N 122 29W
Wheatfield, U.S.A. 157 C9 41 13N 87 4W
Wheatland, Calif., U.S.A. 160 F5 39 1N 121 25W
Wheatland, Ind., U.S.A. 157 F9 38 40N 87 19W
Wheatland, Wyo., U.S.A. 154 D2 42 3N 104 58W
Wheatley, Canada 150 D2 42 6N 82 27W
Wheaton, Ill., U.S.A. 157 C8 41 52N 88 6W
Wheaton, Md., U.S.A. 148 F7 39 3N 77 3W
Wheaton, Minn., U.S.A. 154 C6 45 48N 96 30W
Wheelbarrow Pk., U.S.A. 160 H10 37 26N 116 5W
Wheeler, Oreg., U.S.A. 158 D2 45 41N 123 53W
Wheeler, Tex., U.S.A. 155 H4 35 27N 100 16W
Wheeler →, Canada 141 A6 57 2N 67 13W
Wheeler L., U.S.A. 149 H2 34 48N 87 23W
Wheeler Pk., N. Mex., U.S.A. 159 H11 36 34N 105 25W
Wheeler Pk., Nev., U.S.A. 159 G6 38 57N 114 15W
Wheeler Ridge, U.S.A. 161 L8 35 0N 118 57W
Wheelersburg, U.S.A. 148 F4 38 44N 82 51W
Wheeling, U.S.A. 150 F4 40 4N 80 43W
Whernside, U.K. 20 C5 54 14N 2 24W
Whirlwind Reef, Papua N. G. 132 C5 4 42 S 148 16 E
Whiskey Jack L., Canada 143 B8 58 23N 101 55W
Whiskeytown-Shasta-Trinity ⌓, U.S.A. 158 F2 40 45N 122 15W
Whistleduck Cr. →, Australia 126 C2 20 15 S 135 18 E
Whistler, Canada 142 C4 50 7N 122 58W
Whitby, Canada 150 C6 43 52N 78 56W
Whitby, U.K. 20 C7 54 29N 0 37W
Whitcombe Pass, N.Z. 131 D5 43 13 S 170 55 E
White →, Ark., U.S.A. 155 J9 33 57N 91 5W
White →, Ind., U.S.A. 157 F9 38 25N 87 45W
White →, S. Dak., U.S.A. 154 D5 43 42N 99 27W
White →, Tex., U.S.A. 155 J4 33 14N 100 56W
White →, Utah, U.S.A. 158 F9 40 4N 109 41W
White →, Vt., U.S.A. 151 C12 43 37N 72 20W
White →, Wash., U.S.A. 160 C4 47 12N 122 15W
White, East Fork →, U.S.A. 157 F9 38 33N 87 14W
White, L., Australia 124 D4 21 9 S 128 56 E
White B., Canada 141 C8 50 0N 56 35W
White Bird, U.S.A. 158 D5 45 46N 116 18W
White Butte, U.S.A. 154 B3 46 23N 103 18W
White City, Fla., U.S.A. 152 F4 29 53N 85 13W
White City, Oreg., U.S.A. 158 E2 42 26N 122 51W
White Cliffs, Australia 128 A5 30 50 S 143 10 E
White Hall, U.S.A. 156 E6 39 26N 90 24W
White Haven, U.S.A. 151 E9 41 4N 75 47W
White Horse, Vale of, U.K. 21 F6 51 37N 1 30W
White I., N.Z. 130 D6 37 30 S 177 13 E
White L., Canada 151 A8 45 18N 76 31W
White L., U.S.A. 155 L8 29 44N 92 30W
White Mountain, U.S.A. 144 D7 64 41N 163 24W
White Mountain Peak, U.S.A. 159 G4 37 38N 118 15W
White Mts., Alaska, U.S.A. 144 D11 65 30N 146 30W
White Mts., Calif., U.S.A. 160 H8 37 30N 118 15W
White Mts., N.H., U.S.A. 151 B13 44 15N 71 15W
White Mts. △, Australia 126 C4 20 43 S 145 12 E
White Nile = Nîl el Abyad →, Sudan 107 D3 15 38N 32 31 E
White Nile Dam = Khazzān Jabal al Awliyā, Sudan 107 D3 15 24N 32 20 E
White Oak, U.S.A. 152 D8 31 2N 81 43W
White Otter L., Canada 140 C1 49 5N 91 55W
White Pass, U.S.A. 160 D5 46 38N 121 24W
White Pigeon, U.S.A. 157 C11 41 48N 85 39W
White Plains, Ga., U.S.A. 152 B6 33 28N 83 1W
White Plains, N.Y., U.S.A. 151 E11 41 2N 73 46W
White River, Canada 140 C2 48 35N 85 20W
White River, S. Africa 117 D5 25 20 S 31 0 E
White River, U.S.A. 154 D4 43 34N 100 45W
White Rock, Canada 160 A4 49 2N 122 48W
White Rock, U.S.A. 159 J10 35 50N 106 12W
White Russia = Belarus ■, Europe 58 F4 53 30N 27 0 E
White Sands ⌓, U.S.A. 159 K10 32 46N 106 20W
White Sea = Beloye More, Russia 56 A6 66 30N 38 0 E
White Springs, U.S.A. 152 E7 30 20N 82 45W
White Sulphur Springs, Mont., U.S.A. 158 C8 46 33N 110 54W
White Sulphur Springs, W. Va., U.S.A. 148 G5 37 48N 80 18W
White Swan, U.S.A. 160 D6 46 23N 120 44W
White Volta →, Ghana 113 D4 9 10N 1 15W
Whitecliffs, N.Z. 131 D6 43 26 S 171 55 E
Whitecourt, Canada 142 C5 54 10N 115 45W
Whiteface Mt., U.S.A. 151 B11 44 22N 73 54W
Whitefield, U.S.A. 151 B13 44 23N 71 37W
Whitefish, U.S.A. 158 B6 48 25N 114 20W
Whitefish Bay, U.S.A. 157 A9 43 23N 87 54W
Whitefish L., Canada 143 A7 62 41N 106 48W
Whitefish Point, U.S.A. 148 B3 46 45N 84 59W
Whitegull, L. = Goélands, L. aux, Canada 141 A7 55 27N 64 17W
Whitehall, Mich., U.S.A. 148 D2 43 24N 86 21W
Whitehall, Mont., U.S.A. 158 D7 45 52N 112 6W
Whitehall, N.Y., U.S.A. 151 C11 43 33N 73 24W
Whitehall, Wis., U.S.A. 154 C9 44 22N 91 19W
Whitehaven, U.K. 20 C4 54 33N 3 35W
Whitehorse, Canada 142 A1 60 43N 135 3W
Whiteman Ra., Papua N. G. 132 C5 5 55 S 150 0 E
Whitemark, Australia 127 G4 40 7 S 148 3 E
Whiteplains, Liberia 112 D2 6 28N 10 40W
Whiteriver, U.S.A. 159 K9 33 50N 109 58W
Whitesand →, Canada 142 A5 60 9N 115 45W
Whitesands, S. Africa 116 E3 34 23 S 20 50 E
Whitesboro, N.Y., U.S.A. 151 C9 43 7N 75 18W
Whitesboro, Tex., U.S.A. 155 J6 33 39N 96 54W
Whiteshell ⌓, Canada 143 D9 50 0N 95 40W
Whiteside, Canal, Chile 176 D2 53 55 S 70 15W
Whitesville, U.S.A. 150 D7 42 2N 77 46W
Whiteville, U.S.A. 149 H6 34 20N 78 42W
Whitewater, U.S.A. 157 B8 42 50N 88 44W
Whitewater B., U.S.A. 153 K9 25 15N 81 0W
Whitewater Baldy, U.S.A. 159 K9 33 20N 108 39W
Whitewater L., Canada 140 B2 50 50N 89 10W
Whitewood, Australia 126 C3 21 28 S 143 30 E
Whitewood, Canada 143 C8 50 20N 102 20W
Whitfield, Australia 129 D7 36 42 S 146 24 E
Whithorn, U.K. 22 G4 54 44N 4 26W
Whitianga, N.Z. 130 C4 36 47 S 175 41 E
Whiting, U.S.A. 157 C9 41 41N 87 29W
Whitman, U.S.A. 151 D14 42 5N 70 56W
Whitmore Village, U.S.A. 145 J13 21 31N 158 1W
Whitney, Canada 140 C4 45 31N 78 14W
Whitney, Mt., U.S.A. 160 J8 36 35N 118 18W
Whitney Point, U.S.A. 151 D9 42 20N 75 58W
Whitstable, U.K. 21 F9 51 21N 1 3 E
Whitsunday I., Australia 126 J7 20 15 S 149 4 E
Whitsunday Islands △, Australia 126 J7 20 15 S 149 0 E
Whitsunday Passage, Australia 126 J6 20 16 S 148 51 E
Whittemore, U.S.A. 156 A2 43 4N 94 26W
Whittier, Alaska, U.S.A. 144 F10 60 47N 148 41W
Whittier, Calif., U.S.A. 161 M8 33 58N 118 3W
Whittlesea, Australia 129 D6 37 27 S 145 9 E
Wholdaia L., Canada 143 A8 60 43N 104 20W
Whyalla, Australia 128 B2 33 2 S 137 30 E
Wiang Kosai △, Thailand 86 D2 17 54N 99 29 E
Wiarton, Canada 140 D3 44 40N 81 10W
Wiawso, Ghana 112 D4 6 10N 2 25W
Wiay, U.K. 22 D1 57 24N 7 13W
Wiązów, Poland 55 H4 50 50N 17 10 E
Wibaux, U.S.A. 154 B2 46 59N 104 11W
Wichabai, Guyana 169 C6 2 57N 59 35W
Wichian Buri, Thailand 86 E3 15 39N 101 7 E
Wichita, U.S.A. 155 G6 37 42N 97 20W
Wichita Falls, U.S.A. 155 J5 33 54N 98 30W
Wick, U.K. 22 C5 58 26N 3 5W
Wicked Pt., Canada 150 C7 43 52N 77 15W
Wickenburg, U.S.A. 159 K7 33 58N 112 44W
Wickepin, Australia 125 F2 32 50 S 117 30 E
Wickham, Australia 124 D2 20 42 S 117 11 E
Wickham, C., Australia 127 F3 39 35 S 143 57 E
Wickliffe, U.S.A. 150 E3 41 36N 81 28W
Wicklow, Ireland 23 D5 52 59N 6 3W
Wicklow □, Ireland 23 D5 52 57N 6 25W
Wicklow Hd., Ireland 23 D6 52 58N 6 0W
Wicklow Mts., Ireland 23 C5 52 58N 6 26W
Wicklow Mts. △, Ireland 23 C5 53 6N 6 21W
Widawa, Poland 55 G5 51 27N 18 51 E
Widawka →, Poland 55 G5 51 27N 18 52 E
Wide B., Papua N. G. 132 C7 5 5 S 152 5 E
Widgeegoara Cr. →, Australia 127 D4 28 51 S 146 34 E
Widgiemooltha, Australia 125 F3 31 30 S 121 34 E
Widi, Kepulauan, Indonesia 82 B3 0 33 S 128 24 E
Widnau, Switz. 33 B9 47 24N 9 38 E
Widnes, U.K. 20 D5 53 23N 2 45W
Więcbork, Poland 55 E4 53 21N 17 30 E
Wiehengebirge = Nördlicher Teutoburger Wald-Wiehengebirge ⌓, Germany 30 C4 52 18N 8 10 E
Wiehl, Germany 30 E3 50 56N 7 34 E
Wiek, Germany 30 A9 54 37N 13 17 E
Wielbark, Poland 54 E7 53 24N 20 55 E
Wieleń, Poland 55 F3 52 53N 16 9 E
Wielichowo, Poland 55 F3 52 7N 16 22 E
Wieliczka, Poland 55 J7 50 0N 20 5 E
Wielkopolski △, Poland 55 F3 52 18N 16 45 E
Wielkopolskie □, Poland 55 F4 52 10N 17 30 E
Wieluń, Poland 55 G5 51 15N 18 34 E
Wien, Austria 35 C9 48 12N 16 22 E
Wien ✈ (VIA), Austria 35 C9 48 7N 16 35 E
Wiener Neustadt, Austria 35 D9 47 49N 16 16 E
Wieprz →, Poland 55 G8 51 34N 21 49 E
Wieprza →, Poland 54 D3 54 26N 16 25 E
Wieruszów, Poland 55 G5 51 19N 18 9 E
Wiesbaden, Germany 31 E4 50 4N 8 14 E
Wiesen, Switz. 33 C9 46 42N 9 43 E
Wiesental, Germany 31 F4 49 13N 8 31 E
Wiesloch, Germany 31 F4 49 18N 8 41 E
Wiesmoor, Germany 30 B3 53 24N 7 47 E
Wieżyca, Poland 54 D5 54 14N 18 8 E
Wigan, U.K. 20 D5 53 33N 2 38W
Wiggins, Colo., U.S.A. 154 E2 40 14N 104 4W
Wiggins, Miss., U.S.A. 155 K10 30 51N 89 8W
Wight, I. of □, U.K. 21 G6 50 40N 1 20W
Wigierski △, Poland 54 D10 54 5N 23 5 E
Wigry, Jezioro, Poland 54 D10 54 2N 23 3 E
Wigston, U.K. 21 E6 52 35N 1 6W
Wigton, U.K. 20 C4 54 50N 3 10W
Wigtown, U.K. 22 G4 54 53N 4 27W
Wigtown B., U.K. 22 G4 54 46N 4 15W
Wil, Switz. 33 B8 47 28N 9 3 E
Wilamowice, Poland 55 J6 49 55N 19 9 E
Wilber, U.S.A. 154 E6 40 29N 96 58W
Wilberforce, Canada 150 A6 45 2N 78 13W
Wilberforce, C., Australia 126 A2 11 54 S 136 35 E
Wilburton, U.S.A. 155 H7 34 55N 95 19W
Wilcannia, Australia 128 A5 31 30 S 143 26 E
Wilcox, U.S.A. 150 E6 41 35N 78 41W
Wildbad, Germany 31 G4 48 44N 8 33 E
Wildcat →, U.S.A. 157 D10 40 28N 86 52W
Wildenschwert = Ústí nad Orlicí, Czech Rep. 35 B9 49 58N 16 24 E
Wildeshausen, Germany 30 C4 52 54N 8 27 E
Wildeshauser Geest ⌓, Germany 30 C4 52 54N 8 30 E
Wildhorn, Switz. 32 D4 46 22N 7 21 E
Wildon, Austria 34 E8 46 52N 15 31 E
Wildrose, U.S.A. 161 J9 36 14N 117 11W
Wildspitze, Austria 34 E3 46 53N 10 53 E
Wildstrubel, Switz. 32 D5 46 24N 7 32 E
Wildwood, U.S.A. 153 G7 28 52N 82 2W
Wilga →, Poland 55 G8 51 52N 21 18 E
Wilge →, S. Africa 117 D4 27 3 S 28 20 E
Wilhelm, Mt., Papua N. G. 132 C3 5 50 S 145 1 E
Wilhelm II Coast, Antarctica 7 C7 68 0 S 90 0 E
Wilhelmina Geb., Suriname 169 C6 3 50N 56 30W
Wilhelmina Top = Trikora, Puncak, Indonesia 83 B5 4 15 S 138 45 E
Wilhelmsburg, Austria 34 C8 48 6N 15 36 E
Wilhelmshaven, Germany 30 B4 53 31N 8 7 E
Wilhelmstal, Namibia 116 C2 21 58 S 16 21 E
Wilkes-Barre, U.S.A. 151 E9 41 15N 75 53W
Wilkes Land, Antarctica 7 D9 69 0 S 120 0 E
Wilkie, Canada 143 C7 52 27N 108 42W
Wilkinsburg, U.S.A. 150 F5 40 26N 79 53W
Wilkinson Lakes, Australia 125 E5 29 40 S 132 39 E
Willacoochee, U.S.A. 152 D6 31 20N 83 3W
Willandra △, Australia 129 B6 33 12 S 145 0 E
Willandra Creek →, Australia 128 B6 33 22 S 145 52 E
Willapa B., U.S.A. 158 C2 46 40N 124 0W
Willapa Hills, U.S.A. 160 D3 46 35N 123 25W
Willard, N.Y., U.S.A. 150 D8 42 40N 76 50W

Willard, Ohio, U.S.A. 150 E2 41 3N 82 44W
Willaumez Pen., Papua N. G. 132 C6 5 15 S 150 2 E
Willbriggie, Australia 129 C7 34 28 S 146 2 E
Willcox, U.S.A. 159 K9 32 15N 109 50W
Willemstad, Neth. Ant. 165 D6 12 5N 69 0W
Willenberg = Wielbark, Poland 54 E7 53 24N 20 55 E
Willet, U.S.A. 151 D9 42 28N 75 55W
William →, Canada 143 B7 59 8N 109 19W
William, Mt., Australia 128 D5 37 17 S 142 35 E
William B. Hartsfield International, Atlanta ✕ (ATL), U.S.A. 152 B5 33 38N 84 26W
William 'Bill' Dannelly Res., U.S.A. 149 J2 32 10N 87 10W
William Creek, Australia 127 D2 28 58 S 136 22 E
Williams, Australia 125 F2 33 2 S 116 52 E
Williams, Ariz., U.S.A. 159 J7 35 15N 112 11W
Williams, Calif., U.S.A. 160 F4 39 9N 122 9W
Williams Harbour, Canada 141 B8 52 33N 55 47W
Williams Lake, Canada 142 C4 52 10N 122 10W
Williamsburg, Iowa, U.S.A. 156 C4 41 40N 92 1W
Williamsburg, Ky., U.S.A. 149 G3 36 44N 84 10W
Williamsburg, Pa., U.S.A. 150 F6 40 28N 78 12W
Williamsburg, Va., U.S.A. 148 G7 37 17N 76 44W
Williamsfield, U.S.A. 156 D6 40 55N 90 1W
Williamson, N.Y., U.S.A. 150 C7 43 14N 77 11W
Williamson, W. Va., U.S.A. 148 G4 37 41N 82 17W
Williamsport, Ind., U.S.A. 157 D9 40 17N 87 17W
Williamsport, Pa., U.S.A. 150 E7 41 15N 77 0W
Williamston, Mich., U.S.A. 157 B12 42 41N 84 17W
Williamston, N.C., U.S.A. 149 H7 35 51N 77 4W
Williamstown, Australia 127 F3 37 51 S 144 52 E
Williamstown, Ky., U.S.A. 157 F12 38 38N 84 34W
Williamstown, Mass., U.S.A. 151 D11 42 41N 73 12W
Williamstown, N.Y., U.S.A. 151 C9 43 26N 75 53W
Williamsville, U.S.A. 156 E7 39 57N 89 33W
Willimantic, U.S.A. 151 E12 41 43N 72 13W
Willingboro, U.S.A. 148 F8 40 3N 74 54W
Willisau, Switz. 32 B6 47 7N 8 0 E
Willisburg, U.S.A. 157 G11 37 49N 85 8W
Williston, S. Africa 116 E3 31 20 S 20 53 E
Williston, Fla., U.S.A. 153 F7 29 23N 82 27W
Williston, N. Dak., U.S.A. 154 A3 48 9N 103 37W
Williston, S.C., U.S.A. 152 B8 33 24N 81 25W
Williston L., Canada 142 B4 56 0N 124 0W
Willits, U.S.A. 158 G2 39 25N 123 21W
Willmar, U.S.A. 154 C7 45 7N 95 3W
Willmore Wilderness △, Canada 142 C5 53 45N 119 30W
Willoughby, U.S.A. 150 E3 41 39N 81 24W
Willow, U.S.A. 144 F10 61 45N 150 3W
Willow Bunch, Canada 143 D7 49 20N 105 35W
Willow L., Canada 142 A5 62 10N 119 8W
Willow Tree, Australia 129 A9 31 40 S 150 45 E
Willow Wall, The, China 75 C12 42 10N 122 0 E
Willowick, U.S.A. 150 E3 41 38N 81 28W
Willowlake →, Canada 142 A4 62 42N 123 8W
Willowmore, S. Africa 116 E3 33 15 S 23 30 E
Willows, U.S.A. 160 F4 39 31N 122 12W
Willowvale = Gatyana, S. Africa 117 E4 32 16 S 28 31 E
Wills, L., Australia 124 D4 21 25 S 128 51 E
Wills Cr. →, Australia 126 C3 22 43 S 140 2 E
Willsboro, U.S.A. 151 B11 44 21N 73 24W
Willunga, Australia 128 C3 35 15 S 138 30 E
Wilma, U.S.A. 152 E5 30 9N 84 58W
Wilmette, U.S.A. 157 B9 42 5N 87 42W
Wilmington, Australia 128 B3 32 39 S 138 7 E
Wilmington, Del., U.S.A. 148 F8 39 45N 75 33W
Wilmington, Ill., U.S.A. 157 C8 41 18N 88 9W
Wilmington, N.C., U.S.A. 149 H7 34 14N 77 55W
Wilmington, Ohio, U.S.A. 157 E13 39 27N 83 50W
Wilmington, Vt., U.S.A. 151 D12 42 52N 72 52W
Wilmslow, U.K. 20 D5 53 19N 2 13W
Wilna = Vilnius, Lithuania 15 J21 54 38N 25 19 E
Wilpattu △, Sri Lanka 95 K4 8 20N 79 50 E
Wilpena, Australia 128 A3 31 31 S 138 37 E
Wilpena Cr. →, Australia 128 A3 31 25 S 139 29 E
Wilsall, U.S.A. 158 D8 45 59N 110 38W
Wilson, N.C., U.S.A. 149 H7 35 44N 77 55W
Wilson, N.Y., U.S.A. 150 C6 43 19N 78 50W
Wilson, Pa., U.S.A. 151 F9 40 41N 75 15W
Wilson →, Australia 124 C4 16 48 S 128 16 E
Wilson Bluff, Australia 125 F4 31 41 S 129 0 E
Wilson Inlet, Australia 125 G2 35 0 S 117 22 E
Wilson Str., Solomon Is. 133 M9 8 0 S 156 39 E
Wilsons Promontory, Australia 129 E7 38 55 S 146 25 E
Wilsons Promontory △, Australia 129 D7 37 59 S 146 23 E
Wilster, Germany 30 B5 53 55N 9 23 E
Wilton, Iowa, U.S.A. 156 C5 41 34N 91 4W
Wilton, N. Dak., U.S.A. 154 B4 47 10N 100 47W
Wilton →, Australia 126 A1 14 45 S 134 33 E
Wiltshire □, U.K. 21 F6 51 18N 1 53W
Wiltz, Lux. 24 E5 49 57N 5 55 E
Wiluna, Australia 125 E3 26 36 S 120 14 E
Wimborne Minster, U.K. 21 G6 50 48N 1 59W
Wimereux, France 27 B8 50 45N 1 37 E
Wimmera →, Australia 128 D4 36 8 S 141 56 E
Winam G., Kenya 118 C3 0 20 S 34 15 E
Winamac, U.S.A. 157 C10 41 3N 86 36W
Winburg, S. Africa 116 D4 28 30 S 27 2 E
Winchelsea, Australia 128 E6 38 10 S 144 1 E
Winchendon, U.S.A. 151 D12 42 41N 72 3W
Winchester, N.Z. 131 E6 44 11 S 171 17 E
Winchester, U.K. 21 F6 51 4N 1 18W
Winchester, Conn., U.S.A. 151 E11 41 53N 73 9W
Winchester, Idaho, U.S.A. 158 C5 46 14N 116 38W
Winchester, Ill., U.S.A. 156 E6 39 38N 90 27W
Winchester, Ind., U.S.A. 157 D12 40 10N 84 59W
Winchester, Ky., U.S.A. 157 G12 38 0N 84 11W
Winchester, N.H., U.S.A. 151 D12 42 46N 72 23W
Winchester, Nev., U.S.A. 161 J11 36 6N 115 10W
Winchester, Ohio, U.S.A. 157 F13 38 57N 83 40W
Winchester, Tenn., U.S.A. 149 H2 35 11N 86 7W
Winchester, Va., U.S.A. 148 F6 39 11N 78 10W
Wind →, U.S.A. 158 E9 43 12N 108 12W
Wind Cave △, U.S.A. 154 D3 43 32N 103 17W
Wind Point, U.S.A. 157 B9 42 47N 87 46W
Wind River Range, U.S.A. 158 E9 43 0N 109 30W
Windamere, L., Australia 129 B8 32 42 S 149 44 E
Windau = Ventspils, Latvia 15 H19 57 25N 21 32 E
Windber, U.S.A. 150 F6 40 14N 78 50W
Winder, U.S.A. 152 A6 34 0N 83 45W
Windermere, U.K. 20 C5 54 23N 2 55W
Windermere, U.S.A. 153 G8 28 29N 81 32W
Windfall, U.S.A. 157 D11 40 22N 85 57W
Windhoek, Namibia 116 C2 22 35 S 17 4 E
Windisch, Switz. 32 B6 47 28N 8 14 E
Windisch-Feistritz = Slovenska Bistrica, Slovenia 45 B12 46 24N 15 35 E
Windischgarsten, Austria 34 D7 47 42N 14 21 E
Windischgratz = Slovenj Gradec, Slovenia 45 B12 46 31N 15 5 E
Windom, U.S.A. 154 D7 43 52N 95 7W
Windorah, Australia 126 D3 25 24 S 142 36 E
Window Rock, U.S.A. 159 J9 35 41N 109 3W
Windrush →, U.K. 21 F6 51 43N 1 24W
Windsor, Australia 129 B9 33 37 S 150 50 E
Windsor, N.S., Canada 141 D7 44 59N 64 5W
Windsor, Ont., Canada 140 D3 42 18N 83 0W
Windsor, N.Z. 131 E5 44 59 S 170 49 E
Windsor, U.K. 21 F7 51 29N 0 36W
Windsor, Calif., U.S.A. 158 G2 38 33N 122 49W
Windsor, Colo., U.S.A. 154 E2 40 29N 104 54W
Windsor, Conn., U.S.A. 151 E12 41 50N 72 39W
Windsor, Ill., U.S.A. 157 E8 39 26N 88 36W
Windsor, Mo., U.S.A. 156 F3 38 32N 93 31W
Windsor, N.Y., U.S.A. 151 D9 42 5N 75 37W
Windsor, Vt., U.S.A. 151 C12 43 29N 72 24W
Windsor & Maidenhead □, U.K. 21 F7 51 29N 0 40W
Windsorton, S. Africa 116 D3 28 16 S 24 44 E
Windward Is., W. Indies 165 D7 13 0N 61 0W
Windward Passage = Vientos, Paso de los, Caribbean 165 C5 20 0N 74 0W
Winefred L., Canada 143 B6 55 30N 110 30W
Winejok, Sudan 107 F2 9 1N 27 30 E
Winfield, Iowa, U.S.A. 156 C5 41 7N 91 26W
Winfield, Kans., U.S.A. 155 G6 37 15N 96 59W
Winfield, Mo., U.S.A. 156 F6 39 0N 90 44W
Wingate Mts., Australia 124 B5 14 25 S 130 40 E
Wingham, Australia 129 A10 31 48 S 152 22 E
Wingham, Canada 140 D3 43 55N 81 20W
Winisk, Canada 140 A2 55 20N 85 15W
Winisk →, Canada 140 A2 55 17N 85 5W
Winisk L., Canada 140 B2 52 55N 87 22W
Wink, U.S.A. 155 K3 31 45N 103 9W
Winkler, Canada 143 D9 49 10N 97 56W
Winklern, Austria 34 E5 46 52N 12 52 E
Winlock, U.S.A. 160 D4 46 30N 122 56W
Winneba, Ghana 113 D4 5 25N 0 36W
Winnebago, U.S.A. 156 B7 42 16N 89 15W
Winnebago, L., U.S.A. 148 D1 44 0N 88 26W
Winnecke Cr. →, Australia 124 C5 18 35 S 131 34 E
Winnemucca, U.S.A. 158 F5 40 58N 117 44W
Winnemucca L., U.S.A. 158 F4 40 7N 119 21W
Winner, U.S.A. 154 D5 43 22N 99 52W
Winnett, U.S.A. 158 C9 47 0N 108 21W
Winnfield, U.S.A. 155 K8 31 56N 92 38W
Winnibigoshish, L., U.S.A. 154 B7 47 27N 94 13W
Winnipeg, Canada 143 D9 49 54N 97 9W
Winnipeg →, Canada 143 C9 50 38N 96 19W
Winnipeg, L., Canada 143 C9 52 0N 97 0W
Winnipeg Beach, Canada 143 C9 50 30N 96 58W
Winnipegosis, Canada 143 C9 51 39N 99 55W
Winnipegosis L., Canada 143 C9 52 30N 100 0W
Winnipesaukee, L., U.S.A. 151 C13 43 38N 71 21W
Winnisquam L., U.S.A. 151 C13 43 33N 71 31W
Winnsboro, La., U.S.A. 155 J9 32 10N 91 43W
Winnsboro, S.C., U.S.A. 149 H5 34 23N 81 5W
Winnsboro, Tex., U.S.A. 155 J7 32 58N 95 17W
Winokapau, L., Canada 141 B7 53 15N 62 50W
Winona, Minn., U.S.A. 154 C9 44 3N 91 39W
Winona, Miss., U.S.A. 155 J10 33 29N 89 44W
Winooski, U.S.A. 151 B11 44 29N 73 11W
Winooski →, U.S.A. 151 B11 44 32N 73 17W
Winschoten, Neths. 24 A7 53 9N 7 3 E
Winsen, Germany 30 B6 53 22N 10 13 E
Winsford, U.K. 20 D5 53 12N 2 31W
Winslow, Ariz., U.S.A. 159 J8 35 2N 110 42W
Winslow, Ind., U.S.A. 157 F9 38 23N 87 13W
Winslow, Wash., U.S.A. 160 C4 47 38N 122 31W
Winsted, U.S.A. 151 E11 41 55N 73 4W
Winston-Salem, U.S.A. 149 G5 36 6N 80 15W
Winter Garden, U.S.A. 153 G8 28 34N 81 35W
Winter Haven, U.S.A. 153 G8 28 1N 81 44W
Winter Park, U.S.A. 153 G8 28 36N 81 20W
Winterberg, Germany 30 D4 51 11N 8 33 E
Winterhaven, U.S.A. 161 N12 32 47N 114 39W
Winters, U.S.A. 160 G5 38 32N 121 58W
Winterset, U.S.A. 156 C3 41 20N 94 1W
Wintersville, U.S.A. 150 F4 40 23N 80 42W
Winterswijk, Neths. 24 C6 51 58N 6 43 E
Winterthur, Switz. 33 B7 47 30N 8 44 E
Winthrop, U.S.A. 158 B3 48 28N 120 10W
Winton, Australia 126 C3 22 24 S 143 3 E
Winton, N.Z. 131 G3 46 8 S 168 20 E
Wintua, Vanuatu 133 F5 16 30 S 167 26 E
Wipper →, Germany 30 D7 51 16N 11 12 E
Wirraminna, Australia 128 A2 31 12 S 136 13 E
Wirrulla, Australia 127 E1 32 24 S 134 31 E
Wisbech, U.K. 21 E8 52 41N 0 9 E
Wisconsin □, U.S.A. 154 C10 44 45N 89 30W
Wisconsin →, U.S.A. 156 A5 43 0N 91 15W
Wisconsin Rapids, U.S.A. 154 C10 44 23N 89 49W
Wisdom, U.S.A. 158 D7 45 37N 113 27W
Wiseman, U.S.A. 144 C10 67 25N 150 6W
Wishaw, U.K. 22 F5 55 46N 3 54W
Wishek, U.S.A. 154 B5 46 16N 99 33W
Wisła, Poland 55 J5 49 38N 18 53 E
Wisła →, Poland 54 D5 54 22N 18 55 E
Wisłok →, Poland 55 H9 50 13N 22 32 E
Wisłoka →, Poland 55 H8 50 27N 21 23 E
Wismar, Germany 30 B7 53 54N 11 29 E
Wismar, Guyana 169 B6 5 59N 58 18W
Wisner, U.S.A. 154 E6 41 59N 96 55W
Wissant, France 27 B8 50 52N 1 40 E
Wissembourg, France 27 C14 49 2N 7 57 E
Wisznice, Poland 55 G10 51 48N 23 13 E
Witbank, S. Africa 117 D4 25 51 S 29 14 E
Witdraai, S. Africa 116 D3 26 58 S 20 48 E
Witham, U.K. 21 F8 51 48N 0 40 E
Witham →, U.K. 20 E7 52 59N 0 2W
Withernsea, U.K. 20 D8 53 44N 0 1 E
Withlacoochee →, Fla., U.S.A. 152 E6 30 24N 83 10W
Withlacoochee →, Fla., U.S.A. 153 G7 29 0N 82 45W
Witjira △, Australia 127 D2 26 22 S 135 37 E
Witkowo, Poland 55 F4 52 26N 17 45 E
Witney, U.K. 21 F6 51 48N 1 28W
Witnica, Poland 55 F1 52 40N 14 54 E
Witnossob →, Namibia 116 D3 23 55 S 18 45 E
Wittdün, Germany 30 A4 54 38N 8 23 E
Witten, Germany 30 D3 51 26N 7 20 E
Wittenberge, Germany 30 B7 53 0N 11 45 E
Wittenburg, Germany 30 B7 53 31N 11 4 E
Wittenheim, France 27 E14 47 44N 7 20 E
Wittenoom, Australia 124 D2 22 15 S 118 20 E
Witti, Banjaran, Malaysia 85 A5 5 11N 116 29 E
Wittingau = Třeboň, Czech Rep. 34 B7 49 1N 14 48 E
Wittingen, Germany 30 C6 52 44N 10 44 E
Wittlich, Germany 31 F2 49 59N 6 53 E
Wittmund, Germany 30 B3 53 34N 7 46 E
Wittow, Germany 30 A9 54 38N 13 20 E
Wittstock, Germany 30 B8 53 10N 12 28 E
Witu Is., Papua N. G. 132 C5 4 50 S 149 25 E
Witvlei, Namibia 116 C2 22 23 S 18 32 E
Witzenhausen, Germany 30 D5 51 20N 9 51 E
Wixom, U.S.A. 157 B13 42 32N 83 32W
Wkra →, Poland 55 F7 52 27N 20 44 E
Władysławowo, Poland 54 D5 54 48N 18 25 E
Wleń, Poland 55 G2 51 2N 15 39 E
Wlingi, Indonesia 85 D4 8 5 S 112 25 E
Włocławek, Poland 55 F6 52 40N 19 3 E
Włodawa, Poland 55 G10 51 33N 23 31 E
Włoszczowa, Poland 55 H6 50 50N 19 55 E
Woburn, U.S.A. 151 D13 42 29N 71 9W
Wodian, China 74 H7 32 50N 112 35 E
Wodonga = Albury-Wodonga, Australia 129 D7 36 3 S 146 56 E
Wodonga, Australia 129 D7 36 5 S 146 50 E
Wodzisław Śląski, Poland 55 H5 50 1N 18 26 E
Woerth, France 27 D14 48 57N 7 45 E
Wohlau = Wołów, Poland 55 G3 51 20N 16 38 E
Wohlen, Switz. 33 B6 47 21N 8 17 E
Woinbogoin, China 76 A2 32 51N 98 39 E
Woinui, Selat, Indonesia 83 B4 1 10 S 134 36 E
Woippy, France 27 C13 49 10N 6 8 E
Woitape, Papua N. G. 132 E4 8 33 S 147 15 E
Wojcieszow, Poland 55 H2 50 58N 15 55 E
Wokam, Indonesia 83 C4 5 45 S 134 28 E
Wokha, India 90 B5 26 6N 94 16 E
Woking, U.K. 21 F7 51 19N 0 34W
Wokingham, U.K. 21 F7 51 24N 0 49W
Wokingham □, U.K. 21 F7 51 25N 0 51W
Woko △, Australia 129 A9 31 46 S 151 49 E
Wolbrom, Poland 55 H6 50 24N 19 45 E
Wolcottville, U.S.A. 157 C11 41 32N 85 22W
Wołczyn, Poland 55 G5 51 1N 18 3 E
Woldegk, Germany 30 B9 53 27N 13 34 E
Woldenberg = Dobiegniew, Poland 55 F2 52 59N 15 45 E
Wolf →, Canada 142 A2 60 17N 132 33W
Wolf, Volcán, Ecuador 172 a 0 2N 91 20W
Wolf Creek, U.S.A. 158 C7 47 0N 112 4W
Wolf L., Canada 142 A2 60 24N 131 40W
Wolf Point, U.S.A. 154 A2 48 5N 105 39W
Wolfe I., Canada 140 D4 44 7N 76 20W
Wolfeboro, U.S.A. 151 C13 43 35N 71 13W
Wolfen, Germany 30 D8 51 39N 12 15 E
Wolfenbüttel, Germany 30 C6 52 10N 10 33 E
Wolfratshausen, Germany 31 H7 47 54N 11 24 E
Wolfsberg, Austria 34 E7 46 50N 14 52 E
Wolfsburg, Germany 30 C6 52 25N 10 48 E
Wolfurt, Austria 33 B9 47 28N 9 45 E
Wolgast, Germany 30 A9 54 3N 13 44 E
Wolhusen, Switz. 32 B6 47 4N 8 4 E
Wolin, Poland 54 E1 53 50N 14 37 E
Woliński △, Poland 54 E1 53 57N 14 28 E
Wollaston, Is., Chile 176 E3 55 40 S 67 30W
Wollaston Forland, Greenland 10 C9 74 25N 19 40W
Wollaston L., Canada 143 B8 58 7N 103 10W
Wollaston Lake, Canada 143 B8 58 3N 103 33W
Wollaston Pen., Canada 138 B8 69 30N 115 0W
Wollemi △, Australia 129 B9 33 0 S 150 30 E
Wollongong, Australia 129 C9 34 25 S 150 54 E
Wolmar = Valmiera, Latvia 15 H21 57 37N 25 29 E
Wolmaransstad, S. Africa 116 D4 27 12 S 25 59 E
Wolmirstedt, Germany 30 C7 52 14N 11 37 E
Wołomin, Poland 55 F8 52 19N 21 15 E
Wołów, Poland 55 G3 51 20N 16 38 E
Wolseley, Australia 128 D4 36 23 S 140 54 E
Wolseley, S. Africa 116 E2 33 26 S 19 7 E
Wolsey, U.S.A. 154 C5 44 24N 98 28W
Wolstenholme, C., Canada 136 C12 62 35N 77 30W
Wolsztyn, Poland 55 F3 52 8N 16 5 E
Wolvega, Neths. 24 B6 52 52N 6 0 E
Wolverhampton, U.K. 21 E5 52 35N 2 7W
Wondai, Australia 127 D5 26 20 S 151 49 E
Wonenara, Papua N. G. 132 D3 6 48 S 145 53 E
Wonga Wongué △, Gabon 114 C1 0 29 S 9 25 E
Wongalarroo L., Australia 128 A6 31 32 S 144 0 E
Wongan Hills, Australia 125 F2 30 51 S 116 37 E
Wŏnju, S. Korea 75 F14 37 22N 127 58 E
Wonosari, Indonesia 85 D4 7 58 S 110 36 E
Wonosobo, Indonesia 85 D3 7 22 S 109 54 E
Wonowon, Canada 142 B4 56 44N 121 48W
Wŏnsan, N. Korea 75 E14 39 11N 127 27 E
Wonthaggi, Australia 129 E6 38 37 S 145 37 E
Wood Buffalo △, Canada 142 B6 59 0N 113 41W
Wood Is., Australia 124 C3 16 24 S 123 19 E
Wood L., Canada 143 B8 55 17N 103 17W
Wood River, U.S.A. 156 F6 38 52N 90 5W
Woodah I., Australia 126 A2 13 27 S 136 10 E
Woodbine, U.S.A. 152 E8 30 58N 81 44W
Woodbourne, U.S.A. 151 E10 41 46N 74 36W
Woodbridge, Canada 150 C5 43 47N 79 36W
Woodbridge, U.K. 21 E9 52 6N 1 20 E
Woodburn, U.S.A. 158 D2 45 9N 122 51W
Woodbury, U.S.A. 152 C5 32 59N 84 35W
Woodenbong, Australia 127 D5 28 24 S 152 39 E
Woodend, Australia 128 D6 37 20 S 144 33 E
Woodford, Australia 127 D5 26 58 S 152 47 E
Woodfords, U.S.A. 160 G7 38 47N 119 50W
Woodlake, U.S.A. 160 J7 36 25N 119 6W
Woodland, Calif., U.S.A. 160 G5 38 41N 121 46W
Woodland, Maine, U.S.A. 149 C12 45 9N 67 25W
Woodland, Pa., U.S.A. 150 F6 40 59N 78 21W
Woodland, Wash., U.S.A. 160 E4 45 54N 122 45W
Woodland Caribou △, Canada 143 C10 51 0N 94 45W
Woodlands, Singapore 87 d 1 27N 103 47 E
Woodlark I., Papua N. G. 132 E7 9 10 S 152 50 E
Woodridge, Canada 143 D9 49 20N 96 9W
Woodroffe, Mt., Australia 125 E5 26 20 S 131 45 E
Woods, L., Australia 126 B1 17 50 S 133 30 E
Woods, L. of the, Canada 143 D10 49 15N 94 45W
Woodside, S. Austral., Australia 128 C3 34 58 S 138 52 E
Woodside, Vic., Australia 129 E7 38 31 S 146 52 E
Woodson, U.S.A. 156 E6 39 37N 90 14W
Woodstock, N.S.W., Australia 129 B8 33 45 S 148 53 E
Woodstock, Queens., Australia 126 B4 19 35 S 146 50 E
Woodstock, N.B., Canada 141 C6 46 11N 67 37W
Woodstock, Ont., Canada 140 D3 43 10N 80 45W
Woodstock, U.K. 21 F6 51 51N 1 20W
Woodstock, Ga., U.S.A. 152 A5 34 6N 84 31W
Woodstock, Ill., U.S.A. 154 D10 42 19N 88 27W
Woodstock, Vt., U.S.A. 151 C12 43 37N 72 31W
Woodsville, U.S.A. 151 B13 44 9N 72 2W
Woodville, N.Z. 130 G4 40 20 S 175 53 E
Woodville, Fla., U.S.A. 152 E5 30 19N 84 15W
Woodville, Ga., U.S.A. 152 B6 33 40N 83 7W
Woodville, Miss., U.S.A. 155 K9 31 6N 91 18W
Woodville, Ohio, U.S.A. 157 C13 41 27N 83 22W
Woodville, Tex., U.S.A. 155 K7 30 47N 94 25W
Woodward, U.S.A. 155 G5 36 26N 99 24W
Woody, U.S.A. 161 K8 35 42N 118 50W
Woody →, Canada 143 C8 52 31N 100 51W
Woolacombe, U.K. 21 F3 51 10N 4 13W
Woolamai, C., Australia 129 E6 38 30 S 145 23 E
Woolbrook, Australia 129 A9 30 56 S 151 25 E
Wooler, U.K. 20 B5 55 33N 2 1W
Woolgoolga, Australia 127 E5 30 6 S 153 11 E
Woomera, Australia 128 A2 31 5 S 136 50 E
Woonsocket, R.I., U.S.A. 151 E13 42 0N 71 31W
Woonsocket, S. Dak., U.S.A. 154 C5 44 3N 98 17W
Wooramel →, Australia 125 E1 25 47 S 114 10 E
Wooramel Roadhouse, Australia 125 E1 25 45 S 114 17 E
Wooster, U.S.A. 150 F3 40 48N 81 56W
Worb, Switz. 32 C5 46 56N 7 33 E
Worcester, S. Africa 116 E2 33 39 S 19 27 E
Worcester, U.K. 21 E5 52 11N 2 12W
Worcester, Mass., U.S.A. 151 D13 42 16N 71 48W
Worcester, N.Y., U.S.A. 151 D10 42 36N 74 45W
Worcestershire □, U.K. 21 E5 52 13N 2 10W
Worden, U.S.A. 156 F7 38 56N 89 50W
Wörgl, Austria 34 D5 47 29N 12 3 E
Workai, Indonesia 83 C4 6 40 S 134 40 E
Workington, U.K. 20 C4 54 39N 3 33W
Worksop, U.K. 20 D6 53 18N 1 7W
Workum, Neths. 24 B5 52 59N 5 26 E
Worland, U.S.A. 158 D10 44 1N 107 57W
Wormhout, France 27 B9 50 52N 2 28 E
Worms, Germany 31 F4 49 37N 8 21 E
Worsley, Canada 142 B5 56 31N 119 8W
Wörth, Germany 31 F8 49 1N 12 24 E
Wortham, U.S.A. 155 K6 31 47N 96 28W
Wörther See, Austria 34 E7 46 37N 14 10 E
Worthing, Barbados 165 g 13 5N 59 35W
Worthing, U.K. 21 G7 50 49N 0 21W
Worthington, Ind., U.S.A. 157 E10 39 7N 86 59W
Worthington, Minn., U.S.A. 154 D7 43 37N 95 36W
Worthington, Ohio, U.S.A. 157 D13 40 5N 83 1W
Worthington, Pa., U.S.A. 150 F5 40 50N 79 38W
Wosi, Indonesia 82 B3 0 15 S 128 0 E
Wosimi, Indonesia 83 B4 2 54 S 134 31 E
Wotu, Indonesia 82 B2 2 35 S 120 48 E
Wou-han = Wuhan, China 77 B10 30 31N 114 18 E
Wour, Chad 109 D3 21 14N 16 0 E
Wousi = Wuxi, China 77 B13 31 33N 120 18 E
Wowoni, Indonesia 82 B2 4 5 S 123 5 E
Woy Woy, Australia 129 B9 33 30 S 151 19 E
Wrangel I. = Vrangelya, Ostrov, Russia 67 B19 71 0N 180 0 E
Wrangell, U.S.A. 142 B2 56 28N 132 23W
Wrangell Mts., U.S.A. 144 F12 61 30N 142 0W
Wrangell-St. Elias △, U.S.A. 144 D12 61 0N 142 0W
Wrath, C., U.K. 22 C3 58 38N 5 1W
Wray, U.S.A. 154 E3 40 5N 102 13W
Wrekin, The, U.K. 21 E5 52 41N 2 32W
Wrens, U.S.A. 152 B7 33 12N 82 23W
Wrexham, U.K. 20 D4 53 3N 3 0W
Wrexham □, U.K. 20 D5 53 1N 2 58W
Wriezen, Germany 30 C10 52 42N 14 7 E
Wright = Paranas, Phil. 81 F5 11 42N 125 2 E
Wright, Fla., U.S.A. 149 K2 30 27N 86 38W
Wright, Wyo., U.S.A. 154 D2 43 47N 105 30W
Wright Pt., Canada 150 C3 43 48N 81 44W
Wrightmyo, India 95 J11 11 47N 92 43 E
Wrightson, Mt., U.S.A. 159 L8 31 42N 110 51W
Wrightsville, U.S.A. 152 C7 32 44N 82 43W
Wrightwood, U.S.A. 161 L9 34 21N 117 38W
Wrigley, Canada 138 B7 63 16N 123 37W
Wrocław, Poland 55 G4 51 5N 17 5 E
Wronki, Poland 55 F3 52 41N 16 21 E
Września, Poland 55 F4 52 21N 17 36 E
Wschowa, Poland 55 G3 51 48N 16 20 E
Wu Jiang →, China 76 C6 29 40N 107 20 E
Wu Kau Tang, China 69 F11 22 30N 114 14 E
Wu'an, China 74 F8 36 40N 114 15 E
Wubin, Australia 125 F2 30 6 S 116 37 E
Wubu, China 74 F6 37 28N 110 42 E
Wuchang, China 75 B14 44 55N 127 5 E
Wucheng, China 74 F9 37 12N 116 20 E
Wuchow = Wuzhou, China 77 F8 23 30N 111 18 E
Wuchuan, Guangdong, China 77 G8 21 33N 110 43 E
Wuchuan, Guizhou, China 76 C7 28 25N 108 3 E
Wuchuan, Nei Monggol Zizhiqu, China 74 D6 41 5N 111 28 E
Wuday'ah, Si. Arabia 98 C4 17 2N 47 7 E
Wudi, China 75 F9 37 40N 117 35 E
Wuding, China 76 E4 25 24N 102 21 E
Wuding He →, China 74 F6 37 2N 110 23 E
Wudinna, Australia 127 E2 33 0 S 135 22 E
Wudu, China 74 H3 33 22N 104 54 E
Wufeng, China 77 B8 30 12N 110 42 E
Wugang, China 77 D8 26 44N 110 35 E
Wugong Shan, China 77 D9 27 30N 114 0 E
Wuguishan, China 69 G9 22 25N 113 25 E
Wuhan, China 77 B10 30 31N 114 18 E
Wuhe, China 75 H9 33 10N 117 50 E
Wuhsi = Wuxi, China 77 B13 31 33N 120 18 E
Wuhu, China 77 B12 31 22N 118 21 E
Wujiang, China 77 B13 31 10N 120 38 E
Wukari, Nigeria 113 D6 7 51N 9 42 E
Wulajie, China 75 B14 44 6N 126 33 E
Wulanbulang, China 74 D6 41 5N 110 55 E
Wular L., India 93 B6 34 20N 74 30 E
Wulehe, Ghana 113 D5 8 39N 0 0W
Wulff Land, Greenland 10 A6 82 0N 49 0W
Wulian, China 75 G10 35 40N 119 12 E
Wuliang Shan, China 76 E3 24 30N 100 40 E
Wuliaru, Indonesia 83 C4 7 27 S 131 0 E
Wuling Shan, China 76 C7 30 0N 110 0 E
Wulong, China 76 C6 29 22N 107 43 E
Wuluk'omushih Ling, China 68 C3 36 25N 87 25 E
Wulumuchi = Ürümqi, China 66 E9 43 45N 87 45 E
Wum, Cameroon 113 D7 6 24N 10 2 E
Wuming, China 76 F7 23 12N 108 18 E
Wun Rog, Sudan 107 F2 9 0N 28 20 E
Wuning, China 77 C10 29 17N 115 5 E
Wunna →, India 94 D4 20 18N 78 48 E
Wunnummin L., Canada 140 B2 52 55N 89 10W
Wunsiedel, Germany 31 E8 50 2N 12 0 E
Wunstorf, Germany 30 C5 52 25N 9 26 E
Wuntho, Burma 90 D5 23 55N 95 45 E
Wupatki △, U.S.A. 159 J8 35 35N 111 20W
Wuping, China 77 E11 25 5N 116 5 E
Wuppertal, Germany 30 D3 51 16N 7 12 E
Wuppertal, S. Africa 116 E2 32 13 S 19 12 E
Wuqia, China 65 D7 39 40N 75 7 E
Wuqing, China 75 E9 39 23N 117 4 E
Würenlingen, Switz. 33 A6 47 32N 8 16 E
Wurtsboro, U.S.A. 151 E10 41 35N 74 29W
Würzburg, Germany 31 F5 49 46N 9 55 E
Wurzen, Germany 30 D8 51 22N 12 44 E
Wushan, China 74 G3 34 43N 104 53 E
Wushishi, Nigeria 113 D6 9 46N 6 7 E
Wusi, Vanuatu 133 E4 15 21 S 166 40 E
Wusih = Wuxi, China 77 B13 31 33N 120 18 E
Wutach →, Germany 31 H4 47 37N 8 15 E
Wutai, China 74 E7 38 40N 113 12 E
Wuting = Huimin, China 75 F9 37 27N 117 28 E
Wutong, China 77 E8 25 24N 110 4 E
Wutonghaolai, China 75 C11 42 50N 120 5 E
Wutongqiao, China 76 C4 29 22N 103 50 E
Wutung, Papua N. G. 132 B1 2 37 S 141 1 E
Wuwei, Anhui, China 77 B11 31 18N 117 54 E
Wuwei, Gansu, China 68 C5 37 57N 102 34 E
Wuxi, Jiangsu, China 77 B13 31 33N 120 18 E
Wuxi, Sichuan, China 76 B7 31 23N 109 35 E
Wuxiang, China 74 F7 36 49N 112 50 E
Wuxuan, China 76 F7 23 34N 109 38 E
Wuxue, China 77 C10 29 52N 115 30 E
Wuyang, China 74 H7 33 25N 113 35 E
Wuyi, Hebei, China 74 F8 37 46N 115 56 E
Wuyi, Zhejiang, China 77 C12 28 52N 119 50 E
Wuyi Shan, China 77 D11 27 0N 117 0 E
Wuyishan, China 77 D12 27 45N 118 0 E
Wuyo, Nigeria 113 C7 10 23N 11 50 E
Wuyuan, Jiangxi, China 77 C11 29 15N 117 50 E
Wuyuan, Nei Monggol Zizhiqu, China 74 D5 41 2N 108 20 E
Wuzhai, China 74 E6 38 54N 111 48 E
Wuzhi Shan, China 86 C7 18 45N 109 45 E
Wuzhong, China 74 E4 38 2N 106 12 E
Wuzhou, China 77 F8 23 30N 111 18 E
Wyaaba Cr. →, Australia 126 B3 16 27 S 141 35 E
Wyalkatchem, Australia 125 F2 31 8 S 117 22 E
Wyalusing, U.S.A. 151 E8 41 40N 76 16W
Wyandotte, U.S.A. 157 B13 42 12N 83 9W
Wyandra, Australia 127 D4 27 12 S 145 56 E
Wyangala, L., Australia 129 B8 33 54 S 149 0 E
Wyara, L., Australia 127 D3 28 42 S 144 14 E
Wycheproof, Australia 128 D5 36 5 S 143 17 E
Wye →, U.K. 21 F5 51 38N 2 40W
Wyemandoo, Australia 125 E2 28 28 S 118 29 E
Wyk, Germany 30 A4 54 41N 8 33 E
Wymondham, U.K. 21 E9 52 35N 1 7 E
Wymore, U.S.A. 154 E6 40 7N 96 40W
Wyndham, Australia 124 C4 15 33 S 128 3 E
Wyndham, N.Z. 131 G3 46 20 S 168 51 E
Wynne, U.S.A. 155 H9 35 14N 90 47W
Wynyard, Australia 127 G4 41 5 S 145 44 E
Wynyard, Canada 143 C8 51 45N 104 10W
Wyola L., Australia 125 E5 29 8 S 130 17 E
Wyoming = Plympton-Wyoming, Canada 150 D2 42 57N 82 7W
Wyoming, Ill., U.S.A. 156 C7 41 4N 89 47W
Wyoming, Iowa, U.S.A. 156 B6 42 4N 91 0W
Wyoming, Mich., U.S.A. 157 B11 42 54N 85 42W
Wyoming □, U.S.A. 158 E10 43 0N 107 30W
Wyomissing, U.S.A. 151 F9 40 20N 75 59W
Wyong, Australia 129 B9 33 14 S 151 24 E
Wyperfeld △, Australia 128 C4 35 35 S 141 42 E
Wyrzysk, Poland 55 E4 53 10N 17 17 E
Wyśmierzyce, Poland 55 G7 51 37N 20 50 E
Wysoka, Poland 55 E4 53 13N 17 2 E
Wysokie, Poland 55 H9 50 55N 22 40 E
Wysokie Mazowieckie, Poland 55 F9 52 55N 22 30 E
Wyszków, Poland 55 F8 52 36N 21 25 E
Wyszogród, Poland 55 F7 52 23N 20 9 E
Wytheville, U.S.A. 148 G5 36 57N 81 5W
Wyżyna Małopolska, Poland 55 H7 50 45N 20 0 E

X

Xa-Cassau, Angola 115 D4 9 5 S 20 15 E
Xa-Muteba, Angola 115 D3 9 34 S 17 50 E
Xaafuun, Somali Rep. 120 B4 10 25N 51 16 E
Xaçmaz, Azerbaijan 61 K9 41 31N 48 42 E
Xadded, Somali Rep. 120 C3 9 46N 48 2 E
Xaghra, Malta 38 E7 36 3N 14 16 E
Xai-Xai, Mozam. 117 D5 25 6 S 33 31 E
Xaidulla, China 65 E8 36 28N 77 59 E
Xainza, China 68 C3 30 58N 88 35 E
Xalapa, Mexico 163 D5 19 32N 96 55W
Xambioá, Brazil 170 C2 6 25 S 48 40W
Xangongo, Angola 116 B2 16 45 S 15 5 E
Xankändi, Azerbaijan 101 C12 39 52N 46 49 E
Xanlar, Azerbaijan 61 K8 40 37N 46 12 E
Xanten, Germany 30 D2 51 39N 6 26 E
Xánthi, Greece 51 E8 41 10N 24 58 E
Xánthi □, Greece 51 E8 41 10N 24 58 E
Xanthos, Turkey 49 E11 36 19N 29 18 E
Xanxerê, Brazil 175 B5 26 53 S 52 23W

Xapuri, *Brazil* **172 C4** 10 35 S 68 35W
Xar Moron He →, *China* **75 C11** 43 25N 120 35 E
Xarrë, *Albania* **38 B10** 39 44N 20 3 E
Xátiva, *Spain* **41 G4** 38 59N 0 32W
Xau, L., *Botswana* **116 C3** 21 15 S 24 44 E
Xavantina, *Brazil* **175 A5** 21 15 S 52 48W
Xenia, *U.S.A.* **157 E13** 39 41N 83 56W
Xeropotamos →, *Cyprus* **39 F8** 34 42N 32 33 E
Xertigny, *France* **27 D13** 48 3N 6 24 E
Xewkija, *Malta* **38 E7** 36 2N 14 15 E
Xhora, *S. Africa* **117 E4** 31 55 S 28 38 E
Xhumo, *Botswana* **116 C3** 21 7 S 24 35 E
Xi Jiang →, *China* **77 F9** 22 5N 113 20 E
Xi Xian, *Henan, China* **77 A10** 32 20N 114 43 E
Xi Xian, *Shanxi, China* **74 F6** 36 41N 110 58 E
Xia Xian, *China* **74 G6** 35 8N 111 12 E
Xiachengzi, *China* **75 B16** 44 40N 130 18 E
Xiachuan Dao, *China* **77 G9** 21 40N 112 40 E
Xiaguan, *China* **68 D5** 25 32N 100 16 E
Xiajiang, *China* **77 D10** 27 30N 115 10 E
Xiajin, *China* **74 F9** 36 56N 116 0 E
Xiamen, *China* **77 E12** 24 25N 118 4 E
Xi'an, *China* **74 G5** 34 15N 109 0 E
Xian Xian, *China* **74 E9** 38 12N 116 6 E
Xianfeng, *China* **76 C7** 29 40N 109 8 E
Xiang Jiang →, *China* **77 C9** 28 55N 112 50 E
Xiangcheng, *Henan, China* **74 H8** 33 29N 114 52 E
Xiangcheng, *Henan, China* **74 H7** 33 50N 113 27 E
Xiangcheng, *Sichuan, China* **76 C2** 28 53N 99 47 E
Xiangdu, *China* **76 F6** 23 13N 106 58 E
Xiangfan, *China* **77 A9** 32 2N 112 8 E
Xianggang = Hong Kong □, *China* **77 F10** 22 11N 114 14 E
Xianghuang Qi, *China* **74 C7** 42 2N 113 50 E
Xiangning, *China* **74 G6** 35 58N 110 50 E
Xiangquan, *China* **74 F7** 36 30N 113 1 E
Xiangquan He = Sutlej →, *Pakistan* **91 C3** 29 23N 71 3 E
Xiangshan, *China* **77 C13** 29 29N 121 51 E
Xiangshui, *China* **75 G10** 34 12N 119 33 E
Xiangtan, *China* **77 D9** 27 51N 112 54 E
Xiangxiang, *China* **77 D9** 27 43N 112 28 E
Xiangyin, *China* **77 C9** 28 38N 112 54 E
Xiangyun, *China* **76 E3** 25 34N 100 35 E
Xiangzhou, *China* **76 F7** 23 58N 109 40 E
Xianju, *China* **77 C13** 28 51N 120 44 E
Xianning, *China* **77 C10** 29 51N 114 16 E
Xianshui He →, *China* **76 B3** 30 10N 100 59 E
Xiantao, *China* **77 B9** 30 25N 113 25 E
Xianyang, *China* **74 G5** 34 20N 108 40 E
Xianyou, *China* **77 E12** 25 22N 118 38 E
Xiao Hinggan Ling, *China* **69 B7** 49 0N 127 0 E
Xiao Xian, *China* **74 G9** 34 15N 116 55 E
Xiaofeng, *China* **77 B12** 30 35N 119 32 E
Xiaogan, *China* **77 B9** 30 52N 113 55 E
Xiaojin, *China* **76 B4** 30 59N 102 21 E
Xiaolan, *China* **77 F9** 22 38N 113 13 E
Xiaoshan, *China* **77 B13** 30 12N 120 18 E
Xiaoyi, *China* **74 F6** 37 8N 111 48 E
Xiapu, *China* **77 D12** 26 54N 119 59 E
Xiawa, *China* **75 C11** 42 35N 120 38 E
Xiayi, *China* **74 G9** 34 15N 116 10 E
Xichang, *China* **76 D4** 27 51N 102 19 E
Xichong, *China* **76 B5** 30 57N 105 54 E
Xichou, *China* **76 E5** 23 25N 104 42 E
Xichuan, *China* **74 H6** 33 0N 111 30 E
Xide, *China* **76 C4** 28 8N 102 19 E
Xiemahe, *China* **77 B8** 31 38N 111 12 E
Xieng Khouang, *Laos* **86 C4** 19 17N 103 25 E
Xifei He →, *China* **74 H9** 32 45N 116 40 E
Xifeng, *Gansu, China* **74 G4** 35 40N 107 40 E
Xifeng, *Guizhou, China* **76 D6** 27 7N 106 42 E
Xifeng, *Liaoning, China* **75 C13** 42 42N 124 45 E
Xifengzhen = Xifeng, *China* **74 G4** 35 40N 107 40 E
Xigazê, *China* **68 D3** 29 5N 88 45 E
Xihe, *China* **74 G3** 34 2N 105 20 E
Xihua, *China* **74 H8** 33 45N 114 30 E
Xilaganí, *Greece* **51 F9** 40 58N 25 28 E
Xili Shuiku, *China* **69 F10** 22 36N 113 57 E
Xiliao He →, *China* **75 C12** 43 32N 123 35 E
Xilin, *China* **76 E5** 24 30N 105 6 E
Xilókastron, *Greece* **48 C4** 38 5N 22 38 E
Ximana, *Mozam.* **119 F3** 19 24 S 33 58 E
Xime, *Guinea-Biss.* **112 C2** 11 59N 14 57W
Ximeng, *China* **76 F2** 22 50N 99 27 E
Xin Jiang →, *China* **77 C11** 28 45N 116 35 E
Xin Xian = Xinzhou, *China* **74 E7** 38 22N 112 46 E
Xinavane, *Mozam.* **117 D5** 25 2 S 32 47 E
Xinbin, *China* **75 D13** 41 40N 125 2 E
Xincai, *China* **77 A10** 32 43N 114 58 E
Xinchang, *China* **77 C13** 29 28N 120 52 E
Xincheng, *Guangxi Zhuangzu, China* **76 E7** 24 5N 108 39 E
Xincheng, *Jiangxi, China* **77 D10** 26 48N 114 6 E
Xindu, *China* **76 B5** 30 50N 104 10 E
Xinfeng, *Guangdong, China* **77 E10** 24 5N 114 16 E
Xinfeng, *Jiangxi, China* **77 D11** 27 7N 116 11 E
Xinfeng, *Jiangxi, China* **77 E10** 25 27N 114 58 E
Xinfengjiang Skuiku, *China* **77 F10** 23 52N 114 30 E
Xing Xian, *China* **74 E6** 38 27N 111 7 E
Xing'an, *Guangxi Zhuangzu, China* **77 E8** 25 38N 110 40 E
Xingan, *Jiangxi, China* **77 D10** 27 46N 115 20 E
Xingcheng, *China* **75 D11** 40 40N 120 45 E
Xingguo, *China* **77 D10** 26 21N 115 21 E
Xinghe, *China* **74 D7** 40 55N 113 55 E
Xinghua, *China* **75 H10** 32 58N 119 48 E
Xinghua Wan, *China* **77 E12** 25 15N 119 20 E
Xinglong, *China* **75 D9** 40 25N 117 30 E
Xingning, *China* **77 E10** 24 3N 115 42 E
Xingping, *China* **74 G5** 34 20N 108 28 E
Xingren, *China* **76 E5** 25 24N 105 11 E
Xingshan, *China* **77 B8** 31 15N 110 45 E
Xingtai, *China* **74 F8** 37 3N 114 32 E
Xingu →, *Brazil* **169 D7** 1 30 S 51 53W
Xingwen, *China* **76 C5** 28 22N 104 50 E
Xingyang, *China* **74 G7** 34 45N 112 52 E
Xinhe, *China* **74 F8** 37 30N 115 15 E
Xinhua, *China* **77 D8** 27 42N 111 13 E
Xinhuang, *China* **76 D7** 27 21N 109 12 E
Xinhui, *China* **77 F9** 22 25N 113 0 E
Xining, *China* **68 C5** 36 34N 101 40 E
Xinjian, *China* **77 C10** 28 37N 115 46 E
Xinjiang, *China* **74 G6** 35 34N 111 11 E
Xinjiang Uygur Zizhiqu □, *China* **68 C3** 42 0N 86 0 E
Xinjie, *China* **76 D3** 26 48N 101 15 E
Xinjin = Pulandian, *China* **75 E11** 39 25N 121 58 E
Xinjin, *China* **76 B4** 30 24N 103 47 E
Xinkai He →, *China* **75 C12** 43 32N 123 35 E
Xinken, *China* **69 F10** 22 39N 113 36 E
Xinle, *China* **74 E8** 38 25N 114 40 E
Xinlitun, *China* **75 D12** 42 0N 122 8 E
Xinlong, *China* **76 B3** 30 57N 100 12 E
Xinmin, *China* **75 D12** 41 59N 122 50 E
Xinning, *China* **77 D8** 26 28N 110 50 E
Xinping, *China* **76 E3** 24 5N 101 59 E
Xinshao, *China* **77 D8** 27 21N 111 26 E
Xintai, *China* **75 G9** 35 55N 117 45 E
Xintian, *China* **77 E9** 25 55N 112 13 E
Xinwan, *China* **69 F10** 22 47N 113 40 E
Xinxian, *China* **77 B10** 31 36N 113 51 E
Xinxiang, *China* **74 G7** 35 18N 113 50 E
Xinxing, *China* **77 F9** 22 35N 112 15 E
Xinyang, *China* **77 A10** 32 6N 114 3 E
Xinye, *China* **77 A9** 32 30N 112 21 E
Xinyi, *China* **77 F8** 22 25N 111 0 E
Xinyu, *China* **77 D10** 27 49N 114 58 E
Xinzhan, *China* **75 C14** 43 50N 127 18 E
Xinzheng, *China* **74 G7** 34 20N 113 45 E
Xinzhou, *Hubei, China* **77 B10** 30 50N 114 48 E
Xinzhou, *Shanxi, China* **74 E7** 38 22N 112 46 E
Xinzo de Limia, *Spain* **42 C3** 42 3N 7 47W
Xiongyuecheng, *China* **75 D12** 40 12N 122 5 E
Xiping, *Henan, China* **74 H8** 33 22N 114 5 E
Xiping, *Henan, China* **74 H6** 33 25N 111 8 E
Xiping, *Zhejiang, China* **77 C12** 28 16N 119 29 E
Xique-Xique, *Brazil* **170 D3** 10 50 S 42 40W
Xiruá →, *Brazil* **172 B4** 6 3 S 67 50W
Xisha Qundao = Paracel Is., *S. China Sea* **78 A4** 15 50N 112 0 E
Xishui, *Guizhou, China* **76 C6** 28 19N 106 9 E
Xishui, *Hubei, China* **77 B10** 30 30N 115 15 E
Xitole, *Guinea-Biss.* **112 C2** 11 43N 14 50W
Xiu Shui →, *China* **77 C10** 29 13N 116 0 E
Xiuning, *China* **77 C12** 29 45N 118 10 E
Xiuren, *China* **77 E8** 24 27N 110 12 E
Xiushan, *China* **76 C7** 28 25N 108 57 E
Xiushui, *China* **77 C10** 29 2N 114 33 E
Xiuwen, *China* **76 D6** 26 49N 106 32 E
Xiuyan, *China* **75 D12** 40 18N 123 11 E
Xixia, *China* **74 H6** 33 25N 111 29 E
Xixiang, *China* **74 H4** 33 0N 107 44 E
Xiyang, *China* **74 F7** 37 38N 113 38 E
Xizang Zizhiqu □, *China* **68 C3** 32 0N 88 0 E
Xlendi, *Malta* **38 E6** 36 2N 14 13 E
Xochob, *Mexico* **163 D7** 19 28N 89 45W
Xu Jiang →, *China* **77 D11** 28 0N 116 25 E
Xuan Loc, *Vietnam* **87 G6** 10 56N 107 14 E
Xuan'en, *China* **76 C7** 30 0N 109 30 E
Xuanhan, *China* **76 B6** 31 18N 107 38 E
Xuanhua, *China* **74 D8** 40 40N 115 2 E
Xuanwei, *China* **76 C5** 26 15N 103 59 E
Xuanzhou, *China* **77 B12** 30 56N 118 43 E
Xuchang, *China* **74 G7** 34 2N 113 48 E
Xudat, *Azerbaijan* **61 K9** 41 38N 48 41 E
Xuddur = Oddur, *Somali Rep.* **120 D2** 4 11N 43 52 E
Xuefeng Shan, *China* **77 D8** 27 5N 110 35 E
Xuejiaping, *China* **77 B8** 31 39N 110 16 E
Xun Jiang →, *China* **77 F8** 23 35N 111 30 E
Xun Xian, *China* **74 G8** 35 42N 114 33 E
Xundian, *China* **76 E4** 25 36N 103 15 E
Xunwu, *China* **77 E10** 24 54N 115 37 E
Xunyang, *China* **74 H5** 32 48N 109 22 E
Xunyi, *China* **74 G5** 35 8N 108 20 E
Xupu, *China* **77 D8** 27 53N 110 32 E
Xúquer →, *Spain* **41 F4** 39 5N 0 10W
Xushui, *China* **74 E8** 39 2N 115 40 E
Xuwen, *China* **77 G8** 20 20N 110 10 E
Xuyen Moc, *Vietnam* **87 G6** 10 34N 107 25 E
Xuyong, *China* **76 C5** 28 10N 105 22 E
Xuzhou, *China* **75 G9** 34 18N 117 10 E
Xylophagou, *Cyprus* **39 F9** 34 54N 33 51 E

Y

Ya Xian = Sanya, *China* **86 C7** 18 14N 109 29 E
Yaamba, *Australia* **126 C5** 23 8 S 150 22 E
Ya'an, *China* **76 C4** 29 58N 103 5 E
Yaapeet, *Australia* **128 C5** 35 45 S 142 3 E
Yabassi, *Cameroon* **113 E6** 4 30N 9 57 E
Yabelo, *Ethiopia* **107 G4** 4 50N 38 8 E
Yabelo ⌓, *Ethiopia* **107 F4** 6 0N 37 50 E
Yablanitsa, *Bulgaria* **51 C8** 43 2N 24 5 E
Yablonovy Ra. = Yablonovyy Khrebet, *Russia* **67 D12** 53 0N 114 0 E
Yablonovyy Khrebet, *Russia* **67 D12** 53 0N 114 0 E
Yabluniv, *Ukraine* **53 B9** 48 24N 24 57 E
Yablunytsya, *Ukraine* **53 B9** 48 19N 24 29 E
Yabrai Shan, *China* **74 E2** 39 40N 103 0 E
Yabrūd, *Syria* **103 B5** 33 58N 36 39 E
Yabucoa, *Puerto Rico* **165 d** 18 3N 65 53W
Yacambú △, *Venezuela* **165 E6** 9 42N 69 27W
Yacheng, *China* **69 E5** 18 22N 109 6 E
Yackandandah, *Australia* **129 D7** 36 18 S 146 52 E
Yacuiba, *Bolivia* **174 A3** 22 0 S 63 43W
Yacuma →, *Bolivia* **173 C4** 13 38 S 65 23W
Yadgir, *India* **94 F3** 16 45N 77 5 E
Yadkin →, *U.S.A.* **149 H5** 35 29N 80 9W
Yadrin, *Russia* **60 C8** 55 57N 46 12 E
Yadua, *Fiji* **133 A2** 16 49 S 178 18 E
Yaeyama-Rettō, *Japan* **71 M1** 24 30N 123 40 E
Yafran, *Libya* **108 B2** 32 4N 12 31 E
Yafran □, *Libya* **108 B2** 32 0N 12 20 E
Yagaba, *Ghana* **113 C4** 10 14N 1 20W
Yagasa Cluster, *Fiji* **133 B3** 18 57 S 178 28W
Yağcılar, *Turkey* **49 B10** 39 25N 28 23 E
Yagodnoye, *Russia* **67 C15** 62 33N 149 40 E
Yagoua, *Cameroon* **109 F3** 10 20N 15 13 E
Yaguas →, *Peru* **168 D3** 2 45 S 70 10W
Yahila, *Orientale, Dem. Rep. of the Congo* **114 B4** 1 48N 23 37 E
Yahila, *Orientale, Dem. Rep. of the Congo* **118 B1** 0 13N 24 28 E
Yahk, *Canada* **142 D5** 49 6N 116 10W
Yahotyn, *Ukraine* **59 G6** 50 17N 31 46 E
Yahuma, *Dem. Rep. of the Congo* **114 B4** 1 0N 23 10 E
Yahyalı, *Turkey* **100 C6** 38 5N 35 2 E
Yaita, *Japan* **71 F9** 36 48N 139 56 E
Yaiza, *Canary Is.* **9 e2** 28 57N 13 46W
Yaizu, *Japan* **73 C10** 34 52N 138 20 E
Yajiang, *China* **76 B3** 30 2N 100 57 E
Yajua, *Nigeria* **113 C7** 11 27N 12 49 E
Yakage, *Japan* **72 C5** 34 37N 133 35 E
Yakamba, *Dem. Rep. of the Congo* **114 B3** 2 42N 19 38 E
Yakima, *U.S.A.* **158 C3** 46 36N 120 31W
Yakima →, *U.S.A.* **158 C3** 47 0N 120 30W
Yakkabag, *Uzbekistan* **65 D3** 38 55N 66 51 E
Yako, *Burkina Faso* **112 C4** 12 59N 2 15W
Yakobi I., *U.S.A.* **142 B1** 58 0N 136 30W
Yakoma, *Dem. Rep. of the Congo* **114 B4** 4 5N 22 27 E
Yakoruda, *Bulgaria* **50 D7** 42 1N 23 39 E
Yakossi, *C.A.R.* **114 A4** 5 37N 23 19 E
Yakovlevka, *Russia* **70 B6** 44 26N 133 28 E
Yakovlevskoye = Privolzhsk, *Russia* **60 B5** 57 23N 41 16 E
Yakshur Bodya, *Russia* **64 C4** 57 11N 53 7 E
Yaku-Shima, *Japan* **71 J5** 30 20N 130 30 E
Yakumo, *Japan* **70 C10** 42 15N 140 16 E
Yakutat, *U.S.A.* **144 G13** 59 33N 139 44W
Yakutat B., *U.S.A.* **144 G12** 59 45N 140 45W
Yakutia = Sakha □, *Russia* **67 C13** 66 0N 130 0 E
Yakutsk, *Russia* **67 C13** 62 5N 129 50 E
Yala, *Thailand* **87 J3** 6 33N 101 18 E
Yala △, *Sri Lanka* **95 L5** 6 20N 81 30 E
Yalboroo, *Australia* **126 J6** 20 50 S 148 40 E
Yale, *U.S.A.* **150 C2** 43 8N 82 48W
Yalgoo, *Australia* **125 E2** 28 16 S 116 39 E
Yalgorup △, *Australia* **125 D2** 24 34 S 115 2 E
Yali, *Dem. Rep. of the Congo* **114 B4** 0 4N 21 3 E
Yaligimba, *Dem. Rep. of the Congo* **114 B4** 2 13N 22 56 E
Yalikanda, *Dem. Rep. of the Congo* **114 B4** 0 23N 24 47 E
Yalinga, *C.A.R.* **114 A4** 6 33N 23 10 E
Yalkubul, Punta, *Mexico* **163 C7** 21 32N 88 37W
Yalleroi, *Australia* **126 C4** 24 3 S 145 42 E
Yalobusha →, *U.S.A.* **155 J9** 33 33N 90 10W
Yaloké, *C.A.R.* **114 A3** 5 19N 17 5 E
Yalong Jiang →, *China* **76 D3** 26 40N 101 55 E
Yalova, *Turkey* **51 F13** 40 41N 29 15 E
Yalpuh, Ozero, *Ukraine* **53 E13** 45 30N 28 41 E
Yalta, *Ukraine* **59 K8** 44 30N 34 10 E
Yalu Jiang →, *China* **75 E13** 40 0N 124 22 E
Yalvaç, *Turkey* **100 C4** 38 17N 31 10 E
Yam Ha Melaḥ = Dead Sea, *Asia* **103 D4** 31 30N 35 30 E
Yam Kinneret, *Israel* **103 C4** 32 45N 35 35 E
Yamada, *Japan* **72 D2** 33 33N 130 49 E
Yamaga, *Japan* **72 D2** 33 1N 130 41 E
Yamagata, *Japan* **70 E10** 38 15N 140 15 E
Yamagata □, *Japan* **70 E10** 38 30N 140 0 E
Yamagawa, *Japan* **72 F2** 31 12N 130 39 E
Yamaguchi, *Japan* **72 C3** 34 10N 131 32 E
Yamaguchi □, *Japan* **72 C3** 34 20N 131 40 E
Yamal, Poluostrov, *Russia* **66 B8** 71 0N 70 0 E
Yamal Pen. = Yamal, Poluostrov, *Russia* **66 B8** 71 0N 70 0 E
Yamanaka, *Japan* **73 A8** 36 15N 136 22 E
Yamanashi, *Japan* **73 B10** 35 41N 138 40 E
Yamanashi □, *Japan* **73 B10** 35 40N 138 40 E
Yamanie Falls △, *Australia* **126 B4** 18 29 S 146 9 E
Yamantau, Gora, *Russia* **64 D7** 54 15N 58 6 E
Yamasaki, *Japan* **72 C6** 35 0N 134 32 E
Yamato, *Japan* **73 B11** 35 27N 139 25 E
Yamatotakada, *Japan* **73 C7** 34 31N 135 45 E
Yamba, *Australia* **127 D5** 29 26 S 153 23 E
Yambarran Ra., *Australia* **124 C5** 15 10 S 130 25 E
Yambata, *Dem. Rep. of the Congo* **114 B4** 2 26N 21 58 E
Yambéring, *Guinea* **112 C2** 11 50N 12 18 E
Yâmbiô, *Sudan* **107 G2** 4 35N 28 16 E
Yambol, *Bulgaria* **51 D10** 42 30N 26 30 E
Yamboyo, *Dem. Rep. of the Congo* **114 B4** 0 40N 22 18 E
Yambuya, *Dem. Rep. of the Congo* **114 B4** 1 17N 24 34 E
Yamdena, *Indonesia* **83 C4** 7 45 S 131 20 E
Yame, *Japan* **72 D2** 33 13N 130 35 E
Yamethin, *Burma* **90 E6** 20 29N 96 18 E
Yamma-Yamma, L., *Australia* **127 D3** 26 16 S 141 20 E
Yamoussoukro, *Ivory C.* **112 D3** 6 49N 5 17W
Yampa →, *U.S.A.* **158 F9** 40 32N 108 59W
Yampi Sd., *Australia* **124 C3** 16 8 S 123 38 E
Yampil, *Moldova* **59 H5** 48 15N 28 15 E
Yampol = Yampil, *Moldova* **59 H5** 48 15N 28 15 E
Yamrat, *Nigeria* **113 C6** 10 11N 9 55 E
Yamrukchal = Botev, *Bulgaria* **51 D8** 42 44N 24 52 E
Yamuna →, *India* **93 G9** 25 30N 81 53 E
Yamunanagar, *India* **92 D7** 30 7N 77 17 E
Yamzho Yumco, *China* **68 D4** 28 48N 90 35 E
Yan, *Nigeria* **113 C7** 10 5N 12 11 E
Yan Oya →, *Sri Lanka* **95 K5** 9 0N 81 10 E
Yana →, *Russia* **67 B14** 71 30N 136 0 E
Yanagawa, *Japan* **72 D2** 33 10N 130 24 E
Yanahara, *Japan* **72 C6** 34 58N 134 2 E
Yanai, *Japan* **72 D4** 33 58N 132 7 E
Yan'an, *China* **74 F5** 36 35N 109 26 E
Yanaul, *Russia* **64 C5** 56 25N 55 0 E
Yanbian, *China* **76 D3** 26 47N 101 31 E
Yanbu 'al Baḥr, *Si. Arabia* **96 F3** 24 0N 38 5 E
Yanchang, *China* **74 F6** 36 43N 110 1 E
Yancheng, *Henan, China* **74 H8** 33 35N 114 0 E
Yancheng, *Jiangsu, China* **75 H11** 33 23N 120 8 E
Yanchep Beach, *Australia* **125 F2** 31 33 S 115 37 E
Yanchi, *China* **74 F4** 37 48N 107 20 E
Yanchuan, *China* **74 F6** 36 51N 110 10 E
Yanco, *Australia* **129 C7** 34 38 S 146 27 E
Yanco Cr. →, *Australia* **129 C6** 35 14 S 145 35 E
Yandé, Î., *N. Cal.* **133 T17** 20 3 S 163 49 E
Yandicoogina, *Australia* **124 D2** 22 49 S 119 12 E
Yandina, *Solomon Is.* **133 M10** 9 7 S 159 13 E
Yandja, *Dem. Rep. of the Congo* **114 C3** 1 41 S 17 43 E
Yandongi, *Dem. Rep. of the Congo* **114 B4** 2 51N 22 16 E
Yandoon, *Burma* **90 G5** 17 0N 95 40 E
Yanfeng, *China* **76 E3** 25 52N 101 8 E
Yanfolila, *Mali* **112 C3** 11 11N 8 9W
Yang Xian, *China* **74 H4** 33 15N 107 30 E
Yang-Yang, *Senegal* **112 B1** 15 30N 15 20W
Yangambi, *Dem. Rep. of the Congo* **118 B1** 0 47N 24 24 E
Yangbi, *China* **76 E2** 25 41N 99 58 E
Yangcheng, *China* **74 G7** 35 28N 112 22 E
Yangchow = Yangzhou, *China* **77 A12** 32 21N 119 26 E
Yangch'ü = Taiyuan, *China* **74 F7** 37 52N 112 33 E
Yangchüan = Yangquan, *China* **74 F7** 37 58N 113 31 E
Yangchun, *China* **77 F8** 22 11N 111 48 E
Yanggao, *China* **74 D7** 40 21N 113 55 E
Yanggu, *China* **74 F8** 36 8N 115 43 E
Yangi-Nishan, *Uzbekistan* **65 D2** 38 49N 65 47 E
Yangiabad, *Uzbekistan* **65 C5** 41 7N 70 6 E
Yangibazar = Kofarnikhon, *Tajikistan* **65 D4** 38 34N 69 1 E
Yangikishlak, *Uzbekistan* **65 C3** 40 25N 67 10 E
Yangirabad, *Uzbekistan* **65 C2** 40 2N 65 58 E
Yangiyer, *Uzbekistan* **65 C4** 40 16N 68 49 E
Yangiyul, *Uzbekistan* **65 C4** 41 0N 69 3 E
Yangjiang, *China* **77 G8** 21 50N 111 59 E
Yangliuqing, *China* **75 E9** 39 2N 117 5 E
Yangon = Rangoon, *Burma* **90 G6** 16 45N 96 20 E
Yangonde, *Dem. Rep. of the Congo* **114 B4** 0 3N 22 43 E
Yangping, *China* **77 B8** 31 12N 111 25 E
Yangpingguan, *China* **74 H4** 32 58N 106 5 E
Yangquan, *China* **74 F7** 37 58N 113 31 E
Yangshan, *China* **77 E9** 24 30N 112 40 E
Yangshuo, *China* **77 E8** 24 48N 110 29 E
Yangtse = Chang Jiang →, *China* **77 B13** 31 48N 121 10 E
Yangtze Kiang = Chang Jiang →, *China* **77 B13** 31 48N 121 10 E
Yangudi Rassa △, *Ethiopia* **107 E5** 10 50N 40 42 E
Yangxin, *China* **77 C10** 29 50N 115 12 E
Yangyang, *S. Korea* **75 E15** 38 4N 128 38 E
Yangyuan, *China* **74 D8** 40 1N 114 10 E
Yangzhong, *China* **77 A12** 32 22N 119 22 E
Yangzhou, *China* **77 A12** 32 21N 119 26 E
Yanhe, *China* **76 C7** 28 31N 108 29 E
Yanji, *China* **75 C15** 42 59N 129 30 E
Yanjin, *China* **76 C5** 28 5N 104 18 E
Yanjing, *China* **76 C2** 29 7N 98 33 E
Yankari △, *Nigeria* **113 D7** 9 50N 10 28 E
Yankton, *U.S.A.* **154 D6** 42 53N 97 23W
Yanonge, *Dem. Rep. of the Congo* **118 B1** 0 35N 24 38 E
Yanov = Ivanava, *Belarus* **59 F3** 52 7N 25 29 E
Yanqi, *China* **68 B3** 42 5N 86 35 E
Yanqing, *China* **74 D8** 40 30N 115 58 E
Yanshan, *Hebei, China* **75 E9** 38 4N 117 22 E
Yanshan, *Jiangxi, China* **77 C11** 28 15N 117 41 E
Yanshan, *Yunnan, China* **76 F5** 23 35N 104 20 E
Yanshou, *China* **75 B15** 45 28N 128 22 E
Yantabulla, *Australia* **127 D4** 29 21 S 145 0 E
Yantai, *China* **75 F11** 37 34N 121 22 E
Yantarnyy, *Russia* **54 D6** 54 52N 19 57 E
Yantian, *China* **69 F11** 22 35N 114 16 E
Yanting, *China* **76 B5** 31 11N 105 24 E
Yantra →, *Bulgaria* **51 C9** 43 40N 25 37 E
Yanuca, *Fiji* **133 B1** 18 24 S 178 0 E
Yanwa, *China* **76 D2** 27 35N 98 55 E
Yanykurgan = Zhangaqŭrghan, *Kazakhstan* **65 B4** 43 50N 68 48 E
Yanyuan, *China* **76 D3** 27 25N 101 30 E
Yanzhou, *China* **74 G9** 35 35N 116 49 E
Yao, *Chad* **109 F3** 12 56N 17 33 E
Yao, *Japan* **73 C7** 34 32N 135 36 E
Yao Noi, Ko, *Thailand* **87 a** 8 7N 98 37 E
Yao Xian, *China* **74 G5** 34 55N 108 59 E
Yao Yai, Ko, *Thailand* **87 a** 8 0N 98 35 E
Yao'an, *China* **76 E3** 25 31N 101 18 E
Yaodu, *China* **76 A5** 32 45N 105 22 E
Yaoundé, *Cameroon* **113 E7** 3 50N 11 35 E
Yaowan, *China* **75 G10** 34 15N 118 3 E
Yap, *Pac. Oc.* **134 G5** 9 30N 138 10 E
Yapacana △, *Venezuela* **168 C4** 3 49N 66 44W
Yapehe, *Dem. Rep. of the Congo* **114 C4** 0 13 S 24 28 E
Yapen, *Indonesia* **83 B5** 1 50 S 136 0 E
Yapen, Selat, *Indonesia* **83 B5** 1 20 S 136 10 E
Yapero, *Indonesia* **83 B5** 4 59 S 137 11 E
Yappar →, *Australia* **126 B3** 18 22 S 141 16 E
Yaqaga, *Fiji* **133 A2** 16 35 S 178 36 E
Yaqui →, *Mexico* **162 B2** 27 37N 110 39W
Yar, *Russia* **64 B4** 58 14N 52 5 E
Yar-Sale, *Russia* **66 C8** 66 50N 70 50 E
Yaracuy □, *Venezuela* **168 A4** 10 20N 68 45W
Yaracuy →, *Venezuela* **168 A4** 10 33N 68 15W
Yaraka, *Australia* **126 C3** 24 53 S 144 3 E
Yaransk, *Russia* **60 B8** 57 22N 47 49 E
Yarbasan, *Turkey* **49 C10** 38 59N 28 49 E
Yardımcı Burnu, *Turkey* **49 E12** 36 13N 30 25 E
Yare →, *U.K.* **21 E9** 52 35N 1 38 E
Yaremcha, *Ukraine* **53 B9** 48 27N 24 33 E
Yarensk, *Russia* **56 B8** 62 11N 49 15 E
Yarfa, *Si. Arabia* **106 C4** 24 37N 38 35 E
Yarí →, *Colombia* **168 D3** 0 20 S 72 20W
Yarīm, *Yemen* **98 D4** 14 20N 44 22 E
Yaritagua, *Venezuela* **168 A4** 10 5N 69 8W
Yarkand = Shache, *China* **65 D8** 38 20N 77 10 E
Yarker, *Canada* **151 B8** 44 23N 76 46W
Yarkhun →, *Pakistan* **93 A5** 36 17N 72 30 E
Yarlung Ziangbo Jiang = Brahmaputra →, *Asia* **68 D3** 23 40N 90 35 E
Yarmouth, *Canada* **141 D6** 43 50N 66 7W
Yarmūk →, *Syria* **103 C4** 32 42N 35 40 E
Yaroslavl, *Russia* **58 D10** 57 35N 39 55 E
Yarqa, W. →, *Egypt* **103 F2** 30 0N 33 49 E
Yarra Ranges △, *Australia* **129 D7** 37 40 S 146 3 E
Yarra Yarra Lakes, *Australia* **125 E2** 29 40 S 115 45 E
Yarram, *Australia* **129 E7** 38 29 S 146 39 E
Yarraman, *Australia* **127 D5** 26 50 S 152 0 E
Yarras, *Australia* **129 A10** 31 25 S 152 20 E
Yarrawonga, *Australia* **129 D7** 36 0 S 146 0 E
Yartsevo, *Sib., Russia* **67 C10** 60 20N 90 0 E
Yartsevo, *Smolensk, Russia* **58 E7** 55 6N 32 43 E
Yarumal, *Colombia* **168 B2** 6 58N 75 24W
Yasa, *Dem. Rep. of the Congo* **114 C4** 3 50 S 21 25 E
Yasawa, *Fiji* **133 A1** 16 47 S 177 31 E
Yasawa Group, *Fiji* **133 A1** 17 0 S 177 23 E
Yaselda, *Belarus* **59 F4** 52 7N 26 28 E
Yasen, *Ukraine* **53 B9** 48 45N 24 10 E
Yashbum, *Yemen* **98 D4** 14 19N 46 56 E
Yashi, *Nigeria* **113 C6** 12 23N 7 54 E
Yashikera, *Nigeria* **113 D5** 9 44N 3 29 E
Yashiro-Jima, *Japan* **72 D4** 33 55N 132 15 E
Yashkul, *Russia* **61 G7** 46 11N 45 21 E
Yasin, *Pakistan* **93 A5** 36 24N 73 23 E
Yasinovataya, *Ukraine* **59 H9** 48 7N 37 57 E
Yasinski, L., *Canada* **140 B4** 53 16N 77 35W
Yasinya, *Ukraine* **53 B9** 48 16N 24 21 E
Yasnyy, *Russia* **64 F7** 51 1N 59 58 E
Yasothon, *Thailand* **86 E5** 15 50N 104 10 E
Yass, *Australia* **129 C8** 34 49 S 148 54 E
Yasugi, *Japan* **72 B5** 35 26N 133 15 E
Yāsūj, *Iran* **97 D6** 30 31N 51 31 E
Yasuní △, *Ecuador* **168 D2** 1 19 S 76 3W
Yat, *Niger* **109 D2** 20 28N 13 27 E
Yata →, *Bolivia* **173 C4** 10 29 S 65 26W
Yata →, *C.A.R.* **114 A4** 10 23N 22 45 E
Yata-Ngaya ⌓, *C.A.R.* **114 A4** 9 15N 23 25 E
Yatağan, *Turkey* **49 D10** 37 20N 28 10 E
Yatakala, *Niger* **113 C5** 14 50N 0 22 E
Yaté, *N. Cal.* **133 V20** 22 9 S 166 57 E
Yates Center, *U.S.A.* **155 G7** 37 53N 95 44W
Yates Pt., *N.Z.* **131 E2** 44 29 S 167 49 E
Yathkyed L., *Canada* **143 A9** 62 40N 98 0W
Yathong, *Australia* **129 B6** 32 37 S 145 33 E
Yatolemu, *Dem. Rep. of the Congo* **114 B4** 0 25N 24 35 E
Yatsuo, *Japan* **73 A9** 36 34N 137 8 E
Yatsushiro, *Japan* **72 E2** 32 30N 130 40 E
Yatsushiro-Kai, *Japan* **72 E2** 32 30N 130 25 E
Yatta Plateau, *Kenya* **118 C4** 2 0 S 38 0 E
Yatua →, *Venezuela* **168 C4** 1 30N 66 30W
Yauca, *Peru* **172 D3** 15 39 S 74 35W
Yauco, *Puerto Rico* **165 d** 18 2N 66 51W
Yauri, *Peru* **172 C3** 14 47 S 71 25W
Yauya, *Peru* **172 B2** 8 59 S 77 17W
Yauyos, *Peru* **172 C2** 12 19 S 75 50W
Yaval, *India* **94 D2** 21 10N 75 42 E
Yavan, *Tajikistan* **65 D4** 38 19N 69 2 E
Yavari →, *Peru* **172 A3** 4 21 S 70 2W
Yávaros, *Mexico* **162 B3** 26 42N 109 31W
Yavatmal, *India* **94 D4** 20 20N 78 15 E
Yavero →, *Peru* **172 C3** 12 6 S 72 57W
Yavne, *Israel* **103 D3** 31 52N 34 45 E
Yavoriv, *Ukraine* **55 J10** 49 55N 23 20 E
Yavorov = Yavoriv, *Ukraine* **55 J10** 49 55N 23 20 E
Yavuzeli, *Turkey* **100 D7** 37 18N 37 24 E
Yawatahama, *Japan* **72 D4** 33 27N 132 24 E
Yawnghwe, *Burma* **90 E6** 20 39N 96 56 E
Yawri B., *S. Leone* **112 D2** 8 22N 13 0W
Yaxi, *China* **76 D6** 27 33N 106 41 E
Yaxian = Sanya, *China* **86 C7** 18 14N 109 29 E
Yazagyo, *Burma* **90 D5** 23 30N 94 6 E
Yazd, *Iran* **97 D7** 31 55N 54 27 E
Yazd □, *Iran* **97 D7** 32 0N 55 0 E
Yazd-e Khvāst, *Iran* **97 D7** 31 31N 52 7 E
Yazdān, *Iran* **91 B1** 33 30N 60 50 E
Yazıköy, *Turkey* **49 E9** 36 40N 27 20 E
Yazman, *Pakistan* **92 E4** 29 8N 71 45 E
Yazoo →, *U.S.A.* **155 J9** 32 22N 90 54W
Yazoo City, *U.S.A.* **155 J9** 32 51N 90 25W
Ybbs, *Austria* **34 C8** 48 12N 15 4 E
Ybycuí △, *Paraguay* **174 B4** 26 5 S 56 46W
Ybytyruzú △, *Paraguay* **175 B4** 25 51 S 56 11W
Yding Skovhøj, *Denmark* **17 J3** 55 59N 9 46 E
Ye, *Burma* **86 E1** 15 15N 97 15 E
Ye-ngan, *Burma* **90 E6** 21 9N 96 27 E
Ye-u, *Burma* **90 D5** 22 46N 95 26 E
Ye Xian = Laizhou, *China* **75 F10** 37 8N 119 57 E
Ye Xian, *China* **74 H7** 33 35N 113 25 E
Yea, *Australia* **129 D6** 37 14 S 145 26 E
Yebawmi, *Burma* **90 C5** 25 15N 95 45 E
Yebbi-Souma, *Chad* **109 D3** 21 7N 17 54 E
Yebyu, *Burma* **86 E2** 14 15N 98 13 E
Yecheng, *China* **65 E8** 37 54N 77 26 E
Yechŏn, *S. Korea* **75 F15** 36 39N 128 27 E
Yecla, *Spain* **41 G3** 38 35N 1 5W
Yécora, *Mexico* **162 B3** 28 20N 108 58W
Yedashe, *Burma* **90 F6** 19 10N 96 20 E
Yedebub Biheroch Bihereseboch na Hizboch □, *Ethiopia* **107 F4** 12 0N 36 0 E
Yedintsy = Edineţ, *Moldova* **53 B12** 48 9N 27 18 E
Yedri, *Chad* **109 D3** 22 25N 17 30 E
Yedseram →, *Nigeria* **113 C7** 12 30N 14 5 E
Yefremov, *Russia* **58 F10** 53 8N 38 3 E
Yegguéba, *Niger* **109 E2** 19 59N 12 52 E
Yeghegnadzor, *Armenia* **101 C11** 39 44N 45 19 E
Yegorlyk →, *Russia* **61 G5** 46 35N 41 57 E
Yegorlykskaya, *Russia* **61 G5** 46 35N 40 35 E
Yegoryevsk, *Russia* **58 E10** 55 27N 38 55 E
Yegri-Dere = Ardino, *Bulgaria* **51 E9** 41 34N 25 9 E
Yegros, *Paraguay* **174 B4** 26 20 S 56 25W
Yehbuah, *Indonesia* **79 J17** 8 23 S 114 45 E
Yehuda, Midbar, *Israel* **103 D4** 31 35N 35 15 E
Yei, *Sudan* **107 G3** 4 9N 30 40 E
Yei, Nahr →, *Sudan* **107 F3** 6 15N 30 13 E
Yejmiadzin, *Armenia* **61 K7** 40 12N 44 19 E
Yekaterinburg, *Russia* **64 C8** 56 50N 60 30 E
Yekaterinenshtadt = Marks, *Russia* **60 E8** 51 45N 46 50 E
Yekaterinodar = Krasnodar, *Russia* **61 H4** 45 5N 39 0 E
Yekumbe, *Dem. Rep. of the Congo* **114 C4** 1 2 S 23 27 E
Yelabuga, *Russia* **60 C11** 55 45N 52 4 E
Yelan, *Russia* **60 E6** 50 55N 43 43 E
Yelandur, *India* **95 H3** 12 5N 77 0 E
Yelarbon, *Australia* **127 D5** 28 33 S 150 38 E
Yelatma, *Russia* **60 C5** 55 0N 41 45 E
Yelcho, L., *Chile* **176 B2** 43 18 S 72 18W
Yelenovka = Sevan, *Armenia* **61 K7** 40 33N 44 56 E
Yelenovskiye Karyery = Dokuchayevsk, *Ukraine* **59 J9** 47 44N 37 40 E
Yelets, *Russia* **59 F10** 52 40N 38 30 E
Yélimané, *Mali* **112 B2** 15 9N 10 34W
Yelizavetgrad = Kirovohrad, *Ukraine* **59 H7** 48 35N 32 20 E
Yelizavetgrad = Kirovohrad, *Ukraine* **59 H7** 48 35N 32 20 E
Yelizavetinka, *Russia* **64 F7** 51 46N 59 45 E
Yell, *U.K.* **22 A7** 60 35N 1 5W
Yell Sd., *U.K.* **22 A7** 60 33N 1 15W
Yellamanchilli = Elamanchili, *India* **94 F6** 17 33N 82 50 E
Yellandu, *India* **94 F5** 17 39N 80 23 E
Yellapur, *India* **95 G2** 14 58N 74 43 E
Yellareddi, *India* **94 E4** 18 12N 78 2 E
Yellow →, *U.S.A.* **153 E3** 30 30N 87 0W
Yellow Sea, *China* **75 G12** 35 0N 123 0 E
Yellowhead Pass, *Canada* **142 C5** 52 53N 118 25W
Yellowknife, *Canada* **142 A6** 62 27N 114 29W
Yellowknife →, *Canada* **142 A6** 62 31N 114 19W
Yellowstone △, *U.S.A.* **158 D9** 44 40N 110 30W
Yellowstone →, *U.S.A.* **154 B3** 47 59N 103 59W
Yellowstone L., *U.S.A.* **158 D8** 44 27N 110 22W
Yelnya, *Russia* **58 E7** 54 35N 33 15 E
Yelsk, *Belarus* **59 G5** 51 50N 29 10 E
Yelwa, *Nigeria* **113 C5** 10 49N 4 41 E
Yemanzhelinsk, *Russia* **64 D8** 54 58N 61 18 E
Yemassee, *U.S.A.* **152 C9** 32 41N 80 51W
Yembongo, *Dem. Rep. of the Congo* **114 B3** 3 12N 19 2 E
Yemen ■, *Asia* **98 D4** 15 0N 44 0 E
Yemmiganur = Emmiganuru, *India* **95 G3** 15 44N 77 29 E
Yen Bai, *Vietnam* **76 G5** 21 42N 104 52 E
Yenagoa, *Nigeria* **113 E6** 4 58N 6 16 E
Yenakiyeve, *Ukraine* **59 H10** 48 15N 38 15 E
Yenakiyevo = Yenakiyeve, *Ukraine* **59 H10** 48 15N 38 15 E
Yenangyat, *Burma* **90 E5** 21 6N 94 48 E
Yenangyaung, *Burma* **90 E5** 20 30N 95 0 E
Yenanma, *Burma* **90 F5** 19 46N 94 49 E
Yenbo = Yanbu 'al Baḥr, *Si. Arabia* **96 F3** 24 0N 38 5 E

Yenda, Australia 129 C7 34 13 S 146 14 E
Yende Millimou, Guinea 112 D2 8 55N 10 10W
Yendéré, Burkina Faso 112 C4 10 12N 4 59W
Yendi, Ghana 113 D4 9 29N 0 1W
Yengisar, China 65 D8 38 56N 76 9 E
Yengo, Congo 114 B3 0 22N 15 29 E
Yengo △, Australia 129 B9 33 0 S 150 55 E
Yéni, Niger 113 C5 13 30N 3 1 E
Yeni-Pazar = Novi Pazar, Serbia & M. 50 C4 43 12N 20 28 E
Yenice, Ankara, Turkey 100 C5 39 14N 32 42 E
Yenice, Aydın, Turkey 49 D10 37 49N 28 35 E
Yenice, Çanakkale, Turkey 49 B9 39 55N 27 17 E
Yenice, Edirne, Turkey 51 F10 40 42N 26 9 E
Yenice →, Turkey 100 D6 37 37N 35 33 E
Yenifoça, Turkey 49 C8 38 44N 26 51 E
Yenihisar, Turkey 49 D9 37 22N 27 16 E
Yeniköy, Bursa, Turkey 51 F13 40 31N 29 22 E
Yeniköy, Çanakkale, Turkey 49 B8 39 55N 26 10 E
Yeniköy, Kütahya, Turkey 49 C11 38 52N 29 17 E
Yenipazar, Turkey 49 D10 37 49N 28 11 E
Yenisafa, Greece 51 E8 41 1N 24 57 E
Yenişehir, Turkey 51 F13 40 16N 29 38 E
Yenisey →, Russia 66 B9 71 50N 82 40 E
Yeniseysk, Russia 67 D10 58 27N 92 13 E
Yeniseyskiy Zaliv, Russia 66 B9 72 20N 81 0 E
Yenki = Yanji, China 75 C15 42 59N 129 30 E
Yennádhi, Greece 38 E11 36 2N 27 56 E
Yenne, France 29 C9 45 43N 5 44 E
Yenotayevka, Russia 61 G8 47 15N 47 0 E
Yenyuka, Russia 67 D13 57 57N 121 15 E
Yeo →, U.K. 21 G5 51 2N 2 49W
Yeo, L., Australia 125 E3 28 0 S 124 30 E
Yeo I., Canada 150 A3 45 24N 81 48W
Yeola, India 94 D2 20 2N 74 30 E
Yeoryioúpolis, Greece 39 E5 35 20N 24 15 E
Yeovil, U.K. 21 G5 50 57N 2 38W
Yepes, Spain 42 F7 39 55N 3 39W
Yeppoon, Australia 126 C5 23 5 S 150 47 E
Yérakas, Ákra, Greece 39 D2 37 42N 20 59 E
Yeráki, Greece 48 D4 37 0N 22 42 E
Yerbent, Turkmenistan 66 F6 39 30N 58 50 E
Yerbogachen, Russia 67 C11 61 16N 108 0 E
Yerevan, Armenia 61 K7 40 10N 44 31 E
Yerington, U.S.A. 158 G4 38 59N 119 10W
Yerkesik, Turkey 49 D10 37 7N 28 19 E
Yerköy, Turkey 100 C6 39 38N 34 28 E
Yerla →, India 94 F2 16 50N 74 30 E
Yermak, Kazakhstan 66 D8 52 2N 76 55 E
Yermo, U.S.A. 161 L10 34 54N 116 50W
Yerólakkos, Cyprus 39 E9 35 11N 33 15 E
Yeropol, Russia 67 C17 65 15N 168 40 E
Yeropótamos →, Greece 39 E5 35 3N 24 50 E
Yeroskipos, Cyprus 39 F8 34 46N 32 28 E
Yershov, Russia 60 E9 51 23N 48 27 E
Yerupaja, Cerro, Peru 172 C2 10 16 S 76 55W
Yerushalayim = Jerusalem, Israel 103 D4 31 47N 35 10 E
Yerville, France 26 C7 49 40N 0 53 E
Yerzhar = Gagarin, Uzbekistan 65 C4 40 39N 68 10 E
Yes Tor, U.K. 21 G4 50 41N 4 0W
Yesagyo, Burma 90 E5 21 38N 95 14 E
Yesan, S. Korea 75 F14 36 41N 126 51 E
Yeshin, Burma 90 D5 23 43N 95 6 E
Yeşilhisar, Turkey 100 C6 38 20N 35 5 E
Yeşilırmak →, Turkey 100 B7 41 22N 36 37 E
Yeşilkent, Turkey 100 D7 36 57N 36 12 E
Yeşilköy, Turkey 51 F12 40 57N 28 49 E
Yeşilova, Turkey 49 D11 37 31N 29 46 E
Yeşilyurt, Manisa, Turkey 49 C10 38 22N 28 40 E
Yeşilyurt, Muğla, Turkey 49 D10 37 10N 28 20 E
Yeski Dzhumaya = Tărgovişte, Romania 53 F10 44 55N 25 27 E
Yesnogorsk, Russia 58 E9 54 32N 37 38 E
Yeso, U.S.A. 155 H2 34 26N 104 37W
Yessentuki, Russia 61 H6 44 5N 42 53 E
Yessey, Russia 67 C11 68 29N 102 10 E
Yeste, Spain 41 G2 38 22N 2 19W
Yetman, Australia 127 D5 28 56 S 150 48 E
Yetti, Mauritania 110 C3 26 10N 7 50W
Yeu, Î. d', France 26 F4 46 42N 2 20W
Yevdokimovskoye = Krasnogvardeyskoye, Russia 61 H5 45 52N 41 33 E
Yevlakh = Yevlax, Azerbaijan 61 K8 40 39N 47 7 E
Yevlax, Azerbaijan 61 K8 40 39N 47 7 E
Yevpatoriya, Ukraine 59 K7 45 15N 33 20 E
Yeya →, Russia 59 J10 46 40N 38 40 E
Yeysk, Russia 59 J10 46 40N 38 12 E
Yezd = Yazd, Iran 97 D7 31 55N 54 27 E
Yezerishche, Belarus 58 E5 55 50N 29 59 E
Yhati, Paraguay 174 B4 25 45 S 56 35W
Yhú, Paraguay 175 B4 25 0 S 56 0W
Yi →, Uruguay 174 C4 33 7 S 57 8W
Yi 'Allaq, G., Egypt 103 E2 30 22N 33 32 E
Yi He →, China 75 G10 34 10N 118 8 E
Yi Xian, Anhui, China 77 C11 29 55N 117 57 E
Yi Xian, Hebei, China 74 E8 39 20N 115 30 E
Yi Xian, Liaoning, China 75 D11 41 30N 121 22 E
Yialí, Greece 49 E9 36 41N 27 11 E
Yialiás →, Cyprus 39 E9 35 9N 33 44 E
Yi'allaq, G., Egypt 106 A3 30 21N 33 31 E
Yialousa, Cyprus 39 E10 35 32N 34 10 E
Yiáltra, Greece 48 C4 38 51N 22 59 E
Yianisádhes, Greece 39 E7 35 20N 26 10 E
Yiannitsa, Greece 50 F6 40 46N 22 24 E
Yibin, China 76 C5 28 45N 104 32 E
Yichang, China 77 B8 30 40N 111 20 E
Yicheng, Henan, China 77 B9 31 41N 112 12 E
Yicheng, Shanxi, China 74 G6 35 42N 111 40 E
Yichuan, China 74 F6 36 2N 110 10 E
Yichun, Heilongjiang, China 69 B7 47 44N 128 52 E
Yichun, Jiangxi, China 77 D10 27 48N 114 22 E
Yidu, China 75 F10 36 43N 118 28 E
Yidun, China 76 B2 30 22N 99 21 E
Yifag, Ethiopia 107 E4 12 4N 37 46 E
Yifeng, China 77 C10 28 22N 114 45 E
Yihuang, China 77 D11 27 30N 116 12 E
Yijun, China 74 G5 35 28N 109 8 E
Yıldız Dağları, Turkey 51 E11 41 48N 27 36 E
Yıldızeli, Turkey 100 C7 39 51N 36 36 E
Yilehuli Shan, China 69 A7 51 20N 124 20 E
Yiliang, Yunnan, China 76 D5 27 38N 104 2 E
Yiliang, Yunnan, China 76 E4 24 56N 103 11 E
Yilong, China 76 B6 31 34N 106 23 E
Yimen, China 76 E4 24 40N 102 10 E
Yimianpo, China 75 B15 45 7N 128 2 E
Yinchuan, China 74 E4 38 30N 106 15 E
Yindaik, Burma 90 D5 23 35N 95 22 E
Yindarlgooda, L., Australia 125 F3 30 40 S 121 52 E
Ying He →, China 74 H9 32 30N 116 30 E
Ying Xian, China 74 E7 39 32N 113 10 E
Yingcheng, China 77 B9 30 56N 113 35 E
Yingde, China 77 E9 24 10N 113 25 E
Yingjiang, China 76 E1 24 41N 97 55 E
Yingjing, China 76 C4 29 41N 102 52 E
Yingkou, China 75 D12 40 37N 122 18 E
Yingkow = Yingkou, China 75 D12 40 37N 122 18 E
Yingshan, Henan, China 77 B9 31 35N 113 50 E
Yingshan, Hubei, China 77 B10 30 41N 115 32 E
Yingshan, Sichuan, China 76 B6 31 4N 106 35 E
Yingshang, China 77 A11 32 38N 116 12 E
Yingtan, China 77 C11 28 12N 117 0 E
Yining, China 66 E9 43 58N 81 10 E
Yinjiang, China 76 C7 28 1N 108 21 E
Yinmabin, Burma 90 D5 22 10N 94 55 E
Yiofiros →, Greece 39 E6 35 20N 25 6 E
Yioúra, Nótios Aiyaíon, Greece 48 D6 37 32N 24 40 E
Yioúra, Thessalía, Greece 48 B6 39 23N 24 10 E
Yipinglang, China 76 E3 25 10N 101 52 E
Yirápetra, Ákra, Greece 39 B2 38 51N 20 41 E
Yirba Muda, Ethiopia 107 F4 6 12N 38 42 E
Yirga Alem, Ethiopia 107 F4 6 48N 38 22 E
Yirol, Sudan 107 F3 6 33N 30 30 E
Yirrkala, Australia 126 A2 12 14 S 136 56 E
Yishan, China 76 E7 24 28N 108 38 E
Yishui, China 75 G10 35 47N 118 30 E
Yishun, Singapore 87 d 1 26N 103 50 E
Yíthion, Greece 48 E4 36 46N 22 34 E
Yitong, China 75 C13 43 13N 125 20 E
Yiwu, China 77 C13 29 20N 120 3 E
Yixing, China 77 B12 31 21N 119 48 E
Yiyang, Henan, China 74 G7 34 27N 112 10 E
Yiyang, Hunan, China 77 C9 28 35N 112 18 E
Yiyang, Jiangxi, China 77 C11 28 22N 117 20 E
Yizhang, China 77 E9 25 27N 112 57 E
Yizheng, China 77 A12 32 18N 119 10 E
Yli-Kitka, Finland 14 C23 66 8N 28 30 E
Ylitornio, Finland 14 C20 66 19N 23 39 E
Ylivieska, Finland 14 D21 64 4N 24 28 E
Yngaren, Sweden 17 F10 58 50N 16 35 E
Yoakum, U.S.A. 155 L6 29 17N 97 9W
Yob ⌂, Eritrea 107 D4 17 15N 37 50 E
Yobe □, Nigeria 113 C7 12 0N 11 30 E
Yobuko, Japan 72 D1 33 32N 129 54 E
Yog Pt., Phil. 80 D5 14 6N 124 12 E
Yogan, Togo 113 D5 6 23N 1 30 E
Yoğuntaş, Turkey 51 E11 41 50N 27 4 E
Yogyakarta, Indonesia 85 D4 7 49 S 110 22 E
Yogyakarta □, Indonesia 85 D4 7 48 S 110 22 E
Yoho △, Canada 142 C5 51 25N 116 30W
Yojoa, L. de, Honduras 164 D2 14 53N 88 0W
Yŏju, S. Korea 75 F14 37 20N 127 35 E
Yok Don △, Vietnam 86 F6 12 50N 107 40 E
Yokadouma, Cameroon 114 B2 3 26N 14 55 E
Yōkaichi, Japan 73 B8 35 6N 136 12 E
Yōkaichiba, Japan 73 B12 35 42N 140 33 E
Yokkaichi, Japan 73 C8 34 55N 136 38 E
Yoko, Cameroon 113 D7 5 32N 12 20 E
Yokohama, Japan 73 B11 35 27N 139 28 E
Yokosuka, Japan 73 B11 35 20N 139 40 E
Yokote, Japan 70 E10 39 20N 140 30 E
Yola, Nigeria 113 D7 9 10N 12 29 E
Yolaina, Cordillera de, Nic. 164 D3 11 30N 84 0W
Yolombo, Dem. Rep. of the Congo 114 C4 1 36 S 23 12 E
Yoloten, Turkmenistan 97 B9 37 18N 62 21 E
Yom →, Thailand 78 A2 15 35N 100 1 E
Yombi, Gabon 114 C2 1 26 S 10 37 E
Yonago, Japan 72 B5 35 25N 133 19 E
Yonaguni-Jima, Japan 71 M1 24 27N 123 0 E
Yŏnan, N. Korea 75 F14 37 55N 126 11 E
Yonezawa, Japan 70 F10 37 57N 140 4 E
Yong Peng, Malaysia 87 L4 2 0N 103 3 E
Yong Sata, Thailand 87 J2 7 8N 99 41 E
Yongama, Dem. Rep. of the Congo 114 B4 0 2N 24 35 E
Yongamp'o, N. Korea 75 E13 39 56N 124 23 E
Yong'an, China 77 E11 25 59N 117 25 E
Yongcheng, China 74 H9 33 55N 116 20 E
Yŏngch'ŏn, S. Korea 75 G15 35 58N 128 56 E
Yongchuan, China 76 C5 29 17N 105 55 E
Yongchun, China 77 E12 25 16N 118 20 E
Yongde, China 76 E2 24 5N 99 25 E
Yongdeng, China 74 F2 36 38N 103 25 E
Yongding, China 77 E11 24 43N 116 45 E
Yŏngdŏk, S. Korea 75 F15 36 24N 129 22 E
Yŏngdŭngpo, S. Korea 75 F14 37 31N 126 54 E
Yongfeng, China 77 D10 27 20N 115 22 E
Yongfu, China 76 E7 24 59N 109 59 E
Yonggyap Pass, India 90 A5 29 17N 95 37 E
Yonghe, China 74 F6 36 46N 110 38 E
Yonghong, India 90 B5 26 28N 94 58 E
Yŏnghŭng, N. Korea 75 E14 39 31N 127 18 E
Yongji, China 74 G6 34 52N 110 28 E
Yongjia, China 77 C13 28 10N 120 45 E
Yŏngju, S. Korea 75 F15 36 50N 128 40 E
Yongkang, Yunnan, China 76 E2 24 9N 99 20 E
Yongkang, Zhejiang, China 77 C13 28 55N 120 2 E
Yongnian, China 74 F8 36 47N 114 29 E
Yongning, Guangxi Zhuangzu, China 76 F7 22 44N 108 28 E
Yongning, Ningxia Huizu, China 74 E4 38 15N 106 14 E
Yongping, China 76 E2 25 27N 99 38 E
Yongqing, China 74 E9 39 25N 116 28 E
Yongren, China 76 D3 26 4N 101 40 E
Yongshan, China 76 C4 28 11N 103 35 E
Yongsheng, China 76 D3 26 38N 100 46 E
Yongshun, China 76 C7 29 2N 109 51 E
Yongtai, China 77 E12 25 49N 118 58 E
Yŏngwŏl, S. Korea 75 F15 37 11N 128 28 E
Yongxin = Jinggangshan, China 77 D10 26 58N 114 15 E
Yongxing, China 77 D9 26 9N 113 8 E
Yongxiu, China 77 C10 29 2N 115 42 E
Yongzhou, China 77 D8 26 17N 111 37 E
Yonibana, S. Leone 112 D2 8 30N 12 19W
Yonkers, U.S.A. 151 F11 40 56N 73 54W
Yonne □, France 27 E10 47 50N 3 40 E
Yonne →, France 27 D9 48 23N 2 58 E
Yopal, Colombia 168 B3 5 21N 72 23W
Yopurga, China 65 D8 39 15N 76 45 E
York, Australia 125 F2 31 52 S 116 47 E
York, U.K. 20 D6 53 58N 1 6W
York, Ala., U.S.A. 155 J10 32 29N 88 18W
York, Nebr., U.S.A. 154 E6 40 52N 97 36W
York, Pa., U.S.A. 148 F7 39 58N 76 44W
York, C., Australia 126 A3 10 42 S 142 31 E
York, City of □, U.K. 20 D6 53 58N 1 6W
York, Kap, Greenland 10 B4 75 55N 66 25W
York, Vale of, U.K. 20 C6 54 15N 1 25W
York Haven, U.S.A. 150 F8 40 7N 76 46W
York Sd., Australia 124 C4 15 0 S 125 5 E
Yorke Pen., Australia 128 C2 34 50 S 137 40 E
Yorketown, Australia 128 C2 35 0 S 137 33 E
Yorkshire Dales △, U.K. 20 C5 54 12N 2 10W
Yorkshire Wolds, U.K. 20 C7 54 8N 0 31W
Yorkton, Canada 143 C8 51 11N 102 28W
Yorkville, Calif., U.S.A. 160 G3 38 52N 123 13W
Yorkville, Ga., U.S.A. 152 B5 33 55N 84 58W
Yorkville, Ill., U.S.A. 157 C8 41 38N 88 27W
Yoro, Honduras 164 C2 15 9N 87 7W
Yoron-Jima, Japan 71 L4 27 2N 128 26 E
Yorosso, Mali 112 C4 12 17N 4 55W
Yos Sudarso, Pulau = Dolak, Pulau, Indonesia 83 C5 8 0 S 138 30 E
Yos Sudarso, Teluk, Indonesia 83 B6 2 35 S 140 45 E
Yosemite △, U.S.A. 160 H7 37 45N 119 40W
Yosemite Village, U.S.A. 160 H7 37 45N 119 35W
Yoshida, Japan 72 C4 34 40N 132 42 E
Yoshimatsu, Japan 72 F2 32 0N 130 47 E
Yoshino-Kumano △, Japan 73 C7 34 12N 135 55 E
Yoshkar Ola, Russia 60 B8 56 38N 47 55 E
Yŏsu, S. Korea 75 G14 34 47N 127 45 E
Yotala, Bolivia 173 D4 19 10 S 65 17W
Yotvata, Israel 103 F4 29 55N 35 2 E
You Jiang →, China 76 F6 22 50N 108 6 E
You Xian, China 77 D9 27 1N 113 17 E
Youbou, Canada 160 B2 48 53N 124 13W
Youghal, Ireland 23 E4 51 56N 7 52W
Youghal B., Ireland 23 E4 51 55N 7 49W
Youkounkoun, Guinea 112 C2 12 35N 13 11W
Young, Australia 129 C8 34 19 S 148 18 E
Young, Canada 143 C7 51 47N 105 45W
Young, Uruguay 174 C4 32 44 S 57 36W
Young Ra., N.Z. 131 E4 44 10 S 169 30 E
Younghusband, L., Australia 128 A2 30 50 S 136 5 E
Younghusband Pen., Australia 128 D3 36 0 S 139 25 E
Youngstown, Canada 143 C6 51 35N 111 10W
Youngstown, Fla., U.S.A. 152 E4 30 22N 85 26W
Youngstown, N.Y., U.S.A. 150 C5 43 15N 79 3W
Youngstown, Ohio, U.S.A. 150 E4 41 6N 80 39W
Youngsville, U.S.A. 150 E5 41 51N 79 19W
Youngwood, U.S.A. 150 F5 40 14N 79 34W
Youssoufia, Morocco 110 B3 32 16N 8 31W
Youxi, China 77 D12 26 10N 118 13 E
Youyang, China 76 C7 28 47N 108 42 E
Youyu, China 74 D7 40 10N 112 20 E
Yozgat, Turkey 100 C6 39 51N 34 47 E
Ypacaraí △, Paraguay 174 B4 25 18 S 57 19W
Ypané →, Paraguay 174 A4 23 29 S 57 19W
Yport, France 26 C7 49 45N 0 15 E
Ypres = Ieper, Belgium 24 D2 50 51N 2 53 E
Ypsilanti, U.S.A. 157 B13 42 14N 83 37W
Yreka, U.S.A. 158 F2 41 44N 122 38W
Ysabel Chan., Papua N. G. 132 B5 2 0 S 150 0 E
Yssingeaux, France 29 C8 45 9N 4 8 E
Ystabø, Norway 18 E2 59 3N 5 23 E
Ystad, Sweden 17 J7 55 26N 13 50 E
Ysyk-Köl = Balykchy, Kyrgyzstan 65 B8 42 26N 76 12 E
Ysyk-Köl, Kyrgyzstan 65 B8 42 25N 77 15 E
Ythan →, U.K. 22 D7 57 19N 1 59W
Ytre Arna, Norway 18 D2 60 27N 5 25 E
Ytre Enebakk, Norway 18 E8 59 44N 11 0 E
Ytre Rendal, Norway 18 C8 61 46N 11 8 E
Ytterhogdal, Sweden 16 B8 62 12N 14 56 E
Ytyk-Kyuyel, Russia 67 C14 62 30N 133 45 E
Yu Jiang →, China 76 F7 23 22N 110 3 E
Yu Shan, Taiwan 77 F13 23 30N 120 58 E
Yu Xian = Yuzhou, China 74 G7 34 10N 113 28 E
Yu Xian, Hebei, China 74 E8 39 50N 114 35 E
Yu Xian, Shanxi, China 74 E7 38 5N 113 20 E
Yuan Jiang →, Hunan, China 77 C8 28 55N 111 50 E
Yuan Jiang →, Yunnan, China 76 F4 22 20N 103 59 E
Yuan'an, China 77 B8 31 3N 111 34 E
Yuanjiang, Hunan, China 77 C9 28 47N 112 21 E
Yuanjiang, Yunnan, China 76 F4 23 32N 102 0 E
Yüanli, Taiwan 77 E13 24 27N 120 39 E
Yüanlin, Taiwan 77 F13 23 58N 120 30 E
Yuanling, China 77 C8 28 29N 110 22 E
Yuanmou, China 76 E3 25 42N 101 53 E
Yuanqu, China 74 G6 35 18N 111 40 E
Yuanyang, Henan, China 74 G7 35 3N 113 58 E
Yuanyang, Yunnan, China 76 F4 23 10N 102 43 E
Yuat →, Papua N. G. 132 C2 4 10 S 143 52 E
Yuba →, U.S.A. 160 F5 39 8N 121 36W
Yuba City, U.S.A. 160 F5 39 8N 121 37W
Yūbari, Japan 70 C10 43 4N 141 59 E
Yubdo, Ethiopia 107 F4 8 58N 35 24 E
Yūbetsu, Japan 70 B11 44 13N 143 50 E
Yubo, Sudan 107 F2 5 23N 27 25 E
Yucatán □, Mexico 163 C7 21 30N 86 30W
Yucatán, Canal de, Caribbean 164 B2 22 0N 86 30W
Yucatán, Península de, Mexico 136 H11 19 30N 89 0W
Yucatan Basin, Cent. Amer. 136 H11 19 0N 86 0W
Yucatan Channel = Yucatán, Canal de, Caribbean 164 B2 22 0N 86 30W
Yucca, U.S.A. 161 L12 34 52N 114 9W
Yucca Valley, U.S.A. 161 L10 34 8N 116 27W
Yucheng, China 74 F9 36 55N 116 32 E
Yuci, China 74 F7 37 42N 112 46 E
Yudu, China 77 E10 25 59N 115 30 E
Yuechi, China 76 B6 30 34N 106 25 E
Yuen Long, China 69 G11 22 26N 114 2 E
Yuendumu, Australia 124 D5 22 16 S 131 49 E
Yueqing, China 77 C13 28 9N 120 59 E
Yueqing Wan, China 77 D13 28 5N 121 20 E
Yuexi, Anhui, China 77 B11 30 50N 116 20 E
Yuexi, Sichuan, China 76 C4 28 37N 102 26 E
Yueyang, China 77 C9 29 21N 113 5 E
Yufu-Dake, Japan 72 D3 33 17N 131 33 E
Yugan, China 77 C11 28 43N 116 37 E
Yugoslavia = Serbia & Montenegro ■, Europe 50 C4 43 20N 20 0 E
Yuhuan, China 77 C13 28 9N 121 12 E
Yuhuan Dao, China 77 C13 28 5N 121 15 E
Yujiang, China 77 C11 28 10N 116 43 E
Yukhnov, Russia 58 E8 54 44N 35 15 E
Yūki, Japan 73 A11 36 18N 139 53 E
Yukon, U.S.A. 155 H6 35 31N 97 45W
Yukon →, U.S.A. 144 E7 62 32N 163 54W
Yukon-Charley Rivers ⌂, U.S.A. 144 C12 65 15N 144 0W
Yukon Territory □, Canada 138 B6 63 0N 135 0W
Yüksekova, Turkey 101 D11 37 34N 44 16 E
Yukta, Russia 67 C11 63 26N 105 42 E
Yukuhashi, Japan 72 D2 33 44N 130 59 E
Yulara, Australia 125 E5 25 10 S 130 55 E
Yule →, Australia 124 D2 20 41 S 118 17 E
Yuleba, Australia 127 D4 26 37 S 149 24 E
Yulee, U.S.A. 152 E8 30 38N 81 36W
Yuli, Nigeria 113 D7 9 44N 10 12 E
Yuli, Taiwan 77 F13 23 20N 121 18 E
Yulin, Guangxi Zhuangzu, China 77 F8 22 40N 110 8 E
Yulin, Hainan, China 86 C7 18 10N 109 31 E
Yulin, Shaanxi, China 74 E5 38 20N 109 30 E
Yuma, Ariz., U.S.A. 161 N12 32 43N 114 37W
Yuma, Colo., U.S.A. 154 E3 40 8N 102 43W
Yuma, B. de, Dom. Rep. 165 C6 18 20N 68 35W
Yumali, Australia 128 C3 35 32 S 139 45 E
Yumbe, Uganda 118 B3 3 28N 31 15 E
Yumbi, Équateur, Dem. Rep. of the Congo 114 C3 1 53 S 16 34 E
Yumbi, Maniema, Dem. Rep. of the Congo 118 C2 1 12 S 26 15 E
Yumbo, Colombia 168 C2 3 35N 76 28W
Yumen, China 68 C4 39 50N 97 30 E
Yumurtalık, Turkey 100 D6 36 45N 35 43 E
Yun Gui Gaoyuan, China 76 E3 26 0N 104 0 E
Yun Ho →, China 75 E9 39 10N 117 10 E
Yun Ling, China 76 D2 27 0N 99 20 E
Yun Xian, Hubei, China 77 A8 32 50N 110 46 E
Yun Xian, Yunnan, China 76 E3 24 27N 100 8 E
Yuna, Australia 125 E2 28 20 S 115 0 E
Yunak, Turkey 100 C4 38 49N 31 43 E
Yunan, China 77 F8 23 12N 111 30 E
Yunaska I., U.S.A. 144 K5 52 38N 170 40W
Yuncheng, Henan, China 74 G8 35 36N 115 57 E
Yuncheng, Shanxi, China 74 G6 35 2N 111 0 E
Yunfu, China 77 F9 22 50N 112 5 E
Yungas, Bolivia 173 D4 17 0 S 66 0W
Yungay, Chile 174 D1 37 10 S 72 5W
Yungay, Peru 172 B2 9 2 S 77 45W
Yungki = Jilin, China 75 C14 43 44N 126 30 E
Yungning = Nanning, China 76 F7 22 48N 108 20 E
Yunhe, China 77 C12 28 8N 119 33 E
Yunkai Dashan, China 77 F8 22 30N 111 0 E
Yunlin, Taiwan 77 F13 23 42N 120 30 E
Yunlong, China 76 E2 25 57N 99 13 E
Yunmeng, China 77 B9 31 2N 113 43 E
Yunnan □, China 76 E4 25 0N 102 0 E
Yunotsu, Japan 72 B4 35 5N 132 21 E
Yunquera de Henares, Spain 40 E1 40 47N 3 11W
Yunt Dağı, Turkey 49 C9 38 56N 27 13 E
Yunta, Australia 127 E2 32 34 S 139 36 E
Yunxi, China 74 H6 33 0N 110 22 E
Yunxiao, China 77 F11 23 59N 117 18 E
Yuping, China 76 D7 27 13N 108 56 E
Yupukarri, Guyana 169 C6 3 45N 59 20W
Yupyongdong, N. Korea 75 D15 41 49N 128 53 E
Yuqing, China 76 D6 27 13N 107 53 E
Yuraygir △, Australia 127 D5 29 45 S 153 15 E
Yurga, Russia 66 D9 55 42N 84 51 E
Yurimaguas, Peru 172 B2 5 55 S 76 7W
Yurkiyka, Ukraine 53 B13 48 42N 28 35 E
Yurla, Russia 64 B5 59 22N 54 21 E
Yurubí △, Venezuela 165 D6 10 26N 68 42W
Yurya, Russia 64 B2 59 1N 49 13 E
Yuryev = Tartu, Estonia 15 G22 58 20N 26 44 E
Yuryev-Polskiy, Russia 58 D10 56 30N 39 40 E
Yuryevets, Russia 60 B6 57 25N 43 2 E
Yuryuzan, Russia 64 D7 54 57N 58 28 E
Yuscarán, Honduras 164 D2 13 58N 86 45W
Yûsef, Bahr →, Egypt 106 B3 28 25N 30 35 E
Yushan, China 77 C12 28 42N 118 10 E
Yushanzhen, China 76 C7 29 28N 108 22 E
Yushe, China 74 F7 37 4N 112 58 E
Yushu, Jilin, China 75 B14 44 43N 126 38 E
Yushu, Qinghai, China 68 C4 33 5N 96 55 E
Yusufeli, Turkey 101 B9 40 50N 41 33 E
Yutai, China 74 G9 35 0N 116 45 E
Yutian, China 75 E9 39 53N 117 45 E
Yütze = Yuci, China 74 F7 37 42N 112 46 E
Yuxarı Qarabağ = Nagorno-Karabakh □, Azerbaijan 101 C12 39 55N 46 45 E
Yuxi, China 76 E4 24 30N 102 35 E
Yuyao, China 77 B13 30 3N 121 10 E
Yuzawa, Japan 70 E10 39 10N 140 30 E
Yuzha, Russia 60 B6 56 34N 42 1 E
Yuzhno-Sakhalinsk, Russia 67 E15 46 58N 142 45 E
Yuzhnouralsk, Russia 64 D8 54 26N 61 15 E
Yuzhnyy □, Russia 61 H5 44 0N 40 0 E
Yuzhou, China 74 G7 34 10N 113 28 E
Yuzovka = Donetsk, Ukraine 59 J9 48 0N 37 45 E
Yvelines □, France 27 D8 48 40N 1 45 E
Yverdon-les-Bains, Switz. 32 C3 46 47N 6 39 E
Yvetot, France 26 C7 49 37N 0 44 E
Yvonand, Switz. 32 C3 46 48N 6 44 E
Yzeure, France 27 F10 46 33N 3 22 E

Z

Zaalayskiy Khrebet, Tajikistan 65 D6 39 20N 73 0 E
Zaanstad, Neths. 24 B4 52 27N 4 50 E
Zab, Monts du, Algeria 111 B6 34 55N 5 0 E
Zāb al Kabīr →, Iraq 101 D10 36 1N 43 24 E
Zāb aş Şaghīr →, Iraq 101 E10 35 17N 43 29 E
Žabalj, Serbia & M. 52 E5 45 21N 20 5 E
Žabari, Serbia & M. 50 B5 44 22N 21 15 E
Zabarjad, Egypt 106 C4 23 40N 36 12 E
Zabaykalsk, Russia 67 E12 49 40N 117 25 E
Zabbar, Malta 38 F8 35 53N 14 32 E
Zabid, Yemen 98 D3 14 0N 43 10 E
Zabīd, W. →, Yemen 98 D3 14 7N 43 6 E
Zabki, Poland 55 F8 52 17N 21 7 E
Ząbkowice Śląskie, Poland 55 H3 50 35N 16 50 E
Žabljak, Serbia & M. 50 C3 43 18N 19 5 E
Zabłudów, Poland 55 F9 53 0N 23 19 E
Zabno, Poland 55 H7 50 9N 20 53 E
Zābol, Iran 97 D9 31 0N 61 32 E
Zābol □, Afghan. 91 B2 32 0N 67 0 E
Zābolī, Iran 97 E9 27 10N 61 35 E
Zabolotiv, Ukraine 53 B10 48 28N 25 18 E
Zabolottya, Ukraine 55 G11 51 38N 24 16 E
Zabré, Burkina Faso 113 C4 11 12N 0 36W
Zábřeh, Czech Rep. 35 B9 49 53N 16 52 E
Zabrze, Poland 55 H5 50 18N 18 50 E
Zabuzhzhya, Ukraine 55 G10 51 21N 23 42 E
Zabzuga, Ghana 113 D5 9 20N 0 30 E
Zacapa, Guatemala 164 D2 14 59N 89 31W
Zacapu, Mexico 162 D4 19 50N 101 43W
Zacatecas, Mexico 162 C4 22 49N 102 34W
Zacatecas □, Mexico 162 C4 23 30N 103 0W
Zacatecoluca, El Salv. 164 D2 13 29N 88 51W
Zachary, U.S.A. 155 K9 30 39N 91 9W
Zachodnio-Pomorskie □, Poland 54 E2 53 40N 15 50 E
Zacoalco, Mexico 162 C4 20 14N 103 33W
Zacualtipán, Mexico 163 C5 20 39N 98 36W
Zadar, Croatia 45 D12 44 8N 15 14 E
Zadawa, Nigeria 113 C7 11 33N 10 19 E
Zadetkyi Kyun, Burma 87 G2 10 0N 98 25 E
Zadonsk, Russia 59 F10 52 25N 38 56 E
Zafarqand, Iran 97 C7 33 11N 52 29 E
Zafora, Greece 49 E8 36 5N 26 24 E
Zafra, Spain 43 G4 38 26N 6 30W
Żagań, Poland 55 G2 51 39N 15 22 E
Zagaoua, Chad 109 E4 16 0N 21 10 E
Žagarė, Lithuania 54 B10 56 21N 23 15 E
Zagazig, Egypt 106 H7 30 40N 31 30 E
Zāgheh, Iran 97 C6 33 30N 48 42 E
Zaghouan, Tunisia 108 A2 36 23N 10 10 E
Zaglivérion, Greece 50 F7 40 36N 23 15 E
Zaglou, Algeria 111 C4 27 17N 0 3W
Zagnanado, Benin 113 D5 7 18N 2 28 E
Zagorá, Greece 48 B5 39 27N 23 6 E
Zagora, Morocco 110 B3 30 22N 5 51W
Zagorje, Slovenia 45 B11 46 8N 15 0 E
Zagórów, Poland 55 F4 52 10N 17 54 E
Zagorsk = Sergiyev Posad, Russia 58 D10 56 20N 38 10 E
Zagorsky = Krasnozavodsk, Russia 58 D10 56 27N 38 25 E
Zagórz, Poland 55 J9 49 30N 22 14 E
Zagreb, Croatia 45 C12 45 50N 15 58 E
Zagreb ✈ (ZAG), Croatia 45 C13 45 45N 16 4 E
Zāgros, Kūhhā-ye, Iran 97 C6 33 45N 48 5 E
Zagros Mts. = Zāgros, Kūhhā-ye, Iran 97 C6 33 45N 48 5 E
Žagubica, Serbia & M. 50 B5 44 15N 21 47 E
Zaguinaso, Ivory C. 112 C3 10 1N 6 14W
Zagyva →, Hungary 52 C5 47 5N 20 4 E
Zahamena ⌂, Madag. 117 B8 17 37 S 48 49 E
Zāhedān, Fārs, Iran 97 D7 28 46N 53 52 E
Zāhedān, Sīstān va Balūchestān, Iran 97 D9 29 30N 60 50 E
Zahirabad, India 94 F3 17 43N 77 37 E
Zahlah, Lebanon 103 B4 33 52N 35 50 E
Zahna, Germany 30 D8 51 55N 12 49 E
Záhony, Hungary 52 B7 48 25N 22 11 E
Zahrān, Si. Arabia 98 C3 17 40N 43 30 E
Zainsk, Russia 60 C11 55 18N 52 4 E
Zaïre = Congo →, Africa 115 D2 6 4 S 12 24 E
Zaïre = Congo, Dem. Rep. of the ■, Africa 115 C4 3 0 S 23 0 E
Zaire □, Angola 115 D2 7 0 S 14 0 E
Zaječar, Serbia & M. 50 C6 43 53N 22 18 E
Zaka, Zimbabwe 117 C5 20 20 S 31 29 E
Zakamensk, Russia 67 D11 50 23N 103 17 E
Zakani, Dem. Rep. of the Congo 114 B4 2 33N 23 16 E
Zakarpatska □, Ukraine 53 B8 48 20N 23 20 E
Zakataly = Zaqatala, Azerbaijan 61 K8 41 38N 46 35 E
Zakbayemé, Cameroon 114 B2 4 2N 10 34 E
Zakháro, Greece 48 D3 37 30N 21 39 E
Zakhmatabad = Ayni, Tajikistan 65 D4 39 23N 68 32 E
Zakhodnaya Dzvina = Daugava →, Latvia 15 H21 57 4N 24 3 E
Zākhū, Iraq 101 D10 37 10N 42 50 E
Zákinthos, Greece 39 D2 37 47N 20 54 E
Zákinthos □, Greece 48 D2 37 47N 20 57 E
Zakinthos ✈ (ZTH), Greece 39 D2 37 45N 20 50 E
Zakopane, Poland 55 J6 49 18N 19 57 E
Zakouma, Chad 109 F3 10 54N 19 49 E
Zakouma △, Chad 109 F3 10 52N 19 45 E
Zakroczym, Poland 55 F7 52 26N 20 38 E
Zákros, Greece 39 E7 35 6N 26 10 E
Zakynthos = Zákinthos, Greece 39 D2 37 47N 20 54 E
Zala, Angola 115 D2 7 52 S 13 42 E
Zala, Ethiopia 107 F4 6 28N 37 13 E
Zala □, Hungary 52 D1 46 42N 16 50 E
Zala →, Hungary 52 D2 46 43N 17 16 E
Zalaegerszeg, Hungary 52 D1 46 53N 16 47 E
Zalakomár, Hungary 52 D2 46 33N 17 10 E
Zalalövő, Hungary 52 D1 46 51N 16 35 E
Zalamea de la Serena, Spain 43 G5 38 40N 5 38W
Zalamea la Real, Spain 43 H4 37 41N 6 38W
Zalău, Romania 52 C8 47 12N 23 3 E
Zalazna, Russia 64 B4 58 39N 52 31 E
Žalec, Slovenia 45 B12 46 16N 15 10 E
Zaleshchiki = Zalishchyky, Ukraine 53 B10 48 45N 25 45 E
Zalesye, Russia 54 D8 54 50N 21 31 E
Zalew Wiślany, Poland 54 D6 54 20N 19 50 E
Zalewo, Poland 54 E6 53 50N 19 41 E
Zalim, Si. Arabia 98 B3 22 43N 42 10 E
Zalingei, Sudan 109 F4 12 51N 23 29 E
Zalishchyky, Ukraine 53 B10 48 45N 25 45 E
Zaltan, Ajdābiyā, Libya 108 C3 28 51N 19 52 E
Zaltan, Zuwārah, Libya 108 C2 32 57N 11 52 E
Zaltan, Jabal, Libya 108 C3 28 46N 19 45 E
Zalun, Burma 90 G5 17 29N 95 34 E
Zama L., Canada 142 B5 58 45N 119 5W
Zambales □, Phil. 80 D3 15 20N 120 10 E
Zambales Mts., Phil. 80 D3 15 45N 120 5 E
Zambeke, Dem. Rep. of the Congo 118 B2 2 8N 25 17 E
Zambeze →, Africa 119 F4 18 35 S 36 20 E
Zambezi = Zambeze →, Africa 119 F4 18 35 S 36 20 E
Zambezi, Zambia 115 E4 13 30 S 23 15 E
Zambezi △, Zimbabwe 119 F2 17 54 S 25 41 E
Zambezia □, Mozam. 119 F4 16 15 S 37 30 E
Zambia ■, Africa 119 F2 15 0 S 28 0 E
Zamboanga, Phil. 81 H4 6 59N 122 3 E
Zamboanga del Norte □, Phil. 81 H4 8 0N 123 0 E
Zamboanga del Sur □, Phil. 81 H4 7 40N 123 0 E
Zambrano, Colombia 168 B3 9 45N 74 49W
Zambrów, Poland 55 F9 52 59N 22 14 E
Zametchino, Russia 60 D6 53 30N 42 30 E
Zamfara □, Nigeria 113 C6 12 10N 6 0 E
Zamfara →, Nigeria 113 C5 12 5N 4 2 E
Zamora, Ecuador 168 D2 4 4 S 78 58W
Zamora, Mexico 162 D4 20 0N 102 21W
Zamora, Spain 42 D5 41 30N 5 45W
Zamora □, Spain 42 D5 41 30N 5 46W
Zamora →, Ecuador 168 D2 2 59N 78 13W
Zamora-Chinchipe □, Ecuador 168 D2 4 15 S 78 50W

Zamość, *Poland* **55 H10** 50 43N 23 15 E
Zams, *Austria* **33 B11** 47 9N 10 35 E
Zamtang, *China* **76 A3** 32 26N 101 6 E
Zamuro, Sierra del, *Venezuela* **169 C5** 4 0N 62 30W
Zamzam, W. →, *Libya* **108 B2** 30 58N 14 48 E
Zan, *Ghana* **113 D4** 9 26N 0 17W
Zanaga, *Congo* **114 C2** 2 48 S 13 48 E
Záncara →, *Spain* **41 F1** 39 18N 3 18W
Zanderij, *Suriname* **169 B6** 5 20N 55 16W
Zandu, *Dem. Rep. of the Congo* **115 D3** 5 11 S 18 16 E
Zandvoort, *Neths.* **24 B4** 52 22N 4 32 E
Zanesville, *U.S.A.* **150 G2** 39 56N 82 1W
Zangābād, *Iran* **96 B5** 38 26N 46 44 E
Zangue →, *Mozam.* **119 F4** 17 50 S 35 21 E
Zanjān, *Iran* **97 B6** 36 40N 48 35 E
Zanjān □, *Iran* **97 B6** 37 20N 49 30 E
Zanjān →, *Iran* **97 B6** 37 8N 47 47 E
Zannone, *Italy* **46 B6** 40 58N 13 3 E
Zanow = Sianów, *Poland* **54 D3** 54 13N 16 18 E
Zante = Zákinthos, *Greece* **39 D2** 37 47N 20 54 E
Zanthus, *Australia* **125 F3** 31 2 S 123 34 E
Zanzibar, *Tanzania* **118 D4** 6 12 S 39 12 E
Zanzūr, *Libya* **108 B2** 32 55N 13 1 E
Zaouatallaz, *Algeria* **111 D6** 24 52N 8 30 E
Zaouiet El-Kala = Bordj Omar Driss, *Algeria* **111 C6** 28 10N 6 40 E
Zaouiet Reggâne, *Algeria* **111 C5** 26 32N 0 3 E
Zaoyang, *China* **77 A9** 32 10N 112 45 E
Zaozhuang, *China* **75 G9** 34 50N 117 35 E
Zap Suyu = Zāb al Kabīr →, *Iraq* **101 D10** 36 1N 43 24 E
Zapadna Morava →, *Serbia & M.* **50 C5** 43 38N 21 30 E
Zapadnaya Dvina = Daugava →, *Latvia* **15 H21** 57 4N 24 3 E
Zapadnaya Dvina, *Russia* **58 D7** 56 15N 32 3 E
Západné Beskydy, *Europe* **35 B12** 49 30N 19 0 E
Zapadni Rodopi, *Bulgaria* **50 E7** 41 50N 24 0 E
Západočeský □, *Czech Rep.* **34 B6** 49 35N 13 0 E
Zapala, *Argentina* **176 A2** 39 0 S 70 5W
Zapaleri, Cerro, *Bolivia* **174 A2** 22 49 S 67 11W
Zapata, *U.S.A.* **155 M5** 26 55N 99 16W
Zapatón →, *Spain* **43 F4** 39 0N 6 49W
Zapiga, *Chile* **172 D4** 19 40 S 69 55W
Zapolyarnyy, *Russia* **56 A5** 69 26N 30 51 E
Zaporizhzhya, *Ukraine* **59 J8** 47 50N 35 10 E
Zaporozhye = Zaporizhzhya, *Ukraine* **59 J8** 47 50N 35 10 E
Zaqatala, *Azerbaijan* **61 K8** 41 38N 46 35 E
Zara, *Turkey* **100 C7** 39 58N 37 43 E
Zarafshon, *Uzbekistan* **65 C2** 41 34N 64 12 E
Zaragoza, *Colombia* **168 B3** 7 30N 74 52W
Zaragoza, *Coahuila, Mexico* **162 B4** 28 30N 101 0W
Zaragoza, *Nuevo León, Mexico* **163 C5** 24 0N 99 46W
Zaragoza, *Spain* **40 D4** 41 39N 0 53W
Zaragoza □, *Spain* **40 D4** 41 35N 1 0W
Zarand, *Kermān, Iran* **97 D8** 30 46N 56 34 E
Zarand, *Markazī, Iran* **97 C6** 35 18N 50 25 E
Zărandului, Munţii, *Romania* **52 D7** 46 14N 22 7 E
Zaranj, *Afghan.* **91 C1** 30 55N 61 55 E
Zarasai, *Lithuania* **15 J22** 55 40N 26 20 E
Zárate, *Argentina* **174 C4** 34 7 S 59 0W
Zarautz, *Spain* **40 B2** 43 17N 2 10W
Zaraysk, *Russia* **58 E10** 54 48N 38 53 E
Zaraza, *Venezuela* **169 B4** 9 21N 65 19W
Zarbdar, *Uzbekistan* **65 C4** 40 3N 68 10 E
Zard, Kūh-e, *Iran* **97 C6** 32 22N 50 4 E
Zāreh, *Iran* **97 C6** 35 7N 49 9 E
Zari, *Nigeria* **113 C7** 13 4N 12 45 E
Zaria, *Nigeria* **113 C6** 11 0N 7 40 E
Żarki, *Poland* **55 H6** 50 38N 19 23 E
Zárkon, *Greece* **48 B4** 39 38N 22 6 E
Zarneh, *Iran* **96 C5** 33 55N 46 10 E
Zărneşti, *Romania* **53 E10** 45 33N 25 18 E
Zarós, *Greece* **39 E5** 35 8N 24 54 E
Żarów, *Poland* **55 H3** 50 56N 16 29 E
Zarqā', Nahr az →, *Jordan* **103 C4** 32 10N 35 37 E
Zarrīn, *Iran* **97 C7** 32 46N 54 37 E
Zaruma, *Ecuador* **168 D2** 3 40 S 79 38W
Żary, *Poland* **55 G2** 51 37N 15 10 E
Zarza de Granadilla, *Spain* **42 E4** 40 14N 6 3W
Zarzaïtine, *Algeria* **111 C6** 28 15N 9 34 E
Zarzal, *Colombia* **168 C2** 4 24N 76 4W
Zarzis, *Tunisia* **108 B2** 33 31N 11 2 E
Zas, *Spain* **42 B2** 43 4N 8 53W
Zaskar →, *India* **93 B7** 34 13N 77 20 E
Zaskar Mts., *India* **93 C7** 33 15N 77 30 E
Zastavna, *Ukraine* **53 B10** 48 31N 25 51 E
Zastron, *S. Africa* **116 E4** 30 18 S 27 7 E
Žatec, *Czech Rep.* **34 A6** 50 20N 13 32 E
Zaterechnyy, *Russia* **61 H7** 44 48N 45 11 E
Zatishye = Elektrostal, *Russia* **58 E10** 55 41N 38 32 E
Zator, *Poland* **55 J6** 49 59N 19 28 E
Zatyshshya, *Ukraine* **53 C14** 47 20N 29 51 E
Zavala, *Bos.-H.* **50 D1** 42 50N 17 59 E
Zavāreh, *Iran* **97 C7** 33 29N 52 28 E
Zave, *Zimbabwe* **117 B5** 17 6 S 30 1 E
Zavérdhas, Kólpos, *Greece* **39 B2** 38 47N 20 51 E
Zavetnoye, *Russia* **61 G6** 47 13N 43 50 E
Zavidovići, *Bos.-H.* **52 F3** 44 27N 18 10 E
Zavitaya = Zavitinsk, *Russia* **67 D13** 50 10N 129 20 E
Zavitinsk, *Russia* **67 D13** 50 10N 129 20 E
Zavodovski, I., *Antarctica* **7 B1** 56 0 S 27 45W
Zavodskoy = Komsomolskiy, *Russia* **60 C7** 54 27N 45 33 E
Zavolzhsk, *Russia* **60 B6** 57 30N 42 0 E
Zavolzhye = Zavolzhsk, *Russia* **60 B6** 57 30N 42 0 E
Zavolzhye, *Russia* **60 B6** 56 37N 43 26 E
Zawadzkie, *Poland* **55 H5** 50 37N 18 28 E
Zawichost, *Poland* **55 H8** 50 48N 21 51 E
Zawidów, *Poland* **55 G2** 51 1N 15 1 E
Zawiercie, *Poland* **55 H6** 50 30N 19 24 E
Zāwiyat al Bayḍā = Al Bayḍā, *Libya* **108 B4** 32 50N 21 44 E
Zāwiyat Masūs, *Libya* **108 B4** 31 35N 21 1 E
Zâwyet Shammas, *Egypt* **106 A2** 31 30N 26 37 E
Zâwyet Um el Rakham, *Egypt* **106 A2** 31 18N 27 1 E
Zâwyet Ungeîla, *Egypt* **106 A2** 31 23N 26 42 E
Zāyā, *Iraq* **96 C5** 33 33N 44 13 E
Zāyandeh →, *Iran* **97 C7** 32 35N 52 0 E
Zaymah, *Si. Arabia* **98 B3** 21 37N 40 6 E
Zaysan, *Kazakhstan* **66 E9** 47 28N 84 52 E
Zaysan, Oz., *Kazakhstan* **66 E9** 48 0N 83 0 E
Zayü, *China* **76 C1** 28 48N 97 27 E
Zazafotsy, *Madag.* **117 C8** 21 11 S 46 21 E
Zāzamt, W. →, *Libya* **108 B2** 30 29N 14 30 E
Zazir, O. →, *Algeria* **111 D6** 22 0N 5 40 E
Zázrivá, *Slovak Rep.* **35 B12** 49 16N 19 7 E
Zbarazh, *Ukraine* **59 H3** 49 43N 25 44 E
Zbąszyń, *Poland* **55 F2** 52 14N 15 56 E
Zbąszynek, *Poland* **55 F2** 52 16N 15 51 E
Zblewo, *Poland* **54 E5** 53 56N 18 19 E
Zbruch → **53 B11** 48 32N 26 27 E
Žďár nad Sázavov, *Czech Rep.* **34 B8** 49 34N 15 57 E
Zdolbuniv, *Ukraine* **59 G4** 50 30N 26 15 E
Ždrelo, *Serbia & M.* **50 B5** 44 16N 21 28 E
Zduńska Wola, *Poland* **55 G5** 51 37N 18 59 E
Zduny, *Poland* **55 G4** 51 39N 17 21 E
Zearing, *U.S.A.* **156 B3** 42 10N 93 18W
Zēbāk, *Afghan.* **65 E5** 36 31N 71 20 E
Zeballos, *Canada* **142 D3** 49 59N 126 50W
Zebbug, *Malta* **38 F7** 35 52N 14 26 E
Zebbug, *Gozo, Malta* **38 E6** 36 4N 14 14 E
Zebediela, *S. Africa* **117 C4** 24 20 S 29 17 E
Zebila, *Ghana* **113 C4** 10 55N 0 30W
Zebulon, *U.S.A.* **152 B5** 33 6N 84 21W
Zeebrugge, *Belgium* **24 C3** 51 19N 3 12 E
Zeehan, *Australia* **127 G4** 41 52 S 145 25 E
Zeeland, *U.S.A.* **157 B10** 42 49N 86 1W
Zeeland □, *Neths.* **24 C3** 51 30N 3 50 E
Zeerust, *S. Africa* **116 D4** 25 31 S 26 4 E
Zefat, *Israel* **103 C4** 32 58N 35 29 E
Zegdou, *Algeria* **110 C4** 29 51N 4 45W
Zege, *Ethiopia* **107 E4** 11 43N 37 18 E
Zeggerene, Iracher, *Mali* **113 B5** 16 49N 2 16 E
Zégoua, *Mali* **112 C3** 10 32N 5 35W
Zehden = Cedynia, *Poland* **55 F1** 52 53N 14 12 E
Zehdenick, *Germany* **30 C9** 52 58N 13 20 E
Zeigler, *U.S.A.* **156 G7** 37 54N 89 3W
Zeil, Mt., *Australia* **124 D5** 23 30 S 132 23 E
Zeila, *Somali Rep.* **120 B2** 11 21N 43 30 E
Zeist, *Neths.* **24 B5** 52 5N 5 15 E
Zeitz, *Germany* **30 D8** 51 2N 12 7 E
Zejtun, *Malta* **38 F8** 35 51N 14 32 E
Zelechów, *Poland* **55 G8** 51 49N 21 54 E
Zelena, *Ukraine* **53 B9** 48 3N 24 45 E
Zelengora, *Bos.-H.* **50 C2** 43 22N 18 30 E
Zelenodolsk, *Russia* **60 C9** 55 55N 48 30 E
Zelenogorsk, *Russia* **58 B5** 60 12N 29 43 E
Zelenograd, *Russia* **58 D9** 56 1N 37 12 E
Zelenogradsk, *Russia* **15 J19** 54 53N 20 29 E
Zelenokumsk, *Russia* **61 H6** 44 24N 44 0 E
Železná Ruda, *Czech Rep.* **34 B6** 49 8N 13 15 E
Železnik, *Serbia & M.* **50 B4** 44 43N 20 23 E
Zelfana, *Algeria* **111 B5** 32 27N 4 15 E
Zelienople, *U.S.A.* **150 F4** 40 48N 80 8W
Želiezovce, *Slovak Rep.* **35 C11** 48 3N 18 40 E
Zelina, *Croatia* **45 C13** 45 57N 16 16 E
Zell, *Baden-W., Germany* **31 H3** 47 42N 7 52 E
Zell, *Rhld-Pfz., Germany* **31 E3** 50 1N 7 10 E
Zell am See, *Austria* **34 D5** 47 19N 12 47 E
Zella-Mehlis, *Germany* **30 E6** 50 39N 10 40 E
Zellersee, *Germany* **33 A8** 47 45N 9 2 E
Zelmen = Rovnoye, *Russia* **60 E8** 50 52N 46 3 E
Zelów, *Poland* **55 G6** 51 28N 19 14 E
Zeltweg, *Austria* **34 D7** 47 11N 14 45 E
Zelyony Dol = Zelenodolsk, *Russia* **60 C9** 55 55N 48 30 E
Žemaitijos △, *Lithuania* **54 B8** 56 2N 21 55 E
Zembra, I., *Tunisia* **108 A2** 37 5N 10 56 E
Zemgale = Jelgava, *Latvia* **15 H20** 56 41N 23 49 E
Zémio, *C.A.R.* **118 A2** 5 2N 25 5 E
Zemlya Imperatora Nikolaya II = Severnaya Zemlya, *Russia* **67 B10** 79 0N 100 0 E
Zemmora, *Algeria* **111 A5** 35 44N 0 51 E
Zemmur, *W. Sahara* **110 C2** 25 5N 12 0W
Zemongo ⌓, *C.A.R.* **114 A5** 6 45N 25 5 E
Zemoul, O. →, *Algeria* **110 C3** 29 15N 7 0W
Zempelburg = Sępólno Krajeńskie, *Poland* **54 E4** 53 26N 17 30 E
Zempléni-hegység, *Hungary* **52 B6** 48 25N 21 25 E
Zemplínska šírava, *Slovak Rep.* **35 C15** 48 48N 22 0 E
Zempoala, *Mexico* **163 D5** 19 22N 96 24W
Zemun, *Serbia & M.* **50 B4** 44 51N 20 25 E
Zendeh Jān, *Afghan.* **91 B1** 34 21N 61 45 E
Zengbé, *Cameroon* **113 D7** 5 46N 13 4 E
Zengcheng, *China* **77 F9** 23 13N 113 52 E
Zenica, *Bos.-H.* **52 F2** 44 10N 17 57 E
Zentsūji, *Japan* **72 C5** 34 14N 133 47 E
Zenza →, *Angola* **115 D2** 8 45 S 13 24 E
Zenza do Itombe, *Angola* **115 D2** 9 16 S 14 13 E
Žepče, *Bos.-H.* **52 F3** 44 28N 18 2 E
Zephyrhills, *U.S.A.* **153 G7** 28 14N 82 11W
Zepu, *China* **65 D8** 38 12N 77 18 E
Zeraf, Bahr ez →, *Sudan* **107 F3** 9 42N 30 52 E
Zeravshan, *Tajikistan* **65 D4** 39 10N 68 39 E
Zeravshan →, *Asia* **65 D1** 39 22N 63 45 E
Zeravshanskiy Khrebet, *Tajikistan* **65 D4** 39 20N 69 0 E
Zerbst, *Germany* **30 D8** 51 58N 12 5 E
Żerków, *Poland* **55 F4** 52 4N 17 32 E
Zermatt, *Switz.* **32 D5** 46 2N 7 46 E
Zernez, *Switz.* **33 C10** 46 42N 10 7 E
Zernograd, *Russia* **61 G5** 46 52N 40 19 E
Zernovoy = Zernograd, *Russia* **61 G5** 46 52N 40 19 E
Zerqan, *Albania* **50 E4** 41 27N 20 20 E
Zestaponi, *Georgia* **61 J6** 42 6N 43 0 E
Zetel, *Germany* **30 B3** 53 25N 7 58 E
Zetland = Shetland □, *U.K.* **22 A7** 60 30N 1 30W
Zeulenroda, *Germany* **30 E7** 50 39N 11 59 E
Zeven, *Germany* **30 B5** 53 17N 9 16 E
Zevenaar, *Neths.* **24 C6** 51 56N 6 5 E
Zévio, *Italy* **44 C8** 45 22N 11 8 E
Zeya, *Russia* **67 D13** 53 48N 127 14 E
Zeya →, *Russia* **67 D13** 51 42N 128 53 E
Zeytinbağı, *Turkey* **51 F12** 40 24N 28 47 E
Zeytindağ, *Turkey* **49 C9** 38 58N 27 4 E
Zghartā, *Lebanon* **103 A4** 34 21N 35 53 E
Zgierz, *Poland* **55 G6** 51 50N 19 27 E
Zgorzelec, *Poland* **55 G2** 51 10N 15 0 E
Zgurița, *Moldova* **53 B13** 48 8N 28 1 E
Zhabasak, *Kazakhstan* **64 F8** 50 22N 61 41 E
Zhabinka, *Belarus* **55 F11** 52 13N 24 2 E
Zhabokrych, *Ukraine* **53 B13** 48 23N 28 59 E
Zhailma, *Kazakhstan* **64 F8** 51 37N 61 33 E
Zhalanash, *Kazakhstan* **65 B9** 43 3N 78 38 E
Zhambyl = Taraz, *Kazakhstan* **65 B5** 42 54N 71 22 E
Zhanatas, *Kazakhstan* **65 B4** 43 35N 69 35 E
Zhangaly, *Kazakhstan* **61 G10** 47 1N 50 37 E
Zhangaqazaly, *Kazakhstan* **66 E7** 45 48N 62 6 E
Zhangaqŭrghan, *Kazakhstan* **65 B4** 43 50N 68 48 E
Zhangatas = Zhanatas, *Kazakhstan* **65 B4** 43 35N 69 35 E
Zhangbei, *China* **74 D8** 41 10N 114 45 E
Zhangguangcai Ling, *China* **75 B15** 45 0N 129 0 E
Zhangjiabian, *China* **69 F9** 22 33N 113 28 E
Zhangjiagang, *China* **59 B13** 31 55N 120 30 E
Zhangjiakou, *China* **74 D8** 40 48N 114 55 E
Zhangping, *China* **77 E11** 25 17N 117 23 E
Zhangpu, *China* **77 E11** 24 8N 117 35 E
Zhangshu, *China* **77 C10** 28 4N 115 29 E
Zhangwu, *China* **75 C12** 42 43N 123 52 E
Zhangye, *China* **68 C5** 38 50N 100 23 E
Zhangzhou, *China* **77 E11** 24 30N 117 35 E
Zhanhua, *China* **75 F10** 37 40N 118 8 E
Zhanjiang, *China* **77 G8** 21 15N 110 20 E
Zhannetty, Ostrov, *Russia* **67 B16** 76 43N 158 0 E
Zhanyi, *China* **76 E4** 25 38N 103 48 E
Zhanyu, *China* **75 B12** 44 30N 122 30 E
Zhao Xian, *China* **74 F8** 37 43N 114 45 E
Zhao'an, *China* **77 F11** 23 41N 117 10 E
Zhaocheng, *China* **74 F6** 36 22N 111 38 E
Zhaojue, *China* **76 C4** 28 1N 102 49 E
Zhaoping, *China* **77 E8** 24 11N 110 48 E
Zhaoqing, *China* **77 F9** 23 0N 112 20 E
Zhaotong, *China* **76 D4** 27 20N 103 44 E
Zhaoyuan, *Heilongjiang, China* **75 B13** 45 27N 125 0 E
Zhaoyuan, *Shandong, China* **75 F11** 37 20N 120 23 E
Zharkovskiy, *Russia* **58 E7** 55 56N 32 19 E
Zhashkiv, *Ukraine* **59 H6** 49 15N 30 5 E
Zhashui, *China* **74 H5** 33 40N 109 8 E
Zhayyq →, *Kazakhstan* **57 E9** 47 0N 51 48 E
Zhdanov = Mariupol, *Ukraine* **59 J9** 47 5N 37 31 E
Zhdanovo, *Kazakhstan* **65 B5** 43 40N 71 6 E
Zhecheng, *China* **74 G8** 34 7N 115 20 E
Zhegao, *China* **77 B11** 31 46N 117 45 E
Zhejiang □, *China* **77 C13** 29 0N 120 0 E
Zheleznodorozhny = Qŭnghirot, *Uzbekistan* **66 E6** 43 6N 58 54 E
Zheleznodorozhnyy, *Russia* **54 D8** 54 22N 21 19 E
Zheleznodorozhnyy, *Russia* **56 B9** 62 35N 50 55 E
Zheleznogorsk, *Russia* **59 F8** 52 22N 35 23 E
Zheleznogorsk-Ilimskiy, *Russia* **67 D11** 56 34N 104 8 E
Zheltyye Vody = Zhovti Vody, *Ukraine* **59 H7** 48 21N 33 31 E
Zhen'an, *China* **74 H5** 33 27N 109 9 E
Zhenba, *China* **76 A6** 32 34N 107 58 E
Zhenfeng, *China* **76 E5** 25 22N 105 40 E
Zheng'an, *China* **76 C6** 28 32N 107 27 E
Zhengding, *China* **74 E8** 38 8N 114 32 E
Zhenghe, *China* **77 D12** 27 20N 118 50 E
Zhengyang, *China* **77 A10** 32 37N 114 22 E
Zhengyangguan, *China* **77 A11** 32 30N 116 29 E
Zhengzhou, *China* **74 G7** 34 45N 113 34 E
Zhenhai, *China* **77 C13** 29 59N 121 42 E
Zhenjiang, *China* **77 A12** 32 11N 119 26 E
Zhenkang, *China* **76 F2** 23 58N 99 0 E
Zhenlai, *China* **75 B12** 45 50N 123 5 E
Zhenning, *China* **76 D5** 26 4N 105 45 E
Zhenping, *Henan, China* **74 H7** 33 10N 112 16 E
Zhenping, *Shaanxi, China* **76 B7** 31 59N 109 31 E
Zhenxiong, *China* **76 D5** 27 27N 104 50 E
Zhenyuan, *Gansu, China* **74 G4** 35 35N 107 30 E
Zhenyuan, *Guizhou, China* **76 D7** 27 4N 108 21 E
Zherdevka, *Russia* **60 E5** 51 56N 41 29 E
Zherebkove, *Ukraine* **53 C14** 47 50N 29 52 E
Zherong, *China* **77 D12** 27 15N 119 52 E
Zhetigen, *Kazakhstan* **65 B8** 43 40N 77 6 E
Zhetiqara, *Kazakhstan* **64 E8** 52 11N 61 12 E
Zhetisay, *Kazakhstan* **65 C4** 40 46N 68 19 E
Zhezqazghan, *Kazakhstan* **66 E7** 47 44N 67 40 E
Zhicheng, *China* **77 B8** 30 25N 111 27 E
Zhidan, *China* **74 F5** 36 48N 108 48 E
Zhigansk, *Russia* **67 C13** 66 48N 123 27 E
Zhigulevsk, *Russia* **60 D9** 53 28N 49 30 E
Zhijiang, *Hubei, China* **77 B8** 30 28N 111 45 E
Zhijiang, *Hunan, China* **76 D7** 27 27N 109 42 E
Zhijin, *China* **76 D5** 26 37N 105 45 E
Zhilinda, *Russia* **67 C12** 70 0N 114 20 E
Zhilino, *Russia* **54 D8** 54 54N 21 54 E
Zhirnovsk, *Russia* **60 E7** 50 57N 44 49 E
Zhirnovskiy = Zhirnovsk, *Russia* **60 E7** 50 57N 44 49 E
Zhirnoye = Zhirnovsk, *Russia* **60 E7** 50 57N 44 49 E
Zhitomir = Zhytomyr, *Ukraine* **59 G5** 50 20N 28 40 E
Zhizdra, *Russia* **58 F8** 53 45N 34 40 E
Zhlobin, *Belarus* **59 F6** 52 55N 30 0 E
Zhmerinka = Zhmerynka, *Ukraine* **59 H5** 49 2N 28 2 E
Zhmerynka, *Ukraine* **59 H5** 49 2N 28 2 E
Zhob, *Pakistan* **91 C3** 31 20N 69 31 E
Zhob →, *Pakistan* **92 C3** 32 4N 69 50 E
Zhodino = Zhodzina, *Belarus* **58 E5** 54 5N 28 17 E
Zhodzina, *Belarus* **58 E5** 54 5N 28 17 E
Zhokhova, Ostrov, *Russia* **67 B16** 76 4N 152 40 E
Zholkev = Nesterov, *Ukraine* **59 G2** 50 4N 23 58 E
Zholkva = Nesterov, *Ukraine* **59 G2** 50 4N 23 58 E
Zhongdian, *China* **76 D2** 27 48N 99 42 E
Zhongdong, *China* **76 F6** 22 48N 107 47 E
Zhongdu, *China* **76 E7** 24 40N 109 40 E
Zhongning, *China* **74 F3** 37 29N 105 40 E
Zhongshan, *Antarctica* **7 C6** 69 0 S 39 50 E
Zhongshan, *Guangdong, China* **77 F9** 22 26N 113 20 E
Zhongshan, *Guangxi Zhuangzu, China* **77 E8** 24 29N 111 18 E
Zhongshankong, *China* **69 F9** 22 35N 113 29 E
Zhongtiao Shan, *China* **74 G6** 35 0N 111 10 E
Zhongwei, *China* **74 F3** 37 30N 105 12 E
Zhongxiang, *China* **77 B9** 31 12N 112 34 E
Zhongyang, *China* **74 F6** 37 20N 111 11 E
Zhorany, *Ukraine* **55 G10** 51 19N 23 58 E
Zhoucun, *China* **75 F9** 36 47N 117 48 E
Zhouning, *China* **77 D12** 27 12N 119 20 E
Zhoushan, *China* **77 B14** 30 1N 122 6 E
Zhoushan Dao, *China* **77 C14** 30 5N 122 10 E
Zhouzhi, *China* **74 G5** 34 10N 108 12 E
Zhovti Vody, *Ukraine* **59 H7** 48 21N 33 31 E
Zhovtneve, *Ukraine* **55 H11** 50 42N 24 12 E
Zhovtneve, *Ukraine* **59 J7** 46 54N 32 3 E
Zhovtnevoye = Zhovtneve, *Ukraine* **59 J7** 46 54N 32 3 E
Zhu Jiang →, *China* **77 F9** 22 45N 113 37 E
Zhuanghe, *China* **75 E12** 39 40N 123 0 E
Zhūantöbe, *Kazakhstan* **65 A4** 44 46N 68 49 E
Zhucheng, *China* **75 G10** 36 0N 119 27 E
Zhugqu, *China* **74 H3** 33 40N 104 30 E
Zhuhai, *China* **77 F9** 22 17N 113 34 E
Zhuji, *China* **77 C13** 29 40N 120 10 E
Zhujiang Kou, *China* **69 G10** 22 20N 113 45 E
Zhukovka, *Russia* **58 F7** 53 35N 33 50 E
Zhumadian, *China* **74 H8** 32 59N 114 2 E
Zhuo Xian = Zhuozhou, *China* **74 E8** 39 28N 115 58 E
Zhuolu, *China* **74 D8** 40 20N 115 12 E
Zhuozhou, *China* **74 E8** 39 28N 115 58 E
Zhuozi, *China* **74 D7** 41 0N 112 25 E
Zhushan, *China* **77 A8** 32 15N 110 13 E
Zhuxi, *China* **76 A7** 32 25N 109 40 E
Zhuzhou, *China* **77 D9** 27 49N 113 12 E
Zhvanets, *Ukraine* **53 B11** 48 33N 26 30 E
Zhytomyr, *Ukraine* **59 G5** 50 20N 28 40 E
Zi Shui →, *China* **77 C9** 28 40N 112 40 E
Žiar nad Hronom, *Slovak Rep.* **35 C11** 48 35N 18 53 E
Ziārān, *Iran* **97 B6** 36 7N 50 32 E
Ziarat, *Pakistan* **92 D2** 30 25N 67 49 E
Zibo, *China* **75 F10** 36 47N 118 3 E
Zichang, *China* **74 F5** 37 18N 109 40 E
Zidarovo, *Bulgaria* **51 D11** 42 20N 27 24 E
Zidi = Wandhari, *Pakistan* **92 F2** 27 42N 66 48 E
Ziębice, *Poland* **55 H4** 50 37N 17 2 E
Ziebingen = Cybinka, *Poland* **55 F1** 52 12N 14 46 E
Ziegenhals = Głuchołazy, *Poland* **55 H4** 50 19N 17 24 E
Zielenzig = Sulęcin, *Poland* **55 F2** 52 26N 15 10 E
Zielona Góra, *Poland* **55 G2** 51 57N 15 31 E
Zierikzee, *Neths.* **24 C3** 51 40N 3 55 E
Ziesar, *Germany* **30 C8** 52 16N 12 17 E
Zifta, *Egypt* **106 H7** 30 43N 31 14 E
Zigey, *Chad* **109 F3** 14 43N 15 50 E
Zigon, *Burma* **90 F5** 18 20N 95 37 E
Zigong, *China* **76 C5** 29 15N 104 48 E
Ziguinchor, *Senegal* **112 C1** 12 35N 16 20W
Zihuatanejo, *Mexico* **162 D4** 17 38N 101 33W
Zijin, *China* **77 F10** 23 33N 115 8 E
Zile, *Turkey* **100 B6** 40 15N 35 52 E
Žilina, *Slovak Rep.* **35 B11** 49 12N 18 42 E
Žilinský □, *Slovak Rep.* **35 B12** 49 10N 19 0 E
Zillah, *Libya* **108 C3** 28 30N 17 33 E
Zillertaler Alpen, *Austria* **34 D4** 47 6N 11 45 E
Zima, *Russia* **67 D11** 54 0N 102 5 E
Zimane, Adrar in, *Algeria* **111 D5** 22 10N 4 30 E
Zimapán, *Mexico* **163 C5** 20 54N 99 20W
Zimba, *Zambia* **119 F2** 17 20 S 26 11 E
Zimbabwe, *Zimbabwe* **119 G3** 20 16 S 30 54 E
Zimbabwe ■, *Africa* **119 F3** 19 0 S 30 0 E
Zimi, *S. Leone* **112 D2** 7 20N 11 20W
Zimnicea, *Romania* **53 G10** 43 40N 25 22 E
Zimovniki, *Russia* **61 G6** 47 10N 42 25 E
Zina, *Cameroon* **109 F2** 11 19N 14 54 E
Zinal, *Switz.* **32 D5** 46 8N 7 38 E
Zinave △, *Mozam.* **117 C5** 21 35 S 33 40 E
Zinder, *Niger* **113 C6** 13 48N 9 0 E
Zinga, *C.A.R.* **114 B3** 3 49N 18 34 E
Zinga, *Tanzania* **119 D4** 9 16 S 38 49 E
Zingaro ⌓, *Italy* **46 D5** 38 6N 12 53 E
Zingst, *Germany* **30 A8** 54 26N 12 39 E
Ziniaré, *Burkina Faso* **113 C4** 12 35N 1 18W
Zinnowitz, *Germany* **30 A9** 54 4N 13 54 E
Zinovyevsk = Kirovohrad, *Ukraine* **59 H7** 48 35N 32 20 E
Zion, *U.S.A.* **157 B9** 42 27N 87 50W
Zion △, *U.S.A.* **159 H7** 37 15N 113 5W
Zionsville, *U.S.A.* **157 E10** 39 57N 86 16W
Zipaquirá, *Colombia* **168 C3** 5 0N 74 0W
Zirbitzkogel, *Austria* **34 D7** 47 4N 14 34 E
Zirc, *Hungary* **52 C2** 47 17N 17 52 E
Žiri, *Slovenia* **45 B11** 46 5N 14 5 E
Žirje, *Croatia* **45 E12** 43 39N 15 42 E
Zirke = Sieraków, *Poland* **55 F3** 52 39N 16 2 E
Zirl, *Austria* **34 D4** 47 17N 11 14 E
Zirndorf, *Germany* **31 F6** 49 27N 10 57 E
Ziros, *Greece* **39 E7** 35 5N 26 8 E
Zirreh, Gowd-e, *Afghan.* **91 C1** 29 45N 62 0 E
Zisterdorf, *Austria* **35 C9** 48 33N 16 45 E
Zitácuaro, *Mexico* **162 D4** 19 28N 100 21W
Žitava →, *Slovak Rep.* **35 C11** 48 14N 18 21 E
Žitište, *Serbia & M.* **52 E5** 45 30N 20 32 E
Zitong, *China* **76 B5** 31 37N 105 10 E
Zítsa, *Greece* **48 B2** 39 47N 20 40 E
Zittau, *Germany* **30 E10** 50 53N 14 48 E
Zitundo, *Mozam.* **117 D5** 26 48 S 32 47 E
Živinice, *Bos.-H.* **52 F3** 44 27N 18 36 E
Ziwa Magharibi = Kagera □, *Tanzania* **118 C3** 2 0 S 31 30 E
Ziway, L., *Ethiopia* **107 F4** 8 0N 38 50 E
Zixi, *China* **77 D11** 27 45N 117 4 E
Zixing, *China* **77 E9** 25 59N 113 21 E
Ziyang, *Shaanxi, China* **74 H5** 32 32N 108 31 E
Ziyang, *Sichuan, China* **76 B5** 30 6N 104 40 E
Ziyuan, *China* **77 D8** 26 2N 110 40 E
Ziyun, *China* **76 E6** 25 45N 106 5 E
Ziz, Oued →, *Morocco* **110 B4** 31 40N 4 15W
Zizhong, *China* **76 C5** 29 48N 104 47 E
Zlarin, *Croatia* **45 E12** 43 42N 15 49 E
Zlatar, *Croatia* **45 B13** 46 5N 16 3 E
Zlatar, *Serbia & M.* **50 C3** 43 25N 19 47 E
Zlataritsa, *Bulgaria* **51 C9** 43 2N 25 55 E
Zlaté Moravce, *Slovak Rep.* **35 C11** 48 23N 18 24 E
Zlatibor, *Serbia & M.* **50 C3** 43 45N 19 43 E
Zlatitsa, *Bulgaria* **51 D8** 42 41N 24 7 E
Zlatna, *Romania* **53 D8** 46 8N 23 11 E
Zlatna Panega, *Bulgaria* **51 C8** 43 5N 24 9 E
Zlatni Pyasŭtsi, *Bulgaria* **51 C12** 43 17N 28 3 E
Zlatograd, *Bulgaria* **51 E9** 41 22N 25 7 E
Zlatoust, *Russia* **64 D7** 55 10N 59 40 E
Zletovo, *Macedonia* **50 E6** 41 59N 22 17 E
Zlín, *Czech Rep.* **35 B10** 49 14N 17 40 E
Zlínský □, *Czech Rep.* **35 B10** 49 20N 17 40 E
Zlītan, *Libya* **108 B2** 32 32N 14 35 E
Złocieniec, *Poland* **54 E3** 53 30N 16 1 E
Złoczew, *Poland* **55 G5** 51 24N 18 35 E
Zlot, *Serbia & M.* **50 B5** 44 1N 21 58 E
Złotoryja, *Poland* **55 G2** 51 8N 15 55 E
Złotów, *Poland* **54 E4** 53 22N 17 2 E
Zmeinogorsk, *Kazakhstan* **66 D9** 51 10N 82 13 E
Żmigród, *Poland* **55 G3** 51 28N 16 53 E
Zmiyev, *Ukraine* **59 H9** 49 39N 36 27 E
Znamenka = Znamyanka, *Ukraine* **59 H7** 48 45N 32 30 E
Znamensk, *Russia* **54 D8** 54 36N 21 16 E
Znamyanka, *Ukraine* **59 H7** 48 45N 32 30 E
Żnin, *Poland* **55 F4** 52 51N 17 44 E
Znojmo, *Czech Rep.* **34 C9** 48 50N 16 2 E
Zobeyrī, *Iran* **96 C5** 34 10N 46 40 E
Zobia, *Dem. Rep. of the Congo* **118 B2** 3 0N 25 59 E
Zobten = Sobótka, *Poland* **55 H3** 50 54N 16 44 E
Zoetermeer, *Neths.* **24 B4** 52 3N 4 30 E
Zofingen, *Switz.* **32 B5** 47 17N 7 56 E
Zogang, *China* **76 C1** 29 55N 97 42 E
Zogno, *Italy* **44 C6** 45 48N 9 40 E
Zogqên, *China* **76 A2** 32 13N 98 47 E
Zolfo Springs, *U.S.A.* **153 H8** 27 30N 81 48W
Zollikofen, *Switz.* **32 C4** 47 0N 7 28 E
Zollikon, *Switz.* **33 B7** 47 21N 8 34 E
Zolochev = Zolochiv, *Ukraine* **59 H3** 49 45N 24 51 E
Zolochiv, *Ukraine* **59 H3** 49 45N 24 51 E
Zolotonosha, *Ukraine* **59 H7** 49 39N 32 5 E
Zolotyy Potik, *Ukraine* **53 B10** 48 54N 25 20 E
Zomba, *Malawi* **119 F4** 15 22 S 35 19 E
Zongo, *Dem. Rep. of the Congo* **114 B3** 4 20N 18 35 E
Zonguldak, *Turkey* **100 B4** 41 28N 31 50 E
Zongyang, *China* **77 B11** 30 42N 117 12 E
Zonqor Pt., *Malta* **38 F8** 35 52N 14 34 E
Zonza, *France* **29 G13** 41 45N 9 11 E
Zoo Baba, *Niger* **109 E2** 18 13N 13 2 E
Zorgo, *Burkina Faso* **113 C4** 12 15N 0 35W
Zorita, *Spain* **43 F5** 39 17N 5 39W
Zorleni, *Romania* **53 D12** 46 14N 27 44 E
Zornitsa, *Bulgaria* **51 D10** 42 23N 26 58 E
Zorritos, *Peru* **172 A1** 3 43 S 80 40W
Żory, *Poland* **55 H5** 50 3N 18 44 E
Zorzor, *Liberia* **112 D3** 7 46N 9 28W
Zossen, *Germany* **30 C9** 52 13N 13 27 E
Zou Xiang, *China* **74 G9** 35 30N 116 58 E
Zouan-Hounien, *Ivory C.* **112 D3** 6 55N 8 15W
Zouar, *Chad* **109 D3** 20 30N 16 32 E
Zouérate = Zouîrât, *Mauritania* **110 D2** 22 44N 12 21W
Zouîrât, *Mauritania* **110 D2** 22 44N 12 21W
Zouri, *Gabon* **114 C1** 1 1 S 8 53 E
Zourika, *Niger* **113 B6** 19 16N 7 52 E
Zourma, *Burkina Faso* **113 C4** 11 20N 0 50W
Zousfana, O. →, *Algeria* **111 B4** 31 28N 2 17W
Zoutkamp, *Neths.* **24 A6** 53 20N 6 18 E
Zrenjanin, *Serbia & M.* **52 E5** 45 22N 20 23 E
Zuarungu, *Ghana* **113 C4** 10 49N 0 46W
Zuba, *Nigeria* **113 D6** 9 11N 7 12 E
Zubayr, *Yemen* **98 D3** 15 3N 42 10 E
Zubtsov, *Russia* **58 D8** 56 10N 34 34 E
Zudáñez, *Bolivia* **173 D5** 19 6 S 64 44W
Zuénoula, *Ivory C.* **112 D3** 7 34N 6 3W
Zuera, *Spain* **40 D4** 41 51N 0 49W
Zuetina = Az Zuwaytīnah, *Libya* **108 B4** 30 58N 20 7 E
Zufār, *Oman* **99 C6** 17 40N 54 0 E
Zug, *Switz.* **33 B7** 47 10N 8 31 E
Zug, *W. Sahara* **110 D2** 21 36N 14 9W
Zug □, *Switz.* **33 B7** 47 9N 8 35 E
Zugdidi, *Georgia* **61 J5** 42 30N 41 55 E
Zugersee, *Switz.* **33 B7** 47 7N 8 35 E
Zugspitze, *Germany* **31 H6** 47 25N 10 59 E
Zuid-Holland □, *Neths.* **24 C4** 52 0N 4 35 E
Zuidbeveland, *Neths.* **24 C3** 51 30N 3 50 E
Zuidhorn, *Neths.* **24 A6** 53 15N 6 23 E
Zújar, *Spain* **43 H8** 37 34N 2 50W
Zújar →, *Spain* **43 G5** 39 1N 5 47W
Żukowo, *Poland* **54 D5** 54 21N 18 22 E
Zula, *Eritrea* **107 D4** 15 17N 39 40 E
Zulia □, *Venezuela* **168 B3** 10 0N 72 10W
Züllichau = Sulechów, *Poland* **55 F2** 52 5N 15 40 E
Zülpich, *Germany* **30 E2** 50 41N 6 39 E
Zülz = Biała, *Poland* **55 H4** 50 24N 17 40 E
Zumaia, *Spain* **40 B2** 43 19N 2 15W
Zumárraga, *Spain* **40 B2** 43 5N 2 19W
Zumbo, *Mozam.* **119 F3** 15 35 S 30 26 E
Zummo, *Nigeria* **113 D7** 9 51N 12 59 E
Zumpango, *Mexico* **163 D5** 19 48N 99 6W
Zundi, *Angola* **115 E3** 10 28 S 16 48 E
Zungeru, *Nigeria* **113 D6** 9 48N 6 8 E
Zunhua, *China* **75 D9** 40 18N 117 58 E
Zuni, *U.S.A.* **159 J9** 35 4N 108 51W
Zunyi, *China* **76 D6** 27 42N 106 53 E
Zuo Jiang →, *China* **76 F6** 22 50N 108 6 E
Zuozhou, *China* **76 F6** 22 42N 107 27 E
Županja, *Croatia* **52 E3** 45 4N 18 43 E
Žur, *Serbia & M.* **50 D4** 42 13N 20 34 E
Zura, *Russia* **64 C4** 57 36N 53 24 E
Zurbātīyah, *Iraq* **101 F12** 33 9N 46 3 E
Zürich, *Switz.* **33 B7** 47 22N 8 32 E
Zürich □, *Switz.* **33 B7** 47 26N 8 40 E
Zurich ✈ (ZRH), *Switz.* **33 B7** 47 27N 8 32 E
Zürichsee, *Switz.* **33 B7** 47 18N 8 40 E
Żuromin, *Poland* **55 E6** 53 4N 19 51 E
Zurrieq, *Malta* **38 F7** 35 50N 14 28 E
Zurzach, *Switz.* **33 A6** 47 35N 8 18 E
Žut, *Croatia* **45 E12** 43 52N 15 17 E
Zutphen, *Neths.* **24 B6** 52 9N 6 12 E
Zuurberg △, *S. Africa* **116 E4** 33 12 S 25 32 E
Zuwārah, *Libya* **108 B2** 32 58N 12 1 E
Zuyevka, *Russia* **64 B3** 58 27N 51 10 E
Zūzan, *Iran* **97 C8** 34 22N 59 53 E
Žužemberk, *Slovenia* **45 C11** 45 52N 14 56 E
Zvanka = Volkhov, *Russia* **58 C7** 59 55N 32 15 E
Zvenigorodka = Zvenyhorodka, *Ukraine* **59 H6** 49 4N 30 56 E
Zvenyhorodka, *Ukraine* **59 H6** 49 4N 30 56 E
Zverinogolovskoye, *Russia* **66 D7** 54 26N 64 50 E
Zvezdets, *Bulgaria* **51 D11** 42 6N 27 26 E
Zvishavane, *Zimbabwe* **119 G3** 20 17 S 30 2 E
Zvolen, *Slovak Rep.* **35 C12** 48 33N 19 10 E
Zvonce, *Serbia & M.* **50 D6** 42 57N 22 34 E
Zvornik, *Bos.-H.* **52 F4** 44 26N 19 5 E
Zwedru = Tchien, *Liberia* **112 D3** 5 59N 8 15W
Zweibrücken, *Germany* **31 F3** 49 15N 7 21 E
Zweisimmen, *Switz.* **32 C4** 46 33N 7 22 E
Zwenkau, *Germany* **30 D8** 51 13N 12 20 E
Zwettl, *Austria* **34 C8** 48 35N 15 9 E
Zwickau, *Germany* **30 E8** 50 44N 12 30 E
Zwierzyniec, *Poland* **55 H9** 50 36N 22 58 E
Zwiesel, *Germany* **31 F9** 49 1N 13 13 E
Zwittau = Svitavy, *Czech Rep.* **35 B9** 49 47N 16 28 E
Zwoleń, *Poland* **55 G8** 51 21N 21 36 E
Zwolle, *Neths.* **24 B6** 52 31N 6 6 E
Zwolle, *U.S.A.* **155 K8** 31 38N 93 39W
Żychlin, *Poland* **55 F6** 52 15N 19 37 E
Żyrardów, *Poland* **55 F7** 52 3N 20 28 E
Zyryan, *Kazakhstan* **66 E9** 49 43N 84 20 E
Zyryanka, *Russia* **67 C16** 65 45N 150 51 E
Zyryanovsk = Zyryan, *Kazakhstan* **66 E9** 49 43N 84 20 E
Żywiec, *Poland* **55 J6** 49 42N 19 10 E

World: Regions in the News

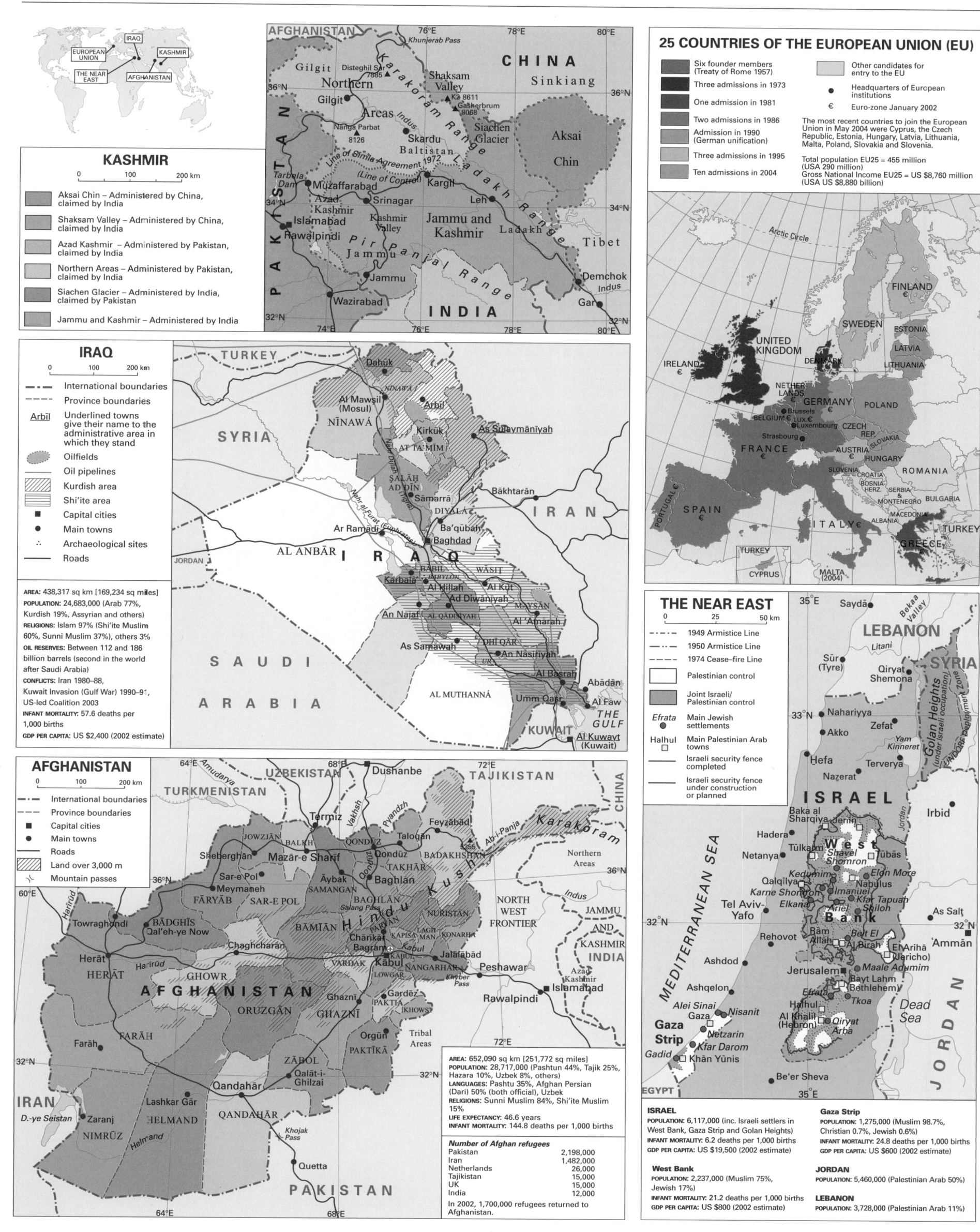

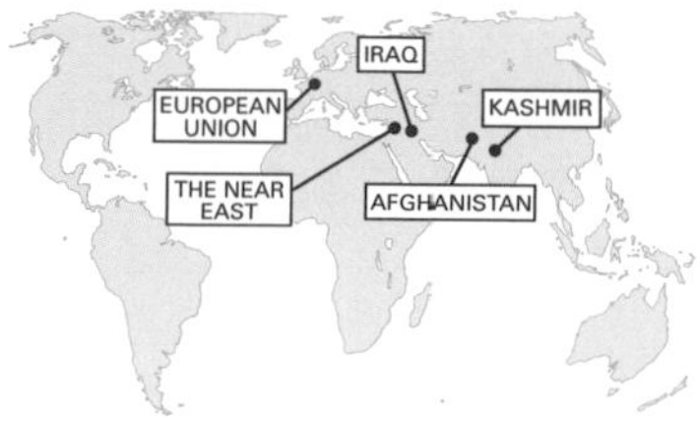

KASHMIR

0 100 200 km

- Aksai Chin – Administered by China, claimed by India
- Shaksam Valley – Administered by China, claimed by India
- Azad Kashmir – Administered by Pakistan, claimed by India
- Northern Areas – Administered by Pakistan, claimed by India
- Siachen Glacier – Administered by India, claimed by Pakistan
- Jammu and Kashmir – Administered by India

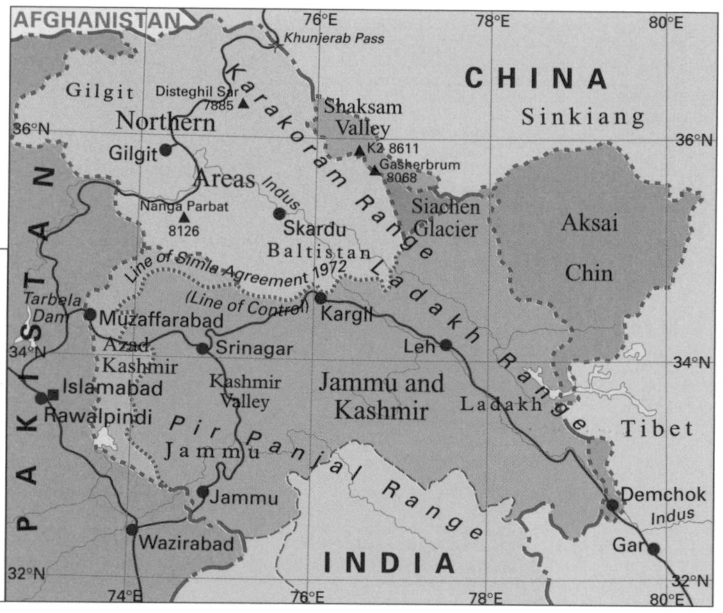

IRAQ

0 100 200 km

- International boundaries
- Province boundaries
- Arbil — Underlined towns give their name to the administrative area in which they stand
- Oilfields
- Oil pipelines
- Kurdish area
- Shi'ite area
- Capital cities
- Main towns
- Archaeological sites
- Roads

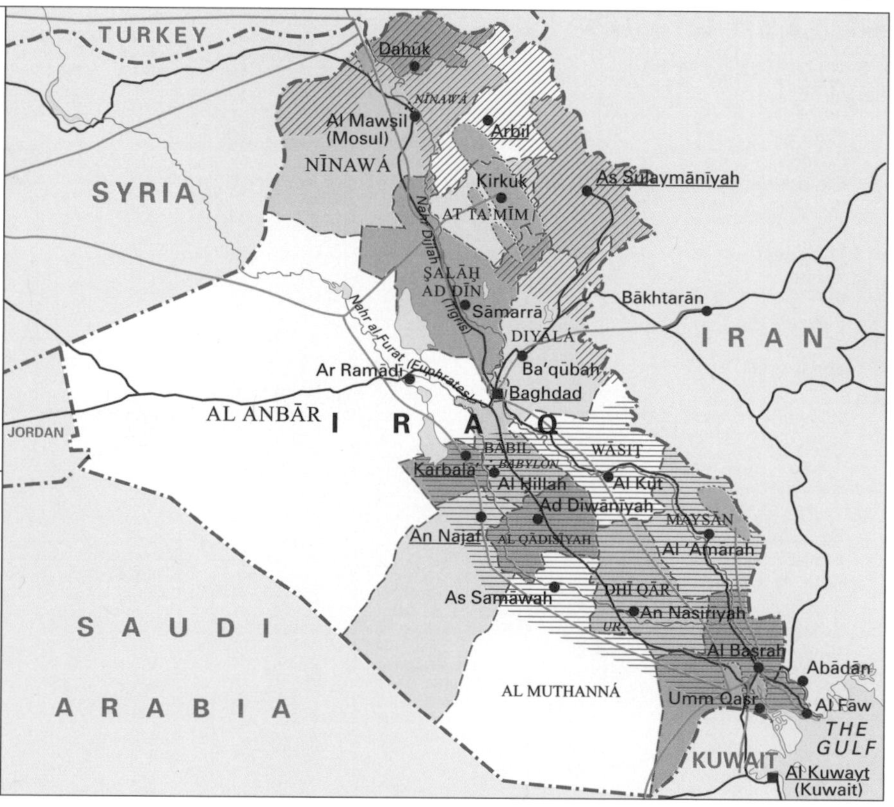

AREA: 438,317 sq km [169,234 sq miles]
POPULATION: 24,683,000 (Arab 77%, Kurdish 19%, Assyrian and others)
RELIGIONS: Islam 97% (Shi'ite Muslim 60%, Sunni Muslim 37%), others 3%
OIL RESERVES: Between 112 and 186 billion barrels (second in the world after Saudi Arabia)
CONFLICTS: Iran 1980–88, Kuwait Invasion (Gulf War) 1990–91, US-led Coalition 2003
INFANT MORTALITY: 57.6 deaths per 1,000 births
GDP PER CAPITA: US $2,400 (2002 estimate)

AFGHANISTAN

0 100 200 km

- International boundaries
- Province boundaries
- Capital cities
- Main towns
- Roads
- Land over 3,000 m
- Mountain passes

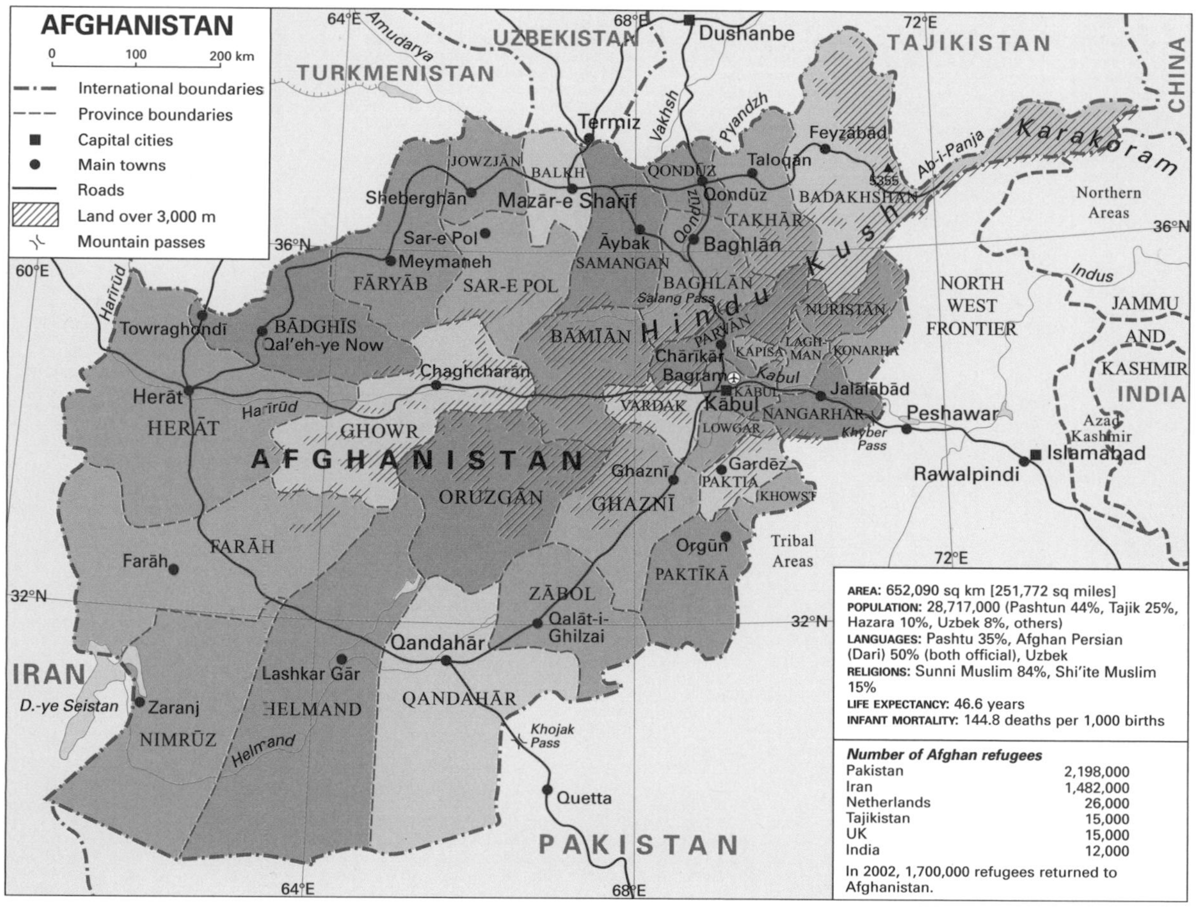

AREA: 652,090 sq km [251,772 sq miles]
POPULATION: 28,717,000 (Pashtun 44%, Tajik 25%, Hazara 10%, Uzbek 8%, others)
LANGUAGES: Pashtu 35%, Afghan Persian (Dari) 50% (both official), Uzbek
RELIGIONS: Sunni Muslim 84%, Shi'ite Muslim 15%
LIFE EXPECTANCY: 46.6 years
INFANT MORTALITY: 144.8 deaths per 1,000 births

Number of Afghan refugees

Pakistan	2,198,000
Iran	1,482,000
Netherlands	26,000
Tajikistan	15,000
UK	15,000
India	12,000

In 2002, 1,700,000 refugees returned to Afghanistan.

25 COUNTRIES OF THE EUROPEAN UNION (EU)

- Six founder members (Treaty of Rome 1957)
- Three admissions in 1973
- One admission in 1981
- Two admissions in 1986
- Admission in 1990 (German unification)
- Three admissions in 1995
- Ten admissions in 2004
- Other candidates for entry to the EU
- ● Headquarters of European institutions
- € Euro-zone January 2002

The most recent countries to join the European Union in May 2004 were Cyprus, the Czech Republic, Estonia, Hungary, Latvia, Lithuania, Malta, Poland, Slovakia and Slovenia.

Total population EU25 = 455 million (USA 290 million)
Gross National Income EU25 = US $8,760 million (USA US $8,880 billion)

THE NEAR EAST

0 25 50 km

- 1949 Armistice Line
- 1950 Armistice Line
- 1974 Cease-fire Line
- Palestinian control
- Joint Israeli/Palestinian control
- Efrata — Main Jewish settlements
- Halhul — Main Palestinian Arab towns
- Israeli security fence completed
- Israeli security fence under construction or planned

ISRAEL
POPULATION: 6,117,000 (inc. Israeli settlers in West Bank, Gaza Strip and Golan Heights)
INFANT MORTALITY: 6.2 deaths per 1,000 births
GDP PER CAPITA: US $19,500 (2002 estimate)

Gaza Strip
POPULATION: 1,275,000 (Muslim 98.7%, Christian 0.7%, Jewish 0.6%)
INFANT MORTALITY: 24.8 deaths per 1,000 births
GDP PER CAPITA: US $600 (2002 estimate)

West Bank
POPULATION: 2,237,000 (Muslim 75%, Jewish 17%)
INFANT MORTALITY: 21.2 deaths per 1,000 births
GDP PER CAPITA: US $800 (2002 estimate)

JORDAN
POPULATION: 5,460,000 (Palestinian Arab 50%)

LEBANON
POPULATION: 3,728,000 (Palestinian Arab 11%)

KEY TO EUROPEAN MAP PAGES

Large scale maps
(>1:3 900 000)

Medium scale maps
(1:4 000 000 – 1:9 900 000)

Small scale maps
(<1:10 000 000)

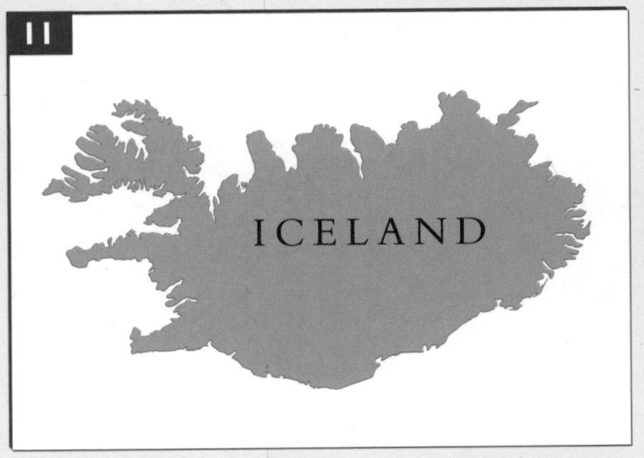

WORLD COUNTRY INDEX

Afghanistan 91
Albania 50
Algeria 110–111
Angola 115
Argentina 174, 176
Armenia 101
Australia 124–129
Austria 34–35
Azerbaijan 101
Azores 9

Bahamas 164–165
Bahrain 99
Bangladesh 90
Barbados 165
Belarus 58–59
Belgium 24
Belize 164
Benin 113
Bhutan 90
Bolivia 172–173
Bosnia-Herzegovina 45, 50
Botswana 116
Brazil 168–175
Brunei 85
Bulgaria 50–51
Burkina Faso 112–113
Burma (Myanmar) 86–87, 90
Burundi 118

Cambodia 86–87
Canary Is. 9
Cameroon 109, 114
Canada 138–143
Cape Verde Is. 9
Central African Republic 114
Chad 109
Chile 172, 174, 176
China 68–69, 74–77
Colombia 168
Comoros 121
Congo 114–115
Congo, Dem. Rep. of the 114–115, 118–119
Costa Rica 164
Croatia 45, 52
Cuba 164–165
Cyprus 39
Czech Republic 34–35

Denmark 17
Djibouti 120
Dominican Republic 165

Ecuador 168
Egypt 106
El Salvador 164
England 20–21
Equatorial Guinea 114
Eritrea 106–107
Estonia 58
Ethiopia 107, 120

Fiji 133
Finland 14–15
France 26–29
French Guiana 169

Gabon 114
Gambia 112
Georgia 101
Germany 30–31
Ghana 112–113
Greece 48–51
Greenland 10
Guadeloupe 164
Guatemala 164
Guinea 112
Guinea-Bissau 112
Guyana 169

Haiti 165
Honduras 164
Hungary 52

Iceland 11
India 90, 92–95
Indonesia 82–85
Iran 96–97
Iraq 96–97
Irish Republic 23
Israel 103
Italy 44–47
Ivory Coast 112

Jamaica 164
Japan 70–73
Jordan 103

Kazakhstan 65, 66
Kenya 118
Korea, North 75
Korea, South 75
Kuwait 96–97
Kyrgyzstan 65

Laos 86
Latvia 58
Lebanon 103
Lesotho 117
Liberia 112
Libya 108
Lithuania 58
Luxembourg 24

Macedonia 50
Madagascar 117
Malawi 119
Malaysia 84–85
Mali 110–111, 112–113
Malta 38
Martinique 164
Mauritania 110, 112
Mauritius 121
Mexico 162–163
Moldova 53
Mongolia 68–69
Morocco 110–111
Mozambique 117, 119

Namibia 116
Nepal 93
Netherlands 24
New Zealand 130–131
Nicaragua 164
Niger 109, 113
Nigeria 113
Northern Ireland 23
Norway 14–15, 18

Oman 99

Pakistan 91
Panama 164
Papua New Guinea 132
Paraguay 174–175
Peru 168, 172
Philippines 80–81
Poland 54–55
Portugal 42–43
Puerto Rico 165

Qatar 99

Réunion 121
Romania 52–53
Russia 56–61, 64, 66–67
Rwanda 118

St. Lucia 165
Samoa 133
Saudi Arabia 96–99
Scotland 22
Senegal 112
Serbia and Montenegro 50, 52
Seychelles 121
Sierra Leone 112
Singapore 87
Slovak Republic 35
Slovenia 45
Solomon Is. 133
Somali Republic 120
South Africa 116–117
Spain 40–43
Sri Lanka 95
Sudan 106–107
Suriname 169
Swaziland 117
Sweden 14–17
Switzerland 32–33
Syria 100–101, 103

Taiwan 77
Tajikistan 65
Tanzania 118–119
Thailand 86–87
Togo 113
Tonga 133
Trinidad and Tobago 169
Tunisia 111
Turkey 100–101
Turkmenistan 65, 66

Uganda 118
Ukraine 59
United Arab Emirates 99
United Kingdom 20–23
USA 144–161
Uruguay 174–175
Uzbekistan 65, 66

Vanuatu 133
Venezuela 168–169
Vietnam 86–87

Wales 20–21

Yemen 98–99

Zambia 115, 119
Zimbabwe 119